W9-BXL-281

THE WORLD ALMANAC®
AND BOOK OF FACTS
2007

Editorial Director: Zoë Kashner
Executive Editor: C. Alan Joyce; **Managing Editor:** Elizabeth J. Lazzara
Editors: Sarah Janssen, Vincent G. Spadafora
Associate Editors: M. L. Liu, Andrew Steinitz
Desktop Publishing Associates: Michael Meyerhofer, Sean Westmoreland
Contributing Editors: Elisheva Coleman, Jennifer Dunham, Jane Flynn, Eric C. Gopel,
Richard Hantula, Geoffrey M. Horn, Chris Larson, William A. McGeveran Jr.,
Cathy Millhauser, Adam Sales, Dr. Lee T. Shapiro, George W. Smith, Donald Young
Research: Martin De Leon, Joseph Fassler, Nick Jackson, Lisette E. Johnson
Cover: Bill SMITH STUDIO

WORLD ALMANAC EDUCATION GROUP
Chief Executive Officer, WRC Media Inc.: Ann W. Jackson
Chief Financial Officer: Robert S. Yingling
President, World Almanac Education Group: Peter M. Esposito
General Manager/Publisher: Ken Park
Associate Publisher/Photo Research: Edward A. Thomas
Director of Indexing Services: Marjorie B. Bank; **Index Editor:** Walter Kronenberg
Facts On File World News Digest: Louise Bloomfield, Publisher; Marion Farrier, Editor in Chief;
Jonathan Taylor, Managing Editor
World Almanac Reference Database@*FACTS.com*: Dennis La Beau

WORLD ALMANAC BOOKS
Vice President, Sales and Marketing: Lola A. Valenciano; **Business Manager:** Babette Romaine
Sales and Marketing Manager: Maria Gonzalez; **Sales and Marketing Coordinator:** Sheena Scott

We acknowledge with thanks the many helpful letters and e-mails from readers of THE WORLD ALMANAC. Because of the volume of mail, it is not possible to reply to each one. However, every communication is read by the editors, and all suggestions receive careful attention. THE WORLD ALMANAC's e-mail address is Walmanac@waegroup.com.

The first edition of THE WORLD ALMANAC, a 120-page volume with 12 pages of advertising, was published by the New York World in 1868. Annual publication was suspended in 1876. Joseph Pulitzer, publisher of the New York World, revived THE WORLD ALMANAC in 1886 with the goal of making it a "compendium of universal knowledge." It has been published annually since then. THE WORLD ALMANAC does not decide wagers.

PHOTOS: COVER: Alexander, Eclipse, Rice: AP Images; Army: U.S. Army; Couric: REUTERS/Mario Anzuoni/Landov; Stock Exchange: Clive Sawyer/eStock Photo; Bridge: Photodisc/Getty; Oil Rig: Corel Stock Library. **YEAR IN PICTURES:** 194, 197, 809-812: AP Images; 193: Cannavaro, Buffett, Bush, Mosque: AP Images, Gas: REUTERS/Robert Galbraith/Landov; 195: Clinton/McCain: REUTERS/Jeffrey Snyder/Landov, DeLay: REUTERS/Evan Sisley/Landov, Supreme Court: REUTERS/Larry Downing/Landov; 196: Gas: REUTERS/Robert Galbraith/Landov, Immigration: AP Images, Minutemen: REUTERS/Jeff Topping/Landov; 198: Couric: REUTERS/Mario Anzuoni/Landov, Stern: AP Images, *An Inconvenient Truth*: Paramount Classics/Photofest; 199: *Brokeback Mountain*: Focus Features/Photofest, *Capote*: Sony Pictures Classics/Photofest, *Walk the Line*: 20th Century Fox/Photofest. 200: Klimt: REUTERS/Shannon Stapleton/Landov, U2: AP Images, *Jersey Boys*: © Joan Marcus 2005; 813: Landis, Cannavaro: AP Images, Zidane: REUTERS/Peter Schola/GPD/HO/Landov; 814: AP Images; 815: Gators: REUTERS/Ryan Mckee/Pool/Landov, Davis, Federer, Woods: AP Images; 816: King: William Lovelace/Express/Getty Images, Knotts: CBS/Photofest, Winters: 20th Century Fox/Photofest, Wasserstein, Parks, Irwin, Weinberger, Cassini, Patterson, Spelling, Friedan, Reeve: AP Images. **TEXT PAGES:** 11: Tami Hecker: Photo by English Mike; 304: Galveston: LOC (Library of Congress), Camille: NOAA; 459, 461, 462, 464, 465-472, 490: LOC; 519-525: U.S. Presidents: LOC, unless otherwise indicated; J. Adams, Jackson, Harrison, Arthur, Harrison, McKinley, Harding, Hoover, Eisenhower © 1967 by Dover Publications; 526: Johnson, Lyndon B. Johnson Library; Ford, Courtesy of Gerald R. Ford Museum; Carter, Courtesy of Jimmy Carter Library; 527: George H.W. Bush, Official White House Photograph; 528: George W. Bush, Eric Draper–The White House; 661, 663, 667-684, 686: LOC.

WORLD ALMANAC BOOKS
A Division of World Almanac Education Group, Inc.
A WRC Media Company
512 Seventh Avenue
New York, NY 10018

THE AUTHORITY SINCE 1868

THE WORLD ALMANAC®

AND BOOK OF FACTS

2007

WORLD ALMANAC BOOKS

CONTENTS

THE TOP TEN NEWS STORIES OF 2006

1. **Sectarian violence in Iraq** and continuing opposition to the U.S. military presence there undermined the elected government of Premier Nouri Kamel al-Maliki, who took office May 20 following elections in Dec. 2005 that gave a plurality to the United Iraq Alliance, a Shiite coalition. Despite the killing of insurgent leader Abu Musab al-Zarqawi in June, violence claimed an average of more than 100 Iraqi civilian lives per day in July and August. As of Oct. 13 the U.S. military had reported 2,752 deaths in Iraq since the 2003 invasion, including 2,198 killed in action. More than 660 deaths in action had come in the last 12 months. U.S. wounded since 2003 totaled 20,895. Estimates of Iraqi civilians killed ranged from 43,850 to 48,693 as of Oct. 9, according to Iraq Body Count, a group monitoring international press reports. Former Iraqi President Saddam Hussein went on trial Aug. 21, for genocide in the deaths of at least 50,000 Kurds in 1988. He was awaiting a verdict in his first trial, which had adjourned in July, in which he was charged in the deaths of 148 Shiite villagers during a 1982 crackdown following a failed assassination attempt. Meanwhile in **Afghanistan**, Taliban rebels stepped up attacks on civilians and NATO forces.

2. **U.S. midterm congressional elections** set for Nov. 7 would decide whether both houses would remain under Republican control—as they had been almost continuously since 1995.

3. The U.S. and allies continued to fight what Pres. George W. Bush called "the decisive ideological struggle of the 21st century" against **fundamentalist Islamic terrorists**. In the U.S., terrorist conspirator Zacarias Moussaoui was sentenced May 4 to life in prison for his involvement in the Sept. 11, 2001 terrorist attacks on the U.S. British officials announced Aug. 10 that they had broken up a potential "major terrorist plot" to use liquid bombs to down transatlantic flights, prompting tighter airport security. Through mid-October, Western nations had not suffered a major terror attack in 2006, but a U.S. intelligence report leaked in September warned that support for Islamic holy war against the West—inspired in part by the invasion and occupation of Iraq—was increasing and spreading. Conflicts between the Islamic and Western world also manifested themselves in the often violent protests in February by Muslims against a Danish newspaper's cartoon caricatures of the Prophet Muhammad, and after Pope Benedict XVI's Sept. 12 speech quoting a denigrating remark about Muhammad and Islam.

4. How to better control **immigration to the U.S.** and how to deal with an estimated 12 million undocumented aliens already in the nation was the focus of debate throughout 2006. The Senate May 25 passed legislation that included processes for current undocumented workers to gain legal status, but the bill was opposed by the leadership of the House. Hundreds of thousands of supporters of immigrant rights rallied in cities across the nation in the late spring. With polls showing most Americans favoring tighter border security, Congress enacted a narrow measure, calling for construction of a 700-mile, double-layered fence along the U.S.-Mexico border, which was signed Oct. 4 by Pres. Bush.

5. The **nuclear programs of Iran and North Korea** continued to cause concern among the nations' neighbors and leading Western powers. North Korea, believed to already possess several weapons, drew global condemnation with its apparent first nuclear test Oct. 9. Ballistic missile tests July 5 had also caused alarm. Six-party talks seeking to persuade North Korea to end its nuclear weapons program had broken off in 2005. Iran, claiming its nuclear program was for peaceful purposes, defied a UN Aug. 31 deadline to suspend uranium enrichment. The European Union was leading negotiations with Iran aimed at halting the enrichment program.

6. Following a July 12 raid into northern Israel by Hezbollah guerrillas, **Israel launched air and ground attacks throughout Lebanon**, where Hezbollah was based. Hezbollah countered with rocket attacks into northern Israel. Before a cease-fire brokered by the UN went into effect Aug. 14, an estimated 150 Israelis and nearly 1,150 Lebanese had been killed. Israel also continued to face resistance in the occupied Palestinian territories. **Hamas**, which continued to oppose the existence of Israel, won parliamentary elections there Jan. 25, but Western cutoffs of funding for the Palestinian Authority were crippling the government's operations.

7. In the U.S., disputes continued over some of the **tactics in the Bush Administration's fight against terrorism**. A secret National Security Administration (NSA) program allowing domestic surveillance without warrants was revealed in late 2005, fueling controversy and sparking legal challenges in 2006. The U.S. Supreme Court in June struck down, as unauthorized under U.S. and international law, the administration's system for prosecuting suspected terrorist detainees using military tribunals. In late September, however, the administration secured passage of new legislation that authorized the use of military tribunals and aggressive interrogation but prohibited the use of evidence gathered using "cruel, unusual or inhumane treatment or punishment." Earlier in September, Pres. Bush had acknowledged the existence of secret CIA prisons abroad, where terrorism suspects had been held. Those prisoners, including alleged Sept. 11 mastermind Khalid Sheikh Mohammed, were moved to the U.S. detention center in Guantanamo Bay, Cuba.

8. Continued rising international demand and political uncertainty in many leading oil-producing nations pushed **oil prices** to a record closing price above $77 a barrel on the New York Mercantile Exchange on July 14 and the average U.S. gas price topped $3.00 a gallon during that month. Prices retreated significantly in the early fall.

9. **The U.S. Supreme Court** in June completed its first term with two new members appointed by Pres. Bush: Chief Justice John G. Roberts Jr., confirmed in 2005, and Associate Justice Samuel A. Alito Jr., confirmed Jan. 31, 2006 by a vote of 58-42 after contentious Senate hearings. They were the first new justices on the Court in 11 years.

10. The UN Security Council Aug. 31 authorized a UN peacekeeping force to take over for an African force and try to curb ongoing violence in the **Sudanese region of Darfur**. It is estimated that at least 200,000 people had died there (and more than 2 million others had been displaced) since 2003 in fighting between government and rebel forces and atrocities by pro-government militias, or Janjaweed. Sudan the same day rejected the deployment of the UN troops.

The World at a Glance

Below is a sampling of facts from *The World Almanac 2007*.

Number Ones

Most popular **car color** in the U.S. . . . . silver, more than 20% of new cars (*p. 83*)
Highest-rated U.S. **television show**, 2005-06 . . . . *American Idol*, Tuesday night (*p. 250*)
Top-spending U.S. **advertiser** in 2005 . . . . Procter & Gamble, $4.61 bil (*p. 252*)
Most prescribed class of **drug** in the U.S. . . . . antidepressants, prescribed 81.2 mil times in 2004 (*p. 170*)
Most popular **dog breed** in U.S. . . . . Labrador retriever, 137,867 new dogs registered in 2005 (*p. 292*)
Leading **cause of death** in U.S. . . . . heart disease, 685,089 deaths (28%) in 2003 (*p. 164*)
Nation with the most **vacation days** per year . . . . Italy, average of 42 days per person (*p. 88*)
Largest **world city** . . . . Tokyo, 2005 population 35.2 mil (*p. 788*)
Largest **army**, by active-duty troop strength . . . . China, 2.3 million (*p. 137*)
Nation hosting the most **refugees** . . . . Pakistan, with 1.1 mil in 2005 (*p. 851*)
Most **densely populated** U.S. state . . . . New Jersey, 1,135 persons per sq. mi. (*p. 592*)
Most **sparsely populated** nation. . . . . Mongolia, 4.7 persons per sq. mi. (*p. 849*)
Nation with most **water per capita** . . . . Iceland, 582,191.8 cubic meters (U.S. has 10,333) (*p. 288*)
Developed nations with highest **federal tax rate**. . . . . Belgium and Germany, 42% (*p. 851*)
Nation with highest **per capita GDP** . . . . Luxembourg, $55,600 (*p. 849*)
Highest temperature recorded on Earth . . . . 136° F in El Azizia, Libya, 9/13/22 (*p. 301*)
Deadliest natural disaster in U.S. . . . . Galveston Hurricane, Sept. 8, 1900; up to 12,000 killed (*p. 302*)
Most **career saves** (baseball) . . . . .Trevor Hoffman, 482 through 2006 (*p. 886*)

Surprising Facts

Young American men (18-24) watch less TV per week than any other group, an average of 23 hours, 1 minute in 2005. (*p. 249*)

Despite rising 2005 domestic **gasoline prices, U.S. prices averaged among the lowest** in the world: 46% lower than in Japan and nearly 60% lower than in Germany and the U.K. (*p. 111*)

Antarctica is considered a desert, with annual precipitation of only 8 inches along the coast and far less inland. (*p. 704*)

The African nation of Equatorial Guinea had the world's **second-highest per capita GDP** in 2005 ($50,200, up from only $2,700 in 2002), thanks to booming oil sales. (*p. 849*)

The **easternmost point in the U.S.** is in Alaska: Pochnoi Point, on Semisopochnoi Island, is at 179° 46' E longitude. (*p. 449*)

All 50 of the **world's tallest mountains** are in Asia. (*p. 701-2*)

U.S. defense spending of $465 billion in 2004 was more than 3 times the combined estimate of spending by Russia, China, North Korea, Iran, and Syria. (*p. 137*)

The **most popular radio format** in the U.S. is country (19% of stations), but rock music sells the most (32% of sales). (*pp. 246-7*)

In the U.S., **firearm deaths by suicide** outnumber those by homicide by more than 40%. (*p. 165*)

Changing Times

1900-2000: The **top country of origin** for foreign-born U.S. residents shifted from Germany (26% of the foreign-born population in 1900) to Italy (13% in 1960) to Mexico (30% in 2000). (*p. 599*)

1940-2005: The **total number of U.S. farms** fell more than 66%, from 6.4 million to 2.10 million. (*p. 94*)

1960-2005: Americans' **average savings**, as a percent of their disposable income, fell from 7.3% to –0.4%. (*p. 49*)

1960-2002: The percentage of **U.S. adults who were clinically overweight** climbed from 45% to 65%, and the number of all U.S. adults considered clinically obese rose from 13% to 31%. (*p. 171*)

1969-2005: **Average annual tuition and fees** for a 4-year private college or university were 10 times higher in 2005 than in 1980, rising from $1,809 to $18,838. (*p. 407*)

1980-2005: The percentage of **high school seniors who had at least one heavy drinking episode** in the previous two weeks fell from 41% to 28%. (*p. 163*)

1990-2005: The median **price for an existing single family home** in the U.S. climbed 138%, from $92,000 to $219,000. (*p. 375*)

1990-2004: The rate of increase of **greenhouse gas emissions** in the U.S. has slowed dramatically in recent years: emissions increased by an annual average of 1.7% from 1990 to 2000, but only 0.4% annually from 2000 to 2004. (*p. 283*)

2006-2050: The population of China, the **most populous nation** in 2006, will climb from 1.3 billion to 1.4 billion in 2050, but India will surpass China by 2030, and is projected to top the list in 2050 with 1.8 billion people. (*pp. 846-7*)

Milestone Birthdays in 2007

90
Sidney Sheldon, Feb. 12
Lena Horne, June 30
Red Auerbach, Sept. 20
Arthur Schlesinger Jr. Oct. 15
Robert Byrd, Nov. 20

80
Eartha Kitt, Jan. 17
Sidney Poitier, Feb. 20
Harry Belafonte, Mar. 1
Pope Benedict XVI, Apr. 16
Neil Simon, July 4

70
Morgan Freeman, Mar. 1
Warren Beatty, Mar. 30
Colin Powell, Apr. 5
Jack Nicholson, Apr. 22
Saddam Hussein, Apr. 28
Thomas Pynchon, May 8
Richard Petty, July 2
Bill Cosby, July 12
Dustin Hoffman, Aug. 8
Robert Redford, Aug. 18
Jane Fonda, Dec. 21

60
David Bowie, Jan. 8
David Letterman, Apr. 12
Carlos Santana, July 20
Stephen King, Sept. 21
Hillary Clinton, Oct. 26

50
Katie Couric, Jan. 7
Osama bin Laden, Mar. 10
Spike Lee, Mar. 20
Lyle Lovett, Nov. 1
Ray Romano, Dec. 21

40
Anderson Cooper, June 7
Nicole Kidman, June 20
Pamela Anderson, July 1
Will Ferrell, July 16
Keith Urban, Oct. 26
Julia Roberts, Oct. 28
Jamie Foxx, Dec. 13

30
Orlando Bloom, Jan. 13
Shakira, Feb. 2
Kanye West, June 8

THE YEAR IN RECORDS

For complete coverage of world records, see *The World Almanac Book of Records: Firsts, Feats, Facts & Phenomena.*

A (Lot of) Mighty Wind. The 2005 Atlantic Hurricane Season stretched into 2006 and brought an unprecedented 27th named storm, named with the Greek letter Zeta, which peaked over the middle of the Atlantic at 65 mph on **Jan. 3, 2006**. It never hit land.

Steelers Supreme. The Pittsburgh Steelers defeated the Seattle Seahawks, 21-10, to win their fifth Super Bowl on **Feb. 5**, tying a league record held by the Dallas Cowboys and San Francisco 49ers. Ben Roethlisberger became the youngest quarterback to lead a team to victory, at the age of 23 years, 340 days. Steelers running back Willie Parker set a Super Bowl record for longest run from scrimmage with a 75-yard touchdown run off right tackle in the third quarter.

Going the Distance, Twice. Steve Fossett set two flight records onboard the single-engine Virgin Atlantic GlobalFlyer in 2006:

First, he flew the longest non-stop distance for an aircraft (25,766 mi.), arriving in Bournemouth, England, on **Feb. 11**, 76 hours, 42 min., 55 sec. after leaving NASA's Kennedy Space Center at Cape Canaveral, FL, and circling the globe twice.

A month later, he set the world record for distance over a closed circuit (same start-end point) without landing. Beginning in Salina, KS, on **March 14**, he flew 25,293.95 miles around the globe back to Salina. The trip took 74 hours, 26 min., 26 sec.

The GlobalFlyer was retired to the Smithsonian's Steven F. Udvar-Hazy Center outside Washington, DC, on **May 23**.

Olympic Golden Oldies. Some elder Olympians taught the "youths" a lesson in Torino. Duff Gibson (Canada) became the oldest athlete to win gold in an individual Winter Olympic event, **Feb. 17**. He won the skeleton at 39 years, 150 days with a combined time of 1:55.88, beating teammate Jeff Pain by 0.26 seconds.

Hilde Pedersen (Norway) placed third in the 10km classical cross-country skiing on **Feb. 16**, becoming the oldest woman ever to medal in a Winter Olympics, at 41 years, 189 days.

Scott Baird (U.S.) became the oldest Winter Games competitor and medalist at 54 years, 293 days, when team America took bronze in curling on **Feb. 24**.

Speedy Shani. Shani Davis (U.S.) won the 1000m speedskating on **Feb. 18** to become the first black person ever to win an individual gold medal in a Winter Olympics.

Millions Want to be Millionaires. Millions of people in 28 states tried to get a piece of the record-setting $365 million Powerball jackpot on **Feb. 18**. A ticket shared by eight coworkers at a ConAgra Foods processing plant in Lincoln, NE, was the only match. The winners, aged 26 to 56, chose the option of splitting $177.3 million cash upfront ($124.1 million after taxes, or $15.5 million each).

iTuning In. The billionth song was downloaded on **Feb. 23** from the Apple iTunes® Music Store since it opened on April 28, 2003. Alex Ostrovsky from West Bloomfield, MI, purchased Coldplay's "Speed of Sound."

Buy Me Some Peanuts and Cracker Jack. For the third year straight, Major League Baseball set a new single-season overall attendance record with 76,043,902 tickets bought to games between **April 1 and Oct. 1**. The New York Yankees set an all-time record with a total attendance of 4,248,067. The St. Louis Cardinals sold out every game (3,407,104). The Boston Red Sox, Chicago White Sox, Los Angeles Angels, Los Angeles Dodgers, and New York Mets all set franchise records.

Like Great-Great-Grandfather, Like Great-Great-Grandson. Prince Albert II of Monaco became the first member of royalty to reach the North Pole, **April 16**. He traveled the 75 miles from Russia's Camp Barneo to honor his great-great-grandfather, Prince Albert I of Monaco, who explored the Arctic 100 years earlier, and to draw attention to the ice cap melting attributed to global warming.

Codger Dinger. New York Mets pinch hitter and first baseman Julio Franco became the oldest person to hit a home run in Major League Baseball, at 47 years, 240 days on **April 20**. In the top of the eighth inning, Franco hit a two-runner deep into right field off of San Diego Padres reliever Scott Linebrink. He beat a record of 46 years, 357 days set by Philadelphia A's pitcher Jack Quinn on June 27, 1930. Franco extended his record to 48 years, 38 days on **Sept. 30**, when he socked a three-run homer.

Finnish Hard Rock Triumphs. Finland's selection for Eurovision, an annual Europop Olympics of sorts whose past winners have included ABBA and Celine Dion, won for the first time on **May 20**. Lordi, the first heavy metal group to win, scored a record high of 292 points. Lordi performed "Hard Rock Hallelujah" as they typically would, masked in grotesque costumes behind a stream of pyrotechnics.

Aaron Will Always Be First in the Alphabet. On **May 28** in San Francisco, Barry Bonds hit his 715th career home run, surpassing Babe Ruth for all-time career home runs. On Sept. 23, Bonds beat Hank Aaron's National League home run record with 734, and finished the season just 21 shy of Aaron's still-standing career homer record of 755.

Bowlin' with the Guys. Kelly Kulick, 29, became the first woman to qualify for one of the ten full-season exemptions for the Professional Bowling Association 2006-07 Tour on **June 4**. In 45 trial games over five days, she averaged a 224, placing her sixth out of 140 bowlers. The Professional Women's Bowling Association, where Kulick was the 2001 Rookie of the Year, closed in 2003. Women were first allowed in the PBA in April 2004.

Nice Legs. It was reported on **June 8** in *Nature* magazine that the leggiest known creature had been rediscovered after an absence of nearly 80 years. Biologists from East Carolina University found seven specimens of *Illacme plenipes* within a 200-acre plot in San Benito County, CA, its only known habitat. While past researchers had counted up to 750 legs on these millipedes, the highest number of legs found on one in the recent batch was "only" 666.

Senior Senator. After 47 years, 160 days in office, Robert Byrd (D, WV) surpassed Strom Thurmond as the longest serving U.S. senator on **June 12**. His tenure began Jan. 3, 1959. In the Senate he has been majority leader, minority leader, whip, and president pro tempore. He was also a U.S. representative from 1953 until 1959.

Pricey Painting. Ronald S. Lauder, son of cosmetics magnate Estée Lauder, paid $135 million on behalf of the Neue Galerie in Manhattan for a 1907 portrait by Austrian Gustav Klimt, the most yet paid for a painting. The sale was reported **June 19**. The portrait of Adele Bloch-Bauer I was purchased from Maria Altmann, whose family had lost it and four other Klimt pieces to the Nazi regime in 1938. Until recently, the pieces had been held by the Austrian government.

Sure-Shot. Los Angeles Sparks center Lisa Leslie became the first WNBA player to score over 5,000 career points, **June 25**. The six-time All-Star and two-time MVP started the game with 4,999 points and quickly topped 5,000 on a 19-foot jump shot just 53 seconds in. She also scored a personal-best 41 points that game. Leslie finished the season with 5,412 career points.

The Most-Golden Foot. Five minutes into a Round of 16 match against Ghana on **June 27**, Brazilian forward Ronaldo (full name: Ronaldo Luís Nazário de Lima) scored a record-setting 15th World Cup tournament goal, 8 years and 11 days after his first goal against Morocco on June 16, 1998. Ronaldo's chance to extend his record ended when France eliminated Brazil in the next match.

Riding High. The section of the Qinghai-Tibet railway connecting most major Chinese cities with Lhasa, Tibet, via Xining in Qinghai Province opened on **July 1**. As it cuts across the mountains of Tibet, it reaches a record altitude of

16,640 feet in the Tanggula Pass. Extra oxygen is generated in the trains to counteract the thin atmosphere. The line includes the world's highest rail tunnel (16,100 ft) and highest station (16,627 ft—at Tanggula).

Tuning Out. Nielsen Media Research reported that **July 3-9, 2006** was the least-watched week for network prime-time TV in recorded history. CBS, ABC, NBC, and Fox averaged 20.8 million viewers, surpassing the low set in the last week of July 2005 of 21.5 million viewers. Only one show was watched by more than 10 million people; *America's Got Talent* (NBC) drew 12 million.

Weiner Winner. Japanese competitive eater Takeru Kobayashi, 27, won his 6th consecutive Nathan's Hot Dog eating contest on **July 4**. He beat his own record by a quarter hot dog, eating 53.75 (buns and all) in 12 minutes, just eking past second-place Joey Chestnut, who finished with 52.

Marathon Tennis. A quarterfinals doubles match at Wimbledon on **July 4-5** was the longest doubles match in any Grand Slam tournament, and the longest match of any sort at Wimbledon. Daniel Nestor (Canada) and Mark Knowles (Bahamas) beat Simon Aspelin (Sweden) and Todd Perry (Australia) after 6 hours, 9 min. The score was 5-7, 6-3, 6-7, 6-3, 23-21. The last set took more than 3 hours. Play was suspended on the first night after 4 hours, 34 min. The previous record for a doubles match was 5 hours, 29 min., set in 1990.

Last Red Mayor. Frank Zeidler, the last Socialist to run a major American city, died on **July 7** at 93. Zeidler was the last of three Socialist mayors of Milwaukee known as the "Sewer Socialists" for their dedication to quality-of-life issues. He served three terms from 1948 through 1960.

Pain at the Pump. Conflict in Nigeria and between Israel and Lebanon sent the price of crude oil futures on the New York Mercantile Exchange to a record close of $77.03 a barrel on **July 14**.

From Paul to Shakira; Pop Plug Pulled. The BBC broadcasted the 2,204th and last episode of its weekly music chart show *Top of the Pops* on **July 30**. TOTP first aired Jan. 1, 1964, and the first Number One on *Top of the Pops* was "I Wanna Hold Your Hand" by The Beatles. The 42-year, 210-day run is the longest for any music television show. The last #1 hit was Shakira's "Hips Don't Lie" featuring Wyclef Jean.

50 by 30. At 30 years, 219 days, Tiger Woods became the youngest golfer to achieve 50 PGA tour wins on **Aug. 6** at the Buick Open, his 210th Tour event. He was only the seventh person to reach the milestone and broke the record set by a 33-year-old Jack Nicklaus back in 1973.

Grand Slams. Cleveland Indians designated hitter Travis Hafner tied Don Mattingly's record for most grand slams in a single season on **Aug. 13**. Hafner hit his sixth grand slam during the first inning of what would be a 13-0 shutout against the Kansas City Royals.

Total Recall. On **Aug. 15** Dell made the largest consumer electronics recall ever announced. The 4.1 million lithium-ion batteries made by Sony for notebook computers distributed internationally since April 2004 were prone to overheat and catch fire.

Tallest Tree. A new record was set for tallest living tree when "Hyperion," a coast redwood (*Sequoia sempervirens*), was found on **Aug. 25** in Redwood National Park near Eureka, CA. Hyperion, discovered by Chris Atkins and Michael Taylor, was measured at 379.1 feet, more than 10 feet taller than the previous record holder, Stratosphere Giant (368.6 ft), which Atkins discovered in Aug. 2000. Atkins and Taylor found two other trees estimated to be taller than Stratosphere Giant: Helios (376.3 ft) and Icarus (371.2 ft).

Hot Hot Hot! The average temperature in the contiguous United States from **January through August** was the warmest yet recorded (57.6° F), passing a 1934 record of 57.2° F. January and April both set record highs. In **January**, the average temperature was 39.5° F, 8.5°F above the normal. In **April**, the average temperature was 56.5° F, 4.5° F above the normal. **July** was the second warmest on record.

Set in Stone. A group of Mexican and American archaeologists discovered the oldest known writing in the Americas, reported in *Science* magazine **Sept. 15**. The stone block was inscribed by the Olmec with 28 distinct symbols, some repeated a few times, presumably with different meanings. It was dated to about 900 BCE and unearthed at Cascajal, Mexico, in 1999.

Saving the Best for Last. In his last home game of the regular season, San Diego Padres pitcher Trevor Hoffman threw his 479th save **Sept. 24**, passing a record set by Lee Smith in 1997. Hoffman retired the Pittsburgh batters 1-2-3 in the ninth, striking out two. He finished his 14th season with 46 saves (482 total).

Records and Firsts to Look for in 2007

Texas Tech Men's college basketball coach Bobby Knight was set to overtake the record for **most NCAA career wins**. He entered the 2006-07 season 10 behind the record of 879 wins (254 losses) held by Dean Smith (North Carolina, 1962-97). Knight, who also coached the Army team (1966-71) and Indiana Univ. (1972-2000), had 869 wins (350 losses) at the beginning of the season, third-most behind Smith and Adolph Rupp (876-190).

For the first time, the NBA will hold its **all-star game in a city that doesn't have a team**. The 56th annual game was scheduled for Feb. 18 at the Univ. of Nevada, Las Vegas's Thomas & Mack Center.

The Simpsons Movie was scheduled to be released in July 2007. *The Simpsons* is already the longest running and most successful animated TV series. The film would need to bring in more than $436.7 million to surpass *Shrek 2* (2004) as the **most lucrative animated movie** at the box office in North America.

San Francisco Giants outfielder Barry Bonds was on track to beat the career **home run record**, which has been held by Hank Aaron since April 8, 1974. Bonds hit 26 home runs in 2006 and was 21 short of Aaron's record of 755.

The Integrated Ocean Drilling Program (IODP) was to start full-scale operations in Sept. 2007. The deep sea drilling vessel *CHIKYU* ("earth" in Japanese), **the largest ocean drilling tool**, will dig 23,000 feet below the seafloor in waters over 8,000 feet deep. It will collect 30-foot core samples at incremental depths from the ocean crust until it reaches the molten mantle (expected in about 2012), where scientists hope to find an environment similar to that of primordial Earth.

The FIFA Women's World Cup was to be held in China Sept. 10-30. Only the U.S. team has won **multiple World Cup championships** (1991, 1999). They also won gold at the 2004 Summer Olympics.

The Large Hadron Collider being built by the European Organization for Nuclear Research (CERN) was to go into operation in November. The ring-shaped tunnel beneath the French-Swiss border measures nearly 17 miles in circumference, making it the **largest scientific instrument in the world**. It will be used to observe what happens when high-energy streams of protons and heavier particles collide.

It was widely believed that the seventh and final Harry Potter book would be released sometime in 2007. Author J.K. Rowling's previous book in the series, *Harry Potter and the Half-Blood Prince*, set a **record for one-day sales** (fiction) on July 16, 2005, when about 6.9 million copies were sold in the U.S.

By the end of 2007, Wisconsin, "America's Dairyland," may no longer be the big cheese. California's **cheese production** had more than doubled since 1995, reaching 2.14 billion pounds in 2005, 270 million pounds shy of Wisconsin's 2.41 billion pounds. California was already the nation's top producer of fluid milk, butter, ice cream, and nonfat dry milk. In the first half of 2006, Wisconsin dairy farms made 1.2 billion pounds of cheese. California made 1.1 billion pounds.

The Oil Price Rollercoaster

By Geoffrey M. Horn

Geoffrey M. Horn, a freelance author and editor, writes frequently on political and economic affairs.

"Gas price panic!" "Pain at the pump!" Headline writers could hardly contain themselves during the spring and summer of 2006, as the price of a barrel of crude oil broke the $75 barrier, U.S. gasoline prices flirted with $3 a gallon, and the $50 fill-up became commonplace. On July 14, as Israeli military operations in Lebanon against the Shiite Muslim group Hezbollah fueled fears of a wider war, the price for a barrel of light sweet crude (the low-sulfur petroleum preferred by refiners as a source of gasoline) settled at $77.03 on the New York Mercantile Exchange—the highest closing price ever. Some analysts predicted $85 or even $90 before the end of the year. But in August, as a truce took hold in Lebanon, oil prices started to sink. By early October, light sweet crude oil prices were around $60 a barrel, less than in January. With gas prices averaging around $2.30 a gallon in the U.S., the short-term spike seemed over—but the long-term problems remained.

Over a Barrel

From the late 1940s through the late 1960s, world oil markets remained relatively stable. Since the early 1970s, however, prices have moved up and down much more rapidly. The first major price spike came in 1973, when Arab oil producers imposed an embargo on the U.S. and other countries that had supported Israel during the Yom Kippur war. A second spike came in the late 1970s and early '80s, when an Islamic revolution in Iran was followed by the outbreak of war between Iran and Iraq. Iraq's 1990 takeover of Kuwait triggered another price spike, as did the U.S.-led invasion that ousted Saddam Hussein in 2003.

The connection between oil price volatility and Middle East upheavals is no accident. Of the world's proved petroleum reserves (estimated at nearly 1.3 trillion barrels at the start of 2006, according to *Oil and Gas Journal*), the Middle East harbors almost 58%. Iran, Iraq, and Kuwait together account for about 27% of the world's proved reserves, and Saudi Arabia—long cultivated as an ally by the U.S., but more recently a breeding ground for Islamic extremists—holds nearly 21%. In second quarter 2006, these four countries produced a combined average of 17.7 million barrels of oil per day, accounting for about 24% of the world oil supply.

Anxiety over Iran's nuclear program, the ongoing insurgency and sectarian violence in Iraq, and Israel's war in Lebanon all roiled the oil markets during spring and summer. And those weren't the only oil-rich countries experiencing political turmoil. Of the five leading U.S. oil import suppliers—Canada, Mexico, Saudi Arabia, Venezuela, and Nigeria—only in Canada did stability prevail.

In Nigeria in July and August, insurgents attacked oil installations and kidnapped foreign petroleum workers. In Saudi Arabia, terrorists tried but failed Feb. 24 to blow up the Abqaiq facility, the world's largest oil-processing plant. In Mexico, hundreds of thousands of demonstrators took to the streets beginning in July, to protest what they claimed was a stolen presidential election. And in Venezuela, the government of leftist Pres. Hugo Chavez faced domestic protests and had stormy relations with the U.S.

Prices respond to environmental changes as well as political events. In late August 2005, for example, Hurricane Katrina hammered oil-drilling and refinery platforms in the Gulf of Mexico. The following week, on Sept. 5, the national average price for a gallon of regular unleaded gasoline hit $3.057 —the highest ever recorded by the American Automobile Association. Conversely, a milder than expected hurricane season contributed to the slide in crude oil and gasoline prices a year later.

Tight Supplies, Big Profits

On an average day in 2005, according to the U.S. Energy Information Administration (EIA), the world produced 84.34 million barrels of crude petroleum and consumed 83.84 million barrels. The net excess of production over consumption averaged less than 1% of the daily world supply. With a margin that slim, even minor uncertainties can have measurable impact on oil markets.

Managing such uncertainties is part of how oil traders and petroleum companies make their money. Traders don't buy oil the way a driver buys a tank of gas. Typically, on the U.S. "spot market," traders buy and sell crude oil in units of 1,000 barrels. Each sales contract specifies the grade of oil, the price, and a physical delivery date, most often within the coming month. Layered on top of these basic oil contracts are a host of other financial investments.

Energy trading has boomed in recent years, propelled by pension fund managers and other large investors who trade in oil contracts as a financial asset. "The idea that speculators can systematically push the price up or down is wrong," Robert J. Weiner, a professor of international business at George Washington University, told *The New York Times* in April. "But they can make it more volatile. They can't raise water levels, but they can create waves."

Oil companies have profited from recent spikes in prices. Exxon Mobil, the top-ranking firm on the Fortune 500, reported a profit of $10.36 billion for April-June 2006, up 36% from the comparable quarter in 2005. Chevron, which ranked 4th on the Fortune 500, had net earnings of $4.35 billion, its highest quarterly profit ever.

Oil Industry Timeline

1848   The first modern oil well is drilled near Baku, Azerbaijan.

1859   The first U.S. commercial oil well begins operations at Titusville (PA).

1882-1911   Through the Standard Oil Trust and its successors, John D. Rockefeller and his partners hold a virtual monopoly over the U.S. oil industry.

1897   The world's first offshore oil well is drilled at Summerland (CA), near Santa Barbara.

1901   The Spindletop gusher near Beaumont sparks a Texas oil boom.

1903   Using a gasoline-powered engine, the Wright Brothers make their first successful airplane flight at Kitty Hawk (NC).

1908   Henry Ford launches the Model T, introducing the era of inexpensive, mass-produced, gasoline-fueled automobiles, which average between 20 and 30 miles per gallon in fuel efficiency.

1913   In Pittsburgh, the Gulf oil company opens the nation's first drive-up gas station.

1939   Commercial production of nylon begins, giving a big boost to the petrochemical industry.

1950   The U.S. is the world's leading source of petroleum, producing 11 barrels of crude oil for every barrel it imports.

1960   Iran, Iraq, Kuwait, Saudi Arabia, and Venezuela form the Organization of Petroleum Exporting Countries (OPEC). Five more countries join in the 1960s, as OPEC's share of world oil production expands to more than 50%.

1973-74   An oil embargo and output cuts by Arab OPEC members produce a fourfold spike in petroleum prices, from $3 to $12 a barrel.

1977   The Trans-Alaska pipeline begins carrying crude oil from Prudhoe Bay.

1994   For the first time, yearly U.S. oil imports exceed domestic output.

2004   The U.S. consumes more than 20.7 million barrels of oil per day, 25% of the world total. China's consumes 6.4 million barrels per day, double the 1994 figure.

2005   Hurricane Katrina damages petroleum installations in the Gulf of Mexico, sending U.S. gasoline prices above $3 a gallon.

2006   Crude oil trades briefly at more than $77 a barrel.

Thirst for Oil

Short-term fluctuations aside, upward pressures on petroleum prices reflect a deeper uncertainty. Most experts believe the world's thirst for oil will eventually outrun supply. The key question is: How soon?

Oil is often called the lifeblood of the modern economy. In the U.S., which consumes about one-fourth of the annual world oil output, refineries and petrochemical complexes transform crude petroleum into an astonishing array of materials. Each 42-gallon barrel of crude oil yields approximately 19.7 gallons of gasoline, 10 gallons of diesel fuel and heating oil, 4 gallons of jet fuel, 1.7 gallons of heavy fuel oil, 1.7 gallons of liquefied petroleum gas, and 7.6 gallons of other products. (The total adds up to more than 44 gallons because refining leads to a reduction in density and a corresponding increase in volume.) The nonfuel products serve as raw materials for thousands of petrochemical items, including crayons, credit cards, perfumes, trash bags, and synthetic rubber tires. The fertilizers and pesticides employed in crop growing, the fuels consumed in mechanical harvesting and transporting, even the plastic bags and cartons used in agricultural packaging require substantial petroleum resources.

Like coal and natural gas, oil is a fossil fuel. Petroleum (literally "rock oil") comes from ancient plant and animal remains on the ocean floor. As these remains were covered by layers of sand and silt, pressure and temperature rose, and the dead organic matter was gradually transformed into the yellow-to-black liquid known as crude oil.

Every barrel of crude oil extracted today took hundreds of millions of years to produce. How fast are we using it up? In 1960, the world consumed about 21 million barrels per day, one-quarter of today's rate. Total worldwide oil consumption has increased at an annual rate of more than 3%. Between 1980 and 2004, China's petroleum use more than tripled and India's nearly quadrupled. The EIA projects that if present trends continue, the world will consume oil at a rate of 118 million barrels a day by 2030. Meeting that demand would mean adding almost the equivalent of four more Saudi Arabias to the world oil supply stream.

"Peaking" into the Future

Concern over the long-term sustainability of an oil-based economy is not new. In March 1956 an American geophysicist, Marion King Hubbert, warned that "the discovery, exploitation, and exhaustion of the fossil fuels will be seen to be but an ephemeral event in the span of recorded history," and predicted that oil production in the U.S. would peak within 25 years. At the time, the U.S. was awash in oil, and Hubbert's fellow scientists greeted his forecast with skepticism. But U.S. crude oil output reached a peak of 3.5 billion barrels in 1970; by 2005, domestic output was less than 1.9 billion barrels, including 315 million from Alaska.

Hubbert's central idea—which he offered as part of a fervent argument in favor of nuclear power—forms the bedrock of what is now generally known as peak-oil theory. Put simply, it holds that at some point in the foreseeable future, world oil output will reach a maximum, after which it will rapidly decline. A global recession, social upheavals, and oil wars could follow.

However, the peak-oil theory is controversial. In a 2005 article in the *Washington Post*, Daniel Yergin, a leading critic of peak oil, pointed to a worldwide expansion of petroleum production capacity that, by 2010, would ease current pressures on petroleum supplies. Yergin, who chairs the Cambridge Energy Research Associates consulting firm, said peak-oil theorists underestimate the extent to which new technologies are making previously inaccessible petroleum resources (such as the vast deposits of bitumen-rich oil sands in Alberta, Canada) more readily available and cost-effective.

Rhetoric and Reality

American politicians have been warning about the nation's fossil-fuel vulnerabilities for more than three decades. In late 1973, in the wake of the Arab oil embargo, the Nixon administration urged voluntary measures, including "gasless Sundays," to conserve gasoline. On Jan. 30, 1977, less than two weeks into his presidency, Jimmy Carter struck a similar note, urging the public to conserve energy during the winter months by turning down thermostats and by wearing "warm clothes indoors, warm underwear, a sweater." Yet, the share of U.S. petroleum supplies represented by imports actually rose from 35% in 1973 to 59% by early 2006.

Pres. George W. Bush joined the chorus in his State of the Union message of Jan. 31, 2006, when he warned that the U.S. was "addicted to oil, which is often imported from unstable parts of the world." He emphasized the need to "move beyond a petroleum-based economy, and make our dependence on Middle Eastern oil a thing of the past."

For years, the Bush administration and some Republican leaders had emphasized dealing with oil-supply problems by expanding domestic drilling, notably in Alaska's Arctic National Wildlife Refuge. In his 2006 State of the Union speech, Bush also endorsed an array of petroleum-substitution measures, including solar and wind power, coal and nuclear technologies, use of ethanol from corn, and, on the more distant horizon, ethanol from wood chips and grass, and hydrogen-powered cars.

Some countries have already taken steps to ease their petroleum addiction. Use of sugarcane waste to produce motor fuel has reduced Brazil's dependence on oil imports; on a visit to Brazil in September, Thomas L. Friedman of *The New York Times* found that a gallon of sugar ethanol in Brazil cost only about half as much at the pump as a gallon of gasoline, enough to make up for ethanol's lower efficiency. In the U.S., switching to smaller, more fuel-efficient vehicles would help. So would increased use of flex-fuel, hybrid, and electric cars, which the Bush administration has endorsed, and tougher mandatory fuel-economy standards, which the administration has opposed. For example, in U.S. government tests of family sedans for the 2007 model year, the Toyota Camry Hybrid averaged 39 miles per gallon in combined city and highway driving, for an estimated annual fuel cost of $887; the Pontiac G6, with its standard gasoline engine, got only 20 mpg, and its estimated fuel cost was almost double that of the hybrid.

Experts differ on when petroleum production will peak and oil prices will spike. But there is broad consensus on the need for a strategy that embraces new extraction technologies, energy conservation, and development of renewable resources as substitutes for fossil fuels. Although such an approach cannot eliminate pain at the pump, it offers a way to avoid the calamitous future that peak-oil theorists fear.

Average Gasoline Prices, 1920-2006

Measured in current dollars, retail gasoline prices on average hit record highs in 2005 and 2006. When the effects of inflation are removed, however, a gallon of gasoline still cost less, on average, than it did in 1981.

Source: U.S. Energy Information Administration

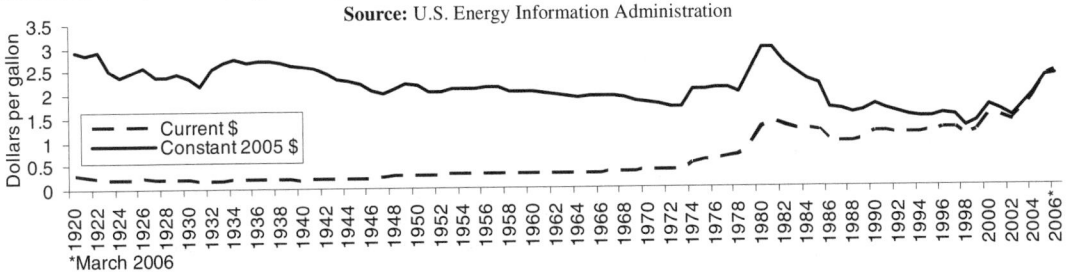

*March 2006

Blogs from Soldiers and Their Families:
Voices of Service to America

Some 12 million Americans keep a blog, according to a 2006 study by the Pew Internet & American Life Project. Blogs are online diaries created by individuals and brought to the Internet through a variety of hosting services such as Blogger and Typepad. At little or no cost to the blogger, text and images—even video—can be uploaded from anywhere. Blogs also provide an opportunity for reader feedback. One entry can inspire arguments, advice, or solidarity from dozens of on-line readers from around the world.

Among the millions who blog are thousands of military personnel and their families who describe day-to-day wartime experiences and thoughts for each other—and for anyone else who might be interested. Milblogging.com, a site that collects, organizes, and features military blogs, was created by J.P. Borda, who blogged from Afghanistan as a National Guard Specialist in 2004-2005. As of Sept. 2006, his site provided links to 1,515 military blogs from writers in 28 countries.

Military bloggers are generally vigilant not to disclose information useful to the enemy, and blogs can be shut down by the military if they compromise operations.

The writings collected here, and used by permission, came from bloggers active as of Sept. 2006. They are the voices of soldiers serving in Iraq and Afghanistan, a recently returned veteran, a "Marine mom" from Indiana, and the wife of a National Guard soldier from South Dakota.

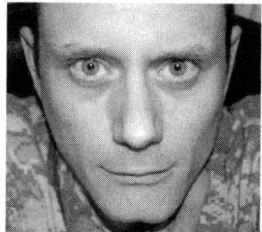

The Will to Exist, *www.willtoexist.com, is a group blog. The author of this entry is Trevor, currently in Baghdad, serving in a public affairs capacity with Multi-National Force—Iraq. He was an active-duty Marine from 1992 to 1996 (Corporal) and has served in the Georgia National Guard (Sergeant) 2005-06. At home in Chattanooga, TN, he is an information technology manager for EMJ Construction.,*

Tuesday, August 1, 2006: BOOOM!!!

This morning I was playing a video game in my hooch (I was awoken early by a boom) when another thunderous BOOOOOOM shook the walls of my trailer. My bed is against the wall, so I moved an inch or so with the concussion blast.

A car bomb had detonated outside a bank in the Karada district just across the river. At last report, we're told, 12 Iraqis died and 18 more were seriously wounded. The victims were Iraqi government employees who were waiting to be paid. Of course, civilians just passing by were also killed. The terrorists here make no attempt whatsoever to limit what military men term collateral damage.

I immediately suited up in full combat gear (which I would have done anyhow in a few minutes) and headed toward the armored humvee we use to get to work. There was no sense continuing to play my video game because immediately after the bomb detonated I heard the distinct crack of AK-47 fire in the nearby area and the thumping vibration of Apache attack helicopters headed for the scene of the carnage. One never knows what will follow the immediate aftermath of such an explosion. Sometimes there are more explosions. Sometimes there are firefights. Always there is chaos. Chaos and I do not get along. I'd rather be moving when the [expletive] hits the fan than sitting still.

As I walked to my vehicle, more small arms fire from very close by emphasized the violence festering in this place where I have made my home for almost a year. A huge cloud of black smoke drifted across the river towards us from the scene of the blast. The area was swarmed with Blackhawks and Apaches. I'm sure our hospital will be busy today.

I've been through so many indirect fire attacks and car bombings now that I've completely lost count. My body's reaction, though, has always been the same. I get a huge rush of adrenaline followed by a few minutes of shaky hands and then I feel exultant because it wasn't me who got blown up. I like being alive. I bet the victims of this morning's attack liked being alive too. I'm sure they had hopes and dreams. Now those have been extinguished. For what? They were fighting for their country, trying to protect their fellow citizens and make a living. They were trying to make Iraq a decent place to live. They died for it.

Missing My Soldier, *www.goedenfamily. blogspot.com, is the blog of Monica Goeden of Vermillion, SD. Her husband Brad, a National Guard SPC who served with the Field Artillery in Iraq, had been on active duty since June 2005, in Baghdad since Oct. 2005, and arrived home Sept. 30, 2006.*

Wednesday, July 19, 2006: A whole lot of random

Today was a whirlwind. I am guessing with all of the stress yesterday and all the stuff I had to do today, things just went by so fast. Hey, it is another day less until Brad is home. Yesterday and today I have received many phone calls from different people. I have had a lot of the "military" people calling to see how I am doing, the battalion commander, a couple of chaplains, and family support people. It seems like I would hang up with one person and someone else would be beeping in or my cell would ring. Then you add family and friends who have heard, and wanted to see how Brad and I were doing. It is great to know so many people care! Brad's work sent out an email so no one would worry more than needed, as rumors spread quite quickly. When Brad called to tell me yesterday that he had gotten hurt, he had asked if I had heard it from anyone else yet. I guess someone made a call out on their cell phone to home and told the news or something. I am very thankful I heard it from Brad first! Brad said he was going to stay in his room to sleep tonight as he had gotten his area cleaned up pretty good he said. He told me he needed to make a trip to the PX though to get a few things, one of the things would be new pillows. His pillows have shrapnel in them I guess. Not too comfy I wouldn't think!

Today I had to explain to Brooke that daddy got hurt. I wasn't even going to tell her, but I guess she had overheard some phone calls today. I tried to explain that daddy was going to be okay, that he just got a cut on his chest. Brooke is our sensitive child and was very upset about her daddy getting hurt. She asked if her daddy was bleeding, and I explained that it was already healing and daddy was not bleeding anymore. I think she feels better about it now. Gracie wanted to send daddy spongebob band aids. How cute would that be? Hopefully he will have some time to use the webcams tomorrow so the girls can see him, and then they will be okay.

Strong Ideas, *majorstrong.blogspot.com, is the work of U.S. Army Major Arnold Strong, currently serving in Kabul, Afghanistan, as a public affairs officer. Major Strong has been in Afghanistan since June 2006 and plans to return to the U.S. in June 2007.*

Thursday, July 06, 2006: Relief in Place, First Loss and Kites

On the Fourth of July, we assumed the mission of CJTF Phoenix. It was a beautiful day preceded by the rarest of Afghan events a double rainbow foreshadowing the polychromatic light of the upcoming leadership of Task Force Phoenix. It was a great day for all of us. On July fifth, almost exactly 24 hours into the mission, we had our first casualty. It made for a serious and unpleasant welcome to the reality of the environment we have now entered. 1st Sgt. (posthumously promoted to Sgt.

It is almost 3 a.m. and Brooke has school in the morning... I better try to get some sleep. Have a good day Bradley and I love you tons! Take care of you always!

Thanks for the great comments! It is good to know others are praying for his safety too!

Maj.) Jeffrey McLochlin had served with Phoenix for ten months as an embedded trainer. He was what we call a "4.25 guy" meaning that he had served with Phoenix IV from about a fourth of the way through the mission and was going to remain with us for about two more months. Like the motto of the 75th Ranger Regiment he once served within, he was leading the way until the end. He was killed by enemy small arms fire. His legacy was that of a beloved leader of soldiers both U.S. and Afghan, a loving father and husband, and professional police officer. He was 42 years old. That evening, several of us joined Lt. Col. Gregory Moore, my predecessor, in his last mission. We drove up to the top of Mausoleum Hill to distribute kites to Afghan children. They were very nice kites, professional quality nylon with a variety of shapes and sizes. The kids loved them and were so happy to fly them in the blistering wind. It was almost too extreme to get them into the air. I thought of First Sergeant Jeffrey McLochlin's spirit flying high over the Afghan countryside where his spirit left this world, and the children he left behind. Fly on, First Sergeant. Fly on.

Daily Life of a Marine Mom, *faefyre.spaces.live.com, is the blog of Tami Becker from Lucerne, IN. She is a mother of three who is an Internet Technology manager at a small Midwestern company. She is an active member of Marine parents/family groups in Indiana as well as ABATE (American Bikers Aimed Towards Education). She writes about issues affecting Marines and Marine families, especially about her youngest son Eric, who has returned from service in the Marine infantry in Iraq. Eric is scheduled to go overseas with the Marine infantry in the near future for his second deployment.*

March 17, 2006: Life of a Marine Mom, entry 99

I heard from another Marine mother once that deployment is similar to being pregnant with that child all over again. Coming to the end of this seemingly endless (at least to me) first deployment of my son has given me a much better insight into the feeling that this mom was describing.

As we near the end of the 3/7s [3rd Battalion, 7th Marines] time in Iraq for now, I have found myself becoming increasingly tired and...well...just plain fried. The first few weeks were frantic. Every time I heard about someone being killed over there I panicked. I came very close to losing it a couple times. Once, a few weeks after they were in place, we lost several young men out of a platoon that my son has ties to. The day after that I ended up in the emergency room of our local hospital with severe chest pains. Well, I kept telling them it was just a combination of stress and asthma (along with a touch of costochondritis, a condition where the cartilage in your chest gets inflamed) but being on the nether side of 40, better safe than sorry. They ran the tests on my heart, and even though it felt like it was breaking, physically it was fine.

After that little incident I gave in and went to my doctor and asked to be prescribed a mild tranquilizer. That got me through the next few panic attacks without a lot of physical symptoms, we won't talk about the heart-ache I still endured though. I am still on that first bottle of tranquilizers that he prescribed me so I did well in maintaining control most of the time. Shoot... I have almost half a bottle left, but I realized that I needed a little help and I was willing to admit it to myself. An important milestone for someone that likes to think that they can handle anything (yes I am a control-freak).

The pressure to write tributes to each and every young man we lost during this tour from the 3/7 in OIF3 (Operation Iraqi Freedom III) is still overwhelming. But it is a pressing need that I can't shake and actually, wouldn't want to if I could. If I can do nothing else for these men that were willing to die for me, I can at least honor their memory in the only way I can. My heart and soul feels deep sorrow for the families of the young men we have lost and my prayers are with those families always. Unfortunately, I still have more to do yet since we in the 3/7 lost two more of these fine and honorable young men in the last couple of week, LCpl Kristen K. Figueroa, 20, of Honolulu, Hawaii and Cpl. Adam Zanutto, 26, of Walker Basin, CA. Their tributes will be posted here soon.

Let's see...I was talking about the similarity to pregnancy that a deployment of your child seems to be originally in this post. In any case... as it draws nearer to the time for these young men who have seen too much and done more than enough already to be birthed from the bus that delivers them back to 29 Palms [Marine Corps Air Ground Combat Center], I think every Marine mother has been overwhelmed and worn down by the constant stress of fearing for their safe delivery. With prayers and determination we have suffered through seven months of fear, fearing the worse too much and yet hoping for the best. There's the similarity of joy, upon hearing the voice of our loved ones on the crackling connection of a SAT phone or a regular phone during (at least in my case) their infrequent opportunities to call home, like a soft movement in the womb; of pain, trying to comfort the ones we know that lost their babies before they could be delivered home safely; of strength, hearing and feeling the pride our sons bear with them on a daily basis, so similar to feeling the hard press of false labor that makes us believe that they will be delivered back to us safely.

And now, as I come so close to the actual arrival home of my son once again, I am exhausted, tired, no longer able to feel the stress so much because it is so close to the end, and I'm just wanting it to be over so I can hold him in my arms again. The fear isn't totally gone yet though. Till the day I see him, he will be held tightly in my prayers with his brothers.

Please keep them all in your prayers during this final transition back to their home. They are still in Iraq and still bored... but for now all is good.

Semper Fi and God bless you all.

Just Another Thunderhorse Roughneck!,
www.pete623.blogspot.com, is the blog of Pete Puebla, an Arizona National Guard Sergeant currently serving in Baghdad.

Friday, March 10, 2006

I am now a combat veteran. We got hit by an IED, and I'm not just talking about the Platoon either. I'm talking about our Humvee. It got hit. Me, I, we. We were within 10 feet of the thing. How we survived without a scratch, I don't know. The Humvee wasn't damaged and no one got hurt. No broken windshield, damaged body, no cuts or concussions. Thank GOD. We all made it in one piece. We pulled up right on the darn thing. We were just sitting there then all of a sudden there it was, POW! I immediately got down. I knew we had got hit but I didn't expect it to be so close. It had our name on it. We were engulfed in a cloud of smoke and debris.

Some of the guys in other trucks that saw it happen thought we were gone for sure. Some said that they couldn't even see our Humvee at the time of the explosion. Some thought that our Humvee had got blown to pieces and thought that the turret was the hood of the vehicle. I couldn't seen anything myself for a few seconds. It was freaking loud too. It was so loud I felt the vibrations in my chest. What can I say about it? It was like something exploded. Obviously.

I don't see why T-Rex didn't see it. I told him after it exploded too, "Didn't you see it! It was right in front of you!" I was alright after a little while though. I regained my composure immediately since this wasn't the first experience in the field. I still can't believe that he drove right up on it. Unbelievable. And to have us all walk away like nothing happened, miracle. I don't know why. That thing had our name on it. Heck we were right next to it and T-Rex and the Lieutenant had front row seats. They were facing the thing when it went off.

Divine intervention is all I thought about. That's all I thought about all day. Hadji [a colloquial military term for an Arab person] must be wondering what happened. I don't know how and I can't explain it myself. We were in a cloud of smoke. How could we just drive away, like nothing happened? Hadji probably thought we were laughing at him. Instead, I think we were all thanking GOD for giving us another day. How unbelievable. A miracle.

It's changed my perspective on life. To be thankful for everyday we have. To cherish what we as Americans take for granted. Thanks be to God.

American Babble: Journey of a Musician,
www.AmericanBabble.com, is the blog of Jami Gibbs, an Illinois National Guard Specialist in a medical unit working in communications. She served in Iraq from Nov. 2005 to Oct. 2006. At home in Chicago, she is a performing and recording musician.

Tower Guard Finale: Journal 08/19/06

This is my triumphant and often dreamt of end of tower guard blog. My total rotation comes to 4 weeks of the year long deployment. This last week wasn't nearly as memorable as some of the others, but I blame that on my lack of caring.

With repetition comes lethargy. This time around, I stripped all non-essential items from my body because every ounce counts when climbing up that God-forsaken ladder. I dumped my neck protector, first aid pouch, extra magazine that is normally strapped to my M-4, and the stupid arm protectors that look like big wings on our body armor. (In my opinion they cause more harm than good because they allow zero arm movement. Try to climb a ladder or raise your weapon without the use of your shoulders.)

I've already mentioned previously how hot it was up there, so I won't reiterate.

Highlights of the week:
• A dead cow floating in the moat in front of the tower.
• Iraqi children jumping in the moat to cool off in the late August heat. They really made me smile. It reminded me of cooling off in the lake during hot Chicago summers.
• Seeing the C-Ram gun go off to defend the base against a mortar attack. It was like the 4th of July. The gun shoots off something like 300 rounds a second and half of those rounds are tracers. It looks like a red laser beam shooting out into the sky. It's so fast that the sound of the rounds being fired are delayed by a good 3 seconds. Then after the tracers fade off, all you hear is "pop pop pop pop pop pop pop". Very cool in a macho sort of "America! [Expletive] yeah!" sort of way.
• Slamming a round into my chamber when they announce "red status". It's so un-cool to get excited over a loaded weapon, but come on! I can admit to it. It got my heart pumping.
• Hearing the Howitzer gun batteries return fire. That deep thud that I may never feel in my stomach again after I leave this place. Watching the flashing of light from the Howitzer rounds landing in the distance through night vision goggles.
• Waving at the little girls who are herding their sheep, goats, and donkeys back to safety. This really amazes me. Every day three little girls would herd 30 or so animals back to their village. I estimated their ages to be between 8 and 10. They liked to stop for a moment in front of our tower to wave and say something in Arabic. My partner and I swore they said something about buying a watch. Who the hell knows.

So... that's the fairly anticlimactic end. For the rest of my life, I'll never have to do anything like that again. I didn't have to fire my weapon once. I only had one life-threatening incident. I did everything I was supposed to do and did it well. My training never failed me once. And now the first chapter is closed in this book of deployment.

American Citizen Soldier, americancitizen soldier.blogspot.com, is the work of "Buck Sargent," an infantry team leader and noncommissioned officer on active duty in Baghdad for the U.S. Army. Previously deployed to Afghanistan from 2003 to 2004 in support of Operation Enduring Freedom, he is currently serving throughout Iraq on a year-plus combat tour.

May 20, 2006: CSI: IRAQ

...The respect for and protection of civil liberties is clearly important within a free society, especially such a fragile one on the brink of civilized adolescence like Iraq. Yet as Justice Robert Jackson once observed, a constitution is not a suicide pact. You won't have a civilization to protect if anarchy is allowed to run rampant.

There are times when it appears we may have exported to the Iraqis some of the more onerous aspects of our system as well as the more enlightened ones; specifically the coddling of criminals. When initially briefed on all the necessary red tape that came with detaining and processing the bad guys before we deployed, the running joke of the company was "take no prisoners—there's less paperwork."*

*(Relax, moonbats. This didn't involve the SecDef or an Executive Order. It was only a joke.)

But the humor recedes when you come to find you're often dealing with a 50/50 chance of conviction in Iraqi courtrooms (at best). Not only do you have to worry about being shot at or blown up again next week, you have to worry about the exact same guy behind the trigger. Same time... same place... same guy.

This revolving door of catch and release is a common frustration among soldiers and Iraqi citizens alike. Nothing is more demoralizing than making a righteous snare of a known terrorist than the knowledge that he was promptly released by a Baghdad magistrate due to "lack of evidence" or an administrative snafu. Three weeks later he's back on the streets planting bombs. The absurdity of it all forces troops in combat to often have to think and act more like Eliot Ness than Audie Murphy. (Has anyone thought to look into Zarqawi's back taxes? I'm just putting that out there...)

Our unit had steeled itself for a brutal year-long experience; something along the lines of Tour of Duty. Yet the reality of what we experienced was closer to a bizarre mix of CSI, CHiPs, and Dragnet, with a nod to "Iraqi Vice" and "Magnum, P.IR." thrown in for good measure.

Sure, there were the midnight raids and hit & run attacks, the intermittent IEDs and too-close-for-comfort sniper fire. Over the previous nine months across the north of Iraq our brigade has suffered over 230 wounded and lost 14 soldiers—10 to hostile fire. But despite what you see on television, the following actions were far more commonplace:

Explosive residue testing. Crime scene photography. Eyewitness sworn statements. Evidence collection. Forensics "cleanup" (of Kentucky Fried Terrorists). Onsite line-ups. Stake-outs, snitches, and sting operations. Electronic surveillance. Prisoner transport. Route overwatch. Counter-propaganda distribution. Get-out-the-vote drives.

Vehicle checkpoints. Dismounted foot patrols. Curfew enforcement.

Traffic direction. Ballot integrity escorts. Bootleg gasoline interdiction. If we could have found one, we may have even "raided" a speakeasy or two.

Technically, it's still a war. Troops are still in contact, and the enemy is still out there. But one can't help but feel at times like a cop with just a really bad beat.

A Soldier's Thoughts, www.misoldierthoughts.blogspot.com is the blog of Zachary Scott-Singley, a veteran who was a Sergeant in the Army's 3rd Infantry Division (as an Arabic translator). He had 2 tours of duty in Iraq and was in the army for 6 years. Married to Tara, he is the father of Jacob and Linnea.

Tuesday, August 29, 2006: Memorial Day

I cried. It was Memorial Day and it hit me so hard, my first Memorial Day since leaving the Army. She watched me and felt helpless as I sat there and quietly broke down in long silent sobs as the memories came flooding back and the guilt started again. My wife didn't know exactly what to do, she made sure my son and daughter were still playing together in the other room and she held me.

She suggested we go to my father's house so that I could talk to him. He had served in Vietnam and I knew he would know what I was going through. I drove without saying a word as I turned on the radio to NPR and listened to vets talk about those they lost, they had one vet for each war since World War I. I drove with big rolling tears quietly so that my children wouldn't know that their father was so weak right then.

I saw my father in his backyard watering the grass and as I walked up to him Tara drove off with the kids. In a heap I crumpled when he turned to me and I couldn't make it stop. Memories I thought I had filed away came flying back hitting me and without control I finally sobbed aloud as he walked over and extended his hand.

The only thing he said just then was, "you feel guilty don't you?" He knew without even needing to ask. I was so very grateful for him at that moment. Not to have to talk about it and try to explain, just being able to have someone understand without asking anything was like gold. After a few minutes I calmed down and asked him if it was ever that hard for him. He told me it was. The memories and feeling that guilt for coming back alive while so many others have died both soldiers and civilians. That was all I could think about that day, why me? God, why did you let me live when you took so many others? But it wasn't God; it was us, mankind that did this.

My father helped me put myself back together piece by piece until I felt complete again and like that it was over. The rest of the day was uneventful, but in the back of my mind I realize that the guilt is still there, it always was I just didn't see it until that day. I love you dad and I know why you came back alive from Vietnam. You came back because I needed you.

2006 WORLD ALMANAC NEWS QUIZ

1. On Sept. 13 the largest known dwarf planet, 2003 UB313, was officially named:

  a. Xena   b. Eris
  c. Sleepy   d. Dysnomia

2. Which country won the most medals in the XX Winter Olympics, held in February?

  a. Germany   b. United States
  c. Russia   d. Jamaica

3. Australian conservationist Steve Irwin, the "Crocodile Hunter," died while filming a documentary on Sept. 4, after being attacked by which creature?

  a. alligator   b. shark
  c. stingray   d. crocodile

4. After two months of controversy, who was named on Sept. 5 the winner in Mexico's presidential race?

  a. Vicente Fox   b. Felipe Calderón
  c. Andrés Manuel   d. Al Gore
     López Obrador

5. Who admitted Sept. 7 to having been the primary source behind leaking the identity of covert CIA officer Valerie Plame?

  a. Richard Armitage   b. Dick Cheney
  c. Libby Lewis   d. I. Lewis "Scooter" Libby

6. A port management company planned to take over key U.S. ports, and then pulled the offer Mar. 9 after many in the U.S. objected. The company is owned by the government of which United Arab Emirate?

  a. Abu Dhabi   b. Dubai
  c. Ajman   d. Shariqah

7. Which of the following national leaders appointed his brother to a top government post?

  a. Cuba's Fidel Castro   b. U.S.'s George W. Bush
  c. Poland's Lech Kaczynski   d. Thailand's Thaksin
                               Shinawatra

8. Newspaper cartoon caricatures of the Prophet Muhammad prompted violent protests across the Muslim world in February. In which country did the cartoons originate?

  a. France   b. Turkey
  c. Denmark   d. Norway

9. In his Jan. 31 State of the Union Address, U.S. President George W. Bush asked America to break an addiction to which of the following?

  a. credit card spending   b. illegal drugs
  c. pretzels   d. oil

10. In May, the Iraqi parliament approved the first elected government under its new constitution. Who was the prime minister, sworn in May 20?

  a. Nouri Kamel al-Maliki   b. Jalal Talabani
  c. Mahmoud Ahmadinejad   d. Tariq Aziz

11. Who was confirmed in May to be the new director of the Central Intelligence Agency?

  a. Bill Nye, Science Guy   b. Lt. Gen. Michael Hayden
  c. Porter Goss   d. John Negroponte

12. Which of these fighters were World Heavyweight title holders in Oct. 2006?

  a. Wladimir Klitschko   b. Nicolay Valuev
  c. Oleg Maskaev   d. Joe Lewis

13. In which nation was Shiloh Nouvel Jolie-Pitt born on May 27?

  a. United States   b. France
  c. Namibia   d. Mauritania

14. On July 19, President Bush exercised the first veto of his presidency. What was the subject of the legislation?

  a. mountain-bike regulation   b. domestic surveillance
  c. immigration   d. stem cell research

15. Match the nation or area with the political party that won an election there in 2006.

  a. Israel   f. Hamas
  b. Mexico   g. National Action Party
  c. Italy   h. Conservative Party
  d. Palestinian Authority   i. Kadima
  e. Canada   j. The Union Coalition

16. Which African nation on July 30 held its first multiparty elections for president and parliament in 46 years?

  a. Republic of the Congo   b. Democratic Republic of
                                     the Congo
  c. Liberia   d. Republican Republic of
                                     the Congo

17. Ford Motor Co. announced on Jan. 23 that it had plans to cut about one-third of its work force. How many jobs were to be cut?

  a. 1,000   b. 35,000
  c. 80,000   d. 200,000

18. On Oct. 3, 2006, the Dow Jones Industrial Average topped a record set in January 2000. What was the new record?

  a. 10,233.22   b. 15,554.36
  c. 11,727.34   d. 12,345.67

19. The leader of which nation referred to President Bush as "the devil" on the floor of the UN on Sept. 20?

  a. Peru   b. Tasmania
  c. Honduras   d. Venezuela

20. Which movie won an Oscar for best director in 2006, and created the catchphrase, "I wish I knew how to quit you"?

  a. *Brokeback Mountain*   b. *Thank You for*
                                    Smoking
  c. *Capote*   d. *Walk the Line*

21. Which No. 1-bestseller was revealed on Jan. 8 by *The Smoking Gun*'s investigation to contain many invented elements, despite purporting to be a realistic memoir?

  a. James Frey's *A Million*   b. Bill Clinton's *My Life*
     Little Pieces
  c. Barbara Bush's   d. John Grogan's
     Millie's Book   *Marley and Me*

22. Kanye West won several Grammys on Feb. 8, 2006. Which two of these four were his award-winning rap songs?

  a. "Bless the Broken Road"   b. "Diamonds from Sierra
                                     Leone"
  c. "Don't Phunk With   d. "Gold Digger"
     My Heart"

23. What did the FBI say it found in Rep. William Jefferson's (D, LA) freezer on May 20?

  a. missing ballots from   b. records of illegally
     his last election   taped conversations
  c. frost-encrusted bagels   d. $90,000

24. What nation declared independence from which other nation as of June 3?

  a. East Timor from   b. Scotland from the U.K.
     Indonesia
  c. Kosovo from Serbia   d. Montenegro from Serbia

25. Italian Marco Materazzi admitted to insulting French soccer star Zinedine Zidane, which then led to the headbutt seen around the world during the final World Cup game in July. Materazzi said in September that after he grabbed Zidane's jersey, Zidane said, "If you want, I'll give you the jersey later." How does Materazzi claim he responded?

  a. "I would prefer your   b. "I don't want your
     sister."   stinking jersey."
  c. "I hate you, your family,   d. "Goooool!"
     and your religion."

Answers: 1 b, 2 a, 3 c, 4 b, 5 a, 6 b, 7 a, 8 c, 9 d, 10 a, 11 b, 12 a, b, c, 13 c, 14 d, 15 a-i, b-g, c-j, d-f, e-h, 16 b, 17 b, 18 c, 19 d, 20 a, 21 a, 22 b, d, 23 d, 24 d, 25 a.

TO DOUBLE-OH-SEVEN
By Cathy Millhauser

Cathy Millhauser's crosswords appear in numerous publications, including The New York Times *and* Wall Street Journal, *and in an original collection,* Humorous Crosswords.

(For answers, see page 1007)

ACROSS

1 Nebraska's biggest city
6 Tony-winning musical, "__ Yankees"
10 Andrew Lloyd Webber hit show
14 Some services under the Dept. of Ed.
15 Actor Morales
16 Taj Mahal site
17 Being a compatriot of Rudolf Nureyev, say
19 "Hud" best actress Patricia
20 "Saturday Night Live" comedian Tina
21 Part of SEATO
22 Homonym for coin-makers
23 HM in HMS
26 Babysitting alternative
30 Great Lakes' __ Locks (St. Marys River bypass)
31 Comrades- __ (soldiers)
32 Almanac lead-in
37 Active Sicilian volcano
38 Honor awarded to Pierce Brosnan: abbr.
39 Cash in __ of commodities (food program feature)
40 Namibian natural resource
43 Famed Boston Street
45 Aniline, e.g.
46 Realm in which stars seem stuck
47 Ophthalmic
52 The troposphere is one
53 It was used by Carter with Begin and Sadat
54 Psychic's claim
57 Food pyramid issuer: abbr.
58 What February has in leap years
61 Traditional Milwaukee industry
62 1996 Tony-winning musical
63 A notable concrete bridge crosses this "rascally" Oregon river
64 Former Estonia, Moldova, etc: abbr.
65 Choice for Ben Roethlisberger
66 Some children's are special

Down

1 "Carmina Burana" composer
2 "Trifling" homophone for strikeout leader Johnny Vander
3 Nabisco cookie brand, Chips __
4 Joe Palooka cartoonist ___ Fisher
5 Husband of Sarah, father of Isaac
6 Last word in a Tennessee Williams title
7 State of India
8 Chiang ___, Thailand
9 Filmdom's Long or Vardalos
10 Astronomer's dog
11 007, e.g., but not 2007
12 Dick created by Chester Gould
13 Wal-Mart is #1 in this
18 Drug-survey group
22 Ragdoll's word?
24 Court king Arthur
25 Football's Montana or Greene
26 Went the way of Milosevic, 2006
27 ___-Vivisection Society
28 Ukraine Olympics swimmer Klochkova
29 Architect Ralph Adams __
32 Popular cable network
33 Norwegian royal name
34 First female African-American Secretary of State
35 Spinks in heavyweight history
36 Bradstreet's partner and kin
38 River that's part of the German/Polish border...
41 ...and its "smelly" homophone
42 Sch. with a Washington Square campus
43 Connecticut lumber source
44 Mid-__ Athletic (NCAA conference)
46 Some "Grand" hotels
47 Gold Glove winners limit these
48 Topographical features of Iran
49 International golf cup
50 Word in long sentences?
51 Jackets named for James Bond's alma mater
54 JFK had a tiny popular-vote one over Nixon
55 Ibn _____, former Mideast ruler
56 1790 British poet laureate and family
58 Dada Artist Jean
59 Fed. funder of creative work
60 Name in a landmark abortion ruling

Themed clues without references in *The World Almanac 2007*: Across: 38. Down: 11, 51
Find related data on these pages. Across: **1** p. 626, **6** p. 264, **10** p. 241, **14** p. 431, **15** p. 224, **16** p. 744, **17** p. 213, **19** p. 267, **20** p. 219, **21** p. 474, **22 p.** 54, **23** p. 725, **26** p. 155, **30** p. 569, **31** p. 10, **32** p. 1, **37** p. 700, **39** p. 93, **40** p. 803, **43** p. 731, **45** p. 278, **46** p. 665, **47** p. 155, **52** p. 339, **53** p. 682, **54** p. 725, **57** p. 150, **58** p. 349, **61** p. 552, **62** p. 264, **63 p.** 739, **64** p. 800, **65** p. 924, **66** p. 403.
Down: 1 p. 209, **2** p. 892, **3** p. 373, **4** p. 182, **5** p. 717, **6** p. 208, **7** p. 781, **8** p. 839, **9** p. 241, **10** p. 330, **12** p. 182, **13** p. 67, **18** p. 360, **22** p 241, **24** p. 948, **25** p. 929, **26** p. 38, **27** p. 393, **28** p. 875, **29** p. 177, **32** p. 371, **33** p. 694, **34** p. 175, **35** p. 877, **36** p. 367, **38 and 41** p. 705, **42** p. 420, **43** p. 560, **44** p. 911, **46** p. 91, **47** p. 890, **48** p. 783, **49** p. 947, **51** p. 123, **54** p. 639, **55** p. 829, **56** p. 208, **58** p. 216, **59** p. 263, **60** p. 509.

Reported Month by Month, Oct. 16, 2005, to Oct. 13, 2006

October 16-31, 2005

National

Rosa Parks, Icon of Civil Rights Movement, Dies— Rosa Parks, whose arrest in 1955 for refusing to yield her seat on a segregated bus led to a boycott by African Americans of the Montgomery, Alabama, bus system and helped spark the civil rights movement, died Oct. 24 at the age of 92. On Oct. 30-31 she became the first woman to lie in honor in the rotunda of the Capitol, and the 31st person overall, in a list that included Abraham Lincoln and 9 other U.S. presidents.

Miers Withdraws as Supreme Court Nominee; Bush Nominates Alito—White House counsel Harriet Miers, who had been nominated earlier in the month to serve as an associate justice on the U.S. Supreme Court replacing Sandra Day O'Connor, withdrew her name in a letter to Pres. George W. Bush Oct. 27.

In her place Bush, Oct. 31, named Circuit Court Judge Samuel A. Alito Jr., a conservative with a long record as a sitting judge. Alito said he would seek to "protect the constitutional rights of all Americans" while keeping in mind "the limited role the courts play in our constitutional system." Some Senate Democrats reacted critically to the appointment; a confirmation battle was expected.

Miers, 60, a lawyer who was the first woman president of the Texas state bar and a close Bush associate, had been nominated Oct. 3. She lacked a public record showing her judicial philosophy or her inclinations on controversial issues such as abortion or prayer in schools. Though few senators had indicated how they might vote on the nomination, many had been skeptical as to her qualifications, and conservatives voiced strong doubts that she would reflect their views or be an advocate of judicial restraint.

On Oct. 19, Sens. Arlen Specter (R, PA) and Patrick Leahy (D, VT), the chairman and ranking Democrat on the Judiciary Committee, had asked Miers to resubmit parts of her questionnaire from the committee, saying that senators had found her previous responses insufficient. Pres. Bush Oct. 24 refused requests from senators that he turn over documents related to her activities as White House counsel, citing executive privilege.

The Supreme Court had opened its new term Oct. 3, with John G. Roberts Jr.—the 17th chief justice of the U.S.—presiding for the first time.

Top Aide to Vice President Is Indicted—I. Lewis ("Scooter") Libby, the chief of staff for Vice Pres. Richard Cheney and an assistant to Pres. Bush, was indicted Oct. 28 by a federal grand jury in Washington, DC, on 5 counts of obstruction of justice, false statements, and perjury. He resigned the same day. No other indictments were handed down, but the investigation remained open.

Special Counsel Patrick Fitzgerald said Libby had obstructed a federal investigation into leaking of the identity of an undercover CIA agent, Valerie Plame Wilson. According to the indictment, Libby said he had heard unsubstantiated reports about Plame from reporters, when in truth he received his information from government sources. The indictment did not, however, charge him with leaking government secrets.

In the wake of the indictment and the collapse of the Miers nomination, Sen. Trent Lott (R, MS), on Oct. 31, and some other Republicans called for a shakeup at the White House that would bring in new blood among the president's advisers. Sen. Harry Reid (NV), the Senate Democratic leader, called for Bush to apologize for the Valerie Plame Wilson leak within his administration and for deputy White House chief of staff Karl Rove to resign because of involvement in the affair.

International

U.S. Troops Battle in Iraq as Insurgent Attacks Continue—After U.S. forces reportedly spotted insurgents rolling artillery shells into a crater near Baghdad on Oct. 16, a U.S. plane fired on them, killing 20, according to the U.S. military. The military said no civilians were killed in the skirmish; some other accounts disputed this. Eight days later, 3 vehicle bombs exploded in succession in Baghdad, damaging 2 hotels popular with foreigners; 6 people were killed and many wounded. On Oct. 30 a series of attacks around Baghdad left at least 11 people dead, including an adviser to Iraqi Prime Min. Ibrahim al-Jaafari.

By Oct. 25, the number of U.S. soldiers who died in action in Iraq since the U.S. invasion had reached 2,000.

Saddam Hussein's Trial Begins in Baghdad—The long-anticipated trial of former Iraqi dictator Saddam Hussein began Oct. 19 in Baghdad; 5 Iraqi judges presided. Although he had been linked to many crimes, he was initially charged with just one incident said to be among the most straightforward: the mass killing of villagers in retaliation for an assassination attempt against him in 1982. Seven former Iraqi officials were also on trial for the same charge. Hussein pleaded not guilty, and refused to recognize the authority of the Iraqi court. The trial was adjourned until late November.

Sadoun al-Janabi, a lawyer for one of the other defendants, was abducted from his office Oct. 21 by a dozen men. His body was found shortly thereafter, with 2 bullet wounds in the head.

Syrian Leadership Linked to Assassination in Lebanon—A UN report made public Oct. 20 implicated Syrian and Lebanese intelligence officers in the Feb. 2005 assassination of former Prime Min. Rafik Hariri of Lebanon. UN investigator Detlev Mehlis's report stated that the assassination had been carefully planned for months. Investigators reportedly were eyeing Syria's military intelligence chief, Asef Shawkat, brother-in-law of Syrian Pres. Bashar al-Assad, as a major figure in the plot.

On Oct. 31 the UN Security Council passed a resolution, 15-0, ordering Syria to cooperate "fully and unconditionally" with the UN investigation; it also ordered Syria not to interfere in Lebanon's politics. The resolution did not specifically call for sanctions in case of noncooperation.

Iraqis Approve Constitution—Iraqi officials announced Oct. 25 that voters by a wide overall margin had approved a draft constitution for Iraq in the Oct. 15 referendum. In all, 79% reportedly voted for the new constitution. However, while Shiites and Kurds voted overwhelmingly in favor of the draft, in 2 of the 3 Sunni-dominated areas it was rejected by more than 2/3 of the voters. Under regulations for the referendum, the constitution would have failed if a 3rd Sunni province had defeated it by a 2/3 vote or more. As a next step, parliamentary elections were to be held in December.

UN Report Links Companies to Oil-for-Food Graft— The 5th and final report of a UN commission looking into the UN-monitored oil-for-food program was issued Oct. 27. The investigation, headed by former Federal Reserve chairman Paul Volcker, found massive corruption associated with what was designed to be a humanitarian program, allowing the Iraqi government under Saddam Hussein to sell oil and use the proceeds to purchase food and medicine for its citizens. The regime, which was allowed to select companies receiving oil or selling goods, reportedly obtained illegal kickbacks totaling more than $1.8 bil.

The regime reportedly gave preference to companies from France and Russia, which were more politically supportive than other countries, but 4,758 companies, from 66 countries in all, participated in the program, and nearly half paid illegal surcharges and kickbacks to the Iraqi government.

Bombs Kill Scores in New Delhi—A series of bomb blasts—2 in a crowded marketplace, 1 in a bus—killed at least 59 people Oct. 29 in the Indian city of New Delhi. More than 200 were wounded. Most of the casualties were among holiday shoppers preparing for the upcoming Hindu Festival of Lights.

General

Hurricane Wilma Strikes Caribbean, Mexico, Florida—On Oct. 17, Hurricane Wilma became the 21st tropical storm of the 2005 hurricane season, the first time storms had reached that number since 1933. On Oct. 19, it was recorded as the most powerful hurricane ever in the Atlantic Basin, with a record-low barometric pressure of 882 millibars. After decreasing in intensity, the storm ripped through Haiti and Jamaica, then struck Mexico's Yucatan Peninsula Oct. 21; some 21,000 tourists were among 71,000 people who crowded into shelters as the storm moved north along Yucatan's resort coast. As the storm moved toward Florida, Gov. Jeb Bush (FL) and local officials Oct. 22 ordered mandatory evacuations of the Florida Keys and adjacent areas to the north.

On Oct. 24, Wilma hit the U.S., cutting eastward across south Florida, soaking Miami and Ft. Lauderdale and heading back out to sea near West Palm Beach. Millions were left without electrical power. Pres. Bush visited devastated areas of Florida Oct. 27. By Oct. 29 the death toll for Wilma was put at 38 in all, including 21 in Florida.

White Sox Win First World Series Since 1917—The Chicago White Sox Oct. 26 became the champions of major league baseball for the first time in 88 years. Managed by Ozzie Guillen, Chicago completed a 4-game World Series sweep of the Houston Astros with a 1-0 victory in Houston. The only run of the final game came in the 8th inning, when right fielder Jermaine Dye, who was named the series MVP, singled home Willie Harris from 2nd base. Freddie Garcia, who threw the first 7 innings, was the winning pitcher.

The last Chicago White Sox World Series championship was in 1917. The team's image faded in 1919, when some Chicago players, including "Shoeless" Joe Jackson, were accused of throwing the World Series to the Cincinnati Reds as part of a betting scandal. Players allegedly involved in the "Black Sox" scandal were banned from baseball for life.

November 2005
National
Bush Seeks to Thwart Bird Flu Pandemic Threat— Pres. Bush Nov. 1 announced a $7.1 bil plan to head off any threat to the U.S. posed by avian influenza, or bird flu. The goal would be to make a vaccine available to every American within 6 months of the onset of a pandemic. No U.S. cases of bird flu had yet been reported, but scores of people in Asia had died since 1997 from the latest strain of the disease, and more than 100,000 chickens had died or been culled.

China said Nov. 15 that it would seek to vaccinate all of its 5.2 bil chickens, ducks, and geese in order to stop bird flu. China Nov. 16 confirmed its first 3 cases of bird flu in humans, 2 of them fatal.

Democrats Elect Governors in New Jersey, Virginia— The Democrats maintained control of governorships in elections in 2 states Nov. 8. In New Jersey, U.S. Sen. John Corzine, with 53% of the vote, defeated his Republican opponent, businessman Douglas Forrester, who won 43%, after a bitter campaign which was estimated to cost a record $70 mil. Corzine succeeded Richard Codey (D), who had led the state since James McGreevey (D) resigned in 2004. In Virginia, Lt. Gov. Timothy Kaine defeated former state Atty. Gen. Jerry Kilgore (R), winning 52% of the vote to Kilgore's 46%.

Democratic mayors were reelected in Atlanta, Boston, Detroit, and Houston, and were elected in Cincinnati, Cleveland, and St. Paul, MN. Billionaire Mayor Michael Bloomberg (R), who ran an expensive self-funded campaign and also had enjoyed high approval ratings, was easily reelected in New York City. Ex-Police Chief Jerry Sanders (R) won in San Diego, where the city was seeking to recover from financial scandals.

Texas voters approved an amendment to the state constitution banning gay marriage. In California, voters rejected a package of reforms proposed by Gov. Arnold Schwarzenegger (R).

Debate Over Iraq War Heats Up—In a Veterans Day speech on Nov. 11, Pres. Bush charged that those who accused him of having manipulated intelligence to win support for the U.S. invasion of Iraq were "irresponsible" and damaging to U.S. troop morale. Pres. Bush said his critics had formerly agreed, based on intelligence, that Iraq did have weapons of mass destruction. In a Nov. 16 speech given in Washington, DC, Vice Pres. Richard Cheney said that those who accused the administration of lying during the buildup to the war were making "one of the most dishonest and rep-

rehensible charges ever aired in this city."

The Senate Nov. 15 defeated, 58-40, a Democratic-supported resolution that would have called on the administration to provide a timetable for pulling U.S. troops out of Iraq. The Senate then passed, 79-19, a GOP resolution asking the administration to provide Congress with a report on the situation in Iraq every 90 days.

Rep. John Murtha (D, PA), a Vietnam combat veteran known as a supporter of the military, called Nov. 17 for a complete withdrawal of U.S. troops from Iraq within 6 months. He said that the war was not winnable and that Americans were "a catalyst for the violence." White House Press Sec. Scott McClellan said Murtha's statement echoed "the extreme liberal wing of the Democratic Party."

CIA Leak Investigation Continues—*Washington Post* reporter Bob Woodward revealed Nov. 16 that a Bush administration official had told him in June 2003 that Valerie Plame Wilson, wife of administration critic Joseph Wilson, worked for the CIA. The statement revealed that Woodward had learned about this before any leak by I. Lewis "Scooter" Libby, who was indicted by a grand jury in Oct. in connection with leaking of the information. Woodward provided sworn testimony Nov. 14 to Patrick Fitzgerald, the special prosecutor investigating the leak.

U.S. Citizen Charged as Supporter of Jihad— Jose Padilla, a former Chicago gang member who had converted to Islam, was charged by the Justice Dept. Nov. 22 with supporting violent jihad campaigns in Afghanistan and elsewhere. The charges came after Padilla had been held in a military prison for more than 3 years on suspicion of terrorist activities. Critics argued that he should not have been held so long as an "enemy combatant" without being charged.

Two Plead Guilty to Corruption Charges— U.S. Rep. Randy Cunningham (R, CA) Nov. 28 pleaded guilty to tax evasion and to conspiring to commit bribery, tax evasion, wire fraud, and mail fraud, and resigned from Congress. He was charged with having taken $2.4 mil in bribes to help friends and supporters get military contracts.

Earlier, on Nov. 21, Michael Scanlon, a former partner of lobbyist Jack Abramoff and former aide to Rep. Tom DeLay (R, TX), pleaded guilty to conspiring to bribe a member of Congress and other public officials. He agreed to repay $19.6 mil to American Indian tribes that had retained his lobbying services.

Bush Defends Iraq War in Speech; Declines to Set Timetable—Pres. Bush defended his Iraq policy Nov. 30 in a speech given at the U.S. Naval Academy in Annapolis, MD, to an audience of midshipmen. In response to polls showing diminished public support, he reiterated his position that the U.S. should not leave until there are enough trained Iraqi forces to secure the country; while not ruling out troop reductions, he vowed not to pull out based on any "artificial timetable set by politicians."

The speech coincided with the release of a 35-page report outlining the Bush administration's plan for winning the war. Democrats renewed calls for deadlines and charged that Bush had not laid out a realistic strategy for success.

International
Insurgent Attacks in Iraq Continue; U.S. Forces Counterattack; Detainees Found Abused in Iraqi Jail— Among other attacks in Iraq, at least 20 died in a bombing at a market and Shiite mosque south of Baghdad Nov. 2. Gunmen Nov. 8 targeted 2 attorneys defending former Baathist officials on trial with ex-Pres. Saddam Hussein; one was killed, the other wounded. A suicide bombing at a Baghdad restaurant Nov. 10 killed at least 34 people.

Later in the month, suicide bombers wearing explosives killed at least 70 worshippers in 2 mosques in Khanaqin, in Kurdish Iraq, Nov. 18. Car bombs killed 18 mourners at a Baghdad funeral Nov. 19, 16 people in Kirkuk Nov. 22, and 30 in Mahmudiya Nov. 24.

On Nov. 5 U.S. and Iraqi forces had opened a new offensive against insurgents in western Iraq, near the Syrian border. Some 50 insurgents were reported killed in that offensive Nov. 14; 2 U.S. Marines were killed the same day, 5 others in an ambush 2 days later. U.S. military deaths were averaging 3 per day in November, the highest level since January.

In other developments, Italy's state-run TV network Nov. 8 exhibited corpses from Fallujah that had been burned by flammable white phosphorous. The U.S. military said Nov. 15 that it had used that substance in its assault on insurgents in Fallujah in 2004 but not against civilians.

On Nov. 13, U.S. forces in Baghdad found a detention facility where at least 160 detainees were being held by Iraqi's Interior Ministry. Some showed evidence of malnutrition or torture. The Iraqi government said it would investigate. Sunni leaders and international human rights groups claimed that Sunnis were being singled out for jailing and mistreatment, and called for an international investigation.

At a reconciliation conference hosted by the Arab League in Cairo, Egypt, Shiite, Sunni, and Kurdish leaders from Iraq condemned attacks on civilians, religious services, and government and humanitarian organizations as terrorism, while calling for the goal of setting a timetable for withdrawal of foreign troops.

Free Trade Debated at Summit of the Americas— Leaders from 34 Western Hemisphere countries attended the Summit of the Americas in Mar del Plata, Argentina, Nov. 4-5 to discuss employment, poverty, and democracy. Pres. Bush advanced a U.S. proposal for a free trade area of the Americas. In a Nov. 5 communiqué, the U.S. and 28 other nations agreed to resume trade talks in 2006. Meanwhile, some 25,000 protesters attended a parallel "people's summit" Nov. 4, at which Pres. Hugo Chavez of Venezuela rebuked Bush on the Iraq war and denounced the free trade proposal, claiming it would mostly benefit U.S. exporters and multinational corporations.

Bush met with leaders in Brazil Nov. 5 and Panama Nov. 6 before returning to the U.S. Nov. 7.

Rioting Sweeps France; Property Damage High—The French government declared a state of emergency Nov. 8, after 12 days of rioting, mostly by disaffected young Muslims of North African descent living in high-unemployment suburbs.

Rioters had battled police and burned thousands of vehicles in more than 300 cities and towns. The protests began in a Paris suburb Oct. 27, following the accidental deaths of 2 teenage boys, electrocuted in a power station where they apparently had been hiding in flight from police. Ten police officers were shot and wounded in the Paris suburb of Grigny Nov. 6. One man died Nov. 7 after being beaten by rioters.

Prem. Dominique de Villepin Nov. 7 announced plans to assist immigrants, including job training, better educational opportunities, and renovated housing. By Nov. 17, the violence mostly ended and the police announced a return to "a normal situation." Nearly 9,000 vehicles had been burned and 3,000 people arrested.

Woman Elected President of Liberia—Ellen Johnson-Sirleaf, a Harvard-educated economist, won the first presidential election in Liberia since the end of the nation's long civil war, with 59.4% of the vote. The voting was held Nov. 8. Although there were allegations of fraud, the Elections Commission, under the protection of U.S. peacekeepers and newly trained Liberian police, found no evidence of tampering, and Johnson-Sirleaf was officially confirmed as the winner, Nov. 23. She is the first woman to be elected as a head of state in modern Africa.

Suicide Bombers Strike 3 Hotels in Jordan—Suicide bombers wearing explosives on their belts set off blasts Nov. 9 that killed at least 57 bystanders and injured 300 in 3 hotels in Amman, the capital of Jordan, a country supportive of U.S. policy in Iraq. Many of the dead and wounded were members of a wedding party. Al-Qaeda operatives claimed responsibility.

On Nov. 13, Jordanian authorities arrested an Iraqi woman, Sajida Mubarak al-Rishawi, who confessed on Jordanian TV that she had accompanied her husband, one of the bombers, to one of the hotels hit, and had tried to detonate a bomb concealed in her belt. Many Jordanians reacted in shock to the bombing and confession, while some said they did not believe the confession or that al-Qaeda could have been involved.

Bush Tours Far East, Presses China and Iran—Pres. Bush began a tour of Asia Nov. 16. During a press conference in Kyoto with Japanese Prime Min. Junichiro Koizumi, he spoke in support of a more free society in China; he also renewed his call for a peaceful re-unification of China and Taiwan. Koizumi avoided saying whether Japan would withdraw its troops from Iraq in 2006.

At a press conference in Kyongju, South Korea, Nov. 17, Pres. Bush and Korean Pres. Roh Moo Hyun discussed their common interest in dealing with North Korea and its nuclear threat. The South Korean government Nov. 18 announced it would withdraw a third of its 3,200 troops from Iraq in 2006.

Pres. Bush and Russian Pres. Vladimir Putin were among leaders attending the annual Asia-Pacific Economic Cooperation summit in Pusan, South Korea. The two leaders Nov. 18 asked Iran to accept a compromise that would allow it to enrich uranium for domestic energy-production use—but in Russia, and using Russian technology.

Bush spoke Nov. 19 to U.S. troops at Osan Air Base, 48 miles south of the border between North and South Korea. In Beijing Nov. 20, he pressed Hu Jintao of China to increase political freedom in China; Chinese authorities did not appear responsive and had placed some dissidents under house arrest or detained them prior to Bush's arrival to stem any demonstrations. On Nov. 21, Bush became the first sitting U.S. president to visit Mongolia.

Israeli Prime Minister Forms New Party—In a political shake-up, Israeli Prime Min. Ariel Sharon Nov. 21 quit the Likud Party, which he had helped found, and formed a new political party, registered Nov. 24 as Kadima, which he said would "lay the foundations for a peace agreement in which we will determine the permanent borders of the state." Sharon had feuded for years with hard-line Likud leaders who resisted steps he had taken or advocated toward a peaceful settlement with Palestinians.

Merkel Becomes Chancellor of Germany—The German Parliament Nov. 22 elected Angela Merkel, leader of the Christian Democratic Party, as chancellor of Germany, after two months of postelection negotiation among parties within her coalition. She took office immediately. The Social Democratic Party of outgoing chancellor Gerhard Schroeder got 8 of the 16 cabinet posts in the new coalition government. Merkel was Germany's first woman chancellor, and the first to have lived under Communism in East Germany.

Saddam Trial Resumes, Briefly—The trial in Baghdad of former Iraqi Pres. Saddam Hussein and codefendants resumed for a few hours Nov. 28. He was charged specifically in the execution of 148 men and boys in Dujail after a 1982 assassination attempt against him. A recess was ordered to give other defendants a chance to meet with lawyers.

Vote in Canadian Parliament Brings Down Government—The government of Canadian Prime Min. Paul Martin was ousted by a no-confidence vote in the House of Commons Nov. 28. The vote, supported by members of 3 opposition parties, came a month after an investigative report charged that the ruling Liberal Party had benefited from kickbacks, money laundering, and other corrupt practices. A new election was to be held in January.

General

Problems Continue in Wake of Hurricane Katrina—Pres. Bush Nov. 1 appointed Donald Powell, chairman of the Federal Deposit Insurance Corp., to coordinate continuing recovery efforts in the Gulf of Mexico region from Hurricane Katrina. The Federal Emergency Management Agency (FEMA) announced Nov. 4 that satellite imagery showed the Aug. 2005 hurricane had left 60,000 homes beyond repair, and hence eligible for $26,200 in aid per household. By late November, Louisiana leaders complained that relief legislation was stalled in Congress and that the national political establishment was losing interest in the state's recovery.

Vatican Bans Gays From Priesthood—The Roman Catholic Church, in a document officially issued Nov. 29, banned most homosexual men from becoming priests. Specifically, it forbade candidates "who are actively homosexual, have deep-seated homosexual tendencies, or support the

World Almanac Editors' Picks
Most Embarrassing Presidential Moments in the Last 35 Years

1. Pres. George H. W. Bush, ill with the flu, vomits on the prime minister of Japan, Kiichi Miyazawa, then faints, during a state dinner in Tokyo. (Jan. 8, 1992)

2. Pres. Bill Clinton quibbles about the meaning of the word "is," during inquiries into his relationship with Monica Lewinsky: "It depends on what the meaning of the word 'is' is. If the—if he—if 'is' means is and never has been that is not—that is one thing . . . Now, if someone had asked me on that day, are you having any kind of sexual relations with Ms. Lewinsky, that is, asked me a question in the present tense, I would have said no. And it would have been completely true." (Grand jury testimony given Aug. 17, 1998)

3. Presidential candidate Gov. Michael Dukakis (D, MA) visits a General Dynamics plant in Michigan for a photo opportunity riding an M1-A1 Abrams tank and clutching a mounted machine gun. Filmed wearing a helmet that seems too large for his head, Dukakis looks awkward, out of place, and decidedly uncomfortable. (Sept. 13, 1988)

4. After finishing third in the 2004 Iowa caucus, with 18%, Democratic presidential candidate Gov. Howard Dean (VT) exults to supporters, "Not only are we going to New Hampshire,. . .we're going to South Carolina and Oklahoma and Arizona and North Dakota and New Mexico, and we're going to California and Texas and New York. . .And then we're going to Washington, DC, to take back the White House! Yeaaaaaggggggh!!!" The televised speech and loud scream strike many viewers as peculiar and unpresidential. (Jan. 19, 2004)

5. Pres. George W. Bush gives a surprise shoulder massage to a shocked German Chancellor Angela Merkel, at a conference meeting during a G-8 Summit in St. Petersburg, Russia. (July 2006)

6. During a microphone check, unaware that he is being recorded, Pres. Ronald Reagan jokes, "My fellow Americans, I'm pleased to tell you today that I've signed legislation that will outlaw Russia forever. We begin bombing in five minutes." (Aug. 11, 1984)

7. Pres. Richard Nixon, while campaigning to mute his Watergate and credibility problems, defends his personal finances at a nationally televised Q&A session with a convention of Associated Press managing editors: "And in all of my years of public life, I have never obstructed justice. . .people have got to know whether or not their President is a crook. Well, I am not a crook. I have earned everything I have got." (Nov. 17, 1973)

8. Presidential candidate Sen. John Kerry (D, MA) tries to defend himself against charges that by failing to vote in favor of funds for the Iraq War he was betraying American troops, but ends up fueling the perception that he has taken inconsistent positions on issues: "I actually did vote for the $87 billion, before I voted against it." (Mar. 16, 2004)

9. In the second presidential campaign debate between incumbent Pres. Gerald Ford and his Democratic rival, Georgia Gov. Jimmy Carter, Ford makes a misstatement widely seen as ridiculous when he declares, ". . .there is no Soviet domination of Eastern Europe and there never will be under a Ford administration." (Oct. 6, 1976)

10. Jimmy Carter loudly bungles the name of a former Democratic vice president and icon during a dramatic part of his acceptance speech for the presidential nomination at the 1980 Democratic National Convention: "And we're the party of a great leader of compassion—Lyndon Baines Johnson, and the party of a great man who should have been president, who would have been one of the greatest presidents in history—Hubert Horatio Hornblower—Humphrey." (Aug. 14, 1980)

so-called 'gay culture.'" The document would allow ordination of candidates who had experienced "transitory" homosexual tendencies that had been "clearly overcome" for at least 3 years.

December 2005

National

Bush Defends Iraq War Policy—Pres. George W. Bush made speeches and other public appearances to boost support for the Iraq war, in Washington, DC, Dec. 7 and 14; Minneapolis, MN, Dec. 9; and Philadelphia, PA, Dec. 12. In a nationally televised address from the White House Dec. 18, he reiterated that U.S. troops would not pull out until insurgents no longer threatened the Iraqi government.

Patriot Act Stalled in Congress—Renewal of the USA Patriot Act met with opposition in Congress. Among 16 provisions scheduled to expire at year's end, a bicameral conference committee had agreed to renew 14 permanently and extend 2 controversial surveillance provisions for 4 years. The House, Dec. 14, approved this compromise, 251-174, but opponents in the Senate proposed only a 3-month extension for the bill, while Pres. Bush said he would veto any temporary extension

A compromise 5-week extension, which Bush said he would accept, was approved by both houses Dec. 22.

Bush Authorized Wiretaps Without Court Approval—Pres. Bush Dec. 17 confirmed media reports from the day before that he had authorized the National Security Agency to monitor international communications—phone calls and emails—between Americans and people with suspected links to al-Qaeda and related terrorist organizations, without approval by a special court after 72 hours as called for under the 1978 Foreign Intelligence Surveillance Act. He argued that as president he had inherent power to authorize warrantless wiretaps given the need for speed in collecting intelligence on terrorist activities.

Sen. Arlen Specter (R, PA), chairman of the Senate Judiciary Committee, Dec. 16 had called warrantless wiretaps inappropriate and said he would conduct hearings.

U.S. District Court Judge James Robertson resigned from the special court Dec. 19, reportedly because he dis-

approved of the Bush policy.

Judge Rejects Promotion of "Intelligent Design"—U.S. District Court Judge John Jones III, in Harrisburg, PA, Dec. 20, struck down a requirement approved 9-0 by the Dover, PA, Area School District that 9th grade biology students be read a statement promoting "intelligent design" as an alternative to evolution.

Eleven parents had challenged the Dover policy, contending that it constituted state sponsorship of religion. Jones's ruling in favor of the parents came six weeks after all 8 school board members up for election had been voted out of office.

New York City Hit by Transit Strike—A strike by the Local 100 of the Transport Workers Union left New York City without bus and subway service for 3 weekdays, Dec. 20-22. Contract negotiations broke down; a key issue was the Metropolitan Transportation Authority's insistence that contributions by new workers to pension funds be increased. A state Supreme Court judge Dec. 20 noted that the strike was illegal and imposed a fine of $1 mil a day on the union. The union sent its workers back on the job without a new contract Dec. 22

On Dec. 27, a deal was struck between the MTA and the TWU; the MTA dropped its demand on pensions, and the union agreed that workers would pay part of their health-insurance premiums.

Cheney Breaks Tie to Pass Budget Cut Bill—Vice Pres. Dick Cheney cut short an international trip to cast the deciding vote in the Senate Dec. 21 in favor of a bill providing for $39.7 bil in federal budget savings over 5 years, mostly through cutbacks in entitlement programs. All 44 Democrats, 1 independent, and 5 Republicans voted against the bill. The measure was aimed at reining in a projected $1.3 tril deficit over the period but provided for savings of only about 2.5% of the amount. Opponents criticized cuts in Medicare, Medicaid, and student loans at a time when Republicans were seeking to extend tax cuts.

The bill had been approved in the House Nov. 18.

Defense Bill Enacted, With Anti-Torture Provision—The Senate Dec. 21 passed a $453 bil defense appropriations bill, 93-0, after an anti-torture amendment had been included. The bill included funds for military operations in

Iraq and Afghanistan and for hurricane and flu pandemic preparedness. Another provision in the Senate bill that would have allowed oil drilling in Alaska's Arctic National Wildlife Refuge had been removed after Republican leaders found it would prevent the bill from coming to a vote.

Despite earlier opposition, Pres. Bush agreed to the anti-torture amendment, barring "cruel and inhumane" treatment of detainees held by the military, as offered by Sen. John McCain (R, AZ); he signed the bill into law Dec. 30. However, in a separate statement Pres. Bush reserved the right to construe various provisions of the prohibition in a manner consistent with his "constitutional role" as commander-in-chief.

Thousands of Acres Burned in Texas and Oklahoma Grassfires—Fast-moving grassfires in northern Texas and Oklahoma ignited Dec. 27, and had killed at least 4 people, consumed tens of thousands of acres, and destroyed at least 250 structures by Dec. 31. High winds and drought conditions made fighting the fire difficult. By New Year's Eve, more fires were reported in NE New Mexico.

Winter Storm Pounds N. California—A strong winter rainstorm hit N. California on Dec. 31 causing extreme flooding and mudslides. As much as 9 inches of rain fell in the wine-producing Napa Valley, the hardest-hit area, and caused the Napa River near St. Helena to rise to a record 21.6 ft (8.6 ft over flood levels). At least 3 people were reported killed.

U.S. Economy at a Glance: Calendar Year 2005	
Unemployment rate	5.1%
Consumer prices (change over 2004)	+3.4%
Trade deficit	$767.5 bil
Dow Jones closing (year end)	10,717.50
Dow Jones highest close (Mar. 4, 2005)	10,854.54
Dow Jones lowest close (Apr. 20, 2005)	10,012.36
GDP (change over 2004)	+3.1%

International

Al-Qaeda Leader Killed in Pakistan—A U.S. missile attack by a predator drone in northern Pakistan Dec. 1 killed Hamza Rabia, believed to be the 3rd-ranking leader in the al-Qaeda terror organization, and 4 others.

Secretary of State Faces Questions on Torture—Responding to critics, Sec. of State Condoleezza Rice, on a European tour, said Dec. 5 that the U.S. did not "authorize or condone torture of detainees" and that the "rendition" of terror suspects to other countries was permissible under international law. Pres. Bush claimed, Dec. 6, "We do not render to countries that torture." At a news conference in Kiev Dec. 7 with Pres. Viktor Yushchenko of Ukraine, Rice said U.S. officials abided by the UN Convention Against Torture.

The European Parliament Dec. 15 asked for an investigation of reports that the CIA had held suspects in secret Eastern European prisons and used airports in Europe to transfer them to places where they faced torture.

President of Iran Calls Holocaust a Myth—Pres. Mahmoud Ahmadinejad Dec. 8 said he doubted that the Holocaust, in which German Nazis and their allies killed millions of Jews during World War II, had taken place. He also suggested that the state of Israel be moved to Europe or North America. Sec. Gen. Kofi Annan condemned the statement the following day, also referring to a General Assembly resolution passed in November rejecting any denial of the Holocaust.

Lebanese Journalist Critical of Syria Is Killed—Gibran Tueni, a Lebanese newspaper editor and member of parliament known as an outspoken opponent of Syria's involvement in Lebanon, was killed by a car bomb in Beirut Dec. 12. He had just returned from France, where he was hiding out of fear of assassination.

Iraqis Vote for a Permanent Government—Despite threats of violence from insurgents, Iraqis voted in large numbers (at least 70% turnout) in Dec. 15 elections for a 275-seat national parliament. The Iraqi election commission released preliminary results Dec. 19-20 showing a strong overall lead, but not a majority, for a Shiite Muslim coalition. Tight security was imposed, including border closings and curfews, and there were only minor scattered instances of violence. Sunni and secular Shiite leaders called for new elections, citing alleged instances of fraud and intimidation. On Dec. 29, the International Mission for Iraqi Elections, a multinational group of election monitors and experts, agreed to review evidence of irregularities.

Among bombings and attacks, 10 U.S. Marines were killed and 11 wounded near Fallujah Dec. 1 when a soldier stepped on planted artillery shells. An attack on an Iraqi convoy north of Baghdad Dec. 3 killed 19 people, and 2 suicide bombers killed at least 27 at a police academy in Baghdad Dec. 6. U.S. and Iraqi forces Dec. 8 found 625 detainees, some of whom showed signs of mistreatment, at a prison in Baghdad run by Iraq's Interior Ministry. That same day, an insurgent group claimed it had killed a U.S. electrician, Ronald Schulz. Terrorists blocked a highway north of Baghdad Dec. 18, and killed 20 truck drivers and others.

The Pentagon Dec. 2 confirmed reports that it had contracted with a private PR firm, the Lincoln Group, to plant pro-American articles in Iraqi newspapers and pay Iraqi journalists to write similar articles.

The trial of Saddam Hussein resumed briefly Dec. 5-7, with 9 witnesses, most of them concealed behind a screen, describing alleged instances of torture, beatings, and executions. Hussein charged Dec. 21 that his U.S. guards had beaten and tortured him and his codefendants.

Prime Minister of Israel Hospitalized After Stroke—Israeli Prime Min. Ariel Sharon was hospitalized Dec. 18 after suffering a severe stroke. Sharon, 77, who was about to run for re-election as leader of a new party that he had formed, Kadima, was released Dec. 20. Former Prime Min. Benjamin Netanyahu Dec. 19 was elected the leader of Likud, the party Sharon had left.

First Indian Elected President of Bolivia—Voters in Bolivia Dec. 18 elected a person from an indigenous minority as president for the first time. Congressman Evo Morales, an Aymara Indian, got 52% in his 2nd try for the presidency. Morales, a cofounder of the Movement Toward Socialism (MAS) party and outspoken critic of the U.S., opposed the U.S.-supported coca-eradication program, while saying he opposed the use of coca in cocaine. He promised to increase state control of the hydrocarbon industry and other resources.

January 2006
National

14 Die in West Virginia Coal Mines—Twelve miners lost their lives as a result of a methane gas explosion in the Sago coal mine in Tallmansville, WV, Jan. 2. Although the men were only about 260 feet below ground level, rescuers had to travel about 2 miles through gas-filled tunnels to reach them. One miner was found dead Jan. 3. The next day 11 miners initially reported to have survived were found dead; a 12th, Randal McCloy Jr., was found alive after 41 hours, but critically injured.

In a separate incident, a fire in a mine in Melville, WV, Jan. 19 took the lives of 2 more miners.

Lobbyist Pleads Guilty, Agrees to Help Investigation—Powerful Washington lobbyist Jack Abramoff struck a deal with prosecutors and pleaded guilty in U.S. District Court in Washington, DC, Jan. 3 to fraud, tax evasion, and conspiring to bribe public officials; he agreed to cooperate in the investigation. Prosecutors recommended that he be imprisoned up to 11 years and be ordered to pay $25 mil in restitution to Indian tribes he had defrauded and $1.7 mil to the IRS.

On Jan. 4, in Miami, in a separate case, Abramoff pleaded guilty to fraud and conspiracy. He admitted having faked a $23 mil wire transfer as part of a 2000 deal to buy SunCruz Casinos. He was sentenced to 5 years, 10 months in prison.

The text of the Washington plea agreement made it clear that prosecutors would move against some as yet unknown members of Congress and others for lobbying abuses. Most of Abramoff's clients were Republicans.

Tom DeLay (R, TX), who had stepped down as House Majority Leader after being indicted in a separate case, said Jan. 7 that he would not seek to return to that post.

On Jan. 15, Rep. Robert Ney (R, OH), who had been alluded to in the Abramoff indictment, temporarily resigned as chairman of the House Administration Committee. Congressional Republicans Jan. 17 and Democrats Jan. 18 both presented legislative proposals to deal with abuses being exposed by the investigation.

Debate Continues Over Surveillance Without Warrants—Former Vice Pres. Al Gore Jan. 16 denounced Pres. Bush's approval of domestic surveillance, without court authorizations, of U.S. citizens communicating with persons abroad alleged to have ties to al-Qaeda, and called for the appointment of a special counsel to investigate. On Jan. 17, the American Civil Liberties Union and the Center for Constitutional Rights filed suits against the National Security Agency, which was conducting the surveillance.

On Jan. 19, the Justice Dept. argued in a 42-page legal analysis that both the U.S. Constitution and a resolution by Congress permitted the surveillance

Supreme Court Upholds Assisted-Suicide Law—The U.S. Supreme Court Jan. 17 upheld, 6-3, Oregon's assisted-suicide law, permitting doctors to help mentally competent terminally ill patients end their lives.

Ford to Cut Up to 30,000 Jobs—Continuing a trend in the downsizing of the U.S. auto industry, the Ford Motor Co. announced Jan. 23 that over the next 6 years it would close as many as 14 factories and reduce its work force by up to 30,000 employees. Ford had posted a loss of $1.6 bil in North America in 2005.

Alito Confirmed to Supreme Court—Judge Samuel A. Alito Jr. was confirmed Jan. 31 by the Senate as an associate justice of the U.S. Supreme Court. Alito, a judge on the 3rd U.S. Court of Appeals, was approved 58-42. All except 1 Republican voted for confirmation, and all but 4 Democrats, along with 1 independent, voted against. Alito was sworn in the same day.

During confirmation hearings Jan. 9-12 before the Senate Judiciary Committee, Democrats focused on what they considered an excessive deference to presidential power and on his abortion views. In a 1985 application for a legal post in the Reagan administration, Alito had maintained that the U.S. Constitution does not provide a right to an abortion. He told questioners he would approach abortion and other cases with an open mind based upon the Constitution and the specifics of each case. He declined to say whether he would vote to overturn *Roe v. Wade*, though he did say he recognized a constitutional right to privacy.

In his 1985 job application, Alito had said he was proud to have contributed to cases opposing racial quotas and had cited his membership in Concerned Alumni of Princeton, known for criticizing the school's admission of women and affirmative action programs. At the hearings, he said he had not been an active member.

The Judiciary Committee Jan. 24 had approved Alito's nomination 10-8, voting along party lines. A last-ditch effort by some Democrats to derail the nomination fizzled when the full Senate, Jan. 30, voted 72-25 to end debate and allow an up or down vote; 24 of the 45 Democrats, and 1 independent, joined in the filibuster attempt.

Bush Denounces "Isolationism," Calls for Less Fossil Fuel Dependence, in State of the Union Speech—Pres. Bush, in his 5th State of the Union address, Jan. 31, continued to defend the Iraq war and denounced "isolationism and protectionism." Saying America was "addicted to oil," he called for reducing U.S. dependence on Mideast oil by 75% and promised more funding of alternative fuel research; he also promised more funding for high school math and science teaching. The president defended his policy of warrantless surveillance of those with suspected terrorist ties and called on Congress to renew elements of the Patriot Act.

The Democratic response, delivered by Gov. Timothy Kaine (VA), derided many of Bush's proposals as recycled. He said Democrats were committed to fighting terrorism, but criticized the president's methods.

Anti-war activist Cindy Sheehan, invited by a House member, was arrested and detained for a time by Capitol police, after showing up in a t-shirt with an anti-war slogan. Police also ejected Beverley Young, the wife of Rep. Bill Young (R, FL) for wearing a "Support the Troops" T-shirt.

International

Sharon Suffers Serious Stroke—Israeli Prime Min. Ariel Sharon suffered a major stroke Jan. 4 and remained hospitalized throughout the month. His powers were transferred to Deputy Prime Min. Ehud Olmert.

Sharon, 77, had previously suffered a mild stroke in December. In November he had formed a new party, Kadima, with the goal of reaching a peace settlement with the Palestinians. Kadima Jan. 16 named Olmert its interim leader.

Attacks Against Troops and Civilians Continue in Iraq—At least 30 Iraqis were killed in a suicide bomb attack at a Shiite Muslim funeral north of Baghdad, Jan. 4, and more than 100 died in bombings Jan. 5 in Karbala and Ramadi. Eleven U.S. military personnel were killed Jan. 5. A helicopter crash in northern Iraq Jan. 7 killed 8 U.S. service members and 4 American civilians. Suicide bombers killed at least 18 people in the Interior Ministry compound in Baghdad Jan. 9.

Jill Carroll, an American freelance journalist on assignment for the *Christian Science Monitor*, was abducted Jan. 7 in Baghdad and her interpreter was killed. In a videotape made public Jan. 17, Carroll's captors threatened to kill her unless the U.S. freed all women it held captive. The demands were refused, although 5 of the 9 women were released. Her fate remained uncertain at the end of the month.

ABC news co-anchor Bob Woodruff and cameraman Doug Vogt were seriously injured Jan. 29 after their vehicle hit a roadside bomb in Iraq. They were airlifted to the U.S. military hospital in Germany and then to the U.S. for treatment.

Italy said Jan. 19 that it would pull its 2,600 troops out of Iraq by the end of 2006.

Iran Resumes Nuclear Activity—Continuing to defy international pressure, Iran Jan. 10 resumed research at its nuclear facilities, for what it claimed were peaceful purposes. The work at its plant at Natanz could lead to the generation of nuclear fuel or weapons-grade uranium. After negotiations with Iran produced no result, foreign ministers of Russia and China Jan. 30 went along with a move by the U.S., Britain, and France to have the International Atomic Energy Agency take Iran to the UN Security Council, which could impose sanctions. Russia and China agreed to the move after it was established that no Security Council action would be taken until after an IEAE meeting in March.

U.S. Launches Missile Attack on al-Qaeda Leader—Using an air-fired missile, the U.S. military Jan. 13 tried to kill Ayman al-Zawahiri, believed to be the No. 2 leader in the al-Qaeda terror network. The missile destroyed 3 houses in the Pakistani town of Damadola, where al-Zawahiri had been believed to be having dinner. Pakistan's provincial government said Jan. 17 that up to 18 people were killed. Pakistani officials said Jan. 18 that 2 top al-Qaeda members and Zawahiri's son-in-law were among the dead.

Earlier, Zawahiri appeared in a videotape, broadcast Jan. 6 by the Arabic television network Al Jazeera. He claimed that by indicating a planned reduction in U.S. troops Pres. Bush had admitted defeat in Iraq. In another tape, broadcast on Al Jazeera Jan. 30, Zawahiri mocked Pres. Bush for not having killed him in the attack.

Woman Elected President of Chile—In a Jan. 15 runoff, Chile elected its first female president. The winner, with 53.5% of the vote, was Michelle Bachelet, who was sworn in Mar. 11 to succeed Pres. Ricardo Lagos. Both are members of a center-left coalition that had governed since 1990. In the 1970s Bachelet and her parents were imprisoned by the Pinochet regime, and her father died after torture. Bachelet was health minister and defense minister under Lagos.

Monitors Validate Iraqi Elections; Official Results Confirm Shiite-Muslim Margin—The International Mission for Iraqi Elections conceded Jan. 19 that there had been instances of "fraud and other irregularities" during the Dec. 15 Iraqi elections, but found the elections had been largely successful, given the unstable situation, and rejected calls by Sunni Muslim and secular Shiite groups for new elections.

Official results released Jan. 20 gave Shiite Muslims 128 seats, a plurality but 10 seats short of a majority. The 2 main Sunni parties had 55 seats, and Kurds had 53. Secular Shiites trailed with 25 seats; minor parties split the rest.

Bin Laden Heard on Tape— In an audiotape, made public by Al Jazeera Jan. 19, No. 1 al-Qaeda leader Osama bin Laden warned that new attacks on the U.S. would occur as soon as preparations were complete. He proposed a truce contingent on a total U.S. military withdrawal from Iraq and Afghanistan.

Conservatives Oust Ruling Liberals in Canadian Election— In a national parliamentary election on Jan. 23, Canada's Conservative Party returned to power after 13 years of Liberal Party rule. The Conservative leader, Stephen Harper, succeeded Prime Min. Paul Martin. The election was precipitated by a Nov. 2005 no-confidence vote in the House of Commons. The Conservatives fell short of an outright majority, receiving 124 out of 308 seats, and would need to govern in a coalition.

Scandals involving kickbacks and insider trading had prompted the no-confidence vote. Harper said he would focus on the economy and corruption. He has supported the U.S. invasion of Iraq, but said he would not send Canadian troops to Iraq.

Hamas Wins Palestinian Election— In a stunning surprise, the radical Islamic party Hamas won the Palestinian parliamentary election Jan. 25. Hamas secured 74 seats in the 132-member legislature of the Palestinian Authority. Fatah, the faction that had dominated Palestinian politics for decades, won only 45. Prime Min. Ahmed Qurei announced his resignation Jan. 26, but Pres. Mahmoud Abbas, of Fatah, remained in office and called for continuing negotiations with Israel. Acting Israeli Prime Min. Ehud Olmert Jan. 26 said talks were not possible until Hamas recognized Israel's right to exist.

The Hamas victory was aided by the widespread belief among Palestinians that the Fatah leadership was corrupt and incompetent. The U.S. and the European Union called on Hamas to renounce terrorism and recognize Israel.

General

Texas Ends Southern California's Reign as Football Champs— The Univ. of Texas Longhorns defeated the Univ. of Southern California Trojans, 41-38, Jan. 4, to take the NCAA Division I-A football title in Pasadena, CA. The Trojans had won 34 straight games, and had been ranked first in the polls, with the Longhorns second. With less than 7 minutes to play in the title game, USC led 38-26, but Longhorn quarterback Vince Young ran for 2 touchdowns to put his team ahead.

Avian Influenza Claims 4 Lives in Turkey— The bird flu virus took its first lives outside of Eastern Asia when, in early January, a brother and his 2 sisters from a town in eastern Turkey died of the disease. The UN Food and Agricultural Organization warned Jan. 11 that bird flu could become endemic in Turkey. A 4th child from the same town died Jan. 15.

Preliminary reports Jan. 30 indicated that bird flu had also killed a teenage girl near Sulaimaniya, Iraq.

345 Killed in Stampede During Pilgrimage— On a pilgrimage to holy sites in Saudi Arabia, at least 345 people were crushed to death Jan. 12 during a stampede in Mina, near Mecca. As many as 1,000 people were injured.

Author Admits to Fabricating Memoir— Daytime television talk show host Oprah Winfrey January 26 rebuked author James Frey, during a live appearance on her show, for having lied in his purported memoir *A Million Little Pieces,* which chronicled his treatment for alcohol and drug addiction. The book had become a best-seller after Winfrey, in Sept. 2005, recommended it for her book club. Controversy had been swirling around Frey since January 8, when *The Smoking Gun* accused him of fabricating many of the book's details.

Coretta Scott King Dies— Coretta Scott King, 78, widow of civil rights leader Dr. Martin Luther King Jr. and an icon of the civil rights movement, died Jan. 30 at a holistic health institute in Baja California, Mexico, where she was seeking to recover from a stroke and other illness.

February 2006
National

Bernanke Becomes Fed Chief, Succeeding Greenspan— Ben Bernanke was sworn in Feb. 1 as chairman of the Federal Reserve Board, replacing longtime Fed chief Alan Greenspan. Bernanke had been nominated by Pres. George W. Bush in Oct. 2005, and was easily confirmed by a voice vote in the Senate, Jan. 31. Previously chairman of the White House Council of Economic Advisers, he had also served as a professor of economics at Princeton University and a governor of the Federal Reserve Board. Greenspan had retired on Jan. 31 as planned, after 18 years in the post; during his tenure he was widely credited for a largely successful strategy focused on containing inflation by raising interest rates.

GOP in U.S. House Chooses a New Leader— Republicans in the U.S. House changed leaders for the 2nd time in 5 months. Tom DeLay (TX) had resigned as majority leader in September after being indicted on a conspiracy charge, and was replaced by majority whip Roy Blunt (MO) as acting leader. Blunt in turn was defeated Feb. 2 in an election for a permanent replacement. The winner, John Boehner (OH), prevailed on the 2nd ballot, 122-109. Speaker J. Dennis Hastert (IL) remained the top-ranking House Republican.

Attorney General Defends Warrantless Surveillance— Atty. Gen. Alberto Gonzales, testifying before the Senate Judiciary Committee Feb. 6, argued that Pres. Bush had the power under the Constitution and a 2001 congressional resolution to approve warrantless surveillance by the National Security Agency of communications between terrorism suspects in the U.S. and abroad. He said that the administration could bypass the Foreign Intelligence Surveillance Act, which required that warrants be obtained.

Congress Continues to Scrutinize Katrina Debacle— Michael Brown, who had been head of the Federal Emergency Management Agency (FEMA) when Hurricane Katrina struck the Gulf Coast in 2005, told a Senate committee Feb. 10 that he had informed a higher official of the seriousness of the situation but did not recall with whom he had spoken. He fixed blame on the decision to make FEMA part of the Dept. of Homeland Security (DHS), arguing that DHS is focused on terrorism, not natural disasters. DHS Sec. Michael Chertoff, testifying Feb. 15, acknowledged that there had been "many lapses" in handling of the affair; he was criticized for having relied on Brown while remaining "curiously disengaged."

The Government Accountability Office Feb. 13 said it had found many examples of waste and fraud in FEMA's relief and reconstruction work. The DHS inspector general, Richard Skinner, testified Feb. 13 that of nearly 25,000 mobile homes bought at $34,000 each, only 2,700 were being utilized. The House Select Committee on Hurricane Katrina Feb. 15 called the relief effort a failure, criticizing national, state, and local governments.

Cheney Shoots Friend in Hunting Accident— Vice Pres. Dick Cheney accidentally shot and wounded a friend while they and others were hunting quail Feb. 11 on a ranch near Corpus Christi, TX. The wounded man, Harry Whittington, was struck in the head and upper body by metal birdshot pellets when Cheney fired his 28-gauge shotgun toward where he thought a bird was taking flight. Whittington, a lawyer and Republican Party activist, was hospitalized. The next morning the ranch owner notified the *Corpus Christi Caller-Times,* and word soon spread. Cheney was criticized for delay in making the accident public.

On Feb. 14, Whittington suffered a mild heart attack after a pellet migrated into his heart. In a Feb. 15 interview, Cheney took responsibility for the accident and expressed his regret; no charges were filed. Whittington left the hospital Feb. 17.

UN Report Calls for U.S. to Close Guantanamo Prison— In a report released Feb. 16, UN officials said that treatment of suspected terrorists in the U.S. prison at Guantanamo Bay, Cuba, violated human rights conventions. The report urged U.S. officials to close the camp immediately and to grant the prisoners fair trials or free them. The report also criticized the force-feeding of hunger strikers. The investigators had declined a U.S. offer to visit Guantanamo after they were denied a request to interview the detainees privately.

UAE Role in Running U.S. Ports Debated—An agreement by the Bush administration to let a United Arab Emirates-based company manage terminals in 6 U.S. maritime ports created an uproar in the U.S. The administration said Feb. 16 that the deal with the company, Dubai Ports World, was final and that U.S. port security would not be compromised as a result. Critics in both parties noted that the UAE had once recognized the Taliban and that 2 of the Sept. 11 hijackers came from the UAE. But in recent years the UAE had supported the war on terror and was considered a U.S. ally in the region.

The Bush administration Feb. 26 accepted an offer by the company to submit to a second, broader U.S. review of the deal's potential security risks, hoping that congressional opposition would abate.

International

Cartoons Depicting Muhammad Spark Muslim Protests and Violence in Several Countries—A series of Muslim protests over cartoons offensive to Islam, beginning in early February, led to violence and sometimes violent reprisals in several countries around the world.

The Danish newspaper *Jyllands-Posten,* on Sept. 30, 2005, had published 12 cartoons depicting Muhammad, including one where he wears a turban containing a bomb. The Islamic religion prohibits depictions of Muhammad. The cartoons attracted little notice until a Norwegian paper reprinted them, Jan. 10; Saudi religious leaders then urged a boycott of Danish goods, and on Jan. 26 Saudi Arabia recalled its ambassador to Denmark. The Danish paper Jan. 26 apologized for offending Muslims, but the Danish and Norwegian premiers said they could not apologize as a government for what had been published by a free press. In early February, some papers and TV stations in other countries began publishing the cartoons, in some cases citing freedom of the press as a principle. In the U.S., the *Philadelphia Inquirer* Feb. 4 printed one of the cartoons.

On Feb. 3, Muslim protesters stormed a building in Jakarta, Indonesia, that housed the Danish embassy. In Damascus, Syria, Feb. 4, protesters set the Danish and Norwegian embassies on fire, and protesters in Beirut, Lebanon, the next day set fire to the Danish embassy there. Between Feb. 6 and 8, 11 people were killed in Afghanistan during protests, one of which occurred outside a U.S. military base. Protesters also set fire to the Danish embassy in Tehran. The editor of the Norwegian paper apologized to Muslims Feb. 10.

Further violence followed. Demonstrations across Pakistan Feb. 14-16 claimed 5 lives and hundreds were arrested. Eleven died during protests in Libya Feb. 17. In Nigeria, scene of the worst violence, the death toll in attacks by Muslims and reprisals by Christians stood at 123 as of late February. Some 50,000 people in all have died in sectarian fighting in Nigeria since 2000.

UN Atomic Energy Agency Moves Against Iran—On Feb. 4, the UN Atomic Energy Agency voted 27-3 to report Iran to the UN Security Council over Iran's nuclear activities. Iran immediately announced that it would end cooperation with the agency. On Feb. 14, an Iranian official announced that Iran had resumed enriching uranium, the first step for production of either nuclear energy or weapons.

Former President Declared Winner in Haiti Election—The Provisional Electoral Council (CEP) declared Feb. 16 that Rene Preval had won the Feb. 7 presidential election in Haiti. Preval, who had been president from 1996 to 2001, won a bare majority after it was decided to exclude blank ballots from the tabulation, avoiding a runoff. The UN and the Organization of American States organized the election, while a Brazilian-led force provided security. There had been widespread instability in Haiti since 2004, when Pres. Jean-Bertrand Aristide was forced to resign.

Mudslide in Philippines Kills Many—A mudslide Feb. 17 caused by excessive rain covered the entire village of Guinsaugon on Leyte island in the central Philippines. Over 1,000 people were buried in up to 30 feet of mud. The 1.2-

sq-mile area included a school with 246 students, which became a focus of the search, but a multinational rescue attempt that included U.S. marines resulted only in the recovery of bodies.

Hamas Takes Over Palestinian Authority—As a result of the January election, Hamas took over the legislature of the Palestinian Authority on Feb. 18. The Israeli cabinet Feb. 19 froze the transfer of about $50 mil in monthly tax and customs receipts to the Authority because Hamas did not recognize Israel's right to exist.

Sectarian Violence Raises Civil War Fears in Iraq; Shiites Pick Candidate—Iraq seemed in danger of civil war Feb. 22 after a suspected Sunni bomb battered the golden dome of an important Shiite shrine in Samarra; Shiites then destroyed or damaged dozens of Sunni mosques. Political and religious leaders pleaded for restraint. By Feb. 28, 379 had died in the new violence in and around Baghdad, and Sunnis had suspended negotiations on formation of a permanent government.

In other Iraqi news, car bombs near a Baghdad market killed 16 and wounded 90 Feb. 2. A car bomb in Baghdad Feb. 21 killed at least 21, and more than 30 people were killed in 3 explosions across Baghdad Feb. 28.

A coalition of Shiite Muslim parties Feb. 12, by a one-vote margin, nominated Ibrahim al-Jaafari to be Iraq's prime minister; he had been made interim prime minister in April 2005.

General

Steelers Win Their 5th Super Bowl—The Pittsburgh Steelers defeated the Seattle Seahawks, 21-10, on Feb. 5 in Detroit to win Super Bowl XL. It was the Steelers' 5th title and their first since 1980. Pittsburgh wide receiver Hines Ward was named the game's most valuable player. It was the first Super Bowl win for coach Bill Cowher, who had been with the Steelers for 14 seasons.

Avian Influenza Virus Found in Africa, Western Europe—The most worrisome strain of avian influenza, the H5N1 virus, was found for the first time in Africa Feb. 8, on a Nigerian chicken farm; officials reported Feb. 9 that they had also detected the virus in 2 other farms. The virus reached Western Europe Feb. 11-12, when it was found in dead swans in Italy, Greece, Bulgaria, and Slovenia. On Feb. 14, Germany, Austria, and Iran also reported the virus in swans.

On Feb. 20-21, in an area of India where avian flu had been reported, government workers slaughtered 130,000 chickens.

Germany Leads Medal Count in Winter Olympics—More than 2,500 athletes from 84 countries took part in the 2006 Winter Olympics, held in and near Turin, Italy, Feb. 10-26. Germany won the most medals of any country, 29, including 11 gold medals. The Germans excelled especially in the biathlon (5 golds) and bobsled (3 golds). The U.S. ranked 2nd overall with 25 medals, 9 of them gold. Canada, Austria, and Russia placed 3rd, 4th, and 5th, respectively. Canadian speed skater Cindy Klassen won the most medals of any athlete at Turin, with 1 gold, 2 silver, and 2 bronze.

The opening ceremony took place in the Olympic stadium Feb. 10. The next day, U.S. speed skater Chad Hedrick won the men's 5,000 meters, but the U.S. suffered a disappointment Feb. 12 when figure skater Michelle Kwan, a 5-time world champion, withdrew from competition because of an injury. Antoine Deneriaz of France won the men's downhill skiing that day. Ted Ligety of the U.S. won the men's combined alpine skiing gold medal Feb. 14. In alpine skiing, Michaela Dorfmeister of Austria won the women's downhill on Feb. 15. (In all the Austrians won 14 medals in alpine skiing, far more than any other country.) The gold medal in men's figure skating went to Yevgeny Plushenko of Russia Feb. 16.

Lindsey Jacobellis of the U.S., leading for the gold in the women's snowboard cross on Feb. 17, fell 100 yards from the finish, and the winner was Tanja Frieden of Switzerland. But on Feb. 18, Shani Davis of the U.S. won the 1,000 meters in men's speedskating, becoming the first black person to win an individual gold medal in any Winter Olympics. Also, Tanith Belbin and Ben Agosto took the silver medal in ice dancing Feb. 20, for the first U.S. medal in that event in 30 years. The gold went to Tatyana Navka and Roman Kostomarov of Russia. Anja Paerson of Sweden won the women's slalom Feb. 22.

In ladies' figure skating, one of the most popular Olympic events, Shizuka Arakawa of Japan took the gold medal Feb. 23. Sasha Cohen of the U.S. won the silver, and Russian Irina Slutskaya took bronze. In a surprise win, the American Julia Mancuso took home the gold in women's giant slalom Feb. 24. American alpine skier Bode Miller, a world champion whose performance on and off the slopes had been widely publicized, failed to win any medals in 5 events.

One of Germany's biggest stars, biathlete Michael Greis, won his 3rd gold medal of the Olympics, Feb. 25, in the 15-km mass start biathlon. In a match between neighbors, Sweden defeated archrival Finland, 3-2, for the men's hockey gold Feb. 26.

March 2006
National
Jury Weighs Fate of Sept. 11 Conspirator—Zacarias Moussaoui, a French citizen of Moroccan descent, who had pleaded guilty in April 2005 to conspiracy charges relating to the Sept. 11, 2001, attacks on the U.S., faced a jury in U.S. District Court in Alexandria, VA, that was considering whether he should be executed or imprisoned for life.

In opening arguments Mar. 6, prosecutors argued that Moussaoui, who had been arrested on immigration charges in August 2001, had lied to federal investigators and withheld information about the 9/11 plot that could have been used to prevent it from being carried out. The defense, while conceding that he had been a member of al-Qaeda, argued that he was an unstable individual who would not have been entrusted with an important role.

Moussaoui, who was still in custody at the time of the attacks, testified Mar. 27 that he had known in advance of the Sept. 11 plot and had originally been slated to fly another plane into the White House that day.

South Dakota Abortion Law Seeks to Force Legal Challenge—A ban on almost all abortions in the state of South Dakota was signed into law Mar. 6 by Gov. Michael Rounds (R). Under the new law, a doctor performing an abortion could face up to 5 years in prison. The law has an exception to allow an abortion if the mother's life is in danger. Supporters of the ban hoped to precipitate a legal challenge that would go to the U.S. Supreme Court.

Dubai Company Bows Out of U.S. Ports Agreement—In the face of broad opposition in the U.S., Dubai Ports World said Mar. 9 that it would transfer to a U.S. company management of 6 U.S. ports on the Atlantic and Gulf of Mexico coasts. The Dubai company would have run the ports after it purchased British company P&O, which had previously controlled the ports. Opposition in Congress was reflected in a 62-2 vote in the House Appropriations Committee Mar. 8 to thwart the deal, which the Bush administration supported.

Bush Signs Extension of Patriot Act—One day before it was to expire, Pres. George W. Bush Mar. 9 signed a renewal of the USA Patriot Act. Disputes in Congress over the privacy rights of U.S. citizens had stalled the renewal. The final compromise bill renewed most provisions of the legislation but incorporated some restrictions favored by civil libertarians, including one that exempted libraries from mandatory cooperation with government requests for records. The Senate, Mar. 2, had approved the compromise bill 89-10, and the House had followed suit on Mar. 7, voting 280-138 (14 abstained).

Interior Secretary Resigns—Sec. of the Interior Gale Norton announced Mar. 10 that she would resign at the end of the month. On Mar. 16, Bush nominated Idaho Gov. Dirk Kempthorne to succeed her. He was confirmed by voice vote, May 26, and was sworn in June 7 after having left office as governor.

Demonstrators Protest as Congress Considers Immigration Measures—As many as 500,000 demonstrators filled the streets of Los Angeles Mar. 25 to protest proposed legislation that would tighten provisions curbing illegal immigration. Other large protests took place in Denver, Milwaukee, and Phoenix. The U.S. Senate began debating new immigration legislation Mar. 29.

The House had already approved a bill that would tighten security along the Mexican border and make illegal immigration a felony. The Senate Judiciary Committee, guided in part by proposals backed by Pres. Bush, on Mar. 27 approved a more lenient bill; it would offer millions of undocumented workers "nonimmigrant visas" that could lead to citizenship after 11 years if they got jobs and paid fines and back taxes. The Senate committee also approved a temporary worker program for additional immigrants.

Bush's Chief of Staff Is Replaced—Pres. Bush announced Mar. 28 that he had accepted the resignation of Andrew Card, his chief of staff for the past 5 years. Bush had been criticized by some for relying too heavily on the same close inner circle of White House advisers, leading to political missteps. Bush said Card would be succeeded by Joshua Bolten, the current budget director.

International
Bush Visits Pakistan and Afghanistan Amid Violence—Pres. Bush Mar. 1 made an unscheduled visit to Afghanistan and met with Pres. Hamid Karzai to discuss security issues. He then traveled to Pakistan for a visit Mar. 3-4. The day before he arrived, a car bomb exploded outside the U.S. Consulate and Marriott Hotel in Karachi killing 4, including a U.S. diplomat. Clashes between security forces and militants on the Afghan-Pakistani border Mar. 4-6 claimed at least 51 lives. At a Mar. 4 press conference, Bush praised Pres. Pervez Musharraf for his efforts in the fight against terrorism.

On Mar 12 in Afghanistan, 4 U.S. soldiers were killed by a roadside bomb.

U.S. and India Reach Nuclear Agreement—At a meeting in New Delhi, India, Pres. Bush and Prime Min. Manmohan Singh announced Mar. 2 that India would be allowed to buy nuclear fuel and reactor components from the U.S. India in return would separate its military and civilian nuclear programs and open its civilian plants to inspection. India, as well as Pakistan and Israel, had been barred by U.S. law from receiving assistance for their nuclear programs because they had not signed the Nuclear Non-Proliferation Treaty. The new agreement required the approval of the U.S. Congress.

Ex-President of Yugoslavia Dies During Genocide Trial—Slobodan Milosevic, who had been on trial since February 2002 at the International War Crimes Tribunal at The Hague, Netherlands, was found dead in his cell Mar. 11. A former president of Yugoslavia, Milosevic was a central figure in a series of violent ethnic struggles that broke out in the 1990s as that country came apart following the collapse of Communist rule in Eastern Europe. Milosevic was charged with genocide and crimes against humanity. His trial had been expected to conclude in late spring.

Results of an autopsy Mar. 12 were said to show that Milosevic, 64, who had a heart condition and other health problems, died of a heart attack. However, some questioned whether he could have been being deliberately poisoned, since the antibiotic rifampicin, which could have countered the action of prescribed drugs he had been taking, was found in his system in January. He was buried Mar. 18 in Pozarevac, Serbia.

New Labor Legislation Sparks Protest in France—Labor-market reform legislation that was being pushed through parliament by Prime Min. Dominique de Villepin sparked widespread student demonstrations and violence throughout France beginning Mar. 11. The new legislation would allow businesses to hire workers under age 26 for a 2-year trial period, with the option to fire them without cause. French law made it difficult for businesses to dismiss young workers. Supporters of the proposed legislation believed it would help ease France's unemployment rate, which stood at around 9%—the highest in Europe. Those against the new law believed it went too far in undermining longstanding laws protecting labor.

On Mar. 14, tens of thousands of students marched in Paris and other cities. About 250,000 took to the streets 2 days later, leading to clashes with French authorities, and as many as 1 mil people joined in demonstrations during a general strike to protest the new legislation Mar. 28. Pres. Jacques Chirac said Mar. 31 that he was signing the legislation but would see that modifications were made in it; on Apr. 10 he scrapped the law completely.

Saddam Hussein Testifies; Insurgents Remain Active— For the first time, former Iraqi Pres. Saddam Hussein Mar. 15 testified at his war crimes trial in Baghdad. Seizing the chance to make a statement, he urged Iraqis to unite and resist the U.S.-led occupation, and claimed he was still president.

As Iraqi leaders continued a contentious effort to form a government, insurgent violence continued. The body of Tom Fox, an American civilian held hostage since November, was found Mar. 10; 3 other members of the Christian Peacemaker Teams, who had been seized with him, were freed Mar. 23 after raids by British and U.S. forces. Britain said Mar. 13 that it would reduce its troop strength, currently about 8,000, in Iraq by 10% beginning in May

Some 1,500 U.S. and Iraqi forces Mar. 16 began an offensive, called Operation Swarmer, aimed at insurgents near Samarra. On Mar. 21, 100 insurgents attacked a jail northeast of Baghdad, killed at least 18 policemen, and freed at least 30 prisoners.

At a Mar. 21 news conference, Pres. Bush said that withdrawal of the last U.S. troops from Iraq "will be decided by future presidents."

Thousands Protest Belarus Elections—A disputed Mar. 19 presidential election in Belarus sparked protests in the capital city of Minsk and throughout the country. Results showed that incumbent Pres. Alexander Yushchenko won with 82.6% of the vote, while the main opposition leader Alexander Milinkevich took only 6%. The results were immediately disputed and protesters took to the streets. International observers declared the election invalid Mar. 20, claiming that Yushchenko had used state authority to intimidate voters and rig the election. The Bush administration called for new elections. Russian Pres. Vladimir Putin, a supporter of Yushchenko, dismissed the allegations.

Protests continued in Minsk until a government crackdown Mar. 24 led to the arrest of at least 400 demonstrators. The move was condemned by the U.S. and European Union. The head prosecutor for the Belarusian government said Mar. 29 that opposition activists who were in custody would be prosecuted for illegally staging demonstrations.

Basque Separatists Announce End to Their Violent Rebellion—In a video broadcast Mar. 22, masked leaders of the Basque separatist group Euzkadi ta Askatasuna (ETA) announced it would end its long violent struggle for independence. The Basque people live in north central Spain and in smaller numbers in southwestern France. Over 3 decades, ETA had killed at least 800 people in terror attacks. Declaring a "permanent cease-fire," the Basque spokesmen called for a "new framework in which our rights...will be recognized."

Kadima Party Finishes First in Israeli Election—The Kadima Party, founded in Nov. 2005 by then-Prime Min. Ariel Sharon, finished in first place in Israeli parliamentary election Mar. 28. The Labor Party finished in 2nd place. Sharon remained in a coma after a stroke in January, leaving the acting prime minister and new Kadima leader, Ehud Olmert, in position to become prime minister. The results made it likely that the government would continue its policy of gradual withdrawal from the West Bank.

Meanwhile, Palestinian Pres. Mahmoud Abbas swore in the Hamas government Mar. 29.

Journalist Released in Iraq—Kidnapped freelance journalist Jill Carroll was released in Baghdad on Mar. 30, by her captors, an obscure radical group, after nearly 3 months in captivity. She said she had been repeatedly threatened and that anti-U.S. statements she had made on 2 videotapes had been coerced.

General

***Crash* Wins Best-Picture Oscar—**In an upset, *Crash*, a film depicting racial conflicts that followed an automobile accident, was voted best picture of 2005 by the Academy of Motion Picture Arts and Sciences. Among other awards handed out at Oscar ceremonies in Hollywood Mar. 5, Ang Lee was named best director, for *Brokeback Mountain*, the widely acclaimed story of 2 gay ranch hands, that had been favored to win best picture. The top 2 acting awards went to Philip Seymour Hoffman, for his performance as author Truman Capote in the biographical film *Capote*, and Reese Witherspoon for her performance as country singer June Carter Cash in the Johnny Cash biopic, *Walk the Line*.

Bird Flu Pandemic Seen as Threat—At a meeting of international health experts in Geneva, Switzerland, Mar. 6-8, Margaret Chan, of the World Health Organization, expressed strong concern that avian flu spreading to humans could cause a massive pandemic and noted that the disease had already cost $10 bil in lost agricultural revenues and impacted some 300 million farmers. As several new countries reported cases in bird populations, WHO on Mar. 13 said that 176 cases of human infection had been documented around the world since 2003, 98 of them fatal.

U.S. Economy at a Glance: March 2006	
Unemployment rate.	4.7%
Consumer prices (change over 2005).	+3.4%
Trade deficit (12 months through Mar.).	$731.8 bil
Dow Jones closing, 1st quarter.	11,109.32
Dow Jones highest close (Mar. 22).	11,317.43
Dow Jones lowest close (Jan. 20)	10,667.39
1st quarter GDP growth (annual rate).	+5.6%

April 2006

National

Retired Generals Call for Rumsfeld Resignation—Defense Sec. Donald Rumsfeld faced growing pressure in April to resign. Beginning Mar. 19, several retired Army and Marine Corps generals had urged him to quit his cabinet post, associating him with errors in conduct of the war. In the Apr. 17 *Time* magazine, Marine Lt. Gen. Gregory Newbold criticized the "casualness and swagger" of civilians who had ordered the invasion. On Apr. 12, retired Army Maj. Gen. John Batiste also had criticized the prewar planning. Pres. George W. Bush declared Apr. 14 that Rumsfeld continued to have his full support.

Jury Finds Moussaoui Eligible for Death Penalty—A federal jury in Alexandria, VA, on Apr. 3, found that Zacarias Moussaoui had lied to the government about the Sept. 11, 2001, terrorist attacks on the U.S, and was responsible for at least one death, and thus eligible for the death penalty. The jury was instructed to consider both mitigating circumstances (such as parental abuse or mental illness) and aggravating circumstances (such as the heinousness of the crime) in deciding whether to actually imprison for life or execute Moussaoui, the only person convicted in connection with the Sept. 11 attacks.

Former House Majority Leader to Leave Congress—Rep. Tom DeLay (R, TX), who had resigned as House majority leader in September 2005 after being indicted for conspiracy in a campaign finance scheme, said Apr. 4 that he would not seek re-election in November and would resign from the House before then. On Mar. 31, DeLay's former deputy chief of staff, Tony Rudy, pleaded guilty in U.S. District Court in Washington to accepting gifts and favors from former lobbyist Jack Abramoff in return for using his influence on behalf of Abramoff and his clients.

Court Filing Brings Bush Into CIA Leak Case—Patrick Fitzgerald, the special prosecutor investigating the leak of the name of an undercover CIA agent, submitted a filing to the U.S. District Court in Washington, DC, Apr. 5 that drew Pres. Bush into the investigation. Fitzgerald said in the filing that I. Lewis (Scooter) Libby, then an aide to Bush and Vice Pres. Dick Cheney and now under indictment, had testified to a grand jury that in 2003 Bush authorized him to leak part of a then-classified intelligence report claiming Iraq was seeking uranium from Niger for use in a nuclear weapons program.

The Iraq-Niger connection had since been proven false. Fitzgerald, in his filing, contended that the purpose of the leak was to strengthen the administration's case for invading Iraq. On Apr. 26, Bush adviser Karl Rove testified before the grand jury for the 5th time.

Immigration Bill Stalls in Senate—The Senate Apr. 7 rejected an immigration reform bill that had been crafted to encourage a bipartisan compromise. The bill, endorsed by the Judiciary Committee, was designed to strengthen border security and create a guest-worker program. Neither the compromise measure nor a more restrictive bill gained enough support to close off debate, with many in both parties wary of coming to an agreement that voters in November might not support,

Echoing the huge turnouts of late March, hundreds of thousands of demonstrators rallied Apr. 9-10 in several U.S. cities including Washington, DC, New York City, and Phoenix in protest against any bill that would take punitive action against illegal immigrants. Renewed debate continued on Apr. 27 after a two-week spring recess.

Former Governor of Illinois Convicted—A U.S. District Court jury in Chicago Apr. 17 convicted ex-Gov. George Ryan (R) of 18 felony counts, including racketeering conspiracy, mail fraud, tax fraud, and lying to the FBI. Ryan's co-defendant Lawrence Warner, a lobbyist, was convicted on 12 counts. The jury concluded that Ryan had steered contracts to Warner and others in return for vacations and gifts. On Sept. 6, Judge Rebecca Pallmeyer sentenced Ryan to 6½ years in prison.

President of China Visits U.S.—Pres. Hu Jintao of China visited the U.S. in April. On his first stop Apr. 18, Hu met with business and political leaders in Washington state, including Microsoft chairman Bill Gates.

At a meeting with Pres. Bush in Washington, DC, Apr. 20, the two leaders pledged to work together against nuclear proliferation and to reduce the trade imbalance, which strongly favored China. However, Hu and Bush failed to come to any agreements on these issues or others, including human rights in China and Iran's nuclear ambitions. On Apr. 21, Hu spoke at Yale University.

More Personnel Changes in the White House—Pres. Bush said Apr. 18 that he would nominate Rob Portman to be director of the Office of Management and Budget (OMB), succeeding Joshua Bolten, the new White House chief of staff. Portman was confirmed May 26.

On Apr. 19 Bolten named Joel Kaplan, who had been his deputy at OMB, as deputy chief of staff. Kaplan was to take over authority for policy from Karl Rove, Bush's top political adviser, who would concentrate on maintaining GOP control of Congress in the 2006 elections.

White House Press Sec. Scott McClellan announced his resignation Apr. 19. Bush announced a week later that McClellan would be succeeded by Fox News commentator Tony Snow.

CIA Officer Fired After Leak Investigation—On Apr. 20, the Central Intelligence Agency dismissed Mary McCarthy, a career officer whose past positions included senior director for intelligence programs at the National Security Council, after conducting an internal investigation into the leaking of classified information to a reporter for the *Washington Post*. McCarthy reportedly failed a lie-detector test. The classified information was a primary basis for a November 2005 article by Dana Priest reporting that the CIA was sending terror suspects to secret detention centers in foreign countries.

Priest had received a Pulitzer Prize Apr. 17 for her articles on the prisons. A lawyer for McCarthy said she denied having leaked classified information.

U.S. Gasoline Prices Cause Concern—Oil prices reached new highs in April, and the cost of gas at the pump in the U.S. was also at a peak compared to the past. The price of a barrel of light crude oil hit $75.35 a barrel on Apr. 21, and a gallon of regular gas cost over $3 in some parts of the country, with average prices about 60 cents a gallon above levels a year earlier.

On Apr. 25 Pres. Bush said he would suspend government shipments to the Strategic Petroleum Reserve to help curb the rising prices. He also called for investigations into corporate price-gouging and price fixing. As gas prices rose, some oil companies were reporting record profits.

Senate Republicans Apr. 28 proposed a measure that would increase taxes on oil industry profits and would open the Arctic National Wildlife Refuge to oil drilling. The latter proposal met with criticism from Senate Democrats. Another proposal, by Sen. Robert Menendez (D, NJ), called for a 60-day suspension of the federal tax on gasoline and diesel to help ease the burden on motorists.

International

Avian Influenza Virus Spreads—The H5N1 strain of avian flu was reported for the first time in the West African nation of Burkina Faso, Apr. 3, and in the U.K., Apr. 6. The virus was found on a poultry farm in Burkina Faso and in a dead swan in eastern Scotland. The World Health Organization Apr. 12 said that there have been 194 human infections worldwide, of which 109 had been fatal.

Genocide Added to Charges Against Hussein—Former Iraqi Pres. Saddam Hussein Apr. 4 was charged with genocide by the Iraqi tribunal trying him for war crimes. He was accused in connection with the so-called Anfal campaign of the late 1980s, during which at least 50,000 Iraqi Kurds were killed. The tribunal called the campaign a systematic effort to persecute the Kurds, who represented about one-fifth of the Iraqi population.

In a separate charge, involving a reprisal for a reported 1982 assassination attempt in the village of Dujail, Hussein admitted Apr. 5 that he had signed death warrants for 148 Shiites in the village, claiming that it was the right of the head of state to do so.

EU and U.S. Cut Off Financial Aid to Palestinians—Both the U.S. and the European Union (EU) Apr. 7 suspended financial aid to the Palestinian Authority (PA), led by the militant Hamas party, because of the Authority's refusal to recognize Israel. The UN, however, continued its financial aid funding. On Apr. 9 Israel broke off relations with the PA.

In new violence, a suicide bombing at a Tel Aviv restaurant Apr. 17 killed 10 people and wounded about 60.

Italian Premier Narrowly Loses Bid for Re-election—Italian Prem. Silvio Berlusconi narrowly lost his bid for another term in Apr. 9-10 elections, to Romano Prodi, a former premier. The tally for the lower house of Parliament, the Chamber of Deputies, gave Prodi's center-left coalition 49.8% of the vote, and Berlusconi's conservative coalition 49.7%. Because additional seats are awarded to the winning party, Prodi's coalition ended up with 348 seats, while 281 went to Berlusconi's party, with 1 independent. The division of seats in the Senate appeared to be virtually even.

Italy's highest judicial body confirmed Apr. 19 that Prodi's coalition had won the Chamber of Deputies by 24,755 votes out of 38 million, and had narrowly won the Senate.

Iran Describes Its Uranium-Enrichment Program—Iranian Pres. Mahmoud Ahmadinejad said Apr. 11 that Iran had nuclear technology and was able to enrich uranium. He claimed, however, that Iran's controversial nuclear program would focus exclusively on energy generation for peaceful purposes. The head of Iran's Atomic Energy Organization, Gholamreza Aghazadeh, said Apr. 11 that the level of enrichment in Iran's program fell far short of the level required for nuclear weapons. On Apr. 13 Mohamed ElBaradei, director of the UN International Atomic Energy Agency, urged Iranian officials to suspend uranium enrichment.

Diplomats from the U.K., China, France, Germany, Russia, and the U.S. met in Moscow Apr. 18-19 but were unable to agree on a response to Iran's nuclear program. China and Russia opposed a U.S. call for sanctions.

Sharon's Prime Ministry Officially Ends—The prime ministry of Ariel Sharon was brought to a formal conclusion in Israel Apr. 11 when the cabinet declared that he was permanently incapacitated. The acting prime minister, Ehud Olmert, whose Kadima Party had finished first in March parliamentary elections, began efforts to form a government.

Iraqi Leaders Choose Prime Minister and Part of Cabinet—Prime Min. Ibrahim al-Jaafari of Iraq Apr. 20 abandoned his hopes of continuing in office in the new permanent government that was being formed. Although the dominant Shiite faction in parliament had chosen him in February to be its candidate for prime minister, Sunnis and Kurds had refused to support him. Many leaders thought he had been ineffectual in curbing sectarian violence and in improving the country's essential services.

Shiite leaders Apr. 21 announced that they would support Jawad al-Maliki, an ally of Jaafari, who had taken tough stands against terrorism and the influence of Saddam Hussein's Baath Party. Iraqi leaders agreed on al-Maliki and 6 other top officials Apr. 22, but completing a full lineup of cabinet ministers was expected to take another month. Sec. of State Condoleezza Rice and Sec. of Defense Donald Rumsfeld visited Iraq Apr. 26 and urged leaders there to speed the process of forming the new government and take steps to restore order and public confidence.

In continuing violence, at least 90 died and 175 were injured Apr. 7 when 3 suicide bombers set off explosives at the Baratha Mosque in Baghdad, which was affiliated with a Shiite Muslim political party. A car bomb in Huwaider, north of Baghdad, killed 26 on Apr. 12. In 2 attacks north of Baghdad Apr. 13, gunmen killed 17 police officers and a bomb killed 15. On Apr. 24, 7 bombs in Baghdad killed 10 and wounded 76. In a video posted on a web site Apr. 25, Abu Musab al-Zarqawi, head of the al-Qaeda terror organization in Iraq, urged insurgents there to press on with the fight against the U.S. forces.

Bombs Explode at Seaside Resort in Egypt—Three bombs exploded within about 15 seconds of each other near a restaurant and supermarket at the small Egyptian seaside resort of Dahab on Apr. 24. More than 20 people were killed. This was the 3rd terror attack on a Sinai resort in 2 years. No group claimed responsibility.

Two suicide bombers unsuccessfully targeted international peacekeepers on Apr. 26 in Egypt's Sinai Peninsula.

General

Florida Wins Its First Men's NCAA Basketball Title—The Florida Gators, led by coach Billy Donovan, won their first men's NCAA Division I basketball championship Apr. 3, defeating UCLA, 73-57, in Indianapolis. Gator center Joakim Noah, who scored 16 points in the title game, was named the outstanding player of the Final Four.

Maryland Wins Women's NCAA Title—The Maryland Terrapins, led by coach Brenda Frese, won the Division I NCAA women's basketball title Apr. 4 in Boston, defeating the Duke Blue Devils, 78-75, in overtime. Maryland's Laura Harper was named the outstanding player of the Final Four.

Duke Athletes Charged With Rape—Two members of the Duke Univ. lacrosse team were arrested Apr. 18 and charged with raping a dancer who had performed at a team party Mar. 13 in an off-campus house in Durham, NC. The case heightened local racial and class tensions. The accuser, a student at North Carolina Central Univ., was black; the students arrested, like most team members, were white. All 46 white team members submitted DNA samples to police, but none matched evidence taken from the woman. On Apr. 5, Duke Univ. Pres. Richard Brodhead canceled the lacrosse team's season, and coach Mike Pressler resigned. A 3rd player was charged with rape May 15.

May 2006

National

Demonstrators Stage a "Day Without Immigrants"—More than 1 million immigrants and their supporters left jobs and schools, boycotted merchants, and took to the streets on a "Day Without Immigrants" May 1 to show their importance to the economy. About 400,000 people demonstrated in both Chicago and Los Angeles. The protests came as part of the ongoing debate on illegal immigration.

Conspirator in U.S. Terror Attacks Gets Life in Prison—Zacarias Moussaoui, who had pleaded guilty to conspiracy in connection with the Sept. 11, 2001, terror attacks on the U.S., was sentenced May 4 to life in prison without parole. Moussaoui, the only person tried in connection with the attacks, had testified that he was proud of his role and still wanted to destroy the U.S.

CIA Director Resigns; Successor Is Confirmed—Porter Goss resigned May 5 as director of the Central Intelligence Agency less than 2 years after he had taken over the agency. Bush May 8 nominated U.S. Air Force Lt. Gen. Michael Hayden, the deputy national intelligence director, to succeed Goss. At confirmation hearings before the Senate Intelligence Committee, May 18, Hayden said that despite his military career he would be independent of the Pentagon and that he had protested Pentagon control of much of the intelligence budget. Hayden also defended the secret eavesdropping program that he had run while director of the National Security Agency (NSA). Hayden was confirmed by the full Senate, 78-15, on May 26.

Congress Approves $70 Bil in Tax Cuts—The House May 10 (244-185) and the Senate May 11 (54-44) gave their final approval to a $70 bil package of tax cuts. The bill extended the 15% rate on capital gains and dividends through 2010. It also exempted about 15 mil taxpayers from the alternative minimum tax for 2006 only. Many Democrats who were opposed to the bill argued that the cuts favored the wealthy. Pres. Bush signed the bill into law May 17.

Paper Says U.S. Got Phone Records of Millions of Americans—*USA Today* reported May 11 that the National Security Agency had obtained the records of phone calls made by millions of Americans since late 2001. According to the newspaper, four companies—AT&T, BellSouth, SBC (which had acquired AT&T in 2004 and adopted its name), and Verizon—responded to government requests for the data, but a 5th, Qwest, refused to divulge usage information without a court order, which the NSA did not provide. The 1934 Communications Act made it illegal for phone companies to divulge customer information or calling patterns. Many members of Congress objected, although the NSA said it did not actually listen in on conversations but merely studied patterns of phone calls to identify possible terrorist activity. Pres. Bush said May 11 that his administration was not "mining or trolling through the personal lives of millions of innocent Americans." BellSouth, May 15, and Verizon, May 16, denied handing over the records.

FBI Finds $90,000 in Congressman's Freezer—FBI agents, during the night of May 20-21, searched the Capitol Hill office suite of Rep. William Jefferson (D, LA) as part of an ongoing corruption investigation. Previously, Vernon Jackson, owner of iGate Inc., an Internet technology company, had pleaded guilty May 3 to paying Jefferson more than $400,000 in bribes via a company controlled by Jefferson's family. The FBI May 21 accused Jefferson of taking hundreds of thousands of dollars in bribes and claimed to have found $90,000 of it in his freezer during an August 2005 raid on his home.

The unprecedented FBI search of Jefferson's offices provoked an outcry by members of Congress who contended that the U.S. Constitution prohibited a search by the executive branch on Congressional property. On May 24, Speaker of the House Dennis Hastert (R, IL) and Minority Leader Nancy Pelosi (D, CA) demanded that the Justice Dept. return materials taken during the search. Pres. Bush, May 25, ordered that the seized files be sealed for 45 days. Hastert May 25 suggested that the Justice Dept. had tried to intimidate him by leaking a claim that he was under investigation.

A district court judge ruled July 10 that the raid was legal since members of Congress were "bound to the operations of the criminal laws as are ordinary persons."

Former Top Enron Executives Convicted of Fraud, Conspiracy—Kenneth Lay and Jeffrey Skilling, both former CEOs of the now-bankrupt Enron Corp., were convicted of conspiracy and securities fraud May 25 in U.S. District Court in Houston, TX, Enron's home base. Lay was also found guilty of wire fraud and bank fraud and Skilling of insider trading and making false statements to auditors. Lay and Skilling denied wrongdoing and were expected to appeal. Judge Simeon T. Lake III scheduled sentencing for September. Jurors, at a press conference, said that the defendants had engaged in fraud by lying to investors and employees about Enron's financial circumstances.

Senate Backs Guest Worker Plan for Immigrants— After a long and intense debate, the Senate passed a bill May 25 (62-36) that would give illegal immigrants a path to citizenship if they had lived in the U.S. for more than 2 years. It also provided for a guest-worker program leading to legal permanent residence while requiring employers to verify the immigration status of their workers. In addition, the bill provided for the construction of 350 miles of fencing and 500 miles of vehicle barriers along the Mexican border. Most Democrats favored the bill and a majority of Republicans opposed it. A Senate-House conference committee was to seek to reconcile bills, passed separately by the 2 bodies, that differed greatly.

In a televised address May 15, Bush had sought to push the Senate toward action, declaring, "We do not yet have full control of the border," and announcing a plan to deploy up to 6,000 National Guard troops to aid Border Patrol operations along the U.S.-Mexico border. He endorsed construction of more detention facilities, said deporting 12 mil illegal immigrants was not feasible, reaffirmed support for a guest-worker program, and backed a procedure by which long-term illegals could become citizens. Some Republican dissenters called this approach amnesty.

Treasury Secretary Resigns— Pres. Bush announced May 30 the resignation of Sec. of the Treasury John Snow. Bush nominated Henry Paulson, CEO of Goldman Sachs, to succeed him. Paulson ws confirmed by voice vote June 28.

International

U.S., European Nations Continue to Pressure Iran— In a draft UN resolution introduced May 3, Britain, France, Germany, and the U.S. asked Iran to suspend its uranium enrichment program and to cease construction of a heavy-water reactor. In response, Pres. Mahmoud Ahmadinejad wrote a letter (made public May 8) to Pres. George W. Bush that criticized U.S. foreign policy but left many observers guessing as to its true purpose. Sec. of State Condoleezza Rice said May 31 that the U.S. would enter direct negotiations if Iran suspended its enrichment program.

Sudanese Government and One Rebel Group Sign Agreement— The government of Sudan and the rebel Sudanese Liberation Army (SLA) signed an agreement in Abuja, Nigeria, May 5 ending their armed conflict in a 3-year civil war in Sudan's Darfur region. However, 2 other rebel groups, a smaller SLA faction and the Justice and Equality Movement (JEM), refused to sign the agreement, threatening prospects for peace in the region. The agreement provided for the disarming of the Janjaweed rebel faction by October and the entry of 5,000 rebels into the armed forces. The rebels also received seats in the National Assembly and in 3 state legislatures in Darfur. The people of Darfur would elect their leaders, and those who fled their homes would be compensated. The government May 6 agreed to let a UN peacekeeping force into Darfur.

As of May 31, an estimated 200,000 people had been killed in the conflict and 2 million more had become refugees.

10 U.S. Soldiers Die in Afghanistan Helicopter Crash— A Chinook helicopter crashed May 5 in the Kunar province of Afghanistan, near the border with Pakistan, killing all 10 U.S. soldiers on board. The crash occurred amid growing evidence of an attempted Taliban military offensive in southeastern Afghanistan. American planes bombed a village May 21-22, killing 20 to 80 Taliban fighters according to the U.S. military; local villagers said at least 16 civilians had been killed. Fighting on May 24 cost the lives of 5 Afghan soldiers and 24 suspected Taliban militants. On May 29, a cargo truck in a U.S. military convoy crashed into automobiles in Kabul, killing several civilians. Afghans then rioted and attacked U.S. vehicles; soon the death toll stood at 20, as strife spread across the capital.

U.S. Restores Relations with Libya— Sec. of State Condoleezza Rice said May 15 that the U.S. would resume full diplomatic relations with Libya and drop Libya from its list of states that sponsor terrorism. Relations had been severed in 1980, after a mob in late 1979 burned down the U.S embassy in Tripoli. Libya renounced weapons of mass destruction in December 2003; as a result of this and other actions a U.S. trade embargo was ended in February 2004. Cuba, Iran, North Korea, Syria, and Sudan remained on the U.S. list of states sponsoring terrorism.

Prodi Becomes Italian Prime Minister After a Delay— Romano Prodi, whose coalition had won a narrow victory in Italy's national election in April, was sworn in May 17 along with his cabinet ministers. Initially, then-Prime Min. Silvio Berlusconi refused to concede. Finally, on May 2, he resigned, allowing Prodi to form a new government. However, Prodi had to wait until members of parliament and regional representatives elected a new president, Giorgio Napolitano, on May 10.

Iraqi Factions Agree on Government— An Iraqi parliament divided along sectarian lines finally agreed on most members of a new government, May 20 in Baghdad. The 275-member body, elected in December, approved a 36-member cabinet headed by Prime Min. Nouri Kamel al-Maliki. However, 3 ministries—Defense, Interior, and National Security—remained unfilled.

Despite this progress, violence across Iraq continued throughout the month. Among other incidents, more than 50 Iraqis were found dead or killed May 3, including 16 men at a police recruiting station. Another 51 murder victims were found in Baghdad May 6 and 7. Car bombs killed 14 in Baghdad and Karbala May 7, and a suicide bomber killed 17 in Tal Afar May 9. Gunmen killed 12 employees of an Iraqi electrical manufacturing firm on a bus near Baqubah May 10; 4 more were killed when a bomb planted on the bus exploded later. Two Iraqi army units, one principally Kurd and the other Shiite, clashed May 12 in Balad.

The U.S. military said it killed 25 insurgents south of Baghdad May 14, and bombs and gunfire killed more than 30 people in Baghdad May 16. A roadside bomb northwest of Baghdad killed 4 U.S. soldiers May 18.

Pres. Bush and Prime Min. Tony Blair of Great Britain, at a joint press conference in Washington, DC, May 25 both acknowledged misjudgments in the conduct of the war, but remained committed to its goals and refused to discuss a timetable for withdrawing troops. A roadside explosion May 29 killed 2 British members of a CBS news crew and critically wounded CBS correspondent Kimberly Dozier. Car bombs and mortars killed more than 40 people on May 30 in and near Baghdad and Hilla, and Prime Min. al-Maliki called for a state of emergency in Basra May 31.

Montenegro Votes for Independence from Serbia— Citizens of Montenegro voted May 21 in favor of seceding from Serbia and becoming an independent nation. In all, 55.4% of the voters in Montenegro chose independence. The government and the European Union had agreed that a vote of at least 55.0% would be required for passage.

Montenegro was the smallest of 6 constituent republics in what was once Yugoslavia. Montenegro and Serbia declared independence as a unit in 1992. The other republics had already broken away, often with great bloodshed.

5,000 Dead in Indonesian Earthquake— An earthquake in central Java, 250 mi east of Jakarta, Indonesia, May 27 killed up to 5,141 people. The quake, of 6.3 magnitude, increased activity in a volcano, Mount Merapi, causing volcanic rocks and clouds of gas to pour down its slopes.

General

Winner of Kentucky Derby Is Injured in Preakness— Barbaro, a thoroughbred horse who entered the Kentucky Derby unbeaten in 5 starts, captured that prize on May 6. Ridden by Edgar Prado and trained by Michael Matz, Barbaro finished first by 6.5 lengths in 2 minutes, 1.36 seconds. However, Barbaro's good fortune came to an end on May 21, at the Preakness in Baltimore, when the horse suffered fractures above and below its right hind ankle about 100 yards from the starting gate.

Bernardini, ridden by Javier Castellano and owned by Sheikh Mohammed bin Rashid al-Maktoum of the royal family of Dubai, won the Preakness by 5.25 lengths.

Defendant Gets 4 Years in Fire that Killed 100—Daniel Biechele was sentenced to 4 years in prison May 10 in connection with a fire at the Station nightclub in West Warwick, RI, in 2003. Beichele had ignited the fireworks that caused the disaster. In passing the sentence, Judge Francis Darigan Jr. said he concluded that the defendant's actions were "totally devoid of any criminal intent."

Explosion in Kentucky Coal Mine Kills 5—Five miners were killed May 20 by an explosion in the Darby Mine No. 1 in Harlan County, Ky. A 6th miner escaped.

Media Focuses on Celebrity Baby—Actress Angelina Jolie, May 27 at a hospital in Namibia gave birth to a baby daughter, who was named Shiloh Nouvel Jolie-Pitt. The girl's father was actor Brad Pitt. The couple had gone to Namibia to avoid media attention during the weeks leading up to their baby's birth.

Six in Indonesia Die of Avian Influenza—Health officials in May investigated the deaths of 6 members of a family in N. Sumatra, Indonesia, who had died of avian influenza, or bird flu. Indonesian officials May 29 confirmed 3 more deaths from the disease.

Barry Bonds Passes Babe Ruth in Home Runs—Barry Bonds, 41-year-old outfielder for the San Francisco Giants, moved into 2nd place among Major League Baseball's career home run leaders May 28, when he hit his 715th 4-bagger, against the Colorado Rockies in San Francisco. Bonds passed Babe Ruth, who had hit 714, but Hank Aaron still held the career record, with 755. Bonds continued to be dogged by allegations of steroid use.

Sam Hornish Jr. Wins the Indy 500 in Close Race—Sam Hornish Jr., who had never finished the 500-mile race in 6 attempts, won the 90th Indianapolis automobile classic May 29 by 1 car length, or 0.0635 second. Hornish, who had started from the pole position as the fastest qualifier, came from behind in the home stretch of the last lap to pass 19-year-old Indy rookie Marco Andretti. Marco's father, Michael Andretti, who had never won the race, finished 3rd, a few seconds later. Michael's father, Mario Andretti, had won the race in 1969. Danica Patrick, the only woman in the race, who had come close to winning in 2005, finished 8th.

June 2006

National

Republicans Hold Onto California House Seat—In a runoff election to fill a vacant U.S. House seat in California, Republican Brian Bilbray prevailed June 6 by a margin of 4 percentage points over Democrat Francine Busby. Rep. Randy (Duke) Cunningham (R) had resigned the seat in 2005 after pleading guilty to taking bribes. Bilbray's relatively narrow margin in what is considered a strong Republican district was seen a sign of likely trouble for the GOP in the November 2006 congressional elections.

Senate Rejects 2 Proposed Constitutional Amendments—The Senate June 7 voted, 49-48, to cut off debate on a proposed constitutional amendment that would have banned same-sex marriage in the U.S. Since 60 votes are needed to end debate, the amendment itself did not come up for a vote. Pres. George W. Bush had publicly supported the measure, after having been accused of being lukewarm on an issue that was popular with his conservative base.

On June 27, the Senate voted, 66-34, for an amendment that would give Congress the power to prohibit desecration of the American flag, just one vote short of the 2/3 margin required for congressional approval of a constitutional amendment.

3 Detainees Commit Suicide at Guantanamo—Three prisoners being held at the U.S. prison camp at Guantanamo Bay, Cuba, hanged themselves June 10. Their suicides were the first reported prisoner deaths at the facility. The incident fueled further international debate over prisoners being held there without trial, amid calls by some for the U.S. to close the prison.

Top Bush Aide Won't Be Indicted In CIA Leak Case—Prosecutor Patrick Fitzgerald, who was investigating the leak of the name of CIA operative Valerie Plame Wilson, June 12 notified the attorney for Karl Rove, Pres. Bush's top political strategist, that Rove did not face indictment. Rove had testified before a grand jury 5 times.

Congress Opposes Timetable for Iraq Withdrawal—Members of Congress, mostly Democrats, who favored setting a timetable for U.S. troop withdrawal from Iraq, were rebuffed in the House and Senate on June 16 and 22, respectively. Pres. Bush strongly opposed a timetable, on the grounds that it could incite further insurgent activity in Iraq. The House approved, 256-153, a resolution saying that the U.S. would complete its mission without setting a timetable for withdrawal. The Senate later defeated, 86-13, a resolution introduced by John Kerry (D, MA) and Russ Feingold (D, WI) that called for pulling out most troops by July 2007. A 2nd resolution, which urged Bush to begin a withdrawal but set no timetable for completing it, also failed, by a 60-39 margin.

Ex-White House Official Convicted of Perjury and Obstruction—David Safavian, a former Bush administration official, was found guilty June 20 of 4 of 5 counts of lying to investigators and obstruction of justice. Safavian had been chief of staff at the General Services Administration and chief procurement officer at the Office of Management and Budget. A witness had testified that Safavian gave inside information to lobbyist Jack Abramoff on 2 real estate parcels that Abramoff wanted to buy. Safavian and others had gone on an expensive golf junket to Scotland on a chartered jet; Safavian acknowledged having paid Abramoff only a small portion of his share of the cost.

U.S. Examines World Bank Data in Pursuit of Terrorists—An article in *The New York Times* reported June 23 that the Bush administration had been scouring international financial transactions in order to identify the sources of financing for terror organizations. The government relied on administrative subpoenas to obtain millions of records from the Society for Worldwide International Financial Telecommunication (SWIFT), based in Brussels, Belgium. The Bush administration, which did not seek court-appointed warrants to examine individual transactions, initiated the secret program within weeks of the Sept. 11, 2001, terror attacks. Wire transfers, a principal means of moving money from one country to another, came under scrutiny.

Vice Pres. Dick Cheney June 23 charged that revelations about the program in the media "were making it more difficult for us to prevent future attacks." Pres. Bush June 26 called the disclosure "disgraceful."

Supreme Court Keeps Most of Texas Redistricting Map—The U.S. Supreme Court in a June 28 ruling said that a U.S. House redistricting map for Texas that had been redrawn by the Republican-controlled legislature in 2004 was done legally, although parts of the map had to be redrawn. The new map superseded one drawn by the legislature after the 2000 census, and favored Republicans, who ousted 4 incumbent Texas House Democrats in the Nov. 2004 election. The remapping had been orchestrated by Tom DeLay (R), then the U.S. House majority leader.

In the complex case, the high court issued 5 separate opinions with shifting coalitions. In one, the majority held that part of the redrawing was in violation of the Voting Rights Act of 1965, which was designed to protect minority voters. The court decreed that one redrawn district weakened the voting strength of Latinos in 2 districts and must be redrawn; however, no timetable was given.

Supreme Court Rebuffs Bush on Guantanamo Detainees—The U.S. Supreme Court ruled June 29 that Pres. Bush had overstepped his authority in ordering military war crimes trials for detainees at the Guantanamo Bay prison. It held 5-3 that the trials for 10 foreign terror suspects violated U.S. law and the Geneva conventions.

Justice John Paul Stevens, writing for the majority, said the administration lacked the authority to take the "extraordinary measure" of scheduling special military trials for inmates, in which defendants have fewer legal protections than in civilian U.S. courts. The ruling left in limbo the legal status of 450 men still being held at the prison.

International

Iran Is Warned, Offered a Package of Incentives—Pres. George W. Bush June 1 warned that Iran could face UN sanctions if it did not stop enriching uranium and enter negotiations aimed at stopping the Iranian nuclear program. The same day, the 5 permanent members of the UN Security Council and Germany agreed to a package of incentives for Iran if it stopped enriching uranium and accepted outside supplies of nuclear fuel. This package, which included light-water nuclear reactors to generate electricity, was presented to Iran June 6 by the European Union.

Canada Arrests 17 for Alleged Terrorist Plot—During the night of June 2-3, Canadian authorities arrested 12 men and 5 teenage boys who had allegedly plotted terror attacks in Canada. The 17 were picked up in Toronto and its suburbs. All the adults were charged June 5 with conspiracy. Charges against the juveniles were not made public.

Former President Returns to Power in Peru—Alan Garcia Perez, who was president of Peru from 1985 to 1990, regained that office June 4 in a runoff election, prevailing by 5 percentage points over his center-left populist opponent, Ollanta Humala Tasso.

Pres. Hugo Chavez of Venezuela had intervened in the election campaign, endorsing Humala for president and calling Garcia a crook. Garcia's first term had been plagued by inflation, insurgency, and corruption, but voters apparently accepted his campaign promises to steer a moderate course and learn from past mistakes.

Islamic Militia Gains Ground in Somalia—The Islamic Courts Union, an Islamic militia in Somalia that supports the imposition of Islamic law, said June 5 that it had gained control of Mogadishu, the capital. The militia was opposed by secular warlords, reportedly financed partially by the CIA. Islamist leaders met in Mogadishu June 24 and chose Hassan Dahir Aweys to head the newly formed Council of Islamic Courts. He had been vice chairman of al-Itihaad, which the Bush administration has labeled a terrorist group.

U.S. Air Attack Kills al-Qaeda Leader in Iraq—Abu Musab al-Zarqawi, leader of the al-Qaeda terrorists in Iraq, was killed June 7 by a U.S. air strike on a house in Hibhib near Baqubah. He was thought to have been responsible for many acts of terror, including hotel bombings in Amman, Jordan, in 2005, and the beheading of U.S. citizen Nicholas Berg in 2004. In all, 6 people were killed in the strike on the house, where Zarqawi had been meeting with other terrorist leaders.

Once U.S. coalition forces gained access to the site of the bombing, Zarqawi was positively identified by fingerprints and scars. A statement on an Islamist web site June 12 said he had been replaced by Abu Hamza al-Muhajir, a name believed to be a pseudonym for Abu Ayyub al-Masri, the Egyptian militant who had established al-Qaeda's first Baghdad cell. The U.S. military said June 15 that since Zarqawi's death U.S. and Iraqi forces had conducted 452 raids, killing 104 insurgents, arresting 759 suspects, and seizing 28 arms caches.

In other Iraq news, the new Iraqi cabinet was completed June 8 with the appointment of ministers of defense, interior, and national security. On June 13, to show his support for the new government, Pres. Bush flew to Baghdad and met with Prem. Nuri Kamal al-Maliki and 12 cabinet ministers during a 5-hour visit. Bush said U.S. military forces would not leave until the Iraqi government could stand on its own.

In major acts of violence, a suicide bomber killed 27 in Basra June 3, gunmen killed at least 19 bus passengers north of Baghdad June 4, 6 bombs killed at least 25 in Kirkuk June 13, bombings and a mortar attack killed at least 35 in Baghdad June 17, and on June 23 a bomb killed 12 at a Sunni mosque in Hibhib, near where Zarqawi was killed. At a U.S. traffic checkpoint south of Baghdad, June 16, insurgents killed one U.S. soldier and captured 2 others; both were found dead June 19. Khamis al-Obeidi June 21 became the third lawyer on ex-Pres. Saddam Hussein's defense team to be assassinated.

Prime Min. Junichiro Koizumi announced June 20 that Japan would withdraw its 550 troops from Iraq.

Death of 8 Palestinians Sets off New Cycle of Mideast Violence—An Israeli shell, aimed at a distant target, went astray and struck and killed 8 Palestinians and wounded 30 on a beach in Gaza June 9; the dead included 7 members of one family. Ending a 15-month truce, Hamas, the ruling Palestinian faction, fired 15 rockets from Gaza into Israel the next day. Hamas supporters also clashed, June 12, with their Fatah adversaries, who set fire to the parliament building in Ramallah. On June 13, 10 Palestinians were killed and 40 wounded in an Israeli missile strike on a van in Gaza. Another Israeli strike June 20 killed 3 children.

On June 25, 8 Palestinian militants killed 2 Israeli soldiers, wounded 3, and kidnapped another whom they brought back to Gaza. Two of the Palestinians were killed. Israel demanded the captive's return, and a cycle of escalating violence ensued. It began when the Israelis June 28 sent troops into Gaza, bombed a Hamas training camp, and arrested several Hamas cabinet ministers and parliament members. On the same day, Israeli warplanes buzzed the seaside home of Pres. Bashar Assad of Syria in a show of force, while Palestinian militants said they had also kidnapped a Jewish settler, whom they then executed.

North Korean Missile Draws Criticism—Japan and the U.S. strongly opposed North Korea's intention to test-launch an intercontinental ballistic missile. The range of the missile was thought to be about 3,750 miles. North Korea had observed a launch moratorium since 1999. Japan said June 18 that in the event of a launch it would invoke economic penalties against North Korea and ask for UN sanctions. Sec. of State Condoleezza Rice said June 19 that the test firing would be "a very serious matter."

General

Gates to Gradually Step Down from Microsoft—Bill Gates, co-founder and head of software giant Microsoft and the wealthiest person in the world, said June 15 that he would gradually retire from Microsoft Corp and over the next few years would take more of a part-time role in the company's operation. Gates had stepped down as chief executive officer in 2002, but still maintained a presence in Microsoft's day to day business. He planned to retire fully in 2008 in order to focus completely on the Bill and Melinda Gates Foundation.

Australian Wins U.S. Open—Geoff Ogilvy of Australia won the U.S. Open golf tournament June 18, after 2 close rivals each double-bogeyed the final hole. Ogilvy finished at 285, 5 over par, on the daunting Winged Foot Golf Club course in Mamaroneck, NY. After stumbling on the 18th hole, Phil Mickelson and Colin Montgomerie ended at 286, along with Jim Furyk. For the first time in his professional career, Tiger Woods missed the cut, having shot 12 over par in 2 rounds.

Miami Heat Win 1st NBA Title—The NBA powerhouse Miami Heat won their first title June 20, defeating the Dallas Mavericks 95-92 in Dallas to take the championship series, 4 games to 2. Series MVP Dwayne Wade and veteran superstar Shaquille O'Neal led the Heat. Winning coach Pat Riley had also coached the championship L.A. Lakers teams in the 1980s.

Buffett to Give Some $30 Bil to Gates Foundation—Warren Buffett, chairman of Berkshire Hathaway Inc., made known June 25 that he would give away 85% of his shares in his company, or about $37 bil at current valuation, to charity, in increments beginning almost immediately. The biggest proportion, currently valued at about $31 bil, would go to the Bill & Melinda Gates Foundation—already by far the largest U.S. philanthropic organization—which focuses primarily on improving health and education in poor nations. The rest would go to 4 private foundations associated with Buffett family members.

Buffett was believed to be the 2nd-wealthiest person in the world, after Gates. His total planned gift amounted to the largest donation ever made by a single individual.

U.S. Economy at a Glance: June 2006	
Unemployment rate.	4.6%
Consumer prices (change over 2005).	+4.3%
Trade deficit (12 months through June)	$761.5 bil
Dow Jones closing 2nd quarter.	11,150.22
Dow Jones highest close, 2nd quarter (May 10). . .	11,642.65
Dow Jones lowest close (June 13)	10,706.14
2nd quarter GDP growth (annual rate)	2.6%

July 2006
National
Record Award in Tobacco Lawsuit Overturned—Upholding a lower court decision, the Florida Supreme Court July 6 rejected a $145 bil class-action judgment, the largest punitive award ever, against 5 tobacco companies. The court found that the award was excessive and that plaintiffs whose health was affected by smoking could not pursue class action suits against tobacco companies. However, the court did agree that tobacco companies had misled the public, and upheld judgments in favor of 2 individual plaintiffs, potentially opening the door to hundreds of individual suits.

3 Held in Alleged Plot to Bomb Tunnel—FBI and New York City police officials said July 7 that 3 men accused of plotting to bomb a commuter rail tunnel under the Hudson River between New York and New Jersey had been taken into custody overseas. The suspects were believed to have had connections to global terrorist networks.

U.S. Oil Prices Peak—Spiking oil prices peaked July 14 at $78.40, with an all-time high closing price of $77.03 for a barrel of light sweet crude on the New York Mercantile Exchange. Analysts speculated that the Israel-Lebanon conflict raised new concerns about the oil-producing region's instability that-along with continually rising demand-prompted the spike.

Bush's First Veto, on Stem Cell Research, Upheld—For the first time in his presidency, Pres. George W. Bush July 19 vetoed a bill passed by Congress. The Senate July 18 had approved a bill, 63-37, that would have ended restrictions on federal funding of human embryonic stem cell research. The House had already passed the bill in 2005. Supporters of the bill said greater funding for research on new stem cell lines was needed to study their possible usefulness in medicine. But Bush agreed with research opponents who oppose the destruction of human embryos that results form stem cell harvesting.. A July 19 House vote fell far short (235-193) of the $2/3$ majority required to override a veto.

International
After Kidnapping, Israel Pounds Gaza—The late-June abduction of an Israeli soldier by Palestinian militants brought a ferocious Israeli response in July. The militant groups were demanding that Israel free 1,000 prisoners and stop attacks in Gaza. On July 2, Israeli bombs destroyed the Gaza City offices of Palestinian Authority (PA) Prime Min. Ismail Haniya. In response, 2 Palestinian rockets hit the city of Ashkelon, Israel, July 4 and 5. Israel July 5 bombed the PA interior ministry building for the 2nd time. In the Gaza Strip July 6, ground fighting reportedly resulted in the deaths of 16 Palestinians and an Israeli soldier.

In further actions, an air strike July 13 badly damaged the foreign ministry building of the PA in Gaza City. Israel bombed Palestinian legislative offices July 14, the PA economy ministry July 15, and the foreign ministry July 17. The PA said July 26 that 155 Palestinians had been killed and 623 wounded thus far in the conflict.

Conservative Appears to Win Mexican Presidency by Tiny Margin—Felipe Calderon, candidate of Mexico's ruling conservative National Action Party (PAN), apparently defeated Andres Manuel Lopez Obrador, candidate of the leftist Democratic Revolutionary Party, in July 2 elections that polarized the nation between left and right. In official results announced July 6, Calderon edged out Lopez Obrador by about 240,000 votes out of more than 41 million cast. The PAN also won a plurality in both houses of Congress.

Lopez Obrador July 9 filed a legal challenge to the Federal Election Tribunal, and promoted mass rallies by his supporters, who occupied the central plaza in Mexico City. On July 16, at least 400,000 people joined in a mass protest there, and on Aug. 5 the tribunal ordered a recount in some polling places.

North Korea Launches Long-Range Missile, 6 Others—North Korea test-launched 7 missiles July 5. One of the missiles, a Taepodong-2 believed to be capable of reaching Alaska, failed within 2 minutes of its launch. North Korea also launched 6 medium- and short-range missiles that fell into the Sea of Japan. North Korea called the launches "routine military exercises." The U.S. joined North Korea's neighbors—China, Japan, and South Korea—in criticizing these exercises.

The UN Security Council July 15 unanimously voted to impose limited sanctions on North Korea in response to the launches, and demanded that the ballistic missile program end immediately. North Korea ignored this decree and said it would continue these missile launches.

Polish President's Twin Brother Named Premier—Jaroslaw Kaczynski, the twin brother of Pres. Lech Kaczynski of Poland, was approved as premier on July 10. Jaroslaw Kaczynski, the successor to Kazimierz Marcinkiewicz who resigned July 7, had been active in the anti-Soviet Solidarity labor movement in the 1970s, and had served in parliament and as minister of state. His conservative party, Law and Justice, won a majority of parliamentary seats in the September 2005 elections.

Russians Kill Chechen Terror Leader—Russian special forces July 10 killed Shamil Basayev, a Chechen rebel leader. Basayev and several other guerrillas were killed in Ekazhevo when a truck laden with dynamite exploded in their convoy. Basayev had claimed responsibility for many terror attacks, including the 2004 seizure of a school in Beslan that resulted in the deaths of 331 civilians and security personnel, as well as all 31 rebel attackers.

Rush Hour Bombings Kill 207 in India—A coordinated terror attack during the evening rush hour on the transit system in Mumbai (Bombay), India, July 11 killed 207 people and left 700 wounded. Explosions occurred on 7 commuter trains and in one station. On July 15 a Muslim extremist group calling itself Lashkar-e-Qahhar ("Army of Terror") claimed responsibility. Indian police July 21 arrested 3 Muslim men in connection with the attacks.

Israel Battles Hezbollah Forces Based in Lebanon—Long-simmering tensions between Israel and the militant Shiite Muslim organization Hezbollah, based in Lebanon, erupted into violence in July. On July 12, Hezbollah fired rockets into northern Israel and also attacked 2 military vehicles inside Israel; 8 Israeli soldiers were killed and 2 captured. Israel responded with air, naval, and artillery bombardments in southern Lebanon, a Hezbollah stronghold.

Hezbollah began a rocket barrage on northern Israel July 13, which included strikes on Haifa, Israel's 3rd-largest city. Israel July 13 widened its bombing in Lebanon, pounding airports and other transportation hubs in and around Beirut, and imposed a naval blockade on Lebanese ports. Israel's aim was to thwart the resupply of Hezbollah by Iran, through Syria. Israel also insisted that Lebanon implement UN Security Council Resolution 1559, which urged Lebanon to disarm Hezbollah. The U.S. July 13 denounced Hezbollah for an "unprovoked act of terrorism" and blamed Iran and Syria for their support of the organization.

The European Union July 13 criticized Israel for a "disproportionate use of force." Israeli ground forces crossed into Lebanon July 19, and bloody fighting raged for the rest of the month along the border. From July 16 to July 25, victims of Israeli bombs included 8 Canadians, 11 Lebanese soldiers, and 4 UN observers from 4 countries. Jan Egeland, head of the UN Office for the Coordination of Humanitarian Affairs, in Beirut July 23, called the Israeli attacks a violation of humanitarian law, but also denounced Hezbollah for mixing its fighters with civilians. Israel estimated July 26 that its forces had killed 200 Hezbollah fighters.

Longer-range and heavier rockets fired by Hezbollah beginning July 28 struck deeper into Israel. Israeli missiles July 30 hit several buildings in the southern Lebanon town of Qana, killing about 50, of whom at least 34 were children. By month's end, according to Lebanese officials, some 600 people had been killed in Lebanon. Israeli deaths as of July 30 stood at 33 soldiers and 18 civilians. Many on both sides became refugees, with 120,000 Lebanese reported in Syria on July 24. By July 31, Lebanese refugees totaled 750,000.

Saudi Arabia July 25 pledged $1 bil in reconstruction aid to Lebanon, in addition to $500 mil already promised. The U.S. promised $30 mil.

With the destruction of roads and bridges, escape from Lebanon was difficult. There were about 25,000 Americans in Lebanon when the fighting broke out. After a slow start, 1,059 citizens were rescued and taken to Cyprus on a cruise ship, July 19. The next day, 1,052 followed on the USS *Nashville*. About 40 U.S. Marines landed in Beirut July 20 to assist the evacuation. By July 28, 15,000 Americans had fled the country.

Efforts Made to Resolve Israeli-Hezbollah War— Leaders of the Group of Eight (G-8) major economic powers, meeting in St. Petersburg, Russia, issued a statement July 16 criticizing both Israel and Hezbollah and urging an end to the fighting between them. UN Sec. Gen. Kofi Annan called for an immediate cease-fire July 20. But U.S. Sec. of State Condoleezza Rice, in a statement criticized by some, said July 21 that she did not want "a cease-fire that I know isn't going to last" and that Hezbollah must be disarmed. In a series of diplomatic meetings, Rice met with Lebanese Prem. Fouad Siniora in Beirut July 24 and with Israeli and Palestinian leaders July 24 and 25.

Diplomats from 18 countries and international organizations met in Rome July 26, and supported the deployment of an international peacekeeping force along the border. However, little progress was made toward this goal.

Civilian Death Toll Climbs in Iraq—A July 18 UN report estimated that 14,338 Iraqi civilians had died in violent acts from January to June 2006. Monthly death tolls had risen sharply over this period, from 1,778 in January to 3,149 in June.

On July 1, a car bomb killed 62 in a Shiite area of Baghdad, and on July 9 gunmen killed 42 in a Sunni neighborhood. At least 50 civilians died in attacks in Baghdad 2 days later. On July 12, northeast of Baghdad, terrorists kidnapped 24 people and killed 20 who were Shiites; 40 others, mostly Shiites, were killed south of the capital July 17. In Kufa, July 18, 53 people died in a suicide bombing that targeted laborers. Bombings in Baghdad and Kirkuk July 23 killed 57 others.

In one sign of progress, Iraq July 13 assumed full responsibility for Muthanna, the first of the country's 18 provinces to pass from coalition to local control since the 2003 invasion. Meanwhile, ex-Pres. Saddam Hussein, who had begun a hunger strike July 7 to demand better security for members of the defense team, was hospitalized to be fed through a tube, July 23; the trial resumed the next day and he was brought back into court July 26.

Iraqi Prem. Nuri Kamal al-Maliki met with Pres. Bush in Washington, DC, July 25. Bush pledged to move more U.S. troops into Baghdad to increase security there.

General

Tour de France Battered by Drug Scandals—The Tour de France was shaken by an investigation into illicit drug use. The Amaury Sport Organization, which ran the Tour, produced documents from the Spanish Cycling Federation that implicated 50 riders and other persons, and 13 riders were banned at the outset from the event, which got underway July 1 with 176 contestants.

The scandal also involved American rider Floyd Landis, who won the race on July 23. On July 27 his Swiss-based team, Phonak, announced that he had tested positive for unnaturally high levels of testosterone, a banned steroid. Results of a backup test, reported Aug. 5, were said to confirm the result, and he was dropped from his team. In several interviews Aug. 7 he denied any illegal steroid use; his title remained in doubt.

Space Shuttle Flight Is First in Nearly a Year—The shuttle *Discovery* was launched from the Kennedy Space Center at Cape Canaveral, FL, July 4. Nearly a year had passed since the previous flight, as technicians focused on safety concerns, notably potential damage caused by liftoff debris. *Discovery* docked July 6 with the International Space Station, and returned to Cape Canaveral on July 17 after a successful flight.

Italy Wins Soccer's World Cup for 4th Time—Italy beat France, 5-3, on penalty kicks to win its 4th FIFA World Cup Championship July 9 at Berlin's Olympic Stadium in Germany. The 2 teams had battled to a 1-1 tie at the end of regulation and overtime play. Marcello Lippi coached the Italians. French midfielder Zinedine Zidane, who had led France to

the 1998 title, was given the red card and tossed out of the game after delivering a vicious head-butt to the chest of Italian midfielder Marco Materazzi—who, according to Zidane, had made an inappropriate slur. Nevertheless, Zidane, who announced he would retire after the competition, received the Golden Ball award (voted on by journalists) as the best player in the competition.

Federer, Mauresmo Win Wimbledon Singles Titles— Roger Federer of Switzerland won his 4th straight men's tennis singles title at Wimbledon, England, July 9, defeating Rafael Nadal of Spain, 6-0, 7-6, 6-7, 6-3. On July 8, the women's singles title went to Amelie Mauresmo of France. She defeated Justine Henin-Hardenne of Belgium, 2-6, 6-3, 6-4.

Heat Breaks Records Across U.S.; Europe Also Hit with Heat Wave—Very high temperatures were recorded across the U.S. throughout July. The need for air conditioning drove demand for power in California to a record high July 17, and by July 28, 126 deaths had been blamed on the heat in California alone. In Death Valley, CA, the mercury hit 125 degrees on July 17. On July 30, the heat wave reached as far north as Bismarck, ND, where temperatures hit 112 degrees

By mid-July, a European heat wave was also beginning to take a human toll. France reported 64 deaths as of July 27. In Britain July 19 the temperature reached 97.3 degrees F, the hottest July day in Britain's history.

Deadly Tsunami in Indonesia—A July 17 earthquake under the Indian Ocean triggered a tsunami that killed 668 people on the Indonesian island of Java. Hardest hit was Pangandaran, a coastal town 110 miles northeast of the quake's epicenter. Some 280 people were reported missing and about 74,000 were displaced from their homes. The quake, measuring 7.7 on the Richter scale, was followed by a 6.2 jolt in the same area on July 19.

Woods Wins British Open Golf Title—Tiger Woods, posting an 18-under-par total of 270, won the British Open golf tournament for the 3rd time in his career July 23. This was his 11th victory in one of the 4 major tournaments.

August 2006

National

Sen. Lieberman Loses Democratic Primary—Sen. Joseph Lieberman (CT), who had served in the U.S. Senate for 18 years and was his party's 2000 vice-presidential nominee, was defeated in the Democratic senatorial primary in Connecticut on Aug. 8. Businessman Ned Lamont won 52% of the vote to Lieberman's 48%. Lieberman's loss was attributed mostly to his support for the war in Iraq, which Lamont opposed. Lieberman filed petition signatures Aug. 9 to run for re-election in November as an independent candidate.

Incumbents Across the Country Face Difficult Challenges—In other primary elections where voter dissatisfaction was running high, incumbents had more difficulty than usual in trying to retain their offices. Two members of the U.S. House, Cynthia McKinney (D, GA) and John Schwarz (R, MI), lost primary elections Aug. 8. Gov. Frank Murkowski (R, AK) Aug. 22 finished last in a 3-way contest after receiving only 19% of the primary vote. U.S. Rep. Bob Ney (R, OH), who had been linked to a scandal involving convicted lobbyist Jack Abramoff, said Aug. 7 that he would not seek re-election.

The U.S. Supreme Court, through Justice Antonin Scalia, Aug. 7 rejected an appeal from former House Majority Leader Tom DeLay (R, TX) to be taken off the November ballot. DeLay had resigned from Congress after being indicted, but had previously been chosen by his party to run on the ballot. The ruling meant that DeLay had to remain on the Texas ballot for re-election, though he claimed that he had moved to Virginia. Texas Republican leaders said they would look for a replacement to serve as a write-in candidate.

Judge Rules NSA Wiretap Program Is Illegal—A National Security Agency wiretapping program was ruled illegal Aug. 17 in U.S. District Court in Detroit, MI, by Judge Anna Diggs Taylor. In an approach backed by Pres. George W. Bush, the NSA had been secretly monitoring telephone conversations between persons in the U.S. with suspected terrorist links and persons in other countries. Taylor, the first judge to strike down the NSA program, said that such wiretaps violated the Foreign Intelligence Surveillance Act of 1978, which required authorities to get warrants from a special court that was set up specifically to facilitate this process. She said the wiretapping had also violated the Constitution's prohibition of unreasonable searches and seizures. The U.S. Justice Dept. appealed the ruling.

International

Lethal Violence Grows in Afghanistan—Combat deaths and terrorist violence claimed a growing number of victims in Afghanistan throughout August. Three British NATO force soldiers were killed in action Aug. 1. In the Panjwai district, 21 civilians died Aug. 3 in a suicide bombing. From Aug. 3 to 11, 7 Canadian soldiers in the NATO force were killed. Three U.S. soldiers were killed in Nuristan Aug. 11. A U.S. air strike in Kunar Aug. 17 resulted in the accidental deaths of 12 Afghan policemen. A suicide bomber killed 17 people in Helmand Province Aug. 28.

Castro Undergoes Surgery After Temporarily Ceding Power—Cuban dictator Fidel Castro underwent intestinal surgery Aug. 1, a day after he formally transferred temporary power to his brother Raul. The state-run television news reported that Fidel Castro was in stable condition after the operation. On Aug. 13, Fidel Castro's 80th birthday, a Cuban newspaper printed photographs of the recuperating leader and a message from him saying Cubans should be prepared for "whatever adverse news." A video on television Aug. 14 showed the Castro brothers meeting with Pres. Hugo Chavez of Venezuela.

Civil War Remains a Concern in Iraq—Testifying before the Senate Armed Services Committee Aug. 3, Gen. John Abizaid, commander of U.S. forces in the Middle East, said, "Sectarian violence is probably as bad as I've seen it in Baghdad," adding that Iraq might be moving toward civil war. At the same hearing, Gen. Peter Pace, chairman of the Joint Chiefs of Staff, said he thought civil war was possible but not probable.

Among other incidents, bombings and shootings across the country led to the deaths of 44 civilians Aug. 1. A suicide bomb attack in Najaf Aug. 10 killed at least 35. About 50 Iraqis were killed in scattered violence Aug. 12. That same day U.S. troops killed 26 insurgents in west Baghdad. Bombings in a Shiite neighborhood of Baghdad Aug. 13 killed 63 and wounded 140. In Karbala, 12 people were killed in battles between Iraqi security forces and insurgents. Seven people were killed and 20 others were wounded Aug. 17 when a car bomb exploded in Sadr City.

At a news conference Aug. 21, Pres. Bush acknowledged that Iraq was "straining the psyche of our country," but he declared, "we're not leaving so long as I'm the president." On Aug. 26, hundreds of tribal chiefs signed a "pact of honor" supporting national reconciliation and opposing sectarian strife. Bombs and gunfire killed 100 Iraqis Aug. 27 and 28. Nine U.S. service personnel were killed Aug. 28. Insurgent bombings on Aug. 30 killed at least 47 people.

Former Pres. Saddam Hussein and 6 other defendants went on trial Aug. 21 for charges—separate from the ongoing proceedings in which Hussein was charged with killing 148 men and boys in retaliation for an attempt on his life—related to the deaths of thousands of Kurds in 1988. The defendants included Ali Hassan al-Majid, known as Chemical Ali, who allegedly ordered chemical gas attacks on Kurds. The prosecutor charged that the campaign against the Kurds amounted to genocide.

Israeli-Palestinian Conflict Continues—Israeli forces launched new air strikes Aug. 4 against Hamas targets in the Gaza Strip. In the West Bank, Israeli troops Aug. 6 seized the speaker of the Palestinian parliament, Aziz Dweik, who was a Hamas official. On Aug. 27, militants in the Gaza Strip released 2 Fox News journalists who had been held captive for 13 days.

British Arrest 24 in Airplane Bomb Plot—British authorities Aug. 9 arrested 24 people in London, Birmingham, and High Wycombe, breaking up a major terrorist plot to bomb airplanes flying from Britain to the U.S. Police said that the suspects, all Muslims born in Britain, were going to set off liquid explosives that they would carry onto the airplanes possibly in shampoo and water bottles; as many as 10 planes were thought to be targets. Evidence seized included chemicals to make liquid explosives and so-called martyrdom videos—taped messages made by would-be suicide bombers to be played after their deaths. Many flights into and out of Britain were cancelled, and many others were delayed.

Pakistani police arrested a British-born man Aug. 9 in the same plot. That same day, Britain released one of the 24 who had been arrested. By Aug. 30, a total of 12 of the suspects had been formally charged with conspiracy to commit murder and preparing acts of terrorism, and 3 others with lesser crimes.

Israel, Hezbollah End Hostilities After 34 Days—The conflict between Israeli forces and Hezbollah ended in a truce effective Aug. 14, after 34 days of fighting.

In an escalation Aug. 1, Israel had sent thousands more troops into Lebanon to attack sites from which Hezbollah was launching rockets. In response, Hezbollah fired more than 200 rockets into northern Israel the next day. Most fell harmlessly, but a similar barrage Aug. 3 killed 8 Israelis. Lebanon said Aug. 4 that 28 farm workers had died in an Israeli air raid. Hezbollah rockets Aug. 6 killed 12 soldiers in northern Israel. On Aug. 7, more than 40 died in an Israeli air attack on southern Beirut.

Israel Aug. 8, announced the evacuation of 15,000 civilians living in the northernmost part of the country; in all, about 250,000 civilians had fled their homes because of the fighting in northern Israel. On Aug. 9, 15 Israeli troops were killed in Lebanon. Israeli's security cabinet Aug. 9 voted to expand the offensive up to the Litani River, 18 miles north of the Israel-Lebanon border.

The UN Security Council Aug. 11 unanimously approved Resolution 1701, which brought the war to an end when it became effective on Aug. 14. It called for "a full cessation of hostilities" by the opposing parties and expanded the UN Interim Force in Lebanon from 2,000 troops to 15,000. Also, Lebanon would deploy 15,000 troops in the Hezbollah-controlled southern part of the country. The resolution also called on all unofficial armed groups to disarm. Before the cease-fire became effective, an Israeli ground offensive pushed deeper into Lebanon while the Israeli air force resumed bombing in Beirut and elsewhere. On Aug. 12, 24 Israeli soldiers were killed, their highest daily total. Hezbollah fired more than 220 rockets Aug. 13.

Hezbollah leader Sheikh Hassan Nasrallah claimed victory Aug. 14, although Hezbollah had sustained heavy losses. Israel did the same, although it had failed to secure the release of the 2 Israeli soldiers whose capture started the conflict. Thousands of refugees on both sides of the border began returning to their homes in the war-torn regions on Aug. 14. Lebanon Aug. 17 began to deploy its army south of the Litani River, and some soldiers reached the Israeli border Aug. 18. On Aug. 22, Italy pledged up to 3,000 troops to the UN force. Pres. Jacques Chirac said Aug. 24 that France would contribute 2,000 troops.

An estimated 843 Lebanese, mostly civilians, were killed during the fighting. A total of 57 Israeli lost their lives, including 39 civilians. The human rights organization Amnesty International charged Aug. 23 that Israel had committed war crimes by targeting civilians and by indiscriminate or disproportionate attacks. The Israeli Foreign Ministry denied Israel had targeted civilians, which it said Hezbollah had done.

Iran Replies to UN on Nuclear Technology—Iranian leader Ayatollah Ali Khamenei said Aug. 21 that Iran would continue its current nuclear technology program without regard to pressure from other nations. The next day, the Iranian government responded to the June UN proposal aimed at turning Iran away from the enrichment of uranium. The text of Iran's response was not immediately made public. The UN had threatened sanctions if Iran did not, by the end of August, halt enrichment, a necessary step in the construction of atomic weapons. Iran expanded its nuclear program Aug. 26 by inaugurating a heavy-water plant.

General

JonBenet Ramsey Murder Suspect Confesses, but Case Against Him Crumbles—Authorities in Bangkok, Thailand, arrested John Mark Karr Aug. 16, for the widely publicized Dec. 1996 murder of JonBenet Ramsey, a 6-year-old beauty queen from Boulder, CO. But 12 days later, the case collapsed when DNA evidence found at the murder scene did not match Karr's. Karr had become a suspect after Michael Terry, a journalism professor who had made documentary films on the murder, alerted Boulder authorities to emails he had received from Karr showing great interest in the crime.

Karr had been arrested in 2001 for possessing child pornography. Speaking to reporters Aug. 17 after his 2006 arrest, he claimed he was with JonBenet when she died but that her death had been an accident. Disputing his statements, Karr's ex-wife, Lara Knutson, said she had no recollection of his having been gone from their Alabama home on the day of the murder, Dec. 26. Karr was flown to Los Angeles Aug. 20 pending trial; after the DNA tests, County Dist. Atty. Mary Lacy, Aug. 28, asked that the arrest warrant be dismissed.

Pluto Demoted to "Dwarf Planet"—Pluto, known since its discovery in 1930 as the smallest and generally most distant planet in the solar system, suffered a hit to its reputation Aug. 24. The International Astronomical Union, meeting in Prague, voted to adopt a definition of "planet" that excluded Pluto. The decision drew a mixed reaction from astronomers and the general public. Pluto differs in a number of ways from other traditional "planets," especially in being much smaller. The recent discovery of other objects orbiting the sun in the outer solar system that are comparable in size to Pluto finally sparked the controversial reconsideration of its status. Two other bodies were categorized as dwarf planets: Ceres—located in the asteroid belt between Mars and Jupiter—and 2003 UB313, a body in the outer solar system formally named Eris Sept. 13.

Tiger Woods Takes PGA Golf Title—Tied for the lead after 54 holes, Tiger Woods shot a 4-under-par 68 in the final round of the PGA tournament to win the title by 5 strokes at the Medinah Country Club in Illinois Aug. 20. With his 12th victory in a major tournament, Woods trailed only Jack Nicklaus, who had won 18 majors tournaments in his career."

September 2006
National

Bush Asks Congress to Act on Trials for Terrorists, Discloses Secret Prisons—Pres. Bush Sept. 6 called on Congress to approve legislation providing for the government to try alleged terrorists using military commissions. He announced the move in a televised speech, following a U.S. Supreme Court decision that prohibited his administration from acting alone to create such commissions for trying accused detainees in the so-called war on terror, The Court held that those being detained were protected by the Geneva Conventions.

Bush also revealed for the first time, Sept. 6, that prisoners had been held at secret prisons in other countries, and that 14 "high-value" detainees, including men linked to the Sept. 11, 2001, terror attacks, were being transferred from CIA custody to the U.S. prison in Guantanamo Bay, Cuba. Also on Sept. 6, the Defense Dept. released a revised edition of the Army Field Manual that established permissible interrogation techniques for captives, including both prisoners of war and so-called unlawful combatants. Several methods that some had called torture were forbidden. The guidelines were for military personnel and government contractors but did not apply to CIA agents.

On Sept. 7, 3 Pentagon lawyers criticized a draft of new legislation from the Bush administration that denied defendants the right to see some evidence used against them. Three Republican senators—Lindsay Graham (SC), John McCain (AZ), and John Warner (VA)—sought changes in Bush's bill. Former Sec. of State Colin Powell, Sept. 14, supported them, writing in a letter to McCain, "The world is beginning to doubt the moral basis of our fight against terrorism."

In a Sept. 21 compromise, the senators and Bush agreed that defendants had the right to see evidence presented to the jury. They also agreed that the legislation would not redefine U.S. obligations under the Geneva Conventions. The House, Sept. 27, approved the compromise draft, 253-168.

Ex-State Dept. Official Was a Source in CIA Leak Case—Richard Armitage confirmed Sept. 7 that, while serving as deputy secretary of state in 2003, he was the primary source for the "outing" of CIA agent Valerie Plame Wilson in a July 2003 newspaper column by Robert Novak. Wilson's husband, Joseph, a former U.S. ambassador, had claimed administration officials leaked his wife's name as punishment for his published criticism of U.S. policy in Iraq. "Scooter" Libby, a former top aide to Vice Pres. Dick Cheney, had been indicted in connection with the incident. *Newsweek* magazine reported Armitage's role on its website Aug. 28, and *The New York Times* website carried his confirmation Sept. 7.

Senators Find No Basis for Link Between Hussein and al-Qaeda—A suspected relationship between the regime of Saddam Hussein and the terror organization al-Qaeda apparently did not exist, according to a Sept. 8 report from the Senate Select Committee on Intelligence. The report said that the CIA had concluded in September 2002 that Iraq had no contact with al-Qaeda's leader Osama bin Laden, and in January 2003 the CIA also reported that Hussein saw al-Qaeda and other militant groups as threats.

That finding by the committee was nearly unanimous. Five of 7 Republicans dissented from another finding—that many administration prewar claims were based on information obtained from the Iraqi National Congress, even after the CIA and the Defense Dept. warned that foreign intelligence services, including Iran's, had penetrated the INC. The committee majority said that the INC had tried to influence U.S. policy with false information that Iraq had weapons of mass destruction and ties to terrorists.

Bush Defends War on Terror—In the days leading up to the 5th anniversary of the Sept. 11, 2001, attacks on the United States, Pres. George W. Bush defended his administration's response to the 9-11 attacks and his decision to invade Iraq. Addressing an American Legion convention in Salt Lake City, Aug. 31, he called the fight against Islamic extremism "the decisive ideological struggle of the 21st century." Speaking to military officers and veterans in Washington, DC, Sept. 5, he likened the fight against terrorists to conflicts with Nazi Germany and the Soviet Union. In Atlanta, GA, Sept. 7, Bush said America was safer 5 years after the attacks because "we've taken action to protect the homeland."

On Sept. 10 and 11, Bush attended memorial ceremonies in New York, Pennsylvania, and Virginia. In a televised address Sept. 11, Bush said that whatever mistakes had been made in Iraq, "the worst mistake would be to think that if we pulled out, the terrorists would leave us alone."

Election-Year Primary Season Concludes—Sen. Lincoln Chafee, a moderate Republican, prevailed in a Republican primary in Rhode Island Sept. 12, winning 54% of the vote against a conservative challenger. In New York, Sept. 12, Sen. Hillary Rodham Clinton, running for a 2nd term, and state Atty. Gen. Eliot Spitzer, running for governor, were big winners in the Democratic primary. In Washington, DC, Sept. 12, City Councilman Adrian Fenty won the Democratic nomination for mayor, in effect guaranteeing his election in November.

House Passes Partial Immigration Bill; Comprehensive Legislation Still Stalled—The U.S. House Sept. 14 passed a measure, 283-138, providing for a 700-mi fence along the U.S.-Mexican border, and sent it to the Senate. But congressional leaders conceded there would be no time for comprehensive immigration legislation before Congress's pre-election recess.

Intelligence Agencies Say Iraq War Increased Terror Threat—Several U.S. newspapers reported Sept. 24 that a classified National Intelligence Estimate completed in April concluded that the Iraq war had made the terror threat worse. The estimate, a consensus view of 16 government agencies, asserted that the war had helped create a new generation of Islamic radicals, many of whom, after fighting in Iraq, may have returned to their home countries to plan acts of terror.

Pres. Bush Sept. 26 condemned the leak of classified information, saying that critics who believed the war had worsened the terror threat were naive and mistaken, and he ordered portions of the report, including a summary, be declassified. The summary concluded that U.S. counterterrosim efforts had "seriously damaged" terrorist leadership, but that a growing threat remained. The summary noted that defeat of the insurgency in Iraq would likely make it more difficult for terror organizations to expand their ranks.

Clinton Says He Tried to Kill Bin Laden—In a contentious interview broadcast on Fox News Sept. 24, former Pres. Bill Clinton said he had "worked hard" to kill or capture the terror leader Osama bin Laden before he left office in January 2001. He charged that the Bush administration, prior to the September 2001 attacks, had not acted on information that bin Laden and al-Qaeda posed an imminent threat. On Sept. 26, Sec. of State Condoleezza Rice defended Pres. Bush's efforts to hunt down bin Laden, while Sen. Hillary Rodham Clinton (D, NY) backed her husband's position.

U.S. Economy at a Glance: September 2006
Unemployment rate 4.6%
Dow Jones closing, 3rd quarter 11,679.07
Dow Jones highest close, 3rd quarter (Sept. 28). . .11,718.45
Dow Jones lowest close, 3rd quarter (July 14) 10,739.45

International

Iraqi Casualties Rise Sharply—A U.S. Defense Dept. report Sept. 1 said that casualties among Iraqi civilians and security forces increased 51% during the period May 20 to Aug. 11, compared with the previous 3-month period. An average of nearly 120 Iraqis died each day in the later period, compared with about 80 per day in the earlier 3 months. On Sept. 7, the U.S.-led coalition formally transferred authority over Iraq's armed forces to Prime Min. Nouri Kamel al-Maliki.

Syria Supports Arms Embargo to Lebanon—UN Sec. Gen. Kofi Annan said Sept. 1 that Pres. Bashar al-Assad of Syria had promised to enforce an embargo on arms shipments from Syria to Lebanon. Israel Sept. 7 lifted its air blockade of Lebanon, and ended its sea blockade Sept. 8. Hundreds of thousands of people attended a pro-Hezbollah rally in Beirut Sept. 22, at which the group's leader, Hassan Nasrallah, claimed that Hezbollah was now stronger than before its fight with Israel, and still had 20,000 missiles.

New Offensive Targets Taliban in Afghanistan, as Violence Continues—Amid evidence of growing Taliban influence in southern Afghanistan, Canadian forces under NATO control and Afghan troops Sept. 2 launched a new offensive, Operation Medusa, in Kandahar Province. A British reconnaissance plane crashed Sept. 2, killing 14.

In Kabul, Sept. 8, in the deadliest attack in the capital since 2002, a car bomb killed 2 U.S. soldiers and 14 Afghans. In Gardez, Sept. 10, a bomber wearing explosives killed the governor of Paktia Province along with 3 others. On Sept. 11, a suicide bomber killed 7 mourners at the governor's funeral and wounded up to 40.

As Operation Medusa wound down Sept. 12, Taliban deaths were estimated at 250 to 500, with 5 Canadians and 1 U.S. soldier killed. A terrorist bomb killed 4 Canadians in a southern village Sept. 18 as they handed out gifts to Afghan children. On Sept. 25, Safia Amajan, head of the women's affairs department in Kandahar Province, was shot to death in Kandahar.

The UN Office on Drugs and Crime said Sept. 2 that the production of opium poppies had risen 50% in Afghanistan in the past year.

Blair Agrees to Resign Within a Year—Prime Min. Tony Blair of Great Britain said Sept. 7 that he would resign within one year, though he declined to set a specific date. Although his government was elected to a 5-year term in 2005, he had been pressed by members of his Labor Party to step aside because of declining Labor Party popularity in polls and widespread opposition especially to Blair's strong support of U.S. policy in Iraq. Eight members of his government, demanding that he leave office immediately, had resigned their positions on Sept. 6.

Conservative Declared Winner in Mexican Presidential Elections—Mexico's Federal Election Tribunal on Sept. 5 unanimously declared conservative candidate Felipe Calderon the winner of the July 2 presidential election by a razor-thin margin, rejecting calls from supporters of leftist candidate Andres Manuel Lopez Obrador for a full recount or new elections. The tribunal had found minor irregularities in a recount of selected polling places but concluded that the overall result was accurate. Public opinion polls found that a majority of Mexicans believed the tribunal was impartial, but many supporters of Lopez Obrador continued to protest that the election had been stolen. At a mass rally in Mexico City Sept. 16, Lopez Obrador was declared the head of a so-called parallel government.

Calderon's inauguration was scheduled for Dec. 1.

Hamas, Fatah Agree on a Unity Palestinian Government—The Palestinian Authority moved closer Sept. 11 to a unity government. Pres. Mahmoud Abbas of the Fatah party and Prem. Ismail Haniya of Hamas, the Islamist movement, agreed on a unity platform that reportedly accepted previous agreements with Israel and supported a final settlement based on Israel's return of territories it took in the 1967 war. Hamas Sept. 12 supported resumption of peace talks with Israel. An Israeli military court Sept. 12 ordered the release of 19 Hamas legislators who had been arrested on terrorism charges, but the prosecution appealed the ruling.

Syrian Guards Help Thwart Attack on U.S. Embassy—Four Muslim men, armed with grenades and rifles and riding in bomb-rigged trucks, attacked the U.S. embassy in Damascus, Syria, Sept. 12. They managed to detonate one bomb. Syrian guards killed 3 and wounded the 4th, who died Sept. 13. One Syrian guard was killed and 10 were wounded.

Military Overthrows Premier of Thailand—Premier Thaksin Shinawatra of Thailand was overthrown in a bloodless coup Sept. 19. The chief of the army, Gen. Sondhi Boonyaratkalin, led the revolt, with tanks and troops surrounding the Government House in Bangkok, the capital. Thaksin was in New York, attending a meeting of the UN General Assembly, at the time of the coup. The new regime suspended the constitution and declared martial law.

President of Sudan Rejects UN Force for Darfur—In an address to the UN General Assembly Sept. 19, Pres. Omar Hassan al-Bashir of Sudan restated a decision not to allow UN peacekeepers to enter Sudan's devastated Darfur region. The UN Security Council had approved a 20,000-member force for Darfur, where 200,000 had died in civil strife. With Bashir's rebuff, the African Union, also meeting in New York, agreed Sept. 20 to extend its Darfur force until the end of the year. The force had, however, proven ineffective thus far in halting the massive violence,

U.S. and Iranian Presidents Give Opposing Speeches Before UN General Assembly—The international debate over Iran's nuclear energy program continued at the United Nations in New York Sept. 19. The annual general debate session of the General Assembly opened that day, with Presidents George Bush and Mahmoud Ahmadinejad among the speakers. In a speech aimed particularly at the Iranian people, Bush said he had no objection to a peaceful nuclear-power program for Iran, and emphasized that he sought a diplomatic solution. Ahmadinejad said international inspectors were watching a "transparent" nuclear program, and he rebuked the Security Council for its ultimatum that Iran end nuclear enrichment by Aug. 31, which Iran had ignored.

Addressing the Assembly Sept. 20, Pres. Hugo Chavez of Venezuela, a vitriolic critic of the Bush administration, called Pres. Bush "the devil himself" and said the United States was attempting to dominate the world.

Pakistani, Afghan Presidents Pay Tense Visits to Washington—Pres. Pervez Musharraf of Pakistan met with Pres. Bush in Washington Sept. 22, and assured him that a deal he had cut with tribal leaders along the border with Afghanistan would curb Taliban influence, not give the militants more freedom.

In a CNN interview Sept. 26, Musharraf said he stood by an assertion in his new book, *In the Line of Fire*, that he had opposed the war in Iraq because it would encourage extremists. Before they both dined with Bush at the White House Sept. 27, Musharraf and Pres. Hamid Karzai of Afghanistan publicly criticized each other's efforts to defeat the terrorist threat, notably as it existed along their common border.

New Japanese Prime Minister Chosen—Shinzo Abe, of the ruling Liberal Democratic Party, was chosen by the lower house of parliament Sept. 26 to be the next prime minister of Japan. He received 339 of 475 votes.

Abe has advocated close alliance with the U.S., a more forceful foreign policy, and pro-growth fiscal policies. At 52 the youngest Japanese premier since World War II, he succeeded Junichiro Koizumi, who had led the government for 5 years.

General

CBS News Appoints First Solo Female Anchor—Katie Couric, host of NBC's *Today* morning show since 1991, debuted as CBS Evening News anchor Sept. 5. Couric took over for Bob Schieffer, the interim replacement for long-time anchor Dan Rather since Mar. 2005.

U.S. Open Tennis Titles Go to Sharapova, Federer—Maria Sharapova of Russia won the women's tennis singles title at the U.S. Open in New York City Sept. 9, defeating Justine Henin-Hardenne of Belgium, 6-4, 6-4. On Sept. 10, Roger Federer of Switzerland defeated the American Andy Roddick 6-2, 4-6, 7-5, 6-1 for his 3rd straight men's title.

Andre Agassi of the United States retired as planned, ending his career Sept. 3 with his defeat in the 3rd round of the Open. He had won 60 tournaments in his career, including 8 Grand Slams. After winning the mixed doubles title with teammate Bob Bryan on Sept. 9, Czech-born American star Martina Navratilova also retired, with a record of 18 Grand Slam singles titles.

Pope Visits Bavaria, Stirs Muslim Anger With Speech at University—Pope Benedict XVI visited his native Bavaria, in Germany, for the first time in his papacy. Masses that he celebrated in Munich, Sept. 10, and Regensburg, Sept. 12, brought out 250,000 and 230,000 people, respectively.

His address Sept. 12 at Regensburg Univ., where he had once taught, made headlines when it created a furor among Muslims. In a scholarly speech defending a concept of God as accessible to reason, and opposing violence in religion, he quoted, but did not endorse, words of a 14th-century Byzantine Christian emperor, who said, "Show me just what Muhammad brought that was new, and there you will find things only evil and inhuman, such as his command to spread by the sword the faith he preached."

Muslims in many countries protested the speech. An Assyrian Catholic church in Basra, Iraq, was bombed Sept. 15. In the West Bank and Gaza, a Palestinian group firebombed 5 churches the next day. The pope, Sept. 17, apologized for any offense caused, saying that the words "do not in any way express my personal thought" and that he sought "frank and sincere dialogue." He said Sept. 20 that he had "deep respect" for Islam.

October 1-13, 2006

National

Dow Hits New High—The Dow Jones Industrial Average closed at 11,727.34 on Oct. 3, surpassing for the first time its record high close of 11,722.98, recorded on Jan. 14, 2000. The current leg of the stock rebound was spurred by a decline in crude oil futures, leading to lower auto gas prices. Oil prices, which had peaked at over $78 a barrel in July, had fallen under $60. However, broader stock market indexes were still below their all-time highs.

U.S.-Mexico Border Bill Signed Into Law—Pres. Bush Oct. 4 signed into law a bill allocating funds to pay for about 700 miles of fence along the U.S.-Mexico border. More complex bills on the contentious immigration issue had stalled, with large, seemingly irreconcilable differences between more comprehensive versions passed separately by the House and Senate.

Scandal Surfaces Over Congressman's Inappropriate Messages to Teenage Pages—The U.S. House Ethics Committee, Oct. 5, began an investigation into the way in which House staff and officials handled indications of misbehavior by former Rep. Mark Foley (R, FL), who had resigned Sept. 29 after ABC News revealed contents of inappropriate and often sexually explicit electronic messages he had sent to teenage male pages on Capitol Hill. An FBI investigation was also in progress.

As the scandal emerged, some called for the resignation of House Speaker J. Dennis Hastert (R, IL), claiming he had learned of or received indications of Foley's inappropriate behavior, but had done little to pursue the matter. Hastert Oct. 4 declared that he would not resign and that he had not known of any of Foley's inappropriate communications before the spring of 2006, although members of his staff reportedly had been warned earlier. He did take full responsibility for what was seen as a serious political problem for Republicans, just a few weeks before congressional elections.

Foley's lawyer, David Roth, said Oct. 3, that Foley had entered a treatment center for alcohol and mental health problems. He said Foley had been abused sexually by clergyman when a teenager.

International

8 U.S. Soldiers Killed in One Day as Iraq War Death Toll Rises—The U.S. Army lost 8 soldiers in Iraq Oct. 3, 4 in a roadside bomb attack and 4 in individual shooting incidents; 17 soldiers and marines in all died in 4 days ending Oct. 3. The U.S. military death toll had reached 74 in September, the highest since 76 were lost in Apr. 2006. Iraqi officials said Oct. 4 that a police brigade had been suspended because of suspicion that some members had allowed or joined in death-squad killings. John Warner (R, VA), chairman of the Senate Armed Services Committee, said that the U.S. should consider a "change of course" in Iraq unless violence was curtailed.

North Korea Reports Underground Nuclear Test—Brushing aside widespread international condemnation, North Korea Oct. 9 announced that it had set off an atomic weapon underground. The official news agency said that the test had been successful and that no radiation had leaked aboveground. Geological instruments in other countries confirmed an explosion, though the cause was not definitely confirmed and some experts believed the test had not been fully successful. Pres. George W. Bush, Oct. 11, said the apparent action by North Korea would have "serious repercussions" but that the U.S. would pursue a diplomatic path. The UN Security Council Oct. 6 had urged North Korea to not carry out the planned test, and was considering its response to North Korea's move. In a joint statement Oct. 8, China and Japan said that a North Korean nuclear test "cannot be tolerated."

Security Council Nominates New UN Secretary General—The UN Security Council Oct. 9 nominated the South Korean foreign minister, Bam Ki-Moon, to succeed Kofi Annan after the latter ends his tenure as secretary general, Dec. 31. Six other candidates for the post had put themselves out of consideration. The nomination then went to the General Assembly which was expected to approve it.

Ki-Moon was regarded as more low-key than the highly activist Annan, who had served for 10 years and was widely admired, though his administration also was touched by financial scandal in the last few years. The nomination was somewhat overshadowed by news of the North Korean nuclear test, which some said might have been deliberately timed in anticipation of the nomination.

Russian Journalist Critical of Kremlin Murdered—Russian journalist Anna Politkovskaya, known for articles exposing alleged Russian atrocities in Chechnya and a tenacious critic of the Russian government, was found murdered execution-style in her Moscow apartment, Oct. 7. Her murder aroused widespread indignation. Russian Pres. Vladimir Putin, who said the crime might have been committed by persons seeking to discredit his administration, vowed that the government would hunt down those responsible.

General

Gunman Kills 5 Girls at Amish Schoolhouse— A 32-year-old dairy truck driver shot 10 girls in a one-room Amish school in Nickel Mines, PA, Oct. 2; 5 died and 5 were seriously wounded. The victims ranged in age from 6 to 13. Charles Roberts had brought a semiautomatic pistol, 2 shotguns, and other weapons into the school, and ordered the boys and adults present to leave; he then tied the girls up and shot them. As police closed in, he shot and killed himself. Roberts, who had a wife and 3 children, lived about a mile from the school, which was in a rural area some 50 miles west of Philadelphia. He left a suicide note saying he was distraught about an incident 2 decades ago, which apparently involved his molestation of two girls.

OBITUARIES

A

Allyson, June, 88, Hollywood leading lady of the 1940s and 1950s; Ojai, CA, July 8, 2006.

Anderson, Jack, 83, muckraking Washington, DC, syndicated columnist; Bethesda, MD, Dec. 18, 2005.

Arnold, Sir Malcolm, 84, British composer of film scores; won an Oscar for *The Bridge on the River Kwai* (1957); Norwich, England, Sept. 23, 2006

B

Ba Jin, 100, novelist and essayist considered the dean of modern Chinese literature; Shanghai, China, Oct.17, 2005.

Barrett, Syd, 60, co-founder of the British psychedelic rock group Pink Floyd; Cambridge, England, July 7, 2006.

Barretto, Ray, 76, master conga drummer who straddled jazz and Latin music; Hackensack, NJ, Feb. 17, 2006.

Bell, Mary Hayley, 94, British playwright and novelist; wife of actor John Mills and mother of actresses Hayley and Juliet Mills; Dec. 1, 2005, England.

Benchley, Peter, 65, author whose best-selling novel *Jaws* (1974) was made into a blockbuster film; Princeton, NJ, Feb. 11, 2006.

Bentsen Jr., Lloyd, 85, long-serving U.S. senator (D, TX, 1971-93) and 1988 vice presidential candidate; U.S. Treasury secretary (1993-94); Houston TX, May 23, 2006.

Berenstain, Stan, 82, co-author and co-illustrator, with wife Jan Berenstain, of the *Berenstain Bears* children's series; Doylestown, PA, Nov. 26, 2005.

Berg, Patty, 88, golf pioneer who won a record 15 women's major championships, including the inaugural U.S. Women's Open (1946); Fort Myers, FL, Sept. 10, 2006

Best, George, 59, first British soccer superstar; battled alcohol problems; London, England, Nov. 25, 2005.

Bujones, Fernando, 50, Cuban-American ballet dancer; Miami, FL, Nov. 10, 2005.

Butcher, Susan, 51, four-time winner (1986-88, 1990) of Alaska's grueling Iditarod dog-sled race; Seattle, WA, Aug. 5, 2006.

Butler, Octavia E., 58, acclaimed black female science-fiction writer; Seattle, WA, Feb. 24, 2006.

Buttons, Red, 87, puckish red-haired comedian, 1950s TV host, movie actor; won an Oscar for *Sayonara* (1959); Los Angeles, CA, July 13, 2006.

C

Caldwell, Sarah, 82, Boston-based opera impresario and conductor; the first woman to conduct at New York City's Metropolitan Opera (1976); Portland, ME, March 23, 2006.

Cameron, James, 92, founded Black Holocaust Museum, documenting racially motivated attacks on African Americans; Milwaukee, WI, June 11, 2006.

Cassini, Oleg, 92, fashion designer who created more than 300 noted ensembles for First Lady Jacqueline Kennedy; Manhasset, NY, March 17, 2006.

Chandler, Otis, 78, newspaper publisher who turned the *Los Angeles Times*, into one of the most respected U.S. papers during his tenure (1960-80); Ojai, CA, Feb. 27, 2006.

Church, Dorothea (née Towles), 83, first black woman to break through as a fashion model in Paris during the early 1950s; New York, NY, July 7, 2006.

Coffin Jr., William Sloane, 81, Protestant minister who became a leading opponent of the Vietnam War as a Yale Univ. chaplain; Strafford, VT, April 12, 2006.

Cummings, Constance, 95, U.S.-born, Britain-based actress; won 1979 Tony Award for *Wings*; Oxfordshire, England, Nov. 23, 2005.

D

D'Aquino, Iva Toguri, 90, Japanese-American citizen better known as Tokyo Rose; convicted of treason for WWII radio broadcasts from Japan to U.S. troops; Pres. Gerald Ford pardoned her in 1977; Chicago, IL, Sept. 26, 2006.

Davis, Ed, 89, high-profile L.A. police chief who pioneered community-based policing (1970s); supported liberal causes as a Republican state senator; San Luis Obispo, CA, April 22, 2006.

Deloria Jr., Vine, 72, Native American activist and author of *Custer Died for Your Sins* (1969); Denver, CO, Nov. 13, 2005.

Douglas, Mike, 81, TV and music impresario; host of syndicated *Mike Douglas Show* (1961-82); Palm Beach Gardens, FL, Aug. 11, 2006.

Drucker, Peter F., 95, pioneering management theorist; wrote *The Future of Industrial Man* (1942) and *The Practice of Management* (1954); Claremont, CA, Nov. 11, 2005.

Dunham, Katherine, 96, dancer and choreographer; introduced new audiences to African and Caribbean forms; New York, NY, May 21, 2006.

E

Edwards, Ralph, 92, radio and TV pioneer who introduced the hit shows *Truth or Consequences*, *This Is Your Life*, *Name That Tune*, and *The People's Court*; West Hollywood, CA, Nov. 16, 2005.

El Din, Hamza, 76, Egyptian composer and musician who adapted traditional Nubian music for the oud, the central instrument in Arab classical music; Berkeley, CA, May 22, 2006.

Epstein, Barbara, 77, co-founder (1963) and co-editor of the the *New York Review of Books*; New York, NY, June 16, 2006.

F

Fallaci, Oriana, 77, Italian journalist; Florence, Italy, Sept. 15, 2006.

Ferguson, Maynard, 78, Canadian-born jazz trumpeter known for his ability to hit exceedingly high notes; Ventura, CA, Aug. 23, 2006.

Feuer, Cy, 95, Broadway producer who, with partner Ernest H. Martin, produced such musicals as *Guys and Dolls* (1950), *Can-Can* (1953) and *How to Succeed in Business Without Really Trying* (1961); New York, NY, May 17, 2006.

Fleischer, Richard, 89, film director; *Doctor Doolittle* (1967), *The Boston Strangler* (1971); Woodland Hills, CA, March 25, 2006.

Ford, Glenn, 90, movie actor; *Cowboy* (1958), *The Courtship of Eddie's Father* (1963), *The Big Heat* (1953); Beverly Hills, CA, Aug. 30, 2006.

Fowles, John, 79, British novelist; *The Collector* (1963), *The Magus* (1965) and *The French Lieutenant's Woman* (1969), many of which were made into films; Lyme Regis, England, Nov. 5, 2005.

Franciosa, Anthony, 77, Method actor, famously difficult to work with, whose Hollywood heyday was in the 1950s and 1960s; Los Angeles, CA, Jan. 19, 2006.

Freed, James Ingo, 75, architect; designed Holocaust Memorial Museum in Washington, DC, and the Jacob K. Javits Convention Center in New York City; New York, NY, Dec. 15, 2005.

Friedan, Betty, 85, feminist leader who wrote the hugely influential book *The Feminine Mystique* (1963); helped found the National Organization for Women (NOW) in 1966 and was its first president; Washington, DC, Feb. 4, 2006.

G

Galbraith, John Kenneth, 97, liberal economist, best-selling author, social critic, Democratic presidential adviser, and U.S. ambassador to India (1961-63); Cambridge, MA, April 29, 2006.

Geoffrion, Bernie (Boom Boom), 75, Hall of Fame hockey player who helped lead the Montreal Canadiens to six Stanley Cup titles between 1953 and 1960; Atlanta, GA, March 11, 2006.

Gigante, Vincent (The Chin), 77, New York City mob boss who for years feigned mental illness to avoid prosecution; prison hospital in Springfield, MO, Dec. 19, 2005.

Gowdy, Curt, 86, radio and TV sportscaster; hosted hunting-and-fishing-oriented *American Sportsman* (1966-86); Palm Beach, FL, Feb. 20, 2006.

H

Harrer, Heinrich, 93, Austrian mountaineer and adventurer; tutored the Dalai Lama; memoir *Seven Years in Tibet* (1953) was an international best-seller; Friesach, Austria, Jan. 7, 2006.

Haughey, Charles, 80, prime minister of Ireland for much of the period between 1979 and 1992; quit amid charges of corruption; Kinsealy, Ireland, June 13, 2006.

Hayden, Melissa, 83, Canadian-born dancer; won acclaim with George Balanchine's New York City Ballet (1955-1973); Winston-Salem, NC, Aug. 9, 2006.

Henderson, Skitch, 87, British-born conductor, pianist, and radio and TV personality; the first music director of NBC's *The Tonight Show*; New Milford, CT, Nov. 1, 2005.

Horn, Shirley, 71, jazz pianist and vocalist known for her mastery of slow tempos and unique phrasing of song lyrics; Cheverly, MD, Oct. 20, 2005.

Hrawi, Elias, 80, president of Lebanon (1989-98), who helped his nation recover from 15 years of civil war; Beirut, Lebanon, July 7, 2006.

I

Irwin, Steve, 44, Australian wildlife handler, conservationist, and zookeeper; attained worldwide fame as TV's "Crocodile Hunter"; from a stingray wound, near Port Douglas, Australia, Sept. 4, 2006.

J

Jacobs, Jane, 89, influential urban-planner, social critic, and activist; author of *The Death and Life of Great American Cities*; Toronto, ON, April 25, 2006.

Jaffe, Rona, 74, author of *The Best of Everything* (1958), among the first of novels addressing the love and sex lives of urban career women; London, England, Dec. 30, 2005.

K

King, Coretta Scott, 78, activist, widow of slain U.S. civil rights leader Dr. Martin Luther King Jr.; Rosarito Beach, Mexico, Jan. 31, 2005.

Kirby, Bruno, 57, character actor; *The Godfather Part II* (1974), *When Harry Met Sally* (1989); Los Angeles, CA, Aug. 14, 2006.

Knotts, Don, 81, comedic actor; best-known role was as bumbling deputy Barney Fife on TV's *Andy Griffith Show*; Los Angeles, CA, Feb. 24, 2006.

Kunitz, Stanley, 100, poet who wrote memorable love poems in his 80s and 90s and was appointed U.S. poet laureate at age 95; New York, NY, May 14, 2006.

L

Lacoste, Bernard, 74, French businessman; expanded the clothing line created by his father, tennis champion René Lacoste; Paris, France, March 21, 2006.

Laker, Sir Freddie, 83, founder of Britain's Laker Airways, which in the late 1970s introduced low-cost transatlantic air travel; Hollywood, FL, Feb. 9, 2006.

Lay, Kenneth, 64, former chief executive of Enron Corp.; central figure in the Enron accounting scandal (2001); convicted of fraud and conspiracy in May 2006; near Aspen, CO, July 5, 2006.

Lem, Stanislaw, 84, Polish author of cerebral science fiction, including the novel *Solaris* (1961); Krakow, Poland, March 27, 2006.

Lewis, Al, 82, actor best known for his role as Grandpa in the 1960s TV sitcom *The Munsters*; New York, NY, Feb. 3, 2006.

Lewis, Edna, 89, renowned chef who wrote *The Taste of Country Cooking* and other definitive works on traditional Southern cuisine; Decatur, GA, Feb. 13, 2006.

Lidle, Cory, 34, journeyman MLB pitcher, most recently for the NY Yankees; died in a plane crash into a building, in New York, NY, Oct. 11, 2006.

Ligeti, Gyorgy, 83, Hungarian-Jewish experimental composer; gained notoriety when his music was used in the film *2001: A Space Odyssey* (1968); Vienna, Austria, June 12, 2006.

Lopez, Al, 97, baseball player and Hall of Fame manager; won pennants with the Cleveland Indians (1954) and the White Sox (1959); Tampa, FL, Oct. 30, 2005.

M

Mahfouz, Naguib, 94, Egyptian novelist (*The Cairo Trilogy*) who in 1988 became the first (and to date only) Arabic-language writer to win the Nobel Prize for Literature; Cairo, Egypt, Aug. 30, 2006.

Maktoum bin Rashid al-Maktoum, Sheik, 62, emir of Dubai, United Arab Emirates, since 1990; Main Beach, Queensland, Australia, Jan. 4, 2006.

Mara, Wellington, 89, longtime owner of the New York Giants football team; one of the last of the NFL's founding generation of owners, Rye, NY, Oct. 25, 2005.

Marcinkus, Archbishop Paul, 84, onetime head of the Vatican Bank, toppled in early 1990 after involvment in Italy's far-reaching Banco Ambrosiano scandal; Sun City, AZ, Feb. 20, 2006.

Mathias, Bob, 75, two-time Olympic decathlon champion (1948, 1952); U.S. congressman (R, CA, 1967-74); Fresno, CA, Sept. 2, 2006.

McCarthy, Eugene, 89, MN senator whose bid for the 1968 Democratic presidential nomination as an anti-Vietnam War candidate helped solidify opposition to the war; Washington, D.C., Dec. 10, 2005.

McGahern, John, 71, Irish author who wrote poignant fiction about Irish farm life; Dublin, Ireland, March 30, 2006.

McGavin, Darren, 83, actor who played TV detective Mike Hammer in the 1950s series of that name (based on stories by Mickey Spillane); Los Angeles, CA, Feb. 25, 2006.

McLean, Jackie, 74, jazz saxophonist, composer, and educator who used music to help rehabilitate drug addicts; Hartford, CT, March 31, 2006.

Meri, Lennart, 76, author and filmmaker who was the first president (1992-2001) of Estonia in the post-Soviet era; Tallinn, Estonia, March 14, 2006.

Merrifield, R. Bruce, 84, Nobel Prize-winning chemist (1984), discovered how to synthesize proteins quickly and efficiently; Creskill, NJ, May 14, 2006.

Milosevic, Slobodan, 64, onetime Yugoslav president and Serbian nationalist leader who had been on trial for genocide since 2002; Scheveningen, Netherlands, March 11, 2006.

Moffo, Anna, 73, soprano who made about 200 appearances at New York's Metropolitan Opera from the late 1950s to the mid-1970s; New York, NY, March 10, 2006.

Montgomery, Sonny, 85, long-time U.S. congressman (D, MS, 1967-97); known as a champion of veterans' rights; Meridian, MS, May 12, 2006.

Morita, Pat, 73, Japanese-American actor; well-known for his portrayals of a diner owner in the TV sitcom *Happy Days* and a wise martial arts instructor in the film *The Karate Kid* (1984) and three sequels; Las Vegas, NV, Nov. 24, 2005.

Murray, Jan, 89, TV personality who hosted 9 game shows in the 1950s and early 1960s, including *Songs for Sale* and *Treasure Hunt*; Beverly Hills, CA, July 2, 2006.

N

Narayanan, K. R., 85, president of India (1977-2002), and India's first head of state from the lowest Hindu caste, the Dalits (formerly known as the "untouchables"); New Delhi, India, Nov. 9, 2005.

Nelson, Byron, 94, golfer; won a record 18 professional tournaments in 1945, including a record 11 in a row, a streak almost twice as long as golf's next-longest winning streak to date; Roanoke, TX, Sept. 26, 2006.

Newman, Arnold, 88, portrait photographer; photographed every U.S. president from Harry Truman to Bill Clinton; New York, NY, June 6, 2006.

Nicholas, Fayard, 91, elder of the Nicholas Brothers tap dancing duo who appeared in 1930s and 1940s movie musicals; Toluca Lake, CA, Jan. 24, 2006.

Nilsson, Birgit, 87, Swedish opera singer who was the preeminent Wagnerian soprano of her time; Vastra Karup, Sweden, Dec. 25, 2005.

Nofziger, Lyn, 81, Republican political operative closely linked to Ronald Reagan, during Reagan's tenure as both governor of California (1967-75) and president of the U.S. (1981-89); Falls Church, VA, March 27, 2006.

North, Sheree, 72, character actress; Los Angeles, CA, Nov. 4, 2005.

Nykvist, Sven, 83, Oscar-winning Swedish cinematographer; worked with director Ingmar Bergman; Stockholm, Sweden, Sept. 20, 2006.

O

O'Neil Jr., John Jordan "Buck", 94, baseball player/manager in the segregated Negro Leagues (1938-1954); first black coach in major leagues (Chicago Cubs, 1962); Kansas City, MO, Oct. 6, 2006.

Owens, Buck, 76, 1960s country music superstar who co-hosted the TV show *Hee Haw* (1969-86); Bakersfield, CA, March 25, 2006.

P

Packer, Kerry, 68, Australian media mogul, worth an estimated $5 bil, who also had gambling and sporting interests; Sydney, Australia, Dec. 26, 2005.

Paik, Nam June, 73, Korean-born video art pioneer; Miami Beach, FL, Jan. 29, 2006.

Parks, Gordon, 93, first black staff photographer for *Life* magazine; later became Hollywood's first major black director; films included *The Learning Tree* (1969) and *Shaft* (1971); New York, NY, March 7, 2006.

Parks, Rosa, 92, iconic figure of the U.S. civil rights movement whose refusal to surrender a seat to a white passenger on a Montgomery, AL, bus sparked the 1955-56 Montgomery bus boycott; Detroit, MI, Oct. 24, 2005.

Patterson, Floyd, 71, two-time world boxing champion (1956-59, 1960-62); won his first title at age 21, making him the youngest heavyweight champion to date; also the first fighter to regain the heavyweight title; New Paltz, NY, May 11, 2006.

Pickett, Wilson, 64, dynamic soul singer who recorded such classic 1960s songs as "Mustang Sally" and "In the Midnight Hour"; Reston, VA, Jan. 19, 2006.

Pitney, Gene, 66, high-voiced singer and songwriter popular in the 1960s; later became more well-known in Britain; Cardiff, Wales, April 5, 2006.

Pointer, June, 52, youngest of the Pointer Sisters singing group and the lead singer in many of their songs, including "Jump (For My Love)" (1984); Santa Monica, CA, April 11, 2006.

Preston, Billy, 59, keyboard player, singer, and songwriter; collaborated with The Beatles and Rolling Stones; made a number of solo recordings; Scottsdale, AZ, June 6, 2006.

Profumo, John, 91, British cabinet minister; center of a 1963 sex scandal that nearly brought down the Tory government of Prime Min. Harold Macmillan; London, England, March 9, 2006.

Proxmire, William, 90, long-time U.S. Senator (D, WI, 1957-89); bestowed monthly "Golden Fleece" awards on what he considered particularly egregious examples of government waste; Sykesville, MD, Dec. 15, 2005.

Pryor, Richard, 65, black comedian who made pioneering comedy concert films and albums; his material dealt with racial, sexual, and drug-use issues with great candor; Los Angeles, CA, Dec. 10, 2005

Puckett, Kirby, 45, star center fielder for the Minnesota Twins; led the team to 2 World Series titles (1987, 1991); retired in 1996 after developing glaucoma; inducted into the Baseball Hall of Fame in 2001; Phoenix, AZ, March 6, 2006.

R

Ramsey, Patricia, 49, onetime Miss West Virginia whose 6-year-old beauty-contestant daughter, JonBenet Ramsey, was murdered in 1996 at the family's Colorado home; Roswell, GA, Jun 24, 2006.

Rau, Johannes, 75, president of Germany (1999-2004); addressed the Israeli Parliament in 2000 asking for forgiveness for the Holocaust; Berlin, Germany, Jan. 27, 2006.

Rawls, Lou, 72, leading pop vocalist in a variety of genres; raised more than $200 million as host of an annual telethon for the United Negro College Fund; Los Angeles, CA, Jan. 6, 2006.

Reeve, Dana, 44, actress and singer, widow of actor Christopher Reeve, who was paralyzed in 1995; she became a leading advocate for spinal paralysis research; New York, NY, March 6, 2006.

Richards, Ann, 73, Texas Democrat; elected governor of Texas in 1990; she was defeated four years later in her bid for reelection by George W. Bush; Austin, TX, Sept. 13, 2006.

Richards, Lloyd, 87, theatre director who first exposed Broadway audiences to the work of black playwrights Lorraine Hansberry and August Wilson; New York, NY, June 29, 2006.

Rimitti, Cheikha, 83, Algerian singer and songwriter known as the mother or queen of rai music; Paris, France, May 15, 2006.

Rosenthal, A. M., 84, top editor of *The New York Times* for 17 years (1969-86) and later a columnist for the *Times* as well as for the *New York Daily News*; New York, NY, May 10, 2006.

Rosenthal, Joe, 94, photojournalist; won 1945 Pulitzer Prize for his iconic WWII photograph of the U.S. flag being raised over the island of Iwo Jima by American servicemen; Novato, CA, Aug. 20, 2006.

Rugova, Ibrahim, 61, ethnic Albanian who had been leader of the UN-administered Serbian province of Kosovo since 2002; Pristina, Kosovo, Jan. 21, 2006.

Rukeyser, Louis, 73, financial commentator who hosted public television's *Wall Street Week* for 32 years (1970-2002); Greenwich, CT, May 2, 2006.

Ruiz, Hilton, 54, jazz pianist and composer, adept at both Latin jazz and bebop, who recorded more than a dozen albums; New Orleans, LA, June 6, 2006.

S

Sabah, Sheik Jaber al-Ahmed al-, 79, emir of Kuwait since 1977, and its premier for a dozen years before then; Kuwait City, Kuwait, Jan. 15, 2006.

Schwarzkopf, Elisabeth, 90, German lyric soprano; leading opera and lieder singers of her time; her image was tarnished by her admission that she had once been a member of the Nazi Party; Schruns, Austria, Aug. 3, 2006.

Scott Jr., Robert L., 97, WWII fighter pilot who wrote a best-selling account of his wartime heroics, *God Is My Co-Pilot*, that was made into a 1945 movie; Warner Robins, GA, Feb. 27, 2006

Shearer, Moira, 80, British ballerina and actress; played the ill-fated heroine of the film *The Red Shoes* (1948); Oxford, England, Jan. 31, 2006.

Sherman, Vincent, 99, Warner Bros. film director; flourished during the heyday of the studio system in the 1940s and 1950s; known as a director of "women's pictures"; Los Angeles, CA, June 18, 2006.

Shumway, Norman E., 83, pioneering U.S. heart transplant surgeon; performed the world's first successful heart-lung transplant (1981); Palo Alto, CA, Feb. 10, 2006

Sjoman, Vilgot, 81, Swedish director of sexual taboo-shattering films such as *I Am Curious (Yellow)* (1967) and *I Am Curious (Blue)* (1968); Stockholm, Sweden, April 9, 2006.

Smalley, Richard E., 62, one of three chemists awarded the Nobel Prize in 1996 for their discovery of "buckminsterfullerenes"; Houston, TX, Oct. 28, 2005.

Spark, Dame Muriel, 88, Scottish author, known for terse, witty, and darkly satirical novels *Memento Mori* (1959) and *The Prime of Miss Jean Brodie* (1961); Florence, Italy, April 13, 2006.

Spelling, Aaron, 83, prolific TV producer of *Charlie's Angels* (1976-81), *The Love Boat* (1977-86), *Dynasty* (1981-89) and *Melrose Place* (1992-99); Los Angeles, CA, June 23, 2006.

Spencer, John, 58, character actor; since 1999 had portrayed Leo McGarry in TV's political drama *The West Wing*; Los Angeles, CA, Dec. 16, 2005.

Spillane, Mickey, 88, crime novelist and one of the best-selling authors of all time; created the hard-fisted detective Mike Hammer; Murrells Inlet, SC, July 17, 2006.

Stapleton, Maureen, 83, Oscar, Emmy, and 2-time Tony Award-winning actress; known for her portrayals of strong-willed, down to earth women; Lenox, MA, March 13, 2006.

Stroessner Matiauda, Alfredo, 93, Paraguayan dicator (1954-89) who ruled his country with an iron fist; overthrown in a coup, he went into exile in Brazil; Brasilia, Brazil, Aug. 16, 2006.

T

Taube, Henry, 89, Nobel laureate in chemistry (1983); discovered the "bridge" transferring electrons between molecules in chemical reactions; Palo Alto, CA, Nov. 16, 2005.

Thomson, Kenneth, 82, Canadian media magnate; holdings included the Toronto *Globe and Mail* newspaper; long ranked as Canada's richest man; Toronto, ON, June 12, 2006.

Tisch, Bob, 79, New York City-based businessman and philanthropist; served as U.S. postmaster general (1986-88); co-owner of the NFL's New York Giants since 1991 (died 3 weeks after Giants co-owner Mara); New York, NY, Nov. 15, 2005.

Touré Ali Farka, 66 or 67, Malian guitarist, songwriter, and singer who fused African traditions with the blues; Bamako, Mali, March 6, 2006.

Tupou IV, King Taufa'ahau, 88, ruler of the Pacific island nation of Tonga since 1965; Auckland, New Zealand, Sept. 10, 2006.

V

Valli, Alida, 84, Italian actress who made more than 100 movies; notably *The Third Man* (1949); Rome, Italy, April 22, 2006.

Van Allen, James, 91, physicist; discovered that Earth was surrounded by two belts of charged particles in the late-1950s; those belts were named after him; Iowa City, IA, Aug. 9, 2006.

W

Warden, Jack, 85, veteran actor often cast in tough-guy roles; won an Emmy for playing football coach George Halas in the TV movie *Brian's Song* (1971); New York, NY, July 19, 2006.

Wasserstein, Wendy, 55, playwright; won the Pulitzer Prize in 1989 for *The Heidi Chronicles*; addressed women's issues; New York, NY, Jan. 30, 2006.

Weaver, Dennis, 81, actor who played Chester Goode in the TV western series *Gunsmoke* (1955-64); starred in *McCloud* (1970-77); Ridgway, CO, Feb. 24, 2006

Weinberger, Caspar W., 88, high-ranking Republican government official; sec. of defense (1981-87), under Pres. Reagan; Bangor, ME, March 28, 2006.

Whitaker, Rodney, 74, author who wrote under the pseudonym Trevanian; *The Eiger Sanction* (1972) and *The Loo Sanction* (1973); Dec. 14, 2005, England

Winters, Shelley, 83, outspoken 2-time Oscar-winning actress who appeared in more than 100 films; Beverly Hills, CA, Jan. 14, 2006.

Offbeat News Stories, 2006

What's in a Name?

"Psycho Path," the name of byways in several U.S. communities, was named the country's weirdest street name on Feb. 24, 2006. Several fans entered the punny thoroughfare in www.thecarconnection.com's Wild, Weird, and Wacky Street Names contest. Psycho Path beat out 2,500 other entries—including runners-up Divorce Court, Farfrompoopen Road, Bucket of Blood Street, and Unexpected Road—to claim first prize. Some entrants found humor in certain intersections, like the junction of Stroke and Acoma streets in a Wisconsin retirement community, and the intersection of Clinton and Fidelity Streets.

Thinking in the Trash

Maybe you would have thrown it away with the garbage, but curators at the National Toy Hall of Fame are honoring an unconventional, low-tech addition to their collection: the cardboard box! "I think every adult has had that disillusioning experience of picking what they think is a wonderful toy for a child, and then finding the kid playing with the box," said chief curator Christopher Bensch. The no-frills plaything joined the collection of 34 classic toys—from Mr. Potato Head and Barbie to Play-Doh and Silly Putty—maintained by the Strong Museum in Rochester, NY. The more conventional jack-in-the-box and Candy Land board game were fellow 2005 inductees.

Soap Opera

Current students and alumni of Yale University are no longer in a lather—because lathering up is finally free. For the first time in its history, the 305-year-old Ivy League university is supplying hand soap to dormitory bathrooms. Previously, students had to buy their own soap or suffer the consequences. But in Jan. 2006, after nearly a decade of lobbying, the student government's Yale College Council (and its "Soap Committee") persuaded the administration to commit to funding a soap dispensing program.

Generations of Yalies had gone without free suds and administrators had seen no reason to alter the tradition until recently. The school, which has a $15.2 billion endowment, had maintained that the $100,000 annual cost of stocking the soap in the bathrooms was too great, even after student lobbying secured bathroom gains of 2-ply toilet paper in the mid-1990s.

Pet Project

Feeling guilty about leaving Fido and Spot alone for the day? Forget about doggie day care: the new solution for bored pets is DogCatRadio.com, an Internet radio station with playlists and programming especially for the four-legged set. The station, broadcasting from a customized RV in a Los Angeles parking lot, has 6 DJs streaming live programming 17 hours a day, including a "Spanish Hour" for "bilingual" animals. "How are all my furry friends doing out there? We hope you're doing great and not chewing on anything but your toys," one DogCatRadio disc jockey purred between sets. Popular requests from listeners (said to number 6.2 million creature-homes every week) include the Baha Men's "Who Let the Dogs Out?" and Elvis Presley's "Hound Dog."

Trading Up, Online

The age-old bartering system, with a high-tech boost, enabled a Canadian man to start a trade with a giant, novelty red paperclip and end up with a home of his own in just one year. Kyle MacDonald set out to achieve his dream of home ownership by using a bartering page on the Website www.craigslist.org. The 26-year-old started small, initially trading the clip for a fish-shaped pen, but the trades quickly progressed to include a camping stove, a small generator, a "party package" (which included a neon beer sign and beer keg, with a promise to fill it). Several steps and television appearances later, MacDonald had traded for a recording contract and then a film role.

Eventually, MacDonald had attracted a cult following, and the town of Kipling, Saskatchewan, offered to trade him a newly renovated 1,100-sq.-ft. house on Main Street for the film role. The deal was finalized July 12, 2006, a year to the day after his first trade. At his housewarming party, at which many of the links in the trade chain gathered, MacDonald proposed to his girlfriend, twisting the original red paperclip into a ring. She accepted the offer.

Toss a Phone, Win a Prize

Have you ever wanted to hurl your cell phone? You're not alone. In Savonlinna, Finland, on Aug. 26, 2006, phone-hurling aficionados competed for prizes at the 7th annual Mobile Phone Throwing World Championships. The Finns aren't known for conventional competition (they originated the World Wife-Carrying Competition, after all), but 100 contestants showed up from as far away as Canada to participate in the phone-recycling promotional event.

Finland's own Lassi Etelatalo, who trained for the competition with a javelin, brought home the gold in the men's competition after chucking a discarded Nokia about 292 ft. The women's champion, who admitted she'd thrown a phone several times—and not to train for a contest—set a new record at 167 ft.

The Gift That Keeps on Giving

Perhaps when shopping for holiday presents we should be considering not what the recipient would like to receive, but what they would like to re-gift. A recent report found that over half of 1,505 Americans surveyed admitted to "re-gifting," or passing on unwanted presents. And a whopping 78% admitted to thinking that it was acceptable to re-gift at least some of the time. At least most of our hearts are in the right places: 77% of respondents re-gifted because the item was suited to the new recipient. But 9% blamed their gift recycling on laziness and 4% re-gifted out of spite.

Humbling Prizes

Nobel Prize winners are recognized for their transformative contributions to literature, peace, and science. Ig Nobel winners, on the other hand, are rewarded for achievements that, while not quite world-altering, "first make people laugh, and then make them think." Past Ig Nobels have been awarded to the inventors of karaoke and pink plastic flamingos.

A few of this year's winners:

• **Acoustics:** D. Lynn Halpern, Randolph Blake, and James Hillenbrand of Northwestern Univ. for a 1986 experiment on why the sound of fingernails on a chalkboard is so irritating.

• **Biology:** Bart Knols and Ruurd de Jong for their study showing that the malaria-carrying female *Anopheles gambiae* mosquito is equally attracted to the smell of human feet and limburger cheese.

• **Ornithology:** Ivan Schwab (Univ. of California Davis) and Philip R.A. May (UCLA) for their explanation of why woodpeckers don't get headaches.

• **Peace:** Howard Stapleton for inventing teenager repellent: a device that makes a high-pitched noise inaudible to adults; and for later marketing the technology as a cell-phone ringer adults can't hear.

Waste Not, Want Not

Most people associate "dumpster diving"—the practice of searching garbage bins for salvageable food and other items—primarily with those who are down on their luck. Of course, most people haven't met the Freegans—a loose-knit group of idealists who try to live entirely on food that others have thrown out. Freegans (a mash-up of "free" and "vegan") pick out their food selectively from dumpsters outside of restaurants and grocery stores, in an effort to effect "a total boycott of an economic system where profit motive has eclipsed ethical considerations."

Aaron Weissman, the 28-year-old Freegan who runs www.freegan.info, claims he hasn't bought food since he was 17. His Website offers a venue for Freegans to share philosophies and tips, as well as a "Dumpster Directory," with reviews of reliable places to scavenge. A review of a Brooklyn bakery warned, "Baker is on site all night long, move fast. Also, vegetarians beware the sausage bread."

There certainly isn't a shortage of wasted food in the U.S: the Dept. of Agriculture estimates that 96 billion lbs—roughly one-third—of the nation's food ends up in trash bins untouched.

Notable Quotes in 2006

Iraq War and Fight Against Terrorism

"The war against this enemy is more than a military conflict. It is the decisive ideological struggle of the 21st century, and the calling of our generation."
—*Pres. George W. Bush*, in an address to the nation on the 5 year anniversary of the Sept. 11, 2001, terrorist attacks.

"I want to fight in a war like World War II. I want to fight an enemy. And this, out here . . . it's a faceless enemy."
—*Sgt. Christopher Dugger*, on fighting Iraqi insurgents, July 26.

"We've got a raid going on right now, and I can't do anything for another 90 minutes. Can I call you then or is it too late?"
—*Marine Maj. Mike McNamara*, in Fallujah, Iraq, to a reporter, on his June 13 election to the Grand Forks, ND, City Council.

"It grieves me so much that we had not told the American people how tough and difficult this task would be."
—*Sen. John McCain*, (R, AZ), accusing the Bush administration Aug. 22 of "underestimating the size of the task" in Iraq.

"I hear the voices, and I read the front page, and I know the speculation. But I'm the decider, and I decide what is best."
—*Pres. Bush*, in support of Def. Sec. Donald Rumsfeld, April 18.

"Everyday we're [in Iraq] the situation is getting worse . . . It's important that we take the American face off this occupation."
—*Ned Lamont*, Connecticut senatorial candidate, who beat the long-time incumbent Joe Lieberman in a heated Democratic primary, speaking Sept. 13 on withdrawing U.S. troops from Iraq.

"Most of the leaders I spoke to felt that the invasion of Iraq and its aftermath has been a real disaster for them. They believe it has destabilized the region."
—*UN Secretary General Kofi Annan*, Sept. 13, on Mideast leaders' response to the U.S. invasion and continued presence in Iraq.

"The world is better off because Saddam Hussein is in jail instead of in power in Baghdad. It was the right thing to do and if we had it to do over again, we'd do exactly the same thing."
—*Vice Pres. Dick Cheney*, challenged on missteps in Iraq by Tim Russert on *Meet the Press*, Sept. 10.

"My friend, whether there's a civil war or not, we don't want you to intervene."
—*Muqtada al-Sadr*, Iraqi Shiite leader, responding Mar. 13 to Defense Sec. Rumsfeld's comment that the U.S. would not intervene in an Iraqi civil war.

"That will be decided by future presidents."
—*Pres. Bush*, Mar. 21, on when he expects American forces to withdraw from Iraq completely.

Other International News

"What we're seeing here, in a sense, is the growing—the birth pangs of a new Middle East."
—*Sec. of State Condoleezza Rice*, July 21, on Israeli military action in Lebanon.

"Had we known that the kidnapping of the soldiers would have led to this, we would definitely not have done it."
—*Sheik Hassan Nasrallah*, leader of Hezbollah, Aug. 27, on his militant group's actions igniting fighting with Israel.

"Everyone was pushing and shoving. Women were crying, saying, 'Here's my passport, here's my children. Take my children, just take them.'"
—*Monika Esseily*, on her family's evacuation from Beirut after Israeli airstrikes began July 13.

"He said, I quote, 'Show me just what Muhammad brought that was new, and there you will find things only evil and inhuman, such as his command to spread by the sword the faith he preached.'"
—*Pope Benedict XVI*, quoting 14th-century Byzantine Emperor Manuel II Paleolgus, in a Sept. 12 speech that sparked uproar in the international Muslim community. He later apologized for causing offense.

"Do you think you are dealing with a 4-year-old child, to whom you can give some walnuts and chocolates and get gold from him?"
—*Mahmoud Ahmadinejad*, Iranian president, rejecting the E.U. offer of non-military nuclear technology in exchange for ceasing the country's uranium enrichment.

"The statements of your vice president . . . are the same as an unsuccessful hunting shot."
—*Russian Pres. Vladimir Putin*, responding July 12 to Dick Cheney's criticisms about Russian restrictions on democracy by alluding to Cheney's shooting accident.

Domestic News

"I'm the guy who pulled the trigger and shot my friend."
—*Vice Pres. Dick Cheney*, admitting Feb. 15 he had accidently shot his friend, Texas attorney Harry Whittington, while hunting quail.

"It's hard to have a debate when you have to debate a bunch of morons."
—*Judy Baar Topinka*, Illinois Republican gubernatorial candidate, Mar. 9. She later apologized.

"I guess you could say in the last few years I've achieved the American Nightmare."
—*Kenneth Lay*, former Enron CEO, at his trial Apr. 24 on charges of fraud and conspiracy.

"We are cleaning up Congress the way teenagers clean up their bedrooms, and the result will be the same mess."
—*Rep. Brian Baird* (D, WA), on the weakness of the Congressional lobbying reform bill passed May 3.

"Mr. Moussaoui, you came here to be a martyr and die in a big bang of glory. But to quote T.S. Eliot, instead, you will die with a whimper."
—*Leonie Brinkema*, U.S. federal judge, sentencing al-Qaeda conspirator Zacarias Moussaoui May 4 to life in prison.

"I exit, as always, stage right."
—*Rep. Tom DeLay* (R, TX), in the former majority leader's farewell speech to Congress June 8.

"This is the Big Easy, and sometimes we lay back a little too much. Get off your duffs."
—*C. Ray Nagin*, New Orleans mayor, encouraging city residents to work harder to rebuild, after being sworn in June 1 to a 2nd term.

"They don't have anything to say to anyone about anything that matters."
—*John Zogby*, pollster, referring to Democrats' struggles to frame a successful political message, June 9.

"Forget perky. Perky is out. She is a serious individual who wants to take on a serious job."
—*Mike Wallace*, *60 Minutes* correspondent, commenting June 22 on Katie Couric's impending move to the anchor desk at CBS Evening News.

Miscellaneous News

"Having a smoking section in a restaurant is like having a peeing section in a swimming pool."
—*Thomas Pfeffer*, of the American Heart Association in Los Angeles, on his support of a Calabasas, CA, law, which went into effect Mar. 17, that bans smoking in public places.

"Probably not. I hate that guy."
—*Tyler Snyder*, baseball fan who caught Barry Bonds's 714th, Babe Ruth-tying home run on May 20, when asked if he would give Bonds the ball.

"I may go down in history as the guy who killed Pluto."
—*Michael Brown*, scientist who helped develop new guidelines that made Pluto a "dwarf planet" on Aug. 24, leaving the solar system with 8 recognized planets.

"Unlike other candidates, I'm not going to hide my evil side."
—*Jonathan "The Impaler" Sharkey*, candidate for Minnesota governor and former pro wrestler, whose platform includes a plan to impale terrorists, Jan. 12.

Historical Anniversaries, 2007

1907 – 100 Years Ago

Congress passes legislation blocking **corporate donations** to candidates campaigning for national offices Jan. 26.

Forty-four nations attend the **Second International Peace Conference** held June 15-Oct. 18 in The Hague, Netherlands.

A **Japan-Korea Convention** is signed July 24, giving Japan considerable power over Korea's government.

New Zealand and Newfoundland Sept. 26 formally gain **dominion** status in the British Commonwealth.

A run on the Knickerbocker Trust Company exhausts its reserves Oct. 21-22, touching off a **financial panic** that is tempered by a bailout by J. P. Morgan and the federal government.

Oklahoma becomes the **46th state** in the Union Nov. 16, activating a state constitution providing for prohibition of alcohol within the state.

Pres. Theodore Roosevelt sends the **"Great White Fleet,"** 14,000 sailors on 16 American battleships, on a round-the-world voyage beginning Dec. 16, in a demonstration of U.S. naval power.

Two coal **mine explosions** Dec. 6 and Dec. 19 in Monongah, WV, and Jacobs Creek, PA, kill 600 people.

An estimated 1.3 million people die in an outbreak of the **Bubonic plague** in India.

Art. Gustav Klimt's *Adele Bloch-Bauer I, Danae*; Pablo Picasso's *Les Demoiselles d'Avignon*; Henri Rousseau's *The Snake Charmer.*

Literature. Joseph Conrad's *The Secret Agent*; E. M. Forster's *The Longest Journey*; Maxim Gorky's *Mother*; Rainer Maria Rilke's *Neue Gedichte*; Rudyard Kipling (*The Jungle Book, Kim*) wins the Nobel Prize in Literature.

Movies. George Méliès' *20,000 Leagues Under the Sea* and *The Eclipse*; *The Golden Beetle.*

Music. Gustav Mahler's *Symphony No. 8*; Richard Strauss's opera *Salomé*, based on Oscar Wilde's play, premieres in New York.

Nonfiction. Henry Adams's *The Education of Henry Adams*; William A. Dunning's *Reconstruction, Political and Economic, 1865-1877*; Henri Bergson's *Creative Evolution*; William James's *Pragmatism: A New Name for Old Ways of Thinking.*

Pop Music. John Bratton's "The Teddy Bears' Picnic"; Scott Joplin's "Gladiolus Rag"; Franz Lehár's "The Merry Widow Waltz."

Science and Technology. Leo Baekeland invents Bakelite, the first synthetic plastic; luxury oceanliner *Mauritania* inaugurates the era of great transatlantic cruise ships.

Sports. The Chicago Cubs, with a roster including the legendary "Tinker to Evers to Chance" double-play turning trio, win the World Series over the Detroit Tigers in 5 games.

Theatre. *Salomy Jane*; *The Warrens of Virginia*; the first "Ziegfield Follies" revue opens on Broadway.

Miscellaneous. Robert Baden-Powell founds the Scouting movement, a precursor to the Boy Scouts, in Britain.

1957 – 50 Years Ago

Pres. Dwight D. Eisenhower announces Jan. 5 that U.S. military and economic aid will be given to Middle East countries requesting help to stave off Communist aggression, in what becomes known as the **"Eisenhower Doctrine."**

The U.S. Supreme Court Apr. 22 rules that **obscenity** is not protected by the First Amendment as a form of free speech.

Great Britain tests its **first thermonuclear bomb** May 15.

Hurricane Audrey and subsequent tidal waves strike coastal Louisiana and Texas June 27-30, leaving 534 people dead.

Sen. **Strom Thurmond** (D, SC) sets a new filibuster record Aug. 28-29, arguing against civil rights legislation (which the Senate passes Aug. 29) for 24 hours, 18 minutes.

More than 10,000 people are evacuated from Chelyabinsk, USSR, after an **explosion** at a nearby nuclear weapons factory in Sept. (The Soviet Union did not confirm the incident until June 1989.)

Arkansas Gov. Orval Faubus and the state's National Guard bar nine African American students Sept. 4 from entering a **Little Rock High School**. Pres. Eisenhower sends federal troops to enforce desegregation Sept. 24.

François Duvalier (a.k.a. **Papa Doc**) is elected president of Haiti Sept. 22, beginning a 14-year dictatorship.

The Soviet Union (Aug. 26) and U.S. (Dec. 17) announce they have successfully tested **intercontinental ballistic missiles**.

The International Atomic Energy Agency (**IAEA**) is created Oct. 1.

The Soviet Union launches *Sputnik*, the first artificial satellite, into orbit Oct. 4.

Under charges of corruption, the **Teamsters Union** is forced out of the AFL-CIO Dec. 6.

U.S. **"baby boom"** peaks at 4.3 million live births.

World Almanac Editors' Picks
2006 Time Capsule

The editors of *The World Almanac* have selected the following items as representative of the year 2006.

1. Receipt for a $50 tank of gas
2. Rubble with gold from the "Golden Mosque" of the Shiite Askariya shrine in Samarra, Iraq, damaged in a Feb. attack believed to have been carried out by Iraqi Sunnis
3. Shani Davis's Winter Olympic Gold Medal—the first won by an African American in an individual winter event
4. Flag for the independent (as of June) nation of Montenegro
5. Flannel shirt belonging to the character Jack Twist in *Brokeback Mountain*
6. A collection of toiletries left behind at airport security in Aug. when rules were tightened to prohibit liquids from being carried aboard planes
7. Zinedine Zidane's jersey, over which comments were exchanged with Italian Marco Materazzi leading to the French star's infamous World Cup head butt
8. Birdshot, fired by Vice President Dick Cheney, that hit hunting partner Harry Whittington
9. mp3 of Coldplay's "Speed of Sound"—the billionth song purchased on iTunes, in Feb.
10. Aug. SEC filing on first tranche of Class B Berkshire Hathaway stock worth $1.6 billion, the first installment of an estimated $31 billion donation by Warren Buffett to the Bill & Melinda Gates Foundation
11. A "Support Our Troops" yellow ribbon auto magnet
12. A copy of *The World Almanac and Book of Facts 2007*

Art. Francis Bacon's *Study of a Nurse*; Alberto Giacometti's *Dog*; Robert Rauschenberg's *Factum I & Factum II*; Mark Rothko's *#20*.

Literature. James Agee's *A Death in the Family*; Samuel Beckett's *Endgame*; John Cheever's *The Wapshot Chronicle*; Jack Kerouac's *On the Road*; Bernard Malamud's *The Assistant*; Albert Camus (*The Fall, The Stranger, The Plague*) wins the Nobel Prize in Literature.

Movies. *An Affair to Remember* starring Cary Grant and Deborah Kerr; *The Bridge on the River Kwai* starring Alec Guinness and William Holden; Elia Kazan's *A Face in the Crowd*; *Jailhouse Rock* starring Elvis Presley; *Old Yeller*; *Pal Joey* starring Kim Novak, Rita Hayworth, and Frank Sinatra; Stanley Kubrick's *Paths of Glory* starring Kirk Douglas; *Peyton Place*; *Sweet Smell of Success* starring Burt Lancaster and Tony Curtis; *The Three Faces of Eve* starring Joanne Woodward; Sidney Lumet's *12 Angry Men*; Ingmar Bergman's *Wild Strawberries*; Billy Wilder's *Witness for the Prosecution* starring Tyrone Power and Marlene Dietrich.

Music. Samuel Barber's *Vanessa*; Francis Poulenc's *Les Dialogues des Carmélites*; Igor Stravinsky's *Agon*.

Nonfiction. Catherine Drinker Bowen's *The Lion and the Throne*; Noam Chomsky's *Syntactic Structures*; Jean-Paul Sartre's *Existentialism and Human Emotions*; Arthur M. Schlesinger Jr.'s *The Crisis of the Old Order: 1919-33*.

Pop Music. Harry Belafonte's "Mary's Boy Child"; Pat Boone's "Love Letters in the Sand"; Patsy Cline's "Walkin'

After Midnight"; Everly Brothers' "All I Have to Do Is Dream" and "Wake Up Little Susie"; Buddy Holly's "Peggy Sue"; Little Richard's "Tutti Frutti"; Frank Sinatra's "Witchcraft"; Elvis Presley has 5 Billboard No. 1 singles, including "All Shook Up," "Jailhouse Rock," and "(Let Me Be Your) Teddy Bear."

Science and Technology. U.S. Surgeon General Leroy E. Burney reports that research has conclusively linked smoking and lung cancer; 67 nations sign on to the International Geophysical Year (July 1 1957-Dec. 31, 1958) and launch coordinated studies of Earth's atmosphere and oceans.

Sports. Althea Gibson becomes the first African American to win the Wimbledon tennis tournament's singles title; the New York Giants and Brooklyn Dodgers baseball franchises leave New York after the 1957 season for San Francisco and Los Angeles, respectively.

Theatre. *The Music Man*; *Look Homeward Angel*; Dylan Thomas's *Under Milk Wood*; Gore Vidal's *A Visit to a Small Planet*; *West Side Story*.

TV. *Leave It to Beaver* premieres; *I Love Lucy* airs its last episode; *Gunsmoke* and *I Love Lucy* are highest-rated programs; Elvis Presley appears on *The Ed Sullivan Show* for the first time.

Miscellaneous. The Southern Christian Leadership Conference forms; Martin Luther King Jr. organizes its first voter registration drive and is awarded the NAACP's Spingarn Medal.

1982 – 25 Years Ago

AT&T agrees Jan. 8 to divest itself of 22 "Baby Bell" phone operating systems, ending a 13-year antitrust lawsuit.

Argentine troops seize the British-held **Falkland Islands** Apr. 2; a British task force recaptures the islands June 14.

Israeli troops **invade Lebanon** June 6; a cease-fire goes into effect there less than a week later.

John W. **Hinckley** Jr. June 21 is found **not guilty** by reason of insanity of shooting Pres. Ronald Reagan and 3 others in Mar. 1981.

The Equal Rights Amendment **(ERA) is defeated** June 30 because only 35 state legislatures (of the required 38) had approved the measure when the ratification deadline arrived.

A **Pan Am** jet crashes July 9 after takeoff in Louisiana, killing 153 people.

Iranian troops invade Iraq July 14 for the first time since the **Iran-Iraq war** began 22 months earlier.

About 800 U.S. Marines join a multinational force Aug. 20 in **Beirut**, Lebanon, overseeing the withdrawal of Palestinian Liberation Organization fighters from the city.

The Chinese Communist Party holds its first national congress in five years Sept. 1-11 and begins making moves to exorcise Mao Zedong's **"personality cult"** from party operations.

The Polish government outlaws the **Solidarity** labor union Oct. 8.

Soviet Premier Leonid **Brezhnev dies** Nov. 10; Yuri Andropov is installed in his place.

The controversial **Vietnam War Memorial**, designed by Maya Lin, is dedicated amid protests in Washington, DC, Nov. 13.

Art. Nan Goldin's *Greer and Robert on the bed, NYC*; Wolf Kahn's *My Barn on a Summer Night*; Julian Schnabel's *Humanity Asleep*; California's J. Paul Getty Museum of Art receives $1.1 billion from the estate of benefactor J. Paul Getty.

Literature. Charles Bukowski's *Ham on Rye*; Thomas Keneally's *Schindler's Ark*; Alice Walker's *The Color Purple*; Gabriel García Márquez (*One Hundred Years of Solitude*) is awarded the Nobel Prize in Literature.

Movies. *Annie*; *Blade Runner* starring Harrison Ford; *Das Boot*; Barry Levinson's *Diner*; Steven Spielberg's *E.T.: The Extra-Terrestrial*; *Fast Times at Ridgemont High*; *Gandhi*;

An Officer and a Gentleman starring Richard Gere and Debra Winger; *Poltergeist*; *Rambo: First Blood*; *Rocky III*; *Sophie's Choice* starring Meryl Streep and Kevin Kline; *Star Trek: The Wrath of Khan*; *Tootsie* starring Dustin Hoffman and Jessica Lange; *Victor/Victoria* starring Julie Andrews and James Garner; *The World According to Garp* starring Robin Williams.

Music. Ellen T. Zwilich's *Three Movements for Orchestra*.

Nonfiction. Russell Baker's *Growing Up*; Fox Butterfield's *China: Alive in the Bitter Sea*; Rhys L. Isaac's *The Transformation of Virginia, 1740-1790*; Susan Sheehan's *Is There No Place on Earth for Me?*

Pop Music. The Clash's "Rock the Casbah"; Marvin Gaye's "Sexual Healing"; Grandmaster Flash's "The Message"; Michael Jackson's *Thriller*; J. Geils Band's "Centerfold"; Joan Jett and the Blackhearts' "I Love Rock 'N Roll"; Paul McCartney and Stevie Wonder's "Ebony and Ivory"; John Cougar Mellencamp's "Jack and Diane"; Willie Nelson's "Always on my Mind"; Prince's *1999*; Survivor's "Eye of the Tiger"; Toto's *Toto IV*.

Science and Technology. The first space shuttle flight is executed by the *Columbia*; doctors successfully install the first permanent artificial heart; *Time* magazine chooses the computer as the "Machine of the Year," rather than the annual "Man of the Year" selection.

Sports. The NCAA sponsors the first major women's college basketball championship; NFL players go on strike for 57 days over a contract dispute.

Theatre. Andrew Lloyd Weber's *Cats* begins its record-setting Broadway run; *Joseph and the Amazing Technicolor Dreamcoat*; *Little Shop of Horrors*; *Nine*; *Torch Song Trilogy*.

TV. *Barney Miller* ends its run; *Cheers* premieres; popular shows include *Dallas, The Dukes of Hazzard, Hill Street Blues*, and *Three's Company*.

Miscellaneous. Seven people die in suburban Chicago after taking Tylenol painkillers that had been laced with cyanide. The Reverend Sun Myung Moon is sentenced to 18 months in prison for tax fraud.

Notable Supreme Court Decisions, 2005-06

During the Supreme Court's 2005-06 term, which ended June 29, 82 decisions were announced; 16, or 20%, were decided by 5-4 votes, compared with 21% in 2004-05 and 28% in 2001-02. Chief Justice John G. Roberts Jr. and Associate Justices Samuel A. Alito Jr., Antonin Scalia, and Clarence Thomas tended to vote as a conservative bloc, often at odds with members of the court's liberal wing—Justices Ruth Bader Ginsburg, Stephen G. Breyer, John Paul Stevens, and David H. Souter. Sandra Day O'Connor, who voted in 20 cases before retiring in Jan., and Anthony M. Kennedy were less clearly aligned but often voted with the conservatives in close cases.

Associate Justice O'Connor had announced her retirement July 1, 2005, pending confirmation of a successor, and Chief Justice Rehnquist died on Sept. 3, 2005. Federal appellate court judge John G. Roberts Jr., who had initially been nominated to take O'Connor's seat on the court, was confirmed by the Senate to replace Rehnquist as chief justice Sept. 29, 2005, and Samuel A. Alito Jr. was sworn in as an associate justice on Jan. 31, 2006.

See also listings of justices on page 438.

Following are some of the major rulings of the 2005-06 term.

Presidential Powers: The Supreme Court June 29 ruled in *Hamdan v. Rumsfeld*, 5-3, that Pres. George W. Bush's system for trying terrorism detainees at the U.S. military base in Guantanamo Bay, Cuba, was unauthorized under both federal law and the international Geneva Conventions.

Redistricting: The Supreme Court June 28 rejected Democrats' claims that a Republican-drawn map of Texas congressional districts amounted to unconstitutional partisan gerrymandering. Another grouping of justices struck one redrawn district for illegally diluting the voting power of Hispanics, in *League of United Latin American Citizens v. Perry*.

Employee Rights: The court June 22 unanimously endorsed a Tennessee railroad worker's claim that her employer had retaliated against her for filing a sexual harassment complaint, in *Burlington Northern & Santa Fe Railway Co. v. White*. The court adopted a broad, worker-friendly definition of employer retaliation.

The court May 30 ruled in *Garcetti v. Ceballos*, 5-4, that the First Amendment guarantee of free speech did not protect statements made by public employees in the course of their official duties.

Campaign Finance: In a 6-3 ruling June 26, the court struck down Vermont's tight restrictions on campaign fund-raising and candidate spending in *Randall v. Sorrell*, calling the limits an infringement on free speech.

Capital Punishment: The court June 26 upheld, 5-4, Kansas's 1994 death penalty statute, which required a death sentence when a jury found the factors for and against a convicted defendant's execution to be equally balanced. The case was *Kansas v. Marsh*.

In *Hill v. McDonough*, the court unanimously ruled June 12 that a Florida death row inmate could challenge the state's lethal injection procedure by claiming that it caused undue pain and suffering.

Consular Access: The court June 28 ruled, 6-3, in *Sanchez-Llamas v. Oregon*, that U.S. courts were not obliged to suppress confessions or set aside procedural rules to remedy violations of the Vienna Convention on Consular Relations, an international treaty that allowed individuals to contact their home country's diplomats when arrested abroad.

Assisted Suicide: The court Jan. 17 ruled, 6-3, that the 1970 Controlled Substances Act did not allow the U.S. attorney general to punish doctors who helped patients end their lives under Oregon's Death With Dignity Act, in *Gonzales v. Oregon*.

Religious Freedom: The court ruled Feb. 21, 8-0, that the U.S. branch of a Brazilian religious sect could continue to use a hallucinogenic tea in its rituals, despite the fact that a key chemical ingredient was banned by the Controlled Substances Act. The case was *Gonzales v. O Centro Espirita Beneficente Uniao do Vegetal*.

Environment: The court June 19 failed to forge a clear majority in a consolidated case involving the scope of federal wetlands regulation under the 1972 Clean Water Act, but 5 of 9 justices agreed to return the matter, *Rapanos v. United States*, to a federal appeals court.

Rules of Evidence: The court June 15 ruled, 5-4, that prosecutors could use evidence seized during the execution of a search warrant even if police had failed to obey the traditional "knock and announce" rule, in *Hudson v. Michigan*.

The court ruled unanimously June 19 in *Davis v. Washington* that evidence from 911 emergency telephone calls could be used by prosecutors even if the caller did not testify in person and face cross-examination.

Campus Military Recruitment: The court March 6 upheld, 8-0, a 2004 law requiring universities to grant military recruiters the same access to their students as other would-be employers, in *Rumsfeld v. Forum for Academic and Institutional Rights*.

The 2006 Nobel Prizes

The 2006 Nobel Prize winners were announced Oct. 3-13. Each prize is worth about $1.4 million.

Chemistry: American Roger D. Kornberg was awarded the chemistry prize for research on the molecular basis of eukaryotic transcription, the process by which cells take information from genes to produce proteins. Disruptions in the process are thought to be involved in illnesses including cancer and heart disease.

Literature: The Nobel Prize committee recognized Turkish novelist Orhan Pamuk, "who in the quest for the melancholic soul of his native city [Istanbul] has discovered new symbols for the clash and interlacing of cultures." Pamuk gained international attention when charges, later dropped, were brought against him in 2005 for "insulting Turkishness" by referencing Armenian genocides of World War I. Pamuk's novels cited by the committee include *The White Castle* (1985), *My Name is Red* (2000), and *Snow* (2002).

Economics: American Edmund S. Phelps was given the economics prize "for his analysis of intertemporal trade-offs in macroeconomic policy"—a model of how wages, unemployment, and inflation interact. He theorized that wages and inflation rise together, until unemployment reaches an "equilibrium" level at which prices stagnate.

Peace: Bangladeshi economist Muhammad Yunus and the Grameen Bank won the prize for their pioneering efforts to extend "microcredit" to the poor. Yunus established the Grameen Bank to provide loans in seemingly insignificant amounts to the poor, especially women, who would be turned away by conventional banks. The small loans (the average amount is $200) are intended to alleviate poverty by providing the opportunity for self-sufficiency.

Physics: Americans John C. Mather and George F. Smoot shared the physics prize for their discovery of the blackbody form of cosmic microwave background radiation theoretically stemming from the "big bang" that formed the universe. Their work provides support for the big-bang theory, which says the universe formed from an explosion about 13.7 bil years ago.

Physiology or Medicine: Americans Andrew Z. Fire and Craig D. Mello shared the award for their 1998 discovery of RNA interference, or gene silencing. Their discovery demonstrated far-reaching potential for research, because it allows scientists to understand the roles of specific genes by suppressing them. The method also has potential for a new class of medications that can switch off unwanted disease processes.

Major Actions of the 109th Congress

The 109th Congress convened Jan. 4, 2005, with Republicans controlling both chambers. In the House of Representatives, Republicans held 232 seats and the Democrats 202, with 1 independent aligned with the Democrats, for a total of 435 voting members. Among the 100 members of the Senate, the GOP held a 55-44 majority, with 1 independent allied with the Democrats. The House had 39 new members, and the Senate 9. A record 65 women served in the House, including 3 non-voting delegates, and 14 held seats in the Senate. Among House legislators were 40 African-Americans, 26 Hispanics including the Resident Commissioner, 5 Asians, and 1 Native American. 1 African-American, 2 Latinos, and 2 Asians held seats in the Senate.

Leadership. The speaker of the House was J. Dennis Hastert (R-IL). Other high-ranking House members at the start of the 109th Congress included Majority Leader Tom DeLay (R-TX) and Minority Leader Nancy Pelosi (D-CA). DeLay surrendered his leadership post Sept. 28, 2005, after he was indicted by a Texas grand jury for allegedly participating in an illegal fundraising scheme during the 2001-02 campaign. On Feb. 2, 2006, House Republicans chose John Boehner (OH) as their new majority leader, replacing Roy Blunt (R), who had been DeLay's interim successor. DeLay, who was also reported under investigation in an influence-peddling scandal involving former lobbyist Jack Abramoff, gave up his House seat June 9, 2006.

In the Senate, Bill Frist (R-TN) was majority leader and Harry Reid (D-NV) minority leader. The president pro tempore was Ted Stevens (R-AK), who became a senator in 1968. The longest-serving member of the Senate was Robert Byrd (D-WV), who took office in 1959; on June 12, 2006, the 88-year-old Byrd became the longest-serving senator in U.S. history.

Ethics. DeLay was not the only House member tainted by scandal. Randy (Duke) Cunningham (R-CA) resigned his seat Nov. 28, 2005, after admitting he took $2.4 million in bribes from defense contractors; a federal judge Mar. 3, 2006, sentenced him to 8 years in prison. In a plea agreement with the Justice Dept. announced Sept. 15, Bob Ney (R-OH) acknowledged receiving illegal gifts from Abramoff and his lobbying associates; he had relinquished his House Administration Committee chairmanship 8 months earlier. On Sept. 29, Mark Foley (R-FL) stepped down amid media reports that he had sent sexually provocative Internet messages to teenage boys who were current and former House pages; the 6-term congressman was founder and co-chair of the Congressional Missing and Exploited Children's Caucus and had championed legislation to combat sexual predators. The Foley affair put intense pressure on House GOP leaders, including Hastert, and triggered an investigation by the House Ethics Committee.

Scandals also snared House Democrats. At about 2:50 A.M. on May 4, Patrick Kennedy (D-RI), the son of Sen. Edward Kennedy (D-MA), crashed his car into a traffic barrier near the Capitol; he announced May 5 that he would seek treatment for addiction to prescription painkillers. For the first time in U.S. history, the Federal Bureau of Investigation on May 20 raided the office of a sitting member of Congress. The FBI justified the raid, which targeted William Jefferson (D-LA), by saying it had previously videotaped Jefferson accepting a $100,000 bribe and had found most of the cash in a freezer in his apartment.

Unfinished Business. Congress left much work undone when it adjourned Sept. 30 so that members could campaign full-time for the Nov. 7 election. Presidential initiatives on Social Security and immigration stalled, and the House and Senate were unable to reconcile their differences on lobbying reform, offshore oil and gas drilling, and warrantless electronic surveillance of suspected terrorists. Of 11 major spending measures, only 2—for defense and homeland security—were enacted. Anticipating a lame-duck session, legislators inserted a stopgap provision into the defense bill to fund other federal agencies through Nov. 17.

For Further Information. Following is a summary of major actions taken by the 109th Congress through Oct. 7, 2006. Measures that have become law are identified by their Public Law (PL) number, when known. Detailed legislative information may be accessed via the Internet at thomas.loc.gov.

2005

Bankruptcy. Tightens requirements for filings by consumers seeking debt relief. Passed by the House Apr. 14, 302-126; passed by the Senate Mar. 10, 74-25; signed by Pres. Bush Apr. 20 (PL 109-8).

Central American Free Trade Agreement (CAFTA). Lowers trade and investment barriers with Costa Rica, El Salvador, Guatemala, Honduras, Nicaragua, and the Dominican Republic. Passed by the House July 28, 217-215; passed by the Senate July 28, 55-45; signed by Pres. Bush Aug. 2 (PL 109-53).

Energy. Provides $14.6 billion in tax breaks for energy producers; sets reliability standards for the national electric power grid, to prevent major blackouts; subsidizes development and purchase of hybrid vehicles; mandates increased use of ethanol as motor fuel; and extends daylight savings time by a month. Passed by the House July 28, 275-156; passed by the Senate July 29, 74-26; signed by Pres. Bush Aug. 8 (PL 109-58).

Transportation. Authorizes $286.5 billion in funding for highways, mass transit, and transportation safety. Passed by the House July 29, 412-8; passed by the Senate July 29, 91-4; signed by Pres. Bush Aug. 10 (PL 109-59).

Hurricane Katrina Disaster. Two measures together providing $62.3 billion for emergency response and relief. PL 109-61: Passed by the House by voice vote, passed by the Senate by unanimous consent, and signed by Pres. Bush, all on Sept. 2. PL 109-62: Passed by the House, 410-11; passed by the Senate, 97-0; signed by Pres. Bush, all on Sept. 8.

Supreme Court. Nomination of John G. Roberts Jr. as U.S. chief justice, confirmed by the Senate Sept. 29, 78-22.

McCain Amendment. Bars "cruel, inhuman, or degrading treatment or punishment" of anyone in U.S. government custody and offers legal protection for U.S. personnel who engage in authorized interrogations; legislation named for Sen. John McCain (R-AZ) and included in the $453.3 billion Defense Dept. appropriations bill. Passed by the House Dec. 19, 308-106; passed by the Senate Dec. 21, 93-0; signed by Pres. Bush Dec. 30 (PL 109-148).

2006

Supreme Court. Nomination of Samuel A. Alito Jr. as associate justice, confirmed by the Senate Jan. 31, 58-42.

National Debt. Raises the U.S. public debt ceiling from $8.2 trillion to $9 trillion. Passed the House under Rule XXVII, avoiding a separate vote on the measure; passed the Senate Mar. 16, 52-48; signed by Pres. Bush Mar. 20 (PL 109-182).

Border Security. Authorizes construction of a 700-mi fence along the SW border with Mexico. Passed by the House Sept. 14, 283-138; passed by the Senate Sept. 29, 80-19; cleared for the White House Sept. 29.

Detainees. Establishes procedures for military commissions to try suspected terrorists, grants wide latitude to the executive branch to detain and interrogate enemy combatants (but without violating the Geneva Convention), and bars detainees from challenging their detention in court through habeas corpus petitions. Passed by the House Sept. 29, 250-170; passed by the Senate Sept. 28, 65-34; presented to Pres. Bush Oct 10.

War Funding. Authorizes $70 billion in emergency spending on military operations in Iraq and Afghanistan, bringing to $507 billion the total approved by Congress for the 2 wars and to beef up security at U.S. bases and embassies since the attacks of Sept. 11, 2001. Funding provided as part of a $44.7.4 billion defense appropriations bill for the 2007 fiscal year. Passed by the House Sept. 26, 394-22; passed by the Senate Sept. 29, 100-0; signed by Pres. Bush Sept. 29 (PL 109-289).

Port Security. Authorizes $3.4 billion over 5 years to protect U.S. seaports from chemical, biological, or nuclear attack. Passed by the House Sept. 30, 409-2; passed by the Senate Sept. 30 by unanimous consent; signed by Pres. Bush Oct. 13.

ECONOMICS

Consumer Price Index

The Consumer Price Index (CPI) is a measure of the change in prices over time of one or more kinds of basic consumer goods and services.

From Jan. 1978, the Bureau of Labor Statistics began publishing CPIs for 2 population groups: (1) a CPI for all urban consumers (CPI-U), which covers about 87% of the total population; and (2) a CPI for urban wage earners and clerical workers (CPI-W), which covers about 32% of the total population. The CPI-U includes, in addition to wage earners and clerical workers, groups such as professional, managerial, and technical workers, the self-employed, short-term workers, the unemployed, retirees, and others not in the labor force.

The CPI is based on prices of food, clothing, shelter, and fuels; transportation fares; charges for doctors' and dentists' services; drug prices; and prices of other goods and services bought for day-to-day living. The index currently measures price changes from a designated reference period, 1982-84, which equals 100.0. Use of this reference period began in Jan. 1988.

U.S. Consumer Price Indexes, 2005-2006

Source: Bureau of Labor Statistics, U.S. Dept. of Labor

(Data are semiannual averages of monthly figures. For all urban consumers; **1982-84 = 100**; unless otherwise noted; % change not annualized)

	1st half 2005	% change 2nd half 2004 to 1st half 2005	2nd half 2005	% change 1st half 2005 to 2nd half 2005	1st half 2006	% change 2nd half 2005 to 1st half 2006
ALL ITEMS	193.2	1.6	197.4	2.2	200.6	1.6
Food, beverages	190.2	1.2	192.2	1.1	194.6	1.2
Housing	193.8	1.5	197.6	2.0	201.6	2.0
Apparel	120.5	0.5	118.6	−1.6	119.7	−0.7
Transportation	169.3	2.8	178.5	5.4	181.4	1.6
Medical care	320.6	2.5	325.9	1.7	333.6	2.4
Recreation[1]	109.1	0.5	109.6	0.5	110.7	1.0
Education and communication[1]	112.8	0.5	114.6	1.6	115.7	1.0
Other goods, services	311.3	1.6	315.4	1.3	319.8	1.4
Services	227.9	1.5	232.3	1.9	236.9	2.0
SPECIAL INDEXES						
All items less food	193.8	1.7	198.3	2.3	201.7	1.7
Commodities less food	142.2	1.9	146.8	3.2	148.4	1.1
Nondurables	176.9	1.9	183.5	3.7	186.4	1.6
Energy	163.3	4.7	190.8	16.8	197.8	3.7
All items less energy	198.0	1.3	199.5	0.8	202.5	1.5

(1) Dec. 1997 = 100.

U.S. Consumer Price Indexes (CPI-U),[1] Annual Percent Change, 1990-2005

Source: Bureau of Labor Statistics, U.S. Dept. of Labor

	1990	1991	1992	1993	1994	1995	1996	1997	1999	2000	2001	2002	2003	2004	2005
ALL ITEMS	5.4	4.2	3.0	3.0	2.6	2.8	3.0	2.3	2.2	3.4	2.8	1.6	2.3	2.7	3.4
Food	5.8	2.9	1.2	2.2	2.4	2.8	3.3	2.6	2.1	2.3	3.2	1.8	2.2	3.4	2.4
Shelter	5.4	4.5	3.3	3.0	3.1	3.2	3.2	3.1	2.9	3.3	3.7	3.7	2.4	2.7	2.6
Rent, residential	5.6	6.1	2.5	2.3	2.5	2.5	2.7	2.9	3.1	3.6	4.5	4.0	2.9	2.7	3.0
Fuel and other utilities	3.5	3.3	2.2	3.0	1.0	0.7	3.1	2.6	0.2	7.1	8.9	−4.4	7.6	4.8	10.6
Apparel and upkeep	4.6	3.7	2.5	1.4	−0.2	−1.0	−0.2	0.9	−1.3	−1.3	−1.8	−2.6	−2.5	−0.4	−0.7
Private transportation	5.2	2.6	2.2	2.3	3.1	3.7	2.7	0.7	1.9	6.1	0.6	−0.8	3.2	3.8	6.8
New cars	1.8	3.8	2.5	2.4	3.4	2.2	1.7	0.2	−0.3	−0.1	−0.5	−1.2	−1.5	−0.6	0.6
Gasoline	14.1	−1.8	−0.2	−1.3	0.5	1.6	6.1	−0.1	9.3	28.5	−3.6	−6.5	16.5	18.2	21.9
Public transportation	10.1	4.4	1.7	10.3	3.0	2.3	3.4	2.6	3.9	6.0	0.5	−1.5	0.9	−0.1	3.9
Medical care	9.0	8.7	7.4	5.9	4.8	4.5	3.5	2.8	3.5	4.1	4.6	4.7	4.0	4.4	4.2
Entertainment, Recreation[2,3]	4.7	4.5	2.8	2.5	2.9	2.5	3.4	2.1	0.9	1.3	1.5	1.2	1.2	1.0	0.7
Education[3]	—	—	—	—	6.3	5.6	5.3	5.0	4.8	5.1	5.3	6.3	1.8	6.9	6.3
Commodities	5.2	4.2	2.0	1.9	1.7	1.9	2.6	1.4	1.8	3.3	1.0	−0.7	1.0	2.3	3.6

(1) The Consumer Price Index CPI-U measures average change in prices of goods and services purchased by all urban consumers. 1982-1984 = 100 unless otherwise noted. (2) The Bureau of Labor Statistics reclassified Entertainment as Recreation in 1997. (3) Dec. 1997 = 100.

Consumer Price Index, 1915-2006

Source: Bureau of Labor Statistics, U.S. Dept. of Labor

(1967 = 100. Annual averages of monthly figures, specified for all urban consumers.)

Prices as measured by the U.S. Consumer Price Index have risen steadily since World War II. What cost $1.00 in 1967 cost about 30 cents in 1915, 54 cents in 1945, and $6.01 by the first half of 2006.

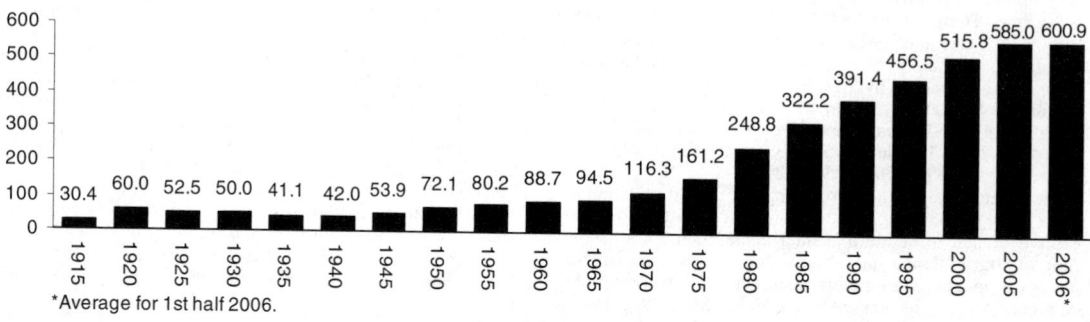

1915	1920	1925	1930	1935	1940	1945	1950	1955	1960	1965	1970	1975	1980	1985	1990	1995	2000	2005	2006*
30.4	60.0	52.5	50.0	41.1	42.0	53.9	72.1	80.2	88.7	94.5	116.3	161.2	248.8	322.2	391.4	456.5	515.8	585.0	600.9

*Average for 1st half 2006.

U.S. Consumer Price Indexes for Selected Items and Groups, 1970-2005

Source: Bureau of Labor Statistics, U.S. Dept. of Labor

(**1982-84 = 100**, unless otherwise noted. Annual averages of monthly figures. For all urban consumers.)

	1970	1975	1980	1985	1990	1995	1999	2000	2001	2002	2003	2004	2005
ALL ITEMS	38.8	53.8	82.4	107.6	130.7	152.4	166.6	172.2	177.1	179.9	184.0	188.9	195.3
Food and beverages	40.1	60.2	86.7	105.6	132.1	148.9	164.6	168.4	173.6	176.8	180.5	186.6	191.2
Food	39.2	59.8	86.8	105.6	132.4	148.4	164.1	167.8	173.1	176.2	180.0	186.2	190.7
Food at home	39.9	61.8	88.4	104.3	132.3	148.8	164.2	167.9	173.4	175.6	179.4	186.2	189.8
Cereals and bakery products	37.1	62.9	83.9	107.9	140.0	167.5	185.0	188.3	193.8	198.0	202.8	206.0	209.0
Meats, poultry, fish, and eggs	44.6	67.0	92.0	100.1	130.0	138.8	147.9	154.5	161.3	162.1	169.3	181.7	184.7
Dairy products	44.7	62.6	90.9	103.2	126.5	132.8	159.6	160.7	167.1	168.1	167.9	180.2	182.4
Fruits and vegetables	37.8	56.9	82.1	106.4	149.0	177.7	203.1	204.6	212.2	220.9	225.9	232.7	241.4
Sugar and sweets	30.5	65.3	90.5	105.8	124.7	137.5	152.3	154.0	155.7	159.0	162.0	163.2	165.2
Fats and oils	39.2	73.5	89.3	106.9	126.3	137.3	148.3	147.4	155.7	155.4	157.4	167.8	167.7
Nonalcoholic beverages	27.1	41.3	91.4	104.3	113.5	131.7	134.3	137.8	139.2	139.2	139.8	140.4	144.4
Other foods	39.6	58.9	83.6	106.4	131.2	151.1	168.9	172.2	176.0	177.1	178.8	179.7	182.5
Food away from home	37.5	54.5	83.4	108.3	133.4	149.0	165.1	169.0	173.9	178.3	182.1	187.5	193.4
Alcoholic beverages	52.1	65.9	86.4	106.4	129.3	153.9	169.7	174.7	179.3	183.6	187.2	192.1	195.9
Housing	36.4	50.7	81.1	107.7	128.5	148.5	163.9	169.6	176.4	180.3	184.8	189.5	195.7
Shelter	35.5	48.8	81.0	109.8	140.0	165.7	187.3	193.4	200.6	208.1	213.1	218.8	224.4
Rent of primary residence	46.5	58.0	80.9	111.8	138.4	157.8	177.5	183.9	192.1	199.7	205.5	211.0	217.3
Fuel and other utilities	29.1	45.4	75.4	106.5	111.6	123.7	128.8	137.9	150.2	143.6	154.5	161.9	179.0
Gas (piped) and electricity	25.4	40.1	71.4	107.1	109.3	119.2	120.9	128.0	142.4	134.4	145.0	150.6	166.5
Household furnishings & operations	46.8	63.4	86.3	103.8	113.3	123.0	126.7	128.2	129.1	128.3	126.1	125.5	126.1
Apparel	59.2	72.5	90.9	105.0	124.1	132.0	131.3	129.6	127.3	124.0	120.9	120.4	119.5
Men's and boys'	62.2	75.5	89.4	105.0	120.4	126.2	131.1	129.7	125.7	121.7	118.0	117.5	116.1
Women's and girls'	71.8	85.5	96.0	104.9	122.6	126.9	123.3	121.5	119.3	115.8	113.1	113.0	110.8
Footwear	56.8	69.6	91.8	102.3	117.4	125.4	125.7	123.8	123.0	121.4	119.6	119.3	122.6
Transportation	37.5	50.1	83.1	106.4	120.5	139.1	144.4	153.3	154.3	152.9	157.6	163.1	173.9
Private	37.5	50.6	84.2	106.2	118.8	136.3	140.5	149.1	150.0	148.8	153.6	159.4	170.2
New vehicles	53.0	62.9	88.4	106.1	121.4	139.0	142.9	142.8	142.1	140.0	137.9	137.1	137.9
Used cars and trucks	31.2	43.8	62.3	113.7	117.6	156.5	152.0	155.8	158.7	152.0	142.9	133.3	139.4
Gasoline	27.9	45.1	97.5	98.6	101.0	99.8	100.1	128.6	124.0	116.0	135.1	159.7	194.7
Public	35.2	43.5	69.0	110.5	142.6	175.9	197.7	209.6	210.6	207.4	209.3	209.1	217.3
Medical care	34.0	47.5	74.9	113.5	162.8	220.5	250.6	260.8	272.8	285.6	297.1	310.1	323.2
Entertainment/Recreation[1]	47.5	62.0	83.6	107.9	132.4	153.9	102.0	103.3	104.9	106.2	107.5	108.6	109.4
Other goods and services	40.9	53.9	75.2	114.5	159.0	206.9	258.3	271.1	282.6	293.2	298.7	304.7	313.4
Tobacco products	43.1	54.7	72.0	116.7	181.5	225.7	355.8	394.9	425.2	461.5	469.0	478.0	502.8
Personal care	43.5	57.9	81.9	106.3	130.4	147.1	161.1	165.6	170.5	154.7	153.5	181.7	185.6
Personal care products	42.7	58.0	79.6	107.6	128.2	143.1	151.8	153.7	155.1	174.7	178.0	153.9	154.4
Personal care services	44.2	57.7	83.7	108.9	132.8	151.5	171.4	178.1	184.3	188.4	193.2	197.6	203.9

(1) Dec. 1997 = 100; Entertainment was reclassified as Recreation in 1997.

Consumer Price Indexes by Region and Selected Cities, 2004-2006[1]

Source: Bureau of Labor Statistics, U.S. Dept. of Labor

(unless otherwise noted; % change not annualized)

	Semiannual averages				Percent change from preceding semiannual average		
	2nd half 2004	1st half 2005	2nd half 2005	1st half 2006	2nd half 2005	1st half 2005	1st half 2006
U.S. CITY AVERAGE	190.2	193.2	197.4	200.6	1.6	2.2	1.6
Northeast urban	201.7	205.3	209.7	213.8	1.8	2.1	2.0
Size A—More than 1,500,000	203.8	207.7	212.0	216.0	1.9	2.1	1.9
Size B/C—50,000 to 1,500,000[2]	119.5	121.0	123.9	126.4	1.3	2.4	2.0
Midwest urban	183.9	186.4	190.5	192.4	1.4	2.2	1.0
Size A—More than 1,500,000	186.1	188.4	192.1	194.0	1.2	2.0	1.0
Size B/C—50,000 to 1,500,000[2]	117.0	118.8	121.5	122.8	1.5	2.3	1.1
Size D—Nonmetro. (less than 50,000)	177.0	180.5	185.2	187.1	2.0	2.6	1.0
South urban	183.1	186.1	190.5	193.8	1.6	2.4	1.7
Size A—More than 1,500,000	184.4	188.0	192.4	195.7	2.0	2.3	1.7
Size B/C—50,000 to 1,500,000[2]	117.1	118.6	121.4	123.5	1.3	2.4	1.7
Size D—Nonmetro. (less than 50,000)	181.4	185.1	190.3	193.7	2.0	2.8	1.8
West urban	194.0	197.1	200.7	204.5	1.6	1.8	1.9
Size A—More than 1,500,000	196.5	199.7	203.5	207.6	1.6	1.9	2.0
Size B/C—50,000 to 1,500,000[2]	118.7	120.6	122.4	124.5	1.6	1.5	1.7
SELECTED AREAS							
Atlanta, GA	183.9	187.1	190.8	192.6	1.7	2.0	0.9
Boston–Brockton–Nashua, MA–NH–ME–CT	210.3	213.9	218.9	222.0	1.7	2.3	1.4
Chicago–Gary–Kenosha, IL–IN–WI	190.1	192.0	196.7	197.9	1.0	2.4	0.6
Cleveland–Akron, OH	183.0	185.8	190.0	191.4	1.5	2.3	0.7
Dallas–Fort Worth, TX	179.6	182.0	187.4	189.7	1.3	3.0	1.2
Detroit–Ann Arbor–Flint, MI	186.6	188.7	193.0	195.9	1.1	2.3	1.5
Houston–Galveston–Brazoria, TX	170.2	174.3	177.0	180.3	2.4	1.5	1.9
L.A.–Riverside–Orange County, CA	194.9	199.2	204.5	209.3	2.2	2.7	2.3
Miami–Fort Lauderdale, FL	186.6	191.8	196.9	202.7	2.8	2.7	2.9
New York, NY–Northern NJ–Long Island, NY–NJ–CT–PA	206.4	210.7	214.8	219.2	2.1	1.9	2.0
Philadelphia–Wilmington–Atlantic City, PA–DE–NJ–MD	199.0	202.1	206.3	210.7	1.6	2.1	2.1
San Francisco–Oakland–San Jose, CA	199.5	201.5	203.9	207.9	1.0	1.2	2.0
Seattle–Tacoma–Bremerton, WA	194.2	199.2	201.3	205.8	1.9	1.1	2.2
Washington–Baltimore, DC–MD–VA–WV[3]	120.7	122.8	125.8	127.7	1.7	2.4	1.5

(1) For all urban consumers. (2) Dec. 1996 = 100. (3) Nov. 1996 = 100.

Index of Leading Economic Indicators

Source: The Conference Board

The index of leading economic indicators is used to project the U.S. economy's performance. The index is made up of 10 measurements of economic activity that tend to change direction in advance of the overall economy. The index has predicted economic downturns from 8 to 20 months in advance and recoveries from 1 to 10 months in advance; however, it can be inconsistent, and has occasionally shown "false signals" of recessions.

Components

Average weekly hours of production workers in manufacturing
Average weekly initial claims for unemployment insurance, state programs
Manufacturers' new orders for consumer goods and materials, adjusted for inflation
Vendor performance (slower deliveries diffusion index)

Manufacturers' new orders, nondefense capital goods industries, adjusted for inflation
New private housing units authorized by local building permits
Stock prices, 500 common stocks
Money supply: M-2, adjusted for inflation
Interest rate spread, 10-yr Treasury bonds less federal funds
Consumer expectations (researched by Univ. of Michigan)

U.S. Gross Domestic Product, Gross National Product, Net National Product, National Income, and Personal Income

Source: Bureau of Economic Analysis, U.S. Dept. of Commerce

(billions of current dollars; revised)

	1960	1970	1980	1990	2000	2002	2003	2004	2005
Gross domestic product	526.4	1,038.5	2,789.5	5,803.1	9,817.0	10,469.6	10,960.8	11,712.5	12,455.8
Gross national product	529.5	1,044.9	2,823.7	5,837.9	9,855.9	10,500.2	11,017.6	11,758.7	12,487.7
Less: Consumption of fixed capital	55.6	106.7	343.0	682.5	1,187.8	1,292.0	1,336.5	1,436.2	1,604.8
Net national product	473.9	938.2	2,480.7	5,155.4	8,668.1	9,208.3	9,681.1	10,322.6	10,882.9
Less: Statistical discrepancy	−0.9	7.3	41.4	66.2	−127.2	−21.0	48.8	66.7	71.0
Equals: National income	474.9	930.9	2,439.3	5,089.1	8,795.2	9,229.3	9,632.3	10,255.9	10,811.8
Less: Corporate profits with inventory valuation and capital consumption adjustments	53.8	83.6	201.1	437.8	817.9	886.3	993.1	1,182.6	1,330.7
Taxes on production and imports less subsidies	43.4	86.7	190.9	398.7	664.6	724.4	759.3	819.4	865.1
Contributions for government social insurance	16.4	46.4	166.2	410.1	702.7	750.0	778.6	826.4	880.6
Net interest and miscellaneous payments on assets	10.6	39.1	181.8	442.2	559.0	520.9	524.7	485.1	483.4
Business current transfer payments (net)	1.9	4.5	14.4	39.4	87.1	84.3	83.8	85.5	74.2
Current surplus of government enterprises	0.9	0.0	−4.8	1.6	5.3	0.9	1.7	-5.0	−15.4
Wage accruals less disbursements	0.0	0.0	0.0	0.1	0.0	0.0	15.0	-15.0	0.0
Plus: Personal income receipts on assets	37.9	93.5	338.7	924.0	1,387.0	1,333.2	1,336.6	1,427.9	1,519.4
Personal current transfer receipts	25.7	74.7	279.5	595.2	1,084.0	1,286.2	1,351.0	1,426.5	1,526.6
Equals: Personal income	411.5	838.8	2,307.9	4,878.6	8,429.7	8,881.9	9,163.6	9,731.4	10,239.2

U.S. Gross Domestic Product, 1995-2006

Source: Bureau of Economic Analysis, U.S. Dept. of Commerce

(billions of current dollars)

	1995	2005	2nd quarter 2006[1]		1995	2005	2nd quarter 2006[1]
Gross domestic product	7,397.7	12,455.8	13,197.3	**Net exports of goods and services**	−91.4	−716.7	− 781.8
Personal consumption expenditures	4,975.8	8,742.4	9,228.1	Exports	812.2	1,303.1	1,448.1
Durable goods	611.6	1,033.1	1,061.8	Goods	583.3	907.5	1,019.1
Nondurable goods	1,485.1	2,539.3	2,721.4	Services	228.9	395.6	429.0
Services	2,879.1	5,170.0	5,444.9	Imports	903.6	2,019.9	2,229.8
Gross private domestic investment	1,144.0	2,057.4	2,237.1	Goods	757.4	1,699.0	1,879.0
Fixed investment	1,112.9	2,036.2	2,174.8	Services	146.1	320.9	350.8
Nonresidential	810.0	1,265.7	1,384.3	**Government consumption expenditures and gross investment**	1,369.2	2,372.8	2,513.9
Structures	207.3	338.6	406.3	Federal	519.2	878.3	919.7
Equipment and software	602.8	927.1	977.9	National defense	348.7	589.3	616.5
Residential	302.8	770.4	790.6	Nondefense	170.5	289.0	303.2
Change in private inventories	31.1	21.3	62.3	State and local	850.0	1,494.4	1,594.2

(1) Seasonally adjusted at annual rates; last revised Sept. 28, 2006

U.S. Gross Domestic Product, 1930-2005

Source: Bureau of Economic Analysis, U.S. Dept. of Commerce

(billions of 2000 dollars)

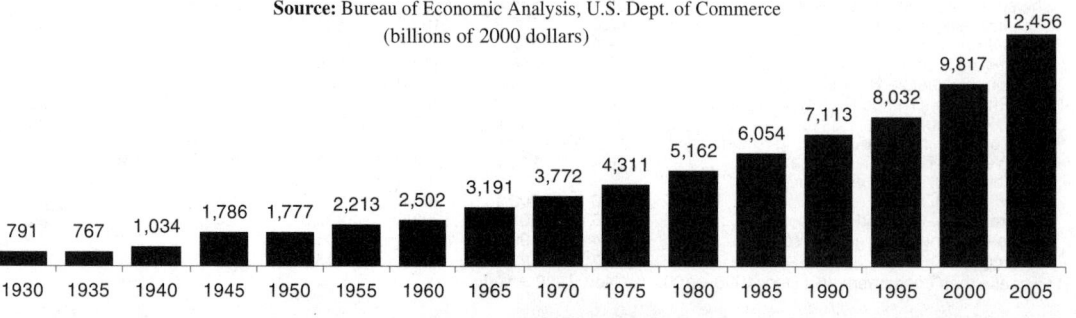

1930	1935	1940	1945	1950	1955	1960	1965	1970	1975	1980	1985	1990	1995	2000	2005
791	767	1,034	1,786	1,777	2,213	2,502	3,191	3,772	4,311	5,162	6,054	7,113	8,032	9,817	12,456

U.S. National Income by Industry[1], 1998-2005

Source: Bureau of Economic Analysis, U.S. Dept. of Commerce; in billions of current dollars; revised Sept. 28, 2006.

	1998	2000	2001	2002	2003	2004	2005
National income without capital consumption adjustment	7,661.4	8,687.4	8,854.9	9,013.5	9,425.3	10,069.5	10,917.9
Domestic industries	7,640.1	8,648.5	8,811.2	8,982.9	9,368.5	10,023.2	10,886.0
Private industries	6,724.6	7,642.8	7,758.4	7,854.7	8,168.2	8,763.1	9,574.6
Agriculture, forestry, fishing, and hunting	78.5	70.1	69.3	65.9	80.7	95.3	87.6
Mining	72.6	93.8	101.0	81.4	104.0	123.7	158.9
Utilities	138.6	144.3	149.2	143.8	148.8	155.9	176.7
Construction	366.6	440.6	463.3	470.8	478.3	522.8	604.2
Manufacturing	1,112.1	1,228.5	1,094.1	1,071.6	1,112.3	1,211.0	1,365.8
Durable goods	672.5	744.0	617.8	613.8	630.4	674.6	746.0
Nondurable goods	439.5	484.5	476.2	457.8	481.9	536.4	619.8
Wholesale trade	505.4	563.8	557.7	553.4	576.0	625.0	689.3
Retail trade	591.1	665.3	689.0	710.1	737.4	766.0	825.3
Transportation and warehousing	235.3	261.2	251.9	250.3	258.8	280.8	306.3
Information	273.7	308.3	305.6	307.3	313.7	359.6	417.1
Finance, insurance, real estate, rental, leasing	1,328.5	1,529.3	1,643.7	1644.7	1,690.7	1,797.4	1,832.9
Professional and business services	975.1	1,151.6	1,171.3	1211.2	1,253.4	1,327.3	1,510.4
Educ. services, health care, social assistance	582.7	664.6	719.2	777.0	823.8	876.1	938.2
Arts, entert., recreation, accommodation, food service	267.9	310.5	316.8	330.3	343.4	366.0	394.2
Other services, except government	196.6	215.8	226.2	237.1	247.1	256.2	267.6
Government	915.5	1,005.7	1,052.8	1,128.2	1,200.2	1,260.2	1,311.4
Rest of the world	21.3	38.9	43.6	30.6	56.8	46.3	31.9

(1) Figures may not add because of rounding. Total national income also includes income from outside the U.S.

U.S. National Income by Type of Income[1], 1930-2005

Source: Bureau of Economic Analysis, U.S. Dept. of Commerce; in billions of current dollars; revised Sept. 28, 2006.

	1930	1950	1960	1970	1980	1990	2000	2004	2005
National income[2]	83.1	264.4	474.9	930.9	2,439.3	5,089.1	8,795.2	10,255.9	10,811.8
Compensation of employees	46.9	155.3	296.4	617.2	1,651.8	3,338.2	5,782.7	6,650.3	7,030.3
Wage and salary accruals	46.2	147.3	272.9	551.6	1,377.6	2754.0	4,829.2	5,377.1	5,664.8
Government	5.2	22.6	49.2	117.2	261.5	517.7	774.7	941.8	977.7
Supplements to wages and salaries	0.7	8.0	23.6	65.7	274.2	584.2	953.4	1,273.2	1,365.5
Employer contributions for employee pension and insurance funds	0.6	4.7	14.3	41.8	185.2	377.8	609.9	866.1	933.2
Employer contributions for government social insurance	0.0	3.4	9.3	23.8	88.9	206.5	343.5	407.1	432.3
Proprietors' income with inventory valuation and capital consumption adjustments	11.1	37.6	50.8	78.4	174.1	380.6	728.4	911.1	970.7
Farm	4.0	12.9	10.5	12.7	11.3	31.9	22.7	36.2	30.2
Nonfarm	7.0	24.7	40.3	65.7	162.8	348.7	705.7	874.9	940.4
Rental income of persons with capital consumption adjustments	5.5	9.2	17.1	21.4	30.0	50.7	150.3	127.0	72.8
Corporate profits with inventory valuation and capital consumption adjustment	7.5	36.0	53.8	83.6	201.1	437.8	817.9	1,182.6	1,330.7
Taxes on corporate income	0.8	17.9	22.8	34.8	87.2	145.4	265.2	300.1	399.3
Profits after tax with inventory valuation and capital consumption adjustments	6.6	18.1	31.0	48.9	113.9	292.4	552.7	882.5	931.4
Net dividends	5.5	8.8	13.4	24.3	64.1	169.1	377.9	539.5	576.9
Undistributed profits with inventory valuation and capital consumption adjustments	1.1	9.3	17.6	24.6	49.9	123.3	174.8	343.0	354.5
Net interest and miscellaneous payments	4.8	3.2	10.6	39.1	181.8	442.2	559.0	485.1	483.4

(1) Figures do not add, because of rounding and incomplete enumeration. (2) National income is the aggregate of labor and property earnings that arises in the production of goods and services. It is the sum of employee compensation, proprietors' income, rental income, adjusted corporate profits, and net interest. It measures the total factor costs of goods and services produced by the economy. Income is measured before deduction of taxes. Total national income figures include adjustments not itemized.

Distribution of U.S. Total Personal Income[1], 1930-2005

Source: Bureau of Economic Analysis, U.S. Dept. of Commerce; in billions of current dollars; revised Sept. 28, 2006.

Year	Personal income	Personal taxes and nontax payments	Disposable personal income	Personal outlays	Personal Savings Amount	Personal Savings As pct. of disposable income
1930	$76.3	$1.6	$74.7	$71.6	$3.1	4.1%
1940	78.5	1.7	76.8	72.4	4.4	5.7
1950	229.0	18.9	210.1	195.0	15.1	7.2
1960	411.5	46.1	365.4	338.8	26.7	7.3
1970	838.8	103.1	735.7	666.2	69.5	9.4
1980	2,307.9	298.9	2,009.0	1,807.5	201.4	10.0
1990	4,878.6	592.8	4,285.8	3,986.4	299.4	7.0
1995	6,152.3	744.1	5,408.2	5,157.3	250.9	4.6
2000	8,429.7	1,235.7	7,194.0	7,025.6	168.5	2.3
2001	8,724.1	1,237.3	7,486.8	7,354.5	132.3	1.8
2002	8,881.9	1,051.8	7,830.1	7,645.3	184.7	2.4
2003	9,163.6	1,001.1	8,162.5	7,987.7	174.9	2.1
2004	9,731.4	1,049.8	8,681.6	8,507.2	174.3	2.0
2005	10,239.2	1,203.1	9,036.1	9,070.9	−34.8	−0.4

(1) Personal income minus taxes/nontax payments=disposable income; disposable income minus outlays=savings. Figures may not add because of rounding.

Selected Personal Consumption Expenditures in the U.S., 1985-2005[1]

Source: Bureau of Economic Analysis, U.S. Dept. of Commerce
(billions of dollars)

	1985	1990	1995	2000	2003	2004	2005
Personal consumption expenditures	2,720.3	3,839.9	4,975.8	6,739.4	7,703.6	8,211.5	8,742.4
Durable goods	363.5	474.2	611.6	863.3	942.7	986.3	1,033.1
Motor vehicles and parts	175.9	212.8	266.7	386.5	431.7	437.9	448.2
New autos	86.3	89.7	82.1	103.6	97.2	97.7	103.7
Tires, tubes, accessories, and other parts	24.3	29.3	37.8	49.0	52.0	54.4	58.7
Furniture and household equipment	128.5	171.6	228.6	312.9	331.5	356.5	377.2
Furniture, including mattresses and bedsprings	29.3	38.4	48.5	67.6	70.2	75.5	79.0
Kitchen and other household appliances	19.8	23.7	26.5	30.4	32.8	34.9	37.2
China, glassware, tableware, and utensils	14.0	17.9	23.4	31.0	33.1	34.9	36.5
Video and audio goods, including musical instruments	33.0	44.1	57.2	72.8	76.5	81.8	85.8
Computers, peripherals, and software	2.9	8.9	24.3	43.8	46.6	51.6	55.4
Ophthalmic products and orthopedic appliances	6.2	13.7	15.0	22.1	22.4	23.4	25.0
Wheel goods, sports and photographic equipment, boats, and pleasure aircraft	21.2	29.7	39.7	57.6	65.6	71.4	81.5
Jewelry and watches	21.1	30.3	38.4	50.6	52.8	56.5	58.9
Books and maps	10.6	16.2	23.2	33.7	38.7	40.6	42.2
Nondurable goods	928.7	1,249.9	1,485.1	1,947.2	2,190.2	2,345.2	2,539.3
Food	467.6	636.8	740.9	925.2	1,046.0	1,114.8	1,201.4
Food purchased for off-premise consumption	310.5	401.6	458.6	566.7	636.0	677.9	734.0
Purchased meals and beverages	150.0	227.7	274.0	348.8	399.0	425.5	455.1
Food furnished to employees (including military) and food produced and consumed on farms	7.1	7.4	8.3	9.7	10.9	11.4	12.3
Alcoholic beverages purchased for off-premise consumption	39.4	48.9	54.6	71.2	78.5	86.2	96.5
Clothing and shoes	152.1	204.1	241.7	297.7	310.9	325.1	341.8
Shoes	22.9	31.5	37.6	47.0	50.3	51.9	54.2
Women's and children's clothing and accessories except shoes	85.3	113.0	129.5	156.7	163.1	171.3	180.5
Men's and boys' clothing and accessories except shoes	43.9	59.6	74.7	94.0	97.5	101.9	107.1
Gasoline, fuel oil, and other energy goods	110.8	124.1	133.3	191.5	209.6	248.8	302.1
Gasoline and oil	97.2	111.2	120.2	175.7	192.7	230.4	280.2
Fuel oil and coal	13.6	12.9	13.1	15.8	16.9	18.4	21.9
Tobacco products	30.8	41.0	49.2	78.5	88.0	87.5	90.0
Toilet articles and preparations	25.7	36.0	45.9	55.0	56.0	58.2	61.7
Semidurable house furnishings	16.4	22.5	29.4	36.5	39.0	41.2	43.5
Cleaning and polishing preparations, misc. household supplies and paper products	30.6	38.9	48.8	61.6	69.0	72.9	77.7
Drug preparations and sundries	38.7	65.4	92.1	169.4	233.6	251.3	265.7
Nondurable toys and sport supplies	21.4	32.8	44.4	56.6	60.6	63.5	67.2
Stationery and writing supplies	8.5	13.2	16.3	19.0	18.4	18.8	19.6
Magazines, newspapers, and sheet music	15.9	21.6	27.5	35.0	36.3	39.6	43.8
Flowers, seeds, and potted plants	6.9	10.9	14.0	18.0	17.9	18.3	19.7
Services	1,428.1	2,115.9	2,879.1	3,928.8	4,570.8	4,880.1	5,170.0
Housing	412.7	597.9	764.4	1,006.5	1,161.8	1,236.1	1,304.1
Owner-occupied nonfarm dwellings—space rent	280.8	412.8	531.2	712.2	846.4	910.1	963.3
Tenant-occupied nonfarm dwellings—rent	108.3	150.7	186.6	227.5	245.3	248.9	257.0
Rental value of farm dwellings	5.1	6.3	9.4	10.7	12.1	12.9	13.8
Household operation	181.8	227.3	298.7	390.1	429.4	450.0	483.0
Electricity	61.2	74.2	91.0	102.3	115.6	121.1	134.2
Gas	29.5	26.8	31.2	41.0	51.7	55.5	65.5
Water and other sanitary services	17.0	27.1	39.3	50.8	57.8	60.7	64.2
Telephone and telegraph	46.0	60.5	85.0	125.1	129.7	132.9	136.0
Domestic service	7.7	10.4	13.8	17.4	18.5	19.6	19.9
Transportation	104.5	147.7	207.7	291.3	297.3	307.8	320.4
User-operated transportation	76.7	110.7	163.6	231.6	241.6	248.9	259.7
Purchased local transportation	6.8	8.4	10.1	12.2	13.0	13.8	14.7
Mass transit systems	4.2	5.8	7.1	9.1	9.5	10.2	10.8
Taxicab	2.6	2.6	3.0	3.1	3.5	3.6	3.9
Purchased intercity transportation	21.0	28.6	33.9	47.4	42.7	45.0	46.0
Railway	0.4	0.6	0.4	0.5	0.6	0.6	0.6
Bus	1.3	1.3	1.8	2.4	2.3	2.3	2.2
Airline	17.6	22.7	25.3	36.7	31.2	33.1	33.8
Medical care	331.5	556.0	797.9	1,026.8	1,300.5	1,395.7	1,493.4
Physicians	78.8	138.6	184.6	236.8	300.6	322.2	342.4
Dentists	22.6	32.4	45.4	61.8	74.6	80.2	85.5
Other professional services	31.8	70.7	126.6	161.6	201.8	217.2	232.0
Hospitals and nursing homes	169.9	270.9	380.5	482.6	610.8	645.8	691.3
Health insurance	28.4	43.4	60.7	84.0	112.8	130.4	142.2
Recreation	77.7	125.9	187.9	268.3	317.7	341.6	360.6
Admissions to specified spectator amusements	9.7	15.1	21.1	30.4	36.0	37.4	38.3
Personal care	28.2	48.1	61.2	87.0	99.5	108.9	114.6
Cleaning, storage, and repair of clothing and shoes	7.3	11.3	12.3	15.7	15.2	15.7	15.8
Barbershops, beauty parlors, and health clubs	13.1	20.9	26.8	38.4	44.4	48.4	50.5
Personal business	177.5	250.9	349.6	539.1	559.7	612.4	647.9
Brokerage charges and investment counseling	15.2	23.2	43.5	100.6	77.4	86.6	90.5
Bank service charges, trust services, and safe deposit box rental	15.6	25.5	37.2	64.2	81.8	89.3	99.9
Expense of handling life insurance and pension plans	39.8	53.2	72.9	96.1	85.9	98.7	106.9
Legal services	24.5	40.9	47.4	63.9	78.1	82.0	85.6
Funeral and burial expenses	6.8	9.5	12.4	14.0	15.9	15.6	16.0
Education and research	53.9	83.7	114.3	163.8	203.1	213.6	226.5
Higher education	28.7	43.8	62.9	86.4	112.6	119.6	126.8
Nursery, elementary, and secondary schools	14.3	21.2	27.0	34.6	40.5	42.5	44.8
Religious and welfare activities	55.7	88.7	120.4	172.3	207.1	219.0	224.5
Net foreign travel	4.6	-10.3	-22.9	-16.2	-5.3	-5.0	-5.0
Foreign travel by U.S. residents	27.9	42.7	54.7	84.4	80.5	91.8	99.9
Less: Expenditures in the United States by nonresidents	23.3	53.0	77.6	100.7	85.8	96.7	104.9

(1) Subtotals may not add to total, due to rounding or incomplete enumeration.

Median Income by Race, Hispanic Origin, and Sex, 1947-2004[1]

Source: U.S. Census Bureau

	Year	Male No. with income (thous.)	Male Median income Current dollars	Male Median income 2004 dollars	Female No. with income (thous.)	Female Median income Current dollars	Female Median income 2004 dollars
All Races	2004	101,777	$30,513	$30,513	103,369	$17,629	$17,629
	2003	100,769	29,931	30,735	102,713	17,259	17,723
	2002	99,788	29,238	30,712	102,487	16,812	17,659
	2001	98,873	29,101	31,054	101,941	16,614	17,729
	2000	98,504	28,343	31,089	101,704	16,063	17,619
	1990	88,220	20,293	28,439	92,245	10,070	14,112
	1980	78,661	12,530	27,206	80,826	4,920	10,683
	1970	65,008	6,670	28,100	51,647	2,237	9,424
	1960	55,172	4,080	22,051	36,526	1,261	6,815
	1950	47,585	2,570	17,077	24,651	953	6,333
	1947	46,813	2,230	16,018	21,479	1,017	7,305
White	2004	85,112	31,335	31,335	84,366	17,648	17,648
	2003	84,405	30,732	31,558	83,852	17,422	17,890
	2002	83,899	30,383	31,914	84,014	16,838	17,687
	2001	83,750	30,240	32,269	84,207	16,652	17,769
	2000	83,372	29,797	32,684	84,123	16,079	17,637
	1990	76,480	21,170	29,668	78,566	10,317	14,459
	1980	69,420	13,328	28,939	70,573	4,947	10,741
	1970	58,447	7,011	29,536	45,288	2,266	9,546
	1960	49,788	4,296	23,219	32,001	1,352	7,307
	1950	NA	2,709	18,001	NA	1,060	7,044
	1947	46,813	2,230	16,018	21,479	1,017	7,529
Black	2004	10,336	22,740	22,740	12,985	17,369	17,369
	2003	10,291	21,935	22,525	12,924	16,540	16,985
	2002	10,096	21,509	22,593	12,665	16,671	17,511
	2001	9,944	21,466	22,907	12,414	16,282	17,375
	2000	9,905	21,343	23,411	12,461	15,881	17,420
	1990	8,820	12,868	18,034	10,687	8,328	11,671
	1980	7,387	8,009	17,390	8,596	4,580	9,944
	1970	5,844	4,157	17,513	5,844	2,063	8,691
	1960	5,384	2,260	12,215	4,525	837	4,524
	1950	NA	1,471	9,775	NA	474	3,150
White not Hispanic	2004	72,768	33,652	33,652	74,810	18,379	18,379
	2003	72,535	32,331	33,200	74,486	18,301	18,793
	2002	72,146	32,034	33,649	74,814	17,389	18,265
	2001	72,649	31,791	33,924	75,117	17,229	18,385
	2000	72,530	31,508	34,561	75,206	16,665	18,280
	1990	69,987	21,958	30,773	72,939	10,581	14,828
	1980	65,564	13,681	29,705	67,084	4,980	10,813
Asian	2004	4,384	32,419	32,419	4,308	20,618	20,618
	2003	4,266	31,737	32,590	4,252	17,879	18,360
	2002	4,139	30,839	32,393	4,137	17,898	18,800
	2001	4,165	31,096	33,183	4,164	18,525	19,768
	2000	4,303	30,833	33,820	4,192	17,356	19,038
	1990	2,235	19,394	27,179	2,333	11,086	15,536
Hispanic	2004	13,255	21,559	21,559	10,389	14,425	14,425
	2003	12,753	21,053	21,619	10,175	13,642	14,009
	2002	12,624	20,702	21,745	10,018	13,364	14,038
	2001	11,766	20,189	21,544	9,691	12,583	13,427
	2000	11,343	19,498	21,387	9,431	12,248	13,435
	1990	6,767	13,470	18,877	5,903	7,532	10,556
	1980	3,996	9,659	20,972	3,617	4,405	9,564

NA = Not available. (1) People 15 years old and over beginning with March 1980, and people 14 years old and over as of March of the following year for previous years.

U.S. Bank Failures, 1934-2005

Source: Federal Deposit Insurance Corp.

Covers all FDIC-insured commercial and savings banks, including savings and loan institutions (S&Ls) 1980 and after.

Year	Closed or assisted	Year	Closed or assisted	Year	Closed or assisted	Year	Closed or assisted
1934	9	1965	5	1981	40	1994	15
1935	26	1966	7	1982	119	1995	8
1936	69	1967	4	1983	99	1996	6
1937	77	1969	9	1984	106	1997	1
1938	74	1970	7	1985	180	1998	3
1939	60	1971	7	1986	204	1999	8
1940	43	1972	2	1987	262	2000	7
1955	5	1973	6	1988	465	2001	4
1959	3	1975	13	1989	534	2002	11
1960	1	1976	17	1990	382	2003	3
1961	5	1978	7	1991	271	2004	4
1963	2	1979	10	1992	181		
1964	7	1980	22	1993	50		

Note: There were no bank failures in 2005, or in 2006 as of Sept. 30.

World's 50 Largest Banking Companies[1]

Source: *American Banker* (as of Dec. 31, 2005)

Assets[2]	(millions)	Assets[2]	(millions)
Barclays PLC, London	$1,587,061	Merrill Lynch, New York	$681,015
UBS AG, Zurich	1,562,254	Dexia, Brussels	600,993
HSBC Holdings PLC, London	1,499,302	Rabobank, Netherlands	599,609
Citigroup Inc., New York	1,493,987	Agricultural Bank of China, Beijing	591,190
BNP Paribas, Paris	1,485,919	Bank of China Ltd., Beijing	587,352
ING Group, Amsterdam	1,372,780	Norinchukin Bank, Tokyo	578,229
Royal Bank of Scotland Group PLC, Edinburgh	1,334,752	China Construction Bank, Beijing	568,232
Mizuho Financial Group, Tokyo	1,325,227	Lloyds TSB Group PLC, London	532,222
Bank of America Corp., Charlotte	1,291,795	Wachovia Corp., Charlotte	520,755
Credit Agricole SA, Paris	1,246,971	Commerzbank AG, Frankfurt	519,766
JPMorgan Chase & Co., New York	1,198,942	Wells Fargo & Co., San Francisco	481,741
Allianz AG, Munich	1,181,940	MetLife, New York	481,645
Deutsche Bank, Frankfurt	1,167,800	BBV Argentaria SA, Spain	456,527
ABN Amro, Amsterdam	1,037,967	Royal Bank of Canada, Toronto	397,517
Mitsubishi UFJ Financial Group, Tokyo	1,024,438	Danske Bank, Copenhagen	385,156
Credit Suisse Group, Zurich	1,012,236	KBC Groupe SA, Brussels	384,545
Societe Generale, Paris	1,001,872	Nordea Bank AB, Stockholm	384,393
Banco Santander Central Hispano SA, Spain	945,857	Resona Holdings Inc., Osaka	368,701
Hbos PLC, Edinburgh	929,333	Washington Mutual Inc., Seattle	343,839
Unicredito Italiano Spa, Milan	922,791	Group Banques Populaires, Paris	340,582
Sumitomo Mitsui Financial Group, Tokyo	915,587	Banca Intesa, Milan	321,641
Morgan Stanley, New York	898,523	National Australia Bank Ltd., Melbourne	318,886
Fortis NV, Netherlands	859,921	West LB, Dusseldorf	312,013
Industrial and Commerical Bank of China, Beijing	799,745	Toronto-Dominion Bank, Toronto	309,585
Groupe Caisse d'Epargne, Paris	700,875	San Paolo IMI, Italy	309,122

(1) Includes bank holding companies and commercial and savings banks. (2) Currency conversion based on Exchange rates on Dec. 31, 2005 or at end of latest fiscal year.

50 Largest U.S. Bank Holding Companies, 2005[1]

Source: *American Banker* (as of Dec. 31, 2005)

Company Name	Total Assets (in thousands)	Company Name	Total Assets (in thousands)
Citigroup Inc. New York	$1,494,037,000	Merrill Lynch & Co. Inc. New York	$71,068,407
Bank of America Corp. Charlotte	1,294,312,241	BNP Paribas Group Paris	66,345,204
JPMorgan Chase & Co. New York	1,198,942,000	Sovereign Bancorp Inc. Philadelphia	63,658,270
Wachovia Corp. Charlotte	520,755,000	MBNA Corp. Wilmington, Del.	61,862,462
Wells Fargo & Co. San Francisco	481,741,000	North Fork Bancorp. Inc. Melville, N.Y.	57,616,871
MetLife Inc. New York	481,645,114	Mitsubishi UFJ Financial Group Inc. Tokyo	58,833,827
HSBC Holdings PLC London	406,673,039	M&T Bank Buffalo	55,146,406
Washington Mutual Inc. Seattle	365,696,006	Comerica Inc. Detroit	53,682,457
Deutsche Bank Frankfurt	364,693,000	Northern Trust Corp. Chicago	53,413,797
U.S. Bancorp Minneapolis	209,465,000	ING USA Holding Wilmington, Del.	53,128,800
SunTrust Banks Inc. Atlanta	179,712,841	AmSouth Bancorp. Birmingham, Ala.	52,619,315
Countrywide Financial Corp. Calabasas, Calif.	175,085,370	Rabobank Nederland Utrecht	51,008,151
Royal Bank of Scotland Group Edinburgh	155,439,714	Harris Financial Chicago	50,006,022
ABN Amro Amsterdam	144,073,691	Popular Inc. Hato Rey, Puerto Rico	48,624,000
National City Corp. Cleveland	142,410,520	Charles Schwab Corp. San Francisco	47,351,142
Golden West Financial Corp. Oakland, Calif.	124,384,506	Marshall & Ilsley Corp. Milwaukee	46,295,972
BB&T Corp. Winston-Salem, N.C.	109,169,759	Zions Bancorp. Salt Lake City	42,762,673
Fifth Third Bancorp Cincinnati	105,225,054	Toronto-Dominion Bank	42,568,606
Bank of New York Co. Inc.	102,157,000	Mellon Financial Corp. Pittsburgh	38,773,216
John Hancock Holding Wilmington	101,335,209	Commerce Bancorp Inc. Cherry Hill, N.J.	38,496,335
State Street Corp. Boston	97,995,766	First Horizon National Corp. Memphis	36,581,677
KeyCorp Cleveland	92,844,997	E-Trade Financial Corp. New York	33,011,722
PNC Financial Services Group Inc. Pittsburgh	91,992,332	Huntington Bancshares Inc. Columbus, Ohio	32,758,006
Capital One Financial Corp. McLean, Va.	88,701,411	Morgan Stanley New York	32,404,076
Regions Financial Corp. Birmingham, Ala.	84,786,331	American Express Co. New York	31,477,594

(1) Includes foreign-owned banks with a strong presence in the U.S.

Banks in the U.S.–Number, Deposits

Source: Federal Deposit Insurance Corp. (as of Dec. 31, 2005)

Comprises all FDIC-insured commercial and savings banks, including savings and loan institutions (S&Ls).

Year	ALL BANKS	TOTAL NUMBER OF BANKS				TOTAL DEPOSITS (millions of dollars)				
		Commercial banks[1]			All savings	ALL DEPOSITS	Commercial banks[1]			All savings
		Natl.	State	Non-members			Natl.	State	Non-members	
1935	15,295	5,386	1,001	7,735	1,173	$45,102[2]	$24,802	$13,653	$5,669	$978[2]
1940	15,772	5,144	1,342	6,956	2,330	67,494	35,787	20,642	7,040	4,025
1950	16,500	4,958	1,912	6,576	3,054	171,963	84,941	41,602	19,726	25,694
1960	17,549	4,530	1,641	6,955	4,423	310,262	120,242	65,487	34,369	90,164
1970	18,205	4,621	1,147	7,743	4,694	686,901	285,436	101,512	95,566	204,367
1980	18,763	4,425	997	9,013	4,328	1,832,716	656,752	191,183	344,311	640,470
1990	15,158	3,979	1,009	7,355	2,815	3,637,292	1,558,915	397,797	693,438	987,142
2000	9,905	2,230	991	5,094	1,590	4,914,808	2,250,464	1,032,110	894,000	738,234
2001	9,631	2,137	972	4,971	1,533	5,189,444	2,384,462	1,079,388	927,772	797,822
2002	9,354	2,077	950	4,861	1,439	5,568,508	2,565,771	1,152,380	971,730	878,627
2003	9,182	2,001	935	4,833	1,413	5,954,288	2,786,756	1,195,914	1,046,195	925,423
2004	8,976	1,907	919	4,805	1,345	6,584,200	3,581,416	872,228	1,139,168	991,388
2005	8,832	1,818	907	4,802	1,305	7,141,178	3,850,051	936,299	1,286,983	1,067,845

(1) "Nonmembers" are banks that are not members of the Federal Reserve System; "National" and "State" institutions are members.
(2) Figures for 1935 do not include data for S&Ls (not available).

Federal Deposit Insurance Corporation (FDIC)

The Federal Deposit Insurance Corporation (FDIC) is the independent deposit insurance agency created by Congress to maintain stability and public confidence in the nation's banking system. In its unique role as deposit insurer of banks and savings associations, and in cooperation with other federal and state regulatory agencies, the FDIC seeks to promote the safety and soundness of insured depository institutions in the U.S. financial system by identifying, monitoring, and addressing risks to the deposit insurance funds. The FDIC aims at promoting public understanding and sound public policies by providing financial and economic information and analyses. It seeks to minimize disruptive effects from the failure of banks and savings associations, and to ensure fairness in the sale of financial products and the provision of financial services.

To maintain its insurance funds, the FDIC assesses depository institutions insurance premiums twice a year. The amount of the premium is based on the institution's balance of insured deposits for the preceding two quarters and the institution's risk to the insurance fund. The Corporation may borrow from the U.S. Treasury, not to exceed $30 bil outstanding, but the agency has made no such borrowings since it was organized in 1933. The FDIC's Bank Insurance Fund was $35.5 bil (unaudited) and the Savings Association Insurance Fund stood at $13.1 bil (unaudited), as of June 30, 2006.

Federal Reserve System

The Federal Reserve System is the central bank for the U.S. The system was established on Dec. 23, 1913, originally to give the country an elastic currency, provide facilities for discounting commercial paper, and improve the supervision of banking. Since then, the system's responsibilities have been broadened. Over the years, stability and growth of the economy, a high level of employment, stability in the purchasing power of the dollar, and reasonable balance in transactions with other countries have come to be recognized as primary objectives of governmental economic policy.

The Federal Reserve System consists of the Board of Governors, the 12 District Reserve Banks and their branch offices, and the Federal Open Market Committee. Several advisory councils help the board meet its varied responsibilities.

The hub of the system is the 7-member **Board of Governors** in Washington, DC. The members of the board are appointed by the president and confirmed by the Senate, to serve 14-year terms. The president also appoints the chairman and vice chairman of the board from among the board members for 4-year terms that may be renewed. As of Oct. 2005 the board members were: Alan Greenspan, chair; Roger W. Ferguson Jr., vice chair; Susan Schmidt Bies; Mark W. Olson; and Donald L. Kohn.

The 12 **District Reserve Banks** and their branch offices serve as the decentralized portion of the system, carrying out day-to-day operations such as circulating currency and coin and providing fiscal agency functions and payments mechanism services. The 12 are in Boston, New York, Philadelphia, Cleveland, Richmond, Atlanta, Chicago, St. Louis, Minneapolis, Kansas City, Dallas, and San Francisco.

The system's principal function is monetary policy, which it controls using 3 tools: reserve requirements, the discount rate, and open market operations.

Uniform **reserve requirements**, set by the board, are applied to the transaction accounts and nonpersonal time deposits of all depository institutions. Responsibility for setting the **discount rate** (the interest rate at which depository institutions can borrow money from the Reserve Banks) is shared by the Board of Governors and the Reserve Banks. Changes in the discount rate are recommended by the individual boards of directors of the Reserve Banks and are subject to approval by the Board of Governors.

The most important tool of monetary policy is **open market operations** (the purchase and sale of government securities). Responsibility for influencing the cost and availability of money and credit through the purchase and sale of government securities lies with the **Federal Open Market Committee** (FOMC), which is composed of the 7 members of the Board of Governors, the president of the Federal Reserve Bank of New York, and 4 other Federal Reserve Bank presidents, who each serve 1-year terms on a rotating basis. The committee bases its decisions on economic and financial developments and outlook, setting yearly growth objectives for key measures of money supply and credit. The decisions of the committee are carried out by the Domestic Trading Desk of the Federal Reserve Bank of New York.

A Federal Advisory Council meets with the Federal Reserve Board 4 times a year to discuss business and financial conditions, as well as to make recommendations.

Website: www.federalreserve.gov

Federal Reserve Board Primary and Secondary Credit Rate

Prior to Jan. 9, 2003, the federal reserve set a single "discount rate," the interest rate that member banks were charged when borrowing money through the Federal Reserve System. The discount rate was replaced with two rates, the *primary credit rate* and *secondary credit rate*. The primary credit rate (listed first) is available to banks in generally sound financial condition. The secondary credit (listed second) rate is given to banks that do not qualify for the primary credit rate. Both are extended for very short terms, usually overnight. Under the new system, financially sound institutions are not required to exhaust all funds before borrowing from the Fed.

Effective date	Rates	Effective date	Rates	Effective date	Rates	Effective date	Rates	Effective date	Rates
1980:		**1984:**		**1991:**		**2000:**		**2004:**	
Feb. 15	13%	April 9	9%	Apr. 30	5½%	Feb. 2	5¼%	Jun. 30	2¼, 2¾%
May 30	12	Nov. 21	8½	Sept. 13	5	Mar. 21	5½	Aug. 10	2½, 3
June 13	11	Dec. 24	8	Nov. 6	4½	May 16	6	Sept. 21	2¾, 3¼
July 28	10	**1985:**		Dec. 20	3½	**2001:**		Nov. 10	3, 3½
Sept. 26	11	May 20	7½	**1992:**		Jan. 3	5¾	Dec. 14	3¼, 3¾
Nov. 17	12	**1986:**		July 2	3	Jan. 31	5	**2005:**	
Dec. 5	13	March 7	7	**1994:**		Mar. 20	4½	Feb. 2	3½, 4
1981:		April 21	6½	May 17	½	Apr. 18	4	Mar. 22	3¾, 4¼
May 5	14	July 11	6	Aug. 16	4	May 15	3½	May 3	4, 4½
Nov. 2	13	Aug. 21	5½	Nov. 15	4¾	June 27	3¼	June 30	4¼, 4¾
Dec. 4	12	**1987:**		**1995:**		Aug. 21	3	Aug. 9	4½, 5
1982:		Sept. 4	6	Feb. 1	5	Sept. 17	2½	Sept. 20	4¾, 5¼
July 20	11½	**1988:**		**1996:**		Oct. 2	2	Nov. 1	5, 5½
Aug. 2	11	Aug. 9	6½	Jan. 31	5	Dec. 11	1¼	Dec. 13	5¼, 5¾
Aug. 16	10	**1989:**		**1998:**		**2002:**		**2006[1]:**	
Aug. 27	10	Feb. 24	7	Oct. 15	4¾	Nov. 6	¾%	Jan. 31	5½, 6
Oct. 12	9½	**1990:**		Nov. 17	4½	**2003:**		Mar. 28	5¾, 6¼
Dec. 15	8½	Dec. 18	6½	**1999:**		Jan. 9	2¼, 2¾	May 10	6, 6½
				Aug. 24	4¾	June 25	2, 2½	Jun. 29	6¼, 6¾
				Nov. 16	5				

(1) Through Oct. 1, 2006.

United States Mint

Source: United States Mint, U.S. Dept. of the Treasury

The United States Mint was created on Apr. 2, 1792, by an act of Congress, which established the U.S. national coinage system. In 1799 the mint became an independent agency reporting directly to the president. It was made a statutory bureau of the Treasury Department in 1873, with a director appointed by the president. The mint manufactures and ships all U.S. coins for circulation to Federal Reserve banks and branches, which in turn issue coins to the public and business community through depository institutions. The mint also safeguards the Treasury Department's stored gold and silver, as well as other monetary assets.

The composition of dimes, quarters, and half dollars, traditionally produced from silver, was changed by the Coinage Act of 1965, which mandated that these coins from then on be minted from a cupronickel-clad alloy and reduced the silver content of the half dollar to 40%. In 1970, legislative action mandated that the half dollar and a dollar coin be minted from the same alloy.

The Eisenhower dollar was minted from 1971 through 1978, when legislation called for the minting of the smaller Susan B. Anthony dollar coin. The Anthony dollar, which was minted through 1981, marked the first time that a woman other than a mythical figure, appeared on a U.S. coin produced for general circulation. This coin was replaced in 2000 by the Golden Dollar Coin. Golden in color, with a smooth edge and wide border, the obverse side depicts Sacagawea (a Shoshone woman who helped guide Lewis and Clark) and her infant son. The reverse shows an American eagle and 17 stars, one for each of the states at the time of the Lewis and Clark expedition.

Mint headquarters are in Washington, DC. Mint production facilities are in Philadelphia, Denver, San Francisco, and West Point, NY. In addition, the mint is responsible for the U.S. Bullion Depository at Fort Knox, KY.

Proof coin sets, silver proof coin sets, and uncirculated coin sets are available from the mint, which also produces medals in honor of significant persons, events, and sites.

Among recent congressionally authorized commemorative coins are: the 2006 Benjamin Franklin Commemorative Coin Program, featuring "Scientist" and "Founding Father" silver dollars; the San Francisco Old Mint Commemorative Coin Program, featuring a $5 gold coin and a silver dollar; the 2006 Westward Journey Nickel Series, commemorating the Lewis and Clark expedition on a redesigned, circulating 5-cent coin; and the 2007 Jamestown 400th Anniversary Commemorative Coin Program, also featuring a $5 gold coin and a silver dollar. In 2007, the mint will also begin issuing circulating $1 coins featuring images of U.S. Presidents. New coins will be issued in the order in which the presidents served, starting with Washington, Adams, Jefferson, and Madison in 2007.

Congressionally authorized American Eagle gold, platinum, and silver bullion coins are also available through dealers worldwide.

The mint offers free public tours and operates sales centers at the U.S. mints in Denver and Philadelphia. Further information is available from the U.S. Mint, Customer Care Center, 801 9th St., NW, Washington, DC 20220; (800) USA-MINT.

Website: www.usmint.gov

New Commemorative State Quarters, 2007-08

Source: United States Mint, U.S. Dept. of the Treasury

Beginning in Jan. 1999, a series of 5 quarter dollars with new reverses are being issued each year through 2008, celebrating each of the 50 states. To make room on the reverse of the commemorative quarters for each state's design, certain design elements have been moved, thereby creating a new obverse design as well. The coins are being issued in the sequence the states became part of the Union (date each state entered the union is shown); listed below are the quarters being issued in 2007-08.

2007	Montana	Washington	Idaho	Wyoming	Utah
	Nov. 8, 1889	Nov. 11, 1889	July 3, 1890	July 10, 1890	Jan. 4, 1896
2008	Oklahoma	New Mexico	Arizona	Alaska	Hawaii
	Nov. 16, 1907	Jan. 6, 1912	Feb. 14, 1912	Jan. 3, 1959	Aug. 21, 1959

The Bureau of Engraving and Printing

Source: Bureau of Engraving and Printing, U.S. Dept. of the Treasury

The Bureau of Engraving and Printing manufactures the financial and other securities of the United States. It designs and prints a variety of products, including Federal Reserve notes (bills in various denominations), Treasury securities, identification cards, naturalization certificates, and other special security documents. Denominations of the various types of printings produced by the bureau range from a 1/5-cent wine stamp to a $100,000,000 International Monetary Fund special note. Among its products are all hand-engraved invitations issued by the White House.

The first general circulation of paper money by the federal government dates back to 1861, prior to the establishment of the bureau, when, to finance the Civil War, Congress authorized the U.S. Treasury to issue non-interest-bearing demand notes, nicknamed "greenbacks" because of their color. A portrait of Pres. Abraham Lincoln appeared on the face of the first $10 notes. By 1862, the design of U.S. currency incorporated fine-line engraving, intricate geometric lathework patterns, a Treasury seal, and engraved signatures, to aid in counterfeit deterrence. All U.S. currency issued since 1861

remains valid and redeemable at full face value.

The Bureau of Engraving and Printing began operations by 1862, originally separating and sealing bank notes that were printed by private companies. In 1877, the bureau became the sole producer of U.S. currency. In 1894, it also began producing Postage Stamps. On June 10, 2005, the bureau printed its last stamps, a roll of 37-cent flag stamps; stamps are now produced by private printers.

The Federal Reserve Act of 1913 created the Federal Reserve as the nation's central bank, and provided for currency called Federal Reserve notes. The first notes, issued the following year, were $10 notes bearing a portrait of Pres. Andrew Jackson. In 1929, the look of U.S. currency was standardized. The national motto, "In God We Trust," began appearing on paper money in 1957.

The Bureau of Engraving and Printing currently operates 2 facilities, one in Washington, DC, opened in 1914, and one in Forth Worth, TX, which began operations in 1991.

More information on the Bureau of Engraving and Printing can be found at www.moneyfactory.com

New U.S. Currency Designs

On Mar. 25, 1996, the U.S. Treasury issued a redesigned $100 note incorporating many new and modified anticounterfeiting features. A new $50 note was issued Oct. 27, 1997, a new $20 bill was released into circulation Sept. 24, 1998, and new $10 and $5 notes were issued May 24, 2000. Old notes are being removed from circulation as they are returned to the Federal Reserve.

The new $100 bill has a larger portrait, moved off-center; a watermark (seen only when held up to the light) to the

right of the portrait, depicting the same person (Benjamin Franklin); a security thread that glows red when exposed to ultraviolet light in a dark environment; color-shifting ink that changes from green to black when viewed at different angles, to appear in the numeral on the lower, front right-hand corner of the bill; microprinting in the numeral in the note's lower, front left-hand corner and on the portrait; and other features for security, machine authentication, and processing of the currency. The redesigned $5, $10, $20, and

$50 bills incorporated the same features as the $100 bill, with the notable addition of a low-vision feature, a large (14-mm high, as compared to 7.8-mm on the old design), dark numeral on a light background on the back of the note. (The security thread glows yellow in the $50, green in the $20, orange in the $10, and blue in the $5. There is no color-shifting ink on the $5 note.)

Beginning in 2003, the Treasury launched another major redesign of U.S. currency: on Oct. 9, 2003, the U.S. Treasury introduced a new $20 note, using background colors for the first time since 1905. The notes have a security thread running vertically up one side, with "USA TWENTY" and a small U.S. flag; the thread glows green under UV light. Other security features include color-shifting ink in the number "20" in the lower right corner on the note's face. A new $50 note with similar security features was released Sept. 28, 2004, followed by a new $10 note on March 2, 2006. A new $5 bill was scheduled for 2008, followed by another redesign of the $100 note.

More new currency information is available on the U.S. Treasury's website: www.ustreas.gov/topics/currency

Denominations of U.S. Currency

Since 1969 the largest denomination of U.S. currency that has been issued is the $100 bill. As larger-denomination bills reach the Federal Reserve Bank, they are removed from circulation. Because some discontinued currency is expected to be in the hands of holders for many years, the description of the various denominations below is continued.

Amt.	Portait	Embellishment on Back	Amt.	Portait	Embellishment on Back
$1	Washington.....	Great Seal of U.S.	$100	Franklin.......	Independence Hall
2	Jefferson.......	Signers of Declaration	500	McKinley......	Ornate denominational marking
5	Lincoln........	Lincoln Memorial	1,000	Cleveland......	Ornate denominational marking
10	Hamilton.......	U.S. Treasury	5,000	Madison.......	Ornate denominational marking
20	Jackson.......	White House	10,000	Salmon Chase..	Ornate denominational marking
50	Grant.........	U.S. Capitol	100,000*	Wilson........	Ornate denominational marking

*For use only in transactions between Federal Reserve System and Treasury Department.

Portraits on U.S. Treasury Bills, Bonds, Notes, and Savings Bonds

Denomination	Savings bonds	Treasury bills*	Treasury bonds*	Treasury notes*
$50..............................	Washington		Jefferson	
75..............................	Adams			
100..............................	Jefferson		Jackson	
200..............................	Madison			
500..............................	Hamilton		Washington	
1,000..............................	B. Franklin	H. McCulloch	Lincoln	Lincoln
5,000..............................	P. Revere	J. G. Carlisle	Monroe	Monroe
10,000..............................	J. Wilson	J. Sherman	Cleveland	Cleveland
50,000..............................	C. Glass			
100,000..............................		A. Gallatin	Grant	Grant
1,000,000..............................		O. Wolcott	T. Roosevelt	T. Roosevelt
100,000,000..............................				Madison
500,000,000..............................				McKinley

*The U.S. Treasury discontinued issuing treasury bill, bond, and note certificates in 1986. Since then, all issues of marketable treasury securities have been available only in book-entry form, although some certificates remain in circulation.

The U.S. $1 Bill

Plate position: Shows where on the 32-note plate this bill was printed.

Serial number Each bill has its own.

Federal Reserve District Number: Shows which district issued the bill.

Federal Reserve District Seal: The name of the Federal Reserve Bank that issued the bill is printed in the seal. The letter tells you quickly where the bill is from. Here are the letter codes for the 12 Federal Reserve Districts:

- **A:** Boston
- **B:** New York
- **C:** Philadelphia
- **D:** Cleveland
- **E:** Richmond
- **F:** Atlanta
- **G:** Chicago
- **H:** St. Louis
- **I:** Minneapolis
- **J:** Kansas City
- **K:** Dallas
- **L:** San Francisco

The Treasury Department seal: The balancing scales represent justice. The pointed stripe across the middle has 13 stars for the original 13 colonies. The key represents authority.

Plate serial number Shows which printing plate was used for the face of the bill.

Treasurer of the U.S. signature

Series indicator (year note's design was first used)

Secretary of the Treasury signature

Plate serial number Shows which plate was used for the back.

Front of the Great Seal of the United States: The bald eagle is the national bird. The shield has 13 stripes for the 13 original colonies. The eagle holds 13 arrows (symbol of war) and an olive branch (symbol of peace). Above the eagle is the motto "E Pluribus Unum," Latin for "out of many, one," and a constellation of 13 stars.

Reverse of the Great Seal of the United States: The pyramid symbolizes something that endures for ages. The eye, known as the "Eye of Providence," probably comes from an ancient Egyptian symbol. The pyramid has 13 levels; at its base are the Roman numerals for 1776, the year of American independence. "Annuit Coeptis" is Latin for "God has favored our undertaking." "Novus Ordo Seclorum" is Latin for "a new order of the ages." Both phrases are from the works of the Roman poet Virgil.

U.S. Currency and Coin

Source: Financial Management Service, U.S. Dept. of the Treasury (June 30, 2006)

Comparative Totals of Money in Circulation — Selected Dates

Date	Dollars (in millions)	Per capita[1]	Date	Dollars (in millions)	Per capita[1]	Date	Dollars (in millions)	Per capita[1]
June 30, 2006	$797,131.0	$2,665.00	Mar. 31, 2000	$562,949.0	$2,050.00	June 30, 1960	$32,064.6	$177.47
June 30, 2005	764,628.2	2,579.00	Mar. 31, 1995	401,610.0	1,531.39	June 30, 1950	27,156.3	179.03
June 30, 2004	733,171.0	2,497.00	Mar. 31, 1990	257,664.4	1,028.71	June 30, 1940	7,847.5	59.40
April 30, 2003	688.772.0	2,368.17	June 30, 1985	185,890.7	778.58	June 30, 1930	4,522.0	36.74
Mar. 31, 2002	641,909.0	2,238.45	June 30, 1980	127,097.2	558.28	June 30, 1920	5,467.6	51.36
Mar. 30, 2001	585,916.0	2,121.82	June 30, 1970	54,351.0	265.39	June 30, 1910	3,148.7	34.07

(1) Based on Bureau of the Census estimates of population. The requirement for a gold reserve against U.S. notes was repealed by Public Law 90-269, approved Mar. 18, 1968. Silver certificates issued on and after July 1, 1929, became redeemable from the general fund on June 24, 1968. The amount of security after those dates has been reduced accordingly.

Amounts Outstanding and in Circulation

Currency	Total currency and coin	Total currency	Federal Reserve notes[1]	U.S. notes	Currency no longer issued
Amounts outstanding	$967,574,436,134	$930,085,744,231	$929,584,877,657	$253,346,466	$247,520,108
Less amounts held by:					
Treasury	194,816,464	23,417,920	23,217,688	7,505	192,727
Federal Reserve banks . . .	170,248,307,709	169,524,346,280	169,524,336,158	—	10,122
Amounts in circulation	797,131,311,961	760,537,980,031	760,037,323,811	253,338,961	247,317,259
Coins[2]		**Total**	**Dollars[3]**	**Fractional coins**	
Amounts outstanding	$37,488,691,903	$3,505,529,008	$33,983,162,895		
Less amounts held by:					
Treasury	171,398,544	115,406,544	55,992,000		
Federal Reserve banks	723,961,429	94,350,818	629,610,611		
Amounts in circulation	36,593,331,930	3,295,771,646	33,297,560,284		

(1) Issued on or after July 1, 1929. (2) Excludes coins sold to collectors at premium prices. (3) Includes $481,781,898 in standard silver dollars.

Currency in Circulation by Denominations

(June 30, 2006)

Denomination	Total currency in circulation	Federal Reserve notes[1]	U.S. notes	Currency no longer issued
$1	$8,727,723,173	$8,583,672,022	$143,503	$143,907,648
$2	1,491,099,638	1,358,878,144	132,208,918	12,576
$5	10,000,017,840	9,862,917,765	109,125,210	27,974,865
$10	15,130,683,610	15,109,379,760	6,300	21,297,550
$20	113,156,355,720	113,136,248,820	3,840	20,103,060
$50	60,897,930,250	60,886,432,200	500	11,497,550
$100	550,820,807,700	550,786,980,100	11,840,100	21,987,500
$500	142,435,500	142,243,000	5,500	187,000
$1,000	165,701,000	165,502,000	5,000	194,000
$5,000	1,765,000	1,710,000	—	55,000
$10,000	3,460,000	3,360,000	—	100,000
Fractional notes[2]	600	—	90	510
TOTAL CURRENCY	**$729,440,444,765**	**$728,936,366,853**	**$255,665,061**	**$248,412,851**

(1) Issued on or after July 1, 1929. (2) Represents the value of certain partial denominations not presented for redemption.

U.S. Budget Receipts and Outlays, Fiscal Years 2001-2005

Source: Congressional Budget Office; Office of Management and Budget, Budget of the United States Government, Fiscal Year 2007

As of Oct. 2006, the estimate from the Congressional Budget Office of the total U.S. budget deficit for the fiscal year 2006 was $250 bil, or 1.9% of GDP, a $68 bil decrease from the $318 bil deficit in 2005.

(in millions of current dollars; many figures do not add to totals because of independent rounding or omitted subcategories, including some subcategories with negative values.)

Function and subfunction	2001	2002	2003	2004	2005
NET RECEIPTS	1,991,426	1,853,395	1,782,532	1,880,279	2,153,859
Individual Income Taxes	994,339	858,345	793,699	808,959	927,222
Corporation Income Taxes	151,075	148,044	131,778	189,371	278,282
Social Insurance and Retirement Receipts	693,967	700,760	712,978	733,407	794,125
Employment and general retirement	661,442	668,547	674,981	689,360	747,664
Old-age and survivors insurance	434,057	440,541	447,806	457,120	493,646
Disability insurance (Off-Budget)	73,462	74,780	76,036	77,625	83,830
Hospital insurance	149,651	149,049	147,186	150,589	166,068
Railroad retirement/pension fund:	2,658	2,525	2,333	2,297	2,284
Railroad social security equivalent account	1,614	1,652	1,620	1,729	1,836
Unemployment insurance	27,812	27,619	33,366	39,453	42,002
Other retirement	4,713	4,594	4,631	4,594	4,459
Excise Taxes	66,232	66,989	67,524	69,855	73,094
Federal funds	24,286	24,017	23,804	24,566	22,547
Alcohol	7,624	7,764	7,893	8,105	8,111
Tobacco	7,396	8,274	7,934	7,926	7,920
Telephone	5,769	5,829	5,788	5,997	6,047
Transportation fuels	1,150	814	920	1,381	−770
Trust funds	41,946	42,972	43,720	45,289	50,547
Highway	31,469	32,603	33,726	34,711	37,892
Airport and airway	9,191	9,031	8,684	9,174	10,314
Black lung disability	522	567	506	566	610
Inland waterway	113	95	90	91	91
Aquatic resources	358	386	392	416	429
Leaking underground storage tank	179	181	184	189	189
Tobacco Assessments	—	—	—	—	899
Vaccine injury compensation	112	109	138	142	123
Other Receipts	85,813	79,257	76,553	78,687	81,136

Function and subfunction	2001	2002	2003	2004	2005
OUTLAYS	1,863,190	2,011,153	2,160,117	2,293,006	2,472,205
National defense	304,880	348,555	404,920	455,908	495,335
Department of Defense—Military:					
Military Personnel	73,977	86,799	106,744	113,576	127,463
Operation and Maintenance	111,964	130,005	151,408	174,045	188,118
Procurement	54,986	62,515	67,926	76,216	82,294
Research, Development, Test, and Evaluation	40,455	44,389	53,098	60,759	65,694
Military Construction	4,977	5,052	5,851	6,312	5,331
Family Housing	3,516	3,736	3,784	3,905	3,720
Subtotal, Department of Defense—Military	290,340	331,951	387,319	436,521	474,163
Atomic energy defense activities	12,931	14,795	16,029	16,625	18,042
Defense-related activities	1,609	1,809	1,572	2,762	3,130
International affairs	16,493	22,351	21,209	26,891	34,592
International development and humanitarian assistance	7,191	7,815	10,332	13,825	17,711
International security assistance	6,560	7,907	8,620	8,369	7,895
Conduct of foreign affairs	5,050	7,068	6,683	7,897	9,149
Foreign information and exchange activities	804	906	959	1,141	1,140
International financial programs	−3,112	−1,345	−5,385	−4,341	−1,303
General science, space and technology	19,784	20,767	20,873	23,053	23,674
General science and basic research	6,548	7,294	7,993	8,416	8,896
Space flight, research, and supporting activities	13,236	13,473	12,880	14,637	14,778
Energy	9	475	−735	−166	429
Energy supply	−1,145	−803	−2,061	−1,555	−940
Energy conservation	760	878	897	926	883
Emergency energy preparedness	159	169	182	158	162
Energy information, policy, and regulation	235	231	247	305	324
Natural resources and environment	25,623	29,454	29,703	30,725	28,023
Water resources	5,240	5,570	5,492	5,571	5,723
Conservation and land management	7,109	9,797	9,739	9,758	6,226
Recreational resources	2,339	2,750	2,872	2,963	3,018
Pollution control and abatement	7,562	7,615	8,208	8,485	8,079
Agriculture	26,253	21,966	22,497	15,440	26,566
Farm income stabilization	22,748	18,371	18,304	11,186	22,048
Agricultural research and services	3,505	3,595	4,193	4,254	4,518
Commerce and housing credit	5,739	−399	735	5,273	7,574
Mortgage credit	−1,164	−7,015	−4,591	2,659	−862
Postal Service	2,395	207	−5,169	−4,070	−1,223
Deposit insurance	−1,569	−1,026	−1,430	−1,976	−1,371
Transportation	54,447	61,833	67,069	64,627	67,894
Ground transportation	35,804	40,158	37,491	40,744	42,317
Air transportation	13,975	16,538	23,343	16,743	18,807
Water transportation	4,401	5,041	5,907	6,898	6,439
Community and regional development	11,773	12,981	18,850	15,822	26,264
Community development	5,313	5,998	6,346	6,167	5,861
Area and regional development	2,634	2,633	2,397	2,351	2,745
Disaster relief and insurance	3,826	4,350	10,107	7,304	17,658
Education, training, employment, and social services	57,143	70,544	82,568	87,948	97,526
Elementary, secondary, and vocational education	22,858	25,879	31,473	34,360	38,271
Higher education	9,568	17,049	22,697	25,264	31,442
Research and general education aids	2,777	2,928	2,973	3,005	3,095
Training and employment	7,192	8,354	8,379	7,918	6,852
Social services	13,480	14,901	15,573	15,855	16,251
Health	172,270	196,544	219,576	240,134	250,612
Health care services	151,911	172,597	192,608	210,092	219,625
Health research and training	17,926	21,356	24,044	27,099	28,050
Consumer and occupational health and safety	2,433	2,591	2,924	2,943	2,937
Medicare	217,384	230,855	249,433	269,360	298,638
Income security	269,774	312,720	334,632	333,059	345,847
Retirement & disability insurance (excluding social security)	5,761	5,741	7,047	6,573	6,976
Federal employee retirement and disability	80,972	83,361	85,154	88,729	93,351
Unemployment compensation	30,242	53,267	57,054	44,994	35,435
Housing assistance	30,250	33,251	35,525	36,790	37,899
Food and nutrition assistance	34,053	38,150	42,526	46,012	50,833
Social security	432,958	455,980	474,680	495,548	523,305
Veterans benefits and services	45,039	50,984	57,022	59,779	70,151
Income security for veterans	22,498	26,720	29,091	30,849	35,767
Veterans education, training, and rehabilitation	1,193	1,726	2,106	2,562	2,790
Hospital and medical care for veterans	20,959	22,290	24,082	26,859	28,754
Veterans housing	−904	−1,006	505	−1,982	860
Administration of justice	30,202	35,061	35,340	45,576	40,019
Federal law enforcement activities	12,542	15,408	15,745	19,131	19,912
Federal litigative and judicial activities	8,299	9,137	9,085	9,685	9,641
Federal correctional activities	4,206	4,748	5,384	5,509	5,862
Criminal justice assistance	5,155	5,768	5,126	11,251	4,604
General government	14,263	16,925	23,054	22,321	16,994
Legislative functions	2,312	2,638	2,840	3,187	3,451
Executive direction and management	457	639	706	503	569
Central fiscal operations	9,146	10,216	11,455	9,302	9,516
General property and records management	−71	−417	201	228	482
Central personnel management	184	47	203	217	101
General purpose fiscal assistance	2,308	2,403	7,464	7,675	3,333
Deductions for offsetting receipts	−1,882	−892	−1,894	−1,136	−2,898
Net interest	206,167	170,949	153,073	160,245	183,986
Undistributed offsetting receipts	−47,011	−47,392	−54,382	−58,537	−65,224
Employer share, employee retirement (on-budget)	−30,883	−33,489	−39,751	−42,100	−47,977
Toal surplus/deficit	128,236	−157,758	−377,585	−412,727	−318,346

Note: Fiscal year ends Sept. 30.

Summary of Receipts, Outlays, and Surpluses or Deficits, 1936-2006

Source: Financial Management Service, U.S. Dept. of the Treasury; Congressional Budget Office

(millions of current dollars)

Fiscal Year[1]	Receipts	Outlays	Surplus or Deficit (−)[2]	Fiscal Year[1]	Receipts	Outlays	Surplus or Deficit (−)[2]
1936	$3,923	$8,228	$−4,304	1972	$207,309	$230,681	$−23,373
1937	5,387	7,580	−2,193	1973	230,799	245,707	−14,908
1938	6,751	6,840	−89	1974	263,224	269,359	−6,135
1939	6,295	9,141	−2,846	1975	279,090	332,332	−53,242
1940	6,548	9,468	−2,920	1976	298,060	371,792	−73,732
1941	8,712	13,653	−4,941	Transition quarter[3]	81,232	95,975	−14,744
1942	14,634	35,137	−20,503	1977	355,559	409,218	−53,659
1943	24,001	78,555	−54,554	1978	399,561	458,746	−59,185
1944	43,747	91,304	−47,557	1979	463,302	504,028	−40,726
1945	45,159	92,712	−47,553	1980	517,112	590,941	−73,830
1946	39,296	55,232	−15,936	1981	599,272	678,241	−78,968
1947	38,514	34,496	4,018	1982	617,766	745,743	−127,977
1948	41,560	29,764	11,796	1983	600,562	808,364	−207,802
1949	39,415	38,835	580	1984	666,486	851,853	−185,367
1950	39,443	42,562	−3,119	1985	734,088	946,396	−212,308
1951	51,616	45,514	6,102	1986	769,215	990,441	−221,227
1952	66,167	67,686	−1,519	1987	854,353	1,004,083	−149,730
1953	69,608	76,101	−6,493	1988	909,303	1,064,481	−155,178
1954	69,701	70,855	−1,154	1989	991,190	1,143,829	−152,639
1955	65,451	68,444	−2,993	1990	1,032,094	1,253,130	−221,036
1956	74,587	70,640	3,947	1991	1,055,093	1,324,331	−269,238
1957	79,990	76,578	3,412	1992	1,091,328	1,381,649	−290,321
1958	79,636	82,405	−2,769	1993	1,154,471	1,409,522	−255,051
1959	79,249	92,098	−12,849	1994	1,258,721	1,461,907	−203,186
1960	92,492	92,191	301	1995	1,351,932	1,515,884	−163,952
1961	94,388	97,723	−3,335	1996	1,453,177	1,560,608	−107,431
1962	99,676	106,821	−7,146	1997	1,579,423	1,601,307	−21,884
1963	106,560	111,316	−4,756	1998	1,721,955	1,652,685	69,270
1964	112,613	118,528	−5,915	1999	1,827,645	1,702,035	125,610
1965	116,817	118,228	−1,411	2000	2,025,457	1,789,216	236,241
1966	130,835	134,532	−3,698	2001	1,991,426	1,863,190	128,236
1967	148,822	157,464	−8,643	2002[R]	1,853,395	2,011,153	−157,758
1968	152,973	178,134	−25,161	2003[R]	1,782,532	2,160,117	−377,585
1969	186,882	183,640	3,242	2004	1,880,279	2,293,006	−412,727
1970	192,807	195,649	−2,842	2005	2,153,859	2,472,205	−318,346
1971	187,139	210,172	−23,033	2006[P]	2,406,681	2,654,379	−247,698

R = Revised. P = Preliminary. (1) Fiscal years 1936 to 1976 end June 30; after 1976, fiscal years end Sept. 30. (2) May not equal difference between figures shown, because of rounding. (3) Transition quarter covers July 1, 1976-Sept. 30, 1976.

Budget Receipts and Outlays, 1789-1935

Source: U.S. Dept. of the Treasury; annual statements for years ending June 30 unless otherwise noted

(thousands of dollars)

Yearly Average	Receipts	Outlays	Yearly Average	Receipts	Outlays	Yearly Average	Receipts	Outlays
1789-1800[1]	$5,717	$5,776	1866-1870	$447,301	$377,642	1901-1905	$559,481	$535,559
1801-1810[2]	13,056	9,086	1871-1875	336,830	287,460	1906-1910	628,507	639,178
1811-1820[2]	21,032	23,943	1876-1880	288,124	255,598	1911-1915	710,227	720,252
1821-1830[2]	21,928	16,162	1881-1885	366,961	257,691	1916-1920	3,483,652	8,065,333
1831-1840[2]	30,461	24,495	1886-1890	375,448	279,134	1921-1925	4,306,673	3,578,989
1841-1850[2]	28,545	34,097	1891-1895	352,891	363,599	1926-1930	4,069,138	3,182,807
1851-1860	60,237	60,163	1896-1900	434,877	457,451	1931-1935	2,770,973	5,214,874
1861-1865	160,907	683,785						

(1) Average for period March 4, 1789, to Dec. 31, 1800. (2) Years from 1801 to 1842 end Dec. 31; average for 1841-1850 is for the period Jan. 1, 1841, to June 30, 1850.

Budget Deficits as Percent of GDP, Selected Countries[1]

Source: Organization of Economic Cooperation and Development

	1990	1995	2000	2005		1990	1995	2000	2005		1990	1995	2000	2005
Australia	−1.7	−3.9	0.9	1.5	Hungary	—	−7.6	−3.0	−6.1	Poland	—	−3.9	−2.4	−2.5
Austria	−2.4	−5.7	−1.6	−1.6	Iceland	−3.3	−3.0	2.5	3.2	Portugal	−6.6	−5.5	−2.9	−6.0
Belgium	−6.8	−4.4	0.2	−0.1	Ireland	−2.8	−2.1	4.4	1.0	Slovak Republic	—	−0.9	−12.3	−2.9
Canada	−5.8	−5.3	2.9	1.7	Italy	−11.8	−7.6	−0.7	−4.3	Spain	−3.9	−6.6	−0.9	1.1
Czech Republic	—	−13.4	−3.7	−2.6	Japan	2.1	−4.7	−7.5	−5.2	Sweden	3.4	−6.9	5.0	2.7
Denmark	−1.2	−2.3	2.5	4.0	Korea	3.2	3.8	5.4	2.7	Switzerland	0.6	−1.2	2.3	−0.5
Finland	5.5	−3.9	7.1	2.4	Luxembourg	4.8	2.5	6.2	−1.9	United Kingdom	−1.6	−5.8	3.8	−3.2
France	−2.1	−5.5	−1.4	−2.9	Netherlands	−5.3	−4.2	2.2	−0.3	United States	−4.2	−3.1	1.6	−3.8
Germany	−2.0	−3.3	1.3	−3.3	New Zealand	−4.3	3.0	3.1	5.8	Euro area	−4.6	−5.1	0.1	−2.4
Greece	−15.7	−10.2	−4.2	−4.4	Norway	2.2	3.4	15.6	15.8	Total OECD	−3.0	−4.0	0.3	−2.7

(1) Financial balances include revenues from the sale of mobile telephone licenses.

Public Debt of the U.S.

Source: Bureau of Public Debt, U.S. Dept. of the Treasury; World Almanac research

Fiscal year	Debt (billions)	Debt per cap. (dollars)	Interest paid (billions)	% of federal outlays	Fiscal year	Debt (billions)	Debt per cap. (dollars)	Interest paid (billions)	% of federal outlays
1870....	$2.4	$61.06	—	—	1986 ...	$2,125.3	$8,774	$190.2	19.2
1880....	2.0	41.60	—	—	1987 ...	2,350.3	9,615	195.4	19.5
1890....	1.1	17.80	—	—	1988 ...	2,602.3	10,534	214.1	20.1
1900....	1.2	16.60	—	—	1989 ...	2,857.4	11,545	240.9	21.0
1910....	1.1	12.41	—	—	1990 ...	3,233.3	13,000	264.8	21.1
1920....	24.2	228	—	—	1991 ...	3,665.3	14,436	285.5	21.6
1930....	16.1	131	—	—	1992 ...	4,064.6	15,846	292.3	21.2
1940....	43.0	325	$1.0	10.5	1993 ...	4,411.5	17,105	292.5	20.8
1950....	256.1	1,688	5.7	13.4	1994 ...	4,692.8	18,025	296.3	20.3
1960....	284.1	1,572	9.2	10.0	1996 ...	5,224.8	19,805	344.0	22.0
1970....	370.1	1,814	19.3	9.9	1997 ...	5,413.1	20,026	355.8	22.2
1976....	620.4	2,852	37.1	10.0	1998 ...	5,526.2	20,443	363.8	22.0
1977....	698.8	3,170	41.9	10.2	1999 ...	5,656.3	20,746	353.5	20.7
1978....	771.5	3,463	48.7	10.6	2000 ...	5,674.2	20,108	362.0	20.3
1979....	826.5	3,669	59.8	11.9	2001 ...	5,807.5	20,370	359.5	19.3
1980....	907.7	3,985	74.9	12.7	2002 ...	6,228.2	21,598	332.5	16.5
1981....	997.9	4,338	95.6	14.1	2003 ...	6,783.2	23,325	318.1	14.7
1982....	1,142.0	4,913	117.4	15.7	2004 ...	7,379.1	25,182	321.6	14.0
1983....	1,377.2	5,870	128.8	15.9	2005 ...	7,932.7	26,763	352.4	14.3
1984....	1,572.3	6,640	153.8	18.1	2006[1]...	8,507.0	28,504	405.9	15.0

Note: As of end of fiscal year. Through 1976, the fiscal year ended June 30. From 1977 on, the fiscal year ends Sept. 30. (1) Estimated.

State Finances: Revenue, Expenditures, Debt, and Taxes

Source: Census Bureau, U.S. Dept. of Commerce

(fiscal year 2004)

STATE	Revenue (thousands)	Expenditures (thousands)	Debt (thousands)	Per capita debt	Per capita taxes	Per capita expenditures
Alabama	$21,568,441	$19,544,560	$6,363,885	$1,406	$1,551	$4,319
Alaska	8,847,705	8,089,240	5,730,403	8,709	2,035	12,294
Arizona	23,753,397	21,748,803	6,773,923	1,180	1,674	3,789
Arkansas	14,225,176	12,674,325	3,749,282	1,363	2,029	4,609
California	229,289,356	203,814,714	102,812,905	2,869	2,392	5,686
Colorado	23,081,951	18,060,533	9,874,764	2,146	1,532	3,925
Connecticut	19,518,768	19,523,465	22,574,585	6,452	2,941	5,580
Delaware	5,697,849	5,387,960	4,158,118	5,010	2,862	6,492
Florida	75,176,415	59,943,442	23,194,784	1,334	1,756	3,448
Georgia	34,814,306	34,196,775	8,664,363	972	1,634	3,835
Hawaii	8,229,259	7,856,134	5,746,194	4,553	3,050	6,225
Idaho	7,112,364	5,762,624	2,383,841	1,709	1,898	4,131
Illinois	61,255,138	53,429,176	48,726,054	3,833	2,005	4,203
Indiana	26,917,365	25,373,330	13,079,818	2,101	1,920	4,075
Iowa	15,291,539	13,424,350	4,857,614	1,645	1,742	4,546
Kansas	11,044,146	11,207,121	4,571,408	1,672	1,933	4,099
Kentucky	20,180,416	20,072,526	8,116,460	1,960	2,043	4,846
Louisiana	23,730,239	20,471,959	10,182,940	2,259	1,782	4,542
Maine	8,309,930	7,322,061	4,643,988	3,532	2,203	5,568
Maryland	28,395,564	25,343,680	13,600,741	2,446	2,214	4,557
Massachusetts	41,615,765	38,405,514	50,981,152	7,957	2,628	5,994
Michigan	57,461,347	52,684,622	20,959,946	2,074	2,381	5,214
Minnesota	29,708,220	28,831,675	6,665,669	1,308	2,891	5,657
Mississippi	15,351,077	14,330,205	4,274,977	1,474	1,767	4,940
Missouri	26,320,416	22,038,965	16,218,362	2,816	1,583	3,826
Montana	5,451,685	4,691,318	3,048,862	3,289	1,754	5,061
Nebraska	8,316,470	6,979,917	1,949,654	1,115	2,082	3,993
Nevada	10,136,127	8,686,071	3,607,292	1,546	2,031	3,723
New Hampshire	6,174,660	5,654,063	5,894,106	4,537	1,544	4,353
New Jersey	50,588,543	46,455,897	35,770,241	4,119	2,416	5,349
New Mexico	11,809,742	11,024,686	5,411,287	2,844	2,103	5,793
New York	136,520,762	132,883,277	95,709,813	4,964	2,377	6,892
North Carolina	44,371,161	37,050,568	14,102,900	1,651	1,971	4,338
North Dakota	5,228,053	3,197,884	1,662,390	2,614	1,932	5,028
Ohio	76,443,362	58,874,466	22,183,360	1,937	1,963	5,142
Oklahoma	17,520,326	14,914,919	6,930,071	1,967	1,824	4,232
Oregon	24,488,705	18,788,196	10,495,671	2,923	1,700	5,232
Pennsylvania	69,212,674	57,353,773	25,995,752	2,097	2,045	4,628
Rhode Island	7,266,196	6,386,602	6,490,701	6,010	2,230	5,914
South Carolina	21,241,956	21,427,748	11,162,865	2,659	1,621	5,104
South Dakota	3,863,621	2,989,366	2,613,067	3,389	1,378	3,877
Tennessee	23,920,818	22,164,577	3,580,940	608	1,617	3,761
Texas	90,570,423	77,338,118	22,925,515	1,020	1,368	3,442
Utah	13,167,850	10,794,264	4,962,141	2,050	1,733	4,459
Vermont	4,302,590	3,913,616	2,537,139	4,086	2,845	6,302
Virginia	35,739,829	30,370,027	15,314,018	2,047	1,903	4,060
Washington	35,085,947	32,510,057	15,773,698	2,541	2,239	5,238
West Virginia	11,633,343	9,879,217	4,745,387	2,617	2,068	5,449
Wisconsin	34,753,272	28,577,240	17,727,318	3,221	2,296	5,192
Wyoming	5,151,978	3,596,174	909,531	1,797	2,974	7,107
ALL STATES[1]	**1,589,856,242**	**1,406,039,800**	**750,409,895**	**2,560**	**2,026**	**4,797**

(1) Totals may not add because of rounding.

State and Local Government Receipts and Current Expenditures

Source: Bureau of Economic Analysis, U.S. Dept. of Commerce

(billions of current dollars; revised)

	2000	2001	2002	2003	2004	2005
RECEIPTS	**$1,319.5**	**$1,373.0**	**$1,410.1**	**$1,494.2**	**$1,592.6**	**$1,700.6**
Current tax receipts	893.2	915.8	929.0	979.4	1,060.9	1,154.4
Personal current taxes	236.6	242.7	221.3	226.6	248.4	275.2
Income taxes	217.3	223.1	200.8	204.5	225.1	250.9
Other	19.4	19.6	20.5	22.2	23.4	24.4
Taxes on production and imports	621.1	642.8	675.5	717.5	769.4	821.2
Sales taxes	316.6	321.1	330.2	347.7	370.3	394.1
Property taxes	254.6	269.3	290.1	307.9	329.8	350.4
Other	49.9	52.4	55.2	61.9	69.3	76.7
Taxes on corporate income	35.5	30.2	32.2	35.3	43.1	58.0
Contributions for government social insurance	11.0	13.6	15.8	19.8	24.2	25.3
Income receipts on assets	92.2	88.8	78.2	72.9	73.3	75.3
Interest receipts	84.0	80.3	69.6	62.9	62.1	63.4
Dividends	1.9	2.0	2.0	2.2	2.4	2.4
Rents and royalties	6.3	6.5	6.6	7.9	8.7	9.5
Current transfer receipts	315.4	350.8	384.7	422.7	438.0	456.1
Federal grants-in-aid	247.3	276.1	304.6	338.5	349.0	361.1
From business (net)	28.8	31.4	32.6	33.5	34.7	36.7
From persons	39.2	43.3	47.5	50.6	54.3	58.3
Current surplus of government enterprises	7.7	4.0	2.5	−0.6	−3.8	−10.5
CURRENT EXPENDITURES	**1,269.5**	**1,368.2**	**1,444.3**	**1,514.5**	**1,605.5**	**1,703.9**
Consumption expenditures	917.8	969.8	1,025.3	1,073.8	1,130.3	1,207.2
Government social benefit payments to persons	271.7	305.2	332.0	353.0	382.9	402.3
Interest payments	79.5	85.5	86.0	87.7	91.8	94.2
Subsidies	0.5	7.7	0.9	0.1	0.4	0.4
Less: Wage accruals less disbursements	0.0	0.0	0.0	0.0	0.0	0.0
Net state and local government saving	50.0	4.8	−34.2	−20.4	−12.9	−3.3
Social insurance funds	2.0	2.6	1.7	3.8	7.5	7.3
Other	47.9	2.2	−35.9	−24.1	−20.4	−10.6
Addenda:						
Total receipts	1,363.2	1,421.6	1,462.2	1,545.8	1,644.5	1,754.6
Current receipts	1,319.5	1,373.0	1,410.1	1,494.2	1,592.6	1,700.6
Capital transfer receipts	43.7	48.6	52.1	51.6	51.9	53.9
Total expenditures	1,393.5	1,502.7	1,588.3	1,659.9	1,749.8	1,849.6
Current expenditures	1,269.5	1,368.2	1,444.3	1,514.5	1,605.5	1,703.9
Gross government investment	225.0	243.0	256.1	262.2	270.0	287.3
Net purchases of nonproduced assets	8.8	9.2	10.6	10.9	11.0	11.6
Less: Consumption of fixed capital	109.8	117.8	122.7	127.8	136.7	153.2
NET LENDING OR NET BORROWING (−)	**−30.4**	**−81.1**	**−126.1**	**−114.1**	**−105.3**	**−95.0**

Consumer Credit Outstanding, 2003-2005

Source: Federal Reserve System

(in billions of dollars, revised)

Estimated amounts of credit outstanding as of end of year. Not seasonally adjusted.

	2003	2004	2005		2003	2004	2005
TOTAL	**$2,119.9**	**$2,232.3**	**$2,323.4**	Credit unions	$22.4	$23.2	$24.7
Major Holders				Fed. government and Sallie Mae	NA	NA	NA
Commercial banks	669.4	704.3	707.0	Savings institutions	23.8	27.9	40.8
Finance companies	393.0	492.3	516.5	Nonfinancial business	20.8	17.2	15.8
Credit unions	205.9	215.4	228.6	Pools of securitized assets[1]	388.9	384.6	384.7
Fed. govt. and Sallie Mae	114.7	98.4	102.1	**Nonrevolving[2]**	**1,333.6**	**1,414.4**	**1,480.0**
Savings institutions	77.9	91.3	109.1	Commercial banks	384.4	389.6	395.8
Nonfinancial business	64.8	64.0	63.5	Finance companies	347.8	442.0	450.2
Pools of securitized assets[1]	594.2	566.7	596.5	Credit unions	183.5	192.1	203.9
Major Types of Credit				Fed. government and Sallie Mae	114.7	98.4	102.1
Revolving[2]	**786.2**	**817.9**	**843.4**	Savings institutions	54.0	63.4	68.3
Commercial banks	285.0	314.6	311.2	Nonfinancial business	44.0	46.8	47.8
Finance companies	45.3	50.4	66.3	Pools of securitized assets[1]	205.4	182.1	211.8

NA = Not available. (1) Outstanding balances of pools upon which securities have been issued; these balances are no longer carried on the balance sheets of the loan originators. (2) Includes estimates for holders that do not separately report consumer credit holding by type.

Global Stock Markets

Source: The Conference Board; not seasonally adjusted

Stock price indexes (1990[1]=100):	June 1, 1960	June 1, 1970	June 1, 1980	June 1, 1990	June 1, 2000	June 1, 2002	June 1, 2003	June 1, 2004	June 1, 2005	June 1, 2006
United States	17.1	21.9	34.3	107.6	437.2	297.5	292.9	342.9	358.1	381.8
Japan	4.4	7.3	23.8	110.8	60.4	36.8	31.5	41.1	40.2	53.8
Germany	36.1	27.5	30.5	111.1	407.9	259.1	190.4	239.6	271.2	336.0
France	16.3	15.6	23.8	112.0	354.7	214.5	169.7	205.4	232.7	273.2
United Kingdom	8.2	11.6	24.9	108.2	279.9	209.1	182.1	205.9	236.5	274.1
Italy	28.9	20.6	15.9	117.3	309.0	196.7	181.1	206.5	241.1	271.5
Canada	14.8	25.0	60.3	103.6	298.0	208.9	204.1	249.8	289.5	339.4

(1) 12-month average.

U.S. Holdings of Foreign Stocks[1]

Source: Bureau of Economic Analysis, U.S. Dept. of Commerce
(billions of dollars)

	2002	2004	2005		2002	2004	2005
Europe....................	$789.4	$1,356.2	$1,582.1	Cayman Islands	$32.9	$69.7	$82.1
United Kingdom............	289.5	461.8	553.7	Brazil	19.7	43.1	61.4
France..................	94.3	164.6	188.5	Mexico	22	37.5	50.8
Switzerland	75.6	138.2	157.4	**Asia**.....................	**258.7**	**565.8**	**739.6**
Netherlands...............	88.1	136.5	156.9	Japan	148.1	330.4	411.2
Germany.................	66.5	123.7	140.4	Korea, Republic of	27.8	66.6	88.9
Spain...................	29.9	63.0	71.7	Taiwan	8.5	34.6	54.5
Italy	28.2	57.5	65.9	Hong Kong	22	35.4	47.5
Sweden..................	19.2	38.3	49.2	**Africa**	**9.6**	**28.9**	**40.0**
Finland	34.3	33.9	38.7	South Africa	7.9	21.6	30.2
Canada	**88.2**	**180.4**	**207.0**	**Other countries**	**37.2**	**65.8**	**79.6**
Latin America and Caribbean ..	**191.6**	**363.3**	**438.2**	Australia	34.6	57.1	68.8
Bermuda	88.6	153.5	175.8	**TOTAL HOLDINGS**	**1,374.7**	**2,560.4**	**3,086.5**

(1) As of year end.

Standard & Poor's 500 Index, 1993-2006

Source: *Facts On File World News Digest;* monthly closing levels; record high daily closing was 1527.46, Mar. 24, 2000.

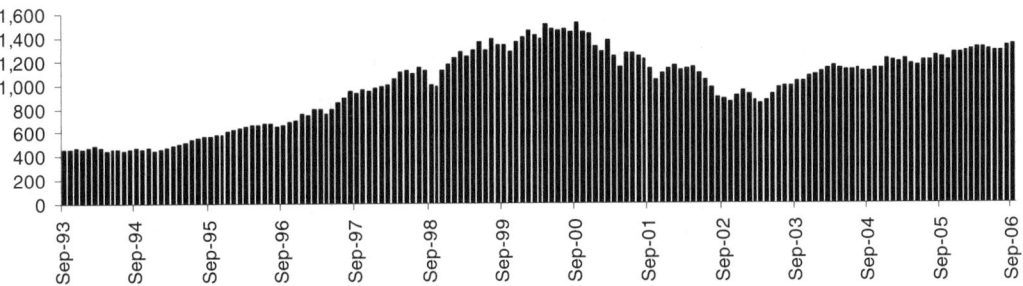

Record One-Day Gains and Losses on the Dow Jones Industrial Average

Source: Dow Jones & Co., Inc.; as of Sept. 30, 2006

	GREATEST POINT GAINS					GREATEST POINT LOSSES			
Rank	Date	Close	Net Chg	% Chg	Rank	Date	Close	Net Chg	% Chg
1.	3/16/2000	10630.60	499.19	4.93	1.	9/17/2001	8920.70	−684.81	−7.13
2.	7/24/2002	8191.29	488.95	6.35	2.	4/14/2000	10305.77	−617.78	−5.66
3.	7/29/2002	8711.88	447.49	5.41	3.	10/27/1997	7161.15	−554.26	−7.18
4.	4/5/2001	9918.05	402.63	4.23	4.	8/31/1998	7539.07	−512.61	−6.37
5.	4/18/2001	10615.83	399.10	3.91	5.	10/19/1987	1738.74	−508.00	−22.61
6.	9/8/1998	8020.78	380.53	4.98	6.	3/12/2001	10208.25	−436.37	−4.10
7.	10/15/2002	8255.68	378.28	4.80	7.	7/19/2002	8019.26	−390.23	−4.64
8.	9/24/2001	8603.86	368.05	4.47	8.	9/20/2001	8376.21	−382.92	−4.37
9.	10/1/2002	7938.79	346.86	4.57	9.	10/12/2000	10034.58	−379.21	−3.64
10.	5/16/2001	11215.92	342.95	3.15	10.	3/7/2000	9796.03	−374.47	−3.68
	GREATEST % GAINS					GREATEST % LOSSES			
Rank	Date	Close	Net Chg	% Chg	Rank	Date	Close	Net Chg	% Chg
1.	3/15/1933	62.10	8.26	15.34	1.	12/12/1914	54.00	−17.42	−24.39
2.	10/6/1931	99.34	12.86	14.87	2.	10/19/1987	1738.74	−508.00	−22.61
3.	10/30/1929	258.47	28.40	12.34	3.	10/28/1929	260.64	−38.33	−12.82
4.	9/21/1932	75.16	7.67	11.36	4.	10/29/1929	230.07	−30.57	−11.73
5.	10/21/1987	2027.85	186.84	10.15	5.	11/6/1929	232.13	−25.55	−9.92
6.	8/3/1932	58.22	5.06	9.52	6.	12/18/1899	58.27	−5.57	−8.72
7.	2/11/1932	78.60	6.80	9.47	7.	8/12/1932	63.11	−5.79	−8.40
8.	11/14/1929	217.28	18.59	9.36	8.	3/14/1907	76.23	−6.89	−8.29
9.	12/18/1931	80.69	6.90	9.35	9.	10/26/1987	1793.93	−156.83	−8.04
10.	2/13/1932	85.82	7.22	9.19	10.	7/21/1933	88.71	−7.55	−7.84

Dow Jones Industrial Average, 1963-2006

High		YEAR		Low	High		YEAR		Low
Dec. 18	767.21	....1963....	Jan. 2	646.79	July 16	2999.75....	1990	... Oct. 11	2365.10
Dec. 31	969.26	....1965....	June 28	840.59	Dec. 31	3168.83....	1991	... Jan. 9	2470.30
Dec. 29	842.00	....1970....	May 6	631.16	June 1	3413.21....	1992	... Oct. 9	3136.58
July 15	881.81	....1975....	Jan. 2	632.04	Dec. 29	3794.33....	1993	... Jan. 20	3241.95
Sept. 21	1014.79	....1976....	Jan. 2	858.71	Jan. 31	3978.36....	1994	... Apr. 4	3593.35
Jan. 3	999.75	....1977....	Nov. 2	800.85	Dec. 13	5216.47....	1995	... Jan. 30	3832.08
Sept. 8	907.74	....1978....	Feb. 28	742.12	Dec. 27	6560.91....	1996	... Jan. 10	5032.94
Oct. 5	897.61	....1979....	Nov. 7	796.67	Aug. 6	8259.31....	1997	... Apr. 11	6391.69
Nov. 20	1000.17	....1980....	Apr. 21	759.13	Nov. 23	9374.27....	1998	... Aug. 31	7539.07
Apr. 27	1024.05	....1981....	Sept. 25	824.01	Dec. 31	11497.12....	1999	... Jan. 22	9120.67
Dec. 27	1070.55	....1982....	Aug. 12	776.92	Jan. 14	11722.98....	2000	... Mar. 7	9796.03
Nov. 29	1287.20	....1983....	Jan. 3	1027.04	May 21	11337.92....	2001	... Sept. 21	8235.81
Jan. 6	1286.64	....1984....	July 24	1086.57	Mar. 19	10635.25....	2002	... Oct. 9	7286.27
Dec. 16	1553.10	....1985....	Jan. 4	1184.96	Dec. 31	10453.90....	2003	... Mar. 11	7524.06
Dec. 2	1955.57	....1986....	Jan. 22	1502.29	Dec. 28	10854.54....	2004	... Oct. 25	9749.99
Aug. 25	2722.42	....1987....	Oct. 19	1738.74	Mar. 4	10940.50....	2005	... Apr. 20	10012.36
Oct. 21	2183.50	....1988....	Jan. 20	1879.14	**Oct. 13, 2006 closing: 11960.51***				
Oct. 9	2791.41	....1989....	Jan. 3	2144.64					

* Record high closing, as of Oct. 15, 2006.

Milestones of the Dow Jones Industrial Average

(as of Oct. 15, 2006)

First close over...	First close over...	First close over...	First close over...	First close over...
100 Jan. 12, 1906	5500 Feb. 8, 1996	8400 Feb. 18, 1998	9300 July 16, 1998	10700 Apr. 22, 1999*
500 Mar. 12, 1956	6000 Oct. 14, 1996	8300 Feb. 12, 1998	9500 Jan. 6, 1999*	10800 Apr. 27, 1999
1000 Nov. 14, 1972	6500 Nov. 25, 1996	8400 Feb. 18, 1998	9600 Jan. 8, 1999	11000 May 3, 1999*
1500 Dec. 11, 1985	7000 Feb. 13, 1997	8500 Feb. 27, 1998	9700 Mar. 5, 1999	11100 May 13, 1999
2000 Jan. 8, 1987	7500 June 10, 1997	8600 Mar. 10, 1998	9800 Mar. 11, 1999	11200 July 12, 1999
2500 July 17, 1987	8000 July 16, 1997	8700 Mar. 16, 1998	9900 Mar. 15, 1999	11300 Aug. 25, 1999
3000 April 17, 1991	8100 July 24, 1997	8800 Mar. 19, 1998	10000 Mar. 29, 1999	11400 Dec. 23, 1999
3500 May 19, 1993	8200 July 30, 1997	8900 Mar. 20, 1998	10100 Apr. 8, 1999	11500 Jan. 7, 2000
4000 Feb. 23, 1995	8100 July 24, 1997	9000 Apr. 6, 1998	10300 Apr. 12, 1999*	11700 Jan. 14, 2000*
4500 June 16, 1995	8200 July 30, 1997	9100 Apr. 14, 1998	10400 Apr. 14, 1999	11800 Oct. 4, 2006
5000 Nov. 21, 1995	8300 Feb. 12, 1998	9200 May 13, 1998	10500 Apr. 21, 1999	11900 Oct. 12, 2006

*9400, 10200, 10600, 10900, and 11600 are not listed because the Dow had risen another 100 points or more by the time the market closed for the day. The all-time record closing was 11960.51 on Oct. 13, 2006.

Components of the Dow Jones Averages

(as of Sept. 30, 2006)

Dow Jones Industrial Average

Alcoa
Altria Group
American Express Co.
American International Group (AIG)
AT&T Inc.
Boeing Co.
Caterpillar, Inc.
Citigroup, Inc.
Coca-Cola, Co.
E.I DuPont de Nemours & Co.

Exxon Mobil Corp.
General Electric Co.
General Motors Corp.
Hewlett-Packard Co.
Home Depot Inc.
Honeywell International, Inc.
IBM
Intel Corp.
J.P. Morgan Chase & Co.
Johnson & Johnson

McDonald's Corp.
Merck & Co. Corp.
Microsoft Corp.
Pfizer, Inc.
Procter & Gamble Co.
3M Co.
United Technologies Corp.
Verizon Communications, Inc.
Wal-Mart Stores, Inc.
Walt Disney Co.

Dow Jones Utility Average

AES Corp.
American Electric Power Co., Inc.
CenterPoint Energy
Consolidated Edison, Inc.
Dominion Resources, Inc. (Virginia)

Duke Energy Corp.
Edison International
Exelon Corp.
FirstEnergy Corp.
NiSource, Inc.

PG&E Corp.
Public Service Enterprise Group, Inc.
Southern Co.
TXU Corp.
Williams Cos.

Dow Jones Transportation Average

Alexander & Baldwin, Inc.
AMR (American Airlines) Corp.
Burlington Northern Santa Fe Corp.
C.H. Robinson Worldwide, Inc.
Con-way Inc.
Continental Airlines C.I.B.

CSX Corp.
Expeditors Int'l of Washington Inc.
FedEx Corp.
GATX Corp.
J.B. Hunt Transportation Services, Inc.
JetBlue Airways Corp.
Landstar System Inc.

Norfolk Southern Corp.
Overseas Shipholding Group, Inc.
Ryder System Inc.
Southwest Airlines Co.
Union Pacific Corp.
United Parcel Service Inc. C.I.B.
YRC Worldwide Inc.

Record One-Day Gains and Losses on the Nasdaq Stock Market

Source: Nasdaq Stock Market; as of Sept. 30, 2005

GREATEST POINT GAINS			GREATEST % GAINS			GREATEST POINT LOSSES			GREATEST % LOSSES		
Rank	Date	Change	Rank	Date	% Change	Rank	Date	Change	Rank	Date	% Change
1.	1/3/2001	324.83	1.	1/3/2001	14.17%	1.	4/14/2000	−355.49	1.	10/19/1987	−11.35%
2.	12/5/2000	274.05	2.	12/5/2000	10.48	2.	4/3/2000	−349.15	2.	4/14/2000	−9.67
3.	4/18/2000	254.41	3.	4/5/2001	8.92	3.	4/12/2000	−286.27	3.	10/20/1987	−9.00
4.	5/30/2000	254.37	4.	4/18/2001	8.12	4.	4/10/2000	−258.25	4.	10/26/1987	−9.00
5.	10/19/2000	247.04	5.	5/30/2000	7.94	5.	1/4/2000	−229.46	5.	8/31/1998	−8.56
6.	10/13/2000	242.09	6.	10/13/2000	7.87	6.	3/14/2000	−200.61	6.	4/3/2000	−7.64
7.	6/2/2000	230.88	7.	10/19/2000	7.79	7.	5/10/2000	−200.28	7.	1/2/2001	−7.23
8.	4/25/2000	228.75	8.	5/8/2002	7.78	8.	5/23/2000	−199.66	8.	12/20/2000	−7.12
9.	4/17/2000	217.87	9.	12/22/2000	7.56	9.	10/25/2000	−190.22	9.	4/12/2000	−7.06
10.	6/1/2000	181.59	10.	10/21/1987	7.34	10.	3/29/2000	−189.22	10.	10/27/1997	−7.02

Nasdaq Stock Market, 1971-2006

High	YEAR	Low	High	YEAR	Low	High	YEAR	Low	High	YEAR	Low
114.12	1971	99.68	208.29	1980	124.09	487.60	1989	376.87	2200.63	1998	1357.09
135.15	1972	113.65	223.96	1981	170.80	470.30	1990	322.93	4090.61	1999	2193.13
136.84	1973	88.67	241.63	1982	158.92	586.35	1991	352.85	5048.62*	2000	2332.78
96.53	1974	54.87	329.11	1983	229.88	676.95	1992	545.85	2892.36	2001	1387.06
88.00	1975	60.70	288.41	1984	223.91	790.56	1993	645.02	2059.38	2002	1114.11
97.88	1976	78.06	325.53	1985	245.82	803.93	1994	691.23	2009.88	2003	1271.47
105.05	1977	93.66	411.21	1986	322.14	1072.82	1995	740.53	2178.00	2004	1752.00
139.25	1978	99.09	456.27	1987	288.49	1328.45	1996	978.17	2273.37	2005	1904.18
152.29	1979	117.84	397.54	1988	329.00	1748.62	1997	1194.39	Oct. 13, 2006 close: 2357.29		

* Record high closing, Mar. 10, 2000.

Milestones of the Nasdaq Stock Market
Source: Nasdaq Stock Market; as of Sept. 30, 2006

First close over...	First close over...	First close over...	First close over...	First close over...
100 Feb. 8, 1971	400 May 30, 1986	1,500 July 11, 1997	3,000 Nov. 3, 1999	4,500 Feb. 17, 2000
200 Nov. 13, 1980	500 Apr. 12, 1991	2,000 July 16, 1998	3,500 Dec. 3, 1999	5,000 Mar. 9, 2000
300 May 6, 1986	1,000 July 17, 1995	2,500 Jan. 29, 1999	4,000 Dec. 29, 1999	

Most Active Common Stocks in 2005

New York Exchange Volume (millions of shares)		NASDAQ Volume (millions of shares)	
Pfizer, Inc.	2,871.0	Microsoft Corp.	17,094,616
Lucent Technologies, Inc.	2,732.1	Intel Corporation	14,936,022
General Electric Co.	2,045.8	Cisco Systems Inc.	14,123,427
Time Warner, Inc.	1,960.6	JDS Uniphase Corporation	11,064,876
Exxon Mobil Corp.	1,905.9	Sirius Satellite Radio Inc.	11,056,705
Citigroup, Inc.	1,657.5	Sun Microsystems Inc.	11,055,162
Motorola, Inc.	1,591.0	Oracle Corp	10,709,597
Texas Instruments, Inc.	1,477.8	Applied Materials Inc.	6,533,329
Wal-Mart Stores	1,427.7	Apple Computer Inc.	5,731,163
Hewlett-Packard Co.	1,371.1	Yahoo! Inc.	4,863,399

Average Yields of Long-Term Treasury, Corporate, and Municipal Bonds
Source: Office of Market Finance, U.S. Dept. of the Treasury; Federal Reserve System

Period	Treasury 30-year bonds[1]	New Aa corporate bonds[2]	New Aa municipal bonds[3]	Period	Treasury 30-year bonds[1]	New Aa corporate bonds[2]	New Aa municipal bonds[3]	Period	Treasury 30-year bonds[1]	New Aa corporate bonds[2]	New Aa municipal bonds[3]
1986				**1993**				**2000**			
June	7.57	9.39	7.87	June	6.81	7.48	5.63	June	5.93	7.75	5.80
Dec.	7.37	8.87	6.87	Dec.	6.25	7.22	5.35	Dec.	5.49	7.21	5.22
1987				**1994**				**2001**			
June	8.57	9.64	7.79	June	7.40	8.16	6.11	June	5.67	7.11	5.20
Dec.	9.12	10.22	7.96	Dec.	7.87	8.66	6.80	Dec.	5.48	6.80	5.25
1988				**1995**				**2002**			
June	9.00	10.08	7.78	June	6.57	7.42	5.84	June	5.65	6.57	5.09
Dec.	9.01	10.05	7.61	Dec.	6.06	7.02	5.45	Dec.	5.01	5.93	4.85
1989				**1996**				**2003**			
June	8.27	9.24	7.02	June	7.06	8.00	6.02	June	4.34	4.97	4.33
Dec.	7.90	9.23	6.98	Dec.	6.55	7.45	5.64	Dec.	5.11	5.62	4.65
1990				**1997**				**2004**			
June	8.46	9.69	7.24	June	6.77	7.71	5.53	June	5.45	6.01	5.05
Dec.	8.24	9.55	7.09	Dec.	5.99	6.68	5.19	Dec.	4.88	5.47	4.49
1991				**1998**				**2005**			
June	8.47	9.37	7.13	Jun	5.70	6.43	5.12	June	4.35	4.96	4.23
Dec.	7.70	8.55	6.69	Dec	5.06	6.13	4.98	Dec.	4.73	5.37	4.46
1992				**1999**				**2006**			
June	7.84	8.45	6.49	Jun.	6.04	7.21	5.37	June	5.15	5.89	4.60
Dec.	7.44	8.12	6.22	Dec.	6.35	7.55	5.95				

NA = Not available. (1) On Feb. 18, 2002, the U.S. treasury discontinued the 30-year constant maturity yield; rates thereafter are for 20-year yields. (2) Treasury series based on 3-week moving average of reoffering yields of new corporate bonds rated Aa by Moody's Investors Service with an original maturity of at least 20 years. Treasury discontinued yield index after Jan. 31, 2003 and reintroduced Feb. 9, 2006. Rates in the interim are for Moody's seasoned Aaa corporate bonds as listed by Federal Reserve. (3) Index of new reoffering yields on 20-year general obligations rated Aa by Moody's Investors Service; discontinued by Treasury Jan. 31, 2003; rates thereafter are from Bond Buyer Index of general obligation, 20-year-to-maturity, mixed quality state and local bonds.

U.S. Capital Gains Tax, 1960-2006
Source: George W. Smith IV, CPA, Partner, George W. Smith & Company, P.C.

The following shows changes in the maximum tax rate on net long-term capital gains for individuals since 1960.

Year	Max %	Year	Max %	Year	Max %	Year	Max %	Year	Max %	Year	Max %
1960	25.0	1972	35.0[1]	1981	20.0	1988	33.0[2]	1997	20.0[4]	2001	20/18[6]
1970	29.5	1978	28.0	1987	28.0	1990	28.0[3]	1999	20.0[5]	2003	20/15[7]
1971	32.5										

(1) From 1972 to 1976, the interplay of minimum tax and maximum tax resulted in a marginal rate of 49.125%. (2) Statutory maximum of 28%, but "phase-out" notch increased marginal rate to 33%; interplay of all "phase-outs" could produce an effective marginal rate to 49.5%. (3) The Budget Act of 1990 increased the statutory rate to 31% and capped the marginal rate at 28%; effective marginal rates could exceed 34% because of the phase-out of personal exemptions and itemized deductions. (4) New rate was for those who, after July 28, 1997, sell capital assets held for more than 18 mos (12 mos for sales after Dec. 31, 1997). A 10% capital gains rate applied to individuals in the 15% income tax bracket. (Those who, after July 28, 1997, but before Jan. 1, 1998, sold capital assets held between 12 and 18 mos to be taxed at the old top rate of 28%. Those who sold capital assets after May 6, 1997, but before July 29, 1997, to be taxed at the 20% rate, so long as such assets were held for at least a year.) (5) The IRS Restructuring and Reform Act of 1998 repealed the more-than-18-month holding period for sales after Dec. 31, 1997. Beginning Jan. 1, 1998, capital assets needed only be held 12 months to have the 20%/10% capital gains rates apply. (6) For capital assets bought after Dec. 31, 2000, and held for more than 5 years, the 20% minimum capital gains rate was lowered to 18%. The 10% rate was lowered to 8%, regardless of when the assets were bought. This provision was repealed in 2003. (7) The maximum capital gains rate for capital assets held more than one year and sold on or after May 6, 2003, was decreased to 15%. The 10% bracket was reduced to 5%. The capital gains rate for the sale of collectibles such as antiques remained at 28%, and the sale of certain depreciable real estate was to be taxed at a maximum of 25%.

2006 Federal Corporate Tax Rates

Taxable Income Amount	Tax Rate	Taxable Income Amount	Tax Rate	Taxable Income Amount	Tax Rate
Not more than $50,000	15%	$100,001 to $335,000	39%	$15,000,001 to $18,333,333	38%
$50,001 to $75,000	25%	$335,001 to $10,000,000	34%	More than $18,333,333	35%
$75,001 to $100,000	34%	$10,000,001 to $15,000,000	35%		

Personal service corporations (used by incorporated professionals such as attorneys and doctors) pay a flat rate of 35%.

Performance of Mutual Funds by Type, 2006

Source: Thomson Financial, Rockville, MD, 800-232-2285

(data for periods ending Sept. 30; all figures are percents)

Fund Type/Fund Objective	AVERAGE ANNUAL RETURN			Fund Type/Fund Objective	AVERAGE ANNUAL RETURN		
	1–year	3–year	5–year		1–year	3–year	5–year
Diversified Stock				Asset Allocation–Global	12.81	14.07	4.65
Aggressive Growth	15.49	16.63	–8.01	Balanced–Domestic	9.32	11.58	2.35
Equity Income	13.33	16.41	3.68	Balanced–Global	16.85	15.49	3.54
Growth–Domestic	13.91	16.16	–2.80	**Bond**			
Growth & Income	12.76	15.90	1.58	Corporate–High Yield	5.79	13.46	5.81
Mid Cap	19.82	20.95	1.60	Corporate–Investment Grade	2.72	4.67	6.14
S&P 500 Index	11.13	14.83	–1.80	Convertible	9.23	14.50	2.22
Small Cap	18.72	22.19	5.30	General Bd–Investment Grade	2.39	4.03	5.77
Specialty Stock				General Bd–Long	3.52	5.25	6.64
Sector–Energy/Natural Res	47.27	36.93	17.36	General Bd–Short & Interm	3.59	5.94	5.91
Sector–Financial Services	8.83	16.55	6.88	General Mortgage	2.26	2.67	4.97
Sector–Health/Biotechnology	15.82	16.40	–0.37	**Global Income**	5.11	8.90	7.76
Sector–Other	0.82	–2.70	0.76	Loan Participation	3.84	5.65	4.76
Sector–Precious Metals	14.56	23.40	28.11	Multi–Sector Bond	3.88	NA	NA
Sector–Real Estate	26.33	25.95	18.63	US Government/Agency	2.46	2.72	5.45
Sector–Tech/Communications	17.77	23.85	–15.63	US Government–Long	3.27	3.08	6.21
Sector–Utilities	32.92	25.28	1.08	US Government–Short & Interm	1.62	2.00	4.71
World Stock				US Treasury	3.18	3.00	6.70
Emerging Market Equity	43.75	37.54	13.75	**Municipal Bond**			
Global Equity	22.57	21.65	1.93	Municipal–High Yield	5.89	5.23	6.04
Non–US Equity	26.93	24.42	3.42	Municipal–Insured	2.63	2.93	5.23
Emerging Market Income	16.51	22.06	15.71	Municipal–National	2.71	2.99	4.98
Hybrid				Municipal–Single State	3.10	3.14	5.23
Asset Allocation–Domestic	10.73	12.28	1.79				

Chicago Board of Trade, Contracts Traded 1995, 2005

Source: Chicago Board of Trade

	1995	2005	% change 1995-2005		1995	2005	% change 1995-2005
FUTURES GROUP				Stock index	—	728,349	NA
Agricultural	41,493,622	75,518,067	82.0	Metals	1,476	—	–100.0
Financial	124,016,379	457,667,874	269.0	**Total options**	45,052,479	113,505,455	151.9
Stock index	—	26,679,733	NA	**COMBINED FUTURES AND OPTIONS**			
Metals	106,176	1,266,251	1092.6	Agricultural	50,260,845	91,872,032	82.8
Total futures	**165,616,177**	**561,145,938**	**238.8**	Financial	160,300,159	554,091,015	245.7
OPTIONS GROUP				Stock index[1]	—	27,408,082	NA
Agricultural	8,767,223	16,353,965	86.5	Metals	107,652	1,266,251	1076.2
Financial	36,283,780	96,423,141	165.7	**GRAND TOTAL**	**210,668,656**	**674,651,393**	**220.2**

(1) Now called the Equity Index, and composed of 6 Dow Jones Indexes; not comparable to Stock Index shown for 1994. A dash indicates item delisted from Board of Trade. NA = not applicable.

U.S. Mutual Fund Shareholders[1]

Source: The Investment Company Institute

Shareholder Characteristics, 2005		Owning:		Households owning mutual funds			
Median age[2]	48	Equity funds	80%	Year	(in mil)[3]	Year	(in mil)[3]
Median annual household income	$68,700	Bond funds	44%	1980 … 4.6		2000 … 51.7	
Median household financial		Hybrid funds	34%	1984 … 10.2		2001 … 56.3	
assets[4]	$125,000	Money market funds	49%	1988 … 22.2		2002 … 54.2	
Median mutual fund assets	$48,000			1992 … 25.8		2003 … 53.3	
Median number of funds owned	4			1994 … 30.2		2004 … 53.7	
Employed[2]	77%			1996 … 36.8		2005 … 54.0	
Married or living with a partner[2]	71%			1999 … 48.4			
Spouse or partner employed	75%						
Four-year college degree or more[2]	56%						

(1) Except where noted, data include mutual funds both inside and outside employer-sponsored retirement plans. (2) Of persons responding to survey. (3) Data from 1980-88 exclude households owning mutual funds solely through employer-sponsored retirement plans. (4) Excluding primary residence.

Distribution of Financial Assets of U.S. Families[1]

Source: Federal Reserve System (by type of asset, in percent of family financial assets)

Type of financial asset	1989	1992	1995	1998	2001	2004	Type of financial asset	1989	1992	1995	1998	2001	2004
Transaction accounts	19.0	17.5	13.9	11.4	11.5	13.2	Retirement accounts	21.5	25.7	28.1	27.6	28.4	32.0
Certificates of deposit	10.2	8.0	5.6	4.3	3.1	3.7	Cash value of life insurance	6.0	5.9	7.2	6.4	5.3	3.0
Savings bonds	1.5	1.1	1.3	0.7	0.7	0.5	Other managed assets	6.6	5.4	5.9	8.6	10.6	8.0
Bonds	10.2	8.4	6.3	4.3	4.6	5.3	Other	4.8	3.8	3.3	1.7	2.0	2.1
Stocks	15.0	16.5	15.6	22.7	21.7	17.6	Financial assets as a						
Mutual funds (excluding money market funds)	5.3	7.6	12.7	12.4	12.2	14.7	percentage of total assets	30.5	31.6	36.7	40.7	42.0	35.7

(1) Data from the triennial *Survey of Consumer Finances*.

The Wealthiest Americans

On Sept. 21, 2006, *Forbes* magazine released its 25th annual roster of the 400 wealthiest Americans. For the first time, all 400 were billionaires.

Here are the top eleven (with *Forbes's* estimate of their net worth):

1. William Henry Gates III, $53.0 bil. (Microsoft)
2. Warren Edward Buffett, $46.0 bil. (Berkshire Hathaway)
3. Sheldon Adelson $20.5 bil. (casinos, hotels)
4. Lawrence Joseph Ellison $19.5 bil. (Oracle)
5. Paul Gardner Allen $16.0 bil. (Microsoft, investments)

6. Jim C. Walton $15.7 bil. (Wal-Mart)
7. Christy Walton & family $15.6 bil. (Wal-Mart heir)
   S. Robson Walton $15.6 bil. (Wal-Mart heir)
9. Robson Walton, $15.6 bil. (Wal-Mart heir)
10. Michael Dell $15.5 bil. (Dell)
    Alice L. Walton $15.5 bil. (Wal-Mart heir)

The total estimated net worth of all 400 came to $1.25 tril., $120 bil. more than 2005.

Stock Ownership of U.S. Families, by Income & Age, 1989, 1998, & 2001, 2004[1]

Source: Federal Reserve System

(in percent, except as noted)

		Families having direct or indirect stock holdings[2]				Median value of portfolios (thousands of 2004 dollars)				Stock holdings as share of financial assets[3]			
		1989	1998	2001	2004	1989	1998	2001	2004	1989	1998	2001	2004
All families		31.7%	48.9%	52.2%	48.6%	$12.5	$29.0	$36.7	$24.4	27.8%	54.0%	56.1%	47.4%
Percentile of income:	Less than 20	3.3	10.0	12.9	11.7	29.3	5.8	8.0	7.0	13.6	20.4	37.4	31.3
	20-39.9	15.2	30.8	34.1	28.8	8.8	11.6	8.3	8.8	10.0	29.8	35.6	29.6
	40-59.9	28.6	50.2	52.5	49.1	6.8	13.9	16.0	11.6	16.7	38.1	46.8	41.0
	60-79.9	44.0	69.3	75.7	66.5	8.5	22.0	30.5	20.0	21.8	45.8	52.0	37.5
	80-89.9	57.6	77.9	82.0	82.5	13.9	52.2	68.8	34.6	26.1	50.4	57.3	43.2
	90-100	76.9	90.4	89.7	91.0	57.9	156.5	263.8	169.9	34.3	62.5	60.5	53.6
By age of family head (years):	Under 35	22.4	40.8	49.0	38.8	4.4	8.1	7.5	5.2	20.2	44.9	52.5	30.0
	35-44	39.0	56.7	59.5	52.3	7.6	23.2	29.3	12.7	29.4	55.0	57.2	47.7
	45-54	41.8	58.6	59.3	54.4	19.3	44.1	53.3	30.6	33.5	55.7	59.1	46.8
	55-64	36.2	55.9	57.4	61.6	27.0	54.5	85.7	59.5	27.7	58.4	56.2	51.1
	65-74	26.7	42.7	40.0	45.7	29.8	64.9	160.1	75.0	26.0	51.3	55.4	51.1
	75+	25.9	29.4	35.7	34.8	36.7	69.6	117.2	85.9	25.0	48.7	51.8	39.1

(1) Data from the triennial *Survey of Consumer Finances*. (2) Indirect holdings are those in mutual funds, retirement accounts, and other managed assets. (3) Among stock-holding families.

Poverty Rate

Source: Bureau of the Census, U.S. Dept. of Commerce

The poverty rate is the proportion of the population whose income falls below the government's official poverty level, and is adjusted each year for inflation. The national poverty rate was 12.6% in 2005, down slightly from the 2004 rate of 12.7%, but above the 2000 rate of 11.3%. About 37.0 million people in the U.S. were in poverty in 2005, nearly 6 million more than in 2000. In 2005 17.1% of children and 9.8% of people aged 65 and older were defined as poor.

Poverty Thresholds by Family Size, 1980-2005[1]

Source: Bureau of the Census, U.S. Dept. of Commerce

	2005	2000	1990	1980		2005	2000	1990	1980
1 person	$9,973	$8,794	$6,652	$4,186	3 persons	$15,577	$13,783	$10,419	$6,570
Under 65 years	10,160	8,959	6,800	4,284	4 persons	19,971	17,603	13,359	8,415
65 years and over	9,367	8,259	6,268	3,950	5 persons	23,613	20,819	15,792	9,967
2 persons	12,755	11,239	8,509	5,361	6 persons	26,683	23,528	17,839	11,272
Householder under 65 . .	13,145	11,590	8,794	5,537	7 persons	30,249	26,754	20,241	12,761
Householder 65 and over	11,815	10,419	7,905	4,982	8 persons	33,610	29,701	22,582	14,199
					9 persons or more	40,288	35,060	26,848	16,896

(1) Weighted average; not used for computing poverty data.

Persons Below Poverty Level, 1960-2005

Source: Bureau of the Census, U.S. Dept. of Commerce

	Number below poverty level (in millions)				Percentage below poverty level				Avg. income cutoffs for family of 4 at poverty level[3]
YEAR	All races[1]	White	Black	Hispanic origin[2]	All races[1]	White	Black	Hispanic origin[2]	
1960	39.9	28.3	NA	NA	22.2	17.8	NA	NA	$3,022
1970	25.4	17.5	7.5	NA	12.6	9.9	33.5	NA	3,968
1980	29.3	19.7	8.6	3.5	13.0	10.2	32.5	25.7	8,414
1990	33.6	22.3	9.8	6.0	13.5	10.7	31.9	28.1	13,359
1991	35.7	23.7	10.2	6.3	14.2	11.3	32.7	28.7	13,924
1992	38.0	25.3	10.8	7.6	14.8	11.9	33.4	29.6	14,335
1993	39.3	26.2	10.9	8.1	15.1	12.2	33.1	30.6	14,763
1994	38.1	25.4	10.2	8.4	14.5	11.7	30.6	30.7	15,141
1995	36.4	24.4	9.9	8.6	13.8	11.2	29.3	30.3	15,569
1996	36.5	24.7	9.7	8.7	13.7	11.2	28.4	29.4	16,036
1997	35.6	24.4	9.1	8.3	13.3	11.0	26.5	27.1	16,400
1998	34.5	23.5	9.1	8.1	12.7	10.5	26.1	25.6	16,660
1999	32.3	21.9	8.4	7.4	11.8	9.8	23.6	22.8	17,029
2000	31.1	21.2	7.9	7.2	11.3	9.4	22.2	21.2	17,063
2002	34.6	23.5	8.6	8.6	12.1	10.2	24.1	21.8	18,556
2003	35.9	24.3	8.8	9.1	12.5	10.5	24.4	22.5	18,979
2004	37.0	25.3	9.0	9.1	12.7	10.8	24.7	21.9	19,307
2005	37.0	24.9	9.2	9.4	12.6	10.6	24.9	21.8	19,971

NA = Not available. **Note:** Because of a change in the definition of poverty, data prior to 1980 are not directly comparable to data since 1980. (1) Includes other races not shown separately. (2) Persons of Hispanic origin may be of any race. (3) Figures for 1960-80 represent only nonfarm families.

Poverty by Family Status, Sex, and Race, 1986-2005

Source: Bureau of the Census, U.S. Dept. of Commerce

(Number. in thousands)

	1986 No.	1986 %[1]	1990 No.	1990 %[1]	1995 No.	1995 %[1]	2000 No.	2000 %[1]	2005 No.	2005 %[1]
TOTAL POOR	32,370	13.6	33,585	13.5	36,425	13.8	31,054	11.3	36,950	12.6
In families	24,754	12.0	25,232	12.0	27,501	12.3	22,015	9.6	26,068	10.8
Head of household	7,023	10.9	7,098	10.7	7,532	10.8	6,222	8.6	7,657	9.9
Related children	12,257	19.8	12,715	19.9	13,999	20.2	11,018	15.6	12,335	17.1
Unrelated individuals	6,846	21.6	7,446	20.7	8,247	20.9	8,503	18.9	10,425	21.1
Families, female householder, no husband present	11,944	38.3	12,578	37.2	14,205	36.5	10,425	27.9	13,153	31.1
Head of household	3,613	34.6	3,768	33.4	4,057	32.4	3,096	24.7	4,044	28.7
Related children	6,943	54.4	7,363	53.4	8,364	50.3	6,116	39.8	7,210	42.8
Unrelated female individuals	4,311	25.1	4,589	24.0	4,865	23.5	5,071	21.6	6,111	24.1
All other families	12,811	7.3	12,654	7.1	13,296	7.2	NA	NA	NA	NA
Head of household	3,410	6.3	3,330	6.0	3,475	6.1	NA	NA	NA	NA
Related children	5,313	10.8	5,352	10.7	5,635	10.7	NA	NA	NA	NA
Unrelated male individuals	2,536	17.5	2,857	16.9	3,382	18.0	3,548	16.0	4,315	17.9
TOTAL WHITE POOR[2]	22,183	11.0	22,326	10.7	24,423	11.2	21,242	9.4	24,872	10.6
In families	16,393	9.4	15,916	9.0	17,593	9.6	14,392	7.7	16,782	8.6
Head of household	4,811	8.6	4,622	8.1	4,994	8.5	4,151	6.9	5,068	8.0
Related children	7,714	15.3	7,696	15.1	8,474	15.5	6,838	12.3	7,652	13.9
Families with female householder, no husband present	2,041	28.2	2,010	26.8	2,200	26.6	1,655	20.0	7,021	27.1
Unrelated individuals	5,198	19.2	5,739	18.6	6,336	19.0	6,402	17.2	7,718	19.2
TOTAL BLACK POOR[2]	8,983	31.1	9,837	31.9	9,872	29.3	7,862	22.0	9,168	24.9
In families	7,410	29.7	8,160	31.0	8,189	28.5	6,108	20.7	7,164	23.8
Head of household	1,987	28.0	2,193	29.3	2,127	26.4	1,685	19.1	1,997	22.1
Related children	4,039	42.7	4,412	44.2	4,644	41.5	3,417	30.4	3,743	34.2
Families with female householder, no husband present	1,488	50.1	1,648	48.1	1,701	45.1	1,301	34.6	5,303	39.3
Unrelated individuals	1,431	38.5	1,491	35.1	1,551	32.6	1,708	28.0	1,949	29.9

NA = Not available. (1) Percentage of total U.S. population in each category who fell below poverty level and are enumerated here. For example, of all persons in families in 2005, 10.8%, or 26,068,000, were poor. (2) Data are for one race only. The Census Bureau revised race categories in 2002; 2005 figures are not directly comparable with previous years.

Persons in Poverty, by State, 2003-2005

Source: Bureau of the Census, U.S. Dept. of Commerce

	2003-04[1]	2004-05[1]		2003-04[1]	2004-05[1]		2003-04[1]	2004-05[1]
Alabama	16.0%	16.8%	Kentucky	16.1%	16.3%	Ohio	11.3%	11.9%
Alaska	9.4	9.5	Louisiana	16.9	17.6	Oklahoma	11.8	13.2
Arizona	13.9	14.8	Maine	11.6	12.1	Oregon	12.2	11.9
Arkansas	16.4	14.5	Maryland	9.3	9.8	Pennsylvania	11.0	11.3
California	13.2	13.2	Massachusetts	9.8	9.7	Rhode Island	11.5	11.8
Colorado	9.8	10.7	Michigan	12.3	12.6	South Carolina	13.8	15.0
Connecticut	9.1	9.7	Minnesota	7.2	7.5	South Dakota	13.1	12.7
Delaware	8.1	9.1	Mississippi	17.4	19.4	Tennessee	15.0	15.4
District of Columbia	16.9	19.1	Missouri	11.5	11.9	Texas	16.7	16.3
			Montana	14.7	14.0	Utah	9.6	9.6
Florida	12.2	11.4	Nebraska	9.6	9.5	Vermont	8.2	7.7
Georgia	12.4	13.7	Nevada	10.9	10.8	Virginia	9.7	9.3
Hawaii	8.9	8.6	New Hampshire	5.6	5.5	Washington	12.0	10.8
Idaho	10.0	9.9	New Jersey	8.3	7.4	West Virginia	15.8	14.8
Illinois	12.5	11.9	New Mexico	17.3	17.2	Wisconsin	11.1	11.3
Indiana	10.8	12.1	New York	14.6	14.8	Wyoming	9.9	10.3
Iowa	9.9	11.1	North Carolina	15.1	13.8			
Kansas	11.1	12.0	North Dakota	9.7	10.4	**U.S. Total**	**12.6**	**12.7**

(1) 2-year average.

Leading U.S. Businesses in 2005

Source: FORTUNE Magazine

(millions of dollars in revenues)

Advertising, Marketing
Omnicom $10,481
Interpublic Group 6,274
Vertis 1,610
Aerospace
Boeing $54,848
United Technologies 42,725
Lockheed Martin 37,213
Northrop Grumman 30,721
Honeywell Intl. 28,862
Raytheon 21,894
General Dynamics 21,290
Textron 11,979
L-3 Communications 9,445
Goodrich 5,405
Airlines
AMR $20,712
UAL 17,379
Delta Air Lines 16,191
Northwest Airlines 12,286
Continental Airlines 11,208

Southwest Airlines $7,584
US Airways Group 5,077
Alaska Air Group 2,975
SkyWest 1,964
Apparel
Nike $13,740
VF 6,502
Jones Apparel Group 5,074
Liz Claiborne 4,848
Levi Strauss 4,125
Polo Ralph Lauren 3,305
Kellwood 2,351
Phillips-Van Heusen 1,909
Quiksilver 1,781
Timberland 1,566
Automotive Retailing, Services
AutoNation $19,468
United Auto Group 10,985
Sonic Automotive 8,378
Group 1 Automotive 5,970
Ashbury Automotive Group 5,874

CarMax $5,260
Banks (commercial and savings)
Citigroup $131,045
Bank of America Corp. 83,980
J.P. Morgan Chase & Co. 79,902
Wells Fargo 40,407
Wachovia Corp. 35,908
U.S. Bancorp 16,596
Capital One Financial 12,085
National City Corp. 11,036
SunTrust Banks 10,886
Bank of New York Co. 8,312
Beverages
Coca-Cola $23,104
Coca-Cola Enterprises 18,706
Anheuser-Busch 15,036
Pepsi Bottling 11,885
Molson Coors Brewing 5,752
Constellation Brands 4,088
PepsiAmericas 3,726
Brown-Forman 2,312

Building Materials, Glass

Owens Corning	$6,323
USG	5,139
Armstrong Holdings	3,558
Vulcan Materials	3,260
Martin Marietta Materials	2,011
Texas Industries	1,951

Chemicals

Dow Chemical	$46,307
DuPont	28,491
Lyondell Chemical	18,606
Huntsman	12,986
PPG Industries	10,201

Computer & Data Services

First Data	$21,033
Fiserv	14,768
SunGard Data Systems	10,101
MasterCard	7,761
DST Systems	7,755
Dun & Bradstreet	5,821

Computers, Office Equipment

Intl. Business Machines	$91,134
Hewlett-Packard	86,696
Dell	55,908
Xerox	15,701
Apple Computer	13,931
Sun Microsystems	11,070
NCR	6,028

Computer Peripherals

EMC	$9,664
Lexmark International	5,222
Maxtor	3,890
Western Digital	3,639
Symbol Technologies	1,766
Network Appliance	1,598

Computer Software

Microsoft	$39,788
Oracle	11,799
Computer Assoc. Intl.	3,530
Electronic Arts	3,129
Symantec	2,583

Diversified Financials

General Electric	$157,153
American Express	30,080
Countrywide Financial	18,537
Marsh & McLennan	12,109
Aon	10,030
SLM	6,518
CIT Group	5,653

Electronics, Electrical Equipment

Emerson Electric	$17,305
Whirlpool	14,317
Rockwell Automation	5,003
Maytag	4,901
SPX	4,787

Energy

Constellation Energy	$17,375
ONEOK	12,811
Williams	12,584
American Electric Power	12,117
Reliant Energy	10,708

Engineering, Construction

Fluor	$13,161
Jacobs Engineering Grp.	5,635
Emcor Group	4,731
Peter Kiewit Sons'	4,145
URS	3,918

Entertainment

Time Warner	$43,652
Walt Disney	31,944
News Corp.	23,859
CBS	14,536
Viacom	9,818

Food

PepsiCo	$32,562
Sara Lee	19,727
ConAgra Foods	15,516
General Mills	11,244
Dean Foods	10,900
Kellogg	10,177
H.J. Heinz	8,912
Land O'Lakes	7,567
Campbell Soup	7,548
Dole Food	5,871
Hormel Foods	$5,414
Hershey	4,836
Wm. Wrigley, Jr.	4,159

Food & Drug Stores

Kroger	$60,553
Walgreen	42,202
Albertson's	40,397
Safeway	38,416
CVS	37,006
Publix Super Markets	20,745
Rite Aid	16,816
Winn-Dixie Stores	10,210

Food Production

Archer Daniels Midland	$35,944
Tyson Foods	26,014
Smithfield Foods	11,354
Pilgrim's Pride	5,666
Chiquita Brands Intl.	3,904
Seaboard	2,689

Food Services

McDonald's	$20,460
Yum Brands	9,349
Starbucks	6,369
Darden Restaurants	5,278
Brinker International	3,913
Wendy's Intl.	3,783

Forest & Paper Products

International Paper	$25,797
Weyerhaeuser	23,000
Bowater	3,484
Louisiana-Pacific	2,742
Universal Forest Prods.	2,692

Furniture

Leggett & Platt	$5,299
Steelcase	2,614
HNI	2,451
Furniture Brands Intl.	2,387
La-Z-Boy	2,048

General Merchandisers

Wal-Mart Stores	$315,654
Target	52,620
Sears Holdings	49,124
Federated Dept. Stores	23,347
J.C. Penney	18,781
Kohl's	13,402
Dollar General	8,582

Health Care: Wholesalers

McKesson	$80,515
Cardinal Health	74,915
AmerisourceBergen	54,590

Health Care: Insurance

UnitedHealth Group	$45,365
Wellpoint	45,136
Aetna	22,885
Cigna	16,684
Humana	14,418
Health Net	11,941
Coventry Health Care	6,611

Health Care: Medical Facilities

HCA	$24,455
Tenet Healthcare	10,052
Triad Hospitals	4,917
Universal Health Svcs.	4,101
Kindred Healthcare	3,979
Community Health Sys.	3,789
Health Management Associates	3,624
Manor Care	3,417
DaVita	3,072
Vanguard Health Systems	2,269

Healthcare: Pharmacy and Other Services

Medco Health Solutions	$37,871
Caremark Rx	32,991
Express Scripts	16,266
Quest Diagnostics	5,504
Omnicare	5,293
Laboratory Corp. of America	3,328

Hotels, Casinos, Resorts

Marriott International	$11,550
Harrah's Entertainment	7,411
MGM Mirage	6,482
Starwood Hotels & Rsrts.	5,977
Hilton Hotels	4,437
Boyd Gaming	2,223

Household & Personal Products

Procter & Gamble	$56,741
Kimberly-Clark	15,903
Colgate-Palmolive	11,397
Avon Products	8,150
Estée Lauder	6,336
Clorox	4,475
Alberto-Culver	3,531

Industrial & Farm Equipment

Caterpillar	$36,339
Deere	21,931
Illinois Tool Works	12,922
Eaton	11,115
American Standard	10,264

Insurance: Life, Health (Mutual)

New York Life Insurance	$28,051
TIAA-CREF	25,917
Mass. Mutual Life Ins.	22,799
Northwestern Mutual	19,221
Guardian Life of America	9,377

Insurance: Life, Health (Stock)

MetLife	$46,983
Prudential Financial	31,708
AFLAC	14,363
UnumProvident	10,437

Insurance: P & C (Mutual)

State Farm Insurance Cos	$59,224
Auto-Owners Insurance	5,014
Country Insurance & Financial Services	3,059

Insurance: P & C (Stock)

American Intl. Group	$108,905
Berkshire Hathaway	81,663
Allstate	35,383
Hartford Financial Services	27,083
St. Paul Travelers Cos.	24,365

Metals

Alcoa	$26,601
United States Steel	14,039
Nucor	12,701
Phelps Dodge	9,030
Commercial Metals	6,593
AK Steel Holding	5,647

Mining, Crude-Oil Production

Occidental Petroleum	$16,286
Devon Energy	10,741
Burlington Resources	7,587
Apache	7,584
Anadarko Petroleum	7,100

Motor Vehicles & Parts

General Motors	$192,604
Ford Motor	177,210
Johnson Controls	28,020
Delphi	27,201
Goodyear Tire & Rubber	19,723

Network & Other Communications Equipment

Motorola	$36,843
Cisco Systems	24,801
Lucent Technologies	9,441
Qualcomm	5,673
Avaya	4,902

Oil and Gas Equipment Services

Halliburton	$20,994
Baker Hughes	7,218
Smith Intl.	5,579

Package, Mail, Freight Delivery

United Parcel Service	$42,581
FedEX	24,710
ABX Air	1,464

Petroleum Refining

Exxon Mobil	$339,938
ChevronTexaco	189,481
ConocoPhillips	166,683
Valero Energy	81,362
Marathon Oil	58,958

Pharmaceuticals

Pfizer	$51,353
Johnson & Johnson	50,514
Abbott Laboratories	22,338
Merck	22,012
Bristol-Myers Squibb	20,222
Wyeth	18,756
Eli Lilly	14,645

Amgen	$12,430	Bear Stearns	$11,552	Robert Half Intl.	$3,338
Schering-Plough	9,508	Charles Schwab	5,151	Volt Info. Sciences	2,178
Forest Laboratories	3,160	**Semiconductors and Other Electronic**		Spherion	1,992
Pipelines		**Components**		MPS Group	1,685
Plains All Amer. Pipeline	$31,177	Intel	$38,826	**Textiles**	
Enterprise Products	12,257	Texas Instruments	13,392	Mohawk Industries	$5,880
Kinder Morgan Energy	9,787	Sanmina-SCI	11,735	WestPoint Stevens	1,655
TEPPCO Partners	8,619	Solectron	10,456	**Tobacco**	
TransMontaigne	8,549	Jabil Circuit	7,524	Altria Group	$69,148
Publishing & Printing		**Specialty Retailers**		Reynolds American	8,256
R.R. Donnelley & Sons	$8,651	Home Depot	$81,511	Universal	3,276
Gannett	7,666	Costco Wholesale	52,935	**Toys, Sporting Goods**	
McGraw-Hill	6,004	Lowe's	43,243	Mattel	$5,179
Tribune	5,596	Best Buy	27,433	Hasbro	3,088
Washington Post	3,554	Staples	16,079	**Transportation Equipment**	
New York Times	3,373	TJX	16,058	Brunswick	$5,924
Knight-Ridder	3,004	Gap	16,023	Harley-Davidson	5,674
E.W. Scripps	2,514	Office Depot	14,279	**Utilities: Gas & Electric**	
Reader's Digest Assn.	2,390	Toys 'R' Us	11,194	Duke Energy	$18,944
Scholastic	2,080	Circuit City Stores	10,472	Dominion Resources	18,041
Railroads		Limited Brands	9,699	Exelon	15,405
Union Pacific	$13,578	**Telecommunications**		Southern	13,554
Burlington No. Santa Fe	12,987	Verizon Communications	$75,112	Public Service Enterprise Group	12,661
CSX	8,632	AT&T	43,862	FirstEnergy	12,195
Norfolk Southern	8,527	Sprint Nextel	34,680	Edison International	11,852
Scientific, Photo, Control Equipment		Comcast	22,255	FPL Group	11,846
Eastman Kodak	$14,268	BellSouth	20,613	Sempra Energy	11,737
Danaher	7,985	Qwest Communications	13,903	Consolidated Edison	11,732
Agilent Technologies	6,935	DIRECTV Group	13,165	**Waste Management**	
Thermo Electron	2,633	Alltell	9,487	Waste Management	$13,074
Securities		Echostar Communications	8,426	Allied Waste Industries	5,735
Morgan Stanley	$52,498	Cox Communications	7,054	Republic Services	2,864
Merrill Lynch	47,783	**Temporary Help**		**Miscellaneous**	
Goldman Sachs Group	43,391	Manpower	$16,080	3M	$21,167
Lehman Brothers Hldgs.	32,420	Kelly Services	5,290	Mohawk Industries	6,620

25 U.S. Corporations with Largest Revenues in 2005

Source: FORTUNE Magazine

(millions of dollars)

Rank, Company (2004 rank)	Revenues	Profits	Rank, Company (2004 rank)	Revenues	Profits
1. Exxon Mobil (2)	$339,938.00	$36,130.00	14. Home Depot (13)	$81,511.00	$5,838.00
2. Wal-Mart Stores (1)	315,654.00	11,231.00	15. Valero Energy (22)	81,362.00	3,590.00
3. General Motors (3)	192,604.00	–10,600.00	16. McKesson (15)	80,514.60	–156.70
4. Chevron Corp. (6)	189,481.00	14,099.00	17. J.P. Morgan Chase & Co. (20)	79,902.00	8,483.00
5. Ford Motor (4)	177,210.00	2,024.00	18. Verizon Communications (14)	75,111.90	7,397.00
6. ConocoPhillips (7)	166,683.00	13,529.00	19. Cardinal Health (16)	74,915.10	1,050.70
7. General Electric (5)	157,153.00	16,353.00	20. Altria Group (17)	69,148.00	10,435.00
8. Citigroup (8)	131,045.00	24,589.00	21. Kroger (21)	60,552.90	958.00
9. American Intl. Group (9)	108,905.00	10,477.00	22. State Farm Insurance Cos (19)	59,223.90	3,241.80
10. Intl. Business Machines (10)	91,134.00	7,934.00	23. Marathon Oil (31)	58,958.00	3,032.00
11. Hewlett-Packard (11)	86,696.00	2,398.00	24. Procter & Gamble (26)	56,741.00	7,257.00
12. Bank of America Corp. (18)	83,980.00	16,465.00	25. Dell (28)	55,908.00	3,572.00
13. Berkshire Hathaway (12)	81,663.00	8,528.00			

Fastest-Growing U.S. Franchises in 2005[1]

Source: *Entrepreneur* Magazine

Company	Type of Business	Minimum start-up cost[2]
1. Subway	Submarine sandwiches & salads	$72-223
2. Quiznos Sub	Submarine sandwiches, soups, salads	$71.7-251.1
3. Curves	Women's fitness & weight-loss centers	$31.4-53.5
4. UPS Store, The	Postal, business & communications services	$153.95-266.8
5. Jackson Hewitt Tax Service	Tax preparation services	$49.8-94
6. Dunkin' Donuts	Donuts & baked goods	$179-1.6
7. Jani-King	Commercial cleaning	$11.3-34.1+
8. RE/MAX Int'l. Inc.	Real estate	$25-199
9. 7-Eleven Inc.	Convenience store	Varies
10. Liberty Tax Service	Income-tax preparation services	$43.8-54.9
11. Domino's Pizza LLC	Pizza, breadsticks, buffalo wings	$141.4-415.1
12. Pizza Hut Inc.	Pizza	$1,100-1,700
13. Sonic Drive In Restaurants	Drive-in restaurant	$710-2,300
14. Century 21 Real Estate LLC	Real estate	$11.8-522.8
15. Jan-Pro Franchising Int'l. Inc.	Commercial cleaning	$3.3-49.9
16. McDonald's	Hamburgers, chicken, salads	$506-1,600
17. ServiceMaster Clean	Comm'l./residential cleaning & disaster restoration	$26-109.2
18. Kumon Math & Reading Centers	Supplemental education	$15.2-37.8
19. Coldwell Banker Real Estate Corp.	Real estate	$23.5-490.5
20. Jiffy Lube Int'l. Inc.	Fast oil change	$214-273
21. Arby's	Roast beef sandwiches, chicken, wraps, salads	$336.5-2,430
22. Baskin-Robbins USA Co.	Ice cream, frozen yogurt, frozen beverages	$135-522
23. KFC Corp.	Chicken	$1,100-1,700
24. Cold Stone Creamery	Ice cream, frozen yogurt, Italian sorbet	$294.3-438.9
25. Jazzercise Inc.	Dance/exercise classes	$3-33.1

(1) Ranked by number of new franchise units added. (2) In thousands; not including franchise fee, which varies.

Largest Corporate Mergers or Acquisitions in U.S.

Source: Securities Data Co.

(as of Sept. 2006; * denotes an announced merger or acquisition not yet complete; year = year effective or announced)

Company	Acquirer	Dollars (in billions)	Year	Company	Acquirer	Dollars (in billions)	Year
Time Warner	America Online, Inc.	$181.6	2001	Electronic Data Syst.	shareholders	$29.7	1996
Warner-Lambert	Pfizer Inc.	88.8	2000	First Chicago NBD	BANC ONE Corp.	29.6	1998
Mobil Corp.	Exxon Corp.	86.4	1999	RJR Nabisco	Kohlberg Kravis Roberts	29.4	1989
*Bell South Corp.	AT&T	72.7	2006	Guidant Corp.	Boston Scientific	27.2	2006
Citicorp	Travelers Group Inc.	72.6	1998	Pharmacia & Upjohn	Monsanto Co.	26.9	2000
Ameritech Corp	SBC Communic. Inc.	72.4	1999	Associates First Capital	shareholders	26.6	1998
GTE Corp.	Bell Atlantic Corp.	71.3	2000	Golden West Fin. Corp.	Wachovia	25.5	2006
Tele-Communications	AT&T	69.9	1999	Conoco	Phillips Petroleum	24.8	2002
AirTouch Communic.	Vodafone Group PLC	65.8	1999	Lucent Technologies (AT&T)	shareholders	24.1	1996
BankAmerica Corp.	NationsBank Corp.	61.6	1998	Bestfoods	Unilever PLC	23.7	2000
Pharmacia Corp.	Pfizer, Inc	61.3	2003	Compaq Computer	Hewlett-Packard	23.5	2002
Bank One Corp.	JP Morgan Chase	58.8	2004	Amer. General Corp.	American Int'l. Group	23.4	2001
US West	Qwest Communication	56.3	2000	AMFM, Inc.	Clear Channel Communications	22.7	2000
Amoco Corp.	British Petroleum Co. PLC	55.0	1998	Pacific Telesis Group	SBC Communications, Inc.	22.4	1997
Gillette	Procter & Gamble	54.9	2005	General Re Corp.	Berkshire Hathaway Inc.	22.3	1998
MediaOne Group	AT&T	51.9	2000	US Bancorp, MN	Firstar Corp.	21.1	2001
FleetBoston Fin. Corp.	Bank of America	47.0	2004	Ascend Communic.	Lucent Technologies	21.1	1999
Liberty Media Group (AT&T)	shareholders	46.0	2001	Network Solutions, Inc.	VeriSign, Inc.	20.8	2000
Texaco	Chevron	43.3	2001	Waste Management	USA Waste Services	20.0	1998
MCI Communications	WorldCom Inc.	41.4	1998	Nabisco Holdings	Philip Morris	19.4	2000
AT&T Wireless Service	Cingular Wireless	41.0	2004	AT&T Wireless Serv.	shareholders	18.8	2001
SDL Inc.	JDS Uniphase Corp.	41.0	2001	Unocal Corp	Chevron Corp.	18.7	2005
CBS Corp.	Viacom	40.9	2000	Capital Cities/ABC Inc	Walt Disney	18.3	1996
Chrysler Corp.	Daimler-Benz AG	40.5	1998	Albertson's Inc.	shareholders	17.1	2006
MBNA	Bank of America	35.8	2005	Pfizer Cons. Healthcare	Johnson & Johnson	16.6	2006
Burlington Resources	Conoco Phillips	35.6	2005	Kerr-McGee Corp.	Anadarko Corp.	16.4	2006
Wells Fargo & Co.	Norwest Corp.	34.4	1998	SunAmerica Inc.	American Int'l. Group	18.1	1999
VoiceStream Wireless Corp.	Deutsche Telekom AG	34.1	2001	May Dept. Stores	Federated Dept. Stores	16.5	2005
ARCO	BP Amoco PLC	33.7	2000	AT&T	SBC Comm	14.7	2005
J.P. Morgan & Co.	Chase Manhattan	33.6	2000	*North Fork Bancorp.	Capital One	14.6	2006
US West Media Group	shareholders	31.7	1998	Vivendi Universal	General Electric	14.0	2003
Agilent Technologies	shareholders	31.2	2000	Travelers Life & Annuity Co	MetLife Inc.	11.7	2005
Associates First Capital	Citigroup	31.0	2000	John Hancock Financial Services	Manulife Financial	11.0	2003
NYNEX	Bell Atlantic	30.8	1997				
AT&T Broadband & Internet Services	Comcast Corp.	30.0	2001				

Economic and Financial Glossary

Source: Reviewed by William M. Gentry, Graduate School of Business, Columbia University

Annuity contract: An investment vehicle sold by insurance companies. Annuity buyers can elect to receive periodic payments for the rest of their lives. Annuities provide insurance against outliving one's wealth.

Arbitrage: A form of hedged investment meant to capture slight differences in the prices of 2 related securities—for example, buying gold in London and selling it at a higher price in New York.

Balanced budget: A budget is balanced when receipts equal expenditures. When receipts exceed expenditures, there is a **surplus;** when they fall short of expenditures, there is a **deficit.**

Balance of payments: The difference between all payments, for some categories of transactions, made to and from foreign countries over a set period of time. A *favorable* balance of payments exists when more payments are coming in than going out; an *unfavorable* balance of payments obtains when the reverse is true. Payments may include gold, the cost of merchandise and services, interest and dividend payments, money spent by travelers, and repayment of principal on loans.

Balance of trade (trade gap): The difference between exports and imports, in both actual funds and credit. A nation's balance of trade is *favorable* when exports exceed imports and *unfavorable* when the reverse is true.

Bear market: A market in which prices are falling.

Bearer bond: A bond issued in bearer form rather than being registered in a specific owner's name. Ownership is determined by possession.

Bond: A written promise, or IOU, by the issuer to repay a fixed amount of borrowed money on a specified date and generally to pay interest at regular intervals in the interim.

Bull market: A market in which prices are on the rise.

Capital gain (loss): An increase (decrease) in the market value of an asset over some period of time. For tax purposes, capital gains are typically calculated from when an asset is bought to when it is sold.

Commercial paper: An extremely short-term corporate IOU, generally due in 270 days or less.

Consumer price index (CPI): A statistical measure of the change in the price of consumer goods.

Convertible bond: A corporate bond (see below) that may be converted into a stated number of shares of common stock. Its price tends to fluctuate along with fluctuations in the price of the stock and with changes in interest rates.

Corporate bond: A bond issued by a corporation. The bond normally has a stated life and pays a fixed rate of interest. Considered safer than the common or preferred stock of the same company.

Cost of living: The cost of maintaining a standard of living measured in terms of purchased goods and services. Inflation typically measures changes in the cost of living.

Cost-of-living adjustments: Changes in promised payments, such as retirement benefits, to account for changes in the cost of living.

Credit crunch (liquidity crisis): A situation in which cash for lending is in short supply.

Debenture: An unsecured bond backed only by the general credit of the issuing corporation.

Deficit spending: Government spending in excess of revenues, generally financed with the sale of bonds. A deficit increases the government debt.

Deflation: A decrease in the level of prices.

Depression: A long period of economic decline marked by low prices, high unemployment, and many business failures.

Derivatives: Financial contracts, such as options, whose values are based on, or *derived* from, the price of an underlying financial asset or indicator such as a stock or an interest rate.

Devaluation: The official lowering of a nation's currency, decreasing its value in relation to foreign currencies.

Discount rate: The rate of interest set by the Federal Reserve that member banks are charged when borrowing money through the Federal Reserve System.

Disposable income: Income after taxes that is available to persons for spending and saving.

Diversification: Investing in more than one asset in order to reduce the riskiness of the overall asset portfolio. By holding more than one asset, losses on some assets may be offset by gains realized on other assets.

Dividend: Discretionary payment by a corporation to its shareholders, usually in the form of cash or stock shares.

Dow Jones Industrial Average: An index of stock market prices, based on the prices of 30 companies, 28 of which are on the New York Stock Exchange.

Econometrics: The use of statistical methods to study economic and financial data.

Federal Deposit Insurance Corp. (FDIC): A U.S. government-sponsored corporation that insures accounts in national banks and other qualified institutions against bank failures.

Federal Reserve System: The entire banking system of the U.S., incorporating 12 Federal Reserve banks (one in each of 12 Federal Reserve districts), 25 Federal Reserve branch banks, all national banks, and state-chartered commercial banks and trust companies that have been admitted to its membership. The governors of the system greatly influence the nation's monetary and credit policies.

Full employment: The economy is said to be at full employment when everyone who wishes to work at the going wage-rate for his or her type of labor is employed, save only for the small amount of unemployment due to the time it takes to switch from one job to another.

Futures: A futures contract is an agreement to buy or sell a specific amount of a commodity or financial instrument at a particular price at a set date in the future. For example, futures based on a stock index (such as the Dow Jones Industrial Average) are bets on the future price of that group of stocks.

Golden parachute: Provisions in contracts of some high-level executives guaranteeing substantial severance benefits if they lose their position in a corporate takeover.

Government bond: A bond issued by the U.S. Treasury, considered a safe investment. These are divided into 2 categories—marketable and not marketable. *Savings bonds* cannot be bought and sold once the original purchase is made. Marketable bonds fall into several categories. *Treasury bills* are short-term U.S. obligations, maturing in 3, 6, or 12 months. *Treasury notes* mature in up to 10 years. *Treasury bonds* mature in 10 to 30 years. *Indexed bonds* are adjusted for inflation.

Greenmail: A company buying back its own shares for more than the going market price to avoid a threatened hostile takeover.

Gross domestic product (GDP): The market value of all goods and services that have been bought for final use during a period of time. It became the official measure of the size of the U.S. economy in 1991, replacing *gross national product (GNP)*, in use since 1941. GDP covers workers and capital employed within the nation's borders. GNP covers production by U.S. residents regardless of where it takes place. The switch aligned U.S. terminology with that of most other industrialized countries.

Hedge fund: A flexible investment fund for a limited number of large investors (the minimum investment is typically $1 million). Hedge funds use a variety of investment techniques, including those forbidden to mutual funds, such as short-selling and heavy leveraging.

Hedging: Taking 2 positions whose gains and losses will offset each other if prices change, in order to limit risk.

Individual retirement account (IRA): A self-funded tax-advantaged retirement plan that allows employed individuals to contribute up to a maximum yearly sum. With a *traditional* IRA, individuals contribute pre-tax earnings and defer income taxes until retirement. With a *Roth* IRA, individuals contribute after-tax earnings but do not pay taxes on future withdrawals (the interest is never taxed). *401(k) plans* are employer-sponsored plans similar to traditional IRAs, but having higher contribution limits.

Inflation: An increase in the level of prices.

Insider information: Important facts about the condition or plans of a corporation that have not been released to the general public.

Interest: The cost of borrowing money.

Investment bank: A financial institution that arranges the initial issuance of stocks and bonds and offers companies advice about acquisitions and divestitures.

Junk bonds: Bonds issued by companies with low credit ratings. They typically pay relatively high interest rates because of the fear of default.

Leading indicators: A series of 11 indicators from different segments of the economy used by the U.S. Commerce Department to predict when changes in the level of economic activity will occur.

Leverage: The extent to which a purchase was paid for with borrowed money. Amplifies the potential gain or loss for the purchaser.

Leveraged buyout (LBO): An acquisition of a company in which much of the purchase price is borrowed, with the debt to be repaid from future profits or by subsequently selling off company assets. A leveraged buyout is typically carried out by a small group of investors, often including incumbent management.

Liquid assets: Assets consisting of cash and/or items that are easily converted into cash.

Margin account: A brokerage account that allows a person to trade securities on credit. A **margin call** is a demand for more collateral on the account.

Money supply: The currency held by the public, plus checking accounts in commercial banks and savings institutions.

Mortgage-backed securities: Created when a bank, builder, or government agency gathers together a group of mortgages and then sells bonds to other institutions and the public. The investors receive their proportionate share of the interest payments on the loans as well as the principal payments. Usually, the mortgages in question are guaranteed by the government.

Municipal bond: Issued by governmental units such as states, cities, local taxing authorities, and other agencies. Interest is exempt from U.S.—and sometimes state and local—income tax. *Municipal bond unit investment trusts* offer a portfolio of many different municipal bonds chosen by professionals. The income is exempt from federal income taxes.

Mutual fund: A portfolio of professionally bought and managed financial assets in which you pool your money along with that of many other people. A share price is based on net asset value, or the value of all the investments owned by the funds, less any debt, and divided by the total number of shares. The major advantage, relative to investing individually in only a small number of stocks, is less risk—the holdings are spread out over many assets and if one or two do badly the remainder may shield you from the losses. *Bond funds* are mutual funds that deal in the bond market exclusively. *Money market mutual funds* buy in the so-called money market—institutions that need to borrow large sums of money for short terms. These funds often offer special checking account advantages.

National debt: The debt of the national government, as distinguished from the debts of political subdivisions of the nation and of private business and individuals.

National debt ceiling: Total borrowing limit set by Congress beyond which the U.S. national debt cannot rise. This limit is periodically raised by congressional vote.

Option: A type of contractual agreement between a buyer and a seller to buy or sell shares of a security. A **call** option contract gives the right to purchase shares of a specific stock at a stated price within a given period of time. A **put** option contract gives the buyer the right to sell shares of a specific stock at a stated price within a given period of time.

Per capita income: The total income of a group divided by the number of people in the group.

Prime interest rate: The rate charged by banks on short-term loans to large commercial customers with the highest credit rating.

Producer price index: A statistical measure of the change in the price of wholesale goods. It is reported for 3 different stages of the production chain: crude, intermediate, and finished goods.

Program trading: Trading techniques involving large numbers and large blocks of stocks, usually used in conjunction with computer programs. Techniques include *index arbitrage*, in which traders profit from price differences between stocks and futures contracts on stock indexes, and *portfolio insurance*, which is the use of stock-index futures to protect stock investors from potentially large losses when the market drops.

Public debt: The total of a nation's debts owed by state, local, and national government. Increases in this sum, reflected in public-sector deficits, indicate how much of the nation's spending is being financed by borrowing rather than by taxation.

Recession: A mild decrease in economic activity marked by a decline in real (inflation-adjusted) GDP, employment, and trade, usually lasting from 6 months to a year, and marked by widespread decline in many sectors of the economy.

Savings Association Insurance Fund (SAIF): Created in 1989 to insure accounts in savings and loan associations up to $100,000.

Seasonal adjustment: Statistical changes made to compensate for regular fluctuations in data that are so great they tend to distort the statistics and make comparisons meaningless. For instance, seasonal adjustments are made for a slowdown in housing construction in midwinter and for the rise in farm income in the fall after summer crops are harvested.

Short-selling: Borrowing shares of stock from a brokerage firm and selling them, hoping to buy the shares back at a lower price, return them, and realize a profit from the decline in prices.

Stagnation: Economic slowdown in which there is little growth in the GDP, capital investment, and real income.

Stock: *Common stocks* are shares of ownership in a corporation. For publicly held firms, the stock typically trades on an exchange, such as the New York Stock Exchange; for closely held firms, the founders and managers own most of the stock. There can be wide swings in the prices of this kind of stock. *Preferred stock* is a type of stock on which a fixed dividend must be paid before holders of common stock are issued their share of the issuing corporation's earnings. Preferred stock is less risky than common stock. *Convertible preferred stock* can be converted into the common stock of the company that issued the preferred. *Over-the-counter stock* is not traded on the major or regional exchanges, but rather through dealers from whom you buy directly. *Blue chip* stocks are so called because they have been leading stocks for a long time. *Growth* stocks are from companies that reinvest their earnings, rather than pay dividends, with the expectation of future stock price appreciation.

Supply-side economics: A school of thinking about economic policy holding that lowering income tax rates will inevitably lead to enhanced economic growth and general revitalization of the economy.

Takeover: Acquisition of one company by another company or group by sale or merger. A *friendly takeover* occurs when the acquired company's management is agreeable to the merger; when management is opposed to the merger, it is a *hostile* takeover.

Tender offer: A public offer to buy a company's stock; usually priced at a premium above the market.

Zero coupon bond: A corporate or government bond that is issued at a deep discount from the maturity value and pays no interest during the life of the bond. It is redeemable at face value.

Minerals

Source: U.S. Geological Survey, U.S. Dept. of the Interior, as of mid-2006; minerals.usgs.gov/minerals

Aluminum: the 2nd most abundant metallic element in the earth's crust. Bauxite is the main source of aluminum. Guinea, Australia, and Jamaica have about 60% of the world's reserves. Main uses in the U.S. are for transportation (37%), packaging (22%), and construction (16%).

Chromium: produced mostly in India, Kazakhstan, and South Africa. The metallurgical industry uses about 91% of the chromite consumed in the world; the chemical industry, 6%; and the refractory and foundry industry, 3%.

Cobalt: used in superalloys for jet engines; cemented carbides for cutting tools; batteries, catalysts, ceramics, and other chemical applications; permanent magnets, tool steels, and other alloys. Australia, Canada, Dem. Rep. of the Congo (Congo-Kinshasa), Cuba, Russia, and Zambia account for most of the world cobalt mine production.

Construction aggregates: construction sand and gravel and crushed stone are two of the most accessible natural resources in the world. Construction sand and gravel is produced in every U.S. state, and crushed stone is mined in every State except Delaware. They are used in construction, agriculture, chemicals, and metallurgy and are produced worldwide.

Copper: main uses of copper and copper alloy products in the U.S. are in building construction (49%), electrical and electronic products (20%), consumer and general products (10%), industrial machinery and equipment (9%), and transportation (11%). The leading mine producers are Chile, the U.S. (mostly in Arizona, Utah, and New Mexico), Indonesia, Peru, Australia, Russia, China, and Canada.

Gold: used in the U.S. in jewelry and the arts (92%), electrical and electronics (4%), dentistry (3%), and other industrial (1%). South Africa has about half of the world's resources; significant quantities are also present in the U.S. (mined in most western states and Alaska), Australia, Russia, Uzbekistan, Canada, and Brazil.

Gypsum: used in wallboard and plaster products, cement production, and agriculture. Leading producers are the U.S., Iran, Canada, Spain, China, and Mexico.

Iron ore: the source of primary iron for the world's iron and steel industries. Major iron ore producers include Brazil, Australia, China, India, Russia, Ukraine, and the U.S.

Lead: Australia, China, the U.S. (mostly in Alaska and Missouri), Peru, Canada, and Mexico are the world's largest producers of lead. The major end use in the U.S. is in lead acid storage batteries (87%). The U.S. produces and consumes about 20% of the world's lead metal. Most U.S. lead production (88%) is recycled material, and 97% of lead acid batteries (mostly automotive) are recycled.

Manganese: essential to iron and steel production. South Africa and Ukraine have over 80% and 10%, respectively, of the world's identified resources.

Nickel: vital to the stainless steel industry, and used to make superalloys. Leading producers are Russia, Canada, Australia, the French overseas territory of New Caledonia, and Indonesia.

Phosphate rock: used in fertilizers, animal feed supplements, chemicals, and food. Phosphorus is an essential element for plant and animal nutrition. The U.S., Morocco, China, Russia, and Tunisia are the world's leading producers.

Platinum-group metals: this group consists of 6 metals: platinum, palladium, rhodium, ruthenium, iridium, and osmium. They commonly occur together in nature and are among the scarcest of the metallic elements. In the U.S., the automotive and chemical industries use PGMs mainly as catalysts. They also are consumed in electrical and electronics, glass, dental, and medical industries. Russia and South Africa have most of the world's reserves.

Salt: used in chemicals, highway deicing, industry, agriculture, food, and water treatment. Leading producers are the U.S., China, Germany, India, and Canada.

Silver: used in industrial and decorative applications, coins, jewelry and silverware, and photography. Silver is mined in more than 60 countries. Alaska and Nevada produce more than 70% of U.S. silver.

Soda ash: a raw material for glass, chemicals, and detergents, it can be mined or produced synthetically. The U.S. is now the world's second leading producer of natural soda ash, having been displaced in 2004 by China.

Sulfur: used in agricultural chemicals production, oil refining, metal mining, and many other industries. It is produced as a byproduct of oil refining, natural gas processing, and nonferrous metal smelting. Leading producers are the U.S., Canada, Russia, China, and Japan.

Titanium: ilmenite and rutile are the major mineral sources of titanium. Titanium minerals are used to produce TiO_2 pigments (95%) and other uses (5%) including alloys, ceramics, chemicals, titanium metal, and welding rod coatings. Major mining operations are in Australia, Canada, China, Norway, and South Africa. U.S. mine production is in Florida, Georgia, and Virginia.

Zinc: used as a protective coating on steel, as diecastings, as an alloying metal with copper to make brass, and as a component of chemical compounds in rubber and paints. Leading producers are China, Australia, Peru, Canada, the U.S. (in Alaska, Missouri, and Tennessee), and Mexico.

U.S. Reliance on Foreign Supplies of Minerals

Source: U.S. Geological Survey, U.S. Dept. of the Interior

Mineral	% Imported in 2005	Major sources (2000-2004)	Major Uses
Arsenic (trioxide)	100%	China, Morocco, Chile, Mexico	Wood preservatives, nonferrous alloys
Asbestos	100	Canada	Roofing products, gaskets, friction products
Bauxite & alumina	100	Jamaica, Australia, Guinea, Suriname	Aluminum production, refractories, abrasives, chemicals
Columbium (niobium)	100	Brazil, Canada, Estonia, China	Steelmaking, superalloys
Fluorspar	100	China, South Africa, Mexico	Hydrofluoric acid, aluminum fluoride, steelmaking
Graphite (natural)	100	China, Mexico, Canada, Brazil	Refractories, batteries, foundry operations, lubricants, brake linings, steelmaking
Indium	100	China, Canada, Japan, Russia	Coatings, electrical components, semicondustors, solders, alloys
Manganese	100	South Africa, Gabon, Australia, China	Iron & steelmaking, batteries, agricultural chemicals
Quartz crystal (industrial)	100	Brazil, Germany, Madagascar, Canada	Electronics, optical applications
Rare earths	100	China, France, Japan, Austria	Catalysts, metallurgy, glass polishing, ceramics, phosphors, magnets
Rubidium	100	Canada	DNA separation, fiber optics, inorganic chemicals, lamps, night vision devices
Strontium	100	Mexico, Germany	Television picture tubes, ferrite magnets, pyrotechnics
Thallium	100	Belgium, Russia, Netherlands, France	Medical imaging, radiation detection, superconductors, glass, alloys
Thorium	100	France	High-temperature ceramics, catalysts, welding electrodes
Vanadium	100	Czech Republic, Canada, South Africa, Swaziland	Steelmaking, catalysts
Yttrium	100	China, Netherlands, Japan, Austria	Lamp & cathode ray tube phosphors, alloys
Gallium	99	China, France, Japan, Russia	Electronic components
Gemstones	99	Israel, India, Belgium	Jewelry, carvings, gem & mineral collections
Bismuth	95	Belgium, Mexico, China, UK	Alloys, solder, ammunition, metallurgy, pharmaceuticals, chemicals
Tin	93	Peru, China, Bolivia, Indonesia	Chemicals, tinplate, solder, alloys
Platinum	91	South Africa, Germany, Canada	Catalysts, jewelry, dental & medical alloys
Tantalum	91	Australia, Canada	Capacitors, superalloys, cemented carbide tools
Stone (dimension)	88	Italy, India, Canada, Spain	Construction, monuments
Diamond (natural industrial)	84	Ireland, Russia, Switzerland, Belgium	Abrasives, stone cutting, highway repair & construction
Antimony	82	China, Mexico, Belgium, South Africa	Flame retardants, transportation, chemicals, ceramics & glass
Barite	82	China, India	Oil & gas well drilling fluids, fillers & extenders, chemicals
Iodine	82	Chile, Japan, Netherlands	Bioides & disinfectants, catalysts, chemicals, nutrition, pharmaceuticals
Rhenium	81	Chile, Kazakhstan, Germany	Petroleum-reforming catalysts, superalloys
Potash	80	Canada, Belarus, Russia, Germany	Fertilizers, chemicals
Cobalt	78	Finland, Norway, Russia, Canada	Superalloys, cemented carbides, magnetic alloys, chemicals
Palladium	78	Russia, South Africa, Belgium, UK	Jewelry, catalysts, dental alloys, chemicals, electronics
Tungsten	70	China, Canada, Germany, Portugal	Cemented carbides, electrical & electronic components, tool steels, alloys
Chromium	69	South Africa, Kazakhstan, Zimbabwe, Russia	Steel, chemicals, refractories
Titanium mineral concentrates	63	South Africa, Australia, Canada, Ukraine	Pigment, metal, welding rod coatings, chemicals, ceramics
Magnesium metal	61	Canada, Russia, China, Israel	Castings & wrought products, aluminum alloys, desulfurization of iron & steel
Titanium (sponge)	60	Kazakhstan, Japan, Russia	High-strength alloys for aerospace and nonaerospace uses
Silver	57	Mexico, Canada, Peru, Chile	Coins & medals, industrial applications, jewelry & silverware, photography
Magnesium compounds	56	China, Canada, Australia, Austria	Refractories, agriculture, chemicals, construction, environment, industry
Peat	55	Canada	Horticulture, absorbents, filter media
Nickel	54	Canada, Russia, Norway, Australia	Nonferrous alloys, superalloys, steel, electroplating
Silicon	52	Brazil, South Africa, Canada, Venezuela	Iron & steel alloys, aluminum & aluminum alloys, specialty chemicals
Zinc	52	Canada, Mexico, Peru	Galvanizing, zinc-base alloys, brass & bronze

World Mineral Reserve Base, 2005

Source: U.S. Geological Survey, U.S. Dept. of the Interior; as of year-end 2004

Mineral	Reserve Base[1]	Mineral	Reserve Base[1]
Aluminum	32,000 mil metric tons[2]	Nickel	140 mil metric tons
Chromium	1,800 mil metric tons[3]	Phosphate Rock	50,000 mil metric tons
Cobalt	13 mil metric tons	Platinum-Group Metals	80,000 metric tons
Copper	940 mil metric tons	Silver	570,000 metric tons
Gold	90,000 metric tons	Soda Ash (Natural)	40,000 mil metric tons
Iron Ore	370,000 mil metric tons	Titanium (ilmenite/rutile)	1,300 mil metric tons[4]
Lead	140 mil metric tons	Zinc	460 mil metric tons
Manganese	5,200 mil metric tons		

(1) Includes demonstrated resources that are currently economic or marginally economic, plus some that are currently subeconomic. (2) Bauxite. (3) Chromite ore, gross weight, marketable product. (4) Titanium dioxide (TiO_2) content of ilmenite and rutile.

World Gold Production, 1980-2005[1]

Source: U.S. Geological Survey, U.S. Dept. of the Interior

(thousands of troy ounces)

Year	World prod.	Africa			North and South America				Other			
		South Africa	Ghana	Congo Dem. Rep.	United States	Canada	Mexico	Colombia	Australia	China	Philip-pines	Russia[2]
1980	39,197	21,669	353	96	970	1,627	196	510	548	NA	753	8,425
1985	49,284	21,565	299	257	2,427	2,815	266	1,142	1,881	1,950	1,063	8,700
1990	70,207	19,454	541	299	9,458	5,447	311	944	7,849	3,215	791	9,710
1991	70,423	19,326	846	283	9,454	5,676	326	1,120	7,530	3,858	833	8,359
1992	73,530	19,743	998	225	10,617	5,189	318	1,033	7,825	4,501	730	8,232
1993	73,300	19,908	1,250	280	10,642	4,917	357	883	7,948	5,144	509	8,228
1994	72,500	16,650	1,400	357	10,500	4,710	447	668	8,237	4,240	870	8,173
1995	71,800	16,800	1,710	322	10,200	4,890	652	680	8,150	4,500	873	4,250
1996	73,600	16,000	1,580	264	10,500	5,350	787	710	9,310	4,660	970	3,960
1997	78,900	15,800	1,760	13	11,600	5,510	836	605	10,100	5,630	1,050	3,990
1998	80,300	15,000	2,330	5	11,800	5,320	817	605	10,000	5,720	1,090	3,690
1999	82,600	14,500	2,570	7	11,000	5,070	764	1,410	9,680	5,560	1,000	4,050
2000	83,300	13,900	2,320	2	11,300	5,020	848	1,190	9,530	5,790	1,170	4,600
2001	82,300	12,700	2,200	196	10,800	5,110	757	701	9,010	5,950	1,090	4,900
2002	82,000	9,600	2,230	244	9,580	4,880	686	669	8,560	6,170	1,150	5,410
2003	82,300	12,000	2,270	132	8,910	4,530	656	1,500	9,070	6,590	1,220	5,470
2004	78,400	11,000	2,030	183	8,290	4,160	701	1,210	8,330	6,910	1,140	5,250
2005[E]	79,800	9,480	2,000	183	8,380	3,810	976	1,150[E]	8,420	7,230	1,210	5,440

(1) Figures are rounded. (2) Figures for 1980-94 are for USSR as constituted prior to Dec. 1991; after 1994, Russia only.
E = Estimated. NA = Not available.

U.S. Nonfuel Minerals Production, 1998-2005

Source: U.S. Geological Survey, U.S. Dept. of the Interior

Production as measured by mine shipments, sales, or marketable production (including consumption by producers).

		1998	2000	2001	2002	2003	2004	2005
Beryllium (metal equivalent)	metric tons	243	180	100	80	85	90	110
Copper (recoverable content of ores, etc.)	thousand metric tons	1,860	1,450	1,340	1,140	1,120	1,160	1,140
Gold (recoverable content of ores, etc.)	metric tons	366	353	335	298	277	258	261[P]
Iron ore, usable	million metric tons	62.9	63.1	46.2	51.6	48.6	54.7	54.3
Lead (recoverable content of ores, etc.)	thousand metric tons	481	449	454	440	449	430	426
Magnesium metal (primary)	thousand metric tons	106	W	W	W	W	W	W
Molybdenum (content of ore and concentrates)	metric tons	53,300	40,900	37,600	32,300	33,500	41,500	58,000
Silver (recoverable content of ores, etc.)	metric tons	2,060	1,860	1,740	1,420	1,240	1,250	1,230
Zinc (recoverable content of ores, etc.)	thousand metric tons	722	805	799	700	738	715	720
Asbestos	thousand metric tons	6	5	5	3	—	—	—
Barite (sold or used)	thousand metric tons	476	392	400	420	468	532	489
Boron minerals (B_2O_3 equivalent)	thousand metric tons	587	546	536	543	605	637	657[E]
Bromine	million kilograms	230	228	212	222	216	222	224
Cement (portland, masonry)	thousand metric tons	83,931	87,846	88,900	89,732	92,843	97,434	99,319
Clays	thousand metric tons	41,900	40,800	39,600	39,300	40,000	41,600	41,800[E]
Diatomite	thousand metric tons	725	677	644	599	625	620	653
Feldspar	thousand metric tons	820[E]	790[E]	800[E]	790[E]	800[E]	770[E]	750[E]
Garnet (industrial)	metric tons	74,000	60,200	52,700	38,500	29,200	28,400	40,100
Gemstones (natural)	million dollars	14.3	17.2	14.9	12.6	12.5	14.5	13.4
Gypsum	thousand metric tons	19,000	19,500	16,300	15,700	16,700	17,200	21,100
Helium (extracted from natural gas)	million cubic meters	114	98	87	87[E]	87	86	84[E]
Helium (Grade A sold)	million cubic meters	114	127	132	127	122	130	133
Iodine	thousand kilograms	1,490	1,470	1,290	1,420	1,090	1,130	1,570
Lime	thousand metric tons	20,100	19,500	18,900	17,900	19,200	20,000	20,000
Mica (scrap & flake)	thousand metric tons	87	101	98	81	79	99	78
Peat	thousand metric tons	685	792	736	642	634	696	685
Perlite (sold and used by producers)	thousand metric tons	685	672	588	521	493	508	508
Phosphate rock (marketable product)	thousand metric tons	44,200	38,600	31,900	36,100	35,000	35,800	36,300
Potash (K_2O equivalent)	thousand metric tons	1,300	1,300	1,200	1,200	1,100	1,300	1,200
Pumice and pumicite	thousand metric tons	872	1,050	920	956	870	1,490	1,270
Salt	thousand metric tons	40,800	43,300	42,200	37,700	41,100	45,000	42,600[E]
Sand and gravel (construction)	million metric tons	1,070	1,120	1,130	1,130	1,160	1,240	1,270[E]
Sand and gravel (industrial)	thousand metric tons	28,200	28,400	27,900	27,300	27,500	29,700	30,600
Soda ash (sodium carbonate)	thousand metric tons	10,100	10,200	10,300	10,500	10,600	11,000	11,000
Sodium sulfate (natural)	thousand metric tons	290	NA	NA	NA	NA	NA	NA
Stone (crushed)	million metric tons	1,510	1,550	1,590	1,510	1,530	1,630	1,690
Stone (dimension)	thousand metric tons	1,140	1,320	1,220	1,260	1,340	1,460	1,510
Sulfur (in all forms)	thousand metric tons	11,700	10,500	9,470	9,270	9,600	10,100	9,460
Talc	thousand metric tons	971	851	863	828	840	833	856
Titanium mineral concentrates (TiO_2 content)	thousand metric tons	400	300	300	300	300	300	300
Vermiculite concentrate[E]	thousand metric tons	W	150[E]	110	100	110	100	100

W = Withheld to avoid disclosing company proprietary data. — = No production. E = Estimated. NA = Not available. P = Preliminary.

TRADE AND TRANSPORTATION

U.S. Trade With Selected Countries and Major Areas, 2005

Source: Office of Trade and Economic Analysis, U.S. Dept. of Commerce
(in millions of dollars; top 25 countries and areas ranked by amount of total trade with U.S.)

COUNTRY	Total Trade with U.S.	U.S. Exports to	Rank[1]	U.S. Imports from	Rank[1]	U.S. Trade Balance with	Rank[2]
Canada	$502,283.0	$211,898.7	1	$290,384.3	1	$−78,485.6	3
Mexico	290,473.4	120,364.8	2	170,108.6	3	−49,743.8	5
China	285,395.4	41,925.3	4	243,470.1	2	−201,544.8	1
Japan	193,488.2	55,484.5	3	138,003.7	4	−82,519.2	2
Federal Republic of Germany	118,934.6	34,183.7	6	84,750.9	5	−50,567.2	4
United Kingdom	89,620.4	38,587.8	5	51,032.6	6	−12,444.8	15
Korea, South	71,546.4	27,765.0	7	43,781.4	7	−16,016.5	12
Taiwan	56,895.0	22,069.2	10	34,825.8	8	−12,756.6	13
France	56,252.5	22,410.4	9	33,842.1	10	−11,431.7	16
Malaysia	44,146.0	10,460.8	18	33,685.2	11	−23,224.3	7
Italy	42,533.6	11,524.3	16	31,009.3	12	−19,484.9	10
Netherlands	41,346.6	26,484.6	8	14,862.0	22	11,622.6	230
Venezuela	40,399.0	6,420.9	27	33,978.1	9	−27,557.2	6
Brazil	39,807.2	15,371.7	15	24,435.5	15	−9,063.8	21
Ireland	38,068.8	9,335.7	20	28,733.1	13	−19,397.4	11
Singapore	35,752.3	20,642.2	11	15,110.1	21	5,532.2	225
Saudi Arabia	34,005.4	6,812.8	26	27,192.6	14	−20,379.8	9
Belgium	31,713.5	18,690.6	12	13,022.9	24	5,667.7	226
Thailand	27,146.4	7,256.6	23	19,889.8	17	−12,633.1	14
India	26,793.6	7,989.4	22	18,804.2	18	−10,814.8	18
Israel	26,567.8	9,737.3	19	16,830.5	19	−7,093.1	25
Nigeria	25,860.6	1,621.2	53	24,239.4	16	−22,618.2	8
Hong Kong	25,242.7	16,351.0	13	8,891.7	30	7,459.3	228
Switzerland	23,719.7	10,719.8	17	12,999.9	25	−2,280.0	39
Australia	23,170.4	15,828.2	14	7,342.2	35	8,486.0	229
Russia	19,269.1	3,962.4	33	15,306.7	20	−11,344.3	17
MAJOR AREA/GROUP							
North America	792,756.4	332,263.5	NA	460,492.9	NA	−128,229.4	NA
Western Europe	566,501.9	211,254.3	NA	355,247.6	NA	−143,993.3	NA
Euro Area	366,377.4	137,496.7	NA	228,880.7	NA	−91,384.0	NA
European Union (EU)	495,212.8	186,437.3	NA	308,775.5	NA	−122,338.2	NA
Africa	80,758.8	15,547.0	NA	65,211.8	NA	−49,664.8	NA
OECD	1,621,192.9	636,648.3	NA	984,544.6	NA	−347,896.2	NA
Pacific Rim Countries	774,734.4	223,334.0	NA	551,400.4	NA	−328,066.4	NA
Asia/Near East	94,337.9	31,893.6	NA	62,444.3	NA	−30,550.8	NA
Asia/NICS	189,436.6	86,827.5	NA	102,609.1	NA	−15,781.6	NA
Asia/South	37,057.0	10,045.2	NA	27,011.8	NA	−16,966.6	NA
ASEAN	148,551.6	49,636.7	NA	98,914.9	NA	−49,278.2	NA
APEC	1,639,695.5	575,440.1	NA	1,064,255.4	NA	−488,815.3	NA
South/Central America	195,286.0	72,413.0	NA	122,873.0	NA	−50,460.1	NA
Twenty Latin American Republics	462,260.4	182,836.4	NA	279,424.0	NA	−96,587.6	NA
Central American Common Market	25,639.0	12,167.5	NA	13,471.5	NA	−1,304.0	NA
LAFTA	423,284.1	162,709.5	NA	260,574.6	NA	−97,865.1	NA
NATO	947,496.5	387,759.4	NA	559,737.1	NA	−171,977.7	NA
OPEC	157,014.2	32,073.8	NA	124,940.4	NA	−92,866.6	NA
WORLD TOTAL	**2,579,432.1**	**905,977.6**	**NA**	**1,673,454.5**	**NA**	**−767,476.9**	**NA**

(1) Rank shown is for column to the left. (2) Ranking includes the territories as well as nations. Rank is by size of U.S. trade deficit. NA = Not applicable. **Note:** Details may not equal totals because of rounding or incomplete enumeration.

Definitions of areas/groups used in the table, as provided by the source: **North America**—Canada, Mexico. **Western Europe**—Albania, Andorra, Armenia, Austria, Azerbaijan, Belarus, Belgium, Bosnia-Herzegovina, Bulgaria, Croatia, Cyprus, Czech Republic, Denmark, Estonia, Faeroe Islands, Finland, France, Georgia, Germany, Gibraltar, Greece, Hungary, Iceland, Ireland, Italy, Liechtenstein, Kazakhstan, Kyrgyzstan, Latvia, Lithuania, Luxembourg, Macedonia, Malta, Moldova, Monaco, Netherlands, Norway, Poland, Portugal, Romania, Russia, San Marino, Serbia and Montenegro, Slovakia, Slovenia, Spain, Svalbard/Jan Mayen Island, Sweden, Switzerland, Tajikistan, Turkey, Turkmenistan, Ukraine, United Kingdom, Uzbekistan, Vatican City. **Euro Area**—Austria, Belgium, Finland, France, Germany, Greece, Ireland, Italy, Luxembourg, Netherlands, Portugal, Spain. **EU**—(European Union) Euro Area plus Denmark, Sweden, United Kingdom. *Not including 10 states that joined 5/1/04.* **EFTA**—(European Free Trade Assoc.) Iceland, Liechtenstein, Norway, Switzerland. **Eastern Europe**—Austria, Belgium, Cyprus, Czech Republic, Denmark, Estonia, Finland, France, Germany, Greece, Hungary, Ireland, Italy, Latvia, Lithuania, Luxembourg, Malta, Netherlands, Poland, Portugal, Slovakia, Slovenia, Spain, Sweden, United Kingdom. **Former Soviet Republics**—Armenia, Azerbaijan, Belarus, Estonia, Georgia, Kazakhstan, Kyrgyzstan, Latvia, Lithuania, Moldova, Russia, Tajikistan, Turkmenistan, Ukraine, Uzbekistan. **Africa**—Algeria, Angola, Benin, Botswana, British Indian Ocean Territories, Burkina, Burundi, Cameroon, Cape Verde, Central African Republic, Chad, Comoros, Congo (Brazzaville), Congo (Kinshasa), Djibouti, Egypt, Equatorial Guinea, Eritrea, Ethiopia, French Southern and Antarctic Lands, Gabon, Gambia, Ghana, Guinea, Guinea-Bissau, Ivory Coast, Kenya, Lesotho, Liberia, Libya, Madagascar, Malawi, Mali, Mauritania, Mauritius, Mayotte, Morocco, Mozambique, Namibia, Niger, Nigeria, Reunion, Rwanda, St. Helena, São Tomé and Príncipe, Senegal, Seychelles, Sierra Leone, Somalia, South Africa, Sudan, Swaziland, Tanzania, Togo, Tunisia, Uganda, Western Sahara, Zambia, Zimbabwe. **OECD**—(Org. for Econ. Cooperation & Development in Europe) Austria, Belgium, Denmark, Finland, France, Germany, Greece, Iceland, Ireland, Italy, Liechtenstein, Luxembourg, Monaco, Netherlands, Norway, Portugal, San Marino, Spain, Svalbard/Jan Mayen Island, Sweden, Switzerland, Turkey, United Kingdom. **Pacific Rim Countries/Territories**—Australia, Brunei, Canada, Chile, China, Hong Kong, Indonesia, Japan, Korea, Macao, Malaysia, New Zealand, Papua New Guinea, Philippines, Singapore, Taiwan. **Asia/Near East**—Bahrain, Iran, Iraq, Israel, Jordan, Kuwait, Lebanon, Oman, Qatar, Saudi Arabia, Syrian Arab Republic, United Arab Emirates, Yemen. **Asia/NICS**—(Newly Industrialized Countries) Hong Kong, S. Korea, Singapore, Taiwan. **Asia/South**—Afghanistan, Bangladesh, India, Nepal, Pakistan, Sri Lanka. **ASEAN**—(Association of Southeast Asian Nations) Brunei, Cambodia, Indonesia, Laos, Malaysia, Myanmar, Philippines, Singapore, Thailand, Vietnam. **APEC**—(Asia-Pacific Economic Cooperation) Australia, Brunei, Canada, Chile, China, Hong Kong, Indonesia, Japan, S. Korea, Malaysia, Mexico, New Zealand, Papua New Guinea, Peru, Philippines, Russia, Singapore, Taiwan, Thailand, Vietnam. **South/Central America**—Anguilla, Antigua and Barbuda, Argentina, Aruba, Bahamas, Barbados, Belize, Bermuda, Bolivia, Brazil, British Virgin Islands, Cayman Islands, Chile, Colombia, Costa Rica, Cuba, Dominica, Dominican Republic, Ecuador, El Salvador, Falkland Islands, French Guiana, Grenada, Guadeloupe, Guatemala, Guyana, Haiti, Honduras, Jamaica, Martinique, Montserrat, Netherlands Antilles, Nicaragua, Panama, Paraguay, Peru, St. Kitts and Nevis, St. Lucia, St. Vincent and the Grenadines, Suriname, Trinidad and Tobago, Turks and Caicos Islands, Uruguay, Venezuela. **Twenty Latin American Republics**—Argentina, Bolivia, Brazil, Chile, Colombia, Costa Rica, Cuba, Dominican Republic, Ecuador, El Salvador, Guatemala, Haiti, Honduras, Mexico, Nicaragua, Panama, Paraguay, Peru, Uruguay, Venezuela. **Central American Common Market**—Costa Rica, El Salvador, Guatemala, Honduras, Nicaragua. **LAFTA**—(Latin American Free Trade Assoc.) Argentina, Bolivia, Brazil, Chile, Colombia, Ecuador, Mexico, Paraguay, Peru, Uruguay, Venezuela. **NATO**—Belgium, Canada, Denmark, France, Germany, Greece, Iceland, Ireland, Italy, Liechtenstein, Luxembourg, Monaco, Netherlands, Norway, Portugal, San Marino, Spain, Svalbard Jan Junean Island, Sweden, Switzerland, Turkey, United Kingdom. **OPEC**—Algeria, Indonesia, Iran, Iraq, Kuwait, Libya, Nigeria, Qatar, Saudi Arabia, United Arab Emirates, Venezuela.

U.S. Exports and Imports by Principal Commodity Groupings, 2005
Source: Office of Trade and Economic Analysis, U.S. Dept. of Commerce
(millions of dollars)

Items	Exports	Imports	Items	Exports	Imports
TOTAL	**$905,978**	**$1,673,455**	Jewelry	$3,029	$9,696
Agricultural commodities	63,139	59,530	Lighting, plumbing	1,694	7,591
Animal feeds	4,029	699	Metal manufactures[1]	13,510	24,777
Cereal flour	2,015	3,010	Metalworking machinery	6,457	7,530
Coffee	5	2,502	Nickel	752	2,178
Corn	5,062	125	Optical goods	3,076	3,789
Cotton, raw and linters	3,929	20	Paper and paperboard	11,457	17,561
Hides and skins	1,629	79	Photographic equipment	3,343	4,481
Live animals	645	2,081	Plastic articles[1]	8,036	13,633
Meat and preparations	6,669	5,747	Platinum	610	3,916
Oils/fats, vegetable	1,003	2,090	Pottery	104	1,688
Rice	1,272	218	Power generating mach.	41,296	41,263
Soybeans	6,282	63	Printed materials	5,445	4,917
Sugar	8	706	Records/magnetic media	5,142	7,258
Tobacco, unmanufactured	990	750	Rubber articles[1]	1,598	2,925
Vegetables and fruits	10,259	14,082	Rubber tires and tubes	2,778	7,725
Wheat	4,410	174	Scientific instruments	34,544	30,242
Manufactured goods	**685,398**	**1,287,376**	Ships, boats	1,913	1,719
ADP equipment; office machines	29,800	98,584	Silver and bullion	287	1,178
Airplane parts	17,538	5,592	Spacecraft	217	0
Airplanes	30,291	10,734	Specialized industrial machinery	33,144	31,076
Aluminum	4,483	11,931	Television, VCR, etc.	20,974	104,079
Artwork/antiques	1,858	5,512	Textile yarn, fabric	11,830	21,249
Basketware, etc.	5,612	8,585	Toys/games/sporting goods	3,756	25,069
Chemicals - cosmetics	8,059	7,922	Travel goods	379	6,183
Chemicals - dyeing	4,901	2,971	Vehicles	71,747	195,926
Chemicals - fertilizers	2,990	3,701	Watches/clocks/parts	256	3,939
Chemicals - inorganic	7,698	10,165	Wood manufactures	1,818	12,847
Chemicals - medicinal	25,012	39,176	**Mineral fuels**	**26,488**	**289,723**
Chemicals - organic	26,765	38,009	Coal	3,471	2,418
Chemicals - plastics	28,861	17,385	Crude oil	595	182,944
Chemicals[1]	15,846	8,939	Liquified propane/butane	587	4,371
Clothing	4,129	76,383	Mineral fuels[1]	3,191	3,055
Copper	2,118	7,040	Natural gas	3,094	34,911
Electrical machinery	74,286	99,121	Petroleum preparations	14,782	59,698
Footwear	508	17,932	**Other commodities**		
Furniture and bedding	4,415	30,633	Alcoholic bev.,distilled	726	4,360
Gem diamonds	2,578	16,238	Cigarettes	1,202	208
General industrial machinery	38,902	52,333	Cork, wood, lumber	4,038	10,939
Glass	2,696	2,782	Crude fertilizers	1,702	1,698
Glassware	784	2,158	Fish and preparations	3,864	11,915
Gold, nonmonetary	5,533	4,430	Metal ores; scrap	11,057	5,335
Iron and steel mill products	10,430	24,632	Pulp and waste paper	5,093	3,049

(1) Those not specified elsewhere. **NOTE:** Not all products are listed in each commodity group, but they are included in totals.

Trends in U.S. Foreign Trade, 1790-2005
Source: Office of Trade and Economic Analysis, U.S. Dept. of Commerce

In 1790, U.S. exports and imports combined came to $43 million and there was a $3 million trade deficit. In 2005, U.S. exports and imports combined amounted to $2.6 trillion, and the trade deficit, which has steadily been climbing since the last recorded surplus in 1975, reached more than $767 billion, the highest dollar total in history.
(in millions of dollars)

Year	Exports	Imports	Trade Balance	Year	Exports	Imports	Trade Balance	Year	Exports	Imports	Trade Balance
1790	$20	$23	$-3	1885	$742	$578	$165	1980	$220,626	$244,871	$-24,245
1795	48	70	-22	1890	858	789	69	1985	213,133	345,276	-132,143
1800	71	91	-20	1895	808	732	76	1990	394,030	495,042	-101,012
1805	96	121	-25	1900	1,394	850	545	1991	421,730	485,453	-63,723
1810	67	85	-19	1905	1,519	1,118	401	1992	448,164	532,665	-84,501
1815	53	113	-60	1910	1,745	1,557	188	1993	465,091	580,659	-115,568
1820	70	74	-5	1915	2,769	1,674	1,094	1994	512,626	683,256	-170,630
1825	91	90	1	1920	8,228	5,278	2,950	1995	584,742	743,445	-158,703
1830	72	63	9	1925	4,910	4,227	683	1996	625,075	795,289	-170,214
1835	115	137	-22	1930	3,843	3,061	782	1997	689,182	870,671	-181,489
1840	124	98	25	1935	2,283	2,047	235	1998	682,138	911,896	-229,758
1845	106	113	-7	1940	4,021	2,625	1,396	1999	695,797	1,024,618	-328,821
1850	144	174	-29	1945	9,806	4,159	5,646	2000	781,918	1,218,022	-436,104
1855	219	258	-39	1950	9,997	8,954	1,043	2001	729,100	1,140,999	-411,899
1860	334	354	-20	1955	14,298	11,566	2,732	2002	693,103	1,161,366	-468,263
1865	166	239	-73	1960	19,659	15,073	4,586	2003	724,771	1,257,121	-532,350
1870	393	436	-43	1965	26,742	21,520	5,222	2004	818,775	1,469,704	-650,930
1875	513	533	-20	1970	42,681	40,356	2,325	2005	905,978	1,673,455	-767,477
1880	836	668	168	1975	107,652	98,503	9,149				

World Trade Organization (WTO)

The World Trade Organization is an international body that seeks to promote free trade by eliminating barriers to trade. Founded in 1995, by 2006 the WTO had grown to include 150 countries with several others, including Russia, seeking membership.

The WTO suspended international negotiations following the July 2006 round of talks in Doha, Qatar, in which the body was unable to make progress on reducing trade barriers, particularly on agricultural products. Developing countries lobbied for the U.S. and the European Union to lower domestic subsidies and foreign import barriers for their agricultural products, while the U.S. and European nations pushed for less developed countries to further open their markets to foreign goods. With the collapse of the Doha talks, representatives from several member nations, including the U.S., said they would pursue bilateral or regional trade deals (such as NAFTA and CAFTA) instead of a multilateral accord.

Foreign Exchange Rates, 1970-2005

Source: International Monetary Fund, Federal Reserve Board; Federal Reserve Board
(National currency units per dollar except as indicated; data are annual averages)

Note: As of 2002, the euro, the European Union's single currency, replaced the national currencies in the EU nations shown (Austria, Belgium, France, Germany, Greece, Ireland, Italy, Netherlands, Portugal, and Spain), as well as in Finland and Luxembourg.

Year	Australia[1] (dollar)	Austria[1] (schilling)	Belgium[1] (franc)	Canada (dollar)	China (yuan)	Denmark (krone)	France[1] (franc)	Germany[1,2] (deutsche mark)	Greece[1] (drachma)
1970	1.1136	25.880	49.680	1.0103	NA	7.489	5.5200	3.6480	30.00
1975	1.3077	17.443	36.799	1.0175	NA	5.748	4.2876	2.4613	32.29
1980	1.1400	12.945	29.237	1.1693	NA	5.634	4.2250	1.8175	42.62
1985	0.7003	20.690	59.378	1.3655	NA	10.596	8.9852	2.9440	138.12
1990	0.7813	11.370	33.418	1.1668	NA	6.189	5.4453	1.6157	158.51
1995	0.7415	10.081	29.480	1.3724	8.3700	5.602	4.9915	1.4331	231.66
2000	0.5815	0.9232[3]	0.9232[3]	1.4855	8.2784	8.095	0.9232[3]	0.9232[3]	365.92
2003	0.6524	1.1321[3]	1.1321[3]	1.4008	8.2772	6.5774	1.1321[3]	1.1321[3]	1.1321[3]
2004	0.7365	1.2438[3]	1.2438[3]	1.3017	8.2768	5.9891	1.2438[3]	1.2438[3]	1.2438[3]
2005	0.7627	1.2449[3]	1.2449[3]	1.2115	8.1936	5.9953	1.2449[3]	1.2449[3]	1.2449[3]

Year	Hong Kong (dollar)	India (rupee)	Ireland[1] (pound)	Italy[1] (lira)	Japan (yen)	Malaysia (ringgit)	Mexico (new peso)	Netherlands[1] (guilder)	Norway (krone)
1970	NA	7.576	2.3959	623	357.60	3.0900	—	3.5970	7.1400
1975	NA	8.409	2.2216	653	296.78	2.4030	—	2.5293	5.2282
1980	NA	7.887	2.0577	856	226.63	2.1767	—	1.9875	4.9381
1985	NA	12.369	1.0656	1,909	238.54	2.4830	—	3.3214	8.5972
1990	NA	17.504	1.6585	1,198	144.79	2.7049	2.8126	1.8209	6.2597
1995	7.7357	32.427	1.6038	1,628.9	94.06	2.5044	6.4194	1.6057	6.3352
2000	7.7925	45.00	0.9232[3]	0.9232[3]	107.80	3.8000	9.4590	0.9232[3]	8.8131
2003	7.7875	46.59	1.1321[3]	1.1321[3]	115.94	3.8000	10.793	1.1321[3]	7.0803
2004	7.7891	45.26	1.2438[3]	1.2438[3]	108.15	3.8000	11.290	1.2438[3]	6.7399
2005	7.7775	44.00	1.2449[3]	1.2449[3]	110.11	3.7869	10.894	1.2449[3]	6.4412

Year	Portugal[1] (escudo)	Singapore (dollar)	South Korea (won)	Spain[1] (peseta)	Sweden (krona)	Switzerland (franc)	Taiwan (dollar)	Thailand (baht)	UK[1] (pound)
1970	28.75	3.0800	310.57	69.72	5.1700	4.3160	NA	21.000	2.3959
1975	25.51	2.3713	484.00	57.43	4.1530	2.5839	NA	20.379	2.2216
1980	50.08	2.1412	607.43	71.76	4.2309	1.6772	NA	20.476	2.3243
1985	170.39	2.2002	870.02	170.04	8.6039	2.4571	NA	27.159	1.2963
1990	142.55	1.8125	707.76	101.93	5.9188	1.3892	NA	25.585	1.7847
1995	151.11	1.4174	771.27	124.69	7.1333	1.1825	26.495	24.915	1.5785
2000	0.9232[3]	1.7250	1,130.90	0.9232[3]	9.1735	1.6904	31.260	40.210	1.5156
2003	1.1321[3]	1.7429	1,192.08	1.1321[3]	8.0787	1.3450	34.405	41.556	1.6347
2004	1.2438[3]	1.6902	1,145.24	1.2438[3]	7.3480	1.2428	33.372	40.271	1.8330
2005	1.2449[3]	1.6639	1,023.75	1.2449[3]	7.471	1.2459	32.131	40.252	1.8204

NA= Not Available. (1) U.S. dollars per unit of national currency. (2) West Germany before 1991. (3) Euro Area member, figures in euros per dollar.

The North American Free Trade Agreement (NAFTA)

NAFTA, a free trade pact between the U.S., Canada, and Mexico, took effect Jan. 1, 1994. Major provisions are:

Agriculture—Tariffs on all farm products to be eliminated over 15 years. Domestic price-support systems may continue provided they do not distort trade.

Automobiles—At least 62.5% of an automobile's value must have been produced in North America for it to qualify for duty-free status. Tariffs were phased out over 10 years.

Disputes—Special judges have jurisdiction to resolve disagreements within strict timetables.

Energy—Mexico continues to bar foreign ownership of its oil fields but, as of 2004, U.S. and Canadian companies could bid on contracts offered by Mexican oil and electricity monopolies.

Environment—The trade agreement cannot be used to overrule national and state environmental, health, or safety laws.

Finance—Limits on ownership of banks, insurance companies, and brokerages eliminated by Jan. 1, 2000.

Immigration—All 3 countries eased restrictions on the movement of business executives and professionals.

Jobs—Barriers to limit Mexican migration to U.S. remain unaffected by NAFTA.

Patent and copyright protection—Mexico strengthened its laws providing protection to intellectual property and agreed to honor pharmaceutical patents for 20 years.

Tariffs—Tariffs on 10,000 customs goods are to be eliminated over 15 years. One-half of U.S. exports to Mexico were considered duty-free by 1999.

Textiles—A "rule of origin" provision requires most garments to be made from yarn and fabric that have been produced in North America. Most tariffs phased out by 1999.

Trucking—Trucks were to have free access on crossborder routes and throughout the 3 countries by 1999, but the U.S. continued to impose restrictions on Mexican trucks. In 2001, an arbitration panel ruled that the U.S. restrictions were in violation of NAFTA. Pres. Bush in Nov. 2002 eased restrictions on Mexican trucks entering the U.S.

U.S. Trade With Mexico and Canada, 1993-2005

Source: Office of Trade and Economic Analysis, U.S. Dept. of Commerce
(U.S. exports to, imports from, Mexico and Canada in millions of dollars)

	With MEXICO				With CANADA		
Year	Exports	Imports	U.S. Trade Balance[1]	Year	Exports	Imports	U.S. Trade Balance[1]
1993	$41,581	$39,917	$1,664	1993	$100,444	$111,216	$-10,772
1994[2]	50,844	49,494	1,350	1994[2]	114,439	128,406	-13,968
1995	46,292	61,685	-15,393	1995	127,226	145,349	-18,123
1996	56,792	74,297	-17,506	1996	134,210	155,893	-21,682
1997	71,388	85,938	-14,549	1997	151,767	167,234	-15,467
1998	78,773	94,629	-15,857	1998	156,603	173,256	-16,653
1999	86,909	109,721	-22,812	1999	166,600	198,711	-32,111
2000	111,349	135,926	-24,577	2000	178,941	230,838	-51,897
2001	101,297	131,338	-30,041	2001	163,424	216,268	-52,844
2002	97,470	134,616	-37,146	2002	160,923	209,088	-48,165
2003	97,412	138,060	-40,648	2003	169,924	221,595	-51,671
2004	110,835	155,902	-45,067	2004	189,880	256,360	-66,480
2005	120,365	170,109	-49,744	2005	211,899	290,384	-78,486

(1) Totals may not add due to rounding. (2) NAFTA provisions began to take effect Jan. 1, 1994.

The Central American Free Trade Agreement (CAFTA)

CAFTA (also known as CAFTA-DR), a free trade agreement between the U.S. and Costa Rica, Dominican Republic, El Salvador, Guatemala, Honduras, and Nicaragua, was signed into law by the U.S. Aug. 2, 2005. Ratification was pending in Costa Rica and the Dominican Republic as of Oct. 2006, but El Salvador, Guatemala, Honduras, Nicaragua, and the U.S. had implemented the agreement's conditions by June 2006.

Some highlights are:

Agriculture: Tariffs on 50% of U.S. farm goods eliminated; other goods deemed "sensitive"—including corn, milk, and potatoes—to have tariffs reduced to zero over 20 years. Sugar imports to the U.S. allowed to rise to 1.2% of annual U.S. production, and to 1.7% over 15 years.

Automobiles: Tariffs to be phased out over 5 years.

Environment and Labor: Party nations agree to enforce local labor and environmental protections (no mechanisms in place to monitor enforcement).

Manufacturing: Tariffs eliminated on 80% of U.S. goods.

Market Barriers: Barriers for services such as telecommunications, insurance, and financial services eliminated or reduced.

Pharmaceuticals: U.S. pharmaceuticals given 5-year patent protection from their date of introduction to CAFTA markets, regardless of date introduced in U.S.

Textiles and Clothing: Open access of CAFTA-nation textiles and clothing to U.S. markets instituted, retroactive to Jan. 1, 2004.

60 Busiest U.S. Ports, 2004

Source: Corps of Engineers, Dept. of the Army, U.S. Dept. of Defense

(ports ranked by tonnage handled; all figures in tons)

Rank Port	Total	Domestic	Foreign	Imports	Exports
1. South Louisiana, LA, Port of	224,187,322	119,416,519	104,770,803	40,087,413	64,683,390
2. Houston, TX	202,047,327	64,510,816	137,536,511	97,713,314	39,823,197
3. New York, NY and NJ	152,377,503	70,177,949	82,199,554	70,748,666	11,450,888
4. Beaumont, TX	91,697,948	20,823,732	70,874,216	65,315,960	5,558,256
5. Long Beach, CA	80,066,130	17,550,722	62,515,408	44,619,556	17,895,852
6. Corpus Christi, TX	78,924,757	25,129,700	53,795,057	44,989,804	8,805,253
7. New Orleans, LA	78,085,209	37,662,499	40,422,710	24,134,664	16,288,046
8. Huntington, WV-KY-OH	77,307,514	77,307,514	0	0	0
9. Texas City, TX	68,282,902	17,477,116	50,805,786	46,384,689	4,421,097
10. Baton Rouge, LA	57,082,823	35,143,834	21,938,989	18,156,227	3,782,762
11. Mobile, AL	56,211,796	26,893,791	29,318,005	19,916,120	9,401,885
12. Lake Charles, LA	54,768,322	23,075,344	31,692,978	27,036,374	4,656,604
13. Plaquemines, LA, Port of	54,404,720	36,710,431	17,694,289	9,307,882	8,386,407
14. Los Angeles, CA	51,931,730	8,059,878	43,871,852	32,420,155	11,451,697
15. Tampa, FL	48,289,134	29,684,171	18,604,963	9,550,970	9,053,993
16. Baltimore, MD	47,399,120	14,618,674	32,780,446	24,950,281	7,830,165
17. Valdez, AK	46,758,499	46,755,392	3,107	582	2,525
18. Duluth-Superior, MN and WI	45,392,619	31,672,144	13,720,475	489,387	13,231,088
19. Pittsburgh, PA	41,034,808	41,034,808	0	0	0
20. Philadelphia, PA	35,219,613	13,782,206	21,437,407	21,123,144	314,263
21. Norfolk Harbor, VA	34,166,269	7,974,156	26,192,113	8,572,099	17,620,014
22. Pascagoula, MS	34,099,989	10,690,429	23,409,560	19,476,237	3,933,323
23. Freeport, TX	33,908,024	5,769,879	28,138,145	25,157,179	2,980,966
24. St. Louis, MO and IL	33,386,972	33,386,972	0	0	0
25. Paulsboro, NJ	30,485,654	11,883,526	18,602,128	18,117,024	485,104
26. Portland, OR	29,995,641	12,337,990	17,657,651	4,433,734	13,223,917
27. Portland, ME	29,709,345	1,875,459	27,833,886	27,614,946	218,940
28. Savannah, GA	28,176,658	2,098,418	26,078,240	16,534,606	9,543,634
29. Port Arthur, TX	27,570,039	8,616,013	18,954,026	13,594,364	5,359,662
30. Tacoma, WA	26,282,033	7,674,132	18,607,901	6,224,746	12,383,155
31. Boston, MA	25,796,721	7,990,857	17,805,864	16,826,384	979,480
32. Port Everglades, FL	24,899,825	11,512,311	13,387,514	11,091,312	2,296,202
33. Richmond, CA	24,743,520	11,850,116	12,893,404	11,440,037	1,453,367
34. Charleston, SC	24,739,212	3,922,856	20,816,356	14,643,483	6,172,873
35. Chicago, IL	24,602,157	20,774,051	3,828,106	2,550,116	1,277,990
36. Marcus Hook, PA	24,568,697	10,452,162	14,116,535	14,116,535	0
37. Seattle, WA	23,501,372	5,889,270	17,612,102	9,133,712	8,478,390
38. Jacksonville, FL	21,451,389	10,021,916	11,429,473	10,198,474	1,230,999
39. Honolulu, HI	19,085,470	13,201,321	5,884,149	5,315,638	568,511
40. Indiana Harbor, IN	18,228,291	17,337,975	890,316	818,487	71,829
41. Memphis, TN	17,520,436	17,520,436	0	0	0
42. Detroit, MI	16,858,179	12,576,616	4,281,563	4,020,693	260,870
43. Anacortes, WA	16,304,725	14,059,026	2,245,699	1,076,109	1,169,590
44. Cleveland, OH	15,774,611	11,855,282	3,919,329	3,567,866	351,463
45. Oakland, CA	15,541,066	2,816,564	12,724,502	5,747,563	6,976,939
46. Newport News, VA	14,280,141	5,798,736	8,481,405	1,050,212	7,431,193
47. San Juan, PR	14,179,070	7,972,123	6,206,947	5,745,944	461,003
48. Cincinnati, OH	13,898,494	13,898,494	0	0	0
49. Two Harbors, MN	13,472,759	13,363,880	108,879	0	108,879
50. Matagorda Ship Channel, TX	12,523,705	3,615,683	8,908,022	7,401,194	1,506,828
51. Ashtabula, OH	10,938,476	5,561,561	5,376,915	450,251	4,926,664
52. New Haven, CT	10,855,934	7,789,159	3,066,775	2,703,512	363,263
53. Presque Isle, MI	10,134,332	8,063,660	2,070,672	0	2,070,672
54. Kalama, WA	10,116,131	1,044,446	9,071,685	435,144	8,636,541
55. Toledo, OH	9,861,562	2,463,657	7,397,905	4,226,229	3,171,676
56. Burns Waterway Harbor, IN	9,801,740	7,947,962	1,853,778	1,407,268	446,510
57. Miami, FL	9,754,577	1,422,677	8,331,900	5,200,899	3,131,001
58. Providence, RI	9,558,978	4,734,276	4,824,702	4,537,200	287,502
59. Calcite, MI	8,949,167	8,004,950	944,217	88,028	856,189
60. Gary, IN	8,531,123	7,962,169	568,954	309,775	259,179

Merchant Fleets of the World, 2004

Source: Maritime Administration, U.S. Dept. of Commerce

Self-propelled oceangoing vessels of 1,000 gross deadweight tons and over, as of July 1, 2004 (tonnage in thousands)

		All Vessels No.	Tons	Tanker No.	Tons	Dry Bulk Carrier No.	Tons	Container No.	Tons	Other[1] No.	Tons
By flag of registry	Panama	4,822	187,164	1,134	58,382	1,503	94,482	587	20,803	1,598	13,497
	Liberia	1,477	81,821	572	46,084	311	18,876	398	13,818	196	3,043
	Greece	730	54,442	301	32,032	295	19,781	43	2,116	91	513
	Bahamas	979	43,513	249	26,362	183	10,085	70	2,042	477	5,024
	Hong Kong	733	38,844	124	9,864	402	23,775	91	3,086	116	2,119
	Malta	1,172	38,798	243	14,841	445	19,011	57	1,296	427	3,651
	Singapore	886	36,843	445	19,834	134	10,187	177	4,616	130	2,206
	Cyprus	975	34,285	142	7,070	396	20,684	120	3,286	317	3,245
	Marshall Islands	456	33,269	231	24,606	80	5,480	78	1,734	67	1,449
	China[2]	1,557	26,490	300	5,088	351	12,499	130	2,683	776	6,220
	Norway (NIS)[3]	575	23,207	285	13,000	77	6,963	4	80	209	3,165
	United States	412	13,035	104	5,618	20	837	84	3,257	204	3,322
	Japan	555	11,871	233	5,940	140	4,628	13	469	169	833
	India	286	11,363	118	7,549	88	3,401	7	131	73	282
	Isle of Man	246	10,604	136	7,623	23	2,175	14	238	73	568
	United Kingdom	378	10,369	87	2,078	16	1,527	135	5,580	140	1,185
	Italy	438	10,197	235	5,300	36	2,613	19	640	148	1,644
	Korea (South)	530	9,861	160	1,783	105	6,139	58	892	207	1,048
	Denmark (DIS)[4]	244	9,034	76	3,648	2	76	81	4,984	85	325
	Iran	123	8,827	34	6,096	40	1,773	10	285	39	673
	All Other	11,461	154,749	2,295	50,402	1,212	45,094	921	21,170	6,973	38,084
By Country[5]	Greece	2,923	160,450	857	71,079	1,334	77,711	157	5,498	575	6,162
	Japan	2,713	111,163	797	40,469	869	54,937	218	8,002	829	7,756
	Germany	2,258	51,351	249	10,295	171	7,709	945	26,750	893	6,596
	China	2,169	48,900	327	9,216	630	26,756	223	4,871	989	8,057
	Norway	1,061	41,844	393	25,658	166	8,636	14	487	488	7,063
	United States	931	39,574	371	28,390	76	3,242	89	3,105	395	4,837
	Hong Kong	542	37,354	154	14,505	233	19,358	41	1,770	114	1,721
	Korea (South)	801	26,093	238	8,566	188	13,524	106	2,361	269	1,642
	United Kingdom	621	24,174	173	8,876	95	8,115	115	4,790	238	2,393
	Singapore	697	23,757	324	14,487	123	5,130	134	3,076	116	1,064
	Taiwan	532	23,730	41	3,741	186	12,351	184	6,654	121	983
	Denmark	492	15,997	154	6,388	29	1,770	130	6,817	179	1,022
	Russia	1,673	15,762	422	9,083	120	1,926	24	329	1,107	4,422
	India	282	12,824	125	8,335	101	4,128	3	87	53	274
	Italy	466	11,971	244	5,925	49	3,499	11	227	162	2,320
	Saudi Arabia	97	11,891	78	11,584	1	2	—	—	18	305
	Malaysia	289	9,524	128	6,373	40	1,946	34	695	87	511
	Iran	127	9,316	36	6,321	45	2,051	10	285	36	659
	Turkey	548	8,769	88	1,406	133	5,277	30	336	297	1,749
	Switzerland	266	8,258	36	1,016	30	1,335	126	5,001	74	906
	All Other	9,547	155,883	2,269	61,486	1,240	50,684	503	12,063	5,535	31,651
TOTAL ALL SHIPS		29,035	848,586	7,504	353,200	5,859	310,088	3,097	93,204	12,575	92,094

(1) Includes roll-on/roll-off, passenger, breakbulk ships, partial container ships, refrigerated cargo ships, barge carriers, and specialized cargo ships. (2) Excluding Hong Kong. (3) NIS = Norwegian International Ship Registry. (4) DIS = Denmark International Shipping Registry. (5) Based on parent company nationality.

U.S. International Transactions, 1970-2005

Source: Bureau of Economic Analysis, U.S. Dept. of Commerce; revised as of June 2006

(millions of dollars)

	1970	1975	1980	1985	1990	1995	2000	2005
Exports of goods, services, and income[1]	$68,387	$157,936	$344,440	$387,612	$706,975	$1,004,631	$1,422,402	$1,749,892
Merchandise, bal. of payments basis[2]	42,469	107,088	224,250	215,915	387,401	575,204	771,994	894,631
Services	14,171	25,497	47,584	73,155	147,832	219,183	299,490	380,614
Income receipts on U.S.-owned assets abroad	11,748	25,351	72,606	98,542	170,570	208,065	348,083	471,722
Imports of goods and services and income payments	−59,901	−132,745	−333,774	−483,769	−759,290	−1,080,124	−1,779,620	−2,455,328
Merchandise, balance of payments basis[2]	−39,866	−98,185	−249,750	−338,088	−498,438	−749,374	−1,224,408	−1,677,371
Services	−14,520	−21,996	−41,491	−72,862	−117,659	−141,397	−225,348	−314,604
Income payments on foreign-owned assets in the U.S.	−5,515	−12,564	−42,532	−72,819	−139,728	−183,090	−322,345	−454,124
Unilateral transfers, net	−6,156	−7,075	−8,349	−21,998	−26,654	−38,177	−58,781	−86,072
Capital acct. transactions, net	NA	NA	NA	315	−6,579	−927	−929	−4,351
U.S.-owned assets abroad, net (increase/financial outflow [−])	−8,470	−39,703	−85,815	−44,752	−81,234	−352,264	−560,523	−426,801
U.S. official reserve assets, net	3,348	−849	−7,003	−3,858	−2,158	−9,742	−290	14,096
U.S. government assets, other than official reserve assets, net	−1,589	−3,474	−5,162	−2,821	2,317	−984	−941	5,539
U.S. private assets, net	−10,229	−35,380	−73,651	−38,074	−81,393	−341,538	−559,292	−446,436
Foreign-owned assets in the U.S., net (increase/financial inflow [+])	6,359	17,170	62,612	146,115	141,571	438,562	1,046,896	1,212,250
Stat. discrepancy (sum of above items with sign reversed)	−219	4,417	20,886	16,478	25,211	28,299	−69,445	10,410
Memorandum: Balance on current account	2,331	18,116	2,317	−118,155	−78,968	113,670	−415,999	−791,508

NA = Not available. (1) Excludes transfers of goods and services under U.S. military grant programs. (2) Excludes exports of goods under U.S. military agency sales contracts identified in Census export documents, excludes imports of goods under direct defense expenditures identified in Census import documents, and reflects various other adjustments.

Foreign Direct Investment[1] in the U.S. by Selected Countries and Territories, 1995, 2000, 2005

Source: Bureau of Economic Analysis; U.S. Dept. of Commerce
(millions of dollars)

	1995	2000	2005		1995	2000	2005
ALL COUNTRIES[2]	**$560,850**	**$1,214,254**	**$1,635,291**	**Other Western Hemisphere[3]**	**$17,362**	**$40,782**	**$52,518**
Canada	48,258	114,599	144,033	Bahamas	−1,780	1,268	703
				Bermuda	1,592	18,502	1,517
Europe[3]	**357,193**	**835,137**	**1,143,614**	Netherlands Antilles	8,481	3,940	4,179
Austria	1,555	3,174	2,502	UK islands, Caribbean	8,417	15,353	26,501
Belgium	3,676	14,585	9,712	**Africa[3]**	**1,164**	**2,756**	**2,564**
Denmark	2,990	4,428	6,255	South Africa	−3	1,218	361
Finland	2,752	9,107	6,205	**Middle East[3]**	**6,008**	**6,189**	**9,965**
France	38,480	131,484	143,378	Israel	1,995	2,690	4,362
Germany	49,269	124,839	184,213	Kuwait	2,527	908	612
Ireland	7,418	23,528	21,898	Lebanon	−9	1	-6
Italy	2,750	5,994	7,716	Saudi Arabia	1,310	NA	NA
Liechtenstein	135	202	NA	United Arab Emirates	98	64	NA
Luxembourg	5,957	53,794	116,736	**Asia and Pacific[3]**	**122,986**	**201,110**	**252,584**
Netherlands	65,806	146,493	170,770	Australia	7,833	20,701	44,061
Norway	2,089	2,241	6,144	Hong Kong	1,557	1,544	2,600
Spain	2,452	5,459	7,114	Japan	107,933	163,577	190,279
Sweden	9,581	22,427	24,774	Korea, South	626	3,287	6,203
Switzerland	35,593	69,240	122,399	Malaysia	402	92	410
United Kingdom	126,177	213,820	282,457	New Zealand	149	385	700
South and Central America[3]	**7,878**	**13,682**	**30,012**	Philippines	75	50	NA
Brazil	751	886	2,551	Singapore	1,548	7,751	2,404
Mexico	1,980	7,832	8,653	Taiwan	2,139	3,131	3,565
Panama	4,721	3,726	11,470	**European Union[4]**	**318,995**	**760,017**	**1,005,672**
Venezuela	−259	802	6,730	**OPEC[5]**	**3,740**	**4,363**	**12,356**

(1) The book value of foreign direct investors' equity in, and net outstanding loans to, their U.S. affiliates. A U.S. affiliate is a U.S. business enterprise in which a single foreign direct investor owns at least 10% of the voting securities or the equivalent. (2) Totals includes sources not reflected in regional subtotals. (3) Totals include countries or territories not shown. (4) Total for the European Union in 2004 includes Austria, Belgium, Denmark, Finland, France, Germany, Greece, Ireland, Italy, Luxembourg, the Netherlands, Portugal, Spain, Sweden, the United Kingdom and 10 additional countries (Cyprus, Czech Republic, Estonia, Hungary, Latvia, Lithuania, Malta, Poland, Slovakia, and Slovenia) in May 2004. (5) Organization of Petroleum Exporting Countries: Algeria, Indonesia, Iran, Iraq, Kuwait, Libya, Nigeria, Qatar, Saudi Arabia, United Arab Emirates, and Venezuela. NA = Not available.

U.S. Direct Investment[1] Abroad in Selected Countries and Territories

Source: Bureau of Economic Analysis, U.S. Dept. of Commerce
(millions of dollars)

	1995	2000	2005		1995	2000	2005
ALL COUNTRIES[2]	**$717,554**	**$1,293,431**	**$2,069,983**	Honduras	$191	$257	$402
Canada	**85,441**	**128,814**	**234,831**	Mexico	15,980	37,332	71,423
Europe	**360,994**	**679,457**	**1,059,443**	Panama	16,216	29,316	5,162
Austria	2,777	2,686	8,762	**Other Western**			
Belgium	17,969	19,527	36,733	**Hemisphere[3]**	**47,650**	**97,377**	**198,684**
Czech Republic	NA		2,786	Bahamas	1,806	2,317	NA
Denmark	2,123	5,363	5,695	Barbados	755	1,170	2,940
Finland	825	1,110	2,493	Bermuda	29,980	56,594	90,358
France	32,950	38,752	60,860	Dominican Republic	394	813	758
Germany	44,226	50,963	86,319	UK islands, Caribbean	8,941	28,514	85,295
Greece	424	637	1,903	**Africa[3]**	**6,383**	**14,417**	**24,257**
Hungary	NA	NA	3,402	Egypt	1,388	2,344	4,839
Ireland	8,400	33,816	61,596	Nigeria	706	1,237	874
Italy	17,587	22,392	25,931	South Africa	1,275	3,245	3,594
Luxembourg	5,857	25,571	61,615	**Middle East[3]**	**7,669**	**11,087**	**21,591**
Netherlands	39,344	117,557	181,384	Israel	1,662	3,386	7,920
Norway	5,133	5,833	8,795	Saudi Arabia	3,245	4,225	3,531
Poland	NA	NA	5,736	United Arab Emirates	660	737	2,663
Portugal	1,755	1,888	2,712	**Asia and Pacific[3]**	**125,834**	**205,317**	**376,849**
Russia	NA	NA	5,545	Australia	25,000	35,364	113,385
Spain	10,770	19,846	43,280	China	2,127	9,861	16,877
Sweden	7,339	22,676	33,398	Hong Kong	14,206	26,621	3,784
Switzerland	33,532	55,854	83,424	India	838	1,431	8,456
Turkey	948	1,356	2,417	Indonesia	6,607	8,514	9,948
United Kingdom	122,767	241,663	323,796	Japan	38,406	59,441	75,491
South America[3]	**46,914**	**84,012**	**74,403**	Korea, South	5,169	8,914	18,759
Argentina	7,496	15,646	13,163	Malaysia	4,200	7,400	9,993
Brazil	23,706	39,033	32,420	New Zealand	4,845	3,854	4,809
Chile	5,878	9,451	9,811	Philippines	2,531	2,735	6,649
Colombia	3,352	4,606	3,393	Singapore	12,689	25,634	48,051
Ecuador	833	763	760	Taiwan	4,210	7,821	13,374
Peru	1,279	3,485	3,900	Thailand	4,315	6,635	8,556
Venezuela	3,220	9,530	9,610	**European Union[4]**	**315,112**	**604,445**	**948,978**
Central America[3]	**33,688**	**70,474**	**79,924**	**Eastern Europe[5]**	**4,739**	**11,149**	**NA**
Costa Rica	870	1,655	1,277	**OPEC[6]**	**16,036**	**28,736**	**37,191**

(1) The book value of U.S. direct investors' equity in, and net outstanding loans to, their foreign affiliates. A foreign affiliate is a foreign business enterprise in which a single U.S. investor owns at least 10% of the voting securities or the equivalent. (2) Totals include countries not reflected in regional totals. (3) Total includes countries not shown. (4) The members of the European Union in 2005 were Austria, Belgium, Cyprus, the Czech Republic, Denmark, Estonia, Finland, France, Germany, Greece, Hungary, Ireland, Italy, Latvia, Lithuania, Luxembourg, Malta, the Netherlands, Poland, Portugal, Slovakia, Slovenia, Spain, Sweden, and the United Kingdom. (5) Eastern Europe is defined to include Albania, Armenia, Azerbaijan, Belarus, Bulgaria, Czech Republic, Estonia, Georgia, Hungary, Kazakhstan, Kyrgyzstan, Latvia, Lithuania, Moldova, Poland, Romania, Russia, Slovakia, Tajikistan, Turkmenistan, Ukraine, and Uzbekistan. (6) Organization of Petroleum Exporting Countries: Algeria, Indonesia, Iran, Iraq, Kuwait, Libya, Nigeria, Qatar, Saudi Arabia, the United Arab Emirates, and Venezuela. NA = not available.

U.S. Railroad Miles, 1830-2004

Source: Association of American Railroads

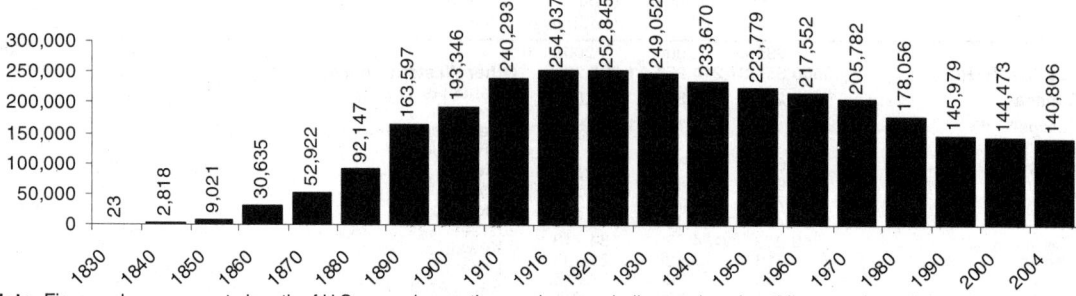

Note: Figures show aggregate length of U.S.-owned operating roadway, excluding yard tracks, sidings, and parallel tracks.

U.S. Railroad Freight, 1890-2005

Source: Association of American Railroads
(in bil ton-miles)

Year	Class I[1]	All	Year	Class I[1]	All	Year	Class I[1]	All	Year	Class I[1]	All	Year	Class I[1]	All
1890...	NA	76	1950...	589	592	1991..	1,039	1,100	1996..	1,356	1,426	2001...	1,495	1,558
1900...	NA	142	1960...	572	575	1992..	1,067	1,138	1997..	1,349	1,421	2002...	1,507	1,564
1910...	NA	255	1970...	765	771	1993..	1,109	1,183	1998..	1,377	1,442	2003...	1,551	1,610
1920...	410	414	1980...	919	932	1994..	1,201	1,275	1999..	1,433	1,499	2004...	1,663	1,719
1930...	383	386	1990...	1,034	1,091	1995..	1,306	1,375	2000..	1,466	1,534	2005...	1,696	NA
1940...	373	375												

Note: A ton-mile equals 1 ton of freight transported 1 statute mile. NA=Not available. (1) Class One, the largest class of freight railroad companies, determined by an annual operating revenue cut-off ($289.4 mil in 2004).

Leading Motor Vehicle Producing Nations, 2005

Source: Automotive News Data Center and R.L. Polk Marketing Systems GmbH

	Total	Passenger Cars	Trucks		Total	Passenger Cars	Trucks
United States	12,018,043	4,325,702	7,692,341	Belgium	924,533	895,740	28,793
Japan	10,799,659	9,016,735	1,782,924	Turkey	879,452	453,663	425,789
Germany.........	5,757,710	5,350,187	407,523	Sweden	710,655	568,484	142,171
China	5,648,972	3,111,103	2,537,869	Poland	643,303	534,605	108,698
Korea, South	3,699,350	3,357,094	342,256	Czech Republic	602,419	597,194	5,225
France	3,547,839	3,112,956	434,883	Malaysia	563,408	404,571	158,837
Spain	2,753,856	2,098,168	655,688	South Africa	520,948	321,950	198,998
Canada..........	2,664,749	1,406,963	1,257,786	Indonesia........	514,179	56,016	458,163
Brazil	2,458,469	1,930,608	527,861	Taiwan..........	446,345	323,819	122,526
United Kingdom	1,806,359	1,596,296	210,063	Australia.........	396,353	316,414	79,939
Mexico	1,691,878	1,052,875	639,003	Argentina........	319,577	182,761	136,816
India...........	1,553,194	1,204,000	349,194	Austria	230,926	208,245	22,681
Russia	1,351,194	1,066,520	284,674	Portugal.........	218,824	137,602	81,222
Thailand	1,097,300	243,200	854,100	Romania	194,802	174,538	20,264
Italy............	1,038,352	725,528	312,824	Slovakia	188,743	188,689	54
Iran.............	1,005,650	901,650	104,000	**World Total[1]**	**67,723,891**	**46,975,785**	**20,748,106**

(1) Total includes countries or territories not shown.

World Motor Vehicle Production, 1950-2005

Source: For 1950-97, American Automobile Manufacturers Assn.; for 1998-2003, Automotive News Data Center and R.L. Polk Marketing Systems GmbH
(in thousands)

Year	United States	Canada	W. Europe	Japan	Other	World total	U.S. % of world total
1950	8,006	388	1,991	32	160	10,577	75.7
1960	7,905	398	6,837	482	866	16,488	47.9
1970	8,284	1,160	13,049	5,289	1,637	29,419	28.2
1980	8,010	1,324	15,496	11,043	2,692	38,565	20.8
1985	11,653	1,933	16,113	12,271	2,939	44,909	25.9
1990	9,783	1,928	18,866	13,487	4,496	48,554	20.1
1991	8,811	1,888	17,804	13,245	5,180	46,928	18.8
1992	9,729	1,961	17,628	12,499	6,269	48,088	20.2
1993	10,898	2,246	15,208	11,228	7,205	46,785	23.3
1994	12,263	2,321	16,195	10,554	8,167	49,500	24.8
1995	11,985	2,408	17,045	10,196	8,349	49,983	24.0
1996	11,799	2,397	17,550	10,346	9,241	51,332	23.0
1997	12,119	2,571	17,773	10,975	10,024	53,463	22.7
1998	12,047	2,568	16,332	10,050	12,844	53,841	22.4
1999	13,107	3,042	17,603	9,985	14,050	57,787	22.7
2000	12,832	2,952	17,678	10,145	16,098	59,704	21.5
2001	11,518	2,535	17,825	9,777	16,170	57,705	19.7
2002	12,328	2,624	17,419	10,240	16,975	59,587	20.7
2003	12,147	2,568	16,943	10,286	20,619	61,562	19.7
2004	12,021	2,621	16,982	10,512	22,175	64,388	18.7
2005	12,018	2,665	20,811[1]	10,800	21,420	67,724	17.7

Note: Data for 1998-2001 not fully comparable with earlier years because derived from different source. (1) Beginning in 2005, data includes all European countries. Total motor vehicle production for the top-producing W. European countries in 2005 was 17,162,484 cars.

New Passenger Cars Imported Into the U.S., by Country of Origin,[1] 1970-2005

Source: Bureau of the Census, Foreign Trade Division

	Japan	Germany[2]	Italy	United Kingdom	Sweden	France	South Korea	Mexico	Canada	Total[3]
1970	381,338	674,945	42,523	76,257	57,844	37,114	NA	NA	692,783	2,013,420
1975	695,573	370,012	102,344	67,106	51,993	15,647	NA	0	733,766	2,074,653
1980	1,991,502	338,711	46,899	32,517	61,496	47,386	NA	1	594,770	3,116,448
1981	1,911,525	234,052	21,635	12,728	68,042	42,477	NA	1	563,943	2,856,286
1982	1,801,185	259,385	9,402	13,023	89,231	50,032	NA	27	702,495	2,926,407
1983	1,871,192	239,807	5,442	17,261	114,726	40,823	NA	2	835,665	3,133,836
1984	1,948,714	335,032	8,582	19,833	114,854	37,788	NA	NA	1,073,425	3,559,427
1985	2,527,467	473,110	8,689	24,474	142,640	42,882	NA	13,647	1,144,805	4,397,679
1986	2,618,711	451,699	11,829	27,506	148,700	10,869	169,309	41,983	1,162,226	4,691,297
1987	2,417,509	377,542	8,648	50,059	138,565	26,707	399,856	126,266	926,927	4,589,010
1988	2,123,051	264,249	6,053	31,636	108,006	15,990	455,741	148,065	1,191,357	4,450,213
1989	2,051,525	216,881	9,319	29,378	101,571	4,885	270,609	133,049	1,151,122	4,042,728
1990	1,867,794	245,286	11,045	27,271	93,084	1,976	201,475	215,986	1,220,221	3,944,602
1991	1,762,347	171,097	2,886	14,862	62,905	1,727	186,740	249,498	1,109,248	3,612,665
1992	1,598,919	205,248	1,791	10,997	76,832	65	130,110	266,111	1,119,223	3,447,200
1993	1,501,953	180,383	1,178	20,029	58,742	23	122,943	299,634	1,371,856	3,604,361
1994	1,488,159	178,774	1,010	28,217	63,867	58	213,962	360,367	1,525,746	3,909,079
1995	1,114,360	204,932	1,031	42,450	82,593	14	131,718	462,800	1,552,691	3,624,428
1996	1,190,896	234,909	1,365	44,373	86,619	27	225,623	550,867	1,690,733	4,069,113
1997	1,387,812	300,489	1,912	43,691	79,780	67	222,568	544,075	1,731,209	4,378,295
1998	1,456,081	373,330	2,104	49,891	84,543	56	211,650	584,795	1,837,615	4,673,418
1999	1,707,277	461,061	1,697	68,394	83,399	186	372,965	639,878	2,170,427	5,639,616
2000	1,839,093	488,323	3,125	81,196	86,707	134	568,121	934,000	2,138,811	6,324,284
2001	1,790,346	494,131	2,580	82,487	92,439	92	633,769	861,853	1,855,789	6,065,138
2002	2,046,902	574,455	3,504	157,563	87,709	150	627,881	845,181	1,882,660	6,477,659
2003	1,770,355	561,482	2,943	207,158	119,773	298	692,863	680,214	1,811,892	6,127,485
2004	1,727,065	547,008	3,373	185,621	98,131	2,417	860,424	652,509	2,035,345	6,521,248
2005	1,832,534	547,191	5,377	184,716	93,736	412	730,500	693,149	1,967,985	6,564,844

(1) Excludes cars assembled in U.S. foreign trade zones. (2) Figures prior to 1991 are for West Germany. (3) Includes countries not shown separately.

Passenger Car Production, U.S. Plants, 2004, 2005

Source: Ward's AutoInfoBank

	2004	2005		2004	2005
TOTAL CARS	4,229,625	4,321,272	Alero	18,906	—
			Oldsmobile Total	**18,906**	**—**
Ford Mustang	41,925	198,416	Bonneville	31,693	5,119
Mazda6	91,339	74,216	G6	42,186	157,414
AUTOALLIANCE TOTAL[1]	**133,264**	**272,632**	Grand Am	116,877	35,089
BMW Z4	35,136	19,830	Grand Prix	—	—
BMW TOTAL	**35,136**	**19,830**	Pursuit	2,575	21,448
Neon	1,844	605	Solstice	—	9,382
Sebring Convertible	39,388	34,439	Sunfire	21,298	—
Sebring Sedan	77,269	62,255	**Pontiac Total**	**214,629**	**228,452**
Chrysler Total	**118,501**	**97,299**	Ion	110,902	110,073
Neon	139,004	125,791	Saturn L	11,729	5
Stratus Sedan	90,792	100,517	**Saturn Total**	**122,631**	**110,078**
Viper	2,469	2,025	**GM TOTAL**	**1,182,933**	**1,153,358**
Dodge Total	**232,265**	**228,333**	Acura TL	82,635	88,545
CHRYSLER GROUP TOTAL	**350,766**	**325,632**	**Acura Total**	**82,635**	**88,545**
Five Hundred	42,782	118,740	Accord	350,337	358,794
Focus	184,805	166,991	Civic	133,995	133,724
Ford GT	500	1,898	**Honda Total**	**484,332**	**492,518**
Mustang	69,704	—	**HONDA GROUP TOTAL**	**566,967**	**581,063**
Taurus	254,842	180,494	Stratus Coupe	23,035	—
Thunderbird	10,716	4,868	Sonata	—	91,218
Ford Total	**563,349**	**472,991**	**HYUNDAI TOTAL**	**—**	**91,218**
Lincoln LS	27,146	15,675	**Dodge Total**	**23,035**	**—**
Town Car	53,958	50,284	Eclipse	11,210	28,220
Lincoln Total	**81,104**	**65,959**	Galant	45,188	34,939
Montego	7,448	32,622	**Mitsubishi Total**	**56,398**	**63,159**
Sable	44,216	13,065	Chrysler Sebring Coupe	12,103	348
Mercury Total	**51,664**	**45,687**	Dodge Stratus Coupe	—	1,427
FORD TOTAL	**696,117**	**584,637**	**MITSUBISHI TOTAL**	**91,536**	**64,934**
LeSabre	103,311	51,673	Altima	279,642	306,479
Lucerne	—	21,895	Maxima	87,129	76,773
Park Ave.	12,601	—	**NISSAN TOTAL**	**366,771**	**383,252**
Buick Total	**115,912**	**73,568**	Pontiac Vibe	69,226	—
CTS	71,518	65,204	Toyota Corolla	167,970	186,119
Deville	63,459	27,554	Toyota Voltz*	201	—
DTS	—	36,360	**Toyota Total**	**—**	**186,119**
Seville	5	—	Pontiac Vibe	—	62,319
STS	20,496	36,559	**NUMMI TOTAL[2]**	**237,397**	**248,438**
XLR	5,314	3,525	Subaru Legacy	98,298	87,151
Cadillac Total	**160,792**	**169,202**	**SUBARU TOTAL**	**98,298**	**87,151**
Cavalier	180,175	—	Avalon	33,074	108,637
Classic	—	42,349	Camry	388,119	356,497
Cobalt	25,994	279,711	Solara	49,247	43,993
Corvette	28,723	37,949	**TOYOTA TOTAL**	**470,440**	**509,127**
Malibu	315,171	212,049			
Chevrolet Total	**550,063**	**572,058**			

* For export only. (1) Company is a joint venture between Ford and Mazda. (2) NUMMI (New United Motor Manufacturing, Inc.) is a joint venture between GM and Toyota.

Domestic and Imported Retail Cars Sales in the U.S., 1980-2005

Source: Ward's Communications

Year	Domestic[1]	Imports Japan	Imports Germany	Imports Other Countries	Imports Total	Total U.S. Sales	Import Percent Total	Import Percent Japan	Import Percent Germany
1980....	6,581,307	1,905,968	305,219	186,700	2,397,887	8,979,194	26.7	21.2	3.3
1981....	6,208,760	1,858,896	282,881	185,502	2,327,279	8,536,039	27.3	21.8	3.3
1982....	5,758,586	1,801,969	247,080	174,508	2,223,557	7,982,143	27.9	22.6	3.0
1983....	6,795,295	1,915,621	279,748	191,403	2,386,772	9,182,067	26.0	20.9	3.0
1984....	7,951,523	1,906,206	344,416	188,220	2,438,842	10,390,365	23.5	18.3	3.8
1985....	8,204,542	2,217,837	423,983	195,925	2,837,745	11,042,287	25.7	20.1	3.8
1986....	8,214,897	2,382,614	443,721	418,286	3,244,621	11,459,518	28.3	20.8	3.9
1987....	7,080,858	2,190,405	347,881	657,465	3,195,751	10,276,609	31.1	21.3	3.4
1988....	7,526,038	2,022,602	280,099	700,991	3,003,692	10,529,730	28.5	19.2	2.7
1989....	7,072,902	1,897,143	248,561	553,660	2,699,364	9,772,266	27.6	19.4	2.5
1990....	6,896,888	1,719,384	265,116	418,823	2,403,323	9,300,211	25.8	18.5	2.9
1991....	6,136,757	1,500,309	192,776	344,814	2,037,899	8,174,656	24.9	18.4	2.4
1992....	6,276,557	1,451,766	200,851	283,938	1,936,555	8,213,112	23.6	17.7	2.4
1993....	6,741,667	1,328,445	186,177	261,570	1,776,192	8,517,859	20.9	15.6	2.2
1994....	7,255,303	1,239,450	192,275	303,489	1,735,214	8,990,517	19.3	13.8	2.1
1995....	7,128,707	981,506	207,482	317,269	1,506,257	8,634,964	17.4	11.4	2.4
1996....	7,253,582	726,940	237,984	308,247	1,273,171	8,526,753	14.9	8.5	2.8
1997....	6,916,769	726,104	297,028	332,173	1,355,305	8,272,074	16.4	8.8	3.6
1998....	6,761,940	691,162	366,724	321,895	1,379,781	8,141,721	16.9	8.5	4.5
1999....	6,979,357	757,568	466,870	494,489	1,718,927	8,698,284	19.8	8.7	5.4
2000....	6,830,505	862,780	516,614	636,726	2,016,120	8,846,625	22.8	9.8	5.8
2001....	6,324,996	836,685	522,659	738,285	2,097,629	8,422,625	24.9	9.9	6.2
2002....	5,877,645	923,182	546,654	755,748	2,225,584	8,103,229	27.5	11.4	6.7
2003....	5,527,430	817,038	543,823	722,190	2,083,051	7,610,481	27.4	10.7	7.1
2004....	5,356,873	798,222	541,940	808,897	2,149,059	7,505,932	28.6	10.6	7.2
2005....	5,480,533	922,934	534,286	729,313	2,186,533	7,667,066	28.5	12.0	7.0

(1) Includes cars manufactured in Canada and Mexico.

U.S. Car Sales by Vehicle Size and Type, 1985-2005

Source: Ward's Communications; percent of total U.S. sales

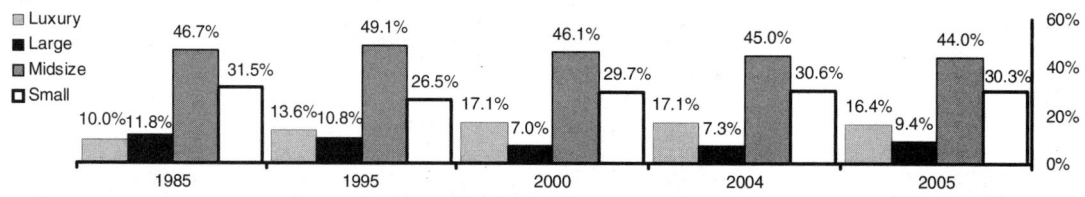

Top-Selling Passenger Cars in the U.S. by Calendar Year, 2002-05

Source: Ward's Communications

2005

1. Toyota Camry 431,703	8. Chevrolet Malibu 203,503	15. Pontiac Grand Prix...... 122,398
2. Honda Accord 369,293	9. Ford Taurus........... 196,919	16. Nissan Sentra 119,489
3. Toyota Corolla/Matrix ... 341,290	10. Ford Focus 184,825	17. Hyundai Elantra........ 116,336
4. Honda Civic........... 308,415	11. Ford Mustang 160,975	18. Dodge Neon........... 113,332
5. Nissan Altima 255,371	12. Chrysler 300 Series..... 144,048	19. Ford Five Hundred...... 107,932
6. Chevrolet Impala....... 246,481	13. Hyundai Sonata........ 130,365	20. Toyota Prius.......... 107,897
7. Chevrolet Cobalt 212,667	14. Pontiac G6........... 124,844	

2004

		2003		**2002**	
1. Toyota Camry 426,990		1. Toyota Camry 413,296		1. Toyota Camry.......... 434,145	
2. Honda Accord 386,770		2. Honda Accord 397,750		2. Honda Accord.......... 398,980	
3. Toyota Corolla/Matrix ... 333,161		3. Toyota Corolla/Matrix ... 325,477		3. Ford Taurus 332,690	
4. Honda Civic........... 309,196		4. Ford Taurus.......... 300,496		4. Honda Civic 313,159	
5. Chevrolet Impala....... 290,259		5. Honda Civic.......... 299,672		5. Toyota Corolla/Matrix ... 254,360	
6. Chevrolet Malibu 268,017		6. Chevrolet Impala...... 267,882		6. Ford Focus 243,199	
7. Ford Taurus........... 248,148		7. Chevrolet Cavalier..... 256,550		7. Chevrolet Cavalier 238,225	
8. Nissan Altima 235,889		8. Ford Focus 229,353		8. Nissan Altima 201,822	
9. Ford Focus 208,339		9. Nissan Altima 201,240		9. Chevrolet Impala....... 198,918	
10. Chevrolet Cavalier...... 195,275		10. Chevrolet Malibu 173,263		10. Chevrolet Malibu........ 169,377	

Top-Selling Light Trucks in the U.S. by Calendar Year, 2003-05

2005		**2004**		**2003**	
1. Ford F Series.......... 854,878		1. Ford F Series 891,482		1. Ford F Series 806,887	
2. Chevrolet Silverado..... 705,980		2. Chevrolet Silverado..... 680,663		2. Chevrolet Silverado 683,889	
3. Dodge Ram Pickup 400,543		3. Dodge Ram Pickup..... 426,289		3. Dodge Ram Pickup......449,371	
4. Chevrolet TrailBlazer.... 244,150		4. Ford Explorer 339,333		4. Ford Explorer 373,118	
5. Ford Explorer.......... 239,788		5. Chevrolet TrailBlazer.... 283,484		5. Chevrolet TrailBlazer ...261,334	
6. GMC Sierra........... 229,488		6. Dodge Caravan........ 242,307		6. Dodge Caravan.........233,394	
7. Dodge Caravan........ 226,771		7. GMC Sierra........... 213,736		7. Ford Ranger...........209,117	
8. Jeep Grand Cherokee... 213,584		8. Chevrolet Tahoe 186,161		8. Jeep Grand Cherokee ...207,479	
9. Chrysler Town & Country 180,759		9. Ford Escape 183,430		9. Chevy Tahoe 199,065	
10. Ford Econoline 179,543		10. Jeep Grand Cherokee... 182,313		10. GMC Sierra............196,429	

Sport Utility Vehicle Sales in the U.S., 1988-2005

Source: Ward's Communications

In 1988, 960,852 sport utility vehicles (SUVs) were sold in the United States, accounting for almost 19% of all light trucks and just over 6% of all sales of light vehicles (cars, SUVs, minivans, vans, pickup trucks, and trucks under 14,000 lbs.). In 2004, that percentage had increased to 28%, but in 2005 SUV sales decreased 2.1% from the previous year to 4,623,960, or 27% of all light vehicles sold (52% of light trucks).

Sales shown here include those for SUVs and lighter SUV models known as crossover or cross utility vehicles, which are generally smaller and get better gas mileage. If separated, SUV sales declined 18.9% since 2002 from 2,974,466 to 2,415,764 in 2005. But crossover vehicle sales increased dramatically to 2,208,196 in 2005, up 78% from 1,237,620 in 2003.

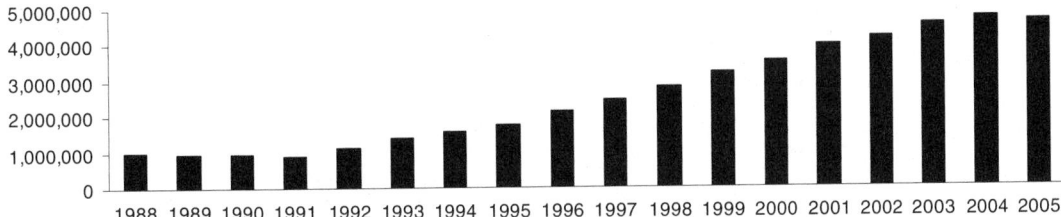

Most Popular Colors, by Type of Vehicle, 2005 Model Year

Source: Ward's Communications; Du Pont Automotive Products

Luxury Cars		Full Size/Intermediate Cars		Compact/Sports Cars		Light Trucks	
Color	Percent	Color	Percent	Color	Percent	Color	Percent
Silver	20	Silver	21	Silver	20	White/White Pearl	21
White/White Pearl	18	Gray	14	Gray	17	Gray	17
Black	16	Red	13	Blue	16	Silver	16
Blue	13	Light Brown	12	Black	14	Blue	12
Light Brown	10	Blue	11	White/White Pearl	10	Red	11
Red	7	White/White Pearl	11	Red	9	Black	10
Yellow/Gold	6	Black	10	Green	6	Light Brown	7
Green	5	Green	4	Light Brown	5	Green	4
Gray	4	Yellow/Gold	3	Yellow/Gold	1	Yellow/Gold	1
Other	1	Other	1	Other	2	Other	1

U.S. Light-Vehicle Fuel Efficiency, 1975-2006

Source: Environmental Protection Agency, Office of Transportation and Air Quality, National Vehicle and Fuel Emissions Laboratory

After showing significant fuel-efficiency improvements from 1974 through 1985, both light-duty trucks (SUVs, minivans, vans, and light trucks) and cars have failed to show consistent gains since then. In addition, light-duty trucks, which are less fuel-efficient than cars, have captured an increasing proportion of the total light vehicle market, rising from only 19% in 1975 to an estimated 50% by 2005. This increase has been a major factor in the leveling off in the fuel efficiency of the average light vehicle sold.

YEAR	Cars (MPG*)	Light-duty Trucks (MPG*)	All Light Vehicles (MPG*)	YEAR	Cars (MPG*)	Light-duty Trucks (MPG*)	All Light Vehicles (MPG*)
1975	13.5	11.6	13.1	1999	24.1	17.5	20.6
1980	20.0	15.8	19.2	2000	24.1	17.7	20.7
1985	23.0	17.5	21.3	2001	24.3	17.6	20.7
1990	23.7	17.7	21.5	2002	24.5	17.6	20.6
1995	24.2	17.5	21.1	2003	24.7	17.8	20.8
1996	24.2	17.8	21.2	2004	24.7	17.7	20.5
1997	24.3	17.6	20.9	2005	25.0	18.1	21.0
1998	24.4	17.8	20.9	2006	24.6	18.4	21.0

*MPG value represents laboratory city and highway fuel efficiency combined in a 55%/45% ratio.

Cars Registered in the U.S., 1900-2004[1]

Source: U.S. Dept. of Transportation, Federal Highway Administration

(includes automobiles for public and private use)

Year	Cars Reg.	Year	Cars Reg.	Year	Cars Reg.	Year	Cars Reg.	Year	Cars Reg.
1900	8,000	1935	22,567,827	1970	89,243,557	1993	127,327,189	2000	133,621,420
1905	77,400	1940	27,465,826	1975	106,705,934	1994	127,883,469	2001	137,633,467
1910	458,377	1945	25,796,985	1980	121,600,843	1995	128,386,775	2002	135,920,677
1915	2,332,426	1950	40,339,077	1985	127,885,193	1996	129,728,311	2003	135,669,897
1920	8,131,522	1955	52,144,739	1990	133,700,497	1997	129,748,704	2004	136,430,651
1925	17,481,001	1960	61,671,390	1991	128,299,601	1998	131,838,538		
1930	23,034,753	1965	75,257,588	1992	126,581,148	1999	132,432,044		

(1) There were no publicly owned vehicles before 1925; statistics also exclude military vehicles for all years. Alaska and Hawaii data included since 1960.

World Almanac Quick Quiz

Rank these countries by the amount of money that they had directly invested in companies in the U.S. in 2005.

(a) Australia   (b) Italy   (c) Luxembourg   (d) United Kingdom

For the answer look in this chapter, or see page 1008.

Licensed Drivers, by Age, 1980-2004

Source: Federal Highway Administration, U.S. Dept. of Transportation

(in thousands)

AGE	1980			1990			2004		
	Male	Female	Total[1]	Male	Female	Total[1]	Male	Female	Total[1]
(under 16).............	52	41	93	23	20	43	13	12	25
16..................	1,001	822	1,823	769	674	1,443	634	616	1,251
17..................	1,530	1,260	2,790	1,136	996	2,132	1,112	1,069	2,181
18..................	1,763	1,484	3,247	1,378	1,217	2,595	1,424	1,343	2,767
19..................	1,900	1,643	3,542	1,608	1,429	3,037	1,596	1,514	3,110
(19 and under)	6,246	5,249	11,496	4,913	4,336	9,249	4,779	4,554	9,333
20..................	1,930	1,706	3,636	1,691	1,538	3,229	1,619	1,558	3,177
21..................	1,961	1,772	3,733	1,694	1,555	3,249	1,671	1,621	3,292
22..................	1,998	1,813	3,811	1,701	1,561	3,262	1,725	1,684	3,410
23..................	2,062	1,876	3,938	1,767	1,631	3,398	1,757	1,724	3,481
24..................	2,047	1,868	3,915	1,951	1,807	3,758	1,788	1,752	3,540
(20-24)	9,998	9,034	19,032	8,804	8,093	16,897	8,560	8,339	16,899
25-29	9,865	9,060	18,925	10.239	9,656	19,895	8,804	8,577	17,381
30-34	9,010	8,359	17,369	10,507	10,071	20,578	9,496	9,188	18,684
35-39	7,113	6,583	13,696	9,684	9,371	19,055	9,850	9,578	19,428
40-44	5,828	5,306	11,134	8,610	8,295	16,905	10,722	10,608	21,330
45-49	5,311	4,765	10,076	6,642	6,378	13,020	10,375	10,374	20,749
50-54	5,351	4,739	10,090	5,376	5,108	10,484	9,198	9,245	18,443
55-59	5,198	4,572	9,770	4,855	4,583	9,438	7,878	7,901	15,779
60-64	4,439	3,793	8,232	4,738	4,497	9,235	5,924	5,962	11,886
65-69	3,631	2,949	6,580	4,266	4,109	8,375	4,474	4,535	9,010
(70 and over)	5,195	3,699	8,894	7,159	6,726	13,885	9,510	10,457	19,965
70-74	NA	NA	NA	NA	NA	NA	3,607	3,748	7,355
75-79	NA	NA	NA	NA	NA	NA	2,876	3,188	6,063
80-84	NA	NA	NA	NA	NA	NA	1,897	2,182	4,079
85 and over	NA	NA	NA	NA	NA	NA	1,129	1,340	2,469
TOTAL...............	**77,187**	**68,108**	**145,295**	**85,792**	**81,223**	**167,015**	**99,571**	**99,318**	**198,889**

(1) These totals may not add due to rounding. NA = not available.

Highway Speed Limits, by State

Source: Insurance Institute for Highway Safety

Under the National Highway System Designation Act of 1995, states are allowed to set their own highway speed limits. Under federal legislation enacted in 1974 during the energy crisis, states had been, in effect, restricted to a National Maximum Speed Limit (NMSL) of 55 miles per hour (raised in 1987 to 65 mph on rural interstates).

Maximum posted speed limits, in miles per hour, are given by state in the table below. (Speeds shown in parentheses are for commercial trucks.) Most data current as of Sept. 2006. For more information visit the Insurance Institute for Highway Safety website at www.hwysafety.org

STATE	Rural Interstate	Urban[1] Interstate	Limited[2] Access Roads	Other Roads	STATE	Rural Interstate	Urban[1] Interstate	Limited[2] Access Roads	Other Roads
AL	70	65	65	65	MT	75 (65)	65	70[3]	70[3]
AK	65	55	65	55	NE	75	65	65	60
AZ	75	55	55	55	NV	75	65	70	70
AR	70 (65)	55	60	55	NH	65	65	55	55
CA	70 (55)	65	70	65	NJ	65	55	65	55
CO	75	65	65	65	NM	75	75	65	55
CT	65	55	65	55	NY	65	65	65	55
DC	–	55	–	25	NC	70	70	70	55
DE	65	55	65	55	ND	75	75	70	65
FL	70	65	70	65	OH	65 (55)[3]	65	55	55
GA	70	65	65	65	OK	75	70	70	70
HI	60	50	45	45	OR	65 (55)	55	55	55
ID	75 (65)	75	65	65	PA	65	55	65	55
IL	65 (55)	55	65	55	RI	65	55	55	55
IN	70 (65)	55	60	55	SC	70	70	60	55
IA	70	55	70	55	SD	75	75	70	70
KS	70	70	70	65	TN	70	70	70	65
KY	65	65	65	55	TX	75 (65)[4]	70[4]	75 (65)[4]	60[5]
LA	70	70	70	65	UT	75	65	75	65
ME	65	65	65	60	VT	65	55	50	50
MD	65	65	65	55	VA	65	65	65	55
MA	65	65	65	55	WA	70 (60)	60	60	60
MI	70 (60)	65	70	55	WV	70	55	65	55
MN	70	65	65	55	WI	65	65	65	55
MS	70	70	70	65	WY	75	60	65	65
MO	70	60	70	65					

(1) Urban interstates are determined from U.S. Census Bureau criteria, which may be adjusted by state and local governments to reflect planning and other issues. (2) Limited access roads are multiple-lane highways with restricted access via exit and entrance ramps rather than intersections. (3) Trucks on the Ohio Turnpike only may travel at 65 mph.(4) Speed limit is 65 mph at night (½ hour after sunset to ½ hour before sunrise). (5) Speed limit is 55 mph at night (½ hour after sunset to ½ hour before sunrise).

Selected Motor Vehicle Statistics

Source: Federal Highway Admin.; U.S. Dept. of Transportation; Insurance Institute for Highway Safety; American Petroleum Institute
Driver's license age requirements, state gas tax, and safety belt laws (incl. laws passed, but not in effect) as of 2006; other figures for 2004.

STATE	Driver's license age requirements Regular[1]	Learner's Permit	State gas tax cents/ gal.	Safety belt use law[11]	Licensed drivers per 1,000 resident pop.	Licensed drivers per motor vehicle	Regist. motor vehicles per 1,000 pop.	Gals. of fuel used per vehicle	Miles per gal.	Annual miles driven per vehicle	Vehicle miles per licensed driver
Alabama	17	15	18	P	798	0.81	976	769	17.26	13,270	16,339
Alaska	16y, 6m	14	8	P	736	0.74	974	793	9.73	7,718	10,341
Arizona	16	15y, 7m	18	P	659	1.01	628	951	16.16	15,365	15,153
Arkansas	16	14	20	P	677	0.99	677	1,101	15.27	16,811	16,993
California	17[2]	15y, 6m	18	P	634	0.77	853	611	17.47	10,666	14,451
Colorado	17	15[3]	22	P	697	1.62	424	1,347	17.24	23,220	14,318
Connecticut	18[2]	16[3]	25	P	769	0.90	852	715	14.79	10,569	11,730
Delaware	17[2]	16[3]	23	P	643	0.76	826	710	18.80	13,355	17,419
Dist. of Col.	18[4]	16	20	P	631	1.54	408	785	21.24	16,668	10,718
Florida	18	15	14.9	P	756	0.89	826	689	19.41	13,362	14,943
Georgia	18	15	10	P	656	0.75	854	849	17.12	14,536	19,440
Hawaii	17[2,4]	15y, 6m	16	P	668	0.91	725	541	19.45	10,517	11,524
Idaho	16[5]	14y, 6m	25	P	677	0.71	922	665	16.80	11,179	15,620
Illinois	17[2]	15[3]	19	P	634	0.88	715	735	16.27	11,958	13,544
Indiana	18	15	18	P	725	0.83	861	836	16.10	13,460	16,082
Iowa	17[2]	14	21	P	678	0.60	1,117	678	14.05	9,519	15,740
Kansas	16	14	24	P	724	0.85	843	763	16.52	12,612	14,735
Kentucky	17[6]	16	19	P	681	0.86	781	981	14.80	14,527	16,760
Louisiana	17[5,7]	15	20	P	702	0.86	811	824	14.76	12,166	14,073
Maine	16y, 6m[2]	15[3]	25.9	P	748	0.94	789	859	16.69	14,331	15,178
Maryland	17y, 9m[2]	15y, 9m[3]	23.5	P	647	0.88	726	796	17.09	13,599	15,381
Massachusetts	18[2]	16	21	P	724	0.86	841	616	16.52	10,174	11,789
Michigan	17[2]	14y, 9m	19	P	702	0.86	813	731	17.19	12,557	14,546
Minnesota	16[2]	15[3]	20	P	604	0.68	882	753	16.60	12,501	18,349
Mississippi	16	15	18	P	653	0.98	658	1,177	17.42	20,506	20,797
Missouri	17y, 11m	15	17	P	703	0.85	822	903	16.03	14,474	17,045
Montana	16	14y, 6m	27	P	769	0.72	1,048	744	15.36	11,427	15,721
Nebraska	17	15	26.1	P	753	0.80	934	784	14.89	11,666	14,570
Nevada	18	15y, 6m[2]	23	S	663	1.23	520	1,146	13.46	15,426	12,502
New Hampshire	17y, 1m	15y, 6m	18	none	759	0.85	884	723	15.79	11,410	13,407
New Jersey	18[8]	16[3]	10.5	P	667	0.96	693	875	13.77	12,049	12,560
New Mexico	16y, 6m[2]	15	17	P	668	0.85	778	969	16.46	15,961	18,832
New York	18	16[9]	23.9	P	585	1.03	562	669	19.06	12,750	12,261
North Carolina	16y, 6m[2]	15	29.9	P	717	1.00	698	918	17.24	15,665	15,665
North Dakota	16	14	23	S	728	0.67	1,073	767	14.49	11,113	16,445
Ohio	17[2]	15y, 6m	28	S	670	0.73	910	659	16.24	10,702	14,548
Oklahoma	16y, 6m	15y, 6m	20	P	673	0.77	861	840	18.11	15,205	19,599
Oregon	17[2]	15	24	P	731	0.90	801	716	17.05	12,211	13,557
Pennsylvania	18[8]	16	32	S	680	0.87	777	696	16.07	11,187	12,819
Rhode Island	17y, 6m[2]	16	30	S(a)	686	0.93	739	558	19.09	10,650	11,422
South Carolina	16y, 6m	15	16	P	708	0.93	749	1,042	14.92	15,538	16,671
South Dakota	16	14	20	S	731	0.69	1,054	755	14.23	10,738	15,594
Tennessee	17	15[3]	20	P	720	0.86	825	829	17.39	14,413	16,701
Texas	16y, 6m	15[3]	20	P	647	0.88	718	924	15.24	14,084	15,884
Utah	17[10]	15	24.5	S(a)	662	0.77	832	690	17.42	12,017	15,605
Vermont	16y, 6m[2]	15	19	S	886	1.08	818	821	18.76	15,404	14,270
Virginia	18[2]	15y, 6m	17.5	P	685	0.80	845	803	15.37	12,340	15,428
Washington	17[2]	15	31	P	726	0.82	867	616	16.58	10,209	12,359
West Virginia	17	15	20.5	S	712	0.96	742	857	17.56	15,054	15,713
Wisconsin	16y, 9m[2]	15y, 6m	32.9	S	710	0.84	835	719	18.19	13,068	15,447
Wyoming	16y, 6m	15	14	S	751	0.61	1,212	1,114	13.47	15,006	24,360
AVERAGE			21		677	0.85	784	768	16.59	12,744	15,195

NOTE: Many states are moving toward graduated licensing systems that phase in full driving privileges. During the learner's phase, driving generally is not permitted unless there is an adult supervisor. In an intermediate phase, young licensees not yet having unrestricted licenses may be allowed to drive unsupervised under certain conditions but not others. (1) Unrestricted operation of private passenger car. (2) Applicants under age 18 (19 in VA) must have completed an approved driver education course (or home training in CT). (3) May not use cell phones during learner's phase (may also extend to intermediate phases). (4) Learner's phase mandatory for all ages. Applicants under age 21 must complete a 6-month intermediate phase. (5) Applicants under age 17 must have completed an approved driver education course. (6) License holders under age 18 must complete a 4-hour course on safe driving within 1 yr. of receiving license. (7) Applicants age 17 and older must have completed an educational program, but doesn't require behind-the-wheel training. (8) 17 after completion of approved drivers' education program. (9) Driving in New York City is prohibited for all licensees under 18, or under 17 if driver has completed an approved driver education course. (10) Regardless of age, applicants must enroll in an approved driver education course. (11) P = officer may stop vehicle for a violation (primary); S = an officer may issue seat belt citation only when vehicle is stopped for another moving violation (secondary). (a) Primary enforcement for children under a specified age: MO-16; RI-18; UT-19.

Road Mileage Between Selected U.S. Cities

	Atlanta	Boston	Chicago	Cincinnati	Cleveland	Dallas	Denver	Des Moines	Detroit	Houston
Atlanta, GA........	...	1,037	674	440	672	795	1,398	870	699	789
Boston, MA........	1,037	...	963	840	628	1,748	1,949	1,280	695	1,804
Chicago, IL........	674	963	...	287	335	917	996	327	266	1,067
Cincinnati, OH	440	840	287	...	244	920	1,164	571	259	1,029
Cleveland, OH	672	628	335	244	...	1,159	1,321	652	170	1,273
Dallas, TX........	795	1,748	917	920	1,159	...	781	684	1,143	243
Denver, CO	1,398	1,949	996	1,164	1,321	781	...	669	1,253	1,019
Detroit, MI........	699	695	266	259	170	1,143	1,253	584	...	1,265
Houston, TX......	789	1,804	1,067	1,029	1,273	243	1,019	905	1,265	...
Indianapolis, IN	493	906	181	106	294	865	1,058	465	278	987
Kansas City, MO ...	798	1,391	499	591	779	489	600	195	743	710
Los Angeles, CA...	2,182	2,979	2,054	2,179	2,367	1,387	1,059	1,727	2,311	1,538
Memphis, TN	371	1,296	530	468	712	452	1,040	599	713	561
Milwaukee, WI	761	1,050	87	374	422	991	1,029	361	353	1,142
Minneapolis, MN ...	1,068	1,368	405	692	740	936	841	252	671	1,157
New Orleans, LA ...	479	1,507	912	786	1,030	496	1,273	978	1,045	356
New York, NY......	841	206	802	647	473	1,552	1,771	1,119	637	1,608
Omaha, NE	986	1,412	459	693	784	644	537	132	716	865
Philadelphia, PA....	741	296	738	567	413	1,452	1,691	1,051	573	1,508
Pittsburgh, PA	687	561	452	287	129	1,204	1,411	763	287	1,313
Portland, OR	2,601	3,046	2,083	2,333	2,418	2,009	1,238	1,786	2,349	2,205
St. Louis, MO	541	1,141	289	340	529	630	857	333	513	779
San Francisco, CA..	2,496	3,095	2,142	2,362	2,467	1,753	1,235	1,815	2,399	1,912
Seattle, WA	2,618	2,976	2,013	2,300	2,348	2,078	1,307	1,749	2,279	2,274
Tulsa, OK	772	1,537	683	736	925	257	681	443	909	478
Washington, DC....	608	429	671	481	346	1,319	1,616	984	506	1,375

	Indianapolis	Kansas City	Los Angeles	Louisville	Memphis	Milwaukee	Minneapolis	New Orleans	New York	Omaha
Atlanta, GA........	493	798	2,182	382	371	761	1,068	479	841	986
Boston, MA........	906	1,391	2,979	941	1,296	1,050	1,368	1,507	206	1,412
Chicago, IL........	181	499	2,054	292	530	87	405	912	802	459
Cincinnati, OH	106	591	2,179	101	468	374	692	786	647	693
Cleveland, OH	294	779	2,367	345	712	422	740	1,030	473	784
Dallas, TX........	865	489	1,387	819	452	991	936	496	1,552	644
Denver, CO	1,058	600	1,059	1,120	1,040	1,029	841	1,273	1,771	537
Detroit, MI........	278	743	2,311	360	713	353	671	1,045	637	716
Houston, TX......	987	710	1,538	928	561	1,142	1,157	356	1,608	865
Indianapolis, IN	...	485	2,073	111	435	268	586	796	713	587
Kansas City, MO ...	485	...	1,589	520	451	537	447	806	1,198	201
Los Angeles, CA...	2,073	1,589	...	2,108	1,817	2,087	1,889	1,883	2,786	1,595
Memphis, TN	435	451	1,817	367	...	612	826	390	1,100	652
Milwaukee, WI	268	537	2,087	379	612	...	332	994	889	493
Minneapolis, MN ...	586	447	1,889	697	826	332	...	1,214	1,207	357
New Orleans, LA ...	796	806	1,883	685	390	994	1,214	...	1,311	1,007
New York, NY......	713	1,198	2,786	748	1,100	889	1,207	1,311	...	1,251
Omaha, NE	587	201	1,595	687	652	493	357	1,007	1,251	...
Philadelphia, PA....	633	1,118	2,706	668	1,000	825	1,143	1,211	100	1,183
Pittsburgh, PA	353	838	2,426	388	752	539	857	1,070	368	895
Portland, OR	2,272	1,809	959	2,320	2,259	2,010	1,678	2,505	2,885	1,654
St. Louis, MO	235	257	1,845	263	285	363	552	673	948	449
San Francisco, CA..	2,293	1,835	379	2,349	2,125	2,175	1,940	2,249	2,934	1,683
Seattle, WA	2,194	1,839	1,131	2,305	2,290	1,940	1,608	2,574	2,815	1,638
Tulsa, OK	631	248	1,452	659	401	757	695	647	1,344	387
Washington, DC....	558	1,043	2,631	582	867	758	1,076	1,078	233	1,116

	Philadelphia	Pittsburgh	Portland	St. Louis	Salt Lake City	San Francisco	Seattle	Toledo	Tulsa	Wash., DC
Atlanta, GA........	741	687	2,601	541	1,878	2,496	2,618	640	772	608
Boston, MA........	296	561	3,046	1,141	2,343	3,095	2,976	739	1,537	429
Chicago, IL........	738	452	2,083	289	1,390	2,142	2,013	232	683	671
Cincinnati, OH	567	287	2,333	340	1,610	2,362	2,300	200	736	481
Cleveland, OH	413	129	2,418	529	1,715	2,467	2,348	111	925	346
Dallas, TX........	1,452	1,204	2,009	630	1,242	1,753	2,078	1,084	257	1,319
Denver, CO	1,691	1,411	1,238	857	504	1,235	1,307	1,218	681	1,616
Detroit, MI........	576	287	2,349	513	1,647	2,399	2,279	59	909	506
Houston, TX......	1,508	1,313	2,205	779	1,438	1,912	2,274	1,206	478	1,375
Indianapolis, IN	633	353	2,272	235	1,504	2,293	2,194	219	631	558
Kansas City, MO ...	1,118	838	1,809	257	1,086	1,835	1,839	687	248	1,043
Los Angeles, CA...	2,706	2,426	959	1,845	715	379	1,131	2,276	1,452	2,631
Memphis, TN	1,000	752	2,259	285	1,535	2,125	2,290	654	401	867
Milwaukee, WI	825	539	2,010	363	1,423	2,175	1,940	319	757	758
Minneapolis, MN ...	1,143	857	1,678	552	1,186	1,940	1,608	637	695	1,076
New Orleans, LA ...	1,211	1,070	2,505	673	1,738	2,249	2,574	986	647	1,078
New York, NY......	100	368	2,885	948	2,182	2,934	2,815	578	1,344	233
Omaha, NE	1,183	895	1,654	449	931	1,683	1,638	681	387	1,116
Philadelphia, PA....	...	288	2,821	868	2,114	2,866	2,751	514	1,264	133
Pittsburgh,, PA	288	...	2,535	588	1,826	2,578	2,465	228	984	221
Portland, OR	2,821	2,535	...	2,060	767	636	172	2,315	1,913	2,754
St. Louis, MO	868	588	2,060	...	1,337	2,089	2,081	454	396	793
San Francisco, CA..	2,866	2,578	636	2,089	752	...	808	2,364	1,760	2,799
Seattle, WA	2,751	2,465	172	2,081	836	808	...	2,245	1,982	2,684
Tulsa, OK	1,264	984	1,913	396	1,172	1,760	1,982	850	...	1,189
Washington, DC....	133	221	2,754	793	2,047	2,799	2,684	447	1,189	...

Air Distances Between Selected World Cities in Statute Miles

Point-to-point measurements are usually from City Hall.

	Bangkok	Beijing	Berlin	Cairo	Cape Town	Caracas	Chicago	Hong Kong	Honolulu	Lima
Bangkok..........	...	2,046	5,352	4,523	6,300	10,555	8,570	1,077	6,609	12,244
Beijing	2,046	...	4,584	4,698	8,044	8,950	6,604	1,217	5,077	10,349
Berlin	5,352	4,584	...	1,797	5,961	5,238	4,414	5,443	7,320	6,896
Cairo.............	4,523	4,698	1,797	...	4,480	6,342	6,141	5,066	8,848	7,726
Cape Town........	6,300	8,044	5,961	4,480	...	6,366	8,491	7,376	11,535	6,072
Caracas	10,555	8,950	5,238	6,342	6,366	...	2,495	10,165	6,021	1,707
Chicago	8,570	6,604	4,414	6,141	8,491	2,495	...	7,797	4,256	3,775
Hong Kong	1,077	1,217	5,443	5,066	7,376	10,165	7,797	...	5,556	11,418
Honolulu..........	6,609	5,077	7,320	8,848	11,535	6,021	4,256	5,556	...	5,947
London...........	5,944	5,074	583	2,185	5,989	4,655	3,958	5,990	7,240	6,316
Los Angeles	7,637	6,250	5,782	7,520	9,969	3,632	1,745	7,240	2,557	4,171
Madrid	6,337	5,745	1,165	2,087	5,308	4,346	4,189	6,558	7,872	5,907
Melbourne	4,568	5,643	9,918	8,675	6,425	9,717	9,673	4,595	5,505	8,059
Mexico City.......	9,793	7,753	6,056	7,700	8,519	2,234	1,690	8,788	3,789	2,639
Montreal..........	8,338	6,519	3,740	5,427	7,922	2,438	745	7,736	4,918	3,970
Moscow	4,389	3,607	1,006	1,803	6,279	6,177	4,987	4,437	7,047	7,862
New York	8,669	6,844	3,979	5,619	7,803	2,120	714	8,060	4,969	3,639
Paris.............	5,877	5,120	548	1,998	5,786	4,732	4,143	5,990	7,449	6,370
Rio de Janeiro	9,994	10,768	6,209	6,143	3,781	2,804	5,282	11,009	8,288	2,342
Rome	5,494	5,063	737	1,326	5,231	5,195	4,824	5,774	8,040	6,750
San Francisco	7,931	5,918	5,672	7,466	10,248	3,902	1,859	6,905	2,398	4,518
Singapore.........	883	2,771	6,164	5,137	6,008	11,402	9,372	1,605	6,726	11,689
Stockholm	5,089	4,133	528	2,096	6,423	5,471	4,331	5,063	6,875	7,166
Tokyo	2,865	1,307	5,557	5,958	9,154	8,808	6,314	1,791	3,859	9,631
Warsaw	5,033	4,325	322	1,619	5,935	5,559	4,679	5,147	7,366	7,215
Washington, DC....	8,807	6,942	4,181	5,822	7,895	2,047	596	8,155	4,838	3,509

	London	Los Angeles	Madrid	Melbourne	Mexico City	Montreal	Moscow	New Delhi	New York	Paris
Bangkok..........	5,944	7,637	6,337	4,568	9,793	8,338	4,389	1,813	8,669	5,877
Beijing	5,074	6,250	5,745	5,643	7,753	6,519	3,607	2,353	6,844	5,120
Berlin	583	5,782	1,165	9,918	6,056	3,740	1,006	3,598	3,979	548
Cairo.............	2,185	7,520	2,087	8,675	7,700	5,427	1,803	2,758	5,619	1,998
Cape Town........	5,989	9,969	5,308	6,425	8,519	7,922	6,279	5,769	7,803	5,786
Caracas	4,655	3,632	4,346	9,717	2,234	2,438	6,177	8,833	2,120	4,732
Chicago	3,958	1,745	4,189	9,673	1,690	745	4,987	7,486	714	4,143
Hong Kong	5,990	7,240	6,558	4,595	8,788	7,736	4,437	2,339	8,060	5,990
Honolulu..........	7,240	2,557	7,872	5,505	3,789	4,918	7,047	7,412	4,969	7,449
London...........	...	5,439	785	10,500	5,558	3,254	1,564	4,181	3,469	214
Los Angeles	5,439	...	5,848	7,931	1,542	2,427	6,068	7,011	2,451	5,601
Madrid	785	5,848	...	10,758	5,643	3,448	2,147	4,530	3,593	655
Melbourne	10,500	7,931	10,758	...	8,426	10,395	8,950	6,329	10,359	10,430
Mexico City.......	5,558	1,542	5,643	8,426	...	2,317	6,676	9,120	2,090	5,725
Montreal..........	3,254	2,427	3,448	10,395	2,317	...	4,401	7,012	331	3,432
Moscow	1,564	6,068	2,147	8,950	6,676	4,401	...	2,698	4,683	1,554
New York	3,469	2,451	3,593	10,359	2,090	331	4,683	7,318	...	3,636
Paris.............	214	5,601	655	10,430	5,725	3,432	1,554	4,102	3,636	...
Rio de Janeiro	5,750	6,330	5,045	8,226	4,764	5,078	7,170	8,753	4,801	5,684
Rome	895	6,326	851	9,929	6,377	4,104	1,483	3,684	4,293	690
San Francisco	5,367	347	5,803	7,856	1,887	2,543	5,885	7,691	2,572	5,577
Singapore.........	6,747	8,767	7,080	3,759	10,327	9,203	5,228	2,571	9,534	6,673
Stockholm	942	5,454	1,653	9,630	6,012	3,714	716	3,414	3,986	1,003
Tokyo	5,959	5,470	6,706	5,062	7,035	6,471	4,660	3,638	6,757	6,053
Warsaw	905	5,922	1,427	9,598	6,337	4,022	721	3,277	4,270	852
Washington, DC....	3,674	2,300	3,792	10,180	1,885	489	4,876	7,500	205	3,840

	Rio de Janeiro	Rome	San Francisco	Singapore	Stockholm	Tehran	Tokyo	Vienna	Warsaw	Wash., DC
Bangkok..........	9,994	5,494	7,931	883	5,089	3,391	2,865	5,252	5,033	8,807
Beijing	10,768	5,063	5,918	2,771	4,133	3,490	1,307	4,648	4,325	6,942
Berlin	6,209	737	5,672	6,164	528	2,185	5,557	326	322	4,181
Cairo.............	6,143	1,326	7,466	5,137	2,096	1,234	5,958	1,481	1,619	5,822
Cape Town........	3,781	5,231	10,248	6,008	6,423	5,241	9,154	5,656	5,935	7,895
Caracas	2,804	5,195	3,902	11,402	5,471	7,320	8,808	5,372	5,559	2,047
Chicago	5,282	4,824	1,859	9,372	4,331	6,502	6,314	4,698	4,679	596
Hong Kong	11,009	5,774	6,905	1,605	5,063	3,843	1,791	5,431	5,147	8,155
Honolulu..........	8,288	8,040	2,398	6,726	6,875	8,070	3,859	7,632	7,366	4,838
London...........	5,750	895	5,367	6,747	942	2,743	5,959	771	905	3,674
Los Angeles	6,330	6,326	347	8,767	5,454	7,682	5,470	6,108	5,922	2,300
Madrid	5,045	851	5,803	7,080	1,653	2,978	6,706	1,128	1,427	3,792
Melbourne	8,226	9,929	7,856	3,759	9,630	7,826	5,062	9,790	9,598	10,180
Mexico City.......	4,764	6,377	1,887	10,327	6,012	8,184	7,035	6,320	6,337	1,885
Montreal..........	5,078	4,104	2,543	9,203	3,714	5,880	6,471	4,009	4,022	489
Moscow	7,170	1,483	5,885	5,228	716	1,532	4,660	1,043	721	4,876
New York	4,801	4,293	2,572	9,534	3,986	6,141	6,757	4,234	4,270	205
Paris.............	5,684	690	5,577	6,673	1,003	2,625	6,053	645	852	3,840
Rio de Janeiro	...	5,707	6,613	9,785	6,683	7,374	11,532	6,127	6,455	4,779
Rome	5,707	...	6,259	6,229	1,245	2,127	6,142	477	820	4,497
San Francisco	6,613	6,259	...	8,448	5,399	7,362	5,150	5,994	5,854	2,441
Singapore.........	9,785	6,229	8,448	...	5,936	4,103	3,300	6,035	5,843	9,662
Stockholm	6,683	1,245	5,399	5,936	...	2,173	5,053	780	494	4,183
Tokyo	11,532	6,142	5,150	3,300	5,053	4,775	...	5,689	5,347	6,791
Warsaw	6,455	820	5,854	5,843	494	1,879	5,689	347	...	4,472
Washington, DC....	4,779	4,497	2,441	9,662	4,183	6,341	6,791	4,438	4,472	...

TRAVEL AND TOURISM

Tourism Trends

World tourist arrivals have grown steadily since 2003, increasing by 10% in 2004 and 5.6% in 2005, according to the World Tourism Organization based in Madrid, Spain. Worldwide, there were 808 mil international tourist arrivals in 2005, 42 mil more than in 2004. Worldwide tourism receipts, as measured in constant U.S. dollars and prices, rose 4.2%. Tourism receipts also reached a record value of $682 bil in 2005 (compared to $633 bil in 2004), but a large part of that gain resulted from the depreciation of the U.S. dollar, causing receipts in other currencies to convert to higher dollar amounts. Europe again commanded the largest share of international arrivals in 2005, 54.7% of the world total, with 441.6 mil international tourist arrivals, an increase of 4.0%. Asia and the Pacific posted the 2nd-largest share of world tourism at 19.4%, with 156.7 mil arrivals in 2005, an increase of 7.8% over 2004. Africa saw 36.8 mil arrivals, up by 10% over 2004. The Middle East had 39.7 mil arrivals, a 9.5% increase from 2004, down from the 20% increase of 2003-04. With 133.6 mil arrivals, the Americas experienced their second straight year of tourist growth, up 6.1% over 2004 overall, with much larger increases, 14.1% and 11.6%, respectively, in Central and South America.

Travel in most regions continued to climb Jan.-June 2006, especially in Africa and the Middle East, both of which posted 11% increases over the same period in 2005. The International Air Transport Assoc., which measures air passenger traffic in revenue passenger kilometers, reported a 6.8% increase in international passenger traffic in Jan.-Apr. 2006, compared with the same period in 2005. The Middle East region had the largest increase, at 18.3%. According to the IATA, air transport growth is expected to continue, especially among low-fare carriers, though cost of fuel presents challenges to air travel, having risen from 14% of operating costs in 2000 to 26% in 2006.

World Tourism Receipts, 1990-2005[1]

Source: World Tourism Organization

(in billions; figures rounded)

1990 . . . . $273	1994 . . . . $356	1998 . . . . $445	2002 . . . . $487
1991 278	1995 413	1999 455	2003 533
1992 317	1996 439	2000 483	2004 633
1993 323	1997 443	2001 472	2005 . . . . 682*

* Preliminary. (1) Tourism receipts are the total of all expenditures made by or on behalf of visitors, for and during the trip and stay.

Top 10 Countries in Tourism Earnings, 2005

Source: World Tourism Organization

International tourism receipts (excluding transportation); in billions of dollars

Rank Country	Receipts 2005*	2004	% change	Rank Country	Receipts 2005*	2004	% change
1. United States	$81.7	$74.5	9.6	6. China[1]	$29.3	$25.7	13.8
2. Spain	47.9	45.2	5.8	7. Germany	29.2	27.7	5.6
3. France	42.3	40.8	3.5	8. Turkey	18.2	15.9	14.2
4. Italy	35.4	35.7	-0.7	9. Austria	15.5	15.3	0.9
5. United Kingdom	30.4	28.2	7.6	10. Australia	14.9	13.6	9.5

* Preliminary. (1) Excluding Hong Kong.

Average Number of Vacation Days per Year, Selected Countries

Source: World Tourism Organization

Country	Days	Country	Days	Country	Days
Italy	42	Brazil	34	Korea	25
France	37	United Kingdom	28	Japan	25
Germany	35	Canada	26	United States	13

World's Top 10 Tourist Destinations, 2005

Source: World Tourism Organization

(number of arrivals in millions; excluding same-day visitors)

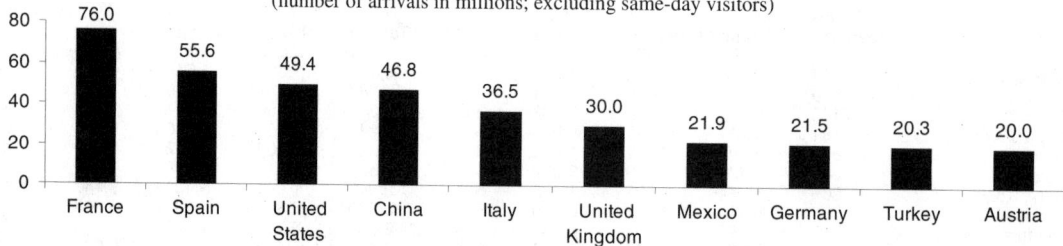

France	Spain	United States	China	Italy	United Kingdom	Mexico	Germany	Turkey	Austria
76.0	55.6	49.4	46.8	36.5	30.0	21.9	21.5	20.3	20.0

International Travel to the U.S., 1986-2005

Source: Office of Travel and Tourism Industries, Dept. of Commerce; World Tourism Organization

(Visitors each year are in millions; some figures are revised and may differ from other sources.)

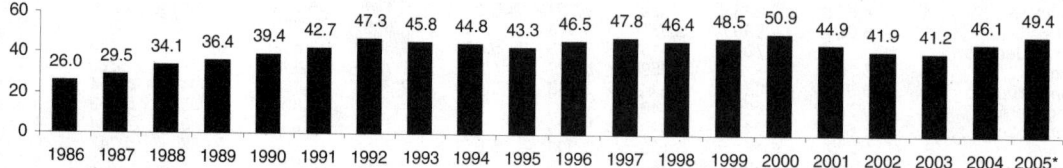

1986	1987	1988	1989	1990	1991	1992	1993	1994	1995	1996	1997	1998	1999	2000	2001	2002	2003	2004	2005*
26.0	29.5	34.1	36.4	39.4	42.7	47.3	45.8	44.8	43.3	46.5	47.8	46.4	48.5	50.9	44.9	41.9	41.2	46.1	49.4

* Preliminary figures

International Visitors to the U.S., 2005[1]

Source: Office of Travel and Tourism Industries, Dept. of Commerce

Country of origin	Visitors (thousands)	Expenditures (millions)[2]	Expenditures per visitor	Country of origin	Visitors (thousands)	Expenditures (millions)[2]	Expenditures per visitor
Canada[3]	14,900	$8,952	$601	Brazil	485	$1,577	$3,252
Mexico[3]	12,900	6,791	526	Netherlands	449	1,015	2,260
United Kingdom . .	4,300	10,684	2,485	China	405	1,628	4,020
Japan	3,900	12,719	3,261	Spain	386	–	–
Germany	1,400	3,810	2,721	Ireland	383	–	–
France	879	2,371	2,697	India	345	1,519	4,403
South Korea	705	2,551	3,618	Venezuela	340	1,135	3,338
Australia	582	2,244	3,856	Colombia	325	–	–
Italy	546	1,594	2,919	All countries	49,400	81,680	1,653

(1) Excludes cruise travel. (2) Excludes international passenger fare payments. (3) Does not include international traveler spending on U.S. carriers for transactions made outside the U.S.

Traveler Spending in the U.S., 1987-2004

Source: Office of Travel and Tourism Industries, Dept. of Commerce
(in billions)

	Domestic Travelers	International Travelers		Domestic Travelers	International Travelers		Domestic Travelers	International Travelers
1987	$235	$31	1993	$323	$58	1999 . . .	$458	$75
1988	258	38	1994	340	58	2000 . . .	488	82
1989	273	47	1995	360	63	2001 . . .	479	72
1990	291	43	1996	385	70	2002 . . .	474	67
1991	296	48	1997	406	73	2003 . . .	491	65
1992	306	55	1998	425	71	2004 . . .	532*	75

*Preliminary figure.

U.S. Domestic Leisure Travel Volume, 1994-2004[1]

Source: Travel Industry Assn. of America, TravelScope

(in millions of person-trips of 50 mi or more, one-way)

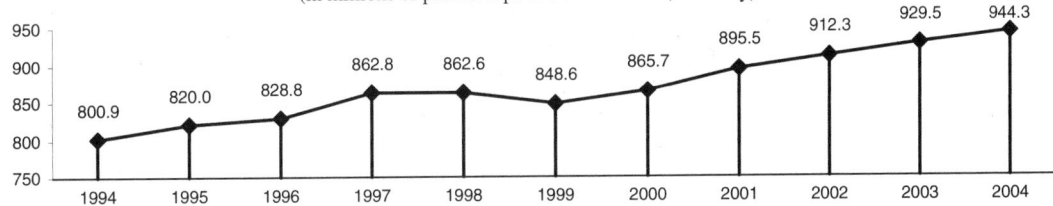

(1) Starting in 2003, based on a survey using revised methods to collect more traveling data; earlier years re-estimated to maintain comparability.

Top U.S. States by Domestic Traveler Spending

Source: Travel Industry Assn. of America
(billions of dollars; in 2004)

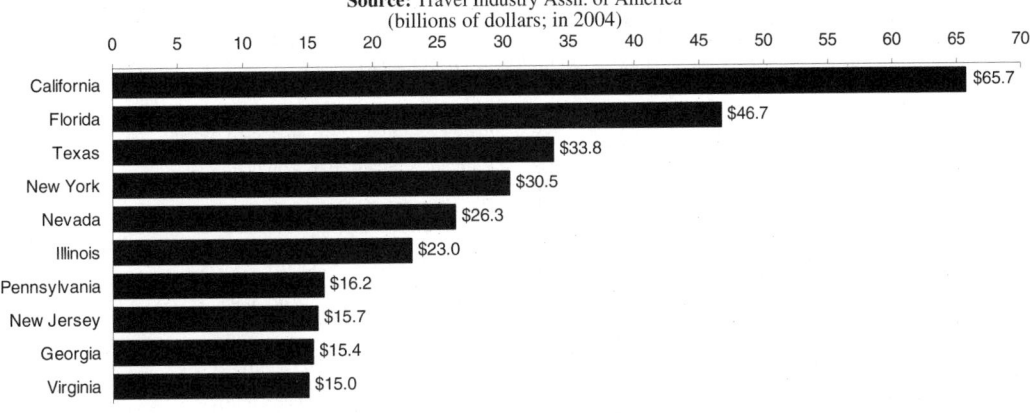

U.S. Airline Safety, Scheduled Commercial Carriers, 1985-2005

Source: Federal Aviation Administration

	Departures (millions)	Fatal accidents	Fatalities	Accident rate[1]		Departures (millions)	Fatal accidents	Fatalities	Accident rate[1]
1985	6.1	4	197	0.066	1998	10.5	1	1[3]	0.009
1990	7.8	6	39	0.077	1999	10.9	2	12	0.018
1991	7.5	4	62	0.053	2000	11.1	2	89	0.018
1992	7.5	4	33	0.053	2001[2]	10.6	6	531	0.019
1993	7.7	1	1	0.013	2002	10.3	0	0	0.000
1994[2]	7.8	4	239	0.051	2003	10.2	2	22	0.020
1995	8.1	1	160	0.012	2004	10.8	1	13	0.009
1996	7.9	3	342	0.038	2005[4]	10.9	3	22	0.027
1997	9.9	3	3	0.030					

(1) Fatal accidents per 100,000 departures. (2) Sabotage-caused accidents are included in the number of fatal accidents and fatalities, but not in the calculation of accident rates. (3) On-ground employee fatality. (4) Preliminary figures.

U.S. Scheduled Airline Traffic, 1995-2005

Source: Courtesy of Air Transport Association of America, Inc. Reprinted with permission.
Copyright © 2006 by Air Transport Association of America, Inc. All rights reserved.
(in thousands, except where otherwise noted)

	1995	2000	2001*	2002*	2003*	2004	2005
Revenue passengers							
enplaned	547,800	666,200	622,100	612,877	646,523	702,900	738,600
Revenue passenger miles ..	540,656,000	692,757,000	651,700,000	641,102,000	655,850,000	733,680,000	779,004,000
Available seat miles	807,078,000	956,950,000	930,511,000	892,554,000	893,902,000	971,466,000	1,003,312,000
% of seating utilized	67.0	72.4	70.0	71.8	73.4	75.5	77.6
Cargo traffic (ton miles)...	16,921,000	23,888,000	22,003,000	23,243,000	24,608,000	27,978,000	28,036,000
Passenger revenue	$69,594,000	$93,622,000	$80,947,000	$73,577,000	$73,281,000	$85,646,000	$93,449,000
Net profit..............	$2,314,000	$2,486,000	–$8,275,000	–$11,312,415	–$3,624,682	–$7,643,000	–$5,673,000
Employees[1]..........	546,987	679,967	671,969	601,355	570,868	569,498	552,857

NA = Not available. (1) Not in thousands. *Revenues and profit measures include aid payments from the U.S. government after Sept. 2001 terrorist attacks.

Leading U.S. Passenger Airlines, 2005

Source: Courtesy of Air Transport Association of America, Inc. Reprinted with permission.
Copyright © 2006 by Air Transport Association of America, Inc. All rights reserved.
(in thousands)

Airline	Passengers	Airline	Passengers	Airline	Passengers	Airline	Passengers
American 98,037		American Eagle 17,534		Comair 13,098		Horizon 6,480	
Southwest 88,379		Alaska........... 16,740		Mesa............ 13,006		Hawaiian.......... 5,786	
Delta.............85,973		AirTran 16,619		Atlantic Southeast... 12,026		Mesaba........... 5,705	
United............66,717		SkyWest.......... 16,561		Pinnacle 8,122		Independence 5,301	
US Airways........63,981		ExpressJet 15,985		Frontier 7,305		ATA.............. 5,287	
Northwest.........56,469		JetBlue 14,680		Air Wisconsin 6,858		Spirit 4,507	
Continental........42,776							

Passenger Traffic at U.S. Airports, 2005

Source: Airports Council International-North America

Airport	Passenger arrivals and departures	Airport	Passenger arrivals and departures
Hartsfield Atlanta (ATL) 85,907,423		Newark (EWR) 33,999,990	
Chicago O'Hare (ORD) 76,510,003		San Francisco (SFO)................. 32,802,363	
Los Angeles (LAX) 61,489,398		Philadelphia (PHL) 31,495,385	
Dallas/Ft Worth (DFW)..................59,176,265		Miami (MIA) 31,008,453	
Las Vegas, (LAS) 43,989,982		Seattle-Tacoma (SEA) 29,289,026	
Denver (DEN).........................43,387,513		Charlotte (CLT) 28,206,052	
New York-JFK (JFK) 41,885,104		Boston Logan (BOS) 27,087,905	
Phoenix Sky Harbor (PHX) 41,213,754		Washington Dulles (IAD)............... 26,842,922	
Houston (IAH) 39,684,640		New York-LaGuardia (LGA) 26,671,787	
Minneapolis/St Paul (MSP) 37,604,373		Cincinnati (CVG) 22,778,785	
Detroit (DTW).........................36,389,294		Ft Lauderdale/Hollywood (FLL)........... 22,390,285	
Orlando (MCO).........................34,128,048		Salt Lake City (SLC) 22,237,176	

Passenger Traffic at World Airports, 2005[1]

Source: Airports Council International

Airport Location (Name)	Passenger arrivals and departures	Airport Location (Name)	Passenger arrivals and departures
London, UK (Heathrow)...................... 67,915,403		Munich, Germany (Franz Josef Strauss)........ 28,619,427	
Tokyo, Japan (Haneda) 63,282,219		Jakarta, Indonesia (Sukarno-Hatta Intl.) 27,947,482	
Paris, France (Charles de Gaulle) 53,798,308		Barcelona, Spain (Barcelona) 27,121,753	
Frankfurt on Main, Germany (Frankfurt Intl.) 52,219,412		Seoul, South Korea (Inchon Intl.) 26,223,291	
Amsterdam, Netherlands (Schiphol) 44,163,098		Paris, France (Orly)..................... 24,860,532	
Madrid (Barajas) 41,940,059		Dubai, United Arab Emirates (Dubai) 24,782,288	
Beijing, China (Beijing Capital Intl.) 41,004,008		Mexico City, Mexico (Benito Juarez Intl.) 24,115,552	
Hong Kong, China (Hong Kong Intl.) 40,269,847		Shanghai, China (Pudong) 23,720,185	
Bangkok, Thailand (Bangkok Intl.) 38,985,043		Guangzhou, China (Baiyun Intl.) 23,558,274	
London, UK (Gatwick) 32,784,330		Kuala Lumpur, Malaysia (KL Intl.)............. 23,213,926	
Singapore (Changi) 32,430,856		Manchester, UK (Manchester Intl.) 22,734,350	
Tokyo, Japan (Narita)...................... 31,451,274		London, UK (Stansted) 22,018,232	
Toronto, Ontario, Canada (Toronto Pearson Intl.) .. 29,914,750		Taipei, Taiwan (Chiang Kai-Shek Intl.) 21,700,702	
Sydney, Australia (Kingsford Smith) 29,234,504		Palma De Mallorca, Spain (Palma de Mallorca) ... 21,237,092	
Rome, Italy (Fiumicino) 28,619,845		Melbourne, Australia (Melbourne).............. 21,191,402	

(1) Excludes U.S. airports (see above), and airports not participating in Airports Council Intl. Airport Traffic Statistics collection.

Top 25 Travel Websites, July 2006

Source: comScore Media Metrix

Rank	Visitors[1]	Rank	Visitors[1]	Rank	Visitors[1]
1. Expedia Inc. 29,724,000		10. InterContinental Hotels		17. About Travel........... 4,206,000	
2. Trip Network Inc....... 16,518,000		Group.............. 5,726,000		18. Sidestep.com 4,135,000	
3. Orbitz.com............ 15,802,000		11. Delta Airlines 5,546,000		19. JetBlue Airways 4,041,000	
4. Travelocity............ 13,527,000		12. Hilton Hotels 5,245,000		20. Travelzoo 3,687,000	
5. Southwest Airlines Co. .. 12,529,000		13. Marriott.............. 5,206,000		21. MSN Travel Central 3,633,000	
6. Yahoo! Travel 11,831,000		14. Walt Disney Parks &		22. Continental Airlines Sites 3,403,000	
7. Priceline.com Inc. 9,513,000		Resorts Online....... 4,357,000		23. Kayak.com Network..... 3,371,000	
8. American Airlines 6,061,000		15. USAirways.com 4,348,000		24. NWA.com............. 2,998,000	
9. AOL Travel 5,758,000		16. United Airlines 4,345,000		25. The Away Network...... 2,959,000	

(1) Number of users who visited at least once in July 2006.

Travel Websites

The following websites are among those that may be of use in planning trips and making arrangements. Websites listed under "Maps" enable the user to plot a route to a destination. Inclusion here does not represent endorsement by *The World Almanac*.

AIRLINES
American Airlines
www.aa.com
Continental Airlines
www.continental.com
Delta Air Lines
www.delta.com
Northwest Airlines
www.nwa.com
Southwest Airlines
www.southwest.com
United Airlines
www.united.com
USAirways
www.usair.com

BUSES
Gray Line Worldwide
www.grayline.com
Greyhound Lines
www.greyhound.com
Peter Pan Bus Lines
www.peterpanbus.com

CAR RENTALS
Alamo Rent A Car
www.alamo.com
Avis Rent-A-Car
www.avis.com
Budget Rent A Car
www.budget.com
Dollar Rent A Car
www.dollar.com

Enterprise Rent-A-Car
www.enterprise.com
Hertz
www.hertz.com
National Car Rental
www.nationalcar.com
Rent-A-Wreck
www.rentawreck.com
Thrifty Rent-A-Car
www.thrifty.com

TRAINS
Amtrak
www.amtrak.com
BC Rail (Canada)
www.bcrco.com
Rail Europe
www.raileurope.com

CRUISE LINES
Carnival Cruise Lines
www.carnival.com
Celebrity Cruises
www.celebritycruises.com
Costa Cruise Lines
www.costacruise.com
Cunard Line
www.cunardline.com
Holland America Line
www.hollandamerica.com
Norwegian Cruise Line
www.ncl.com
Princess Cruises
www.princess.com

Royal Caribbean Int'l.
www.royalcaribbean.com
Windjammer Barefoot Cruises
www.windjammer.com

HOTELS/RESORTS
Best Western Int'l.
www.bestwestern.com
Choice Hotels Int'l.,
Clarion Hotels & Resorts,
Comfort Inns,
Econo Lodges,
MainStay Suites,
Quality Inns,
Rodeway Inns,
Sleep Inns
www.hotelchoice.com
Days Inn of America
www.daysinn.com
Doubletree Hotels
www.doubletree.com
Embassy Suites
www.embassysuites.com
Four Seasons Hotels
www.fourseasons.com
Hilton Hotels
www.hilton.com
Holiday Inn Worldwide
www.holidayinn.com
Hyatt Hotels and Resorts
www.hyatt.com
Inter-Continental Hotels
www.ichotelsgroup.com

Loews Hotels
www.loewshotels.com
Marriott Int'l.
www.marriott.com
Radisson Hotels Int'l.
www.radisson.com
Sheraton Hotels & Resorts
www.starwood.com/
sheraton
Westin Hotels & Resorts
www.starwood.com/westin
Wyndham Hotels & Resorts
www.wyndham.com

TRAVEL PLANNING
www.bestfares.com
www.cheaptickets.com
www.expedia.com
www.fodors.com
www.frommers.com
www.hotels.com
www.itn.net (American Express)
www.libertytravel.com
www.lowestfare.com
www.orbitz.com
www.priceline.com
www.travelocity.com

MAPS
www.freetrip.com
maps.google.com
www.mapquest.com
www.mapsonus.com
maps.yahoo.com

Passports, Health Regulations, and Travel Warnings for Foreign Travel

Source: Bureau of Consular Affairs, U.S. Dept. of State; www.travel.state.gov

Passports, Visas

Passports are issued by the U.S. Department of State to citizens and nationals of the U.S. to provide documentation for foreign travel. It is important to apply well in advance of need; receiving a passport may take up to 6 weeks. Fees for a new passport for persons age 16 and older total $97; passport renewals cost $67, provided certain criteria are met.

For U.S. citizens traveling on business or as tourists, especially in Europe, a U.S. passport is often sufficient to gain admission for a limited stay. For many countries, however, a **visa** must also be obtained before entering. It is the responsibility of the traveler to check in advance and obtain any required visas from the appropriate embassies or nearest consulates.

Each country has its own specific guidelines concerning length and purpose of visit, etc. Some may require visitors to display proof that they have (1) sufficient funds to stay for the intended time period, (2) onward/return tickets, and/or (3) at least 6-months remaining validity on their U.S. passports.

Some countries, including **Canada, Mexico,** and some **Caribbean** islands, do not (as of Sept. 2006) require a passport or a visa for limited stays. However, they do require proof of U.S. citizenship, and may have other requirements. Apart from governmental requirements, some airlines and cruiselines to these locations require passengers to have passports in order to board. For further information, check with the embassy or nearest consulate of the country you plan to visit and the airline or cruiseline you plan to use.

For up-to-date passport and international travel information, visit the Consular Affairs website (www.travel.state.gov), or call the National Passport Information Center at (877) 487-2778 (TDD/TYY: (888) 874-7793). Customer service representatives are available from 7 AM to midnight, Eastern Time, Mon.-Fri., excluding federal holidays.

Health Regulations

Under World Health Organization regulations, a country may require International Certificates of Vaccination against yellow fever. Cholera immunization may be required for travelers from infected areas. Check with health care providers or your records to see that other immunizations (e.g., for tetanus and polio) are up-to-date.

Other preventative measures, including prophylactic medication for malaria, are advisable for travel to some countries. No immunizations are needed to return to the U.S. Many countries have regulations regarding AIDS testing, particularly for longtime visitors.

Detailed information and recommendations are included in *Health Information for International Travel*, the "Yellow Book" published every 2 years by the Centers for Disease Control (CDC). It can be ordered from the Public Health Foundation for $25.95 by calling (800) 545-2500 and asking for ISBN number 032303716X. Portions of the book are available online at www.cdc.gov/travel/yb

Information may also be obtained from your local health department or physician, or by calling the Centers for Disease Control and Prevention's Travelers Health Information Line at (877) 394-8747. The more technical *International Travel and Health* is available from the World Health Organization for $22.50, with portions of the book accessible online, at www.who.int/ith

Travel Warnings

The State Dept. issues travel warnings when it decides, based on relevant information, to recommend that Americans avoid travel to certain countries; these are subject to change. As of Sept. 15, 2006, travel warnings are in effect for: Afghanistan, Algeria, Bosnia and Herzegovina, Burundi, Central African Rep., Chad, Colombia, Côte d'Ivoire, Dem. Rep. of the Congo, East Timor, Eritrea, Haiti, Indonesia, Iran, Iraq, Israel (incl. West Bank and Gaza), Kenya, Lebanon, Liberia, Nepal, Nigeria, Pakistan, Philippines, Saudi Arabia, Somalia, Sri Lanka, Sudan, Syria, Uzbekistan, Yemen, and Zimbabwe. For the most current information, visit www.travel.state.gov

The Depts. of State and Homeland Security announced in 2005 that they would be imposing new restrictions on travelers returning to the U.S. If new federal regulations go into effect as scheduled, by Dec. 31, 2006, all U.S. citizens returning to the U.S. or its territories after air or sea travel anywhere outside the country—including, for the first time, Mexico, Canada, and the Caribbean—will be required to have a passport to reenter. These stricter regulations were also expected to apply to land-border crossing after Dec. 31, 2007, but federal officials were considering possible alternatives to requiring passports for land travels.

Some Notable Roller Coasters
Source: American Coasters Network; as of Sept. 2006

Fastest Roller Coasters

Name	Speed	Location
Kingda Ka	128 mph	Six Flags Great Adventure; Jackson, NJ
Top Thrill Dragster	120 mph	Cedar Point; Sandusky, OH
Dodonpa	107 mph	Fujikyu Highland; Yamanashi, Japan
Tower of Terror	100 mph	Dreamworld; Coomera, Queensland, Australia
Superman: The Escape	100 mph	Six Flags Magic Mountain; Valencia, CA

Longest Roller Coasters

Name	Length	Location
Steel Dragon 2000	8,133 ft	Nagashima Spaland; Mie, Japan
Daidarasaurus	7,677 ft	Expoland; Osaka, Japan
The Ultimate	7,442 ft	Lightwater Valley; North Yorkshire, UK
Beast	7,400 ft	Paramount's Kings Island; Kings Mills, OH
Son of Beast	7,032 ft	Paramount's Kings Island; Kings Mills, OH

Tallest Roller Coasters

Name	Height	Location
Kingda Ka	456 ft	Six Flags Great Adventure; Jackson, NJ
Top Thrill Dragster	420 ft	Cedar Point; Sandusky, OH
Superman: The Escape	415 ft	Six Flags Magic Mountain; Valencia, CA
Tower of Terror	377 ft	Dreamworld; Coomera, Queensland, Australia
Steel Dragon 2000	318 ft	Nagashima Spaland; Mie, Japan

Roller Coasters With Longest Drop

Name	Drop	Location
Kingda Ka	418 ft	Six Flags Great Adventure; Jackson, NJ
Top Thrill Dragster	400 ft	Cedar Point; Sandusky, OH
Superman: The Escape	328 ft	Six Flags Magic Mountain; Valencia, CA
Tower of Terror	328 ft	Dreamworld; Coomera, Queensland, Australia
Steel Dragon 2000	307 ft	Nagashima Spaland; Mie, Japan

Top 50 Amusement/Theme Parks Worldwide, Year-end 2005
(ranked by estimated attendance)
Source: Amusement Business

Rank	Park and Location	Country	Attendance
1.	Magic Kingdom at Walt Disney World, Lake Buena Vista, FL	United States	16,160,000
2.	Disneyland, Anaheim, CA	United States	14,550,000
3.	Tokyo Disneyland	Japan	13,000,000
4.	Tokyo Disney Sea	Japan	12,000,000
5.	Disneyland Paris, Marne-La-Vallee	France	10,200,000
6.	Epcot at Walt Disney World, Lake Buena Vista, FL	United States	9,917,000
7.	Disney-MGM Studios at Walt Disney World, Lake Buena Vista, FL	United States	8,670,000
8.	Disney's Animal Kingdom at Walt Disney World, Lake Buena Vista, FL	United States	8,210,000
9.	Universal Studios Japan, Osaka	Japan	8,000,000
10.	Everland, Kyonggi-Do	South Korea	7,500,000
11.	Lotte World, Seoul	South Korea	6,200,000
12.	Universal Studios at Universal Orlando, Orlando, FL	United States	6,130,000
13.	Blackpool Pleasure Beach, Blackpool, England	United Kingdom	6,000,000
14.	Disney's California Adventure, Anaheim, CA	United States	5,830,000
15.	Islands of Adventure at Universal Orlando, Orlando, FL	United States	5,760,000
16.	SeaWorld Florida, Orlando, FL	United States	5,600,000
17.	Yokohama Hakkeijima Sea Paradise, Yokohama	Japan	5,300,000
18.	Universal Studios Hollywood, Universal City, CA	United States	4,700,000
19.	Adventuredome at Circus Circus, Las Vegas, NV	United States	4,500,000
20.	Busch Gardens, Tampa Bay, FL	United States	4,300,000
21.	Tivoli Gardens, Copenhagen	Denmark	4,100,000
	SeaWorld California, San Diego, CA	United States	4,100,000
23.	Ocean Park, Hong Kong	China	4,030,000
24.	Europa-Park, Rust	Germany	3,950,000
25.	Nagashima Spa Land, Kuwana	Japan	3,800,000
26.	Paramount Canada's Wonderland, Maple, Ontario	Canada	3,660,000
27.	Knott's Berry Farm, Buena Park, CA	United States	3,470,000
28.	Port Aventura, Salou	Spain	3,350,000
29.	Paramount's Kings Island, Kings Island, OH	United States	3,330,000
30.	De Efteling, Kaatsheuvel	The Netherlands	3,300,000
31.	Liseburg, Gothenburg	Sweden	3,150,000
32.	Morey's Piers, Wildwood, NJ	United States	3,130,000
33.	Cedar Point, Sandusky, OH	United States	3,110,000
34.	Gardaland, Castelnuovo del Garda	Italy	3,100,000
35.	Santa Cruz Beach Boardwalk, Santa Cruz, CA	United States	3,000,000
36.	Six Flags Great Adventure, Jackson, NJ	United States	2,968,000
37.	Six Flags Great America, Gurnee, IL	United States	2,852,000
38.	Six Flags Magic Mountain, Valencia, CA	United States	2,835,000
39.	HersheyPark, Hershey, PA	United States	2,700,000
40.	Busch Gardens (The Old Country), Williamsburg, VA	United States	2,600,000
	Suzuka Circuit, Suzuka	Japan	2,600,000
	Bakken, Klampenborg	Denmark	2,600,000
	Happy Valley, Shenzhen	China	2,600,000
44.	Alton Towers, Staffordshire, England	United Kingdom	2,400,000
45.	Window of the World, Shenzhen	China	2,390,000
46.	Dollywood, Pigeon Forge, TN	United States	2,360,000
47.	Six Flags Over Texas, Arlington, TX	United States	2,310,000
48.	Six Flags Mexico, Mexico City	Mexico	2,279,000
49.	Camp Snoopy at Mall of America, Bloomington, MN	United States	2,200,000
50.	Paramount's Carowinds, Charlotte, NC	United States	2,130,000

AGRICULTURE

U.S. Farms—Number and Acreage by State, 2000, 2005

Source: National Agricultural Statistics Service, U.S. Dept. of Agriculture

STATE	No. of farms (1,000) 2005	2000[1]	Acreage in farms (mil.) 2005	2000	Acreage per farm 2005	2000
AL....	43.5	47	8.6	9	198	191
AK ...	0.64	0.58	0.9	0.91	1,406	1,569
AZ....	10.1	10.7	26.2	26.9	2,594	2,518
AR ...	47	48	14.4	14.6	306	304
CA ...	76.5	83.1	26.4	28	345	337
CO ...	30.5	30	30.7	31.6	1,007	1,060
CT ...	4.2	4.2	0.36	0.36	86	86
DE ...	2.3	2.6	0.52	0.56	226	215
FL....	42.5	44	10	10.4	235	239
GA ...	49	49.1	10.5	10.9	214	223
HI	5.5	5.5	1.3	1.38	236	251
ID	25	24.5	11.8	11.9	472	486
IL	72.5	77	27.3	27.5	377	357
IN	59	63.4	15	15.2	254	240
IA	89	94	31.6	32.5	355	346
KS	64.5	64.5	47.2	47.5	732	736
KY ...	84	90	13.8	13.7	164	152
LA....	26.8	29	7.8	8.03	291	277
ME ...	7.1	7.1	1.37	1.35	193	190
MD ...	12.1	12.4	2.04	2.13	169	172
MA ...	6.1	6.1	0.52	0.54	85	89
MI	53	53	10.1	10.15	191	192
MN ...	79.6	81	27.5	27.9	345	344
MS ...	42.2	42	11.05	11.16	262	266
MO ...	105	109	30.1	30.2	287	277
MT ...	28	27.8	60.1	59.3	2,146	2,133
NE	48	46.1	45.7	46.1	952	887
NV	3	3.1	6.3	6.4	2,100	2,065
NH	3.4	3.3	0.45	0.44	132	133
NJ	9.8	9.7	0.79	0.83	81	86
NM....	17.5	18	44.5	44.9	2,543	2,494
NY	35.6	37.5	7.6	7.67	212	205
NC....	50	55.5	8.9	9.21	178	166
ND....	30.3	30.8	39.4	39.4	1,300	1,279
OH....	76.5	79	14.3	14.77	187	187
OK....	83	84.5	33.7	33.8	406	401
OR....	40	40	17.1	17.3	428	433
PA	58.2	59	7.7	7.69	132	130
PR[2]....	13.6	NA	0.6	NA	45	NA
RI....	0.85	0.8	0.06	0.06	71	75
SC....	24.3	24.2	4.84	4.91	199	203
SD....	31.4	32.4	43.7	44	1,392	1,358
TN....	84	88	11.6	11.8	138	134
TX....	230	228.3	129.8	130.9	564	573
UT....	15.2	15.5	11.6	11.6	763	747
VT....	6.3	6.6	1.25	1.27	198	192
VA....	47	48.5	8.5	8.71	181	180
WA....	34.5	37	15.1	15.55	438	420
WV....	20.8	20.8	3.6	3.6	173	173
WI	76.5	77.5	15.4	16	201	206
WY....	9.2	9.2	34.4	34.5	3,739	3,750
U.S....	**2,101.0**	**2,166.78**	**933.4**	**945.08**	**444**	**436**

(1) Figs. for 2000 are revised. (2) Puerto Rico. Not included in U.S. total.

U.S. Farms, Number and Average Size, 1940-2005

Source: National Agricultural Statistics Service, U.S. Dept. of Agriculture

The number of farms in the United States in 2005 was estimated at 2.1 million, 0.6% fewer than in 2004. Total land in farms decreased 2.9 million acres from 2004, to 933.4 million acres. The average farm size during 2005 was 444 acres, an increase of 1 acre from the previous year. The continuing decline in the number of farms and land being farmed reflected consolidation in farming operations and use of agricultural land for other purposes.

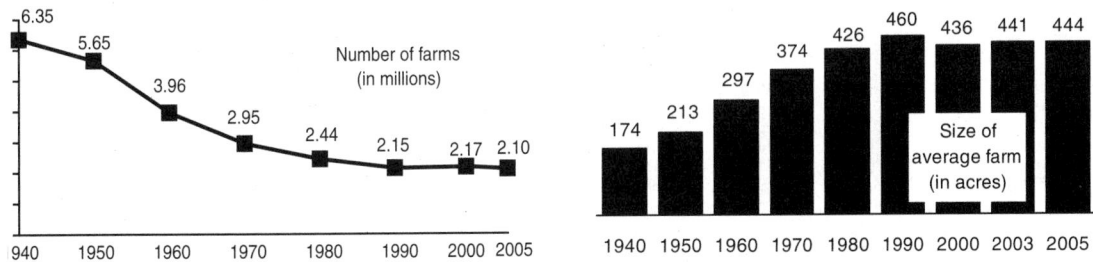

U.S. Federal Food Assistance Programs, 1990-2005[1]

Source: Food and Nutrition Service, U.S. Dept. of Agriculture

(in millions of dollars)

	1990	1995	2000	2001	2002	2003	2004	2005
Food stamps[2]	$15,491	$24,620	$17,054	$17,789	$20,643	$23,821	$27,140	$31,131
Puerto Rico nutrition asst.[3]	937	1,131	1,268	1,296	1,351	1,395	1,413	1,495
Natl. school lunch[4]	3,834	5,160	6,149	6,475	6,853	7,189	7,625	8,028
School breakfast[4,5]	596	1,048	1,393	1,450	1,567	1,652	1,775	1,926
WIC[6]	2,122	3,440	3,982	4,151	4,342	4,526	4,891	4,995
Summer food service[7]	164	237	267	270	263	257	263	267
Child/adult care[8]	813	1,464	1,683	1,737	1,853	1,926	2,019	2,113
Special milk[9]	19	17	15	16	16	14	14	17
Nutrition for the elderly (NSIP)[10]	142	148	137	152	150	3	4	4
Food distrib. to Indian reserv.[11]	66	65	76	72	76	75	77	76
Commodity supp. food prog.[11]	85	99	98	106	115	122	146	150
Food dist. to charitable inst.[12]	104	64	2	7	16	6	10	4
Emergency food assistance[13]	334	135	225	377	435	456	420	372
TOTAL[14]	**$24,707**	**$37,628**	**$32,317**	**$33,905**	**$37,719**	**$41,442**	**$45,797**	**$50,578**

(1) Data are for fiscal years, ending Sept. 30. All 2005 data are preliminary; all data subject to revision by the FNS. (2) Includes benefits and admin. expenses. (3) Puerto Rico does not participate in the Food Stamp Program. (4) Data are 9-month averages (summer months excluded). (5) Costs are cash payments (federal reimbursements to states). (6) Includes food benefits, nutrition services and admin. funds, Farmers' Market Nutrition Program, infrastructure, program evaluation, and technical assistance. (7) Includes cash payments, commodity costs, and admin. expenditures. Similar services provided by Natl. School Lunch & Breakfast Program. (8) Includes cash payments, entitlement and bonus commodities, cash-in-lieu of commodities, sponsor admin. costs, start-up costs and audits. (9) Costs are cash payments. (10) Cash grants administered by the Agency on Aging; Food and Nutrition Service costs limited to value of commodities distributed. (11) Includes commodity distribution costs and admin. expenses. (12) Includes summer camps. (13) Food made available to hunger relief orgs. such as food banks and soup kitchens. (14) Totals may not add because of rounding.

Total U.S. Government Agricultural Payments, by State, 1990-2005

Source: Economic Research Service, U.S. Dept. of Agriculture; in thousands of dollars

STATE	1990	1995	2000	2001	2002	2003	2004	2005
Alabama	$82,226	$54,140	$170,852	$230,126	$263,127	$219,214	$128,668	201,718
Alaska	1,117	1,735	1,672	2,173	1,762	1,830	5,434	3,773
Arizona	43,349	9,456	107,066	99,254	70,241	135,261	82,256	116,230
Arkansas	312,696	383,783	900,648	832,135	450,038	819,994	404,890	441,349
California	252,333	239,809	667,466	586,699	461,041	645,272	381,353	443,509
Colorado	236,723	167,661	351,116	319,271	210,367	316,893	216,185	354,637
Connecticut	2,123	2,382	18,143	7,540	4,940	7,237	4,312	7,534
Delaware	3,213	3,150	25,028	24,963	11,944	17,096	13,067	21,837
Florida	37,155	55,778	56,741	107,311	82,651	109,824	206,157	392,588
Georgia	130,593	67,332	380,057	426,534	656,717	549,155	278,131	475,947
Hawaii	519	947	11,927	3,860	1,911	1,294	1,706	3,454
Idaho	133,431	89,482	261,297	207,636	165,391	151,620	150,504	176,191
Illinois	506,603	543,753	1,943,916	1,849,734	614,734	854,099	1,154,266	1,732,742
Indiana	244,170	246,026	938,464	925,249	334,330	438,053	521,365	860,064
Iowa	753,733	786,652	2,302,094	1,971,615	739,864	1,045,632	1,251,809	2,217,602
Kansas	834,746	422,226	1,231,923	1,068,601	456,622	807,415	640,189	1,049,611
Kentucky	81,610	67,382	448,473	293,367	138,254	145,219	140,215	211,983
Louisiana	154,631	164,251	451,831	434,012	253,108	422,076	230,532	294,438
Maine	6,982	14,114	13,851	7,794	13,740	11,494	9,485	16,777
Maryland	17,386	15,241	88,470	86,543	48,848	66,299	48,307	71,779
Massachusetts	3,023	2,490	10,973	10,129	6,064	11,439	4,099	7,878
Michigan	168,831	151,055	381,056	352,730	190,536	251,608	208,631	363,951
Minnesota	511,759	467,807	1,502,230	1,242,073	466,801	781,677	694,197	1,336,534
Mississippi	185,969	133,544	463,901	516,314	251,315	470,694	297,698	383,202
Missouri	299,065	256,629	869,390	817,027	398,355	506,049	426,638	638,428
Montana	299,599	189,809	490,002	475,972	261,998	353,350	276,013	353,820
Nebraska	624,646	507,302	1,406,971	1,297,564	537,903	722,620	720,919	1,367,729
Nevada	5,347	4,264	3,918	5,860	11,288	11,953	6,379	8,425
New Hampshire	1,856	1,216	4,768	2,774	3,642	4,762	2,619	2,394
New Jersey	15,744	5,491	22,481	16,399	6,446	12,041	8,371	15,005
New Mexico	63,840	55,134	79,495	93,560	73,726	92,390	76,908	99,156
New York	59,304	43,563	159,876	114,009	159,105	160,276	79,775	133,235
North Carolina	73,255	41,476	447,096	330,312	277,739	357,543	176,422	323,217
North Dakota	545,378	296,215	1,170,234	944,546	383,452	651,484	464,508	810,306
Ohio	197,006	167,351	678,104	681,519	280,826	395,322	326,313	570,082
Oklahoma	319,040	164,662	439,851	391,712	317,124	355,332	209,142	294,644
Oregon	89,137	52,145	137,401	104,725	80,081	106,595	73,414	86,460
Pennsylvania	41,414	41,096	147,848	103,435	129,275	182,426	87,143	128,844
Rhode Island	191	317	1,218	292	651	611	877	548
South Carolina	62,637	34,586	144,499	129,742	65,264	126,461	63,907	115,759
South Dakota	332,851	245,016	789,895	714,936	333,439	547,920	395,774	780,050
Tennessee	91,029	47,405	298,873	247,454	108,144	175,199	124,594	194,272
Texas	974,702	643,119	1,647,066	1,702,477	998,215	1,661,141	998,199	1,607,027
Utah	34,897	25,045	36,181	39,689	54,278	55,479	34,473	41,070
Vermont	5,793	4,334	26,093	7,863	36,294	28,479	14,991	17,054
Virginia	32,378	25,967	152,452	116,801	181,891	175,585	63,744	111,070
Washington	205,425	116,062	352,503	298,547	215,689	263,950	192,665	219,860
West Virginia	6,049	5,268	23,509	9,807	5,640	12,962	6,206	8,193
Wisconsin	181,243	184,350	603,213	414,981	332,068	475,696	291,465	549,187
Wyoming	31,283	31,432	34,302	50,171	65,792	51,042	33,867	63,413
UNITED STATES[1]	**$9,298,030**	**$7,279,451**	**$22,896,433**	**$20,990,842**	**$11,365,194**	**$16,177,044**	**$12,581,287**	**$19,977,473**

(1) Total includes disbursements to territories not shown.

Production of Principal U.S. Crops, by State, 2005

Source: National Agricultural Statistics Service, U.S. Dept. of Agriculture

STATE	Barley (1,000 bu)	Corn, grain (1,000 bu)	Upland Cotton (1,000 b)	All hay (1,000 t)	Oats (1,000 bu)	Potatoes (1,000 cwt)	Soybeans (1,000 bu)	Tobacco (1,000 lb)	All wheat (1,000 bu)
Alabama	—	23,800	850	1,971	1,100	202	4,785	—	2,250
Alaska	208,000	—	—	30	58	166	—	—	—
Arizona	3,000	4,290	620	2,324	—	1,183	—	—	8,060
Arkansas	—	30,130	2,190	2,239	—	—	102,000	—	8,320
California	3,780	18,920	1,050	8,935	1,500	14,964	—	—	28,155
Colorado	7,670	140,600	—	4,085	1,125	24,044	—	—	54,035
Connecticut	—	NE	—	118	—	—	—	4,067	—
Delaware	2,187	22,022	—	39	—	806	4,732	—	3,570
Florida	—	2,632	129	711	—	7,919	256	5,500	360
Georgia	—	29,670	2,150	1,650	1,200	—	4,550	27,760	7,280
Hawaii	—	—	—	—	—	—	—	—	—
Idaho	52,200	10,200	—	5,382	1,280	116,975	—	—	100,590
Illinois	—	1,708,850	—	2,159	3,160	1,462	444,150	—	36,600
Indiana	—	888,580	—	2,067	621	NE	263,620	NE	24,480
Iowa	—	2,162,500	—	5,860	9,875	—	532,650	—	750
Kansas	588	465,750	90	6,680	2,360	1,440	105,450	—	380,000
Kentucky	747	155,760	—	5,777	—	—	53,750	167,260	20,400
Louisiana	—	44,880	1,120	805	—	—	28,900	—	4,800
Maine	1,320	NE	—	240	1,960	15,736	—	—	—
Maryland	3,526	54,000	—	531	—	884	15,980	NE	9,240
Massachusetts	—	NE	—	189	—	624	—	1,800	—
Michigan	517	288,860	—	3,290	4,575	13,920	77,610	—	38,940
Minnesota	3,870	1,191,900	—	6,055	12,710	17,630	306,000	—	71,470
Mississippi	—	47,085	2,160	2,117	—	—	58,830	—	3,250
Missouri	—	329,670	885	6,718	1,300	1,972	183,520	2,800	29,160
Montana	39,200	2,516	—	5,850	1,855	3,434	—	—	192,480
Nebraska	NE	1,270,500	—	6,945	4,380	8,245	235,330	—	68,640
Nevada	170	NE	—	1,609	—	2,338	—	—	805

STATE	Barley (1,000 bu)	Corn, grain (1,000 bu)	Upland Cotton (1,000 b)	All hay (1,000 t)	Oats (1,000 bu)	Potatoes (1,000 cwt)	Soybeans (1,000 bu)	Tobacco (1,000 lb)	All wheat (1,000 bu)
New Hampshire	—	NE	—	105	—	—	—	—	—
New Jersey	142	7,564	—	212	—	536	2,548	—	1,219
New Mexico	—	9,625	100	1,413	—	1,764	—	—	9,720
New York	735	57,040	—	2,625	4,050	5,226	7,896	—	5,130
North Carolina	1,482	84,000	1,430	1,660	1,679	2,850	39,420	278,900	24,795
North Dakota	57,240	154,800	—	5,646	14,160	20,500	107,300	—	303,765
Ohio	300	464,750	—	3,630	3,600	864	201,600	6,732	58,930
Oklahoma	—	28,750	365	5,084	410	—	7,930	—	128,000
Oregon	2,025	4,000	—	3,140	1,404	22,023	—	—	53,560
Pennsylvania	3,384	117,120	—	3,397	6,050	2,750	17,220	10,700	7,830
Rhode Island	—	NE	—	20	—	105	—	—	—
South Carolina	—	33,060	420	783	1,180	—	8,610	42,000	8,580
South Dakota	2,303	470,050	—	7,560	12,960	NE	138,600	—	133,420
Tennessee	—	77,350	1,120	4,367	—	—	41,800	51,670	8,400
Texas	—	210,900	8,200	9,140	4,730	6,094	5,980	—	96,000
Utah	1,920	1,956	—	2,594	511	NE	—	—	7,099
Vermont	—	NE	—	374	—	—	—	—	—
Virginia	3,915	42,480	185	3,542	183	1,029	15,300	39,840	10,080
Washington	12,505	16,400	—	3,210	600	95,480	—	—	139,300
West Virginia	—	3,052	—	1,070	—	—	595	680	300
Wisconsin	1,590	429,200	—	4,470	13,760	27,880	69,520	NE	10,262
Wyoming	5,580	6,860	—	2,202	600	—	—	—	4,665
UNITED STATES	211,896	11,112,072	23,064	150,590	114,878	420,879	3,086,432	639,709	2,104,690

NE = Not estimated; bu = bushels; b = bales (480-lbs); t = tons; cwt = hundredweight.

Production of Principal U.S. Crops, 1990-2005

Source: National Agricultural Statistics Service, U.S. Dept. of Agriculture

Year	Corn for grain (1,000 bu)	Oats (1,000 bu)	Barley (1,000 bu)	Sorghum for grain (1,000 bu)	All wheat (1,000 bu)	Rye (1,000 bu)	Flaxseed (1,000 bu)	Upland Cotton (1,000 b)	Cottonseed (1,000 t)
1990	7,934,028	357,654	422,196	573,303	2,729,778	10,176	3,812	15,505.4	5,968.5
1991	7,474,765	243,851	464,326	584,860	1,980,139	9,734	6,200	17,614.3	6,925.5
1992	9,476,698	294,229	455,090	875,022	2,466,798	11,440	3,288	16,219.5	6,230.1
1993	6,336,470	206,770	398,041	534,172	2,396,440	10,340	3,480	16,134.6	6,343.2
1994	10,102,735	229,008	374,862	649,206	2,320,981	11,341	2,922	19,662.0	7,603.9
1995	7,373,876	162,027	359,562	460,373	2,182,591	10,064	2,211	17,532.2	6,848.7
1996	9,293,435	155,273	395,751	802,974	2,285,133	9,016	1,602	18,413.5	7,143.5
1997	9,206,832	167,246	359,878	633,545	2,481,466	8,132	2,420	18,245.0	6,934.6
1998	9,758,685	165,981	352,125	519,933	2,547,321	12,161	6,708	13,475.9	5,365.4
1999	9,430,612	146,193	280,292	595,166	2,299,010	11,038	7,864	16,293.7	6,354.0
2000	9,915,051	149,545	318,728	470,526	2,232,460	8,386	10,730	16,799.2	6,435.6
2001	9,506,840	117,024	249,420	514,524	1,957,043	6,971	11,455	19,602.4	7,452.2
2002	8,966,787	116,002	226,906	360,713	1,605,878	6,488	11,863	16,530.3	6,183.9
2003[1]	10,089,222	144,383	278,283	411,237	2,344,760	8,634	10,516	17,822.9	6,664.6
2004[1]	11,807,086	115,695	279,743	453,654	2,158,245	8,255	10,368	22,505.1	8,242.1
2005	11,112,072	114,878	211,896	393,893	2,104,690	7,537	19,695	23,064.0	8,501.0

Year	Tobacco (1,000 lb)	All hay (1,000 t)	Beans, dry edible (1,000 cwt)	Peas, dry edible (1,000 cwt)	Peanuts[2] (1,000 lb)	Soybeans[3] (1,000 bu)	Potatoes (1,000 cwt)	Sweet potatoes (1,000 cwt)
1990	1,626,380	146,212	32,379	2,372	3,602,770	1,925,947	402,110	12,594
1991	1,664,372	152,073	33,765	3,715	4,926,570	1,986,539	417,622	11,203
1992	1,721,671	146,903	22,615	2,535	4,284,416	2,190,354	425,367	12,005
1993	1,613,319	146,799	21,913	3,292	3,392,415	1,870,958	428,693	11,053
1994	1,582,896	150,060	29,028	2,255	4,247,455	2,516,694	467,054	13,395
1995	1,268,538	154,166	30,812	4,765	4,247,455	2,176,814	443,606	12,906
1996	1,517,334	149,457	27,960	2,671	3,661,205	2,382,364	498,633	13,456
1997	1,787,399	152,536	29,370	5,752	3,539,380	2,688,750	467,091	13,327
1998	1,479,867	151,780	30,418	5,934	3,963,440	2,741,014	475,771	12,382
1999	1,292,692	159,707	33,085	4,773	3,829,490	2,653,758	478,216	12,234
2000	1,052,999	151,921	26,409	3,474	3,265,505	2,757,810	513,621	13,794
2001	991,223	156,764	19,583	3,763	4,276,704	2,890,682	437,888	14,637
2002	871,122	149,467	30,312	4,727	3,321,040	2,756,147	458,171	12,799
2003[1]	802,560	157,585	22,492	5,202	4,144,150	2,453,665	457,814	15,891
2004[1]	881,973	158,247	17,788	11,419	4,288,200	3,123,686	456,041	16,112
2005	639,709	150,590	27,222	14,003	4,821,250	3,086,432	420,879	15,747

Year	Rice (1,000 cwt)	Sugarcane (1,000 t)	Sugar beets (1,000 t)	Pecans[4] (1,000 lb)	Apples (1,000 t)	Grapes (1,000 t)	Peaches (1,000 t)	Oranges[5] (1,000 bx)	Grapefruit[5] (1,000 bx)
1990	156,088	28,136	27,513	205,000	4,828.4	5,659.9	1,121.1	184,415	49,300
1991	159,367	30,252	28,203	299,000	4,853.4	5,555.9	1,347.8	178,950	55,500
1992	179,658	30,363	29,143	166,000	5,284.3	6,052.1	1,336.0	209,610	55,265
1993	156,110	31,101	26,249	365,000	5,342.4	6,023.2	1,330.1	255,760	68,375
1994	197,779	30,929	31,853	199,000	5,667.8	5,870.6	1,253.3	240,450	65,100
1995	173,871	30,944	27,954	268,000	5,292.5	5,922.3	1,150.8	263,605	71,050
1996	171,321	29,462	26,680	209,500	5,196.0	5,554.3	1,058.2	263,890	66,200
1997	182,992	31,709	29,886	335,000	5,161.9	7,290.9	1,312.3	292,620	70,200
1998	184,443	32,743	32,499	146,400	5,381.3	5,816.4	1,162.8	315,525	63,150
1999	206,027	35,299	33,420	406,100	5,223.3	6,234.8	1,216.7	224,580	61,200
2000	190,872	36,114	32,541	209,850	5,291.9	7,688.0	1,289.9	299,760	66,980
2001	215,270	34,587	25,764	338,500	4,711.5	6,569.3	1,203.9	280,935	59,750
2002	210,960	35,553	27,707	172,900	4,262.0	7,338.9	1,267.5	283,760	58,660
2003[1]	199,897	33,858	30,710	282,100	4,396.0	6,643.5	1,259.5	267,040	50,080
2004[1]	232,342	29,013	30,021	185,800	5,209.5	6,240.0	1,307.1	294,620	52,540
2005	223,235	27,897	27,654	259,600	4,689.2	6,974.9	1,182.6	216,500	25,640

(1) Some totals revised. (2) Harvested for nuts. (3) Harvested for beans. (4) Utilized production only. (5) Crop year ending in year cited.

Eggs: U.S. Production, Price, and Value, 2004-05[1]

Source: National Agricultural Statistics Service, U.S. Dept. of Agriculture

STATE	Eggs produced 2004	2005	Price[2] per dozen 2004	2005	Value of production 2004	2005	STATE	Eggs produced 2004	2005	Price[2] per dozen 2004	2005	Value of production 2004	2005
	(mil)		(dollars)		(1,000 dollars)			(mil)		(dollars)		(1,000 dollars)	
AL.....	2,099	2,071	1.650	1.630	287,956	281,595	NE....	3,174	3,217	0.525	0.310	138,851	82,989
AR	3,526	3,416	1.220	1.240	358,280	352,645	NH....	42	39	0.952	0.736	3,333	2,391
CA	5,352	5,082	0.644	0.429	287,392	181,655	NJ	558	495	0.622	0.494	28,912	20,373
CO	1,105	1,071	0.653	0.472	60,103	42,141	NY	1,163	1,190	0.617	0.368	59,844	36,461
CT	818	846	0.675	0.475	46,038	33,458	NC....	2,523	2,573	1.140	1.160	239,062	249,368
FL.....	3,068	2,980	0.625	0.406	159,878	100,723	OH....	7,355	7,506	0.545	0.365	333,750	228,182
GA	5,038	4,850	0.939	0.843	394,120	340,680	OK....	764	731	1.050	0.983	67,102	59,862
HI	119	115	1.080	0.941	10,670	8,979	OR....	818	823	0.714	0.447	48,693	30,626
ID	238	241	0.730	0.572	14,479	11,492	PA	6,585	6,608	0.619	0.389	339,744	214,188
IL	1,044	1,210	0.592	0.377	51,478	38,058	PR	226	236	0.912	0.908	17,179	17,863
IN	6,256	6,254	0.560	0.369	291,841	192,327	SC	1,351	1,289	0.735	0.578	82,772	62,133
IA	11,615	12,978	0.508	0.310	491,656	335,318	SD	933	816	0.517	0.301	40,178	20,460
KY	1,232	1,228	0.858	0.709	88,099	72,568	TN	319	316	1.340	1.310	35,511	34,478
LA.....	465	469	0.902	0.795	34,966	31,073	TX	4,825	4,684	0.762	0.607	306,322	236,843
ME	1,156	1,025	0.737	0.545	70,988	46,594	UT	831	878	0.520	0.318	36,012	23,248
MD	843	798	0.651	0.467	45,737	31,069	VT	55	50	0.746	0.584	3,418	2,434
MA	75	71	0.812	0.607	5,078	3,591	VA	761	823	1.100	0.983	69,703	67,421
MI	2,009	2,142	0.563	0.347	94,313	61,870	WA....	1,332	1,343	0.697	0.400	77,348	44,791
MN	2,927	2,985	0.583	0.365	142,183	90,899	WV....	273	261	1.420	1.400	32,325	30,473
MS	1,606	1,627	1.290	1.250	172,166	169,834	WI	1,206	1,321	0.564	0.361	56,679	39,702
MO	1,865	1,910	0.652	0.469	101,395	74,570	WY....	4	4	0.607	0.397	182	119
MT	107	106	0.657	0.374	5,862	3,300	**U.S.[3]** ..	**89,091**	**89,960**	**0.714**	**0.539**	**5,299,185**	**4,042,282**

(1) Estimates cover the 12-month period from Dec. 1 of the previous year through Nov. 30. (2) Average of all eggs sold by producers, including hatching eggs. (3) U.S. total includes other states not listed separately. Puerto Rico (PR) not included in total.

Livestock on Farms in the U.S., 1900-2006

Source: National Agricultural Statistics Service, U.S. Dept. of Agriculture
(in thousands)

Year (On Jan. 1)	All cattle[1]	Milk cows	Sheep and lambs	Hogs and pigs[2]	Year (On Jan. 1)	All cattle[1]	Milk cows	Sheep and lambs	Hogs and pigs[2]
1900	59,739	16,544	48,105	51,055	1980	111,242	10,758	12,699	67,318
1910	58,993	19,450	50,239	48,072	1985	109,582	10,777	10,716	54,073
1920	70,400	21,455	40,743	60,159	1990	95,816	10,015	11,358	53,788
1930	61,003	23,032	51,565	55,705	1995	102,755	9,487	8,886	57,150
1940	68,309	24,940	52,107	61,165	2000	98,199	9,183	7,036	59,335
1950	77,963	23,853	29,826	58,937	2001	97,298	9,172	6,908	59,110
1955	96,592	23,462	31,582	50,474	2002	96,723	9,106	6,623	59,722
1960	96,236	19,527	33,170	59,026	2003	96,100	9,142	6,321	59,554
1965	109,000	16,981	25,127	56,106	2004	94,888	8,990	6,105	60,444
1970	112,369	12,091	20,423	57,046	2005	95,838	9,005	6,135	60,975
1975	132,028	11,220	14,515	54,693	2006[3]	97,102	9,058	6,230	61,197

(1) From 1970, includes milk cows and heifers that have calved. (2) As of Dec. 1 of preceding year. (3) Preliminary.

U.S. Meat Production and Consumption, 1940-2006

Source: Economic Research Service, U.S. Dept. of Agriculture
(in millions of pounds)

Year	Beef Prod.	Cons.	Veal Prod.	Cons.	Lamb and mutton Prod.	Cons.	Pork Prod.	Cons.	All red meats[1] Prod.	Cons.	All Poultry Prod.	Cons.
1940	7,175	7,257	981	981	876	873	10,044	9,701	19,076	18,812	NA	NA
1950	9,534	9,529	1,230	1,206	597	596	10,714	10,390	22,075	21,721	3,174	3,097
1960	14,728	15,465	1,109	1,118	769	857	13,905	14,057	30,511	31,497	6,310	6,168
1970	21,684	23,451	588	613	551	669	14,699	14,957	37,522	39,689	10,193	9,981
1980	21,643	23,560	400	420	318	351	16,617	16,838	38,978	41,170	14,173	13,525
1990	22,743	24,030	327	325	363	397	15,354	16,025	38,787	40,778	23,468	22,152
1995	25,222	25,534	319	319	285	346	17,849	17,768	43,675	43,967	30,393	25,944
2000	26,888	27,338	225	225	234	354	18,952	18,643	46,299	46,560	36,073	30,508
2001	26,212	27,026	205	204	227	368	19,160	18,492	45,804	46,089	38,942	30,823
2002	27,192	27,878	205	204	223	381	19,685	19,144	47,305	47,608	38,079	32,575
2003	26,339	26,999	202	204	203	367	19,966	19,436	46,710	47,006	38,477	33,131
2004	24,650	27,750	176	177	200	372	20,529	19,437	45,555	47,735	39,585	34,139
2005	24,784	27,760	165	164	191	355	20,705	19,118	45,845	47,397	40,935	35,002
2006*	26,127	28,563	164	166	206	378	21,345	19,449	47,842	48,556	41,814	35,854

* Preliminary. (1) Meats may not add to total because of rounding. (2) Consumption (also called total disappearance) is estimated as: production plus beginning stocks, plus imports, minus exports, minus ending stocks. NA = Not available.

U.S. Annual Per Capita Consumption of Selected Foods, 1910-2004

Source: USDA/Economic Research Service

Year	Whole milk[1]	Low-fat & skim milk[1]	Butter[2]	Margarine[2]	Total fat[2, 3]	Red meat[2, 4]	Poultry[2, 5]	Fish & shellfish[2]
1910...	25.2	7.1	18.4	1.6	37.7	96.0	11.8	11.2
1940...	29.2	4.7	17.0	2.4	50.1	92.4	12.3	11.0
1970...	25.5	5.8	5.4	10.8	55.7	131.9	33.8	11.7
2000...	8.1	14.4	4.5	7.5	84.5	113.7	67.9	15.0
2004...	7.3	13.9	4.6	5.3	87.5	112.0	72.7	16.5

(1) Gallons. (2) Pounds. (3) Includes edible rapeseed (canola) oil beginning in 1985. Includes specialty fats used mainly in confectionary products and non-dairy creamers. (4) Figures are calculated on the basis of raw and edible meat. Excludes edible offals, bones, and viscera. Excludes game consumption. (5) Figures are calculated on the basis of raw and edible meat. Includes skin, neck, and giblets. Excludes chicken for commercially prepared pet food.

U.S. Farm Business Real Estate Debt Outstanding, by Lender Groups,[1] 1960-2005

Source: Economic Research Service, U.S. Dept. of Agriculture
(in millions of dollars)

Dec. 31	Total farm real estate debt[2]	AMOUNTS HELD BY PRINCIPAL LENDER GROUPS				
		Farm Credit System[2]	Farm Service Agency[3]	Life insurance companies[4]	All operating banks	Other[5]
1960	$11,310	$2,222	$624	$2,652	$1,356	$4,456
1970	27,506	6,420	2,180	5,123	3,329	10,455
1980	89,692	33,225	7,435	11,998	7,765	27,813
1985	100,076	42,169	9,821	11,273	10,732	25,775
1990	74,732	25,924	7,639	9,704	16,288	15,169
1991	74,944	25,305	7,041	9,546	17,417	15,632
1992	75,421	25,408	6,394	8,765	18.757	16,095
1993	76,036	24,900	5,837	8,985	19,595	16,719
1994	77,680	24,597	5,465	9,025	21,079	17,514
1995	79,287	24,851	5,055	9,092	22,277	18,012
1996	81,657	25,730	4,702	9,468	23,276	18,481
1997	85,359	27,098	4,373	9,699	25,240	18,950
1998	89,615	28,888	4,073	10,723	27,168	18,763
1999	94,226	30,302	3,872	11,490	29,799	18,763
2000	91,109	29,692	3,418	11,053	29,757	17,188
2001	96,008	32,855	3,347	11,205	31,082	17,519
2002	103,357	37,815	3,181	11,421	33,060	17,880
2003	107,982	40,095	2,848	11,597	35,126	18,316
2004	107,402	41,057	2,369	11,631	34,548	17,796
2005[6]	114,338	44,340	2,221	10,536	40,019	17,222

(1) Excludes debt for non-farm purposes. (2) Includes data for joint stock land banks and real estate loans by Agricultural Credit Association. (3) Includes loans made directly by Farm Services Agency for farm ownership, soil, and water loans to individuals, Native American tribe land acquisition, grazing associations, and half of economic emergency loans. Also includes loans for rural housing on farm tracts and labor housing. (4) American Council of Life Insurance members. (5) Estimated by ERS, USDA. Includes Commodity Credit Corporation storage and drying facility loans. (6) Preliminary.

U.S. Farm Marketings by State, 2004-05

Source: Economic Research Service, U.S. Dept. of Agriculture; in thousands of dollars

STATE	2004 FARM MARKETINGS			2005 FARM MARKETINGS		
	Total	Crops	Livestock and products	Total	Crops	Livestock and products
Alabama	$4,103,235	$734,696	$3,368,539	$3,885,257	$715,827	$3,169,430
Alaska	52,987	24,329	28,658	52,987	24,329	28,658
Arizona	3,065,604	1,628,576	1,437,028	3,183,757	1,698,679	1,485,078
Arkansas	6,604,401	2,431,732	4,172,669	6,080,740	2,105,249	3,975,491
California	31,835,183	23,212,043	8,623,140	31,942,154	23,653,330	8,288,824
Colorado	5,501,154	1,345,001	4,156,153	5,646,838	1,369,358	4,277,481
Connecticut	526,580	348,651	177,929	523,382	358,301	165,081
Delaware	933,842	191,185	742,657	894,674	172,211	722,464
Florida	6,843,731	5,359,595	1,484,136	7,484,273	6,006,992	1,477,281
Georgia	6,107,025	2,036,173	4,070,852	5,907,916	2,066,193	3,841,723
Hawaii	549,830	457,079	92,751	553,234	459,987	93,248
Idaho	4,349,255	1,818,681	2,530,574	4,548,634	1,883,592	2,665,041
Illinois	9,708,305	7,769,390	1,938,915	8,702,010	6,866,953	1,835,057
Indiana	6,043,191	3,978,204	2,064,987	5,417,475	3,532,832	1,884,643
Iowa	14,652,945	7,368,773	7,284,172	14,217,966	6,686,445	7,531,521
Kansas	9,502,727	3,082,658	6,420,069	9,785,403	3,098,724	6,686,679
Kentucky	4,126,186	1,387,682	2,738,504	3,918,663	1,187,898	2,730,765
Louisiana	2,225,802	1,347,809	877,993	2,102,082	1,190,351	911,730
Maine	553,830	223,221	330,609	546,149	237,041	309,108
Maryland	1,743,357	732,691	1,010,666	1,666,477	688,018	978,459
Massachusetts	413,954	319,810	94,144	390,289	295,913	94,375
Michigan	4,312,320	2,566,437	1,745,883	3,971,758	2,390,062	1,581,696
Minnesota	9,794,911	4,860,595	4,934,316	9,072,149	4,313,638	4,758,512
Mississippi	4,089,158	1,377,005	2,712,153	3,852,258	1,241,506	2,610,752
Missouri	5,818,728	2,756,149	3,062,579	5,568,724	2,516,038	3,052,686
Montana	2,238,980	960,935	1,278,045	2,379,257	1,037,820	1,341,437
Nebraska	11,779,728	4,441,545	7,338,183	11,241,083	3,913,566	7,327,518
Nevada	454,343	147,274	307,069	477,780	172,143	305,638
New Hampshire	168,871	95,222	73,649	168,295	94,633	73,661
New Jersey	866,719	680,053	186,666	861,907	675,234	186,672
New Mexico	2,564,862	565,345	1,999,517	2,671,842	625,287	2,046,555
New York	3,653,430	1,351,115	2,302,315	3,525,686	1,332,814	2,192,872
North Carolina	8,210,496	2,859,152	5,351,344	7,682,649	2,595,523	5,087,126
North Dakota	4,090,863	3,152,582	938,281	3,957,785	2,968,669	989,116
Ohio	5,459,380	3,387,276	2,072,104	5,105,359	3,136,743	1,968,616
Oklahoma	5,054,570	1,172,866	3,881,704	5,035,418	1,026,835	4,008,583
Oregon	3,691,554	2,647,919	1,043,635	3,712,632	2,655,981	1,056,651
Pennsylvania	4,859,335	1,544,652	3,314,683	4,717,995	1,546,409	3,171,586
Rhode Island	63,826	54,014	9,812	62,619	52,815	9,804
South Carolina	1,909,098	833,134	1,075,964	1,749,951	742,481	1,007,470
South Dakota	4,877,484	2,455,300	2,422,184	4,818,306	2,261,593	2,556,712
Tennessee	2,561,984	1,263,003	1,298,981	2,536,031	1,218,365	1,317,667
Texas	16,498,398	5,391,411	11,106,987	16,893,968	5,585,436	11,308,532
Utah	1,253,154	270,028	983,126	1,252,738	291,925	960,813
Vermont	581,773	84,927	496,846	560,831	81,808	479,023
Virginia	2,684,392	902,271	1,782,121	2,615,907	833,483	1,782,424
Washington	5,868,195	4,132,390	1,735,805	5,681,268	3,999,039	1,682,230
West Virginia	422,872	74,359	348,513	424,294	76,067	348,227
Wisconsin	6,864,150	1,781,723	5,082,427	6,621,948	1,734,878	4,887,071
Wyoming	1,104,702	153,746	950,956	1,130,813	146,452	984,361
UNITED STATES	**$241,241,400**	**$117,760,407**	**$123,480,993**	**$235,801,611**	**$113,565,466**	**$122,236,148**

Average Prices Received by U.S. Farmers, 1940-2005

Source: National Agricultural Statistics Service, U.S. Dept. of Agriculture

Figures below represent dollars per 100 lb for hogs, beef cattle, veal calves, sheep, lamb, and milk (wholesale); dollars per head for milk cows; cents per lb for chickens, broilers, turkeys, and wool; cents per dozen for eggs; weighted calendar year prices for livestock and livestock products other than wool. For 1943-63, wool prices are weighted on marketing year basis. The marketing year was changed in 1964 from a calendar year to a Dec.-Nov. basis for hogs, chickens, broilers, and eggs.

Year	Broilers	Calves (veal)	Cattle (beef)	Chickens (excl. broilers)	Eggs	Hogs	Lambs	Milk cows	Milk	Sheep	Turkeys	Wool
1940...	17.3	8.83	7.56	13.0	18.0	5.39	8.10	61	1.82	3.95	15.2	28.4
1950...	27.4	26.30	23.30	22.2	36.3	18.00	25.10	198	3.89	11.60	32.8	62.1
1960...	16.9	22.90	20.40	12.2	36.1	15.30	17.90	223	4.21	5.61	25.4	42.0
1970...	13.6	34.50	27.10	9.1	39.1	22.70	26.40	332	5.71	7.51	22.6	35.4
1975...	26.3	27.20	32.20	9.9	54.5	46.10	42.10	412	8.75	11.30	34.8	44.8
1980...	27.7	76.80	62.40	11.0	56.3	38.00	63.60	1,190	13.05	21.30	41.3	88.1
1985...	30.1	62.10	53.70	14.8	57.1	44.00	67.70	860	12.76	23.90	49.1	63.3
1990...	32.6	95.60	74.60	9.3	70.9	53.70	55.50	1,160	13.74	23.20	39.4	80.0
1991...	30.8	98.00	72.70	7.1	67.8	49.10	52.20	1,100	12.27	19.70	38.4	55.0
1992...	31.8	89.00	71.30	8.6	57.6	41.60	59.50	1,130	13.15	25.80	37.7	74.0
1993...	34.0	91.20	72.60	10.0	63.4	45.20	64.40	1,160	12.84	28.60	39.0	51.0
1994...	35.0	87.20	66.70	7.6	61.4	39.90	65.60	1,170	13.01	30.90	40.4	78.0
1995...	34.4	73.10	61.80	6.5	62.4	40.50	78.20	1,130	12.78	28.00	41.6	104.0
1996...	38.1	58.40	58.70	6.6	74.9	51.90	82.20	1,090	14.75	29.90	43.3	70.0
1997...	37.7	78.90	63.10	7.7	70.3	52.90	90.30	1,100	13.36	37.90	39.9	84.0
1998...	39.3	78.80	59.60	8.0	65.5	34.40	72.30	1,120	15.41	30.60	38.0	60.0
1999...	37.1	87.70	63.40	7.1	62.2	30.30	74.50	1,280	14.38	31.10	40.8	38.0
2000...	33.6	104.00	68.60	5.7	61.8	42.30	79.80	1,340	12.40	34.30	40.7	33.0
2001...	39.3	106.00	71.30	4.5	62.2	44.30	66.90	1,500	15.04	34.60	39.0	36.0
2002...	30.5	96.40	66.50	4.8	58.9	33.40	73.80	1,600	12.18	27.90	36.5	53.0
2003...	34.6	102.00	79.70	4.9	73.2	37.20	94.40	1,340	12.55	34.90	36.1	73.0
2004[1]..	44.6	119.00	85.80	5.8	71.4	49.30	101.00	1,580	16.13	38.80	42.0	80.0
2005...	43.6	135.00	89.70	6.5	53.9	50.20	110.00	1,770	15.20	45.10	44.9	71.0

Figures below represent cents per lb for cotton, apples, and peanuts; dollars per bushel for oats, wheat, corn, barley, and soybeans; dollars per 100 lb for rice, sorghum, and potatoes; dollars per ton for cottonseed and baled hay; weighted crop year prices. The marketing year is described as follows: apples, June-May; wheat, oats, barley, hay, and potatoes, July-June; cotton, rice, peanuts, and cottonseed, Aug.-July; soybeans, Sept.-Aug.; and corn and sorghum grain, Oct.-Sept.

Year	Apples	Barley	Corn	Cotton-seed	Cotton (upland)*	Hay	Oats	Peanuts	Pota-toes	Rice	Sor-ghum	Soy-beans	Wheat
1940...	NA	0.39	0.62	21.70	9.8	9.78	0.30	3.7	0.85	1.80	0.87	0.89	0.67
1950...	NA	1.19	1.52	86.60	39.9	21.10	0.79	10.9	1.50	5.09	1.88	2.47	2.00
1960...	2.7	0.84	1.00	42.50	30.1	21.70	0.60	10.0	2.00	4.55	1.49	2.13	1.74
1970...	6.5	0.97	1.33	56.40	21.9	26.10	0.62	12.8	2.21	5.17	2.04	2.85	1.33
1975...	8.8	2.42	2.54	97.00	51.1	52.10	1.45	19.0	4.48	8.35	4.21	4.92	3.55
1980...	12.1	2.86	3.11	129.00	74.4	71.00	1.79	25.1	6.55	12.80	5.25	7.57	3.91
1985...	17.3	1.98	2.23	66.00	56.8	67.60	1.23	24.4	3.92	6.53	3.45	5.05	3.08
1990...	20.9	2.14	2.28	121.00	67.1	80.60	1.14	34.7	6.08	6.68	3.79	5.74	2.61
1991...	25.1	2.10	2.37	71.00	56.8	71.20	1.21	28.3	4.96	7.58	4.01	5.58	3.00
1992...	19.5	2.04	2.07	97.50	53.7	74.30	1.32	30.0	5.52	5.89	3.38	5.56	3.24
1993...	18.4	1.99	2.50	113.00	58.1	84.70	1.36	30.4	6.18	7.98	4.13	6.40	3.26
1994...	18.6	2.03	2.26	101.00	72.0	86.70	1.22	28.9	5.58	6.78	3.80	5.48	3.45
1995...	24.0	2.89	3.24	106.00	75.4	82.20	1.67	29.3	6.77	9.15	5.69	6.72	4.55
1996...	20.8	2.74	2.71	126.00	69.3	95.80	1.96	28.1	4.93	9.96	4.17	7.35	4.30
1997...	22.1	2.38	2.43	121.00	65.2	100.00	1.60	28.3	5.62	9.70	3.95	6.47	3.38
1998...	17.1	1.98	1.90	129.00	64.2	84.60	1.10	25.7	5.24	8.50	3.10	5.35	2.65
1999...	21.3	2.13	1.82	89.00	45.0	76.90	1.12	25.4	5.77	5.93	2.80	4.63	2.48
2000...	17.8	2.11	1.85	105.00	49.8	84.60	1.10	27.4	5.08	5.61	3.37	4.54	2.62
2001...	22.9	2.22	1.97	90.50	29.8	96.50	1.59	23.4	6.99	4.25	4.25	4.38	2.78
2002...	25.6	2.72	2.32	101.00	44.5	92.40	1.81	18.2	6.69	4.49	4.14	5.53	3.56
2003...	29.4	2.83	2.42	117.00	61.8	85.50	1.48	19.3	5.89	8.08	4.26	7.34	3.40
2004[1]...	21.8	2.48	2.06	107.00	41.6	92.00	1.48	18.9	5.67	7.33	3.19	5.74	3.40
2005...	27.6	2.53	1.90	95.50	46.9	98.00	1.63	17.4	6.90	7.80	3.04	5.50	3.42

*Beginning in 1964, 480-lb net weight bales. NA = Not available. (1) Revised.

Value of U.S. Agricultural Exports and Imports, 1978-2005

Source: Economic Research Service, U.S. Dept. of Agriculture

(in billions of dollars, except percent)

Year[1]	Agric. Trade surplus	Agric. exports	% of all exports	Agric. imports	% of all imports	Year[1]	Agric. Trade surplus	Agric. exports	% of all exports	Agric. imports	% of all imports
1978.....	13.4	27.3	21	13.9	8	1992	18.3	43.1	10	24.8	5
1979.....	15.8	32.0	19	16.2	8	1993	17.7	42.9	10	25.1	4
1980.....	23.2	40.5	19	17.3	7	1994	19.2	46.2	10	27.0	4
1981.....	26.4	43.8	19	17.3	7	1995	26.0	56.3	10	30.3	4
1982.....	23.6	39.1	18	15.5	6	1996	26.8	60.3	10	33.5	4
1983.....	18.5	34.8	18	16.3	7	1997	21.0	57.2	9	36.1	4
1984.....	19.1	38.0	18	18.9	6	1998	14.9	51.8	9	36.9	4
1985.....	11.5	31.2	15	19.7	6	1999	10.7	48.4	8	37.7	4
1986.....	5.4	26.3	13	20.9	6	2000	12.2	51.2	7	39.0	3
1987.....	7.2	27.9	12	20.7	5	2001	14.3	53.7	8	39.4	4
1988.....	14.3	35.3	12	21.0	5	2002	11.2	53.1	8	41.9	4
1989.....	18.1	39.7	12	21.6	5	2003	10.3	56.0	9	45.7	4
1990.....	16.6	39.5	11	22.9	5	2004[2].....	9.7	62.4	9	52.7	4
1991.....	16.4	39.3	10	22.9	5	2005[3].....	4.8	62.5	8	57.7	4

(1) Fiscal year (Oct.-Sept.). (2) Revised. (3) Preliminary.

World Wheat, Rice, and Corn Production, 2005

Source: UN Food and Agriculture Organization; in metric tons

Country	Corn	Rice[1]	Wheat
Afghanistan	250,000	448,000	3,000,000
Albania	220,000	—	260,000
Algeria	1,000	300	2,600,000
Argentina	19,500,000	1,027,000	16,000,000
Australia	312,000	323,000	25,090,000
Austria	1,604,818	—	1,453,000
Bangladesh	526,000	41,104,000	1,000,000
Belgium	553,775	—	1,768,410
Brazil	34,859,600	13,140,900	5,200,840
Bulgaria	1,585,700	20,163	3,478,070
Cambodia	258,000	4,200,000	—
Cameroon	950,000	50,000	400
Canada	8,392,000	—	25,546,900
Chile	1,507,766	116,832	1,851,940
China	135,000,000	181,900,000	97,000,000
Colombia	1,441,501	2,602,300	40,018
Congo, Dem Rep.	1,155,260	315,480	11,000
Côte d'Ivoire	910,000	1,150,000	850,000
Croatia	2,100,000	—	—
Cuba	400,000	650,000	13,000
Cyprus	—	—	4,145,039
Czech Republic	702,900	—	4,887,200
Denmark	—	—	14,366
Ecuador	750,727	1,375,502	8,140,961
Egypt	6,800,000	6,200,000	1,650,000
Ethiopia	2,740,000	15,500	36,877,964
France	13,711,964	102,466	23,693,000
Germany	4,083,000	—	—
Ghana	1,157,621	241,807	2,044,149
Greece	2,534,077	167,247	11,339
Guatemala	1,072,310	34,926	5,079,000
Hungary	9,017,000	10,900	72,000,000
India	14,500,000	130,513,000	—
Indonesia	12,013,707	53,984,592	14,500,000
Iran	1,500,000	3,500,000	2,200,000
Iraq	300,000	125,000	798,000
Israel	80,000	—	213,626
Italy	10,509,830	1,412,957	7,717,129
Japan	150	11,342,000	877,400
Kazakhstan	510,000	307,000	11,100,000
Kenya	2,200,000	50,000	380,000
Korea, North	1,600,000	2,500,000	175,000
Korea, South	63,000	6,435,000	7,000
Kuwait	800	—	—
Laos	210,000	2,350,000	—
Madagascar	349,646	3,030,000	10,000
Malaysia	75,000	2,215,000	—
Mexico	20,500,000	191,540	3,000,000
Moldova	1,695,000	—	822,800
Morocco	224,130	16,900	3,043,000
Mozambique	1,450,000	201,000	2,100
Myanmar	820,000	24,500,000	145,000
Nepal	1,716,042	4,100,000	1,442,442
Netherlands	270,000	—	1,253,000
Nigeria	4,779,000	3,542,000	71,000
Pakistan	3,560,000	7,351,000	21,591,400
Paraguay	830,000	102,000	630,000
Peru	1,242,653	2,466,135	179,348
Philippines	5,250,000	14,615,000	—
Poland	1,917,388	—	8,556,248
Portugal	700,000	120,000	275,000
Romania	9,965,000	5,000	7,027,000
Russia	3,179,000	572,000	47,608,000
Saudi Arabia	43,697	—	2,200,000
Serbia and Montenegro	6,600,000	—	2,008,000
Slovakia	943,000	—	1,700,000
South Africa	11,996,000	3,200	2,034,300
Spain	3,950,700	845,900	3,820,000
Sri Lanka	40,000	3,126,000	—
Sweden	—	—	2,246,800
Syria	—	—	4,668,750
Tanzania	3,230,000	680,000	—
Thailand	4,180,000	27,000,000	800
Turkey	3,500,000	525,000	21,000,000
Turkmenistan	16,000	120,000	2,834,000
Uganda	1,350,000	140,000	15,000
Ukraine	7,100,000	70,000	18,690,000
United Kingdom	—	—	14,877,000
U.S.	282,259,584	10,125,770	57,280,272
Uruguay	251,000	1,214,500	387,500
Uzbekistan	154,500	152,000	5,745,000
Venezuela	2,050,000	950,000	150
Vietnam	3,500,000	36,341,000	—
Zambia	820,000	12,000	135,000
Zimbabwe	900,000	600	140,000
World[2]	**702,036,208**	**618,036,734**	**631,297,791**

— Production is small or nonexistent. (1) Paddy rice only. (2) Includes countries not listed.

Wheat, Rice, and Corn—Exports/Imports of 10 Leading Countries, 2004, 1995

Source: UN Food and Agriculture Organization; in metric tons

TOP EXPORTERS

Wheat

2004		1995	
U.S.	31,581,449	U.S.	32,420,000
Australia	18,450,822	Canada	16,960,000
Canada	15,118,679	France	16,310,000
France	14,891,804	Australia	7,818,000
Argentina	9,976,599	Argentina	6,913,286
Russia	4,672,189	Germany	3,681,597
Germany	3,926,949	Hungary	2,764,541
Ukraine	2,553,931	U.K.	2,669,090
U.K.	2,523,344	Kazakhstan	2,485,588
Kazakhstan	2,360,062	Denmark	1,540,179

Rice

2004		1995	
Thailand	10,130,073	Thailand	6,197,990
India	4,904,271	India	4,913,156
Vietnam	4,087,143	U.S.	3,083,609
U.S.	3,625,457	Vietnam	1,988,000
Pakistan	1,828,028	Pakistan	1,852,267
China	938,924	Australia	541,848
Egypt	837,611	Italy	523,898
Italy	682,447	Uruguay	462,471
Uruguay	660,502	Argentina	390,091
Spain	346,348	Myanmar	353,800

Corn

2004		1995	
U.S.	48,741,188	U.S.	60,240,000
Argentina	10,692,005	France	6,474,138
France	6,155,982	Argentina	6,000,873
Brazil	5,030,999	South Africa	1,508,450
China	2,318,232	Hungary	600,950
Hungary	1,237,488	Canada	443,612
Ukraine	1,233,853	Belgium-Lux.	442,645
India	1,068,677	Zimbabwe	287,818
Thailand	951,310	Germany	244,000
Germany	947,474	Paraguay	203,430

TOP IMPORTERS

Wheat

2004		1995	
China	8,331,604	China	12,601,814
Italy	6,482,655	Brazil	6,135,235
Japan	5,490,227	Japan	5,965,296
Algeria	5,034,447	Italy	5,078,844
Brazil	4,847,805	Egypt	5,069,599
Indonesia	4,545,590	Indonesia	4,054,203
Spain	4,367,919	Algeria	3,504,679
Egypt	4,366,841	Iran	3,100,000
Mexico	3,585,471	Spain	2,757,498
Malaysia	3,378,088	Belgium-Lux.	2,719,024

Rice

2004		1995	
Nigeria	1,398,657	Indonesia	3,157,700
China	1,324,850	China	1,645,837
Saudi Arabia	1,208,594	Iran	1,633,000
Philippines	1,076,923	Bangladesh	995,946
Bangladesh	994,592	Brazil	870,506
Iran	991,545	North Korea	587,000
Brazil	927,915	U. Arab Em.	540,888
Côte d'Ivoire	868,334	Saudi Arabia	522,942
Senegal	822,610	Côte d'Ivoire	483,688
Mexico	797,302	South Africa	466,154

Corn

2004		1995	
Japan	16,479,436	Japan	16,580,000
South Korea	8,371,012	China	11,702,350
Mexico	5,518,690	South Korea	9,035,169
China	4,942,472	Spain	2,912,371
Malaysia	2,977,594	Mexico	2,686,921
Spain	2,750,923	Egypt	2,425,162
Egypt	2,429,278	Malaysia	2,383,267
Netherlands	2,204,731	Belgium-Lux.	1,815,945
Canada	2,055,270	Netherlands	1,589,800
Colombia	1,909,354	U.K.	1,501,563

World Commercial Catch of Fish, Crustaceans, and Mollusks, by Major Fishing Areas, 1990-2004

Source: Food and Agriculture Organization of the United Nations (FAO) Fishery Information (2006)
(in thousands of metric tons; live weight)

AREA	1990	1995	2000	2001	2002	2003	2004
Marine							
Pacific Ocean..........	52,868	61,839	65,556	63,708	65,037	63,320	57,047
Atlantic Ocean..........	23,205	25,054	25,906	26,455	25,834	25,070	25,606
Indian Ocean..........	6,609	8,365	9,473	9,376	9,967	10,280	8,940
Total Marine..........	**83,187**	**95,406**	**101,073**	**99,659**	**100,984**	**98,813**	**104,123**
Inland Waters							
Asia.................	10,432	17,337	25,527	26,455	28,047	29,575	31,450
Africa...............	1,938	2,081	2,445	2,452	2,529	2,650	2,785
Europe..............	1,294	838	886	826	822	836	788
N. America[1]...........	490	538	594	588	613	642	639
S. America.............	330	445	553	594	655	673	703
Oceania..............	24	21	24	25	22	20	21
Total Inland...........	**14,508**	**21,261**	**30,028**	**31,356**	**32,688**	**34,396**	**36,386**
GRAND TOTAL........	**97,695**	**116,667**	**131,100**	**131,015**	**133,672**	**133,209**	**140,509**

(1) N. America includes figures for Central America. **Note:** Data for marine mammals and aquatic plants are excluded. Totals include areas or territories not shown. Figures may be revised. Includes weight of clam, oyster, scallop and other mollusk shells.

Commercial Catch of Fish, Crustaceans, and Mollusks, for 20 Leading Countries, 2000-04[1]

Source: FishSTAT Plus, Food and Agriculture Organization of the United Nations (FAO), 2006
(in thousands of metric tons; live weight; ranked for 2004)

COUNTRY	2004	2003	2002	2001	2000	COUNTRY	2004	2003	2002	2001	2000
China......	58,601	55,740	53,427	51,006	49,636	Russia.....	3,110	3,429	3,389	3,747	4,104
Peru.......	9,643	6,108	8,783	7,996	10,665	Vietnam....	3,108	2,824	2,531	2,333	2,137
Indonesia...	6,350	5,920	5,517	5,354	5,121	S. Korea ...	2,537	2,488	2,476	2,674	2,506
India......	6,097	6,034	5,933	5,937	5,669	Bangladesh..	2,102	1,998	1,890	1,781	1,661
Chile......	6,021	4,525	5,134	4,663	4,973	Myanmar...	1,987	1,596	1,474	1,309	1,192
Japan......	5,778	6,085	5,875	6,139	6,398	Iceland.....	1,758	2,006	2,148	2,005	2,004
U.S........	5,602	5,533	5,482	5,461	5,216	Mexico.....	1,567	1,569	1,555	1,522	1,404
Thailand....	4,018	3,914	3,797	3,648	3,736	Malaysia ...	1,542	1,483	1,464	1,416	1,461
Philippines ..	3,932	3,618	3,372	3,172	3,000	Canada	1,336	1,281	1,250	1,209	1,160
Norway.....	3,309	3,285	3,473	3,373	3,383	Spain......	1,167	1,210	1,216	1,419	1,372

(1) Includes aquaculture. Includes weight of aquatic plants, clam, oyster, scallop, and other mollusk shells; this weight is not included in U.S. landings statistics shown elsewhere.

U.S. Commercial Landings of Fish and Shellfish, 1990-2004[1]

Source: U.S. Dept. of Commerce, Natl. Oceanic and Atmospheric Admin., Natl. Marine Fisheries Service
(in millions)

YEAR	Landings for human food Weight (lbs)	Value	Landings for industrial purposes[2] Weight (lbs)	Value	TOTAL · Weight (lbs)	Value
1990	7,041	$3,366	2,363	$156	9,404	$3,522
1991	7,031	3,169	2,453	139	9,484	3,308
1992	7,618	3,531	2,019	147	9,637	3,678
1993	8,214	3,317	2,253	154	10,467	3,471
1994	7,936	3,751	2,525	95	10,461	3,846
1995	7,667	3,625	2,121	145	9,788	3,770
1996	7,474	3,355	2,091	132	9,565	3,487
1997	7,244	3,285	2,598	163	9,842	3,448
1998	7,173	3,009	2,021	119	9,194	3,128
1999	6,832	3,265	2,507	202	9,339	3,467
2000	6,912	3,398	2,157	152	9,069	3,550
2001	7,314	3,074	2,178	154	9,492	3,228
2002	7,205	2,940	2,192	152	9,397	3,092
2003	7,521	3,185	1,986	157	9,507	3,347
2004	7,768	3,510	1,875	142	9,643	3,652

Note: Data do not include products of aquaculture, except oysters and clams. (1) Statistics on landings are shown in round (live) weight for all items except univalve and bivalve mollusks such as clams, oysters, and scallops, which are shown in weight of meats (excluding the shell). (2) Processed into meal, oil, solubles, and shell products or used as bait or animal food.

U.S. Domestic Landings, by Region, 2003-04[1]

Source: U.S. Dept. of Commerce, Natl. Oceanic and Atmospheric Admin., Natl. Marine Fisheries Service

REGION	2003[2] Weight (1,000 lbs)	Value ($1,000)	2004[3] Weight (1,000 lbs)	Value ($1,000)
New England.........................	660,835	$690,726	685,873	$757,566
Middle Atlantic.......................	214,552	177,494	223,644	191,272
Chesapeake..........................	496,178	179,702	531,062	209,470
South Atlantic........................	196,722	152,757	197,048	151,726
Gulf................................	1,600,481	683,277	1,474,421	667,315
Pacific Coast incl. Alaska..............	6,291,194	1,382,374	6,483,345	1,587,115
Great Lakes.........................	17,471	13,174	16,620	12,381
Hawaii..............................	23,556	52,433	24,265	57,202
TOTAL.............................	**9,506,986**	**$3,347,530**	**9,643,291**	**$3,652,281**

(1) Landings reported in round (live) weight items except for univalve and bivalve mollusks (e.g., clams, oysters, scallops), which are reported in weight of meats (excluding shell). Landings for Mississippi River Drainage Area states not included (not available). (2) Revised. (3) Preliminary.

> ▶ **IT'S A FACT:** Aquaculture, or fish farming, has grown explosively worldwide in the last 50 years. Production of aquaculture, which includes aquatic plants, was less than 1 mil metric tons in 1950. In 2004, production was 59.4 mil metric tons—about 42% of total commercial fish production—with a value of $70.3 bil.

EMPLOYMENT

Employment and Unemployment in the U.S., 1900-2005

Source: Bureau of Labor Statistics, U.S. Dept. of Labor

(civilian labor force, persons 16 years of age and older; annual averages; in thousands)

Year[1]	Employed	Unemployed	Unemployment rate	Year[1]	Employed	Unemployed	Unemployment rate
1900[2]	26,956	1,420	5.0%	1990[3]	118,793	7,047	5.6%
1910[2]	34,599	2,150	5.9	1991	117,718	8,628	6.8
1920[2]	39,208	2,132	5.2	1992	118,492	9,613	7.5
1930[2]	44,183	4,340	8.9	1993	120,259	8,940	6.9
1940[2]	47,520	8,120	14.6	1994[4]	123,060	7,996	6.1
1950	58,918	3,288	5.0	1995	124,900	7,404	5.6
1955	62,170	2,852	4.4	1996	126,708	7,236	5.4
1960	65,778	3,852	5.5	1997[5]	129,558	6,739	4.9
1965	71,088	3,366	4.5	1998[5]	131,463	6,210	4.5
1970	78,678	4,093	4.9	1999[6]	133,488	5,880	4.2
1975	85,846	7,929	8.5	2000[7]	136,891	5,692	4.0
1980	99,303	7,637	7.1	2001[7]	136,933	6,801	4.7
1985	107,150	8,312	7.2	2002[7]	136,485	8,378	5.8
1986	109,597	8,237	7.0	2003[7]	137,736	8,774	6.0
1987	112,440	7,425	6.2	2004[7]	139,252	8,149	5.5
1988	114,968	6,701	5.5	2005[7]	141,730	7,591	5.1
1989	117,342	6,528	5.3				

(1) **Other unemployment rates (1905-1945): 1905**, 4.3; **1915**, 8.5; **1925**, 3.2; **1935**, 20.3; **1936**, 16.9; **1937**, 14.3; **1938**, 19.0; **1939**, 17.2; **1945**, 1.9; all for 14 years of age and older. (2) Persons 14 years of age and older. (3) Beginning in 1990, data incorporate 1990 census-based population controls, adjusted for estimated undercount. (4) Beginning in 1994, not strictly comparable with prior years, because of major redesign of the survey used. (5) From 1997 not strictly comparable with 1994-96 because of revisions in population controls used in household survey. (6) From 1999 not strictly comparable with 1998 and earlier years because of further revisions in population controls used in household survey. (7) From 2000, not strictly comparable with earlier years because of revisions to the controls used in the survey.

Unemployment Insurance Data, by State, 2005

Source: Employment and Training Admin., U.S. Dept. of Labor; state programs only

STATE	Monetarily eligible claimants	First payments	Final payments	Initial claims	Benefits paid	Average weekly benefit	Employers subject to state law
AL	133,137	106,762	29,512	245,173	205,787,760	182.01	87,659
AK	49,221	43,944	17,847	89,863	107,109,372	193.91	16,972
AZ	104,397	75,887	32,743	180,979	224,909,334	194.76	114,991
AR	109,535	78,718	29,459	191,017	213,364,632	229.61	62,502
CA	1,273,974	974,979	456,782	2,172,541	4,199,894,142	277.46	1,074,566
CO	102,525	73,893	35,379	130,652	310,275,520	301.77	149,070
CT	140,007	121,538	41,114	217,142	522,611,175	295.42	97,551
DE	31,053	24,337	7,088	53,724	94,035,294	247.47	25,959
FL	17,223	16,619	8,788	15,495	81,581,623	266.67	27,729
GA	349,233	244,017	120,164	533,558	842,089,368	226.35	463,627
HI	262,700	194,114	75,572	446,370	502,072,423	244.65	206,408
ID	27,509	19,832	4,868	53,973	82,253,373	337.42	30,227
IL	54,887	43,759	13,777	100,065	114,049,601	235.25	45,416
IN	410,879	351,963	141,819	702,725	1,702,911,777	285.38	287,711
IA	235,246	184,931	73,358	385,563	630,735,656	278.07	126,249
KS	112,218	91,540	22,399	173,402	288,574,871	271.26	70,047
KY	73,601	61,002	24,242	125,908	199,976,729	278.47	69,634
LA	155,861	110,724	24,968	284,403	361,103,852	259.56	84,704
ME	327,818	299,088	31,189	378,649	582,857,489	192.29	96,760
MD	43,272	31,936	10,657	67,572	105,986,002	240.24	40,790
MA	139,978	99,387	33,232	209,441	364,790,386	256.64	139,278
MI	260,053	218,287	80,165	391,991	1,223,055,850	356.64	181,360
MN	545,634	449,917	150,889	900,734	1,728,177,058	290.13	214,230
MS	177,264	144,233	43,189	283,975	593,199,737	321.59	132,046
MO	132,247	102,598	18,644	212,753	207,527,517	186.34	54,837
MT	205,734	137,165	52,318	378,043	415,191,046	205.79	135,417
NE	30,891	21,366	6,879	50,167	60,757,640	220.58	35,286
NV	53,759	38,822	17,211	75,073	107,886,498	225.65	46,723
NH	77,251	59,393	20,179	133,009	216,430,937	258.31	53,579
NJ	32,785	24,183	3,796	50,323	71,004,691	252.12	40,151
NM	359,689	315,037	146,149	535,913	1,731,312,161	336.04	259,049
NY	32,861	28,951	12,912	56,955	104,663,522	217.70	43,064
NC	615,115	488,443	192,197	1,047,468	2,253,483,124	276.05	483,001
ND	334,404	250,486	94,240	667,145	665,623,613	257.71	185,431
OH	16,435	12,529	4,183	24,533	38,515,429	238.41	19,429
OK	368,996	285,738	83,704	654,032	1,063,140,092	260.99	231,875
OR	70,167	47,385	20,238	120,127	147,147,410	221.49	77,594
PA	170,222	132,813	45,960	332,813	490,272,812	261.26	105,600
RI	575,053	461,257	139,872	1,094,401	1,917,176,158	291.89	279,482
SC	97,356	105,595	48,439	185,987	205,828,121	108.28	61,610
SD	47,434	38,442	14,737	78,090	200,100,120	336.42	33,575
TN	163,086	115,916	44,549	308,901	321,083,419	216.66	94,726
TX	12,743	9,380	1,458	21,023	25,776,148	211.49	24,055
UT	183,513	154,046	55,001	340,304	416,992,502	212.11	110,757
VT	631,188	356,906	144,693	829,923	1,175,246,927	261.34	410,040
VA	51,747	35,897	12,591	64,162	110,794,951	263.37	61,614
WA	27,030	22,880	3,892	40,036	73,699,224	267.14	21,428
WV	1,990	1,553	657	2,359	5,667,121	237.00	3,382
WI	161,547	110,188	39,083	260,630	327,078,433	245.74	176,199
WY	253,486	183,530	43,199	449,266	705,978,011	296.86	191,210
DC	53,619	40,685	10,156	72,674	135,386,003	225.12	36,736
PR	306,462	262,724	66,174	612,406	751,844,757	252.82	126,932
VI	24,052	11,979	3,499	19,924	32,782,729	241.52	20,504
U.S.	**10,228,087**	**7,917,294**	**2,855,810**	**17,053,355**	**29,259,794,140**	**266.62**	**7,268,763**

Unemployed Persons[1] by Industry and Duration of Unemployment, Sept. 2006

Source: Bureau of Labor Statistics, U.S. Dept. of Labor

				15 weeks and over			Weeks of Unemployment	
OCCUPATION	Total	Less than 5 weeks	5 to 14 weeks	Total	15 to 26 weeks	27 weeks and over	Average (mean) duration	Median duration
Management, professional, and related	1,094	429	307	358	173	185	16.5	8.4
Service	1,359	617	352	391	163	228	15.9	5.7
Sales and office	1,707	604	510	593	246	347	19.0	9.2
Natural resources, construction, and maintenance	932	402	224	305	113	192	17.6	7.2
Production, transportation, and material moving	927	340	277	310	121	189	18.9	8.3
INDUSTRY[2]								
Agriculture and related industries	79	46	9	23	11	12	13.4	3.7
Mining	14	8	3	3	1	2	(3)	(3)
Construction	603	286	134	183	68	115	16.5	6.0
Manufacturing	636	236	181	220	97	122	18.5	8.4
Wholesale and retail trade	1,014	358	327	329	128	202	18.3	8.7
Transportation and utilities	202	70	59	73	36	37	16.1	9.4
Information	180	64	48	68	26	42	21.8	8.7
Financial activities	241	74	83	83	43	41	18.3	9.1
Professional and business services	757	259	215	283	108	175	20.1	9.5
Education and health services	749	289	184	276	115	161	19.2	9.3
Leisure and hospitality	839	397	235	207	91	116	13.8	5.2
Other services	311	122	88	100	43	57	17.5	7.1
Public administration	97	37	32	27	13	14	15.1	9.4
No previous work experience	590	215	196	180	87	93	16.5	8.2

(1) Numbers are in thousands. (2) Includes wage and salary workers only. (3) Data not shown where base is less than 75,000.

Persons Not in the Labor Force, 2005

Source: Bureau of Labor Statistics, U.S. Dept. of Labor

The Labor Department's unemployment rate, based on its household survey, shows the number of people out of work as a percentage of U.S. adults in the labor force. Millions of other adults are considered not to be in the labor force.

(in thousands)

		Age			Sex	
	Total	16 to 24 years	25 to 54 years	55 years and over	Men	Women
Total not in the labor force	**76,762**	**14,383**	**21,403**	**40,976**	**29,119**	**47,643**
Do not want a job now[1]	71,777	12,585	19,238	39,954	26,926	44,851
Want a job[1]	4,985	1,798	2,165	1,022	2,193	2,792
Did not search for work in previous year	2,841	963	1,163	715	1,173	1,668
Searched for work in previous year[2]	2,144	836	1,002	307	1,020	1,124
Not available to work now	599	285	260	54	231	368
Available to work now	1,545	551	742	252	789	756
Reason not currently looking:						
Discouragement over job prospects[3]	436	141	217	78	260	176
Reasons other than discouragement	1,109	410	525	175	529	580
Family responsibilities	159	32	105	22	36	123
In school or training	217	179	35	2	118	99
Ill health or disability	119	16	69	34	64	55
Other[4]	614	182	316	116	311	302

(1) Includes some persons who are not asked if they want a job. (2) Persons who had a job in the prior 12 months must have searched since the end of that job. (3) Includes believes no work available, could not find work, lacks necessary schooling or training, employer thinks too young or old, and other types of discrimination. (4) Includes those who did not actively look for work in the prior 4 weeks for such reasons as child care and transportation problems, as well as a small number for which reason for nonparticipation was not ascertained.

Displaced Workers, Jan. 2006

Source: Bureau of Labor Statistics, U.S. Dept. of Labor

		Percent distribution by reason of job loss		
	Total (thousands)	Plant or company closed down or moved	Insufficient work	Position or shift abolished
Total, 20 years and over	**3,815**	**49.0**	**22.2**	**28.8**
20 to 24 years	111	39.1	42.8	18.1
25 to 54 years	2,841	48.5	22.6	28.9
55 to 64 years	728	53.2	16.5	30.2
65 years and over	135	44.1	28.8	27.1
Men	2,076	48.8	24.8	26.5
Women	1,739	49.2	19.2	31.6
White	3,169	49.5	22.1	28.4
Black or African American	452	42.5	19.7	37.8
Asian	113	52.3	25.9	21.8
Hispanic or Latino ethnicity	416	59.6	26.1	14.3

Note: Displaced workers are persons 20 years or older who lost or left jobs they had held for at least 3 years. Workers in this table were displaced between Jan. 2003 and Dec. 2005.

U.S. Unemployment Rates by Selected Characteristics, 1995-2006[1]

Source: Bureau of Labor Statistics, U.S. Dept. of Labor

	1995	2000	2001	2002	2003	2004	2005 Jan.	2005 June	2005 Annual	2006 Jan.	2006 June
Total (all civilian workers)	5.6	4.0	4.7	5.8	6.0	5.5	5.7	5.2	5.1	5.1	4.8
Men, 20 years and older	4.8	3.3	4.2	5.3	5.6	5.0	5.6	4.1	4.4	4.8	3.8
Women, 20 years and older	4.9	3.6	4.1	5.1	5.1	4.9	4.8	4.8	4.6	4.4	4.3
Both sexes, 16 to 19 years	17.3	13.1	14.7	16.5	17.5	17.0	16.6	19.1	16.6	15.5	18.4
White	4.9	3.5	4.2	5.1	5.2	4.8	5.0	4.4	4.4	4.6	4.2
Black	10.4	7.6	8.6	10.2	10.8	10.4	11.0	10.8	10.0	9.1	9.4
Hispanic origin	9.3	5.7	6.6	7.5	7.7	7.0	6.9	5.6	6.0	6.4	5.1
Asian	—	3.6	4.5	5.9	6.0	4.4	4.2	4.0	4.0	3.2	3.5
Married men, spouse present	3.3	—	—	—	—	—	3.0	2.6	—	2.4	2.5
Married women, spouse present	3.9	—	—	—	—	—	3.2	3.3	—	3.0	2.9
Women who maintain families	8.0	5.9	6.6	8.0	8.5	8.0	8.2	8.2	7.8	8.2	7.2
OCCUPATION											
Management, professional, and related occupations	2.4	1.8	2.3	3.0	3.1	2.7	2.4	2.6	2.3	2.1	2.4
Service occupations	7.5	5.2	5.8	6.6	7.1	6.6	7.3	6.3	6.4	6.4	5.8
Sales and office occupations	5.0	3.8	4.4	5.6	5.5	5.2	5.3	4.9	4.8	4.7	4.7
Nat. resources, constr., maint. occupations	—	5.3	6.4	7.8	8.1	7.3	9.4	5.5	6.5	7.8	4.8
Prod., trans., material moving occupations	—	5.1	6.4	7.6	7.9	7.2	7.3	6.3	6.5	7.1	5.2
INDUSTRY											
Nonagricultural, private wage, and salary workers	5.8	4.1	5.0	6.2	6.3	5.7	6.0	5.1	5.2	5.3	4.7
Mining	5.2	4.4	4.2	6.3	6.7	3.9	4.9	4.0	3.1	3.9	4.3
Construction	11.5	6.2	7.1	9.2	9.3	8.4	11.8	5.7	7.4	9.0	5.6
Manufacturing	4.9	3.5	5.2	6.7	6.6	5.7	5.3	4.4	4.9	4.6	3.8
Durable goods	4.4	3.2	5.2	6.9	6.9	5.5	5.1	4.3	4.6	4.1	3.6
Non durable goods	5.7	4.0	5.2	6.2	6.1	5.9	5.7	4.6	5.3	5.4	4.2
Wholesale and retail trade	6.5	4.3	4.9	6.1	6.0	5.8	6.3	5.7	5.4	5.7	5.1
Transportation and utilities	4.5	3.4	4.3	4.9	5.3	4.4	5.0	4.5	4.1	5.0	3.9
Information	—	3.2	4.9	6.9	6.8	5.7	5.4	5.0	5.0	3.3	3.4
Financial activities	3.3	2.4	2.9	3.5	3.5	3.6	2.7	3.3	2.9	2.4	3.1
Professional and business services	—	4.8	6.1	7.9	8.2	6.8	7.6	5.8	6.2	6.5	5.7
Education and health services	—	2.5	2.8	3.4	3.6	3.4	3.4	3.6	3.4	3.2	3.3
Leisure and hospitality	—	6.6	7.5	8.4	8.7	8.3	8.7	7.6	7.8	8.1	7.4
Other services	8.4	3.9	4.0	5.1	5.7	5.3	4.7	4.6	4.8	4.9	4.3
Agriculture and related	11.1	9.0	11.2	10.1	10.2	9.9	13.2	5.2	8.3	11.5	2.4
Government	2.9	2.1	2.2	2.5	2.8	2.7	2.6	3.2	2.6	2.2	2.8
Self-employed and unpaid family workers	—	2.1	2.1	2.6	2.7	2.8	3.2	2.4	2.7	3.2	2.2

(1) All monthly rates unadjusted, except for married men and women, which are seasonally adjusted. — = Not available.

Employed Persons in the U.S., by Occupation and Sex, 2004 and 2005

Source: Bureau of Labor Statistics, U.S. Dept. of Labor

(in thousands)

	Total 16 years and older 2004	Total 16 years and older 2005	Men 16 years and older 2004	Men 16 years and older 2005	Women 16 years and older 2004	Women 16 years and older 2005
Total	139,252	141,730	74,524	75,973	64,728	65,757
Management, professional, and related	48,532	49,245	24,136	24,349	24,396	24,896
Management, business, and financial operations	20,235	20,450	11,718	11,761	8,517	8,689
Management	14,555	14,685	9,210	9,220	5,344	5,466
Business and financial operations	5,680	5,765	2,508	2,541	3,172	3,223
Professional and related	28,297	28,795	12,418	12,588	15,879	16,207
Computer and mathematical	3,140	3,246	2,292	2,371	848	875
Architecture and engineering	2,760	2,793	2,380	2,407	380	385
Life, physical, and social science	1,365	1,406	777	808	588	598
Community and social services	2,170	2,138	845	827	1,325	1,311
Legal	1,554	1,614	795	817	759	797
Education, training, and library	7,900	8,114	2,104	2,125	5,796	5,989
Arts, design, entertainment, sports, and media	2,687	2,736	1,425	1,427	1,262	1,309
Healthcare practitioner and technical	6,721	6,748	1,799	1,806	4,922	4,942
Service	22,720	23,133	9,826	9,882	12,894	13,251
Healthcare support	2,921	3,092	311	339	2,609	2,753
Protective service	2,847	2,894	2,230	2,246	616	648
Food preparation and serving related	7,279	7,374	3,196	3,202	4,084	4,173
Building and grounds cleaning and maintenance	5,185	5,241	3,085	3,111	2,100	2,130
Personal care and service	4,488	4,531	1,004	984	3,484	3,548
Sales and office	35,464	35,962	12,805	13,190	22,660	22,772
Sales and related	15,983	16,433	8,105	8,362	7,878	8,072
Office and administrative support	19,481	19,529	4,700	4,829	14,781	14,700
Natural resources, construction, and maintenance	14,582	15,348	13,930	14,635	652	713
Farming, fishing, and forestry	991	976	786	756	204	220
Construction and extraction	8,522	9,145	8,306	8,871	216	274
Installation, maintenance, and repair	5,069	5,226	4,838	5,008	231	219
Production, transportation, and material moving	17,954	18,041	13,827	13,917	4,126	4,124
Production	9,462	9,378	6,587	6,540	2,875	2,838
Transportation and material moving	8,491	8,664	7,240	7,377	1,251	1,286

Note: Beginning in Jan. 2005, data reflect revised population controls used in the household survey. Totals may not add because of independent rounding.

► **IT'S A FACT:** According to the 2006 National Association of Colleges and Employers' Job Outlook survey, employers are more strongly influenced by handshakes (33%) than by body piercings (31%) or visible tattoos (29%). Non-traditional attire strongly influences 49% of those surveyed, with 73% reporting that an applicant's grooming strongly influences their impression of the candidate.

Elderly in U.S. Labor Force, 1890-2005

Source: Bureau of the Census, U.S. Dept. of Commerce

The percentage of men 65 years of age and older in the U.S. labor force steadily declined between 1890 and 1990, dropping 76% in 100 years, but since 1990 the rate has risen. The percentage of women 65 or older in the work force has always been much lower than that of men; after ranging from around 6% to 10% from 1890 to 1950, it has increased to 9%-12% in recent years.

(labor force participation rate; figs. for 1910 not available)

Year	Men	Women
1890	68.3	7.6
1900	63.1	8.3
1920	55.6	7.3
1930	54.0	7.3
1940	41.8	6.1
1950	45.8	9.7
1960	33.1	10.8
1970	26.8	9.7
1980	19.0	8.1
1990	16.3	8.6
2000	17.7	9.4
2005	19.8	11.5

Projected Openings for Selected High-Paying Occupations, 2002-2012

Source: Bureau of Labor Statistics, U.S. Dept. of Labor

Job openings shown below represent the average number expected each year for workers in the U.S. who are entering these occupations for the first time.

Occupation	Annual avg. job openings[1]	Median annual earnings[2]	Occupation	Annual avg. job openings[1]	Median annual earnings[2]
Registered nurses	110,119	$48,090	First-line office superv. or mgrs	40,909	$38,820
Postsecondary teachers	95,980	49,090	Accountants and auditors	40,465	47,000
Gen. & operations mgrs.	76,245	68,210	Carpenters	31,917	34,190
Sales representatives[3]	66,239	42,730	Auto mechanics/technicians	31,887	30,590
Truck drivers, heavy & tractor trailer	62,517	33,210	Police & Sheriff's patrol officers	31,290	42,270
Elementary school teachers	54,701	41,780	Lic. practical and voc. nurses	29,480	31,440
First-line retail superv. or mgrs.	48,645	29,700	Electricians	28,485	41,390
Secondary school teachers[4]	45,761	43,950	Management analysts	25,470	60,340
Gen. maintenance & repair wkrs	44,978	29,370	Computer systems analysts	23,735	62,890
Exec. secretaries, admin. assists.	42,444	33,410	Special education teachers	23,297	43,450

(1) As a result of growth and net replacement needs. (2) Median earnings are for 2002. (3) Wholesale and manufacturing, except technical and scientific products. (4) Except special and vocational education.

Top-Paying U.S. Counties by Average Weekly Wage, 4th Quarter 2005

Source: Bureau of Labor Statistics

County	Avg. weekly wage	% change 4th qtr. 2004-2005	County	Avg. weekly wage	% change 4th qtr. 2004-2005
New York, NY	1,684	4.3	Westchester, NY	1,173	5.4
Fairfield, CT	1,496	4.3	Middlesex, MA	1,158	1.0
Santa Clara, CA	1,490	1.8	Fulton, GA	1,139	7.6
Suffolk, MA	1,412	3.7	Marin, CA	1,133	6.7
San Francisco, CA	1,378	7.5	Montgomery, MD	1,109	4.0
San Mateo, CA	1,365	3.5	Mercer, NJ	1,085	1.9
Washington, DC	1,354	4.9	Union, NJ	1,078	0.7
Arlington, VA	1,345	4.2	Alexandria City, VA	1,077	2.4
Somerset, NJ	1,296	4.5	Bergen, NJ	1,072	0.5
Fairfax, VA	1,247	0.4	**United States**	**$825**	**1.5**
Morris, NJ	1,239	1.7			

Note: Cameron County, TX, recorded the lowest average weekly earnings among the 323 largest counties with an average weekly wage of $506 in the fourth quarter of 2005 It was followed by: Hidalgo County, TX ($512); Web County, TX ($548); Yakima County, WA ($553); and Horry County, SC ($556). (1) The top ten were derived from a list of the 322 largest U.S. counties, which comprise 70.8% of the total covered workers. Data includes all workers covered by state and federal unemployment insurance programs.

Federal Minimum Hourly Wage Rates Since 1950

Source: Bureau of Labor Statistics, U.S. Dept. of Labor

The Fair Labor Standards Act of 1938 and subsequent amendments provide for minimum wage-coverage applicable to nonprofessional workers in specified nonsupervisory employment categories.

EFFECTIVE DATE	NONFARM WORKERS Under laws prior to 1966[1]	Percent of avg. earnings[2]	Under 1966 and later provis.[3]	FARM WORKERS[4]	EFFECTIVE DATE	NONFARM WORKERS Under laws prior to 1966[1]	Percent of avg. earnings[2]	Under 1966 and later provis.[3]	FARM WORKERS[4]
Jan. 25, 1950	$0.75	54	NA	NA	Jan. 1, 1976	$2.30	46	$2.20	$2.00
Mar. 1, 1956	1.00	52	NA	NA	Jan. 1, 1977	2.30	(5)	2.30	2.20
Sept. 3, 1961	1.15	50	NA	NA	Jan. 1, 1978	2.65	44	2.65	2.65
Sept. 3, 1963	1.25	51	NA	NA	Jan. 1, 1979	2.90	45	2.90	2.90
Feb. 1, 1967	1.40	50	$1.00	$1.00	Jan. 1, 1980	3.10	43	3.10	3.10
Feb. 1, 1968	1.60	54	1.15	1.15	Jan. 1, 1981	3.35	42	3.35	3.35
Feb. 1, 1969	(5)	(5)	1.30	1.30	Apr. 1, 1990	3.80[6]	35	3.80	3.80[6]
Feb. 1, 1970	(5)	(5)	1.45	(5)	Apr. 1, 1991	4.25[6]	38	4.25	4.25[6]
Feb. 1, 1971	(5)	(5)	1.60	(5)	Oct. 1, 1996	4.75[7]	37	4.75	4.75[7]
May 1, 1974	2.00	46	1.90	1.60	Sept. 1, 1997	5.15[7]	39[8]	5.15	5.15[7]
Jan. 1, 1975	2.10	45	2.00	1.80					

NA = not applicable. (1) Applies to workers covered prior to 1961 Amendments and, after Sept. 1965, to workers covered by 1961 Amendments. Rates set by 1961 Amendments were: Sept. 1961, $1.00; Sept. 1964, $1.15; and Sept. 1965, $1.25. (2) Percent of gross average hourly earnings of production workers in manufacturing. (3) Applies to workers newly covered by Amendments of 1966, 1974, and 1977, and Title IX of Education Amendments of 1972. (4) Included in coverage as of 1966, 1974, and 1977 Amendments. (5) No change in rate. (6) Training wage for workers age 16-19 in first 6 months of first job: Apr. 1, 1990, $3.35; Apr. 1, 1991, $3.62. The training wage expired Mar. 31, 1993. (7) Under 1996 legislation, a subminimum training wage of $4.25 an hour was established for employees under 20 years of age during their first 90 consecutive calendar days of employment with an employer. For workers receiving gratuities, the minimum wage remained $2.13 per hour. (8) Minimum wage was 32-7% by this measure in 2003.

Fatal Occupational Injuries, 2005

Source: Bureau of Labor Statistics, U.S. Dept. of Labor

	FATALITIES Number	Percent		FATALITIES Number	Percent
TRANSPORTATION INCIDENTS	**2,480**	**43**	Caught in or compressed by equipment or		
Highway	1,428	25	objects	277	5
Collision between vehicles, mobile equipment	716	13	Caught in running equipment or machinery	121	2
Vehicle struck stationary object, equipment	342	6	Caught in or crushed in collapsing materials	109	2
Worker struck by a vehicle	390	7	**FALLS**	**767**	**13**
Water vehicle	86	2	**EXPOSURE TO HARMFUL SUBSTANCES**		
Aircraft	147	3	**OR ENVIRONMENTS**	**496**	**9**
ASSAULTS AND VIOLENT ACTS	**787**	**14**	Contact with electric current	250	4
Homicides	564	10	Contact with overhead power lines	110	2
Shooting	439	8	Contact with temperature extremes	55	1
Stabbing	60	1	Exposure to caustic, noxious, or allergenic		
Self-inflicted injuries	177	3	substances	132	2
CONTACT WITH OBJECTS & EQUIPMENT	**1,001**	**18**	Inhalation of substance	65	1
Struck by object	604	11	Oxygen deficiency	59	1
Struck by falling object	383	7	Drowning, submersion	48	1
Struck by flying object	52	1	**FIRES AND EXPLOSIONS**	**158**	**3**
			TOTAL	**5,702**	**100**

Note: Totals for categories may include subcategories not shown separately. Percentages based on incidence rate per total fatalities.

U.S. Occupational Injuries or Illnesses, by Industry, 2004

Source: Bureau of Labor Statistics, U.S. Dept. of Labor

(percent distribution)

	Private Industry	Goods Producing Natural Resources & Mining[2,3]	Construction	Manufacturing	Service Providing Trade, Trans. & Utilities[4]	Info.	Financial	Prof. & Business	Edu & Health	Leisure and Hospitality
Total [1,259,320 cases]	100.0	100.0	100.0	100.0	100.0	100.0	100.0	100.0	100.0	100.0
Nature of injury or illness:										
Sprains, strains	41.7	32.7	37.4	35.7	45.7	44.0	39.4	36.7	52.5	34.3
Bruises, contusions	9.1	9.7	6.8	8.3	10.1	9.7	8.1	10.5	9.1	9.9
Cuts, lacerations	7.8	10.0	11.3	9.5	6.8	3.7	6.3	7.6	2.3	14.4
Fractures	7.5	14.9	10.3	8.2	6.7	6.0	9.0	7.2	5.4	6.2
Heat burns	1.5	0.6	1.1	1.7	0.7	0.2	0.7	0.5	1.0	6.8
Carpal tunnel syndrome	1.5	1.2	0.7	2.9	1.0	2.6	3.8	2.0	1.1	0.8
Tendonitis	0.6	0.4	0.3	1.1	0.5	1.1	0.8	0.5	0.4	0.2
Chemical burns	0.6	0.5	0.5	0.9	0.5	—	0.5	0.6	0.6	0.5
Amputations	0.6	1.0	1.0	1.6	0.4	0.4	0.1	0.3	-5.0	0.2
Multiple traumatic injuries	4.0	6.3	4.1	3.4	3.8	6.0	5.6	5.0	3.6	3.9
Part of body affected by the injury or illness:										
Head	6.5	8.7	7.6	7.0	6.2	4.7	5.8	7.2	5.2	5.9
Eye	2.9	4.3	4.3	4.3	2.3	1.8	1.6	2.8	1.8	2.1
Neck	1.7	1.3	1.4	1.2	2.0	2.2	1.5	1.8	2.3	1.0
Trunk	35.5	32.0	32.6	32.6	38.6	34.0	32.8	31.2	42.8	27.2
Shoulder	6.5	5.4	5.3	7.1	7.0	7.8	5.6	5.5	7.0	5.4
Back	22.4	18.1	21.0	17.9	24.5	21.7	21.8	19.4	30.1	16.5
Upper extremities	23.1	22.4	24.2	32.5	19.2	19.0	20.7	24.1	15.9	29.9
Wrist	4.6	3.1	3.6	6.2	3.9	5.5	7.8	5.3	4.6	4.4
Hand, except finger	4.0	5.4	4.7	4.7	3.4	2.5	2.9	4.6	2.1	6.9
Finger	8.6	8.9	9.6	14.3	6.7	5.1	4.9	7.3	4.2	12.5
Lower extremities	21.4	24.0	24.4	18.3	23.1	18.8	23.7	20.6	18.7	22.3
Knee	7.9	8.0	8.8	6.5	8.0	8.3	9.7	7.5	8.2	8.5
Foot, except toe	3.6	3.4	3.6	3.6	4.5	2.1	3.6	3.1	2.3	3.5
Toe	1.0	1.5	0.9	1.1	1.3	0.7	0.9	0.5	0.6	1.3
Body systems	1.1	0.7	0.7	0.9	0.9	1.8	2.4	1.8	1.6	1.1
Multiple parts	10.0	9.9	8.2	6.9	9.5	18.8	12.9	12.2	12.9	11.9
Source of injury or illness:										
Chemicals and chemical products	1.4	2.5	1.1	2.0	1.0	0.6	1.2	1.7	1.7	1.3
Containers	12.8	7.6	4.4	12.3	20.6	13.0	9.1	12.1	5.6	15.5
Furniture and fixtures	3.6	0.6	1.3	2.6	4.3	2.2	5.1	3.2	4.9	4.9
Machinery	6.5	8.8	6.7	12.5	5.5	5.2	5.5	5.1	2.2	6.4
Parts and materials	10.1	9.7	21.3	18.0	8.9	6.3	5.7	6.7	1.2	2.2
Worker motion or position	14.5	10.5	13.5	17.6	14.0	19.6	16.5	13.1	13.4	13.0
Floors, walkways, ground surfaces	18.6	19.5	20.8	12.3	17.1	23.5	27.2	20.3	20.2	26.2
Tools, instruments, and equipment	6.7	7.7	12.2	6.9	4.9	8.8	6.8	5.7	4.1	9.2
Vehicles	8.8	7.5	5.4	5.3	14.0	10.3	8.9	12.6	5.0	5.1
Health care patient	4.5	—	—	—	(5)	—	0.4	1.0	29.4	—
Event or exposure leading to injury or illness:										
Contact with objects and equipment	26.6	37.0	33.8	35.7	26.0	18.6	18.7	23.7	13.1	27.1
Struck by object	13.5	20.1	18.2	15.4	14.3	9.2	10.3	10.5	6.4	14.9
Struck against object	6.6	8.3	8.3	7.3	6.5	4.9	6.0	6.5	4.5	7.6
Caught in equipment or object	4.4	6.6	3.4	10.1	3.5	3.4	1.5	4.2	1.5	2.5
Fall to lower level	6.3	9.4	13.7	4.1	6.1	8.9	10.5	6.6	3.1	4.2
Fall on same level	13.3	12.0	8.3	9.1	11.8	15.5	18.7	15.5	17.7	23.6
Slip, trip, loss of balance-without fall	3.0	2.0	2.9	2.2	3.1	3.7	3.3	3.0	3.1	4.0
Overexertion	25.1	17.0	19.9	23.8	28.1	22.2	20.6	19.2	35.7	16.2
Overexertion in lifting	13.8	7.4	11.0	12.4	16.4	11.8	11.8	12.1	16.9	10.2

	Private Industry	Goods Producing			Service Providing					
		Natural Resources & Mining[2,3]	Con-struc-tion	Manu-facturing	Trade, Trans. & Utilities[4]	Info.	Financial	Prof. & Business	Edu & Health	Leisure and Hos-pitality
Repetitive motion.....	3.9	1.9	2.1	7.8	2.7	7.8	7.4	3.9	3.0	2.2
Exposure to harmful substances........	4.2	3.3	3.4	4.7	2.7	4.1	3.3	4.9	4.6	9.3
Transportation accidents	5.0	3.9	3.7	2.2	7.2	8.5	6.2	9.3	3.1	3.1
Fires and explosions..	0.2	0.3	0.3	0.3	0.1	—	0.1	0.2	-5.0	0.2
Assaults and violent acts by person......	1.4	0.5	0.2	0.2	0.6	0.3	1.1	1.0	6.4	0.9

Note: Dashes (—) indicate data are not available. Because of rounding and classifications not shown, percentages may not add to 100. All injuries and illnesses reported involved days away from work. (1) Excludes farms with fewer than 11 employees. (2) Agriculture includes forestry and fishing, but excludes farms with fewer than 11 employees. (3) Data conforming to OSHA definitions for mining operators in coal, metal, and nonmetal mining are provided by the Mine Safety and Health Administration, U.S. Dept. of Labor. Independent mining contractors are excluded from the coal, metal, and nonmetal industries. Data for mining include establishments not governed by Mine Safety and Health Administration rules, such as those in oil and gas extraction. (4) Data for employers in railroad transportation are provided by the Federal Railroad Administration, U.S. Department of Transportation. (5) Less than 0.1%.

Civilian Employment of the Federal Government, November 2005

Source: Statistical Analysis and Services Division, U.S. Office of Personnel Management

(monthly payroll in thousands of dollars)

	ALL AREAS		UNITED STATES		WASH., D.C., MSA[2]		OVERSEAS	
	Employ-ment*	Payroll*	Employ-ment	Payroll	Employ-ment	Payroll	Employ-ment	Payroll
TOTAL, all agencies[1].............	2,677,999	12,526,488	2,586,169	12,095,755	327,270	1,996,683	91,830	430,733
Legislative Branch[1]..............	30,090	167,722	30,083	167,653	29,094	161,332	7	69
Congress	17,439	94,436	17,439	94,436	17,439	94,436	—	—
U.S. Senate	6,866	36,378	6,866	36,378	6,866	36,378	—	—
House of Representatives	10,573	58,058	10,573	58,058	10,573	58,058	—	—
Architect of the Capitol...........	2,158	9,828	2,158	9,828	2,157	9,819	—	—
Congressional Budget Ofc........	232	1,813	232	1,813	232	1,813	—	—
Govt. Accountability Ofc..........	3,204	22,848	3,203	22,836	2,393	17,362	1	12
Govt. Printing Ofc...............	2,362	12,424	2,362	12,424	2,220	11,737	—	—
Library of Congress	4,200	23,322	4,194	23,265	4,167	23,153	6	57
U.S. Tax Court	231	1,541	231	1,541	231	1,541	—	—
Judicial Branch	34,433	166,777	33,996	164,926	1,960	11,139	437	1,851
Supreme Court................	464	1,385	464	1,385	464	1,385	—	—
U.S. Courts....................	33,969	165,392	33,532	163,541	1,496	9,754	437	1,851
Executive Branch.................	2,613,476	12,191,989	2,522,090	11,763,176	296,216	1,824,212	91,386	428,813
Exec Ofc of the President	1,697	11,707	1,684	11,637	1,684	11,637	13	70
White House Office	409	2,041	409	2,041	409	2,041	—	—
Ofc of Vice President..........	18	183	18	183	18	183	—	—
Ofc of Mgmt & Budget	473	3,775	473	3,775	473	3,775	—	—
Ofc of Administration	221	1,380	221	1,380	221	1,380	—	—
Council Economic Advisors	23	140	23	140	23	140	—	—
Council Environmental Quality...	22	146	22	146	22	146	—	—
Ofc of Policy Development......	26	151	26	151	26	151	—	—
National Security Council........	61	418	61	418	61	418	—	—
Ofc of Natl Drug Control Policy ..	110	801	110	801	110	801	—	—
Ofc of U.S. Trade Rep	213	1,866	200	1,796	200	1,796	13	70
Executive Departments	1,668,955	7,936,512	1,583,906	7,543,401	231,628	1,404,653	85,049	393,111
State........................	33,945	267,812	13,181	78,515	11,299	65,000	20,764	189,297
Treasury....................	109,077	540,560	108,400	537,890	14,491	103,407	677	2,670
Defense, Total	675,111	2,454,584	623,956	2,314,323	64,420	255,918	51,155	140,261
Defense, Mil Function	652,552	2,393,440	601,444	2,253,241	63,610	253,845	51,108	140,199
Defense, Civ Function	22,559	61,144	22,512	61,082	810	2,073	47	62
Dept of the Army	244,272	676,577	222,378	613,442	19,587	42,352	21,894	63,135
Army, Mil Function.........	221,714	615,434	199,867	552,361	18,777	40,279	21,847	63,073
Army, Civil Function.......	22,558	61,143	22,511	61,081	810	2,073	47	62
Corps of Engineers	22,479	60,942	22,432	60,880	731	1,872	47	62
Dept of the Navy	175,959	712,232	168,760	682,942	23,911	96,759	7,199	29,290
Dept of the Air Force	158,281	640,148	152,286	615,914	5,691	23,008	5,995	24,234
Defense Logist. Agency......	21,077	93,922	20,245	89,381	1,683	11,452	832	4,541
Other Defense Activities......	75,522	331,705	60,287	312,644	13,548	82,347	15,235	19,061
Justice	105,873	652,566	104,055	640,986	22,943	173,637	1,818	11,580
Interior	67,138	310,985	66,798	309,831	7,563	44,592	340	1,154
Agriculture	95,289	441,315	94,040	436,847	11,367	71,550	1,249	4,468
Commerce	39,184	217,144	38,405	212,954	20,566	135,295	779	4,190
Labor	15,279	93,494	15,243	93,266	5,120	34,424	36	228
Health & Human Services	60,375	370,156	60,123	368,460	27,561	190,218	252	1,696
Housing & Urban Dev	9,685	65,214	9,609	64,738	3,141	22,977	76	476
Transportation	53,337	404,459	53,020	402,415	8,939	69,129	317	2,044
Energy	14,759	110,695	14,746	110,577	4,969	43,070	13	118
Education....................	4,230	28,715	4,223	28,678	3,065	21,367	7	37
Veterans Affairs	235,654	1,221,154	232,069	1,206,467	7,324	49,095	3,585	14,687
Homeland Security.............	150,019	757,659	146,038	737,454	18,860	124,974	3,981	20,205
Independent Agencies.............	942,824	4,243,770	936,500	4,208,138	62,904	407,922	6,324	35,632
Bd of Govt, Fed Rsrv Sys........	1,861	15,584	1,861	15,584	1,861	15,584	—	—
Environmtl Protect Agcy..........	18,201	123,605	18,149	123,244	5,331	35,315	52	361
Equal Employ Opp Comm	2,322	13,991	2,312	13,946	560	3,852	10	45
Federal Communic Comm........	1,854	14,312	1,852	14,295	1,550	12,229	2	17
Federal Deposit Ins Corp.........	4,554	34,575	4,543	34,512	1,548	13,192	11	63

	ALL AREAS		UNITED STATES		WASH., D.C., MSA[2]		OVERSEAS	
	Employ-ment*	Payroll*	Employ-ment	Payroll	Employ-ment	Payroll	Employ-ment	Payroll
Federal Trade Comm............	1,011	7,675	1,011	7,675	863	6,504	—	—
General Svcs Admin	12,465	78,574	12,391	78,192	4,405	30,284	74	382
Natl Aero & Space Admin	18,347	132,676	18,333	132,543	4,335	32,413	14	133
Natl Fnd Arts & Humanities	368	2,474	368	2,474	368	2,474	—	—
Natl Science Foundation	1,291	9,423	1,285	9,370	1,279	9,328	6	53
Nuclear Regulatory Comm........	3,227	24,776	3,226	24,764	2,262	17,908	1	12
Ofc Personnel Mangement	4,860	23,859	4,844	23,831	1,753	10,935	16	28
Peace Corps	1,050	5,367	666	3,640	542	3,115	384	1,727
Securities & Exch. Comm	3,792	34,370	3,792	34,370	2,246	20,041	—	—
Small Business Adm.............	6,417	35,330	6,366	35,033	794	6,097	51	297
Smithsonian Inst...............	4,895	23,866	4,867	23,671	4,487	21,636	28	195
Social Security Admin	64,848	321,125	64,411	319,292	1,605	8,692	437	1,833
Tennessee Valley Authority	12,566	79,995	12,566	79,995	3	16	—	—
U.S. Postal Service	758,035	3,130,045	754,602	3,113,686	15,144	78,968	3,433	16,359

Note: *Denotes figures that are preliminary or are based in whole or part on figures for the previous month. (1) Totals include agencies not listed. (2) Metropolitan Statistical Area.

U.S Median Weekly Earnings, 2nd Quarter 2006*

Source: Bureau of Labor Statistics, U.S. Dept. of Labor

	Total		Men		Women	
	Number of workers (in thousands)	Median weekly earnings	Number of workers (in thousands)	Median weekly earnings	Number of workers (in thousands)	Median weekly earning
Age, Race, Hispanic or Latino ethnicity						
ALL WORKERS, BY AGE						
16 years and over	105,881	659	59,983	731	45,897	593
16 to 24 years	11,394	410	6,684	421	4,710	395
16 to 19 years	1,804	330	1,055	355	749	307
20 to 24 years	9,590	427	5,629	438	3,961	416
25 years and over	94,487	705	53,299	783	41,188	619
25 to 54 years	78,777	700	44,689	772	34,088	619
25 to 34 years	25,350	617	14,703	647	10,647	583
35 to 44 years	27,273	735	15,639	815	11,634	638
45 to 54 years	26,153	766	14,347	897	11,807	646
55 years and over	15,710	728	8,611	858	7,100	619
55 to 64 years	13,617	749	7,341	900	6,276	633
65 years and over	2,093	559	1,270	614	823	629
WHITE[1]						
16 years and over	85,831	678	49,804	753	36,026	602
16 to 24 years	9,273	414	5,591	427	3,682	396
25 years and over	76,558	727	44,213	814	32,345	630
25 to 54 years	63,423	723	36,883	800	26,540	630
55 years and over	13,134	746	7,330	889	5,804	628
BLACK OR AFRICAN AMERICAN[1]						
16 years and over	12,748	534	6,084	573	6,664	511
16 to 24 years	1,388	386	679	394	709	375
25 years and over	11,360	570	5,405	595	5,955	530
25 to 54 years	9,768	575	4,640	596	5,128	535
55 years and over	1,592	546	765	592	826	517
ASIAN[1]						
16 years and over	4,858	765	2,780	843	2,078	688
16 to 24 years	304	487	174	483	130	496
25 years and over	4,553	803	2,605	897	1,948	714
25 to 54 years	3,840	810	2,246	893	1,594	724
55 years and over	713	761	359	912	354	664
HISPANIC AND LATINO[2]						
16 years and over	15,715	485	10,044	504	5,671	434
16 to 24 years	2,266	378	1,517	384	749	362
25 years and over	13,449	507	8,526	533	4,922	454
25 to 54 years	12,065	507	7,671	535	4,394	450
55 years and over	1,383	506	855	522	528	485
Occupation						
Managerial, professional, and related occupations	37,095	967	18,713	1,159	18,381	829
Management, business, and financial operations occupations	15,267	1,091	8,669	1,254	6,598	899
Professional and related occupations	21,827	911	10,044	1,090	11,783	781
Service occupations......................	14,933	421	7,237	492	7,696	389
Sales and office occupations	25,860	581	9,827	669	16,032	534
Sales and related occupations..............	10,682	615	5,952	735	4,730	491
Office and administrative support occupations .	15,177	561	3,875	600	11,302	551
Natural resources, construction, and maintenance occupations........................	12,430	643	11,947	648	483	504
Farming, fishing, and forestry occupations	739	388	542	411	197	305
Construction and extraction occupations......	7,204	610	7,071	611	133	542
Installation, maintenance, and repair occupations...................	4,487	736	4,334	734	153	837
Production, transportation, and material moving occupations	15,564	554	12,259	598	3,305	424
Production occupations	8,576	549	6,153	615	2,423	427
Transportation and material moving occupations	6,988	565	6,105	587	883	415

*Not seasonally adjusted; figures are for median usual weekly earnings of full-time wage and salary workers. (1) Persons who selected this race group only; persons who selected more than one race group are not included. (2) May be of any race.

Average Hours and Earnings of U.S. Production Workers, 1969-2005[1]

Source: Bureau of Labor Statistics, U.S. Dept. of Labor

(annual averages)

	Weekly hours	Hourly earnings	Weekly earnings		Weekly hours	Hourly earnings	Weekly earnings		Weekly hours	Hourly earnings	Weekly earnings
1969...	37.5	$3.22	$120.75	1982....	34.7	$7.86	$272.74	1994 ...	34.5	$11.32	$390.73
1970...	37.0	3.40	125.80	1983....	34.9	8.19	285.83	1995 ...	34.3	11.64	399.53
1971...	36.8	3.63	133.58	1984....	35.1	8.48	297.65	1996 ...	34.3	12.03	412.74
1972...	36.9	3.90	143.91	1985....	34.9	8.73	304.68	1997 ...	34.5	12.49	431.25
1973...	36.9	4.14	152.77	1986....	34.7	8.92	309.52	1998 ...	34.5	13.00	448.04
1974...	36.4	4.43	161.25	1987....	34.7	9.13	316.81	1999 ...	34.3	13.47	462.49
1975...	36.0	4.73	170.28	1988....	34.6	9.43	326.28	2000 ...	34.3	14.00	480.41
1976...	36.1	5.06	182.67	1989....	34.5	9.80	338.10	2001 ...	34.0	14.53	493.20
1977...	35.9	5.44	195.30	1990....	34.3	10.19	349.29	2002 ...	33.9	14.95	506.07
1978...	35.8	5.87	210.15	1991....	34.1	10.50	358.06	2003 ...	33.7	15.35	517.30
1979...	35.6	6.33	225.35	1992....	34.2	10.76	367.83	2004 ...	33.7	15.67	528.36
1980...	35.2	6.84	240.77	1993....	34.3	11.03	378.40	2005 ...	33.8	16.11	543.65
1981...	35.2	7.43	261.54								

(1) Data refer to production workers in natural resources, mining and manufacturing, construction workers, and non-supervisory workers in the service industries. Figures may be revised.

Union Affiliation and Median Weekly Earnings of Wage and Salary Workers in the U.S., 1996, 2005

Source: Bureau of Labor Statistics, U.S. Dept. of Labor

	1996				2005			
SEX AND AGE	TOTAL	Members of unions[1]	Represented by unions[2]	Non-union	TOTAL	Members of unions[1]	Represented by unions[2]	Non-union
Total, 16 years and older..	$490	$615	$610	$462	$651	$801	$795	$622
16 to 24 years	298	371	362	294	397	502	502	392
25 years and older	520	625	621	498	696	820	815	669
25 to 34 years	463	554	548	447	610	735	729	595
35 to 44 years	559	636	632	530	731	844	837	708
45 to 54 years	594	687	686	552	748	854	851	722
55 to 64 years	535	620	616	505	742	852	851	716
65 years and older	384	510	510	367	569	679	683	551
Men, 16 years and older....	557	653	651	520	722	857	855	692
16 to 24 years	307	375	369	303	409	513	511	403
25 years and older	599	669	668	580	771	876	876	749
25 to 34 years	499	591	587	485	644	763	760	624
35 to 44 years	632	683	683	617	822	921	918	800
45 to 54 years	698	718	721	682	853	911	912	831
55 to 64 years	643	667	664	633	855	888	895	840
65 years and older	477	589	593	424	644	758	768	625
Women, 16 years and older	418	549	543	398	585	731	726	559
16 to 24 years	284	358	339	280	381	484	487	377
25 years and older	444	560	555	420	612	743	738	593
25 to 34 years	415	497	495	405	573	693	682	548
35 to 44 years	463	561	556	439	621	740	735	603
45 to 54 years	481	620	616	445	644	760	758	619
55 to 64 years	420	524	523	395	639	795	785	610
65 years and older	334	417	413	321	492	610	599	480

Note: Data refer to the sole or principal job of full-time workers. Excluded are self-employed workers regardless of whether or not their businesses are incorporated. (1) Including members of an employee association similar to a union. (2) Including members of a labor union or employee association similar to a union, and others whose jobs are covered by a union or an employee-association contract.

Work Stoppages (Strikes and Lockouts) in the U.S., 1950-2005[1]

Source: Bureau of Labor Statistics, U.S. Dept. of Labor; involving 1,000 workers or more

Year	Number[1]	Workers (thous.)	Days idle (thous.)	Year	Number[1]	Workers (thous.)	Days idle (thous.)	Year	Number[1]	Workers (thous.)	Days idle (thous.)
1950....	424	1,698	30,390	1980.....	187	795	20,844	1993	35	182	3,981
1955....	363	2,055	21,180	1981.....	145	729	16,908	1994	45	322	5,020
1960....	222	896	13,260	1982.....	96	656	9,061	1995	31	192	5,771
1965....	268	999	15,140	1983.....	81	909	17,461	1996	37	273	4,889
1970....	381	2,468	52,761	1984.....	62	376	8,499	1997	29	339	4,497
1971....	298	2,516	35,538	1985.....	54	324	7,079	1998	34	387	5,116
1972....	250	975	16,764	1986.....	69	533	11,861	1999	17	73	1,996
1973....	317	1,400	16,260	1987.....	46	174	4,481	2000	39	394	20,419
1974....	424	1,796	31,809	1988.....	40	118	4,381	2001	29	99	1,151
1975....	235	965	17,563	1989.....	51	452	16,996	2002	19	46	660
1976....	231	1,519	23,962	1990.....	44	185	5,926	2003	14	129	4,091
1977....	298	1,212	21,258	1991.....	40	392	4,584	2004	17	171	3,344
1978....	219	1,006	23,774	1992.....	35	364	3,989	2005	22	100	1,736
1979....	235	1,021	20,409								

(1) Numbers cover stoppages that began in the year indicated. Workers are counted more than once if they are involved in more than 1 stoppage during the year. For work stoppages ongoing at the end of a calendar year, days idle include only the days for the calendar year.

Work Stoppages Involving 5,000 Workers or More Beginning in 2005

The number of work stoppages increased in 2005, but the number of workers idled because of strikes and lockouts in the U.S. and the number of days of idleness declined. There were 22 major work stoppages beginning in 2005, idling 170,700 workers and resulting in 1.7 mil workdays lost. There were 4 stoppages in which more than 5,000 workers participated. The largest work stoppage in terms of worker participation in 2005 involved the Transit Workers Union, Local 100 and the New York City Metropolitan Transit Authority. It began on Dec. 20, 2005 and ended Dec. 22. It involved 35,000 workers and accounted for about 105,000 days lost.

U.S. Union Membership, 1930-2005[1]

Source: Bureau of Labor Statistics, U.S. Dept. of Labor; figures in thousands

Year	Total employed[1]	% in unions	Union members[2]	Year	Total employed[1]	% in unions	Union members[2]	Year	Total employed[1]	% in unions	Union members[2]
1930....	29,424	11.6	3,401	1980....	90,564	21.9	19,843	1997....	114,533	14.1	16,110
1935....	27,053	13.2	3,584	1985....	94,521	18.0	16,996	1998....	116,730	13.9	16,211
1940....	32,376	26.9	8,717	1990....	103,905	16.1	16,740	1999....	118,963	13.9	16,477
1945....	40,394	35.5	14,322	1991....	102,786	16.1	16,568	2000....	120,786	13.5	16,258
1950....	45,222	31.5	14,267	1992....	103,688	15.8	16,390	2001....	122,482	13.4	16,387
1955....	50,675	33.2	16,802	1993....	105,067	15.8	16,598	2002[3]...	121,826	13.3	16,145
1960....	54,234	31.4	17,049	1994....	107,989	15.5	16,748	2003[4]...	122,358	12.9	15,776
1965....	60,815	28.4	17,299	1995....	110,038	14.9	16,360	2004[4]...	123,554	12.5	15,472
1970....	70,920	27.3	19,381	1996....	111,960	14.5	16,269	2005[4]...	125,889	12.5	15,685
1975....	76,945	25.5	19,611								

(1) Does not include agricultural employment; from 1985, does not include self-employed or unemployed persons. (2) From 1930 to 1980, includes dues-paying members of traditional trade unions, regardless of employment status; after that includes employed only. From 1985, includes members of employee associations that engage in collective bargaining with employers. (3) Revised to incorporate changes to the class of worker status associated with the introduction of the 2002 Census industry and occupational classification systems into the Current Population Survey. (4) Data reflect revised population controls used in the household survey.

Labor Union Directory

Source: Bureau of Labor Statistics, U.S. Dept. of Labor; AFL-CIO; *World Almanac* research.

(#) Member of Change to Win Coalition formed in 2005 by unions disaffiliated from AFL-CIO. (*) Independent union. All others are affiliated with AFL-CIO. Year established in parenthesis.

Air Line Pilots Association, (1931); 61,000+ members, 39 U.S. and Canadian airlines; www.alpa.org

American Federation of Labor & Congress of Industrial Organizations (AFL-CIO), (1955); 9 mil members; www.aflcio.org

Automobile, Aerospace & Agricultural Implement Workers of America, International Union, United (UAW), (1935); 640,000 active (500,000 ret.) members, 800 locals; www.uaw.org

Bakery, Confectionery, Tobacco Workers and Grain Millers International Union (BCTGM), (1881); 120,000 members; www.bctgm.org

Bricklayers and Allied Craftworkers, International Union of (BAC), (1865); 100,000 members, 50 locals; www.bacweb.org

#Carpenters and Joiners of America, United Brotherhood of, (1881); 520,000 members, 1,000 locals; www.carpenters.org

#Change to Win Coalition, (2005); 7 unions, 6 ex-affiliates unions of AFL-CIO, 1 independent; www.changetowin.org

*Communications Workers of America (IUE-CWA), (1938); 700,000+ members, 1,200 locals; www.cwa-union.org

*Education Association, National, (1857); 2.7 mil members, 14,000+ affiliates; www.nea.org

Electrical Workers, International Brotherhood of (IBEW), (1891); 750,000 members, 1,019 locals; www.ibew.org

Engineers, International Union of Operating (IUOE), (1896); 400,000 members, 170 locals; www.iuoe.org

#Farm Workers of America, United (UFW), (1962); 27,000+ members; www.ufw.org

*Federal Employees, Federal District 1, National Federation of (NFFE FD1, IAMAW, AFL-CIO), (1917); 90,000 members, 200 locals; www.nffe.org

Fire Fighters, International Association of, (1918); 263,000 members, 2,900 locals; www.iaff.org

Flight Attendants, Association of, (1945); 46,000 members, 20 carriers; www.afanet.org

#Food and Commercial Workers International Union, United (UFCW), (1979); 1.4 mil members, 500 locals; www.ufcw.org

Glass, Molders, Pottery, Plastics & Allied Workers Intl. Union (GMP), (1842); 51,000 members, 290+ locals; www.gmpiu.org

Government Employees, American Federation of (AFGE), (1932); 600,000 members, 1,100 locals; www.afge.org

Graphic Communications International Union (GCIU), (1983); 150,000 members, 321 locals; www.gciu.org

Iron Workers, International Association of Bridge, Structural, Ornamental and Reinforcing, (1896); 126,975 members, 213 locals; www.ironworkers.org

#Laborers' International Union of North America (LIUNA), (1903); more than 700,000 members, 500+ locals; www.liuna.org

Letter Carriers, National Association of (NALC), (1889); 300,000+ members, 2,500+ locals; www.nalc.org

Locomotive Engineers and Trainmen, Brotherhood of (BLET), (1863); 53,386 members, 524 divisions; www.ble.org

Longshoremen's Association, International (ILA), (1892); 50,000 members; www.ilaunion.org

Machinists and Aerospace Workers, International Association of (IAMAW), (1888); 730,000 members (current and retired, 1,174 locals; merged with TCU in 2006; www.iamaw.org

Maintenance of Way Employees, Brotherhood of (BMWE), (1887); 35,000 members, 770 locals; www.bmwe.org

Mine Workers of America, United (UMWA), (1890); 110,000 members, 600 locals; www.umwa.org

Musicians of the United States and Canada, American Federation of (AFM), (1896); 100,000 members, 249 locals; www.afm.org

Newspaper Guild-Communications Workers of America (CWA), The, (1933); 34,000 members, 90 locals; www.news-guild.org

*Nurses Association, American (ANA), (1897); 2.6 mil members, 54 constituent state & territorial assns; www.nursing-world.org

Office and Professional Employees International Union (OPEIU), (1945); 145,000 members, 200 locals; www.opeiu.org

Painters and Allied Trades, International Union of (IUPAT), (1887); 140,000 members, 425 locals; www.ibpat.org

Plumbing and Pipe Fitting Industry of the United States and Canada, United Association of Journeymen and Apprentices of the, (1889); 320,000 members, 317 locals; www.ua.org

*Police, National Fraternal Order of, 321,000 members, 2,100+ affiliates; www.grandlodgefop.org

Police Associations, International Union of, (1979); 80,000 members, 500 locals; www.iupa.org

Postal Workers Union, American (APWU), (1971); 333,000+ members, 1,600+ locals; www.apwu.org

Roofers, Waterproofers & Allied Workers, United Union of, (1906); 22,000 members; www.unionroofers.com

*Rural Letter Carriers' Association, National, (1903); 100,000+ members; 50 state org; www.nrlca.org

*Security, Police, and Fire Professionals of America (SPFPA), (1948); 27,000 members, 200 locals; www.spfpa.org

#Service Employees International Union (SEIU), (1921); 1.8 million members, 350 locals; www.seiu.org

Sheet Metal Workers' International Association (SMWIA), (1888); 150,000 members, 350 locals; www.smwia.org

State, County, and Municipal Employees, American Federation of (AFSCME), 1.6 mil members, 3,617 locals; www.afscme.org

Steelworkers of America, United (USWA), (1936); 850,000 active members, 2,700 locals; merged with PACE union in 2005; www.uswa.or

Teachers, American Federation of (AFT), (1916); 1.3 mil members, 3,000 locals; www.aft.org

#Teamsters, International Brotherhood of (IBT), (1903); 1.4 mil. members, 521 locals; www.teamsters.org

Theatrical Stage Employees, Moving Picture Technicians, Artists and Allied Crafts of the United States, Its Territories, and Canada, International Alliance of (IATSE), (1893); 105,000+ members, 555+ locals; www.iatse-intl.org

Transit Union, Amalgamated (ATU), (1892); 180,000+ members, 270 locals; www.atu.org

Transportation-Communications International Union (TCU), (1899); merged with IAMAW in 2006.

Transportation Union, United (UTU), (1969); 135,000 members, 620 locals; www.utu.org

Transport Workers Union of America, (1934); 126,000 members, 92 locals; www.twu.org

*Treasury Employees Union, National (NTEU), (1938); 150,000+ represented, 270+ chapters; www.nteu.org

#UNITE HERE, UNITE, (1900), HERE, (1891); unions merged 2004; 450,000 members, www.unitehere.org

ENERGY

U.S. Energy Overview, 1960-2005

Source: Energy Information Administration, U.S. Dept. of Energy, *Annual Energy Review 2005*; in quadrillion Btu

	1960	1965	1970	1975	1980	1985	1990	1995	2000	2004	2005P
Production	42.80	50.68	63.50	61.36	67.23	67.76	70.79	71.13	71.29	70.39	69.17
Fossil fuels	39.87	47.23	59.19	54.73	59.01	57.54	57.44	57.44	57.25	55.95	54.97
Coal	10.82	13.06	14.61	14.99	18.60	19.33	22.46	22.03	22.62	22.71	23.05
Natural gas (dry)	12.66	15.78	21.67	19.64	19.91	16.98	18.33	19.08	19.66	19.26	18.76
Crude oil[1]	14.93	16.52	20.40	17.73	18.25	18.99	15.57	13.89	12.36	11.50	10.84
Natural gas plant liquids (NGPL)	1.46	1.88	2.51	2.37	2.25	2.24	2.18	2.44	2.61	2.47	2.32
Nuclear electric power	0.01	0.04	0.24	1.90	2.74	4.08	6.10	7.08	7.86	8.22	8.13
Hydroelectric pumped storage[2]	(3)	(3)	(3)	(3)	(3)	(3)	−0.04	−0.03	−0.06	(3)	(3)
Renewable energy	2.93	3.40	4.08	4.72	5.49	6.14	6.16	6.62	6.17	6.22	6.06
Conventional hydroelectric power[4]	1.61	2.06	2.63	3.15	2.90	2.97	3.05	3.21	2.81	2.69	2.71
Biomass[5]	1.32	1.33	1.43	1.50	2.48	2.98	2.69	3.02	2.92	2.98	2.78
Geothermal energy	(*)	(*)	0.01	0.07	0.11	0.20	0.34	0.29	0.32	0.34	0.35
Solar	NA	NA	NA	NA	NA	(*)	0.06	0.07	0.07	0.06	0.06
Wind	NA	NA	NA	NA	NA	(*)	0.03	0.03	0.06	0.14	0.15
Imports	4.19	5.89	8.34	14.03	15.80	11.78	18.82	22.26	28.97	33.54	34.26
Coal	0.01	(*)	(*)	0.02	0.03	0.05	0.07	0.24	0.31	0.68	0.76
Natural gas	0.16	0.47	0.85	0.98	1.01	0.95	1.55	2.90	3.87	4.37	4.39
All crude oil and petroleum prods.[6]	4.00	5.40	7.47	12.95	14.66	10.61	17.12	18.88	24.53	28.21	28.87
Other[7]	0.02	0.01	0.02	0.08	0.10	0.17	0.08	0.24	0.26	0.24	0.29
Exports	1.48	1.83	2.63	2.32	3.69	4.20	4.75	4.51	4.01	4.43	4.64
Coal	1.02	1.38	1.94	1.76	2.42	2.44	2.77	2.32	1.53	1.25	1.27
Natural gas	0.01	0.03	0.07	0.07	0.05	0.06	0.09	0.16	0.25	0.86	0.79
All crude oil and petroleum prods.[6]	0.43	0.39	0.55	0.44	1.16	1.66	1.82	1.99	2.15	2.21	2.46
Other[7]	0.01	0.03	0.08	0.05	0.07	0.04	0.07	0.05	0.08	0.11	0.11
Consumption	45.09	54.02	67.84	72.00	78.28	76.58	84.73	91.20	98.98	100.41	99.89
Fossil fuels	42.14	50.58	63.52	65.35	69.98	66.22	72.46	77.49	84.96	86.23	85.96
Coal	9.84	11.58	12.26	12.66	15.42	17.48	19.17	20.09	22.58	22.47	22.83
Coal coke net imports	−0.01	−0.02	−0.06	0.01	−0.04	−0.01	0.00	0.06	0.07	0.14	0.04
Natural gas[8]	12.39	15.77	21.80	19.95	20.39	17.83	19.73	22.78	23.92	23.04	22.64
Petroleum[9]	19.92	23.25	29.52	32.73	34.20	30.92	33.55	34.55	38.40	40.59	40.44
Nuclear electric power	0.01	0.04	0.24	1.90	2.74	4.08	6.10	7.08	7.86	8.22	8.13
Hydroelectric pumped storage[2]	(3)	(3)	(3)	(3)	(3)	(3)	−0.04	−0.03	−0.06	(3)	(3)
Renewable energy	2.93	3.40	4.08	4.72	5.49	6.14	6.16	6.62	6.17	6.22	6.06
Conventional hydroelectric power[4]	1.61	2.06	2.63	3.15	2.90	2.97	3.05	3.21	2.81	2.69	2.71
Geothermal energy	(*)	(*)	0.01	0.07	0.11	0.20	0.34	0.29	0.32	0.34	0.35
Biomass[5]	1.32	1.33	1.43	1.50	2.48	2.98	2.69	3.02	2.92	2.98	2.78
Solar energy	NA	NA	NA	NA	NA	(*)	0.06	0.07	0.07	0.06	0.06
Wind energy	NA	NA	NA	NA	NA	(*)	0.03	0.03	0.06	0.14	0.15

(1) Incl. lease condensate. (2) Total pumped storage facility production minus energy used for pumping. (3) Included in conventional hydroelectric power. (4) Starting in 1990, pumped storage is removed and expanded coverage of industrial use of hydroelectric power is included. (5) Substituted in 2000 for former "Wood, waste, and alcohol" category. Includes wood, waste, and alcohol fuels (ethanol blended into motor gasoline). Ethanol is included in both "Petroleum" and "Biomass" categories, but is only counted once in totals. (6) Incl. imports of crude oil for the Strategic Petroleum Reserve, which began in 1977. (7) Coal coke and small amts. of electricity transmitted across borders with Canada and Mexico. (8) Incl. supplemental gaseous fuels. (9) Petroleum products supplied, incl. natural gas plant liquids and crude oil burned as fuel. NA = Not available. P = preliminary. (*) = Less than 0.005 quadrillion Btu. **Note:** Some figures here have been revised. Some totals may not add because of rounding.

U.S. Energy Flow, 2005[1]

Source: Energy Information Administration, U.S. Dept. of Energy, *Annual Energy Review 2005*; in quadrillion Btu

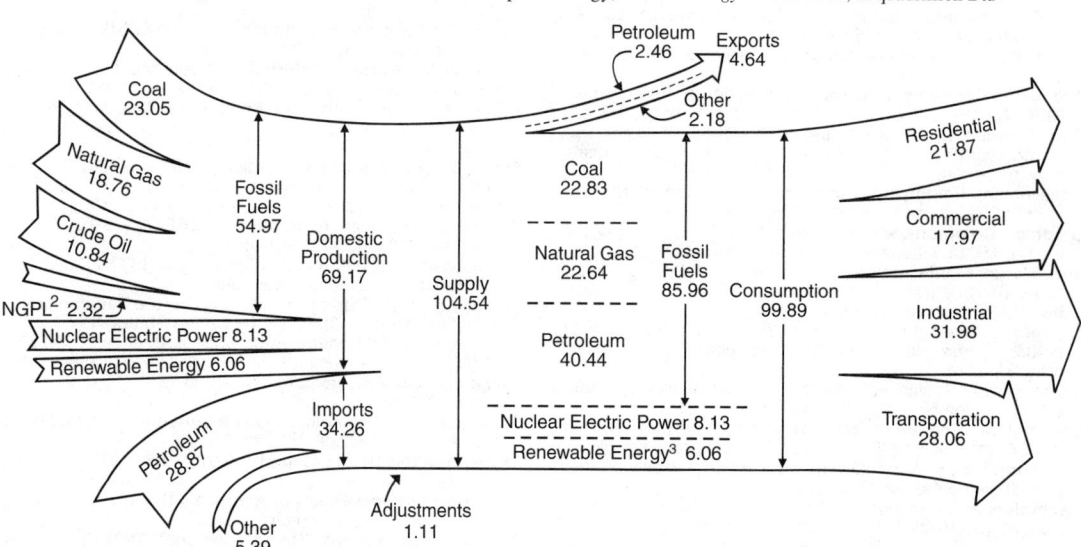

(1) Preliminary figures. (2) Natural Gas Plant Liquids. (3) Conventional hydroelectric power; wood, waste, and ethanol blended into gasoline; geothermal; solar; and wind power. Note: Some totals may not add because of rounding.

World Energy Consumption and Production Trends, 2004

Source: Energy Information Administration, U.S. Dept. of Energy, *International Energy Annual 2004*, May-July 2006

The world's **consumption** of primary energy—petroleum, natural gas, coal, net hydroelectric, nuclear, geothermal, solar, wind, and wood and waste electric power increased to 446 quadrillion Btu in 2004, up from 397 quadrillion Btu in 2000, 404 in 2001, 412 in 2002, and 422 in 2003.

World **production** of primary energy increased to 443 quadrillion Btu in 2004 from 418 quadrillion Btu in 2003, a 6% rise. World production of petroleum, both the most consumed and most produced primary energy source, was about 79.9 million barrels per day in 2004, rising 20% over 1994 production levels.

Five countries—U.S., China, Russia, Japan, and India—consumed over half of the world's primary energy in 2004, accounting for 51.1% of world consumption. Energy consumption in China has increased rapidly in recent years, from 38.8 quadrillion Btu in 2000 to 59.6 in 2004, a 54% increase, and more than double the 27.0 quadrillion Btu China consumed in 1990.

World's Major Consumers of Primary Energy, 2004

Source: Energy Information Administration, Dept. of Energy, *International Energy Annual 2004*, July 2006; quadrillion Btu

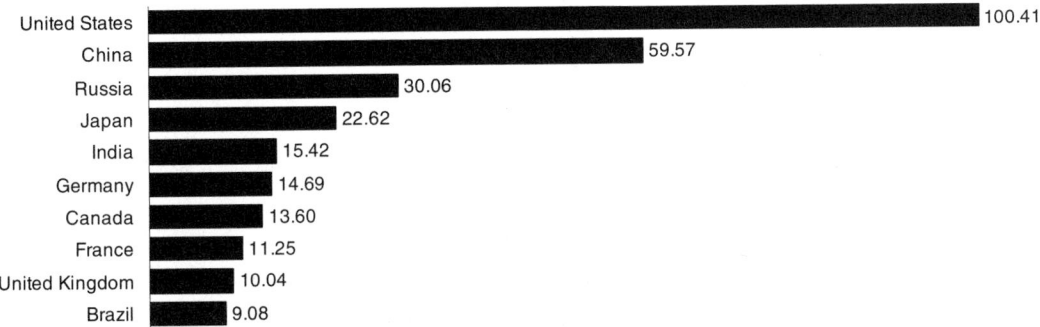

United States	100.41
China	59.57
Russia	30.06
Japan	22.62
India	15.42
Germany	14.69
Canada	13.60
France	11.25
United Kingdom	10.04
Brazil	9.08

World's Major Producers of Primary Energy, 2004

Source: Energy Information Administration, Dept. of Energy, *International Energy Annual 2004*, July 2006; quadrillion Btu

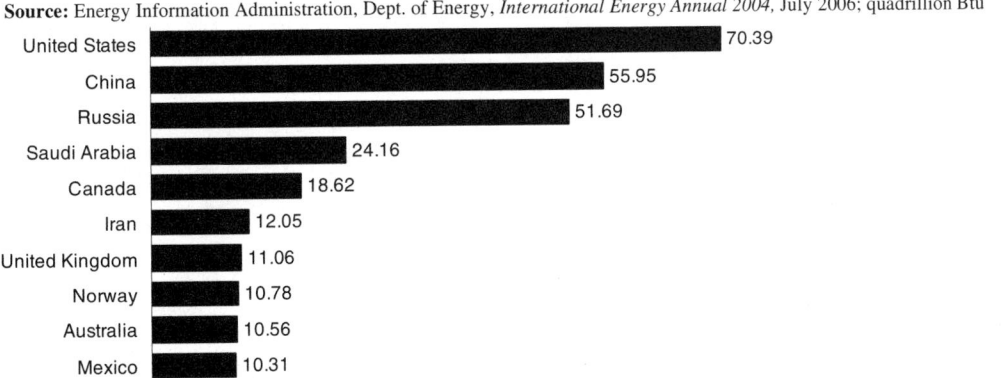

United States	70.39
China	55.95
Russia	51.69
Saudi Arabia	24.16
Canada	18.62
Iran	12.05
United Kingdom	11.06
Norway	10.78
Australia	10.56
Mexico	10.31

Gasoline Retail Prices in Selected Countries, 1990-2005

Source: Energy Information Administration, U.S. Dept. of Energy
(average price of unleaded regular gas unless otherwise noted; in dollars per gallon, including taxes)

Year	Australia	Brazil	Canada	China	Germany	Japan	Mexico	S. Korea	Taiwan	U.S.	France*	Italy*	S. Africa*	Spain*	Thailand*	UK*	U.S.*
1990	NA	$3.82	$1.87	NA	$2.65	$3.16	$1.00	$2.05	$2.49	$1.16	$3.63	$4.59	NA	NA	NA	$2.82	$1.35
1991	$1.96	2.91	1.92	NA	2.90	3.46	1.30	2.49	2.39	1.14	3.45	4.50	NA	NA	NA	3.01	1.32
1992	1.89	2.92	1.73	NA	3.27	3.59	1.50	2.65	2.42	1.13	3.57	4.53	NA	$3.50	$1.35	3.06	1.32
1993	1.73	2.40	1.57	NA	3.07	4.02	1.56	2.88	2.27	1.11	3.41	3.68	NA	3.01	1.26	2.84	1.30
1994	1.84	2.80	1.45	$0.96	3.52	4.39	1.48	2.87	2.14	1.11	3.59	3.70	NA	2.99	1.21	2.99	1.31
1995	1.95	2.16	1.53	1.03	3.96	4.43	1.11	2.94	2.23	1.15	4.26	4.00	NA	3.24	1.26	3.21	1.34
1996	2.12	2.31	1.61	1.03	3.94	3.65	1.25	3.18	2.15	1.23	4.41	4.39	NA	3.32	1.49	3.34	1.41
1997	2.05	2.61	1.62	1.07	3.53	3.27	1.47	3.34	2.23	1.23	4.00	4.07	$1.72	3.01	1.27	3.83	1.42
1998	1.63	2.80	1.38	0.95	3.34	2.83	1.49	3.04	1.86	1.06	3.87	3.84	1.51	2.80	1.09	4.06	1.25
1999	1.72	NA	1.52	0.95	3.42	3.27	1.79	3.80	1.86	1.17	3.85	3.87	1.55	2.82	1.22	4.29	1.36
2000	1.94	NA	1.86	1.06	3.45	3.65	2.01	4.18	2.15	1.51	3.80	3.77	1.78	2.86	1.38	4.58	1.69
2001	1.71	NA	1.72	NA	3.40	3.27	2.20	3.76	2.02	1.46	3.51	3.57	1.59	2.74	1.33	4.14	1.66
2002	1.76	NA	1.70	NA	3.67	3.15	2.24	3.84	1.93	1.36	3.62	3.74	1.41	2.90	1.35	4.16	1.56
2003	2.20	NA	1.99	NA	4.59	3.47	2.04	4.12	2.16	1.59	4.35	4.53	1.91	3.50	1.52	4.70	1.78
2004	2.72	NA	2.37	NA	5.24	3.93	2.03	4.51	2.46	1.88	4.99	5.30	2.58	4.09	1.76	5.56	2.07
2005	3.23	NA	2.87	NA	5.60	4.28	2.22	5.28	2.79	2.30	5.46	5.74	NA	4.49	1.92	5.97	2.49

NA = Not available. *Premium unleaded gasoline. Note: Some countries report only premium averages and some do not sell unleaded regular gasoline.

Gasoline Retail Prices, U.S. City Average, 1974-2006

Source: Energy Information Administration, U.S. Dept. of Energy, *Monthly Energy Review,* Aug. 2006

(cents per gallon, including taxes)

AVERAGE	Leaded regular	Unleaded regular	Unleaded premium	All types[1]	AVERAGE	Leaded regular	Unleaded regular	Unleaded premium	All types[1]
1974	53.2	NA	NA	NA	1991	NA	114.0	132.1	119.6
1975	56.7	NA	NA	NA	1992	NA	112.7	131.6	119.0
1976	59.0	61.4	NA	NA	1993	NA	110.8	130.2	117.3
1977	62.2	65.6	NA	NA	1994	NA	111.2	130.5	117.4
1978	62.6	67.0	NA	65.2	1995	NA	114.7	133.6	120.5
1979	85.7	90.3	NA	88.2	1996	NA	123.1	141.3	128.8
1980	119.1	124.5	NA	122.1	1997	NA	123.4	141.6	129.1
1981[2]	131.1	137.8	147.0	135.3	1998	NA	105.9	125.0	111.5
1982	122.2	129.6	141.5	128.1	1999	NA	116.5	135.7	122.1
1983	115.7	124.1	138.3	122.5	2000	NA	151.0	169.3	156.3
1984	112.9	121.2	136.6	119.8	2001	NA	146.1	165.7	153.1
1985	111.5	120.2	134.0	119.6	2002	NA	135.8	157.8	144.1
1986	85.7	92.7	108.5	93.1	2003	NA	159.1	177.7	163.8
1987	89.7	94.8	109.3	95.7	2004	NA	188.0	206.8	192.3
1988	89.9	94.6	110.7	96.3	2005	NA	229.5	249.1	233.8
1989	99.8	102.1	119.7	106.0	2006 (Jan.-June)	NA	260.8	282.0	265.2
1990	114.9	116.4	134.9	121.7					

Until unleaded gas became available in 1976, leaded was the only type used in automobiles. Average retail prices (in cents per gallon) for selected years preceding those in the table above were as follows: 1950: 27; 1955: 29; 1960: 31; 1965: 31; 1970: 36. (1) Also includes types of motor gasoline not shown separately. (2) In Sept. 1981, the Bureau of Labor Statistics changed the weights in the calculation of average motor gasoline prices. Starting in Sept. 1981, gasohol is included in average for all types, and unleaded premium is weighted more heavily. (3) Based on Sept. through Dec. data only. **Note:** Geographic coverage for 1974-77 is 56 urban areas; for 1978 and later, 85 urban areas. NA = Not applicable.

U.S. Petroleum Trade, 1976-2006

Source: Energy Information Administration, U.S. Dept. of Energy, *Monthly Energy Review,* Aug. 2006

(in thousands of barrels per day; average for the year)

Year	Imports from Persian Gulf[1]	Total imports	Total exports	Net imports[2]	Petroleum products supplied[3]	Year	Imports from Persian Gulf[1]	Total imports	Total exports	Net imports[2]	Petroleum products supplied[3]
1976	1,840	7,313	223	7,090	17,461	1992	1,778	7,888	950	6,938	17,033
1977	2,448	8,807	243	8,565	18,431	1993	1,782	8,620	1,003	7,618	17,237
1978	2,219	8,363	362	8,002	18,847	1994	1,728	8,996	942	8,054	17,718
1979	2,069	8,456	471	7,985	18,513	1995	1,573	8,835	949	7,886	17,725
1980	1,519	6,909	544	6,365	17,056	1996	1,604	9,478	981	8,498	18,309
1981	1,219	5,996	595	5,401	16,058	1997	1,755	10,162	1,003	9,158	18,620
1982	696	5,113	815	4,298	15,296	1998	2,136	10,708	945	9,764	18,917
1983	442	5,051	739	4,312	15,231	1999	2,464	10,852	940	9,912	19,519
1984	506	5,437	722	4,715	15,726	2000	2,488	11,459	1,040	10,419	19,701
1985	311	5,067	781	4,286	15,726	2001	2,761	11,871	971	10,900	19,649
1986	912	6,224	785	5,439	16,281	2002	2,269	11,530	984	10,546	19,761
1987	1,077	6,678	764	5,914	16,665	2003	2,501	12,264	1,027	11,238	20,034
1988	1,541	7,402	815	6,587	17,283	2004	2,493	13,145	1,048	12,097	20,731
1989	1,861	8,061	859	7,202	17,325	2005	2,298	13,527	1,174	12,353	20,656
1990	1,966	8,018	857	7,161	16,988	2006[4]	2,185	13,587	1,274	12,313	20,441
1991	1,845	7,627	1,001	6,626	16,714						

(1) Bahrain, Iran, Iraq, Kuwait, Qatar, Saudi Arabia, and United Arab Emirates. (2) Net imports are total imports minus total exports. (3) Includes domestic production and imports minus change in stocks, refinery imports, and exports. (4) Annualized 6-month average, for Jan.-June 2006. **Notes:** Beginning in Oct. 1977, imports for the Strategic Petroleum Reserves are included. U.S. exports include shipments to U.S. territories; imports include receipts from U.S. territories. Totals may not add because of rounding. Some figures are revised.

Energy Consumption, Total and Per Capita, by State, 2002

Source: Energy Information Administration, U.S. Dept. of Energy, State Energy Data Report 2002; latest available

Total Consumption				Consumption Per Capita			
Rank/State	Trillion Btu	Rank/State	Trillion Btu	Rank/State	Million Btu	Rank/State	Million Btu
1. Texas	12,489.3	27. Colorado	1,348.6	1. Alaska	1,149.1	27. Ohio	347.1
2. California	7,984.4	28. Iowa	1,192.7	2. Wyoming	883.9	28. Dist. of Columbia	329.5
3. Florida	4,261.0	29. Mississippi	1,184.7	3. Louisiana	824.2	29. Missouri	324.7
4. New York	4,123.4	30. Arkansas	1,146.9	4. North Dakota	629.5	30. Virginia	320.5
5. Ohio	3,959.4	31. Oregon	1,076.2	5. Texas	574.6	31. Pennsylvania	317.7
6. Illinois	3,938.0	32. Kansas	1,073.2	6. Kentucky	486.4	32. Washington	317.3
7. Pennsylvania	3,916.3	33. Connecticut	849.1	7. Indiana	467.8	33. North Carolina	317.1
8. Louisiana	3,689.1	34. West Virginia	777.0	8. Alabama	451.8	34. Michigan	314.3
9. Michigan	3,156.8	35. Alaska	737.1	9. West Virginia	430.5	35. Illinois	312.9
10. Georgia	3,035.7	36. Utah	694.0	10. Arkansas	423.8	36. Oregon	305.7
11. Indiana	2,880.4	37. New Mexico	673.9	11. Montana	419.1	37. Colorado	299.6
12. North Carolina	2,633.8	38. Nebraska	641.1	12. Oklahoma	418.7	38. Utah	299.3
13. New Jersey	2,519.9	39. Nevada	640.9	13. Mississippi	413.2	39. Nevada	295.7
14. Virginia	2,335.1	40. Idaho	491.5	14. Iowa	406.3	40. New Jersey	293.9
15. Tennessee	2,252.6	41. Maine	467.7	15. Kansas	395.8	41. Maryland	276.5
16. Alabama	2,023.6	42. Wyoming	440.9	16. Tennessee	389.1	42. New Hampshire	256.0
17. Kentucky	1,989.4	43. North Dakota	399.0	17. South Carolina	387.6	43. Vermont	255.7
18. Washington	1,925.0	44. Montana	381.6	18. Delaware	382.1	44. Florida	255.3
19. Wisconsin	1,889.4	45. New Hampshire	326.3	19. Nebraska	371.1	45. Arizona	250.2
20. Missouri	1,841.1	46. Delaware	307.9	20. Idaho	366.0	46. Connecticut	245.5
21. Minnesota	1,782.2	47. Hawaii	291.8	21. New Mexico	363.8	47. Massachusetts	243.1
22. South Carolina	1,590.7	48. South Dakota	266.8	22. Maine	361.2	48. Hawaii	235.2
23. Massachusetts	1,561.4	49. Rhode Island	219.6	23. Georgia	355.3	49. California	228.1
24. Maryland	1,506.8	50. Dist. of Columbia	187.5	24. Minnesota	354.7	50. New York	215.5
25. Oklahoma	1,461.3	51. Vermont	157.6	25. South Dakota	350.8	51. Rhode Island	205.6
26. Arizona	1,361.4	**U.S.**	**98,142.5**	26. Wisconsin	347.3	**U.S.**	**340.8**

World Crude Oil and Natural Gas Reserves, Jan. 1, 2005

Sources: Energy Information Administration, U.S. Dept. of Energy, *U.S. Crude Oil, Natural Gas, and Natural Gas Liquids Reserves,* Nov. 2005; *Oil and Gas Journal (OGJ),* Dec. 2004; *World Oil (WO),* Sept. 2005

Region/Country	Crude oil (billion barrels) OGJ	WO	Natural gas (trillion cubic feet) OGJ	WO	Region/Country	Crude oil (billion barrels) OGJ	WO	Natural gas (trillion cubic feet) OGJ	WO
North America	214.8	40.9	264.0	273.7	**Middle East**	77.8	89.9	1,952.6	2,823.3
Canada	178.8[1]	4.7	56.6	60.7	Azerbaijan	7.0	NA	30.0	NA
Mexico	14.6	14.8	14.9	20.4	Belarus	0.2	NA	0.1	NA
United States	21.4	21.4	192.5	192.5	Georgia	(2)	NA	0.3	NA
Central & South America	100.6	76.0	250.5	241.4	Kazakhstan	9.0	NA	65.0	NA
Argentina	2.7	2.3	21.6	18.9	Kyrgyzstan	(2)	NA	0.2	NA
Bolivia	0.4	0.5	24.0	27.2	Russia	60.0	67.1	1,680.0	2,361.1
Brazil	10.6	11.2	8.8	11.5	Tajikistan	(2)	NA	0.2	NA
Chile	0.2	(2)	3.5	0.9	Turkmenistan	0.5	NA	71.0	NA
Colombia	1.5	1.5	4.0	4.0	Ukraine	0.4	NA	39.6	NA
Cuba	0.8	0.6	2.5	0.6	Uzbekistan	0.6	NA	66.2	NA
Ecuador	4.6	5.5	0.3	0.4	**Africa**	100.8	112.4	476.5	500.8
Guatemala	0.5	NA	0.1	NA	Algeria	11.8	15.3	160.5	171.5
Peru	1.0	1.0	8.7	8.7	Angola	5.4	9.0	1.6	4.0
Suriname	0.1	NA	(2)	NA	Cameroon	0.4	NA	3.9	NA
Trinidad and Tobago	1.0	0.8	25.9	18.8	Congo, Rep. of the	1.5	1.8	3.2	4.2
Venezuela	77.2	52.4	151.0	150.5	Congo, Dem. Rep. of the	0.2	NA	(2)	NA
Europe	17.6	18.1	194.0	191.3	Côte d'Ivoire	0.1	NA	1.0	NA
Albania	0.2	0.2	0.1	0.1	Egypt	3.7	3.6	58.5	66.0
Austria	0.1	0.1	0.5	0.8	Equatorial Guinea	(2)	1.8	1.3	3.4
Bulgaria	(2)	(2)	0.2	0.1	Ethiopia	(2)	NA	0.9	NA
Croatia	0.1	0.1	0.9	1.0	Gabon	2.5	2.2	1.2	3.4
Czech Republic	(2)	(2)	0.1	0.1	Ghana	(2)	NA	0.8	NA
Denmark	1.3	1.3	3.5	2.6	Libya	39.0	33.6	52.0	51.5
France	0.1	0.2	0.5	0.4	Mozambique	(2)	(2)	4.5	(2)
Germany	0.4	0.2	9.9	7.1	Namibia	(2)	(2)	2.2	(2)
Hungary	0.1	0.2	1.2	2.4	Nigeria	35.3	36.6	176.0	180.0
Ireland	(2)	NA	0.7	NA	Rwanda	(2)	NA	2.0	NA
Italy	0.6	0.7	8.0	6.3	Somalia	(2)	NA	0.2	NA
Netherlands	0.1	0.2	62.0	55.5	Sudan	0.6	6.4	3.0	4.0
Norway	8.5	9.9	73.6	84.3	Tanzania	(2)	NA	0.8	NA
Poland	0.1	0.3	5.8	5.3	Tunisia	0.3	0.7	2.8	3.9
Romania	1.0	0.5	3.6	4.8	**Asia & Oceania**	36.2	36.2	383.9	424.7
Serbia and Montenegro	0.1	NA	1.7	NA	Afghanistan	(2)	NA	3.5	NA
Slovakia	(2)	NA	0.5	NA	Australia	1.5	3.6	29.0	128.6
Spain	0.2	NA	0.1	NA	Bangladesh	0.1	NA	10.6	NA
Turkey	0.3	0.3	0.3	0.3	Brunei	1.4	1.1	13.8	8.5
United Kingdom	4.5	3.9	20.8	18.8	Burma	0.1	0.2	10.0	8.9
Middle East	729.3	708.3	2,522.1	2,542.7	China	18.3	15.4	53.3	51.4
Bahrain	0.1	NA	3.3	NA	India	5.4	4.9	30.1	28.6
Iran	125.8	130.8	940.0	944.7	Indonesia	4.7	5.3	90.3	63.0
Iraq	115.0	115.0	110.0	112.6	Japan	0.1	NA	1.4	NA
Israel	(2)	NA	1.4	NA	Malaysia	3.0	3.0	75.0	56.6
Jordan	(2)	NA	0.2	NA	New Zealand	0.1	0.1	1.2	1.4
Kuwait	101.5	99.7	55.5	56.6	Pakistan	0.3	0.3	26.8	30.1
Oman	5.5	4.8	29.3	24.2	Papua New Guinea	0.2	0.2	12.2	13.6
Qatar	15.2	20.0	910.0	913.4	Philippines	0.2	0.1	3.8	2.0
Saudi Arabia	261.9	262.1	235.0	238.5	Taiwan	(2)	NA	2.7	NA
Syria	2.5	2.3	8.5	18.0	Thailand	0.6	0.5	13.3	12.5
United Arab Emirates	97.8	69.9	212.1	204.1	Vietnam	0.6	1.4	6.8	7.2
Yemen	4.0	3.0	16.9	17.0	**World Total**	1,277.2	1,081.8	6,043.7	6,997.8

Note: NA=Not reported seperately, amounts included in totals. Totals may not add because of rounding. Some countries omitted for lack of appreciable reserves. Data for Kuwait and Saudi Arabia include one-half of the reserves in the Neutral Zone between Kuwait and Saudi Arabia. All reserve figures except those for the former USSR and natural gas reserves in Canada are *proved reserves.* Former USSR and Canadian natural gas figures include amounts understood as *proved,* and some *probable reserves.* Totals may include small amounts not listed. (1) Figure includes 4.3 bil barrels of conventional crude oil and 174.5 bil barrels contained in Alberta's oil sands. (2) Less than 50 mil barrels of crude oil or less than 50 mil cubic feet of natural gas.

U.S. Production of Crude Oil by State, 2005

Source: Energy Information Administration, *Petroleum Supply Monthly, April 2006*

(thousand barrels)

State	Total	State	Total	State	Total	State	Total
1. Texas	385,144	9. Kansas	33,635	17. Michigan	5,935	25. South Dakota	1,441
2. Alaska	315,420	10. Montana	33,011	18. Ohio	5,731	26. Nevada	447
3. California	229,963	11. Colorado	20,117	19. Pennsylvania	2,758	27. Tennessee	278
4. Louisiana	72,823	12. Mississippi	17,516	20. Florida	2,585	28. New York	197
5. Oklahoma	61,543	13. Utah	15,852	21. Nebraska	2,415	29. Missouri	59
6. New Mexico	60,603	14. Illinois	10,608	22. Kentucky	2,399	30. Arizona	50
7. Wyoming	50,900	15. Alabama	7,813	23. Indiana	1,727	31. Virginia	8
8. North Dakota	34,744	16. Arkansas	6,318	24. West Virginia	1,598	**U.S. Total**[1]	**1,868,990**

(1) Includes 484,738 thousand bbls offshore production.

U.S. Crude Oil Imports by Selected Country, 1988-2006

Source: Energy Information Administration, *Petroleum Supply Monthly*, Aug. 2006; ranked by 2006 totals
(thousand barrels per day)

The United States has become increasingly dependent on foreign oil. From 1990 to 2006 (based on annualized Jan-June data for the latter year), total U.S. oil imports went up about 70%. Over the same period, oil imports from OPEC countries increased 36%. The proportion of U.S. oil imports from OPEC nations has been declining; in 1990 they accounted for 60% of U.S. oil imports, while in 2006 they accounted for 48%. Although OPEC countries, especially in the Persian Gulf region, have a significant production advantage because of the relatively low cost of developing their oil resources, non-OPEC oil production has been rising; North America dominated this growth in the early 1970s, the North Sea and Mexico became major producers in the 1980s, and more recent production increases have come from oil supplies in Latin America, West Africa, and the former Soviet Union. Sanctions, imposed originally by Pres. Bill Clinton, do not permit the U.S. to import oil from Iran.

	2006[1]	2005	2004	2003	2002	2001	2000	1995	1990	1988
Canada.................	1,736	1,602	1,587	1,535	1,418	1,297	1,267	1,040	643	681
Mexico.................	1,679	1,550	1,597	1,589	1,490	1,379	1,301	1,027	689	674
Saudi Arabia#.........	1,423	1,438	1,494	1,724	1,521	1,610	1,521	1,260	1,195	911
Venezuela#...........	1,156	1,231	1,294	1,193	1,195	1,281	1,223	1,151	666	439
Nigeria#..............	1,111	1,060	1,062	838	567	813	865	621	784	607
Iraq#.................	547	520	651	470	442	778	613	0	514	343
Angola...............	448	450	306	361	315	314	289	360	236	203
Algeria#..............	297	228	214	113	30	11	1	27	63	58
Ecuador[4]...........	280	276	228	138	99	108	126	96	38	33
Colombia.............	169	156	138	163	233	245	308	207	140	106
Kuwait#..............	163	215	241	205	212	233	261	213	79	80
United Kingdom......	132	219	235	347	406	226	272	341	155	254
Brazil................	109	94	51	48	57	13	5	0	0	0
Russia[2].............	92	193	150	149	86	0	7	14	1	0
Norway..............	87	119	146	164	335	267	292	258	96	62
Trinidad and Tobago	72	62	59	54	68	55	53	NA	NA	NA
Libya#...............	54	44	18	0	0	0	0	0	0	0
Gabon[3].............	52	127	142	131	143	138	142	229	64	15
Argentina............	36	56	49	67	68	51	56	62	76	71
China................	20	24	12	13	21	13	34	53	77	82
Indonesia#...........	12	19	34	26	50	40	36	64	98	186
Australia.............	3	10	21	26	51	36	42	16	47	59
United Arab Emirates#......	1	9	5	10	16	21	1	5	9	23
Malaysia.............	4	10	18	21	9	15	29	6	40	19
Non-OPEC.............	**5,242**	**5,252**	**4,994**	**5,055**	**4,996**	**4,336**	**4,361**	**3,889**	**2,381**	**2,411**
OPEC.................	**4,764**	**4,762**	**5,018**	**4,579**	**4,042**	**4,787**	**4,520**	**3,341**	**3,514**	**2,696**
Arab-OPEC[5]........	**2,485**	**2,454**	**2,628**	**2,522**	**2,230**	**2,653**	**2,396**	**1,505**	**1,864**	**1,415**
TOTAL........	**10,006**	**10,015**	**10,012**	**9,633**	**9,038**	**9,123**	**8,882**	**7,230**	**5,894**	**5,107**

# Denotes OPEC members. NA=Not available. (1) Jan.-June average annualized. (2) May include oil from USSR states before 1992. (3) Gabon withdrew from OPEC Dec. 31, 1994. Imports after Jan. 1, 1995, appear in Non-OPEC totals. (4) Ecuador withdrew from OPEC Dec. 31, 1992. Imports after Jan. 1, 1993, appear in Non-OPEC totals. (5) Includes Algeria, Iraq, Kuwait, Libya, Qatar, Saudi Arabia, and United Arab Emirates.

World Nuclear Power Summary, 2005

Source: International Atomic Energy Agency, Power Reactor Information System, Dec. 31, 2005

Country	Reactors in operation		Reactors under construction		Nuclear electricity supplied in 2005		Total operating experience[2]	
	No. of units	Total MW(e)	No. of units	Total MW(e)	TW(e).h[1]	% of nation's total	Years	Months
Argentina	2	935	1	692	6.37	6.92	54	7
Armenia	1	376	—	—	2.50	42.74	38	3
Belgium	7	5,801	—	—	45.34	55.63	205	7
Brazil	2	1,901	—	—	9.85	2.46	29	3
Bulgaria	4	2,722	2	1,906	17.34	44.10	137	3
Canada	18	12,599	—	—	86.83	14.63	534	7
China	9	6,572	3	3,000	50.33	2.03	56	11
Czech Republic	6	3,368	—	—	23.25	30.52	86	10
Finland	4	2,676	1	1,600	22.33	32.91	107	4
France	59	63,363	—	—	430.90	78.46	1,464	2
Germany	17	20,339	—	—	154.61	30.98	683	5
Hungary	4	1,755	—	—	13.02	37.15	82	2
India	15	3,040	8	3,602	15.73	2.83	252	0
Iran	—	—	1	915	—	—	0	0
Japan	56	47,839	1	866	280.67	29.33	1,231	8
Korea, South	20	16,810	—	—	139.29	44.67	259	8
Lithuania	1	1,185	—	—	10.30	69.59	39	6
Mexico	2	1,310	—	—	10.80	5.01	27	11
Netherlands	1	449	—	—	3.77	3.91	61	0
Pakistan	2	425	1	300	2.41	2.80	39	10
Romania	1	655	1	655	5.11	8.58	9	6
Russia	31	21,743	4	3,775	137.27	15.78	870	6
Slovakia	6	2,442	—	—	16.34	56.06	112	6
Slovenia	1	656	—	—	5.61	42.36	24	3
South Africa	2	1,800	—	—	12.24	5.52	42	3
Spain	9	7,588	—	—	54.70	19.56	237	2
Sweden	10	8,910	—	—	70.00	46.67	332	6
Switzerland	5	3,220	—	—	22.11	32.09	153	10
Taiwan	6	4,904	2	2,600	38.40	20.25	146	1
Ukraine	15	13,107	2	1,900	83.29	48.48	308	6
United Kingdom	23	11,852	—	—	75.17	19.86	1,377	8
United States	104	99,210	—	—	780.47	19.33	3,079	8
TOTAL	**443**	**369,552**	**27**	**21,811**	**2,626.35**	**19.28**	**12,086**	**2**

(1) 1 terawatt-hour [TW(e).h] = 10^6 megawatt-hour [MW(e).h]. For an average power plant, 1 TW(e).h = 0.39 megatons of coal equivalent (input) and 0.23 megatons of oil equivalent (input). (2) Through Dec. 31, 2005.

Nations Most Reliant on Nuclear Energy, 2005

Source: International Atomic Energy Agency

(Nuclear electricity generation as % of total electricity generated)

Country	%	Country	%	Country	%	Country	%
1. France	78.5	8. Bulgaria	44.1	14. Germany	31.0	20. Russia	15.8
2. Lithuania	69.6	9. Armenia	42.7	15. Czech Republic	30.5	21. Canada	14.6
3. Slovakia	56.1	10. Slovenia	42.4	16. Japan	29.3	22. Romania	8.6
4. Belgium	55.6	11. Hungary	37.2	17. United Kingdom	19.9	23. Argentina	6.9
5. Ukraine	48.5	12. Finland	32.9	18. Spain	19.6	24. South Africa	5.5
6. Sweden	44.9	13. Switzerland	32.1	19. **United States**	**19.3**	25. Mexico	5.0
7. South Korea	44.7						

U.S. Nuclear Reactors and Power Plant Operations, 1955-2005

Source: Energy Information Administration, U.S. Dept. of Energy, Annual Energy Review 2005

	Number of Reactor Units								Nuclear electricity generation (million net KW-hrs)	Nuclear share of domestic electricity generation (percent)
	Ordered[1]	Cancelled	Construction permits[2]	Low-power licensed[3]	Full-power licensed[4]	Shutdown[5]	Operable units	Capacity factor[6] (percent)		
1955	3	0	1	0	0	0	0	NA	NA	NA
1960	1	0	7	1	1	0	3	NA	518	0.1
1965	7	0	1	0	0	0	13	NA	3,657	0.3
1970	14	0	10	4	3	0	20	NA	21,804	1.4
1971	21	0	4	5	2	0	22	NA	38,105	2.4
1972	38	7	8	6	6	1	27	NA	54,091	3.1
1973	42	0	14	12	15	0	42	53.5	83,479	4.5
1974	28	9	23	14	15	2	55	47.8	113,976	6.1
1975	4	13	9	3	2	0	57	55.9	172,505	9.0
1980	0	15	0	5	2	0	71	56.3	251,116	11.0
1985	0	2	0	7	9	0	96	58.0	383,691	15.5
1990	0	1	0	1	2	1	112	66.0	576,862	19.0
1995	0	2	0	1	0	0	109	77.4	673,402	20.1
2000	0	0	0	0	0	0	104	88.1	753,893	19.8
2005	0	0	0	0	0	0	104	89.4	780,465	19.3
Total[7]	259	124	177	132	132	28				

Note: Revised permit/license procedures eliminate the historical categories shown. According to Senate testimony, the Nuclear Regulatory Commission anticipates 16 or more new "combined license applications" over the next few years, which may amount to 25 or more new reactor units. (1) Order placed by a utility or government agency for a nuclear steam supply system. (2) Numbers show permits issued in a given year, not extant permits. (3) Licenses granted to conduct testing. (4) Licenses granted for full power operation. (5) Permanently ceased operation. (6) The ratio of electric energy produced to the amount that could be produced at continuous full power operation. (7) Totals include years not shown.

Major U.S. Coal Producers[1]

Source: Energy Information Administration, U.S. Dept. of Energy, 2005

Rank	Company Name	Production (thousand short tons)	Percent of total production	Rank	Company Name	Production (thousand short tons)	Percent of total production
1.	Peabody Coal Co.	201,410	17.8	13.	International Coal Group Inc. (ICG)	18,505	1.6
2.	Rio Tinto Energy America, Inc.	123,876	10.9	14.	BHP Minerals Group	17,701	1.6
3.	Arch Coal, Inc.	117,402	10.4	15.	Alpha Natural Resources., LLC	14,172	1.3
4.	CONSOL Energy, Inc.	65,626	5.8	16.	Magnum Coal Co.	10,842	1.0
5.	Foundation Coal Corp.	64,071	5.7	17.	Pittsburg & Midway Coal Mining Co.	10,120	0.9
6.	A.T. Massey Coal Co., Inc.	42,272	3.7	18.	PacifiCorp	9,302	0.8
7.	North American Coal Corp.	30,909	2.7	19.	James River Coal Co.	7,729	0.7
8.	Westmoreland Coal Co.	29,911	2.6	20.	Peter Kiewit/Kennecott	6,916	0.6
9.	TXU Corp.	23,158	2.0		**All Other Coal Producers**	**276,236**	**24.4**
10.	Alliance Coal, LLC	21,897	1.9		**U.S. TOTAL**	**1,131,498**	**100.0**
11.	Robert Murray	19,878	1.8				
12.	Peter Kiewit Sons, Inc.	19,568	1.7				

Note: The company is the firm controlling the coal, particularly the sale of the coal. (1) Preliminary.

Major U.S. Coal Mines[1]

Source: Energy Information Administration, U.S. Dept. of Energy, 2005

Rank	Mine Name/Company	Mine Type	State	Production (short tons)
1.	Black Thunder/Thunder Basin Coal Company LLC	Surface	Wyoming	87,586,375
2.	North Antelope Rochelle Comple/Powder River Coal Company	Surface	Wyoming	82,688,918
3.	Cordero Mine/Cordero Mining Co.	Surface	Wyoming	37,836,811
4.	Jacobs Ranch Mine/Jacobs Ranch Coal Company	Surface	Wyoming	37,277,820
5.	Caballo Mine/Caballo Coal Company	Surface	Wyoming	30,532,313
6.	Antelope Coal Mine/Antelope Coal Company	Surface	Wyoming	29,953,375
7.	Eagle Butte Mine/Rag Coal West, Inc.	Surface	Wyoming	24,133,324
8.	Buckskin Mine/Triton Coal Company	Surface	Wyoming	19,568,058
9.	Belle Ayr Mine/Foundation Coal West Incorporation	Surface	Wyoming	19,326,943
10.	Freedom Mine/Coteau Properties Company	Surface	North Dakota	15,007,352
	All Other Mines			**687,164,925**
	U.S. TOTAL			**1,131,498,099**

Note: The company is the firm operating the mine. (1) Preliminary.

Measuring Crime

The U.S. Dept. of Justice administers two statistical programs to measure trends in crime in the U.S. Because of differences in focus and methodology, their results are not strictly comparable.

The Federal Bureau of Investigation conducts the **Uniform Crime Report (UCR)** program, which aims to provide statistics for law enforcement administration, operation, and management. It collects actual counts on the crimes of homicide, forcible rape, robbery, aggravated assault, burglary, larceny-theft, motor vehicle theft, and arson as they are reported to law enforcement authorities. Each year, the program releases a preliminary report in the spring, followed by a more detailed, final report in the fall.

The **National Crime Victimization Survey (NCVS)** is conducted annually by the Bureau of Justice Statistics through interviews with members of a nationally representative sample of households about their experiences with crime. The survey complements the UCR by providing alternative and previously unavailable information, including information about the victims of crime and their offenders (e.g., age, sex, ethnicity, victim-offender relationship) and information on crimes not reported to law enforcement. In contrast to the UCR, the NCVS does not cover homicide, arson, commercial crimes, or crimes against children under age 12.

Further explanation of the UCR and NCVS is available at www.ojp.usdoj.gov/bjs/abstract/ntmc.htm

Uniform Crime Report for 2005

Source: *Crime in the United States, 2005,* Uniform Crime Reporting Program, FBI, U.S. Dept. of Justice

The number of violent crimes in the U.S. increased by 2.3%, and the number of property crimes fell by 1.5% between 2004 and 2005. Within the category of violent crime, murder rose by 3.4%, robbery by 3.9%, and aggravated assault by 1.8%. Forcible rapes, however, decreased by 1.2%. The 2005 increase in violent crimes was only the second in 14 years. The rate of violent crimes per 100,000 residents has dropped 17.6% between 1995 and 2005.

Among property crimes reported in 2005, the number of larceny-thefts (e.g. pocket-picking, purse-snatching) decreased by 2.3% from the previous year. Burglary increased by 0.5% while motor vehicle theft numbers showed a decrease of 0.2%. Reports of arson, considered a property crime but not included in the property crime total, declined 2.7%.

Violent crime reports increased in all regions, rising by 0.8% in the Northeast, 5.6% in the Midwest, 1.7% in the South, and 1.6% in the West. Property crime declined in all regions, falling by 3.1% in the Northeast, 0.2% in the Midwest, 2.2% in the South, and 0.6% in the West.

Cities with populations between 500,000 and 999,999 showed the greatest increase in violent crime (9.2%) followed by cities of 100,000 to 249,999 people (3.7%). Violent crime numbers decreased slightly—by 0.4%—in cities with 1 mil or more residents.

In metropolitan counties, violent crime rose by 2.3%, while in nonmetropolitan counties, it rose by 1.5% from 2004 levels.

In cities of all population sizes, property crime decreased by 1.7%. Cities with populations over 1 mil showed the steepest declines in property crime, with figures dropping 3.3% between 2004 and 2005.

In 2003, use of the Crime Index was suspended, and in 2004, an FBI advisory board approved its discontinuation. The Crime Index was an aggregate of the figures for the seven main offense categories: murder, forcible rape, aggravated assault, robbery, burglary, larceny-theft, and motor vehicle theft. Because property crimes predominate, however, the advisory board recommended the development of an index that more accurately reflects trends in crime.

National Crime Victimization Survey for 2005

Source: *Criminal Victimization, 2005,* Bureau of Justice Statistics, U.S. Dept. of Justice

The NCVS estimated that there were 23.4 mil victimizations of U.S. residents ages 12 and up in 2005 (including unreported crimes), about the same as in 2004. Victimization rates—21.2 per 1,000 persons over age 12 for violent crime and 154 per 1,000 households for property crimes—continued their decline to record low levels since the NCVS began in 1973, when there were about 44 mil victimizations.

Based on the NCVS, the victimization rates for violent crimes decreased 57.7% between 1993 and 2005. During that same period, the percentage of crimes reported to the police increased (with the exception of rape/sexual assault

and robbery)—from 42% to 47% for violent crimes and from 34% to 40% for property crimes, according to the NCVS.

Comparisons between the two-year average annual rates for 2002-03 and 2004-05 show drops in violent crime. Rates of violent crimes against women dropped 11.7% (to 17.6 per 1,000 persons in 2004-05), though violent crimes against men fell by only 2.6% (to 25.2 per 1,000). In suburban areas, the violent crime rate decreased by 11.7%, more than in urban areas (–3.9%). Violent crime rates went up in rural areas by 0.7%.

Criminal Victimization, 2004-05

Source: *Criminal Victimization, 2005,* Bureau of Justice Statistics, U.S. Dept. of Justice

Type of crime	Number of victimizations		Victimization rates[1]	
	2004	2005	2004	2005
All crimes	**24,061,140**	**23,440,720**	NA	NA
Violent crimes[2]	**5,182,670**	**5,173,720**	**21.4**	**21.2**
Rape/sexual assault[3]	209,880	191,670	0.9	0.8
Robbery	501,820	624,850	2.1	2.6
Assault	4,470,960	4,357,190	18.5	17.8
Aggravated[4]	1,030,080	1,052,260	4.3	4.3
Simple[5]	3,440,880	227,070	14.2	13.5
Property crimes	**18,654,400**	**18,039,930**	**161.1**	**154.0**
Household burglary	3,427,690	3,456,220	29.6	29.5
Motor vehicle theft	1,014,770	978,120	8.8	8.4
Theft[6]	14,211,940	13,605,590	122.8	116.2

NA = not applicable. (1) Per 1,000 persons age 12 or older (est. 241,703,710 in 2004; est. 244,493,430 in 2005) or per 1,000 households (115,775,570 in 2004; 117,110,800 in 2005). (2) This survey does not measure murder. (3) Includes male as well as female victims and both heterosexual and homosexual rape. (4) Attack with a weapon or including serious injury. (5) Attack without a weapon resulting in no injury, minor injury, or undetermined injury requiring less than 2 days' hospitalization. (6) Purse snatching and pocket picking.

Crime in the U.S., 1986-2005[1]

Source: *Crime in the United States, 2005*, Uniform Crime Reporting Program, FBI, U.S. Dept. of Justice; additional data may be available at www.fbi.gov/ucr/ucr.htm

Year	Population[2]	Crime Index (total)	Violent crime[3]	Property crime[3]	Murder & nonnegligent manslaughter[1]	Forcible rape[4]	Robbery	Aggravated assault	Burglary	Larceny-theft
1986—	240,132,887	13,211,869	1,489,169	11,722,700	20,613	91,459	542,775	834,322	3,241,410	7,257,153
1987—	242,288,918	13,508,708	1,483,999	12,024,709	20,096	91,111	517,704	855,088	3,236,184	7,499,851
1988—	244,498,982	13,923,086	1,566,221	12,356,865	20,675	92,486	542,968	910,092	3,218,077	7,705,872
1989—	246,819,230	14,251,449	1,646,037	12,605,412	21,500	94,504	578,326	951,707	3,168,170	7,872,442
1990—	249,464,396	14,475,613	1,820,127	12,655,486	23,438	102,555	639,271	1,054,863	3,073,909	7,945,670
1991—	252,153,092	14,872,883	1,911,767	12,961,116	24,703	106,593	687,732	1,092,739	2,979,884	8,142,228
1992—	255,029,699	14,438,191	1,932,274	12,505,917	23,760	109,062	672,478	1,126,974	2,979,884	7,915,199
1993—	257,782,608	14,144,794	1,926,017	12,218,777	24,526	106,014	659,870	1,135,607	2,834,808	7,820,909
1994—	260,327,021	13,989,543	1,857,670	12,131,873	23,326	102,216	618,949	1,113,179	2,712,774	7,879,812
1995—	262,803,276	13,862,727	1,798,792	12,063,935	21,606	97,470	580,509	1,099,207	2,593,784	7,997,710
1996—	265,228,572	13,493,863	1,688,540	11,805,323	19,645	96,252	535,594	1,037,049	2,506,400	7,904,685
1997—	267,783,607	13,194,571	1,636,096	11,558,475	18,208	96,153	498,534	1,023,201	2,460,526	7,743,760
1998—	270,248,003	12,485,714	1,533,887	10,951,827	16,974	93,144	447,186	976,583	2,332,735	7,376,311
1999—	272,690,813	11,634,378	1,426,044	10,208,334	15,522	89,411	409,371	911,740	2,100,739	6,955,520
2000—	281,421,906	11,608,070	1,425,486	10,182,584	15,586	90,178	408,016	911,706	2,050,992	6,971,590
2001—	285,317,559	11,876,669	1,439,480	10,437,189	16,037	90,863	423,557	909,023	2,116,531	7,092,267
2002—	287,973,924	11,877,218	1,423,677	10,455,277	16,229	95,235	420,806	891,407	2,151,252	7,057,379
2003—	290,788,976	(6)	1,383,676	10,442,862	16,528	93,883	414,235	859,030	2,154,834	7,026,802
2004—	293,656,842	(6)	1,360,088	10,319,386	16,148	95,089	401,470	847,381	2,144,446	6,937,089
2005[5]—	296,410,404	(6)	1,390,695	10,166,159	16,692	93,934	417,122	862,947	2,154,126	6,776,807
PERCENT CHANGE: NUMBER OF OFFENSES										
2005/2004		(6)	2.3	−1.5	3.4	−1.2	3.9	1.8	0.5	−2.3
2005/2001		(6)	−3.4	−2.6	4.1	3.4	−1.5	−5.1	1.8	−4.4
2005/1996		(6)	−17.6	−13.9	−15.0	−2.4	−22.1	−16.8	−14.1	−14.3
RATE PER 100,000 INHABITANTS										
1986		5,501.9	620.1	4,881.8	8.6	38.1	226.0	347.4	1,349.8	3,022.1
1987		5,575.5	612.5	4,963.0	8.3	37.6	213.7	352.9	1,335.7	3,095.4
1988		5,694.5	640.6	5,054.0	8.5	37.8	222.1	372.2	1,316.2	3,151.7
1989		5,774.0	666.9	5,107.1	8.7	38.3	234.3	385.6	1,283.6	3,189.6
1990		5,802.7	729.6	5,073.1	9.4	41.1	256.3	422.9	1,232.2	3,185.1
1991		5,898.4	758.2	5,140.2	9.8	42.3	272.7	433.4	1,252.1	3,229.1
1992		5,661.4	757.7	4,903.7	9.3	42.8	263.7	441.9	1,168.4	3,103.6
1993		5,487.1	747.1	4,740.0	9.5	41.1	256.0	440.5	1,099.7	3,033.9
1994		5,373.8	713.6	4,660.2	9.0	39.3	237.8	427.6	1,042.1	3,026.9
1995		5,274.9	684.5	4,590.5	8.2	37.1	220.9	418.3	987.0	3,043.2
1996		5,087.6	636.6	4,451.0	7.4	36.3	201.9	391.0	945.0	2,980.3
1997		4,927.3	611.0	4,316.3	6.8	35.9	186.2	382.1	918.8	2,891.8
1998		4,620.1	567.6	4,052.5	6.3	34.5	165.5	361.4	863.2	2,729.5
1999		4,266.5	523.0	3,743.6	5.7	32.8	150.1	334.3	770.4	2,550.7
2000		4,124.8	506.5	3,618.3	5.5	32.0	145.0	324.0	728.8	2,477.3
2001		4,162.6	504.5	3,658.1	5.6	31.8	148.5	318.6	741.8	2,485.7
2002		4,118.8	494.4	3,630.6	5.6	33.1	146.1	309.5	747.0	2,450.7
2003		(6)	475.8	3,591.2	5.7	32.3	142.5	295.4	741.0	2,416.5
2004		(6)	463.2	3,514.1	5.5	32.4	136.7	288.6	730.3	2,362.3
2005[5]		(6)	469.2	3,429.8	5.6	31.7	140.7	291.1	726.7	2,286.3
PERCENT CHANGE: RATE PER 100,000 INHABITANTS										
2005/2004		(6)	1.3	−2.4	2.4	−2.1	2.9	0.9	−0.5	−3.2
2005/2001		(6)	−7.0	−6.2	0.2	−0.5	−5.2	−8.6	−2.0	−8.0
2005/1996		(6)	−26.3	−22.9	−24.0	−12.7	−30.3	−25.5	−23.1	−23.3

(1) The murder and nonnegligent homicides that occurred as a result of the attacks of Sept. 11, 2001, are not included in this table. (2) Populations are U.S. Census Bureau provisional estimates as of July 1 for each year except 1990 and 2000, which are decennial census counts. (3) Violent crimes are offenses of murder, forcible rape, robbery, and aggravated assault. Property crimes are offenses of burglary, larceny-theft, and motor vehicle theft. (4) Does not include statutory rape (without force) and other sex offenses. Does not include sexual attacks on male, which are counted as aggravated assaults or sex offenses. (5) 2004 crime figures have been adjusted. (6) The use of the Crime Index in the Uniform Crime Reports Program was discontinued beginning with the report of 2003 data.

Law Enforcement Officers, 2005

Source: *Crime in the United States, 2005*, Uniform Crime Reporting Program, FBI, U.S. Dept. of Justice
Later data may be available at www.fbi.gov/ucr/ucr.htm

In 2005, the national full-time law enforcement employee rate (civilian employees in addition to sworn officers) was 3.5 per 1,000 inhabitants, a rate that remained unchanged from 2004. Nationally, 14,291 city, county, state, college and university, and tribal enforcement agencies collectively employed 673,146 officers and 295,924 civilians, who provided service to an estimated 279.2 mil people. The national rate of sworn law enforcement officers was 2.4 for every 1,000 inhabitants, a rate also unchanged from 2004.

The law enforcement employee average for all cities nationwide was 3.0 per 1,000 inhabitants. The highest rate— 4.2 per 1,000 inhabitants—was in cities with populations of less than 10,000. Cities with populations between 25,000 and 99,999 had the lowest rate (2.3). County law enforcement agencies averaged 4.4 employees per 1,000 inhabitants. Regionally, the law enforcement employee rate was highest for agencies in the Northeast, with 3.5 full-time employees per 1,000 inhabitants, and lowest in the West, with a rate of 2.4. Law enforcement agencies in the Midwest had 2.7, and agencies in the South had 3.4 employees per 1,000 people.

Nationally, males constituted 88.4% of all sworn law enforcement officers; in metropolitan counties, males accounted for 86.8% of sworn officers, and in nonmetropolitan counties, the figure was 92.3%.

Civilian employees, including clerks, radio dispatchers, and correctional officers, made up 30.5% of the nation's law enforcement personnel. Among all civilian employees, 61.8% were female.

Fifty-seven law enforcement officers in the U.S. were slain in the line of duty in 2004 (the latest year for which data is available), 5 more than in 2003 and 1 more than in 2002. Another 82 were accidentally killed while on duty, 1 more than in 2003. In 2004, 59,373 officers were assaulted while on duty, 1,532 more than in 2003.

Federal Bureau of Investigation

The Federal Bureau of Investigation was created July 26, 1908, as the Office of Chief Examiner. It later became the Bureau of Investigation (Mar. 16, 1909), United States Bureau of Investigation (July 1, 1932), the Division of Investigation (Aug. 10, 1933), and finally, the Federal Bureau of Investigation (July 1, 1935).

Director	Assumed office	Director	Assumed office	Director	Assumed office
Stanley W. Finch	July 26, 1908	L. Patrick Gray, acting	May 3, 1972	John E. Otto, acting	May 26, 1987
A. Bruce Bielaski	Apr. 30, 1912	William D. Ruckelshaus,		William S. Sessions	Nov. 2, 1987
William E. Allen, acting	Feb. 10, 1919	acting	Apr. 30, 1973	Floyd I. Clarke, acting	July 19, 1993
William J. Flynn	July 1, 1919	Clarence M. Kelley	July 9, 1973	Louis J. Freeh	Sept. 1, 1993
William J. Burns	Aug. 22, 1921	James B. Adams, acting	Feb. 15, 1978	Thomas J. Pickard, acting	June 25, 2001
J. Edgar Hoover, acting	May 10, 1924	William H. Webster	Feb. 23, 1978	Robert S. Mueller III	Sept. 4, 2001
J. Edgar Hoover	Dec. 10, 1924				

U.S. Crime Rates by Region, Geographic Division, and State, 2005

Source: *Crime in the United States, 2005*, Uniform Crime Reporting Program, FBI, U.S. Dept. of Justice
(rate per 100,000 population)

	Violent crime[1]	Murder & nonnegligent manslaughter	Forcible rape	Robbery	Aggravated assault	Property crime[2]	Burglary	Larceny-theft	Motor vehicle theft
U.S. TOTAL	469.2	5.6	31.7	140.7	291.1	3,429.8	726.7	2,286.3	416.7
Northeast	393.6	4.4	22.1	147.7	219.4	2,287.2	424.5	1,625.0	237.6
New England	319.8	2.5	25.5	92.1	199.7	2,387.2	483.3	1,643.8	260.0
Connecticut	274.5	2.9	20.0	113.0	138.6	2,558.0	437.1	1,824.1	296.8
Maine	112.2	1.4	24.7	24.4	61.7	2,413.1	478.5	1,832.6	102.0
Massachusetts	456.9	2.7	27.1	119.0	308.1	2,363.6	541.1	1,527.4	295.1
New Hampshire	132.0	1.4	30.9	27.4	72.3	1,796.4	317.0	1,377.3	102.1
Rhode Island	251.2	3.2	29.8	72.1	146.1	2,718.9	494.2	1,816.0	408.7
Vermont	119.7	1.3	23.3	11.7	83.5	2,280.7	491.8	1,686.1	102.9
Middle Atlantic	419.6	5.1	20.9	167.3	226.3	2,251.9	403.8	1,618.4	229.7
New Jersey	354.7	4.8	13.9	151.6	184.4	2,333.0	447.1	1,568.4	317.5
New York	445.8	4.5	18.9	182.7	239.7	2,108.5	353.3	1,569.6	185.6
Pennsylvania	424.5	6.1	28.9	154.6	235.0	2,417.2	451.6	1,729.1	236.5
Midwest	412.7	4.9	36.2	125.3	246.2	3,259.9	666.2	2,251.9	341.8
East North Central	433.8	5.5	36.9	144.3	247.1	3,228.0	685.1	2,189.2	353.7
Illinois	551.5	6.0	33.7	181.7	330.2	3,080.3	606.9	2,164.8	308.6
Indiana	323.7	5.7	29.6	108.6	179.9	3,456.3	697.6	2,412.0	346.7
Michigan	552.1	6.1	51.3	131.8	362.9	3,091.1	696.8	1,917.8	476.5
Ohio	351.3	5.1	39.8	163.1	143.4	3,662.7	872.8	2,429.0	360.9
Wisconsin	241.5	3.5	20.6	82.2	135.2	2,660.2	440.8	1,992.8	226.6
West North Central	363.5	3.7	34.6	81.2	244.0	3,334.2	622.3	2,397.8	314.1
Iowa	291.3	1.3	27.9	38.9	223.3	2,833.7	606.4	2,042.7	184.6
Kansas	387.4	3.7	38.4	65.3	280.0	3,787.0	689.2	2,758.1	339.6
Minnesota	297.0	2.2	44.0	92.0	158.7	3,084.1	578.9	2,226.9	278.2
Missouri	525.4	6.9	28.0	124.1	366.4	3,927.5	738.3	2,746.2	443.1
Nebraska	287.0	2.5	32.9	59.1	192.5	3,423.2	532.4	2,574.3	316.5
North Dakota	98.2	1.1	24.2	7.4	65.5	1,978.2	311.9	1,500.3	166.0
South Dakota	175.7	2.3	46.7	18.6	108.1	1,776.4	324.4	1,343.7	108.4
South	542.6	6.6	33.1	148.4	354.5	3,883.1	898.1	2,601.7	383.3
South Atlantic	567.5	6.5	29.7	160.5	370.8	3,788.3	858.7	2,522.8	406.8
Delaware	632.1	4.4	44.7	154.8	428.2	3,111.4	688.9	2,144.0	278.5
District of Columbia	1,459.0	35.4	30.2	672.1	721.3	4,747.0	649.7	2,694.9	1,402.3
Florida	708.0	5.0	37.1	169.4	496.6	4,007.9	926.3	2,658.3	423.3
Georgia	448.9	6.2	23.6	154.8	264.3	4,172.3	931.0	2,751.1	490.2
Maryland	703.0	9.9	22.6	256.7	413.8	3,544.1	641.4	2,294.3	608.4
North Carolina	468.1	6.7	26.5	145.5	289.4	4,075.1	1,201.1	2,546.2	327.8
South Carolina	761.1	7.4	42.5	132.1	579.0	4,339.4	1,000.9	2,954.1	384.4
Virginia	282.8	6.1	22.7	99.2	154.8	2,638.2	392.1	2,035.0	211.1
West Virginia	272.8	4.4	17.7	44.6	206.1	2,625.2	621.2	1,794.0	210.0
East South Central	475.9	6.9	35.8	127.8	305.4	3,594.5	897.1	2,388.0	309.4
Alabama	431.7	8.2	34.3	141.4	247.8	3,892.1	953.8	2,650.0	288.3
Kentucky	266.8	4.6	34.0	88.4	139.8	2,530.5	634.0	1,685.8	210.8
Mississippi	278.4	7.3	39.3	82.3	149.4	3,260.1	919.7	2,083.9	256.5
Tennessee	752.8	7.2	36.4	167.3	541.9	4,275.5	1,026.9	2,828.1	420.6
West South Central	536.0	6.6	37.4	139.1	352.9	4,191.8	964.2	2,844.9	382.7
Arkansas	527.5	6.7	42.9	91.1	386.8	4,057.9	1,084.6	2,711.2	262.1
Louisiana	594.4	9.9	31.4	118.0	435.1	3,683.1	870.6	2,494.5	318.1
Oklahoma	508.6	5.3	41.7	91.0	370.5	4,042.0	1,006.0	2,644.2	391.8
Texas	529.7	6.2	37.2	156.6	329.8	4,332.0	961.6	2,961.7	408.7
West	468.7	5.8	32.7	137.9	292.3	3,794.5	757.3	2,352.1	685.1
Mountain	444.8	5.4	39.5	102.3	297.7	4,128.8	811.9	2,676.1	640.8
Arizona	513.2	7.5	33.8	144.4	327.4	4,838.0	948.4	2,965.2	924.4
Colorado	396.5	3.7	43.4	84.6	264.7	4,039.5	744.8	2,735.2	559.5
Idaho	256.8	2.4	40.4	18.6	195.4	2,697.9	564.4	1,931.7	201.8
Montana	281.5	1.9	32.2	18.9	228.5	3,142.9	389.2	2,543.0	210.7
Nevada	606.8	8.5	42.1	194.7	361.5	4,241.5	972.4	2,153.9	1,115.2
New Mexico	702.2	7.4	54.1	98.7	541.9	4,148.3	1,093.9	2,639.9	414.5
Utah	227.2	2.3	37.3	44.3	143.4	3,868.9	602.2	2,918.8	343.9
Wyoming	230.1	2.7	24.0	15.3	188.1	3,155.3	476.3	2,533.9	145.1
Pacific	478.5	5.9	29.9	153.0	290.0	3,653.1	734.2	2,215.1	703.8
Alaska	631.9	4.8	81.1	80.9	465.1	3,612.5	622.5	2,599.1	391.0
California	526.3	6.9	26.0	176.1	317.3	3,322.6	693.3	1,916.5	712.8
Hawaii	255.1	1.9	26.9	78.5	147.8	4,792.6	767.9	3,308.4	716.4
Oregon	286.8	2.2	34.8	68.1	181.8	4,399.8	758.6	3,112.2	529.0
Washington	345.8	3.3	44.7	92.1	205.8	4,893.0	959.7	3,149.5	783.9
Puerto Rico	244.9	19.6	4.3	141.9	79.1	1,417.8	439.4	740.7	237.7

Note: Offense totals are based on all reporting agencies and estimates for unreported areas. Totals may not add because of rounding. (1) Violent crimes are murder, forcible rape, robbery, and aggravated assault. (2) Property crimes are burglary, larceny-theft, and motor vehicle theft. Data not included for property crime of arson.

State and Federal Prison Population, Death Penalty, 2004-05

Source: *Prison and Jail Inmates at Midyear 2005, Capital Punishment, 2004*, Bureau of Justice Statistics, U.S. Dept. of Justice

As of June 30, 2005, there were 1,512,823 prisoners under the jurisdiction of federal or state adult correctional authorities. The total prison population grew 1.4%, which was less than the average annual growth rate of 3% between 1995 and 2005. As of mid-2005, these two systems housed two-thirds of the incarcerated population. Jails, which are locally operated and typically hold persons awaiting trial and those with sentences of a year or less, held most of the remainder (747,529), not including those supervised through community-based programs (71,905).

As of mid-2005, the incarceration rate in state and federal prisons for those with sentences over one year was 488 per 100,000 U.S. residents, up from 486 in mid-2004 and 411 at year-end 1995; sentenced prisoners numbered 64 out of every 100,000 women and 925 out of every 100,000 men. The number of persons under sentence of death at the end of 2004 was 3,314, down from 3,374 the year before. In 2004, 59 prisoners were executed—6 fewer than in the previous year. Also in 2004, 129 death sentences were overturned or removed, including 6 inmates' death sentences that were declared unconstitutional by the Kansas Supreme Court.

	SENTENCED PRISONERS[1], 2004-05			DEATH PENALTY, 2004		
	Mid-2005	Mid-2004	% change 2004-05	Under sentence of death	Executions	Death penalty
U.S. TOTAL	1,512,823	1,491,834	1.4	3,314	59	—
Federal institutions	184,484	179,210	2.9	33	0	Yes
State institutions	1,328,339	1,312,624	1.2	3,281	59	38
Northeast	173,125	173,967	−0.5	242	0	—
Connecticut[2]	19,744	20,018	−1.4	7	0	Yes
Maine	2,084	2,014	3.5	—	—	No
Massachusetts[3]	10,495	10,365	1.3	—	—	No
New Hampshire	2,561	2,441	4.9	0	0	Yes
New Jersey[4]	28,124	28,107	0.1	11	0	Yes
New York	62,963	64,596	−2.5	2	0	(6)
Pennsylvania	41,540	40,692	2.1	222	0	Yes
Rhode Island[2]	3,639	3,701	−1.7	—	—	No
Vermont[2]	1,975	2,033	−2.9	—	—	No
Midwest	252,406	249,732	1.1	298	7	—
Illinois[4]	44,669	44,379	0.7	6	0	Yes
Indiana	24,244	23,760	2.0	27	0	Yes
Iowa	8,578	8,611	−0.4	—	—	No
Kansas[4]	9,042	9,152	−1.2	0	0	(6)
Michigan	49,014	48,591	0.9	—	—	No
Minnesota	9,187	8,613	6.7	—	—	No
Missouri	31,066	30,542	1.7	52	0	Yes
Nebraska	4,284	4,042	6.0	8	0	Yes
North Dakota	1,338	1,266	5.7	—	—	No
Ohio[4]	44,976	44,770	0.5	201	7	Yes
South Dakota	3,344	3,101	7.8	4	0	Yes
Wisconsin	22,664	22,905	−1.1	—	—	No
South	606,361	596,763	1.6	1,833	50	—
Alabama	27,740	26,521	4.6	193	2	Yes
Arkansas	13,469	13,477	−0.1	39	1	Yes
Delaware[2]	7,180	6,973	3.0	17	0	Yes
Florida	87,545	84,733	3.3	364	2	Yes
Georgia[5]	47,682	48,625	−1.9	109	2	Yes
Kentucky	18,897	17,763	6.4	34	0	Yes
Louisiana	37,254	36,745	1.4	87	0	Yes
Maryland	23,276	23,727	−1.9	9	1	Yes
Mississippi	20,856	20,429	2.1	70	0	Yes
North Carolina	36,399	34,917	4.2	181	4	Yes
Oklahoma	23,702	23,284	1.8	91	6	Yes
South Carolina	23,896	24,173	−1.1	71	4	Yes
Tennessee	26,208	25,834	1.4	99	0	Yes
Texas	171,338	169,110	1.3	446	23	Yes
Virginia	35,667	35,472	0.5	23	5	Yes
West Virginia	5,252	4,980	5.5	—	—	No
West	296,447	292,162	1.5	908	2	—
Alaska[2]	4,630	4,515	2.5	—	—	No
Arizona[5]	32,664	31,631	3.3	105	0	Yes
California	166,532	166,053	0.3	637	0	Yes
Colorado[4]	20,841	19,756	5.5	3	0	Yes
Hawaii[2]	6,071	5,946	2.1	—	—	No
Idaho	6,136	6,312	−2.8	22	0	Yes
Montana	3,369	3,123	7.9	4	0	Yes
Nevada	11,565	10,971	5.4	83	2	Yes
New Mexico	6,595	6,352	3.8	2	0	Yes
Oregon	13,317	13,219	0.7	30	0	Yes
Utah	6,013	5,802	3.6	10	0	Yes
Washington	16,688	16,559	0.8	10	0	Yes
Wyoming	2,026	1,923	5.4	2	0	Yes

Note: District of Columbia inmates sentenced to more than 1 year are under the jurisdiction of the Federal Bureau of Prisons. Numbers excludes persons held under Armed Forces jurisdiction with a military death sentence for murder. (1) The number of prisoners with a sentence of more than 1 year per 100,000 residents. (2) Prisons and jails form one integrated system. Data include total inmate population. (3) The incarceration rate includes an estimated 6,200 inmates sentenced to more than 1 year per 100,000 residents but held in local jails or houses of corrections. (4) Includes some inmates sentenced to 1 year or less. (5) Population figures are based on custody counts. (6) The New York (June 24) and Kansas (Dec. 17) death penalty statutes were declared unconstitutional in 2004.

Prison Situation Among the States and in the Federal System, Mid-2005

Source: *Prison and Jail Inmates at Midyear 2005*, Bureau of Justice Statistics, U.S. Dept. of Justice

10 largest prison popula-tions, 2005	No. of inmates	10 highest incarceration rates, 2005	Prisoners per 100,000 residents[1]	Growth[2] 2004-05	% annual increase	Growth since 1995	% increase
1. Federal	184,484	1. Louisiana	824	1. Montana	7.9	1. North Dakota	119.3
2. Texas	171,338	2. Texas	703	2. South Dakota	7.8	2. West Virginia	115.4
3. California	166,532	3. Mississippi	682	3. Minnesota	6.7	3. Wisconsin	113.2
4. Florida	87,545	4. Oklahoma	655	4. Nebraska	6.0	4. Colorado	93.7
5. New York	62,963	5. Alabama	587	5. North Dakota	5.7	5. Minnesota	92.8
6. Michigan	49,014	6. South Carolina	538	6. West Virginia	5.5	6. Idaho	89.4
7. Georgia	47,682	7. Missouri	535	Colorado	5.5	7. South Dakota	87.9
8. Ohio	44,976	8. Georgia	526	8. Nevada	5.4	8. Montana	87.1
9. Illinois	44,669	9. Arizona	502	Wyoming	5.4	9. Vermont	86.7
10. Pennsylvania	41,540	10. Florida	492	10. New Hampshire	4.9	10. Utah	83.8

(1) Prisoners with sentences of more than 1 year. As of Dec. 31, 2002, the District of Columbia had transferred all sentenced felons to federal prison system. (2) Comparisons are drawn from mid-year figures.

Inmate Population by Gender, Race, Hispanic Origin, and Age, Mid-2005

Source: *Prison and Jail Inmates at Midyear 2005*, Bureau of Justice Statistics, U.S. Dept. of Justice

(Number of inmates per 100,000 residents of each group)

Age	Males				Females			
	Total[1]	White[2]	Black[2]	Hispanic	Total[1]	White[2]	Black[2]	Hispanic
18-19	1,739	905	5,306	2,072	116	76	257	168
20-24	3,291	1,627	10,486	3,878	277	206	611	317
25-29	3,462	1,682	11,955	3,884	299	220	720	287
30-34	3,122	1,693	10,472	3,640	342	255	855	312
35-39	2,765	1,562	9,425	3,111	364	260	957	322
40-44	2,240	1,299	7,575	2,649	264	177	751	264
45-54	1,214	658	4,401	1,873	110	70	323	138
55 or older	260	167	879	562	12	9	26	26
Total	1,371	709	4,682	1,856	129	88	347	144

Note: Based on U.S. resident population for Jan. 1, 2005, by gender, race, and Hispanic origin. Detailed categories exclude persons identifying with two or more races. (1) Includes American Indians, Alaska Natives, Asians, Native Hawaiians, and other Pacific Islanders not listed separately. (2) Non-Hispanic.

Executions, by State and Method, 1977-2005[1]

Source: *Capital Punishment 2004*, Nov. 2005, Bureau of Justice Statistics, U.S. Dept. of Justice

	No. Executed	Lethal injection	Electro-cution	Lethal gas	Firing squad	Hang-ing		No. Executed	Lethal injection	Electro-cution	Lethal gas	Firing squad	Hang-ing
TOTAL U.S.	1,004	836	152	11	2	3	Montana	2	2	0	0	0	0
Federal govt.	3	3	0	0	0	0	Nebraska	3	0	3	0	0	0
Alabama	34	10	24	0	0	0	Nevada	11	10	0	1	0	0
Arizona	22	20	0	2	0	0	New Mexico	1	1	0	0	0	0
Arkansas	27	26	1	0	0	0	North						
California	12	10	0	2	0	0	Carolina	39	37	0	2	0	0
Connecticut	1	0	0	0	0	0	Ohio	19	19	0	0	0	0
Colorado	1	1	0	0	0	0	Oklahoma	79	79	0	0	0	0
Delaware	14	13	0	0	0	1	Oregon	2	2	0	0	0	0
Florida	60	16	44	0	0	0	Pennsylvania	3	3	0	0	0	0
Georgia	39	16	23	0	0	0	South						
Idaho	1	1	0	0	0	0	Carolina	35	29	6	0	0	0
Illinois	12	12	0	0	0	0	Tennessee	1	1	0	0	0	0
Indiana	16	13	3	0	0	0	Texas	355	355	0	0	0	0
Kentucky	2	1	1	0	0	0	Utah	6	4	0	0	2	0
Louisiana	27	7	20	0	0	0	Virginia	94	67	27	0	0	0
Maryland	5	5	0	0	0	0	Washington	4	2	0	0	0	2
Mississippi	7	3	0	4	0	0	Wyoming	1	1	0	0	0	0
Missouri	66	66	0	0	0	0							

Note: Table shows methods used since the 1976 reinstatement of the death penalty by the Supreme Court. Lethal injection was used in 83% of total executions. 17 states—Alabama, Arizona, Arkansas, California, Delaware, Florida, Georgia, Indiana, Kentucky, Louisiana, Mississippi, Nevada, North Carolina, South Carolina, Utah, Virginia, and Washington—have used 2 methods. 17 states had no executions during the period. (1) Includes preliminary data on executions in 2005.

Total Estimated Arrests, 2005

Source: *Crime in the United States, 2005*, Uniform Crime Reporting Program, FBI, U.S. Dept. of Justice

Total[1]	14,094,186	Vandalism	279,562
Violent crime[2]	**603,503**	Weapons; carrying, possessing, etc.	193,469
Murder and nonnegligent manslaughter	14,062	Prostitution and commercialized vice	84,891
Forcible rape	25,528	Sex offenses (except forcible rape and prostitution)	91,625
Robbery	114,616	Drug abuse violations	1,846,351
Aggravated assault	449,297	Gambling	11,180
Property crime[2]	**1,609,327**	Offenses against the family and children	129,128
Burglary	298,835	Driving under the influence	1,371,919
Larceny-theft	1,146,696	Liquor laws	597,838
Motor vehicle theft	147,459	Drunkenness	556,167
Arson	16,337	Disorderly conduct	678,231
Other assaults[3]	1,301,392	Vagrancy	33,227
Forgery and counterfeiting	118,455	All other offenses	3,863,785
Fraud	321,521	Suspicion	3,764
Embezzlement	18,970	Curfew and loitering law violations	140,835
Stolen property; buying, receiving, possessing	133,856	Runaways	108,954

(1) Does not include suspicion. (2) Violent crimes are offenses of murder, forcible rape, robbery, and aggravated assault. Property crimes are offenses of burglary, larceny-theft, motor vehicle theft, and arson. (3) Other assaults are simple assaults where no weapons are used and where the victim doesn't sustain serious injury.

Hate Crimes

Hate crimes are defined as crimes where the victims are chosen because of one or more of their personal characteristics, such as race, ethnicity, or religion. Congress enacted the Hate Crime Statistics Act of 1990, which led to the collection of hate crime data as part of the FBI's Uniform Crime Report (UCR) beginning in 1992. However, not all agencies that submit reports for the UCR include hate crime data. For the 2004 report, only 16% of reporting agencies included bias motivation as part of their reports. The table below gives a breakdown of the hate crimes that were reported through the UCR.

The National Criminal Victimization Survey (NCVS) has also tracked bias crimes since 2000, and through their general-population survey, they estimate that an average of 210,000 hate crime victimizations occurred annually between July 2000 and Dec. 2003 (approximately 66% were unreported). Most hate crimes reported through NCVS (84%) were crimes against persons; the remaining 16% were property crimes.

Hate Crime Offenses by Bias Motivation, 2004

Source: *Hate Crime Statistics, 2004*, Uniform Crime Reporting Program, FBI, U.S. Dept. of Justice

Bias motivation	Total offenses	Crime against Persons[1]	Property[2]	Society[3]
Total..................................	9,035	5,642	3,333	60
Single-bias incidents....................	9,021	5,631	3,330	60
Race	4,863	3,273	1,545	45
Anti-White...........................	998	704	272	22
Anti-Black...........................	3,281	2,221	1,045	15
Anti-Amer. Indian/Alaskan Native	97	69	25	3
Anti-Asian/Pacific Islander	252	148	101	3
Anti-multiple races, group	235	131	102	2
Religion.............................	1,480	473	1,003	4
Anti-Jewish..........................	1,003	297	706	0
Anti-Catholic.........................	57	11	46	0
Anti-Protestant	43	11	32	0
Anti-Islamic..........................	193	114	79	0
Anti-other religion	140	31	106	3
Anti-mult. religions, group	37	7	30	0
Anti-Atheism/etc.	7	2	4	1
Sexual orientation	1,406	979	421	6
Anti-male homosexual	855	624	229	2
Anti-female homosexual................	201	145	54	2
Anti-homosexual	297	180	117	0
Anti-heterosexual	35	19	14	2
Anti-bisexual.........................	18	11	7	0
Ethnicity/national origin	1,201	863	334	4
Anti-Hispanic	611	458	151	2
Anti-other ethnicity/natl. origin	590	405	183	2
Disability............................	71	43	27	1
Anti-physical	23	11	12	0
Anti-mental..........................	48	32	15	1
Multiple-bias incidents[4].................	14	11	3	0

(1) Includes offense types murder and nonnegligent manslaughter, forcible rape, aggravated assault, simple assault, intimidation, and additional offenses collected in the National Incident-Based Reporting System (NIBRS). (2) Includes offense types robbery, burglary, larceny-theft, motor vehicle theft, arson, destruction/damage/vandalism, and additional offenses collected in the NIBRS. (3) The NIBRS includes a third category, "Crimes Against Society," which includes drug or narcotic offenses, gambling and prostitution offenses, and weapon law violations where society as a whole is considered the victim. (4) In a multiple-bias incident, two conditions must be met: more than one offense type must occur and at least two offense types must be motivated by different biases.

Notable Assassinations Since 1865

1865—Apr. 14: U.S. Pres. Abraham Lincoln shot by John Wilkes Booth, a well-known actor with Confederate sympathies, at Ford's Theater in Washington, DC; died Apr. 15.

1881—Mar. 13: Alexander II of Russia.   **July 2:** U.S. Pres. James A. Garfield shot by Charles J. Guiteau, a disappointed office seeker, in Washington, DC; died Sept. 19.

1894—June 24: Pres. Sadi Carnot of France, by Italian anarchist, Sante Caserio, in Lyon.

1898—Sept. 10: Empress Elizabeth of Austria, stabbed by Italian anarchist Luigi Luccheni.

1900—July 29: Umberto I, king of Italy.

1901—Sept. 6: U.S. Pres. William McKinley in Buffalo, NY; died Sept. 14; Leon Czolgosz executed for the crime.

1908—Feb. 1: King Carlos I of Portugal and his son Luis Felipe, in Lisbon.

1913—Feb. 23: Mexican Pres. Francisco I. Madero and Vice Pres. Jose Pino Suarez.   **Mar. 18:** George, king of Greece.

1914—June 28: Archduke Francis Ferdinand of Austria-Hungary and his wife in Sarajevo, Bosnia, by Gavrilo Princip.

1916—Dec. 30: Grigori Rasputin, powerful Russian monk.

1918—July 12: Grand Duke Michael of Russia, at Perm. **July 16:** Nicholas II, former (abdicated) czar of Russia; his wife, the Czarina Alexandra; their son, Czarevitch Alexis; their daughters, Grand Duchesses Olga, Tatiana, Marie, Anastasia; and 4 members of their household, executed by Bolsheviks at Ekaterinburg.

1920—May 20: Mexican Pres. Gen. Venustiano Carranza in Tlaxcalantongo.

1922—Aug. 22: Michael Collins, Irish revolutionary.   **Dec. 16:** Polish Pres. Gabriel Narutowicz in Warsaw.

1923—July 20: Gen. Francisco "Pancho" Villa, ex-rebel leader, in Parral, Mexico.

1928—July 17: Gen. Alvaro Obregon, president-elect of Mexico, in San Angel.

1932—May 6: Pres. Paul Doumer of France shot by Russian émigré, Pavel Gorgulov, in Paris.

1934—July 25: Austrian Chancellor Engelbert Dollfuss by Nazis, in Vienna.

1935—Sept. 8: U.S. Sen. Huey P. Long shot in Baton Rouge, LA, by Dr. Carl Austin Weiss; died Sept. 10.

1940—Aug. 20: Leon Trotsky (Lev Bronstein), exiled Soviet war minister, near Mexico City.

1948—Jan. 30: Mohandas K. Gandhi, shot in New Delhi, India, by Nathuram Vinayak Godse.   **Sept. 17:** Count Folke Bernadotte, UN mediator for Palestine, by Jewish extremists in Jerusalem.

1951—July 20: King Abdullah ibn Hussein of Jordan.   **Oct. 16:** Prime Min. Liaquat Ali Khan of Pakistan shot in Rawalpindi.

1956—Sept. 21: Pres. Anastasio Somoza of Nicaragua shot in Leon; died Sept. 29.

1957—July 26: Pres. Carlos Castillo Armas of Guatemala, in Guatemala City by one of his own guards.

1958—July 14: King Faisal of Iraq, Crown Prince Abdullah, and July 15, Prem. Nuri as-Said, by rebels in Baghdad.

1959—Sept. 25: Prime Min. Solomon Bandaranaike of Ceylon, by Buddhist monk in Colombo.

1961—Jan. 17: Ex-Prem. Patrice Lumumba of the Congo, in Katanga Province.   **May 30:** Dominican dictator Rafael Leonidas Trujillo Molina, near Ciudad Trujillo.

1963—June 12: Medgar W. Evers, NAACP's Mississippi field secretary, shot by Byron De La Beckwith in Jackson, MS.   **Nov. 2:** Pres. Ngo Dinh Diem of South Vietnam and his brother, Ngo Dinh Nhu, in a military coup.   **Nov. 22:** U.S. Pres. John F. Kennedy shot while riding in motorcade in Dallas, TX; accused gunman Lee Harvey Oswald murdered by Jack Ruby while awaiting trial.

1965—Jan. 21: Iranian Prem. Hassan Ali Mansour in Tehran; 4 executed. **Feb. 21:** Malcolm X, black nationalist, shot in New York City.
1966—Sept. 6: Prime Min. Hendrik F. Verwoerd of South Africa stabbed to death in parliament at Cape Town.
1968—Apr. 4: Rev. Dr. Martin Luther King Jr. fatally shot in Memphis, TN; James Earl Ray convicted of crime. **June 5:** Sen. Robert F. Kennedy (D-NY) shot in Los Angeles; Sirhan Sirhan convicted of crime.
1971—Nov. 28: Prime Min. Wasfi Tal of Jordan in Cairo, by Palestinian guerrillas.
1973—Mar. 2: U.S. Amb. Cleo A. Noel Jr., U.S. Charge d'Affaires George C. Moore, and Belgian Charge d'Affaires Guy Eid, by Palestinian guerrillas in Khartoum, Sudan. **Dec. 20:** Spanish Premier Luis Carrero Blanco, in car explosion by Basque separatist group ETA, in Madrid.
1974—Aug. 19: U.S. Amb. to Cyprus, Rodger P. Davies, by sniper's bullet in Nicosia.
1975—Feb. 11: Pres. Richard Ratsimandrava of Madagascar shot in Tananarive. **Mar. 25:** Saudi Arabian King Faisal shot by nephew Prince Musad Abdel Aziz, in Riyadh. **Aug. 15:** Bangladesh Pres. Sheik Mujibur Rahman killed in coup.
1976—Feb. 13: Nigerian head of state, Gen. Murtala Ramat Mohammed, by self-styled "young revolutionaries."
1977—Mar. 16: Kamal Jumblat, Lebanese Druse chieftain, shot near Beirut. **Mar. 18:** Congo Pres. Marien Ngouabi shot in Brazzaville.
1978—May 9: Former Italian Prem. Aldo Moro killed by Red Brigades terrorists who abducted him Mar. 16 in Rome, held him hostage for several weeks. **July 9:** Former Iraqi Prem. Abdul Razak Al-Naif shot in London.
1979—Feb. 14: U.S. Amb. Adolph Dubs shot by Afghan Muslim extremists in Kabul. **Aug. 27:** Lord Mountbatten, WWII hero, and 2 others killed when a bomb exploded on his fishing boat off the coast of Co. Sligo, Ireland. IRA claimed responsibility. **Oct. 26:** S. Korean Pres. Park Chung Hee and 6 bodyguards fatally shot by Kim Jae Kyu, head of S. Korean CIA.
1980—Apr. 12: Liberian Pres. William R. Tolbert slain in military coup. **Sept. 17:** Former Nicaraguan Pres. Anastasio Somoza Debayle shot in Paraguay.
1981—Oct. 6: Egyptian Pres. Anwar al-Sadat shot by commandos while reviewing a military parade in Cairo; 7 others killed, 28 wounded; 4 convicted as assassins and executed.
1982—Sept. 14: Lebanese Pres.-elect Bashir Gemayel killed by bomb in east Beirut.
1983—Aug. 21: Philippine opposition leader Benigno Aquino Jr. shot by gunman at Manila International Airport.
1984—Oct. 31: Indian Prime Min. Indira Gandhi shot and killed by 2 Sikh bodyguards, in New Delhi.
1986—Feb. 28: Swedish Prem. Olof Palme shot by gunman on Stockholm street.
1987—June 1: Lebanese Prem. Rashid Karami killed when bomb exploded aboard a helicopter.
1988—Apr. 16: PLO military chief Khalil Wazir (Abu Jihad) gunned down by Israeli commandos in Tunisia.
1989—Aug. 18: Colombian pres. candidate Luis Carlos Galan killed by Medellín cartel drug traffickers at campaign rally in Bogotá. **Nov. 22:** Lebanese Pres. Rene Moawad killed when bomb exploded next to his motorcade.
1990—Mar. 22: Colombian pres. candidate Bernardo Jaramillo Ossa shot by gunman at an airport in Bogotá.
1991—May 21: Rajiv Gandhi, former Prime Min. of India, killed by bomb during election rally in Madras.
1992—June 29: Algerian Pres. Mohammed Boudiaf shot by gunman in Annaba.
1993—May 1: Sri Lankan Pres. Ranasinghe Premadasa killed by bomb in Colombo.
1994—Mar. 23: Mexican pres. candidate Luis Donaldo Colosio Murrieta shot by gunman Mario Aburto Martinez. **Apr. 6:** Burundian Pres. Cyprien Ntaryamira and Rwandan Pres. Juvenal Habyarimana killed with 8 others when their plane was apparently shot down.
1995—Nov. 4: Israeli Prime Min. Yitzhak Rabin shot by gunman Yigal Amir at peace rally in Tel Aviv.
1996—Oct. 2: Andrei Lukanov, former Bulgarian Prime Min., shot outside his home by an unidentified gunman.
1998—Feb. 6: Prefect of Corsica, Claude Erignac, shot in the back while walking to a concert, by 2 unidentified gunmen. **Apr. 26:** Guatemalan Rom. Catholic Bishop Juan Gerardi Conedera, human rights champion, found beaten to death in Guatemala City; 4 persons convicted, June 8, 2001.
1999—Mar. 23: Paraguayan Vice-Pres. Luis Maria Argaña, ambushed and shot to death, along with his driver, by 4 unidentified assailants. **Apr. 9:** Niger's Pres. Ibrahim Bare Mainassara ambushed and killed by dissident soldiers. **Oct. 27:** Armenian Prime Min. Vazgen Sarkissian, along with 7 others, shot to death during a session of parliament.

2000—Jan. 15: Serbian paramilitary leader Zeljko Raznjatovic (alias Arkan), with 2 others, shot and killed by unidentified gunman in Belgrade hotel lobby; 4 suspects later charged with the killing. **June 8:** Brig. Gen. Stephen Saunders, Britain's senior military representative in Greece, shot and killed by 2 men on motorcycle, while driving a car in an Athens suburb.
2001—Jan. 16: Congolese Pres. Laurent Kabila shot to death by bodyguard at pres. palace in Kinshasa. **June 1:** Nepal's King Birendra, Queen Aiswarya, and 7 other royals fatally shot by Crown Prince Dipendra, who also fatally wounded himself. **Sept. 9:** Afghan Northern Alliance (anti-Taliban) guerrilla leader Ahmed Shah Massoud, injured in suicide-attack bombing in N. Afghanistan by 2 Arabs posing as journalists; died Sept. 15. **Oct. 14:** Abdel Rahman Hamad, a leader of Palestinian militant group Hamas, shot by Israeli military snipers. **Oct. 17:** Israeli tourism min. Rehavam Zeevi, fatally shot. Popular Front for the Liberation of Palestine claimed responsibility.
2002—Mar. 16: Colombian cleric Isaias Duarte Cancino, critic of Colombian guerrillas and drug traffickers, shot by unidentified gunmen outside of church in Cali. **May 6:** Dutch right-wing politician Pim Fortuyn shot outside a radio station in Hilversum, Netherlands. **July 6:** Afghan Vice Pres. Haji Abdul Qadir shot outside his office in Kabul. **July 23:** Salah Sherhada, a founder of the armed wing of Hamas, killed with 14 others in an assassination air strike on Gaza City by an Israeli fighter jet.
2003—Mar. 12: Serbian Prime Min. Zoran Djindjic shot by snipers outside government headquarters in Belgrade. **Apr. 10:** Shiite Muslim cleric Abdul Majid al-Khoei attacked by crowd, hacked to death at Imam Ali mosque, Najaf, Iraq. **Apr. 17:** Sergei Yushenkov, former Russian legislator and Liberal Party head, shot outside apartment in Moscow. **Aug. 29:** Prominent Shiite Muslim cleric Bakir al-Hakim killed in car bombing at Imam Ali mosque in Najaf, Iraq. **Sept. 10:** Swedish Foreign Min. Anna Lindh stabbed in dept. store in Stockholm; died Sept. 11.
2004—Feb. 13: Former Chechen Pres. Zelimkhan Yandarbiyev killed after car exploded in Qatar. **Mar. 22:** Sheik Ahmed Yassin, spiritual leader of Hamas, by Israeli missile attack in Gaza City. **Apr. 17:** Hamas leader Abdel Aziz Rantisi, by Israeli missile strike in Gaza City. **May 9:** Chechen Pres. Akhmad Kadyrov, by bomb explosion at WWII memorial service in Grozny. **May 17:** Iraqi Gov. Council Pres. Ezzedine Salim, by car bomb explosion at Green Zone checkpoint in Baghdad. **June 12:** Iraqi Dep. Foreign Min. Bassam Salih Kubba gunned down outside home in Baghdad. **Nov. 2:** Controversial filmmaker Theo van Gogh, critic of Islam and a great-grandnephew of painter Vincent van Gogh, shot and stabbed by Muslim militant in Amsterdam.
2005—Jan. 4: Baghdad Gov. Ali al-Haidari gunned down by insurgents in Baghdad, Iraq. **Feb. 14:** Former Lebanese Prime Min. Rafik al-Hariri killed when motorcade bombed in Beirut. **Mar. 8:** Former Chechen President Aslan Maskhadov killed in raid by Russian special forces, in village outside of Grozny. **June 21:** Lebanese Communist Party leader George Hawi killed after car bombed in Beirut. **July 1:** Sheik Kamaledding al-Ghuraifi, senior aide to Grand Ayatollah Ali Sistani shot and killed on his way to Friday prayers, in Baghdad. **July 7:** Egyptian Amb.-designate Ihab al-Sherif was killed in Iraq, by kidnappers who had abducted him July 2 in Baghdad. **Aug. 12:** Sri Lankan Foreign Minister Lakshman Kadirgamar, an ethnic Tamil, shot to death at his home in Colombo; Liberation Tigers of Tamil Eelam suspected.
2006—Feb. 11: Leading Kazakhstan opposition politician Altynbek Sarsenbayev (also known as Sarsenbaiuly) kidnapped, later found murdered outside Almaty. **Apr. 22:** Guyana's Agriculture Minister Satyadeow Sawh shot by unidentified gunmen, near Georgetown. **July 10:** Shamil Basayev, a leader of the Chechen separatist movement who had claimed responsibility for many of Russia's worst terrorist attacks, killed in a massive explosion near the village of Ekazhevo. Chechen rebel website said explosion was accidental, but Russian security director said killing was result of special forces operation. **Jul. 14:** Prominent Shiite Muslim cleric Allama Hassan Turabi killed in suicide bombing at his home in Karachi, Pakistan. **Jul. 28:** Somali transitional government's Constitution and Federalism Minister Abdallah Deerow Isaq shot in Baidoa. **Sept. 10:** Hakim Taniwal, governor of eastern Afghan province, killed by suicide bomber outside of his office; Taliban claimed responsibility. **Sept. 14:** Andrei Kozlov, Russian central banker active in reforming industry, shot by unidentified gunmen in Moscow. **Sept. 25:** Safia Amajan, women's affairs official in Afghanistan, killed by gunmen in Kandahar; Taliban claimed responsibility. **Oct. 7:** Anna Politkovskaya, reporter critical of Kremlin's Chechnya policies, was shot dead by unidentified gunman in her apartment building in central Moscow.

Assassination Attempts Since 1912

1912—Oct. 14: Former U.S. Pres. Theodore Roosevelt shot and wounded by demented man in Milwaukee, WI.

1933—Feb. 15: In Miami, FL, Joseph Zangara, anarchist, shot at Pres.-elect Franklin D. Roosevelt, but a woman seized his arm; bullet fatally wounded Chicago Mayor Anton J. Cermak, who died Mar. 6.

1944—July 20: Adolf Hitler injured when a bomb, planted by a German officer, exploded in his headquarters; 1 aide killed and 12 injured.

1950—Nov. 1: In an attempt to assassinate Pres. Harry Truman, 2 members of a Puerto Rican nationalist movement—Griselio Torresola and Oscar Collazo—tried to shoot their way into Blair House, across the street from the White House. Torresola killed, a White House policeman, Pvt. Leslie Coffelt, fatally shot.

1970—Nov. 27: Pope Paul VI unharmed by knife-wielding assailant who attempted to attack him in Manila airport in Philippines.

1972—May 15: Alabama Gov. George Wallace shot in Laurel, MD, by Arthur Bremer; seriously crippled.

1975—Sept. 5: Pres. Gerald R. Ford unharmed when a Secret Service agent grabbed a pistol aimed at him by Lynette (Squeaky) Fromme, a Charles Manson follower, in Sacramento, CA. **Sept. 22:** Pres. Ford again unharmed when Sara Jane Moore fired a revolver at him in San Francisco; a bystander helped deflect the shot.

1980—May 29: Civil rights leader Vernon E. Jordan Jr. shot and wounded in Ft. Wayne, IN.

1981—Jan. 16: Irish political activist Bernadette Devlin McAliskey and her husband shot and seriously wounded by 3 members of a Protestant paramilitary group in Co. Tyrone, Ireland. **Mar. 30:** Pres. Ronald Reagan, along with Press Sec. James Brady, Secret Service agent Timothy J. McCarthy, and Washington, DC, policeman Thomas Delahanty shot and seriously wounded by John W. Hinckley Jr. in Washington, DC. **May 13:** Pope John Paul II and 2 bystanders shot and wounded by Mehmet Ali Agca, an escaped Turkish prisoner, in St. Peter's Square, Rome.

1982—May 12: Pope John Paul II unharmed after guards overpowered a man with a knife, in Fatima, Portugal.

1984—Oct. 12: British Prime Min. Margaret Thatcher unharmed when a bomb, said to have been planted by the IRA, exploded at the Grand Hotel in Brighton, England, during a Party conference. Four died, including a member of Parliament.

1986—Sept. 7: Chilean Pres. Gen. Augusto Pinochet Ugarte unharmed after motorcade was attacked by rebels.

1995—June 26: Egyptian Pres. Hosni Mubarak unharmed when gunmen fired on his motorcade in Addis Ababa, Ethiopia. Four died, including 2 Ethiopian police officers.

1997—Feb. 12: Colombian Pres. Ernesto Samper Pizano unharmed when a bomb exploded on a runway in Barranquilla as his plane was preparing to land. **Apr. 30:** Tajik Pres. Imamali Rakhmanov injured when a grenade was thrown at him.

1998—Feb. 9: Georgian Pres. Eduard A. Shevardnadze unharmed when gunmen fired on his motorcade in Tbilisi. Three died, including 2 bodyguards and 1 assailant.

2000—Sept. 18: Armed men attempted to assassinate Côte d'Ivoire military leader Gen. Robert Guei in predawn raid.

2002—Apr. 14: Leading Colombian pres. candidate Alvaro Uribe Velez unharmed after bomb exploded under parked bus as his motorcade passed in Barranquilla; 3 bystanders killed. **July 14:** French Pres. Jacques Chirac unharmed after Maxime Brunerie, gunman with ties to neo-Nazi groups, fired at his open-top jeep during a Bastille Day parade in Paris. **Sept. 5:** Afghan Pres. Hamid Karzai unharmed after militant shot at car in Kandahar. **Nov. 25:** Turkmenistan Pres. Saparmurat Niyazov unharmed after gunmen opened fire on his motorcade in Ashgabat.

2003—Dec. 14: Pakistani Pres. Pervez Musharraf unharmed after bomb detonated on bridge in Rawalpindi seconds after his motorcade crossed over.

2004—Mar. 19: Taiwanese Pres. Chen Shui-bian shot while campaigning in motorcade; minor injuries. **July 13:** Separatists bombed motorcade of Sergei Abramov, Chechnya's acting pres. **Sept. 16:** Rocket fired at helicopter carrying Afghan Pres. Hamid Karzai, near Gardez.

2005—Mar. 15: Kosovo Pres. Ibrahim Rugova survived after a bomb damaged the vehicle he was in as his motorcade traveled through Pristina. **July 12:** Lebanon's pro-Syrian defense min. Elias Murr wounded by a car explosion in Beirut suburb.

2006—Apr. 12: Pro-democracy activist Edil Baisalov was beaten as he left his office in Bishkek, Kyrgyzstan. He had sought to block the parliamentary candidacy of a reputed crime boss. **Sept. 5:** Lt. Col. Samir Shehade, involved in investigation of 2005 assassination of former Lebanese Prime Min. Rafik al-Hariri, wounded by bomb as he drove in village near Sidon.

Notable U.S. Kidnappings Since 1924

Robert Franks, 13, in Chicago, **May 22, 1924**, by 2 youths, Richard Loeb and Nathan Leopold, who killed boy. Demand for $10,000 ignored. Loeb died in prison; Leopold paroled 1958.

Charles A. Lindbergh Jr., 20 mos. old, in Hopewell, NJ, **Mar. 1, 1932**; found dead **May 12**. Ransom of $50,000 paid to man identified as Bruno Richard Hauptmann, 35, paroled German convict who entered U.S. illegally. Hauptmann convicted after spectacular trial at Flemington; electrocuted in Trenton, NJ, prison, **Apr. 3, 1936**.

William A. Hamm Jr., 39, in St. Paul, **June 15, 1933**. $100,000 paid. Alvin Karpis given life, paroled in 1969.

Charles F. Urschel, in Oklahoma City, **July 22, 1933**. Released **July 31** after $200,000 paid. George "Machine Gun" Kelly and 5 others sentenced to life.

Brooke L. Hart, 22, in San Jose, CA. Thomas Thurmond and John Holmes arrested after demanding $40,000. When Hart's body was found in San Francisco Bay, **Nov. 26, 1933**, a mob attacked the jail and lynched the 2 kidnappers.

June Robles, 6, abducted in Tucson, AZ, **Apr. 25, 1934**. Missing for 19 days after ransom note sent to parents. Found alive in iron cage buried in the desert. No arrests made.

George Weyerhaeuser, 9, in Tacoma, WA, **May 24, 1935**. Returned home **June 1** after $200,000 paid. Kidnappers given 20 to 60 years.

Charles Mattson, 10, in Tacoma, WA, **Dec. 27, 1936**. Found dead **Jan. 11, 1937**. Kidnapper asked $28,000 but failed to contact for delivery.

Arthur Fried, in White Plains, NY, **Dec. 4, 1937**. Body not found. Two kidnappers executed.

Robert C. Greenlease, 6, taken from Kansas City, MO, school **Sept. 28, 1953**, held for $600,000. Body was found **Oct. 7**. Bonnie Brown Heady and Carl A. Hall pleaded guilty, were executed.

Peter Weinberger, 32 days old, Westbury, NY, **July 4, 1956**, for $2,000 ransom, not paid. Child found dead. Angelo John LaMarca, 31, convicted, executed.

Lee Crary, 8, in Everett, WA, **Sept. 22, 1957**; $10,000 ransom, not paid. Escaped after 3 days, led police to George E. Collins, who was convicted.

Frank Sinatra Jr., 19, from hotel room in Lake Tahoe, CA, **Dec. 8, 1963**. Released **Dec. 11** after his father paid $240,000 ransom. Three men sentenced to prison.

Barbara Jane Mackle, 20, abducted **Dec. 17, 1968**, from Atlanta, GA, motel; found unharmed 3 days later, buried in a coffin-like box 18 in. underground, after her father had paid $500,000 ransom; Gary Steven Krist sentenced to life, Ruth Eisenmann-Schier to 7 years.

Mrs. Roy Fuchs, 35, and 3 children held hostage 2 hours, **May 14, 1969**, in Long Island, NY. Released after her husband, a bank manager, paid kidnappers $129,000 in bank funds; 4 men arrested, ransom recovered.

Virginia Piper, 49, abducted **July 27, 1972**, from her home in suburban Minneapolis; found unharmed near Duluth 2 days later after husband paid $1 mil ransom.

J. Paul Getty III, 17, grandson of the oil billionaire, disappeared **July 10, 1973**, in Italy. Reported payment of $2.8 mil ransom not made until after Getty's ear was sent to a newspaper with a warning that other parts of his body would be mutilated unless ransom was paid. Getty freed **Dec. 15**; 2 men sentenced to prison.

Patricia "Patty" Hearst, 19, taken from her Berkeley, CA, apartment **Feb. 4, 1974**, "Symbionese Liberation Army" captors demanded her father, publisher Randolph Hearst, give millions to the area's poor. Patricia implicated in a San Francisco bank holdup, **Apr. 15**. The FBI, **Sept. 18, 1975**, captured her and others; they were indicted on various charges. Patricia convicted of bank robbery, **Mar. 20, 1976**; released from prison under executive clemency, **Feb. 1, 1979**. In 1978, William and Emily Harris were sentenced to 10 years to life for the kidnapping; both were paroled in 1983.

J. Reginald Murphy, 40, an editor of *Atlanta* (GA) *Constitution*, kidnapped **Feb. 20, 1974**; freed **Feb. 22** after newspaper paid $700,000 ransom. William A. H. Williams arrested; most of the money recovered.

E. B. Reville, Hepzibah, GA, banker, and wife, Jean, kidnapped **Sept. 30, 1974**. $30,000 ransom paid. He was found alive; Jean Reville was found dead **Oct. 2**.

Jack Teich, Kings Point, NY, steel executive, seized **Nov. 12, 1974**; released **Nov. 19** after payment of $750,000.

Adam Walsh, 6, abducted from a Hollywood, FL, dept. store, **July 27, 1981**. Severed head found 2 weeks later. John Walsh, Adam's father, became active in raising awareness about missing children.

Sidney J. Reso, oil company executive, seized **Apr. 29, 1992**; died **May 3**. Arthur D. Seale and wife, Irene, arrested **June 19**. Arthur pleaded guilty, sentenced to life in prison; Irene sentenced to 20-year prison term.

Polly Klaas, 12, Petaluma, CA, abducted at knife point, **Oct. 1, 1993**, during a slumber party at her home. Police arrested Richard Allen Davis on **Nov. 30**; he led them to her body, found **Dec. 4** in wooded area of Cloverdale, CA. Davis found guilty **June 18, 1996**, and sentenced to death **Sept. 26**.

Marshall I. Wais, 79, owner of 2 San Francisco steel companies, kidnapped **Nov. 19, 1996**, from his San Francisco home. Released unharmed the same day after $500,000 ransom paid; Thomas William Taylor and Michael K. Robinson arrested same day.

Tionda Z. Bradley, 10, and sister **Diamond Yvette Bradley**, 3, went missing **July 6, 2001**, in Chicago, IL. Note left by Tionda at home stated that the 2 girls were going to the store and the playground. Police believed girls kidnapped.

Daniel Pearl, 38, reporter for *Wall Street Journal*, disappeared **Jan. 23, 2002**, while researching story in Karachi, Pakistan. British-born militant Ahmad Omar Saeed Sheikh **Feb. 14** admitted to organizing the kidnapping and said Pearl was dead. Sheikh and 3 others convicted **July 15** of kidnapping and murder by a judge in Hyderabad.

Elizabeth Smart, 14, abducted from her home in Salt Lake City, UT, **June 5, 2002**, allegedly by Brian D. Mitchell, and forced to live with Mitchell and wife Wanda for 9 months in various U.S. cities; found walking down street with captors in Sandy, UT, 15 miles from Smart family home, **Mar. 12, 2003**. Mitchell found incompetent to stand trial, **July 26, 2005**, with review to be held after 90 days' treatment.

Natalee Holloway, 18, of Birmingham, AL, vanished **May 30, 2005**, on high school graduation trip to Aruba. Officials believed she was kidnapped and murdered. Several suspects were detained but later released.

Jill Carroll, 28, freelance journalist, in Baghdad by group called the Revenge Brigade, **Jan. 7, 2006**. She was on assignment for the *Christian Science Monitor* when she was seized. She was released **Mar. 30**; 4 Iraqis arrested in connection with her kidnapping in Aug.

Steve Centanni, 60, a Fox News reporter released **Aug. 26, 2006** (along with a colleague), after being kidnapped and held hostage for 13 days by Palestinian militant group Holy Jihad Brigades. The group had demanded that the U.S. release all Muslims held in its prisons.

Notable Terrorist Incidents Worldwide, 1971-Sept. 2006

Note: Selected noteworthy incidents, excluding most assassinations, kidnappings, and military targets. Not including all 2005 and 2006 incidents in Iraq; *see* Chronology of the Year's Events.

Source: U.S. Dept. of State; *Facts On File World News Digest @ Facts.com*; World Almanac research

1971—Mar. 1: Senate wing of U.S. Capitol Building in Wash., DC, bombed by Weather Underground; no deaths.

1972—July 21: "Bloody Friday." Provisional IRA exploded 20+ bombs across Belfast, N. Ireland; 9 killed, hundreds injured.   **Sept. 5:** Members of Palestinian group Black September killed 2 Israeli athletes and seized 9 others at Olympic Village in Munich, W. Germany, during Summer Olympics. 9 hostages, 5 militants, 1 Ger. officer died in botched rescue.

1973—Dec. 17: Palestinian gunmen attacked Rome airport and bombed plane on tarmac; hijacked Lufthansa plane with 5 Italian hostages to Athens, then to Kuwait; 31 killed in all.

1974—June 17: Houses of Parliament in London, England, bombed by Provisional IRA; 11 injured.

1975—Jan. 27: Puerto Rican FALN nationalists bombed Fraunces Tavern in New York City; 4 killed, 53 injured.   **Jan. 29:** U.S. State Dept. building in Wash., DC, bombed by Weather Underground; no deaths.

1976—June 27: Palestinian and Baader-Meinhof militants forced Air France jet to land at Entebbe, Uganda. Israeli army rescued 103 hostages from airport terminal in battle with terrorists and Ugandan troops, July 3-4; 32 killed in all.

1978—Mar. 11: Palestinian militants landed on beach near Haifa, Israel. Shot civilians and hijacked bus with hostages to Tel Aviv; exploded at roadblock; 43 killed.

1979—Nov. 4: Iranian radicals seized U.S. embassy in Tehran, taking 66 Americans hostage. 52 were held until Jan. 20, 1981.   **Nov. 20:** 200 Islamic terrorists seized Grand Mosque in Mecca, Saudi Arabia, and held hundreds of pilgrims hostage. Saudi forces retook mosque Dec. 4; about 250 died.

1980—Feb. 27: Members of leftist guerrilla group April 19 Movement (M-19) seized Dominican Republic embassy in Bogota, Colombia; 80 hostages taken. 18 held until Apr. 27.

1983—April 18: Hezbollah suicide truck bomb at the U.S. embassy in Beirut, Lebanon, killed 63.   **Oct. 9:** N. Korean agents ambushed a S. Korean govt. delegation in Rangoon, Burma, killing 21.   **Oct. 23:** Hezbollah suicide truck bombings of U.S. and French military bases, Beirut, Lebanon; 242 Americans, 58 French killed.

1984—Sept. 20: U.S. embassy annex near Beirut, Lebanon, bombed, killing approx. 20.

1985—June 14: Hezbollah members hijacked TWA Flight 847 with 153 passengers and crew to Beirut; 39 held for 17 days; 1 U.S. Navy sailor killed.   **June 23:** Air India Flight 182 destroyed by bomb off coast of Ireland; 329 killed. Blamed on Sikh terrorists.   **Apr. 12:** 18 killed in bomb blast at restaurant near Air Force base in Torrejon, Spain.   **Oct. 7:** 4 Palestinians hijacked Italian cruise ship *Achille Lauro*; 1 passenger killed.   **Nov. 23:** EgyptAir Flight 648 from Athens to Cairo hijacked to Malta by Palestinian group Abu Nidal; 60 killed in rescue.   **Dec. 27:** Palestinian militants opened fire at El-Al airline counters at Rome and Vienna airports; 19 killed.

1986—Apr. 5: Nightclub in Berlin, W. Germany, bombed; 3 killed, incl. 2 U.S. servicemen, 200+ hurt. 3 Libyan embassy workers in Germany convicted in bombing.

1987—Apr. 17: Bomb in Sri Lankan capital killed 100+; blamed on Tamil rebels who, 4 days later, attacked Sinhalese travelers on highway, killing 127.   **June 19:** Basque group ETA bombed supermarket garage in Barcelona, Spain; 21 killed, 45 injured.   **Nov. 29:** Bomb planted by N. Korean agents exploded on Korean Air Lines Flight 858 over Indian Ocean; 115 killed.

1988—Dec. 21: Pan Am Flight 103 exploded over Lockerbie, Scotland, killing all 259 aboard and 11 on the ground; Libya took responsibility for bombing in Aug. 2003.

1989—Sept. 19: French UTA Flight 722 from Congo to Paris destroyed by bomb in midair over Niger; 171 killed. Several Libyan officials convicted in absentia; no official admission.

1992—Mar. 17: Israeli embassy in Buenos Aires, Argentina, bombed; 28 killed, 200+ injured. Hezbollah suspected.

1993—Feb. 2: Truck bomb exploded in World Trade Center garage in New York City; 6 killed. Blast later linked to al-Qaeda.   **Mar. 12-19:** At least 11 bombs ripped through Bombay and Calcutta, India; 300+ killed.

1994—Feb. 25: U.S.-born Israeli settler Baruch Goldstein opened fire in mosque in Hebron, West Bank; about 30 Muslim worshippers killed.   **July 18:** Buenos Aires Jewish center bombed; 87 killed. Blamed on Hezbollah.

1995—Mar. 20: Twelve killed and over 5,000 injured when Japanese Aum Shinri-kyu cult members released Sarin nerve gas in several Tokyo subway cars.   **Apr. 19:** Murrah Federal Building in Oklahoma City bombed, killing 168 and injuring 500+. Timothy McVeigh and Terry Nichols convicted in bombing. McVeigh executed, June 11, 2001; Nichols sentenced to life in prison, 1998 on state charges, 2004 on federal charges.   **Nov. 13:** U.S. miltary compound in Riyadh, Saudi Arabia, bombed by Islamic Movement of Change; 7 killed.   **Nov. 19:** Suicide bomber drove into Egyptian embassy in Islamabad, Pakistan; at least 16 killed, 60 injured.

1996—Jan. 31: Tamil Tigers drove explosives-laden truck into Central Bank in Colombo, Sri Lanka; 90 killed.   **Feb. 25:** Hamas suicide bombers hit 2 buses in Jerusalem; 26 killed.   **Mar. 4:** Bomb outside Tel Aviv shopping mall killed 14, injured 130.   **June 25:** Bomb-laden fuel truck exploded outside Khobar Towers, a U.S. military complex in Dhahran, Saudi Arabia; killed 19.   **June 27:** Bomb exploded at Centennial Olympic Park in Atlanta, GA, during Summer Games; killed 2, injured 100+. Suspect Eric Robert Rudolph arrested in 2003, pleaded guilty; sentenced to life in prison, Aug. 22, 2005.   **Dec. 3:** Bomb exploded on subway train in Paris; 4 killed, 86 injured. Blamed on Algerian extremists.

1997—Nov. 17: Gamaa al-Islamiya gunmen killed 58 tourists and 4 Egyptians in Valley of the Kings near Luxor, Egypt.

1998—Aug. 7: U.S. embassies in Nairobi, Kenya, and Dar-es-Salaam, Tanzania, bombed; 257 people killed. Al-Qaeda blamed.   **Aug. 15:** IRA car bomb exploded outside courthouse in Omagh, N. Ireland; killed 29, injured 300+.   **Oct. 18:** National Liberation Army of Colombia blew up Ocensa oil pipeline; about 71 killed, 100+ injured.

1999—Sept. 9-16: Three apt. buildings bombed in Moscow and Volgodonsk, Russia; about 300 killed. Chechen rebels blamed.

2000—Oct. 12: Small boat assisting in docking of U.S.S. *Cole* exploded while alongside it in Aden, Yemen; 17 U.S. sailors killed, 39 injured. Blamed on al-Qaeda.

2001—Sept. 11: 19 al-Qaeda terrorists hijacked 4 U.S. domestic flights, including 2 planes that crashed into World Trade Center towers and 1 into Pentagon. Total dead minus hijackers: 2,973; deadliest attack of terrorism yet on U.S.

soil.   **Sept.-Nov. 7:** letters tainted with deadly anthrax bacteria mailed through U.S. postal system killed 5; unsolved.
2002—Mar. 27: Suicide bombing at hotel in Netanya, Israel, during Passover celebration; 27 killed.   **Oct 12:** Resort in Bali, Indonesia, bombed; 202 dead. Jemaah Islamiah blamed.   **Oct. 23:** Chechen guerrillas seized theater in Moscow, held 700+ hostages. Russian authorities gassed theater; most guerrillas and about 128 hostages were killed.   **Nov. 28:** Suicide bombers destroyed Israeli-owned hotel near Mombasa, Kenya; 13 killed. At the same time, 2 missiles narrowly missed Israeli plane taking off from Mombasa airport; blamed on al-Qaeda.   **Dec. 27:** Chechen rebels plowed truck bomb into pro-Russian gov. headquarters in Grozny, Chechnya; 80 killed, 152 injured.
2003—May 12: Truck bombing near gov. buildings in Znamenskoye, Chechnya; 59 killed.   **May 12-13:** Al-Qaeda militants detonated car bombs at 3 residential complexes used by Westerners in Riyadh, Saudi Arabia; 34 killed.   **May 16:** 5 explosions in Casablanca, Morocco; 44 killed, 100+ wounded. Blamed on al-Qaeda.   **May 17-19:** Five suicide bombings in Israel; 17 killed. Hamas and al-Aqsa Martyrs brigade blamed.   **Aug. 1:** Truck bomb hit military hospital in Mozdok, Russia, near Chechnya; 50 killed. Blamed on Chechen rebels.   **Aug. 5:** Car bomb hit Marriott hotel in Jakarta, Indonesia; 12 killed, 150 injured. Blamed on Jemaah Islamiah.   **Aug. 19:** UN headquarters in Baghdad bombed by truck; 22 killed, including UN envoy to Iraq.   **Aug. 25:** Two bombs exploded in taxis in Mumbai (Bombay), India; 46 killed, 100+ injured. Islamic militants suspected.   **Oct. 27:** Suicide bombings at Intl. Red Cross and police stations; 40 killed.   **Nov. 15:** Two synagogues in Istanbul, Turkey, bombed; 25 killed.   **Nov. 20:** British consulate and offices of British bank HSBC bombed in Istanbul, Turkey; 27 killed incl. Br. cons. gen. Blamed on al-Qaeda.   **Dec. 5:** Suicide bombing on commuter train in Yessentuki, Russia; 44 killed, 150 injured. Blamed on Chechen rebels.   **Dec. 9:** Chechen suicide bombing outside National Hotel in Red Square, Moscow; 5 killed.
2004—Feb. 6: Bomb exploded on Moscow subway; 39 killed, 130 injured. Chechen rebels blamed.   **Mar. 11:** Al-Qaeda cell bombed 4 commuter trains during morning rush hour in Madrid, Spain; 191 killed, about 1,200 injured.   **Mar. 28-29:** Suicide bombings by Muslim militants hit Tashkent, Uzbekistan; 19 killed.   **Apr. 21:** Car bomb destroyed Saudi govt. security building in Riyadh; 4 killed, 148 injured.   **May 29:** Al-Qaeda militants stormed foreigner compound in Khobar, Saudi Arabia, taking hostages; 22 killed.   **July 30:** U.S. and Israeli embassies in Tashkent, Uzbekistan, bombed simultaneously; 2 killed.   **Aug. 24:** Two Russian passenger planes crashed nearly simultaneously in diff. parts of Russia; 90 killed. Blamed on Chechen rebels.   **Sept. 1:** Militants seized school in Beslan, in northern Ossetia, Russia; held 1,000+ hostage for 3 days before Russian troops stormed school. About 330 killed, incl. 27 hostage-takers. Blamed on Chechen militants.   **Sept. 9:** Australian embassy in Jakarta, Indonesia, bombed; 9 killed. Blamed on Jemaah Islamiah.
2005—July 7: Four bombs exploded on 3 separate subways and a bus in central London, UK; 52 killed, incl. bombers, about 700 injured.   **July 21:** Four bombs placed on 3 subways and a bus in London malfunction.   **July 23:** Three car bombs explode near resorts at Sharm el Sheik, Egypt; about 90 killed.   **Aug. 17:** More than 400 small bombs exploded in cities and towns across Bangladesh, killing 2 and injuring at least 125. Jamaat ul-Mujahedeen Bangladesh claimed responsibility.   **Aug. 19:** Three rockets fired from Jordan hit cities of Eilat, Israel, and Aqaba, Jordan. One missile flies over a docked U.S. naval ship; 1 death.   **Nov. 9:** Three suicide bombings targeting hotels in Amman, Jordan; killed 56+, injured about 100. Al-Qaeda in Iraq took responsibility.
2006—Apr. 24: Three deadly bombs within 5 minutes struck Egyptian Red Sea resort town of Dahab; 18 killed, 85 injured. Nasser Khamis el-Mallah, supposed "mastermind and leader" of Tawhid wal Jihad (Unity and Holy War), the terrorist cell that launched the attack, reported killed during gun battle in May.   **July 11:** Eight explosions struck 7 different trains and 1 station of public commuter rail system in Mumbai, India; 207 killed, 700+ wounded. Lashkar-e-Qahhar (Army of Terror) claimed responsibility.

Genocide

by Aram A. Schvey, former Crowley Fellow and Adjunct Professor at Fordham University School of Law

Sources: Convention on the Prevention and Punishment of the Crime of Genocide, United Nations Treaty Series 277; Rome Statute of the International Criminal Court.

The term "genocide" (literally "murder of a race") was coined by Professor Raphael Lemkin (1900-59) in 1944 and refers to the intentional destruction or attempted destruction of a national, ethnic, racial, or religious group, whether in wartime or peacetime. Genocide is defined as killing members of the group, causing serious bodily harm to members of the group, or otherwise attempting to bring about its destruction, including preventing births or transferring children away from the group. Although the legal definition of genocide does not extend to political groups, the term is often used colloquially to refer to large-scale political violence.

The prohibition against genocide is part of customary international law and is codified in the Convention on the Prevention and Punishment of the Crime of Genocide ("Genocide Convention"), entered into force in 1951. To-

day, more than 130 nations, including the United States, are parties to it. Genocide is also prohibited by the domestic laws of many nations.

The first modern trials for genocide were conducted by the victorious Allies after WWII. Although the charter of the Nuremberg Tribunal (the international court set up to try Nazi war criminals) did not use the term "genocide," its definition of "crimes against humanity" included persecution on racial or religious grounds. More recently, the UN Security Council created ad hoc tribunals to try those responsible for genocide and other serious crimes in the former Yugoslavia and in Rwanda. The International Criminal Court (ICC), which began functioning on July 1, 2002, also has jurisdiction to try perpetrators of genocide. In Mar. 2005, the UN Security Council referred the situation in Darfur, Sudan, to the ICC prosecutor.

Examples of Genocides Since 1900

Year	Event	Location	Estimated deaths
1915	Extermination of Armenians by the Young Turks	Turkey/Ottoman Empire	1,000,000+
1930s	Intentional infliction of famine on Ukraine	Soviet Union (Ukraine)	6,000,000-7,000,000
1933-45	Attempted destruction of European Jewry (Holocaust)	Europe	6,000,000
1975-79	Khmer Rouge campaign of extermination under Pol Pot	Cambodia	1,500,000-2,000,000
1988	Anfal Campaign (named by the Iraqi government) against Iraqi Kurds	Iraq	100,000-200,000
1992-95	Ethnic killings during the breakup of Yugoslavia, chiefly Serbs against Bosnian Muslims	Bosnia-Herzegovina, Serbia, Croatia	200,000
1994	Hutu massacre of Tutsis	Rwanda	800,000
2003-present	Rebel group and government-backed Arab militia attacks on non-Arab southern tribes, black population[1]	Darfur region, Sudan	200,000-400,000

Note: Estimates based on historical evidence. (1) On Oct. 9, 2006, the UN Office of the High Commissioner for Human Rights called on Sudan's goverment to investigate recent militia attacks on civilians. It has not, however, called the situation in Darfur a genocide.

The legal definition of "genocide" does not include politically motivated mass killings. Therefore, instances of mass violence against political or class enemies, such as Josef Stalin's purges in the 1930s, which killed some 20 mil Soviets, and Mao Zedong's Cultural Revolution, which killed several million Chinese, are not included. The mass killings of an estimated 1.7 mil during the Khmer Rouge regime in Cambodia are often spoken of as a genocide, despite the fact that many of the murders were politically or class motivated.

MILITARY AFFAIRS

Timeline of Major Wars Since 1066

Norman Conquest
1066-1071

William I, duke of Normandy, landed on the English coast near Hastings on Sept. 28, 1066, and defeated Harold II, Saxon king of England, at **Battle of Hastings** Oct. 14. William crowned king Dec. 25 in Westminster Abbey. Most revolts were suppressed by 1071. **Conquest linked England's interests with those of the continent and led to its rise as a powerful monarchy.**

Crusades
1095-1270/1291

Military expeditions undertaken by Western European Christians usually at the behest of the papacy, to recover Jerusalem and other Biblical places of pilgrimage from Muslim control; **in the long term, stimulated trade and flow of ideas between East and West.** Pope Urban II called Nov. 27, 1095 for the **First Crusade**; Crusaders took Jerusalem on July 15, 1099, massacred inhabitants, and founded four temporary states: Antioch, Edessa, Jerusalem, and Tripoli. The failed **Second Crusade** was prompted by Muslims' capture of Edessa in 1144. Jerusalem was captured by Ayyubid sultan Saladin on Oct. 2, 1187, launching the **Third Crusade**, which involved the Holy Roman emperor, Frederick I (Barbarossa); the French king, Philip II (Augustus); and the English king, Richard I (Lion-Heart), but did not lead to a Crusader victory. The **Fourth Crusade** sacked Constantinople on Apr. 13, 1204. The **Fifth Crusade** began with capture of Damietta in Egypt (1219) but failed at Cairo. A **Sixth Crusade** led to the treaty of Jaffa in 1229, giving Jerusalem to the Crusaders until 1244, when it was taken by the Templars, launching a **Seventh Crusade**. The last crusade abruptly ended when its leader, French King Louis IX, died in 1270. The last major Crusader stronghold, Acre (now Akko, Israel), was lost on May 18, 1291.

Hundred Years War
1337-1453

Series of armed conflicts over rival claims to the French throne, broken by a number of truces and peace treaties. Edward III declared himself King of France in 1338 and invaded, with victories at **Crécy** in 1346 and **Poitiers** in 1356. Treaty of Brétigny signed May 8, 1360, but French king Charles V renewed fighting in 1369. Truce from 1396 until Henry V of England invaded in 1415 and defeated French army at **Agincourt**, capturing land north of Loire river including Paris. Treaty of Troyes in 1420 made Henry VI heir of both thrones. The siege of French stronghold **Orléans**, lifted in 1429 with help from Joan of Arc, turned the tide in favor of the French. **War ended English claims to France, paved the way for French absolute monarchy.**

Wars of the Roses
1455-1485

Series of dynastic civil wars in England fought by the rival houses of Lancaster and York for the throne. Richard, third duke of York, in conflict with the Lancastrian King Henry VI, won victories at **St. Albans** (1455) and **Northampton** (1460); Richard died at battle of **Wakefield** on Dec. 30, 1460, before coronation, leaving his son to become King Edward IV. Henry VI imprisoned in tower of London, 1465. Edward died in 1483; his brother became Richard III, after usurping throne from Edward V. Henry Tudor defeated Richard III at the **Battle of Bosworth Field** (1485). As Henry VII, he married Edward's daughter Elizabeth, 1486, **finally uniting the houses.**

Thirty Years War
1618-1648

A series of religious and political conflicts involving most countries of western Europe; most fighting in Germany, devastating it. Major conflicts included the **"Defenestration of Prague"** (May 23, 1618); defeat of King Christian IV of Denmark and Norway by Catholic League (1626); victories by Lutheran King Gustav II Adolph of Sweden at Breitenfeld (1631) and Lützen (1632). France, under cardinal and statesman Richelieu, chief minister of King Louis XIII, declared war on the Hapsburgs in May 1635; defeated Austro-Bavarian army (Aug. 3, 1645), leading to Truce of Ulm. Peace of Westphalia signed at Münster on Oct. 24, 1648, **bringing peace by recognizing the rulers' sovereignty within their lands** and their right to determine the religious beliefs of their subjects.

English Civil Wars
1638-60

Series of conflicts between followers of King Charles (Cavaliers) and Parliament (Roundheads), over divine right of king versus Parliament's right to control national finances. Presbyterian Scots, allied with Parliament, rioted and in 1640 occupied the northern counties of England. Oliver Cromwell, second in command of Parliament's New Model Army, destroyed the king's army at the **Battle of Naseby** (June 14, 1645); first civil war ended May 1646 when Charles surrendered to the Scots. Charles later allied with Scots, but was defeated by Cromwell at **Preston**, Aug. 17-19, 1648, and executed Jan. 30, 1649. Parliament abolished monarchy and House of Lords. Cromwell suppressed Irish and Scottish rebellions, was briefly succeeded by son Richard after death (1658); **Charles II restored to the throne** by "The Long Parliament," May 1660.

War of the Spanish Succession
1701-1714

War fought by the Grand Alliance (originally England, Netherlands, Denmark, and Austria; later also Portugal), against a coalition of France, Spain, and a number of small Italian and German principalities to preserve balance of power after death of Spanish King Charles II. Opened with invasion of Italy, via Venice, by an Austrian army under Prince Eugène of Savoy in May 1701. French forced to withdraw from Netherlands and Italy in 1706, and finally defeated 1709 in bloodiest battle of the war at the French village of **Malplaquet**. Treaty of Rastatt and Baden signed in 1714; gave **Austria control of Spanish Netherlands and settled peace between Austria and France.**

War of the Austrian Succession
1740-48

Conflict over rival claims for the hereditary dominions of the Habsburg family, following death (1740) of Charles VI, Holy Roman emperor and archduke of Austria. An alliance of Bavaria, France, Spain, Sardinia, Prussia, and Saxony fought against Austria, allied with Holland and Great Britain. King Frederick the Great of Prussia captured Silesia from Austria in the **First** (1740-42) and **Second Silesian Wars** (1744-45). British King George II defeated French army at **Battle of Dettingen am Main** (June 27, 1743). French conquered Austrian Netherlands. Treaty of Aix-la-Chapelle Oct. 18, 1748 **restored most original borders, and Prussia became a significant force.**

Seven Years War
1756-63

Worldwide conflicts fought for the control of Germany and for supremacy in colonial North America and India. French defeated Gen. Edward Braddock on the Monongahela in 1754, leading to undeclared declaration of **French-Indian War**, May 1756. Frederick II of Prussia invaded Saxony on Aug. 29, 1756; defeated French at **Rossbach** (1757), Austrians at **Leuthen** (1757), Russians at **Zorndorf** (1758). By 1760, British conquered French Canada. Peter III signed armistice with Prussia, 1762. Treaty of Paris signed Feb. 10, 1763; Peace of Hubertusburg Feb. 15, 1763, between Prussia and Austria. **England emerged as leading world naval power.**

American Revolution
1775-83

Conflict between 13 British colonies on the eastern seaboard of America and Great Britain. George Washington took command of the Continental Army, July 2, and King George III declared colonies traitors on Aug. 23. Independence of colonies declared July 4, 1776. France recognized the colonies' independence Feb. 6, 1778, followed by Spain on June 21, 1779; both pledged support. French fleet drove British fleet under Adm. Thomas Grave from the Chesapeake Bay on Sept. 5, 1781. French and Americans laid siege to **Yorktown** Sept. 28-Oct. 19, forcing British Gen. Cornwallis to surrender. Treaty of Paris (Sept. 3, 1783) recognized **U.S. independence.**

Wars of French Revolution & Napoleonic Wars
1792-1815

Large-scale wars fought between France and two multinational coalitions. France declared war on the Austrian part of the Holy Roman Empire for aiding King Louis XVI, Apr. 20, 1792. Newly created French Republic declared war on monarchs of Britain and Holland, Feb. 1, 1793, and Spain, Mar. 7. Napoleon Bonaparte defeated Austria in N Italy (1796-1797), captured Egypt from Britain (1798-1799; Battle of the Pyramids, July 21, 1798), and became First Consul after coup d'état of Nov. 9-10, 1799. French Grande Armée later swept through Europe using innovative and aggressive tactics. French navy defeated by British under Adm. Horatio Nelson at **Trafalgar** (Oct. 21, 1805), but Napoleon defeated Austro-Russian forces at **Austerlitz** (Dec. 2) and controlled most of Europe except Russia and Great Britain by 1808. France suffered its first major defeat by Austria at **Aspern-Essling**, May 21-22, 1809. Napoleon invaded Russia, captured **Moscow** Sept. 14, 1812, but was forced to flee the bitter Russian winter and abandoned Germany after defeat at **Leipzig**, Oct. 16-19, 1813. **Paris** captured by Allied armies Mar. 30-31, 1814. Napoleon exiled to Elba May 4 but returned for "Hundred Days" reign, Mar. 20-June 28, 1815; final defeat at **Waterloo** by British and Prussian troops (June 18). The **Bourbon monarchy was restored under Louis XVIII** and Britain, Prussia, Russia, and Austria maintained European peace.

Crimean War 1853-56	Conflict between Russia and a coalition of Great Britain, France, Sardinia, and Turkey for influence over Balkans and the straits between the Black Sea and the Mediterranean. Russia destroyed Turkish fleet at **Sinope** on Nov. 30, 1853. Britain and France declared war in Mar. 1854, and with Turkish troops defeated Russians at **Battle of Alma River** on Sept. 20. Lord Lucan of Britain prevented Russia from capturing Balaklava on Oct. 25 (the **"Charge of the Light Brigade"**). **Siege of Sevastopol** ended when Russia evacuated Sept. 8, 1855. Treaty of Paris signed Mar. 30, 1856; **curbed Russian expansion and loosened European power alignments.**
American Civil War 1861-65	Conflict between the United States (the Union) and 11 secessionist Southern states, organized as the Confederate States of America. Union garrison at Fort Sumter off Charleston, S.C. surrendered to Brig. Gen. Pierre Beauregard (Apr. 12-13, 1861). 22,000 Confederates under Beauregard repelled 35,000 Union troops under Gen. Irvin McDowell along **Bull Run** stream near Manassas, VA (July 21). The *Merrimack* (renamed the *Virginia*) battled the *Monitor* Mar. 9, 1862. In **Battle of Antietam** (Sept. 17), some 12,000 Northerners and 12,700 Southerners were killed or wounded. Pres. Abraham Lincoln announced Emancipation Proclamation on Sept. 22. Confederate Gen. Robert E. Lee's forces numbering 75,000 battled 88,000 Union troops under Gen. George Meade at **Gettysburg** July 1-3, 1863, forcing Lee's army back across the Potomac River. Lee surrendered to Ulysses S. Grant at Appomattox Court House (Apr. 9, 1865). **The Union was preserved and slavery abolished.**
Franco-Prussian War 1870-71	German states led by Prussia defeated France, seizing Alsace and part of Lorraine. French defeated in several major battles, culminating at **Sedan** Sept. 1, 1870 when Prussian forces decisively defeated the French army and captured emperor Napoleon III. Prussian king crowned William I, emperor of a unified Germany, Jan 18, 1871. **France surrendered** Jan. 28. Final treaty signed May 10; set the stage for later **German imperialistic expansion.**
Spanish-American War 1898	War waged by the U.S. to liberate Cuba from Spanish rule. A mysterious explosion, blamed on Spain by American newspapers, sank the U.S. battleship *Maine* in Havana's harbor (Feb. 15, 1898), killing 260. The U.S. called for Spain's withdrawal from Cuba, and Spain declared war (Apr. 24). 17,000 U.S. troops rode from Daiquirí to Santiago de Cuba, taking **San Juan Hill** with help of the Rough Riders under Teddy Roosevelt. Santiago de Cuba surrendered July 17. The Treaty of Paris (Dec. 10, 1898) provided for the **independence of Cuba; the cession by Spain to the U.S. of Puerto Rico, Guam, and for a $20 mil payment, the Philippine Islands.**
World War I 1914-18	Local European war that grew into a global war involving 32 nations: the Allies and the Associated Powers—28 nations including Great Britain, France, Russia, Italy, and the U.S.—versus the Central Powers of Germany, Austria-Hungary, Turkey, and Bulgaria. Archduke Francis Ferdinand assassinated at Sarajevo, Bosnia (June 28, 1914). Germany invaded France through Belgium and the Netherlands; advance on Paris halted by the French under Gen. Joseph Jacques Césaire Joffre at the **First Battle of the Marne**, Sept. 5-12. Germany checked the Russian army at the **Battle of Tannenberg**, Aug. 26-30. The British suffered 57,470 casualties (19,240 dead) in the opening day of the First **Battle of the Somme** (July 1-Nov. 18), first of 12 battles that forced Germany back to the Hindenburg Line. U.S. declared war on Germany Apr. 6, 1917. Russian involvement ended when Bolshevik party seized power on Nov. 7; signed armistice Dec. 15. German offensive halted by U.S. and French troops at **Second Battle of the Marne** (July 15-Aug. 5, 1918), the turning point of the war. Allied counter-offensive broke the Hindenburg line and an armistice was signed on Nov. 11. **Inadequate enforcement of resulting peace treaties led to resurgence of militarism in Germany and social disorder in Europe.**

World War II
1939-45
	Global military conflict stemming from European unrest after World War I and Japan's aggressive expansion into Asia and the Pacific.
	    The War in Europe: The Nazi-Soviet nonaggression pact (Aug. 23, 1939) freed Germany to attack Poland (Sept. 1). Britain and France declared war on Germany Sept. 3. German forces raced through Europe (Apr.-June), capturing Paris June 14. Italy declared war on France and Britain June 10; German-Italian campaigns won the Balkans and N Africa by June 1941. U.S. entered war Dec. 1941. Three million Axis troops invaded Russia June 22, 1941, but Russian counterthrusts stopped the German advance at **Stalingrad**, Aug. 20, 1942-Feb. 2, 1943), and Allies took N Africa (Nov. 8, 1942-May 13, 1943), Italy (July 10, 1943-May 2, 1945). Normandy invaded on **D-Day**, June 6, 1944; Paris liberated Aug. 25. Yalta Conference (Feb. 4-11, 1945) launched "race for Berlin." Adolf Hitler committed suicide Apr. 30. **Germany surrendered unconditionally May 7.**
	    The War in the Pacific: Japan invaded China (July 7, 1937), joined alliance with Germany and Italy (1940) and signed non-aggression pact with Russia (1941); attacked Hawaii's **Pearl Harbor**, Dec. 7, 1941; U.S. declared war on Japan Dec. 8. **Battle of Midway** (June 4-7, 1942) repulsed the Japanese advance. Marines landed on Guadalcanal Aug. 7, defeated Japanese fleet at **Battle of Leyte Gulf**, Oct. 23-26. B-29 bombing raids on Japan began in Nov.; Marines invaded **Iwo Jima** (Feb. 19-Mar. 16, 1945) with heavy casualties, then **Okinawa** (Apr. 1-June 21). U.S. atom bombs dropped on Hiroshima (Aug. 6) and Nagasaki (Aug 9) and the Soviet invasion of Manchuria (Aug. 8) **forced Japan to agree, on Aug. 14, to surrender**; formal surrender was on Sept. 2, 1945.

Korean War 1950-53	Military struggle fought on the Korean Peninsula between the Democratic Peoples' Republic of Korea (N Korea) and the Republic of Korea (S Korea) that developed into an international war involving China allied with North Korea against the U.S. and other nations under the UN flag. DPRK army crossed the 38th parallel and invaded S Korea (June 25, 1950), entering Seoul (June 26). Amphibious assault launched at **Inchon** by Gen. Douglas MacArthur (Sept. 15) helped U.S. forces rout DPRK close to the Yalu River by Nov. 24. Chinese counterattack retook Seoul (Jan. 4, 1951), but forced back to the 38th parallel by Apr. 22. Armistice was signed (July 27, 1953) by the UN, DPRK, and China, but not ROK, **leaving the peninsula partitioned at 38th parallel.**
Vietnam War 1959-75	Struggle primarily in S Vietnam that widened into a war between S Vietnam supported mainly by the U.S. and N Vietnam supported by the USSR and China. Viet Minh, led by Communist leader Ho Chi Minh, formed the Democratic Republic of Vietnam (Sept. 2, 1945). Colonial power France withdrew after fortress at Dien Bien Phu fell (May 8, 1954). Pres. John F. Kennedy pledged U.S. commitment to S Vietnamese independence Dec. 14, 1961. USS *Maddox* destroyer sunk in Gulf of Tonkin (Aug. 2, 1964) prompted Congress to increase involvement. Regular bombing of N Vietnam began (Feb. 24, 1965) and the first U.S. combat ground-forces arrived (Mar. 6). North Vietnamese Army siege of **Khe Sanh** (Jan. 21-Apr. 7, 1968) and the **"Tet" offensive** (Jan. 30) aimed to cause insurrection in the south. **My Lai Massacre** by U.S. soldiers against civilians (Mar. 16, 1968) created scandal, fueled U.S. disaffection with war. U.S. forces peaked at 543,400 in Apr., 1969. NVA **"Easter Offensive"** (Mar. 30, 1972) rebuffed and U.S. responded with aerial bombings in May and Dec. U.S. withdrew after cease-fire, Jan. 1973. **NVA offensive captured Saigon, Apr. 30, 1975, and unified Vietnam under Communist rule.**
Persian Gulf Wars 1991, 2003	Conflicts fought principally between Iraq and the U.S. concerning Iraq's influence in the Middle East and its supposed development of weapons of mass destruction. **First Gulf War:** Iraq under dictator Saddam Hussein invaded Kuwait Aug 2, 1990, and annexed it; UN Security Council ordered Iraqi forces to withdraw by Jan. 15, 1991. Beginning Jan. 17, a multinational force (**Operation Desert Storm**) led by the U.S. bombed military targets in Iraq and Kuwait. A coordinated air-land offensive (**Operation Desert Sabre**, begun Feb. 24) retook Kuwait City Feb. 26, and permanent cease-fire was signed on Apr. 6. Iraq was ordered to pay reparations to Kuwait, reveal locations of biological and chemical weapons, and eliminate weapons of mass destruction. **Second Gulf War:** The U.S. and U.K. asserted that Iraq was producing WMD (later proved false) and posed an imminent threat. The UN passed Resolution 1441, Nov. 8, 2002, warning Iraq of "serious consequences" if it failed to cooperate fully and unconditionally with UN weapons inspectors. Iraq rejected a Mar. 17 U.S. ultimatum, demanding Hussein and his sons leave Iraq; U.S. launched Operation Iraqi Freedom Mar. 19, 2003, with support from U.K. and other allies but without full UN Security Council support. Baghdad fell Apr. 9, and major combat operations declared over May 1. Saddam Hussein was captured Dec. 13, but **guerrilla opposition to U.S. troops and violence between Iraqi Shiites and Sunnis continued.**

Chief Commanding Officers of the U.S. Military

Chairman, Joint Chiefs of Staff: Gen. Peter Pace (USMC)
Vice Chairman: Adm. Edmund P. Giambastiani Jr. (USN)

The **Joint Chiefs of Staff** consists of the Chairman and Vice Chairman of the Joint Chiefs of Staff; the Chief of Staff, U.S. Army; the Chief of Naval Operations; the Chief of Staff, U.S. Air Force; and the Commandant of the Marine Corps. Date of rank is date when the individual achieved his or her current rank.

Army

Chief of Staff	Date of rank
Schoomaker, Gen. Peter J.	Oct. 31, 1997

Other Generals

Abizaid, John	Aug. 1, 2003
Bell, Burwell B.	Dec. 3, 2002
Brown, Bryan D.	Nov. 1, 2003
Casey, George W., Jr.	Dec. 1, 2003
Cody, Richard	June 28, 2004
Craddock, Bantz J.	Jan. 1, 2005
Griffin, Benjamin S.	Jan. 1, 2005
McKiernan, David	Dec. 14, 2005
McNeill, Dan K.	July 1, 2004
Wallace, William S.	Oct. 13, 2005
Ward, William E.	May 3, 2006

Air Force

Chief of Staff	Date of rank
Moseley, T. Michael	Oct. 1, 2003

Other Generals

Carlson, Bruce	Sept. 1, 2005
Corley, John D. W.	Nov. 1, 2005
Hester, Paul V.	Aug. 1, 2004
Keys, Ronald E.	May 27, 2005
Looney III, William R.	Aug. 1, 2005
Lord, Lance W.	Apr. 19, 2002
Schwartz, Norton	Oct. 1, 2005
Wald, Charles F.	Jan. 1, 2003

Navy

Chief of Naval Operations	Date of rank
Mullen, Michael G. (surface warfare)	Aug. 28, 2003

Other Admirals

Donald, Kirkland H. (submariner)	Jan. 1, 2005
Fallon, William J. (aviator)	Nov. 1, 2000
Giambastiani, Edmund P., Jr. (submariner)	Oct. 2, 2002
Keating, Timothy J. (aviator)	Jan. 1, 2005
Nathman, John B. (aviator)	Dec. 1, 2004
Roughead, Gary (surface warfare)	Sept. 1, 2005
Stavridis, James, G.	Oct. 19, 2006
Ulrich III, H. G. (surface warfare)	July 22, 2005
Willard, Robert F. (aviator)	Mar. 18, 2005

Marine Corps

Commandant of the Marine Corps (CMC)	Date of Rank
Hagee, Gen. Michael W.	Jan. 13, 2003

Other Generals

Cartwright, James E.	July 9, 2004
Jones, James L.	June 30, 1999
Magnus, Robert	Sept. 8, 2005
Pace, Peter	Sept. 8, 2000

Coast Guard

Commandant, with rank of Admiral	Date of rank
Allen, Thad W.	May 30, 2006

Vice Commandant, with rank of Vice Admiral

Crea, Vivian S.	July 16, 2004

Unified Combatant Commands Commanders-in-Chief

U.S. European Command, Stuttgart-Vaihingen, Germany—Gen. James L. Jones (USMC)
U.S. Pacific Command, Honolulu, HI—Adm. William J. Fallon (USN)
U.S. Joint Forces Command, Norfolk, VA—Gen. Lance L. Smith (U.S. Army) (Acting Commander)
U.S. Special Operations Command, MacDill AFB, Florida—Gen. Bryan D. Brown (U.S. Army)
U.S. Transportation Command, Scott AFB, Illinois—Gen. Norton Schwartz (USAF)
U.S. Central Command, MacDill AFB, Florida—Gen. John Abizaid (U.S. Army)
U.S. Southern Command, Miami, FL—Admiral James. G. Stavridis (USN)
U.S. Northern Command, Peterson AFB, Colorado—Adm. Timothy J. Keating (USN)
U.S. Strategic Command, Offutt AFB, Nebraska—Gen. James E. Cartwright (USMC)

North Atlantic Treaty Organization (NATO) International Commands

NATO Headquarters: Chairman, NATO Military Committee—Gen. Raymond Henault (Canada)
Strategic Commands:
Allied Command Operations (ACO)—Gen. James L. Jones (USMC), Supreme Allied Commander, Europe
Allied Command Transformation (ACT)—Gen. Lance L. Smith (USAF), Supreme Allied Commander Transformation
Allied Command Operations (ACO) Subordinate Commands:
Joint Force Command Brunssum (JFC Brunnsum)—Gen. Gerhard W. Back (German Luftwaffe), Commander, Brunssum
Joint Force Command Naples (JFC Naples)—Adm. H.G. Ulrich III (USN), Commander, Naples
Joint Headquarters Lisbon (JHQ Lisbon)—Vice Adm. John Stufflebeem (USN), Commander, Lisbon

Chairmen of the Joint Chiefs of Staff, 1949-2006

Gen. of the Army Omar N. Bradley, USA	8/16/49–8/15/53	Gen. David C. Jones, USAF	6/21/78–6/18/82
Adm. Arthur W. Radford, USN	8/15/53–8/15/57	Gen. John W. Vessey Jr., USA	6/18/82–9/30/85
Gen. Nathan F. Twining, USAF	8/15/57–9/30/60	Adm. William J. Crowe Jr., USN	10/1/85–9/30/89
Gen. Lyman L. Lemnitzer, USA	10/1/60–9/30/62	Gen. Colin L. Powell, USA	10/1/89–9/30/93
Gen. Maxwell D. Taylor, USA	10/1/62–7/1/64	Gen. John M. Shalikashvili, USA.	10/25/93–9/30/97
Gen. Earle G. Wheeler, USA	7/3/64–7/2/70	Gen. Henry H. Shelton, USA.	9/30/97–9/30/01
Adm. Thomas H. Moorer, USN	7/2/70–7/1/74	Gen. Richard B. Myers, USAF	10/1/01–9/30/05
Gen. George S. Brown, USAF	7/1/74–6/20/78	Gen. Peter Pace, USMC	9/30/05–

Military Units, U.S. Army and Air Force

ARMY UNITS. Squad: In infantry usually 4-10 enlisted personnel under a staff sergeant. **Platoon:** In infantry 3-4 squads under a lieutenant. **Company:** Headquarters section and 3-4 platoons under a captain. (Company-size unit in the artillery is a battery; in the cavalry, a troop.) **Battalion:** Hdqts. and 3-5 companies under a lieutenant colonel. (Battalion-size unit in the cavalry is a squadron.) **Brigade:** Hdqts. and 3 or more battalions under a colonel. **Division:** Hdqts. and 3 brigades with artillery, combat support, and combat service support units under a major general. **Army Corps:** Two or more divisions with corps troops under a lieutenant general. **Field Army:** Hdqts. and 2 or more corps with field Army troops under a general.

AIR FORCE UNITS. Flight: Numerically designated flights are the lowest level unit in the Air Force. They are used primarily where there is a need for small mission elements to be incorporated into an organized unit. **Squadron:** A squadron is the basic unit in the Air Force. It is used to designate the mission units in operational commands. **Group:** The group is a flexible unit composed of 2 or more squadrons whose functions may be operational, support, or administrative in nature. **Wing:** An operational wing normally has 2 or more assigned mission squadrons in an area such as combat, flying training, or airlift. **Numbered Air Forces:** Normally an operationally oriented agency, the numbered air force is designed for the control of 2 or more wings with the same mission and/or geographical location. **Major Command:** A major subdivision of the Air Force that is assigned a major segment of the USAF mission. Major Command is composed of 3 or more numbered air forces.

Principal U.S. Military Training Centers

Air Force

Name, PO address	ZIP	Nearest city
Columbus AFB, MS	39701	Tupelo
Goodfellow AFB, TX	76908	San Angelo
Keesler AFB, MS	39534	Biloxi
Lackland AFB, TX	78236	San Antonio
Maxwell AFB, AL	36112	Montgomery
Sheppard AFB, TX	76311	Wichita Falls

All are Air Education and Training Command Bases.

Army

Name, PO address	ZIP	Nearest city
Aberdeen Proving Ground, MD	21005	Aberdeen
Carlisle Barracks, PA	17013	Carlisle
Fort Benning, GA	31905	Columbus
Fort Bliss, TX	79916	El Paso
Fort Bragg, NC	28307	Fayetteville
Fort Gordon, GA	30905	Augusta
Fort Huachuca, AZ	85613	Sierra Vista
Fort Jackson, SC	29207	Columbia
Fort Knox, KY	40121	Radcliff
Fort Leavenworth, KS	66027	Leavenworth
Fort Lee, VA	23801	Petersburg
Fort Leonard Wood, MO	65473	Waynesville
Fort Rucker, AL	36362	Dothan
Fort Sill, OK	73503	Lawton
Joint Readiness Training Center, Fort Polk, LA	71459	Leesville
National Training Center, Fort Irwin, CA	92310	Barstow
The Judge Advocate General's Legal Center and School, VA	22903	Charlottesville

Marine Corps

Name, PO address	ZIP	Nearest city
MCB Camp Lejeune, NC	28547	Jacksonville
MCB Camp Pendleton, CA	92055	Oceanside
MCB Kaneohe Bay, HI	96863	Kailua
MCAGCC Twentynine Palms, CA	92278	Palm Springs
MCCDC Quantico, VA	22134	Quantico
MCRD Parris Island, SC	29905	Beaufort
MCRD San Diego, CA	92140	San Diego
MCAS Cherry Point, NC	28533	Havelock
MCAS Miramar, CA	92145	San Diego
MCAS New River, NC	28545	Jacksonville
MCAS Beaufort, SC	29904	Beaufort
MCAS Yuma, AZ	85369	Yuma
MCMWTC Bridgeport, CA	93517	Bridgeport

MCB = Marine Corps Base. MCAGCC = Marine Corps Air-Ground Combat Center. MCCDC = Marine Corps Combat Development Command. MCRD = Marine Corps Recruit Depot. MCAS = Marine Corps Air Station. MCMWTC = Marine Corps Mountain Warfare Training Center.

Navy

Name, PO address	ZIP	Nearest city
Naval Education & Training Ctr.	32508	Pensacola, FL
Naval Air Training Center	78419	Corpus Christi,TX
Training Command Fleet	92113	San Diego, CA
Naval Aviation Schools Command	32508	Pensacola, FL
Naval Education & Training Ctr.	02841	Newport, RI
Naval Post Graduate School	93943	Monterey, CA
Naval Submarine School	06349	Groton, CT
Naval Training Ctr., Great Lakes	60088	N. Chicago, IL
Naval War College	02841	Newport, RI
Naval Air Tech. Training Ctr.	32508	Pensacola, FL
Fleet Antisubmarine Warfare	92147	San Diego, CA

The Federal Service Academies

U.S. Military Academy, West Point, NY. Founded 1802. Awards BS degree and Army commission for a 5-year service obligation. For admissions information, write USMA Admissions, Bldg. 606, USMA, West Point, NY 10996. www.usma.edu

U.S. Naval Academy, Annapolis, MD. Founded 1845. Awards BS degree and Navy or Marine Corps commission for a 5-year service obligation. For admissions information, write Candidate Guidance Office, United States Naval Academy, 117 Decatur Rd., Annapolis, MD 21402-5018. www.usna.edu

U.S. Air Force Academy, Colorado Springs, CO. Founded 1954. Awards BS degree and Air Force commission for a 6-year service obligation. For admissions information, write HQ USAFA/RRS, 2304 Cadet Dr., Ste. 200, USAF Academy, CO 80840. www.usafa.edu

U.S. Coast Guard Academy, New London, CT. Founded 1876. Awards BS degree and Coast Guard commission for a 5-year service obligation. For admissions information, write Director of Admissions, U.S. Coast Guard Academy, 31 Mohegan Ave., New London, CT 06320-8103. www.cga.edu

U.S. Merchant Marine Academy, Kings Point, NY. Founded 1943. Awards BS degree, a license as a deck, engineer, or dual officer, and a U.S. Naval Reserve commission. Service obligations vary according to options taken by the graduate. For admissions information, write Admissions Office, U.S. Merchant Marine Academy, 300 Steamboat Rd., Kings Point, NY 11024. www.usmma.edu

Personal Salutes and Honors, U.S.

The U.S. **national salute**, 21 guns, is also the salute to a national flag. U.S. independence is commemorated by the salute to the Union—one gun for each state—fired at noon July 4, at all military posts provided with suitable artillery.

A 21-gun salute on arrival and departure, with 4 ruffles and flourishes, is rendered to the **president** of the United States, to a former president, and to a president-elect. The national anthem or "Hail to the Chief," as appropriate, is played for the president, and the national anthem for the others. A 21-gun salute on arrival and departure, with 4 ruffles and flourishes, also is rendered to the **sovereign or chief of state of a foreign country** or a member of a reigning royal family, and the national anthem of his or her country is played. The music is considered an inseparable part of the salute and immediately follows the ruffles and flourishes without pause. For the Honors March, generals receive the "General's March," admirals receive the "Admiral's March," and all others receive the 32-bar medley of "The Stars and Stripes Forever."

GRADE, TITLE, OR OFFICE	SALUTE (IN GUNS) Arriving	Leaving	Ruffles and flourishes	Music
Vice president of U.S.	19		4	Hail, Columbia
Speaker of the House	19		4	Honors March
U.S. or foreign ambassador	19		4	Nat. anthem of official
Premier or prime minister	19		4	Nat. anthem of official
Secretary of Defense, Army, Navy, or Air Force	19	19	4	Honors March
Other cabinet members, Senate president pro tempore, governor, or chief justice of U.S.	19		4	Honors March
Chairman, Joint Chiefs of Staff	19	19	4	
Army chief of staff, chief of naval operations, Air Force chief of staff, Marine commandant	19	19	4	Honors March
General of the Army, general of the Air Force, fleet admiral	19	19	4	
Generals, admirals	17	17	4	
Assistant secretaries of Defense, Army, Navy, or Air Force	17	17	4	Honors March
Chair of a committee of Congress	17		4	Honors March

OTHER SALUTES (on arrival only) include 15 guns, with 3 ruffles and flourishes, for U.S. envoys or ministers and foreign envoys or ministers accredited to the U.S.; 15 guns, for a lieutenant general or vice admiral; 13 guns, with 2 ruffles and flourishes, for a major general or rear admiral (upper half) and for U.S. ministers resident and ministers resident accredited to the U.S.; 11 guns, with 1 ruffle and flourish, for a brigadier general or rear admiral (lower half) and for U.S. chargés d'affaires and like officials accredited to the U.S.; 11 guns, no ruffles and flourishes, for consuls general accredited to the U.S.

U.S. Army, Navy, Air Force, Marine Corps, and Coast Guard Insignia

Source: Dept. of the Army, Dept. of the Navy, Dept. of the Air Force, U.S. Dept. of Defense, U.S. Coast Guard, U.S. Dept. of Homeland Security

Army

General of the Armies—Gen. John J. Pershing (1860-1948), the only person to have held this rank while living, was authorized to prescribe his own insignia but never wore in excess of four stars. The rank originally was established posthumously by Congress for George Washington in 1799, and he was promoted to the rank by joint resolution of Congress, approved by Pres. Gerald Ford, Oct. 19, 1976.

General of the Army—Five silver stars fastened together in a circle and the coat of arms of the United States in gold color metal with shield and crest enameled. Reserved for wartime use only.

General	Four silver stars
Lieutenant General	Three silver stars
Major General	Two silver stars
Brigadier General	One silver star
Colonel	Silver eagle
Lieutenant Colonel	Silver oak leaf
Major	Gold oak leaf
Captain	Two silver bars
First Lieutenant	One silver bar
Second Lieutenant	One gold bar

Warrant Officers

Grade Five—Silver bar with enamel black line.
Grade Four—Silver bar with 4 enamel black squares.
Grade Three—Silver bar with 3 enamel black squares.
Grade Two—Silver bar with 2 enamel black squares.
Grade One—Silver bar with 1 enamel black square.

Noncommissioned Officers

Sergeant Major of the Army (E-9)—Three chevrons above 3 arcs, with a U.S. Coat of Arms centered on the chevrons, flanked by 2 stars—one star on each side of the eagle. Also wears distinctive red and white shield collar insignia.

Command Sergeant Major (E-9)—Three chevrons above 3 arcs with a 5-pointed star with a wreath around the star between the chevrons and arcs.

Sergeant Major (E-9)—Three chevrons above 3 arcs with a 5-pointed star between the chevrons and arcs.

First Sergeant (E-8)—Three chevrons above 3 arcs with a lozenge between the chevrons and arcs.

Master Sergeant (E-8)—Three chevrons above 3 arcs.

Sergeant First Class (E-7)—Three chevrons above 2 arcs.

Staff Sergeant (E-6)—Three chevrons above 1 arc.

Sergeant (E-5)—Three chevrons.

Corporal (E-4)—Two chevrons.

Specialists

Specialist (E-4)—Eagle device only.

Other Enlisted

Private First Class (E-3)—One chevron above one arc.

Private (E-2)—One chevron.

Private (E-1)—None.

Air Force

Insignia for Air Force officers are identical to those of the Army. Insignia for enlisted personnel are worn on both sleeves and consist of a star and an appropriate number of rockers. Chevrons appear above 5 rockers for the top 3 noncommissioned officer ranks, as follows (in ascending order): Master Sergeant, 1 chevron; Senior Master Sergeant, 2 chevrons; and Chief Master Sergeant, 3 chevrons. The insignia of the Chief Master Sergeant of the Air Force has 3 chevrons and a wreath around the star design. General of the Air Force is reserved for wartime use only.

Navy

The following stripes are worn on the lower sleeves of the Service Dress Blue uniform. They are of gold embroidery.

Rank	Insignia
Fleet Admiral*	1 two inch with 4 one-half inch
Admiral	1 two inch with 3 one-half inch
Vice Admiral	1 two inch with 2 one-half inch
Rear Admiral (upper half) . .	1 two inch with 1 one-half inch
Rear Admiral (lower half) . .	1 two inch
Captain	4 one-half inch
Commander	3 one-half inch
Lieutenant Commander . . .	2 one-half inch with 1 one-quarter inch between
Lieutenant	2 one-half inch
Lieutenant (j.g.)	1 one-half inch with one-quarter inch above
Ensign	1 one-half inch
Warrant Officer-W-4	½" stripe with 1 break
Warrant Officer W-3	½" stripe with 2 breaks, 2" apart
Warrant Officer W-2	½" stripe with 3 breaks, 2" apart

Enlisted personnel (noncommissioned petty officers)—A rating badge worn on the upper left sleeve, consisting of a spread eagle, appropriate number of chevrons, and centered specialty mark.

*The rank of Fleet Admiral is reserved for wartime use only.

Marine Corps

Marine Corps' distinctive cap and collar ornament is the Marine Corps Emblem—a combination of the American eagle, a globe, and an anchor. Marine Corps and Army officer insignia are similar. Marine Corps enlisted insignia, although basically similar to the Army's, feature crossed rifles beneath the chevrons. Marine Corps enlisted rank insignia are as follows:

Sergeant Major of the Marine Corps (E-9)—Same as Sergeant Major (below) but with Marine Corps emblem in the center with a 5-pointed star on both sides of the emblem.

Sergeant Major (E-9)—Three chevrons above 4 rockers with a 5-pointed star in the center.

Master Gunnery Sergeant (E-9)—Three chevrons above 4 rockers with a bursting bomb insignia in the center.

First Sergeant (E-8)—Three chevrons above 3 rockers with a diamond in the middle.

Master Sergeant (E-8)—Three chevrons above 3 rockers with crossed rifles in the middle.

Gunnery Sergeant (E-7)—Three chevrons above 2 rockers with crossed rifles in the middle.

Staff Sergeant (E-6)—Three chevrons above 1 rocker with crossed rifles in the middle.

Sergeant (E-5)—Three chevrons above crossed rifles.

Corporal (E-4)—Two chevrons above crossed rifles.

Lance Corporal (E-3)—One chevron above crossed rifles.

Private First Class (E-2)—One chevron.

Private (E-1)—None.

Coast Guard

Coast Guard insignia follow Navy custom, with certain minor changes such as the officer cap insignia. The Coast Guard shield is worn on both sleeves of officers and on the right sleeve of all enlisted personnel.

For Further Information on the U.S. Armed Forces

Army—Office of the Chief of Public Affairs, Attn: Media Relations Division—MRD, 1500 Army Pentagon, Washington, DC 20310-1500. **Website:** www.army.mil

Navy—Chief of Information, 1200 Navy Pentagon, Washington, DC 20350-1200. **Website:** www.navy.mil

Air Force—Office of Public Affairs, 1690 Air Force Pentagon, Washington, DC 20330-1690. **Website:** www.af.mil

Marine Corps—Marine Corps Headquarters, Division of Public Affairs, U.S. Marine Corps, Washington, DC 20380-1775. **Website:** www.usmc.mil

Coast Guard—Commandant (G-IPA-2), U.S. Coast Guard Headquarters, 2100 Second St. SW, Washington, DC 20593. **Website:** www.uscg.mil

Additional information on all the U.S. Armed Forces branches, as well as many other related organizations, can be accessed through DefenseLINK, the official Internet site of the Dept. of Defense: www.defenselink.mil

 IT'S A RECORD: The largest naval battle to have ever occurred in the Pacific Ocean is the Battle of Leyte Gulf, which took place near the Philippines on Oct. 23-26, 1944. It involved 282 ships (218 Allied, 64 Japanese). Nearly all of Japan's surviving fleet was engaged—including 7 battleships and 16 cruisers. The Japanese used organized *kamikaze* (suicide airplane attacks) for the first time on Oct. 25.

U.S. Army Personnel on Active Duty[1]

Source: Dept. of the Army, U.S. Dept. of Defense
(as of mid-year, except where noted)

Date	Total strength[2]	Commissioned officers Total	Male	Female[3]	Warrant officers Male[4]	Female	Enlisted personnel Total	Male	Female
1940	267,767	17,563	16,624	939	763	—	249,441	249,441	—
1942	3,074,184	203,137	190,662	12,475	3,285	—	2,867,762	2,867,762	—
1943	6,993,102	557,657	521,435	36,222	21,919	—	6,413,526	6,358,200	55,325
1944	7,992,868	740,077	692,351	47,726	36,893	10	7,215,888	7,144,601	71,287
1945	8,266,373	835,403	772,511	62,892	56,216	44	7,374,710	7,283,930	90,780
1946	1,889,690	257,300	240,643	16,657	9,826	18	1,622,546	1,605,847	16,699
1950	591,487	67,784	63,375	4,409	4,760	22	518,921	512,370	6,551
1955	1,107,606	111,347	106,173	5,174	10,552	48	985,659	977,943	7,716
1960	871,348	91,056	86,832	4,224	10,141	39	770,112	761,833	8,279
1965	967,049	101,812	98,029	3,783	10,285	23	854,929	846,409	8,520
1970	1,319,735	143,704	138,469	5,235	23,005	13	1,153,013	1,141,537	11,476
1975	781,316	89,756	85,184	4,572	13,214	22	678,324	640,621	37,703
1980 (Sept. 30)	772,661	85,339	77,843	7,496	13,265	113	673,944	612,593	61,351
1985 (Sept. 30)	776,244	94,103	83,563	10,540	15,296	288	666,557	598,639	67,918
1990 (Mar. 31)	746,220	91,330	79,520	11,810	15,177	470	639,713	567,015	72,698
1995	521,036	72,646	62,250	10,396	12,053	599	435,807	377,832	57,975
1996 (May 31)	493,330	68,850	58,875	9,975	11,456	660	408,511	351,669	56,842
1997 (May 31)	487,297	67,986	58,270	9,716	11,021	719	403,072	342,817	60,255
1998	491,707	67,048	56,650	10,398	10,989	661	402,000	345,149	56,851
1999	479,100	66,613	56,952	9,661	10,767	757	388,211	329,803	58,408
2000	471,633	66,344	56,391	9,953	10,608	781	393,900	333,947	59,953
2001	478,918	64,809	54,570	10,239	10,575	795	398,983	336,264	62,719
2002	485,536	66,446	55,715	10,731	10,900	812	404,363	341,794	62,569
2003 (Sept. 30)	499,301	68,198	56,980	11,218	11,273	854	414,769	351,921	62,848
2004 (Sept. 30)	499,543	68,640	57,245	11,395	11,414	914	414,438	354,043	60,395
2005 (Sept. 30)	492,728	69,174	57,675	11,499	11,506	976	406,923	346,194	57,354
2006	496,362	69,588[5]	NA	NA	12,837[5]	NA	409,531	NA	NA

NA = not available. (1) Represents strength of the active Army, including Philippine Scouts, retired Regular Army personnel on extended active duty, and National Guard and Reserve personnel on extended active duty; excludes U.S. Military Academy cadets, contract surgeons, and National Guard and Reserve personnel not on extended active duty. (2) Includes categories not listed, e.g. West Point Cadets. Data for 1940 to 1946 include personnel in the Army Air Forces and its predecessors (Air Service and Air Corps). (3) Includes women doctors, dentists, and Medical Service Corps officers for 1946 and subsequent years, women in the Army Nurse Corps for all years, and the Women's Army Corps and Women's Medical Specialists Corps (dietitians, physical therapists, and occupational specialists) for 1943 and subsequent years. (4) Act of Congress approved Apr. 27, 1926, directed the appointment as warrant officers of field clerks still in active service. Includes flight officers as follows: 1943, 5,700; 1944, 13,615; 1945, 31,117; 1946, 2,580. (5) Total male and female.

U.S. Navy Personnel on Active Duty

Source: Dept. of the Navy, U.S. Dept. of Defense
(as of mid-year, except where noted)

Date	Officers	Nurses	Enlisted	Officer Candidates	Total[1]	Date	Officers	Nurses	Enlisted	Officer Candidates	Total[1]
1940	13,162	442	144,824	2,569	160,997	1997	57,341	—	340,616	—	397,957
1945	320,293	11,086	2,988,207	61,231	3,380,817	1998 (Sept.)	55,007	—	326,196	—	381,203
1950	42,687	1,964	331,860	5,037	381,538	1999	55,726	—	322,372	—	378,098
1960	67,456	2,103	544,040	4,385	617,984	2000 (Oct.)	53,698	—	320,212	—	373,910
1970	78,488	2,273	605,899	6,000	692,660	2001 (Aug.)	54,177	—	317,100	—	375,618
1980[2]	63,100	—	464,100	—	527,200	2002	55,506	—	324,712	—	384,576
1990 (Sept.)	74,429	—	530,133	—	604,562	2003	55,852	—	324,927	—	380,779
1993 (Mar.)	66,787	—	445,409	—	512,196	2004	55,592	—	319,929	—	375,521
1994 (Apr.)	64,430	—	418,378	—	482,808	2005	54,039	—	305,368	—	363,858
1995 (May)	61,075	—	402,626	—	463,701	2006	53,209	—	295,773	—	353,496
1996	60,013	—	376,595	—	436,608						

(1) May include categories not shown, e.g. midshipmen. (2) Starting in 1980, "Nurses" are included with "Officers," and "Officer Candidates" are included with "Enlisted."

U.S. Air Force Personnel on Active Duty

Source: Dept. of the Air Force, U.S. Dept. of Defense
(as of mid-year)

Year[1]	Strength	Year[1]	Strength	Year[1]	Strength	Year[1]	Strength	Year[1]	Strength	Year[1]	Strength
1918	195,023	1943	2,197,114	1970	791,078	1992	470,315	1997	378,681	2002	369,721
1920	9,050	1944	2,372,292	1980	557,969	1993	444,351	1998	363,479	2003	373,116
1930	13,531	1945	2,282,259	1986	608,200	1994	426,327	1999	357,929	2004	379,887
1940	51,165	1950	411,277	1990	535,233	1995	400,051	2000	357,777	2005	358,705
1941	152,125	1960	814,213	1991	510,432	1996	389,400	2001	351,935	2006	352,620
1942	764,415										

(1) Prior to 1947, data are for U.S. Army Air Corps and Air Service of the Signal Corps.

U.S. Marine Corps Personnel on Active Duty

Source: Dept. of the Marines, U.S. Dept. of Defense
(as of mid-year)

Year	Officers	Enlisted	Total	Year	Officers	Enlisted	Total	Year	Officers	Enlisted	Total
1940	1,800	26,545	28,345	1992	19,132	165,397	184,529	2000	17,897	154,744	172,641
1945	37,067	437,613	474,680	1993	18,878	161,205	180,083	2001	18,072	152,559	170,631
1950	7,254	67,025	74,279	1994	18,430	159,949	178,379	2002	18,472	154,913	173,385
1960	16,203	154,418	170,621	1995	18,017	153,929	171,946	2003	18,908	160,814	179,722
1970	24,941	234,796	259,737	1996	18,146	154,141	172,287	2004	19,052	157,150	176,202
1980	18,198	170,271	188,469	1997	18,089	154,240	172,329	2005	19,118	159,113	178,231
1990	19,958	176,694	196,652	1998	17,984	154,648	172,632	2006	19,218	159,705	178,923
1991	19,753	174,287	194,040	1999	17,892	155,250	173,142				

U.S. Coast Guard Personnel on Active Duty

Source: U.S. Coast Guard, U.S. Dept. of Defense

(as of mid-year)

Year	Total	Officers	Cadets	Enlisted	Year	Total	Officers	Cadets	Enlisted	Year	Total	Officers	Cadets	Enlisted
1970	37,689	5,512	653	31,524	1995	36,731	7,489	841	28,401	2001	35,328	7,112	631	27,585
1980	39,381	6,463	877	32,041	1996	35,229	7,270	830	27,129	2002	37,166	7,267	694	29,205
1985	38,595	6,775	733	31,087	1997	34,717	7,079	868	26,770	2003	39,000	7,532	983	30,859
1990	37,308	6,475	820	29,860	1998	34,890	7,140	805	26,945	2004	40,151	7,835	1,030	31,286
1992	39,185	7,348	919	30,918	1999	35,266	7,135	880	27,251	2005	40,814	7,908	1,006	31,900
1993	38,832	7,724	691	30,417	2000	35,712	7,154	863	27,695	2006	40,639	8,032	1,004	32,001
1994	37,284	7,401	881	29,002										

Women in the U.S. Armed Forces

Source: U.S. Dept. of Defense, U.S. Census Bureau

Women in the Army, Navy, Air Force, Marines, and Coast Guard are fully integrated with male personnel. Expansion of military women's programs began in the Dept. of Defense in fiscal year 1973. Admission of women to the service academies began in the fall of 1976. Under rules instituted in 1993, women were allowed to fly combat aircraft and serve aboard warships. Women remained restricted from service in ground combat units.

Between Apr. 1993 and July 1994, almost 260,000 positions in the armed forces were opened to women. By the mid-1990s, 80% of all jobs and more than 90% of all career fields in the military had been opened to women. In 1975, women made up 4.6% of the armed forces. This figure had grown to 14.6% by Sept. 2005, with about 203,000 women on active duty.

Women Active Duty Troops in 2005

Service	% Women
Army	14.3
Navy	14.4
Marines	6.1
Air Force	19.6
Coast Guard	11.0

Note: (As of mid-year)

Women on Active Duty, All Services: 1973-2005

Year	% Women	Year	% Women
1973	2.5	1993	11.6
1975	4.6	1997	13.6
1981	8.9	2000	14.4
1987	10.2	2004	15.2
		2005	14.6

African American Service in U.S. Wars

Source: U.S. Dept. of Defense, U.S. Census Bureau

American Revolution. About 5,000 African Americans served in the Continental Army, mostly in integrated units, some in all-black combat units.

Civil War. Some 200,000 African Americans served in the Union Army; about 38,000 died, mainly from disease; and 22 won the Medal of Honor (the nation's highest award).

World War I. About 367,000 African Americans served in the armed forces, 100,000 in France.

World War II. Over 1 mil African Americans served in the armed forces; all-black fighter and bomber AAF units and infantry divisions gave distinguished service. (By 1954, armed forces were completely desegregated.)

Korean War. Approximately 3,100 African Americans lost their lives in combat.

Vietnam War. 274,937 African Americans served in the armed forces (1965-74); 5,681 were killed in combat.

Persian Gulf War. About 104,000 African Americans served in the Kuwaiti theater—20% of all U.S. troops, compared with 8.7% of all troops for World War II and 9.8% for Vietnam.

Iraq War. 266 African-American military deaths (as of Sept. 30, 2006), making up about 9.8% of all military deaths in this war.

Veterans Compensation and Pension Case Payments, 1900-2005

Source: U.S. Dept. of Veterans Affairs

Fiscal year	Living veteran cases	Deceased veteran cases	Total cases	Total expenditures (in thousands)	Fiscal year	Living veteran cases	Deceased veteran cases	Total cases	Total expenditures (in thousands)
1900	752,510	241,019	993,529	$138,462	1996	2,671,026	637,232	3,308,258	$18,489,468
1910	602,622	318,461	921,083	159,974	1997	2,666,785	613,976	3,280,761	19,307,852
1920	419,627	349,916	769,543	316,418	1998	2,668,030	594,782	3,262,812	20,199,306
1930	542,610	298,223	840,833	418,433	1999	2,673,167	578,508	3,251,675	21,069,431
1940	610,122	239,176	849,298	429,138	2000	2,672,407	563,754	3,236,161	22,011,965
1950	2,368,238	658,123	3,026,361	2,009,462	2001	2,669,156	548,589	3,217,745	23,275,902
1960	3,008,935	950,802	3,959,737	3,314,761	2002	2,744,866	539,796	3,284,662	25,572,913
1970	3,127,338	1,487,176	4,614,514	5,251,902	2003	2,831,784	537,513	3,369,297	27,995,345
1980	3,195,395	1,450,785	4,646,180	11,044,453	2004	2,898,599	533,482	3,432,081	29,936,868
1990	2,746,329	837,596	3,583,925	14,674,411	2005	2,938,370	537,512	3,475,882	32,025,372
1995	2,668,576	661,679	3,330,255	17,765,044					

U.S. Veteran Population, 2006

Source: U.S. Dept. of Veterans Affairs

(projection of population, as of Sept. 30, 2006)

TOTAL VETERANS IN CIVILIAN LIFE[1]	**23,977,000**
Total wartime veterans[2]	**17,835,000**
Total Gulf War[3]	4,647,000
Gulf War with no prior wartime service	4,297,000
Gulf War with service in Vietnam era	343,000
Gulf War, with service in Vietnam and Korea	6,000
Gulf War with service in Vietnam, Korea, and WWII	1,000
Total Vietnam era[3]	7,956,000
Vietnam era with no prior wartime service	7,287,000
Vietnam era with service in Korean conflict	221,000
Vietnam era with service in Korea and WWII	99,000
Total Korean conflict[3]	3,086,000
Korean conflict with no prior wartime service	2,531,000
Korean conflict with service in WWII	230,000
Total World War II[3]	3,152,000
WWII only	2,822,000
Total peacetime veterans[4]	**6,142,000**
Service between Vietnam era and Gulf War only	3,448,000
Service between Korean conflict and Vietnam era only	2,538,000
Pre-Korean conflict without service in WWII	156,000

Note: Figures are for U.S. veterans worldwide. (1) Includes those who served on active duty in Army, Navy, Air Force, Marines, Coast Guard, uniformed Public Health Service and NOAA, and reservists called to federal active duty. Excludes those dishonorably discharged, those whose only active duty was training, and those currently on active duty. (2) Veterans serving in more than one period are counted only once in total. (3) Total includes veterans who also served in previous periods. (4) Veterans with both wartime and peacetime service are counted only as "wartime veterans."

▶ *IT'S A FACT:* Some of the highest military honors given in other countries include the Order of Leopold (Belgium), the Victoria Cross (UK), the Croix de Guerre ("War Cross," France), the Taeguk Order of Military Merit (South Korea), the Virtuti Militari (Lat. "for military virtue," Poland), the Order of the Redeemer (Greece), and the Order of Rama (Thailand).

U.S. Military Awards
The Medal of Honor
Source: Congressional Medal of Honor Society; Army, U.S. Dept of Defense

The Medal of Honor is the highest military award for bravery that can be given to any individual in the United States. The first Army Medals were awarded on Mar. 25, 1863, and the first Navy Medals went to sailors and Marines on Apr. 3, 1863.

On Dec. 21, 1861, Pres. Abraham Lincoln signed into law a bill to create the Navy Medal of Honor. Lincoln, on July 14, 1862, approved a resolution providing for the presentation of Medals of Honor to enlisted men of the Army and Voluntary Forces, making it a law. The law was amended on March 3, 1863, to extend its provisions to include officers as well as enlisted men.

The Medal of Honor is awarded in the name of Congress to a person who, while a member of the armed forces, distinguishes himself or herself conspicuously by gallantry and intrepidity at the risk of life above and beyond the call of duty while engaged in an action against any enemy of the United States; while engaged in military operations involving conflict with an opposing foreign force; or while serving with friendly foreign forces engaged in an armed conflict against an opposing armed force in which the United States is not a belligerent party.

The deed performed must have been one of personal bravery or self-sacrifice so conspicuous as to clearly distinguish the individual above his or her comrades and must have involved risk of life. Incontestable proof of the performance of service is required, and each recommendation for award of this decoration is considered on the standard of extraordinary merit.

Prior to World War I, the 2,625 Army Medal of Honor awards up to that time were reviewed to determine which past awards met new stringent criteria. The Army removed 911 names from the list, most of them former members of a volunteer infantry group during the Civil War who had been induced to extend their enlistments when they were promised the medal. However, in 1977 a medal was restored to Dr. Mary Walker, and in 1989 medals were restored to Buffalo Bill Cody and 7 other Indian scouts.

Seven African-American soldiers were awarded Medals of Honor for service in World War II (6 of them posthumously) in Jan. 1997. Previously, no black soldier had received the medal for World War II service; an Army inquiry begun in 1993 concluded that the prevailing political climate and Army practices of the time had prevented proper recognition of heroism on the part of black soldiers in that war. In June 2002, 22 Asian Americans received the award for World War II service.

The most recent recipient was Corporal Tibor Rubin, who was awarded the medal on Sept. 23, 2005. While serving in North Korea, 1950-53, Cpl. Rubin distinguished himself in combat and by refusing release from a Chinese POW camp in order to secretly obtain food and medical care for his fellow prisoners, ultimately saving up to 40 lives.

As of Sept. 30, 2006, one Medal of Honor had been awarded for actions in Operation Iraqi Freedom. On April 4, 2003, Sergeant First Class Paul R. Smith distinguished himself during the defense of a prisoner of war holding area near Baghdad International Airport. Sgt. Smith was mortally wounded as he personally engaged the enemy from an exposed position atop a damaged personnel carrier, helping to defeat the enemy attack and secure the evacuation of numerous wounded U.S. troops.

Other Selected Awards
Source: U.S. Army Institute of Heraldry; Navy Department Awards Web Service; Air Force Personnel Center

Distinguished Service Cross. Established in Congress July 9, 1918, on recommendation of Gen. John J. "Black Jack" Pershing, and awarded for extraordinary heroism not justifying the award of a Medal of Honor. The act or acts of heroism must have been so notable and have involved risk of life so extraordinary as to set the individual apart from his or her comrades.

Silver Star. An earlier version of this award, the Citation Star, was established by Congress on July 19, 1918, and retroactively awarded to soldiers for "gallantry in action," back to the Spanish-American War. The Silver Star medal replaced the Citation Star in 1932 and is awarded for gallantry in action which, while of a lesser degree than that required for award of the Distinguished Service Cross, must nevertheless have been performed with marked distinction.

Legion of Merit. Established by Congress on July 20, 1942, and awarded to individuals who have distinguished themselves by exceptionally meritorious conduct in the performance of outstanding services. There are different designs depending on the level of command of the award recipient.

Distinguished Flying Cross. Established by Congress July 2, 1926, and awarded for heroism or extraordinary achievement while participating in aerial flight. Awards are made only to recognize single acts of heroism or extraordinary achievement, not sustained operational activities against an armed enemy. Initial awards were given to persons who made record breaking long distance and endurance flights or who set altitude records. The first DFC was awarded to Cpt. Charles A. Lindbergh on May 31, 1927, and DFCs were awarded retroactively to Orville and Wilbur Wright.

Soldier's Medal. Established by Congress July 2, 1926, to recognize acts of heroism not involving actual conflict with an enemy. The same degree of heroism is required as for the award of the Distinguished Flying Cross. The performance must have involved personal hazard or danger and the voluntary risk of life under conditions not involving conflict with an armed enemy. Awards are not made solely on the basis of having saved a life.

Bronze Star. Established by Executive Order Feb. 4, 1944, largely to raise the morale of ground troops in WWII, on the recommendation of Gen. George C. Marshall. It is awarded to any person who, while serving in any capacity in or with the U.S. military, distinguishes himself or herself by heroic or meritorious achievement or service, not involving participation in aerial flight.

Purple Heart. The original Purple Heart, designated as the Badge of Military Merit, was established by Gen. George Washington on Aug. 7, 1782. Following the American Revolution, the badge fell into disuse until 1932, the 200th anniversary of Washington's birth. During WWII, the Order of the Purple Heart was awarded for both wounds received in action and for meritorious service; following the introduction of the Legion of Merit, it was awarded only for combat wounds. Today, the Purple Heart is awarded to any member of an armed force who, while serving with the U.S. Armed Services, has been wounded or killed, or who has died or may hereafter die after being wounded in action against an enemy of the U.S. or in an armed conflict in which the U.S. or friendly foreign forces are engaged; as the result of an act of any hostile foreign force; as a result of an international terrorist attack against the U.S. or a friendly foreign nation; as a result of military operations outside the U.S. as part of a peacekeeping force. Wounds must be inflicted by weapon fire while directly engaged in armed conflict, regardless of the fire causing the wound; or while held as a prisoner of war or while being taken captive.

Air Medal. Authorized by President Roosevelt on May 11, 1942, and awarded for heroism or meritorious achievement while participating in aerial flight. Awards may be made to recognize single acts of merit or heroism, or for meritorious service. Awards are not made to individuals who use air transportation solely for the purpose of moving from point to point in a combat zone.

Army Commendation. Established Dec. 18, 1945, and awarded for heroism, meritorious achievement or meritorious service. It may also be awarded to a member of the Armed Forces of a friendly foreign nation who distinguishes him or herself by an act of heroism, extraordinary achievement, or meritorious service which has been of mutual benefit to a friendly nation and the United States.

U.S. Military Awards in Selected Wars and Conflicts
Source: U.S. Army Human Resources Command, U.S. Dept. of Defense

AWARD	Civil War	WWI	WWII	Korea	Vietnam	Gulf War	OEF[1]	OIF[2]
Medal of Honor	1,522	124	464	131	245	0	0	1
Distinguished Service Cross	NA	6,430	4,434	723	846	0	1	3
Silver Star	NA	(3)	73,651	10,061	21,630	75	48	201
Legion of Merit	NA	NA	20,273	(3)	10,356	158	4	26
Distinguished Flying Cross	NA	NA	126,318	(3)	21,697	108	57	38
Soldier's Medal	NA	NA	12,485	581	5,402	43	17	75
Bronze Star (Total)[4]	NA	NA	395,379	30,358	719,960	27,967	11,945	41,429
Purple Heart	NA	NA	(3)	(3)	220,516	504	1,032	12,912
Air Medal (Total)[4]	NA	NA	1,166,471	0	1,039,124	6,399	3,161	9,162
Army Commendation (Total)[4]	NA	NA	0	0	837,036	81,979	18,114	118,502

(1) Operation Enduring Freedom (primarily Afghanistan). (2) Operation Iraqi Freedom. (3) Numbers for the individual decorations shown on these charts represent only those awards that were properly processed and reported to Headquarters, Department of the Army. The actual number of individual decorations awarded under combat conditions, when award approval authority is delegated to field commanders, cannot be stated with absolute certainty. These charts reflect the current statistics recorded by the Military Awards Branch, as of Sept. 30, 2006. (4) Includes awards for valor/heroism and for meritorious service or achievement.

Active Duty U.S. Military Personnel Strengths, Worldwide, 2006
Source: U.S. Dept. of Defense
(as of Mar. 31, 2006)

TOTAL WORLDWIDE[1]...... 1,378,963

U.S. TERRITORIES & SPEC. LOCATIONS

U.S., 48 contiguous states	881,346
Alaska	19,579
Hawaii	34,167
Guam	2,931
Puerto Rico	198
Transients	44,576
Afloat	101,722
Regional Total[2]	**1,084,552**

OTHER WESTERN HEMISPHERE

Canada	143
Cuba (Guantánamo)	982
Honduras	432
Afloat	28
Regional Total[2]	**2,115**

FORMER SOVIET UNION

Total	140

EUROPE

Belgium	1,379
Bosnia and Herzegovina	255
Germany	65,917
Greece	403
Iceland	1,089
Italy	11,257
Netherlands	567
Portugal	980
Serbia (incl. Kosovo)	1,844
Spain	1,591
Turkey	1,734
United Kingdom	10,525
Afloat	1,727
Regional Total[2]	**99,875**

SUB-SAHARAN AFRICA

Djibouti	1,462
Regional Total[2]	**1,756**

EAST ASIA & PACIFIC

Australia	135
Japan	33,969
Korea, South	30,506
Philippines	126
Singapore	171
Thailand	114
Afloat	15,073
Regional Total[2]	**80,254**

NORTH AFRICA, NEAR EAST, & SOUTH ASIA*

Afghanistan[3]	23,200
Bahrain	1,415
Diego Garcia	808
Egypt	392
Iraq[3]	170,700
Qatar	395
Saudi Arabia	261
Afloat	363
Regional Total[2, 3]	**197,939**

*Special Forces personnel involved in Operation Enduring Freedom in Afghanistan not reported by Dept. of Defense. (1) Total worldwide also includes undistributed personnel. (2) Most countries and areas with fewer than 100 assigned U.S. military members not listed; regional totals include personnel stationed in those countries and areas not shown. (3) Rounded strengths for OEF/OIF deployment; includes troops in surrounding areas and deployed Reserve/National Guard.

Monthly Military Pay Scale[1]
Source: U.S. Dept. of Defense
(effective Jan. 1, 2006)

Years of Service: Grade	<2	2	3	4	6	8	10	12	14	16	18	20	22	24	26
Commissioned officers															
O-10	NA	NA	NA	NA	NA	NA	NA	NA	NA	NA	NA	$13,365	$13,430	$13,710	$14,196
O-9	NA	NA	NA	NA	NA	NA	NA	NA	NA	NA	NA	11,690	11,858	12,101	12,526
O-8	$8,271	$8,542	$8,722	$8,772	$8,996	$9,371	$9,458	$9,814	$9,916	$10,223	$10,666	11,075	11,349	11,349	11,349
O-7	6,873	7,192	7,340	7,457	7,670	7,880	8,123	8,365	8,608	9,371	10,016	10,016	10,016	10,016	10,067
O-6	5,094	5,596	5,963	5,963	5,986	6,243	6,277	6,277	6,633	7,264	7,634	8,004	8,215	8,428	8,841
O-5	4,247	4,784	5,115	5,177	5,384	5,507	5,779	5,979	6,236	6,631	6,818	7,004	7,214	7,214	7,214
O-4	3,664	4,241	4,524	4,588	4,850	5,132	5,482	5,756	5,945	6,054	6,118	6,118	6,118	6,118	6,118
O-3	3,221	3,652	3,942	4,298	4,503	4,729	4,875	5,116	5,241	5,241	5,241	5,241	5,241	5,241	5,241
O-2	2,783	3,170	3,651	3,774	3,852	3,852	3,852	3,852	3,852	3,852	3,852	3,852	3,852	3,852	3,852
O-1	2,416	2,515	3,040	3,040	3,040	3,040	3,040	3,040	3,040	3,040	3,040	3,040	3,040	3,040	3,040
Commissioned officers with over 4 years' active duty service as enlisted member or warrant officer															
O-3E	NA	NA	NA	$4,298	$4,503	$4,729	$4,875	$5,116	$5,318	$5,435	$5,593	$5,593	$5,593	$5,593	$5,593
O-2E	NA	NA	NA	3,774	3,852	3,975	4,181	4,342	4,461	4,461	4,461	4,461	4,461	4,461	4,461
O-1E	NA	NA	NA	3,040	3,246	3,366	3,489	3,609	3,774	3,774	3,774	3,774	3,774	3,774	3,774
Warrant officers															
W-5	NA	NA	NA	NA	NA	NA	NA	NA	NA	NA	NA	$5,720	$5,916	$6,113	$6,311
W-4	$3,329	$3,581	$3,684	$3,785	$3,959	$4,131	$4,306	$4,476	$4,652	$4,927	5,104	5,276	5,455	5,631	5,811
W-3	3,040	3,167	3,296	3,339	3,476	3,632	3,837	4,040	4,256	4,418	4,580	4,649	4,721	4,877	5,033
W-2	2,674	2,827	2,960	3,057	3,141	3,370	3,545	3,674	3,801	3,888	3,962	4,101	4,239	4,379	4,379
W-1	2,361	2,555	2,684	2,768	2,990	3,125	3,244	3,377	3,465	3,545	3,675	3,773	3,773	3,773	3,773
Enlisted members															
E-9	NA	NA	NA	NA	NA	NA	$4,022	$4,113	$4,228	$4,364	$4,499	$4,718	$4,902	$5,097	$5,394
E-8	NA	NA	NA	NA	NA	$3,293	3,438	3,528	3,636	3,753	3,965	4,072	4,254	4,355	4,604
E-7	$2,289	$2,498	$2,594	$2,721	$2,819	2,990	3,085	3,180	3,350	3,436	3,516	3,566	3,733	3,841	4,114
E-6	1,980	2,178	2,274	2,368	2,465	2,685	2,771	2,865	2,949	2,978	2,999	2,999	2,999	2,999	2,999
E-5	1,814	1,935	2,029	2,125	2,274	2,402	2,497	2,527	2,527	2,527	2,527	2,527	2,527	2,527	2,527
E-4	1,663	1,748	1,843	1,936	2,018	2,018	2,018	2,018	2,018	2,018	2,018	2,018	2,018	2,018	2,018
E-3	1,501	1,596	1,692	1,692	1,692	1,692	1,692	1,692	1,692	1,692	1,692	1,692	1,692	1,692	1,692
E-2	1,427	1,427	1,427	1,427	1,427	1,427	1,427	1,427	1,427	1,427	1,427	1,427	1,427	1,427	1,427
E-1 >4.	1,274	1,274	1,274	1,274	1,274	1,274	1,274	1,274	1,274	1,274	1,274	1,274	1,274	1,274	1,274
E-1 <4.	1,178	NA	NA	NA	NA	NA	NA	NA	NA	NA	NA	NA	NA	NA	NA

NA = not applicable. (1) Basic pay is limited for O-7 to O-10 to $12,667 per month, and for O-6 and below to $11,158 per month. (2) E-1>4 = E-1 grade personnel with 4 or more months service. E-1<4 = E-1 grade personnel with less than 4 months service.

Casualties in Principal Wars of the U.S.

Source: U.S. Dept. of Defense, U.S. Coast Guard

Data prior to World War I are based on incomplete records in many cases. Casualty data are confined to dead and wounded personnel and, therefore, exclude personnel captured or missing in action who were subsequently returned to military control. Dash (—) indicates information is not available. off. = officers.

WAR / Branch of service	Number serving	Battle deaths	Other deaths	Wounds not mortal[7]	Total[13]
Revolutionary War . . . . Total	—	4,435	—	6,188	10,623
1775-83 Army	184,000	4,044	—	6,004	10,048
Navy	to	342	—	114	456
Marines	250,000	49	—	70	119
War of 1812 . . . . Total	286,730[8]	2,260	—	4,505	6,765
1812-15 Army	—	1,950	—	4,000	5,950
Navy	—	265	—	439	704
Marines	—	45	—	66	111
Mexican War . . . . Total	78,789[8]	1,733	11,550	4,152	17,435
1846-48 Army	—	1,721	11,550	4,102	17,373
Navy	—	1	—	3	4
Marines	—	11	—	47	58
Coast Guard[12]	71 off.	—	—	—	—
Civil War					
Union forces . . . . Total	2,213,363[8]	140,415	224,097	281,881	646,392
1861-65 Army	2,128,948	138,154	221,374	280,040	639,568
Navy	—	2,112	2,411	1,710	6,233
Marines	84,415	148	312	131	591
Confederate forces . . . . Total	—	74,524	59,297	—	133,821
(estimate)[1] Army	600,000	—	—	—	—
1863-66 Navy	to	—	—	—	—
Marines	1,500,000	—	—	—	—
Coast Guard[12]	219 off.	1	—	—	1
Spanish-American War . . . . Total	307,420	385	2,061	1,662	4,108
1898 Army[3]	280,564	369	2,061	1,594	4,024
Navy	22,875	10	0	47	57
Marines	3,321	6	0	21	27
Coast Guard[12]	660	0	—	—	—
World War I . . . . Total	4,743,826	53,513	63,195	204,002	320,710
April 6, 1917 - Nov. 11, 1918 Army[4]	4,057,101	50,510	55,868	193,663	300,041
Navy	599,051	431	6,856	819	8,106
Marines	78,839	2,461	390	9,520	12,371
Coast Guard	8,835	111	81	—	192
World War II . . . . Total	16,353,659	292,131	115,185	671,846	1,079,162
Dec. 7, 1941 - Dec. 31, 1946[2] Army[5]	11,260,000	234,874	83,400	565,861	884,135
Navy[6]	4,183,466	36,950	25,664	37,778	100,392
Marines	669,100	19,733	4,778	68,207	91,718
Coast Guard	241,093	574	1,343	—	1,917
Korean War[9] . . . . Total	5,764,143	33,667	3,249	103,284	140,200
June 25, 1950 - July 27, 1953 Army	2,834,000	27,709	2,452	77,596	107,757
Navy	1,177,000	493	160	1,576	2,226
Marines	424,000	4,267	339	23,744	28,353
Air Force	1,285,000	1,198	298	368	1,864
Coast Guard	44,143	—	—	—	—
Vietnam War[10] . . . . Total	8,752,000	47,393	10,800	153,363	211,556
Aug. 4, 1964 - Jan. 27, 1973 Army	4,368,000	30,929	7,272	96,802	135,003
Navy	1,842,000	1,631	931	4,178	6,740
Marines	794,000	13,085	1,753	51,392	66,230
Air Force	1,740,000	1,741	842	931	3,514
Coast Guard	8,000	7	2	60	69
Persian Gulf War . . . . Total	467,939[11]	148	151	467	766
1991 Army	246,682	98	105	—	203
Navy	98,852	6	14	—	20
Marines	71,254	24	26	—	50
Air Force	50,751	20	6	—	26
Coast Guard	400	—	—	—	—
Iraq War[14] . . . . Total	269,363[15]	2,099	542	19,945	22,586
Mar. 19, 2003-Sept. 2, 2006 Army	99,664[15]	1,406	388	12,883	27,340
Navy	61,018[15]	36	19	434	489
Marines	66,166[15]	644	123	6,390	7,646
Air Force	42,515[15]	13	12	230	255
Coast Guard	1,250[15]	1	—	—	1

(1) Authoritative statistics for the Confederate forces are not available. An estimated 26,000-31,000 Confederate personnel died in Union prisons. (2) Data are for Dec. 1, 1941, through Dec. 31, 1946, when hostilities were officially terminated by presidential proclamation; few battle deaths or wounds not mortal were incurred after Japanese acceptance of Allied peace terms on Aug. 14, 1945. Numbers serving Dec. 1, 1941-Aug. 31, 1945, were: Total—14,903,213; Army—10,420,000; Navy—3,883,520; Marine Corps—599,693. (3) Number serving covers the period April 21-Aug. 13, 1898, while dead and wounded data are for the period May 1-Aug. 31, 1898. Active hostilities ceased on Aug. 13, 1898, but ratifications of the treaty of peace were not exchanged between the U.S. and Spain until April 11, 1899. (4) Includes Army Air Forces battle deaths and wounds not mortal, as well as casualties suffered by American forces in northern Russia to Aug. 25, 1919, and in Siberia to April 1, 1920. Other deaths covered the period April 1, 1917-Dec. 31, 1918. (5) Includes Army Air Forces. (6) Battle deaths and wounds not mortal include casualties incurred in Oct. 1941 due to hostile action. (7) For Iraq War, World War II, the Spanish-American War, and prior wars represent the number of individuals wounded, whereas all other data in this column represent the total number (incidence) of wounds. (8) As reported by Commissioner of Pensions in his Annual Report for Fiscal Year 1903. (9) As a result of an ongoing Dept. of Defense review of available Korean War casualty record information, updates to previously reported figures for battle deaths and other deaths are reflected in this table. (10) Number serving covers the period Aug. 4, 1964-Jan. 27, 1973 (date of ceasefire). Includes casualties incurred in Mayaguez incident. Wounds not mortal exclude 150,332 persons not requiring hospital care. (11) Estimated. (12) Includes the U.S. Revenue Cutter Services, predecessor to the U.S. Coast Guard. (13) Totals do not include categories for which no data are listed. (14) Including deaths from May 1, 2003 (declared end of major combat) through Sept. 2, 2006. Military deaths through Apr. 30, 2003 only totaled 115 combat-related and 23 other. As of Sept. 2, 2006, there were 2,641 total military deaths. (15) Number serving figures for the Iraq War are current as of Mar. 31, 2003, and do not include numbers of troops deployed since then. **NOTE:** As of Sept. 2, 2006, there have been 328 military deaths in Op. Enduring Freedom, mostly in Afghanistan and the Persian Gulf area.

Homeland Security

On Nov. 25, 2002, Pres. George W. Bush signed a measure creating a cabinet-level **Department of Homeland Security (DHS)**. It became operational on Jan. 24, 2003, headed by Sec. Tom Ridge, a former Pennsylvania governor (1995-2001). On Feb. 15, 2005, Michael Chertoff, a federal judge, replaced Ridge becoming the 2nd DHS secretary.

The main **objectives** of the DHS are to prevent terrorist attacks within the U.S., reduce the vulnerability to attacks, and minimize the effects of such attacks should they occur. The DHS is responsible for border and transportation security, protecting critical infrastructure, coordinating emergency response activities, and overseeing research and development for homeland security efforts. The new department also responds to natural disasters.

Following the attacks of Sept. 11, 2001, Pres. Bush created a small-scale advisory office known as the Office of Homeland Security. When a congressional inquiry in the summer of 2002 revealed extensive failures in intelligence gathering and communication, sentiment grew in favor of creating a large agency that could coordinate anti-terrorism efforts. The final plan passed by Congress in Nov. 2002 called for the integration of 22 federal agencies from many different departments.

The DHS is organized into 5 directorates: Border and Transportation Security, Emergency Preparedness, Science and Technology, Information Analysis and Infrastructure Protection, and Management, the administrative arm of the department. The U.S. Coast Guard, Secret Service, and Bureau of Citizenship and Immigration Services (formerly part of the INS) became part of DHS as discrete entities, separate from the directorates. The fiscal year 2007 budget for DHS was $42.7 billion.

Emergency Preparedness

In Feb. 2003, the DHS launched its public service "Ready" campaign in association with the Ad Council and the Sloan Foundation. People are advised to take 3 steps.

1. Make a Kit.

Make a home emergency supply kit with at least 3 days' worth of essential provisions for "sheltering-in-place," and assemble a lightweight version in case evacuation is necessary. Kits should include 1 gallon of water per person per day. Provide enough easily prepared canned or dried foods, warm clothes and sleeping bags.

Kits should contain a first-aid kit, flashlight, battery-powered or hand crank radio, extra batteries, a whistle, local maps, toiletries, and any needed medical prescriptions. They should include a filter mask (available in hardware stores) or other covering to use as a filter when breathing. Duct tape and heavy-duty garbage bags or plastic sheeting should be available in case it is necessary to seal windows and doors.

2. Make a Plan.

Form a communication plan, with designated contacts for each family member. Provisions should be made both for staying in place and for evacuating.

Shelter-in-place. Designate in advance an interior room, or one with the fewest windows and doors, for shelter. In an emergency, if there is heavy debris in the air or authorities deem the air contaminated, close windows, doors, vents, and fireplace dampers, and turn off air conditioners, forced-air heating systems, exhaust fans, and clothes dryers. Take family members and emergency supplies to a selected room and seal doors and windows as needed. Follow TV or radio broadcasts, or the Internet, for further instructions.

Evacuation. Create an evacuation plan with a specific meeting place for family members. Keep at least half a tank of gas in the car at all times, and learn alternate driving routes, as well as alternate means of transportation in your area. If the air is contaminated, drive with the windows and vents closed and keep the air conditioning or heater off.

Work and School. Talk to schools and employers about emergency plans and how they will communicate with families in emergencies.

3. Be Informed.

What to do depends partly on the nature of the threat.

Biological Threat. If a biological danger is reported, keep in contact with the media for news and advice. If you become aware of a release of an unknown substance nearby, get away and cover your mouth and nose with layers of fabric that can filter the air but still allow breathing. Wash with soap and water, and seek medical attention.

Chemical Threat. In the event of a chemical attack, leave the contaminated area immediately, if you can safely do so. Signs of a chemical attack in the area may include people with symptoms such as watery eyes, twitching, choking, difficulty breathing, or loss of coordination. Listen to news reports. If you believe you may have been exposed to a chemical agent, remove clothes promptly and wash with soap and water. Do not scrub chemical into skin. Be sure to seek medical attention.

Explosions. If there is an explosion, take shelter from the blast under a desk or table. Leave the building or area when feasible; check for fire and never use elevators.

Nuclear Blast. In case of a nuclear blast, take cover immediately, preferably below ground. Decide whether to shelter in-place or evacuate; bear in mind that the more shielding and distance between you and the blast, and the less time of exposure, the more you reduce your risk.

For Further Information.

FEMA publishes a handbook, *Are You Ready? A Guide to Citizen Preparedness*, which can be obtained electronically at www.fema.gov/areyouready, or in print by calling 1-800-480-2520. You can also visit www.ready.gov or call 1-800-BE-READY.

Security Advisories

The Homeland Security Advisory System, established on Mar. 12, 2002, indicates the estimated threat level for a terrorist attack in the U.S.; state and local authorities may have separate alert systems and criteria.

Low (Green) Governments should refine and exercise pre-planned protective measures and train personnel, assess and update vulnerabilities, and take steps to reduce them.

Guarded (Blue) In addition to the above, authorities should check communications with emergency response and command locations, review emergency response procedures, and provide public information as needed.

Elevated (Yellow) Authorities should also increase surveillance of critical locations, coordinate emergency plans with nearby jurisdictions, implement response plans as appropriate.

High (Orange) Authorities should coordinate with federal, state, and local law enforcement agencies, or National Guard or other armed service; take additional precautions at public events, including possible cancellation; prepare to execute contingency procedures and move to alternate locations; restrict access to threatened facilities.

Severe (Red) Authorities should increase or redirect personnel to address critical emergency needs; assign or pre-position emergency response and specialty teams; monitor, redirect, or limit access to transportation systems; close public and government facilities.

As of Oct. 2, 2006, the national threat level had reached "high" 5 times: Sept. 10-24, 2002, around the anniversary of Sept. 11; Feb. 7-27, 2003, based on threats of attacks during the Haj pilgrimage in Mecca; Mar. 17-Apr. 16, 2003, during the beginning of the Iraq War; May 20-30, following bombings in Saudi Arabia and Morocco and as a precaution for Memorial Day; and Dec. 21, 2003-Jan. 15, 2004, based on threats specific to the holiday season. Since Aug. 2004, the Dept. of Homeland Security has changed alert levels only for particular industry sectors or geographic locations. New intelligence information caused a rise from "elevated" to "high" for the financial section in New York City, northern New Jersey, and Washington, DC, for several months (Aug. 1-Nov. 10, 2004). In response to the London railway bombings, the administration raised threat levels to "high" for mass transit (July 7-Aug. 12, 2005). On Aug. 10, 2006, the administration raised threat levels to "severe" for the first time for flights originating in the U.K. bound for the U.S. This followed the arrest by British authorities of 21 individuals allegedly involved in a plot to detonate liquid explosives on board U.S.-bound commercial aircraft. The threat level was raised to "high" for all other commercial flights destined for or operating within the U.S. On Aug. 13, 2006, the threat level of U.S.-bound flights from the United Kingdom was lowered to "high." As of Sept. 2006, the rest of the nation was on "elevated" alert except for New York City, which has remained on "high" alert since the creation of the security advisory system.

World Almanac Quick Quiz

What do five of the world's top six arms suppliers for the period 1997-2004 have in common?

(a) They are all members of the European Union.

(b) They are all permanent members of the UN Security Council.

(c) They have the five largest economies in the world.

(d) They are the five most populous nations in the world.

For the answer look in this chapter, or see page 1008.

Directors of the Central Intelligence Agency

In 1942, Pres. Franklin D. Roosevelt established the Office of Strategic Services (OSS); it was disbanded in 1945. In 1946, Pres. Harry Truman established the Central Intelligence Group (CIG) to operate under the National Intelligence Authority (NIA). A 1947 law replaced the NIA with the National Security Council and the CIG with the Central Intelligence Agency.

Director	Served	Appointed by President	Director	Served	Appointed by President
Adm. Sidney W. Souers	1946	Truman	George H. W. Bush	1976-1977	Ford
Gen. Hoyt S. Vandenberg	1946-1947	Truman	Adm. Stansfield Turner	1977-1981	Carter
Adm. Roscoe H. Hillenkoetter	1947-1950	Truman	William J. Casey	1981-1987	Reagan
Gen. Walter Bedell Smith	1950-1953	Truman	William H. Webster	1987-1991	Reagan
Allen W. Dulles	1953-1961	Eisenhower	Robert M. Gates	1991-1993	Bush
John A. McCone	1961-1965	Kennedy	R. James Woolsey	1993-1995	Clinton
Adm. William F. Raborn Jr.	1965-1966	Johnson	John M. Deutch	1995-1997	Clinton
Richard Helms	1966-1973	Johnson	George J. Tenet	1997-2004	Clinton
James R. Schlesinger	1973	Nixon	Porter Goss	2004-2006	Bush
William E. Colby	1973-1976	Nixon	Gen. Michael V. Hayden[*]	2006-	Bush

*Took office May 30, 2006.

Nations with Largest Armed Forces, by Active-Duty Troop Strength[1,2]

Source: *The Military Balance. 2005-06* (International Institute for Strategic Studies, published by Routledge Journals, Taylor Francis, UK)

	Troop strength				Navy		Combat aircraft	
	Active troops (thousands)	Reserve troops (thousands)	Defense expend. ($ bil)	Tanks (MBT) (army only)	Cruisers/ Frigates/ Destroyers	Sub-marines	FGA	Fighters (air force only)
1. China	2,255	800	62.5	7,580+	42F/21D	69	1,169	1,252
2. United States	1,474	1,291	465.0	7,620+	27C/30F/49D*	80	1,382	865
3. India	1,325	1,155	19.6	3,978	17F/8D*	19	380	386
4. N. Korea	1,106	4,700	5.5	3,500+	3F	88	211	299
5. Russia	1,037	20,000	61.9	22,800+	6C/19F*	54	757	1,094
6. S. Korea	688	4,500	20.7[2]	2,330	9F/6D	20	283	210
7. Pakistan	619	—	3.3	2,461+	7F	11	51+	143
8. Turkey	515	379	10.1	4,205	19F	13	358	87
9. Vietnam	484	3-4,000	3.5[2]	1,315	6F	2	—	204
10. Egypt	469	479	3.5	3,855	10F/1D	4	223	218
11. Myanmar	428	—	6.9[2]	150	—	—	22	58
12. Iran	420	350	4.4[2]	1,613+	3F	3	102	153
13. Syria	308	354	1.7[2]	4,600	2F	—	136	390
14. Thailand	307	200	2.0[2]	333	12F*	—	87 FGA/FTR	
15. Brazil	303	1,340	9.2	178	14F*	4	33	57
16. Indonesia	302	400	7.6	—	13F	2	18	26
17. Taiwan	290	1,654	8.3[2]	926+	21F/11D	4	128	293
18. Germany	285	359	37.7	2,398	14F	13	145	12
19. France	255	22	51.6	926	20F/12D*	10	137	32
20. Japan	240	44	44.7[2]	980	9F/44D*	16	130	150
21. Colombia	207	61	3.9	—	—	4	17+	—
22. United Kingdom	206	273	49.6	543	20F/11D	15	74	128
23. Eritrea	202	120	74 mil[2]	150	—	—	—	13
24. Morocco	201	150	2.1[2]	540	3F	—	—	66
25. Saudi Arabia	200	—	21.3[2]	1,055	7F	—	—	191
26. Mexico	193	300	2.8	—	10F/1D	—	17	10
27. Italy	192	57	30.5	320	12F/2D*	6	79	52
28. Ukraine	188	1,000	6.0	3,784	1C/2F	1	187	280
29. Ethiopia	183	—	229 mil[2]	250+	—	—	15	31
30. Israel	168	408	9.68	3,657	—	3	177+	199

— = not available. MBT = main battle tank. FGA = fighter, ground attack. *Denotes navies with aircraft carriers, as follows: United States 12, United Kingdom 3, France 2, India 1, Italy 1, Russia 1, Brazil 1, Thailand 1. (1) All figures are for Aug. 2005, except Defense Expenditure, which is for 2004, unless otherwise noted. Iraq's security forces were estimated to be about 180,000 at this time but were not a fully developed military force. (2) 2005 budget.

Nuclear Arms Treaties and Negotiations: A Historical Overview

Aug. 5, 1963—Limited Test Ban Treaty signed in Moscow by U.S., USSR, and Britain; prohibited testing of nuclear weapons in space, above ground, and under water.

Jan. 27, 1967—Outer Space Treaty banned the introduction of other weapons of mass destruction in space.

July 1, 1968—Nuclear Nonproliferation Treaty, with U.S., USSR, and Great Britain as major signers, limited spread of nuclear material for military purposes by agreement not to help nonnuclear nations get or make nuclear weapons. In 1995, the treaty was extended indefinitely. As of Sept. 2006, 188 countries had signed the treaty; Israel, India, and Pakistan were not signatories. In Jan. 2003, N. Korea withdrew from the treaty.

May 26, 1972—Strategic Arms Limitation Treaty (SALT I) signed in Moscow by U.S. and USSR. This short-term agreement imposed a 5-year freeze on both testing and deployment of intercontinental ballistic missiles (ICBMs) as well as submarine-launched ballistic missiles (SLBMs). In the area of defensive nuclear weapons, the separate **ABM Treaty,** signed on the same occasion, limited antiballistic missiles to 2 sites of 100 antiballistic missile launchers in each country (amended in 1974 to 1 site in each country).

July 3, 1974—ABM Treaty Revision (protocol on antiballistic missile systems) and **Threshold Test Ban Treaty** on limiting underground testing of nuclear weapons to 150 kilotons were signed by the U.S. and USSR in Moscow.

Sept. 1977—The U.S. and USSR agreed to continue to abide by **SALT I,** despite its expiration date.

June 18, 1979—SALT II, signed in Vienna by the U.S. and USSR, constrained offensive nuclear weapons, limiting each side to 2,400 missile launchers and heavy bombers; ceiling to apply until Jan. 1, 1985. Treaty also set a subceiling of 1,320 ICBMs and SLBMs with multiple warheads on each side. SALT II never reached the Senate floor for ratification because Pres. Jimmy Carter withdrew support following Dec. 1979 Soviet invasion of Afghanistan.

Dec. 8, 1987—Intermediate-Range Nuclear Forces (INF) Treaty signed in Washington, DC, by U.S. and USSR, eliminating all U.S. and Soviet intermediate- and shorter-range nuclear missiles from Europe and Asia. Ratified, with conditions, by U.S. Senate May 27, 1988, by USSR June 1, 1988. Entered into force June 1, 1988.

July 31, 1991—Strategic Arms Reduction Treaty (START I) signed in Moscow by USSR and U.S. to reduce strategic offensive arms by about 30% in 3 phases over 7 years. START I was the first treaty to mandate reductions by the superpowers. Treaty was approved by U.S. Senate Oct. 1, 1992.

With the Soviet Union breakup in Dec. 1991, 4 former Soviet republics became independent nations with strategic nuclear weapons—Russia, Ukraine, Kazakhstan, and Belarus. The last 3 agreed in principle in 1992 to transfer their nuclear weapons to Russia and ratify START I. The Russian Supreme Soviet voted to ratify, Nov. 4, 1992, but Russia decided not to provide instruments of ratification until the other 3 republics ratified START I and acceded to the Nuclear Nonproliferation Treaty (NPT) as nonnuclear nations. By late 1994, all 3 nations had done so, and NPT entered into force on Dec. 5, 1994.

Jan. 3, 1993—START II signed in Moscow by U.S. and Russia, called for both sides to reduce their long-range nuclear arsenals to about one-third of their then-current levels within a decade and disable and dismantle launching systems. The U.S. ratified START II Jan. 26, 1996; Russia ratified it Apr. 13, 2000. On Sept. 26, 1997, the U.S. and Russia signed an agreement that would delay the dismantling of launching systems under START II to the end of 2007.

Sept. 24, 1996—Comprehensive Test Ban Treaty (CTBT), signed by U.S. and Russia. The CTBT banned all nuclear weapons tests and other nuclear explosions. It was intended to help prevent the nuclear powers from developing more advanced weapons, while limiting the ability of other states to acquire such devices. As of Sept. 2006, the CTBT had been signed by 176 nations, including China, Russia, the U.S., the U.K., and France. It has been ratified by 135, including France, Russia, and the U.K., but not the U.S. or China. Enters into force after 44 nuclear-capable states ratify it. As of Sept. 25, 2006, only 34 of the 44 had done so.

Sept. 1997—ABM Treaty amended to allow greater flexibility in development of shorter-range nuclear weapons.

May 24, 2002—Nuclear Arms Reduction Pact (Treaty of Moscow) signed by U.S. and Russia in Moscow, committed both countries to cutting nuclear arsenals to 1,700 to 2,200 warheads each, down from about 6,000, by 2012. No intermediate timetable established, but joint committee set up for monitoring implementation; either side allowed to back out with 90 days notice. Ratified by U.S. Senate, Mar. 6, 2003.

June 2002—U.S. formally withdrew from the **ABM Treaty,** effective June 13, with the intent of developing a defensive missile system. Russia, June 14, announced its withdrawal from **START II,** stating that U.S. withdrawal from the ABM Treaty effectively invalidated START II.

April 13, 2005—International Convention for the Suppression of Acts of Nuclear Terrorism adopted unanimously by UN General Assembly, provides legal basis for international cooperation in the event of terrorist act involving nuclear material. As of Oct. 3, 2006, 107 countries have signed and 7 have ratified the convention, which will go into force after 22 nations have ratified it.

Leading Purchasers of U.S. Defense Articles and Services

Source: Congressional Research Service

(in current U.S. dollars)

Worldwide Deliveries[1]

1997-2000		2001-04	
1. Saudi Arabia	$16.0 billion	1. Egypt	$5.3 billion
2. Taiwan	7.7 billion	2. Saudi Arabia	4.7 billion
3. Israel	3.8 billion	3. Japan	4.2 billion
4. South Korea	3.5 billion	4. Taiwan	4.0 billion
5. Turkey	3.4 billion	5. Israel	3.6 billion
6. Egypt	3.2 billion	6. Greece	3.4 billion
7. Japan	2.6 billion	7. South Korea	2.6 billion
8. Finland	2.5 billion	8. U.K.	2.4 billion
9. Greece	2.1 billion	9. Italy	1.6 billion
10. U.K.	1.8 billion	10. Turkey	1.6 billion

(1) Total dollar value of all U.S. defense articles and services actually delivered to top 10 purchasers worldwide. Figures include government-to-government sales through the Foreign Military Sales (FMS) system (which accounts for the overwhelming majority of U.S. conventional arms deliveries) concluded in calendar years listed, as well as commercially licensed exports concluded in pertinent fiscal years.

Arms Deliveries to Near East, by Supplier, 1997-2004[1]

Source: Congressional Research Service

(in millions of current U.S. dollars)

Destination	Total	U.S.	Russia	China	Major West European[2]	All other European	All others
Saudi Arabia	$54,700	$20,700	$0	$0	$31,000	$3,000	$0
U.A.E.	11,600	1,000	600	0	9,000	1,000	0
Egypt	9,700	8,500	600	300	200	0	100
Israel	8,400	7,100	0	0	1,000	100	200
Kuwait	4,400	2,400	100	400	1,200	100	200
Iran	2,400	0	1,100	500	100	400	300
Algeria	1,800	100	600	200	$0	800	100
Qatar	1,800	0	0	0	1,800	0	0
Yemen	1,100	0	400	100	200	300	100
Jordan	1,000	600	0	0	100	100	200
Bahrain	900	900	0	0	0	0	0
Morocco	900	200	0	0	200	200	300
Syria	800	0	400	0	100	100	200
Libya	600	0	100	0	0	200	300
Oman	500	100	0	0	300	0	100
Iraq	200	0	0	0	0	100	100
Lebanon	200	100	0	0	100	0	0
Tunisia	100	100	0	0	0	0	0

(1) Figures for all supplies except U.S. represent government-to-government sales. U.S. figures include sales through the government-to-government Foreign Military Sales (FMS) system (which accounts for the overwhelming majority of U.S. conventional arms transfer agreements and deliveries), as well as the licensed commercial export system. (2) Major West European includes France, United Kingdom, Germany, and Italy totals as an aggregate figure.

Defense Contracts, 2005

Source: U.S. Dept. of Defense

(in thousands of dollars)

Listed are the 50 companies or organizations receiving the largest dollar volume of prime contract awards from the U.S. Dept. of Defense during fiscal year 2005.

Company	Total[1]	Company	Total[1]
Lockheed Martin	$19,447,131	Renco Group	$1,406,264
Boeing	18,317,887	Fedex Corp	1,369,725
Northrop Grumman	13,512,356	Stewart & Stevenson	1,295,813
General Dynamics	10,640,762	Alliant Techsystems	1,274,541
Raytheon	9,109,329	Bell Boeing Joint Program	1,204,290
Halliburton	5,827,623	Booz Allen Hamilton	1,162,990
Bae Systems Plc	5,582,581	N.V. Koninklijke Nederlandsche	1,069,504
United Technologies	5,021,703	Exxon Mobil	1,046,077
L-3 Communications Holding	4,713,814	Amerisourcebergen	1,020,843
Computer Sciences	2,827,727	Evergreen International Airlines	985,088
Science Applications Intl.	2,795,942	Anteon International	938,637
Itt Industries	2,493,318	Washington Group International	879,146
Humana	2,260,685	Engineered Support Systems	769,274
General Electric	2,196,664	Cardinal Health	765,863
Health Net	2,031,991	Caci International	764,655
Triwest Healthcare Alliance	1,803,646	Rockwell Collins	759,010
Textron	1,599,949	Harris	736,701
Urs	1,522,958	Mckesson Delaware	686,451
Gm Gdls Defense Group	1,513,312	Massachusetts Institute Of Tech	611,330
Honeywell International	1,504,768	Aerospace	611,298
B P Plc	1,502,106	Mitre	585,391
Bechtel Group	1,486,860	Dell	583,606
Oshkosh Truck	1,473,876	General Atomic Technologies Co	573,641
Electronic Data Systems	1,450,518	A P Moller Gruppen	572,383
Public Warehousing	1,425,343	Valero Energy	564,413

(1) Totals include subsidiaries of each company.

Arms Transfer Agreements with the World, by Supplier, 1997-2004

Source: Congressional Research Service

(in millions of current U.S. dollars)

Supplier	1997	1998	1999	2000	2001	2002	2003	2004	1997-2004
United States	$7,069	$9,555	$11,805	$17,705	$11,639	$13,175	$14,570	$12,391	$97,909
Russia	3,500	2,500	4,200	6,300	5,500	5,700	4,200	6,100	38,000
France	1,300	6,100	1,700	4,300	4,000	1,200	600	4,800	24,000
Germany	600	5,000	4,400	1,200	1,200	900	2,700	200	16,200
United Kingdom	1,000	2,000	1,400	600	500	700	300	5,500	12,000
China	1,300	700	3,100	500	1,000	400	300	600	7,900
Italy	300	600	700	200	1,100	300	600	600	4,400
All other European	1,600	1,900	5,800	4,200	3,200	4,400	2,900	4,300	28,300
All others	800	1,300	2,000	2,300	2,500	2,400	1,300	2,500	15,100
TOTAL	$17,469	$29,655	$35,105	$37,305	$30,639	$29,175	$27,470	$36,991	$243,809

Note: All data are for the calendar year given, except for U.S. MAP (Military Assistance Program) and IMET (International Military Education and Training), excess defense articles, which are included for the particular fiscal year. All amounts given include the values of all categories of weapons and ammunition, military spare parts, military construction, excess defense articles, military assistance and training programs, and all associated services. Statistics for foreign countries are based upon estimated selling prices. All foreign data are rounded to the nearest $100 mil. The U.S. total in 2000 includes a $6.432 bil licensed commercial agreement with the United Arab Emirates for 80 F-16 aircraft.

HEALTH

Health News 2006

New Vaccine for Children

The Advisory Committee on Immunization Practices of the Centers for Disease Control and Prevention (CDC) Feb. 21, recommended that a vaccine developed to treat rotavirus be administered to all U.S. children. The recommendation came after the Food and Drug Administration (FDA) Feb. 3 approved the orally administered vaccine as a prevention measure against rotavirus infections, which infects nearly every child in the U.S. by age 5. These infections result in about 410,000 physician visits each year and direct and indirect costs of about $1 billion. The vaccine, called RotaTeq, was developed by drug manufacturer Merck & Co. Glaxo-SmithKline developed a vaccine for the same purpose, Rotarix, concurrently.

"Moderately Inactive" Outlive "Inactive"

A review by the European Prospective Investigation of Cancer (EPIC) of collected studies of the eating habits of more than 500,000 people in 10 European countries, found that people who were moderately inactive (sedentary job with up to 30 minutes of recreational activity per day or standing job with no recreational activity) had a 20% lower rate of death than people classified as inactive (sedentary job and no recreational activity)—equivalent to about three additional years of life for the moderately inactive group. (*International Journal of Epidemiology*, Aug. 2006)

Second-Hand Smoke

Surgeon General Richard Carmona June 27, released a report which found that secondhand tobacco smoke presented a "serious health hazard," and that evidence to that effect was "indisputable." The report found that secondhand smoke exposure increased nonsmokers' risk of developing lung cancer by 20% to 30%, and their chances of developing heart disease by 25% to 30%. Children were especially susceptible to ailments caused by secondhand smoke. An estimated 430 newborns died annually of smoke-caused sudden infant death syndrome (SIDS), according to the report. The report was an updated version of one first released in 1986.

Hospital Medication Errors

The Institute of Medicine (IOM), a federal health care policy advisory group, July 20, reported that medication errors caused an estimated 1.5 mil injuries annually in the U.S. The IOM report found that, on average, each hospitalized patient was exposed to one medication error per day. The IOM recommended that all health-care providers by 2010 institute electronic systems for doctors and pharmacists to use in prescribing and dispensing medications.

Inhaled Insulin Approved

The FDA Jan. 27, approved a form of inhaled insulin for use in treating diabetes. The approval of the drug heralded a potential sea change in the treatment of diabetes, a chronic disease estimated to afflict roughly 20 million people in the U.S.

The new form of insulin, sold under the brand name Exubera by Pfizer Inc., was produced in a powdered form. Exubera was administered with an inhaler roughly double the size of an eyeglass case, and absorbed into the body through the lungs. Some doctors said they believed an alternative to frequent, inconvenient insulin injections would encourage more diabetics to maintain healthy blood sugar levels.

Because of the concerns regarding the long-term use of Exubera, the FDA had not approved its use in children. Analysts predicted that the market for the drug could result in worldwide annual sales of $1.8 billion by 2010.

Cervical Cancer Vaccine

The FDA June 8, approved a vaccine that prevented the cause of most cases of cervical cancer, for use in women and girls aged nine to 26. The vaccine, Gardasil, prevented infection by four types of the sexually transmitted human papillomavirus (HPV), which caused an estimated 70% of cervical cancer cases, and 90% of genital warts cases. The vaccine was one of the most expensive ever created; Merck & Co., the vaccine's manufacturer, said a three-shot course of the vaccine would cost $360.

Autism Estimates Revised

The Centers for Disease Control and Prevention (CDC) May 4, released the results of two surveys which found that about 300,000 children in the U.S. suffered from autism. The figure roughly translated to 5.5 autism diagnoses per 1,000 school-aged children. They were the first comprehensive surveys of autism in children. The surveys also found that boys were four times more likely to have autism than girls. Autism was defined as a developmental disorder characterized by social, verbal and emotional difficulties.

FDA Panel Advises ADHD Drug Warnings

A FDA advisory panel Feb. 9, voted, 8-7, in favor of adding the agency's most serious label alert to several stimulant drugs commonly used to treat attention-deficit hyperactivity disorder (ADHD). These included methylphenidate drugs Ritalin, Methylin, Metadate and Concerta, and amphetamines Adderall and Adderall XR. The panel reportedly based its recommendations on reports of dozens of people taking ADHD drugs who had suffered sudden death or serious health problems. Several panel members also said their vote had been influenced by concerns that the drugs were being overprescribed in the U.S. The FDA approved label requirements for some of these drugs, including Ritalin, Aug. 21.

No Benefit Found in Low-Fat Diet for Older Women

A federal study published in the Feb. 8 issue of the *Journal of the American Medical Association* found that women who followed a low-fat diet for eight years experienced the same rate of various kinds of cancer, heart attacks and strokes as those women who ate uncontrolled diets. The results failed to support popularly held theories that a low-fat diet had a wide range of health benefits.

The study was the largest ever commissioned to examine the impact of a low-fat diet on the health of women, and was considered the most authoritative ever completed. Researchers had enrolled a total of 48,835 women aged 50 to 79 who had gone through menopause to participate in the study.

Some diet experts said that the study did not follow participants for a long-enough period of time to witness the benefits of a low-fat diet. Others said study participants had not lowered their fat intake enough.

Some experts also noted that the study did not differentiate between fats believed to be less healthy, such as trans fats, and healthier fats such as those found in olive oil.

No Benefit Found in Calcium Pills for Older Women

A study funded by the Women's Health Initiative, published in the Feb. 16 issue of the *New England Journal of Medicine*, found that women taking calcium and vitamin D supplements had only slightly increased their hip bone density. The supplements had been regarded by doctors as the best measure to prevent osteoporosis, a weakening of the bones common among the elderly, especially women over 50.

The study, which examined 36,282 women aged 50 to 79, found that the supplements offered no protection from colorectal cancer, and that those taking them were also at higher risk of kidney stones.

Avian Flu

Avian influenzas (also known as bird flu) are a group of viruses carried by birds. They are usually harmless in wild birds, but can be fatal to domesticated birds. The H5N1 subtype of the virus is the most deadly to humans, which has killed almost 60% of those infected. Symptoms include common flu ailments such as fever, cough, sore throat, or muscle aches, and can progress to pneumonia or acute respiratory distress. The human form of H5N1 was first reported in Hong Kong in 1997, where 18 people were hospitalized, 6 of whom died. According to the World Health Organization, between 2003 and Sept. 2006, out of a total of 251 people infected, more than half died: 51 in Indonesia, 42 in Vietnam, 17 in Thailand, 14 in China, 6 in Cambodia, 6 in Egypt, 5 in Azerbaijan, 4 in Turkey, and 2 in Iraq. Poultry workers in the U.S. and Canada have come down with other avian flu strains, but not H5N1.

In 2006, the WHO reported evidence of human-to-human spread. In this situation, 8 people in one family were infected. The first family member is thought to have become ill through contact with infected poultry. This person then infected six family members. Then one of those six people (a child) then infected another family member (his father). No further spread outside of the exposed family was documented or suspected. But because viruses like the H5N1 are constantly mutating, scientists worry the bird flu may merge with a common human influenza virus and spread rapidly. The WHO predicted in Sept. 2005 that such an outbreak could cause between 5 mil and 150 mil deaths. In the U.S. as many as 2 mil people could die. Risks are highest in affected agricultural areas or open-air markets where contact with sick chickens or their eggs is likely.

Public health officials around the world, in an effort to prevent the spread of H5N1, have exterminated millions of birds, including small flocks in the U.S, that may have been or had been exposed. In Feb. 2004, the U.S. Dept. of Agriculture issued a ban on poultry imports from affected Asian countries. The virus is resistant to some antiviral medications. However, neuraminidase inhibitors such as oseltamavir and zanamavir may be effective in fighting the flu.

In response to the new threat, Pres. George W. Bush announced in May 2006 a plan to stop or slow the spread of a possible pandemic into the U.S., and to limit the domestic spread of a pandemic (which may include quarantining). The U.S. government under the plan would follow the lead of the WHO, which would coordinate an international response to a potential outbreak. The plan also stipulated that the U.S. government could reroute international flights to a limited number of airports and restrict domestic travel if an outbreak were to occur. Also in May 2006, the U.S. Dept. of Health and Human Services awarded more than $1 bil to drug companies to develop new methods of quickly producing influenza vaccines.

Experimental vaccines showed promise in 2006. In one experiment, doctors vaccinated birds using weakened versions of H5N1. The vaccine was effective in protecting birds from infection; however, researchers do not know if it will produce adequate immunity in humans. In another experiment in 2006, a clinical trial involving 96 humans, half were given an experimental vaccine using the H9N2 strain of avian flu (a strain closely related to H5N1) combined with an immune-boosting substance called an adjuvant. The results showed a positive immune response in those given the vaccine, which may give researchers a better idea of how to develop a similar vaccine for H5N1.

Trends in Daily Use of Cigarettes, for U.S. 8th, 10th, and 12th Graders[1]

Source: *Monitoring the Future*, Univ. of Michigan Inst. for Social Research and National Inst. on Drug Abuse
(percent who smoked daily in last 30 days; change 2004-2005 in percentage points)

	8th grade						10th grade						12th grade					
	1995	2000	2003	2004	2005	'04-'05 change	1995	2000	2003	2004	2005	'04-'05 change	1995	2000	2003	2004	2005	'04-'05 change
TOTAL.........	9.3	7.4	4.5	4.4	4.0	−0.3	16.3	14.0	8.9	8.3	7.5	−0.7	21.6	20.6	15.8	15.6	13.6	−1.9
Sex																		
Male	9.2	7.0	4.4	4.3	3.9	−0.4	16.3	13.7	8.6	8.2	7.2	−1.0	21.7	20.9	17.0	15.4	14.6	−0.8
Female	9.2	7.5	4.5	4.3	4.0	−0.2	16.1	14.1	9.0	8.2	7.7	−0.5	20.8	19.7	14.0	15.0	11.9	−3.1
College plans																		
None or under 4 yrs........	22.5	21.7	16.1	15.4	14.4	−1.0	32.7	28.8	22.1	21.4	19.2	−2.2	33.7	31.7	27.9	26.9	24.9	−2.0
Complete 4 yrs..	7.5	5.6	3.2	3.1	2.9	−0.2	13.3	11.6	6.7	6.4	5.9	−0.5	17.4	16.6	12.1	12.2	10.5	−1.7
Region																		
Northeast	9.2	6.9	2.9	3.3	3.2	−0.1	15.8	14.1	8.6	8.5	7.6	−0.9	22.5	22.8	16.4	16.2	13.3	−2.8
North central...	11.0	9.0	5.5	5.7	4.8	−0.9	17.6	16.3	10.2	7.4	8.6	1.2	25.7	23.6	18.2	18.5	16.3	−2.3
South	9.4	7.8	5.7	4.7	5.0	0.3	19.3	15.7	10.1	11.0	8.8	−2.2	21.7	19.4	16.3	15.8	15.4	−0.4
West	7.0	4.9	2.4	3.3	2.4	−0.9	9.4	7.8	6.0	5.2	4.0	−1.2	14.5	16.9	11.8	10.1	7.6	−2.5
Race/Ethnicity[2]																		
White.........	10.5	9.0	5.3	4.7	4.6	−0.1	17.6	17.7	11.4	10.0	9.1	−0.9	23.9	25.7	19.5	18.3	17.1	−1.2
Black.........	2.8	3.2	2.9	2.7	2.1	−0.6	4.7	5.2	4.3	4.4	3.9	−0.5	6.1	8.0	5.4	5.2	5.6	0.5
Hispanic	9.2	7.1	3.7	3.5	3.1	−0.4	9.9	8.8	6.0	6.0	5.9	−0.1	11.6	15.7	8.0	8.2	7.7	−0.5

(1) Totals and percentage changes may not add up due to rounding. (2) For each of these groups, data for the specified year and previous year have been combined to increase sample size and thus provide a more reliable estimate.

Spending on Health in the 50 Most Populous Countries

Source: *The World Health Report 2006*, The World Health Organization

Country	As % of GDP	Per capita[1]	Country	As % of GDP	Per capita[1]	Country	As % of GDP	Per capita[1]	Country	As % of GDP	Per capita[1]
Afghanistan ..	6.5	$11	Germany	11.1	$3,204	Nepal	5.3	$12	Sudan.......	4.3	$21
Algeria	4.1	89	Ghana	4.5	16	Nigeria	5.0	22	Tanzania	4.3	12
Argentina	8.9	305	India........	4.8	27	North Korea ..	5.8	<1	Thailand.....	3.3	76
Bangladesh ..	3.4	14	Indonesia	3.1	30	Pakistan.....	2.4	13	Turkey	7.6	257
Brazil	7.6	212	Iran.........	6.5	131	Peru	4.4	98	Uganda	7.3	18
Canada......	9.9	2,669	Iraq.........	2.7	23	Philippines ...	3.2	31	Ukraine......	5.7	60
China	5.6	61	Italy........	8.4	2,139	Poland	6.5	354	United		
Colombia	7.6	138	Japan	7.9	2,662	Romania.....	6.1	159	Kingdom...	8.0	2,428
Congo, Dem.			Kenya.......	4.3	20	Russia.......	5.6	167	**United States**	**15.2**	**5,711**
Rep. of the .	4.0	4	Malaysia.....	3.8	163	Saudi Arabia..	4.0	366	Uzbekistan...	5.5	21
Egypt	5.8	55	Mexico	6.2	372	South Africa ..	8.4	295	Venezuela ...	4.5	146
Ethiopia	5.9	5	Morocco	5.1	72	South Korea ..	5.6	705	Vietnam	5.4	26
France	10.1	2,981	Myanmar	2.8	394	Spain	7.7	1,514	Yemen	5.5	32

(1) At average exchange rates.

Heart and Blood Vessel Disease

Sources: American Heart Association, 7272 Greenville Ave., Dallas, TX 75231-4596; phone: (800) 242-8721; Centers for Disease Control and Prevention; National Center for Health Statistics; National Institutes of Health; National Heart, Blood, and Lung Institute

Warning Signs

Of Heart Attack

- Chest discomfort. Most heart attacks involve discomfort in the center of the chest that lasts more than a few minutes, or that goes aways and comes back. It can feel like uncomfortable pressure, squeezing, fullness, or pain.
- Discomfort in other areas of the upper body. Symptoms can include pain or discomfort in one or both arms, the back, neck, jaw, or stomach.
- Shortness of breath. This feeling may occur with or without chest discomfort.
- Other signs: These may include breaking out in a cold sweat, nausea, or lightheadedness.
- The American Heart Assoc. advises immediate action at onset of symptoms, as more than half of heart attack victims die witin an hour of symptoms.

Of Stroke

- Sudden numbness or weakness of face, arm or leg, especially on one side of the body
- Sudden confusion, trouble speaking or understanding
- Sudden trouble seeing in one or both eyes
- Sudden trouble walking, dizziness, loss of balance or coordination
- Sudden severe headache with no known cause

Prompt treatment of stroke can be a major factor in controlling the effects.

Some Major Modifiable Risk Factors

High Blood pressure—High blood pressure, or hypertension, increases the risk of stroke, heart attack, kidney failure, and heart failure. It affects people of all races, sexes, ethnic origins, and ages. Obesity, physical inactivity, and an unhealthy diet can contribute to this **often symptomless** disease, and it is recommended that individuals have a blood pressure reading at least once every 2 years (more often if advised by a physician).

A blood pressure reading is really two measurements in one, with one written over the other, such as 122/78. The **upper number (systolic pressure)** represents the amount of pressure in the blood vessels when the heart contracts (beats) and pushes blood through the circulatory system. The **lower number (diastolic pressure)** represents the pressure in the blood vessels between beats, when the heart is resting. According to recent National Institutes of Health guidelines, a blood pressure reading below 120/80 is considered normal, while readings from 120/80 to 139/89 are considered "prehypertension."

High blood pressure is divided into 2 stages:
Stage 1 is 140-159 (systolic) over 90-99 (diastolic);
Stage 2 is 160+ (systolic) over 100+ (diastolic).

Individuals with diabetes or chronic kidney disease are considered to have high blood pressure if they have a reading of 130/80 or higher. The diagnosis can be based on either the systolic or the diastolic reading.

High blood pressure usually cannot be cured, but it can be controlled in a variety of ways, including lifestyle modifications and medication. Treatment always should be at the direction and under the supervision of a physician.

High Blood Cholesterol—Cholesterol is a waxy fat-like substance found in all cells of the body. It is produced by the body and also comes in some foods. The body needs some cholesterol, but excess levels increase the risk of heart disease. High cholesterol itself **does not cause symptoms**, so many people are unaware that they have a problem.

There are 2 kinds of cholesterol: **LDL (low-density lipoprotein)**, often called "bad" cholesterol, leads to narrowing of the arteries; **HDL (high-density lipoprotein)**, known as "good" cholesterol, helps reduce this risk.

National Institutes of Health guidelines classify total cholesterol levels (determined by a blood test) of less than 200 mg/dl as desirable, 200-239 as borderline high, and 240 and above as high. About 37 mil Americans have a cholesterol level of 240 mg/dl or higher. LDL levels of less than 100 are considered optimal, 130-159 as borderline high, 160-189 as high, and 190 and over as very high. For HDL, levels of 60 mg/dl and above are considered protective against heart disease, while levels under 40 mg/dl are considered a risk factor for heart disease.

Like high-blood pressure, high cholestrol can be controlled by life-style modification and medication, and should be treated under supervision of a physician.

Triglycerides, another form of fat in the blood, can also raise the risk of heart disease. Levels that are borderline high (150-199) or high (200 or more) may need treatment.

Diabetes—Diabetes is a major risk factor for heart disease; at least 65% of people with diabetes mellitus die of some form of heart or blood vessel disease. *See also* "Diabetes" on page 147.

Smoking—Cigarette smokers are 2-4 times more likely to develop CHD. Smoking is also associated with the risk of sudden cardiac death.

Obesity—Using a body mass index (BMI) of 25 and higher for overweight and 30 and higher for obesity, an estimated 140 mil Americans age 20 and over are overweight and more than 66 mil are obese. *See also* "Weight Guidelines for Adults" on page 153.

Physical Inactivity—An infactive lifestyle is a risk factor for coronary heart disease (CHD). This increase in risk is comparable to that observed for high blood cholesterol, high blood pressure, or cigarette smoking.

Women and Cardiovascular Disease

The American Heart Association reports that diseases of the heart and stroke, respectively, are the No. 1 and No. 3 killers of women over the age of 25 (cancer is the 2nd); one in 2.6 women die of some form of cardiovascular disease. Because heart disease was long viewed as a "man's" disease, many of the major cardiovascular studies were conducted only on men. Much recent attention has been directed toward understanding the influence of gender on cardiovascular disease risk and prevention, but important gaps in knowledge remain.

Women often present some of the same "classic" symptoms of heart attack that men feel, such as chest pain that spreads to the shoulders and arms, but they may more often report atypical chest pain or complain of abdominal pain, difficulty breathing (dyspnea), and nausea. Another problem in diagnosis is that women tend to have heart attacks later in life than men, so symptoms may more often be masked by other age-related diseases such as arthritis or osteoporosis. Even certain diagnostic tests and procedures such as the exercise stress test may not be as accurate in women, with the result that the disease process that leads to heart attack or stroke may not be detected early on, with potentially serious consequences.

World Almanac Quick Quiz

Which of these four infectious diseases has the largest number of annual U.S. cases?

(a) Measles   (b) Hepatitis A   (c) Chlamydia   (d) Salmonella

For the answer look in this chapter, or see page 1008.

Cancer Prevention

Source: American Cancer Society, 1599 Clifton Road NE, Atlanta, GA 30329-4251; phone: (800) 227-2345

PRIMARY PREVENTION: Modifiable determinants of cancer risk.

Smoking	Lung cancer mortality rates are about 23 times higher for current male smokers, and 13 times higher for current female smokers, than for those who have never smoked. Smoking accounts for about 30% of all cancer deaths in the U.S. Tobacco use is responsible for nearly 1 in 5 deaths in the U.S. Smoking is associated with cancer of the lung, mouth, nasal cavities, pharynx, larynx, esophagus, stomach, pancreas, uterine cervix, kidney, bladder, and myeloid leukemia.
Nutrition and Diet	Risk for colon, breast (among postmenopausal women), kidney, prostate, and endometrial cancers increases in obese people. While a diet high in fat may be a factor in the development of certain cancers, the link between obesity and cancer is more the result of an imbalance between caloric intake and energy expenditure than fat per se. Eating 5 or more servings of fruits and vegetables each day, and eating other foods from plant sources (especially grains and beans), may reduce risk for many cancers. Physical activity can help protect against some cancers .
Sunlight	Many of the 1 million skin cancers that are diagnosed annually in the U.S. could have been prevented by protection from the sun's rays. Epidemiological evidence shows that sun exposure is a major factor in the development of melanoma and that the incidence rates are increasing around the world.
Alcohol	Heavy drinking, especially when accompanied by cigarette smoking or smokeless tobacco use, increases risk of cancers of the mouth, larynx, pharynx, esophagus, and liver. Studies have also noted an association between regular alcohol consumption and an increased risk of breast cancer.
Smokeless Tobacco	Use of chewing tobacco or snuff increases risk of cancers of the mouth and pharynx. The excess risk of cancer of the cheek and gum may reach nearly 50-fold among long-term snuff users.
Estrogen	Estrogen replacement therapy (ERT) to control menopausal symptoms can increase the risk of endometrial cancer. However, adding progesterone to estrogen (hormone replacement therapy, or HRT) helps to minimize this risk. Most studies suggest that long-term use (5 years or more) of HRT after menopause increases the risk of breast cancer, and recent studies suggest that risks from taking HRT exceed benefits. The benefits and risks of the use of HRT or ERT by menopausal women should be discussed carefully by the woman and her doctor.
Radiation	Excessive exposure to ionizing radiation can increase cancer risk. Medical and dental X rays are adjusted to deliver the lowest dose possible without sacrificing image quality. Excessive radon exposure in the home may increase lung cancer risk, especially in cigarette smokers.
Environmental Hazards	Exposure to various chemicals (including benzene, asbestos, vinyl chloride, arsenic, and aflatoxin) increases risk of various cancers. Risk of lung cancer from asbestos is greatly increased when combined with smoking.

Cancer-Detection Guidelines

SECONDARY PREVENTION: Steps to diagnose a cancer or precursor as early as possible after it has developed.

In addition to indicated screening for cancers of the breast, colon, and rectum, prostate, and uterine cervix, a cancer-related checkup should include health counseling and, depending on a person's age, might include examinations for cancers of the thyroid, oral cavity, skin, lymph nodes, testes, and ovaries, as well as for some nonmalignant diseases. Special tests for certain cancer sites for individuals at average risk are recommended as outlined below:

Breast Cancer	Women should start getting annual mammograms beginning at age 40. Women who are at increased risk because of family history, genetic predisposition, or past breast cancer should discuss the benefits and limitations of initiating screening at an earlier age. Clinical breast exam should be part of a periodic health exam, about every 3 years for women in their 20's and 30's, and every year for women 40 and older. Women should be aware of any changes in their breasts and report these promptly to their health care provider.
Cervical Cancer	Women should begin cervical cancer screening about 3 years after they begin having vaginal intercourse, but no later than when they are 21 years old. Screening should be done every year with the regular Pap test or every 2 years using the newer liquid-based Pap test. Beginning at age 30, women who have had 3 normal Pap test results in a row may get screened every 2 to 3 years. Women who have certain risk factors such as diethylstilbestrol (DES) exposure before birth, HIV infection, or a weakened immune system due to organ transplant, chemotherapy, or chronic steroid use should continue to be screened annually. Another reasonable option for women over 30 is to get screened every 3 years (but no more frequently) with either the conventional or liquid-based Pap test, *plus* the HPV DNA test. Women 70 years of age or older who have had 3 or more normal Pap tests in a row and no abnormal Pap test results in the last 10 years may choose to stop having cervical cancer screening. Women with a history of cervical cancer, DES exposure before birth, HIV infection or a weakened immune system should continue to have screening as long as they are in good health. Women who have had a total hysterectomy (removal of the uterus and cervix) may also choose to stop having cervical cancer screening, unless the surgery was done as a treatment for cervical cancer or precancer. Women who have had a hysterectomy without removal of the cervix should continue to follow the guidelines above.
Colorectal Cancer	Beginning at age 50, both men and women should follow one of these testing schedules: • Yearly fecal occult blood test; or flexible sigmoidoscopy every five years; or • yearly fecal occult blood test plus flexible sigmoidoscopy every 5 years; or • colonoscopy every 10 years; or • double-contrast barium enema every 5-10 years. **Note:** Persons known to be at increased risk for colorectal cancer (due to inflammatory bowel disease, personal or family history, etc.) need to begin screening at an early age and may need more frequent screening.
Endometrial Cancer	For women with or at high risk of hereditary nonpolyposis colon cancer (HNPCC), annual screening including endometrial biopsy should be obtained beginning at age 35.
Prostate Cancer	The prostate specific antigen (PSA) test and the digital rectal examination should offered annually, beginning at age 50, by men who have a 10-year life expectancy. Men at high risk such as African-American men and men with a strong family history of one or more first-degree relatives (father, brother, or son) diagnosed with prostate cancer at an early age, should start getting tested at age 45. For both men at average risk and high risk, information should be provided about what is known and what is uncertain about the benefits and limitations of early detection and treatment of prostate cancer so that they can make an informed decision about testing.
Skin Cancer	Adults should practice skin self-exam regularly. Suspicious lesions and moles should be evaluated promptly by a physician.

Breast Cancer

Source: American Cancer Society, Inc., 1599 Clifton Road NE, Atlanta, GA 30329-4251; phone: (800) 227-2345

In 2006, an estimated 212,920 women and 1,690 men in the U.S. will have been diagnosed with breast cancer, and about 40,970 women and 460 men will have died from it. Currently, an estimated 2.4 mil women are living with a history of breast cancer, the 2nd biggest cause of cancer death for women in the U.S. (lung cancer ranks first). But mortality rates have been declining, especially among younger women, probably because of earlier detection and improved treatment.

The **risk** for breast cancer increases with age. It is higher for women with a personal or family history of cancer, a long menstrual history (menstrual periods that started early and ended late in life), recent use of birth control pills, long-term use of postmenopausal hormone replacement therapy, and no children or no live birth until age 30 or older. Other risk factors include alcohol consumption and obesity. Inherited mutations such as in the BRCA1 and BRCA2 genes greatly increase risk, but these probably account for 5% to 10% of all breast cancers. By far the majority of women who develop breast cancer have no family history of it.

Breast cancer is often **manifested** first as an abnormality on a mammogram, a type of X-ray. Physical symptoms that show up later, which may be detectable by a woman or her doctor, include a breast lump and, less commonly, breast thickening, swelling, distortion, or tenderness; skin irritation or dimpling; or pain, scaliness, or retraction of the nipple. Breast pain is more commonly associated with benign (non-cancerous) conditions.

Studies show that **early detection** increases survival and treatment options (*See* "Cancer Prevention" above). Although most breast lumps that are detected are noncancerous, any suspicious lump needs to be biopsied.

Treatment for breast cancer may involve lumpectomy (local removal of a tumor), mastectomy (surgical removal of the breast), radiation therapy, chemotherapy, hormone therapy, immunotherapy, or some combination. For early-stage breast cancer, long-term survival rates following lumpectomy plus radiation therapy are similar to survival rates after mastectomy.

Prostate Cancer

Source: Prostate Cancer Foundation, 1250 Fourth Street Santa Monica, CA 90401

The **prostate** is a male gland located between the bladder and scrotum that secretes seminal fluid. Prostate cancer is the most common form of cancer among American men after skin cancer, and the most common cause of cancer death among American men after lung cancer. The American Cancer Society estimates that 234,000 men will be diagnosed with the disease in 2006, and over 27,000 will die from it. Over the course of a lifetime, 1 in 6 men will develop prostate cancer, but only 1 in 34 will die from it.

The exact **cause** of prostate cancer is unknown. The most identifiable risk factors are age, family history, and race. About 65% of all prostate cancers are diagnosed in men over the age of 65, and the chances of developing the disease rise dramatically with age. Men with a single relative with a history of prostate cancer are twice as likely to develop the disease, and those with two or more relatives are more than four times as likely to get it. African-American men are 65% more likely to get the disease than white men and are twice as likely to die from it. The cause for this disparity remains unknown; it is likely that both socioeconomic and biologic differences are involved.

Usually, the disease has no **symptoms** in its early stages. If symptoms arise, they may include: a need to urinate frequently; difficulty starting urination; weak or interrupted flow; pain during urination; difficulty having an erection; painful ejaculation; blood in urine or semen; frequent pain or stiffness in lower back, hips or upper thighs.

White men over 50 with no family history of prostate cancer are typically encouraged to be screened annually for the disease with both a prostate specific antigen (**PSA**) **blood test** and a **digital rectal exam** (DRE). African-American men or those with a family history of the disease may be encouraged to undergo screening beginning at age 40 or 45. Men under 40 seldom get prostate cancer.

Treatment may include surgery, radiation, hormone deprivation therapy, chemotherapy, or a combination. If caught early, while tumor cells are localized within the prostate, the cure rate is over 90%.

Acquired Immune Deficiency Syndrome (AIDS)

Source: Centers for Disease Control and Prevention; www.cdc.gov

AIDS (Acquired Immune Deficiency Syndrome) is caused by the human immunodeficiency virus (**HIV**). HIV kills or disables crucial cells of the immune system, progressively destroying the body's ability to fight disease.

HIV is commonly spread through unprotected sexual contact with an infected partner. It is also spread through contact with infected blood. Where modern screening techniques are used it is rare to contract HIV from transfusion, but it can be contracted when intravenous drug users share syringes with others. Though HIV can be spread through semen, vaginal fluids, and breast milk, there is no evidence it can be spread through saliva. The rate of transmission from a pregnant woman to her infant is about 25% without treatment, but can be reduced to less than 2% with treatment. Studies have indicated no evidence of HIV transmission through casual contact such as the sharing of food utensils, towels and bedding, telephones, or toilet seats.

Some people experience flu-like symptoms a short time after infection with HIV, and scientists estimate that about half of those infected with HIV develop more serious, often chronic symptoms within ten years. Even when symptoms are not present, HIV is active in the body, multiplying, infecting, and killing CD4+ T cells, or "T-helper cells," the crucial immune cells that signal other cells in the immune system to perform their functions.

The term **AIDS** applies to the most advanced stages of HIV infection. According to the official definition set by the Centers for Disease Control and Prevention (CDC), an HIV–infected person with fewer than 200 CD4+ T cells can be said to have AIDS. (Healthy adults usually have 1,000 or more). An HIV-infected person, regardless of T cell count, is diagnosed with AIDS if he or she develops one of 26 conditions that typically affect people with advanced HIV. Most of these conditions are "opportunistic infections" that occur when the immune system is so ravaged by HIV that the body cannot fight off certain bacteria, viruses and microbes.

Months or years prior to the onset of AIDS, many people experience such symptoms as swollen glands, lack of energy, fevers and sweats, and skin rashes. People with full-blown AIDS may develop infections of the intestinal tract, lungs, brain, eyes, and other organs, with a variety of symptoms, and may become severely debilitated. They also are prone to developing certain cancers, especially those caused by viruses, such as Kaposi's sarcoma, cervical cancer, and lymphoma. Children with AIDS may have delayed development or failure to thrive.

HIV is primarily **detected** by testing a person's blood for the presence of antibodies (disease-fighting proteins) to HIV. In about 5% of infected individuals, HIV antibodies may take more than 6 months after exposure to reach detectable levels, but in most cases the antibodies are detectable in about 6 weeks. HIV testing may also be performed on oral fluid and urine samples. New rapid HIV tests can provide preliminary results in about 20 minutes.

Patients are typically given a combination of different drugs, because HIV can much more easily become resistant to a single drug. While these drugs extend the period between HIV infection and serious illness, they do not prevent the spread of the disease to others, and can have severe side effects.

The **U.S. Food and Drug Administration** has approved a number of **drugs** that may slow down the growth of HIV in the body and treat the infections and cancers associated with AIDS. The first group of drugs used to treat HIV, called nucleoside analog reverse transcriptase inhibitors (NRTIs), include the drug zidovudine (commonly known as AZT). Non-nucleoside reverse transcriptase inhibitors (NNRTIs) have also been approved to treat HIV. A third class of drugs, called protease inhibitors, are also approved for HIV. In 2003 the FDA granted accelerated approval of Fuzeon for use with other anti-HIV drugs to treat advanced cases of infection. Fuzeon was the first among a new class of medications called fusion inhibitors; drugs in this class interfered with HIV's entry into cells by hindering the fusion of viral and cellular membranes. The FDA in July 2006 approved the first once-a-day, single-pill drug combination treatment for AIDS. The development was regarded as a significant milestone in treatment of the disease, which often required the daily administration of several drugs. Two drug companies, Bristol-Myers Squibb Co. and Gilead Sciences Inc., had cooperated to develop the drug, called Atripla. The pill combined three drugs—Sustiva, Viread and Emtriva—and would cost roughly $1,100 per month in the U.S. FDA officials said complicated AIDS drug regimens had often dissuaded patients from taking their pills as directed. They said the new drug would simplify drug regimens and help prevent HIV, the virus that caused AIDS, from gaining resistance to drugs. Health experts expect the drug to dramatically improve AIDS treatment in the developing world.

Since there is no vaccine or cure for AIDS, the only **protection** is to avoid activities that carry a risk. When it cannot be known with certainty whether a sexual partner has HIV, the CDC recommends abstinence (the only certain protection), mutual monogamy with an uninfected partner, or correct and consistent use of male latex condoms.

Allergies and Asthma

Source: Asthma and Allergy Foundation of America, 1233 20th St., NW, Suite 402, Wash., DC 20036; phone: (800) 7-ASTHMA; www.aafa.org

One out of five Americans suffers from **allergies** of some kind. People with allergies have extra-sensitive immune systems that react to normally harmless substances. Common allergens that may produce this reaction include plant pollens, dust mites, or animal dander; plants such as poison ivy; certain drugs, such as penicillin; and certain foods such as eggs, milk, nuts, or seafood.

The **tendency to develop allergies** is usually inherited, and allergies usually begin to appear in childhood, but they can show up at any age. **Common allergies** for infants include food allergies and eczema (patches of dry skin). Older children and adults may often develop allergic rhinitis (hay fever), a reaction to an inhaled allergen; common symptoms include nasal congestion, runny nose, and sneezing.

It is best to avoid contact with the allergen, if feasible. In some cases, **medications** such as antihistamines are used to decrease the reaction, and there are treatments aimed at gradually desensitizing the patient to the allergen. Other effective allergy treatments include decongestants, eye drops, and ointments.

Some people with allergies also have **asthma**, and allergens are a common asthma trigger. Asthma is a disease of chronic inflammation affecting the passages that carry air into and out of the lungs. It can develop at any age.

People with asthma have inflamed, supersensitive airways that tighten and become filled with mucus during an asthma episode. Wheezing, difficulty in breathing, tightening of the chest, and coughing are common symptoms. Asthma can progress through stages to become life-threatening if not controlled. **Emergency symptoms** include: no improvement minutes after initial treatment; struggling to breathe, with patient hunched over and/or chest and neck pulled in; trouble walking or talking; stopping activity and not starting activity again; gray or blue lips or fingernails.

Besides common allergens, tobacco smoke, cold air, and pollution can trigger an asthma attack, as can viral infections or physical exercise. An accurate diagnosis by a physician is important. Although there is no cure for asthma or allergies, they can be controlled with medications and lifestyle changes. *See* "Health News" on page 379.

Alzheimer's Disease

Source: Alzheimer's Association, 225 N Michigan Ave., 17th Fl., Chicago, IL 60601-7633; phone: (800) 272-3900; www.alz.org

Alzheimer's disease, the most common form of dementia, is a progressive, degenerative disease of the brain in which nerve cells deteriorate and die for unknown reasons. Its first symptoms usually involve impaired memory and confusion about recent events. As the disease advances, it results in greater impairment of memory, thinking, judgement, language, behavior, and physical health.

The **rate of progression** of Alzheimer's varies, ranging from 3 to 20 years; the average length of time from onset of symptoms until death is 8 years. Eventually, affected individuals lose their ability to care for themselves and become susceptible to infections of the lungs, urinary tract, or other organs as they grow progressively debilitated.

Alzheimer's disease affects an estimated 4.5 mil Americans, striking men and women of all ethnic groups. Although most people diagnosed with Alzheimer's are older than age 60, some cases occur in people in their 40s and 50s. An estimated 10% of the population over age 65 have Alzheimer's, and the disease affects almost half of those over 85. In the United States, annual costs of diagnosis, treatment, and long-term care are estimated at $100 billion.

Diagnosis involves a comprehensive evaluation that may include a complete health history, a physical examination, neurological and mental status assessments, and other testing as needed. Skilled health care professionals can generally diagnose Alzheimer's with about 90% accuracy. Other conditions that can cause similar symptoms include depression, drug interactions, nutritional imbalances, infections such as AIDS, meningitis, and syphilis, and other forms of dementia, such as those associated with stroke, Huntington's disease, Parkinson's disease, frontotemporal dementia, and vascular disease. Absolute confirmation of diagnosis requires a brain biopsy or autopsy.

Treatments for cognitive and behavioral symptoms are available, but no intervention has yet been developed that prevents Alzheimer's or reverses its course. Some research suggests that risk factors for heart disease, such as high blood pressure, elevated cholesterol, diabetes and excess body weight may also increase risk of developing Alzheimer's. Studies also suggest that staying physically and mentally active and socially connected may be associated with a lower risk for the disease.

Providing care for people with Alzheimer's is physically and psychologically demanding. Nearly 70% of affected individuals live at home, where family or friends care for them. In advanced stages of the disease, many individuals require long-term residential care. Nearly half of all nursing home residents in the U.S. have Alzheimer's.

People with Alzheimer's need a safe, stable environment and a regular daily schedule offering appropriate stimulation. Physical exercise and social interaction are important, as are proper nutritionand adequate pain management. Security is also a consideration, because many people with Alzheimer's tend to wander. An identification bracelet listing the person's name, address, and condition may help ensure the safe return of an individual who wanders.

Warning Signs of Alzheimer's Disease

- Forgetting recently learned information or inability to learn new information
- Difficulty with everyday tasks such as cooking or dressing
- Inability to remember simple words
- Use of inappropriate words when communicating
- Disorientation to time and place
- Poor or decreased judgment
- Problems with abstract thinking
- Putting objects in inappropriate places
- Rapid changes in mood or behavior
- Increased irritability, anxiety, depression, confusion, and restlessness
- Prolonged loss of initiative

Arthritis

Source: Arthritis Foundation, P.O. Box 7669, Atlanta, GA 30357-0669; phone: (800) 568-4045; www.arthritis.org

The term "arthritis" refers to more than 100 different diseases that cause pain, stiffness, swelling, and restricted movement in joints. The condition is usually chronic. The Centers for Disease Control and Prevention (CDC) estimates that nearly 70 million adults suffer from arthritis and/or chronic joint symptoms. The cause for most types of arthritis is unknown; scientists are studying the roles played by genetics, lifestyle, and the environment.

Symptoms of arthritis may develop either slowly or suddenly. A visit to the doctor is indicated when pain, stiffness, or swelling in a joint or difficulty in moving a joint persists for more than two weeks. To make a diagnosis of arthritis, the doctor records the patient's symptoms and examines joints, looking for any swelling or limited movement. In addition, the doctor checks for other signs often seen with arthritis, such as rashes, mouth sores, or eye involvement. Finally, the doctor may test the blood, urine, or joint fluid, or take X-rays of the joints.

Of the 3 most prevalent forms of arthritis, **osteoarthritis** is the most common, affecting more than 21 mil Americans; it usually occurs after age 45. In this type, which is also called degenerative arthritis, the protective cartilage of joints is lost and changes occur in the bone, leading to pain and stiffness. It usually occurs in the fingers, knees, feet, hips, and back.

Fibromyalgia, another common arthritis condition, affects more than 2 million Americans and affects more women than men. In this form, widespread pain and tenderness occur in muscles and their attachments to the bone. Common symptoms include fatigue, disturbed sleep, stiffness, and psychological distress.

Rheumatoid arthritis, which also affects more than 2 million people in the U.S., is one of the most serious and disabling forms of the disease. In this type, which is also more common and more degenerative in women, inflammation of the joints leads to damage of the cartilage and bone. The areas of the body that can be affected are the hands, wrists, feet, knees, ankles, shoulders, neck, jaw, and elbows.

Other forms of arthritis and related conditions include lupus, gout, ankylosing spondylitis, and scleroderma; also related are bursitis and tendinitis, which may result from injuring or overusing a joint.

Medications to treat arthritis include drugs that relieve pain and swelling such as analgesics, anti-inflammatory drugs, biologic response modifiers, glucocorticoids and antirheumatic drugs that also tend to slow the disease process. Most treatment programs call for exercise, use of heat or cold, and joint-protection techniques, such as avoiding excess stress on joints, using assistive devices, and controlling weight. In some cases, surgery can help.

Depression

Source: National Institute of Mental Health (NIMH)

Depression is a serious illness that affects thoughts, feelings, and the ability to function in everyday life. It strikes across all age groups, and often goes unrecognized or inadequately treated. The National Institutes of Health estimates that about 19 million Americans suffer from depression in any given year and that more than 16% of all Americans will have had depression at some point in life. Young people are among those at risk; in a one-year period, 3 times as many persons with depression were 18 to 29 years old as were 60 or older.

Nearly twice as many women as men suffer from a depressive illness in a given year. Although conventional wisdom holds that depression is most closely associated with menopause, in fact, the childbearing years are marked by the highest rates of depression, followed by the years prior to menopause. The influence of hormones on depression in women has been an active area of NIMH research.

In a given year, 1-2% of people over age 65 living in the community (outside of institutions) suffer from major depression. Depression frequently occurs with other physical illnesses, including heart disease, stroke, cancer, and diabetes. It is not a normal part of aging.

The **treatments** that are now available can alleviate symptoms, and with awareness growing, more people with depression are seeking the help they need. But many depressed people—and those around them—still fail to realize that they have an illness or could benefit from medical help. According to the NIH, more than half of those seeking help do not get adequate treatment, often because they consult family practioners who do not deal aggressively enough with the problem.

Symptoms and Types of Depression

- persistent sad mood
- loss of interest or pleasure in activities once enjoyed, including sex
- significant change in appetite or body weight
- difficulty sleeping or oversleeping
- lethargy or agitation
- loss of energy
- feelings of worthlessness or inappropriate guilt
- difficulty thinking or concentrating
- recurrent thoughts of death or suicide

A diagnosis of **major depressive disorder** (or **unipolar major depression**) is made if an individual has 5 or more of these symptoms during the same two-week period. Unipolar

major depression typically comes to the fore in episodes that recur during a person's lifetime.

Bipolar disorder (or **manic-depressive illness**) is characterized by episodes of major depression as well as episodes of mania—abnormally and persistently elevated mood or irritability, accompanied by such symptoms as inflated self-esteem, less need for sleep, increased talkativeness, racing thoughts, distractibility, agitation, and excessive involvement in pleasurable activities that have a high potential for painful consequences. While sharing some of the features of major depression, bipolar disorder is a distinct illness.

Dysthymic disorder (or **dysthymia**), a less severe yet typically more chronic form of depression, is diagnosed when a depressed mood persists for at least two years in adults (one year in children or adolescents) and is accompanied by at least 2 other depressive symptoms. Many people with dysthymic disorder also experience major depressive episodes.

In contrast to the normal experiences of sadness, or passing moods, depression is extreme and persistent and can interfere significantly with an individual's ability to function. A recent study sponsored by the World Health Organization and the World Bank found unipolar major depression to be the leading cause of disability in the U.S. and worldwide.

Treatments for Depression

A variety of **medicines** are used to treat depression. These drugs influence the functioning of certain neurotransmitters in the brain, primarily serotonin and norepinephrine, known as monoamines. Older drugs—so-called tricyclic antidepressants (TCAs) and monoamine oxidase inhibitors (MAOIs)—affect the functioning of both of these neurotransmitters. But they can have strong side effects or, in the case of MAOIs, require dietary restrictions. Newer medications, such as the selective serotonin reuptake inhibitors (SSRIs), have fewer side effects. All of these medications can be effective, but some people respond to one type and not another.

NIMH research has shown that certain types of **psychotherapy**, particularly cognitive-behavioral therapy (CBT) and interpersonal therapy (IPT), can help relieve depression. CBT helps patients change the negative styles of thinking and behaving often associated with depression. IPT focuses on working through disturbed personal relationships that may contribute to depression. Studies of adults have shown that a combination of psychotherapy and antidepressant medication is most effective in treating moderate-to-severe depression.

Electroconvulsive therapy (ECT) has been found effective in treating 80-90% of cases of severe depression, particularly those that have not responded to other forms of treatment. ECT involves producing a seizure in the brain of a patient under general anesthesia by applying electrical stimulation through electrodes placed on the scalp. Memory loss and other cognitive problems are common, but typically short-lived, side effects.

For more information, start with the website www.nimh. nih.gov/healthinformation/depressionmenu.cfm

Diabetes

Source: American Diabetes Association, 1701 N Beauregard St., Alexandria, VA 22311; phone: (800) 342-2383

Diabetes is a chronic disease in which the body does not produce or properly use **insulin**, a hormone needed to convert sugar, starches, and other foods into energy necessary for daily life. Both genetics and environment appear to play roles in the onset of diabetes. This disease, which has no cure, is the 5th-leading cause of death by disease in the U.S. According to death certificate data, diabetes contributed to 224,092 deaths in 2002.

It is estimated that there are 20.8 mil Americans with diabetes, 6.2 mil of whom are undiagnosed.

The American Diabetes Association recommends the following **guidelines for diagnosing diabetes**: lowering the acceptable level of blood sugar in a fasting glucose test from 140 mg of glucose/deciliter of blood to 126 mg/deciliter; testing all adults 45 years and older, and then every 3 years if normal; and testing at a younger age, or more frequently, in high-risk individuals. The American Diabetes Association supports studies that have proven that detection at an earlier stage and modest lifestyle changes, such as eating better and exercising more, will help prevent or delay complications. (*See* "Health News," on p. 140).

There are 2 major types of diabetes:

Type 1 (formerly known as insulin dependent, or juvenile diabetes). The body produces very little or no insulin; disease most often begins in childhood or early adulthood. People with type 1 diabetes must take daily insulin injections to stay alive.

Type 2 (formerly known as non-insulin dependent, or adult-onset diabetes). The body does not produce enough or cannot properly use insulin. It is the most common form of the disease (90-95% of cases in people over age 20) and often begins later in life.

Warning Signs of Diabetes

Type 1 Diabetes (usually occurs suddenly):

frequent urination	unusual weight loss
unusual thirst	extreme fatigue
extreme hunger	irritability

Type 2 Diabetes (occurs less suddenly):

any type 1 symptoms	cuts/bruises slow to heal
frequent infections	tingling/numbness in hands or feet
blurred vision	recurring skin, gum, or bladder infections

Pre-Diabetes

Among U.S. adults 40-74 years of age, 41 mil (40.1% of the population) have **pre-diabetes**, the state that occurs when a person's blood glucose levels are higher than normal but not high enough for a diagnosis of diabetes.

About 11% of people with pre-diabetes developed type 2 diabetes during each year of the study. Other studies show that most people with pre-diabetes develop type 2 diabetes in 10 years.

Complications of Diabetes

People often have diabetes many years before it is diagnosed. During that time, serious complications have a chance to develop. Potential complications include:

Blindness. Diabetes is the leading cause of blindness in people ages 20-74. Each year, from 12,000 to 24,000 people lose their sight because of diabetes.

Kidney disease. 10% to 21% of all people with diabetes develop kidney disease. In 2002, more than 44,400 people initiated treatment for end-stage renal disease (kidney failure) because of diabetes.

Amputations. Diabetes is the most frequent cause of non-traumatic lower limb amputations. The risk of a leg amputation is 15 to 40 times greater for a person with diabetes than for the average American. Each year, an estimated 80,000 people lose a foot or leg as a result of complications brought on by diabetes.

Heart disease and stroke. People with diabetes are 2 to 4 times more likely to have heart disease. And they are 2 to 4 times more likely to suffer a stroke. About 65% of deaths among people with diabetes are due to heart disease and stroke.

Eating Disorders

Source: National Institute of Mental Health

Eating disorders involve serious disturbances in eating behavior, usually in the form of extreme and unhealthy reduction of food intake or severe overeating. They are not due to a failure of will; rather, they are real and treatable medical illnesses in which certain patterns of behavior get out of control. The **main types** are anorexia nervosa, bulimia nervosa, and binge-eating disorder. These disorders usually develop in adolescence or early adulthood and often occur with other illnesses such as depression, substance abuse, and anxiety disorders. They are much more common among females; only about 5% to 15% of anorexia or bulimia patients and 35% of binge eaters are male.

If not treated, eating disorders can lead serious complications, including heart conditions and kidney failure, which may lead to death.

Anorexia nervosa affects an estimated 0.5% to 3.7% of females during their lifetime. Symptoms include resistance to maintaining weight at even minimally normal levels, intense fear of gaining weight, exaggerated importance of body weight or shape in one's self image, and infrequent or absent menstrual periods. Anorexics see themselves as overweight even though they are dangerously thin. In response, they avoid food, and often takes other extreme measures to lose weight, such as compulsive exercise or purging by means of vomiting or laxatives and enemas. While some anorexics fully recover after a single episode, others may relapse frequently or experience chronic deterioration.

Bulimia nervosa affects an estimated 1.1% to 4.2% of females. It is characterized by recurrent uncontrolled binge-eating episodes followed by a compensatory behavior to prevent weight gain, such as self-induced vomiting, excessive exercise, or fasting. Persons with bulimia usually end up weighing within a normal range for their age and height, but they may fear gaining weight and feel intensely dissatisfied with their bodies. They often perform their behaviors in secret, feeling ashamed when they binge and relieved when they purge.

Binge-eating disorder (not officially approved as a psychiatric diagnosis) affects an estimated 2% to 5% of Americans in any given 6-month period. Like bulimia, a binge-eating disorder involves episodes of excessive eating during which the sufferer may lose all control, but individuals with this disorder do not compensate by purging, exercising, or fasting. Many are thus overweight, and the shame associated with the illness can lead to further bingeing.

Eating disorder sufferers may not admit they are ill and may resist treatment. Early diagnosis and a comprehensive treatment program are essential to recovery. Some patients may need immediate hospitalization. For anorexia, treatment usually follows 3 established steps: weight restoration (usually in an inpatient hospital setting), treatment of any accompanying psychological disturbances, and achieving long-term remission or recovery. Medications may be helpful in treating underlying depression or anxiety. Families are sometimes involved in the therapeutic process.

Irritable Bowel Syndrome

Source: National Institutes of Health, 9000 Rockville Pike Bethesda, MD 20892

Irritable Bowel Syndrome (IBS) is a functional disorder, not a disease, that occurs in the large intestine and is one of the most common disorders diagnosed by physicians. Nearly 1 in 5 Americans has symptoms of IBS, and it accounts for more than one out of every 10 doctor visits in the U.S. IBS occurs more frequently in women than in men and it usually begins before the age of 35 for about 50% those affected. Though IBS causes discomfort and may even be painful, it does not damage the bowel.

Most people are not comfortable discussing IBS because of its embarrassing symptoms. They include:
- bloating
- gas
- diarrhea
- constipation
- abdominal pain or cramping
- mucus in the stool
- feeling like you have not finished with a bowel movement

For most people, IBS is a chronic condition and there will likely be times where the symptoms are worse than during other times, or they may disappear altogether only to reappear again in the future. Most complications are derived from the symptoms such as hemorrhoids, which may form as a result of the diarrhea and constipation. Often people with chronic IBS may feel discouraged and go through periods of depression partly because of the constant discomfort, but also because the symptoms can interfere with work and personal relationships.

The specific causes for IBS are unknown. The walls of the intestines are lined with layers of muscle that contract and relax in a coordinated manner as they move food through the digestive system. When a person has IBS, the contractions cause food to either speed up or slow down as it moves though the bowel, subsequently causing the gas, bloating, diarrhea, and/or constipation. Some researchers believe that people who suffer from IBS have a colon that is particularly sensitive to certain foods. In particular, milk products, alcohol, caffeine, carbonated drinks, chocolate, and fatty foods can trigger IBS symptoms. Another common factor is a low tolerance for stretching of the large intestine. Women tend to get IBS more often than men and they usually have more severe symptoms during menstrual periods, leading researchers to believe that IBS may have a hormonal trigger. Recent research has shown that serotonin, a neurotransmitter hormone, may be linked with gastrointestinal functioning.

IBS can sometimes be the result of infection or other problems in the body. Researchers have found that people who have had gastroenteritis have later developed IBS. But because symptoms of IBS can match those many serious diseases, it is important for chronic sufferers to consult their doctors. If symptoms began early in life and have been stable, a patient may require a colonoscopy to rule out any inflammatory bowel diseases, such as Crohn's, or even colon cancer. Patients over 50 should be regularly screened for colon cancer.

Despite the uncertainty over the cause of IBS, there are known precautionary measures that people with sensitive digestive systems can take. Having a well-balanced diet is the best possible prevention. High fiber foods such as bread and cereal reduce IBS symptoms, particularly constipation. In addition, vegetables, beans and bran can reduce symptoms if part of a daily diet. Eating large meals has been shown to worsen the condition, so eating smaller meals can also help reduce symptoms.

There is no particular cure for IBS, and treatment usually involves lessening the symptoms so that the sufferer may lead a more normal life.

Common Infectious Diseases

Sources: National Institutes of Health; Centers for Disease Control; World Health Organization

The following is a list of major infectious diseases. It is meant to be used for reference purposes only and not as a tool for diagnosis. If you think you may have a serious disease, you should see your doctor immediately. Statistics may appear uneven because of different methods of reporting by the various agencies, and because not all diseases are surveyed in the same year.

Chicken Pox *(Varicella simplex)*. Usually non-threatening viral disease commonly associated with children. In adults, the disease can be serious. **Transmission:** Highly contagious; transmitted by direct contact with rash, coughing, or sneezing of infected persons. **Symptoms:** blister-like rash, discomfort, high fever. Infected people may develop shingles later in life. **Vaccine:** became available 1995. **Treatment:** none; antibiotics in some severe cases. **Annual U.S. cases:** before 1995, about 4 mil, mostly children; in 2004, 32,931 reported cases.

Chlamydia *(Chlamydia trachomatis)*. One of the most widely spread sexually transmitted diseases. **Transmission:** Sexually transmitted. **Symptoms:** 70% of those infected have no symptoms. In women, vaginal discharge, infection of the cervix and urinary tract, can cause pelvic inflammatory disease; in men, infection of urinary tract and epididymitis (inflammation of testicular duct); can also infect the throat, rectum, and eye. **Treatment:** curable with antibiotics. **Annual U.S. cases:** 2.8 mil (CDC estimate).

Common Cold (more than 200 different viruses). An upper respiratory viral infection. **Transmission:** touching your nose, eyes, or mouth after touching something contaminated by the virus; inhalation of airborne virus. **Symptoms:** irritated nose or scratchy throat, sneezing and watery nasal discharge; green or yellow nasal discharge, cough, muscle aches, headache, postnasal drip, decreased appetite. **Treatment:** no cure, over-the-counter remedies can relieve symptoms; effectiveness of anti-viral drugs is debated. **Annual U.S. cases:** about 1 billion.

Gonorrhea *(Neisseria Gonorhoeae)*. Common bacterial STD. **Transmission:** sexually transmitted. **Symptoms:** in men, discomfort in urethra, yellow or green discharge, burning during urination; in women, pelvic pain, bleeding associated with intercourse, burning during urination, yellow or bloody discharge. **Treatment:** highly curable with antibiotics. **Annual U.S. cases:** 330,132 (2004)

Hepatitis A viral disease that causes inflammation of the liver. In the U.S., five forms are endemic: A, B, C, D, and E; A, B, and C are the most common. **Symptoms:** all forms have generally similar symptoms including jaundice, fatigue, abdominal pain, loss of appetite, nausea, mild flu like symptoms; many cases cause no symptoms; in extreme cases, liver transplants may be necessary.
- **Hepatitis A** *(Hepatovirus Picornaviridae)*. **Transmission:** food or water contaminated with feces from infected persons. **Vaccine:** Effective; travelers are advised to not drink tap water in countries where disease is common. **Treatment:** disease usually resolves itself on its own; alcohol consumption should be avoided. **Est. Annual U.S. cases:** 24,000; 5,683 acute lab-confirmed cases in 2004
- **Hepatitis B** *(Orthohepadnavirus Hepadnaviridae)*. **Transmission:** unsterilized needle sharing; contaminated blood transfusions; sexual contact. **Vaccine:** highly effective **Treatment:** for chronic cases, drug treatment is necessary; for acute cases, disease usually resolves itself, severe cases treated with lamivudine. **Est. Annual U.S. cases:** 17,000; 6,212 lab-confirmed cases in 2004
- **Hepatitis C** *(Hepacivirus Flavinviridae)*. **Transmission:** unsterilized needle sharing, contaminated blood transfusions; sexual contact. **Vaccine:** none. **Treatment:** chronic cases treated with drugs, eliminating virus in about 50% of patients; for acute cases, treatment recommended if disease present after 2-3 months. **Est. Annual U.S. cases:** 4,200

HPV Infection (more than 100 strains of human papillomavirus). Common viral infection; leading cause of cervical cancer. **Transmission:** sexually transmitted. **Symptoms:**

Most of those infected have no symptoms but can still transmit virus; in some cases, genital warts; pre-cancerous bumps on anus, cervix or vulva (women), or penis (men). **Treatment:** No cure for virus; warts may recur even with treatment; cervical cancer treated with surgery, chemotherapy, and/or radiation. Women with HPV should have pap smear and pelvic exam every 6 months. **Annual U.S. cases:** 6.8 million new cases of sexually transmitted HPV; approximately 20 million Americans currently infected with HPV.

Influenza (various influenza viruses). Highly contagious viral respiratory infection. **Transmission:** Airborne transmission; contact with face after touching infected surface. **Symptoms:** chills, fatigue, fever, headache, sore throat, sinus congestion, coughing. "Stomach flu" is not influenza. **Vaccine:** Yearly vaccinations recommended. **Treatment:** Antiviral drugs; disease normally runs its course in a matter of days. **Annual U.S. Cases:** 5-20% of U.S. population; 200,000 hospitalized and 36,000 killed annually.

Lyme Disease *(borrelia burgdorferi).* Bacterial inflammatory disease, first identified 1975 in Old Lyme, CT. Found across the U.S., usually in areas with large deer populations. **Transmission:** Bite of infected deer ticks. Mice and deer are most common hosts. **Symptoms**: Mimic those of other diseases: flu-like symptoms; fatigue; stiff neck, joint inflammation; skin rash may appear at site of tick bite. **Treatment:** Antibiotics in early stages; anti-inflammation drugs to relieve symptoms; without treatment, long-term complications (some fatal) involving joints, heart, and nervous system. **Annual U.S. cases:** about 16,000

Malaria *(plasmodium* parasite). Infectious disease known from as early as 2700 BCE. Virtually eradicated in developed countries; still a major killer in tropical regions. **Transmission:** bite from an infected mosquito. **Symptoms:** high fever, shaking chills, heavy sweating, headache, fatigue, enlarged spleen; if left untreated, organ damage and death. **Treatment:** Antimalarial drugs, including chloroquine for treatment and prevention. **Annual U.S. Cases:** 1,458 (2004); worldwide, as many as 2.7 million people killed each year, 75% of them African children.

Measles *(rubeola* virus). Once-common viral infection; today almost nonexistent in U.S. and Canada. **Transmission:** Airborne transmission by infected people. **Symptoms:** itchy and raised rash, sore throat, cough, pink-eye, high fever, high fever; in rare cases, encephalitis, seizures, permanent deafness, death. **Vaccine:** Highly effective. **Treatment:** no specific treatment; symptoms relieved with bed rest, acetaminophen, humidified air. **Annual U.S. cases:** 56 in 2003

Mumps (mumps virus). Acute and contagious viral infection. **Transmission:** direct contact with mucus or saliva of infected persons. **Symptoms:** Painful, visible swelling of the salivary or parotid glands in the face; chills, headache, fever, painful swallowing; in some cases, inflammation of testes, pancreas, ovaries; in severe cases, brain swelling and symptoms ranging from nausea and drowsiness to seizures and permanent deafness. **Vaccine**: MMR vaccine is effective. **Treatment:** No specific treatment; symptoms may be relieved by applying ice or heat to swollen glands. **Annual U.S. cases:** 258 in 2004

Peptic Ulcer (most from *Helicobacter pylori* [*H. pylori*] bacteria; also overuse of aspirin or other anti-inflammatory drugs) Weakening of the stomach's protective mucous coating, allowing stomach acid and bacteria to irritate stomach lining. **Transmission:** *H. Pylori* may be transmitted through food and water. **Symptoms:** Indigestion; bloating; dull, transient abdominal pain or discomfort; nausea; vomiting. **Treatment:** antibiotics, acid-suppressing drugs. **Annual U.S. cases:** About 20% of Americans under 40 and half of those over 60 years may be infected with *H. pylori*. An estimated 500,000 to 850,000 develop peptic ulcers each year.

Pertssis or Whooping cough *(Bordetella pertussis* or *B. parepertussis).* Upper respiratory bacterial infection. **Transmission:** Highly contagious; airborne transmission by infected people. **Symptoms:** initially, mild cold-like symptoms, fever, diarrhea, difficulty breathing; later, violent coughing with characteristic "whooping" heard when patient tries to breathe between coughs, vomiting; in severe cases, apnea, pneumonia, seizures, encephalopathy. **Vaccine:** TDaP vaccine or pertussis only vaccine. **Treatment:** Antibiotics in early cases, otherwise disease must run its course. **Annual U.S. Cases:** 11,647 in 2003; annual infections have been increasing since 1980s.

Salmonella or Salmonellosis *(Salmonella enteritidis).* Bacterial infection. **Transmission:** Eating foods contaminated by feces carrying the bacteria; undercooked meats or raw eggs contaminated by bacteria; contact with feces of infected animal/pet. **Symptoms:** fever, diarrhea, abdominal cramps 12 to 72 hours after infection. **Treatment:** no standard treatment; runs its course in 4 to 7 days; antibiotics in severe cases. **Annual U.S. cases:** about 40,000; about 600 are fatal.

Shigellosis (Four species of *Shigella: boydii, dysenteriae, flexneri,* and *sonnei*). Bacterial infection and a form of dysentery (an intestinal disease). **Transmission:** Food contaminated by infected feces; vegetables grown in fields containing contaminated sewage; swimming in contaminated water. **Symptoms:** watery or bloody diarrhea 1 to 4 days after infection, high fever, vomiting, painful bowel movements, severe diarrhea; in extreme cases, seizures in children, intestinal perforation. **Treatment:** mild infection allowed to run its course; replacement of fluids and salts lost through excessive diarrhea; antibiotics in severe cases. Although severe diarrhea is symptomatic, antidiarrheal medicines may make illness worse. **Annual U.S. Cases:** 400,000 estimated; about 18,000 reported.

Syphilis *(Treponema pallidum).* Bacterial infection known since ancient times, and spread rampantly throughout Europe in the Middle Ages. **Transmission:** Sexually transmitted. **Symptoms:** Primary stage: painless ulcer where bacteria enters the body; usually heals in 3 to 12 weeks with or without treatment. Without treatment, disease enters secondary stage: skin rash 2-10 weeks after chancre. Without treatment, enters tertiary stage: mouth sores, fever, fatigue, loss of appetite, weight loss, hair loss, jaundice, syphilitic meningitis, aortal aneurysms, lesions, damage to nervous system, heart, and eyes. Most infected do not progress beyond primary or secondary stage. **Treatment:** Curable with antibiotics (mostly penicillin). **Annual U.S. Cases:** 33,407 total cases (2004); 7,980 primary and secondary (2004)

Tetanus or Lockjaw *(Clostridium tetani).* Bacterial infection. **Transmission**: Bacteria, found in soil, enters body through broken skin. **Symptoms:** muscle stiffness and spasm or "locking" of muscles of the jaw, neck, and limbs. **Vaccine:** 4 forms of tetanus immunization. **Treatment:** tetanus immune globulin can fight infection; with treatment, less than 10% of cases are fatal. **Annual U.S. Cases:** Approx. 100 cases per year, most due to lack of immunization.

Tuberculosis *(Mycobacterium tuberculosis).* Bacterial infection that primarily affects the lungs. **Transmission:** Airborne transmission by people with active TB infection. **Symptoms:** weight loss, fever, cough with discharge (sometimes with bloody sputum), night sweats, growing shortness of breath over time, chest pains. **Vaccine:** BCG (Bacille Calmette Guerin) vaccine only effective in protecting young children and used where TB is common; not recommended by health experts in U.S. **Treatment:** Difficult to cure and fatal if untreated. Treated with cocktail of antibiotics given over 6-12 months or longer. **Annual U.S. Cases:** 14,093 (2005); worldwide, about 2 bil people are thought to be infected.

Yellow Fever (Yellow fever virus, in *flavivirus* group). Viral infection that has caused large epidemics in S. America, the Caribbean and Africa. **Transmission:** bite from mosquitoes carrying the virus. **Symptoms:** headaches, muscle aches, fever, jaundice (yellowing skin), nausea and vomiting, kidney failure, severe generalized pain; in severe cases, shock, coma, and death. **Vaccine:** Available, safe and effective. **Treatment:** symptoms are treated until disease runs its course. **Annual U.S. cases:** 0; 200,000 estimated new cases worldwide per year, with 30,000 deaths.

Food Guide Pyramid

In 2005 the U.S. Dept. of Agriculture issued a revised food guide pyramid called MyPyramid, along with new dietary guidelines for Americans. The new pyramid represents the latest findings in health and nutrition, with a focus on reducing calorie consumption and increasing physical activity. More specifically, the new system factors in weight, age, gender, physical activity in putting together a nutrition plan and distinguishes between necessary and unnecessary types of fats and sugars. In addition, the new pyramid allows for variation and personalization according to an individual's caloric needs. The guidelines below are general guidelines for better health and nutrition. To get a personalized nutrition and exercise assessment and for dietary recommendations visit MyPyramid.gov

2005 Dietary Guidelines for Americans—Some Key Recommendations:

- Choose nutrient-dense foods and beverages among the basic food groups, while limiting the intake of foods with saturated and trans fats, cholesterol, added sugars, salt, and alcohol.
- To maintain a healthy body weight, balance calories consumed with calories expended.
- To prevent gradual weight gain over time, make small decreases in calories and increase physical activity.
- Engage in regular physical activity and cut down on sedentary activities.
- Keep fit through cardiovascular conditioning, stretching exercises for flexibility, and resistance exercises or calisthenics for muscle strength and endurance.
- Eat a sufficient amount of fruits and vegetables each day.
- Choose from all 5 vegetable subgroups, dark greens, orange, legumes, starchy vegetables, and other vegetables.

- Consume 3 cups per day of fat-free or low-fat milk or equivalent milk products.
- Consume less than 10% of calories from saturated fatty acids and less than 300 mg/day of cholesterol, and keep trans fatty acid consumption as low as possible.
- Keep total fat intake between 20%-35% of calories, with most fats coming from sources of polyunsaturated and monounsaturated fatty acids, such as fish, nuts, and vegetable oils.
- Choose lean, low-fat, or fat-free meat, poultry, dry beans, and milk or milk products.
- Eat fiber-rich fruits, vegetables, and whole grains often.
- Consume less than 2,300 mg (approx. 1 teaspoon of salt) of sodium per day. Eat potassium-rich foods, such as fruits and vegetables.
- If you drink alcoholic beverages, do so in moderation: up to 1 drink per day for women and up to 2 drinks per day for men.

Estimated Calorie Requirements[1]

Estimated amounts of calories, rounded to the nearest 200, needed to maintain energy balance for various gender, age groups, and levels of physical activity.

	Age (years)	Sedentary[2]	Moderately[3] Active	Active[4]		Age (years)	Sedentary[2]	Moderately[3] Active	Active[4]
Child	2–3	1,000	1,000–1,400	1,000–1,400					
Female	4–8	1,200	1,400–1,600	1,400–1,800	**Male**	4–8	1,400	1,400–1,600	1,600–2,000
	9–13	1,600	1,600–2,000	1,800–2,200		9–13	1,800	1,800–2,200	2,000–2,600
	14–18	1,800	2,000	2,400		14–18	2,200	2,400–2,800	2,800–3,200
	19–30	2,000	2,000–2,200	2,400		19–30	2,400	2,600–2,800	3,000
	31–50	1,800	2,000	2,200		31–50	2,200	2,400–2,600	2,800–3,000
	51+	1,600	1,800	2,000–2,200		51+	2,000	2,200–2,400	2,400–2,800

(1) Based on median height and weight for ages up to age 18 years and Body Mass Index (BMI) of 21.5 for adult females and 22.5 for adult males. (2) Engaging only in minimal activities associated with ordinary day-to-day life. (3) Includes physical activity equivalent to walking 1.5 to 3 miles per day at 3-4 mph. (4) Includes physical activity equivalent to walking more than 3 miles per day at 3-4 mph.

Food Ingredients

PROTEIN

Proteins, composed of amino acids, are essential to good nutrition. They build, maintain, and repair the body. Best sources: eggs, milk, fish, meat, poultry, soybeans, nuts. High-quality proteins such as eggs, meat, or fish supply all 8 amino acids needed in the diet. Plant foods can be combined to meet protein needs as well: whole grain breads and cereals, rice, oats, soybeans, other beans, split peas, and nuts.

FATS

Fats provide energy by furnishing calories to the body, and they also carry vitamins A, D, E, and K. They are the most concentrated source of energy in the diet. Best sources of polyunsaturated and monounsaturated fats: margarine, vegetable/plant oils, nuts. Meats, cheeses, butter, cream, egg yolks, lard are concentrated sources of saturated fats.

CARBOHYDRATES

Carbohydrates provide energy for body function and activity by supplying immediate calories. The carbohydrate group includes sugars, starches, fiber, and starchy vegetables. Best sources: grains, legumes, potatoes, vegetables, fruits.

FIBER

The portion of plant foods that our bodies cannot digest is known as fiber. There are 2 basic types: *insoluble* ("roughage") and *soluble*. Insoluble fibers help move food materials through the digestive tract; soluble fibers tend to slow them down. Both types absorb water, thus prevent and treat constipation by softening and increasing the bulk of the undigested food components passing through the digestive tract. Soluble fibers have also been reported to be helpful in reducing blood cholesterol levels. Best sources: beans, bran, fruits, whole grains, vegetables.

WATER

Water dissolves and transports other nutrients throughout the body, aiding the processes of digestion, absorption, circulation, and excretion. It helps regulate body temperature.

VITAMINS

Vitamin A—promotes good eyesight and helps keep the skin and mucous membranes resistant to infection. Best sources: liver, sweet potatoes, carrots, kale, cantaloupe, turnip greens, collard greens, broccoli, fortified milk.

Vitamin B_1 (thiamine)—prevents beriberi. Essential to carbohydrate metabolism and health of nervous system. Best sources: pork, enriched cereals, grains, soybeans, nuts.

Vitamin B_2 (riboflavin)—protects the skin, mouth, eyes, eyelids, and mucous membranes. Essential to protein and energy metabolism. Best sources: milk, meat, poultry, cheese, broccoli, spinach.

Vitamin B_6 (pyridoxine)—important in the regulation of the central nervous system and in protein metabolism. Best sources: whole grains, meats, fish, poultry, nuts, brewers' yeast.

Vitamin B_{12} (cobalamin)—needed to form red blood cells. Best sources: meat, fish, poultry, eggs, dairy products.

Niacin—maintains health of skin, tongue, digestive system. Best sources: poultry, peanuts, fish, enriched flour and bread.

Folic acid (folacin)—required for normal blood cell formation, growth, and reproduction and for important chemical reactions in body cells. Best sources: yeast, orange juice, green leafy vegetables, wheat germ, asparagus, broccoli, nuts.

Other B vitamins—biotin, pantothenic acid.

Vitamin C (ascorbic acid)—maintains collagen, a protein necessary for the formation of skin, ligaments, and bones. It helps heal wounds and mend fractures and aids in resisting some types of viral and bacterial infections. Best sources: citrus fruits and juices, cantaloupe, broccoli, brussels sprouts, potatoes and sweet potatoes, tomatoes, cabbage.

Vitamin D—important for bone development. Best sources: sunlight, fortified milk and milk products, fish-liver oils, egg yolks.

Vitamin E (tocopherol)—helps protect red blood cells. Best sources: vegetable oils, wheat germ, whole grains, eggs, peanuts, margarine, green leafy vegetables.

Vitamin K—necessary for formation of prothrombin, which helps blood to clot. Also made by intestinal bacteria. Best dietary sources: green leafy vegetables, tomatoes.

MINERALS

Calcium—works with phosphorus in building and maintaining bones and teeth. Best sources: milk and milk products, cheese, blackstrap molasses, some types of tofu.

Phosphorus—performs more functions than any other mineral, and plays a part in nearly every chemical reaction in the body. Best sources: cheese, milk, meats, poultry, fish, tofu.

Iron—Necessary for the formation of myoglobin, which is a reservoir of oxygen for muscle tissue, and hemoglobin, which transports oxygen in the blood. Best sources: lean meats, beans, green leafy vegetables, shellfish, enriched breads and cereals, whole grains.

Other minerals—chromium, cobalt, copper, fluorine, iodine, magnesium, manganese, molybdenum, potassium, selenium, sodium, sulfur, and zinc.

Understanding Food Label Claims

Source: U.S. Food and Drug Admin., Center for Food Safety and Applied Nutrition

The federal Nutrition Labeling and Education Act of 1990 provides that manufacturers can make certain claims on processed food labels only if they meet the definitions specified here:

SUGAR

Sugar free: less than 0.5g per serving

No added sugar; Without added sugar; No sugar added: No sugars added during processing or packing, including ingredients that contain sugars (for example, fruit juices, applesauce, or dried fruit).

Processing does not increase sugar content above the amount naturally in the ingredients. (A functionally insignificant increase in sugars is acceptable from processes used for purposes other than increasing sugar content.)

Food for which it substitutes normally contains added sugars.

Reduced sugar: at least 25% less sugar than reference food

FAT

Fat free: less than 0.5g of fat per serving

Saturated fat free: less than 0.5g of saturated fat per serving, and the level of trans fatty acids does not exceed 1% of total fat

Low fat: 3g or less per serving and, if the serving is 30g or less or 2 tbs or less, per 50g of the food

Low saturated fat: 1g or less per serving and not more than 15% of calories from saturated fatty acids

Reduced or Less fat: at least 25% less per serving than reference food

FIBER

High fiber: 5g or more per serving. (Also, must meet low-fat definition, or must state level of total fat.)

Good source of fiber: 2.5g to 4.9g per serving

More or Added fiber: at least 2.5g more per serving than reference food

SODIUM

Sodium free: less than 5mg per serving

Low sodium: 140 mg or less per serving and, if the serving is 30g or less or 2 tbs or less, per 50g of the food

Very low sodium: 35 mg or less per serving and, if the serving is 30g or less or 2 tbs or less, per 50g of the food

Reduced or Less sodium: at least 25% less per serving than reference food

CALORIES

Low calorie: 40 calories or less per serving; if the serving is 30g or less or 2 tablespoons or less, 40 calories or less per 50g of food

Calorie free: under 5 calories per serving

Reduced or Fewer calories: at least 25% fewer calories than reference food

CHOLESTEROL

Cholesterol free: less than 2mg of cholesterol and 2g or less of saturated fat per serving

Low cholesterol: 20mg or less and 2g or less of saturated fat per serving and, if the serving is 30g or less or 2 tbs or less, per 50g of the food

Reduced or Less cholesterol: at least 25% less than reference food

Other Food Label Claims

Source: Food Safety and Inspection Service, U.S. Department of Agriculture

The FDA allows food producers and marketers to use language on their packaging that advertises the health benefits and production methods of their products. Products marked as "certified" have been formally evaluated for class, grade, or other quality characteristics by the USDA's Food Safety and Inspection Service. Below are some common packaging terms and their meanings.

Organic: Produced by farmers who use environmentally friendly methods to raise their crops or animals. Before a product can be labeled "organic," the farm where the food is grown must pass a special inspection by a USDA official. Organic foods must be produced without conventional pesticides; fertilizers made with synthetic ingredients, sewage or sludge; bioengineering; or ionizing radiation.

The official *USDA Organic* label may appear on vegetables, fruit, packages of meat, cartons of milk, eggs, cheese, and other single-ingredient foods. Foods with more than one ingredient can place the official seal on their packaging if at least 95% of the ingredients are organic. Products with at least 70% organic ingredients may advertise prominently on the front of the package that the item contains organic ingredients. Products with some organic ingredients, but less than 70%, may not make any organic claims on the front of the package, but may list organic ingredients on the side panel. Foods that contain 100% organic ingredients may advertise that fact on the front of the packaging along with the organic seal.

Natural: A product that does not contain any artificial ingredient or added color, and which has been minimally pro-

cessed. The label must explain the specific use of the term natural with regard to the product, such as: no added colorings, no artificial ingredients, minimally processed.

Free-range: Generally means that the product comes from an animal that was given access to the outdoors to roam for an unspecified amount of time each day. Animals raised in slaughterhouses are not considered free range. Free range products do not necessarily mean healthier or more disease-free.

Halal and **Zabiah Halal:** Produced in federally inspected meat packing plants and handled in accordance with Islamic law and under Islamic authority.

Kosher: Only used on meat and poultry products prepared under Rabbinical supervision.

Minimal Processing: Produced using only traditional physical processes which do not fundamentally alter the raw products, in order to make food edible, to preserve it, or to make it safe for human consumption. Includes smoking, roasting, freezing, drying, and fermenting; applies mostly to meat and poultry.

No Hormones: Hormones are not allowed in raising hogs or poultry, so those products may not make this claim. If sufficient documentation is provided to the USDA to prove that hormones were not used, this term may be used on packages of beef.

No Antibiotics: This claim may be made on a package if sufficient documentation is provided to the USDA that shows the animals were raised without being administered antibiotics.

Recommended Levels for Vitamins

Source: Food and Nutrition Board, National Academy of Sciences—Institute of Medicine, 2005
in milligrams per day (mg/d) or in micrograms per day (µg/d); asterisks denote levels defined as "adequate intake" (AI).

		Vitamin A (µg/d)[1]	Vitamin C (mg/d)	Vitamin D (µg/d)[2]	Vitamin E (mg/d)	Vitamin K (µg/d)	Thiamin (mg/d)	Riboflavin (mg/d)	Niacin (mg/d)[3]	Vitamin B6 (mg/d)	Folate (µg/d)[4]	Vitamin B12 (µg/d)	Pantothenic Acid (mg/d)	Biotin (µg/d)	Choline (mg/d)[5]
Infants	0-6 mos	400*	40*	5*	4*	2.0*	0.2*	0.3*	2*	0.1*	65*	0.4*	1.7*	5*	125*
	7-12 mos	500*	50*	5*	5*	2.5*	0.3*	0.4*	4*	0.3*	80*	0.5*	1.8*	6*	150*
Children	1-3 yrs	300	15	5*	6	30*	0.5	0.5	6	0.5	150	0.9	2*	8*	200*
	4-8 yrs	400	25	5*	7	55*	0.6	0.6	8	0.6	200	1.2	3*	12*	250*
Males	9-13 yrs	600	45	5*	11	60*	0.9	0.9	12	1.0	300	1.8	4*	20*	375*
	14-18 yrs	900	75	5*	15	75*	1.2	1.3	16	1.3	400	2.4	5*	25*	550*
	19-30 yrs	900	90	5*	15	120*	1.2	1.3	16	1.3	400	2.4	5*	30*	550*
	31-50 yrs	900	90	5*	15	120*	1.2	1.3	16	1.3	400	2.4	5*	30*	550*
	51-70 yrs	900	90	10*	15	120*	1.2	1.3	16	1.7	400	2.4[6]	5*	30*	550*
	over 70 yrs ...	900	90	15*	15	120*	1.2	1.3	16	1.7	400	2.4[6]	5*	30*	550*
Females	9-13 yrs	600	45	5*	11	60*	0.9	0.9	12	1.0	300	1.8	4*	20*	375*
	14-18 yrs	700	65	5*	15	75*	1.0	1.0	14	1.2	400[7]	2.4	5*	25*	400*
	19-30 yrs	700	75	5*	15	90*	1.1	1.1	14	1.3	400[7]	2.4	5*	30*	425*
	31-50 yrs	700	75	5*	15	90*	1.1	1.1	14	1.3	400[7]	2.4	5*	30*	425*
	51-70 yrs	700	75	10*	15	90*	1.1	1.1	14	1.5	400	2.4[6]	5*	30*	425*
	over 70 yrs ...	700	75	15*	15	90*	1.1	1.1	14	1.5	400	2.4[6]	5*	30*	425*
Pregnancy	18 yrs. or less.	750	80	5*	15	75*	1.4	1.4	18	1.9	600[8]	2.6	6*	30*	450*
	19-30 yrs.....	770	85	5*	15	90*	1.4	1.4	18	1.9	600[8]	2.6	6*	30*	450*
	31-50 yrs.....	770	85	5*	15	90*	1.4	1.4	18	1.9	600[8]	2.6	6*	30*	450*
Lactation	18 yrs. or less.	1,200	115	5*	19	75*	1.4	1.6	17	2.0	500	2.8	7*	35*	550*
	19-30 yrs.....	1,300	120	5*	19	90*	1.4	1.6	17	2.0	500	2.8	7*	35*	550*
	31-50 yrs.....	1,300	120	5*	19	90*	1.4	1.6	17	2.0	500	2.8	7*	35*	550*

NOTE: For healthy breastfed infants, the AI is the mean intake. The AI for other life stage and gender groups is believed to cover needs of all individuals in the group, but lack of data or uncertainty in the data prevent being able to specify with confidence the percentage of individuals covered by this intake. (1) As retinol activity equivalents. (2) In the absence of adequate exposure to sunlight. (3) As niacin equivalents (NE). 1 mg of niacin = 60 mg of tryptophan; 0-6 months = preformed niacin (not NE). (4) As dietary folate equivalents (DFE). 1 DFE = 1 µg food folate = 0.6 µg of folic acid from fortified food or as a supplement consumed with food = 0.5 µg of a supplement taken on an empty stomach. (5) Although AIs have been set for choline, there are few data to assess whether a dietary supply of choline is needed at all stages of the life cycle, and it may be that the choline requirement can be met by endogenous synthesis at some of these stages. (6) Because 10-30% of older people may malabsorb food-bound B_{12}, it is advisable for those older than 50 years to meet their RDA mainly by consuming foods fortified with B_{12} or a supplement containing B_{12}. (7) In view of evidence linking folate intake with neural tube defects in the fetus, it is recommended that all women capable of becoming pregnant consume 400 µg from supplements or fortified foods in addition to intake of food folate from a varied diet. (8) It is assumed that women will continue consuming 400 µg from supplements or fortified food until their pregnancy is confirmed and they enter prenatal care, which ordinarily occurs after the end of the periconceptional period—the critical time for formation of the neural tube.

Recommended Levels for Elements (Minerals)

Source: Food and Nutrition Board, National Academy of Sciences—Institute of Medicine, 2005
in milligrams per day (mg/d) or in micrograms per day (µg/d); asterisks denote levels defined as "adequate intake" (AI).

		Calcium (mg/d)	Chromium (µg/d)	Copper (µg/d)	Fluoride (mg/d)	Iodine (µg/d)	Iron (mg/d)	Magnesium (mg/d)	Manganese (mg/d)	Molybdenum (µg/d)	Phosphorus (mg/d)	Selenium (µg/d)	Zinc (mg/d)
Infants	0-6 mos......	210*	0.2*	200*	0.01*	110*	0.27*	30*	0.003*	2*	100*	15*	2*
	7-12 mos.....	270*	5.5*	220*	0.5*	130*	11	75*	0.6*	3*	275*	20*	3
	1-3 yrs.......	500*	11*	340	0.7*	90	7	80	1.2*	17	460	20	3
	4-8 yrs.......	800*	15*	440	1*	90	10	130	1.5*	22	500	30	5
Males	9-13 yrs......	1,300*	25*	700	2*	120	8	240	1.9*	34	1,250	40	8
	14-18 yrs.....	1,300*	35*	890	3*	150	11	410	2.2*	43	1,250	55	11
	19-30 yrs.....	1,000*	35*	900	4*	150	8	400	2.3*	45	700	55	11
	31-50 yrs.....	1,000*	35*	900	4*	150	8	420	2.3*	45	700	55	11
	51-70 yrs.....	1,200*	30*	900	4*	150	8	420	2.3*	45	700	55	11
	over 70 yrs ...	1,200*	30*	900	4*	150	8	420	2.3*	45	700	55	11
Females	9-13 yrs......	1,300*	21*	700	2*	120	8	240	1.6*	34	1,250	40	8
	14-18 yrs.....	1,300*	24*	890	3*	150	15	360	1.6*	43	1,250	55	9
	19-30 yrs.....	1,000*	25*	900	3*	150	18	310	1.8*	45	700	55	8
	31-50 yrs.....	1,000*	25*	900	3*	150	18	320	1.8*	45	700	55	8
	51-70 yrs.....	1,200*	20*	900	3*	150	8	320	1.8*	45	700	55	8
	over 70 yrs ...	1,200*	20*	900	3*	150	8	320	1.8*	45	700	55	8
Pregnancy	18 yrs. or less.	1,300*	29*	1,000	3*	220	27	400	2.0*	50	1,250	60	12
	19-30 yrs.....	1,000*	30*	1,000	3*	220	27	350	2.0*	50	700	60	11
	31-50 yrs.....	1,000*	30*	1,000	3*	220	27	360	2.0*	50	700	60	11
Lactation	18 yrs. or less.	1,300*	44*	1,300	3*	290	10	360	2.6*	50	1,250	70	13
	19-30 yrs.....	1,000*	45*	1,300	3*	290	9	310	2.6*	50	700	70	12
	31-50 yrs.....	1,000*	45*	1,300	3*	290	9	320	2.6*	50	700	70	12

Dietary Requirements

The Food and Nutrition Board of the National Academy of Sciences' Institute of Medicine, in reports published from 1997 to 2005, set **Dietary Reference Intakes (DRIs)** for vitamins and elements (often called minerals). The DRIs, based on recent scientific research, establish daily consumption values that aim to optimize health at all stages of life, not just to guard against nutritional deficiencies.

The DRIs include 4 categories of values. The **Recommended Dietary Allowance (RDA)** gives an intake that meets the nutrient requirements of almost all (97-98%) healthy individuals in a specified group. The **Estimated Average Requirement (EAR)** is the intake that meets the estimated nutrient need of half the individuals in a specified group, while the **Adequate Intake (AI)** is the value given

when adequate scientific evidence is not available to calculate an EAR. For healthy breastfed infants, the AI is the mean intake; for other life stage groups the AI is thought to cover the needs of all individuals in the group, but lack of data or uncertainty in the data prevents the percentage of individuals covered from being specified with confidence. The **Tolerable Upper Intake Level (UL)** designates the maximum intake that is unlikely to pose risks of adverse health effects in almost all healthy individuals in a specified group; taking the nutrient above that level could be bad for one's health. RDAs and AIs may both be used as goals for individual intake.

The tables, give the RDA or, where not available, the AI, followed by an asterisk(*).

Weight Guidelines for Adults

Source: *Dietary Guidelines for Americans, 2005, U.S. Dept. of Agriculture.*

Guidelines on identification, evaluation, and treatment of overweight and obesity in adults were released in June 1998 by the National Heart, Lung, and Blood Institute (NHLBI), in cooperation with the National Institute of Diabetes and Digestive and Kidney Diseases. The guidelines, based on research into risk factors in heart disease, stroke, and other conditions, define degrees of overweight and obesity in terms of **body mass index (BMI)**, which is based on weight and height and is strongly correlated with total body fat content. A BMI of 25-29 is said to indicate **overweight**; a BMI of 30 or above is said to indicate **obesity**. Weight reduction is advised for persons with a BMI of 25 or higher. (Previous guidelines have been less stringent.) Factors such as large waist circumference, high blood pressure or cholesterol, and a family history of obesity-related disease may increase risk.

Despite growing awareness of the health problems associ-

ated, nearly 1/3 of Americans adults are obese (have a BMI of 30 or greater) and the number is growing, according to the National Center for Health Statistics. A high prevalence of overweight and obesity is a huge public health concern because excess body fat has been associated with type 2 diabetes, hypertension, dyslipidemia, cardiovascular disease, stroke, gall bladder disease, respiratory dysfunction, gout, osteoarthritis, and certain kinds of cancers. Over the last 2 decades, the prevalence of overweight children has doubled, and among adolescents it has tripled. It is estimated that, in 2005, as many as 16% of children and adolescents were overweight.

The table below shows the BMI for certain heights and weights. For weight reduction tips, contact the Weight-control Information Network, 1 WIN Way, Bethesda, MD 20892-3665. Phone: 1-877-946-4627. Website: win.niddk.nih.gov

Weight (lbs)

Height	HEALTHY						OVERWEIGHT					OBESE						
4'10"	91	96	100	105	110	115	119	124	129	134	138	143	148	153	158	162	167	172	177 181
4'11"	94	99	104	109	114	119	124	128	133	138	143	148	153	158	163	168	173	178	183 188
5'0"	97	102	107	112	118	123	128	133	138	143	148	153	158	163	168	174	179	184	189 194
5'1"	100	106	111	116	122	127	132	137	143	148	153	158	164	169	174	180	185	190	195 201
5'2"	104	109	115	120	126	131	136	142	147	153	158	164	169	175	180	186	191	196	202 207
5'3"	107	113	118	124	130	135	141	146	152	158	163	169	175	180	186	191	197	203	208 214
5'4"	110	116	122	128	134	140	145	151	157	163	169	174	180	186	192	197	204	209	215 221
5'5"	114	120	126	132	138	144	150	156	162	168	174	180	186	192	198	204	210	216	222 228
5'6"	118	124	130	136	142	148	155	161	167	173	179	186	192	198	204	210	216	223	229 235
5'7"	121	127	134	140	146	153	159	166	172	178	185	191	198	204	211	217	223	230	236 242
5'8"	125	131	138	144	151	158	164	171	177	184	190	197	203	210	216	223	230	236	243 249
5'9"	128	135	142	149	155	162	169	176	182	189	195	203	209	216	223	230	236	243	250 257
5'10"	132	139	146	153	160	167	174	181	188	195	202	209	216	222	229	236	243	250	257 264
5'11"	136	143	150	157	165	172	179	186	193	200	208	215	222	229	236	243	250	257	265 272
6'0"	140	147	154	162	169	177	184	191	199	206	213	221	228	235	242	250	258	265	272 279
6'1"	144	151	159	166	174	182	189	197	204	212	219	227	235	242	250	257	265	272	280 288
6'2"	148	155	163	171	179	186	194	202	210	218	225	233	241	249	256	264	272	280	287 295
6'3"	152	160	168	176	184	192	200	208	216	224	232	240	248	256	264	272	279	287	295 303
6'4"	156	164	172	180	189	197	205	213	221	230	238	246	254	263	271	279	287	295	304 312
BMI[1]	19	20	21	22	23	24	25	26	27	28	29	30	31	32	33	34	35	36	37 38

(1) The BMI numbers apply to both men and women. Some very muscular people may have a high BMI without health risks.

Finding Your Target Heart Rate

Source: Carole Casten, EdD, *Aerobics Today;* Peg Jordan, RN, Aerobics and Fitness Assoc. of America

The target heart rate is the heartbeat rate a person should have during aerobic exercise (such as running, fast walking, cycling, or cross-country skiing) to get the full benefit of the exercise for cardiovascular conditioning.

First, determine the intensity level at which one would like to exercise. A sedentary person may want to begin an exercise regimen at the 60% level and work up gradually to the 70% level. Athletes and highly fit individuals must work at an 85% or higher level to receive benefits.

Second, calculate the target heart rate. One common way is by using the American College of Sports Medicine Method.

To obtain cardiovascular fitness benefits from aerobic exercise, it is recommended that an individual participate in an aerobic activity at least 3-5 times a week for 20-30 minutes per session, although cardiac patients and very sedentary individuals can obtain benefits with shorter periods (15-20 minutes). Generally, training changes occur in 4-6 weeks, but they can occur in as little as 2 weeks.

Using the American College of Sports Medicine Method to calculate one's target heart rate, an individual should subtract his or her age from 220, then multiply by the desired intensity level of the workout. Then divide the answer by 6 for a 10-second pulse count. (The 10-second pulse count is useful for checking whether the target heart rate is being achieved during the workout. One can easily check one's pulse—at the wrist or side of the neck—counting the number of beats in 10 seconds.)

For example, a 20-year-old wishing to exercise at 70% intensity would employ the following steps:

Maximum Heart Rate	220 − 20 = 200
Target Heart Rate	200 × .70 = 140
10-second Pulse Count	140/6 = 23

To work at the desired level of intensity, this 20-year-old would strive for a target heart rate of 140 beats per minute, or a 10-second pulse count of 23.

Calories Used During Physical Activity

Source: U.S. Dept. of Agriculture

Amounts of calories burned during physical activities are estimates for a 154-pound person. The more an individual weighs the more calories he or she will burn up with the same degree of exercise.

Moderate physical activities	In 1 hour	In 30 min.	Vigorous physical activities	In 1 hour	In 30 min.
Hiking	370	185	Running/jogging (5 miles per hour)	590	295
Light gardening/yard work	330	165	Bicycling (more than 10 miles per hour)	590	295
Dancing	330	165	Swimming (slow freestyle laps)	510	255
Golf (walking and carrying clubs)	330	165	Aerobics	480	240
Bicycling (less than 10 miles per hour)	290	145	Walking (4 ½ miles per hour)	460	230
Walking (3 ½ miles per hour)	280	140	Heavy yard work (e.g., chopping wood)	440	220
Weight training (general light workout)	220	110	Weight lifting (vigorous effort)	440	220
Stretching	180	90	Basketball (vigorous)	440	220

Basic First Aid

Source: Courtesy of the American National Red Cross. All rights reserved in all countries.

NOTE: This information is not intended to be a substitute for formal training. It is recommended that you contact your local American Red Cross chapter (www.redcross.org) to sign up for a First Aid/CPR/AED course.

It is important to get medical assistance as soon as possible, but knowing what to do until a doctor or other trained person gets to the scene can save a life, especially in cases of severe bleeding, choking, poisoning, and shock.

People with special medical problems, such as diabetes, cardiovascular disease, epilepsy, or allergies, are urged to wear some sort of emblem identifying the problem, as a safeguard against receiving medication that might be harmful or even fatal. Emblems may be obtained from Medic Alert Foundation, 2323 Colorado Ave., Turlock, CA 95382; 888-633-4298.

Animal bite — Call 9-1-1 or the local emergency number if the wound is bleeding seriously or if you suspect the animal might have rabies. Control any bleeding. Wash minor wounds with soap under running water and apply triple antibiotic ointment and a dressing. When possible, proper authorities should test the animal for rabies.

Asphyxiation — Call 9-1-1, or the local emergency number. Give care for any life-threatening conditions.

Bleeding — Use a barrier between your hand and the wound to help prevent infection. Cover wound with a sterile compress. Apply direct pressure until bleeding stops. Cover compress with a bandage. Call 9-1-1, or the local emergency number if bleeding is severe.

Burn — Check for life-threatening conditions. If the burn is mild, with skin unbroken and no blisters, flush with cold running water until pain subsides. Apply a loose, sterile, dry dressing to prevent infection. If severe, call 9-1-1 or the local emergency number. Care for shock (see below). Keep the person from getting chilled or overheated until advanced medical assistance arrives. Do not try to clean a severe burn or break blisters.

Chemical in eye — Call 9-1-1 or the local emergency number. With the victim's head turned to the side with the affected eye lower than the unaffected eye, continuously flush the injured eye with water.

Choking — See **First Aid for Choking**, below.

Convulsions (seizures) — Remove nearby objects that might cause injury. Protect the person's head by placing a thin folded towel or clothing under it. If there is fluid in the person's mouth, roll him or her on one side so that the fluid may drain from the mouth. Do not place anything between the person's teeth. Stay with the person until he or she is fully conscious. If convulsions do not stop, get medical attention immediately.

Cut (minor) — Use a clean barrier between your hand and the wound to prevent infection. Apply direct pressure for a few minutes to control any bleeding. Wash the wound thoroughly with soap and water and apply triple-antibiotic ointment or cream. Cover the wound with a sterile compress and a bandage (or an adhesive bandage).

Fainting — If the victim feels faint, lower him or her to the ground. Lay the victim down on his or her back. If fainted, elevate the victim's legs 8 to 12 inches. Care for any life-threatening conditions. Loosen any restrictive clothing and check for any other signs of injury. Call 9-1-1 or the local emergency number.

Foreign object in eye — If an object is embedded in someone's eye do not remove it. If not embedded, try to remove the object by having the victim blink several times. If the object doesn't come out, try gently flushing the eye with water. Do not rub the eye. If the object still doesn't come out, the victim should receive professional medical attention.

Frostbite — Handle frostbitten area gently. Do not rub., Soak affected area in warm water (not warmer than 105°F), if there is no danger of area refreezing. Do not allow frostbitten area to touch the container. Keep the frostbitten part in the water until normal color returns and it feels warm. Loosely bandage the area with dry, sterile dressings. If fingers or toes are frostbitten, put sterile gauze between them. Call 9-1-1 or seek emergency help as soon as possible.

Heat Stroke and Heat Exhaustion — Remove the victim from the heat. Loosen any tight clothing. Fan the person and apply cool, wet cloths to the skin. If the victim is conscious, give him or her cool water to drink slowly. Call 9-1-1 if the victim's condition does not improve or if you suspect heat stroke.

Heart Attack and Stroke — See page 142.

Hypothermia — Call 9-1-1 or the local emergency number. Move victim to a warm place. Remove wet clothing and dry victim, if necessary. Warm victim gradually by wrapping the person in warm blankets or clothing. Apply heat pads or other heat sources if available, but not directly to the body. If the person is alert, give the victim warm, non-alcoholic and decaffeinated liquids to drink.

Loss of Limb — Call 9-1-1 or the local emergency number and care for any life-threatening conditions. If a limb is severed, it is important to properly protect the limb so that it can possibly be reattached. After the victim is cared for, the limb should be wrapped in a sterile gauze or clean material and placed in a clean plastic bag, garbage can, or other suitable container. Pack ice around the limb on the OUTSIDE of the bag to keep the limb cold. Be sure the limb is taken to the hospital with the person.

Poisoning — Care for any life-threatening conditions. Call the National Poison Control Center (800-222-1222) , 9-1-1 or the local emergency number and follow their directions. Do not give the victim any food or drink or induce vomiting, unless specified by medical professionals.

Shock (injury-related) — Monitor breathing and consciousness. Have the victim lie down and keep him or her as comfortable as possible. Elevate legs 8 to 12 in. if you do not suspect a head, neck or back injury or broken bones in the hips or legs. Maintain normal body temperature; if the weather is cold or damp, place blankets or extra clothing over and under the victim; if weather is hot, provide shade. Do not attempt to move victim if spinal injury is suspected.

Snakebite — Call 9-1-1 or the local emergency number. Wash the injury. Keep the area still and at a lower level than the heart. Keep the victim calm. If the victim cannot get professional medical help within 30 minutes, consider using a snakebite kit if available. Care for a bite from an elapid snake, such as a coral snake, the same except that after washing the wound you should apply an elastic roller bandage.

Sprains and fractures — Apply ice to reduce swelling and pain. Do not try to straighten or move broken limbs. Apply a splint to immobilize the injured area only if you have to move or transport the victim to seek medical attention and if it does not cause more pain. If you suspect a serious injury, call 9-1-1 or the local emergency number.

Sting from insect — If possible, remove stinger by scraping it away with your finger, a plastic card (like a credit card) or using tweezers. If you use tweezers, grasp the stinger, not the venom sac. Wash the area with soap and water; cover it to keep it clean. Apply a cold pack to reduce pain and swelling. Call 9-1-1 or the local emergency number immediately if body swells, patient collapses, or you know that the victim is allergic to the sting.

Unconsciousness — Call 9-1-1 or the local emergency number immediately. Care for any life-threatening conditions. If the person shows signs of life (movement and breathing), place him or her in the recovery position (i.e., lying on a side, with head supported, so that the airway is open). Do not move the person if a spinal injury is suspected.

First Aid for Choking

The recommended first aid for a conscious choking victim who is unable to speak, cough or breathe, is to deliver a series of 5 back blows and 5 abdominal thrusts. Have someone call 9-1-1 or the local emergency number. Obtain consent. Lean the victim forward and give 5 back blows with the heel of your hand. Stand or kneel behind the victim and wrap your arms around his or her waist. Make a fist with one hand and place the thumb side against the middle of the person's abdomen, just above the navel and well below the lower tip of the breastbone. Grasp the fist with the other hand and give 5 quick, upward thrusts into the abdomen. Continue back blows and abdominal thrusts until the object is dislodged and the person can breathe or cough forcefully, or becomes unconscious.

Where to Get Help

Source: Based on *Health & Medical Year Book.* © by Collier Newfield, Inc.; additional data, World Almanac research

Listed here are some of the major U.S. and Canadian organizations providing information about good health practices generally, or about specific conditions and how to deal with them. (Canadian sources are identified as such.) Where a toll-free number is not available, an address is given when possible.

Some entries conclude with an e-mail address for the organization and/or an address for its Internet site, where you can also obtain useful information. In addition to these selected sites, there is a vast array of medical information on the Internet; however, it is very important to be certain that the source of information is reliable and accurate. Always check with a physician before embarking on any new health-related undertaking.

General Sources

Centers for Disease Control and Prevention Voice Information System
800-311-3435
Recorded information about public health topics, such as AIDS and Lyme disease. Also, you can request to talk with a CDC expert or have information faxed to you.
Website: www.cdc.gov

National Health Information Center
800-336-4797; in Maryland, 301-565-4167
Phone numbers for more than 1,000 health-related organizations in the United States. Printed materials offered.
E-mail: info@nhic.org
Website: www.health.gov/NHIC

National Institutes of Health
301-496-4000
Free information, including the latest research findings, on many diseases.
E-mail: NIHinfo@OD.NIH.GOV
Website: www.nih.gov

Aging

Administration on Aging's Eldercare Locator Line
800-677-1116
Information and assistance on a wide range of services and programs including adult day-care and respite services, consumer fraud, hospital and nursing home information, legal services, elder abuse/protective services, Medicaid/Medigap information, tax assistance, and transportation.
E-mail: eldercarelocator@apherix.gov
Website: www.eldercare.gov

National Institute on Aging
800-222-2225
Information and publications about disabling conditions, support groups, and community resources.
Website: www.nia.nih.gov

AIDS

AIDSinfo
800-HIV-0440
Information on federally and privately sponsored clinical trials for patients with AIDS or HIV; treatment information for people with AIDS, their families and health care providers
E-mail: ContactUs@aidsinfo.nih.gov
Website: www.aidsinfo.nih.gov

Canadian AIDS Society
613-230-3580
Written materials and referrals.
Website: www.cdnaids.ca
E-mail: CASinfo@cdnaids.ca

CDC-INFO
1-800 CDC-INFO (232-4636);
TTY: 1-818-232-6348
Information on the prevention and spread of AIDS, along with referrals.
E-mail: cdcinfo@cdc.gov
Website: www.cdc.gov/hiv/hivinfo/nah.htm

Alcoholism and Drug Abuse

Alcoholics Anonymous
212-870-3400
Worldwide support groups for alcoholics. Check phone book for local chapters.
Websites: www.alcoholics-anonymous.org or www.AA.org

American Council on Alcoholism
800-527-5344
Treatment referrals and counseling for recovering alcoholics.
E-mail: info@aca-usa.org
Website: www.aca-usa.org

Phoenix House
Answers questions on substance abuse and provides referrals to treatment centers.
Website: www.drughelp.org

National Clearinghouse for Alcohol and Drug Information
800-729-6686
Provides written materials on alcohol and drug-related subjects.
Website: www.health.org

National Council on Alcoholism and Drug Dependence Hopeline
800-622-2255
Advisory and referral service.
E-mail: national@ncadd.org
Website: www.ncadd.org

Wellplace
800-821-4357, 24 hours
Referrals to local facilities
Website: www.wellplace.com

Alzheimer's Disease

Alzheimer's Association
800-272-3900
Gives referrals to local chapters and support groups; offers information on publications available from the association.
E-mail: info@alz.org
Website: www.alz.org

Alzheimer's Society of Canada
416-488-8772
Gives phone numbers for local support chapters. Publishes support materials.
E-mail: info@alzheimer.ca
Website: www.alzheimer.ca

Amyotrophic Lateral Sclerosis (ALS)

ALS Association 818-880-9007
Information about ALS (Lou Gehrig's Disease) and referrals to ALS specialists, local chapters and support groups.
Website: www.alsa.org

Arthritis

Arthritis Foundation
800-283-7800
Information, publications, and referrals to local groups.
Website: www.arthritis.org

Arthritis Society (Canada)
393 University Ave., Suite 1700
Toronto, ON M5G 1E6
416-979-7228; in Ontario only, 800-321-1433
Phone numbers for local chapters.
E-mail: info@arthritis.ca
Website: www.arthritis.ca

National Institute of Arthritis and Musculoskeletal and Skin Diseases
877-226-4267 or 301-495-4484
Subject searches and resource referrals.
E-mail: niamsweb–l@mail.nih.gov
Website: www.niams.nih.gov

Asthma and Allergies
See also Lung Diseases

Asthma and Allergy Foundation of America
800-7-ASTHMA
Information; education; links to support groups.
E-mail: info@aafa.org
Website: www.aafa.org

American Academy of Allergy, Asthma, and Immunology Referral Line
800-822-ASMA, 24 hours; 414-272-6071
Patient information and referrals for asthma and allergies.
E-mail: info@aaaai.org
Website: www.aaaai.org

Autism

Autism Society of America
301-657-0881 or 800-3AUTISM
Information about autism, referral to local chapters.
E-mail: chapters@autism-society.org
Website: www.autism-society.org

Blindness and Eye Care

Canadian National Institute for the Blind
416-486-2500
National office offers training and library with braille books and audiotapes. Local chapters provide core services: orientation in mobility, sight enhancement, counseling, referrals, career aid, technology services.
Website: www.cnib.ca

Foundation Fighting Blindness
888-394-3937; TDD 800-683-5555
Answers questions about retinal degenerative diseases; has written materials.
E-mail: info@blindness.org
Website: www.blindness.org

Library of Congress National Library Service for the Blind and Physically Handicapped
800-424-8567; in Washington, DC, 202-707-5100; for the hearing impaired, TDD 202-707-0744
Information on libraries that offer talking books and books in **braille**.
E-mail: nls@loc.gov
Website: www.loc.gov/nls

National Association for Parents of Children with Visual Impairments
800-562-6265 or 617-972-7441
Support and information for parents of individuals who are visually impaired.
E-mail: napvi@perkins.org
Website: www.napvi.org

Blood Disorders

Cooley's Anemia Foundation
800-522-7222
Information on patient care and support groups; makes referrals to local chapters.
E-mail: info@cooleysanemia.org
Website: www.thalassemia.org

Sickle Cell Disease Association of America
800-421-8453; 310-216-6363
Referrals for genetic counseling and information packet.
E-mail: scdaa@sicklecelldisease.org
Website: www.sicklecelldisease.org

Burns

Phoenix Society
800-888-2876; 616-458-2773
Counseling network for burn survivors and information on self-help services for burn survivors and their families.
E-mail: info@phoenix-society.org
Website: www.phoenix-society.org

Cancer
American Cancer Society
800-ACS-2345
Publications and information about cancer and coping with cancer; makes referrals to local chapters for support services.
Website: www.cancer.org

Canadian Cancer Information Service
888-939-3333 or 416-961-7223
Information on prevention, treatment, drugs, clinical trails, local services.
E-mail: info@cis.cancer.ca
Website: www.cancer.ca

National Cancer Institute's Cancer Information Service
800-4-CANCER
Information about clinical trials, treatments, symptoms, prevention, referrals to support groups, and screening.
Website: cis.nci.nih.gov

Y-Me Breast Cancer Support Program
800-221-2141, 24 hours;
800-986-9505, Spanish, 24-hours
Information and literature on breast cancer, counseling, and referrals.
Website: www.y-me.org

Cerebral Palsy
Ontario Federation for Cerebral Palsy
Ontario only: 877-244-9686; 416-244-9686
Canada does not have a national cerebral palsy organization, but the provincial organizations offer information on housing, services, and coping with life, and each one will provide contact numbers for the others.
E-mail: info@ofcp.on.ca
Website: www.ofcp.on.ca

United Cerebral Palsy Associations
800-872-5827, (TTY) 202-973-7197; in Washington, DC, 202-776-0406
Written materials.
Website: www.ucpa.org

Child Abuse
See Domestic Violence

Children
American Academy of Pediatrics
847-434-4000
Child-care publications and materials; referrals to pediatricians.
E-mail: kidsdocs@aap.org
Website: www.aap.org

National Center for Missing and Exploited Children
800-843-5678; 703-274-3900. Operates 24 hours.
Hotline for reporting missing children and sightings of missing children.
Website: www.missingkids.com

National Runaway Switchboard
800-786-2929 (Runaway)
Crisis intervention and referrals for runaways. Runaways can leave messages for parents, and vice versa. Operates 24 hours.
E-mail: info@nrscrisisline.org
Website: www.nrscrisisline.org

Chronic Fatigue Syndrome
CFIDS Association of America
704-365-2343
Literature and a list of support groups.
E-mail: cfids@cfids.org
Website: www.cfids.org

Cystic Fibrosis
Canadian Cystic Fibrosis Foundation
416-485-9149;
800-378-2233 in Canada only,
Information and brochures; makes referrals to local chapters.
E-mail: info@cysticfibrosis.ca
Website: www.cysticfibrosis.ca

Cystic Fibrosis Foundation
800-FIGHT-CF or 301-951-4422
Answers questions and offers literature and referrals to local clinics.
E-mail: info@cff.org
Website: www.cff.org

Diabetes
American Diabetes Association
800-342-2383
Information about diabetes, nutrition, exercise, and treatment; offers referrals.
E-mail: askADA@diabetes.org
Website: www.diabetes.org

Canadian Diabetes Association
416-363-0177;
800-226-8464 in Canada only.
Information about diabetes and its management.
E-mail: info@diabetes.ca
Website: www.diabetes.ca

Juvenile Diabetes Research Foundation Hotline
800-533-2873
Answers questions, provides literature (some in Spanish). Offers referrals to local chapters, physicians, and clinics.
E-mail: info@jdf.org
Website: www.jdf.org

Digestive Diseases
Crohn's and Colitis Foundation of America
800-932-2423
Educational materials; offers referrals to local chapters, which can provide referrals to support groups and physicians.
E-mail: info@ccfa.org
Website: www.ccfa.org

Crohn's and Colitis Foundation of Canada
416-920-5035;
in Canada only, 800-387-1479
Will send out educational materials upon request.
E-mail: ccfc@ccfc.ca
Website: www.ccfc.ca

Domestic Violence
Childhelp's USA National Child Abuse Hotline
800-4-A-CHILD
Crisis intervention, professional counseling, referrals to local groups and shelters for runaways, and literature. Operates 24 hours.
Website: www.childhelpusa.org

National Council on Child Abuse and Family Violence
800-422-4453, (TTY) 800-787-3244
Information and referrals.
Website: www.nccafv.org

National Domestic Violence Hotline
800-799-7233; (TTY) 800-787-3224

Down Syndrome
National Down Syndrome Congress
800-232-6372; in Georgia, 770-604-9500
Answers questions on all aspects of Down syndrome. Provides referrals.
E-mail: info@ndsccenter.org
Website: www.ndsccenter.org

National Down Syndrome Society
800-221-4602; 212-460-9330 (NYC)
E-mail: info@ndss.org
Website: www.ndss.org

Drug Abuse
See Alcoholism and Drug Abuse

Dyslexia
International Dyslexia Association
800-ABCD-123; in Maryland, 410-296-0232
Information on testing, tutoring, and computers used to aid people with dyslexia and related disorders.
E-mail: info@interdys.org
Website: www.interdys.org

Eating Disorders
National Association of Anorexia Nervosa and Associated Disorders
847-831-3438
Written materials, referrals to health professionals treating eating disorders, telephone counseling, offers self-help groups and information on how to set up a self-help group.
E-mail: anad20@aol.com
Website: www.anad.org

Endometriosis
Endometriosis Association
800-992-ENDO, an answering machine for callers to request information; 414-355-2200
Website: www.endometriosisassn.org

Epilepsy
Epilepsy Foundation's Answer Place
800-332-1000, Mon. through Thurs.
Information and referrals to local chapters.
Website: www.epilepsyfoundation.org

Erectile Dysfunction
American Urological Association
866-746-4282.
Information on various urological disorders and referrals.
E-mail: aua@auanet.org
Website: www.auanet.org

Food Safety and Nutrition
Meat and Poultry Hotline of the U.S. Department of Agriculture's Food, Safety, and Inspection Service
888-674-6854; TTY 800-256-7072
Information on prevention of food-borne illness and the proper handling, preparation, storage, labeling, and cooking of meat, poultry, and eggs.
E-mail: MPHotline.fsis@usda.gov
Website: www.foodsafety.gov

FDA Center for Food Safety and Applied Nutrition Outreach & Information Center
888-SAFE-FOOD
Information on how to buy and use food products and on their proper handling and storage, women's health, and cosmetics & colors. Callers may speak to food specialists, Mon. through Fri., 10 am to 4 PM (EST).
Website: www.cfsan.fda.gov

Headaches
National Headache Foundation
888-NHF-5552
Literature on headaches and treatment.
E-mail: info@headaches.org
Website: www.headaches.org

Heart Disease and Stroke
American Heart Association
800-242-8721
Information, publications, and referrals to organizations.
Website: www.americanheart.org

National Institute of Neurological Disorders and Stroke
800-352-9424, 301-496-5751;
TTY 301-468-5981
Literature and information.
Website: www.ninds.nih.gov

National Stroke Association
800-787-6537; in Colorado, 303-649-9299
Information on support networks for stroke victims and their families; referrals to local support groups.
Website: www.stroke.org

Hospices
Children's Hospice International
800-242-4453, in Virginia, 703-684-0330
Information, referrals to children's hospices.
E-mail: info@chionline.org
Website: www.chionline.org

Hospice Education Institute Hospicelink
800-331-1620; in Maine, 207-255-8800
Information, referrals to local programs.
E-mail: info@hospiceworld.org
Website: www.hospiceworld.org

Huntington's Disease
Huntington's Disease Society of America
800-345-4372; in New York, 212-242-1968
Information and referrals to physicians and support groups.
E-mail: hdsainfo@hdsa.org
Website: www.hdsa.org

Kidney Diseases
Kidney Foundation of Canada
514-369-4806; in Canada only, 800-361-7494
Educational materials and general information.
Website: www.kidney.ca

National Kidney and Urologic Diseases Information Clearinghouse
800-891-5390
Information, referrals to organizations.
Website: www.kidney.niddk.nih.gov

National Kidney Foundation
800-622-9010, 212-889-2210
Information and referrals.
E-mail: info@kidney.org
Website: www.kidney.org

Lead Exposure
National Lead Information Center
800-424-LEAD
Recommendations (in English and Spanish) for reducing a child's exposure to lead. Referrals to state and local agencies.
Website: www.epa.gov/lead

Liver Diseases
American Liver Foundation
800-465-4837; 800-443-7872
Information on hepatitis, liver, and gallbladder diseases.
E-mail: info@liverfoundation.org
Website: www.liverfoundation.org

Lung Diseases
See also Asthma and Allergies
American Lung Association
Check the phone book for local listings or call the national office at 800-LUNG-USA for automatic connection to the office nearest you. Answers questions about asthma and lung diseases; publications and referrals.
Website: www.lungusa.org
Lung Line Information Service at the National Jewish Medical and Research Center
800-222-LUNG; outside the U.S.: 303-388-4461
Answers questions on asthma, emphysema, allergies, smoking, and other respiratory and immune system disorders.
E-mail: lungline@njc.org
Website: www.njc.org

Lupus
Lupus Foundation of America
800-558-0121; 202-349-1155
Sends information to those who leave name and address on answering machine.
E-mail: info@lupus.org
Website: www.lupus.org

Lyme Disease
Lyme Disease Foundation
860-870-0070
Written information; doctor referrals.
E-mail: lymefnd@aol.com
Website: www.lyme.org

Mental Health
Depression and Bipolar Support Alliance
800-826-3632
Support for patients and families, provides publications, and makes referrals to affiliated organizations.
E-mail: questions@dbsalliance.org
Website: www.dbsalliance.org
National Institute of Mental Health
301-443-4513, toll free 866-615-6464; TTY 301-443-8431
Information on a range of topics, from children's mental disorders to schizophrenia, depression, eating disorders, and others.
E-mail: nimhinfo@nih.gov
Website: www.nimh.nih.gov
National Mental Health Association
800-969-6642
Referrals to mental health groups.
Website: www.nmha.org

Multiple Sclerosis
Multiple Sclerosis Society of Canada
416-922-6065, 800-268-7582 in Canada only. Counseling, literature, and referrals to local chapters.
E-mail: info@mssociety.ca
Website: www.mssociety.ca
National Multiple Sclerosis Society
800-344-4867
Information about local chapters.
Website: www.nationalmssociety.org

Muscular Dystrophy
Muscular Dystrophy Association
800-572-1717
Written materials on 40 neuromuscular diseases, including muscular dystrophy. Will give information over the phone about such matters as MDA clinics, support groups, summer camps, and wheelchair purchase assistance.
E-mail: mda@mdausa.org
Website: www.mdausa.org

Nutrition
See Food Safety and Nutrition

Organ Donation
Living Bank
800-528-2971, 24 hours
A registry and referral service for people wanting to commit organs to transplantation or research.
E-mail: info@livingbank.org
Website: www.livingbank.org

Osteoporosis
National Osteoporosis Foundation
800-223-9994; in Washington, DC, 202-223-2226
Information packet available on request.
Website: www.nof.org

Pain
National Chronic Pain Outreach Association
540-862-9437
Information packet available on request.
Website: www.chronicpain.org

Parkinson's Disease
National Parkinson Foundation
800-327-4545; in Miami, 305-547-6666
Answers questions, makes physician referrals, and provides written information in English and Spanish.
E-mail: contact@parkinson.org
Website: www.parkinson.org
Parkinson Society Canada
800-565-3000, Canada only; 416-227-9700
Information; referrals to support groups.
E-mail: General.info@parkinson.ca
Website: www.parkinson.ca

Plastic Surgery
Plastic Surgery Refferal Service
888-475-2784
Referrals to board-certified plastic surgeons in the U.S. and Canada; general information.
Website: www.plasticsurgery.org

Polio
Post-Polio Health International
314-534-0475
Information on coping with the late effects of polio; referrals to other organizations.
E-mail: info@post-polio.org
Website: www.post-polio.org

Prostate Problems
American Urological Association Foundation
800-828-7866, 410-689-3990
Information and publications.
Website: www.urologyhealth.org

Rare Disorders
National Organization for Rare Disorders
800-999-6673, 203-744-0100
Information on diseases and networking programs; referrals to organizations for specific disorders.
E-mail: orphan@rarediseases.org
Website: www.rarediseases.org

Rehabilitation
National Rehabilitation Information Center
800-34-NARIC; in Maryland, 301-459-5900; TTY 301-459-5984
Research referrals and information on rehabilitation issues.
E-mail: naricinfo@heitechservices.com
Website: www.naric.com

Scleroderma
United Scleroderma Foundation
800-722-4673
Referrals to local support groups and treatment centers, as well as information on scleroderma and related skin disorders.
E-mail: sfinfo@scleroderma.org
Website: www.scleroderma.org

Sexually Transmitted Diseases
See also AIDS
National STD Hotline
800-227-8922; Spanish 800-344-7432
Information; confidential referrals.
E-mail: std-hivnet@ashastd.org
Website: www.ashastd.org

Sjogren's Syndrome
Sjogren's Syndrome Foundation
800-475-6473;
Provides an answering machine for callers to request treatment literature.
Website: www.sjogrens.org

Skin Problems
National Psoriasis Foundation
800-723-9166
Information and referrals.
E-mail: getinfo@psoriasis.org
Website: www.psoriasis.org

Speech and Hearing
American Speech-Language-Hearing Association Action Center
800-638-8255 (also TTY)
Materials on speech and language disorders and hearing impairment; referrals.
E-mail: actioncenter@asha.org
Website: www.asha.org
Canadian Hard of Hearing Association
800-263-8068, Canada only; TTY 613-526-2692; 613-526-1584
Publications; answers general questions.
E-mail: chhanational@chha.ca
Website: www.chha.ca
Dial a Hearing Screening Test
800-222-EARS
Answers questions on hearing problems. Makes referrals to local telephone numbers for a two-minute hearing test. Also to ear, nose, and throat specialists and to organizations that can provide specialized ear and hearing aid information. 9 AM-5 PM EST
Hearing Aid Helpline
800-521-5247, ext. 333
Information and distributes a directory of hearing aid specialists certified by the International Hearing Society.
Website: www.ihsinfo.org
National Center for Stuttering
800-221-2483; 212-532-1460
Information on stuttering in all age groups.
E-mail: martin.schwartz@nyu.edu
Website: www.stuttering.com
Stuttering Foundation of America
800-992-9392
Referrals to speech pathologists; resource lists, publications.
E-mail: info@stutteringhelp.org
Website: www.stutteringhelp.org

Spinal Injuries
National Spinal Cord Injury Association
800-962-9629; 301-214-4006
Peer counseling; referrals to local chapters and other organizations.
E-mail: info@spinalcord.org
Website: www.spinalcord.org

Stroke
See Heart Disease and Stroke

Sudden Infant Death Syndrome
American Sudden Infant Death Syndrome Institute
800-232-SIDS; in Georgia, 770-426-8746
Answers questions; literature; referrals to other organizations.
E-mail: prevent@sids.org
Website: www.sids.org

Tourette Syndrome
Tourette Syndrome Association
718-224-2999
Printed information.
E-mail: ts@tsa-usa.org
Website: tsa-usa.org

Urinary Incontinence
National Association for Continence
800-BLADDER, 843-377-0900
Information on bladder control, services available for incontinence, and assistive devices.
E-mail: memberservices@nafc.org
Website: www.nafc.org
Simon Foundation for Continence
800-23-SIMON
Support and literature on incontinence.
E-mail: Simoninfo@simonfoundation.org; jasmineschmidt@simonfoundation.org
Website: www.simonfoundation.org

Women's Health
National Women's Health Network
202-347-1140; 202-628-7814
Information and referrals on more than 70 women's health concerns.
E-mail: nwhn@nwhn.org
Website: www.nwhn.org
National Women's Health Resource Center
877-986-9472
A national clearinghouse for women's health information.
E-mail: snelson@healthywomen.org
Website: www.healthywomen.org

VITAL STATISTICS

Recent Trends in Vital Statistics

Source: National Center for Health Statistics, U.S. Dept. of Health and Human Services; latest years available

Highlights

Final U.S. data for 2004 reported by the National Center for Health Statistics show that birth rates declined slightly from 2003. The teen birth rate declined in 2004 for the 13th straight year, dropping to 41.2 births per 1,000 women aged 15-19 years; this was a one-third reduction since 1991.

According to provisional 2005 data, marriage rates and divorce rates both declined slightly from 2004, after a slight increase in 2003 and 2004. Life expectancy for all Americans at birth was 77.5 years in 2003, an all-time high and an increase of more than 2 years since 1990.

Births

An estimated 4,143,000 babies were born in the U.S. in 2005, a rise from 4,121,000 births in 2004. (The birth rate held steady at 14.0 per 1,000 total population, only lightly above the record low of 13.9 in 2002.)

The fertility rate (number of live births per 1,000 women aged 15-44 years) rose to an estimated 66.7 for 2005, up from the 2004 rate of 66.4; this marked the highest rate since 1993, but was still low by historical standards.

Deaths

The number of deaths during 2005 was estimated at 2,432,000 according to provisional data, up from 2,393,000 in 2004. The 2005 data showed a death rate of 8.2 per 1,000 population, up from 8.1 in 2004. The infant mortality rate was 6.8 infant deaths per 1,000 live births in 2005, up from 6.6 in 2004.

Natural Increase

As a result of natural increase (the excess of births over deaths), an estimated 1,711,000 persons were added to the population in 2005. The rate of increase (5.8 per 1,000 population) was down slightly from 5.9 for 2004.

Marriages

An estimated 2,230,000 marriages were performed in 2005, compared to 2,279,000 in 2004. The provisional marriage rate for 2005 (7.5 per 1,000 population) was down from the 2004 rate of 7.8.

Divorces

The provisional 2005 data give a divorce rate of 3.6 per 1,000 population, down from 3.7 in 2004. Data are incomplete, however. The NCHS no longer includes divorce data for California, Hawaii, Indiana, Louisiana, and Oklahoma.

Births and Deaths in the U.S.

Source: National Center for Health Statistics, U.S. Dept. of Health and Human Services

Year	BIRTHS Total number	Rate	DEATHS Total number	Rate	Year	BIRTHS Total number	Rate	DEATHS Total number	Rate
1960	4,257,850	23.7	1,711,982	9.5	1997	3,880,894	14.2	2,314,245	8.5
1970	3,731,386	18.4	1,921,031	9.5	1998	3,941,553	14.3	2,337,256	8.5
1980	3,612,258	15.9	1,989,841	8.8	1999	3,959,417	14.2	2,391,399	8.6
1990	4,092,994	16.7	2,148,463	8.6	2000	4,058,814	14.4	2,403,351	8.5
1991	4,094,566	16.2	2,169,518	8.6	2001	4,025,933	14.1	2,416,425	8.5
1992	4,049,024	15.8	2,175,613	8.5	2002	4,021,726	13.9	2,443,387	8.5
1993	4,000,240	15.4	2,268,553	8.7	2003	4,089,950	14.1	2,448,288	8.3
1994	3,952,767	15.0	2,278,994	8.7	2004	4,121,000	14.0	2,393,000	8.1
1995	3,899,589	14.6	2,312,132	8.7	2005	4,143,000(P)	14.0(P)	2,432,000(P)	8.2(P)
1996	3,891,494	14.4	2,314,690	8.6					

(P) = provisional data. **NOTE:** Statistics cover only events occurring within the U.S. and exclude fetal deaths. Rates per 1,000 population; enumerated as of Apr. 1 for 1960 and 1970; estimated as of July 1 for all other years. Beginning 1970 statistics exclude births and deaths occurring among nonresidents of the U.S. Data include revisions. Birth and death rates for years in the 1990s revised on basis of the 2000 Census.

Marriage and Divorce Rates, 1920-2005

Source: National Center for Health Statistics, U.S. Dept. of Health and Human Services

The U.S. marriage rate dipped during the Depression and peaked sharply just after World War II; the trend after that has been more gradual. The divorce rate generally rose from the 1920s through 1981, when it peaked at 5.3 per 1,000 population, before declining somewhat. The graph below shows marriage and divorce rates since 1920. (Recent divorce rates are calculated excluding data and populations from the non-reporting states California, Hawaii, Indiana, Louisiana, and Oklahoma; incomplete reporting from Oklahoma may lead to slight underestimation of marriage rate. Some data are provisional.)

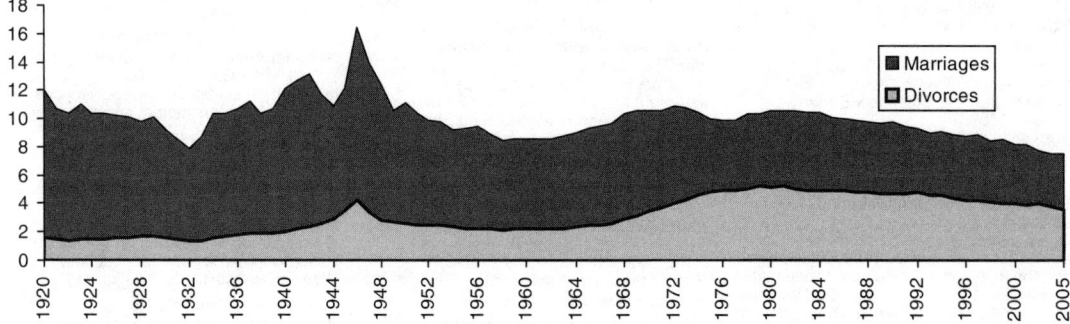

U.S. Median Age at First Marriage, 1890-2004

Source: Bureau of the Census, U.S. Dept. of Commerce

Year[1]	Men	Women	Year[1]	Men	Women	Year[1]	Men	Women	Year[1]	Men	Women	Year[1]	Men	Women
1890	26.1	22.0	1950	22.8	20.3	1985	25.5	23.3	1995	26.9	24.5	2000	26.8	25.1
1900	25.9	21.9	1960	22.8	20.3	1990	26.1	23.9	1996	27.1	24.8	2001	26.9	25.1
1910	25.1	21.6	1965	22.8	20.6	1991	26.3	24.1	1997	26.8	25.0	2002	26.9	25.3
1920	24.6	21.2	1970	23.2	20.8	1992	26.5	24.4	1998	26.7	25.0	2003	27.1	25.3
1930	24.3	21.3	1975	23.5	21.1	1993	26.5	24.5	1999	26.9	25.1	2004	27.1	25.8
1940	24.3	21.5	1980	24.7	22.0	1994	26.7	24.5						

(1) Figures after 1940 based on Current Population Survey data; earlier figures based on decennial censuses.

Birth Rates; Fertility Rates by Age of Mother, 1950-2004

Source: National Center for Health Statistics, U.S. Dept. of Health and Human Services

	Birth rate[1]	Fertility rate[2]	10-14 years	15-19 years Total	15-17	18-19	20-24 years	25-29 years	30-34 years	35-39 years	40-44 years	45-49 years
						Live births per 1,000 women by age group						
1950	24.1	106.2	1.0	81.6	40.7	132.7	196.6	166.1	103.7	52.9	15.1	1.2
1960	23.7	118.0	0.8	89.1	43.9	166.7	258.1	197.4	112.7	56.2	15.5	0.9
1970	18.4	87.9	1.2	68.3	38.8	114.7	167.8	145.1	73.3	31.7	8.1	0.5
1980	15.9	68.4	1.1	53.0	32.5	82.1	115.1	112.9	61.9	19.8	3.9	0.2
1990	16.7	70.9	1.4	59.9	37.5	88.6	116.5	120.2	80.8	31.7	5.5	0.2
1991	16.2	69.3	1.4	61.8	38.6	94.0	115.3	117.2	79.2	31.9	5.5	0.2
1992	15.8	68.4	1.4	60.3	37.6	93.6	113.7	115.7	79.6	32.3	5.9	0.3
1993	15.4	67.0	1.4	59.0	37.5	91.1	111.3	113.2	79.9	32.7	6.1	0.3
1994	15.0	65.9	1.4	58.2	37.2	90.2	109.2	111.0	80.4	33.4	6.4	0.3
1995	14.6	64.6	1.3	56.0	35.5	87.7	107.5	108.8	81.1	34.0	6.6	0.3
1996	14.4	64.1	1.2	53.5	33.3	84.7	107.8	108.6	82.1	34.9	6.8	0.3
1997	14.2	63.6	1.1	51.3	31.4	82.1	107.3	108.3	83.0	35.7	7.1	0.4
1998	14.3	64.3	1.0	50.3	29.9	80.9	108.4	110.2	85.2	36.9	7.4	0.4
1999	14.2	64.4	0.9	48.8	28.2	79.1	107.9	111.2	87.1	37.8	7.4	0.4
2000	14.4	65.9	0.9	47.7	26.9	78.1	109.7	113.5	91.2	39.7	8.0	0.5
2001	14.1	65.3	0.8	45.3	24.7	76.1	106.2	113.4	91.9	40.6	8.1	0.5
2002	13.9	64.8	0.7	43.0	23.2	72.8	103.6	113.6	91.5	41.4	8.3	0.5
2003	14.1	66.1	0.6	41.6	22.4	70.7	102.6	115.6	95.1	43.8	8.7	0.5
2004	14.0	66.3	0.7	41.2	22.1	70.0	101.8	115.5	95.5	45.4	9.0	0.6

(1) Live births per 1,000 population. (2) Live births per 1,000 women 15-44 years of age.

Numbers of Multiple Births in the U.S., 1990-2004

Source: National Center for Health Statistics, U.S. Dept. of Health and Human Services

The general upward trend in multiple births reflects greater numbers of births to older women and increased use of fertility drugs.

Year	Twins	Triplets	Quadruplets	Quintuplets and higher	Year	Twins	Triplets	Quadruplets	Quintuplets and higher
1990	93,865	2,830	185	13	1998	110,670	6,919	627	79
1992	95,372	3,547	310	26	1999	114,307	6,742	512	67
1993	96,445	3,834	277	57	2000	118,916	6,742	506	77
1994	97,064	4,233	315	46	2001	121,246	6,885	501	85
1995	96,736	4,551	365	57	2002	125,134	6,898	434	69
1996	100,750	5,298	560	81	2003	128,665	7,110	468	85
1997	104,137	6,148	510	79	2004	132,219	6,750	439	86

Top 15 Countries for U.S. Foreign Adoptions, 1998-2005[1]

Source: Dept. of Homeland Security, Office of Immigration Statistics.

Country	2005	2004	2003	2002	2001	2000	1999	1998
China	7,096	7,044	6,859	5,053	4,629	4,943	4,009	3,988
Russia	4,639	5,865	5,209	4,939	4,210	4,210	4,250	4,320
Guatemala	3,783	3,264	2,328	2,219	1,601	1,504	987	938
South Korea	1,630	1,716	1,790	1,779	1,863	1,711	1,956	1,705
Ukraine	821	723	702	1,106	1,227	645	307	168
Kazakhstan	755	826	825	819	664	392	108	54
Ethiopia	441	289	135	105	160	103	100	88
India	323	406	472	466	540	491	486	462
Colombia	291	287	272	334	261	246	226	221
Philippines	271	196	214	221	220	176	185	189
Haiti	231	356	250	187	187	136	93	113
Liberia	182	86	22	23	50	20	20	9
Taiwan	141	89	104	41	44	24	26	18
Mexico	98	89	61	61	105	115	145	170
Poland	73	102	97	101	89	81	97	70
Total[2]	**22,728**	**22,884**	**21,616**	**21,100**	**19,237**	**17,718**	**16,363**	**15,774**

Note: Totals are for U.S. government fiscal years. (1) Ranked by 2005 totals. (2) Total includes countries not shown.

10 Leading Causes of Infant Death in the U.S., 2003

Source: National Center for Health Statistics, U.S. Dept. of Health and Human Services

Cause	Number	Percent of total deaths	Mortality rate
Congenital malformations, deformations, and chromosomal abnormalities	5,612	20.1	137.4
Disorders relating to short gestation and low birthweight, not elsewhere classified	4,849	17.3	118.6
Sudden infant death syndrome	2,162	7.7	52.9
Newborn affected by maternal complications of pregnancy	1,710	6.1	41.8
Newborn affected by complications of placenta, cord, and membranes	1,099	3.9	26.9
Accidents (unintentional injuries)	945	3.4	26.9
Respiratory distress of newborn	831	3.0	23.1
Bacterial sepsis[3] of newborn	772	2.8	18.9
Diseases of the circulatory system	649	2.3	15.9
Intrauterine hypoxia and birth asphyxia	591	2.1	14.5
All other causes	8,796	31.3	215.0
All causes	**28,025**	**100.0**	**685.0**

NA = Not available. (1) Infant deaths per 100,000 live births. (3) Toxic condition resulting from the spread of bacteria.

Nonmarital Childbearing in the U.S., 1970-2003

Source: National Center for Health Statistics, U.S. Dept. of Health and Human Services

Race of Mother	1970	1975	1980	1985	1990	1995	1997	1998	1999	2000	2001	2002	2003
	Percent of live births to unmarried mothers												
All races	10.7	14.3	18.4	22.0	28.0	32.2	32.4	32.8	33.0	33.2	33.5	34.0	34.6
White	5.5	7.1	11.2	14.7	20.4	25.3	25.8	26.3	26.8	27.1	27.7	28.5	29.4
Black	37.5	49.5	56.1	61.2	66.5	69.9	69.2	69.1	68.9	68.5	68.4	68.2	68.2
American Indian or Alaska Native	22.4	32.7	39.2	46.8	53.6	57.2	58.7	59.3	58.9	58.4	59.7	59.7	61.3
Asian or Pacific Islander.	—	—	7.3	9.5	13.2	16.3	15.6	15.6	15.4	14.8	14.9	14.9	15.0
Hispanic origin (selected states)[1,2] . . .	—	—	23.6	29.5	36.7	40.8	40.9	41.6	42.2	42.7	42.5	43.5	45.0
White, non-Hispanic (selected states)[1]	—	—	9.6	12.4	16.9	21.2	21.5	21.9	22.1	22.1	22.5	23.0	23.6
Black, non-Hispanic (selected states)[1]	—	—	57.3	62.1	66.7	70.0	69.4	69.3	69.1	68.7	68.6	68.4	68.5
Births to unmarried mothers (1,000s). . . .	399	448	666	828	1,165	1,254	1,257	1,294	1,309	1,347	1,349	1,366	1,416
Maternal age	Percent distribution of live births to unmarried mothers												
Under 20 years.	50.1	52.1	40.8	33.8	30.9	30.9	30.7	30.1	29.3	28.0	26.6	25.4	24.3
20–24 years	31.8	29.9	35.6	36.3	34.7	34.5	34.9	35.6	36.4	37.4	38.2	38.6	38.8
25 years and over	18.1	18.0	23.5	29.9	34.4	34.7	34.4	34.3	34.3	34.6	35.2	34.7	36.9
	Live births per 1,000 unmarried women 15–44 years of age[3]												
All races and origins.	26.4	24.5	29.4	32.8	43.8	45.1	44.0	44.3	44.4	45.2	45.0	43.7	44.9
White[4]	13.9	12.4	18.1	22.5	32.9	37.5	37.0	37.5	38.1	38.9	39.2	38.9	40.4
Black[4]	95.5	84.2	81.1	77.0	90.5	75.9	73.4	73.3	71.5	72.5	70.1	66.2	66.3
Hispanic origin (selected states)[1,2] . . .	—	—	—	—	89.6	95.0	91.4	90.1	93.4	97.3	98.0	87.9	92.2
White, non-Hispanic.	—	—	—	—	—	28.2	27.0	27.4	27.9	27.9	27.7	27.8	28.6

— Data not available. (1) Data for Hispanics and non-Hispanics are affected by expansion of the reporting area for an Hispanic-origin item on the birth certificate and by immigration. The states in the reporting area increased from 22 in 1980, to 23 and the District of Columbia in 1983, 48 and DC by 1990, and 50 and DC by 1993. (2) Includes mothers of all races. (3) Rates computed by relating births to unmarried mothers, regardless of mother's age, to unmarried women 15–44 years of age. (4) For 1970 and 1975, birth rates are by race of child.

U.S. Infant Mortality Rates, by Race and Sex, 1960-2004[1]

Source: National Center for Health Statistics, U.S. Dept. of Health and Human Services

Year	ALL RACES			WHITE			BLACK		
	Total	Male	Female	Total	Male	Female	Total	Male	Female
1960	26.0	29.3	22.6	22.9	26.0	19.6	44.3	49.1	39.4
1970	20.0	22.4	17.5	17.8	20.0	15.4	32.6	36.2	29.0
1980	12.6	13.9	11.2	11.0	12.3	9.6	21.4	23.3	19.4
1985	10.6	11.9	9.3	9.3	10.6	8.0	18.2	19.9	16.5
1988	10.0	11.0	8.9	8.5	9.5	7.4	17.6	19.0	16.1
1989	9.8	10.8	8.8	8.1	9.0	7.1	18.6	20.0	17.2
1990	9.2	10.3	8.1	7.6	8.5	6.6	18.0	19.6	16.2
1991	8.9	10.0	7.8	7.3	8.3	6.3	17.6	19.4	15.7
1992	8.5	9.4	7.6	6.9	7.7	6.1	16.8	18.4	15.3
1993	8.4	9.3	7.4	6.8	7.6	6.0	16.5	18.3	14.7
1994	8.0	8.8	7.2	6.6	7.2	5.9	15.8	17.5	14.1
1995	7.6	8.3	6.8	6.3	7.0	5.6	15.1	16.3	13.9
1996	7.3	8.0	6.6	6.1	6.7	5.4	14.7	16.0	13.3
1997	7.2	8.0	6.5	6.0	6.7	5.4	14.2	15.5	12.8
1998	7.2	7.8	6.5	6.0	6.5	5.4	14.3	15.7	12.8
1999	7.1	7.7	6.4	5.8	6.4	5.2	14.6	15.9	13.2
2000	6.9	7.6	6.2	5.7	6.2	5.1	14.1	15.5	12.6
2001	6.8	7.5	6.1	5.7	6.2	5.1	14.0	15.5	12.5
2002	7.0	7.6	6.3	5.8	6.4	5.1	14.4	15.4	13.3
2003	6.9	7.6	6.1	5.7	6.3	5.0	14.0	15.5	12.4
2004	6.8	NA	NA	5.7	NA	NA	13.7	NA	NA

NA = Not available. (1) Rates per 1,000 live births. (2) Preliminary.

Years of Life Expected at Birth in U.S., 1900-2003

Source: National Center for Health Statistics, U.S. Dept. of Health and Human Services

Year[1]	ALL RACES			WHITE			BLACK		
	Total	Male	Female	Total	Male	Female	Total	Male	Female
1900	47.3	46.3	48.3	47.6	46.6	48.7	NA	NA	NA
1910	50.0	48.4	51.8	50.3	48.6	52.0	NA	NA	NA
1920	54.1	53.6	54.6	54.9	54.4	55.6	NA	NA	NA
1930	59.7	58.1	61.6	61.4	59.7	63.5	NA	NA	NA
1940	62.9	60.8	65.2	64.2	62.1	66.6	NA	NA	NA
1950	68.2	65.6	71.1	69.1	66.5	72.2	NA	NA	NA
1960	69.7	66.6	73.1	70.6	67.4	74.1	NA	NA	NA
1970	70.8	67.1	74.7	71.7	68.0	75.6	64.1	60.0	68.3
1975	72.6	68.8	76.6	73.4	69.5	77.3	68.8	62.4	71.3
1980	73.7	70.0	77.5	74.4	70.7	78.1	68.1	63.8	72.5
1985	74.7	71.2	78.2	75.3	71.9	78.7	69.3	65.0	73.4
1990	75.4	71.8	78.8	76.1	72.9	79.4	69.1	64.5	73.6
1991	75.5	72.0	78.9	76.3	72.9	79.2	69.3	64.6	73.8
1992	75.5	72.1	78.9	76.4	73.0	79.5	69.6	65.0	73.9
1993	75.5	72.1	78.9	76.3	73.0	79.5	69.2	64.6	73.7
1994	75.7	72.4	79.0	76.5	73.3	79.6	69.5	64.9	73.9
1995	75.8	72.5	78.9	76.5	73.4	79.6	69.6	65.2	73.9
1996	76.1	73.1	79.1	76.8	73.9	79.7	70.2	66.1	74.2
1997	76.5	73.6	79.4	77.1	74.3	79.9	71.1	67.2	74.7
1998	76.7	73.8	79.5	77.3	74.5	80.0	71.3	67.6	74.8
1999	76.7	73.9	79.4	77.3	74.6	79.9	71.4	67.8	74.7
2000	76.9	74.1	79.5	77.4	74.8	80.0	71.7	68.2	74.9
2001	77.2	74.4	79.8	77.7	75.0	80.2	72.2	68.6	75.5
2002	77.3	74.5	79.9	77.7	75.1	80.3	72.3	68.8	75.6
2003	77.5	74.8	80.1	78.0	75.3	80.5	72.7	69.0	76.1

NA = Not available. (1) Data prior to 1940 for death-registration states only.

U.S. Life Expectancy at Selected Ages, 2003

Source: National Center for Health Statistics, U.S. Dept. of Health and Human Services

Exact age in years	ALL RACES[1] Both sexes	Male	Female	WHITE Both sexes	Male	Female	BLACK Both sexes	Male	Female
0	77.5	74.8	80.1	78.0	75.3	80.5	72.7	69.0	76.1
1	77.0	74.3	79.6	77.4	74.8	79.9	72.7	69.1	76.0
5	73.1	70.4	75.7	73.5	70.9	76.0	68.9	65.3	72.2
10	68.2	65.5	70.7	68.5	66.0	71.0	63.9	60.3	67.2
15	63.2	60.6	65.8	63.6	61.0	66.1	59.0	55.4	62.3
20	58.4	55.8	60.9	58.8	56.3	61.2	54.2	50.7	57.4
25	53.7	51.2	56.0	54.1	51.6	56.3	49.6	46.3	52.6
30	48.9	46.5	51.2	49.3	46.9	51.5	45.0	41.8	47.8
35	44.2	41.9	46.4	44.5	42.2	46.6	40.4	37.3	43.1
40	39.5	37.3	41.6	39.8	37.6	41.9	36.0	32.9	38.6
45	35.0	32.8	37.0	35.2	33.1	37.2	31.6	28.7	34.1
50	30.6	28.5	32.4	30.8	28.8	32.6	27.6	24.8	29.9
55	26.3	24.4	28.0	26.5	24.6	28.1	23.8	21.2	25.9
60	22.2	20.4	23.8	22.3	20.6	23.8	20.2	17.9	22.1
65	18.4	16.8	19.8	18.5	16.9	19.8	17.0	14.9	18.5
70	14.9	13.5	16.0	14.9	13.5	16.0	14.0	12.1	15.3
75	11.8	10.5	12.6	11.7	10.5	12.6	11.4	9.8	12.4
80	9.0	8.0	9.6	9.0	8.0	9.6	9.2	7.9	9.8
85	6.8	6.0	7.2	6.7	5.9	7.1	7.4	6.4	7.8
90	5.0	4.4	5.2	4.9	4.3	5.1	5.7	5.0	6.0
95	3.6	3.2	3.7	3.5	3.1	3.6	4.4	3.8	4.5
100	2.6	2.3	2.6	2.5	2.2	2.5	3.4	3.0	3.4

(1) Includes races other than white and black.

Number, Ratio, and Rate of Legal Abortions in U.S., 1970-2002

Source: Centers for Disease Control, *Abortion Surveillance, U.S., 2002*

Year	Legal Abortions	Ratio[1]	Rate[2]	Year	Legal Abortions	Ratio[1]	Rate[2]	Year	Legal Abortions	Ratio[1]	Rate[2]
1970	193,491	52	5	1981	1,300,760	358	24	1992	1,359,146	334	23
1971	485,816	137	11	1982	1,303,980	354	24	1993	1,330,414	333	23
1972	586,760	180	13	1983	1,268,987	349	23	1994	1,267,415	321	21
1973	615,831	196	14	1984	1,333,521	364	24	1995	1,210,883	311	20
1974	763,476	242	17	1985	1,328,570	354	24	1996	1,225,937	315	21
1975	854,853	272	18	1986	1,328,112	354	23	1997	1,186,039	306	20
1976	988,267	312	21	1987	1,353,671	356	24	1998[3]	884,273	264	17
1977	1,079,430	325	22	1988	1,371,285	352	24	1999[3]	861,789	256	17
1978	1,157,776	347	23	1989	1,396,658	346	24	2000[3]	857,475	245	16
1979	1,251,921	358	24	1990	1,429,247	344	24	2001[4]	853,485	246	16
1980	1,297,606	359	25	1991	1,388,937	338	24	2002[4]	854,122	246	16

(1) Number of abortions per 1,000 live births. (2) Number of abortions per 1,000 women aged 15-44 years. (3) Without estimates for AK, CA, NH, and OK. (4) Without estimates for AK, CA, and NH

Cigarette Use in the U.S., 1985-2005

Source: Substance Abuse and Mental Health Services Administration (SAMHSA), U.S. Dept. of Health and Human Services

(percentage reporting use in the month prior to the survey; figures exclude persons under age 12)

	1985	2000	2003	2004	2005		1985	2000	2003	2004	2005
TOTAL	38.7	24.9	25.4	24.9	24.9	**Race/Ethnicity**					
Sex						White	38.9	25.9	27.6	26.4	27.3
Male	43.4	26.9	28.1	27.7	27.4	Black	38.0	23.3	26.2	23.5	27.3
Female	34.5	23.1	23.0	22.3	22.5	Hispanic	40.0	20.7	23.2	21.3	24.2
Age group						**Education**[2]					
12-17	29.4	13.4	12.2	11.9	10.8	Non-high school graduate	37.3	32.4	35.3	34.8	34.8
18 and older	47.4	38.3	40.2	39.5	39.0	High school graduate	37.0	31.1	31.5	30.4	31.8
26 and older	45.7[1]	24.2	24.7	24.1	24.3	Some college	32.6	27.7	28.9	29.0	28.1
						College graduate	23.0	13.9	14.0	13.6	13.8

NA = Not available. (1) Figures are for all persons aged 26 to 34 only. (2) Estimates for education are for persons aged 18 and older.

Contraceptive Use in the U.S.

Source: National Center for Health Statistics, U.S. Dept. of Health and Human Services; as of 2002; latest data available.

	Percent of women in each age group 15-44	15-19	20-24	25-29	30-34	35-39	40-44		Percent of women in each age group 15-44	15-19	20-24	25-29	30-34	35-39	40-44
Using any method	61.9	31.5	60.7	68.0	69.2	70.8	69.1	Intrauterine device (IUD)	1.3	0.1	1.1	2.5	2.2	1.0	0.8
Female sterilization	16.7	—	2.2	10.3	19.0	29.2	34.7	Diaphragm	0.2	–	0.1	0.3	0.1	–	0.4
Male sterilization	5.7	—	0.5	2.8	6.4	10.0	12.7	Condom	11.1	8.5	14.0	14.0	11.8	11.1	8.0
Pill	18.9	16.7	31.9	25.6	21.8	13.2	7.6	Periodic abstinence	0.7	—	0.8	0.3	0.9	1.1	1.2
Implant	0.8	0.4	0.9	1.7	0.9	0.5	0.2	Natural family planning	0.2	—	—	0.4	0.2	0.3	0.4
Injectable	3.3	4.4	6.1	4.4	2.9	1.5	1.1	Withdrawal	2.5	0.8	3.1	5.3	2.6	2.4	1.0
								Other methods[1]	0.6	0.6	0.2	0.4	0.4	0.5	1.1

(1) These include morning-after pill, foam, cervical cap, Today sponge, suppository, jelly or cream (without diaphragm), and other methods not shown separately.

Sexual Behavior in the U.S.

Data released by the National Center for Health Statistics in 2005 show that about 90% of U.S. men and women 18-44 years of age think of themselves as heterosexual; 2.3% of men and 1.3% of women as homosexual; and 1.8% of men and 2.8% of women as bisexual. However, 6.2% of men 18-44 years of age reported ever having had sex with another male as of 2002 (up from 2.3% in 1991) and 11.5% of women reported ever having had a sexual experience with another woman (up from 4.1% in 1992).

Ten percent of males age 15-44 had never had sex with a female, but this percentage varied greatly with age: more than half (52%) of males age 15-17 had never had sex with a female, but only 1.8% of males age 40-44 had not done so.

Percentages were slightly lower for women, with only 8.4% of females age 15-44 having never had sex with a male, with specific percentages ranging from 50.2% for females age 15-17 to only 1.3% for females age 40-44.

Among men age 15-44 who had sex with at least one partner in the previous year, 39% reported using a condom in their most recent sexual encounter (24% of married men and 65% of never-married men). Among women, only 22% reported using a condom (13% of married and 42% of never-married women). Condom use was also more frequent among younger men and women: in the 15-19 age group, 66% of males and 44% of females used a condom in their most recent sexual encounter.

Median Number of Opposite-Sex Partners in Past Year

Source: National Center for Health Statistics, *Sexual Behavior and Selected Health Measures, 2002*
Note: U.S. males and females 15-44 years of age

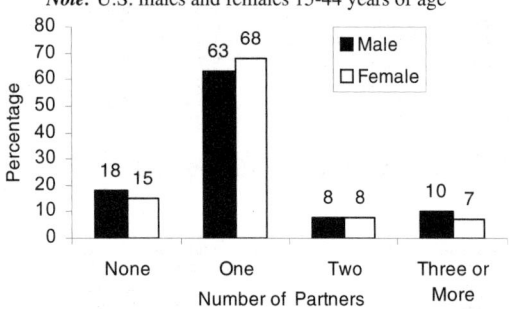

Median Number of Opposite-Sex Partners in Lifetime

Source: National Center for Health Statistics, *Sexual Behavior and Selected Health Measures, 2002*

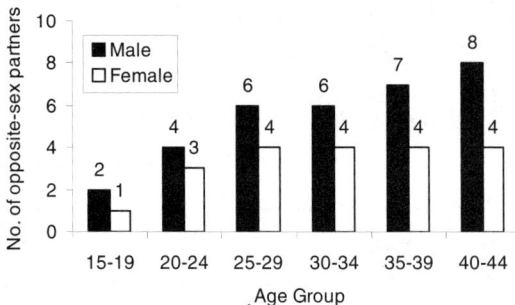

Sexual Activity of High School Students, 2004
Source: CDC, *Youth Risk Behavior Surveillance—United States, 2004*

		Ever had sexual intercourse			First sexual intercourse before age 13			Currently sexually active[1]			Responsible sexual behavior[2]		
		Female	Male	Total	Female	Male	Total	Female	Male	Total	Female	Male	Total
Race/	White[3] . . .	43.7	42.2	43.0	2.9	5.0	4.0	33.5	30.6	32.0	55.6	70.1	62.6
Ethnicity	Black[3] . . .	61.2	74.6	67.6	7.1	26.8	16.5	43.8	51.3	47.4	62.1	76.6	68.9
	Hispanic. .	44.4	57.6	51.0	3.6	11.1	7.3	33.7	36.3	35.0	49.8	65.3	57.7
Grade	9	29.3	39.3	34.3	5.4	12.0	8.7	19.5	24.5	21.9	71.5	77.1	74.5
	10	44.0	41.5	42.8	4.1	7.7	5.9	31.1	27.2	29.2	57.1	74.4	65.3
	11	52.1	50.6	51.4	2.6	8.0	5.2	40.8	37.9	39.4	57.8	66.0	61.7
	12	62.4	63.8	63.1	2.0	6.2	4.1	51.7	47.0	49.4	57.8	65.8	55.4
Total.		45.7	47.9	46.8	3.7	8.8	6.2	34.6	33.3	33.9	55.9	70.0	62.8

(1) Sexual intercourse during the 3 months preceding the survey. (2) Used condom during last sexual intercourse. (3) Non-Hispanic.

Lifetime and Median Number of Sexual Partners, by Age and Race, 2002
Source: National Center for Health Statistics, Sexual Behavior and Selected Health Measures, 2002

Number of opposite-sex partners in lifetime, percent distribution								Number of opposite-sex partners in lifetime, percent distribution							
	0	1	2	3-6	7-14	15+	Median[1]		0	1	2	3-6	7-14	15+	Median[1]
Males 15-44 years[2] . . .	9.6	12.5	8.0	27.2	19.5	23.2	5.6	**Females 15-44 years[2]**	8.6	22.5	10.8	32.6	16.3	9.2	3.3
Age								**Age**							
15-19	43.5	23.4	9.0	17.0	4.9	2.3	1.6	15-19	37.8	27.2	9.0	19.1	5.0	1.9	1.4
20-24	9.9	15.7	11.6	33.1	13.9	15.8	3.8	20-24	8.9	24.6	13.0	32.2	14.4	6.9	2.8
25-44	2.9	9.5	6.9	27.7	23.7	29.2	6.7	25-44	1.7	20.9	10.7	36.0	19.4	11.4	3.8
Race								**Race**							
White, non-Hispanic .	9.8	13.4	8.3	27.0	19.2	22.3	5.3	White, non-Hispanic. .	7.8	21.0	10.6	32.1	18.2	10.2	3.6
Black, non-Hispanic. .	8.6	5.8	5.9	24.0	22.1	33.7	8.3	Black, non-Hispanic. .	7.7	12.4	8.4	44.8	18.0	8.8	4.1
Hispanic or Latino. . .	9.1	13.5	8.5	32.5	18.4	17.9	4.5	Hispanic or Latina . .	10.5	34.6	14.9	27.2	8.2	4.6	1.7

(1) Excludes people who have never had intercourse with an opposite-sex partner. (2) Includes people of other or multiple race and origin groups, not shown separately.

Drug Use in the General U.S. Population, 2005
Source: Substance Abuse and Mental Health Services Administration (SAMHSA), U.S. Dept. of Health and Human Services

According to the Substance Abuse and Mental Health Services Administration's 2005 National Survey on Drug Use and Health, an estimated 112 mil Americans 12 years of age and older (46.1%) had used an illicit drug at least once during their lifetimes, 14.4% had used one during the previous year, and 8.1% had used one in the most recent month.

The rate of current illicit drug use (in the past month) in 2005 was 10.2% for men; for women it was 6.1%. An estimated 29.5% of Americans 12 or older (71.8 mil) had used

an illicit drug other than marijuana at least once in their life. The overall rate of illicit drug use between 2004 and 2005 increased slightly.

The Substance Abuse and Mental Health Services Administration's Drug Abuse Warning Network (DAWN) reported 1.3 mil drug abuse or misuse related episodes in hospital emergency departments in the coterminous U.S in 2004. Cocaine was a factor in 19% of these. Alcohol in combination with illegal drug use was a factor in 23%.

Drug Use: America's High School Seniors, 1980-2005

Source: *Monitoring the Future*, Univ. of Michigan Inst. for Social Research and National Inst. on Drug Abuse

Class of:	1975	1980	1985	1990	1995	2000	2001	2002	2003	2004	2005	'04-'05 change[7]
Marijuana/hashish	47.3%	60.3%	54.2%	40.7%	41.7%	48.8%	49.0%	47.8%	46.1%	45.7%	44.8%	−0.9
Inhalants[1]	—	17.3	18.1	18.5	17.8	14.2	13.0	11.7	11.2	11.4	11.9	+0.4
Amyl & butyl nitrites	—	11.1	7.9	2.1	1.5	0.8	1.9	1.5	1.6	1.3	1.1	−0.1
Hallucinogens[2]	—	15.6	12.1	9.7	12.7	13.0	14.7	12.0	10.6	9.9	9.3	−0.7
LSD	11.3	9.3	7.5	8.7	11.7	11.1	10.9	8.4	5.9	4.6	3.5	−1.1
PCP	—	9.6	4.9	2.8	2.7	3.4	3.5	3.1	2.5	1.6	2.4	+0.8
Ecstasy	—	—	—	—	—	11.0	11.7	10.5	8.3	7.5	5.4	−2.1
Cocaine	9.0	15.7	17.3	9.4	6.0	8.6	8.2	7.8	7.7	8.1	8.0	−0.1
Crack	—	—	—	3.5	3.0	3.9	3.7	3.8	3.6	3.9	3.5	−0.4
Heroin[3]	2.2	1.1	1.2	1.3	1.6	2.4	1.8	1.7	1.5	1.5	1.5	0.0
Other opiates[4]	9.0	9.8	10.2	8.3	7.2	10.6	9.9	13.5	13.2	13.5	12.8	−0.7
Amphetamines[4,5]	22.3	26.4	26.2	17.5	15.3	15.6	16.2	16.8	14.4	15.0	13.1	−1.9
Methamphetamine	—	—	—	—	—	7.9	6.9	6.7	6.2	6.2	4.5	−1.7
Crystal Meth.	—	—	—	2.7	3.9	4.0	4.0	4.7	3.9	4.0	4.0	0.0
Barbiturates[4]	16.9	11.0	9.2	6.8	7.4	9.2	8.7	9.5	8.8	9.9	10.5	+0.7
Methaqualone[4]	8.1	9.5	6.7	2.3	1.2	0.8	1.1	1.5	1.0	1.3	1.3	+0.1
Tranquilizers[4]	17.0	15.2	11.9	7.2	7.1	8.9	10.3	11.4	10.2	10.6	9.9	−0.7
Alcohol[6]	90.4	93.2	92.2	89.5	80.7	80.3	79.7	78.4	76.6	76.8	75.1	−1.7
Cigarettes	73.6	71.0	68.8	64.4	64.2	62.5	61.0	57.2	53.7	52.8	50.0	−2.8
Steroids	—	—	—	2.9	2.3	2.5	3.7	4.0	3.5	3.4	2.6	−0.7

— Data not available. (1) Adjusted for underreporting of amyl and butyl nitrites. (2) Adjusted for underreporting of PCP. (3) Reflects use with or without injection. (4) Includes only drug use that was not under a doctor's orders. (5) Data for 1990-2005 are not directly comparable to prior years. (6) Data for 1995-2005 are not directly comparable to prior years. (7) In percentage points.

Alcohol Use by 8th and 12th Graders, 1980-2005

Source: *Monitoring the Future*, Univ. of Michigan Inst. for Social Research and National Inst. on Drug Abuse

	1980	1990	1994	1995	1996	1997	1998	1999	2000	2001	2002	2003	2004	2005
ALCOHOL[1]			Percent using alcohol in the month before the survey											
All 12th graders	72.0	57.1	50.1	51.3	50.8	52.7	52.0	51.0	50.0	49.8	48.6	47.5	48.0	47.0
Male	77.4	61.3	55.5	55.7	54.8	56.2	57.3	55.3	54.0	54.7	52.3	51.7	51.1	50.7
Female	66.8	52.3	45.2	47.0	46.9	48.9	46.9	46.8	46.1	45.1	45.1	43.8	45.1	43.3
White	75.4	63.8	54.0	54.5	54.8	56.4	57.7	56.3	55.1	55.3	54.0	52.3	52.2	52.3
Black	47.6	35.8	33.8	35.2	36.5	34.3	33.3	32.2	30.0	29.4	30.1	29.9	29.2	29.0
Hispanic	63.6	49.1	45.9	48.7	47.5	48.2	49.8	50.2	51.2	48.9	47.5	46.4	45.4	43.3
All 8th graders	—	—	25.5	24.6	26.2	24.5	23.0	24.0	22.4	21.5	19.6	19.7	18.6	17.1
Male	—	—	26.5	25.0	26.6	25.2	24.0	24.8	22.5	22.3	19.1	19.4	17.9	16.2
Female	—	—	24.7	24.0	25.8	23.9	21.9	23.3	22.0	20.6	20.0	19.8	19.0	17.9
White	—	—	25.3	25.4	26.6	26.7	24.8	24.7	24.7	23.2	21.5	20.1	19.2	17.9
Black	—	—	19.4	18.7	18.1	17.9	16.1	16.0	16.0	15.0	14.8	15.5	16.2	14.9
Hispanic	—	—	33.5	32.4	29.7	29.8	29.5	29.0	26.7	25.7	26.5	25.3	23.5	20.6
HEAVY ALCOHOL[2]			Percent heavily using the 2 weeks before the survey											
All 12th graders	41.2	32.2	28.2	29.8	30.2	31.3	31.5	30.8	30.0	29.7	28.6	27.9	29.2	28.1
Male	52.1	39.1	37.0	36.9	37.0	37.9	39.2	38.1	36.7	36.0	34.2	34.2	34.3	33.4
Female	30.5	24.4	20.2	23.0	23.5	24.4	24.0	23.6	23.5	23.7	23.0	22.1	24.2	22.7
White	44.3	36.6	31.5	32.3	33.4	35.1	36.4	35.7	34.6	34.5	33.7	32.4	32.5	33.0
Black	17.7	14.4	14.4	14.9	15.3	13.4	12.3	12.3	11.5	11.8	11.5	10.8	11.4	11.6
Hispanic	33.1	25.6	24.3	26.6	27.1	27.6	28.1	29.3	31.0	28.4	26.4	25.9	26.0	24.7
All 8th graders	—	—	14.5	14.5	15.6	14.5	13.7	15.2	14.1	13.2	12.4	11.9	11.4	10.5
Male	—	—	16.0	15.1	16.5	15.3	14.4	16.4	14.4	13.7	12.5	12.2	10.8	10.2
Female	—	—	13.0	13.9	14.5	13.5	12.7	13.9	13.6	12.4	12.1	11.6	11.8	10.6
White	—	—	12.9	13.9	15.1	15.1	14.1	14.3	14.9	13.8	12.7	11.8	11.3	10.8
Black	—	—	11.8	10.8	10.4	9.8	9.0	9.9	10.0	9.0	9.4	10.4	9.8	8.2
Hispanic	—	—	22.3	22.0	21.0	20.7	20.4	20.9	19.1	17.6	17.8	16.6	16.1	14.8

— Data not available. **Note:** *Monitoring the Future* study excludes high school dropouts (about 3-6% of the class group, according to a 1996 report) and absentees (about 16-17% of 12th graders and about 9-10% of 8th graders). High school dropouts and absentees have higher alcohol usage than those included in the survey. (1) In 1993 the alcohol question was changed to indicate that a "drink" meant "more than a few sips." (2) Five or more drinks in a row at least once in the prior 2-week period.

Risk Behaviors in High School Students, 2005

Source: CDC, *Youth Risk Behavior Surveillance—United States, 2005*

		Percent rarely or never wear seatbelts[1]			Percent rarely or never wear bicycle helmets[2]			Percent who rode with a driver who had been drinking alcohol[3]		
		Female	Male	Total	Female	Male	Total	Female	Male	Total
Race	Non-Hispanic White	7.2	11.5	9.4	77.9	84.4	81.5	30.4	26.2	28.3
	Non-Hispanic Black	9.4	17.7	13.4	90.1	93.5	92.0	24.0	24.3	24.1
	Hispanic	8.7	12.5	10.6	83.4	88.6	86.5	34.7	37.4	36.1
Grade	9	8.7	13.0	10.9	78.6	86.7	83.0	30.1	25.8	27.9
	10	7.7	9.5	8.6	80.4	87.1	84.3	29.5	26.2	27.8
	11	7.1	13.2	10.1	78.4	85.1	82.2	28.1	27.7	28.0
	12	7.5	14.1	10.8	83.3	84.5	84.0	30.7	29.5	30.1
Total		7.8	12.5	10.2	79.9	86.1	83.4	29.6	27.2	28.5

(1) When riding in a car or truck driven by someone else. (2) Among the 62.3% of students who rode bicycles during the 12 months preceding the survey. (3) In a car or truck one or more times during the 30 days preceding the survey.

> **IT'S A FACT:** According to the National Safety Council, basketball playing accounted for 561,444 injuries in the U.S. in 2004—more than three times the number of injuries suffered by baseball players (162,527) and nearly five times the number suffered by skateboarders (113,329)

U.S. Motor Vehicle Accidents

Source: National Safety Council

A total of 46,200 people in the U.S. were killed in motor vehicle accidents in 2004, according to preliminary figures, up 5% from the revised total for 2003. The number of drivers and vehicle miles driven also increased, and the fatality rate per motor vehicle declined, as has happened most years since the introduction of the automobile. Motor-vehicle deaths per 10,000 registered vehicles went from 2.43 in 1990 to 1.92 in 2004, a decrease of 21% over 14 years, and the rate in 2004 was a decline of 0.5% from 1.88 the year before. The rate of fatalities per 100,000 population has declined 18% from 1990 to 2003, but it showed an increase from 2003 to 2004 (see table below).

Among the estimated 198.1 mil licensed drivers in 2004, there were slightly more male drivers than female (99.1 mil male vs. 99 mil female; slightly more than 50% male), but males accounted for 62% of all miles driven. About 11.6 mil male drivers and 8.4 mil female drivers were involved in an accident in 2004. Male drivers were also involved in many more fatal accidents than female drivers; about 46,200 male

drivers compared to 16,800 females. The rate was also substantially higher for males (26 fatal accidents per bil miles) than for females (15).

In 2003, 34% of all traffic fatalities involved an intoxicated (blood alcohol concentration of 0.08 or greater) driver or nonoccupant (pedestrian, bicyclist, etc.) and 40% involved a driver or nonoccupant who had been drinking. Alcohol was a factor in about 7% of all traffic accidents.

	Deaths 2004	% change from 2003	Rate 2004[1]
All motor vehicle accidents	46,200	+5	15.7
Collision between motor vehicles	20,600	+4	7.0
Collision with fixed object	13,300	+7	4.5
Pedestrian accidents	5,900	+4	2.0
Noncollision accidents	5,200	+2	1.8
Collision with pedal cycle	900	+12	0.3
Collision with railroad train	200	0	0.1
Other collision (animal, animal-drawn vehicles)	100	0	(2)

(1) Deaths per 100,000 population. (2) Less than 0.05.

Improper Driving Reported in Accidents, 2000, 2002, 2004

Source: National Safety Council

Type	Percentage of fatal accidents			Percentage of injury accidents			Percentage of all accidents		
	2004	2002	2000	2004	2002	2000	2004	2002	2000
Improper driving	**66.0**	**59.5**	**61.6**	**67.1**	**54.7**	**60.3**	**61.0**	**50.3**	**57.8**
Speed too fast or unsafe	17.6	21.9	18.6	13.7	12.6	16.3	12.5	10.1	13.6
Right of way	13.1	17.4	10.1	19.1	18.9	19.9	15.7	16.4	20.1
Failed to yield	9.0	10.1	4.6	14.6	14.3	15.0	12.0	11.4	12.7
Disregarded signal	2.1	4.0	8.2	1.8	3.3	1.3	1.2	3.4	2.2
Passed stop sign	1.9	3.3	3.8	3.6	1.3	3.6	2.5	1.6	5.3
Drove left of center	7.3	5.7	0.7	1.7	0.9	1.1	1.3	0.7	1.0
Improper overtaking	3.9	1.0	0.9	4.6	0.5	2.0	4.6	0.8	2.4
Made improper turn	1.3	0.5	0.7	0.9	1.2	0.6	0.9	1.7	0.9
Followed too closely	0.8	0.4	0.9	7.2	2.8	4.3	8.0	3.8	5.7
Other improper driving	22.0	12.5	9.0	19.9	17.9	16.1	18.0	16.8	14.1
No improper driving stated	**34.0**	**40.5**	**38.4**	**32.9**	**45.3**	**39.7**	**39.0**	**49.7**	**42.2**

Note: Based on reports from state traffic authorities. When a driver was under the influence of alcohol or drugs, the accident was considered a result of the driver's physical condition—not a driving error. For this reason, accidents in which the driver was reported to be under the influence are included under "no improper driving stated."

Death Rates[1] for Suicide at Selected Ages, 1960, 1980, 2000, 2003

Source: *Health, United States, 2004*, National Center for Health Statistics, U.S. Dept. of Health and Human Services

	2003			2000			1980			1960		
AGE	Both sexes	Male	Female	Both sexes	Male	Female	Both sexes	Male	Female	Both sexes	Male	Female
15-24	9.7	16.0	3.0	10.2	17.1	3.0	12.3	20.2	4.3	5.2	8.2	2.2
25-44	13.8	21.9	5.7	13.4	21.3	5.4	15.6	24.0	7.7	12.2	17.9	6.6
45-64	15.0	23.5	7.0	13.5	21.3	6.2	15.9	23.7	8.9	22.0	34.4	10.2
65 and older	14.6	29.8	3.8	15.2	31.1	4.0	17.6	35.0	6.1	24.5	44.0	8.4
All ages	**10.8**	**18.0**	**4.2**	**10.4**	**17.7**	**4.0**	**12.2**	**19.9**	**5.7**	**12.5**	**20.0**	**5.6**

(1) Per 100,000 population.

The Leading Causes of Death in the U.S., 2003

Source: National Center for Health Statistics, U.S. Dept. of Health and Human Services

	Number	Death rate[1]	% of deaths		Number	Death rate[1]	% of deaths
ALL CAUSES	**2,448,288**	**841.9**	**100.0**	9. Kidney disease	42,453	14.6	1.7
1. Heart disease	685,089	235.6	28.0	10. Blood poisoning	34,069	11.7	1.4
2. Cancer	556,902	191.5	22.7	11. Intentional self-harm	31,484	10.8	1.3
3. Stroke	157,689	54.2	6.4	12. Chronic liver disease and cirrhosis	27,503	9.5	1.1
4. Chronic lower respiratory diseases	126,382	43.5	5.2	13. Hypertension and hypertensive renal disease	21,940	7.5	0.9
5. Accidents	109,277	37.6	4.5	14. Parkinson's disease	17,997	6.2	0.7
6. Diabetes mellitus	74,219	25.5	3.0	15. Assault homicide	17,732	6.1	0.7
7. Influenza and pneumonia	65,163	22.4	2.7	All other causes	416,932	143.4	17.0
8. Alzheimer's disease	63,457	21.8	2.6				

(1) Per 100,000 population.

Principal Types of Accidental Deaths in the U.S., 1970-2004

Source: National Safety Council

Year	Total	Motor vehicle	Falls	Poisoning	Drowning	Fires, flames, smoke	Suffocation: Ingestion of food, object	Firearms	Mechanical Suffocation
1970...	NA	54,633	16,926	5,299	7,860	6,718	2,753	2,406	NA
1980...	105,718	53,172	13,294	4,331	7,257	5,822	3,249	1,955	NA
1985...	93,457	45,901	12,001	5,170	5,316	4,938	3,551	1,649	NA
1990...	91,983	46,814	12,313	5,803	4,685	4,175	3,303	1,416	NA
1991...	89,347	43,536	12,662	6,434	4,818	4,120	3,240	1,441	NA
1992...	86,777	40,982	12,646	7,082	3,542	3,958	3,182	1,409	NA
1993...	90,437	41,893	13,141	8,537	3,807	3,900	3,160	1,521	NA
1994...	91,437	42,524	13,450	8,994	3,942	3,986	3,065	1,356	NA
1995...	93,320	43,363	13,986	9,072	4,350	3,761	3,185	1,225	NA
1996...	94,948	43,649	14,986	9,510	3,959	3,741	3,206	1,134	NA
1997...	95,644	43,458	15,447	10,163	4,051	3,490	3,275	981	NA
1998...	97,835	43,501	16,274	10,801	4,406	3,255	3,515	866	NA
1999[1]...	97,860	42,401	13,162	12,186	3,529	3,348	3,885	824	1,618
2000...	97,900	43,354	13,322	12,757	3,482	3,377	4,313	776	1,335
2001...	101,537	43,788	15,019	14,078	3,281	3,309	4,185	802	1,370
2002[2]..	106,742	45,380	16,257	18,550	3,447	3,159	4,128	762	1,389
2003[2]..	108,900	44,100	19,800	14,900	3,700	3,400	4,500	700	1,300
2004[3]..	111,000	46,200	20,200	13,300	3,800	3,900	4,900	700	1,300

				Death rates per 100,000 population					
1970...	NA	26.8	8.3	2.6	3.9	3.3	1.4	1.2	NA
1980...	47.8	23.4	5.9	1.9	3.2	2.6	1.4	0.9	NA
1985...	39.3	19.3	5.0	2.2	2.2	2.1	1.5	0.7	NA
1990...	3639	18.8	4.9	2.3	1.9	1.7	1.3	0.6	NA
1991...	35.4	17.3	5.0	2.6	1.8	1.6	1.3	0.6	NA
1992...	34.0	16.1	5.0	2.7	1.4	1.6	1.2	0.6	NA
1993...	35.1	16.3	5.1	3.4	1.5	1.5	1.2	0.6	NA
1994...	35.1	16.3	5.2	3.5	1.5	1.5	1.2	0.5	NA
1995...	35.5	16.5	5.3	3.4	1.7	1.4	1.2	0.5	NA
1996...	35.8	16.5	5.6	3.5	1.5	1.4	1.2	0.4	NA
1997...	35.7	16.2	5.8	3.8	1.5	1.3	1.2	0.4	NA
1998...	36.2	16.1	6.0	4.0	1.6	1.2	1.3	0.3	NA
1999[1]...	35.9	15.5	4.8	4.5	1.3	1.2	1.4	0.3	0.6
2000...	35.6	15.7	4.8	4.6	1.3	1.2	1.6	0.3	0.5
2001...	35.6	15.4	5.3	4.9	1.2	1.2	1.5	0.3	0.5
2002[2]..	37.1	15.8	5.6	6.4	1.2	1.1	1.4	0.3	4.7
2003[2]..	37.4	15.2	6.8	5.1	1.3	1.2	1.5	0.2	5.7
2004[3]..	37.8	15.7	6.9	4.5	1.3	1.3	1.7	0.2	5.7

NA = Not available. **Note:** There were 16,700 other accidental deaths in 2004. All figures include on-the-job deaths. (1)   Data   for 1999 and later not comparable with earlier data because of classification changes. (2) Revised data. (3) Preliminary data.

Worldwide Airline Fatalities, 1986-2004

Source: National Safety Council

Year	Aircraft accidents[1]	Passenger deaths	Death rate[2]	Year	Aircraft accidents[1]	Passenger deaths	Death rate[2]	Year	Aircraft accidents[1]	Passenger deaths	Death rate[2]
1986.....	24	641	0.04	1993.....	33	864	0.04	1999	21	499	0.02
1987.....	25	900	0.06	1994.....	27	1,170	0.05	2000	18	757	0.03
1988.....	29	742	0.04	1995.....	25	711	0.03	2001[3]....	13	577	0.02
1989.....	29	879	0.05	1996.....	24	1,146	0.05	2002[4]....	13	791	0.03
1990.....	27	544	0.03	1997.....	25	921	0.04	2003	7	466	0.02
1991.....	29	638	0.03	1998.....	20	904	0.03	2004[5]....	9	203	0.01
1992.....	28	1,070	0.06								

(1) Involving 1 or more passenger fatalities and an aircraft with a maximum take-off mass greater than 2,250 kg. (2) Passenger deaths per 100 mil passenger kilometers. (3) Excluding accidents caused by terrorism or sabotage. (4) Revised data. (5) Preliminary.

Deaths in the U.S. Involving Firearms, by Age, 2002

Source: National Safety Council

	All ages	Under 5	5-14	15-19	20-24	25-44	45-64	65-74	75 & over
Total firearms deaths.......	30,242	71	348	2,474	4,306	11,586	7,040	1,993	2,424
Male...................	26,098	42	242	2,209	3,887	9,850	5,875	1,768	2,225
Female................	4,144	29	106	265	419	1,736	1,165	225	199
Unintentional	762	12	48	107	103	266	151	36	39
Male...................	667	8	39	101	94	227	134	32	32
Female................	95	4	9	6	9	39	17	4	7
Suicide.................	17,108	—	86	742	1,346	5,556	5,370	1,776	2,232
Male...................	15,045	—	68	668	1,229	4,750	4,607	1,620	2,103
Female................	2,063	—	18	74	117	806	763	156	129
Homicide	11,829	58	205	1,567	2,750	5,507	1,434	161	147
Male...................	9,899	33	127	1,384	2,467	4,640	1,062	101	85
Female................	1,930	25	78	183	283	867	372	60	62
Legal Intervention..........	300	0	3	23	63	161	44	5	1
Male...................	288	0	3	22	60	155	42	5	1
Female................	12	0	0	1	3	6	2	0	0
Undetermined[1].............	243	1	6	35	44	96	41	15	5
Male...................	199	1	5	34	37	78	30	10	4
Female................	44	0	1	1	7	18	11	5	1

Note: There were 28,663 firearms deaths in 2000. (1) "Undetermined" means that the intention involved (whether accident, suicide, or homicide) could not be determined.

U.S. Fires, 2005

Source: National Fire Protection Assn.

Fires

- Public fire departments responded to 1,602,000 fires in 2005, an increase of 3.3% from 2004.
- Every 20 seconds, a fire department responds to a fire somewhere in the United States.
- There were 511,000 structure fires in 2005, a decrease of 3.0% from the 2004 figure.
- 75% of all structure fires, or 381,000 fires, occurred in homes.
- Fires in vehicles dropped 2.4% from the previous year, totaling 290,000 in 2005.
- There were 801,000 fires in outside properties, an increase of 10.1% from 2004.

Civilian deaths

- There were 3,695 civilian fire deaths in 2005. This was a decrease of 5.8% from the year before.
- The number of civilian fire deaths that occurred in home structure fires decreased by 5.0%, to 3,030.
- 82% (3,030) of all fire deaths were caused by fires in the home.
- Home fires caused an average of one civilian death every 3 hours.

Civilian injuries

- There were an estimated 17,925 civilian fire injuries reported in 2005, a slight increase of 0.3% from 2004.

- Home structure fires were the site of 13,300 civilian fire injuries in 2005, and non-home structure fires accounted for 2,025 civilian injuries.
- Nationwide, a civilian was injured in a fire every half hour.

Property damage

- Direct property damage from fires amounted to an estimated $10,672,000,000 in 2005, a significant increase of 9.0% from 2004. Structure fires accounted for $9,193,000,000 of property damage.
- Property loss associated with home fires came to $6,729,000,000 for 2005.

Intentionally set fires

- There were an estimated 31,500 intentionally set structure fires in 2005, a significant decrease of 13.7% from the 2004 number.
- Intentionally set structure fires resulted in 315 civilian deaths in 2005, a slight decrease of 1.6% from the year before. Property damage from intentionally set structure fires totaled $664,000,000, a decrease of 7.0% from the 2004 figure.
- The number of intentionally set vehicle fires in 2005 was 21,000, a significant decrease of 41.4% from 2004. The 2005 intentionally set vehicle fires caused an estimated $113,000,000 in property damage, a decrease of 31.5% from 2004.

Physicians by Age, Sex, and Specialty, 2004

Source: American Medical Assn., as of Dec. 31, 2004

	Male	Female		Male	Female
All Specialties[1]	649,347	235,627	Obstetrics/Gynecology	24,801	17,258
Aerospace Medicine.	442	33	Occupational Medicine	2,172	502
Allergy & Immunology	3,056	1,050	Ophthalmology	15,529	3,177
Anaesthesiology.	30,452	8,370	Orthopedic Surgery	22,775	1,021
Cardiovascular Disease	20,060	2,054	Otolaryngology	8,777	1,084
Child Psychiatry	3,829	3,019	Pathology-Anat./Clin.	12,523	6,037
Colon/Rectal Surgery	1,116	149	Pediatric Cardiology	1,276	480
Dermatology.	6,535	3,906	Pediatrics.	33,515	36,636
Diagnostic Radiology	18,527	5,126	Physical Med./Rehab.	4,812	2,478
Emergency Medicine	21,877	5,987	Plastic Surgery	6,075	777
Family Practice.	54,022	26,305	Psychiatry	27,213	13,079
Forensic Pathology	413	207	Public Health	1,091	464
Gastroenterology	10,473	1,255	Pulmonary Diseases	8,385	1,422
General Practice	9,544	2,120	Radiation Oncology	3,271	1,017
General Preventive Med.	1,297	751	Radiology	7,465	1,270
General Surgery.	32,329	5,173	Thoracic Surgery.	4,750	166
Internal Medicine	104,688	46,245	Transplantation Surgery	94	10
Medical Genetics	250	226	Urology	10,060	508
Neurological Surgery	4,976	312	Vascular	17	5
Neurology.	10,396	3,266	Other Speciality.	4,427	908
Nuclear Medicine	1,164	283	Unspecified	3,813	1,720

(1) Includes "Inactive," "Address Unknown," and certain specialties with very few practitioners.

Persons Not Covered by Health Insurance, by Selected Characteristics, 2005

Source: Bureau of the Census, U.S. Dept. of Commerce

	Number[1]	% of specified population		Number[1]	% of specified population
Sex			**Age**		
Male	24,854	17.2	Under 18 years	8,310	11.2
Female	21,723	14.5	18 to 24 years	8,556	30.6
Race and Ethnicity			25 to 34 years	10,412	26.4
White	35,340	15.0	35 to 44 years	8,090	18.8
Non-Hispanic	21,144	11.3	45 to 64 years	10,740	14.6
Black	7,228	19.6	65 years and over	459	8.5
Asian and Pacific Islander	2,257	17.9	**Region**		
Hispanic[2]	14,122	32.7	Northeast.	6,657	12.3
Education (18 years and older)			Midwest	7,777	11.9
No high school diploma	10,175	30.1	South.	19,793	18.6
High school graduate only	14,113	20.3	West	12,352	18.1
Some college, no degree	7,006	16.5	**Household Income**		
Associate degree	2,312	12.7	Less than $25,000.	14,561	24.4
Bachelor's degree or higher	4,661	8.3	$25,000 to $49,999	14,977	20.6
Nativity			$50,000 to $74,999	8,300	14.1
Native.	34,608	13.4	$75,000 or more	8,740	8.5
Foreign born.	11,969	33.6	**TOTAL**	46,577	15.9
Naturalized citizen	2,482	17.9			
Not a citizen	9,487	43.6			

(1) In thousands. (2) Persons of Hispanic origin may be of any race.

U.S. Health Expenditures, 1960-2003

Source: *Health, United States, 2005,* National Center for Health Statistics, U.S. Dept. of Health and Human Services

	1960	1970	1980	1990	1995	2000	2001	2002	2003
					Amount in billions				
National health expenditures	$26.7	$73.1	$245.8	$696.0	$990.2	$1,309.9	$1,426.4	$1,559.0	$1,678.9
					Percent distribution				
Health services and supplies	93.6	92.2	95.0	96.2	96.7	96.3	96.3	96.2	96.1
Personal health care	87.6	86.5	87.3	87.6	87.4	86.7	86.6	86.1	85.8
Hospital care	34.4	37.8	41.3	36.5	34.7	31.5	31.3	31.1	30.7
Professional services..............	31.3	28.3	27.4	31.2	32.0	32.6	32.6	32.3	32.3
Physician and clinical services.....	20.1	19.1	19.2	22.6	22.3	22.2	22.1	21.9	22.0
Other professional services	1.5	1.0	1.5	2.6	2.9	3.0	3.0	3.0	2.9
Dental services	7.4	6.4	5.4	4.5	4.5	4.6	4.6	4.5	4.4
Other personal health care	2.4	1.7	1.3	1.4	2.3	2.8	2.9	2.9	2.9
Nursing home and home health......	3.4	6.1	8.2	9.4	10.6	9.7	9.5	9.2	9.0
Home health care..............	0.2	0.3	1.0	1.8	3.1	2.4	2.4	2.3	2.4
Nursing home care.............	3.2	5.8	7.2	7.6	7.5	7.3	7.1	6.8	6.6
Retail outlet sales of medical products.	18.6	14.3	10.5	10.5	10.2	13.0	13.3	13.6	13.8
Prescription drugs	10.0	7.5	4.9	5.8	6.1	9.3	9.9	10.4	10.7
Other medical products	8.5	6.8	5.6	4.7	4.0	3.7	3.4	3.3	3.1
Government administration and net cost of private health insurance.....	4.5	3.8	4.9	5.7	6.1	6.2	6.4	6.8	7.1
Government public health activities[1]	1.5	1.9	2.7	2.9	3.2	3.3	3.3	3.3	3.2
Investment	6.4	7.8	5.0	3.8	3.3	3.7	3.7	3.8	3.9
Research	2.6	2.7	2.2	1.8	1.7	2.2	2.3	2.3	2.4
Construction.....................	3.8	5.2	2.8	2.0	1.6	1.5	1.4	1.5	1.5
			Average annual percent change from previous year shown						
National health expenditures	—	10.6	12.9	11.0	7.3	7.1	8.5	9.3	7.7
Health services and supplies	—	10.4	13.2	11.1	7.4	6.8	8.6	9.2	7.6
Personal health care	—	10.5	13.0	11.0	7.3	6.6	8.5	8.8	7.3
Hospital care	—	11.7	13.9	9.6	6.2	5.0	7.5	9.5	6.5
Professional services..............	—	9.5	12.5	12.4	7.9	7.3	8.8	8.0	7.8
Physician and clinical services.....	—	10.1	12.9	12.8	7.0	7.2	8.6	7.7	8.5
Other professional services	—	6.6	17.1	17.5	9.5	5.8	9.9	7.6	4.8
Dental services	—	9.1	11.1	9.0	7.1	7.7	8.0	7.2	9.2
Other personal health care	—	7.2	10.0	11.4	18.9	9.0	11.3	12.1	9.2
Nursing home and home health......	—	17.2	16.3	12.5	10.0	3.0	5.8	4.9	9.2
Home health care..............	—	14.5	26.9	18.1	19.4	-1.8	6.2	7.2	9.5
Nursing home care.............	—	17.4	15.4	11.5	7.2	4.7	5.7	4.1	4.0
Retail outlet sales of medical products.	—	7.8	9.4	11.1	6.5	11.9	11.7	12.0	9.2
Prescription drugs	—	7.5	8.2	12.8	8.6	16.4	15.9	15.3	10.7
Other medical products	—	8.1	10.6	9.2	3.8	2.1	1.3	2.6	4.2
Government administration and net cost of private health insurance	—	8.6	15.9	12.7	8.6	10.0	12.5	16.2	13.2
Government public health activities[1]	—	13.2	17.4	11.6	9.2	4.8	5.5	5.9	5.1
Investment	—	12.9	7.9	8.0	4.3	17.3	5.5	11.9	9.1
Research	—	10.9	10.8	8.8	6.2	23.1	9.4	8.9	10.0
Construction.....................	—	14.1	6.1	7.3	2.4	9.5	-0.3	16.8	7.7

Note: Numbers may not add to totals because of rounding. (1) Includes personal care services delivered by government public health agencies.

Health Coverage for Persons Under 65, by Characteristics, 1984, 2000-2003

Source: *Health, United States, 2004,* National Center for Health Statistics, U.S. Dept. of Health and Human Services

	PRIVATE INSURANCE				MEDICAID[1]				NOT COVERED[2]			
	1984	2000[3]	2002	2003	1984	2000[3]	2002	2003	1984	2000[3]	2002	2003
					Percent of each population group							
Total......................	76.8	71.5	69.4	68.9	6.8	9.5	11.8	12.3	14.5	17.0	16.8	16.5
Age												
Under 18 years...........	72.6	66.6	63.5	63.0	11.9	19.6	24.8	26.0	13.9	12.6	10.9	9.8
18-44 years	76.5	70.5	68.7	67.7	5.1	5.6	7.1	7.4	17.1	22.4	23.0	23.5
45-64 years	83.3	78.7	77.3	77.3	3.4	4.5	5.3	5.3	9.6	12.6	13.1	12.5
Race and Hispanic origin[4,5]												
White, non-Hispanic........	82.3	79.5	77.9	77.8	3.7	6.1	7.7	8.0	12.0	12.5	12.5	11.9
Black, non-Hispanic........	58.3	56.0	55.2	55.5	20.7	21.0	23.2	23.4	19.6	19.5	18.7	18.1
All Hispanic	55.7	47.8	44.4	41.9	13.3	15.5	20.8	21.8	29.5	35.6	33.9	34.7
Percent of poverty level[4]												
Below 100%..............	32.2	25.2	25.2	23.9	33.0	38.4	42.8	43.2	33.9	34.2	30.3	31.1
100-149%...............	62.2	41.7	38.4	37.5	7.7	20.7	27.6	26.9	27.2	34.9	32.2	31.9
150-199%...............	77.2	58.5	56.2	52.2	3.2	11.5	16.1	17.1	17.3	27.0	25.2	27.6
200% or more............	91.5	85.7	83.9	84.6	0.6	2.3	3.1	3.3	6.0	10.1	11.1	10.0
Geographic region[4]												
Northeast	80.5	76.3	73.9	74.7	8.6	10.6	12.5	12.9	10.2	12.2	12.8	11.3
Midwest	80.6	78.8	76.4	75.9	7.4	8.0	10.3	10.8	11.3	12.3	12.5	12.4
South	74.3	66.8	64.6	64.0	5.1	9.4	12.0	12.6	17.7	20.5	20.5	19.8
West	71.9	66.5	66.1	64.7	7.0	10.4	12.7	12.8	18.2	20.7	19.1	19.9

Note: Data based on household interviews of a sample of the civilian noninstitutionalized population. Percents do not add to 100 because other types of health insurance (e.g., Medicare, military) are not shown and persons with both private insurance and Medicaid appear in both sections. (1) Includes Medicaid or other public assistance. In 2002, the age-adjusted percent of the population under 65 covered by Medicaid was 9.2%; 1.2% were covered by state-sponsored health plans and 1.4% were covered by State Children's Health Insurance Program (SCHIP). (2) Includes persons not covered by private insurance, Medicaid or other public assistance, Medicare, or military plans. (3) In 1997 the questionnaire changed compared with previous years. (4) Age adjusted. (5) Changed reporting methods make percentages for race before 1999 not strictly comparable with those from 1999 on.

Health Insurance Coverage,[1] by State, 1990, 2000, 2005

Source: Bureau of the Census, U.S. Dept. of Commerce

	2005 Not covered[2]	2005 % not covered	2000 Not covered[2]	2000 % not covered	1990 Not covered[2]	1990 % not covered		2005 Not covered[2]	2005 % not covered	2000 Not covered[2]	2000 % not covered	1990 Not covered[2]	1990 % not covered
AL..	696	15.4	582	13.3	710	17.4	MT..	162	17.4	150	16.8	115	14.0
AK.	117	17.7	117	18.7	77	15.4	NE..	208	11.8	154	9.1	138	8.5
AZ..	1,219	20.2	869	16.7	547	15.5	NV..	425	17.4	344	16.8	201	16.5
AR.	494	17.9	379	14.3	421	17.4	NH..	135	10.3	103	8.4	107	9.9
CA.	6,961	19.4	6,299	18.5	5,683	19.1	NJ..	1,324	15.2	1,021	12.2	773	10.0
CO.	788	17	620	14.3	495	14.7	NM..	396	20.4	435	24.2	339	22.2
CT.	394	11.3	330	9.8	226	6.9	NY..	2,559	13.5	3,056	16.3	2,176	12.1
DE.	110	13	72	9.3	96	13.9	NC..	1,371	16	1,084	13.6	883	13.8
DC.	73	NA	78	14.0	109	19.2	ND..	76	12.2	71	11.3	40	6.3
FL..	3,703	20.7	2,829	17.7	2,376	18.0	OH..	1,394	12.3	1,248	11.2	1,123	10.3
GA.	1,709	18.9	1,166	14.3	971	15.3	OK..	647	18.4	641	18.9	574	18.6
HI..	116	9.1	113	9.4	81	7.3	OR..	579	16	433	12.7	360	12.4
ID..	222	15.4	199	15.4	159	15.2	PA..	1,287	10.5	1,047	8.7	1,218	10.1
IL..	1,802	14.3	1,704	13.9	1,272	10.9	RI...	125	11.8	77	7.4	105	11.1
IN..	871	14.2	674	11.2	587	10.7	SC..	741	17.7	480	12.1	550	16.2
IA..	251	8.6	253	8.8	225	8.1	SD..	95	12.4	81	11.0	81	11.6
KS.	290	10.8	289	10.9	272	10.8	TN..	836	14.2	615	10.9	673	13.7
KY.	514	12.7	545	13.6	480	13.2	TX..	5,516	24.2	4,748	22.9	3,569	21.1
LA..	767	18.8	789	18.1	797	19.7	UT..	420	16.6	281	12.5	156	9.0
ME.	143	10.8	138	10.9	139	11.2	VT..	73	NA	52	8.6	54	9.5
MD.	788	14.2	547	10.4	601	12.7	VA..	1,011	13.6	814	11.6	996	15.7
MA.	618	9.8	549	8.7	530	9.1	WA..	866	13.8	792	13.5	557	11.4
MI..	1,133	11.4	901	9.2	865	9.4	WV..	322	17.9	250	14.1	249	13.8
MN.	431	8.4	399	8.1	389	8.9	WI..	534	9.8	406	7.6	321	6.7
MS.	495	17.4	380	13.6	531	19.9	WY..	82	16.1	76	15.7	58	12.5
MO.	691	12.1	524	9.5	665	12.7	**U.S..**	**46,577**	**15.9**	**39,804**	**14.2**	**34,719**	**13.9**

NA = Not available. (1) For population, all ages, including those 65 or over, an age group largely covered by Medicare. (2) In thousands.

Enrollment in Health Maintenance Organizations (HMOs), 1976-2004

Source: *Health, United States, 2004,* National Center for Health Statistics, U.S. Dept. of Health and Human Services

	1976	1980	1990	1995	1997	1998	1999	2000	2001	2002	2003	2004
					Number of enrolled in millions							
TOTAL	6.0	9.1	33.0	50.9	66.8	76.6	81.3	80.9	79.5	76.1	71.6	68.8
Model type[1]												
Individual practice assoc.[2]	0.4	1.7	13.7	20.1	26.7	32.6	32.8	33.4	33.1	31.6	27.9	24.6
Group[3]	5.6	7.4	19.3	13.3	11.0	13.8	15.9	15.2	15.6	15.0	16.1	15.3
Mixed	—	—	—	17.6	29.0	30.1	32.6	32.3	30.9	29.6	27.8	28.9
Federal program[4]												
Medicaid[5]	—	0.3	1.2	3.5	5.6	7.8	10.4	10.8	11.4	12.8	14.5	14.3
Medicare	—	0.4	1.8	2.9	4.8	5.7	6.5	6.1	6.1	5.4	4.9	4.9
					Percent of population enrolled in HMOs							
TOTAL	2.8	4.0	13.4	19.4	25.2	28.6	30.1	30.0	28.3	26.4	24.6	23.4
Geographic region												
Northeast	2.0	3.1	14.6	24.4	32.4	37.8	36.7	36.5	35.1	33.4	31.8	30.1
Midwest	1.5	2.8	12.6	16.4	19.5	22.7	23.3	23.2	21.7	20.6	19.7	18.7
South	0.4	0.8	7.1	12.4	17.9	21.0	23.9	22.6	21.0	19.8	17.1	16.0
West	9.7	12.2	23.2	28.6	36.4	39.1	41.4	41.7	40.7	38.2	35.8	34.4

— = Not available. **Note:** Data as of June 30 in 1976-80, Jan. 1 from 1990 onwards. HMOs in Guam included starting in 1994; Puerto Rico, 1998; Guam HMO enrollment was 32,000 in 2003 and Puerto Rico enrollment was 1,726,000 in 2003. Open-ended enrollment in HMO plans, amounting to 7.6 mil on Jan. 1, 2003, included from 1994 onwards. (1) Enrollment may not equal total because some plans did not report these characteristics. (2) This type of HMO contracts with an association of physicians from various settings (a mixture of solo and group practices) to provide health services. (3) Group includes staff, group, and network model types. (4) Enrollment by Medicaid or Medicare beneficiaries, where the Medicaid or Medicare program contracts directly with the HMO to pay the premium. (5) Data for 1990 and later include enrollment in managed-care health insuring organizations.

Top 20 Reasons Given by Patients for Physicians' Office Visits, 2004

Source: National Center for Health Statistics, U.S. Dept. of Health and Human Services

Rank	Number of visits (1,000)	Percent Distribution Total	Rank	Number of visits (1,000)	Percent Distribution Total
ALL VISITS	910,857	100.0	11. For other and unspecified test results	13,159	1.4
1. General medical examination	56,703	6.2	12. Stomach pain, cramps, and spasms	13,080	1.4
2. Progress visit, not otherwise specified	48,302	5.3	13. Diabetes mellitus	13,053	1.4
3. Postoperative visit	26,299	2.9	14. Depression	12,110	1.3
4. Cough	25,951	2.8	15. Back symptoms	11,892	1.3
5. Prenatal examination, routine	24,816	2.7	16. Skin rash	11,548	1.3
6. Medication, other and unspecified kinds	16,483	1.8	17. Vision dysfunctions	11,364	1.2
7. Gynecological examination	14,716	1.6	18. Well-baby examination	11,023	1.2
8. Hypertension	14,510	1.6	19. Ache, pain in head	10,780	1.2
9. Symptoms referable to throat	14,470	1.6	20. Earache or ear infection	10,125	1.1
10. Knee symptoms	14,241	1.6	All other reasons	536,232	58.9

(1) Based on 529,075,000 visits by women and 360,905,000 by men.

Hospitals and Nursing Homes in the U.S., 2002

Source: *Hospital Statistics™ 2003* ed., Health Forum, LLC, An American Hospital Assoc. Company, © 2003; *Health, United States, 2004*
For information on choosing a nursing home, go to the website www.medicare.gov/nursing/overview.asp

STATE	Hospitals[1]	% of beds occupied[1]	Nursing homes	% of beds occupied	STATE	Hospitals[1]	% of beds occupied[1]	Nursing homes	% of beds occupied
AL......	107	56	230	90.3	MT	53	69	102	77.3
AK	19	60	15	79.4	NE	84	58	230	82.7
AZ......	61	64	134	79.4	NV	24	68	44	79.9
AR	83	58	247	72.1	NH	28	62	83	90.3
CA	384	69	1,347	81.6	NJ	78	70	360	86.7
CO	66	62	224	80.3	NM.....	35	65	82	84.1
CT	35	80	252	91.9	NY	212	77	674	93.0
DE	5	74	42	83.7	NC.....	111	69	415	88.0
DC	10	77	21	90.5	ND.....	40	60	84	94.1
FL.......	202	66	704	85.6	OH.....	166	62	994	76.6
GA	147	65	362	91.2	OK.....	108	58	373	68.4
HI	23	74	45	93.6	OR.....	60	61	145	70.2
ID	40	53	82	75.5	PA	205	70	757	88.0
IL	192	63	848	74.7	RI.......	11	73	97	87.9
IN	110	59	545	76.1	SC.....	62	72	176	89.2
IA	116	60	463	77.8	SD.....	50	59	112	92.1
KS	133	55	376	79.0	TN	123	60	339	89.5
KY	103	62	303	88.7	TX	411	64	1,139	70.3
LA......	125	59	321	77.3	UT	42	55	90	72.1
ME	37	66	121	90.7	VT	14	61	44	90.5
MD	49	73	245	86.8	VA	87	68	277	84.5
MA	80	74	499	89.4	WA.....	84	60	267	82.5
MI.......	145	66	431	84.3	WV.....	57	62	137	90.2
MN	133	68	425	92.2	WI	121	64	407	84.6
MS	96	57	204	88.2	WY.....	24	54	39	82.3
MO	117	61	538	69.2	**U.S.....**	**4,908**	**66**	**16,491**	**82.4**

(1) Community hospitals (excludes federal hospitals, hospital units of institutions, facilities for the mentally retarded, and alcoholism and chemical dependency hospitals).

Health Care Visits, by Selected Characteristics, 1997, 2000, 2003

Source: Centers for Disease Control and Prevention, National Center for Health Statistics.
National Health Interview Survey, family core and sample adult questionnaires.

	No visits			1-3 visits			4-9 visits			10 or more visits		
	1997	2000	2003	1997	2000	2003	1997	2000	2003	1997	2000	2003
					Percent distribution							
All persons	16.5	16.6	15.8	46.2	45.4	45.8	23.6	24.7	24.8	13.7	13.3	13.6
Age												
Under 6 years............	5.0	6.3	5.5	44.9	44.3	46.0	37.0	38.3	39.0	13.0	11.2	9.4
6–17 years.............	15.3	15.1	14.0	58.7	58.2	58.7	19.3	20.7	20.8	6.8	6.0	6.6
18–24 years.............	22.0	24.3	23.6	46.8	45.6	47.2	20.0	18.8	18.2	11.2	11.2	11.0
25–44 years.............	21.6	22.9	22.0	46.7	45.2	46.6	18.7	19.3	19.4	13.0	12.6	12.0
45–54 years.............	17.9	16.4	16.9	43.9	45.3	44.2	23.4	23.7	24.5	14.8	14.6	14.3
55–64 years.............	15.3	12.8	11.4	41.3	40.6	39.2	26.7	28.8	29.8	16.7	17.8	19.6
65–74 years.............	9.8	9.0	7.1	36.9	34.5	34.0	31.6	34.4	35.7	21.6	22.1	23.3
75 years and over	7.7	5.8	5.4	31.8	29.3	28.6	33.8	39.3	36.0	26.6	25.6	30.0
Sex												
Male..................	21.3	21.5	20.6	47.1	46.0	46.8	20.6	22.4	21.9	11.0	10.1	10.7
Female................	11.8	11.9	11.1	45.4	44.8	44.9	26.5	27.0	27.7	16.3	16.4	16.3
Race and Hispanic origin												
White, non-Hispanic.......	14.7	14.5	13.5	46.6	45.4	46.2	24.4	26.0	26.1	14.3	14.1	14.2
Black, non-Hispanic	16.9	17.2	14.6	46.1	46.9	45.9	23.1	23.4	25.3	13.8	12.6	14.2
Hispanic[1]	24.9	26.5	25.3	42.3	41.8	42.9	20.3	20.0	20.3	12.5	11.7	11.5
Geographic region												
Northeast...............	13.2	12.4	10.4	45.9	46.2	47.6	26.0	27.3	27.0	14.9	14.0	15.0
Midwest................	15.9	14.4	14.2	47.7	46.2	47.2	22.8	25.6	25.4	13.6	13.9	13.2
South	17.2	18.4	16.5	46.1	44.7	45.1	23.3	24.1	24.8	13.5	12.9	13.6
West..................	19.1	20.0	21.0	44.8	44.9	44.2	22.8	22.2	22.2	13.3	12.8	12.6

NOTE: Covers visits to doctor's offices, emergency departments, and home visits. (1) Persons of Hispanic origin may be of any race.

Top 20 Reasons Given by Patients for Emergency Room Visits, 2004

Source: National Center for Health Statistics, U.S. Dept. of Health and Human Services

Rank	Principal reason for visit	Number (thous.)	%
	ALL VISITS	110,216	100.0
1.	Stomach and abdominal pain, cramps, and spasms	7,502	6.8
2.	Chest pain and related symptoms	6,005	5.4
3.	Fever	4,167	3.8
4.	Back symptoms	2,895	2.6
5.	Headache, pain in head	2,895	2.6
6.	Cough	2,702	2.5
7.	Shortness of breath	2,553	2.3
8.	Vomiting	2,524	2.3
9.	Pain, site not referable to a specific body system	2,312	2.1
10.	Lacerations and cuts-upper extremity	2,069	1.9
11.	Accident, not otherwise specified	2,057	1.9
12.	Symptoms referable to throat	2,005	1.8
13.	Motor vehicle accident, type of injury unspecified	1,843	1.7
14.	Earache or ear infection	1,737	1.6
15.	Vertigo-dizziness	1,595	1.4
16.	Nausea	1,552	1.4
17.	Skinrash	1,535	1.4
18.	Legsymptoms	1,467	1.3
19.	Injury,other and unspecified type—head, neck, and face	1,423	1.3
20.	Labored or difficult breathing (dyspnea)	1,362	1.2

Drugs Most Frequently Prescribed in Physicians' Offices, 2004

Source: National Center for Health Statistics, *Health, United States, 2005*

Rank	Therapeutic Classification[1]	Times prescribed (thous.)	% distrib.[2]
1.	Antidepressants	81,185	5.1
2.	NSAIDs[3]	73,737	4.7
3.	Antiasthmatics or bronchodilators	69,507	4.4
4.	Antihypertensive agents	69,113	4.4
5.	Hyperlipidemia	63,996	4.1
6.	Antihistamines	58,163	3.7
7.	Acid or peptic disorders	56,906	3.6
8.	Antiarthritics	54,783	3.5
9.	Blood glucose regulators	53,069	3.4
10.	Non-narcotic analgesics	51,918	3.3
11.	Antipyretics	46,700	3.0
12.	ACE inhibitors[4]	46,329	2.9
13.	Narcotic analgesics	46,053	2.9
14.	Vitamins or minerals	44,066	2.8
15.	Diuretics	43,555	2.8
16.	Betablockers	43,518	2.8
17.	Vaccines or antisera	42,735	2.7
18.	Adrenal corticosteroids	31,716	2.0
19.	Calcium channel blockers	31,480	2.0
20.	Anticonvulsants	30,273	1.9

(1) Based on the standard classification used in National Drug Code Directory. (2) Based on an estimated 1,577,208,000 drug prescriptions at office visits in 2004. (3) Nonsteroidal anti-inflammatory drugs (4) Angiotensin-converting enzyme.

Expected New Cancer Cases and Deaths, by Sex, for Leading Sites, 2006

Source: American Cancer Society

The estimates of expected new cases are offered as a rough guide only. They exclude basal and squamous cell skin cancers and in situ carcinomas, except urinary bladder. Carcinoma in situ of the breast accounts for about 54,890 new cases annually, melanoma carcinoma in situ for about 46,170. More than 1 mil cases of basal cell and squamous cell cancer, which are highly curable forms of skin cancer, occur annually.

EXPECTED NEW CASES

Both sexes		Women		Men	
Lung	174,470	Breast	212,920	Prostate	234,460
Colorectal	148,610	Lung	81,770	Lung	92,700
Urinary bladder	61,420	Colorectal	75,810	Colorectal	72,800
Non-Hodgkin lymphoma	58,870	Uterine corpus (endometrium)	41,200	Urinary bladder	44,690
Pancreas	33,730	Ovary	20,180	Non-Hodgkin's lymphoma	30,680
ALL SITES	1,372,910	ALL SITES	679,510	ALL SITES	720,280

EXPECTED DEATHS

Both sexes		Women		Men	
Lung	162,460	Lung	72,130	Lung	90,330
Colorectal	55,170	Breast	40,970	Colorectal	27,870
Non-Hodgkin's lymphoma	18,840	Colorectal	27,300	Prostate	27,350
Pancreas	32,300	Ovary	15,310	Pancreas	16,090
Liver	16,200	Pancreas	16,210	Liver	10,840
ALL SITES	564,830	ALL SITES	273,560	ALL SITES	291,270

U.S. Cancer Incidence for Top 15 Sites, 1992-2002

Source: Surveillance, Epidemiology, and End Results (SEER) Program, National Cancer Institute

	Rate[1]	Average yearly % change[2]		Rate[1]	Average yearly % change[2]
ALL SITES	475.4	−0.6	Melanoma of the skin	16.2	2.4
Prostate.....................	180.1	−2.0	Ovary	14.2	−0.9
Breast (female only)	132.4	0.4	Leukemia	12.5	−0.9
Lung	63.2	−1.3	Pancreas...................	11.1	−0.3
Colon and rectum	53.9	−0.8	Kidney and renal pelvis........	11.1	1.5
Corpus and uterus...........	24.4	−0.2	Oral cavity and pharynx	11.0	−1.5
Urinary bladder	20.3	−0.2	Cervix Uteri.................	9.7	−2.8
Non-Hodgkin's lymphoma	19.2	0.1	Stomach	9.1	−1.5

(1) Per 100,000 population; rates for prostate, breast, corpus and uterus, and ovary are sex-specific; rates age-adjusted to the 2000 population, and so not comparable with previously published rates. (2) For 1992-2002.

U.S. Cancer Mortality for Top 15 Sites, 1992-2002

Source: Surveillance, Epidemiology, and End Results (SEER) Program, National Cancer Institute

	Rate[1]	Average yearly % change[2]		Rate[1]	Average yearly % change[2]
ALL SITES.................	204.0	−1.0	Leukemia..................	7.7	−0.6
Lung.......................	57.1	−0.8	Stomach	4.9	−3.0
Prostate	33.9	−3.6	Brain and other nervous system ...	4.7	−0.9
Breast (female only)...........	28.5	−2.4	Liver and intrahepatic bile duct ...	4.4	1.9
Colon and rectum...........	21.6	−1.8	Urinary bladder	4.4	−0.3
Pancreas	10.6	−0.1	Esophagus	4.3	0.6
Ovary	9.0	−0.5	Kidney and renal pelvis.........	4.2	−0.1
Non-Hodgkin's lymphoma	8 4	−0.8	Corpus and uterus............	4.1	−0.1

(1) Per 100,000 population; rates age-adjusted to the 2000 population, and so not comparable with previously published rates; annual average for 8-year period; rates for prostate, breast, and ovary are sex-specific. (2) For 1992-2002.

Cardiovascular Diseases Statistical Summary, 2003

Source: American Heart Association

Prevalence — An estimated 71,300,000 Americans had one or more forms of heart and blood vessel disease in 2003.
• hypertension (high blood pressure)—65,000,000
• coronary heart disease—13,200,000
• stroke—500,000
• heart failure—5,000,000
Mortality — 910,614* in 2003 (37.3% of all deaths).
• Someone in the U.S. dies from cardiovascular disease every 35 seconds.
Congenital or inborn heart defects — Mortality from such heart defects was 4,178 in 2002.

* Preliminary data

Coronary heart disease (heart attack and angina pectoris) — caused 479,305* deaths in 2003.
• 13,200,000 Americans had a history of heart attack and/or angina pectoris.
• As many as 1,200,000 Americans have coronary attacks every year.
Heart failure — killed 57,218* in 2003.
Stroke — killed 157,804* Americans in 2003.
Rheumatic fever/rheumatic heart disease — killed 3,554* in 2003.
High blood pressure — killed 52,602* in 2003

Transplant Waiting List, Sept. 2006*

Source: United Network for Organ Sharing

Type of transplant	Patients waiting
Kidney..............	67,817
Liver	17,142
Lung	2,870
Heart...............	2,867
Kidney-pancreas......	2,422
Pancreas	1,751
Intestine	233
Heart-lung...........	147
Total[1]	**92,588**

Transplants Performed, 2005

Type of transplant	Number
Kidney	16,477
Liver	6,443
Heart	2,125
Lung................	1,406
Kidney-pancreas	903
Pancreas	541
Intestine	178
Heart-lung	35
Total	**28,108**

* As of Sept. 22, 2006. (1) Some patients are waiting for more than one organ; therefore total number of patients waiting is less than the sum of patients waiting for each organ.

Overweight, Obesity, and Healthy Weight in the U.S.[1], 1960-2002

Source: National Center for Health Statistics, National Health and Nutrition Examination Survey

	1960-62	1971-74	1976-80	1988-94	1999-2002
			Percent of population		
Overweight[2]					
Both sexes[3,4] ..	44.8	47.7	47.4	56.0	65.2
Male	49.5	54.7	52.9	61.0	68.8
Female[3]	40.2	41.1	42.0	51.2	61.7
Obese[5]					
Both sexes[3,4] ..	13.3	14.6	15.1	23.3	31.1
Male.	10.7	12.2	12.8	20.6	28.1
Female[3]	15.7	16.8	17.1	26.0	34.0
Healthy weight[6] .					
Both sexes[3,4] ..	51.2	48.8	49.6	41.7	32.9
Male	48.3	43.0	45.4	37.9	30.2
Female[3]	54.1	54.3	53.7	45.3	35.6

NOTE: Percents do not sum to 100 because the percent of persons with BMI less than 18.5 is not shown and the percent of persons with obesity is a subset of the percent with overweight. Height was measured without shoes; two pounds were deducted from data for 1960-62 to allow for weight of clothing. (1) In persons age 20-74, age-adjusted to 2000 standard population group; Data based on measured height and weight of a sample of the civilian noninstitutionalized population. (2) Body mass index (BMI) greater than or equal to 25. (3) Excludes pregnant women. (4) Includes persons of all races and Hispanic origins. (5) Body mass index (BMI) greater than or equal to 30. (6) BMI of 18.5 to less than 25. See pg. 153 for tables to calculate BMI.

AIDS Deaths and New AIDS Cases in the U.S., 1985-2003

Source: *Health, United States, 2004;* National Center for Health Statistics, U.S. Dept. of Health and Human Services

	Percent Distribu- tion	All Years[1]	1985	1990	1995	2000	2001	2002	2003	2003 rate[2]
TOTAL DEATHS	—	524,060	6,981	31,988	52,254	17,741	18,524	17,557	18,017	4.7
					NEW AIDS CASES					
All races	—	874,230	8,131	41,449	70,373	40,165	41,312	42,478	44,232	14.7
All males, 13 years and over	100.0	708,452	7,484	36,180	56,650	30,047	30,570	31,425	32,781	27.4
Race White, non-Hispanic	47.1	333,873	4,743	20,818	25,972	11,224	10,971	11,069	11,831	13.6
Black, non-Hispanic	35.7	253,078	1,695	10,244	20,812	13,041	13,720	14,214	13,820	109.2
Hispanic[3]	15.8	112,101	989	4,746	9,128	5,295	5,329	5,550	6,344	37.2
American Indian or Alaska Native[4]	0.3	2,353	9	81	196	135	145	146	169	16.0
Asian or Pacific Islander[4]	0.8	5,875	47	254	463	275	325	351	458	7.2
Age 13-19 years	0.4	2,861	27	106	223	142	179	197	249	1.3
20-29 years	15.2	107,651	1,497	6,917	8,387	3,327	3,280	3,418	3,570	17.1
30-39 years	44.4	314,224	3,575	16,670	25,680	12,510	12,041	12,011	12,214	55.8
40-49 years	28.1	199,248	1,632	8,832	16,120	9,614	10,234	10,593	11,257	48.4
50-59 years	8.9	62,905	596	2,645	4,691	3,372	3,629	3,926	4,239	23.9
60 years and over	3.0	21,563	157	1,010	1,549	1,082	1,207	1,280	1,252	6.3
All females, 13 years and over	100.0	156,837	519	4,544	12,978	9,932	10,572	10,914	11,297	9.0
Race White, non-Hispanic	21.5	33,766	143	1,230	3,031	1,841	1,977	1,893	1,923	2.2
Black, non-Hispanic	61.4	96,338	275	2,557	7,581	6,455	6,927	7,304	7,373	49.0
Hispanic[4]	15.9	24,997	98	724	2,244	1,476	1,547	1,579	1,776	11.3
American Indian or Alaska Native[4]	0.4	562	2	9	38	68	41	41	61	4.3
Asian or Pacific Islander[4]	0.6	905	1	20	69	71	64	67	105	1.3
Age 13-19 years	1.4	2,177	5	67	157	168	167	195	209	1.4
20-29 years	20.2	31,748	175	1,117	2,676	1,749	1,720	1,815	1,774	9.5
30-39 years	43.1	67,523	230	2,088	5,937	3,965	4,125	3,977	4,075	18.6
40-49 years	24.7	38,685	45	780	3,055	2,851	3,123	3,375	3,547	15.1
50-59 years	7.3	11,483	26	273	818	859	998	1,147	1,253	6.6
60 years and over	3.3	5,221	38	219	335	340	439	405	439	1.5
All children, under 13 years	100.0	8,939	128	725	745	186	170	139	153	0.7
Race White, non-Hispanic	18.0	1,613	26	156	117	30	29	21	23	0.2
Black, non-Hispanic	61.6	5,504	84	390	483	121	111	92	93	3.0
Hispanic[4]	19.2	1,714	18	169	135	30	27	22	34	0.6
American Indian or Alaska Native[4]	0.3	31	—	5	2	1	—	—	—	0.0
Asian or Pacific Islander[4]	0.6	57	—	4	5	3	3	4	1	0.5
Age Under 5 years	76.2	6,812	108	586	553	116	105	87	85	0.4
5-12 years	23.8	2,127	20	139	192	70	65	52	68	0.2

Note: The definition of AIDS cases for reporting purposes was expanded in 1985, 1987, and 1993, as more was learned about the spectrum of human immunodeficiency virus-associated diseases. Data exclude residents of U.S. territories. Figures were updated Dec. 31, 2002 to include delayed case reports and may differ from previous reports of *Health, United States*. (1) Revised figures; includes cases and deaths prior to 1985 and for years not shown. Through 2003. (2) Rate is per 100,000 pop. (3) Persons of Hispanic origin may be of any race. (4) Excludes persons of Hispanic origin.

New AIDS Cases in the U.S., 1985-2003, by Transmission Category

Source: *HIV/AIDS Surveillance Report, 2003,* CDC, National Center for HIV, STD, and TB Prevention, Div. of HIV/AIDS Prevention

TRANSMISSION CATEGORY	Percent distribu- tion	All years[1]	1985	1990	2000	2001	2002	2003
All males 13 years and older	100	729,478	7,504	36,193	30,251	31,901	32,513	33,250
Men who have sex with men	55	401,392	5,348	23,658	13,648	13,265	14,545	15,859
Injecting drug use	21	156,575	1,103	6,923	5,554	5,261	5,121	4,866
Men who have sex with men and injecting drug use	8	57,998	661	2,943	1,587	1,502	1,510	1,695
Hemophilia/coagulation disorder	1	5,130	68	332	93	97	79	74
Heterosexual contact[2]	6	40,947	32	715	2,537	2,762	3,213	3,371
Sex with injecting drug user	1	10,930	25	454	514	549	519	477
Transfusion[3]	1	5,219	102	440	146	105	147	111
Undetermined[4]	9	62,217	190	1,182	6,686	8,909	7,898	7,274
All females 13 years and older	100	163,396	524	4,547	9,979	11,082	11,279	11,561
Injecting drug use	38	61,621	287	2,347	2,545	2,212	2,381	2,262
Hemophilia/coagulation disorder	<1	318	3	15	5	9	11	11
Heterosexual contact[2]	43	70,200	119	1,538	4,025	4,142	4,740	5,234
Sex with injecting drug user	15	24,148	82	1,030	976	937	985	985
Transfusion[3]	2	4,076	63	330	151	113	118	108
Undetermined[4]	17	27,181	52	317	3,253	4,606	4,029	3,946

Note: The definition of AIDS cases for reporting purposes was expanded in 1985, 1987, and 1993, as more was learned about the spectrum of human immunodeficiency virus-associated diseases. Data exclude residents of U.S. territories. (1) Includes cases prior to 1985 and for years not shown. (2) Includes persons who have had heterosexual contact with a person with immunodeficiency virus (HIV) infection or at risk of HIV infection. (3) Receipt of blood transfusion, blood components, or tissue. (4) Includes persons for whom risk information is incomplete, persons still under investigation, men reported only to have had heterosexual contact with prostitutes, and interviewed persons for whom no specific risk is identified.

NOTED PERSONALITIES

Widely Known Americans of the Present

Political leaders, journalists, other prominent living persons. As of Sept. 2006. Excludes most who fall in categories listed elsewhere in Noted Personalities, such as Writers of the Present and Entertainment Personalities of the Present, or in Sports Personalities. Includes some figures active in American life but not U.S. citizens.

Jack Abramoff, b 2/28/58 (Atlantic City, NJ), former lobbyist; convicted in 2006 of crimes including bribing public officials.
Samuel Alito, b 4/1/50 (Trenton, NY), Supreme Court justice.
Roger Ailes, b 5/15/40 (Warren, OH), TV exec.
Madeleine K. Albright, b 5/15/37 (Prague, Czech.), former sec. of state.
Edwin "Buzz" Aldrin, b 1/20/30 (Montclair, NJ), former astronaut; 2nd person on the Moon.
Paul Allen, b 1/21/53 (Mercer Is., WA), co-founder of Microsoft.
Christiane Amanpour, b 1/12/58 (London, Eng.), TV journalist.
Richard K. Armey, b 7/7/40 (Cando, ND), former U.S. rep., House majority leader.
Neil Armstrong, b 8/5/30 (Wapakoneta, OH), former astronaut, 1st person on Moon.
John Ashcroft, b 5/9/42 (Chicago, IL), former MO gov., attorney gen.
Kathleen Babineaux Blanco, b 12/15/42 (Coteau, LA), LA governor.
F. Lee Bailey, b 6/10/33 (Waltham, MA), attorney.
Russell Baker, b 8/14/25 (Loudoun Co., VA), columnist.
Haley Barbour, b 10/22/47 (Yazoo City, MS), MS governor.
Dave Barry, b 7/3/47 (Armonk, NY), humorist.
Marion Barry, b 3/6/36 (Itta Bena, MS), former Wash., DC, mayor; DC city council member.
William Bennett, b 7/31/43 (Brooklyn, NY), author, former education secretary.
Chris Berman, b 5/10/55 (Greenwich, CT), sportscaster.
Ben Bernanke, b 12/13/53 (Augusta, GA), Federal Reserve Chairman, appointed in 2006.
Carl Bernstein, b 2/14/44 (Washington, DC), journalist; with Woodward cracked Watergate scandal.
Jeff Bezos, b 1/12/64 (Albuquerque, NM), founder and CEO of Amazon.com.
Joseph R. Biden Jr., b 11/20/42 (Scranton, PA), senator (DE).
James H. Billington, b 6/1/29 (Bryn Mawr, PA), librarian of Congress.
Wolf Blitzer, b 3/22/48 (Buffalo, NY), TV journalist.
Harold Bloom, b 7/11/30 (New York City), literary critic.
Michael R. Bloomberg, b 2/14/42 (Medford, MA), NYC mayor; financial information/media entrepreneur.
Roy Blunt, b 1/10/50 (Niangua, MO), U.S. House majority whip, interim House majority leader.
Samuel W. Bodman, b 11/26/38 (Chicago, IL), sec. of energy.
John Bolton, b 11/20/48 (Baltimore), U.S. amb. to UN.
Julian Bond, b 1/14/40 (Nashville), civil rights leader; NAACP chairman
Barbara Boxer, b 11/11/40 (Brooklyn, NY), senator (CA).
Bill Bradley, b 7/28/43 (Crystal City, MO), former senator (NJ), basketball player, presid. candidate.
Ed Bradley, b 6/22/41 (Philadelphia), TV journalist.
James Brady, b 8/29/40 (Centralia, IL), former presid. press sec.; gun control advocate.
L. Paul Bremer III, b 9/30/41 (Hartford, CT), diplomat, former top U.S. civilian administrator in Iraq.
Jimmy Breslin, b 10/17/30 (Queens, NY), columnist, author.
Stephen Breyer, b 8/15/38 (San Francisco), Sup. Ct. justice.
Sergey Brin, b 3/26/73 (Moscow, Russia), co-founder of Google.
David Broder, b 9/11/29 (Chicago Heights, IL), journalist.
Tom Brokaw, b 2/6/40 (Webster, SD), TV journalist, retired NBC anchor.
David Brooks, b 8/11/61 (NYC), columnist, political commentator.
Joyce Brothers, b 10/20/28 (NYC), psychologist.
Aaron Brown, b 11/10/48 (Hopkins, MN), CNN anchor.

Michael Brown, b 11/11/54 (Guymon, OK), former FEMA head, resigned under fire after Hurricane Katrina.
Jerry (Edmund G.) Brown Jr., b 4/7/38 (San Francisco), Oakland mayor; former CA gov., pres. candidate.
Pat Buchanan, b 11/2/38 (Washington, DC), journalist, former presid. candidate.
Art Buchwald, b 10/20/25 (Mt. Vernon, NY), humorist.
William F. Buckley Jr., b 11/24/25 (NYC), columnist, author.
Warren Buffett, b 8/30/30 (Omaha), investor, leading philanthropist.
Barbara Bush, b 6/8/25 (Rye, NY), former first lady.
Barbara Bush, b 11/25/81 (Dallas, TX), daughter of Pres. George W. Bush.
George H. W. Bush, b 6/12/24 (Milton, MA), former president.
George W. Bush, b 7/6/46 (New Haven, CT), U.S. president.
Jeb Bush, b 2/11/53 (Midland, TX), FL governor.
Jenna Bush, b 11/25/81(Dallas, TX), daughter of Pres. George W. Bush.
Laura Bush, b 11/4/46 (Midland, TX), first lady.
Robert Byrd, b 11/20/17 (N. Wilkesboro, NC), senator (WV), former majority leader.
Andrew Card, b 5/10/47 (Brockton, MA), former White House chief of staff.
Tucker Carlson, b 5/16/69 (San Francisco), journalist, TV commentator.
Jimmy Carter, b 10/1/24 (Plains, GA), former president; won 2002 Nobel Peace Prize.
James Carville Jr., b 10/25/44 (Fort Benning, GA), TV political commentator.
Steve Case, b 8/21/58 (Honolulu, HI), former AOL Time Warner chairman.
Elaine Chao, b 3/26/53 (Taipei, Taiwan), labor sec.
Dick Cheney, b 1/30/41 (Lincoln, NE), U.S. vice president.
Lynne Cheney, b 8/14/41 (Casper, WY), political commentator, wife of Dick Cheney.
Michael Chertoff, b 11/28/53 (Elizabeth, NJ), sec. of homeland security.
Noam Chomsky, b 12/7/28 (Philadelphia), linguist; activist.
Connie Chung, b 8/20/46 (Washington, DC), TV journalist.
Liz Claiborne, b 3/31/29 (Brussels, Belg.), fashion designer.
Wesley Clark, b 12/23/44 (Chicago), retired general, former NATO commander in Europe; 2004 presid. contender.
Bill Clinton, b 8/19/46 (Hope, AR), former U.S. president.
Chelsea Clinton, b 2/27/80 (Little Rock, AR), daughter of Pres. Clinton and Sen. Hillary Rodham Clinton.
Hillary Rodham Clinton, b 10/26/47 (Chicago), senator (NY), former first lady.
Anderson Cooper, b 6/3/67 (NYC), CNN anchor.
Bob Costas, b 3/22/52 (Queens, NY), TV sports journalist.
Ann Coulter, b 12/8/61 (New Canaan, CT), political commentator, author.
Katie Couric, b 1/7/57 (Arlington, VA), TV journalist; former NBC morning anchor; anchor of CBS Evening News.
Walter Cronkite, b 11/4/16 (St. Joseph, MO), former CBS news anchor.
Mario Cuomo, b 6/15/32 (Queens, NY), former NY gov.
Richard M. Daley, b 4/24/42 (Chicago), Chicago mayor.
John Danforth, b 9/5/36 (St. Louis, MO), former senator; former ambassador to the UN.
Thomas Daschle, b 12/9/47 (Aberdeen, SD), former senator and Senate minority leader.
Patti Davis, b 10/21/52 (LA county), daughter of Pres. Reagan.
Howard Dean, b 11/17/48 (NYC), former VT gov., 2004 pres. contender; Democratic National Committee chair.
Oscar de la Renta, b 7/22/36 (Santo Domingo, Dominican Rep.), fashion designer.

Tom DeLay, b 4/8/47 (Laredo, TX), former House Majority leader.
Michael Dell, b 2/23/65 (Houston, TX), founder, chairman, and CEO of Dell computers.
Alan Dershowitz, b 9/1/38 (Brooklyn, NY), attorney.
Barry Diller, b 2/2/42 (San Francisco), TV exec.
Lou Dobbs, b 9/24/45 (Childress, TX), TV journalist.
Christopher Dodd, b 5/27/44 (Willimantic, CT), senator.
Elizabeth Hanford Dole, b 7/29/36 (Salisbury, NC), senator; former Red Cross pres., cabinet member.
Robert Dole, b 7/22/23 (Russell, KS), former Senate majority leader, presid. nominee.
Sam Donaldson, b 3/11/34 (El Paso, TX), TV journalist.
Elizabeth Drew, b 11/16/35 (Cincinnati), journalist.
Matt Drudge, b 10/27/66 (Tacoma Park, MD), internet journalist.
Michael S. Dukakis, b 11/3/33 (Brookline, MA), former MA gov., presid. nominee.
Dick Durbin, b 11/21/44 (East. St. Louis, IL), Senate minority whip.
Bernard Ebbers, b 8/27/41 (Edmonton, Alberta, Can.), former WorldCom CEO, jailed for fraud.
Roger Ebert, b 6/18/42 (Urbana, IL), film critic.
Marian Wright Edelman, b 6/6/39 (Bennettsville, SC), pres. and founder of the Children's Defense Fund.
John Edwards, b 6/10/53 (Seneca, SC), former senator; 2004 vice-presid. candidate.
Edward Egan, b 4/2/32 (Oak Park, IL), Rom. Cath. cardinal, archbishop of New York.
Michael Eisner, b 3/7/42 (Mt. Kisco, NY), former Disney Co. CEO.
Lawrence J. Ellison, b 8/17/44 (NYC), Oracle Corp. founder, CEO.
Rev. Jerry Falwell, b 8/11/33 (Lynchburg, VA), TV evangelist, religious commentator.
Louis Farrakhan, b 5/11/33 (Roxbury, MA), Nation of Islam leader.
Russell Feingold, b 3/2/53 (Janesville, WI), senator.
Dianne Feinstein, b 6/22/33 (San Francisco), senator.
W. Mark Felt, b 8/17/13 (Twin Falls, ID), former No. 2 person at FBI, revealed (2005) as "Deep Throat" Watergate informant.
Geraldine Ferraro, b 8/26/35 (Newburgh, NY), former U.S. rep., vice-presid. nominee.
Bobby Fischer, b 3/9/43 (Chicago, IL), former chess champion.
Larry Flynt, b 11/1/42 (Salyersville, KY), publisher.
Steve (Malcolm) Forbes Jr., b 7/18/47 (Morristown, NJ), publisher, former presid. contender.
Betty Ford, b 4/8/18 (Chicago), former first lady.
Gerald R. Ford, b 7/14/13 (Omaha), former president.
Steve Fossett, b 4/22/1944 (Jackson, TN), adventurer, balloonist.
Al Franken, b 5/21/51 (NYC), humorist, political writer, radio host.
Tommy R. Franks, b 6/17/45 (Wynnewood, OK), former commander in chief U.S. Central Command.
Milton Friedman, b 7/31/12 (Brooklyn, NY), economist.
Thomas Friedman, b 7/20/53 (Minneapolis), columnist, author.
Bill Frist, b 8/19/42 (Nashville, TN), Senate majority leader; physician.
Bill Gates, b 10/28/55 (Seattle), software pioneer; Microsoft exec.
Henry Louis Gates Jr., b 9/16/50 (Keyser, WV), African American studies scholar.
David Geffen, b 2/21/43 (Brooklyn, NY), entertainment exec.
Richard Gephardt, b 1/31/41 (St. Louis, MO), former House party leader; 2004 presid. contender.
Louis Gerstner, b 3/1/42 (Mineola, NY), retired IBM exec.
Charles Gibson, b 3/4/43 (Evanston, IL), TV journalist; host of ABC World News Tonight.
Newt Gingrich, b 6/17/43 (Harrisburg, PA), former House Speaker.
Ruth Bader Ginsburg, b 3/15/33 (Brooklyn, NY), Sup. Ct. justice.
Rudolph Giuliani, b 5/28/44 (Brooklyn, NY), former NYC mayor.
John Glenn, b 7/18/21 (Cambridge, OH), former senator, astronaut.
Alberto Gonzales, b 8/4/55 (San Antonio, TX), attorney gen.
Roger Goodell, b 2/19/59 (Jamestown, NY), NFL commissioner.
Ellen Goodman, b 4/11/41 (Newton, MA), columnist.
Doris Kearns Goodwin, b 1/4/43 (Rockville Centre, NY), historian, TV commentator.
Berry Gordy, b 11/28/29 (Detroit), Motown record label founder.
Al Gore Jr., b 3/31/48 (Washington, DC), former senator, U.S. vice president, presid. candidate.
Tipper Gore, b 8/19/48 (Washington, DC), wife of Al Gore.
Porter Goss, b 11/26/38 (Waterbury, CT), former CIA director; former U.S. rep. (FL).
Rev. Billy Graham, b 11/7/18 (Charlotte, NC), evangelist.

Bob Graham, b 4/9/36 (Coral Gables, FL), former U.S. senator, FL gov; 2004 pres. contender.
(William) Franklin Graham III, b 7/14/52 (Asheville, NC), evangelist, son of Billy Graham.
Andrew Greeley, b 2/5/28 (Oak Park, IL), Rom. Cath. priest, sociologist, writer.
Jeff Greenfield, b 6/10/43 (NYC), TV journalist.
Alan Greenspan, b 3/6/26 (NYC), former Fed chairman.
Michael Griffin, b 11/1/99 (Aberdeen, MD), NASA head.
Andrew Grove, b 9/2/36 (Budapest, Hungary), Intel chairman.
Bryant Gumbel, b 9/29/48 (New Orleans), TV journalist.
Greg Gumbel, b 5/3/46 (New Orleans), sportscaster.
Carlos Gutierrez, b 11/4/52 (Havana, Cuba), sec. of commerce.
Chuck Hagel, b 10/4/46 (North Platte, NE), U.S. senator.
David Halberstam, b 4/10/34 (NYC), journalist, author.
Pete Hamill, b 6/24/35 (Brooklyn, NY), journalist, author.
Lee Hamilton, b 4/20/31 (Daytona Beach, FL), 9-11 commission vice-chair; former U.S. rep. from Indiana.
Paul Harvey, b 9/4/18 (Tulsa, OK), radio journalist.
J. Dennis Hastert, b 1/2/42 (Aurora, IL), House Speaker.
Orrin Hatch, b 3/22/34 (Homestead Park, PA), senator (UT).
Hugh Hefner, b 4/9/26 (Chicago), publisher.
Jesse Helms, b 10/18/21 (Monroe, NC), former senator.
Leona Helmsley, b 7/4/20 (NYC), real estate exec.
Tommy Hilfiger, b 3/24/51 (Elmira, NY), fashion designer.
Anita Hill, b 7/30/56 (Morris, OK), legal scholar, complainant against Clarence Thomas.
Christopher Hitchens, b 4/13/49 (Portsmouth, England), journalist, author.
James P. Hoffa, b 5/19/41, (Detroit), Teamsters Union head.
Richard Holbrooke, b 4/24/41 (Scarsdale, NY), former U.S. rep. to UN.
Russel Honoré, b 1947 (Lakeland, LA), lt. gen. commander U.S. 1st Army, in charge of Army Hurricane Katrina relief.
David Horowitz, b 1/10/39 (NYC), consumer advocate, columnist, author.
Steny H. Hoyer, b 6/14/39 (NYC), U.S. House minority whip.
Arianna Huffington, b 7/15/50 (Athens, Greece), political commentator.
H. Wayne Huizenga, b 12/29/39 (Evergreen Park, IL), entrepreneur, sports exec.
Brit Hume, b 6/22/43 (Washington DC), TV journalist (FOX).
Kay Bailey Hutchison, b 7/22/43 (Galveston, TX), senator.
Henry J. Hyde, b 4/18/24 (Chicago), U.S. rep.
Lee Iacocca, b 10/15/24 (Allentown, PA), former auto exec.
Carl Icahn, b 1936 (Queens, NY), financier.
Gwen Ifil, b 9/29/55 (Queens, NY), TV journalist, moderator (PBS).
Jeffrey Immelt, b 2/19/56 (Cincinnati, OH), General Electric CEO.
Don Imus, b 7/23/40 (Riverside, CA), talk-show host.
Patricia Ireland, b 10/19/45 (Oak Park, IL), feminist leader.
Molly Ivins, b 8/30/44 (Monterey, CA), author, columnist.
Alphonso Jackson, b 1947 (Marshall, TX), sec. of housing and urban development.
Rev. Jesse Jackson, b 10/8/41 (Greenville, SC), civil rights leader, former presid. contender.
Steve Jobs, b 2/24/55 (San Francisco), Apple Computer exec.; Pixar exec.
Mike Johanns, b 6/18/50 (Osage, IA), sec. of agriculture.
Jasper Johns, b 5/15/30 (Augusta, GA), artist.
Lady Bird Johnson, b 12/22/12 (Karnack, TX), former first lady.
Vernon E. Jordan Jr., b 8/15/35 (Atlanta), attorney, former presid. adviser, civil rights leader.
Donna Karan, b 10/2/48 (Queens, NY), fashion designer.
Jeffrey Katzenberg, b 12/21/50 (NYC), entertainment exec.
Thomas Kean, b 4/21/35 (NYC), 9-11 commission chair, Drew Univ. pres., former NJ gov.
Garrison Keillor, b 8/7/42 (Anoka, MN), author, broadcaster.
Jack Kemp, b 7/13/35 (Los Angeles), former vice-presid. nominee, HUD sec., pro football quarterback.
Anthony M. Kennedy, b 7/23/36 (Sacramento, CA), Sup. Ct. justice.
Edward M. Kennedy, b 2/22/32 (Brookline, MA), senator.
Robert ("Bob") Kerrey, b 8/27/43 (Lincoln, NE), former senator.
Teresa Heinz Kerry, b 10/5/38 (Mozambique), heiress, philanthropist; wife of John Kerry.
John Kerry, b 12/11/43 (Aurora, CO), senator (MA), 2004 presid. candidate.
Jack Kevorkian, b 5/26/28 (Pontiac, MI), physican, assisted-suicide activist; imprisoned on murder charges.
Larry King, b 11/19/33 (Brooklyn, NY), TV talk show host.
Michael Kinsley, b 3/9/51 (Detroit), editor, pol. commenator.
Jeane J. Kirkpatrick, b 11/19/26 (Duncan, OK), political scientist, former ambassador to UN.
Henry Kissinger, b 5/27/23 (Fuerth, Germany), former sec. of state, nat. security adviser; won 1973 Nobel Peace Prize.

Calvin Klein, b 11/19/42 (Bronx, NY), fashion designer.

Philip H. Knight, b 2/24/38 (Portland, OR), founder and chairman of the board of Nike.

Edward I. Koch, b 12/12/24 (NYC), former NYC mayor.

Ted Koppel, b 2/8/40 (Lancashire, England), former ABC network TV journalist; former anchor of *Nightline*.

Larry Kramer, b 6/25/35 (Bridgeport, CT), AIDS activist, writer.

William Kristol, b 12/23/52 (NYC), editor, columnist.

Steve Kroft, b 8/22/45 (Kokomo, IN), TV journalist.

Dennis Kucinich, b 10/8/46 (Cleveland, OH), U.S. repr., 2004 pres. contender.

Brian Lamb, b 10/9/41 (Lafayette, IN), cable TV exec., journalist.

Matt Lauer, b 12/30/57 (NYC), TV journalist; NBC morning anchor.

Ralph Lauren, b 10/14/39 (Bronx, NY), fashion designer.

Bernard F. Law, b 11/4/31 (Torreon, Mexico), cardinal, former Rom. Cath. archbishop of Boston, figure in church scandal.

Patrick Leahy, b 3/31/40 (Montpelier, VT), senator.

Norman Lear, b 7/27/22 (New Haven, CT), TV producer, political activist.

Michael O. Leavitt, b 2/11/51 (Cedar City, UT), sec. of health and human services.

Jim Lehrer, b 5/19/34 (Wichita, KS), TV journalist, author.

Carl Levin, b 6/28/34 (Detroit), senator.

Monica Lewinsky, b 7/23/73 (San Francisco), former White House intern, key figure in Clinton White House scandal.

Joseph Lieberman, b 2/24/42 (Stamford, CT), senator, former vice presid. candidate; 2004 presid. contender.

Rush Limbaugh, b 1/12/51 (Cape Girardeau, MO), radio talk-show host.

Trent Lott, b 10/9/41 (Grenada, MS), senator, former Senate majority leader.

Shannon Lucid, b 1/14/43 (Shanghai, China), NASA scientist, astronaut.

Richard Lugar, b 4/4/32 (Indianapolis), senator.

Roger Mahony, b 2/27/36 (Hollywood, CA), Rom. Cath. cardinal, archbishop of Los Angeles.

Mary Matalin, b 8/19/53 (Chicago), political commentator.

Chris Matthews, b 12/18/45 (Philadelphia), TV journalist.

John McCain, b 8/29/36 (Panama Canal Zone), senator (AZ); former presid. contender.

Scott McClellan, b 2/14/68 (Austin, TX), former White House press sec.

Mitch McConnell, b 2/20/42 (Tuscumbia, AL), senator (KY); majority whip.

David McCullough, b 7/7/33 (Pittsburgh, PA), historian, biographer.

George McGovern, b 7/19/22 (Avon, SD), former senator, presid. nominee.

Dr. Phil McGraw, b 9/1/50 (Vinita, OK), talk-show host, motivational speaker, author.

James McGreevey, b 8/6/57 (Jersey City, NY), former NJ governor; resigned amid allegations of sexual harassment and admitted he was gay.

John McLaughlin, b 3/29/27 (Providence, RI), TV journalist.

Robert S. McNamara, b 6/9/16 (San Francisco), former defense sec., World Bank head.

Russell Means, b 11/10/39 (Pine Ridge Indian Reserv., SD), Native American activist.

Kate Michelman, b 8/4/42 (NJ), abortion-rights activist.

Ken Mehlman, b. 1967 (Baltimore, MD), Republican National Committee chair.

Kate Millett, b 9/14/34 (St. Paul, MN), author, feminist.

Norman Mineta, b 11/12/31 (San Jose, CA), former transportation sec.

George Mitchell, b 8/20/33, (Waterville, ME), former Senate majority leader; diplomat, Disney Co. chairman.

Walter Mondale, b 1/5/28 (Ceylon, MN), former vice pres., senator, presid. nominee.

Michael Moore, b 4/23/54 (Davison, MI), activist, documentary filmmaker; author.

Bill Moyers, b 6/5/34 (Hugo, OK), TV journalist, author.

Robert S. Mueller III, b 8/7/44 (NYC), FBI director.

Rupert Murdoch, b 3/11/31 (Melbourne, Aus.), media exec.

John Murtha, b 6/17/32 (New Martinsville, WV), Congressman (PA); Vietnam War hero; outspoken critic of Iraq War.

Richard B. Myers, b 3/1/42 (Kansas City, MO), former chairman of Joint Chiefs of Staff.

Ralph Nader, b 2/27/34 (Winsted, CT), consumer advocate, 2000, 2004 independent presid. cand.

(Clarence) Ray Nagin, b 6/11/56 (New Orleans, LA), New Orleans mayor.

John Negroponte, b 7/21/39 (London, Eng.), director of National Intelligence; former U.S. rep. to UN.

Craig Newmark, b 12/6/52 (Morristown, NY), founder of Craigslist.com.

Peggy Noonan, b 9/7/50 (Brooklyn, NY), columnist, speechwriter.

Oliver North, b 10/7/43 (San Antonio, TX), talk-show host, former Nat. Sec. Council aide, fig. in Iran-contra scandal.

Eleanor Holmes Norton, b 6/13/37 (Washington, DC), U.S. House delegate.

Gale Norton, b 3/11/54 (Wichita, KS), former interior sec.

Robert Novak, b 2/26/31 (Joliet, IL), journalist.

Sam Nunn, b 9/8/38 (Perry, GA), former senator.

Barack Obama, b 8/4/61 (Hawaii), senator (IL); 2004 Dem. convention keynote speaker.

Soledad O'Brien, b 9/19/66 (Smithtown, NY), CNN morning anchor.

Sandra Day O'Connor, b 3/26/30 (El Paso, TX), former Sup. Ct. justice.

Joel Olsteen, b 3/5/63 (Houston, TX), televangelist, author.

Paul O'Neill, b 12/4/35 (St. Louis, MO), former treasury sec.

Bill O'Reilly, b 9/10/49 (NYC), TV commentator, host.

Michael Ovitz, b 12/14/46 (Encino, CA), entertainment exec.

Clarence Page, b 6/2/47 (Dayton, OH), journalist, TV commentator.

Lawrence Page, b 9/26/73 (East Lansing, MI), co-founder of Google.

Camille Paglia, b 4/2/47 (Endicott, NY), scholar, author.

Leon F. Panetta, b 6/28/38 (Monterey, CA), former White House chief of staff, U.S. rep.

Richard Parsons, b 4/4/48 (NYC), Time Warner CEO.

George Pataki, b 6/24/45 (Peekskill, NY), NY gov.

Jane Pauley, b 10/31/50 (Indianapolis), TV journalist.

Nancy Pelosi, b 3/26/40 (Baltimore, MD), U.S. rep. (CA); House minority leader.

Ross Perot, b 6/27/30 (Texarkana, TX), entrepreneur, former presid. nominee.

Rob Portman, b 12/19/55 (Cincinnati), Director of the Office of Management and Budget.

Colin Powell, b 4/5/37 (NYC), former sec. of state, nat. security adviser, Joint Chiefs of Staff chairman.

Dan Quayle, b 2/4/47 (Indianapolis), former U.S. vice pres., senator, presid. contender.

Anna Quindlen, b 7/8/53 (Philadelphia), author, columnist.

Dan Rather, b 10/31/31 (Wharton, TX), TV journalist, retired CBS anchor.

Nancy Reagan, b 7/6/21 (NYC), former first lady.

Michael Reagan, b 3/18/45, talk-show host, adopted son of Pres. Reagan and his 1st wife.

Ron Reagan, b 5/20/58 (Los Angeles), journalist, TV and radio talk show host, son of Pres. Reagan.

Sumner Redstone, b 5/27/23 (Boston), Viacom chairman, CEO.

Ralph Reed, Jr., b 6/24/61 (Portsmouth, VA), political adviser.

Robert B. Reich, b 6/24/46 (Scranton, PA), economist, author, former labor sec.

Harry Reid, b 12/2/39 (Searchlight, NV), Senate minority leader.

Janet Reno, b 7/21/38 (Miami, FL), former attorney gen.

Condoleezza Rice, b 11/14/54 (Birmingham, AL), sec. of state, former nat. security advisor.

Bill Richardson, b 11/15/47 (Pasadena, CA), NM gov.; former energy sec., UN ambassador, U.S. rep.

Sally K. Ride, b 5/26/51 (Encino, CA), former astronaut, 1st U.S. woman in space.

Tom (Thomas Joseph) Ridge, b 8/26/45 (Munhall, PA) former sec. of homeland security; former PA gov.

Geraldo Rivera, b 7/4/43 (NYC), TV journalist.

Cokie Roberts, b 12/27/43 (New Orleans), TV journalist.

John G. Roberts, b 1/27/55 (Buffalo, NY), Sup. Ct. chief justice.

Rev. Oral Roberts, b 1/24/18 (nr. Ada, OK), TV evangelist, educator.

Rev. Pat Robertson, b 3/22/30 (Lexington, VA), religious broadcasting exec., former presid. contender.

V. Gene Robinson, b 5/29/47 (Lexington, KY), first openly gay Episcopal bishop.

David Rockefeller, b 6/12/15 (NYC), banker.

John D. "Jay" Rockefeller 4th, b 6/18/37 (NYC), senator (WV), former WV gov.

Al Roker, b 8/20/54 (Queens, NY), TV weather person.

Mitt Romney, b 3/12/47 (Detroit), MA gov, former Olympics organizer.

Andy Rooney, b 1/14/19 (Albany, NY), TV commentator.

Charlie Rose, b 1/5/42 (Henderson, NC), TV journalist.

Karl Rove, b 12/25/50 (Denver, CO) White House senior domestic policy advisor.

Donald Rumsfeld, b 7/9/32 (Chicago), defense sec.

Tim Russert, b 5/7/50 (Buffalo, NY), TV journalist, moderator *Meet the Press* (NBC).

Morley Safer, b 11/8/31 (Toronto, Can.), TV journalist.

Diane Sawyer, b 12/22/45 (Glasgow, KY), TV journalist; ABC morning anchor.

Antonin Scalia, b 3/11/36 (Trenton, NJ), Sup. Ct. justice.

Bob Schieffer, b 2/25/37 (Austin, TX), CBS TV news anchor.

Phyllis Schlafly, b 8/15/24 (St. Louis, MO), political activist.

Arthur Schlesinger Jr., b 10/15/17 (Columbus, OH), historian.

Caroline Kennedy Schlossberg, b 11/27/57 (NYC), author, daughter of Pres. Kennedy.
Patricia Schroeder, b 7/30/40 (Portland, OR), former U.S. rep.
Rev. Robert Schuller, b 9/16/26 (Alton, IA), TV evangelist.
Charles Schumer, b 11/23/50 (Brooklyn, NY), senator.
Arnold Schwarzenegger, b 7/30/47 (Thal, Styria, Austria), CA governor; former actor.
H. Norman Schwarzkopf, b 8/22/34 (Trenton, NJ), former military leader.
Willard Scott, b 3/7/34 (Alexandria, VA), TV weather person.
Allan H. ("Bud") Selig, b 7/30/34 (Milwaukee), MLB comm.
Richard Serra, b 11/2/39 (San Francisco), sculptor.
Rev. Al Sharpton, b 10/3/54 (Brooklyn, NYC), activist, civil rights leader; 2004 presid. contender.
Cindy Sheehan, b 7/10/57 (Bellflower, CA), anti-Iraq-War activist.
Maria Shriver, b 11/6/55 (Chicago), TV journalist
George P. Shultz, b 12/13/20 (NYC), former sec. of state; other cabinet posts.
Russell Simmons, b 10/4/57 (Queens, NY), music producer.
O. J. Simpson, b 7/9/47 (San Francisco), former football star, murder defendant.
Harry Smith, b 8/21/51 (Lansing, IL), TV journalist; CBS morning anchor.
Liz Smith, b 2/2/23 (Ft. Worth, TX), gossip columnist.
John Snow, b 8/2/39 (Toledo, OH), former treasury sec, former CSX CEO.
Tony Snow, b 6/1/55 (Berea, KY), White House press sec.
George Soros, b 8/12/30 (Budapest, Hungary), financier, philanthropist.
David H. Souter, b 9/17/39 (Melrose, MA), Sup. Ct. justice.
Arlen Specter, b 2/12/30 (Wichita, KS), senator (PA), Judiciary Committee chair.
Margaret Spellings, b 11/30/57 (Michigan), sec of education.
Steven Spielberg, b 12/18/46 (Cincinnati, OH), movie director, producer.
Lesley Stahl, b 12/16/41 (Swampscott, MA), TV journalist.
Kenneth Starr, b 7/21/46 (Vernon, TX), former Whitewater indep. counsel.
Shelby Steele, b 1/1/46 (Chicago), scholar, critic.
George Steinbrenner, b 7/4/30 (Rocky River, OH), NY Yankees owner.
Gloria Steinem, b 3/25/34 (Toledo, OH), author, feminist.
Frank Stella, b 5/12/36 (Malden, MA), painter.
George Stephanopoulos, b 2/10/61 (Fall River, MA), TV journalist, former presid. adviser.
David J. Stern, b 9/22/42 (NYC), NBA comm.
Howard Stern, b 1/12/54 (Roosevelt, NY), radio talk show host.
John Paul Stevens, b 4/20/20 (Chicago), Sup. Ct. justice.
Ted Stevens, b 11/18/23 (Indianapolis, IN), senator (AK), Senate pres. pro tempore.
Martha Stewart, b 8/3/41 (Nutley, NJ), homemaking adviser, entrepreneur; TV personality.
Arthur Ochs Sulzberger Jr., b 9/22/51 (Mt. Kisco, NY), newspaper publisher.
Lawrence H. Summers, b 11/30/54 (New Haven, CT), former Harvard Univ. pres.
John J. Sweeney, b 5/5/34 (NYC), AFL-CIO pres.

Paul Tagliabue, b 11/24/40 (Jersey City, NJ), former NFL comm.
George Tenet, b 1/5/53 (Queens, NY), former CIA director.
Clarence Thomas, b 6/23/48 (Savannah, GA), Sup. Ct. justice.
Helen Thomas, b 8/4/20 (Winchester, KY), journalist.
Fred Thompson, b 8/19/42 (Sheffield, AL), former senator; actor.
Tommy G. Thompson, b 11/19/41 (Elroy, WI), former sec. of health and human services, former WI gov.
Margaret Truman (Daniel), b 2/17/24 (Independence, MO), author, daughter of Pres. Truman.
Donald Trump, b 6/14/46 (NYC), real estate exec.; TV personality.
Ted Turner, b 11/19/38 (Cincinnati), TV exec, philanthropist.
Peter Ueberroth, b 9/2/37 (Evanston, IL), sports & travel exec.; former MLB comm.
Jack Valenti, b 9/5/21 (Houston), former White House aide, movie industry exec.
Abigail Van Buren, b 7/4/18 (Sioux City, IA), retired advice columnist.
Gloria Vanderbilt, 2/20/24 (NYC), fashion designer, heiress.
Jesse Ventura, b 7/15/51 (Minneapolis), former wrestler, former MN governor; radio talk show host.
Antonio Villaraigosa, b 1/23/53 (East LA), 1st Hispanic mayor of LA since 1870s.
Paul Volcker, b 9/5/27 (Cape May, NJ), economist, former Fed chairman; chair of inquiry into UN Oil for Food scandal.
Mike Wallace, b 5/9/18 (Brookline, MA), TV journalist.
Barbara Walters, b 9/25/31 (Boston), TV journalist.
James Watson, b 4/6/28 (Chicago), biochemist, DNA pioneer, co-winner 1962 Nobel Prize.
Dr. Andrew Weil, b 6/8/42 (Philadelphia), health adviser.
Harvey Weinstein, b 3/19/52 (NYC), movie exec.
Jack Welch, b 11/19/35 (Peabody, MA), former General Electric CEO.
Jann Wenner, b 1/7/46 (NYC), publisher, founder *Rolling Stone.*
Cornel West, b 6/23/53 (Tulsa, OK), African American scholar, critic.
Ruth Westheimer, b 6/4/28 (Frankfurt am Main, Germany), human sexuality expert.
Christine Todd Whitman, b 9/26/46 (NYC), former EPA head, NJ gov.
Meg Whitman, b 8/4/56 (Cold Spring Harbor, NY), eBay pres. and CEO.
Elie Wiesel, b 9/30/28 (Sighet, Romania), scholar, author, 1986 Nobel Peace Prize winner.
George Will, b 5/4/41 (Champaign, IL), journalist, author.
Brian Williams, b 5/5/59 (Elmira, NY), NBC TV news anchor.
Oprah Winfrey, b 1/29/54 (Kosciusko, MS), TV and media personality, businesswoman, actress.
Paul Wolfowitz, b 12/22/43 (NYC), World Bank head.
Bob Woodward, b 3/26/43 (Geneva, IL), journalist; with Bernstein cracked Watergate scandal.
Steve Wynn, b 1/27/42 (New Haven, CT), casino developer.
Paula Zahn, b 2/24/56 (Omaha, NE), TV journalist.
Mortimer Zuckerman, b 6/4/37 (Montreal, Quebec, Can.), publisher, columnist.

Widely Known World Personalities of the Present

Living Non-Americans only. Generally excludes current heads of state or government (see Nations chapter) and excludes most others covered elsewhere, such as in Widely Known Americans, Entertainers and Writers lists or Sports Personalities.

Mahmoud Abbas (Abu Mazen), b 3/26/35 (Safed, Palestine [now Israel]), President of the Palestinian National Authority.
Gerry Adams, b 10/6/48 (Belfast, N. Ireland), Sinn Fein leader.
Theo Albrecht, b 3/28/22 (Schonebeck, Ger.), German billionaire, CEO of Aldi.
Giulio Andreotti, b 1/14/19 (Rome, Italy), former Italian premier.
Prince Andrew, b 2/19/60 (London, Eng.), Duke of York (2nd son of Queen Elizabeth II).
Kofi Annan, b 4/8/38 (Kumasi, Ghana), UN sec.-gen.; 2001 Nobel laureate.
Princess Anne, b 8/15/50 (London, Eng.), Princess Royal (daughter of Queen Elizabeth II).
Corazon Aquino, b 1/25/33 (Manila, Philip.), former pres. of Philippines.
Oscar Arias Sánchez, b 9/13/41 (Heredia, Costa Rica), former Costa Rican pres., peace negotiator, 1987 Nobel laureate.
Giorgio Armani, b 7/30/34 (Piacenza, Italy), fashion designer.
Ehud Barak, b 2/12/42 (Mishmar Ha-Sharon Kibbutz, Israel), former Israeli prime min.
Ahmed Ben Bella, b 12/25/18 (Marnia, Algeria), 1st Algerian prime min.; revolutionary leader.
Benedict XVI (Joseph Ratzinger), b 4/16/27 (Marktl am Inn, Germany), pope of Rom. Cath. Church, elected 2005.
Boris Berezovsky, b 1/23/46 (Moscow, USSR), businessman, politician.

Tim Berners-Lee, b 6/8/55 (London, Eng.), World Wide Web inventor.
Benazir Bhutto, b 6/21/53 (Karachi, Pak.), former prime min. of Pakistan.
Osama bin Laden, b 3/10/57 (Riyadh, Saudi Ar.), leader of al-Qaeda terrorist organization.
Hans Blix, b 6/28/28 (Uppsala, Sweden), former UN weapons inspector.
Fernando Botero, b 4/19/32 (Medellín, Col.), Colombian artist.
Boutros Boutros-Ghali, b 11/14/22 (Cairo, Egypt), former UN sec.-gen.
Richard Branson, b 7/18/50 (S. London, Eng.), British Virgin Records and Airways founder.
Gordon Brown, b 2/20/51 (Glasgow, Scot.), Brit. chancellor of the exchequer.
Mark Burnett, b 7/17/60 (Myland, England), reality TV producer.
Kim Campbell, b 3/10/47 (Port Alberni, British Columbia, Can.), former Canadian prime min.
Pierre Cardin, b 7/7/22 (Venice, Italy), fashion designer.
Princess Caroline, b 1/23/57 (Monte Carlo, Monaco), Monaco royal (eldest daughter of Prince Rainier and Princess Grace).
Prince Charles, b 11/14/48 (London, Eng.), Prince of Wales (eldest son of Queen Elizabeth II); heir to British throne.
Jean Chrétien, b 1/11/34 (Shawinigan, Que., Can.), former Canadian prime min.
Christo (Javacheff), b 6/13/35 (Gabrovo, Bulg.), artist.

Joe (Charles Joseph) Clark, b 6/5/39 (High River, Alberta, Can.), former Canadian prime min.

King Constantine II, b 6/2/40 (Psychiko, Greece), former king of Greece.

Dalai Lama (Tenzin Gyatso), b 7/6/35 (Taktser, Amdo, Tibet), Buddhist leader; 1989 Nobel laureate.

Jean Claude Duvalier ("Baby Doc"), b 7/3/51 (Port-au-Prince, Haiti), former Haitian dictator.

Shirin Ebadi, b 6/21/47 (Hamadan, Iran), human rights activist, 2003 Nobel laureate.

Prince Edward, b 3/10/64 (London, Eng.), Earl of Essex (3rd son of Queen Elizabeth II).

Mohammed ElBaradei, b 6/17/42 (Cairo, Egypt), Director general of the International Atomic Energy Agency (IAEA).

Prince Felipe, b 1/30/68 (Madrid, Spain), heir to Spanish throne.

Sarah Ferguson, b 10/15/58 (London, Eng.), Duchess of York; ex-wife of Prince Andrew.

John Galliano, b 11/28/60 (Gibraltar), fashion designer.

Valery Giscard d'Estaing, b 2/2/26 (Koblenz, Ger.), former French pres.

Jane Goodall, b 4/3/34 (London, Eng.), British anthropologist and primatologist.

Mikhail Gorbachev, b 3/2/31 (Privolnoye, USSR), former Soviet pres.; 1990 Nobel laureate.

Jurgen Habermas, b 6/18/29 (Dusseldorf, Ger.), philosopher.

Prince Henry ("Harry") of Wales, b 9/15/84 (London, Eng.), son of Prince Charles; 3rd in line to British throne.

Vaclav Havel, b 10/5/36 (Prague, Czech.), former Czech pres.; playwright.

Stephen Hawking, b 1/8/42 (Oxford, Eng.), physicist; author.

Sir Edmund Hillary, b 7/20/19 (Auckland, New Zeal.), 1st to reach summit of Mt. Everest, with Tenzing Norgay, 1953.

David Hockney, b 7/9/37 (Bradford, Eng.), artist.

Saddam Hussein, b 4/28/37 (Tikrit, Iraq), captured former Iraqi ruler.

Jiang Zemin, b 8/17/26 (Yangzhou, Jiangsu Prov., China), former pres. of China.

Kim Dae Jung, b 12/3/25 (near Mokpo, S. Korea), former S. Korean dissident, opposition leader, pres.; 2000 Nobelist.

Garry Kasparov, b 4/13/63 (Baku, Azerbaijan, USSR), former world chess champion; Russian pro-democracy leader.

Mikhail Khodorkovsky, b 6/26/63 (Moscow, Russia), oil oligarch, jailed for tax evasion (2005).

F.W. (Frederik Willem) de Klerk, b 3/18/36 (Johannesburg, S. Africa), former S. African pres.; 1993 Nobel laureate.

Helmut Kohl, b 4/3/30 (Ludwigshafen, Ger.), former German chancellor.

Vladimir Kramnik, b 7/25/75 (Tuapse, Russia, USSR), world chess champion.

Hans Kung, b 3/19/28 (Sursee, Switz.), Rom. Cath. theologian.

Richard Leakey, b 12/19/44 (Nairobi, Kenya), anthropologist, paleontologist, conservationist.

Claude Lévi-Strauss, b 11/28/08 (Brussels, Belg.), French anthropologist, developed structuralism.

John Major, b 3/29/43 (Wimbledon, Eng.), former British prime min.

Nelson Mandela, b 7/18/18 (Transkei, S. Africa), former pres. of S. Africa; 1993 Nobel laureate.

Imelda Marcos, b 7/2/29 (Manila, Philip.), former first lady of Philippines.

Paul Martin, b 8/28/38 (Windsor, Ont., Can.), former Canadian Prime Min.

Peter Max, b 10/19/37 (Berlin, Ger.), artist, designer.

Angela Merkel, b 7/17/54 (Hamburg, Ger.), Chancellor of Germany; 1st female to hold the office.

Jean-Marie Messier, b 12/13/56 (Grenoble, Fr.), former CEO of Vivendi Universal.

Empress Michiko, b 10/20/34 (Tokyo, Jap.), empress of Japan.

Rev. Sun Myung Moon, b 1/6/20 (Kwangju Sangsa Ri, N. Korea), Unification Church founder.

Brian Mulroney, b 3/20/39 (Baie-Corneau, Quebec, Can.), former Canadian prime min.

Prince Naruhito, b 2/23/60 (Tokyo, Jap.), crown prince of Japan.

Hassan Nasrallah, b 1960 (Beirut, Lebanon), leader of the Hezbollah in Lebanon.

Benjamin Netanyahu, b 10/21/49 (Tel-Aviv, Israel), former Israeli prime min. 1996-1999.

Queen Noor (Lisa Halaby), b 8/23/51 (Washington, DC), American-born widow of Jordan's King Hussein.

Manuel Noriega, b 2/11/34 (Panama City, Pan.), ousted Panamanian pres., jailed in Miami.

Daniel Ortega Saavedra, b 11/11/45 (La Libertad, Nicar.), former Nicaraguan pres., Sandinista leader.

Camilla Parker-Bowles, Duchess of Cornwall, b 7/17/47 (London, Eng.) wife of Prince Charles.

Jean-Marie le Pen, b 6/20/28 (La Trinite-sur-Mer, Fr.), French right-wing politician.

Shimon Peres, b 8/21/23 (Wolozyn, Pol.), former Israeli prime min.; 1994 Nobel laureate.

Javier Perez de Cuellar, b 1/19/20 (Lima, Peru), former UN sec. gen.

Prince Philip, b 6/10/21 (Corfu, Greece), Duke of Edinburgh (husband of Queen Elizabeth II).

Augusto Pinochet Ugarte, b 11/25/15 (Valparaiso, Chile), former Chilean ruler; indicted for crimes in office.

Gerhard Richter, b 2/9/32 (Dresden, Ger.), artist.

Mary Robinson, b 5/21/44 (Ballina, Co. Mayo, Ireland), former Irish pres.; UN High Commissioner for Human Rights.

Moqtada al-Sadr, b 1974 (Iraq), extremist Shiite cleric.

Yves Saint Laurent, b 8/1/36 (Oran, Algeria), fashion designer.

Carlos Salinas de Gortari, b 4/3/48 (Mexico City, Mex.), former Mexican pres.

Ariel Sharon, b 2/26/28 (Kfar Malal, Palestine), former Israeli prime min. 2000-2006.

Eduard Shevardnadze, b 1/25/28 (Mamati, Georgia, USSR), former Georgian pres.

Ayatollah Ali al-Sistani, b 8/4/30 (Mashhad, Iran), major Iraqi Shiite religious leader.

Princess Stephanie, b 2/1/65 (Monte Carlo, Monaco), youngest daughter and child of Prince Rainier and Princess Grace.

Suharto, b 6/8/21 (Kemusa Argamulja, Java), former longtime Indonesian ruler.

Aung San Suu Kyi, b 6/19/45 (Rangoon, Myanmar), political activist, 1991 Nobel laureate, under effective house arrest.

Valentina Tereshkova, b 3/6/37 (Maslennikovo, Russia, USSR), 1st woman in space.

Margaret Thatcher, b 10/13/25 (Grantham, Eng.), former British prime min.

John Napier Turner, b 6/7/29 (Richmond, Surrey, Eng.), former Canadian prime min.

Desmond Tutu, b 10/7/31 (Klerksdorp, Transvaal, S. Africa), former S. African archbishop; 1984 Nobel laureate.

Kurt Waldheim, b 12/21/18 (St. Andra-Wordern, Austria), former UN sec.-gen. and Austrian pres.

Lech Walesa, b 9/29/43 (Popowo, Pol.), Solidarity leader; 1983 Nobel laureate; former president of Poland.

Prince William (of Wales), b 6/21/82 (London, Eng.), son of Prince Charles; 2nd in line to British throne.

Rowan Williams, b 6/14/50 (Ystradgynlais, Wales), Archbishop of Canterbury.

Boris Yeltsin, b 2/1/31 (Butka, USSR), former Russian pres.

Ayman al-Zawahri, b 6/19/51 (Cairo, Egypt), reputed high-ranking al-Qaeda leader.

Architects and Some of Their Projects

Max Abramovitz, 1908-2004, Avery Fisher Hall, NYC; U.S. Steel Bldg. (now USX Towers), Pittsburgh, PA.

Henry Bacon, 1866-1924, Lincoln Memorial, Washington, DC.

Benjamin Banneker, 1731-1806, African American inventor, astronomer, mathematician; helped design and lay out Washington, D.C.

Pietro Belluschi, 1899-1994, Juilliard School, Lincoln Center, Pan Am, now MetLife, Bldg. (with Walter Gropius), NYC.

Marcel Breuer, 1902-81, Whitney Museum of American Art (with Hamilton Smith), NYC.

Charles Bulfinch, 1763-1844, State House, Boston; Capitol (part), Washington, DC.

Gordon Bunshaft, 1909-90, Lever House, Park Ave, NYC; Hirshhorn Museum, Washington, DC.

Daniel H. Burnham, 1846-1912, Union Station, Washington DC; Flatiron Bldg., NYC.

Irwin Chanin, 1892-1988, theaters, skyscrapers, NYC.

David Childs, b 1941, Washington Mall Master Plan/Constitution Gardens, Washington, DC; WTC Freedom Tower, NYC.

Lucio Costa, 1902-98, master plan for city of Brasilia, with Oscar Niemeyer.

Ralph Adams Cram, 1863-1942, Cath. of St. John the Divine, NYC; U.S. Military Acad. (part), West Point, NY.

Norman Foster, b 1935, Commerzbank Headquarters, Frankfurt-am-Main, Ger.; London Millennium Bridge, London.

James Ingo Freed, 1930-2005, Holocaust Memorial Museum, Washington, DC; Jacob K. Javits Center, NYC.

R. Buckminster Fuller, 1895-1983, U.S. Pavilion (geodesic domes), Expo 67, Montreal.

Frank O. Gehry, b 1929, Guggenheim Museum, Bilbao, Spain; Experience Music Project, Seattle, WA.

Cass Gilbert, 1859-1934, Custom House, Woolworth Bldg., NYC; Supreme Court Bldg., Washington, DC.

Bertram G. Goodhue, 1869-1924, Capitol, Lincoln, NE; St. Thomas's Church, St. Bartholomew's Church, NYC.

Michael Graves, b 1934, Portland Bldg., Portland, OR; Humana Bldg., Louisville, KY.

World Almanac Editors' Picks
Top 10 Twentieth Century U.S. Entertainers Known by a Pseudonym

1. Marilyn Monroe / Norma Jeane Mortensen (later Baker)
2. John Wayne / Marion Robert Morrison
3. Bob Dylan / Robert Zimmerman
4. Billie Holiday / Eleanora Fagan
5. Judy Garland / Frances Gumm
6. Tom Cruise / Thomas Cruise Mapother IV
7. Madonna / Madonna Louise Veronica Ciccone
8. Prince / Prince Rogers Nelson
9. Patsy Cline / Virginia Patterson Hensley
10. Woody Allen / Allen Konigsberg

Walter Gropius, 1883-1969, Pan Am Bldg. (now MetLife Bldg.) (with Pietro Belluschi), NYC.

Lawrence Halprin, b 1916, Ghirardelli Sq., San Francisco; Nicollet Mall, Minneapolis; FDR Memorial, Washington, DC.

Peter Harrison, 1716-75, Touro Synagogue, Redwood Library, Newport, RI.

Wallace K. Harrison, 1895-1981, Metropolitan Opera House, Lincoln Center, NYC.

Thomas Hastings, 1860-1929, NY Public Library (with John Carrère), Frick Mansion, NYC.

James Hoban, 1762-1831, White House, Washington, DC.

Raymond Hood, 1881-1934, Rockefeller Center (part), Daily News, NYC; Tribune, Chicago, IL.

Richard M. Hunt, 1827-95, Metropolitan Museum (part), NYC; National Observatory, Washington, DC.

Helmut Jahn, b 1940, United Airlines Terminal, O'Hare Airport, Chicago.

William Le Baron Jenney, 1832-1907, Home Insurance (demolished 1931), Chicago, IL.

Philip C. Johnson, 1906-2005, AT&T headquarters (now 550 Madison Ave.), NYC; Transco Tower, Houston, TX.

Albert Kahn, 1869-1942, General Motors Bldg., Detroit, MI.

Louis Kahn, 1901-74, Salk Laboratory, La Jolla, CA; Yale Art Gallery, New Haven, CT.

Christopher Grant LaFarge, 1862-1938, Roman Catholic Chapel, West Point, NY.

Benjamin H. Latrobe, 1764-1820, Capitol (part), Washington, DC; State Capitol Bldg., Richmond, VA.

Le Corbusier, (Charles-Edouard Jeanneret), 1887-1965, Salvation Army Hostel and Swiss Dormitory, both Paris; master plan for cities of Algiers and Buenos Aires.

William Lescaze, 1896-1969, Philadelphia Savings Fund Society; Borg-Warner Bldg., Chicago.

Maya Lin, b 1959, Vietnam Veterans Mem., Washington, DC.

Charles Rennie Mackintosh, 1868-1928, Glasgow School of Art; Hill House, Helensburgh.

Bernard R. Maybeck, 1862-1957, Hearst Hall, Univ. of CA, Berkeley; First Church of Christ Scientist, Berkeley, CA.

Charles F. McKim, 1847-1909, Public Library, Boston; Columbia Univ. (part), NYC.

Charles M. McKim, b 1920, KUHT-TV Transmitter Bldg., Lutheran Church of the Redeemer, Houston, TX.

Richard Meier, b 1934, Getty Center Museum, Los Angeles, CA; High Museum of Art, Atlanta, GA.

Ludwig Mies van der Rohe, 1886-1969, Seagram Bldg. (with Philip C. Johnson), NYC; National Gallery, Berlin.

Robert Mills, 1781-1855, Washington Monument, Wash., DC.

Charles Moore, 1925-93, Sea Ranch, near San Francisco; Piazza d'Italia, New Orleans, LA.

Richard J. Neutra, 1892-1970, Mathematics Park, Princeton, NJ; Orange Co. Courthouse, Santa Ana, CA.

Oscar Niemeyer, b 1907, government buildings, Brasilia Palace Hotel, all Brasilia.

Gyo Obata, b 1923, Natl. Air & Space Museum, Smithsonian Inst., Washington, DC; Dallas-Ft. Worth Airport.

Frederick L. Olmsted, 1822-1903, Central Park, NYC; Fairmount Park, Philadelphia, PA.

I(eoh) M(ing) Pei, b 1917, East Wing, Natl. Gallery of Art, Washington, DC; Pyramid, The Louvre, Paris; Rock & Roll Hall of Fame and Museum, Cleveland, OH.

Cesar Pelli, b 1926, World Financial Center, Carnegie Hall Tower, NYC; Petronas Twin Towers, Malaysia.

William Pereira, 1909-85, Cape Canaveral; Transamerica Bldg., San Francisco, CA.

John Russell Pope, 1874-1937, National Gallery, Wash., DC.

John Portman, b 1924, Peachtree Center, Atlanta, GA.

George Browne Post, 1837-1913, NY Stock Exchange; Capitol, Madison, WI.

James Renwick Jr., 1818-95, Grace Church, St. Patrick's Cath., NYC.; Corcoran (Renwick) Gallery, Washington, DC.

Henry H. Richardson, 1838-86, Trinity Church, Boston, MA.

Kevin Roche, b 1922, Oakland Museum, Oakland, CA; Fine Arts Center, University of Massachusetts, Amherst.

James Gamble Rogers, 1867-1947, Columbia-Presbyterian Medical Center, NYC; Northwestern Univ., Evanston, IL.

John Wellborn Root, 1887-1963, Palmolive Bldg., Chicago; Hotel Statler, Washington, DC.

Paul Rudolph, 1918-97, Jewitt Art Center, Wellesley Colllege, MA; Art & Architecture Bldg., Yale Univ., New Haven, CT.

Eero Saarinen, 1910-61, Gateway to the West Arch, St. Louis, MO; Trans World Airlines Flight Center, NYC.

Louis Skidmore, 1897-1962, Atomic Energy Commission town site, Oak Ridge, TN; Terrace Plaza Hotel, Cincinnati, OH.

Clarence S. Stein, 1882-1975, Temple Emanu-El, NYC.

Edward Durell Stone, 1902-78, U.S. Embassy, New Delhi, India; (H. Hartford) Gallery of Modern Art, NYC.

Louis H. Sullivan, 1856-1924, Auditorium Bldg., Chicago, IL.

Kenzo Tange, 1913-2005, Hiroshima Peace Park, 1964 Tokyo Olympics twin stadiums.

Richard Upjohn, 1802-78, Trinity Church, NYC.

Max O. Urbahn, 1912-95, Vehicle Assembly Bldg., Cape Canaveral, FL.

Robert Venturi, b 1925, Gordon Wu Hall, Princeton, NJ; Mielparque Nikko Kirifuri Resort, Japan.

Ralph T. Walker, 1889-1973, NY Telephone Bldg. (now NYNEX); IBM Research Lab, Poughkeepsie, NY.

Roland A. Wank, 1898-1970, Cincinnati Union Terminal, OH; head architect (1933-44), Tennessee Valley Authority.

Stanford White, 1853-1906, Washington Arch in Washington Square Park, first Madison Square Garden, NYC.

Frank Lloyd Wright, 1867-1959, Imperial Hotel, Tokyo; Guggenheim Museum, NYC; Marin County Civic Center, San Rafael; Kaufmann "Fallingwater" house, Bear Run, PA.; Taliesin West, Scottsdale, AZ.

William Wurster, 1895-1973, Ghirardelli Sq., San Francisco.

Minoru Yamasaki, 1912-86, World Trade Center, NYC.

Artists, Photographers, and Sculptors of the Past
Artists are painters unless otherwise indicated.

Berenice Abbott, 1898-1991, (U.S.) photographer. Documentary of New York City, *Changing New York* (1939).

Ansel Easton Adams, 1902-84, (U.S.) photographer. Landscapes of the American Southwest.

Washington Allston, 1779-1843, (U.S.) landscapist. *Belshazzar's Feast.*

Albrecht Altdorfer, 1480-1538, (Ger.) landscapist.

Andrea del Sarto, 1486-1530, (It.) frescoes. *Madonna of the Harpies.*

Fra Angelico, c1400-55, (It.) Renaissance muralist. *Madonna of the Linen Drapers' Guild.*

Diane Arbus, 1923-71, (U.S.) photographer. Disturbing images.

Alexsandr Archipenko, 1887-1964, (U.S.) sculptor. *Boxing Match, Medranos.*

Jean Arp, 1887-1966, (Fr.) sculptor and painter, founder of Dada movement.

Eugène Atget, 1856-1927, (Fr.) photographer. Paris life.

John James Audubon, 1785-1851, (U.S.) *Birds of America.*

Hans Baldung-Grien, 1484-1545, (Ger.) *Todentanz.*

Ernst Barlach, 1870-1938, (Ger.) Expressionist sculptor. *Man Drawing a Sword.*

Frederic-Auguste Bartholdi, 1834-1904, (Fr.) *Liberty Enlightening the World, Lion of Belfort.*

Fra Bartolommeo, 1472-1517, (It.) *Vision of St. Bernard.*

Romare Bearden, 1911-88, (U.S.) collage and other media. *The Visitation.*

Aubrey Beardsley, 1872-98, (Br.) illustrator. *Salome, Lysistrata, Morte d'Arthur, Volpone.*

Max Beckmann, 1884-1950, (Ger.) Expressionist. *The Descent From the Cross.*

Gentile Bellini, 1426-1507, (It.) Renaissance. *Procession in St. Mark's Square.*

Giovanni Bellini, 1428-1516, (It.) *St. Francis in Ecstasy.*

Jacopo Bellini, 1400-70, (It.) *Crucifixion.*

George Wesley Bellows, 1882-1925, (U.S.) sports artist, portraitist, landscapist. *Stag at Sharkey's, Edith Clavell.*

Thomas Hart Benton, 1889-1975, (U.S.) American regionalist. *Threshing Wheat, Arts of the West.*

Gianlorenzo Bernini, 1598-1680, (It.) Baroque sculpture. *The Assumption.*

Albert Bierstadt, 1830-1902, (U.S.) landscapist. *The Rocky Mountains, Mount Corcoran.*

George Caleb Bingham, 1811-79, (U.S.) *Fur Traders Descending the Missouri.*

William Blake, 1752-1827, (Br.) engraver. *Book of Job, Songs of Innocence, Songs of Experience.*

Rosa Bonheur, 1822-99, (Fr.) *The Horse Fair.*

Pierre Bonnard, 1867-1947, (Fr.) Intimist. *The Breakfast Room, Girl in a Straw Hat.*

Gutzon Borglum, 1871-1941, (U.S.) sculptor. Mt. Rushmore Memorial.

Hieronymus Bosch, 1450-1516, (Flem.) religious allegories. *The Crowning With Thorns.*

Sandro Botticelli, 1444-1510, (It.) Renaissance. *Birth of Venus, Adoration of the Magi, Guiliano de'Medici.*

Margaret Bourke-White, 1906-71, (U.S.) photographer, photojournalist. WW2, USSR, rural South during the Depression.

Mathew Brady, c1823-96, (U.S.) photographer. Official photographer of the Civil War.

Constantin Brancusi, 1876-1957, (Romanian-Fr.) Nonobjective sculptor. *Flying Turtle, The Kiss.*

Georges Braque, 1882-1963, (Fr.) Cubist. *Violin and Palette.*

Pieter Bruegel the Elder, c1525-69, (Flem.) *The Peasant Dance, Hunters in the Snow, Magpie on the Gallows.*

Pieter Bruegel the Younger, 1564-1638, (Flem.) *Village Fair, The Crucifixion.*

Edward Burne-Jones, 1833-98, (Br.) Pre-Raphaelite artist-craftsman. *The Mirror of Venus.*

Alexander Calder, 1898-1976, (U.S.) sculptor. *Lobster Trap and Fish Tail.*

Julia Cameron, 1815-79, (Br.) photographer. Considered one of the most important portraitists of the 19th cent.

Robert Capa (Andrei Friedmann), 1913-54, (Hung.-U.S.) photographer. War photojournalist; invasion of Normandy.

Michelangelo Merisi da Caravaggio, 1573-1610, (It.) Baroque. *The Supper at Emmaus.*

Emily Carr, 1871-1945, (Can.) landscapist. *Blunden Harbour, Big Raven, Rushing Sea of Undergrowth.*

Carlo Carrà, 1881-1966, (It.) Metaphysical school. *Lot's Daughters, The Enchanted Room.*

Henri Cartier-Bresson, 1908-2004, (Fr.) photographer. *Imagenes à la sauvette.*

Mary Cassatt, 1844-1926, (U.S.) Impressionist. *The Cup of Tea, Woman Bathing, The Boating Party.*

Oleg Cassini, 1913-2006, (Fr.-U.S.) fashion designer.

George Catlin, 1796-1872, (U.S.) American Indian life. *Gallery of Indians, Buffalo Dance.*

Benvenuto Cellini, 1500-71, (It.) Mannerist sculptor, goldsmith. *Perseus and Medusa.*

Paul Cézanne, 1839-1906, (Fr.) *Card Players, Mont-Sainte-Victoire With Large Pine Trees.*

Marc Chagall, 1887-1985, (Russ.) Jewish life and folklore. *I and the Village, The Praying Jew.*

Jean Simeon Chardin, 1699-1779, (Fr.) still lifes. *The Kiss, The Grace.*

Giorgio de Chirico, 1888-1978, (It.) painter, founded the metaphysical school. *Enigma of an Autumn Night.*

Frederick Church, 1826-1900, (U.S.) Hudson River school. *Niagara, Andes of Ecuador.*

Giovanni Cimabue, 1240-1302, (It.) Byzantine mosaicist. *Madonna Enthroned With St. Francis.*

Claude Lorrain (Claude Gellée), 1600-82, (Fr.) ideal-landscapist. *The Enchanted Castle.*

Thomas Cole, 1801-48, (U.S.) Hudson River school. *The Ox-Bow, In the Catskills.*

John Constable, 1776-1837, (Br.) landscapist. *Salisbury Cathedral From the Bishop's Grounds.*

John Singleton Copley, 1738-1815, (U.S.) portraitist. *Samuel Adams, Watson and the Shark.*

Lovis Corinth, 1858-1925, (Ger.) Expressionist. *Apocalypse.*

Jean-Baptiste-Camille Corot, 1796-1875, (Fr.) landscapist. *Souvenir de Mortefontaine, Pastorale.*

Correggio, 1494-1534, (It.) Renaissance muralist. *Mystic Marriages of St. Catherine.*

Gustave Courbet, 1819-77, (Fr.) Realist. *The Artist's Studio.*

Lucas Cranach the Elder, 1472-1553, (Ger.) Protestant Reformation portraitist. *Luther.*

Imogen Cunningham, 1883-1976, (U.S.) photographer, portraitist. Plant photography.

Nathaniel Currier, 1813-88, and **James M. Ives,** 1824-95, (both U.S.) lithographers. *A Midnight Race on the Mississippi, American Forest Scene—Maple Sugaring.*

John Steuart Curry, 1897-1946, (U.S.) Americana, murals. *Baptism in Kansas.*

Salvador Dalí, 1904-89, (Sp.) Surrealist. *Persistence of Memory, The Crucifixion.*

Honoré Daumier, 1808-79, (Fr.) caricaturist. *The Third-Class Carriage.*

Jacques-Louis David, 1748-1825, (Fr.) Neoclassicist. *The Oath of the Horatii.*

Arthur Davies, 1862-1928, (U.S.) Romantic landscapist. *Unicorns, Leda and the Dioscuri.*

Aaron Douglas, 1900-79, Harlem Renaissance artist.

Willem de Kooning, 1904-1997, (Dutch-U.S.) abstract expressionist. *Excavation, Woman I, Door to the River.*

Edgar Degas, 1834-1917, (Fr.) *The Ballet Class.*

Eugène Delacroix, 1798-1863, (Fr.) Romantic. *Massacre at Chios, Liberty Leading the People.*

Paul Delaroche, 1797-1856, (Fr.) historical themes. *Children of Edward IV.*

Luca Della Robbia, 1400-82, (It.) Renaissance terracotta artist. *Cantoria* (singing gallery), Florence cathedral.

Donatello, 1386-1466, (It.) Renaissance sculptor. *David, Gattamelata.*

Jean Dubuffet, 1902-85, (Fr.) painter, sculptor, printmaker. *Group of Four Trees.*

Marcel Duchamp, 1887-1968, (Fr.) Dada artist. *Nude Descending a Staircase, No. 2.*

Raoul Dufy, 1877-1953, (Fr.) Fauvist. *Chateau and Horses.*

Asher Brown Durand, 1796-1886, (U.S.) Hudson River school. *Kindred Spirits.*

Albrecht Dürer, 1471-1528, (Ger.) Renaissance painter, engraver, woodcuts. *St. Jerome in His Study, Melencolia I.*

Anthony van Dyck, 1599-1641, (Flem.) Baroque portraitist. *Portrait of Charles I Hunting.*

Thomas Eakins, 1844-1916, (U.S.) Realist. *The Gross Clinic.*

Alfred Eisenstaedt, 1898-1995, (Ger.-U.S.) photographer, photojournalist. Famous photo, V-J Day, Aug. 14, 1945.

Peter Henry Emerson, 1856-1936, (Br.) photographer. Promoted photography as an independent art form.

Jacob Epstein, 1880-1959, (Br.) religious and allegorical sculptor. *Genesis, Ecce Homo.*

Erté, 1892-1990, (Fr.) b. Romain de Tiertoff; painter, fashion and stage designer.

Jan van Eyck, c1390-1441, (Flem.) naturalistic panels. *Adoration of the Lamb.*

Roger Fenton, 1819-68, (Br.) photographer. Crimean War.

Anselm Feuerbach, 1829-80, (Ger.) Romantic Classicist. *Judgment of Paris, Iphigenia.*

John Bernard Flannagan, 1895-1942, (U.S.) animal sculptor. *Triumph of the Egg.*

Jean-Honoré Fragonard, 1732-1806, (Fr.) Rococo. *The Swing.*

Daniel Chester French, 1850-1931, (U.S.) *The Minute Man of Concord;* seated *Lincoln,* Lincoln Memorial, Washington, DC.

Caspar David Friedrich, 1774-1840, (Ger.) Romantic landscapes. *Man and Woman Gazing at the Moon.*

Thomas Gainsborough, 1727-88, (Br.) portraitist. *The Blue Boy, The Watering Place, Orpin the Parish Clerk.*

Alexander Gardner, 1821-82, (U.S.) photographer. Civil War; railroad construction; Great Plains Indians.

Paul Gauguin, 1848-1903, (Fr.) Post-impressionist. *The Tahitians, Spirit of the Dead Watching.*

Lorenzo Ghiberti, 1378-1455, (It.) Renaissance sculptor. Gates of Paradise baptistery doors, Florence.

Alberto Giacometti, 1901-66, (Swiss) attenuated sculptures of solitary figures. *Man Pointing.*

Giorgione, c1477-1510, (It.) Renaissance. *The Tempest.*

Giotto di Bondone, 1267-1337, (It.) Renaissance. *Presentation of Christ in the Temple.*

François Girardon, 1628-1715, (Fr.) Baroque sculptor of classical themes. *Apollo Tended by the Nymphs.*

Vincent van Gogh, 1853-90, (Dutch) *The Starry Night, L'Arlesienne, Bedroom at Arles, Self-Portrait.*

Edward Gorey, 1925-2000, (U.S.) artist, illustrator. *The Doubtful Guest.*

Arshile Gorky, 1905-48, (U.S.) Surrealist. *The Liver Is the Cock's Comb.*

Francisco de Goya y Lucientes, 1746-1828, (Sp.) *The Naked Maja, The Disasters of War* (etchings).

El Greco, 1541-1614, (Sp.) *View of Toledo, Assumption of the Virgin.*

Horatio Greenough, 1805-52, (U.S.) Neo-classical sculptor.

Matthias Grünewald, 1480-1528, (Ger.) mystical religious themes. *The Resurrection.*

Frans Hals, c1580-1666, (Dutch) portraitist. *Laughing Cavalier, Gypsy Girl.*

Austin Hansen, 1910-96, (U.S.) photographer. Harlem, NY, life.

Childe Hassam, 1859-1935, (U.S.) Impressionist. *Southwest Wind, July 14 Rue Daunon.*

Edward Hicks, 1780-1849, (U.S.) folk painter. *The Peaceable Kingdom.*

Lewis Wickes Hine, 1874-1940, (U.S.) photographer. Studies of immigrants, children in industry.

Hans Hofmann, 1880-1966, (U.S.) early abstract Expressionist. *Spring, The Gate.*

William Hogarth, 1697-1764, (Br.) caricaturist. *The Rake's Progress.*

Katsushika Hokusai, 1760-1849, (Jpn.) printmaker. *Crabs.*

Hans Holbein the Elder, 1460-1524, (Ger.) late Gothic. *Presentation of Christ in the Temple.*

Hans Holbein the Younger, 1497-1543, (Ger.) portraitist. *Henry VIII, The French Ambassadors.*

Winslow Homer, 1836-1910, (U.S.) naturalist painter, marine themes. *Marine Coast, High Cliff.*

Edward Hopper, 1882-1967, (U.S.) realistic urban scenes. *Nighthawks, House by the Railroad.*

Horst P. Horst, 1906-99, (Ger.) fashion, celebrity photographer.

Jean-Auguste-Dominique Ingres, 1780-1867, (Fr.) Classicist. *Valpincon Bather.*

George Inness, 1825-94, (U.S.) luminous landscapist. *Delaware Water Gap.*

William Henry Jackson, 1843-1942, (U.S.) photographer. American West, building of Union Pacific Railroad.

Donald Judd, 1928-94, (U.S.) sculptor, major Minimalist.

Frida Kahlo, 1907-54, (Mex.) painter. *Self-Portrait With Monkey.*

Vasily Kandinsky, 1866-1944, (Russ.) Abstractionist. *Capricious Forms, Improvisation 38 (second version).*

Paul Klee, 1879-1940, (Swiss) Abstractionist. *Twittering Machine, Pastoral, Death and Fire.*

Gustav Klimt, 1862-1918, (Austrian) cofounder of Vienna Secession Movement, *The Kiss.*

Oscar Kokoschka, 1886-1980, (Austrian) Expressionist. *View of Prague, Harbor of Marseilles.*

Kathe Kollwitz, 1867-1945, (Ger.) printmaker, social justice themes. *The Peasant War.*

Gaston Lachaise, 1882-1935, (U.S.) figurative sculptor. *Standing Woman.*

John La Farge, 1835-1910, (U.S.) muralist. *Red and White Peonies, The Ascension.*

Sir Edwin (Henry) Landseer, 1802-73, (Br.) painter, sculptor. *Shoeing, Rout of Comus.*

Dorothea Lange, 1895-1965, (U.S.) photographer. Depression photographs, migrant farm workers.

Fernand Léger, 1881-1955, (Fr.) machine art. *The Cyclists.*

Leonardo da Vinci, 1452-1519, (It.) *Mona Lisa, Last Supper, The Annunciation.*

Emanuel Leutze, 1816-68, (U.S.) historical themes. *Washington Crossing the Delaware.*

Roy Lichtenstein, 1923-97, (U.S.) pop artist.

Jacques Lipchitz, 1891-1973, (Fr.) Cubist sculptor. *Harpist.*

Filippino Lippi, 1457-1504, (It.) Renaissance.

Fra Filippo Lippi, 1406-69, (It.) Renaissance. *Coronation of the Virgin, Madonna and Child With Angels.*

Morris Louis, 1912-62, (U.S.) abstract Expressionist. *Signa, Stripes, Alpha-Phi.*

René Magritte, 1898-1967, (Belgian) Surrealist. *The Descent of Man, The Betrayal of Images.*

Aristide Maillol, 1861-1944, (Fr.) sculptor. *L'Harmonie.*

Édouard Manet, 1832-83, (Fr.) forerunner of Impressionism. *Luncheon on the Grass, Olympia.*

Andrea Mantegna, 1431-1506, (It.) Renaissance frescoes. *Triumph of Caesar.*

Franz Marc, 1880-1916, (Ger.) Expressionist. *Blue Horses.*

John Marin, 1870-1953, (U.S.) Expressionist seascapes. *Maine Island.*

Reginald Marsh, 1898-1954, (U.S.) satirical artist. *Tattoo and Haircut.*

Agnes Martin, 1912-2004, (U.S.) abstract artist. *Night Sea.*

Masaccio, 1401-28, (It.) Renaissance. *The Tribute Money.*

Henri Matisse, 1869-1954, (Fr.) Fauvist. *Woman With the Hat.*

Michelangelo Buonarroti, 1475-1564, (It.) *Pietà, David, Moses, The Last Judgment,* Sistine Chapel ceiling.

Jean-Francois Millet, 1814-75, (Fr.) painter of peasant subjects. *The Gleaners, The Man With a Hoe.*

Joan Miró, 1893-1983, (Sp.) Exuberant colors, playful images. Catalan landscape, *Dutch Interior.*

Amedeo Modigliani, 1884-1920, (It.) *Reclining Nude.*

Piet Mondrian, 1872-1944, (Dutch) Abstractionist. *Composition With Red, Yellow and Blue.*

Claude Monet, 1840-1926, (Fr.) Impressionist. *The Bridge at Argenteuil, Haystacks.*

Henry Moore, 1898-1986, (Br.) sculptor of large-scale, abstract works. *Reclining Figure* (several).

Gustave Moreau, 1826-98, (Fr.) Symbolist. *The Apparition, Dance of Salome.*

James Wilson Morrice, 1865-1924, (Can.) landscapist. *The Ferry, Quebec, Venice, Looking Over the Lagoon.*

William Morris, 1834-1896, (Br.) decorative artist, leader of the Arts and Crafts movement.

Grandma Moses, 1860-1961, (U.S.) folk painter. *Out for the Christmas Trees, Thanksgiving Turkey.*

Edvard Munch, 1863-1944, (Nor.) Expressionist. *The Cry.*

Bartolome Murillo, 1618-82, (Sp.) Baroque religious artist. *Vision of St. Anthony, The Two Trinities.*

Eadweard Muybridge, 1830-1904, (Br.-U.S.) photographer. Studies of motion, *Animal Locomotion.*

Nadar (Gaspar-Félix Tournachon), 1820-1910, (Fr.) photographer, caricaturist, portraitist. Invented photo-essay.

Barnett Newman, 1905-70, (U.S.) abstract Expressionist. *Stations of the Cross.*

Isamu Noguchi, 1904-88, (U.S.) abstract sculptor, designer. *Kouros, BirdC(MU),* sculptural gardens.

Georgia O'Keeffe, 1887-1986, (U.S.) Southwest motifs. *Cow's Skull: Red, White, and Blue, The Shelton With Sunspots.*

José Clemente Orozco, 1883-1949, (Mex.) frescoes. *House of Tears, Pre-Columbian Golden Age.*

Timothy H. O'Sullivan, 1840-82, (U.S.) Civil War photographer.

Gordon Parks, 1912-2006, (U.S.) African American photographer and film maker. *Life* photographer 1948-68.

Charles Willson Peale, 1741-1827, (U.S.) Amer. Revolutionary portraitist. *The Staircase Group,* U.S. presidents.

Rembrandt Peale, 1778-1860, (U.S.) portraitist. Thomas Jefferson.

Pietro Perugino, 1446-1523, (It.) Renaissance. *Delivery of the Keys to St. Peter.*

Pablo Picasso, 1881-1973, (Sp.) painter, sculptor. *Guernica; Dove; Head of a Woman; Head of a Bull, Metamorphosis.*

Piero della Francesca, c1415-92, (It.) Renaissance. *Duke of Urbino, Flagellation of Christ.*

Camille Pissarro, 1830-1903, (Fr.) Impressionist. *Boulevard des Italiens, Morning, Sunlight; Bather in the Woods.*

Jackson Pollock, 1912-56, (U.S.) abstract Expressionist. *Autumn Rhythm.*

Nicolas Poussin, 1594-1665, (Fr.) Baroque pictorial classicism. *St. John on Patmos.*

Maurice B. Prendergast, c1860-1924, (U.S.) Post-impressionist water colorist. *Umbrellas in the Rain.*

Pierre-Paul Prud'hon, 1758-1823, (Fr.) Romanticist. *Crime Pursued by Vengeance and Justice.*

Pierre Cecile Puvis de Chavannes, 1824-98, (Fr.) muralist. *The Poor Fisherman.*

Raphael Sanzio, 1483-1520, (It.) Renaissance. *Disputa, School of Athens, Sistine Madonna.*

Man Ray, 1890-1976, (U.S.) Dada artist. *Observing Time, The Lovers, Marquis de Sade.*

Odilon Redon, 1840-1916, (Fr.) Symbolist painter, lithographer. *In the Dream, Vase of Flowers.*

Rembrandt van Rijn, 1606-69, (Dutch) *The Bridal Couple, The Night Watch.*

Frederic Remington, 1861-1909, (U.S.) painter, sculptor. Portrayer of the American West, *Bronco Buster.*

Pierre-Auguste Renoir, 1841-1919, (Fr.) Impressionist. *The Luncheon of the Boating Party, Dance in the Country.*

Joshua Reynolds, 1723-92, (Br.) portraitist. *Mrs. Siddons as the Tragic Muse.*

Herb Ritts, 1952-2002, (U.S.) photographer. Nudes, celebrities.

Diego Rivera, 1886-1957, (Mex.) frescoes. *The Fecund Earth.*

Larry Rivers, 1923-2002, (U.S.) painter, sculptor, often realistic; Dutch Masters series.

Henry Peach Robinson, 1830-1901 (Br.) photographer. A leader of "high art" photography.

Norman Rockwell, 1894-1978, (U.S.) painter, illustrator. *Saturday Evening Post* covers.

Auguste Rodin, 1840-1917, (Fr.) sculptor. *The Thinker.*

Mark Rothko, 1903-70, (U.S.) abstract Expressionist. *Light, Earth and Blue.*

Georges Rouault, 1871-1958, (Fr.) Expressionist. *Three Judges.*

Henri Rousseau, 1844-1910, (Fr.) primitive exotic themes. *The Snake Charmer.*

Theodore Rousseau, 1812-67, (Swiss-Fr.) landscapist. *Under the Birches, Evening.*

Peter Paul Rubens, 1577-1640, (Flem.) Baroque. *Mystic Marriage of St. Catherine.*

Jacob van Ruisdael, c1628-82, (Dutch) landscapist. *Jewish Cemetery.*

Charles M. Russell, 1866-1926, (U.S.) Western life.

Salomon van Ruysdael, c1600-70, (Dutch) landscapist. *River With Ferry-Boat.*

Albert Pinkham Ryder, 1847-1917, (U.S.) seascapes and allegories. *Toilers of the Sea.*

Augustus Saint-Gaudens, 1848-1907, (U.S.) memorial statues. *Farragut, Mrs. Henry Adams (Grief).*

Andrea Sansovino, 1460-1529, (It.) Renaissance sculptor. *Baptism of Christ.*

Jacopo Sansovino, 1486-1570, (It.) Renaissance sculptor. *St. John the Baptist.*

John Singer Sargent, 1856-1925, (U.S.) Edwardian society portraitist. *The Wyndham Sisters, Madam X.*

George Segal, 1924-2000, (U.S.) sculptor of life-sized figures realistically depicting daily life.

Georges Seurat, 1859-91, (Fr.) Pointillist. *Sunday Afternoon on the Island of La Grande Jatte.*

Gino Severini, 1883-1966, (It.) Futurist and Cubist. *Dynamic Hieroglyph of the Bal Tabarin.*

Ben Shahn, 1898-1969, (U.S.) social and political themes. Sacco and Vanzetti series, *Seurat's Lunch, Handball.*

Charles Sheeler, 1883-1965, (U.S.) abstractionist.

David Alfaro Siqueiros, 1896-1974, (Mex.) political muralist. *March of Humanity.*

David Smith, 1906-65, (U.S.) welded metal sculpture. *Hudson River Landscape, Zig, Cubi* series.

Edward Steichen, 1879-1973, (U.S.) photographer. Credited with transforming photography into an art form.

Alfred Stieglitz, 1864-1946, (U.S.) photographer, editor; helped create acceptance of photography as art.

Paul Strand, 1890-1976, (U.S.) photographer. People, nature, landscapes.

Gilbert Stuart, 1755-1828, (U.S.) portraitist. George Washington, Thomas Jefferson, James Madison.

Thomas Sully, 1783-1872, (U.S.) portraitist. *Col. Thomas Handasyd Perkins, The Passage of the Delaware.*

William Henry Fox Talbot, 1800-77, (Br.) photographer. *Pencil of Nature,* early photographically illustrated book.

George Tames, 1919-94, (U.S.) photographer. Chronicled presidents, political leaders.

Yves Tanguy, 1900-55, (Fr.) Surrealist. *Rose of the Four Winds, Mama, Papa Is Wounded!*

Giovanni Battista Tiepolo, 1696-1770, (It.) Rococo frescoes. *The Crucifixion.*

Jacopo Tintoretto, 1518-94, (It.) Mannerist. *The Last Supper.*

Titian, c1485-1576, (It.) Renaissance. *Venus and the Lute Player, The Bacchanal.*

Jose Rey Toledo, 1916-94, (U.S.) Native American artist. Captured the essence of tribal dances on canvas.

Henri de Toulouse-Lautrec, 1864-1901, (Fr.) *At the Moulin Rouge.*

John Trumbull, 1756-1843, (U.S.) historical themes. *The Declaration of Independence.*

J(oseph) M(allord) W(illiam) Turner, 1775-1851, (Br.) Romantic landscapist. *Snow Storm.*

Paolo Uccello, 1397-1475, (It.) Gothic-Renaissance. *The Rout of San Romano.*

Maurice Utrillo, 1883-1955, (Fr.) Impressionist. *Sacre-Coeur de Montmartre.*

John Vanderlyn, 1775-1852, (U.S.) Neo-classicist. *Ariadne Asleep on the Island of Naxos.*

Diego Velázquez, 1599-1660, (Sp.) Baroque. *Las Meninas, Portrait of Juan de Pareja.*

Jan Vermeer, 1632-75, (Dutch) interior genre subjects. *Young Woman With a Water Jug.*

Paolo Veronese, 1528-88, (It.) devotional themes, vastly peopled canvases. *The Temptation of St. Anthony.*

Andrea del Verrocchio, 1435-88, (It.) Floren. sculptor. *Colleoni.*

Maurice de Vlaminck, 1876-1958, (Fr.) Fauvist landscapist. *Red Trees.*

Andy Warhol, 1928-87, (U.S.) Pop Art. *Campbell's Soup Cans, Marilyn Diptych.*

Antoine Watteau, 1684-1721, (Fr.) Rococo painter of "scenes of gallantry." *The Embarkation for Cythera.*

George Frederic Watts, 1817-1904, (Br.) painter and sculptor of grandiose allegorical themes. *Hope.*

Benjamin West, 1738-1820, (U.S.) realistic historical themes. *Death of General Wolfe.*

Edward Weston, 1886-1958, (U.S.) photographer. Landscapes of American West.

James Abbott McNeill Whistler, 1834-1903, (U.S.) *Arrangement in Grey and Black, No. 1: The Artist's Mother.*

Archibald M. Willard, 1836-1918, (U.S.) *The Spirit of '76.*

Grant Wood, 1891-1942, (U.S.) Midwestern regionalist. *American Gothic, Daughters of Revolution.*

Ossip Zadkine, 1890-1967, (Russ.) School of Paris sculptor. *The Destroyed City, Musicians, Christ.*

Business Leaders and Philanthropists of the Past

Giovanni Agnelli, 1921-2003, (It.) industrialist, principal shareholder of Fiat.

Walter Annenberg, 1908-2002, (U.S.) publisher, founder *TV Guide,* philanthropist.

Elizabeth Arden (F. N. Graham), 1884-1966, (U.S.) Canadian-born founder of cosmetics empire.

Philip D. Armour, 1832-1901, (U.S.) industrialist; streamlined meatpacking.

John Jacob Astor, 1763-1848, (U.S.) German-born fur trader, banker, real estate magnate; at death, richest in U.S.

Francis W. Ayer, 1848-1923, (U.S.) ad industry pioneer.

August Belmont, 1816-90, (U.S.) German-born financier.

James B. (Diamond Jim) Brady, 1856-1917, (U.S.) financier, philanthropist, legendary bon vivant.

Adolphus Busch, 1839-1913, (U.S.) German-born businessman; established brewery empire.

Asa Candler, 1851-1929, (U.S.) founded Coca-Cola Co.

Andrew Carnegie, 1835-1919, (U.S.) Scottish-born industrialist; philanthropist; founded Carnegie Steel Co.

Tom Carvel, 1908-89, (Gr.-U.S.) founded ice cream chain.

William Colgate, 1783-1857, (Br.-U.S.) Br.-born businessman, philanthropist; founded soap-making empire.

Jay Cooke, 1821-1905, (U.S.) financier; sold $1 billion in Union bonds during Civil War.

Peter Cooper, 1791-1883, (U.S.) industrialist, inventor, philanthropist; founded Cooper Union (1859).

Ezra Cornell, 1807-74, (U.S.) businessman, philanthropist; headed Western Union, established university.

Erastus Corning, 1794-1872, (U.S.) financier; headed N.Y. Central.

Charles Crocker, 1822-88, (U.S.) railroad builder, financier.

Samuel Cunard, 1787-1865, (Can.) pioneered trans-Atlantic steam navigation.

Marcus Daly, 1841-1900, (U.S.) Irish-born copper magnate.

W. Edwards Deming, 1900-93, (U.S.) quality-control expert who revolutionized Japanese manufacturing.

Walt Disney, 1901-66, (U.S.) pioneer in cinema animation; built entertainment empire.

Herbert H. Dow, 1866-1930, (U.S.) founder of chemical co.

James Duke, 1856-1925, (U.S.) founded American Tobacco, Duke Univ.

Eleuthere I. du Pont, 1771-1834, (Fr.-U.S.) gunpowder manufacturer; founded one of the largest business empires.

Thomas C. Durant, 1820-85, (U.S.) railroad official, financier.

William C. Durant, 1861-1947, (U.S.) industrialist; formed General Motors.

George Eastman, 1854-1932, (U.S.) inventor; manufacturer of photographic equipment.

Marshall Field, 1834-1906, (U.S.) merchant; founded Chicago's largest department store.

Harvey Firestone, 1868-1938, (U.S.) founded tire company.

Avery Fisher, 1906-94, (U.S.) industrialist, philanthropist, founded Fisher electronics.

Henry M. Flagler, 1830-1913, (U.S.) financier; helped form Standard Oil; developed Florida as resort state.

Malcolm Forbes, 1919-90, (U.S.) magazine publisher.

Henry Ford, 1863-1947, (U.S.) auto maker; developed first popular low-priced car.

Henry Ford 2nd, 1917-87, (U.S.) headed auto company founded by grandfather.

Henry C. Frick, 1849-1919, (U.S.) steel and coke magnate; had prominent role in development of U.S. Steel.

Jakob Fugger (Jakob the Rich), 1459-1525, (Ger.) headed leading banking, trading house, in 16th-cent. Europe.

Alfred C. Fuller, 1885-1973, (U.S.) Canadian-born businessman; founded brush company.

Elbert H. Gary, 1846-1927, (U.S.) one of the organizers of U.S. Steel; chaired board of directors, 1903-27.

Jean Paul Getty, 1892-1976, (U.S.) founded oil empire.

Amadeo Giannini, 1870-1949, (U.S.) founded Bank of America.

Stephen Girard, 1750-1831, (U.S.) French-born financier, philanthropist; richest man in U.S. at his death.

Leonard H. Goldenson, 1905-99, (U.S.) turned ABC into major TV network.

Jay Gould, 1836-92, (U.S.) railroad magnate, financier.

Hetty Green, 1834-1916, (U.S.) financier, the "witch of Wall St."; richest woman in U.S. in her day.

William Gregg, 1800-67, (U.S.) launched textile industry in S.

Meyer Guggenheim, 1828-1905, (U.S.) Swiss-born merchant, philanthropist; built merchandising, mining empires.

Armand Hammer, 1898-1990, (U.S.) headed Occidental Petroleum; promoted U.S.-Soviet ties.

Edward H. Harriman, 1848-1909, (U.S.) railroad financier, administrator; headed Union Pacific.

Henry J. Heinz, 1844-1919, (U.S.) founded food empire.

Milton Snavely Hershey, 1857-1945, (U.S.) chocolate co. founder, philanthropist.

James J. Hill, 1838-1916, (U.S.) Canadian-born railroad magnate, financier; founded Great Northern Railway.

Conrad N. Hilton, 1888-1979, (U.S.) hotel chain founder.

Howard Hughes, 1905-76, (U.S.) industrialist, aviator, movie maker.

H. L. Hunt, 1889-1974, (U.S.) oil magnate.

Collis P. Huntington, 1821-1900, (U.S.) railroad magnate.

Henry E. Huntington, 1850-1927, (U.S.) railroad builder, philanthropist.

Walter L. Jacobs, 1898-1985, (U.S.) founder of the first rental car agency, which later became Hertz.

Howard Johnson, 1896-1972, (U.S.) founded restaurants.

John H. Johnson, 1918-2005; built publishing empire based on *Ebony* and *Jet.*

Samuel Curtis Johnson, 1928-2004, (U.S.) headed S.C. Johnson & Sons.

Henry J. Kaiser, 1882-1967, (U.S.) industrialist; built empire in steel, aluminum.

Minor C. Keith, 1848-1929, (U.S.) railroad magnate; founded United Fruit Co.

Will K. Kellogg, 1860-1951, (U.S.) businessman, philanthropist; founded breakfast food co.

Richard King, 1825-85, (U.S.) cattleman; founded half-million-acre King Ranch in Texas.

William S. Knudsen, 1879-1948, (U.S.) Danish-born auto industry executive.

Samuel H. Kress, 1863-1955, (U.S.) businessman, art collector, philanthropist; founded "dime store" chain.

Ray A. Kroc, 1902-84, (U.S.) original CEO of McDonald's Corp.; oversaw company's vast expansion.

Alfred Krupp, 1812-87, (Ger.) armaments magnate.

Kenneth L. Lay, 1942-2006, (U.S.), former CEO of Enron, indicted on fraud charges.

William Levitt, 1907-94, (U.S.) industrialist, "suburb maker".

Thomas Lipton, 1850-1931, (Scot.) merchant, tea empire.

James McGill, 1744-1813, (Scot.-Can.) founded university.

Andrew W. Mellon, 1855-1937, (U.S.) financier, industrialist; benefactor of National Gallery of Art.

Charles E. Merrill, 1885-1956, (U.S.) financier; developed firm of Merrill Lynch.

John Pierpont Morgan, 1837-1913, (U.S.) most powerful figure in finance and industry at the turn of the cent.

Akio Morita, 1921-99, (Japan) co-founded Sony Corp.

Malcolm Muir, 1885-1979, (U.S.) created *Business Week* magazine; headed *Newsweek,* 1937-61.

Samuel Newhouse, 1895-1979, (U.S.) publishing and broadcasting magnate; built communications empire.

Aristotle Onassis, 1906-75, (Gr.) shipping magnate.

William S. Paley, 1901-90, (U.S.) built CBS communic. empire.

Frederick D. Patterson, 1901-88, founder of United Negro College Fund, 1944.

George Peabody, 1795-1869, (U.S.) merchant, financier, philanthropist.

James C. Penney, 1875-1971, (U.S.) businessman; developed department store chain.

William C. Procter, 1862-1934, (U.S.) headed soap co.

Frank Perdue, 1920-2005, (U.S.) founder of Perdue Farms, chicken-processing company.

John D. Rockefeller, 1839-1937, (U.S.) industrialist; established Standard Oil.

John D. Rockefeller Jr., 1874-1960, (U.S.) philanthropist; established foundation; provided land for UN.

Laurance S. Rockefeller, 1910-2004, (U.S.) philanthropist, conservationist.

Meyer A. Rothschild, 1743-1812, (Ger.) founded international banking house.

Thomas Fortune Ryan, 1851-1928, (U.S.) financier; a founder of American Tobacco.

Edmond J. Safra, 1932-99, (U.S.), banker.

David Sarnoff, 1891-1971, (U.S.) broadcasting pioneer; established first radio network, NBC.

Richard Sears, 1863-1914, (U.S.) founded mail-order co.

Werner von Siemens, 1816-92, (Ger.) industrialist; inventor.

Alfred P. Sloan, 1875-1966, (U.S.) industrialist, philanthropist; headed General Motors.

A. Leland Stanford, 1824-93, (U.S.) railroad official, philanthropist; founded university.

Nathan Straus, 1848-1931, (U.S.) German-born merchant, philanthropist; headed Macy's.

Levi Strauss, c1829-1902, (U.S.) pants manufacturer.

Clement Studebaker, 1831-1901, (U.S.) wagon, carriage maker.

Gustavus Swift, 1839-1903, (U.S.) pioneer meatpacker.

Gerard Swope, 1872-1957, (U.S.) industrialist, economist; headed General Electric.

Dave Thomas, 1932-2002, (U.S.) Wendy's founder.

James Walter Thompson, 1847-1928, (U.S.) ad executive.

Alice Tully, 1902-93, (U.S.) philanthropist, arts patron.

Theodore N. Vail, 1845-1920, (U.S.) organized Bell Telephone system; headed AT&T.

Cornelius Vanderbilt, 1794-1877, (U.S.) financier; established steamship, railroad empires.

Henry Villard, 1835-1900, (U.S.) German-born railroad executive, financier.

George Westinghouse, 1846-1914, (U.S) inventor, manufacturer; organized Westinghouse Electric Co., 1886.

Charles R. Walgreen, 1873-1939, (U.S.) founded drugstore chain.

DeWitt Wallace, 1889-1981, (U.S.) and **Lila Wallace,** 1889-1984, (U.S.) cofounders of *Reader's Digest* magazine.

Sam Walton, 1918-92, (U.S.) founder of Wal-Mart stores.

John Wanamaker, 1838-1922, (U.S.) pioneered department-store merchandising.

Aaron Montgomery Ward, 1843-1913, (U.S.) established first mail-order firm.

Thomas J. Watson, 1874-1956, (U.S.) IBM head, 1914-56.

John Hay Whitney, 1905-82, (U.S.) publisher, sportsman, philanthropist.

Charles E. Wilson, 1890-1961, (U.S.) auto exec., public official.

Frank W. Woolworth, 1852-1919, (U.S.) created 5 & 10 chain.

William Wrigley Jr., 1861-1932, (U.S.) founded Wrigley chewing gum company.

American Cartoonists

Reviewed by Lucy Shelton Caswell, Professor and Curator, Cartoon Research Library, Ohio State University

Scott Adams, b 1957, Dilbert.

Charles Addams, 1912-88, macabre cartoons.

Brad Anderson, b 1924, Marmaduke.

Sergio Aragones, b 1937, *MAD Magazine.*

Peter Arno, 1904-68, *The New Yorker.*

Tex Avery, 1908-80, animator, Bugs Bunny, Porky Pig.

George Baker, 1915-75, The Sad Sack.

Carl Barks, 1901-2000, Donald Duck comic books.

C. C. Beck, 1910-89, Captain Marvel.

Dave Berg, 1920-2002, *Mad Magazine.*

Jim Berry, b 1932, Berry's World.

Herb Block (Herblock), 1909-2001, political cartoonist.

George Booth, b 1926, *The New Yorker.*

Berkeley Breathed, b 1957, Bloom County.

Dik Browne, 1917-89, Hi & Lois, Hagar the Horrible.

Marjorie Buell, 1904-93, Little Lulu.

Ernie Bushmiller, 1905-82, Nancy.

Milton Caniff, 1907-88, Terry & the Pirates, Steve Canyon.

Al Capp, 1909-79, Li'l Abner.

Roz Chast, b 1954, *The New Yorker.*

Paul Conrad, 1924, political cartoonist.

Roy Crane, 1901-77, Captain Easy, Buz Sawyer.

Robert Crumb, b 1943, underground cartoonist.

Shamus Culhane, 1908-96, animator.

Jay N. Darling (Ding), 1876-1962, political cartoonist.

Jack Davis, b 1926, *MAD Magazine.*

Jim Davis, b 1945, Garfield.

Billy DeBeck, 1890-1942, Barney Google.

Rudolph Dirks, 1877-1968, The Katzenjammer Kids.

Walt Disney, 1901-66, produced animated cartoons, created Mickey Mouse, Donald Duck.

Steve Ditko, b 1927, Spider-Man.

Mort Drucker, b 1929, *MAD Magazine.*

Will Eisner, 1917-2005, The Spirit.

Jules Feiffer, b 1929, political cartoonist.

Bud Fisher, 1884-1954, Mutt & Jeff.

Ham Fisher, 1900-55, Joe Palooka.

Max Fleischer, 1883-1972, Betty Boop.

Hal Foster, 1892-1982, Tarzan, Prince Valiant.

Fontaine Fox, 1884-1964, Toonerville Folks.

Isadore "Friz" Freleng, 1905-95, animator, Yosemite Sam, Porky Pig, Sylvester and Tweety Bird.

Rube Goldberg, 1883-1970, Boob McNutt.

Chester Gould, 1900-85, Dick Tracy.

Harold Gray, 1894-1968, Little Orphan Annie.

Matt Groening, b 1954, Life in Hell, The Simpsons.

Cathy Guisewite, b 1950, Cathy.

Bill Hanna, 1910-2001, & **Joe Barbera,** b 1911, animators, Tom & Jerry, Yogi Bear, Flintstones.

Johnny Hart, b 1931, BC, Wizard of Id.

Oliver Harrington, 1912-95, Bootsie.

Alfred Harvey, 1913-94, created Casper the Friendly Ghost.

Jimmy Hatlo, 1898-1963, Little Iodine.

John Held Jr., 1889-1958, Jazz Age.

George Herriman, 1881-1944, Krazy Kat.

Harry Hershfield, 1885-1974, Abie the Agent.

Al Hirschfeld, 1903-2003, *N.Y. Times* theater caricaturist.

Burne Hogarth, 1911-96, Tarzan.

Helen Hokinson, 1900-49, *The New Yorker.*

Nicole Hollander, b 1939, Sylvia.

Chuck Jones, 1912-2002, animator, Bugs Bunny, Porky Pig.

Mike Judge, b. 1962, Beavis and Butt-head, King of the Hill.

Bob Kane, 1916-98, Batman.

Bil Keane, b 1922, The Family Circus.

Walt Kelly, 1913-73, Pogo.

Hank Ketcham, 1920-2001, Dennis the Menace.

Ted Key, b 1912, Hazel.

Frank King, 1883-1969, Gasoline Alley.

Jack Kirby, 1917-94, Fantastic Four, The Incredible Hulk.

Rollin Kirby, 1875-1952, political cartoonist.

B(ernard) Kliban, 1935-91, cat books.

Edward Koren, b 1935, *The New Yorker.*

Harvey Kurtzman, 1921-93, *MAD Magazine.*

Walter Lantz, 1900-94, Woody Woodpecker.

Gary Larson, b 1950, The Far Side.

Mell Lazarus, b 1929, Momma, Miss Peach.

Stan Lee, b 1922, Marvel Comics.

David Levine, b 1926, *N.Y. Review of Books* caricatures.

Doug Marlette, b 1949, political cartoonist, Kudzu.

Don Martin, 1931-2000, *MAD Magazine.*

Bill Mauldin, 1921-2003, political cartoonist.

Jeff MacNelly, 1947-2000, political cartoonist, Shoe.

Winsor McCay, 1872-1934, Little Nemo.

John T. McCutcheon, 1870-1949, political cartoonist.

Aaron McGruder, b 1974, The Boondocks.
George McManus, 1884-1954, Bringing Up Father.
Dale Messick, 1906-2005, Brenda Starr.
Norman Mingo, 1896-1980, Alfred E. Neuman.
Bob Montana, 1920-75, Archie.
Dick Moores, 1909-86, Gasoline Alley.
Willard Mullin, 1902-78, sports cartoonist; Dodgers "Bum," Mets "Kid."
Russell Myers, b 1938, Broom Hilda.
Thomas Nast, 1840-1902, political cartoonist; Republican elephant and Democratic donkey.
Pat Oliphant, b 1935, political cartoonist.
Frederick Burr Opper, 1857-1937, Happy Hooligan.
Richard Outcault, 1863-1928, Yellow Kid, Buster Brown.
Brant Parker, b 1920, Wizard of Id.
Trey Parker, b 1969, animator, co-creator of *South Park.*
Mike Peters, b 1943, cartoonist, Mother Goose & Grimm.
George Price, 1901-95, *The New Yorker.*
Antonio Prohias, 1921-98, Spy vs. Spy.
Alex Raymond, 1909-56, Flash Gordon, Jungle Jim.
Forrest (Bud) Sagendorf, 1915-94, Popeye.
Art Sansom, 1920-91, The Born Loser.
Charles Schulz, 1922-2000, Peanuts.

Elzie C. Segar, 1894-1938, Popeye.
Joe Shuster, 1914-92, & **Jerry Siegel,** 1914-96, Superman.
Sidney Smith, 1887-1935, The Gumps.
Otto Soglow, 1900-75, Little King.
Art Spiegelman, b 1948, Raw, Maus.
William Steig, b 1907-2003, *The New Yorker.*
Matt Stone, b 1971, animator, co-creator of South Park.
Paul Szep, b 1941, political cartoonist.
James Swinnerton, 1875-1974, Little Jimmy, Canyon Kiddies.
Paul Terry, 1887-1971, animator of Mighty Mouse.
Bob Thaves, b 1924, Frank and Ernest.
James Thurber, 1894-61, *The New Yorker.*
Garry Trudeau, b 1948, Doonesbury.
Mort Walker, b 1923, Beetle Bailey.
Bill Watterson, b 1958, Calvin and Hobbes.
Russ Westover, 1887-1966, Tillie the Toiler.
Signe Wilkinson, b 1950, political cartoonist.
Frank Willard, 1893-1958, Moon Mullins.
J. R. Williams, 1888-1957, The Willets Family, Out Our Way.
Gahan Wilson, b 1930, *The New Yorker.*
Tom Wilson, b 1931, Ziggy.
Art Young, 1866-1943, political cartoonist.
Chic Young, 1901-73, Blondie.

Economists, Educators, Historians, and Social Scientists of the Past

For Psychologists see Scientists of the Past.

Brooks Adams, 1848-1927, (U.S.) historian, political theoretician; *The Law of Civilization and Decay.*
Henry Adams, 1838-1918, (U.S.) historian, autobiographer; *The Education of Henry Adams.*
Francis Bacon, 1561-1626, (Eng.) philosopher, essayist, and statesman; championed observation and induction.
George Bancroft, 1800-91, (U.S.) historian; wrote 10-volume *History of the United States.*
Jack Barbash, 1911-94, (U.S.) labor economist who helped create the AFL-CIO.
Henry Barnard, 1811-1900, (U.S.) public school reformer.
Charles A. Beard, 1874-1948, (U.S.) historian; *The Economic Basis of Politics.*
(St.) Bede (the Venerable), c673-735, (Br.) scholar, historian; *Ecclesiastical History of the English People.*
Ruth Benedict, 1887-1948, (U.S.) anthropologist; studied Indian tribes of the Southwest.
Sir Isaiah Berlin, 1909-97, (Br.) philosopher, historian; *The Age of Enlightenment.*
Leonard Bloomfield, 1887-1949, (U.S.) linguist; *Language.*
Franz Boas, 1858-1942, (U.S.) German-born anthropologist; studied American Indians.
Van Wyck Brooks, 1886-1963, (U.S.) historian; critic of New England culture, especially literature.
William Edward Burghardt (W.E.B.) Du Bois, 1868-1963, (U.S.) historian, sociologist; and NAACP founder, 1909.
Edmund Burke, 1729-97, (Ir.) British parliamentarian and political philosopher; *Reflections on the Revolution in France.*
Nicholas Murray Butler, 1862-1947, (U.S.) educator; headed Columbia Univ., 1902-45; Nobel Peace Prize, 1931.
Joseph Campbell, 1904-87, (U.S.) author, editor, teacher; wrote books on mythology, folklore.
Thomas Carlyle, 1795-1881, (Sc.) historian, critic; *Sartor Resartus, Past and Present, The French Revolution.*
Edward Channing, 1856-1931, (U.S.) historian; wrote 6-volume *History of the United States.*
Henry Steele Commager, 1902-98, (U.S.) historian, educator; wrote *The Growth of the American Republic.*
John R. Commons, 1862-1945, (U.S.) economist, labor historian; *Legal Foundations of Capitalism.*
James B. Conant, 1893-1978, (U.S.) educator, diplomat; *The American High School Today.*
Benedetto Croce, 1866-1952, (It.) philosopher, statesman, and historian; *Philosophy of the Spirit.*
Bernard A. De Voto, 1897-1955, (U.S.) historian; wrote trilogy on American West; edited Mark Twain manuscripts.
Melvil Dewey, 1851-1931, (U.S.) devised decimal system of library-book classification.
St. Clair Drake, 1911-90, (U.S.) Sociologist, black studies pioneer, *Black Metropolis* (1945), with Horace R. Cayton.
Emile Durkheim, 1858-1917, (Fr.) a founder of modern sociology; *The Rules of Sociological Method.*
Jean Baptiste Point du Sable, c1750-1818, (U.S.) pioneer trader and first settler of Chicago, 1779.
Charles Eliot, 1834-1926, (U.S.) educator, Harvard president.
Friedrich Engels, 1820-95, (Ger.) political writer; with Marx wrote the *Communist Manifesto.*
Irving Fisher, 1867-1947, (U.S.) economist; contributed to the development of modern monetary theory.
John Fiske, 1842-1901, (U.S.) historian and lecturer; popularized Darwinian theory of evolution.
Charles Fourier, 1772-1837, (Fr.) utopian socialist.
John Kenneth Galbraith, 1908-2006, (Can.-U.S.) economist, author, professor, former amb. to India.

Giovanni Gentile, 1875-1944, (It.) philosopher, educator; reformed Italian educational system.
Sir James George Frazer, 1854-1941, (Br.) anthropologist; studied myth in religion; *The Golden Bough.*
Henry George, 1839-97, (U.S.) economist, reformer; led single-tax movement.
Edward Gibbon, 1737-94, (Br.) historian; *The History of the Decline and Fall of the Roman Empire.*
Francesco Guicciardini, 1483-1540, (It.) historian; *Storia d'Italia,* principal historical work of the 16th cent.
Thomas Hobbes, 1588-1679, (Eng.) philosopher, political theorist; *Leviathan.*
Richard Hofstadter, 1916-70, (U.S.) historian; *The Age of Reform.*
Charles Hamilton Houston, 1895-1950, (U.S.) African American lawyer, Howard University instructor, champion of minority rights,
George F. Kennan, 1904-2005, (U.S.) diplomat, historian; main architect of the U.S. Cold War "containment" strategy.
John Maynard Keynes, 1883-1946, (Br.) economist; principal advocate of deficit spending.
Alfred Kinsey, 1894-1956, (U.S.) zoologist; pioneering human sex researcher.
Russell Kirk, 1918-94, (U.S.), social philosopher; *The Conservative Mind.*
Alfred L. Kroeber, 1876-1960, (U.S.) cultural anthropologist; studied Indians of North and South America.
Elisabeth Kubler-Ross, 1926-2004, (Swiss) psychiatrist, author. *On Death and Dying.*
Christopher Lasch, 1932-94, (U.S.) social critic, historian; *The Culture of Narcissism.*
James L. Laughlin, 1850-1933, (U.S.) economist; helped establish Federal Reserve System.
Lucien Lévy-Bruhl, 1857-1939, (Fr.) philosopher; studied the psychology of primitive societies; *Primitive Mentality.*
John Locke, 1632-1704, (Eng.) philosopher and political theorist; *Two Treatises of Government.*
Thomas B. Macaulay, 1800-59, (Br.) historian, statesman.
Niccolò Machiavelli, 1469-1527, (It.) writer, statesman. *The Prince.*
Bronislaw Malinowski, 1884-1942, (Pol.) considered the father of social anthropology.
Thomas R. Malthus, 1766-1834, (Br.) economist; famed for *Essay on the Principle of Population.*
Horace Mann, 1796-1859, (U.S.) pioneered modern public school system.
Karl Mannheim, 1893-1947, (Hung.) sociologist, historian; *Ideology and Utopia.*
Harriet Martineau, 1802-76, (Eng.) writer, feminist; *Society in America*
Karl Marx, 1818-83, (Ger.) political theorist, proponent of Communism; *Communist Manifesto, Das Kapital.*
Benjamin Mays, 1895-1984, (U.S.) minister, educator, civil rights leader; headed Morehouse College, 1940-67.
Giuseppe Mazzini, 1805-72, (It.) political philosopher.
William H. McGuffey, 1800-73, (U.S.) whose *Reader* was a mainstay of 19th-cent. U.S. public education.
George H. Mead, 1863-1931, (U.S.) philosopher, social psychologist.
Margaret Mead, 1901-78, (U.S.) cultural anthropologist; popularized field; *Coming of Age in Samoa.*
Alexander Meiklejohn, 1872-1964, (U.S.) Br.-born educator; championed academic freedom and experimental curricula.

James Mill, 1773-1836, (Sc.) philosopher, historian, economist; a proponent of utilitarianism.

John Stuart Mill, 1806-73, (Eng.) philosopher, economist, *Utilitarianism*; eldest son of James Mill.

Perry G. Miller, 1905-63, (U.S.) historian; interpreted 17th-cent. New England.

Theodor Mommsen, 1817-1903, (Ger.) historian; *The History of Rome.*

Ashley Montagu, 1905-99, (Eng.) anthropologist; *The Natural Superiority of Women.*

Charles-Louis Montesquieu, 1689-1755, (Fr.) social philosopher; *The Spirit of Laws.*

Maria Montessori, 1870-1952, (It.) educator, physician; started Montessori method of student self-motivation.

Samuel Eliot Morison, 1887-1976, (U.S.) historian; chronicled voyages of early explorers.

Lewis Mumford, 1895-1990, (U.S.) sociologist, critic; *The Culture of Cities.*

Gunnar Myrdal, 1898-1987, (Swed.) economist, social scientist; *Asian Drama: An Inquiry Into the Poverty of Nations.*

Allan Nevins, 1890-1971, (U.S.) historian, biographer; *The Ordeal of the Union.*

José Ortega y Gasset, 1883-1955, (Sp.) philosopher; advocated control by elite, *The Revolt of the Masses.*

Robert Owen, 1771-1858, (Br.) political philosopher, reformer; pioneer in cooperative movement.

Thomas (Tom) Paine, 1737-1809, (U.S.) political theorist, writer. *Common Sense.*

Vilfredo Pareto, 1848-1923, (It.) economist, sociologist.

Francis Parkman, 1823-93, (U.S.) historian; *France and England in North America.*

Elizabeth P. Peabody, 1804-94, (U.S.) education pioneer; founded 1st kindergarten in U.S., 1860.

William Prescott, 1796-1859, (U.S.) early American historian; *The Conquest of Peru.*

Pierre Joseph Proudhon, 1809-65, (Fr.) social theorist; father of anarchism; *The Philosophy of Property.*

François Quesnay, 1694-1774, (Fr.) economic theorist.

David Ricardo, 1772-1823, (Br.) economic theorist; advocated free international trade.

David Riesman, 1909-2002, (U.S.) sociologist, coauthor *The Lonely Crowd.*

Jean-Jacques Rousseau, 1712-78, (Fr.) social philosopher; the father of romantic sensibility; *Confessions.*

Edward Sapir, 1884-1939, (Ger.-U.S.) anthropologist; studied ethnology and linguistics of U.S. Indian groups.

Ferdinand de Saussure, 1857-1913, (Swiss) a founder of modern linguistics.

Joseph Schumpeter, 1883-1950, (Czech.-U.S.) economist, sociologist.

Elizabeth Seton, 1774-1821, (U.S.) nun; est. parochial school education in U.S.; first native-born American saint.

George Simmel, 1858-1918, (Ger.) sociologist, philosopher; helped establish German sociology.

Adam Smith, 1723-90, (Br.) economist; advocated laissez-faire economy, free trade; *The Wealth of Nations.*

Jared Sparks, 1789-1866, (U.S.) historian, educator, editor; *The Library of American Biography.*

Oswald Spengler, 1880-1936, (Ger.) philosopher and historian; *The Decline of the West.*

William G. Sumner, 1840-1910, (U.S.) social scientist, economist; laissez-faire economy, Social Darwinism.

Hippolyte Taine, 1828-93, (Fr.) historian; basis of naturalistic school; *The Origins of Contemporary France.*

A(lan) J(ohn) P(ercivale) Taylor, 1906-89, (Br.) historian; *The Origins of the Second World War.*

Nikolaas Tinbergen, 1907-88, (Dutch-Br.) ethologist; pioneer in study of animal behavior.

Alexis de Tocqueville, 1805-59, (Fr.) political scientist, historian; *Democracy in America.*

Francis E. Townsend, 1867-1960, (U.S.) led old-age pension movement, 1933.

Arnold Toynbee, 1889-1975, (Br.) historian; *A Study of History,* sweeping analysis of hist. of civilizations.

George Trevelyan, 1838-1928, (Br.) historian, statesman; favored "literary" over "scientific" history; *History of England.*

Frederick J. Turner, 1861-1932, (U.S.) historian, educator; *The Frontier in American History.*

Thorstein B. Veblen, 1857-1929, (U.S.) economist, social philosopher; *The Theory of the Leisure Class.*

Giovanni Vico, 1668-1744, (It.) historian, philosopher; regarded by many as first modern historian; *New Science.*

Izaak Walton, 1593-1683, (Eng.) wrote biographies; political-philosophical study of fishing, *The Compleat Angler.*

Booker T. Washington, 1856-1915, (U.S.) founder, 1881, and first pres. of Tuskegee Institute; *Up From Slavery.*

Sidney J., 1859-1947, and **Beatrice,** 1858-1943, **Webb,** (Br.) leading figures in Fabian Society and Labor Party.

Max Weber, 1864-1920, (Ger.) sociologist; *The Protestant Ethic and the Spirit of Capitalism.*

Walter White, 1893-1955, (U.S.) exec. sec., NAACP, 1931-55.

Roy Wilkins, 1901-81, (U.S.) exec. director, NAACP, 1955-77.

Emma Hart Willard, 1787-1870, (U.S.) pioneered higher education for women.

Carter G. Woodson, 1875-1950, (U.S.) historian; founded Assn. for the Study of Negro Life and History.

C. Vann Woodward, 1908-99, (U.S.) historian; *The Strange Career of Jim Crow.*

American Journalists of the Past

Reviewed by Dean Mills, Dean, Missouri School of Journalism

See also Business Leaders, Cartoonists, Writers of the Past.

Franklin P. Adams (F.P.A.), 1881-1960, humorist; wrote column "The Conning Tower."

Joseph W. Alsop, 1910-89, and **Stewart Alsop,** 1914-74, Washington-based political analysts, columnists.

Jack Anderson, 1922-2006, muckraking Washington, DC, syndicated columnist.

Brooks Atkinson, 1894-1984, theater critic.

Bartley, Robert L., 1937-2003, editorial-page editor for *Wall Street Journal.*

James Gordon Bennett, 1795-1872, editor and publisher; founded *NY Herald.*

James Gordon Bennett, 1841-1918, succeeded father, financed expeditions; founded afternoon paper.

Elias Boudinot, d 1839, founding editor of first Native American newspaper in U.S., *Cherokee Phoenix* (1828-34).

David Brinkley, 1920-2003, co-anchor of NBC's *Huntley-Brinkley Report,* host of ABC's *This Week With David Brinkley.*

Margaret Bourke-White, 1904-71, photojournalist.

Arthur Brisbane, 1864-1936, editor; helped introduce "yellow journalism" with sensational, simply written articles.

Heywood Broun, 1888-1939, author, columnist; founded American Newspaper Guild.

Herb Caen, 1916-97, longtime columnist for *San Francisco Chronicle* and *Examiner.*

John Campbell, 1653-1728, published *Boston News-Letter,* first continuing newspaper in the American colonies.

Jimmy Cannon, 1909-73, syndicated sports columnist.

John Chancellor, 1927-96, NBC TV reporter, anchor.

Harry Chandler, 1864-1944, *Los Angeles Times* publisher, 1917-41; made it a dominant force.

Otis Chandler, 1928-2006, *Los Angeles Times* publisher, 1960-80.

Marquis Childs, 1903-90, reporter and columnist for *St. Louis Post-Dispatch* and United Feature syndicate.

Craig Claiborne, 1920-2000, *NY Times* food editor and critic; key in internationalizing American taste.

Elizabeth Cochrane (Nellie Bly), pioneer woman journalist, investig. reporter, noted for series on trip around the world.

Charles Collingwood, 1917-85, CBS news correspondent.

Alistair Cooke, 1908-2004, journalist, TV narrator, naturalized American citizen, "Letter from America" series.

Howard Cosell, 1920-95, TV and radio sportscaster.

Gardner Cowles, 1861-1946, founded newspaper chain.

Cyrus Curtis, 1850-1933, publisher of *Saturday Evening Post, Ladies' Home Journal, Country Gentleman.*

John Charles Daly, 1914-91, war correspondent; TV journalist; Voice of America head.

Charles Anderson Dana, 1819-97, editor, publisher; made *NY Sun* famous for its news reporting.

Elmer (Holmes) Davis, 1890-1958, *NY Times* editorial writer; radio commentator.

Richard Harding Davis, 1864-1916, war correspondent, travel writer, fiction writer.

Benjamin Day, 1810-89, published *NY Sun* beginning in 1833, introducing penny press to the U.S.

Finley Peter Dunne, 1867-1936, humorist, social critic, wrote "Mr. Dooley" columns.

Mary Baker Eddy, 1821-1910, founded Christian Science movement and *Christian Science Monitor.*

Rowland Evans Jr., 1921-2001, Washington columnist.

Fanny Fern (Sarah Willis Parton), 1811-1872, newspaper columnist, author.

Marshall Field III, 1893-1956, retail magnate, *Chicago Sun* founder.

Doris Fleeson, 1901-70, war correspondent, columnist.

James Franklin, 1697-1735, printer, pioneer journalist, publisher of *New England Courant* and *Rhode Island Gazette.*

Fred W. Friendly, 1915-98, radio, TV reporter, producer, executive, collaborator with Edward R. Murrow.

Margaret Fuller, 1810-50, social reformer, transcendentalist, critic and foreign correspondent for *NY Tribune.*

Frank E. Gannett, 1876-1957, founded newspaper chain.

William Lloyd Garrison, 1805-79, abolitionist; publisher of *The Liberator.*

Elizabeth Meriwether Gilmer (Dorothy Dix), 1861-1951, reporter, pioneer of the advice column genre.

Edwin Lawrence Godkin, 1831-1902, founder of *The Nation,* editor of *N.Y. Evening Post.*

Katharine Graham,1917-2001, *Washington Post* publisher.

Sheilah Graham, 1904-89, Hollywood gossip columnist.

Horace Greeley, 1811-72, editor and politician; founded *NY Tribune.*

Meg Greenfield, 1930-1999, *Newsweek* columnist, editorial page editor *Washington Post.*

Gilbert Hovey Grosvenor, 1875-1966, longtime editor of *National Geographic* magazine.

John Gunther, 1901-70, *Chicago Daily News* foreign correspondent, author.

Sarah Josepha Buell Hale, 1788-1879, first female magazine editor, (Ladies' Magazine, later Godey's Lady's Book)

William Randolph Hearst, 1863-1951, founder of Hearst newspaper chain and one of the pioneer yellow journalists.

Gabriel Heatter, 1890-1972, radio commentator.

John Hersey, 1914-98, foreign correspondent for *Time, Life,* and *The New Yorker;* author.

Marguerite Higgins, 1920-66, reporter, war correspondent.

Hedda Hopper, 1885-1966, Hollywood gossip columnist.

Roy Howard, 1883-1964, editor, executive, Scripps-Howard papers and United Press (later United Press International).

Chet (Chester Robert) Huntley, 1911-74, co-anchor of NBC's *Huntley-Brinkley Report.*

Ralph Ingersoll, 1900-85, editor, *Fortune, Time, Life* exec.

Peter Jennings, 1938-2005, ABC TV correspondent, anchor.

H. V. (Hans von) Kaltenborn, 1878-1965, radio commentator, reporter.

Murray Kempton, 1917-97, reporter, columnist for magazines and newspapers, including *NY Post.*

Dorothy Kilgallen, 1913-65, crime reporter; columnist.

John S. Knight, 1894-1981, editor, publisher; founded Knight newspaper group, which merged into Knight-Ridder.

Joseph Kraft, 1942-86, foreign policy columnist.

Arthur Krock, 1886-1974, *NY Times* political writer, Washington bureau chief.

Charles Kuralt, 1934-97, TV anchor and host of CBS "On the Road" featuring stories about life in the U.S.

Ann Landers (Eppie Lederer), 1918-2002, advice columnist.

David Lawrence, 1888-1973, reporter, columnist, publisher; founded *U.S. News & World Report.*

Frank Leslie, 1821-80, engraver and publisher of newspapers and magazines, notably *Leslie's Illustrated Newspaper.*

Alexander Liberman, 1912-99, editorial director for Conde Nast magazines.

A(bbott) J(oseph) Liebling, 1904-63, foreign correspondent, critic, principally with *The New Yorker.*

Walter Lippmann, 1889-1974, political analyst, social critic, columnist, author.

Peter Lisagor, 1915-76, Washington bureau chief, *Chicago Daily News;* broadcast commentator.

David Ross Locke, 1833-88, humorist, satirist under pseudonym P.V. Nasby; owned *Toledo (Ohio) Blade.*

Elijah Parish Lovejoy, 1802-37, abolitionist editor in St. Louis and in Alton, IL; killed by proslavery mob.

Clare Booth Luce, 1903-87, war correspondent for *Life;* diplomat, playwright.

Henry R. Luce, 1898-1967, founded *Time, Fortune, Life, Sports Illustrated.*

C(harles) K(enny) McClatchy, 1858-1936, founder of McClatchy newspaper chain.

Sarah McClendon, 1910-2003, veteran White House correspondent.

Samuel McClure, 1857-1949, founder (1893) of *McClure's Magazine,* famous for its investigative reporting.

Anne O'Hare McCormick, 1889-1954, foreign correspondent, first woman on *NY Times* editorial board.

Robert R. McCormick, 1880-1955, editor, publisher, executive of *Chicago Tribune* and *NY Daily News.*

Dwight Macdonald, 1906-1982, reporter, social critic.

Ralph McGill, 1893-1969, crusading editor and publisher of *Atlanta Constitution.*

Mary McGrory, 1918-2004, Washington, DC, columnist.

O(scar) O(dd) McIntyre, 1884-1938, feature writer, syndicated columnist on everyday life in New York City.

Don Marquis, 1878-1937, humor columnist for *NY Sun* and *N.Y. Tribune;* wrote "archy and mehitabel" stories.

Robert Maynard, 1937-97, first African American editor and then owner of major U.S. paper, the *Oakland Tribune.*

Joseph Medill, 1823-99, longtime *editor of Chicago Tribune.*

H(enry) L(ouis) Mencken, 1880-1956, reporter, editor, columnist with *Baltimore Sun* papers; anti-establishment viewpoint.

Edwin Meredith, 1876-1928, founder of magazine company.

Frank A. Munsey, 1854-1925, owner, editor, and publisher of newspapers and magazines, including *Munsey's Magazine.*

Edward R. Murrow, 1908-65, broadcast reporter, executive; reported from Britain in WW2; hosted *See It Now, Person to Person.*

Louella Parsons, 1881-1972, Hollywood gossip columnist.

Drew (Andrew Russell) Pearson, 1897-1969, investigative reporter and columnist.

(James) Westbrook Pegler, 1894-1969, reporter, columnist.

Shirley Povich, 1905-98, sports columnist.

Joseph Pulitzer, 1847-1911, *NY World* publisher; founded Columbia Journalism School, Pulitzer Prizes.

Joseph Pulitzer II, 1885-1955, longtime *St. Louis Post-Dispatch* editor, publisher; built it into major paper.

Ernie (Ernest Taylor) Pyle, 1900-45, reporter, war correspondent; killed in WW2.

Henry Raymond, 1820-69, cofounder, editor, *NY Times.*

Harry Reasoner, 1923-91, ABC and CBS news reporter, anchor.

John Reed, 1887-1920, reporter, foreign correspondent famous for coverage of Bolshevik Revolution; buried at the Kremlin.

Whitelaw Reid, 1837-1912, longtime editor, *NY Tribune.*

James Reston, 1909-95 *NY Times* political reporter, columnist.

Frank Reynolds, 1923-83, ABC reporter, anchor.

(Henry) Grantland Rice, 1880-1954, sportswriter.

Jacob Riis, 1849-1914, reporter, photographer; exposed slum conditions in *How the Other Half Lives.*

Max Robinson, 1939-88, first African American to anchor network news (ABC), 1978.

Harold Ross, 1892-1951, founder, editor, The *New Yorker.*

Carl T. Rowan, 1925-2000, reporter, columnist, author.

Mike Royko, 1932-97, Chicago newspaper columnist; wrote *Boss,* biography of Mayor Richard Daley.

(Alfred) Damon Runyon, 1884-1946, sportswriter, columnist; stories collected in *Guys and Dolls.*

John B. Russwurm, 1799-1851, cofounded (1827) nation's first black newspaper, *Freedom's Journal,* in NYC.

Adela Rogers St. Johns, 1894-1988, reporter, sportswriter for Hearst newspapers.

Joe Rosenthal, 1911-2006, (U.S.) photojournalist; photographed six marines raising the U.S. flag over Iwo Jima in WWII.

A. M. Rosenthal, 1922-2006, reporter and editor for the *New York Times* (1943-99).

Louis Rukeyser, 1933-2006, TV journalist, financial analyst, hosted "Wall Street Week" on public television.

Pierre Salinger, 1925-2004, press secretary under Pres. Kennedy and Johnson; foreign correspondent.

Harrison Salisbury, 1908-93, reporter, foreign correspondent; a Soviet specialist.

E(dward) W(yllis) Scripps, 1854-1926, founded first large U.S. newspaper chain, pioneered syndication.

Eric Sevareid, 1912-92, war correspondent, radio newscaster, CBS commentator.

William L. Shirer, 1904-93, broadcaster, foreign correspondent; wrote *The Rise and Fall of the Third Reich.*

Howard K. Smith, 1914-2002, ABC TV reporter, anchor.

Red (Walter) Smith, 1905-82, sportswriter.

Edgar P. Snow, 1905-71, correspondent, expert on Chinese Communist movement.

Lawrence Spivak, 1900-94, co-creator, moderator, producer of *Meet the Press.*

(Joseph) Lincoln Steffens, 1866-1936, muckraking journalist.

I(sidor) F(einstein) Stone, 1907-89, one-man editor of *I.F. Stone's Weekly.*

Arthur Hays Sulzberger, 1891-1968, longtime publisher of *N.Y. Times.*

C(yrus) L(eo) Sulzberger, 1912-93, *N.Y. Times* foreign correspondent and columnist.

David Susskind, 1920-87, TV producer, public affairs talk-show host (*Open End*).

John Cameron Swayze, 1906-95, early TV newscaster (NBC).

Herbert Bayard Swope, 1882-1958, war correspondent and editor of *N.Y. World.*

Ida Tarbell, 1857-1944, muckraking journalist.

Isaiah Thomas, 1750-1831, printer, publisher, cofounder of revolutionary journal, *Massachusetts Spy.*

Lowell Thomas, 1892-1981, radio newscaster, world traveler.

Dorothy Thompson, 1894-1961, foreign correspondent, columnist, radio commentator.

Hunter S. Thompson, 1937-2005, political journalist, author *Fear and Loathing* on the Campaign Trail (1972).

Kenneth Thompson, 1923-2006, Canadian media magnate; owned Toronto *Globe and Mail* newspaper.

Ida Bell Wells-Barnett, 1862-1931, African American reporter, editor, anti-lynching crusader.

William Allen White, 1868-1944, newspaper editor, publisher.

Walter Winchell, 1897-1972, reporter, columnist, broadcaster of celebrity news.

John Peter Zenger, 1697-1746, printer and journalist; acquitted in precedent-setting libel suit (1735).

Military and Naval Leaders of the Past
Reviewed by Alan C. Aimone, USMA Library

Alexander the Great, 356-323 BCE, (Maced.) conquered Persia and much of the world known to Europeans.

Harold Alexander, 1891-1969, (Br.) led Allied invasion of Italy, 1943, WW2.

Ethan Allen, 1738-89, (U.S.) headed Green Mountain Boys; captured Ft. Ticonderoga, 1775, Amer. Rev.

Edmund Allenby, 1861-1936, (Br.) in Boer War, WW1; led Egyptian expeditionary force, 1917-18.

Benedict Arnold, 1741-1801, (U.S.) victorious at Saratoga; tried to betray West Point to British, Amer. Rev.

Henry "Hap" Arnold, 1886-1950, (U.S.) commanded Army Air Force in WW2.

Ashurnasirpal II, 884-859 BCE, (Assyria) king, began Assyrian conquest of Middle East.

John Barry, 1745-1803, (U.S.) won numerous sea battles during Amer. Rev.

Belisarius, c505-565, (Byzant.) won remarkable victories for Byzantine Emperor Justinian I.

Pierre Beauregard, 1818-93, (U.S.) Confed. general, ordered bombardment of Ft. Sumter that began Civil War.

Gebhard von Blücher, 1742-1819, (Ger.) helped defeat Napoleon at Waterloo.

Simón Bolívar, 1783-1830, (Venez.) S. Amer. Revolutionary who liberated much of the continent from Spanish rule.

Napoleon Bonaparte, 1769-1821, (Fr.) defeated Russia and Austria at Austerlitz, 1805; invaded Russia, 1812; defeated at Waterloo, 1815.

Edward Braddock, 1695-1755, (Br.) commanded forces in French and Indian War.

Omar N. Bradley, 1893-1981, (U.S.) headed U.S. ground troops in Normandy invasion, 1944, WW2.

John Burgoyne, 1722-92, (Br.) general, defeated at Saratoga, Amer. Rev.

Julius Caesar, 100-44 BCE, (Rom.) general and politician; conquered northern Gaul; overthrew Roman Republic.

Charlemagne, 742-814, (Fr.) king of the Franks, Holy Roman Emperor, conqured most of Western Europe.

El Cid (Rodrigo Diaz de Vivar), 1040-99, (Sp.) renowned knight, captured Valencia (1094); hero of "Song of Cid" epic.

Claire Lee Chennault, 1893-1958, (U.S.) headed Flying Tigers in WW2.

Mark W. Clark, 1896-1984, (U.S.) helped plan N. African invasion in WW2; commander of UN forces, Korean War.

Karl von Clausewitz, 1780-1831, (Pruss.) military theorist.

Lucius D. Clay, 1897-1978, (U.S.) led Berlin airlift, 1948-49.

Henry Clinton, 1738-95, (Br.) commander of forces in Amer. Rev., 1778-81.

Cochise, c1815-74, (Nat. Am.) chief of Chiricahua band of Apache Indians in Southwest.

Charles Cornwallis, 1738-1805, (Br.) victorious at Brandywine, 1777; surrendered at Yorktown, Amer. Rev.

Hernán Cortés, 1485-1547, (Sp.) led Spanish conquistadors in the defeat of the Aztec empire, 1519-28.

Crazy Horse, 1849-77, (Nat. Am.) Sioux war chief victorious at battle of Little Bighorn.

George Armstrong Custer, 1839-76, (U.S.) U.S. army officer defeated and killed at battle of Little Bighorn.

Moshe Dayan, 1915-81, (Isr.) directed campaigns in the 1967, 1973 Arab-Israeli wars.

Benjamin O. Davis Jr., 1912-2002, leader of World War II black aviators, first African American general in U.S. Air Force.

Benjamin O. Davis Sr., 1877-1970, first African American general, 1940, in U.S. Army.

Stephen Decatur, 1779-1820, (U.S.) naval hero of Barbary wars, War of 1812.

Anton Denikin, 1872-1947, (Russ.) led White forces in Russian civil war.

George Dewey, 1837-1917, (U.S.) destroyed Spanish fleet at Manila, 1898, Span.-Amer. War.

Karl Doenitz, 1891-1980, (Ger.) submarine com. in chief and naval commander, WW2.

Jimmy Doolittle, 1896-1993, (U.S.) led 1942 air raid on Tokyo and other Japanese cities in WW2.

Hugh C. Dowding, 1883-1970, (Br.) headed RAF, 1936-40, WW2.

Jubal Early, 1816-94, (U.S.) Confed. general, led raid on Washington, 1864, Civil War.

Dwight D. Eisenhower, 1890-1969, (U.S.) commanded Allied forces in Europe, WW2.

Erich von Falkenhayn, 1861-1922, (Ger.) minister of war, general, commander at Verdun in WW1.

David Farragut, 1801-70, (U.S.) Union admiral, captured New Orleans, Mobile Bay, Civil War.

John Arbuthnot Fisher, 1841-1920, (Br.) WW1 admiral, naval reformer.

Ferdinand Foch, 1851-1929, (Fr.) headed victorious Allied armies, 1918, WW1.

Nathan Bedford Forrest, 1821-77, (U.S.) Confed. general, led raids against Union supply lines, Civil War.

Frederick the Great, 1712-86, (Pruss.) led Prussia in Seven Years War.

Horatio Gates, 1728-1806, (U.S.) commanded army at Saratoga, Amer. Rev.

Daniel James Jr., 1920-78, first black 4-star general, 1975; commander, North American Air Defense Command.

Genghis Khan, 1162-1227, (Mongol) unified Mongol tribes and subjugated much of Asia, 1206-21.

Geronimo, 1829-1909, (Nat. Am.) leader of Chiricahua band of Apache Indians.

Charles G. Gordon, 1833-85, (Br.) led forces in China, Crimean War; killed at Khartoum.

Ulysses S. Grant, 1822-85, (U.S.) headed Union army, Civil War, 1864-65; forced Lee's surrender, 1865.

Nathanael Greene, 1742-86, (U.S.) defeated British in Southern campaign, 1780-81, Amer. Rev.

Heinz Guderian, 1888-1953, (Ger.) tank theorist, led panzer forces in Poland, France, Russia, WW2.

Gustavus Adolphus, 1594-1632, (Swed.) King; military tactician; reformer; led forces in Thirty Years' War.

Douglas Haig, 1861-1928, (Br.) led British armies in France, 1915-18, WW1.

William F. Halsey, 1882-1959, (U.S.) defeated Japanese fleet at Leyte Gulf, 1944, WW2.

Hannibal, 247-183 BCE, (Carthage) invaded Rome, crossing Alps, in Second Punic War, 218-201 BCE

Sir Arthur Travers Harris, 1895-1984, (Br.) led Britain's WW2 bomber command.

Paul von Hindenburg, 1847-1934, (Ger.) chief of general staff, WW1; 2nd pres. of Weimar Republic.

Richard Howe, 1726-99, (Br.) commanded navy in Amer. Rev., 1776-78; June 1 victory against French, 1794.

William Howe, 1729-1814, (Br.) commanded forces in Amer. Rev., 1776-78.

Isaac Hull, 1773-1843, (U.S.) sunk British frigate *Guerriere,* War of 1812.

Thomas (Stonewall) Jackson, 1824-63, (U.S.) Confed. general, led Shenandoah Valley campaign, Civil War.

Joseph Joffre, 1852-1931, (Fr.) headed Allied armies, won Battle of the Marne, 1914, WW1.

Chief Joseph, c1840-1904, (Nat. Am.) chief of the Nez Percé, forced by army to retreat and surrender.

John Paul Jones, 1747-92, (U.S.) commanded *Bonhomme Richard* in victory over *Serapis,* Amer. Rev., 1779.

Stephen Kearny, 1794-1848, (U.S.) headed Army of the West in Mexican War.

Albert Kesselring, 1885-1960 (Ger.) field marshal who led the defense of Italy in WW2.

Ernest J. King, 1878-1956, (U.S.) key WW2 naval strategist.

Horatio H. Kitchener, 1850-1916, (Br.) led forces in Boer War; victorious at Khartoum; organized army in WW1.

Henry Knox, 1750-1806, (U.S.) general in Amer. Rev.; first sec. of war under U.S. Constitution.

Lavrenti Kornilov, 1870-1918, (Russ.) commander-in-chief, 1917; led counter-revolutionary march on Petrograd.

Thaddeus Kosciusko, 1746-1817, (Pol.) aided Amer. Rev.

Walter Krueger, 1881-1967, (U.S.) led Sixth Army in WW2 in Southwest Pacific.

Mikhail Kutuzov, 1745-1813, (Russ.) fought at Borodino, Napol. Wars, 1812; abandoned Moscow; forced French retreat.

Marquis de Lafayette, 1757-1834, (Fr.) fought in, secured French aid for Amer. Rev.

T(homas) E. Lawrence (of Arabia), 1888-1935, (Br.) organized revolt of Arabs against Turks in WW1.

William Daniel Leahy, 1875-1959, (U.S.) chief of staff to Pres. Roosevelt in WWII, Fleet Admiral.

Henry (Light-Horse Harry) Lee, 1756-1818, (U.S.) cavalry officer in Amer. Rev.

Robert E. Lee, 1807-70, (U.S.) Confed. general defeated at Gettysburg, Civil War; surrendered to Grant, 1865.

Curtis LeMay, 1906-90, (U.S.) Air Force commander in WW2, Korean War, and Vietnam War.

Lyman Lemnitzer, 1899-1988, (U.S.) WW2 hero, later general, chairman of Joint Chiefs of Staff.

James Longstreet, 1821-1904, (U.S.) aided Lee at Gettysburg, Civil War.

Erich Ludendorff, 1865-1937, (Ger.) general, victor at Tannenberg, WW1.

Maurice, Count of Nassau, 1567-1625, (Dutch) military innovator; led forces in Thirty Years' War.

Douglas MacArthur, 1880-1964, (U.S.) commanded forces in SW Pacific in WW2; headed occupation forces in Japan, 1945-51; UN commander in Korean War.

Erich von Manstein, 1887-1973, (Ger.) served WW1–2, planned inv. of France (1940), convicted of war crimes.

Carl Gustaf Mannerheim, 1867-1951, (Finn.) army officer and pres. of Finland 1944-46.

Francis Marion, 1733-95, (U.S.) led guerrilla actions in South Carolina during Amer. Rev.

Duke of Marlborough, 1650-1722, (Br.) led forces against Louis XIV in War of the Spanish Succession.

George C. Marshall, 1880-1959, (U.S.) chief of staff in WW2; authored Marshall Plan.

George B. McClellan, 1826-85, (U.S.) Union general, commanded Army of the Potomac, 1861-62, Civil War.

George Meade, 1815-72, (U.S.) commanded Union forces at Gettysburg, Civil War.

Dorie Miller, 1919-43, Navy hero of Pearl Harbor attack.

Billy Mitchell, 1879-1936, (U.S.) WW1 air-power advocate; court-martialed for insubordination, later vindicated.

Helmuth von Moltke, 1800-91, (Ger.) victorious in Austro-Prussian, Franco-Prussian wars.

Louis de Montcalm, 1712-59, (Fr.) headed troops in Canada, French and Indian War; defeated at Quebec, 1759.

Bernard Law Montgomery, 1887-1976, (Br.) stopped German offensive at Alamein, 1942, WW2; helped plan Normandy.

Daniel Morgan, 1736-1802, (U.S.) victorious at Cowpens, 1781, Amer. Rev.

Louis Mountbatten, 1900-79, (Br.) Supreme Allied Commander of SE Asia, 1943-46, WW2.

Joachim Murat, 1767-1815, (Fr.) led cavalry at Marengo, Austerlitz, and Jena, Napoleonic Wars.

Horatio Nelson, 1758-1805, (Br.) naval commander, destroyed French fleet at Trafalgar.

Michel Ney, 1769-1815, (Fr.) commanded forces in Switz., Aust., Russ., Napoleonic Wars; defeated at Waterloo.

Chester Nimitz, 1885-1966, (U.S.) commander of naval forces in Pacific in WW2.

George S. Patton, 1885-1945, (U.S.) led assault on Sicily, 1943, Third Army invasion of Europe, WW2.

Oliver Perry, 1785-1819, (U.S.) won Battle of Lake Erie in War of 1812.

John Pershing, 1860-1948, (U.S.) commanded Mexican border campaign, 1916, Amer. Expeditionary Force, WW1.

Henri Philippe Pétain, 1856-1951, (Fr.) defended Verdun, 1916; headed Vichy government in WW2.

George E. Pickett, 1825-75, (U.S.) Confed. general famed for "charge" at Gettysburg, Civil War.

Charles Portal, 1893-1971, (Br.) chief of staff, Royal Air Force, 1940-45, led in Battle of Britain.

Manfred Frieherr von Richthofen (Red Baron), 1892-1918, (Ger.) WW1 flying ace, led elite fighter squadron.

Hyman Rickover, 1900-86, (U.S.) father of nuclear navy.

Matthew Bunker Ridgway, 1895-1993, (U.S.) commanded Allied ground forces in Korean War.

Erwin Rommel, 1891-1944, (Ger.) headed Afrika Korps, WW2.

Gerd von Rundstedt, 1875-1953, (Ger.) supreme commander in West, 1942-45, WW2.

Saladin, 1138-93, (Kurdish Muslim) recaptured Jerusalem from Crusaders.

Aleksandr Samsonov, 1859-1914, (Russ.) led invasion of E Prussia, WW1, defeated at Tannenberg, 1914.

Antonio Lopez de Santa Anna, 1794-1876, (Mex.) defeated Texans at the Alamo; defeated in Mexican War.

Maurice, Count of Saxe, 1696-1750, (Fr.) general, War of Aust. Succession, War of Pol. Succession; noted tactician.

Scipio Africanus the Elder, 234?-183, (Rom.) hero of 2nd Punic War, defeated Hannibal, invaded N. Africa.

Winfield Scott, 1786-1866, (U.S.) hero of War of 1812; headed forces in Mexican War, took Mexico City.

Philip Sheridan, 1831-88, (U.S.) Union cavalry officer, headed Army of the Shenandoah, 1864-65, Civil War.

William T. Sherman, 1820-91, (U.S.) Union general, sacked Atlanta during "march to the sea," 1864, Civil War.

Carl Spaatz, 1891-1974, (U.S.) directed strategic bombing against Germany, later Japan, in WW2.

Raymond Spruance, 1886-1969, (U.S.) victorious at Midway Island, 1942, WW2.

Joseph W. Stilwell, 1883-1946, (U.S.) headed forces in the China, Burma, India theater in WW2.

J.E.B. Stuart, 1833-64, (U.S.) Confed. cavalry commander, Civil War.

Sun Tzu, 6th? cent. BCE, (Chin.) general, author of *The Art of War.*

Aleksandr Suvorov, 1729-1800, (Rus.) commanded Allied Russian and Austrian armies, Russo-Turkish War.

Tamerlane, 1336-1405, (Turkoman Mongol) conqueror, established empire from India to Mediterranean Sea.

George H. Thomas, 1816-70, (U.S.) saved Union army at Chattanooga, 1863; won at Nashville, 1864, Civil War.

Semyon Timoshenko, 1895-1970, (USSR) defended Moscow, Stalingrad, WW2; led winter offensive, 1942-43.

Alfred von Tirpitz, 1849-1930, (Ger.) responsible for submarine blockade in WW1.

Henri de la Tour d'Auvergne, Viscount of Turenne, 1611-75, (Fr.) marshal, Thirty Years' War, Fronde, War of Devolution.

Sebastien Le Prestre de Vauban, 1633-1707, (Fr.) innovative military engineer and theorist.

Jonathan M. Wainwright, 1883-1953, (U.S.) forced to surrender on Corregidor, 1942, WW2.

George Washington, 1732-99, (U.S.) led Continental army, 1775-83, Amer. Rev.

Archibald Wavell, 1883-1950, (Br.) commanded forces in N and E Africa, and SE Asia in WW2.

Anthony Wayne, 1745-96, (U.S.) captured Stony Point, 1779, Amer. Rev.

Duke of Wellington, 1769-1852, (Br.) defeated Napoleon at Waterloo, 1815.

William Westmoreland, 1914-2005, (U.S.) commanded forces in Vietnam 1964-68.

William I (The Conqueror), 1027-87, (Br.) victor Battle of Hastings 1066, became first Norman king of England.

James Wolfe, 1727-59, (Br.) captured Quebec from French, 1759, French and Indian War.

Isoroku Yamamoto, 1884-1943, (Jpn.) com. in chief of Japanese fleet and naval planner before and during WW2.

Georgi Zhukov, 1895-1974, (Russ.) defended Moscow, 1941, led assault on Berlin, 1945, WW2.

Philosophers and Religious Figures of the Past

Excludes most biblical figures and popes (see Religion). For Greeks and Romans, see also Historical Figures chapter.

Lyman Abbott, 1835-1922, (U.S.) clergyman, reformer; advocate of Christian Socialism.

Pierre Abelard, 1079-1142, (Fr.) philosopher, theologian, teacher; used dialectic method to support Christian beliefs.

Mortimer Adler, 1902-2001, (U.S.) philosopher, helped create "Great Books" program.

Felix Adler, 1851-1933, (U.S.) German-born founder of the Ethical Culture Society.

(St.) Anselm, c1033-1109, (It.) philosopher-theologian, church leader; "ontological argument" for God's existence.

(St.) Thomas Aquinas, 1225-74, (It.) preeminent medieval philosopher-theologian; *Summa Theologica.*

Aristotle, 384-322 BCE, (Gr.) pioneering wide-ranging philosopher, logician, ethician, naturalist.

(St.) Augustine, 354-430, (N Africa) philosopher, theologian, bishop; *Confessions, City of God, On the Trinity.*

J. L. Austin, 1911-60, (Br.) ordinary-language philosopher.

Averroes (Ibn Rushd), 1126-98, (Sp.) Islamic philosopher, physician.

Avicenna (Ibn Sina), 980-1037, (Iran.) Islamic philosopher, scientist.

A(lfred) J(ules) Ayer, 1910-89, (Br.) philosopher; logical positivist; *Language, Truth, and Logic.*

Roger Bacon, c1214-94, (Eng.) philosopher and scientist.

Bahaullah (Mirza Husayn Ali), 1817-92, (Pers.) founder of Bahá'í faith.

Karl Barth, 1886-1968, (Swiss) theologian; a leading force in 20th-cent. Protestantism.

Thomas à Becket, 1118-70, (Eng.) archbishop of Canterbury; opposed Henry II; murdered by King's men.

(St.) Benedict, c480-547, (It.) founded the Benedictines.

Jeremy Bentham, 1748-1832, (Br.) philosopher, reformer; enunciated utilitarianism.

Henri Bergson, 1859-1941, (Fr.) philosopher of evolution.

George Berkeley, 1685-1753, (Ir.) idealist philosopher, bishop.

John Biddle, 1615-62, (Eng.) founder of English Unitarianism.

Jakob Boehme, 1575-1624, (Ger.) theosophist and mystic.

Dietrich Bonhoeffer, 1906-1945 (Ger.) Lutheran theologian, pastor; executed as opponent of Nazis.

William Brewster, 1567-1644, (Eng.) headed Pilgrims.

Emil Brunner, 1889-1966, (Swiss) Protestant theologian.

Giordano Bruno, 1548-1600, (It.) philosopher, pantheist.

Martin Buber, 1878-1965, (Ger.) Jewish philosopher, theologian; *I and Thou.*

Buddha (Siddhartha Gautama), c563-c483 BCE, (Indian) philosopher; founded Buddhism.

John Calvin, 1509-64, (Fr.) theologian; a key figure in the Protestant Reformation.

Rudolph Carnap, 1891-1970, (U.S.) German-born analytic philosopher; a founder of logical positivism.

William Ellery Channing, 1780-1842, (U.S.) clergyman; early spokesman for Unitarianism.

Auguste Comte, 1798-1857, (Fr.) philosopher; originated positivism.

Confucius, 551-479 BCE, (Chin.) founder of Confucianism.

John Cotton, 1584-1652, (Eng.) Puritan theologian.

Thomas Cranmer, 1489-1556, (Eng.) Anglican churchman; wrote much of *Book of Common Prayer.*

Jacques Derrida, 1930-2004 (Fr.), deconstructionist philosopher.

René Descartes, 1596-1650, (Fr.) philosopher, mathematician; "father of modern philosophy." *Discourse on Method, Meditations on First Philosophy.*

John Dewey, 1859-1952, (U.S.) philosopher, educator; instrumentalist theory of knowledge; progressive education.

Denis Diderot, 1713-84, (Fr.) philosopher, encyclopedist.

John Duns Scotus, c1266-1308, (Sc.) Franciscan philosopher and theologian.

Mary Baker Eddy, 1821-1910, (U.S.) founder of Christian Science; *Science and Health.*

Jonathan Edwards, 1703-58, (U.S.) preacher, theologian; "Sinners in the Hands of an Angry God."

(Desiderius) Erasmus, c1466-1536, (Dutch) Renaissance humanist; *On the Freedom of the Will.*

Johann Fichte, 1762-1814, (Ger.) idealist philosopher.

Michel Foucault, 1926-84, (Fr.) structuralist philosopher, historian.

George Fox, 1624-91, (Br.) founder of Society of Friends.

(St.) Francis of Assisi, 1182-1226, (It.) espoused voluntary poverty; founded Franciscans.

al-Ghazali, 1058-1111, Islamic philosopher.

Billy James Hargis, 1925-2004, (U.S.) anti-Communist televangelist; founder of the Church of the Christian Crusade.

Georg W. F. Hegel, 1770-1831, (Ger.) idealist philosopher; *Phenomenology of Mind.*

Martin Heidegger, 1889-1976, (Ger.) existentialist philosopher; affected many fields; *Being and Time.*

Johann G. Herder, 1744-1803, (Ger.) philosopher, cultural historian; a founder of German Romanticism.

Thomas Hobbes, 1588-1679, (Eng.) philosopher, political theorist; *Leviathan.*

David Hume, 1711-76, (Sc.) empiricist philosopher; *Enquiry Concerning Human Understanding.*

Jan Hus, 1369-1415, (Czech.) religious reformer.

Edmund Husserl, 1859-1938, (Ger.) philosopher; founded the phenomenological movement.

Thomas Huxley, 1825-95, (Br.) philosopher, educator.

William Inge, 1860-1954, (Br.) theologian; explored mystic aspects of Christianity.

William James, 1842-1910, (U.S.) philosopher, psychologist; pragmatist; studied religious experience.

Karl Jaspers, 1883-1969, (Ger.) existentialist philosopher.

Joan of Arc, 1412-1431, (Fr.) national heroine and a patron saint of France; key figure in the Hundred Years' War.

Immanuel Kant, 1724-1804, (Ger.) philosopher; founder of modern critical philosophy; *Critique of Pure Reason.*

Thomas à Kempis, c1380-1471, (Ger.) monk, devotional writer; *Imitation of Christ* attributed to him.

Soren Kierkegaard, 1813-55, (Dan.) religious philosopher; pre-existentialist; *Either/Or, The Sickness Unto Death.*

John Knox, 1505-72, (Sc.) leader of the Protestant Reformation in Scotland.

Lao-Tzu, 604-531 BCE, (Chin.) philosopher; considered the founder of the Taoist religion.

Gottfried von Leibniz, 1646-1716, (Ger.) rationalistic philosopher, logician, mathematician.

John Locke, 1632-1704, (Eng.) political theorist, empiricist philosopher; *Essay Concerning Human Understanding.*

(St.) Ignatius Loyola, 1491-1556, (Sp.) founder of the Jesuits; *Spiritual Exercises.*

Martin Luther, 1483-1546, (Ger.) leader of the Protestant Reformation, founded Lutheran church.

Jean-Francois Lyotard, 1924-98, (Fr.) postmodern philosopher, lecturer; *The Post-Modern Condition.*

Maimonides, 1135-1204, (Sp.) major Jewish philosopher.

Gabriel Marcel, 1889-1973, (Fr.) Rom. Cath. existentialist philosopher, dramatist,

Jacques Maritain, 1882-1973, (Fr.) Neo-Thomist philosopher.

Cotton Mather, 1663-1728, (U.S.) defender of orthodox Puritanism; founded Yale, 1701.

Philipp Melanchthon, 1497-1560, (Ger.) theologian, humanist; an important voice in the Reformation.

Maurice Merleau-Ponty, 1908-61, (Fr.) existentialist philosopher; *Phenomenology of Perception.*

Thomas Merton, 1915-68, (U.S.) Trappist monk, spiritual writer; *The Seven Storey Mountain.*

Dwight Moody, 1837-99, (U.S.) evangelist.

G(eorge) E(dward) Moore, 1873-1958, (Br.) philosopher; *Principia Ethica,* "A Defense of Common Sense."

Muhammad, c570-632, (Arab) the prophet of Islam.

Elijah Muhammad, 1897-1975, (U.S.) Black Muslim sect leader.

Heinrich Muhlenberg, 1711-87, (Ger.) organized the Lutheran Church in America.

John H. Newman, 1801-90, (Br.) Rom. Cath. convert, cardinal; led Oxford Movement; *Apologia pro Vita Sua.*

Reinhold Niebuhr, 1892-1971, (U.S.) Protestant theologian.

Richard Niebuhr, 1894-1962 (U.S.) Protestant theologian.

Friedrich Nietzsche, 1844-1900, (Ger.) philosopher; *The Birth of Tragedy, Beyond Good and Evil, Thus Spake Zarathustra.*

Robert Nozick, 1938-2002, (U.S.) political philosopher; *Anarchy, State, and Utopia.*

Blaise Pascal, 1623-62, (Fr.) philosopher, mathematician; *Pensées.*

(St.) Patrick, c389-c461, (Br.) brought Christianity to Ireland.

Norman Vincent Peale, 1898-1993, (U.S.) minister, author; *The Power of Positive Thinking.*

C(harles) S. Peirce, 1839-1914, (U.S.) philosopher, logician; originated concept of pragmatism, 1878.

Plato, c428-347 BCE, (Gr.) philosopher; wrote Socratic dialogues; argued for immortality of soul, indep. reality of ideas or forms; *Republic, Meno, Phaedo, Apology.*

Plotinus, 205-70, (Rom.) a founder of neo-Platonism; *Enneads.*

W(illard) V(an) O(rman) Quine, 1908-2001, (U.S.) philosopher, logician; "On What There Is."

John Rawls, 1922-2002, (U.S.) political philosopher; *A Theory of Justice* (1971).

Josiah Royce, 1855-1916, (U.S.) idealist philosopher

Bertrand Russell, 1872-1970, (Br.) philosopher, logician; one of the founders of modern logic; a prolific popular writer.

Charles T. Russell, 1852-1916, (U.S.) founder of Jehovah's Witnesses.

Gilbert Ryle, 1900-76, (Br.) analytic philosopher; *The Concept of Mind.*

George Santayana, 1863-1952, (U.S.) philosopher, writer, critic; *The Sense of Beauty, The Realms of Being.*

Jean-Paul Sartre, 1905-80, (Fr.) philosopher, novelist, playwright. *Nausea, No Exit, Being and Nothingness.*

Friedrich von Schelling, 1775-1854, (Ger.) philosopher of romantic movement.

Friedrich Schleiermacher, 1768-1834, (Ger.) theologian; a founder of modern Protestant theology.

Arthur Schopenhauer, 1788-1860, (Ger.) philosopher; *The World as Will and Idea.*

Albert Schweitzer, 1875-1965, (Ger.) theologian, social philosopher, medical missionary.

Joseph Smith, 1805-44, (U.S.) founded Latter-Day Saints (Mormon) movement, 1830.

Socrates, 469-399 BCE, (Gr.) philosopher immortalized by Plato.

Herbert Spencer, 1820-1903, (Br.) philosopher of evolution.

Baruch de Spinoza, 1632-77, (Dutch) rationalist philosopher; *Ethics.*

Billy Sunday, 1862-1935, (U.S.) evangelist.

Emanuel Swedenborg, 1688-1772, (Swed.) philosopher, mystic; *Principia.*

Pierre Teilhard de Chardin, 1881-1955, (Fr.) Jesuit priest, paleontologist, philosopher-theologian; *The Divine Milieu.*

Daisetz Teitaro Suzuki, 1870-1966, (Jpn.) Buddhist scholar.

(St.) Therese of Lisieux, 1873-97, (Fr.) Carmelite nun ("Little Flower"), revered for everyday sanctity; *The Story of a Soul.*

Paul Tillich, 1886-1965, (U.S.) German-born philosopher and theologian; brought depth psychology to Protestantism.

John Wesley, 1703-91, (Br.) theologian, evangelist; founded Methodism.

Alfred North Whitehead, 1861-1947, (Br.) philosopher, mathematician; *Process and Reality.*

William of Occam, c1285-c1349 (Eng.) medieval scholastic philosopher; nominalist.

Roger Williams, c1603-83, (U.S.) clergyman; championed religious freedom and separation of church and state.

Ludwig Wittgenstein, 1889-1951, (Austrian) philosopher; major influence on contemporary language philosophy; *Tractatus Logico-Philosophicus, Philosophical Investigations.*

John Woolman, 1720-72, (U.S.) Quaker social reformer, abolitionist, writer; *The Journal.*

John Wycliffe, 1320-84, (Eng.) theologian, reformer.

(St.) Francis Xavier, 1506-52, (Sp.) Jesuit missionary, "Apostle of the Indies."

Brigham Young, 1801-77, (U.S.) Mormon leader after Smith's assassination; colonized Utah.

Huldrych Zwingli, 1484-1531, (Swiss) theologian; led Swiss Protestant Reformation.

Political Leaders of the Past

(U.S. presidents, vice presidents, Supreme Ct. justices, signers of Decl. of Indep. listed elsewhere.)

Abu Bakr, 573-634, Muslim leader, first caliph, chosen successor to Muhammad.

Dean Acheson, 1893-1971, (U.S.) sec. of state; architect of cold war foreign policy.

Samuel Adams, 1722-1803, (U.S.) patriot, Boston Tea Party firebrand.

Konrad Adenauer, 1876-1967, (Ger.) first West German chancellor.

Emilio Aguinaldo, 1869-1964, (Philip.) revolutionary; fought against Spain and the U.S.

Akbar, 1542-1605, greatest Mogul emperor of India.

Carl Albert, 1908-2000 (U.S.) House rep. from OK, Speaker, 1971-76.

Salvador Allende Gossens, 1908-1973, (Chilean) Marxist pres. 1970-73; ousted and died in coup.

Idi Amin, 1925-2003 (Uganda), Ugandan ruler from 1971 to 1979, blamed for hundreds of thousands of deaths.

Hafez al Assad, 1930-2000 (Syr.), Syrian ruler from 1970.

Herbert H. Asquith, 1852-1928, (Br.) liberal prime min.; instituted major social reform.

Atahualpa, ?-1533, Inca (ruling chief) of Peru.

Kemal Ataturk, 1881-1938, (Turk.) founded modern Turkey.

Clement Attlee, 1883-1967, (Br.) Labour party leader, prime min.; enacted natl. health, nationalized many industries.

Stephen F. Austin, 1793-1836, (U.S.) led Texas colonization.

Mikhail Bakunin, 1814-76, (Rus.) revolutionary; leading exponent of anarchism.

Arthur J. Balfour, 1848-1930, (Br.) foreign sec. under Lloyd George; issued Balfour Declaration backing Zionism.

Bernard M. Baruch, 1870-1965, (U.S.) financier, govt. adviser.

Fulgencio Batista y Zaldívar, 1901-73, (Cub.) Cuban pres. (1940-44, 1952-59), overthrown by Castro.

Lord Beaverbrook, 1879-1964, (Br.) financier, statesman, newspaper owner.

Menachem Begin, 1913-92, (Isr.) Israeli prime min., shared 1978 Nobel Peace Prize.

Eduard Benes, 1884-1948, (Czech.) pres. during interwar and post-WW2 eras.

David Ben-Gurion, 1886-1973, (Isr.) first prime min. of Israel, 1948-53, 1955-63.

Thomas Hart Benton, 1782-1858, (U.S.) Missouri senator; championed agrarian interests and westward expansion.

Lloyd Bentsen, 1921-2006 (U.S.), former senator, treasury sec., vice-pres. nominee.

Aneurin Bevan, 1897-1960, (Br.) Labour party leader.

Ernest Bevin, 1881-1951, (Br.) Labour party leader, foreign minister; helped lay foundation for NATO.

Otto von Bismarck, 1815-98, (Ger.) statesman known as the Iron Chancellor; uniter of Germany, 1870.

James G. Blaine, 1830-93, (U.S.) Republican politician, diplomat; influential in Pan-American movement.

Léon Blum, 1872-1950, (Fr.) socialist leader, writer; headed first Popular Front government.

William E. Borah, 1865-1940, (U.S.) isolationist senator; helped block U.S. membership in League of Nations.

Cesare Borgia, 1476-1507, (It.) soldier, politician; an outstanding figure of the Italian Renaissance.

Tom Bradley, 1917-98, (U.S.) first African American LA mayor.

Willy Brandt, 1913-92, (Ger.) statesman, chancellor of West Germany, 1969-74; promoted East/West peace, *Ostpolitik.*

Leonid Brezhnev, 1906-82, (USSR) Soviet leader, 1964-82.

Aristide Briand, 1862-1932, (Fr.) foreign min.; chief architect of Locarno Pact and anti-war Kellogg-Briand Pact.

William Jennings Bryan, 1860-1925, (U.S.) Democratic, populist leader, orator; 3 times lost race for presidency.

Ralph Bunche, 1904-71, (U.S.) first black person to win the Nobel Peace Prize, 1950; undersecretary of the UN, 1950.

John C. Calhoun, 1782-1850, (U.S.) political leader; champion of states' rights and a symbol of the Old South.

James Callaghan (Baron Callaghan), 1912-2005 (Br.) Labour Party politican, prime min. 1976-79.

Robert Castlereagh, 1769-1822, (Br.) foreign sec.; guided Grand Alliance against Napoleon.

Camillo Benso Cavour, 1810-61, (It.) statesman; largely responsible for uniting Italy under the House of Savoy.

Nicolae Ceausescu, 1918-89, (Roman.) Communist leader, head of state 1967-89; executed.

Austen Chamberlain, 1863-1937, (Br.) statesman; helped finalize Locarno Treaties, both 1925.

Neville Chamberlain, 1869-1940, (Br.) Conservative prime min. whose appeasement of Hitler led to Munich Pact.

Chiang Kai-shek, 1887-1975, (Chin.) Nationalist Chinese pres. whose government was driven from mainland to Taiwan.

Chiang Kai-shek, Madame, 1898-2003, (Chin.) highly influential wife of Nationalist Chinese leader Chiang Kai-shek.

Shirley Chisholm, 1924-2005, first black woman elected to U.S. House (1968); pres. contender, 1972.

Winston Churchill, 1874-1965, (Br.) prime min., soldier, author; guided Britain through WW2.

Galeazzo Ciano, 1903-44, (It.) fascist foreign minister; helped create Rome-Berlin Axis, executed by Mussolini.

Henry Clay, 1777-1852, (U.S.) "The Great Compromiser," one of the most influential pre-Civil War political leaders.

Georges Clemenceau, 1841-1929, (Fr.) twice prem., Wilson's antagonist at Paris Peace Conference after WW1.

DeWitt Clinton, 1769-1828, (U.S.) political leader; responsible for promoting the Erie Canal.

Robert Clive, 1725-74, (Br.) first administrator of Bengal; laid foundation for British Empire in India.

Jean Baptiste Colbert, 1619-83, (Fr.) statesman; influential under Louis XIV, created the French navy.

Bettino Craxi, 1934-2000, (It.) Italy's first post-WWII Socialist premier.

David Crockett, 1786-1836, (U.S.) frontiersman, congressman, died defending the Alamo.

Oliver Cromwell, 1599-1658, (Br.) Lord Protector of England, led parliamentary forces during Civil War.

Curzon of Kedleston, 1859-1925, (Br.) viceroy of India, foreign sec.; major force in post-WW1 world.

Édouard Daladier, 1884-1970, (Fr.) Radical Socialist politician, arrested by Vichy, interned by Germans until 1945.

Richard J. Daley, 1902-1976, (U.S.) Chicago mayor.

Georges Danton, 1759-94, (Fr.) leading French Rev. figure.

Jefferson Davis, 1808-89, (U.S.) pres. of the Confederacy.

Charles G. Dawes, 1865-1951, (U.S.) statesman, banker; advanced plan to stabilize post-WW1 German finances.

William L. Dawson, 1886-1970, Illinois congressman, first black chairman of a major U.S. House committee.

Alcide De Gasperi, 1881-1954, (It.) prime min.; founder of Christian Democratic party.

Charles De Gaulle, 1890-1970, (Fr.) general, statesman; first pres. of the Fifth Republic.

Deng Xiaoping, 1904-97, (Chin.) "paramount leader" of China; backed economic modernization.

Eamon De Valera, 1882-1975, (Ir.-U.S.) statesman; led fight for Irish independence.

Thomas E. Dewey, 1902-71, (U.S.) NY governor; twice loser in try for presidency.

Ngo Dinh Diem, 1901-63, (Viet.) South Vietnamese pres.; assassinated in government takeover.

Everett M. Dirksen, 1896-1969, (U.S.) Senate Republican minority leader, orator.

Benjamin Disraeli, 1804-81, (Br.) prime min.; considered founder of modern Conservative party.

Engelbert Dollfuss, 1892-1934, (Austrian) chancellor; assassinated by Austrian Nazis.

Andrea Doria, 1466-1560, (It.) Genoese admiral, statesman; called "Father of Peace" and "Liberator of Genoa."

Stephen A. Douglas, 1813-61, (U.S.) Democratic leader, orator; opposed Lincoln for the presidency.

Alexander Dubcek, 1921-92, (Czech.) statesman whose attempted liberalization was crushed, 1968.

John Foster Dulles, 1888-1959, (U.S.) sec. of state under Eisenhower, cold war policy-maker.

Abba Eban, 1915-2002, (Isr.) diplomat, foreign min. 1966-74.

Friedrich Ebert, 1871-1925, (Ger.) Social Democratic movement leader; 1st pres., Weimar Republic, 1919-25.

Sir Anthony Eden, 1897-1977, (Br.) foreign sec., prime min. during Suez invasion of 1956.

Ludwig Erhard, 1897-1977, (Ger.) economist, West German chancellor; led nation's economic rise after WW2.

King Fahid, 1921-2005, (Saudi Arab.) monarch since 1982, but inactive since 1995 stroke; encouraged U.S. relations.

Joao Baptista de Figueiredo, 1918-99, (Braz.) president of Brazil, restored the nation's democracy.

Hamilton Fish, 1808-93, (U.S.) sec. of state, successfully mediated disputes with Great Britain, Latin America.

James V. Forrestal, 1892-1949, (U.S.) sec. of navy, first sec. of defense.

Francisco Franco, 1892-1975, (Sp.) leader of rebel forces during Spanish Civil War and longtime ruler of Spain.

Benjamin Franklin, 1706-90, (U.S.) printer, publisher, author, inventor, scientist, diplomat.

Louis de Frontenac, 1620-98, (Fr.) governor of New France (Canada); encouraged explorations, fought Iroquois.

J. William Fulbright, 1905-95, (U.S.) U.S. senator; leading figure in U.S. foreign policy during cold war years.

Hugh Gaitskell, 1906-63, (Br.) Labour party leader; major force in reversing its stand for unilateral disarmament.

Albert Gallatin, 1761-1849, (U.S.) sec. of treasury; instrumental in negotiating end of War of 1812.

Léon Gambetta, 1838-82, (Fr.) statesman, politician; one of the founders of the Third Republic.

Indira Gandhi, 1917-84, (In.) daughter of Jawaharlal Nehru, prime min. of India, 1966-77, 1980-84; assassinated.

Mohandas K. Gandhi, 1869-1948, (In.) political leader, ascetic; led movement against British rule; assassinated.

Giuseppe Garibaldi, 1807-82, (It.) patriot, soldier; a leader in the Risorgimento, Italian unification movement.

William E. Gladstone, 1809-98, (Br.) prime min. 4 times; dominant force of Liberal party from 1868 to 1894.

Paul Joseph Goebbels, 1897-1945, (Ger.) Nazi propagandist, master of mass psychology.

Barry Goldwater, 1909-98 (U.S.) conservative U.S. senator and 1964 Republican presid. nominee.

Klement Gottwald, 1896-1953, (Czech.) Communist leader; ushered Communism into his country.

Alexander Hamilton, 1755-1804, (U.S.) first treasury sec.; champion of strong central government.

Dag Hammarskjold, 1905-61, (Swed.) statesman; UN sec.-general.

Barbara Jordan, 1936-96, (U.S) congresswoman, orator, educator; first black woman to win a seat in the Texas senate, 1966.

Hassan II, King, 1929-99, (Moroc.), ruler of Morocco,1962-99.

John Hay, 1838-1905, (U.S.) sec. of state; primarily associated with Open Door Policy toward China.

Sir Edward Heath, 1916-205, (Br.) Conservative prime min., 1970-74; promoted European unity.

Patrick Henry, 1736-99, (U.S.) major Revolutionary War figure; remarkable orator.

Édouard Herriot, 1872-1957, (Fr.) Radical Socialist leader; twice prem., pres. of National Assembly.

Theodor Herzl, 1860-1904, (Hung.) founded modern Zionism.

Heinrich Himmler, 1900-45, (Ger.) head of Nazi SS and Gestapo.

Paul von Hindenburg, 1847-1934, (Ger.) field marshal, WW1; 2nd pres. of Weimar Republic, 1925-34.

Adolf Hitler, 1889-1945, (Ger.) dictator; built Nazism, launched WW2, presided over the Holocaust.

Ho Chi Minh, 1890-1969, (Viet.) N Vietnamese pres., Vietnamese Communist leader.

Harry L. Hopkins, 1890-1946, (U.S.) New Deal administrator; closest adviser to FDR during WW2.

Edward M. House, 1858-1938, (U.S.) diplomat; confidential adviser to Woodrow Wilson.

Samuel Houston, 1793-1863, (U.S.) leader of struggle for Texas independence.

Cordell Hull, 1871-1955, (U.S.) sec. of state, 1933-44; initiated reciprocal trade to lower tariffs, helped organize UN.

Hubert H. Humphrey, 1911-78, (U.S.) MN Democrat; senator, vice pres., pres. candidate.

Hussein, King, 1935-99 (Jordan), peacemaker; ruler of Jordan, 1952-99.

Jinnah, Muhammad Ali, 1876-1948, (Pak.) founder, first governor-general of Pakistan.

Benito Juarez, 1806-72, (Mex.) rallied his country against foreign threats, sought to create democratic, federal republic.

Constantine Karamanlis, 1907-98, (Gr.) Greek prime min., restored democracy; later president.

Frank B. Kellogg, 1856-1937, (U.S.) sec. of state; negotiated Kellogg-Briand Pact to outlaw war.

Robert F. Kennedy, 1925-68, (U.S.) attorney general, senator, assassinated while seeking presidency.

Aleksandr Kerensky, 1881-1970, (Russ.) headed provisional government after Feb. 1917 revolution.

Ayatollah Ruhollah Khomeini, 1900-89, (Iranian), religious-political leader, spearheaded overthrow of shah, 1979.

Nikita Khrushchev, 1894-1971, (USSR) prem., first sec. of Communist party; initiated de-Stalinization.

Kim Il Sung, 1912-94, (Korean) N Korean dictator, 1948-94.

Lajos Kossuth, 1802-94, (Hung.) principal figure in 1848 Hungarian revolution.

Pyotr Kropotkin, 1842-1921, (Russ.) anarchist; championed the peasants but opposed Bolshevism.

Kublai Khan, c1215-94, (Mongol) emperor; founder of Yüan dynasty in China.

Béla Kun, 1886-c1939, (Hung.) member of 3rd Communist Internat.; tried to foment worldwide revolution.

Robert M. LaFollette, 1855-1925, (U.S.) Wisconsin public official; leader of progressive movement.

Fiorello La Guardia, 1882-1947, (U.S.) colorful NYC reform mayor.

Pierre Laval, 1883-1945, (Fr.) politician, Vichy foreign min.; executed for treason.

Andrew Bonar Law, 1858-1923, (Br.) Conservative party politician; led opposition to Irish home rule.

Vladimir Ilyich Lenin (Ulyanov), 1870-1924, (Russ.) revolutionary; founded Bolshevism; Soviet leader 1917-24.

Ferdinand de Lesseps, 1805-94, (Fr.) diplomat, engineer; conceived idea of Suez Canal.

Rene Levesque, 1922-87, (Can.) prem. of Quebec, 1976-85; led unsuccessful separartist campaign.

Maxim Litvinov, 1876-1951, (Pol.-Russ.) revolutionary, commissar of foreign affairs; favored cooperation with West.

Liu Shaoqi, c1898-1974, (Chin.) Communist leader; fell from grace during Cultural Revolution.

David Lloyd George, 1863-1945, (Br.) Liberal party prime min.; laid foundations for modern welfare state.

Henry Cabot Lodge, 1850-1924, (U.S.) Republican senator; led opposition to participation in League of Nations.

Huey P. Long, 1893-1935, (U.S.) Louisiana political demagogue, governor, U.S. senator; assassinated.

Rosa Luxemburg, 1871-1919, (Ger.) revolutionary; leader of the German Social Democratic party and Spartacus party.

J. Ramsay MacDonald, 1866-1937, (Br.) first Labour party prime min. of Great Britain.

Harold Macmillan, 1895-1986, (Br.) prime min. of Great Britain, 1957-63.

Eugene McCarthy, 1916-2005, (U.S.) political leader and author; 1968 presidential contender.

Joseph R. McCarthy, 1908-57, (U.S.) senator, extremist in searching out alleged Communists and pro-Communists.

Makarios III, 1913-77, (Cypriot) Greek Orthodox archbishop; first pres. of Cyprus.

Mao Zedong, 1893-1976, (Chin.) chief Chinese Marxist theorist, revolutionary, political leader; led Chinese revolution establishing his nation as Communist state.

Jean Paul Marat, 1743-93, (Fr.) revolutionary, politician; identified with radical Jacobins; assassinated.

Thurgood Marshall, 1908-93, (U.S.) first black U.S. solicitor general, 1965; first black justice of U.S. Sup. Ct., 1967-91.

José Martí, 1853-95, (Cub.) patriot, poet; leader of Cuban struggle for independence.

Jan Masaryk, 1886-1948, (Czech.) foreign min.; died by mysterious alleged suicide following Communist coup.

Thomas G. Masaryk, 1850-1937, (Czech.) statesman, philosopher; first pres. of Czechoslovak Republic.

Jules Mazarin, 1602-61, (Fr.) cardinal, statesman; prime min. under Louis XIII and queen regent Anne of Austria.

Giusseppe Mazzini, 1805-72, (It.), reformer dedicated to Risorgimento movement for renewal of Italy.

Tom Mboya, 1930-69, (Kenyan) political leader; instrumental in securing independence for Kenya.

Cosimo I de' Medici, 1519-74, (It.) Duke of Florence, grand duke of Tuscany.

Lorenzo de' Medici, the Magnificent, 1449-92, (It.) merchant prince; a towering figure in Italian Renaissance.

Catherine de Médicis, 1519-89, (Fr.) queen consort of Henry II, regent of France; influential in Catholic-Huguenot wars.

Golda Meir, 1898-1978, (Isr.) a founder of the state of Israel and prime min., 1969-74.

Klemens W. N. L. Metternich, 1773-1859, (Austrian) statesman; arbiter of post-Napoleonic Europe.

Slobodan Milosevic, 1941-2006, (Serbian/Yugoslavian), former Yugoslav pres.; tried for war crimes.

François Mitterrand, 1916-96, (Fr.) pres. of France, 1981-95.

Mobutu Sese Seko, 1930-97, (Zaire) longtime ruler of Zaire (now Congo) (1965-97); exiled after rebellion.

Guy Mollet, 1905-75, (Fr.) socialist politician, resistance leader.

Henry Morgenthau Jr., 1891-1967, (U.S.) sec. of treasury; fund-raiser for New Deal and U.S. WW2 activities.

Gouverneur Morris, 1752-1816, (U.S.) statesman, diplomat. financial expert, helped plan decimal coinage.

Daniel Patrick Moynihan 1927-2003, (U.S.) senator, diplomat, social scientist and author.

Benito Mussolini, 1883-1945, (It.) leader of the Italian fascist state; assassinated.

Imre Nagy, c1896-1958, (Hung.) Communist prem.; assassinated after Soviets crushed 1956 uprising.

Gamal Abdel Nasser, 1918-70, (Egypt.) leader of Arab unification, 2nd Egyptian pres.

Jawaharlal Nehru, 1889-1964, (In.) prime min.; guided India through its early years of independence.

Kwame Nkrumah, 1909-72, (Ghan.) 1st prime min., 1957-60, and pres., 1960-66, of Ghana.

Frederick North, 1732-92, (Br.) prime min.; his inept policies led to loss of American colonies.

Julius K. Nyerere, 1923?-99, (Tanz.) founding father, 1st pres., 1962-85, of Tanzania.

Daniel O'Connell, 1775-1847, (Ir.) nationalist political leader; known as The Liberator.

Omar, c581-644, Muslim leader; 2nd caliph, led Islam to become an imperial power.

Thomas P. (Tip) O'Neill Jr., 1912-94, (U.S.) U.S. congressman, Speaker of the House, 1977-86.

Ignace Paderewski, 1860-1941, (Pol.) statesman, pianist; composer, briefly prime min., an ardent patriot.

Viscount Palmerston, 1784-1865, (Br.) Whig-Liberal prime min., foreign min.; embodied British nationalism.

Andreas George Papandreou, 1919-1996, (Gk.) leftist politician, served 2 times as prem. (1981-89, 1993-96).

Georgios Papandreou, 1888-1968, (Gk.) Republican politician; served 3 times as prime min.

Franz von Papen, 1879-1969, (Ger.) politician; major role in overthrow of Weimar Republic and rise of Hitler.

Charles Stewart Parnell, 1846-1891, (Ir.) nationalist leader; "uncrowned king of Ireland."

Lester Pearson, 1897-1972, (Can.) diplomat, Liberal party leader, prime min.

Robert Peel, 1788-1850, (Br.) reformist prime min., founder of Conservative party.

Eva (Evita) Perón, 1919-52 (Arg.) highly influential 2nd wife of Juan Perón.

Juan Perón, 1895-1974, (Arg.) dynamic pres. of Argentina (1946-55, 1973-74).

Joseph Pilsudski, 1867-1935, (Pol.) statesman; instrumental in reestablishing Polish state in the 20th cent.

Charles Pinckney, 1757-1824, (U.S.) founding father; his Pinckney plan largely incorporated into Constitution.

Christian Pineau, 1905-95, (Fr.) leader of French Resistance during WW2; French foreign min., 1956-58.

William Pitt, the Elder, 1708-78, (Br.) statesman; the "Great Commoner," transformed Britain into imperial power.

William Pitt, the Younger, 1759-1806, (Br.) prime min. during French Revolutionary wars.

Georgi Plekhanov, 1857-1918, (Russ.) revolutionary, social philosopher; called "father of Russian Marxism."

Raymond Poincaré, 1860-1934, (Fr.) 9th pres. of the Republic; advocated harsh punishment of Germany after WW1.

Pol Pot, 1925-98, (Camb.) leader of Khmer Rouge; ruled Cambodia, 1975-79; responsible for mass deaths.

Georges Pompidou, 1911-74, (Fr.) Gaullist political leader; pres. 1969-74.

Grigori Potemkin, 1739-91, (Russ.) field marshal; favorite of Catherine II.

Adam Clayton Powell Jr., 1908-72, (U.S.) civil rights leader, congressman, 1945-69.

Yitzhak Rabin, 1922-95, (Isr.) military, political leader; prime min. of Israel, 1974-77, 1992-95; assassinated.

Joseph H. Rainey, 1832-87, (U.S.) first black person elected to U.S. House, 1869, from South Carolina.

Edmund Randolph, 1753-1813, (U.S.) attorney; prominent in drafting, ratification of constitution.

John Randolph, 1773-1833, (U.S.) Southern planter; strong advocate of states' rights.

Jeannette Rankin, 1880-1973, (U.S.) pacifist; first woman member of U.S. Congress.

Walter Rathenau, 1867-1922, (Ger.) industrialist, statesman.

Sam Rayburn, 1882-1961, (U.S.) Democratic leader; representative for 47 years, House Speaker for 17.

Hiram R. Revels, 1822-1901, (U.S.) first African American U.S. senator, elected in Mississippi, served 1870-71.

Paul Reynaud, 1878-1966, (Fr.) statesman; prem. in 1940 at the time of France's defeat by Germany.

Syngman Rhee, 1875-1965, (Korean) first pres. of S Korea.

Cecil Rhodes, 1853-1902, (Br.) imperialist, industrial magnate; established Rhodes scholarships in his will.

Ann Richards, 1933-2006, (U.S.) former TX gov.

Cardinal de Richelieu, 1585-1642, (Fr.) statesman, known as "red eminence;" chief minister to Louis XIII.

Maximilien Robespierre, 1758-94, (Fr.) leading figure in French Revolution and Reign of Terror.

Nelson Rockefeller, 1908-79, (U.S.) Republican governor of NY, 1959-73; U.S. vice pres., 1974-77.

George W. Romney, 1907-95, (U.S.) auto exec.; 3-term Republican governor of Michigan.

Eleanor Roosevelt, 1884-1962, (U.S.) influential First Lady, humanitarian, UN diplomat.

Elihu Root, 1845-1937, (U.S.) lawyer, statesman, diplomat; leading Republican supporter of the League of Nations.

Dean Rusk, 1909-95, (U.S.) statesman; sec. of state, 1961-69.

John Russell, 1792-1878, (Br.) Liberal prime min. during the Irish potato famine.

Anwar al-Sadat, 1918-81, (Egypt.) pres., 1970-1981; promoted peace with Israel; Nobel laureate; assassinated.

António de Oliveira Salazar, 1889-1970, (Port.) longtime dictator.

José de San Martin, 1778-1850, S Amer. revolutionary; protector of Peru.

Eisaku Sato, 1901-75, (Jpn.) prime min.; presided over Japan's post-WW2 emergence as major world power.

Abdul Aziz Ibn Saud, c1880-1953, (Saudi Arabia) king of Saudi Arabia, 1932-53.

Robert Schuman, 1886-1963, (Fr.) statesman; founded European Coal and Steel Community.

Carl Schurz, 1829-1906, (U.S.) German-American political leader, journalist, orator, dedicated reformer.

Kurt Schuschnigg, 1897-1977, (Austrian) chancellor; unsuccessful in stopping Austria's annexation by Germany.

William H. Seward, 1801-72, (U.S.) anti-slavery activist; as U.S. sec. of state purchased Alaska.

Carlo Sforza, 1872-1952, (It.) foreign min., anti-fascist.

Sitting Bull, c1831-90, (Nat. Am.) Sioux leader in Battle of Little Bighorn over George A. Custer, 1876.

Alfred E. Smith, 1873-1944, (U.S.) NY Democratic governor; first Roman Catholic to run for presidency.

Margaret Chase Smith, 1897-1995, (U.S.) congresswoman, senator; 1st woman elected to both houses of Congress.

Jan C. Smuts, 1870-1950, (S. African) statesman, philosopher, soldier, prime min.

Paul Henri Spaak, 1899-1972, (Belg.) statesman, socialist leader.

Joseph Stalin, 1879-1953, (USSR) Soviet dictator, 1924-53; instituted forced collectivization, massive purges, and labor camps, causing millions of deaths.

Edwin M. Stanton, 1814-69, (U.S.) sec. of war, 1862-68.

Edward R. Stettinius Jr., 1900-49, (U.S.) industrialist, sec. of state who coordinated aid to WW2 allies.

Adlai E. Stevenson, 1900-65, (U.S.) Democratic leader, diplomat, Illinois governor, presidenial candidate.

Henry L. Stimson, 1867-1950, (U.S.) statesman; served in 5 administrations, foreign policy adviser in 30s and 40s.

Carl Stokes, 1927-1996, (U.S.) first black mayor of a major American city (Cleveland), 1967-72.

Sukarno, 1901-70, (Indon.) dictatorial first pres. of the Indonesian republic.

Sun Yat-sen, 1866-1925, (Chin.) revolutionary; leader of Kuomintang, regarded as the father of modern China.

Robert A. Taft, 1889-1953, (U.S.) conservative Senate leader, called "Mr. Republican."

Charles de Talleyrand, 1754-1838, (Fr.) statesman, diplomat; the major force of the Congress of Vienna of 1814-15.

U Thant, 1909-74 (Bur.) statesman, UN sec.-general.

Norman M. Thomas, 1884-1968, (U.S.) social reformer; 6 times Socialist party presidential candidate.

Josip Broz Tito, 1892-1980, (Yug.) pres. of Yugoslavia from 1953, WW2 guerrilla chief, postwar rival of Stalin.

Palmiro Togliatti, 1893-1964, (It.) major Italian Communist leader.

Hideki Tojo, 1885-1948, (Jpn.) statesman, soldier; prime min. during most of WW2.

François Toussaint L'Ouverture, c1744-1803, (Haitian) patriot, martyr; thwarted French colonial aims.

Leon Trotsky, 1879-1940, (Russ.) revolutionary, founded Red Army, expelled from party in conflict with Stalin; assassinated.

Pierre Elliott Trudeau, 1919-2000, (Can.) longtime liberal prime minister of Canada, 1968-79, 1980-84; achieved native Canadian constitution.

Rafael L. Trujillo Molina, 1891-1961, (Dom.) dictator of Dominican Republic, 1930-61; assassinated.

Moise K. Tshombe, 1919-69, (Cong.) pres. of secessionist Katanga, prem. of Congo.

William M. Tweed, 1823-78, (U.S.) politicial boss of Tammany Hall, NYC's Democratic political machine.

Walter Ulbricht, 1893-1973, (Ger.) Communist leader of German Democratic Republic.

Arthur H. Vandenberg, 1884-1951, (U.S.) senator; proponent of bipartisan anti-Communist foreign policy.

Eleutherios Venizelos, 1864-1936, (Gk.) most prominent Greek statesman of early 20th cent.

Hendrik F. Verwoerd, 1901-66, (S. African) prime min.; rigorously applied apartheid policy despite protest.

George Wallace, 1919-98, (U.S.) former segregationist governor of Alabama and presid. candidate.

Robert Walpole, 1676-1745, (Br.) statesman; generally considered Britain's first prime min.

Harold Washington, 1922-87, (U.S.) first black mayor of Chicago.

Robert C. Weaver, 1907-97, (U.S.) first African American appointed to cabinet; secretary of HUD.

Daniel Webster, 1782-1852, (U.S.) orator, politician; advocate of business interests during Jacksonian agrarianism.

Caspar Weinberger, 1917-2006 (U.S.), business exec, former defense sec., other cabinet posts.

Chaim Weizmann, 1874-1952, (Russ.-Isr.) Zionist leader, scientist; first Israeli pres.

Wendell L. Willkie, 1892-1944, (U.S.) Republican who tried to unseat FDR when he ran for his 3d term.

Harold Wilson, 1916-95, (Br.) Labour party leader; prime min., 1964-70, 1974-76.

Coleman A. Young, 1918-97, (U.S.) first Afr.-Amer. mayor of Detroit, 1974-93.

Emiliano Zapata, c1879-1919, (Mex.) revolutionary; major influence on modern Mexico.

Todor Zhivkov, 1911-98, (Bulg.) Communist ruler of Bulgaria from 1954 until ousted in a 1989 coup.

Zhou Enlai, 1898-1976, (Chin.) diplomat, prime min.; a leading figure of the Chinese Communist party.

Scientists of the Past

Revised by Peter Barker, Prof. & Chair, Dept. of the Hist. of Science, Univ. of Oklahoma

For pre-modern scientists see also Philosophers and Religious Figures of the Past and Historical Figures chapter.

Albertus Magnus, c1200-1280, (Ger.) theologian, philosopher; helped found medieval study of natural science.

Alhazen (Ibn al-Haytham), c965-c1040, mathematician, astronomer; optical theorist.

Andre-Marie Ampère, 1775-1836, (Fr.) mathematician, chemist; founder of electrodynamics.

John V. Atanasoff, 1903-95, (U.S.) physicist; co-invented Atanasoff-Berry Computer (1939-41).

Amedeo Avogadro, 1776-1856, (It.) chemist, physicist; proposed that equal volumes of gas contain equal numbers of molecules, permitting determination of molecular weights.

John Bardeen, 1908-91, (U.S.) double Nobel laureate in physics (transistor, 1956; superconductivity, 1972).

A. H. Becquerel, 1852-1908, (Fr.) physicist; discovered radioactivity in uranium (1896).

Alexander Graham Bell, 1847-1922, (U.S.) inventor; first to patent and commercially exploit the telephone (1876).

Daniel Bernoulli, 1700-82, (Swiss) mathematician; developed fluid dynamics and kinetic theory of gases.

Clifford Berry, 1918-1963, (U.S.) collaborated with Atanasoff on the ABC Computer (1939-41).

Jöns Jakob Berzelius, 1779-1848, (Swed.) chemist; developed modern chemical symbols and formulas.

Henry Bessemer, 1813-98, (Br.) engineer; invented Bessemer steel-making process.

Hans Bethe, 1906-2005, (Ger.-U.S.) physicist; won Nobel Prize in 1967 for describing how stars generate energy.

Bruno Bettelheim, 1903-90, (Austrian-U.S.) psychoanalyst; studied disturbed children; *Uses of Enchantment* (1976).

Louis Blériot, 1872-1936, (Fr.) engineer; monoplane pioneer, first Channel flight (1909).

Franz Boas, 1858-1942, (Ger.-U.S.) founded modern anthropology; studied Pacific Coast tribes.

Niels Bohr, 1885-1962, (Dan.) atomic and nuclear physicist; founded quantum mechanics.

Max Born, 1882-1970, (Ger.) atomic and nuclear physicist; helped develop quantum mechanics.

Satyendranath Bose, 1894-1974, (Indian) physicist; forerunner of modern quantum theory for integral-spin particles.

Louis de Broglie, 1892-1987, (Fr.) physicist; proposed quantum wave-particle duality.

Robert Bunsen, 1811-99, (Ger.) chemist; pioneered spectroscopic analysis; discovered rubidium, caesium.

Luther Burbank, 1849-1926, (U.S.) naturalist; developed plant breeding into a modern science.

Vannevar Bush, 1890-1974, (U.S.) electrical engineer; developed differential analyzer, an early analogue computer; headed WWII Office of Scientific Res. and Dev.

Marvin Camras, 1916-95, (U.S.) inventor, electrical engineer; invented magnetic tape recording.

Alexis Carrel, 1873-1944, (Fr.) surgeon, biologist; developed methods of suturing blood vessels and transplanting organs.

Rachel Carson, 1907-64, (U.S.) marine biologist, environmentalist; *Silent Spring* (1962).

James Chadwick, 1891-1974, (Br.) physicist; discovered the neutron (1932); led Brit. Manhattan Project group in U.S..

Albert Claude, 1898-1983, (Belg.-U.S.) a founder of modern cell biology; determined role of mitochondria.

Nicolaus Copernicus, 1473-1543, (Pol.) first modern astronomer to propose sun as center of the planets' motions.

Jacques Yves Cousteau, 1910-1997, (Fr.) oceanographer; co-inventor, with E. Gagnan, of the Aqualung (1943).

Seymour Cray, 1925-96, (U.S.) computer industry pioneer; developed supercomputers.

Francis Crick, 1916-2004, (Br.) biophysicist; co-discoverer of genetic code; shared 1962 Nobel Prize.

Marie, 1867-1934 (Pol.-Fr.) and **Pierre Curie**, 1859-1906, (Fr.) physical chemists; pioneer investigators of radioactivity, discovered radium and polonium (1898).

Gottlieb Daimler, 1834-1900, (Ger.) engineer, inventor; pioneer automobile manufacturer.

John Dalton, 1766-1844, (Br.) chemist, physicist; formulated atomic theory, made first table of atomic weights.

Charles Darwin, 1809-82, (Br.) naturalist; established theory of organic evolution; *Origin of Species* (1859).

Lee De Forest, 1873-1961, (U.S.) inventor of triode, pioneer in wireless telegraphy, sound pictures, television.

Max Delbruck, 1906-81, (Ger.-U.S.) founded molecular biology.

Rudolf Diesel, 1858-1913, (Ger.) mechanical engineer; patented Diesel engine (1892).

Theodosius Dobzhansky, 1900-75, (Russ.-U.S.) biologist; reconciled genetics and natural selection.

Christian Doppler, 1803-53, (Austrian) physicist; showed change in wave frequency caused by motion of source, now known as Doppler effect.

J. Presper Eckert Jr., 1919-95, (U.S.) co-inventor, with Mauchly, of the ENIAC computer (1943-45).

Thomas A. Edison, 1847-1931, (U.S.) inventor; held more than 1,000 patents, including incandescent electric lamp.

Paul Ehrlich, 1854-1915, (Ger.) medical researcher in immunology and bacteriology; pioneered antitoxin production.

Albert Einstein, 1879-1955, (Ger.-U.S.) theoretical physicist; founded relativity theory.

John F. Enders, 1897-1985, (U.S.) virologist, helped discover vaccines against polio, measles, mumps and chicken pox.

Erik Erikson, 1902-94, (U.S.) psychoanalyst, author; theory of developmental stages of life, *Childhood and Society* (1950).

Leonhard Euler, 1707-83, (Swiss) mathematician, physicist; pioneer of calculus, revived ideas of Fermat.

Gabriel Fahrenheit, 1686-1736, (Ger.) physicist; improved thermometers and introduced Fahrenheit temperature scale.

Michael Faraday, 1791-1867, (Br.) chemist, physicist; discovered electrical induction and invented dynamo (1831).

Philo T. Farnsworth, 1906-71, (U.S.) inventor; built first television system (San Francisco, 1928).

Pierre de Fermat, 1601-65, (Fr.) mathematician; founded modern theory of numbers.

Enrico Fermi, 1901-54, (It.-U.S.) nuclear physicist; demonstrated first controlled chain reaction (Chicago, 1942).

Richard Feynman, 1918-88, (U.S.) theoretical physicist, author; founder of Quantum Electrodynamics (QED).

Alexander Fleming, 1881-1955, (Br.) bacteriologist; discovered penicillin (1928).

Jean B. J. Fourier, 1768-1830, (fr.) introduced method of analysis in math and physics known as Fourier Series.

Sigmund Freud, 1856-1939, (Austrian) psychiatrist; founder of psychoanalysis. *Interpretation of Dreams* (1901).

Erich Fromm, 1900-1980, (U.S.) psychoanalyst. *Man for Himself* (1947).

Galileo Galilei, 1564-1642, (It.) physicist; used telescope to vindicate Copernicus, founded modern science of motion.

Carl Friedrich Gauss, 1777-1855, (Ger.) math. physicist; completed work of Fermat and Euler in number theory.

Josiah W. Gibbs, 1839-1903, (U.S.) theoretical physicist, chemist; founded chemical thermodynamics.

Robert H. Goddard, 1882-1945, (U.S.) physicist; invented liquid fuel rocket (1926).

George W. Goethals, 1858-1928, (U.S.) chief engineer who completed Panama Canal (1907-14).

William C. Gorgas, 1854-1920, (U.S.) physician; pioneer in prevention of yellow fever and malaria.

Stephen Jay Gould, 1941-2002, (U.S.) paleontologist, evolutionary biologist, writer.

Ernest Haeckel, 1834-1919, (Ger.) zoologist, evolutionist; early Darwinist, introduced concept of "ecology."

Otto Hahn, 1879-1968, (Ger.) chemist; with Meitner discovered nuclear fission (1938).

Edmund Halley, 1656-1742, (Br.) astronomer; predicted return of 1682 comet ("Halley's Comet") in 1759.

William Harvey, 1578-1657, (Br.) physician, anatomist; discovered circulation of the blood (1628).

Werner Heisenberg, 1901-76, (Ger.) physicist; developed matrix mechanics and uncertainty principle (1927).

Hermann von Helmholtz, 1821-94, (Ger.) physicist, physiologist; formulated principle of conservation of energy.

William Herschel, 1738-1822, (Ger.-Br.) astronomer; discovered Uranus (1781).

Heinrich Hertz, 1857-94, (Ger.) physicist; discovered radio waves and photo-electric effect (1886-7).

David Hilbert, 1862-1943, (Ger.) mathematician; contributed to algebra, calculus and foundational studies (formalism).

Edwin P. Hubble, 1889-1953, (U.S.) astronomer; discovered observational evidence of expanding universe.

Alexander von Humboldt, 1769-1859, (Ger.) naturalist, author; explored S America, created ecology.

Edward Jenner, 1749-1823, (Br.) physician; pioneered vaccination, introduced term "virus."

James Joule, 1818-89, (Br.) physicist; found relation between heat and mechanical energy (conservation of energy).

Carl Jung, 1875-1961, (Swiss) psychiatrist; founder of analytical psychology.

Ernest Everett Just, 1883-1941, (U.S.) marine biologist; studied egg development; author, *Biology of Cell Surfaces,* 1941.

Johannes Kepler, 1571-1630, (Ger.) astronomer; discovered laws of planetary motion.

Al-Khawarizmi, early 9th cent., (Arab.), mathematician; regarded as founder of algebra.

Robert Koch, 1843-1910 (Ger.) bacteriologist; isolated bacterial causes of tuberculosis and other diseases.

Georges Köhler, 1946-95, (Ger.) immunologist; with Cesar Milstein he developed monoclonal antibody technique.

Year *in* Pictures

National

WAR VETERAN
In June, President Bush jogged with Army Staff Sgt. Christian Bagge, 23, who lost both legs in a roadside bombing while serving in Iraq.

SURVEILLANCE
In Feb., Attorney General Alberto Gonzales defended the Bush administration's domestic electronic surveillance program to the Senate Judiciary Committee.

CO-CONSPIRATOR
Zacarias Moussaoui was sentenced in May to life in prison for his role in the 9/11 terrorist plot.

DELAY RESIGNS
Former House Majority Leader Tom DeLay (R-TX) resigned from office, effective June 9, after being indicted on charges of money laundering.

2008 CONTENDERS?
New York Senator Hillary Rodham Clinton (D) and Arizona Senator John McCain (R). Both are assumed to be candidates for the 2008 presidential nomination in their respective parties.

NEW SUPREME COURT
In Mar., the justices of the Supreme Court posed for their 2006 class portrait with a new chief justice, John Roberts Jr. (front row, center), and a new associate justice, Samuel Alito (back row, right).

National

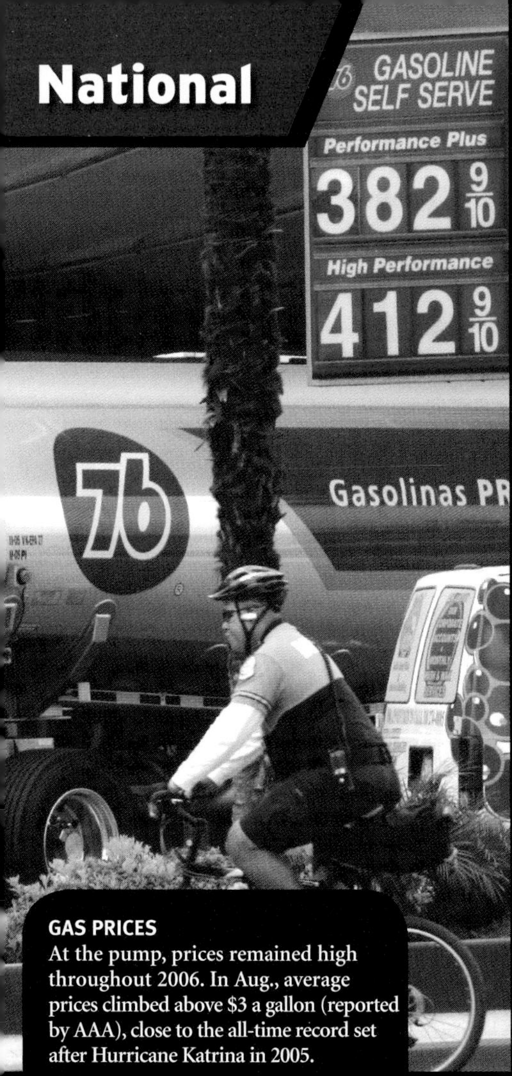
GASOLINE
SELF SERVE
Performance Plus
382 9/10
High Performance
412 9/10
76
Gasolinas PR

GAS PRICES
At the pump, prices remained high throughout 2006. In Aug., average prices climbed above $3 a gallon (reported by AAA), close to the all-time record set after Hurricane Katrina in 2005.

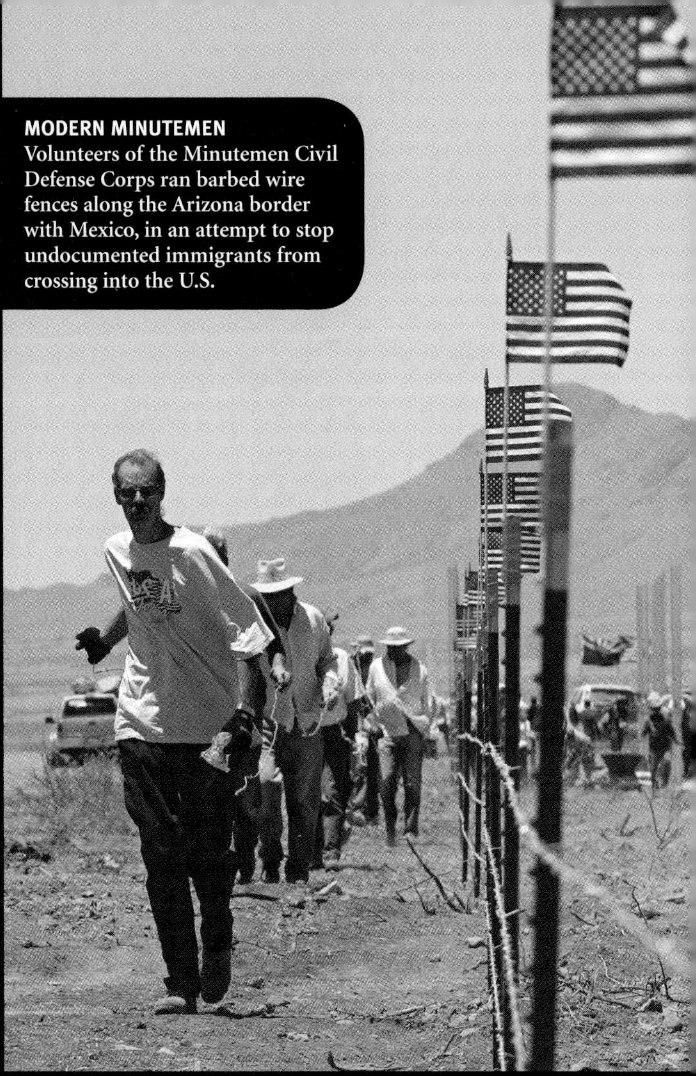

MODERN MINUTEMEN
Volunteers of the Minutemen Civil Defense Corps ran barbed wire fences along the Arizona border with Mexico, in an attempt to stop undocumented immigrants from crossing into the U.S.

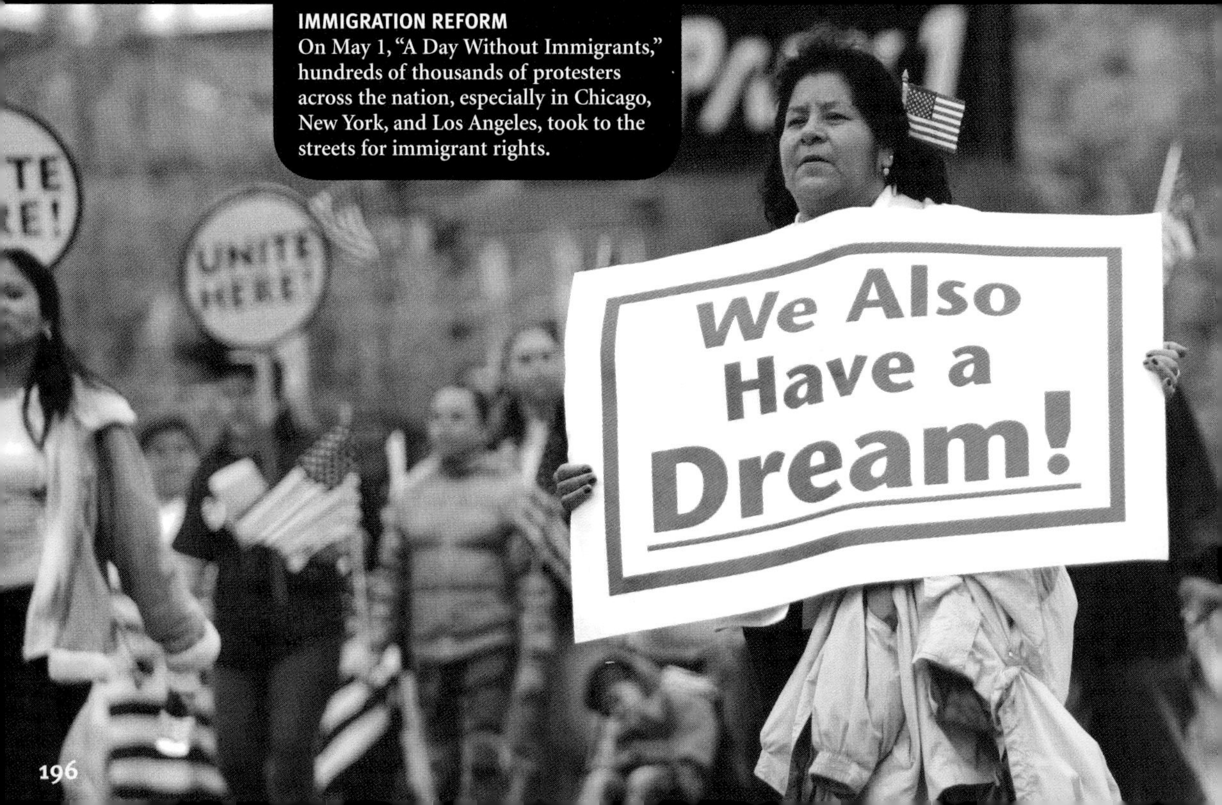
UNITE HERE!
We Also Have a Dream!

IMMIGRATION REFORM
On May 1, "A Day Without Immigrants," hundreds of thousands of protesters across the nation, especially in Chicago, New York, and Los Angeles, took to the streets for immigrant rights.

ENRON ON TRIAL
Co-defendants Jeffrey Skilling (background) and Ken Lay, former leaders of Enron, were convicted of fraud and conspiracy in May. Lay died of a heart attack in July.

FIRST NEW FACE
Isabelle Dinoire of France received the first-ever partial face transplant in late 2005. She had been mauled by her dog and received a new nose, chin, and mouth.

HUNTING ACCIDENT
Harry Whittington, an Austin attorney, was accidentally shot by his hunting partner, Vice President Dick Cheney. The incident in Feb. caused a furor when, after a day's delay, it was first reported by local press, rather than by the White House.

CHAMPIONS OF CHARITY
On June 25, Warren Buffett (right) made a pledge valued at about $31 bil to the Bill and Melinda Gates Foundation, which donates money to learning and health programs worldwide. This was the largest philanthropic gift in history.

197

People

SIRIUS STERN
Radio personality Howard Stern moved to Sirius Satellite Radio in Jan. 2006.

FIRST FEMALE ANCHOR
In Sept. 2006, Katie Couric started as the anchor of CBS Evening News.

GORE GOES GLO
Sharing *An Inconvenient Truth* about global warm former vice president Al Gore's documentary m over $20 mil in box-office sa

Hurricane Katrina
August 29, 2005

Photo: NOAA

BREAKING DOWN BARRIERS
The tragic love story of two cowboys—*Brokeback Mountain*, starring Heath Ledger (left) and Jake Gyllenhaal—won three Oscars in Mar. 2006.

LEAD ACTOR
Philip Seymour Hoffman won a 2006 Oscar for his portrayal of Truman Capote in *Capote*.

LEAD ACTRESS
Reese Witherspoon took an Oscar in Mar. 2006 for her performance as June Carter in *Walk the Line*.

NEUE

PRICEY PORTRAIT
Gustav Klimt's 1907 portrait of Adele Bloch-Bauer was auctioned in June for $135 mil to Ronald S. Lauder. It now hangs in New York's Neue Galerie.

U2 WINS FIVE
Rock group U2 (members The Edge and Bono pictured here) won five Grammy Awards in Feb. 2006, including Album of the Year for *How to Dismantle an Atomic Bomb* and Song of the Year for "Sometimes You Can't Make It on Your Own."

OH *BOYS!*
The musical *Jersey Boys*, which tells the story of pop group The Four Seasons, won the 2006 Tony for Best Musical.

Jacques Lacan, 1901-81, (Fr.) influential psychoanalyst.

Joseph Lagrange, 1736-1813, (Fr.) geometer, astronomer; showed that gravity of earth and moon cancels creating stable points in space around them.

Jean B. Lamarck, 1744-1829, (Fr.) naturalist; forerunner of Darwin in evolutionary theory.

Pierre Simon de Laplace, 1749-1827, (Fr.) astronomer, physicist; proposed nebular origin for solar system.

Lewis H. Latimer, 1848-1928, (U.S.) African American scientist; associate of Edison; supervised installation of first electric street lighting in NYC.

Antoine Lavoisier, 1743-94, (Fr.) a founder of mod. chemistry.

Ernest O. Lawrence, 1901-58, (U.S.) physicist; invented the cyclotron.

Jerome Lejeune, 1927-94, (Fr.) geneticist; discovered chromosomal cause of Down syndrome (1959).

Louis 1903-72, and **Mary Leakey,** 1913-96, (Br.) early hominid paleoanthropologists; discovered remains in Africa.

Anton van Leeuwenhoek, 1632-1723, (Dutch) founder of microscopy.

Kurt Lewin, 1890-1947, (Ger.-U.S.) social psychologist; studied human motivation and group dynamics.

Justus von Liebig, 1803-73, (Ger.) founded quantitative organic chemistry.

Joseph Lister, 1827-1912, (Br.) physician; pioneered antiseptic surgery.

Hendrik Lorentz, 1853-1928 (Neth.), physicist, developed electron theory of matter, contrib. to relativity theory.

Konrad Lorenz, 1903-89, (Austrian) ethologist; pioneer in study of animal behavior.

Percival Lowell, 1855-1916, (U.S.) astronomer; predicted the existence of Pluto.

Louis, 1864-1948, and **Auguste Lumière,** 1862-1954, (Fr.) invented cinematograph and made first motion picture (1895).

Guglielmo Marconi, 1874-1937, (It.) physicist; developed wireless telegraphy.

John W. Mauchly, 1907-80, (U.S.) co-inventor, with Eckert, of computer ENIAC (1943-45).

James Clerk Maxwell, 1831-79, (Br.) physicist; unified electricity and magnetism; electromagnetic theory of light.

Maria Goeppert Mayer, 1906-72, (Ger.-U.S.) physicist; developed shell model of atomic nuclei.

Barbara McClintock, 1902-92, (U.S.) geneticist; showed that some genetic elements are mobile.

Lise Meitner, 1878-1968, (Austrian) co-discoverer, with Hahn, of nuclear fission (1938).

Gregor J. Mendel, 1822-84, (Austrian) botanist, monk; his experiments became the foundation of modern genetics.

Dmitri Mendeleyev, 1834-1907, (Russ.) chemist; established Periodic Table of the Elements.

Bruce R. Merrifield, 1921-2006, (U.S.) chemist; discovered how to synthesize proteins quickly and efficiently.

Franz Mesmer, 1734-1815, (Ger.) physician; introduced hypnotherapy.

Albert A. Michelson, 1852-1931, (U.S.) physicist; invented interferometer.

Robert A. Millikan, 1868-1953, (U.S.) physicist; measured electronic charge.

Thomas Hunt Morgan, 1866-1945, (U.S.) geneticist, embryologist; established role of chromosomes in heredity.

Isaac Newton, 1642-1727, (Br.) natural philosopher; discovered laws of gravitation, motion; with Leibniz, founded calculus.

Robert N. Noyce, 1927-90, (U.S.) invented microchip.

J. Robert Oppenheimer, 1904-67, (U.S.) physicist; scientific director of Manhattan project.

Wilhelm Ostwald, 1853-1932, (Ger.) chemist, philosopher; main founder of modern physical chemistry.

Louis Pasteur, 1822-95, (Fr.) chemist; showed that germs cause disease and fermentation, originated pasteurization.

Linus C. Pauling, 1901-94, (U.S.) chemist; studied chemical bonds; campaigned for nuclear disarmament.

Jean Piaget, 1896-1980, (Swiss) psychologist; four-stage theory of intellectual development in children.

Max Planck, 1858-1947, (Ger.) physicist; introduced quantum hypothesis (1900).

Jules Henri Poincaré, 1854-1912 (Fr.), mathematician, founded algebraic topology, many other discoveries.

Walter S. Reed, 1851-1902, (U.S.) army physician; proved mosquitoes transmit yellow fever.

Theodor Reik, 1888-1969, (Austrian-U.S.) psychoanalyst, major Freudian disciple.

Bernhard Riemann, 1826-66, (Ger.) mathematician; developed non-Euclidean geometry used by Einstein.

Norbert Rillieux, 1806-94, (U.S.) African American inventor of a vacuum pan evaporator, 1846, revolutionized sugar-refining industry.

Wilhelm Roentgen, 1845-1923, (Ger.) physicist; discovered X-rays (1895).

Carl Rogers, 1902-87, (U.S.) psychotherapist, author; originated nondirective therapy.

Ernest Rutherford, 1871-1937, (Br.) physicist; pioneer investigator of radioactivity, identified the atomic nucleus.

Albert B. Sabin, 1906-93, (Russ.-U.S.), developed oral polio live-virus vaccine.

Carl Sagan, 1934-96, (U.S.) astronomer, author.

Jonas Salk, 1914-95, (U.S.) developed first successful polio vaccine, widely used in U.S. after 1955.

Giovanni Schiaparelli, 1835-1910, (It.) astronomer; reported canals on Mars.

Erwin Schrödinger, 1887-1961, (Austrian) physicist; developed wave equation for quantum systems.

Glenn T. Seaborg, 1912-99, (U.S.) chemist, Nobel Prize winner (1951); codiscoverer of plutonium.

Harlow Shapley, 1885-1972, (U.S.) astronomer; mapped galactic clusters and position of Sun in our own galaxy.

Norman E. Shumway, 1923-2006, (U.S.) surgeon; performed the world's first successful heart-lung transplant.

B(urrhus) F(rederick) Skinner, 1904-89, (U.S.) psychologist; leading advocate of behaviorism.

Richard E. Smalley, 1943-2006, (U.S.) chemist; along with three other scientists, discovered "buckminsterfullerenes," a previously unknown class of carbon molecules.

Roger W. Sperry, 1913-94, (U.S.) neuorobiologist; established different functions of right and left sides of brain.

Benjamin Spock, 1903-98, (U.S.) pediatrician, child care expert; *Common Sense Book of Baby and Child Care.*

Charles P. Steinmetz, 1865-1923, (Ger.-U.S.) electrical engineer; developed basic ideas on alternating current.

Leo Szilard, 1898-1964, (Hung.-U.S.) physicist; helped on Manhattan project, later opposed nuclear weapons.

Edward Teller, 1908-2003, (Hung.-U.S.) physicist, aided on Manhattan project, had key role in development of H-bomb.

Nikola Tesla, 1856-1943, (Serb.-U.S.) invented electrical devices including a.c. dynamos, transformers and motors.

William Thomson (Lord Kelvin), 1824-1907, (Br.) physicist; aided in success of transatlantic telegraph cable (1865); proposed Kelvin absolute temperature scale.

Alan Turing, 1912-54, (Br.) mathematician; helped develop basis for computers.

Rudolf Virchow, 1821-1902, (Ger.) pathologist; pioneered the modern theory that diseases affect the body through cells.

James Van Allen, 1914-2006, (U.S.) physicist; discovered the presence of radiation belts around Earth (Van Allen belts).

Alessandro Volta, 1745-1827, (It.) physicist; electricity pioneer.

Werner von Braun, 1912-77, (Ger.-U.S.) developed rockets for warfare and space exploration.

John Von Neumann, 1903-57, (Hung.-U.S.) mathematician; originated game theory; basic design for modern computers.

Alfred Russell Wallace, 1823-1913, (Br.) naturalist; proposed concept of evolution independently of Darwin.

John B. Watson, 1878-1958, (U.S.) psychologist; a founder of behaviorism.

James E. Watt, 1736-1819, (Br.) mechanical engineer, inventor; invented modern steam engine (1765).

Alfred L. Wegener, 1880-1930, (Ger.) meteorologist, geophysicist; postulated continental drift.

Norbert Wiener, 1894-1964, (U.S.) mathematician; founder of cybernetics.

Daniel Hale Williams, 1858-1931, (U.S.) African American surgeon; performed one of first two open-heart operations, 1893.

Sewall Wright, 1889-1988, (U.S.) evolutionary theorist; helped found population genetics.

Wilhelm Wundt, 1832-1920, (Ger.) founder of experimental psychology.

Ferdinand von Zeppelin, 1838-1917, (Ger.) soldier, aeronaut, airship designer.

Social Reformers, Activists, and Humanitarians of the Past

Ralph David Abernathy, 1926-90, (U.S.) black civil rights activist; pres., 1968, Southern Christian Leadership Conf.

Jane Addams, 1860-1935, (U.S.) cofounder of Hull House; won Nobel Peace Prize, 1931.

Susan B. Anthony, 1820-1906, (U.S.) a leader in temperance, anti-slavery, and woman suffrage movements.

Thomas Barnardo, 1845-1905, (Br.) social reformer; pioneered in care of destitute children.

Clara Barton, 1821-1912, (U.S.) organized American Red Cross.

Daisy Bates, 1914-99, (U.S.) black civil rights leader who fought for school integration; leading advocate for the "Little Rock 9" during the Arkansas desegregation crisis in 1957.

Henry Ward Beecher, 1813-87, (U.S.) clergyman, abolitionist.

Peter Benenson, 1921-2005, (Br.) activist, founded Amnesty International in 1961.

Mary McCleod Bethune, 1875-1955, (U.S.) black educator and civil rights activist; adviser to FDR and Truman; founder, pres., Bethune-Cookman College.

Amelia Bloomer, 1818-94, (U.S.) suffragette, social reformer.

William Booth, 1829-1912, (Br.) founded Salvation Army.

John Brown, 1800-59, (U.S.) abolitionist who led murder of 5 pro-slavery men, was hanged.

Frances Xavier (Mother) Cabrini, 1850-1917, (It.-U.S.) Italian-born nun; founded charitable institutions; first American canonized as a saint, 1946.

Stokely Carmichael (Kwame Toure), 1941-98, (U.S.) black power activist, major proponent of Pan-Africanism. Prime Min. Black Panthers.

Carrie Chapman Catt, 1859-1947, (U.S.) suffragette.

Eldridge Cleaver, 1935-98, (U.S.) revolutionary social critic; former "minister of information" for Black Panthers; *Soul on Ice.*

Cesar Chavez, 1927-93, (U.S.) labor leader; helped establish United Farm Workers of America.

Clarence Darrow, 1857-1938, (U.S.) lawyer; defender of "underdog," opponent of capital punishment.

Ossie Davis, 1917-2005, (U.S.) black civil rights activist, actor, director.

Dorothy Day, 1897-1980, (U.S.) founder of Catholic Worker movement.

Eugene V. Debs, 1855-1926, (U.S.) labor leader; led Pullman strike, 1894; 4-time Socialist presidential candidate.

Vine Deloria, Jr., 1933-2005, (U.S) Native American activist and author; wrote *Custer Died for Your Sins.*

Dorothea Dix, 1802-87, (U.S.) crusader for mentally ill.

Thomas Dooley, 1927-61, (U.S.) "jungle doctor," noted for efforts to supply medical aid to developing countries.

Frederick Douglass, 1817-95, (U.S.) slave, author, editor, orator, diplomat; edited abolitionist weekly *The North Star.*

Marjory Stoneman Douglas, 1890-1998, (U.S.) writer and environmentalist; campaigned to save Florida Everglades.

Andrea Dworkin, 1946-2005, (U.S.) radical feminist and anti-pornography crusader.

Betty Friedan, 1921-2006 (U.S.), author, feminist; wrote *The Feminine Mystique.*

Medgar Evers, 1925-63, (U.S.) black civil rights leader; campaigned to register black voters; assassinated.

James Farmer, 1920-99, (U.S.) black civil rights leader; founded Congress of Racial Equality (CORE).

William Lloyd Garrison, 1805-79, (U.S.) abolitionist.

Emma Goldman, 1869-1940, (Russ.-U.S.) published anarchist *Mother Earth,* birth-control advocate.

Samuel Gompers, 1850-1924, (U.S.) labor leader. First president of the American Federation of Labor (AFL).

Prince Hall, 1735-1807, (U.S.) activist; founded black Freemasonry; served in American Revolutionary war.

Michael Harrington, 1928-89, (U.S.) exposed poverty in affluent U.S. in *The Other America,* 1963.

Sidney Hillman, 1887-1946, (U.S.) labor leader; helped organize CIO.

Samuel G. Howe, 1801-76, (U.S.) social reformer; changed public attitudes toward the handicapped.

Helen Keller, 1880-1968, (U.S.) crusader for better treatment for the handicapped; deaf and blind herself.

Coretta Scott King, 1927-2006, (U.S.) black civil rights leader; wife of Rev. Martin Luther King Jr.

Rev. Martin Luther King Jr., 1929-68, (U.S.) civil rights leader; led 1955-56 Montgomery, AL, boycott; founder, pres., Southern Christian Leadership Conference, 1957; Nobel laureate (1964); assassinated.

Malcolm X (Little), 1925-65, (U.S.) Black Muslim, black nationalist leader; promoted black pride; assassinated.

Maggie Kuhn, 1905-95, (U.S.) founded Gray Panthers, 1970.

William Kunstler, 1919-95, (U.S.) civil liberties attorney.

John L. Lewis, 1880-1969, (U.S.) labor leader; headed United Mine Workers, 1920-60.

Karl Menninger, 1893-1990, (U.S.) with brother William founded Menninger Clinic and Menninger Foundation.

Lucretia Mott, 1793-1880, (U.S.) reformer, pioneer feminist.

Philip Murray, 1886-1952, (U.S.) Scottish-born labor leader.

Huey P. Newton, 1942-89, (U.S.) co-founded Black Panther Party, 1966.

Florence Nightingale, 1820-1910, (Br.) founder of modern nursing.

Rosa Parks,1913-2005, (U.S.), black civil rights activist; her actions sparked 1955-56 Montgomery bus boycott.

Emmeline Pankhurst, 1858-1928, (Br.) woman suffragist.

A. Philip Randolph, 1889-1979, (U.S.) organized Brotherhood of Sleeping Car Porters, 1925; an organizer of 1941 and 1963 March on Washington movements.

Walter Reuther, 1907-70, (U.S.) labor leader; headed UAW.

Jacob Riis, 1849-1914, (U.S.) crusader for urban reforms.

Paul Robeson, 1898-1976, (U.S.) actor, singer, black civil rights activist.

Bayard Rustin, 1910-87, (U.S.) an organizer of the 1963 March on Washington; exec. director, A. Philip Randolph Institute.

Margaret Sanger, 1883-1966, (U.S.) social reformer; pioneered the birth-control movement.

Earl of Shaftesbury (A. A. Cooper), 1801-85, (Br.) social reformer.

Elizabeth Cady Stanton, 1815-1902, (U.S.) woman suffrage pioneer.

Lucy Stone, 1818-93, (U.S.) feminist, abolitionist.

Mother Teresa of Calcutta, 1910-97, (Alban.) nun; founded order to care for sick, dying poor; 1979 Nobel Peace Prize.

Willard Townsend, 1895-1957, (U.S.) organized the United Transport Service Employees (redcaps), 1935.

Sojourner Truth (Isabella Baumfree), 1797-1883, (U.S.) preacher, abolitionist; worked for black educ. opportunity.

Harriet Tubman, 1823-1913, (U.S.) prominent figure in the Underground Railroad, which helped runaway slaves in the south reach safety in the north; nurse and spy for Union Army in the Civil War.

Nat Turner, 1800-31, (U.S.) slave who led the most significant of more than 200 slave revolts in U.S., in Southampton, VA; hanged.

Philip Vera Cruz, 1905-94, (Filipino-U.S.) helped to found the United Farm Workers Union.

William Wilberforce, 1759-1833, (Br.) social reformer; prominent in struggle to abolish the slave trade.

Frances E. Willard, 1839-98, (U.S.) temperance, women's rights leader.

Mary Wollstonecraft, 1759-97, (Br.) wrote *Vindication of the Rights of Women.*

Writers of the Present

Name (Birthplace)	Birthdate	Name (Birthplace)	Birthdate
Chinua Achebe (Ogidi, Nigeria)	11/16/30	Ray Bradbury (Waukegan, IL)	8/22/20
Richard Adams (Newbury, Eng.)	5/9/20	Barbara Taylor Bradford (Leeds, Eng.)	5/10/33
Edward Albee (Wash., DC)	3/12/28	Dan Brown (Exeter, NH)	6/22/64
Isabel Allende (Lima, Peru)	8/2/42	Rita Mae Brown (Hanover, PA)	11/28/44
Dorothy Allison (Greenville, SC)	4/11/49	Christopher Buckley (NYC)	9/28/52
Martin Amis (Oxford, Eng.)	8/25/49	James Lee Burke (Houston, TX)	12/5/36
Maya Angelou (St. Louis, MO)	4/4/28	Augusten Burroughs (Pittsburgh, PA)	1965
Piers Anthony (Oxford, Eng.)	8/6/34	Robert Olen Butler (Granite City, IL)	1/20/45
Jeffrey Archer (Somerset, Eng.)	4/15/40	A. S. Byatt (Sheffield, England)	8/24/36
Oscar Arias Sanchez (Heredia, Costa Rica)	9/13/41	Hortense Calisher (NYC)	12/20/11
John Ashbery (Rochester, NY)	7/28/27	Ethan Canin (Ann Arbor, MI)	7/19/60
Margaret Atwood (Ottawa, Ont.)	11/18/39	Peter Carey (Bacchus-Marsh, Victoria, Australia)	5/7/43
David Auburn (Chicago)	1969	Caleb Carr (NYC)	5/19/63
Louis Auchincloss (Lawrence, NY)	9/27/17	Michael Chabon (Wash., DC)	5/19/63
Jean Auel (Chicago)	2/18/36	Tracy Chevalier (Wash., DC)	10/62
Paul Auster (Newark, NJ)	2/3/47	Sandra Cisneros (Chicago)	12/20/54
Alan Ayckbourn (Hampstead, Eng.)	4/12/39	Tom Clancy (Baltimore, MD)	4/12/47
Nicholson Baker (Rochester, NY)	1/7/57	Mary Higgins Clark (NYC)	12/24/29
Russell Banks (Newton, MA)	3/28/40	Arthur C. Clarke (Minehead, Eng.)	12/16/29
John Barth (Cambridge, MD)	5/27/30	Beverly Cleary (McMinnville, OR)	4/12/16
Ann Beattie (Wash., DC)	9/8/47	Paulo Coelho (Rio de Janeiro, Brazil)	8/24/47
John Berendt (Syracuse, NY)	12/5/39	J(ohn) M(axwell) Coetzee (Capetown, S. Africa)	2/9/40
Thomas Berger (Cincinnati, OH)	7/20/24	Billy Collins (NYC)	3/22/41
Maeve Binchy (Dalkey, Ireland)	3/28/40	Jackie Collins (London, Eng.)	10/4/41
Judy Blume (Elizabeth, NJ)	2/12/38	Evan S. Connell (Kansas City, MO)	8/17/24
T. Coraghessan Boyle (Peekskill, NY)	12/2/48	Pat Conroy (Atlanta, GA)	10/26/45

Name (Birthplace)	Birthdate
Robin Cook (NYC)	5/4/40
Patricia Cornwell (Miami, FL)	6/9/56
Harry Crews (Alma, GA)	6/6/35
Michael Crichton (Chicago)	10/23/42
Michael Cunningham (Cincinnati, Ohio)	11/6/52
Don DeLillo (NYC)	11/20/36
Nelson DeMille (NYC)	8/23/43
Joan Didion (Sacramento, CA)	12/5/34
E. L. Doctorow (NYC)	1/6/31
Takako Doi (Hyogo, Jap.)	11/30/28
Rita Dove (Akron, OH)	8/28/52
Roddy Doyle (Dublin, Ireland)	5/5/58
Umberto Eco (Alessandria, Italy)	1/5/32
Bret Easton Ellis (Los Angeles,)	3/7/64
Dave Eggers (Chicago)	3/12/70
James Ellroy (Los Angeles)	3/4/48
Louise Erdrich (Little Falls, MN)	7/6/54
Laura Esquivel (Mexico City, Mexico)	9/30/51
Jeffrey Eugenides (Detroit, MI)	1960
Lawrence Ferlinghetti (Yonkers, NY)	3/24/19
Helen Fielding (Morley, Yorkshire, Eng.)	2/19/58
Ken Follet (Cardiff, Wales)	6/5/49
Dario Fo (San Giano, Italy)	3/26/26
Horton Foote (Wharton, TX)	3/14/16
Richard Ford (Jackson, MS)	2/16/44
Frederick Forsyth (Ashford, Eng.)	8/25/38
Paula Fox (NYC)	4/22/23
Dick Francis (Tenby, Pembrokeshire, Wales)	10/31/20
Jonathan Franzen (Western Springs, IL)	8/17/59
Michael Frayn (London, Eng.)	9/8/33
Charles Frazier (Asheville, NC)	11/4/50
Marilyn French (NYC)	11/21/29
Brian Friel (Omagh, County Tyrone, N. Ireland)	1/9/29
Carlos Fuentes (Panama City, Panama)	11/11/28
Ernest J. Gaines (Oscar, LA)	1/15/33
Gabriel Garcia Marquez (Aracataca, Colombia)	3/6/28
Frank Gilroy (Bronx, NY)	10/13/25
Gail Godwin (Birmingham, AL)	6/18/37
William Goldman (Highland Park, IL)	8/12/31
Nadine Gordimer (Springs, S. Africa)	11/20/23
Mary Gordon (Far Rockaway, Long Island, NY)	12/8/49
Sue Grafton (Louisville, KY)	4/24/40
Günter Grass (Danzig, now Gdansk, Poland)	10/16/27
Shirley Ann Grau (New Orleans, LA)	7/8/29
John Grisham (Jonesboro, AR)	2/8/55
John Guare (NYC)	2/5/38
David Handler (Los Angeles)	9/14/52
David Hare (St. Leonards, Sussex, Eng.)	6/5/47
Jim Harrison (Grayling, MI)	12/11/37
Robert Hass (San Francisco, CA)	3/1/41
Vaclav Havel (Prague, Czech.)	10/5/36
Seamus Heaney (Mossbaum, Cty. Derry, N. Ire.)	4/13/39
Mark Helprin (NYC)	6/28/47
Carl Hiaasen (S. Florida)	3/12/53
Oscar Hijuelos (NYC)	8/24/51
Tony Hillerman (Sacred Heart, OK)	5/27/25
S. E. Hinton (Tulsa, OK)	7/22/50
Alice Hoffman (NYC)	3/16/52
John Irving (Exeter, NH)	3/2/42
Kazuo Ishiguro (Nagasaki, Japan)	11/8/54
John Jakes (Chicago)	3/31/32
P. D. James (Oxford, Eng.)	8/3/20
Ha Jin (Liaoning, China)	2/21/56
Erica Jong (NYC)	3/26/42
Garrison Keillor (Anoka, MN)	8/7/42
Thomas Keneally (Sydney, Austral.)	10/7/35
William Kennedy (Albany, NY)	1/16/28
Jamaica Kincaid (St. Johns, Antigua)	5/25/49
Stephen King (Portland, ME)	9/21/47
Barbara Kingsolver (Annapolis, MD)	4/8/55
Maxine Hong Kingston (Stockton, CA)	10/27/40
Galway Kinnell (Providence, RI)	2/1/27
Dean Koontz (Everett, PA)	7/9/45
Ted Kooser (Ames, IA)	4/25/39
Judith Krantz (NYC)	1/9/28
Maxine Kumin (Philadelphia, PA)	6/6/25
Milan Kundera (Brno, Czechoslovakia)	4/1/29
Tony Kushner (NYC)	7/16/56
David Leavitt (Pittsburgh, PA)	6/23/61
John Le Carré (Poole, Eng.)	10/19/31
Harper Lee (Monroeville, AL)	4/28/26
Ursula K. Le Guin (Berkeley, CA)	10/21/29
Madeleine L'Engle (NYC)	11/29/18
Elmore Leonard (New Orleans, LA)	10/11/25
Doris Lessing (Kermanshah, Persia)	10/22/19
Jonathan Lethem (Bklyn, NY)	2/19/64
Ira Levin (NYC)	8/27/29
David Lodge (South London, Eng.)	1/28/35
Alison Lurie (Chicago)	9/3/26
Gregory Maguire (Albany, NY)	6/9/54
Norman Mailer (Long Branch, NJ)	1/31/23
David Mamet (Chicago)	11/30/47
Yann Martel (Salamanca, Spain)	6/25/63
Bobbie Ann Mason (nr. Mayfield, KY)	5/1/40
Peter Matthiessen (NYC)	5/22/27
Armistead Maupin (Wash., DC)	4/13/44
Cormac McCarthy (Providence, RI)	7/20/33
Frank McCourt (Bklyn, NY)	8/19/30
Colleen McCullough (Wellington, N.S.W., Austral.)	6/1/37
Alice McDermott (Bklyn, NY)	6/27/53
Ian McEwan (Aldershot, England)	6/21/48
Thomas McGuane (Wyandotte, MI)	12/11/39
Terry McMillan (Port Huron, MI)	10/18/51
Larry McMurtry (Wichita Falls, TX)	6/3/36
Terrence McNally (St. Petersburg, FL)	11/3/39
John McPhee (Princeton, NJ)	3/8/31
W(illiam) S(tanley) Merwin (NYC)	9/30/27
Toni Morrison (Lorain, OH)	2/18/31
Walter Mosley (Los Angeles, CA)	1/12/52
Andrew Motion (London)	10/26/52
Bharati Mukherjee (Calcutta, India)	7/27/40
Alice Munro (Wingham, Ont.)	7/10/31
Haruki Murakami (Kyoto, Japan)	1/12/49
V. S. Naipaul (Chaguanas, Trinidad)	8/17/32
Joyce Carol Oates (Lockport, NY)	6/16/38
Edna O'Brien (Tuamgraney, Ir.)	12/15/32
Tim O'Brien (Austin, MN)	10/1/46
Kenzaburo Oe (Uchiko, Japan)	1/31/35
Michael Ondaatje (Colombo, Sri Lanka)	9/12/43
Cynthia Ozick (NYC)	4/17/28
Grace Paley (NYC)	12/11/22
Robert B. Parker (Springfield, MA)	9/17/32
Suzan-Lori Parks (Fort Knox, KY)	5/10/63
Marge Piercy (Detroit, MI)	3/31/36
Robert Pinsky (Long Branch, NJ)	10/20/40
Harold Pinter (Hackney, East London, Eng.)	10/10/30
Reynolds Price (Macon, NC)	2/1/33
Richard Price (Bronx, NY)	10/12/49
E. Annie Proulx (Norwich, CT)	8/22/35
Philip Pullman (Norwich, Eng.)	10/19/46
Thomas Pynchon (Glen Cove, Long Island, NY)	5/8/37
David Rabe (Dubuque, IA)	3/10/40
Ishmael Reed (Chattanooga, TN)	2/22/38
Ruth Rendell (London, England)	2/17/30
Anne Rice (New Orleans, LA)	10/4/41
Adrienne Rich (Baltimore, MD)	5/16/29
Nora Roberts (Wash., DC)	10/10/50
Marilyn Robinson (Sandpoint, IL)	1944
Philip Roth (Newark, NJ)	3/19/33
J.K. Rowling (Chipping Sodbury, Eng.)	7/31/65
Norman Rush (Oakland, CA)	10/24/33
Salman Rushdie (Bombay, India)	6/19/47
Richard Russo (Johnstown, NY)	7/15/49
J. D. Salinger (NYC)	1/1/19
Jose Saramago (Azinhaga, Portugal)	11/16/22
Alice Sebold (Madison, WI)	1963
David Sedaris (Johnson City, NY)	12/26/56
Vikram Seth (Calcutta, India)	6/20/52
Sidney Sheldon (Chicago)	2/11/17
Sam Shepard (Ft. Sheridan, IL)	11/5/43
Neil Simon (Bronx, NY)	7/4/27
Jane Smiley (Los Angeles, CA)	9/26/49
Aleksandr Solzhenitsyn (Kislovodsk, Russia)	12/11/18
Wole Soyinka (Abeokuta, Nigeria)	7/13/34
Danielle Steel (NYC)	8/14/47
Richard Stern (NYC)	2/25/28
Mary Stewart (Sunderland, Eng.)	9/17/16
R(obert) L(awrence) Stine (Columbus, OH)	10/8/43
Tom Stoppard (Zlin, Czech.)	7/3/37
Mark Strand (P.E.I., Can.)	4/11/34
William Styron (Newport News, VA)	6/11/25
Wislawa Szymborska (Kornik, Pol.)	7/2/23
Amy Tan (Oakland, CA)	2/19/52
Donna Tartt (Greenwood, MS)	12/23/63
Paul Theroux (Medford, MA)	4/10/41
Calvin Trillin (Kansas City, MO)	12/5/35
Scott F. Turow (Chicago)	4/12/49
Anne Tyler (Minneapolis, MN)	10/25/41
John Updike (Shillington, PA)	3/18/32
Mario Vargas Llosa (Arequipa, Peru)	3/28/36
Gore Vidal (West Point, NY)	10/3/25
Paula Vogel (Wash., DC)	11/16/51
Kurt Vonnegut Jr. (Indianapolis, IN)	11/11/22
Derek Walcott (Castries, Saint Lucia)	1/23/30
Alice Walker (Eatonton, GA)	2/9/44
Robert James Waller (Rockford, IA)	8/1/39
Joseph Wambaugh (East Pittsburgh, PA)	1/22/37
Eli Wiesel (Sighet, Romania)	9/30/28
Edmund White (Cincinnati, OH)	1/19/40
Lanford Wilson (Lebanon, MO)	4/13/37
Tom Wolfe (Richmond, VA)	3/2/31
Tobias Wolff (Birmingham, AL)	6/19/45
Herman Wouk (NYC)	5/27/15
Yevgeny Yevtushenko (Irkutsk, Russia)	7/18/33

Writers of the Past

See also Journalists of the Past, and Greeks and Romans in Historical Figures chapter.

Alice Adams, 1926-99, (U.S.) novelist, short-story writer. *Superior Woman.*

James Agee, 1909-55, (U.S.) novelist. *A Death in the Family.*

S(hmuel) Y(osef)Agnon, 1888-1970, (Is.) Hebrew novelist. *Only Yesterday.*

Conrad Aiken, 1889-1973, (U.S.) poet, critic. *Ushant.*

Anna Akhmatova, 1889-1966, (Russ.) poet. *Requiem.*

Louisa May Alcott, 1832-88, (U.S.) novelist. *Little Women.*

Sholom Aleichem, 1859-1916, (Russ.) Yiddish writer. *Tevye's Daughters, The Old Country.*

Vicente Aleixandre, 1898-1984, (Sp.) poet. *La destrucción o el amor, Dialogolos del conocimiento.*

Horatio Alger, 1832-1899, (U.S.) "rags-to-riches" books.

Jorge Amado, 1912-2001, (Brazil) novelist. *Dona Flor and Her Two Husbands, The Violent Land.*

Eric Ambler, 1909-98, (Br.) suspense novelist. *A Coffin for Dimitrios.*

Kingsley Amis, 1922-95, (Br.) novelist, critic. *Lucky Jim.*

Hans Christian Andersen, 1805-75, (Dan.) author of fairy tales. *The Ugly Duckling.*

Maxwell Anderson, 1888-1959, (U.S.) playwright. *What Price Glory?, High Tor, Winterset, Key Largo.*

Sherwood Anderson, 1876-1941, (U.S.) short-story writer. *"Death in the Woods;" Winesburg, Ohio.*

Reinaldo Arenas, 1943-1990, (Cuba) short-story writer, novelist. *Before Night Falls.*

Ludovico Ariosto, 1474-1533, (It.) poet. *Orlando Furioso.*

Matthew Arnold, 1822-88, (Br.) poet, critic. *"Thrysis," "Dover Beach," "Culture and Anarchy."*

Isaac Asimov, 1920-92, (U.S.) versatile writer, espec. of science-fiction. *I Robot.*

Miguel Angel Asturias, 1899-1974, (Guatemala) novelist. *El Señor Presidente.*

W(ystan) H(ugh) Auden, 1907-73, (Br.) poet, playwright, literary critic. *"The Age of Anxiety."*

Jane Austen, 1775-1817, (Br.) novelist. *Pride and Prejudice, Sense and Sensibility, Emma, Mansfield Park.*

Isaac Babel, 1894-1941, (Russ.) short-story writer, playwright. *Odessa Tales, Red Cavalry.*

James Baldwin, 1924-87, (U.S.) author, playwright. *The Fire Next Time, Blues for Mister Charlie.*

Honoré de Balzac, 1799-1850, (Fr.) novelist. *Le Père Goriot, Cousine Bette, Eugénie Grandet.*

James M. Barrie, 1860-1937, (Br.) playwright, novelist. *Peter Pan, Dear Brutus, What Every Woman Knows.*

Charles Baudelaire, 1821-67, (Fr.) poet. *Les Fleurs du Mal.*

L(yman) Frank Baum, 1856-1919, (U.S.) *Wizard of Oz* series.

Simone de Beauvoir, 1908-86, (Fr.) novelist, essayist. *The Second Sex, Memoirs of a Dutiful Daughter.*

Samuel Beckett, 1906-89, (Ir.) novelist, playwright. *Waiting for Godot, Endgame* (plays); *Murphy, Watt, Molloy* (novels).

Brendan Behan, 1923-64, (Ir.) playwright. *The Quare Fellow, The Hostage, Borstal Boy.*

Saul Bellow,1915-2005, (U.S.) novelist. *The Adventures of Augie March, Humboldt's Gift.*

Robert Benchley, 1889-1945, (U.S.) humorist.

Stephen Vincent Benét, 1898-1943, (U.S.) poet, novelist. *John Brown's Body.*

Stan Berenstain 1923-2005, (U.S.) co-writer and illustrator of *Berenstain Bears* series of children's books.

John Berryman, 1914-72, (U.S.) poet. *Homage to Mistress Bradstreet.*

Ambrose Bierce, 1842-1914, (U.S.) short-story writer, journalist. *In the Midst of Life, The Devil's Dictionary.*

Elizabeth Bishop, 1911-79, (U.S.) poet. *North and South—A Cold Spring.*

William Blake, 1757-1827, (Br.) poet, artist. *Songs of Innocence, Songs of Experience.*

Aleksandr Blok, 1880-1921, (Russ.) poet. *"The Twelve", "The Scythians."*

Giovanni Boccaccio, 1313-75, (It.) poet. *Decameron.*

Heinrich Böll, 1917-85, (Ger.) novelist, short-story writer. *Group Portrait With Lady.*

Jorge Luis Borges, 1900-86, (Arg.) short-story writer, poet, essayist. *Labyrinths.*

James Boswell, 1740-95, (Sc.) biographer. *The Life of Samuel Johnson.*

Pierre Boulle, 1913-94, (Fr.) novelist. *The Bridge Over the River Kwai, Planet of the Apes.*

Paul Bowles, 1910-99, (U.S.) novelist, short-story writer. *The Sheltering Sky.*

Anne Bradstreet, c1612-72, (U.S.) poet. *The Tenth Muse Lately Sprung Up in America.*

Bertolt Brecht, 1898-1956, (Ger.) dramatist, poet. *The Threepenny Opera, Mother Courage and Her Children.*

Charlotte Brontë, 1816-55, (Br.) novelist. *Jane Eyre.*

Emily Brontë, 1818-48, (Br.) novelist. *Wuthering Heights.*

Elizabeth Barrett Browning, 1806-61, (Br.) poet. *Sonnets From the Portuguese, Aurora Leigh.*

Joseph Brodsky, 1940-96, (Russ.-U.S.) poet. *A Part of Speech, Less Than One, To Urania.*

Sterling A. Brown, 1901-89, (U.S.) poet, literature professor. *Southern Road.*

William Wells Brown, 1815-84, (U.S.) writer, memoirist, first African American to publish a novel, *Clotel,* 1853.

Robert Browning, 1812-89, (Br.) poet. "My Last Duchess," "Fra Lippo Lippi," *The Ring and The Book.*

Pearl S. Buck, 1892-1973, (U.S.) novelist. *The Good Earth.*

Mikhail Bulgakov, 1891-1940, (Russ.) novelist, playwright. *The Heart of a Dog, The Master and Margarita.*

John Bunyan, 1628-88, (Br.) writer. *Pilgrim's Progress.*

Anthony Burgess, 1917-93, (Br.) author. *A Clockwork Orange.*

Frances Hodgson Burnett, 1849-1924, (Br.-U.S.) novelist. *The Secret Garden.*

Robert Burns, 1759-96, (Sc.) poet. "Flow Gently, Sweet Afton," "My Heart's in the Highlands," "Auld Lang Syne."

Edgar Rice Burroughs, 1875-1950, (U.S.) "Tarzan" books.

William S. Burroughs, 1914-97, (U.S.) novelist. *Naked Lunch.*

George Gordon, Lord Byron, 1788-1824, (Br.) poet. *Don Juan, Childe Harold, Manfred, Cain.*

Pedro Calderon de la Barca, 1600-81, (Sp.) playwright. *Life Is a Dream.*

Italo Calvino, 1923-85, (It.) novelist, short-story writer. *If on a Winter's Night a Traveler.*

Luis Vaz de Camoes, 1524?-80 (Port.) poet. *The Lusiads.*

Albert Camus, 1913-60, (Fr.) writer. *The Stranger, The Fall.*

Elias Canetti, 1905-94, (Bulg.) novelist, essayist. *Auto-Da-Fe.*

Karel Capek, 1890-1938, (Czech.) playwright, novelist, essayist. *R.U.R. (Rossum's Universal Robots).*

Truman Capote, 1924-84, (U.S.) author. *Other Voices, Other Rooms, Breakfast at Tiffany's, In Cold Blood.*

Lewis Carroll (Charles Dodgson), 1832-98, (Br.) writer, mathematician. *Alice's Adventures in Wonderland.*

Giacomo Casanova, 1725-98, (It.) adventurer, memoirist.

Willa Cather, 1873-1947, (U.S.) novelist. *O Pioneers!, My Ántonia, Death Comes for the Archbishop.*

Constantine Cavafy, 1863-1933, (Gr.) poet. "Ithaka", "Sensual Pleasures."

Camilo Jose Cela, 1916-2001, (Sp.) novelist. *The Family of Pascual Duarte, The Hive.*

Miguel de Cervantes Saavedra, 1547-1616, (Sp.) novelist, dramatist, poet. *Don Quixote.*

Raymond Chandler, 1888-1959, (U.S.) writer of detective fiction. Philip Marlowe series.

Geoffrey Chaucer, c1340-1400, (Br.) poet. *The Canterbury Tales, Troilus and Criseyde.*

John Cheever, 1912-82, (U.S.) novelist, short-story writer. *The Wapshot Scandal,* "The Country Husband."

Anton Chekhov, 1860-1904, (Russ.) short-story writer, dramatist. *Uncle Vanya, The Cherry Orchard, The Three Sisters.*

Charles Waddell Chesnutt, 1858-1932, (U.S.) author known for his short stories, such as in *The Conjure Woman (1899).*

G(ilbert) K(eith) Chesterton, 1874-1936, (Br.) critic, novelist, relig. apologist. Father Brown series of mysteries.

Kate Chopin, 1851-1904, (U.S.) writer. *The Awakening.*

Agatha Christie, 1890-1976, (Br.) mystery writer; created Miss Marple, Hercule Poirot; *And Then There Were None, Murder on the Orient Express, Murder of Roger Ackroyd.*

James Clavell, 1924-94, (Br.-U.S.) novelist. *Shogun, King Rat.*

Jean Cocteau, 1889-1963, (Fr.) writer, visual artist, filmmaker. *The Beauty and the Beast, Les Enfants Terribles.*

Samuel Taylor Coleridge, 1772-1834, (Br.) poet, critic. "Kubla Khan," "The Rime of the Ancient Mariner."

(Sidonie) Colette, 1873-1954, (Fr.) novelist. *Claudine, Gigi.*

Wilkie Collins, 1824-89, (Br.) novelist. *The Moonstone.*

Joseph Conrad, 1857-1924, (Br.) novelist. *Lord Jim, Heart of Darkness, The Secret Agent.*

James Fenimore Cooper, 1789-1851, (U.S.) novelist. *Leatherstocking Tales, The Last of the Mohicans.*

Pierre Corneille, 1606-84, (Fr.) dramatist. *Medeé, Le Cid.*

Hart Crane, 1899-1932, (U.S.) poet. "The Bridge."

Stephen Crane, 1871-1900, (U.S.) novelist, short-story writer. *The Red Badge of Courage,* "The Open Boat."

Countee Cullen, 1903-46, (U.S.) poet, prominent in the Harlem Renaissance of the 1920s; *The Black Christ.*

E. E. Cummings, 1894-1962, (U.S.) poet. *Tulips and Chimneys.*

Roald Dahl, 1916-90, (Br.-U.S.) writer. *Charlie and the Chocolate Factory, James and the Giant Peach.*

Gabriele D'Annunzio, 1863-1938, (It.) poet, novelist, dramatist. *The Child of Pleasure, The Intruder, The Victim.*

Dante Alighieri, 1265-1321, (It.) poet. *The Divine Comedy.*

Robertson Davies, 1913-95, (Can.) novelist, playwright, essayist. Salterton, Deptford, and Cornish trilogies.

Daniel Defoe, 1660-1731, (Br.) writer. *Robinson Crusoe, Moll Flanders, Journal of the Plague Year.*

Charles Dickens, 1812-70, (Br.) novelist. *David Copperfield, Oliver Twist, Great Expectations, A Tale of Two Cities.*

Philip K. Dick, 1928-82, (U.S.) science fiction writer. *Do Androids Dream of Electric Sheep?*

James Dickey, 1923-1997, (U.S.) poet, novelist. *Deliverance.*

Emily Dickinson, 1830-86, (U.S.) lyric poet. "Because I could not stop for Death . . .," "Success is counted sweetest . . ."

Isak Dinesen (Karen Blixen), 1885-1962, (Dan.) author. *Out of Africa, Seven Gothic Tales, Winter's Tales.*

John Donne, 1573-1631, (Br.) poet. *Songs and Sonnets.*

José Donoso, 1924-96, (Chil.) surreal novelist and short-story writer. *The Obscene Bird of Night.*

John Dos Passos, 1896-1970, (U.S.) novelist. *U.S.A.*

Fyodor Dostoyevsky, 1821-81, (Russ.) novelist. *Crime and Punishment, The Brothers Karamazov, The Possessed.*

Arthur Conan Doyle, 1859-1930, (Br.) novelist. Sherlock Holmes mystery stories.

Theodore Dreiser, 1871-1945, (U.S.) novelist. *An American Tragedy, Sister Carrie.*

John Dryden, 1631-1700, (Br.) poet, dramatist, critic. *All for Love, Mac Flecknoe, Absalom and Achitophel.*

Alexandre Dumas, 1802-70, (Fr.) novelist, dramatist. *The Three Musketeers, The Count of Monte Cristo.*

Alexandre Dumas (fils), 1824-95, (Fr.) dramatist, novelist. *La Dame aux Camélias, Le Demi-Monde.*

Paul Laurence Dunbar, 1872-1906, (U.S.) poet, novelist; won fame with *Lyrics of Lowly Life,* 1896.

Lawrence Durrell, 1912-90, (Br.) novelist, poet. *Alexandria Quartet.*

Ilya G. Ehrenburg, 1891-1967, (Russ.) writer. *The Thaw.*

George Eliot (Mary Ann Evans or Marian Evans), 1819-80, (Br.) novelist. *Silas Marner, Middlemarch.*

T(homas) S(tearns) Eliot, 1888-1965, (Br.) poet, critic. *The Waste Land,* "The Love Song of J. Alfred Prufrock."

Stanley Elkin, 1930-95, (U.S.) novelist, short story writer. *George Mills.*

Ralph Ellison, 1914-94, (U.S.), writer. *Invisible Man.*

Ralph Waldo Emerson, 1803-82, (U.S.) poet, essayist. "Brahma," "Nature," "The Over-Soul," "Self-Reliance."

James T. Farrell, 1904-79, (U.S.) novelist. *Studs Lonigan.*

William Faulkner, 1897-1962, (U.S.) novelist. *Sanctuary, Light in August, The Sound and the Fury, Absalom, Absalom!*

Edna Ferber, 1887-1968, (U.S.) novelist, short-story writer, playwright. *So Big, Cimarron, Show Boat.*

Henry Fielding, 1707-54, (Br.) novelist. *Tom Jones.*

F(rancis) Scott Fitzgerald, 1896-1940, (U.S.) short-story writer, novelist. *The Great Gatsby, Tender Is the Night.*

Gustave Flaubert, 1821-80, (Fr.) novelist. *Madame Bovary.*

Ian Fleming, 1908-64, (Br.) novelist; James Bond spy thrillers. *Dr. No, Goldfinger.*

Ford Madox Ford, 1873-1939, (Br.) novelist, critic, poet. *The Good Soldier.*

C(ecil) S(cott) Forester, 1899-1966, (Br.) writer. Horatio Hornblower books.

E(dward) M(organ) Forster, 1879-1970, (Br.) novelist. *A Passage to India, Howards End.*

Anatole France, 1844-1924, (Fr.) writer. *Penguin Island, My Friend's Book, The Crime of Sylvestre Bonnard.*

Robert Frost, 1874-1963, (U.S.) poet. "Birches," "Fire and Ice," "Stopping by Woods on a Snowy Evening."

William Gaddis, 1922-98, (U.S.) novelist. *The Recognitions.*

John Galsworthy, 1867-1933, (Br.) novelist, dramatist. *The Forsyte Saga.*

Federico Garcia Lorca, 1898-1936, (Sp.) poet, dramatist. *Blood Wedding.*

Erle Stanley Gardner, 1889-1970, (U.S.) mystery writer; created Perry Mason.

Jean Genet, 1911-86, (Fr.) playwright, novelist. *The Maids.*

Kahlil Gibran, 1883-1931, (Lebanese-U.S.) mystical novelist, essayist, poet. *The Prophet.*

André Gide, 1869-1951, (Fr.) writer. *The Immoralist, The Pastoral Symphony, Strait Is the Gate.*

Allen Ginsberg, 1926-1997, (U.S.) Beat poet. "Howl."

Jean Giraudoux, 1882-1944, (Fr.) novelist, dramatist. *Electra, The Madwoman of Chaillot, Ondine, Tiger at the Gate.*

Johann Wolfgang von Goethe, 1749-1832, (Ger.) poet, dramatist, novelist. *Faust, Sorrows of Young Werther.*

Nikolai Gogol, 1809-52, (Russ.) short-story writer, dramatist, novelist. *Dead Souls, The Inspector General.*

William Golding, 1911-93, (Br.) novelist. *Lord of the Flies.*

Oliver Goldsmith, 1728-74, (Br.-Ir.) dramatist, novelist. *The Vicar of Wakefield, She Stoops to Conquer.*

Maxim Gorky, 1868-1936, (Russ.) dramatist, novelist. *The Lower Depths.*

Robert Graves, 1895-1985, (Br.) poet, classical scholar, novelist. *I, Claudius; The White Goddess.*

Thomas Gray, 1716-71, (Br.) poet. "Elegy Written in a Country Churchyard," "The Progress of Poesy."

Julien Green, 1900-98, (U.S.-Fr.) expatriate American, French novelist. *Moira, Each Man in His Darkness.*

Graham Greene, 1904-91, (Br.) novelist. *The Power and the Glory, The Heart of the Matter, The Ministry of Fear.*

Zane Grey, 1872-1939, (U.S.) writer of Western stories.

Jakob Grimm, 1785-1863, (Ger.) philologist, folklorist; with brother **Wilhelm,** 1786-1859, collected *Grimm's Fairy Tales.*

Alex Haley, 1921-92, (U.S.) author. *Roots.*

Dashiell Hammett, 1894-1961, (U.S.) detective-story writer; created Sam Spade. *The Maltese Falcon, The Thin Man.*

Jupiter Hammon, c1720-1800, (U.S.) poet; first African American to have his works published, 1761.

Knut Hamsun, 1859-1952 (Nor.) novelist. *Hunger.*

Lorraine Hansberry, 1930-65, (U.S.) playwright; won New York Drama Critics Circle Award, 1959; *A Raisin in the Sun.*

Thomas Hardy, 1840-1928, (Br.) novelist, poet. *The Return of the Native, Tess of the D'Urbervilles, Jude the Obscure.*

Joel Chandler Harris, 1848-1908, (U.S.) Uncle Remus stories.

Moss Hart, 1904-61, (U.S.) playwright. *Once in a Lifetime, You Can't Take It With You, The Man Who Came to Dinner.*

Bret Harte, 1836-1902, (U.S.) short-story writer, poet. *The Luck of Roaring Camp.*

Jaroslav Hasek, 1883-1923, (Czech.) writer, playwright. *The Good Soldier Schweik.*

John Hawkes, 1925-98, (U.S.) experimental fiction writer. *The Goose on the Grave, Blood Oranges.*

Nathaniel Hawthorne, 1804-64, (U.S.) novelist, short-story writer. *The Scarlet Letter,* "Young Goodman Brown."

Heinrich Heine, 1797-1856, (Ger.) poet. *Book of Songs.*

Robert Heinlein, 1907-88, (U.S.) science fiction writer. *Stranger in a Strange Land.*

Joseph Heller, 1923-99, (U.S.) novelist. *Catch-22.*

Lillian Hellman, 1905-84, (U.S.) playwright, author of memoirs. *The Little Foxes, An Unfinished Woman, Pentimento.*

Ernest Hemingway, 1899-1961, (U.S.) novelist, short-story writer. *A Farewell to Arms, For Whom the Bell Tolls.*

O. Henry (W. S. Porter), 1862-1910, (U.S.) short-story writer. "The Gift of the Magi."

George Herbert, 1593-1633, (Br.) poet. "The Altar," "Easter Wings."

Zbigniew Herbert, 1924-98, (Pol.) poet. "Apollo and Marsyas."

Robert Herrick, 1591-1674, (Br.) poet. "To the Virgins to Make Much of Time."

John Hersey, 1914-93, (U.S.) novelist, journalist. *Hiroshima, A Bell for Adano.*

Hermann Hesse, 1877-1962, (Ger.) novelist, poet. *Death and the Lover, Steppenwolf, Siddhartha.*

James Hilton, 1900-54, (Br.) novelist. *Lost Horizon.*

Chester Himes, 1909-84, (U.S.) novelist; *Cotton Comes to Harlem.*

Oliver Wendell Holmes, 1809-94, (U.S.) poet, novelist. *The Autocrat of the Breakfast-Table.*

Gerard Manley Hopkins, 1844-89, (Br.) poet. "Pied Beauty," "God's Grandeur."

A(lfred) E. Housman, 1859-1936, (Br.) poet. *A Shropshire Lad.*

William Dean Howells, 1837-1920, (U.S.) novelist, critic. *The Rise of Silas Lapham.*

Langston Hughes, 1902-67, (U.S.) poet, lyric writer, author; a major influence in 1920s Harlem Renaissance.

Ted Hughes, 1930-98, (Br.) British poet laureate, 1984-98. *Crow, The Hawk in the Rain.*

Victor Hugo, 1802-85, (Fr.) poet, dramatist, novelist. *Notre Dame de Paris, Les Misérables.*

Zora Neale Hurston, 1903-60, (U.S.) novelist, folklorist. *Their Eyes Were Watching God, Mules and Men.*

Aldous Huxley, 1894-1963, (Br.) writer. *Brave New World.*

Henrik Ibsen, 1828-1906, (Nor.) dramatist, poet. *A Doll's House, Ghosts, The Wild Duck, Hedda Gabler.*

William Inge, 1913-73, (U.S.) playwright. *Picnic; Come Back, Little Sheba; Bus Stop.*

Eugene Ionesco, 1910-94, (Fr.) surrealist dramatist. *The Bald Soprano, The Chairs.*

Washington Irving, 1783-1859, (U.S.) writer. "Rip Van Winkle," "The Legend of Sleepy Hollow."

Christopher Isherwood, 1904-1986, (Br.) novelist, playwright. *The Berlin Stories.*

Shirley Jackson, 1919-65, (U.S.) short-story writer. "The Lottery."

Henry James, 1843-1916, (U.S.) novelist, short-story writer, critic. *The Portrait of a Lady, The Ambassadors, Daisy Miller.*

Robinson Jeffers, 1887-1962, (U.S.) poet, dramatist. *Tamar and Other Poems, Medea.*

Samuel Johnson, 1709-84, (Br.) author, scholar, critic. *Dictionary of the English Language, Vanity of Human Wishes.*

Ben Jonson, 1572-1637, (Br.) dramatist, poet. *Volpone.*

James Weldon Johnson, 1871-1938, (U.S.) poet, novelist, diplomat; lyricist for *Lift Every Voice and Sing.*

James Joyce, 1882-1941, (Ir.) writer. *Ulysses, Dubliners, A Portrait of the Artist as a Young Man, Finnegans Wake.*

Ernst Junger, 1895-1998, (Ger.) novelist, essayist. *The Peace, On the Marble Cliff.*

Franz Kafka, 1883-1924, (Austro-Hung./Czech) novelist, short-story writer. *The Trial, The Castle,* "The Metamorphosis."

George S. Kaufman, 1889-1961, (U.S.) playwright. *The Man Who Came to Dinner, You Can't Take It With You.*

Yasunari Kawabata, 1899-1972, (Japan) novelist. *The Sound of the Mountains.*

Nikos Kazantzakis, 1883-1957, (Gk.) novelist. *Zorba the Greek, A Greek Passion.*

Alfred Kazin, 1915-98 (U.S.) author, critic, teacher. *On Native Grounds.*

John Keats, 1795-1821, (Br.) poet. "Ode on a Grecian Urn," "Ode to a Nightingale," "La Belle Dame Sans Merci."

Jack Kerouac, 1922-1969, (U.S.), author, Beat poet. *On the Road, The Dharma Bums,* "Mexico City Blues."

Joyce Kilmer, 1886-1918, (U.S.) poet. "Trees."

Rudyard Kipling, 1865-1936, (Br.) author, poet. "The White Man's Burden," "Gunga Din," *The Jungle Book.*

Jean de la Fontaine, 1621-95, (Fr.) poet. *Fables choisies.*

Pär Lagerkvist, 1891-1974, (Swed.) poet, dramatist, novelist. *Barabbas, The Sybil.*

Selma Lagerlöf, 1858-1940, (Swed.) novelist. *Jerusalem, The Ring of the Lowenskolds.*

Alphonse de Lamartine, 1790-1869, (Fr.) poet, novelist, statesman. *Méditations poétiques.*

Charles Lamb, 1775-1834, (Br.) essayist. *Specimens of English Dramatic Poets, Essays of Elia.*

Giuseppe di Lampedusa, 1896-1957, (It.) novelist. *The Leopard.*

William Langland, c1332-1400, (Eng.) poet. *Piers Plowman.*

Ring Lardner, 1885-1933, (U.S.) short-story writer, humorist.

Louis L'Amour, 1908-88, (U.S.) western author, screenwriter. *Hondo, The Cherokee Trail.*

D(avid) H(erbert) Lawrence, 1885-1930, (Br.) novelist. *Sons and Lovers, Women in Love, Lady Chatterley's Lover.*

Halldor Laxness, 1902-98, (Icelandic) novelist. *Iceland's Bell.*

Mikhail Lermontov, 1814-41, (Russ.) novelist, poet. "Demon," *Hero of Our Time.*

Alain-René Lesage, 1668-1747, (Fr.) novelist. *Gil Blas de Santillane.*

Gotthold Lessing, 1729-81, (Ger.) dramatist, philosopher, critic. *Miss Sara Sampson, Minna von Barnhelm.*

C(live) S(taples) Lewis, 1898-1963, (Br.) critic, novelist, religious writer. *Allegory of Love; The Lion, the Witch and the Wardrobe; Out of the Silent Planet.*

Sinclair Lewis, 1885-1951, (U.S.) novelist. *Babbitt, Main Street, Arrowsmith, Dodsworth.*

Li Po, 701-762, (China) poet. "Song Before Drinking," "She Spins Silk."

Vachel Lindsay, 1879-1931, (U.S.) poet. *General William Booth Enters Into Heaven, The Congo.*

Hugh Lofting, 1886-1947, (Br.) writer. Dr. Doolittle series.

Jack London, 1876-1916, (U.S.) novelist, journalist. *Call of the Wild, The Sea-Wolf, White Fang.*

Henry Wadsworth Longfellow, 1807-82, (U.S.) poet. *Evangeline, The Song of Hiawatha.*

Lope de Vega, 1562-1635, (Sp.) playwright. *Noche de San Juan, Maestro de Danzar.*

H(oward) P(hillips) Lovecraft, 1890-1937, (U.S.), novelist, short-story writer. "At the Mountains of Madness."

Amy Lowell, 1874-1925, (U.S.) poet, critic. "Lilacs."

James Russell Lowell, 1819-91, (U.S.) poet, editor. *Poems, The Biglow Papers.*

Robert Lowell, 1917-77, (U.S.) poet. "Lord Weary's Castle."

Joaquim Maria Machado de Assis, 1839-1908, (Brazil) novelist, poet. *The Posthumous Memoirs of Bras Cubas.*

Archibald MacLeish, 1892-1982, (U.S.) poet. *Conquistador.*

Naguib Mahfouz, 1911-2006, (Egypt) novelist; first Arabic-language writer to win the Nobel Prize for Literature. *Cairo Trilogy.*

Bernard Malamud, 1914-86, (U.S.) short-story writer, novelist. "The Magic Barrel," *The Assistant, The Fixer.*

Stéphane Mallarmé, 1842-98, (Fr.) poet. *Poésies.*

Sir Thomas Malory, ?-1471, (Br.) writer. *Morte d'Arthur.*

Andre Malraux, 1901-76, (Fr.) novelist. *Man's Fate.*

Osip Mandelstam, 1891-1938, (Russ.) poet. *Stone, Tristia.*

Thomas Mann, 1875-1955, (Ger.) novelist, essayist. *Buddenbrooks, The Magic Mountain,* "Death in Venice."

Katherine Mansfield, 1888-1923, (Br.) short-story writer. "Bliss."

Christopher Marlowe, 1564-93, (Br.) dramatist, poet. *Tamburlaine the Great, Dr. Faustus, The Jew of Malta.*

Andrew Marvell, 1621-78, (Br.) poet. "To His Coy Mistress."

John Masefield, 1878-1967, (Br.) poet. "Sea Fever," "Cargoes," *Salt Water Ballads.*

Edgar Lee Masters, 1869-1950, (U.S.) poet, biographer. *Spoon River Anthology.*

W(illiam) Somerset Maugham, 1874-1965, (Br.) author. *Of Human Bondage, The Moon and Sixpence.*

Guy de Maupassant, 1850-93, (Fr.) novelist, short-story writer. "A Life," "Bel-Ami," "The Necklace."

François Mauriac, 1885-1970, (Fr.) novelist, dramatist. *Viper's Tangle, The Kiss to the Leper.*

Vladimir Mayakovsky, 1893-1930, (Russ.) poet, dramatist. *The Cloud in Trousers.*

Mary McCarthy, 1912-89, (U.S.) critic, novelist, memoirist. *Memories of a Catholic Girlhood.*

Carson McCullers, 1917-67, (U.S.) novelist. *The Heart Is a Lonely Hunter, Member of the Wedding.*

Herman Melville, 1819-91, (U.S.) novelist, poet. *Moby-Dick, Typee, Billy Budd, Omoo.*

George Meredith, 1828-1909, (Br.) novelist, poet. *The Ordeal of Richard Feverel, The Egoist.*

Prosper Mérimée, 1803-70, (Fr.) author. *Carmen.*

James Merrill, 1926-95, (U.S.) poet. *Divine Comedies.*

James Michener, 1907-97, (U.S.) novelist. *Tales of the South Pacific.*

Edna St. Vincent Millay, 1892-1950, (U.S.) poet. *The Harp Weaver and Other Poems.*

Arthur Miller, 1915-2005, (U.S.) playwright. *The Crucible, After the Fall, Death of a Salesman.*

Henry Miller, 1891-1980, (U.S.) erotic novelist. *Tropic of Cancer.*

A(lan) A(lexander) Milne, 1882-1956, (Br.) author. *Winnie-the-Pooh.*

Czeslaw Milosz, 1911-2004, (Pol.) essayist, poet. "Esse," "Encounter."

John Milton, 1608-74, (Br.) poet, writer. *Paradise Lost, Comus, Lycidas, Areopagitica.*

Mishima Yukio (Hiraoka Kimitake), 1925-70, (Jpn.) writer. *Confessions of a Mask.*

Gabriela Mistral, 1889-1957, (Chil.) poet. *Sonnets of Death.*

Margaret Mitchell, 1900-49, (U.S.) novelist. *Gone With the Wind.*

Jean Baptiste Molière, 1622-73, (Fr.) dramatist. *Tartuffe, Le Misanthrope, Le Bourgeois Gentilhomme.*

Ferenc Molnár, 1878-1952, (Hung.) dramatist, novelist. *Liliom, The Guardsman, The Swan.*

Michel de Montaigne, 1533-92, (Fr.) essayist. *Essais.*

Eugenio Montale, 1896-1981, (It.) poet.

Brian Moore, 1921-99, (Ir.-U.S.) novelist. *The Lonely Passion of Judith Hearne.*

Clement C. Moore, 1779-1863, (U.S.) poet, educator. "A Visit From Saint Nicholas."

Marianne Moore, 1887-1972, (U.S.) poet.

Alberto Moravia, 1907-90, (It.) novelist, short-story writer. *The Time of Indifference.*

Sir Thomas More, 1478-1535, (Br.) writer, statesman, saint. *Utopia.*

Wright Morris, 1910-98 (U.S.) novelist. *My Uncle Dudley.*

Murasaki Shikibu, c978-1026, (Jpn.) novelist. *The Tale of Genji.*

Iris Murdoch, 1919-99 (Br.), novelist, philosopher. *The Sea, The Sea.*

Alfred de Musset, 1810-57, (Fr.) poet, dramatist. *La Confession d'un Enfant du Siècle.*

Vladimir Nabokov, 1899-1977, (Russ.-U.S.) novelist. *Lolita, Pale Fire.*

R.K. Narayan, 1906-2001, (India), novelist, *The Guide.*

Ogden Nash, 1902-71, (U.S.) poet of light verse.

Pablo Neruda, 1904-73, (Chil.) poet. *Twenty Love Poems and One Song of Despair, Toward the Splendid City.*

Patrick O'Brian, 1914-2000, (Br.) historical novelist. *Master and Commander, Blue at the Mizzen.*

Sean O'Casey, 1884-1964, (Ir.) dramatist. *Juno and the Paycock, The Plough and the Stars.*

Frank O'Connor (Michael Donovan), 1903-66, (Ir.) short-story writer. "Guests of a Nation."

Flannery O'Connor, 1925-64, (U.S.) novelist, short-story writer. *Wise Blood,* "A Good Man Is Hard to Find."

Clifford Odets, 1906-63, (U.S.) playwright. *Waiting for Lefty, Awake and Sing, Golden Boy, The Country Girl.*

John O'Hara, 1905-70, (U.S.) novelist, short-story writer. *From the Terrace, Appointment in Samarra, Pal Joey.*

Omar Khayyam, c1028-1122, (Per.) poet. *Rubaiyat.*

Eugene O'Neill, 1888-1953, (U.S.) playwright. *Emperor Jones, Anna Christie, Long Day's Journey Into Night.*

George Orwell (Eric Arthur Blair), 1903-50, (Br.) novelist, essayist. *Animal Farm, Nineteen Eighty-Four.*

John Osborne, 1929-95, (Br.) dramatist, novelist. *Look Back in Anger, The Entertainer.*

Wilfred Owen, 1893-1918 (Br.) poet. "Dulce et Decorum Est."

Dorothy Parker, 1893-1967, (U.S.) poet, short-story writer. *Enough Rope, Laments for the Living.*

Boris Pasternak, 1890-1960, (Russ.) poet, novelist. *Doctor Zhivago.*

Alan Paton, 1903-88, (S. Africa) novelist. *Cry, the Beloved Country.*

Octavio Paz, 1914-98, (Mex.) poet, essayist. *The Labyrinth of Solitude, They Shall Not Pass!, The Sun Stone.*

Samuel Pepys, 1633-1703, (Br.) public official, diarist.

S(idney) J(oseph) Perelman, 1904-79, (U.S.) humorist. *The Road to Miltown, Under the Spreading Atrophy.*

Charles Perrault, 1628-1703, (Fr.) writer. *Tales From Mother Goose* (*Sleeping Beauty, Cinderella*).

Petrarch (Francesco Petrarca), 1304-74, (It.) poet. *Africa, Trionfi, Canzoniere.*

Luigi Pirandello, 1867-1936, (It.) novelist, dramatist. *Six Characters in Search of an Author.*

Sylvia Plath, 1932-63, (U.S.) author, poet. *The Bell Jar.*

Edgar Allan Poe, 1809-49, (U.S.) poet, short-story writer, critic. "Annabel Lee," "The Raven," "The Purloined Letter."

Alexander Pope, 1688-1744, (Br.) poet. *The Rape of the Lock, The Dunciad, An Essay on Man.*

Katherine Anne Porter, 1890-1980, (U.S.) novelist, short-story writer. *Ship of Fools.*

Chaim Potok, 1929-2002, (U.S.) novelist. *The Chosen.*

Ezra Pound, 1885-1972, (U.S.) poet. *Cantos.*

Anthony Powell, 1905-2000, (Br.) novelist. *A Dance to the Music of Time* series.

J(ohn) B. Priestley, 1894-1984, (Br.) novelist, dramatist. *The Good Companions.*

Marcel Proust, 1871-1922, (Fr.) novelist. *Remembrance of Things Past.*

Aleksandr Pushkin, 1799-1837, (Russ.) poet, novelist. *Boris Godunov, Eugene Onegin.*

Mario Puzo, 1920-99, (U.S.) novelist. *The Godfather.*

François Rabelais, 1495-1553, (Fr.) writer. *Gargantua.*

Jean Racine, 1639-99, (Fr.) dramatist. *Andromaque, Phèdre, Bérénice, Britannicus.*

Ayn Rand, 1905-82, (Russ.-U.S.) novelist, moral theorist. *The Fountainhead, Atlas Shrugged.*

Terence Rattigan, 1911-77, (Br.) playwright. *Separate Tables, The Browning Version.*

Erich Maria Remarque, 1898-1970, (Ger.-U.S.) novelist. *All Quiet on the Western Front.*

Samuel Richardson, 1689-1761, (Br.) novelist. *Pamela; or Virtue Rewarded.*

Rainer Maria Rilke, 1875-1926, (Ger.) poet. *Life and Songs, Duino Elegies, Poems From the Book of Hours.*

Arthur Rimbaud, 1854-91, (Fr.) poet. *A Season in Hell.*

Edwin Arlington Robinson, 1869-1935, (U.S.) poet. "Richard Cory," "Miniver Cheevy," *Merlin.*

Theodore Roethke, 1908-63, (U.S.) poet. *Open House, The Waking, The Far Field.*

Romain Rolland, 1866-1944, (Fr.) novelist, biographer. *Jean-Christophe.*

Pierre de Ronsard, 1524-85, (Fr.) poet. *Sonnets pour Hélène, La Franciade.*

Christina Rossetti, 1830-94, (Br.) poet. "When I Am Dead, My Dearest."

Dante Gabriel Rossetti, 1828-82, (Br.) poet, painter. "The Blessed Damozel."

Edmond Rostand, 1868-1918, (Fr.) poet, dramatist. *Cyrano de Bergerac.*

Damon Runyon, 1880-1946, (U.S.) short-story writer, journalist. *Guys and Dolls, Blue Plate Special.*

John Ruskin, 1819-1900, (Br.) critic, social theorist. *Modern Painters, The Seven Lamps of Architecture.*

François Sagan, (Françoise quoirez) 1935-2004, (Fr.) novelist *Bonjour Tristesse.*

Antoine de Saint-Exupéry, 1900-44, (Fr.) writer. *Wind, Sand and Stars, The Little Prince.*

Saki, or H(ector) H(ugh) Munro, 1870-1916, (Br.) writer. *The Chronicles of Clovis.*

George Sand (Amandine Lucie Aurore Dupin), 1804-76, (Fr.) novelist. *Indiana, Consuelo.*

Carl Sandburg, 1878-1967, (U.S.) poet. *The People, Yes; Chicago Poems, Smoke and Steel, Harvest Poems.*

William Saroyan, 1908-81, (U.S.) playwright, novelist. *The Time of Your Life, The Human Comedy.*

Nathalie Sarraute, 1900-99, (Fr.) Nouveau Roman novelist. *Tropismes.*

May Sarton, 1914-95, (Belg.-U.S.) poet, novelist. *Encounter in April, Anger.*

Dorothy L. Sayers, 1893-1957, (Br.) mystery writer; created Lord Peter Wimsey.

Richard Scarry, 1920-94, (U.S.) author of children's books. *Richard Scarry's Best Story Book Ever.*

Friedrich von Schiller, 1759-1805, (Ger.) dramatist, poet, historian. *Don Carlos, Maria Stuart, Wilhelm Tell.*

Sir Walter Scott, 1771-1832, (Sc.) novelist, poet. *Ivanhoe.*

Jaroslav Seifert, 1902-86, (Czech.) poet.

Dr. Seuss (Theodor Seuss Geisel), 1904-91, (U.S.) children's book author and illustrator. *The Cat in the Hat.*

William Shakespeare, 1564-1616, (Br.) dramatist, poet. *Romeo and Juliet, Hamlet, King Lear, Julius Caesar,* sonnets.

Karl Shapiro, 1913-2000, (U.S.) poet. "Elegy for a Dead Soldier."

George Bernard Shaw, 1856-1950, (Ir.-Br.) playwright, critic. *St. Joan, Pygmalion, Major Barbara, Man and Superman.*

Mary Wollstonecraft Shelley, 1797-1851, (Br.) novelist, feminist. *Frankenstein. The Last Man.*

Percy Bysshe Shelley, 1792-1822, (Br.) poet. *Prometheus Unbound, Adonais,* "Ode to the West Wind," "To a Skylark."

Richard B. Sheridan, 1751-1816, (Br.) dramatist. *The Rivals, School for Scandal.*

Robert Sherwood, 1896-1955, (U.S.) playwright, biographer. *The Petrified Forest, Abe Lincoln in Illinois.*

Mikhail Sholokhov, 1906-84, (Russ.) writer. *The Silent Don.*

Georges Simenon (Georges Sims), 1903-89, (Belg.-Fr.) mystery writer; created Inspector Maigret.

Upton Sinclair, 1878-1968, (U.S.) novelist. *The Jungle.*

Isaac Bashevis Singer, 1904-91, (Pol.-U.S.) novelist, short-story writer, in Yiddish. *The Magician of Lublin.*

C(harles) P(ercy) Snow, 1905-80, (Br.) novelist, scientist. *Strangers and Brothers, Corridors of Power.*

Susan Sontag, 1933-2004, (U.S.) critic, essayist, novelist. *Notes on Camp, The Volcano Lover, In America.*

Stephen Spender, 1909-95, (Br.) poet, critic, novelist. *Twenty Poems,* "Elegy for Margaret."

Edmund Spenser, 1552-99, (Br.) poet. *The Faerie Queen.*

Mickey Spillane, 1918-2006, (U.S.) novelist; series of novels with the character detective Mike Hammer. *The Killing Man.*

Johanna Spyri, 1827-1901, (Swiss) children's author. *Heidi.*

Christina Stead, 1903-83, (Austral.) novelist, short-story writer. *The Man Who Loved Children.*

Richard Steele, 1672-1729, (Br.) essayist, playwright, began the *Tatler* and *Spectator. The Conscious Lovers.*

Gertrude Stein, 1874-1946, (U.S.) writer. *Three Lives.*

John Steinbeck, 1902-68, (U.S.) novelist. *The Grapes of Wrath, Of Mice and Men, The Winter of Our Discontent.*

Stendhal (Marie Henri Beyle), 1783-1842, (Fr.) novelist. *The Red and the Black, The Charterhouse of Parma.*

Laurence Sterne, 1713-68, (Br.) novelist. *Tristram Shandy.*

Wallace Stevens, 1879-1955, (U.S.) poet. *Harmonium, The Man With the Blue Guitar, Notes Toward a Supreme Fiction.*

Robert Louis Stevenson, 1850-94, (Br.) novelist, poet, essayist. *Treasure Island, A Child's Garden of Verses.*

Bram Stoker, 1845-1910, (Br.) writer. *Dracula.*

Rex Stout, 1886-1975, (U.S.) mystery writer; created Nero Wolfe.

Harriet Beecher Stowe, 1811-96, (U.S.) novelist. *Uncle Tom's Cabin.*

Lytton Strachey, 1880-1932, (Br.) biographer, critic. *Eminent Victorians. Queen Victoria, Elizabeth and Essex.*

August Strindberg, 1849-1912, (Swed.) dramatist, novelist. *The Father, Miss Julie, The Creditors.*

Jonathan Swift, 1667-1745, (Br.) satirist, poet. *Gulliver's Travels,* "A Modest Proposal."

Algernon C. Swinburne, 1837-1909, (Br.) poet, dramatist. *Atalanta in Calydon.*

John M. Synge, 1871-1909, (Ir.) poet, dramatist. *Riders to the Sea, The Playboy of the Western World.*

Rabindranath Tagore, 1861-1941, (In.) author, poet. *Sadhana, The Realization of Life, Gitanjali.*

Booth Tarkington, 1869-1946, (U.S.) novelist. *Seventeen.*

Peter Taylor, 1917-94, (U.S.) novelist. *A Summons to Memphis.*

Sara Teasdale, 1884-1933, (U.S.) poet. *Helen of Troy and Other Poems, Rivers to the Sea.*

Alfred, Lord Tennyson, 1809-92, (Br.) poet. *Idylls of the King, In Memoriam,* "The Charge of the Light Brigade."

William Makepeace Thackeray, 1811-63, (Br.) novelist. *Vanity Fair, Henry Esmond, Pendennis.*

Dylan Thomas, 1914-53, (Welsh) poet. *Under Milk Wood, A Child's Christmas in Wales.*

Hunter S. Thompson, 1937-2005, (U.S.) author, journalist. *Hell's Angels, Fear and Loathing in Las Vegas.*

Henry David Thoreau, 1817-62, (U.S.) writer, philosopher, naturalist. *Walden,* "Civil Disobedience."

James Thurber, 1894-1961, (U.S.) humorist; "The Secret Life of Walter Mitty," *My Life and Hard Times.*

J(ohn) R(onald) R(euel) Tolkien, 1892-1973, (Br.) writer. *The Hobbit, Lord of the Rings* trilogy.

Leo Tolstoy, 1828-1910, (Russ.) novelist, short-story writer. *War and Peace, Anna Karenina,* "The Death of Ivan Ilyich."

Lionel Trilling, 1905-75 (U.S.) critic, author, teacher. *The Liberal Imagination.*

Anthony Trollope, 1815-82, (Br.) novelist. *The Warden, Barchester Towers,* the Palliser novels.

Ivan Turgenev, 1818-83, (Russ.) novelist, short-story writer. *Fathers and Sons, First Love, A Month in the Country.*

Amos Tutuola, 1920-97, (Nigerian) novelist. *The Palm-Wine Drunkard, My Life in the Bush of Ghosts.*

Mark Twain (Samuel Clemens), 1835-1910, (U.S.) novelist, humorist. *The Adventures of Huckleberry Finn.*

Sigrid Undset, 1881-1949, (Nor.) novelist, *Kristin Lavransdatter.*

Paul Valéry, 1871-1945, (Fr.) poet, critic. *La Jeune Parque, The Graveyard by the Sea.*

Paul Verlaine, 1844-96, (Fr.) Symbolist poet. *Songs Without Words.*

Jules Verne, 1828-1905, (Fr.) novelist. *Twenty Thousand Leagues Under the Sea.*

François Villon, 1431-63?, (Fr.) poet. *The Lays, The Grand Testament.*

Voltaire (F.M. Arouet), 1694-1778, (Fr.) writer of "philosophical romances"; philosopher, historian; *Candide.*

Robert Penn Warren, 1905-89, (U.S.) novelist, poet, critic. *All the King's Men.*

Wendy Wasserstein, 1950-2006, (U.S.) playwright; *The Heidi Chronicles.*

Evelyn Waugh, 1903-66, (Br.) novelist. *The Loved One, Brideshead Revisited, A Handful of Dust.*

H(erbert) G(eorge) Wells, 1866-1946, (Br.) novelist. *The Time Machine, The Invisible Man, The War of the Worlds.*

Eudora Welty, 1909-2001, (U.S.) Southern short story writer, novelist. "Why I Live at the P.O.," "The Ponder Heart."

Rebecca West, 1893-1983, (Br.) novelist, critic, journalist. *Black Lamb and Grey Falcon.*

Edith Wharton, 1862-1937, (U.S.) novelist. *The Age of Innocence, The House of Mirth, Ethan Frome.*

Phillis Wheatley, c1753-84, (U.S.) poet; 2nd American woman and first black woman to be published, 1770.

E(lwyn) B(rooks) White, 1899-1985, (U.S.) essayist, novelist. *Charlotte's Web, Stuart Little.*

Patrick White, 1912-90, (Austral.) novelist. *The Tree of Man.*

T(erence) H(anbury) White, 1906-64, (Br.) author. *The Once and Future King, A Book of Beasts.*

Walt Whitman, 1819-92, (U.S.) poet. *Leaves of Grass.*

John Greenleaf Whittier, 1807-92, (U.S.) poet, journalist. *Snow-Bound.*

Oscar Wilde, 1854-1900, (Ir.) novelist, playwright. *The Picture of Dorian Gray, The Importance of Being Earnest.*

Laura Ingalls Wilder, 1867-1957, (U.S.) novelist. Little House on the Prairie series of children's books.

Thornton Wilder, 1897-1975, (U.S.) playwright. *Our Town, The Skin of Our Teeth, The Matchmaker.*

Tennessee Williams, 1911-83, (U.S.) playwright. *A Streetcar Named Desire, Cat on a Hot Tin Roof, The Glass Menagerie.*

William Carlos Williams, 1883-1963, (U.S.) poet, physician. *Tempers, Al Que Quiere! Paterson,* "This Is Just to Say."

Edmund Wilson, 1895-1972, (U.S.) critic, novelist. *Axel's Castle, To the Finland Station.*

P(elham) G(renville) Wodehouse, 1881-1975, (Br.-U.S.) humorist. The "Jeeves" novels, *Anything Goes.*

Thomas Wolfe, 1900-38, (U.S.) novelist. *Look Homeward, Angel; You Can't Go Home Again.*

Virginia Woolf, 1882-1941, (Br.) novelist, essayist. *Mrs. Dalloway, To the Lighthouse, A Room of One's Own.*

William Wordsworth, 1770-1850, (Br.) poet. "Tintern Abbey," "Ode: Intimations of Immortality," *The Prelude.*

Richard Wright, 1908-60, (U.S.) novelist, short-story writer. *Native Son, Black Boy, Uncle Tom's Children.*

Elinor Wylie, 1885-1928, (U.S.) poet. *Nets to Catch the Wind.*

William Butler Yeats, 1865-1939, (Ir.) poet, playwright. "The Second Coming," *The Wild Swans at Coole.*

Frank Yerby, 1916-91, (U.S.) first best-selling African American novelist; *The Foxes of Harrow.*

Émile Zola, 1840-1902, (Fr.) novelist. *Nana, Thérèsè Raquin.*

Poets Laureate

There is no record of the origin of the office of Poet Laureate of England. Henry III (1216-72) reportedly had a Versificator Regis, or King's Poet, paid 100 shillings per year. Other poets said to have filled the role include Geoffrey Chaucer (d 1400), Edmund Spenser (d 1599), Ben Jonson (d 1637), and Sir William d'Avenant (d 1668). The first official English poet laureate was John Dryden, appointed 1668, for life (as was customary). Then came Thomas Shadwell, in 1689; Nahum Tate, 1692; Nicholas Rowe, 1715; Rev. Laurence Eusden, 1718; Colley Cibber, 1730; William Whitehead, 1757; Rev. Thomas Warton, 1785; Henry James Pye, 1790; Robert Southey, 1813; William Wordsworth, 1843; Alfred, Lord Tennyson, 1850; Alfred Austin, 1896; Robert Bridges, 1913; John Masefield, 1930; C. Day Lewis, 1968; Sir John Betjeman, 1972; Ted Hughes, 1984; Andrew Motion, 1999.

In U.S., appointment is by Librarian of Congress and is not for life: Robert Penn Warren, appointed 1986; Richard Wilbur, 1987; Howard Nemerov, 1988; Mark Strand, 1990; Joseph Brodsky, 1991; Mona Van Duyn, 1992; Rita Dove, 1993; Robert Hass, 1995; Robert Pinsky, 1997; Stanley Kunitz, 2000; Billy Collins, 2001; Louise Gluck, 2003; Ted Kooser, 2004; Donald Hall, 2006.

Composers of Classical and Avant Garde Music

Carl Philipp Emanuel Bach, 1714-88, (Ger.) Cantatas, passions, numerous keyboard and instrumental works.

Johann Christian Bach, 1735-82, (Ger.) Concertos, operas, sonatas. Known as the "English" Bach.

Johann Sebastian Bach, 1685-1750, (Ger.) *St. Matthew Passion, The Well-Tempered Clavier.*

Samuel Barber, 1910-81, (U.S.) *Adagio for Strings, Vanessa.*

Béla Bartók, 1881-1945, (Hung.) *Concerto for Orchestra, The Miraculous Mandarin.*

Amy Beach (Mrs. H. H. A. Beach), 1867-1944, (U.S.) *The Year's at the Spring, Fireflies, The Chambered Nautilus.*

Ludwig van Beethoven, 1770-1827, (Ger.) Concertos (*Emperor*), sonatas (*Moonlight, Pathetique*), 9 symphonies.

Vincenzo Bellini, 1801-35, (It.) *I Puritani, La Sonnambula, Norma.*

Alban Berg, 1885-1935, (Austrian) *Wozzeck, Lulu.*

Hector Berlioz, 1803-69, (Fr.) *Damnation of Faust, Symphonie Fantastique, Requiem.*

Leonard Bernstein, 1918-90, (U.S.) *Chichester Psalms, Jeremiah Symphony, Mass.*

Georges Bizet, 1838-75, (Fr.) *Carmen, Pearl Fishers.*

Ernest Bloch, 1880-1959, (Swiss-U.S.) *Macbeth* (opera), *Schelomo, Voice in the Wilderness.*

Luigi Boccherini, 1743-1805, (It.) Chamber music and guitar pieces.

Alexander Borodin, 1833-87, (Russ.) *Prince Igor, In the Steppes of Central Asia, Polovtzian Dances.*

Pierre Boulez, b 1925, (Fr.) *LeVisage* nuptial, *Edats/Multiple, Domaines.*

Johannes Brahms, 1833-97, (Ger.) *Liebeslieder Waltzes, Acad. Festival Overture,* chamber music, 4 symphonies.

Benjamin Britten, 1913-76, (Br.) *Peter Grimes, Turn of the Screw, A Ceremony of Carols, War Requiem.*

Anton Bruckner, 1824-96, (Austrian) 9 symphonies.

Dietrich Buxtehude, 1637-1707, (Dan.) Organ works, vocal music.

William Byrd, 1543-1623, (Br.) Masses, motets.

John Cage, 1912-92, (U.S.) *Winter Music, Fontana Mix.*

Emmanuel Chabrier, 1841-94, (Fr.) *Le Roi Malgré Lui, España.*

Gustave Charpentier, 1860-1956, (Fr.) *Louise.*

Frédéric Chopin, 1810-49, (Pol.) Mazurkas, waltzes, etudes, nocturnes, polonaises, sonatas.

Aaron Copland, 1900-90, (U.S.) *Appalachian Spring, Fanfare for the Common Man, Lincoln Portrait.*

Claude Debussy, 1862-1918, (Fr.) *Pelleas et Melisande, La Mer, Prelude to the Afternoon of a Faun.*

Gaetano Donizetti, 1797-1848, (It.) Elixir of Love, Lucia di Lammermoor, Daughter of the Regiment.

Paul Dukas, 1865-1935, (Fr.) *Sorcerer's Apprentice.*

Antonín Dvorak, 1841-1904, (Czech.) *Songs My Mother Taught Me, Symphony in E Minor (From the New World).*

Edward Elgar, 1857-1934, (Br.) *Enigma Variations, Pomp and Circumstance.*

Manuel de Falla, 1876-1946, (Sp.) *El Amor Brujo, La Vida Breve, The Three-Cornered Hat.*

Gabriel Fauré, 1845-1924, (Fr.) *Requiem,* Elègie for Cello and Piano.

Cesar Franck, 1822-90, (Belg.) Symphony in D minor, Violin Sonata.

George Gershwin, 1898-1937, (U.S.) *Rhapsody in Blue, An American in Paris, Porgy and Bess.*

Philip Glass, b 1937, (U.S.) *Einstein on the Beach, The Voyage.*

Mikhail Glinka, 1804-57, (Russ.) *A Life for the Tsar, Ruslan and Ludmilla.*

Christoph W. Gluck, 1714-87, (Ger.) *Alceste, Iphigènie en Tauride.*

Charles Gounod, 1818-93, (Fr.) *Faust, Romeo and Juliet.*

Edvard Grieg, 1843-1907, (Nor.) *Peer Gynt Suite,* Concerto in A minor for piano.

George Frideric Handel, 1685-1759, (Ger.-Br.) *Messiah, Water Music.*

Howard Hanson, 1896-1981, (U.S.) Symphonies No. 1 (Nordic) and No. 2 (Romantic).

Roy Harris, 1898-1979, (U.S.) Symphonies.

(Franz) Joseph Haydn, 1732-1809, (Austrian) Symphonies (*Clock, London, Toy*), chamber music, oratorios.

Paul Hindemith, 1895-1963, (U.S.) *Mathis der Maler.*

Gustav Holst, 1874-1934, (Br.) *The Planets.*

Arthur Honegger, 1892-1955, (Fr.) *Judith, Le Roi David, Pacific 231.*

Alan Hovhaness, 1911-2000, (U.S.) Symphonies, *Magnificat.*
Engelbert Humperdinck, 1854-1921, (Ger.) *Hansel and Gretel.*
Charles Ives, 1874-1954, (U.S.) *Concord Sonata*, symphonies.
Aram Khachaturian, 1903-78, (Russ.) Ballets, piano pieces, *Sabre Dance.*
Zoltán Kodaly, 1882-1967, (Hung.) *Háry János, Psalmus Hungaricus.*
Fritz Kreisler, 1875-1962, (Austrian) *Caprice Viennois, Tambourin Chinois.*
Edouard Lalo, 1823-92, (Fr.) *Symphonie Espagnole.*
Ruggero Leoncavallo, 1857-1919, (It.) *Pagliacci.*
Franz Liszt, 1811-86, (Hung.) 20 Hungarian rhapsodies, symphonic poems.
Edward MacDowell, 1861-1908, (U.S.) *To a Wild Rose.*
Gustav Mahler, 1860-1911, (Austrian) *Das Lied von der Erde*; 9 complete symphonies.
Pietro Mascagni, 1863-1945, (It.) *Cavalleria Rusticana.*
Jules Massenet, 1842-1912, (Fr.) *Manon, Le Cid, Thaïs.*
Felix Mendelssohn, 1809-47, (Ger.) *A Midsummer Night's Dream*, Songs *Without Words*, violin concerto.
Gian-Carlo Menotti, b 1911, (It.-U.S.) *The Medium, The Consul, Amahl and the Night Visitors.*
Claudio Monteverdi, 1567-1643, (It.) Opera, masses, madrigals.
Modest Moussorgsky, 1839-81, (Russ.) *Boris Godunov, Pictures at an Exhibition.*
Wolfgang Amadeus Mozart, 1756-91, (Austrian) Chamber music, concertos, operas (*Magic Flute, Marriage of Figaro*), 41 symphonies.
Jacques Offenbach, 1819-80, (Fr.) *Tales of Hoffmann.*
Carl Orff, 1895-1982, (Ger.) *Carmina Burana.*
Johann Pachelbel, 1653-1706, (Ger.) *Canon and Fugue in D major.*
Ignacy Paderewski, 1860-1941, (Pol.) *Minuet in G.*
Niccolò Paganini, 1782-1840, (It.) *Caprices for violin solo.*
Giovanni Palestrina, c1525-94, (It.) *Masses, madrigals.*
Krzysztof Penderecki, b 1933, (Pol.) *Psalmus, Polymorphia, De natura sonoris.*
Francis Poulenc, 1899-1963, (Fr.) *Dialogues des Carmèlites.*
Mel Powell, 1923-98, (U.S.) *Duplicates: A Concerto for Two Pianos and Orchestra, Cantilena Concertante.*
Sergei Prokofiev, 1891-1953, (Russ.) *Classical Symphony, Love for Three Oranges, Peter and the Wolf.*
Giacomo Puccini, 1858-1924, (It.) *La Boheme, Manon Lescaut, Tosca, Madama Butterfly.*
Henry Purcell, 1659-95, (Eng.) *Dido and Aeneas.*
Sergei Rachmaninoff, 1873-1943, (Russ.) Concertos, preludes (Prelude in C sharp minor), symphonies.
Maurice Ravel, 1875-1937, (Fr.) *Bolèro, Daphnis et Chloè,* Piano Concerto in D for Left Hand Alone.

Nikolai Rimsky-Korsakov, 1844-1908, (Russ.) *Golden Cockerel, Scheherazade, Flight of the Bumblebee.*
Gioacchino Rossini, 1792-1868, (It.) *Barber of Seville, Otello, William Tell.*
Camille Saint-Saëns, 1835-1921, (Fr.) *Carnival of Animals (The Swan), Samson and Delilah, Danse Macabre.*
Alessandro Scarlatti, 1660-1725, (It.) Cantatas, oratorios, operas.
Domenico Scarlatti, 1685-1757, (It.) Harpsichord works.
Alfred Schnittke, 1934-98, (Sov.-Ger.) *Life With an Idiot.*
Arnold Schoenberg, 1874-1951, (Austrian) *Pelleas and Melisande, Pierrot Lunaire, Verklärte Nacht.*
Franz Schubert, 1797-1828, (Austrian) Chamber music (*Trout Quintet*), lieder, symphonies (*Unfinished*).
Robert Schumann, 1810-56, (Ger.) *Die Frauenliebe und Leben, Träumerei.*
Dimitri Shostakovich, 1906-75, (Russ.) Symphonies, *Lady Macbeth of the District Mzensk.*
Jean Sibelius, 1865-1957, (Finn.) *Finlandia.*
Bedrich Smetana, 1824-84, (Czech.) *The Bartered Bride.*
Karlheinz Stockhausen, b 1928, (Ger.) *Kontra-Punkte, Kontakte for Electronic Instruments.*
Richard Strauss, 1864-1949, (Ger.) *Salome, Elektra, Der Rosenkavalier, Thus Spake Zarathustra.*
Igor Stravinsky, 1882-1971, (Russ.) *Noah and the Flood, The Rake's Progress, The Rite of Spring.*
Toru Takemitsu, 1930-96, (Jpn.) *Requiem for Strings, Dorian Horizon.*
Peter I. Tchaikovsky, 1840-93, (Russ.) *Nutcracker, Swan Lake, The Sleeping Beauty.*
Georg Philipp Telemann, 1681-1767, (Ger.) church music, orchestral suites, chamber music.
Virgil Thomson, 1896-1989, (U.S.) Opera, film music, *Four Saints in Three Acts.*
Dmitri Tiomkin, 1894-1979, (Russ.-U.S.) film scores, including *High Noon.*
Sir Michael Tippett, 1905-98, (Br.) *A Child of Our Time, The Midsummer Marriage, The Knot Garden.*
Ralph Vaughan Williams, 1872-1958, (Eng.) *Fantasiz on a Theme by Thomas Tallis,* symphonies, vocal music.
Giuseppe Verdi, 1813-1901, (It.) *Aida, Rigoletto, Don Carlo, Il Trovatore, La Traviata, Falstaff, Macbeth.*
Heitor Villa-Lobos, 1887-1959, (Brazil) *Bachianas Brasileiras.*
Antonio Vivaldi, 1678-1741, (It.) Concerto grossos (*The Four Seasons*).
Richard Wagner, 1813-83, (Ger.) *Rienzi, Tannhäuser, Lohengrin, Tristan and Isolde.*
Carl Maria von Weber, 1786-1826, (Ger.) *Der Freischutz.*

Composers of Operettas, Musicals, and Popular Music

Richard Adler, b 1921, (U.S.) *Pajama Game; Damn Yankees.*
Milton Ager, 1893-1979, (U.S.) I Wonder What's Become of Sally; Hard-Hearted Hannah; Ain't She Sweet?
Arthur Altman, 1910-94, (U.S.) All or Nothing at All.
Leroy Anderson, 1908-75, (U.S.) Sleigh Ride, Blue Tango, Syncopated Clock.
Paul Anka, b 1941, (Can.) My Way; *Tonight Show* theme.
Harold Arlen, 1905-86, (U.S.) Stormy Weather; Over the Rainbow; Blues in the Night; That Old Black Magic.
Burt Bacharach, b 1928, (U.S.) Raindrops Keep Fallin' on My Head; Walk on By; What the World Needs Now Is Love.
Ernest Ball, 1878-1927, (U.S.) Mother Machree; When Irish Eyes Are Smiling.
Irving Berlin, 1888-1989, (U.S.) *Annie Get Your Gun; Call Me Madam;* God Bless America; White Christmas.
Leonard Bernstein, 1918-90, (U.S.) *On the Town; Wonderful Town; Candide; West Side Story.*
Eubie Blake, 1883-1983, (U.S.) *Shuffle Along;* I'm Just Wild About Harry.
Jerry Bock, b 1928, (U.S.) *Mr. Wonderful; Fiorello; Fiddler on the Roof; The Rothschilds.*
Carrie Jacobs Bond, 1862-1946, (U.S.) I Love You Truly.
Nacio Herb Brown, 1896-1964, (U.S.) Singing in the Rain; You Were Meant for Me; All I Do Is Dream of You.
Hoagy Carmichael, 1899-1981, (U.S.) Stardust; Georgia on My Mind; Old Buttermilk Sky.
James Cleveland, 1931-91, (U.S.) composer, musician, singer; first black gospel artist to appear at Carnegie Hall.
George M. Cohan, 1878-1942, (U.S.) Give My Regards to Broadway; You're a Grand Old Flag; Over There.
Cy Coleman, b 1929, (U.S.) *Sweet Charity;* Witchcraft.
John Frederick Coots, 1895-1985, (U.S.) Santa Claus Is Coming to Town; You Go to My Head; For All We Know.
Noel Coward, 1899-1973, (Br.) *Bitter Sweet;* Mad Dogs and Englishmen; Mad About the Boy.
Neil Diamond, b 1941, (U.S.) I'm a Believer; Sweet Caroline.
Walter Donaldson, 1893-1947, (U.S.) My Buddy; Carolina in the Morning; Makin' Whoopee.

Vernon Duke, 1903-69, (U.S.) April in Paris.
Bob Dylan, b 1941, (U.S.) Blowin' in the Wind.
Gus Edwards, 1879-1945, (U.S.) School Days; By the Light of the Silvery Moon; In My Merry Oldsmobile.
Sherman Edwards, 1919-81, (U.S.) See You in September; Wonderful! Wonderful!
Duke Ellington, 1899-1974, (U.S.) Sophisticated Lady; Satin Doll; It Don't Mean a Thing; Solitude.
Sammy Fain, 1902-89, (U.S.) I'll Be Seeing You; Love Is a Many-Splendored Thing.
Fred Fisher, 1875-1942, (U.S.) Peg O' My Heart; Chicago.
Stephen Collins Foster, 1826-64, (U.S.) My Old Kentucky Home; Old Folks at Home, Beautiful Dreamer.
Rudolf Friml, 1879-1972, (Czech-U.S.) *The Firefly; Rose Marie; Vagabond King; Bird of Paradise.*
John Gay, 1685-1732, (Br.) *The Beggar's Opera.*
George Gershwin, 1898-1937, (U.S.) Someone to Watch Over Me; I've Got a Crush on You; Embraceable You.
Morton Gould, 1913-96, (U.S.) Fall River Suite, Holocaust Suite, Spirituals for Orchestra, Stringmusic.
Ferde Grofe, 1892-1972, (U.S.) Grand Canyon Suite.
Marvin Hamlisch, b 1944, (U.S.) The Way We Were; Nobody Does It Better; *A Chorus Line.*
Ray Henderson, 1896-1970, (U.S.) *George White's Scandals;* That Old Gang of Mine; Five Foot Two, Eyes of Blue.
Victor Herbert, 1859-1924, (Ir.-U.S.) *Mlle. Modiste; Babes in Toyland; The Red Mill; Naughty Marietta; Sweethearts.*
Jerry Herman, b 1931, (U.S.) *Hello Dolly; Mame.*
Brian Holland, b 1941, **Lamont Dozier,** b 1941, **Eddie Holland,** b 1939, (all U.S.) Heat Wave; Stop! In the Name of Love; Baby, I Need Your Loving.
Antonio Carlos Jobim, 1927-94, (Brazil) The Girl From Ipanema; Desafinado; One Note Samba.
Billy (William Martin) Joel, b 1949, (U.S.) Just the Way You Are; Honesty; Piano Man.
Scott Joplin, 1868-1917, (U.S.) Maple Leaf Rag; *Treemonisha.*
John Kander, b 1927, (U.S.) *Cabaret; Chicago; Funny Lady.*
Jerome Kern, 1885-1945, (U.S.) *Sally; Sunny; Show Boat.*

Carole King, b 1942, (U.S.) Will You Love Me Tomorrow?; Natural Woman; One Fine Day; Up on the Roof.

Burton Lane, 1912-1997, (U.S.) *Finian's Rainbow.*

Franz Lehar, 1870-1948, (Hung.) *Merry Widow.*

Jerry Leiber, & **Mike Stoller,** both b 1933, (both U.S.) Hound Dog; Searchin'; Yakety Yak; Love Me Tender.

Mitch Leigh, b 1928, (U.S.) *Man of La Mancha.*

John Lennon, 1940-80, & **Paul McCartney,** b 1942, (both Br.) I Want to Hold Your Hand; She Loves You.

Jay Livingston, 1915-2001 (U.S.) Mona Lisa; Que Sera, Sera.

Andrew Lloyd Webber, b 1948, (Br.) *Jesus Christ Superstar; Evita; Cats; The Phantom of the Opera.*

Frank Loesser, 1910-69, (U.S.) *Guys and Dolls; Where's Charley?; The Most Happy Fella; How to Succeed....*

Frederick Loewe, 1901-88, (Austrian-U.S.) *Brigadoon; Paint Your Wagon; My Fair Lady; Camelot.*

Henry Mancini, 1924-94, (U.S.) Moon River; Days of Wine and Roses; Pink Panther Theme.

Barry Mann, b 1939, & **Cynthia Weil,** b 1937, (both U.S.) You've Lost That Loving Feeling.

Jimmy McHugh, 1894-1969, (U.S.) Don't Blame Me; I'm in the Mood for Love; I Feel a Song Coming On.

Alan Menken, b 1949, (U.S.) *Little Shop of Horrors, Beauty and the Beast.*

Joseph Meyer, 1894-1987, (U.S.) If You Knew Susie; California, Here I Come; Crazy Rhythm.

Chauncey Olcott, 1858-1932, (U.S.) Mother Machree.

Jerome "Doc" Pomus, 1925-91, (U.S.) Save the Last Dance for Me; A Teenager in Love.

Cole Porter, 1893-1964, (U.S.) *Anything Goes; Kiss Me Kate; Can Can; Silk Stockings.*

Smokey Robinson, b 1940, (U.S.) Shop Around; My Guy; My Girl; Get Ready.

Richard Rodgers, 1902-79, (U.S.) *Oklahoma!; Carousel; South Pacific; The King and I; The Sound of Music.*

Sigmund Romberg, 1887-1951, (Hung.) *Maytime; The Student Prince; Desert Song; Blossom Time.*

Harold Rome, 1908-93, (U.S.) *Pins and Needles; Call Me Mister; Wish You Were Here; Fanny; Destry Rides Again.*

Vincent Rose, b 1880-1944, (U.S.) Avalon; Whispering; Blueberry Hill.

Harry Ruby, 1895-1974, (U.S.) Three Little Words; Who's Sorry Now?

Arthur Schwartz, 1900-84, (U.S.) *The Band Wagon;* Dancing in the Dark; By Myself; That's Entertainment.

Neil Sedaka, b 1939, (U.S.) Breaking Up Is Hard to Do.

Paul Simon, b 1942, (U.S.) Sounds of Silence; I Am a Rock; Mrs. Robinson; Bridge Over Troubled Waters.

Stephen Sondheim, b 1930, (U.S.) *A Little Night Music; Company; Sweeney Todd; Sunday in the Park With George.*

John Philip Sousa, 1854-1932, (U.S.) *El Capitan;* Stars and Stripes Forever.

Oskar Straus, 1870-1954, (Austrian) *Chocolate Soldier.*

Johann Strauss, 1825-99, (Austrian) *Gypsy Baron; Die Fledermaus;* waltzes: Blue Danube; Artist's Life.

Charles Strouse, b 1928, (U.S.) *Bye Bye, Birdie; Annie.*

Jule Styne, 1905-94, (Br.-U.S.) *Gentlemen Prefer Blondes; Bells Are Ringing; Gypsy; Funny Girl.*

Arthur S. Sullivan, 1842-1900, (Br.) *H.M.S. Pinafore; Pirates of Penzance; The Mikado.*

Deems Taylor, 1885-1966, (U.S.) *Peter Ibbetson.*

Harry Tobias, 1905-94, (U.S.) *I'll Keep the Lovelight Burning.*

Egbert van Alstyne, 1882-1951, (U.S.) In the Shade of the Old Apple Tree; Memories; Pretty Baby.

Jimmy Van Heusen, 1913-90, (U.S.) Moonlight Becomes You; Swinging on a Star; All the Way; Love and Marriage.

Albert von Tilzer, 1878-1956, (U.S.) I'll Be With You in Apple Blossom Time; Take Me Out to the Ball Game.

Harry von Tilzer, 1872-1946, (U.S.) Only a Bird in a Gilded Cage; On a Sunday Afternoon.

Fats Waller, 1904-43, (U.S.) Honeysuckle Rose; Ain't Misbehavin'.

Harry Warren, 1893-1981, (U.S.) You're My Everything; We're in the Money; I Only Have Eyes for You.

Jimmy Webb, b 1946, (U.S.) Up, Up and Away; By the Time I Get to Phoenix; Didn't We?; Wichita Lineman.

Kurt Weill, 1900-50, (Ger.-U.S.) *Threepenny Opera; Lady in the Dark; Knickerbocker Holiday; One Touch of Venus.*

Percy Wenrich, 1887-1952, (U.S.) When You Wore a Tulip; Moonlight Bay; Put On Your Old Gray Bonnet.

Richard A. Whiting, 1891-1938, (U.S.) Till We Meet Again; Sleepytime Gal; Beyond the Blue Horizon; My Ideal.

John Williams, b 1932, (U.S.) *Jaws; E.T.; Star Wars* series; *Raiders of the Lost Ark* series.

Meredith Willson, 1902-84, (U.S.) *The Music Man.*

Stevie Wonder, b 1950, (U.S.) You Are the Sunshine of My Life; Signed, Sealed, Delivered, I'm Yours.

Vincent Youmans, 1898-1946, (U.S.) *Two Little Girls in Blue; Wildflower; No, No, Nanette; Hit the Deck; Rainbow; Smiles.*

Lyricists

Howard Ashman, 1950-91, (U.S.) Little Shop of Horrors; The Little Mermaid.

Johnny Burke, 1908-84, (U.S.) Misty; Imagination.

Irving Caesar, 1895-1996, (U.S.) Swanee; Tea for Two; Just a Gigolo.

Sammy Cahn, 1913-93, (U.S.) High Hopes; Love and Marriage; The Second Time Around; It's Magic.

Leonard Cohen, b 1934, (Can.) Suzanne; Stranger Song.

Betty Comden, b 1919, (U.S.) and **Adolph Green,** 1915-2002, (U.S.) The Party's Over; Just in Time; New York, New York.

Hal David, b 1921, (U.S.) *What the World Needs Now Is Love.*

Buddy De Sylva, 1895-1950, (U.S.) When Day Is Done; Look for the Silver Lining; April Showers.

Howard Dietz, 1896-1983, (U.S.) Dancing in the Dark; You and the Night and the Music; That's Entertainment.

Al Dubin, 1891-1945, (U.S.) Tiptoe Through the Tulips; Anniversary Waltz; Lullaby of Broadway.

Fred Ebb, b 1936-2004, (U.S.) Cabaret; Zorba; Woman of the Year, Chicago.

Ray Evans, b 1915 (U.S.) Mona Lisa; Que Sera, Sera.

Dorothy Fields, 1905-74, (U.S.) On the Sunny Side of the Street; Don't Blame Me; The Way You Look Tonight.

Ira Gershwin, 1896-1983, (U.S.) The Man I Love; Fascinating Rhythm; S'Wonderful; Embraceable You.

William S. Gilbert, 1836-1911, (Br.) The Mikado; H.M.S. Pinafore; Pirates of Penzance.

Gerry Goffin, b 1939, (U.S.) Will You Love Me Tomorrow; Take Good Care of My Baby; Up on the Roof.

Mack Gordon, 1905-59, (Pol.-U.S.) You'll Never Know; The More I See You; Chattanooga Choo-Choo.

Oscar Hammerstein II, 1895-1960, (U.S.) Ol' Man River; Oklahoma!; Carousel.

E. Y. (Yip) Harburg, 1898-1981, (U.S.) Brother, Can You Spare a Dime; April in Paris; Over the Rainbow.

Sheldon Harnick, b 1924, (U.S.) Fiddler on the Roof, She Loves Me.

Lorenz Hart, 1895-1943, (U.S.) .) Isn't It Romantic; Blue Moon; Lover; Manhattan; My Funny Valentine.

DuBose Heyward, 1885-1940, (U.S.) Summertime.

Gus Kahn, 1886-1941, (U.S.) Memories; Ain't We Got Fun.

Alan J. Lerner, 1918-86, (U.S.) Brigadoon; My Fair Lady; Camelot; Gigi; On a Clear Day You Can See Forever.

Johnny Mercer, 1909-76, (U.S.) Blues in the Night; Come Rain or Come Shine; Laura; That Old Black Magic.

Bob Merrill, 1921-98, (U.S.) People; (How Much Is That) Doggie in the Window.

Jack Norworth, 1879-1959, (U.S.) Take Me Out to the Ball Game; Shine On Harvest Moon.

Mitchell Parish, 1901-93, (U.S.) Stardust; Stairway to the Stars.

Andy Razaf, 1895-1973, (U.S.) Honeysuckle Rose; Ain't Misbehavin'; S'posin'.

Leo Robin, 1900-84, (U.S.) Thanks for the Memory; Hooray for Love; Diamonds Are a Girl's Best Friend.

Paul Francis Webster, 1907-84, (U.S.) Secret Love; The Shadow of Your Smile; Love Is a Many-Splendored Thing.

Jack Yellen, 1892-1991, (U.S.) Down by the O-HI-O; Ain't She Sweet; Happy Days Are Here Again.

Blues and Jazz Artists of the Past

Julian "Cannonball" Adderley, 1928-75, alto sax

Nat Adderley, 1931-2000, cornet

Henry "Red" Allen, 1908-67, trumpet

Louis "Satchmo" Armstrong, 1901-71, trumpet, singer, bandleader

Albert Ayler, 1936-70, tenor sax, alto sax

Mildred Bailey, 1907-51, singer

Chet Baker, 1929-88, trumpet, singer

Ray Barretto, 1930-2006, conga drummer

Count Basie, 1904-84, bandleader, piano, composer

Sidney Bechet, 1897-1959, soprano sax, clarinet

Bix Beiderbecke, 1903-31, cornet, composer, piano

Bunny Berigan, 1908-42, trumpet

Barney Bigard, 1906-80, clarinet

Eubie Blake, 1883-1983, composer, piano

Art Blakey, 1919-90, drums, bandleader

Jimmy Blanton, 1921-42, bass

Charles "Buddy" Bolden, 1877-1931, cornet, pioneer bandleader

Lester Bowie, 1941-99, trumpet, composer, bandleader

Big Bill Broonzy, 1893-1958, blues singer, guitar

Clarence "Gatemouth" Brown, 1924 -2006, guitar, singer

Clifford Brown, 1930-56, trumpet
Ray Brown, 1926-2002, bass
Don Byas, 1912-72, tenor sax
Charlie Byrd, 1925-99, guitarist; popularized bossa nova
Cab Calloway, 1907-94, bandleader, singer
Harry Carney, 1910-74, baritone sax, clarinet
Betty Carter, 1930-98, jazz singer
Sidney "Big Sid" Catlett, 1910-51, drums
Doc Cheatham, 1905-97, trumpet
Don Cherry, 1936-95, trumpet
Charlie Christian, 1916-42, guitar
Kenny "Klook" Clarke, 1914-85, drums
Buck Clayton, 1911-91, trumpet
Al Cohn, 1925-88, tenor sax
Cozy Cole, 1909-81, drums
John Coltrane, 1926-67, tenor sax, soprano sax, composer
Eddie Condon, 1905-73, guitar, bandleader
Tadd Dameron, 1917-65, piano, composer
Eddie "Lockjaw" Davis, 1921-86, tenor sax
Miles Davis, 1926-91, trumpet, composer
Wild Bill Davison, 1906-89, cornet
Paul Desmond, 1924-77, alto sax
Vic Dickenson, 1906-84, trombone
Willie Dixon, 1915-92, blues composer, bass
Johnny Dodds, 1892-1940, clarinet
Warren "Baby" Dodds, 1898-1959, drums
Eric Dolphy, 1928-64, alto sax, bass clarinet, flute
Jimmy Dorsey, 1904-57, alto sax, bandleader
Tommy Dorsey, 1905-56, trombone, bandleader
Billy Eckstine, 1914-93, singer, bandleader
Harry "Sweets" Edison, 1915-99, trumpet
Roy Eldridge, 1911-89, trumpet, singer
Duke Ellington, 1899-1974, piano, bandleader, composer
Bill Evans, 1929-80, piano
Gil Evans, 1912-88, composer, arranger, piano
Art Farmer, 1928-99, trumpet, flugelhorn
Maynard Ferguson, 1926-2006, trumpeter, bandleader
Ella Fitzgerald, 1917-96, singer
Tommy Flanagan, 1930-2001, piano
Erroll Garner, 1921-77, piano, composer
Stan Getz, 1927-91, tenor sax
Dizzy Gillespie, 1917-93, trumpet, composer, singer
Benny Goodman, 1909-86, clarinet, bandleader
Dexter Gordon, 1923-90, tenor sax
Stéphane Grappelli, 1908-97, violin
Bobby Hackett, 1915-76, trumpet, cornet
Lionel Hampton, 1908-2002, vibraphone, bandleader
W. C. Handy, 1873-1958, composer
Jimmy Harrison, 1900-31, trombone
Coleman Hawkins, 1904-69, tenor sax
Percy Heath, 1923-2005, bass
Fletcher Henderson, 1898-1952, bandleader, arranger
Woody Herman, 1913-87, clarinet, alto sax, bandleader
Jay C. Higginbotham, 1906-73, trombone
Ruiz Hilton, 1952-2006, piano, composer
Earl "Fatha" Hines, 1903-83, piano
Milt Hinton, 1910-2000, bass
Al Hirt, 1922-99, trumpet
Johnny Hodges, 1906-70, alto sax
Billie Holiday, 1915-59, singer
John Lee Hooker, 1917-2001, blues guitar, singer
Sam "Lightnin'" Hopkins, 1912-82, blues singer, guitar
Shirley Horn, 1934-2005, piano, singer
Howlin' Wolf, 1910-1976, blues singer, harmonica, guitar
Alberta Hunter, 1895-1984, singer
Mahalia Jackson, 1911-72, gospel singer
Milt Jackson, 1923-99, vibraphone
Elmore James, 1918-63, blues singer, guitar
Blind Lemon Jefferson, 1897-1930, blues singer, guitar
Bunk Johnson, 1879-1949, trumpet
J.J. Johnson, 1924-2001, trombone
James P. Johnson, 1891-1955, piano, composer
Robert Johnson, 1912-38, blues singer, guitar
Elvin Jones, 1927-2004, drums
Jo Jones, 1911-85, drums
Philly Joe Jones, 1923-85, drums
Thad Jones, 1923-86, cornet, bandleader, composer
Scott Joplin, 1868-1917, ragtime composer
Louis Jordan, 1908-75, singer, alto sax
Stan Kenton, 1911-79, bandleader, composer, piano
Barney Kessel, 1923-2004, guitar
Albert King, 1923-92, blues guitar
John Kirby, 1908-52, bandleader, bass
Rahsaan Roland Kirk, 1936-77, saxophones, composer
Gene Krupa, 1909-73, drums, bandleader
Scott LaFaro, 1936-61, bass
Huddie Ledbetter (Lead Belly), 1888-1949, folk and blues singer, guitar

John Lewis, 1920-2001, piano, Modern Jazz Quartet founder
Mel Lewis, 1929-90, drums, bandleader
Jimmie Lunceford, 1902-47, bandleader
Machito (Frank Grillo), 1912-84, Latin percussion, singer, bandleader
Shelly Manne, 1920-84, drums, bandleader
Jackie McLean, 1931-2006, saxophone, composer
Jimmy McPartland, 1907-91, trumpet
Carmen McRae, 1920-94, singer
Glenn Miller, 1904-44, trombone, bandleader
Charles Mingus, 1922-79, bass, composer, bandleader
Thelonious Monk, 1917-82, piano, composer
Wes Montgomery, 1925-68, guitar
"Jelly Roll" Morton, 1885-1941, composer, piano
Bennie Moten, 1894-1935, piano, bandleader
Gerry Mulligan, 1927-96, baritone sax, composer
"Fats" Navarro, 1923-50, trumpet
Red Nichols, 1905-65, cornet, bandleader
Red Norvo, 1908-99, vibraphone, xylophone, bandleader
Arturo "Chico" O'Farrill, 1921-2001, Latin composer, arranger
King Oliver, 1885-1938, cornet, band leader
Sy Oliver, 1910-88, arranger, composer
Kid Ory, 1886-1973, trombone, bandleader
Oran "Hot Lips" Page, 1908-54, trumpet, singer
Charlie "Bird" Parker, 1920-55, alto sax, composer
Joe Pass, 1929-94, guitar
Art Pepper, 1925-82, alto sax
Oscar Pettiford, 1922-60, bass
Bud Powell, 1924-66, piano
Chano Pozo, 1915-48, Cuban percussion, singer
Louis Prima, 1911-78, singer, bandleader
Tito Puente, 1923-2000, Latin percussion, bandleader
Gertrude "Ma" Rainey, 1886-1939, blues singer
Lou Rawls, 1933- 2006, singer
Dewey Redman, 1931-2006, tenor saxophone
Don Redman, 1900-64, composer, arranger
Django Reinhardt, 1910-53, guitar
Buddy Rich, 1917-87, drums
Red Rodney, 1928-94, trumpet
Jimmy Rowles, 1918-96, piano
Jimmy Rushing, 1903-72, blues and jazz singer
Pee Wee Russell, 1906-69, clarinet
Artie Shaw, 1910-2004, swing-era bandleader, clarinet
Zoot Sims, 1925-85, tenor sax
Zutty Singleton, 1898-1975, drums
Bessie Smith, 1894-1937, blues singer
Clarence "Pinetop" Smith, 1904-29, piano, singer; boogie woogie pioneer
Willie "The Lion" Smith, 1897-1973, piano, composer
Muggsy Spanier, 1906-67, cornet
Sonny Stitt, 1924-82, tenor sax, alto sax
Billy Strayhorn, 1915-67, composer, piano; Duke Ellington collaborator
Sun Ra, 1915?-93, bandleader, piano, composer
Art Tatum, 1910-56, piano
Art Taylor, 1929-95, drums
Jack Teagarden, 1905-64, trombone, singer
Mel Torme, 1925-99, singer ("the Velvet Fog")
Dave Tough, 1908-48, drums
Lennie Tristano, 1919-78, piano, composer
Joe Turner, 1911-85, blues singer
Sarah Vaughan, 1924-90, singer
Joe Venuti, 1904-78, violin
T-Bone Walker, 1910-75, blues guitar
Thomas "Fats" Waller, 1904-43, piano, singer, composer
Dinah Washington, 1924-63, singer
Grover Washington Jr., 1943-99, pop-jazz sax, composer
Ethel Waters, 1896-1977, jazz and blues singer
Muddy Waters, 1915-83, blues singer, songwriter
Julius Watkins, 1921-77, French horn
Chick Webb, 1902-39, bandleader, drums
Ben Webster, 1909-73, tenor sax
Junior Wells, 1934-98, blues singer, harmonica
Paul Whiteman, 1890-1967, bandleader
Charles "Cootie" Williams, 1910-85, trumpet, bandleader
Joe Williams, 1918-99, singer
Mary Lou Williams, 1910-81, piano, composer
Tony Williams, 1945-97, drums
John Lee "Sonny Boy" Williamson, 1914-48, blues singer, harmonica
Sonny Boy Williamson ("Rice" Miller), 1900?-65, blues singer, harmonica
Teddy Wilson, 1912-86, piano
Kai Winding, 1922-83, trombone
Jimmy Yancey, 1894-1951, piano
Lester "Pres" Young, 1909-59, tenor sax

Noted Country Music Artists of the Past and Present

Roy Acuff, 1903-92, fiddler, singer, songwriter; "Wabash Cannon Ball"

Alabama (Randy Owen, b 1949 ; Jeff Cook, b 1949 ; Teddy Gentry, b 1952 ; Mark Herndon, b 1955) "Feels So Right"

Eddy Arnold, b 1918 , singer, guitarist, the "Tennessee Plowboy"

Chet Atkins, 1924-2001, guitarist, composer, producer, helped create the "Nashville sound"

Gene Autry, 1907-98, first great singing movie cowboy; "Back in the Saddle Again"

Garth Brooks, b 1962, singer, songwriter; "Friends in Low Places"

Brooks & Dunn (Kix Brooks, b 1955 ; Ronnie Dunn, b 1953) "Hard Workin' Man"

Boudleaux and Felice Bryant (Boudleau, 1920-87; Felice, 1925-2003), songwriting team; "Hey Joe"

Mary Chapin Carpenter, b 1958 , singer, songwriter; "I Feel Lucky"

Carter Family (original members, **"Mother" Maybelle** 1909-78; **A.P.,** 1891-1960, **Sara,** 1898-1979) "Wildwood Flower"

Johnny Cash, 1932-2003 , singer, songwriter; "I Walk the Line," "Ring of Fire," "Folsom Prison Blues"

Kenny Chesney, b 1968, guitar, singer, songwriter; "You Had Me from Hello"

Patsy Cline, 1932-63, singer; "Walkin' After Midnight," "Crazy," "Sweet Dreams"

John Denver, 1943-97, singer, songwriter; "Rocky Mountain High"

Dixie Chicks (Natalie Maines, b 1974 ; Martie Seidel, b 1969 ; Emily Erwin Robison, b 1972) "Wide Open Spaces," "Fly"

Dale Evans (Lucille Wood Smith), 1912-2001, singer, actress, married Roy Rogers

Flatt & Scruggs (Lester Flatt, 1914-79; Earl Scruggs, b 1924), guitar-banjo duo and soloists; "Foggy Mountain Breakdown"

Red Foley, 1910-68, singer; "Chattanoogie Shoe Shine Boy"

Tennessee Ernie Ford, 1919-91, singer, TV host; "Sixteen Tons"

Lefty Frizzell, 1928-75, singer, guitarist; "Long Black Veil"

Vince Gill, b 1957, singer, songwriter; "When I Call Your Name"

Merle Haggard, b 1937, singer, songwriter; "Okie from Muskogee"

Emmylou Harris, b 1947, singer, songwriter, folk-country crossover artist; "If I Could Only Win Your Love"

Faith Hill, b 1967, singer, songwriter, married Tim McGraw; "Wild One," "This Kiss," "Breathe"

Alan Jackson, b 1958, singer, songwriter, "Where Were You (When the World Stopped Turning)"

Waylon Jennings, 1937-2002, singer, songwriter, "outlaw country" pioneer; "Luckenbach, Texas"

George Jones, b 1931, singer; "He Stopped Loving Her Today"

The Judds (Naomi, 1946- ; Wynonna, 1964-), mother-daughter duo; Wynonna also a solo act

Alison Krauss, b 1971, bluegrass fiddler, singer, bandleader; "When You Say Nothing at All"

Kris Kristofferson, b 1936, singer, songwriter, actor; "Me and Bobby McGee"

Patty Loveless, b 1957, singer, songwriter; "How Can I Help You Say Goodbye"

Lyle Lovett, b 1957, singer, songwriter, bandleader, actor; "Cowboy Man"

Loretta Lynn, b 1935, singer, songwriter; "Coal Miner's Daughter"

Kathy Mattea, b 1959, singer, songwriter; "Eighteen Wheels and a Dozen Roses"

Martina McBride, b 1966, singer, songwriter; "Independence Day"

Reba McEntire, b 1955, singer, songwriter, actress; "Whoever's in New England"

Tim McGraw, b 1967, singer; "It's Your Love," with wife, Faith Hill

Roger Miller, 1936-92, singer, songwriter; "King of the Road"

Ronnie Milsap, b 1944, singer, songwriter; "There's No Gettin' Over Me"

Bill Monroe, 1911-96, singer, songwriter, mandolin player, "father of bluegrass music"; "Mule Skinner Blues"

Willie Nelson, b 1933, singer, songwriter, actor; "On the Road Again"

Mark O'Connor, b 1961, fiddler, country-classical crossover composer

Dolly Parton, b 1946, singer, songwriter, actress; "Dollywood" theme park; "Here You Come Again," "9 to 5"

Minnie Pearl, 1912-96, comedienne, Grand Ole Opry star

Charley Pride, b 1938, singer, 1st African American country star; "Kiss an Angel Good Mornin'"

Jim Reeves, 1923-64, singer, songwriter; "Four Walls"

Charlie Rich, 1932-95, singer, songwriter called the "Silver Fox"; "The Most Beautiful Girl"

LeAnn Rimes, b 1982, singer; "Blue"

Tex Ritter, 1905-74, singer, songwriter; "Jingle, Jangle, Jingle"

Marty Robbins, 1925-82, singer, songwriter; "A White Sport Coat and a Pink Carnation"

Jimmie Rodgers, 1897-1933, singer, songwriter; "T for Texas"

Kenny Rogers, b 1938, singer, songwriter; "The Gambler"

Roy Rogers (Leonard Slye), 1911-98, singer, actor, "King of the Cowboys," sang with Sons of the Pioneers.

Fred Rose, 1898-1954, songwriter, singer, producer; "Blue Eyes Cryin' in the Rain"

Ricky Skaggs, b 1954, singer, songwriter, bandleader; "Don't Cheat in Our Hometown"

Ralph Stanley, b 1927, singer, banjo player, "Man of Constant Sorrow"

George Strait, b 1952, singer, bandleader; "Ace in the Hole"

Merle Travis, 1917-83, singer, guitarist, songwriter; "Divorce Me C.O.D."

Randy Travis, b 1959, singer, songwriter; "Forever and Ever, Amen"

Ernest Tubb, 1914-84, singer, songwriter, guitarist; "Walking the Floor Over You"

Shania Twain, b 1965, singer, songwriter; "You're Still the One"

Conway Twitty, 1933-93, singer, songwriter; "Hello Darlin' "

Keith Urban, b 1967, guitar, singer, songwriter; "It's a Love Thing"

Dottie West, 1932-91, singer, songwriter; "Here Comes My Baby"

Hank Williams Jr., b 1949, singer, songwriter; "Bocephus"; "All My Rowdy Friends (Have Settled Down)"

Hank Williams Sr., 1923-53, singer, songwriter; "Your Cheatin' Heart"

Bob Wills, 1905-75, Western Swing fiddler, singer, bandleader, songwriter; "New San Antonio Rose"

Tammy Wynette, 1942-98, singer; "Stand By Your Man"

Trisha Yearwood, b 1964, singer, songwriter; "How Do I Live"

Dwight Yoakam, b 1957, singer, songwriter, actor; "Ain't That Lonely Yet"

Dance Figures of the Past

Source: Reviewed by Gary Parks, Reviews editor, *Dance* magazine

Alvin Ailey, 1931-89, (U.S.) modern dancer, choreographer; melded modern dance and Afro-Caribbean techniques.

Frederick Ashton, 1904-88, (Br.) ballet choreographer; director of Great Britain's Royal Ballet, 1963-70.

Fred Astaire, 1899-1987, (U.S.) dancer, actor; teamed with dancer/actress **Ginger Rogers** 1911-95, (U.S.) in movie musicals.

George Balanchine, 1904-83, (Russ.-U.S.) ballet choreographer, teacher; most influential exponent of the neoclassical style; founded, with Lincoln Kirstein, School of American Ballet and New York City Ballet.

Carlo Blasis, 1803-78, (It.) ballet dancer, choreographer, writer; his teaching methods are standards of classical dance.

August Bournonville, 1805-79, (Dan.) ballet dancer, choreographer, teacher; exuberant, light style.

Fernando Bujones, 1955-2005, (Cuba-U.S.) ballet dancer.

Gisella Caccialanza, 1914-97, (U.S.) ballerina, charter member of Balanchine's American Ballet.

Enrico Cecchetti, 1850-1928, (It.) ballet dancer, leading dancer of Russia's Imperial Ballet; his technique was basis for Britain's Imperial Soc. of Teachers of Dancing.

Gower Champion, 1921-80, (U.S.) dancer, choreographer, director; with his wife **Marge,** b 1923, (U.S.) choreographed, danced in Broadway musicals and films.

John Cranko, 1927-73, (S. African) choreographer; created narrative ballets based on literary works.

Agnes de Mille, 1909-93, (U.S.) ballerina, choreographer; known for using American themes, she choreographed the ballet *Rodeo* and the musical *Oklahoma!*

Dame Ninette DeValois, 1898-2001, (Br.) choreographer, founding director London's Royal Ballet; *The Rake's Progress.*

Sergei Diaghilev, 1872-1929, (Russ.) impresario; founded Les Ballet Russes; saw ballet as an art unifying dance, drama, music, and decor.

Alexandra Danilova, 1903-97, (Russ.) ballerina; noted teacher at the School of American Ballet.

Isadora Duncan, 1877-1927, (U.S.) expressive dancer who united free movement with serious music; one of the founders of modern dance.

Katherine Dunham, 1910-2006, (U.S.) dancer, choreographer; internationally known for African, Caribbean, and African American dance forms.

Fanny Elssler, 1810-84, (Austrian) ballerina of the Romantic era; known for dramatic skill, sensual style.

Michel Fokine, 1880-1942, (Russ.) ballet dancer, choreographer, teacher; rejected strict classicism in favor of dramatically expressive style.

Margot Fonteyn, 1919-91, (Br.) prima ballerina, Royal Ballet of Great Britain; famed performance partner of Rudolf Nureyev.

Bob Fosse, 1927-87, (U.S.) jazz dancer, choreographer, director; Broadway musicals and film.

Serge Golovine, 1924-98, (Fr.) ballet dancer with Grand Ballet du Marquis de Cuevas; choreographer.

Martha Graham, 1893-1991, (U.S.) modern dancer, choreographer; created and codified her own dramatic technique.

Melissa Hayden, 1923-2006, (Canada) ballet dancer.

Martha Hill, 1901-95, (U.S.) educator; leading figure in modern dance; founded American Dance Festival.

Gregory Hines, 1946-2003, (U.S.) tap-dance innovator and master of improvisation.

Doris Humphrey, 1895-1958, (U.S.) modern dancer, choreographer, writer, teacher.

Robert Joffrey, 1930-88, (U.S.) ballet dancer, choreographer; cofounded with **Gerald Arpino,** b 1928, (U.S.), the Joffrey Ballet.

Kurt Jooss, 1901-79, (Ger.) choreographer, teacher; created expressionist works using modern and classical techniques.

Tamara Karsavina, 1885-1978, (Russ.) prima ballerina of Russia's Imperial Ballet and Diaghilev's Ballets Russes; partner of Nijinsky.

Nora Kaye, 1920-87, (U.S.) ballerina with Metropolitan Opera Ballet and Ballet Theater (now American Ballet Theatre).

Lincoln Kirstein, 1907-96 (U.S.) brought ballet as an art form to U.S.; founded, with George Balanchine, School of American Ballet and New York City Ballet.

Serge Lifar, 1905-86, (Russ.-Fr.) prem. danseur, choreographer; director of dance at Paris Opera, 1930-45, 1947-58.

José Limón, 1908-72, (Mex.-U.S.) modern dancer, choreographer, teacher; developed technique based on Humphrey.

Catherine Littlefield, 1908-51, (U.S.) ballerina, choreographer, teacher; pioneer of American ballet.

Léonide Massine, 1896-1979, (Russ.-U.S.) ballet dancer, choreographer; known for his "symphonic ballet."

Kenneth MacMillan, 1929-92, (Br.) dancer, choreographer; directed Royal Ballet of Great Britain 1970-77.

Dame Alicia Markova, 1910-2004, (Br.) ballerina; helped popularize ballet in U.S. and Britain; known for title role in *Giselle*.

Fayard Nicholas, 1914-2006, (U.S.) tap dancer, choreographer, actor; together with brother **Harold Nicholas,** 1921-2000, (U.S.) formed the "Nicholas Brothers."

Vaslav Nijinsky, 1890-50, (Russ.) prem. danseur, choreographer; leading member of Diaghilev's Ballets Russes; his ballets were revolutionary for their time.

Alwin Nikolais, 1910-93, (U.S.) modern choreographer; created dance theater utilizing mixed media effects.

Jean-George Noverre, 1727-1810, (Fr.) ballet choreographer, teacher, writer; "Shakespeare of the Dance."

Rudolf Nureyev, 1938-93, (Russ.) prem. danseur, choreographer; leading male dancer of his generation; director of dance at Paris Opera, 1983-89.

Ruth Page, 1903-91, (U.S.) ballerina, choreographer; danced and directed ballet at Chicago Lyric Opera.

Anna Pavlova, 1881-1931, (Russ.) prima ballerina; toured with her own company to world acclaim.

Marius Petipa, 1818-1910, (Fr.) ballet dancer, choreographer; ballet master of the Imperial Ballet; established Russian classicism as leading style of late 19th cent.

Pearl Primus, 1919-95, (Trinidad-U.S.) modern dancer, choreographer, scholar; combined African, Caribbean, and African American styles.

Jerome Robbins, 1918-98, (U.S.) choreographer, director, dancer; *The King and I, West Side Story, Fiddler on the Roof*

Bill (Bojangles) Robinson, 1878-1949, (U.S.) famed tap dancer; called King of Tapology on stage and screen.

Ruth St. Denis, 1877-1968, (U.S.) influential interpretive dancer, choreographer, teacher.

Ted Shawn, 1891-1972, (U.S.) modern dancer, choreographer; formed dance company and school with Ruth St. Denis; established Jacob's Pillow Dance Festival.

Marie Taglioni, 1804-84, (It.) ballerina, teacher; in title role of *La Sylphide* established image of the ethereal ballerina.

Antony Tudor, 1908-87, (Br.) choreographer, teacher; exponent of the "psychological ballet."

Galina Ulanova, 1910-98, (Russ.) revered ballerina with Bolshoi Ballet.

Agrippina Vaganova, 1879-1951, (Russ.) ballet teacher, director; codified Soviet ballet technique that developed virtuosity; called "queen of variations."

Mary Wigman, 1886-1973, (Ger.) modern dancer, choreographer, teacher; influenced European expressionist dance.

Opera Singers of the Past

Frances Alda, 1883-1952, (N.Z.) soprano
Pasquale Amato, 1878-1942, (It.) baritone
Marian Anderson, 1897-1993, (U.S.) contralto
Jussi Björling, 1911-60, (Swed.) tenor
Lucrezia Bori, 1887-1960, (It.) soprano
Maria Callas, 1923-77, (U.S.) soprano
Emma Calvé, 1858-1942, (Fr.) soprano
Enrico Caruso, 1873-1921, (It.) tenor
Feodor Chaliapin, 1873-1938, (Russ.) bass
Boris Christoff, 1914-93, (Bulg.) bass
Franco Corelli, 1921-2003, (It.) tenor
Victoria De Los Angeles, 1923-2005, (Sp.) soprano
Giuseppe De Luca, 1876-1950, (It.) baritone
Fernando De Lucia, 1860-1925, (It.) tenor
Edouard De Reszke, 1853-1917, (Pol.) bass
Jean De Reszke, 1850-1925, (Pol.) tenor
Emmy Destinn, 1878-1930, (Czech.) soprano
Emma Eames, 1865-1952, (U.S.) soprano
(Carlo Broschi) Farinelli, 1705-82, (It.) castrato
Geraldine Farrar, 1882-1967, (U.S.) soprano
Eileen Farrell, 1920-2002, (U.S.) soprano
Kathleen Ferrier, 1912-53, (Eng.) contralto
Kirsten Flagstad, 1895-1962, (Nor.) soprano
Olive Fremstad, 1871-1951, (Swed.-U.S.) soprano
Amelita Galli-Curci, 1882-1963, (It.) soprano
Mary Garden, 1874-1967, (Br.) soprano
Nicolai Ghiaurov, 1929-2004, (Bulg.) bass
Beniamino Gigli, 1890-1957, (It.) tenor
Tito Gobbi, 1913-84, (It.) baritone
Giulia Grisi, 1811-69, (It.) soprano
Frieda Hempel, 1885-1955, (Ger.) soprano
Jerome Hines, 1921-2003, (U.S.) bass
Hans Hotter, 1909-2003, (Ger.) bass-baritone
Maria Jeritza, 1887-1982, (Czech.) soprano
Alexander Kipnis, 1891-1978, (Russ.-U.S.) bass
Dorothy Kirsten, 1910-1992, (U.S.) soprano
Alfredo Kraus, 1927-99, (Sp.) tenor
Luigi Lablache, 1794-1858, (It.) bass
Lilli Lehmann, 1848-1929, (Ger.) soprano

Lotte Lehmann, 1888-1976, (Ger.-U.S.) soprano
Jenny Lind, 1820-87, (Swed.) soprano
Maria Malibran, 1808-36, (Sp.) mezzo-soprano
Giovanni Martinelli, 1885-1969, (It.) tenor
John McCormack, 1884-1945, (Ir.) tenor
Nellie Melba, 1861-1931, (Austral.) soprano.
Lauritz Melchior, 1890-1973, (Dan.) tenor
Robert Merrill, 1919-2004, (U.S.) baritone
Zinka Milanov, 1906-89, (Yugo.) soprano
Birgit Nilsson, 1918-2005, (Swed.) soprano
Lillian Nordica, 1857-1914, (U.S.) soprano
Giuditta Pasta, 1797-1865, (It.) soprano
Adelina Patti, 1843-1919, (It.) soprano
Peter Pears, 1910-86, (Eng.) tenor
Jan Peerce, 1904-84, (U.S.) tenor
Ezio Pinza, 1892-1957, (It.) bass
Lily Pons, 1898-1976, (Fr.) soprano
Rosa Ponselle, 1897-1981, (U.S.) soprano
Hermann Prey, 1929-98, (Ger.) baritone.
Elisabeth Rethberg, 1894-1976, (Ger.) soprano
Giovanni Battista Rubini, 1794-1854, (It.) tenor
Leonie Rysanek, 1926-1998, (Austrian) soprano
Bidú Sayão, 1902-99, (Braz.) soprano
Friedrich Schorr, 1888-1953, (Hung.) bass-baritone
Elisabeth Schwarzkopf, 1915-2006, (Ger.) soprano
Marcella Sembrich, 1858-1935, (Pol.) soprano
Eleanor Steber, 1916-90, (U.S.) soprano
Ferrucio Tagliavini, 1913-95, (It.) tenor
Renata Tebaldi, 1922-2004 (It.) soprano
Luisa Tetrazzini, 1871-1940, (It.) soprano
Lawrence Tibbett, 1896-1960, (U.S.) baritone
Tatiana Troyanos, 1938-93, (U.S.) mezzo-soprano
Richard Tucker, 1913-75, (U.S.) tenor
Pauline Viardot, 1821-1910, (Fr.) mezzo-soprano
William Warfield, 1920-2002, (U.S.) bass-baritone
Leonard Warren, 1911-60, (U.S.) baritone
Ljuba Welitsch, 1913-96, (Bulg.) soprano
Wolfgang Windgassen, 1914-74, (Ger.) tenor

World Almanac Quick Quiz

Which three of these four military leaders were alive at the same time?

(a) Robert E. Lee   (b) Napoleon Bonaparte   (c) Chief Joseph   (d) Simon Bolivar

For the answer look in this chapter, or see page 1008.

Selected Rock and Roll, Rhythm and Blues, Rap Artists

Titles in quotation marks are singles; others are albums. *Inducted into Rock and Roll Hall of Fame as performer between 1986 and 2006; year is in parentheses.

Aaliyah: "More than a Woman"
Paula Abdul: "Straight Up"
*AC/DC (2003): "Back in Black"
Bryan Adams: "Cuts Like a Knife"
*Aerosmith (2001): "Sweet Emotion"
Christina Aguilera: "What a Girl Wants"
Alice In Chains: "Heaven Beside You"
*The Allman Brothers Band (1995): "Ramblin' Man"
*The Animals (1994): "House of the Rising Sun"
Paul Anka: "Lonely Boy"
Fiona Apple: "Criminal"
Ashanti: "Foolish"
Frankie Avalon: "Venus"
The B-52s: "Love Shack"
Bachman Turner Overdrive: "Takin' Care of Business"
Backstreet Boys: "I Want it That Way"
Bad Company: "Can't Get Enough"
Erykah Badu: "On and On"
*La Vern Baker (1991): "I Cried a Tear"
*Hank Ballard and the Midnighters (1990): "Work With Me, Annie"
*The Band (1994): "The Weight"
Barenaked Ladies: "One Week"
*The Beach Boys (1988): "Good Vibrations"
Beastie Boys: "(You Gotta) Fight for Your Right (to Party)"
*The Beatles (1988): *Sgt. Pepper's Lonely Hearts Club Band*
Beck: "Loser"
*The Bee Gees (1997): "Stayin' Alive"
Pat Benatar: "Hit Me With Your Best Shot"
Beyoncé: "Crazy in Love"
Ben Folds Five: "Brick"
*Chuck Berry (1986): "Johnny B. Goode"
The Big Bopper: "Chantilly Lace"
Björk: "Human Behavior"
The Black Crowes: "Hard to Handle"
Black Eyed Peas: *Elephunk*
*Black Sabbath (2006): "Paranoid"
*Bobby "Blue" Bland (1992): "Turn On Your Love Light"
Mary J. Blige: *My Life*
Blind Faith: "Can't Find My Way Home"
Blink-182: "All the Small Things"
*Blondie (2006): "Heart of Glass"
Blood, Sweat, and Tears: "Spinning Wheel"
Blues Traveler: "Run-Around"
Gary "U.S." Bonds: "Quarter to Three"
Bon Jovi: "Livin' on a Prayer"
*Booker T. and the M.G.'s (1992): "Green Onions"
Earl Bostic: "Flamingo"
Boston: "More Than A Feeling"
*David Bowie (1996): "Space Oddity"
Boyz II Men: "I'll Make Love to You"
Toni Braxton: "Un-Break My Heart"
*James Brown (1986): "Papa's Got a Brand New Bag"
*Ruth Brown (1993): "Lucky Lips"
*Jackson Browne (2004): "Doctor My Eyes"
*Buffalo Springfield (1997): "For What It's Worth"
*Jimmy Buffett: "Margaritaville"
*Solomon Burke (2001): "Over and Over (Huggin' and Lovin')"
Bush: "Glycerine"
*The Byrds (1991): "Turn! Turn! Turn!"
Mariah Carey: "Vision of Love"
The Carpenters: "(They Long to Be) Close to You"
The Cars: "Shake It Up"
*Johnny Cash (1992): "I Walk the Line"
*Ray Charles (1986): "Georgia on My Mind"
Cheap Trick: "Surrender"
Chicago: "Saturday in the Park"
Chubby Checker: "The Twist"
*Eric Clapton (2000): "Layla"
Kelly Clarkson: "Since U Been Gone"
*The Clash (2003): "Rock the Casbah"
*The Coasters (1987): "Yakety Yak"
*Eddie Cochran (1987): "Summertime Blues"
Joe Cocker: "With a Little Help From My Friends"
Coldplay: "Clocks"
Collective Soul: "The World I Know"
Phil Collins: "Against All Odds"
*Sam Cooke (1986): "You Send Me"
Coolio: "Gangsta's Paradise"
Alice Cooper: "School's Out"
*Elvis Costello and the Attractions (2003): "Alison"
Counting Crows: "Mr. Jones"
*Cream (1993): "Sunshine of Your Love"
Creed: "Arms Wide Open"
*Creedence Clearwater Revival (1993): "Proud Mary"
*Crosby, Stills, and Nash (1997): "Suite: Judy Blue Eyes"
Sheryl Crow: "All I Want to Do"

The Cure: "Boys Don't Cry"
The Crystals: "Da Doo Ron Ron"
Cypress Hill: "Insane in the Brain"
Danny and the Juniors: "At the Hop"
*Bobby Darin (1990): "Splish Splash"
*Miles Davis (2006): *Bitches Brew*
Spencer Davis Group: "Gimme Some Lovin' "
Deep Purple: "Smoke on the Water"
Def Leppard: "Photograph"
*The Dells (2004): "Oh, What a Night"
Depeche Mode: "Strange Love"
Destiny's Child: "Survivor"
*Bo Diddley (1987): "Who Do You Love?"
*Dion and the Belmonts (1989): "A Teenager in Love"
Celine Dion: "Because You Loved Me"
Dire Straits: "Money for Nothing"
DMX: "What's My Name"
*Fats Domino (1986): "Blueberry Hill"
Donovan: "Mellow Yellow"
The Doobie Brothers: "What a Fool Believes"
*The Doors (1993): "Light My Fire"
Dr. Dre: "Nothin' But a 'G' Thang"
*The Drifters (1988): "Save the Last Dance for Me"
Duran Duran: "Hungry Like the Wolf"
*Bob Dylan (1988): "Like a Rolling Stone"
*The Eagles (1998): "Hotel California"
*Earth, Wind, and Fire (2000): "Shining Star"
*Duane Eddy (1994): "Rebel-Rouser"
Missy Elliott: "Sock It 2 Me"
Eminem: "The Real Slim Shady"
En Vogue: "Hold On"
The Eurythmics: "Sweet Dreams (Are Made of This)"
Everclear: "Father Of Mine"
*The Everly Brothers (1986): "Wake Up, Little Susie"
50 Cent (Curtis Jackson): *Get Rich Or Die Tryin'*
The Five Satins: "In the Still of the Night"
*The Flamingos (2001): "I Only Have Eyes for You"
*Fleetwood Mac (1998): *Rumours*
The Foo Fighters: "I'll Stick Around"
Foreigner: "Double Vision"
*The Four Seasons (1990): "Sherry"
*The Four Tops (1990): "I Can't Help Myself (Sugar Pie, Honey Bunch)"
*Aretha Franklin (1987): "Respect"
Nelly Furtado: "I'm Like a Bird"
Peter Gabriel: "Shock the Monkey"
*Marvin Gaye (1987): "I Heard It Through the Grapevine"
Genesis: "No Reply at All"
Goo Goo Dolls: "Iris"
Grand Funk Railroad: "We're an American Band"
Grand Master Flash and the Furious Five: "The Message"
*The Grateful Dead (1994): "Uncle John's Band"
*Al Green (1995): "Let's Stay Together"
Green Day: "Boulevard of Broken Dreans"
The Guess Who: "American Woman"
Guns N' Roses: "Sweet Child o' Mine"
*Buddy Guy (2005): *A Man and His Blues*
*Bill Haley and His Comets (1987): "Rock Around the Clock"
Hall and Oates: "Kiss on My List"
Hanson: "MMMBop"
*Isaac Hayes (2002): "Theme from 'Shaft'"
Heart: "Barracuda"
*Jimi Hendrix (1992): "Purple Haze"
Lauryn Hill: "Doo-Wop (That Thing)"
Hole: "Doll Parts"
The Hollies: "Long Cool Woman (In a Black Dress)"
*Buddy Holly (1986): "Peggy Sue"
*John Lee Hooker (1991): "Boogie Chillen"
Hootie and the Blowfish: *Cracked Rear View*
Whitney Houston: "I Will Always Love You"
*The Impressions (1991): "For Your Precious Love"
Indigo Girls: "Closer to Fine"
INXS: "Need You Tonight"
*The Isley Brothers (1992): "It's Your Thing"
*The Jackson Five (1997): "ABC"
Janet Jackson: *Rhythm Nation*
*Michael Jackson (2001): *Thriller*
*Etta James (1993): "At Last"
Tommy James & The Shondells: "Crimson and Clover"
Jane's Addiction: "Jane Says"
Ja Rule: *Venni, Vetti, Vecci*
Jay and the Americans: "This Magic Moment"
Jay-Z: "Can I Live"
*Jefferson Airplane (1996): "White Rabbit"
Jethro Tull: *Aqualung*
Joan Jett: "I Love Rock 'n' Roll"

Jewel: "You Were Meant for Me"
*Billy Joel (1999): "Piano Man"
*Elton John (1994): "Candle in the Wind"
*Little Willie John (1996): "Sleep"
Norah Jones: *Come Away With Me*
*Janis Joplin (1995): "Me and Bobby McGee"
Journey: "Don't Stop Believin'"
K.C. and the Sunshine Band: "Get Down Tonight"
R. Kelly: "I Can't Sleep Baby (If I)"
Alicia Keys: "Fallin'"
Kid Rock: "Cowboy"
*B.B. King (1987): "The Thrill Is Gone"
Carole King: *Tapestry*
*The Kinks (1990): "You Really Got Me"
Kiss: "Rock 'n' Roll All Night"
*Gladys Knight and the Pips (1996): "Midnight Train to Georgia"
Korn: "Blind"
Lenny Kravitz: "Are You Gonna Go My Way?"
*Led Zeppelin (1995): "Stairway to Heaven"
*Brenda Lee (2002): "I'm Sorry"
*John Lennon (1994): "Imagine"
*Jerry Lee Lewis (1986): "Whole Lotta Shakin' Going On"
Lil' Kim: "No Matter What They Say"
Limp Bizkit: "Break Stuff"
Linkin Park: "One Step Closer"
Little Anthony and the Imperials: "Tears on My Pillow"
*Little Richard (1986): "Tutti Frutti"
Live: "Lightning Crashes"
L. L. Cool J: "Mama Said Knock You Out"
Jennifer Lopez: "Love Don't Cost a Thing"
*The Lovin' Spoonful (2000): "Summer in the City"
*Frankie Lymon and the Teenagers (1993): "Why Do Fools Fall in Love?"
*Lynyrd Skynyrd (2006): "Free Bird"
Madonna: "Material Girl"
Taj Mahal: "Going up to the Country, Paint My Mailbox Blue"
*The Mamas and the Papas (1998): "Monday, Monday"
Aimee Mann: "Save Me"
Marilyn Manson: "Beautiful People"
*Bob Marley (1994): *Exodus*
Maroon 5: *Songs About Jane*
*Martha and the Vandellas (1995): "Dancin' in the Streets"
The Marvelettes: "Please, Mr. Postman"
Matchbox 20: "Push"
Dave Matthews Band: "Don't Drink the Water"
John Mayer: "Daughters"
*Curtis Mayfield (1999): "Superfly"
*Paul McCartney (1999): "Band on the Run"
Don McLean: "American Pie"
*Clyde McPhatter (1987): "A Lover's Question"
Meat Loaf: "Paradise by the Dashboard Light"
John (Cougar) Mellencamp: "Jack and Diane"
Men at Work: "Who Can It Be Now?"
Metallica: "Enter Sandman"
George Michael: "Faith"
*Joni Mitchell (1997): "Both Sides Now"
Moby: "Bodyrock"
The Monkees: "I'm a Believer"
Moody Blues: "Nights in White Satin"
*The Moonglows (2000): "Blue Velvet"
Alanis Morissette: "Ironic"
*Van Morrison (1993): "Brown-Eyed Girl"
Nelly: *Country Grammar*
*Ricky Nelson (1987): "Hello, Mary Lou"
Nine Inch Nails: "Closer"
Nirvana: *Nevermind*
No Doubt: *Rock Steady*
The Notorious B.I.G.: "Mo Money Mo Problems"
'N Sync: "Bye, Bye, Bye"
Oasis: "Wonderwall"
The Offspring: "Pretty Fly (for a White Guy)"
*The O'Jays (2005): "Back Stabbers"
*Roy Orbison (1987): "Oh, Pretty Woman"
Outkast: *Speakerboxxx*
Ozzy Osbourne: "Crazy Train"
*Parliament/Funkadelic (1997): "One Nation Under a Groove"
Pearl Jam: "Jeremy"
*Carl Perkins (1987): "Blue Suede Shoes"
Peter, Paul, and Mary: "Leaving on a Jet Plane"
*Tom Petty and the Heartbreakers (2002): "Refugee"
Liz Phair: *Exile in Guyville*
Phish: "Sample in a Jar"
*Wilson Pickett (1991): "Land of 1,000 Dances"
Pink: *Missundaztood!*
*Pink Floyd (1996): *The Wall*
*Gene Pitney (2002): "Only Love Can Break a Heart"
*The Platters (1990): "The Great Pretender"
*The Police (2003): "Every Breath You Take"
Iggy Pop: "Lust for Life"
*Elvis Presley (1986): "Love Me Tender"

*The Pretenders (2005): "Back on the Chain Gang"
*Lloyd Price (1998): "Stagger Lee"
*Prince (The Artist) (2004): "Purple Rain"
Public Enemy: "Fight the Power"
Puff Daddy and the Family: *No Way Out*
*Queen (2001): "Bohemian Rhapsody"
Radiohead: "Creep"
Rage Against the Machine: "Bulls on Parade"
*Bonnie Raitt (2000): "Something to Talk About"
*The Ramones (2002): "I Wanna Be Sedated"
*Otis Redding (1989): "(Sittin' on) the Dock of the Bay"
Red Hot Chili Peppers: "Under the Bridge"
*Jimmy Reed (1991): "Ain't That Loving You, Baby?"
Lou Reed: "Walk on the Wild Side"
R.E.M.: "Losing My Religion"
REO Speedwagon: "Can't Fight This Feeling"
Busta Rhymes: "What's It Gonna Be?"
*The Righteous Brothers (2003): "You've Lost That Lovin' Feelin'"
Johnny Rivers: "Poor Side of Town"
*Smokey Robinson and the Miracles (1987): "Shop Around"
*The Rolling Stones (1989): "Satisfaction"
The Ronettes: "Be My Baby"
Linda Ronstadt: "You're No Good"
Run-D.M.C.: "Raisin' Hell"
Rush: "Tom Sawyer"
Sade: "Smooth Operator"
Salt-N-Pepa: "Shoop"
*Sam and Dave (1992): "Soul Man"
*Santana (1998): "Black Magic Woman"
Seal: "Kiss From a Rose"
Neil Sedaka: "Breaking Up Is Hard to Do"
*Bob Seger (2004): "Old Time Rock & Roll"
*Sex Pistols (2006): "Anarchy in the U.K."
Shaggy: "It Wasn't Me"
Shakira: "Whenever, Wherever"
Tupac Shakur: "How Do U Want It"
*Del Shannon (1999): "Runaway"
*The Shirelles (1996): "Soldier Boy"
Carly Simon: "You're So Vain"
*Paul Simon (2001): "50 Ways to Leave Your Lover"
*Simon and Garfunkel (1990): "Bridge Over Troubled Water"
*Percy Sledge (2005): "When a Man Loves a Woman"
*Sly and the Family Stone (1993): "Everyday People"
Smashing Pumpkins: "Today"
Patti Smith: "Because the Night"
Will Smith: "Gettin' Jiggy With It"
The Smiths: "This Charming Man"
Snoop Dogg: "Gin and Juice"
Sonic Youth: "Bull in the Heather"
Soundgarden: "Black Hole Sun"
Britney Spears: "Hit Me Baby One More Time"
Spice Girls: "Wannabe"
*Dusty Springfield (1999): "I Only Want to Be With You"
*Bruce Springsteen (1999): "Born to Run"
*Staple Singers (1999): "I'll Take You There"
*Steely Dan (2001): "Rikki Don't Lose That Number"
Gwen Stefani: "Hollaback Girl"
Steppenwolf: "Born to Be Wild"
*Rod Stewart (1994): "Maggie Mae"
Sting: "If You Love Somebody, Set Them Free"
Stone Temple Pilots: "Plush"
Styx: "Come Sail Away"
Sublime: "What I Got"
The Sugar Hill Gang: "Rapper's Delight"
Donna Summer: "Bad Girls"
*The Supremes (1988): "Stop! In the Name of Love"
*Talking Heads (2002): "Once in a Lifetime"
*James Taylor (2001): "You've Got a Friend"
*The Temptations (1989): "My Girl"
Three Dog Night: "Joy to the World"
TLC: "Waterfalls"
T. Rex: "Bang a Gong (Get It On)"
*Traffic (2004): *Traffic*
*Big Joe Turner (1987): "Shake, Rattle & Roll"
*Ike and Tina Turner (1991): "Proud Mary"
*Tina Turner: "What's Love Got to Do With It?"
The Turtles: "Happy Together"
*U2 (2005): "With or Without You"
Usher: "You Make Me Wanna"
*Ritchie Valens (2001): "La Bamba"
Van Halen: "Running With the Devil"
Stevie Ray Vaughan: "Crossfire"
*The Velvet Underground (1996): "Sweet Jane"
*Gene Vincent[1] (1998): "Be-Bop-A-Lula"
Tom Waits: "Downtown Train"
The Wallflowers: "One Headlight"
Dionne Warwick: "I Say a Little Prayer"
*Muddy Waters (1987): "I Can't Be Satisfied"
Mary Wells: "My Guy"

Kanye West: "Gold Digger"
The White Stripes: "Seven Nation Army"
***The Who (1990):** *Tommy*
Lucinda Williams: *Car Wheels on a Gravel Road*
***Jackie Wilson (1987):** "That's Why"
***Stevie Wonder (1989):** "You Are the Sunshine of My Life"
Wu-Tang Clan: "Protect Ya Neck"
Weird Al Yankovic: Dare to Be Stupid

***The Yardbirds (1992):** "For Your Love"
Yes: "Roundabout"
***Neil Young (1995):** "Down by the River"
***The Young Rascals/The Rascals (1997):** "Good Lovin' "
***Frank Zappa[1]/Mothers of Invention (1995):** *Hot Rats*
John Zorn: *News for Lulu*
***ZZ Top (2004):** "Legs"

(1) Only individual performer is in Rock and Roll Hall of Fame.

Entertainment Personalities of the Present
Living actors, musicians, dancers, singers, producers, directors, radio-TV performers.

Name	Birthplace	Birthdate
Abbado, Claudio	Milan, Italy	6/26/33
Abdul, Paula	San Fernando, CA	6/19/62
Abraham, F. Murray	Pittsburgh, PA	10/24/39
Adams, Bryan	Kingston, Ontario	11/5/59
Adams, Edie	Kingston, PA	4/16/29
Adjani, Isabelle	Paris, France	6/27/55
Ad-rock	South Orange, NJ	10/31/66
Affleck, Ben	Berkeley, CA	8/15/72
Aghdashloo, Shohreh	Tehran, Iran	1952
Aguilera, Christina	Staten Is., New York, NY	12/18/80
Agutter, Jenny	Taunton, Somerset, Eng.	12/20/52
Aiello, Danny	New York, NY	6/20/33
Aiken, Clay	Raleigh, NC	11/30/78
Aimee, Anouk	Paris, France	4/27/32
Albanese, Licia	Bari, Italy	7/22/13
Alberghetti, Anna Maria	Pesaro, Italy	5/15/36
Albert, Marv	Brooklyn, New York, NY	6/12/41
Alda, Alan	New York, NY	1/28/36
Alexander, Jane	Boston, MA	10/28/39
Alexander, Jason	Newark, NJ	9/23/59
Allen, Debbie	Houston, TX	1/16/50
Allen, Joan	Rochelle, IL	8/20/56
Allen, Karen	Carrollton, IL	10/5/51
Allen, Krista	Ventura, CA	04/5/71
Allen, Ted	Carmel, IN	5/20/65
Allen, Tim	Denver, CO	6/13/53
Allen, Woody	Brooklyn, NY	12/1/35
Alley, Kirstie	Wichita, KS	1/12/51
Allman, Gregg	Nashville, TN	12/8/47
Allyson, June	Bronx, New York, NY	10/7/17
Alonso, Maria Conchita	Cienfuegos, Cuba	6/29/57
Alpert, Herb	Los Angeles, CA	3/31/35
Altman, Robert	Kansas City, MO	2/20/25
Almodóvar, Pedro	Calzada de Calatrava, Spain	9/25/51
Ambrose, Lauren	New Haven, CT	2/20/78
Ames, Ed	Malden, Boston, MA	7/9/27
Amos, John	Newark, NJ	12/27/41
Amos, Tori	Newton, NC	8/22/63
Andre 3000	Atlanta, GA	5/27/75
Anderson, Gillian	Chicago, IL	8/9/68
Anderson, Harry	Newport, RI	10/14/52
Anderson, Ian	Dunfermline, Scotland	8/10/47
Anderson, Kevin	Gurnee, IL	1/13/60
Anderson, Loni	St. Paul, MN	8/5/46
Anderson, Lynn	Grand Forks, ND	9/26/47
Anderson, Melissa Sue	Berkeley, CA	9/26/62
Anderson, Pamela	Comox, Vancouver Isl., BC	7/1/67
Anderson, Richard	Long Branch, NJ	8/8/26
Anderson, Richard Dean	Minneapolis, MN	1/23/50
Anderson, Wes	Houston, TX	5/1/69
Andersson, Bibi	Stockholm, Sweden	11/11/35
Andress, Ursula	Bern, Switzerland	3/19/36
Andrews, Julie	Walton-on-Thames, Surrey, England	10/1/35
Andrews, Patty	Minneapolis, MN	2/16/20
Aniston, Jennifer	Sherman Oaks, CA	2/11/69
Anka, Paul	Ottawa, Ontario	7/30/41
Ann-Margret	Stockholm, Sweden	4/28/41
Anthony, Marc	New York, NY	9/16/68
Antonioni, Michelangelo	Ferrara, Italy	9/29/12
Apple, Fiona	New York, NY	9/13/77
Applegate, Christina	Los Angeles, CA	11/25/71
Archer, Anne	Los Angeles, CA	8/25/47
Arkin, Adam	Brooklyn, NY	8/19/56
Arkin, Alan	New York, NY	3/26/34
Arnaz, Desi, Jr.	Hollywood, CA	1/19/53
Arnaz, Lucie	Hollywood, CA	7/17/51
Arness, James	Minneapolis, MN	5/26/23
Arnold, Eddy	Henderson, TN	5/15/18
Arnold, Tom	Ottumwa, IA	3/6/59
Arquette, David	Winchester, VA	9/8/71
Arquette, Patricia	Chicago, IL	4/8/68
Arquette, Rosanna	New York, NY	8/10/59
Arroyo, Martina	Harlem, New York, NY	2/2/37
Arthur, Beatrice	New York, NY	5/13/23
Ashanti (Douglas)	Glen Cove, NY	10/13/80
Ashley, Elizabeth	Ocala, FL	8/30/39
Asner, Ed	Kansas City, KS	11/15/29
Assante, Armand	New York, NY	10/4/49

Name	Birthplace	Birthdate
Astin, John	Baltimore, MD	3/30/30
Atkins, Eileen	London, England	6/16/34
Atkins, Sharif	Pittsburgh, PA	1/29/75
Atkinson, Rowan	Newcastle-Upon-Tyne, Eng.	1/6/55
Attenborough, Richard	Cambridge, England	8/29/23
Auberjonois, Rene	New York, NY	6/1/40
Austin, Patti	New York, NY	8/10/48
Autry, Alan	Shreveport, LA	7/31/52
Avalon, Frankie	Philadelphia, PA	9/18/39
Aykroyd, Dan	Ottawa, Ontario	7/1/52
Azaria, Hank	Forest Hills, Queens, NY	4/25/64
Aznavour, Charles	Paris, France	5/22/24
Babyface (Kenneth Edmonds)	Indianapolis, IN	4/10/59
Bacall, Lauren	Bronx, New York, NY	9/16/24
Bacon, Kevin	Philadelphia, PA	7/8/58
Badalucco, Michael	Brooklyn, NY	12/20/54
Bader, Diedrich	Alexandria, VA	12/24/66
Badu, Erykah	Dallas, TX	2/26/71
Baez, Joan	Staten Island, NY	1/9/41
Bain, Conrad	Lethbridge, Alberta	2/4/23
Baio, Scott	Brooklyn, NY	9/22/61
Baker, Anita	Toledo, OH	1/26/58
Baker, Carroll	Johnstown, PA	5/28/31
Baker, Diane	Hollywood, CA	2/25/38
Baker, Joe Don	Groesbeck, TX	2/12/36
Baker, Kathy	Midland, TX	6/8/50
Bakula, Scott	St. Louis, MO	10/9/54
Baldwin, Alec	Massapequa, NY	4/3/58
Baldwin, Daniel	Massapequa, NY	10/5/60
Baldwin, Stephen	Massapequa, NY	5/12/66
Baldwin, William	Massapequa, NY	2/21/63
Bale, Christian	Pembrokeshire, Wales	1/30/74
Ballard, Kaye	Cleveland, OH	11/20/26
Bana, Eric	Melbourne, Australia	8/9/68
Banderas, Antonio	Málaga, Spain	8/10/60
Banks, Elizabeth	Pittsfield, MA	2/10/75
Banks, Tyra	Los Angeles, CA	12/4/73
Bannon, Jack	Los Angeles, CA	6/14/40
Baranski, Christine	Buffalo, NY	5/2/52
Barbeau, Adrienne	Sacramento, CA	6/11/45
Bardem, Javier	Las Palmas, Canary Isl.	3/1/69
Bardot, Brigitte	Paris, France	9/28/34
Barker, Bob	Darrington, WA	12/12/23
Barkin, Ellen	Bronx, New York, NY	4/16/55
Barrie, Barbara	Chicago, IL	5/23/31
Barrino, Fantasia	High Point, NC	6/30/84
Barry, Gene	New York, NY	6/14/19
Barrymore, Drew	Los Angeles, CA	2/22/75
Bartoli, Cecilia	Rome, Italy	6/4/66
Barton, Misha	London, Eng.	1/24/86
Baryshnikov, Mikhail	Riga, Latvia	1/28/48
Basinger, Kim	Athens, GA	12/8/53
Bass, Lance	Laurel, MS	5/4/79
Bassett, Angela	Harlem, New York, NY	8/16/58
Bassey, Shirley	Cardiff, Wales	1/8/37
Bateman, Jason	Rye, NY	1/14/69
Bateman, Justine	Rye, NY	2/19/66
Bates, Kathy	Memphis, TN	6/28/48
Battle, Kathleen	Portsmouth, OH	8/13/48
Baxter, Meredith	Los Angeles, CA	6/21/47
Bean, Orson	Burlington, VT	7/22/28
Bean, Sean	Sheffield, England	4/17/59
Beatty, Ned	Louisville, KY	7/6/37
Beatty, Warren	Richmond, VA	3/30/37
Beauvais, Garcelle	St. Marc, Haiti	11/26/66
Beck (Hansen)	Los Angeles, CA	7/8/70
Beck, Jeff	Wallington, Surrey, Eng.	6/24/44
Beckinsale, Kate	London, England	7/26/73
Bedelia, Bonnie	New York, NY	3/25/48
Begley, Ed, Jr.	Los Angeles, CA	9/16/49
Behar, Joy	Brooklyn, NY	10/7/43
Belafonte, Harry	Harlem, New York, NY	3/1/27
Bell, Art	Camp Lejeune, NC	6/17/45
Bell, Catherine	London, England	8/14/68
Bello, Maria	Norristown, PA	4/18/67
Belmondo, Jean-Paul	Neuilly-sur-Seine, France	4/9/33
Belushi, Jim	Chicago, IL	6/15/54
Belzer, Richard	Bridgeport, CT	8/4/44

Name	Birthplace	Birthdate
Benatar, Pat	Brooklyn, NY	1/10/53
Benedict, Dirk	Helena, MT.	3/1/45
Benigni, Roberto	Misericordia, Italy	10/27/52
Bening, Annette	Topeka, KS	5/29/58
Benjamin, Richard	New York, NY	5/22/38
Bennett, Alan	Leeds, England	5/9/34
Bennett, Tony	Astoria, Queens, NY	8/3/26
Benson, George	Pittsburgh, PA	3/22/43
Benson, Robby	Dallas, TX	1/21/56
Berenger, Tom	Chicago, IL	5/31/50
Berfield, Justin	Ventura County, CA	2/25/86
Bergen, Candice	Beverly Hills, CA	5/9/46
Bergen, Polly	Knoxville, TN.	7/14/30
Bergeron, Tom	Haverhill, MA.	5/6/55
Bergman, Ingmar	Uppsala, Sweden	7/14/18
Berlinger, Warren	Brooklyn, NY.	8/31/37
Berman, Shelley	Chicago, IL	2/3/26
Bernard, Crystal	Dallas, TX	9/30/64
Bernhard, Sandra	Flint, MI	6/6/55
Bernsen, Corbin	N. Hollywood, CA	9/7/54
Berry, Chuck	St. Louis, MO	10/18/26
Berry, Halle	Cleveland, OH.	8/14/66
Berry, Ken	Moline, IL	11/3/33
Bertinelli, Valerie	Wilmington, DE	4/23/60
Bertolucci, Bernardo	Parma, Italy	3/16/40
Bettany, Paul	London, England.	5/27/71
Biafra, Jello	Boulder, CO	6/17/58
Bialik, Mayim	San Diego, CA	12/12/75
Big Boi	Savanah, GA.	2/1/75
Biggs, Jason	Pompton Plains, NJ	5/12/78
Bikel, Theodore	Vienna, Austria	5/2/24
Billingsley, Barbara	Los Angeles, CA	12/22/22
Bilson, Rachel	Los Angeles, CA	8/25/81
Binoche, Juliette	Paris, France.	3/9/64
Birch, Thora	Beverly Hills, CA	3/11/82
Birney, David	Washington, DC	4/23/39
Bishop, Joey	Bronx, NY	2/3/18
Bisset, Jacqueline	Weybridge, England	9/13/44
Bissett, Josie	Seattle, WA.	10/5/70
Björk (Gudmundsdottir)	Reykjavik, Iceland	11/21/65
Black, Clint	Long Branch, NJ	2/4/62
Black, Jack	Los Angeles, CA	4/7/69
Black, Karen	Park Ridge, IL	7/1/42
Blades, Ruben	Panama City, Panama	7/16/48
Blair, Janet	Altoona, PA	4/23/21
Blair, Linda	St. Louis, MO	1/22/59
Blair, Selma	Southfield, MI	6/23/72
Blake, Robert	Nutley, NJ	9/18/33
Blanchett, Cate	Melbourne, Australia	5/14/69
Bledsoe, Tempestt	Chicago, IL	8/1/73
Bleeth, Yasmine	New York, NY	6/14/68
Blethyn, Brenda	Ramsgate, Kent, England	2/20/46
Blige, Mary J.	Bronx, NY	1/11/71
Bloom, Claire	London, England.	2/15/31
Bloom, Orlando	Canterbury, England.	1/13/77
Blyth, Ann	Mt. Kisco, NY	8/16/28
Bochco, Steven	New York, NY	12/16/43
Bocelli, Andrea	Lajatico, Italy	9/22/58
Bogdanovich, Peter	Kingston, NY	7/30/39
Bogosian, Eric	Woburn, MA	4/24/53
Bologna, Joseph	Brooklyn, NY	12/30/38
Bolton, Michael	New Haven, CT.	2/26/53
Bonet, Lisa	San Francisco, CA	11/16/67
Bonham Carter, Helena	London, England.	5/26/66
Bon Jovi, Jon	Sayreville, NJ	3/2/62
Bono (Vox)	Dublin, Ireland.	5/10/60
Boone, Debby	Hackensack, NJ	9/22/56
Boone, Pat	Jacksonville, FL	6/1/34
Boreanaz, David	Buffalo, NY	5/16/71
Borgnine, Ernest	Hamden, CT	1/24/17
Bosco, Philip	Jersey City, NJ	9/26/30
Bosley, Tom	Chicago, IL	10/1/27
Bosson, Barbara	Charleroi, PA.	11/1/39
Bostwick, Barry	San Mateo, CA	2/24/45
Bosworth, Kate	Los Angeles, CA.	1/2/83
Bottoms, Timothy	Santa Barbara, CA	8/30/51
Bowen, Julie	Baltimore, MD	3/3/70
Bowie, David	London, England.	1/8/47
Bowles, Peter	London, England.	10/16/36
Boxleitner, Bruce	Elgin, IL	5/12/50
Boy George	Bexleyheath, England.	6/14/61
Boyle, Lara Flynn	Davenport, IA	3/24/70
Boyle, Peter	Philadelphia, PA	10/18/33
Bracco, Lorraine	Brooklyn, NY.	10/2/55
Brady, Wayne	Orlando, FL.	6/2/72
Braff, Zach	S. Orange, NJ	4/6/75
Branagh, Kenneth	Belfast, N. Ireland	12/10/60
Brandauer, Klaus Maria	Steiermark, Austria	6/22/44
Brandy (Norwood)	McComb, MS	2/11/79
Braschi, Nicoletta	Cesena, Italy	8/10/60
Bratt, Benjamin	San Francisco, CA	12/16/63
Braugher, Andre	Chicago, Il.	7/1/62
Braxton, Toni	Severn, MD.	10/7/66

Name	Birthplace	Birthdate
Bremner, Ewen	Edinburgh, Scotland	1971
Brendon, Nicholas	Los Angeles, CA	4/12/71
Brennan, Eileen	Los Angeles, CA	9/3/35
Brenneman, Amy	Glastonbury, CT	6/22/64
Brenner, David	Philadelphia, PA	2/4/45
Brewer, Teresa	Toledo, OH	5/7/31
Bridges, Beau	Hollywood, CA.	12/9/41
Bridges, Jeff	Los Angeles, CA.	12/4/49
Brightman, Sarah	Berkhamstead, England	8/14/60
Brimley, Wilford	Salt Lake City, UT	9/27/34
Brinkley, Christie	Malibu, CA.	2/2/54
Broadbent, Jim	Lincolnshire, England	5/24/49
Brochtrup, Bill	Inglewood, CA.	3/7/63
Broderick, Matthew	New York, NY	3/21/62
Brody, Adam	San Diego, CA	12/15/79
Brody, Adrien	New York, NY	4/14/73
Brolin, James	Los Angeles, CA	7/18/40
Brooks, Albert	Beverly Hills, CA	7/22/47
Brooks, Garth	Tulsa, OK	2/7/62
Brooks, James L	North Bergen, NJ	5/9/40
Brooks, Mel	Brooklyn, NY.	6/28/26
Brosnan, Pierce	Navan, Co. Meath, Ireland	5/16/53
Brown, Blair	Washington, DC	4/23/46
Brown, Bobby	Roxbury, Boston, MA	2/5/69
Brown, Bryan	Panania, Australia	6/23/47
Brown, James	Barnwell, SC	5/3/33
Browne, Jackson	Heidelberg, Germany	10/9/48
Browne, Roscoe Lee	Woodbury, NJ	5/2/25
Brubeck, Dave	Concord, CA	12/6/20
Bryson, Peabo	Greenville, SC	4/13/51
Buckley, Betty	Ft. Worth, TX.	7/3/47
Buffett, Jimmy	Pascagoula, MS	12/25/46
Bujold, Genevieve	Montreal, Quebec	7/1/42
Bullock, Sandra	Arlington, VA.	7/26/64
Bumbry, Grace	St. Louis, MO	1/4/37
Bundchen, Gisele	Horizontina, Brazil	7/20/80
Burghoff, Gary	Bristol, CT	5/24/43
Burke, Delta	Orlando, FL	7/30/56
Burnett, Carol	San Antonio, TX	4/26/33
Burns, Edward	Woodside, Queens, NY.	1/29/68
Burrows, Darren E.	Winfield, KS.	9/12/66
Burstyn, Ellen	Detroit, MI	12/7/32
Burton, LeVar	Landstuhl, W Germany	2/16/57
Burton, Tim	Burbank, CA	8/25/58
Buscemi, Steve	Brooklyn, NY	12/13/57
Busey, Gary	Goose Creek, TX	6/29/44
Busfield, Timothy	Lansing, MI	6/12/57
Butler, Brett	Montgomery, AL	1/30/58
Buzzi, Ruth	Westerly, RI.	7/24/36
Bynes, Amanda	Thousand Oaks, CA	4/3/86
Byrne, David	Dumbarton, Scotland	5/14/52
Byrne, Gabriel	Dublin, Ireland.	5/12/50
Caan, James	Bronx, NY	3/26/40
Caballe, Montserrat	Barcelona, Spain.	4/12/33
Caesar, Sid	Yonkers, NY	9/8/22
Cage, Nicolas	Long Beach, CA	1/7/64
Cain, Dean	Mt. Clemens, MI	7/31/66
Caine, Michael	London, England.	3/14/33
Caldwell, Zoe	Hawthorne, Australia.	9/14/33
Cameron, James	Kapuskasing, Ontario	8/16/54
Cameron, Kirk	Panorama City, CA	10/12/70
Campanella, Joseph	New York, NY	11/21/27
Campbell, Bruce	Royal Oak, MI	6/22/58
Campbell, Glen	Delight, AR	4/22/36
Campbell, Naomi	South London, England.	5/22/70
Campbell, Neve	Guelph, Ontario	10/3/73
Campion, Jane	Waikanae, New Zealand	4/30/54
Cannell, Stephen J.	Pasadena, CA.	5/2/41
Cannon, Dyan	Tacoma, WA.	1/4/37
Capshaw, Kate	Ft. Worth, TX.	11/3/53
Cara, Irene	New York, NY	3/18/64
Carell, Steve	Concord, MA.	8/16/62
Cardellini, Linda	Redwood City, CA.	6/25/75
Cardinale, Claudia	Tunis, Tunisia	4/15/39
Carey, Drew	Cleveland, OH.	5/23/58
Carey Jr., Harry	Saugus, CA.	5/16/21
Carey, Mariah	Huntington, NY	3/27/70
Cariou, Len	Winnipeg, Canada.	9/30/39
Carlin, George	Bronx, New York, NY	5/12/37
Carlisle Hart, Kitty	New Orleans, LA.	9/3/10
Carlton, Vanessa	Milford, PA.	8/16/80
Carlyle, Robert	Glasgow, Scotland	4/14/61
Carmen, Eric	Cleveland, OH.	8/11/49
Caron, Leslie	Boulogne, France	7/1/31
Carpenter, John	Carthage, NY	1/16/48
Carpenter, Mary Chapin	Princeton, NJ.	2/21/58
Carr, Vikki	El Paso, TX.	7/19/41
Carradine, David	Hollywood, CA.	12/8/36
Carradine, Keith	San Mateo, CA.	8/8/49
Carreras, Jose	Barcelona, Spain.	12/5/46
Carrere, Tia	Honolulu, HI	1/2/67
Carrey, Jim	Newmarket, Ontario	1/17/62
Carroll, Diahann	Bronx, NY	7/17/35

Name	Birthplace	Birthdate
Carroll, Pat	Shreveport, LA	5/5/27
Carson, Lisa Nicole	Brooklyn, NY	7/12/69
Carter, Dixie	McLemoresville, TN	5/25/39
Carter, Jack	Brooklyn, New York, NY	6/24/23
Carter, Lynda	Phoenix, AZ	7/24/51
Carter, Nick	Jamestown, NY	1/28/80
Carter, Ron	Ferndale, MI	5/4/37
Cartwright, Nancy	Kettering, OH	10/25/59
Caruso, David	Forest Hills, Queens, NY	1/17/56
Carvey, Dana	Missoula, MT.	6/2/55
Case, Sharon	Detroit, MI	2/9/71
Cash, Rosanne	Memphis, TN.	5/24/55
Cassidy, David	New York, NY	4/12/50
Castellaneta, Dan	Chicago, IL	9/10/58
Castle-Hughes, Keisha	Donnybrook, W. Australia, Australia	3/24/90
Cates, Phoebe	New York, NY	7/16/63
Cattrall, Kim	Liverpool, England	8/21/56
Cavanagh, Tom	Ottawa, Canada	10/26/68
Cavett, Dick	Gibbon, NE	11/19/36
Cedric the Entertainer	Jefferson City, MO	4/24/64
Chabert, Lacey	Purvis, MS.	9/30/82
Chalke, Sarah	Ottawa, Ontario	8/27/76
Chamberlain, Richard	Beverly Hills, CA	3/31/34
Chan, Jackie	Hong Kong	4/7/54
Channing, Carol	Seattle, WA	1/31/21
Channing, Stockard	New York, NY	2/13/44
Chaplin, Geraldine	Santa Monica, CA	7/31/44
Chapman, Tracy	Cleveland, OH.	3/30/64
Chappelle, Dave	Washington, DC	8/24/73
Charisse, Cyd	Amarillo, TX	3/8/21
Charo	Murcia, Spain	1/15/41
Chase, Chevy	New York, NY	10/8/43
Chasez, Joshua (J.C.)	Washington, DC	8/8/76
Cheadle, Don	Kansas City, MO	11/29/64
Checker, Chubby	Spring Gulley, SC	10/3/41
Cher	El Centro, CA	5/20/46
Chianese, Dominic	Bronx, NY	2/24/31
Chiba, Sonny	Fukuoka, Kyushu, Japan	1/23/39
Chiklis, Michael	Lowell, MA	8/30/63
Cho, Margaret	San Francisco	12/5/68
Chong, Rae Dawn	Vancouver, B. C. Can.	2/28/61
Chong, Thomas	Edmonton, Alberta, Can..	5/24/38
Chow Yun-Fat	Hong Kong	5/18/55
Christensen, Hayden	Vancouver, B. C. Can.	4/19/81
Christensen, Helena	Copenhagen, Denmark.	12/25/68
Christie, Julie	Chukua, Assam, India.	4/14/40
Christopher, William	Evanston, IL	10/20/32
Chuck D	New York, NY	8/1/60
Church, Charlotte	Llandaff, Cardiff, Wales.	2/21/86
Church, Thomas Haden	El Paso, TX.	6/17/61
Clapp, Gordon	North Conway, NH	9/24/48
Clapton, Eric	Surrey, England	3/30/45
Clark, Anthony	Lynchburg, VA	4/4/64
Clark, Dick	Mt. Vernon, NY	11/30/29
Clark, Petula	Ewell, Surrey, England	11/15/32
Clark, Roy	Meherrin, VA	4/15/33
Clarkson, Kelly	Burleson, TX	4/24/82
Clarkson, Patricia	New Orleans, LA.	12/29/59
Clay, Andrew Dice	Brooklyn, NY	9/29/58
Clayburgh, Jill	New York, NY	4/30/44
Cleese, John	Weston-super-Mare, Eng.	10/27/39
Cliburn, Van	Shreveport, LA	7/12/34
Clooney, George	Lexington, KY	5/6/61
Close, Glenn	Greenwich, CT	3/19/47
Coen, Ethan	St. Louis Park, MN	9/21/57
Coen, Joel	St. Louis Park, MN	11/29/54
Cohen, Leonard	Montreal, Canada	9/21/34
Cohen, Sacha Baron	London, England.	10/13/71
Colbert, Stephen	Charleston, SC	5/13/64
Cole, Gary	Park Ridge, IL	9/20/57
Cole, Natalie	Los Angeles, CA	2/6/50
Cole, Olivia	Memphis, TN.	11/26/42
Cole, Paula	Manchester, CT	4/5/68
Coleman, Dabney	Austin, TX	1/3/32
Coleman, Gary	Zion, IL	2/8/68
Coleman, Ornette	Fort Worth, TX	3/19/30
Collette, Toni	Blacktown, Australia	11/1/72
Collins, Joan	London, England	5/23/33
Collins, Judy	Seattle, WA.	5/1/39
Collins, Pauline	Exmouth, England.	9/3/40
Collins, Phil	London, England.	1/30/51
Collins, Stephen	Des Moines, IA	10/1/47
Colvin, Shawn	Vermillion, SD.	1/10/56
Combs, Sean "Diddy"	Harlem, NY	11/4/69
Comden, Betty	Brooklyn, NY.	5/3/19
Connelly, Jennifer	Catskill Mountains, NY	12/12/70
Connery, Sean	Edinburgh, Scotland	8/25/30
Connick, Harry, Jr.	New Orleans, LA.	9/11/67
Connolly, Kevin	New York, NY	3/5/74
Connors, Mike	Fresno, CA	8/15/25
Conrad, Robert	Chicago, IL	3/1/35
Conroy, Frances	Monroe, GA.	11/13/53

Name	Birthplace	Birthdate
Constantine, Michael	Reading, PA	5/22/27
Conti, Tom	Paisley, Scotland.	11/22/41
Conway, Tim	Willoughby, OH	12/15/33
Cook, Barbara	Atlanta, GA	10/25/27
Coolidge, Rita	Nashville, TN.	5/1/45
Coolio	Los Angeles, CA	8/1/63
Cooper, Alice	Detroit, MI	2/4/48
Cooper, Jackie	Los Angeles, CA	9/15/21
Copperfield, David	Metuchen, NJ	9/16/56
Coppola, Francis Ford	Detroit, MI	4/7/39
Coppola, Sofia	New York, NY	5/12/71
Corbett, John	Wheeling, WV	5/9/61
Corbin, Barry	Lamesa, TX.	10/16/40
Cord, Alex	Floral Park, NY	5/3/33
Corea, Chick	Chelsea, MA	6/12/41
Corgan, Billy	Elk Grove, IL	3/17/67
Corley, Pat	Dallas, TX.	6/1/30
Cornell, Chris	Seattle, WA.	7/20/64
Corwin, Jeff	Halifax, Nova Scotia	7/11/67
Cosby, Bill	Philadelphia, PA	7/12/37
Costas, Bob	Queens, New York, NY	3/22/52
Costello, Elvis	London, England.	8/25/54
Costner, Kevin	Compton, CA.	1/18/55
Courtenay, Tom	Hull, England.	2/25/37
Cowell, Simon	London, England.	10/7/59
Cox, Brian	Dundee, Scotland	6/1/46
Cox, Nikki	Los Angeles, CA	6/2/78
Cox, Ronny	Cloudcroft, NM	7/23/38
Cox Arquette, Courteney	Birmingham, AL.	6/15/64
Coyote, Peter	New York, NY.	10/10/42
Craig, Daniel	Chester, England	3/2/68
Cranston, Bryan	San Fernando Valley, CA	3/7/56
Crawford, Cindy	DeKalb, IL	2/20/66
Crawford, Michael	Salisbury, England	1/19/42
Crespin, Regine	Marseilles, France.	2/23/26
Crosby, David	Los Angeles, CA	8/14/41
Cross, Ben	London, England.	12/16/47
Cross, Marcia	Marlborough, MA.	3/25/62
Crouse, Lindsay	New York, NY	5/12/48
Crow, Sheryl	Kennett, MO	2/11/62
Crowe, Cameron	Palm Springs, CA	7/13/57
Crowe, Russell	Wellington, New Zealand	4/7/64
Crowell, Rodney	Houston, TX	8/17/50
Crudup, Billy	Manhasset, NY	7/8/68
Cruise, Tom	Syracuse, NY	7/3/62
Cruz, Penelope	Madrid, Spain	4/28/74
Crystal, Billy	Long Beach, NY	3/14/47
Culkin, Kieran	New York, NY.	9/30/82
Culkin, Macaulay	New York, NY	8/26/80
Culkin, Rory	New York, NY	7/21/89
Cullum, John	Knoxville, TN.	3/2/30
Culp, Robert	Oakland, CA	8/16/30
Curry, Tim	Cheshire, England.	4/19/46
Curtin, Jane	Cambridge, MA	9/6/47
Curtis, Jamie Lee	Los Angeles, CA	11/22/58
Curtis, Tony	New York, NY	6/3/25
Cusack, Joan	New York, NY.	10/11/62
Cusack, John	Evanston, IL	6/28/66
Cyrus, Billy Ray	Flatwoods, KY.	8/25/61
Dafoe, Willem	Appleton, WI	7/22/55
Dahl, Arlene	Minneapolis, MN	8/11/28
Dale, Jim	Rothwell, England.	8/15/35
Dalton, Abby	Las Vegas, NV	8/15/32
Dalton, Timothy	Colwyn Bay, Wales.	3/21/44
Daltrey, Roger	London, England.	3/1/44
Daly, Carson	Santa Monica, CA	6/22/73
Daly, Timothy	New York, NY.	3/1/56
Daly, Tyne	Madison, WI	2/21/46
Damon, Matt	Cambridge, MA.	10/8/70
Damone, Vic	Brooklyn, NY.	6/12/28
Danes, Claire	New York, NY.	4/12/79
D'Angelo	Richmond, VA	2/11/74
D'Angelo, Beverly	Columbus, OH.	11/15/54
Daniels, Anthony	Salisbury, England	2/21/46
Daniels, Charlie	Wilmington, NC	10/28/36
Daniels, Jeff	Athens, GA	2/19/55
Daniels, William	Brooklyn, NY	3/31/27
Danner, Blythe	Rosemont, PA.	2/3/43
Danson, Ted	San Diego, CA	12/29/47
Danza, Tony	Brooklyn, New York, NY	4/21/51
Darby, Kim	Hollywood, CA.	7/8/48
David, Larry	Brooklyn, NY.	7/2/47
Davidson, John	Pittsburgh, PA.	12/13/41
Davis, Ann B.	Schenectady, NY	5/5/26
Davis, Clifton	Chicago, IL	10/4/45
Davis, Geena	Wareham, MA.	1/21/56
Davis, Hope	Englewood, NJ	3/23/64
Davis, Judy	Perth, Australia	4/23/55
Davis, Kristin	Boulder, CO	2/24/65
Davis, Mac	Lubbock, TX.	1/21/42
Dawber, Pam	Farmington Hills, MI	10/18/51
Dawson, Richard	Gosport, Hampshire, Eng..	11/20/32
Dawson, Rosario	Bronx, New York, NY	5/9/79

Name	Birthplace	Birthdate
Day, Doris	Cincinnati, OH.	4/3/24
Day, Laraine	Roosevelt, UT.	10/13/17
Day-Lewis, Daniel	London, England.	4/29/57
Dean, Jimmy	Plainview, TX	8/10/28
Dearie, Blossom	E. Durham, NY	4/28/26
DeCarlo, Yvonne	Vancouver, BC	9/1/22
Dee, Ruby	Cleveland, OH.	10/27/24
DeFranco, Buddy.	Camden, NJ	2/17/23
DeGeneres, Ellen	Metairie, LA.	1/26/58
DeHaven, Gloria	Los Angeles, CA.	7/23/25
De Havilland, Olivia	Tokyo, Japan	7/1/16
Delaney, Kim	Philadelphia, PA	11/29/61
Delany, Dana	New York, NY	3/13/56
De la Rocha, Zack	Long Beach, CA	1/12/70
DeLaurentiis, Dino	Torre Annunziata, Italy	8/8/19
Delon, Alain	Sceaux, France.	11/8/35
Del Toro, Benicio	Santurce, Puerto Rico.	2/19/67
DeLuise, Dom	Brooklyn, NY.	8/1/33
Demme, Jonathan	Baldwin, NY	2/22/44
De Mornay, Rebecca	Santa Rosa, CA	8/29/62
Dempsey, Patrick.	Lewiston, ME	1/13/66
Dench, Judi	York, England.	12/9/34
Deneuve, Catherine.	Paris, France.	10/22/43
De Niro, Robert	New York, NY	8/17/43
Dennehy, Brian	Bridgeport, CT.	7/9/38
DePalma, Brian	Newark, NJ	9/11/40
Depardieu, Gerard	Chateauroux, France	12/27/48
Depp, Johnny.	Owensboro, KY.	6/9/63
Derek, Bo.	Long Beach, CA	11/20/56
De Rossi, Portia.	Melbourne, Victoria, Aust.	1/31/73
Dern, Bruce	Winnetka, IL	6/4/36
Dern, Laura	Santa Monica, CA.	2/10/67
DeVito, Danny	Neptune, NJ	11/17/44
DeWitt, Joyce.	Wheeling, WV	4/23/49
Dey, Susan	Pekin, IL	12/10/52
Diamond, Neil	Brooklyn, NY.	1/24/41
Diaz, Cameron.	San Diego, CA.	8/30/72
DiCaprio, Leonardo	Hollywood, CA	11/11/74
Dick, Andy	Charleston, SC	12/21/65
Dickinson, Angie	Kulm, ND.	9/30/31
Diddley, Bo	McComb, MS	12/30/28
Diesel, Vin	New York, NY	7/18/67
Diggs, Taye	Essex Co., NJ	1/2/72
Diller, Phyllis	Lima, OH.	7/17/17
Dillman, Bradford	San Francisco, CA	4/14/30
Dillon, Kevin	Mamaroneck, NY	8/16/65
Dillon, Matt.	New Rochelle, NY.	2/18/64
Dinklage, Peter	Mendham, NJ	6/11/69
Dion, Celine	Charlemagne, Quebec	3/30/68
Djalili, Omad	London, England.	1965
Dobson, Kevin	Queens, New York, NY	3/18/43
Dogg, Snoop	Long Beach, CA	10/20/71
Doherty, Shannen	Memphis, TN.	4/12/71
Dolenz, Mickey	Los Angeles, CA.	3/8/45
Domingo, Placido.	Madrid, Spain	1/21/41
Domino, Fats	New Orleans, LA.	2/26/28
Donahue, Phil	Cleveland, OH.	12/21/35
D'Onofrio, Vincent	Brooklyn, NY.	6/30/59
Donovan (Leitch)	Glasgow, Scotland	5/10/46
Donovan, Tate	Tenafly, NJ	9/25/63
Dorn, Michael.	Luling, TX	12/9/52
Dorough, Howie	Orlando, FL	8/22/73
Dotrice, Roy.	Guernsey, England	5/26/23
Douglas, Kirk	Amsterdam, NY.	12/9/16
Douglas, Michael	New Brunswick, NJ.	9/25/44
Dourdan, Gary	Philadelphia, PA	12/11/66
Dow, Tony	Hollywood, CA	4/13/45
Down, Lesley-Ann	London, England.	3/17/54
Downey, Robert, Jr.	New York, NY	4/4/65
Downey, Roma	Derry, Northern Ireland	5/6/60
Downs, Hugh	Akron, OH.	2/14/21
Drescher, Fran.	Flushing, Queens, NY.	9/30/57
Dreyfuss, Richard	Brooklyn, NY.	10/29/47
Driver, Minnie.	London, England.	1/31/70
Dryer, Fred.	Hawthorne, CA.	7/6/46
Duchovny, David	New York, NY	8/7/60
Duff, Haylie	Houston, TX.	2/19/85
Duff, Hilary.	Houston, TX.	9/28/87
Duffy, Julia	Minneapolis, MN.	6/27/51
Duffy, Patrick	Townsend, MT	3/17/49
Duhamel, Josh.	Minot, ND.	11/14/72
Dukakis, Olympia.	Lowell, MA	6/20/31
Duke, Patty	Elmhurst, NY.	12/14/46
Dullea, Keir	Cleveland, OH.	5/30/36
Dunaway, Faye	Bascom, FL.	1/14/41
Duncan, Lindsay	Edinburgh, Scotland	11/7/50
Duncan, Sandy	Henderson, TX	2/20/46
Dunne, Griffin.	New York, NY	6/8/55
Dunst, Kirsten	Point Pleasant, NJ	4/30/82
Durbin, Deanna	Winnipeg, Manitoba	12/4/21
Durning, Charles	Highland Falls, NY	2/28/23
Dussault, Nancy.	Pensacola, FL.	6/30/36
Dutton, Charles S.	Baltimore, MD.	1/30/51

Name	Birthplace	Birthdate
Duvall, Robert	San Diego, CA	1/5/31
Duvall, Shelley	Houston, TX	7/7/49
Dylan, Bob	Duluth, MN	5/24/41
Dylan, Jakob	New York, NY	12/9/69
Dysart, Richard	Brighton, MA.	3/30/29
Dzundza, George.	Rosenheim, Germany	7/19/45
Eads, George.	Fort Worth, TX.	3/1/67
Easton, Sheena	Bellshill, Scotland	4/27/59
Eastwood, Clint	San Francisco, CA	5/31/30
Ebert, Roger.	Urbana, IL	6/18/42
Eden, Barbara	Tucson, AZ	8/23/34
Edwards, Anthony	Santa Barbara, CA.	7/19/62
Edwards, Blake	Tulsa, OK	7/26/22
Ehle, Jennifer.	Winston-Salem, NC.	12/29/69
Eichhorn, Lisa	Reading, PA	2/4/52
Eikenberry, Jill	New Haven, CT.	1/21/47
Ekberg, Anita	Malmo, Sweden	9/29/31
Ekland, Britt	Stockholm, Sweden	10/6/42
Electra, Carmen	Cincinnati, OH.	4/20/72
Elfman, Jenna	Los Angeles, CA.	9/30/71
Elizabeth, Shannon	Houston, TX.	9/7/73
Elizondo, Hector.	New York, NY	12/22/36
Elliott, Bob	Boston, MA	3/26/23
Elliott, Chris	New York, NY	5/31/60
Elliott, Sam.	Sacramento, CA	8/9/44
Elvira	Manhattan, KS	9/17/51
Eminem	St. Joseph, MO	10/17/72
Enberg, Dick	Mt. Clemens, MI	1/9/35
Englund, Robert.	Glendale, CA.	6/6/49
Enya.	Gweedore, Ireland.	5/17/61
Ephron, Nora	New York, NY	5/19/41
Ermey, R. Lee	Emporia, KS	3/24/44
Estefan, Gloria	Havana, Cuba	9/1/57
Estevez, Emilio	New York, NY	5/12/62
Estrada, Erik	New York, NY	3/16/49
Etheridge, Melissa	Leavenworth, KS.	5/29/61
Evans, Linda	Hartford, CT	11/18/42
Evans, Robert	New York, NY	6/29/30
Everett, Chad.	South Bend, IN	6/11/36
Everett, Rupert.	Norfolk, England	5/29/59
Everly, Don	Brownie, KY	2/1/37
Everly, Phil.	Chicago, IL	1/19/39
Evigan, Greg	South Amboy, NJ	10/14/53
Fabares, Shelley	Santa Monica, CA.	1/19/44
Fabian (Forte)	Philadelphia, PA	2/6/43
Fabio	Milan, Italy	3/15/61
Fairchild, Morgan	Dallas, TX	2/3/50
Faison, Donald.	New York, NY	6/22/74
Falana, Lola	Philadelphia, PA	9/11/43
Falco, Edie.	Brooklyn, NY.	7/5/63
Falk, Peter	New York, NY	9/16/27
Fallon, Jimmy	Brooklyn, NY.	9/19/74
Farentino, James	Brooklyn, NY.	2/24/38
Fargo, Donna	Mt. Airy, NC.	11/10/49
Farina, Dennis	Chicago, IL	2/29/44
Farr, Jamie.	Toledo, OH.	7/1/34
Farrell, Colin	Dublin, Ireland.	5/31/76
Farrell, Mike.	St. Paul, MN	2/6/39
Farrell, Perry	Queens, NY.	3/29/59
Farrelly, Bob.	Cumberland, RI.	6/17/58
Farrelly, Peter	Phoenixville, PA	12/17/56
Farrow, Mia	Los Angeles, CA.	2/9/45
Fatone, Joey	Brooklyn, New York, NY	1/28/77
Fawcett, Farrah	Corpus Christi, TX.	2/2/47
Feinstein, Michael	Columbus, OH.	9/7/56
Feldon, Barbara	Pittsburgh, PA.	3/12/41
Feldshuh, Tovah	New York, NY.	12/27/52
Feliciano, Jose.	Lares, Puerto Rico	9/10/45
Fenn, Sherilyn	Detroit, MI	2/1/65
Ferrara, Jerry	Brooklyn, NY.	11/29/79
Ferrell, Conchata	Charleston, WV	3/28/43
Ferrell, Will.	Irvine, CA	7/16/67
Ferrer, Mel	Elberon, NJ	8/25/17
Feuerstein, Mark	New York, NY	6/8/71
Fey, Tina	Upper Darby, PA	5/18/70
Field, Sally	Pasadena, CA.	11/6/46
Fiennes, Joseph.	Salisbury, England	5/27/70
Fiennes, Ralph.	Suffolk, England	12/22/62
Fierstein, Harvey	Brooklyn, NY.	6/6/54
50 Cent	Queens, NY.	7/6/76
Filicia, Thom.	Syracuse, NY	5/17/69
Fincher, David	Denver, CO	5/10/62
Finney, Albert.	Salford, England	5/9/36
Fiorentino, Linda	Philadelphia, PA	3/9/60
Firth, Colin	Grayshott, England	9/10/60
Firth, Peter.	Bradford, Yorkshire, Eng.	10/27/53
Fischer-Dieskau, Dietrich	Berlin, Germany	5/28/25
Fischer, Jenna	Ft. Wayne, IN	3/7/74
Fishburne, Laurence	Augusta, GA.	7/30/61
Fisher, Carrie	Beverly Hills, CA.	10/21/56
Fisher, Eddie	Philadelphia, PA	8/10/28
Flack, Roberta	Black Mountain, NC	2/10/39
Flanagan, Fionnula	Dublin, Ireland.	12/10/41

Name	Birthplace	Birthdate
Flavor Flav	New York, NY	3/16/59
Fleetwood, Mick	Redruth, Cornwall, Eng.	6/24/42
Fleming, Rhonda	Hollywood, CA	8/10/23
Fletcher, Louise	Birmingham, AL	7/22/34
Flockhart, Calista	Freeport, IL	11/11/64
Florek, Dann	Flat Rock, MI	5/1/50
Foch, Nina	Leyden, Netherlands	4/20/24
Fogelberg, Dan	Peoria, IL	8/13/51
Fogerty, John	Berkeley, CA	5/28/45
Foley, Dave	Etobicoke, Ontario	1/4/63
Fonda, Bridget	Los Angeles, CA	1/27/64
Fonda, Jane	New York, NY	12/21/37
Fonda, Peter	New York, NY	2/23/40
Fontaine, Joan	Tokyo, Japan	10/22/17
Ford, Faith	Alexandria, LA	9/14/64
Ford, Glenn	Sainte-Christine, Quebec	5/1/16
Ford, Harrison	Des Plaines, IL	7/13/42
Forman, Milos	Caslav, Czechoslovakia	2/18/32
Forsythe, John	Penns Grove, NJ	1/29/18
Foster, Jodie	Los Angeles, CA	11/19/62
Fox, James	London, England	5/19/39
Fox, Jorja	New York, NY	7/7/68
Fox, Matthew	Crowheart, WY	7/14/66
Fox, Michael J.	Edmonton, Alberta	6/9/61
Fox, Vivica A.	Indianapolis, IN	7/30/64
Foxworth, Robert	Houston, TX	11/1/41
Foxworthy, Jeff	Atlanta, GA	9/6/58
Foxx, Jamie	Terrell, TX	12/13/67
Frampton, Peter	Kent, England	4/22/50
Francis, Anne	Ossining, NY	9/16/30
Francis, Connie	Newark, NJ	12/12/38
Franco, James	Palo Alto, CA	4/19/78
Franken, Al	New York, NY	5/21/51
Franklin, Aretha	Memphis, TN	3/25/42
Franklin, Bonnie	Santa Monica, CA	1/6/44
Franz, Dennis	Maywood, IL	10/28/44
Fraser, Brendan	Indianapolis, IN	12/3/68
Freeman, Al, Jr.	San Antonio, TX	3/21/34
Freeman, Mona	Baltimore, MD	6/9/26
Freeman, Morgan	Memphis, TN	6/1/37
French, Dawn	Holyhead, Wales	10/11/57
Fricker, Brenda	Dublin, Ireland	2/17/45
Friedkin, William	Chicago, IL	8/29/39
Frost, David	Tenterden, England	4/7/39
Fry, Stephen	London, England	8/24/57
Fuentes, Daisy	Havana, Cuba	11/17/66
Fuller, Robert	Troy, NY	7/29/34
Funicello, Annette	Utica, NY	10/22/42
Furlong, Edward	Pasadena, CA	8/2/77
Furtado, Nelly	Victoria, British Columbia	12/2/78
Gabor, Zsa Zsa	Budapest, Hungary	2/6/17
Gabriel, John	Niagara Falls, NY	5/25/31
Gabriel, Peter	Surrey, England	2/13/50
Gallagher, Peter	Armonk, NY	8/19/55
Gallo, Vincent	Buffalo, NY	4/11/62
Galway, James	Belfast, N. Ireland	12/8/39
Gandolfini, James	Westwood, NJ	9/18/61
Garagiola, Joe	St. Louis, MO	2/12/26
Garber, Victor	London, Ont.	3/16/49
Garcia, Andy	Havana, Cuba	4/12/56
Garfunkel, Art	Queens, New York, NY	11/5/41
Garland, Beverly	Santa Cruz, CA	10/17/26
Garner, James	Norman, OK	4/7/28
Garner, Jennifer	Houston, TX	4/17/72
Garofalo, Janeane	Newton, NJ	9/28/64
Garr, Teri	Lakewood, OH	12/11/49
Garrett, Betty	St. Joseph, MO	5/23/19
Garrett, Brad	Woodland Hills, CA	4/14/60
Garth, Jennie	Urbana, IL	4/3/72
Gatlin, Larry	Seminole, TX	5/2/48
Gavin, John	Los Angeles, CA	4/8/31
Gayle, Crystal	Paintsville, KY	1/9/51
Gaynor, Mitzi	Chicago, IL	9/4/31
Gazzara, Ben	New York, NY	8/28/30
Geary, Anthony	Coalville, UT	5/29/47
Geary, Cynthia	Jackson, MS	3/21/65
Gedda, Nicolai	Stockholm, Sweden	7/11/25
Gellar, Sarah Michelle	New York, NY	4/14/77
Gere, Richard	Philadelphia, PA	8/31/49
Gervais, Ricky	Reading, England	6/25/61
Getty, Estelle	New York, NY	7/25/23
Ghostley, Alice	Eve, MO	8/14/26
Giannini, Giancarlo	La Spezia, Italy	8/1/42
Gibb, Barry	Isle of Man, England	9/1/46
Gibb, Robin	Isle of Man, England	12/22/49
Gibbons, Leeza	Irmo, SC	3/26/57
Gibbs, Marla	Chicago, IL	6/14/31
Gibson, Deborah	Brooklyn, New York, NY	8/31/70
Gibson, Henry	Germantown, PA	9/21/35
Gibson, Mel	Peekskill, NY	1/3/56
Gibson, Thomas	Charleston, SC	7/3/62
Gifford, Frank	Santa Monica, CA	8/16/30
Gifford, Kathie Lee	Neuilly-sur-Seine, France	8/16/53

Name	Birthplace	Birthdate
Gilbert, Sara	Santa Monica, CA	1/29/75
Gilbert, Melissa	Los Angeles, CA	5/8/64
Gilberto, Astrud	Salvador, Brazil	3/30/40
Gill, Vince	Norman, OK	4/12/57
Gillette, Anita	Baltimore, MD	8/16/36
Gilley, Mickey	Natchez, MS	3/9/36
Gilliam, Terry	Minneapolis, MN	11/22/40
Gilmour, David	Cambridge, England	3/6/44
Gilpin, Peri	Waco, TX	5/27/61
Ginty, Robert	New York, NY	11/14/48
Givens, Robin	New York, NY	11/27/64
Glaser, Paul Michael	Cambridge, MA	3/25/43
Gleeson, Brendan	Belfast, N. Ireland	11/9/55
Glenn, Scott	Pittsburgh, PA	1/26/42
Gless, Sharon	Los Angeles, CA	5/31/43
Glover, Crispin	New York, NY	9/20/64
Glover, Danny	San Francisco, CA	7/22/47
Glover, Julian	London, England	3/27/35
Glover, Savion	Newark, NJ	11/19/73
Godard, Jean Luc	Paris, France	12/3/30
Goldberg, Whoopi	New York, NY	11/13/55
Goldblum, Jeff	Pittsburgh, PA	10/22/52
Goldthwait, Bobcat	Syracuse, NY	5/26/62
Goldwyn, Tony	Los Angeles, CA	5/20/60
Gooding, Cuba, Jr.	Bronx, NY	1/2/68
Goodman, John	Affton, MO	6/20/52
Gordon-Levitt, Joseph	Los Angeles, CA	2/17/81
Gorme, Eydie	Bronx, NY	8/16/32
Gosselaar, Mark-Paul	Panorama City, CA	3/1/74
Gossett, Louis, Jr.	Brooklyn, NY	5/27/36
Gould, Elliott	Brooklyn, NY	8/29/38
Gould, Harold	Schenectady, NY	12/10/23
Goulet, Robert	Lawrence, MA	11/26/33
Grace, Topher	New York, NY	7/19/78
Graham, Heather	Milwaukee, WI	1/29/70
Grammer, Kelsey	St. Thomas, Virgin Isl.	2/21/55
Granger, Farley	San Jose, CA	7/1/25
Grant, Amy	Augusta, GA	11/25/60
Grant, Hugh	London, England	9/9/60
Grant, Lee	New York, NY	10/31/27
Graves, Peter	Minneapolis, MN	3/18/26
Gray, Linda	Santa Monica, CA	9/12/40
Gray, Macy	Canton, OH	9/9/70
Grayson, Kathryn	Winston-Salem, NC	2/9/22
Green, Al	Forrest City, AR	4/13/46
Green, Seth	Overbrook Park, PA	2/8/74
Green, Tom	Pembroke, Ontario	7/30/71
Greene, Shecky	Chicago, IL	4/8/26
Greenwood, Bruce	Noranda, Quebec	8/12/56
Gregory, Cynthia	Los Angeles, CA	7/8/46
Gregory, Dick	St. Louis, MO	10/12/32
Grenier, Adrian	Brooklyn, NY	7/10/76
Grey, Jennifer	New York, NY	3/26/60
Grey, Joel	Cleveland, OH	4/11/32
Grier, David Alan	Detroit, MI	6/30/55
Grier, Pam	Winston-Salem, NC	5/26/49
Gries, Jon	Glendale, CA	6/17/57
Griffin, Merv	San Mateo, CA	7/6/25
Griffith, Andy	Mount Airy, NC	6/1/26
Griffith, Melanie	New York, NY	8/9/57
Griffiths, Rachel	New Castle, Australia	2/20/68
Grimes, Tammy	Lynn, MA	1/30/34
Grint, Rupert	Hertfordshire, England	8/24/88
Grizzard, George	Roanoke Rapids, NC	4/1/28
Groban, Josh	Los Angeles, CA	2/27/81
Grodin, Charles	Pittsburgh, PA	4/21/35
Grohl, David	Warren, OH	1/14/69
Grosbard, Ulu	Antwerp, Belgium	1/9/29
Gross, Michael	Chicago, IL	6/21/47
Guest, Christopher	New York, NY	2/5/48
Guillaume, Robert	St. Louis, MO	11/30/37
Gumbel, Greg	New Orleans, LA	5/3/46
Guthrie, Arlo	Brooklyn, New York, NY	7/10/47
Guttenberg, Steve	Brooklyn, New York, NY	8/24/58
Guy, Buddy	Lettsworth, LA	7/30/36
Guy, Jasmine	Boston, MA	3/10/64
Gyllenhaal, Jake	Los Angeles, CA	12/19/80
Gyllenhaal, Maggie	New York, NY	11/16/77
Hackman, Gene	San Bernardino, CA	1/30/30
Hagerty, Julie	Cincinnati, OH	6/15/55
Haggard, Merle	Bakersfield, CA	4/6/37
Hagman, Larry	Fort Worth, TX	9/21/31
Haid, Charles	San Francisco, CA	6/2/43
Haines, Connie	Savannah, GA	1/20/22
Hale, Barbara	DeKalb, IL	4/18/22
Hall, Anthony Michael	West Roxbury, MA	4/14/68
Hall, Arsenio	Cleveland, OH	2/12/55
Hall, Daryl	Pottstown, PA	10/11/49
Hall, Deidre	Milwaukee, WI	10/31/47
Hall, Michael C.	Raleigh, NC	2/1/71
Hall, Monty	Winnipeg, Manitoba	8/25/21
Hall, Tom T.	Olive Hill, KY	5/25/36
Halliwell, Geri	Watford, England	8/6/72

Name	Birthplace	Birthdate	Name	Birthplace	Birthdate
Hamill, Mark	Oakland, CA	9/25/51	Ho, Don	Kakaako, HI	8/13/30
Hamilton, George	Memphis, TN	8/12/39	Hodgman, John	Cambridge, MA	6/3/71
Hamilton, Linda	Salisbury, MD	9/26/56	Hoffman, Dustin	Los Angeles, CA	8/8/37
Hamlin, Harry	Pasadena, CA	10/30/51	Hoffman, Philip Seymour	Fairport, NY	7/23/67
Hammer	Oakland, CA	3/29/63	Hogan, Paul	Lightning Ridge, New South	
Hammond, Darrell	Melbourne, FL	10/8/60		Wales, Australia	10/8/39
Hampshire, Susan	London, England	5/12/37	Holbrook, Hal	Cleveland, OH	2/17/25
Hancock, Herbie	Chicago, IL	4/12/40	Holder, Geoffrey	Port of Spain, Trinidad	8/1/30
Hanks, Tom	Concord, CA	7/9/56	Holliday, Polly	Jasper, AL	7/2/37
Hannah, Daryl	Chicago, IL	12/3/60	Holliman, Earl	Delhi, LA	9/11/28
Hannigan, Alyson	Washington, DC	3/24/74	Holly, Lauren	Bristol, PA	10/28/63
Hanson, Curtis	Reno, NV	3/24/45	Holm, Celeste	New York, NY	4/29/19
Hanson, Isaac	Tulsa, OK	11/17/80	Holm, Ian	Ilford, England	9/12/31
Hanson, Taylor	Tulsa, OK	3/14/83	Holmes, Katie	Toledo, OH	12/18/78
Hanson, Zac	Tulsa, OK	10/22/85	Hooks, Jan	Decatur, GA	4/23/57
Harden, Marcia Gay	La Jolla, CA	8/14/59	Hopkins, Anthony	Port Talbot, South Wales	12/31/37
Hardison, Kadeem	New York, NY	7/24/66	Hopkins, Bo	Greenville, SC	2/2/42
Harewood, Dorian	Dayton, OH	8/6/50	Hopkins, Telma	Louisville, KY	10/28/48
Hargitay, Mariska	Los Angeles, CA	1/23/64	Hopper, Dennis	Dodge City, KS	5/17/36
Harmon, Angie	Highland Park, TX	8/10/72	Horne, Lena	Brooklyn, NY	6/30/17
Harmon, Mark	Burbank, CA	9/2/51	Horne, Marilyn	Bradford, PA	1/16/34
Harper, Ben	Claremont, CA	10/28/69	Hornsby, Bruce	Williamsburg, VA	11/23/54
Harper, Jessica	Chicago, IL	10/10/49	Horsley, Lee	Muleshoe, TX	5/15/55
Harper, Tess	Mammoth Springs, AR	8/15/50	Horton, Robert	Los Angeles, CA	7/29/24
Harper, Valerie	Suffern, NY	8/22/40	Hoskins, Bob	Suffolk, England	10/26/42
Harrelson, Woody	Midland, TX	7/23/61	Hounsou, Djimon	Benin	4/24/64
Harrington, Pat	New York, NY	8/13/29	Houston, Whitney	Newark, NJ	8/9/63
Harris, Barbara	Evanston, IL	7/25/35	Howard, Ken	El Centro, CA	3/28/44
Harris, Ed	Tenafly, NJ	11/28/50	Howard, Ron	Duncan, OK	3/1/54
Harris, Emmylou	Birmingham, AL	4/2/47	Howell, C. Thomas	Van Nuys, CA	12/7/66
Harris, Julie	Grosse Pte. Park, MI	12/2/25	Howes, Sally Ann	London, England	7/20/30
Harris, Neil Patrick	Albuquerque, NM	6/15/73	Hudson, Kate	Los Angeles, CA	4/19/79
Harris, Rosemary	Ashby, England	9/19/30	Huffman, Felicity	Bedford, NY	12/6/62
Harris, Steve	Chicago, IL	12/3/65	Hughes, Barnard	Bedford Hills, NY	7/16/15
Harrison, Gregory	Avalon, CA	5/31/50	Hughley, D.L.	Los Angeles, CA	3/6/63
Harry, Deborah	Miami, FL	7/1/45	Hulce, Tom	Whitewater, WI	12/6/53
Hart, Mary	Madison, SD	11/8/50	Humperdinck, Engelbert	Madras, India	5/2/36
Hart, Melissa Joan	Sayville, NY	4/18/76	Humphries, Barry	Melbourne, Australia	2/17/34
Hartley, Hal	Lindenhurst, NY	11/3/59	Hunt, Bonnie	Chicago, IL	9/22/64
Hartley, Mariette	New York, NY	6/21/40	Hunt, Helen	Culver City, CA	6/15/63
Hartman, David	Pawtucket, RI	5/19/35	Hunt, Linda	Morristown, NJ	4/2/45
Hartman Black, Lisa	Houston, TX	6/1/56	Hunter, Holly	Conyers, GA	3/20/58
Hartnett, Josh	San Francisco, CA	7/21/78	Hunter, Tab	New York, NY	7/11/31
Harvey, P.J.	Yeovil, Somerset, England	10/9/69	Hurley, Elizabeth	Hampshire, England	6/10/65
Harvey, Steve	Welch, WV	11/23/56	Hurt, John	Chesterfield, England	1/22/40
Hasselhoff, David	Baltimore, MD	7/17/52	Hurt, Mary Beth	Marshalltown, IA	9/26/48
Hatcher, Teri	Sunnyvale, CA	12/8/64	Hurt, William	Washington, DC	3/20/50
Hatfield, Juliana	Wiscasset, ME	7/27/67	Huston, Anjelica	Santa Monica, CA	7/8/51
Hathaway, Anne	Brooklyn, NY	11/12/82	Hutton, Betty	Battle Creek, MI	2/26/21
Hauer, Rutger	Breukelen, Netherlands	1/23/44	Hutton, Lauren	Charleston, SC	11/17/43
Havoc, June	Seattle, WA	11/8/16	Hutton, Timothy	Malibu, CA	8/16/60
Hawke, Ethan	Austin, TX	11/6/70	Hyman, Earle	Rocky Mount, NC	10/11/26
Hawn, Goldie	Washington, DC	11/21/45	Ian, Janis	New York, NY	4/7/51
Hayek, Salma	Coatzacoalcos, Mexico	9/2/66	Ice Cube	Los Angeles, CA	6/15/69
Hayes, Isaac	Covington, TN	8/20/42	Ice-T	Newark, NJ	2/16/58
Hayes, Sean	Glen Ellyn, IL	6/26/70	Idle, Eric	S. Shields, England	3/29/43
Haynes, Roy	Roxbury, Boston, MA	3/13/26	Idol, Billy	Middlesex, England	11/30/55
Hays, Robert	Bethesda, MD	7/24/47	Iglesias, Enrique	Madrid, Spain	5/8/75
Head, Anthony Stewart	North London, England	2/20/54	Iglesias, Julio	Madrid, Spain	9/23/43
Heard, John	Washington, DC	3/7/46	Iler, Robert	New York, NY	3/2/85
Hearn, George	St. Louis, MO	6/18/34	Iman	Mogadishu, Somalia	7/25/55
Heaton, Patricia	Bay Village, OH	3/4/58	Imbruglia, Natalie	Sydney, Australia	2/4/75
Heche, Anne	Aurora, OH	5/25/69	Imperioli, Michael	Mount Vernon, NY	1/1/66
Heder, Jon	Fort Collins, CO	10/26/77	Imus, Don	Riverside, CA	7/23/40
Hedren, Tippi	Lafayette, MN	1/19/31	Ingram, James	Akron, OH	2/16/56
Helfgott, David	Melbourne, Australia	5/19/47	Innes, Laura	Pontiac, MI	8/16/59
Helgenberger, Marg	Fremont, NE	11/16/58	Ireland, Kathy	Glendale, CA	3/20/63
Helmond, Katherine	Galveston, TX	7/5/34	Irons, Jeremy	Isle of Wight, England	9/19/48
Hemingway, Mariel	Mill Valley, CA	11/22/61	Irving, Amy	Palo Alto, CA	9/10/53
Hemsley, Sherman	Philadelphia, PA	2/1/38	Irving, George S.	Springfield, MA	11/1/22
Henderson, Florence	Dale, IN	2/14/34	Irwin, Bill	Santa Monica, CA	4/11/50
Henley, Don	Gilmer, TX	7/22/47	Irwin, Steve	Beerwah, Queensl., Aust.	2/22/62
Henner, Marilu	Chicago, IL	4/6/52	Ivey, Judith	El Paso, TX	9/4/51
Hennessy, Jill	Edmonton, Alberta	11/25/68	Ivory, James	Berkeley, CA	6/7/28
Henry, Buck	New York, NY	12/9/30	Jackee (Harry)	Winston-Salem, NC	8/14/56
Herman, Pee-Wee	Peekskill, NY	8/27/52	Jackman, Hugh	Sydney, Australia	10/12/68
Herrmann, Edward	Washington, DC	7/21/43	Jackson, Anne	Allegheny, PA	9/3/26
Hershey, Barbara	Hollywood, CA	2/5/48	Jackson, Glenda	Birkenhead, England	5/9/36
Hesseman, Howard	Lebanon, OR	2/27/40	Jackson, Janet	Gary, IN	5/16/66
Heston, Charlton	Evanston, IL	10/4/24	Jackson, Jermaine	Gary, IN	12/11/54
Hetfield, James	Downey, CA	8/3/63	Jackson, Jonathan	Orlando, FL	5/11/82
Hewitt, Jennifer Love	Waco, TX	2/21/79	Jackson, Joshua	Vancouver, Brit. Columbia	6/11/78
Hicks, Catherine	Scottsdale, AZ	8/6/51	Jackson, Kate	Birmingham, AL	10/29/48
Hill, Arthur	Melfort, Sask.	8/1/22	Jackson, La Toya	Gary, IN	5/29/56
Hill, Dulé	Orange, NJ	5/3/74	Jackson, Michael	Gary, IN	8/29/58
Hill, Faith	Jackson, MS	9/21/67	Jackson, Peter	Wellington, New Zealand	10/31/61
Hill, Lauryn	South Orange, NJ	5/25/75	Jackson, Samuel L.	Chattanooga, TN	12/21/48
Hill, Steven	Seattle, WA	2/24/22	Jacobi, Derek	London, England	10/22/38
Hillerman, John	Denison, TX	12/20/32	Jagger, Mick	Dartford, England	7/26/43
Hilton, Paris	New York, NY	2/17/81	James, Etta	Los Angeles, CA	1/25/38
Hines, Cheryl	Miami Beach, FL	9/21/65	James, Kevin	Mineola, NY	4/26/65
Hingle, Pat	Denver, CO	7/19/24	Janis, Conrad	New York, NY	2/11/28
Hirsch, Judd	New York, NY	3/15/35	Janney, Allison	Boston, MA	11/19/60

Name	Birthplace	Birthdate
Janssen, Famke	Amsterdam, Netherlands	11/5/65
Jardine, Al	Lima, OH	9/3/42
Jarmusch, Jim	Akron, OH	1/22/53
Jarreau, Al	Milwaukee, WI	3/12/40
Jarrette, Keith	Allentown, PA	5/8/45
Jay Z	Brooklyn, NY	12/4/69
Jeffreys, Anne	Goldsboro, NC	1/26/23
Jett, Joan	Philadelphia, PA	9/22/60
Jewel (Kilcher)	Payson, UT	5/23/74
Jewison, Norman	Toronto, Ontario	7/21/26
Jillian, Ann	Cambridge, MA	1/29/50
Jillette, Penn	Greenfield, MA	3/5/55
Joel, Billy	Bronx, NY	5/9/49
Johansson, Scarlett	New York, NY	11/22/84
John, Elton	Pinner, Middlesex, Eng.	3/25/47
Johns, Glynis	Durban, S Africa	10/5/23
Johnson, Arte	Benton Harbor, MI.	1/20/34
Johnson, Beverly	Buffalo, NY	10/13/52
Johnson, Don	Flatt Creek, MO.	12/15/49
Johnson, Van	Newport, RI	8/25/16
Johnston, Bruce	Chicago, IL	6/24/44
Johnston, Kristen	Washington, DC	9/20/67
Jolie, Angelina	Los Angeles, CA	6/4/75
Jones, Charlie	Ft. Smith, AR	11/9/30
Jones, Cherry	Paris, TN	11/21/56
Jones, Davy	Manchester, England	12/30/45
Jones, Dean	Morgan City, AL	1/25/31
Jones, Elvin	Pontiac, MI	9/9/27
Jones, Gemma	London, England	12/4/42
Jones, George	Saratoga, TX	9/12/31
Jones, Grace	Spanishtown, Jamaica	5/19/52
Jones, Jack	Hollywood, CA	1/14/38
Jones, James Earl	Arkabutla, MS	1/17/31
Jones, Jennifer	Tulsa, OK	3/2/19
Jones, Mick	London, England	6/26/55
Jones, Norah	New York, NY	3/30/79
Jones, Quincy	Chicago, IL	3/14/33
Jones, Shirley	Smithton, PA	3/31/34
Jones, Star	Badin, NC	3/24/62
Jones, Tom	Pontypridd, Wales	6/7/40
Jones, Tommy Lee	San Saba, TX	9/15/46
Jonze, Spike	Rockville, MD	10/22/69
Jourdan, Louis	Marseilles, France	6/19/19
Jovovich, Milla	Kiev, Ukraine	12/17/75
Judd, Ashley	Granada Hills, CA	4/19/68
Judd, Naomi	Ashland, KY	1/11/46
Judd, Wynonna	Ashland, KY	5/30/64
Kaczmarek, Jane	Milwaukee, WI	12/21/55
Kanaly, Steve	Burbank, CA	3/14/46
Kane, Carol	Cleveland, OH	6/18/52
Kaplan, Gabe	Brooklyn, NY	3/31/45
Karlen, John	Brooklyn, NY	5/28/33
Karn, Richard	Seattle, WA	2/17/56
Karras, Alex	Gary, IN	7/15/35
Kasem, Casey	Detroit, MI	4/27/32
Kattan, Chris	Sherman Oaks, CA	10/19/70
Kavner, Julie	Burbank, CA	9/7/51
Kazan, Lainie	New York, NY	5/15/42
Keach, Stacy	Savannah, GA	6/2/41
Keaton, Diane	Santa Ana, CA	1/5/46
Keaton, Michael	Pittsburgh, PA	9/9/51
Keener, Catherine	Miami FL	3/23/59
Keitel, Harvey	Brooklyn, NY	5/13/39
Keith, David	Knoxville, TN	5/8/54
Keith, Penelope	Sutton, Surrey, England	4/2/40
Kellerman, Sally	Long Beach, CA	6/2/37
Kelly, Jean Louisa	Worcester, MA	3/9/72
Kelly, R(obert)	Chicago, IL	1/8/67
Kennedy, George	New York, NY	2/18/25
Kennedy, Jamie	Upper Darby, PA	5/25/70
Kennedy, Jayne	Washington, DC	10/27/51
Kenny G	Seattle, WA	6/5/56
Kent, Allegra	Santa Monica, CA	8/11/37
Kercheval, Ken	Wolcottville, IN	7/15/35
Kerns, Joanna	San Francisco, CA	2/12/53
Kerr, Deborah	Helensburgh, Scotland	9/30/21
Keys, Alicia	New York, NY	1/25/81
Khan, Chaka	Great Lakes, IL	3/23/53
Kidder, Margot	Yellowknife, N.W.T.	10/17/48
Kidman, Nicole	Honolulu, HI	6/20/67
Kiel, Richard	Detroit, MI	9/13/39
Kilborn, Craig	Kansas City, KS	8/24/62
Kilmer, Val	Los Angeles, CA	12/31/59
Kimmel, Jimmy	Brooklyn, NY	11/13/67
King, B. B.	Itta Bena, MS	9/16/25
King, Carole	Brooklyn, NY	2/9/42
King, Larry	Brooklyn, NY	11/19/33
King, Perry	Alliance, OH	4/30/48
Kingsley, Ben	Scarborough, England	12/31/43
Kingston, Alex	London, England	3/11/63
Kinnear, Greg	Logansport, IN	6/17/63
Kinney, Kathy	Stevens Point, WI	11/3/53
Kinski, Nastassja	Berlin, W. Germany	1/24/60

Name	Birthplace	Birthdate
Kirkland, Gelsey	Bethlehem, PA	12/29/52
Kirkpatrick, Chris	Clarion, PA	10/17/71
Kirshner, Mia	Toronto, Canada	1/25/75
Kitt, Eartha	North, SC	1/17/27
Klein, Robert	Bronx, New York, NY	2/8/42
Kline, Kevin	St. Louis, MO	10/24/47
Klugman, Jack	Philadelphia, PA	4/27/22
Knight, Gladys	Atlanta, GA	5/28/44
Knight, Shirley	Goessel, KS	7/5/36
Knight, Wayne	New York, NY	8/7/55
Knightley, Keira	Teddington, England	3/26/85
Knopfler, Mark	Glasgow, Scotland	8/12/49
Knowles, Beyoncé	Houston, TX	9/4/81
Knoxville, Johnny	Knoxville, TN	3/11/71
Konitz, Lee	Chicago, IL	10/13/27
Kopell, Bernie	New York, NY	6/21/33
Korman, Harvey	Chicago, IL	2/15/27
Kotto, Yaphet	New York, NY	11/15/37
Krakowski, Jane	Parsippany, NJ	10/11/68
Krasinski, John	Newton, MA.	10/20/79
Krause, Peter	Alexandria, MN	8/12/65
Kressley, Carson	Allentown, PA	11/11/69
Kretschmann, Thomas	Dessau, E. Germany	9/8/62
Kristofferson, Kris	Brownsville, TX	6/22/36
Kudrow, Lisa	Encino, CA	7/30/63
Kunis, Mila	Kiev, Ukraine, Soviet Union	8/14/83
Kuriyama, Chiaki	Tsuchiura, Ibaraki, Japan	10/10/84
Kurtz, Swoosie	Omaha, NE	9/6/44
Kutcher, Ashton	Cedar Rapids, IA	2/7/78
Kwan, Nancy	Hong Kong	5/19/39
LaBelle, Patti	Philadelphia, PA	5/24/44
LaBeouf, Shia	Los Angeles, CA	6/11/86
Ladd, Cheryl	Huron, SD	7/12/51
Ladd, Diane	Meridian, MS	11/29/32
Lagasse, Emeril	Fall River, MA	10/15/59
Lahti, Christine	Royal Oak, MI	4/4/50
Laine, Cleo	Southall, England	10/28/27
Laine, Frankie	Chicago, IL	3/30/13
Lake, Ricki	Hastings-on-Hudson, NY	9/21/68
Lamas, Lorenzo	Santa Monica, CA	1/20/58
Lambert, Christopher	Great Neck, NY	3/29/57
Landau, Martin	Brooklyn, NY	6/20/28
Landis, John	Chicago, IL	8/3/50
Lane, Diane	New York, NY	1/22/65
Lane, Nathan	Jersey City, NJ	2/3/56
lang, k.d.	Consort, Alberta	11/2/61
Lang, Stephen	Queens, New York, NY	7/11/52
Lange, Jessica	Cloquet, MN	4/20/49
Langella, Frank	Bayonne, NJ	1/1/40
Lansbury, Angela	London, England	10/16/25
LaPaglia, Anthony	Adelaide, Australia	1/31/59
Larroquette, John	New Orleans, LA	11/25/47
LaSalle, Eriq	Hartford, CT	6/23/62
Lauper, Cyndi	Brooklyn, NY	6/20/53
Laurie, Hugh	Oxford, England	6/11/59
Laurie, Piper	Detroit, MI	1/22/32
Lavigne, Avril	Napanee, Ontario	9/27/84
Lavin, Linda	Portland, ME	10/15/37
Law, Jude	London, England	12/29/72
Lawless, Lucy	Mount Albert, New Zealand	3/29/68
Lawrence, Carol	Melrose Park, IL	9/5/34
Lawrence, Joey	Montgomery, PA	4/20/76
Lawrence, Martin	Frankfurt, Germany	4/16/65
Lawrence, Steve	Brooklyn, NY	7/8/35
Lawrence, Vicki	Inglewood, CA.	3/26/49
Leach, Robin	London, England	8/29/41
Leachman, Cloris	Des Moines, IA	4/30/26
Lear, Norman	New Haven, CT.	7/27/22
Learned, Michael	Washington, DC	4/9/39
Leary, Denis	Worcester, MA	8/18/57
LeBlanc, Matt	Newton, MA.	7/25/67
LeBon, Simon	Bushey, England	10/27/58
Ledger, Heath	Perth, Australia	4/4/79
Lee, Ang	Pingtung, Taiwan	10/23/54
Lee, Brenda	Lithonia, GA	12/11/44
Lee, Christopher	London, England	5/27/22
Lee, Jason	Huntington Beach, CA.	4/25/70
Lee, Michele	Los Angeles, CA	6/24/42
Lee, Spike	Atlanta, GA	3/20/57
Leeves, Jane	London, England	4/18/61
Legrand, Michel	Paris, France	2/24/32
Leguizamo, John	Bogotá, Colombia	7/22/64
Leibman, Ron	New York, NY	10/11/37
Leigh, Jennifer Jason	Hollywood, CA.	2/5/62
Leighton, Laura	Iowa City, IA	7/24/68
Lennox, Annie	Aberdeen, Scotland	12/25/54
Leno, Jay	New Rochelle, NY	4/28/50
Leonard, Robert Sean	Westwood, NJ	2/28/69
Leoni, Tea	New York, NY	2/25/66
Leslie, Joan	Detroit, MI	1/26/25
Leto, Jared	Bossier City, LA.	12/26/71
Letterman, David	Indianapolis, IN	4/12/47
Levine, James	Cincinnati, OH.	6/23/43

Name	Birthplace	Birthdate
Levine, Ted	Parma, OH	5/29/58
Levinson, Barry	Baltimore, MD	4/6/42
Levy, Eugene	Hamilton, Ontario	12/17/46
Lewis, Huey	New York, NY	7/5/50
Lewis, Jason	Newport Beach, CA	6/25/71
Lewis, Jerry	Newark, NJ	3/16/26
Lewis, Jerry Lee	Ferriday, LA	9/29/35
Lewis, Juliette	San Fernando Valley, CA	6/21/73
Lewis, Richard	Brooklyn, NY	6/29/47
Li, Jet	Beijing, China	4/26/63
Light, Judith	Trenton, NJ	2/9/49
Lightfoot, Gordon	Orillia, Ontario	11/17/38
Lil' Kim	Brooklyn, NY	7/11/75
Linden, Hal	Bronx, New York, NY	3/20/31
Ling, Lisa	Sacramento, CA	8/30/73
Linkletter, Art	Moose Jaw, Sask., Can	7/17/12
Linn-Baker, Mark	St. Louis, MO	6/17/54
Linney, Laura	New York, NY	2/5/64
Liotta, Ray	Newark, NJ	12/18/55
Lithgow, John	Rochester, NY	10/19/45
Little, Rich	Ottawa, Ontario	11/26/38
Little Richard	Macon, GA	12/5/32
Littrell, Brian	Lexington, KY	2/20/75
Liu, Lucy	Queens, NY	12/2/68
L. L. Cool J.	St. Albans, Queens, NY	1/14/68
Lloyd, Christopher	Stamford, CT	10/22/38
Lloyd, Emily	North London, England	9/29/70
Lloyd Webber, Andrew	London, England	3/22/48
Locke, Sondra	Shelbyville, TN	5/28/47
Lockhart, June	New York, NY	6/25/25
Locklear, Heather	Westwood, CA	9/25/61
Loggia, Robert	Staten Island, NY	1/3/30
Loggins, Kenny	Everett, WA	1/7/48
Logue, Donal	Ottawa, Canada	2/27/66
Lohan, Lindsay	New York, NY	7/2/86
Lollobrigida, Gina	Subiaco, Italy	7/4/27
Lom, Herbert	Prague, Czechoslovakia	1/9/17
Lonergan, Kenneth	New York, NY	10/16/62
Long, Nia	Brooklyn, NY	10/30/70
Long, Shelley	Ft. Wayne, IN	8/23/49
Longoria, Eva	Corpus Christi, TX	3/15/75
Lopez, George	Mission Hills, CA	4/23/61
Lopez, Jennifer	Bronx, NY	7/24/70
Loren, Sophia	Rome, Italy	9/20/34
Loring, Gloria	New York, NY	12/10/46
Louis-Dreyfus, Julia	New York, NY	1/13/61
Love, Courtney	San Francisco, CA	7/9/64
Love, Mike	Baldwin Hills, CA	3/15/41
Lovett, Lyle	Klein, TX	11/1/57
Lovitz, Jon	Tarzana, CA	7/21/57
Loveless, Patty	Pikeville, KY	1/4/57
Lowe, Rob	Charlottesville, VA	3/17/64
Lowell, Carey	Huntington, NY	2/11/61
Lucas, George	Modesto, CA	5/14/44
Lucci, Susan	Scarsdale, NY	12/23/46
Luckinbill, Laurence	Ft. Smith, AR	11/21/34
Ludwig, Christa	Berlin, Germany	3/16/24
Luhrmann, Baz	Sydney, Australia	9/17/62
Lumet, Sidney	Philadelphia, PA	6/25/24
LuPone, Patti	Northport, NY	4/21/49
Lynch, David	Missoula, MT	1/20/46
Lynch, Susan	Corrinshego, N. Ireland,UK	6/5/71
Lynley, Carol	New York, NY	2/13/42
Lynn, Loretta	Butcher Hollow, KY	4/14/35
Lynn, Vera	London, England	3/20/17
Lynne, Shelby	Quantico, VA	10/22/68
Lyonne, Natasha	Great Neck, NY	4/4/79
Ma, Yo-Yo	Paris, France	10/7/55
Maazel, Lorin	Neuilly-sur-Seine, France	3/6/30
Mac, Bernie	Chicago, IL	10/5/58
MacArthur, James	Los Angeles, CA	12/8/37
Macchio, Ralph	Huntington, NY	11/4/62
MacCorkindale, Simon	Ely, England	2/12/52
MacDonald, Kelly	Glasgow, Scotland	2/23/76
MacDowell, Andie	Gaffney, SC	4/21/58
MacFarlane, Seth	Kent, CT	11/26/73
MacGraw, Ali	Pound Ridge, NY	4/1/38
MacGowan, Shane	Tunbridge, Kent, England	12/25/57
MacLachlan, Kyle	Yakima, WA	2/22/59
MacLaine, Shirley	Richmond, VA	4/24/34
MacLeod, Gavin	Mt. Kisco, NY	2/28/31
MacNee, Patrick	London, England	2/6/22
MacNeil, Cornell	Minneapolis, MN	9/24/22
MacNicol, Peter	Dallas, TX	4/10/54
MacPherson, Elle	Sydney, Australia	3/29/64
Macy, Bill	Revere, MA	5/18/22
Macy, William H.	Miami, FL	3/13/50
Madden, John	Austin, MN	4/10/36
Madigan, Amy	Chicago, IL	9/11/50
Madonna (Ciccone)	Bay City, MI	8/16/58
Madsen, Michael	Chicago, IL	9/25/58
Maguire, Tobey	Santa Monica, CA	6/27/75
Maher, Bill	New York, NY	1/20/56

Name	Birthplace	Birthdate
Mahoney, John	Manchester, England	6/20/40
Majors, Lee	Wyandotte, MI	4/23/39
Malden, Karl	Gary, IN	3/22/12
Malick, Terrence	Ottawa, IL	11/30/43
Malick, Wendie	Buffalo, NY	12/13/50
Malina, Joshua	New York, NY	1/17/66
Malkovich, John	Christopher, IL	12/9/53
Malone, Dorothy	Chicago, IL	1/30/25
Mamet, David	Chicago, IL	11/30/47
Manchester, Melissa	Bronx, NY	2/15/51
Mandel, Howie	Toronto, Ontario	11/29/55
Mandrell, Barbara	Houston, TX	12/25/48
Mangione, Chuck	Rochester, NY	11/29/40
Manheim, Camryn	Caldwell, NJ	3/8/61
Manilow, Barry	Brooklyn, NY	6/17/46
Mann, Aimee	Richmond, VA	8/9/60
Manoff, Dinah	New York, NY	1/25/58
Manson, Marilyn	Canton, OH	1/5/69
Mantegna, Joe	Chicago, IL	11/13/47
Marceau, Marcel	Strasbourg, France	3/22/23
Marcil, Vanessa	Indio, CA	10/15/69
Margulies, Julianna	Spring Valley, NY	6/8/66
Marie, Constance	Hollywood, CA	9/9/69
Marin, Cheech	Los Angeles, CA	7/13/46
Marinaro, Ed	New York, NY	3/31/50
Markova, Alicia	London, England	12/1/10
Marriner, Neville	Lincoln, England	4/15/24
Marsalis, Branford	New Orleans, LA	8/26/60
Marsalis, Wynton	New Orleans, LA	10/18/61
Marsh, Jean	London, England	7/1/34
Marshall, Garry	Bronx, New York, NY	11/13/34
Marshall, Penny	Bronx, New York, NY	10/15/42
Marshall, Peter	Huntington, WV	3/30/27
Martin, Chris	Devon, England	3/22/77
Martin, Dick	Detroit, MI	1/30/22
Martin, Jesse L.	Rocky Mount, VA	1/18/69
Martin, Kellie	Riverside, CA	10/16/75
Martin, Ricky	San Juan, Puerto Rico	12/24/71
Martin, Steve	Waco, TX	8/14/45
Martin, Tony	Oakland, CA	12/25/13
Martins, Peter	Copenhagen, Denmark	10/27/46
Mason, Jackie	Sheboygan, WI	6/9/34
Mason, Marsha	St. Louis, MO	4/3/42
Masterson, Christopher	Long Island, NY	1/22/80
Masterson, Mary Stuart	New York, NY	6/28/66
Mastrantonio, Mary Elizabeth	Lombard, IL	11/17/58
Masur, Kurt	Brieg, Germany	7/18/27
Masur, Richard	New York, NY	11/20/48
Mathers, Jerry	Sioux City, IA	6/2/48
Matheson, Tim	Glendale, CA	12/31/47
Mathis, Johnny	Gilmer, TX	9/30/35
Matlin, Marlee	Morton Grove, IL	8/24/65
Matthews, Dave	Johannesburg, S. Africa	1/9/67
May, Elaine	Philadelphia, PA	4/21/32
Mayer, John	Bridgeport, CT	10/16/77
Mazar, Debi	Queens, NY	8/15/64
Mazursky, Paul	Brooklyn, NY	4/25/30
MCA	Brooklyn, NY	11/20/65
McAdams, Rachel	London, Ontario, Canada	10/7/86
McArdle, Andrea	Abington, PA	11/5/63
McBride, Patricia	Teaneck, NJ	8/23/42
McCallum, David	Glasgow, Scotland	9/19/33
McCarthy, Andrew	Westfield, NJ	11/29/62
McCarthy, Jenny	Chicago, IL	11/1/72
McCarthy, Kevin	Seattle, WA	2/15/14
McCartney, Paul	Liverpool, England	6/18/42
McCarver, Tim	Memphis, TN	10/16/41
McClanahan, Rue	Healdton, OK	2/21/34
McConaughey, Matthew	Uvalde, Texas	11/4/69
McCoo, Marilyn	Jersey City, NJ	9/30/43
McCormack, Eric	Toronto, Canada	4/18/63
McCormack, Mary	Plainsfield, NJ	2/8/69
McCrane, Paul	Philadelphia, PA	1/19/61
McDaniel, James	Washington, DC	3/25/58
McDermott, Dylan	Waterbury, CT	10/26/61
McDiarmid, Ian	Carnoustie, Tayside, Scotland	4/17/47
McDonald, Audra	Berlin, Germany	7/3/70
McDonnell, Mary	Wilkes-Barre, PA	4/28/52
McDormand, Frances	Illinois	6/23/57
McDowell, Malcolm	Leeds, England	6/13/43
McEntire, Reba	McAlester, OK	3/28/55
McFerrin, Bobby	New York, NY	3/11/50
McGillis, Kelly	Newport Beach, CA	7/9/57
McGoohan, Patrick	Astoria, Queens, NY	3/19/28
McGovern, Elizabeth	Evanston, IL	7/18/61
McGovern, Maureen	Youngstown, OH	7/27/49
McGraw, Tim	Delhi, LA	5/1/67
McGregor, Ewan	Crieff, Scotland	3/31/71
McGuire, Al	New York, NY	9/7/31
McKean, Michael	New York, NY	10/17/47
McKechnie, Donna	Pontiac, MI	11/16/42

Name	Birthplace	Birthdate
McKellen, Ian	Burnley, England	5/25/39
McKenzie, Benjamin	Austin, TX	9/12/78
McLachlan, Sarah	Halifax, Nova Scotia	1/28/68
McLean, A.J.	West Palm Beach, FL	1/9/78
McMahon, Ed.	Detroit, MI	3/6/23
McNichol, Kristy	Los Angeles, CA	9/11/62
McPartland, Marian	Stough, England	3/20/20
McRaney, Gerald	Collins, MS	8/19/47
McShane, Ian	Blackburn, England	9/29/42
Meadows, Jayne	Wu Chang, China	9/27/20
Meara, Anne	Brooklyn, NY	9/20/29
Meat Loaf	Dallas, TX	9/27/51
Mehta, Zubin	Bombay, India	4/29/36
Mellencamp, John	Seymour, IN	10/7/51
Meloni, Christopher	Washington, DC	4/2/61
Mendes, Sam	Redding, England	8/1/65
Mendes, Sergio	Niteroi, Brazil	2/11/41
Mercer, Marian	Akron, OH	11/26/35
Merchant, Natalie	Jamestown, NY	10/26/63
Merkerson, S. Epatha	Saginaw, MI	11/28/52
Merrill, Dina	New York, NY	12/9/25
Messing, Debra	Brooklyn, NY	8/15/68
Metcalf, Laurie	Carbondale, IL	6/16/55
Michael, George	London, England	6/25/63
Michaels, Al	Brooklyn, NY	11/12/44
Michaels, Lorne	Toronto, Canada	11/17/44
Midler, Bette	Honolulu, HI	12/1/45
Midori	Osaka, Japan	10/25/71
Mike D	Brooklyn, NY	11/20/65
Milano, Alyssa	Brooklyn, NY	12/19/72
Miles, Sarah	Ingatestone, England	12/31/41
Miles, Vera	near Boise City, OK	8/23/29
Miller, Dennis	Pittsburgh, PA	11/3/53
Miller, Mitch	Rochester, NY	7/4/11
Miller, Penelope Ann	Santa Monica, CA	1/13/64
Mills, Donna	Chicago, IL	12/11/43
Mills, Hayley	London, England	4/18/46
Milner, Martin	Detroit, MI	12/28/27
Milnes, Sherrill	Downers Grove, IL	1/10/35
Milsap, Ronnie	Robinsville, NC	1/16/44
Mimieux, Yvette	Hollywood, CA	1/8/42
Minghella, Anthony	Isle of Wight, England	1/6/54
Ming-Na	Macao	11/20/63
Minnelli, Liza	Los Angeles, CA	3/12/46
Minogue, Kylie	Melbourne, Australia	5/28/68
Mirren, Helen	London, England	7/26/45
Mitchell, Brian	Seattle, WA	10/31/58
Mitchell, Elizabeth	Los Angeles, CA	3/27/70
Mitchell, Joni	Fort McLeod, Alberta	11/7/43
Moby	Harlem, New York, NY	9/11/65
Modine, Matthew	Loma Linda, CA	3/22/59
Moffat, Donald	Plymouth, England	12/26/30
Molina, Alfred	London, England	5/24/53
Molinaro, Al	Kenosha, WI	6/24/19
Moll, Richard	Pasadena, CA	1/13/43
Moloney, Janel	Woodland Hills, CA	10/3/69
Monica (Arnold)	College Park, GA	10/24/80
Mo'Nique	Woodlawn, MD	12/11/67
Montalban, Ricardo	Mexico City, Mexico	11/25/20
Moody, Ron	London, England	1/8/24
Moore, Demi	Roswell, NM	11/11/62
Moore, Julianne	Fort Bragg, NC	12/3/60
Moore, Mandy	Nashua, NH	4/10/84
Moore, Mary Tyler	Brooklyn, NY	12/29/36
Moore, Melba	New York, NY	10/29/45
Moore, Michael	Flint, MI	4/23/54
Moore, Roger	London, England	10/14/27
Moore, Terry	Los Angeles, CA	1/7/29
Morales, Esai	Brooklyn, NY	10/1/62
Moranis, Rick	Toronto, Ontario	4/18/54
Moreau, Jeanne	Paris, France	1/23/28
Moreno, Rita	Humacao, PR	12/11/31
Morgan, Harry	Detroit, MI	4/10/15
Moriarty, Michael	Detroit, MI	4/5/41
Morissette, Alanis	Ottawa, Ontario	6/1/74
Morris, Garrett	New Orleans, LA	2/1/37
Morrison, Van	Belfast, N. Ireland	8/31/45
Morrissey	Manchester, England	5/22/59
Morrow, Rob	New Rochelle, NY	9/21/62
Morse, David	Beverly, MA	10/11/53
Morse, Robert	Newton, MA	5/18/31
Mortensen, Viggo	New York, NY	10/20/58
Mortimer, Emily	London, England	12/1/71
Morton, Joe	Brooklyn, NY	10/18/47
Morton, Samantha	Nottingham, Enlgand	5/13/77
Moses, William	Los Angeles, CA	11/17/59
Moss, Carrie-Anne	Vancouver, B.C., Can.	8/21/67
Moss, Kate	Croydon, Surrey, England	1/16/74
Mueller-Stahl, Armin	Tilsit, E. Prussia	12/17/30
Muldaur, Diana	Brooklyn, NY	8/19/38
Mulgrew, Kate	Dubuque, IA	4/29/55
Mull, Martin	Chicago, IL	8/18/43
Mullally, Megan	Los Angeles, CA	11/12/58
Mullan, Peter	Peterhead, Scotland	1960
Mulroney, Dermot	Alexandria, VA	10/31/63
Muniz, Frankie	Ridgewood, NJ	12/5/85
Munsel, Patrice	Spokane, WA	5/14/25
Murphy, Ben	Jonesboro, AR	3/6/42
Murphy, Brittany	Atlanta, GA	11/10/77
Murphy, Donna	Queens, NY	3/7/58
Murphy, Eddie	Brooklyn, NY	4/3/61
Murphy, Michael	Los Angeles, CA	5/5/38
Murray, Anne	Springhill, Nova Scotia	6/20/45
Murray, Bill	Wilmette, IL	9/21/50
Murray, Don	Hollywood, CA	7/31/29
Musburger, Brent	Portland, OR	5/26/39
Muti, Riccardo	Naples, Italy	7/28/41
Myers, Mike	Scarborough, Ontario	5/25/63
Nabors, Jim	Sylacauga, AL	6/12/30
Nagra, Parminder	Leicester, England	10/5/75
Nash, Graham	Blackpool, England	2/2/42
Naughton, James	Middletown, CT	12/6/45
Navarro, Dave	Santa Monica, CA	6/7/67
Neal, Patricia	Packard, KY	1/20/26
Nealon, Kevin	Bridgeport, CT	11/18/53
Neeson, Liam	Ballymena, N. Ireland	6/7/52
Neill, Sam	Ulster, N. Ireland	9/14/47
Nelligan, Kate	London, Ontario	3/16/51
Nelly	Austin, TX	11/2/74
Nelson, Craig T.	Spokane, WA	4/4/46
Nelson, Ed	New Orleans, LA	12/21/28
Nelson, Judd	Portland, ME	11/28/59
Nelson, Tracy	Santa Monica, CA	10/25/63
Nelson, Willie	Abbott, TX	4/30/33
Nero, Peter	Brooklyn, NY	5/22/34
Nesmith, Mike	Houston, TX	12/30/42
Nettleton, Lois	Oak Park, IL	8/16/29
Neuwirth, Bebe	Newark, NJ	12/31/58
Neville, Aaron	New Orleans, LA	1/24/41
Newhart, Bob	Oak Park, IL	9/5/29
Newman, Paul	Cleveland, OH	1/26/25
Newman, Randy	New Orleans, LA	11/28/43
Newton, Wayne	Norfolk, VA	4/3/42
Newton-John, Olivia	Cambridge, England	9/26/48
Nicholas, Denise	Detroit, MI	7/12/44
Nichols, Mike	Berlin, Germany	11/6/31
Nicholson, Jack	Neptune, NJ	4/22/37
Nicks, Stevie	Phoenix, AZ	5/26/48
Nielsen, Connie	Copenhagen, Denmark	7/3/65
Nielsen, Leslie	Regina, Sask.	2/11/26
Nighy, Bill	Caterham, Surrey, Eng.	12/12/49
Nimoy, Leonard	Boston, MA	3/26/31
Nixon, Cynthia	New York, NY	4/9/66
Nolte, Nick	Omaha, NE	2/8/41
Noone, Peter	Manchester, England	11/5/47
Norman, Jessye	Augusta, GA	9/15/45
Norris, Chuck	Ryan, OK	3/10/40
Northam, Jeremy	Cambridge, Enlgand	12/1/61
Norton, Edward	Columbia, MD	8/18/69
Noth, Christopher	Madison, WI	11/13/54
Novak, Kim	Chicago, IL	2/13/33
Nuyen, France	Marseilles, France	7/31/39
Oates, John	New York, NY	4/7/49
Obradors, Jacqueline	San Fernando Valley, CA	10/6/66
O'Brian, Hugh	Rochester, NY	4/19/25
O'Brien, Conan	Brookline, MA	4/18/63
O'Brien, Margaret	Los Angeles, CA	1/15/37
Ocean, Billy	Fyzabad, Trinidad	1/21/50
O'Connor, Frances	Oxford, England	6/12/69
O'Connor, Sinead	Glenageary, Ireland	12/8/66
Odetta	Birmingham, AL	12/31/30
O'Donnell, Chris	Winnetka, IL	6/26/70
O'Donnell, Rosie	Commack, NY	3/21/62
O'Grady, Gail	Detroit, MI	1/23/63
Oh, Sandra	Nepean, Ontario	7/20/71
O'Hara, Catherine	Toronto, Canada	3/4/54
O'Hara, Maureen	Dublin, Ireland	8/17/20
Oldman, Gary	South London, England	3/21/58
Olin, Ken	Chicago, IL	7/30/54
Olin, Lena	Stockholm, Sweden	3/22/55
Olmos, Edward James	E. Los Angeles, CA	2/24/47
Olsen, Ashley	Sherman Oaks, CA	6/13/86
Olsen, Mary-Kate	Sherman Oaks, CA	6/13/86
Olsen, Merlin	Logan, UT	9/15/40
Olson, Nancy	Milwaukee, WI.	7/14/28
O'Malley, Mike	Boston, MA	10/31/69
O'Neal, Ryan	Los Angeles, CA	4/20/41
O'Neal, Tatum	Los Angeles, CA	11/5/63
O'Neill, Ed	Youngstown, OH	4/12/46
Ontkean, Michael	Vancouver, B.C.	1/24/46
Orlando, Tony	New York, NY	4/3/44
Ormond, Julia	Epsom, England	1/4/65
Osbourne, Jack	London, England	11/8/85
Osbourne, Kelly	London, England	10/27/84
Osbourne, Ozzy	Birmingham, England	12/3/48
Osbourne, Sharon	London, England	10/10/52

Name	Birthplace	Birthdate
O'Shea, Milo	Dublin, Ireland	6/2/26
Oslin, K.T.	Crossett, AR	5/15/42
Osment, Haley Joel	Los Angeles, CA	4/10/88
Osmond, Donny	Ogden, UT	12/9/57
Osmond, Marie	Ogden, UT	10/13/59
O'Toole, Annette	Houston, TX	4/1/53
O'Toole, Peter	Connemara, Ireland	8/2/32
Otto, Miranda	Brisbane, Australia	12/16/67
Oz, Frank	Herford, England	5/25/44
Ozawa, Seiji	Shenyang, China	9/1/35
Pacino, Al	East Harlem, NY	4/25/40
Packer, Billy	Wellsville, NY	2/25/40
Page, Bettie	Nashville, TN	4/22/23
Page, Jimmy	Heston, England	1/9/44
Page, Patti	Claremore, OK	11/8/27
Paget, Debra	Denver, CO	8/19/33
Paige, Janis	Tacoma, WA	9/16/22
Palance, Jack	Lattimer, PA	2/18/20
Palin, Michael	Sheffield, England	5/5/43
Palmer, Betsy	East Chicago, IN	11/1/29
Palmer, Geoffrey	London, England	6/4/27
Palminteri, Chazz	Bronx, NY	5/15/51
Paltrow, Gwyneth	Los Angeles, CA	9/28/72
Pantoliano, Joe	Hoboken, NJ	9/12/51
Papas, Irene	Chiliomodion, Greece	9/3/26
Paquin, Anna	Wellington, New Zealand	7/24/82
Parker, Alan	London, England	2/14/44
Parker, Eleanor	Cedarville, OH	6/26/22
Parker, Fess	Ft. Worth, TX	8/16/25
Parker, Jameson	Baltimore, MD	11/18/47
Parker, Jean	Dear Lodge, MT	8/11/15
Parker, Mary-Louise	Fort Jackson, SC	8/2/64
Parker, Sarah Jessica	Nelsonville, OH	3/25/65
Parsons, Estelle	Marblehead, MA	11/20/27
Parton, Dolly	Sevierville, TN	1/19/46
Patinkin, Mandy	Chicago, IL	11/30/52
Patric, Jason	Queens, NY	6/17/66
Patton, Will	Charleston, SC	6/14/54
Paul, Adrian	London, England	5/29/59
Paul, Les	Waukesha, WI	1/9/15
Paulson, Sarah	Tampa, FL	12/17/75
Pavarotti, Luciano	Modena, Italy	10/12/35
Paxton, Bill	Fort Worth, TX	5/17/55
Pearce, Guy	Ely, England	10/5/67
Peet, Amanda	New York, NY	1/11/72
Pendergrass, Teddy	Philadelphia, PA	3/26/50
Penn, Arthur	Philadelphia, PA	9/27/22
Penn, Sean	Burbank, CA	8/17/60
Perez, Rosie	Brooklyn, NY	9/6/64
Perkins, Elizabeth	Queens, NY	11/18/60
Perlman, Itzhak	Tel Aviv, Israel	8/31/45
Perlman, Rhea	Brooklyn, NY	3/31/48
Perlman, Ron	New York, NY	4/13/50
Perrine, Valerie	Galveston, TX	9/3/43
Perry, Luke	Fredericktown, OH	10/11/66
Perry, Mathew	Williamstown, MA	8/19/69
Persoff, Nehemiah	Jerusalem, Israel	8/2/20
Pesci, Joe	Newark, NJ	2/9/43
Peters, Bernadette	Queens, NY	2/28/48
Peters, Roberta	Bronx, NY	5/4/30
Petersen, Wolfgang	Emden, Germany	3/14/41
Peterson, Oscar	Montreal, Quebec	8/15/25
Petty, Lori	Chattanooga, TN	3/23/63
Petty, Tom	Gainesville, FL	10/20/50
Pfeiffer, Michelle	Santa Ana, CA	4/29/58
Philbin, Regis	New York, NY	8/25/31
Phair, Liz	New Haven, CT	4/17/67
Phillippe, Ryan	New Castle, DE	9/10/74
Phillips, Lou Diamond	Subic Bay, Philippines	2/17/62
Phillips, Mackenzie	Alexandria, VA	11/10/59
Phillips, Michelle	Long Beach, CA	6/4/44
Phillips, Sian	Bettws, Wales, UK	5/14/34
Phoenix, Joaquin	San Juan, Puerto Rico	10/28/74
Pierce, David Hyde	Albany, NY	4/3/59
Pinchot, Bronson	New York, NY	5/20/59
Pink (Alecia Moore)	Doylestown, PA	9/8/79
Pinkett Smith, Jada	Baltimore, MD	9/18/71
Pirner, David	Green Bay, WI	4/16/64
Piscopo, Joe	Passaic, NJ	6/17/51
Pitt, Brad	Shawnee, OK	12/18/63
Piven, Jeremy	New York, NY	7/26/65
Plant, Robert	W. Bromwich, England	8/20/48
Pleshette, Suzanne	New York, NY	1/31/37
Plowright, Joan	Brigg, England	10/28/29
Plummer, Amanda	New York, NY	3/23/57
Plummer, Christopher	Toronto, Ontario	12/13/27
Poitier, Sidney	Miami, FL	2/20/27
Polanski, Roman	Paris, France	8/18/33
Pollack, Sydney	Lafayette, IN	7/1/34
Pompeo, Ellen	Everett, MA	11/10/69
Ponti, Carlo	Milan, Italy	12/11/12
Pop, Iggy	Muskegon, MI	4/21/47
Portman, Natalie	Jerusalem, Israel	6/9/81
Posey, Parker	Baltimore, MD	11/8/68
Post, Markie	Palo Alto, CA	11/4/50
Poston, Tom	Columbus, OH	10/17/21
Potente, Franka	Dulmen, Germany	7/22/74
Potts, Annie	Nashville, TN	10/28/52
Povich, Maury	Bethesda, MD	1/17/39
Powell, Jane	Portland, OR	4/1/28
Powers, Stefanie	Hollywood, CA	11/2/42
Prentiss, Paula	San Antonio, TX	3/4/39
Prepon, Laura	Watchung, NJ	3/7/80
Presley, Priscilla	Brooklyn, NY	5/24/45
Previn, Andre	Berlin, Germany	4/6/29
Price, Leontyne	Laurel, MS	2/10/27
Price, Molly	North Plainfield, NJ	12/15/66
Price, Ray	Perryville, TX	1/12/26
Pride, Charley	Sledge, MS	3/18/38
Priestley, Jason	Vancouver, Brit. Columbia	8/28/69
Prince (The Artist)	Minneapolis, MN	6/7/58
Prince, Faith	Augusta, GA	8/5/57
Principal, Victoria	Fukuoka, Japan	1/3/50
Prinze, Freddie, Jr.	Albuquerque, NM	3/8/76
Probst, Jeff	Wichita, KS	11/1/61
Proctor, Emily	Raleigh, NC	10/18/68
Prosky, Robert	Philadelphia, PA	12/13/30
Provine, Dorothy	Deadwood, SD	1/20/37
Pryce, Jonathan	Holywell, N. Wales	6/1/47
Puck, Wolfgang	St. Veit, Austria	1/8/49
Pulliam, Keshia Knight	Newark, NJ	4/9/79
Pullman, Bill	Hornell, NY	12/17/53
Purcell, Sarah	Richmond, IN	10/8/48
Quaid, Dennis	Houston, TX	4/9/54
Quaid, Randy	Houston, TX	10/1/50
Queen Latifah	Newark, NJ	3/18/70
Quinn, Aidan	Chicago, IL	3/8/59
Quinn, Colin	Brooklyn, NY	8/15/59
Quinn, Martha	Albany, NY	5/11/59
Rachins, Alan	Cambridge, MA	10/3/42
Radcliffe, Daniel	London, England	7/23/89
Rae, Charlotte	Milwaukee, WI	4/22/26
Raffi	Cairo, Egypt	7/8/48
Rainer, Luise	Vienna, Austria	1/12/10
Raitt, Bonnie	Burbank, CA	11/8/49
Ramey, Samuel	Colby, KS	3/28/42
Ramirez, Efren	Los Angeles, CA	10/2/83
Ramone, Tommy	Budapest, Hungary	1/29/52
Randolph, Joyce	Detroit, MI	10/21/25
Raphael, Sally Jessy	Easton, PA	2/25/35
Rashad, Phylicia	Houston, TX	6/19/48
Ratzenberger, John	Bridgeport, CT.	4/6/47
Raver, Kim	New York, NY	3/15/69
Reddy, Helen	Melbourne, Australia	10/25/41
Redford, Robert	Santa Monica, CA	8/18/37
Redgrave, Lynn	London, England	3/8/43
Redgrave, Vanessa	London, England	1/30/37
Reed, Jerry	Atlanta, GA	3/20/37
Reed, Lou	Brooklyn, NY	3/2/42
Reed, Rex	Ft. Worth, TX	10/2/38
Reese, Della	Detroit, MI	7/6/31
Reeves, Keanu	Beirut, Lebanon	9/2/64
Reeves, Martha	Eufaula, AL	7/18/41
Regalbuto, Joe	Brooklyn, NY	8/24/49
Reid, Tara	Wyckoff, NJ	11/8/75
Reid, Tim	Norfolk, VA	12/19/44
Reid, Vernon	London, England	8/22/58
Reilly, Charles Nelson	New York, NY	1/13/31
Reilly, John C.	Chicago, IL	5/24/65
Reiner, Carl	Bronx, NY	3/20/22
Reiner, Rob	Bronx, NY	3/6/47
Reinhold, Judge	Wilmington, DE	5/21/57
Reinking, Ann	Seattle, WA	11/10/49
Reiser, Paul	New York, NY	3/30/57
Reitman, Ivan	Komarno, Czechoslovakia	10/26/46
Remini, Leah	Brooklyn, NY	6/15/70
Resnik, Regina	New York, NY	8/30/22
Reynolds, Burt	Waycross, GA	2/11/36
Reynolds, Debbie	El Paso, TX	4/1/32
Reznor, Trent	Mercer, PA	5/17/65
Rhames, Ving	Harlem, New York, NY	5/12/59
Rhymes, Busta	Brooklyn, NY	5/20/72
Ribisi, Giovanni	Los Angeles, CA	12/17/74
Ricci, Christina	Santa Monica, CA	2/12/80
Richards, Denise	Downers Grove, IL	2/17/71
Richards, Keith	Dartford, Kent, England	12/18/43
Richards, Michael	Culver City, CA	7/24/49
Richardson, Ian	Edinburgh, Scotland	4/7/34
Richardson, Kevin	Lexington, KY	10/3/71
Richardson, Miranda	Lancashire, England	3/3/58
Richardson, Natasha	London, England	5/11/63
Richardson, Patricia	Bethesda, MD	2/23/51
Richie, Lionel	Tuskegee, AL	6/20/49
Richter, Andy	Grand Rapids, MI	8/28/66
Rickles, Don	Queens, NY	5/8/26
Rickman, Alan	Hammersmith, England	2/21/46

Name	Birthplace	Birthdate
Riegert, Peter.	New York, NY	4/11/47
Rigg, Diana	Doncaster, England	7/20/38
Rimes, LeAnn	Flowood, MS	8/28/82
Ringwald, Molly	Roseville, CA	2/18/68
Ripa, Kelly	Stratford, NJ	10/2/70
Rivera, Chita	Washington, DC	1/23/33
Rivera, Geraldo	New York, NY	7/4/43
Rivers, Joan.	Brooklyn, NY	6/8/33
Roach, Max	New Land, NC	1/10/25
Robbins, Tim	W. Covina, CA	10/16/58
Roberts, Doris	St. Louis, MO	11/4/29
Roberts, Eric	Biloxi, MS	4/18/56
Roberts, Julia.	Smyrna, GA	10/28/67
Roberts, Pernell	Waycross, GA	5/18/28
Roberts, Tony	New York, NY	10/22/39
Robertson, Cliff	La Jolla, CA.	9/9/25
Robertson, Dale.	Harrah, OK	7/14/23
Robinson, Smokey.	Detroit, MI	2/19/40
Rochon, Lela	Torrance, CA.	4/17/64
Rock, Chris	South Carolina	2/7/66
Rock, The	Hayward, CA.	5/2/72
Rodgers, Jimmy	Camas, WA.	9/18/33
Rodriguez, Jai	Brentwood, NY	6/22/77
Rodriguez, Johnny.	Sabinal, TX	12/10/51
Rogan, Joe	Newark, NJ	8/11/67
Rogers, Kenny	Houston, TX	8/21/38
Rogers, Mimi	Coral Gables, FL	1/27/56
Rogers, Wayne	Birmingham, AL	4/7/33
Rohm, Elisabeth	Dusseldorf, Germany	4/28/73
Rollins, Henry	Washington, DC	2/13/61
Rollins, Sonny	Harlem, NY	9/7/30
Romano, Ray.	Queens, NY	12/21/57
Romijn, Rebecca	Berkeley, CA.	11/6/72
Ronstadt, Linda	Tucson, AZ	7/15/46
Rooney, Mickey	Brooklyn, NY	9/23/20
Root, Stephen	Sarasota, FL	11/17/51
Rose, Axl	Lafayette, IN	2/6/62
Rose Marie	New York, NY	8/15/23
Roseanne	Salt Lake City, UT	11/3/52
Ross, Charlotte	Winnetka, IL	1/21/68
Ross, Diana.	Detroit, MI	3/26/44
Ross, Katharine	Hollywood, CA	1/29/40
Rossdale, Gavin	London, England.	10/30/67
Ross, Marion	Albert Lea, MN	10/25/28
Rossellini, Isabella.	Rome, Italy	6/18/52
Rossum, Emmy	New York, NY	9/12/86
Rostropovich, Mstislav.	Baku, Azerbaijan	3/27/27
Roth, David Lee.	Bloomington, IN	10/10/55
Roth, Tim	London, England.	5/14/61
Rotten, Johnny.	London, England.	1/31/56
Rourke, Mickey	Schenectady, NY	9/16/56
Routh, Brandon	Des Moines, IA	10/9/79
Routledge, Patricia	Birkenhead, England.	2/17/29
Rowan, Kelly	Ottawa, Canada.	1967
Rowlands, Gena	Cambria, WI	6/19/36
Rubinstein, John	Beverly Hills, CA	12/8/46
Rudner, Rita.	Miami, FL	9/17/56
Ruehl, Mercedes	Queens, NY	2/28/48
Ruffalo, Mark	Kenosha, WI	11/22/67
Rupp, Debra Jo	Glendale, CA.	2/24/51
Rush, Barbara	Denver, CO.	1/4/27
Rush, Geoffrey.	Toowoomba, Australia	7/6/51
Russell, Jane	Bemidji, MN.	6/21/21
Russell, Ken.	Southampton, England	7/3/27
Russell, Keri.	Fountain Valley, CA	3/23/76
Russell, Kurt	Springfield, MA	3/17/51
Russell, Leon.	Lawton, OK.	4/2/41
Russell, Mark.	Buffalo, NY	8/23/32
Russell, Theresa	San Diego, CA	3/20/57
Russo, Rene	Burbank, CA.	2/17/54
Rutherford, Ann	Toronto, Ontario	11/2/20
Ruttan, Susan	Oregon City, OR	9/16/50
Ryan, Meg.	Fairfield, CT	11/19/61
Ryan, Roz	Detroit, MI	7/7/51
Rydell, Bobby.	Philadelphia, PA	4/26/42
Ryder, Winona.	Winona, MN.	10/29/71
Sabato, Antonio, Jr.	Rome, Italy	2/29/72
Sade	Ibadan, Nigeria	1/16/59
Sagal, Katey	Hollywood, CA	1/19/53
Saget, Bob.	Philadelphia, PA	5/17/56
Sagnier, Ludivine	La Celle-St.-Cloud, France	7/3/79
Sahl, Mort	Montreal, Quebec	5/11/27
Saint, Eva Marie	Newark, NJ	7/4/24
St. James, Susan.	Hollywood, CA	8/14/46
St. John, Jill	Los Angeles, CA	8/19/40
St. Patrick, Mathew	Philadelphia, PA	3/17/69
Sajak, Pat	Chicago, IL	10/26/46
Saks, Gene	New York, NY	11/8/21
Sales, Soupy	Franklinton, NC	1/8/26
Salonga, Lea	Manila, Philippines	2/22/71
Samms, Emma	London, England	8/28/60
Sandler, Adam	Brooklyn, NY	9/9/66
Sands, Julian	West Yorkshire, England	1/15/58

Name	Birthplace	Birthdate
San Giacomo, Laura	West Orange, NJ.	11/14/61
Santana, Carlos	Autlan, Mexico.	7/20/47
Sara, Mia	Brooklyn, NY.	6/19/67
Sarandon, Susan	New York, NY	10/4/46
Sarnoff, Dorothy.	New York, NY	5/25/17
Sartain, Gailard	Tulsa, OK	9/18/46
Savage, Ben	Highland Park, IL.	9/13/80
Savage, Fred	Highland Park, IL.	7/9/76
Sawa, Devon	Vancouver, B.C., Can.	9/7/78
Saxon, John.	Brooklyn, NY	8/5/35
Sayles, John	Schenectady, NY	9/28/50
Scacchi, Greta	Milan, Italy	2/18/60
Scaggs, Boz.	Canton, OH.	6/8/44
Scales, Prunella.	Sutton Abinger, England	6/22/32
Scalia, Jack	Brooklyn, NY	11/10/51
Schallert, William	Los Angeles, CA	7/6/22
Scheider, Roy	Orange, NJ	11/10/35
Schell, Maximilian	Vienna, Austria	12/8/30
Schenkel, Chris	Bippus, IN	8/21/23
Schiff, Richard	Bethesda, MD.	5/27/55
Schiffer, Claudia.	Rheinbach, Germany	8/25/70
Schneider, John.	Mt. Kisco, NY	4/8/54
Schneider, Rob	San Francisco, CA	10/31/63
Schram, Bitty	New York, NY	7/17/68
Schreiber, Liev.	San Francisco, CA	10/4/67
Schroder, Rick	Staten Island, NY	4/13/70
Schwarzenegger, Arnold	Thal, Austria	7/30/47
Schwimmer, David.	Astoria, Queens, NY	11/2/66
Sciorra, Annabella	New York, NY	3/24/64
Scofield, Paul	Hurstpierpoint, England.	1/21/22
Scolari, Peter	New Rochelle, NY	9/12/54
Scorsese, Martin	Flushing, Queens, NY.	11/17/42
Scott, Lizabeth	Scranton, PA.	9/29/22
Scott, Ridley.	South Shields, England.	11/30/37
Scott, Seann William	Cottage Grove, MN	10/3/76
Scott-Heron, Gil	Chicago, IL	4/1/49
Scott Thomas, Kristin.	Redruth, England	5/24/60
Scotto, Renata	Savona, Italy	2/24/35
Scram, Bitty	New York, NY	7/17/68
Scully, Vin	Bronx, NY	11/29/27
Seacrest, Ryan	Atlanta, GA	12/24/74
Seagal, Steven.	Lansing, MI	4/10/51
Secor, Kyle.	Tacoma, WA	5/31/58
Sedaka, Neil.	Brooklyn, NY	3/13/39
Seeger, Pete	New York, NY	5/3/19
Segal, George	Great Neck, NY	2/13/34
Seidelman, Susan	Abington, PA	12/11/52
Seinfeld, Jerry	Brooklyn, NY	4/29/54
Sellecca, Connie	Bronx, NY	5/25/55
Selleck, Tom	Detroit, MI	1/29/45
Severinsen, Doc.	Arlington, OR.	7/7/27
Sevigny, Chloë	Springfield, MA	11/18/74
Sewell, Rufus	London, England.	10/29/67
Seymour, Jane.	Hillingdon, England	2/15/51
Shackelford, Ted	Oklahoma City, OK	6/23/46
Shaffer, Paul	Thunder Bay, Ontario	11/28/49
Shakira	Barranquilla, Colombia	2/2/77
Shalhoub, Tony	Green Bay, WI.	10/9/53
Shandling, Garry	Chicago, IL	11/29/49
Shankar, Ravi	Benares, India.	4/7/20
Shannon, Molly	Shaker Heights, OH	9/16/64
Sharif, Omar.	Alexandria, Egypt	4/10/32
Shatner, William	Montreal, Quebec.	3/22/31
Shaughnessy, Charles.	London, England.	2/9/55
Shaver, Helen	St. Thomas, Ontario	2/24/51
Shea, John.	N. Conway, NH	4/14/49
Shearer, Harry	Los Angeles, CA	12/23/43
Shearing, George.	London, England	8/13/19
Sheedy, Ally	New York, NY	6/13/62
Sheen, Charlie.	Los Angeles, CA	9/3/65
Sheen, Martin.	Dayton, OH.	8/3/40
Sheindlin, Judge Judy	Brooklyn, NY.	10/21/42
Shelley, Carole.	London, England.	8/16/39
Shepard, Sam	Ft. Sheridan, IL	11/5/43
Shepherd, Cybill.	Memphis, TN.	2/18/50
Sheridan, Nicollette	Worthing, England.	11/21/63
Shields, Brooke	New York, NY	5/31/65
Shire, Talia.	Lake Success, NY.	4/25/46
Short, Martin	Hamilton, Ontario	3/26/50
Shortz, Will.	Crawfordsville, IN	8/26/52
Show, Grant	Detroit, MI	2/27/62
Shue, Andrew	Washington, DE	2/20/67
Shue, Elisabeth	Wilmington, DE	10/6/63
Shyamalan, M. Night.	Pondicherry, India	8/6/70
Siepi, Cesare	Milan, Italy.	2/14/23
Sigler, Jamie-Lynn	Jericho, NY	5/15/81
Sikking, James B.	Los Angeles, CA	3/5/34
Sills, Beverly	Brooklyn, NY	5/25/29
Silver, Ron	New York, NY	7/2/46
Silverman, Jonathan	Beverly Hills, CA	8/5/66
Silverman, Sarah	Bedford, NH	12/70
Silverstone, Alicia.	Hillsborough, CA	10/4/76
Simmons, Gene	Haifa, Israel	8/25/49

Name	Birthplace	Birthdate
Simmons, Henry	Stamford, CT	7/1/70
Simmons, Jean	London, England	1/31/29
Simmons, Richard	New Orleans, LA	7/12/48
Simon, Carly	Riverdale, NY	6/25/45
Simon, Paul	Newark, NJ	10/13/41
Simpson, Ashlee	Waco, TX	10/3/84
Simpson, Jessica	Abilene, TX	7/10/80
Sinatra, Nancy	Jersey City, NJ	6/8/40
Sinbad	Benton Harbor, MI	11/10/56
Singleton, John	Los Angeles, CA	1/6/68
Sinise, Gary	Blue Island, IL	3/17/55
Sirico, Tony	Brooklyn, NY	7/29/42
Sisto, Jeremy	Grass Valley, CA	10/6/74
Sizemore, Tom	Detroit, MI	9/29/64
Skerritt, Tom	Detroit, MI	8/25/33
Skye, Ione	Hertfordshire, England	9/4/70
Slater, Christian	New York, NY	8/18/69
Slater, Helen	Massapequa, NY	12/15/63
Slezak, Erika	Hollywood, CA	8/5/46
Slick, Grace	Evanston, IL	10/30/39
Smirnoff, Yakov	Odessa, Ukraine	1/24/51
Smith, Allison	Bronx, NY	12/9/69
Smith, Jaclyn	Houston, TX	10/26/47
Smith, Keely	Norfolk, VA	3/9/32
Smith, Kevin	Red Bank, NJ	8/2/70
Smith, Maggie	Ilford, England	12/28/34
Smith, Patti	Chicago, IL	12/30/46
Smith, Robert	Blackpool, England	4/21/59
Smith, Will	West Philadelphia, PA	9/25/68
Smits, Jimmy	New York, NY	7/9/55
Smothers, Dick	Governor's Island, NY	11/20/38
Smothers, Tom	Governor's Island, NY	2/2/37
Snipes, Wesley	Orlando, FL	7/31/62
Snyder, Tom	Milwaukee, WI	5/12/36
Soderbergh, Steven	Atlanta, GA	1/14/63
Somers, Suzanne	San Bruno, CA	10/16/46
Sommer, Elke	Berlin, Germany	11/5/40
Sorbo, Kevin	Mound, MN	9/24/58
Sorvino, Mira	Tenafly, NJ	9/28/67
Sorvino, Paul	Brooklyn, NY	4/13/39
Soul, David	Chicago, IL	8/28/43
Spacek, Sissy	Quitman, TX	12/25/49
Spacey, Kevin	S. Orange, NJ	7/26/59
Spade, David	Birmingham, MI	7/22/64
Spader, James	Boston, MA	2/7/60
Spano, Joe	San Francisco, CA	7/7/46
Spears, Britney	Kentwood, LA	12/2/81
Spector, Phil	Bronx, NY	12/26/40
Spelling, Tori	Los Angeles, CA	5/16/73
Spielberg, Steven	Cincinnati, OH	12/18/46
Spiner, Brent	Houston, TX	2/2/49
Springer, Jerry	London, England	2/13/44
Springfield, Rick	Sydney, Australia	8/23/49
Springsteen, Bruce	Freehold, NJ	9/23/49
Spurlock, Morgan	Parksburg, WV	11/7/70
Stafford, Jo	Coalinga, CA	11/12/17
Stahl, Nick	Harlingen, TX	12/5/79
Stallone, Sylvester	New York, NY	7/6/46
Stamos, John	Cypress, CA	8/19/63
Stamp, Terence	Stepney, England	7/22/39
Stang, Arnold	Chelsea, MA	9/28/25
Stanton, Harry Dean	West Irvine, KY	7/14/26
Stapleton, Jean	New York, NY	1/19/23
Starr, Ringo	Liverpool, England	7/7/40
Steenburgen, Mary	Newport, AR	2/8/53
Stefani, Gwen	Anaheim, CA	10/3/69
Stein, Ben	Washington, DC	11/25/44
Stephens, James	Mt. Kisco, NY	5/18/51
Stern, Daniel	Bethesda, MD	8/28/57
Stern, Howard	Roosevelt, NY	1/12/54
Sternhagen, Frances	Washington, DC	1/13/30
Stevens, Andrew	Memphis, TN	6/10/55
Stevens, Cat	London, England	7/21/48
Stevens, Connie	Brooklyn, NY	8/8/38
Stevens, Rise	Bronx, NY	6/11/13
Stevens, Stella	Hot Coffee, MS	10/1/36
Stevenson, Parker	Philadelphia, PA	6/4/52
Stewart, French	Albuquerque, NM	2/20/64
Stewart, Jon	Trenton, NY	11/28/62
Stewart, Patrick	Mirfield, England	7/13/40
Stewart, Rod	London, England	1/10/45
Stiers, David Ogden	Peoria, IL	10/31/42
Stiles, Julia	New York, NY	3/28/81
Stiller, Ben	New York, NY	11/30/65
Stiller, Jerry	Brooklyn, NY	6/8/27
Stills, Stephen	Dallas, TX	1/3/45
Sting	Newcastle, England	10/2/51
Stipe, Michael	Decatur, GA	1/4/60
Stockwell, Dean	North Hollywood, CA	3/5/36
Stoltz, Eric	Whittier, CA	9/30/61
Stone, Dee Wallace	Kansas City, KS	12/14/48
Stone, Oliver	New York, NY	9/15/46
Stone, Sharon	Meadville, PA	3/10/58
Stookey, Paul	Baltimore, MD	12/30/37
Storch, Larry	New York, NY	1/8/23
Storm, Gale	Bloomington, TX	4/5/22
Stowe, Madeleine	Eagle Rock, CA	8/18/58
Strait, George	Pearsall, TX	5/18/52
Strasser, Robin	New York, NY	5/7/45
Stratas, Teresa	Toronto, Ontario	5/26/38
Strathairn, David	San Francisco, CA	1/26/49
Strauss, Peter	Croton-on-Hudson, NY	2/20/47
Streep, Meryl	Summit, NJ	6/22/49
Streisand, Barbra	Brooklyn, NY	4/24/42
Stringfield, Sherry	Colorado Springs, CO	6/24/67
Stritch, Elaine	Detroit, MI	2/2/26
Stroman, Susan	Wilmington, DE	10/17/54
Struthers, Sally	Portland, OR	7/28/48
Stuart, Gloria	Santa Monica, CA	7/4/10
Stuarti, Enzo	Rome, Italy	3/3/25
Studdard, Ruben	Birmingham, AL	9/12/78
Suchet, David	London, England	5/2/46
Sullivan, Erik Per	Worcester, MA	7/12/91
Sullivan, Susan	New York, NY	11/18/42
Sumac, Yma	Ichocan, Peru	9/10/27
Summer, Donna	Dorchester, MA	12/31/48
Sutherland, Donald	St. John, New Brunswick	7/17/34
Sutherland, Joan	Sydney, Australia	11/7/26
Sutherland, Kiefer	London, England	12/21/66
Suvari, Mena	Newport, RI	2/9/79
Swank, Hilary	Bellingham, WA	7/30/74
Swayze, Patrick	Houston, TX	8/18/52
Swinton, Tilda	London, England	11/5/60
Swit, Loretta	Passaic, NJ	11/4/37
Sykes, Wanda	Portsmouth, VA	3/7/64
Szmanda, Eric	Milwaukee, WI	7/24/75
T, Mr.	Chicago, IL	5/21/52
Takei, George	Los Angeles, CA	4/20/37
Tallchief, Maria	Fairfax, OK	1/24/25
Tamblyn, Amber	Santa Monica, CA	5/14/83
Tamblyn, Russ	Los Angeles, CA	12/30/34
Tarantino, Quentin	Knoxville, TN	3/27/63
Tautou, Audrey	Beaumont, France	8/9/78
Taylor, Billy	Greenville, NC	7/21/21
Taylor, Buck	Hollywood, CA	5/13/38
Taylor, Elizabeth	London, England	2/27/32
Taylor, James	Boston, MA	3/12/48
Taylor, Rip	Washington, DC	1/13/34
Taylor, Rod	Sydney, Australia	1/11/30
Taymor, Julie	Newton, MA	12/15/52
Te Kanawa, Kiri	Gisborne, New Zealand	3/6/44
Teller	Philadelphia, PA	2/14/48
Temple Black, Shirley	Santa Monica, CA	4/23/28
Tennant, Victoria	London, England	9/30/50
Tennille, Toni	Montgomery, AL	5/8/43
Tesh, John	Garden City, NY	7/9/52
Tharp, Twyla	Portland, IN	7/1/41
Thaxter, Phyllis	Portland, ME	11/20/21
Theron, Charlize	South Africa	8/7/75
Thicke, Alan	Kirkland Lake, Ontario	3/1/47
Thiessen, Tiffani	Long Beach, CA	1/23/74
Thomas, Jay	Kermit, TX	7/12/48
Thomas, Jonathan Taylor	Bethlehem, PA	9/8/81
Thomas, Marlo	Deerfield, MI	11/21/38
Thomas, Michael Tilson	Hollywood, CA	12/21/44
Thomas, Philip Michael	Columbus, OH	5/26/49
Thomas, Richard	New York, NY	6/13/51
Thomas, Sean Patrick	Wilmington, DE	12/17/70
Thompson, Emma	London, England	4/15/59
Thompson, Jack	Sydney, Australia	8/31/40
Thompson, Lea	Rochester, MN	5/31/61
Thompson, Sada	Des Moines, IA	9/27/29
Thorne-Smith, Courtney	San Francisco, CA	11/8/67
Thornton, Billy Bob	Hot Springs, AR	8/4/55
Thurman, Uma	Boston, MA	4/29/70
Tiegs, Cheryl	Breckenridge, MN	9/25/47
Tierney, Maura	Boston, MA	2/3/65
Tillis, Mel	Tampa, FL	8/8/32
Tilly, Jennifer	Harbor City, CA	9/16/58
Tilly, Meg	Long Beach, CA	2/14/60
Timberlake, Justin	Memphis, TN	1/31/81
Todd, Richard	Dublin, Ireland	6/11/19
Tomei, Marisa	Brooklyn, NY	12/4/64
Tomlin, Lily	Detroit, MI	9/1/39
Tork, Peter	Washington, DC	2/13/42
Torn, Rip	Temple, TX	2/6/31
Townsend, Robert	Chicago, IL	2/6/57
Townshend, Peter	Chiswick, England	5/19/45
Travanti, Daniel J.	Kenosha, WI	3/7/40
Travers, Mary	Louisville, KY	11/7/37
Travis, Nancy	Astoria, Queens, NY	9/21/61
Travis, Randy	Marshville, NC	5/4/59
Travolta, John	Englewood, NJ	2/18/54
Trebek, Alex	Sudbury, Ontario	7/22/40
Tripplehorn, Jean	Tulsa, OK	6/10/63
Tritt, Travis	Marietta, GA	2/9/63

Name	Birthplace	Birthdate
Tucci, Stanley	Katonah, NY	1/11/60
Tucker, Chris	Decatur, GA	8/31/72
Tucker, Michael	Baltimore, MD	2/6/44
Tucker, Tanya	Seminole, TX	10/10/58
Tune, Tommy	Wichita Falls, TX	2/28/39
Turlington, Christy	Walnut Creek, CA	1/2/69
Turner, Ike	Clarksdale, MS	11/5/31
Turner, Janine	Lincoln, NE	12/6/62
Turner, Kathleen	Springfield, MO	6/19/54
Turner, Tina	Brownsville, TN	11/26/39
Turturro, John	Brooklyn, NY	2/28/57
Twain, Shania	Windsor, Ontario	8/28/65
Twiggy (Lawson)	London, England	9/19/49
Tyler, Liv	New York, NY	7/1/77
Tyler, Steven	Yonkers, NY	3/26/48
Tyson, Cicely	Harlem, NY	12/19/33
Uecker, Bob	Milwaukee, WI	1/26/35
Uggams, Leslie	New York, NY	5/25/43
Ullman, Tracey	Slough, England	12/30/59
Ullmann, Liv	Tokyo, Japan	12/16/39
Ulrich, Skeet	New York, NY	1/20/69
Underwood, Carrie	Checotah, OK	3/10/83
Underwood, Blair	Tacoma, WA	8/25/64
Usher (Raymond IV)	Chattanooga,TN	10/14/78
Vaccaro, Brenda	Brooklyn, NY	11/18/39
Vale, Jerry	Bronx, NY	7/8/32
Valente, Caterina	Paris, France	1/14/31
Valley, Mark	Ogdensburg, NY	12/24/64
Valli, Frankie	Newark, NJ	5/3/37
Van Ark, Joan	New York, NY	6/16/43
Vance, Courtney B.	Birmingham, MI	3/12/60
Van Damme, Jean-Claude	Brussels, Belgium	10/18/60
Van Der Beek, James	Chesire, CT	3/8/77
Van Doren, Mamie	Rowena, SD	2/6/31
Van Dyke, Dick	West Plains, MO	12/13/25
Van Dyke, Jerry	Danville, IL	7/27/31
Van Halen, Eddie	Nijmegen, Netherlands	1/26/55
Van Patten, Dick	Queens, NY	12/9/28
Van Peebles, Mario	Mexico City, Mexico	1/15/57
Van Sant, Gus	Louisville, KY	7/24/52
Van Zandt, Steven	Boston, MA	11/22/50
Vardalos, Nia	Winnipeg, Manit, Can	9/24/62
Vaughn, Robert	New York, NY	11/22/32
Vaughn, Vince	Minneapolis, MN	3/28/70
Vedder, Eddie	Evanston, IL	12/23/64
Vega, Alexa	Miami, FL	8/27/88
Vereen, Ben	Miami, FL	10/10/46
Verrett, Shirley	New Orleans, LA	5/31/31
Vickers, Jon	Prince Albert, Sask.	10/29/26
Vieira, Meredith	Providence, RI	12/30/53
Vigoda, Abe	New York, NY	2/24/21
Vincent, Jan-Michael	Denver, CO	7/15/44
Vinton, Bobby	Canonsburg, PA	4/16/35
Visnjic, Goran	Sibenik, Yugo. (Croatia)	9/9/72
Vitale, Dick	East Rutherford, NJ	6/9/39
Voight, Jon	Yonkers, NY	12/29/38
Von Stade, Frederica	Somerville, NJ	6/1/45
Von Sydow, Max	Lund, Sweden	4/10/29
Von Trier, Lars	Copenhagen, Denmark	4/30/56
Wagner, Jack	Washington, MO	10/3/59
Wagner, Lindsay	Los Angeles, CA	6/22/49
Wagner, Robert	Detroit, MI	2/10/30
Wahl, Ken	Chicago, IL	2/14/56
Wahlberg, Mark	Dorchester, MA	6/5/71
Wain, Bea	Bronx, NY	4/30/17
Waite, Ralph	White Plains, NY	6/22/28
Waits, Tom	Pomona, CA	12/7/49
Walden, Robert	New York, NY	9/25/43
Walken, Christopher	Astoria, Queens, NY	3/31/43
Wallace, Marcia	Creston, IA	11/1/42
Wallach, Eli	Brooklyn, NY	12/7/15
Walter, Jessica	Brooklyn, NY	1/31/40
Ward, Fred	San Diego, CA	12/30/42
Ward, Sela	Meridian, MS	7/11/56
Ward, Simon	Kent, London, England	10/19/41
Warfield, Marsha	Chicago, IL	3/5/54
Warner, Malcolm-Jamal	Jersey City, NJ	8/18/70
Warren, Lesley Ann	New York, NY	8/16/46
Warwick, Dionne	East Orange, NJ	12/12/40
Washington, Denzel	Mt. Vernon, NY	12/28/54
Washington, Isaiah	Houston, TX	8/3/63
Watanabe, Ken	Koide, Niigata, Japan	10/21/59
Waters, John	Baltimore, MD	4/22/46
Waters, Roger	Great Bookham, England	9/6/44
Waterston, Sam	Cambridge, MA	11/15/40
Watson, Emily	London, England	1/14/67
Watson, Emma	Oxford, England	4/15/90
Watts, Andre	Nuremberg, Germany	6/20/46
Watts, Naomi	Shoreham, England	9/28/68
Wayans, Damon	New York, NY	9/4/60
Wayans, Keenen Ivory	Brooklyn, NY	6/8/58
Wayans, Marlon	New York, NY	723/72
Wayans, Shawn	New York, NY	1/19/71
Weathers, Carl	New Orleans, LA	1/14/48
Weaver, Fritz	Pittsburgh, PA	1/19/26
Weaver, Sigourney	New York, NY	10/8/49
Weiland, Scott	Santa Cruz, CA	10/27/67
Weir, Peter	Sydney, Australia	8/8/44
Weisz, Rachel	London, England	3/7/71
Weitz, Bruce	Norwalk, CT	5/27/43
Welch, Raquel	Chicago, IL	9/5/40
Weld, Tuesday	New York, NY	8/27/43
Weller, Peter	Stevens Point, WI	6/24/47
Wells, Kitty	Nashville, TN	8/30/19
Wendt, George	Chicago, IL	10/17/48
West, Adam	Walla Walla, WA	9/19/28
West, Kayne	Atlanta, GA	6/8/77
West, Shane	Baton Rouge, LA	6/10/78
Wettig, Patricia	Cincinnati, OH	12/4/51
Whalley, Joanne	Manchester, England	8/25/64
Wheaton, Wil	Burbank, CA	7/29/72
Whitaker, Forest	Longview, TX	7/15/61
White, Betty	Oak Park, IL	1/17/22
White, Jack	Detroit, MI	7/9/75
White, Jaleel	Pasadena, CA	11/27/76
White, Vanna	N. Myrtle Beach, SC	2/18/57
Whitford, Bradley	Madison, WI	10/10/59
Whiting, Margaret	Detroit, MI	7/22/24
Whitman, Stuart	San Francisco, CA	2/1/26
Whitmore, James	White Plains, NY	10/1/21
Widmark, Richard	Sunrise, MN	12/26/14
Wiest, Dianne	Kansas City, MO	3/28/48
Wilder, Gene	Milwaukee, WI	6/11/33
Wilkinson, Tom	Leeds, England	12/12/48
Williams, Andy	Wall Lake, IA	12/3/27
Williams, Armstong	Marion, SC	2/5/59
Williams, Barry	Santa Monica, CA	9/30/54
Williams, Billy Dee	Harlem, NY	4/6/37
Williams, Cindy	Van Nuys, CA	8/22/47
Williams, Esther	Los Angeles, CA	8/8/23
Williams, Hal	Columbus, OH	12/14/38
Williams, Hank, Jr.	Shreveport, LA	5/26/49
Williams, JoBeth	Houston, TX	12/6/48
Williams, Kimberly	Rye, NY	9/14/71
Williams, Lucinda	Lake Charles, LA	1/26/53
Williams, Michelle	Kalispell, MT	9/9/80
Williams, Montel	Baltimore, MD	7/3/56
Williams, Paul	Omaha, NE	9/19/40
Williams, Robin	Chicago, IL	7/21/51
Williams, Treat	Rowayton, CT	12/1/51
Williams, Vanessa	Tarrytown, NY	3/18/63
Williamson, Kevin	New Bern, NC	3/14/65
Williamson, Nicol	Hamilton, Scotland	9/14/38
Willis, Bruce	Idar-Oberstein, W. Germ.	3/19/55
Wilson, Brian	Hawthorne, CA	6/20/42
Wilson, Cassandra	Jackson, MS	12/4/55
Wilson, Demond	Valdosta, GA	10/13/46
Wilson, Elizabeth	Grand Rapids, MI	4/4/21
Wilson, Luke	Dallas, TX	9/21/71
Wilson, Nancy	Chillicothe, OH	2/20/37
Wilson, Owen	Dallas, TX	11/18/68
Wilson, Rainn	Seattle, WA	1/20/66
Windom, William	New York, NY	9/28/23
Winfrey, Oprah	Kosciusko, MS	1/29/54
Winger, Debra	Cleveland, OH	5/16/55
Winkler, Henry	New York, NY	10/30/45
Winningham, Mare	Phoenix, AZ	5/16/59
Winokur, Marissa Jaret	New York, NY	2/2/73
Winslet, Kate	Reading, England	10/5/75
Winter, Johnny	Beaumont,TX	2/23/44
Winters, Jonathan	Dayton, OH	11/11/25
Winwood, Steve	Birmingham, England	5/12/48
Wiseman, Joseph	Montreal, Quebec	5/15/18
Withers, Jane	Atlanta, GA	4/12/26
Witherspoon, Reese	Nashville, TN	3/22/76
Witt, Alicia	Worcester, MA	8/21/75
Wolf, Scott	Boston, MA	6/4/68
Wonder, Stevie	Saginaw, MI	5/13/50
Wong, Faye	Beijing, China	8/8/69
Woo, John	Guangzhou, China	5/1/46
Wood, Elijah	Cedar Rapids, IA	1/28/81
Woodard, Alfre	Tulsa, OK	11/8/53
Woods, James	Vernal, UT	4/18/47
Woodward, Edward	Croyden, England	6/1/30
Woodward, Joanne	Thomasville, GA	2/27/30
Wopat, Tom	Lodi, WI	9/9/51
Wright, Jeffrey	Washington, DC	12/7/65
Wright, Max	Detroit, MI	8/2/43
Wright, Steven	New York, NY	12/6/55
Wright Penn, Robin	Dallas, TX	4/8/66
Wyatt, Jane	Campgaw, NJ	8/12/11
Wyle, Noah	Hollywood, CA	6/4/71
Wyman, Bill	London, England	10/24/36
Wyman, Jane	St. Joseph, MO	1/4/14
Yankovic, Weird Al	Lynwood, CA	10/23/59
Yanni	Kalamata, Greece	11/14/54

Name	Birthplace	Birthdate	Name	Birthplace	Birthdate
Yarrow, Peter	New York, NY	5/31/38	Zellweger, Renee	Katy, TX	4/25/69
Yearwood, Trisha	Monticello, GA	9/19/64	Zemeckis, Robert	Chicago, IL	5/14/52
Yoakam, Dwight	Pikesville, KY	10/23/56	Zerbe, Anthony	Long Beach, CA	5/20/36
York, Michael	Fulmer, England	3/27/42	Zeta-Jones, Catherine	Swansea, Wales	9/25/69
York, Susannah	London, England	1/9/41	Zimbalist, Efrem, Jr.	New York, NY	11/30/18
Young, Alan	North Shields, England	11/19/19	Zimbalist, Stephanie	New York, NY	10/8/56
Young, Burt	New York, NY	4/30/40	Zimmer, Kim	Grand Rapids, MI	2/2/55
Young, Neil	Toronto, Ontario	11/12/45	Zhang, Ziyi	Beijing, China	2/9/79
Young, Sean	Louisville, KY	11/20/59	Zukerman, Pinchas	Tel Aviv, Israel	7/16/48
Zane, Billy	Chicago, IL	2/24/66	Zuniga, Daphne	San Francisco, CA	10/28/62
Zeffirelli, Franco	Florence, Italy	2/12/23			

Entertainment Personalities of the Past

See also other lists for some deceased entertainers not included here.

Name	Born	Died	Name	Born	Died	Name	Born	Died
Aaliyah	1979	2001	Barnum, Phineas T.	1810	1891	Booth, Junius Brutus	1796	1852
Abbott, Bud	1895	1974	Barrett, Syd	1946	2006	Booth, Shirley	1898	1992
Abbott, George	1887	1995	Barrymore, Ethel	1879	1959	Borge, Victor	1909	2000
Acuff, Roy	1903	1992	Barrymore, John	1882	1942	Bow, Clara	1905	1965
Adams, Don	1923	2005	Barrymore, Lionel	1878	1954	Bowes, Maj. Edward	1874	1946
Adams, Joey	1911	1999	Barrymore, Maurice	1848	1905	Bowman, Lee	1914	1979
Adams, Maude	1872	1953	Bartel, Paul	1938	2000	Brown, Les	1912	2001
Adams, Mason	1919	2005	Barthelmess, Richard	1897	1963	Boxcar Willie	1931	1999
Adler, Jacob P.	1855	1926	Bartholomew, Freddie	1924	1992	Boyd, Stephen	1928	1977
Adler, Luther	1903	1984	Bartok, Eva	1926	1998	Boyd, William	1898	1972
Adoree, Renee	1898	1933	Barty, Billy	1924	2000	Boyer, Charles	1899	1978
Agar, John	1921	2002	Basehart, Richard	1914	1984	Bracken, Eddie	1915	2002
Aherne, Brian	1902	1986	Basie, Count	1904	1984	Brady, Alice	1893	1939
Ailey, Alvin	1931	1989	Bates, Alan	1934	2003	Brand, Neville	1921	1992
Akins, Claude	1918	1994	Bates, Clayton (Peg Leg)	1907	1998	Brando, Marlon	1924	2004
Albert, Eddie	1908	2005	Bates, Florence	1888	1954	Branigan, Laura	1957	2004
Albertson, Frank	1909	1964	Bavier, Francis	1902	1989	Brazzi, Rossano	1916	1994
Albertson, Jack	1907	1981	Baxter, Anne	1923	1985	Brennan, Walter	1894	1974
Alda, Robert	1914	1986	Baxter, Warner	1889	1951	Brent, George	1904	1979
Alexander, Ben	1911	1969	Beatty, Clyde	1904	1965	Brett, Jeremy	1935	1995
Allen, Fred	1894	1956	Beaumont, Hugh	1909	1982	Brice, Fanny	1891	1951
Allen, Gracie	1906	1964	Beavers, Louise	1902	1962	Bridges, Lloyd	1913	1998
Allen, Mel	1913	1996	Beery, Noah, Sr.	1884	1946	Broderick, Helen	1891	1959
Allen, Peter	1944	1992	Beery, Noah, Jr.	1913	1994	Bronson, Charles	1921	2003
Allen, Steve	1921	2000	Beery, Wallace	1889	1949	Brooks, Foster	1912	2001
Allgood, Sara	1883	1950	Begley, Ed	1901	1970	Brown, Joe E.	1892	1973
Ameche, Don	1908	1993	Bel Geddes, Barbara	1922	2005	Brown, Les	1912	2001
Ames, Leon	1903	1993	Bellamy, Ralph	1904	1991	Bruce, Lenny	1925	1966
Amsterdam, Morey	1908	1996	Belushi, John	1949	1982	Bruce, Nigel	1895	1953
Anderson, Judith	1897	1992	Benaderet, Bea	1906	1968	Bruce, Virginia	1910	1982
Anderson, Marian	1902	1993	Bendix, William	1906	1964	Brynner, Yul	1915	1985
Andre the Giant	1946	1993	Bennett, Constance	1904	1965	Buchanan, Edgar	1903	1979
Andrews, Dana	1909	1992	Bennett, Joan	1910	1990	Buchholz, Horst	1933	2003
Andrews, Laverne	1913	1967	Bennett, Michael	1943	1987	Buñuel, Luis	1900	1983
Andrews, Maxine	1918	1995	Benny, Jack	1894	1974	Buono, Victor	1938	1982
Angeli, Pier	1933	1971	Benzell, Mimi	1924	1970	Burke, Billie	1885	1970
Anita Louise	1915	1970	Berg, Gertrude	1899	1966	Burnette, Smiley	1911	1967
Arbuckle, Fatty (Roscoe)	1887	1933	Bergen, Edgar	1903	1978	Burns, George	1896	1996
Arden, Eve	1908	1990	Bergman, Ingrid	1915	1982	Burr, Raymond	1917	1993
Arlen, Richard	1900	1976	Berkeley, Busby	1895	1976	Burton, Richard	1925	1984
Arliss, George	1868	1946	Berle, Milton	1908	2002	Busch, Mae	1897	1946
Armetta, Henry	1888	1945	Bernardi, Herschel	1923	1986	Bushman, Francis X.	1883	1966
Armstrong, Louis	1901	1971	Berman, Lazar	1930	2005	Butterworth, Charles	1896	1946
Arnaz, Desi	1917	1986	Bernhardt, Sarah	1844	1923	Buttons, Red	1919	2006
Arnold, Edward	1890	1956	Bernie, Ben	1893	1943	Byington, Spring	1893	1971
Arquette, Cliff	1905	1974	Berry, Jan	1941	2004	Cabot, Bruce	1904	1972
Arthur, Jean	1900	1991	Bessell, Ted	1939	1996	Cabot, Sebastian	1918	1977
Ashcroft, Peggy	1907	1991	Bickford, Charles	1889	1967	Cagney, James	1899	1986
Astaire, Fred	1899	1987	Big Bopper, The	1930	1959	Caldwell, Sarah	1924	2006
Astor, Mary	1906	1987	Bing, Rudolf	1902	1997	Calhern, Louis	1895	1956
Atkins, Chet	1924	2001	Bissell, Whit	1909	1996	Calhoun, Rory	1923	1999
Atwill, Lionel	1885	1946	Bixby, Bill	1934	1993	Callas, Maria	1923	1977
Auer, Mischa	1905	1967	Bjoerling, Jussi	1911	1960	Calloway, Cab	1907	1994
Aumont, Jean-Pierre	1911	2001	Blackmer, Sidney	1895	1973	Cambridge, Godfrey	1933	1976
Austin, Gene	1900	1972	Blackstone, Harry	1885	1965	Camp, Hamilton	1934	2005
Autry, Gene	1907	1998	Blake, Amanda	1931	1989	Campbell, Mrs. Patrick	1865	1940
Axton, Hoyt	1938	1999	Blaine, Vivian	1921	1995	Candy, John	1950	1994
Ayres, Lew	1908	1996	Blanc, Mel	1908	1989	Cantinflas	1911	1993
Backus, Jim	1913	1989	Blocker, Dan	1928	1972	Cantor, Eddie	1892	1964
Bailey, Pearl	1918	1990	Blondell, Joan	1909	1979	Capra, Frank	1897	1991
Bainter, Fay	1892	1968	Blore, Eric	1888	1959	Carey, Harry	1878	1947
Baker, Josephine	1906	1975	Blue, Ben	1901	1975	Carey, Macdonald	1913	1994
Baker, Stanley	1927	1976	Blyden, Larry	1925	1975	Carle, Frankie	1903	2001
Balanchine, George	1904	1983	Bogarde, Dirk	1920	1999	Carney, Art	1918	2003
Ball, Lucille	1911	1989	Bogart, Humphrey	1899	1957	Carpenter, Karen	1950	1983
Balsam, Martin	1919	1996	Boland, Mary	1880	1965	Carradine, John	1906	1988
Bancroft, Anne	1931	2005	Boles, John	1895	1969	Carrillo, Leo	1880	1961
Bancroft, George	1882	1956	Bolger, Ray	1904	1987	Carroll, Leo G.	1892	1972
Bankhead, Tallulah	1903	1968	Bond, Ward	1903	1960	Carroll, Madeleine	1906	1987
Banks, Leslie	1890	1952	Bondi, Beulah	1892	1981	Carroll, Nancy	1905	1965
Bara, Theda	1890	1955	Bono, Sonny	1935	1998	Carson, Jack	1910	1963
Barnes, Binnie	1903	1998	Boone, Richard	1917	1981	Carson, Jean	1923	2005
Barnett, Etta Moten	1902	2004	Booth, Edwin	1833	1893	Carson, Johnny	1925	2005

Name	Born	Died
Carter, Benny	1907	2003
Carter, Nell	1948	2003
Caruso, Enrico	1873	1921
Casadesus, Gaby	1901	1999
Casals, Pablo	1876	1973
Cash, Johnny	1932	2003
Cash, June Carter	1929	2003
Cass, Peggy	1924	1999
Cassidy, Jack	1927	1976
Cassavetes, John	1929	1989
Castle, Irene	1893	1969
Castle, Vernon	1887	1918
Caulfield, Joan	1922	1991
Chaliapin, Feodor	1873	1938
Champion, Gower	1919	1980
Chandler, Jeff	1918	1961
Chaney, Lon	1883	1930
Chaney, Lon, Jr.	1905	1973
Chapin, Harry	1942	1981
Chaplin, Charles	1889	1977
Chapman, Graham	1941	1989
Charles, Ray	1930	2004
Chase, Ilka	1905	1978
Chatterton, Ruth	1893	1961
Cherrill, Virginia	1908	1996
Chevalier, Maurice	1888	1972
Child, Julia	1912	2004
Clair, René	1898	1981
Clark, Bobby	1888	1960
Clark, Dane	1913	1998
Clark, Fred	1914	1968
Clayton, Jan	1917	1983
Clift, Montgomery	1920	1966
Cline, Patsy	1932	1963
Clooney, Rosemary	1928	2002
Clyde, Andy	1892	1967
Cobain, Kurt	1967	1994
Cobb, Lee J.	1911	1976
Coburn, Charles	1877	1961
Coburn, James	1928	2002
Coca, Imogene	1908	2001
Cochran, Steve	1917?	1965
Coco, James	1930	1987
Cody, Buffalo Bill	1846	1917
Cody, Iron Eyes	1907	1999
Cohan, George M.	1878	1942
Cohen, Myron	1902	1986
Colbert, Claudette	1903	1996
Cole, Nat "King"	1919	1965
Collins, Ray	1890	1965
Colman, Ronald	1891	1958
Columbo, Russ	1908	1934
Como, Perry	1912	2001
Conniff, Ray	1916	2002
Connors, Chuck	1921	1992
Conrad, William	1920	1994
Conried, Hans	1917	1982
Conte, Richard	1911	1975
Convy, Bert	1933	1991
Conway, Tom	1904	1967
Coogan, Jackie	1914	1984
Cook, Elisha, Jr.	1904	1995
Cooke, Alistair	1908	2004
Cooke, Sam	1935	1964
Cooper, Gary	1901	1961
Cooper, Gladys	1888	1971
Cooper, Melville	1896	1973
Corby, Ellen	1913	1999
Corelli, Franco	1923	2003
Corey, Jeff	1914	2002
Corio, Ann	1914	1999
Cornell, Katharine	1893	1974
Correll, Charles ("Andy")	1890	1972
Costello, Dolores	1905	1979
Costello, Lou	1906	1959
Cotten, Joseph	1905	1994
Coward, Noel	1899	1973
Cox, Wally	1924	1973
Crabbe, Buster	1908	1983
Crain, Jeanne	1925	2003
Crane, Bob	1928	1978
Crawford, Broderick	1911	1986
Crawford, Joan	1904	1977
Cregar, Laird	1914	1944
Crenna, Richard	1926	2003
Crews, Laura Hope	1880	1942
Crisp, Donald	1880	1974
Croce, Jim	1942	1973
Cronyn, Hume	1911	2003

Name	Born	Died
Crosby, Bing	1903	1977
Crothers, Scatman	1910	1986
Cruz, Celia	1925	2003
Cugat, Xavier	1900	1990
Cukor, George	1899	1983
Cullen, Bill	1920	1990
Cummings, Constance	1910	2005
Cummings, Robert	1908	1990
Currie, Finlay	1878	1968
Curtis, Keene	1923	2002
Curtis, Ken	1916	1991
Cushing, Peter	1913	1994
Dailey, Dan	1914	1978
Dandridge, Dorothy	1923	1965
Dangerfield, Rodney	1921	2004
Daniell, Henry	1894	1963
Daniels, Bebe	1901	1971
Darin, Bobby	1936	1973
Darnell, Linda	1921	1965
Darwell, Jane	1879	1967
Da Silva, Howard	1909	1986
Davenport, Harry	1866	1949
Davies, Marion	1897	1961
Davis, Bette	1908	1989
Davis, Joan	1907	1961
Davis, Sammy Jr.	1925	1990
Davis, Ossie	1917	2005
Day, Dennis	1917	1988
Dean, James	1931	1955
Dee, Frances	1907	2004
Dee, Sandra	1942	2005
Defore, Don	1917	1993
Dekker, Albert	1905	1968
Del Rio, Dolores	1908	1983
Demarest, William	1892	1983
DeMille, Agnes	1905	1993
DeMille, Cecil B.	1881	1959
Denison, Michael	1915	1998
Denning, Richard	1914	1998
Dennis, Sandy	1937	1992
Denny, Reginald	1891	1967
Denver, Bob	1935	2005
Denver, John	1943	1997
Derek, John	1926	1998
DeSica, Vittorio	1901	1974
Devine, Andy	1905	1977
Dewhurst, Colleen	1924	1991
De Wilde, Brandon	1942	1972
De Wolfe, Billy	1907	1974
Diamond, Selma	1920	1985
Dietrich, Marlene	1901	1992
Digges, Dudley	1879	1947
Disney, Walt	1901	1966
Dix, Richard	1894	1949
Dmytryk, Edward	1908	1999
Donahue, Troy	1936	2001
Donat, Robert	1905	1958
Donlevy, Brian	1901?	1972
Dors, Diana	1931	1984
Dorsey, Tommy	1905	1956
Douglas, Melvyn	1901	1981
Douglas, Paul	1907	1959
Dove, Billie	1900	1998
Downey, Morton, Jr.	1933	2001
Doyle, David	1929	1997
Drake, Alfred	1914	1992
Draper, Ruth	1889	1956
Dresser, Louise	1881	1965
Dressler, Marie	1869	1934
Drew, Ellen	1915	2003
Drew, Mrs. John	1820	1897
Dru, Joanne	1923	1996
Duchin, Eddy	1909	1951
Duff, Howard	1917	1990
Duggan, Andrew	1923	1988
Dumbrille, Douglass	1890	1974
Dumont, Margaret	1889	1965
Duncan, Isadora	1878	1927
Dunham, Katherine	1910	2006
Dunn, James	1905	1967
Dunne, Irene	1898	1990
Dunnock, Mildred	1904	1991
Durante, Jimmy	1893	1980
Duryea, Dan	1907	1968
Duse, Eleanora	1858	1924
Dvorak, Ann	1912	1979
Eagels, Jeanne	1894	1929
Ebsen, Buddy	1908	2003
Eckstine, Billy	1914	1993

Name	Born	Died
Eddington, Paul	1927	1995
Eddy, Nelson	1901	1967
Edelman, Herb	1933	1996
Edwards, Cliff	1897	1971
Edwards, Gus	1879	1945
Edwards, Ralph	1913	2005
Edwards, Vince	1928	1996
Egan, Richard	1923	1987
Eisenstein, Sergei	1898	1948
Elam, Jack	1916	2003
Ellington, Duke	1899	1974
Elliot, Cass	1941	1974
Elliott, Denholm	1922	1992
Ellis, Mary	1897	2003
Elman, Mischa	1891	1967
Errol, Leon	1881	1951
Evans, Dale	1912	2001
Evans, Edith	1888	1976
Evans, Maurice	1901	1989
Ewell, Tom	1909	1994
Fadiman, Clifton	1904	1999
Fairbanks, Douglas	1883	1939
Fairbanks, Douglas, Jr.	1909	2000
Falkenburg, Jinx	1919	2003
Farley, Chris	1964	1997
Farmer, Frances	1914	1970
Farnsworth, Richard	1920	2000
Farnum, Dustin	1870	1929
Farnum, William	1876	1953
Farrar, Geraldine	1882	1967
Farrell, Charles	1901	1990
Farrell, Eileen	1920	2002
Farrell, Glenda	1904	1971
Fassbinder, Rainer Werner	1946	1982
Fay, Frank	1897	1961
Faye, Alice	1912	1998
Fazenda, Louise	1895	1962
Feld, Fritz	1900	1993
Feldman, Marty	1933	1982
Fell, Norman	1924	1998
Fellini, Federico	1920	1993
Fenneman, George	1919	1997
Ferrer, Jose	1912	1992
Fetchit, Stepin	1898	1985
Fiedler, Arthur	1894	1979
Fiedler, John	1925	2005
Field, Betty	1918	1973
Fields, Gracie	1898	1979
Fields, W.C.	1879	1946
Fields, Totie	1931	1978
Finch, Peter	1916	1977
Fine, Larry	1902	1975
Firkusny, Rudolf	1912	1994
Fiske, Minnie Maddern	1865	1932
Fitzgerald, Barry	1888	1961
Fitzgerald, Ella	1917	1996
Fitzgerald, Geraldine	1913	2005
Flagstad, Kirsten	1895	1962
Fleischer, Richard	1916	2006
Fleming, Art	1924	1995
Fleming, Eric	1925	1966
Flippen, Jay C.	1900	1971
Flynn, Errol	1909	1959
Flynn, Joe	1925	1974
Foley, Red	1910	1968
Fonda, Henry	1905	1982
Fontaine, Frank	1920	1978
Fontanne, Lynn	1887	1983
Fonteyn, Margot	1919	1991
Ford, John	1895	1973
Ford, Paul	1901	1976
Ford, Tennessee Ernie	1919	1991
Ford, Wallace	1899	1966
Forrest, Helen	1918	1999
Fosse, Bob	1927	1987
Foster, Phil	1914	1985
Foster, Preston	1901	1970
Foxx, Redd	1922	1991
Foy, Eddie	1857	1928
Franchi, Sergio	1933?	1990
Franciosa, Anthony	1929	2006
Francis, Arlene	1908	2001
Francis, Kay	1903	1968
Franciscus, James	1934	1991
Frankenheimer, John	1930	2002
Frann, Mary	1943	1998
Frawley, William	1887	1966
Frederick, Pauline	1885	1938
French, Victor	1934	1989

Name	Born	Died
Kirby, Durward	1912	2000
Kirsten, Dorothy	1910	1992
Klemperer, Werner	1919	2000
Knight, Ted	1923	1986
Knotts, Don	1924	2006
Kostelanetz, Andre	1901	1980
Kovacs, Ernie	1919	1962
Kramer, Stanley	1913	2001
Kruger, Otto	1885	1974
Kubrick, Stanley	1928	1999
Kulp, Nancy	1921	1991
Kurosawa, Akira	1910	1998
Kyser, Kay	1906	1985
Ladd, Alan	1913	1964
Lahr, Bert	1895	1967
Lake, Arthur	1905	1987
Lake, Veronica	1919	1973
Lamarr, Hedy	1913	2000
Lamas, Fernando	1915	1982
Lamour, Dorothy	1914	1996
Lancaster, Burt	1913	1994
Lanchester, Elsa	1902	1986
Lane, Pricilla	1917	1995
Landis, Carole	1919	1948
Landis, Jessie Royce	1904	1972
Landon, Michael	1936	1991
Lang, Fritz	1890	1976
Langdon, Harry	1884	1944
Lange, Hope	1931	2003
Langford, Frances	1914	2005
Langtry, Lillie	1853	1929
Lanza, Mario	1921	1959
LaRue, Lash (Alfred)	1917	1996
Lauder, Harry	1870	1950
Laughton, Charles	1899	1962
Laurel, Stan	1890	1965
Lawford, Peter	1923	1984
Lawrence, Gertrude	1898	1952
Lean, David	1908	1991
Lee, Bernard	1908	1981
Lee, Bruce	1940	1973
Lee, Canada	1907	1952
Lee, Gypsy Rose	1914	1970
Lee, Anna	1913	2004
Lee, Peggy	1920	2002
LeGallienne, Eva	1899	1991
Lehmann, Lotte	1888	1976
Leigh, Janet	1927	2004
Leigh, Vivien	1913	1967
Leighton, Margaret	1922	1976
Lemmon, Jack	1925	2001
Lennon, John	1940	1980
Lenya, Lotte	1898	1981
Leonard, Eddie	1870	1941
Leonard, Sheldon	1907	1997
LeRoy, Mervyn	1900	1987
Levant, Oscar	1906	1972
Levene, Sam	1905	1980
Levenson, Sam	1911	1980
Lewis, Al	1923	2006
Lewis, Joe E.	1902	1971
Lewis, Shari	1934	1998
Lewis, Ted	1892	1971
Liberace	1919	1987
Lillie, Beatrice	1894	1989
Lind, Jenny	1820	1887
Lindfors, Viveca	1920	1995
Lindley, Audra	1918	1997
Linville, Larry	1939	2000
Little, Cleavon	1939	1992
Llewelyn, Desmond	1914	1999
Lloyd, Harold	1893	1971
Lloyd, Marie	1870	1922
Lockhart, Gene	1891	1957
Logan, Ella	1913	1969
Lombard, Carole	1909	1942
Lombardo, Guy	1902	1977
Long, Richard	1927	1974
Lopes, Lisa	1971	2002
Lopez, Vincent	1895	1975
Lord, Jack	1920?	1998
Lorne, Marion	1888	1968
Lorre, Peter	1904	1964
Loudon, Dorothy	1933	2003
Lovejoy, Frank	1912	1962
Lowe, Edmund	1890	1971
Loy, Myrna	1905	1993
Lubitsch, Ernst	1892	1947
Ludden, Allen	1918	1981
Lugosi, Bela	1882	1956
Lukas, Paul	1894	1971
Lundigan, William	1914	1975
Lunt, Alfred	1892	1977
Lupino, Ida	1918	1995
Lymon, Frankie	1942	1968
Lynde, Paul	1926	1982
Lynn, Diana	1926	1971
MacDonald, Jeanette	1903	1965
Mack, Ted	1904	1976
MacKenzie, Gisele	1927	2003
MacLane, Barton	1902	1969
MacMurray, Fred	1908	1991
MacRae, Gordon	1921	1986
Macready, George	1909	1973
Madison, Guy	1922	1996
Magnani, Anna	1908	1973
Main, Marjorie	1890	1975
Malle, Louis	1932	1995
Mann, Herbie	1930	2003
Mansfield, Jayne	1932	1967
Mantovani, Annunzio	1905	1980
Marais, Jean	1913	1998
March, Fredric	1897	1975
March, Hal	1920	1970
Marchand, Nancy	1928	2000
Marley, Bob	1945	1981
Marshall, Brenda	1915	1992
Marshall, E.G.	1910	1998
Marshall, Herbert	1890	1966
Martin, Barney	1923	2005
Martin, Dean	1917	1995
Martin, Mary	1913	1990
Martin, Ross	1920	1981
Marvin, Lee	1924	1987
Marx, Arthur (Harpo)	1888	1964
Marx, Herbert (Zeppo)	1901	1979
Marx, Julius (Groucho)	1890	1977
Marx, Leonard (Chico)	1886	1961
Marx, Milton (Gummo)	1893	1977
Mason, James	1909	1984
Massey, Daniel	1933	1998
Massey, Raymond	1896	1983
Mastroianni, Marcello	1924	1996
Matthau, Walter	1920	2000
Mature, Victor	1916	1999
Maxwell, Marilyn	1921	1972
Mayer, Louis B.	1885	1957
Mayfield, Curtis	1942	1999
Maynard, Ken	1895	1973
Mayo, Virginia	1920	2005
Mazurki, Mike	1909	1990
McCambridge, Mercedes	1916	2004
McCartney, Linda	1941	1998
McClure, Doug	1935	1995
McCormack, John	1884	1945
McCrary, Tex	1910	2003
McCrea, Joel	1905	1990
McDaniel, Hattie	1895	1952
McDowall, Roddy	1928	1998
McFarland, George "Spanky"	1928	1993
McGavin, Darren	1922	2006
McGuire, Dorothy	1916	2001
McHugh, Frank	1899	1981
McIntire, John	1907	1991
McKay, Gardner	1932	2001
McKern, Leo	1920	2002
McLaglen, Victor	1883	1959
McMahon, Horace	1907	1971
McNally, Stephen	1913	1994
McNeill, Don	1907	1996
McQueen, Butterfly	1911	1995
McQueen, Steve	1930	1980
Meader, Vaughn	1936	2004
Meadows, Audrey	1924	1996
Medford, Kay	1920	1980
Meek, Donald	1880	1946
Meeker, Ralph	1920	1988
Melba, Nellie	1861	1931
Melchior, Lauritz	1890	1973
Menjou, Adolphe	1890	1963
Menken, Helen	1902	1966
Menuhin, Yehudi	1916	1999
Mercouri, Melina	1925	1994
Mercury, Freddie	1946	1991
Meredith, Burgess	1909	1997
Merman, Ethel	1908	1984
Merrick, David	1911	2000
Merrill, Gary	1915	1990
Mifune, Toshiro	1920	1997
Milland, Ray	1905	1986
Miller, Ann	1923	2004
Miller, Glenn	1904	1944
Miller, Marilyn	1898	1936
Miller, Roger	1936	1992
Mills, Harry	1913	1982
Mills, Sir John	1908	2005
Minnevitch, Borrah	1903	1955
Mineo, Sal	1939	1976
Miner, Jan	1917	2004
Mingus, Charles	1922	1979
Miranda, Carmen	1913	1955
Mitchell, Cameron	1918	1994
Mitchell, Thomas	1892	1962
Mitchum, Robert	1917	1997
Mix, Tom	1880	1940
Monica, Corbett	1930	1998
Moffo, Anna	1934	2006
Monroe, Marilyn	1926	1962
Monroe, Vaughn	1911	1973
Montand, Yves	1921	1991
Montez, Maria	1917	1951
Montgomery, Elizabeth	1933	1995
Montgomery, George	1916	2000
Montgomery, Robert	1904	1981
Moore, Clayton	1914	1999
Moore, Colleen	1900	1988
Moore, Dudley	1935	2002
Moore, Grace	1901	1947
Moore, Garry	1914	1993
Moore, Victor	1876	1962
Moorehead, Agnes	1906	1974
Moreland, Mantan	1902	1973
Morgan, Dennis	1910	1994
Morgan, Frank	1890	1949
Morgan, Helen	1900	1941
Morgan, Henry	1915	1994
Morita, Pat	1932	2005
Morley, Robert	1908	1992
Morris, Chester	1901	1970
Morris, Greg	1934	1996
Morris, Howard	1919	2005
Morris, Wayne	1914	1959
Morrison, Jim	1943	1971
Morrow, Vic	1932	1982
Mostel, Zero	1915	1977
Mowbray, Alan	1897	1969
Mulhare, Edward	1923	1997
Mulligan, Gerry	1927	1996
Mulligan, Richard	1932	2000
Muni, Paul	1895	1967
Munshin, Jules	1915	1970
Murphy, Audie	1924	1971
Murphy, George	1902	1992
Murray, Arthur	1895	1991
Murray, Kathryn	1906	1999
Murray, Mae	1885	1965
Nagel, Conrad	1896	1970
Naish, J. Carroll	1900	1973
Naldi, Nita	1898	1961
Nance, Jack	1943	1997
Natwick, Mildred	1908	1994
Negri, Pola	1897	1987
Nelson, Harriet (Hilliard)	1909	1994
Nelson, Ozzie	1906	1975
Nelson, Rick	1940	1985
Nesbit, Evelyn	1885	1967
Newley, Anthony	1931	1999
Newton, Robert	1905	1956
Nicholas, Harold	1924	2000
Nijinsky, Vaslav	1890	1950
Nilsson, Anna Q.	1893	1974
Niven, David	1910	1983
Nolan, Lloyd	1902	1985
Normand, Mabel	1894	1930
North, Sheree	1933	2005
Notorious B.I.G.	1972	1997
Novarro, Ramon	1899	1968
Nureyev, Rudolf	1938	1993
Oakie, Jack	1903	1978
Oakley, Annie	1860	1926
Oates, Warren	1928	1982
Oberon, Merle	1911	1979
O'Brien, Edmond	1915	1985
O'Brien, Pat	1899	1983
O'Connell, Arthur	1908	1981

Name	Born	Died
O'Connell, Helen	1921	1993
O'Connor, Carroll	1924	2001
O'Connor, Donald	1925	2003
O'Connor, Una	1880	1959
O'Keefe, Dennis	1908	1968
O'Herlihy, Daniel	1919	2005
Oland, Warner	1880	1938
Olcott, Chauncey	1860	1932
Oliver, Edna May	1883	1942
Olivier, Laurence	1907	1989
Olsen, Ole	1892	1963
O'Neill, James	1849	1920
O'Neal, Ron	1937	2004
Orbach, Jerry	1935	2004
Orbison, Roy	1936	1988
Ormandy, Eugene	1899	1985
O'Sullivan, Maureen	1911	1998
Ouspenskaya, Maria	1876	1949
Owen, Reginald	1887	1972
Owens, Buck	1929	2006
Paar, Jack	1918	2004
Paderewski, Ignace	1860	1941
Page, Geraldine	1924	1987
Pakula, Alan	1928	1998
Pallette, Eugene	1889	1954
Palmer, Lilli	1914	1986
Palmer, Robert	1949	2003
Pangborn, Franklin	1894	1958
Parks, Bert	1914	1992
Parks, Larry	1914	1975
Pasternack, Josef A.	1881	1940
Pastor, Tony (vaudevillian)	1837	1908
Pastor, Tony (bandleader)	1907	1969
Patti, Adelina	1843	1919
Patti, Carlotta	1840	1889
Patrick, Gail	1911	1980
Pavlova, Anna	1885	1931
Paycheck, Johnny	1938	2003
Payne, John	1912	1989
Pearl, Minnie	1912	1996
Peck, Gregory	1916	2003
Peerce, Jan	1904	1984
Penn, Chris	1965	2006
Penner, Joe	1905	1941
Peppard, George	1928	1994
Perkins, Anthony	1932	1992
Perkins, Carl	1932	1998
Perkins, Marlin	1905	1986
Peters, Brock	1927	2005
Peters, Jean	1926	2000
Peters, Susan	1921	1952
Phillips, John	1935	2001
Phoenix, River	1970	1993
Piaf, Edith	1915	1963
Pickens, Slim	1919	1983
Pickett, Wilson	1941	2006
Pickford, Mary	1893	1979
Picon, Molly	1898	1992
Pidgeon, Walter	1897	1984
Pinza, Ezio	1892	1957
Pitney, Gene	1941	2006
Pitts, Zasu	1898	1963
Plato, Dana	1964	1999
Pleasence, Donald	1919	1995
Pons, Lily	1904	1976
Ponselle, Rosa	1897	1981
Porter, Eric	1928	1995
Porter, Nyree Dawn	1940	2001
Powell, Dick	1904	1963
Powell, Eleanor	1912	1982
Powell, William	1892	1984
Power, Tyrone	1913	1958
Preminger, Otto	1905	1986
Presley, Elvis	1935	1977
Preston, Billy	1946	2006
Preston, Robert	1918	1987
Price, Vincent	1911	1993
Prima, Louis	1911	1978
Prinze, Freddie	1954	1977
Prowse, Juliet	1936	1996
Pryor, Richard	1940	2005
Puente, Tito	1923	2000
Pyle, Denver	1920	1997
Quayle, Anthony	1913	1989
Questel, Mae	1908	1998
Quinn, Anthony	1915	2001
Quintero, José	1924	1999
Rabb, Ellis	1930	1998
Rabbit, Eddie	1941	1998

Name	Born	Died
Radner, Gilda	1946	1989
Raft, George	1895	1980
Rains, Claude	1890	1967
Ralston, Esther	1902	1994
Raitt, John	1917	2005
Ramone, Dee Dee	1952	2002
Ramone, Joey	1951	2001
Ramone, Johnny	1951	2004
Rampal, Jean-Pierre	1922	2000
Randall, Tony	1920	2004
Randolph, John	1915	2004
Rathbone, Basil	1892	1967
Ratoff, Gregory	1897	1960
Rawls, Lou	1933	2006
Ray, Aldo	1926	1991
Ray, Johnnie	1927	1990
Rayburn, Gene	1917	1999
Raye, Martha	1916	1994
Raymond, Gene	1908	1998
Reagan, Ronald	1911	2004
Redding, Otis	1941	1967
Redgrave, Michael	1908	1985
Reed, Donna	1921	1986
Reed, Oliver	1938	1999
Reed, Robert	1932	1992
Reeve, Christopher	1952	2004
Reeves, George	1914	1959
Reeves, Steve	1926	2000
Reinhardt, Max	1873	1943
Remick, Lee	1935	1991
Renaldo, Duncan	1904	1980
Rennie, Michael	1909	1971
Renoir, Jean	1894	1979
Rettig, Tommy	1941	1996
Reynolds, Marjorie	1923	1997
Rich, Charlie	1932	1995
Richardson, Ralph	1902	1983
Riddle, Nelson	1921	1985
Riefenstahl, Leni	1902	2003
Ripperton, Minnie	1947	1979
Ritchard, Cyril	1898	1977
Ritter, John	1948	2003
Ritter, Tex	1907	1974
Ritter, Thelma	1905	1969
Ritz, Al	1901	1965
Ritz, Harry	1906	1986
Ritz, Jimmy	1903	1985
Robards, Jason	1922	2000
Robbins, Jerome	1918	1998
Robbins, Marty	1925	1982
Robeson, Paul	1898	1976
Robinson, Bill	1878	1949
Robinson, Edward G.	1893	1973
Roche, Eugene	1928	2004
Rochester (E. Anderson)	1905	1977
Roddenberry, Gene	1921	1991
Rodgers, Jimmie	1897	1933
Rogers, Buddy	1904	1999
Rogers, Fred	1928	2003
Rogers, Ginger	1911	1995
Rogers, Roy	1911	1998
Rogers, Will	1879	1935
Roland, Gilbert	1905	1994
Rolle, Esther	1920?	1998
Rollins, Howard	1950	1996
Roman, Ruth	1924	1999
Romero, Cesar	1907	1994
Rooney, Pat	1880	1962
Rose, Billy	1899	1966
Rossellini, Roberto	1906	1977
Rowan, Dan	1922	1987
Rubinstein, Artur	1887	1982
Ruggles, Charles	1886	1970
Russell, Gail	1924	1961
Russell, Harold	1914	2002
Russell, Lillian	1861	1922
Russell, Nipsey	1923	2005
Russell, Rosalind	1911	1976
Rutherford, Margaret	1892	1972
Ryan, Irene	1903	1973
Ryan, Robert	1909	1973
Sabu	1924	1963
Sanford, Isabel	1917	2004
Sargent, Dick	1933	1994
St. Cyr, Lili	1917	1999
St. Denis, Ruth	1877	1968
Sakall, S.Z.	1884	1955
Sale (Chic), Charles	1885	1936
Sanders, George	1906	1972

Name	Born	Died
Savalas, Telly	1924	1994
Schell, Maria	1926	2005
Schiavelli, Vincent	1948	2005
Schildkraut, Joseph	1895	1964
Schipa, Tito	1889	1965
Schlesinger, John	1926	2003
Schnabel, Artur	1882	1951
Schneider, Romy	1938	1982
Schwartzkopf, Elizabeth	1915	2006
Scott, George C.	1927	1999
Scott, Hazel	1920	1981
Scott, Martha	1914	2003
Scott, Randolph	1898	1987
Scott, Zachary	1914	1965
Scott-Siddons, Mrs.	1843	1896
Seberg, Jean	1938	1979
Seeley, Blossom	1892	1974
Segovia, Andres	1893	1987
Selena	1971	1995
Sellers, Peter	1925	1980
Selznick, David O.	1902	1965
Sennett, Mack	1884	1960
Senor Wences	1896	1999
Serling, Rod	1924	1975
Shakur, Tupac	1971	1996
Shaw, Robert (actor)	1927	1978
Shaw, Robert (conductor)	1916	1999
Shawn, Ted	1891	1972
Shean, Al	1868	1949
Shearer, Moira	1926	2006
Shearer, Norma	1902	1983
Sheridan, Ann	1915	1967
Shore, Dinah	1917	1994
Short, Bobby	1924	2005
Shubert, Lee	1875	1953
Shull, Richard B.	1929	1999
Siddons, Mrs. Sarah	1755	1831
Sidney, Sylvia	1910	1999
Signoret, Simone	1921	1985
Silverheels, Jay	1912	1980
Silvers, Phil	1912	1985
Sim, Alastair	1900	1976
Simmons, Richard	1913	2003
Simone, Nina	1933	2003
Sims, Irene	1930	2001
Sinatra, Frank	1915	1998
Sinclair, Madge	1938	1995
Singleton, Penny	1908	2003
Siskel, Gene	1946	1999
Sitka, Emil	1914	1998
Sjostrom, Victor	1879	1960
Skelton, Red	1913	1997
Skinner, Otis	1858	1942
Smith, Alexis	1921	1993
Smith, Buffalo Bob	1917	1998
Smith, C. Aubrey	1863	1948
Smith, Elliott	1969	2003
Smith, Jeff	1939	2004
Smith, Kate	1907	1986
Smith, Kent	1907	1985
Snodgress, Carrie	1946	2004
Snow, Hank	1914	1999
Solti, George	1912	1997
Sondergaard, Gale	1899	1985
Sothern, Ann	1909	2001
Sousa, John Philip	1854	1932
Sparks, Ned	1884	1957
Spelling, Aaron	1928	2006
Spencer, John	1946	2005
Sperber, Wendy Jo.	1958	2005
Springfield, Dusty	1939	1999
Stack, Robert	1919	2003
Stander, Lionel	1908	1994
Stanley, Kim	1925	2001
Stanwyck, Barbara	1907	1990
Stapleton, Maureen	1925	2006
Steiger, Rod	1925	2002
Sterling, Jan	1921	2004
Stern, Isaac	1920	2001
Stevens, Craig	1918	2000
Stevens, Inger	1934	1970
Stevens, Mark	1916	1994
Stevenson, McLean	1929	1996
Stewart, James	1908	1997
Stickney, Dorothy	1896	1998
Stokowski, Leopold	1882	1977
Stone, Lewis	1879	1953
Stone, Milburn	1904	1980

Name	Born	Died	Name	Born	Died	Name	Born	Died
Straight, Beatrice	1918	2001	Turpin, Ben	1874	1940	Weston, Jack	1924	1996
Strasberg, Lee	1901	1982	Twelvetrees, Helen	1908	1958	Whale, James	1889	1957
Strasberg, Susan	1938	1999	Twitty, Conway	1933	1993	Wheeler, Bert	1895	1968
Strode, Woody	1914	1994	Urich, Robert	1947	2002	White, Barry	1944	2003
Strummer, Joe	1952	2002	Ustinov, Peter	1921	2004	White, Jesse	1919	1997
Sturges, Preston	1898	1959	Valens, Ritchie	1941	1959	White, Pearl	1889	1938
Sullavan, Margaret	1911	1960	Valentino, Rudolph	1895	1926	Whiteman, Paul	1891	1967
Sullivan, Barry	1912	1994	Vallee, Rudy	1901	1986	Whitty, May	1865	1948
Sullivan, Ed	1902	1974	Van, Bobby	1928	1980	Wickes, Mary	1910	1995
Sullivan, Francis L.	1903	1956	Vance, Vivian	1912	1979	Wilde, Cornel	1918	1989
Summerville, Slim	1892	1946	Van Cleef, Lee	1925	1989	Wilder, Billy	1906	2002
Swanson, Gloria	1899	1983	Vandross, Luther	1951	2005	Wilding, Michael	1912	1979
Swarthout, Gladys	1904	1969	Van Fleet, Jo	1922	1996	Williams, Bert	1877	1922
Switzer, Carl "Alfalfa"	1926	1959	Varney, Jim	1949	2000	Williams, Guy	1924	1989
Talbot, Lyle	1904	1996	Vaughan, Sarah	1924	1990	Williams, Hank Sr.	1923	1953
Talmadge, Norma	1893	1957	Veidt, Conrad	1893	1943	Wills, Bob	1905	1975
Tamiroff, Akim	1899	1972	Velez, Lupe	1908	1944	Wills, Chill	1903	1978
Tandy, Jessica	1909	1994	Vera-Ellen	1926	1981	Wilson, Carl	1946	1998
Tanguay, Eva	1878	1947	Verdon, Gwen	1925	2000	Wilson, Dennis	1944	1983
Tati, Jacques	1908	1982	Vernon, Jackie	1925	1987	Wilson, Dooley	1894	1953
Taylor, Deems	1885	1966	Vernon, John	1932	2005	Wilson, Flip	1933	1998
Taylor, Dub	1907	1994	Villechaize, Herve	1943	1993	Wilson, Jackie	1934	1984
Taylor, Estelle	1899	1958	Vincent, Gene	1935	1971	Wilson, Marie	1917	1972
Taylor, Laurette	1887	1946	Vicious, Sid	1957	1979	Windsor, Marie	1919	2000
Taylor, Robert	1911	1969	Vinson, Helen	1907	1999	Winfield, Paul	1941	2004
Tebaldi, Renata	1922	2004	Von Stroheim, Erich	1885	1957	Winninger, Charles	1884	1969
Terry, Ellen	1847	1928	Von Zell, Harry	1906	1981	Winters, Shelley	1920	2006
Thalberg, Irving	1899	1936	Walker, Junior	1942	1995	Wise, Robert	1914	2005
Thaw, John	1942	2002	Walker, Nancy	1922	1992	Withers, Grant	1904	1959
Thigpen, Lynne	1948	2003	Walker, Robert	1918	1951	Wong, Anna May	1907	1961
Thomas, Danny	1912	1991	Wallenda, Karl	1905	1978	Wood, Natalie	1938	1981
Thomas, John Charles	1892	1960	Walsh, J. T.	1943	1998	Wood, Peggy	1892	1978
Thorndike, Sybil	1882	1976	Walsh, Raoul	1887	1980	Wooley, Sheb	1921	2003
Thulin, Ingrid	1926	2004	Walston, Ray	1914	2001	Woolley, Monty	1888	1963
Tibbett, Lawrence	1896	1960	Walter, Bruno	1876	1962	Worth, Irene	1916	2002
Tierney, Gene	1920	1991	Ward, Helen	1916	1998	Wray, Fay	1907	2004
Tiny Tim	1923	1996	Warden, Jack	1914	2006	Wright, Teresa	1918	2005
Tippett, Sir Michael	1905	1998	Waring, Fred	1900	1984	Wyler, William	1902	1981
Todd, Michael	1909	1958	Warner, H. B.	1876	1958	Wynette, Tammy	1942	1998
Tomlinson, David	1917	2000	Warrick, Ruth	1915	2005	Wynn, Ed	1886	1966
Tone, Franchot	1903	1968	Washington, Dinah	1924	1963	Wynn, Keenan	1916	1986
Torme, Mel	1925	1999	Waters, Ethel	1896	1977	Yankovic, Frank	1915	1998
Toscanini, Arturo	1867	1957	Waxman, Al	1935	2001	York, Dick	1929	1992
Tracy, Lee	1898	1968	Wayne, David	1914	1995	Young, Clara Kimball	1890	1960
Tracy, Spencer	1900	1967	Wayne, John	1907	1979	Young, Gig	1913	1978
Traubel, Helen	1903	1972	Weaver, Dennis	1924	2006	Young, Loretta	1913	2000
Travers, Henry	1874	1965	Webb, Clifton	1891	1966	Young, Robert	1907	1998
Treacher, Arthur	1894	1975	Webb, Jack	1920	1982	Young, Roland	1887	1953
Tree, Herbert Beerbohm	1853	1917	Weems, Ted	1901	1963	Youngman, Henny	1906	1998
Trevor, Claire	1909	2000	Weissmuller, Johnny	1904	1984	Zanuck, Darryl F.	1902	1979
Truex, Ernest	1890	1973	Welk, Lawrence	1903	1992	Zapa, Frank	1940	1993
Truffaut, Francois	1932	1984	Welles, Orson	1915	1985	Zevon, Warren	1947	2003
Tucker, Forrest	1919	1986	Wellman, William	1896	1975	Zinneman, Fred	1907	1997
Tucker, Richard	1913	1975	Werner, Oskar	1922	1984	Ziegfeld, Florenz	1869	1932
Tucker, Sophie	1884	1966	West, Mae	1893	1980	Zukor, Adolph	1873	1976
Turner, Lana	1920	1995						

Original Names of Selected Entertainers

ALI G: Sacha Baron Cohen
EDIE ADAMS: Elizabeth Edith Enke
EDDIE ALBERT: Edward Albert Heimberger
ALAN ALDA: Alphonso D'Abruzzo
JASON ALEXANDER: Jay Greenspan
FRED ALLEN: John Sullivan
WOODY ALLEN: Allen Konigsberg
JUNE ALLYSON: Ella Geisman
ANDRE 3000: Andre Benjamin
JULIE ANDREWS: Julia Wells
EVE ARDEN: Eunice Quedens
BEATRICE ARTHUR: Bernice Frankel
JEAN ARTHUR: Gladys Greene
FRED ASTAIRE: Frederick Austerlitz
BABYFACE: Kenneth Edmonds
LAUREN BACALL: Betty Joan Perske
ERYKAH BADU: Erica Wright
ANNE BANCROFT: Anna Maria Italiano
GENE BARRY: Eugene Klass
PAT BENATAR: Patricia Andrejewski
TONY BENNETT: Anthony Benedetto
IRVING BERLIN: Israel Baline
JACK BENNY: Benjamin Kubelsky
BIG BOI: Antwan Patton
JOEY BISHOP: Joseph Gottlieb
THE BIG BOPPER: Jiles Perry "J.P." Richardson

BONO (VOX): Paul Hewson
VICTOR BORGE: Borge Rosenbaum
DAVID BOWIE: David Robert Jones
BOY GEORGE: George Alan O'Dowd
FANNY BRICE: Fanny Borach
CHARLES BRONSON: Charles Buchinski
ALBERT BROOKS: Albert Einstein
MEL BROOKS: Melvin Kaminsky
GEORGE BURNS: Nathan Birnbaum
ELLEN BURSTYN: Edna Gilhooley
RICHARD BURTON: Richard Jenkins
RED BUTTONS: Aaron Chwatt
NICOLAS CAGE: Nicholas Coppola
MICHAEL CAINE: Maurice Micklewhite
MARIA CALLAS: Maria Kalogeropoulos
CEDRIC THE ENTERTAINER: Cedric Kyles
JACKIE CHAN: Chan Kwong-Sung
CYD CHARISSE: Tula Finklea
RAY CHARLES: Ray Charles Robinson
CHUBBY CHECKER: Ernest Evans
CHUCK D: Carlton Ridenhour
CHER: Cherilyn Sarkisian
PATSY CLINE: Virginia Patterson Hensley
LEE J. COBB: Leo Jacoby
CLAUDETTE COLBERT: Lily Chauchoin

ALICE COOPER: Vincent Furnier
DAVID COPPERFIELD: David Kotkin
HOWARD COSELL: Howard Cohen
ELVIS COSTELLO: Declan McManus
LOU COSTELLO: Louis Cristillo
PETER COYOTE: Peter Cohon
MICHAEL CRAWFORD: Michael Dumble-Smith
TOM CRUISE: Thomas Mapother IV
TONY CURTIS: Bernard Schwartz
VIC DAMONE: Vito Farinola
RODNEY DANGERFIELD: Jacob Cohen
BOBBY DARIN: Walden Robert Cassotto
DORIS DAY: Doris von Kappelhoff
YVONNE DE CARLO: Peggy Middleton
SANDRA DEE: Alexandra Zuck
JOHN DENVER: Henry John Deutschendorf Jr.
BO DEREK: Mary Cathleen Collins
DANNY DEVITO: Daniel Michaeli
ANGIE DICKINSON: Angeline Brown
BO DIDDLEY: Elias Bates
PHYLLIS DILLER: Phyllis Driver
DMX: Earl Simmons
EARL TROY DONAHUE: Merle Johnson Jr.
KIRK DOUGLAS: Issur Danielovitch

MELVYN DOUGLAS: Melvyn Hesselberg
BOB DYLAN: Robert Zimmerman
BARBARA EDEN: Barbara Huffman
ELVIRA: Cassandra Peterson
EMINEM: Marshall Mathers
ENYA: Eithne Ni Bhraonian
DALE EVANS: Frances Smith
CHAD EVERETT: Raymond Cramton
DOUGLAS FAIRBANKS: Douglas Ullman
MORGAN FAIRCHILD: Patsy McClenny
JAMIE FARR: Jameel Farah
ALICE FAYE: Alice Jeanne Leppert
STEPIN FETCHIT: Lincoln Perry
W.C. FIELDS: William Claude Dukenfield
50 CENT: Curtis Jackson
BARRY FITZGERALD: William Shields
FLAVOR FLAV: William Drayton
JOAN FONTAINE: Joan de Havilland
JODIE FOSTER: Alicia Christian Foster
REDD FOXX: John Sanford
ANTHONY FRANCIOSA: Anthony Papaleo
ARLENE FRANCIS: Arlene Kazanjian
CONNIE FRANCIS: Concetta Franconero
GRETA GARBO: Greta Gustafsson
VINCENT GARDENIA: Vincent Scognamiglio
JOHN GARFIELD: Julius Garfinkle
JUDY GARLAND: Frances Gumm
JAMES GARNER: James Bumgarner
CRYSTAL GAYLE: Brenda Gayle Webb
KATHIE LEE GIFFORD: Kathie Epstein
WHOOPI GOLDBERG: Caryn Johnson
EYDIE GORME: Edith Gormezano
STEWART GRANGER: James Stewart
CARY GRANT: Archibald Leach
LEE GRANT: Lyova Rosenthal
ROBERT GUILLAUME: Robert Williams
BUDDY HACKETT: Leonard Hacker
HAMMER: Stanley Kirk Burrell
JEAN HARLOW: Harlean Carpentier
REX HARRISON: Reginald Carey
LAURENCE HARVEY: Larushka Skikne
HELEN HAYES: Helen Brown
SUSAN HAYWARD: Edythe Marriner
RITA HAYWORTH: Margarita Cansino
PEE-WEE HERMAN: Paul Reubenfeld
CHARLTON HESTON: John Charlton Carter
WILLIAM HOLDEN: William Beedle
BILLIE HOLIDAY: Eleanora Fagan
JUDY HOLLIDAY: Judith Tuvim
BOB HOPE: Leslie Townes Hope
HARRY HOUDINI: Ehrich Weiss
LESLIE HOWARD: Leslie Stainer
HOWLIN' WOLF: Chester Burnett
ROCK HUDSON: Roy Scherer Jr. (later Fitzgerald)
ENGELBERT HUMPERDINCK: Arnold Dorsey
KIM HUNTER: Janet Cole
BETTY HUTTON: Betty Thornberg
ICE CUBE: O'Shea Jackson
ICE-T: Tracy Morrow
BILLY IDOL: William Broad
JAY-Z: Shawn Carter
ANN JILLIAN: Anne Nauseda
ELTON JOHN: Reginald Dwight
DON JOHNSON: Donald Wayne
AL JOLSON: Asa Yoelson
JENNIFER JONES: Phylis Isley
TOM JONES: Thomas Woodward
SPIKE JONZE: Adam Spiegel
LOUIS JOURDAN: Louis Gendre
WYNONNA JUDD: Christina Ciminella
BORIS KARLOFF: William Henry Pratt
DANNY KAYE: David Kaminsky
DIANE KEATON: Diane Hall

MICHAEL KEATON: Michael Douglas
CHAKA KHAN: Yvette Stevens
CAROLE KING: Carole Klein
LARRY KING: Larry Zeiger
BEN KINGSLEY: Krishna Banji
TED KNIGHT: Tadeus Wladyslaw Konopka
CHERYL LADD: Cheryl Stoppelmoor
VERONICA LAKE: Constance Ockleman
HEDY LAMARR: Hedwig Kiesler
DOROTHY LAMOUR: Mary Leta Dorothy Slaton
MICHAEL LANDON: Eugene Orowitz
MARIO LANZA: Alfredo Cocozza
QUEEN LATIFAH: Dana Owens
STAN LAUREL: Arthur Jefferson
STEVE LAWRENCE: Sidney Leibowitz
BRENDA LEE: Brenda Mae Tarpley
GYPSY ROSE LEE: Rose Louise Hovick
MICHELLE LEE: Michelle Dusiak
PEGGY LEE: Norma Egstrom
JANET LEIGH: Jeanette Morrison
VIVIEN LEIGH: Vivian Hartley
HUEY LEWIS: Hugh Cregg
JERRY LEWIS: Joseph Levitch
LIL' KIM: Kimberly Denise Jones
CAROLE LOMBARD: Jane Peters
SOPHIA LOREN: Sophia Scicolone
PETER LORRE: Laszio Lowenstein
MYRNA LOY: Myrna Williams
BELA LUGOSI: Bela Ferenc Blasko
MOMS MABLEY: Loretta Mary Aitken
SHIRLEY MACLAINE: Shirley Beaty
ELLE MACPHERSON: Eleanor Gow
MADONNA: Madonna Louise Veronica Ciccone
LEE MAJORS: Harvey Lee Yeary
KARL MALDEN: Mladen Sekulovich
BARRY MANILOW: Barry Alan Pincus
JAYNE MANSFIELD: Vera Jane Palmer
MARILYN MANSON: Brian Warner
FREDRIC MARCH: Frederick Bickel
PETER MARSHALL: Pierre LaCock
WALTER MATTHAU: Walter Matuschanskayasky
DEAN MARTIN: Dino Crocetti
MEAT LOAF: Marvin Lee Aday
FREDDIE MERCURY: Frederick Bulsara
ETHEL MERMAN: Ethel Zimmerman
GEORGE MICHAEL: Georgios Panayiotou
RAY MILLAND: Reginald Truscott-Jones
ANN MILLER: Lucille Collier
HELEN MIRREN: Ilynea Lydia Mironoff
JONI MITCHELL: Roberta Joan Anderson
MOBY: Richard Melville Hall
MARILYN MONROE: Norma Jean Mortenson (later Baker)
YVES MONTAND: Ivo Livi
RON MOODY: Ronald Moodnick
DEMI MOORE: Demetria Guynes
GARRY MOORE: Thomas Garrison Morfit
RITA MORENO: Rosita Alverio
HARRY MORGAN: Harry Bratsburg
MR. T: Lawrence Tero
PAUL MUNI: Muni Weisenfreund
MIKE NICHOLS: Michael Igor Peschowsky
CHUCK NORRIS: Carlos Ray
NOTORIOUS B.I.G.: Christopher Wallace
HUGH O'BRIAN: Hugh Krampke
MAUREEN O'HARA: Maureen Fitzsimons
OZZY OSBOURNE: John Michael Osbourne
PATTI PAGE: Clara Ann Fowler
JACK PALANCE: Walter Palanuik
BERT PARKS: Bert Jacobson

MINNIE PEARL: Sarah Ophelia Cannon
BERNADETTE PETERS: Bernadette Lazzaro
EDITH PIAF: Edith Gassion
SLIM PICKENS: Louis Lindley
MARY PICKFORD: Gladys Smith
PAULA PRENTISS: Paula Ragusa
ROBERT PRESTON: Robert Preston Meservey
PRINCE: Prince Rogers Nelson
DEE DEE RAMONE: Douglas Colvin
JOEY RAMONE: Jeffrey Hyman
JOHNNY RAMONE: John Cummings
TOMMY RAMONE: Tom Erdelyi
TONY RANDALL: Leonard Rosenberg
MARTHA RAYE: Margaret O'Reed
DONNA REED: Donna Belle Mullenger
DELLA REESE: Delloreese Patricia Early
BUSTA RHYMES: Trevor Smith Jr.
JOAN RIVERS: Joan Sandra Molinsky
EDWARD G. ROBINSON: Emmanuel Goldenberg
THE ROCK: Dwayne Johnson
GINGER ROGERS: Virginia McMath
ROY ROGERS: Leonard Franklin Slye
MICKEY ROONEY: Joe Yule Jr.
JOHNNY ROTTEN: John Lydon
LILLIAN RUSSELL: Helen Leonard
MEG RYAN: Margaret Hyra
WINONA RYDER: Winona Horowitz
SADE: Helen Folsad Abu
SOUPY SALES: Milton Hines
SUSAN SARANDON: Susan Tomaling
SEAL: Samuel Sealhenry
RANDOLPH SCOTT: George Randolph Crane
JANE SEYMOUR: Joyce Frankenberg
OMAR SHARIF: Michael Shalhoub
CHARLIE SHEEN: Carlos Irwin Estevez
MARTIN SHEEN: Ramon Estevez
TALIA SHIRE: Talia Coppola
BEVERLY SILLS: Belle Silverman
GENE SIMMONS: Haim Witz
PHIL SILVERS: Philip Silversmith
SINBAD: David Atkins
SNOOP DOGGY DOG: Calvin Broadus
ANN SOTHERN: Harriette Lake
ROBERT STACK: Robert Modini
BARBARA STANWYCK: Ruby Stevens
JEAN STAPLETON: Jeanne Murray
RINGO STARR: Richard Starkey
CONNIE STEVENS: Concetta Ingolia
STING: Gordon Sumner
JOE STRUMMER: John Graham Mellor
DONNA SUMMER: La Donna Gaines
RIP TAYLOR: Charles Elmer Jr.
ROBERT TAYLOR: Spangler Brugh
DANNY THOMAS: Muzyad Yakhoob, later Amos Jacobs
TINY TIM: Herbert Khaury
RIP TORN: Elmore Rual Torn Jr.
RANDY TRAVIS: Randy Traywick
SOPHIE TUCKER: Sophia Kalish
TINA TURNER: Annie Mae Bullock
TWIGGY: Leslie Hornby
CONWAY TWITTY: Harold Lloyd Jenkins
RUDOLPH VALENTINO: Rudolpho D'Antonguolla
FRANKIE VALLI: Frank Castelluccio
SID VICIOUS: John Simon Ritchie
JOHN WAYNE: Marion Morrison
CLIFTON WEBB: Webb Hollenbeck
RAQUEL WELCH: Raquel Tejada
GENE WILDER: Jerome Silberman
SHELLEY WINTERS: Shirley Schrift
STEVIE WONDER: Stevland Morris
JANE WYMAN: Sarah Jane Fulks
GIG YOUNG: Byron Barr
LORETTA YOUNG: Gretchen Michaels

World Almanac Quick Quiz

Which of the following entertainment personalities is not originally from Canada?

(a) Michael J. Fox   (b) Pamela Anderson   (c) William Shatner   (d) Vince Vaughn

For the answer look in this chapter, or see page 1008.

ARTS AND MEDIA

Some Notable Movies, Sept. 2005 – Aug. 2006

Film	Stars	Director
Barnyard	Courteney Cox, Sam Elliot, Danny Glover, Kevin James	Steve Oedekerk
The Break-Up	Jennifer Aniston, Vince Vaughn	Peyton Reed
Brokeback Mountain	Jake Gyllenhaal, Heath Ledger	Ang Lee
Capote	Chris Cooper, Philip Seymour Hoffman, Catherine Keener	Bennett Miller
Cars	George Carlin, Bonnie Hunt, Paul Newman, Owen Wilson	John Lasseter
Chicken Little	Zach Braff, Joan Cusack, Garry Marshall	Mark Dindal
The Chronicles of Narnia: The Lion, the Witch and the Wardrobe	Jim Broadbent, Tilda Swinton	Andrew Adamson
Clerks II	Jeff Anderson, Rosario Dawson, Brian O'Halloran	Kevin Smith
Click	Kate Beckinsale, Adam Sandler, Christopher Walken	Frank Coraci
The Da Vinci Code	Tom Hanks, Ian McKellen, Audrey Tautou	Ron Howard
Dave Chappelle's Block Party	Dave Chappelle, Mos Def, Kanye West	Michel Gondry
Derailed	Jennifer Aniston, Clive Owen	Mikael Håfström
The Devil Wears Prada	Anne Hathaway, Meryl Streep, Stanley Tucci	David Frankel
Eight Below	Jason Biggs, Paul Walker	Frank Marshall
Failure to Launch	Kathy Bates, Terry Bradshaw, Matthew McConaughey, Sarah Jessica Parker	Tom Dey
The Family Stone	Claire Danes, Diane Keaton, Rachel McAdams, Sarah Jessica Parker, Luke Wilson	Thomas Bezucha
Firewall	Paul Bettany, Harrison Ford, Virginia Madsen	Richard Loncraine
Flightplan	Jodie Foster, Peter Sarsgaard	Robert Schwentke
Fun With Dick & Jane	Alec Baldwin, Jim Carrey, Tea Léoni	Dean Parisot
Good Night, and Good Luck	Patricia Clarkson, George Clooney, David Strathairn	George Clooney
Harry Potter & The Goblet of Fire	Rupert Grint, Daniel Radcliffe, Emma Watson	Mike Newell
A History of Violence	Maria Bello, William Hurt, Viggo Mortensen	David Cronenberg
Hostel	Jay Hernandez, Derek Richardson	Eli Roth
Ice Age: The Meltdown	Queen Latifah, Denis Leary, John Leguizamo, Jay Leno, Ray Romano	Carlos Saldanha
The Illusionist	Jessica Biel, Paul Giamatti, Edward Norton	Neil Burger
In Her Shoes	Toni Collette, Cameron Diaz, Shirley MacLaine	Curtis Hanson
An Inconvenient Truth	Al Gore (Documentary)	Davis Guggenheim
Inside Man	Willem Dafoe, Jodie Foster, Clive Owen, Denzel Washington	Spike Lee
Invincible	Greg Kinnear, Mark Wahlberg	Ericson Core
Jarhead	Jamie Foxx, Jake Gyllenhaal, Peter Sarsgaard	Sam Mendes
King Kong	Jack Black, Adrien Brody, Naomi Watts	Peter Jackson
The Legend of Zorro	Antonio Banderas, Catherine Zeta-Jones	Martin Campbell
Little Miss Sunshine	Alan Arkin, Steve Carell, Toni Collette, Greg Kinnear	Jonathan Dayton & Valerie Faris
Lucky Number Slevin	Morgan Freeman, Josh Hartnett, Ben Kingsley, Lucy Liu, Stanley Tucci, Bruce Willis	Paul McGuigan
Madea's Family Reunion	Tyler Perry, Blair Underwood, Lynn Whitfield	Tyler Perry
Match Point	Scarlett Johansson, Jonathan Rhys Meyers	Woody Allen
Memoirs of a Geisha	Ken Watanabe, Michelle Yeoh, Ziyi Zhang	Rob Marshall
Miami Vice	Colin Farrell, Jamie Foxx	Michael Mann
Mission Impossible 3	Tom Cruise, Philip Seymour Hoffman, Ving Rhames	J.J. Abrams
Monster House	Steve Buscemi, Maggie Gyllenhaal, Jon Heder, Kevin James, Kathleen Turner	Gil Kenan
Munich	Eric Bana, Daniel Craig, Geoffrey Rush	Steven Spielberg
Nacho Libre	Jack Black, Ana de la Reguera, Héctor Jiménez	Jared Hess
North Country	Sean Bean, Frances McDormand, Charlize Theron	Niki Caro
The Omen	Mia Farrow, Liev Schreiber, Julia Stiles	John Moore
Over the Hedge	Steve Carell, Garry Shandling, Wanda Sykes, Bruce Willis	Tim Johnson & Karey Kirkpatrick
Pirates of the Caribbean: Dead Man's Chest	Orlando Bloom, Johnny Depp, Keira Knightley, Bill Nighy	Gore Verbinski
Poseidon	Richard Dreyfuss, Josh Lucas, Emmy Rossum, Kurt Russell	Wolfgang Petersen
A Prairie Home Companion	Garrison Keillor, Kevin Kline, Lindsay Lohan, John C. Reilly, Meryl Streep, Lily Tomlin	Robert Altman
The Squid and the Whale	Jeff Daniels, Laura Linney	Noah Baumbach
Superman Returns	Kate Bosworth, Brandon Routh, Kevin Spacey	Bryan Singer
Syriana	George Clooney, Chris Cooper, Matt Damon, Jeffrey Wright	Stephen Gaghan
Talladega Nights: The Ballad of Ricky Bobby	Sacha Baron Cohen, Will Ferrell, John C. Reilly	Adam McKay
Thank You for Smoking	Maria Bello, Robert Duvall, Aaron Eckhart, Katie Holmes, Rob Lowe, William H. Macy	Jason Reitman
Transamerica	Felicity Huffman, Kevin Zegers	Duncan Tucker
Underworld: Evolution	Kate Beckinsale, Tony Curran, Scott Speedman	Len Wiseman
United 93	David Alan Basche, Richard Bekins, Susan Blommaert	Paul Greengrass
V for Vendetta	Natalie Portman, Hugo Weaving	James McTeigue
Walk the Line	Joaquin Phoenix, Reese Witherspoon	James Mangold
Wallace & Gromit in The Curse of the Were-Rabbit	Ralph Fiennes, Peter Sallis	Nick Park & Steve Box
The Wild	Jim Belushi, Janeane Garofalo, William Shatner, Kiefer Sutherland	Steve Williams
Wordplay	Bill Clinton, Bob Dole, Will Shortz, Jon Stewart (documentary)	Patrick Creadon
World Trade Center	Maria Bello, Nicolas Cage, Maggie Gyllenhaal, Michael Pena	Oliver Stone
X-Men: The Last Stand	Halle Berry, Kelsey Grammer, Hugh Jackman, Famke Janssen, Ian McKellen, Rebecca Romijn, Patrick Stewart	Brett Ratner
You, Me and Dupree	Matt Dillon, Kate Hudson, Owen Wilson	Anthony & Joe Russo
Zathura	Jonah Bobo, Josh Hutcherson, Tim Robbins	Jon Favreau

50 Top-Grossing Movies, 2005

Source: *Variety*, box-office grosses in the U.S. and Canada during calendar year 2005

Rank	Title	Gross (millions)	Rank	Title	Gross (millions)
1.	Star Wars: Episode III—Revenge of the Sith	$380.3	26.	March of the Penguins	$77.4
2.	Harry Potter and the Goblet of Fire	278.7	27.	The Ring Two	75.9
3.	War of the Worlds	234.3	28.	Constantine	75.5
4.	The Chronicles of Narnia: The Lion, the Witch and the Wardrobe	232.1	29.	The Exorcism of Emily Rose	75.1
5.	Wedding Crashers	209.2	30.	Four Brothers	74.5
6.	Charlie and the Chocolate Factory	206.5	31.	Sin City	74.1
7.	Batman Begins	205.3	32.	The Interpreter	72.6
8.	Madagascar	193.2	33.	Fun With Dick and Jane	69.2
9.	Mr. and Mrs. Smith	186.3	34.	Sahara	68.7
10.	King Kong	180.1	35.	Guess Who	68.0
11.	Hitch	177.6	36.	The Aviator	67.3
12.	The Longest Yard	158.1	37.	Coach Carter	67.3
13.	Fantastic Four	154.7	38.	Herbie: Fully Loaded	66.0
14.	Chicken Little	132.5	39.	The Amityville Horror	64.5
15.	Robots	128.2	40.	Sky High	63.9
16.	The Pacifier	113.1	41.	Jarhead	62.5
17.	The 40 Year-Old Virgin	109.3	42.	Bewitched	62.3
18.	Meet the Fockers	103.4	43.	Cinderella Man	61.6
19.	Million Dollar Baby	99.2	44.	Cheaper by the Dozen 2	58.1
20.	Walk the Line	93.3	45.	Red Eye	57.9
21.	Flightplan	89.2	46.	Wallace & Gromit: The Curse of the Were-Rabbit	56.1
22.	Saw II	87.0	47.	White Noise	55.9
23.	Monster-In-Law	82.9	48.	Be Cool	55.8
24.	Are We There Yet?	82.3	49.	Crash	53.4
25.	The Dukes of Hazzard	80.3	50.	Tim Burton's Corpse Bride	53.4

All-Time Top-Grossing American Movies[1]

Source: *Variety* magazine

Rank	Title (original release)	Gross[2]	Rank	Title (original release)	Gross[2]
1.	Titanic (1997)	$600.8	25.	Star Wars: Episode V—The Empire Strikes Back (1980)	$290.3
2.	Star Wars: Episode IV—A New Hope (1977)	461.0	26.	Harry Potter and the Goblet of Fire (2005)	290.0
3.	Shrek 2 (2004)	436.7	27.	Home Alone (1990)	285.8
4.	E.T.: The Extra-Terrestrial (1982)	435.0	28.	The Matrix: Reloaded (2003)	281.5
5.	Star Wars: Episode I—The Phantom Menace (1999)	431.1	29.	Meet the Fockers (2004)	279.2
6.	Pirates of the Carribbean: Dead Man's Chest (2006)	409.1	30.	Shrek (2001)	267.7
7.	Spider-Man (2002)	403.7	31.	Harry Potter and the Chamber of Secrets (2002)	262.0
8.	Star Wars: Episode III—Revenge of the Sith (2005)	380.3	32.	The Incredibles (2004)	261.4
9.	The Lord of the Rings: The Return of the King (2003)	377.0	33.	Dr. Seuss' How the Grinch Stole Christmas (2000)	260.0
10.	Spider-Man 2 (2004)	373.4	34.	Jaws (1975)	260.0
11.	The Passion of the Christ (2004)	370.3	35.	Monsters, Inc. (2001)	255.9
12.	Jurassic Park (1993)	357.1	36.	Batman (1989)	251.2
13.	The Lord of the Rings: The Two Towers (2002)	341.7	37.	Men in Black (1997)	250.7
14.	Finding Nemo (2003)	339.7	38.	Harry Potter and the Prisoner of Azkaban (2004)	249.5
15.	Forrest Gump (1994)	329.7	39.	Toy Story 2 (1999)	245.9
16.	The Lion King (1994)	328.5	40.	Raiders of the Lost Ark (1981)	245.0
17.	Harry Potter and the Sorcerer's Stone (2001)	317.6	41.	Bruce Almighty (2003)	242.7
18.	The Lord of the Rings: The Fellowship of the Ring (2001)	314.8	42.	Twister (1996)	241.7
19.	Star Wars: Episode II—Attack of the Clones (2002)	310.7	43.	My Big Fat Greek Wedding (2002)	241.4
20.	Star Wars: Episode VI—Return of the Jedi (1983)	309.2	44.	Cars (2006)	240.9
21.	Independence Day (1996)	306.2	45.	Ghostbusters (1984)	238.6
22.	Pirates of the Caribbean: The Curse of the Black Pearl (2003)	305.4	46.	Beverly Hills Cop (1984)	234.8
23.	The Sixth Sense (1999)	293.5	47.	War of the Worlds (2005)	234.3
24.	The Chronicles of Narnia: The Lion, the Witch and the Wardrobe (2005)	291.7	48.	X-Men: The Last Stand (2006)	234.3
			49.	Cast Away (2000)	233.6
			50.	The Exorcist (1973)	232.7

(1) Through Sept. 1, 2006. (2) Gross is in millions of absolute dollars based on box office sales in the U.S. and Canada. Rising ticket prices favor newer films. Revenues from re-releases are included.

Top Movie Quotes of All Time

In 2005, the American Film Institute published its list of top (American) movie quotes of all time, based on a jury of 1,500 film artists, critics, and historians.

	Quote	Movie	Year
1.	"Frankly, my dear, I don't give a damn."	*Gone With the Wind*	1939
2.	"I'm going to make him an offer he can't refuse."	*The Godfather*	1972
3.	"You don't understand! I coulda had class. I coulda been a contender. I could've been somebody, instead of a bum, which is what I am."	*On the Waterfront*	1954
4.	"Toto, I've got a feeling we're not in Kansas anymore."	*The Wizard of Oz*	1939
5.	"Here's looking at you, kid."	*Casablanca*	1942
6.	"Go ahead, make my day."	*Sudden Impact*	1983
7.	"All right, Mr. DeMille, I'm ready for my close-up."	*Sunset Blvd.*	1950
8.	"May the Force be with you."	*Star Wars: Episode IV—A New Hope*	1977
9.	"Fasten your seatbelts. It's going to be a bumpy night."	*All About Eve*	1950
10.	"You talking to me?"	*Taxi Driver*	1976

100 Best American Movies of All Time

Source: American Film Institute

Compiled in 1998 based on ballots sent to 1,500 figures, mostly from the film world. Criteria for judging included historical significance, critical recognition and awards, and popularity. The year each film was first released is in parentheses.

1. Citizen Kane (1941)
2. Casablanca (1942)
3. The Godfather (1972)
4. Gone With the Wind (1939)
5. Lawrence of Arabia (1962)
6. The Wizard of Oz (1939)
7. The Graduate (1967)
8. On the Waterfront (1954)
9. Schindler's List (1993)
10. Singin' in the Rain (1952)
11. It's a Wonderful Life (1946)
12. Sunset Boulevard (1950)
13. The Bridge on the River Kwai (1957)
14. Some Like It Hot (1959)
15. Star Wars (1977)
16. All About Eve (1950)
17. The African Queen (1951)
18. Psycho (1960)
19. Chinatown (1974)
20. One Flew Over the Cuckoo's Nest (1975)
21. The Grapes of Wrath (1940)
22. 2001: A Space Odyssey (1968)
23. The Maltese Falcon (1941)
24. Raging Bull (1980)
25. E.T.: The Extra-Terrestrial (1982)
26. Dr. Strangelove (1964)
27. Bonnie and Clyde (1967)
28. Apocalypse Now (1979)
29. Mr. Smith Goes to Washington (1939)
30. Treasure of the Sierra Madre (1948)
31. Annie Hall (1977)
32. The Godfather, Part II (1974)
33. High Noon (1952)
34. To Kill a Mockingbird (1962)
35. It Happened One Night (1934)
36. Midnight Cowboy (1969)
37. The Best Years of Our Lives (1946)
38. Double Indemnity (1944)
39. Doctor Zhivago (1965)
40. North by Northwest (1959)
41. West Side Story (1961)
42. Rear Window (1954)
43. King Kong (1933)
44. The Birth of a Nation (1915)
45. A Streetcar Named Desire (1951)
46. A Clockwork Orange (1971)
47. Taxi Driver (1976)
48. Jaws (1975)
49. Snow White and the Seven Dwarfs (1937)
50. Butch Cassidy and the Sundance Kid (1969)
51. The Philadelphia Story (1940)
52. From Here to Eternity (1953)
53. Amadeus (1984)
54. All Quiet on the Western Front (1930)
55. The Sound of Music (1965)
56. M*A*S*H (1970)
57. The Third Man (1949)
58. Fantasia (1940)
59. Rebel Without a Cause (1955)
60. Raiders of the Lost Ark (1981)
61. Vertigo (1958)
62. Tootsie (1982)
63. Stagecoach (1939)
64. Close Encounters of the Third Kind (1977)
65. The Silence of the Lambs (1991)
66. Network (1976)
67. The Manchurian Candidate (1962)
68. An American in Paris (1951)
69. Shane (1953)
70. The French Connection (1971)
71. Forrest Gump (1994)
72. Ben-Hur (1959)
73. Wuthering Heights (1939)
74. The Gold Rush (1925)
75. Dances With Wolves (1990)
76. City Lights (1931)
77. American Graffiti (1973)
78. Rocky (1976)
79. The Deer Hunter (1978)
80. The Wild Bunch (1969)
81. Modern Times (1936)
82. Giant (1956)
83. Platoon (1986)
84. Fargo (1996)
85. Duck Soup (1933)
86. Mutiny on the Bounty (1935)
87. Frankenstein (1931)
88. Easy Rider (1969)
89. Patton (1970)
90. The Jazz Singer (1927)
91. My Fair Lady (1964)
92. A Place in the Sun (1951)
93. The Apartment (1960)
94. Goodfellas (1990)
95. Pulp Fiction (1994)
96. The Searchers (1956)
97. Bringing Up Baby (1938)
98. Unforgiven (1992)
99. Guess Who's Coming to Dinner (1967)
100. Yankee Doodle Dandy (1942)

National Film Registry, 1989-2005

Source: National Film Registry, Library of Congress

"Culturally, historically, or aesthetically significant" American films placed on the registry. * = selected in 2005.

Abbott and Costello Meet Frankenstein (1948)
Adam's Rib (1949)
The Adventures of Robin Hood (1938)
The African Queen (1951)
Alien (1979)
All About Eve (1950)
All My Babies (1953)
All That Heaven Allows (1955)
All That Jazz (1979)
All Quiet on the Western Front (1930)
All the King's Men (1949)
An American in Paris (1951)
America, America (1963)
American Graffiti (1973)
A Movie (1958)
Annie Hall (1977)
Antonia: A Portrait of the Woman (1974)
The Apartment (1960)
Apocalypse Now (1979)
Atlantic City (1980)
The Awful Truth (1937)
Baby Face (1933)*
The Bad and the Beautiful (1952)
Badlands (1973)
The Band Wagon (1953)
The Bank Dick (1940)
The Battle of San Pietro (1945)
Beauty and the Beast (1991)
Ben-Hur (1926)
Ben-Hur (1959)
The Best Years of Our Lives (1946)
Big Business (1929)
The Big Parade (1925)
The Big Sleep (1946)
The Birth of a Nation (1915)
The Black Pirate (1926)
Blacksmith Scene (1893)
The Black Stallion (1979)
Blade Runner (1982)
The Blood of Jesus (1941)
The Blue Bird (1918)
Bonnie and Clyde (1967)
Boyz N the Hood (1991)
Bride of Frankenstein (1935)
The Bridge on the River Kwai (1957)
Bringing Up Baby (1938)
Broken Blossoms (1919)
A Bronx Morning (1931)
The Buffalo Creek Flood: An Act of Man (1975)*
Butch Cassidy and the Sundance Kid (1969)
Cabaret (1972)

The Cameraman (1928)*
Carmen Jones (1954)
Casablanca (1942)
Castro Street (1966)
Cat People (1942)
Chan Is Missing (1982)
The Cheat (1915)
The Chechahcos (1924)
Chinatown (1974)
Chulas Fronteras (1976)
Citizen Kane (1941)
The City (1939)
City Lights (1931)
Civilization (1916)
Clash of the Wolves (1925)
Cologne: From the Diary of Ray and Esther (1939)
Commandment Keeper Church, Beaufort South Carolina, May 1940 (1940)*
The Conversation (1974)
Cool Hand Luke (1967)*
The Cool World (1963)
Cops (1922)
A Corner in Wheat (1909)
The Court Jester (1956)
The Crowd (1928)
Czechoslovakia 1968 (1968)
Daughters of the Dust (1991)
David Holzman's Diary (1968)
The Day the Earth Stood Still (1951)
Dead Birds (1964)
The Deer Hunter (1978)
Destry Rides Again (1939)
Detour (1946)
Dickson Experimental Sound Film (1894-95)
D.O.A. (1950)
Dodsworth (1936)
The Docks of New York (1928)
Dog Star Man (1964)
Don't Look Back (1967)
Do the Right Thing (1989)
Double Indemnity (1944)
Dracula (1931)
Dr. Strangelove (or, How I Learned to Stop Worrying and Love the Bomb) (1964)
Duck Amuck (1953)
Duck and Cover (1951)
Duck Soup (1933)
Easy Rider (1969)
Eaux D'Artifice (1953)
El Norte (1983)
The Emperor Jones (1933)

Empire (1964)
The Endless Summer (1966)
Enter the Dragon (1973)
Eraserhead (1978)
E.T.: The Extra-Terrestrial (1982)
Evidence of the Film (1913)
The Exploits of Elaine (1914)
The Fall of the House of Usher (1928)
Fantasia (1940)
Fast Times at Ridgemont High (1982)*
Fatty's Tintype Tangle (1915)
Film Portrait (1970)
Five Easy Pieces (1970)
Flash Gordon serial (1936)
Footlight Parade (1933)
Force of Evil (1948)
The Forgotten Frontier (1931)
42nd Street (1933)
The Four Horsemen of the Apocalypse (1921)
Fox Movietone News: Jenkins Orphanage Band (1928)
Frankenstein (1931)
Frank Film (1973)
Freaks (1932)
The French Connection (1971)*
The Freshman (1925)
From Here to Eternity (1953)
From the Manger to the Cross (1912)
From Stump to Ship (1930)
Fuji (1974)
Fury (1936)
Garlic is as Good as Ten Mothers (1980)
The General (1927)
Gerald McBoing Boing (1951)
Gertie the Dinosaur (1914)
Giant (1956)*
Gigi (1958)
The Godfather (1972)
The Godfather, Part II (1974)
Going My Way (1944)
Gold Diggers of 1933 (1933)
The Gold Rush (1925)
Gone With the Wind (1939)
GoodFellas (1990)
The Graduate (1967)
The Grapes of Wrath (1940)
Grass (1925)
The Great Dictator (1940)
The Great Train Robbery (1903)
Greed (1924)
Gun Crazy (1949)
Gunga Din (1939)

H2O (1929)*
Hands Up (1926)*
Harlan County, U.S.A. (1976)
Harold and Maude (1972)
The Heiress (1949)
Hell's Hinges (1916)
High Noon (1952)
High School (1968)
Hindenburg Disaster Newsreel Footage (1937)
His Girl Friday (1940)
The Hitch-Hiker (1953)
Hoop Dreams (1994)*
Hoosiers (1986)
Hospital (1970)
The Hospital (1971)
The House in the Middle (1954)
House of Usher (1960)*
How Green Was My Valley (1941)
How the West Was Won (1962)
The Hunters (1957)
The Hustler (1961)
I Am a Fugitive from a Chain Gang (1932)
Imitation of Life (1934)*
The Immigrant (1917)
In the Heat of the Night (1967)
In the Land of the Head-Hunters aka In the
    Land of the War Canoes (1914)
Intolerance (1916)
Invasion of the Body Snatchers (1956)
It (1927)
It Happened One Night (1934)
It's a Wonderful Life (1946)
The Italian (1915)
Jailhouse Rock (1957)
Jammin' the Blues (1944)
Jam Session (1942)
Jaws (1975)
Jazz on a Summer's Day (1959)
The Jazz Singer (1927)
Jeffries-Johnson World's Championship
    Boxing Contest (1910)*
Kannapolis, NC (1941)
Killer of Sheep (1977)
King: A Filmed Record . . . Montgomery to
    Memphis (1970)
King Kong (1933)
The Kiss (1896)
Kiss Me Deadly (1955)
Knute Rockne, All American (1940)
Koyaanisqatsi (1983)
The Lady Eve (1941)
Lady Helen's Escapade (1909)
Lady Windermere's Fan (1925)
Lambchops (1929)
The Land Beyond the Sunset (1912)
Lassie Come Home (1943)
The Last of the Mohicans (1920)
The Last Picture Show (1972)
Laura (1944)
Lawrence of Arabia (1962)
The Learning Tree (1969)
Let's All Go to the Lobby (1957)
Letter From an Unknown Woman (1948)
The Life and Death of 9413—A Hollywood
    Extra (1928)
Life and Times of Rosie the Riveter (1980)
The Life of Emile Zola (1937)
Little Caesar (1930)
The Little Fugitive (1953)
Little Miss Marker (1934)
The Living Desert (1953)
The Lost World (1925)
Louisiana Story (1948)
Love Finds Andy Hardy (1938)
Love Me Tonight (1932)
Magical Maestro (1952)
The Magnificent Ambersons (1942)
Making of an American (1920)*
The Maltese Falcon (1941)
The Manchurian Candidate (1962)
Manhattan (1921)
Manhattan (1979)
March of Time: Inside Nazi Germany—1938
    (1938)
Marian Anderson: The Lincoln Memorial
    Concert (1939)
Marty (1955)
M*A*S*H (1970)
Master Hands (1936)
Matrimony's Speed Limit (1913)
Mean Streets (1973)
Medium Cool (1969)
Meet Me in St. Louis (1944)
Melody Ranch (1940)
Memphis Belle (1944)
Meshes of the Afternoon (1943)

Midnight Cowboy (1969)
Mildred Pierce (1945)
The Miracle of Morgan's Creek (1944)
Miracle on 34th Street (1947)*
Miss Lulu Bett (1921)
Modern Times (1936)
Modesta (1956)
Mom and Dad (1944)*
Morocco (1930)
Motion Painting No. 1 (1947)
Mr. Smith Goes to Washington (1939)
Multiple Sidosis (1970)
The Music Box (1932)
The Music Man (1962)*
My Darling Clementine (1946)
My Man Godfrey (1936)
The Naked Spur (1953)
Nanook of the North (1922)
Nashville (1975)
National Lampoon's Animal House (1978)
National Velvet (1944)
Naughty Marietta (1935)
Network (1976)
A Night at the Opera (1935)
The Night of the Hunter (1955)
Night of the Living Dead (1968)
Ninotchka (1939)
North by Northwest (1959)
Nostalgia (1971)
Nothing but a Man (1964)
The Nutty Professor (1963)
OffOn (1968)
One Flew Over the Cuckoo's Nest (1975)
One Froggy Evening (1956)
On the Waterfront (1954)
The Outlaw Josey Wales (1976)
Out of the Past (1947)
The Ox-Bow Incident (1943)
Pass the Gravy (1928)
Paths of Glory (1957)
Patton (1970)
The Pearl (1948)
Peter Pan (1924)
Phantom of the Opera (1925)
The Philadelphia Story (1940)
Pinocchio (1940)
A Place in the Sun (1951)
Planet of the Apes (1968)
The Plow That Broke the Plains (1936)
Point of Order (1964)
The Poor Little Rich Girl (1917)
Popeye the Sailor Meets Sindbad the Sailor
    (1936)
Porky in Wackyland (1938)
Power of the Press (1928)*
Powers of Ten (1978)
President McKinley Inauguration Footage
    (1901)
Primary (1960)
Princess Nicotine; or The Smoke Fairy (1909)
The Prisoner of Zenda (1937)
The Producers (1968)
Psycho (1960)
The Public Enemy (1931)
Pull My Daisy (1959)
Punch Drunks (1934)
Pups is Pups (Our Gang) (1930)
Raging Bull (1980)
Raiders of the Lost Ark (1981)
A Raisin in the Sun (1961)*
Rear Window (1954)
Rebel Without a Cause (1955)
Red River (1948)
Regeneration (1915)
Republic Steel Strike Riots Newsreel
    Footage (1937)
Return of the Secaucus 7 (1980)
Ride the High Country (1962)
Rip Van Winkle (1896)
The River (1937)
Road to Morocco (1942)
The Rocky Horror Picture Show (1975)*
Roman Holiday (1953)
Rose Hobart (1936)
Sabrina (1954)
Safety Last (1923)
Salesman (1969)
Salomé (1922)
Salt of the Earth (1954)
San Francisco Earthquake and Fire, April
    18,1906 (1906)*
Scarface (1932)
Schindler's List (1993)
The Searchers (1956)
Serene Velocity (1970)

Seven Brides for Seven Brothers (1954)
Seventh Heaven (1927)
Shadow of a Doubt (1943)
Shadows (1959)
Shaft (1971)
Shane (1953)
She Done Him Wrong (1933)
Sherlock, Jr. (1924)
Sherman's March (1986)
Shock Corridor (1963)
The Shop Around the Corner (1940)
Show Boat (1936)
Show People (1928)
Singin' in the Rain (1952)
Sky High (1922)
Snow White (1933)
Snow White and the Seven Dwarfs (1937)
Some Like It Hot (1959)
The Son of the Sheik (1926)
The Sound of Music (1965)
Stagecoach (1939)
A Star Is Born (1954)
Star Theatre (1901)
Star Wars (1977)
Steamboat Willie (1928)
Stranger Than Paradise (1984)
A Streetcar Named Desire (1951)
The Sting (1973)*
Stormy Weather (1943)
Sullivan's Travels (1941)
Sunrise (1927)
Sunset Boulevard (1950)
Sweet Smell of Success (1957)
Swing Time (1936)
Tabu (1931)
Tacoma Narrows Bridge Collapse (1940)
The Tall T (1957)
Tarzan and His Mate (1934)
Taxi Driver (1976)
The Ten Commandments (1956)
The Tell-Tale Heart (1953)
Tevye (1939)
Theodore Case Sound Tests: Gus Visser
    and His Singing Duck (1925)
There It Is (1928)
The Thief of Bagdad (1924)
The Thin Blue Line (1988)
The Thing From Another World (1951)
The Thin Man (1934)
This Is Cinerama (1952)
This Is Spinal Tap (1984)
Through Navajo Eyes (series) (1966)
A Time for Burning (1966)*
Tin Toy (1988)
To Be or Not To Be (1942)
To Fly (1976)
To Kill a Mockingbird (1962)
Tootsie (1982)
Topaz (1943-45)
Top Hat (1935)
Touch of Evil (1958)
Toy Story (1995)*
Trance and Dance in Bali (1936-39)
The Treasure of the Sierra Madre (1948)
Trouble in Paradise (1932)
Tulips Shall Grow (1942)
Twelve O'Clock High (1949)
2001: A Space Odyssey (1968)
Unforgiven (1992)
Verbena Tragica (1939)
Vertigo (1958)
The Wedding March (1928)
Westinghouse Works 1904 (1904)
West Side Story (1961)
What's Opera, Doc? (1957)
Where Are My Children? (1916)
White Heat (1949)
Why Man Creates (1968)
Why We Fight (Series/1943-45)
Wild and Wooly (1917)
The Wild Bunch (1969)
Wild River (1960)
Will Success Spoil Rock Hunter? (1957)
The Wind (1928)
Wings (1927)
Within Our Gates (1920)
The Wizard of Oz (1939)
Woman of the Year (1942)
A Woman Under the Influence (1974)
Woodstock (1970)
Yankee Doodle Dandy (1942)
Young Frankenstein (1974)
Young Mr. Lincoln (1939)
Zapruder Film (1963)

Most Popular Movie Videos/DVDs

Source: Compiled industry sources, provided by Alexander & Associates, New York, NY.
Note: Year given to distinguish from other films with the same title.

All-Time Top Ten Rentals VHS [1]

1. Top Gun
2. Pretty Woman
3. The Little Mermaid
4. Cinderella
5. Home Alone
6. Ghost
7. The Lion King
8. Forrest Gump
9. Terminator II: Judgment Day
10. Dances With Wolves

All-Time Top Ten Rentals DVD [3]

1. The Fast and the Furious
2. The Matrix
3. Gladiator (2000)
4. The Lord of the Rings: The Fellowship of the Ring
5. Shrek
6. Training Day
7. Pearl Harbor (2001)
8. Black Hawk Down
9. Spider-Man (2002)
10. My Big Fat Greek Wedding

2005 Top Ten Rental Titles DVD/VHS [4]

1. National Treasure
2. Meet the Fockers
3. Hitch
4. Ladder 49
5. The Notebook
6. Without a Paddle
7. The Longest Yard (2005)
8. Guess Who
9. The Pacifier
10. Monster-in-Law

All-Time Top Ten Purchase Titles VHS [2]

1. The Lion King
2. Cinderella
3. Snow White and the Seven Dwarfs
4. Forrest Gump
5. Aladdin
6. Toy Story
7. Jurassic Park
8. Pocahontas
9. Beauty and the Beast
10. The Little Mermaid

All-Time Top Ten Purchase Titles DVD [3]

1. The Lord of the Rings: The Fellowship of the Ring
2. Shrek
3. Harry Potter and the Sorcerer's Stone
4. Spider-Man (2002)
5. Gladiator (2000)
6. Monsters Inc.
7. The Fast and the Furious
8. The Matrix
9. Finding Nemo
10. A Knight's Tale

2005 Top Ten Purchase Titles DVD/VHS [4]

1. The Incredibles
2. Madagascar
3. Star Wars: Episode III—Revenge of the Sith
4. Shark Tale
5. The Polar Express
6. National Treasure
7. Meet the Fockers
8. Batman Begins
9. War of the Worlds (2005)
10. Ray

(1) March 1, 1987, to Dec. 31, 2004. (2) Feb. 16, 1988, to Dec. 31, 2004. (3) Jan. 1, 2000, to Dec. 31, 2004. (4) Jan. 1, 2005-Dec. 31, 2005. Due to the shrinking VHS market share, VHS and DVD figures are combined.

Top-Selling Video Games, 2005

Source: The NPD Group / NPD Funworld / Point-of-Sale; ranked by units sold.

Title, Platform

1. Madden NFL 2006, Sony PlayStation 2
2. Pokemon Emerald, Nintendo Game Boy Advance
3. Gran Turismo 4, Sony PlayStation 2
4. Madden NFL 2006, Microsoft Xbox
5. NCAA Football 2006, Sony PlayStation 2

Title, Platform

6. Star Wars: Battlefront II, Sony PlayStation 2
7. MVP Baseball 2005, Sony PlayStation 2
8. Star Wars Episode III: Revenge of the Sith, Sony PlayStation 2
9. NBA Live 2006, Sony PlayStation 2
10. Lego Star Wars, Sony PlayStation 2

Broadway Season Statistics, 1959-2006

Source: The League of American Theatres and Producers, Inc., New York, NY

Season	Gross (mil $)	Attendance (mil)	Playing Weeks	New Productions	Season	Gross (mil $)	Attendance (mil)	Playing Weeks	New Productions
1959-1960	46	7.9	1,156	58	1983-1984	227	7.9	1,097	36
1960-1961	44	7.7	1,210	48	1984-1985	209	7.3	1,078	33
1961-1962	44	6.8	1,166	53	1985-1986	190	6.5	1,041	34
1962-1963	44	7.4	1,134	54	1986-1987	208	7.1	1,039	41
1963-1964	40	6.8	1,107	63	1987-1988	253	8.1	1,113	30
1964-1965	50	8.2	1,250	67	1988-1989	262	8.1	1,108	33
1965-1966	54	9.6	1,295	68	1989-1990	282	8.0	1,070	40
1966-1967	55	9.3	1,269	69	1990-1991	267	7.3	971	28
1967-1968	59	9.5	1,259	74	1991-1992	293	7.4	905	37
1968-1969	58	8.6	1,209	67	1992-1993	328	7.9	1,019	34
1969-1970	53	7.1	1,047	62	1993-1994	356	8.1	1,066	39
1970-1971	55	7.4	1,107	49	1994-1995	406	9.0	1,120	33
1971-1972	52	6.5	1,157	55	1995-1996	436	9.5	1,146	38
1972-1973	45	5.4	889	55	1996-1997	499	10.6	1,349	37
1973-1974	46	5.7	907	43	1997-1998	558	11.5	1,442	33
1974-1975	57	6.6	1,101	54	1998-1999	588	11.7	1,441	39
1975-1976	71	7.3	1,136	55	1999-2000	603	11.4	1,464	37
1976-1977	93	8.8	1,349	54	2000-2001	666	11.9	1,484	28
1977-1978	114	9.6	1,433	42	2001-2002	643	11.0	1,434	28
1978-1979	134	9.6	1,542	50	2002-2003	721	11.4	1,544	36
1979-1980	146	9.6	1,540	61	2003-2004	771	11.6	1,451	39
1980-1981	197	11.0	1,544	60	2004-2005	769	11.5	1,494	39
1981-1982	223	10.1	1,455	48	2005-2006	862	12.0	1,501	39
1982-1983	209	8.4	1,258	50					

IT'S A FACT: Americans watched a record amount of television during the 2005-06 TV season: the average household had a television on for 8 hours, 11 minutes per day, according to Nielsen Media Research. Individual viewers watched a record 4 hours and 35 minutes of television each day. Many media observers and critics had predicted that television viewing time would be eroded by time spent on new media. Since 1995-96, however, average household television viewing is up by nearly an hour per day, from 7 hours and 15 minutes.

Top 50 Record Long-Run Broadway Plays[1]

Source: The League of American Theatres and Producers, Inc., New York, NY

Title (Run) Performances	Title (Run) Performances	Title (Run) Performances
1. *The Phantom of the Opera (1988-) 7,755	18. Annie (1977-83) 2,377	35. Hair (1968-72) 1,750
2. Cats (1982-2000) 7,485	Cabaret (revival, 1998-2004) . 2,377	36. *Hairspray (2002-) 1,685
3. Les Misérables (1987-2003) . . 6,680	20. Man of La Mancha (1965-71) . . 2,328	37. The Wiz (1975-79) 1,672
4. A Chorus Line (1975-90) 6,137	21. Abie's Irish Rose (1922-27) . . 2,327	38. Born Yesterday (1946-49) 1,642
5. Oh! Calcutta! (revival, 1976-89) 5,959	22. *The Producers (2001-) 2,235	39. Crazy For You (1992-96) 1,622
6. *Beauty and the Beast (1994-) 5,080	23. Oklahoma! (1943-48) 2,212	40. Ain't Misbehavin' (1978-82) . . 1,604
7. *Rent (1996-) 4,301	24. Smokey Joe's Cafe (1995- 2000). 2,036	41. The Best Little Whorehouse in Texas (1978-82) 1,584
8. Miss Saigon (1991-2001) 4,092	25. *Mamma Mia! (2001-) 2,026	42. Mary, Mary (1961-64) 1,572
9. *Chicago (revival, 1996-) . . . 4,080	26. Pippin (1972-77) 1,944	43. Evita (1979-83) 1,567
10. *The Lion King (1997-) 3,633	27. South Pacific (1949-54) 1,925	44. The Voice of the Turtle (1943- 48) 1,557
11. 42nd Street (1980-89) 3,486	28. The Magic Show (1974-78) . . 1,920	
12. Grease (1972-80) 3,388	29. Aida (2000-04) 1,852	45. Jekyll & Hyde (1997-2001) . . 1,543
13. Fiddler on the Roof (1964-72) . 3,242	30. Gemini (1977-81) 1,819	46. Barefoot in the Park (1963-67) 1,530
14. Life With Father (1939-47) . . . 3,224	31. Deathtrap (1978-82) 1,793	47. 42nd Street (revival, 2001-05) 1,524
15. Tobacco Road (1933-41) 3,182	32. Harvey (1944-49) 1,775	48. Dreamgirls (1981-85) 1,521
16. Hello, Dolly! (1964-70). 2,844	33. Dancin' (1978-82) 1,774	49. Mame (1966-70) 1,508
17. My Fair Lady (1956-62). 2,717	34. La Cage aux Folles (1983-87) 1,761	50. Grease (revival, 1994-98). . . . 1,505

*Still running Sept. 1, 2006. (1) Unless noted, listings reflect a play's first run on Broadway. (2) Number of performances through Sept. 1, 2006.

U.S. Symphony Orchestras[1]

Source: American Symphony Orchestra League

Symphony Orchestra[2]	Music Director[3]	Symphony Orchestra[2]	Music Director[3]
Akron (OH)	Christopher P. Wilkins	Memphis (TN)	David Loebel
Alabama (Birmingham)	Justin Brown	Milwaukee (WI)	Andreas Delfs
American (New York, NY)	Leon Botstein	Minnesota Orch. (Minneapolis)	Osmo Vänskä
Arkansas (Little Rock)	David Itkin	Modesto Assn. (CA)	Darryl One
Atlanta (GA)	Robert Spano	Monterey Symphony (Carmel, CA)	Max Bragado-Darman
Austin (TX)	Peter Bay	Music of the Baroque (Chicago, IL)	Jane Glover
Baltimore (MD)	Marin Alsop	Napa Valley Symphony (CA)	Asher Raboy
Baton Rouge Symphony (LA)	Timothy Muffitt	Naples Philharmonic (FL)	Jorge Mester
Boston (MA)	James Levine	Nashville Symphony (TN)	Leonard Slatkin
Brooklyn Philharmonic Orch. (NY)	Michael Christie	National (Washington, DC)	Leonard Slatkin
Buffalo Philharmonic Orch. (NY)	JoAnn Falletta	New Haven (CT)	Jung-Ho Pak
Chamber Orch. of Philadelphia (PA)	Ignat Solzhenitsyn	New Jersey (Newark)	Neeme Järvi
Charleston (SC)	David Stahl	New Mexico (Albuquerque)	Guillermo Figueroa
Charlotte Symphony (NC)	Christof Perick	New West (Thousand Oaks, CA)	Boris Brott
Chattanooga Symphony and Opera Assn. (TN)	Robert E. Bernhardt	New World Symphony (Miami Beach, FL)	Michael Tilson Thomas
Chicago (IL)	Bernard Haitink & Pierre Boulez	New York Philharmonic (NYC)	Lorin Maazel
		New York Pops (NYC)	vacant
Chicago Sinfonietta (IL)	Paul Freeman	North Carolina Symphony (Raleigh)	Grant Llewellyn
Cincinnati (OH)	Paavo Järvi	Oklahoma City Philharmonic (OK)	Joel A. Levine
Cleveland Orch. (OH)	Franz Welser-Möst	Omaha Symphony (NE)	Thomas A. Wilkins
Colorado (Denver)	Jeffrey Kahane	Orch. of St. Luke's (NYC)	Donald Runnicles
Colorado Springs Philharmonic (CO)	Lawrence L. Smith	Oregon Symphony (Portland)	Carlos Kalmar
Columbus (OH)	Gunther Herbig	Orlando Philharmonic Orch. (FL)	Christopher P. Wilkins
Dallas (TX)	vacant	Orpheus Chamber Orch. (NYC)	Committee
Dayton Philharmonic Orch. (OH)	Neal Gittleman	Pacific Symphony (Santa Ana, CA)	Carl St. Clair
Delaware (Wilmington)	David Amado	Pasadena Symphony (CA)	Jorge Mester
Des Moines Symphony (IA)	Joseph S. Giunta	Philadelphia (PA)	Christoph Eschenbach
Detroit (MI)	Thomas A. Wilkins	Philharmonia Baroque Orch (CA)	Nicholas McGegan
Elgin (IL)	Robert Hanson	Phoenix Symphony (AZ)	Michael Christie
Evansville Philharmonic Orch. (IN)	Alfred Savia	Pittsburgh (PA)	Sir Andrew Davis
Florida (Tampa)	Stefan Sanderling	Portland (ME)	Toshiyuki Shimada
Florida West Coast (Sarasota)	Andrew D. Lane	Puerto Rico (PR)	Guillermo Figueroa
Fort Wayne Philharmonic Orch. (IN)	Edvard Tchivzhel	Quad City (IA)	Donald Schleicher
Fort Worth (TX)	Miguel Harth-Bedoya	Rhode Island Philharmonic (RI)	Larry Rachleff
Grand Rapids Symphony (MI)	David Lockington	Richmond Symphony (VA)	Mark Russell Smith
Grant Park Orch. and Chorus (Chicago, IL)	Carlos Kalmar	Roanoke (VA)	David S. Wiley
		Rochester Philharmonic Orch. (NY)	Christopher Seaman
Greenville (SC)	Edvard Tchivzhel	St. Louis (MO)	David Robertson
Handel & Haydn Society Orch. (Boston)	Christopher Hogwood	St. Paul Chamber Orchestra (MN)	Committee
Harrisburg Symphony Assn. (PA)	Stuart Malina	San Antonio Symphony (TX)	Larry Rachleff
Hartford (CT)	Edward Cumming	San Diego Symphony (CA)	Jahja Ling
Honolulu (HI)	vacant	San Francisco Symphony (CA)	Michael Tilson Thomas
Houston Symphony (TX)	Hans Graf	Santa Barbara (CA)	Nir Kabaretti
Indianapolis (IN)	Mario Venzago	Santa Rosa Symphony (CA)	Bruno Ferrandis
Jacksonville (FL)	Fabio Mechetti	Seattle Symphony (WA)	Gerard Schwarz
Jazz Arts Group/Columbus Jazz Orch. (OH)	Byron Stripling	Shreveport (LA)	Michael Butterman
		Spokane (WA)	Eckart Preu
Kalamazoo (MI)	Raymond C. Harvey	Springfield (MA)	Kevin Rhodes
Kansas City Symphony (MO)	Michael Stern	Symphony Silicon Valley (San Jose, CA)	vacant
Knoxville (TN)	Lucas Richman	Syracuse (NY)	Daniel Hege
Long Beach (CA)	Enrique Arturo Diemecke	Toledo (OH)	Stefan Sanderling
		Tucson (AZ)	George Hanson
Long Island Philharmonic (NY)	David S. Wiley	Utah Symphony and Opera (Salt Lake City)	Keith Lockhart
Los Angeles Chamber Orch. (CA)	Jeffrey Kahane	Virginia Symphony (VA)	JoAnn Falletta
Los Angeles Philharmonic (CA)	Esa-Pekka Salonen	West Virginia (Charleston)	Grant Cooper
Louisiana Philharmonic Orch (New Orleans)	Carlos Miguel Prieto	Wichita (KS)	Andrew Sewell
Louisville (KY)	vacant	Wisconsin Chamber Orch (Madison)	Andrew Sewell
Madison (WI)	John DeMain	Youngstown (OH)	vacant

(1) As of Sept. 2006. Includes only orchestras with annual expenses $1.8 mil or greater. (2) If only place name is given, add Symphony Orchestra. (3) General title; listed is highest-ranking member of conducting personnel.

U.S. Opera Companies[1]

Source: OPERA America; as of Sept. 2006.

Anchorage Opera (AK); Ed Bourgeois, gen. dir.
Arizona Opera (Tucson/Phoenix); Joel Revzen, gen./art. dir.
Atlanta Opera (GA); Dennis Hanthorn, gen. dir.
Austin Lyric Opera (TX); Richard Buckley, art. dir.
Baltimore Opera Company (MD); Michael Harrison, gen. dir.
Boston Lyric Opera (MA); Janice Mancini Del Sesto, gen. dir.
Central City Opera (CO); Pelham G. Pearce, gen. dir.
Chautauqua Opera (NY); Jay Lesenger, gen./art. dir.
Chicago Opera Theater (IL); Brian Dickie, gen. dir.
Cincinnati Opera (OH); Evans Mirageas, art. dir.
Cleveland Opera (OH); Robert Chumbley, gen. dir.
Connecticut Opera (Hartford); Willie Anthony Waters, gen./art. dir.
Dallas Opera (TX); Karen Stone, gen. dir.
Dayton Opera Association (OH); Thomas Bankston, gen./art. dir.
Des Moines Metro Opera, Inc. (IA); Robert L. Larsen, art. dir.
Florentine Opera Company, Inc. (Milwaukee, WI); William Florescu, gen. dir.
Florida Grand Opera (Miami, FL); Robert M. Heuer, gen. dir.
Fort Worth Opera Association (TX); Darren K. Woods, gen. dir.
Glimmerglass Opera (Cooperstown, NY); Michael McLeod, gen./art. dir.
Hawaii Opera Theatre (Honolulu); Henry G. Akina, gen./art. dir.
Houston Grand Opera (TX); Anthony Freud, gen. dir.
Indianapolis Opera (IN); James Caraher, art. dir.
Kentucky Opera (Louisville); David Roth, gen. dir.
Knoxville Opera Company (TN); Brian Salesky, gen. dir.
Los Angeles Opera (CA); Plácido Domingo, gen. dir.
Lyric Opera of Chicago (IL); William Mason, gen. dir.
Lyric Opera of Kansas City (MO); Evan R. Luskin, gen. dir.
Madison Opera (WI); Allan Naplan, gen. dir.
Metropolitan Opera (New York, NY); James Levine, art. dir.

Michigan Opera Theatre (Detroit); David DiChiera, gen. dir.
Minnesota Opera Company (Minneapolis); Dale Johnson, art. dir.
Nashville Opera Assn. (TN); John Hoomes, gen. art. dir.
New Orleans Opera Association (LA); Robert Lyall, gen./art. dir.
New York City Opera (NY); Paul Kellogg, gen./art. dir.
Opera Boston (MA); Carole Charnow, gen. dir.
Opera Carolina (Charlotte, NC); James Meena, gen. dir.
Opera Colorado (Denver); Peter Russell, gen. dir.
Opera Columbus (OH); William Boggs, art. dir.
Opera Company of Philadelphia (PA); Robert B. Driver, gen./art. dir.
Opera Memphis (TN); Michael Ching, art. dir.
Opera Omaha, Inc. (NE); Joan Desens, gen. dir.
Opera Pacific (Irvine, CA); John DeMain, art. dir.
Opera Theatre of Saint Louis (MO); Charles MacKay, gen. dir.
Orlando Opera (FL); Robert Swedberg, gen. dir.
Palm Beach Opera, Inc. (FL); William Ryberg, gen. dir.
Pittsburgh Opera (PA); Mark Weinstein, gen. dir.
Portland Opera (OR); Christopher Mattaliano, gen. dir.
Sacramento Opera (CA); Timm Rolek, art. dir.
San Diego Opera Association (CA); Ian D. Campbell, gen. dir.
San Francisco Opera (CA); David Gockley, gen. dir.
Santa Fe Opera (NM); Richard Gaddes, gen. dir.
Sarasota Opera (FL); Victor DeRenzi, art. dir.
Seattle Opera (WA); Speight Jenkins, gen. dir.
Skylight Opera Theatre (Milwaukee, WI); Bill Theisen, art. dir.
Syracuse Opera (NY); Catherine Wolff, gen. dir.
Tulsa Opera (OK); Carol I. Crawford, gen. dir.
Utah Symphony & Opera (Salt Lake City); Christopher McBeth, art. dir.
Virginia Opera (Norfolk, Richmond, Fairfax); Peter Mark, art. dir.
Washington National Opera (DC); Plácido Domingo, gen. dir.

(1) Includes only opera companies with budgets of $1 mil or more.

Some Notable U.S. Museums

This unofficial list of some of the largest (by budget) museums in the U.S. was compiled with the assistance of the American Association of Museums, a national association representing the concerns of the museum community. Association members also include zoos, aquariums, arboretums, botanical gardens, and planetariums, but these are not included in *The World Almanac* listing.

Museum	City	State	Museum	City	State
American Museum of Natural History	New York	NY	Minneapolis Institute of Art	Minneapolis	MN
Amon Carter Museum of Western Art	Ft. Worth	TX	Museum of African American History	Detroit	MI
The Art Institute of Chicago	Chicago	IL	Museum of the American West	Los Angeles	CA
Brooklyn Museum of Art	Brooklyn	NY	Museum of Contemporary Art	Los Angeles	CA
Busch-Reisinger Museum	Cambridge	MA	Museum of Fine Arts	Boston	MA
California Academy of Sciences	San Francisco	CA	Museum of Fine Arts	Houston	TX
California Science Center	Los Angeles	CA	Museum of Modern Art	New York	NY
Carnegie Museums of Pittsburgh	Pittsburgh	PA	Museum of New Mexico	Santa Fe	NM
Chicago Historical Society	Chicago	IL	Museum of Science	Boston	MA
Children's Museum of Indianapolis	Indianapolis	IN	Mystic Seaport Museum	Mystic	CT
Cincinnati Art Museum	Cincinnati	OH	National Air & Space Museum	Washington	DC
Cincinnati Museum Center	Cincinnati	OH	National Baseball Hall of Fame and		
Cleveland Museum of Art	Cleveland	OH	Museum, Inc.	Cooperstown	NY
Colonial Williamsburg	Williamsburg	VA	National Gallery of Art	Washington	DC
Corning Museum of Glass	Corning	NY	National Museum of American History	Washington	DC
Dallas Museum of Art	Dallas	TX	National Museum of the American Indian	Washington	DC
Denver Art Museum	Denver	CO	National Museum of Natural History	Washington	DC
Denver Museum of Nature and Science	Denver	CO	Nelson-Atkins Museum of Art	Kansas City	MO
Detroit Institute of Arts	Detroit	MI	New York Historical Society	New York	NY
Exploratorium	San Francisco	CA	New York State Museum	Albany	NY
The Field Museum	Chicago	IL	Peabody Essex Museum	Salem	MA
Fine Arts Museums of San Francisco	San Francisco	CA	Pennsylvania Historical & Museum		
Franklin Institute	Philadelphia	PA	Commission	Harrisburg	PA
The Frick Collection	New York	NY	Philadelphia Museum of Art	Philadelphia	PA
J. Paul Getty Museum	Los Angeles	CA	Public Museum of Grand Rapids	Grand Rapids	MI
Harvard University Art Museums	Cambridge	MA	Rock & Roll Hall of Fame and Museum,		
Henry F. Dupont Winterthur Museum	Winterthur	DE	Inc.	Cleveland	OH
Henry Ford Museum/Greenfield Village	Dearborn	MI	San Diego Museum of Art	San Diego	CA
High Museum of Art	Atlanta	GA	San Francisco Museum of Modern Art	San Francisco	CA
Houston Museum of Natural Science	Houston	TX	Science Museum of Minnesota	Saint Paul	MN
Jamestown-Yorktown Foundation	Williamsburg	VA	Scottsdale Museum of Contemp. Art	Scottsdale	AZ
Jewish Museum	New York	NY	St. Louis Science Center	St. Louis	MO
L.A. County Museum of Art	Los Angeles	CA	Toledo Museum of Art	Toledo	OH
Liberty Science Center, Liberty State Pk.	Jersey City	NJ	U.S. Holocaust Memorial Museum	Washington	DC
Maryland Science Center	Baltimore	MD	Univ. of Pennsylvania Museum of		
Mashantucket Pequot Museum and			Archaeology and Anthropology	Philadelphia	PA
Research Center	Mashantucket	CT	Virginia Museum of Fine Arts	Richmond	VA
Metropolitan Museum of Art	New York	NY	Wadsworth Atheneum	Hartford	CT
Milwaukee Public Museum	Milwaukee	WI	Walker Art Center	Minneapolis	MN
			Whitney Museum of American Art	New York	NY

Best-Selling U.S. Magazines, 2005

Source: Audit Bureau of Circulations, Schaumburg, IL

General magazines, exclusive of comics; also excluding magazines that failed to file reports to ABC by press time. Based on total average paid circulation during the 6 months ending Dec. 31, 2005.

Publication	Paid circ.	Publication	Paid circ.	Publication	Paid circ.
1. AARP The Magazine...	22,791,354	34. Martha Stewart Living..	1,972,337	68. Country Home	1,307,303
2. AARP Bulletin	22,113,496	35. Parenting	1,933,929	69. Rolling Stone	1,302,600
3. Reader's Digest.......	10,094,602	36. ESPN The Magazine ..	1,894,193	70. Vogue...............	1,301,468
4. Better Homes And		37. Real Simple	1,862,069	71. Teen Vogue	1,293,227
Gardens	7,607,694	38. Game Informer	1,832,966	72. FHM (For Him Magazine)	1,262,788
5. TV Guide............	7,349,619	39. FamilyFun...........	1,800,584	73. Weight Watchers	1,262,621
6. National Geographic...	5,376,750	40. Men's Health.........	1,775,503	74. Popular Mechanics....	1,210,126
7. Good Housekeeping...	4,662,725	41. In Style	1,772,568	75. Vanity Fair	1,208,644
8. Family Circle	4,294,841	42. Entertainment Weekly..	1,760,815	76. In Touch Weekly.....	1,178,015
9. Ladies' Home Journal ..	4,112,010	43. Country Living........	1,741,462	77. National Enquirer	1,159,245
10. Woman's Day	4,086,381	44. Cooking Light	1,720,168	78. Family Handyman	1,154,969
11. Time	4,026,891	45. Endless Vacation	1,719,861	79. Boys' Life	1,130,526
12. People.............	3,691,167	46. VFW Magazine.......	1,690,904	80. More...............	1,120,313
13. AAA Westways	3,676,453	47. US Weekly	1,662,003	81. Motor Trend	1,108,501
14. Prevention...........	3,345,214	48. Shape..............	1,650,815	82. Lucky	1,094,876
15. Sports Illustrated	3,238,101	49. Golf Digest	1,600,655	83. Elle	1,077,786
16. Newsweek..........	3,117,562	50. Home & Away........	1,574,027	84. Allure	1,071,700
17. Cosmopolitan	3,007,349	51. Woman's World	1,547,809	85. Essence	1,054,981
18. Playboy	3,005,753	52. Field & Stream	1,543,678	86. National Geographic	
19. Via Magazine........	2,745,095	53. Teen People	1,500,119	International	1,054,218
20. Southern Living	2,736,389	54. Fitness	1,488,657	87. New Yorker.........	1,051,919
21. Guideposts	2,628,767	55. Popular Science	1,467,894	88. Scouting	1,018,370
22. American Legion	2,525,838	56. Sunset............	1,457,745	89. Home	1,002,391
23. Maxim	2,503,218	57. Ebony	1,457,340	90. BusinessWeek	988,068
24. AAA Going Places.....	2,476,832	58. First for Women	1,437,020	91. Gourmet	984,813
25. Redbook	2,429,127	59. Star Magazine........	1,430,373	92. Traditional Home	981,752
26. O, The Oprah Magazine	2,403,917	60. Self	1,420,543	93. American Hunter	971,441
27. Glamour............	2,403,013	61. Golf Magazine........	1,416,047	94. Marie Claire	970,617
28. AAA Living..........	2,395,611	62. Cosmo Girl!.........	1,371,108	95. This Old House.......	964,601
29. Parents	2,050,920	63. American Rifleman	1,362,112	96. Travel + Leisure	957,849
30. Smithsonian.........	2,047,582	64. Health	1,360,786	97. Midwest Living	954,614
31. U.S. News & World		65. Car and Driver	1,357,956	98. Outdoor Life	948,410
Report............	2,034,848	66. Bon Appetit.........	1,326,198	99. Jet.................	941,530
32. Seventeen...........	2,031,466	67. Stuff	1,310,900	100. Forbes	927,202
33. Money	1,993,890				

Some Notable New Books, 2005

Source: Reference and User Services Assn. and Young Adult Library Services Assn., divisions of the American Library Association, for books published in 2005

Fiction

Midnight at the Dragon Café, Judy Fong Bates
Extremely Loud and Incredibly Close, Jonathan Safran Foer
Veronica, Mary Gaitskill
The Hungry Tide, Amitav Ghosh
Never Let Me Go, Kazuo Ishiguro
Beasts of No Nation, Uzodinma Iweala
No Country for Old Men, Cormac McCarthy
Saturday, Ian McEwan
Kafka on the Shore, Haruki Murakami
Gilead, Marilynne Robinson
The Hummingbird's Daughter, Luis Alberto Urrea

Nonfiction

Voices from Chernobyl, Svetlana Alexievich
A Woman in Berlin: Eight Weeks in the Conquered City, Anonymous
Bound for Canaan: The Underground Railroad and the War for the Soul of America, Fergus Bordewich
The Fly in the Cathedral: How a Group of Cambridge Scientists Won the International Race to Split the Atom, Brian Cathcart
Collapse: How Societies Choose to Fail or Succeed, Jared M. Diamond
Conspiracy of Fools, Kurt Eichenwald
New York Burning: Liberty, Slavery and Conspiracy in Eighteenth-Century Manhattan, Jill Lepore
Human Cargo: A Journey Among Refugees, Caroline Moorehead
The Assassins' Gate: America in Iraq, George Packer
The Orientalist: Solving the Mystery of a Strange and Dangerous Life, Tom Reiss
John Brown, Abolitionist: The Man Who Killed Slavery, Sparked the Civil War, and Seeded Civil Rights, David S. Reynolds
Shockwave: Countdown to Hiroshima, Stephen Walker
The Glass Castle, Jeannette Walls

Poetry

American Sublime, Elizabeth Alexander
Streets in Their Own Ink, Stuart Dybeck

Young Adult Nonfiction

Come Back to Afghanistan: A California Teenager's Story, Said Hyder Akbar and Susan Burton
Hitler Youth: Growing Up in Hitler's Shadow, Susan Campbell Bartoletti
Let Me Play: The Story of Title IX: The Law That Changed the Future of Girls in America, Karen Blumenthal
Maritcha: A Nineteenth Century American Girl, Tonya Bolden

Bodies From the Ash: Life and Death in Ancient Pompeii, James M. Deem
Pyongyang: A Journey in North Korea, Guy Delisle
Guinea Pig Scientists: Bold Self-Experimenters in Science and Medicine, Leslie Dendy and Mel Boring
The Plot: The Secret Story of the Protocols of the Elders of Zion, Will Eisner
Invisible Allies: Microbes That Shape Our Lives, Jeanette Farrell
Our Eleanor: A Scrapbook Look at Eleanor Roosevelt's Remarkable Life, Candace Fleming
Understanding the Holy Land: Answering Questions About the Israeli-Palestinian Conflict, Mitch Frank
Good Brother, Bad Brother: The Story of Edwin Booth and John Wilkes Booth, James Cross Giblin
Growing Up in Slavery: Stories of Young Slaves as Told By Themselves, Yuval Taylor, ed.
The Forbidden Schoolhouse: The True and Dramatic Story of Prudence Crandall and Her Students, Suzanne Jurmain
Lessons in Taxidermy, Bee Lavender
Fortune's Bones: The Manumission Requiem, Marilyn Nelson
A Wreath for Emmett Till, Marilyn Nelson
Japan 1945: A U.S. Marine's Photographs From Ground Zero, Joe O'Donnell
John Lennon: All I Want Is the Truth, Elizabeth Partridge
When I Was a Soldier: A Memoir, Valérie Zenatti

Young Adult Fiction

The Diary of Pelly D. Greenwillow, L.J. Adlington
Spacer and Rat, Margaret Bechard
Valiant: A Modern Tale of Faerie, Holly Black
Rebel Angels, Libba Bray
Code Talker: A Novel About the Navajo Marines of World War II, Joseph Bruchac
Upstate, Kalisha Buckhanon
Boy Proof, Cecil Castellucci
LoveSick, Jake Coburn
Red Kayak, Priscilla Cummings
Revenge of the Witch, Joseph Delaney
Every Man for Himself: Ten Short Stories About Being a Guy, ed. by Nancy E. Mercado
Bang!, Sharon G. Flake
Zap, Paul Fleischman
Wrecked, E.R. Frank
Anansi Boys, Neil Gaiman
As Simple as Snow, Gregory Galloway
Looking for Alaska, John Green
Where I Want to Be, Adele Griffin

Dark Sons, Nikki Grimes
The Witch's Boy, Michael Gruber
Siberia: A Novel, Ann Halam
Stripes of the Sidestep Wolf, Sonya Hartnett
Invisible, Pete Hautman
The Minister's Daughter, Julie Hearn
Flush, Carl Hiaasen
An Innocent Soldier, Joseph Holub
Stained, Jennifer Richard Jacobson
13 Little Blue Envelopes, Maureen Johnson
Real Time, Pnina Moed Kass
Daisy Kutter: The Last Train, Kazu Kibuishi
Heavy Metal and You, Christopher Krovatin
Black Juice, Margo Lanagan
Magic or Madness, Justine Larbalestier
Absolutely Positively Not, David Larochelle
Day of Tears: A Novel in Dialogue, Julius Lester
Are We There Yet?, David Levithan
Sleeping Freshman Never Lie, David Lubar
Inexcusable, Chris Lynch
The Highest Tide: A Novel, Jim Lynch
Gil's All Fright Diner, A. Lee Martinez
All Rivers Flow to the Sea, Alison McGhee
Twilight: A Novel, Stephanie Meyer
Autobiography of My Dead Brother, Walter Dean Myers
Skybreaker, Kenneth Oppel
A Room on Lorelai Street, Mary E. Pearson

Keeper, Mal Peet
Ball Don't Lie, Matt de la Peña
Criss Cross, Lynne Rae Perkins
Just Like That, Marsha Qualey
The Lightning Thief: Percy Jackson and the Olympians, Rick Riordan
Harry Potter and the Half-Blood Prince, J.K. Rowling
Eyes of the Emperor, Graham Salisbury
Kipling's Choice, Geert Spillebeen
Under the Persimmon Tree, Suzanne Fisher Staples
Light Years: A Novel, Tammar Stein
Mimus, Lilli Thal
Ariel, Grace Tiffany
Far Traveler, Rebecca Tingle
Red Sea, Diane Tullson
Runaways: Volume 1, Brian K. Vaughan
Stormwitch, Susan Vaught
Black and White, Paul Volponi
Superman: Birthright, Mark Waid and others
Full Service, Will Weaver
Peeps, Scott Westerfeld
Uglies, Scott Westerfeld
A Certain Slant of Light, Laura Whitcomb
Sandpiper, Ellen Wittlinger
Poison, Chris Wooding
A Thief in the House of Memory, Tim Wynne-Jones
I Am the Messenger, Markus Zusak

Some Notable New Books for Children, 2005

Source: Association for Library Service to Children, a division of the American Library Association, for books published in 2005.

Younger Readers

Terrific, Jon Agee
Elephants Can Paint Too!, Katya Arnold
Hi! Fly Guy, Tedd Arnold
I Ain't Gonna Paint No More!, Karen Beaumont
A Splendid Friend, Indeed, Suzanne Bloom
Willa and the Wind, Janice Del Negro
Mercy Watson to the Rescue, Kate DiCamillo
Leaf Man, Lois Ehlert
Oscar's Half Birthday, Bob Graham
Traction Man is Here!, Mini Grey
Siesta, Ginger Foglesong Guy
Jitterbug Jam: A Monster Tale, Barbara Jean Hicks
The Hello, Goodbye Window, Norton Juster
On Earth, G. Brian Karas
You and Me Together: Moms, Dads, and Kids Around the World, Barbara Kerley
Doña Flor: A Tall Tale About a Giant Woman With a Great Big Heart, Pat Mora
Zen Shorts, John J. Muth
Yum! Yuck! A Foldout Book of People Sounds, Linda Sue Park & Julia Durango
Hot Air: The (Mostly) True Story of the First Hot-Air Balloon Ride, Marjorie Priceman
And Tango Makes Three, Justin Richardson and Peter Parnell
Clara and Asha, Eric Rohmann
Henry and Mudge and the Great Grandpas, Cynthia Rylant
Stars Beneath Your Bed: The Surprising Story of Dust, April Pulley Sayre
Walter Was Worried, Laura Vaccaro Seeger
White is for Blueberry, George Shannon
Cowgirl Kate and Cocoa, Erica Silverman
Amanda Pig and the Really Hot Day, Jean Van Leeuwen
Leonardo the Terrible Monster, Mo Willems
Squashed in the Middle, Elizabeth Winthrop

Middle Readers

Poems to Dream Together/Poemas para soñar juntos, Francisco X. Alarcón
Whales on Stilts, M.T. Anderson
Whittington, Alan Armstrong
The Penderwicks: A Summer Tale of Four Sisters, Two Rabbits, and a Very Interesting Boy, Jeanne Birdsall
The Journey That Saved Curious George: The True Wartime Escape of Margret and H.A. Rey, Louise Borden
Toulouse-Lautrec: The Moulin Rouge and the City of Light, Robert Burleigh
The Prairie Builders: Reconstructing America's Lost Grasslands, Sneed B. Collard
Genius: A Photobiography of Albert Einstein, Marfé Ferguson Delano
The Game of Silence, Louise Erdrich
Rosa, Nikki Giovanni
Nicholas, René Goscinny
Queen Sophie Hartley, Stephanie Greene
The Trouble Begins, Linda Himelblau
Babymouse: Queen of the World!, Jennifer L. Holm and Matthew Holm
Goha the Wise Fool, Denys Johnson-Davies
Martin Bridge, Ready for Takeoff!, Jessica Scott Kerrin
A Kick in the Head: An Everyday Guide to Poetic Forms, Paul B. Janeczko, ed.

Precious and the Boo Hag, Patricia C. McKissack & Onawumi Jean Moss
The Girl from Chimel, Rigoberta Menchú with Dante Liano
The King of Mulberry Street, Donna Jo Napoli
Always Remember Me: How One Family Survived World War II, Marisabina Russo
Dinosaurs: Encyclopedia Prehistorica, Robert Sabuda & Matthew Reinhart
Kamishibai Man, Allen Say
Song of the Water Boatman and Other Pond Poems, Joyce Sidman
Central Heating: Poems About Fire and Warmth, Marilyn Singer
Kibitzers and Fools: Tales My Zayda Told Me, Simms Taback
Gorilla Doctors: Saving Endangered Great Apes, Pamela S. Turner
Brothers in Hope: The Story of the Lost Boys of Sudan, Mary Williams
The Librarian of Basra: A True Story from Iraq, Jeanette Winter
Roberto Clemente: Pride of the Pittsburgh Pirates, Jonah Winter
Show Way, Jacqueline Woodson

Older Readers

Photo by Brady: A Picture of the Civil War, Jennifer Armstrong
Hitler Youth: Growing Up in Hitler's Shadow, Susan Campbell Bartoletti
Let Me Play: The Story of Title IX: The Law That Changed the Future of Girls in America, Karen Blumenthal
Shakespeare's Secret, Elise Broach
Code Talker: A Novel About the Navajo Marines of World War Two, Joseph Bruchac
The Tequila Worm, Viola Canales
Sweetgrass Basket, Marlene Carvell
Chicken Boy, Frances O'Roark Dowell
Our Stories, Our Songs: African Children Talk About AIDS, Deborah Ellis
Children of the Great Depression, Russell Freedman
Inkspell, Cornelia Funke
The Legend of the Wandering King, Laura Gallego García
The Witch's Boy, Michael Gruber
Guys Write for Guys Read, ed. by Jon Scieszka
Princess Academy, Shannon Hale
An Innocent Soldier, Josef Holub
Totally Joe, James Howe
Leonardo da Vinci, Kathleen Krull
Day of Tears: A Novel in Dialogue, Julius Lester
The Mzungu Boy, Meja Mwangi
A Maze Me: Poems for Girls, Naomi Shihab Nye
The Lightning Thief, Rick Riordan
Under the Persimmon Tree, Suzanne Fisher Staples
Harry Sue, Sue Stauffacher
Hans Christian Andersen: His Fairy Tale Life, Hjørdis Varmer
Secrets of a Civil War Submarine: Solving the Mysteries of the H.L. Hunley, Sally M. Walker
The Illustrated Mum, Jacqueline Wilson
Stanford Wong Flunks Big-Time, Lisa Yee
When I Was a Soldier, Valérie Zenatti
Elsewhere, Gabrielle Zevin

All Ages

A Family of Poems: My Favorite Poetry for Children, ed. by Caroline Kennedy

World Almanac Quick Quiz

Of the bands ranking in the 10 top-grossing North American concert tours, how many acts are actually from North America?

    (a) 10   (b) 7   (c) 5   (d) 1

For the answer look in this chapter, or see page 1008.

Best-Selling Books, 2005

Source: Publishers Weekly

Hardcover Fiction
1. *The Broker*, John Grisham
2. *The Da Vinci Code*, Dan Brown
3. *Mary, Mary*, James Patterson
4. *At First Sight*, Nicholas Sparks
5. *Predator*, Patricia Cornwell
6. *True Believer*, Nicholas Sparks
7. *Light from Heaven*, Jan Karon
8. *The Historian*, Elizabeth Kostova
9. *The Mermaid Chair*, Sue Monk Kidd
10. *Eleven on Top*, Janet Evanovich

Hardcover Nonfiction
1. *Natural Cures "They" Don't Want You to Know*, Kevin Trudeau
2. *Your Best Life Now: 7 Steps to Living at Your Full Potential*, Joel Osteen
3. *The Purpose-Driven® Life*, Rick Warren
4. *You: The Owner's Manual*, Michael F. Roizen and Mehmet Oz
5. *1776*, David McCullough
6. *The World is Flat*, Thomas L. Friedman
7. *Love Smart: Find the One You Want—Fix the One You Got*, Dr. Phil McGraw
8. *Blink: The Power of Thinking Without Thinking*, Malcolm Gladwell
9. *Freakonomics: A Rogue Economist Explores the Hidden Side of Everything*, Steven D. Levitt and Stephen J. Dubner
10. *Guinness World Records 2006*, Guinness World Records

Trade Paperback
1. *A Million Little Pieces*, James Frey
2. *The Kite Runner*, Khaled Hosseini
3. *Guns, Germs, and Steel*, Jared Diamond
4. *Rachael Ray 365*, Rachael Ray
5. *Wicked*, Gregory Maguire
6. *The Secret Life of Bees*, Sue Monk Kidd
7. *The Curious Incident of the Dog in the Night-Time*, Mark Haddon

8. *The Tipping Point*, Malcolm Gladwell
9. *South Beach Diet*, Arthur Agatston, M.D.
10. *My Sister's Keeper*, Jodi Picoult

Mass Market
1. *The Broker*, John Grisham
2. *Red Lily*, Nora Roberts
3. *Black Rose*, Nora Roberts
4. *Angels and Demons*, Dan Brown
5. *3rd Degree*, James Patterson and Andrew Gross
6. *Life Expectancy*, Dean Koontz
7. *South Beach Diet*, Arthur Agatston, M.D.
8. *Trace*, Patricia Cornwell
9. *State of Fear*, Michael Crichton
10. *London Bridges*, James Patterson

Children's Hardcover
1. *Harry Potter and the Half-Blood Prince*, J.K. Rowling
2. *The Penultimate Peril (A Series of Unfortunate Events #12)*, Lemony Snicket
3. *Eldest*, Christopher Paolini
4. *Girls in Pants: The Third Summer of the Sisterhood*, Ann Brashares
5. *If You Give a Pig a Party*, Laura Numeroff
6. *Runny Babbit*, Shel Silverstein
7. *Artemis Fowl: The Opal Deception*, Eoin Colfer
8. *10 Little Rubber Ducks*, Eric Carle
9. *Snowmen at Christmas*, Caralyn Buehner
10. *Jingle Bells, Batman Smells! (P.S. So Does May) (Junie B. Jones #25)*, Barbara Park

Almanacs, Atlases, & Annuals
1. *The World Almanac and Book of Facts 2006*, ed. Ken Park
2. *J.K. Lasser's Your Income Tax 2006*, J.K. Lasser
3. *The Old Farmer's Almanac 2006*, Old Farmer's Almanac
4. *Turbotax 2006 Income Tax Guide*, Intuit
5. *Europe TravelBook*, AAA
6. *2006 AAA North American Road Atlas*, AAA
7. *What Color Is Your Parachute? 2006*, Richard Nelson Bolles

Note: Bestseller calculations are based on shipped-and-billed figures supplied by publishers and reflect 2005 sales only.

Leading U.S. Daily Newspapers, 2005

Source: 2006 *Editor & Publisher International Yearbook*

(Circulation as of Sept. 30, 2005; m = morning, e = evening, d=all day)

As of Feb. 1, 2006, the number of U.S. daily newspapers had fallen to 1,452, for a net loss of 5 since Feb. 1, 2005. Average daily circulation fell by 1.3 mil, from 54.6 mil in 2005 to 53.3 mil in 2006. The overall number of Sunday papers dipped by 1, to 914. Average Sunday circulation as of Feb. 1, 2006, fell 2.5 mil, or about 4.3%, from 57.8 mil to 55.3 mil.

Newspaper	Circulation	Newspaper	Circulation
1. Arlington (VA) *USA Today* (m)	2,222,745	34. Indianapolis (IN) *Star* (m)	252,862
2. New York (NY) *Wall Street Journal* (m)	2,083,653	35. San Jose (CA) *Mercury News* (m)	249,090
3. New York (NY) *Times* (m)	1,126,190	36. Baltimore (MD) *Sun* (m)	247,193
4. Los Angeles (CA) *Times* (m)	843,432	37. Milwaukee (WI) *Journal Sentinel* (m)	237,333
5. New York (NY) *Daily News* (m)	688,584	38. Orlando (FL) *Sentinel* (d)	235,918
6. Washington (DC) *Post* (m)	678,779	39. Fort Lauderdale *South Florida Sun-Sentinel* (m)	234,688
7. New York (NY) *Post* (m)	662,681	40. Pittsburgh (PA) *Post-Gazette* (m)	232,584
8. Chicago (IL) *Tribune* (m)	586,122	41. Boston (MA) *Herald* (m)	230,543
9. Houston (TX) *Chronicle* (m)	521,419	42. Columbus (OH) *Dispatch* (m)	230,501
10. Dallas (TX) *Morning News* (m)	465,469	43. Tampa (FL) *Tribune* (m)	225,676
11. Long Island (NY) *Newsday* (m)	439,708	44. San Antonio (TX) *Express-News* (m)	222,838
12. San Francisco (CA) *Chronicle* (d)	419,358	45. Fort Worth (TX) *Star-Telegram* (m)	220,515
13. Boston (MA) *Globe* (m)	414,225	46. Charlotte (NC) *Observer* (m)	218,960
14. Phoenix *Arizona Republic* (m)	411,043	47. Detroit (MI) *News* (m)	216,711
15. Newark (NJ) *Star-Ledger* (m)	400,092	48. Seattle (WA) *Times* (m)	215,502
16. Chicago (IL) *Sun-Times* (m)	382,796	49. Louisville (KY) *Courier-Journal* (m)	208,943
17. Minneapolis (MN) *Star Tribune* (m)	374,528	50. Norfolk (VA) *Virginian-Pilot* (m)	196,913
18. Philadelphia (PA) *Inquirer* (m)	357,679	51. Oklahoma City (OK) *Daily Oklahoman* (m)	190,655
19. Atlanta (GA) *Journal Constitution* (m)	351,999	52. Cincinnati (OH) *Enquirer* (m)	189,210
20. Detroit (MI) *Free Press* (m)	341,248	53. Hartford (CT) *Courant* (m)	186,518
21. Cleveland (OH) *Plain Dealer* (m)	339,055	54. Buffalo (NY) *News* (d)	185,799
22. Portland (OR) *Oregonian* (d)	333,515	55. Omaha (NE) *World-Herald* (d)	185,039
23. St. Petersburg (FL) *Times* (m)	319,349	56. St. Paul (MN) *Pioneer Press* (m)	184,497
24. San Diego (CA) *Union-Tribune* (m)	314,279	57. Walnut Creek (CA) *Contra Costa Times* (m)	182,834
25. Miami (FL) *Herald* (m)	302,005	58. Richmond (VA) *Times-Dispatch* (m)	179,958
26. Orange County (CA) *Register* (m)	298,456	59. Riverside (CA) *Press-Enterprise* (m)	177,857
27. Sacramento (CA) *Bee* (m)	290,553	60. Little Rock (AR) *Democrat-Gazette* (m)	176,917
28. St. Louis (MO) *Post-Dispatch* (m)	271,386	61. Austin (TX) *American-Statesman* (m)	176,604
29. New York (NY) *am New York* (m)	266,852	62. Nashville (TN) *Tennessean* (m)	169,924
30. Denver (CO) *Post* (m)	264,301	63. Los Angeles (CA) *Daily News* (m)	169,379
31. Denver (CO) *Rocky Mountain News* (m)	263,425	64. Los Angeles (CA) *Investors Business Daily* (m)	168,876
32. New Orleans (LA) *Times-Picayune* (m)	261,573	65. West Palm Beach (FL) *Post* (m)	168,213
33. Kansas City (MO) *Star* (m)	258,658		

Newspaper		Circulation
66. Bergen County (NJ) *Record*	(m)	166,373
67. Raleigh (NC) *News & Observer*	(m)	165,604
68. Memphis (TN) *Commercial Appeal*	(m)	162,327
69. Jacksonville *Florida Times-Union*	(m)	161,758
70. Rochester (NY) *Democrat and Chronicle*	(m)	161,303
71. Las Vegas (NV) *Review-Journal*	(m)	158,116
72. Fresno (CA) *Bee*	(m)	157,136
73. Providence (RI) *Journal*	(m)	157,031
74. Neptune (NJ) *Asbury Park Press*	(m)	154,396
75. San Francisco (CA) *Examiner*	(m)	154,104
76. Chicago (IL) *Daily Herald*	(m)	151,028
77. Des Moines (IA) *Register*	(m)	150,201
78. Birmingham (AL) *News*	(m)	144,171
79. Honolulu (HI) *Advertiser*	(d)	140,327
80. Grand Rapids (MI) *Press*	(e)	135,902
81. Toledo (OH) *Blade*	(m)	133,498
82. Seattle (WA) *Post-Intelligencer*	(m)	132,694
83. Dayton (OH) *Daily News*	(m)	132,081
84. Salt Lake City (UT) *Tribune*	(m)	130,615
85. Westchester Co. (NY) *Journal News*	(m)	130,531
86. Akron (OH) *Beacon Journal*	(m)	128,949
87. Tacoma (WA) *News Tribune*	(m)	128,213
88. Tulsa (OK) *World*	(m)	127,429
89. Los Angeles (CA) *La Opinion*	(m)	124,647
90. Philadelphia (PA) *Daily News*	(m)	121,093
91. Syracuse (NY) *Post-Standard*	(m)	117,226
92. Knoxville (TN) *News-Sentinel*	(m)	115,123
93. Wilmington (DE) *News Journal*	(d)	114,406
94. Columbia (SC) *State*	(m)	112,884
95. Allentown (PA) *Morning Call*	(m)	112,724
96. Sarasota (FL) *Herald-Tribune*	(m)	111,535
97. Albuquerque (NM) *Journal*	(m)	106,878
98. Lexington (KY) *Herald-Leader*	(m)	106,612
99. Daytona Beach (FL) *News-Journal*	(m)	105,336
100. Tucson (AZ) *Daily Star*	(m)	104,130

Leading Canadian Daily Newspapers, 2005

Source: 2005 *Editor & Publisher International Yearbook*
(Circulation as of Sept. 30, 2005; all morning papers)

Rank	Circulation	Rank	Circulation	Rank	Circulation
1. Toronto (ON) *Star*	451,972	4. Toronto (ON) *National Post*	232,508	8. Vancouver (BC) *Province*	148,244
2. Toronto (ON) *Globe and*		5. Montreal (QC) *La Presse*	194,183	9. Montreal (QC) *Gazette*	136,818
Mail	330,706	6. Toronto (ON) *Sun*	191,146	10. Ottawa (ON) *Citizen*	127,792
3. Montreal (QC) *Le Journal*	269,520	7. Vancouver (BC) *Sun*	165,437		

Top 25 News/Information Websites, July 2006

Source: comScore Media Metrix, Inc.

Rank	Visitors[1]	Rank	Visitors[1]	Rank	Visitors[1]
1. New York Times Digital	38,133,000	10. Tribune Newspapers	8,547,000	18. FoxNews.com	5,315,000
2. The Weather Channel	35,021,000	11. ABCNews Digital	7,113,000	19. WashingtonPost.com	5,193,000
3. Yahoo! News	31,061,000	12. McClatchey Corp.	7,012,000	20. Lee Enterprises, Inc.	5,087,000
4. MSNBC	24,430,000	13. CBS News Digital	6,943,000	21. Wunderground.com	4,559,000
5. AOL News	22,119,000	14. Military.com	6,720,000	22. Discovery.com	4,519,000
6. CNN	20,648,000	15. USA Today Sites	6,380,000	23. Slate.com	4,260,000
7. Weatherbug Property	16,016,000	16. Legacy.com	5,555,000	24. Accuweather.com	3,859,000
8. IBS Sites	9,280,000	17. MSN News & Weather	5,508,000	25. AP.org	3,815,000
9. WorldNow Sites	9,111,000				

(1) Number of unique visitors who visited Website at least once in July 2006.

U.S. Commercial Radio Stations, by Format, 1997-2006[1]

Source: The M Street Radio Directory, M Street Corporation, Littleton, NH © 2006; counts are for June of each year

Primary format	2006	2005	2004	2003	2002	2001	1999	1998
1. Country	2,097	2,019	2,047	2,088	2,131	2,190	2,306	2,368
2. News/Talk	1,403	1,324	1,282	1,224	1,179	1,139	1,159	1,131
3. Oldies	755	773	816	807	813	786	766	799
4. Spanish	744	703	665	628	603	574	536	493
5. Adult Contemporary (AC)	681	684	703	692	713	709	775	844
6. Sports	551	497	469	429	388	338	256	251
7. Top 40	545	502	497	491	474	468	401	379
8. Classic Rock	489	461	450	425	384	338	314	282
9. Hot AC	398	380	416	399	395	369	325	281
10. Adult Standards	376	405	460	497	547	569	595	561
11. Religion (Teaching, Variety)	320	318	336	347	332	356	363	356
12. Soft AC	319	324	322	336	340	375	382	368
13. Rock	300	270	280	273	278	282	280	266
14. Classic Hits	293	262	229	237	258	265	222	192
15. Black Gospel	282	286	273	253	254	264	257	238
16. Southern Gospel	207	207	208	207	240	255	269	273
17. Urban AC	184	153	136	128	121	118	112	127
18. Adult Hits	163	54	0	0	0	0	0	0
19. R&B	163	150	159	189	193	183	166	171
20. Modern Rock	158	152	165	169	147	140	136	145
Off Air	92	70	79	123	110	113	96	102
TOTAL OPERATING STATIONS[2]	11,297	10,661	10,648	10,605	10,569	10,516	10,444	10,292

(1) Data for 2000 unavailable. (2) Totals include stations that are changing or did not report format.

Top-Grossing North American Concert Tours, 1985-2005

Source: Pollstar, Fresno, CA

Rank	Artist (Year)	Total gross[1]	Cities/ Shows	Rank	Artist (Year)	Total gross[1]	Cities/ Shows
1.	The Rolling Stones (2005)	$162.0	38/42	11.	Prince (2004)	$87.4	69/96
2.	U2 (2005)	138.9	43/78	12.	'N Sync (2001)	86.8	36/43
3.	The Rolling Stones (1994)	121.2	43/60	13.	Backstreet Boys (2001)	82.1	73/98
4.	Bruce Springsteen & The E Street			14.	Celine Dion (2005)	81.3	1/155
	Band (2003)	115.9	30/47	15.	Celine Dion (2003)	80.5	1/145
5.	U2 (2001)	109.7	56/80	16.	Celine Dion (2004)	80.4	1/154
6.	Pink Floyd (1994)	103.5	39/59	17.	Tina Turner (2000)	80.2	88/95
7.	Paul McCartney (2002)	103.3	43/53	18.	U2 (1997)	79.9	37/46
8.	The Rolling Stones (1989)	98.0	33/60	19.	Madonna (2004)	79.5	14/39
9.	The Rolling Stones (1997)	89.3	26/33	20.	The Eagles (1994)	79.4	32/54
10.	The Rolling Stones (2002)	87.9	33/34				

(1) In millions. Not adjusted for inflation.

Top-Selling Albums of All-Time[1]

Source: Recording Industry Assn. of America, Washington, DC

Rank	Title, Artist	Sales (in millions)
1.	*Eagles/Their Greatest Hits 1971-1975*, Eagles	29.0
2.	*Thriller*, Michael Jackson	27.0
3.	*Led Zeppelin IV*, Led Zeppelin	23.0
	The Wall, Pink Floyd	23.0
5.	*Back in Black*, AC/DC	21.0
	Greatest Hits Volume I & Volume II, Billy Joel	21.0
7.	*Double Live*, Garth Brooks	20.0
	Come on Over, Shania Twain	20.0
9.	*The Beatles*, The Beatles	19.0
	Rumours, Fleetwood Mac	19.0
11.	*Boston*, Boston	17.0
	The Bodyguard (soundtrack), Whitney Houston	17.0
13.	*The Beatles 1967-1970*, The Beatles	16.0
	No Fences, Garth Brooks	16.0
	Hotel California, Eagles	16.0
	Cracked Rear View, Hootie & the Blowfish	16.0
	Greatest Hits, Elton John	16.0
	Physical Graffiti, Led Zeppelin	16.0
	Jagged Little Pill, Alanis Morissette	16.0
20.	*The Beatles 1962-1966*, The Beatles	15.0
	Saturday Night Fever (soundtrack), Bee Gees	15.0
	Appetite for Destruction, Guns N' Roses	15.0
	Dark Side of the Moon, Pink Floyd	15.0
	Supernatural, Santana	15.0
	Born in the U.S.A., Bruce Springsteen	15.0

(1) As of Aug. 2006; sales figures represent RIAA multi-platinum certifications, albums ranked by latest sales certification.

Sales of Recorded Music and Music Videos, by Units Shipped and Value, 1994-2005

Source: Recording Industry Assn. of America, Washington, DC

(in millions, net after returns)

FORMAT	1994	1995	1998	2000	2001	2002	2003	2004	2005	CHANGE 2004-05
Compact disc (CD)										
Units shipped	662.1	722.9	847.0	942.5	881.9	803.3	746.0	767.0	705.4	−8.0%
Dollar value	8,464.5	9,377.4	11,416.0	13,214.5	12,909.4	12,044.1	11,232.9	11,446.5	10,520.2	−8.1
CD single										
Units shipped	9.3	21.5	56.0	34.2	17.3	4.5	8.3	3.1	2.8	−12.1
Dollar value	56.1	110.9	213.2	142.7	79.4	19.6	36.0	15.0	10.9	−27.0
Download album										
Units shipped	—	—	—	—	—	—	—	4.6	13.6	198.5
Dollar value	—	—	—	—	—	—	—	45.5	135.7	198.5
Download single										
Units shipped	—	—	—	—	—	—	—	139.4	366.9	163.3
Dollar value	—	—	—	—	—	—	—	138.0	363.3	163.3
Cassette										
Units shipped	345.4	272.6	158.5	76.0	45.0	31.1	17.2	5.2	2.5	−52.6
Dollar value	2,976.4	2,303.6	1,419.9	626.0	363.4	209.8	108.1	23.7	13.1	−44.9
Cassette single										
Units shipped	81.1	70.7	26.4	1.3	−1.5	−0.5	NA	NA	NA	NA
Dollar value	274.9	236.3	94.4	4.6	−5.3	−1.6	NA	NA	NA	NA
LP/EP										
Units shipped	1.9	2.2	3.4	2.2	2.3	1.7	1.5	1.4	1.0	−25.0
Dollar value	17.8	25.1	34.0	27.7	27.4	20.5	21.7	19.3	14.2	−26.2
Vinyl single										
Units shipped	11.7	10.2	5.4	4.8	5.5	4.4	3.8	3.5	2.3	−35.4
Dollar value	47.2	46.7	25.7	26.3	31.4	24.9	21.5	19.9	13.2	−33.4
Music video										
Units shipped	11.2	12.6	27.2	18.2	17.7	14.7	19.9	32.8	33.8	3.2
Dollar value	231.1	220.3	508.0	281.9	329.2	288.4	399.9	607.2	602.2	−0.8
DVD audio										
Units shipped	—	—	—	—	0.3	0.4	0.4	0.3	0.5	31.8
Dollar value	—	—	—	—	6.0	8.5	8.0	6.5	11.2	72.2
DVD video*										
Units shipped	—	—	0.5	3.3	7.9	10.7	17.5	29.0	27.8	−4.1
Dollar value	—	—	12.2	80.3	190.7	236.3	369.6	561.0	539.8	−3.8
TOTAL UNITS	1,122.7	1,112.7	1,123.9	1,079.2	968.5	859.7	798.4	814.1	748.7	−8.0%
TOTAL VALUE	12,068.0	12,320.3	13,711.2	14,323.7	13,740.9	12,614.2	11,854.4	12,154.7	11,195.0	−7.9%

* While broken out for this chart, DVD Video Product is included in the Music Video totals. Note: Figures for mobile sales (including ringtones, ringbacks, music videos, full downloads, and other mobile) became available in 2005; 170 mil units (worth $421.6 mil) shipped that year. Digital download and mobile figures not included in totals.

Sales of Recorded Music and Music Videos, by Genre and Format, 2000-05

Source: Recording Industry Assn. of America, Washington, DC

Breakdown is by percentage of sales revenue for all recorded music sold, ranked for 2005.

GENRE	2005	2004	2003	2002	2001	2000	FORMAT	2005	2004	2003	2002	2001	2000
Rock	31.5%	23.9%	25.2%	24.7%	24.4%	24.8%	Compact disc						
Rap/Hip-Hop	13.3	12.1	13.3	13.8	11.4	12.9	(CD)	87.0%	90.3%	87.8%	90.5%	89.2%	89.3%
Country	12.5	13.0	10.4	10.7	10.5	10.7	Digital						
R&B/Urban[1]	10.2	11.3	10.6	11.2	10.6	9.7	download[4]	5.7	0.9	1.3	0.5	0.2	NA
Pop	8.1	10.0	8.9	9.0	12.1	11.0	Singles						
Religious[2]	5.3	6.0	5.8	6.7	6.7	4.8	(all types)	2.7	2.4	2.4	1.9	2.4	2.5
Classical	2.4	2.0	3.0	3.1	3.2	2.7	Cassette	1.1	1.7	2.2	2.4	3.4	4.9
Children's	2.3	2.8	0.6	0.4	0.5	0.6	DVD audio	0.8	1.7	2.7	1.3	1.1	NA
Jazz	1.8	2.7	.9	3.2	3.4	2.9	Music Videos/						
Oldies	1.1	1.4	1.3	0.9	0.8	0.9	DVDs[4]	0.7	1.0	0.6	0.7	1.1	0.8
Soundtracks	0.9	1.1	1.4	1.1	1.4	0.7	LPs	0.7	0.9	0.5	0.7	0.6	0.5
New Age	0.4	1.0	0.5	0.5	1.0	0.5							
Other[3]	8.5	8.9	7.6	8.1	7.9	8.3							

(1) Includes R&B, blues, dance, disco, funk, fusion, Motown, reggae, soul. (2) Includes Christian, Gospel, Inspirational, Religious, and Spiritual. (3) "Other" includes big band, Broadway, comedy, contemporary, electronic, emo, ethnic, exercise, folk, gothic, grunge, holiday music, house music, humor, instrumental, language, latin, love songs, mix, mellow, modern, ska, spoken-word, standards, swing, Top-40, trip-hop. (4) 2001 is the first year that data were collected on digital download purchases, and that music video/DVD was recorded separately from audio DVD.

Multi-Platinum and Platinum Awards for Recorded Music and Music Videos, 2005

Source: Recording Industry Assn. of America, Washington, DC

To achieve platinum status, an **album** must reach a minimum sale of 1 mil units in LPs, tapes, and CDs, with a manufacturer's dollar volume of at least $2 mil based on one-third of the suggested retail list price for each record, tape, or CD sold. To achieve multi-platinum status, an album must reach a minimum sale of at least 2 mil units in LPs, tapes, and CDs, with a manufacturer's dollar volume of at least $4 mil based on one-third of the list price.

Singles must sell 1 mil units to achieve a platinum award (created in 1976) and 2 mil to achieve a multi-platinum award (created in 1984). In 1999, the Diamond Award, honoring sales of 10 mil or more copies of an album or single, was introduced. EP singles count as 2 units. Double-CD sets count as 2 units. **Music videos** (long form) must sell 100,000 units to qualify for a platinum award, more than 200,000 units for a multi-platinum award, and are recertified with each additional 100,000 sold. **Video singles**, which must have a maximum running time of 15 minutes and no more than 2 songs per title, must sell 50,000 units to qualify for a platinum award, at least 100,000 units to qualify for a multi-platinum award, and are recertified with each additional 50,000 sold. In Oct. 2004, digital gold (100,000 sold), platinum (200,000 sold), and multi-platinum (400,000 sold) awards were introduced.

Awards listed were for albums (released Sept. 2004–Sept. 2005) and for music videos (released at any time) that were certified Jan.-Sept. 2005. Numbers in parentheses = millions sold. Alphabetized by artist's name.

Albums, Multi-Platinum

The Emancipation of Mimi, Mariah Carey (3)
Goodies, Ciara
Breakaway, Kelly Clarkson (3)
X & Y, Coldplay (2)
Destiny Fulfilled, Destiny's Child (3)
The Massacre, 50 Cent (4)
The Documentary, The Game (2)
American Idiot, Green Day (4)
Crunk Juice, Lil' Jon & The Eastside Boyz (2)
The Red Light District, Ludacris (2)
Suit, Nelly (3)
Feels Like Today, Rascal Flatts (2)
Love, Angel, Music, Baby, Gwen Stefani (2)
Be Here, Keith Urban (2)
Now That's What I Call Music! Vol. 19, Various Artists (2)
Late Registration, Kanye West (2)

Albums, Platinum

Merry Christmas With Love, Clay Aiken
Out of Exile, Audioslave
Never Gone, Backstreet Boys
Monkey Business, The Black Eyed Peas
Wanted, Bow Wow
It's Time, Michael Bublé
Be as You Are, Kenny Chesney
Powerballin', Chingy
Retaliation, Dane Cook
Greatest Hits, Creed
Stand Up, Dave Matthews Band
Miracle, Celine Dion
Most Wanted, Hilary Duff
From Under the Cork Tree, Fall Out Boy
Free Yourself, Fantasia
In Your Honor, Foo Fighters
Demon Days, Gorillaz
Il Divo, Il Divo
In Between Dreams, Jack Johnson
Collision Course, Jay-Z and Linkin Park
Who is Mike Jones?, Mike Jones
Honkytonk University, Toby Keith
TP.3 Reloaded, R. Kelly
Get Lifted, John Legend
Speak, Lindsay Lohan
Rebirth, Jennifer Lopez

Christmas Celebration, Mannheim Steamroller
Turning Point, Mario
Beautiful Soul, Jesse McCartney
Red, White & Crüe, Mötley Crüe
Karma & Effect, Seether
Still Not Getting Any, Simple Plan
Phantom of the Opera Soundtrack, Various Artists
Devils & Dust, Bruce Springsteen
The Very Best of Sting and The Police, Sting and The Police
Mind, Body and Soul, Joss Stone
Somewhere Down in Texas, George Strait
Twice the Speed of Life, Sugarland
Mezmerize, System of a Down
A Christmas Album, James Taylor
Something to Be, Rob Thomas
Seventeen Days, 3 Doors Down
Greatest Hits '93-'03, 311
Urban Legend, T.I.
Loyal to the Game, 2Pac
All the Best, Tina Turner
Vans Warped Tour 2005, Various Artists
U.S.A.: United States of Atlanta, Ying Yang Twins
Let's Get It, Young Jeezy

Music Videos, Multi-Platinum

Family Jewels, AC/DC
Live at Donington, AC/DC
You Gotta Move, Aerosmith
One Night Only, Bee Gees
The Complex Rock Tour Live, Blue Man Group
Action Bible Songs/Bible Songs/Preschool Songs/Silly Songs/Sunday School Songs/Toddler Tunes, Cedarmont Kids
The Gorge, Dave Matthews Band
Farewell Tour: Live From Melbourne, Eagles
Here's Your Sign: Live!, Bill Engvall
You Might Be a Redneck If...And Check Your Neck, Jeff Foxworthy
I Might Need Security, Jamie Foxx
The Greatful Dead Movie, Greatful Dead
Welcome to the Videos, Guns N' Roses

Visions of the Beast, Iron Maiden
Git-R-Done, Larry the Cable Guy
Any Given Thursday, John Mayer
Afterglow Live, Sarah McLachlan
Dark Side of the Moon, Pink Floyd
Disasterpieces, Slipknot
Comedy Video Classics, Ray Stevens
The Complete Masterworks, Tenacious D
Live at the Astoria, Steve Vai
Live Without a Net, Van Halen
Eric Clapton Crossroads Guitar Festival, Various Artists
They Call Me Tater Salad, Ron White

Music Videos, Platinum

Thug Angel: The Life of an Outlaw, 2Pac
Gold, Abba
Video Hits, Trace Adkins
Super Galactic Fan Pack, Big & Rich
The Crush Tour, Bon Jovi
Reality Tour, David Bowie
#1s, Mariah Carey
In Concert With the Edmonton Symphony, Ray Charles
Live at the Greek Theatre, Chicago and Earth, Wind & Fire
Goodies: The Videos & More, Ciara
Trilogy: Live in Berlin, The Cure
Live in Buffalo, July 4, 2004, Goo Goo Dolls
Live Inside Job, Don Henley
Alive at Red Rocks, Incubus
The Early Days, Iron Maiden
The Work of Director Spike Jonze, Spike Jonze
Texican Style: Live From Austin, Los Lonely Boys
Greatest Video Hits, Mötley Crüe
The Videos, Nickelback
Nevermind, Nirvana
No Quarter, Jimmy Page & Robert Plant
It, Phish
Reality Tour Live, Jessica Simpson
Video Hits, Keith Urban
Maybe Memories, The Used
Live Evolution, Usher
Live at the Royal Albert Hall, The Who
Brian Wilson Presents Smile, Brian Wilson

World Almanac Editors' Picks
Most Memorable TV Families

1. **The Simpsons** (1989-): Homer, Marge, Bart, Lisa & Maggie
2. **The Huxtables** (The Cosby Show, 1984-92): Cliff, Clair, Sondra, Denise, Theo, Vanessa, & Rudy
3. **The Bunkers** (All in the Family, 1971-79): Archie, Edith, Meathead (Michael), & Gloria
4. **The Bradys** (The Brady Bunch, 1969-74): Mike, Carol, Greg, Marcia, Peter, Jan, Bobby, & Cindy
5. **The Barones** (Everybody Loves Raymond, 1996-2005): Debra, Ray, Frank, Marie, Robert, Ally, Geoffrey, & Michael
6. **The Cleavers** (Leave it to Beaver, 1957-63): Ward, June, Wally, & Beaver (Theodore)
7. **The Cunninghams** (Happy Days, 1974-84): Howard, Marion, Joanie, & Richie
8. **The Sopranos** (1999-2007): Tony, Carmela, Meadow, & A.J.
9. **The Ingalls** (Little House on the Prairie, 1974-83): Charles, Caroline, Laura, Mary, Carrie, Grace, & Albert
10. **The Bluths** (Arrested Development, 2003-06): George Sr., Lucille, Michael, Gob (George II), Lindsay Bluth Fünke, Tobias Fünke, Buster, George-Michael, & Maeby Fünke

U.S. Households With Cable Television, 1977-2006

Source: Nielsen Media Research

Year	Subscribers[1] (mil)	As % of house-holds with TVs	Year	Subscribers[1] (mil)	As % of house-holds with TVs	Year	Subscribers[1] (mil)	As % of house-holds with TVs
1977	12.2	16.6%	1988	46.3	52.0%	1998	65.9	67.2%
1978	13.4	17.9	1989	50.2	55.6	1999[2]	76.4	76.9
1979	14.9	19.4	1990	53.9	58.6	2000[2]	78.6	77.9
1980	17.7	22.6	1991	56.1	60.3	2001[2]	81.5	79.8
1981	23.2	28.3	1992	56.2	61.1	2002[2]	87.8	83.8
1982	27.4	33.4	1993	57.6	61.9	2003[2]	88.4	82.9
1983	31.8	37.9	1994	59.7	63.4	2004[2]	92.4	85.3
1984	35.8	42.5	1995	62.1	65.1	2005[2]	94.0	85.7
1985	38.7	45.3	1996	63.6	66.3	2006[2]	95.0	86.2
1986	40.9	47.4	1997	65.1	67.2			
1987	43.3	49.2						

(1) Households that subscribe to basic cable service. (2) After 1998, figures include wired-cable households as well as households that receive TV programming via an alternate delivery systems (including satellite receivers, SMATV, MMDS).

Number of Cable TV Systems, 1975-2006

Source: 2005 Television and Cable Factbook, Warren Communications News, Inc., Washington, DC; estimates as of Jan. 1

Year	Systems[1]	Year	Systems[1]	Year	Systems[1]	Year	Systems[1]	Year	Systems[1]	Year	Systems[1]
1975	3,506	1984	6,200	1989	9,050	1994	11,214	1999	10,700	2003	9,339*
1980	4,225	1985	6,600	1990	9,575	1995	11,218	2000	10,400	2004	8,869*
1981	4,375	1986	7,500	1991	10,704	1996	11,119	2001	9,924	2005	8,409*
1982	4,825	1987	7,900	1992	11,035	1997	10,950	2002	9,947	2006	7,926*
1983	5,600	1988	8,500	1993	11,108	1998	10,845				

(1) The satellite-signal-receiving hardware, cable lines, and cable boxes that provide cable programming to homes within a geographic area. *Figures as of March of the year noted.

Top 20 Cable TV Networks, 2005

Source: Natl. Cable Television Assn., Dec. 2005; ranked by number of subscribers

1. Discovery Channel (1985) 90.3
2. ESPN (1979) 90.1
3. CNN (Cable News Network) (1980) 89.9
4. TNT (Turner Network Television) (1988) 89.8
   QVC (1986) 89.8
6. USA Network (1980). 89.7
   C-SPAN (Cable Satellite Public Affairs Network)
   (1979) 89.7
8. Spike TV[2] (2003) 89.6
9. Lifetime Television (LIFE) (1984). 89.5
   Nickelodeon (1979) 89.5
   TBS (Superstation) (1976). 89.5
13. A&E Networks 89.3
    ESPN2 (1993) 89.3
15. TLC (The Learning Channel) (1980) 89.1
16. Home Shopping Network (HSN) (1985) 88.9
    Headline News (1982). 88.9
19. MTV (Music Television) (1981) 88.8
20. ABC Family Channel[3] (2001) 88.7

Note: Data include noncable affiliates. (1) Date in parentheses is year service began. (2) Formerly The Nashville Network (1983-2000); The National Network (2000-2003); The New TNN (2003). (3) Began 1977 as the Family Channel; FOX Family Channel (1998-2000).

U.S. Television Set Owners, 2005

Source: Nielsen Media Research; Sept. 2005

Of the 110.2 million U.S. households that owned at least one TV set in 2005:

81% had 2 or more TV sets	89% had a VCR	86% received basic cable
50% had 3 or more TV sets	84% had a DVD player	45% received premium cable

Average U.S. Television Viewing Time, November 2005

Source: Nielsen Media Research (hours: minutes per week)

Group	Age	Total per week	M-F 7-10 AM	M-F 10 AM-4:00 PM	M-Sun. 8-11 PM	Sat. 7 AM-1 PM	M-F 11:30 PM-1 AM	Sunday 1-7:00 PM
Men	18+	33:16	1:53	4:05	8:43	0:56	1:33	1:58
	18-24	23:01	1:04	3:07	5:11	0:34	1:24	1:12
	25-54	31:35	1:41	3:27	8:28	0:56	1:36	1:55
	55+	41:30	2:38	5:46	10:53	1:06	1:31	2:27
Women	18+	38:18	2:39	5:42	9:37	1:02	1:43	1:42
	18-24	27:13	1:34	4:17	6:14	0:43	1:28	1:09
	25-54	35:37	2:28	4:55	9:13	1:01	1:43	1:37
	55+	46:52	3:25	7:34	11:36	1:12	1:50	2:05
Children	2-11	23:41	1:59	3:32	5:06	1:12	0:39	1:15
Teens	12-17	24:01	0:57	2:19	6:07	0:50	1:10	1:17
ALL VIEWERS		33:06	2:07	4:30	8:20	1:00	1:27	1:42

TV Viewing Shares, Broadcast Years 1990-2005[1]

Source: Cable TV Facts, Cable Advertising Bureau, New York, NY

	All Television Households[2]					All Cable Households[2]					Pay Cable Households[2]				
	'90	'95	'00	'04	'05		'90	'95	'00	'04	'05		'90	'95	'00	'04	'05
Network Affiliates[3]	55	48	44	37	30		46	41	40	33	27		43	38	37	30	24
Indep. TV Stations[4]	20	22	12	10	9		16	17	9	8	7		16	17	9	8	6
Public TV Stations	3	3	3	2	2		3	3	2	2	2		2	2	1	1	1
Basic Cable[5]	21	30	46	53	48		32	42	55	60	54		30	41	55	60	52
Pay Cable	6	6	6	6	5		10	8	7	7	5		18	15	11	13	10

(1) Broadcast years represent the 12-month period October-September. (2) Share figures refer to percentage of the viewing audience for all television viewing, 24 hours/day. As a result of multiset use and rounding, share figures add to more than 100. (3) Includes CBS, NBC, ABC, and FOX after 1998. (4) Includes WB, UPN, and PAX. (5) Includes ad-supported cable and all other cable (non-pay and non-ad-supported channels).

Favorite Prime-Time Television Programs, 2005-06

Source: Nielsen Media Research

Data are for regularly scheduled network programs in 2005-06 season through May 24; ranked by average audience percentage. Average audience percentages, or ratings, are estimates of the percentage of all TV-owning households that are watching a particular program. Audience share percentages are estimates of the percentage of those watching TV that are tuned into a particular program. Tied programs are given the same rank.

Rank	Programs	Avg. audience	Audience share	Rank	Programs	Avg. audience	Audience share
1.	American Idol-Tuesday	17.6%	27%	27.	The New Adventures of Old		
2.	American Idol-Wednesday	17.2	26		Christine	8.3%	12%
3.	CSI	15.6	24		Unan1mous	8.3	12
4.	Desperate Housewives	13.8	20	29.	Criminal Minds	8.2	12
5.	Grey's Anatomy	12.5	20	30.	24	8.1	12
6.	Without a Trace	12.3	20		E.R.	8.1	13
7.	Dancing With the Stars	12.0	18	32.	Out of Practice	7.8	12
8.	CSI: Miami	11.8	19	33.	Numb3rs	7.6	13
9.	Survivor: Guatemala	10.9	17	34.	Law and Order	7.5	12
10.	NFL Monday Night Football	10.7	18		Medium	7.5	12
11.	House	10.5	16	36.	Courting Alex	7.3	11
12.	NCIS	9.8	15		Crumbs	7.3	11
13.	Survivor Panama—Exile Island	9.7	15	38.	The Apprentice	7.2	11
	Two and a Half Men	9.7	14		Crossing Jordan	7.2	11
	The Unit	9.7	14		Deal Or No Deal-Friday	7.2	13
16.	Dancing With the Stars (Results)	9.6	16		Law and Order: Criminal Intent	7.2	11
	Deal or No Deal-Monday	9.6	15	42.	Skating With Celebrities	7.1	10
	Cold Case	9.3	14	43.	Las Vegas	7.0	11
19.	CSI: NY	9.2	15		The OC	7.0	12
	Law and Order: SVU	9.2	15	45.	Boston Legal	6.9	11
	Lost	9.2	14		Close to Home	6.9	12
22.	60 Minutes	9.0	15	47.	CBS Sunday Movie	6.8	11
	Deal or No Deal-Wednesday	9.0	15		My Name is Earl	6.8	10
24.	NFL Monday Showcase	8.8	14	49.	The Amazing Race	6.7	10
25.	Extreme Makeover: Home Edition	8.6	13	50.	Ghost Whisperer	6.6	12
26.	Commander in Chief	8.4	13		King of Queens	6.6	10

Favorite Syndicated Programs, 2005-06

Source: Nielsen Media Research, Aug. 29, 2005-Aug. 27, 2006

Average audience percentages, or ratings, are estimates of the percentage of TV-owning households watching a program.

Rank	Program	Avg. audience	Rank	Program	Avg. audience
1.	Wheel of Fortune	8.1%	17.	Inside Edition	3.4%
2.	Oprah Winfrey Show	6.6		Live With Regis and Kelly	3.4
3.	Jeopardy	6.4	19.	Century 19*	3.2
	ESPN NFL Regular Season	6.4	20.	Who Wants to Be a Millionaire?	3.1
5.	Everybody Loves Raymond	5.9		Judge Joe Brown	3.1
6.	Seinfeld	5.3		Warner Bros. Vol 35*	3.1
7.	Dr. Phil Show	5.0	23.	Entertainment Tonight (weekend)	2.8
	ESPN NFL Regular Season 2	5.0		People's Court	2.8
9.	Entertainment Tonight	4.9		Buena Vista VI*	2.8
10.	CSI	4.8	24.	Maury	2.7
11.	Seinfeld (weekend)	4.7		King of the Hill	2.7
	Judge Judy	4.7		Revolution 1*	2.7
13.	Friends	4.6		Insider	2.7
14.	That 70s Show	3.9		Warner Bros. Vol 33*	2.7
15.	Wheel of Fortune (weekend)	3.7		Legacy I*	2.7
16.	Everybody Loves Raymond (weekend)	3.5			

* Represents a package of films or programs sold for syndication.

Selected Reality TV Show Winners

Numbers in parentheses represent the season/edition of the show.

The Amazing Race. Debuted Aug. 2001 on CBS. (1) Rob Frisbee & Brennan Swain; (2) Chris Luca & Alex Boylan; (3) Flo Pesenti & Zach Behr; (4) Reichen Lehmkuhl & Chip Arndt; (5) Chip & Kim McAllister; (6) Freddy Holliday & Kendra Bentley; (7) Uchenna & Joyce Agu; (8) The Linz Family; (9) B.J. Averell & Tyler MacNiven.

American Idol. Debuted July 2002 on Fox. (1) Kelly Clarkson; (2) Ruben Studdard; (3) Fantasia Barrino; (4) Carrie Underwood; (5) Taylor Hicks.

America's Next Top Model. Debuted May 2003. (1) Adrianne Curry; (2) Yoanna House; (3) Eva Pigford; (4) Naima Mora; (5) Nicole Linkletter; (6) Danielle Evans.

The Apprentice. Debuted Jan. 2004 on NBC. (1) Bill Rancic; (2) Kelly Perdew; (3) Kendra Todd; (4) Randal Pinkett; (5) Sean Yazbeck.

The Bachelor. Debuted Mar. 2002 on ABC. (1) Alex Michel chose Amanda Marsh; (2) Aaron Buerge chose Helene Eksterowicz; (3) Andrew Firestone chose Jen Schefft; (4) Bob Guiney chose Estella Gardinier; (5) Jesse Palmer chose Jessica Bowlin; (6) Byron Velvick chose Mary Delgado; (7) Charlie O'Connell chose Sarah Brice; (8) Travis Stork chose Sarah Stone.

The Bachelorette. Debuted Jan. 2003 on ABC. (1) Trista Rehn chose Ryan Sutter; (2) Meredith Phillips chose Ian McKee; (3) Jen Schefft chose Jerry Ferris.

Big Brother. Debuted July 2000 on CBS. (1) Eddie McGee; (2) Will Kirby; (3) Lisa Donahue; (4) Jun Song; (5) Drew Daniel; (6) Maggie Ausburn; (7) Mike Malin.

The Contender. Debuted Mar. 2005 on NBC; 2nd season aired on ESPN. (1) Sergio Mora; (2) Grady Brewer.

Dancing With the Stars. Debuted June 2005 on ABC. (1) John O'Hurley & Charlotte Jorgensen; (2) Drew Lachey & Cheryl Burke.

Hell's Kitchen. Debuted Mar. 2005 on FOX. (1) Michael Wray; (2) Heather West.

Last Comic Standing. Debuted June 2003 on NBC. (1) Dat Phan; (2) John Heffron; (3) Alonzo Bodden; (4) Josh Blue.

Nashville Star. Debuted Mar. 2003 on USA Network. (1) Buddy Jewell; (2) Brad Cotter; (3) Erika Jo Heriges; (4) Chris Young.

Project Runway. Debuted Dec. 2004 on Bravo. (1) Jay McCarroll; (2) Chloe Dao.

Rock Star. Debuted July 2005 on CBS. INXS (1) J.D. Fortune; Supernova (2), Lukas Rossi.

Survivor. Debuted May 2000 on CBS. Borneo (1), Richard Hatch; Outback (2), Tina Wesson; Africa (3), Ethan Zohn; Marquesas (4), Vecepia Towery; Thailand (5), Brian Heidik; The Amazon (6), Jenna Morasca; Pearl Islands (7), Sandra Diaz-Twine; All-Stars (Panama) (8), Amber Brkich; Vanuatu (9), Chris Daugherty; Palau (10), Tom Westman; Guatemala (11), Danni Boatwright; Panama (12), Aras Baskauskas.

Top Chef. Debuted Mar. 2006 on Bravo. (1) Harold Dieterle.

Highest-Rated TV Shows of Each Season, 1950-51 to 2005-06

Source: Nielsen Media Research; regular series programs, Sept.-May season

Season	Program	Rating[1]	TV-owning households (in thousands)	Season	Program	Rating[1]	TV-owning households (in thousands)
1950-51	Texaco Star Theatre	61.6	10,320	1978-79	Laverne & Shirley	30.5	74,500
1951-52	Godfrey's Talent Scouts	53.8	15,300	1979-80	60 Minutes	28.2	76,300
1952-53	I Love Lucy	67.3	20,400	1980-81	Dallas	31.2	79,900
1953-54	I Love Lucy	58.8	26,000	1981-82	Dallas	28.4	81,500
1954-55	I Love Lucy	49.3	30,700	1982-83	60 Minutes	25.5	83,300
1955-56	$64,000 Question	47.5	34,900	1983-84	Dallas	25.7	83,800
1956-57	I Love Lucy	43.7	38,900	1984-85	Dynasty	25.0	84,900
1957-58	Gunsmoke	43.1	41,920	1985-86	Cosby Show	33.8	85,900
1958-59	Gunsmoke	39.6	43,950	1986-87	Cosby Show	34.9	87,400
1959-60	Gunsmoke	40.3	45,750	1987-88	Cosby Show	27.8	88,600
1960-61	Gunsmoke	37.3	47,200	1988-89	Roseanne	25.5	90,400
1961-62	Wagon Train	32.1	48,555	1989-90	Roseanne	23.4	92,100
1962-63	Beverly Hillbillies	36.0	50,300	1990-91	Cheers	21.6	93,100
1963-64	Beverly Hillbillies	39.1	51,600	1991-92	60 Minutes	21.7	92,100
1964-65	Bonanza	36.3	52,700	1992-93	60 Minutes	21.6	93,100
1965-66	Bonanza	31.8	53,850	1993-94	Home Improvement	21.9	94,200
1966-67	Bonanza	29.1	55,130	1994-95	Seinfeld	20.5	95,400
1967-68	Andy Griffith	27.6	56,670	1995-96	E.R.	22.0	95,900
1968-69	Rowan & Martin's Laugh-In	31.8	58,250	1996-97	E.R.	21.2	97,000
1969-70	Rowan & Martin's Laugh-In	26.3	58,500	1997-98	Seinfeld	22.0	98,000
1970-71	Marcus Welby, MD	29.6	60,100	1998-99	E.R.	17.8	99,400
1971-72	All in the Family	34.0	62,100	1999-2000	Who Wants to Be a Millionaire	18.6	100,800
1972-73	All in the Family	33.3	64,800	2000-01	Survivor II	17.4	102,200
1973-74	All in the Family	31.2	66,200	2001-02	Friends	15.3	105,500
1974-75	All in the Family	30.2	68,500	2002-03	CSI	16.1	106,700
1975-76	All in the Family	30.1	69,600	2003-04	CSI	15.9	108,400
1976-77	Happy Days	31.5	71,200	2004-05	CSI	16.3	106,900
1977-78	Laverne & Shirley	31.6	72,900	2005-06	American Idol-Tuesday	17.6	110,200

(1) Rating is percent of TV-owning households tuned in to the program. Data prior to 1988-89 exclude Alaska and Hawaii.

All-Time Highest-Rated Television Programs

Source: Nielsen Media Research, Jan. 1961-May 2006

Estimates exclude unsponsored or joint network telecasts (e.g., presidential addresses) or programs under 30 minutes long. Ranked by rating (percentage of TV-owning households tuned in to the program).

Rank	Program	Telecast date	Network	Rating (%)	Avg. households (in thousands)
1.	M*A*S*H (last episode)	2/28/83	CBS	60.2	50,150
2.	Dallas (Who Shot J.R.?)	11/21/80	CBS	53.3	41,470
3.	Roots-Pt. 8	1/30/77	ABC	51.1	36,380
4.	Super Bowl XVI	1/24/82	CBS	49.1	40,020
5.	Super Bowl XVII	1/30/83	NBC	48.6	40,480
6.	XVII Winter Olympics - 2nd Wed	2/23/94	CBS	48.5	45,690
7.	Super Bowl XX	1/26/86	NBC	48.3	41,490
8.	Gone With the Wind-Pt. 1	11/7/76	NBC	47.7	33,960
9.	Gone With the Wind-Pt. 2	11/8/76	NBC	47.4	33,750
10.	Super Bowl XII	1/15/78	CBS	47.2	34,410
11.	Super Bowl XIII	1/21/79	NBC	47.1	35,090
12.	Bob Hope Christmas Show	1/15/70	NBC	46.6	27,260
13.	Super Bowl XIX	1/20/85	ABC	46.4	39,390
	Super Bowl XVIII	1/22/84	CBS	46.4	38,800
15.	Super Bowl XIV	1/20/80	CBS	46.3	35,330
16.	Super Bowl XXX	1/28/96	NBC	46.0	44,150
	ABC Theater (The Day After)	11/20/83	ABC	46.0	38,550
18.	Roots-Pt. 6	1/28/77	ABC	45.9	32,680
	The Fugitive	8/29/67	ABC	45.9	25,700
20.	Super Bowl XXI	1/25/87	CBS	45.8	40,030
21.	Roots-Pt. 5	1/27/77	ABC	45.7	32,540
22.	Super Bowl XXVIII	1/30/94	NBC	45.5	42,860
	Cheers (last episode)	5/20/93	NBC	45.5	42,360
24.	Ed Sullivan	2/9/64	CBS	45.3	23,240
25.	Super Bowl XXVII	1/31/93	NBC	45.1	41,990
26.	Bob Hope Christmas Show	1/14/71	NBC	45.0	27,050
27.	Roots-Pt. 3	1/25/77	ABC	44.8	31,900
28.	Super Bowl XXXII	1/25/98	NBC	44.5	43,630
29.	Super Bowl XV	1/25/81	NBC	44.4	34,540
	Super Bowl XI	1/9/77	NBC	44.4	31,610
31.	Super Bowl VI	1/16/72	CBS	44.2	27,450
32.	XVII Winter Olympics - 2nd Fri	2/25/94	CBS	44.1	41,540
	Roots-Pt. 2	1/24/77	ABC	44.1	31,400
34.	Beverly Hillbillies	1/8/64	CBS	44.0	22,570
35.	Roots-Pt. 4	1/26/77	ABC	43.8	31,190
	Ed Sullivan	2/16/64	CBS	43.8	22,445
37.	Super Bowl XXIII	1/22/89	NBC	43.5	39,320
38.	Academy Awards	4/7/70	ABC	43.4	25,390
39.	Super Bowl XXXI	1/26/97	FOX	43.3	42,000
	Super Bowl XXXIV	1/30/00	ABC	43.3	43,620
41.	Thorn Birds-Pt. 3	3/29/83	ABC	43.2	35,990
42.	Thorn Birds-Pt. 4	3/30/83	ABC	43.1	35,900
43.	CBS NFC Championship	1/10/82	CBS	42.9	34,960
44.	Beverly Hillbillies	1/15/64	CBS	42.8	21,960
45.	Super Bowl VII	1/14/73	NBC	42.7	27,670

100 Leading U.S. Advertisers, 2005

Source: Reprinted with permission from Ad Age (www.adage.com). © 2006, Crain Communications Inc.

(in millions of dollars)

Rank	Advertiser	Ad Spending	Rank	Advertiser	Ad Spending	Rank	Advertiser	Ad Spending
1.	Procter & Gamble Co.	$4,609	35.	Citigroup	$1,004	69.	Kroger Co.	$489
2.	General Motors Corp.	4,353	36.	Wal-Mart Stores.	973	70.	Capital One Financial Corp.	489
3.	Time Warner	3,494	37.	Microsoft Corp.	945	71.	Doctor's Associates.	487
4.	Verizon Communications	2,484	38.	Dell	939	72.	Eli Lilly & Co.	475
5.	AT&T	2,471	39.	General Mills	922	73.	Campbell Soup Co.	469
6.	Ford Motor Co.	2,398	40.	Anheuser-Busch Cos.	919	74.	MasterCard International.	466
7.	Walt Disney Co.	2,279	41.	Wyeth	919	75.	Burger King Corp.	464
8.	Johnson & Johnson	2,209	42.	Berkshire Hathaway	909	76.	Wendy's International	462
9.	GlaxoSmithKline.	2,194	43.	Cendant Corp.	869	77.	Mattel	460
10.	DaimlerChrysler	2,179	44.	Yum Brands.	863	78.	Sara Lee Corp.	459
11.	Pfizer	2,153	45.	Schering-Plough Corp.	853	79.	ConAgra Foods.	456
12.	General Electric Co.	1,917	46.	Hewlett-Packard Co.	833	80.	SABMiller	453
13.	Toyota Motor Corp.	1,785	47.	Best Buy Co.	812	81.	State Farm Mutual Auto Insurance Co.	449
14.	Sony Corp.	1,778	48.	AstraZeneca	796	82.	JP Morgan Chase & Co.	448
15.	Sears Holdings Corp.	1,713	49.	Merck & Co.	769	83.	Comcast Corp.	425
16.	Sprint Nextel Corp.	1,663	50.	Deutsche Telekom.	721	84.	Cadbury Schweppes.	417
17.	McDonald's Corp.	1,662	51.	Kellogg Co.	715	85.	Abbott Laboratories.	415
18.	Unilever	1,522	52.	Coca-Cola Co.	703	86.	Vonage Holdings Corp.	414
19.	Viacom	1,497	53.	Lowe's Cos.	695	87.	Circuit City Stores	406
20.	Altria Group	1,486	54.	Sanofi-Aventis	687	88.	Molson Coors Brewing Co.	401
21.	PepsiCo	1,467	55.	Mars Inc.	629	89.	United Parcel Service	397
22.	L'Oreal	1,456	56.	Nike	609	90.	Allstate Corp.	394
23.	Federated Department Stores	1,453	57.	Hyundai Motor Co.	608	91.	Limited Brands	393
24.	Nissan Motor Co.	1,441	58.	IBM Corp.	606	92.	Kimberly-Clark Corp.	369
25.	Honda Motor Co.	1,325	59.	Diageo	599	93.	Adidas.	363
26.	Nestle.	1,219	60.	Kohl's Corp.	595	94.	Supervalu	361
27.	U.S. Government	1,218	61.	Volkswagen	590	95.	Kia Motors Corp.	357
28.	Novartis	1,163	62.	Bristol-Myers Squibb Co.	582	96.	Bank of America Corp.	356
29.	News Corp.	1,160	63.	Bayer.	572	97.	Philips Electronics.	337
30.	Home Depot	1,114	64.	Clorox Co.	571	98.	Reckitt Benckiser	329
31.	Estee Lauder Cos.	1,093	65.	SC Johnson.	546	99.	Joh. A. Benckiser	327
32.	J.C. Penney Co.	1,072	66.	Safeway.	528	100.	TD Ameritrade Holding Corp.	322
33.	American Express Co.	1,067	67.	Visa International.	515			
34.	Target Corp.	1,020	68.	Gap Inc.	500			

U.S. Ad Spending Categories, 2005

Source: Reprinted with permission from Ad Age (www.adage.com). © 2006, Crain Communications Inc.

(in millions of dollars)

Category	Total	Mag.	Bus. Pub.	News-paper	Out door	Network	Spot	Cable	Spanish Lang.	Syndi-cated	Radio	Inter-net
Automotive	$20,959	$2,360	$84	$6,294	$351	$3,015	$4,925	$1,461	$280	$190	$1,578	$422
Retail	18,630	1,684	127	6,958	359	2,021	2,721	994	280	268	2,184	1,035
Telecommunications, internet and ISP.	9,896	627	229	2,159	219	1,693	1,019	980	218	429	798	1,525
Financial services.	8,477	1,053	242	1,832	246	1,547	543	948	70	177	787	1,032
Medicine & remedies	8,442	2,242	59	221	18	2,719	359	1,388	132	621	291	390
General services	7,868	629	346	2,136	498	149	1,741	335	12	110	1,197	715
Food, beverages & candy.	7,313	1,843	107	61	80	2,052	529	1,415	243	524	351	109
Personal care.	5,648	2,209	42	25	25	1,470	191	883	152	515	58	79
Movies, recorded video & music	5,583	325	98	1,140	105	1,637	428	934	320	217	263	116
Airlines, hotels, car rental, travel	5,546	1,168	293	1,574	294	336	412	510	25	35	387	513
Restaurants	5,062	177	3	179	226	1,539	1,329	704	139	210	513	45
Media	4,912	1,487	252	1,253	268	35	187	58	15	37	780	543
Government, politics, religion.	4,602	328	43	447	124	1,385	842	390	485	33	353	172
Insurance	2,894	219	61	289	97	496	571	501	39	131	331	162
Apparel.	2,727	1,998	91	46	34	233	20	221	13	25	19	27
Real estate	2,722	259	16	1,763	197	89	104	68	11	24	121	70
Computers, software	2,303	441	798	211	28	170	21	195	0	6	76	358
Beer, wine & liquor.	2,208	498	15	73	186	553	99	392	81	30	238	43
Home furnishings, appliances & electronics.	2,055	851	230	91	7	324	78	291	11	40	55	79
Home supplies & cleaners	1,861	333	11	7	4	626	103	458	88	181	37	14
Education	1,791	147	275	303	62	8	451	115	6	14	157	254
Toys & games	1,297	135	110	5	3	234	15	602	7	55	9	123
Hardware & home building supplies	1,039	377	179	82	7	83	76	165	9	9	37	15
Pet food & pet care	576	143	2	3	0	149	24	86	0	42	8	120
Gas & oil.	545	86	8	70	44	94	30	87	2	5	109	8
Sporting goods	533	374	3	18	4	68	9	40	0	1	8	10
Office equipment	369	126	54	25	1	76	3	44	0	23	11	5
Shipping & freight.	359	42	35	16	5	163	1	42	0	0	49	7
Cigarettes & tobacco	155	139	5	1	1	1	0	0	0	0	1	6
Direct response advertising	6,101	2,241	158	506	12	267	184	1,845	431	249	64	154
Miscellaneous	4,373	871	1,062	1,217	34	407	99	302	4	22	180	174
Total.	**146,844**	**25,408**	**5,038**	**29,004**	**3,529**	**23,635**	**17,115**	**16,453**	**3,072**	**4,223**	**11,045**	**8,323**

AWARDS — MEDALS — PRIZES

The Alfred B. Nobel Prize Winners, 1901-2005

Alfred B. Nobel (1833-96) bequeathed $9 mil, the interest on which was to be distributed yearly to those judged to have most benefited humankind in physics, chemistry, medicine-physiology, literature, and promotion of peace. Prizes were first awarded in 1901. The 1st prize in economics was awarded in 1969, funded by Sweden's central bank. Each prize is now worth 10 mil Swedish kroner (about $1.3 mil). If year is omitted, no award was given. For 2006 winners, see page 44.

Physics

1901 Wilhelm C. Röntgen, Ger.
1902 Hendrik A. Lorentz, Pieter Zeeman, Neth.
1903 Antoine Henri Becquerel, Pierre Curie, Fr.; Marie Curie, Pol.-Fr.
1904 Lord Rayleigh (John W. Strutt), UK
1905 Philipp E. A. von Lenard, Ger.
1906 Sir Joseph J. Thomson, UK
1907 Albert A. Michelson, U.S.
1908 Gabriel Lippmann, Fr.
1909 Carl F. Braun, Ger.; Guglielmo Marconi, It.
1910 Johannes D. van der Waals, Neth.
1911 Wilhelm Wien, Ger.
1912 Nils G. Dalén, Swed.
1913 Heike Kamerlingh Onnes, Neth.
1914 Max von Laue, Ger.
1915 Sir William H. Bragg, Sir William L. Bragg, UK
1917 Charles G. Barkla, UK
1918 Max K. E. L. Planck, Ger.
1919 Johannes Stark, Ger.
1920 Charles E. Guillaume, Fr.-Switz.
1921 Albert Einstein, Ger.-U.S.
1922 Niels Bohr, Den.
1923 Robert A. Millikan, U.S.
1924 Karl M. G. Siegbahn, Swed.
1925 James Franck, Gustav Hertz, Ger.
1926 Jean B. Perrin, Fr.
1927 Arthur H. Compton, U.S.; Charles T. R. Wilson, UK
1928 Owen W. Richardson, UK
1929 Prince Louis-Victor de Broglie, Fr.
1930 Sir Chandrasekhara V. Raman, India
1932 Werner Heisenberg, Ger.
1933 Paul A. M. Dirac, UK; Erwin Schrödinger, Austria
1935 Sir James Chadwick, UK
1936 Carl D. Anderson, U.S.; Victor F. Hess, Austria
1937 Clinton J. Davisson, U.S.; Sir George P. Thomson, UK
1938 Enrico Fermi, It.-U.S.
1939 Ernest O. Lawrence, U.S.
1943 Otto Stern, U.S.
1944 Isidor Isaac Rabi, U.S.
1945 Wolfgang Pauli, U.S.-Austria
1946 Percy W. Bridgman, U.S.
1947 Sir Edward V. Appleton, UK
1948 Patrick M. S. Blackett, UK

1949 Hideki Yukawa, Jpn.
1950 Cecil F. Powell, UK
1951 Sir John D. Cockcroft, UK; Ernest T. S. Walton, Ire.
1952 Felix Bloch, Edward M. Purcell, U.S.
1953 Frits Zernike, Neth.
1954 Max Born, UK; Walter Bothe, Ger.
1955 Polykarp Kusch, Willis E. Lamb, U.S.
1956 John Bardeen, Walter H. Brattain, William Shockley, U.S.
1957 Tsung-dao Lee, Chen Ning Yang, U.S.-China
1958 Pavel Cherenkov, Il'ja Frank, Igor Y. Tamm, USSR
1959 Owen Chamberlain, Emilio G. Segre, U.S.
1960 Donald A. Glaser, U.S.
1961 Robert Hofstadter, U.S.; Rudolf L. Mossbauer, Ger.
1962 Lev D. Landau, USSR
1963 Maria Goeppert-Mayer, Eugene P. Wigner, U.S.; J. Hans D. Jensen, Ger.
1964 Nicolay G. Basov, Aleksandr M. Prokhorov, USSR; Charles H. Townes, U.S.
1965 Richard P. Feynman, Julian S. Schwinger, U.S.; Sin-Itiro Tomonaga, Jpn.
1966 Alfred Kastler, Fr.
1967 Hans A. Bethe, U.S.
1968 Luis W. Alvarez, U.S.
1969 Murray Gell-Mann, U.S.
1970 Louis Néel, Fr.; Hannes Alfvén, Swed.
1971 Dennis Gabor, UK
1972 John Bardeen, Leon N. Cooper, John R. Schrieffer, U.S.
1973 Ivar Giaever, U.S.; Leo Esaki, Jpn.; Brian D. Josephson, UK
1974 Sir Martin Ryle, Antony Hewish, UK
1975 Leo James Rainwater, U.S.; Ben Mottelson, U.S.-Den.; Aage Bohr, Den.
1976 Burton Richter, Samuel C.C. Ting, U.S.
1977 John H. van Vleck, Philip W. Anderson, U.S.; Sir Nevill F. Mott, UK
1978 Pyotr Kapitsa, USSR; Arno Penzias, Robert Wilson, U.S.
1979 Steven Weinberg, Sheldon L. Glashow, U.S.; Abdus Salam, Pakistan

1980 James W. Cronin, Val L. Fitch, U.S.
1981 Nicolaas Bloembergen, Arthur Schawlow, U.S.; Kai M. Siegbahn, Swed.
1982 Kenneth G. Wilson, U.S.
1983 Subramanyan Chandrasekhar, William A. Fowler, U.S.
1984 Carlo Rubbia, It.; Simon van der Meer, Neth.
1985 Klaus von Klitzing, Ger.
1986 Ernest Ruska, Ger.; Gerd Binnig, Ger.; Heinrich Rohrer, Switz.
1987 K. Alex Müller, Switz.; J. Georg Bednorz, Ger.
1988 Leon M. Lederman, Melvin Schwartz, Jack Steinberger, U.S.
1989 Norman F. Ramsey, U.S.; Hans G. Dehmelt, Ger.-U.S.; Wolfgang Paul, Ger.
1990 Richard E. Taylor, Can.; Jerome I. Friedman, Henry W. Kendall, U.S.
1991 Pierre-Gilles de Gennes, Fr.
1992 Georges Charpak, Pol.-Fr.
1993 Joseph H. Taylor, Russell A. Hulse, U.S.
1994 Bertram N. Brockhouse, Can.; Clifford G. Shull, U.S.
1995 Martin Perl, Frederick Reines, U.S.
1996 David M. Lee, Douglas D. Osheroff, Robert C. Richardson, U.S.
1997 Steven Chu, William D. Phillips, U.S.; Claude Cohen-Tannoudji, Fr.
1998 Robert B. Laughlin, U.S.; Horst L. Störmer, Ger.-U.S.; Daniel C. Tsui, China-U.S.
1999 Gerardus't Hooft and Martinus J. G. Veltman, Netherlands
2000 Jack S. Kilby, U.S.; Herbert Kroemer, Ger.-U.S.; Zhores I. Alferov, Russ.
2001 Eric A. Cornell, Carl E. Wieman, U.S.; Wolfgang Ketterle, Ger.
2002 Raymond Davis Jr., Riccardo Giacconi, U.S.; Masatoshi Koshiba, Jpn.
2003 Vitaly L. Ginzburg, Alexei A. Abrikosov, Russ., Anthony J. Leggett, U.S.
2004 David J. Gross, H. David Politzer, Frank Wilczek, U.S.
2005 Roy J. Glauber, John L. Hall, U.S.; Theodor W. Hänsch, Ger.

Chemistry

1901 Jacobus H. van't Hoff, Neth.
1902 Emil Fischer, Ger.
1903 Svante A. Arrhenius, Swed.
1904 Sir William Ramsay, UK
1905 Adolf von Baeyer, Ger.
1906 Henri Moissan, Fr.
1907 Eduard Buchner, Ger.
1908 Ernest Rutherford, UK
1909 Wilhelm Ostwald, Ger.
1910 Otto Wallach, Ger.
1911 Marie Curie, Pol.-Fr.
1912 Victor Grignard, Paul Sabatier, Fr.
1913 Alfred Werner, Switz.
1914 Theodore W. Richards, U.S.
1915 Richard M. Willstätter, Ger.
1918 Fritz Haber, Ger.
1920 Walther H. Nernst, Ger.
1921 Frederick Soddy, UK
1922 Francis W. Aston, UK
1923 Fritz Pregl, Austria
1925 Richard A. Zsigmondy, Ger.
1926 Theodor Svedberg, Swed.
1927 Heinrich O. Wieland, Ger.
1928 Adolf O. R. Windaus, Ger.
1929 Sir Arthur Harden, UK; Hans von Euler-Chelpin, Swed.
1930 Hans Fischer, Ger.
1931 Friedrich Bergius, Carl Bosch, Ger.
1932 Irving Langmuir, U.S.
1934 Harold C. Urey, U.S.
1935 Frédéric & Irene Joliot-Curie, Fr.
1936 Peter J. W. Debye, Neth.
1937 Walter N. Haworth, UK; Paul Karrer, Switz.

1938 Richard Kuhn, Ger.
1939 Adolf F. J. Butenandt, Ger.; Leopold Ruzicka, Switz.
1943 George de Hevesy, Hung.
1944 Otto Hahn, Ger.
1945 Artturi I. Virtanen, Fin.
1946 James B. Sumner, John H. Northrop, Wendell M. Stanley, U.S.
1947 Sir Robert Robinson, UK
1948 Arne W. K. Tiselius, Swed.
1949 William F. Giauque, U.S.
1950 Kurt Alder, Otto P. H. Diels, Ger.
1951 Edwin M. McMillan, Glenn T. Seaborg, U.S.
1952 Archer J. P. Martin, Richard L. M. Synge, UK
1953 Hermann Staudinger, Ger.
1954 Linus C. Pauling, U.S.
1955 Vincent du Vigneaud, U.S.
1956 Sir Cyril N. Hinshelwood, UK; Nikolay N. Semenov, USSR
1957 Lord (Alexander R.) Todd, UK
1958 Frederick Sanger, UK
1959 Jaroslav Heyrovsky, Czech.
1960 Willard F. Libby, U.S.
1961 Melvin Calvin, U.S.
1962 John C. Kendrew, Max F. Perutz, UK
1963 Giulio Natta, It.; Karl Ziegler, Ger.
1964 Dorothy C. Hodgkin, UK
1965 Robert B. Woodward, U.S.
1966 Robert S. Mulliken, U.S.
1967 Manfred Eigen, Ger.; Ronald G. W. Norrish, George Porter, UK
1968 Lars Onsager, U.S.

1969 Derek H. R. Barton, UK; Odd Hassel, Nor.
1970 Luis F. Leloir, Arg.
1971 Gerhard Herzberg, Can.
1972 Christian B. Anfinsen, Stanford Moore, William H. Stein, U.S.
1973 Ernst Otto Fischer, Ger.; Geoffrey Wilkinson, UK
1974 Paul J. Flory, U.S.
1975 John Cornforth, Austral.-UK; Vladimir Prelog, Bosnia-Switz.
1976 William N. Lipscomb, U.S.
1977 Ilya Prigogine, Belg.
1978 Peter Mitchell, UK
1979 Herbert C. Brown, U.S.; Georg Wittig, Ger.
1980 Paul Berg, Walter Gilbert, U.S.; Frederick Sanger, UK
1981 Kenichi Fukui, Jpn.; Roald Hoffmann, U.S.
1982 Aaron Klug, UK-Lith.
1983 Henry Taube, Can.
1984 Robert Bruce Merrifield, U.S.
1985 Herbert A. Hauptman, Jerome Karle, U.S.
1986 Dudley Herschbach, Yuan T. Lee, U.S.; John C. Polanyi, Can.
1987 Donald J. Cram, Charles J. Pedersen, U.S.; Jean-Marie Lehn, Fr.
1988 Johann Deisenhofer, Robert Huber, Hartmut Michel, Ger.
1989 Thomas R. Cech, Sidney Altman, U.S.
1990 Elias James Corey, U.S.

1991 Richard R. Ernst, Switz.	1997 Paul D. Boyer, U.S., & John E. Walker, UK; Jens C. Skou, Den.	2002 John B. Fenn, U.S.; Koichi Tanaka, Jpn.; Kurt Wüthrich, Switz.
1992 Rudolph A. Marcus, Can.-U.S.		
1993 Kary B. Mullis, U.S.; Michael Smith, UK-Can.	1998 Walter Kohn, U.S.; John A. Pople, UK	2003 Peter Agre, Roderick MacKinnon, U.S.
	1999 Ahmed H. Zewail, U.S.	2004 Aaron Ciechanover, Avram Hershko, Isr.; Irwin Rose, U.S.
1994 George A. Olah, U.S.	2000 Alan J. Heeger, U.S.; Alan G. MacDiarmid, N. Zea.-U.S.; Hideki Shirakawa, Jpn.	
1995 Paul Crutzen, Neth.; Mario Molina, Mex.-U.S.; Sherwood Rowland, U.S.		2005 Yves Chauvin, Fr.; Robert H. Grubbs, Richard R. Schrock, U.S.
1996 Sir Harold W. Kroto, UK; Robert F. Curl Jr., Richard E. Smalley, U.S.	2001 K. Barry Sharpless, U.S.; William S. Knowles, U.S., Ryoji Noyori, Jpn.	

Physiology or Medicine

1901 Emil A. von Behring, Ger.	1950 Philip S. Hench, Edward C. Kendall, U.S.; Tadeus Reichstein, Switz.	1978 Daniel Nathans, Hamilton O. Smith, U.S.; Werner Arber, Switz.
1902 Sir Ronald Ross, UK		
1903 Niels R. Finsen, Den.	1951 Max Theiler, U.S.	1979 Allan M. Cormack, U.S.; Godfrey N. Hounsfield, UK
1904 Ivan P. Pavlov, Russ.	1952 Selman A. Waksman, U.S.	
1905 Robert Koch, Ger.	1953 Hans A. Krebs, UK; Fritz A. Lipmann, U.S.	1980 Baruj Benacerraf, George Snell, U.S.; Jean Dausset, Fr.
1906 Camillo Golgi, It.; Santiago Ramon y Cajal, Spain		
1907 Charles L. A. Laveran, Fr.	1954 John F. Enders, Frederick C. Robbins, Thomas H. Weller, U.S.	1981 Roger W. Sperry, David H. Hubel, Torsten N. Wiesel, U.S.
1908 Paul Ehrlich, Ger.; Ilya Mechnikov, Fr.	1955 Alex H. T. Theorell, Swed.	
1909 Emil T. Kocher, Switz.	1956 André F. Cournand, Dickinson W. Richards, U.S.; Werner Forssmann, Ger.	1982 Sune Bergström, Bengt Samuelsson, Swed.; John R. Vane, UK
1910 Albrecht Kossel, Ger.		
1911 Allvar Gullstrand, Swed.		1983 Barbara McClintock, U.S.
1912 Alexis Carrel, Fr.	1957 Daniel Bovet, It.	1984 César Milstein, UK-Arg.; Georges J. F. Köhler, Ger.; Niels K. Jerne, UK-Den.
1913 Charles R. Richet, Fr.	1958 George W. Beadle, Edward L. Tatum, Joshua Lederberg, U.S.	
1914 Robert Bárány, Austria		
1919 Jules Bordet, Belg.	1959 Arthur Kornberg, Severo Ochoa, U.S.	1985 Michael S. Brown, Joseph L. Goldstein, U.S.
1920 Schack A. S. Krogh, Den.	1960 Sir F. MacFarlane Burnet, Austral.; Peter B. Medawar, UK	
1922 Archibald V. Hill, UK; Otto F. Meyerhof, Ger.		1986 Rita Levi-Montalcini, It.-U.S., Stanley Cohen, U.S.
	1961 Georg von Békésy, U.S.	1987 Susumu Tonegawa, Jpn.
1923 Frederick G. Banting, Can.; John J. R. Macleod, Scot.	1962 Francis H. C. Crick, Maurice H. F. Wilkins, UK; James D. Watson, U.S.	1988 Gertrude B. Elion, George H. Hitchings, U.S; Sir James Black, UK
1924 Willem Einthoven, Neth.	1963 Sir John C. Eccles, Austral.; Alan L. Hodgkin, Andrew F. Huxley, UK	1989 J. Michael Bishop, Harold E. Varmus, U.S.
1926 Johannes A. G. Fibiger, Den.		
1927 Julius Wagner-Jauregg, Austrian	1964 Konrad E. Bloch, U.S.; Feodor Lynen, Ger.	1990 Joseph E. Murray, E. Donnall Thomas, U.S.
1928 Charles J. H. Nicolle, Fr.		
1929 Christiaan Eijkman, Neth.; Sir Frederick G. Hopkins, UK	1965 François Jacob, André Lwoff, Jacques Monod, Fr.	1991 Edwin Neher, Bert Sakmann, Ger.
1930 Karl Landsteiner, U.S.	1966 Charles B. Huggins, Peyton Rous, U.S.	1992 Edmond H. Fisher, Edwin G. Krebs, U.S.
1931 Otto H. Warburg, Ger.		
1932 Edgar D. Adrian, Sir Charles S. Sherrington, UK	1967 Ragnar Granit, Swed.; Haldan Keffer Hartline, George Wald, U.S.	1993 Phillip A. Sharp, U.S.; Richard J. Roberts, UK
		1994 Alfred G. Gilman, Martin Rodbell, U.S.
1933 Thomas H. Morgan, U.S.	1968 Robert W. Holley, H. Gobind Khorana, Marshall W. Nirenberg, U.S.	1995 Edward B. Lewis, Eric F. Wieschaus, U.S.; Christiane Nüsslein-Volhard, Ger.
1934 George R. Minot, William P. Murphy, G. H. Whipple, U.S.		
1935 Hans Spemann, Ger.	1969 Max Delbrück, Alfred D. Hershey, Salvador Luria, U.S.	
1936 Sir Henry H. Dale, UK; Otto Loewi, U.S.	1970 Julius Axelrod, U.S.; Sir Bernard Katz, UK; Ulf von Euler, Swed.	1996 Peter C. Doherty, Austral.; Rolf M. Zinkernagel, Switz.
1937 Albert Szent-Gyorgyi, Hung.-U.S.		1997 Stanley B. Prusiner, U.S.
1938 Corneille J. F. Heymans, Belg.	1971 Earl W. Sutherland Jr., U.S.	1998 Robert F. Furchgott, Louis J. Ignarro, Ferid Murad, U.S.
1939 Gerhard Domagk, Ger.	1972 Gerald M. Edelman, U.S.; Rodney R. Porter, UK	
1943 Henrik C. P. Dam, Den.; Edward A. Doisy, U.S.		1999 Günter Blobel, U.S.
	1973 Karl von Frisch, Ger.; Konrad Lorenz, Austria; Nikolaas Tinbergen, UK	2000 Arvid Carlsson, Swed.; Paul Greengard, U.S.; Eric R. Kandel, Austria-U.S.
1944 Joseph Erlanger, Herbert S. Gasser, U.S.		
1945 Ernst B. Chain, Sir Alexander Fleming, Sir Howard W. Florey, UK	1974 Albert Claude, Lux.-U.S.; George Emil Palade, Rom.-U.S.; Christian de Duve, Belg.	2001 Leland H. Hartwell, U.S.; R. Timothy (Tim) Hunt, Sir Paul M. Nurse, UK
1946 Hermann J. Muller, U.S.		2002 Sydney Brenner, John E. Sulston, UK; H. Robert Horvitz, U.S.
1947 Carl F. Cori, Gerty T. Cori, U.S.; Bernardo A. Houssay, Arg.	1975 David Baltimore, Howard Temin, U.S.; Renato Dulbecco, It.-U.S.	
	1976 Baruch S. Blumberg, Daniel Carleton Gajdusek, U.S.	2003 Paul C. Lauterbur, U.S.; Sir Peter Mansfield, UK
1948 Paul H. Müller, Switz.		
1949 Walter R. Hess, Switz.; Antonio Moniz, Port.	1977 Rosalyn S. Yalow, Roger C.L. Guillemin, Andrew V. Schally, U.S.	2004 Richard Axel, Linda B. Buck, U.S.
		2005 Barry J. Marshall, J. Robin Warren, Australia

Literature

1901 Rene F. A. Sully Prudhomme, Fr.	1932 John Galsworthy, UK	1967 Miguel Angel Asturias, Guat.
1902 Theodor Mommsen, Ger.	1933 Ivan A. Bunin, USSR	1968 Yasunari Kawabata, Jpn.
1903 Bjørnstjerne Bjørnson, Nor.	1934 Luigi Pirandello, It.	1969 Samuel Beckett, Ire.
1904 Fréderic Mistral, Fr.; José Echegaray y Eizaguirre, Spain	1936 Eugene O'Neill, U.S.	1970 Aleksandr I. Solzhenitsyn, USSR
	1937 Roger Martin du Gard, Fr.	1971 Pablo Neruda, Chile
1905 Henryk Sienkiewicz, Pol.	1938 Pearl S. Buck, U.S.	1972 Heinrich Böll, Ger.
1906 Giosuè Carducci, It.	1939 Frans E. Sillanpää, Fin.	1973 Patrick White, Austral.
1907 Rudyard Kipling, UK	1944 Johannes V. Jensen, Den.	1974 Eyvind Johnson, Harry Edmund Martinson, Swed.
1908 Rudolf C. Eucken, Ger.	1945 Gabriela Mistral, Chile	
1909 Selma Lagerlöf, Swed.	1946 Hermann Hesse, Ger.-Switz.	1975 Eugenio Montale, It.
1910 Paul J. L. Heyse, Ger.	1947 André Gide, Fr.	1976 Saul Bellow, U.S.
1911 Maurice Maeterlinck, Belg.	1948 T.S. Eliot, UK	1977 Vicente Aleixandre, Spain
1912 Gerhart Hauptmann, Ger.	1949 William Faulkner, U.S.	1978 Isaac Bashevis Singer, U.S.
1913 Rabindranath Tagore, India	1950 Bertrand Russell, UK	1979 Odysseus Elytis, Greece
1915 Romain Rolland, Fr.	1951 Pär F. Lagerkvist, Swed.	1980 Czeslaw Milosz, Pol.-U.S.
1916 Verner von Heidenstam, Swed.	1952 François Mauriac, Fr.	1981 Elias Canetti, Bulg.-UK
1917 Karl A. Gjellerup, Henrik Pontoppidan, Den.	1953 Sir Winston Churchill, UK	1982 Gabriel García Márquez, Colombia-Mex.
	1954 Ernest Hemingway, U.S.	
1919 Carl F. G. Spitteler, Switz.	1955 Halldór K. Laxness, Ice.	1983 William Golding, UK
1920 Knut Hamsun, Nor.	1956 Juan Ramón Jiménez, Spain	1984 Jaroslav Siefert, Czech.
1921 Anatole France, Fr.	1957 Albert Camus, Fr.	1985 Claude Simon, Fr.
1922 Jacinto Benavente, Spain	1958 Boris L. Pasternak, USSR (declined)	1986 Wole Soyinka, Nigeria
1923 William Butler Yeats, Ire.	1959 Salvatore Quasimodo, It.	1987 Joseph Brodsky, USSR-U.S.
1924 Wladyslaw S. Reymont, Pol.	1960 Saint-John Perse, Fr.	1988 Naguib Mahfouz, Egypt
1925 George Bernard Shaw, Ire.-UK	1961 Ivo Andric, Yugo.	1989 Camilo José Cela, Spain
1926 Grazia Deledda, It.	1962 John Steinbeck, U.S.	1990 Octavio Paz, Mex.
1927 Henri Bergson, Fr.	1963 Giorgos Seferis, Greece	1991 Nadine Gordimer, S. Afr.
1928 Sigrid Undset, Nor.	1964 Jean-Paul Sartre, Fr. (declined)	1992 Derek Walcott, W. Ind.
1929 Thomas Mann, Ger.	1965 Mikhail Sholokhov, USSR	1993 Toni Morrison, U.S.
1930 Sinclair Lewis, U.S.	1966 Shmuel Yosef Agnon, Isr.; Nelly Sachs, Swed.	1994 Kenzaburo Oe, Jpn.
1931 Erik A. Karlfeldt, Swed.		1995 Seamus Heaney, Ire.

1996 Wislawa Szymborska, Pol.	2000 Gao Xingjian, China-Fr.	2003 J.M. Coetzee, S. Afr.
1997 Dario Fo, It.	2001 Sir V.S. Naipaul, UK	2004 Elfriede Jelinek, Austria
1998 Jose Saramago, Por.	2002 Imre Kertész, Hung.	2005 Harold Pinter, UK
1999 Günter Grass, Ger.		

Peace

1901 Jean H. Dunant, Switz.; Frédéric Passy, Fr.	1936 Carlos Saavedra Lamas, Arg.	1979 Mother Teresa of Calcutta, Alb.-Ind.
1902 Élie Ducommun, Charles A. Gobat, Switz.	1937 Viscount Cecil of Chelwood, UK	1980 Adolfo Pérez Esquivel, Arg.
1903 Sir William R. Cremer, UK	1938 Nansen International Office for Refugees	1981 Office of UN High Com. for Refugees
1904 Institute of International Law	1944 International Red Cross	1982 Alva Myrdal, Swed.; Alfonso García Robles, Mex.
1905 Baroness Bertha von Suttner, Austria	1945 Cordell Hull, U.S.	1983 Lech Walesa, Pol.
1906 Theodore Roosevelt, U.S.	1946 Emily G. Balch, John R. Mott, U.S.	1984 Bishop Desmond Tutu, S. Afr.
1907 Ernesto T. Moneta, It.; Louis Renault, Fr.	1947 Friends Service Council, UK; Amer. Friends Service Committee, U.S.	1985 Intl. Physicians for the Prevention of Nuclear War, U.S.
1908 Klas P. Arnoldson, Swed.; Fredrik Bajer, Den.	1949 Lord John Boyd Orr of Brechin, UK	1986 Elie Wiesel, Rom.-U.S.
1909 Auguste M. F. Beernaert, Belg.; Paul H. B. B. d'Estournelles de Constant, Fr.	1950 Ralph J. Bunche, U.S.	1987 Oscar Arias Sánchez, Costa Rica
1910 Permanent Intl. Peace Bureau	1951 Léon Jouhaux, Fr.	1988 UN Peacekeeping Forces
1911 Tobias M.C. Asser, Neth.; Alfred H. Fried, Austria	1952 Albert Schweitzer, Fr.	1989 Dalai Lama (Tenzin Gyatso), Tibet
1912 Elihu Root, U.S.	1953 George C. Marshall, U.S.	1990 Mikhail S. Gorbachev, USSR
1913 Henri La Fontaine, Belg.	1954 Office of UN High Com. for Refugees	1991 Aung San Suu Kyi, Burm.
1917 International Red Cross	1957 Lester B. Pearson, Can.	1992 Rigoberta Menchú Tum, Guat.
1919 Woodrow Wilson, U.S.	1958 Georges Pire, Belg.	1993 Frederik W. de Klerk, Nelson Mandela, S. Afr.
1920 Léon V.A. Bourgeois, Fr.	1959 Philip J. Noel-Baker, UK	1994 Yasser Arafat, Pal.; Shimon Peres, Yitzhak Rabin, Isr.
1921 Karl H. Branting, Swed.; Christian L. Lange, Nor.	1960 Albert J. Lutuli, S. Afr.	1995 Joseph Rotblat, Pol.-UK; Pugwash Conference
1922 Fridtjof Nansen, Nor.	1961 Dag Hammarskjöld, Swed.	1996 Bishop Carlos Ximenes Belo, José Ramos-Horta, Timor-Leste
1925 Sir J. Austen Chamberlain, UK; Charles G. Dawes, U.S.	1962 Linus C. Pauling, U.S.	1997 Jody Williams, U.S.; International Campaign to Ban Landmines
1926 Aristide Briand, Fr.; Gustav Stresemann, Ger.	1963 International Red Cross, League of Red Cross Societies	1998 John Hume, David Trimble, N. Ire.
1927 Ferdinand E. Buisson, Fr.; Ludwig Quidde, Ger.	1964 Martin Luther King Jr., U.S.	1999 Doctors Without Borders (Médecins Sans Frontières), Fr.
1929 Frank B. Kellogg, U.S.	1965 UN Children's Fund (UNICEF)	2000 Kim Dae-Jung, S. Kor.
1930 Nathan Söderblom, Swed.	1968 René Cassin, Fr.	2001 UN; Kofi Annan, Ghana
1931 Jane Addams, Nicholas Murray Butler, U.S.	1969 Intl. Labor Organization	2002 Jimmy Carter, U.S.
1933 Sir Norman Angell, UK	1970 Norman E. Borlaug, U.S.	2003 Shirin Ebadi, Iran
1934 Arthur Henderson, UK	1971 Willy Brandt, Ger.	2004 Wangari Maathai, Kenya
1935 Carl von Ossietzky, Ger.	1973 Henry Kissinger, U.S.; Le Duc Tho, N. Viet. (Tho declined)	2005 Mohamed ElBaradei, Egypt; International Atomic Energy Agency, Austria
	1974 Eisaku Sato, Jpn.; Seán MacBride, Ire.	
	1975 Andrei Sakharov, USSR	
	1976 Mairead Corrigan, Betty Williams, N. Ire.	
	1977 Amnesty International	
	1978 Anwar al-Sadat, Egypt; Menachem Begin, Isr.	

Nobel Memorial Prize in Economic Science

1969 Ragnar Frisch, Nor.; Jan Tinbergen, Neth.	1981 James Tobin, U.S.	1996 James A. Mirrlees, UK; William Vickrey, Can.-U.S.
1970 Paul A. Samuelson, U.S.	1982 George J. Stigler, U.S.	1997 Robert C. Merton, U.S.; Myron S. Scholes, Can.-U.S.
1971 Simon Kuznets, U.S.	1983 Gerard Debreu, Fr.-U.S.	1998 Amartya Sen, India
1972 Kenneth J. Arrow, U.S.; John R. Hicks, UK	1984 Richard Stone, UK	1999 Robert A. Mundell, Can.
1973 Wassily Leontief, U.S.	1985 Franco Modigliani, It.-U.S.	2000 James J. Heckman, Daniel L. McFadden, U.S.
1974 Gunnar Myrdal, Swed.; Friedrich A. von Hayek, Austria	1986 James M. Buchanan, U.S.	2001 George A. Akerlof, A. Michael Spence, Joseph E. Stiglitz, U.S.
1975 Tjalling Koopmans, Neth.-U.S.; Leonid Kantorovich, USSR	1987 Robert M. Solow, U.S.	2002 Daniel Kahneman, U.S.-Isr.; Vernon L. Smith, U.S.
1976 Milton Friedman, U.S.	1988 Maurice Allais, Fr.	2003 Robert F. Engle, U.S.; Clive W.J. Granger, UK
1977 Bertil Ohlin, Swed.; James E. Meade, UK	1989 Trygve Haavelmo, Nor.	2004 Finn E. Kydland, Nor.; Edward C. Prescott, U.S.
1978 Herbert A. Simon, U.S.	1990 Harry M. Markowitz, William F. Sharpe, Merton H. Miller, U.S.	2005 Robert J. Aumann, Israel-U.S.; Thomas C. Schelling, U.S.
1979 Theodore W. Schultz, U.S.; Sir Arthur Lewis, UK	1991 Ronald H. Coase, UK-U.S.	
1980 Lawrence R. Klein, U.S.	1992 Gary S. Becker, U.S.	
	1993 Robert W. Fogel, Douglass C. North, U.S.	
	1994 John C. Harsanyi, John F. Nash, U.S.; Reinhard Selten, Ger.	
	1995 Robert E. Lucas Jr., U.S.	

Pulitzer Prizes in Journalism, Letters, and Music

Endowed by Joseph Pulitzer (1847-1911), publisher of the *New York World*, in a bequest to Columbia Univ. and awarded annually, in years shown, for work the previous year. Prizes are now $10,000 in each category, except Public Service (in Journalism), for which a medal is given. For letters and music, prizes in past years are listed; if a year is omitted, no award was given that year.

Journalism, 2006

Public Service: *Times-Picayune* (New Orleans, LA) and *Sun Herald* (Biloxi-Gulfport, MS), for heroic and comprehensive coverage of Hurricane Katrina and its aftermath.

Breaking News Reporting: *Times-Picayune* (New Orleans, LA) staff for coverage of Hurricane Katrina, overcoming desperate conditions facing the city and newspaper.

Investigative Reporting: Susan Schmidt, James V. Grimaldi, and R. Jeffrey Smith of *Washington Post*, for a probe of Washington lobbyist Jack Abramoff that exposed congressional corruption.

Explanatory Reporting: David Finkel, *Washington Post*, for his study of the U.S. government's attempt to bring democracy to Yemen.

Beat Reporting: Dana Priest, *Washington Post*, for persistent reports on secret "black site" prisons and other controversial counterterrorism measures.

National Reporting: James Risen and Eric Lichtblau, *NY Times*, for carefully sourced stories on secret domestic eavesdropping program.

San Diego Union-Tribune and Copley News Service staffs, with notable work by Marcus Stern and Jerry Kammer, for their disclosure of bribery that sent former Congressman Randy Cunningham to prison.

International Reporting: Joseph Kahn and Jim Yardley, *NY Times*, for ambitious stories on ragged justice in China's evolving legal system.

Feature Writing: Jim Sheeler, *Rocky Mountain News* (Denver, CO), for a poignant story on a Marine major who helps families of Marines killed in Iraq cope.

Commentary: Nicholas D. Kristof, *NY Times*, for graphic columns that focus attention on genocide in Darfur at personal risk and gave voice to the voiceless in other parts of the world.

Criticism: Robin Givhan, *Washington Post*, for witty essays that transform fashion criticism into cultural criticism."

Editorial Writing: Rick Attig and Doug Bates, *Oregonian* (Portland, OR), for persuasive editorials on abuses in a forgotten Oregon mental hospital.

Editorial Cartooning: Mike Luckovich, *Atlanta Journal-Constitution*.

Breaking News Photog.: *Dallas Morning News* staff, for vivid photographs depicting chaos and pain in New Orleans after Hurricane Katrina.

Feature Photog.: Todd Heisler, *Rocky Mountain News* (Denver, CO), for a haunting look at funerals for Colorado Marines who return from Iraq in caskets.

Letters

Fiction

1918 Ernest Poole, *His Family*
1919 Booth Tarkington, *The Magnificent Ambersons*
1921 Edith Wharton, *The Age of Innocence*
1922 Booth Tarkington, *Alice Adams*
1923 Willa Cather, *One of Ours*
1924 Margaret Wilson, *The Able McLaughlins*
1925 Edna Ferber, *So Big*
1926 Sinclair Lewis, *Arrowsmith* (refused prize)
1927 Louis Bromfield, *Early Autumn*
1928 Thornton Wilder, *Bridge of San Luis Rey*
1929 Julia M. Peterkin, *Scarlet Sister Mary*
1930 Oliver LaFarge, *Laughing Boy*
1931 Margaret Ayer Barnes, *Years of Grace*
1932 Pearl S. Buck, *The Good Earth*
1933 T. S. Stribling, *The Store*
1934 Caroline Miller, *Lamb in His Bosom*
1935 Josephine W. Johnson, *Now in November*
1936 Harold L. Davis, *Honey in the Horn*
1937 Margaret Mitchell, *Gone With the Wind*
1938 John P. Marquand, *The Late George Apley*
1939 Marjorie Kinnan Rawlings, *The Yearling*
1940 John Steinbeck, *The Grapes of Wrath*
1942 Ellen Glasgow, *In This Our Life*
1943 Upton Sinclair, *Dragon's Teeth*
1944 Martin Flavin, *Journey in the Dark*
1945 John Hersey, *A Bell for Adano*
1947 Robert Penn Warren, *All the King's Men*
1948 James A. Michener, *Tales of the South Pacific*
1949 James Gould Cozzens, *Guard of Honor*
1950 A. B. Guthrie Jr., *The Way West*
1951 Conrad Richter, *The Town*
1952 Herman Wouk, *The Caine Mutiny*
1953 Ernest Hemingway, *The Old Man and the* Sea
1955 William Faulkner, *A Fable*
1956 MacKinlay Kantor, *Andersonville*
1958 James Agee, *A Death in the Family*
1959 Robert Lewis Taylor, *The Travels of Jaimie McPheeters*
1960 Allen Drury, *Advise and Consent*
1961 Harper Lee, *To Kill a Mockingbird*
1962 Edwin O'Connor, *The Edge of Sadness*
1963 William Faulkner, *The Reivers*
1965 Shirley Ann Grau, *The Keepers of the House*
1966 Katherine Anne Porter, *Collected Stories*
1967 Bernard Malamud, *The Fixer*
1968 William Styron, *The Confessions of Nat Turner*
1969 N. Scott Momaday, *House Made of Dawn*
1970 Jean Stafford, *Collected Stories*
1972 Wallace Stegner, *Angle of Repose*
1973 Eudora Welty, *The Optimist's Daughter*
1975 Michael Shaara, *The Killer Angels*
1976 Saul Bellow, *Humboldt's Gift*
1978 James Alan McPherson, *Elbow Room*
1979 John Cheever, *The Stories of John Cheever*
1980 Norman Mailer, *The Executioner's Song*
1981 John Kennedy Toole, *A Confederacy of Dunces*
1982 John Updike, *Rabbit Is Rich*
1983 Alice Walker, *The Color Purple*
1984 William Kennedy, *Ironweed*
1985 Alison Lurie, *Foreign Affairs*
1986 Larry McMurtry, *Lonesome Dove*
1987 Peter Taylor, *A Summons to Memphis*
1988 Toni Morrison, *Beloved*
1989 Anne Tyler, *Breathing Lessons*
1990 Oscar Hijuelos, *The Mambo Kings Play Songs of Love*
1991 John Updike, *Rabbit at Rest*
1992 Jane Smiley, *A Thousand Acres*
1993 Robert Olen Butler, *A Good Scent From a Strange Mountain*
1994 E. Annie Proulx, *The Shipping News*
1995 Carol Shields, *The Stone Diaries*
1996 Richard Ford, *Independence Day*
1997 Steven Millhauser, *Martin Dressler: The Tale of an American Dreamer*
1998 Philip Roth, *American Pastoral*
1999 Michael Cunningham, *The Hours*
2000 Jhumpa Lahiri, *Interpreter of Maladies*
2001 Michael Chabon, *The Amazing Adventures of Kavalier & Clay*
2002 Richard Russo, *Empire Falls*
2003 Jeffrey Eugenides, *Middlesex*
2004 Edward P. Jones, *The Known World*
2005 Marilynne Robinson, *Gilead*
2006 Geraldine Brooks, *March*

Drama

1918 Jesse Lynch Williams, *Why Marry?*
1920 Eugene O'Neill, *Beyond the Horizon*
1921 Zona Gale, *Miss Lulu Bett*
1922 Eugene O'Neill, *Anna Christie*
1923 Owen Davis, *Icebound*
1924 Hatcher Hughes, *Hell-Bent for Heaven*
1925 Sidney Howard, *They Knew What They Wanted*
1926 George Kelly, *Craig's Wife*
1927 Paul Green, *In Abraham's Bosom*
1928 Eugene O'Neill, *Strange Interlude*
1929 Elmer Rice, *Street Scene*
1930 Marc Connelly, *The Green Pastures*
1931 Susan Glaspell, *Alison's House*
1932 George S. Kaufman, Morrie Ryskind, and Ira Gershwin, *Of Thee I Sing*
1933 Maxwell Anderson, *Both Your Houses*
1934 Sidney Kingsley, *Men in White*
1935 Zoe Akins, *The Old Maid*
1936 Robert E. Sherwood, *Idiot's Delight*
1937 George S. Kaufman and Moss Hart, *You Can't Take It With You*
1938 Thornton Wilder, *Our Town*
1939 Robert E. Sherwood, *Abe Lincoln in Illinois*
1940 William Saroyan, *The Time of Your Life*
1941 Robert E. Sherwood, *There Shall Be No Night*
1943 Thornton Wilder, *The Skin of Our Teeth*
1945 Mary Chase, *Harvey*
1946 Russel Crouse and Howard Lindsay, *State of the Union*
1948 Tennessee Williams, *A Streetcar Named Desire*
1949 Arthur Miller, *Death of a Salesman*
1950 Richard Rodgers, Oscar Hammerstein 2nd and Joshua Logan, *South Pacific*
1952 Joseph Kramm, *The Shrike*
1953 William Inge, *Picnic*
1954 John Patrick, *Teahouse of the August Moon*
1955 Tennessee Williams, *Cat on a Hot Tin Roof*
1956 Frances Goodrich and Albert Hackett, *The Diary of Anne Frank*
1957 Eugene O'Neill, *Long Day's Journey Into Night*
1958 Ketti Frings, *Look Homeward, Angel*
1959 Archibald MacLeish, *J. B.*
1960 George Abbott, Jerome Weidman, Sheldon Harnick, and Jerry Bock, *Fiorello!*
1961 Tad Mosel, *All the Way Home*
1962 Frank Loesser and Abe Burrows, *How to Succeed in Business Without Really Trying*
1965 Frank D. Gilroy, *The Subject Was Roses*
1967 Edward Albee, *A Delicate Balance*
1969 Howard Sackler, *The Great White Hope*
1970 Charles Gordone, *No Place to Be Somebody*
1971 Paul Zindel, *The Effect of Gamma Rays on Man-in-the-Moon Marigolds*
1973 Jason Miller, *That Championship Season*
1975 Edward Albee, *Seascape*
1976 Michael Bennett, James Kirkwood, Nicholas Dante, Marvin Hamlisch, and Edward Kleban, *A Chorus Line*
1977 Michael Cristofer, *The Shadow Box*
1978 Donald L. Coburn, *The Gin Game*
1979 Sam Shepard, *Buried Child*
1980 Lanford Wilson, *Talley's Folly*
1981 Beth Henley, *Crimes of the Heart*
1982 Charles Fuller, *A Soldier's Play*
1983 Marsha Norman, *'night, Mother*
1984 David Mamet, *Glengarry Glen Ross*
1985 Stephen Sondheim and James Lapine, *Sunday in the Park With George*
1987 August Wilson, *Fences*
1988 Alfred Uhry, *Driving Miss Daisy*
1989 Wendy Wasserstein, *The Heidi Chronicles*
1990 August Wilson, *The Piano Lesson*
1991 Neil Simon, *Lost in Yonkers*
1992 Robert Schenkkan, *The Kentucky Cycle*
1993 Tony Kushner, *Angels in America: Millennium Approaches*
1994 Edward Albee, *Three Tall Women*
1995 Horton Foote, *The Young Man From Atlanta*
1996 Jonathan Larson, *Rent*
1998 Paula Vogel, *How I Learned to Drive*
1999 Margaret Edson, *Wit*
2000 Donald Margulies, *Dinner With Friends*
2001 David Auburn, *Proof*
2002 Suzan-Lori Parks, *Topdog/Underdog*
2003 Nilo Cruz, *Anna in the Tropics*
2004 Doug Wright, *I Am My Own Wife*
2005 John Patrick Shanley, *Doubt, a parable*
2006 No award given

History (U.S.)

1917 J. J. Jusserand, *With Americans of Past and Present Days*
1918 James Ford Rhodes, *History of the Civil War*
1920 Justin H. Smith, *The War With Mexico*
1921 William Sowden Sims, *The Victory at Sea*
1922 James Truslow Adams, *The Founding of New England*
1923 Charles Warren, *The Supreme Court in United States History*

1924 Charles Howard McIlwain, *The American Revolution: A Constitutional Interpretation*
1925 Frederick L. Paxton, *A History of the American Frontier*
1926 Edward Channing, *A History of the U.S.*
1927 Samuel Flagg Bemis, *Pinckney's Treaty*
1928 V. L Parrington, *Main Currents in American Thought*
1929 Fred A. Shannon, *The Organization and Administration of the Union Army, 1861-65*
1930 Claude H. Van Tyne, *The War of Independence*
1931 Bernadotte E. Schmitt, *The Coming of the War, 1914*
1932 Gen. John J. Pershing, *My Experiences in the World War*
1933 Frederick J. Turner, *The Significance of Sections in American History*
1934 Herbert Agar, *The People's Choice*
1935 Charles McLean Andrews, *The Colonial Period of American History*
1936 Andrew C. McLaughlin, *The Constitutional History of the United States*
1937 Van Wyck Brooks, *The Flowering of New England*
1938 Paul Herman Buck, *The Road to Reunion, 1865-1900*
1939 Frank Luther Mott, *A History of American Magazines*
1940 Carl Sandburg, *Abraham Lincoln: The War Years*
1941 Marcus Lee Hansen, *The Atlantic Migration, 1607-1860*
1942 Margaret Leech, *Reveille in Washington*
1943 Esther Forbes, *Paul Revere and the World He Lived In*
1944 Merle Curti, *The Growth of American Thought*
1945 Stephen Bonsal, *Unfinished Business*
1946 Arthur M. Schlesinger Jr., *The Age of Jackson*
1947 James Phinney Baxter III, *Scientists Against Time*
1948 Bernard De Voto, *Across the Wide Missouri*
1949 Roy F. Nichols, *The Disruption of American Democracy*
1950 O. W. Larkin, *Art and Life in America*
1951 R. Carlyle Buley, *The Old Northwest: Pioneer Period 1815-1840*
1952 Oscar Handlin, *The Uprooted*
1953 George Dangerfield, *The Era of Good Feelings*
1954 Bruce Catton, *A Stillness at Appomattox*
1955 Paul Horgan, *Great River: The Rio Grande in North American History*
1956 Richard Hofstadter, *The Age of Reform*
1957 George F. Kennan, *Russia Leaves the War*
1958 Bray Hammond, *Banks and Politics in America—From the Revolution to the Civil War*
1959 Leonard D. White and Jean Schneider, *The Republican Era; 1869-1901*
1960 Margaret Leech, *In the Days of McKinley*
1961 Herbert Feis, *Between War and Peace: The Potsdam Conference*
1962 Lawrence H. Gibson, *The Triumphant Empire: Thunderclouds Gather in the West*
1963 Constance McLaughlin Green, *Washington: Village and Capital, 1800-1878*
1964 Sumner Chilton Powell, *Puritan Village: The Formation of a New England Town*
1965 Irwin Unger, *The Greenback Era*
1966 Perry Miller, *Life of the Mind in America*
1967 William H. Goetzmann, *Exploration and Empire: The Explorer and Scientist in the Winning of the American West*
1968 Bernard Bailyn, *The Ideological Origins of the American Revolution*
1969 Leonard W. Levy, *Origin of the Fifth Amendment*
1970 Dean Acheson, *Present at the Creation: My Years in the State Department*
1971 James McGregor Burns, *Roosevelt: The Soldier of Freedom*
1972 Carl N. Degler, *Neither Black nor White*
1973 Michael Kammen, *People of Paradox: An Inquiry Concerning the Origins of American Civilization*
1974 Daniel J. Boorstin, *The Americans: The Democratic Experience*
1975 Dumas Malone, *Jefferson and His Time*
1976 Paul Horgan, *Lamy of Santa Fe*
1977 David M. Potter, *The Impending Crisis*
1978 Alfred D. Chandler Jr., *The Visible Hand: The Managerial Revolution in American Business*
1979 Don E. Fehrenbacher, *The Dred Scott Case: Its Significance in American Law and Politics*
1980 Leon F. Litwack, *Been in the Storm So Long*
1981 Lawrence A. Cremin, *American Education: The National Experience, 1783-1876*
1982 C. Vann Woodward, ed., *Mary Chesnut's Civil War*
1983 Rhys L. Issac, *The Transformation of Virginia, 1740-1790*
1985 Thomas K. McCraw, *Prophets of Regulation*
1986 Walter A. McDougall, *The Heavens and the Earth*
1987 Bernard Bailyn, *Voyagers to the West*
1988 Robert V. Bruce, *The Launching of Modern American Science, 1846-1876*
1989 Taylor Branch, *Parting the Waters: America in the King Years, 1954-63*; and James M. McPherson, *Battle Cry of Freedom: The Civil War Era*

1990 Stanley Karnow, *In Our Image: America's Empire in the Philippines*
1991 Laurel Thatcher Ulrich, *A Midwife's Tale: The Life of Martha Ballard,* based on her diary, 1785-1812
1992 Mark E. Neely Jr., *The Fate of Liberty: Abraham Lincoln and Civil Liberties*
1993 Gordon S. Wood, *The Radicalism of the American Revolution*
1995 Doris Kearns Goodwin, *No Ordinary Time: Franklin and Eleanor Roosevelt: The Home Front in World War II*
1996 Alan Taylor, *William Cooper's Town: Power and Persuasion on the Frontier of the Early American Republic*
1997 Jack N. Rakove, *Original Meanings: Politics and Ideas in the Making of the Constitution*
1998 Edward J. Larson, *Summer for the Gods: The Scopes Trial and America's Continuing Debate Over Science and Religion*
1999 Edwin G. Burrows and Mike Wallace, *Gotham: A History of New York City to 1898*
2000 David M. Kennedy, *Freedom From Fear: The American People in Depression and War, 1929-1945*
2001 Joseph J. Ellis, *Founding Brothers: The Revolutionary Generation*
2002—Louis Menand, *The Metaphysical Club: A Story of Ideas in America*
2003 Rick Atkinson, *An Army at Dawn: The War in North Africa, 1942-1943*
2004 Steven Hahn, *A Nation Under Our Feet: Black Political Struggles in the Rural South from Slavery to the Great Migration*
2005 David Hackett Fischer, *Washington's Crossing*
2006 David M. Oshinsky, *Polio: An American Story*

Biography or Autobiography

1917 Laura E. Richards and Maude Howe Elliott, assisted by Florence Howe Hall, *Julia Ward Howe*
1918 William Cabell Bruce, *Benjamin Franklin, Self-Revealed*
1919 Henry Adams, *The Education of Henry Adams*
1920 Albert J. Beveridge, *The Life of John Marshall*
1921 Edward Bok, *The Americanization of Edward Bok*
1922 Hamlin Garland, *A Daughter of the Middle Border*
1923 Burton J. Hendrick, *The Life and Letters of Walter H. Page*
1924 Michael Pupin, *From Immigrant to Inventor*
1925 M. A. DeWolfe Howe, *Barrett Wendell and His Letters*
1926 Harvey Cushing, *Life of Sir William Osler*
1927 Emory Holloway, *Whitman: An Interpretation in Narrative*
1928 Charles Edward Russell, *The American Orchestra and Theodore Thomas*
1929 Burton J. Hendrick, *The Training of an American: The Earlier Life and Letters of Walter H. Page*
1930 Marquis James, *The Raven (Sam Houston)*
1931 Henry James, *Charles W. Eliot*
1932 Henry F. Pringle, *Theodore Roosevelt*
1933 Allan Nevins, *Grover Cleveland*
1934 Tyler Dennett, *John Hay*
1935 Douglas Southall Freeman, *R. E. Lee*
1936 Ralph Barton Perry, *The Thought and Character of William James*
1937 Allan Nevins, *Hamilton Fish: The Inner History of the Grant Administration*
1938 Divided between Odell Shepard, *Pedlar's Progress* (Bronson Alcott) and Marquis James, *Andrew Jackson*
1939 Carl Van Doren, *Benjamin Franklin*
1940 Ray Stannard Baker, *Woodrow Wilson, Life and Letters*
1941 Ola Elizabeth Winslow, *Jonathan Edwards*
1942 Forrest Wilson, *Crusader in Crinoline* (Harriet Beecher Stowe)
1943 Samuel Eliot Morison, *Admiral of the Ocean Sea* (Christopher Columbus)
1944 Carleton Mabee, *The American Leonardo: The Life of Samuel F. B. Morse*
1945 Russell Blaine Nye, *George Bancroft: Brahmin Rebel.*
1946 Linny Marsh Wolfe, *Son of the Wilderness* (John Muir)
1947 William Allen White, *Autobiography of William Allen White*
1948 Margaret Clapp, *Forgotten First Citizen: John Bigelow*
1949 Robert E. Sherwood, *Roosevelt and Hopkins*
1950 Samuel Flagg Bemis, *John Quincy Adams and the Foundations of American Foreign Policy*
1951 Margaret Louise Coit, *John C. Calhoun: American Portrait*
1952 Merlo J. Pusey, *Charles Evans Hughes*
1953 David J. Mays, *Edmund Pendleton, 1721-1803*
1954 Charles A. Lindbergh, *The Spirit of St. Louis*
1955 William S. White, *The Taft Story*
1956 Talbot F. Hamlin, *Benjamin Henry Latrobe*
1957 John F. Kennedy, *Profiles in Courage*
1958 Douglas Southall Freeman (I-VI), John Alexander Carroll and Mary Wells Ashworth (VII), *George Washington*
1959 Arthur Walworth, *Woodrow Wilson: American Prophet*
1960 Samuel Eliot Morison, *John Paul Jones*
1961 David Donald, *Charles Sumner and the Coming of the Civil War*

1963 Leon Edel, *Henry James: Vols. 2-3*
1964 Walter Jackson Bate, *John Keats*
1965 Ernest Samuels, *Henry Adams*
1966 Arthur M. Schlesinger Jr., *A Thousand Days*
1967 Justin Kaplan, *Mr. Clemens and Mark Twain*
1968 George F. Kennan, *Memoirs (1925-1950)*
1969 B. L. Reid, *The Man From New York: John Quinn and His Friends*
1970 T. Harry Williams, *Huey Long*
1971 Lawrence Thompson, *Robert Frost: The Years of Triumph, 1915-1938*
1972 Joseph P. Lash, *Eleanor and Franklin*
1973 W. A. Swanberg, *Luce and His Empire*
1974 Louis Sheaffer, *O'Neill, Son and Artist*
1975 Robert A. Caro, *The Power Broker: Robert Moses and the Fall of New York*
1976 R.W.B. Lewis, *Edith Wharton: A Biography*
1977 John E. Mack, *A Prince of Our Disorder: The Life of T. E. Lawrence*
1978 Walter Jackson Bate, *Samuel Johnson*
1979 Leonard Baker, *Days of Sorrow and Pain: Leo Baeck and the Berlin Jews*
1980 Edmund Morris, *The Rise of Theodore Roosevelt*
1981 Robert K. Massie, *Peter the Great: His Life and World*
1982 William S. McFeely, *Grant: A Biography*
1983 Russell Baker, *Growing Up*
1984 Louis R. Harlan, *Booker T. Washington*
1985 Kenneth Silverman, *The Life and Times of Cotton Mather*
1986 Elizabeth Frank, *Louise Bogan: A Portrait*
1987 David J. Garrow, *Bearing the Cross: Martin Luther King Jr. and the Southern Christian Leadership Conference*
1988 David Herbert Donald, *Look Homeward: A Life of Thomas Wolfe*
1989 Richard Ellmann, *Oscar Wilde*
1990 Sebastian de Grazia, *Machiavelli in Hell*
1991 Steven Naifeh and Gregory White Smith, *Jackson Pollock: An American Saga*
1992 Lewis B. Puller Jr., *Fortunate Son: The Healing of a Vietnam Vet*
1993 David McCullough, *Truman*
1994 David Levering Lewis, *W.E.B. DuBois: Biography of a Race, 1868-1919*
1995 Joan D. Hedrick, *Harriet Beecher Stowe: A Life*
1996 Jack Miles, *God: A Biography*
1997 Frank McCourt, *Angela's Ashes: A Memoir*
1998 Katharine Graham, *Personal History*
1999 A. Scott Berg, *Lindbergh*
2000 Stacy Schiff, *Véra (Mrs. Vladimir Nabokov)*
2001 David Levering Lewis, *W.E.B. Du Bois: The Fight for Equality and the American Century, 1919-1963*
2002 David McCullough, *John Adams*
2003 Robert Caro, *The Years of Lyndon Johnson: Master of the Senate*
2004 William Taubman, *Khrushchev: The Man and His Era*
2005 Mark Stevens and Annalyn Swan, *de Kooning: An American Master*
2006 Kai Bird and Martin J. Sherwin, *American Prometheus: The Triumph and Tragedy of J. Robert Oppenheimer*

American Poetry

Before 1922, awards were funded by the Poetry Society.

1918 *Love Songs*, by Sara Teasdale;
1919 *Old Road to Paradise*, by Margaret Widdemer; *Corn Huskers*, by Carl Sandburg.
1922 Edwin Arlington Robinson, *Collected Poems*
1923 Edna St. Vincent Millay, *The Ballad of the Harp-Weaver; A Few Figs From Thistles; other works*
1924 Robert Frost, *New Hampshire: A Poem With Notes and Grace Notes*
1925 Edwin Arlington Robinson, *The Man Who Died Twice*
1926 Amy Lowell, *What's O'Clock*
1927 Leonora Speyer, *Fiddler's Farewell*
1928 Edwin Arlington Robinson, *Tristram*
1929 Stephen Vincent Benet, *John Brown's Body*
1930 Conrad Aiken, *Selected Poems*
1931 Robert Frost, *Collected Poems*
1932 George Dillon, *The Flowering Stone*
1933 Archibald MacLeish, *Conquistador*
1934 Robert Hillyer, *Collected Verse*
1935 Audrey Wurdemann, *Bright Ambush*
1936 Robert P. Tristram Coffin, *Strange Holiness*
1937 Robert Frost, *A Further Range*
1938 Marya Zaturenska, *Cold Morning Sky*
1939 John Gould Fletcher, *Selected Poems*
1940 Mark Van Doren, *Collected Poems*
1941 Leonard Bacon, *Sunderland Capture*
1942 William Rose Benet, *The Dust Which Is God*
1943 Robert Frost, *A Witness Tree*
1944 Stephen Vincent Benet, *Western Star*
1945 Karl Shapiro, *V-Letter and Other Poems*
1947 Robert Lowell, *Lord Weary's Castle*

1948 W. H. Auden, *The Age of Anxiety*
1949 Peter Viereck, *Terror and Decorum*
1950 Gwendolyn Brooks, *Annie Allen*
1951 Carl Sandburg, *Complete Poems*
1952 Marianne Moore, *Collected Poems*
1953 Archibald MacLeish, *Collected Poems*
1954 Theodore Roethke, *The Waking*
1955 Wallace Stevens, *Collected Poems*
1956 Elizabeth Bishop, *Poems, North and South*
1957 Richard Wilbur, *Things of This World*
1958 Robert Penn Warren, *Promises: Poems 1954-1956*
1959 Stanley Kunitz, *Selected Poems 1928-1958*
1960 W. D. Snodgrass, *Heart's Needle*
1961 Phyllis McGinley, *Times Three: Selected Verse From Three Decades*
1962 Alan Dugan, *Poems*
1963 William Carlos Williams, *Pictures From Breughel*
1964 Louis Simpson, *At the End of the Open Road*
1965 John Berryman, *77 Dream Songs*
1966 Richard Eberhart, *Selected Poems*
1967 Anne Sexton, *Live or Die*
1968 Anthony Hecht, *The Hard Hours*
1969 George Oppen, *Of Being Numerous*
1970 Richard Howard, *Untitled Subjects*
1971 William S. Merwin, *The Carrier of Ladders*
1972 James Wright, *Collected Poems*
1973 Maxine Winokur Kumin, *Up Country*
1974 Robert Lowell, *The Dolphin*
1975 Gary Snyder, *Turtle Island*
1976 John Ashbery, *Self-Portrait in a Convex Mirror*
1977 James Merrill, *Divine Comedies*
1978 Howard Nemerov, *Collected Poems*
1979 Robert Penn Warren, *Now and Then: Poems 1976-1978*
1980 Donald Justice, *Selected Poems*
1981 James Schuyler, *The Morning of the Poem*
1982 Sylvia Plath, *The Collected Poems*
1983 Galway Kinnell, *Selected Poems*
1984 Mary Oliver, *American Primitive*
1985 Carolyn Kizer, *Yin*
1986 Henry Taylor, *The Flying Change*
1987 Rita Dove, *Thomas and Beulah*
1988 William Meredith, *Partial Accounts*
1989 Richard Wilbur, *New and Collected Poems*
1990 Charles Simic, *The World Doesn't End*
1991 Mona Van Duyn, *Near Changes*
1992 James Tate, *Selected Poems*
1993 Louise Glück, *The Wild Iris*
1994 Yusef Komunyakaa, *Neon Vernacular*
1995 Philip Levine, *The Simple Truth*
1996 Jorie Graham, *The Dream of the Unified Field*
1997 Lisel Mueller, *Alive Together: New and Selected Poems*
1998 Charles Wright, *Black Zodiac*
1999 Mark Strand, *Blizzard of One*
2000 C. K. Williams, *Repair*
2001 Stephen Dunn, *Different Hours*
2002 Carl Dennis, *Practical Gods*
2003 Paul Muldoon, *Moy Sand and Gravel*
2004 Franz Wright, *Walking to Martha's Vineyard*
2005 Ted Kooser, *Delights & Shadows*
2006 Claudia Emerson, *Late Wife*

General Nonfiction

1962 Theodore H. White, *The Making of the President 1960*
1963 Barbara W. Tuchman, *The Guns of August*
1964 Richard Hofstadter, *Anti-Intellectualism in American Life*
1965 Howard Mumford Jones, *O Strange New World*
1966 Edwin Way Teale, *Wandering Through Winter*
1967 David Brion Davis, *The Problem of Slavery in Western Culture*
1968 Will and Ariel Durant, *Rousseau and Revolution*
1969 Norman Mailer, *The Armies of the Night;* Rene Jules Dubos, *So Human an Animal: How We Are Shaped by Surroundings and Events*
1970 Eric H. Erikson, *Gandhi's Truth*
1971 John Toland, *The Rising Sun*
1972 Barbara W. Tuchman, *Stilwell and the American Experience in China, 1911-1945*
1973 Frances FitzGerald, *Fire in the Lake: The Vietnamese and the Americans in Vietnam;* Robert Coles, *Children of Crisis,* Volumes II & III
1974 Ernest Becker, *The Denial of Death*
1975 Annie Dillard, *Pilgrim at Tinker Creek*
1976 Robert N. Butler, *Why Survive? Being Old in America*
1977 William W. Warner, *Beautiful Swimmers*
1978 Carl Sagan, *The Dragons of Eden*
1979 Edward O. Wilson, *On Human Nature*
1980 Douglas R. Hofstadter, *Gödel, Escher, Bach: An Eternal Golden Braid*
1981 Carl E. Schorske, *Fin-de-Siecle Vienna: Politics and Culture*
1982 Tracy Kidder, *The Soul of a New Machine*
1983 Susan Sheehan, *Is There No Place on Earth for Me?*

1984 Paul Starr, *Social Transformation of American Medicine*
1985 Studs Terkel, *The Good War*
1986 Joseph Lelyveld, *Move Your Shadow;* J. Anthony Lukas, *Common Ground*
1987 David K. Shipler, *Arab and Jew*
1988 Richard Rhodes, *The Making of the Atomic Bomb*
1989 Neil Sheehan, *A Bright Shining Lie: John Paul Vann and America in Vietnam*
1990 Dale Maharidge and Michael Williamson, *And Their Children After Them*
1991 Bert Holldobler and Edward O. Wilson, *The Ants*
1992 Daniel Yergin, *The Prize: The Epic Quest for Oil*
1993 Garry Wills, *Lincoln at Gettysburg*
1994 David Remnick, *Lenin's Tomb: The Last Days of the Soviet Empire*
1995 Jonathan Weiner, *The Beak of the Finch: A Story of Evolution in Our Time*
1996 Tina Rosenberg, *The Haunted Land: Facing Europe's Ghosts After Communism*
1997 Richard Kluger, *Ashes to Ashes: America's Hundred-Year Cigarette War, the Public Health, and the Unabashed Triumph of Philip Morris*
1998 Jared Diamond, *Guns, Germs, and Steel: The Fates of Human Societies*
1999 John McPhee, *Annals of the Former World*

2000 John W. Dower, *Embracing Defeat: Japan in the Wake of World War II*
2001 Herbert P. Bix, *Hirohito and the Making of Modern Japan*
2002 Diane McWhorter, *Carry Me Home: Birmingham, Alabama, the Climactic Battle of the Civil Rights Revolution*
2003 Samantha Power, *A Problem From Hell: America and the Age of Genocide*
2004 Anne Applebaum, *Gulag: A History*
2005 Steve Coll, *Ghost Wars*
2006 Caroline Elkins, *Imperial Reckoning: The Untold Story of Britain's Gulag in Kenya*

Special Citation in Letters

1944 Richard Rodgers and Oscar Hammerstein II, for *Oklahoma!*
1957 Kenneth Roberts, for his historical novels
1960 *The Armada*, by Garrett Mattingly
1961 *American Heritage Picture History of the Civil War*
1973 *George Washington, Vols. I-IV*, by James Thomas Flexner
1977 Alex Haley, for *Roots*
1978 E.B. White
1984 Theodore Seuss Geisel (Dr. Seuss)
1992 Art Spiegelman, for *Maus*
2006 Edmund S. Morgan

Music

1943 William Schuman, *Secular Cantata No. 2, A Free Song*
1944 Howard Hanson, *Symphony No. 4, Op. 34*
1945 Aaron Copland, *Appalachian Spring*
1946 Leo Sowerby, *The Canticle of the Sun*
1947 Charles E. Ives, *Symphony No. 3*
1948 Walter Piston, *Symphony No. 3*
1949 Virgil Thomson, *Louisiana Story*
1950 Gian-Carlo Menotti, *The Consul*
1951 Douglas Moore, *Giants in the Earth*
1952 Gail Kubik, *Symphony Concertante*
1954 Quincy Porter, *Concerto for Two Pianos and Orchestra*
1955 Gian-Carlo Menotti, *The Saint of Bleecker Street*
1956 Ernest Toch, *Symphony No. 3*
1957 Norman Dello Joio, *Meditations on Ecclesiastes*
1958 Samuel Barber, *Vanessa*
1959 John La Montaine, *Concerto for Piano and Orchestra*
1960 Elliott Carter, *Second String Quartet*
1961 Walter Piston, *Symphony No. 7*
1962 Robert Ward, *The Crucible*
1963 Samuel Barber, *Piano Concerto No. 1*
1966 Leslie Bassett, *Variations for Orchestra*
1967 Leon Kirchner, *Quartet No. 3*
1968 George Crumb, *Echoes of Time and The River*
1969 Karel Husa, *String Quartet No. 3*
1970 Charles W. Wuorinen, *Time's Encomium*
1971 Mario Davidovsky, *Synchronisms No. 6*
1972 Jacob Druckman, *Windows*
1973 Elliott Carter, *String Quartet No. 3*
1974 Donald Martino, *Notturno*
1975 Dominick Argento, *From the Diary of Virginia Woolf*
1976 Ned Rorem, *Air Music*
1977 Richard Wernick, *Visions of Terror and Wonder*
1978 Michael Colgrass, *Deja Vu for Percussion and Orchestra*
1979 Joseph Schwantner, *Aftertones of Infinity*
1980 David Del Tredici, *In Memory of a Summer Day*
1982 Roger Sessions, *Concerto for Orchestra*

1983 Ellen T. Zwilich, *Three Movements for Orchestra*
1984 Bernard Rands, *Canti del Sole*
1985 Stephen Albert, *Symphony, RiverRun*
1986 George Perle, *Wind Quintet IV*
1987 John Harbison, *The Flight Into Egypt*
1988 William Bolcom, *12 New Etudes for Piano*
1989 Roger Reynolds, *Whispers Out of Time*
1990 Mel Powell, *Duplicates: A Concerto for Two Pianos and Orchestra*
1991 Shulamit Ran, *Symphony*
1992 Wayne Peterson, *The Face of the Night, The Heart of the Dark*
1993 Christopher Rouse, *Trombone Concerto*
1994 Gunther Schuller, *Of Reminiscences and Reflections*
1995 Morton Gould, *Stringmusic*
1996 George Walker, *Lilacs*
1997 Wynton Marsalis, *Blood on the Fields*
1998 Aaron Jay Kernis, *String Quartet No. 2*
1999 Melinda Wagner, *Concerto for Flute, Strings and Percussion*
2000 Lewis Spratlan, *Life is a Dream, Opera in Three Acts: Act II, Concert Version*
2001 John Corigliano, *Symphony No. 2 for String Orchestra*
2002 Henry Brant, *Ice Field*
2003 John Adams, *On the Transmigration of Souls*
2004 Paul Moravec, *Tempest Fantasy*
2005 Steven Stucky, *Second Concerto for Orchestra*
2006 Yehudi Wyner, *Piano Concerto: 'Chiavi in Mano'*

Special Citation in Music

1974 Roger Sessions
1976 Scott Joplin
1982 Milton Babbitt
1985 William Schuman
1998 George Gershwin
1999 Edward Kennedy "Duke" Ellington
2006 Thelonious Monk

National Book Awards, 1950-2005

The National Book Awards (known as American Book Awards 1980–86) are administered by the National Book Foundation and have been given annually in the years shown, since 1950. The prizes, each valued at $10,000, are awarded to U.S. citizens for works published in the U.S. In some years, multiple awards were given for nonfiction in various categories; in such cases, the history and biography (if any) or biography winner is listed. Selected additional awards in nonfiction and other 2005 awards are listed in footnotes. **Other National Book Awards, 2005**: Poetry: W.S. Merwin, *Migration: New and Selected Poems*; Young People's Literature: Jeanne Birdsall, *The Penderwicks*. Medal for Distinguished Contribution to American Letters: Norman Mailer.

Fiction

Year Author, Title
1950 Nelson Algren, *The Man With the Golden Arm*
1951 William Faulkner, *The Collected Stories*
1952 James Jones, *From Here to Eternity*
1953 Ralph Ellison, *Invisible Man*
1954 Saul Bellow, *The Adventures of Augie March*
1955 William Faulkner, *A Fable*
1956 John O'Hara, *Ten North Frederick*
1957 Wright Morris, *The Field of Vision*
1958 John Cheever, *The Wapshot Chronicle*
1959 Bernard Malamud, *The Magic Barrel*
1960 Philip Roth, *Goodbye, Columbus*
1961 Conrad Richter, *The Waters of Kronos*
1962 Walker Percy, *The Moviegoer*
1963 J.F. Powers, *Morte d'Urban*
1964 John Updike, *The Centaur*

Year Author, Title
1965 Saul Bellow, *Herzog*
1966 Katherine Anne Porter, *The Collected Stories*
1967 Bernard Malamud, *The Fixer*
1968 Thornton Wilder, *The Eighth Day*
1969 Jerzy Kosinski, *Steps*
1970 Joyce Carol Oates, *Them*
1971 Saul Bellow, *Mr. Sammler's Planet*
1972 Flannery O'Connor, *The Complete Stories*
1973 John Barth, *Chimera*
1974 Thomas Pynchon, *Gravity's Rainbow*
1974 Isaac Bashevis Singer, *A Crown of Feathers*
1975 Robert Stone, *Dog Soldiers*
1976 William Gaddis, *JR*
1977 Wallace Stegner, *The Spectator Bird*
1978 Mary Lee Settle, *Blood Ties*
1979 Tim O'Brien, *Going After Cacciato*
1980 William Styron, *Sophie's Choice*

Year	Author, Title
1981	Wright Morris, *Plains Song*
1982	John Updike, *Rabbit Is Rich*
1983	Alice Walker, *The Color Purple*
1984	Ellen Gilchrist, *Victory Over Japan*
1985	Don DeLillo, *White Noise*
1986	E.L. Doctorow, *World's Fair*
1987	Larry Heinemann, *Paco's Story*
1988	Pete Dexter, *Paris Trout*
1989	John Casey, *Spartina*
1990	Charles Johnson, *Middle Passage*
1991	Norman Rush, *Mating*
1992	Cormac McCarthy, *All the Pretty Horses*
1993	E. Annie Proulx, *The Shipping News*
1994	William Gaddis, *A Frolic of His Own*
1995	Philip Roth, *Sabbath's Theater*
1996	Andrea Barrett, *Ship Fever and Other Stories*
1997	Charles Frazier, *Cold Mounatin*
1998	Alice McDermott, *Charming Billy*
1999	Ha Jin, *Waiting*
2000	Susan Sontag, *In America*
2001	Jonathan Franzen, *The Corrections*
2002	Julia Glass, *Three Junes*
2003	Shirley Hazzard, *The Great Fire*
2004	Lily Tuck, *The News from Paraguay*
2005	William T. Vollmann, *Europe Central*

Nonfiction

Year	Author, Title
1950	Ralph L. Rusk, *Ralph Waldo Emerson*
1951	Newton Arvin, *Herman Melville*
1952	Rachel Carson, *The Sea Around Us*
1953	Bernard A. De Voto, *The Course of an Empire*
1954	Bruce Catton, *A Stillness at Appomattox*
1955	Joseph Wood Krutch, *The Measure of Man*
1956	Herbert Kubly, *An American in Italy*
1957	George F. Kennan, *Russia Leaves the War*
1958	Catherine Drinker Bowen, *The Lion and the Throne*
1959	J. Christopher Herold, *Mistress to an Age: A Life of Madame De Stael*
1960	Richard Ellman, *James Joyce*
1961	William L. Shirer, *The Rise and Fall of the Third Reich*
1962	Lewis Mumford, *The City in History: Its Origins, Its Transformations, and Its Prospects*
1963	Leon Edel, *Henry James: Vol. II: The Conquest of London; Vol. III: The Middle Years*
1964	William H. McNeill, *The Rise of the West: A History of the Human Community*
1965	Louis Fisher, *The Life of Lenin*
1966	Arthur M. Schlesinger, Jr., *A Thousand Days: John F. Kennedy in the White House*
1967	Peter Gay, *The Enlightenment, An Interpretation Vol I: The Rise of Modern Paganism*
1968	George F. Kennan, *Memoirs: 1925–1950*[1]
1969	Winthrop D. Jordan, *White Over Black: American Attitudes Toward the Negro, 1550-1812*[2]
1970	T. Harry Williams, *Huey Long*[3]

Year	Author, Title
1971	James MacGregor Burns, *Roosevelt: The Soldier of Freedom*
1972	Joseph P. Lash, *Eleanor and Franklin: The Story of Their Relationship, Based on Eleanor Roosevelt's Private Papers*
1973	James Thomas Flexner, *George Washington, Vol. IV: Anguish and Farewell, 1793-1799*[4]
1974	John Clive, *Macaulay, The Shaping of the Historian*; Douglas Day, *Malcolm Lowry: A Biography*[5]
1975	Richard B. Sewall, *The Life of Emily Dickinson*[6]
1976	David Brion Davis, *The Problem of Slavery in the Age of Revolution, 1770-1823*
1977	W.A. Swanberg, *Norman Thomas: The Last Idealist*[7]
1978	W. Jackson Bate, *Samuel Johnson*
1979	Arthur M. Schlesinger, Jr., *Robert Kennedy and His Times*
1980	Tom Wolfe, *The Right Stuff*
1981	Maxine Hong Kingston, *China Men*
1982	Tracy Kidder, *The Soul of a New Machine*
1983	Fox Butterfield, *China: Alive in the Bitter Sea*
1984	Robert V. Remini, *Andrew Jackson and the Course of American Democracy, 1833-1845*
1985	J. Anthony Lukas, *Common Ground: A Turbulent Decade in the Lives of Three American Families*
1986	Barry Lopez, *Arctic Dreams*
1987	Richard Rhodes, *The Making of the Atom Bomb*
1988	Neil Sheehan, *A Bright Shining Lie: John Paul Vann and America in Vietnam*
1989	Thomas L. Friedman, *From Beirut to Jerusalem*
1990	Ron Chernow, *The House of Morgan: An American Banking Dynasty and the Rise of Modern Finance*
1991	Orlando Patterson, *Freedom*
1992	Paul Monette, *Becoming a Man: Half a Life Story*
1993	Gore Vidal, *United States: Essays 1952-1992*
1994	Sherwin B. Nuland, *How We Die: Reflections on Life's Final Chapter*
1995	Tina Rosenberg, *The Haunted Land: Facing Europe's Ghosts After Communism*
1996	James Carroll, *An American Requiem: God, My Father, and the War That Came Between Us*
1997	Joseph J. Ellis, *American Sphinx: The Character of Thomas Jefferson*
1998	Edward Ball, *Slaves in the Family*
1999	John W. Dower, *Embracing Defeat: Japan in the Wake of World War II*
2000	Nathaniel Philbrick, *In the Heart of the Sea: The Tragedy of the Whaleship Essex*
2001	Andrew Solomon, *The Noonday Demon: An Atlas of Depression*
2002	Robert A. Caro, *Master of the Senate: The Years of Lyndon Johnson*
2003	Carlos Eire, *Waiting for Snow in Havana: Confessions of a Cuban Boy*
2004	Kevin Boyle, *Arc of Justice: A Saga of Race, Civil Rights, and Murder in the Jazz Age*
2005[8]	Joan Didion, *The Year of Magical Thinking*

(1) Science, Philosophy, and Religion: Jonathan Kozol, *Death at an Early Age*. (2) Arts & Letters: Norman Mailer, *The Armies of the Night: History as a Novel, The Novel as History*. (3) Arts & Letters: Lillian Hellman, *An Unfinished Woman: A Memoir*. (4) Contemp. Affairs: Frances FitzGerald, *Fire in the Lake: The Vietnamese and the Americans in Vietnam*. (5) Arts & Letters: Pauline Kael, *Deeper Into the Movies*. (6) Arts & Letters: Roger Shattuck, *Marcel Proust*; Lewis Thomas, *The Lives of a Cell: Notes of a Biology Watcher*. (7) Contemp. Thought: Bruno Bettelheim, *The Uses of Enchantment: The Meaning and Importance of Fairy Tales*.

The Man Booker Prize for Fiction, 1969-2005

The Booker Prize for fiction, established in 1968, is awarded annually in October for what is judged the best full-length novel written in English by a citizen of the UK, the Commonwealth, or the Irish Republic. In 2002 sponsorship of the award was taken over by Man Group PLC, the name was changed to the Man Booker Prize, and the amount was increased from £20,000 to £50,000.

Year	Author, Title
1969	P. H. Newby, *Something to Answer For*
1970	Bernice Rubens, *The Elected Member*
1971	V. S. Naipaul, *In a Free State*
1972	John Berger, *G*
1973	J. G. Farrell, *The Siege of Krishnapur*
1974	Nadine Gordimer, *The Conservationist*; Stanley Middleton, *Holiday*
1975	Ruth Prawer Jhabvala, *Heat & Dust*
1976	David Storey, *Saville*
1977	Paul Scott, *Staying On*
1978	Iris Murdoch, *The Sea, The Sea*
1979	Penelope Fitzgerald, *Offshore*
1980	William Golding, *Rites of Passage*
1981	Salman Rushdie, *Midnight's Children*
1982	Thomas Keneally, *Schindler's Ark*
1983	J. M. Coetzee, *Life and Times of Michael K*
1984	Anita Brookner, *Hotel du Lac*
1985	Keri Hulme, *The Bone People*
1986	Kingsley Amis, *The Old Devils*
1987	Penelope Lively, *Moon Tiger*

Year	Author, Title
1988	Peter Carey, *Oscar and Lucinda*
1989	Kazuo Ishiguro, *The Remains of the Day*
1990	A. S. Byatt, *Possession*
1991	Ben Okri, *The Famished Road*
1992	Michael Ondaatje, *The English Patient*; Barry Unsworth, *Sacred Hunger*
1993	Roddy Doyle, *Paddy Clarke Ha Ha Ha*
1994	James Kelman, *How Late It Was, How Late*
1995	Pat Barker, *The Ghost Road*
1996	Graham Swift, *Last Orders*
1997	Arundhati Roy, *The God of Small Things*
1998	Ian McEwan, *Amsterdam*
1999	J. M. Coetzee, *Disgrace*
2000	Margaret Atwood, *The Blind Assassin*
2001	Peter Carey, *True History of the Kelly Gang*
2002	Yann Martel, *Life of Pi*
2003	DBC Pierre, *Vernon God Little*
2004	Alan Hollinghurst, *The Line of Beauty*
2005	John Banville, *The Sea*

Newbery Medal Books, 1922-2006

The Newbery Medal was awarded annually in the years shown, by the Association for Library Service to Children, a division of the American Library Association, to the author of the most distinguished contribution to American literature for children.

Year	Book, Author
1922	*The Story of Mankind*, Hendrik Willem van Loon
1923	*The Voyages of Dr. Dolittle*, Hugh Lofting
1924	*The Dark Frigate*, Charles Boardman Hawes
1925	*Tales From Silver Lands*, Charles Joseph Finger
1926	*Shen of the Sea*, Arthur Bowie Chrisman
1927	*Smoky, the Cowhorse*, Will James
1928	*Gay-Neck*, Dhan Gopal Mukerji
1929	*The Trumpeter of Krakow*, Eric P. Kelly
1930	*Hitty, Her First Hundred Years*, Rachel Field
1931	*The Cat Who Went to Heaven*, Elizabeth Coatsworth
1932	*Waterless Mountain*, Laura Adams Armer
1933	*Young Fu of the Upper Yangtze*, Elizabeth Foreman Lewis
1934	*Invincible Louisa*, Cornelia Lynde Meigs
1935	*Dobry*, Monica Shannon
1936	*Caddie Woodlawn*, Carol Ryrie Brink
1937	*Roller Skates*, Ruth Sawyer
1938	*The White Stag*, Kate Seredy
1939	*Thimble Summer*, Elizabeth Enright
1940	*Daniel Boone*, James Daugherty
1941	*Call It Courage*, Armstrong Sperry
1942	*The Matchlock Gun*, Walter D. Edmonds
1943	*Adam of the Road*, Elizabeth Janet Gray
1944	*Johnny Tremain*, Esther Forbes
1945	*Rabbit Hill*, Robert Lawson
1946	*Strawberry Girl*, Lois Lenski
1947	*Miss Hickory*, Carolyn S. Bailey
1948	*Twenty-One Balloons*, William Pène Du Bois
1949	*King of the Wind*, Marguerite Henry
1950	*The Door in the Wall*, Marguerite de Angeli
1951	*Amos Fortune, Free Man*, Elizabeth Yates
1952	*Ginger Pye*, Eleanor Estes
1953	*Secret of the Andes*, Ann Nolan Clark
1954	*. . . And Now Miguel*, Joseph Krumgold
1955	*The Wheel on the School*, Meindert DeJong
1956	*Carry On, Mr. Bowditch*, Jean Lee Latham
1957	*Miracles on Maple Hill*, Virginia Sorensen
1958	*Rifles for Watie*, Harold Keith
1959	*The Witch of Blackbird Pond*, Elizabeth George Speare
1960	*Onion John*, Joseph Krumgold
1961	*Island of the Blue Dolphins*, Scott O'Dell
1962	*The Bronze Bow*, Elizabeth George Speare
1963	*A Wrinkle in Time*, Madeleine L'Engle
1964	*It's Like This, Cat*, Emily Cheney Neville
1965	*Shadow of a Bull*, Maja Wojciechowska
1966	*I, Juan de Pareja*, Elizabeth Borton de Trevino
1967	*Up a Road Slowly*, Irene Hunt
1968	*From the Mixed-Up Files of Mrs. Basil E. Frankweiler*, E. L. Konigsburg
1969	*The High King*, Lloyd Alexander
1970	*Sounder*, William H. Armstrong
1971	*The Summer of the Swans*, Betsy Byars
1972	*Mrs. Frisby and the Rats of NIMH*, Robert C. O'Brien
1973	*Julie of the Wolves*, Jean George
1974	*The Slave Dancer*, Paula Fox
1975	*M. C. Higgins the Great*, Virginia Hamilton
1976	*Grey King*, Susan Cooper
1977	*Roll of Thunder, Hear My Cry*, Mildred D. Taylor
1978	*Bridge to Terabithia*, Katherine Paterson
1979	*The Westing Game*, Ellen Raskin
1980	*A Gathering of Days*, Joan Blos
1981	*Jacob Have I Loved*, Katherine Paterson
1982	*A Visit to William Blake's Inn: Poems for Innocent and Experienced Travelers*, Nancy Willard
1983	*Dicey's Song*, Cynthia Voigt
1984	*Dear Mr. Henshaw*, Beverly Cleary
1985	*The Hero and the Crown*, Robin McKinley
1986	*Sarah, Plain and Tall*, Patricia MacLachlan
1987	*The Whipping Boy*, Sid Fleischman
1988	*Lincoln: A Photobiography*, Russell Freedman
1989	*Joyful Noise: Poems for Two Voices*, Paul Fleischman
1990	*Number the Stars*, Lois Lowry
1991	*Maniac Magee*, Jerry Spinelli
1992	*Shiloh*, Phyllis Reynolds Naylor
1993	*Missing May*, Cynthia Rylant
1994	*The Giver*, Lois Lowry
1995	*Walk Two Moons*, Sharon Creech
1996	*The Midwife's Apprentice*, Karen Cushman
1997	*The View From Saturday*, E. L. Konigsburg
1998	*Out of the Dust*, Karen Hesse
1999	*Holes*, Louis Sachar
2000	*Bud, Not Buddy*, Christopher Paul Curtis
2001	*A Year Down Yonder*, Richard Peck
2002	*A Single Shard*, Linda Sue Park
2003	*Crispin: The Cross of Lead*, Avi
2004	*The Tale of Despereaux: Being the Story of a Mouse, a Princess, Some Soup, and a Spool of Thread*, by Kate DiCamillo, illustrated by Timothy Basil Ering
2005	*Kira-Kira*, Cynthia Kadohata
2006	*Criss Cross*, Lynne Rae Perkins

Caldecott Medal Books, 1938-2006

The Caldecott Medal was awarded annually in the years shown, by the Association for Library Service to Children, a division of the American Library Association, to the illustrator of the most distinguished American picture book for children.

Year	Book, Illustrator
1938	*Animals of the Bible*, Dorothy P. Lathrop
1939	*Mei Li*, Thomas Handforth
1940	*Abraham Lincoln*, Ingri & Edgar Parin d'Aulaire
1941	*They Were Strong and Good*, Robert Lawson
1942	*Make Way for Ducklings*, Robert McCloskey
1943	*The Little House*, Virginia Lee Burton
1944	*Many Moons*, Louis Slobodkin
1945	*Prayer for a Child*, Elizabeth Orton Jones
1946	*The Rooster Crows*, Maude & Miska Petersham
1947	*The Little Island*, Leonard Weisgard
1948	*White Snow, Bright Snow*, Roger Duvoisin
1949	*The Big Snow*, Berta & Elmer Hader
1950	*Song of the Swallows*, Leo Politi
1951	*The Egg Tree*, Katherine Milhous
1952	*Finders Keepers*, Nicolas, pseud. (Nicholas Mordvinoff)
1953	*The Biggest Bear*, Lynd Ward
1954	*Madeline's Rescue*, Ludwig Bemelmans
1955	*Cinderella, or the Little Glass Slipper*, Marcia Brown
1956	*Frog Went A-Courtin'*, Feodor Rojankovsky
1957	*A Tree Is Nice*, Marc Simont
1958	*Time of Wonder*, Robert McCloskey
1959	*Chanticleer and the Fox*, Barbara Cooney
1960	*Nine Days to Christmas*, Marie Hall Ets
1961	*Baboushka and the Three Kings*, Nicolas Sidjakov
1962	*Once a Mouse*, Marcia Brown
1963	*The Snowy Day*, Ezra Jack Keats
1964	*Where the Wild Things Are*, Maurice Sendak
1965	*May I Bring a Friend?*, Beni Montressor
1966	*Always Room for One More*, Nonny Hogrogian
1967	*Sam, Bang, and Moonshine*, Evaline Ness
1968	*Drummer Hoff*, Ed Emberley
1969	*The Fool of the World and the Flying Ship*, Uri Shulevitz
1970	*Sylvester and the Magic Pebble*, William Steig
1971	*A Story A Story*, Gail E. Haley
1972	*One Fine Day*, Nonny Hogrogian
1973	*The Funny Little Woman*, Blair Lent
1974	*Duffy and the Devil*, Margot Zemach
1975	*Arrow to the Sun*, Gerald McDermott
1976	*Why Mosquitoes Buzz in People's Ears*, Leo & Diane Dillon
1977	*Ashanti to Zulu: African Traditions*, Leo & Diane Dillon
1978	*Noah's Ark*, Peter Spier
1979	*The Girl Who Loved Wild Horses*, Paul Goble
1980	*Ox-Cart Man*, Barbara Cooney
1981	*Fables*, Arnold Lobel
1982	*Jumanji*, Chris Van Allsburg
1983	*Shadow*, Marcia Brown
1984	*The Glorious Flight: Across the Channel with Louis Bleriot*, Alice and Martin Provensen
1985	*Saint George and the Dragon*, Trina Schart Hyman
1986	*The Polar Express*, Chris Van Allsburg
1987	*Hey, Al*, Richard Egielski
1988	*Owl Moon*, John Schoenherr
1989	*Song and Dance Man*, Stephen Grammell
1990	*Lon Po Po: A Red-Riding Hood Story From China*, Ed Young
1991	*Black and White*, David Macaulay
1992	*Tuesday*, David Wiesner
1993	*Mirette on the High Wire*, Emily Arnold McCully
1994	*Grandfather's Journey*, Allen Say
1995	*Smoky Night*, David Diaz
1996	*Officer Buckle and Gloria*, Peggy Rathmann
1997	*Golem*, David Wisniewski
1998	*Rapunzel*, Paul O. Zelinsky
1999	*Snowflake Bentley*, Mary Azarian

Year	Book, Illustrator
2000	*Joseph Had a Little Overcoat,* Simms Taback
2001	*So You Want to be President?,* David Small
2002	*The Three Pigs,* David Wiesner
2003	*My Friend Rabbit,* Eric Rohmann

Year	Book, Illustrator
2004	*The Man Who Walked Between the Towers,* Mordicai Gerstein
2005	*Kitten's First Full Moon,* Kevin Henkes
2006	*The Hello, Goodbye Window,* Chris Raschka

Miscellaneous Book Awards

(Awarded in 2006, unless otherwise noted)

Academy of American Poets Awards. Wallace Stevens Award, for poetry mastery, $100,000 (2005): Gerald Stern. Academy Fellowship, $25,000 (2005): Claudia Rankine. James Laughlin Award, $5,000: Barbara Jane Reyes, *Poeta en San Francisco.* Walt Whitman Award, $5,000: Anne Pierson Wiese, *Floating City.* Harold Morton Landon Trans. Award, $1,000: Richard Zenith, *Education by Stone: Selected Poems* (works of Brazilian poet João Cabral de Melo Neto). Lenore Marshall Poetry Prize, $25,000 (2005): Anne Winters, *The Displaced of Capital.* Raiziss/de Palchi Trans. Prize, $5,000: John DuVal, *Tales of Trilussa* by Carlo Alberto Salustri.

American Academy of Arts and Letters. Academy Awards in Literature ($7,500 each): Dan Chaon, Charles Edward Eaton, Daniel Mark Epstein, Michael Fried, Mary Gordon, Stephen Sandy, Stacy Schiff, John Patrick Shanley. E. M. Forster Award, $15,000: Geoff Dyer. Sue Kaufman Prize for First Fiction, $5,000: Uzodinma Iweala, *Beasts of No Nation.* Katherine Anne Porter Award, $20,000: Arturo Vivante. Morton Dauwen Zabel Award, $10,000: Jean Valentine. Richard and Hinda Rosenthal Foundation Awards, $5,000: Nick Arvin, *Articles of War.* Harold D. Vursell Memorial Award, $10,000: Peter Pouncey, *Rules for Old Men Waiting.* Rome Fellowships in Literature: Tom Bissell, Dave King. Michael Braude Award, $5,000: John Fuller. Gold Medal for Biography: Robert A. Caro.

Bollingen Prize in Poetry, $75,000, by the Yale Univ. Library (2005): Jay Wright.

Edgar Awards, by the Mystery Writers of America: Grand Master award: Stuart Kaminsky. Best novel: *Citizen Vince,* Jess Walter. First novel by an American author: *Officer Down,* Theresa Schwegel. Best paperback original: *Girl in the Glass,* Jeffrey Ford. Best Critical/Biographical: *Girl Sleuth: Nancy Drew and the Women Who Created Her,* Melanie Rehak.

Golden Kite Awards, by Society of Children's Book Writers and Illustrators. Fiction: Mary E. Pearson, *A Room on Lorelai Street.* Nonfiction: Russell Freedman, *Children of the Great Depression.* Picture book illustration: Melissa Sweet, *Baby Bear's Chairs* (Jane Yolen, text). Picture book text: Pat Mora, *Doña Flor* (Raul Colón, illus.).

Le Prix Goncourt, by Académie Goncourt (2005): François Weyergans, *Trois jours chez ma mère (Three Days at My Mother's House).*

Hugo Awards, by the World Science Fiction Convention. Novel: *Jonathan Strange & Mr. Norrell,* Susanna Clarke. Novella: *The Concrete Jungle,* Charles Stross. Novelette: *The Faery Handbag,* Kelly Link. Short story: "Travels with My Cats," Mike Resnick. John W. Campbell Award for Best New Writer (not a Hugo): Elizabeth Bear.

Coretta Scott King Award, by American Library Assn., for African American authors and illustrators of outstanding books for children and young adults. Author: Julius Lester, *Day of Tears: A Novel in Dialogue.* Illustrator: Bryan Collier, *Rosa,* by Nikki Giovanni. New Talent Award: Jaime Adoff, *Jimi & Me.*

Lincoln Prize, by Lincoln and Soldiers Institute at Gettysburg College, for contribution to Civil War studies, $50,000 and bust of Lincoln: Doris Kearns Goodwin, *Team of Rivals: The Political Genius of Abraham Lincoln.*

National Book Critics Circle Awards. Fiction: E. L. Doctorow, *The March.* Nonfiction: Svetlana Alexievich, *Voices from Chernobyl: The Oral History of a Nuclear Disaster.* Criticism: William Logan, *The Undiscovered Country: Poetry in the Age of Tin.* Autobiography: Francine du Plessix Gray, *Them: A Memoir of Parents.* Biography: Kai Bird & Martin J. Sherwin, *American Prometheus: The Triumph and Tragedy of J. Robert Oppenheimer.* Poetry: Jack Gilbert, *Refusing Heaven.* Nona Balakian Citation for Excellence in Reviewing: Wyatt Mason. Ivan Sandrof Lifetime Achievement Award: Bill Henderson.

Nebula Awards, by the Science Fiction Writers of America. Novel: *Camouflage,* Joe Haldeman. Novella: *Magic for Beginners,* Kelly Link. Novelette: *The Faery Handbag,* Kelly Link. Short story: "I Live With You," Carol Emshwiller.

PEN/Faulkner Award, for fiction, $15,000: E. L. Doctorow, *The March.*

Whitbread Book of the Year Award, by Whitbread PLC: £25,000: Hilary Spurling, *Matisse the Master.*

Journalism Awards, 2006

National Journalism Awards, by Scripps Howard Foundation. Investigative Reporting: *Los Angeles Times.* Public Service Reporting: *South Florida Sun-Sentinel* (Fort Lauderdale). Editorial Writing: Tony Biffle, *The Sun Herald* (Gulfport, MS). Commentary: Steve Lopez, *Los Angeles Times.* Human Interest Writing: Brady Dennis, *St. Petersburg Times* (FL). Web Reporting: roanoke.com, *The Roanoke Times* (VA). Environmental Reporting: Ken Ward, *The Charleston Gazette* (WV). Washington Reporting: Knight Ridder Washington Bureau. Editorial Cartooning: Michael Ramirez, *Los Angeles Times.* Distinguished Service to the First Amendment: *Post Register* (Idaho Falls, ID). Photojournalism: Damon Winter, *Los Angeles Times.* Business/Economics Reporting: *The Seattle Times.* Excellence in Electronic Media: BBC World Service/Public Radio Intl./WGBH Boston (Radio); WCCO-TV, Minneapolis (TV-Cable). College Cartooning: Russell Gottwaldt, *F Newsmagazine,* School of the Art Institute of Chicago. Journalism Teacher of the Year: Dr. Louis A. Day, Louisiana State Univ. Journalism Administrator of the Year: Thomas Kunkel, Univ. of Maryland.

National Magazine Awards, by American Society of Magazine Editors and Columbia Univ. Graduate School of Journalism. Gen. excel., circ. over 2 mil: *Time;* 1 mil-2 mil: *ESPN The Magazine;* 500,000 to 1 mil: *Esquire;* 250,000-500,000: *New York;* 100,000-250,000: *Harper's;* under 100,000: *Virginia Quarterly Review.* Personal Service: *Self.* Leisure Interests: *Golf.* Reporting: *Rolling Stone.* Public Interest: *The New Yorker.* Feature Writing: *The American Scholar.* Profile Writing: *Esquire.* Essays: *Vanity Fair.* Columns and Commentary: *The New Yorker.* Reviews and Criticism: *Harper's.* Magazine Section: *Backpacker.* Single-Topic Issue: *Time.* Design: *New York.* Photography: *W.* Photo Portfolio/Essay: *Rolling Stone.* Fiction: *Virginia Quarterly Review.* General Excellence Online: National Geographic Online, www.ngm.com.

George Foster Peabody Awards, by Univ. of Georgia. "Hurricane Katrina," WLOX-TV (Biloxi, MS). "Preparation and Coverage of Hurricane Katrina," WWL-TV (New Orleans). "After the Storm: The Long Road Back," *NBC Nightly News with Brian Williams.* "Hurricane Katrina and Aftermath," CNN. "China: A Million Steps Ahead," TVE (Madrid, Spain). "Two Days in October," *American Experience,* PBS. "Bad Medicine," *This World BBC,* BBC 2. "Chisolm '72: Unbought and Unbossed," *P.O.V.,* PBS. *Boston Legal,* ABC. *House,* FOX. *Edge of America,* Showtime. *South Park,* Comedy Central. "No Direction Home: Bob Dylan," *American Masters,* PBS. *The Wire: The Impact of Electricity on Music,* CBC. *BBC DoNation Season: Life on the List,* BBC. *Classical Baby,* HBO. *A Room Nearby,* PRI. "Burning Questions," KNBC-TV (Los Angeles). "How Far Will the Army Go?" KNCC-TV (Denver). "A Place of Our Own (Los Ninon en Su Casa)," KCET-TV (Los Angeles). *Radio Rookies Project,* WNYC Radio (New York City). *15% of the United States,* KMEX-Univision 34 (Los Angeles). *Save Our History: Voices of Civil Rights,* History Channel. "What if Winter Never Comes?" CBC/Radio-Canada. *Viva Blackpool,* BBC America. *The Staircase,* Sundance Channel. *Yesterday,* HBO. *The Queen of Trees,* BBC 2. *Children of Beslan,* HBO. *Bleak House,* BBC. *The Shield,* FX. *Battlestar Gallactica,* SCI FI Channel.

Selected National Press Club Awards, by National Press Club. John Aubuchon Freedom of the Press Award: Tom Curley, Associated Press, & Akbar Ganji. Arthur Rowse Award for Press Criticism: (single entry) Susan Paterno, "The Sad Saga of Gary Webb," *American Journalism Review;* (broadcast) Howard Kurtz, *Reliable Sources,* CNN. Angele Gingras Humor Award: Mary Roach, "My Planet," *Reader's Digest.*

Reuben Award, by National Cartoonists Society. For best cartoonist of 2005: Mike Luckovich.

The Spingarn Medal, 1915-2006

The Spingarn Medal has been awarded annually since 1915 (except in 1938) by the National Assoc. for the Advancement of Colored People for outstanding achievement by an African American.

1915 Ernest E. Just	1939 Marian Anderson	1961 Kenneth B. Clark	1984 Thomas Bradley
1916 Charles Young	1940 Louis T. Wright	1962 Robert C. Weaver	1985 Bill Cosby
1917 Harry T. Burleigh	1941 Richard Wright	1963 Medgar W. Evers	1986 Dr. Benjamin L. Hooks
1918 William S. Braithwaite	1942 A. Philip Randolph	1964 Roy Wilkins	1987 Percy E. Sutton
1919 Archibald H. Grimké	1943 William H. Hastie	1965 Leontyne Price	1988 Frederick D. Patterson
1920 W. E. B. Du Bois	1944 Charles Drew	1966 John H. Johnson	1989 Jesse Jackson
1921 Charles S. Gilpin	1945 Paul Robeson	1967 Edward W. Brooke	1990 L. Douglas Wilder
1922 Mary B. Talbert	1946 Thurgood Marshall	1968 Sammy Davis Jr.	1991 Gen. Colin L. Powell
1923 George W.Carver	1947 Dr. Percy L. Julian	1969 Clarence M. Mitchell Jr.	1992 Barbara Jordan
1924 Roland Hayes	1948 Channing H. Tobias	1970 Jacob Lawrence	1993 Dorothy I. Height
1925 James W. Johnson	1949 Ralph J. Bunche	1971 Leon H. Sullivan	1994 Maya Angelou
1926 Carter G. Woodson	1950 Charles H. Houston	1972 Gordon Parks	1995 John Hope Franklin
1927 Anthony Overton	1951 Mabel K. Staupers	1973 Wilson C. Riles	1996 A. Leon Higginbotham
1928 Charles W. Chesnutt	1952 Harry T. Moore	1974 Damon Keith	1997 Carl T. Rowan
1929 Mordecai W. Johnson	1953 Paul R. Williams	1975 Henry (Hank) Aaron	1998 Myrlie Evers-Williams
1930 Henry A. Hunt	1954 Theodore K. Lawless	1976 Alvin Ailey	1999 Earl G. Graves Sr.
1931 Richard B. Harrison	1955 Carl Murphy	1977 Alex Haley	2000 Oprah Winfrey
1932 Robert R. Moton	1956 Jack R. Robinson	1978 Andrew Young	2001 Vernon E. Jordan Jr.
1933 Max Yergan	1957 Martin Luther King Jr.	1979 Rosa L. Parks	2002 John Lewis
1934 William T. B. Williams	1958 Daisy Bates and the Little	1980 Dr. Rayford W. Logan	2003 Constance Baker Motley
1935 Mary McLeod Bethune	Rock Nine	1981 Coleman Young	2004 Robert L. Carter
1936 John Hope	1959 Duke Ellington	1982 Dr. Benjamin E. Mays	2005 Oliver W. Hill
1937 Walter White	1960 Langston Hughes	1983 Lena Horne	2006 Dr. Benjamin S. Carson

Miscellaneous Awards, 2006

(unless otherwise noted)

American Academy of Arts and Letters: Gold Medal for Music: Stephen Sondheim. Award for Distinguished Service to the Arts: Barbara Epstein, Robert Silvers. Award of Merit for Painting: Thomas Nozkowski. Arnold W. Brunner Memorial Prize in Architecture, $5,000: Jean Nouvel. Academy Awards, $7,500 each, in Architecture: Marwan al-Sayed, Yung Ho Chang, Jeanne Gang; in Art: Elizabeth King, Glenn Ligon, Arthur Simms, Merrill Wagner, Yuriko Yamaguchi; in Music: Derek Bermel, Margaret Brouwer, Tamar Diesendruck, David Froom. Benjamin H. Danks Award, $20,000 (split): Marta Ptaszynska, Scott Wheeler. Jimmy Ernst Award (Art), $5,000: Lynda Benglis. Walter Hinrichsen Award (Music): Philip Lasser. Charles Ives Fellowships (Music), $15,000: Anthony Cheung, Yevgeniy Sharlat. Goddard Charles Ives Scholarships (Music), $7,500: Jacob Cooper, Shawn Crouch, Steven Hoey, Robinson McClellan, Justin Messina, Adam Schoenberg. Wladimir & Rhoda Lakond Award (Music), $10,000: John Musto. Goddard Lieberson Fellowships (Music), $15,000: Michael Hersch, Jonathan Pieslak. Addison M. Metcalf Award (Art), $10,000: Gedi Sibony. Richard Rodgers Awards for the Musical Theater: (production) *Grey Gardens*, Scott Frankel, Michael Korie, Doug Wright; (staged readings) *The Yellow Wood*, Michelle Elliott, Danny Larsen; *True Fans*, Chris Miller, Bill Rosenfield, Nathan Tysen. Richard and Hinda Rosenthal Foundation Award (Art), $5,000: Ellen Altfest.

Congressional Gold Medal, by Congress: Jackie Robinson, March 2, 2005.

Intel Science Talent Search (formerly given by Westinghouse): First ($100,000 schol.): Shannon Lisa Babb, Highland, UT; second ($75,000 schol.): Yi Sun, San Jose, CA; third ($50,000 schol.): Yuan Zhang, Derwood, MD.

John F. Kennedy Center for the Performing Arts Awards (Dec. 2005): Tony Bennett, Suzanne Farrell, Julie Harris, Robert Redford, Tina Turner.

John W. Kluge Prize, by Library of Congress, 2004: Jaroslav Pelikan & Paul Ricoeur.

Library of the Year Award, by Thomson Gale and *Library Journal*, $10,000: Salt Lake City Public Library.

National Humanities Medal (Charles Frankel Prize), by National Endowment for the Humanities. $5,000 each (2005): Walter Berns, Matthew Bogdanos, Eva Brann, John Lewis Gaddis, Richard Gilder, Mary Ann Glendon, Leigh Keno, Leslie Keno, Alan Charles Kors, Lewis Lehrman, Judith Martin, The Papers of George Washington.

National Inventor of the Year Awards, by Intellectual Property Owners Education Foundation. Philip Frank Souter and Colin Ure, Proctor & Gamble.

National Medal of the Arts, by the National Endowment for the Arts and the White House. Louis Auchincloss, James DePreist, Paquito D'Rivera, Robert Duvall, Leonard Garment, Ollie Johnston, Wynton Marsalis, Dolly Parton, Pennsylvania Academy of Fine Arts, Tina Ramirez.

Presidential Medal of Freedom, by the White House (Nov. 2005): Muhammad Ali, Carol Burnett, Vinton Cerf & Robert Kahn, Robert Conquest, Aretha Franklin, Alan Greenspan, Andy Griffith, Paul Harvey, Sonny Montgomery, Gen. Richard B. Myers, Jack Nicklaus, Frank Robinson, Paul Rusesabagina.

Pritzker Architecture Prize, by the Hyatt Foundation, $100,000: Paulo Mendes da Rocha, Brazil.

Teacher of the Year, by Council of Chief State School Officers, ING, and and Scholastic, Inc.: Kimberly Oliver, Broad Acres Elementary School, Silver Spring, MD.

Templeton Prize for Progress Toward Research or Discoveries about Spiritual Realities, by Templeton Foundation, £795,000 (about $1.4 million): John D. Barrow.

Miss America Winners, 1921-2006

The Sept. 2005 Miss America Pageant and award were postponed until Jan. 2006, when the pageant was broadcast from Las Vegas, NV, by Country Music Television (CMT) (rather than from Atlantic City by ABC).

1921	Margaret Gorman, Washington, DC	1954	Evelyn Margaret Ay, Ephrata, Pennsylvania
1922-23	Mary Campbell, Columbus, Ohio	1955	Lee Meriwether, San Francisco, California
1924	Ruth Malcolmson, Philadelphia, Pennsylvania	1956	Sharon Ritchie, Denver, Colorado
1925	Fay Lamphier, Oakland, California	1957	Marian McKnight, Manning, South Carolina
1926	Norma Smallwood, Tulsa, Oklahoma	1958	Marilyn Van Derbur, Denver, Colorado
1927	Lois Delander, Joliet, Illinois	1959	Mary Ann Mobley, Brandon, Mississippi
1933	Marion Bergeron, West Haven, Connecticut	1960	Lynda Lee Mead, Natchez, Mississippi
1935	Henrietta Leaver, Pittsburgh, Pennsylvania	1961	Nancy Fleming, Montague, Michigan
1936	Rose Coyle, Philadelphia, Pennsylvania	1962	Maria Fletcher, Asheville, North Carolina
1937	Bette Cooper, Bertrand Island, New Jersey	1963	Jacquelyn Mayer, Sandusky, Ohio
1938	Marilyn Meseke, Marion, Ohio	1964	Donna Axum, El Dorado, Arkansas
1939	Patricia Donnelly, Detroit, Michigan	1965	Vonda Kay Van Dyke, Phoenix, Arizona
1940	Frances Marie Burke, Philadelphia, Pennsylvania	1966	Deborah Irene Bryant, Overland Park, Kansas
1941	Rosemary LaPlanche, Los Angeles, California	1967	Jane Anne Jayroe, Laverne, Oklahoma
1942	Jo-Caroll Dennison, Tyler, Texas	1968	Debra Dene Barnes, Moran, Kansas
1943	Jean Bartel, Los Angeles, California	1969	Judith Anne Ford, Belvidere, Illinois
1944	Venus Ramey, Washington, D.C.	1970	Pamela Anne Eldred, Birmingham, Michigan
1945	Bess Myerson, New York City, New York	1971	Phyllis Ann George, Denton, Texas
1946	Marilyn Buferd, Los Angeles, California	1972	Laurie Lea Schaefer, Columbus, Ohio
1947	Barbara Walker, Memphis, Tennessee	1973	Terry Anne Meeuwsen, DePere, Wisconsin
1948	BeBe Shopp, Hopkins, Minnesota	1974	Rebecca Ann King, Denver, Colorado
1949	Jacque Mercer, Litchfield, Arizona	1975	Shirley Cothran, Fort Worth, Texas
1951	Yolande Betbeze, Mobile, Alabama	1976	Tawney Elaine Godin, Yonkers, New York
1952	Coleen Kay Hutchins, Salt Lake City, Utah	1977	Dorothy Kathleen Benham, Edina, Minnesota
1953	Neva Jane Langley, Macon, Georgia	1978	Susan Perkins, Columbus, Ohio

1979	Kylene Barker, Galax, Virginia		1993	Leanza Cornett, Jacksonville, Florida
1980	Cheryl Prewitt, Ackerman, Mississippi		1994	Kimberly Aiken, Columbia, South Carolina
1981	Susan Powell, Elk City, Oklahoma		1995	Heather Whitestone, Birmingham, Alabama
1982	Elizabeth Ward, Russellville, Arkansas		1996	Shawntel Smith, Muldrow, Oklahoma
1983	Debra Maffett, Anaheim, California		1997	Tara Dawn Holland, Overland Park, Kansas
1984	Vanessa Williams*, Milwood, New York		1998	Kate Shindle, Evanston, Illinois
	Suzette Charles, Mays Landing, New Jersey		1999	Nicole Johnson, Roanoke, Virginia
1985	Sharlene Wells, Salt Lake City, Utah		2000	Heather Renee French, Maysville, Kentucky
1986	Susan Akin, Meridian, Mississippi		2001	Angela Perez Baraquio, Honolulu, Hawaii
1987	Kellye Cash, Memphis, Tennessee		2002	Katie Harman, Gresham, Oregon
1988	Kaye Lani Rae Rafko, Monroe, Michigan		2003	Erika Harold, Urbana, Illinois
1989	Gretchen Carlson, Anoka, Minnesota		2004	Ericka Dunlap, Orlando, Florida
1990	Debbye Turner, Columbia, Missouri		2005	Deidre Downs, Birmingham, Alabama
1991	Marjorie Vincent, Oak Park, Illinois		2006	Jennifer Berry, Tulsa, Oklahoma
1992	Carolyn Suzanne Sapp, Honolulu, Hawaii			

* Resigned July 23, 1984.

Entertainment Awards

Tony (Antoinette Perry) Awards, 2006

Play: *The History Boys*, by Alan Bennett
Musical: *Jersey Boys*
Book of a musical: Bob Martin & Don McKellar, *The Drowsy Chaperone*
Original score: Lisa Lambert & Greg Morrison, *The Drowsy Chaperone*
Play revival: *Awake and Sing!*
Musical revival: *The Pajama Game*
Actor, play: Richard Griffiths, *The History Boys*
Actress, play: Cynthia Nixon, *Rabbit Hole*
Actor, musical: John Lloyd Young, *Jersey Boys*
Actress, musical: LaChanze, *The Color Purple*
Featured actor, play: Ian McDiarmid, *Faith Healer*
Featured actress, play: Frances de la Tour, *The History Boys*
Featured actor, musical: Christian Hoff, *Jersey Boys*

Featured actress, musical: Beth Leavel, *The Drowsy Chaperone*
Director, play: Nicholas Hytner, *The History Boys*
Director, musical: John Doyle, *Sweeney Todd*
Choreography: Kathleen Marshall, *The Pajama Game*
Orchestrations: Sarah Travis, *Sweeney Todd*
Scenic design, play: Bob Crowley, *The History Boys*
Scenic design, musical: David Gallo, *The Drowsy Chaperone*
Costume design, play: Catherine Zuber, *Awake and Sing!*
Costume design, musical: Gregg Barnes, *The Drowsy Chaperone*
Lighting design, play: Mark Henderson, *The History Boys*
Lighting design, musical: Howell Binkley, *Jersey Boys*
Lifetime achievement: Harold Prince
Regional Theater: Intiman Theatre, Seattle
Special Tony: Sarah Jones

Tony Awards, 1948-2006

Year	Play	Musical	Year	Play	Musical
1948	*Mister Roberts*	No Award	1977	*The Shadow Box*	*Annie*
1949	*Death of a Salesman*	*Kiss Me Kate*	1978	*Da*	*Ain't Misbehavin'*
1950	*The Cocktail Party*	*South Pacific*	1979	*The Elephant Man*	*Sweeney Todd*
1951	*The Rose Tattoo*	*Guys and Dolls*	1980	*Children of a Lesser God*	*Evita*
1952	*The Fourposter*	*The King and I*	1981	*Amadeus*	*42nd Street*
1953	*The Crucible*	*Wonderful Town*	1982	*The Life and Adventures of Nicholas Nickelby*	*Nine*
1954	*The Teahouse of the August Moon*	*Kismet*	1983	*Torch Song Trilogy*	*Cats*
1955	*The Desperate Hours*	*The Pajama Game*	1984	*The Real Thing*	*La Cage aux Folles*
1956	*The Diary of Anne Frank*	*Damn Yankees*	1985	*Biloxi Blues*	*Big River*
1957	*Long Day's Journey Into Night*	*My Fair Lady*	1986	*I'm Not Rappaport*	*The Mystery of Edwin Drood*
1958	*Sunrise at Campobello*	*The Music Man*	1987	*Fences*	*Les Miserables*
1959	*J.B.*	*Redhead*	1988	*M. Butterfly*	*Phantom of the Opera*
1960	*The Miracle Worker*	(tie) *Fiorello!*, *The Sound of Music*	1989	*The Heidi Chronicles*	*Jerome Robbins' Broadway*
1961	*Becket*	*Bye, Bye Birdie*	1990	*The Grapes of Wrath*	*City of Angels*
1962	*A Man for All Seasons*	*How to Succeed in Business Without Really Trying*	1991	*Lost in Yonkers*	*The Will Rogers Follies*
1963	*Who's Afraid of Virginia Woolf?*	*A Funny Thing Happened on the Way to the Forum*	1992	*Dancing at Lughnasa*	*Crazy for You*
			1993	*Angels in America: Millennium Approaches*	*Kiss of the Spider Woman*
1964	*Luther*	*Hello, Dolly!*	1994	*Angels in America: Perestroika*	*Passion*
1965	*The Subject Was Roses*	*Fiddler on the Roof*	1995	*Love! Valour! Compassion!*	*Sunset Boulevard*
1966	*Marat/Sade*	*Man of La Mancha*	1996	*Master Class*	*Rent*
1967	*The Homecoming*	*Cabaret*	1997	*The Last Night of Ballyhoo*	*Titanic*
1968	*Rosencrantz and Guildenstern Are Dead*	*Hallelujah, Baby!*	1998	*Art*	*The Lion King*
1969	*The Great White Hope*	*1776*	1999	*Side Man*	*Fosse*
1970	*Borstal Boy*	*Applause*	2000	*Copenhagen*	*Contact*
1971	*Sleuth*	*Company*	2001	*Proof*	*The Producers*
1972	*Sticks and Bones*	*Two Gentleman of Verona*	2002	*Edward Albee's The Goat or Who Is Sylvia?*	*Thoroughly Modern Millie*
1973	*That Championship Season*	*A Little Night Music*	2003	*Take Me Out*	*Hairspray*
1974	*The River Niger*	*Raisin*	2004	*I Am My Own Wife*	*Avenue Q*
1975	*Equus*	*The Wiz*	2005	*Doubt*	*Monty Python's Spamalot*
1976	*Travesties*	*A Chorus Line*	2006	*The History Boys*	*Jersey Boys*

Selected Daytime Emmy Awards, 2006

Drama series: *General Hospital*, ABC
Actress: Kim Zimmer, *Guiding Light*, CBS
Actor: Anthony Geary, *General Hospital*, ABC
Sup. actress: Gina Tognoni, *Guiding Light*, CBS
Sup. actor: Jordan Clarke, *Guiding Light*, CBS
Younger actress: Jennifer Landon, *As the World Turns*, CBS
Younger actor: Tom Pelphrey, *Guiding Light*, CBS
Game show host: Alex Trebek, *Jeopardy!*, synd.

Talk show host: Ellen DeGeneres, *The Ellen DeGeneres Show*, synd.
Talk show: *The Ellen DeGeneres Show*, synd.
Outstanding service show host: Suze Orman, *Suze Orman: For the Young, Fabulous, and Broke*, PBS
Pre-School Series: *Sesame Street*, PBS
Special Class series: *A Baby Story*, TLC
Drama series directing team: *General Hospital*, ABC
Drama series writing team: *The Young and the Restless*, CBS

▶ **IT'S A FACT:** *The Office*, which won the Emmy Award for Best Comedy series in 2006, is based on a British show of the same name, broadcast on the BBC (2001-03). Many other popular American sitcoms were originally British shows, including *Sanford and Son* (in Britain, *Steptoe and Son*), *Three's Company* (*Man About the House*), and *All in the Family* (*Till Death Us Do Part*), which won 4 Best Comedy Emmys between 1971 and 1979.

Selected 2006 Prime-Time Emmy Awards (for 2005-06 TV season)

Drama series: *24*, Fox
Comedy series: *The Office*, NBC
Miniseries: *Elizabeth I*, HBO
Variety, music, or comedy series: *The Daily Show With Jon Stewart*, Comedy Central
Made-for-television movie: *The Girl in the Cafe*, HBO
Lead actor, drama: Kiefer Sutherland, *24*, Fox
Lead actress, drama: Mariska Hargitay, *Law & Order: Special Victims Unit*, NBC
Lead actor, comedy: Tony Shalhoub, *Monk*, USA
Lead actress, comedy: Julia Louis-Dreyfus, *The New Adventures of Old Christine*, CBS

Lead actor, miniseries/movie: Andre Braugher, *Thief*, FX
Lead actress, miniseries/movie: Helen Mirren, *Elizabeth I*, HBO
Sup. actor, drama: Alan Alda, *The West Wing*, NBC
Sup. actress, drama: Blythe Danner, *Huff*, Showtime
Sup. actor, comedy: Jeremy Piven, *Entourage*, HBO
Sup. actress, comedy: Megan Mullally, *Will & Grace*, NBC
Sup. actor, miniseries/movie: Jeremy Irons, *Elizabeth I*, HBO
Sup. actress, miniseries/movie: Kelly MacDonald, *The Girl in the Cafe*, HBO
Individual performance, variety series/music program: Barry Manilow, *Barry Manilow, Music and Passion*, PBS
Reality/competition program: *The Amazing Race*, CBS

Prime-Time Emmy Awards, 1952-2006

The National Academy of Television Arts and Science presented the first Emmy Awards in 1949. Through the years, award categories have changed, but since 1952, the Academy has given out an outstanding comedy and drama award each year.

Year	Comedy	Drama	Year	Comedy	Drama
1952	*Red Skelton Show*, NBC	*Studio One*, CBS	1976	*Mary Tyler Moore Show*, CBS	*Police Story*, NBC
1953	*I Love Lucy*, CBS	*Robert Montgomery Presents*, NBC	1977	*Mary Tyler Moore Show*, CBS	*Masterpiece Theatre: Upstairs, Downstairs;* PBS
1954	*I Love Lucy*, CBS	*The U.S. Steel Hour*, ABC	1978	*All in the Family*, CBS	*The Rockford Files*, NBC
1955	*Make Room for Daddy*, ABC	*The U.S. Steel Hour*, ABC	1979	*Taxi*, ABC	*Lou Grant*, CBS
1956	*Phil Silvers Show*, CBS	*Producer's Showcase*, NBC	1980	*Taxi*, ABC	*Lou Grant*, CBS
1957	*Phil Silvers Show*, CBS	*Requiem for a Heavyweight*, CBS[1]	1981	*Taxi*, ABC	*Hill Street Blues*, NBC
			1982	*Barney Miller*, ABC	*Hill Street Blues*, NBC
1958	*Phil Silvers Show*, CBS	*Gunsmoke*, CBS	1983	*Cheers*, NBC	*Hill Street Blues*, NBC
1959[2]	*Jack Benny Show*, CBS	*	1984	*Cheers*, NBC	*Hill Street Blues*, NBC
1960	*Art Carney Special*, NBC	*Playhouse 90*, CBS	1985	*The Cosby Show*, NBC	*Cagney & Lacey*, CBS
1961	*Jack Benny Show*, CBS	*Hallmark Hall of Fame: Macbeth*, NBC	1986	*Golden Girls*, NBC	*Cagney & Lacey*, CBS
			1987	*Golden Girls*, NBC	*L.A. Law*, NBC
1962	*Bob Newhart Show*, CBS	*The Defenders*, CBS	1988	*The Wonder Years*, ABC	*thirtysomething*, ABC
1963	*Dick Van Dyke Show*, CBS	*The Defenders*, CBS	1989	*Cheers*, NBC	*L.A. Law*, NBC
1964	*Dick Van Dyke Show*, CBS	*The Defenders*, CBS	1990	*Murphy Brown*, CBS	*L.A. Law*, NBC
1965	*Dick Van Dyke Show*, CBS	*Hallmark Hall of Fame: The Magnificent Yankee*, NBC	1991	*Cheers*, NBC	*L.A. Law*, NBC
			1992	*Murphy Brown*, CBS	*Northern Exposure*, CBS
1966	*Dick Van Dyke Show*, CBS	*The Fugitive*, ABC	1993	*Seinfeld*, NBC	*Picket Fences*, CBS
1967	*The Monkees*, NBC	*Mission: Impossible*, CBS	1994	*Frasier*, NBC	*Picket Fences*, CBS
1968	*Get Smart*, NBC	*Mission: Impossible*, CBS	1995	*Frasier*, NBC	*NYPD Blue*, ABC
1969	*Get Smart*, NBC	*NET Playhouse*, NET	1996	*Frasier*, NBC	*ER*, NBC
1970	*My World and Welcome to It*, NBC	*Marcus Welby, M.D.*, ABC	1997	*Frasier*, NBC	*Law & Order*, NBC
			1998	*Frasier*, NBC	*The Practice*, ABC
1971	*All in the Family*, CBS	*The Bold Ones: "The Senator,"* NBC	1999	*Ally McBeal*, Fox	*The Practice*, ABC
			2000	*Will & Grace*, NBC	*The West Wing*, NBC
1972	*All in the Family*, CBS	*Masterpiece Theatre: Elizabeth R*, PBS	2001	*Sex and the City*, HBO	*The West Wing*, NBC
			2002	*Friends*, NBC	*The West Wing*, NBC
1973	*All in the Family*, CBS	*The Waltons*, CBS	2003	*Everybody Loves Raymond*, CBS	*The West Wing*, NBC
1974	*M*A*S*H*, CBS	*Masterpiece Theatre: Upstairs, Downstairs;* PBS	2004	*Arrested Development*, Fox	*The Sopranos*, HBO
			2005	*Everybody Loves Raymond*, CBS	*Lost*, ABC
1975	*Mary Tyler Moore Show*, CBS	*Masterpiece Theatre: Upstairs, Downstairs;* PBS	2006	*The Office*, NBC	*24*, Fox

(1) "Best Single Program of the Year," shown on *Playhouse 90*, which was named "Best New Series." (2) Beginning in 1959, Emmys awarded for work in the season encompassing the previous and current year. (*) *Playhouse 90* (CBS) was best drama of 1 hour or longer; *Alcoa-Goodyear Theatre* (NBC) was best drama of less than 1 hour.

2006 Golden Globe Awards

Film

Drama: *Brokeback Mountain*
Musical/comedy: *Walk the Line*
Actress, drama: Felicity Huffman, *Transamerica*
Actor, drama: Philip Seymour Hoffman, *Capote*
Actress, musical/comedy: Reese Witherspoon, *Walk the Line*
Actor, musical/comedy: Joaquin Phoenix, *Walk the Line*
Sup. actress: Rachel Weisz, *The Constant Gardner*
Sup. actor: George Clooney, *Syriana*
Director: Ang Lee, *Brokeback Mountain*
Screenplay: Larry McMurtry & Diana Ossana, *Brokeback Mountain*
Foreign-language film: *Paradise Now* (Palestine)
Original score: John Williams, *Memoirs of a Geisha*
Original song: "A Love That Will Never Grow Old," *Brokeback Mountain*
Cecil B. DeMille award for lifetime achievement: Anthony Hopkins

Television

Series, drama: *Lost*, ABC
Actress, drama: Geena Davis, *Commander in Chief*, ABC
Actor, drama: Hugh Laurie, *House*, FOX
Series, musical/comedy: *Desperate Housewives*, ABC
Actress, musical/comedy: Mary-Louise Parker, *Weeds*, Showtime
Actor, musical/comedy: Steve Carell, *The Office*, NBC
Miniseries, movie made for TV: *Empire Falls*, HBO
Actress, miniseries/movie: S. Epatha Merkerson, *Lackawanna Blues*, HBO
Actor, miniseries/movie: Jonathan Rhys Meyers, *Elvis*, CBS
Sup. actress, series/miniseries/movie: Sandra Oh, *Grey's Anatomy*, ABC
Sup. actor, series/miniseries/movie: Paul Newman, *Empire Falls*, HBO

2006 People's Choice Awards

Film

Picture: *Star Wars: Episode III—Revenge of the Sith*
Drama: *Star Wars: Episode III—Revenge of the Sith*
Comedy: *Wedding Crashers*
Family Movie: *Charlie and the Chocolate Factory*
Movie stars: Sandra Bullock, Johnny Depp
Action movie stars: Matthew McConaughey, Jennifer Garner

Music

Male performer: Tim McGraw
Female performer: Kelly Clarkson
Group or band: Green Day

Television

Drama: *CSI: Crime Scene Investigation*
Comedy: *Everybody Loves Raymond*
Male TV star: Ray Romano
Female TV star: Jennifer Garner
New comedy: *My Name is Earl*
New drama: *Prison Break*
Talk show host, daytime: Ellen DeGeneres
Talk show host, late-night: Jay Leno
Reality program (competition): *American Idol*
Reality program (other): *Extreme Makeover: Home Edition*

Academy Awards (Oscars) for 1927-2005

Year	Picture	Actor	Actress	Sup. Actor[1]	Sup. Actress[1]	Director
1927-28	Wings	Emil Jannings, *The Way of All Flesh*	Janet Gaynor, *Seventh Heaven*			Frank Borzage, *Seventh Heaven*; Lewis Milestone, *Two Arabian Knights*
1928-29	Broadway Melody	Warner Baxter, *In Old Arizona*	Mary Pickford, *Coquette*			Frank Lloyd, *The Divine Lady*
1929-30	All Quiet on the Western Front	George Arliss *Disraeli*	Norma Shearer *The Divorcee*			Lewis Milestone *All Quiet on the Western Front*
1930-31	Cimarron	Lionel Barrymore *Free Soul*	Marie Dressler *Min and Bill*			Norman Taurog *Skippy*
1931-32	Grand Hotel	Fredric March *Dr. Jekyll and Mr. Hyde;* Wallace Beery *The Champ* (tie)	Helen Hayes *The Sin of Madelon Claudet*			Frank Borzage *Bad Girl*
1932-33	Cavalcade	Charles Laughton *The Private Life of Henry VIII*	Katharine Hepburn *Morning Glory*			Frank Lloyd *Cavalcade*
1934	It Happened One Night	Clark Gable *It Happened One Night*	Claudette Colbert *It Happened One Night*			Frank Capra *It Happened One Night*
1935	Mutiny on the Bounty	Victor McLaglen *The Informer*	Bette Davis *Dangerous*			John Ford *The Informer*
1936	The Great Ziegfeld	Paul Muni *Story of Louis Pasteur*	Luise Rainer *The Great Ziegfeld*	Walter Brennan *Come and Get It*	Gale Sondergaard *Anthony Adverse*	Frank Capra *Mr. Deeds Goes to Town*
1937	Life of Emile Zola	Spencer Tracy *Captains Courageous*	Luise Rainer *The Good Earth*	Joseph Schildkraut *Life of Emile Zola*	Alice Brady *In Old Chicago*	Leo McCarey *The Awful Truth*
1938	You Can't Take It With You	Spencer Tracy *Boys Town*	Bette Davis *Jezebel*	Walter Brennan *Kentucky*	Fay Bainter *Jezebel*	Frank Capra *You Can't Take It With You*
1939	Gone With the Wind	Robert Donat *Goodbye Mr. Chips*	Vivien Leigh *Gone With the Wind*	Thomas Mitchell *Stage Coach*	Hattie McDaniel *Gone With the Wind*	Victor Fleming *Gone With the Wind*
1940	Rebecca	James Stewart *The Philadelphia Story*	Ginger Rogers *Kitty Foyle*	Walter Brennan *The Westerner*	Jane Darwell *The Grapes of Wrath*	John Ford *The Grapes of Wrath*
1941	How Green Was My Valley	Gary Cooper *Sergeant York*	Joan Fontaine *Suspicion*	Donald Crisp *How Green Was My Valley*	Mary Astor *The Great Lie*	John Ford *How Green Was My Valley*
1942	Mrs. Miniver	James Cagney *Yankee Doodle Dandy*	Greer Garson *Mrs. Miniver*	Van Heflin *Johnny Eager*	Teresa Wright *Mrs. Miniver*	William Wyler *Mrs. Miniver*
1943	Casablanca	Paul Lukas *Watch on the Rhine*	Jennifer Jones *The Song of Bernadette*	Charles Coburn *The More the Merrier*	Katina Paxinou *For Whom the Bell Tolls*	Michael Curtiz *Casablanca*
1944	Going My Way	Bing Crosby *Going My Way*	Ingrid Bergman *Gaslight*	Barry Fitzgerald *Going My Way*	Ethel Barrymore *None But the Lonely Heart*	Leo McCarey *Going My Way*
1945	The Lost Weekend	Ray Milland *The Lost Weekend*	Joan Crawford *Mildred Pierce*	James Dunn *A Tree Grows in Brooklyn*	Anne Revere *National Velvet*	Billy Wilder *The Lost Weekend*
1946	The Best Years of Our Lives	Fredric March *The Best Years of Our Lives*	Olivia de Havilland *To Each His Own*	Harold Russell *The Best Years of Our Lives*	Anne Baxter *The Razor's Edge*	William Wyler *The Best Years of Our Lives*
1947	Gentleman's Agreement	Ronald Colman *A Double Life*	Loretta Young *The Farmer's Daughter*	Edmund Gwenn *Miracle on 34th Street*	Celeste Holm *Gentleman's Agreement*	Elia Kazan *Gentleman's Agreement*
1948	Hamlet	Laurence Olivier *Hamlet*	Jane Wyman *Johnny Belinda*	Walter Huston *Treasure of Sierra Madre*	Claire Trevor *Key Largo*	John Huston *Treasure of Sierra Madre*
1949	All the King's Men	Broderick Crawford *All the King's Men*	Olivia de Havilland *The Heiress*	Dean Jagger *Twelve O'Clock High*	Mercedes McCambridge *All the King's Men*	Joseph L. Mankiewicz *Letter to Three Wives*
1950	All About Eve	Jose Ferrer *Cyrano de Bergerac*	Judy Holliday *Born Yesterday*	George Sanders *All About Eve*	Josephine Hull *Harvey*	Joseph L. Mankiewicz *All About Eve*
1951	An American in Paris	Humphrey Bogart *The African Queen*	Vivien Leigh *A Streetcar Named Desire*	Karl Malden *A Streetcar Named Desire*	Kim Hunter *A Streetcar Named Desire*	George Stevens *A Place in the Sun*
1952	The Greatest Show on Earth	Gary Cooper *High Noon*	Shirley Booth *Come Back Little Sheba*	Anthony Quinn *Viva Zapata!*	Gloria Grahame *The Bad and the Beautiful*	John Ford *The Quiet Man*
1953	From Here to Eternity	William Holden *Stalag 17*	Audrey Hepburn *Roman Holiday*	Frank Sinatra *From Here to Eternity*	Donna Reed *From Here to Eternity*	Fred Zinnemann *From Here to Eternity*
1954	On the Waterfront	Marlon Brando *On the Waterfront*	Grace Kelly *The Country Girl*	Edmond O'Brien *The Barefoot Contessa*	Eva Marie Saint *On the Waterfront*	Elia Kazan *On the Waterfront*
1955	Marty	Ernest Borgnine *Marty*	Anna Magnani *The Rose Tattoo*	Jack Lemmon *Mister Roberts*	Jo Van Fleet *East of Eden*	Delbert Mann *Marty*
1956	Around the World in 80 Days	Yul Brynner *The King and I*	Ingrid Bergman *Anastasia*	Anthony Quinn *Lust for Life*	Dorothy Malone *Written on the Wind*	George Stevens *Giant*
1957	The Bridge on the River Kwai	Alec Guinness *The Bridge on the River Kwai*	Joanne Woodward *The Three Faces of Eve*	Red Buttons *Sayonara*	Miyoshi Umeki *Sayonara*	David Lean *The Bridge on the River Kwai*
1958	Gigi	David Niven *Separate Tables*	Susan Hayward *I Want to Live*	Burl Ives *The Big Country*	Wendy Hiller *Separate Tables*	Vincente Minnelli *Gigi*
1959	Ben-Hur	Charlton Heston *Ben-Hur*	Simone Signoret *Room at the Top*	Hugh Griffith *Ben-Hur*	Shelley Winters *Diary of Anne Frank*	William Wyler *Ben-Hur*

Year	Picture	Actor	Actress	Sup. Actor[1]	Sup. Actress[1]	Director
1960	The Apartment	Burt Lancaster *Elmer Gantry*	Elizabeth Taylor *Butterfield 8*	Peter Ustinov *Spartacus*	Shirley Jones *Elmer Gantry*	Billy Wilder *The Apartment*
1961	West Side Story	Maximilian Schell *Judgment at Nuremberg*	Sophia Loren *Two Women*	George Chakiris *West Side Story*	Rita Moreno *West Side Story*	Jerome Robbins, Robert Wise *West Side Story*
1962	Lawrence of Arabia	Gregory Peck *To Kill a Mockingbird*	Anne Bancroft *The Miracle Worker*	Ed Begley *Sweet Bird of Youth*	Patty Duke *The Miracle Worker*	David Lean *Lawrence of Arabia*
1963	Tom Jones	Sidney Poitier *Lilies of the Field*	Patricia Neal *Hud*	Melvyn Douglas *Hud*	Margaret Rutherford *The V.I.P.s*	Tony Richardson *Tom Jones*
1964	My Fair Lady	Rex Harrison *My Fair Lady*	Julie Andrews *Mary Poppins*	Peter Ustinov *Topkapi*	Lila Kedrova *Zorba the Greek*	George Cukor *My Fair Lady*
1965	The Sound of Music	Lee Marvin *Cat Ballou*	Julie Christie *Darling*	Martin Balsam *A Thousand Clowns*	Shelley Winters *A Patch of Blue*	Robert Wise *The Sound of Music*
1966	A Man for All Seasons	Paul Scofield *A Man for All Seasons*	Elizabeth Taylor *Who's Afraid of Virginia Woolf?*	Walter Matthau *The Fortune Cookie*	Sandy Dennis *Who's Afraid of Virginia Woolf?*	Fred Zinnemann *A Man for All Seasons*
1967	In the Heat of the Night	Rod Steiger *In the Heat of the Night*	Katharine Hepburn *Guess Who's Coming to Dinner*	George Kennedy *Cool Hand Luke*	Estelle Parsons *Bonnie and Clyde*	Mike Nichols *The Graduate*
1968	Oliver!	Cliff Robertson *Charly*	Katharine Hepburn *The Lion in Winter;* Barbra Streisand *Funny Girl* (tie)	Jack Albertson *The Subject Was Roses*	Ruth Gordon *Rosemary's Baby*	Sir Carol Reed *Oliver!*
1969	Midnight Cowboy	John Wayne *True Grit*	Maggie Smith *The Prime of Miss Jean Brodie*	Gig Young *They Shoot Horses, Don't They?*	Goldie Hawn *Cactus Flower*	John Schlesinger *Midnight Cowboy*
1970	Patton	George C. Scott *Patton* (refused)	Glenda Jackson *Women in Love*	John Mills *Ryan's Daughter*	Helen Hayes *Airport*	Franklin Schaffner *Patton*
1971	The French Connection	Gene Hackman *The French Connection*	Jane Fonda *Klute*	Ben Johnson *The Last Picture Show*	Cloris Leachman *The Last Picture Show*	William Friedkin *The French Connection*
1972	The Godfather	Marlon Brando *The Godfather* (refused)	Liza Minnelli *Cabaret*	Joel Grey *Cabaret*	Eileen Heckart *Butterflies Are Free*	Bob Fosse *Cabaret*
1973	The Sting	Jack Lemmon *Save the Tiger*	Glenda Jackson *A Touch of Class*	John Houseman *The Paper Chase*	Tatum O'Neal *Paper Moon*	George Roy Hill *The Sting*
1974	The Godfather Part II	Art Carney *Harry and Tonto*	Ellen Burstyn *Alice Doesn't Live Here Anymore*	Robert DeNiro *The Godfather Part II*	Ingrid Bergman *Murder on the Orient Express*	Francis Ford Coppola *The Godfather Part II*
1975	One Flew Over the Cuckoo's Nest	Jack Nicholson *One Flew Over the Cuckoo's Nest*	Louise Fletcher *One Flew Over the Cuckoo's Nest*	George Burns *The Sunshine Boys*	Lee Grant *Shampoo*	Milos Forman *One Flew Over the Cuckoo's Nest*
1976	Rocky	Peter Finch *Network*	Faye Dunaway *Network*	Jason Robards *All the President's Men*	Beatrice Straight *Network*	John G. Avildsen *Rocky*
1977	Annie Hall	Richard Dreyfuss *The Goodbye Girl*	Diane Keaton *Annie Hall*	Jason Robards *Julia*	Vanessa Redgrave *Julia*	Woody Allen *Annie Hall*
1978	The Deer Hunter	Jon Voight *Coming Home*	Jane Fonda *Coming Home*	Christopher Walken *The Deer Hunter*	Maggie Smith *California Suite*	Michael Cimino *The Deer Hunter*
1979	Kramer vs. Kramer	Dustin Hoffman *Kramer vs. Kramer*	Sally Field *Norma Rae*	Melvyn Douglas *Being There*	Meryl Streep *Kramer vs. Kramer*	Robert Benton *Kramer vs. Kramer*
1980	Ordinary People	Robert DeNiro *Raging Bull*	Sissy Spacek *Coal Miner's Daughter*	Timothy Hutton *Ordinary People*	Mary Steenburgen *Melvin & Howard*	Robert Redford *Ordinary People*
1981	Chariots of Fire	Henry Fonda *On Golden Pond*	Katharine Hepburn *On Golden Pond*	John Gielgud *Arthur*	Maureen Stapleton *Reds*	Warren Beatty *Reds*
1982	Gandhi	Ben Kingsley *Gandhi*	Meryl Streep *Sophie's Choice*	Louis Gossett Jr. *An Officer and a Gentleman*	Jessica Lange *Tootsie*	Richard Attenborough *Gandhi*
1983	Terms of Endearment	Robert Duvall *Tender Mercies*	Shirley MacLaine *Terms of Endearment*	Jack Nicholson *Terms of Endearment*	Linda Hunt *The Year of Living Dangerously*	James L. Brooks *Terms of Endearment*
1984	Amadeus	F. Murray Abraham *Amadeus*	Sally Field *Places in the Heart*	Haing S. Ngor *The Killing Fields*	Peggy Ashcroft *A Passage to India*	Milos Forman *Amadeus*
1985	Out of Africa	William Hurt *Kiss of the Spider Woman*	Geraldine Page *The Trip to Bountiful*	Don Ameche *Cocoon*	Anjelica Huston *Prizzi's Honor*	Sydney Pollack *Out of Africa*
1986	Platoon	Paul Newman *The Color of Money*	Marlee Matlin *Children of a Lesser God*	Michael Caine *Hannah and Her Sisters*	Dianne Wiest *Hannah and Her Sisters*	Oliver Stone *Platoon*
1987	The Last Emperor	Michael Douglas *Wall Street*	Cher *Moonstruck*	Sean Connery *The Untouchables*	Olympia Dukakis *Moonstruck*	Bernardo Bertolucci *The Last Emperor*
1988	Rain Man	Dustin Hoffman *Rain Man*	Jodie Foster *The Accused*	Kevin Kline *A Fish Called Wanda*	Geena Davis *The Accidental Tourist*	Barry Levinson *Rain Man*
1989	Driving Miss Daisy	Daniel Day-Lewis *My Left Foot*	Jessica Tandy *Driving Miss Daisy*	Denzel Washington *Glory*	Brenda Fricker *My Left Foot*	Oliver Stone *Born on the Fourth of July*
1990	Dances With Wolves	Jeremy Irons *Reversal of Fortune*	Kathy Bates *Misery*	Joe Pesci *Goodfellas*	Whoopi Goldberg *Ghost*	Kevin Costner *Dances With Wolves*
1991	The Silence of the Lambs	Anthony Hopkins *The Silence of the Lambs*	Jodie Foster *The Silence of the Lambs*	Jack Palance *City Slickers*	Mercedes Ruehl *The Fisher King*	Jonathan Demme *The Silence of the Lambs*
1992	Unforgiven	Al Pacino *Scent of a Woman*	Emma Thompson *Howards End*	Gene Hackman *Unforgiven*	Marisa Tomei *My Cousin Vinny*	Clint Eastwood *Unforgiven*
1993	Schindler's List	Tom Hanks *Philadelphia*	Holly Hunter *The Piano*	Tommy Lee Jones *The Fugitive*	Anna Paquin *The Piano*	Steven Spielberg *Schindler's List*

Year	Picture	Actor	Actress	Sup. Actor[1]	Sup. Actress[1]	Director
1994	*Forrest Gump*	Tom Hanks *Forrest Gump*	Jessica Lange *Blue Sky*	Martin Landau *Ed Wood*	Dianne Wiest *Bullets Over Broadway*	Robert Zemeckis *Forrest Gump*
1995	*Braveheart*	Nicolas Cage *Leaving Las Vegas*	Susan Sarandon *Dead Man Walking*	Kevin Spacey *The Usual Suspects*	Mira Sorvino *Mighty Aphrodite*	Mel Gibson *Braveheart*
1996	*The English Patient*	Geoffrey Rush *Shine*	Frances McDormand *Fargo*	Cuba Gooding Jr. *Jerry Maguire*	Juliette Binoche *The English Patient*	Anthony Minghella *The English Patient*
1997	*Titanic*	Jack Nicholson *As Good As It Gets*	Helen Hunt *As Good As It Gets*	Robin Williams *Good Will Hunting*	Kim Basinger *L.A. Confidential*	James Cameron *Titanic*
1998	*Shakespeare in Love*	Roberto Benigni *Life Is Beautiful*	Gwyneth Paltrow *Shakespeare in Love*	James Coburn *Affliction*	Judi Dench *Shakespeare in Love*	Steven Spielberg *Saving Private Ryan*
1999	*American Beauty*	Kevin Spacey *American Beauty*	Hilary Swank *Boys Don't Cry*	Michael Caine *The Cider House Rules*	Angelina Jolie *Girl, Interrupted*	Sam Mendes *American Beauty*
2000	*Gladiator*	Russell Crowe *Gladiator*	Julia Roberts *Erin Brockovich*	Benicio Del Toro *Traffic*	Marcia Gay Harden *Pollock*	Steven Soderbergh *Traffic*
2001	*A Beautiful Mind*	Denzel Washington *Training Day*	Halle Berry *Monster's Ball*	Jim Broadbent *Iris*	Jennifer Connelly *A Beautiful Mind*	Ron Howard *A Beautiful Mind*
2002	*Chicago*	Adrien Brody *The Pianist*	Nicole Kidman *The Hours*	Chris Cooper *Adaptation*	Catherine Zeta-Jones *Chicago*	Roman Polanski *The Pianist*
2003	*The Lord of the Rings: The Return of the King*	Sean Penn, *Mystic River*	Charlize Theron, *Monster*	Tim Robbins, *Mystic River*	Renée Zellweger, *Cold Mountain*	Peter Jackson, *The Lord of the Rings: The Return of the King*
2004	*Million Dollar Baby*	Jamie Foxx, *Ray*	Hilary Swank, *Million Dollar Baby*	Morgan Freeman, *Million Dollar Baby*	Cate Blanchett, *The Aviator*	Clint Eastwood, *Million Dollar Baby*
2005	*Crash*	Philip Seymour Hoffman, *Capote*	Reese Witherspoon, *Walk the Line*	George Clooney, *Syriana*	Rachel Weisz, *The Constant Gardener*	Ang Lee, *Brokeback Mountain*

(1) These awards not given until 1936.

OTHER 2005 OSCAR WINNERS: Animated film: *Wallace & Gromit in The Curse of the Were-Rabbit*. Foreign film: *Tsotsi*, South Africa. Original screenplay: Paul Haggis & Bobby Moresco, *Crash*. Adapted screenplay: Larry McMurtry & Diana Ossana, *Brokeback Mountain*. Cinematography: Dion Beebe, *Memoirs of a Geisha*. Art direction: John Myhre (art direction), Gretchen Rau (set decoration), *Memoirs of a Geisha*. Film editing: Hughes Winborne, *Crash*. Original song: "It's Hard Out There for a Pimp," *Hustle & Flow*, music and lyrics by Jordan Houston, Cedric Coleman, & Paul Beauregard. Original score: Gustavo Santaolalla, *Brokeback Mountain*. Costume design: Colleen Atwood, *Memoirs of a Geisha*. Makeup: Howard Berger & Tami Lane, *The Chronicles of Narnia: The Lion, the Witch and the Wardrobe*. Sound mixing: Christopher Boyes, Michael Semanick, Michael Hedges, & Hammond Peek; *King Kong*. Documentary feature: Luc Jacquet & Yves Darondeau, *March of the Penguins*. Documentary short subject: Corinne Marrinan & Eric Simonson, *A Note of Triumph: The Golden Age of Norman Corwin*. Short film, live: Martin McDonagh, *Six Shooter*. Short film, animated: John Canemaker & Peggy Stern, *The Moon and the Son: An Imagined Conversation*. Visual effects: Joe Letteri, Brian Van't Hul, Christian Rivers, & Richard Taylor; *King Kong*. Sound editing: Mike Hopkins & Ethan Van der Ryn, *King Kong*. Honorary Oscars: Robert Altman.

Other 2006 Film Awards

Cannes Film Festival Awards: Feature Films—Palme d'Or (Golden Palm): *The Wind That Shakes the Barley*, Ken Loach, Britain; Grand Prix: *Flanders*, Bruno Dumont, France; Best Actress(es): Penélope Cruz, Carmen Maura, Lola Dueñas, Blanca Portillo, Yohana Cobo, Chus Lampreave, *Volver* (*Return*), Spain; Best Actor(s): Jamel Debbouze, Samy Nacéri, Roschdy Zem, Sami Bouajila, Bernard Blancan, *Indigènes* (*Days of Glory*), France; Best Director: Alejandro Gonzáles Iñárrtu, *Babel*, Mexico; Best Screenplay: Pedro Almodóvar, *Volver*, Spain; Jury Prize: *Red Road*, Andrea Arnold, Britain. Caméra d'Or (Golden Camera; first-time director's prize): *A Fost Sau n-a Fost?*, Corneliu Porumboiu, Romania.

Short Films—Palme d'Or: *Sniffer*, Bobbie Peers, Norway; Jury Prize: *Primera Nieve*, Pablo Aguero, Argentina; Mention Spéciale: *Conte de Quartier*, Florence Miailhe, France.

Director's Guild of America Awards: Feature film: Ang Lee, *Brokeback Mountain*; Documentary: Werner Herzog, *Grizzly Man*; Lifetime Achievement: Clint Eastwood.

Sundance Film Festival Awards: Grand Jury Prizes: (drama) *Quinceañera*, Wash Westmoreland & Richard Glatzer; (documentary) *God Grew Tired of Us*, Christopher Quinn. Directing Awards: (drama) Dito Montiel, *A Guide to Recognizing Your Saints*; (doc.) James Longley, *Iraq in Fragments*. Waldo Salt Screenwriting Award: Hilary Brougher, *Stephanie Daley*. Audience Awards: (drama) *Quinceañera*, Wash Westmoreland & Richard Glatzer; (documentary) *God Grew Tired of Us*, Christopher Quinn. Cinematography Awards: (drama) Tom Richmond, *Right at Your Door*; (doc.) James Longley, *Iraq in Fragments*. World Cinema Jury Prizes: (drama) *13 Tzameti*, Géla Babluani, France; (doc.) *In the Pit*, Juan Carlos Rulfo, Mexico. World Cinema Audience Awards: (drama) *No. 2*, Toa Fraser, New Zealand; (doc.) *De Nadie*, Tin Dirdamal, Mexico. Alfred P. Sloan Prize: Andrucha Waddington, *The House of Sand*. Internat. Filmmakers Award: Patrice Toy, *The Spring Ritual* (Europe); Fernando Eimbcke, *Lake Tahoe* (Latin Amer.); Cruz Angeles, *Don't Let Me Drown* (U.S.); Kanji Nakajima, *The Clone Returns to the Homeland* (Japan). Short Filmmaking Jury Prizes: *Bugcrush*, Carter Smith; *The Wraith of Cobble Hill*, Adam Parrish King.

2006 MTV Video Music Awards

Video of the Year: Panic! at the Disco, "I Write Sins Not Tragedies"
Best Male Video: James Blunt, "You're Beautiful"
Best Female Video: Kelly Clarkson, "Because of You"
Best Group Video: The All-American Rejects, "Move Along"
Best Dance Video: Pussycat Dolls feat. Snoop Dogg, "Buttons"
Best Hip-Hop Video: Black Eyed Peas, "My Humps"
Best Pop Video: Pink, "Stupid Girls"
Best R&B Video: Beyoncé feat. Slim Thug, "Check on It"
Best Rap Video: Chamillionaire, "Ridin'"
Best Rock Video: AFI, "Miss Murder"
Best New Artist: Avenged Sevenfold, "Bat Country"
Best MTV2 Video: 30 Seconds to Mars, "The Kill"
Best Direction: Robert Hales for Gnarls Barkley, "Crazy"
Best Choreography: Shakira feat. Wyclef Jean, "Hips Don't Lie"
Best Special Effects: Missy Elliott, "We Run This"
Best Art Direction: Red Hot Chili Peppers, "Dani California"
Best Editing: Gnarls Barkley, "Crazy"
Best Cinematography: James Blunt, "You're Beautiful"
Best Soundtrack From a Video Game: "Mark Ecko's Getting Up," Atari
Best Score From a Video Game: "Elder Scrolls IV: Oblivion" (Jeremy Soule)
Viewers' Choice: Fall Out Boy, "Dance, Dance"
Ringtone of the Year: Fort Minor, "Where'd You Go"

2006 Academy of Country Music Awards

Entertainer of the Year: Kenny Chesney
Album of the Year: *Time Well Wasted*, Brad Paisley; Chris DuBois & Frank Rogers, prod.
Single of the Year: "Jesus Take the Wheel," Carrie Underwood; Mark Bright, prod.
Top Female Vocalist: Sara Evans
Top Male Vocalist: Keith Urban
Top Vocal Duo: Brooks & Dunn
Top Vocal Group: Rascal Flatts
Top New Female Vocalist: Carrie Underwood
Top New Male Vocalist: Jason Aldean
Top New Duo/Group: Sugarland
Song of the Year: "Believe," Brooks & Dunn; written by Ronnie Dunn & Craig Wiseman
Video of the Year: "When I Get Where I'm Going," Brad Paisley & Dolly Parton; Mark Kalbfeld & Peter Tilden, prod.; Jim Shea, dir.
Vocal Event of the Year: "When I Get Where I'm Going," Brad Paisley & Dolly Parton; Chris DuBois & Frank Rogers, prod.
Humanitarian Award: Vince Gill

Grammy Awards

Source: National Academy of Recording Arts & Sciences

Selected Grammy Awards for 2005

Record of the Year (single): "Boulevard of Broken Dreams," Green Day
Album of the Year: *How to Dismantle an Atomic Bomb*, U2
Song of the Year: "Sometimes You Can't Make It on Your Own," U2
New artist: John Legend
Short Form Music Video: "Lose Control," Missy Elliott feat. Ciara & Fat Man Scoop
Pop vocal perf., female: "Since U Been Gone," Kelly Clarkson
Pop vocal perf., male: "From the Bottom of My Heart," Stevie Wonder
Pop vocal perf., duo/group: "This Love," Maroon 5
Pop vocal perf., collaboration: "Feel Good Inc.," Gorillaz feat. De La Soul
Pop instrumental album: *At This Time*, Burt Bacharach
Pop vocal album, traditional: *The Art of Romance*, Tony Bennett
Pop vocal album: *Breakaway*, Kelly Clarkson
Dance recording: "Galvanize," The Chemical Brothers feat. Q-Tip
Electric/Dance album: *Push the Button*, The Chemical Brothers
Rock vocal perf., solo: "Devils & Dust," Bruce Springsteen
Rock vocal perf., duo/group: "Sometimes You Can't Make It on Your Own," U2
Rock instrumental perf.: "'69 Freedom Special," Les Paul & Friends
Hard rock perf.: "B.Y.O.B.," System of a Down
Metal perf.: "Before I Forget," Slipknot
Rock song: "City of Blinding Lights," U2
Rock album: *How to Dismantle an Atomic Bomb*, U2
Alternative album: *Get Behind Me Satan*, The White Stripes
R&B vocal perf., female: "We Belong Together," Mariah Carey
R&B vocal perf., male: "Ordinary People," John Legend

R&B vocal perf., duo/group: "So Amazing," Beyoncé & Stevie Wonder
R&B song: "We Belong Together," Mariah Carey
R&B album: *Get Lifted*, John Legend
R&B album, contemporary: *The Emancipation of Mimi*, Mariah Carey
Rap perf., solo: "Gold Digger," Kanye West
Rap perf., duo/group: "Don't Phunk With My Heart" The Black Eyed Peas
Rap song: "Diamonds From Sierra Leone," Kanye West
Rap album: *Late Registration*, Kanye West
Country vocal perf., female: "The Connection," Emmylou Harris
Country vocal perf., male: "You'll Think of Me," Keith Urban
Country vocal perf., duo/group: "Restless," Alison Krauss & Union Station
Country song: "Bless the Broken Road," Rascal Flatts
Country album: *Lonely Runs Both Ways*, Alison Krauss & Union Station
Bluegrass album: *The Company We Keep*, The Del McCoury Band
Jazz album, vocal: *Good night, and Good Luck*, Dianne Reeves
Jazz album, instr.: *Beyond the Sound Barrier*, Wayne Shorter Quartet
Jazz album, contemporary: *The Way Up*, Pat Metheny Group
Blues album, contemporary: *Cost of Living*, Delbert McClinton
Blues album, traditional: *80*, B.B. King and Friends
Folk album, contemporary: *Fair & Square*, John Prine
Folk album, traditional: *Fiddler's Green*, Tim O'Brien
Latin pop album: *Escucha*, Laura Pausini
Producer, non-classical: Steve Lillywhite (U2)
Classical album: *Bolcom: Songs of Innocence and of Experience*, Leonard Slatkin
Classical vocal perf.: *Bach: Cantata*, Thomas Quasthoff

Grammy Awards for 1958-2005

Record of the Year (single)	Year	Album of the Year
Domenico Modugno, "Nel Blu Dipinto Di Blu (Volare)"	1958	Henry Mancini, *The Music From Peter Gunn*
Bobby Darin, "Mack the Knife"	1959	Frank Sinatra, *Come Dance With Me*
Percy Faith, "Theme From a Summer Place"	1960	Bob Newhart, *Button Down Mind*
Henry Mancini, "Moon River"	1961	Judy Garland, *Judy at Carnegie Hall*
Tony Bennett, "I Left My Heart in San Francisco"	1962	Vaughn Meader, *The First Family*
Henry Mancini, "The Days of Wine and Roses"	1963	Barbra Streisand, *The Barbra Streisand Album*
Stan Getz, Astrud Gilberto, "The Girl From Ipanema"	1964	Stan Getz, Astrud Gilberto, *Getz/Gilberto*
Herb Alpert, "A Taste of Honey"	1965	Frank Sinatra, *September of My Years*
Frank Sinatra, "Strangers in the Night"	1966	Frank Sinatra, *A Man and His Music*
5th Dimension, "Up, Up and Away"	1967	The Beatles, *Sgt. Pepper's Lonely Hearts Club Band*
Simon & Garfunkel, "Mrs. Robinson"	1968	Glen Campbell, *By the Time I Get to Phoenix*
5th Dimension, "Aquarius/Let the Sunshine In"	1969	Blood Sweat and Tears, *Blood, Sweat and Tears*
Simon & Garfunkel, "Bridge Over Troubled Water"	1970	Simon & Garfunkel, *Bridge Over Troubled Water*
Carole King, "It's Too Late"	1971	Carole King, *Tapestry*
Roberta Flack, "The First Time Ever I Saw Your Face"	1972	George Harrison and friends, *The Concert for Bangla Desh*
Roberta Flack, "Killing Me Softly With His Song"	1973	Stevie Wonder, *Innervisions*
Olivia Newton-John, "I Honestly Love You"	1974	Stevie Wonder, *Fulfillingness' First Finale*
Captain & Tennille, "Love Will Keep Us Together"	1975	Paul Simon, *Still Crazy After All These Years*
George Benson, "This Masquerade"	1976	Stevie Wonder, *Songs in the Key of Life*
Eagles, "Hotel California"	1977	Fleetwood Mac, *Rumours*
Billy Joel, "Just the Way You Are"	1978	Bee Gees, *Saturday Night Fever*
The Doobie Brothers, "What a Fool Believes"	1979	Billy Joel, *52nd Street*
Christopher Cross, "Sailing"	1980	Christopher Cross, *Christopher Cross*
Kim Carnes, "Bette Davis Eyes"	1981	John Lennon, Yoko Ono, *Double Fantasy*
Toto, "Rosanna"	1982	Toto, *Toto IV*
Michael Jackson, "Beat It"	1983	Michael Jackson, *Thriller*
Tina Turner, "What's Love Got to Do With It"	1984	Lionel Richie, *Can't Slow Down*
USA for Africa, "We Are the World"	1985	Phil Collins, *No Jacket Required*
Steve Winwood, "Higher Love"	1986	Paul Simon, *Graceland*
Paul Simon, "Graceland"	1987	U2, *The Joshua Tree*
Bobby McFerrin, "Don't Worry, Be Happy"	1988	George Michael, *Faith*
Bette Midler, "Wind Beneath My Wings"	1989	Bonnie Raitt, *Nick of Time*
Phil Collins, "Another Day in Paradise"	1990	Quincy Jones, *Back on the Block*
Natalie Cole, with Nat "King" Cole, "Unforgettable"	1991	Natalie Cole, with Nat "King" Cole, *Unforgettable*
Eric Clapton, "Tears in Heaven"	1992	Eric Clapton, *Unplugged*
Whitney Houston, "I Will Always Love You"	1993	Whitney Houston, *The Bodyguard*
Sheryl Crow, "All I Wanna Do"	1994	Tony Bennett, *MTV Unplugged*
Seal, "Kiss From a Rose"	1995	Alanis Morissette, *Jagged Little Pill*
Eric Clapton, "Change the World"	1996	Celine Dion, *Falling Into You*
Shawn Colvin, "Sunny Came Home"	1997	Bob Dylan, *Time Out of Mind*
Celine Dion, "My Heart Will Go On"	1998	Lauryn Hill, *The Miseducation of Lauryn Hill*
Santana featuring Rob Thomas, "Smooth"	1999	Santana, *Supernatural*
U2, "Beautiful Day"	2000	Steely Dan, *Two Against Nature*
U2, "Walk On"	2001	Various Artists, *O Brother, Where Art Thou?*
Norah Jones, "Don't Know Why"	2002	Norah Jones, *Come Away With Me*
Coldplay, "Clocks"	2003	OutKast, *Speakerboxxx/The Love Below*
Ray Charles & Norah Jones, "Here We Go Again"	2004	Ray Charles & Various Artists, *Genius Loves Company*
Green Day, "Boulevard of Broken Dreams"	2005	U2, *How to Dismantle an Atomic Bomb*

Science News 2006

Earth Science news and glossary entries reviewed by Prof. Maura C. Flannery, St. John's Univ., Queens, NY. Earth Science developments written by Phill Jones. Physical science developments written by Philip Downey.

The following were some of the more newsworthy developments in Science in the past year. (See also the chapters on Astronomy, Computers and Telecommunications, and Health.)

Earth and Life Science Developments

Hydrology: Subglacial Rivers in Antarctica

Deep beneath the Antarctic ice pack, rivers the size of the Thames move water hundreds of miles between subglacial lakes, according to Univ. College of London climate physicist Duncan Wingham and colleagues. Using ice-penetrating radar aboard a research satellite, the scientists recorded ice sinking above one subglacial lake and rising above two other subglacial lakes, both more than 180 mi away. These shifts indicate that water flowed downstream from the first lake into the two others. The discovery of connected lakes suggests that in the past, huge flood waters might have flowed from interior ice and into the ocean—and that **massive flooding could occur again, disrupting ocean circulation and influencing global climate**. In light of this discovery, scientists may have to take new precautions when drilling into subglacial lakes to search for unique microbial life. An accidental contamination of one lake could spread to other lakes via the river network and affect the subglacial ecosystem. [University College London; reported in *Nature,* Apr. 20]

New Species Discovered in New Guinea, Israel, and a Mile Undersea

Dozens of new animal and plant species were discovered in late 2005 and 2006. In a remote area of the Foja Mountains in New Guinea, biologist Bruce Beehler and his team of explorers discovered a wealth of new animal species during a research trip to New Guinea in Dec. 2005. Of the new species, scientists found **an orange-faced honeyeater bird, four species of butterfly, five types of palm, and more than 20 new species of frogs,** including one measuring less than half an inch long. It is believed that few if any humans had ever previously visited the area. [Conservation International, Feb. 7]

Hebrew Univ. of Jerusalem researchers discovered **8 new arthropod species** in a limestone cave located 328 ft below the surface of a quarry between Jerusalem and Tel Aviv. Geologist Amos Frumkin and his group found 4 terrestrial species, and 4 seawater and freshwater crustaceans. The invertebrate species had been isolated from the outside world in their underground ecosystem and may be millions of years old. [Hebrew Univ. of Jerusalem, June 1]

An international scientific team discovered **a blind deep-sea crab with legs covered in long, pale yellow hairs**. *Kiwa hirsuta,* dubbed the Yeti crab, was eating mussels near a hydrothermal vent about 7,200 ft under the ocean, south of Easter Island. The scientists, led by Bob Vrijenhoek of California's Monterey Bay Aquarium Research Institute, speculated that the Yeti crab may use its arm hairs to farm colonies of filamentous bacteria, perhaps as an additional food source. [Monterey Bay Research Institute; reported *Nature,* Mar. 13]

Conservation: Panda Population May be Twice Previous Estimates

There may be twice as many giant pandas in the wild as previously estimated, according to Chinese researchers. Scientists have traditionally estimated panda populations by visually identifying and counting unique animals in the wild, or using survey populations to estimate overall counts, but pandas' timid nature makes it difficult to achieve accurate counts using these techniques. However, by using a new genetic profiling technique based on DNA from panda fecal samples, Chinese Academy of Sciences researchers estimated that Wanglang Nature Reserve's giant panda population could be as high as 72, or more than double the previous estimate. Fu-wen Wei, senior author of the report, said that if higher estimates hold true for China's other panda sanctuaries, which are ecologically similar to Wanglang, there may be as many as 2,500 to 3,000 giant pandas living in the wild. [Chinese Academy of Sciences; reported in *Current Biology,* June 20]

Global Warming: Surprising Sources of Methane

Land plants may emit as much as 30% of the world's atmospheric methane, according to a team of geochemists led by Frank Keppler from the Max Planck Institute. Keppler and his team found that living plants naturally generate methane, which may be a by-product of plants' regular metabolic cycle. Previously, anaerobic microorganisms and ruminant animals (such as cows) were thought to be the most important biological producers of the greenhouse gas. The findings may provide insight into many unexplained natural phenomena, such as the high concentrations of methane observed in the air over tropical rain forests. In addition, these results may force scientists to reconsider the role of plant-generated methane in past climate change. [*Nature,* Jan. 12]

A team of scientists led by biogeochemist Katey Walter from the University of Alaska Fairbanks have found that carbon, which had been **trapped in permafrost** under Siberian lakes since the Pleistocene epoch (about 40,000 years ago), is being **released in the form of methane as the permafrost melts.** The team measured the amount of methane being released in two Siberian lakes by measuring gas collected by "bubble traps" placed beneath the surface of frozen lake ice, which caught methane bubbling from the lake bottoms. Using historical area data, researchers found that methane emissions in the area increased 58% between 1975 and 2000; they warn that as global warming causes more permafrost under northern lakes to melt, emissions of methane from this source may further exacerbate the problem. [*Nature,* Sept. 7]

Plant Life: Increased Runoff and Lost Species

Plants may be a major contributor to a worldwide phenomenon whereby **rivers are delivering increasing amounts of fresh water to the ocean**. According to a team of hydrologists and meteorologists led by Nicola Gedney at the Hadley Centre for Climate Prediction and Research in the UK, this increased runoff cannot be explained by increased precipitation over land. Rather, rising atmospheric concentrations of the greenhouse gas carbon dioxide stimulate plants to constrict small pores in their leaves; the plants thus lose less water to evaporation and require less water from the ground. The increased moisture left in the soil winds up in streams and rivers, and eventually, the ocean. This could affect ocean salinity, which could in turn affect ocean ecosystems. [*Nature,* Feb. 16]

Six rare, 40-ft-tall, healthy, American chestnut trees were found in May on Pine Mountain near Warm Springs, GA. An estimated 4 bil American chestnut trees grew in eastern U.S. forests until 1904, when a chestnut blight fungus wiped out almost every mature chestnut tree in the U.S. The discovery, made by Nathan Klaus, a biologist with Georgia's Department of Natural Resources, represents the southernmost American chestnut trees able to produce flowers and nuts. Scientists can only speculate as to how these newly found trees escaped the blight, but they hope to spread the trees' pollen and breed blight-resistant chestnut trees. [*Associated Press,* May 18]

Evolution: Missing Links and Family Ties

Discoveries made in 2006 may shed light on the evolutionary development of both animals and plants. Paleontologists from the Univ. of Chicago, the Academy of Natural Sciences of Philadelphia, and Harvard Univ. discovered in Arctic Canada 375 mil-year-old fossils of what may be the **missing evolutionary link between fish and the first land animals**. *Tiktaalik roseae* had been a four- to nine-foot-long predator with sharp teeth in a crocodile-like head. Although the animal had fins and fish-like scales, its skull, neck, ribs and parts of its limbs resembled those of four-legged land-living animals known as tetrapods. [*Nature,* Apr. 6]

Woo Suk Hwang's Stem Cell Fraud

Most of the groundbreaking stem cell research by teams led by geneticist Woo Suk Hwang of Seoul National Univ. proved to be false in 2006. Last year, in a May 2005 *Science* online report, Hwang claimed that his team created 11 patient-specific stem cell lines. This embryonic stem cell breakthrough would have paved the way for therapies with cells genetically tailored to match a patient's DNA. Yet doubt soon arose about the report's veracity. During January 2006, a Seoul National Univ. investigation committee reported that they had found no evidence to support the claim that the patient-specific cell lines existed. The researchers had fabricated the breakthrough. In May 2006, the Korean public prosecutor's office charged Hwang with fraud, embezzlement, and violations of bioethics law.

Some recently discovered 4 mil-year-old fossils may bolster the controversial proposition that **the human family's early members did not branch into numerous species, but rather evolved in a single lineage,** according a team of evolutionary biologists led by Univ. of California's Tim White. *Homo sapien's* ancestor, the small-brained *Australopithecus,* lived about 3.5 mil years ago, whereas the more ape-like *Ardipithecus* lived 1 mil years earlier. Due to a gap in the fossil record, the relationship between the two has been unclear, but the new fossils, discovered in the desert of eastern Ethiopia, belong to the most primitive species of *Australopithecus* and may bridge the gap, suggesting a rapid evolutionary shift from *Ardipithecus* to *Australopithecus* in this region. [*Nature,* Apr. 13]

DNA analysis of human, chimpanzee, gorilla, orangutan, and macaque genomes suggests that **the evolutionary split between humans and chimpanzees occurred about 1 to 2 mil years more recently than previous estimates,** which had placed the split at approximately 7 mil years ago. According to geneticist David Reich of Harvard Medical School and colleagues, the new timeline raises questions about fossils previously classified as early human precursors. Even more controversially, the researchers proposed that after human and chimp lineages first separated, the different species continued to interbreed for thousands, or even millions, of years before separating permanently. [online edition of *Nature,* May 17]

Human and Animal Physiology and Behavior

Research by Univ. of California psychologist Aaron Blaisdell and his group may indicate that rats can understand complex cause and effect relationships and make correct inferences for actions by observational learning. The researchers designed a series of experiments using levers that would emit a flash of light, make a high-pitched ring, and release a sweet liquid when pulled. After exposure to these levers, the rats were separated into groups where pulling the levers would produce various combinations of these effects. After repeated experimentation, the researchers found that the rats were able to distinguish cause from coincidence. This new research contradicts the long-held belief that animals can only reason by association. [*Science,* Feb. 17]

Hans-Reimer Rodewald at the Univ. of Ulm and colleagues found **a previously unknown, pinhead-sized thymus,** an immune-system organ that produces T-cells, **hidden in the necks of common laboratory mice.** Scientists previously thought that mice only had a thymus in their chests, so for years, researchers have performed immunological studies in mice by removing the thoracic thymus. The new discovery calls into question their results, which could have been affected by the presence of a functioning neck thymus. [Univ. of Ulm; reported in *Science,* Apr. 14]

Researchers at the Université libre de Bruxelles were able to **influence cockroach behavior using tiny robots** according to robotics engineers led by Jean-Louis Deneubourg. The team used thumbnail-sized, cubic insect-like robots, or "insbots," equipped with two motors, wheels, a rechargeable battery, several computer processors, a light-sensing camera, infrared proximity sensors, and a coating of cockroach pheromones. The cockroaches followed the insbots into bright beams of light, despite their preference for the dark. [Université libre de Bruxelles; reported by *IST Results,* May 8]

Humans may have core geometrical knowledge embedded in their brains according to a team of psychologists led by Stanislas Dehaene of the Collège de France in Paris. The researchers tested volunteers from the Munduruku, an isolated Amazonian group whose members had little or no schooling and did not use maps, rulers, or other artifacts that rely on geometric or metric concepts. Nevertheless, children and adults could understand and use distance relationships and basic geometric concepts, such as lines, parallelism, and right angles to solve puzzles and perform tasks designed by the researchers. These findings may lead to a better understanding of human cognitive development and brain function. [Collège de France in Paris; reported in *Science,* Jan. 20]

In the **first brain imaging study of dread,** a group of Emory University neuroscientists led by Gregory Berns found that some subjects were so uncomfortable waiting for an electric shock that, given the choice, they preferred to receive more pain sooner, rather than less pain later. Brain scans of the subjects showed that the areas of the brain most affected by the anticipation of pain were those areas ruled by attention, and not those areas ruled by fear. Therefore, people who chose to take more pain sooner— rather than less pain later—did so not out of fear of the outcome, but out of the desire to end the sensation of dread. This discomfort appears to partly originate from attention devoted to anticipated pain, suggesting that dread can be diminished by diverting attention. These findings may form the foundation to future brain studies involving dread, notably the study of drug abusers who use drugs despite the expectation of negative effects. [*Science,* May 5]

Geology: Ocean's Crust Penetrated

Scientists drilling off the coast of Costa Rica reported the **first successful drilling into a fossil magma chamber under intact ocean crust.** The team recovered samples of coarse-grained, black rocks known as gabbro, which forms when molten magma becomes trapped beneath the Earth's surface and slowly cools. Analysis of the rock should shed light on the mechanisms of ocean crust formation—information that would increase understanding of earthquakes, volcanoes, and other phenomena associated with plate tectonics. [reported on the *Science Express* web site, Apr. 20]

Physical Sciences Developments

Particle Physics: First Signs of Ghostly Axion, and a New Form of Radiation

An Italian team led by physicist Emilio Zavattini may have found the **first signs of the axion, a theoretical neutral particle that was predicted nearly 30 years ago to fill in holes in the Standard Model of particle physics,** which describes all the known particles. The Italian physicists found that a magnetic field can rotate the polarization of a light wave traveling in a vacuum. When they analyzed the rotated light's properties, they detected a signal that matched some of the axion's predicted properties. [*Physical Review Letters,* Mar. 24]

A rare form of silver that displays a new type of radioactivity has been found. Physicist Ivn Mukha and colleagues created a silver atom with fewer neutrons than usual and found that it could radioactively decay in multiple ways. When sped up in a particle accelerator, the silver atoms assumed an elongated cigar shape. Instead of radioactively decaying by emitting one proton, which occurs in regular silver atoms, the scientists found that these atoms sometimes emitted two. The protons could be spit out the same side of the atom, or opposite sides, but the release was always perfectly coordinated. This type of decay is only expected in atoms with proton-rich nuclei and an even number of protons in them, but the silver isotope has an odd number. The discovery may one day lead to a fuller understanding of radioactive decay and will help physicists understand the nuclear reactions that power stars. [*Nature,* Jan. 19]

Thermodynamics: A Glimpse of Perpetual Motion

A team of physicists led by David Weiss at Penn. State Univ. have created a system where two clouds of atomic gases do not settle into equilibrium. The result is **a temporary exception to the second law of thermodynamics**, which states that the energy in all systems must run down, and that there can be no perpetual motion machines. After trapping two thin clouds of rubidium atoms in a narrow channel created by lasers, the team of physicists found that when each cloud was given a push by a laser towards the other, the two clouds bounced off each other without losing any energy and sometimes passed straight through each other. In either case they then bounced off the end of the channel and repeated the cycle again and again without losing any energy. The clouds, which behave as single atoms, could repeat this cycle more than 1,000 times before losing any of their energy. [*Nature,* Apr. 13]

Fluid Mechanics: Icy Hazards at Nano Scales

Water can turn into ice at room temperature at microscopic scales, according to researchers at Leiden Univ. in the Netherlands. Materials scientists K. B. Jinesh and J. W. M. Frenken found that water can turn to ice at the nano level when sandwiched between a tungsten metal tip and a graphite surface. Surfaces that appear flat to the naked eye are always rough and bumpy at the molecular scale; water can collect between the bumps. As the researchers moved the tungsten tip over the graphite, they found that nanometer-sized ice bridges, each lasting a few seconds, froze the tungsten to the graphite. Instead of acting as a lubricant, the water acted as a glue. The findings raise questions about the forces at work behind freezing at extremely small levels. In addition, they raise the possibility that freezing could happen between other surfaces, and that tiny mechanical devices, or nanomachines, currently under development may be susceptible to such freezing. [*Physical Review Letters,* Apr. 27]

Robotics: New Fuel for Artificial Muscles

Scientists have developed **artificial muscles that run on fuel and oxygen instead of an external electrical supply**. Led by chemistry professor Ray H. Baughman, researchers at the University of Texas at Dallas developed two sets of artificial muscles. The first was made of a thin metal wire coated with a catalyst that burned methanol as a fuel. The resulting heat caused the wire to contract, generating muscle force that could lift a one-pound weight. Despite their thin size, they were 100 times stronger than biological muscles of equal thickness. The second muscle, made of sheets of carbon nanotubes, expanded when an electrical charge was generated by the combustion of oxygen and hydrogen on its surface and contracted when the charge dissipated. The new muscles could lead to the development of assistive devices for people and robots that do not require external power sources or lengthy recharging. [*Science,* Mar. 11]

Materials and Fabrication: Spray-on Circuits, Groundbreaking LEDs

Creating silicon patterns for microchips may one day be as easy as hitting the "print" button on your computer. Materials scientists in Japan led by Tatsuya Shimoda and Yasuo Matsuki have developed a technique that would allow engineers to **spray liquid silicon in controlled patterns onto a surface**. The liquid is prepared by baking a silicon-rich molecule and exposing it to ultraviolet light; the resulting form of liquid silicon could then be sprayed through a machine like an ink-jet printer. The technique could be used to make computer chips, which depend on precise patterning to work properly. Aside from chip manufacturing, spraying liquid silicon could find applications in printing circuits for flexible displays, LCD computer screens, solar cells, and X-ray detectors. [*Nature,* Apr. 6]

Incandescent light bulb may give way to a **new generation of light-emitting diodes (LEDs)** sooner than previously believed. Chemist Mark Thompson of USC, engineer Stephen Forrest of Princeton Univ., and colleagues invented a white light LED that may be three times more efficient than normal light bulbs. Scientists usually create white light

LEDs using a mix of phosphorescent materials, which results in a light that doesn't last long enough to be useful in consumer applications. The new model combines phosphorescent and florescent materials, which results in an LED that can shine for about 10,000 hours. A regular incandescent light bulb burns out after about 1,000 hours and consumes more energy. [*Nature,* Apr. 2006]

Physicists have invented an ultraviolet LED that emits light at **the shortest wavelength ever emitted by an LED**. Yoshitaka Taniyasu and colleagues at NTT Basic Research Laboratories in Japan made the LED from a substance called aluminum nitride, which has been found to be of use in emitting ultraviolet light. Although certain chemical properties of aluminum nitride make it difficult to produce, the scientists were able to control the LED's molecular structure precisely during the fabrication stage, resulting in a material that effectively produced ultraviolet light. If developed further, ultraviolet LEDs could have uses in medicine, public health, photolithography, computer chip fabrication, and other applications. [*Nature,* May 18]

Aerodynamics: Bumps May Make the Ride Smoother

A smooth surface may not always produce the least turbulent air or liquid flow, According to a team of physicists led by Jens Fransson at the Royal Institute of Technology in Stockholm, Sweden, **small bumps on a surface can sometimes keep air and liquid flowing smoothly**. At low speeds liquids and gases can flow smoothly over a surface. But at higher speeds, the flow may become turbulent, which can reduce performance in aircraft and other vehicles. In wind tunnel experiments, the scientists found that by carefully controlling the shape and number of small bumps on the surface of a plane to increase its roughness, they could delay the onset of turbulence. The findings, which run somewhat counter to conventional thought, could lead to more aerodynamic cars and airplanes and quieter submarines. [*Physical Review Letters,* Feb. 17]

Cosmology: New Addition to Neutron Star Family

A new kind of neutron star was discovered by a team of astronomers led by Maura McLaughlin of the University of Manchester. Neutron stars are the collapsed cores of heavy stars and are made entirely of neutrons. They are small and incredibly dense, and spin rapidly. Some, called pulsars, shoot out regularly repeating radio waves many times per second. McLaughlin and her group have found **neutron stars that give off irregular radio waves**. The bursts lasted from two to 30 milliseconds, and could then be separated by minutes or hours. These neutron stars seem to be isolated and do not have companion stars, like many others do. The team says the new stars could be related to other isolated neutron stars that emit x-and gamma-ray radiation. They predict that many more of these irregular neutron stars, which they call rotating radio transients (RRATs) will be discovered in the future. [*Nature,* Feb. 16]

Plasma Physics: Lightning in a Microwave

Two teams of scientists have succeeded in **creating ball lightning in the lab using the generator taken from a household microwave**. The rare type of lightning forms small, slow moving balls about a foot wide at ground level during storms. Physicists Eli Jerby and Vladimir Dikhtyar working at Tel Aviv Univ. in Israel created what is called a "microwave drill," which concentrates microwaves through a rod forcing them into a small spot in solid glass or other ceramics. The intense rays created a molten hot spot which was pulled out with the drill. The hot spot expanded to a little over an inch and lasted a few hundredths of a second. A team of German physicists led by Gerd Fussmann produced ball lightning a different way: they sent a very large electrical current through a tank of water, with one electrode insulated by clay. The water between the clay and electrode heated enough to become a ball of hot plasma similar to ball-lightning. The scientists think the fireballs will be useful for studying lightning and could be applied to various industrial techniques. [Tel Aviv Univ., Feb. 9; Max Planck Institute for Plasma Physics, reported in *New Scientist,* June 7]

> **IT'S A FACT:** Nikola Tesla displayed the first remote-controlled device to group of onlookers at an electrical exhibition at Madison Square Garden in 1898. Tesla's device was a small boat he controlled using radio waves through a primitive wireless remote control. Many in the audience were frightened by the boat, which seemed to be moving independently; some even thought that Tesla was controlling the boat with his mind.

Science Glossary

This glossary covers some concepts that come up frequently in the news, in biology, chemistry, geology, and physics. See also Astronomy, Computers and Telecommunications, Environment, Health, Meteorology, Weights and Measures.

Biology

Note: For classification terms such as *kingdom, phylum,* etc., see Environment chapter.

Amino acid: one of about 20 similar small molecules that are the building blocks of proteins.

Antibiotic: a drug made from a substance produced by a bacterium, fungus, or other organism that battles bacterial infections and diseases, killing the bacteria or halting their growth.

Autoimmunity: a condition in which an individual's immune system reacts against his or her own tissues; leads to diseases such as lupus, diabetes, inflammatory bowel disease, rheumatoid arthritis.

Bacteriophage: a virus that infects or lyses bacteria. Also called "phage."

Bacterium (plural, bacteria): one of a large, varied class of microscopic and simple, single-celled organisms; bacteria live almost everywhere—some forms cause disease, while others are useful in digestion and other natural processes.

Biodiversity: richness of variety of life forms—both plant and animal—in a given environment.

Cell: the smallest unit of life capable of living independently, or with other cells; usually bounded by a membrane; may include a nucleus and other specialized parts.

Cholesterol: a fatty substance in animal tissues; it is produced by the liver in humans, and is found in foods such as butter, eggs, and meat, and is an essential body constituent.

Chromosome: one of the rod-like structures in the nuclei of cells that carry genetic material (DNA).

Cloning: the process of copying a particular piece of DNA to allow it to be sequenced, studied, or used in some other way; can also refer to producing a genetic copy of an organism.

DNA (deoxyribonucleic acid): the chemical substance that carries genetic information, which determines the form and functioning of all living things.

Ecosystem: an interdependent community of living organisms and their climatic and geographical habitat.

Enzyme: a protein that promotes a particular chemical reaction in the body.

Estrogen: one of a group of hormones that promote development of female secondary sex characteristics and the growth and health of the female reproductive system; males also produce small amounts of estrogen.

Eukaryote: single- or multi-celled organisms whose cells have distinct nuclei.

Evolution: the process of gradual change that may occur as a species adapts to its environment; natural selection is the process by which evolution occurs.

Gene: a portion of a DNA molecule that provides the blueprint for the assembly of a protein.

Gene pool: the collection and total diversity of genes in an interbreeding population.

Gene therapy: a treatment in which scientists try to implant functioning genes into a person's cells so the genes can produce proteins that the person lacks or that help the person fight disease.

Genetic sequencing: the process of determining the order of subunits within a gene or even the order of all genes for an organism.

Genome: the complete set of an organism's genetic material.

Hormone: a substance secreted in one part of an organism that regulates the functioning of other tissues or organs.

Meiosis: the process of cell division that results in gametes (sperm or egg cells), all of which contain half the number of chromosomes as their precursor.

Metabolism: the sum total of the body's chemical processes providing energy for vital functions, and enabling new material to be synthesized.

Mitosis: the process by which a cell divides its nucleus and other cell materials into two duplicate daughter cells with the same DNA.

Neuron: a nerve cell, of the type found in the brain or spinal cord, that sends electrical and chemical messages to other cells.

Nucleus (plural: nuclei): the center of an atom; or the portion of a cell containing the chemical directions for functioning.

Organism: a living being.

Phenotype: the observable properties and characteristics of an organism arising at least in part from its genetic makeup.

Pheromone: a chemical secreted by an animal to influence the behavior of other members of its own species.

Placebo effect: a phenomenon in which patients show improvements even though they have taken a medically inactive substance, called a placebo.

Prokaryote: a single-celled organism that does not have a distinct nucleus, such as bacteria, cyanobacteria, and blue-green algae.

Protein: a complex molecule made up of one or more chains of amino acids; essential to the structure and function of all cells.

RNA (ribonucleic acid): a complex molecule similar to the genetic material DNA, but usually single-stranded; several forms of RNA translate the genetic code of DNA and use that code to assemble proteins for structural and biological functions in the body.

Species: a population of organisms that breed with each other in nature and produce fertile offspring; other definitions of species exist to accommodate the diversity of life on Earth.

Stem cell: a cell that can give rise to other types of cells; for instance, bone marrow stem cells divide and produce different types of blood cells.

Steroid: type of hormone that freely enters cells (other hormones bind to cell surfaces); different varieties can suppress immune response or influence stress reaction, blood pressure, or sexual development; includes testosterone- and estrogen-related compounds.

Testosterone: a hormone that stimulates the development and maintenance of male sexual characteristics and the production of sperm; women also produce small amounts of testosterone.

Virus: a microscopic, often disease-causing, organism made of genetic material surrounded by a protein shell; can only reproduce inside a living cell.

Chemistry

Acid: a class of compound that contrasts with bases. Acids taste sour, turn litmus red/pink, and often produce hydrogen gas in contact with some metals. Acids donate protons (hydrogen atoms minus the electron) in chemical reactions.

Base: a substance that yields hydroxyl ions (OH-) when dissolved in water; any of a class of compounds whose aqueous solutions taste bitter, feel slippery, turn litmus blue, and react with acids to form salts; also known as **alkaline**.

Carbon fiber: an extremely strong, thin fiber made by pyrolyzing (decomposing by heat) synthetic fibers, such as rayon, until charred; used to make high-strength composites

Chlorofluorocarbon (CFC): one of a group of industrial chemicals that contain chlorine, fluorine, and carbon and have been found to damage Earth's ozone layer.

Element: a substance that cannot be chemically decomposed into simpler substances; the atoms of an element all have the same number of protons and electrons.

Isotope: an atom of a chemical element with the same number of protons in its nucleus as other atoms of that element, but with a different number of neutrons.

Molecule: the basic unit of a chemical compound, composed of two or more atoms bound together.

Noble gases: a group of gasses including helium, neon, argon, krypton, xenon, and radon that are not reactive except in rare and limited instances. Also called "inert gases."

Osmosis: the transfer of a fluid from an area of higher concentration to an area of lower concentration, usually through a membrane.

Phase: any of the possible states of matter—solid, liquid, gas, or plasma—that change according to temperature and pressure.

Polymer: a huge molecule containing hundreds or thousands of smaller molecules arranged in repeating units.

Salt: a neutral compound produced by the reaction of an acid and a base.

Geology

Fault, tectonic: a crack or break in Earth's crust, often due to the slippage of tectonic plates past or over one another; usually geologically unstable.

Igneous: a type of rock formed by solidification from a molten state, especially from molten magma.

Magma: hot liquid rock material under Earth's crust, from which igneous rock is formed by cooling.

Metamorphic: in geology, the name given to sedimentary rocks or minerals that have recrystallized under the influence of heat and pressure since their original deposition.

Pangaea: a single super-continent that scientists believe broke apart about 170 mil years ago to form the current continents.

Plate tectonics: theory that Earth's crust is made up of many separate rigid plates of rock that float on top of hot semi-liquid rock.

Sedimentary rock: rock formed by the buildup of material at the bottoms of bodies of water.

Physics

Absolute zero: the theoretical temperature at which all motion within a molecule stops, corresponding to −273.15° C (−459.67° F).

Antimatter: matter that consists of antiparticles, such as antiprotons, that have an opposite charge from normal particles; when matter meets antimatter, both are destroyed and their combined mass is converted to energy. Antimatter is created in certain radioactive decay processes, but appears to be present in only small amounts in the universe.

Atom: the basic unit of a chemical element.

Atomic mass: the total mass of an atom of a given element; atoms of the same element with different atomic masses (different numbers of neutrons, not protons) are called isotopes.

Atomic number: the number of protons in an atom of a given element of the periodic table; the characteristic that sets atoms of different elements apart.

Axion: a hypothetical subatomic particle with low mass and energy that is thought to exist because of the properties of the strong nuclear force.

Bose-Einstein condensate: a "super-atom" comprised of thousands of atoms super-cooled to within a few billionths of a degree of absolute zero and thus condensed into the lowest energy state; atoms bound in the BEC behave synchronously, giving the BEC wavelike properties.

Boson: force-carrying particles including photons, gluons, and the W and Z particles; one of the two primary categories of particles in the Standard Model, the other being fermions.

Dark energy: a mysterious, undefined energy leading to a repulsive force pervading all of space-time; proposed by cosmologists as counteracting gravity and accelerating the expansion of the universe; predicted to make up 65% of the universe's composition.

Dark matter: hypothetical, invisible matter that some scientists believe makes up 90% of the matter in the universe; its existence was proposed to account for otherwise inexplicable gravitational forces observed in space.

Doppler effect: a change in the frequency of sound, light, or radio waves caused by the motion of the source emitting the waves or the motion of the person or instrument perceiving the waves.

Electron: negatively charged particle that is the least massive electrically charged fundamental particle; the most common charged lepton in the Standard Model.

Energy: capacity to perform work. Energy can take various forms, such as potential energy, kinetic energy, chemical energy, etc.

Entropy: A measure of disorder in a system.

Fermion: any one of a number of matter particles including electrons, protons, neutrons, and quarks; one of the two primary categories of particles in the Standard Model, the other being bosons.

Field: the effects of forces (gravitational, electric, etc.) are visualized and described mathematically by physicists in terms of fields, which show the strength and direction of a force at a given position.

Fission: a nuclear reaction that occurs when the nuclei of large, unstable atoms break apart, releasing large amounts of energy.

Fluorescence: luminescence that is caused by the absorption of radiation at one wavelength followed by an immediate reradiation, usually at a different wavelength, that stops almost immediately when the radiation stops.

Force: In classical physics, a force is something that causes acceleration in a body, and can be thought of as a push or pull.

Fusion: a nuclear reaction occurring when atomic nuclei collide at high temperatures and combine to form one heavier atomic nucleus, releasing enormous energy in the process.

Gravity: an attractive force between any 2 objects or particles, proportional to the mass (or energy) of the objects; strength of the force decreases with greater distance; the only fundamental force still unaccounted for by the Standard Model.

Half-life: the time it takes for half of a given amount of a radioactive element to decay.

Hertz: a measure of frequency, or how many times a given event occurs per second; applied to sound waves, electrical current, microchip clock speeds; abbreviated as Hz.

Laser: light consisting of a cascade of photons all having the same wavelength; *laser* stands for Light Amplification by Stimulated Emission of Radiation.

Light-emitting diode (LED): A semiconductor that emits light when an electrical current is passed through it. The color of the light depends on the material used in making the diode.

Neutrino: a tiny fundamental particle with no electrical charge and very small mass that moves very quickly through the universe; comes in three varieties, or flavors, called electron, muon, and tau.

Neutron: a neutral particle found in the nuclei of atoms.

Particle accelerator: a large machine with a long tunnel in which atoms smash into each other at high speeds; physicists use these machines to study subatomic particles.

Phosphorescence: luminescence that is caused by the absorption of radiation at one wavelength followed by a delayed reradiation, usually at a different wavelength, that continues for a noticeable time after the radiation stops.

Photon: the elementary unit, or quantum, of light or electromagnetic radiation, having no mass or electrical charge; one of the fundamental force-carrying particles, or bosons, described by the Standard Model.

Plasma: a high-energy state of matter different from solid, liquid or gas in which atomic nuclei and the electrons orbiting them separate from each other.

Proton: a positively charged subatomic particle found in the nuclei of atoms.

Quantum: a natural unit of some physically measurable property, such as energy or electrical charge.

Quark: a fermion and a fundamental matter particle that makes up neutrons and protons, forming atomic nuclei; there are 6 different "flavors" of quarks grouped in pairs; up and down, charm and strange, top and bottom.

Radiation: energy emitted as rays or particles; radiation includes heat, light, ultraviolet rays, gamma rays, X rays, cosmic rays, alpha particles, beta particles, and the protons, neutrons, and electrons of radioactive atoms.

Relativity, general theory of: a theory of space-time proposed by Albert Einstein in 1915; gravitational and other forces are transmitted through the effects of the curvature of space-time.

Relativity, special theory of: Einstein's theory of space and time: all laws of physics are valid in all uniformly moving frames of reference and the speed of light in a vacuum is always the same, so long as the source and the observer are moving uniformly (not accelerating).

Standard Model: prevailing theory of fundamental particles and forces of matter; matter particles are fermions: either leptons or quarks; force-carrying particles are bosons: either gluons, W or Z bosons or photons; gravity has not yet been worked into the model.

String theory: a theory that seeks to unify quantum mechanics and general relativity, positing that the basic constituents of matter can best be understood not as point objects but as tiny closed loops ("strings").

Subatomic particle: one of the small particles, such as electrons, neutrons, and protons, which make up an atom.

Superconductivity: the property of certain materials, usually metals and chemically complex ceramics, to conduct electricity without resistance, generally at very cold temperatures.

Thermodynamics: the branch of physics that describes how energy, heat, and temperature flow in physical systems.

Ultraviolet radiation: a form of light, invisible to the human eye, that has a shorter wavelength and greater energy than visible light but a longer wavelength and less energy than X rays.

Virtual particle: subatomic particles that rapidly pop into and out of existence and can exert real forces; usually occur in particle-antiparticle pairs and are rapidly annihilated.

▶ **IT'S A FACT:** Isaac Newton will always be remembered as one of the world's greatest physicists, but the scientific genius dabbled in other careers as well. After publishing *Principia*, Newton served as a member of the English Parliament from 1689-70. In 1696, Newton was appointed Warden of the London Mint, of which he became Master in 1699, and spent his time coming up with anti-counterfeit measures to protect English money. Newton returned to academic life in 1703 when he was elected president of the Royal Society.

Mohs Scale of Hardness

Hardness is the ability of a solid substance to resist abrasion or deformation on the surface. Soft minerals scratch easier than hard ones. For example, a diamond will scratch graphite because the graphite is softer. In 1812, German mineralogist Frederich Mohs (1773-1839) created the arbitrary scale shown below to measure relative hardness using ten minerals that were readily available at that time. The numbers in the Mohs scale are arranged in order of increasing hardness. A mineral's hardness is obtained by determining which mineral in the Mohs scale will scratch the specimen.

Mohs Scale

1.	Talc	6.	Orthoclase Feldspar
2.	Gypsum	7.	Quartz
3.	Calcite	8.	Topaz
4.	Fluorite	9.	Corundum
5.	Apatite	10.	Diamond

Selected items and their relative hardness include:

2.5	Fingernails	5.5	Knife Blade
2.5-3	Gold, Silver	6-7	Glass
3	Copper Penny	6.5	Iron pyrite
4-4.5	Platinum	7+	Hardened steel file
4-5	Iron		

Chemical Elements, Atomic Numbers, Year Discovered

Reviewed by Darleane C. Hoffman, Ph.D., Lawrence Berkeley National Laboratory and Department of Chemistry, Univ. of California, Berkeley.

See Periodic Table of the Elements on page 276 for atomic weights.

Element	Symbol	Atomic number	Year discov.	Element	Symbol	Atomic number	Year discov.	Element	Symbol	Atomic number	Year discov.
Actinium	Ac	89	1899	Gold	Au	79	BCE	Promethium	Pm	61	1945
Aluminum	Al	13	1825	Hafnium	Hf	72	1923	Protactinium	Pa	91	1917
Americium	Am	95	1944	Hassium	Hs	108	1984	Radium	Ra	88	1898
Antimony	Sb	51	1450	Helium	He	2	1868	Radon	Rn	86	1900
Argon	Ar	18	1894	Holmium	Ho	67	1878	Rhenium	Re	75	1925
Arsenic	As	33	c. 13th	Hydrogen	H	1	1766	Rhodium	Rh	45	1803
Astatine	At	85	1940	Indium	In	49	1863	Roentgenium	Rg	111	1995
Barium	Ba	56	1808	Iodine	I	53	1811	Rubidium	Rb	37	1861
Berkelium	Bk	97	1949	Iridium	Ir	77	1804	Ruthenium	Ru	44	1845
Beryllium	Be	4	1798	Iron	Fe	26	BCE	Rutherfordium	Rf	104	1969
Bismuth	Bi	83	c. 15th	Krypton	Kr	36	1898	Samarium	Sm	62	1879
Bohrium	Bh	107	1981	Lanthanum	La	57	1839	Scandium	Sc	21	1879
Boron	B	5	1808	Lawrencium	Lr	103	1961	Seaborgium	Sg	106	1974
Bromine	Br	35	1826	Lead	Pb	82	BCE	Selenium	Se	34	1817
Cadmium	Cd	48	1817	Lithium	Li	3	1817	Silicon	Si	14	1823
Calcium	Ca	20	1808	Lutetium	Lu	71	1907	Silver	Ag	47	BCE
Californium	Cf	98	1950	Magnesium	Mg	12	1829	Sodium	Na	11	1807
Carbon	C	6	BCE	Manganese	Mn	25	1774	Strontium	Sr	38	1790
Cerium	Ce	58	1803	Meitnerium	Mt	109	1982	Sulfur	S	16	BCE
Cesium	Cs	55	1860	Mendelevium	Md	101	1955	Tantalum	Ta	73	1802
Chlorine	Cl	17	1774	Mercury	Hg	80	BCE	Technetium	Tc	43	1937
Chromium	Cr	24	1797	Molybdenum	Mo	42	1782	Tellurium	Te	52	1782
Cobalt	Co	27	1735	Neodymium	Nd	60	1885	Terbium	Tb	65	1843
Copper	Cu	29	BCE	Neon	Ne	10	1898	Thallium	Tl	81	1861
Curium	Cm	96	1944	Neptunium	Np	93	1940	Thorium	Th	90	1828
Darmstadtium	Ds	110	1995	Nickel	Ni	28	1751	Thulium	Tm	69	1879
Dubnium (Hahnium)[1]	Db (Ha)	105	1970	Niobium[2]	Nb	41	1801	Tin	Sn	50	BCE
Dysprosium	Dy	66	1886	Nitrogen	N	7	1772	Titanium	Ti	22	1791
Einsteinium	Es	99	1952	Nobelium	No	102	1958	Tungsten (Wolfram)	W	74	1783
Erbium	Er	68	1843	Osmium	Os	76	1804	Uranium	U	92	1789
Europium	Eu	63	1901	Oxygen	O	8	1774	Vanadium	V	23	1830
Fermium	Fm	100	1953	Palladium	Pd	46	1803	Xenon	Xe	54	1898
Fluorine	F	9	1771	Phosphorus	P	15	1669	Ytterbium	Yb	70	1878
Francium	Fr	87	1939	Platinum	Pt	78	1735	Yttrium	Y	39	1794
Gadolinium	Gd	64	1886	Plutonium	Pu	94	1941	Zinc	Zn	30	BCE
Gallium	Ga	31	1875	Polonium	Po	84	1898	Zirconium	Zr	40	1789
Germanium	Ge	32	1886	Potassium	K	19	1807				
				Praseodymium	Pr	59	1885				

Note: 111 elements are listed here. The discovery of element 111 with a mass number of 272 was reported by S. Hofmann *et al.* in 1995 and was approved by a Joint Working Party of the International Unions of Pure & Applied Chemistry (IUPAC) and Pure and Applied Physics (IUPAP) in 2003. The discoverers proposed the name Roentgenium with symbol Rg in early 2004 and it was confirmed by IUPAC in Nov. 2004. The discovery of element 112 by S. Hofmann *et al.* in 1996 still awaits confirmation. Between 1999 and 2006, a multinational group and a Dubna/Lawrence Livermore National Laboratory group working in Dubna, Russia, have published evidence in refereed journals for observation of many isotopes of elements 112 through 116 and 118 has been reported. These reports all await confirmation and are shown in Italics in the periodic table. Evidence for Element 117 has not been published in refereed journals and is shown in parentheses. (1) The name Dubnium (Db) has been approved by IUPAC for element 105, but the name Hahnium (Ha) is used in most of the scientific literature before 1998 and is still sometimes used in the U.S. (2) Formerly Columbium.

> **IT'S A FACT:** By listening to crickets chirping, it's possible to get an idea of what the temperature is in degrees Fahrenheit. Count the number of chirps in 14 seconds and then add 40. This will give you a very rough estimate of the temperature. Scientists believe that a cricket's chirping speed is closely related to its metabolism, which speeds up at higher temperatures and slows down at lower ones.

Periodic Table of the Elements

Source: © 1996 Lawrence Berkeley National Laboratory

Parentheses indicate undiscovered elements.

Legend:
- atomic number: 14
- atomic weight: 28.09
- symbol: **Si**
- name: Silicon

alkali metals | alkaline earth metals | transitional metals | other metals | nonmetals | noble gases

1 1.01 **H** Hydrogen																	2 4.003 **He** Helium
3 6.94 **Li** Lithium	4 9.01 **Be** Beryllium											5 10.81 **B** Boron	6 12.01 **C** Carbon	7 14.01 **N** Nitrogen	8 15.999 **O** Oxygen	9 18.998 **F** Fluorine	10 20.18 **Ne** Neon
11 22.99 **Na** Sodium	12 24.31 **Mg** Magnesium											13 26.98 **Al** Aluminum	14 28.09 **Si** Silicon	15 30.97 **P** Phosphorus	16 32.06 **S** Sulfur	17 35.45 **Cl** Chlorine	18 39.95 **Ar** Argon
19 39.10 **K** Potassium	20 40.08 **Ca** Calcium	21 44.96 **Sc** Scandium	22 47.90 **Ti** Titanium	23 50.94 **V** Vanadium	24 51.996 **Cr** Chromium	25 54.94 **Mn** Manganese	26 55.85 **Fe** Iron	27 58.93 **Co** Cobalt	28 58.70 **Ni** Nickel	29 63.55 **Cu** Copper	30 65.37 **Zn** Zinc	31 69.72 **Ga** Gallium	32 72.59 **Ge** Germanium	33 74.92 **As** Arsenic	34 78.96 **Se** Selenium	35 79.90 **Br** Bromine	36 83.80 **Kr** Krypton
37 85.47 **Rb** Rubidium	38 87.62 **Sr** Strontium	39 88.91 **Y** Yttrium	40 91.22 **Zr** Zirconium	41 92.91 **Nb** Niobium	42 95.94 **Mo** Molybdenum	43 98 **Tc** Technetium	44 101.07 **Ru** Ruthenium	45 102.91 **Rh** Rhodium	46 106.40 **Pd** Palladium	47 107.87 **Ag** Silver	48 112.41 **Cd** Cadmium	49 114.82 **In** Indium	50 118.69 **Sn** Tin	51 121.75 **Sb** Antimony	52 127.60 **Te** Tellurium	53 126.90 **I** Iodine	54 131.30 **Xe** Xenon
55 132.91 **Cs** Cesium	56 137.33 **Ba** Barium	57 138.91 **La** Lanthanum	72 178.49 **Hf** Hafnium	73 180.95 **Ta** Tantalum	74 183.85 **W** Tungsten	75 186.21 **Re** Rhenium	76 190.20 **Os** Osmium	77 192.22 **Ir** Iridium	78 195.09 **Pt** Platinum	79 196.97 **Au** Gold	80 200.59 **Hg** Mercury	81 204.37 **Tl** Thallium	82 207.19 **Pb** Lead	83 208.98 **Bi** Bismuth	84 209 **Po** Polonium	85 210 **At** Astatine	86 222 **Rn** Radon
87 223 **Fr** Francium	88 226.03 **Ra** Radium	89 227.03 **Ac** Actinium	104 261 **Rf** Rutherfordium	105 262 **Db (Ha)** Dubnium (Hahnium)	106 266 **Sg** Seaborgium	107 267 **Bh** Bohrium	108 269 **Hs** Hassium	109 268 **Mt** Meitnerium	110 271 **Ds** Darmstadtium	111 272 **Rg** Roentgenium	112 **112**	113 **113**	114 **114**	115 **115**	116 **116**	85 (117) **(117)**	118 **118**

Lanthanide series

| 58 140.12 **Ce** Cerium | 59 140.91 **Pr** Praseodymium | 60 144.24 **Nd** Neodymium | 61 145 **Pm** Promethium | 62 150.35 **Sm** Samarium | 63 151.96 **Eu** Europium | 64 157.25 **Gd** Gadolinium | 65 158.93 **Tb** Terbium | 66 162.50 **Dy** Dysprosium | 67 164.93 **Ho** Holmium | 68 167.26 **Er** Erbium | 69 168.93 **Tm** Thulium | 70 173.04 **Yb** Ytterbium | 71 174.97 **Lu** Lutetium |

Actinide series

| 90 232.04 **Th** Thorium | 91 231.04 **Pa** Protactinium | 92 238.03 **U** Uranium | 93 237.05 **Np** Neptunium | 94 244 **Pu** Plutonium | 95 243 **Am** Americium | 96 247 **Cm** Curium | 97 247 **Bk** Berkelium | 98 251 **Cf** Californium | 99 252 **Es** Einsteinium | 100 257 **Fm** Fermium | 101 258 **Md** Mendelevium | 102 259 **No** Nobelium | 103 262 **Lr** Lawrencium |

Basic Laws of Physics

Isaac Newton's Laws of Motion

1. An object in motion moves at a constant velocity in a straight line unless acted upon by a force. Likewise, an object at rest will stay at rest. This is known as inertia.

2. The acceleration of an object is proportional to the force acting on it and inversely proportional to the mass of an object.

Force (F) equals mass (m) times acceleration (a)

$$F = ma$$

3. For every action, there is an equal and opposite reaction.

Law of Gravity

In common usage, gravity only refers to the gravitational force between the Earth and objects on or near it. More specifically, gravitation is one of four basic forces controlling the interactions of matter, the others being strong and weak nuclear forces and electromagnetic force. The gravitational force (F) between objects is proportional to the product of their masses (m_1 and m_2) and inversely proportional to the square of the distance (d) between them. G represents the "gravitational constant" in Newton's law of gravity, a fixed ratio measured in metric terms as, $G = 6.67390 \times 10^{-11}$ newton m^2/kg^2.

The basic law of gravity is:

$$F = G \frac{m_1 \, m_2}{d^2}$$

Excluding factors such as high winds and wind resistance, objects close to the Earth's surface will fall at constant acceleration of 32.174 ft/sec² (9.8 m/sec²), which is usually written as g. Using g will yield the velocity (v) and the distance travelled by a falling object (d) after any amount of time, (t) in seconds. (Positive numbers represent up, negative numbers down.)

$$v = -g\,t$$
$$d = -\tfrac{1}{2}g(t^2)$$

If an object has an initial velocity of v_0 and an initial height above ground called a, the equations become:

$$v = v_0 - g\,t$$
$$d = -\tfrac{1}{2}g(t^2) + v_0 t + a$$

The maximum height (H) reached by an object with a positive initial velocity (v_0) and initial height (a) is expressed as:

$$H = a + \frac{v_0{}^2}{64}$$

The force of gravity on Earth is lessened by the centrifugal force caused by the Earth's rotation. This counteracts the gravitational effect to a small degree. At the poles, where technically there is no centrifugal force, acceleration due to gravity is greater.

The force of gravity decreases slightly with an increase in distance from the Earth's center; gravity is weaker on a mountaintop than it is at sea level.

Conservation Laws

In physics, laws of conservation state that in a closed system certain measurable quantities remain constant. Anything added from outside the system could affect the quantity of the entity being conserved.

Conservation of Mass: Mass is neither created nor destroyed within a closed system except when converted to energy.

Conservation of Momentum: All moving objects have momentum, and in a closed system, momentum is always conserved. Linear momentum is the product of the mass of an object and its velocity. In the following equation, M and V represent the initial total mass and velocity of objects within a closed system. After a collision between those objects, the mass and velocity of individual objects may change (for example, one object could break into smaller pieces, each traveling at a different velocity) but the product of the total mass and velocity in the system after the collision (mv) will remain the same.

$$MV = mv$$

Any object moving in a circle has *angular momentum*. Motion in a circle requires acceleration which is directed towards the center of the circle and which depends on the speed of the object and the square of the radius of the circle. [Angular momentum is the product of this speed, the mass of the object and the square of the radius.]

Conservation of Energy: The amount of energy of a closed system will not change except when converted to mass.

Conservation of Mass-energy: According to Einstein, as part of his special theory of relativity, mass and energy are related. Because they can be converted into one another, mass and energy alone cannot be conserved. However, the total amount of mass and energy together must be conserved. This is reflected in the following equation where m is mass, E is energy, and c is the speed of light in a vacuum (which is constant):

$$E = mc^2$$

Einstein also discovered that mass increases with velocity. The following equation—where m is the mass of a moving object, m_0 is the object's mass when not moving, v is its velocity in relation to a stationary observer, and c is the speed of light—shows how mass is related to velocity in this context.

$$m = \frac{m_0}{\sqrt{1 - \dfrac{v^2}{c^2}}}$$

This equation accounts for the theory that no object can travel faster than the speed of light. As an object approaches c, so much energy is converted to mass that it no longer accelerates.

Laws of Thermodynamics

1. Heat is a form of energy. Within a closed system energy must be conserved except in nuclear reactions or other extreme conditions. It is neither created nor destroyed.

2. Within a self-sustaining system, heat can never go from an area of low temperature to an area of high temperature. Disorder, or entropy, can only increase in closed system.

3. Absolute zero cannot be attained by any procedure in a finite number of steps. Absolute zero can be approached arbitrarily closely, but it can never be reached.

Laws of Current Electricity

Electricity is the result of electrons flowing through a conductor. When electrons flow through a conductor, the amount of current generated, measured in amperes, is defined in terms of the coulomb (an amount of electric charge equal to about 6.25 quintillion or 6.25×10^{18} electrons) and the time it takes for electrons to pass through the conductor. One ampere is equal to 1 coulomb of charge moving past a point in 1 second. As an electric current moves through a conductor, energy can vary depending on varying charges within the conductor. This variation is known as the *potential difference* and is measured in volts.

Certain substances are more prone to conductivity. The resistance to conductivity is measured in ohms.

Ohm's law: Electric current is directly proportional to the potential difference and inversely proportional to the total resistance of the circuit. I is electric current (measured in amperes), and V is the potential difference (measured in volts), and R is resistance (measured in ohms):

$$I = \frac{V}{R}$$

Law of electric power: The rate at which electricity is used is electric power. If electric power (P) is measured in watts, then P is the product of current and potential difference.

$$P = IV$$

Two Basic Laws of Quantum Physics

1. Heisenberg's uncertainty principle: Certain pairs of observable quantities like energy and time, or position and momentum cannot be measured with complete accuracy simultaneously. Also known as indeterminacy principle.

2. Pauli's exclusion principle: Two electrons in an atom cannot simultaneously occupy the same quantum or energy state. This has since been shown to be true for many subatomic particles.

Breaking the Sound Barrier; Speed of Sound

The prefix **Mach** is used to describe supersonic speed. It was named for Ernst Mach (1838-1916), a Czech-born Austrian physicist. When a plane moves at the speed of sound, it is Mach 1. When the plane is moving at twice the speed of sound, it is Mach 2. Mach may be defined as the ratio of the velocity of a rocket or a jet to the velocity of sound in the medium being considered.

When a plane passes the sound barrier—flying faster than sound travels—listeners in the area hear thunderclaps, but the pilot of the plane does not hear them.

Sound is produced by vibrations of an object and is transmitted by alternate increase and decrease in pressures that radiate outward through a material media of molecules—somewhat like waves spreading out on a pond after a rock has been tossed into it.

The **frequency of sound** is determined by the number of times the vibrating waves undulate per second and is measured in cycles per second. The slower the cycle of waves, the lower the frequency. As frequencies increase, the sound is higher in pitch. The human ear is usually not sensitive to frequencies of fewer than 20 vibrations per second or greater than about 20,000 vibrations per second—although this range varies among individuals.

Intensity, or loudness, is the strength of the pressure of these radiating waves and is measured in decibels. (See Weights and Measures.)

The **speed of sound** is generally defined as 1,088 feet per second at sea level at 32° F. It varies in other temperatures and in different media. Sound travels faster in water than in air, and even faster in iron and steel.

Light; Colors of the Spectrum

Light, a form of electromagnetic radiation similar to radiant heat, radio waves, and X rays, is emitted from a source in straight lines and spreads out over larger areas as it travels; light per unit area diminishes as the square of the distance.

The English mathematician and physicist Sir Isaac Newton (1642-1727) described light as an **emission of particles**; the Dutch astronomer, mathematician, and physicist Christiaan Huygens (1629-95) developed the theory that light travels by a **wave motion**. It is now believed that these 2 theories are essentially complementary, and the development of quantum theory has led to results where light acts like a series of particles in some experiments and like a wave in others.

The **speed of light** was first measured in a laboratory experiment by the French physicist Armand Hippolyte Louis Fizeau (1819-96). Today the speed of light is known very precisely as 299,792.458 km per sec (or 186,282.396 mi per sec) in a vacuum; in water the speed of light is about 25% less, and in glass, 33% less.

Color sensations are produced through the excitation of the retina of the eye by light vibrating at different frequencies. The different colors of the spectrum may be produced by viewing a light beam that is refracted by passage through a prism, which breaks the light into its wavelengths.

Customarily, the **primary colors** are taken to be the 6 monochromatic colors that occupy relatively large areas of the spectrum: red, orange, yellow, green, blue, and violet. Scientists have differed, however, in how many and which primary colors they recognized. The color sensation of **black** is due to complete lack of stimulation of the retina, that of **white** to complete stimulation.

The **infrared and ultraviolet rays**, below the red (long) end of the spectrum and above the violet (short) end of the spectrum, respectively, are invisible to the naked eye. Heat is the principal effect of the infrared rays, and chemical action that of the ultraviolet rays.

Discoveries and Innovations: Chemistry, Physics, Biology, Medicine

	Date	Discoverer	Nationality
Acetylene gas	1862	Berthelot	French
ACTH	1927	Evans, Long	U.S.
Adrenaline	1901	Takamine	Japan
Aluminum, electrolytic process	1886	Hall	U.S.
Aluminum, isolated	1825	Oersted	Danish
Anesthesia, ether	1842	Long	U.S.
Anesthesia, local	1885	Koller	Austrian
Anesthesia, spinal	1898	Bier	German
Aniline dye	1856	Perkin	English
Anti-rabies	1885	Pasteur	French
Antiseptic surgery	1867	Lister	English
Antitoxin, diphtheria	1891	Von Behring	German
Argyrol	1897	Bayer	German
Arsphenamine	1910	Ehrlich	German
Aspirin	1853	Gerhardt	French
Atabrine	1932	Mietzsch, et al.	German
Atomic numbers	1913	Moseley	English
Atomic theory	1803	Dalton	English
Atomic time clock	1948	Lyons	U.S.
Atomic time clock, cesium beam	1948	Essen	English
Atom-smashing theory	1919	Rutherford	English
Bacitracin	1943	Johnson, Meleneyl	U.S.
Bacteria, description	1676	Leeuwenhoek	Dutch
Bleaching powder	1798	Tennant	English
Blood, circulation	1628	Harvey	English
Blood plasma storage (blood banks)	1940	Drew	U.S.
Bordeaux mixture	1885	Millardet	French
Bromine from the sea	1826	Balard	French
Calcium carbide	1888	Wilson	U.S.
Calculus	1670	Newton	English
Camphor synthetic	1896	Haller	French
Canning (food)	1804	Appert	French
Carbon oxides	1925	Fisher	German
Chemotherapy	1909	Ehrlich	German
Chloamphenicol	1947	Burkholder	U.S.
Chlorine	1774	Scheele	Swedish
Chloroform	1831	Guthrie, S.	U.S.
Chlortetracycline	1948	Duggen	U.S.
Classification of plants and animals	1735	Linnaeus	Swedish
Cloning, DNA	1973	Boyer, Cohen	U.S.
Cloning, mammal	1996	Wilmut, et al.	Scottish
Cocaine	1860	Niermann	German

	Date	Discoverer	Nationality
Combustion explained	1777	Lavoisier	French
Conditioned reflex	1914	Pavlov	Russian
Cortisone	1936	Kendall	U.S.
Cortisone, synthesis	1946	Sarett	U.S.
Cosmic rays	1910	Gockel	Swiss
Cyanamide	1905	Frank, Caro	German
Cyclotron	1930	Lawrence	U.S.
DDT (not applied as insecticide until 1939)	1874	Zeidler	German
Deuterium	1932	Urey, Brickwedde, Murphy	U.S.
DNA (structure)	1953	Crick	English
		Watson	U.S.
		Wilkins	English
Electric resistance, law of	1827	Ohm	German
Electric waves	1888	Hertz	German
Electrolysis	1852	Faraday	English
Electromagnetism	1819	Oersted	Danish
Electron	1897	Thomson, J.	English
Electron diffraction	1936	Thomson	English
		Davisson, G.	U.S.
Electroshock treatment	1938	Cerletti, Bini	Italian
Erythromycin	1952	McGuire	U.S.
Evolution, natural selection	1858	Darwin	English
Falling bodies, law of	1590	Galileo	Italian
Gases, law of combining volumes	1808	Gay-Lussac	French
Geometry, analytic	1619	Descartes	French
Gold, cyanide process for extraction	1887	MacArthur, Forest	British
Gravitation, law	1687	Newton	English
HIV (human immuno-deficiency virus)	1984	Montagnier	French
		Gallo	U.S.
Holograph	1948	Gabor	British
Human heart transplant	1967	Barnard	S. African
Indigo, synthesis of	1880	Baeyer	German
Induction, electric	1830	Henry	U.S.
Insulin	1922	Banting, Best	Canadian
		Macleod	Scottish
Intelligence testing	1905	Binet, Simon	French
In vitro fertilization	1978	Steptoe, Edwards	English
Isotopes, theory	1912	Soddy	English
Laser	1957	Gould	U.S.
Light, velocity	1675	Roemer	Danish

	Date	Discoverer	Nationality
Light, wave theory	1690	Huygens	Dutch
Lithography	1796	Senefelder	Bohemian
Logarithms	1614	Napier	Scottish
LSD-25	1943	Hoffman	Swiss
Mendelian laws	1866	Mendel	Austrian
Mercator projection (map)	1568	Mercator (Kremer)	Flemish
Methanol	1661	Boyle	Irish
Milk condensation	1853	Borden	U.S.
Molecular hypothesis	1811	Avogadro	Italian
Motion, laws of	1687	Newton	English
Neomycin	1949	Waksman, Lechevalier	U.S.
Neutron	1932	Chadwick	English
Nitric acid	1648	Glauber	German
Nitric oxide	1772	Priestley	English
Nitroglycerin	1846	Sobrero	Italian
Oil cracking process	1891	Dewar	U.S.
Oxygen	1774	Priestley	English
Oxytetracycline	1950	Finlay, et al.	U.S.
Ozone	1840	Schonbein	German
Paper, sulfite process	1867	Tilghman	U.S.
Paper, wood pulp, sulfate process	1884	Dahl	German
Penicillin	1928	Fleming	Scottish
practical use	1941	Florey, Chain	English
Periodic law and table of elements	1869	Mendeleyev	Russian
Physostigmine synthesis	1935	Julian	U.S.
Pill, birth-control	1954	Pincus, Rock	U.S.
Planetary motion, laws	1609	Kepler	German
Plutonium fission	1940	Kennedy, Wahl, Seaborg, Segre	U.S.
Polymyxin	1947	Ainsworth	English
Positron	1932	Anderson	U.S.
Proton	1919	Rutherford	N. Zealand
Psychoanalysis	1900	Freud	Austrian
Quantum theory	1900	Planck	German
Quasars	1963	Matthews, Sandage	U.S.
Quinine synthetic	1946	Woodward, Doering	U.S.
Radioactivity	1896	Becquerel	French
Radiocarbon dating	1947	Libby	U.S.
Radium	1898	Curie, Pierre	French
		Curie, Marie	Pol.-Fr.

	Date	Discoverer	Nationality
Relativity theory	1905	Einstein	German
Reserpine	1949	Jal Vaikl.	Indian
Schick test	1913	Schick	U.S.
Silicon	1823	Berzelius	Swedish
Smallpox eradication	1979	World Health Org.	UN
Streptomycin	1944	Waksman, et al.	U.S.
Sulfanilamide	1935	Bovet, Trefouel	French
Sulfanilamide theory	1908	Gelmo	German
Sulfapyridine	1938	Ewins, Phelps	English
Sulfathiazole	1939	Fosbinder, Walter	U.S.
Sulfuric acid	1831	Phillips	English
Sulfuric acid, lead	1746	Roebuck	English
Syphilis test	1906	Wassermann	German
Tuberculin	1890	Koch	German
Uranium fission theory	1939	Hahn, Meitner, Strassmann	German
		Bohr	Danish
		Fermi	Italian
		Einstein, Pegram, Wheeler	U.S.
Uranium fission, atomic reactor	1942	Fermi, Szilard	U.S.
Vaccine, measles	1963	Enders	U.S.
Vaccine, meningitis (first conjugate)	1987	Gordon, et al., Connaught Lab.	U.S.
Vaccine, polio	1954	Salk	U.S.
Vaccine, polio, oral	1960	Sabin	U.S.
Vaccine, rabies	1885	Pasteur	French
Vaccine, smallpox	1796	Jenner	English
Vaccine, typhus	1909	Nicolle	French
Vaccine, varicella	1974	Takahashi	Japan
Van Allen belts, radiation	1958	Van Allen	U.S.
Vitamin A	1913	McCollum, Davis	U.S.
Vitamin B	1916	McCollum	U.S.
Vitamin C	1928	Szent-Gyorgyi	Hungarian
		King	U.S.
Vitamin D	1922	McCollum	U.S.
Vitamin K	1935	Dam, Doisy	U.S.
Xerography	1938	Carlson	U.S.
X ray	1895	Roentgen	German

Inventions

Invention	Date	Inventor	Nationality
Adding machine	1642	Pascal	French
Adding machine	1885	Burroughs	U.S.
Aerosol spray	1926	Rotheim	Norwegian
Airbag	1952	Hetrick	U.S.
Air brake	1868	Westinghouse	U.S.
Air conditioning	1902	Carrier	U.S.
Air pump	1654	Guericke	German
Airplane, automatic pilot	1912	Sperry	U.S.
Airplane, experimental	1896	Langley	U.S.
Airplane, hydro	1911	Curtiss	U.S.
Airplane jet engine	1939	Ohain	German
Airplane with motor	1903	Wright Bros.	U.S.
Airship	1852	Giffard	French
Arc welder	1919	Thomson	U.S.
Aspartame	1965	Schlatter	U.S.
Autogyro	1920	de la Cierva	Spanish
Automobile, differential gear	1885	Benz	German
Automobile, electric	1892	Morrison	U.S.
Automobile, exp'mtl	1864	Marcus	Austrian
Automobile, gasoline	1889	Daimler	German
Automobile, gasoline	1892	Duryea	U.S.
Automobile magneto	1897	Bosch	German
Automobile muffler	1904	Pope	U.S.
Automobile self-starter	1911	Kettering	U.S.
Bakelite	1907	Baekeland	Belgian, U.S.
Balloon	1783	Montgolfier	French
Barometer	1643	Torricelli	Italian
Bicycle, modern	1885	Starley	English
Bifocal lens	1780	Franklin	U.S.
Bottle machine	1895	Owens	U.S.
Braille printing	1829	Braille	French
Bubble gum	1928	Diemer	U.S.
Burner, gas	1855	Bunsen	German
Calculating machine	1833	Babbage	English
Calculator, electronic pocket	1972	Merryman, Van Tassel	U.S.
Camera, Kodak	1888	Eastman, Walker	U.S
Camera, Polaroid Land	1948	Land	U.S.
Car coupler	1873	Janney	U.S.
Carburetor, gasoline	1893	Maybach	German
Carding machine	1797	Whittemore	U.S.
Carpet sweeper	1876	Bissell	U.S.

Invention	Date	Inventor	Nationality
Cash register	1879	Ritty	U.S.
Cassette, audio	1963	Philips Co.	Dutch
Cassette, videotape	1969	Sony	Japanese
Cathode-ray tube	1897	Braun	German
CAT, or CT, scan	1973	Hounsfield	English
Cellophane	1908	Brandenberger	Swiss
Celluloid	1870	Hyatt	U.S.
Cement, Portland	1824	Aspdin	English
Chronometer	1735	Harrison	English
Circuit breaker	1925	Hilliard	U.S.
Circuit, integrated	1959	Kilby, Noyce, Texas Instr.	U.S.
Clock, pendulum	1657	Huygens	Dutch
Coaxial cable system	1929	Affel, Espensched	U.S.
Coffeemaker, automatic drip	1963	Bunn Corp.	U.S.
Compressed air rock drill	1871	Ingersoll	U.S.
Comptometer	1887	Felt	U.S.
Computer, automatic sequence	1944	Aiken, et al.	U.S.
Computer, electronic	1942	Atanasoff, Berry	U.S.
Computer, laptop	1987	Sinclair	English
Computer, mini	1960	Digital Corp	U.S.
Condenser microphone (telephone)	1916	Wente	U.S.
Contact lens, corneal	1948	Tuohy	U.S.
Contraceptive, oral	1954	Pincus, Rock	U.S.
Corn, hybrid	1917	Jones	U.S.
Cotton gin	1793	Whitney	U.S.
Cream separator	1878	DeLaval	Swedish
Cultivator, disc	1878	Mallon	U.S.
Cystoscope	1878	Nitze	German
Diapers, disposable	1950	Donovan	U.S.
Diesel engine	1895	Diesel	German
Disc, compact	1972	RCA	U.S.
Disc player, compact	1979	Sony, Philips Co.	Japan, Dutch
Dishwasher	1893	Cochrane	U.S.
Disk, floppy	1970	IBM	U.S.
Disk, video	1972	Philips Co.	Dutch
Dynamite	1866	Nobel	Swedish
Dynamo, contin. current	1871	Gramme	Belgian
Electric battery	1800	Volta	Italian
Electric fan	1882	Wheeler	U.S.

Invention	Date	Inventor	Nationality
Electrocardiograph	1903	Einthoven	Dutch
Electroencephalograph	1929	Berger	German
Electromagnet	1824	Sturgeon	English
Electron spectrometer	1944	Deutsch, Elliott, Evans	U.S.
Electron tube multigrid	1913	Langmuir	U.S.
Electroplating	1805	Brugnatelli	Italian
Electrostatic generator	1929	Van de Graaff	U.S.
Elevator brake	1852	Otis	U.S.
Elevator, push button	1922	Larson	U.S.
Engine, automatic transmission	1910	Fottinger	German
Engine, coal-gas 4-cycle	1876	Otto	German
Engine, compression ignition	1883	Daimler	German
Engine, electric ignition	1883	Benz	German
Engine, gas, compound	1926	Eickemeyer	U.S.
Engine, gasoline	1872	Brayton, Geo.	U.S.
Engine, gasoline	1889	Daimler	German
Engine, jet	1930	Whittle	English
Engine, steam, piston	1705	Newcomen	English
Engine, steam, piston	1769	Watt	Scottish
Engraving, half-tone	1852	Talbot	U.S.
Fiberglass	1938	Owens-Corning	U.S.
Fiber optics	1955	Kapany	English
Fiber optic wire	1970	Keck, Maurer Schulz	U.S.
Filament, tungsten	1913	Coolidge	U.S.
Flanged rail	1831	Stevens	U.S.
Flatiron, electric	1882	Seely	U.S.
Food, frozen	1923	Birdseye	U.S.
Freon	1930	Midgley, et al.	U.S.
Furnace (for steel)	1858	Siemens	German
Galvanometer	1820	Sweigger	German
Garbage bag, polyethylene	1950	Wasylyk	Canadian
Gas discharge tube	1922	Hull	U.S.
Gas lighting	1792	Murdoch	Scottish
Gas mantle	1885	Welsbach	Austrian
Gasoline (lead ethyl)	1922	Midgley	U.S.
Gasoline, cracked	1913	Burton	U.S.
Gasoline, high octane	1930	Ipatieff	Russian
Geiger counter	1913	Geiger	German
Glass, laminated safety	1909	Benedictus	French
Glider	1853	Cayley	English
Gun, breechloader	1811	Thornton	U.S.
Gun, Browning	1897	Browning	U.S.
Gun, magazine	1875	Hotchkiss	U.S.
Gun, silencer	1908	Maxim, H.P.	U.S.
Guncotton	1847	Schoenbein	German
Gyrocompass	1911	Sperry	U.S.
Gyroscope	1852	Foucault	French
Harvester-thresher	1818	Lane	U.S.
Heart, artificial	1982	Jarvik	U.S.
Helicopter	1939	Sikorsky	U.S.
Hydrometer	1768	Baume	French
Iron lung	1928	Drinker, Slaw	U.S.
Kaleidoscope	1817	Brewster	Scottish
Kevlar	1965	Kwolek, Blades	U.S.
Kinetoscope	1889	Edison	U.S.
Lamp, arc	1847	Staite	English
Lamp, fluorescent	1938	General Electric, Westinghouse	U.S.
Lamp, incandescent	1879	Edison	U.S.
Lamp, incand., gas	1913	Langmuir	U.S.
Lamp, klieg	1911	Kliegl, A. & J.	U.S.
Lamp, mercury vapor	1912	Hewitt	U.S.
Lamp, miner's safety	1816	Davy	English
Lamp, neon	1909	Claude	French
Lathe, turret	1845	Fitch	U.S.
Launderette	1934	Cantrell	U.S.
Lens, achromatic	1758	Dollond	English
Lens, fused bifocal	1908	Borsch	U.S.
Leyden jar (condenser)	1745	von Kleist	German
Lightning rod	1752	Franklin	U.S.
Linoleum	1860	Walton	English
Linotype	1884	Mergenthaler	U.S.
Liquid Paper	c.1951	Graham	U.S.
Lock, cylinder	1851	Yale	U.S.
Locomotive, electric	1851	Vail	U.S.
Locomotive, exp'mtl	1802	Trevithick	English
Locomotive, exp'mtl	1812	Fenton, et al.	English
Locomotive, exp'mtl	1814	Stephenson	English
Locomotive, practical	1829	Stephenson	English
Locomotive, 1st U.S.	1830	Cooper, P.	U.S.
Loom, power	1785	Cartwright	English
Loudspeaker, dynamic	1924	Rice, Kellogg	U.S.
Machine gun	1862	Gatling	U.S.
Machine gun, improved	1872	Hotchkiss	U.S.
Machine gun (Maxim)	1883	Maxim, H.S.	U.S., Eng.
Magnet, electro	1828	Henry	U.S.
Magnetic Resonance Imaging (MRI)	1971	Damadian	U.S.
Mason jar	1858	Mason, J.	U.S.
Match, friction	1827	Walker, J.	English
Mercerized textiles	1843	Mercer, J.	English
Meter, induction	1888	Shallenberger	U.S.
Metronome	1816	Malezel	German
Microcomputer	1973	Truong, et al.	French
Micrometer	1636	Gascoigne	English
Microphone	1877	Berliner	U.S.
Microprocessor	1971	Intel Corp.	U.S.
Microscope, compound	1590	Janssen	Dutch
Microscope, electronic	1931	Knoll, Ruska	German
Microscope, field ion	1951	Mueller	German
Microwave oven	1947	Spencer	U.S.
Monitor, warship	1861	Ericsson	U.S.
Monotype	1887	Lanston	U.S.
Motor, AC	1892	Tesla	U.S.
Motor, DC	1837	Davenport	U.S.
Motor, induction	1887	Tesla	U.S.
Motorcycle	1885	Daimler	German
Movie machine	1894	Jenkins	U.S.
Movie, panoramic	1952	Waller	U.S.
Movie, talking	1927	Warner Bros.	U.S.
Mower, lawn	1831	Budding, Ferrabee	English
Mowing machine	1822	Bailey	U.S.
Neoprene	1930	Carothers	U.S.
Nylon	1937	Du Pont lab	U.S.
Nylon synthetic	1930	Carothers	U.S.
Oil cracking furnace	1891	Gavrilov	Russian
Oil filled power cable	1921	Emanueli	Italian
Oleomargarine	1869	Mege-Mouries	French
Ophthalmoscope	1851	Helmholtz	German
Pacemaker	1952	Zoll	U.S.
Paper	105	Ts'ai	Chinese
Paper clip	1900	Waaler	Norwegian
Paper machine	1809	Dickinson	U.S.
Parachute	1785	Blanchard	French
Pen, ballpoint	1888	Loud	U.S.
Pen, fountain	1884	Waterman	U.S.
Pen, steel	1780	Harrison	English
Pendulum	1583	Galileo	Italian
Percussion cap	1807	Forsythe	Scottish
Phonograph	1877	Edison	U.S.
Photo, color	1892	Ives	U.S.
Photo film, celluloid	1893	Reichenbach	U.S.
Photo film, transparent	1884	Eastman, Goodwin	U.S.
Photoelectric cell	1895	Elster	German
Photocopier	1938	Carlson	U.S.
Photographic paper	1835	Talbot	English
Photography	1816	Niepce	French
Photography	1835	Talbot	English
Photography	1835	Daguerre	French
Photophone	1880	Bell	U.S.-Scot.
Phototelegraphy	1925	Bell Labs	U.S.
Piano	1709	Cristofori	Italian
Piano, player	1863	Fourneaux	French
Pin, safety	1849	Hunt	U.S.
Pistol (revolver)	1836	Colt	U.S.
Plow, cast iron	1785	Ransome	English
Plow, disc	1896	Hardy	U.S.
Pneumatic hammer	1890	King	U.S.
Post-it note	1980	Spencer Silver, 3M	U.S.
Powder, smokeless	1884	Vieille	French
Printing press, rotary	1845	Hoe	U.S.
Printing press, web	1865	Bullock	U.S.
Propeller, screw	1804	Stevens	U.S.
Propeller, screw	1837	Ericsson	Swedish
Pulsars	1967	Bell	English
Punch card accounting	1889	Hollerith	U.S.
Radar	1940	Watson-Watt	Scottish
Radio, magnetic detector	1902	Marconi	Italian
Radio, signals	1895	Marconi	Italian
Radio amplifier	1906	De Forest	U.S.
Radio beacon	1928	Donovan	U.S.
Radio crystal oscillator	1918	Nicolson	U.S.
Radio receiver, cascade tuning	1913	Alexanderson	U.S.
Radio receiver, heterodyne	1913	Fessenden	Canadian
Radio transmitter triode modulation	1914	Alexanderson	U.S.
Radio tube diode	1904	Fleming	English
Radio tube oscillator	1915	De Forest	U.S.
Radio tube triode	1906	De Forest	U.S.
Radio FM, 2-path	1933	Armstrong	U.S.
Rayon (acetate)	1895	Cross	English

Invention	Date	Inventor	Nationality
Rayon (cuprammonium)	1890	Despeissis	French
Rayon (nitrocellulose)	1884	Chardonnet	French
Razor, electric	1917	Schick	U.S.
Razor, safety	1895	Gillette	U.S.
Reaper	1834	McCormick	U.S.
Record, cylinder	1887	Bell, Tainter	U.S.
Record, disc	1887	Berliner	U.S.
Record, long playing	1947	Goldmark	U.S.
Record, wax cylinder	1888	Edison	U.S.
Refrigerator car	1868	David	U.S.
Remote Control	1898	Tesla	U.S.
Resin, synthetic	1931	Hill	English
Richter scale	1935	Richter	U.S.
Rifle, repeating	1860	Henry	U.S.
Rocket, liquid fuel	1926	Goddard	U.S.
Rollerblades	1980	Olson	U.S.
Rubber, vulcanized	1839	Goodyear	U.S.
Saccharin	1879	Remsen, Fahlberg	U.S.
Saw, circular	1777	Miller	English
Scotch tape	1930	Drew	U.S.
Seat belt	1959	Volvo	Swedish
Sewing machine	1846	Howe	U.S.
Shoe-lasting machine	1883	Matzeliger	U.S.
Shoe-sewing machine	1860	McKay	U.S.
Shrapnel shell	1784	Shrapnel	English
Shuttle, flying	1733	Kay	English
Sleeping-car	1865	Pullman	U.S.
Slide rule	1620	Oughtred	English
Smoke detector	1969	Smith, House	U.S.
Soap, hardwater	1928	Bertsch	German
Spectroscope	1859	Kirchoff, Bunsen	German
Spectroscope (mass)	1918	Dempster	U.S.
Spinning jenny	c.1764	Hargreaves	English
Spinning mule	1779	Crompton	English
Steamboat, exp'mtl	1778	Jouffroy	French
Steamboat, exp'mtl	1785	Fitch	U.S.
Steamboat, exp'mtl	1787	Rumsey	U.S.
Steamboat, exp'mtl	1803	Fulton	U.S.
Steamboat, exp'mtl	1804	Stevens	U.S.
Steamboat, practical	1802	Symington	Scottish
Steamboat, practical	1807	Fulton	U.S.
Steam car	1770	Cugnot	French
Steam turbine	1884	Parsons	English
Steel (converter)	1856	Bessemer	English
Steel alloy	1891	Harvey	U.S.
Steel alloy, high-speed	1901	Taylor, White	U.S.
Steel, manganese	1884	Hadfield	English
Steel, stainless	1916	Brearley	English
Stereoscope	1838	Wheatstone	English
Stethoscope	1819	Laennec	French
Stethoscope, binaural	1840	Cammann	U.S.
Stock ticker	1870	Edison	U.S.
Storage battery, rechargeable	1859	Plante	French
Stove, electric	1896	Hadaway	U.S.
Submarine	1891	Holland	U.S.
Submarine, even keel	1894	Lake	U.S.
Submarine, torpedo	1776	Bushnell	U.S.
Superconductivity	1957	Bardeen, Cooper, Schreiffer	U.S.
Superconductivity in ceramics at high temp	1986	Bednorz, Muller	German Swiss
Synthesizer	1964	Moog	U.S.
Tank, military	1914	Swinton	English
Tape recorder, magnetic	1899	Poulsen	Danish
Teflon	1938	Du Pont	U.S.
Telegraph, magnetic	1837	Morse	U.S.
Telegraph, quadruplex	1864	Edison	U.S.

Invention	Date	Inventor	Nationality
Telegraph, railroad	1887	Woods	U.S.
Telegraph, wireless high frequency	1895	Marconi	Italian
Telephone[1]	1871	Meucci	U.S.-Italian
Telephone[1]	1876	Bell	U.S.-Scot.
Telephone answering machine (1st practical)	1954	Hashimoto	Japanese
Telephone, automatic	1891	Strowger	U.S.
Telephone, cellular	1947	Bell Labs	U.S.
Telephone, cordless[2]	1950	Gross	U.S.
Telephone, radio	1900	Poulsen Fessenden	Danish Canadian
Telephone, radio	1906	De Forest	U.S.
Telephone, radio, long dist.	1915	AT&T	U.S.
Telephone, recording	1898	Poulsen	Danish
Telephone amplifier	1912	De Forest	U.S.
Telescope	1608	Lippershey	Neth.
Telescope	1609	Galileo	Italian
Telescope, astronomical	1611	Kepler	German
Teletype	1928	Morkrum, Kleinschmidt	U.S.
Television, color	1928	Baird	Scottish
Television, electronic	1927	Farnsworth	U.S.
Television, iconoscope	1923	Zworykin	U.S.
Television, mech. scanner	1923	Baird	Scottish
Tesla Coil	1891	Tesla	U.S.
Thermometer	1593	Galileo	Italian
Thermometer	1730	Reaumur	French
Thermometer, mercury	1714	Fahrenheit	German
Time recorder	1890	Bundy	U.S.
Tire, double-tube	1845	Thomson	Scottish
Tire, pneumatic	1888	Dunlop	Scottish
Toaster, automatic	1918	Strite	U.S.
Toilet, flush	1589	Harington	English
Tool, pneumatic	1865	Law	English
Torpedo, marine	1804	Fulton	U.S.
Tractor, crawler	1904	Holt	U.S.
Transformer, AC	1885	Stanley	U.S.
Transistor	1947	Shockley, Brattain, Bardeen	U.S.
Trolley car, electric	1884-87	Van DePoele, Sprague	U.S.
Tungsten, ductile	1912	Coolidge	U.S.
Tupperware®	1945	Tupper	U.S.
Turbine, gas	1849	Bourdin	French
Turbine, hydraulic	1849	Francis	U.S.
Turbine, steam	1884	Parsons	English
Type, movable	1447	Gutenberg	German
Typewriter	1867	Sholes, Soule, Glidden	U.S.
Vacuum cleaner, electric	1907	Spangler	U.S.
Vacuum evaporating pan	1846	Rillieux	U.S.
Velcro	1948	de Mestral	Swiss
Video game ("Pong")	1972	Bushnell	U.S.
Video home system (VHS)	1975	Matsushita, JVC	Japanese
Washer, electric	1901	Fisher	U.S.
Welding, atomic hydrogen	1924	Langmuir, Palmer	U.S.
Welding, electric	1877	Thomson	U.S.
Windshield wiper	1903	Anderson	U.S.
Wind tunnel	1912	Eiffel	French
Wire, barbed	1874	Glidden	U.S.
Wrench, double-acting	1913	Owen	U.S.
X-ray tube	1913	Coolidge	U.S.
Zeppelin	1900	Zeppelin	German
Zipper, early model	1893	Judson	U.S.
Zipper, improved	1913	Sundback	Canadian

(1) While Alexander Graham Bell has traditionally been credited with invention of the telephone, which he patented, Antonio Meucci developed a working model before Bell. (2) Al Gross held a number of important early patents in the field of wireless communication; other people were also involved in the development of practical cordless telephones.

Top 20 Corporations Receiving U.S. Patents in 2005

Source: U.S. Patent and Trademark Office, U.S. Department of Commerce

Rank	Company	Number of patents
1.	International Business Machines Corporation	2,941
2.	Canon Kabushiki Kaisha	1,829
3.	Hewlett-Packard Development Company, L.P.	1,790
4.	Matsushita Electric Industrial Co., Ltd.	1,688
5.	Samsung Electronics Co., Ltd.	1,641
6.	Micron Technology, Inc.	1,561
7.	Intel Corporation	1,549
8.	Hitachi, Ltd.	1,271
9.	Toshiba Corporation	1,258
10.	Fujitsu Limited	1,154
11.	Sony Corporation	1,135
12.	General Electric Company	904
13.	Seiko Epson Corporation	884
14.	Infineon Technologies Ag	787
15.	Koninklijke Philips Electronics N.V.	763
16.	Robert Bosch GMBH.	756
17.	Fuji Photo Film Co., Ltd.	750
18.	Microsoft Corporation	746
19.	Texas Instruments, Incorporated	734
20.	Honda Giken Kogyo Kabushiki Kaisha (Honda Motor Co., Ltd.)	698

Geologic Time Scale

Our understanding of Earth's ancient history is largely a result of geoscientists' study of climate, rock strata, ice samples, mineral deposits, and fossils from around the world; clues to the planet's origin have also been found through the study of extraterrestrial bodies. Geologists divide Earth's history into the following units (mya = million years ago):

PRECAMBRIAN TIME (4,600-542 mya)

HADEAN EON (4,600-3,800 mya) Earth has no continents, oceans, or life; surface conditions are defined by intense volcanic activity and widespread meteorite impact. Oldest known minerals and rocks, many of meteoric origin, date to this era.

ARCHEAN EON (3,800-2,500 mya) Earth's surface cools and water vapor in atmosphere condenses to form early oceans, which define small protocontinents; the first single-celled organisms, primarily bacteria, appear in these oceans.

PROTEROZOIC EON (2,500-542 mya) Protocontinents merge into larger landmasses as Earth's crust continues to shift. Atmospheric oxygen levels increase, and first known multicellular life (a form of algae) appears. Later, soft-bodied marine animals emerge.

PHANEROZOIC EON

Paleozoic Era (542-251 mya)

Cambrian Period (542-488 mya) Collisions between Earth's plates create a supercontinent of the southern hemisphere known as Gondwanaland. Seas experience an explosion of invertebrate animal life, including thousands of species of trilobites; there is no life on land.

Ordovician Period (488-443 mya) Gondwanaland extends from South Pole to tropic regions; northern hemisphere is mostly open ocean. Average global temperatures are warmer than present era. First primitive land plants, early ancestors of starfish and mollusks, and first known vertebrates (armored, jawless fishes) appear. The period ends in extinction of a majority of species, possibly a result of a global drop in sea level due to glaciation.

Silurian Period (443-416 mya) South Pole remains covered by supercontinent, but precursors of present-day N America, Europe, and Asia coalesce around the equator and middle latitudes. Appearance of first known vascular land plants, first freshwater fish, first jawed fish, first coral reefs, and first air-breathing animals (*eurypterids,* a scorpion-like creature).

Devonian Period (416-359 mya) Collisions between Gondwanaland and ancestral landmasses of N America and Eurasia produce mountains visible today as northern Appalachians. Newly-formed ozone layer offers protection from sun's rays, allowing first air-breathing spiders and mites to appear on dry land; emergence of first jawed fish, fish with fins and scales, and first amphibians.

Carboniferous Period (359-299 mya) Precursors of modern N America and Northern Europe lie in tropical latitudes north of the Equator; warm and humid conditions there facilitate spread of lush forests and peat swamps that later form most of the world's coal and limestone. Later period sees emergence of first true conifers, *lepidodendrales* ("scale trees") as tall as 100 ft, and first true reptiles.

Permian Period (299-251 mya) All major landmasses collide to form the supercontinent Pangaea, surrounded by the world ocean Panthalassa. Gradual warming throughout the Permian allows for initial flourishing of species—including dinosaur precursors (up to 10 ft in length) and marine species in shallow inland seas—but later precipitates mass extinction of as much as 95% of all species.

Mesozoic Era (251-65.5 mya)

Triassic Period (251-199 mya) Pangea separates into supercontinents of Laurasia and Gondwana; subtropical conditions extend as far north as present-day Wyoming and New England. Emergence of *icthyosaurs* and *plesiosaurs* (large marine reptiles), several species of dinosaurs (up to 15 ft long), first true mammals, and first insects to undergo metamorphosis from larva to pupa to adult.

Jurassic Period (199-145 mya) North American continent drifts westward, opening Gulf of Mexico; rift forms between South America and Africa. Warm, moist climate contributes to flourishing of coral reefs and temperate and subtropical forests. Appearance of first *angiosperms* (flowering plants), *pterosaurs* (winged reptiles), earliest known bird (*Archaeopteryx*), and huge dinosaurs such as the carnivorous *Allosaurus* and herbivorous *Apatosaurus*.

Cretaceous Period (145-65.5 mya) African continental plate drifts north, creating roots of European Alps; gap between S America and Africa broadens; western movement of N America drives formation of Sierra Nevada and Rocky Mountains, turning the western interior of continent into a vast swamp. Later, sea levels rise and cover about one-third of Earth's present land area; global climate is warm and mild. The period ends in a mass extinction of plant and animal species (including dinosaurs), possibly caused by volcanic activity or impact of one or more asteroids or comet fragments.

Cenozoic Era (65.5 mya-present)

Paleogene Period (65.5-23 mya)

• Paleocene Epoch (65.5-55.8 mya) Australia separates from Antarctica; N America and Greenland spread apart. Mammalian life predominates, including early marsupials, insectivores, creodonts (carnivorous ancestors to both cats and dogs), and primitive hoofed mammals.

• Eocene Epoch (55.8-33.9 mya) Australia drifts farther from Antarctica; the Indian subcontinent becomes welded to Asia, and tectonic forces drive the upheaval of the Alpine-Himalayan system. Climate in N America and Europe is subtropical and moist, with temperate forests as far north as Greenland and Siberia. Ancestors of modern horse, rhinoceros, camel, bats, primates, and squirrel-like rodents emerge; earliest known marine mammals appear in later Eocene.

• Oligocene Epoch (33.9-23 mya) San Andreas fault develops between N American and Pacific plates. Mammalian species continue to diversify, producing the first elephants, modern horses, and multiple rodent, camel, and rhinoceros-like species, as well as first known species of great ape. Long-term cooling trend begins that would later cause Pleistocene ice ages.

Neogene Period (23 mya-present)

• Miocene Epoch (23-5.3 mya) Crustal plate collisions continue to drive uplift of Alps, Himalayas, and Cordilleran Ranges in Americas; eroded sediment is deposited in shallow marine basins, forming reservoirs for oil fields of California, Romania, and Caspian Sea. Ocean currents prevent Antarctica from receiving warmer waters, fostering growth of Antarctic ice sheet; northern forests become grassy prairies. Elephants give rise to first mastodons, and large apes related to the orangutan live in Asia and southern Europe; oldest hominid fossils from Africa date to this epoch.

• Pliocene Epoch (5.3-1.8 mya) Alps continue to rise in Europe, and subduction of the Pacific tectonic plate elevates the Sierra Nevada and volcanic Cascade Range. Climate becomes cooler and drier, driving formation of permanent Arctic ice cap. Rapid primate evolution produces *Australopithecus,* earliest direct ancestor of *Homo sapiens.*

• Pleistocene Epoch (1.8 mya-11,800 years ago) Glacier ice covers as much as 25% of more of Earth's land surface, carving numerous present-day features including the Great Lakes; increased rainfall in lower latitudes allows plant and animal life to flourish in northern and eastern Africa. Late Pleistocene brings worldwide extinction of many large mammals, including the mastodon, saber-toothed tiger, and ground sloth.

• Holocene Epoch (11,800 years ago to the present) Melting ice caused sea levels to rise 100 ft or more in early Holocene, covering large areas of land and extending continental shelf of North America. Humans proliferate, and civilization begins.

ENVIRONMENT AND NATURE

Greenhouse Effect and Global Warming
Source: U.S. Environmental Protection Agency

The Earth absorbs incoming solar radiation and emits thermal radiation back into space, but some of this thermal radiation is trapped by atmospheric "greenhouse gases" that warm Earth's surface and atmosphere (**"greenhouse effect"**). Naturally occurring greenhouse gases include carbon dioxide (CO_2), water vapor, methane (CH_4), nitrous oxide (N_2O), and ozone (O_3). Mostly artificial greenhouse gases include chlorofluorocarbons (CFCs), hydrochlorofluorocarbons (HCFCs), hydrofluorocarbons (HFCs), perfluorocarbons (PFCs), and sulfur hexafluoride (SF_6). (Several non-greenhouse gases—carbon monoxide [CO], oxides of nitrogen [NOX], and nonmethane volatile organic compounds [NMVOCs]—contribute indirectly to the greenhouse effect by producing greenhouse gases during chemical transformations and by influencing their atmospheric lifetimes.)

Levels of CO_2 are higher now than at any time in the past 400,000 years. They began rising over the past 2 centuries as a result of human activities such as the burning of fossil fuels (coal, oil, natural gas) and deforestation. During this time, atmospheric concentrations of CO_2, CH_4, and N_2O have risen sharply. Scientists believe this buildup is a major cause of higher-than-normal average global temperatures since the 1990s. Over the 20th century **Earth's average temperature** rose about 1°F, and since the 1970s it has been rising at a faster rate. Some scientists believe the global temperature could rise by 2°F to 6°F over the 21st century. This could speed the melting of polar ice caps, inundate coastal lowlands, promote stronger hurricanes, and cause major changes in crop production and natural habitats.

Delegates from over 150 nations adopted a proposal to limit emissions of CO_2, CH_4, N_2O, HFCs, PFCs, and SF_6 at a UN summit in Kyoto, Japan (Dec. 1997). Under the so-called **Kyoto Protocol**, the 38 participating industrial nations agreed to cut emissions by a collective 5.2% from 1990 levels by 2012. High-emissions nations could meet their targets by purchasing pollution credits from nations that exceed targeted cuts, and gain credits for "sinks," such as forests and croplands, that absorb CO_2 from the atmosphere. Cuts by developing nations were voluntary.

By 1999, 84 nations had signed the protocol, but the agreement could not be implemented until it was ratified by at least 55 countries responsible for at least 55% of developed nations' greenhouse emissions. This threshold was reached with Russia's Nov. 2004 ratification, and the protocol took effect on Feb. 16, 2005. By February 2006, 160 parties to the treaty had ratified and the UN estimated that many of these nations would be achieving emissions reductions of 3.5% below 1990 levels by 2012. Among countries absent from the Kyoto Protocol were U.S. and Australia and developing nations such as China and India. Pres. Bill Clinton signed the agreement in 1998; however, it was not sent to the Senate for ratification because of dim prospects for approval.

Pres. George W. Bush opposed the agreement on the grounds that it did not bind developing nations and would hurt the U.S. economy. The Bush administration has advocated urging technological innovations and providing tax incentives for companies, rather than mandatory limits. The U.S. accounts for 22% of world carbon dioxide emissions from fossil fuels. For new scientific findings related to global warming, see Science News, p. 270.

U.S. Greenhouse Gas Emissions from Human Activities, 1990-2004
Source: U.S. Environmental Protection Agency

GAS AND MAJOR SOURCE(S)	1990	1995	2000	2001	2002	2003	2004	Percent Change
Carbon dioxide (CO_2)	5,005.3	5,325.3	5,864.5	5,795.2	5,815.9	5,877.7	5,988.0	20%
Fossil fuel combustion	4,696.6	4,996.7	5,533.7	5,486.9	5,501.8	5,571.1	5,656.6	20
Methane (CH_4)	618.1	608.9	566.9	560.3	559.8	564.4	556.7	−10
Landfills	81.9	65.8	56.3	55.5	52.5	54.8	56.3	−31
Natural gas systems	126.7	128.1	126.7	125.6	125.4	124.7	118.8	−6
Enteric fermentation[1]	117.9	123.0	115.6	114.6	114.7	115.1	112.6	−4
Coal mining	172.3	163.2	139.0	136.2	139.8	142.4	140.9	−18
Nitrous oxide (N_2O)	394.9	454.2	416.2	412.8	407.4	386.1	386.7	−2
Agricultural soil management	266.1	308.1	278.2	282.9	277.8	259.2	261.5	−2
Hydrofluorocarbons (HFCs), perfluorocarbons (PFCs), and sulfur hexafluoride (SF_6)	90.8	94.8	134.7	124.9	132.7	131.0	143.0	58
TOTAL U.S. EMISSIONS	6,109.0	6,483.3	6,982.3	6,893.1	6,915.8	6,959.1	7,074.4	16
NET U.S. EMISSIONS[2]	5,198.6	5,868.4	6,222.8	6,125.1	6,147.2	6,184.3	6,294.3	21

Note: Emissions given in terms of equivalent emissions of carbon dioxide (CO_2), using units of teragrams of carbon dioxide equivalents (Tg CO_2 Eq.). (1) Digestive process of ruminant animals, such as cattle and sheep, producing methane as a by-product. (2) Total emissions minus carbon dioxide absorbed by forests or other means.

Top 15 Nations Producing Carbon Dioxide Emissions, Ranked by 2004 Totals, 1980-2004
Source: U.S. Department of Energy
(million metric tons of carbon dioxide emitted from fossil fuel consumption)

Region/Country	1980	1985	1990	1995	2000	2004	Percent Change 1980-2004	Percent Change 1990-2004
United States	4,754.52	4,585.20	5,013.45	5,292.67	5,815.50	5,912.21	24%	18%
China	1,454.65	1,838.47	2,241.17	2,873.10	3,030.88	4,707.28	224	110
Russia	3,027.53	3,496.77	3,792.16	1,590.82	1,556.27	1,684.84	NA	NA
Japan	937.50	892.96	1,014.85	1,075.84	1,190.06	1,262.10	35	24
India	299.76	439.34	588.24	867.08	1,000.69	1,112.84	271	89
Germany	751.02	689.20	693.90	875.85	847.08	862.23	NA	NA
Canada	452.51	434.73	478.57	504.93	568.23	587.98	30	23
United Kingdom	608.30	588.25	598.48	555.00	551.02	579.68	−5	−3
Korea, South	126.48	165.05	237.87	393.35	442.51	496.76	293	109
Italy	366.75	374.00	413.38	427.52	443.95	484.98	32	17
South Africa	234.19	298.81	295.48	344.04	378.59	429.56	83	45
France	487.89	394.61	368.64	372.65	399.79	405.66	−17	10
Iran	119.52	164.72	201.79	260.13	318.27	401.91	236	99
Australia	198.31	224.59	262.77	284.84	353.20	386.18	95	47
Mexico	231.43	270.46	300.09	318.70	379.99	385.46	67	28
World Total[3]	**18,333.26**	**19,412.76**	**21,426.12**	**22,033.53**	**23,851.46**	**27,043.57**	**48**	**26**

(1) Numbers for 1980-90 are for the former Soviet Union. (2) Numbers for 1980-90 are for the former West Germany. (3) Includes nations not listed

U.S. Greenhouse Gas Emissions, 2004
Source: U.S. Environmental Protection Agency

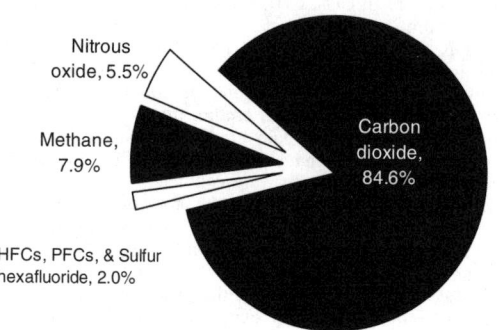

Nitrous oxide, 5.5%
Methane, 7.9%
HFCs, PFCs, & Sulfur hexafluoride, 2.0%
Carbon dioxide, 84.6%

World Carbon Dioxide Emissions from the Use of Fossil Fuels, 2004
Source: U.S. Energy Information Administration

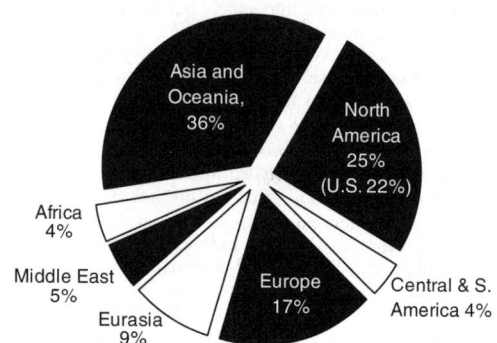

Asia and Oceania, 36%
North America 25% (U.S. 22%)
Africa 4%
Middle East 5%
Eurasia 9%
Europe 17%
Central & S. America 4%

Atmospheric Concentration of CO_2, 1744-2005
Sources: Carbon Dioxide Information Analysis Center, Dept. of Energy

Year[1]	Concentration in ppm[2]	Year[1]	Concentration in ppm[2]	Year[1]	Concentration in ppm[2]
1744	277	1903	295	1980	339
1791	280	1915	301	1990	354
1816	284	1927	306	2000	369
1843	287	1943	308	2004	377
1869	289	1960	317	2005	377
1878	290	1970	326		

(1) Measurements for the years 1744-1943 were derived from a 200m ice core sample drilled near Siple Station in Antarctica between 1983-84. Measurements from 1960-2004 were taken directly from the atmosphere at Mauna Loa Observatory in Hawaii. Measurements for 2005 were taken directly from the atmosphere at Jubany Station, Antarctica. (2) parts per million.

Air Pollution in Selected World Cities
Source: World Bank, *World Development Indicators 2006*

Particulate matter in the following table refers to smoke, soot, dust, and liquid droplets from combustion that are in the air—specifically, to particulates less than 10 microns in diameter capable of reaching deep into the respiratory tract. The level of particulates, an important indicator of air quality, is significantly affected by the state of technology and pollution controls. Particulate pollution causes an estimated 500,000 premature deaths each year. **Sulfur dioxide** is a pollutant formed when fossil fuels containing sulfur are burned. **Nitrogen dioxide** is a poisonous, pungent gas formed when nitric oxide combines with hydrocarbons and sunlight, producing a photochemical reaction. Nitrogen oxides are emitted by bacteria, nitrogenous fertilizers, aerobic decomposition of organic matter, biomass combustion, and, especially, burning fuel for vehicles and industrial activities. Emissions of sulfur dioxide and nitrogen oxides lead to **acid rain.**

Data in the following table are average concentrations based on reports from urban monitoring sites, measured in micrograms per cubic meter, mpcm; the figures give a general indication of air quality, but results should be interpreted with caution. World Health Organization standards for acceptable air quality are 50 mpcm for sulfur dioxide and 40 mpcm for nitrogen dioxide; the WHO has set no guidelines for acceptable levels of suspended particulate matter.

City and Country	Particulate matter[1]	Sulfur dioxide[2]	Nitrogen dioxide[2]	City and Country	Particulate matter[1]	Sulfur dioxide[2]	Nitrogen dioxide[2]
Accra, Ghana	40	NA	NA	Montreal, Canada	20	10	42
Amsterdam, Netherlands	40	10	58	Moscow, Russia	25	109	NA
Athens, Greece	51	34	64	Mumbai, India	74	33	39
Bangkok, Thailand	83	11	23	Nairobi, Kenya	42	NA	NA
Barcelona, Spain	43	11	43	New York City, US	22	26	79
Beijing, China	99	90	122	Oslo, Norway	19	8	43
Berlin, Germany	25	18	26	Paris, France	12	14	57
Cairo, Egypt, Arab Rep.	159	69	NA	Prague, Czech Republic	25	14	33
Calcutta, India	145	49	34	Quito, Ecuador	33	22	NA
Capetown, South Africa	15	21	72	Rio de Janeiro, Brazil	42	129	NA
Caracas, Venezuela, RB	17	33	57	Rome	35	NA	NA
Chicago, United States	26	14	57	Sao Paulo, Brazil	49	43	83
Delhi, India	177	24	41	Seoul, South Korea	46	44	60
Jakarta, Indonesia	115	NA	NA	Shanghai, China	81	53	73
London, England	23	25	77	Sofia, Bulgaria	76	39	122
Los Angeles, U.S.	36	9	74	Tokyo, Japan	42	18	68
Manila, Philippines	42	33	NA	Toronto, Canada	24	17	43
Mexico City, Mexico	55	74	130	Warsaw, Poland	43	16	32
Milan, Italy	36	31	248				

NA = Not available. (1) Data was collected in 2002. (2) Average of data collected between 1995 and 2001.

World Almanac Quick Quiz
Which of these nations did not lose 10% or more of its forest area between 1990 and 2005?
(a) Russian Federation   (b) Myanmar (Burma)   (c) Zambia   (d) Indonesia

For the answer look in this chapter, or see page 1008.

Emissions of Principal Air Pollutants in the U.S., 1970-2005

Source: U.S. Environmental Protection Agency, Office of Air Quality Planning and Standards; in million tons; estimated

Polluant Emitted	1970	1975	1980	1985	1990	1995	2000	2005[1]
Carbon monoxide........	197.3	184.0	177.8	169.6	143.6	120.0	102.4	89
Nitrogen oxides[2]........	26.9	26.4	27.1	25.8	25.2	24.7	22.3	19
Particulate matter[3]								
PM $_{10}$...............	12.2	7.0	6.2	3.6	3.2	3.1	2.3	2
PM $_{2.5}$	NA	NA	NA	NA	2.3	2.2	1.8	2
Sulfur dioxide..........	32.1	28.0	25.9	23.3	23.1	18.6	16.3	15
Volatile org. compounds[2]..	3.7	30.2	30.1	26.9	23.1	21.6	16.9	16
Lead.................	0.221	0.16	0.074	0.022	0.005	0.004	0.003	0.003
TOTAL[4]	301.5	275.8	267.2	249.2	218.2	188.0	160.2	141

(1) Preliminary. (2) Ozone, a major air pollutant and the primary constituent of smog, is not emitted directly to the air but is formed by sunlight acting on emissions of nitrogen oxides and volatile organic compounds. (3) PM$_{10}$, particulates 10 microns or smaller in diameter. PM$_{2.5}$, particulates 2.5 microns or smaller diameter. (4) Totals are rounded, as are components of totals.

Carbon Monoxide Emission Estimates, 1970-2003

Source: U.S. Environmental Protection Agency, Office of Air Quality Planning and Standards; in thousand tons; estimated

Source	1970	1975	1980	1985	1990	1995	2000	2001	2002	2003
Fuel combustion, elec. util..	237	276	322	291	363	372	484	485	660	674
Industrial processes[1]	10,610	8,304	7,700	5,894	5,572	5,631	3,628	3,781	3,399	3,440
Transportation	174,602	167,884	160,512	153,216	131,702	107,755	92,239	88,153	85,297	82,403
Fires..................	6,766	4,433	7,622	7,289	10,583	6,705	12,049	7,744	16,118	(3)
TOTAL[2]	204,043	188,398	185,407	176,844	154,186	126,777	114,467	106,262	113,447	94,435

(1) Includes industrial fuel combustion, chemical and allied manufacturing, metals processing, and petroleum and other industrial sectors. (2) Totals may not add because of rounding or because all categories are not listed. (3) 2003 numbers do not include fire related emissions.

Nitrogen Oxides Emission Estimates, 1970-2003

Source: U.S. Environmental Protection Agency, Office of Air Quality Planning and Standards; in thousand tons; estimated

Source	1970	1975	1980	1985	1990	1995	2000	2001	2002	2003
Fuel combustion, elec. util.	4,900	5,694	7,024	6,127	6,663	6,384	5,330	4,917	4,725	4,270
Industrial processes[1]	5,100	4,546	4,110	4,009	3,831	3,909	3,518	3,587	2,991	2,996
Transportation	15,276	15,029	14,846	14,508	13,373	12,989	12,560	11,930	12,530	12,052
TOTAL[2]	26,883	26,371	27,079	25,757	25,529	24,956	22,598	21,549	21,343	20,281

(1) Includes industrial fuel combustion, chemical and allied manufacturing, metals processing, and petroleum and other industrial sectors. (2) Totals may not add because of rounding or because all categories are not listed.

Sulfur Dioxide Emissions, 1970-2003

Source: U.S. Environmental Protection Agency, Office of Air Quality Planning and Standards; in thousand tons; estimated

Source	1970	1975	1980	1985	1990	1995	2000	2001	2002	2003
Fuel combustion, elec. util.	17,398	18,268	17,469	16,272	15,909	12,080	11,396	10,850	10,455	10,595
Industrial processes[1]	11,661	7,993	6,725	5,597	5,402	4,945	3,515	3,665	3,055	3,084
Transportation	551	635	717	809	874	741	697	688	751	692
TOTAL[2]	31,218	28,043	25,925	23,307	23,076	18,619	16,347	15,932	15,293	15,044

(1) Includes industrial fuel combustion, chemical and allied manufacturing, metals processing, and petroleum and other industrial sectors. (2) Totals include miscellaneous sources not determined.

Air Quality of Selected U.S. Metropolitan Areas, 1990-2005

Source: U.S. Environmental Protection Agency, Office of Air Quality Planning and Standards

Data indicate the number of days metropolitan statistical areas failed to meet acceptable air-quality standards.

Metropolitan Statistical Area	1990	1995	2000	2001	2002	2003	2004	2005
Atlanta,GA	42	35	39	24	20	12	11	11
Bakersfield,CA	99	105	132	124	150	141	133	87
Baltimore,MD	28	36	23	33	42	20	16	27
Baton Rouge,LA...............................	28	15	29	5	5	15	11	12
Boston,MA–NH	0	0	0	3	7	6	1	1
Chicago,IL	5	23	13	33	23	10	9	23
Cincinnati,OH–KY–IN...........................	12	19	15	15	31	10	4	14
Cleveland-Lorain–Elyria,OH.....................	10	24	21	29	30	17	18	25
Dallas,TX	0	20	20	14	7	5	9	10
Denver,CO....................................	9	3	2	8	7	16	0	1
Detroit,MI	11	14	16	31	28	19	9	23
Fresno,CA	62	61	131	139	152	127	48	64
Greensboro-Winston Salem-High Point,NC...........	12	6	14	11	24	4	2	2
Houston,TX	51	65	42	27	21	31	22	28
Indianapolis,IN	9	19	8	14	24	11	1	18
Las Vegas,NV–AZ	4	0	0	1	2	3	1	2
Los Angeles–Long Beach,CA	161	103	63	81	81	88	65	45
Miami,FL	1	2	2	1	1	1	3	1
Minneapolis-St. Paul,MN-WI	4	3	4	6	1	1	0	2
New Haven-Meriden,CT..........................	15	14	9	15	25	16	3	13
New York,NY	15	17	19	21	26	14	6	15
Orange County,CA..............................	42	8	5	6	4	5	3	0
Philadelphia,PA-NJ	39	30	21	35	35	20	14	26
Phoenix-Mesa,AZ..............................	12	16	11	7	8	8	1	4
Riverside-San Bernardino,CA	158	124	144	156	146	138	118	103
Sacramento,CA	56	41	41	46	57	35	26	39
St. Louis,MO-IL	22	34	20	20	34	13	2	29
Salt Lake City-Ogden,UT	5	4	20	27	33	10	37	26
San Diego,CA	96	48	31	30	20	20	16	7
San Francisco,CA	0	2	3	5	1	0	0	0
Seattle–Bellevue-Everett,WA.....................	2	0	7	6	6	2	1	1
Washington,DC-MD-VA-WV	25	32	22	28	34	13	10	19

Average Global Temperatures, 1900-2005

Source: National Oceanic and Atmospheric Administration; in degrees Fahrenheit

1900-09 . . . . . .56.5	1940-49 . . . . . .57.1	1980-89 . . . . . .57.4	2002 . . . . .57.9
1910-19 . . . . . .56.6	1950-59 . . . . . .57.1	1990-99 . . . . . .57.6	2003 . . . . .57.9
1920-29 . . . . . .56.7	1960-69 . . . . . .57.1	2000 . . . . .57.6	2004 . . . . .57.9
1930-39 . . . . . .57.0	1970-79 . . . . . .57.0	2001 . . . . .57.8	2005 . . . . .58.0

Note: The warmest year on record was 1998, when the average global temperature reached 58.1°F. The second warmest year on record was 2005.

Toxics Release Inventory, U.S., 2003-2004

Source: U.S. Environmental Protection Agency

Releases of toxic chemicals into the environment, by manner of release and industry sector; pollutant transfers by destination of transfer. Totals below may not add because of rounding.

	2003 mil lb	2004 mil lb		2003 %	2004 %
Pollutant releases			**Top industries, total releases**		
Air releases.	1,570	1,545	Metal mining.	28	25
Surface water discharges	219	240	Electric utilities	24	25
Underground injection.	220	228	Primary metals	11	12
On-site land releases	1,420	1,224	Chemicals.	12	13
Off-site releases	473	499	Hazardous waste/solvent recovery	5	5
TOTAL on- and off-site releases.	**3,903**	**3,735**	Paper	5	5
			All others	15	15
Pollutant transfers					
To recycling.	1,883	2,272	**Top carcinogens, air/water/land releases**	**mil lb**	**mil lb**
To energy recovery.	650	654	Styrene	51	55
To treatment	279	326	Formaldehyde	21	30
To publicly owned treatment works.	271	260	Acetaldehyde	14	15
Other transfers	1	72	Dichloromethane	9	8
Off-site to disposal	587	606	Trichloroethylene	7	7
TOTAL.	**3,671**	**4,190**	Ethylbenzene	7	6

Note: This information does not indicate whether (or to what degree) the public has been exposed to toxic chemicals.

Top 10 States, Total Toxics Releases, 2004

Source: U.S. Environmental Protection Agency

State	2004 lb	State	2004 lb	State	2004 lb
Alaska	512,278,274	Indiana.	239,456,035	Illinois	135,318,299
Texas.	276,043,628	Utah.	167,845,367	North Carolina.	133,417,120
Nevada.	269,308,749	Pennsylvania.	160,746,259		
Ohio	242,479,503	Tennessee.	157,754,861	**U.S. Total*. . . . . . .**	**4,235,300,325**

*Total includes District of Columbia, Puerto Rico, American Samoa, Guam, Northern Marianas, and the Virgin Islands.

Hazardous Waste Sites in the U.S., 2006

Source: U.S. Environmental Protection Agency, *National Priorities List,* Sept. 2006

State/Territory	Proposed Gen	Proposed Fed	Final Gen	Final Fed	Total Number	State/Territory	Proposed Gen	Proposed Fed	Final Gen	Final Fed	Total Number
Alabama.	2	0	10	3	15	Nevada	0	0	1	0	1
Alaska	0	0	1	5	6	New Hampshire. . . .	1	0	19	1	21
Arizona.	0	0	7	2	9	New Jersey	4	0	105	8	117
Arkansas	0	0	10	0	10	New Mexico.	1	0	11	1	13
California	2	0	69	24	95	New York.	1	0	82	4	87
Colorado.	2	0	14	3	19	North Carolina	0	0	29	2	31
Connecticut	1	0	13	1	16	North Dakota	0	0	0	0	0
Delaware	0	0	13	1	15	Ohio.	5	2	27	3	37
District of Columbia .	0	0	0	1	1	Oklahoma	1	0	9	1	11
Florida	1	0	43	6	50	Oregon	0	0	9	2	11
Georgia	1	0	14	2	17	Pennsylvania.	2	0	88	6	96
Hawaii	0	0	1	2	3	Rhode Island	0	0	10	2	12
Idaho	3	0	4	2	9	South Carolina	0	0	24	2	26
Illinois	6	1	37	4	48	South Dakota	0	0	1	1	2
Indiana	1	0	29	0	30	Tennessee.	0	1	10	3	14
Iowa	1	0	10	1	12	Texas.	2	0	38	4	44
Kansas	1	0	9	1	11	Utah.	4	0	10	4	18
Kentucky	0	0	13	1	14	Vermont.	0	0	11	0	11
Louisiana	3	0	10	1	14	Virginia	0	0	18	11	28
Maine	0	0	9	3	12	Washington	0	0	34	13	47
Maryland	1	0	8	9	18	West Virginia	0	0	7	2	9
Massachusetts	1	0	25	7	33	Wisconsin	1	0	37	0	38
Michigan.	1	1	66	0	68	Wyoming	0	0	1	1	2
Minnesota.	0	0	22	2	24	Guam.	0	0	1	1	2
Mississippi	2	0	3	0	5	Puerto Rico	2	0	9	1	12
Missouri	0	0	23	3	26	Virgin Islands.	0	0	2	0	2
Montana	1	0	14	0	15						
Nebraska	0	0	13	1	14	**Total . . . .**	**55**	**5**	**1,083**	**158**	**1,300**

Note: Fed. = for hazardous waste produced by federal agency; Gen. = non-Fed./ sites. Proposed = proposed for federal Superfund financing; Final = qualified for Superfund financing.

Renewable Energy Sources

Source: U.S. Department of Energy

Concern over the environmental impact of burning fossil fuels has helped spur interest in alternative fuels that are less polluting. And since the supply of fossil fuels is finite and diminishing, there is interest in "renewable" sources that do not deplete existing supplies. However, renewable energy sources still make up only a small share of U.S. domestic energy production (about 6%, or excluding hydropower about 3.5%). The major reason for this is their relatively higher cost (in some cases 2 to 4 times that of power obtained from traditional fuels). The following are the major renewable energy sources available.

Biomass is plant-derived material usable as a renewable energy source, including wood energy crops such as hybrid poplars and willow trees, agricultural crops including soybeans and corn, and animal and other wastes. Biomass is one of the two most common energy sources in the U.S. today along with hydropower. Forms of biomass such as wood can be burned to produce heat and generate electricity. Agricultural crops can be chemically converted into fuels such as ethanol and biodiesel; these are the only known renewable liquid energy sources, and may one day replace petroleum and fossil-fuel produced diesel. But bringing ethanol and biodiesel into wide use would require more energy-efficient methods of production and transportation. Overall, biomass fuels are much cleaner-burning than fossil fuels, though biomass fuels do produce carbon dioxide and other pollutants.

Geothermal energy is generated from heat from inside Earth. This form of energy is both clean and renewable. The technology has caught on in countries with substantial geothermal activity such as Iceland, where it accounts for 16% of electricity output and 86% of all energy used for home heating. In the U.S. the best sources for geothermal power are in the west, where there are many underground lakes of heated water; however, large-scale access would require drilling. A major goal in this field is to find a way to harness energy directly from magma (molten rock material), which has great potential because of its high temperature.

Hydrogen is the 3rd most abundant element on Earth. It does not naturally occur on Earth as a pure gas or liquid, but is always combined with other elements (such as with oxygen to form water or carbon to form methane). For energy use it is produced from hydrocarbons using heat, bacteria or algae through photosynthesis, or by using sunlight or electricity to split water into hydrogen and oxygen. Hydrogen batteries or "fuel cells" are already used by NASA on the space shuttle. In a fuel cell, electrons are released from the hydrogen atoms in a chemical reaction and flow through an external circuit as electricity. The protons then combine with oxygen (and some of the electrons in the electric current) to make heat and water suitable for drinking. Fuel cells do not run down, but work as long as hydrogen is supplied. Some experts think hydrogen will be the power source of the future. However, an infrastructure would need to be created for safe and cost-effective transportation and storage of hydrogen.

Hydropower, or hydroelectric power, is generated by water flowing through turbines. With biomass fuels, it is one of the two most common renewable energy sources in the U.S. today. A dam on a river is a common hydropower producer. No harmful greenhouse gases are produced, but the dams needed to generate the power can harm river ecosystems. Researchers are working on turbine technologies that may maximize use of hydropower and reduce adverse environmental effects.

Ocean energy is generated in two ways. Thermal ocean energy uses the heat that the ocean absorbs from the sun to power generators, and sometimes drinkable desalinated water is a by-product. Mechanical ocean energy is generated by the movement of tides and waves through a turbine. In both cases, power generation is not very efficient with current technology. Much more research is needed to make thermal ocean energy generation a reality. Mechanical ocean energy requires large dams or breakwater-type structures called "tidal barrages" to be built, which could cause harm to coastal ecosystems.

Solar energy is generated using heat and light from the sun. Solar energy is an increasingly common source of electricity. Photovoltaic (PV) solar cells are made of semi-conducting materials that can directly convert sunlight to electricity without any harmful waste product. Solar collectors are made more efficient by using arrays of mirrors to concentrate the sun's rays onto PV panels. Another way of using sunlight is to heat water directly. According to the DOE, homes incorporating solar heating designs can save as much as 50% on heating bills. The downside to solar energy is that it depends heavily on a range of factors including location, time of year, and weather.

Wind energy uses wind turbines to produce energy. They are perched on high towers, usually 100 feet or higher, and often placed in large groups ("farms") to generate electricity for towns and cities. On a much smaller scale, stand-alone turbines are sometimes used by farmers and homeowners to generate supplemental electricity. In the past 20 years, government incentives in the form of tax credits to producers and incentives for homeowners have helped lower the price of wind power by 85%, making it a more feasible option. Some people object to wind farms because of their appearance or the noise the turbines make. Wind power raises few other environmental problems; but the turbines can pose a danger to birds. In addition, because weather is involved, consistent generation is a challenge.

IT'S A RECORD: In accordance with a new program to dispose of decommissioned ships, the Navy used explosives to sink USS *Oriskany* to the bottom of the Gulf of Mexico on May 17, 2006, to create the world's largest intentionally created reef. The 888-foot former aircraft carrier, commissioned in 1950 and decommissioned in 1976, is now to being used as a reef for sport fishing and diving about 24 miles off Pensacola Beach, FL. The Environmental Protection Agency estimated that any chemical toxins in the ship's infrastructure would leech into surrounding water so slowly that they would pose no threat to the natural habitat.

Renewable Water Resources

Source: Food and Agriculture Organization, United Nations, 2005

Globally, water supplies are abundant, but they are unevenly distributed among and within countries. In some areas, water withdrawals are so high, relative to supply, that surface water supplies are shrinking and groundwater reserves are being depleted faster than they can be replenished by precipitation. The U.S. has a total of 2,818 cubic kilometers of internal renewable water resources, an actual total (which takes into account incoming water flow from outside the country) of 3,069 cubic kilometers, and 10,333 cubic meters per capita. Totals for all countries are 43,219 cubic kilometers of internal resources, 55,273 cubic kilometers of actual resources, and 8,549 cubic meters per capita.

These numbers, and those in the tables below, were published by the Food and Agriculture Organization in 2005; the tables draw upon studies done over a number of years and use 2000 population data.

Countries With Most Resources Per Capita
(ranked by per capita resources)

Country	Cubic meters per capita	Total cubic km
Iceland	582,191.8	170.0
Guyana	314,211.2	241.0
Suriname	277,904.3	122.0
Congo, Republic of	217,915.1	832.0
Papua New Guinea	137,251.5	801.0
Gabon	121,391.6	164.0
Canada	91,418.9	2,902.0
Solomon Islands	91,038.7	44.7
Norway	83,919.2	382.0
New Zealand	83,760.2	327.0

Countries With Least Resources Per Capita*
(ranked by per capita resources, starting with the lowest)

Country/Territory	Cubic meters per capita	Total cubic km
Kuwait	7.7	(1)
United Arab Emirates	49.2	0.2
Bahamas	63.1	(1)
Qatar	85.6	0.1
Maldives	91.5	(1)
Saudi Arabia	96.3	2.4
Libya	106.0	0.6
Malta	127.5	0.1
Singapore	139.0	0.6
Jordan	156.8	0.9

* Data not available from all nations. (1) Less than 0.1 cubic km.

Forest Area Top 50 Countries, 1990–2005*

Source: World Resources Institute; United Nations

Units: Thousand hectares

Country	Total Forest Area (thousand hectares)			Percent change in forest area 1990–2005	Country	Total Forest Area (thousand hectares)			Percent change in forest area 1990–2005
	2005	2000	1990			2005	2000	1990	
Russian Federation	808,790	809,268	808,950	0	Congo	22,471	22,556	22,726	−1
Brazil	477,698	493,213	520,027	−8	Gabon	21,775	21,826	21,927	−1
Canada	310,134	310,134	310,134	0	Cameroon	21,245	22,345	24,545	−13
United States	303,089	302,294	298,648	1	Malaysia	20,890	21,591	22,376	−7
China	197,290	177,001	157,141	26	Mozambique	19,262	19,512	20,012	−4
Australia	163,678	164,645	167,904	−3	Paraguay	18,475	19,368	21,157	−13
Congo, Dem Rep	133,610	135,207	140,531	−5	Spain	17,915	16,436	13,479	33
Indonesia	88,495	97,852	116,567	−24	Zimbabwe	17,540	19,105	22,234	−21
Peru	68,742	69,213	70,156	−2	Lao People's Dem Rep	16,142	16,532	17,314	−7
India	67,701	67,554	63,939	6	Chile	16,121	15,834	15,263	6
Sudan	67,546	70,491	76,381	−12	France	15,554	15,351	14,538	7
Mexico	64,238	65,540	69,016	−7	Guyana	15,104	15,104	15,104	0
Colombia	60,728	60,963	61,439	−1	Suriname	14,776	14,776	14,776	0
Angola	59,104	59,728	60,976	−3	Thailand	14,520	14,814	15,965	−9
Bolivia	58,740	60,091	62,795	−6	Ethiopia	13,000	13,705	15,114	−14
Venezuela	47,713	49,151	52,026	−8	Viet Nam	12,931	11,725	9,363	38
Zambia	42,452	44,676	49,124	−14	Madagascar	12,838	13,023	13,692	−6
Tanzania	35,257	37,318	41,441	−15	Mali	12,572	13,072	14,072	−11
Argentina	33,021	33,770	35,262	−6	Botswana	11,943	12,535	13,718	−13
Myanmar	32,222	34,554	39,219	−18	Chad	11,921	12,317	13,110	−9
Papua New Guinea	29,437	30,132	31,523	−7	Nigeria	11,089	13,137	17,234	−36
Sweden	27,528	27,474	27,367	−1	Germany	11,076	11,076	10,741	3
Japan	24,868	24,876	24,950	0	Iran, Islamic Rep	11,075	11,075	11,075	0
Central African Rep.	22,755	22,903	23,203	−2	Ecuador	10,853	11,841	13,817	−21
Finland	22,500	22,475	22,194	1	Cambodia	10,447	11,541	12,946	−19
					World	**3,952,025**	**3,988,610**	**4,077,291**	**−3**

*Ranked by hectares of forest

Some Endangered Animal Species

Source: Fish and Wildlife Service, U.S. Dept. of the Interior

Common name	Scientific name	Range
Albatross, Amsterdam	Diomedia amsterdamensis	Amsterdam Island, Indian Ocean
Antelope, giant sable	Hippotragus niger variani	Angola
Armadillo, giant	Pridontes maximus	Venezuela, Guyana to Argentina
Babirusa	Babyrousa babyrussa	Indonesia
Bandicoot, desert	Perameles eremiana	Australia
Bat, gray	Myotis grisescens	Central, southeastern U.S.
Bear, Mexican grizzly	Ursus aretos	Mexico
Bison, wood	Bison bison athabascae	Canada, northwestern U.S.
Bobcat, Mexican	Felis rufus escuinapae	Central Mexico
Caiman, black	Melanosuchus niger	Amazon basin
Camel, Bactrian	Camelus bactrianus	Mongolia, China
Caribou, woodland	Rangifer tarandus caribou	Canada, Northwestern U.S.
Cheetah	Acinonyx jubatus	Africa to India

Common name	Scientific name	Range
Chimpanzee, pygmy	Pan paniscus	Congo (formerly Zaire)
Condor, California	Gymnogyps californianus	U.S. (AZ, CA, OR), Mexico (Baja California)
Crane, whooping	Grus americana	Canada, Mexico, U.S. (Rocky Mts. to Carolinas)
Crocodile, American	Crocodylus acutus	U.S. (FL), Mexico, Caribbean Sea, Central and S America
Deer, Columbian white-tailed	Odocoileus virginianus leucurus	U.S. (OR, WA)
Dolphin, Chinese river	Lipotes vexillifer	China
Dugong	Dugong dugon	East Africa to southern Japan
Elephant, Asian	Elephas maximus	S central and southeastern Asia
Fox, northern swift	Vulpes velox hebes	Canada
Frog, mountain yellow-legged	Rano capito sevosa	Western U.S. (CA, NV)
Gorilla	Gorilla gorilla	Central and W Africa
Hartebeest, Tora	Alcelaphus buselaphus tora	Egypt, Ethiopia, Sudan
Hawk, Hawaiian	Buteo solitarius	U.S. (HI)
Hyena, brown	Hyaena brunnea	Southern Africa
Impala, black-faced	Aepyceros melampus petersi	Angola, Namibia
Kangaroo, Tasmanian forester	Macropus giganteus tasmaniensis	Australia (Tasmania)
Leopard	Panthera pardus	Africa and Asia
Lion, Asiatic	Panthera leo persica	Turkey to India
Manatee, West Indian	Trichechus manatus	Southeastern U.S., Caribbean Sea, Mexico
Monkey, spider	Ateles geoffroyi frontatus	Costa Rica, Nicaragua
Ocelot	Felis pardalis	U.S. (AZ, TX) to Central and S America
Orangutan	Pongo pygmaeus	Borneo, Sumatra
Ostrich, West African	Struthio camelus spatzi	W Sahara
Otter, marine	Lutra felina	Peru south to Straits of Magellan
Panda, giant	Ailuropoda melanoleuca	China
Panther, Florida	Felis concolor coryi	U.S. (FL)
Parakeet, golden	Aratinga guarouba	Brazil
Parrot, imperial	Amazona imperialis	West Indies (Dominica)
Penguin, Galapagos	Spheniscus mendiculus	Ecuador (Galapagos Islands)
Puma, eastern	Felis concolor couguar	Eastern N America (presumed extinct in wild)
Python, Indian	Python molurus molurus	Sri Lanka, India
Rat-kangaroo, brush-tailed	Bettongia penicillata	Australia
Rhinoceros, black	Diceros bicornis	Sub-Saharan Africa
Rhinoceros, northern white	Ceratotherium simum cottoni	Congo, Sudan, Uganda, Central African Rep.
Salamander, Chinese giant	Andrias davidianus	Western China
Sea-lion, Steller	Eumetopias jubatus	Alaska, Russia
Sheep, bighorn	Ovis canadensis	California
Squirrel, Carolina northern flying	Glaucomys sabrinus coloratus	U.S. (NC, TN)
Tiger	Panthera tigris	Asia
Tortoise, Galapagos	Geochelone elephantopus	Ecuador (Galapagos Islands)
Turtle, Plymouth red-bellied	Pseudemys rubriventris bangsi	U.S. (MA)
Whale, gray	Eschrichtius robustus	N Pacific Ocean
Whale, humpback	Megaptera novaeangliae	Oceania
Wolf, red	Canis rufus	U.S. (FL, NC, SC)
Woodpecker, ivory-billed	Campephilus principalis	Cuba
Yak, wild	Bos grunniens mutus	China (Tibet), India
Zebra, mountain	Equus zebra zebra	South Africa

U.S. List of Endangered and Threatened Species, 2006

Source: Fish and Wildlife Service, U.S. Dept. of Interior; as of Sept. 2006

Group	Endangered U.S.	Endangered Foreign	Threatened U.S.	Threatened Foreign	Total species[1]	Species with recovery plans
Mammals	69	255	13	20	357	55
Birds	76	175	15	6	272	80
Reptiles	14	65	23	16	118	34
Amphibians	13	8	10	1	32	16
Fishes	75	11	62	1	149	98
Clams	62	2	8	0	72	69
Snails	24	1	12	0	37	29
Insects	47	4	10	0	61	32
Arachnids	12	0	0	0	12	6
Crustaceans	19	0	3	0	22	18
Animal subtotal	411	521	156	44	1,132	437
Flowering plants	570	1	143	0	714	599
Conifers & cycads	2	0	1	2	5	3
Ferns and allies	24	0	2	0	26	26
Lichens	2	0	0	0	2	2
Plant subtotal	598	1	146	2	747	630
GRAND TOTAL	1,009	522	302	46	1,879	1,067

(1) Some species are classified as both endangered and threatened. The table tallies these "dual status" species only once, as endangered, except for the olive ridley sea turtle, which is dual status but tallied as a U.S. threatened species. The other dual status species, all tallied as endangered, are: (U.S.) California tiger salamander, chinook salmon, gray wolf, green sea turtle, piping plover, roseate tern, sockeye salmon, steelhead, Steller sea lion; (non-U.S.) argali, chimpanzee, leopard, saltwater crocodile.

 IT'S A RECORD: The trap-jaw ant has the fastest jaw in the animal kingdom. The tiny ant can clamp shut its mandibles at a speed between 78 and 145 mph, over a period of 0.13 milliseconds. The ant's jaws slam shut with such force that it can throw the ant sideways to an average distance of 15.6 inches. That's the equivalent of a human jumping 132 feet.

Classification

Source: *Funk & Wagnalls New Encyclopedia*

In biology, classification is the identification, naming, and grouping of organisms into a formal system. The 2 fields that are most directly concerned with classification are taxonomy and systematics. Although the 2 disciplines overlap considerably, taxonomy is more concerned with nomenclature (naming) and with constructing hierarchical systems, and systematics with uncovering evolutionary relationships. Two kingdoms of living forms, Plantae and Animalia, have been recognized since Aristotle established the first taxonomy in the 4th century BC. In addition, there are the following 3 kingdoms: Protista (one-celled organisms), Monera (bacteria and blue-green algae; also known as the kingdom Procaryotae), and Fungi. The 7 basic categories of classification (from most general to most specific) are: kingdom, phylum (or division), class, order, family, genus, and species. Below are 2 examples:

ZOOLOGICAL HIERARCHY

Kingdom	Phylum	Class	Order	Family	Genus	Species name	Common name
Animalia	Chordata	Mammalia	Primates	Hominidae	Homo	Homo sapiens	Human

BOTANICAL HIERARCHY

Kingdom	Division*	Class	Order	Family	Genus	Species name	Common name
Plantae	Magnoliophyta	Magnoliopsida	Magnoliales	Magnoliaceae	Magnolia	M. virginiana	Sweet Bay

* In botany, the division is generally used in place of the phylum.

Gestation, Longevity, and Incubation of Animals

Information reviewed by Ronald M. Nowak, author *Walker's Mammals of the World* (6th ed., Johns Hopkins University Press, 1999). Average longevity figures supplied by Ronald T. Reuther. These apply to animals in captivity; the potential life span of animals is rarely attained in nature. Figures on gestation and incubation are averages based on estimates.

ANIMAL	Gestation (days)	Average longevity (years)	Maximum longevity (yr-mo)	ANIMAL	Gestation (days)	Average longevity (years)	Maximum longevity (yr-mo)
Ass	365	12	47	Leopard	98	12	23
Baboon	187	20	45	Lion	100	15	30
Bear: Black	219	18	36-10	Monkey (rhesus)	166	15	37
Grizzly	225	25	50	Moose	240	12	27
Polar	240	20	45	Mouse (meadow)	21	3	4
Beaver	105	5	50	Mouse (dom. white)	19	3	6
Bison	285	15	40	Opossum (American)	13	1	5
Camel	406	12	50	Pig (domestic)	112	10	27
Cat (domestic)	63	12	28	Puma	90	12	20
Chimpanzee	230	20	60	Rabbit (domestic)	31	5	13
Chipmunk	31	6	10	Rhinoceros (black)	450	15	45-10
Cow	284	15	30	Rhinoceros (white)	480	20	50
Deer (white-tailed)	201	8	20	Sea lion (California)	350	12	34
Dog (domestic)	61	12	20	Sheep (domestic)	154	12	20
Elephant (African)	660	35	70	Squirrel (gray)	44	10	23-6
Elephant (Asian)	645	40	77	Tiger	105	16	26-3
Elk	250	15	26-8	Wolf (maned)	63	5	15-8
Fox (red)	52	7	14	Zebra (Grant's)	365	15	50
Giraffe	457	10	36-2				
Goat (domestic)	151	8	18				
Gorilla	258	20	54				
Guinea pig	68	4	8				
Hippopotamus	238	41	61				
Horse	330	20	50				
Kangaroo (gray)	36	7	24				

Incubation time (days)

Chicken	21
Duck	30
Goose	30
Pigeon	18
Turkey	26

Major Venomous Animals

Snakes

Asian pit viper — from 2 ft to 5 ft long; throughout Asia; reactions and mortality vary, but most bites cause tissue damage, and mortality is generally low.

Australian brown snake — 4 ft to 7 ft long; very slow onset of cardiac or respiratory distress; moderate mortality, but because death can be sudden and unexpected, it is the most dangerous of the Australian snakes; antivenom.

Barba Amarilla or fer-de-lance — up to 7 ft long; from tropical Mexico to Brazil; severe tissue damage common; moderate mortality; antivenom.

Black mamba — up to 14 ft long, fast-moving; S and C Africa; rapid onset of dizziness, difficulty breathing, erratic heart-beat; mortality high, nears 100% without antivenom.

Boomslang — less than 6 ft long; in African savannahs; rapid onset of nausea and dizziness, often followed by slight recovery and then sudden death from internal hemorrhaging; bites rare, mortality high; antivenom.

Bushmaster — up to 12 ft long; wet tropical forests of C and S America; few bites occur, but mortality rate is high.

Common or Asian cobra — 4 ft to 8 ft long; throughout southern Asia; considerable tissue damage, sometimes paralysis; mortality probably not more than 10%; antivenom.

Copperhead — less than 4 ft long; from New England to Texas; pain and swelling; very seldom fatal; antivenom seldom needed.

Coral snake — 2 ft to 5 ft long; in Americas south of Canada; bite may be painless; slow onset of paralysis, impaired breathing; mortalities rare, but high without antivenom and mechanical respiration.

Cottonmouth water moccasin — up to 5 ft long; wetlands of southern U.S. from Virginia to Texas. Rapid onset of severe pain, swelling; mortality low, but tissue destruction can be extensive; antivenom.

Death adder — less than 3 ft long; Australia; rapid onset of faintness, cardiac and respiratory distress; at least 50% mortality without antivenom.

Desert horned viper — in dry areas of Africa and western Asia; swelling and tissue damage; low mortality; antivenom.

European viper — 1 ft to 3 ft long; bleeding and tissue damage; mortality low; antivenom.

Gaboon viper — more than 6 ft long; fat; 2-in. fangs; south of the Sahara; massive tissue damage, internal bleeding; few recorded bites.

King cobra — up to 16 ft long; throughout southern Asia; rapid swelling, dizziness, loss of consciousness, difficulty breathing, erratic heartbeat; mortality varies sharply with amount of venom involved, but most bites involve nonfatal amounts; antivenom.

Krait — up to 5 ft long; in SE Asia; rapid onset of sleepiness; numbness; up to 50% mortality even with use of antivenom.

Puff adder — up to 5 ft long; fat; south of the Sahara and throughout the Middle East; rapid large swelling, great pain, dizziness; moderate mortality, often from internal bleeding; antivenom.

Rattlesnake — 2 ft to 6 ft long; throughout W Hemisphere; rapid onset of severe pain, swelling; mortality low, but amputation of affected digits is sometimes necessary; antivenom. Mojave rattler may produce temporary paralysis.

Ringhals, or spitting, cobra — 5 ft to 7 ft long; southern Africa; squirts venom through holes in front of fangs as a defense; venom is severely irritating, can cause blindness.

Russell's viper or tic-polonga — more than 5 ft long; throughout Asia; internal bleeding; bite reports common; moderate mortality rate; antivenom.

Saw-scaled or carpet viper — as much as 2 ft long; in dry areas from India to Africa; severe bleeding, fever; high mortality, causes more human fatalities than any other snake; antivenom.

Sea snakes — throughout Pacific, Indian oceans except NE Pacific; almost painless bite, variety of muscle pain, paralysis; mortality rate low, many bites not envenomed; some antivenoms.

Sharp-nosed pit viper or one hundred pace snake — up to 5 ft long; in S Vietnam, Taiwan, and China; the most toxic of Asian pit vipers; very rapid onset of swelling and tissue damage, internal bleeding; moderate mortality; antivenom.

Taipan — up to 11 ft long; in Australia and New Guinea; rapid paralysis with severe breathing difficulty; mortality nears 100% without antivenom.

Tiger snake — 2 ft to 6 ft long; S Australia; pain, numbness, mental disturbances with rapid paralysis; may be deadliest of all land snakes, but antivenom is quite effective.

Yellow or Cape cobra — 7 ft long; in S Africa; most toxic venom of any cobra; rapid onset of swelling, breathing and cardiac difficulties; mortality is high without treatment; antivenom.

Note: Not all bites by venomous snakes are actually envenomed. Any animal bite, however, carries the danger of tetanus, and anyone suffering a venomous snake bite should seek medical attention. Antivenoms do not cure; they are only an aid in the treatment of bites. Mortality rates above are for envenomed bites; low mortality, c. 2% or less; moderate, 2%-5%; high, 5%-15%.

Lizards

Gila monster — as much as 24 in. long, with heavy body and tail; in high desert in SW U.S. and N Mexico; immediate severe pain and transient low blood pressure; no recent mortality.

Mexican beaded lizard — similar to Gila monster, Mexican west coast; reaction and mortality rate similar to Gila monster.

Insects

Ants, bees, wasps, hornets, etc. Global distribution. Usual reaction is piercing pain in area of sting. Not directly fatal, except in cases of massive multiple stings. However, many people suffer allergic reactions — swelling and rashes — and a few may die within minutes from severe sensitivity to the venom (anaphylactic shock).

Spiders, Scorpions

Atrax spider — also known as funnel web spider; several varieties, often large; in Australia; slow onset of breathing, circulation difficulties; low mortality; antivenom.

Black widow — small, round-bodied with red hourglass marking; the widow and its relatives are found in tropical and temperate zones; severe musculoskeletal pain, weakness, breathing difficulty, convulsions; may be more serious in small children; low mortality; antivenom. The **redback** spider of Australia has the hourglass marking on its back, rather than on its front, but is otherwise identical to the black widow.

Brown recluse, or fiddleback, spider — small, oblong body; throughout U.S.; pain with later ulceration at place of bite; in severe cases fever, nausea, and stomach cramps; ulceration may last months; very low mortality.

Scorpion — crablike body with stinger in tail, various sizes, many varieties throughout tropical and subtropical areas; various symptoms may include severe pain spreading from the wound, numbness, severe agitation, cramps; severe reaction may include respiratory failure; low mortality, usually in children; antivenoms.

Tarantula — large, hairy spider found around the world; the American tarantula, and probably all other tarantulas, are harmless to humans, though their bite may cause some pain and swelling.

Sea Life

Cone-shell — mollusk in small, beautiful shell; in the S Pacific and Indian oceans; shoots barbs into victims; paralysis; low mortality.

Octopus — global distribution, usually in warm waters; all varieties produce venom, but only a few can cause death; rapid onset of paralysis with breathing difficulty.

Portuguese man-of-war — jellyfishlike, with tentacles up to 100 ft long; in most warm water areas; immediate severe pain; not directly fatal, though shock may cause death in rare cases.

Sea wasp — jellyfish, with tentacles up to 30 ft long, in the S Pacific; very rapid onset of circulatory problems; high mortality because of speed of toxic reaction; antivenom.

Stingray — several varieties of differing sizes; found in tropical and temperate seas and some fresh water; severe pain, rapid onset of nausea, vomiting, breathing difficulties; wound area may ulcerate, gangrene may appear; seldom fatal.

Stonefish — brownish fish that lies motionless as a rock on bottom in shallow water; throughout S Pacific and Indian oceans; extraordinary pain, rapid paralysis; low mortality; antivenom available, amount determined by number of puncture wounds; warm water relieves pain.

Speeds of Animals

Source: Natural History magazine. © American Museum of Natural History

ANIMAL	mph	ANIMAL	mph	ANIMAL	mph
Cheetah	70	Greyhound	39.35	Black mamba snake	20
Pronghorn antelope	61	Whippet	35.50	Six-lined race runner	
Wildebeest	50	Rabbit (domestic)	35	(lizard)	18
Lion	50	Mule deer	35	Wild turkey	15
Thomson's gazelle	50	Jackal	35	Squirrel	12
Quarterhorse	47.5	Reindeer	32	Pig (domestic)	11
Elk	45	Giraffe	32	Chicken	9
Cape hunting dog	45	White-tailed deer	30	Spider (Tegenaria	
Coyote	43	Wart hog	30	atrica)	1.17
Gray fox	42	Grizzly bear	30	Giant tortoise	0.17
Hyena	40	Cat (domestic)	30	Three-toed sloth	0.15
Zebra	40	Human	27.89	Garden snail	0.03
Mongolian wild ass	40	Elephant	25		

Note: Most of these measurements are for maximum speeds over approximate quarter-mile distances. Exceptions are the lion and elephant, whose speeds were clocked in the act of charging; the whippet, which was timed over a 200-yd course; the cheetah, timed over a 100-yd distance; humans timed over a 15-yard segment of a 100-yard run; and the black mamba, six-lined race runner, spider, giant tortoise, three-toed sloth, and garden snail, which were measured over various small distances.

Top 50 American Kennel Club Registrations

Source: American Kennel Club, New York, NY; covers (new) dogs registered during calendar year shown

Breed	2005 Rank	2005 Number registered	2004 Rank	2004 Number registered	Breed	2005 Rank	2005 Number registered	2004 Rank	2004 Number registered
Retrievers (Labrador)	1.	137,867	1.	146,714	Basset Hounds	27.	8,890	25.	9,815
Retrievers (Golden)	2.	48,509	2.	52,560	Spaniels (English Springer)	28.	8,749	28.	9,376
Yorkshire Terriers	3.	47,238	5.	43,527	Weimaraners	29.	8,623	29.	9,013
German Shepherd Dogs	4.	45,014	3.	46,054	Brittanys	30.	7,853	30.	8,152
Beagles	5.	42,592	4.	44,557	Cavalier King Charles Spaniels	31.	7,678	32.	7,101
Dachshunds	6.	38,566	6.	40,774	West Highland White Terriers	32.	7,597	31.	7,746
Boxers	7.	37,268	7.	37,744	Mastiffs	33.	6,799	33.	6,442
Poodles	8.	31,638	8.	32,673	Australian Shepherds	34.	6,221	34.	6,116
Shih Tzu	9.	28,087	9.	28,960	Papillons	35.	6,005	35.	6,020
Miniature Schnauzers	10.	24,144	11.	24,083	Collies	36.	5,098	36.	5,486
Chihuahuas	11.	23,575	10.	24,853	St. Bernards	37.	4,352	37.	4,491
Pugs	12.	22,064	12.	23,156	French Bulldogs	38.	4,210	49.	3,380
Bulldogs	13.	20,556	14.	19,396	Lhasa Apsos	39.	3,921	40.	4,316
Pomeranians	14.	19,511	13.	21,273	Scottish Terriers	40.	3,795	42.	3,855
Spaniels (Cocker)	15.	16,343	15.	18,556	Cairn Terriers	41.	3,739	43.	3,751
Rottweilers	16.	15,916	16.	17,502	Bullmastiffs	42.	3,668	47.	3,433
Boston Terriers	17.	15,852	17.	16,465	Havanese	43.	3,595	52.	2,950
Shetland Sheepdogs	18.	14,278	18.	15,608	Vizslas	44.	3,559	44.	3,616
Maltese	19.	13,676	19.	13,684	Chinese Shar-Pei	45.	3,544	41.	3,924
Pointers (German Shorthaired)	20.	13,273	20.	12,801	Newfoundlands	46.	3,493	45.	3,505
Doberman Pinschers	21.	11,662	22.	11,725	Bernese Mountain Dogs	47.	3,479	48.	3,431
Miniature Pinschers	22.	11,454	21.	12,702	Pekingese	48.	3,441	39.	4,335
Welsh Corgis (Pembroke)	23.	10,648	23.	11,232	Retrievers (Chesapeake Bay)	49.	3,332	46.	3,454
Great Danes	24.	9,640	27.	9,510	Bloodhounds	50.	3,112	50.	3,113
Siberian Huskies	25.	9,452	24.	10,569					
Bichons Frises	26.	9,184	26.	9,797					

Breed Registration for Top 10 Pedigreed Cats, 1979-2005

Source: The Cat Fanciers' Association, Manasquan, NJ; ranked by new registrations, 2005.

Breed	2005	2004	2000	1995	1990	1979	Breed	2005	2004	2000	1995	1990	1979
Persian	16,657	18,176	25,524	44,735	60,661	25,819	Birman	991	945	998	990	969	258
Maine Coon	3,932	4,162	4,539	4,332	2,727	401	American Shorthair	802	846	885	1,050	1,176	738
Exotic	3,006	2,838	2,094	1,610	1,311	289	Oriental	764	854	1,085	1,237	1,288	260
Siamese	1,445	1,621	2,131	3,025	3,860	3,607	Tonkinese	704	717	803	780	618	—
Abyssinian	1,344	1,462	1,683	2,469	2,702	1,524	TOTAL	NA	41,606	49,551	70,288	84,729	37,630
Ragdoll	1,215	981	—	—	—	—							

Trees of the U.S.

Source: American Forests, Washington, DC

Approximately 826 native and naturalized species of trees are grown in the U.S. The oldest living tree is believed to be a bristlecone pine tree in California named Methuselah, estimated to be 4,700 years old. The world's largest known living tree*, the General Sherman giant sequoia in California, weighs more than 6,167 tons—as much as 41 blue whales or 740 elephants. California naturalists in Septemberare reported finding three redwood trees topping 370 feet in height, including "Hyperion," estimated at 378.1 feet.

Listed here are 10 largest National Champion trees as listed by American Forests.

10 Largest National Champion Trees

Tree Type	Girth at 4.5 ft. (in.)	Height (ft.)	Crown Spread (ft.)	Total Points*	Location
Giant sequoia (Gen. Sherman tree)	1,020	274	107	1,321	Sequoia National Park, CA
Coast redwood	950	321	75	1,290	Jedidiah Smith State Park, CA
Coast redwood	895	307	83	1,223	Jedidiah Smith State Park, CA
Coast redwood	867	311	101	1,203	Prairie Creek State Park, CA
Western red cedar	761	159	45	931	Olympic National Park, WA
Sitka spruce	668	191	96	883	Olympic National Forest, WA
Sitka spruce	629	204	93	856	Kloochy Creek Park, OR
Douglas-fir	512	301	65	829	Jedidiah Smith State Park, CA
Douglas-fir	505	281	71	804	Olympic National Forest, WA
Common Baldcypress	644	83	85	762	Cat Island, LA

* American Forests uses a point system to determine the largest trees. The following calculation to determine a tree's total points: Trunk Circumference (in inches) + Height (in feet) + ¼ Average Crown Spread (in feet) = Total Points

> **IT'S A FACT:** A creature discovered in central Laos in 2005, nicknamed the Laotian rock rat, was hailed as a new species—until scientists discovered that it had been extinct for 11 million years. Comparisons of the new-found species to the fossil record, published in *Science* in March 2006, proved the squirrel-like rodent to be a member of the family *Diatomyidae*, which had been previously thought extinct. Researchers are now trying to calculate how many exist in order to determine whether or not the formerly-extinct species should be considered endangered.

METEOROLOGY

National Weather Service Watches and Warnings

Source: Natl. Weather Service, Natl. Oceanic and Atmospheric Admin.,
U.S. Dept. of Commerce; *Glossary of Meteorology,* American Meteorological Society

The **National Weather Service** issues watches, warnings, and advisories for specific geographic areas to alert people to the possibility or imminent arrival of various forms of severe weather. A severe thunderstorm or tornado watch is issued when a severe convective storm that usually covers a relatively small geographic area or moves in a narrow path is sufficiently intense to threaten life and/or property. Examples include thunderstorms with large hail, damaging winds, and tornadoes. Excessive localized convective rains are not classified as severe storms but are often the product of severe local storms. Such rainfall may result in phenomena that threaten life and property, such as flash floods. Lightning occurs with all thunderstorms and, along with flash floods, is a leading cause of storm deaths and injuries.

Severe Thunderstorm—a thunderstorm that produces a tornado, winds of at least 50 knots (58 mph), and/or hail at least ¾ inch in diameter. A *severe thunderstorm watch* is issued for an area where such storms are most likely to develop. A *severe thunderstorm warning* indicates that a severe thunderstorm has been sighted or indicated by radar.

Tornado—a violent rotating column of air, usually extending down from a cumulonimbus cloud, with circulation reaching the ground. A tornado nearly always starts as a funnel cloud and may be accompanied by a loud roaring noise. On a local scale, it is the most destructive of all atmospheric phenomena. Tornado paths range from a few feet to more than 100 mi long (avg. 5 mi) and from a few feet to more than 1 mile in diameter (avg. 220 yd). The average forward speed is 30 mph. Tornado watches and warnings follow the same criteria as those for thunderstorms.

Cyclone—an atmospheric circulation of winds rotating counterclockwise in the Northern Hemisphere and clockwise in the Southern Hemisphere. Tornadoes, hurricanes, and the lows shown on weather maps are all examples of cyclones of various size and intensity. Cyclones are usually accompanied by precipitation or stormy weather.

Subtropical Storm—a cyclone that develops over subtropical waters (N of 20° lat.) with one-minute sustained surface winds of 34 knots (39 mph) or more. It may form over warm or cold water and can develop into a tropical storm or a hurricane.

Tropical Storm—a cyclone that develops over tropical waters (23.5° N-23.5° S lat.), with one-minute sustained surface winds between 34 and 63 knots (39-73 mph). A *tropical storm watch* is issued when tropical storm conditions pose a threat to specified coastal areas within 36 hours. A *tropical storm warning* is issued when tropical storm conditions are expected in a specified coastal area in 24 hours or less.

Hurricane—a severe cyclone originating over tropical ocean waters and having one-minute sustained surface winds of 64 knots (74 mph) or higher. (West of the international date line, in the western Pacific, such storms are known as typhoons.) The hurricane-force winds form a circle or an oval, sometimes as wide as 300 mi in diameter. In the lower latitudes, hurricanes usually move west or northwest at 10 to 15 mph. When the center approaches 25° to 30° N lat., the direction of motion often changes to northeast, with increased forward speed. In the western Atlantic and eastern Pacific, hurricane season is June 1-Nov. 30. Hurricane watches and warnings follow the same criteria as those for tropical storms.

Winter Storm and Blizzard—A *winter storm watch* is issued when conditions are favorable for hazardous winter weather, such as heavy snow, sleet, or freezing rain. A *winter storm warning* is issued when hazardous winter weather conditions are imminent. A *blizzard warning* is issued for winter storm conditions with winds of 35 mph or higher and sufficient falling and/or blowing snow to frequently reduce visibility to less than ¼ mi for at least 3 hours.

Flood—Flooding takes many forms. *River flooding:* This occurs when rains, sometimes coupled with melting snow, fill river basins with too much water too quickly. Torrential rains from decaying hurricanes or tropical systems can also be a major cause of river flooding. *Coastal flooding:* Winds from tropical storms and hurricanes or intense offshore low pressure systems can drive ocean water inland and cause significant flooding. Coastal floods can also be produced by sea waves called tsunamis, sometimes referred to as tidal waves. These waves are produced by earthquakes or volcanic activity. *Flash flooding:* Usually due to copious amounts of rain falling in a short time, flash flooding typically occurs within 6 hours of the rain event. Flash floods account for the majority of flood deaths in the U.S. and are the leading cause of deaths associated with thunderstorms. *Urban flooding:* Urbanization significantly increases runoff over what would occur on natural terrain, making flash flooding in these areas extremely dangerous. Streets can become swift-moving rivers, and basements can fill with water. *Ice jam flooding:* Ice can accumulate at natural or artificial obstructions and stop the flow of water. As the water flow is stopped, water builds up, and flooding can occur upstream. If the jam suddenly gives way, the gush of ice and water can cause downstream flash flooding.

A *flash flood watch* or *flood watch* means that flash flooding or flooding is possible within a designated area. A *flash flood warning* or *flood warning* means that flash flooding or flooding has been reported or is imminent. All necessary precautions should be taken immediately.

National Weather Service Marine Warnings and Advisories

Small Craft Advisory—alerts mariners to sustained (exceeds 2 hours) weather and/or sea conditions, present or forecast, potentially hazardous to small boats, including winds 18-33 knots and/or dangerous wave conditions. The advisory is also issued for lower wind speeds that may affect small craft. Criteria vary depending on region and type of marine environment. Upon receiving a small craft advisory, the mariner should immediately obtain the latest marine forecast for details.

Gale Warning—indicates that winds of 34-47 knots, not directly associated with a tropical storm, are forecast for the area.

Tropical Storm Warning—indicates that winds 34-63 knots associated with a tropical storm are forecast to occur within 24 hours or less.

Storm Warning—indicates that winds 48 knots or above, not directly associated with a tropical storm, are forecast for the area.

Hurricane Warning—indicates that winds 64 knots or greater associated with a hurricane are forecast for the area within 24 hours.

Special Marine Warning—indicates potentially hazardous weather conditions, usually of short duration (2 hours or less) and producing wind speeds of 34 knots or more, not adequately covered by existing marine warnings.

Primary sources of dissemination are commercial radio, TV, U.S. Coast Guard radio stations, and NOAA VHF-FM broadcasts. These NOAA broadcasts on 162.40 to 162.55 MHz can usually be received 20-40 mi from the transmitting antenna site.

> ▶ *IT'S A FACT:* On Aug. 6, 2000, the English port town of Great Yarmouth experienced an unusual downpour: sprats (a small fish of the herring family). The British Meteorological Office confirmed that the shower of fish was caused by a small tornado at sea that drew up the fish along with seawater.

Monthly Normal Mean Temperatures, Normal Precipitation, U.S. Cities

Source: Natl. Climatic Data Center, NESDIS, NOAA, U.S. Dept. of Commerce

Normals are averages covering a 30-year period. The temperature and precipitation normals given here are based on records for 1971-2000. Temperatures listed below represent means of the normal daily maximum and normal daily minimum temperatures for each month. For stations that did not have continuous records from the same site for the entire 30 years, the means have been adjusted to the record at the present site. (*) = city station. Other figures are for airport stations. T = temp. in Fahrenheit; P = precipitation in inches.

	Jan.		Feb.		Mar.		Apr.		May		June		July		Aug.		Sept.		Oct.		Nov.		Dec.	
Station	T	P	T	P	T	P	T	P	T	P	T	P	T	P	T	P	T	P	T	P	T	P	T	P
Albany, NY	22	2.7	25	2.3	35	3.2	47	3.3	58	3.7	66	3.7	71	3.5	69	3.7	61	3.3	49	3.2	39	3.3	28	2.8
Albuquerque, NM	36	0.5	41	0.4	48	0.6	56	0.5	65	0.6	75	0.7	79	1.3	76	1.7	69	1.1	57	1.0	44	0.6	36	0.5
Anchorage, AK	16	0.7	19	0.7	26	0.7	36	0.5	47	0.7	55	1.1	58	1.7	56	2.9	48	2.9	34	2.1	22	1.1	18	1.1
Asheville, NC	36	3.1	39	3.2	46	3.9	54	3.2	62	3.5	69	3.2	73	3.0	72	3.3	66	3.0	55	2.4	46	2.9	39	2.6
Atlanta, GA	43	5.0	47	4.7	54	5.4	62	3.6	70	4.0	77	3.6	80	5.1	79	3.7	73	4.1	63	3.1	53	4.1	45	3.8
Atlantic City, NJ	32	3.6	34	2.9	42	4.1	51	3.5	61	3.4	70	2.7	75	3.9	74	4.3	66	3.1	55	2.9	46	3.3	37	3.2
Baltimore, MD	32	3.5	36	3.0	44	3.9	53	3.0	63	3.9	72	3.4	77	3.9	75	3.7	67	4.0	55	3.2	46	3.1	37	3.4
Barrow, AK	–14	0.1	–16	0.1	–14	0.1	–1	0.1	20	0.1	35	0.3	40	0.9	39	1.0	31	0.7	15	0.4	–1	0.2	–11	0.1
Birmingham, AL	43	5.5	47	4.2	55	6.1	61	4.7	69	4.8	76	3.8	80	5.1	80	3.5	74	4.1	63	3.2	53	4.6	46	4.5
Bismarck, ND	10	0.5	18	0.5	30	0.9	43	1.5	56	2.2	65	2.6	70	2.6	69	2.2	58	1.6	45	1.3	28	0.7	15	0.4
Boise, ID	30	1.4	37	1.1	44	1.4	51	1.3	59	1.3	67	0.7	75	0.4	74	0.3	64	0.8	53	0.8	40	1.4	31	1.4
Boston, MA	29	3.9	32	3.3	39	3.9	48	3.6	59	3.2	68	3.2	74	3.1	72	3.4	65	3.5	54	3.8	45	4.0	35	3.7
Buffalo, NY	25	3.2	26	2.4	34	3.0	45	3.0	57	3.4	66	3.8	71	3.1	69	3.9	62	3.8	51	3.2	40	3.9	30	3.8
Burlington, VT	18	2.2	20	1.7	31	2.3	44	2.9	57	3.3	66	3.4	71	4.0	68	4.0	59	3.8	48	3.1	37	3.1	25	2.2
Caribou, ME	10	3.0	13	2.1	25	2.6	38	2.6	52	3.3	61	3.3	66	3.9	63	4.2	54	3.3	43	3.0	31	3.1	16	3.2
Charleston, SC	48	4.1	51	3.1	58	4.0	64	2.8	72	3.7	78	5.9	82	6.1	81	6.9	76	6.0	66	3.1	58	2.7	51	3.2
Charleston, WV	33	3.3	37	3.2	45	3.9	54	3.3	62	4.3	70	4.1	74	4.9	73	4.1	66	3.5	55	2.7	46	3.7	38	3.3
Chicago, IL	22	1.8	27	1.6	37	2.7	48	3.7	59	3.4	68	3.6	73	3.5	72	4.6	64	3.3	52	2.7	39	3.0	27	2.4
Cleveland, OH	26	2.5	28	2.3	38	2.9	48	3.4	59	3.5	68	3.9	72	3.5	70	3.7	63	3.8	52	2.7	42	3.4	31	3.1
Columbus, OH	28	2.5	32	2.2	42	2.9	52	3.3	63	3.9	71	4.1	75	4.6	74	3.7	67	2.9	55	2.3	44	3.2	34	2.9
Dallas–Ft. Worth, TX	44	1.9	49	2.4	57	3.1	65	3.2	73	5.2	81	3.2	85	2.1	84	2.0	78	2.4	67	4.1	55	2.6	47	2.6
Denver, CO	29	0.5	33	0.5	40	1.3	48	1.9	57	2.3	68	1.6	73	2.2	72	1.8	62	1.1	51	1.0	38	1.0	30	0.6
Des Moines, IA	20	1.0	27	1.2	38	2.2	51	3.6	62	4.3	71	4.6	76	4.2	74	4.5	65	3.2	53	2.6	38	2.1	25	1.3
Detroit, MI	25	1.9	27	1.9	37	2.5	48	3.1	60	3.1	69	3.6	74	3.2	72	3.1	64	3.3	52	2.2	41	2.7	30	2.5
Dodge City, KS	30	0.6	36	0.7	44	1.8	54	2.3	64	3.0	74	3.2	80	3.2	78	2.7	69	1.7	57	1.5	42	1.0	33	0.8
Duluth, MN	8	1.1	15	0.8	25	1.7	39	2.1	52	3.0	60	4.3	66	4.2	64	4.2	55	4.1	44	2.5	28	2.1	14	0.9
Fairbanks, AK	–10	0.6	–4	0.4	11	0.3	32	0.2	49	0.6	60	1.4	62	1.7	56	1.7	45	1.1	24	1.0	2	0.7	–6	0.7
Fresno, CA	46	2.2	51	2.1	56	2.2	61	0.8	69	0.4	76	0.2	81	0.0	80	0.0	75	0.3	65	0.7	53	1.1	45	1.3
Galveston, TX*	56	4.1	58	2.6	64	2.8	70	2.6	77	3.7	82	4.0	84	3.5	84	4.2	81	5.8	74	3.5	65	3.6	58	3.5
Grand Rapids, MI	22	2.0	25	1.5	35	2.6	46	3.5	58	3.4	67	3.7	71	3.6	69	3.8	61	4.3	50	2.8	38	3.4	28	2.7
Hartford, CT	26	3.8	29	3.0	38	3.9	49	3.9	60	4.4	69	3.9	74	3.7	72	4.0	63	4.1	52	3.9	42	4.1	31	3.6
Helena, MT	20	0.5	26	0.4	35	0.6	44	0.9	53	1.8	61	1.8	68	1.3	67	1.3	56	1.1	45	0.7	31	0.5	21	0.5
Honolulu, HI	73	2.7	73	2.4	74	1.9	76	1.1	77	0.8	80	0.4	81	0.5	82	0.5	82	0.7	80	2.2	78	2.3	75	2.9
Houston, TX	52	3.7	55	3.0	62	3.4	69	3.6	76	5.2	81	5.4	84	3.2	83	3.8	79	4.3	70	4.5	61	4.2	54	3.7
Huron, SD	14	0.5	21	0.6	33	1.7	46	2.3	58	3.0	68	3.3	73	2.9	72	2.1	61	1.8	48	1.6	31	0.9	19	0.4
Indianapolis, IN	27	2.5	31	2.4	42	3.4	52	3.6	63	4.4	72	4.1	75	4.4	74	3.8	66	2.9	55	2.8	43	3.6	32	3.0
Jackson, MS	45	5.7	49	4.5	57	5.7	63	6.0	72	4.9	79	3.8	81	4.7	81	3.7	76	3.2	64	3.4	55	5.0	48	5.3
Jacksonville, FL	53	3.7	56	3.2	62	3.9	67	3.1	73	3.5	79	5.4	82	6.0	81	6.9	78	7.9	69	3.9	62	2.3	55	2.6
Juneau, AK	26	4.8	29	4.0	34	3.5	41	3.0	48	3.5	54	3.4	57	4.1	56	5.4	50	7.6	42	8.3	33	5.4	29	5.4
Kansas City, MO	27	1.2	33	1.3	44	2.4	54	3.4	64	5.4	74	4.4	79	4.4	77	3.5	68	4.6	57	3.3	43	2.3	31	1.6
Knoxville, TN	38	4.6	42	4.0	50	5.2	58	4.0	66	4.7	74	4.0	78	4.7	77	2.9	71	3.0	59	2.7	49	4.0	41	4.5
Lander, WY	20	0.5	26	0.5	36	1.2	44	2.1	53	2.4	64	1.2	71	0.8	69	0.6	59	1.1	46	1.4	30	1.0	21	0.6
Lexington, KY	32	3.3	36	3.3	46	4.4	55	3.7	64	4.8	72	4.6	76	4.8	75	3.8	68	3.1	57	2.7	46	3.4	36	4.0
Little Rock, AR	40	3.6	45	3.3	53	4.9	61	5.5	70	5.1	78	4.0	82	3.3	81	2.9	74	3.7	63	4.3	52	5.7	43	4.7
Los Angeles, CA*	57	3.0	58	3.1	58	2.4	61	0.6	63	0.2	66	0.1	69	0.0	71	0.1	70	0.3	67	0.4	62	1.1	58	1.8
Louisville, KY	33	3.3	38	3.3	47	4.4	56	3.9	66	4.9	74	3.8	78	4.3	77	3.4	70	3.1	59	2.8	48	3.8	38	3.7
Marquette, MI*	12	2.6	15	1.9	24	3.1	36	2.8	50	3.1	59	3.2	64	3.0	62	3.6	54	3.7	43	3.7	29	3.3	17	2.4
Memphis, TN	40	4.2	45	4.3	54	5.6	62	5.8	71	5.2	79	4.3	83	4.2	81	3.0	75	3.3	64	3.3	52	5.8	43	5.7
Miami, FL	68	1.9	69	2.1	72	2.6	76	3.4	80	5.5	82	8.5	84	5.8	84	8.6	82	8.4	79	6.2	74	3.4	70	2.2
Milwaukee, WI	21	1.9	25	1.7	35	2.6	45	3.8	56	3.1	66	3.6	72	3.6	71	4.0	63	3.3	51	2.5	38	2.7	26	2.2
Minneapolis, MN	13	1.0	20	0.8	32	1.9	47	2.3	59	3.2	68	4.3	73	4.0	71	4.1	61	2.7	49	2.1	33	1.9	19	1.0
Mobile, AL	61	5.8	65	5.1	71	7.2	77	5.1	84	6.1	89	5.0	91	6.5	91	6.2	87	6.0	79	3.3	70	5.4	63	4.7
Moline, IL	21	1.6	27	1.5	39	2.9	51	3.8	62	4.3	71	4.6	75	4.0	73	4.4	65	3.2	53	2.8	39	2.7	26	2.2
Nashua, NH	23	3.9	26	3.1	35	4.1	46	3.9	57	3.7	66	3.9	71	3.7	69	3.8	61	3.6	49	3.9	39	4.2	28	3.7
Nashville, TN	37	4.0	41	3.7	50	4.9	59	3.9	67	5.1	75	4.1	79	3.8	78	3.3	71	3.6	60	2.9	49	4.5	41	4.5
Newark, NJ	31	4.0	34	3.0	42	4.2	52	3.9	63	4.5	72	3.4	77	4.7	76	4.0	68	4.0	56	3.2	46	3.9	36	3.6
New Orleans, LA	53	5.9	56	5.5	62	5.2	68	5.0	76	4.6	81	6.8	83	6.2	83	6.2	79	5.6	70	3.1	61	5.1	55	5.1
New York, NY*	33	3.6	35	2.8	42	3.9	52	3.7	62	4.2	72	3.6	77	4.4	76	4.1	69	3.8	58	3.3	48	3.7	38	3.5
Norfolk, VA	40	3.9	42	3.3	49	4.1	57	3.4	66	3.7	75	3.8	79	5.2	77	4.8	72	4.1	61	3.5	52	3.0	44	3.0
Oklahoma City, OK	37	1.3	42	1.6	51	2.9	60	3.0	68	5.4	77	4.6	82	2.9	81	2.5	73	4.0	62	3.6	49	2.1	40	1.9
Omaha, NE	22	0.8	28	0.8	39	2.1	51	2.9	62	4.4	72	4.0	77	3.9	75	3.2	65	3.2	53	2.2	38	1.8	26	0.9
Philadelphia, PA	32	3.5	35	2.7	43	3.8	53	3.5	64	3.9	72	3.3	78	4.4	76	3.8	69	3.9	57	2.8	47	3.2	37	3.3
Phoenix, AZ	54	0.8	58	0.8	63	1.1	70	0.3	79	0.2	89	0.1	93	1.0	91	0.9	86	0.8	75	0.8	62	0.7	54	0.9
Pittsburgh, PA	28	2.7	31	2.4	40	3.2	50	3.0	60	3.8	68	4.1	73	4.0	71	3.4	64	3.2	53	2.3	42	3.0	33	2.9
Portland, ME	22	4.1	25	3.1	34	4.1	44	4.3	54	3.8	63	3.3	69	3.3	67	3.1	59	3.4	48	4.4	38	4.7	28	4.2
Portland, OR	40	5.1	43	4.2	47	3.7	51	2.6	57	2.4	63	1.6	68	0.7	69	0.9	64	1.7	54	2.9	46	5.6	40	5.7
Providence, RI	29	4.4	31	3.5	39	4.4	49	4.2	59	3.7	68	3.4	73	3.2	72	3.9	64	3.7	53	3.7	44	4.4	34	4.1
Raleigh, NC	40	4.0	43	3.5	51	4.0	59	2.8	67	3.8	75	3.4	79	4.3	77	3.8	71	4.3	60	3.2	51	3.0	43	3.0
Rapid City, SD	22	0.4	27	0.5	35	1.0	45	1.9	55	3.0	65	2.8	72	2.0	71	1.6	61	1.1	48	1.4	33	0.6	25	0.4
Reno, NV	34	1.1	39	1.1	43	0.9	49	0.4	56	0.6	65	0.5	71	0.2	70	0.3	62	0.5	52	0.4	41	0.8	34	0.9
Richmond, VA	36	3.6	40	3.0	48	4.1	57	3.2	65	4.0	74	3.5	78	4.7	76	4.2	70	4.0	58	3.6	49	3.1	40	3.1
St. Louis, MO	30	2.1	35	2.3	46	3.6	57	3.7	67	4.1	77	3.8	80	3.9	78	3.0	70	3.0	58	2.8	45	3.7	34	2.9
Salt Lake City, UT	29	1.4	35	1.3	43	1.9	50	2.0	59	2.1	69	0.8	77	0.7	76	0.8	65	1.3	53	1.6	40	1.4	30	1.2
San Antonio, TX	51	1.7	55	1.8	63	1.9	69	2.6	76	4.7	81	4.3	84	2.0	84	2.6	79	3.0	71	3.9	60	2.6	53	2.0
San Diego, CA	58	2.3	59	2.0	60	2.3	63	0.8	65	0.2	67	0.1	71	0.0	73	0.1	72	0.2	68	0.4	62	1.1	58	1.3
San Francisco, CA	49	4.5	52	4.0	54	3.3	56	1.2	59	0.4	61	0.1	63	0.0	64	0.1	64	0.2	61	1.0	55	2.5	50	2.9
San Juan, PR	77	3.0	77	2.3	78	2.1	79	3.7	81	5.3	82	3.5	82	4.2	82	5.2	82	5.6	82	5.1	80	6.2	78	4.6
Santa Fe, NM	29	0.6	35	0.5	41	0.8	48	0.7	57	1.3	66	1.2	70	2.3	68	2.1	62	1.7	51	1.3	38	1.1	30	0.7
Savannah, GA	49	4.0	53	2.9	59	3.6	65	3.3	73	3.6	79	5.5	82	6.0	81	7.2	77	5.1	67	3.1	59	2.4	51	2.8
Seattle, WA	41	5.1	43	4.2	46	3.8	50	2.6	56	1.8	61	1.5	65	0.8	66	1.0	61	1.6	53	3.2	45	5.9	41	5.6
Spokane, WA	27	1.8	33	1.5	40	1.5	47	1.3	54	1.6	62	1.2	69	0.8	69	0.7	59	0.8	47	1.1	35	2.2	27	2.3
Springfield, MO	32	2.1	37	2.3	46	3.8	56	4.3	65	4.6	73	5.0	79	3.6	78	3.4	69	4.8	58	3.5	46	4.5	36	3.2
Tampa, FL	61	2.3	63	2.7	67	2.9	72	1.8	78	2.9	82	5.5	83	6.5	83	7.6	82	6.5	76	2.3	69	1.6	63	2.3
Washington, DC	34	3.6	36	2.8	44	3.9	54	3.3	64	4.3	73	3.6	78	4.2	76	3.9	69	4.1	57	3.4	47	3.3	38	3.2
Wilmington, DE	32	3.4	34	2.8	43	4.0	52	3.4	63	4.1	72	4.0	77	4.3	75	3.5	68	4.0	56	3.0	46	3.2	36	3.4

Normal High and Low Temperatures, Precipitation, U.S. Cities

Source: Natl. Climatic Data Center, NESDIS, NOAA, U.S. Dept. of Commerce

The **normal** temperatures and precipitation data given here are based on records for the period 1971-2000. The **extreme** temperatures are based on records from time of each station's installation. (*) = city station. Other figures are for airport stations. Temperatures are Fahrenheit.

State	Station	NORMAL TEMPERATURE January Max.	January Min.	July Max.	July Min.	EXTREME TEMPERATURE Highest	Lowest	AVG. ANNUAL PRECIPITATION (inches)
Alabama	Mobile	61	40	91	72	105	3	66.29
Alaska	Anchorage	22	9	65	52	85	−34	16.08
Alaska	Barrow	−8	−20	47	34	79	−56	4.16
Alaska	Juneau	31	21	64	49	90	−22	58.33
Arizona	Phoenix	65	43	104	81	122	17	8.29
Arkansas	North Little Rock	49	31	94	73	111	−6	49.19
California	Los Angeles*	66	49	75	63	110	23	13.15
California	San Francisco	56	43	71	55	106	20	20.11
Colorado	Denver	43	15	88	59	101	−19	15.81
Connecticut	Hartford	34	17	85	62	102	−26	46.16
Delaware	Wilmington	39	24	86	67	102	−14	42.81
District of Columbia	Washington–National	43	27	89	67	105	−5	39.35
Florida	Jacksonville	64	42	91	72	105	7	52.34
Florida	Miami	77	60	91	77	98	30	58.53
Georgia	Atlanta	52	34	89	71	105	−8	50.20
Georgia	Savannah	60	38	92	72	105	3	49.58
Hawaii	Honolulu	80	66	88	74	95	53	18.29
Idaho	Boise	37	24	89	60	111	−25	12.19
Illinois	Chicago	30	14	84	63	104	−27	36.27
Indiana	Indianapolis	35	19	86	65	104	−27	40.95
Iowa	Des Moines	29	12	86	66	108	−26	34.72
Kansas	Dodge City	41	19	93	67	110	−21	22.35
Kentucky	Lexington	40	24	86	66	103	−21	45.91
Kentucky	Louisville	41	25	87	70	106	−22	44.54
Louisiana	New Orleans	62	43	91	74	102	11	64.16
Maine	Caribou	19	0	76	55	96	−41	37.44
Maine	Portland	31	13	79	59	103	−39	45.83
Maryland	Baltimore	41	24	87	66	105	−7	41.94
Massachusetts	Boston	37	22	82	66	102	−12	42.53
Michigan	Detroit	31	18	83	64	104	−21	32.89
Michigan	Grand Rapids	29	16	82	61	100	−22	37.13
Michigan	Sault Ste. Marie*	22	5	76	52	98	−36	34.67
Minnesota	Duluth	18	−1	76	55	97	−39	31.00
Minnesota	Minneapolis-St. Paul	22	4	83	63	105	−34	29.41
Mississippi	Jackson	55	35	91	71	107	2	55.95
Missouri	Kansas City	36	18	89	68	109	−23	37.98
Missouri	St. Louis	38	21	90	71	107	−18	38.75
Montana	Helena	31	10	83	52	105	−42	11.32
Nebraska	Omaha	32	12	87	66	114	−23	30.22
Nevada	Reno	46	22	91	51	108	−16	7.48
New Hampshire	Concord	31	10	83	57	102	−37	37.60
New Jersey	Atlantic City	41	23	85	65	106	−11	40.59
New Mexico	Albuquerque	48	24	92	65	107	−17	9.47
New York	Albany	31	13	82	60	100	−28	38.60
New York	Buffalo	31	18	80	62	99	−20	40.54
New York	New York–Central Park*	38	26	84	69	106	−15	49.69
North Carolina	Raleigh	50	30	89	69	105	−9	43.05
North Dakota	Bismarck	21	−1	85	56	111	−44	16.84
Ohio	Cleveland	33	19	81	62	104	−20	38.71
Ohio	Columbus	36	20	85	65	102	−22	38.52
Oklahoma	Oklahoma City	47	26	93	71	110	−8	35.85
Oregon	Portland	46	34	79	57	107	−3	37.07
Pennsylvania	Philadelphia	39	26	86	70	104	−7	42.05
Pennsylvania	Pittsburgh	35	20	83	62	103	−22	37.85
Puerto Rico	San Juan	82	71	87	77	98	46	50.76
Rhode Island	Providence	37	20	83	64	104	−13	46.45
South Carolina	Charleston	59	37	91	73	105	6	51.53
South Dakota	Huron	25	4	86	61	112	−41	20.90
South Dakota	Rapid City	34	11	86	58	110	−31	16.64
Tennessee	Memphis	49	31	92	73	108	−13	54.65
Tennessee	Nashville	46	28	89	70	107	−17	48.11
Texas	Dallas-Fort Worth	54	34	95	75	109	17	34.73
Texas	Houston	62	41	94	74	109	17	47.84
Utah	Salt Lake City	37	21	91	63	107	−30	16.50
Vermont	Burlington	27	9	81	60	101	−30	36.05
Virginia	Norfolk	48	32	87	71	104	−3	45.74
Virginia	Richmond	45	28	88	68	105	−12	43.91
Washington	Seattle-Tacoma	46	36	75	55	100	0	37.07
Washington	Spokane	33	22	83	55	108	−25	16.67
West Virginia	Charleston	43	24	85	63	104	−16	44.05
Wisconsin	Milwaukee	28	13	81	63	103	−26	34.81
Wyoming	Lander	32	9	86	55	101	−37	13.42

Mean Annual Snowfall (inches): based on climate normals 1971-2000: Boston, MA, 41.8; Sault Ste. Marie, MI, 132.6; Albany, NY, 62.7; Burlington, VT, 83.1; Lander, WY, 102.9; Anchorage, AK, 69.5.

Wettest Spot: Mount Waialeale, HI, on the island of Kauai, is the rainiest place in the world and in the U.S., according to the National Geographic Society; it has an average annual rainfall of 460 ins.

Temperature Extremes: A temperature of 136° F observed at El Azizia (Al Aziziyah), near Tripoli, Libya, on Sept. 13, 1922, is generally accepted as the world's highest temperature recorded under standard conditions. The record high in the U.S. was 134° F in Death Valley, CA, July 10, 1913. A record low of −129° F was recorded at the Soviet Antarctica station of Vostok on July 21, 1983. The record low in the U.S. was −80° F at Prospect Creek, AK, Jan. 23, 1971.

Annual Climatological Data for U.S. Cities, 2005

Source: Natl. Climatic Data Center, NESDIS, NOAA, U.S. Dept. of Commerce

Station	Elev. (ft)	Temperature °F Highest	Date	Lowest	Date	Precipitation[1] Total (in.)	Greatest in 24 hrs (in.)	Date	Sleet or snow Total (in.)	Greatest in 24 hrs (in.)	Date	Fastest[2] wind MPH	Date	No. of days Prec. .01 in. or more	Snow, sleet 1" or more
Albany, NY	278	94	6/26	−16	1/28	47.72	2.70	10/8-9	75.4	10.7	3/1	38	6/06	142	18
Albuquerque, NM	5,305	99	7/19+	9	12/8	11.42	1.53	9/28-29	5.6	3.3	3/14	45	10/5	61	1
Anchorage, AK	130	77	8/12	−8	2/5+	15.91	1.18	9/6	62.3	7.2	2/10	37	4/22	118	16
Asheville, NC	2,171	93	7/26	8	1/24	47.26	3.22	6/26-27	6.0	3.2	2/28	46	4/3	126	2
Atlanta, GA	971	94	8/21	16	1/24	56.43	6.73	7/10-11	0.5	0.5	1/29	43	7/6	118	—
Atlantic City, NJ	114	99	7/27	3	1/28	43.95	2.24	10/12-13	18.6	4.9	2/24	41	4/2	123	6
Baltimore, MD	193	96	7/27	9	1/24	49.13	5.98	10/7-8	24.5	5.2	2/24	38	11/24	106	8
Barrow, AK	35	67	8/14	−38	1/16	4.86	0.89	8/8-9	41.9	3.1	12/25	43	9/22	82	14
Birmingham, AL	636	97	8/21	18	1/24	49.20	2.56	5/29-30	T	T	4/22	36	8/29	112	0
Bismarck, ND	1,651	100	7/19+	−27	1/16+	19.22	2.79	6/7	29.7	5.2	12/29-30	47	6/1	93	10
Boise, ID	2,858	107	7/21	7	12/8	13.66	0.88	5/5	9.0	2.6	12/1	36	9/16	90	3
Boston, MA	19	97	8/5	−2	1/28	43.67	3.69	10/14-15	87.3	13.4	1/23	44	10/25	135	19
Buffalo, NY	714	95	7/27	−6	1/28	39.07	3.00	8/30-31	124.3	10.2	11/25	59	9/29	147	43
Burlington, VT	345	93	6/27	−17	1/22	39.41	2.44	8/30-31	91.6	8.0	2/10	36	1/2	148	27
Caribou, ME	627	90	7/19	−20	2/21	54.31	2.83	10/15-16	158.1	20.7	12/26	37	5/12	163	37
Charleston, SC	45	100	7/27	18	1/24	46.16	3.03	8/23-24	T	T	1/29	40	3/18	116	0
Chicago, IL	655	102	7/24	−1	12/19	24.09	1.35	8/20	46.0	6.7	12/8	48	7/25	117	15
Cleveland, OH	802	95	7/26	0	1/28	39.87	3.55	8/20	108.4	9.1	1/16	43	11/6	159	31
Columbus, OH	846	97	8/13	−1	1/24	40.26	2.88	8/30-31	35.5	3.0	4/24	41	6/29	149	15
Dallas-Ft. Worth, TX	559	104	9/28	15	12/9	18.97	2.03	1/2-3	—	—	—	43	9/28	60	—
Denver, CO	5,379	105	7/20	−13	12/7	12.79	1.42	10/9-10	—	—	—	54	12/29	74	—
Des Moines, IA	968	98	7/23	−8	12/7	28.05	2.39	5/12-13	33.3	8.0	1/5	47	11/12	105	10
Detroit, MI	628	95	6/25	−2	1/28+	28.30	2.30	11/15	75.3	12.2	1/22	46	11/6	120	23
Duluth, MN	1,426	92	7/17	−28	1/17	32.39	2.82	10/3-4	118.8	13.2	12/14	43	6/8	134	27
Fairbanks, AK	461	84	8/13	−47	1/12	11.80	1.04	7/17-18	57.2	4.2	1/5	32	3/21+	116	22
Fresno, CA	372	109	7/16	33	12/5	11.68	1.02	5/5	—	—	—	38	1/7	61	—
Grand Rapids, MI	785	94	7/24	−9	1/27+	36.53	2.23	6/13	104.5	12.3	1/22	44	11/13	147	34
Hartford, CT	162	97	8/13	−8	1/29	57.12	5.81	10/14-15	82.9	10.5	12/9	39	8/5	133	23
Helena, MT	3,864	100	8/6	−25	1/15	12.16	1.46	6/1	32.9	5.2	1/12	46	7/22	95	10
Honolulu, HI	15	93	9/3+	71.9	3/16	15.60	1.95	1/29	—	—	—	32	3/15	90	—
Houston, TX	118	101	7/6+	3	2/26	41.21	5.64	12/14	T	T	1/31	45	9/24	87	0
Huron, SD	1,281	109	7/23	−25	1/14	25.78	3.46	11/27-28	37.8	14.8	11/28	53	7/19	96	10
Indianapolis, IN	794	95	7/25	−2	1/18	43.73	3.10	6/12-13	29.3	7.7	12/8	46	11/6	122	10
Jackson, MS	293	101	8/21	21	1/24	52.17	4.10	8/29-30	—	—	—	47	8/29	97	—
Jacksonville, FL	31	97	7/22	23	1/24	64.45	5.96	6/29-30	—	—	—	35	11/21	125	—
Kansas City, MO	1,005	99	8/3	−5	12/9	44.14	3.84	8/12-13	17.6	7.3	12/7	40	7/3	97	6
Knoxville, TN	979	95	8/5	11	1/24	38.43	2.54	7/6-7	0.4	0.4	3/1	46	7/27	124	0
Lander, WY	5,557	101	7/13	−18	12/8	12.09	2.17	5/10-11	75.2	9.2	4/19	48	3/28	59	20
Lexington, KY	977	98	8/12	6	1/23	33.52	2.06	8/30-31	6.0	1.3	1/22	39	11/28	125	2
Los Angeles, CA	323	96	9/29	42	12/4	18.81	1.98	2/11	—	—	—	38	4/8	45	—
Louisville, KY	481	98	7/25	10	1/18+	39.86	2.89	5/19-20	4.9	1.7	1/29	44	8/5	122	3
Marquette, MI	1,415	95	7/17	−17	1/16	33.64	1.71	9/19	203.5	15.1	11/15-16	—	—	172	52
Memphis, TN	283	100	8/21+	18	12/9	40.01	3.33	8/29-30	—	—	—	41	4/22	100	—
Miami, FL	26	95	8/4	43	1/24	68.21	4.89	6/20-21	—	—	—	69	10/24	137	—
Milwaukee, WI	677	97	7/24	−1	12/7	25.92	2.31	9/25	61.8	9.0	1/22	40	11/24+	121	22
Minn.-St. Paul, MN	871	97	7/17+	−14	1/14	33.41	4.83	10/4-5	42.8	5.5	1/21	47	6/8	114	13
Mobile, AL	209	97	9/19	25	1/24+	73.83	8.30	4/31-30	T	T	4/1	66	8/29	105	0
Moline, IL	604	103	7/24	−11	12/7	17.86	1.00	7/26	27.7	4.9	1/5	43	11/5	94	9
Nashville, TN	571	98	8/20+	13	1/18	39.31	3.22	8/29	—	—	—	37	11/28	97	—
Newark, NJ	25	102	8/13	3	1/28	44.14	4.24	10/7-8	52.8	13.4	1/22-23	48	6/22	122	12
New Orleans, LA	4	98	7/25	31	1/23	53.00	4.50	8/29	—	—	—	77	—	109	—
New York, NY	158	99	8/13	5	1/28	55.97	4.78	10/12-13	47.7	8.5	1/22	29	3/23	123	14
Norfolk, VA	66	101	7/27	16	1/19	46.11	3.02	10/7-8	2.7	0.9	3/8	39	5/6	119	0
North Little Rock, AR	563	100	8/21+	15	12/9	37.83	3.45	9/24-25	0.1	0.1	12/8	—	—	90	0
Oklahoma City, OK	1,281	100	7/27	6	12/9+	23.60	1.99	6/16-17	5.1	2.5	1/28	48	11/27	77	2
Philadelphia, PA	10	98	7/27	3	1/24	42.22	5.94	10/7-8	37.0	10.8	1/22	52	5/28	116	11
Phoenix, AZ	1,103	116	7/17	35	12/17	7.04	1.05	2/18-19	—	—	—	47	7/18	37	—
Pittsburgh, PA	1,172	94	8/13+	−1	1/24	41.23	1.99	1/5-6	57.5	5.6	2/24	39	7/26	157	20
Portland, ME	69	94	6/25	−13	1/22	66.40	5.05	10/8-9	116.0	13.9	12/9	40	3/9	142	23
Portland, OR	220	96	8/4	24	12/16	36.10	1.80	3/26-27	—	—	—	41	12/18+	150	—
Providence, RI	50	100	8/13	−2	1/24	57.92	6.38	10/14-15	71.3	16.4	1/23	45	1/23	124	19
Raleigh, NC	427	102	7/27	11	1/24	37.55	2.23	7/28-29	0.9	0.7	1/19	33	4/30	118	0
Rapid City, SD	3,150	109	7/16	−15	1/6	14.41	1.29	5/7-8	—	—	—	54	12/5	85	—
Reno, NV	4,404	104	7/16+	6	1/13	9.39	1.72	12/30-31	24.7	10.5	1/8	47	4/3	60	5
Richmond, VA	164	100	7/27	8	1/24	41.54	3.08	7/7-8	8.8	4.2	12/5	38	3/8	114	3
St. Louis, MO	707	103	7/24	4	1/17	37.85	3.07	1/4-5	14.8	3.6	1/13	45	8/13	104	4
Salt Lake City, UT	4,221	103	7/20+	5	12/7	16.88	1.15	5/10-11	28.8	7.6	2/7	41	6/28	97	7
San Antonio, TX	818	105	9/25	27	12/8+	16.54	1.65	1/27-28	T	T	6/1	35	7/18	64	0
San Diego, CA	78	89	10/6	44	12/6+	14.11	2.28	2/21-22	—	—	—	28	1/7	50	—
San Francisco, CA	86	89	8/31	38	12/6	26.99	2.83	12/17-18	—	—	—	47	6/5	82	—
San Juan, PR	7	95	5/21	64	1/22	77.28	4.94	4/21-22	0.0	0.0	—	29	1/1	215	—
Sault Ste. Marie, MI	724	94	7/11	−20	1/18	25.48	1.40	7/30-31	—	—	—	43	11/13	153	—
Savannah, GA	48	99	7/27	21	1/24	46.03	4.40	10/5-6	0.0	0.0	—	38	5/20	117	0
Scottsbluff, NE	3,946	105	7/20	−20	12/8	19.64	2.73	6/3-4	31.1	5.7	1/4	48	11/28	86	10
Seattle, WA	447	89	5/27+	23	12/16	35.44	2.39	1/17	—	—	—	39	12/18	152	—
Spokane, WA	2,381	95	7/28	−6	1/15	17.38	0.93	5/9-10	29.6	5.2	11/29	62	6/21	108	12
Springfield, MO	1,277	104	7/23	4	12/9	35.32	3.72	1/4-5	6.8	2.9	2/2	39	11/27	96	2
Tampa, FL	8	95	9/19+	31	1/24	38.95	3.39	6/29-29	0.0	0.0	—	35	10/24	102	0
Washington, DC[3]	10	97	8/5+	12	1/24	44.38	5.91	10/7-8	17.2	3.0	1/22	43	10/24	108	7
Wilmington, DE	92	96	8/14+	1	1/28	40.25	3.31	10/7-8	33.9	8.1	1/22	45	10/24	110	9

In some cases the value for the extreme also occurred on an earlier date in 2004. (+) First reading; matched on later dates. (T) Trace. (—) Data not available or incomplete. (1) Where one date is shown, it is the starting date of the storm. (2) Sustained for at least 2 minutes, not peak gust. (3) As measured at Reagan Nat'l. Airport.

Record Temperatures by State

Source: National Climatic Data Center, NESDIS, NOAA, U.S. Dept. of Commerce, through May 2004.

State	°F	Latest date	Station	Approx. elevation in feet	°F	Latest date	Station	Approx. elevation in feet
		LOWEST TEMPERATURE				**HIGHEST TEMPERATURE**		
Alabama	−27	Jan. 30,1966	New Market	760	112	Sept. 5,1925	Centerville	345
Alaska	−80	Jan. 23,1971	Prospect Creek Camp	1,100	100	June 27,1915	Fort Yukon	c. 420
Arizona	−40	Jan. 7,1971	Hawley Lake	8,180	128	June 29,1994	Lake Havasu City	505
Arkansas	−29	Feb. 13,1905	Pond	1,250	120	Aug. 10,1936	Ozark	396
California	−45	Jan. 20,1937	Boca	5,532	134	July 10,1913	Greenland Ranch	−178
Colorado	−61	Feb. 1,1985	Maybell	5,920	118	July 11,1888	Bennett	5,484
Connecticut	−32	Jan. 22,1961[1]	Coventry	480	106	July 15,1995	Danbury	450
Delaware	−17	Jan. 17,1893	Millsboro	20	110	July 21,1930	Millsboro	20
Florida	−2	Feb. 13,1899	Tallahassee	193	109	June 29,1931	Monticello	207
Georgia	−17	Jan. 27,1940	CCC Camp F-16	1,000	112	Aug. 20,1983[1]	Greenville	860
Hawaii	12	May 17,1979	Mauna Kea Obs.	13,770	100	Apr. 27,1931	Pahala	850
Idaho	−60	Jan. 18,1943	Island Park Dam	6,285	118	July 28,1934	Orofino	1,027
Illinois	−36	Jan. 5,1999	Congerville	635	117	July 14,1954	East St. Louis	410
Indiana	−36	Jan. 19,1994	New Whiteland	785	116	July 14,1936	Collegeville	672
Iowa	−47	Feb. 3,1996[1]	Elkader	770	118	July 20,1934	Keokuk	614
Kansas	−40	Feb. 13,1905	Lebanon	1,812	121	July 24,1936[1]	Alton (near)	1,651
Kentucky	−37	Jan. 19,1994	Shelbyville	730	114	July 28,1930	Greensburg	581
Louisiana	−16	Feb. 13,1899	Minden	194	114	Aug. 10,1936	Plain Dealing	268
Maine	−48	Jan. 19,1925	Van Buren	510	105	July 10,1911[1]	North Bridgton	450
Maryland	−40	Jan. 13,1912	Oakland	2,461	109	July 10,1936[1]	Cumberland	623
							Frederick	325
Massachusetts	−35	Jan. 12,1981	Chester	640	107	Aug. 2,1975	Chester	640
							New Bedford	120
Michigan	−51	Feb. 9,1934	Vanderbilt	785	112	July 13,1936	Mio	963
Minnesota	−60	Feb. 2,1996	Tower	1,460	114	July 6,1936[1]	Moorhead	904
Mississippi	−19	Jan. 30,1966	Corinth	420	115	July 29,1930	Holly Springs	600
Missouri	−40	Feb. 13,1905	Warsaw	700	118	July 14,1954[1]	Warsaw	705
							Union	560
Montana	−70	Jan. 20,1954	Rogers Pass	5,470	117	July 5,1937	Medicine Lake	1,950
Nebraska	−47	Dec. 22,1989[1]	Oshkosh	3,379	118	July 24,1936[1]	Minden	2,169
Nevada	−50	Jan. 8,1937	San Jacinto	5,200	125	June 29,1994[1]	Laughlin	605
New Hampshire	−47	Jan. 29,1934	Mt. Washington	6,262	106	July 4,1911	Nashua	125
New Jersey	−34	Jan. 5,1904	River Vale	70	110	July 10,1936	Runyon	18
New Mexico	−50	Feb. 1,1951	Gavilan	7,350	122	June 27,1994	Waste Isolat. Pilot Plt.	3,418
New York	−52	Feb. 18,1979	Old Forge	1,720	108	July 22,1926	Troy	35
North Carolina	−34	Jan. 21,1985	Mt. Mitchell	6,525	110	Aug. 21,1983	Fayetteville	213
North Dakota	−60	Feb. 15,1936	Parshall	1,929	121	July 6,1936	Steele	1,857
Ohio	−39	Feb. 10,1899	Milligan	800	113	July 21,1934[1]	Gallipolis (near)	673
Oklahoma	−27	Jan. 18,1930[1]	Watts	958	120	June 27,1994[1]	Tipton	1,350
Oregon	−54	Feb. 10,1933[1]	Seneca	4,700	119	Aug. 10,1898[1]	Pendleton	1,074
Pennsylvania	−42	Jan. 5,1904	Smethport	1,500	111	July 10,1936[1]	Phoenixville	100
Rhode Island	−25	Feb. 5,1996	Greene	425	104	Aug. 2,1975	Providence	51
South Carolina	−19	Jan. 21,1985	Caesars Head	3,115	111	June 28,1954[1]	Camden	170
South Dakota	−58	Feb. 17,1936	McIntosh	2,277	120	July 5,1936	Gannvalley	1,750
Tennessee	−32	Dec. 30,1917	Mountain City	2,471	113	Aug. 9,1930[1]	Perryville	377
Texas	−23	Feb. 8,1933[1]	Seminole	3,275	120	June 28,1994[1]	Monahans	2,660
Utah	−69	Feb. 1,1985	Peter's Sink	8,092	117	Jul. 5,1985	Saint George	2,880
Vermont	−50	Dec. 30,1933	Bloomfield	915	105	July 4,1911	Vernon	310
Virginia	−30	Jan. 22,1985	Mountain Lake Bio. Station	3,870	110	July 15,1954	Balcony Falls	725
Washington	−48	Dec. 30,1968	Mazama	2,120				
			Winthrop	1,755	118	Aug. 5,1961[1]	Ice Harbor Dam	475
West Virginia	−37	Dec. 30,1917	Lewisburg	2,200	112	July 10,1936[1]	Martinsburg	435
Wisconsin	−55	Feb. 4,1996	Couderay	1,300	114	July 13,1936	Wisconsin Dells	900
Wyoming	−66	Feb. 9,1933	Riverside R.S.	6,500	115	Aug. 8,1983	Basin	3,500

(1) Also on earlier dates at the same or other places.

Hurricane and Tornado Classifications

Source: Natl. Weather Service, NOAA, U.S. Dept. of Commerce

The Saffir-Simpson Hurricane Scale is a 1-5 rating based on a hurricane's intensity. The scale is used to give an estimate of the potential property damage and flooding expected along the coast from a hurricane landfall. Wind speed is the determining factor in the scale. The Fujita (or F) Scale, created by T. Theodore Fujita, is used to classify tornadoes. The F Scale uses rating numbers from 0 to 5, based on the amount and type of wind damage. The Enhanced Fujita Scale, an update to the original, is scheduled to be implemented in the U.S. on Feb. 1, 2007.

Saffir-Simpson Scale (Hurricanes)				Enhanced Fujita Scale (Tornadoes)			
Category	Wind speed	Severity	Storm surge[1]	Rank	3-sec. gust	Damage	Strength
1	74-95 mph	Weak	4-5 ft	EF-0	65-85 mph	Light	Weak
2	96-110 mph	Moderate	6-8 ft	EF-1	86-110 mph	Moderate	Weak
3	111-130 mph	Strong	9-12 ft	EF-2	111-135 mph	Considerable	Strong
4	131-155 mph	Very Strong	13-18 ft	EF-3	136-165 mph	Severe	Strong
5	over 155 mph	Devastating	above 18 ft	EF-4	166-200 mph	Devastating	Violent
(1) Above normal tides.				EF-5	over 200 mph	Incredible	Violent

Atlantic Hurricane Names in 2007

Source: Natl. Weather Service, NOAA, U.S. Dept. of Commerce

Names for Atlantic hurricanes in 2007 are Andrea, Barry, Chantal, Dean, Erin, Felix, Gabrielle, Humberto, Ingrid, Jerry, Karen, Lorenzo, Melissa, Noel, Olga, Pablo, Rebekah, Sebastien, Tanya, Van, and Wendy. If there are more than 21 named Atlantic storms in one season, remaining storms take names from the Greek alphabet, starting with Alpha.

World Temperature and Precipitation

Source: World Meteorological Organization

Average daily maximum and minimum temperatures and annual precipitation based on records for the period 1961-90. Records of extreme temperatures include all available years of data for a given location and are usually for a longer period. Surface elevations are supplied by the WMO and may differ from figures in other sections of *The World Almanac*. NA = not available.

Station	Surface elevation (ft)	January Max.	January Min.	July Max.	July Min.	EXTREME Max.	EXTREME Min.	Average annual precipitation (in.)
Algiers, Algeria	82	61.7	42.6	87.1	65.3	NA	NA	27.0
Athens, Greece	49	56.1	44.6	88.9	73.0	NA	NA	14.6
Auckland, New Zealand	20	74.8	61.2	58.5	46.4	NA	NA	49.4
Bangkok, Thailand	66	89.6	69.8	90.9	77.0	104	51	59.0
Berlin, Germany	190	35.2	26.8	73.6	55.2	107	−4	23.3
Bogotá, Colombia	8,357	67.3	41.7	64.6	45.5	75	21	32.4
Bombay (Mumbai), India	36	85.3	66.7	86.2	77.5	110	46	85.4
Bucharest, Romania	298	34.7	22.1	83.8	60.1	105	−18	23.4
Budapest, Hungary	456	34.2	24.8	79.7	59.7	103	−10	20.3
Buenos Aires, Argentina	82	85.8	67.3	59.7	45.7	104	22	45.2
Cairo, Egypt	243	65.8	48.2	93.9	71.1	118	34	1.0
Cape Town, South Africa	138	79.0	60.3	63.3	44.6	105	28	20.5
Caracas, Venezuela	2,739	79.9	60.8	81.3	66.0	96	45	36.1
Casablanca, Morocco	203	62.8	47.1	77.7	66.7	NA	NA	16.8
Copenhagen, Denmark	16	35.6	28.4	68.9	55.0	NA	NA	NA
Damascus, Syria	2,004	54.3	32.9	97.2	61.9	NA	NA	5.6
Dublin, Ireland	279	45.7	36.5	66.0	52.5	86	8	28.8
Geneva, Switzerland	1,364	38.3	27.9	76.3	53.2	101	−3	35.6
Havana, Cuba	164	78.4	65.5	88.3	74.8	NA	NA	46.9
Hong Kong, China	203	65.5	56.5	88.7	79.9	97	32	87.2
Istanbul, Turkey	108	47.8	37.2	82.8	65.3	105	7	27.4
Jerusalem, Israel	2,483	53.4	39.4	83.8	63.0	107	26	23.2
Lagos, Nigeria	125	90.0	72.3	82.8	72.1	NA	NA	59.3
Lima, Peru	43	79.0	66.9	66.4	59.4	NA	NA	0.2
London, England	203	44.1	32.7	71.1	52.3	99	2	29.7
Manila, Philippines	79	85.8	74.8	89.1	76.8	NA	NA	49.6
Mexico City, Mexico	7,570	70.3	43.7	73.8	53.2	NA	NA	33.4
Montreal, Canada	118	21.6	5.2	79.2	59.7	100	−36	37.0
Nairobi, Kenya	5,897	77.9	50.9	71.6	48.6	NA	NA	41.9
Paris, France	213	42.8	33.6	75.2	55.2	105	−1	25.6
Prague, Czech Republic	1,197	32.7	22.5	73.9	53.2	98	−16	20.7
Reykjavik, Iceland	200	35.4	26.6	55.9	46.9	76	−3	31.5
Rome, Italy	79	53.8	35.4	88.2	62.1	NA	NA	33.0
San Salvador, El Salvador	2,037	86.5	61.3	86.2	66.4	105	45	68.3
São Paulo, Brazil	2,598	81.1	65.7	71.2	53.1	NA	NA	57.4
Shanghai, China	23	45.9	32.9	88.9	76.6	104	10	43.8
Singapore	52	85.8	73.6	87.4	75.6	NA	NA	84.6
Stockholm, Sweden	171	30.7	23.0	71.4	56.1	97	−26	21.2
Sydney, Australia	10	79.5	65.5	62.4	43.9	114	32	46.4
Tehran, Iran	3,906	45.0	30.0	98.2	75.2	109	−5	9.1
Tokyo, Japan	118	49.1	34.2	83.8	72.1	NA	NA	55.4
Toronto, Canada	567	27.5	12.0	80.2	57.6	105	−26	30.8

Speed of Winds in the U.S.

Source: Natl. Climatic Data Center, NESDIS, Ntl. Oceanic and Atmospheric Admin (NOAA), U.S. Dept. of Commerce

In miles per hour; based on available records through 2005. Average and max. speeds are annual. Max. speeds are highest one-minute average values, except where noted.

Station	Avg.	Max.	Station	Avg.	Max.	Station	Avg.	Max.
Albuquerque, NM	8.9	53	Helena, MT[2]	7.7	73	Oklahoma City, OK	12.2	74
Anchorage, AK[1]	7.1	75	Honolulu, HI	11.3	46	Omaha (Eppley Airfield), NE	10.5	58
Atlanta, GA	9.1	60	Houston, TX	7.6	51	Philadelphia, PA[2]	9.5	73
Baltimore, MD[2]	8.8	80	Indianapolis, IN	9.6	49	Phoenix, AZ	6.2	51
Bismarck, ND	10.2	64	Jackson, MS	6.9	55	Pittsburgh, PA	9.0	58
Boise, ID	8.7	84	Jacksonville, FL	7.8	57	Portland, ME	8.7	57
Boston, MA	12.4	54	Las Vegas, NV	9.2	56	Portland, OR[2]	7.9	88
Buffalo, NY	11.8	91	Little Rock, AR[2]	7.8	65	Providence, RI	10.4	90
Burlington, VT	9.0	39	Los Angeles, CA[2]	5.5	49	Richmond, VA	7.7	46
Cape Hatteras, NC	10.8	66	Louisville, KY	8.3	56	St. Louis, MO	9.6	52
Charleston (Intl. Airport), SC	8.6	52	Miami, FL	9.2	86	Salt Lake City, UT[2]	8.8	71
Charleston, WV	5.8	55	Milwaukee, WI	11.5	54	San Francisco, CA[2]	8.7	47
Cheyenne, WY	12.9	71	Minn.-St. Paul, MN	10.5	51	Seattle (Sea-Tac Intl. Airport), WA[2]	8.8	66
Chicago, IL	10.3	58	Mobile, AL	8.8	66	Sioux Falls, SD	11.0	70
Cleveland, OH	10.5	53	Mt. Washington, NH[1]	35.1	231	Washington (Natl. Airport), DC	9.4	49
Denver, CO	8.7	54	Nashville, TN	8.0	58	Wichita, KS	12.2	70
Des Moines, IA[2]	10.7	76	Newark, NJ	10.2	82	Wilmington, DE	9.0	58
Detroit, MI	10.2	61	New Orleans, LA	8.2	69			
Hartford, CT	8.4	46	New York (Central Park), NY	9.3	40			

(1) Max. speed is based on short gusts. (2) Calculated from minimum time during which one mile of wind passed station.

IT'S A RECORD: The windiest place in the world is around Cape Dennison and Port Martin on Commonwealth Bay, Antarctica, where wind speeds average 50 mph. Winds of more than 200 mph have been recorded there.

Tides and Their Causes

Source: NOAA, Natl. Ocean Service, U.S. Dept. of Commerce

The tides are a natural phenomenon involving the alternating rise and fall in the large fluid bodies of the Earth caused by the combined gravitational attraction of the Sun and Moon. The combination of these 2 variable influences produces the complex recurrent cycle of the tides. Tides may occur in both oceans and seas, to a limited extent in large lakes, in the atmosphere, and, to a very minute degree, in the Earth itself. The length of time between succeeding tides varies as the result of many factors.

The tide-generating force represents the difference between (1) the centrifugal force produced by the revolution of the earth around the common center-of-gravity of the earth-moon system and (2) the gravitational attraction of the moon acting upon the earth's overlying waters. The Moon is about 400 times closer than the Sun; so despite its smaller mass, the Moon's tide-raising force is 2.5 times greater.

The tide-generating forces of the Moon and Sun acting tangentially to the Earth's surface tend to cause a maximum accumulation of waters at 2 diametrically opposite positions on the surface of the Earth and to withdraw compensating amounts of water from all points 90° removed from these tidal bulges. As the Earth rotates beneath the maxima and minima of these tide-generating forces, a sequence of 2 high tides, separated by 2 low tides, ideally is produced each day (semidiurnal tide). Each ocean basin reacts differently to this tidal forcing.

Twice in each month, when the Sun, Moon, and Earth are directly aligned, with the Moon between the Earth and Sun (at New Moon) or on the opposite side of the Earth from the Sun (at Full Moon), the Sun and Moon exert gravitational force in a mutual or additive fashion. The highest high tides and lowest low tides are produced at these times. These are called spring tides. At 2 positions 90° in between, the gravitational forces of the Moon and Sun—imposed at right angles—counteract each other to the greatest extent, and the range between high and low tides is reduced. These are called neap tides.

The inclination to the equator of the moon's monthly orbit and the inclination of the Sun to the equator during the Earth's yearly orbit produce a difference in the height of succeeding high tides and in the extent of depression of succeeding low tides that is known as the diurnal inequality. In most cases, this produces a so-called mixed tide. In extreme cases, these phenomena may result in only one high tide and one low tide each (diurnal tide). There are other monthly and yearly variations in the tide because of the elliptical shape of the orbits themselves.

U.S. convention distinguishes between mean higher high water (MHHW), mean high water (MHW), mean tide level (MTL), mean sea level (MSL), mean low water (MLW), and mean lower low water (MLLW). Diurnal range of tide is the difference in height between MHHW and MLLW. Mean range of tide is the difference between MHW and MLW.

The range of tide in the open ocean is generally less than in the coastal regions, as the range of the incoming tide can be augmented by the continental shelves, as well as by bays and estuaries. In some shallow inlets and bays, the range may be diminished. In the Bay of Fundy in Nova Scotia, the range of tide, or difference between high and low waters, may reach 43½ feet or more (under spring tide conditions).

At New Orleans, the periodic rise and fall of the diurnal tide is affected by the seasonal stages of the Mississippi River, being about 10 inches at low stage and zero at high. The Canadian Tide Tables for 1972 gave a maximum range of nearly 50 feet at Leaf Basin, Ungava Bay, Quebec.

In every case, actual high or low tide can vary considerably from the average, as a result of weather conditions such as strong winds, abrupt barometric pressure changes, or prolonged periods of extreme high or low pressure.

Average Rise and Fall of Tides[1]

Place	Ft	In.	Place	Ft	In.	Place	Ft	In.
Baltimore, MD	1	8	Hampton Roads, VA	2	10	St. John's, Nfld., Can.	2	7
Boston, MA	10	4	Key West, FL	1	10	St. Petersburg, FL	2	3[2]
Charleston, SC	5	10	Mobile, AL	1	6[2]	San Diego, CA	5	9
Cristobal, Panama	1	1	New London, CT	3	1	Sandy Hook, NJ	5	2
Eastport, ME	19	4	Newport, RI	3	11	San Francisco, CA	5	10
Ft. Pulaski, GA	7	6	New York, NY	5	1	Seattle, WA	11	4
Galveston, TX	1	5[2]	Philadelphia, PA	6	9	Vancouver, BC, Can.	10	6
Halifax, NS, Can.	4	5[2]	Portland, ME	9	11	Washington, DC	3	2

(1) Mean ranges, except where noted. (2) Diurnal range.

El Niño and La Niña

Source: Natl. Weather Service, NOAA, U.S. Dept. of Commerce

El Niño is a climatically significant disruption of the ocean-atmosphere system characterized by large-scale weakening of trade winds and warming of the surface layers in the central and eastern equatorial Pacific. The term *El Niño*, Spanish for "the Christ Child," was originally used by fishermen to refer to a warm ocean current appearing around Christmas off the west coasts of Ecuador and Peru and lasting several months. The term has come to be reserved for exceptionally strong, warm currents that bring heavy rains.

El Niño events generally occur at irregular intervals of 2 to 7 years, at an average of once every 3 to 4 years. They typically last 12 to 18 months. The intensity of El Niño events varies; some are strong, such as the 1982-83 and 1997-98 events; others are considerably weaker, such as the 2004-05 event, all depending on the intensity of and area encompassed by the abnormally warm ocean temperatures. The eastward extent of warmer than normal water varies from episode to episode.

El Niño influences weather around the globe, and its impacts are most clearly seen in the winter. During El Niño years, winter temperatures in the continental U.S. tend to be warmer than normal in the north and west coast states and cooler than normal in the southeast. Conditions tend to be wetter than normal over central and southern California, the Southwest states and across much of the South, and drier than normal over the northern portions of the Rocky Mountains and in the Ohio valley. Globally, El Niño brings wetter than normal conditions to Peru and Chile and dry conditions to Australia and Indonesia. It should be noted that El Niño is only one of a number of factors influencing seasonal variations of climate.

The opposite of El Niño is La Niña ("The Little Girl"), characterized by colder than normal sea surface temperatures in the equatorial Pacific. La Niña typically brings wetter, cooler conditions to the Pacific Northwest and drier, warmer conditions to much of the southern U.S. El Niño and La Niña are opposite phases of the El Niño-Southern Oscillation (ENSO) cycle, a shift in tropical sea-level pressure between the Eastern and Western hemispheres.

The events are monitored by the National Weather Service's Climate Prediction Center, using satellites and buoys in the Pacific Ocean. Highly sophisticated numerical computer models of the ocean and atmosphere use these data to predict the onset and evolution of El Niño and La Niña. In Sept. 2006, the NOAA reported that El Niño conditions had developed in the tropical Pacific and were likely to continue into early 2007.

IT'S A RECORD: The summer of 2006 was the second warmest in the continental U.S. since recordkeeping began in 1895. Based on preliminary data from the National Oceanic and Atmospheric Administration, the average June-Aug. 2006 temperature in the contiguous U.S. was 74.5° F. The warmest summer on record was set in 1936, when the average was 74.7° F. The average summer temperature in the 20th century was 72.1° F.

Wind Chill Table
Source: Natl. Weather Service, NOAA, U.S. Dept. of Commerce

Temperature and wind combine to cause heat loss from body surfaces. The following table shows that, for example, a temperature of 5° F, plus a wind of 10 miles per hour, causes body heat loss equal to that in minus 10°F with no wind. In other words, a 10-mph wind makes 5° F feel like –10° F.

The National Weather Service issued new wind chill calculations in 2001 for the 2001-02 winter season. The top line of figures shows actual temperatures in degrees Fahrenheit. The column at far left shows wind speeds up to 45 mph. (Wind speeds greater than 45 mph have little additional chilling effect.) When the wind chill temperature falls within the shaded area, frostbite occurs in 30 minutes or less.

Calm	40	35	30	25	20	15	10	5	0	–5	–10	–15	–20	–25	–30	–35	–40	–45
5	36	31	25	19	13	7	1	–5	–11	–16	–22	–28	–34	–40	–46	–52	–57	–63
10	34	27	21	15	9	3	–4	–10	–16	–22	–28	–35	–41	–47	–53	–59	–66	–72
15	32	25	19	13	6	0	–7	–13	–19	–26	–32	–39	–45	–51	–58	–64	–71	–77
20	30	24	17	11	4	–2	–9	–15	–22	–29	–35	–42	–48	–55	–61	–68	–74	–81
25	29	23	16	9	3	–4	–11	–17	–24	–31	–37	–44	–51	–58	–64	–71	–78	–84
30	28	22	15	8	1	–5	–12	–19	–26	–33	–39	–46	–53	–60	–67	–73	–80	–87
35	28	21	14	7	0	–7	–14	–21	–27	–34	–41	–48	–55	–62	–69	–76	–82	–89
40	27	20	13	6	–1	–8	–15	–22	–29	–36	–43	–50	–57	–64	–71	–78	–84	–91
45	26	29	12	5	–2	–9	–16	–23	–30	–37	–44	–51	–58	–65	–72	–79	–86	–93

Heat Index
Source: Natl. Weather Service, NOAA, U.S. Dept. of Commerce

The heat index is a measure of the contribution high humidity makes, in combination with abnormally high temperatures, to reducing the body's ability to cool itself. For example, the index shows that an air temperature of 100° F with a relative humidity of 50% has the same effect on the human body as a temperature of 120° F. Sunstroke and heat exhaustion are likely when the heat index reaches 105. This index is a measure of what hot weather "feels like" to the average person.

| Relative humidity | Air temperature (°F) | | | | | | | | | | |
| | 70 | 75 | 80 | 85 | 90 | 95 | 100 | 105 | 110 | 115 | 120 |
	Apparent temperature (°F)										
0%	64	69	73	78	83	87	91	95	99	103	107
10%	65	70	75	80	85	90	95	100	105	111	116
20%	66	72	77	82	87	93	99	105	112	120	130
30%	67	73	78	84	90	96	104	113	123	135	148
40%	68	74	79	86	93	101	110	123	137	151	
50%	69	75	81	88	96	107	120	135	150		
60%	70	76	82	90	100	114	132	149			
70%	70	77	85	93	106	124	144				
80%	71	78	86	97	113	136					
90%	71	79	88	102	122						
100%	72	80	91	108							

Ultraviolet (UV) Index Forecast
Source: Natl. Weather Service, NOAA, U.S. Dept. of Commerce; U.S. Environmental Protection Agency

The National Weather Service (NWS), Environmental Protection Agency (EPA), and Centers for Disease Control and Prevention (CDC) developed and began offering a UV index on June 28, 1994, in response to increasing incidences of skin cancer, cataracts, and other effects from exposure to the sun's harmful rays. In 2004, a new version of the index—the Global Solar UV Index—was released. The UV Index is now a regular element of NWS atmospheric forecasts.

UV Index number and forecast. The UV Index number, ranging from 0 to 11+, is an indication of the expected intensity of UV radiation reaching the Earth's surface during the solar noon hour (11:30 AM-2:30 PM standard time). The lower the number, the less the radiation. The UV Index forecast is produced daily for 58 cities by the NWS Climate Prediction Center and uses the following scale.

UV index	Exposure	Minimum precautions
0-2	Low	Sunscreen with an SPF of at least 15
3-5	Moderate	Sunscreen, covering up
6-7	High	Sunscreen, hat, UV-blocking sunglasses, avoid sun 10 AM-4 PM
8-10	Very High	Same as above
11+	Extreme	Same as above

The index number is valid for a radius of about 30 miles around a listed city and is based on several factors:

Ozone. Ozone, a form of oxygen, the molecules of which consist of three atoms rather than two, blocks UV radiation. The more ozone, the lower the UV radiation at the surface.

Cloudiness. Clear skies allow 100% UV transmission to the surface, broken clouds allow about 73%, and overcast conditions allow 32%.

Reflectivity. Reflective surfaces intensify UV exposure. Grass reflects 2.5% to 3% of UV radiation reaching the surface; sand, 20% to 30%; snow and ice, 80% to 90%; water, up to 100% (depending on reflection angle).

Elevation. At higher elevations, UV radiation travels a shorter distance to reach the surface so there is less atmosphere to absorb the rays. For every 4,000 ft one travels above sea level, the UV Index increases by 1 unit. Snow and lack of pollutants intensify UV exposure at higher altitudes.

Latitude. The closer to the equator, the higher the UV radiation level.

SPF number. The UV Index is not linked in any way to the SPF number on suntan lotions and sunscreens. For an explanation of the SPF factor, contact the product's manufacturer or the Food and Drug Administration.

Further information. For precautions to take after learning the UV Index number, call the EPA's stratospheric ozone hotline (800-296-1996) or your doctor. For questions on scientific aspects, call the NWS at 301-713-0622.

Lightning

Source: Natl. Weather Service, NOAA, U.S. Dept. of Commerce

There are an estimated 25 mil cloud-to-ground lightning bolts in the U.S. each year, killing an annual average of 67 people. This is a small number compared to U.S. deaths from fire (about 4,000 a year) and motor vehicle accidents (about 40,000), but still significant. In comparison, tornadoes cause an average of 65 deaths a year, and hurricanes an average of 16. Documented injuries from lightning number about 300 a year; probably many more injuries occur.

Lightning is a result of ice in storm clouds. As ice particles rise and sink in a cloud, numerous collisions between them cause a separation of electrical charge. Positively charged crystals rise to the top, while negatively charged crystals drop. As the storm travels, a pool of positive charges gathers in the ground below and follows along, traveling up objects like trees and telephone poles. In a common form of lightning, the negatively charged area in a storm sends charges downward, which are attracted to positively charged objects. A channel develops and the electrical transfer that you see is lightning. Lightning can travel miles away from the area of a storm.

The transfer of charges in lightning generates a huge amount of heat, sending the temperature in the channel to 50,000° F and causing the air within it to expand rapidly. The sound of that expansion is thunder. Sound travels more slowly than light, so you usually see lightning before you hear thunder.

To (very roughly) gauge one's danger, use the 30-30 rule. In good visibility, count the time between a lightning flash and the crack of thunder. If it's less than 30 seconds, the storm is within 6 miles of you. Find shelter immediately. The threat of more lightning does not stop right away; you need to wait about 30 minutes after the last flash of the storm to be sure.

Most lightning deaths and injuries occur in the summer months when people are outdoors. When a storm threatens people need to move to a safe place promptly. Even while indoors, people are advised to stay away from windows and avoid contact with anything conducting electricity.

For more information about lightning, try the website www.lightningsafety.noaa.gov/overview.htm

Global Measured Extremes of Temperature and Precipitation Records

Source: Natl. Climatic Data Center, NESDIS, NOAA, U.S. Dept. of Commerce; based on latest available rdata records

Highest Temperature Extremes

Continent	Highest temp. (°F)	Place	Elevation (ft)	Date
Africa	136	El Azizia, Libya	367	Sept. 13, 1922
North America	134	Death Valley, CA (Greenland Ranch)	−178	July 10, 1913
Asia	129	Tirat Tsvi, Israel	−722	June 22, 1942
Australia	128	Cloncurry, Queensland	622	Jan. 16, 1889
Europe	122	Seville, Spain	26	Aug. 4, 1881
South America	120	Rivadavia, Argentina	676	Dec. 11, 1905
Oceania	108	Tuguegarao, Philippines	72	Apr. 29, 1912
Antarctica	59	Vanda Station, Scott Coast	49	Jan. 5, 1974

Lowest Temperature Extremes

Continent	Lowest temp. (°F)	Place	Elevation (ft)	Date
Antarctica	−129	Vostok	11,220	July 21, 1983
Asia	−90	Oimekon, Russia	2,625	Feb. 6, 1933
Asia	−90	Verkhoyansk, Russia	350	Feb. 7, 1892
Greenland	−87	Northice	7,687	Jan. 9, 1954
North America	−81.4	Snag, Yukon, Canada	2,120	Feb. 3, 1947
Europe	−67	Ust'Shchugor, Russia	279	Jan.*
South America	−27	Sarmiento, Argentina	879	June 1, 1907
Africa	−11	Ifrane, Morocco	5,364	Feb. 11, 1935
Australia	−9.4	Charlotte Pass, NSW	5,758	June 29, 1994
Oceania	12	Mauna Kea Observatory, HI	13,773	May 17,1979

* Exact day and year unknown.

Greatest Measured Average Annual Precipitation Extremes

Continent	Highest avg. (in.)	Place	Elevation (ft)	Years of data
South America	523.6[1,2]	Lloro, Colombia	520[3]	29
Asia	467.4[1]	Mawsynram, India	4,597	38
Oceania	460[1]	Mt. Waialeale, Kauai, HI	5,148	30
Africa	405	Debundscha, Cameroon	30	32
South America	354[2]	Quibdo, Colombia	120	16
Australia	340	Bellenden Ker, Queensland	5,102	9
North America	256	Henderson Lake, British Columbia	12	14
Europe	183	Crkvica, Bosnia-Herzegovina	3,337	22

(1) The value given is the continent's highest and possibly the world's, depending on measurement practices, procedures, and period of record variations. (2) The official greatest average annual precipitation for South America is 354 in. at Quibdo, Colombia. The 523.6 in. average at Lloro, Colombia (14 mi SE and at a higher elevation than Quibdo) is an estimate. (3) Approx. elevation.

Lowest Measured Average Annual Precipitation Extremes

Continent	Lowest avg. (in.)	Place	Elevation (ft)	Years of data
South America	0.03	Arica, Chile	95	59
Africa	<0.1	Wadi Halfa, Sudan	410	39
Antarctica	0.8[1]	Amundsen-Scott South Pole Station	9,186	10
North America	1.2	Batagues, Mexico	16	14
Asia	1.8	Aden, Yemen	22	50
Australia	4.1	Mulka (Troudaninna), South Australia	160[2]	42
Europe	6.4	Astrakhan, Russia	45	25
Oceania	8.9	Puako, HI	5	13

(1) The value given is the average amount of solid snow accumulating in one year as indicated by snow markers. The amount of liquid content of the snow is undetermined. (2) Approx. elevation.

Notorious U.S. Storms, 1859-2005

Note: Damage estimates are not adjusted for inflation. The current convention of naming hurricanes began in 1953.

1859 Solar superstorm: Intense magnetic fields (coronal mass ejections) projected from the Sun reached the Earth Sept. 1-2, creating a geomagnetic storm witnessed as aurora borealis as far south as Panama but which also disabled telegraph wires around the world. Scientists estimate that if an event of this magnitude occurs during the peak of the next sunspot cycle, about 2012, satellites could sustain up to $70 bil in damages and geomagnetically-induced currents could cause blackouts of the electrical grids.

1888 NE blizzard: A Nor'easter Mar. 11-14 covered the northeast from the Chesapeake Bay to Maine and Canada. Snow fell 20-30 in deep as winds reached more than 80 mph. At least 400 died. Damage was estimated at $20+ mil.

1900 Galveston (TX) hurricane: A Category 4 storm Sept. 8 flooded the island with 15 ft high waves and winds over 130 mph; estimates of fatalities ranged from 6,000 to 12,000, making this the nation's most deadly natural disaster. Damage was estimated at $20 mil.

Damage from Galveston hurricane

1925 Tri-state tornado: The longest-traveling and deadliest tornado in U.S. history set down Mar. 18 and cut though 219 mi of southeast Missouri, southern Illinois, and southwest Indiana. In 3.5 hours, the F5 tornado leveled entire towns (about 15,000 homes), killed 695 people (including 234 in Murphysboro, IL), and caused $16.5 mil in damages.

1935 Labor Day Hurricane: A Category 5 storm Sept. 2 hit the Florida Keys. The storm made landfall with a U.S. record low pressure of 892 millibars and with winds estimated to be over 160 mph. It killed more than 400 people, mostly veteran soldiers escaping relief work camps on the islands by train. An official estimate put the damages at $6 mil.

1938 Long Island Express: The U.S. Weather Bureau was relieved when a Category 5 hurricane turned north, away from Florida, Sept. 19. Nearly everyone was surprised when it hit Long Island, NY, Sept. 21 as a category 3 with winds over 110 mph and storm surges over 10 ft. The eye went directly over New Haven, CT. Providence, RI was battered as floodwaters rose to nearly 14 feet. In Massachusetts, sustained winds were recorded at 121 mph and storm surges were measured up to 25 ft. More than 600 died. Damages were estimated at $306 mil, including about 7,000 damaged or destroyed boats.

1962 Columbus Day Windstorm: A low pressure system (the remnants of Typhoon Freda) Oct. 12 off the coast of Crescent City, CA created sustained winds of up to 150 mph that blew through N. California, Oregon, and Washington to British Columbia. The strongest non-tropical windstorm in U.S. history killed 46 and caused at least $235 mil in damages. Hundreds of thousands of trees, equaling 15 bil board feet, were also destroyed—an amount greater than the total lumber harvest of Oregon and Washington in 2005 (13.1 bil board feet).

1969 Hurricane Camille: A Category 5 storm with an intensity second only to the 1935 Labor Day hurricane hit Mississippi near the Bay of St. Louis on Aug. 17. Winds at the coast were estimated to be near 200 mph but specific numbers were unavailable because measurement equipment was destroyed by the wind. The winds weakened as the storm moved from western Tennessee to Virginia but the rain intensified, dropping over 20 in on towns along its path. Overall, the storm killed 256 people and caused $1.42 bil in damages.

1972 Rapid City Floods: Within six hours on June 9, thunderstorms near the eastern Black Hills of South Dakota deposited more than 10 in of rain across 60 sq mi, including 15 in at Nemo, SD, resulting in the deadliest flash flood in U.S. history. The runoff raised Rapid Creek (which runs through Rapid City) 13 ft in five hours, and Canyon Lake Dam failed; the flood killed 238, injured 3,057, and caused more than $160 mil in damages.

1974 Super tornado outbreak: A storm system resulted in 148 tornadoes (including 1 in Canada) in 24 hours Apr. 3-4 across 13 states from Mississippi to Michigan. The tornados traveled 18.7 mi on average; 30 were rated F4 or F5 including an F5 that killed 34 people in Xenia, OH. Ten states were declared disaster areas, at least 310 people died, about 5,500 were injured, and the twisters left behind $600 mil in damages.

1992 Hurricane Andrew: A Category 5 hurricane (the third in U.S. history) hit S Florida Aug. 24. The small storm blew across the peninsula in about four hours with sustained winds up to 145 mph, crossed the Gulf of Mexico, and hit Louisiana as a Category 3 on Aug. 26 before quickly degrading. The rain did not cause much flooding but high winds leveled towns, leaving about 250,000 people homeless and with $26.5 billion in damages. The storm caused 65 deaths directly and indirectly, including 4 in the Bahamas.

1993 NE superstorm: A storm buried the eastern seaboard as far south as Alabama in 10-60 in of snow Mar. 12-14. The "Storm of the Century" subjected about 90 mil people to high winds and below freezing temperatures, causing 270 deaths, and $5-6 bil in damage. A low-pressure system also caused a derecho (a damaging straight-line wind) in Florida and Cuba with hurricane-like winds in excess of 90 mph accompanied by storm surges and tornados. For the first time, every airport on the east coast was closed.

1999 Hurricane Floyd: A Category 2 hurricane spanned 580 mi across when it hit the eastern seaboard Sept. 16 near Cape Fear, NC. Floyd poured over 10 in across the state, including 19 in onto Wilmington. Combined with the 6 in of rain N Carolina received from Tropical Storm Dennis earlier that month, rivers along its eastern coast rose to record levels. Record rainfall was reported across the eastern seaboard as the storm blew through New England. Ten states were declared major disaster areas. Floyd caused 56 deaths, mostly from drowning, and left $6 billion in damages.

2005 Hurricane Katrina: The costliest storm in U.S. history first made landfall Aug. 25 as a Category 1 hurricane in SE Florida. It strengthened to a Category 5 with winds up to 175 mph in the Gulf of Mexico but then weakened to a Category 3 with winds at 125 mph just before it hit near Buras, LA Aug. 29. A U.S. record storm surge of 25-29 ft flooded much of SE Louisiana, S Mississippi, and SW Alabama, including 80% of New Orleans after the city's levees failed. Thirty-three tornadoes were also reported. Although the hurricane was downgraded to a tropical storm by the next day, at least 1,833 people died and about a mil were displaced from their homes. As of Aug. 2006, NOAA estimated the damages at $125 bil.

Damage from Hurricane Camille

DISASTERS

Some Notable Aircraft Disasters Since 1937

Source: National Transportation Safety Board; World Almanac research; most notable in bold.

Date	Aircraft	Site of accident	Deaths
1937, May 6	**German zeppelin Hindenburg**	**Burned at mooring, Lakehurst, NJ**	**36***
1944, Aug. 23	U.S. Air Force B-24 Liberator bomber	Hit school, Freckleton, England	61*
1945, July 28	U.S. Army B-25	Hit Empire State Building, New York, NY	14*
1952, Dec. 20	U.S. Air Force C-124	Fell, burned, Moses Lake, WA	87
1953, Mar. 3	**Canadian Pacific Comet Jet**	**Karachi, Pakistan**	**11[1]**
1953, June 18	U.S. Air Force C-124	Crashed, burned near Tokyo	129
1955, Oct. 6	United Airlines DC-4	Crashed in Medicine Bow Peak, WY	66
1955, Nov. 1	United Airlines DC-6B	Exploded, crashed near Longmont, CO	44[2]
1956, June 20	Venezuelan Super-Constellation	Crashed in Atlantic off Asbury Park, NJ	74
1956, June 30	TWA Super-Const., United DC-7	Collided over Grand Canyon, AZ	128
1960, Dec. 16	United DC-8, TWA Super-Const.	Collided over New York City	134[3]
1962, Mar. 16	Flying Tiger Super-Constellation	Vanished in W Pacific	107
1962, June 3	Air France Boeing 707	Crashed on takeoff from Paris	130
1962, June 22	Air France Boeing 707	Crashed in storm, Guadeloupe, W.I.	113
1963, Feb. 1	Lebanese Middle East Airlines Vickers Viscount 754, Turkish Mil. Douglas C-47	Collided in over Ankara, Turkey, killing all 17 on planes, 87 on ground.	104
1963, June 3	Chartered Northwest Airlines DC-7	Crashed in Pacific off British Columbia	101
1963, Nov. 29	Trans-Canada Airlines DC-8F	Crashed after takeoff from Montreal	118
1964, Mar. 1	Paradise Airlines Constellation	Crashed on approach in heavy weather	85
1965, May 20	Pakistani Boeing 720-B	Crashed at Cairo, Egypt, airport	121
1965, Sept. 17	Pan Am Boeing 707-121B	Crashed in Montserrat, West Indies, on approach to Antigua	30
1966, Jan. 24	Air India Boeing 707	Crashed on Mont Blanc, France-Italy	117
1966, Feb. 4	All-Nippon Boeing 727	Plunged into Tokyo Bay	133
1966, Mar. 5	BOAC Boeing 707	Crashed on Mount Fuji, Japan	124
1966, Dec. 24	U.S. military-chartered CL-44	Crashed into village in South Vietnam	129*
1967, Apr. 20	Swiss Britannia turboprop	Crashed at Nicosia, Cyprus	126
1967, July 19	Piedmont Boeing 727, Cessna 310	Collided in air, Hendersonville, NC	82
1968, Apr. 20	S. African Airways Boeing 707	Crashed on takeoff, Windhoek, South-West Africa	122
1968, May 3	Braniff International Electra	Crashed in storm near Dawson, TX	85
1969, Mar. 16	Venezuelan DC-9	Crashed after takeoff from Maracaibo, Venezuela	155[4]
1969, Dec. 8	Olympic Airways DC-6B	Crashed near Athens in storm	93
1970, Feb. 15	Dominican DC-9	Crashed into sea on takeoff from Santo Domingo	102
1970, July 3	British chartered jetliner	Crashed near Barcelona, Spain	112
1970, July 5	Air Canada DC-8	Crashed near Toronto International Airport	108
1970, Aug. 9	Peruvian turbojet	Crashed after takeoff from Cuzco, Peru	101*
1970, Nov. 14	Southern Airways DC-9	Crashed in mountains near Huntington, WV	75[5]
1971, July 30	All-Nippon Boeing 727, Jap. AF F-86	Collided over Morioka, Japan	162[6]
1971, Sept. 4	Alaska Airlines Boeing 727	Crashed into mountain near Juneau, AK	111
1972, Aug. 14	East German IL-62	Crashed on takeoff, East Berlin	156
1972, Oct. 13	Aeroflot IL-62	Crashed near Moscow	176
1972, Dec. 3	Chartered Spanish airliner	Crashed on takeoff, Canary Islands	155
1972, Dec. 29	Eastern Airlines Lockheed Tristar	Crashed on approach to Miami Intl. Airport	101
1973, Jan. 22	Chartered Boeing 707	Burst into flames during landing, Kano Airport, Nigeria	176
1973, Feb. 21	**Libyan jetliner**	**Shot down by Israeli fighter planes over Sinai**	**108**
1973, Apr. 10	British Vanguard turboprop	Crashed during snowstorm at Basel, Switzerland	104
1973, June 3	Soviet Supersonic TU-144	Crashed near Goussainville, France	14[7]
1973, July 11	Brazilian Boeing 707	Crashed on approach to Orly Airport, Paris	122
1973, July 31	Delta Airlines DC-9	Crashed, landing in fog at Logan Airport, Boston	89
1973, Dec. 23	French Caravelle jet	Crashed in Morocco	106
1974, Mar. 3	Turkish DC-10	Crashed at Ermenonville near Paris	346
1974, Apr. 22	Pan American Boeing 707	Crashed in Bali, Indonesia	107
1974, Dec. 1	TWA-727	Crashed in storm, Upperville, VA	92
1974, Dec. 4	Dutch-chartered DC-8	Crashed in storm near Colombo, Sri Lanka	191
1975, Apr. 4	Air Force Galaxy C-5A	Crashed near Saigon, S Viet., after takeoff (carrying orphans)	172
1975, June 24	Eastern Airlines 727	Crashed in storm, JFK Airport, NY	113
1975, Aug. 3	Chartered 707	Hit mountainside, Agadir, Morocco	188
1976, Sept. 10	Brit. Airways Trident, Yug. DC-9	Collided near Zagreb, Yugoslavia	176
1976, Sept. 19	Turkish 727	Hit mountain, S Turkey	155
1976, Oct. 13	Bolivian 707 cargo jet	Crashed in Santa Cruz, Bolivia	100[8]
1977, Mar. 27	**KLM 747, Pan American 747**	**Collided on runway, Tenerife, Canary Islands**	**583[9]**
1977, Nov. 19	TAP Boeing 727	Crashed on Madeira	130
1977, Dec. 4	Malaysian Boeing 737	Hijacked, then exploded in mid-air over Straits of Johore	100
1977, Dec. 13	U.S. DC-3	Crashed after takeoff at Evansville, IN	29[10]
1978, Jan. 1	Air India 747	Exploded, crashed into sea off Bombay	213
1978, Sept. 25	Boeing 727, Cessna 172	Collided in air, San Diego, CA	150
1978, Nov. 15	Chartered DC-8	Crashed near Colombo, Sri Lanka	183
1979, May 25	**American Airlines DC-10**	**Crashed after takeoff at O'Hare Intl. Airport, Chicago**	**275[11]**
1979, Aug. 17	Two Soviet Aeroflot jetliners	Collided over Ukraine	173
1979, Nov. 26	Pakistani Boeing 707	Crashed near Jidda, Saudi Arabia	156
1979, Nov. 28	New Zealand DC-10	Crashed into mountain in Antarctica	257
1980, Mar. 14	Polish IL-62	Crashed making emergency landing, Warsaw	87[12]
1980, Aug. 19	Saudi Arabian Tristar	Burned after emergency landing, Riyadh	301
1981, Dec. 1	Yugoslavian DC-9	Crashed into mountain in Corsica	178
1982, Jan. 13	Air Florida Boeing 737	Crashed into Potomac R. after takeoff	78
1982, July 9	Pan Am Boeing 727	Crashed after takeoff in Kenner, LA	153[13]
1983, Sept. 1	**S. Korean Boeing 747**	**Shot down after violating Soviet airspace**	**269**
1983, Nov. 27	Colombian Boeing 747	Crashed near Barajas Airport, Madrid	183
1985, Feb. 19	Spanish Boeing 727	Crashed into Mt. Oiz, Spain	148
1985, June 23	Air-India Boeing 747	Crashed into Atlantic Ocean S of Ireland	329
1985, Aug. 2	Delta Airlines L-1011	Crashed at Dallas-Ft. Worth Intl. Airport	137
1985, Aug. 12	**Japan Air Lines Boeing 747**	**Crashed into Mt. Ogura, Japan**	**520[14]**
1985, Dec. 12	Arrow Air DC-8	Crashed after takeoff in Gander, Newfoundland	256[15]
1986, Mar. 31	Mexican Boeing 727	Crashed NW of Mexico City	166
1986, Aug. 31	Aeromexico DC-9	Collided with Piper PA-28 over Cerritos, CA	82[16]
1987, May 9	Polish IL-62M	Crashed after takeoff in Warsaw, Poland	183
1987, Aug. 16	Northwest Airlines MD-82	Crashed after takeoff in Romulus, MI	156
1987, Nov. 28	S. African Boeing 747	Crashed into Indian Ocean near Mauritius	159

Date	Aircraft	Site of accident	Deaths
1987, Nov. 29	S. Korean Boeing 707	Exploded over Thai-Burmese border	155
1988, Mar. 17	Colombian Boeing 707	Crashed into mountainside near Venezuela border	137
1988, July 3	**Iranian A300 Airbus**	**Shot down by U.S. Navy warship *Vincennes* over Pers. Gulf**	**290**
1988, Dec. 21	**Pan Am Boeing 747**	**Bomb on board; exploded over Lockerbie, Scot.**	**270**[17]
1989, Feb. 8	U.S. Boeing 707	Crashed into mountain in Azores Islands off Portugal	144
1989, June 7	Suriname DC-8	Crashed near Paramaribo Airport, Suriname	168
1989, July 19	United Airlines DC-10	Crashed while landing in Sioux City, IA	111
1989, Sept. 19	**French DC-10**	**Bomb on board; exploded in air over Niger**	**171**
1990, Jan. 25	Avianca Air Boeing 707	Crashed on landing, JFK Airport, NY	73
1990, Feb. 14	Indian Airlines Airbus 320	Crashed and burned landing in Bangalore, India	91
1990, Oct. 2	Chinese airline Boeing 737, 707	Hijacked; 737 jet landing in Guangzhou, crashed into 707	132
1991, May 26	Lauda-Air Boeing 767-300	Exploded over rural Thailand	223
1991, July 11	Nigerian DC-8	Crashed while landing at Jidda, Saudi Arabia	261
1991, Oct. 5	Indonesian military transport	Crashed after takeoff from Jakarta	137*
1992, July 31	Thai Airbus A-300-310	Crashed into mountain S. of Kathmandu, Nepal	113
1992, Oct. 4	**El Al Boeing 747-200F**	**Crashed into 2 apartment bldgs., Amsterdam, Netherlands**	**120***
1993, Feb. 8	Iran Air TU-154	Collided in air with military plane	132
1993, Mar. 5	Macedonian Pal Air Fokker 100	Crashed after takeoff in snowstorm in Skopje, Macedonia	83
1994, Jan. 3	Aeroflot TU-154	Crashed and exploded after takeoff in Irkhutsk, Russia	125[18]
1994, Apr. 26	China Airlines Airbus A-300-600R	Crashed at Japan's Nagoya Airport	264
1994, June 16	China Northwest Airlines TU-154	Crashed 10 min. after takeoff	160
1994, Sept. 8	USAir Boeing 737-300	Crashed in Aliquippa, PA, near Pittsburgh Intl. Airport	132
1994, Oct. 31	American Eagle ATR-72-210	Crashed in field near Roselawn, IN	68
1995, Aug. 11	Aviateca Boeing 737	Crashed into Chichontepec volcano, El Salvador	65
1995, Dec. 18	Zairian passenger jet	Crashed in Angola, location disputed	136
1995, Dec. 20	American Airlines Boeing 757	Crashed into mountain 50 mi N of Cali, Colombia	160
1996, Jan. 8	Antonova 32 cargo jet	Crashed into central market, Kinshasa, Zaire	350+*
1996, Feb. 6	Turkish Boeing 757	Crashed into Atlantic Ocean, off Dominican Republic	189
1996, Apr. 25	T-43, a military version of a Boeing 737	Crashed into mountain near Dubrovnik, Croatia	35[19]
1996, May 11	ValuJet DC-9	Crashed into the Florida Everglades after takeoff	110
1996, July 17	Trans World Airlines Boeing 747	Exploded and crashed in Atlantic Ocean, off Long Isl., NY	230
1996, Aug. 29	Vnukovo TU-154	Crashed into mountain on Arctic island of Spitsbergen	141
1996, Oct. 2	Aeroperu Boeing 757	Crashed in Pacific after takeoff from Lima, Peru	70
1996, Oct. 31	Brazilian TAM Fokker-100	Crashed into houses in São Paulo, Brazil	98[20]
1996, Nov. 7	Nigerian Boeing 727	Crashed into a lagoon 40 mi SE of Lagos, Nigeria	143
1996, Nov. 12	**Saudi Arabian Boeing 747, Kazakh IL-76 cargo plane**	**Collided in midair near New Delhi, India**	**349**[21]
1996, Nov. 23	Ethiopian Boeing 767	Hijacked, then crashed in Indian Ocean off the Comoros	127
1997, Jan. 9	Comair Embraer 120	Crashed on approach into Detroit Metro. Airport	29
1997, Feb. 4	2 Sikorsky CH-53 transport helicopters	Collided in midair over northern Galilee, Israel	73
1997, May 8	China Southern Airlines Boeing 737	Crashed on approach into Shenzhen's Huangtian Airport	35
1997, July 11	Cubana de Aviación Antonov-24	Crashed into the Caribbean off SE Cuba	44
1997, Aug. 6	Korean Air Boeing 747-300	Crashed into jungle on Guam on approach into airport	228
1997, Sept. 3	Vietnamese Airlines TU-134	Crashed on approach into Phnom Penh airport	64
1997, Sept. 14	U.S. C-141 cargo plane, Ger. TU-154	Collided in midair off SW Africa	33
1997, Sept. 26	Indonesian Airbus A-300	Crashed near Medan, Indonesia, airport	234
1997, Oct. 10	Austral Airlines DC-9-32	Crashed and exploded near Neuvo Berlin, Uruguay	74
1997, Dec. 6	Russian AN-124 transport cargo plane	Crashed into apartment complex near Irkutsk, Siberia	67*
1997, Dec. 15	Chartered TU-154 from Tajikistan	Crashed in desert near Sharja, U.A.E., airport	85
1997, Dec. 17	Chartered Yakovlev-42 from Ukraine	Crashed in mountains near Katerini, Greece	70
1997, Dec. 19	SilkAir Boeing 737-300	Crashed in Musi River, Sumatra, Indonesia	104
1998, Jan. 14	Afghan cargo plane	Crashed into mountain, SW Pakistan	50+
1998, Feb. 2	Cebu Pacific Air DC-9-32	Crashed into mountain near Cagayan de Oro, Philippines	104
1998, Feb. 16	China Airlines Airbus 300-622R	Crashed on approach to airport, Taipei, Taiwan	203[22]
1998, Apr. 20	Air France Boeing 727-200	Crashed into mountain after takeoff from Bogotá, Colombia	53
1998, Sept. 2	Swissair MD-11	Crashed into Atlantic Ocean off Halifax, Nova Scotia	229
1998, Sept. 25	Pauknair BAE146	Crashed into hillside in Morocco	38
1998, Oct. 11	Congo Air Lines Boeing 727	Shot down by rebels in Kindu, Congo	40
1998, Dec. 11	Thai Airways Airbus A310-200	Crashed short of runway at Surat Thani airport, S Thailand	101
1999, Feb. 24	China Southwest Airlines TU-154	Crashed on approach to Wenzhou airport, eastern China	61
1999, Sept. 1	LAPA Boeing 737-200	Crashed on takeoff from Jorge Newbery Airport, Buenos Aires	74[23]
1999, Oct. 31	EgyptAir Boeing 767-300	Crashed off Nantucket, MA	217
2000, Jan. 31	Alaska Airlines MD-83	Crashed into Pacific Ocean NW of Malibu, CA	88
2000, Apr. 19	Air Philippines Boeing 737-200	Crashed by Davao airport	131
2000, May 21	Chartered Jetstream 31	Crashed near Wilkes-Barre, PA	19
2000, July 25	Air France Concorde	Crashed into hotel after takeoff from Paris	113[24]
2000, Aug. 23	Gulf Air Airbus A320	Crashed into Persian Gulf near Manama, Bahrain	143
2000, Oct. 31	Singapore Airlines Boeing 747-400	Crashed immediately after takeoff, Taipei, Taiwan	81
2000, Oct. 31	Chartered Antonov 26	Exploded after takeoff in northern Angola	50
2000, Nov. 15	Chartered Antonov 24	Crashed after takeoff from Luanda, Angola	40+
2001, Jan. 27	Chartered Beechcraft King Air 200	Crashed after takeoff from Boulder, CO	10[25]
2001, Mar. 3	C23 Sherpa military transport	Crashed in storm, central GA	21
2001, Apr. 7	M-17 helicopter	Crashed into mountain S. of Hanoi, Vietnam	16[26]
2001, July 3	Vladivostokavia TU-154	Crashed on approach to landing at Irkutsk, Russia	145
2001, Sept. 11	**2 Boeing 767s, 2 Boeing 757s**	**See below**[27]	**265**[27]
2001, Oct. 4	Sibir Airlines Tupelov TU-154	Crashed into Black Sea, struck by errant Ukrainian missile	78
2001, Oct. 8	Twin-engine Cessna, Scandinavian Airlines System (SAS) jetliner	Collided in heavy fog during takeoff from Milan, Italy	118*
2001, Nov. 12	**American Airlines Airbus A-300**	**Crashed after takeoff from JFK Airport, New York, NY**	**265***
2002, Jan. 28	Ecuadoran Airlines Boeing 727-100	Crashed in Andes mountains in southern Colombia	92
2002, Feb. 12	Iran Air Tours TU-154	Crashed before landing in Khorramabad, Iran	119
2002, Apr. 15	Air China Boeing 767-200	Crashed into hillside amid rain and fog near Pusan, South Korea	122
2002, Apr. 18	4-seat Rockwell Commander	Crashed into Pirelli building, tallest skyscraper in Milan, Italy	3*
2002, May 4	EAS Airlines BAC 1-11-500	Crashed in suburb of Kano, Nigeria, shortly after takeoff	148+*
2002, May 7	China Northern MD-82	Plunged into Yellow Sea near Dalian, China, after fire in cabin	112
2002, May 25	China Airlines Boeing 747-200	Broke apart in mid-air and plunged into Taiwan Strait	225
2002, July 1	Bashkirian Airlines TU-154, DHL (Ger. cargo) Boeing 757	Collided over S Germany	71
2002, July 4	Prestige Airlines Cargo Boeing B-707	Crashed short of runway in Bangui, Central African Rep.	25
2002, July 27	Ukraine Air Force Sukhoi SU-27	Crashed into spectators at airshow in Lviv, Ukraine	85

Date	Aircraft	Site of accident	Deaths
2002, Aug. 19	Russian MI-26 helicopter	Troop-carrier hit by Chechen missile near Grozny	127
2002, Dec. 23	Aeromist Kharkiv Antonov AN-140	Crashed into mountain in fog approaching Isfahan, Iran	46
2003, Jan. 8	Air Midwest, Beechcraft 1900D	Crashed after takeoff at Charlotte, N.C.	21
2003, Jan. 8	Turkish Airlines Avro RJ-100	Crashed on landing in Diyarbakir, Turkey	75
2003, Jan. 9	TANS Airlines Fokker 28 Fellowship	Crashed into mountain near Chachopoyas, Peru	46
2003, Feb. 19	Iranian Guard IL-76	Troop-carrying plane crashed into mountain near Kerman, Iran	275
2003, Mar. 6	Air Algerie Boeing 737	Crashed on takeoff at Tamanrasset, Algeria	102
2003, May 8	Congolese Army IL-76	On flight from Kinshasa door opened, passengers sucked out	160
2003, May 26	Ukrain.-Medit. Airlines Yak. 42D	Crashed into mountain in fog approaching Trabzon, Turkey	75
2003, July 8	Sudan Airways, Boeing 737-2J8C	Crashed into hillside after takeoff from Port Sudan Airport	116
2003, Aug. 24	Tropical Airways Let 410UVP-E	Crashed after takeoff in Haiti, because of overloading	21
2003, Nov. 29	Congolese Air Force Antonov 26	Crashed on takeoff attempt from Boendo, Dem. Rep. of Congo	33
2003, Dec. 25	Union Transp. Africaines Boeing B-727	Crashed after takeoff from Cotonou, Benin	140
2004, Jan. 3	Flash Airlines Boeing B-737	Crashed after takeoff from Sharm el-Sheik, Egypt	148
2004, Jan. 13	Uzbekistan Airways Yakovlev YAK-40	Crashed on landing attempt in fog at Tashkent, Uzbekistan	37
2004, Jan. 17	Cessna 208B Grand Caravan	Crashed into L. Erie after takeoff from island nr. Can	10
2004, Feb. 10	Iranian Kish Airline Fokker-50	Crashed on approach to Sharjah, UAE	43
2004, Mar. 21	Med-Trans Corp. Bell 407 helicopter	Crashed in Pyote, TX, enroute to Lubbock, TX	4
2004, May 15	Rico Linhas Aereas Embraer 120ER Brasilia	Crashed in Amazon jungle near Manaus, Brazil	33
2004, June 8	Gabon Express Hawker Siddeley HS-748	Crashed into sea after takeoff from Libreville, Gabon	19
2004, June 29	UN MI-8 helicopter	Crashed in forest in Sierra Leone	24[28]
2004, Aug. 24	Volga-Aviaexpress TU-134A-3, Sibir Airlines TU-154B2	2 planes crashed after takeoff from Moscow, Russia; brought down by Chechen terrorists	90
2005, Jan. 13	Colombian Black Hawk helicopter	Crashed in Narino prov. in bad weather	20
2005, Jan. 26	CH-53-Super Stallion Marine helicopter	Crashed in Iraq's western desert	31
2005, Feb. 3	Kam Air Boeing 737	Crashed after attempting to land at Kabul airport, Afghan.	104
2005, Mar. 16	Russian Antonov-24	Crashed in Varandei, Russia, near Barents Sea	29
2005, Apr. 7	Russian AN-24 turboprop	Crashed into hill near Barents Sea port	28+
2005, July 14	Ugandan mil. helicopter	Crashed in mountains; among the killed was former Sudan rebel leader John Garang	14
2005, Aug. 6	Tunisian ATR-72 turboprop	Crashed off Sicilia Coast after engine fail	16
2005, Aug. 14	Helios Airways Boeing 737	Crashed near Athens, Greece	121
2005, Aug. 16	West Caribbean Airways MD-82	Crashed into mountains after engine failure, near Machiques, Venezuela	160
2005, Aug. 23	TANS Peru Boeing 737	Crashed near Pucallpa, Peru, during emergency landing	41
2005, Sept. 5	Mandala Airlines Boeing 737-200	Crashed after takeoff from Medan, Sumatra, Indon.	145
2005, Oct. 22	Bellview Airlines Boeing 737-200	Crashed after takeoff in heavy electrical storm near Lagos, Nigeria	117
2005, Dec. 6	Lockheed Martin C-130	Crashed into apartment building after reportedly attempting emergency landing shortly after takeoff in Tehran, Iran	115+[29]
2005, Dec. 10	Sosoliso Airlines DC-9	Crashed during severe storm near Port Harcourt, Nigeria	107[30]
2006, Aug. 27	Comair Bombardier CRJ-100	Crashed after takeoff from airport in Lexington, KY	49

*Including those on ground and in buildings. (1) First fatal crash of commercial jet. (2) Caused by bomb planted by John G. Graham in insurance plot to kill his mother, a passenger. (3) Incl. all 128 aboard planes and 6 on ground. (4) Killed 84 on plane and 71 on ground. (5) Incl. 43 Marshall Univ. football players and coaches. (6) Airliner-fighter crash; pilot of fighter parachuted to safety, was arrested for negligence. (7) First supersonic plane crash; killed 8 on ground. (8) Crew of 3 killed; 97 killed on the ground. (9) World's worst airline disaster. (10) Incl. Univ. of Evansville basketball team. (11) Incl. 2 on ground. Highest death toll in U.S. aviation history. (12) Incl. 22 members of U.S. boxing team. (13) Incl. 8 on ground. (14) Worst single-plane disaster. (15) Incl. 248 members of U.S. 101st Airborne Division. (16) Incl. 15 on ground. (17) Incl. 11 on ground. (18) Incl. 1 on ground. (19) Incl. U.S. Sec. of Commerce Ron Brown. (20) Incl. 2 on ground. (21) World's worst midair collision. (22) Incl. 6 on ground. (23) Incl. 10 on ground. (24) World's first Concorde crash; deaths incl. 5 on ground. (25) Incl. 7 players and staff of Oklahoma State Univ. men's basketball team. (26) Carried U.S. mil. personnel, searching for MIAs from Vietnam War. (27) 4 planes were hijacked and crashed, with all on board (265, incl. 19 hijackers) killed: American Airlines Flight 11, a Boeing 767-200, with 81 passengers, 11 crew, crashed into Tower 1 of the World Trade Center in NYC; United Airlines Flight 175, a Boeing 767-200, with 56 passengers, 9 crew, crashed into Tower 2 of the World Trade Center; American Airlines Flight 77, a Boeing 757-200, with 58 passengers, 6 crew, crashed into the Pentagon outside Washington, DC; United Air Lines Flight 93, a Boeing 757-200, with 37 passengers, 7 crew, crashed near Shanksville, PA. About 2,600 people on ground died at the 2 World Trade Center towers, and 125 in the Pentagon. (28) Incl. 14 Pakistani UN Peacekeepers. (29) 92 on plane plus 23+ on ground. (30) Incl. 50+ children.

Some Notable Shipwrecks Since 1854

(Figures indicate estimated lives lost. Does not include most wartime disasters.)

1854, Mar.—City of Glasgow; Brit. steamer missing in N Atlantic; 480.

1854, Sept. 27—Arctic; U.S. (Collins Line) steamer sunk in collision with French steamer *Vesta* near Cape Race; 285-351.

1856, Jan. 23—Pacific; U.S. (Collins Line) steamer missing in N Atlantic; 186-286.

1858, Sept. 23—Austria; German steamer destroyed by fire in N Atlantic; 471.

1863, Apr. 27—Anglo-Saxon; Brit. steamer wrecked at Cape Race; 238.

1865, Apr. 27—Sultana; Mississippi R. steamer blew up near Memphis, TN; 1,450.

1869, Oct. 27—Stonewall; steamer burned on Mississippi R. below Cairo, IL; 200.

1870, Jan. 25—City of Boston; Brit. (Inman Line) steamer vanished between New York and Liverpool; 177.

1870, Oct. 19—Cambria; Brit. steamer off N Ireland; 196.

1872, Nov. 7—Mary Celeste; U.S. half-brig sailed from New York for Genoa; found abandoned; loss of life unknown.

1873, Jan. 22—Northfleet; Brit. steamer foundered off Dungeness, England; 300.

1873, Apr. 1—Atlantic; Brit. (White Star) steamer off Nova Scotia; 585.

1873, Nov. 23—Ville du Havre; French steamer sank after collision with Brit. sailing ship *Loch Earn*; 226.

1875, May 7—Schiller; German steamer off Scilly Isles; 312.

1875, Nov. 4—Pacific; U.S. steamer sank after collision off Cape Flattery; 236.

1878, Sept. 3—Princess Alice; Brit. steamer sank after collision in Thames River; 700.

1878, Dec. 18—Byzantin; French steamer sank after collision in Dardanelles; 210.

1881, May 24—Victoria; steamer capsized in Thames R., Canada; 200.

1883, Jan. 19—Cimbria; German steamer sank in collision with Brit. steamer *Sultan* in North Sea; 389.

1887, Nov. 15—Wah Yeung; Brit. steamer burned at sea; 400.

1890, Feb. 17—Duburg; Brit. steamer wrecked, China Sea; 400.

1890, Sept. 19—Ertogrul; Turkish frigate off Japan; 540.

1891, Mar. 17—Utopia; Brit. steamer sank in collision with Brit. ironclad *Anson* off Gibraltar; 562.

1895, Jan. 30—Elbe; German steamer sank in collision with Brit. steamer *Craithie* in North Sea; 332.

1895, Mar. 11—Reina Regenta; Spanish cruiser foundered near Gibraltar; 400.

1898, Feb. 15—Maine; U.S. battleship blown up in Havana Harbor; 260.

1898, July 4—La Bourgogne; French steamer sank in collision with Brit. sailing ship *Cromartyshire* off Nova Scotia; 549.

1898, Nov. 26—Portland; U.S. steamer off Cape Cod; 157.

1904, June 15—General Slocum; excursion steamer burned in East R., New York City; 1,030.

1904, June 28—Norge; Danish steamer wrecked on Rockall Island, Scotland; 620.

1906, Aug. 4—Sirio; Italian steamer wrecked off Cape Palos, Spain; 350.

1908, Mar. 23—Matsu Maru; Japanese steamer sank in collision near Hakodate, Japan; 300.

1909, Aug. 1—Waratah; Brit. steamer, Sydney to London, vanished; 300.

1910, Feb. 9—General Chanzy; French steamer wrecked off Minorca, Spain; 200.

1911, Sept. 25—Liberté; French battleship exploded at Toulon; 285.

1912, Mar. 5—Principe de Asturias; Spanish steamer wrecked off Spain; 500.

1912, Apr. 14-15—Titanic; Brit. (White Star) steamer hit iceberg in N Atlantic; 1,503.

1912, Sept. 28—Kichemaru; Japanese steamer sank off Japanese coast; 1,000.

1914, May 29—Empress of Ireland; Brit. (Canadian Pacific) steamer collided with Norw. collier in St. Lawrence R.; 1,014.

1915, May 7—Lusitania; Brit. (Cunard Line) steamer torpedoed and sunk by German submarine off Ireland; 1,198.

1915, July 24—Eastland; steamer capsized in Chicago R.; 844.

1916, Feb. 26—Provence; French cruiser sank in Medit.; 3,100.

1916, Mar. 3—Principe de Asturias; Spanish steamer wrecked near Santos, Brazil; 558.

1916, Aug. 29—Hsin Yu; Chinese steamer sank off Chinese coast; 1,000.

1917, Dec. 6—Mont Blanc and **Imo;** French ammunition ship and Belgian steamer collided in Halifax Harbor; 1,600.

1918, Apr. 25—Kiang-Kwan; Chinese steamer sank in collision off Hankow; 500.

1918, July 12—Kawachi; Japanese battleship blew up in Tokayama Bay; 500.

1918, Oct. 25—Princess Sophia; Canadian steamer sank off Alaskan coast; 398.

1919, Jan. 17—Chaonia; French steamer lost in Straits of Messina, Italy; 460.

1919, Sept. 9—Valbanera; Spanish steamer lost off Florida coast; 500.

1921, Mar. 18—Hong Kong; steamer wrecked in South China Sea; 1,000.

1922, Aug. 26—Niitaka; Japanese cruiser sank in storm off Kamchatka, USSR; 300.

1924, June 12—USS Mississippi; explosions in gun turret of U.S. battleship, off San Pedro, CA; 48.

1927, Oct. 25—Principessa Mafalda; Italian steamer blew up, sank off Porto Seguro, Brazil; 314.

1928, Nov. 12—Vestris; Brit. steamer sank off Virginia; 113.

1934, Sept. 8—Morro Castle; U.S. steamer, Havana to New York, burned off Asbury Park, NJ; 134.

1939, May 23—Squalus; U.S. submarine sank off Portsmouth, NH; 26.

1939, June 1—Thetis; submarine sank, Liverpool Bay; 99.

1942, Feb. 18—Truxtun and **Pollux;** U.S. destroyer and cargo ship ran aground, sank off Newfoundland; 204.

1942, Oct. 2—Curacao; Brit. cruiser sank after collision with liner *Queen Mary;* 338.

1944, Dec. 17-18—3 U.S. Third Fleet destroyers sank during typhoon in Philippine Sea; 790.

1945, Jan. 30—Wilhelm Gustloff; Liner with German refugees, soldiers sunk by Soviet submarine in Baltic; 5,000-9,000.

1945, Apr. 16—Goya; Cargo ship carrying German refugees, soldiers sunk by Soviet submarine in Baltic; 6,000-7,000.

1945, May 3—Cap Arcona and **Thielbek;** German liners carrying concentration camp inmates sunk by British warplanes in Lubeck Bay; 7,000-8,000.

1947, Jan. 19—Himera; Greek steamer hit a mine off Athens; 392.

1947, Apr. 16—Grandcamp; French freighter exploded in Texas City, TX, harbor, started fires; 576+.

1948, Nov.—Chinese army evacuation ship exploded and sank off S Manchuria; 6,000.

1948, Dec. 3—Kiangya; Chinese refugee ship wrecked in explosion S of Shanghai; 1,100+.

1949, Sept. 17—Noronic; Canadian Great Lakes Cruiser burned at Toronto dock; 130.

1952, Apr. 26—Hobson and **Wasp;** U.S. destroyer and aircraft carrier collided in Atlantic; 176.

1954, May 26—Bennington; U.S. carrier damaged by explosions off Rhode Island; 103.

1954, Sept. 26—Toya Maru; Japanese ferry sank in Tsugaru Strait, Japan; 1,172.

1956, July 26—Andrea Doria and **Stockholm;** Italian liner and Swedish liner collided off Nantucket; 51.

1957, July 14—Eshghabad; Soviet ship ran aground in Caspian Sea; 270.

1960, Dec. 19—Constellation; U.S. aircraft carrier caught fire in Brooklyn Navy Yard, NY; 49.

1961, Apr. 8—Dara; British liner exploded in Persian Gulf; 236.

1961, July 8—Save; Portuguese ship ran aground off Mozambique; 259.

1963, Apr. 10—Thresher; U.S. Navy atomic submarine sank in N Atlantic; 129.

1964, Feb. 10—Voyager; Australian destroyer sank after collision with aircraft carrier *Melbourne* off New South Wales; 82.

1965, Nov. 13—Yarmouth Castle; Panamanian registered cruise ship burned and sank off Nassau; 89.

1967, July 29—Forrestal; U.S. aircraft carrier caught fire off N Vietnam; 134.

1968, Jan. 25—Dakar; Israeli submarine vanished in Medit.; 69.

1968, late May—Scorpion; U.S. nuclear submarine sank in Atlantic near Azores; 99 (located Oct. 31).

1969, June 2—Evans; U.S. destroyer cut in half by Australian carrier *Melbourne,* S China Sea; 74.

1970, Mar. 4—Eurydice; French submarine sank in Mediterranean near Toulon; 57.

1970, Dec. 15—Namyong-Ho; South Korean ferry sank in Korea Strait; 308.

1974, May 1—Motor launch capsized off Bangladesh; 250.

1974, Sept. 26—Soviet destroyer sank in Black Sea; 200+.

1975, Nov. 10—Edmund Fitzgerald; U.S. cargo ship sank during storm on Lake Superior; 29.

1976, Oct. 20—George Prince and **Frosta;** ferryboat and Norwegian tanker collided on Mississippi R. at Luling, LA; 77.

1976, Dec. 25—Patria; Egyptian liner caught fire and sank in the Red Sea; 100.

1979, Aug. 14—23 yachts competing in Fastnet yacht race sank or abandoned during storm in south Irish Sea; 18.

1980, Apr. 22—Don Juan; sank off Mindoro Is., Philippines, after colliding with a barge; 1,000+.

1981, Jan. 27—Tamponas II; Indonesian passenger ship caught fire and sank in Java Sea; 580.

1981, May 26—Nimitz; U.S. Marine combat jet crashed on deck of U.S. aircraft carrier; 14.

1983, Feb. 12—Marine Electric; coal freighter sank during storm off Chincoteague, VA; 33.

1983, May 25—10th of Ramadan; Nile steamer caught fire and sank in Lake Nasser; 357.

1986, Apr. 20—Ferry sank near Barisal, Bangladesh; 262.

1986, May 25—Samia; double-decker ferry capsized in storm on Bangladesh's Meghna R.; 600+.

1986, Sept. 1—Admiral Nakhimov and **Pyotr Vasev;** Soviet cruise ship collided with Soviet freighter in the Black Sea; 425.

1987, Mar. 6—The Herald of Free Enterprise; British ferry capsized off Zeebrugge, Belgium; 189.

1987, Dec. 20—Dona Paz and **Victor;** Philippine ferry and oil tanker collided in Tablas Strait; 4,341.

1988, Aug. 6—Indian ferry capsized on Ganges R.; 400+.

1989, Apr. 19—USS Iowa; explosion in gun turret; 47.

1989, Apr. 7—Komsolets; Soviet submarine sank after fire off Norwegian coast; 42.

1989, Aug. 20—Bowbelle and **Marchioness;** Brit. barge struck Brit. pleasure cruiser on Thames R. in central London; 56.

1989, Sept. 10—Romanian pleasure boat and Bulgarian barge collided on Danube R.; 161.

1991, Apr. 10—Auto ferry and oil tanker collided outside Livorno Harbor, Italy; 140.

1991, Dec. 14—Salem Express; ferry rammed coral reef near Safaga, Egypt; 462.

1993, Feb. 17—Neptune; ferry capsized off Port-au-Prince, Haiti; 500+.

1993, Oct. 10—Seohae; capsized in Yellow Sea near W South Korea during storm; 285.

1994, Sept. 28—Estonia; ferry sank in Baltic Sea; 1,049.

1996, May 21—Bukoba; ferry sank in Lake Victoria (Africa); 500.

1997, Feb. 20—Tamil refugee boat sank off Sri Lanka; 165.

1997, Mar. 28—Albanian refugee boat sank in Adriatic Sea after being rammed by Italian navy warship Sibilla; 83.

1997, Sept. 8—Pride of la Gonâve; Haitian ferry sank off Montrouis, Haiti; 200+.

1998, Apr. 4—Passenger boat capsized off coast near Ibaka beach, Nigeria; 280.

1998, Sept. 2—2 passenger boats capsized on Lake Kivu, near Bukavu, Congo; 200+.

1998, Sept. 18—Ferry sank south of Manila; 97.

1999, Feb. 6—Harta Rimba; cargo ship sank off Indonesia; 280+.

1999, Mar. 26—Passenger boat overturned off coast, Sierra Leone; 150+.

1999, Apr. 2—Passenger ferry sank off coast of Nigeria; 100+.

1999, May 1—Excursion boat sank in Lake Hamilton, AR; 13.

1999, May 8—Passenger ferry capsized off Bangladesh; 200+.

1999, Nov. 24—Dashun; passenger ferry capsized near Yantai, China; 280.

2000, May 3—2 ferries capsized, Meghna R., Bangladesh; 72+.

2000, June 29—Overloaded ferry capsized in storm off Sulawesi Is., Indonesia; 500+.

2000, Aug. 12—Kursk; Russian sub sank in Barents Sea; 118.

2000, Sept. 26—Express Samina; Greek ferry sank off Paros, Greece; 81+.

2001, Feb. 9—Ehime Maru; Japanese trawler sunk by surfacing U.S. submarine *Greeneville,* near Hawaii; 9.

2001, Oct. 19—Indonesian fishing boat overloaded with asylum-seekers sank off Java's south coast; 350+.

2001, Dec. 22—North Korean spy ship sank after exchanging fire with Japanese coast guard; 15.

2002, May 4—Bangladesh ferry sank, Meghna R.; 370+.

2002, May 26—Barge struck Interstate highway bridge over Arkansas R. in Oklahoma; 13+.

2002, Sept. 26—**Joola;** overloaded Senegalese ferry capsized in ocean off The Gambia; 1,863.
2003, Mar. 23—**Kashowgwe;** overloaded ferry capsized in Lake Tanganyika off Burundi; 111+.
2003, Apr. 21—2 ferries capsized in storms in Bangladesh on Meghna and Buriganga rivers; 180+.
2003, Apr. 4—Ferry sank near Chhatak in Bangladesh; 80+.
2003, July 8—**MV-Nasrin 1;** overcrowded ferry sank near Chandpur in the Bangladesh River; 400.
2003, Oct. 15—**Andrew J. Barberi;** NYC ferry crashed into dock on approaching Staten Is.; 11.
2003, Nov. 25—**Dieu Merci;** overloaded ferry sank on Lake Mayi Ndombe, Dem. Rep. of Congo; 130-200.
2004, Jan. 26—**Convoi Lengi**; ferry caught fire on Congo R. in Dem. Rep. of Congo; 200.
2004, Feb. 28—**Bow Mariner**; tanker carrying ethanol caught fire and exploded off Virginia coast; 21.

2004, Mar 6—**Lady D;** water taxi capsized in storm in Baltimore's Inner Harbor; 5.
2004, Mar. 11—**Samson;** ferry sank off Madagascar during cyclone; 113.
2004, May 24—**Lightning Sun;** ferry sank in Meghna R. in Bangladesh; 60+.
2004, Dec. 8—**Selendang Ayu;** Malaysian freighter ran aground, Aleutian Islands; 6.
2005, July 7—**KMP Digul;** ferry capsized in rough waters near Merauke, Indonesia; 150+.
2005, Aug. 12—Fishing boat overloaded with Ecuadorans attempting to migrate to the U.S. sank off Columbia; 94.
2005, Oct. 2—**Ethan Allen;** glass boat carrying senior citizens capsized on tour, Lake George, in NY; 20.
2006, Feb. 3—**Al-Salam Boccaccio 98;** ferry caught fire and sank in Red Sea off Egypt; 1,000+.

Some Notable Railroad Disasters Since 1925

Date	Location	Deaths	Date	Location	Deaths
1925, June 16	Hackettstown, NJ	50	1983, Feb. 19	Empalme, Mexico	100
1925, Oct. 27	Victoria, MS	21	1985, Feb. 23	Madhya Pradesh, India	50
1926, Sept. 5	Waco, CO	30	1985, Aug. 3	southern France	35
1937, July 16	Bhita, India	107	1987, July 2	Kasumbalesha Shaba, Zaire	125
1938, June 19	Saugus, MT	47	1988, June 27	Paris train station, Gare de Lyon	57
1939, Aug. 12	Harney, NV	24	1988, Dec. 12	London, England	35
1939, Dec. 22	Near Magdeburg, Germany	132	1989, Jan. 15	Maizdi Khan, Bangladesh	110+
1939, Dec. 22	Near Friedrichshafen, Germany	99	1989, June 9	train collided with bus in S Russia	31
1940, Apr. 19	Little Falls, NY	31	1990, Jan. 4	Sindh Prov., Pakistan	210+
1940, July 31	Cuyahoga Falls, OH	43	1991, May 14	Shigaraki, Japan	42
1943, Aug. 29	Wayland, NY	27	1993, Sept. 22	Big Bayou Conot, AL	47
1943, Sept. 6	Frankford Junction, Philad. PA	79	1994, Mar. 8	Nr. Durban, South Africa	63
1943, Dec. 16	Between Rennert and Buie, NC	72	1994, Sept. 22	Tolunda, Angola	300
1944, Jan. 16	León Prov., Spain	500	1995, Aug. 20	Firozabad, India	358
1944, Mar. 2	Salerno, Italy	521	1996, Feb. 16	Silver Spring, MD	11
1944, July 6	High Bluff, TN	35	1997, Mar. 3	Punjab State, Pakistan	125
1944, Aug. 4	Near Stockton, GA	47	1997, Mar. 31	Huarte Arakil, Spain	21
1944, Sept. 14	Dewey, IN	29	1997, Apr. 29	Hunan, China	58
1944, Dec. 31	Bagley, UT	50	1997, May 4	Rwanda	100+
1945, Aug. 9	Michigan, ND	34	1997, Sept. 14	Central India	77
1946, Mar. 20	Aracaju, Mexico	185	1998, June 3	Eschede, Germany	102
1946, Apr. 25	Naperville, IL	45	1998, Feb. 19	Yaounde, Cameroon	100+
1947, Feb. 18	Gallitzin, PA	24	1998, Nov. 26	Khanna, India	200+
1949, Oct. 22	Nr. Dwor, Poland	200+	1999, Mar. 15	Bourbonnais, IL	11
1950, Feb. 17	Rockville Centre, NY	31	1999, Mar. 24	Nairobi, Kenya	32+
1950, Sept. 11	Coshocton, OH	33	1999, Aug. 2	Gauhati, India	285+
1950, Nov. 22	Richmond Hill, NY	79	1999, Oct. 5	London, England	31
1951, Feb. 6	Woodbridge, NJ	84	2000, Jan. 4	Rena, Norway	35
1952, Mar. 4	Nr. Rio de Janeiro, Brazil	119	2000, July 28	São Paulo, Brazil	12
1952, July 9	Rzepin, Poland	160	2000, Nov. 11	Kaprun, Austria	155
1952, Oct. 8	Harrow, England	112	2001, Feb. 28	Great Heck, England	13
1953, Mar. 27	Conneaut, OH	21	2001, June 22	Cochin, India	64
1955, Apr. 3	Guadalajara, Mexico	300	2001, Sept. 1	Indonesia	40
1956, Jan. 22	Los Angeles, CA	30	2002, Feb. 20	South of Cairo, Egypt	373
1957, Sept. 1	Kendal, Jamaica	178	2002, Apr. 18	Seville, FL	4
1957, Sept. 29	Montgomery, W Pakistan	250	2002, Apr. 23	Placentia, CA	2
1957, Dec. 4	London, England	90	2002, May 25	Muamba, Mozambique	196+
1958, May 8	Rio de Janeiro, Brazil	128	2002, June 24	Igandu, Tanzania	281+
1958, Sept. 15	Elizabethport, NJ	48	2002, Sept. 10	Bihar, India	118
1960, Nov. 14	Pardubice, Czech.	110	2002, Nov. 6	Nancy, France	12
1962, Jan. 8	Woerden, Netherlands	91	2003, Jan. 3	Maharashtra, India	18
1962, May 3	Tokyo, Japan	163	2003, Feb. 1	NW Zimbabwe	46
1963, Nov. 9	Yokohama, Japan	120+	2003, May 8	Near Lake Balaton in Hungary	33
1964, July 26	Porto, Portugal	94	2003, May 15	Ludhiana, India	36
1967, July 6	Madgeburg, Germany	94	2003, June 3	Spain, Albacete province	19
1970, Feb. 1	Buenos Aires, Argentina	236	2003, June 22	Rajapur, India	33
1972, June 16	Vierzy, France	107	2003, July 2	Andhra Pradesh, India	22
1972, July 21	Seville, Spain	76	2004, Feb. 18	Neyshabur, NE Iran	300+
1972, Oct. 6	Saltillo, Mexico	208	2004, Apr. 22	Ryongchon, North Korea	161
1972, Oct. 30	Chicago, IL	45	2004, July 22	Mekece, NW Turkey	36
1974, Aug. 30	Zagreb, Yugoslavia	153	2005, Jan. 6	Graniteville, SC	8
1975, Feb. 28	London subway train	41	2005, Jan. 26	Glendale, CA	11
1977, Jan. 18	Granville, Australia	83	2005, Apr. 25	Near Amagasaki, Japan	107+
1981, June 6	Bihar, India	800+	2005, July 13	Ghotki, Pakistan	133
1982, Jan. 27	El Asnam, Algeria	130	2005, Oct. 29	Near Veligonda, India	114+
1982, July 11	Tepic, Mexico	120	2006, Jan. 23	Podgorica, Montenegro	46

Some Notable U.S. Tornadoes Since 1925

Date	Location	Deaths	Date	Location	Deaths
1925, Mar. 18	MO, IL, IN	689	1944, June 23	OH, PA, WV, MD	150
1927, Apr. 12	Rock Springs, TX	74	1945, Apr. 12	OK-AR	102
1927, May 9	AR, Poplar Bluff, MO	92	1947, Apr. 9	TX, OK, KS	169
1927, Sept. 29	St. Louis, MO	90	1948, Mar. 19	Bunker Hill and Gillespie, IL	33
1930, May 6	Hill, Navarro, Ellis Co., TX	41	1949, Jan. 3	LA and AR	58
1932, Mar. 21	AL	268	1952, Mar. 21	AR, MO, TN	208
1936, Apr. 5	MS, GA	455	1953, May 11	Waco, TX	114
1936, Apr. 6	Gainesville, GA	203	1953, June 8	MI, OH	142
1938, Sept. 29	Charleston, SC	32	1953, June 9	Worcester and vicinity, MA	90
1942, Mar. 16	Central to NE Mississippi	75	1953, Dec. 5	Vicksburg, MS	38
1942, Apr. 27	Rogers and Mayes Co., OK	52	1955, May 25	KS, MO, OK, TX	115

Date	Location	Deaths	Date	Location	Deaths
1957, May 20	KS, MO	48	1991, Apr. 26	KS, OK	23
1958, June, 4	NW Wisconsin	30	1992, Nov. 21-23	South, Midwest	26
1959, Feb. 10	St. Louis, MO	21	1994, Mar. 27-28	AL, TN, GA, NC, SC	52
1960, May 5, 6	Southeastern OK, AR	30	1995, May 6-7	Southern OK, northern TX	23
1962, Mar. 31	Milton, FL	17	1997, Mar. 1	Central AR	26
1965, Apr. 11	IN, IL, OH, MI, WI	271	1997, May 27	Jarrell, TX	27
1966, Mar. 3	Jackson, MS	57	1998, Feb. 22-23	Central FL	42
1966, Mar. 3	MS, AL	61	1998, Mar. 20	Northeast GA	12
1967, Apr. 21	IL, MI	33	1998, Mar. 24	Eastern India	145
1968, May 15	Midwest	71	1998, Apr. 8	AL, GA, MS	39
1969, Jan. 23	MS	32	1999, May 3-4	OK, KS	42
1971, Feb. 21	Mississippi delta	110	2000, Feb. 14	Southwest GA	22+
1973, May 26-27	South, Midwest	47	2000, July 14	Alberta	11
1974, Apr. 3-4	AL, GA, IN, KY, OH, TN, et al.	315	2000, Dec. 16	AL	12
1977, Apr. 4	AL, MS, GA	22	2001, Nov. 23-24	AL, AR, MS	13
1979, Apr. 10	TX, OK	60	2002, Nov. 9-11	AL, MS, OH, PA, TN	36
1984, Mar. 28	NC, SC	57	2003, Mar. 20	GA	6
1985, May 31	NY, PA, OH, Ont.	75	2003, May 4-11	TN, MO, KS, IL, OK, WV, AL	48
1987, May 22	Saragosa, TX	29	2004, Apr. 20-21	IL, IN	8
1989, Nov. 15	Huntsville, AL	18	2005, Nov. 6	KY, IN	22
1990, Aug. 28	Northern IL	25	2006, Apr. 7-8	Central U.S., from TX to WV	12

Principal U.S. Mine Disasters Since 1900

Source: Bureau of Mines, U.S. Dept. of the Interior; Mine Safety and Health Admin., U.S. Dept. of Labor; World Almanac research
(All are bituminous-coal mines unless otherwise noted.)

Date	Location	Deaths	Date	Location	Deaths	Date	Location	Deaths
1900, May 1	Scofield, UT	200	1913, Oct. 22	Dawson, NM	263	1940, Jan. 10	Bartley, WV	91
1902, May 19	Coal Creek, TN	184	1914, Apr. 28	Eccles, WV	181	1940, Mar. 16	St. Clairesville, OH	72
1902, July 10	Johnstown, PA	112	1915, Mar. 2	Layland, WV	112	1942, Mar. 26	Allentown, PA[3]	31
1903, June 30	Hanna, WY	169	1917, Apr. 27	Hastings, CO	121	1947, Mar. 25	Centralia, IL	111
1904, Jan. 25	Cheswick, PA	179	1917, June 8	Butte, MT[1]	163	1951, Dec. 21	West Frankfort, IL	119
1905, Feb. 26	Virginia City, AL	112	1919, June 5	Wilkes-Barre, PA[2]	92	1959, Jan. 22	Port Griffith, PA	12
1907, Jan. 29	Stuart, WV	84	1922, Nov. 6	Spangler, PA	77	1968, Nov. 20	Farmington, WV	78
1907, Dec. 6	Monongah, WV	361	1922, Nov. 22	Dolomite, AL	90	1970, Dec. 30	Hyden, KY	38
1907, Dec. 19	Jacobs Creek, PA	239	1923, Feb. 8	Dawson, NM	120	1972, May 2	Kellogg, ID[1]	91
1908, Nov. 28	Marianna, PA	154	1923, Aug. 14	Kemmerer, WY	99	1976, Mar. 9	Oven Fork, KY	15
1909, Nov. 13	Cherry, IL	259	1924, Mar. 8	Castle Gate, UT	171	1981, Apr. 15	Redstone, CO	15
1910, Jan. 31	Primero, CO	75	1924, Apr. 28	Benwood, WV	119	1981, Dec. 8	Whitwell, TN	13
1910, May 5	Palos, AL	90	1926, Jan. 13	Wilburton, OK	91	1984, Dec. 19	Orangeville, UT	27
1910, Nov.8	Delagua, CO	79	1926, Nov. 3	Ishpeming, MI[1]	51	1989, Sept. 13	Wheatcroft, KY	10
1911, Apr. 8	Littleton, AL	128	1927, Apr. 30	Everettville, WV	97	2001, Sept. 23	Brookwood, AL	13
1911, Dec. 9	Briceville, TN	84	1928, May 19	Mather, PA	195	2006, Jan. 2	Sago, WV	12
1912, Mar. 26	Jed, WV	83	1930, Nov. 5	Millfield, OH	82			
1913, Apr. 23	Finleyville, PA	96						

Note: World's worst mine disaster killed 1,549 workers in Manchuria, Apr. 25, 1942. (1) Metal mine. (2) Anthracite mine. (3) Limestone mine.

Some Notable Hurricanes, Typhoons, Blizzards, Other Storms

As of Sept. 26, 2006.
H.—hurricane; T.—typhoon

Date	Location	Deaths	Date	Location	Deaths
1881, Aug. 24-29	H., GA, SC	700	1962, Sept. 1	T. *Wanda*, Hong Kong	130-200
1888, Mar. 11-14	Blizzard, eastern U.S.	400	1963, May 28-29	Windstorm, Bangladesh	22,000
1893, Aug. 15-Sept. 2	H., GA, SC	1,000+	1963, Oct. 4-8	H. *Flora*, Caribbean.	6,000
1893, Oct. 1	H., LA	1,100+	1964, June 30	T. *Winnie*, N Philippines	107
1900, Sept. 8	H., Galveston, TX.	8,000+	1964, Sept. 5	T. *Ruby*, Hong Kong and China	735
1906, Sept. 19-24	H., LA, MS	350	1965, May 11-12	Windstorm, Bangladesh	17,000
1906, Sept. 18	T., Hong Kong	10,000+	1965, June 1-2	Windstorm, Bangladesh	30,000
1909, Sept. 20	H., LA	350+	1965, Sept. 7-12	H. *Betsy*, FL, MS, LA	74
1915, Aug. 16	H., Galveston, TX.	275	1965, Dec. 15	Windstorm, Bangladesh	10,000
1915, Sept. 29	H., LA	275	1966, June 4-10	H. *Alma*, Honduras, SE U.S.	51
1919, Sept. 6-14	Carib., Florida Keys, Gulf, TX	600+[1]	1966, Sept. 24-30	H. *Inez*, Carib., FL, Mexico	293
1926, Sept. 11-22	H., FL, AL, MS	370+	1967, July 9	T. *Billie*, SW Japan	347
1926, Oct. 20	H., Cuba	600	1967, Sept. 5-23	H. *Beulah*, Carib., Mex., TX	54
1928, Sept. 6-20	H., southern FL	2,500+	1967, Dec. 12-20	Blizzard, SW U.S.	51
1930, Sept. 3	H., Dominican Republic	2,000	1968, Nov. 18-28	T. *Nina*, Philippines	63
1935, Aug. 29-Sept. 10	H., Caribbean, southeastern U.S.	400+	1969, Aug. 17-18	H. *Camille*, MS, LA	256
1937, Sept. 2	T., "The Great Typhoon," Hong Kong	10,000+	1970, Sept. 15	T. *Georgia*, Philippines	300
1938, Sept. 21	H., Long Island, NY; New England	287[2]	1970, Oct. 14	T. *Sening*, Philippines	583
			1970, Oct. 15	T. *Titang*, Philippines	526
1940, Nov. 11-12	Blizzard, NE, Midwest U.S.	144	1970, Nov. 13	Cyclone, Bangladesh	300,000
1942, Oct. 15-16	H., Bengal, India.	40,000	1971, Aug. 1	T. *Rose*, Hong Kong	130
1947, Dec. 26	Blizzard, NYC, N Atlan. states	55	1972, June 19-29	H. *Agnes*, FL to NY	118
1952, Oct. 22	T., Philippines.	440	1972, Dec. 3	T. *Theresa*, Philippines	169
1954, Aug. 30	H. *Carol*, northeastern U.S.	68	1973, June-Aug.	Monsoon rains, India.	1,217
1954, Oct. 5-18	H. *Hazel*, E Canada, U.S.; Haiti	347	1974, June 11	Storm *Dinah*, Luzon Is., Phil.	71
1955, Aug. 12-13	H. *Connie*, NC, SC, VA, MD	43	1974, July 11	T. *Gilda*, Japan, S. Korea	108
1955, Aug. 7-21	H. *Diane*, eastern U.S.	400	1974, Sept. 19-20	H. *Fifi*, Honduras	2,000
1955, Sept. 19	H. *Hilda*, Mexico	200	1974, Dec. 25	Cyclone leveled Darwin, Austral.	50
1956, Feb. 1-29	Blizzard, W Europe	1,000	1975, Sept. 13-27	H. *Eloise*, Caribbean, NE U.S.	71
1957, June 25-30	H. *Audrey*, TX to AL	390	1976, May 20	T. *Olga*, floods, Philippines	215
1958, Feb. 15-16	Blizzard, NE U.S.	171	1978, Oct. 27	T. *Rita*, Philippines	400
1959, Sept. 17-19	T. *Sarah*, Japan, South Korea	2,000	1979, Aug. 30-Sept. 7	H. *David*, Caribbean, E U.S.	1,100
1959, Sept. 26-27	T. *Vera*, Honshu, Japan	4,466	1980, Aug. 4-11	H. *Allen*, Caribbean, TX	272
1960, Sept. 4-12	H. *Donna*, Caribbean, E U.S.	148	1981, Nov. 25	T. *Irma*, Luzon Is., Philippines	176
1961, Oct. 31	H. *Hattie*, Br. Honduras	400	1983, June	Monsoon, India	900
			1984, Sept. 2	T. *Ike*, S Philippines	1,363

IT'S A RECORD: The largest storm surge ever recorded in the North Sea occurred Jan. 31-Feb. 1, 1953, along the coasts of the Netherlands and southeastern England. The storm surge—water swept inland as the result of a storm's winds—reached a height of nearly 10 ft in England and 11 ft in the Netherlands. Over 2,000 people drowned, and 1,940 sq mi. of land were flooded.

Date	Location	Deaths	Date	Location	Deaths
1985, May 25	Cyclone, Bangladesh	10,000	2001, July 30	T. *Toraji*, Taiwan	200
1985, Oct. 26-Nov. 6	H. *Juan*, SE U.S.	97	2001, Oct. 8-9	H. *Iris*, Belize	22
1987, Nov. 25	T. *Nina*, Philippines	650	2001, Nov. 2-5	H. *Michelle*, Cuba, Jamaica	17
1988, Sept. 10-17	H. *Gilbert*, Carib., Gulf of Mex.	260	2001, Nov. 6-12	T. *Lingling*, S Philip., Vietnam	220+
1989, Sept. 16-22	H. *Hugo*, Caribbean, SE U.S.	504	2002, July 1-11	T. *Chata'an*, Micron., Philip., Jap.	70+
1990, May 6-11	Cyclones, SE India	450	2002, Aug.-Sept.	T. *Rusa*, North & South Korea	115+
1991, Apr. 30	Cyclone, Bangladesh	139,000	2003, Feb. 16-17	Blizzard, E seaboard U.S.	59
1991, Nov. 5	Tropical storm, Philippines	7,000+	2003, Sept. 2	T. *Dujuan*, S China	32
1992, Aug. 24-26	H. *Andrew*, southern FL, LA	65	2003, Sept. 12	T. *Maemi*, South Korea	130
1993, Mar. 13-14	Blizzard, E U.S.	200	2003, Sept. 7-19	H. *Isabel*, NC, VA, MD	
1993, June	Monsoon, Bangladesh	2,000		E seaboard, U.S.	40+
1994, Nov. 8-18	Storm *Gordon*, Caribbean, FL	830	2003, Dec. 17	Cyclone, southern India	50
1995, Oct. 2-4	H. *Opal*, S Mexico, FL, AL	59	2004, Jan. 26-Feb. 4	Cyclone *Elita*, Madagascar	29
1995, Nov. 2-3	T. *Angela*, Philippines	600+	2004, Mar. 7-19	Cyclone *Gafilo*, Madagascar	198
1996, Jan. 7-8	Blizzard, NE U.S.	100	2004, Apr. 8	Cyclone 22P, Fiji	22
1996, Aug. 22	Blizzard, Himalayas, N India	239	2004, May 18	T. *Nida*, Philippines	19+
1996, Aug. 29- Sept. 6	H. *Fran*, Carib., NC, VA, WV	30	2004, May 19	Cyclone, Myanmar	220
1996, Sept. 9-10	H. *Hortense*, Caribbean	24	2004, Aug. 12-15	T. *Rananim*, E China	164
1996, Sept. 9	T. *Sally*, S China	114	2004, Aug. 13-14	H.*Charley*, Fl, SC	36
1996, Nov. 6	Cyclone, Andhra Pradesh, India	1,000+	2004, Aug. 24-Sept. 10	T. *Aere*, China, Taiwan, Philip.	67
1996, Nov. 24-25	Ice storms, TX to MO	26	2004, Sept. 5-6	H. *Frances*, Bahamas, Florida	35
1996, Dec. 25	Tropical storm, E Malaysia	100+	2004, Sept. 7-16	H. *Ivan*, Barbados, Grenada,	
1997, May 19	Cyclone, Bangladesh	108		Jamaica, Cuba, U.S. Gulf	
1997, Aug. 18	T. Taiwan	24		Coast	115
1997, Oct. 8-10	H. *Pauline*, SW Mexico	230	2004, Sept. 16-26	H. *Jeanne*, Dom. Rep., Haiti, FL.	1,500+
1998, Feb. 4-6	Blizzard, KY, WV	10+	2005, July 7-11	H. *Dennis*, Jamaica, Haiti, Cuba,	
1998, June 9	Cyclone, Gujarat, India	1,320		FL.	50
1998, Aug.	Monsoon, Bangladesh	326	2005, Aug. 25-29	H. *Katrina*, LA, MS, FL, AL, GA	1,833+3
1998, Sept. 21-23	H. *Georges*, Caribbean, FL Keys,		2005, Aug. 31-Sept. 1	T. *Talim*, Taiwan; E China	129+
	U.S. Gulf Coast	600+	2005, Sept. 21-24	H. *Rita*, TX, LA	624
1998, Oct. 27-29	H. *Mitch*, Honduras, Nicaragua,		2005, Sept. 21-28	T. *Damrey*, SE Asia, Philippines,	
	Guatemala, El Salvador	10,866+		Hainan (China)	145
1999, Sept. 4-17	H. *Floyd*, Baha., E seaboard, U.S	56	2005, Oct. 4	H. *Stan*, Central Amer., Mex.	1,000+5
1999, Oct. 29	Cyclone, E India	9,392	2006, Feb. 17	Landslides from heavy rain,	
1999, Dec. 26-29	Gales, France, Switz., Germany	120		Leyte Is., Philippines	137+
2000, Dec. 27	Winter storm, TX, OK, AR	40+	2006, Jul. 14	Tropical Storm *Bilis*, SE China	612
2001, June 6-17	Tropical storm *Allison*, SE U.S.	47	2006, Aug. 10	T. *Saomai*, SE China	295

(1) Incl. about 500 lost on ships at sea. (2) 600 incl. offshore deaths and deaths from flooding that started Sept. 12. (3) Official toll as of Aug. 2006 was 1,577 in LA, 238 in MS, 14 in FL, and 2 each in AL and GA. (4) Incl. 55 indirect deaths, among them 20 people, mostly elderly evacuees froma nursing home, whose bus exploded and caught fire oustide Dallas. (5) Incl. deaths from floods and landslides generated by heavy rainstorms.

Some Notable Floods, Tidal Waves

Date	Location	Deaths	Date	Location	Deaths
1703	Awa, Japan	100,000+	1971, Feb. 26	Rio de Janeiro, Brazil	130
1889, May 31	Johnstown, PA	2,200+	1972, Feb. 26	Buffalo Creek, WV	118
1903, June 15	Heppner, OR	325	1972, June 9	Rapid City, SD	238
1911	Chang Jiang River, China	100,000	1972, Aug. 7	Luzon Isl., Philippines	454
1913, Mar. 25-27	OH, IN	732	1972, Aug. 19-31	Pakistan	1,500
1915, Aug. 17	Galveston, TX	275	1974, Mar. 29	Tubaro, Brazil	1,000
1927, Jan.-July	Mississippi Valley	246+	1974, Aug. 12	Monty-Long, Bangladesh	2,500
1928, Mar. 13	Dam collapse, Saugus, CA	450	1976, June 5	Teton Dam collapse, ID	11
1928, Sept. 16	Lake Okeechobee, FL	1,770+	1976, July 31	Big Thompson Canyon, CO	140
1931, Aug.	Huang He River, China	3,700,000	1976, Nov. 17	East Java, Indonesia	136
1937, Jan. 22	OH, MS Valleys	250	1977, July 19-20	Johnstown, PA	68
1939	N China	200,000	1977, Nov. 6	Toccoa, GA	39
1946, Apr. 1	HI, AK	159	1978, June-Sept.	N India	1,200
1947, Sept. 20	Honshu Island, Japan	1,900	1979, Jan.-Feb.	Brazil	204
1951, Aug.	Manchuria	1,800	1979, July 17	Lomblem Isl., Indonesia	539
1953, Jan. 31	W Europe	2,000	1979, Aug. 11	Morvi, India	15,000
1954, Aug. 17	Farahzad, Iran	2,000	1980, Feb. 13-22	Southern CA, AZ	26
1955, Oct. 7-12	India, Pakistan	1,700	1981, Apr.	N China	550
1959, Nov. 1	W Mexico	2,000	1981, July	Sichuan, Hubei Prov., China	1,300
1959, Dec. 2	Frejus, France	412	1982, Jan. 23	Nr. Lima, Peru	600
1960, Oct. 10	Bangladesh	6,000	1982, May 12	Guangdong, China	430
1960, Oct. 31	Bangladesh	4,000	1982, Sept. 17-21	El Salvador, Guatemala	1,300+
1962, Feb. 17	North Sea coast, Germany	343	1984, Aug-Sept.	South Korea	200+
1962, Sept. 27	Barcelona, Spain	445	1985, July 19	Dam collapse, N Italy	361
1963, Oct. 9	Dam collapse, Vaiont, Italy	1,800	1987, Aug.-Sept.	N Bangladesh	1,000+
1966, Nov. 3-4	Florence, Venice, Italy	113	1988, Sept.	N India	1,000+
1967, Jan. 18-24	E Brazil	894	1990, June 14	Shadyside, OH	26
1967, Mar. 19	Rio de Janeiro, Brazil	436	1993, July-Aug.	Midwest	48
1967, Nov. 26	Lisbon, Portugal	464	1994, July	GA, AL	32
1968, Aug. 7-14	Gujarat State, India	1,000	1995, Jan. 30-Feb. 9	NW Europe	40
1968, Oct. 7	NE India	780	1995, July	NE China	1,200
1969, Jan. 18-26	Southern CA	100	1995, Aug. 19	SW Morocco	136
1969, Mar. 17	Mundau Valley, Alagoas,		1995, Dec. 25	KwaZulu Natal, South Africa	166
	Brazil.	218	1996, Feb. 17	Biak Isl., Indonesia	105
1969, Aug. 20-22	Western VA	189	1996, April	Afghanistan	100+
1969, Sept. 15	South Korea	250	1996, June-July	S China	950+
1969, Oct. 1-8	Tunisia	500	1996, Aug. 7	Pyrenees Mts., Spain	71
1970, May 20	Central Romania	160	1996, Dec.-Jan. 1997	NW U.S.	29
1970, July 22	Himalayas, India	500	1997, Mar.	Ohio R. Valley	35

Date	Location	Deaths	Date	Location	Deaths
1997, July	Poland, Czech Republic	98	2002, Apr.-May	E Africa	150+
1997, Nov.	Spanish-Portuguese border . . .	31+	2002, early May	MO, IL, IN, WV, VA KY	20
1997, Nov.	Bardera, Somalia	1,300+	2002, Apr.-Aug.	China	800+
1998, Jan.	Kenya	86	2002, July-Aug.	India, Nepal, Bangladesh	1,100+
1998, Feb.	California to Tijuana, Mexico. . .	30+	2002, Aug.	Russia	110
1998, Mar.	SW Pakistan	300+	2002, Aug.	Germany, Hungary, Austria,	
1998, July-Aug.	China.	4,150		Czech Rep.	100+
1998, July-Sept.	Bangladesh	1,441	2003, May 17-27	Sri Lanka	250
1998, July 17	Papua New Guinea	3,000	2003, Aug.-mid-Sept.	E India	200+
1999, Aug. 1-4	Philippines, SE Asia	188+	2003, early Nov.	Sumatra, Indonesia	65+
1999, Sept.-Oct.	NE Mexico.	350+	2003, Dec. 10-		
1999, Oct.-Dec.	Central Vietnam	700+	Jan. 23, 2004	Sumatra, Indonesia	148
1999, Feb. 6-11	Botswana	70+	2003, Dec. 19-		
1999, Dec.	Venezuela	9,000+	Jan. 7, 2004	Central Philippines.	200
2000, Feb.-Mar.	Madagascar	150+	2004, Jan. 10-Mar. 8	Brazil	161
2000, Feb.-Mar.	Mozambique	700	2004, Apr. 4-6	Coahuila, N Mexico	37
2000, May 17	Timor Island	50+	2004, Apr. 9-May 11	W Kenya	50
2000, Aug. 2	Himachal Pradesh, India.	120+	2004, Apr. 12-16	Djibouti City, Djibouti	53
2000, Aug. 2	Bhutan.	200+	2004, May 23-25	Dom. Repubiic and Haiti	2,000
2000, Sept. 19-30	India, Bangladesh	1,000+	2004, June-Sept.	Banglad., India, Myan., Nepal	2,000+
2000, Oct. 12-17	France, Brit., Italy, Switz.	35	2004, June-Sept.	China	500
2001, Jan.-Feb.	Mozambique	84+	2004, Aug. 8-12	NE Nigeria	65
2001, Aug.-Nov.	S Vietnam and Cambodia	360+	2004, Nov-Dec.	Philippines	1,060+
2001, Aug. 1-6	Taiwan.	100+	2004, Dec. 26	12 Indian Ocean nations,	
2001, Aug. 10-12	NE Iran	247		espec. Indonesia, Sri Lanka,	
2001, Aug.	Northern Thailand	170		India, Thailand	226,328[1]
2001, Nov. 9-10	Northern Algeria	711+	2005, July 26-Aug. 2	India	1,000+
2001, Dec. 23-31	Rio de Janeiro	66	2005, Aug. 21-23	Central Europe, espec.	
2002, Jan. 30-Feb. 15	Java Isl., Indonesia	147		Romania	67
2002, Feb. 19	La Paz, Bolivia	65	2006, July 17	South of Java, Indonesia	530+

(1) Based on official estimates assembled by the Intl. Fed. of Red Cross and Red Crescent Societies, including 50,773 missing; as reported Dec. 15, 2005. The nearly 176,300 listed as dead include 128,645 from Indonesia; 31,147 from Sri Lanka; 10,749 from India; and 5,395 from Thailand.

Some Major Earthquakes

Source: Global Volcanism Network, Smithsonian Institution; U.S. Geological Survey, Dept. of the Interior; World Almanac research

Magnitude of earthquakes (Mag.) is measured on the Richter scale; an increase of one whole point represents a release of about 30 times more energy. Adopted in 1935, the scale is applied to earthquakes as far back as reliable seismograms are available, but those earlier figures should be considered estimates.

Date	Location	Deaths	Mag.	Date	Location	Deaths	Mag.
526, May 20	Antioch, Syria.	250,000	NA	1950, Aug. 15	Assam, India.	1,530	8.7
856	Corinth, Greece	45,000	NA	1953, Mar. 18	NW Turkey	1,200	7.2
856, Dec. 22	Damghan, Iran.	200,000	NA	1956, June 10-17	N Afghanistan.	2,000	7.7
893, Mar. 23	Ardabil, Iran	150,000	NA	1957, July 2	N Iran	1,200	7.4
1057	Chihli, China.	25,000	NA	1957, Dec. 13	W Iran.	1,130	7.3
1138, Aug. 9	Aleppo, Syria	230,000	NA	1960, Feb. 29	Agadir, Morocco	12,000	5.9
1169, Feb. 11	Near Mt. Etna, Sicily	15,000	NA[1]	1960, May 21-30	S Chile	5,000	9.5[4]
1268	Cilicia, Asia Minor	60,000	NA	1962, Sept. 1	NW Iran	12,230	7.3
1290, Sept. 27	Chihli, China.	100,000	NA	1963, July 26	Skopje, Yugoslavia	1,100	6.0
1293, May 20	Kamakura, Japan.	30,000	NA	1964, Mar. 27	Alaska.	131	9.2[5]
1531, Jan. 26	Lisbon, Portugal.	30,000	NA	1966, Aug. 19	E Turkey	2,520	7.1
1556, Jan. 24	Shaanxi, China.	830,000	NA	1968, Aug. 31	NE Iran	12,000	7.3
1667, Nov.	Shemakha, Caucasia.	80,000	NA	1970, Jan. 5	Yunnan Prov., China	15,621	7.7
1693, Jan. 11	Catania, Italy	60,000	NA	1970, Mar. 28	W Turkey	1,100	7.3
1737, Oct. 11	India, Calcutta	300,000	NA	1970, May 31	N Peru	66,000	7.8
1755, June 7	N Persia	40,000	NA	1971, Feb. 9	San Fernando Val., CA. . . .	65	6.6
1755, Nov. 1	Lisbon, Portugal.	60,000	8.75[2]	1972, Apr. 10	S Iran	5,054	7.1
1783, Feb. 4	Calabria, Italy.	30,000	NA	1972, Dec. 23	Managua, Nicaragua	5,000	6.2
1797, Feb. 4	Quito, Ecuador.	41,000	NA	1974, Dec. 28	Pakistan (9 towns)	5,200	6.3
1822, Sept. 5	Asia Minor, Aleppo.	22,000	NA	1975, Sept. 6	Turkey (Lice, etc.).	2,300	6.7
1828, Dec. 28	Echigo, Japan	30,000	NA	1976, Feb. 4	Guatemala	23,000	7.5
1868, Aug. 13-15	Peru, Ecuador.	40,000	NA	1976, May 6	NE Italy.	1,000	6.5
1875, May 16	Venezuela, Colombia.	16,000	NA	1976, June 25	Irian Jaya, New Guinea . . .	422	7.1
1886, Aug. 31	Charleston, SC.	60	6.6	1976, July 27	Tangshan, China	255,000	8.0
1896, June 15	Japan, sea wave	27,120	NA	1976, Aug. 16	Mindanao, Philippines. . . .	8,000	7.8
1905, Apr. 4	Kangra, India	19,000	8.6	1976, Nov. 24	NW Iran-USSR border	5,000	7.3
1906, Apr. 18-19	San Francisco, CA.	3,000	7.7[3]	1977, Mar. 4	Romania	1,500	7.2
1906, Aug. 17	Valparaiso, Chile	20,000	8.6	1977, Aug. 19	Indonesia	200	8.0
1907, Oct. 21	Central Asia	12,000	8.1	1978, Sept. 16	NE Iran	15,000	7.8
1908, Dec. 28	Messina, Italy.	83,000	7.5	1979, Sept. 12	Indonesia	100	8.1
1915, Jan. 13	Avezzano, Italy.	29,980	7.5	1979, Dec. 12	Colombia, Ecuador.	800	7.9
1918, Oct. 11	Mona Passage, PR	116	7.5	1980, Oct. 10	NW Algeria	3,500	7.7
1920, Dec. 16	Gansu, China.	200,000	8.6	1980, Nov. 23	S Italy	3,000	7.2
1923, Sept. 1	Yokohama, Japan	143,000	8.3	1981, June 11	S Iran	3,000	6.9
1925, Mar. 16	Yunnan, China.	5,000	7.1	1981, July 28	S Iran	1,500	7.3
1927, May 22	Tsinghai, China	200,000	8.3	1982, Dec. 13	W Arabian Peninsula	2,800	6.0
1932, Dec. 25	Gansu, China.	70,000	7.6	1983, Oct. 30	E Turkey	1,342	6.9
1933, Mar. 2	Japan.	2,990	8.9	1985, Mar. 3	Chile	146	7.8
1933, Mar. 10	Long Beach, CA.	115	6.2	1985, Sept. 19	Michoacan, Mexico.	9,500	8.1
1934, Jan. 15	India, Bihar-Nepal	10,700	8.4	1986, Oct. 10	El Salvador	1,000+	5.5
1935, Apr. 21	Taiwan (Formosa)	3,276	7.4	1987, Mar. 6	Colombia-Ecuador.	4,000+	7.0
1935, May 30	Quetta, Pakistan	50,000	7.5	1988, Aug. 20	India-Nepal border	1,450	6.6
1939, Jan. 25	Chillan, Chile	28,000	8.3	1988, Nov. 6	China-Burma border	1,000	7.3
1939, Dec. 26	Erzincan, Turkey	30,000	8.0	1988, Dec. 7	Soviet Armenia	55,000	7.0
1946, Dec. 20	Honshu, Japan.	1,330	8.4	1989, Oct. 17	San Francisco Bay area . . .	63	6.9
1948, June 28	Fukui, Japan	5,390	7.3	1990, May 30	N Peru	115	6.3
1948, Oct. 5	Ashgabat, Turkmenistan . . .	110,000	7.3	1990, June 20	W Iran.	40,000+	7.7
1949, Aug. 5	Pelileo, Ecuador.	6,000	6.8	1990, July 16	Luzon, Philippines	1,621	7.8

Date	Location	Deaths	Mag.
1991, Feb. 1	Pakistan, Afgh. border	1,200	6.8
1991, Oct. 19	N India	2,000	7.0
1992, Mar. 13, 15	E Turkey.	4,000	6.2/6.0
1992, June 28	S California	1	7.5/6.6
1992, Sept. 1	SW Nicaragua	116	7.0
1992, Oct. 12	Cairo, Egypt.	450	5.9
1992, Dec. 12	Flores Isl., Indonesia	2,500	7.5
1993, July 12	off Hokkaido, Japan.	200+	7.7
1993, Sept. 30	Maharashtra, S India	9,748	6.3[6]
1994, Jan. 17	Northridge, CA.	61	6.8
1994, Feb. 15	S Sumatra, Indon.	215	7.0
1994, June 6	Cauca, SW Colombia.	1,000	6.8
1994, Aug. 19	N Algeria	164	6.0
1995, Jan. 16	Kobe, Japan.	5,502	6.9
1995, May 27	Sakhalin Isl., Russia.	1,989	7.5
1996, Feb. 3	SW China.	200+	7.0
1997, Feb. 27	W Pakistan.	100+	7.3
1997, Feb. 28	NW Iran	1,000+	6.1
1997, May 10	N Iran	1,560	7.5
1998, Feb. 4, 8	Takhar province, NE		6.1
	Afghanistan.	2,323	
1998, May 22	Central Bolivia	105	6.5
1998, May 30	NE Afghanistan	4,700+	6.9
1998, June 27	Adana, Turkey	144	6.3
1999, Jan. 25	Armenia, Colombia	1,185+	6.0
1999, Aug. 17	Western Turkey	17,200+	7.4
1999, Sept. 7	Athens, Greece	143	5.9
1999, Sept. 21	Taichung, Taiwan.	2,474	7.6
1999, Nov. 12	Duzce, Turkey	675+	7.2

Date	Location	Deaths	Mag.
2000, June 4	Sumatra, Indonesia	103	7.9
2001, Jan. 13	San Vicente, El Salv.	800+	7.6
2001, Jan. 26	Gujarat, India	20,000+	7.9
2001, Feb. 13	San Vicente, El Salv.	255	6.6
2001, June 23	Arequipa, Peru	102	8.1
2002, Feb. 3	Central Turkey	44+	6.5
2002, Mar. 3	N Afghanistan	166	7.4
2002, Mar. 25-26	Nahrin, N Afghanistan	1,000+	6.1
2002, Apr. 1	E New Guinea	36	5.0
2002, Apr. 12	Hindu Kush, Afghanistan . .	50+	5.9
2002, June 22	W Iran	261+	6.5
2002, Oct. 31	S Italy	29	5.9
2003, Jan. 22	Colima, Mexico	29	7.6
2003, Feb. 24	S Xinjiang prov., China.	261	6.4
2003, May 1	E Turkey	177	6.4
2003, May 21	N Algeria	2,200+	6.8
2003, Dec. 26	Bam, SE Iran	26,271	6.6
2004, Feb. 4	Papua, Indonesia	37	7.0
2004, Feb. 14	NW Pakistan.	24	5.5
2004, Feb. 24	Al Hoceima, NE Morocco . .	629	6.4
2004, May 28	N Iran	35	6.3
2004, Dec. 26	Nr. Sumatra, Indon.	226,328	9.3[7]
2005, Feb. 22	Central Iran.	549	6.4
2005, Mar. 28	Islands off Sumatra,		8.7
	Indonesia.	1,000+	
2005, June 13	N Chile	10+	7.9
2005, Oct. 8	Kashmir, Pakistan, India. . .	80,000+	7.6
2006, Mar. 31	W Iran	70+	6.1
2006, May 27	Java, Indonesia	6,200+	6.3

*Estimated from earthquake intensity. NA = not available. (1) Once thought to have been a volcanic eruption; evidence indicates a destructive earthquake and tsunami occurred on this date. (2) This earthquake caused the most deadly Tsunami to have occurred to date in the Atlantic Ocean. (3) Total estimate includes deaths from resulting fires; revised estimates of magnitude range from 7.7 to 7.9. (4) This, the largest recorded earthquake ever, caused a deadly Tsunami that spread across the Pacific Ocean as far as Japan. (5) The "Good Friday" earthquake sent a tsunami that hit British Columbia, Canada and the U.S. Pacific coast. (6) Official death toll from Indian government. Other sources reported estimates of about 30,000 deaths. (7) This undersea earthquake triggered devastating tsunamis that hit 12 Indian Ocean nations. See listing above under Floods; see also Nations of the World.

Some Notable Fires Since 1930

(See also Some Notable Explosions Since 1920.)

Date	Location	Deaths	Date	Location	Deaths
1930, Apr. 21	Penitentiary, Columbus, OH	320	1973, June 24	Bar, New Orleans, LA.	32
1931, July 24	Home for aged, Pittsburgh, PA	48	1973, Aug. 3	Amusement park, Isle of Man, Eng.	51
1934, Dec. 11	Hotel Kerns, Lansing, MI	34	1973, Sept. 1	Hotel, Copenhagen, Denmark	35
1938, May 16	Terminal Hotel, Atlanta, GA.	35	1973, Nov. 29	Dept. store, Kumamoto, Japan.	107
1940, Apr. 23	Nightclub, Natchez, MS	198	1973, Dec. 2	Theater, Seoul, South Korea	50
1942, Nov. 28	Cocoanut Grove Nightclub, Boston, MA	491	1974, Feb. 1	Bank building, São Paulo, Brazil	189
1942, Dec. 12	Hostel, St. John's, Nfld.	100	1974, June 30	Discotheque, Port Chester	24
1943, Sept. 7	Gulf Hotel, Houston, TX.	55	1974, Nov. 3	Hotel, disco, Seoul, S. Korea	88
1944, July 6	Ringling Circus, Hartford, CT.	168	1975, Dec. 12	Tent city, Mina, Saudi Arabia	138
1946, June 5	LaSalle Hotel, Chicago, IL	61	1976, Oct. 24	Social club, Bronx, NY	25
1946, Dec. 7	Winecoff Hotel, Atlanta, GA	119	1977, Feb. 25	Rossiya hotel, Moscow, Russia	45
1946, Dec. 12	Ice plant, tenement, New York, NY	37	1977, May 28	Nightclub, Southgate, KY	164
1949, Apr. 5	Hospital, Effingham, IL.	77	1977, June 9	Nightclub, Abidjan, Ivory Coast	41
1950, Jan. 7	Mercy Hospital, Davenport, IA	41	1977, June 26	Jail, Columbia, TN	42
1953, Mar. 29	Nursing home, Largo, FL	35	1977, Nov. 14	Hotel, Manila, Philippines	47
1953, Apr. 16	Metalworking plant, Chicago, IL.	35	1978, Jan. 28	Coates House Hotel, Kansas City, MO . .	16
1957, Feb. 17	Home for aged, Warrenton, MO.	72	1978, Aug. 19	Movie theater, Abadan, Iran	425+
1958, Mar. 19	Loft building, New York, NY.	24	1979, July 14	Hotel, Saragossa, Spain	80
1958, Dec. 1	Parochial school, Chicago, IL	95	1979, Dec. 31	Social club, Chapais, Quebec	42
1958, Dec. 16	Store, Bogotá, Colombia	83	1980, May 20	Nursing home, Kingston, Jamaica	157
1959, June 23	Resort hotel, Stalheim, Norway	34	1980, Nov. 21	MGM Grand Hotel, Las Vegas, NV . .	84
1960, Mar. 12	Chemical plant, Pusan, Korea	68	1980, Dec. 4	Stouffer Inn, Harrison, NY	26
1960, July 14	Mental hospital, Guatemala City	225	1981, Jan. 9	Boarding home, Keansburg, NJ	30
1960, Nov. 13	Movie theater, Amude, Syria	152	1981, Feb. 10	Las Vegas Hilton, Las Vegas, NV	8
1961, Jan. 6	Thomas Hotel, San Francisco, CA. . . .	20	1981, Feb. 14	Discotheque, Dublin, Ireland	44
1961, Dec. 8	Hospital, Hartford, CT	16	1982, Sept. 4	Apt. house, Los Angeles, CA	24
1961, Dec. 17	Circus, Niteroi, Brazil	323	1982, Nov. 8	County jail, Biloxi, MS.	29
1963, May 4	Theater, Diourbel, Senegal	64	1983, Feb. 13	Movie theater, Turin, Italy	64
1963, Nov. 18	Surfside Hotel, Atlantic City, NJ.	25	1983, Dec. 17	Discotheque, Madrid, Spain	83
1963, Nov. 23	Rest home, Fitchville, OH	63	1984, May 11	Great Adventure Amusement Pk., NJ . .	8
1963, Dec. 29	Roosevelt Hotel, Jacksonville, FL	22	1985, Apr. 21	Movie theaters, Tabaco, Philippines. . . .	44
1964, May 8	Apt. bldg., Manila, Philippines	30	1985, Apr. 26	Hospital, Buenos Aires, Argentina	79
1964, Dec. 18	Nursing home, Fountaintown, IN	20	1985, May 11	Soccer stadium, Bradford, England	53
1965, Mar. 1	Apartment, LaSalle, Quebec	28	1985, May 13	MOVE hdqrtrs, row houses,	
1965, Aug. 11-16	Watts riot fires, Los Angeles, CA	30+		Philadelphia, PA	11
1966, Mar. 11	2 ski resorts, Numata, Japan.	31	1986, Dec. 31	Dupont Plaza Hotel, Puerto Rico	96
1966, Oct. 17	Bldg. (firefighters), New York, NY	12	1987, May 6-June 2	Forest fire, N China	193
1966, Dec. 7	Barracks, Erzurum, Turkey	68	1987, Nov. 17	Subway, London, England	30
1967, Feb. 7	Restaurant, Montgomery, AL	25	1988, Mar. 20	2000 buildings, Lashio, Burma	134
1967, May 22	Store, Brussels, Belgium	322	1990, Mar. 25	Social club, Bronx, NY	87
1967, July 16	State prison, Jay, FL	37	1991, Mar. 3	Munitions dump, Addis Ababa, Ethiopia .	260+
1968, May 11	Wedding hall, Vijayawada, India	58	1991, Sept. 3	Processing plant, Hamlet, NC	25
1969, Dec. 2	Nursing home, Notre Dame, Can.	54	1991, Oct. 20-21	Wildfire, Oakland, Berkeley, CA	24
1970, Jan. 9	Nursing home, Marietta, OH	27	1993, Apr. 19	Cult compound, Waco, TX	72
1970, Nov. 1	Dance hall, Grenoble, France	145	1994, May 10	Toy factory, Bangkok, Thailand	213
1970, Dec. 20	Hotel, Tucson, AZ	28	1994, July 4-10	(Firefighters), Glenwood Springs, CO . .	14
1971, Dec., 25	Hotel, Seoul, South Korea	162	1994, Nov. 2	Burning fuel flood, Durunka, Egypt.	500
1972, May 13	Nightclub, Osaka, Japan	116	1994, Dec. 10	Theater, Karamay, China	300
1972, July 5	Hospital, Sherborne, England	30	1995, Oct. 28	Subway train, Baku, Azerbaijan	300

Date	Location	Deaths
1995, Dec. 23	School, Mandi Dabwali, India	500+
1996, Mar. 19	Nightclub, Quezon City, Philippines	150+
1996, Mar. 28	Shopping mall, Bogor, Indonesia	78
1996, Oct. 22	Jail, Caracas, Venezuela	25
1996, Nov. 20	Building, Hong Kong	39
1997, Feb. 23	Worship site, Baripada, India	164
1997, Apr. 15	Encampment, Mina, Saudi Arabia	343
1997, June 7	Temple, Thanjavur, India	60+
1997, June 13	Movie theater, New Delhi, India	60
1997, July 11	Hotel, Pattaya, Thailand	90
1997, Sept. 29	Children's home, nr. Colina, Chile	30
1998, Dec. 3	Orphanage, Manila, Philippines	28
1999, Mar. 24	Mt. Blanc tunnel, France and Italy	40
1999, Oct. 30	Karaoke salon, Inchon, S. Korea	55+
2000, Mar. 17	Church, Kanungu, Uganda	530
2000, Oct. 20	Nightclub, Mexico City, Mexico	20
2000, Nov. 11	Cable car, Kaprun, Austria	155
2000, Dec. 25	Shopping center, Luoyang, China	309
2001, Jan. 1	Cafe, Volendam, Netherlands	10
2001, Mar. 6	School, Central China	41
2001, Mar. 26	School, Machakos, Kenya	64
2001, Aug. 6	Home for mentally ill, Madras, India	27
2001, Aug. 18	Hotel, Quezon City, Philippines	73
2001, Sept. 1	Nightclub, Tokyo, Japan	44
2001, Oct. 24	St. Gotthard Tunnel, Swiss Alps	11
2001, Dec. 29	Fireworks accident, Lima, Peru	291
2002, Mar. 11	Girls' school, Mecca, Saudi Arabia	15
2002, June 16	Internet cafe, Beijing, China	24
2002, July 7	Coal mine, Donetsk region, Ukraine	34+
2002, July 20	Disco, Lima, Peru	25+
2002, July 31	Coal mine, Donetsk region, Ukraine	20
2003, Feb. 18	Subway train, Taegu, S. Korea	198
2003, Feb. 20	Warwick, RI, nightclub (pyrotechnics)	100
2003, Sept. 15	Prison, Riyadh, Saudi Arabia	94
2003, Nov. 24	Students' hostel, Moscow, Russ.	36
2004, May 17	Prison, San Pedro Sula, Honduras	104
2004, July 16	Pvt. school, Kumbakonam, India	80+
2004, Aug. 1	Market, Asunción, Paraguay	400+
2004, Dec. 30	Club, Buenos Aires, Argentina	194
2005, Feb. 14	Mosque, Tehran, Iran	59
2005, Mar. 7	Prison, Higuey, Dom. Republic	159
2005, Apr. 15	Hotel, Paris, France	22
2005, Sept. 5	Beni Suef, Egypt, theater fire	32
2006, Jan. 8	Orphanage, Dushanbe, Tajikistan	13

Some Notable Explosions Since 1920

(See also Principal U.S. Mine Disasters Since 1900.) Note: Some bombings related to political conflicts and terrorism are not included.

Date	Location	Deaths
1920, Sept. 16	Wall Street, New York, NY	30
1921, Sept. 21	Chem. storage facility, Oppau, Ger.	561
1924, Jan. 3	Food plant, Pekin, IL	42
1927, May 18	Bath school, Lansing, MI	38
1928, April 13	Dance hall, West Plains, MO	40
1937, Mar. 18	School, New London, TX	311
1940, Sept. 12	Hercules Powder factory, Kenvil, NJ	55
1942, June 5	Ordnance plant, Elwood, IL	49
1944, Apr. 14	Harbor, Bombay, India	700
1944, July 17	Munitions ships and depot, Port Chicago, CA	322
1944, Oct. 21	Liquid gas tank, Cleveland, OH.	135
1947, Apr. 16	Freighter and chemical co. plant, Texas City, TX	576
1948, July 28	Farben works, Ludwigshafen, Ger.	184
1950, May 19	Munitions barges, S. Amboy, NJ	30
1956, Aug. 7	Dynamite trucks, Cali, Colombia	1,100
1958, Apr. 18	Sunken munitions ship, Okinawa, Japan	40
1958, May 22	Nike missiles, Leonardo, NJ	10
1959, Apr. 10	WWII bomb, Philippines	38
1959, June 28	Rail tank cars, Meldrim, GA	25
1959, Aug. 7	Dynamite truck, Roseburg, OR	13
1959, Nov. 2	Explosives, Jamuri Bazar, India	46
1959, Dec. 13	2 apt. bldgs., Dortmund, Ger.	26
1960, Mar. 4	Belgian munitions ship, Havana, Cuba	100
1962, Oct. 3	Telephone Co. office, New York, NY	23
1963, Jan. 2	Packing plant, Terre Haute, IN	17
1963, Mar. 9	Dynamite plant, S. Africa	45
1963, Aug. 13	Explosives dump, Gauhaiti, India	32
1963, Oct. 31	State Fair Coliseum, Indianapolis, IN	73
1964, July 23	Harbor munitions, Bone, Algeria	100
1965, Mar. 4	Gas pipeline, Natchitoches, LA	17
1965, Aug. 9	Missile silo, Searcy, AR	53
1965, Oct. 21	Bridge, Tila Bund, Pakistan	80
1965, Nov. 24	Armory, Keokuk, IA	20
1967, Dec. 25	Apartment bldg., Moscow, USSR	20
1968, Apr. 6	Sports store, Richmond, IN	43
1969, Mar. 31	Coal mine, near Barroteran, Mexico	180
1970, Apr. 8	Subway construction, Osaka, Japan	73
1971, June 24	Tunnel, Sylmar, CA	17
1973, Feb., 10	Liquid gas tank, Staten Island, NY	40
1975, Dec. 27	Coal mine, Chasnala, India	431
1976, Apr. 13	Munitions works, Lapua, Finland	40
1977, Nov. 11	Freight train, Iri, South Korea	57
1977, Dec. 22	Grain elevator, Westwego, LA	35
1978, Feb. 24	Derailed tank car, Waverly, TN	12
1978, July 11	Propylene tank truck, Tarragona, Spain	150
1980, Oct. 23	School, Ortuella, Spain	64
1982, Apr. 25	Antiques exhibition, Todi, Italy	33
1982, Nov. 2	Salang Tunnel, Afghanistan	1,000+
1984, Feb. 25	Oil pipeline, Cubatao, Brazil	508
1984, June 21	Naval supply depot, Severomorsk, USSR	200+
1984, Nov. 19	Gas storage area, NE Mexico City	334
1984, Dec. 3	Chemical plant, Bhopal, India	3,849
1984, Dec. 5	Coal mine, Taipei, Taiwan	94
1985, June 25	Fireworks factory, Hallett, OK	21
1988, Apr. 10	Army ammunitions dump nr. Rawalpindi and Islamabad, Pakistan	100
1988, July 6	Oil rig, North Sea off NE Scotland	167
1989, June 3	Gas pipeline, between Ufa, Asha, USSR	650+
1992, Mar. 3	Coal mine, Kozlu, Turkey	270+
1992, Apr. 22	Sewer, Guadalajara, Mexico	190
1992, May 9	Coal mine, Plymouth, Nova Scotia	26
1993, Feb. 26	World Trade Center, New York, NY	6
1994, July 18	Jewish com. center, Buenos Aires, Arg.	100
1995, Apr. 19	Fed. office building, Oklahoma City	168
1995, Apr. 29	Subway construction, South Korea	110
1995, Nov. 13	Military facility, Riyadh, Saudi Arabia	7
1996, Jan. 31	Bank, Colombo, Sri Lanka	53
1996, Feb. 25	Jerusalem and Ashkelon, Israel	27
1996, Mar. 3-4	Jerusalem and Tel Aviv, Israel	33
1996, June 25	U.S. military housing complex, near Dhahran, Saudi Arabia	19
1996, July 24	Train, Colombo, Sri Lanka	86
1996, Nov. 16	Russian military apt., Dagestan region, Russia	68
1996, Nov. 21	Building, San Juan, Puerto Rico	29
1996, Nov. 27	Coal mine, Shanxi province, China	91+
1996, Dec. 30	Train, Assam, India	59+
1997, Jan. 18	Near courthouse, Lahore, Pakistan	25
1997, Mar. 19	Ammunition depot, Jalalabad, Afgh.	16
1997, July 8	Train, Punjab, India	36
1997, Nov. 19	Car, Hyderabad, India	23
1997, Dec. 2	Coal mine, Novokuznetsk, Siberia	68
1998, Jan. 17	Coal mine, Sokobanja, Serbia	29
1998, Feb. 14	Oil tankers (2), Yaounde, Cameroon	120
1998, Feb. 14	17 bombs, Coimbatore, India	50
1998, Mar. 5	Bus, Colombo, Sri Lanka	32
1998, Apr. 4	Coal mine, Donetsk, Ukraine	63
1998, Aug. 7	Bomb, U.S. emb., Nairobi, Kenya	213
	Bomb, U.S. emb., Dar-es-Salaam, Tanz.	11
1998, Aug. 15	Car bomb, Omagh, Ireland	29
1998, Sept. 8	Two buses, São Paulo, Brazil	59
1998, Oct. 17	Oil pipeline, Jesse, Nigeria	700+
1999, May 16	Fuel truck, Punjab province, Pakistan	75
1999, July 29	Gold mine, Carletonville, S. Africa	17
1999, Sept. 10	Apartment building, Moscow, Russia	94
1999, Sept. 13	Apartment building, Moscow, Russia	118
1999, Sept. 16	Apartment building, Moscow, Russia	18
1999, Sept. 26	Fireworks factory, Celaya, Mexico	56
2000, Feb. 25	Bombs on 2 buses, Ozamis, Philippines	41
2000, Mar. 11	Coal mine, Krasnodon, Ukraine	80
2000, Apr. 16	Airport hangar, Congo, Dem. Rep. of	100+
2000, July 16	Oil pipeline, Warri, Nigeria	30
2000, Aug. 19	Train derailment, Nairobi, Kenya	25
2000, Aug. 20	Natural gas pipeline, Carlsbad, NM	10
2000, Sept. 9	Truck explosion, Urumqi, China	60
2000, Sept. 13	Bomb, Jakarta, Indonesia	15
2000, Sept. 19	Bomb, Islamabad, Pakistan	16
2000, Oct. 12	U.S. destroyer, Yemen	17
2001, Mar. 6	School, Wanzai Co., China	41
2001, Apr. 21	Coal mine, Shaanxi, China	51
2001, June 1	Dance club, Tel Aviv, Israel	21
2001, July 17	Coal mine, Guanxi, China	76+
2001, Aug. 19	Coal mine, Donetsk region, Ukraine	52
2001, Sept. 21	Chem. plant, Toulouse, France	29
2002, Jan. 21	Volcanic lava causes gas station blast, Goma, Dem. Rep. of the Congo	50+
2002, Jan. 27	Munitions dump, Lagos, Nigeria	1,000+
2002, Mar. 21	Car bomb near U.S. embassy, Lima, Peru	9
2002, Apr. 11	Truck nr. synagogue, Djerba, Tunisia	17
2002, Apr. 21	Bomb, dept. store, Mindanao, Philip.	14
2002, Apr. 26	Bomb at mosque, central Pakistan	12

Date	Location	Deaths
2002, May 8	Bomb on bus outside hotel, Karachi, Pak.	14
2002, May 9	Land mine at parade, Kaspiisk, Russia..	34+
2002, June 14	Car bomb outside U.S. consulate, Karachi, Pak.	12
2002, June 18	Bomb on bus, Jerusalem, Israel	20
2002, July 5	Bomb in market, Larba, Algeria.	35+
2002, Aug. 9	Explosion, Jalalabad, Afghanistan	25+
2002, Sept. 5	Car bomb, Kabul, Afghanistan	30
2002, Oct. 12	Bombings of nightclubs, Bali, Indon..	202
2003, Aug. 5	Car bomb at hotel, Jakarta, Indon.	12
2003, Aug. 19	Truck bomb, UN headquarters, Baghdad	22
2003, Aug. 25	Bombs in 2 taxis, Mumbai, India	52
2003, Dec. 5	Bomb on train, Yessentuki, Russia	45
2003, Dec. 23	Gas well explosion, Chongqing, China..	233
2004, Jan. 19	Natural gas facility, Skikda, Algeria..	27
2004, Feb. 6	Bomb on subway car, Moscow, Russia	39

Date	Location	Deaths
2004, Mar. 11	Commuter trains bombed, Madrid, Spain .	191
2004, Apr. 17	Chemical factory, China.	9+
2004, May 6-7	Ammunition dump, Ukraine	5
2004, May 11	Plastics factory, Glasgow, Scotland	4+
2004, July 19	Coal mine, Ukraine	31
2005, Feb. 14	Coal mine, NE China	214
2005, Mar. 23	Oil refinery, Texas City, Texas.	15
2005, May 2	Arms cache, Baghlan prov., Afghanistan..	34+
2005, May 3	Accidental detonation of hand grenade, Mogadishu, Somalia	15+
2005, July, 7	Bombs in mass transit, London, Eng.	56
2005, Oct. 1	Bombings of restaurants, Bali, Indonesia .	26
2005, Nov. 27	Coal mine, NE China	161+
2006, May 12	Oil pipeline, near Lagos, Nigeria	200
2006, July 1	Bombings of trains and a station, Mumbai, India	207

Notable Nuclear Accidents

Oct. 7, 1957—A fire in the Windscale plutonium production reactor N of Liverpool, England, released radioactive material; later blamed for 39 cancer deaths.

Jan. 3, 1961—A reactor at a federal installation near Idaho Falls, ID, killed 3 workers. Radiation contained.

Oct. 5, 1966—A sodium cooling system malfunction caused a partial core meltdown at the Enrico Fermi demonstration breeder reactor, near Detroit, MI. Radiation contained.

Jan. 21, 1969—A coolant malfunction from an experimental underground reactor at Lucens Vad, Switzerland, released radiation into a cavern, which was then sealed.

Mar. 22, 1975—Fire at the Brown's Ferry reactor in Decatur, AL, caused dangerous lowering of cooling water levels.

Mar. 28, 1979—The worst commercial nuclear accident in the U.S. occurred as equipment failures and human mistakes led to a loss of coolant and a partial core meltdown at the Three Mile Island reactor in Middletown, PA.

Feb. 11, 1981—8 workers were contaminated when 100,000 gallons of radioactive coolant fluid leaked into containment building of TVA's Sequoyah 1 plant in Tennessee.

Apr. 25, 1981—Some 100 workers were exposed to radiation during repairs of a nuclear plant at Tsuruga, Japan.

Jan. 6, 1986—A cylinder of nuclear material burst after being improperly heated at a Kerr-McGee plant at Gore, OK. One worker died; 100 were hospitalized.

Apr. 26, 1986—In the worst nuclear accident in the history of nuclear power, fires and explosions resulting from an unauthorized experiment at the Chernobyl nuclear power plant near Kiev, USSR (now in Ukraine), left at least 31 dead in the immediate aftermath and spread radioactive material over much of Europe. An estimated 135,000 people were evacuated from the region, some of which was uninhabitable for years. As a result of the radiation released, tens of thousands of excess cancer deaths (as well as increased birth defects) were expected.

Sept. 30, 1999—Japan's worst nuclear accident ever occurred at a uranium-reprocessing facility in Tokaimura, NE of Tokyo, when workers accidentally overloaded a container with uranium, thereby exposing workers and area residents to extremely high radiation levels.

Record Oil Spills

The number of tons can be multiplied by 7 to estimate roughly the number of barrels spilled; the exact number of barrels in a ton varies with the type of oil. Each barrel contains 42 gallons.

Name, place	Date	Cause	Tons
Ixtoc I oil well, S Gulf of Mexico	June 3, 1979	Blowout	600,000
Nowruz oil field, Persian Gulf	Feb. 1983	Blowout	600,000 (est.)
Atlantic Empress and *Aegean Captain*, off Trinidad and Tobago.	July 19, 1979	Collision	300,000
Castillo de Bellver, off Cape Town, South Africa	Aug. 6, 1983	Fire	250,000
Amoco Cadiz, near Portsall, France	Mar. 16, 1978	Grounding	223,000
Torrey Canyon, off Land's End, England	Mar. 18, 1967	Grounding	119,000
Sea Star, Gulf of Oman	Dec. 19, 1972	Collision	115,000
Urquiola, La Coruna, Spain	May 12, 1976	Grounding	100,000

Other Notable Oil Spills

Name, place	Date	Cause	Gallons
Persian Gulf	began Jan. 23, 1991	Spillage by Iraq	130,000,000[1]
Braer, off Shetland Islands	Jan. 5, 1993	Grounding	26,000,000
Prestige, off N Spain	Nov. 13-19, 2002	Ship broke in half.	22,600,000
Aegean Sea, off N Spain	Dec. 3, 1992	Unknown	21,500,000
Sea Empress, off SW Wales	Feb. 15, 1996	Grounding	18,000,000
World Glory, off South Africa	June 13, 1968	Hull failure	13,524,000
Exxon Valdez, Prince William Sound, AK.	Mar. 24, 1989	Grounding	10,080,000

(1) Est. by Saudi Arabia. Some estimates as low as 25 mil gal.

Some Notable Miscellaneous Disasters Since 1950

Date	Event	Location	Details	Est. deaths
1952, Dec.	Pollution	London, England	Heavy smog blanketed city; caused difficulty breathing	4,000
1973-74	Drought and famine	Ethiopia	Caused by a 6-year drought	200,000
1974	Famine	Bangladesh	Caused by flooding	26,000+
1974-75	Famine	Sub-Saharan Africa	Drought in some regions, torrential rains in others, compounded by government mismanagement	40,000+
1980, summer	Heat wave	United States	June through Sept.	1,265
1984, Dec. 3	Industrial accident	Bhopal, India	Toxic gas leaked from a Union Carbide factory	3,000+
1984	Famine	Africa, chiefly Ethiopia	Several years of drought compounded by government mismanagement	800,000-1 mil
1986, Aug. 21	Gas	Near Lake Nyos, Cameroon	Volcanic lake released toxic gas	1,700
1990, July 2	Stampede	Mecca, Saudi Arabia	Pilgrims panicked in tunnel leading to the holy city	1,426
2003, summer	Heat wave	Europe	Abnormally high temperatures from Russia to Britain; France suffered most, with 14,800 dead	35,000
2005, Aug. 31	Stampede	Baghdad, Iraq	Fear of suicide bomber caused bridge stampede	1,000

▶ **IT'S A FACT:** The first nuclear reactor accident occurred at an experimental facility in Chalk River, Ontario, Can., on Dec. 12, 1952, as a result of human error. Because of built up pressure, the reactor's 4-ton lid blew off and radioactive water began spurting out. No one was killed, but the reactor core could not be decontaminated and had to be buried. A trained nuclear engineer, future U.S. Pres. Jimmy Carter was among hundreds who aided in the cleanup.

Memorable Moments in Human Spaceflight

Sources: National Aeronautics and Space Administration; Congressional Research Service; World Almanac research

The spaceflights listed are a selection of notable U.S. missions by the National Aeronautics and Space Administration (NASA), unless otherwise noted, plus non-U.S. missions (shown with an asterisk). The non-U.S missions were sponsored by the USSR (later, the Commonwealth of Independent States and, from 1997, Russia) or by China. Dates are Eastern standard time. EVA = extravehicular activity. ASTP = Apollo-Soyuz Test Project. STS = Space Transportation System, NASA's name for the overall Shuttle program. Number of total flights by each crew member is given in parentheses when flight listed is not the first.

Launch Date	Mission[1]	Crew (no. of flights)	Duration (hr:min)	Remarks
4/12/61	*Vostok 1	Yuri A. Gagarin	1:48	**1st human orbital flight**
5/5/61	Mercury-Redstone 3	Alan B. Shepard Jr.	0:15	**1st American in space**
7/21/61	Mercury-Redstone 4	Virgil I. Grissom	0:15	Spacecraft sank, Grissom rescued
8/6/61	*Vostok 2	Gherman S. Titov	25:18	1st spaceflight of more than 24 hrs
2/20/62	Mercury-Atlas 6	John H. Glenn Jr.	4:55	**1st American in orbit;** 3 orbits
5/24/62	Mercury-Atlas 7	M. Scott Carpenter	4:56	Manual retrofire error caused 250-mi landing overshoot
8/11/62	*Vostok 3	Andrian G. Nikolayev	94:22	Vostok 3 and 4 made 1st group flight
8/12/62	*Vostok 4	Pavel R. Popovich	70:57	On 1st orbit, it came within 3 mi of Vostok 3
10/3/62	Mercury-Atlas 8	Walter M. Schirra Jr.	9:13	Landed 5 mi from target
5/15/63	Mercury-Atlas 9	L. Gordon Cooper	34:19	1st U.S. evaluation of effects of one day in space on a person; 22 orbits
6/14/63	*Vostok 5	Valery F. Bykovsky	119:06	Vostok 5 and 6 made 2nd group flight
6/16/63	*Vostok 6	Valentina V. Tereshkova	70:50	**1st woman in space;** passed within 3 mi of Vostok 5
10/12/64	*Voskhod 1	Vladimir M. Komarov, Konstantin P. Feoktistov, Boris B. Yegorov	24:17	1st 3-person orbital flight; 1st without space suits
3/18/65	*Voskhod 2	Pavel I. Belyayev, Aleksei A. Leonov	26:02	Leonov made **1st "space walk"** (10 min)
3/23/65	Gemini-Titan 3	Grissom (2), John W. Young	4:53	1st piloted spacecraft to change its orbital path
6/3/65	Gemini-Titan 4	James A. McDivitt, Edward H. White 2nd	97:56	White was 1st American to "walk in space" (36 min)
8/21/65	Gemini-Titan 5	Cooper (2), Charles Conrad Jr.	190:55	Longest-duration human flight to date
12/15/65	Gemini-Titan 6A	Schirra (2), Thomas P. Stafford	25:51	Completed 1st U.S. space rendezvous, with Gemini 7
12/4/65	Gemini-Titan 7	Frank Borman, James A. Lovell	330:35	Longest-duration Gemini flight
3/16/66	Gemini-Titan 8	Neil A. Armstrong, David R. Scott	10:41	**1st docking of one space vehicle with another;** mission aborted, control malfunction; 1st Pacific landing
6/3/66	Gemini-Titan 9A	Stafford (2), Eugene A. Cernan	72:21	Performed simulation of lunar module rendezvous
7/18/66	Gemini-Titan 10	Young (2), Michael Collins	70:47	1st use of Agena target vehicle's propulsion systems; 1st orbital docking
9/12/66	Gemini-Titan 11	Conrad (2), Richard F. Gordon Jr.	71:17	1st tethered flight; highest Earth-orbit altitude (850 mi)
11/11/66	Gemini-Titan 12	Lovell (2), Edwin E. "Buzz" Aldrin Jr.	94:34	Final Gemini mission; 5-hr EVA
4/23/67	*Soyuz 1	Komarov (2)	26:40	Crashed on reentry, killing Komarov
10/11/68	Apollo-Saturn 7	Schirra (3), Donn F. Eisele, R. Walter Cunningham	260:09	1st piloted flight of Apollo spacecraft command-service module only; live TV footage of crew
12/21/68	Apollo-Saturn 8	Borman (2), Lovell (3), William A. Anders	147:00	**1st lunar orbit** and piloted lunar return reentry (command-service module only); views of lunar surface televised to Earth
1/14/69	*Soyuz 4	Vladimir A. Shatalov	71:21	Docked with Soyuz 5
1/15/69	*Soyuz 5	Boris V. Volyanov, Aleksei S. Yeliseyev, Yevgeny V. Khrunov	72:54	Docked with 4; Yeliseyev and Khrunov transferred to Soyuz 4 via a spacewalk
3/3/69	Apollo-Saturn 9	McDivitt (2), D. Scott (2), Russell L. Schweickart	241:00	1st piloted flight of lunar module
5/18/69	Apollo-Saturn 10	Stafford (3), Young (3), Cernan (2)	192:03	1st lunar module orbit of Moon, 50,000 ft from Moon surface
7/16/69	Apollo-Saturn 11	Armstrong (2), Collins (2), Aldrin (2)	195:18	**1st lunar landing** made by Armstrong and Aldrin (7/20); collected 48.5 lb of soil, rock samples; lunar stay time 21:36:21
10/11/69	*Soyuz 6	Georgi S. Shonin, Valery N. Kubasov	118:43	1st welding of metals in space
10/12/69	*Soyuz 7	Anatoly V. Flipchenko, Vladislav N. Volkov, Viktor V. Gorbatko	118:40	Space lab construction test made; Soyuz 6, 7, and 8: 1st time 3 spacecraft, 7 crew members orbited the Earth at once
10/13/69	*Soyuz 8	Shatalov (2), Yeliseyev (2)	118:51	Part of space lab construction team
11/14/69	Apollo-Saturn 12	Conrad (3), Richard F. Gordon Jr. (2), Alan L. Bean	244:36	Conrad and Bean made **2nd Moon landing** (11/18); collected 74.7 lb of samples, lunar stay 31:31
4/11/70	Apollo-Saturn 13	Lovell (4), Fred W. Haise Jr., John L. Swigert Jr.	142:54	Aborted after service module oxygen tank ruptured; crew returned in lunar module
6/1/70	*Soyuz 9	Nikolayev (2), Vitaliy I. Sevastyanov	424:59	Longest human spaceflight to date
1/31/71	Apollo-Saturn 14	A. Shepard (2), Stuart A. Roosa, Edgar D. Mitchell	216:01	Shepard and Mitchell made **3rd Moon landing** (2/3); collected 96 lb of lunar samples; lunar stay 33:31
4/19/71	*Salyut 12	(Occupied by Soyuz 11 crew)		**1st space station**
4/22/71	*Soyuz 10	Shatalov (3), Yeliseyev (3), Nikolay N. Rukavishnikov	47:46	**1st successful docking with a space station;** failed to enter space station
6/6/71	*Soyuz 11	Georgi T. Dobrovolskiy, V. Volkov (2), Viktor I. Patsayev	570:22	Docked and entered Salyut 1 space station; **crew died** during reentry from loss of pressurization
7/26/71	Apollo-Saturn 15	D. Scott (3), James B. Irwin, Alfred M. Worden	295:12	Scott and Irwin made **4th Moon landing** (7/30); 1st lunar rover use; 1st deep space walk; 170 lb of samples; 66:55 stay
4/16/72	Apollo-Saturn 16	Young (4), Charles M. Duke Jr., Thomas K. Mattingly 2nd	265:51	Young and Duke made **5th Moon landing** (4/20); collected 213 lb of lunar samples; lunar stay 71:2

Launch Date	Mission[1]	Crew (no. of flights)	Duration (hr:min)	Remarks
12/7/72	Apollo-Saturn 17	Cernan (3), Ronald E. Evans, Harrison H. Schmitt	301:51	Cernan and Schmitt made 6th and **last lunar landing** (12/11); collected 243 lb of samples; record lunar stay over 75 hrs
5/14/73[2]	Skylab 1	(Occupied by Skylab 2, 3, and 4 crews)		**1st U.S. space station**; fell out of orbit 7/11/79
5/25/73	Skylab 2	Conrad (4), Joseph P. Kerwin, Paul J. Weitz	672:49	1st Amer. piloted orbiting space station; crew repaired damage caused in boost
7/28/73	Skylab 3	Bean (2), Owen K. Garriott, Jack R. Lousma	1,427:09	Crew systems and operational tests; scientific activities; 3 EVAs· 13:44
11/16/73	Skylab 4	Gerald P. Carr, Edward G. Gibson, William Pogue	2,017:15	Final Skylab mission
7/15/75	*Soyuz 19 (ASTP)	Leonov (2), Kubasov (2)	143:31	U.S.-USSR joint flight; crews linked up in space (7/17), conducted experiments, shared meals, held a joint news conf.
7/15/75	Apollo (ASTP)	Vance Brand, Stafford (4), Donald K. Slayton	217:28	Joint flight with Soyuz 19
12/10/77	*Soyuz 26	Yuri V. Romanenko, Georgiy M. Grechko (2)	2,314:00	1st multiple docking to a space station (Soyuz 26 and 27 docked at Salyut 6)
1/10/78	*Soyuz 27	Vladimir A. Dzhanibekov (2)	142:59	*See Soyuz 26*
3/2/78	*Soyuz 28	Aleksei A. Gubarev (2), Vladimir Remek	190:16	1st international crew launch; Remek was 1st Czech in space
4/12/81	Columbia (STS-1)	Young (5), Robert L. Crippen	54:21	**1st space shuttle** to fly into Earth's orbit
11/12/81	Columbia (STS-2)	Joe H. Engle, Richard H. Truly	54:13	1st scientific payload; 1st reuse of space shuttle
11/11/82	Columbia (STS-5)	Brand (2), Robert Overmyer, William Lenoir, Joseph Allen	122:14	1st 4-person crew
6/18/83	Challenger (STS-7)	Crippen (2), Frederick Hauck, Sally K. Ride, John M. Fabian, Norman Thagard	146:24	Ride was **1st U.S. woman in space**; 1st 5-person crew
6/27/83	*Soyuz T-9	Vladimir A. Lyakhov (2), Aleksandr Pavlovich	3,585:46	Docked at Salyut 7; 1st construction in space
8/30/83	Challenger (STS-8)	Truly (2), Daniel Brandenstein, William Thornton, Guion Bluford, Dale Gardner	145:09	Bluford was **1st African-American in space**
11/28/83	Columbia (STS-9)	Young (6), Brewster Shaw Jr., Robert Parker, Garriott (2), Byron Lichtenberg, Ulf Merbold	247:47	1st 6-person crew; 1st Spacelab mission
2/3/84	Challenger (41-B)	Brand (3), Robert Gibson, Ronald McNair, Bruce McCandless, Robert Stewart	191:16	1st untethered EVA
2/8/84	*Soyuz T-10B	Leonid Kizim, Vladimir Solovyov, Oleg Atkov	1,510:43	Docked with Salyut 7; crew set space duration record of 237 days
4/3/84	*Soyuz T-11	Yury Malyshev (2), Gennady Strekalov (3), Rakesh Sharma	4,365:48	Docked with Salyut 7; Sharma 1st Indian in space
4/6/84	Challenger (41-C)	Crippen (3), Francis R. Scobee, George D. Nelson, Terry J. Hart, James D. van Hoften	167:40	1st in-orbit satellite repair
7/17/84	*Soyuz T-12	Dzhanibekov (4), Svetlana Y. Savitskaya (2), Igor P. Volk	283:14	Docked at Salyut 7; Savitskaya was 1st woman to perform EVA
8/30/84	Discovery (41-D)	Henry W. Hartsfield (2), Michael L. Coats, Richard M. Mullane, Steven A. Hawley, Judith A. Resnik, Charles D. Walker	144:56	1st flight of U.S. nonastronaut (Walker)
10/5/84	Challenger (41-G)	Crippen (4), Jon A. McBride, Kathryn D. Sullivan, Ride (2), Marc Garneau, David C. Leestma, Paul D. Scully-Power	197:24	1st 7-person crew
11/8/84	Discovery (51-A)	Hauck (2); David M. Walker, Dr. Anna L. Fisher, J. Allen (2), D. Gardner (2)	191:45	1st satellite retrieval/repair
4/12/85	Discovery (51-D)	Karol J. Bobko, Donald E. Williams, Jake Garn, C. Walker (2), Jeffrey A. Hoffman, S. David Griggs, M. Rhea Seddon	167:55	Garn (R, UT) was **1st U.S. senator in space**
6/17/85	Discovery (51-G)	Brandenstein (2), John O. Creighton, Shannon W. Lucid, Steven R. Nagel, Fabian (2), Prince Sultan Salman al-Saud, Patrick Baudry	169:39	Launched 3 satellites; Salman al-Saud was 1st Arab in space; Baudry was 1st French person on U.S. mission
10/3/85	Atlantis (51-J)	Bobko (3), Ronald J. Grabe, David C. Hilmers, Stewart (2), William A. Pailes	97:47	1st Atlantis flight
10/30/85	Challenger (61-A)	Hartsfield (3), Nagel (2), Buchli (2), Bluford (2), Bonnie J. Dunbar, Wubbo J. Ockels, Richard Furrer, Ernst Messerschmid	168:45	1st 8-person crew; 1st German Spacelab mission
1/12/86	Columbia (61-C)	R. Gibson (2), Charles F. Bolden Jr., Hawley (2), G. Nelson (2), Franklin R. Chang-Diaz, Robert J. Cenker, Bill Nelson	146:04	B. Nelson was 1st U.S. representative in space; material and astronomy experiments conducted
1/28/86	Challenger (51-L)	Scobee (2), Michael J. Smith, Resnik (2), Ellison S. Onizuka (2), Ronald E. McNair, Gregory B. Jarvis, Christa McAuliffe	—	**Exploded 73 sec after liftoff**; all aboard were killed
2/20/86	*Mir[2]	—	—	*Mir* **space station** with 6 docking ports **launched**
3/13/86	*Soyuz T-15	Kizim (3), Solovyov (2)	3,000:01	Ferry between stations; docked at *Mir*
2/5/87	*Soyuz TM-2	Romanenko (3), Aleksandr I. Laveikin	7,835:38	Romanenko set endurance record, since broken
7/22/87	*Soyuz TM-3	Aleksandr Viktorenko, Aleksandr Pavlovich Aleksandrov (2), Mohammed Faris	3,847:13	Docked with *Mir*; Faris 1st Syrian in space
9/29/88	Discovery (STS-26)	Hauck (3), Richard O. Covey (2), Hilmers (2), G. Nelson (2), John M. Lounge (2)	97:00	**1st shuttle flight since *Challenger* explosion** 1/28/86
5/4/89	Atlantis (STS-30)	D. Walker (2), Grabe (2), Thagard (2), Mary L. Cleave (2), Mark C. Lee	96:56	Launched Venus orbiter *Magellan*
10/18/89	Atlantis (STS-34)	Donald E. Williams (2), Michael J. McCulley, Lucid (2), Chang-Diaz (2), Ellen S. Baker	119:39	Launched Jupiter probe and orbiter *Galileo*
4/24/90	Discovery (STS-31)	McCandless (2), Sullivan (2), Loren J. Shriver (2), Bolden (2), Hawley (3)	121:16	**Launched Hubble Space Telescope**
10/6/90	Discovery (STS-41)	Richard N. Richards (2), Robert D. Cabana, Bruce E. Melnick, William M. Shepherd (2), Thomas D. Akers	98:10	Launched *Ulysses* spacecraft to investigate interstellar space and the Sun
5/18/91	*Soyuz TM-12	Anatoly Artsebarskiy, Sergei Krikalev (2) (to *Mir*), Helen Sharman	3,471:22	Docked with *Mir*; Sharman 1st from United Kingdom in space

Launch Date	Mission[1]	Crew (no. of flights)	Duration (hr:min)	Remarks
3/17/92	*Soyuz TM-14	Viktorenko (3) (to *Mir*), Alexandr Kaleri (to *Mir*), Klaus-Dietrich Flade, Aleksandr Volkov (3) (from *Mir*), Krikalev (2) (from *Mir*)	3,495:11	First human CIS space mission; docked with *Mir* 3/19; Viktorenko and Kaleri to *Mir*; Volkov and Krikalev from *Mir*; Krikalev was in space 313 days
5/7/92	Endeavour (STS-49)	Brandenstein (4), Kevin C. Chilton, Melnick (2), Pierre J. Thuot (2), Richard J. Hieb (2), Kathryn Thornton (2), Akers (2)	213:30	1st 3-person EVA; satellite recovery and redeployment
9/12/92	Endeavour (STS-47)	R. Gibson (4), Curtis L. Brown Jr., Lee (2), Jay Apt (2), N. Jan Davis, Mae Carol Jemison, Mamoru Mohri	190:30	**Jemison was 1st black woman in space; Lee and Davis 1st married couple to travel together in space;** 1st Japanese Spacelab
6/21/93	Endeavour (STS-57)	Grabe (4), Brian J. Duffy (2), G. David Low (3), Nancy J. Sherlock, Peter J. K. Wisoff, Janice E. Voss	239:46	Carried Spacelab commercial payload module
12/2/93	Endeavour (STS-61)	Covey (3), Kenneth D. Bowersox (2), Claude Nicollier (2), Story Musgrave (5), Akers (3), K. Thornton (3), Hoffman (4)	259:58	Hubble Space Telescope repaired; Akers set new U.S. EVA duration record (29 hr, 40 min)
2/3/94	Discovery (STS-60)	Bolden (3), Kenneth S. Reightier Jr. (2), Davis (2), Chang-Diaz (3), Ronald M. Sega, Krikalev (3)	199:10	Krikalev was 1st Russian on U.S. shuttle
7/1/94	*Soyuz TM-19	Yuri I. Malenchenko, Talgat A. Musabayev, Merbold (2) (from *Mir*)	3,022:53	Docked with *Mir*; Merbold from *Mir*
9/9/94	Discovery (STS-64)	Richards (4), L. Blaine Hammond Jr. (2), Jerry M. Linenger, Susan J. Helms (2), Carl J. Meade (3), Lee (3)	262:50	Performed atmospheric research; 1st untethered EVA in over 10 years
2/3/95	Discovery (STS-63)	James D. Wetherbee (3), Eileen M. Collins, Bernard A. Harris (2), C. Michael Foale (3), Janice E. Voss (2), V. Titov (4)	198:29	*Discovery* and Russian space station rendezvous
3/2/95	Endeavour (STS-67)	Stephen S. Oswald (3), William G. Gregory, Samuel T. Durrance (2), Ronald Parise (2), Wendy B. Lawrence, Tamara E. Jernigan (3), John M. Grunsfeld	399:09	Shuttle data made available on the Internet; astronomy research conducted
3/14/95	*Soyuz TM-21	Thagard (2), Vladimir Dezhurov, Strekalov (5)	2,688[3]	Docked with *Mir* 3/16/95; Thagard was 1st Amer. on the Russ. spacecraft; Valery Polyakov returned to Earth, 3/22/95, after record stay in space (439 days)
6/27/95	Atlantis (STS-71)	R. Gibson (5), Charles J. Precourt (2), E. Baker (3), Gregory J. Harbaugh (3), Dunbar (4), Anatoly Solovyev (4) (to *Mir*), Nikolai M. Budarin (to *Mir*), Thagard (5) (from *Mir*), Strekalov (from *Mir*), Dezhurov (from *Mir*)	269:47	**1st shuttle-*Mir* docking;** exchanged crew members with *Mir*; Thagard, with his stay on *Mir*, had spent 115 days in space
11/12/95	Atlantis (STS-74)	Kenneth D. Cameron (3), James D. Halsell Jr. (2), Chris Hadfield, Jerry L. Ross (5), William S. McArthur (2)	196:30	2nd shuttle-*Mir* docking (11/15-11/18); erected a 15-ft permanent docking tunnel to *Mir* for future use by U.S. orbiters
2/22/96	Columbia (STS-75)	Andrew M. Allen (3), Scott J. Horowitz, Chang-Diaz (5), Umberto Guidoni, Hoffman (5), Maurizio Cheli, Nicollier (3)	377:40	Lost an Italian satellite when its tether was severed; microgravity experiments performed; singe marks found on 2 O-rings
3/22/96	Atlantis (STS-76)	Chilton (2), Richard A. Searfoss (2), Sega (2), Michael R. Clifford (3), Linda Godwin (3), Lucid (5) (to *Mir*)	221:15	3rd shuttle-*Mir* docking (5 days); Lucid to *Mir*, 2-person EVA
9/16/96	Atlantis (STS-79)	Apt (4), Terry Wilcutt (2), William Readdy (3), Akers (4), Carl E. Walz (3), Lucid (5) (from *Mir*), John E. Blaha (5) (to *Mir*)	243:19	Docked with *Mir* 9/18/96; exchanged crew members; **Lucid set U.S. and women's duration in space record (188 days)**
11/19/96	Columbia (STS-80)	Kenneth D. Cockrell (3), Kent V. Rominger (2), Jernigan (4), Thomas D. Jones (3), Musgrave (6)	423:53	Longest-duration shuttle flight; Musgrave 61, oldest thus far to fly in space; 2 science satellites deployed, retrieved
1/12/97	Atlantis (STS-81)	Michael A. Baker (4), Brent W. Jett (2), Wisoff (3), Grunsfeld (2), Marsha Ivins (4), Linenger (2) (to *Mir*), Blaha (5) (from *Mir*)	243:30	Docked with *Mir* 1/14-1/19/97; Linenger to *Mir*; Blaha from *Mir*, spent 128 days in space
2/11/97	Discovery (STS-82)	Bowersox (4), Horowitz (2), Joe Tanner (2), Hawley (4), Harbaugh (4), Lee (4), Steve Smith (2)	238:47	Increased capabilities of Hubble Space Telescope; 5 EVAs used to service it
5/15/97	Atlantis (STS-84)	Precourt (3), E. Collins (2), Jean-François Clervoy (2), Carlos Noriega, Ed Lu, Elena Kondakova, Foale (4) (to *Mir*), Linenger (2) (from *Mir*)	221:20	Docked with *Mir* 5/16-5/21; Foale to *Mir*; Linenger from *Mir*, 132 days in space, 2nd-longest time for an American; stay on *Mir* marked by troubles incl. fire 2/23
8/5/97	*Soyuz TM-26	Solovyev (5), Pavel Vinogradov	4,743:35	Docked with *Mir* 8/7/97; repaired damaged space station
8/7/97	Discovery (STS-85)	Brown (4), Rominger (3), Davis (3), Robert L. Curbeam Jr., Stephen K. Robinson, Bjarni V. Tryggvason	284:27	Deployed and retrieved satellite designed to study Earth's middle atmosphere; demonstrated robotic arm
9/25/97	Atlantis (STS-86)	Wetherbee (4), Michael J. Bloomfield, V. Titov (4), Scott Parazynski (2), Jean-Loup Chrétien (3), Lawrence (2), David A. Wolf (2) (to *Mir*), Foale (4) (from *Mir*)	236:24	Docked with *Mir* 9/27-10/3/97; delivered new computer to *Mir*; Wolf to *Mir*; Foale from *Mir*; stay on *Mir* marked by major collision with cargo ship 6/25
4/17/98	Columbia (STS-90)	Searfoss (3), Scott D. Altman, Richard M. Linnehan (2), Dafydd Rhys Williams, Kathryn P. Hire, Jay C. Buckey, James A. Pawelczyk	381:50	Studied effects of microgravity on the nervous systems of the crew and over 2,000 live animals; 1st surgery in space on animals meant to survive
6/2/98	Discovery (STS-91)	Precourt (4), Dominic L. Gorie, Lawrence (3), Chang-Diaz (6), Janet L. Kavandi, Valery Ryumin (4), A. Thomas (2) (from *Mir*)	235:53	Final docking mission with *Mir*; Thomas from *Mir*, 141 days in space
10/29/98	Discovery (STS-95)	Brown (5), Steven W. Lindsey (2), Parazynski (3), Robinson (2), Pedro Duque, Chiaki Mukai (2), Glenn (2)	213:44	Sen. John Glenn (D, OH), 77, was **oldest person to fly in space**; Duque was 1st Spaniard in space; experiments to study aging performed on Glenn
12/4/98	Endeavour (STS-88)	Cabana (4), Frederick W. Sturckow, Nancy J. Currie (3), Ross (6), James H. Newman (3), Krivalev (4)	283:18	**1st assembly of International Space Station (ISS)**; attached U.S.-built *Unity* connecting module to Russian-built *Zarya* control module; 1st crew to enter ISS
7/23/99	Columbia (STS-93)	E. Collins (3), Jeffrey S. Ashby, Hawley (5), Catherine G. Coleman (2), Michel Tognini (2)	118:50	Collins was **1st woman to command a space shuttle**; deployed Chandra X-ray Observatory telescope

Launch Date	Mission[1]	Crew (no. of flights)	Duration (hr:min)	Remarks
12/19/99	Discovery (STS-103)	Brown (6), Scott Kelly, S. Smith (3), Foale (5), Grunsfeld (3), Nicollier (4), Clervoy (3)	191:10	Replaced equipment on and upgraded Hubble Space Telescope; 3 EVAs
2/11/00	Endeavour (STS-99)	Kevin Kregel (4), Gorie (2), Kavandi (2), Janice E. Voss (5), Mohri (2), Gerhard P.J. Thiele	269:38	Used radar to make most complete topographic map of Earth's surface ever produced
5/19/00	Atlantis (STS-101)	Halsell (5), Horowitz (3), Helms (4), Yury Usachev (3), James S. Voss (4), Mary Ellen Weber (2), Jeffrey N. Williams	236:09	Serviced and resupplied ISS; boosted orbit of ISS to an altitude of about 238 mi; 1 EVA
9/8/00	Atlantis (STS-106)	Wilcutt (4), Altman (2), Lu (2), Richard A. Mastracchio, Daniel C. Burbank, Malenchenko (2), Boris V. Morukov	283:10	Prepared ISS for 1st permanent crew; 1 EVA by all 7 crew members
10/11/00	Discovery (STS-92)	Duffy (4), Pamela A. Melroy, Koichi Wakata (2), Leroy Chiao (3), Wisoff (4), Michael Lopez-Alegria (4), McArthur (3)	309:43	Installed framework structure on ISS, setting the stage for future additions; 4 EVAs
10/31/00	*Soyuz TM-204	Shepherd (4), Yuri Gidzenko (2), Krikalev (5)	—	Established **1st permanent manning of ISS** with 3-person crew for a 4-month stay
11/30/00	Endeavour (STS-97)	Jett (3), Bloomfield (2), Tanner (3), Marc Garneau (3), Noriega (2)	259:57	Delivered 17-ton solar arrays, batteries, and radiators to ISS; 3 EVAs
2/7/01	Atlantis (STS-98)	Cockrell (4), Ivins (5), Jones (4), Curbeam (2), Mark L. Polansky	309:20	Installed U.S. Destiny Laboratory Module on the ISS; 3 EVAs
3/8/01	Discovery (STS-102)	Wetherbee (5), James M. Kelly, Helms (4) (to ISS), James S. Voss (5) (to ISS), Paul Richards, Andrew S.W. Thomas (2), Usachev (4) (to ISS), Shepherd (4) (from ISS), Gidzenko (2) (from ISS), Krikalev (5) (from ISS)	307:49	Transported 2nd permanent crew (Voss, Helms, Usachev) to ISS and returned 1st crew to Earth; 2 EVAs
4/19/01	Endeavour (STS-100)	Rominger (5), John L. Phillips, Hadfield (2), Ashby (2), Parazynski (4), Guidoni (2), Yuri V. Lonchakov	285:30	Installed the Canadarm2, a robotic arm, and delivered supplies to ISS; 2 EVAs
7/12/01	Atlantis (STS-104)	Lindsey (4), Charles O. Hobaugh, Michael L. Gernhardt (3), Kavandi (3), James F. Reilly II(2)	259:58	Installed a Joint Airlock, with nitrogen and oxygen tanks to permit future spacewalks from the ISS; 3 EVAs
8/10/01	Discovery (STS-105)	Horowitz (4), Sturckow (2), Daniel Barry (3), Patrick G. Forrester, Culbertson (3) (to ISS), Dezhurov (2) (to ISS), Mikhail Tyurin (to ISS), Usachev, (4), Voss (5) (from ISS), Helms (5) (from ISS)	285:13	Transported Expedition 3 crew to ISS (Culbertson, Tyurin, Dezhurov) and returned Expedition 2 crew to Earth; 2 EVAs
12/5/01	Endeavour (STS-108)	Gorie (3), Mark Kelly, Godwin (4), Daniel Tani, Yury Onufrienko (2) (to ISS), Daniel Bursch (4) (to ISS), Walz (4) (to ISS), Culbertson (3) (from ISS), Dezhurov (2) (from ISS), Tyurin (from ISS)	283:36	Transported Expedition 4 crew to ISS (Onufrienko, Bursch, Walz) and returned Expedition 3 crew to Earth; deployed STARSHINE 2 satellite; 1 EVA
3/1/02	Columbia (STS-109)	Altman (3), Duane G. Carey, Grunsfeld (4), Currie (4), Linnehan (3), Newman (4), Michael J. Massimino	262:10	Installed powerful new camera and upgraded other equipment on Hubble Space Telescope; 5 EVAs
4/8/02	Atlantis (STS-110)	Bloomfield (3), Stephen N. Frick, Rex J. Walheim, Ellen Ochoa (4), Lee M.E. Morin, Ross (7), S. Smith (4)	259:42	Installed S0 Truss, backbone for expansion of ISS; Ross set records with 7th spaceflight, 9th spacewalk; 4 EVAs
6/5/02	Endeavour (STS-111)	Cockrell (5), Paul Lockhart, Chang-Diaz (7), Philippe Perrin, Valery Korzun (2) (to ISS), Peggy Whitson (to ISS), Sergei Treschev (to ISS), Onufrienko (2) (from ISS), Bursch (4) (from ISS), Walz (4) (from ISS)	332:35	Transported Expedition 5 crew to ISS (Korzun, Whitson, Treschev) and returned Expedition 4 crew to Earth; brought platform for ISS robot arm; 3 EVAs
10/7/02	Atlantis (STS 112)	Ashby (3), Melroy (2), Wolf (3), Sandy Magnus, Piers Sellers, Fyodor Yurchikhin	259:58	Installed S1 Truss to ISS; 3 EVAs
10/30/02	*Soyuz TMA-1	Sergei Zalyotin (2), Frank De Winne, Yuri Lonchakov (2)	—	1st launch of Soyuz TMA (Crew returned 11/10/02 on Soyuz TM-34 already docked at ISS)
11/23/02	Endeavour (STS 113)	Wetherbee (6), Lockhart (2), Lopez-Alegria (3), John Herrington, Bowersox (5) (to ISS), Budarin (3) (to ISS), Don Pettit (to ISS), Korzun (2) (from ISS), Whitson (from ISS), Treschev (from ISS)	330:47	Delivered Expedition 6 crew to ISS (Bowersox, Budarin, Pettit) and returned Expedition 5 crew to Earth; installed P1 Truss to ISS; 3 EVAs
1/16/03	Columbia (STS 107)	Rick Husband (2), William McCool, Michael Anderson (2), David Brown, Kalbana Chawla (2), Laurel Clark, Ilan Ramon	382:20	**Entire crew lost when** *Columbia* **burned up** during reentry, 2/1/03
10/15/03	*Shenzhou 5	Yang Liwei	21:00	**1st Chinese manned spacecraft**
6/21/04	SpaceShipOne	Mike Melvill	0:90	**1st privately funded manned spaceflight[4]**
7/26/05	Discovery (STS-114)	Charles Camarda, E. Collins (4), J. Kelly (2), Lawrence (4), Soichi Noguchi, Robinson (3), A.Thomas (3)		**1st space shuttle flight since** *Columbia* **disaster**; tested new safety modifications to craft; delivered supplies to ISS
7/4/06	Discovery (STS-121)	Lindsey (5), J. Kelly (2), Michael E. Fossum, Sellers (2), Lisa M. Nowak, Thomas Reiter (to ISS), Stephanie D. Wilson	306:36	**1st shuttle to launch on Independence Day.** Conducted more safety tests to craft; brought supplies to and performed maintenance on ISS.
9/9/06	Atlantis (STS-115)	Burbank (2), Christopher J. Ferguson, Jett (4), Steven G. MacLean (3), Heidemarie M. Stefanyshyn-Piper, Tanner (4)	283:07	Continued ISS construction; installed a new truss segment, two solar arrays, and a solar alpha rotary joint (used to orient the station's solar arrays).

Note: As of Sept. 2006, there have been 116 space shuttle flights, 90 since the 1986 *Challenger* explosion, 3 since the 2003 loss of *Columbia*. Totals include the final (28th) *Columbia* flight. There are 3 remaining shuttles: *Discovery* (32 flights), *Atlantis* (27), and *Endeavour* (19); the *Challenger* completed 9 missions in all. Four Soviets have died during spaceflight: Vladimir Komarov was killed on *Soyuz 1* (1967) when parachute lines tangled during descent; the 3-person *Soyuz 11* crew (1971) was asphyxiated. Six Americans and an Israeli astronaut died aboard the *Columbia*; 7 Americans died in the *Challenger* explosion, and 3 astronauts—Virgil I. Grissom, Edward H. White, and Roger B. Chaffee—died in the Jan. 27, 1967, *Apollo 1* fire on the ground at Cape Canaveral, FL.

(1) For shuttle flights, mission name is in parentheses following name of orbiter. (2) Space stations, such as the *Salyuts* and *Mir*, were used to house crews starting in 1971. (3) Approx. crew duration for Thagard's stay. Crew did not return together. (4) Date of first successful flight; later, SpaceShipOne flew at least 100 km (62 mi) into space, 9/29/04, piloted by Mike Melvill, and 10/4/04, piloted by Brian Binnie, winning the $10 mil Ansari Prize for 1st private venture to accomplish this feat twice within 2 weeks.

World Almanac Editors' Picks
Top 10 Celestial and Space Exploration Events of 2007

1. **Perseid Meteor Shower:** Aug. 13 peak coincides with the new Moon; excellent viewing throughout the night.
2. *New Horizons* **(NASA):** probe slingshots past Jupiter, en route to Pluto in 2015; closest Jupiter approach on Feb. 28.
3. *Phoenix Mars Lander* **(NASA):** scheduled to launch Aug 3, arriving on Mars in May 2008.
4. *Planck/Herschel* **(ESA):** two new orbiting observatories, scheduled to launch July 2007.
5. *Chang'e-1* **(China):** first Chinese lunar orbiter, scheduled to launch in 2007.
6. **Waxing Crescent Moon paired with Jupiter,** Nov. 12: One of the best dates to view this pretty pairing, due to close proximity of the two bodies and visibility soon after sunset.
7. *GLAST* **(NASA):** Gamma Ray Large Area Space Telescope, launch set for Aug. 7; will study extremely energetic objects and phenomena.
8. **Waxing Crescent Moon between Venus and Saturn,** June 18: One of the best dates to view this celestial grouping.
9. *NOAA-N Prime* **(NASA):** new weather and climate satellite, scheduled to launch Dec. 6.
10. **Saturn at Opposition,** Feb. 10: Saturn's closest approach to Earth, and the best time to view and photograph the planet and its moons throughout the night.

U.S. Manned Space Program

Following the Feb. 1, 2003, *Columbia* disaster, when the craft broke up on re-entry, all space shuttle flights were grounded. Improvements to future spacecrafts were made, including a redesigned external tank, new sensors to register impact, and a boom with a camera to allow astronauts to inspect the shuttle in flight for potential damage. On July 26, 2005, a modified *Discovery* made it into orbit, but onboard cameras showed that foam insulation broke off from the external fuel tank during launch—the same problem that caused the *Columbia* disaster. Despite a successful return, the shuttle program was grounded again until July 4, 2006, when *Discovery* lifted off with new safety features in place. The crew visited the International Space Station and returned to Earth without incident. Following *Discovery*'s successful flight, a modified *Atlantis* blasted off Sept. 9 and delivered new components to the ISS.

Even before the *Columbia* disaster it was clear that that a new vehicle was needed to replace the space shuttle, which is due to be retired in 2010. President George W. Bush in 2004 outlined his vision for future space exploration: Following the retirement of the space shuttle fleet, NASA will employ a new space vessel to aid not only in finishing the ISS, but also in sending astronauts to the moon and eventually to Mars. In August 2006, NASA unveiled plans for the new spacecraft, a multi-purpose orbital capsule called *Orion*, developed by Lockheed Martin. *Orion* will be designed to carry astronauts into orbit, ferry personnel and equipment to the ISS, serve as the orbital vehicle for missions to the Moon, and eventually to help with the construction of a vehicle to carry the first astronauts to Mars.

The reusable *Orion* craft abandons the 25-year old space shuttle design and returns to an *Apollo*-style design which will launch with the aid of new type of expendable rocket called *Ares* (also currently under development). *Orion*, costing $3.9 bil, will incorporate the latest technology in electronics, life support, computers, propulsion and heat protection systems. At 16.5 ft in diameter, *Orion* will have 2.5 times the interior volume of the original *Apollo* capsules, and like the Russian *Soyuz* capsules, *Orion* will use parachutes to touch down on land (the *Apollo* capsules landed in water). Like the *Apollo* craft, *Orion* will launch on top of its booster rocket, which will prevent ice or insulating foam from the booster rocket from hitting the capsule. In addition, the capsule will be able to jettison from its booster in the event of launch failure—a safety mechanism unavailable to space shuttle crews.

The earliest *Orion* flight is scheduled for 2014, with a manned Moon mission expected by 2020.

International Space Station

The International Space Station (ISS) is considered the largest cooperative scientific project in history.

16 cooperating nations: U.S., Russia, Canada, Belgium, Denmark, France, Germany, Italy, Netherlands, Norway, Spain, Sweden, Switzerland, United Kingdom, Japan, and Brazil.

Impact of *Columbia* disaster: The grounding of U.S. space shuttles after the *Columbia* disaster and then after complications with *Discovery* in 2005 interrupted further assembly of the station. Since lower-capacity Russian *Soyuz* and *Progress* craft were the usual means of ferrying provisions and crew to and from Earth, the size of the crew aboard the ISS was reduced to 2.

In 2006, the flights resumed, allowing operations on the station to move forward and bringing the ISS crew back up to 3. Over the course of the year, the crew tested new equipment and safety procedures and performed maintenance on the station, notably the station's mobile transporter (a device that moves along exterior rails and facilitates repair, maintenance, and module additions). New and updated research equipment was installed inside the Leonardo Multi-Purpose Logistics Module. In September, the space shuttle *Atlantis* arrived with a new truss segment, two solar arrays, and a rotary joint that is used to position the solar panels so that they face the sun as the ISS moves through its orbit.

The station when completed:
- mass of 1,040,000 lb
- 356' x 290', with almost an acre of solar panels
- internal volume roughly equivalent to passenger cabin of a 747 jumbo jet
- 6 laboratories; living space for up to 7 people

Examples of research conducted or planned:
- growing living cells in a gravity-free environment
- studying the effects on humans of long-term exposure to reduced gravity
- studying large-scale long-term changes in Earth's environment by observing Earth from orbit

Summary of Worldwide Successful Launches, 1957-2006
Source: National Aeronautics and Space Administration

Year	Total[1]	Russia[2]	U.S.	ESA[3]	China	Japan	France	India	U.K.	Germany	Canada	Israel
1957-59	24	6	18	—	—	—	—	—	—	—	—	—
1960-69	1,035	399	614	2	—	—	4	—	1	—	—	—
1970-79	1,366	1,028	247	5	8	18	14	1	6	3	4	—
1980-89	1,431	1,132	191	14	16	26	5	9	4	7	5	—
1990-99	1,045	542	300	55	33	23	16	11	7	6	4	—
2000-06[4]	317	165	142	44	30	12	0	6	0	0	0	2
TOTAL	5,303	3,272	1,512	120	87	79	39	27	18	16	13	2

(1) Includes launches sponsored by countries not shown. (2) Data for 1957-91 apply to the Soviet Union, for 1992-96 to the Commonwealth of Independent States, after 1996 to Russia. (3) European Space Agency. Member States are Austria, Belgium, Denmark, Finland, France, Germany, Greece, Ireland, Italy, Luxembourg, the Netherlands, Norway, Portugal, Spain, Sweden, Switzerland and the United Kingdom. Canada, Hungary and the Czech Republic also participate in some projects under cooperation agreements. (4) As of Sept. 22, 2006.

Notable Proposed U.S. Space Missions

Source: National Aeronautics and Space Administration

Planned Launch	Mission	Purpose
June 20, 2007	Dawn	Orbit and study the asteroid Vesta and the newly designated dwarf planet Ceres.
Aug. 2007	Gamma-ray Large Area Space Telescope (GLAST)	High-energy gamma-ray observatory designed to study celestial gamma-ray sources.
Aug. 2007	Phoenix Mars Lander	Land on or near Martian polar ice cap; study soil composition for chemical make-up and signs of life; monitor climate.
Oct. 2008	Lunar Reconnaissance Orbiter	Accurately map the surface of the moon; surface temperature mapping; assess lunar surface features for future landing sites.
2009	Mars Science Laboratory	Roving, long-range, long-duration science lab to study the Martian surface.

Notable Lunar and Planetary Science Missions

Source: National Aeronautics and Space Administration

Spacecraft	Launch date[1]	Mission	Remarks
Mariner 2	Aug. 27, 1962	Venus	Passed within 22,000 mi of Venus 12/14/62; confirmed high surface temperature on planet; contact lost 1/3/63 at 54 million mi
Ranger 7	July 28, 1964	Moon	Yielded over 4,000 photos of lunar surface
Mariner 4	Nov. 28, 1964	Mars	1st probe to fly by mars; passed behind planet 7/14/65; took 22 photos from 6,000 mi above surface
Ranger 8	Feb. 17, 1965	Moon	Yielded over 7,000 photos of lunar surface
Surveyor 3	Apr. 17, 1967	Moon	Scooped and tested lunar soil
Venera 3	Nov. 16, 1965	Venus	Soviet probe; first artificial probe to impact on the surface of another planet 3/1/66; probe failed to send back data.
Mariner 5	June 14, 1967	Venus	In solar orbit; closest Venus flyby 10/19/67; allowed scientists to obtain accurate readings on the composition of the Venusian atmosphere.
Mariner 6	Feb. 24, 1969	Mars	Came within 2,000 mi of Mars 7/31/69; collected data, photos
Mariner 7	Mar. 27, 1969	Mars	Came within 2,000 mi of Mars 8/5/69
Venera 7	Aug. 17, 1970	Venus	Soviet probe; first probe to land safely on the surface of another planet; because of high atmospheric temperatures, probe is thought to have melted.
Mariner 9	May 30, 1971	Mars	First craft to orbit Mars 11/13/71; sent back over 7,000 photos
Pioneer 10	Mar. 2, 1972	Jupiter	Passed Jupiter 12/4/73; took readings on Jupiter's composition, found that the planet is composed mostly of hydrogen; exited the planetary system 6/13/83; transmission ended 3/31/97 at 6.39 bil mi
Pioneer 11	Apr. 5, 1973	Jupiter, Saturn	Passed Jupiter 12/3/74, Saturn 9/1/79; discovered an additional ring and 2 moons around Saturn; operating in outer solar system; transmission ended 9/95
Mariner 10	Nov. 3, 1973	Venus, Mercury	Passed Venus 2/5/74; arrived Mercury 3/29/74. 1st time gravity of 1 planet (Venus) used to whip spacecraft toward another (Mercury). 1st probe to visit 2 planets. Took readings of cloud and wind patterns in Venusian atmosphere.
Viking 1	Aug. 20, 1975	Mars	Landed on Mars 7/20/76; 1st probe to land safely on Mars; performed chemical analysis of soil; functioned 6 years
Viking 2	Sept. 9, 1975	Mars	Sister probe of *Viking 1*; landed on Mars 9/3/76; functioned 3 years
Voyager 1	Sept. 5, 1977	Jupiter, Saturn	Encountered Jupiter 3/5/79, provided evidence of rings around Jupiter ring; passed near Saturn 11/12/80; passed *Pioneer 10* to become most distant human-made object 2/17/98; 8/15/06 reached a distance of 100 AUs from sun
Voyager 2	Aug. 20, 1977	Jupiter, Saturn, Uranus, Neptune	Encountered Jupiter 7/9/79; Saturn 8/25/81; Uranus 1/24/86; Neptune 8/25/89; confirmed existence of rings around Neptune; observed Neptune's "great dark spot," whicn has since dissipated.
Pioneer Venus 1	May 20, 1978	Venus	Entered Venus orbit 12/4/78; spent 14 years studying atmosphere, magnetic field, weather and surface; fuel ran out and probe was destroyed in atomospheric entry, 8/92
Pioneer Venus 2 (multiprobe)	Aug. 8, 1978	Venus	Consisted of a "bus" which carried 1 large and 3 small atmospheric probes. All four probes entered the Venus atmosphere 12/9, followed by the bus; took readings of Venusian atompshere; probes impacted on surface
Magellan	May 4, 1989	Venus	Landed on Venus 8/10/90; monitored geological activity; mapped more than 99% of planet surface, observed more than 1,600 volcanoes and volcanic features, enabling creation of a 3 dimensional map; showed that about 85% of the surface is covered by volcanic flows; ceased operating 10/11/94
Galileo	Oct. 18, 1989	Jupiter	Used Earth's gravity to propel it toward Jupiter; encountered Venus Feb. 1990; encountered Jupiter 12/7/95; encountered moons; released probe into Jovian atmosphere; intentionally flown into Jupiter 9/21/03 to prevent accidental contamination of Jupiter's moon Europa.
Mars Global Surveyor	Nov. 7, 1996	Mars	Began orbiting Mars 9/11/97; began mapping survey of entire surface 3/9/99; discovered a weak magnetic field on planet; observed Martian moon Phobos; found evidence of liquid water in past 6/22/00
Mars Pathfinder	Dec. 4, 1996	Mars	Landed on Mars 7/4/97; rover *Sojourner* made measurements of climate and soil composition, sending thousands of surface images; ceased operating 9/27/97
Cassini-Huygens	Oct. 15, 1997	Saturn	Began orbiting Saturn 6/30/04; 4-year mission to study planet's atmosphere, rings, and moons; spotted a 270-mi-wide crater and 300-mi-wide hot spot region on Titan; and detected an atmosphere on Saturn's moon Enceladus. *Huygens* probe landed on Titan 1/14/05; found a muddy surface, possible deposits of water ice, channels carved by liquid methane springs, possible evidence of a coastline.
Lunar Prospector	Jan. 6, 1998	Moon	Began orbiting Moon 1/11/98; mapped abundance of 11 elements on Moon's surface; discovered evidence of water-ice at both lunar poles; made 1st precise gravity map of entire lunar surface; crashed into crater near Moon's south pole 7/31/99 to end mission
Deep Space 1	Oct. 24, 1998	Comet Borrelly	Flew within 1,500 mi of comet, sent back photos showing a 6 mi long nucleus.
Stardust	Feb. 7, 1999	Comet Wild-2	Reached comet 1/2/04; gathered dust samples; returned samples to Earth Jan. 15, 2006.
2001 Mars Odyssey	Apr. 7, 2001	Mars	Reached Mars 10/24/01; detected evidence of water ice near South Pole; primary mission to study climate and geologic history completed 8/04; began extended mission.
Genesis	Aug. 8, 2001	Sun	Orbited Sun, collected particles from solar wind. Capsule containing specimens crashed to Earth 9/8/04; some samples survived.

Spacecraft	Launch date[1]	Mission	Remarks
Mars Express/ Beagle 2 lander	June 3, 2003	Mars	First European Space Agency probe to another planet; arrived at Mars 12/03; performing remote sensing including high-resolution photography in a search for subsurface water; *Beagle 2* lander was deployed 12/19/03 but contact was lost soon after.
Mars Exploration Rovers	June 7 & July 10, 2003	Mars	Rovers *Spirit* and *Opportunity* landed on Mars Jan. 2004, found further evidence that water existed on surface; *Spirit* took first photo of a Martian meteor; both rovers still functioning more than 2 ½ years after primary missions ended; in 9/06, both rovers got a software upgrade
MESSENGER	Mar. 2, 2004	Mercury	Due to fly by Mercury in 2008, enter orbit in 2011. Probe will map and study Mercury's surface.
Deep Impact	Jan. 12, 2005	Comet Tempel 1	Reached Tempel 1; deployed an impact probe which slammed into the comet on 7/4/05, impacting with a force equivalent to roughly 5 tons of TNT; orbiter probe sent back pictures and analysis is due to return to Earth at the end of 2007.
Mars Reconnaissance Orbiter	Aug. 12, 2005	Mars	Reached Mars March 10, 2006 and began taking detailed images of the Martian surface. In Sept. 2006, craft deployed ground-penetrating radar to look for evidence of water ice more than 1 meter below the surface.
New Horizons (Pluto)	Jan. 19, 2006	Pluto & Charon	The craft will fly by Jupiter between Feb. and March 2007. Due to reach dwarf planet Pluto and its moon Charon in July 2015, and may examine other Kuiper Belt Objects

(1) Coordinated Universal Time

General Aviation and Air Taxi Active Aircraft, 2004

Source: Federal Aviation Administration; Aircraft not associated with major airlines or the military.

	Total Active	Personal	Business	Corporate	Instructional	Aerial Apps	External Load	Other Work	Sight Seeing	Air Medical	Other	On Demand Operations
Fixed Wing ...	182,867	122,672	23,060	9,594	11,819	6,231	0	619	407	303	2,272	5,890
Piston	165,189	120,384	19,770	1,750	11,759	5,506	0	530	402	250	1,942	2,896
Turboprop ...	8,379	1,603	1,993	2,395	57	694	0	77	2	38	160	1,359
Turbojet ...	9,298	685	1,296	5,449	3	30	0	12	2	15	170	1,635
Rotorcraft	7,821	1,360	514	484	721	2,389	215	50	96	165	171	716
Piston	2,315	989	220	33	623	342	8	8	47	0	38	7
Turbine	5,506	370	295	452	98	2,046	208	41	49	165	133	1,649
Other Aircraft .	5,939	4,972	6	6	258	3	0	112	545	0	34	3
Gliders......	2,116	1,853	6	6	197	0	0	0	21	0	34	0
Lighter-than-air	3,823	3,119	0	0	61	3	0	112	524	0	0	3
Experimental..	22,800	20,696	609	128	301	174	0	149	2	59	626	56
Amateur.....	19,165	18,024	438	0	272	12	0	61	0	59	299	0
Exhibition....	2,070	1,813	15	0	14	4	0	44	0	0	181	0
Other.......	1,565	859	156	128	15	159	0	44	2	0	147	56
Total All Aircraft ...	219,426	149,700	24,189	10,212	13,099	8,796	215	930	1,050	527	3,103	7,605

Note: Columns may not add to totals due to rounding. **Personal**—Flying for personal reasons; **Business**—Individual or group use for business transportation without a paid, professional crew; **Corporate**—Individual or group business transportation with a paid, professional crew (includes fractional ownership); **Instructional**—Flying under the supervision of a flight instructor; **Aerial Applications**—Includes observation (Aerial mapping/photography, patrol, search and rescue, hunting, traffic advisory, ranching, surveillance, oil and mineral exploration, etc.), agriculture, forestry, public health, fire fighting, and other applications; **External Load**—Operations such as helicopter hoists, hauling logs, etc.; **Other Work Use**—Construction work, parachuting, aerial advertising, towing gliders, etc.; **Sight-seeing**—Commercial sight-seeing; **Air Medical Services**—Air ambulance services, rescue, human organ transportation, emergency medical services; **Other**—Positioning flights, proficiency flights, training, ferrying, sales demos; **On Demand Operations**—On-demand air taxi, air tours, commuter, and air medical services.

Estimated Active Airmen Certificates Held, 2005

Source: U.S. Dept. of Transportation, Federal Aviation Administration

CATEGORY		CATEGORY		CATEGORY	
Pilot Total	609,737	Airline Transport........	141,992	Ground Instructor.........	74,378
Student	87,213	Rotorcraft only (helicopters..	9,518	Dispatcher	18,079
Recreational	278	Glider	21,369	Flight Navigator	298
Sport	134	**Nonpilot—Total**	**644,016**	Flight Attendant	125,032
Airplane[1]		Mechanic	320,293	Flight Engineer...........	57,756
Private	228,619	Repairmen	40,030		
Commercial	120,614	Parachute Rigger	8,150		

Note: The term airmen includes men and women certified as pilots, mechanics or other aviation technicians. (1) Includes pilots with an airplane only certificate as well as those with an airplane and a helicopter and/or glider certificate.

Aircraft Operating Statistics

Source: Courtesy of Air Transport Association of America, Inc. Reprinted with permission. © 2003 by Air Transport Association of America, Inc. All rights reserved. Figures are averages for most commonly used models.

	No. of seats	Speed airborne (mph)	Flight length (mi)	Fuel (gal per hr)	Operating cost per hr		No. of seats	Speed airborne (mph)	Flight length (mi)	Fuel (gal per hr)	Operating cost per hr
B747-200/300* ..	370	520	3,148	3,625	$9,153	B767-200ER ...	175	487	1,987	1,404	$3,873
B747-400	367	534	3,960	3,411	8,443	A321	169	454	1,094	673	1,347
B747-100*	—	503	2,022	1,762	3,852	B737-800/900 ..	151	454	1,035	770	2,248
B747-F*	—	506	2,512	3,593	7,138	MD-90	150	446	886	825	2,716
L-1011	325	494	2,023	1,981	8,042	B727-200*	148	430	644	1,289	4,075
DC-10*	286	497	1,637	2,405	7,374	B727-100*	—	417	468	989	13,667
B767-400	265	495	1,682	1,711	3,124	A320	146	454	1,065	767	2,359
B-777	263	525	3,515	2,165	5,105	B737-400.....	141	409	646	703	2,595
A330..........	261	509	3,559	1,407	3,076	MD-80	134	432	791	953	2,718
MD-11*	261	515	2,485	2,473	7,695	B737-700LR ...	132	441	879	740	1,692
A300-600*	235	460	947	1,638	6,518	B737-300/700 ..	132	403	542	723	2,388
B757-300	235	472	1,309	985	2,345	A319	122	442	904	666	1,913
B767-300ER* ...	207	497	2,122	1,579	4,217	A310-200*	—	455	847	1,561	8,066
DC-8*	—	437	686	1,712	8,065	B737-100/200 ..	119	396	465	824	2,377
B757-200*	181	464	1,175	1,045	3,312	B717-200......	112	339	175	573	3,355

	No. of seats	Speed airborne (mph)	Flight length (mi)	Fuel (gal per hr)	Operating cost per hr		No. of seats	Speed airborne (mph)	Flight length (mi)	Fuel (gal per hr)	Operating cost per hr
B737-500	110	407	576	756	$2,347	ERJ-145	50	360	343	280	$1,142
DC-9.	101	387	496	826	2,071	CRJ-145	49	397	486	369	1,433
F-100	87	398	587	662	2,303	ERJ-135	37	357	382	267	969
B737-200C	55	387	313	924	3,421	SD 340B	33	230	202	84	644

* Data include cargo operations.

Some Notable Aviation Firsts[1]

1903 — On Dec. 17, near Kitty Hawk, NC, brothers Wilbur and Orville Wright made the 1st human-carrying, powered flight. Each made 2 flights; the longest, about 852 ft, lasted 59 sec.

1907 — U.S. airplane manufacturing company formed by Glenn H. Curtiss.

1908 — 1st airplane passenger, Lt. Frank P. Lahm, rode with Wilbur Wright in a brief (6 min, 24 sec) flight.

1911 — 1st transportation of mail by airplane officially approved by the U.S. Postal Service began on Sept. 23. It lasted one week. In 1918, limited scheduled airmail service began. By 1921, scheduled transcontinental airmail service began between New York City and San Francisco.

1914 — 1st scheduled passenger airline service began. It operated between St. Petersburg and Tampa, FL.

1919 — 1st airline food, a basket lunch, was served as part of a commercial airline service.

1930 — Ellen Church became 1st flight attendant.

1939 — On Aug. 27, the German Heinkel He 178 made the 1st successful flight powered by a jet engine.

1947 — Mach 1, the sound barrier was broken by Amer. Chuck Yeager in a Bell X-1 rocket-powered aircraft.

(1) Excludes notable around-the-world and international trips.

1947 — Largest airplane ever flown, Howard Hughes's "Spruce Goose," flew 1 mi at an altitude of 80 ft.

1953 — Jacqueline Cochran became 1st woman to fly faster than sound.

1960 — Convair B-58, 1st supersonic bomber, was introduced.

1968 — The supersonic speed of Mach 2 was accomplished for 1st time, in a Tupolev Tu-144. The plane had an approximate maximum speed of 1,200 mph.

1970 — The Tupolev Tu-144, during commercial transport, exceeded Mach 2. It reached about 1,335 mph at 53,475 ft.

1976 — The Concorde began 1st scheduled supersonic commercial service.

1977 — The Gossamer Condor successfully demonstrated human-powered flight, completing figure-8 course of 1.15 miles.

1979 — The human-powered Gossamer Albatross crossed the English Channel in 2 hr, 49 min.

1981 — Solar Challenger became the 1st solar-powered airplane to cross the English Channel.

2005 — The Airbus 380, the biggest-ever commercial jet, was unveiled. It was 240 ft. long, had a wingspan of 262 ft., and could seat a maximum of 840 passengers.

Some Notable Around-the-World and Intercontinental Trips

Aviator or Craft	From/To	Miles	Time	Date
J. Alcock-A.W. Brown[1]	Newfoundland/Ireland	1,960	16h 12m	June 14-15, 1919
2 U.S. Army airplanes	Seattle/Seattle	26,103	35d 01h 11m	1924
Richard E. Byrd, Floyd Bennett[2]	Spitsbergen (Nor.)/N. Pole	1,545	15h 30m	May 9, 1926
Amundsen-Ellsworth-Nobile Polar Expedition (in a dirigible)	Spitsbergen (Nor.)/over N. Pole to Teller, Alaska		80h	May 11-14, 1926
E.S. Evans and L. Wells (New York World)	New York/ New York	18,410[3]	28d 14h 36m 05s	June 16-July 14, 1926
Charles Lindbergh[4]	New York/Paris.	3,610	33h 29m 30s	May 20-21, 1927
Amelia Earhart, W. Stultz, L. Gordon	Newfoundland/Wales		20h 40m	June 17-18, 1928
Graf Zeppelin	Friedrichshafen, Ger./Lakehurst, NJ. .	6,630	4d 15h 46m	Oct. 11-15, 1928
Graf Zeppelin	Friedrichshafen, Ger./Lakehurst, NJ. .	21,700	20d 04h	Aug. 14-Sept. 4, 1929
Wiley Post and Harold Gatty (Monoplane Winnie Mae)	New York/New York.	15,474	8d 15h 51m	July 1, 1931
C. Pangborn-H. Herndon Jr.[5]	Misawa, Japan./Wenatchee, WA . . .	4,458	41h 34m	Oct. 3-5, 1931
Amelia Earhart [6]	Newfoundland/Ireland	2,026	14h 56m	May 20-21, 1932
Wiley Post (Monoplane Winnie Mae)[7]	New York/New York.	15,596	115h 36m 30s	July 15-22, 1933
Hindenburg Zeppelin.	Lakehurst, NJ/Frankfort, Ger..		42h 53m	Aug. 9-11, 1936
Howard Hughes and 4 assistants	New York/New York.	14,824	3d 19h 08m 10s	July 10-13, 1938
America, Pan American 4-engine Lockheed Constellation[8]	New York/New York.	22,219	101h 32m	June 17-30, 1947
Col. Edward Eagan.	New York/New York.	20,559	147h 15m	Dec. 13, 1948
USAF B-50 Lucky Lady II (Capt. James Gallagher)[9]	Ft. Worth, TX/Ft. Worth, TX	23,452	94h 01m	Mar. 2, 1949
Col. D. Schilling, USAF [10]	England/Limestone, ME.	3,300	10h 01m	Sept. 22, 1950
C.F. Blair Jr.	Norway/Alaska	3,300	10h 29m	May 29, 1951
Canberra Bomber[11]	N. Ireland/Newfoundland	2,073	04h 34m	Aug. 26, 1952
	Newfoundland/N. Ireland	2,073	03h 25m	Aug. 26, 1952
3 USAF B-52 Strato-fortresses[12]	Merced, CA/CA	24,325	45h 19m	Jan. 15-18, 1957
USSR TU-114[13]	Moscow/New York	5,092	11h 06m	June 28, 1959
Peter Gluckmann (solo)	San Francisco/San Francisco	22,800	29d	Aug. 22-Sept. 20, 1959
Robert & Joan Wallick	Manila/Manila.	23,129	5d 06h 17m 10s	June 2-7, 1966
Trevor K. Brougham	Darwin, Australia/Darwin	24,800	5d 05h 57m	Aug. 5-10, 1972
Arnold Palmer.	Denver/Denver.	22,985	57h 7m 12s	May 17-19, 1976
Boeing 747[14]	San Francisco/San Francisco	26,382	57h 25m 42s	Oct. 28-31, 1977
Richard Rutan & Jeana Yeager[15]	Edwards AFB, CA	24,986	09d 03m 44s	Dec. 14-23, 1986
Concorde	New York/New York	1,114 mph	31h 27m 49s	Aug. 15-16, 1995
Col. Douglas L. Raaberg and crew, B1 bomber[16]	Dyess AFB, Abilene, TX/ Dyess AFB.	6,250	36h 13m 36s	June 3, 1995
Linda Finch[17]	Oakland, CA/Oakland, CA	26,000	73d	Mar. 17-May 28, 1997
Bertrand Piccard, Brian Jones[18]	Switzerland/Egypt.	29,054.6	19d 21h 55m	Mar. 1-21, 1999
Steve Fossett[19]	Australia/Australia	21,109.6	14d 20h 01m	June 19-July 4, 2002
Steve Fossett[20]	Salina, KS/Salina, KS.	26,366	67h 2m 38s	Mar. 1-Mar. 3, 2005
Steve Fossett[21]	Cape Canaveral, FL/Bournemouth, UK	26,389.3	76h 45m	Feb. 8-11, 2006

(1) Nonstop transatlantic flight. (2) Claim of reaching N. Pole in dispute; if claim is untrue, then Amundsen-Ellsworth-Nobile were the first to fly over N. Pole. (3) Includes mileage by train and auto, 4,110; by plane, 6,300; by steamship, 8,000. (4) Solo transatlantic flight in the Ryan monoplane "Spirit of St. Louis." (5) Nonstop transpacific flight. (6) First woman to complete a transoceanic solo flight. Earhart disappeared in the Pacific in 1937 while attempting an around-the-world flight. (7) First to fly solo around N circumference of the world and first to fly twice around the world. (8) Inception of regular commercial global air service. (9) First nonstop round-the-world flight, refueled 4 times in flight. (10) Nonstop jet transatlantic flight. (11) Transatlantic round trip on same day. (12) First nonstop global flight by jet planes; refueled in flight by KC-97 aerial tankers; average speed approx. 525 mph. (13) Nonstop between Moscow and New York. (14) Speed record around the world over both Earth's poles. (15) Circled Earth nonstop without refueling. (16) Refueled in flight 6 times. Tested B-1B bomber by bombing 3 pre-arranged target sites on 3 continents. (17) Followed the intended around-the-world flight route (1937) of Amelia Earhart. (18) First to circumnavigate the globe nonstop in a balloon. (19) First solo circumnavigation of globe nonstop in a balloon; time, dates, and distance are for complete flight, which exceeded circumnavigation because winds prevented landing. (20) First non-stop solo circumnavigation in an airplane without refueling. (21) Longest-distance non-stop flight.

ASTRONOMY

Edited by Lee T. Shapiro, Ph.D., Fellow of the Royal Astronomical Society

Celestial Events Summary, 2007

There are 4 **eclipses** in 2007: two partial solar eclipses and two total lunar eclipses. However, in N America, neither solar eclipse is viewable and only portions of the two lunar eclipses can be seen. *See* page 331.

The most likely viewing successes for **meteor showers** will be the Lyrids in April, the Perseids in August, the Orionids in October, the Leonids in November, and the Geminids in December. *See* page 325.

At the start of the year Saturn is up most of the night and can be seen rising a few hours after sunset. Jupiter and Mars rise a couple hours before dawn, and Venus is low in the southwest after sunset. Venus gradually gets higher and stays in the evening sky through July, emerging in the morning sky in September for the remainder of the year. Jupiter gradually extends in visibility from just the morning sky until June when it is up all night. In July, it continues moving into the evening sky, eventually disappearing from view after November. Mars moves gradually from the morning sky early in the year to all-night visibility in December. Saturn is up all night long in February, then begins its move into the evening sky; by August it is lost in the glare of the Sun, reappearing in the morning sky in mid-September. By December, Saturn is visible more than half the night. The best opportunities for seeing Mercury occur in early February and late May in the evening sky and in the first half of November in the morning sky.

The crescent **Moon**, with its subdued light, regularly makes pretty pairings with the 2 brightest planets, Venus and Jupiter. Waxing crescent **pairings** are visible in the early evening soon after sunset, while waning crescent pairings are visible in the early morning before sunrise. The waxing crescent Moon pairs with Venus in each of the months from January through July and then with Jupiter during September, October and November, The waning crescent Moon pairs with Jupiter in the morning in January and February, and then with Venus each month from September through December. Venus passes Saturn 3 times between July and October.

Astronomical Positions and Constants

Two celestial bodies are in **conjunction** when they are due North and South of each other, either in **right ascension** (with respect to the North celestial pole) or in **celestial longitude** (with respect to the North ecliptic pole). Celestial bodies in conjunction will rise and set at nearly the same time. For the inner planets—Mercury and Venus—**inferior conjunction** occurs when either planet passes between Earth and the Sun, while **superior conjunction** occurs when either Mercury or Venus is on the far side of the Sun. Celestial bodies are in **opposition** when their Right Ascensions differ by exactly 12 hours, or when their Celestial Longitudes differ by 180 . In this case one of the 2 objects in opposition will rise while the other is setting. **Quadrature** refers to the arrangement where the coordinates of 2 bodies differ by exactly 90°. These terms may refer to the relative positions of any 2 bodies as seen from Earth, but one of the bodies is so frequently the Sun that mention of the Sun is omitted in that case.

When objects are in conjunction, the alignment is not perfect, and one is usually passing above or below the other.

The geocentric angular separation between the Sun and an object is termed **elongation**. Elongation is limited only for Mercury and Venus; the greatest elongation for each of these bodies is approximately the time for longest observation. **Perihelion** is the point in an orbit that is nearest to the Sun, and **aphelion**, the point farthest from the Sun. **Perigee** is the point in an orbit that is nearest Earth, **apogee** the point that is farthest from Earth. An **occultation** of a planet or a star is an eclipse of it by some other body, usually the Moon. A **transit** of the Sun occurs when Mercury or Venus passes directly between Earth and the Sun, appearing to cross the disk of the Sun.

The following were adopted as part of the International Astronomical Union System of Astronomical Constants (1976): **Speed of light,** 299,792.458 km per sec., or about 186,282 statute mi per sec.; **solar parallax,** 8".794148; Astronomical Unit (the mean distance between the Earth and the Sun), 149,597,870 km, or 92,955,807 mi; **constant of nutation,** 9".2025; and **constant of aberration,** 20".49552.

Celestial Events Highlights, 2007

(Coordinated Universal Time, or UTC—the standard time of the prime meridian)

January

Mercury is visible low in the SW near the end of the month.

Venus, low in the SW after sunset, passes Neptune on the 18th.

Mars is very low in the SE before sunrise.

Jupiter is low in the SE before sunrise.

Saturn, rising a couple of hours after sunset, is up most of the night.

Moon passes Saturn on 6th, Jupiter on the 15th, Mars on the 17th, Neptune and Venus on the 20th, and Uranus on the 22nd. **Watch for the waning crescent Moon near Jupiter on the 15th and the waxing crescent Moon near Venus on the 20th.**

Jan. 1—Neptune in Capricornus, Uranus in Aquarius, and Saturn in Leo all year. Jupiter and Mars in Ophiuchus. Venus and Sun in Sagittarius.

Jan. 3—Earth at perihelion, closest approach to the Sun. Venus enters Capricornus.

Jan. 5—Jupiter passes 5° N of Antares in the constellation Scorpius.

Jan. 6—Moon passes 0.9° N of Saturn, occults Saturn. (Like all occultations, this one is only visible from some parts of the Earth.)

Jan. 7—Moon passes 1.2° N of Regulus in the constellation Leo, occults Regulus. Mercury at superior conjunction.

Jan. 11—Moon passes 1.1° S of Spica in the constellation Virgo, occults Spica. Mars enters Sagittarius.

Jan. 15—Moon passes 0.5° S of Antares and 6° S of Jupiter, occults Antares.

Jan. 17—Moon passes 4.5° S of Mars.

Jan. 18—Venus passes 1.4° S of Neptune.

Jan. 20—Moon passes 2° S of Neptune and 0.8° S of Venus, occults Venus. Sun enters Capricornus.

Jan. 22—Moon passes 0.4° N of Uranus, occults Uranus.

Jan. 25—Venus enters Aquarius.

February

Mercury is visible low in the SW after sunset during the first half of the month.

Venus is low in the SW after sunset and passes Uranus on the 7th.

Mars is low in the SE at sunrise.

Jupiter, rising a couple of hours after midnight, is in the S before sunrise.

Saturn, rising around sunset, is up most of the night.

Moon passes Saturn on 2nd, Jupiter on the 12th, Mars on the 15th, and Venus on the 19th. In the morning watch for the waning quarter Moon below Jupiter on the 12th. Look for the thin waxing crescent Moon paired with Venus on the 19th.

Feb. 2—Moon passes 0.9° N of Saturn, occults Saturn.

Feb. 3—Moon passes 1.1° N of Regulus, occults Regulus.

Feb. 7—Venus passes 0.7° S of Uranus. (E of the Sun and sets after the Sun).

Feb. 8—Moon passes 1.3° S of Spica, occults, Spica. Neptune at conjunction.

Feb. 9—Mercury at perihelion, closest to the Sun.

Feb. 10—Saturn at opposition.
Feb. 11—Moon passes 0.7° S of Antares, occults Antares.
Feb. 12—Moon passes 6° S of Jupiter.
Feb. 13—Mercury stationary, begins retrograde motion.
Feb. 15—Moon passes 4° S of Mars.
Feb. 16—Venus enters Pisces. Sun enters Aquarius.
Feb. 19—Moon passes 2° N of Venus.
Feb. 23—Mercury at inferior conjunction, passes between the Earth and the Sun.
Feb. 25—Mars enters Capricornus.
Feb. 27—Venus enters Cetus.
Feb. 28—Venus enters Pisces.

March

Mercury is in the morning sky all month.
Venus is bright in the W after sunset.
Mars, low in the SE before sunrise, passes Neptune on the 25th.
Jupiter, rising about midnight, is prominent in the S at sunrise.
Saturn is high in the E at sunset.
Moon passes Saturn on the 2nd and 29th, Jupiter on the 11th, Mars and Neptune on the 16th, Mercury on the 17th, Venus on the 21st. Look for the waning crescent Moon between Mercury and Mars on the 16th, and the waxing crescent Moon above Venus on the 21st.
Mar. 2—Moon passes 1.1° N of Saturn and 1.1° N of Regulus, occults Saturn and Regulus.
Mar. 3—Total eclipse of the Moon, see details under Eclipses.
Mar. 5—Uranus at conjunction.
Mar. 7—Mercury stationary, resumes direct motion.
Mar. 11—Moon passes 0.7° S of Antares and 6° S of Jupiter, occults Antares.
Mar. 12—Sun enters Pisces.
Mar. 16—Moon passes 1.9° S of Mars and 2° S of Neptune.
Mar. 17—Moon passes 1.4° S of Mercury, occults Mercury. Venus enters Aries.
Mar. 19—Partial eclipse of the Sun, see details under Eclipses.
Mar. 20—Vernal Equinox at 7:07 p.m. EST (00:07 UTC March 21), spring begins in the northern hemisphere, autumn in the southern hemisphere.
Mar. 21—Moon passes 4.0° N of Venus.
Mar. 22—Mercury at greatest western elongation of 28° (W of the Sun, rises before the Sun). Ceres at conjunction.
Mar. 25—Mars passes 1.0° S of Neptune. Mercury at aphelion, greatest distance from the Sun.
Mar. 28—Sun barely touches constellation of Cetus.
Mar. 29—Moon passes 1.2° N of Saturn, occults Saturn.
Mar. 30—Moon passes 1.1° N of Regulus, occults Regulus.

April

Mercury passes Uranus on the first and disappears from the morning sky before the end of the month.
Venus is prominent in the W after sunset.
Mars is low in the SE before sunrise.
Jupiter, rising about midnight, is in the SW at sunrise.
Saturn, high in the S at sunset, sets after midnight.
Moon passes Jupiter on the 8th, Neptune on the 13th, Mars and Uranus on the 14th, Mercury on the 16th, Venus on the 20th, Saturn on the 25th, and Uranus on the 28th. Use the waning crescent Moon to find Mercury alongside the morning of the 16th and look for the waxing crescent Moon above Venus on the 20th.
Apr. 1—Mercury passes 1.6° S of Uranus.
Apr. 2—Mars enters Aquarius.
Apr. 6—Jupiter stationary, begins retrograde motion. Venus enters Taurus.
Apr. 7—Moon passes 0.6° S of Antares, occults Antares.
Apr. 8—Moon passes 6° S of Jupiter.
Apr. 13—Moon passes 2° S of Neptune.
Apr. 14—Moon passes 0.5° N of Mars and 1.0° N of Uranus, occults Mars and Uranus.

Apr. 16—Moon passes 5° N of Mercury.
Apr. 19—Venus at perihelion. Sun enters Aries.
Apr. 20—Saturn stationary, resumes direct motion. Moon passes 3° N of Venus.
Apr. 21—Venus passes 7° N of Aldebaran in the constellation of Taurus.
Apr. 22—Lyrid meteor shower from the setting of the waxing crescent moon in the middle of the night until dawn.
Apr. 25—Moon passes 1.1° N of Saturn, occults Saturn.
Apr. 26—Moon passes 1.0° N of Regulus.
Apr. 28—Mars passes 0.7° S of Uranus.

May

Mercury is low in W after sunset during the second half of the month.
Venus is higher in the sky in W at sunset.
Mars is low in the SE before sunrise.
Jupiter, rising before midnight, is low in the SW at dawn.
Saturn, getting lower in the SW at sunset, sets a few hours later.
Moon passes Jupiter on the 5th, Neptune on the 10th, Uranus on the 12th, Mars on the 13th, Mercury on the 18th, Venus on the 20th, and Saturn on the 22nd. On the 17th look for the Moon near Mercury, and on the 19th use the Moon to find Venus nearby in the daytime.
May 3—Mercury at superior conjunction.
May 4—Moon passes 0.5° S of Antares, occults Antares.
May 5—Moon passes 6° S of Jupiter.
May 8—Mercury at perihelion. Venus enters Gemini.
May 9—Mars enters Pisces.
May 10—Moon passes 1.8° S of Neptune.
May 12—Moon passes 1.3° N of Uranus, occults Uranus.
May 13—Moon passes 3° N of Mars.
May 14—Sun enters Taurus.
May 16—Mercury passes 7° N of Aldebaran.
May 18—Moon passes 3° N of Mercury.
May 20—Moon passes 1.7° N of Venus.
May 22—Moon passes 0.8° N of Saturn, occults Saturn.
May 23—Moon passes 0.7° N of Regulus, occults Regulus.
May 24—Mars enters Cetus.
May 25—Neptune stationary, begins retrograde motion.
May 29—Mars enters Pisces.
May 30—Venus passes 4° S of Pollux in the constellation of Gemini.

June

Mercury is visible in the W after sunset during the first half of the month.
Venus, prominent in the early evening sky, is getting higher in the W. Watch as Venus approaches and eventually passes Saturn next month.
Mars is getting higher in the SE before sunrise.
Jupiter is in the SE at sunset, setting before sunrise
Saturn, very low in the W after sunset, sets a couple of hours later.
Moon passes Jupiter on the 2nd and the 28th, Neptune on the 6th, Uranus on the 8th, Mars on the 10th, Mercury on the 16th, Venus on the 18th, and Saturn on the 19th. Watch for the waxing crescent Moon between Venus and Saturn on the 18th.
June 1—Moon passes 0.4° S of Antares, occults Antares.
June 2—Moon passes 6° S of Jupiter. **Mercury at greatest eastern elongation of 23°.**
June 3—Venus enters Cancer.
June 4—Mars at perihelion.
June 5—Jupiter at opposition.
June 6—Moon passes 1.5° S of Neptune.
June 8—Moon passes 1.6° N of Uranus.
June 9—Venus at greatest eastern elongation of 45°.
June 10—Moon passes 5° N of Mars.
June 15—Mercury stationary, begins retrograde motion.
June 16—Moon passes 6° N of Mercury.
June 18—Moon passes 0.6° N of Venus, occults Venus.
June 19—Moon passes 0.4° N of Saturn, occults Saturn.
June 20—Moon passes 0.4° N of Regulus, occults Regulus.

June 21—Northern solstice at 2:06 p.m. EDT (18:06 UTC), summer begins in the northern hemisphere, winter in the southern hemisphere. Mercury at aphelion. Sun enters Taurus.

June 23—Uranus stationary, begins retrograde motion.

June 25—Venus enters Leo.

June 26—Mars enters Aries.

June 28—Moon passes 0.5° S of Antares and 6° S of Jupiter, occults Antares. Mercury at inferior conjunction.

July

Mercury returns to the morning sky in the NE and remains visible for the remainder of the month.

Venus passes Saturn on the 2nd and Regulus on the 16th, while remaining prominent in the W at sunset.

Mars is now rising in the E an hour or so after midnight.

Jupiter, in the SE at sunset, sets a few hours after midnight.

Saturn is getting very low in the W at sunset.

Moon passes Neptune on the 2nd and the 31st, Uranus on the 4th, Mars on the 9th, Mercury on the 13th, Saturn on the 16th, Venus on the 17th, and Jupiter on the 25th. **Watch for triple grouping of the Moon, Venus, and Saturn on the 16th.**

July 2—Venus passes 0.8° S of Saturn.

July 3—Moon passes 1.3° S of Neptune, occults Neptune.

July 4—Moon passes 1.9° N of Uranus.

July 6—Earth at aphelion.

July 9—Moon passes 6° N of Mars.

July 10—Mercury stationary, resumes direct motion.

July 13—Moon passes 9° N of Mercury.

July 16—Venus passes 2° S of Regulus. Moon passes 0.04° S of Saturn, occults Saturn.

July 17—Moon passes 0.3° N of Regulus and 3° N of Venus, occults Regulus.

July 20—Mercury at greatest Western elongation of 20°.

July 21—Sun enters Cancer.

July 25—Venus stationary, begins retrograde motion. Moon passes 0.6° S of Antares and 6° S of Jupiter, occults Antares.

July 27—Mars enters Taurus.

July 29—Venus enters Sextans.

July 31—Moon passes 1.3° S of Neptune, occults Neptune.

August

Mercury, passing Pollux on the 1st, disappears from the morning sky early in the month and re-emerges in the evening sky at the end of the month.

Venus disappears from evening sky early in the month, passes Regulus on the 3rd and re-emerges in the morning sky at the end of the month.

Mars, rising in the NE soon after midnight, is high in the south E at sunrise.

Jupiter in the S at sunset sets shortly after midnight.

Saturn disappears into the glow of the Sun early in the month.

Moon passes Uranus on the 2nd and the 29th, Mars on the 7th, Jupiter on the 22nd, and Neptune on the 27th.

Aug. 1—Mercury passes 6° S of Pollux.

Aug. 2—Moon passes 2° N of Uranus.

Aug. 3—Venus passes 6° S of Regulus.

Aug. 4—Mercury at perihelion.

Aug. 7—Moon passes 6° N of Mars. Jupiter stationary, resumes direct motion.

Aug. 9—Venus at aphelion.

Aug. 11—Sun enters Leo.

Aug. 13—Perseid meteor shower peaks this morning. Neptune at opposition.

Aug. 15—Mercury at superior conjunction.

Aug. 16—Venus enters Hydra.

Aug. 18—Venus at inferior conjunction.

Aug. 21—Saturn at conjunction.

Aug. 22—Moon passes 0.7° S of Antares and 6° S of Jupiter, occults Antares.

Aug. 23—Venus enters Leo.

Aug. 24—Mars passes 5° N of Aldebaran.

Aug. 25—Venus enters Cancer.

Aug. 27—Moon passes 1.4° S of Neptune.

Aug. 28—Total eclipse of the Moon, see details under Eclipses.

Aug. 29—Moon passes 2° N of Uranus.

September

Mercury in the evening sky all month long, passes Spica on the 22nd.

Venus is low in the E before sunrise.

Mars, rising in the NE about midnight, is high in the S at dawn.

Jupiter is in the SW at sunset, setting a few hours later.

Saturn reappears in the morning sky very low in the E.

Moon passes Mars on the 4th, Venus on the 8th, Saturn on the 10th, Mercury on the 13th, Jupiter on the 18th, and Uranus on the 25th. Watch the waxing crescent Moon pair with Jupiter on the 18th. Look for the waning crescent Moon above Venus in the morning sky on the 8th, then between Venus and Saturn on the 9th.

Sept. 4—Moon passes 6° N of Mars.

Sept. 7—Venus stationary, resumes direct motion.

Sept. 8—Moon passes 9° N of Venus.

Sept. 9—Uranus at opposition.

Sept. 10—Moon passes 0.2° N of Regulus and 0.8° S of Saturn, occults Regulus and Saturn.

Sept. 11—Partial eclipse of the Sun, see details under Eclipses.

Sept. 13—Moon passes 2° S of Mercury.

Sept. 17—Mercury at aphelion. Sun enters Virgo.

Sept. 18—Moon passes 0.7° S of Antares and 6° S of Jupiter, occults Antares.

Sept. 21—Venus enters Leo.

Sept. 22—Mercury passes 0.09° N of Spica.

Sept. 23—Autumnal Equinox at 5:51 a.m. EDT (9:51 UTC), autumn begins in the northern hemisphere, spring begins in the southern hemisphere. Moon passes 1.4° S of Neptune.

Sept. 25—Moon passes 1.9° N of Uranus.

Sept. 29—Mercury at greatest eastern elongation of 26°. Mars enters Gemini.

October

Mercury is visible in the early evening sky low in the SW during the first half of the month.

Venus, paired with Saturn all month in the morning in the SE, passes Regulus on the 9th and Saturn on the 16th.

Mars, rising before midnight, is very high in the SW at dawn.

Jupiter is getting lower in the SW before sunset.

Saturn is low in the sky in the E before sunrise.

Moon passes Mars on the 2nd and the 30th, Venus and Saturn on the 7th, Mercury on the 13th, Jupiter on the 16th, Neptune on the 21st, and Uranus on the 23rd. Watch the thin waning crescent Moon between Venus and Saturn on the morning of the 7th and the waxing crescent Moon below Jupiter on the 15th.

Oct. 2—Moon passes 5° N of Mars.

Oct. 7—Moon passes 3° N of Venus, 0.2° N of Regulus, and 1.3° S of Saturn; occults Regulus and Saturn.

Oct. 9—Venus passes 3° S of Regulus.

Oct. 12—Mercury stationary, begins retrograde motion.

Oct. 13—Moon passes 1.3° S of Mercury.

Oct. 15—Venus passes 3° S of Saturn. Moon passes 0.5° S of Antares, occults Antares.

Oct. 16—Moon passes 5° S of Jupiter.

Oct. 21—Moon passes 1.3° S of Neptune.

Oct. 22—Orionid meteor shower this morning from a couple of hours after midnight, when the waxing quarter moon sets, until dawn.

Oct. 23—Moon passes 1.8° N of Uranus.

Oct. 24—Mercury at inferior conjunction.

Oct. 28—Venus at greatest western elongation of 46°.

Oct. 30—Moon passes 3° N of Mars.

Oct. 31—Neptune stationary, resumes direct motion. Mercury at perihelion. Sun enters Libra.

November

Mercury is visible in the morning sky low in the SE all month long.

Venus, prominent in the morning sky in the SE, passes Spica on 28th.

Mars, rising in the NE a few hours after sunset, is in the west at dawn.

Jupiter is very low in SW at dusk.

Saturn, rising about midnight, is in the S at dawn.

Moon passes Saturn on the 4th, Venus on the 5th, Mercury on the 8th, Jupiter on the 12th, Neptune on the 17th, Uranus on the 19th, and Mars on the 27th. **In the early morning from the 3rd through 7th watch the Moon move from Saturn, to Venus, to Mercury.** Watch for the thin waxing crescent Moon paired with Jupiter on the 12th.

Nov. 1—Mercury stationary, resumes direct motion.

Nov. 2—Venus enters Virgo.

Nov. 3—Moon passes 0.03° S of Regulus, occults Regulus.

Nov. 4—Moon passes 1.8° S of Saturn.

Nov. 5—Moon passes 3° S of Venus.

Nov. 8—Moon passes 7° S of Mercury. **Mercury at greatest western elongation of 19°.**

Nov. 9—Ceres at opposition.

Nov. 11—Moon passes 0.4° S of Antares, occults Antares.

Nov. 12—Moon passes 5° S of Jupiter.

Nov. 15—Mars stationary, begins retrograde motion.

Nov. 17—Moon passes 1.0° S of Neptune, occults Neptune.

Nov. 18—Leonid meteor shower this morning from the middle of the night until dawn.

Nov. 19—Moon passes 2° N of Uranus.

Nov. 23—Sun enters Scorpius.

Nov. 24—Uranus stationary, resumes direct motion.

Nov. 27—Moon passes 1.7° N of Mars.

Nov. 28—Venus passes 4° N of Spica.

Nov. 30—Moon passes 0.3° S of Regulus, occults Regulus. Venus at perihelion. Sun enters Ophiuchus.

December

Mercury is too close to the Sun's direction to be seen this month.

Venus is still prominent in the morning sky in the SE.

Mars, in the NE at sunset, reaches the NW by dawn and is up the whole night.

Jupiter is too close to the Sun's direction to be seen this month.

Saturn, rising before midnight, is high in the SW at dawn.

Moon passes Saturn the 1st and the 28th, Venus on the 6th, Neptune on the 14th, Uranus on the 16th, and Mars on the 24th. Watch for the thin waning crescent Moon paired with Venus on the 5th.

Dec. 1—Moon passes 2° S of Saturn.

Dec. 2—Jupiter enters Sagittarius.

Dec. 6—Moon passes 7° S of Venus.

Dec. 11—Venus enters Libra.

Dec. 13-14—Geminid meteor shower most of the night from the setting of the waxing crescent moon until dawn.

Dec. 14—Moon passes 0.7° S of Neptune, occults Neptune. Mercury at aphelion.

Dec. 16—Moon passes 2° N of Uranus.

Dec. 17—Mercury at superior conjunction.

Dec. 18—Sun enters Sagittarius.

Dec. 19—Mars at closest approach to the Earth this year.

Dec. 20—Saturn stationary, begins retrograde motion.

Dec. 22—Southern Solstice at 1:08 a.m. EST (6:08 UTC), winter begins in the northern hemisphere, summer begins in the southern hemisphere.

Dec. 23—Jupiter at conjunction.

Dec. 24—Moon passes 0.9° N of Mars, occults Mars. **Mars at opposition.**

Dec. 28—Moon passes 0.6° S of Regulus and 3° S of Saturn, occults Regulus.

Dec. 31—Mars enters Taurus.

Meteorites and Meteor Showers

When a chunk of material, ice or rock, plunges into Earth's atmosphere and burns up in a fiery display, the event is a **meteor**. While the chunk of material is still in space, it is a **meteoroid**. If a portion of the material survives passage through the atmosphere and reaches the ground, the remnant on the ground is a **meteorite**.

Meteorites found on Earth are classified into types, depending on their composition: **irons**, those composed chiefly of iron, a small percentage of nickel, and traces of other metals such as cobalt; **stones**, stony meteors consisting of silicates; and **stony irons**, containing varying proportions of both iron and stone.

Serious study of meteorites as non-earth objects began in the 20th century. Scientists use sophisticated chemical analysis, X rays, and mass spectrography in determining their origin and composition. Although most meteorites are now believed to be fragments of asteroids or comets, geochemical studies have shown that a few Antarctic stones came from the Moon or from Mars, presumably ejected by the explosive impact of asteroids.

The **largest known meteorite**, estimated to weigh about 55 metric tons, is situated at Hoba West near Grootfontein, Namibia. The Manicouagan impact crater in Quebec, Canada, with an estimated diameter of 60 mi, is one of the largest crater structures still visible on the surface of the Earth. Although not visible to the eye, other still larger impact craters identified include the Vredefort crater in South Africa at 185 mi across and the Sudbury crater in Ontario, Canada, estimated at 125 mi across. The Bedout impact site off the NW coast of Australia gained attention in 2004, when scientists identified further evidence in support of the idea that it may be linked to the Permian extinction event 250 million years ago.

Meteor showers vary in strength, but usually the 3 best meteor showers of the year are the **Perseids**, around Aug. 13, the **Orionids**, around Oct. 21, and the **Geminids**, around Dec. 14. These showers feature meteors at the rate of about 60 per hour. Best observing conditions occur with the absence of moonlight, usually when the Moon's phase is between waning crescent Moon and waxing quarter Moon.

For most meteor showers the cometary debris is relatively uniformly scattered along the comet's orbit. However, in the case of the **Leonid** meteor shower, which occurs every year around Nov. 17-18, the cometary debris, from Comet Temple-Tuttle, seems to be bunched up in one stretch. Hence, most years when Earth crosses the orbit of this comet, the meteor shower produced is relatively weak. However, about every 33 years, Earth encounters the bunched-up debris. Sometimes the storm is a disappointment, as it was in 1899 and 1933; at other times it is a roaring success, as in 1833 and 1866. The Leonids stormed again more recently, producing rates of 1,000-3,000 meteors per hour in 2001. Best showers in 2007 are the Lyrids in April after the waxing quarter Moon sets, the Perseids in mid-August at new moon, the Orionids in October after the waxing quarter moon sets, the Leonids in November after the waxing quarter moon sets, and the Geminids in December most of the night after the waxing crescent moon sets.

Rising and Setting of Planets, 2007

In Coordinated Universal Time (0 in the *h* col. designates 12 am).

Venus, 2007

Date	20° N Rise	20° N Set	30° N Rise	30° N Set	40° N Rise	40° N Set	50° N Rise	50° N Set	60° N Rise	60° N Set
	h m	h m	h m	h m	h m	h m	h m	h m	h m	h m
Jan. 1	8 29	17 57	9 05	17 22	10 05	16 21	8 29	17 57	9 05	17 22
11	8 31	18 21	9 01	17 51	9 50	17 02	8 31	18 21	9 01	17 51
21	8 28	18 46	8 51	18 23	9 29	17 46	8 28	18 46	8 51	18 23
31	8 21	19 10	8 37	18 54	9 02	18 29	8 21	19 10	8 37	18 54
Feb. 10	8 11	19 34	8 20	19 25	8 34	19 12	8 11	19 34	8 20	19 25
20	8 00	19 57	8 01	19 56	8 03	19 54	8 00	19 57	8 01	19 56
Mar. 2	7 47	20 19	7 41	20 26	7 32	20 35	7 47	20 19	7 41	20 26
12	7 35	20 42	7 22	20 56	7 01	21 17	7 35	20 42	7 22	20 56
22	7 24	21 05	7 03	21 26	6 30	22 01	7 24	21 05	7 03	21 26
Apr. 1	7 15	21 28	6 47	21 57	6 00	22 45	7 15	21 28	6 47	21 57
11	7 10	21 51	6 34	22 27	5 33	23 29	7 10	21 51	6 34	22 27
21	7 08	22 12	6 27	22 53	5 11	0 07	7 08	22 12	6 27	22 53
May 1	7 12	22 29	6 26	23 14	4 58	0 41	7 12	22 29	6 26	23 14
11	7 20	22 41	6 33	23 28	4 59	1 00	7 20	22 41	6 33	23 28
21	7 31	22 46	6 46	23 31	5 18	0 59	7 31	22 46	6 46	23 31
31	7 44	22 44	7 03	23 25	5 47	0 42	7 44	22 44	7 03	23 25
June 10	7 56	22 36	7 20	23 11	6 18	0 15	7 56	22 36	7 20	23 11
20	8 05	22 20	7 36	22 49	6 47	23 37	8 05	22 20	7 36	22 49
30	8 09	21 58	7 46	22 21	7 08	22 58	8 09	21 58	7 46	22 21
July 10	8 05	21 29	7 47	21 46	7 19	22 14	8 05	21 29	7 47	21 46
20	7 49	20 51	7 37	21 04	7 16	21 24	7 49	20 51	7 37	21 04
30	7 18	20 04	7 09	20 13	6 54	20 27	7 18	20 04	7 09	20 13
Aug. 9	6 28	19 07	6 20	19 15	6 08	19 27	6 28	19 07	6 20	19 15
19	5 24	18 06	5 15	18 15	5 01	18 29	5 24	18 06	5 15	18 15
29	4 18	17 12	4 07	17 24	3 50	17 42	4 18	17 12	4 07	17 24
Sept. 8	3 26	16 33	3 12	16 47	2 51	17 08	3 26	16 33	3 12	16 47
18	2 52	16 06	2 36	16 21	2 12	16 45	2 52	16 06	2 36	16 21
28	2 32	15 47	2 17	16 03	1 52	16 27	2 32	15 47	2 17	16 03
Oct. 8	2 24	15 33	2 10	15 47	1 48	16 09	2 24	15 33	2 10	15 47
18	2 25	15 21	2 14	15 32	1 56	15 50	2 25	15 21	2 14	15 32
28	2 32	15 10	2 24	15 17	2 12	15 29	2 32	15 10	2 24	15 17
Nov. 7	2 42	14 59	2 40	15 01	2 35	15 06	2 42	14 59	2 40	15 01
17	2 56	14 48	2 59	14 45	3 02	14 41	2 56	14 48	2 59	14 45
27	3 13	14 38	3 21	14 29	3 33	14 17	3 13	14 38	3 21	14 29
Dec. 7	3 31	14 28	3 45	14 14	4 06	13 53	3 31	14 28	3 45	14 14
17	3 50	14 22	4 10	14 02	4 41	13 30	3 50	14 22	4 10	14 02
27	4 11	14 18	4 36	13 52	5 18	13 11	4 11	14 18	4 36	13 52

Mars, 2007

Date	20° N Rise	20° N Set	30° N Rise	30° N Set	40° N Rise	40° N Set	50° N Rise	50° N Set	60° N Rise	60° N Set
	h m	h m	h m	h m	h m	h m	h m	h m	h m	h m
Jan. 1	5 02	15 55	5 23	15 33	5 49	15 07	6 27	14 29	7 33	13 23
11	4 55	15 46	5 17	15 24	5 44	14 57	6 23	14 18	7 32	13 09
21	4 48	15 37	5 10	15 17	5 37	14 49	6 16	14 10	7 26	13 00
31	4 40	15 32	5 02	15 10	5 29	14 43	6 07	14 05	7 16	12 56
Feb. 10	4 32	15 26	4 53	15 05	5 19	14 39	5 56	14 02	7 01	12 58
20	4 23	15 21	4 43	15 01	5 07	14 36	5 42	14 02	6 41	13 03
Mar. 2	4 13	15 16	4 31	14 57	4 54	14 35	5 25	14 03	6 18	13 10
12	4 02	15 10	4 18	14 54	4 38	14 34	5 06	14 06	5 52	13 20
22	3 50	15 05	4 04	14 51	4 22	14 33	4 46	14 09	5 25	13 31
Apr. 1	3 37	15 00	3 49	14 48	4 03	14 33	4 24	14 13	4 55	13 41
11	3 23	14 54	3 32	14 44	3 44	14 32	4 00	14 17	4 25	13 52
21	3 08	14 47	3 15	14 40	3 24	14 32	3 36	14 20	3 54	14 02
May 1	2 53	14 41	2 58	14 36	3 03	14 31	3 11	14 24	3 22	14 12
11	2 37	14 34	2 39	14 32	2 42	14 30	2 45	14 27	2 50	14 22
21	2 22	14 27	2 21	14 27	2 20	14 28	2 19	14 29	2 18	14 31
31	2 05	14 19	2 03	14 22	1 59	14 26	1 54	14 32	1 46	14 40
June 10	1 49	14 12	1 44	14 17	1 37	14 24	1 28	14 34	1 14	14 48
20	1 34	14 04	1 26	14 12	1 16	14 22	1 03	14 35	0 42	14 57
30	1 18	13 56	1 08	14 06	0 55	14 19	0 38	14 36	0 10	15 04
July 10	1 02	13 48	0 50	14 00	0 35	14 15	0 14	14 37	23 37	15 11
20	0 47	13 39	0 33	13 53	0 15	14 11	23 48	14 36	23 07	15 17
30	0 32	13 30	0 16	13 46	23 54	14 06	23 25	14 34	22 38	15 21
Aug. 9	0 17	13 20	23 57	13 38	23 35	14 00	23 04	14 31	22 10	15 24
19	0 01	13 09	23 41	13 28	23 17	13 52	22 43	14 26	21 44	15 25
29	23 44	12 57	23 24	13 17	22 59	13 42	22 23	14 18	21 19	15 22
Sept. 8	23 28	12 43	23 07	13 04	22 41	13 31	22 03	14 08	20 56	15 16
18	23 11	12 28	22 49	12 49	22 22	13 16	21 43	13 55	20 33	15 06
28	22 52	12 10	22 30	12 32	22 02	13 00	21 23	13 39	20 10	14 52
Oct. 8	22 31	11 50	22 09	12 12	21 41	12 40	21 00	13 20	19 47	14 34
18	22 07	11 27	21 44	11 49	21 16	12 17	20 36	12 58	19 21	14 12
28	21 39	10 59	21 16	11 22	20 48	11 50	20 07	12 31	18 51	13 47
Nov. 7	21 06	10 28	20 43	10 51	20 14	11 19	19 33	12 01	18 15	13 19
17	20 28	9 51	20 04	10 14	19 35	10 44	18 52	11 27	17 31	12 48
27	19 43	9 09	19 19	9 33	18 49	10 03	18 04	10 47	16 39	12 13
Dec. 7	18 52	8 20	18 27	8 45	17 56	9 16	17 09	10 03	15 38	11 34
17	17 56	7 27	17 30	7 52	16 58	8 25	16 10	9 12	14 33	10 50
27	16 58	6 31	16 33	6 57	15 59	7 30	15 10	8 19	13 28	10 01

Jupiter, 2007

Date	20° N Latitude Rise h m	20° N Latitude Set h m	30° N Latitude Rise h m	30° N Latitude Set h m	40° N Latitude Rise h m	40° N Latitude Set h m	50° N Latitude Rise h m	50° N Latitude Set h m	60° N Latitude Rise h m	60° N Latitude Set h m
Jan. 1	4 14	15 14	4 33	14 55	4 56	14 31	5 29	13 59	6 25	13 03
11	3 44	14 42	4 03	14 23	4 27	13 59	5 00	13 26	5 57	12 29
21	3 13	14 11	3 32	13 51	3 56	13 27	4 30	12 53	5 28	11 55
31	2 41	13 38	3 01	13 19	3 25	12 54	4 00	12 20	4 59	11 21
Feb. 10	2 09	13 05	2 29	12 46	2 53	12 21	3 28	11 46	4 28	10 46
20	1 36	12 32	1 56	12 12	2 21	11 47	2 56	11 12	3 56	10 11
Mar. 2	1 01	11 57	1 21	11 37	1 47	11 12	2 22	10 37	3 23	9 36
12	0 26	11 21	0 46	11 01	1 11	10 36	1 47	10 01	2 48	9 00
22	23 46	10 44	0 10	10 24	0 35	9 59	1 10	9 24	2 12	8 22
Apr. 1	23 08	10 06	23 28	9 46	23 53	9 21	0 32	8 46	1 34	7 44
11	22 28	9 27	22 48	9 07	23 14	8 42	23 49	8 06	0 54	7 05
21	21 47	8 46	22 07	8 26	22 33	8 01	23 08	7 26	0 13	6 24
May 1	21 05	8 04	21 25	7 44	21 50	7 19	22 26	6 44	23 27	5 43
11	20 22	7 22	20 42	7 02	21 07	6 37	21 42	6 01	22 43	5 01
21	19 38	6 38	19 58	6 18	20 23	5 53	20 58	5 18	21 58	4 18
31	18 53	5 53	19 13	5 34	19 38	5 09	20 12	4 34	21 12	3 35
June 10	18 08	5 09	18 28	4 49	18 52	4 25	19 27	3 50	20 26	2 51
20	17 23	4 24	17 43	4 05	18 07	3 41	18 42	3 06	19 40	2 08
30	16 39	3 41	16 59	3 21	17 23	2 57	17 57	2 23	18 55	1 25
July 10	15 56	2 58	16 15	2 38	16 39	2 14	17 13	1 40	18 11	0 43
20	15 14	2 15	15 33	1 56	15 57	1 32	16 30	0 59	17 28	0 01
30	14 33	1 34	14 52	1 15	15 16	0 51	15 49	0 18	16 47	23 16
Aug. 9	13 53	0 55	14 12	0 35	14 36	0 11	15 10	23 34	16 07	22 37
19	13 15	0 16	13 34	23 53	13 58	23 29	14 32	22 55	15 30	21 57
29	12 38	23 35	12 57	23 16	13 21	22 51	13 56	22 17	14 54	21 19
Sept. 8	12 02	22 59	12 22	22 39	12 46	22 15	13 20	21 41	14 19	20 42
18	11 28	22 24	11 47	22 04	12 12	21 40	12 47	21 05	13 46	20 05
28	10 54	21 50	11 14	21 30	11 39	21 05	12 14	20 30	13 15	19 29
Oct. 8	10 22	21 17	10 42	20 57	11 07	20 31	11 43	19 56	12 44	18 54
18	9 50	20 44	10 10	20 24	10 36	19 59	11 12	19 23	12 14	18 20
28	9 19	20 13	9 39	19 52	10 05	19 26	10 41	18 50	11 45	17 47
Nov. 7	8 48	19 42	9 09	19 21	9 35	18 55	10 12	18 18	11 16	17 14
17	8 18	19 11	8 39	18 50	9 05	18 24	9 42	17 47	10 47	16 42
27	7 49	18 41	8 10	18 20	8 36	17 54	9 13	17 16	10 19	16 11
Dec. 7	7 19	18 11	7 40	17 50	8 07	17 24	8 44	16 46	9 50	15 40
17	6 50	17 42	7 11	17 21	7 37	16 54	8 15	16 16	9 21	15 10
27	6 20	17 12	6 41	16 51	7 08	16 25	7 46	15 47	8 52	14 41

Saturn, 2007

Date	20° N Latitude Rise h m	20° N Latitude Set h m	30° N Latitude Rise h m	30° N Latitude Set h m	40° N Latitude Rise h m	40° N Latitude Set h m	50° N Latitude Rise h m	50° N Latitude Set h m	60° N Latitude Rise h m	60° N Latitude Set h m
Jan. 1	20 40	9 30	20 27	9 43	20 11	9 59	19 48	10 22	19 12	10 58
11	19 58	8 49	19 45	9 02	19 29	9 19	19 06	9 41	18 29	10 18
21	19 16	8 08	19 03	8 21	18 46	8 38	18 23	9 01	17 45	9 38
31	18 33	7 26	18 20	7 39	18 03	7 56	17 39	8 20	17 01	8 58
Feb. 10	17 50	6 44	17 36	6 58	17 19	7 15	16 55	7 39	16 16	8 18
20	17 07	6 02	16 53	6 16	16 36	6 34	16 11	6 58	15 31	7 38
Mar. 2	16 25	5 20	16 10	5 34	15 52	5 52	15 27	6 17	14 47	6 58
12	15 43	4 38	15 28	4 53	15 10	5 11	14 44	5 36	14 03	6 18
22	15 01	3 57	14 46	4 12	14 27	4 30	14 02	4 56	13 20	5 38
Apr. 1	14 20	3 16	14 05	3 31	13 46	3 50	13 20	4 16	12 38	4 58
11	13 39	2 36	13 24	2 51	13 06	3 10	12 40	3 36	11 57	4 18
21	13 00	1 57	12 45	2 11	12 26	2 30	12 00	2 56	11 17	3 39
May 1	12 21	1 18	12 06	1 32	11 47	1 51	11 21	2 17	10 39	3 00
11	11 43	0 39	11 28	0 54	11 09	1 13	10 44	1 38	10 01	2 21
21	11 06	0 01	10 51	0 16	10 33	0 34	10 07	1 00	9 25	1 42
31	10 29	23 20	10 14	23 35	9 56	23 53	9 31	0 22	8 50	1 03
June 10	9 53	22 44	9 39	22 58	9 21	23 16	8 56	23 40	8 16	0 25
20	9 18	22 07	9 04	22 21	8 46	22 39	8 22	23 03	7 43	23 42
30	8 43	21 31	8 29	21 45	8 12	22 02	7 48	22 26	7 10	23 04
July 10	8 08	20 56	7 55	21 09	7 38	21 26	7 15	21 49	6 38	22 26
20	7 34	20 20	7 21	20 33	7 05	20 49	6 42	21 12	6 06	21 48
30	7 00	19 45	6 47	19 58	6 31	20 13	6 10	20 35	5 35	21 10
Aug. 9	6 26	19 10	6 14	19 22	5 58	19 37	5 37	19 58	5 04	20 32
19	5 52	18 35	5 40	18 47	5 26	19 01	5 05	19 22	4 33	19 54
29	5 18	18 00	5 07	18 11	4 53	18 25	4 33	18 45	4 02	19 16
Sept. 8	4 45	17 24	4 33	17 36	4 20	17 49	4 01	18 08	3 31	18 38
18	4 11	16 49	4 00	17 00	3 47	17 13	3 28	17 31	2 59	18 00
28	3 36	16 14	3 26	16 24	3 13	16 37	2 56	16 54	2 28	17 22
Oct. 8	3 02	15 38	2 52	15 48	2 40	16 00	2 22	16 17	1 56	16 44
18	2 27	15 02	2 17	15 12	2 05	15 24	1 49	15 40	1 23	16 06
28	1 52	14 26	1 42	14 35	1 31	14 47	1 15	15 03	0 49	15 28
Nov. 7	1 16	13 49	1 07	13 58	0 55	14 10	0 40	14 25	0 15	14 50
17	0 39	13 12	0 30	13 21	0 19	13 32	0 04	13 47	23 36	14 11
27	0 02	12 34	23 50	12 43	23 39	12 54	23 24	13 09	23 00	13 33
Dec. 7	23 20	11 56	23 12	12 05	23 01	12 16	22 46	12 31	22 22	12 54
17	22 42	11 17	22 33	11 26	22 22	11 37	22 07	11 52	21 44	12 15
27	22 02	10 38	21 53	10 47	21 42	10 58	21 27	11 13	21 04	11 36

Brightest Stars

This table lists **stars of greatest visual magnitude** as seen in the night sky (the lower the number, the brighter the star). The common name of the star is in parentheses. Stars of variable magnitude are designated by v. Coordinates are for mid-2007. Greek letters in the star names indicate perceived degree of brightness within the constellation, alpha generally being the brightest, though there are some exceptions.

To find when the star is on the meridian, subtract Right Ascension of Mean Sun (*see* the table Greenwich Sidereal Time for 0h UTC) from the star's Right Ascension, first adding 24h to the latter if necessary. Mark this result PM if less than 12h; if greater than 12, subtract 12h and mark the remainder AM.

Star	Magni-tude	Paral-lax "	Light-yrs	Right ascen. h m	Decli-nation ° '
α Canis Majoris (Sirius)	−1.44v	0.379	8.6	6 45.5	−16 44
α Carinae (Canopus)	−0.62v	0.010	313	6 24.1	−52 42
α Bootis (Arcturus)	−0.05v	0.089	37	14 16.0	+19 09
α Centauri (Rigel Kentaurus)	−0.01	0.742	4.4	14 40.1	−60 52
α Lyrae (Vega)	0.03v	0.129	25.3	18 37.2	+38 48
α Aurigae (Capella)	0.08v	0.077	42	5 17.2	+46 00
β Orionis (Rigel)	0.18v	0.004	773	5 14.9	−8 12
α Canis Minoris (Procyon)	0.40	0.286	11.4	7 39.7	+5 12
α Eridani (Achernar)	0.45v	0.023	144	1 38.0	−57 12
α Orionis (Betelgeuse)	0.45v	0.008	427	5 55.6	+7 24
β Centauri (Hadar)	0.61v	0.006	525	14 4.3	−60 25
α Aquilae (Altair)	0.76v	0.194	16.8	19 51.1	+8 53
α Crucis (Acrux)	0.77	0.010	321	12 27.0	−63 08
α Tauri (Aldebaran)	0.87v	0.050	65	4 36.4	+16 31
α Virginis (Spica)	0.98v	0.012	262	13 25.6	−11 12
α Scorpii (Antares)	1.06v	0.005	604	16 29.9	−26 27
β Geminorum (Pollux)	1.16v	0.097	33.7	7 45.7	+28 00
α Piscis Austrinis (Fomalhaut)	1.17	0.130	25.1	22 58.1	−29 35
β Crucis (Becrux)	1.25v	0.009	352	12 48.2	−59 44
α Cygni (Deneb)	1.25v	0.001	3230	20 41.7	+45 18
α Leonis (Regulus)	1.36	0.042	77	10 08.8	+11 56
ε Canis Majoris (Adhara)	1.50v	0.008	431	6 58.9	−28 59
α Geminorum (Castor)	1.58	0.063	52	7 35.1	+31 52
γ Crucis (Gacrux)	1.59v	0.037	88	12 31.6	−57 09
λ Scorpii (Shaula)	1.62v	0.005	703	17 34.1	−37 07
γ Orionis (Bellatrix)	1.64v	0.013	243	5 25.5	+6 21
β Tauri (Elnath)	1.65	0.025	131	5 26.8	+28 37
β Carinae (Miaplacidus)	1.67v	0.029	111	9 13.3	−69 45
ε Orionis (Alnilam)	1.69v	0.002	1340	5 36.6	−1 12
α Gruis (Al Nair)	1.73v	0.032	101	22 08.7	−46 55
ζ Orionis (Alnitak)	1.74	0.004	817	5 41.1	−1 56
γ Velorum (Al Suhail)	1.75v	0.004	840	8 09.8	−47 22
ε Ursae Majoris (Alioth)	1.76v	0.040	81	12 54.4	+55 55
ε Sagittarii (Kaus Australis)	1.79	0.023	145	18 24.7	−34 23
α Persei (Mirfak)	1.79v	0.006	592	3 24.9	+49 53
α Ursae Majoris (Dubhe)	1.81	0.026	124	11 04.2	+61 43
δ Canis Majoris (Wezen)	1.83v	0.002	1790	7 08.7	−26 24
η Ursae Majoris (Alkaid)	1.85v	0.032	101	13 47.8	+49 17
ε Carinae (Avior)	1.86v	0.005	632	8 22.7	−59 32
θ Scorpii	1.86	0.012	272	17 37.9	−43 00
β Aurigae (Menkalinan)	1.90v	0.040	82	6 00.1	+44 57
α Trianguli Australis (Atria)	1.91v	0.008	415	16 49.5	−69 02
γ Geminorum (Alhena)	1.93	0.031	105	6 38.1	+16 24
δ Velorum	1.93	0.041	80	8 44.9	−54 42
α Pavonis (Peacock)	1.94v	0.018	183	20 26.2	−56 43
α Ursae Minoris (Polaris)	1.97v	0.008	431	2 40.6	+89 18
β Canis Majoris (Mirzam)	1.98v	0.007	499	6 23.0	−17 58
α Hydrae (Alphard)	1.99v	0.018	177	9 27.9	−8 41
α Arietis (Hamal)	2.01	0.049	66	2 07.6	+23 30
γ Leonis (Algieba)	2.01v	0.026	126	10 20.4	+19 48
β Ceti (Deneb Kaitos)	2.04v	0.034	96	0 43.9	−17 57
σ Sagittarii (Nunki)	2.05v	0.015	224	18 55.7	−26 17
θ Centauri (Menkent)	2.06	0.054	61	14 07.1	−36 24
α Andromedae (Alpheratz)	2.07v	0.034	97	0 08.8	+29 08
β Andromedae (Mirach)	2.07v	0.016	199	1 10.2	+35 40
κ Orionis (Saiph)	2.07v	0.005	721	5 48.1	−9 40
β Ursae Minoris (Kochab)	2.07v	0.026	126	14 50.7	+74 07
β Gruis	2.07v	0.019	170	22 43.1	−46 51
α Ophiuchi (Rasalhague)	2.08	0.070	47	17 35.3	+12 33
β Persei (Algol)	2.09v	0.035	93	3 08.7	+40 59
γ Andromedae (Almaak)	2.10	0.009	355	2 04.4	+42 22
β Leonis (Denebola)	2.14	0.090	36.2	11 49.4	+14 32
γ Cassiopeiae	2.15v	0.005	613	0 57.2	+60 45
γ Centauri	2.20	0.025	130	12 41.9	−49 00
ζ Puppis (Naos)	2.21v	0.002	1400	8 03.8	−40 01
ι Carinae (Tureis)	2.21	0.005	692	9 17.3	−59 18
α Coronae Borealis (Alphecca)	2.22v	0.044	75	15 35.0	+26 41
λ Velorum (Suhail)	2.23v	0.006	573	9 08.3	−43 28
ζ Ursae Majoris (Mizar)	2.23	0.042	78	13 24.2	+54 53
γ Cygni (Sadr)	2.23v	0.002	1520	20 22.5	+40 17
γ Draconis (Eltanin)	2.24v	0.022	148	17 56.8	+51 29
δ Orionis (Mintaka)	2.25v	0.004	916	5 32.4	−0 18
β Cassiopeiae (Caph)	2.28v	0.060	54	0 09.6	+59 12
ε Scorpii	2.29	0.050	65	16 50.7	−34 18
ε Centauri	2.29v	0.009	376	13 40.4	−53 30
δ Scorpii (Dschubba)	2.29v	0.008	401	16 00.8	−22 39
α Lupi	2.30v	0.006	548	14 42.4	−47 25
η Centauri	2.33v	0.011	308	14 36.0	−42 11
β Ursae Majoris (Merak)	2.34	0.041	79	11 02.3	+56 21
ε Bootis (Izar)	2.35	0.016	210	14 45.3	+27 03
κ Scorpii	2.39v	0.007	464	17 43.0	−39 02

Morning and Evening "Stars," 2007

(Coordinated Universal Time)

	Morning	Evening		Morning	Evening
Jan.	Mercury to Jan. 4 Mars Jupiter Saturn	Mercury from Jan 5 Venus Uranus Neptune	**Apr.**	Mercury Mars Jupiter Uranus Neptune	Venus Saturn
Feb.	Mercury from Feb 24 Mars Jupiter Saturn to Feb. 14 Neptune from Feb. 12	Mercury to Feb. 23 Venus Saturn from Feb. 15 Uranus Neptune to Feb. 11	**May**	Mercury to May 3 Mars Jupiter Uranus Neptune	Mercury from May 4 Venus Saturn
Mar.	Mercury Mars Jupiter Uranus from Mar. 9 Neptune	Venus Saturn Uranus to Mar. 8	**June**	Mercury from June 29 Mars Jupiter to June 5 Uranus Neptune	Mercury to June 28 Venus Jupiter from June 6 Saturn

	Morning	Evening		Morning	Evening
July	Mercury	Venus	Oct.	Mercury from Oct. 22	Mercury to Oct. 21
	mars	Jupiter		Venus	Jupiter
	Uranus	Saturn		Mars	Uranus
	Neptune			Saturn	Neptune
Aug.	Mercury to Aug. 13	Mercury from Aug. 14	Nov.	Mercury	Jupiter
	Venus from Aug. 17	Venus to Aug. 16		Venus	Uranus
	Mars	Jupiter		Mars	Neptune
	Saturn from Aug. 23	Saturn to Aug. 22		Saturn	
	Uranus	Neptune from Aug. 16	Dec.	Mercury to Dec. 18	Mercury from Dec. 19
	Neptune to Aug. 15			Venus	Mars from Dec. 25
Sept.	Venus	Mercury		Mars to Dec. 24	Jupiter to Dec. 22
	Mars	Jupiter		Jupiter from Dec. 23	Uranus
	Saturn	Uranus from Sept. 10		Saturn	Neptune
	Uranus to Sept. 9	Neptune			

Greenwich Sidereal Time for 0ʰ UTC*, 2007

(Add 12 hours to obtain Right Ascension of Mean Sun)

Date	d	h	m	Date	d	h	m	Date	d	h	m	Date	d	h	m
Jan.	1	6	41.0	Apr.	1	12	35.9	July	10	19	10.2	Oct.	8	1	05.0
	11	7	20.5		11	13	15.3		20	19	49.6		18	1	44.4
	21	7	59.9		21	13	54.8		30	20	29.0		28	2	23.9
	31	8	39.4	May	1	14	34.2	Aug.	9	21	08.4	Nov.	7	3	03.3
Feb.	10	9	18.8		11	15	13.6		19	21	47.9		17	3	42.7
	20	9	58.2		21	15	53.0		29	22	27.3		27	4	22.1
Mar.	2	10	37.6		31	16	32.5	Sept.	8	23	06.7	Dec.	7	5	01.5
	12	11	17.1	June	10	17	11.9		18	23	46.2		17	5	41.0
	22	11	56.5		20	17	51.3		28	0	25.6		27	6	20.4
					30	18	30.7								

* Universal coordinated Time.

Aurora Borealis and Aurora Australis

The **Aurora Borealis,** also called the **Northern Lights**, is a broad display of rather faint light in the northern skies at night. The **Aurora Australis**, a similar phenomenon, appears at night in southern skies. The auroras are the result of particles from the Sun reacting with those in the Earth's atmosphere. The Sun produces a stream of charged particles, called the **solar wind**. These particles, mainly electrons and protons, approach Earth at speeds of up to 300 mi per second. In addition, there are interplanetary coronal mass ejections—large-scale, high-speed releases of as much as 10 bil tons of coronal material. Some of these particles are trapped by Earth's magnetic field, forming the **Van Allen belts**—2 donut-shaped radiation bands around Earth. Excess amounts of these charged particles, often produced by solar flares, follow Earth's magnetic lines of force toward Earth's magnetic poles. High in the atmosphere, collisions between these solar particles and terrestrial particles result in the glow in the upper atmosphere called the **aurora**. The glow may be vivid where the lines of magnetic force converge near the magnetic poles.

The aurora appears in a wide variety of forms. Sometimes it is seen as a quiet glow, almost foglike in character; sometimes as vertical streamers in which there may be considerable motion; sometimes as a series of luminous expanding arcs. There are many colors, with white, yellow, and red predominating. The auroras are most vivid and most frequently seen at about 20° from the magnetic poles. The Aurora Borealis is commonly seen along the northern coast of North America and eastern Europe. It has occasionally been seen as far south as Key West, FL, while the Aurora Australis has occasionally been seen as far north as Australia and New Zealand.

The auroral displays appear at heights ranging from 50 mi to about 600 mi and have given us a means of estimating the extent of Earth's atmosphere. The auroras are often accompanied by **magnetic storms** whose forces, also guided by the lines of force of Earth's magnetic field, disrupt electrical communication.

Largest Telescopes

Astronomers indicate the size of telescopes not by length or magnification, but by the diameter of the primary light-gathering component of the system—such as the lens or mirror. This measurement is a direct indication of the telescope's light-gathering power. The bigger the diameter, the fainter the objects you are able to detect. The Earth's atmosphere limits the resolution of what you see. That is why the Hubble Space Telescope, which is outside the atmosphere, can have better resolution than larger telescopes on the Earth.

Refracting (lens) telescopes are currently not made with lens diameters of more than 40 in. Mirror telescopes can be made less expensively than lens telescopes, so all modern large optical telescopes are made with mirrors. **Radio telescopes**, also reflecting telescopes, view at wavelengths not visible to optical telescopes or to the human eye. Radio telescopes are made larger than optical telescopes because larger diameters are required at longer wavelengths to obtain equivalent resolution. Arrays of telescopes are used to achieve even better resolution through a technique called interferometry. Originally developed for radio telescopes, the technique is now also used with optical and infrared telescopes.

Largest Refracting (lens) Optical Telescope: Yerkes Observatory—1 m (40 in), at Williams Bay, WI

Largest Reflecting (mirror) Optical/Infrared Telescope: Keck—9.8 m (32 ft), on Mauna Kea in Hawaii (segmented mirror; 2 equal-size telescopes)

Largest Infrared Interferometer: Four 8.2-m (27-ft) telescopes of the Very Large Telescope Interferometer (VLTI) with a 200-m (656-ft) baseline on Cerro Paranal in Chile

Largest Fully Steerable Radio Dish: Robert C. Byrd Green Bank Telescope—100 m x 110 m (328 ft x 361 ft), in West Virginia

Largest Single Radio Dish: Arecibo Observatory—305 m (1,000 ft), in Puerto Rico

Largest Radio Interferometer: Ten 25-m (82-ft) diameter telescopes of the Very Long Baseline Array (VLBA), dispersed from Hawaii to the Virgin Islands with a resolution equal to a radio dish of 8,600 km (5,000 mi), making it the highest resolution telescope in the solar system

Constellations

Culturally, constellations are imagined patterns among the stars that, in some cases, have been recognized through millennia. Knowledge of constellations was once necessary in order to function as an astronomer. For today's astronomers, constellations are simply areas on the entire sky in which interesting objects await observation and interpretation.

Because Western culture has prevailed in establishing modern science, equally viable and interesting constellations and celestial traditions of other cultures are not well known outside their regions of origin. Even the patterns with which we are most familiar today have undergone considerable change over the centuries.

Today, **88 constellations** are officially recognized. Although many have ancient origins, some are "modern," devised out of unclaimed stars by astronomers a few centuries ago. Unclaimed stars were those too faint or inconveniently placed to be included in the more prominent constellations. Stars in a constellation are not necessarily near each other; they are just located in the same direction on the celestial sphere.

When astronomers began to travel to South Africa in the 16th and 17th centuries, they found an unfamiliar sky that showed numerous brilliant stars. Thus, we find constellations in the southern hemisphere that depict technological marvels of the time, as well as some arguably traditional forms, such as the "fly."

Many of the commonly recognized constellations had their **origins** in ancient Asia Minor. These were adopted by the Greeks and Romans, who translated their names and stories into their own languages, modifying some details in the process. After the declines of these cultures, most such knowledge entered oral tradition or remained hidden in monastic libraries. From the 8th century, the Muslim explosion spread through the Mediterranean world. Wherever possible, every-

thing was translated into Arabic to be taught in the universities the Muslims established all over their new-found world.

In the 13th century, Alfonso X of Castile, an avid student of astronomy, had Ptolemy's *Almagest* translated into Latin. It thus became widely available to European scholars. In the process, the constellation names were translated, but the star names were retained in their Arabic forms. Thus the names of many stars—e.g., Altair, Alnitak, Mirfak—have Arabic roots, although linguistic adaptation and the inaccuracies of transliteration have wrought changes.

Until the 1920s, astronomers used curved boundaries for the constellation areas. As these were rather arbitrary at best, the International Astronomical Union adopted new constellation boundaries that ran due north-south and east-west, filling the sky much as the contiguous states fill up the area of the "lower 48" United States.

Common names of stars often referred to parts of the traditional figures they represented: Deneb, the tail of the swan; Betelgeuse, the armpit of the giant. Avoiding traditional names, astronomers may label stars by using Greek letters, generally to denote order of brightness. Thus, the "alpha star" would generally be the brightest star of that constellation. The "of" implies possession, so the genitive (possessive) form of the constellation name is used, as in Alpha Orionis, the first star of Orion (Betelgeuse). Astronomers usually use a 3-letter abbreviation for the constellation name, as indicated here.

Within these boundaries, and occasionally crossing them, popular "asterisms" are recognized: the so-called Big Dipper is a small part of the constellation Ursa Major, the big bear; the Sickle is the traditional head and mane of Leo, the lion; the three stars of the Summer Triangle are each in a different constellation, with Vega in Lyra the lyre, Deneb in Cynus the swan, and Altair in Aquila the eagle; the northeast star of the Great Square of Pegasus is Alpha Andromedae.

Name	Genitive Case	Abbr.	Meaning
Andromeda	Andromedae	And	Chained Maiden
Antlia	Antliae	Ant	Air Pump
Apus	Apodis	Aps	Bird of Paradise
Aquarius	Aquarii	Aqr	Water Bearer
Aquila	Aquilae	Aql	Eagle
Ara	Arae	Ara	Altar
Aries	Arietis	Ari	Ram
Auriga	Aurigae	Aur	Charioteer
Boötes	Boötis	Boo	Herdsmen
Caelum	Caeli	Cae	Chisel
Camelopardalis	Camelopardalis	Cam	Giraffe
Cancer	Cancri	Cnc	Crab
Canes Venatici	Canum Venaticorum	CVn	Hunting Dogs
Canis Major	Canis Majoris	CMa	Greater Dog
Canis Minor	Canis Minoris	CMi	Littler Dog
Capricornus	Capricorni	Cap	Sea-goat
Carina	Carinae	Car	Keel
Cassiopeia	Cassiopeiae	Cas	Queen
Centaurus	Centauri	Cen	Centaur
Cepheus	Cephei	Cep	King
Cetus	Ceti	Cet	Whale
Chamaeleon	Chamaeleontis	Cha	Chameleon
Circinus	Circini	Cir	Compasses (art)
Columba	Columbae	Col	Dove
Coma Berenices	Comae Berenices	Com	Berenice's Hair
Corona Australis	Coronae Australis	CrA	Southern Crown
Corona Borealis	Coronae Borealis	CrB	Northern Crown
Corvus	Corvi	Crv	Crow
Crater	Crateris	Crt	Cup
Crux	Crucis	Cru	Cross (southern)
Cygnus	Cygni	Cyg	Swan
Delphinus	Delphini	Del	Dolphin
Dorado	Doradus	Dor	Goldfish
Draco	Draconis	Dra	Dragon
Equuleus	Equulei	Equ	Little Horse
Eridanus	Eridani	Eri	River
Fornax	Fornacis	For	Furnace
Gemini	Geminorum	Gem	Twins
Grus	Gruis	Gru	Crane (bird)
Hercules	Herculis	Her	Hercules
Horologium	Horologii	Hor	Clock
Hydra	Hydrae	Hya	Water Snake (female)
Hydrus	Hydri	Hyi	Water Snake (male)
Indus	Indi	Ind	Indian

Name	Genitive Case	Abbr.	Meaning
Lacerta	Lacertae	Lac	Lizard
Leo	Leonis	Leo	Lion
Leo Minor	Leonis Minoris	LMi	Littler Lion
Lepus	Leporis	Lep	Hare
Libra	Librae	Lib	Balance
Lupus	Lupi	Lup	Wolf
Lynx	Lyncis	Lyn	Lynx
Lyra	Lyrae	Lyr	Lyre
Mensa	Mensae	Men	Table Mountain
Microscopium	Microscopii	Mic	Microscope
Monoceros	Monocerotis	Mon	Unicorn
Musca	Muscae	Mus	Fly
Norma	Normae	Nor	Square (rule)
Octans	Octantis	Oct	Octant
Ophiuchus	Ophiuchi	Oph	Serpent Bearer
Orion	Orionis	Ori	Hunter
Pavo	Pavonis	Pav	Peacock
Pegasus	Pegasi	Peg	Flying Horse
Perseus	Persei	Per	Hero
Phoenix	Phoenicis	Phe	Phoenix
Pictor	Pictoris	Pic	Painter
Pisces	Piscium	Psc	Fishes
Piscis Austrinus	Piscis Austrini	PsA	Southern Fish
Puppis	Puppis	Pup	Stern (deck)
Pyxis	Pyxidis	Pyx	Compass (sea)
Reticulum	Reticuli	Ret	Reticle
Sagitta	Sagittae	Sge	Arrow
Sagittarius	Sagittarii	Sgr	Archer
Scorpius	Scorpii	Sco	Scorpion
Sculptor	Sculptoris	Scl	Sculptor
Scutum	Scuti	Sct	Shield
Serpens	Serpentis	Ser	Serpent
Sextans	Sextantis	Sex	Sextant
Taurus	Tauri	Tau	Bull
Telescopium	Telescopii	Tel	Telescope
Triangulum	Trianguli	Tri	Triangle
Triangulum Australe	Trianguli Australis	TrA	Southern Triangle
Tucana	Tucanae	Tuc	Toucan
Ursa Major	Ursae Majoris	UMa	Greater Bear
Ursa Minor	Ursae Minoris	UMi	Littler Bear
Vela	Velorum	Vel	Sail
Virgo	Virginis	Vir	Maiden
Volans	Volantis	Vol	Flying Fish
Vulpecula	Vulpeculae	Vul	Fox

Eclipses, 2007
(in Coordinated Universal Time, standard time of the prime meridian)

There are 4 eclipses in 2007: a total eclipse of the Moon, a partial eclipse of the Sun, a total eclipse of the Moon, and a partial eclipse of the Sun. During a partial eclipse of the sun, only the penumbra, or outside part of the Moon's shadow, is visible. When this happens, the sun is only partly obscured.

I. Total eclipse of the Moon, March 3-4
The beginning of the eclipse will be visible in the far western Pacific Ocean, Asia, Australia, Russia, Europe, Africa, the eastern Atlantic Ocean, Greenland, and the Arctic region. The end of the eclipse will be visible in Europe, Africa, North and South America, the eastern Pacific Ocean, and the Arctic region.

Event	Date	h	m
Penumbral Eclipse Begins	Mar. 3	20	18.2
Partial eclipse begins	3	21	30.4
Total eclipse begins	3	22	44.2
Greatest eclipse	3	23	20.9
Total eclipse ends	3	23	57.6
Partial eclipse ends	4	1	11.5
Penumbral; Eclipse Ends	4	2	23.7

II. Partial eclipse of the Sun, March 19
The partial eclipse of the Sun is visible from western Alaska, Eastern Russia, parts of western Japan, China, southeast Asia, Mongolia, India, and parts of the Middle East.

Event	Date	h	m
Partial eclipse begins	Mar. 19	0	38.4
Greatest eclipse	19	2	31.9
End of eclipse	19	4	25.0

III. Total eclipse of the Moon, August 28
The beginning of the eclipse will be visible in the western Atlantic Ocean, North and South America, the Pacific Ocean, New Zealand, and most of Antarctica. The end will be visible on the west coast of North America, Alaska, New Zealand, Australia, east Asia, Russia, and India.

Event	Date	h	m
Penumbral Eclipse Begins	Aug. 28	7	53.6
Partial eclipse begins	28	8	51.3
Total eclipse begins	28	9	52.4
Greatest eclipse	28	10	37.4
Total eclipse ends	28	11	22.4
Partial eclipse ends	28	12	23.5
Penumbral; Eclipse Ends	28	13	20.0

IV. Partial eclipse of the Sun, September 11
The partial eclipse will be visible in Antarctica, the southern Atlantic Ocean, Argentina, Chile, Uraguay, Paraguay, Bolivia, and most of southern Brazil.

Event	Date	h	m
Partial eclipse begins	Sept. 11	10	25.8
Greatest eclipse	11	12	31.4
Partial eclipse ends	11	14	36.6

Total Solar Eclipses, 2000-2030

Total solar eclipses actually take place nearly as often as total lunar eclipses. Total lunar eclipses are visible over at least half of the Earth, while total solar eclipses can be seen only along a very narrow path up to a few hundred miles wide and a few thousand miles long. Observing a total solar eclipse is thus a rarity for most people.

Solar eclipses can be dangerous to observe. This is not because the Sun emits more potent rays, but because the Sun is always dangerous to observe directly and people are particularly likely to stare at it during a solar eclipse.

Date	Duration[1] m	s	Width (mi)	Path of Totality
2001, June 21	4	56	125	Atlantic Ocean, Africa, Madagascar
2002, Dec. 4	2	4	54	S Africa, Indian Ocean, Australia
2003, Nov. 23	1	57	338	Antarctica
2005, Apr. 8[h]	0	42	17	Pacific Ocean, northwestern S America
2006, Mar. 29	4	7	118	Atlantic Ocean, Africa, Asia
2008, Aug. 1	2	27	157	Arctic Ocean, Asia
2009, July 22	6	39	160	Asia, Pacific Ocean
2010, July 11	5	20	164	Pacific Ocean, southern S America
2012, Nov. 13	4	2	112	N Australia, Pacific Ocean
2013, Nov. 3[h]	1	40	36	Atlantic Ocean, Africa
2015, Mar. 20	2	47	304	N Atlantic Ocean, Arctic Ocean
2016, Mar. 9	4	10	96	Indonesia, Pacific Ocean
2017, Aug. 21	2	40	71	Pacific Ocean, U.S., Atlantic Ocean
2019, July 2	4	33	125	S Pacific Ocean, S America
2020, Dec. 14	2	10	56	S Pacific Ocean, S America, S Atlantic Ocean
2021, Dec. 4	1	55	282	Antarctica, S Atlantic Ocean
2023, Apr. 20[h]	1	16	31	Indian Ocean, New Guinea, Pacific Ocean
2024, Apr. 8	4	28	127	Pacific Ocean, Mexico, N America, Atlantic Ocean
2026, Aug. 12	2	18	198	Arctic Ocean, Greenland, N Atlantic Ocean, Indian Ocean, Australia, New Zealand
2027, Aug. 2	6	23	161	N Atlantic Ocean, N Africa, Middle East, Indian Ocean
2028, July 22	5	9	145	Indian Ocean, Australia, New Zealand
2030, Nov. 25	3	44	105	S Pacific Ocean, S Africa, Indian Ocean, Australia

h = indicates annular-total hybrid eclipse. (1) Duration refers to length of time at optimal viewing area.

Total Solar Eclipses in the U.S. in the 21st Century

During the 21st century there will be 8 total solar eclipses visible somewhere in the continental U.S. The first comes after a long gap; the last total solar eclipse was on Feb. 26, 1979, in the northwestern U.S.

Date	Path of Totality	Date	Path of Totality
Aug. 21, 2017	Oregon to South Carolina	Mar. 30, 2052	Florida to Georgia
Apr. 8, 2024	Mexico to Texas and up through Maine	May 11, 2078	Louisiana to North Carolina
Aug. 23, 2044	Montana to North Dakota	May 1, 2079	New Jersey to the lower edge of New England
Aug. 12, 2045	N California to Florida	Sept. 14, 2099	North Dakota to Virginia

Beginnings of the Universe

One of the dominating astronomical discoveries of the 20th century was that the galaxies of the universe all seem to be moving away from us. Doppler redshifts were observed for the spiral nebulae around 1920, even though they were not yet known to be galaxies. By the early 1930s, Edwin Hubble and M.L. Humason had established that the more distant a galaxy, the faster it was receding. It turned out that they are moving away not just from us but from one another—that is, **the universe is expanding**. Scientists conclude that the universe must once, very long ago, have been extremely compact and dense, until an explosion or a similar event caused the matter to spread out. The explosion that gave birth to the universe is called the **Big Bang**.

On the subatomic level, according to this theory, there were vast changes of energy and matter and the way physical laws operated during the first few minutes. After those early minutes the percentages of the basic matter of the universe—hydrogen, helium, and lithium—were set. Everything was so compact and so hot that **radiation dominated the early universe** and there were no stable, un-ionized atoms. At first, the universe was opaque, in the sense that any energy emitted was quickly absorbed and then re-emitted by free electrons. **As the universe expanded, density and temperature continued to drop.** A few hundred thousand years after the Big Bang, the temperature dropped far enough that electrons and nuclei could combine to form stable atoms as the universe became transparent. Once that occurred, the radiation that

had been trapped was free to escape.

In the 1940s, George Gamov and others predicted that astronomers should be able to see remnants of this escaped radiation. They were starting to search for this background radiation when physicists Arno Penzias and Robert Wilson, using a radio telescope, inadvertently beat them to the punch (the 2 were later awarded a Nobel Prize).

In 2003, NASA's Wilkinson Microwave Anisotropy Probe made measurements of the temperature of this **cosmic microwave background** radiation to within millionths of a degree. From these measurements, scientists were able to deduce that our universe is **13.7 bil years old** and that first-generation stars began to form a mere 200 mil years after the Big Bang.

A related mystery is that evidence suggests there is hidden matter and hidden energy that cannot be directly observed. This **dark matter** may be composed of gas, large numbers of cool, small objects, or even sub-atomic particles. The presence of dark matter is indicated by the rotation curves of galaxies and the dynamics of clusters of galaxies. Evidence for **dark energy** is derived from studies of distant Type Ia supernovae in far galaxies indicating that the expansion of the universe is accelerating, rather than slowing. The visible matter we see seems to constitute only about 4% of the total mass of the universe, while the rest of the mass of the universe is in the form of dark matter (23%) and dark energy (73%). Dark energy is a mysterious force that seems to work on the very fabric of the universe, spreading it apart.

Galaxies

The 20th century might be called the century of the galaxy. By the start of the century, more than 10,000 **nebulae**—cloud-like luminous objects in the sky—had been discovered. Some were correctly identified as star clusters and others as clouds of gas and dust. Those nebulae which were spiral or elliptical in shape were found in regions of the sky far from the glowing band that is our own Milky Way Galaxy. Immanuel Kant had written in 1775 that some of these fuzzy objects might be **"island universes"** apart from our own. But the idea remained speculative until 1923-24, when Edwin Hubble discovered the existence of variable stars in some of these nebulae. This provided conclusive evidence that these systems were outside our own "island universe," the Milky Way Galaxy.

Galaxies range in **size** from small dwarf elliptical ones, with perhaps 1 mil stars, to spiral galaxies containing 300

billion stars, to giant elliptical galaxies that may be home to more than 10 tril stars. The diameters of galaxies range from 3,000 light-years in dwarf elliptical galaxies to over 500,000 light-years in giant elliptical galaxies. It is estimated that the Milky Way galaxy is about 100,000 light-years in diameter with about 400 bil stars.

Galaxies also congregate into **clusters**. The smallest are poor clusters of only a few dozen galaxies, while the largest rich clusters may contain thousands of galaxies. The Milky Way is part of a poor cluster of about 3 dozen galaxies called the **Local Group**. The largest member of the Local Group is the Andromeda Galaxy, a spiral galaxy visible to the unaided eye in the constellation of Andromeda on a very dark night away from lights. The Milky Way is the second largest galaxy in this group; most other galaxies in our Local Group are small.

The Solar System

The major planets of the solar system, in order of mean distance from the Sun, are **Mercury, Venus, Earth, Mars, Jupiter, Saturn, Uranus,** and **Neptune.** The dwarf planets in order of distance from the Sun are **Ceres** (located between Mars and Jupiter), **Pluto,** and **Eris** (formerly known as UB313). All planets orbit counterclockwise around the Sun.

Because **Mercury and Venus** are nearer to the Sun than is Earth, their motions about the Sun appear from Earth as wide swings first to one side of the Sun then to the other, though both planets move continuously around the Sun in almost circular orbits. When their passage takes them either between Earth and the Sun or beyond the Sun as seen from Earth, they cannot be seen.

The **planets that lie farther from the Sun** than does Earth may be seen for longer periods and are invisible only when so located in our sky so that they rise and set at about the same time as the Sun—and thus become overwhelmed by the Sun's light.

The giant planets emit their own energy. On occasion, radio emissions from Jupiter exceed even those emitted by the Sun in intensity.

Mercury and Venus, because they are between Earth and the Sun, show phases much as the Moon does. The planets farther from the Sun are always seen as full, although Mars does occasionally present a slightly gibbous phase—like the Moon when not quite full.

The **planets appear to move rapidly among the stars** because they are relatively closer to Earth than the stars. The stars are also in motion, some at tremendous speeds, but they are so far away that their motion does not change their apparent positions in the heavens enough to be perceived. The nearest star is about 9,000 times farther away than Neptune. The count for identified **moons** in the solar system orbiting planets and dwarf planets stood at 166 in late 2006.

Planet Superlatives			
Largest, most massive planet	Jupiter	Smallest, least massive planet	Mercury
Fastest orbiting planet	Mercury	Slowest orbiting planet	Neptune
Fastest sidereal rotation	Jupiter	Slowest sidereal rotation	Venus
Longest (synodic) day	Mercury	Shortest (synodic) day	Jupiter
Rotational pole closest to ecliptic	Uranus	Hottest planet	Venus
Most moons	Jupiter	No moons	Mercury, Venus
Planet with largest moon	Jupiter	Planet with moon with most eccentric orbit	Neptune
Greatest average density	Earth	Lowest average density	Saturn
Tallest mountain	Mars	Deepest oceans	Jupiter
Strongest magnetic fields	Jupiter	Greatest amount of liquid, surface water	Earth
Most circular orbit	Venus		

New Definition of "Planet"

The International Astronomical Union (IAU) on August 24, 2006, at their General Assembly in Prague, agreed on a new definition for "planet," and in the process effectively removed Pluto's planet status. The ruling came after years of debate as to whether Pluto, discovered in 1930, should still be considered the ninth planet in our Solar System because of its size, orbit, and other characteristics. New discoveries of other Pluto-like objects in the Solar System, such as the 2003 discovery of UB313, a Kuiper Belt object (KBO) bigger than Pluto, also contributed to the debate.

Under the IAU's new definition, Mercury, Venus, Earth, Mars, Jupiter, Saturn, Uranus, and Neptune are regarded as "classical" planets. A planet is now defined as a celestial body that (a) is in orbit around the Sun, (b) has sufficient mass for its self-gravity to overcome rigid body forces so that it assumes a hydrostatic equilibrium (nearly round) shape, and (c) has cleared the neighborhood around its orbit.

Pluto, UB313 (officially named Eris in Sept. 2006), and Ceres are now regarded as "dwarf planets," with the status of Pluto's moon, Charon, to be determined at a later date. A **dwarf planet** is a celestial body that (a) is in orbit around the Sun, (b) has sufficient mass for its self-gravity to overcome rigid body forces so that is assumed a hydrostatic equilibrium (nearly round) shape, (c) has not cleared the neighborhood around its orbit, and (d) is not a satellite.

The IAU also created a new category, **Small Solar System Bodies**, for all other objects orbiting the Sun, including comets, asteroids, KBOs, and other small objects, although it has not yet established a process by which other Solar System objects will be classified.

Planets and the Sun, by Selected Characteristics

Sun and Planets	Radius: at unit distance[1] "	at mean least distance[2] "	in mi mean radius	Volume[3]	Mass[3]	Density[3]	Sidereal period d	h	m	s	Gravity at surface[3]	Reflecting power Pct°	Daytime surface temp. °F
Sun	959.5	976	432,500	1,304,000	333,000	0.26	25	9	7		28.0		+9,941
Mercury	3.36	6.5	1,516	0.0562	0.0553	0.98	58	15	36		0.38	0.11	845
Venus	8.34	33.0	3,760	0.857	0.815	0.95	243		30R		0.91	0.65	867
Earth	8.78	—	3,959	1.000	1.000	1.00		23	56	4.2	1.00	0.37	59
Moon	2.40	986.2	1,079	0.0203	0.0123	0.61	27	7	43	40	0.16	0.12	260
Mars	4.67	12.8	2,106	0.151	0.107	0.71		24	37	22	0.38	0.15	−24
Jupiter	96.40	24.5	43,441	1,321	317.8	0.24		9	55	30	2.53	0.52	−162
Saturn	80.29	10.05	36,184	764	95.16	0.12		10	39	20	1.06	0.47	−218
Uranus	34.97	2.05	15,759	63.1	14.54	0.23		17	14	20R	0.90	0.51	−323
Neptune	33.95	1.2	15,301	57.7	17.15	0.30		16	6	40	1.14	0.41	−330

(1) Angular radius, in seconds of arc, if object were seen at a distance of 1 astronomical unit. (2) Angular radius, in seconds of arc, when object is closest to Earth. (3) Earth = 1. R = Retrograde rotation.

The Planets: Motion, Distance, and Brightness

Planet	Mean daily motion[1]	Orbital velocity mi per sec.[2]	Sidereal revolution days[3]	Synodic revolution days[4]	Distance from Sun in millions of mi Max.	Min.	Distance from Earth in millions of mi Max.	Min.	Light at[5] perihelion	aphelion
Mercury	14,732	29.75	87.97	115.9	43.4	28.6	137.9	48.0	10.56	4.59
Venus	5,768	21.76	224.7	583.9	67.7	66.8	162.2	23.7	1.94	1.89
Earth	3,548	18.50	365.256	—	94.5	91.4	—	—	1.03	0.97
Mars	1,887	15.00	686.98	779.9	154.9	128.4	249.4	33.9	0.52	0.36
Jupiter	299	8.12	4,332.6	398.9	507.4	460.1	602	366	0.041	0.034
Saturn	120	6.02	10,759.2	378.1	941.1	840.4	1,031	743	0.012	0.0098
Uranus	42	4.23	30,685.4	369.7	1,866	1,703	1,962	1,605	0.0030	0.0025
Neptune	22	3.37	60,189.0	367.5	2,824	2,762	2,913	2,676	0.0011	0.0011

(1) Average angular motion measured in seconds of arc per day. (2) Speed of revolution around Sun. (3) Number of Earth days to orbit Sun with respect to background stars. (4) Number of Earth days to get back to the same position in its orbit around Sun, relative to Earth. (5) Light at perihelion and aphelion is solar illumination measured in units of mean illumination at Earth.

Planets of the Solar System

Note: AU = astronomical unit (92.96 mil mi, mean distance of Earth from the Sun); **d** = 1 Earth synodic (solar) day (24 hrs); **synodic day** = rotation period of a planet measured with respect to the Sun (the "true" day, i.e. the time from midday to midday, or from sunrise to sunrise); **sidereal day** = the rotation period of a planet with respect to the stars

Mercury

Distance from Sun	
Perihelion	28.6 mil mi
Aphelion	43.4 mil mi
Semi-major axis (mean distance)	36.0 mil mi (0.387 AU)
Period of revolution around Sun	87.97 d
Orbital eccentricity	0.2056
Orbital inclination	7.00°
Synodic day (midday to midday)	175.94 d
Sidereal day	58.65 d
Rotational inclination	0.01°
Mass (Earth = 1)	0.0553
Mean radius	1,516 mi
Mean density (Earth = 1)	0.984
Natural satellites	0
Average surface temperature	333°F

Mercury, named for the Roman gods' messenger, is the closest planet to the Sun and the 2nd-smallest in the Solar System. Mercury is too much in line with the Sun to be observed against a dark sky; therefore it is always seen during morning or evening twilight.

Orbit and Rotation. Mercury moves with great speed around the Sun, averaging about 30 mi per second to complete its orbit, which takes about 88 Earth days. Mercury takes nearly 59 days to rotate on its axis. Because its orbital period is only about 50% longer than its sidereal rotation, the time from one sunrise to the next on Mercury is about 176 days—twice as long as a Mercurial year. Oddly, Mercury has a magnetic field, albeit very weak. It has been held that both a fluid core and rapid rotation—neither of which Mercury is believed to have—are necessary for the generation of a planetary magnetic field. Mercury may demonstrate the contrary.

Atmosphere. Mercury's atmosphere is almost non-existent. What very little it has is composed of 42% oxygen, 29% sodium, 22% hydrogen, 6% helium, 0.5% potassium, and 0.5% other particles. Because of Mercury's lack of atmosphere to regulate temperatures between day and night, the surface during the day may reach a temperature of about 845°F, while the temperature at night may fall as low as − 300°F. Earth-based observation has provided evidence of water ice near the poles.

Surface and Composition. Mercury's surface is rocky and cratered similar to that of the Earth's Moon. The most imposing feature on Mercury, the Caloris Basin, is a huge impact crater more than 800 mi in diameter. Mercury has a huge iron core that takes up about 75% of the planet's radius; it has higher percentage of iron than any other planet.

Venus

Distance from Sun	
Perihelion	66.8 mil mi
Semi-major axis (mean distance)	67.2 mil mi (0.723 AU)
Aphelion	67.7 mil mi
Period of revolution around Sun	224.70 d
Orbital eccentricity	0.0067
Orbital inclination	3.39°
Synodic day (midday to midday)	116.75 d (retrograde)
Sidereal day	243.02 d (retrograde)
Rotational inclination	177.4°
Mass (Earth = 1)	0.815
Mean radius	3,760 mi
Mean density (Earth = 1)	0.951
Natural satellites	0
Average surface temperature	867°F

Venus, named for the Roman goddess of love, is the second planet out from the Sun. Almost the same size as Earth, it is believed that the two planets were formed at the same time by the same general process and from the same mixture of chemical elements. Venus can easily be seen from Earth with the naked eye; it is the 3rd-brightest object in the sky, exceeded only by the Sun and the Moon.

Orbit and Rotation. It takes Venus 225 Earth days to complete its orbit around the sun. Its synodic revolution—its return to the same relationship with Earth and the Sun, which is a result of the combination of its own motion with that of Earth—is 584 days. Because of this, every 19 months Venus is closer to Earth than any other planet. The rotation period of Venus appears to be 243 days clockwise—in other words, contrary to the spin of the other planets and contrary to its own motion around the Sun. This rate and sense of rotation makes for a solar day (sunrise to sunrise) on Venus of 116.8 Earth days; nighttime lasts 58 days and daytime lasts 58 days. Venus has no detectible magnetic field.

Atmosphere. The Venusian atmosphere is very thick and toxic. It is composed primarily of 96.5% carbon dioxide, 3.5% nitrogen, trace concentrations of sulfur dioxide, argon, water, carbon monoxide, helium, and neon. In addition, it exerts an atomspheric pressure at the surface more than 90 times Earth's normal sea-level pressure. The planet is covered with a dense, white, cloudy atmosphere that conceals whatever is below it. These clouds are believed to contain sulfuric acid, meaning that when it rains on Venus, it may rain sulfuric acid. Due to the thickness of the atmosphere and resulting extreme greenhouse effect, the temperature is essentially the same day and night; the planet has an average surface temperature of about 867°F making it the hottest planet in the solar system. Winds of about 200 mph in the clouds may account for the transfer of heat into the night side despite the low rotation speed of the planet. However, at the surface, the winds are very slow.

Surface and Composition. Radar-produced maps of the entire planet show large craters, continent-sized highlands, and extensive dry lowlands. No tectonic activity has been found similar to Earth's moving tectonic plates, but a system of global rift zones and numerous broad, low, dome-like structures, called coronae, may have been produced by the upwelling and subsidence of magma from the mantle. Volcanic surface features, such as vast lava plains, fields of small lava domes, and large shield volcanoes, are common. About 1,600 volcanoes and volcanic features appear on the Venusian surface; more than 85% of the surface is covered by volcanic flows. Theia Mons, a huge shield volcano, has a diameter of over 600 mi and a height of over 3.5 mi. (The largest Hawaiian volcano is only about 125 mi in diameter, but rises nearly 5.5 mi from the ocean floor.) Aside from volcanoes, there are highly deformed mountain belts across

Venus along with a few meteor-impact craters more than 20 mi wide. Erosion is a very slow process on Venus due to the lack of water. There are indications of some wind movement of dust and sand. The few impact craters on Venus suggest that the surface is generally geologically young—less than 800 million years old. Despite the fact that probes have landed on Venus, there are very few pictures because the probes themselves couldn't survive the high temperature and atmospheric pressure.

Mars

Distance from Sun	
Perihelion	128.4 mil mi
Semi-major axis (mean distance)	141.6 mil mi (1.524 AU)
Aphelion	154.9 mil mi
Period of revolution around Sun	686.98 d (1.88 y)
Orbital eccentricity	0.0935
Orbital inclination	1.85°
Synodic day (midday to midday)	24h 39m 35s
Sidereal day	24h 37m 22s
Rotational inclination	25.19°
Mass (Earth = 1)	0.107
Mean radius	2,106 mi
Mean density (Earth = 1)	0.713
Natural satellites	2
Average surface temperature	−81° F

Named for the Roman god of war, the "Red Planet" has some features much like Earth. Mars has climate, seasons, volcanoes, and possibly once had liquid water flowing across its surface. Mars can easily be seen with the naked eye on most clear nights, which is why it was one of the first planets to be studied by ancient astronomers. Later, when telescopes came into use, many observers claimed that canals made by Martians existed on the planet's surface, which led to speculation as to whether there was intelligent life there. Unmanned probes have since put all those theories to rest; the canals turned out to be topographic patterns and dust storms.

Orbit and Rotation. Although Mars' orbital path is nearly circular, it is somewhat more eccentric than that of most other planets; Mars is more than 26 mil mi farther from the Sun at its most distant point compared to its closest approach. Its orbit and speed in relation to Earth's bring it fairly close to Earth about every 2 years. Every 15-17 years the close approaches are especially favorable for observation.

Mars rotates in 24 hours and 37 minutes, almost the same period of time as Earth. Mars' mean distance from the Sun is 142 mil mi. Because Mars' axis of rotation is inclined by about 25° from the vertical to the plane of its solar orbit about the Sun, the planet has seasons.

Unlike Earth's global magnetic field, the Martian magnetic field is small, weak, and localized and m.ay be the remnant of a stronger field from the planet's past.

Atmosphere. The Martian atmosphere is composed primarily of 95.32% carbon dioxide, 2.7% nitrogen, 1.6% argon, 0.13% oxygen, 0.08% carbon monoxide, and in very minor quantities, water, hydrogen oxide, and neon. The atmosphere on Mars is very thin; it has an atmospheric pressure between 1% and 2% of Earth's (if Earth's atmosphere were that thin, we would not have enough oxygen to breathe). Because the Martian atmosphere is so thin and because of the planet's weak magnetic field, its surface is bombarded by cosmic radiation about 100 times as intense as on Earth.

Martian weather systems consist mainly of huge dust storms. On the poles, white caps (believed to be both water ice and carbon dioxide ice) grow in winter and shrink in summer. It is mainly the carbon dioxide that comes and goes with the seasons. The water ice is apparently in many layers with dust between them, indicating climatic cycles.

Surface and Composition. Mars is an alien world with rust-red sand and pink skies. In the planet's beginning stages when it was much hotter, Mars' surface melted to a sufficient extent to separate into dense and lighter layers. At some point later, Mars cooled enough to allow liquid water to possibly flow across its surface. Today, Mars is very dry.

Natural Satellites. Mars has 2 satellites called Phobos and Deimos, each discovered in 1877 by Asaph Hall. (Phobos measures about 11 by 17 mi and Deimos about 7 by 9 mi.) Deimos, the outer satellite, revolves around the planet in about 31 hours. Phobos, the inner satellite, whips around Mars in a little more than 7 hours, making 3 trips each Martian day. Since it orbits Mars faster than the planet rotates, Phobos rises in the west and sets in the east, opposite to what other bodies appear to do in the Martian sky. Both moons are irregularly shaped and pitted with numerous craters. Their origins are not known; however, some astronomers consider them to be asteroid-like objects that were captured by Mars very early in its history.

Jupiter

Distance from Sun	
Perihelion	460.1 mil mi
Semi-major axis (mean distance)	483.8 mil mi (5.204 AU)
Aphelion	507.4 mil mi
Period of revolution around Sun	11.862 y
Orbital eccentricity	0.0489
Orbital inclination	1.304°
Synodic day (midday to midday)	9h 55m 33s
Sidereal day	9h 55m 30s
Rotational inclination	3.13°
Mass (Earth = 1)	317.8
Mean radius	43,441 mi
Mean density (Earth = 1)	0.24
Natural satellites	63
Average temperature*	−162°F

*i.e., temperature where atmosphere pressure equals 1 Earth atmosphere.

Jupiter, named for the Roman ruler of the gods, is the largest planet in the solar system (11 times the diameter of Earth). Its mass is more than twice the mass of all the other planets, moons, and asteroids put together. Visible to the naked eye and known to the ancients, it was a focus of the Italian scientist Galileo Galilei who viewed the planet and its 4 largest moons through a homemade telescope.

Orbit and Rotation. Jupiter is at an average distance of 484 mil mi from the Sun and takes almost 12 Earth years to make a complete revolution. The largest of the planets, Jupiter has an equatorial diameter of 88,846 mi; however, its polar diameter is more than 5,700 mi shorter. This noticeable oblateness is a result of the liquidity of the planet and its extremely rapid rotation rate—a Jupiter day is less than 10 Earth hours long. For a planet this size, this rotational speed is amazing. A point on Jupiter's equator moves at a speed of 22,000 mph, as compared with 1,000 mph for a point on Earth's equator. Jupiter's magnetic field is by far the strongest of any planet. Electrical activity caused by this field is so strong that it discharges billions of watts into Earth's magnetic field daily.

Atmosphere. Jupiter's atmosphere is primarily composed of 90% molecular hydrogen and 10% helium. Minor constituents include methane, ammonia, hydrogen deuteride, ethane, and water. Jupiter has a turbulent atmosphere characterized by thick clouds, high winds, and huge lightning storms many times larger than those on Earth. The atmospheric temperature varies but the temperature at the tops of clouds may be about −280°F. The Great Red Spot seen prominently on Jupiter is a huge hurricane-like storm that is three times the diameter of Earth. In 2006, the Hubble Space Telescope detected the appearance of a second, smaller red spot.

Surface and Composition. Gas giant planets like Jupiter, Saturn, and Neptune do not have a surface like Earth or any of the other rocky planets. The gases become denser with depth, until they may turn into a slush or slurry. Jupiter has a liquid hydrogen ocean more than 35,000 mi deep. It likely has a rocky core about the size of Earth, but 13 times more massive. There is no sharp interface between the gaseous atmosphere and the hydrogen ocean that accounts for most of Jupiter's volume. At lower depths, under enormous pressure, the liquid hydrogen takes on the properties of a metal. It is likely that this liquid metallic hydrogen is the source for

both Jupiter's persistent radio noise and for its improbably strong magnetic field.

Natural Satellites. Jupiter has 63 known satellites, 23 of which were found as recently as 2003. Four of the moons (in order from Jupiter), Io, Europa, Ganymede, and Callisto—all discovered by Galileo in 1610—are large and bright and are close in diameter to Earth's Moon and Mercury. Because they move so rapidly around Jupiter, their change in position from night to night can be seen from Earth using binoculars.

Io is one of the most intriguing moons because it is the most volcanically active body in the Solar System. A gaseous, doughnut-shaped ring, or torus, enveloping Io's orbit around Jupiter may have been formed by material ejected from Io's active volcanoes. (This is not to be confused with Jupiter's rings.) These volcanoes, hotter than Earth's volcanoes, erupt mainly molten sulfur.

Europa may have a 30-mi-deep salty, liquid ocean beneath its icy crust, perhaps a small metallic core, and a very tenuous atmosphere. Ganymede is the biggest moon in the Solar System. With a diameter of 3,120 mi, it is bigger than both Mercury and Pluto. Ganymede also has it own magnetic field produced by a molten core perhaps of iron sulfide. Callisto has the oldest, most heavily cratered surface in the solar system, a very thin atmosphere of carbon dioxide, and possibly a subsurface liquid ocean.

The other satellites are much smaller, with 4 closer to Jupiter than Io, 5 between Ganymede and Callisto, and the rest farther out. Most of Jupiter's moons revolve around Jupiter clockwise as seen from the north, contrary to the motions of most satellites in the solar system and to the direction of revolution of planets around the Sun. These moons may be captured asteroids.

Jupiter has a set of rings that cannot be seen from Earth without powerful telescopes. They are composed of small dust grains possibly blasted off the 4 innermost moons by meteoroid impacts.

Saturn

Distance from Sun	
Perihelion	840.44 mil mi
Semi-major axis (mean distance)	890.8 mil mi (9.582 AU)
Aphelion	941.07 mil mi
Period of revolution around Sun	29.458 y
Orbital eccentricity	0.0565
Orbital inclination	2.485°
Synodic day (midday to midday)	10h 39m 23s
Sidereal day	10h 39m 22s
Rotational Inclination	26.73°
Mass (Earth = 1)	95.159
Mean radius	36,184 mi
Mean density (Earth = 1)	0.125
Natural satellites	56
Average temperature*	−218° F

*i.e., temperature where atmosphere pressure equals 1 Earth atmosphere.

Saturn, named for the Roman ruler of the Titans, is the 6th planet from the sun and most distant of the planets visible to the unaided eye. Saturn is 2nd in size to Jupiter, but its mass is much smaller. Saturn is the only planet less dense than water, meaning that Saturn would float if there were a pool of water gigantic enough to hold it.

Orbit and Rotation. Saturn's diameter is almost 74,900 mi at the equator, while its polar diameter is more than 7,300 mi shorter. Like Jupiter, its noticeable oblateness is a result of the liquidity of the planet and its extremely rapid rate of rotation; a day is little more than 10 Earth hours long.

Atmosphere. Saturn's atmosphere is composed primarily of 96.3% hydrogen, 3.3% helium, and traces of methane, ammonia, hydrogen deuteride, ethane, and water. Saturn's atmosphere is much like that of Jupiter, except that the temperature at the top of its cloud layer is at least 50°F colder.

Surface and Composition. Saturn's atmosphere resembles Jupiter's; it likely has a small dense center surrounded by a deep ocean of hydrogen.

Natural Satellites. Saturn has many natural satellites, most of which were not discovered until space probes reached the planet. Saturn's moon Mimas has an impact crater 81 miles across (the moon itself is only 249 miles across). Enceladus has an atmosphere and shows evidence of geysers that spit water ice and vapor. Two tiny moons orbit within the rings, plowing through and making gaps in the rings along their orbits. Pan, the innermost satellite creates the Encke Gap of Saturn's A-ring. 2005 S1 creates the Keeler Gap. The most intriguing Saturnian moon is Titan. The second biggest moon in the Solar System, Titan is bigger than Mercury. Its atmosphere is similar to Earth's atmosphere of long ago; it is made up of approximately 95% nitrogen with traces of methane. Titan's atmosphere extends about 360 mi into space whereas Earth's atmosphere extends about 37 mi. Photographs from the surface show a muddy terrain, with possible deposits of water ice, channels carved by liquid methane springs, and an interesting boundary between light and dark material on the surface. In addition, in 2006, scientists found sand dunes on Titan's surface. The "sand" is believed to be tiny water ice crystals or organic compounds. Surface phenomenon such as sand dunes are signs of erosion and wind. However, unlike on Earth or Mars, Titan's winds are not the result of uneven solar heating on the moon's surface, but rather the strong gravitational pull from Saturn that creates atmospheric "tides" almost in the same way Earth's moon does to the oceans.

Rings. Saturn's ring system is the planet's most recognizable feature. It begins about 4,000 mi above the visible disk of Saturn lying above its equator and extends about 260,000 mi into space. The diameter of the ring system visible from Earth is about 170,000 mi; the rings are estimated to be about 700 feet thick. The rings are composed of rock and ice and range in size from tiny particles to large chunks of material the size of a bus. There are several divisions in the rings. The 2,920 mi Cassini division, the gap between the A and B rings, is the largest division.

Uranus

Distance from Sun	
Perihelion	1,703.4 mil mi
Semi-major axis (mean distance) 1,784.8 mil mi	(19.201 AU)
Aphelion	1,866.4 mil mi
Period of revolution around Sun	84.01 y
Orbital eccentricity	0.0457
Orbital inclination	0.772°
Synodic day (midday to midday)	17h 14m 23s (retrograde)
Sidereal day	17h 14m 24s (retrograde)
Rotational inclination	97.77°
Mass (Earth = 1)	14.536
Mean radius	15,759mi
Mean density (Earth = 1)	0.230
Natural satellites	27
Average temperature*	−323° F

*i.e., temperature where atmosphere pressure equals 1 Earth atmosphere.

Uranus, discovered by Sir William Herschel in 1781, was the first planet discovered using a telescope. It was named for the father of the Titans in Roman mythology.

Rotation and Orbit. Uranus has a diameter of over 31,000 mi and spins once in approximately 17.23 hours, according to flyby magnetic data. One of the most fascinating features of Uranus is how far over it is tipped. Its north pole lies 98° from being directly up and down to its orbit plane. Thus, its seasons are extreme. Over its 84 year orbit, when the Sun rises at the north pole, it shines there for about 42 Earth years; then it sets, and the north pole is in darkness for 42 Earth years. In addition to its rotational tilt, Uranus's magnetic field axis is tipped an incredible 58.6° from its rotational axis and is displaced about 30% of its radius away from the planet's center.

Atmosphere. The atmosphere is composed primarily of 82.5% hydrogen, 15.2 % helium, 2.3% methane, with small amounts of hydrogen deuteride, ammonia ice, water ice, ammonia hydrosulfide, and methane ice.

Surface and Composition. Uranus has no solid surface, and likely no rocky core but rather a mixture of rocks and assorted ices with about 15% hydrogen and some helium.

Natural Satellites. Uranus has 27 known moons, which have orbits lying in the plane of the planet's equator. Five moons are relatively large, while 22 are very small and were only discovered with the *Voyager 2* mission or in later observations. Miranda has grooved markings, reminiscent of Jupiter's Ganymede, but often arranged in a chevron pattern. Rifts and channels on Ariel provide evidence of liquid flowing over its surface in the past. Umbriel is extremely dark, prompting some observers to regard its surface as among the oldest in the system. Titania has rifts and fractures, but not the evidence of flow found on Ariel. Oberon's main feature is its surface saturated with craters, unrelieved by other formations.

In the equatorial plane there is also a complex of 11 rings, 9 of which were discovered in 1978 by observers watching Uranus pass before a star.

Neptune

Distance from the Sun	
Perihelion	2,761.7 mil mi
Semi-major axis (mean distance)	2,793.1 (30.047 AU)
Aphelion	2,824.5 mil mi
Period of revolution around Sun	164.79 y
Orbital eccentricity	0.0113
Orbital inclination	1.769°
Synodic day (midday to midday)	16h 6m 37s
Sidereal day	16h 6m 36s
Rotational inclination	28.32°
Mass (Earth = 1)	17.147
Mean radius	15,301 mi
Mean density (Earth = 1)	0.297
Natural satellites	13
Average temperature*	−330° F

*i.e., temperature where atmosphere pressure equals 1 Earth atmosphere.

Named for the Roman god of the sea, Neptune was the first planet discovered through mathematical calculations and not observation. Its approximate orbit and position was first calculated independently by John Couch Adams and Urbain Le Verrier in 1845. In 1846, Johann Galle first observed Neptune through a telescope.

Orbit and Rotation. Neptune orbits the Sun in 164.8 years in a nearly circular orbit. It's magnetic field is considerably asymmetric to the planet's structure, similar to, but not so extreme as, that found at Uranus. Neptune's magnetic field axis is tipped 46.9 from its rotational axis and is displaced more than 55% of its radius away from the planet's center.

Atmosphere. The Neptunian atmosphere is composed primarily of 80.0% hydrogen, 19.0% helium, 1.5% methane, and small amounts of hydrogen deuteride, ethane, ammonia ice, water ice, ammonia hydrosulfide, and methane ice. Neptune's atmosphere is quite blue, with quickly changing white clouds often suspended high above an apparent surface. A Great Dark Spot was discovered in 1989 when *Voyager 2* visited the planet, reminiscent of the Great Red Spot of Jupiter. Observations with the *Hubble Space Telescope* have shown that the Great Dark Spot originally seen by *Voyager* has apparently dissipated, but a new dark spot has since appeared. Lightning and auroras have been found on other giant planets, but only the aurora phenomenon has been seen on Neptune. As with the other giant planets, Neptune is emitting more energy than it receives from the Sun. The excess has been found to be 2.7 times the solar contribution.

Surface and Composition. As with other giant planets, Neptune may have no solid surface, or exact diameter. However, a mean value of 30,600 mi may be assigned to a diameter between atmosphere levels where the pressure is about the same as sea level on Earth.

Natural Satellites. Largest of Neptune's 13 satellites is Triton. It is the only large moon in a retrograde orbit, which suggests that it was captured rather than having been there from the beginning. Triton's large size, sufficient to raise significant tides on the planet, may one day, billions of years from now, cause Triton to come close enough to Neptune for it to be torn apart. Triton has a tenuous atmosphere of nitrogen with a trace of hydrocarbons and evidence of active geysers injecting material into it. Triton is the coldest object yet measured in the Solar System with a surface temperature of –391° F . Only about half of Triton has been observed, but its terrain shows cratering and a strange regional feature described as resembling the skin of a cantaloupe. Nereid has the highest orbital eccentricity (0.75) of any moon. Its long looping orbit suggests that it was also captured. In 2003, 2 more moons, which orbit farther from their parent planet than any other moons, were discovered. The *Voyager 2* probe in 1989 confirmed the existence of 6 rings around Neptune composed of very fine particles. There may be some clumpiness in the rings' structure. It is not known whether Neptune's satellites influence the formation or maintenance of the rings.

Dwarf Planets

Note: See page 333 for the definition of a dwarf planet.

Ceres

Distance from Sun	
Perihelion	237 mil mi (2.55 AU)
Semi-major axis (mean distance)	257 mil mi (2.77 AU)
Period of revolution around Sun	4.6 y
Orbital eccentricity	0.0789
Orbital inclination	10.58°
Sidereal day	9.075 hours
Mean radius	300 mi

Ceres was the first asteroid ever discovered, on January 1, 1801, by Guiseppe Piazzi. In the 1800s, it was considered a planet, but as more asteroids were discovered, it lost that designation. In August of 2006, it was designated a "dwarf planet" by the International Astronomical Union.

No probe has ever visited Ceres. NASA's DAWN space probe, due to launch in june 2007, may become the first. The DAWN probe's mission is to Vesta and Ceres, the solar system's two largest asteroids. When DAWN arrives at Ceres in February 2015, months before the New Horizons probe arrives at Pluto, it will be the first mission to study a dwarf planet.

Orbit and rotation. Ceres orbits the sun in the asteroid belt region between Mars and Jupiter.

Atmosphere. It is not known if Ceres has an atmosphere. However, it may be similar to the atmosphere on Mercury or the Earth's moon.

Surface and Composition. Ceres is in a class of stony meteorites known as carbonaceous chondrites. These are considered to be the oldest materials in the solar system, with a composition reflecting that of the primitive solar nebula. Extremely dark in color, probably because of their hydrocarbon content, they show evidence of having absorbed water of hydration. Thus, unlike the earth and the moon, they have never either melted or been reheated since they first formed.

Pluto

Distance from Sun	
Perihelion	2,756.9 mil mi
Semi-major axis (mean distance)	3,647.2 (39.482 AU)
Aphelion	4,583.2 mil mi
Period of revolution around Sun	247.68 y
Orbital eccentricity	0.2488
Orbital inclination	17.16°
Synodic day (midday to midday)	6d 9h 17m (retrograde)
Sidereal day	6d 9h 18m (retrograde)
Rotational inclination	122.53°
Mass (Earth = 1)	0.0021
Mean radius	742.5 mi
Mean density (Earth = 1)	0.317
Natural satellites	3
Average surface temperature	–369°

Pluto, named for the Roman god of the underworld, is the second largest known KBO (Kuiper Belt Object) in the Solar System. It was first discovered in 1930 by Clyde Tombaugh, and was classified as a planet until 2006 when the International Astronomical Union changed its designation to dwarf planet.

Orbit and Rotation. Pluto's orbit is highly irregular. Although Pluto on the average stays about 3.6 bil mi from the Sun, it may get as close as 2.76 bil mi, and for about 20 years of its orbit, it is closer to the Sun than Neptune. Currently, it is beyond Neptune's orbit.

Atmosphere and Surface. Because no probes have visited Pluto, it is difficult for astronomers to accurately take readings of the planet's atmospheric composition. It is believed that an atmosphere of methane, nitrogen, and carbon monoxide exists when the planet is closer to the Sun. When Pluto is farther away from the sun during its orbit, the atmosphere freezes and becomes part of the surface. Large regions on Pluto are dark, others light; Pluto has spots and perhaps polar caps. There is also evidence of temperature fluctuations on the planet that may indicate primitive weather. Its core may be rocky with a mantle of water ice surrounding it.

Natural Satellites. Pluto has 3 natural satellites. Charon, the biggest, has a diameter of 737 mi—about half of Pluto's diameter of 1,485 mi. No other planet of any kind has a moon so close to its size. Discovered in 1978, Charon orbits Pluto at a distance of 12,200 mi and takes 6.39 days to move around the planet. In this same length of time, Pluto and Charon both rotate once around their axes, meaning that a person standing on Pluto would always see the same face of Charon in the same part of the sky, everyday and night. The Pluto-Charon system thus appears to rotate as virtually a rigid body. Both worlds are roughly spherical and have comparable densities. Because of these similarities and their peculiar relationship, there is a debate as to whether Charon should one day be designated a dwarf planet.

The 2 other moons were discovered in 2005 and as yet have not been named.

Eris (formerly known as UB313)

Distance from Sun	
Semi-major axis (mean distance)	67.6681 AU
Period of revolution around Sun	560 years
Mean radius	925 mi
Orbital eccentricity	0.44177
Orbital inclination	44.177°
Natural satellites	1

Eris is a dwarf planet formerly referred to only as a KBO, but that is larger than Pluto. Discovered in 2003 by astronomers at the California Institute of Technology, it is the most distant object ever seen in orbit around the sun. Little is known about Eris.

Orbit and Rotation. Eris has a highly elliptical orbit and takes about 560 years to go around the sun—more than twice the time it takes Pluto. Its inclination is steep, tilted at 44° to the planetary plane. It also has an extremely eccentric orbit. It will be at its closest, actually coming inside part of Pluto's orbit, in about 280 years.

Atmosphere. As of yet, nothing is known about Eris's atmosphere, however, it may be similar to Pluto's.

Surface and Composition. Eris, with a surface covered in frozen methane, may be similar to Pluto and the Neptunian moon Triton. Observations made by the Hubble Space Telescope show that Eris's surface is almost white and uniform, reflecting 86% of the light that hits it. This makes it the most reflective body in the Solar System. The dwarf planet's interior is likely a mixture of rock and ice.

Natural Satellites. Eris has one moon. It is officially called S/2005 (2003 UB313) 1. Unofficially, it is referred to as Gabrielle. Little is known about this object.

Small Solar System Bodies: Asteroids, Comets, Kuiper Belt, and the Oort Cloud

Asteroids

Besides planets and moons, there are many smaller objects that orbit the sun. In 2006, the IAU officially designated these objects "small Solar System bodies." **Asteroids** or minor planets are found mainly in a belt between the orbits of Mars and Jupiter, but some may be found outside this region. Within this belt there may be millions of asteroids of varying sizes. Most of asteroids are very small, however, some such as Ceres, which can be classified both as an asteroid and a dwarf planet, is 588 mi in diameter is about one-quarter the diameter of our Moon.

Some of these objects, or asteroids, are gravitationally locked with Jupiter and the Sun so that they have roughly the same orbit as Jupiter but either 60° ahead or behind the planet. These are the **Trojan asteroids.** Many of the smaller moons of the solar system, especially those in retrograde orbits, may be captured asteroids. Asteroids whose orbits either cross or come close to the Earth's orbit are labeled **Near Earth Asteroids** or NEAs. A handful of asteroids have actually been imaged by the Arecibo and Goldstone radio telescopes, and by the NEAR Shoemaker space probe, while the *Galileo* spacecraft imaged the asteroids Gaspra and Ida (including its moon Dactyl) on its way to Jupiter.

Comets

Comets are small icy bodies that orbit the Sun. When they approach the Sun, the energy from the Sun boils off material from the comet's icy nucleus, producing an enlarged head (or **coma**), and in many cases an extended tail. Because of the proximity to the Sun and the expanded head and tail, comets are brighter when near the Sun. For large comets, the head may be a 100,000 mi across and the tail more than a million mi long, though both are mainly empty space.

Comets have been known since ancient times; ultimately, British astronomer Edmund Halley (1656-1742) realized that a group of historical reports were just repeated visits of the same object. Comets are the only astronomical objects named after their discoverers. In 1986, the European spacecraft *Giotto* took the first close-up images of a comet's nucleus, specifically of Comet Halley, showing it had a peanut-shaped nucleus whose longest dimension was about 10 mi.

In 1995, Alan Hale and Thomas Bopp independently discovered a comet that was then beyond the orbit of Jupiter. It was the farthest comet ever discovered by amateurs and one of the brightest of all time. It also holds the record for length of naked-eye visibility—19 months—and is the most photographed comet in history.

Kuiper Belt

The **Kuiper Belt** is a donut-shaped region that extends to about 50 AU from the Sun and is thought to be the source for short-period comets such as Comet Halley or Comet Swift-Tuttle. It is filled with icy bodies that are in solar orbit. The more than 800 objects found in this region in recent years are called Kuiper Belt Objects (KBOs). It is estimated that there are more than 70,000 objects 60 mi in diameter or larger within the Kuiper Belt. Dwarf planets Pluto and UB313 are considered KBOs. There are at least 6 KBOs larger than 500 mi in diameter.

Oort Cloud

The Oort Cloud is a vast spherical shell hypothesized to exist around the Sun. Astronomer Jan Oort proposed its existence as the origin for long-period comets that enter the inner part of the solar system where the planets orbit. As of yet, our technology is not sufficient to detect any members of the Oort Cloud, other than those comets that have been observed that indicate the most distant parts of their orbits may reach out to 50,000 AU. Recent examples of such long-period comets are Comet Hale-Bopp and Comet Hyakutake.

The Sun

Distance from Earth, mean	92.96 mil mi (1 AU)
Sidereal day	25.38 d
Mass (Earth=1)	332,900
Mean Radius	432,200 mi
Mean Density	(Earth=1) 0.255
Average surface temperature	9,941°F

The Sun is the Earth's primary source of light and heat, and its closest star. The biggest object in the solar system, the sun is 332,900 times more massive than Earth and contains 99.86 percent of the mass of the entire solar system. On the whole, the sun is made up of about 92.1% hydrogen and 7.8 % helium, with trace amounts of other elements. It has a mass and luminosity greater than that of 90% of the stars in the Milky Way galaxy. Although most of the stars that can be easily seen on a clear night are bigger and brighter than the Sun, its proximity to Earth that makes it appear tremendously large and bright. The Sun is 400,000 times as bright as the full moon and it gives Earth 6 mil times as much light as do all other stars put together. Because of the great distance between the Sun and Earth, it takes about 499 seconds, or slightly more than 8 minutes, for light from the Sun to reach Earth.

Composition. The Sun has six regions. The first three from the inside out are the core, the radiative zone, and the convective zone. Together they form the interior. The others, which comprise the visible surface, are photosphere, the chromosphere, and the outermost region, the corona.

The Sun's core is where its heat and energy is produced. Through a series of nuclear fusion reactions, hydrogen nuclei are converted to helium nuclei. Temperatures in the core are theorized to be 28 mil° F. From the core photons transport the energy outward through the radiative zone. It can take photons several millions of years to pass through this area. In the convective zone, gases move energy outward at a faster rate. Like a boiling pot, bubbles of gasses bring energy to the surface.

The photosphere is the visible surface of the sun, that is, the light from here is what we see as sunlight. When sunlight is analyzed with a spectroscope, it is found to consist of a continuous spectrum composed of all the colors of the rainbow in order, crossed by many dark lines. The dark "absorption lines" are produced by gaseous materials in the outer layers of the Sun. More than 60 of the natural terrestrial elements have been identified in the Sun, all in gaseous form because of the Sun's intense heat.

Just above the photosphere is the chromosphere, which is visible to the naked eye only at total solar eclipses, appearing then to be a pinkish-violet layer with occasional great prominences projecting above its general level. With proper instruments, the chromosphere can be seen or photographed whenever the Sun is visible. Above the chromosphere is the corona, also visible to the naked eye only at times of total eclipse or with instruments that permit the brighter portions of the corona to be seen. The light of the corona surges millions of miles from the Sun, where atoms of which it is composed are all in a state of extreme attenuation and high ionization that indicates temperatures nearly 2 mil° F.

Sunspots. These dark, irregularly shaped regions may reach diameters of thousands of miles. There is an intimate connection between sunspots and the corona. At times of low sunspot activity, the fine streamers of the corona are longer above the Sun's equator than over the polar regions of the Sun; during periods of high sunspot activity, the corona extends fairly evenly outward from all regions of the Sun, but to a much greater distance in space. The average life of a sunspot group is 2 months, but some have lasted for more than a year.

Sunspots reach a low point, on average, every 11.3 years, with a maximum peak of activity occurring irregularly between 2 successive periods of minimal activity. Currently, the number of sunspots is declining. We will be heading towards a solar minimum sometime possibly in late 2006, or 2007.

Solar Wind and Magnetic Field. Magnetic arches, called prominences, may extend tens of thousands of miles into the corona, and may release enormous amounts of energy heating the corona. Coronal mass ejections are enormous releases of solar energy. Coronal holes are regions where the corona appears dark in X rays, and are associated with open magnetic field lines, where the magnetic field lines project out into space instead of back towards the Sun. It is in these regions where the high-speed solar wind originates.

The solar wind carries the Sun's magnetic field, which extends beyond the planets. This is called the Interplanetary Magnetic Field (IMF). Far past Pluto and the Kuiper Belt, the solar wind and the IMF lose their influence, and the boundary between them and interstellar space is called the heliopause.

Searching for Extrasolar Planets

During the last 10 years of the 20th century, astronomers began to detect the presence of planets orbiting stars other than the Sun. Except for a few possible instances, they have not seen those objects, but merely inferred their existence by their effect on their parent star. The Sun is a typical star in many respects. With over 200 billion stars in the Milky Way, it seems plausible that many other stars might have planets.

As of mid-2006, astronomers had found a total of 193 planets in 96 star systems. Of those, 110 where more massive than Jupiter, which is about 318 times more massive than the Earth. About 79 star systems may have planets less massive than Jupiter. In June 2005, astronomers reported detecting a planet that is only about 6 times the mass of the Earth. The planet orbits much closer to its parent star; Gliese 876 takes less than 2 days to complete one orbit.

Using the Doppler Effect to detect radial velocity changes in the motions of individual stars, astronomers are more likely to find high-mass planets in close and eccentric orbits around stars, because that situation produces larger and more noticeable changes.

In addition to the radial velocity method, astronomers are now using an optical gravitational lensing means of detecting extrasolar planets. Using this technique, Southern hemisphere astronomers found the most distant planet yet detected, about halfway to the center of our own Milky Way galaxy.

In 2005, astronomers obtained the first direct photograph of an extra-solar planet. The unnamed planet orbits a star called GQ Lupi, which is a star like our Sun but younger. The planet is about 100 AUs away from its star, and it is estimated to be about twice as massive as Jupiter.

In 2006, astronomers discovered what they call a "super Earth" orbiting a red dwarf star 9,000 light-years away. The planet appears to have about 13 times the mass of Earth and may be composed of rock and ice. Although the planet is similar in structure to the Earth, it is believed to orbit too far from its star for there to be any liquid on the surface.

Earth: Size, Computation of Time, Seasons

Distance from the Sun	
Perihelion	91.4 mil mi
Semi-major axis	93.0 mil mi (1.0000 AU)
Aphelion	94.5 mil mi
Period of revolution	365.256 d
Orbital eccentricity	0.0167
Orbital inclination	0.0°
Sidereal day (rotation period)	23h 56m 4.2s
Synodic day (midday to midday)	24h 0m 0s
Rotational inclination	23.45°
Mass (Earth = 1)	1.00
Mean radius	3,958.8 mi
Mean density (Earth = 1)	1.00
Natural satellites	1
Average surface temperature	59° F

Earth is the 5th-largest planet and the 3rd from the Sun. Its mass is 5.9736 x 10^{24} kg. Earth's equatorial diameter is 7,926 miles while its polar diameter is only 7,900 mi.

Size and Dimensions. Earth is considered a solid mass, yet it has a large, liquid iron, **magnetic core** with a radius of about 2,160 mi. Surprisingly, it has a solid **inner core** that may be a large iron crystal, with a radius of 760 mi. Around the core is a thick shell, or **mantle**, of dense rock. This mantle is composed of materials rich in iron and magnesium. It is somewhat plastic-like, and under slow steady pressure, it can flow like a liquid. The mantle, in turn, is covered by a thin **crust** forming the solid granite and basalt base of the continents and ocean basins. Over broad areas of Earth's surface, the crust has a thin cover of sedimentary rock such as sandstone, shale, and limestone formed by weathering and by deposits of sands, clays, and plant and animal remains.

The **temperature** inside the Earth increases about 1° F with every 100 to 200 feet in depth, in the upper 100 km of Earth, and reaches nearly 8,000-9,000° F at the center. The heat is believed to come from radioactivity in rocks, pressures within Earth, and the original heat of formation.

Atmosphere of Earth. Earth's atmosphere is a blanket composed of 78% nitrogen, 21% oxygen, and 1% argon. Present in minute quantities are carbon dioxide, hydrogen, neon, helium, krypton, and xenon. Water vapor displaces other gases and varies from nearly zero to about 4% by volume. The atmosphere rests on Earth's surface with a weight equivalent to a layer of water 34 ft deep. For about 300,000 ft upward, the gases remain in the proportions stated. Gravity holds the gases to Earth. The weight of the air compresses it at the bottom so that the greatest density is at Earth's surface. Pressure and density decrease as height increases.

The lowest layer of the atmosphere extending up about 7.5 mi is the **troposphere**, which contains 90% of the air and the tallest mountains. This is also where most weather phenomena occur. The temperature drops with increasing height throughout this layer. The atmosphere for about 23 mi above the troposphere is the **stratosphere**, where the temperature generally increases with height. The stratosphere contains **ozone**, which prevents ultraviolet rays from reaching Earth's surface. Since there is very little convection in the stratosphere, jets regularly cruise in the lower parts to provide a smoother ride for passengers.

Above the stratosphere is the **mesosphere**, where the temperature again decreases with height for another 19 mi. Extending above the mesosphere to the outer fringes of the atmosphere is the **thermosphere**, a region where temperature once more increases with height to a value measured in thousands of degrees Fahrenheit. The lower portion of this region, extending from 50 to about 400 mi in altitude, is characterized by a high ion density and is thus called the **ionosphere**. Most meteors are in the lower thermosphere or the mesosphere at the time they are observed.

Longitude, Latitude. Position on the globe is measured by meridians and parallels. Meridians, which are imaginary lines drawn around Earth through the poles, determine **longitude**. The meridian running through Greenwich, England, is the **prime meridian** of longitude, and all others are either E or W. Parallels, which are imaginary circles parallel with the equator, determine **latitude**. The length of a degree of longitude varies as the cosine of the latitude. At the equator a degree of longitude is 69.171 statute mi; this is gradually reduced toward the poles. Value of a longitude degree at the poles is zero.

Latitude is reckoned by the number of degrees N or S of the **equator**, an imaginary circle on Earth's surface everywhere equidistant between the two poles. According to the International Astronomical Union, the length of a degree of latitude is 68.708 statute mi at the equator and varies slightly N and S because of the oblate form of the globe; at the poles it is 69.403 statute mi.

Definitions of Time. Earth rotates on its axis and follows an elliptical orbit around the Sun. The rotation makes the Sun appear to move across the sky from E to W. This rotation determines day and night, and the complete rotation, in relation to the Sun, is called the **apparent** or **true solar day.** A sundial thus measures **apparent solar time.** This length of time varies, but an average determines the mean solar day of 24 hours.

The mean solar day and **mean solar time** are in universal use for civil purposes. Mean solar time may be obtained from apparent solar time by correcting observations of the Sun for the **equation of time.** Mean solar time may be up to 16 minutes different from apparent solar time.

Sidereal time is the measure of time defined by the diurnal motion of the vernal equinox and is determined from observation of the meridian transits of stars. One complete rotation of Earth relative to the equinox is called the **sidereal day.** The **mean sidereal day** is 23 hours, 56 minutes, 4.091 seconds of mean solar time.

The interval required for Earth to make one absolute revolution around the Sun is a **sidereal** year; it consisted of 365 days, 6 hours, 9 minutes, and 9.5 seconds of mean solar time (approximately 24 hours per day) in 1900 and has been increasing at the rate of 0.0001 second annually.

The **tropical year,** upon which our calendar is based, is the interval between 2 consecutive returns of the Sun to the vernal equinox. The tropical year consisted of 365 days, 5 hours, 48 minutes, and 46 seconds in 1900. It has been decreasing at the rate of 0.530 second per century. The **calendar year** begins at 12 o'clock midnight precisely, local clock time, on the night of Dec. 31-Jan. 1. The day and the calendar month also begin at midnight by the clock.

On Jan. 1, 1972, the Bureau International des Poids et Mesures in Paris introduced **International Atomic Time** (TAI) as the most precisely determined time scale for astronomical usage. The fundamental unit of TAI in the international system of units is the second, defined as the duration of 9,192,631,770 periods of the radiation corresponding to the transition between 2 hyperfine levels of the ground state of the cesium 133 atom. **Coordinated Universal Time** (UTC), which serves as the basis for civil timekeeping and is the standard time of the prime meridian, is officially defined by a formula which relates UTC to mean sidereal time in Greenwich, England. (UTC has replaced GMT as the basis for standard time for the world.)

The Zones and Seasons. The 5 zones of Earth's surface are the Torrid, lying between the Tropics of Cancer and Capricorn; the N Temperate, between Cancer and the Arctic Circle; the S Temperate, between Capricorn and the Antarctic Circle; and the 2 Frigid Zones, between the Polar Circles and the Poles.

The inclination, or **tilt,** of Earth's axis, 23° 27′ away from a perpendicular to Earth's orbit of the Sun, determines the seasons. These are commonly marked in the N Temperate Zone, where spring begins at the vernal equinox, summer at the summer solstice, autumn at the autumnal equinox, and winter at the winter solstice. In the S Temperate Zone, the seasons are reversed. Spring begins at the autumnal equinox, summer at the winter solstice, etc.

The points at which the Sun crosses the equator are the **equinoxes,** when day and night are most nearly equal. The points at which the Sun is at a maximum distance from the equator are the **solstices.** Days and nights are then most unequal. However, at the equator, day and night are equal throughout the year.

In June, the North Pole is tilted 23° 27′ toward the Sun, and the days in the northern hemisphere are longer than the nights, while the days in the southern hemisphere are shorter than the nights. In Dec., the North Pole is tilted 23°27′ away from the Sun, and the situation is reversed.

The Seasons in 2007. In 2007, the 4 seasons begin in the northern hemisphere as shown. (Add 1 hour to Eastern Standard Time for Atlantic Time; subtract 1 hour for Central, 2 for Mountain, 3 for Pacific, 4 for Alaska, 5 for Hawaii-Aleutian. Also shown is Coordinated Universal Time.)

Seasons	Date	UTC	EST/EDT*
Vernal Equinox (spring)	Mar. 21	00:07	19:07*
Northern Solstice (summer)	June 21	18:06	12:06
Autumnal Equinox (autumn)	Sept. 23	09:51	05:51
Southern Solstice (winter)	Dec. 22	06:08	01:08

* Previous Day

Poles of Earth. The geographic (rotation) poles, or points where Earth's axis of rotation cuts the surface, are not absolutely fixed in the body of Earth. The pole of rotation describes an irregular curve about its mean position.

Two periods have been detected in this motion: (1) an annual period due to seasonal changes in barometric pressure, to load of ice and snow on the surface, and to other seasonal phenomena; (2) a period of about 14 months due to the shape and constitution of Earth. In addition, there are small but as yet unpredictable irregularities. The whole motion is so small that the actual pole at any time remains within a circle of 30 or 40 feet in radius centered at the mean position of the pole.

The pole of rotation for the time being is of course the pole having a latitude of 90° and an indeterminate longitude.

Magnetic Poles. Although Earth's magnetic field resembles that of an ordinary bar magnet, this magnetic field is probably produced by electric currents in the liquid currents of the Earth's outer core. The **north magnetic pole** of Earth is that region where the magnetic force is vertically downward, and the **south magnetic pole** is that region where the magnetic force is vertically upward. A compass placed at the magnetic poles experiences no directive force in azimuth (i.e., direction).

There are slow changes in the distribution of Earth's magnetic field. This slow temporal change is referred to as the secular change of the main magnetic field, and the magnetic poles shift due to this. The location of the N magnetic pole was first measured in 1831 at Cape Adelaide on the west coast of Boothia Peninsula in Canada's Northwest Territories (about latitude 70° N and longitude 96° W). Since then it has moved over 500 mi. It is now estimated to be at 82.7° N and 114.4° W, northwest of Ellef Ringnes Island in N Canada. Measurement for several decades by Canadian scientists indicates the motion of the pole has accelerated, now averaging about 25 mi per year.

The direction of the horizontal components of the magnetic field at any point is known as magnetic N at that point, and the angle by which it deviates E or W of true N is known as the magnetic declination.

A compass without error points in the direction of magnetic north. (In general, this is not the direction of the true rotational north pole.) If you follow the direction indicated by the N end of the compass, you will go along an irregular curve that eventually reaches the north magnetic pole (though not usually by a great-circle route). However, the action of the compass should not be thought of as due to any influence of the distant pole, but simply as an indication of the distribution of Earth's magnetism at the place of observation.

Rotation of Earth. The speed of rotation of Earth about its axis is slightly variable. The variations may be classified as:

(A) **Secular.** Tidal friction acts as a brake on the rotation and causes a slow secular increase in the length of the day, about 1 millisecond per century.

(B) **Irregular.** The speed of rotation may increase for a number of years, about 5 to 10, and then start decreasing. The maximum difference from the mean in the length of the day during a century is about 5 milliseconds. The accumulated difference in time has amounted to approximately 44 seconds since 1900. The cause is probably motion in the interior of Earth.

(C) **Periodic.** Seasonal variations exist with periods of 1 year and 6 months. The cumulative effect is such that each year, Earth is late about 30 milliseconds near June 1 and is ahead about 30 milliseconds near Oct. 1. The maximum seasonal variation in the length of the day is about 0.5 millisecond. It is believed that the principal cause of the annual variation is the seasonal change in the wind patterns of the northern and southern hemispheres. The semiannual variation is due chiefly to tidal action of the Sun, which distorts the shape of Earth slightly.

The Moon

Distance from Earth	
Perigee	225,744 mi
Semi-major axis	238,855 mi
Apogee	251,966 mi
Period of revolution	27.322 d
Synodic orbital period (period of phases)	29.53 d
Orbital eccentricity	0.0549
Orbital inclination	5.145°
Sidereal day (rotation period)	27.322 d
Rotational inclination	6.68°
Mass (Earth = 1)	0.0123
Mean radius	1,079 mi
Mean density (Earth = 1)	0.607
Average surface temperature	−100° F

The Moon is the second brightest object in the sky (the sun is the first). Earth's only natural satellite, the Moon is the force behind the rising and falling of tides, and it helps to regulate the Earth's orbit around the sun. Many probes have been sent to the moon and between 1969 and 1972, 12 U.S. astronauts walked on its surface.

Orbit and Rotation. The Moon completes a circuit around Earth in a period that averages 27 days, 7 hours, 43.2 minutes. This is the Moon's sidereal period. Because of the motion of the Moon in common with Earth around the Sun, the mean duration of the lunar month—the period from one New Moon to the next New Moon—is 29 days, 12 hours, 44.05 minutes. This is the Moon's synodic period.

The mean distance of the Moon from Earth is 238,855 mi, but its orbit about Earth is elliptical, and thus the actual distance varies considerably. The maximum distance from Earth that the Moon may reach is 251,966 mi and the least distance is 225,744 mi.

The Moon rotates on its axis in a period of time that is exactly equal to its sidereal revolution about Earth—27.322 days. Thus the backside or farside of the Moon always faces away from Earth. But this does not mean that the backside is always dark. The farside of the Moon gets just as much direct sunlight as the nearside; at New Moon phase, the farside of the Moon is fully lit, but not visible from Earth.

The Moon's revolution about Earth is irregular because of its elliptical orbit. The Moon's rotation, however, is regular, and this, together with the irregular revolution, produces what is called "libration in longitude," which permits an observer on Earth to see first farther around the E side and then farther around the western side of the Moon. The Moon's variation north or south of the ecliptic permits one to see farther over first one pole and then the other of the Moon; this is called "libration in latitude." These two libration effects permit observers on Earth to see a total of about 60% of the Moon's surface over a period of time.

Atmosphere and Surface. The Moon, like the planet Mercury, has no real atmosphere to speak of. What little exists is variable and tenuous. With its long day and night, the daytime temperature can reach 260° F, while the coldest nighttime temperature may reach −280° F. This day-to-night contrast is exceeded only by that on Mercury.

The lunar surface has not changed much since humans have been observing it. The side visible from Earth has large craters and vast dark areas called maria that were once lava. The farside has almost no maria but is pockmarked with craters.

Recent findings show that up to 300 mil metric tons of water ice may exist in craters at the lunar poles. In its interior, the Moon may have a small core, which supports the idea that most of the mass of the Moon was ripped away from the early Earth when a Mars-size object collided with Earth. The hidden side of the Moon was first photographed in 1959 by the Soviet space probe *Lunik III*.

Harvest Moon and Hunter's Moon. The Harvest Moon, the full Moon nearest the autumnal equinox, ushers in a period of several successive days when the Moon rises soon after sunset. This phenomenon gives farmers in temperate latitudes extra hours of light in which to harvest their crops before frost and winter. The 2007 Harvest Moon falls on Sept. 26 UTC. Harvest Moon in the southern hemisphere temperate latitudes falls on Apr. 12.

The next full Moon after Harvest Moon is called the Hunter's Moon; it is accompanied by a similar but less marked phenomenon. In 2007, the Hunter's Moon occurs on Oct. 26 in the northern hemisphere and on May 2 in the southern hemisphere.

Moon's Perigee and Apogee, 2007

Perigee is the point in the moon's orbit where it is closest to the Earth. Apogee is the point where it is farthest.

(Coordinated Universal Time, standard time of the prime meridian)

Perigee Date	Hour	Perigee Date	Hour	Apogee Date	Hour	Apogee Date	Hour
Jan. 22	12	Aug. 31	0	Jan. 10	16	July 24	14
Feb. 19	10	Sept. 28	2	Feb. 7	13	Aug. 22	9
Mar. 19	19	Oct. 26	12	Mar. 7	4	Sept. 19	3
Apr. 17	6	Nov. 24	0	Apr. 3	9	Oct. 15	21
May 15	15	Dec. 22	10	May 30	11	Nov. 13	10
June 12	17			June 27	22	Dec. 9	13
July 9	22						
Aug. 3	24						

Moon Phases, 2007

(Coordinated Universal Time, standard time of the prime meridian)

New Moon Month	d	h	m	Waxing Quarter Month	d	h	m	Full Moon Month	d	h	m	Waning Quarter Month	d	h	m
Jan.	19	4	01	Jan.	25	23	01	Jan.	3	13	57	Jan.	11	12	45
Feb.	17	16	14	Feb.	24	7	56	Feb.	2	5	45	Feb.	10	9	51
Mar.	19	2	43	Mar.	25	18	16	Mar.	3	23	17	Mar.	12	3	54
Apr.	17	11	36	Apr.	24	6	35	Apr.	2	17	15	Apr.	10	18	04
May	16	19	27	May	23	21	02	May	2	10	09	May	10	4	27
June	15	3	13	June	22	13	15	June	1	1	04	June	8	11	43
								June	30	13	49				
July	14	12	04	July	22	6	29	July	30	0	48	July	7	16	54
Aug.	12	23	02	Aug.	20	23	54	Aug.	28	10	35	Aug.	5	21	20
				Aug.	19	16	48								
Sept.	11	12	44	Sept.	19	8	33	Sept.	26	19	45	Sept.	4	2	32
Oct.	11	5	01	Oct.	17	22	33	Oct.	26	4	52	Oct.	3	10	06
Nov.	9	23	03	Nov.	17	10	17	Nov.	24	14	30	Nov.	1	21	18
Dec.	9	17	40	Dec.	22	6	29	Dec.	24	1	16	Dec.	1	12	44
												Dec.	31	7	51

CALENDAR

Julian and Gregorian Calendars; Leap Year; Century

The **Julian calendar**, under which all Western nations measured time until 1582 CE, was authorized by Julius Caesar in 46 BCE. It called for a year of 365¼ days, starting in January, with every 4th year being a **leap year** of 366 days. St. Bede, an Anglo-Saxon monk also known as the Venerable Bede, announced in 730 CE that the Julian year was 11 min, 14 sec too long, a cumulative error of about a day every 128 years, but nothing was done about this for centuries.

By 1582 the accumulated error was estimated at 10 days. In that year Pope Gregory XIII decreed that the day following Oct. 4, 1582, should be called Oct. 15, thus dropping 10 days and initiating the **Gregorian calendar**.

The Gregorian calendar continued a system devised by the monk Dionysius Exiguus (6th century), starting from the first year following the birth of Jesus Christ, which was inaccurately taken to be year 753 in the Roman calendar. Leap years were continued but, to prevent further displacements, centesimal years (years ending in 00) were made common years, not leap years, unless divisible by 400. Under this plan, **1600** and **2000** were leap years (as was **2004**); 1700, 1800, and 1900 were not.

The Gregorian calendar was adopted at once by France, Italy, Spain, Portugal, and Luxembourg. Within 2 years most German Catholic states, Belgium, and parts of Switzerland and the Netherlands were brought under the new calendar, and Hungary followed in 1587. The rest of the Netherlands, along with Denmark and the German Protestant states, made the change in 1699-1700.

The British government adopted the Gregorian calendar and imposed it on all its possessions, including the American colonies, in 1752, decreeing that the day following Sept. 2, 1752, should be called Sept. 14, a loss of 11 days. All dates preceding were marked OS, for Old Style. In addition, New Year's Day was moved to Jan. 1 from Mar. 25 (under the old reckoning, for example, Mar. 24, 1700, had been followed by Mar. 25, 1701). Thus George Washington's birthdate, which was Feb. 11, 1731, OS, became Feb. 22, 1732, NS (New Style). In 1753 Sweden also went Gregorian.

In 1793 the French revolutionary government adopted a calendar of 12 months of 30 days with 5 extra days in September of each common year and a 6th every 4th year. Napoleon reinstated the Gregorian calendar in 1806.

The Gregorian system later spread to non-European regions, replacing traditional calendars at least for official purposes. Japan in 1873, Egypt in 1875, China in 1912, and Turkey in 1925 made the change, usually in conjunction with political upheaval. In China, the republican government began reckoning years from its 1911 founding. After 1949, the People's Republic adopted the Common, or Christian Era, year count, even for the traditional lunar calendar, which is also retained. In 1918 the Soviet Union decreed that the day after Jan. 31, 1918, OS, would be Feb. 14, 1918, NS. Greece changed over in 1923. For the first time in history, all major nations had one calendar. The Russian Orthodox church and some other Christian sects retained the Julian calendar.

To convert from the Julian to the Gregorian calendar, add 10 days to dates Oct. 5, 1582, through Feb. 28, 1700; after that date add 11 days through Feb. 28, 1800; 12 days through Feb. 28, 1900; and 13 days through Feb. 28, 2100.

A **century** consists of 100 consecutive years. The 1st century CE may be said to have run from the years 1 through 100. The 20th century by this reckoning consisted of the years 1901 through 2000 and technically ended Dec. 31, 2000, as did the 2nd millennium CE. The 21st century thus technically began Jan. 1, 2001.

For a **Perpetual Calendar,** see pages 348-49.

Gregorian Calendar

Choose the desired year from the table below or from the Perpetual Calendar (for years 1803 to 2080). The number after each year designates which calendar to use for that year, as shown in the Perpetual Calendar. (The Gregorian calendar was inaugurated Oct. 15, 1582. From that date to Dec. 31, 1582, use calendar 6.)

1583-1802

1583	7	1603	4	1623	1	1643	5	1663	2	1683	6	1703	2	1723	6	1743	3	1763	7	1783	4
1584	8	1604	12	1624	9	1644	13	1664	10	1684	14	1704	10	1724	14	1744	11	1764	8	1784	12
1585	3	1605	7	1625	4	1645	1	1665	5	1685	2	1705	5	1725	2	1745	6	1765	3	1785	7
1586	4	1606	1	1626	5	1646	2	1666	6	1686	3	1706	6	1726	3	1746	7	1766	4	1786	1
1587	5	1607	2	1627	6	1647	3	1667	7	1687	4	1707	7	1727	4	1747	1	1767	5	1787	2
1588	13	1608	10	1628	14	1648	11	1668	8	1688	12	1708	8	1728	12	1748	9	1768	13	1788	10
1589	1	1609	5	1629	2	1649	6	1669	3	1689	7	1709	3	1729	7	1749	4	1769	1	1789	5
1590	2	1610	6	1630	3	1650	7	1670	4	1690	1	1710	4	1730	1	1750	5	1770	2	1790	6
1591	3	1611	7	1631	4	1651	1	1671	5	1691	2	1711	5	1731	2	1751	6	1771	3	1791	7
1592	11	1612	8	1632	12	1652	9	1672	13	1692	10	1712	13	1732	10	1752	14	1772	11	1792	8
1593	6	1613	3	1633	7	1653	4	1673	1	1693	5	1713	1	1733	5	1753	2	1773	6	1793	3
1594	7	1614	4	1634	1	1654	5	1674	2	1694	6	1714	2	1734	6	1754	3	1774	7	1794	4
1595	1	1615	5	1635	2	1655	6	1675	3	1695	7	1715	3	1735	7	1755	4	1775	1	1795	5
1596	9	1616	13	1636	10	1656	14	1676	11	1696	8	1716	11	1736	8	1756	12	1776	9	1796	13
1597	4	1617	1	1637	5	1657	2	1677	6	1697	3	1717	6	1737	3	1757	7	1777	4	1797	1
1598	5	1618	2	1638	6	1658	3	1678	7	1698	4	1718	7	1738	4	1758	1	1778	5	1798	2
1599	6	1619	3	1639	7	1659	4	1679	1	1699	5	1719	1	1739	5	1759	2	1779	6	1799	3
1600	14	1620	11	1640	8	1660	12	1680	9	1700	6	1720	9	1740	13	1760	10	1780	14	1800	4
1601	2	1621	6	1641	3	1661	7	1681	4	1701	7	1721	4	1741	1	1761	5	1781	2	1801	5
1602	3	1622	7	1642	4	1662	1	1682	5	1702	1	1722	5	1742	2	1762	6	1782	3	1802	6

The Julian Period

How many days have you lived? To determine this, multiply your age by 365, add the number of days since your last birthday, and account for all leap years. Chances are your calculations will go wrong somewhere. Astronomers, however, find it convenient to express dates and time intervals in days rather than in years, months, and days. This is done by placing events within the Julian period.

The Julian period was devised in 1582 by the French classical scholar Joseph Scaliger (1540-1609), and it was named after his father, Julius Caesar Scaliger, not after the Julian calendar as might be supposed.

Scaliger began with a zero hour, or starting time, of noon on Jan. 1, 4713 BCE (on the Julian calendar). This was the most recent time that 3 major chronological cycles began on the same day: (1) the 28-year solar cycle, after which dates in the Julian calendar (e.g., Feb. 11) return to the same days of the week (e.g., Monday); (2) the 19-year lunar cycle, after which the phases of the moon return to the same dates of the year; and (3) the 15-year indiction cycle, used in ancient Rome to regulate taxes.

It will take 7,980 years to complete the period, the product of 28, 19, and 15.

Noon of Dec. 31, 2006 will be Julian date (JD) 2,454,101; that many days will have passed since the start of the Julian period. The JD at noon of any date in 2007 may be found by adding to this figure the day of the year for that date, which can be obtained from the left half of the "How Far Apart Are Two Dates?" chart on the next page.

Julian Calendar

To find which of the 14 calendars of the Perpetual Calendar (pages 362-63) applies to any year under the Julian system, find the century for the desired year in the 3 leftmost columns below. Read across and find the year in the 4 top rows. Then read down. The number in the intersection is the calendar designation for that year. For some years and countries the Julian new year did not start Jan. 1; to find the correct Perpetual Calendar for Britain and its possessions, you can generally add one year for dates from Jan. 1-Mar. 24. For example, to look up Feb. 2, 1705, Old Style, use the year 1706.

Year (last 2 figures of desired year)

Century			01 02 03 04 05 06 07 08 09 10 11 12 13 14 15 16 17 18 19 20 21 22 23 24 25 26 27 28
			29 30 31 32 33 34 35 36 37 38 39 40 41 42 43 44 45 46 47 48 49 50 51 52 53 54 55 56
			57 58 59 60 61 62 63 64 65 66 67 68 69 70 71 72 73 74 75 76 77 78 79 80 81 82 83 84
	Century	00	85 86 87 88 89 90 91 92 93 94 95 96 97 98 99
0	700 1400	12	7 1 2 10 5 6 7 8 3 4 5 13 1 2 3 11 6 7 1 9 4 5 6 14 2 3 4 12
100	800 1500	11	6 7 1 9 4 5 6 14 2 3 4 12 7 1 2 10 5 6 7 8 3 4 5 13 1 2 3 11
200	900 1600	10	5 6 7 8 3 4 5 13 1 2 3 11 6 7 1 9 4 5 6 14 2 3 4 12 7 1 2 10
300	1000 1700	9	4 5 6 14 2 3 4 12 7 1 2 10 5 6 7 8 3 4 5 13 1 2 3 11 6 7 1 9
400	1100 1800	8	3 4 5 13 1 2 3 11 6 7 1 9 4 5 6 14 2 3 4 12 7 1 2 10 5 6 7 8
500	1200 1900	14	2 3 4 12 7 1 2 10 5 6 7 8 3 4 5 13 1 2 3 11 6 7 1 9 4 5 6 14
600	1300 2000	13	1 2 3 11 6 7 1 9 4 5 6 14 2 3 4 12 7 1 2 10 5 6 7 8 3 4 5 13

How Far Apart Are Two Dates?

This table covers a range of 2 years. To use, **find the numbers in the tables for each date and subtract** the smaller from the larger. Example—to find the number of days from Mar. 15, 2006, to Sept. 22, 2007, subtract 74 from 630; the result is 556. For leap years, such as 2008, where Feb. 29 intervenes, one day must be then added; thus Feb. 4, 2007, and Mar. 13, 2008, are 403 days apart.

First Year

Date	Jan.	Feb.	Mar.	April	May	June	July	Aug.	Sept.	Oct.	Nov.	Dec.
1	1	32	60	91	121	152	182	213	244	274	305	335
2	2	33	61	92	122	153	183	214	245	275	306	336
3	3	34	62	93	123	154	184	215	246	276	307	337
4	4	35	63	94	124	155	185	216	247	277	308	338
5	5	36	64	95	125	156	186	217	248	278	309	339
6	6	37	65	96	126	157	187	218	249	279	310	340
7	7	38	66	97	127	158	188	219	250	280	311	341
8	8	39	67	98	128	159	189	220	251	281	312	342
9	9	40	68	99	129	160	190	221	252	282	313	343
10	10	41	69	100	130	161	191	222	253	283	314	344
11	11	42	70	101	131	162	192	223	254	284	315	345
12	12	43	71	102	132	163	193	224	255	285	316	346
13	13	44	72	103	133	164	194	225	256	286	317	347
14	14	45	73	104	134	165	195	226	257	287	318	348
15	15	46	74	105	135	166	196	227	258	288	319	349
16	16	47	75	106	136	167	197	228	259	289	320	350
17	17	48	76	107	137	168	198	229	260	290	321	351
18	18	49	77	108	138	169	199	230	261	291	322	352
19	19	50	78	109	139	170	200	231	262	292	323	353
20	20	51	79	110	140	171	201	232	263	293	324	354
21	21	52	80	111	141	172	202	233	264	294	325	355
22	22	53	81	112	142	173	203	234	265	295	326	356
23	23	54	82	113	143	174	204	235	266	296	327	357
24	24	55	83	114	144	175	205	236	267	297	328	358
25	25	56	84	115	145	176	206	237	268	298	329	359
26	26	57	85	116	146	177	207	238	269	299	330	360
27	27	58	86	117	147	178	208	239	270	300	331	361
28	28	59	87	118	148	179	209	240	271	301	332	362
29	29	—	88	119	149	180	210	241	272	302	333	363
30	30	—	89	120	150	181	211	242	273	303	334	364
31	31	—	90	—	151	—	212	243	—	304	—	365

Second Year

Date	Jan.	Feb.	Mar.	April	May	June	July	Aug.	Sept.	Oct.	Nov.	Dec.
1	366	397	425	456	486	517	547	578	609	639	670	700
2	367	398	426	457	487	518	548	579	610	640	671	701
3	368	399	427	458	488	519	549	580	611	641	672	702
4	369	400	428	459	489	520	550	581	612	642	673	703
5	370	401	429	460	490	521	551	582	613	643	674	704
6	371	402	430	461	491	522	552	583	614	644	675	705
7	372	403	431	462	492	523	553	584	615	645	676	706
8	373	404	432	463	493	524	554	585	616	646	677	707
9	374	405	433	464	494	525	555	586	617	647	678	708
10	375	406	434	465	495	526	556	587	618	648	679	709
11	376	407	435	466	496	527	557	588	619	649	680	710
12	377	408	436	467	497	528	558	589	620	650	681	711
13	378	409	437	468	498	529	559	590	621	651	682	712
14	379	410	438	469	499	530	560	591	622	652	683	713
15	380	411	439	470	500	531	561	592	623	653	684	714
16	381	412	440	471	501	532	562	593	624	654	685	715
17	382	413	441	472	502	533	563	594	625	655	686	716
18	383	414	442	473	503	534	564	595	626	656	687	717
19	384	415	443	474	504	535	565	596	627	657	688	718
20	385	416	444	475	505	536	566	597	628	658	689	719
21	386	417	445	476	506	537	567	598	629	659	690	720
22	387	418	446	477	507	538	568	599	630	660	691	721
23	388	419	447	478	508	539	569	600	631	661	692	722
24	389	420	448	479	509	540	570	601	632	662	693	723
25	390	421	449	480	510	541	571	602	633	663	694	724
26	391	422	450	481	511	542	572	603	634	664	695	725
27	392	423	451	482	512	543	573	604	635	665	696	726
28	393	424	452	483	513	544	574	605	636	666	697	727
29	394	—	453	484	514	545	575	606	637	667	698	728
30	395	—	454	485	515	546	576	607	638	668	699	729
31	396	—	455	—	516	—	577	608	—	669	—	730

Signs of the Zodiac

The **zodiac** is the apparent yearly path of the sun among the stars as viewed from earth, and was divided by the ancients into 12 equal sections or signs, each named for the constellation situated within its limits in ancient times. Astrologers claim that the temperament and destiny of each individual depend on the zodiac sign under which the person was born and the relationships between the planets at that time and throughout life.

Below are the 12 traditional signs and the traditional range of dates pertaining to each:

♈ **Aries** (Ram), March 21 – April 19
♉ **Taurus** (Bull), April 20 – May 20
♊ **Gemini** (Twins), May 21 – June 21
♋ **Cancer** (Crab), June 22 – July 22
♌ **Leo** (Lion), July 23 – August 22
♍ **Virgo** (Maiden), August 23 – September 22

♎ **Libra** (Balance), September 23 – October 23
♏ **Scorpio** (Scorpion), October 24 – November 21
♐ **Sagittarius** (Archer), November 22 – December 21
♑ **Capricorn** (Goat), December 22 – January 19
♒ **Aquarius** (Water Bearer), January 20 – February 18
♓ **Pisces** (Fishes), February 19 – March 20

WORLD ALMANAC QUICK QUIZ

Tom DeLay, Stephen King, David Letterman, Arnold Schwarzenegger, and O.J. Simpson were all born in 1947, which is what year (the same as 2007) according to the Chinese calendar?
(a) Year of the Pig
(b) Year of the Ox
(c) Year of the Bamboo
(d) Year of the Rooster

For the answer look in this chapter, or see page 1008.

Calendar for the Year 2007

JANUARY
S M T W T F S
1 2 3 4 5 6
7 8 9 10 11 12 13
14 15 16 17 18 19 20
21 22 23 24 25 26 27
28 29 30 31

FEBRUARY
S M T W T F S
1 2 3
4 5 6 7 8 9 10
11 12 13 14 15 16 17
18 19 20 21 22 23 24
25 26 27 28

MARCH
S M T W T F S
1 2 3
4 5 6 7 8 9 10
11 12 13 14 15 16 17
18 19 20 21 22 23 24
25 26 27 28 29 30 31

APRIL
S M T W T F S
1 2 3 4 5 6 7
8 9 10 11 12 13 14
15 16 17 18 19 20 21
22 23 24 25 26 27 28
29 30

MAY
S M T W T F S
1 2 3 4 5
6 7 8 9 10 11 12
13 14 15 16 17 18 19
20 21 22 23 24 25 26
27 28 29 30 31

JUNE
S M T W T F S
1 2
3 4 5 6 7 8 9
10 11 12 13 14 15 16
17 18 19 20 21 22 23
24 25 26 27 28 29 30

JULY
S M T W T F S
1 2 3 4 5 6 7
8 9 10 11 12 13 14
15 16 17 18 19 20 21
22 23 24 25 26 27 28
29 30 31

AUGUST
S M T W T F S
1 2 3 4
5 6 7 8 9 10 11
12 13 14 15 16 17 18
19 20 21 22 23 24 25
26 27 28 29 30 31

SEPTEMBER
S M T W T F S
1
2 3 4 5 6 7 8
9 10 11 12 13 14 15
16 17 18 19 20 21 22
23 24 25 26 27 28 29
30

OCTOBER
S M T W T F S
1 2 3 4 5 6
7 8 9 10 11 12 13
14 15 16 17 18 19 20
21 22 23 24 25 26 27
28 29 30 31

NOVEMBER
S M T W T F S
1 2 3
4 5 6 7 8 9 10
11 12 13 14 15 16 17
18 19 20 21 22 23 24
25 26 27 28 29 30

DECEMBER
S M T W T F S
1
2 3 4 5 6 7 8
9 10 11 12 13 14 15
16 17 18 19 20 21 22
23 24 25 26 27 28 29
30 31

Federal Holidays and Other Notable Dates, 2007

Some dates may be subject to change.

The days marked on the calendar above and shown below *in italics* are U.S. federal holidays, designated by the president or Congress and applicable to federal employees and the District of Columbia. Most U.S. states also observe these holidays, and many states observe others; practices vary from state to state. In most states the secretary of state's office can provide details.

January
1   *New Year's Day*; Fiesta Bowl; Rose Bowl
2   Orange Bowl
3   Sugar Bowl
8   BCS Football Championship Game (Phoenix, AZ)
15   *Martin Luther King Jr. Day* (3rd Mon. in Jan.)
15-28   Australian Open tennis tournament
26   Australia Day, Australia
20   Muharram 1 (Islamic New Year), 1st full day

February
2   Groundhog Day
4   Super Bowl XLI (Miami, FL)
10   NFL Pro Bowl (Honolulu, HI)
12   Lincoln's Birthday
12-13   Westminster Dog Show
14   Valentine's Day
18   Chinese New Year; Daytona 500; NBA All-Star Game
19   *Washington's Birthday* (observed), *Presidents' Day*, or *Washington-Lincoln Day* (3rd Mon. in Feb.)
17-20   Carnival, Brazil
20   Mardi Gras
21   Ash Wednesday
25   Academy Awards

March
3   Iditarod Trail Sled Dog Race begins
4   Purim (Feast of Lots), 1st full day
11   Daylight Saving Time begins in U.S.
12   Commonwealth Day, Canada
17   St. Patrick's Day
20   First day of spring (Northern Hemisphere)
21   Benito Juárez's Birthday, Mexico

April
1   April Fool's Day
2   NCAA men's basketball championship
3   NCAA women's basketball championship; first full day of Passover
5-8   Masters golf tournament
6   Good Friday
8   Easter
16   Patriots' Day; Boston Marathon
22   Earth Day
25   Administrative Professionals Day
26   Take Our Daughters and Sons to Work Day
27   Arbor Day, U.S.

May
1   May Day
5   Kentucky Derby; Cinco de Mayo (Battle of Puebla Day), Mexico
8   National Teacher Day, U.S.
13   Mother's Day
19   Armed Forces Day; Preakness Stakes
21   Victoria Day, Canada
24   Buddha's Birthday, Korea, Hong Kong
27-June 10   French Open tennis tournament
28   *Memorial Day*, or *Decoration Day* (last Mon. in May)

June
9   Belmont Stakes
14   Flag Day, U.S.
14-17   U.S. Open golf tournament
17   Father's Day
19   Dragon Boat Festival, China
21   First day of summer (Northern Hemisphere)
25-July 8   Wimbledon tennis tournament

July
1   Canada Day
4   *Independence Day*
7–14   Running of the Bulls (Pamplona, Spain)
14   Bastille Day, France
19-22   British Open golf tournament

August
9-12   PGA Championship

September
3   *Labor Day*, U.S. (1st Monday in Sept.); Labor Day, Canada
9   Grandparents' Day, U.S.
10-30   Women's World Cup soccer (China)
12   Ramadan (Islamic month of fasting), 1st full day
13   Rosh Hashanah (New Year), 1st full day
16   Independence Day, Mexico
17   Citizenship Day, U.S.
19   San Gennaro, Italy
22   Yom Kippur (Day of Atonement), 1st full day
23   First day of autumn (Northern Hemisphere)

October
1   U.S. Supreme Court session begins
3   German Unification Day, Germany
8   *Columbus Day* (2nd Mon. in Oct.); Thanksgiving Day, Canada
12   Día de la Raza, Spain, Mexico
24   United Nations Day
31   Halloween

November
1   All Saints' Day
1-2   Día de los Muertos, Mexico
4   Daylight Saving Time ends in U.S.; New York City Marathon
5   Guy Fawkes Day, UK
6   Election Day (1st Tues. after 1st Mon. in Nov.)
11   Veterans Day; Remembrance Day, Canada, UK
12   *Veterans Day* (observed)
15   Shichi-Go-San (Seven-Five-Three), Japan
22   *Thanksgiving Day*, (4th Thurs. in Nov.)

December
5-12   Hanukkah (Festival of Lights)
10   Nobel Prizes awarded (winners announced in Oct.)
12   Día de la Virgen de Guadalupe, Mexico
22   First day of winter (Northern Hemisphere)
25   *Christmas Day*
26   Boxing Day, Australia, Canada, New Zealand, UK
26-Jan. 1   Kwanzaa

IT'S A FACT: The tradition of presidential pardons for Thanksgiving turkeys dates back half a century. The birds that are spared are no common gobblers, though. The toms are raised in an air-conditioned barn and hand-selected for photogenic qualities, such as plumage and girth. Caregivers also condition the turkeys to be comfortable in a ceremonial atmosphere by wearing dark blue overalls (in imitation of formal blue suits) while they clap and chatter at, hand feed, and pet the birds in preparation for a crowd of admirers.

Chinese Calendar, Asian Festivals

Source: Chinese Information and Culture Center, New York, NY

The Chinese calendar, like the Jewish and Islamic calendars (see the Religion chapter), is a lunar calendar. It is divided into 12 months of 29 or 30 days (compensating for the lunar month's mean duration of 29 days, 12 hr, 44.05 min). This calendar is synchronized with the solar year by the addition of extra months at fixed intervals.

The Chinese calendar runs on a 60-year cycle. The cycles 1876-1935 and 1936-95, with the years grouped under their 12 animal designations, are printed below, along with the first 24 years of the current cycle. This cycle began in 1996 and will last until 2055. Feb. 18, 2007, marks the beginning of the year 4705 in the Chinese calendar, and is designated the Year of the Pig. Readers can find the animal name for the year of their birth in the chart below. (Note: The first 3-7 weeks of each Western year belong to the previous Chinese year and animal designation.)

Both the Western (Gregorian) and traditional lunar calendars are used publicly in China and in North and South Korea, and 2 New Year's celebrations are held. In Taiwan, in overseas Chinese communities, and in Vietnam, the lunar calendar is used only to set the dates for traditional festivals, with the Gregorian system in general use.

The 4-day Chinese New Year, Hsin Nien, the 3-day Vietnamese New Year festival, Tet, and the 3-to-4-day Korean festival, Suhl, begin at the 2nd new moon after the winter solstice. The new moon in the Far East, which is west of the International Date Line, may be a day later than the new moon in the U.S. The festivals may start, therefore, anywhere between Jan. 21 and Feb. 19 of the Gregorian calendar.

Rat	Ox	Tiger	Hare (Rabbit)	Dragon	Snake	Horse	Sheep (Goat)	Monkey	Rooster	Dog	Pig (Boar)
1876	1877	1878	1879	1880	1881	1882	1883	1884	1885	1886	1887
1888	1889	1890	1891	1892	1893	1894	1895	1896	1897	1898	1899
1900	1901	1902	1903	1904	1905	1906	1907	1908	1909	1910	1911
1912	1913	1914	1915	1916	1917	1918	1919	1920	1921	1922	1923
1924	1925	1926	1927	1928	1929	1930	1931	1932	1933	1934	1935
1936	1937	1938	1939	1940	1941	1942	1943	1944	1945	1946	1947
1948	1949	1950	1951	1952	1953	1954	1955	1956	1957	1958	1959
1960	1961	1962	1963	1964	1965	1966	1967	1968	1969	1970	1971
1972	1973	1974	1975	1976	1977	1978	1979	1980	1981	1982	1983
1984	1985	1986	1987	1988	1989	1990	1991	1992	1993	1994	1995
1996	1997	1998	1999	2000	2001	2002	2003	2004	2005	2006	2007
2008	2009	2010	2011	2012	2013	2014	2015	2016	2017	2018	2019

Other Calendars: Year and New Year's in 2007

Era	Year	Begins in 2007	Era	Year	Begins in 2007
Byzantine	7516	Sept. 14	Grecian (Seleucidae)	2319	Sept. 14 or Oct. 14
Jewish	5768	Sept. 13[1]	Diocletian	1724	Sept. 11
Roman (Ab Urbe Condita)	2760	Jan. 14	Indian (Saka)	1929	Mar. 22
Nabonassar (Babylonian)	2756	Apr. 23	Islamic/Muslim (Hijra)	1428	Jan. 19/20[2]
Japanese (starts at 0 with new emperor)	19	Jan. 1	Chinese (Year of the Pig)	4705	Feb. 18

(1) Year begins at sunset. (2) Year begins at moon crescent.

Chronological Cycles, 2007

Dominical Letter	G	Roman Indiction	15	Solar Cycle	28
Golden Number (Lunar Cycle)	13	Epact	11	Julian Period (year of)	6720

Special Months

Every year there are many thousands of special months, days, and weeks as a result of anniversaries, official proclamations, and promotional events, both trivial and serious. Here are a few of the special months:

January: Jump Out of Bed Month, National Mentoring Month, National Poverty in America Awareness Month

February: Black History Month, American Heart Month, Library Lovers Month, Youth Leadership Month, Return Shopping Carts to the Supermarket Month

March: Irish-American Heritage Month, Women's History Month, American Red Cross Month, National Frozen Foods Month, National Talk With Your Teen About Sex Month

April: National Child Abuse Prevention Month, National Humor Month, Stress Awareness Month, Grange Month

May: Clean Air Month, Get Caught Reading Month, National Barbecue Month, Asian Pacific American Heritage Month, National Mental Health Month

June: National Candy Month, Gay and Lesbian Pride Month, Potty Training Awareness Month, National Safety Month

July: Cell Phone Courtesy Month, National Hot Dog Month, Women's Motorcycle Month

August: Black Business Month, National Inventors' Month, Happiness Happens Month, National Toddler Month

September: Library Card Sign-Up Month, National Hispanic Heritage Month (Sept. 15-Oct. 15), National Biscuit Month

October: National Domestic Violence Awareness Month, National Breast Cancer Awareness Month, Diversity Awareness Month, National Popcorn Poppin' Month

November: National AIDS Awareness Month, National American Indian Heritage Month, National Adoption Month, American Diabetes Month, Peanut Butter Lovers' Month

December: Universal Human Rights Month, National Drunk and Drugged Driving Prevention Month, National Tie Month, Colorectal Cancer Education and Awareness Month

Wedding Anniversaries

The traditional names for wedding anniversaries go back many years in social usage and have been used to suggest types of appropriate anniversary gifts. Traditional products for gifts are listed here in CAPITAL letters, with a few allowable revisions in parentheses, followed by common modern gifts in each category.

1st	PAPER, clocks	9th	POTTERY (CHINA), leather goods	25th	SILVER, sterling silver
2nd	COTTON, china	10th	TIN, ALUMINUM, diamond	30th	PEARL, diamond
3rd	LEATHER, crystal, glass	11th	STEEL, fashion jewelry	35th	CORAL (JADE), jade
4th	LINEN (SILK), appliances	12th	SILK, pearls, colored gems	40th	RUBY, ruby
5th	WOOD, silverware	13th	LACE, textiles, furs	45th	SAPPHIRE, sapphire
6th	IRON, wood objects	14th	IVORY, gold jewelry	50th	GOLD, gold
7th	WOOL (COPPER), desk sets	15th	CRYSTAL, watches	55th	EMERALD, emerald
8th	BRONZE, linens, lace	20th	CHINA, platinum	60th	DIAMOND, diamond

Birthstones

Source: Jewelry Industry Council

MONTH	Ancient	Modern	MONTH	Ancient	Modern
January	Garnet	Garnet	July	Onyx	Ruby
February	Amethyst	Amethyst	August	Carnelian	Sardonyx or Peridot
March	Jasper	Bloodstone or Aquamarine	September	Chrysolite	Sapphire
April	Sapphire	Diamond	October	Aquamarine	Opal or Tourmaline
May	Agate	Emerald	November	Topaz	Topaz
June	Emerald	Pearl, Moonstone, or Alexandrite	December	Ruby	Turquoise or Zircon

Standard Time, Daylight Saving Time, and Others

Source: National Imagery and Mapping Agency; U.S. Dept. of Transportation
See also Time Zone map, page 476.

Standard Time

Standard Time is reckoned from the Prime Meridian of Longitude in Greenwich, England. The world is divided into 24 zones, each 15 deg of arc, or one hour in time apart. The Greenwich meridian (0 deg) extends through the center of the initial zone, and the zones to the east are numbered from 1 to 12, with the prefix "minus" indicating the number of hours to be subtracted to obtain Greenwich Time. Each zone extends 7.5 deg on either side of its central meridian.

Westward zones are similarly numbered, but prefixed "plus," showing the number of hours that must be added to get Greenwich Time. Although these zones apply generally to sea areas, the Standard Time maintained in many countries does not coincide with zone time. A graphical representation of the zones is shown on the Standard Time Zone Chart of the World (WOBZC76) published by the National Imagery and Mapping Agency. This chart is available by calling (800) 638-8972.

The U.S. and possessions are divided into 10 Standard Time zones. Each zone is approximately 15 deg of longitude in width. All places in each zone use, instead of their own local time, the time counted from the transit of the "mean sun" across the Standard Time meridian that passes near the middle of that zone. These time zones are designated as Atlantic, Eastern, Central, Mountain, Pacific, Alaska, Hawaii-Aleutian, Samoa, Wake Island, and Guam; the time in these zones is reckoned from the 60th, 75th, 90th, 105th, 120th, 135th, 150th, and 165th meridians west of Greenwich and the 165th and 150th meridians east of Greenwich. The time zone line wanders to conform to local geographical regions. The time in the various zones in the U.S. and U.S. territories west of Greenwich is earlier than Greenwich Time by 4, 5, 6, 7, 8, 9, 10, and 11 hours, respectively. However, Wake Island and Guam cross the International Date Line and are 12 and 10 hours later than Greenwich Time, respectively.

24-Hour Time

Twenty-four-hour time is widely used in scientific work throughout the world. In the U.S. it is also used in operations of the armed forces. In Europe it is frequently used by the transportation networks in preference to the 12-hour AM and PM system. With the 24-hour system the day begins at midnight, and times are designated 00:00 through 23:59.

International Date Line

The Date Line, approximately coinciding with the 180th meridian, separates the calendar dates. The date must be advanced one day when crossing in a westerly direction and set back one day when crossing in an easterly direction. The Date Line frequently deviates from the 180th meridian because of decisions made by individual nations affected. The line is deflected eastward through the Bering Strait and westward of the Aleutians to prevent separating these areas by date. The line is deflected eastward of the Tonga and New Zealand Islands in the South Pacific for the same reason. More recently it was deflected much farther eastward to include all of Kiribati. The line is established by international custom; there is no international authority prescribing its exact course.

Daylight Saving Time

Daylight Saving Time is achieved by advancing the clock one hour. Daylight Saving Time in the U.S. has traditionally begun each year at 2 AM on the first Sunday in Apr. and ended at 2 AM on the last Sunday in Oct. In accordance with a 2005 energy bill passed by Congress, which takes effect in 2007, daylight saving time will be extended by 4 weeks, and will be observed from the 2nd Sunday in Mar. to the first Sunday in Nov.

Daylight Saving Time was first observed in the U.S. during World War I, and then again during World War II. In the intervening years, some states and communities observed Daylight Saving Time, using whatever beginning and ending dates they chose. In 1966, Congress passed the Uniform Time Act, which provided that any state or territory that chooses to observe Daylight Saving Time must begin and end on the federal dates. Any state could, by law, exempt itself; a 1972 amendment to the act authorized states split by time zones to observe Daylight Saving Time in one time zone and standard time in the other time zone. Currently, Arizona, Hawaii, Puerto Rico, the U.S. Virgin Islands, and American Samoa do not observe Daylight Saving Time. On Apr. 2, 2006, all of Indiana observed Daylight Saving Time for the first time.

Congress and the secretary of transportation both have authority to change time zone boundaries. Since 1966 there have been a number of changes to U.S. time zone boundaries. In addition, efforts to conserve energy have prompted various changes in the times that Daylight Saving Time is observed.

Daylight Saving Time: International Usage

Adjusting clock time so as to gain the added daylight on summer evenings is common throughout the world.

Canada, which extends over 6 time zones, generally observes Daylight Saving Time during the same period as the U.S. Most provincial governments—with the exceptions of Newfoundland, Nunavut, and Yukon Territory—pledged to observe the 4 week extension to Daylight Saving Time that goes into effect in 2007. Most of Saskatchewan remains on standard time all year. Communities elsewhere in Canada also may exempt themselves from Daylight Saving Time. Except for the state of Sonora, which shares a border with Arizona, most of Mexico observes Daylight Saving Time.

Member nations of the European Union (EU) observe a "summer-time period," the EU's version of Daylight Saving Time, from the last Sunday of Mar. until the last Sunday in Oct.

Russia, which extends over 11 time zones, maintains its Standard Time 1 hour fast for its zone designation. Additionally, it proclaims Daylight Saving Time from the last Sunday in Mar. until the 4th Sunday in Oct.

China, which extends across 5 time zones, has decreed that the entire country be placed on Greenwich Time plus 8 hours. Daylight Saving Time is not observed. Japan, which lies within one time zone, also does not modify its legal time during the summer months.

Many countries in the Southern Hemisphere maintain Daylight Saving Time, generally from Oct. to Mar.; however, most countries near the equator do not deviate from Standard Time.

> **IT'S A FACT:** The energy bill approved by Congress in 2005 stipulates that Daylight Saving Time be extended by four weeks beginning in 2007. Accordingly, from 2 AM on Sun., Mar. 11, until 2 AM on Sun., Nov. 4, most states in the U.S. will set their clocks an hour ahead of local standard time.

Standard Time Differences—World Cities

The time indicated in the table is fixed by law and is called the legal time or, more generally, Standard Time. Use of Daylight Saving Time varies widely. *Indicates morning of the following day. At 12:00 noon, Eastern Standard Time, the Standard Time (in 24-hour time) in selected cities is as follows:

Addis Ababa...... 20 00	Caracas 13 00	Lima 12 00	St. Petersburg...... 20 00
Amsterdam........ 18 00	Casablanca....... 17 00	Lisbon 17 00	Santiago 13 00
Ankara 19 00	Copenhagen....... 18 00	London 17 00	Sarajevo 18 00
Athens 19 00	Dhaka........... 23 00	Madrid........... 18 00	Seoul 2 00*
Auckland 5 00*	Dublin 17 00	Manila 1 00*	Shanghai......... 1 00*
Baghdad.......... 20 00	Edinburgh........ 17 00	Mecca 20 00	Singapore 1 00*
Bangkok.......... 0 00*	Geneva.......... 18 00	Melbourne........ 3 00*	Stockholm........ 18 00
Beijing 1 00*	Helsinki.......... 19 00	Montevideo....... 14 00	Sydney 3 00*
Belfast 17 00	Ho Chi Minh City.... 0 00*	Moscow.......... 20 00	Taipei 1 00*
Belgrade.......... 18 00	Hong Kong 1 00*	Munich 18 00	Tashkent.......... 22 00
Berlin 18 00	Islamabad........ 22 00	Nagasaki......... 2 00*	Tehran........... 20 30
Bogotá 12 00	Istanbul.......... 19 00	Nairobi 20 00	Tel Aviv.......... 19 00
Bombay (Mumbai) .. 22 30	Jakarta 0 00*	New Delhi 22 30	Tokyo 2 00*
Brussels 18 00	Jerusalem........ 19 00	Oslo 18 00	Vladivostok 3 00*
Bucharest........ 19 00	Johannesburg...... 19 00	Paris 18 00	Vienna........... 18 00
Budapest 18 00	Kabul 21 50	Prague 18 00	Warsaw.......... 18 00
Buenos Aires 14 00	Karachi.......... 22 00	Quito 12 00	Wellington 5 00*
Cairo........... 19 00	Kathmandu....... 22 45	Rio de Janeiro...... 14 00	Yangon (Rangoon) .. 23 30
Calcutta (Kolkata)... 22 30	Kiev............ 19 00	Riyadh........... 20 00	Yokohama......... 2 00*
Cape Town........ 19 00	Lagos 18 00	Rome 18 00	Zurich 18 00

Standard Time Differences—North American Cities

At 12:00 noon, Eastern Standard Time, the Standard Time in selected North American cities is as follows:

Akron, OH .... 12 00 Noon	Fort Wayne, IN[1] .... 12 00 Noon	Ottawa, Ont............. 12 00 Noon
Albuquerque, NM....... 10 00 AM	Frankfort, KY .... 12 00 Noon	*Panama City, Panama ... 12 00 Noon
Anchorage, AK......... 8 00 AM	Havana, Cuba .... 12 00 Noon	Peoria, IL .... 11 00 AM
Atlanta, GA............ 12 00 Noon	Helena, MT............. 10 00 AM	*Phoenix, AZ .... 10 00 AM
Austin, TX............. 11 00 AM	*Honolulu, HI .... 7 00 AM	Pierre, SD............. 11 00 AM
Baltimore, MD .... 12 00 Noon	Houston, TX............ 11 00 AM	Pittsburgh, PA .... 12 00 Noon
Birmingham, AL .... 11 00 AM	Indianapolis, IN[1] .... 12 00 Noon	*Regina, Sask........... 11 00 AM
Bismarck, ND.......... 11 00 AM	Jackson, MS............ 11 00 AM	Reno, NV .... 9 00 AM
Boise, ID.............. 10 00 AM	Jacksonville, FL .... 12 00 Noon	Richmond, VA .... 12 00 Noon
Boston, MA............ 12 00 Noon	Juneau, AK............. 8 00 AM	Rochester, NY .... 12 00 Noon
Buffalo, NY............ 12 00 Noon	Kansas City, MO .... 11 00 AM	Sacramento, CA........ 9 00 AM
Butte, MT .... 10 00 AM	*Kingston, Jamaica ...... 12 00 Noon	St. John's, Nfld......... 1 30 PM
Calgary, Alta........... 10 00 AM	Knoxville, TN .... 12 00 Noon	St. Louis, MO .... 11 00 AM
Charleston, SC......... 12 00 Noon	Las Vegas, NV .... 9 00 AM	St. Paul, MN............ 11 00 AM
Charleston, WV........ 12 00 Noon	Lexington, KY........... 12 00 Noon	Salt Lake City, UT ...... 10 00 AM
Charlotte, NC.......... 12 00 Noon	Lincoln, NE............. 11 00 AM	San Antonio, TX........ 11 00 AM
Charlottetown, PEI....... 1 00 PM	Little Rock, AR .... 11 00 AM	San Diego, CA .... 9 00 AM
Chattanooga, TN .... 12 00 Noon	Los Angeles, CA .... 9 00 AM	San Francisco, CA ...... 9 00 AM
Cheyenne, WY.......... 10 00 AM	Louisville, KY .... 12 00 Noon	San Jose, CA.......... 9 00 AM
Chicago, IL............. 11 00 AM	Madison, WI .... 11 00 AM	*San Juan, PR .... 1 00 PM
Cincinnati, OH .... 12 00 Noon	Mexico City, Mexico...... 11 00 AM	Santa Fe, NM........... 10 00 AM
Cleveland, OH .... 12 00 Noon	Memphis, TN .... 11 00 AM	Savannah, GA .... 12 00 Noon
Colorado Spr., CO ...... 10 00 AM	Miami, FL.............. 12 00 Noon	Seattle, WA .... 9 00 AM
Columbus, OH .... 12 00 Noon	Milwaukee, WI .... 11 00 AM	Shreveport, LA.......... 11 00 AM
Dallas, TX............. 11 00 AM	Minneapolis, MN .... 11 00 AM	Sioux Falls, SD......... 11 00 AM
*Dawson, Yuk. .... 9 00 AM	Mobile, AL .... 11 00 AM	Spokane, WA.......... 9 00 AM
Dayton, OH .... 12 00 Noon	Montreal, Que .... 12 00 Noon	Tampa, FL .... 12 00 Noon
Denver, CO .... 10 00 AM	Nashville, TN .... 11 00 AM	Toledo, OH............ 12 00 Noon
Des Moines, IA......... 11 00 AM	Nassau, Bahamas ...... 12 00 Noon	Topeka, KS .... 11 00 AM
Detroit, MI............. 12 00 Noon	New Haven, CT .... 12 00 Noon	Toronto, Ont............ 12 00 Noon
Duluth, MN .... 11 00 AM	New Orleans, LA .... 11 00 AM	*Tucson, AZ .... 10 00 AM
Edmonton, Alta......... 10 00 AM	New York, NY.......... 12 00 Noon	Tulsa, OK............. 11 00 AM
El Paso, TX .... 10 00 AM	Nome, AK............. 8 00 AM	Vancouver, BC......... 9 00 AM
Erie, PA .... 12 00 Noon	Norfolk, VA............ 12 00 Noon	Washington, DC........ 12 00 Noon
Evansville, IN[1] .... 11 00 AM	Oklahoma City, OK ...... 11 00 AM	Wichita, KS............ 11 00 AM
Fairbanks, AK.......... 8 00 AM	Omaha, NE .... 11 00 AM	Wilmington, DE .... 12 00 Noon
Flint, MI .... 12 00 Noon	Orlando, FL .... 12 00 Noon	Winnipeg, Man......... 11 00 AM

(1) While most of Indiana is in the Eastern Time Zone, as of April 2, 2006, 18 counties in the southwestern and northwestern parts of the state observe Central Time. Note: This same table can be used for Daylight Saving Time when it is in effect, but allowance must be made for cities that do not observe it; they are marked with an asterisk (*). Daylight Saving Time is one hour later than Standard Time.

 IT'S A RECORD: A Louis XVI clock, the most expensive clock ever sold at auction, performs more functions than the average wristwatch. Made for the Duc de Choiseul (the French foreign minister from 1758 to 1770), it sold for $3,001,294 in 1999. The golden clock displays seconds, minutes, hours, sunrise, sunset, moon phases, date, day of the week, and position of the sun in the zodiac.

Perpetual Calendar

The number shown for each year indicates which Gregorian calendar to use. For 1583-1802, see "Gregorian Calendar" on page 342. For 1803-20, use numbers for 1983-2000, respectively. For Julian Calendar, see "Julian Calendar" on page 343.

Year reference table

Year	No.	Year	No.	Year	No.	Year	No.	Year	No.	Year	No.	Year	No.	Year	No.	Year	No.	Year	No.
1821	2	1847	6	1873	4	1899	1	1925	5	1951	2	1977	7	2003	4	2029	2	2055	6
1822	3	1848	14	1874	5	1900	2	1926	6	1952	10	1978	1	2004	12	2030	3	2056	14
1823	4	1849	2	1875	6	1901	3	1927	7	1953	5	1979	2	2005	7	2031	4	2057	2
1824	12	1850	3	1876	14	1902	4	1928	8	1954	6	1980	10	2006	1	2032	12	2058	3
1825	7	1851	4	1877	2	1903	5	1929	3	1955	7	1981	5	2007	2	2033	7	2059	4
1826	1	1852	12	1878	3	1904	13	1930	4	1956	8	1982	6	2008	10	2034	1	2060	12
1827	2	1853	7	1879	4	1905	1	1931	5	1957	3	1983	7	2009	5	2035	2	2061	7
1828	10	1854	1	1880	12	1906	2	1932	13	1958	4	1984	8	2010	6	2036	10	2062	1
1829	5	1855	2	1881	7	1907	3	1933	1	1959	5	1985	3	2011	7	2037	5	2063	2
1830	6	1856	10	1882	1	1908	11	1934	2	1960	13	1986	4	2012	8	2038	6	2064	10
1831	7	1857	5	1883	2	1909	6	1935	3	1961	1	1987	5	2013	3	2039	7	2065	5
1832	8	1858	6	1884	10	1910	7	1936	11	1962	2	1988	13	2014	4	2040	8	2066	6
1833	3	1859	7	1885	5	1911	1	1937	6	1963	3	1989	1	2015	5	2041	3	2067	7
1834	4	1860	8	1886	6	1912	9	1938	7	1964	11	1990	2	2016	13	2042	4	2068	8
1835	5	1861	3	1887	7	1913	4	1939	1	1965	6	1991	3	2017	1	2043	5	2069	3
1836	13	1862	4	1888	8	1914	5	1940	9	1966	7	1992	11	2018	2	2044	13	2070	4
1837	1	1863	5	1889	3	1915	6	1941	4	1967	1	1993	6	2019	3	2045	1	2071	5
1838	2	1864	13	1890	4	1916	14	1942	5	1968	9	1994	7	2020	11	2046	2	2072	13
1839	3	1865	1	1891	5	1917	2	1943	6	1969	4	1995	1	2021	6	2047	3	2073	1
1840	11	1866	2	1892	13	1918	3	1944	14	1970	5	1996	9	2022	7	2048	11	2074	2
1841	6	1867	3	1893	1	1919	4	1945	2	1971	6	1997	4	2023	1	2049	6	2075	3
1842	7	1868	11	1894	2	1920	12	1946	3	1972	14	1998	5	2024	9	2050	7	2076	11
1843	1	1869	6	1895	3	1921	7	1947	4	1973	2	1999	6	2025	4	2051	1	2077	6
1844	9	1870	7	1896	11	1922	1	1948	12	1974	3	2000	14	2026	5	2052	9	2078	7
1845	4	1871	1	1897	6	1923	2	1949	7	1975	6	2001	2	2027	6	2053	4	2079	1
1846	5	1872	9	1898	7	1924	10	1950	1	1976	12	2002	3	2028	14	2054	5	2080	9

The remainder of the page consists of fourteen reference calendar grids, each labelled with a key number and a sample year, showing all twelve months (JANUARY–DECEMBER) with weekday columns S M T W T F S.

Calendar keys and sample years shown:

- 1 — 2006
- 2 — 2001/2007
- 3 — 2002
- 4 — 2003
- 5 — 2009
- 6 — 2010

7 2005	8	9	10 2008
11	12 2004	13	14 2000

Each cell contains a full year's calendar with the months:

JANUARY, FEBRUARY, MARCH, APRIL, MAY, JUNE, JULY, AUGUST, SEPTEMBER, OCTOBER, NOVEMBER, DECEMBER

Each month laid out in columns:

S M T W T F S

WEIGHTS AND MEASURES

Source: National Institute of Standards and Technology, U.S. Dept. of Commerce

The International System of Units (SI)

Two systems of weights and measures coexist in the U.S. today: the **U.S. Customary System** and the **International System of Units** (SI, after the initials of Système International). SI, **commonly identified with the metric system,** is actually a more complete, coherent version of it. Throughout U.S. history, the Customary System (inherited from, but now different from, the British Imperial System) has been generally used; federal and state legislation has given it, through implication, standing as the primary weights and measures system. The metric system, however, is the only system that Congress has ever specifically sanctioned. An 1866 law reads:

"It shall be lawful throughout the United States of America to employ the weights and measures of the metric system; and no contract or dealing, or pleading in any court, shall be deemed invalid or liable to objection because the weights or measures expressed or referred to therein are weights or measures of the metric system."

Since that time, use of the metric system in the U.S. has slowly and steadily increased, particularly in the scientific community, the pharmaceutical industry, and the manufacturing sector—the last motivated by the practice in international commerce, in which the metric system is now predominantly used.

On Feb. 10, 1964, the National Bureau of Standards (now known as the National Institute of Standards and Technology) issued the following statement:

"Henceforth it shall be the policy of the National Bureau of Standards to use the units of the International System (SI), as adopted by the 11th General Conference on Weights and Measures (October 1960), except when the use of these units would obviously impair communication or reduce the usefulness of a report."

On Dec. 23, 1975, Pres. Gerald R. Ford signed the Metric Conversion Act of 1975. It defines the metric system as being the International System of Units as interpreted in the U.S. by the secretary of commerce. The Trade Act of 1988 and other legislation declare the metric system the preferred system of weights and measures for U.S. trade and commerce, call for the federal government to adopt metric specifications, and mandate the Commerce Dept. to oversee the program. However, the metric system has still not become the system of choice for most Americans' daily use.

The following 7 units serve as the base units for the system: **length**—meter; **mass**—kilogram; **time**—second; **electric current**—ampere; **thermodynamic temperature**—kelvin; **amount of substance**—mole; and **luminous intensity**—candela.

Frequently Used Conversions

Boldface indicates exact values. For greater accuracy, use the "multiply by" number in parentheses. For weights, *avdp* is an abbreviation for avoirdupois weight, the system of weights applied to all goods except medicines, precious metals, and precious stones (see p. 353). For more detailed tables, see pp. 352-355.

U.S. Customary to Metric

	If you have:	Multiply by:	To get:
Length	inches	**25.4**	millimeters
	inches	**2.54**	centimeters
	inches	**0.0254**	meters
	feet	0.3 (**0.3048**)	meters
	yards	0.9 (**0.9144**)	meters
	miles[1]	1.6 (**1.609344**)	kilometers
Area	sq. inches	6.5 (**6.4516**)	sq. cm.
	sq. feet	0.09 (0.09290341)	sq. meters
	sq. yards	0.84 (0.83612736)	sq. meters
	acres	0.4 (0.4046873)	hectares
	sq. miles	2.6 (2.58998811)	sq. kilometers
Weight	ounces (avdp)	28 (**28.349523125**)	grams
	pounds (avdp)	454 (**453.59237**)	grams
	pounds (avdp)	0.45 (**0.45359237**)	kilograms
	short tons[2]	0.91 (**0.90718474**)	metric tons
	long tons[3]	1 (**1.0160469088**)	metric tons
Liquid meas.	ounces	0.03 (0.02957353)	liters
	cups	0.24 (0.23658824)	liters
	pints	0.47 (0.473176473)	liters
	quarts	0.95 (0.946352946)	liters
	gallons	3.79 (3.785411784)	liters

Metric to U.S. Customary

	If you have:	Multiply by:	To get:
Length	millimeters	0.04 (0.03937)	inches
	centimeters	0.4 (0.3937)	inches
	meters	39 (39.37)	inches
	meters	3.3 (3.280840)	feet
	meters	1.1 (1.093613)	yards
	kilometers	0.6 (0.621371)	miles
Area	sq. cm.	0.16 (0.15500)	sq. inches
	sq. meters	10.8 (10.76391)	sq. feet
	sq. meters	1.2 (1.195990)	sq. yards
	hectares	2.5 (2.471044)	acres
	sq. kilometers	0.39 (0.386102)	sq. miles
Weight	grams	0.035 (0.03527396)	ounces (avdp)
	grams	0.002 (0.00220462)	pounds (avdp)
	kilograms	2.2 (2.204623)	pounds (avdp)
	metric tons	1.1 (1.102311)	short tons[2]
	metric tons	0.98 (0.9842065)	long tons[3]
Liquid meas.	liters	33.8 (33.81402)	ounces
	liters	4.2 (4.226752)	cups
	liters	2.1 (2.113376)	pints
	liters	1.1 (1.056688)	quarts
	liters	0.26 (0.264172)	gallons

(1) Statute mile. (2) A short ton is 2,000 pounds. (3) A long ton is 2,240 pounds.

Temperature Conversions

The left-hand column below gives a temperature according to the **Celsius** scale, and the right-hand gives the same temperature according to the **Fahrenheit** scale. The lowest number on each scale is equivalent to absolute zero, the temperature at which all motion within a molecule would stop.

For temperatures not shown: To convert Fahrenheit to Celsius by formula, subtract 32 degrees and divide by 1.8; to convert Celsius to Fahrenheit, multiply by 1.8 and add 32 degrees.

Note: Although the term *centigrade* is still frequently used, the International Committee on Weights and Measures and the National Institute of Standards and Technology have recommended since 1948 that this scale be called *Celsius*.

Celsius	Fahrenheit	Celsius	Fahrenheit	Celsius	Fahrenheit	Celsius	Fahrenheit	Celsius	Fahrenheit
−273.15	−459.67	−45.6	−50	−1.1	30	30	86	66	150
−250	−418	**−40**	**−40**	**0**	**32**	32.2	90	70	158
−200	−328	−34.4	−30	4.4	40	35	95	80	176
−184	−300	−30	−22	10	50	37	98.6	90	194
−157	−250	−28.9	−20	15.6	60	37.8	100	93	200
−150	−238	−23.3	−10	**20**	**68**	40	104	**100**	**212**
−129	−200	−20	−4	21.1	70	43	110	121	250
−101	−150	−17.8	0	23.9	75	49	120	149	300
−100	−148	−12.2	10	25	77	50	122	150	302
−73.3	−100	−10	14	26.7	80	54	130	200	392
−50	−58	−6.7	20	29.4	85	60	140	300	572

> **IT'S A FACT:** Pres. George W. Bush's physical in Aug. 2006 showed him to be in excellent health, but he was measured at 5 feet, 11½ inches tall—shorter by a quarter of an inch over the previous year's measurement. People generally lose height as they age, due to flattening of fluid-filled discs that separate spinal vertebrae. These discs also effect height measurements in general: people who are measured in the morning tend to be slightly taller than they would be in the afternoon or evening. Gravity flattens the intervertebral discs as people walk around over the course of the day.

Boiling and Freezing Points

Water boils at 212° F (100° C) at sea level. For every 550 feet above sea level, boiling point of water is lower by about 1° F. Methyl alcohol boils at 148° F. Average human oral temperature, 98.6° F. **Water freezes** at 32° F (0° C).

Mathematical Formulas

Note: The value of π (the Greek letter pi) is approximately 3.14159265 (equal to the ratio of the circumference of a circle to the diameter). The equivalence is typically rounded further to 3.1416 or 3.14.

To find the CIRCUMFERENCE of a:
Circle — Multiply the diameter by π.

To find the AREA of a:
Circle — Multiply the square of the radius (equal to ½ the diameter) by π.
Rectangle — Multiply the length of the base by the height.
Sphere (surface) — Multiply the square of the radius by π and multiply by 4.
Square — Square the length of one side.
Trapezoid — Add the 2 parallel sides, multiply by the height, and divide by 2.
Triangle — Multiply the base by the height, divide by 2.

To find the VOLUME of a:
Cone — Multiply the square of the radius of the base by π, multiply by the height, and divide by 3.
Cube — Cube the length of one edge.
Cylinder — Multiply the square of the radius of the base by π and multiply by the height.
Pyramid — Multiply the area of the base by the height and divide by 3.
Rectangular Prism — Multiply the length by the width by the height.
Sphere — Multiply the cube of the radius by π, multiply by 4, and divide by 3.

Playing Cards and Dice Chances

5-Card Poker Hands

Hand	Number possible	Odds against
Royal flush	4	649,739 to 1
Other straight flush	36	72,192 to 1
Four of a kind	624	4,164 to 1
Full house	3,744	693 to 1
Flush	5,108	508 to 1
Straight	10,200	254 to 1
Three of a kind	54,912	46 to 1
Two pairs	123,552	20 to 1
One pair	1,098,240	4 to 3 (1.37 to 1)
Nothing	1,302,540	1 to 1
TOTAL	**2,598,960**	

Bridge

The odds—against suit distribution in a hand of 4-4-3-2 are about 4 to 1, against 5-4-2-2 about 8 to 1, against 6-4-2-1 about 20 to 1, against 7-4-1-1 about 254 to 1, against 8-4-1-0 about 2,211 to 1, and against 13-0-0-0 about 158,753,389,899 to 1.

Dice
(probabilities on 2 dice)

Total	Odds against (single toss)	Total	Odds against (single toss)
2	35 to 1	8	31 to 5
3	17 to 1	9	8 to 1
4	11 to 1	10	11 to 1
5	8 to 1	11	17 to 1
6	31 to 5	12	35 to 1
7	5 to 1		

Large Numbers

No. of zeros	U.S.	British[1], French, German	No. of zeros	U.S.	British[1], French, German
6	million	million	42	tredecillion	septillion
9	billion	milliard	45	quattuordecillion	1,000 septillion
12	trillion	billion	48	quindecillion	octillion
15	quadrillion	1,000 billion	51	sexdecillion	1,000 octillion
18	quintillion	trillion	54	septendecillion	nonillion
21	sextillion	1,000 trillion	57	octodecillion	1,000 nonillion
24	septillion	quadrillion	60	novemdecillion	decillion
27	octillion	1,000 quadrillion	63	vigintillion	1,000 decillion
30	nonillion	quintillion	100	googol	googol
33	decillion	1,000 quintillion	303	centillion	—
36	undecillion	sextillion	600	—	centillion
39	duodecillion	1,000 sextillion	googol	googolplex	googolplex

(1) In recent years, it has become more common in Britain to use U.S. terminology for large numbers.

Prime Numbers

A prime number is a positive integer that is divisible only by two positive integers, 1 and itself.

Prime Numbers to 1,009

	2	3	5	7	11	13	17	19	23
29	31	37	41	43	47	53	59	61	67
71	73	79	83	89	97	101	103	107	109
113	127	131	137	139	149	151	157	163	167
173	179	181	191	193	197	199	211	223	227
229	233	239	241	251	257	263	269	271	277
281	283	293	307	311	313	317	331	337	347
349	353	359	367	373	379	383	389	397	401
409	419	421	431	433	439	443	449	457	461
463	467	479	487	491	499	503	509	521	523
541	547	557	563	569	571	577	587	593	599
601	607	613	617	619	631	641	643	647	653
659	661	673	677	683	691	701	709	719	727
733	739	743	751	757	761	769	773	787	797
809	811	821	823	827	829	839	853	857	859
863	877	881	883	887	907	911	919	929	937
941	947	953	967	971	977	983	991	997	1,009

Common Fractions Reduced to Decimals

8ths	16ths	32nds	64ths		8ths	16ths	32nds	64ths		8ths	16ths	32nds	64ths		8ths	16ths	32nds	64ths	
			1 = 0.015625					17 = 0.265625					33 = 0.515625					49 = 0.765625	
		1	2 = 0.03125				9	18 = 0.28125				17	34 = 0.53125				25	50 = 0.78125	
			3 = 0.046875					19 = 0.296875					35 = 0.546875					51 = 0.796875	
	1	2	4 = 0.0625			5	10	20 = 0.3125				18	36 = 0.5625			13	26	52 = 0.8125	
			5 = 0.078125					21 = 0.328125					37 = 0.578125					53 = 0.828125	
		3	6 = 0.09375				11	22 = 0.34375				19	38 = 0.59375				27	54 = 0.84375	
			7 = 0.109375					23 = 0.359375					39 = 0.609375					55 = 0.859375	
1	2	4	8 = 0.125		3	6	12	24 = 0.375		5	10	20	40 = 0.625		7	14	28	56 = 0.875	
			9 = 0.140625					25 = 0.390625					41 = 0.640625					57 = 0.890625	
		5	10 = 0.15625				13	26 = 0.40625				21	42 = 0.65625				29	58 = 0.90625	
			11 = 0.171875					27 = 0.421875					43 = 0.671875					59 = 0.921875	
	3	6	12 = 0.1875			7	14	28 = 0.4375			11	22	44 = 0.6875			15	30	60 = 0.9375	
			13 = 0.203125					29 = 0.453125					45 = 0.703125					61 = 0.953125	
		7	14 = 0.21875				15	30 = 0.46875				23	46 = 0.71875				31	62 = 0.96875	
			15 = 0.234375					31 = 0.484375					47 = 0.734375					63 = 0.984375	
2	4	8	16 = 0.25		4	8	16	32 = 0.5		6	12	24	48 = 0.75		8	16	32	64 = 1.0	

Roman Numerals

I — 1	IV — 4	VII — 7	X — 10	XX — 20	L — 50	C — 100	D — 500
II — 2	V — 5	VIII — 8	XI — 11	XXX — 30	LX — 60	CC — 200	CM — 900
III — 3	VI — 6	IX — 9	XIX — 19	XL — 40	XC — 90	CD — 400	M — 1,000

Note: The numerals V, X, L, C, D, or M shown with a horizontal line on top denote 1,000 times the original value.

Ancient Measures

Biblical
Cubit . . . .= 21.8 inches
Omer. . . . .= 0.45 peck
                        = 3.964 liters
Ephah . . . .= 10 omers
Shekel. . . . .= 0.497 ounce
                        = 14.1 grams

Greek
Cubit . . . .= 18.3 inches
Stadion . . . .= 607.2 or 622 feet
Obolos. . . . .= 715.38 milligrams
Drachma . . . .= 4.2923 grams
Mina . . . .= 0.9463 pound
Talent . . . .= 60 mina

Roman
Cubit . . . .= 17.5 inches
Stadium. . . . .= 202 yards
As, libra,
  pondus . . . .= 325.971 grams
                        = 0.71864 pound

Metric System Prefixes

The following prefixes, in combination with the basic unit names, provide the multiples and submultiples in the metric system. For example, the unit name *meter*, with the prefix *kilo* added, produces *kilometer*, meaning "1,000 meters."

Prefix	Symbol	Multiples	Equivalent		Prefix	Symbol	Multiples	Equivalent
yotta	Y	10^{24}	septillionfold		deci	d	10^{-1}	tenth part
zetta	Z	10^{21}	sextillionfold		centi	c	10^{-2}	hundredth part
exa	E	10^{18}	quintillionfold		milli	m	10^{-3}	thousandth part
peta	P	10^{15}	quadrillionfold		micro	μ	10^{-6}	millionth part
tera	T	10^{12}	trillionfold		nano	n	10^{-9}	billionth part
giga	G	10^{9}	billionfold		pico	p	10^{-12}	trillionth part
mega	M	10^{6}	millionfold		femto	f	10^{-15}	quadrillionth part
kilo	k	10^{3}	thousandfold		atto	a	10^{-18}	quintillionth part
hecto	h	10^{2}	hundredfold		zepto	z	10^{-21}	sextillionth part
deka	da	10	tenfold		yocto	y	10^{-24}	septillionth part

Tables of Metric Weights and Measures

(**Note:** The metric system generally uses the term *mass* instead of *weight*. Mass is a measure of an object's inertial property, or the amount of matter it contains. Weight is a measure of the force exerted on an object by gravity or the force needed to support it. Also, the metric system does not make a distinction between "dry volume" and "liquid volume.")

Length
10 millimeters (mm) . . . .= 1 centimeter (cm)
10 centimeters . . . .= 1 decimeter (dm)
                                      = 100 millimeters
10 decimeters. . . . .= 1 meter (m)
                                      = 1,000 millimeters
10 meters. . . . .= 1 dekameter (dam)
10 dekameters . . . .= 1 hectometer (hm)
                                      = 100 meters
10 hectometers . . . .= 1 kilometer (km)
                                      = 1,000 meters

Area
100 square millimeters (mm²) = 1 square centimeter (cm²)
10,000 square centimeters. . . .= 1 square meter (m²)
                                      = 1,000,000 square millimeters
100 square meters . . . .= 1 are (a)
100 ares. . . . .= 1 hectare (ha)
                                      = 10,000 square meters
100 hectares . . . .= 1 square kilometer (km²)
                                      = 1,000,000 square meters

Volume
10 milliliters (mL) . . . .= 1 centiliter (cL)
10 centiliters. . . . .= 1 deciliter (dL)
                                      = 100 milliliters
10 deciliters . . . .= 1 liter (L)
                                      = 1,000 milliliters

10 liters . . . .= 1 dekaliter (daL)
10 dekaliters . . . .= 1 hectoliter (hL)
                                      = 100 liters
10 hectoliters. . . . .= 1 kiloliter (kL)
                                      = 1,000 liters

Volume (Cubic Measure)
1,000 cubic millimeters (mm³) = 1 cubic centimeter (cm³)
1,000 cubic centimeters . . . . .= 1 cubic decimeter (dm³)
                                      = 1,000,000 cubic millimeters
1,000 cubic decimeters . . . . . .= 1 cubic meter (m³)
                                      = 1 stere
                                      = 1,000,000 cubic centimeters
                                      = 1,000,000,000 cubic millimeters

Weight (Mass)
10 milligrams (mg). . . . .= 1 centigram (cg)
10 centigrams . . . .= 1 decigram (dg)
                                      = 100 milligrams
10 decigrams. . . . .= 1 gram (g)
                                      = 1,000 milligrams
10 grams . . . .= 1 dekagram (dag)
10 dekagrams . . . .= 1 hectogram (hg)
                                      = 100 grams
10 hectograms. . . . .= 1 kilogram (kg)
                                      = 1,000 grams
1,000 kilograms. . . . .= 1 metric ton (t)

Table of U.S. Customary Weights and Measures

Length

12 inches (in)	= 1 foot (ft)
3 feet	= 1 yard (yd)
5½ yards	= 1 rod (rd), pole, or perch (16½ feet)
40 rods	= 1 furlong (fur)
	= 220 yards
	= 660 feet
8 furlongs	= 1 statute mile (mi)
	= 1,760 yards
	= 5,280 feet
3 miles	= 1 league (land)
	= 5,280 yards
	= 15,840 feet
6076.11549 feet	= 1 international nautical mile

Volume (Liquid Measure)

When necessary to distinguish the liquid pint or quart from the dry pint or quart, the word *liquid* or the abbreviation *liq* is used in combination with the name or abbreviation of the liquid unit.

4 gills (gi)	= 1 pint (pt)
	= 28.875 cubic inches
2 pints	= 1 quart (qt)
	= 57.75 cubic inches
4 quarts	= 1 gallon (gal)
	= 231 cubic inches
	= 8 pints
	= 32 gills

Volume (Dry Measure)

When necessary to distinguish the dry pint or quart from the liquid pint or quart, the word *dry* is used in combination with the name or abbreviation of the dry unit.

2 pints (pt)	= 1 quart (qt)
	= 67.2006 cubic inches
8 quarts	= 1 peck (pk)
	= 537.605 cubic inches
	= 16 pints
4 pecks	= 1 bushel (bu)
	= 2,150.42 cubic inches
	= 32 quarts

Area

Squares and cubes of units are sometimes abbreviated by using superscripts. For example, ft^2 means square foot, and ft^3 means cubic foot.

144 square inches	= 1 square foot (ft^2)
9 square feet	= 1 square yard (yd^2)
	= 1,296 square inches
30 ¼ square yards	= 1 square rod (rd^2)
	= 272 ¼ square feet
160 square rods	= 1 acre
	= 4,840 square yards
	= 43,560 square feet

640 acres	= 1 square mile (mi^2)
1 mile square	= 1 section (of land)
6 miles square	= 1 township
	= 36 sections
	= 36 square miles

Cubic Measure

1 cubic foot (ft^3)	= 1,728 cubic inches (in^3)
27 cubic feet	= 1 cubic yard (yd^3)

Gunter's, or Surveyor's, Chain Measure

7.92 inches (in)	= 1 link
100 links	= 1 chain (ch)
	= 4 rods
	= 66 feet
80 chains	= 1 statute mile (mi)
	= 320 rods
	= 5,280 feet

Avoirdupois Weight

When necessary to distinguish the avoirdupois ounce or pound from the troy ounce or pound, the word *avoirdupois* or the abbreviation *avdp* is used in combination with the name or abbreviation of the avoirdupois unit. The *grain* is the same in avoirdupois and troy weight.

27 $^{11}/_{32}$ grains	= 1 dram (dr)
16 drams	= 1 ounce (oz)
	= 437 ½ grains
16 ounces	= 1 pound (lb)
	= 256 drams
	= 7,000 grains
100 pounds	= 1 hundredweight (cwt)*
20 hundredweights	= 1 ton
	= 2,000 pounds*

In *gross* or *long* measure, the following values are recognized.

112 pounds	= 1 gross or long hundredweight*
20 gross or long hundredweights	= 1 gross or long ton
	= 2,240 pounds*

*When the terms *hundredweight* and *ton* are used unmodified, they are commonly understood to mean the 100-pound hundredweight and the 2,000-pound ton, respectively; these units may be designated *net* or *short* when necessary to distinguish them from the corresponding units in gross or long measure.

Troy Weight

24 grains	= 1 pennyweight (dwt)
20 pennyweights	= 1 ounce troy (oz t)
	= 480 grains
12 ounces troy	= 1 pound troy (lb t)
	= 240 pennyweights
	= 5,760 grains

Tables of Equivalents

In this table it is necessary to distinguish between the *international* and the *survey* foot. The international foot, defined in 1959 as exactly equal to 0.3048 meter, is shorter than the old survey foot by exactly 2 parts in 1 million. The survey foot is still used in data expressed in feet in geodetic surveys within the U.S. In this table the survey foot is indicated with capital LETTERS.

When the name of a unit is enclosed in brackets, e.g., [1 hand], either (1) the unit is not in general current use in the U.S. or (2) the unit is believed to be based on custom and usage rather than on formal definition.

Equivalents involving decimals are, in most instances, rounded to the 3rd decimal place; exact equivalents are so designated.

Lengths

1 angstrom (Å)	= 0.1 nanometer (exactly)
	= 0.000 1 micrometer (exactly)
	= 0.000 000 1 millimeter (exactly)
	= 0.000 000 004 inch
1 cable's length	= 120 fathoms (exactly)
	= 720 FEET (exactly)
	= 219 meters
1 centimeter (cm)	= 0.3937 inch
1 chain (ch) (Gunter's or surveyor's)	= 66 FEET (exactly)
	= 20.1168 meters
1 chain (engineer's)	= 30.48 meters (exactly)
	= 100 feet
1 decimeter (dm)	= 3.937 inches
1 degree (geographical)	= 364,566.929 feet
	= 69.047 miles (avg.)
	= 111.123 kilometers (avg.)
of latitude	= 68.708 miles at equator
	= 69.403 miles at poles
of longitude.	= 69.171 miles at equator

1 dekameter (dam)	= 32.808 feet
1 fathom	= 6 FEET (exactly)
	= 1.8288 meters
1 foot (ft)	= 0.3048 meters (exactly)
	= 0.015 chains (surveyors)
1 furlong (fur)	= 660 FEET (exactly)
	= ⅛ statute mile (exactly)
	= 201.168 meters
[1 hand] (height measure for horses from ground to top of shoulders)	= 4 inches
1 inch (in)	= 2.54 centimeters (exactly)
1 kilometer (km)	= 0.621371 mile
	= 3,280.8 feet
1 league (land)	= 3 statute miles (exactly)
	= 4.828 kilometers
1 link (Gunter's or surveyor's)	= 7.92 inches (exactly)
	= 0.201 meter
1 link (engineer's)	= 1 foot
	= 0.305 meter
1 meter (m)	= 39.37 inches
	= 1.09361 yards

1 micrometer (μm) . . . . = 0.001 millimeter (exactly)
  = 0.00003937 inch
1 mil . . . . = 0.001 inch (exactly)
  = 0.0254 millimeter (exactly)
1 mile (mi) (statute or land) . . . = 5,280 FEET (exactly)
  = 1.609344 kilometers (exactly)
1 international nautical mile
  (nmi) . . . . = 1.852 kilometers (exactly)
  = 1.150779 statute miles
  = 6,076.11549 feet
1 millimeter (mm) . . . . = 0.03937 inch
1 nanometer (nm) . . . . = 0.001 micrometer (exactly)
  = 0.00000003937 inch
1 pica (typography) . . . . = 12 points
1 point (typography) . . . . = 0.013 837 inch (exactly)
  = 0.351 millimeter
1 rod (rd), pole, or perch . . . . . = 16½ FEET (exactly)
  = 5.029 meters
1 yard (yd) . . . . = 0.9144 meter (exactly)

Areas or Surfaces

1 acre . . . . = 43,560 square FEET (exactly)
  = 4,840 square yards
  = 0.405 hectare
1 are (a) . . . . = 119.599 square yards
  = 0.025 acre
1 bolt (cloth measure):
  length . . . . = 100 yards (on modern looms)
  width . . . . = 45 or 60 inches
1 hectare (ha) . . . . = 2.471 acres
[1 square (building)] . . . . = 100 square feet
1 square centimeter (cm²) . . . . = 0.155 square inch
1 square decimeter (dm²). . . . . = 15.500 square inches
1 square foot (ft²) . . . . = 929.030 square centimeters
1 square inch (in²) . . . . = 6.4516 square centimeters
  (exactly)
1 square kilometer (km²) . . . . . = 247.104 acres
  = 0.386102 square mile
1 square meter (m²) . . . . = 1.196 square yards
  = 10.764 square feet
1 square mile (mi²) . . . . = 258.999 hectares
1 square millimeter (mm²) . . . . = 0.002 square inch
1 square rod (rd²), sq. pole,
  or sq. perch . . . . = 25.293 square meters
1 square yard (yd²) . . . . = 0.836127 square meter

Capacities or Volumes

1 barrel (bbl), liquid . . . . = 31 to 42 gallons*
*There are a variety of "barrels" established by law or usage. For
example: federal taxes on fermented liquors are based on a
barrel of 31 gallons; many state laws fix the "barrel for liquids" as
31½ gallons; one state fixes a 36-gallon barrel for cistern
measurement; federal law recognizes a 40-gallon barrel for
"proof spirits"; by custom, 42 gallons constitute a barrel of crude
oil or petroleum products for statistical purposes, and this
equivalent is recognized "for liquids" by 4 states.

1 barrel (bbl), standard for
  fruits, vegetables, and other
  dry commodities except dry
  cranberries . . . . = 7,056 cubic inches
  = 1 barrel (bbl), standard for
    fruits
1 barrel (bbl), standard,
  cranberry . . . . = 86 ⁴⁵/₆₄ dry quarts
  = 2.709 bushels, struck measure
  = 5,826 cubic inches
1 board foot (lumber measure) = a foot-square board 1 inch
    thick
1 bushel (bu) (U.S.) (struck
  measure) . . . . = 2,150.42 cu in (exactly)
  = 35.239 liters
[1 bushel, heaped (U.S.)] . . . . . = 2,747.715 cubic inches
  = 1.278 bushels, struck
    measure*
*Frequently recognized as 1¼ bushels, struck measure.
[1 bushel (bu) (British Imperial)
  (struck measure)] . . . . = 1.032 U.S. bushels, struck
    measure
  = 2,219.36 cubic inches
1 cord (cd) firewood . . . . = 128 cubic feet (exactly)
1 cubic centimeter (cm³) . . . . . = 0.061 cubic inch
1 cubic decimeter (dm³) . . . . . . = 61.024 cubic inches
1 cubic inch (in³) . . . . = 0.554 fluid ounce
  = 4.433 fluid drams
  = 16.387 cubic centimeters
1 cubic foot (ft³) . . . . = 7.481 gallons
  = 28.317 cubic decimeters

1 cubic meter (m³) . . . . = 1.308 cubic yards
1 cubic yard (yd³) . . . . = 0.765 cubic meter
1 cup, measuring . . . . = 8 fluid ounces (exactly)
  = ½ liquid pint (exactly)
[1 dram, fluid (fl dr) (British)] . . = 0.961 U.S. fluid dram
  = 0.217 cubic inch
  = 3.552 milliliters
1 dekaliter (daL) . . . . = 2.642 gallons
  = 1.135 pecks
1 gallon (gal) (U.S.) . . . . = 231 cubic inches (exactly)
  = 3.785 liters
  = 0.833 British gallon
  = 128 U.S. fluid ounces (exactly)
[1 gallon (gal) British Imperial]. = 277.42 cubic inches
  = 1.201 U.S. gallons
  = 4.546 liters
  =160 British fluid ounces
    (exactly)
1 gill (gi). . . . . = 7.219 cubic inches
  = 4 fluid ounces (exactly)
  = 0.118 liter
1 hectoliter (hL) . . . . = 26.418 gallons
  = 2.838 bushels
1 liter (L) (1 cubic decimeter
  exactly) . . . . = 1.057 liquid quarts
  = 0.908 dry quart
  = 61.024 cubic inches
1 milliliter (mL) (1 cu cm
  exactly) . . . . = 0.271 fluid dram
  = 16.231 minims
  = 0.061 cubic inch
1 ounce, liquid (U.S.) . . . . = 1.805 cubic inches
  = 29.574 milliliters
  = 1.041 British fluid ounces
[1 ounce, fluid (fl oz) (British)] . = 0.961 U.S. fluid ounce
  = 1.734 cubic inches
  = 28.412 milliliters
1 peck (pk). . . . . = 8.810 liters
1 pint (pt), dry . . . . = 33.600 cubic inches
  = 0.551 liter
1 pint (pt), liquid. . . . . = 28.875 cubic inches (exactly)
  = 0.473 liter
1 quart (qt), dry (U.S.) . . . . = 67.201 cubic inches
  = 1.101 liters
  = 0.969 British quart
1 quart (qt), liquid (U.S.) . . . . . = 57.75 cubic in (exactly)
  = 0.946 liter
  = 0.833 British quart
[1 quart (qt) (British)] . . . . = 69.354 cubic inches
  = 1.032 U.S. dry quarts
  = 1.201 U.S. liquid quarts
1 tablespoon . . . . = 3 teaspoons*(exactly)
  = 4 fluid drams
  = ½ fluid ounce (exactly)
1 teaspoon. . . . . = ⅓ tablespoon*(exactly)
  = 1⅓ fluid drams*
*The equivalent "1 teaspoon = 1 ⅓ fluid drams" has been found
to correspond more closely with the actual capacities of
teaspoons in use than the equivalent "1 teaspoon = 1 fluid dram"
which is given by many dictionaries.

Weights or Masses

1 assay ton** (AT) . . . . = 29.167 grams
**Used in assaying. The assay ton bears the same relation to
the milligram that a ton of 2,000 pounds avoirdupois bears to the
ounce troy; hence, the weight in milligrams of precious metal
obtained from one assay ton of ore gives directly the number of
troy ounces to the net ton.

1 bale (cotton measure) . . . . . = 500 pounds in U.S.
  = 750 pounds in Egypt
1 carat (c) . . . . = 200 milligrams (exactly)
  = 3.086 grains
1 dram avoirdupois (dr avdp) . = 27 ¹¹/₃₂ (= 27.344) grains
  = 1.772 grams
1 gamma (g) . . . . = 1 microgram (exactly),
    see below
1 grain . . . . = 64.7989 milligrams
1 gram . . . . = 15.432 grains
  = 0.035 ounce, avoirdupois
1 hundredweight, gross or
  long*** (gross cwt) . . . . = 112 pounds (exactly)
  = 50.802 kilograms
1 hundredweight, net or
  short (cwt or net cwt) . . . . . = 100 pounds (exactly)
  = 45.359 kilograms
1 kilogram (kg). . . . . = 2.20462 pounds
1 microgram (μg) . . . . = 0.000001 gram (exactly)

1 milligram (mg) . . . . = 0.015 grain	
1 ounce, avoirdupois (oz avdp) = 437.5 grains (exactly)	
= 0.911 troy ounce	
= 28.3495 grams	
1 ounce, troy (oz t). . . . . = 480 grains (exactly)	
= 1.097 avoirdupois ounces	
= 31.103 grams	
1 pennyweight (dwt) . . . . = 1.555 grams	
1 pound, avoirdupois (lb avdp) = 7,000 grains (exactly)	
= 1.215 troy pounds	
= 453.59237 grams (exactly)	
1 pound, troy (lb t) . . . . = 5,760 grains (exactly)	
= 0.823 pound, avoirdupois	
= 373.242 grams	

1 stone, (avdp) . . . . = 14 pounds avdp (exactly)
= 6.350 kilograms
1 ton, gross or long***(gross = 2,240 pounds (exactly)
ton) . . . . = 1.12 net tons (exactly)
= 1.016 metric tons

***The gross or long ton and hundredweight are used commercially in the U.S. to only a limited extent, usually in restricted industrial fields. These units are the same as the British ton and hundredweight.

1 ton, metric (t) . . . . = 2,204.623 pounds
= 0.984 gross ton
= 1.102 net tons
1 ton, net or short (sh ton). . . . = 2,000 pounds (exactly)
= 0.893 gross ton
= 0.907 metric ton

Electrical Units

The **watt** is the unit of power (electrical, mechanical, thermal, etc.). Electrical power is given by the product of the voltage and the current.

Energy is sold by the **joule,** but in common practice the billing of electrical energy is expressed in terms of the **kilowatt-hour,** which is 3,600,000 joules or 3.6 megajoules.

The **horsepower** is a nonmetric unit sometimes used in mechanics. It is equal to 746 watts.

The **ohm** is the unit of electrical resistance and represents the physical property of a conductor that offers a resistance to the flow of electricity, permitting just 1 ampere to flow at 1 volt of pressure.

Measures of Force and Pressure

Dyne = force necessary to accelerate a 1-gram mass 1 centimeter per second squared = 0.000072 poundal

Poundal = force necessary to accelerate a 1-pound mass 1 foot per second squared = 13,825.5 dynes = 0.138255 newtons

Newton = force needed to accelerate a 1-kilogram mass 1 meter per second squared

Pascal (pressure) = 1 newton per square meter = 0.020885 pound per square foot

Atmosphere (air pressure at sea level) = 2,116.102 pounds per square foot = 14.6952 pounds per square inch = 1.0332 kilograms per square centimeter = 101,323 newtons per square meter

Spirits Measures

Pony.	= 0.5 jigger	Quart	= 32 shots	For champagne only:	
Shot	= 0.667 jigger		= 1.25 fifths	Rehoboam.	= 3 magnums
	= 1.0 ounce	Magnum.	= 2 quarts	Methuselah	= 4 magnums
Jigger	= 1.5 shots		= 2.49797 bottles	Salmanazar.	= 6 magnums
Pint	= 16 shots		(wine)	Balthazar.	= 8 magnums
	= 0.625 fifth	For champagne and brandy only:		Nebuchadnezzar. . . .	= 10 magnums
Fifth	= 25.6 shots	Jeroboam	= 6.4 pints	Wine bottle	
	= 1.6 pints		= 1.6 magnum	(standard)	= 0.800633 quart
	= 0.8 quart		= 0.8 gallon		= 0.7576778 liter
	= 0.75706 liter				

Miscellaneous Modern Measures

Caliber—the diameter of a gun bore. In the U.S., caliber is traditionally expressed in hundredths of inches, e.g., .22. In Britain, caliber is often expressed in thousandths of inches, e.g., .270. Now it is commonly expressed in millimeters, e.g., the 5.56 mm M16 rifle. Heavier weapons' caliber has long been expressed in millimeters, e.g., the 155 mm howitzer. Naval guns' caliber refers to the barrel length as a multiple of the bore diameter. A 5-inch, 50-caliber naval gun has a 5-inch bore and a barrel length of 250 inches.

Decibel (dB)—a measure of the relative loudness or intensity of sound. A 20-decibel sound is 10 times louder than a 10-decibel sound; 30 decibels is 100 times louder; 40 decibels is 1,000 times louder, etc.
One decibel is the smallest difference between sounds detectable by the human ear. A 120-decibel sound is painful.

10 decibels	– a light whisper
20	– quiet conversation
30	– normal conversation
40	– light traffic
50	– typewriter, loud conversation
60	– noisy office
70	– normal traffic, quiet train
80	– rock music, subway
90	– heavy traffic, thunder
100	– jet plane at takeoff

Em—a printer's measure designating the square width of any given type size. Thus, an em of 10-point type is 10 points. An en is half an em.

Gauge—a measure of shotgun bore diameter. Gauge numbers originally referred to the number of lead balls just fitting the gun barrel diameter required to make a pound. Thus, a 16-gauge shotgun's bore was smaller than a 12-gauge shotgun's. Today, an international agreement assigns millimeter measures to each gauge, e.g.:

Gauge	Bore diameter (in mm)	Gauge	Bore diameter (in mm)
6. . . .	23.34	14 . . .	17.60
10. . . .	19.67	16 . . .	16.81
12. . . .	18.52	20 . . .	15.90

Horsepower—the power needed to lift 550 pounds 1 foot in 1 second or to lift 33,000 pounds 1 foot in 1 minute. Equivalent to 746 watts or 2,546.0756 Btu/h.

Karat or carat—a measure of fineness for gold equal to $1/24$ part of pure gold in an alloy. Thus 24-karat gold is pure; 18-karat gold is ¼ alloy. The *carat* is also used as a unit of weight for precious stones; it is equal to 200 milligrams or 3.086 grains.

Knot—a measure of the speed of ships. A knot equals 1 nautical mile per hour.

Quire—25 sheets of paper

Ream—500 sheets of paper

World Almanac Quick Quiz

For every 550 feet above sea level, the boiling point of water is lower by about 1 degree Fahrenheit. If you were trying to boil water at the summit of Mount Everest (29,035 ft above sea level), to what temperature would you theoretically have to bring the water?

(a) about 159°F   (b) about 200°F   (c) about 77°F   (d) about 272°F

For the answer, see page 1008.

COMPUTERS AND TELECOMMUNICATIONS

Computer Milestones

1623: German mathematician Wilhelm Schickard developed the **1st mechanical calculator**, capable of adding, subtracting, multiplying, and dividing.

1642: French mathematician Blaise Pascal built the 1st of more than 4 dozen copies of an **adding and subtracting machine** that he invented.

1801: French inventor Joseph Marie Jacquard demonstrated a new control system for looms. He **"programmed"** the loom, communicating desired weaving operations to the machine via patterns of holes in paper cards.

1833-71: British mathematician and scientist Charles Babbage used the Jacquard punch-card system in his design for a sophisticated, programmable **"Analytical Engine"** that foreshadowed basic features of today's computers. Babbage's conception was beyond the capabilities of the technology of his time, and the machine remained unfinished at his death in 1871.

1889: American engineer Herman Hollerith patented an electromechanical **punch-card tabulating system** that facilitated the handling of large amounts of statistical data and quickly found use in censuses in the U.S. and other countries.

1911: Hollerith's Tabulating Machine Company merged with 2 other enterprises to form the Computing-Tabulating-Recording Company, renamed in 1924 the International Business Machines Corporation (**IBM**).

1941: German engineer Konrad Züse completed the Z3, the **1st fully functional digital computer** to be **controlled by a program;** the Z3 was not electronic—it was based on electrical switches called relays.

1942: Iowa State College physicist John Vincent Atanasoff and his assistant Clifford Berry completed a working model of the **1st fully electronic computer,** using vacuum tubes, which could operate much more quickly than relays; the rudimentary machine was not programmable.

1943: IBM and Harvard Professor Howard Aiken completed the **1st large-scale automatic digital computer**, the Mark I, a relay-based machine 55 ft long and 8 ft high.

1943: British scientists built the **Colossus,** an electronic computer designed specifically for breaking German codes.

1946: **Eniac** (for Electronic Numerical Integrator and Computer), a 30-ton room-sized electronic computer with over 18,000 vacuum tubes, was completed by physicist John Mauchly and engineer J. Presper Eckert at the University of Pennsylvania for the U.S. Army. Eniac could be programmed to do different tasks, although programming could take a couple of days, since cables had to be plugged in and switches set by hand.

1951: Eckert and Mauchly's **Univac** ("Universal Automatic Computer") became the 1st computer commercially available in the U.S.; the 1st customer: the Census Bureau. CBS-TV used a Univac in 1952 to predict election results.

1969-71: The powerful **Unix operating system** was developed at Bell Laboratories; later versions became widely used on large computers and formed the basis for the popular Linux and Macintosh OS X operating systems for personal computers.

1971: Intel released the 4004, the 1st commerical **microprocessor** (an entire computer processing unit on a chip).

1973: The Alto computer, developed at Xerox's Palo Alto Research Center, became operational, implementing many features used years later in commerical personal computers, including a **graphical user interface** (GUI) featuring windows, icons, a mouse, and pointers.

1975: The **1st widely marketed personal computer**, the MITS Altair 8800, was introduced in kit form, with no keyboard, video display, or printer, for under $400.

1975: **Microsoft** was founded by college dropouts Bill Gates and Paul Allen.

1976: The **1st word-processing program** for personal computers, the Electric Pencil, was written.

1976: **Apple** Computer Company was founded by Steven Jobs and Stephen Wozniak.

1977: Apple introduced the **Apple II;** capable of displaying text and graphics in color, the machine enjoyed phenomenal success.

1981: **IBM** unveiled its **"Personal Computer,"** which used Microsoft's DOS (disk operating system).

1984: Apple introduced the 1st **Macintosh**. The easy-to-use Macintosh came with a proprietary operating system and was the 1st popular computer to have a GUI and a mouse.

1990: Microsoft released **Windows** 3.0, the 1st workable version of its own GUI.

1991: **Linux** was invented for the personal computer by Helsinki Univ. student Linus Torvalds and made available for free.

1996: The **Palm Pilot**, the 1st widely successful handheld computer and personal information manager, arrived.

1997: The IBM computer **Deep Blue** beat world chess champion Garry Kasparov in a 6-game match, 3.5-2.5.

2000: **Microsoft** was found guilty of **antitrust violations** by a a federal district judge, who ordered the company split into 2 parts, an outcome later avoided through a settlement in which Microsoft accepted certain restrictions on its competitive practices.

2001: Apple introduced the **Unix-based operating system** OS X for the **Macintosh**.

2002: The total number of **personal computers** (PCs), including desktop and laptop machines of all types, shipped by manufacturers since 1975 reached 1 bil, according to computer industry research firm Gartner Dataquest.

2004: The European Union (EU) found **Microsoft** guilty of **anticompetitive practices** and fined the company 497 mil euros (over $600 mil); Microsoft was also ordered to share certain details of its Windows operating system with other software producers and to introduce a stripped-down version of Windows. In mid-2006 the EU, saying Microsoft failed to provide all required information, levied an additional penalty of 280.5 mil euros ($357 mil) and threatened further fines if the software maker continued to show noncompliance.

2006: **Apple** started using **Intel microprocessors** in its Macintosh computers. The Macintosh traditionally used microprocessors of a different design than the chips made by Intel and other companies that were found in more than 90% of PCs running Microsoft Windows.

About the Internet

Internet Milestones

The **Internet** is a vast and rapidly growing computer network of computer networks. In 1994, a total of 3 mil people (most of them in the U.S.) made use of it; by the end of 2005 he number of users worldwide exceeded 1 bil (Computer Industry Almanac Inc.).

The Internet is not owned or funded by any one institution, organization, or government. It has no CEO and is not a commercial service. Its development is guided by the Internet Society (ISOC), composed of volunteers. The ISOC appoints the Internet Architecture Board (IAB), which oversees issues of standards, network resources, etc.

Major historical highlights:

1969: **ARPANET**, an experimental 4-computer network, was established by the Advanced Research Projects Agency (ARPA) of the U.S. Defense Dept. 2 years later, ARPANET linked about 2 dozen computers ("hosts") at 15 sites, including MIT and Harvard.

1978: The 1st **spam**, or junk e-mail, message was sent over ARPANET.

1983: The protocol, or set of communications rules, known as **TCP/IP**, became the main networking protocol of ARPANET. TCP/IP facilitates connection between networks, and its adoption was tantamount to the birth of the Internet.

1983: The military portion of ARPANET was moved onto the MILNET.

1986: The U.S. National Science Foundation (NSF) launched **NSFNET**, the 1st large-scale network using Internet technology.

1988: **Internet Relay Chat** (IRC) was developed by Finnish student Jarkko Oikarinen, enabling people to communicate via the Internet in "real time."

1988: A **"worm"** crafted by Cornell Univ. graduate student Robert Morris, Jr., infected thousands of computers, shutting many down and causing millions of dollars of damage—the 1st known case of large-scale damage caused by a computer virus spread via the Internet.

1989: The World—the **1st commercial Internet service** provider supplying dial-up access—appeared.

1989-90: Tim Berners-Lee invented the **World Wide Web.** Begun as an environment in which scientists at the European Center for Nuclear Research in Switzerland could share information, it gradually evolved into a medium with text, graphics, audio, animation, and video.

1990: ARPANET was disbanded.

1991: The NSFNET was opened to commercial traffic.

1991: Berners-Lee introduced the **1st browser**, or software for accessing the Web.

1993: The U.S. National Center for Supercomputing Applications released versions of **Mosaic**, the 1st Web browser able to present both text and images in a single page, for Microsoft Windows, Unix systems running the X Window GUI, and the Apple Macintosh.

1994: Netscape Communications released the **Netscape Navigator** browser.

1995: Microsoft released its **Internet Explorer** browser but initially failed to make a dent in Netscape's dominance of the browser market. By 1998, Netscape's market share had fallen below 50%, while Internet Explorer's exceeded 25% and was growing rapidly.

1996: A group of universities launched **Internet2**, an advanced, high-performance network for the research community and a test bed for development of new capabilities that might find use in the commercial Internet.

1998: Under a contract with the U.S. Dept. of Commerce, the nonprofit Internet Corporation for Assigned Numbers and Names (ICANN) took over the management of such basic Internet functions as assignment of **domain names** and Internet (IP) addresses.

1999: Release of the free **Napster** file-sharing service enabled users to easily exchange files containing music or other content without regard to copyright restrictions. In 2001, a court ordered Napster to suspend operations; Napster users, however, switched to other file-sharing services, such as Morpheus and KaZaA. (Napster was later reconstituted as a for-pay music download service.)

2003: Niue, a self-governing Pacific island associated with New Zealand, became the 1st "country" to offer free **nationwide wireless access** to the Internet (using Wi-Fi technology).

2004: The Mozilla Foundation released the first official version of the open-source browser Mozilla Firefox, which quickly became popular. By mid-2006, Firefox held nearly 16% of the U.S. browser market, according to Dutch Web analysis firm OneStat.com, which put the Internet Explorer share at about 80%.

Internet Addresses
The fundamental part of an address on the Internet is called the domain. The final part of a domain name, known as the **top-level domain**, is its most basic part. For example, in *The World Almanac*'s web address—www. worldalmanac.com—com is the top-level domain.

So-called generic top-level domains, consisting of 3 or more letters, include:

Domain	What It Is
.aero	an organization in the air-transport industry
.biz	a business
.cat	a site associated with Catalan language and culture
.com	generally a commercial organization, business, or company
.coop	a nonprofit business cooperative, such as a rural electric coop
.edu	a 4-year higher-educational institution
.gov	a nonmilitary U.S. governmental entity, usually federal
.info	an informational site for an individual or organization, without restriction
.int	an international organization
.jobs	information about employment, such as job openings
.mil	a U.S. military organization
.mobi	a site providing content for mobile devices
.museum	a museum
.name	an individual
.net	suggested for a network administration, but actually used by a wide variety of sites
.org	suggested for a nonprofit organization, but actually used by a wide variety of sites
.pro	a professional, such as an accountant, lawyer, or physician
.tel	Internet communications identifier for an individual or organization
.travel	information about travel

Domain names with 2 letters are generally for countries or regions. The **top-level domain** .us, for instance, is available to persons, organizations, and entities in the U.S. More examples: .eu (European Union), .jp (Japan), .ru (Russia), .uk (United Kingdom).

As of mid-2006, discussions were under way to establish additional generic top-level domains, such as .post (for postal services) and .xxx (sexually explicit sites).

Safety and Security on the Internet
Common sense dictates some basic security rules:
• Pick passwords that are difficult to guess, preferably consisting of both letters and numbers, and perhaps also other symbols (if permitted). It's a bad idea to use the same password at multiple websites.
• Do not give out your phone number, address, credit card number, or other personal information, unless needed for a transaction at a site you trust.
• If you feel someone is being threatening or dangerous, inform your Internet service provider.
• Use protective "firewall," antivirus, and antispyware software to guard your system against attacks by hackers. Be sure to keep the software up to date.
• Be careful about opening e-mail from unknown correspondents.
• If you have programs that can make use of macros—bits of auxiliary coding that are meant to play a helpful role but can be taken advantage of by some viruses—make sure the programs' macro virus protection (if any) is turned on. Keep macros disabled if you do not know what you might want to use them for.
• Users of so-called **peer-to-peer** (P2P) file-sharing networks, such as KaZaA, should open up only part of their computer system to sharing—not the entire hard drive.
• Security flaws turn up from time to time in operating systems, Web browsers, and other software, and when the manufacturers provide **patches** to solve the problem, it is usually advisable to install these fixes. If a fix is not available for a serious security problem, you may want to consider switching to an alternative program.

Malware. Software designed to harm a computer system—such as a virus (malicious code carried within a program) or a worm (a self-contained malicious program)—may be picked up from the Internet or elsewhere, received on a disk, or communicated via e-mail.

IT'S A RECORD: The first "spam" e-mail message was sent by Digital Equipment Corporation (DEC) marketing representative Gary Thuerk on May 1, 1978. The e-mail, advertising new DEC computers, was mailed to 593 users of the Advanced Research Projects Agency Network (ARPANET), the forerunner of the Internet.

Some malicious software may install a "back door" on an infected system, giving access to a hacker; may attempt to turn off any antivirus program on the system; or may try to log the user's keystrokes.

A **Trojan horse** is computer code concealed within harmless code or data that is capable of taking control and causing damage. It can be used to mount a massive **"denial-of-service"** attack, which overwhelms targeted computers by inundating them with messages. The infected computers, acting under hacker control without their owners' knowledge, are called **zombies**, and the network of zombie computers that carry out the attack is called a **botnet**.

Spyware—software that observes your computer activity without your knowledge—is often regarded as a type of malware. Spyware programs may gain entry to your machine via a Trojan horse. They may record your keystrokes and report passwords or other personal information to a hacker. Some may flood your screen with ads.

Phishing. A popular scam is **phishing**—the use of a forged e-mail message purportedly from a respectable organization, such as a bank, to elicit such personal data. The e-mail typically contains a hyperlink that leads to a fabricated website resembling the site of the ostensible sender. A simple way to avoid falling victim to a phishing scam is to refuse to click on links in e-mails from companies where you have an account. If you want to visit such a company's website, open your browser and manually enter the site's normal address.

Spam. Junk e-mail, or **spam**, can be a time-wasting annoyance or worse—spam may hawk pornography or products dangerous to health, seek to defraud the recipient, may carry a destructive virus, or turn the recipient's machine into a zombie that stores illicit material, takes part in a denial-of-service attack, or distributes spam. Net administrators worry that the flood of spam may cause delays or even a breakdown in the flow of Internet traffic.

In 2003 Congress enacted a law that attempted to restrict spam, but it had little effect on the ever-increasing volume of spam received on e-mail accounts.

While filtering software can help reduce the deluge of spam—some e-mail programs include filters—it is not completely accurate. Experts recommend that you be wary of revealing your e-mail address as you surf the Web.

Emerging Computer Technologies

Progress in miniaturization and computing power in recent decades has been impressive. But there are physical limits to the ways electrons can be shunted around tiny circuits in a wafer of silicon. For this reason, researchers have been looking into alternative technologies that might someday deliver performance unthinkable with traditional semiconductors. Some of the most interesting approaches deal with the very small—the **world of molecules** and the even more minuscule **subatomic realm** where the strange laws of quantum mechanics come into play.

Molecules

Among molecules with a high profile in computer-technology research, the two most intriguing are the **carbon nanotube** and **DNA** (deoxyribonucleic acid), the basic vehicle of heredity in the biological world.

Nanotube Devices: Carbon nanotubes have a simple structure and astounding physical characteristics. They consist of carbon atoms, which may be arranged in a hexagonal pattern—like chicken wire. This chicken wire structure is rolled up to form a tube that may be as narrow as 1 nanometer. (A nanometer is one-billionth of a meter, or 0.0000000000254 inch, that is, about 50,000 times thinner than a human hair.) Carbon nanotubes are extraordinarily strong and hard. They are resistant to heat, cold, magnetism, and radiation. Depending on how their atoms are arranged, they can be fine conductors of electricity or, conversely, they may resist its flow. The tiny tubes potentially offer a way to **overcome the limitations of** the **silicon chips and copper wires** used in today's computers.

Engineers have already developed carbon nanotube transistors that can carry as much as 1,000 times the current accommodated by the copper wires used in silicon chips. Today's computer processors, however, may have a billion transistors or more. Still to be solved are the problems of how to make similarly enormous numbers of high-quality nanotubes and how to arrange them in circuits—while keeping costs down.

Nanotubes' potential is enormous. Their use in computer storage and memory devices raises the prospect of ultra-high capacity hard drives as well as fast random-access memory (RAM) that, unlike today's RAM chips, would not lose its contents when the power is turned off. Such storage devices could make possible instant-booting computers, handheld computers with upwards of 10 gigabytes of memory, and MP3 players that hold exponentially more songs than today's devices.

DNA Computing: DNA carries a living organism's genetic code. Instead of the 0 and 1 used in computers' binary code, the genetic code uses four basic units called bases, which pack a lot of information into a single strand of DNA. They are usually symbolized A, C, G, and T. In an organism, this information is used, with the help of RNA (ribonucleic acid, a molecule related to DNA) and enzymes, to make proteins as well as replicate DNA molecules. Researchers who would like to employ DNA in computing see particularly great potential in using multiple DNA molecules "in parallel," thereby generating enormous computing power, since a trillion or more strands of DNA could be contained in a space as small as a drop of water.

The **first demonstration of the manipulation of DNA** to solve a simple mathematical problem was made in 1994 by Univ. of Southern California computer scientist Leonard M. Adleman. In 2001, researchers at the Weizmann Institute of Science in Israel created a test-tube computer able to do elementary computations; DNA played the role of software governing the action of enzymes (the "hardware").

Aside from its rudimentary capabilities, this test-tube computer was rather impractical because accessing the results required substantial equipment. To get around this limitation, the Israeli scientists developed a computer that would not only compute but would act on the results. In 2004, they reported the creation of a DNA test-tube computer that could detect the presence of cancer genes and thereupon release a drug. Meanwhile, in 2003 a pair of U.S. scientists developed the first interactive DNA computing system, an enzyme-driven device called MAYA that played unbeatable tic-tac-toe. Its human opponent made moves by putting DNA into little wells making up the game board; each well contained enzymes that acted as "logic gates" controlling the device's response to the input data.

Quantum Effects

Much of the buzz associated with quantum computing in recent years has been about computing systems that take advantage of the peculiarities of quantum mechanics to implement parallel processing on an extravagantly huge scale. Conventional computers operate in a binary universe where statements are either true or false, switches are either on or off. In this universe, the bit, the basic unit of information, has a value of either 1 or 0. In the quantum world, a quantum bit, or qubit, can be both on and off at the same time. The two states are said to be "superposed." Because of this simultaneity of values, a quantum computer using 300 qubits could, in theory, speedily carry out more calculations than the number of atoms in the known universe.

Scientists **working to build a practical quantum computer** have to confront a number of difficulties. For example, there is the question of how to physically implement qubits. Another big issue is how to extract the results; in the quantum world, the mere act of observing or measuring can cause superposed states to collapse into one state.

The first demonstration of a working quantum computer was carried out by California researchers in 1998. The experimental device had just two qubits: the carbon and hydrogen atoms in a molecule of chloroform, which were manipulated with a variation on the magnetic resonance imaging used in medicine. Subsequent quantum computing experiments have been done with slightly more qubits (as many as 12 by mid-2006), but the problems solved by the devices have been only rudimentary. A variety of methods have been proposed for constructing quantum computers, including the use of carbon nanotubes as mechanical cubits.

Cryptography of the Future

Today's encryption systems for protecting information transmitted via such channels as the Internet tend to rely on mathematical problems that would take an enormous—hopefully unfeasible—amount of time and effort to solve. For example, one of the most popular encryption methods, called **RSA** (from the initials of its inventors), depends on the fact that it is very hard to find the prime factors of a very large number—that is, the prime numbers that produce the number when multiplied by each other.

This approach works for now, but **what if mathematicians make a breakthrough?** As it happens, one of the most celebrated unsolved problems in mathematics, the so-called Riemann hypothesis, deals with the pattern that might lurk behind the seeming randomness of prime numbers. The Clay Mathematics Institute of Cambridge, MA, has promised $1 mil to anyone who can prove the hypothesis. A successful proof could lead to development of an easy way to find the factors of large primes, thereby bringing, notes British mathematician Marcus du Sautoy, "the whole of e-commerce to its knees overnight." A proof was proposed by U.S. mathematician Louis de Branges in 2004, but it is exceedingly abstruse and as of mid-2006 had not won acceptance.

Another potential threat to secure encryption comes from **quantum computing**. In 1994, Bell Laboratories computer scientist Peter Shor demonstrated that a sizable quantum computer, because of its unconventional properties, could find the factors of a large number reasonably quickly.

Paradoxically, quantum physics could also become the savior of secure encryption. So-called quantum cryptography, whose origins date back to the late 1980s, utilizes such fundamental quantum concepts as the **Heisenberg uncertainty principle** (it is impossible to measure one property of a quantum system without perturbing a second one) and the principle of entanglement (two separate quantum systems that interacted at one time may still share some information). The keys required for encrypting and decrypting messages are represented in this instance by a pattern of particles of light, or photons, with certain characteristics. Interception by an eavesdropper will leave obvious traces, revealing that the key has been detected. In theory, surreptitious eavesdropping would be impossible.

The **first commercial quantum-cryptographic systems** came on the market in 2003, for communication between two points. Transmission over large distances remained a major hurdle—as of early 2006, 90 mi or so was the farthest achieved. The first network to use quantum cryptography went into operation in 2004, connecting several sites in the Boston area by underground optical fiber links, over which encryption keys are sent. A wireless link was added in 2005. Called the DARPA Quantum Network, the project was funded by the Pentagon's Defense Advanced Research Projects Agency (DARPA) and built by BBN Technologies, the company that played the lead role in the creation of ARPANET, the forerunner of the Internet. The purpose of the project was to foster the development of hardware and software facilitating quantum cryptography over a network and to demonstrate its practicality.

New Wave of Microprocessors

Microprocessors are the brains of computers. For decades the semiconductor industry has steadily raised the capabilities of its most up-to-date microprocessors, more or less reflecting a prediction originally made in 1965 by Gordon Moore, a co-founder of leading chip maker Intel. In its most common version, "Moore's law" holds that the number of transistors on a chip will double every 18 months or so. Industry pundits say technological advances may permit this pattern to continue for a while longer, but at some point it will become impossible to cram any more transistors into a finite space. In 2005 and 2006 the two leading chip makers—Intel and AMD—introduced new ways of enhancing microprocessor capabilities.

Energy Efficiency. Gains in chip speed and performance have often come at a high cost: increased electricity consumption and heat production. One way manufacturers can try to get around the problem is to revamp their microprocessors' internal design, or "microarchitecture," to make the chips run more efficiently. Since the new chips are more energy efficient, they should generate less heat, which means fewer fans are needed for cooling. This can translate into machines that occupy less space and run more quietly. Greater energy efficiency should mean longer battery life for laptop users.

Multi-core Processors. Both AMD and Intel also introduced microprocessors with dual cores—two processors united on a single chip. Intel's new chips are based on a next-generation design trademarked under the name "Core" and have supplanted older Pentiums in desktops, laptops, servers, and workstations. This doubling of processor power is good for multitasking—the running of multiple programs at the same time—and it also can enable more efficient operation of individual programs, specifically those that are written to take advantage of the dual-core feature. Computers with more than one processor were first introduced years ago, but they were too costly for general use. The new microprocessors with two "cores" on a single chip are just a little more expensive than traditional single-core chips. Looking down the road, both AMD and Intel plan to roll out four-core, or quad-core, chips by 2007. Consumers contemplating getting a new computer with a dual-core chip should, however, keep in mind the slightly higher cost of such chips and also the fact that it will be a while before most software on the market is optimized to take advantage of dual-core

processing. Individuals who do little multitasking but need fast performance may find it makes more sense to buy a machine with a top-level single-core chip, which is likely to operate at a higher speed than the dual-core chips on the immediate horizon.

Hyperthreading. In some of Intel's new chips there is a feature called hyperthreading. This enables software to use different parts of the processor at the same time, in effect turning a single-core chip into two virtual cores (or a dual-core chip into four virtual cores). This allows, for example, video and sound enthusiasts to edit digital video or audio while running a virus scan in the background, with little or no slow-down in software performance.

Graphics and Physics Processing. Game players and other PC users who use graphic-intensive programs favor machines equipped with a special graphics processing unit (GPU), or video card, which frees up the CPU for other tasks. Over the years graphics processors have grown more powerful and sophisticated, capable of generating better and better pictures. But a truly realistic depiction of an action scene would convey the complex physical interactions involved in, say, an explosion, or the way a garment hangs on a person's body. In early 2006, Ageia Technologies introduced a special chip for PCs called PhysX that serves as a "physics processing unit" capable of handling the massive calculations required for such scenes. Meanwhile, companies such as Sony and Microsoft released new models of their dedicated gaming machines, (Xbox 360 and Playstation 3 respectively) that also offered enhanced processing capabilities, including improved physics rendering.

Asynchronous Processors. One processor that appeared in 2006 had little or no immediate relevance for PCs but huge potential long-term significance. PCs are typically synchronous machines; they operate at a fixed speed in accordance with a clock circuit. The new product, from the Dutch company Handshake Solutions and the English firm ARM, was the world's first commercial asynchronous, or clockless, processor. It was expected to one day find use in consumer electronics and automobiles. Since an asynchronous processor lacks a fixed clock speed, its circuits operate only when busy, and only at the speed needed. This may make the chip extremely efficient, with very low power consumption.

> **IT'S A FACT:** According to a July 2006 report by the Pew Internet & American Life Project, 39% of internet users, or 57 mil American adults, read online weblogs (blogs), and about 12 mil American adults, or 8% of all internet users, say they maintain their own blog. The highest percentage of bloggers, 37%, said that the main focus of their blog was to "share personal experiences." Coming in second, 11% of bloggers said that reporting and commenting on politics and government was their main focus.

Internet Lingo

The following abbreviations are sometimes used on the Internet documents and in e-mail.

BTW	By the way	**GOK**	God only knows	**LOL**	Laughing out loud
CBLO	See below	**GTG**	Got to go	**PLS**	Please
F2F	Face to face; a personal meeting	**HHOK**	Ha, ha—only kidding	**ROTFL**	Rolling on the floor laughing
FCOL	For crying out loud	**IMHO**	In my humble opinion	**TAFN**	That's all for now
FWIW	For what it's worth	**IMO**	In my opinion	**TTFN**	Ta-ta for now

Emoticons, or **smileys,** are a series of typed characters that, when turned sideways, resemble a face and express an emotion. Here are some smileys often encountered on the Internet.

:-)	Smile	:-D	Laugh	:-(	Unhappy	:-b..	Drooling
;-)	Wink	:-*	Kiss	:-o	Surprised	{*}	A hug and a kiss

Nations With the Most Personal Computers in Use

Source: Computer Industry Almanac, Inc., for year end 2005

Rank	Country	PCs In Use[1]	% of Worldwide Total
1.	United States	230.4	25.5
2.	Japan	73.7	8.2
3.	China	63.5	7.0
4.	Germany	50.4	5.6
5.	United Kingdom	38.6	4.3
6.	France	32.4	3.6
7.	South Korea	28.4	3.1
8.	Italy	26.0	2.9
9.	Canada	23.8	2.6
10.	Russia	22.8	2.5
11.	Brazil	22.4	2.5
12.	India	17.0	1.9
13.	Australia	14.6	1.6
14.	Mexico	12.9	1.4
15.	Spain	12.0	1.3
	Top 15 Total	**668.9**	**74.0**
	Worldwide Total	**903.9**	**100.0**

(1) In millions.

Nations With the Most Internet Users

Source: Computer Industry Almanac, Inc., for year end 2005

Rank	Country	Internet Users[1]	% of Worldwide Users
1.	United States	197.8	18.3
2.	China	119.5	11.1
3.	Japan	86.3	8.0
4.	India	50.6	4.7
5.	Germany	46.3	4.3
6.	United Kingdom	35.8	3.3
7.	South Korea	33.9	3.1
8.	Italy	28.8	2.7
9.	France	28.8	2.7
10.	Brazil	25.9	2.4
11.	Russia	23.7	2.2
12.	Canada	21.9	2.0
13.	Indonesia	18.0	1.7
14.	Mexico	16.9	1.6
15.	Spain	15.8	1.5
	Top 15 Total	**750.0**	**69.4**
	Worldwide Total	**1,081.0**	**100.0**

(1) In millions.

U.S. Broadband Internet Access

Changes in the percentage of each group who have broadband connections at home

Source: Horrigan, John B., Home Broadband Adoption 2006, Pew Internet & American Life Project, May 28, 2006, URL: www.pew internet.org/PPF/r/184/report_display.asp

	% with broadband at home (2005)	% with broadband at home (2006)	Percentage increase, 2005-06
Total	30	42	40
Gender			
Male	31	45	45
Female	27	38	41
Age			
18-29	38	55	45
30-49	36	50	39
50-64	27	38	41
65+	8	13	63
Race/ethnicity			
White (not hispanic)	31	42	35
Black (not hispanic)	14	31	121
Hispanic (English speaking)	28	41	46

	% with broadband at home (2005)	% with broadband at home (2006)	Percentage increase, 2005-06
Educational attainment			
Less than High School	10	17	70
High School grad	20	31	55
Some college	35	47	34
College +	47	62	32
Household income			
Under $30K	15	21	40
$30K-$50K	27	43	59
$50K-$75	35	48	37
Over $75	57	68	19
Community type			
Urban	31	44	42
Suburban	33	46	39
Rural	18	25	39

Note: 2005 Data comes from the Pew Internet Project's combined January-March tracking survey of 4,402 adults; 1,265 were home broadband users. 2006 data comes from the Pew Internet Project's February 15 through April 6 survey of 4,001 adults; 1,562 were home broadband users.

Most-Visited Websites, July 2006

Source: comScore Media Metrix, Inc.

Rank	Website*	Visitors[1]	Rank	Website*	Visitors[1]
1.	Yahoo! Sites	129,439	11.	Weather Channel, The	35,021
2.	Time Warner Network	121,068	12.	Apple Computer, Inc.	31,102
3.	Microsoft Sites	117,791	13.	Viacom Digital	30,767
4.	Google Sites	103,860	14.	CNET Networks	30,468
5.	eBay	75,814	15.	Adobe Sites	30,122
6.	MYSPACE.COM	54,522	16.	Expedia Inc.	29,724
7.	Ask Network	52,061	17.	Monster Worldwide	28,409
8.	Amazon Sites	46,788	18.	Wikipedia Sites	28,121
9.	New York Times Digital	38,133	19.	United Online, Inc	26,788
10.	Verizon Communications Corporation	36,605	20.	Wal-Mart	26,550

*In some cases, represents an aggregation of commonly owned domain names. (1) Number of visitors, in thousands, who visited Website at least once in June 2006.

Internet Directory to Selected Sites

The Websites listed are but a sampling of what is available. For some others, see; the Where to Get Help directory (Health), Business Directory (Consumer Information), Sports Directory, Travel and Tourism, Associations and Societies, 100 Most Populous U.S. Cities, States of the U.S., U.S. Government, and Nations of the World.

Online Service Providers

America Online
www.aol.com
CompuServe
www.compuserve.com
EarthLink
www.earthlink.net
Juno
www.juno.com
Microsoft Network
www.msn.com
Road Runner
www.rr.com
SBC Yahoo!
sbc.yahoo.com

Directories

Addresses.com
www.addresses.com
Bigfoot (e-mail addresses and white page listings)
www.bigfoot.com
InfoSpace, the Ultimate Directory
www.infospace.com
People Search
people.yahoo.com
Switchboard, the People and Business Directory
www.switchboard.com

Security and Screening

Anti-Phishing Working Group
www.antiphishing.org
National Cyber Security Alliance
www.staysafeonline.org
The National Fraud Information Center
www.fraud.org
U.S. Computer Emergency Readiness Team (CERT)
www.us-cert.gov

Auctions

eBay
www.ebay.com
uBid Online Auction
www.ubid.com
Yahoo! Auctions
auctions.shopping.yahoo.com

Bookstores

AddAll Book Search
www.addall.com
Barnes and Noble
www.barnesandnoble.com
Powell's City of Books
www.powells.com

Chat Sites

America Online
www.aim.com
Excite
communicate.excite.com
IVILLAGE: The Women's Network
www.ivillage.com
MYSPACE
myspace.com
Yahoo
chat.yahoo.com

Children's Sites

American Library Association-Great Web Sites for Kids
www.ala.org/greatsites

FirstGov for Kids
www.kids.gov
Nick.com (Nickelodeon)
www.nick.com
Scholastic
www.scholastic.com/kids
Sports Illustrated for Kids
www.siforkids.com
Time for Kids
www.timeforkids.com
Weekly Reader
www.weeklyreader.com
World Almanac for Kids
www.worldalmanacforkids.com
Yahooligans (for homework help sites)
www.yahooligans.com

Economic Data

Bureau of Economic Analysis
www.bea.gov
Bureau of Labor Statistics
www.bls.gov
Economics Statistics Briefing Room
www.whitehouse.gov/fsbr/esbr.html
Economy at a Glance
stats.bls.gov/eag/
Office of Management and Budget
www.gpoaccess.gov/usbudget
Statistical Abstract of the United States
www.census.gov/compendia/statab
STAT-USA/Internet (a subscription-based government service)
www.stat-usa.gov

Entertainment

Eonline
www.eonline.com
Boing Boing
boingboing.net
The Internet Movie Database
www.imdb.com
Movies.com
www.movies.go.com
The Movie Times
www.the-movie-times.com
Variety
www.variety.com
YouTube
www.youtube.com

Family Resources

Babies Online
www.babiesonline.com
BabyCenter
www.babycenter.com
FamilyFun.Com
familyfun.go.com
KidsHealth.org
www.kidshealth.org
KidSource Online
www.kidsource.com
Parenthood.com
parenthood.com
Parenting on iVillage
www.parenting.ivillage.com
Screen It! Entertainment Reviews for Parents
www.screenit.com

Greeting Cards, Electronic

123 Greetings
www.123greetings.com
1001 Postcards
www.postcards.org
Blue Mountain Arts
www.bluemountain.com
E-CARDS
www.ecards.com
Egreetings Network
www.egreetings.com
Zero to Three
www.zerotothree.org

Health

Drugstore.com
www.drugstore.com
Healthfinder
www.healthfinder.gov
MayoClinic.com
www.mayoclinic.com
The Merck Manual
www.merck.com
National Institutes of Health
health.nih.gov
WebMD
www.webmd.com

Job Search Sites

CareerBuilder.com
www.careerbuilder.com
Hotjobs
hotjobs.yahoo.com
Monster
www.monster.com

Money Management

American Stock Exchange
www.amex.com
E*TRADE
www.etrade.com
Internal Revenue Service
www.irs.gov
MarketWatch
www.marketwatch.com
NASDAQ
www.nasdaq.com
New York Stock Exchange
www.nyse.com

Music

All Music Guide
www.allmusic.com
BBC Music
www.bbc.co.uk/music
Classical Net
www.classical.net
MusicMoz (the open music project)
www.musicmoz.org

Online Maps/Directions

Google Maps
maps.google.com
MapQuest
www.mapquest.com
Multimap.com
www.multimap.com

News

The Associated Press
www.ap.org
BBC Online
news.bbc.co.uk
Cable News Network
www.cnn.com

Fox News
www.foxnews.com
Los Angeles Times
www.latimes.com
MSNBC
www.msnbc.com
The New York Times
www.nytimes.com
NPR
www.npr.org
Reuters
www.reuters.com
USA Today
www.usatoday.com
Wall Street Journal
www.wsj.com
Washington Post
www.washingtonpost.com
World Press Review Online
www.worldpress.org

Reference

CIA Publications and Reports
www.cia.gov/cia/publications
Dictionary.com
www.dictionary.com
Explore the Internet; The Library of Congress
www.loc.gov
Great Books Online
www.bartleby.com
Libweb: Library Servers via WWW
sunsite.berkeley.edu/Libweb
Merriam-Webster Online
www.m-w.com
Refdesk
www.refdesk.com
Roget's Thesaurus
www.thesaurus.com
Snopes.com (evaluates rumors, urban legends)
www.snopes.com
Wikipedia
www.wikipedia.org

Shopping Sites

Amazon.com Inc.
www.amazon.com
Buy.com
www.buy.com
Overstock.com
www.overstock.com

Sports

ESPN
www.espn.go.com
Sports Illustrated
www.sportsillustrated.cnn.com
Sports Network
www.sportsnetwork.com
Sporting News
www.sportingnews.com

Weather

National Center for Environmental Prediction (includes links to Storm Prediction Center sites)
www.ncep.noaa.gov
National Weather Service
www.nws.noaa.gov
Weather Channel
www.weather.com

Weddings/Registries

The Knot
www.theknot.com

Selected Fun and Odd Websites[1]

The following is a sampling of odd or humorous Websites selected by the editors of *The World Almanac*.

Name	URL	Description
Bathroom Diaries	www.thebathroomdiaries.com	Bathroom stories from around the world
Googlism	www.googlism.com	Type in your name and see what the Internet has to say about you
History Buff	www.historybuff.com/audio/index.html	Audio files of famous people from history
Mug Shots	www.mugshots.net	Mug shots of naughty celebrities
Pointless Web Sites	www.pointlesssites.com	From the mildly interesting to the most mundane
Roadside America	www.roadsideamerica.com	Offbeat Tourist Attractions in America
Seat Guru	www.seatguru.com	Find out where NOT to sit when you book your next flight
Snap Bubbles	www.snapbubbles.com	Pop some virtual bubble wrap
Straight Dope	www.straightdope.com	Answers to life's many pointless questions
UFO Center	www.ufocenter.com	Want to report a UFO sighting?
Where's George?	www.wheresgeorge.com	Tracking $1 bills
World Beard Championships	www.worldbeardchampionships.com	See some of the finest facial hair in the world
World License Plates	www.worldlicenseplates.com	Ever wondered what a license plate from Burundi looks like?

(1) These sites were viewed by the editors, but content is subject to change and *The World Almanac* cannot take responsibility for contents.

The monthly World Almanac e-newsletter provides updates on interesting Websites, as well as on current events, offbeat news, celebrity birthdays, and obituaries, among other features. To subscribe, visit www.worldalmanac.com or e-mail newsletter@waegroup.com.

Top-Selling Software, 2005-2006

Source: The NPD Group/Retail Tracking Service
(based on unit U.S. sales, June 2005-2006[1])

All Software
1. TurboTax 2005 Deluxe w/State, Intuit
2. Spy Sweeper, Webroot
3. Norton Antivirus 2006, Symantec
4. MS Office 2003 Student/Teacher Ed, Microsoft
5. Norton Internet Security 2006, Symantec
6. Taxcut 2005 Deluxe w/State, H&R Block
7. Norton Antivirus 2005, Symantec
8. World Of Warcraft, Vivendi
9. TurboTax 2005 Premier w/State, Intuit
10. PC-Cillin AntiVirus 11.0, Trend Micro

Business
1. MS Office 2003 Student/Teacher Ed, Microsoft
2. MS Office 2004 Student/Teacher Ed, Microsoft
3. Quicktime 7.0 Pro (PC), Apple
4. Quicktime 7.0 Pro (Mac), Apple
5. .Mac 4.0, Apple
6. MS Office 2003 Pro Upgr, Microsoft
7. MS Office 2003 Pro, Microsoft
8. MS Office 2003, Microsoft
9. iWork 2006, Apple
10. .Mac 3.5, Apple

Home Education
1. Dora The Explorer Dance To The Rescue, Atari
2. I Spy Fantasy, Scholastic
3. MS Student 2006, Microsoft
4. Instant Immersion Spanish 2.0, Topics Entertainment
5. I Spy Spooky Mansion Deluxe, Scholastic
6. Kid Pix 4 Deluxe, Riverdeep Interactive
7. Dora The Explorer Fairytale Adventure 3-Pk, Atari
8. Elementary School Success 2006 Deluxe, Topics Entertainment
9. Mavis Beacon Teaches Typing 17.0, Riverdeep Interactive
10. Nickelodeon Toon Twister, Scholastic

Finance
1. TurboTax 2005 Deluxe w/State, Intuit
2. Taxcut 2005 Deluxe w/State, H&R Block
3. TurboTax 2005 Premier w/State, Intuit
4. TurboTax 2005 Basic, Intuit
5. TurboTax 2005 Deluxe, Intuit
6. Quicken 2006, Intuit
7. QuickBooks 2006 Pro, Intuit
8. Quicken 2006 Deluxe, Intuit
9. MS Money 2006 Deluxe, Microsoft
10. Taxcut 2005 Standard, H&R Block

Imaging/Graphics
1. Adobe Photoshop Elements 4.0, Adobe
2. iLife 2006, Apple
3. Print Shop 21.0 Deluxe, Riverdeep Interactive
4. MS Digital Image 2006 Suite, Microsoft
5. Photo Explosion 2.0 Deluxe, Nova Development
6. Print Workshop 2006, Valusoft (THQ)
7. Adobe Photoshop Elements 4.0/Premiere Elements 2.0 Bundle, Adobe
8. Art Explosion Scrapbook Factory 3.0 Deluxe, Nova Development
9. Printmaster 16.0 Gold, Riverdeep Interactive
10. Print Shop 20.0 JC, Riverdeep Interactive

Operating System
1. MS Windows XP Home Ed Upgr, Microsoft
2. MS Windows XP Pro Upgr, Microsoft
3. Mac OS X 10.4 Tiger, Apple
4. MS Windows XP Home Ed, Microsoft
5. MS Windows XP Pro, Microsoft
6. MS Plus Super Pack, Microsoft
7. Mac OS X 10.4 Tiger Family Pack 5User, Applet
8. MS Virtual PC 7.0, Microsoft
9. Linux 10.0 Pro Ed, Novell
10. MS Windows Svr 2003 Clnt Acc OPEN Lic, Microsoft

PC Games
1. World Of Warcraft, Vivendi
2. MS Age Of Empires III, Microsoft
3. The Sims 2 Nightlife Expansion Pack, Electronic Arts
4. The Sims 2, Electronic Arts
5. Battlefield 2, Electronic Arts
6. Civilization IV, 2K Games (Take 2)
7. Call Of Duty 2, Activision
8. Roller Coaster Tycoon 3, Atari
9. The Sims 2 Open For Business Expansion Pack, Electronic Arts
10. Guild Wars, NCsoft

Personal Productivity
1. PSP Max Media Manager w/USB Link Cable, Datel
2. MS Streets & Trips 2006, Microsoft
3. MS Streets & Trips 2006 w/GPS Locator, Microsoft
4. Nero 7.0 Ultra Edition, Nero Inc
5. Easy CD & DVD Burning, Roxio
6. Easy Media Creator 8.0 Suite, Roxio
7. Street Atlas USA w/LT-20 GPS, DeLorme
8. MS Works 8.0, Microsoft
9. MS Streets & Trips 2005, Microsoft
10. Marine Aquarium 2.0, Encore

System Utilities
1. Spy Sweeper, Webroot
2. Norton Antivirus 2006, Symantec
3. Norton Internet Security 2006, Symantec
4. Norton Antivirus 2005, Symantec
5. PC-Cillin AntiVirus 11.0, Trend Micro
6. Norton Antivirus 2006 Upgr, Symantec
7. Norton Internet Security 2006 Upgr/Norton Goback 4.0 Upgr Bundle
8. Symantec, Norton Internet Security 2006/System Works 2006 Upgr Bundle, Symantec
9. Norton Internet Security 2005, Symantec
10. VirusScan 10.0, McAfee Inc.

(1) Some widely used software is often bundled with computers when sold; these are not included in sales figures above.

▶ **IT'S A FACT:** How often does online dating lead to long-term commitment? According a March 2006 survey by the Pew Internet & American Life Project, of the 16 mil adults who had ever gone online in search of romance, 17%, or 3 mil people, had either married or entered into long-term relationships with people they met through online dating sites.

TELECOMMUNICATIONS

Worldwide Telecommunications: Market Data (1990-2004)

Source: © International Telecommunication Union

	1990	1999	2000	2001	2002	2003	2004[3]
Total market revenue (billions of U.S. $)[1]	$508	$1,123	$1,210	$1,232	$1,314	$1,426	NA
Intl. phone traffic (billions of minutes)[2]	33	100	118	127	131	142	$145
Main telephone lines (millions)	520	905	983	1,053	1,086	1,140	1,207
Mobile cellular subscriptions (millions)	11	490	740	955	1,166	1,414	1,758

NA=not available. (1) Revenue from installation, subscription, and local, trunk, and international call charges. (2) From 1994 including traffic between countries of the former Soviet Union. (3) Preliminary.

Worldwide Use of Cellular Telephones, Year-End 2005

Source: © International Telecommunication Union, estimated; top countries or regions ranked by subscriptions per 100 pop.

Country/Region	Subscriptions (thousands)	per 100 pop.	Country/Region	Subscriptions (thousands)	per 100 pop.	Country/Region	Subscriptions (thousands)	per 100 pop.
Luxembourg	720.0	154.8	Taiwan, China	22,170.7	97.4	Korea (Rep.)	38,342.3	79.4
Lithuania	4,353.4	127.1	Netherlands	15,834.0	97.2	France	48,058.4	79.4
Italy	72,200.0	124.3	Spain	41,327.9	96.8	Guernsey	43.8	78.5
Hong Kong, China	8,693.4	123.5	Germany	79,200.0	95.8	Barbados	206.2	76.7
Macao, China	532.8	115.8	Jersey	83.9	95.3	Bermuda	49.0	76.6
Czech Republic	11,775.9	115.2	Sweden	8,436.5	93.3	Poland	29,166.0	75.7
Israel	7,757.0	112.4	Hungary	9,320.0	92.3	Réunion	579.2	75.5
Portugal	11,447.7	109.1	Qatar	716.8	92.2	Malaysia	19,545.0	75.2
Estonia	1,445.3	108.8	Switzerland	6,847.0	91.8	Martinique	295.4	74.8
Singapore	4,384.6	103.4	Australia	18,420.0	91.4	Japan	94,745.0	74.0
Iceland	304.0	103.4	Belgium	9,460.0	90.8	South Africa	33,960.0	71.6
Bahrain	748.7	103.0	Greece	10,042.6	90.3	Guadeloupe	314.7	71.0
Norway	4,754.5	102.9	Neth. Antilles	200.0	90.1	Seychelles	57.0	70.7
United Kingdom	61,091.0	102.2	Slovenia	1,759.2	89.4	Puerto Rico	2,682.0	68.8
Jamaica	2,700.0	101.9	Kuwait	2,379.8	88.6	Chile	10,569.6	67.8
Ireland	4,210.0	101.5	New Zealand	3,530.0	87.6	United States	201,650.0	67.6
United Arab Emirates	4,534.5	100.9	Cyprus	718.8	86.1	Antigua & Barbuda	54.0	67.1
Denmark	5,469.3	100.7	Slovak Republic	4,540.4	84.1	Croatia	2,983.9	65.6
Aruba	98.4	100.2	Russia	120,000.0	83.6	Serbia and Montenegro	5,229.0	64.0
Austria	8,160.0	99.8	Latvia	1,871.6	81.1			
Finland	5,231.0	99.7	Bulgaria	6,244.7	80.8	**World**	**2,168,433.6**	**34.0**
			Malta	324.0	80.8			

U.S. Cellular Telephone Subscribership, 1985–2005[1]

Source: The CTIA Semi-Annual Wireless Industry Survey. Used with permission of CTIA; in thousands of subscriptions[2]

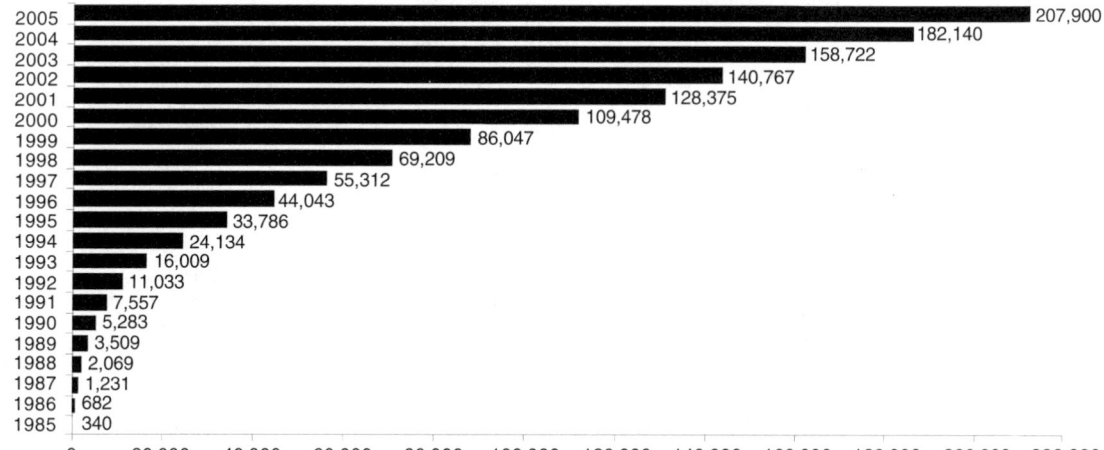

Year	Subscriptions (thousands)
2005	207,900
2004	182,140
2003	158,722
2002	140,767
2001	128,375
2000	109,478
1999	86,047
1998	69,209
1997	55,312
1996	44,043
1995	33,786
1994	24,134
1993	16,009
1992	11,033
1991	7,557
1990	5,283
1989	3,509
1988	2,069
1987	1,231
1986	682
1985	340

(1) In December. (2) Data may differ slightly from other sources.

U.S. Sales and Household Penetration, Selected Products[1], 1985-2004

Source: Consumer Electronics Association

	1985		1990		1995		2000		2003		2004	
	Sales[2]	% of all house- holds	Sales[2]	% of all house- holds	Sales[2]	% of all house- holds	Sales[2]	% of all house- holds	Sales[2]	% of all house- holds	Sales[2]	% of all house- holds
Cordless telephones	$280	11	$842	28	$1,141	55	$1,307	80	$1,268	82	$1,134	83
Pagers	—	—	118	1	300	11	750	23	729	17	675	13
Modems/Fax modems	10	0	191	2.7	770	16	1,564	55	1,419	64	1,386	64
Telephone answering devices	325	7	827	35	1,077	57	984	75	1,210	78	1,274	78
Cellular phones	116	0.1	1,098	5	2,574	29	8,995	60	9,163	70	10,538	70

(1) Data may differ slightly from other sources. (2) In millions of dollars.

Telephone Area Codes, by Number

As of Aug. 2006. For area codes listed by place, see pages 607-640.

Area Code	Location or Service	Area Code	Location or Service	Area Code	Location or Service	Area Code	Location or Service
201	New Jersey	403	Alberta	615	Tennessee	810	Michigan
202	District of Columbia	404	Georgia	616	Michigan	811	Pipeline excavation
203	Connecticut	405	Oklahoma	617	Massachusetts		damage prevention
204	Manitoba	406	Montana	618	Illinois	812	Indiana
205	Alabama	407	Florida	619	California	813	Florida
206	Washington	408	California	620	Kansas	814	Pennsylvania
207	Maine	409	Texas	623	Arizona	815	Illinois
208	Idaho	410	Maryland	626	California	816	Missouri
209	California	411	Directory Assistance	630	Illinois	817	Texas
210	Texas	412	Pennsylvania	631	New York	818	California
211	Community Info.	413	Massachusetts	636	Missouri	819	Quebec
212	New York	414	Wisconsin	641	Iowa	828	North Carolina
213	California	415	California	646	New York	829	Dominican Republic
214	Texas	416	Ontario	647	Ontario	830	Texas
215	Pennsylvania	417	Missouri	649	Turks & Caicos Islands	831	California
216	Ohio	418	Quebec	650	California	832	Texas
217	Illinois	419	Ohio	651	Minnesota	843	South Carolina
218	Minnesota	423	Tennessee	660	Missouri	845	New York
219	Indiana	425	Washington	661	California	847	Illinois
224	Illinois	430	Texas	662	Mississippi	848	New Jersey
225	Louisiana	432	Texas	664	Montserrat	850	Florida
226	Ontario	434	Virginia	670	N. Mariana Islands	856	New Jersey
228	Mississippi	435	Utah	671	Guam	857	Massachusetts
229	Georgia	440	Ohio	678	Georgia	858	California
231	Michigan	441	Bermuda	682	Texas	859	Kentucky
234	Ohio	443	Maryland	684	American Samoa	860	Connecticut
239	Florida	450	Quebec	700	IC Services	862	New Jersey
240	Maryland	456	Inbound International	701	North Dakota	863	Florida
242	Bahamas	469	Texas	702	Nevada	864	South Carolina
246	Barbados	473	Grenada	703	Virginia	865	Tennessee
248	Michigan	478	Georgia	704	North Carolina	866	Toll-Free Service
250	British Columbia	479	Arkansas	705	Ontario	867	Yukon, NW Terr., Nunavut
251	Alabama	480	Arizona	706	Georgia	868	Trinidad & Tobago
252	North Carolina	484	Pennsylvania	707	California	869	St. Kitts & Nevis
253	Washington	500	Personal Comm. Serv.	708	Illinois	870	Arkansas
254	Texas	501	Arkansas	709	Newfoundland	876	Jamaica
256	Alabama	502	Kentucky	710	U.S. Government	877	Toll-Free Service
260	Indiana	503	Oregon	711	Telecommunications	878	Pennsylvania
262	Wisconsin	504	Louisiana		Relay Service (TRS)	881	Toll-Free Service
264	Anguilla	505	New Mexico	712	Iowa	882	Toll-Free Service
267	Pennsylvania	506	New Brunswick	713	Texas	888	Toll-Free Service
268	Antigua/Barbuda	507	Minnesota	714	California	900	Premium Service
269	Michigan	508	Massachusetts	715	Wisconsin	901	Tennessee
270	Kentucky	509	Washington	716	New York	902	Nova Scotia
276	Virginia	510	California	717	Pennsylvania	903	Texas
281	Texas	511	Traffic Info.	718	New York	904	Florida
284	British Virgin Islands	512	Texas	719	Colorado	905	Ontario
289	Ontario	513	Ohio	720	Colorado	906	Michigan
301	Maryland	514	Quebec	724	Pennsylvania	907	Alaska
302	Delaware	515	Iowa	727	Florida	908	New Jersey
303	Colorado	516	New York	731	Tennessee	909	California
304	West Virginia	517	Michigan	732	New Jersey	910	North Carolina
305	Florida	518	New York	734	Michigan	911	Emergency
306	Saskatchewan	519	Ontario	740	Ohio	912	Georgia
307	Wyoming	520	Arizona	754	Florida	913	Kansas
308	Nebraska	530	California	757	Virginia	914	New York
309	Illinois	540	Virginia	758	St. Lucia	915	Texas
310	California	541	Oregon	760	California	916	California
311	Non-Emergency Access	551	New Jersey	763	Minnesota	917	New York
312	Illinois	559	California	765	Indiana	918	Oklahoma
313	Michigan	561	Florida	767	Dominica	919	North Carolina
314	Missouri	562	California	769	Mississippi	920	Wisconsin
315	New York	563	Iowa	770	Georgia	925	California
316	Kansas	567	Ohio	772	Florida	928	Arizona
317	Indiana	570	Pennsylvania	773	Illinois	931	Tennessee
318	Louisiana	571	Virginia	774	Massachusetts	936	Texas
319	Iowa	573	Missouri	775	Nevada	937	Ohio
320	Minnesota	574	Indiana	778	British Columbia	939	Puerto Rico
321	Florida	580	Oklahoma	780	Alberta	940	Texas
323	California	585	New York	781	Massachusetts	941	Florida
325	Texas	586	Michigan	784	St. Vincent & Gren.	947	Michigan
330	Ohio	600	(Canadian Services)	785	Kansas	949	California
334	Alabama	601	Mississippi	786	Florida	951	California
336	North Carolina	602	Arizona	787	Puerto Rico	952	Minnesota
337	Louisiana	603	New Hampshire	800	Toll-Free Service	954	Florida
339	Massachusetts	604	British Columbia	801	Utah	956	Texas
340	U.S. Virgin Islands	605	South Dakota	802	Vermont	970	Colorado
345	Cayman Islands	606	Kentucky	803	South Carolina	971	Oregon
347	New York	607	New York	804	Virginia	972	Texas
351	Massachusetts	608	Wisconsin	805	California	973	New Jersey
352	Florida	609	New Jersey	806	Texas	978	Massachusetts
360	Washington	610	Pennsylvania	807	Ontario	979	Texas
361	Texas	611	Repair Service	808	Hawaii	980	North Carolina
386	Florida	612	Minnesota	809	Dominican Republic	985	Louisiana
401	Rhode Island	613	Ontario			989	Michigan
402	Nebraska	614	Ohio				

CONSUMER INFORMATION

Business Directory

Listed below are major U.S. corporations offering products and services to consumers. Information as of Sept. 2006. Alphabetization is by first key word. Listings generally include examples of products offered.

Company Name (NYSE/NASDAQ symbol); Address; Telephone Number; Website; Top Executive; Business, Products, or Services.

A&P: *see* Great Atlantic & Pacific Tea Co.

Abbott Laboratories (ABT); 100 Abbott Park Rd., Abbott Park, IL 60064; (847) 937-6100; www.abbott.com; Miles D. White; develops and manuf. pharmaceutical, nutritional, and hospital prods.

Aetna, Inc. (AET); 151 Farmington Ave., Hartford, CT 06156; (860) 273-0123; www.aetna.com; John W. Rowe; health insurance, financial services.

AFLAC, Inc. (AFL); 1932 Wynnton Rd., Columbus, GA 31999; (706) 323-3431; www.aflac.com; Daniel P. Amos; supplemental health and life insurance.

Alaska Air Group (ALK); 19300 International Blvd., Seattle, WA 98188; (206) 392-5040; www.alaskaair.com; William S. Ayer; air travel (Alaska Air, Horizon Air).

Alberto-Culver (ACV); 2525 Armitage Ave., Melrose Park, IL 60160; (708) 450-3000; www.alberto.com; Carol Lavin Bernick; hair care (VO5), consumer prods. (Mrs. Dash, Sugar Twin), personal care prods. (St. Ives), Sally Beauty Supply stores.

Albertson's LLC; 250 Parkcenter Blvd., Boise, ID 83706; (208) 395-6200; www.albertsons.com; Robert Miller; supermarkets.

Alcoa Inc. (AA); 201 Isabella St., Pittsburgh, PA 15212; (412) 553-4545; www.alcoa.com; Alain J.P. Belda; aluminum products; aerospace & automotive components; industrial materials/tools.

Allegheny Technologies, Inc. (ATI); 1000 Six PPG Place, Pittsburgh, PA 15222; (412) 394-2800; www.allegheny techologies.com; L. Patrick Hassey; electronics, aerospace, and industrial metals mfgr.

Allied Waste Industries (AW); 15880 N. Greenway-Hayden Loop, Suite 100, Scottsdale, AZ 85260; (480) 627-2700; www.allied waste.com; John J. Zillmer; solid waste management.

Allstate Corp. (ALL); 2775 Sanders Rd., Northbrook, IL 60062; (847) 402-5000; www.allstate.com; Edward M. Liddy; property/casualty, life insurance; financial services.

Altria Group, Inc. (MO); 120 Park Ave., NY, NY 10017; (917) 663-4000; www.altria.com; www.kraft.com. Louis C. Camilleri; cigarettes (largest U.S. tobacco company; Marlboro, Merit, Virginia Slims); Kraft Foods products (Jell-O, Maxwell House, Kool-Aid, Oscar Mayer, Tang, Cheez Whiz and Velveeta, Post cereals, Tombstone Pizza, and Toblerone chocolate); Nabisco products (Oreo, Chips Ahoy! cookies, Ritz, Triscuit crackers, Mallomars). (Philip Morris Companies, Inc., changed its name to Altria, 1/27/03).

Amazon.com, Inc. (AMZN); 1200 12th Ave. S., Suite 1200, Seattle, WA 98144; (206) 266-1000; www.amazon.com; Jeff Bezos; online books, music, electronics, photo, and home and garden products.

American Electric Power (AEP); 1 Riverside Plaza, Columbus, OH 43215; (614) 716-1000; www.aep.com; Michael G. Morris; utilities.

American Express Co. (AXP); 200 Vesey St., NY, NY 10285; (212) 640-2000; www.americanexpress.com; Kenneth I. Chenault; travel, financial, and information services.

American Greetings Corp. (AM); 1 American Rd., Cleveland, OH 44144; (216) 252-7300; www.americangreetings.com; Zev Weiss; greeting cards, stationery, party goods, gift items.

American Home Products: *see* Wyeth.

American Intl. Group (AIG); 70 Pine St., NY, NY 10270; (212) 770-7000; www.aig.com; Martin J. Sullivan; insurance, financial services.

American Standard (ASD); One Centennial Ave., P.O. Box 6820, Piscataway, NJ 08855; (732) 980-6000; www.american standard. com; Frederic M. Poses; bathroom and kitchen fixtures and fittings, air conditioning systems, vehicle control systems.

AMR Corp. (AMR); 4333 Amon Carter Blvd., Ft. Worth, TX 76155; (817) 963-1234; www.aa.com; Gerard J. Arpey; world's largest air carrier (American Airlines, American Eagle); acquired assets of Trans World Air Lines Inc. in 2001.

Anheuser-Busch Cos., Inc. (BUD); 1 Busch Pl., St. Louis, MO 63118; (314) 577-2000; www.anheuser-busch.com; Patrick T. Stokes; world's largest brewer (Budweiser, Michelob, Busch, O'Doul's), aluminum can manuf. and recycling, theme parks.

AOL Time Warner Inc.: *see* Time Warner, Inc.

Apple Computer, Inc. (AAPL); 1 Infinite Loop, Cupertino, CA 95014; (408) 996-1010; www.apple.com; Steve Jobs; manuf. of personal computers, software, digital media players (iPod); distrib. digital media (iTunes store).

Aramark Corp. (RMK); Aramark Tower, 1101 Market St., Philadelphia, PA 19107; (215) 238-3000; www.aramark.com; Joseph Neubauer; food and support services, uniforms and career apparel, child care and early education.

Archer Daniels Midland Co. (ADM); 4666 Faries Pkwy., Decatur, IL 62525; (217) 424-5200; www.admworld.com; G. Allen Andreas; agricultural commodities and prods.

Armstrong World Industries, Inc.; 2500 Columbia Ave., Lancaster, PA 17604; (717) 397-0611; www.armstrong.com; Michael D. Lockhart; carpeting, flooring, interior furnishings, specialty prods; began Chapt. 11 restructuring, 2000.

Arvinmeritor Inc. (ARM); 2135 W. Maple Road, Troy, MI 48084; (248) 435-1000; www.arvinmeritor.com; Charles G. McClure; auto ride control systems; vehicle components.

Ashland Inc. (ASH); 50 E. RiverCenter Blvd., P.O. Box 391, Covington, KY 41012; (859) 815-3333; www.ashland.com; James J. O'Brien Jr.; petroleum producer and refiner (Valvoline, plastics), chemicals, road construction.

AT&T Inc. (T); 175 E. Houston, San Antonio, TX 78205; (210) 821-4105; att.sbc.com; Edward E. Whitmore Jr.; telecommunications, global information management. Created by merger of SBC Communications and AT&T Corp., finalized 11/19/05; announced agreement to merge with BellSouth, 3/5/06.

AutoNation (AN); 110 SE 6th St., Ft. Lauderdale, FL 33301; (954) 769-6000; www.autonation.com; Michael J. Jackson; new and used auto vehicles; auto parts, maintenance, and repair; auto protection products.

Avon Prods., Inc. (AVP); 1345 Ave. of Americas, NY, NY 10015; (212) 282-5000; www.avon.com; Andrea Jung; cosmetics, fragrances, toiletries, fashion jewelry, gift items, casual apparel, lingerie.

Bank of America Corp. (BAC); Bank of America Corporate Center, 100 N. Tryon St., Charlotte, NC 28255; (704) 386-5681; www.bankofamerica.com; Kenneth D. Lewis; 2nd-largest U.S. bank; acquired FleetBoston, 4/1/2004; acquired credit card co. MBNA, 1/1/06.

Barnes & Noble, Inc. (BKS); 122 Fifth Ave., New York, NY 10011; (212) 633-3300; www.bn.com; Steve Riggio; leading U.S. bookstore chain (Barnes & Noble, B. Dalton stores), publishing (Sterling Pub. Co.).

Bausch & Lomb Inc. (BOL); One Bausch & Lomb Place, Rochester, NY 14604; (585) 338-6000; www.bausch.com; Ronald L. Zarrella; vision and health-care prods., surgical equip.

Baxter International Inc. (BAX); 1 Baxter Pkwy., Deerfield, IL 60015; (847) 948-2000; www.baxter.com; Robert Parkinson Jr.; health care prods. & services.

Bear Stearns Cos. Inc. (BSC); 383 Madison Ave., NY, NY 10179; (212) 272-2000; www.bearstearns.com; James E. Cayne; investment banking, securities trading, brokerage.

Becton, Dickinson & Co. (BDX); 1 Becton Dr., Franklin Lakes, NJ 07417; (201) 847-6800; www.bd.com; E.J. Ludwig; medical, laboratory, diagnostic prods.

BellSouth Corp. (BLS); 1155 Peachtree St. NE, Atlanta, GA 30309; (404) 249-2000; www.bellsouth.com; F. Duane Ackerman; telephone service in southern U.S. Agreed to merge with AT&T, 3/5/06.

Berkshire Hathaway Inc. (BRK); 1440 Kiewit Plaza, Omaha, NE 68131; (402) 346-1400; www.berkshirehathaway.com; Warren E. Buffett; subsidiaries include GEICO Direct insurance, Johns Manville building materials, Fruit of the Loom apparel, Dairy Queen restaurants/desserts, Benjamin Moore paints, Shaw carpeting.

Bertelsmann AG; Carl-Bertelsmann-Strasse 270, D-33311 Gütersloh, Germany; +49-5241-80-0; www.bertelsmann.de; Gunter Thielen; largest trade book publisher (Random House: Knopf, Ballantine, Bantam, Crown, Doubleday), 2nd-largest music company.

Best Buy Co., Inc. (BBY); 7601 Penn Ave. S., Richfield, MN 55423; (612) 291-1000; www.bestbuy.com; Richard Schulze; retailer of software, appliances, consumer electronics, cameras, music, DVDs.

Black & Decker Corp. (BDK); 701 E. Joppa Rd., Towson, MD 21286; (410) 716-3900; www.bdk.com; Nolan D. Archibald; manuf. power tools (DeWalt, Black & Decker), household prods. (Kwikset locks, Price Pfister faucets, Black & Decker small appliances).

H & R Block, Inc. (HRB); 4400 Main St., Kansas City, MO 64111; (816) 753-6900; www.hrblock.com; Mark A. Ernst; tax return preparation, software; residential mortgages.

Blockbuster Inc. (BBI); 1201 Elm St., Dallas, TX 75270; (214) 854-3000; www.blockbuster.com; John F. Antioco; DVD rentals.

Boeing Co. (BA); 100 N. Riverside Plaza, Chicago, IL 60606; (312) 544-2000; www.boeing.com; W. James McNerney Jr.; world's 2nd-largest mfgr. of commercial jet aircraft; 2nd-largest U.S. defense contractor.

The Brink's Co. (BCO); 1801 Bayberry Ct., Richmond, VA 23226; (804) 289-9600; www.brinkscompany.com; Michael T. Dan; security (alarm systems, armored cars).

Bristol-Myers Squibb Co. (BMY); 345 Park Ave., NY, NY 10154; (212) 546-4000; www.bms.com; Peter R. Dolan; drugs (Bufferin, Comtrex, Pravachol, TAXOL), nutritionals (Enfamil infant formula, Boost energy drink).

Brown-Forman Corp. (BFB); 850 Dixie Hwy., Louisville, KY 40210; (502) 585-1100; www.brown-forman.com; Owsley Brown II; distilled spirits (Jack Daniel's, Southern Comfort), wines (Bolla, Fetzer, Korbel), china, crystal (Dansk, Lenox), silver prods., Hartmann luggage.

Brown Shoe Co., Inc. (BWS); 8300 Maryland Ave., P.O. Box 29, St. Louis, MO 63105; (314) 854-4000; www.brownshoe.com; Ronald A. Fromm; mfgr. and retailer (Famous Footwear) of women's, men's, and children's shoes (Buster Brown, Naturalizer, Dr. Scholl's).

Brunswick Corp. (BC); 1 N. Field Ct., Lake Forest, IL 60045; (847) 735-4700; www.brunswick.com; Dustan McCoy; largest U.S. maker of leisure and recreation prods., incl. marine, camping, billiards, fitness, and fishing equip.; bowling centers and equip.

Burger King Corp. (BKC); 5505 Blue Lagoon Dr., Miami, FL 33126; (305) 378-3000; www.burgerking.com; John W. Chidsey; fast-food restaurants.

Burlington Northern Santa Fe Inc. (BNI); 2650 Lou Menk Dr., Ft. Worth, TX 76131; (800) 795-2673; www.bnsf.com; Matthew Rose; 2nd-largest U.S. rail transportation co.

Cablevision Systems Corp. (CVC); 1111 Stewart Ave., Bethpage, NY 11714; (516) 803-2300; www.cablevision.com; James L. Dolan; cable & VoIP provider. CATV (AMC, Fuse, IFC, WE); sports teams (NY Knicks, NY Rangers); arenas.

Cadbury Schweppes plc (CSG); 25 Berkeley Sq., London, W1J 6HB, UK; +44 20 7409 1313; www.cadburyschweppes.com; Todd Stitzer; 3rd-largest beverage producer; candies, gum.

Campbell Soup Co. (CPB); One Campbell Pl., Camden, NJ 08103; (856) 342-4800; www.campbellsoup.com; Douglas R. Conant; soups, sauces (Pace, Prego), V8 juice, Pepperidge Farm baked goods, Godiva chocolates,.

Caterpillar Inc. (CAT); 100 NE Adams St., Peoria, IL 61629; (309) 675-1000; www.cat.com; James W. Owens; world's largest producer of earth moving equip.

CBS Corp. (CBS); 51 W. 52nd St., New York, NY 10019; www.cbscorporation.com; Leslie Moonves; TV stations, networks (CBS, Showtime); distrib. TV shows (Paramount, King World); radio stations; book publishing (Simon & Schuster). Split from parent co. Viacom, 1/1/06.

Chase Manhattan Corp.: see JPMorgan Chase & Co. Inc.

Chevron Corp. (CVX); 6001 Bollinger Canyon Rd., San Ramon, CA 94583; (925) 842-1000; www.chevron.com; David J. O'Reilly; 2nd-largest U.S.-based oil co; acquired Unocal, 8/10/05.

Chiquita Brands International, Inc. (CQB); 250 E. 5th St., Cincinnati, OH 45202; (513) 784-8000; www.chiquita.com; Fernando Aguirre; bananas, fruits, vegetables.

Church & Dwight Co., Inc. (CHD); 469 N. Harrison St., Princeton, NJ 08543; (609) 683-5900; www.churchdwight.com; R.A. Davies III; world's largest producer of sodium bicarbonate (Arm & Hammer); household products (Brillo, Fresh'n Soft, other Arm & Hammer products); personal care products (Arrid antiperspirant, Nair, Trojan condoms, First Response pregnancy tests).

CIGNA Corp. (CI); 2 Liberty Pl., Philadelphia, PA 19192; (215) 761-1000; www.cigna.com; H. Edward Hanway; accident, health, life insurance provider.

Cintas Corp. (CTAS); 6800 Cintas Blvd., Cincinnati, OH 45262; (513) 459-1200; www.cintas-corp.com; Scott D. Farmer; largest U.S. uniform supplier; laundry services.

Circuit City Stores, Inc. (CC); 9950 Mayland Dr., Richmond, VA 23233; (804) 527-4000; www.circuitcity.com; Philip J. Schoonover; retailer of electronics, audio/video equip., consumer appliances.

Cisco Systems (CSCO); 170 West Tasman Dr., San Jose, CA 95134; (408) 526-4000; www.cisco.com; John Chambers; networking and communication products.

Citigroup (C); 399 Park Ave., NY, NY 10043; (212) 559-1000; www.citigroup.com; Charles O. Prince III; diversified financial services.

Clear Channel Communications, Inc. (CCU); 200 E. Basse Rd., San Antonio, TX 78209; (210) 822-2828; www.clearchannel.com; Mark P. Mays; largest radio station owner in U.S. (1,200 stations); outdoor advertising (billboards, mass transit ads); TV stations.

Clorox Co. (CLX); 1221 Broadway, Oakland, CA 94612; (510) 271-7000; www.clorox.com; Robert W. Matschullat; retail consumer prods. (Clorox, Formula 409, Pine-Sol, S.O.S., Soft Scrub cleansers; Armor All, STP, Rain Dance automotive prods.; Scoop Away, Fresh Step cat litters; Kingsford charcoal briquets; Hidden Valley dressing; Glad plastic bags; Brita water systems)

Coca-Cola Co. (KO); 1 Coca-Cola Plaza, Atlanta, GA 30313; (404) 676-2121; www.cocacola.com; E. Neville Isdell; world's largest soft drink co. (Coca-Cola, Sprite, Nestea, POWERade), world's largest dist. of juice prods. (Minute Maid).

Colgate-Palmolive Co. (CL); 300 Park Ave., NY, NY 10022; (212) 310-2000; www.colgate.com; Reuben Mark; soap (Palmolive, Irish Spring), detergent (Fab, Ajax), toothpaste (Colgate, Tom's of Maine), pet food (Hill's, Science Diet).

Comcast Corp.; 1500 Market St., Philadelphia, PA 19102; 215-665-1700; www.comcast.com; Brian L. Roberts; largest U.S. cable company; broadband cable, internet, and voice services. Some programming, incl. E!, Golf Channel, et al.

Compaq Computer Corp.: see Hewlett-Packard Co.

CompUSA Inc.; 14951 N. Dallas Pkwy., Dallas, TX 75254; (972) 982-4000; www.compusa.com; Anthony Weiss; retailer of computers and peripherals.

Computer Sciences Corp. (CSC); 2100 E. Grand Ave., El Segundo, CA 90245; (310) 615-0311; www.csc.com; Van B. Honeycutt; technology services.

ConAgra Foods, Inc. (CAG); 1 ConAgra Dr., Omaha, NE 68102; (402) 595-4000; www.conagra.com; Gary M. Rodkin; 2nd-largest U.S. food processor (Armour, Bumble Bee, Butterball, Chef Boyardee, Healthy Choice frozen dinners, Egg Beaters, Reddi-Wip); food service supplier.

ConocoPhillips Co. (COP); 600 North Dairy Ashford, P.O. Box 2197, Houston, TX 77079; (281) 293-1000; www.conocophillips.com; James J. Mulva; 3rd-largest U.S. oil and gas company. Formed by merger of Conoco and Phillips Petroleum, 8/30/02.

Consolidated Edison (ED); 4 Irving Pl., NY, NY 10003; (212) 460-4600; www.conedison.com; Kevin Burke; electric utility holding co.

Continental Airlines, Inc. (CAL); 1600 Smith St., Dept. HQSEO, Houston, TX 77002; (713) 324-2950; www.continental.com; Larry Kellner; air transportation.

Corning Inc. (GLW); 1 Riverfront Plaza, Corning, NY 14831; (607) 974-9000; www.corning.com; James R. Houghton; telecommunications, specialty equipment, fiber optics.

Costco Wholesale Corp. (COST); 999 Lake Dr., Issaquah, WA 98027; (425) 313-8100; www.costco.com; James D. Sinegal; wholesale warehouse stores.

Crane Co. (CR); 100 First Stamford Place, Stamford, CT 06902; (203) 363-7300; www.craneco.com; Eric C. Fast; manuf. fluid control devices, vending machines, aircraft components.

A. T. Cross Co. (ATX); 1 Albion Rd., Lincoln, RI 02865; (401) 333-1200; www.cross.com; David Whalen; writing instruments.

Crown Holdings, Inc. (CCK); 1 Crown Way, Philadelphia, PA 19154; (215) 698-5100; www.crowncork.com; John W. Conway; leading producer of packaging prods.

CSX Corp. (CSX); 500 Water St., 15th Fl., Jacksonville, FL 32202; (904) 359-3200; www.csx.com; Michael J. Ward; rail and road freight transport.

CVS Corp. (CVS); 1 CVS Dr., Woonsocket, RI 02895; (401) 765-1500; www.cvs.com; Thomas M. Ryan; acquired Eckerd Corp. in August 2004, to become nation's largest drugstore chain.

Dana Corp.; 4500 Dorr St., Toledo, OH 43615; (419) 535-4500; www.dana.com; Michael Burns; truck and auto parts, supplies; began Chapter 11 reorganization, 3/3/06.

Darden Restaurants, Inc. (DRI); 5900 Lake Ellenor Dr., Orlando, FL 32809; (407) 245-4000; www.dardenrestaurants.com; Clarence Otis Jr.; chain restaurants (Red Lobster, Olive Garden, Bahama Breeze, Smokey Bones BBQ Sports Bar).

Dean Foods Co. (DF); 2515 McKinney Ave., Ste. 1200, Dallas, TX 75201; (214) 303-3400; www.deanfoods.com; Gregg L. Engles; milk and specialty dairy products (Land O'Lakes, Horizon Organic, Silk soymilk), salad dressings (Marie's), pickles.

Deere & Co. (DE); One John Deere Pl., Moline, IL 61265; (309) 765-8000; www.deere.com; Robert W. Lane; world's largest manuf. of farm equip.; also makes industrial equip., and lawn and garden tractors.

Dell Inc. (DELL); 1 Dell Way, Round Rock, TX 78682; (512) 338-4400; www.dell.com; Kevin B. Rollins; laptop and desktop computers, network accessories, peripherals.

Del Monte Foods Co. (DLM); One Market @ The Landmark, San Francisco, CA 94105; (415) 247-3000; www.delmonte.com; Richard G. Wolford; canned food (College Inn, Del Monte, StarKist), pet food (9Lives, Gravy Train, Milk-Bone, Meow Mix).

Delphi Corp.; 5725 Delphi Dr., Troy, MI 48098; (248) 813-2000; www.delphi.com; Robert S. Miller Jr.; automotive systems, audio systems, mobile electronics; began Chapter 11 reorganization, 10/8/05.

Delta Air Lines, Inc.; 1030 Delta Blvd., Atlanta, GA 30320; (404) 715-2600; www.delta.com; Gerald Grinstein; air transportation; began Chapter 11 reorganization, 9/14/05.

Dial Corp.; 15501 N. Dial Blvd., Scottsdale, AZ 85260; (480) 754-3425; www.dialcorp.com; Bradley A. Casper; consumer prods. (Dial soap, Purex detergent, Armour Star meats, Renuzit air fresheners); U.S. subsidiary of Germany's Henkel company.

Diebold, Inc. (DBD); 5995 Mayfair Rd., North Canton, OH 44720; (330) 490-4000; www.diebold.com; Thomas W. Swidarski; manuf. ATMs, security systems and prods.

Dillard's (DDS); 1600 Cantrell Rd., Little Rock, AR 72201; (501) 376-5200; www.dillards.com; William Dillard II; 2nd-largest dept. store chain in U.S.

The Walt Disney Co. (DIS); 500 S. Buena Vista St., Burbank, CA 91521; (818) 560-1000; www.disney.com; Robert A. Iger; motion pictures (Touchstone, Pixar, Miramax); television (ESPN, ABC, SoapNet, Disney Channel); radio stations; theme parks (Walt Disney World, Disneyland); resorts; publishing; recordings; retailing (Disney Stores).

Dole Food Co., Inc.; One Dole Drive, Westlake Village, CA 91362; (818) 879-6600; www.dole.com; David H. Murdock; food prods., fresh fruits and vegetables.

R. R. Donnelley & Sons Co. (RRD); 111 S. Wacker Dr., Chicago, IL 60606; (312) 326-8000; www.rrdonnelley.com; Mark A. Angelson; largest commercial printer in N. America; photo/graphics, translation; printer of *The World Almanac*.

Dow Chemical Co. (DOW); 2030 Dow Center, Midland, MI 48674; (989) 636-1000; www.dow.com; Andrew N. Liveris; chemicals, plastics (world's 2nd-largest chemical co.).

Dow Jones & Co., Inc. (DJ); 200 Liberty St., NY, NY 10281; (212) 416-2000; www.dj.com; Richard F. Zannino; financial news service, publishing (*Wall Street Journal, Barron's*, Ottaway Newspapers).

Duke Energy Corp. (DUK); 526 S. Church St., Charlotte, NC 28202; (704) 594-6200; www.duke-energy.com; James E. Rogers; natural gas, uilities, pipelines, fiber optics.

Dun & Bradstreet Corp. (DNB); 103 JFK Parkway, Short Hills, NJ 07078; (973) 921-5500; www.dnb.com; Steven Alesio; business information, supplies, research.

Duracell: *see* Gillette.

E. I. du Pont de Nemours & Co. (Dupont) (DD); 1007 Market St., Wilmington, DE 19898; (302) 774-1000; www.dupont.com; Charles Holliday Jr.; 3rd-largest U.S. chemical co.; petroleum, consumer prods.

Eastman Kodak Co. (EK); 343 State St., Rochester, NY 14650; (800) 698-3324; www.kodak.com; Antonio Perez; world's largest producer of photographic film; digital cameras; printers.

Eaton Corp. (ETN); 1111 Superior Ave., Cleveland, OH 44114; (216) 523-5000; www.eaton.com; Alexander Cutler; manuf. of vehicle powertrain components, controls.

eBay Inc. (EBAY); 2145 Hamilton Ave., San Jose, CA 95125; (408) 376-7400; www.ebay.com; Meg C. Whitman; online auctions.

Eckerd Corp.: *see* CVS Corp.

Edison Intl. (EIX); 2244 Walnut Grove Ave., Rosemead, CA 91770; (626) 302-2222; www.edison.com; John Bryson; electric utilities.

Electronic Arts Inc. (ERTS); 209 Redwood Shores Pkwy., Redwood City, CA 94065; (650) 628-1500; www.ea.com; Larry Probst III; leading U.S. video game publisher.

Electronic Data Systems (EDS); 5400 Legacy Dr., Plano, TX 75024; (972) 604-6000; www.eds.com; Michael H. Jordan; systems management and services; software.

Eli Lilly and Co. (LLY); Lilly Corporate Center, Indianapolis, IN 46285; 317-276-2000; www.lilly.com; Sidney Taurel; pharmaceutical research, development, and manufacturing (Prozac, Stratera, Evista, Cialis).

El Paso Corp. (EP); 1001 Louisiana Street, Houston, TX 77002; (713) 420-2600; www.elpaso.com; Ronald L. Kuehn Jr.; natural gas/oil transportation, storage, exploration, production.

EMC Corp. (EMC); 176 South St., Hopkinton, MA 01748; (877) 362-6973; www.emc.com; Joseph M. Tucci; data storage and protection.

Emerson Electric Co. (EMR); 8000 W. Florissant Avenue, St. Louis, MO 63136; (314) 553-2000; www.gotoemerson.com; David Farr; electrical, electronics prods. & systems.

Energizer Holdings Inc. (ENR); 533 Maryville Univ. Dr., St. Louis, MO 63141; (314) 985-2000; www.energizer.com; Ward M. Klein; batteries, flashlights, lanterns, razors (Schick).

Estée Lauder Cos. Inc. (EL); 767 5th Ave., NY, NY 10153; (212) 572-4200; www.elcompanies.com; William P. Lauder; cosmetics (Clinique, Bobbi Brown), fragrance prods. (Aramis, Aveda, Tommy Hilfiger).

Exelon Corp. (EXC); 10 S. Dearborn St., 37th Fl., Chicago, IL 60680; (312) 394-7398; www.exeloncorp.com; John W. Rowe; electricity generation and distribution; nat. gas.

Exxon Mobil Corp. (XOM); 5959 Las Colinas Blvd., Irving, TX 75039; (972) 444-1000; www.exxon.mobil.com; Rex W. Tillerson; world's largest integrated oil co.

Fannie Mae (FNM); 3900 Wisconsin Ave. NW, Washington, DC 20016; (202) 752-7000; www.fanniemae.com; Daniel H. Mudd; largest U.S. provider of residential mortgage funds.

Fedders Corp. (FJC); 505 Martinsville Road, Liberty Corner, NJ 07938; (908) 604-8686; www.fedders.com; Salvatore Giordano Jr.; manuf. air conditioners (Fedders, Airtemp), dehumidifiers.

Federated Dept. Stores (FD); 7 W. 7th St., Cincinnati, OH 45202; (513) 579-7000; www.Federated-fds.com; Terry J. Lundgren; dept. stores (Macy's, Bloomingdale's); acquired May Dept. Stores (Lord & Taylor, Marshall Field's), 2/28/05.

FedEx Corp. (FDX); 942 S. Shady Grove Rd., Memphis, TN 38120; (901) 818-7500; www.fedex.com; F. W. Smith; world's largest express delivery service.

First Data Corp. (FDC); 6200 S. Quebec St., Greenwood Village, CO, 80111; (303) 967-8000; www.firstdatacorp.com; Henry C. Duques; financial transaction processing.

FirstEnergy Corp. (FE); 76 S. Main St., Akron, OH 44308; (800) 633-4766; www.firstenergycorp.com; Anthony J. Alexander; public utility company; provides electricity and natural gas.

FleetBoston Financial Corp.: *see* Bank of America.

Fleetwood Enterprises, Inc. (FLE); 3125 Myers St., Riverside, CA 92503; (951) 351-3500; www.fleetwood.com; Elden L. Smith; manufactured homes, recreational vehicles.

Fluor Corp. (FLR); Las Colinas Blvd., Irving, TX 75039; (469) 398-7000; www.fluor.com; Alan L. Boeckmann; largest international engineering and construction co. in U.S.

Foot Locker, Inc. (FL); 112 West 34th St., NY, NY 10120; (212) 720-3700; www.footlocker-inc.com; Matthew D. Serra; operates retail athletic stores: Eastbay, Foot Locker, Champs.

Ford Motor Co. (F); 1 American Rd., Dearborn, MI 48126; (313) 322-3000; www.ford.com; William Clay Ford Jr.; 2nd-largest auto manufacturer; motor vehicle sales (Ford, Lincoln, Jaguar, Mercury, Volvo), rentals (Hertz); largest U.S. auto finance co. (Ford Motor Credit).

Fortune Brands, Inc. (FO); 520 Lake Cook Rd., Deerfield, IL 60015; (847) 484-4400; www.fortunebrands.com; Craig Omtvedt; spirits and wine (Jim Beam, Absolut, Sauza), hardware, office prods., golf and leisure prods. (Titleist, Cobra, FootJoy).

Freddie Mac (FRE); 8200 Jones Branch Dr., McLean, VA 22102; (703) 903-2000; www.freddiemac.com; Dick Syron; residential mortgage provider.

Fruit of the Loom, Inc.; *see* Berkshire Hathaway.

Gannett Co., Inc. (GCI); 7950 Jones Branch Dr., McLean, VA 22107; (703) 854-6000; www.gannett.com; Craig A. Dubow; largest U.S. newspaper publisher (*USA Today*), network and cable TV.

Gap Inc. (GPS); Two Folsom St., San Francisco, CA 94105; (650) 952-4400; www.gap.com; Robert Fisher; casual apparel retailer (Gap, Banana Republic, Old Navy).

Gateway Inc. (GTW); 7565 Irvine Ctr. Dr., Irvine, CA 92618; (949) 471-7000; www.gateway.com; Richard D. Snyder; personal computers, network servers, peripherals.

General Dynamics (GD); 2941 Fairview Park Dr., Ste. 100, Falls Church, VA 22042; (703) 876-3000; www.gendyn.com; Nicholas D. Chabraja; nuclear submarines , armored vehicles, combat systems, computing devices, defense systems.

General Electric Co. (GE); 3135 Easton Tpke., Fairfield, CT 06828; (203) 373-2211; www.ge.com; Jeffrey Immelt; electrical, electronic equip., radio and TV broadcasting (NBC, Bravo, USA, Telemundo), aircraft engines, power generation, appliances.

General Mills, Inc. (GIS); One General Mills Blvd., Minneapolis, MN 55426; (763) 764-7600; www.generalmills.com; Steven W. Sanger; foods (Total, Wheaties, Cheerios, Chex, Hamburger Helper, Betty Crocker, Bisquick, Pillsbury).

General Motors Corp. (GM); 300 Renaissance Center, Detroit, MI 48265; (313) 556-5000; www.gm.com; G. Richard Wagoner Jr.; world's largest auto manuf. (Chevrolet, Pontiac, Cadillac, Buick, Saab, Saturn).

Genuine Parts Co. (GPC); 2999 Circle 75 Pkwy., Atlanta, GA 30339; (770) 953-1700; www.genpt.com; Thomas C. Gallagher; distributes auto replacement parts (NAPA).

Georgia-Pacific Corp.; 133 Peachtree St. NE, Atlanta, GA 30303; (404) 652-4000; www.gp.com; Joseph W. Moeller; manuf. of paper and wood prods; subsidiary of Koch Industries.

Gillette; *see* Proctor & Gamble.

The Goldman Sachs Group, Inc. (GS); 85 Broad Street, NY, NY 10004; (212) 902-1000; www.goldmansachs.com; Lloyd F. Blankfein; investment banking, asset management, securities services.

The Goodyear Tire & Rubber Co. (GT); 1144 E. Market St., Akron, OH 44316; (330) 796-2121; www.goodyear.com; Robert Keegan; world's largest rubber manuf.; tires and other auto prods.

Google, Inc. (GOOG); 1600 Amphitheatre Pkwy., Mountain View, CA 94043; (650) 253-0000; www.google.com; Eric E. Schmidt; leading internet search engine.

W. R. Grace & Co. (GRA); 7500 Grace Dr., Columbia, MD 21044; (410) 531-4000; www.grace.com; Alfred E. Festa; chemicals, construction prods.

Great Atlantic & Pacific Tea Co. (A&P) (GAP); 2 Paragon Dr., Montvale, NJ 07645; (201) 573-9700; www.aptea.com; Christian Haub; supermarkets (A&P, Farmer Jack, Super Fresh, Waldbaum's).

Halliburton Co. (HAL); 5 Houston Center, 1401 McKinney, Ste. 2400, Houston, TX 77010; (713) 759-2600; www.halliburton.com; Dave Lesar; energy, engineering, and construction services.

Harley-Davidson, Inc. (HOG); 3700 W. Juneau Ave., Milwaukee, WI 53208; (414) 342-4680; www.harley-davidson.com; James L. Ziemer; manuf. of motorcycles, parts, and accessories.

Harrah's Entertainment, Inc. (HET); One Harrah's Court, Las Vegas, NV 89119; (702) 407-6000; www.harrahs.com; Gary W. Loveman; casino-hotels (Bally's, Caesars) and riverboats (Showboat); merged with Park Place Entertainment, Jan. 2005.

Hartford Financial Services Group, Inc. (HIG); Hartford Plaza, 690 Asylum Ave., Hartford, CT 06115; (860) 547-5000; www.thehartford.com; Ramani Ayer; insurance, financial services.

Hartmarx (HMX); 101 N. Wacker Dr., Chicago, IL 60606; (312) 372-6300; www.hartmarx.com; Homi B. Patel; apparel manuf. (Hart Schaffner & Marx, Hickey Freeman, Claiborne, Tommy Hilfiger, Pierre Cardin, Perry Ellis).

Hasbro, Inc. (HAS); 1027 Newport Ave., Pawtucket, RI 02862; (401) 431-8697; www.hasbro.com; Alfred J. Verrecchia; toy and game manuf. (Milton Bradley, Playskool, G.I. Joe, Parker Bros., Tiger Electronics, Play-Doh).

HCA Inc. (HCA); 1 Park Plaza, Nashville, TN 37203; (615) 344-9551; www.hcahealthcare.com; Jack O. Bovender Jr.; largest hospital mgmt. co. in the U.S.

H. J. Heinz Co. (HNZ); 600 Grant St., Pittsburgh, PA 15219; (412) 456-5700; www.heinz.com; William R. Johnson; foods (StarKist, Ore-Ida, 57 Varieties ketchup), pet food (Kibbles 'n Bits, 9 Lives), Weight Watchers.

Hershey Co. (HSY); 100 Crystal A Dr., Hershey, PA 17033; (717) 534-6799; www.hersheys.com; Richard H. Lenny; largest U.S. producer of chocolate and confectionary prods. (Reese's, Kit Kat, Mounds, Almond Joy, Cadbury, Jolly Rancher, Twizzlers, Milk Duds, Good & Plenty).

Amerada Hess Corp. (HES); 1185 Ave. of the Americas, NY, NY 10036; (212) 997-8500; www.hess.com; John B. Hess; integrated international oil co.

Hewlett-Packard Co. (HPQ); 3000 Hanover St., Palo Alto, CA 94304; (650) 857-1501; www.hp.com; Mark V. Hurd; manuf. computers, electronic prods. and systems. (On 5/3/02 Hewlett-Packard acquired Compaq Computer Co.)

Hillenbrand Industries, Inc. (HB); 700 State Rte. 46 E., Batesville, IN 47006; (812) 934-7000; www.hillenbrand.com; Peter H. Soderberg; manuf. caskets, adjustable hospital beds.

Hilton Hotels Corp. (HLT); 9336 Civic Center Dr., Beverly Hills, CA 90210; (310) 278-4321; www.hiltonworldwide.com; Stephen F. Bollenbach; hotels, casinos.

Home Depot, Inc. (HD); 2455 Paces Ferry Rd. NW, Atlanta, GA 30339; (770) 433-8211; www.homedepot.com; Robert L. Nardelli; 2nd-largest U.S. retailer, home improvement warehouse stores.

Honeywell Intl. Inc. (HON); 101 Columbia Road, Morristown, NJ 07962; (973) 455-2000; www.honeywell.com; David Cote; industrial and home control systems, aerospace guidance systems.

Hormel Foods Corp. (HRL); 1 Hormel Pl., Austin, MN 55912; (507) 437-5611; www.hormel.com; Joel W. Johnson; meat processor; pork, turkey, and beef prods. (SPAM, Dinty Moore, Jennie-O).

Houghton Mifflin Co.; 222 Berkeley St., Boston, MA 02116; (617) 351-5000; www.hmco.com; Anthony Lucki; publisher of textbooks, reference, general interest books.

Huffy Corp.; 225 Byers Rd., Miamisburg, OH 45342; (937) 866-6251; www.huffy.com; Jay Muskovich; bicycle manuf.; sports and hardware equip.

Humana, Inc. (HUM); 500 W. Main Street, Louisville, KY 40202; (502) 580-1000; www.humana.com; Michael B. McCallister; managed healthcare service provider, related specialty products.

Illinois Tool Works Inc. (ITW); 3600 West Lake Ave., Glenview, IL 60026; (847) 724-7500; www.itw.com; David B. Speer; food equip. (Hobart), home appliances and cookware (West Bend).

Ingersoll-Rand Co. Ltd. (IR); 155 Chestnut Ridge Road, Montvale, NJ 07645; (201) 573-0123; www.irco.com; Herbert L. Henkel; industrial and construction equip.; locks and security systems.

Intel Corp. (INTC); 2200 Mission College Blvd., Santa Clara, CA 95052-8119; (408) 765-8080; www.intel.com; Paul S. Otellini; manuf. microprocessors (Pentium, Celeron).

International Business Machines Corp. (IBM); One New Orchard Rd., Armonk, NY 10504; (914) 499-1900; www.ibm.com; Samuel Palmisano; world's largest supplier of advanced information processing technology equip., services.

International Paper Co. (IP); 6400 Poplar Ave., Memphis, TN 38197; (901) 419-9000; www.paper.com; John V. Faraci Jr.; world's largest paper/forest prods. co.; chemicals, packaging.

Interstate Bakeries Corp.; 12 E. Armour Blvd., Kansas City, MO 64111; (816) 502-4000; www.interstatebakeries corp.com; Antonio C. Alvarez II; baked goods wholesaler, distributor (Wonder, Hostess, Dolly Madison, Drake's, Home Pride); began Chapter 11 reorganization, 9/22/04.

J. Crew Group, Inc. (JCG); 770 Broadway, NY, NY 10003; (212) 209-2500; www.jcrew.com; Millard S. Drexler; retail and mail order apparel and accessories.

JetBlue Airways (JBLU); 118-29 Queens Blvd., Forest Hills, NY 11375; (800) JETBLUE; www.jetblue.com; David Neeleman; air transportation.

Jo-Ann Stores, Inc (JAS).; 5555 Darrow Rd., Hudson, OH 44236; (330) 656-2600; www.joann.com; Darrell D. Webb; nation's largest specialty fabric and craft stores.

Johnson & Johnson (JNJ); 1 Johnson & Johnson Plaza, New Brunswick, NJ 08933; (732) 524-0400; www.jnj.com; William Weldon; health care prods. (Band-Aid), pharmaceuticals (Tylenol, Motrin), toiletries (Neutrogena); announced plans to acquire Pfizer's consumer prods. division (Neosporin, Listerine, Sudafed), 6/26/06.

S.C. Johnson & Son, Inc.; 1525 Howe St., Racine, WI 53403; (262) 260-2000; www.scjohnson.com; H. Fisk Johnson; cleaning and other household prods. (Johnson's Wax, Windex, Pledge, Fantastik, Raid, Off!, Shout, Glade, Scrubbing Bubbles, Ziploc bags).

Johnson Controls, Inc. (JCI); 5757 N. Green Bay Ave., Milwaukee, WI 53201; (414) 524-1200; www.johnsoncontrols.com; John Barth; fire protection services, auto interiors, and batteries.

Jones Apparel Group, Inc. (JNY).; 250 Rittenhouse Circle, Bristol, PA 19007; (215) 785-4000; www.jny.com; Peter Boneparth; apparel (Jones New York, Gloria Vanderbilt), shoes (Nine West, Anne Klein); luxury (Barney's New York), retail, and outlet stores.

JPMorgan Chase & Co. (JPM); 270 Park Ave., NY, NY 10017; (212) 270-6000; www.jpmorganchase.com; William Harrison Jr.; global financial firm; merged with Bank One Corp., 7/1/04.

Kellogg Co. (K); One Kellogg Sq., Battle Creek, MI 49016; (269) 961-2000; www.kelloggcompany.com; James M. Jenness; world's largest mfgr. of ready-to-eat cereals, other food prods. (Frosted Flakes, Rice Krispies, Froot Loops, Pop-Tarts, Nutri-Grain, Keebler, Eggo).

Kelly Services, Inc.; 999 West Big Beaver Rd., Troy, MI 48084; (248) 362-4444; www.kellyservices.com; Carl T. Camden; temporary staffing services.

Kimberly-Clark Corp. (KMB); 351 Phelps Dr., Irving, TX 75038; (972) 281-1200; www.kimberly-clark.com; Thomas Falk; personal care prods. (Kleenex, Scott, Cottonelle, Huggies, Kotex).

Kmart Corp.: *see* Sears Holdings.

Knight Ridder, Inc.; *see* McClatchy Co..

Kraft Foods, Inc.: *see* Altria Group, Inc.

Kroger Co. (KR); 1014 Vine St., Cincinnati, OH 45202; (513) 762-4000; www.kroger.com; David Dillon; largest U.S. retail grocery chain, convenience stores, mall jewelry stores.

La-Z-Boy Inc. (LZB); 1284 N. Telegraph Rd., Monroe, MI 48162; (734) 242-1444; www.lazboy.com; Kurt L. Darrow; reclining chairs, other furniture.

Leggett & Platt, Inc. (LEG); No. 1 Leggett Rd., Carthage, MO 64836; (417) 358-8131; www.leggett.com; David S. Haffner; furniture and furniture components, industrial materials, automotive seating suspension, train and cable control systems.

Lehman Bros. Holdings, Inc. (LEH); 745 7th Ave., NY, NY 10019; (212) 526-7000; www.lehman.com; Richard S. Fuld Jr.; investment bank.

Levi Strauss & Co; 1155 Battery St., San Francisco, CA 94111; (415) 501-6000; www.levistrauss.com; Philip A. Marineau; blue jeans, casual sportswear (Dockers).

Lexmark Intl., Inc. (LXK); 740 W. New Circle Rd., Lexington, KY 40550; (800) 539-6275; www.lexmark.com; John W. Gamble Jr.; computer printers and peripherals.

Liberty Mutual Holding Co. Inc.; 175 Berkeley St., Boston, MA 02116; (617) 357-9500; www.libertymutual.com; Edmund F. Kelly; auto, home, and life insurance.

Limited Brands Inc. (LTD); 3 Limited Pkwy., Columbus, OH 43230; (614) 415-7000; www.limitedbrands.com; Leslie H. Wexner; apparel stores (Lane Bryant, Lerner, Limited, Express, Victoria's Secret, Henri Bendel), home decor (White Barn Candle Co.), personal care (Bath & Body Works).

Liz Claiborne, Inc. (LIZ); 1441 Bway., New York, NY 10018; (212) 354-4900; www.lizclaiborne.com; Paul R. Charron; women's apparel (Ellen Tracy, Laundry, Crazy Horse, Dana Buchman).

L.L. Bean, Inc.; 15 Casco St., Freeport, ME 04033; (207) 865-4761; www.llbean.com; Chris McCormick; catalog and retail outdoor apparel and footwear.

Lockheed Martin Corp. (LMT); 6801 Rockledge Dr., Bethesda, MD 20817; (301) 897-6000; www.lockheedmartin.com; Robert J. Stevens; leading U.S. defense contractor; commercial and military aircraft, electronics, missiles, information tech., and communications.

Loews Corp. (LTR); 667 Madison Ave., NY, NY 10021; (212) 521-2000; www.loews.com; James S. Tisch; tobacco prods. (Kent, True, Newport), watches (Bulova), hotels, insurance (CNA Financial), offshore drilling (Diamond).

Longs Drug Stores Corp. (LDG); 141 N. Civic Dr., Walnut Creek, CA 94596; (925) 937-1170; www.longs.com; Warren Bryant; drug store chain.

Lowe's Cos., Inc. (LOW); 1000 Lowe's Blvd. Mooresville, NC 28117; (704) 758-1000; www.lowes.com; Robert A. Niblock; building materials and home improvement superstores.

Luby's, Inc. (LUB); 13111 Northwest Fwy., Ste. 600, Houston, TX 77040; (713) 329-6800; www.lubys.com; Christopher Pappas; operates cafeterias in S and SW.

Lucent Technologies, Inc. (LU); 600 Mountain Ave., Murray Hill, NJ 07974; (908) 582-8500; www.lucent.com; Patricia Russo; leading developer, designer, and manuf. of telecommunications systems, software, and prods. Agreed to merge with France-based Alcatel, 4/2/06.

Mandalay Resort Group: *see* MGM MIRAGE.

Manpower Inc. (MAN); 5301 N. Ironwood Rd., Milwaukee, WI 53217; (414) 961-1000; www.manpower.com; Jeffrey A. Joerres; 2nd-largest non-gov't. employment services co. in the world.

Marathon Oil Corp. (MRO); 5555 San Felipe Rd., Houston, TX 77056; (713) 629-6600; www.marathon.com; Clarence P. Cazalot Jr.; integrated oil co. (Became independent co. 1/1/02 after being separated from USX-Marathon Group; United States Steel Corp. created as a result of a spin-off from USX.)

Marriott International, Inc. (MAR); 10400 Fernwood Rd., Bethesda, MD 20817; (301) 380-3000; www.marriott.com; J.W. Marriott Jr; hotels (Renaissance, Courtyard, Fairfield, Ritz-Carlton.

Masco Corp. (MAS); 21001 Van Born Rd., Taylor, MI 48180; (313) 274-7400; www.masco.com; Richard A. Manoogian; manuf. kitchen, bathroom prods. (Delta, Peerless faucets; Fieldstone, Merillat cabinets), paints (Behr).

MassMutual Financial Group; 1295 State St., Springfield, MA 01111; (800) 767-1000; www.massmutual.com; James R. Birle; financial planning and investment, life insurance.

Mattel, Inc. (MAT); 333 Continental Blvd., El Segundo, CA 90245; (310) 252-2000; www.mattel.com; Robert A. Eckert; largest U.S. toymaker (Barbie, Fisher-Price, Hot Wheels, Matchbox, American Girls).

May Department Stores Co.: *see* Federated Dept. Stores.

Maytag Corp.; *see* Whirlpool Corp.

MBNA Corp.; *see* Bank of America.

McClatchy Co. (MNI); 2100 Q St., Sacramento, CA 95816; (916) 321-1846; www.mcclatchy.com; Gary B. Pruitt; 2nd-largest newspaper publisher; acquired Knight Ridder papers, 6/27/06.

McDonald's Corp. (MCD); McDonald's Plaza, Oak Brook, IL 60523; (630) 623-3000; www.mcdonalds.com; James A. Skinner; fast-food restaurants.

McGraw-Hill Cos. (MHP); 1221 Ave. of the Americas, NY, NY 10020; (212) 512-2000; www.mcgraw-hill.com; Harold (Terry) McGraw III; book, textbook, magazine publishing (*Business Week*); information and financial services (Standard & Poor's); TV stations.

MCI, Inc.; *see* Verizon Communications Inc.

McKesson Corp. (MCK); 1 Post St., San Francisco, CA 94104; (415) 983-8300; www.mckesson.com; John Hammergren; distributor of drugs and toiletries; provides mgmt. software and services.

MeadWestvaco Corp. (MWV); One High Ridge Park, Stamford, CT 06905; (203) 461-7400; www.meadwestvaco.com; John A. Luke Jr.; paperboard, packaging, shipping containers; school supplies, consumer office prods.

Medco Health Solutions, Inc. (MHS); 100 Parsons Pond Dr., Franklin Lakes, NJ 07417; (201) 269-3400; www.medco.com; David B. Snow Jr.; pharmacy benefits management.

Medtronic, Inc. (MDT); 710 Medtronic Pkwy. NE, Minneapolis, MN 55432; (763) 514-4000; www.medtronic.com; Art Collins Jr.; world's largest manuf. of implantable biomedical devices.

Merck & Co., Inc. (MRK); 1 Merck Dr., Whitehouse Station, NJ 08889-0100; (908) 423-1000; www.merck.com; Richard T. Clark; pharmaceuticals (Pepcid, Propecia, Singulair, Zocor).

Meredith Corp. (MDP); 1716 Locust St., Des Moines, IA 50309; (515) 284-3000; www.meredith.com; Steven M. Lacy; magazine publishing (*Better Homes and Gardens, Ladies' Home Journal, Parents, Family Circle*), book publishing, broadcasting.

Merrill Lynch & Co., Inc. (MER); 4 World Financial Ctr., NY, NY 10080; (212) 449-1000; www.merrilllynch.com; Stan O'Neal; securities broker, financial services.

MetLife, Inc. (MET); 200 Park Ave., NY, NY 10166; (212) 578-2211; www.metlife.com; C. Robert Henrikson; insurance, financial services.

MGM MIRAGE (MGM); 3600 Las Vegas Blvd. S., Las Vegas, NV 89109; (702) 693-7111; www.mgmmirage.com; J. Terrence Lanni; hotel-casino operator (Mirage, Treasure Island, Golden Nugget); acquired Mandalay Resort Group, 4/25/05.

Microsoft Corp. (MSFT); One Microsoft Way, Redmond, WA 98052; (425) 882-8080; www.microsoft.com; William H. Gates; largest independent software maker (Windows, Word, Excel).

Mobil Corp.: *see* Exxon Mobil Corp.

Miller Brewing Co.: 3939 W. Highland Blvd. Milwaukee, WI 53208; (414) 931-2000; www.millerbrewing.com; 2nd-largest U.S. brewer (Miller, sharps); subsidiary of SABMiller plc.

Mittal Steel USA; 3210 Watling St., East Chicago, IN 46312; (219) 399-1200; www.mittalsteel.com; Michael G. Rippey; subsidiary of Netherlands-based Mittal Steel Co., N.V., world's largest steel co.

Molson Coors Brewing Co. (TAP); 311 Tenth St., Golden, CO 80401; (303) 279-6565; www.molsoncoors.com; W. Leo Kiely III; brewer (Coors, Killian's, Molson, Zima). Formed by merger of Adolph Coors and Molson, 2/9/05.

Morgan Stanley (MS); 1585 Broadway, NY, NY 10036; (212) 761-4000; www.morganstanley.com; John J. Mack; diversified financial services, major U.S. credit-card issuer.

Motorola, Inc. (MOT); 1303 E. Algonquin Rd., Schaumburg, IL 60196; (847) 576-5000; www.motorola.com; Edward Zander; electronic equipment and components; integrated communication devices.

Nabisco: *see* Altria Group., Inc.

National Semiconductor Corp. (NSM); 2900 Semiconductor Dr., P.O. Box 58090; Santa Clara, CA 95052; (408) 721-5000; www.national.com; Brian L. Halla; manuf. of semiconductors, integrated circuits.

Nationwide Mutual Insurance Co.; One Nationwide Plaza, Columbus, OH 43215; (800) 882-2822; www.nationwide.com; W.G. Jurgensen; life insurance and financial services.

Navistar Intl. Corp.; 4201 Winfield Rd., Warrenville, IL 60555; (630) 735-5000; www.navistar.com; Daniel Ustian; manuf. heavy-duty trucks, parts, school buses.

NCR Corp. (NCR); 1700 S. Patterson Blvd., Dayton, OH 45479; (937) 445-5000; www.ncr.com; William R. Nuti; manuf ATMs, computer hardware and software; computer services and supplies.

Nestlé USA, Inc.; 800 North Brand Blvd., Glendale, CA 91203; (818) 549-6000; www.nestleusa.com; Joe Weller; candy (Baby Ruth, Raisinets), beverages (Nestea, Juicy Juice, Perrier), frozen foods (Stouffer's), pet foods (Purina, Alpo, Friskies). Subsidiary of Nestlé SA in Switzerland; world's largest food co.

Netflix, Inc. (NFLX); 100 Winchester Cir., Los Gatos, CA 95032; (408) 540-3700; www.netflix.com; Reed Hastings; online DVD rentals.

New York Life Insurance Co.; 51 Madison Ave., New York, NY 10010; (212) 576-7000; www.newyorklife.com; Seymour Sternberg; life insurance, annuities, mutual funds.

New York Times Co. (NYT); 229 W. 43rd St., NY, NY 10036; (212) 556-1234; www.nytco.com; A. O. Sulzberger Jr.; newspapers (*New York Times, Boston Globe*), radio and TV stations.

Newell Rubbermaid Inc. (NWL); 10 B Glenlake Pkwy., Ste. 600, Atlanta, GA 30328; (770) 407-3800; www.newellco.com; Mark D. Ketchum; housewares (Anchor Hocking, Rubbermaid); hair accessories (Goody); writing utensils (Eberhard Faber, Sharpie); childrens' prods. (Little Tikes, Graco).

News Corp. (NWS); 1211 Ave. of the Americas, 8th fl., New York, NY 10036; (212) 852-7017; www.newscorp.com; K. Rupert Murdoch; newspaper, magazine, book publishing (Harper Collins); TV and CATV stations (FOX, Fox News Channel, FX); film (20th Century Fox, Fox Searchlight); websites (MySpace.com, RottenTomatoes.com).

Nextel Communications, Inc.: *see* Sprint Nextel Corp.

NIKE, Inc. (NKE); 1 Bowerman Dr., Beaverton, OR 97005; (503) 671-6453; www.nikebiz.com; Mark G. Parker; #1 world athletic footwear mfgr.

Nordstrom, Inc. (JWN); 1617 6th Ave., Seattle, WA 98101; (206) 628-2111; www.nordstrom.com; Enrique Hernandez Jr.; upscale dept. store chain.

Norfolk Southern Corp. (NSC); Three Commercial Pl., Norfolk, VA 23510; (757) 629-2600; www.nscorp.com; Charles W. Moorman IV; operates railway, freight carrier.

Northrop Grumman Corp (NOC); 1840 Century Park East, Los Angeles, CA 90067; (310) 553-6262; www.northgrum.com; Ronald D. Sugar; world's largest shipbuilder; aircraft, electronics, data systems, information systems, missiles.

Northwest Airlines Corp.; 2700 Lone Oak Pkwy., Eagan, MN 55121; (612) 726-2111; www.nwa.com; Gary L. Wilson; air transportation; began Chapter 11 reorganization, 9/14/05.

Northwestern Mutual Life Insurance Co.; 720 E. Wisconsin Ave., Milwaukee, WI 53202; (414) 271-1444; www.north westernmutual.com; Edward J. Zore; life insurance, investment products and services, annuities.

Occidental Petroleum Corp. (OXY); 10889 Wilshire Blvd., Los Angeles, CA 90024; (310) 208-8800; www.oxy.com; Ray R. Irani; oil, natural gas, chemicals, plastics, fertilizers.

Office Depot, Inc. (ODP); 2200 Old Germantown Rd., Delray Beach, FL 33445; (561) 438-4800; www.officedepot.com; Steve Odland; office supply retail stores.

Omnicom Group Inc. (OMC); 437 Madison Ave., NY, NY 10022; (212) 415-3600; www.omnicomgroup.com; John D. Wren; advertising, market services, interactive/digital media.

Oracle Corp. (ORCL); 500 Oracle Pkwy., Redwood Shores, CA 94065; (650) 506-7000; www.oracle.com; Lawrence J. Ellison; database and file management software.

Owens Corning; 1 Owens Corning Parkway, Toledo, OH 43659; (419) 248-8000; www.owenscorning.com; David T. Brown; world leader in advanced glass, composite materials.

Owens-Illinois (OI); 1 SeaGate, Toledo, OH 43666; (419) 247-5000; Steven McCracken; www.o-i.com; one of the world's largest producers of glass and plastic packaging.

Oxford Health Plans: see UnitedHealth Group.

Park Place Entertainment: see Harrah's Entertainment.

J.C. Penney Co. (JCP); 6501 Legacy Dr., Plano, TX 75024; (972) 431-1000; www.jcpenney.com; Myron E. Ulman III; dept. stores, catalog sales, insurance.

Pepsi Bottling Group, Inc. (PBG); 1 Pepsi Way; Somers, NY 10589; (914) 767-6000; www.pbg.com; Eric J. Foss; world's #1 mfgr. & distrib. of PepsiCo prods.

PepsiCo, Inc. (PEP); 700 Anderson Hill Rd., Purchase, NY 10577; (914) 253-2000; www.pepsico.com; Steven S. Reinemund; soft drinks (Pepsi-Cola, Mountain Dew), fruit juice (Tropicana), sports drinks (Gatorade), FritoLay snacks (Ruffles, Lay's, Fritos, Doritos, Rold Gold), Quaker Oats.

Petters Group Worldwide LLC; 4400 Baker Rd., Minnetonka, MN 55343; (952) 934-9918; www.pettersgroup.com; Stuart R. Romenesko; conglomeration of consumer prod. mfgrs (Polaroid) and retailers (Fingerhut, uBid.com).

Pfizer, Inc. (PFE); 235 E. 42nd St., NY, NY 10017; (212) 573-2323; www.pfizer.com; Jeffrey B. Kinler; pharmaceuticals (Diflucan, Viagra, Zithromax), hospital, agricultural, chemical prods. Agreed consumer prods. div. (Visine, Desitin, Benadryl, Listerine, Lubriderm, Schick, Sudafed, Zantac 75, BenGay) to Johnson & Johnson, 6/26/06.

PG&E Corp. (PCG); One Market St., Spear Tower, Ste. 2400, San Francisco, CA 94105; (415) 267-7000; www.pgecorp.com; Peter E. Darbee; energy supplier.

Philip Morris Cos. Inc.: see Altria Group, Inc.

Phillips-Van Heusen Corp. (PVH); 200 Madison Ave., NY, NY 10016; (212) 381-3500; www.pvh.com; Emanuel Chirico; designer of apparel (Calvin Klein, IZOD, Geoffrey Beene, DKNY, Kenneth Cole).

Pitney Bowes, Inc. (PBI); 1 Elmcroft Rd., Stamford, CT 06926; (203) 356-5000; www.pb.com; Michael J. Critelli; world's largest mfgr. of postage meters and mailing equip.

Plains All American Pipeline, L.P. (PAA); 333 Clay St., Ste. 1600, Houston, TX 77002; (800) 564-3036; www.plainsallameri can.com; Greg L. Armstrong; oil transportation, storage.

Polaroid Corp.; see Petters Group Worldwide.

Polo Ralph Lauren Corp. (RL); 650 Madison Ave., NY, NY 10022; (212) 318-7000; www.polo.com; Ralph Lauren; men's and women's apparel.

PPG Industries, Inc. (PPG); 1 PPG Place, Pittsburgh, PA 15272; (412) 434-3131; www.ppg.com; Charles E. Bunch; glass prods., silicas, fiberglass, chemicals, sealants; world's leading supplier of automobile/industrial coatings.

The Procter & Gamble Co. (PG); 1 Procter & Gamble Plaza, Cincinnati, OH 45202; (513) 983-1100; www.pg.com; Alan Lafley; soaps and detergents (Ivory, Cheer, Tide, Mr. Clean, Comet, Zest); toiletries (Crest, Scope, Head & Shoulders, Noxzema, Oil of Olay, Old Spice); pharmaceuticals (NyQuil, Pepto-Bismol, Vicks cough medicines); foods (Folgers coffee, Pringles); paper prods. (Charmin toilet tissues, Bounty towels, Tampax tampons, Pampers & Luvs disposable diapers); Cover Girl and Max Factor cosmetics, Clairol haircare. Acquired Gillette (razors, batteries), 10/1/06.

Prudential Financial, Inc. (PRU); 751 Broad St., Newark, NJ 07102; (973) 802-6000; www.prudential.com; Arthur F. Ryan; insurance, financial services.

Publix Super Markets Inc.; 3300 Publix Corporate Pkwy., Lakeland, FL 33811; (863) 688-1188; www.publix.com; Charles H. Jenkins Jr.; chain of supermarkets.

Quaker Oats Co.: see PepsiCo, Inc.

Qwest Communications, Inc. (Q); 1801 California St., Denver, CO 80202; (303) 992-1400; www.qwest.com; Richard Notebaert; telecommunications, wireless, and directory services for most of western and southwestern U.S.

RadioShack Corp (RSH); 300 Radio Shack Circle, Fort Worth, TX 76102; (817) 415-3011; www.radioshack.com; Julian C. Day; consumer electronics retailer.

Ralcorp Holdings, Inc. (RAH); 800 Market St., St. Louis, MO 63101; (314) 877-7000; www.ralcorp.com; William Stiritz; private-label breakfast cereals, snack foods, baby food (Beech-Nut).

Ralston Purina: see Nestlé USA.

Raytheon Co. (RTN); 870 Winter St., Waltham, MA 02451; (781) 522-3000; www.raytheon.com; William Swanson; defense systems, electronics.

The Reader's Digest Assn., Inc. (RDA); Reader's Digest Road, Pleasantville, NY 10570; (914) 238-1000; www.rd.com; Thomas Ryder; world's best-selling gen. interest magazines; direct-mail marketer of magazines, books.

Reebok Intl., Ltd.; 1895 J.W. Foster Blvd., Canton, MA 02021; (781) 401-5000; www.reebok.com; Paul Harrington; athletic and leisure footwear, apparel; acquired by Germany's adidas AG, 1/31/06.

Revlon, Inc. (REV); 237 Park Ave., NY, NY 10017; (212) 527-4000; www.revlon.com; Jack L. Stahl; cosmetics, skin care.

Reynolds American Inc.; 401 N. Main St., Winston-Salem, NC 27102; (336) 741-2000; www.reynoldsamerican.com; Andrew J. Schindler; 2nd-largest U.S. producer of cigarettes (Winston, Salem, Camel, Lucky Strike). RJ Reynolds merged with Brown & Williamson Tobacco Corp. to form co., 7/30/04.

Rite Aid Corp. (RAD); 30 Hunter Lane, Camp Hill, PA 17011-2404; (717) 761-2633; www.riteaid.com; Mary F. Sammons; 3rd-largest U.S. drugstore chain.

Rockwell Automation, Inc. (ROK); 777 E. Wisconsin Ave., Suite 1400, Milwaukee, WI 53202; (414) 212-5200; www.rockwell.com; Keith D. Nosbusch; diversified industrial automation co. (world leader in electronic controls).

Rohm & Haas Co.; (ROH) 100 Independence Mall West, Philadelphia, PA 19106; (215) 592-3000; www.rohmhaas.com; Rajiv Gupta; adhesives and sealants, performance chemicals, automotive coatings; salt (Morton, Windsor).

Ryder System, Inc. (R); 11690 NW 105th St., Miami, FL 33178; (305) 500-3726; www.ryder.com; Gregory T. Swienton; truck-leasing service.

Safeway Inc. (SWY); 5918 Stoneridge Mall Rd., Pleasanton, CA 94588; (925) 467-3000; www.safeway.com; Steven A. Burd; supermarkets.

Sara Lee Corp. (SLE); Three First National Plaza, Chicago, IL 60602; (312) 726-2600; www.saralee.com; Brenda Barnes; baked goods, fresh and processed meats (Ball Park, Jimmy Dean, Hillshire Farms, Kahn's), hosiery, intimate apparel, and knitwear (Hanes, L'eggs, Playtex, Wonderbra).

SBC Communications, Inc.: see AT&T, Inc.

Schering-Plough Corp. (SGP); 2000 Galloping Hill Rd., Kenilworth, NJ 07033; (908) 298-4000; www.sch-plough.com; Fred Hassan; pharmaceuticals (Clarinex, Nasonex, Proventil), consumer prods. (Afrin, Claritin, Coppertone), animal health prods.

Sears Holdings Co. (SHLD); 3333 Beverly Rd., Hoffman Estates, IL 60179; (847) 286-2500; www.searshc.com; Eddie Lampert; 3rd largest U.S. retailer; formed by merger of Kmart and Sears, 3/24/05.

Sears, Roebuck and Co.: see Sears Holdings.

Shaw Industries, Inc.: see Berkshire Hathaway Inc.

The Shell Oil Co.; 1 Shell Plaza, 910 Louisiana St., Houston, TX 77002; (713) 241-6161; www.shellus.com; John D. Hofmeister; subsidiary of Royal Dutch Shell, world's 3rd-largest oil co.; natural gas; chemicals.

Sherwin-Williams Co. (SHW); 101 Prospect Ave. NW, Cleveland, OH 44115; (216) 566-2000; www.sherwin-williams.com; Christopher Connor; largest North American paint and varnish producer (Dutch Boy, Pratt & Lambert, Martha Stewart, Minwax).

Smithfield Foods, Inc. (SFD); 200 Commerce St., Smithfield, VA 23430; (757) 365-3000; www.smithfieldfoods.com; C. Larry Pope; pork and processed meat products.

The J. M. Smucker Co. (SJM); One Strawberry Lane, Orrville, OH 44667; (330) 682-3000; www.smuckers.com; Timothy P. Smucker; largest U.S. producer of preserves, jams, jellies; toppings (Magic Shell), Jif peanut butter; Crisco oil.

Smurfit-Stone Container Corp. (SSCC); 150 N. Michigan Ave., Chicago, IL 60601; (312) 346-6600; www.smurfit-stone.com; Patrick J. Moore; industry leader for corrugated containers, paper bags and sacks.

Southwest Airlines Co. (LUV); 2702 Love Field Dr., Dallas, TX 75235; (214) 792-4000; www.southwest.com; Gary Kelly; air transportation.

Sprint Nextel Corp. (S); 2001 Edmund Halley Dr., Reston, VA 20191; (703) 433-4000; www.sprint.com; Gary D. Forsee; wireless and long-distance telecommunications; merged with Nextel, 8/12/05.

Staples, Inc (SPLS); 500 Staples Dr., Framingham, MA 01702; (508) 253-5000; www.staples.com; Ron Sargent; largest U.S. office-supply retailer.

Starbucks Corp. (SBUX); 2401 Utah Ave. S., Seattle, WA 98134; (206) 447-1575; www.starbucks.com; James L. Donald; coffee and tea producers, retail coffee and tea stores.

Starwood Hotels & Resorts Worldwide, Inc. (HOT); 1111 Westchester Ave., White Plains, NY 10604; (914) 640-8100; www.starwoodhotels.com; Steven J. Heyer; hotels and leisure company (Westin, Sheraton, W Hotels).

State Farm Mutual Automobile Ins. Co.; 1 State Farm Plaza, Bloomington, IL 61710; (309) 766-2311; www.statefarm.com; Edward B. Rust Jr.; largest U.S. provider of auto/homeowners insurance.

The Stride Rite Corp. (SRR); 191 Spring St., Lexington, MA 02420; (617) 824-6000; www.strideritecorp.com; David Chamberlain; children's footwear (Keds, Sperry Top-Sider) and eyewear.

Sun Microsystems, Inc. (SUNW); 4150 Network Circle, Santa Clara, CA 95054; (800) 555-9SUN; www.sun.com; Jonathan I. Schwartz; supplier of network computer systems.

Sunoco, Inc. (SUN); Ten Penn Ctr., 1801 Market St., Philadelphia, PA 19103; (215) 977-3000; www.sunocoinc.com; John G. Drosdick; energy resources co., markets Sunoco gasoline.

SUPERVALU Inc. (SVU); 11840 Valley View Rd., Eden Prairie, MN 55344; (952) 828-4000; www.supervalu.com; Jeffrey Noddle; food wholesaler, retailer.

Sysco Corp. (SYY); 1390 Enclave Pkwy., Houston, TX 77077-2099; (281) 584-1390; www.sysco.com; Richard J. Schnieders; leading U.S. food-service distributor.

Target Corp.; 1000 Nicollet Mall, Minneapolis, MN 55403; (612) 304-6073; www.targetcorp.com; Robert J. Ulrich; 2nd-largest U.S. discount retailer.

Tenneco, Inc. (TEN); 500 N. Field Drive, Lake Forest, IL 60045; (847) 482-5000; www.tenneco.com; Paul T. Stecko; automotive parts (Monroe, Walker).

Texas Instruments Inc. (TXN); 12500 TI Blvd., Dallas, TX 75266; (800) 336-5236; www.ti.com; Thomas Engibous; electronics, semiconductors, software, handheld calculators.

Intl. Textile Group; 804 Green Valley Rd., Ste. 300, Greensboro, NC 27408; (336) 379-6220; www.itg-global.com; Joseph L. Gorga; apparel and home textiles/fabrics.

Textron, Inc. (TXT); 40 Westminster St., Providence, RI 02903; (401) 421-2800; www.textron.com; Lewis B. Campbell; aerospace, industrial, automotive prods.; financial services.

3M Company (MMM); 3M Center, St. Paul, MN 55144-1000; (612) 733-1110; www.mmm.com; George W. Morrison; abrasives, adhesives, electrical, health care, cleaning (Scotch-Brite, O-Cel-O sponges, Scotchgard), printing, consumer prods. (Scotch Tape, Post-it).

TIAA-CREF; 730 Third Ave., NY, NY 10017; (212) 490-9000; www.tiaa-cref.org; Herb Allison; financial services provider.

The Timberland Company (TBL); 200 Domain Dr., Stratham, NH 03885; (603) 772-9500; www.timberland.com; Jeffrey Swartz; footwear, apparel, accessories.

Time Warner Inc. (TWX); One Time Warner Ctr., New York, NY 10019; (212) 484-8000; www.timewarner.com; Richard D. Parsons; Internet service provider; magazine publishing (*Time, Sports Illustrated, Fortune, Money, People,* DC Comics), TV and CATV (Cartoon Network, HBO, CNN, TBS, TNT), book publishing (Little, Brown; Warner Books), motion pictures (Warner Bros., New Line Cinema), recordings, sports teams (Atlanta Braves). America Online and Time Warner completed the largest corporate merger in history in 2001, becoming the largest media company in the U.S. Dropped "AOL" from name, 9/18/03.

The TJX Cos., Inc. (TJX); 770 Cochituate Rd., Framingham, MA 01701; (508) 390-1000; www.tjx.com; Bernard Cammarata; world's largest off-price apparel retailer (T.J. Maxx, Marshalls).

Tootsie Roll Industries, Inc. (TR); 7401 S. Cicero Ave., Chicago, IL 60629; (773) 838-3400; www.tootsie.com; Melvin Gordon; candy (Tootsie Roll, Mason Dots, Charms, Sugar Daddy, Charleston Chew, Junior Mints); world's largest producer of lollipops.

The Toro Co. (TTC); 8111 Lyndale Ave. S, Bloomington, MN 55420; (952) 888-8801; www.thetorocompany.com; Michael J. Hoffman; lawn and turf maintenance (Lawn-Boy), snow removal equipment, lighting and irrigation systems.

Toys "R" Us Inc.; 1 Geoffrey Way, Wayne, NJ 07470; (973) 617-3500; www.toysrus.com; Gerald L. Storch; children's specialty retailer (Toys "R" Us, Babies "R" Us).

Trans World Airlines, Inc.: *see* AMR Corp.

Triarc Cos., Inc. (TRY); 280 Park Ave., NY, NY 10017; (212) 451-3000; www.triarc.com; Nelson Peltz; fast-food restaurants (Arby's).

Tribune Co. (TRB); 435 N. Michigan Ave., Chicago, IL 60611; (312) 222-9100; www.tribune.com; Dennis J. FitzSimons; newspapers (*Los Angeles Times, Chicago Tribune, Newsday, Hoy*), broadcasting (incl. WGN and 25 other stations), Chicago Cubs baseball team.

Trinity Industries, Inc. (TRN); 2525 Stemmons Fwy., Dallas, TX 75207; (214) 631-4420; www.trin.net; Timothy R. Wallace; manufactures metal prods., rail and freight prods.

Tyco Intl., Ltd. (TYC); 9 Roszel Rd., Princeton, NJ 08540; (609) 720-4200; www.tyco.com; Edward D. Breen Jr.; fire protection systems, pipes, power cables, medical supplies, packaging.

Tyson Foods, Inc. (TSN); 2210 West Oaklawn Dr., Springdale, AR 72762; (479) 290-4000 www.tysonfoodsinc.com; Richard L. Bond; fresh and processed poultry and beef, pork, and seafood prods. (Holly Farms, Weaver, Louis Kemp, IBP).

UAL Corp. (UAUA); 1200 E. Algonquin Rd., Elk Grove Twp., IL 60007; (847) 700-4000; www.united.com; Glenn Tilton; air transportation (United Airlines).

UBS Financial Services Inc.; 1285 Ave. of the Americas, New York, NY 10019; (212) 713-2000; www.ubs.com; Marten Hoekstra; financial services; subsidiary of Switzerland's UBS AG.

Unilever US (UN/UL); 800 Sylvan Ave., Englewood Cliffs, NJ 07632; (877) 995-4483; www.unilever.com; Patrick Cescau; food (Hellmann's mayonnaise, Knorr soups, Ragu pasta sauce, Wish-Bone salad dressing, Lipton Tea, Skippy Peanut Butter, Slim-Fast), hygiene prods. (Dove, Q-Tips, Vaseline). Subsidiary of Unilever NV (Neth.) and Unilever PLC (UK).

Union Pacific Corp. (UNP); 1400 Douglas St., Omaha, NE, 68179; (402) 544-5000; www.up.com; James R. Young; largest railroad, trucking co. in U.S.

Unisys Corp. (UIS); Unisys Way, Blue Bell, PA 19424; (215) 986-4011; www.unisys.com; Joseph W. McGrath; designs, manuf. computer information systems and related prods..

UnitedHealth Group Corp. (UNH); UHG Center, Bren Rd. E., Minnetonka, MN 55343; (952) 936-1300; www.unitedhealthgroup.com; William W. McGuire; 2nd-largest U.S. health insurer; acquired Oxford Health Plans, 7/29/04; acquired PacifiCare, 12/21/05.

United Parcel Service, Inc. (UPS); 55 Glenlake Pkwy. NE, Atlanta, GA 30328; (404) 828-6000; www.ups.com; Michael L. Eskew; world's largest package delivery co.

United States Steel Corp. (X); 600 Grant St., Pittsburgh, PA 15219; (412) 433-1121; www.ussteel.com; John P. Surma Jr.; steel, tin prods. (Became separate co. 1/1/02 as a result of a spin-off from USX-Marathon Group; rest of corp. became Marathon Oil Corp.)

United Technologies Corp. (UTX); One Financial Plaza, Hartford, CT 06103; (860) 728-7000; www.utc.com; George David; aerospace, industrial prods. and services (Carrier, Otis Elevator, Pratt & Whitney, Sikorsky Aircraft).

Unocal Corp.: *see* Chevron Corp.

US Airways Group, Inc. (LCC); 111 W. Rio Salado Pkwy., Tempe, AZ 85281; (480) 693-0800; www.usairways.com; William Douglas Parker; air transportation.

UST Inc. (UST); 100 W. Putnam Ave., Greenwich, CT 06830; (203) 661-1100; www.ustinc.com; Vincent A. Gierer Jr.; smokeless tobacco (Copenhagen, Skoal), pipe tobacco, wine (Chateau St. Michelle, Conn Creek, Columbia Crest).

Verizon Communications Inc. (VZ); 140 West St., New York, NY 10036; (212) 395-2121; www.verizon.com; Ivan Seidenberg; largest U.S. wireline and 2nd-lgst. wireless provider. Acquired MCI, Inc., 1/6/06.

VF Corp. (VFC); 105 Corporate Center Blvd., Greensboro, NC 27408; (336) 424-6000; www.vfc.com; Mackey J. McDonald; apparel (Lee, Wrangler, Vanity Fair, Jantzen, North Face).

Viacom, Inc. (VIA); 1515 Broadway, NY, NY 10036; (212) 258-6000; www.viacom.com; Philippe Dauman; CATV (TNN, BET, Comedy Central, MTV, VH1, Nickelodeon); produces, distributes movies (Paramount); theme parks. (Co. split into 2 separately traded entities, 1/1/06. *See* CBS Corp.)

Visteon Corp. (VC); One Village Ctr. Dr., Van Buren Twp., MI 48111; (313) 755-2800; www.visteon.com; Mike Johnston; automotive parts manufacturing, architectural glass.

Wachovia Corp. (WB); One Wachovia Center, Charlotte, NC 28288; (704) 374-6565; www.wachovia.com; G. Kennedy Thompson; financial services provider.

Walgreen Co. (WAG); 200 Wilmot Rd., Deerfield, IL 60015; (847) 914-2500; www.walgreens.com; Jeffrey A. Rein; 2nd-largest U.S. drugstore chain.

Wal-Mart Stores, Inc. (WMT); 702 SW 8th St., Bentonville, AR 72716; (479) 273-4000; www.walmartstores.com; H. Lee Scott Jr.; world's largest retailer; discount stores, wholesale clubs.

The Washington Post Co. (WPO); 1150 15th St. NW, Washington, DC 20071; (202) 334-6000; www.washpostco.com; Donald E. Graham; newspapers, *Newsweek* magazine, Salon.com, TV and CATV stations, Kaplan Educational Centers.

Waste Management, Inc. (WMI); 1001 Fannin St., Suite 4000, Houston, TX 77002; (713) 512-6200; www.wm.com; David P. Steiner; N. America's largest solid waste collection and disposal co.

WellPoint Inc. (WLP); 120 Monument Circle, Indianapolis, IN 46204; (317) 488-6000; www.wellpoint.com; Larry C. Glasscock; largest U.S. health insurer; HMOs and PPOs, incl. Blue Cross Blue Shield (in CA, GA, MI, WI), HealthLink, UNICARE, and WellChoice. Merged with Anthem, Inc., 11/30/04.

Wells Fargo & Co. (WFC); 420 Montgomery St., San Francisco, CA 94104; (800) 869-3557; www.wellsfargo.com; Dick Kovacevich; financial services.

Wendy's Intl., Inc (WEN); One Dave Thomas Blvd., Dublin, OH 43017; (614) 764-3100; www.wendys.com; Kerrii B. Anderson; quick-serve restaurants (Tim Horton's, Baja Fresh, Wendy's).

Weyerhaeuser Co. (WY); 33663 Weyerhaeuser Way S., Federal Way, WA 98003; (253) 924-2345; www.weyerhaeuser.com; Steven R. Rogel; produces and distributes. paper and wood prods.

Whirlpool Corp. (WHR); 2000 N. M-63, Benton Harbor, MI 49022; (269) 923-5000; www.whirlpoolcorp.com; Jeff M. Fettig; world's largest manuf. of major home appliances (KitchenAid, Kenmore, Roper). Acquired Maytag Corp. appliances, 3/31/06.

Whole Foods Market, Inc. (WFMI); 550 Bowie St., Austin, TX 78703; (512) 477-4455; www.wholefoodsmarket.com; John P. Mackey; world's largest natural food market chain.

Winn-Dixie Stores, Inc.; 5050 Edgewood Ct., Jacksonville, FL 32254; (904) 783-5000; www.winn-dixie.com; Peter Lynch; supermarkets (Winn Dixie, Save Rite); began Chapter 11 reorganization, 2/21/05.

Winnebago Industries, Inc. (WGO); 605 W. Crystal Lake Rd., Forest City, IA 50436; (641) 585-3535; www.winnebago-ind.com; Bruce D. Hertzke; manuf. of motor homes, recreational vehicles.

WRC Media Inc.; 512 Seventh Ave., New York, NY 10018; (212) 768-1150; www.wrcmedia.com; Ann Jackson; publisher of educational and reference media: *World Almanac*, Facts On File News Services, Funk & Wagnalls, Gareth Stevens Publishing, CompassLearning, *Weekly Reader*.

Wm. Wrigley Jr. Co. (WWY); 410 N. Michigan Ave., Chicago, IL 60611; (312) 644-2121; www.wrigley.com; William Wrigley Jr.; world's largest mfgr. of chewing gum.

Wyeth; 5 Giralda Farms, Madison, NJ 07940; (973) 660-5000; www.wyeth.com; Robert Essner; manuf. prescription (Alavert, Effexor) and over-the-counter drugs (Advil, Centrum, Chap Stick, Robitussin).

Xerox Corp.; 800 Long Ridge Road, Stamford, CT 06904; (203) 968-3000; www.xerox.com; Anne Mulcahy; copiers, printers, document publishing equip.

Yahoo! Inc. (YHOO); 701 First Ave. Sunnyvale, CA 94089; (408) 349-3300; www.yahoo.com; Terry Semel; internet media company.

Yum! Brands, Inc. (YUM); 1441 Gardiner Lane, Louisville, KY 40213; (502) 874-8300; www.yum.com; David C. Novak; quick-serve restaurants (Pizza Hut, KFC, Taco Bell).

Who Owns What: Familiar Consumer Products and Services

The following is a partial list of well-known consumer brands with their (U.S.) parent companies. Among brands not listed are many brands whose parent companies have the same or a similar name (e.g., Colgate is product of Colgate-Palmolive Co.). For company contact information, see Business Directory on previous pages.

A&W Rootbeer: Cadbury Schweppes
ABC broadcasting: Walt Disney
Admiral appliances: Maytag
Advil: Wyeth
Ajax cleanser: Colgate-Palmolive
Almond Joy candy bar: Hershey
American Girl: Mattel
Arm & Hammer: Church & Dwight
Arrid antiperspirant: Church & Dwight
Aunt Jemima Pancake mix: PepsiCo
Banana Republic stores: Gap Inc.
Band-Aids: Johnson & Johnson
Barbie dolls: Mattel
BENGAY: Pfizer
Betty Crocker prods.: General Mills
Boston Market: McDonald's
Bounty paper towels: Procter & Gamble
Brillo soap pads: Church & Dwight
Brita water systems: Clorox
Budweiser beer: Anheuser-Busch
Bulova watches: Loews
Business Week magazine: McGraw-Hill
Butterball: ConAgra
Cap'n Crunch cereal: PepsiCo
Calphalon cookware: Newell Rubbermaid
Camel cigarettes: Reynolds American
Charmin toilet tissue: Procter & Gamble
Cheer detergent: Procter & Gamble
Cheerios cereal: General Mills
Cheez Whiz: Altria (Kraft)
Chef Boyardee: ConAgra
Chipotle Mexican Grill restaurants: McDonald's
Chips Ahoy!: Altria (Nabisco)
Cingular wireless: AT&T
Clairol hair prods.: Procter & Gamble
Clinique: Estée Lauder
CNN: Time Warner
Combat insecticides: Henkel
Coppertone sun care prods.: Schering-Plough
Crest toothpaste: Procter & Gamble
Crisco shortening: J.M. Smucker
DC Comics: Time Warner
Dr. Pepper: Cadbury Schweppes

Doritos chips: PepsiCo
Dove soaps: Unilever
Duracell batteries: Proctor & Gamble
Dutch Boy paints: Sherwin-Williams
Efferdent dental cleanser: Pfizer
ESPN: Walt Disney
Fab detergent: Colgate-Palmolive
Fantastik: S.C. Johnson
Febreeze: Proctor & Gamble
Fisher Price Toys: Mattel
Folger's coffee: Procter & Gamble
Formula 409 spray cleaner: Clorox
Fox News Channel: News Corp.
Fortune magazine: Time Warner
Friskies Cat Food: Nestlé
Frito-Lays snacks: PepsiCo
Fruit of the Loom apparel: Berkshire Hathaway
Gatorade: PepsiCo
Gilette razors: Proctor & Gamble
Glade air fresheners: SC Johnson
Glad Prods.: Clorox
Godiva chocolate: Campbell Soup
Haagen-Dazs: General Mills
Halcion: Pfizer
Halls coughdrops: Cadbury Schweppes
Hamburger Helper: General Mills
Hanes apparel: Sara Lee
HBO: Time Warner
Head and Shoulders shampoo: Procter & Gamble
Hellmann's mayonnaise: Unilever
Hi-C fruit drinks: Coca-Cola
Hidden Valley prods.: Clorox
Hillshire Farm meats: Sara Lee
Hot Wheels/Matchbox cars: Mattel
Hostess cupcakes: Interstate Bakeries
Huggies diapers: Kimberly-Clark
Irish Spring: Colgate-Palmolive
Ivory soap: Procter & Gamble
Jack Daniel's whiskey: Brown-Forman
Jell-O: Altria (Kraft)
Jennie-O turkey: Hormel
Jif peanut butter: J.M. Smucker
Jim Beam bourbon: Fortune Brands
Keds footwear: Stride Rite

Kent cigarettes: Loews
KFC restaurants: Yum! Brands
Kibbles 'n Bits pet foods: Del Monte
KitchenAid appliances: Whirlpool
Kit Kat candy: Hershey
Kleenex: Kimberly-Clark
Kmart: Sears Holdings Co.
Knorr soups: Unilever
Kool-Aid: Altria (Kraft)
Ladies Home Journal magazine: Meredith
Lee jeans: V.F. Corp.
L'eggs hosiery: Sara Lee
Lenox china: Brown-Forman
LifeSavers candy: Altria (Kraft)
Lipton tea: Unilever
Listerine mouthwash: Pfizer
Lord & Taylor: Federated Dept. Stores
Macy's: Federated Dept. Stores
Marlboro cigarettes: Altria (Philip Morris)
Max Factor beauty products: Procter & Gamble
Maxwell House coffee: Altria (Kraft)
Maytag appliances: Whirlpool
Metamucil: Procter & Gamble
Michelob beer: Anheuser-Busch
Miller beer: Miller Brewing (SABMiller)
Milton Bradley games: Hasbro
Minute Maid juices: Coca-Cola
Mr. Clean: Procter & Gamble
Monroe automotive parts: Tenneco Automotive
Mountain Dew soda: PepsiCo
MTV: Viacom
Nature Valley granola bars: General Mills
NBC broadcasting: General Electric
Neutrogena soap: Johnson & Johnson
Newport cigarettes: Loews
Newsweek magazine: Washington Post
Nickelodeon TV: Viacom
9 Lives cat food: Del Monte
Olay: Procter & Gamble
Old Navy clothing: Gap Inc.
Oreo cookies: Altria (Nabisco)
Oscar Mayer meats: Altria (Kraft)
Pampers: Procter & Gamble

Pantene Shampoos: Procter & Gamble
Parker Bros. games: Hasbro
People magazine: Time Warner
Pepperidge Farm prods.: Campbell Soup
Pepto-Bismol: Procter & Gamble
Philadelphia Cream Cheese: Altria (Kraft)
Pillsbury: General Mills
Pine-Sol cleaner: Clorox
Pizza Hut restaurants: Yum! Brands
Planters nuts: Altria (Kraft)
Playskool toys: Hasbro
PlayStation: Sony
Playtex apparel: Sara Lee
Post cereals: Altria (Kraft)
Post-it notes: 3M
Prego pasta sauce: Campbell Soup
Prozac: Eli Lilly
Purina pet foods: Nestlé
Q-Tips: Unilever
Ragu sauce: Unilever
Reese's candy: Hershey
Rice-A-Roni: PepsiCo
Rice Krispies: Kellogg Co.
Right Guard deodorant: Proctor & Gamble
Ritz crackers: Altria (Nabisco)

Robitussin: Wyeth
Rogaine hair growth aide: Pfizer
Ruffles chips: PepsiCo
Schick razors: Energizer
Scope mouthwash: Procter & Gamble
Scotch tape: 3M
Scott tissue: Kimberly-Clark
Simon & Schuster publishing: CBS Corp.
Skippy peanut butter: Unilever
Slimfast: Unilever
SnackWell's cookies: Altria (Nabisco)
S.O.S. cleanser: Clorox
Southern Comfort liquor: Brown-Forman
SPAM meat: Hormel Foods
Sports Illustrated magazine: Time Warner
Sprite soda: Coca-Cola
StarKist tuna: Del Monte
Swanson broth: Campbell Soup
Swiffer: Procter & Gamble
Taco Bell restaurants: Yum! Brands
Tampax tampons: Procter & Gamble
Thomas' English muffins: Unilever
Tide detergent: Procter & Gamble
Time magazine: Time Warner
Titleist: Fortune Brands
Tombstone pizza: Altria (Kraft)

Triscuits: Altria (Nabisco)
Trojan condoms: Church & Dwight
Tropicana juice: PepsiCo
Tylenol: Johnson & Johnson
USA Today newspaper: Gannett
V8 vegetable juice: Campbell Soup
Vanity Fair apparel: V.F. Corp.
Vaseline: Unilever
Velveeta cheese prods.: Altria (Kraft)
VH-1: Viacom
Viagra: Pfizer
Vicks cold medicines: Procter & Gamble
Victoria's Secret stores: Limited Brands
Visine eye drops: Pfizer
Wall Street Journal: Dow Jones
Weekly Reader: WRC Media
Weight Watchers: H.J. Heinz
Wheaties cereal: General Mills
Windex: S.C. Johnson
Windows software applications: Microsoft
Wonderbra: Sara Lee
Wonder bread: Interstate Bakeries
The World Almanac: WRC Media
Xbox: Microsoft
Zest soap: Procter & Gamble
Ziploc storage bags: S.C. Johnson

Top Brands in Selected Categories, 2005-06[1]

Source: Information Resources, Inc., a Chicago-based marketing research company; figures for 12-month period ending 7/16/05.

Beer

	Sales	Market Share (%)
Bud Light	$1,350,503,936	15.4%
Budweiser	777,537,792	8.8
Miller Lite	712,481,152	8.1
Coors Light	606,930,944	6.9
Corona Extra	471,151,808	5.4

Chocolate Candies

	Sales	Market Share (%)
Hersheys	$87,414,740	10.8%
Reeses	83,097,940	10.2
M & Ms	82,516,670	10.2
Snickers	65,616,470	8.1
Kit Kat	40,605,600	5.0

Ready-to-Eat Cold Cereals

	Sales	Market Share (%)
Private Label	$549,454,200	9.0%
General Mills Cheerios	281,006,000	4.6
Post Honey Bunches of Oats	255,028,000	4.2
Kelloggs Frosted Flakes	242,048,100	4.0
General Mills Honey Nut Cheerios	241,237,700	4.0

Ground Coffee (excluding Decaf)

	Sales	Market Share (%)
Folgers	$421,031,000	21.9%
Maxwell House	283,510,500	14.7
Starbucks	184,439,500	9.6
Private Label	157,311,200	8.2
Folgers Coffee House	113,328,900	5.9

Cookies

	Sales	Market Share (%)
Nabisco Oreo	$473,924,300	14.0%
Nabisco Chips Ahoy	308,880,300	9.1
Private Label	293,015,500	8.6
Keebler Chips Deluxe	102,024,500	3.0
Nabisco Newtons	97,450,860	2.9

Ice Cream

	Sales	Market Share (%)
Private Label	$809,885,200	20.1%
Breyers	638,508,500	15.8
Dreyers Edy's Grand	449,843,800	11.2
Haagen Dazs	277,766,200	6.9
Blue Bell	252,952,500	6.3

Paper Towels

	Sales	Market Share (%)
Bounty	$876,025,200	39.6%
Private Label	421,530,200	19.1
Brawny	238,806,800	10.8
Scott	206,095,800	9.3
Kleenex Viva	188,112,700	8.5

Frozen Pizza

	Sales	Market Share (%)
Di Giorno	$459,271,700	18.0%
Red Baron	254,999,400	10.0
Tombstone	251,550,100	9.9
Private Label	186,940,200	7.3
Freschetta	152,183,400	6.0

Salad Dressing

	Sales	Market Share (%)
Kraft	$239,660,300	17.9%
Wishbone	160,008,200	11.9
Ken's Steakhouse	134,088,400	10.0
Private Label	128,336,400	9.6
Hidden Valley Ranch	113,855,700	8.5

Toothpaste

	Sales	Market Share (%)
Crest	$142,536,500	12.1%
Colgate Total	95,180,320	8.1
Colgate	93,757,980	8.0
Crest Whitening Plus Scope	93,522,290	8.0
Crest Whitening Expressions	67,632,900	5.8

(1) For all categories brands are ranked by dollar sales at supermarkets, drugstores, and mass merchandisers, excluding Wal-Mart.

Most Visited Shopping Websites, July 2006

Source: comScore Media Metrix, Inc.

Rank	Website[1]	Visitors[2]	Rank	Website[1]	Visitors[2]
1.	eBay	75,814,000	11.	Moviefone	13,998,000
2.	Amazon Sites	46,788,000	12.	Hewlett Packard	13,665,000
3.	Apple Computer, Inc.	31,102,000	13.	Cingular.com	12,437,000
4.	Wal-Mart	26,550,000	14.	Best Buy Sites	12,143,000
5.	Target Corp.	23,394,000	15.	Netflix.com	11,209,000
6.	Shopzilla.com	18,602,000	16.	JCPenney Sites	11,140,000
7.	Dell	14,745,000	17.	The Home Depot, Inc.	10,142,000
8.	Yahoo! Shopping	14,439,000	18.	Circuit City Stores, Inc.	8,780,000
9.	Overstock.com	14,335,000	19.	Sears.com	8,407,000
10.	Ticketmaster	14,190,000	20.	AmericanGreetings Property	8,093,000

(1) May include affiliated Websites not shown; e.g. Apple Computer, Inc. sites include the iTunes digital media store. (2) Unique visitors (visited Website at least once in July 2006).

Median Price of Existing Single-Family Homes, by Metropolitan Area, 2004-2006

Source: National Association of REALTORS®

Median prices are in thousands and based on all transactions within the time period shown.

Metropolitan Area	2004	2005	2nd Qtr. 2006	Metropolitan Area	2004	2005	2nd Qtr. 2006
Akron, OH	$116.9	$120.5	$123.4	Madison, WI	$200.8	$218.3	$221.4
Albany-Schenectady-Troy, NY	161.3	183.5	193.0	Memphis, TN/MS/AR	136.2	141.2	145.6
Albuquerque, NM	145.4	169.2	185.4	Miami-Fort Lauderdale-Miami Beach, FL.	286.4	370.1	376.2
Allentown-Bethlehem-Easton, PA/NJ	207.3	243.4	243.4	Milwaukee-Waukesha-West Allis, WI.	197.1	215.7	227.7
Amarillo, TX.	97.1	107.1	118.6	Minneapolis-St. Paul-Bloomington, MN/WI	217.4	234.8	233.0
Anaheim-Santa Ana, CA (Orange Co.)	627.3	691.9	726.2	Mobile, AL	115.2	130.5	138.2
Atlanta-Sandy Springs-Marietta, GA	156.9	167.2	173.9	Montgomery, AL.	116.6	133.3	150.7
Atlantic City, NJ.	197.9	256.1	257.3	Nashville-Davidson-Murfreesboro, TN.	145.4	161.8	177.9
Austin-Round Rock, TX.	154.7	163.8	176.7	New Haven-Milford, CT	249.2	279.1	292.6
Baltimore-Towson, MD	217.0	265.3	285.1	New Orleans-Metairie-Kenner, LA	137.4	159.2	178.0
Baton Rouge, LA.	127.7	146.2	172.3	New York City-Northern New Jersey-Long			
Beaumont-Port Arthur, TX.	93.5	98.5	114.2	Island, NY/NJ/PA	385.9	445.2	473.7
Birmingham-Hoover, AL	146.6	157.0	169.7	NY: Nassau-Suffolk, NY.	413.5	465.2	478.0
Bloomington-Normal, IL	147.8	159.2	151.0	NY: Newark-Union, NJ/PA	375.8	416.8	443.8
Boise City-Nampa, ID	135.9	147.0	NA	Norwich-New London, CT	231.5	255.9	274.0
Boston-Cambridge-Quincy, MA	389.7	413.2	421.2	Ocala, FL	110.1	143.5	169.5
Boulder, CO	325.3	348.4	373.2	Oklahoma City, OK	112.4	114.7	125.4
Bridgeport-Stamford-Norwalk, CT.	441.3	482.4	495.5	Omaha, NE/IA	131.3	136.2	142.9
Buffalo-Niagara Falls, NY	95.0	99.0	96.8	Orlando, FL	169.6	243.6	271.7
Canton-Massillon, OH.	115.2	102.2	114.4	Pensacola-Ferry Pass-Brent, FL	131.1	162.1	169.0
Cedar Rapids, IA.	129.5	131.8	133.4	Peoria, IL	96.3	109.3	115.4
Champaign-Urbana, IL	127.2	137.7	143.5	Philadelphia-Camden-Wilmington, PA/NJ/			
Charleston-North Charleston, SC	183.5	197.0	213.8	DE/MD	185.1	215.3	235.1
Charleston, WV.	111.3	118.4	123.1	Phoenix-Mesa-Scottsdale, AZ	169.4	247.4	272.2
Charlotte-Gastonia-Concord, NC/SC	168.0	180.9	191.4	Pittsburgh, PA	113.4	116.1	120.3
Chattanooga, TN/GA.	125.4	131.9	142.3	Portland-South Portland-Biddeford, ME.	224.8	246.6	242.7
Chicago-Naperville-Joliet, IL.	240.1	264.2	278.5	Portland-Vancouver-Beaverton, OR/WA	206.5	244.9	283.4
Cincinnati-Middletown, OH/KY/IN	142.5	145.9	149.1	Providence-New Bedford-Fall River, RI/MA	276.9	293.4	291.1
Cleveland-Elyria-Mentor, OH	136.4	138.9	139.0	Raleigh-Cary, NC.	169.9	194.9	207.7
Colorado Springs, CO.	187.6	205.9	218.3	Reno-Sparks, NV	284.3	349.9	353.4
Columbia, SC	123.4	135.0	145.1	Richmond, VA	170.7	201.9	227.3
Columbus, OH.	146.7	152.0	155.7	Riverside-San Bernardino-Ontario, CA	296.4	374.2	395.7
Corpus Christi, TX.	112.7	125.2	138.5	Rochester, NY	106.5	113.5	115.3
Cumberland, MD/WV	72.7	87.4	100.0	Rockford, IL	103.6	118.2	115.9
Dallas-Fort Worth-Arlington, TX	138.2	147.6	153.9	Sacramento-Arden-Arcade-Roseville, CA	317.0	375.9	380.6
Davenport-Moline-Rock Island, IA/IL	107.8	117.9	118.5	Saint Louis, MO/IL	128.7	141.0	153.0
Dayton, OH	115.8	119.7	120.6	Salem, OR	154.6	177.7	195.3
Denver-Aurora, CO	239.1	247.1	255.2	Salt Lake City, UT	158.0	173.9	191.2
Des Moines, IA	140.8	145.5	147.8	San Antonio, TX.	122.7	133.9	NA
Detroit-Warren-Livonia, MI	161.0	134.5	155.7	San Diego-Carlsbad-San Marcos, CA	551.6	604.3	613.1
Dover, DE	150.1	180.4	200.0	San Francisco-Oakland-Fremont, CA	641.7	715.7	751.9
Durham, NC	149.0	NA	177.9	San Jose-Sunnyvale-Santa Clara, CA.	698.5	744.5	748.2
El Paso, TX.	94.7	111.8	126.7	Sarasota-Bradenton-Venice, FL.	255.7	354.2	350.9
Erie, PA.	98.6	100.0	102.3	Seattle-Tacoma-Bellevue, WA	284.6	316.8	NA
Eugene-Springfield, OR	164.9	197.6	227.6	Shreveport-Bossier City, LA.	110.6	124.3	136.1
Fargo-Moorhead, ND/MN	124.2	132.8	137.2	Sioux Falls, SD.	129.2	135.8	140.3
Farmington, NM	135.0	155.0	177.1	South Bend-Mishawaka, IN	93.6	96.6	100.6
Fort Myers-Cape Coral, FL	187.2	269.2	271.6	Spartanburg, SC	110.8	121.2	132.3
Ft. Wayne, IN	96.6	102.3	100.8	Spokane, WA	128.5	156.4	179.0
Gainesville, FL	159.0	184.0	214.1	Springfield, IL	103.3	106.4	112.1
Gary-Hammond, IN.	122.6	129.8	128.4	Springfield, MA.	180.3	201.8	208.6
Grand Rapids, MI	132.9	137.8	136.4	Springfield, MO	114.1	121.1	122.1
Green Bay, WI.	143.3	154.8	152.6	Syracuse, NY	98.4	110.6	116.8
Greensboro-High Point, NC	139.8	147.8	150.6	Tallahassee, FL	152.5	167.6	174.7
Gulfport-Biloxi, MS	113.9	131.4	144.6	Tampa-St.Petersburg-Clearwater, FL	159.7	205.3	231.6
Hartford, CT	231.6	253.3	256.6	Toledo, OH.	113.5	117.3	115.8
Honolulu, HI	460.0	590.0	640.0	Topeka, KS	102.1	105.7	105.1
Houston-Baytown-Sugar Land, TX	136.0	143.0	152.7	Trenton-Ewing, NJ	234.2	261.1	290.4
Indianapolis, IN	121.7	123.8	122.4	Tucson, AZ.	177.3	231.6	247.3
Jackson, MS	118.1	133.8	149.3	Tulsa, OK.	113.1	118.2	135.0
Jacksonville, FL.	150.7	175.2	198.0	Virginia Beach-Norfolk-Newport News, VA/			
Kalamazoo-Portage, MI	123.1	121.1	NA	NC	163.0	197.2	237.3
Kansas City, MO/KS	150.0	156.7	158.8	Washington-Arlington-Alexandria, DC/VA/			
Knoxville, TN.	132.2	143.7	152.9	MD/WV	339.8	425.8	443.4
Lansing-E.Lansing, MI	137.9	142.2	141.5	Waterloo/Cedar Falls, IA	95.2	102.2	108.2
Las Vegas-Paradise, NV.	266.4	304.7	319.1	Wichita, KS.	103.9	108.0	111.5
Lexington-Fayette, KY.	138.7	146.9	150.0	Worcester, MA.	275.9	290.7	285.7
Lincoln, NE	134.4	137.2	138.7	Yakima, WA.	129.9	133.9	130.2
Little Rock-N. Little Rock, AR	108.4	119.0	128.2	Youngstown-Warren-Boardman, OH/PA	86.0	85.6	78.7
Los Angeles-Long Beach-Santa Ana, CA	446.4	529.0	576.3				
Louisville, KY/IN	131.5	135.8	138.1	**United States**	**$195.2**	**$219.0**	**$227.5**

NA = Not available.

U.S. Home Ownership Rates, by Selected Characteristics, 1997, 2006[1]

Source: Bureau of the Census, U.S. Dept. of Commerce

Region	1997	2006	Age	1997	2006	Race/Ethnicity[2]	1997	2006	Income	1997	2006
Northeast	62.4%	65.4%	Under 35	38.6%	42.4%	White, non-			Median family		
Midwest	70.3	72.5	35-44	66.3	68.9	Hispanic	72.1%	75.9%	income or more	80.8%	84.1%
South	68.1	70.4	45-54	75.6	76.3	Black	44.4	47.2	Below median		
West	59.9	64.7	55-64	80.3	81.0	Hispanic	43.3	50.0	family income	50.0	52.6
			65+	79.1	80.6	Other	52.7	59.3	**TOTAL U.S.**	**65.7%**	**68.7%**

(1) In 2006, figures are for 2nd quarter of the year. Not seasonally-adjusted. (2) Hispanic householders may be of any race. "Other" includes householders reporting Asian, Native Hawaiian/Pacific Islander, and Native American/AK Native, as well as combinations of two or more races/ethnicities.

Housing Affordability, U.S., 1990-2006

Source: National Association of REALTORS®

Year	Median priced existing home	Average mortgage rate[1]	Monthly principal & interest payment	Payment as percentage of median monthly income	Year	Median priced existing home	Average mortgage rate[1]	Monthly principal & interest payment	Payment as percentage of median monthly income
1990...	$92,000	10.04%	$648	22.0%	1999 ..	$133,300	7.33%	$733	18.0%
1991...	97,100	9.30	642	21.4	2000 ..	139,000	8.03	818	19.3
1992...	99,700	8.11	591	19.3	2001 ..	147,800	7.03	789	18.4
1993...	103,100	7.16	558	18.1	2002 ..	158,100	6.55	804	18.3
1994...	107,200	7.47	598	18.5	2003 ..	180,200	5.74	840	19.1
1995...	110,500	7.85	639	18.9	2004 ..	195,200	5.73	909	20.2
1996...	115,800	7.71	661	18.8	2005 ..	219,000	5.91	1,040	21.8
1997...	121,800	7.68	693	18.7	2006[2]..	227,500	6.63	1,166	23.6
1998...	128,400	7.10	690	17.4					

(1) All figures assume a down payment of 20% of the home price. Based on effective rate on loans closed on existing homes for the period shown. (2) Preliminary, as of the 2nd quarter of fiscal year 2006.

Average Insurance Costs by State, 2003

Source: National Association of Insurance Commissioners

	Automobile Insurance			Homeowners Insurance		
	Avg. annual expenditure[1]	Rank	% Change, 2002-03	Avg. annual premium	Rank	% Change, 2002-03
Alabama	$656	40	4.9%	$681	14	27.8%
Alaska	938	10	6.1	731	9	9.4
Arizona	920	13	4.9	614	23	13.1
Arkansas	698	33	4.2	721	11	17.0
California	821	20	7.6	753	7	14.1
Colorado	923	12	0.9	762	6	15.5
Connecticut	983	8	1.9	714	12	9.5
Delaware	973	9	7.2	442	41	13.3
District of Columbia[2]	1,129	3	8.6	806	44	15.6
Florida	1,015	5	8.7	810	45	3.1
Georgia	759	25	2.6	570	50	10.3
Hawaii	774	23	5.2	687	13	21.6
Idaho	585	48	4.5	433	43	13.4
Illinois	761	24	4.9	610	48	18.2
Indiana	670	38	3.7	594	24	16.9
Iowa	580	49	6.1	542	34	20.4
Kansas	610	46	4.2	772	5	12.9
Kentucky	737	27	7.6	559	28	16.5
Louisiana	1,014	6	9.5	975	2	16.1
Maine	631	42	7.9	462	39	11.1
Maryland	891	15	6.4	584	49	22.4
Massachusetts[3]	1,052	4	6.9	671	18	9.8
Michigan	931	11	7.0	673	16	16.6
Minnesota	836	18	4.5	733	8	24.2
Mississippi	709	31	4.5	793	4	18.7
Missouri	702	32	5.3	650	47	18.2
Montana	674	36	7.4	628	19	14.8
Nebraska	624	43	6.0	690	46	15.8
Nevada	913	14	2.9	582	26	9.6
New Hampshire	776	22	6.3	539	35	11.8
New Jersey [2]	1,188	1	6.8	585	25	8.7
New Mexico	730	30	4.4	551	31	12.4
New York	1,161	2	6.8	721	10	9.1
North Carolina	605	47	2.9	576	27	9.3
North Dakota	536	51	6.4	625	20	18.4
Ohio	671	37	5.0	476	37	16.1
Oklahoma	689	34	5.9	925	3	15.6
Oregon	735	28	7.8	461	40	15.8
Pennsylvania	811	21	3.5	543	33	13.8
Rhode Island	992	7	5.9	673	15	11.1
South Carolina	745	26	6.0	672	17	11.3
South Dakota	563	50	4.2	557	29	18.8
Tennessee	650	41	2.9	622	21	16.0
Texas[4]	837	17	5.8	1,328	1	7.3
Utah	732	29	4.6	463	38	11.3
Vermont	683	35	6.0	552	30	12.0
Virginia	657	39	5.1	560	51	17.6
Washington	824	19	4.7	549	32	9.6
West Virginia	842	16	8.5	534	36	19.5
Wisconsin	620	44	1.8	434	42	27.6
Wyoming	617	45	6.4	621	22	12.7
United States	**$821**		**5.7%**	**$668**		**12.6%**

(1) Average expenditure is equal to the total written premium for combined liability, collision and comprehensive coverages divided by the liability written car-years (A car-year is equal to 365 days of insured coverage for a single vehicle.) in that state. This assumes that all insured vehicles carry liability coverage but do not necessarily carry the physical damage coverages—collision and/or comprehensive. (2) The District of Columbia is entirely urban and New Jersey is predominantly urban. Their results cannot be directly compared with states with large rural areas. (3) Data incorporates Safe Driver Plan credits and surcharges. (4) Due to the exclusion of county mutuals, which had 43 percent of the market in 2003, Texas results are not comparable with results from other states.

Auto Insurance Premiums by City, 2006[1]

Source: Insurance Information Institute; Runzheimer International

	Most expensive cities			Least expensive cities	
Rank	City	Avg. annual premium	Rank	City	Avg. annual premium
1.	Detroit, MI	$5,894	1.	Roanoke, VA	$912
2.	Philadelphia, PA	4,440	2.	Chattanooga, TN	980
3.	Newark, NJ	3,977	3.	Nashville, TN	1,040
4.	New York City, NY	3,430	4.	Green Bay, WI	1,042
5.	Los Angeles, CA	3,303	5.	Raleigh, NC	1,057

(1) Assumes $100/$300/$50 liability limits, collision and comprehensive with $500 deductibles, and $100/$300 uninsured coverage.

Leading Auto Insurers, 2005[1]

Source: National Association of Insurance Commissioners

Rank	Company/Group	Direct premiums written[2]	% Market Share
1.	State Farm Mutual Group	$29,471,232	18.0%
2.	Allstate Insurance Co. Group	18,131,607	11.1
3.	Progressive Casualty Group	12,052,274	7.4
4.	National Indemnity Co. Group (Berkshire Hathaway)	10,101,325	6.2
5.	Farmers Insurance Group	8,022,571	4.9

(1) By direct premiums written. (2) After reinsurance transactions, excluding state funds, as of 2005.

Leading Home Insurers, 2005[1]

Source: National Association of Insurance Commissioners

Rank	Company/Group	Direct premiums written[2]	% Market share
1.	State Farm Mutual Group	$12,835,980	22.2%
2.	Allstate Insurance Co. Group	7,054,405	12.2
3.	Farmers Insurance Group	3,936,087	6.8
4.	Nationwide Group	2,703,828	4.7
5.	St. Paul Travelers Companies and Affiliates	2,416,817	4.2

(1) By direct premiums written for homeowners insurance. (2) Before reinsurance transactions, excluding state funds.

Top U.S. Charities by Donations[1]

Source: The Chronicle of Philanthropy, 2006

(ranked by private support; in millions of dollars)

Rank	Organization	Private Support[2]	Total Income[3]
1.	United Way of America (Alexandria, VA)	$3,884	$4,037
2.	Salvation Army (Alexandria, VA)	1,545	3,104
3.	Feed the Children (Oklahoma City, OK)	888	959
4.	American Cancer Society (Atlanta, GA)	868	926
5.	AmeriCares Foundation (Stamford, CT)	801	802
6.	YMCA (Chicago, IL)	773	4,832
7.	Gifts In Kind International (Alexandria, VA)	750	754
8.	Lutheran Services in America (Baltimore, MD)	723	8,031
9.	Fidelity Charitable Gift Fund (Boston, MA)	683	768
10.	Catholic Charities USA (Alexandria, VA)	581	3,139
11.	American National Red Cross (Washington, DC)	557	3,066
12.	Harvard University (Cambridge, MA.)	540	4,343
13.	Food for the Poor (Deerfield Beach, FL)	536	643
14.	Stanford University (CA)	524	NA
15.	World Vision (Federal Way, WA)	514	804
16.	Boys & Girls Clubs of America (Atlanta, GA)	510	1,186
17.	America's Second Harvest (Chicago, IL)	482	489
18.	Nature Conservancy (Arlington, VA)	436	732
19.	American Heart Association (Dallas, TX)	436	593
20.	Goodwill Industries International (Rockville, MD)	397	2,351
21.	Cornell University (Ithaca, NY)	386	NA
22.	Campus Crusade for Christ International (Orlando, FL)	383	421
23.	American Lebanese Syrian Associated Charities/St. Jude Children's Research Hospital (Memphis, TN)	376	641
24.	Habitat for Humanity International (Americus, GA)	359	844
25.	University of Pennsylvania (Philadelphia, PA)	333	NA
26.	University of Southern California (Los Angeles, CA)	322	NA
27.	Johns Hopkins University (Baltimore, MD)	312	2,789
28.	Vanguard Charitable Endowment Program (Southeastern, PA)	310	316
29.	Boy Scouts of America (Irving, TX)	296	771
30.	Columbia University (New York, NY)	291	NA

(1) Fiscal year 2004 data used, except: 2005 data used for organizations with fiscal years ending in Jan.–March; 2003 data used for organizations with incomplete 2004 data. (2) Private support consists of donations from individuals, foundations, and corporations. (3) Total income includes private support as well as government funding, fees charged, and revenue or losses from investments made by the charity. NA = not available.

How to Obtain Birth, Death, Marriage, Divorce Records

The pamphlet "Where to Write for Vital Records: Births, Deaths, Marriages, and Divorces" (Stock # 017-022-01597-8) is available from the U.S. Government Printing Office (GPO) at a cost of $4.25. Orders can also be placed by calling (866) 512-1800 or (202) 512-1800; by mail at Superintendent of Documents, P.O. Box 371954, Pittsburgh, PA 15250; or on the Website bookstore.gpo.gov.

The complete pamphlet and other vital records information can also be accessed online at www.cdc.gov/nchs/howto/w2w/w2welcom.htm

IT'S A FACT: According to the U.S. Dept. of Labor, the average American consumer spends 32 cents of every dollar on housing. Transportation accounts for about 18 cents, and food costs about 13 cents. Health care and entertainment respectively make up about 6 and 5 cents on the dollar.

Annual Cost of Raising a Child Born in 2005

Source: Center for Nutrition Policy and Promotion, U.S. Dept. of Agriculture

Estimated annual expenditures in 2005 dollars for a child born in 2005, by income group, for each year to age 17, assuming an average inflation rate of 3.1%. Estimates are for the younger child in a 2-parent family with 2 children, for the overall U.S.

Year (Age)	Lowest	Income group[1] Middle	Highest	Year (Age)	Lowest	Income group[1] Middle	Highest
2005 (<1)	$7,300	$10,220	$15,190	2015 (10)........	$10,090	$13,830	$20,200
2006 (1)	7,520	10,530	15,650	2016 (11)........	10,400	14,250	20,810
2007 (2)	7,750	10,850	16,130	2017 (12)........	11,900	15,740	22,630
2008 (3)	8,180	11,490	17,010	2018 (13)........	12,270	16,220	23,320
2009 (4)	8,430	11,840	17,530	2019 (14)........	12,640	16,710	24,030
2010 (5)	8,690	12,200	18,060	2020 (15)........	12,990	17,690	25,680
2011 (6)	8,990	12,460	18,250	2021 (16)........	13,390	18,230	26,470
2012 (7)	9,260	12,840	18,810	2022 (17)........	13,790	18,780	27,270
2013 (8)	9,540	13,230	19,380				
2014 (9)	9,790	13 420	19,600	**TOTAL**	**$182,920**	**$250,530**	**$366,020**

(1) In 2005, the lowest annual income group included those households earning less than $43,200 (average in this range = $26,900); middle income covered those earning $43,200-72,600 (average = $57,400); highest income group had earnings of $72,600 or more (average = $108,700).

Identity Theft

Source: Federal Trade Commission; Dept. of Justice

Identity theft and fraud are crimes in which a person wrongfully obtains and uses deception or fraud to take advantage of another person's personal data, usually for financial gain. Identifying information—such as Social Security, bank account, and credit card numbers—can be used without permission to remove funds from bank and other financial accounts. In the worst-case scenario, an identity thief could mirror a person's identity altogether, creating new accounts and vast debts, and even committing other crimes in the victim's name.

In 2005, the Federal Trade Commission (FTC) received 255,565 identity theft complaints from U.S. law enforcement and consumers, up 4% from 2004. The U.S. Dept. of Justice made identity theft and identity fraud federal offenses in 1998.

Identity Theft Prevention

You can take these simple steps (acronym, **SCAM**) to reduce your vulnerability to identity theft.

Be stingy about revealing personal information to others unless you have a reason to trust them. Adopt a "need to know" basis for revealing personal data. Keep information printed on personal bank checks to a minimum. If someone contacts you via telephone or the Internet and offers a prize but asks for personal data, ask them to mail you a form, and check the company with the Better Business Bureau (www.bbb.org). When traveling, have mail held at the post office or have a trusted person collect your mail. Be careful when throwing out documents; shredding documents containing personal or financial information is advised. Never click on links in unsolicited emails; type addresses into web browsers. Use firewalls, anti-spyware, and anti-virus software to protect your computer and the information it stores.

Check financial information often for irregular activity, and review statements for any charges or transactions that should not be there. Statements for your bank and credit card accounts should arrive monthly; if not, contact the company or financial institution.

Ask for a copy of your credit report periodically, and review it to confirm that no unknown accounts have been opened in your name. Free annual credit reports are now available by visiting www.annualcreditreport.com, calling 877-322-8228, or writing Annual Credit Report Request Service, P.O. Box 105283, Atlanta, GA 30348. Note: Do not contact the credit bureaus directly for this.

Maintain careful records. Keep monthly statements and cancelled checks or their copies for at least a year. These can be useful if you need to dispute a transaction.

Identity Theft Recovery

If you think you have become a victim of identity theft or fraud, take action immediately.

Contact one of the three major credit bureaus to have them place a fraud alert in your file. This will require that creditors contact you before opening new accounts in your name or changing information on existing accounts. Once the alert is activated, the other two credit bureaus will be notified.

Get a copy of your credit report and review it closely. Close any accounts that have been tampered with or opened fraudulently. Speak with someone in the fraud/security department of each creditor, and follow up in writing, with copies of supporting documents. Victims of identity theft have the right to request that those debts incurred through fraud are blocked from future credit reports. An ID Theft affidavit, accepted by most credit companies, is available online at www.consumer.gov/idtheft/pdf/affidavit.pdf

Report the crime to local police or police in the community where the theft took place. Report the theft to the FTC at www.consumer.gov/idtheft or 877-IDTHEFT. You can also report to the FTC in writing at the Identity Theft Clearinghouse, Federal Trade Commission, 600 Pennsylvania Ave. NW, H-130, Washington, DC 20580.

Obtain copies of fraudulent credit and account applications from the three major credit bureaus and give copies to the police.

Contact the Social Security Administration (www.ssa.gov) if you suspect your social security number is being used.

Credit Bureau Contacts

If you think you have become a victim of identity theft or fraud, take action immediately.

Equifax. Reports: 800-685-1111; fraud alerts: 800-525-6285. P.O. Box 740241, Atlanta, GA 30374-0241. www.equifax.com

Experian (formerly TRW). Reports and fraud alerts: 888-EXPERIAN. P.O. Box 2002, Allen, TX 75013. www.experian.com

Trans Union. Reports: 800-888-4213; P.O. Box 1000, Chester, PA 19022. Fraud alerts: 800-680-7289; P.O. Box 6790, Fullerton, CA 92834. www.transunion.com

POSTAL INFORMATION

Basic U.S. Postal Service

The Postal Reorganization Act, creating a government-owned postal service under the executive branch and replacing the old Post Office Department, was signed into law by Pres. Richard Nixon, Aug. 12, 1970. The service officially came into being on July 1, 1971. The U.S. Postal Service is governed by an 11-person Board of Governors. Nine of the members are appointed by the president, with Senate approval. These 9 choose a postmaster general. The board and the postmaster general choose the 11th member, who serves as deputy postmaster general. An independent Postal Rate Commission of 5 members, appointed by the president, reviews and rules on proposed postal rate increases submitted by the Board of Governors.

U.S. Domestic Rates

(Domestic rates apply to the U.S., to its territories and possessions, and to APOs and FPOs. Many changes in domestic postal rates, fees, and services took effect January 8, 2006.)

First-Class Mail

First-Class Mail includes written matter such as letters, postal cards, and postcards (private mailing cards), plus all other matter wholly or partly in writing, whether sealed or unsealed, except book manuscripts, periodical articles and music, manuscript copy accompanying proofsheets or corrected proofsheets of the same, and the writing authorized by law on matter of other classes. Also included: matter sealed or closed against inspection, bills, and statements of accounts.

Written letters and matter sealed against inspection cost 37¢ for first ounce or fraction, 24¢ for each additional ounce or fraction up to and including 13 ounces. U.S. Postal Service cards cost 24¢ for postage, with a 2¢ fee for the card. Private postcards postage is 24¢. Presort and automation-compatible mail can qualify for lower rates if certain piece minimums, mailing permits, and other requirements are met.

Express Mail

Express Mail provides guaranteed expedited service for any mailable article (up to 70 lbs and not over 108 in. in combined length and girth). Offers next day delivery by noon to most destinations; no extra charge for Saturday, Sunday, or holiday delivery. Second-day service is available to locations not on the Next Day Delivery Network. The basic rate for Express Mail weighing up to 8 oz is **$14.40**. All rates include insurance up to $100, shipment receipt, record of delivery at the destination post office, and free tracking on the USPS Web site (www.usps.com).

Express Mail Flat Rate: $14.40, regardless of weight, if matter fits into a special Postal Service flat-rate envelope.

Scheduled pickup service is available for **$13.25** per stop, regardless of the number of pieces or service used (e.g., Express Mail, Priority Mail, or Parcel Post can be picked up together).

Contact your local post office for further information.

Standard Mail

Standard Mail is limited to items less than 16 ounces such as solicitations, newsletters, advertising materials, books, cassettes, and other merchandise. A minimum volume of 200 pieces or 50 lbs of such items is necessary, and specific bulk mail preparation and sortation requirements apply.

The minimum rate per piece for pieces 3.3 ounces or less is $0.282 for basic letters and $0.363 for flats/nonletters. Contact your post office for the discounts offered for automation, presorted, carrier route, destination entry, and other discounts. Separate rates are available for some nonprofit organizations.

Any mailer who uses a permit imprint is required to pay a one-time $160 application fee plus an annual (calendar year) fee of $160. Additional standards apply to mailings of non-identical-weight pieces.

Priority Mail

Due to expeditious handling and transportation, Priority Mail is delivered in 1-3 days, on average. Priority Mail may include any mailable article up to 70 lbs and not over 108 in. in length and girth combined, whether sealed or unsealed, including written and other First Class material.

Packages weighing less than 15 lbs and measuring over 84 in. (but less than 108 in.) in length and girth combined cost the same as the zoned rate for a 15-lb parcel. Scheduled pickup service costs an additional $13.25 per stop, regardless of the number of pieces or service used (e.g. Express Mail, Priority Mail, or Parcel Post can be picked up together).

Priority Mail Flat Rate: $4.05, regardless of weight, if matter fits into a special Postal Service flat-rate envelope. **$8.10**, regardless of weight (under 70 lbs), if matter fits into a special Postal Service flat-rate box.

Priority Mail Rates

Weight not over (lbs)	ZONES 1-3	4	5	6	7	8
1	$4.05	$4.05	$4.05	$4.05	$4.05	$4.05
2	4.20	4.80	5.15	5.30	5.70	6.05
3	5.00	6.40	7.20	7.55	8.25	9.00
4	5.60	7.45	8.50	8.95	9.95	10.90
5	6.15	8.45	9.80	10.40	11.60	12.80
6	6.65	9.35	10.45	10.60	11.90	12.95
7	7.15	10.35	11.25	11.60	13.25	14.80
8	7.75	11.35	12.05	12.60	14.55	16.60
9	8.35	12.35	12.85	13.60	15.85	18.45
10	8.85	13.30	13.70	14.75	17.20	20.25
11	9.45	14.05	14.50	15.95	18.50	22.05
12	10.00	14.80	15.30	17.20	19.80	23.85
13	10.55	15.55	16.15	18.45	21.15	25.65
14	11.10	16.30	16.90	19.60	22.40	27.45
15[1]	11.65	17.05	17.75	20.80	23.70	29.30

(1) See postmaster for pieces over 15 lbs.

Periodicals

Periodicals include newspapers and magazines.

For the general public, the applicable Package Services or First-Class postage is paid for periodicals.

For publishers, rates vary according to:
 (1) whether item is sent to same county,
 (2) percentage of editorial and advertising matter,
 (3) whether the publishing org. is nonprofit or produces educational material for use in classrooms,
 (4) weight,
 (5) distance,
 (6) level of presort,
 (7) automation compatibility.

Package Services

Package Services, formerly "Standard Mail (B)," is any mailable matter that is not included in First-Class or Periodicals (unless permitted or required by regulations). There are currently four subclasses of Package Services: Parcel Post, Bound Printed Matter, Media Mail (formerly "Special Standard Mail"), and Library Mail.

The post office determines charges for Package Services according to the weight of the package in pounds and the zone distance shipped (Media Mail and Library Mail rates are determined by weight alone). There is no minimum weight; see separate headings for maximum weight. Presort and automation-compatible mail for all Package Services can qualify for lower rates if certain piece minimums, mailing permits, and other requirements are met. Contact your local post office for further information. Package Services is not sealed against postal inspection.

Parcel Post

Parcel Post is any Package Services not mailed as Bound Print Matter, Media Mail, or Library Mail. Any Package Services matter may be mailed at the Parcel Post rates, subject to these basic standards: not to exceed 70 lbs or 130 in. in combined length and girth (packages over 84 in., but not more than 130 in. in combined length and girth and under 15 lbs are subject to the 15 lb "balloon rate"). All fractions of a pound are counted as a full pound. Parcel Post subclass consists of two basic retail rate categories and three drop-shipped categories, the latter collectively known as Parcel Select.

Parcel Post Basic Rate Schedule

(Inter BMC/ASF ZIP codes only, machinable[1] parcels, no discount, no surcharge)

Weight not over	ZONES						
	1 & 2	3	4	5	6	7	8
1 lb.	$3.89	$3.95	$3.95	$3.95	$3.95	$3.95	$3.95
2	4.06	4.06	4.36	4.36	4.73	4.73	4.73
3	4.90	4.90	5.85	5.96	6.02	6.08	6.66
4	5.12	5.48	6.63	7.30	7.53	7.59	8.29
5	5.30	6.02	7.31	8.17	9.04	9.11	9.94
6	5.93	6.33	7.84	8.96	10.03	10.43	12.11
7	6.11	6.62	8.34	9.70	10.91	12.01	13.52
8	6.30	6.88	8.75	10.37	11.71	13.22	15.85
9	6.44	7.13	9.21	11.01	12.47	14.10	17.96
10	6.62	7.98	9.59	11.60	13.18	14.94	19.12
11	6.76	8.22	9.98	12.16	13.84	15.73	20.18
12	6.89	8.44	10.33	12.69	14.46	16.46	21.19
13	7.03	8.63	10.67	13.19	15.05	17.15	22.12
14	7.17	8.87	10.99	13.65	15.61	17.81	23.02
15	7.29	9.07	11.31	14.10	16.14	18.43	23.86
16	7.40	9.26	11.59	14.52	16.64	19.02	24.67
17	7.54	9.42	11.89	14.92	17.12	19.59	25.43
18	7.64	9.60	12.14	15.30	17.58	20.12	26.16
19	7.77	9.78	12.41	15.67	18.01	20.64	26.86
20[2]	7.86	9.94	12.63	16.02	18.42	21.13	27.53

(1) Machinable parcels must be: not less than 6 in. long, 3 in. high, and .25 in. thick or more than 34 in. long, 17 in. high, and 17 in. thick; at least 6 oz. but not more than 35 lbs. (2) Consult postmaster for pieces greater than 20 lbs.

Library Mail

(minimum weight: none; maximum weight: 70 lbs)

Applies to books, printed music, bound academic theses, periodicals, sound recordings, museum materials, and other library materials mailed between schools, colleges, universities, public libraries, museums, veteran and fraternal organizations, and nonprofit religious, educational, scientific, and labor organizations or associations (or to or from these organizations). Advertising restrictions apply. All packages must be marked "Library Mail," and may not exceed 108 in.

in combined length and girth. Contact your local post office for further information.

Rates are calculated by weight only. Single-piece rates are: $1.20, up to 1 lb; 46¢ for each additional pound or fraction, to 7 lbs; additional pounds thereafter, 32¢ each.

Media Mail

(minimum weight: none; maximum weight: 70 lbs)

Formerly "Special Standard Mail." Applies to books of at least 8 printed pages; 16-mm or narrower-width films; printed music; printed test materials; sound recordings, playscripts, and manuscripts for books; printed educational charts; loose-leaf pages and binders consisting of medical information; computer-readable media. Advertising restrictions apply. Packages must be marked "Media Mail" and may not exceed 108 in. in combined length and girth. Contact your local post office for further information.

Rates are calculated by weight only. Single-piece rates are: $1.59, up to 1 lb; 48¢ for each additional pound or fraction, to 7 lbs; additional pounds thereafter, 34¢ each.

Bound Printed Matter

(minimum weight: none; maximum weight: 15 lbs)

Applies to advertising, promotional, directory, or editorial material that is bound by permanent fastening and consists of sheets of which at least 90% are imprinted by any process other than handwriting or typewriting. Does not include stationery (or pads of blank forms) or personal correspondence. Packages may not exceed 108 in. in combined length and girth, and must be marked "Bound Printed Matter" or "BPM."

Bound Printed Matter Rates

(zone rate for parcels; flat single pieces pay 8¢ less)

Weight not over	ZONES						
	1 & 2	3	4	5	6	7	8
1.0 lb.	$1.97	$2.02	$2.07	$2.15	$2.22	$2.32	$2.50
1.5	1.97	2.02	2.07	2.15	2.22	2.32	2.50
2.0	2.04	2.11	2.17	2.28	2.38	2.51	2.74
2.5	2.12	2.20	2.28	2.41	2.54	2.70	2.99
3.0	2.19	2.29	2.38	2.54	2.70	2.89	3.24
3.5	2.27	2.38	2.49	2.68	2.86	3.08	3.49
4.0	2.34	2.47	2.59	2.80	3.01	3.27	3.73
4.5	2.41	2.56	2.70	2.94	3.17	3.46	3.98
5.0	2.49	2.65	2.80	3.07	3.33	3.65	4.23
6.0	2.64	2.82	3.01	3.33	3.65	4.03	4.72
7.0	2.78	3.00	3.23	3.59	3.96	4.41	5.22
8.0	2.93	3.18	3.44	3.86	4.28	4.79	5.71
9.0	3.08	3.36	3.65	4.12	4.60	5.16	6.21
10.0	3.23	3.54	3.86	4.38	4.91	5.54	6.70
11.0	3.37	3.72	4.07	4.65	5.23	5.92	7.20
12.0	3.52	3.90	4.28	4.91	5.54	6.30	7.69
13.0	3.67	4.08	4.49	5.18	5.86	6.68	8.19
14.0	3.82	4.26	4.70	5.44	6.18	7.06	8.68
15.0	3.96	4.44	4.91	5.70	6.49	7.44	9.18

Domestic Mail Special Services

Insured Mail

Applicable to Standard Mail, Package Services, and First-Class or Priority Mail items eligible to be mailed as Package Services. Matter for sale addressed to prospective purchasers who have not ordered it or authorized its sending cannot be insured. **Note:** for Express Mail, insurance is included up to $100. Add $1.05 per $100 or fraction thereof over $100 up to $5,000.

Declared Value	Insured Mail Fee[1]
$0.01 to $50.00	$1.35
$50.01 to $100.00	2.30
$100.01 to $200.00	3.35
$200.01 to $300.00	4.40
$300.01 to $400.00	5.45
$400.01 to $500.00	6.50
$500.01 to $600.00	7.55
$600.01 to $700.00	8.60
$700.01 to $800.00	9.65
$800.01 to $900.00	10.70
$900.01 to $1,000.00	11.75
$1,000.01 to $5,000.00	12.30 plus $1.05 per

each $100 or fraction thereof over $1,000 in desired coverage
(1) In addition to postage. (Maximum liability is $5,000.) See postmaster for details on bulk discounts.

Special Handling

Provides preferential handling, but not preferential delivery, to the extent practicable in dispatch and transportation. Available for First-Class Mail, Priority Mail, and Package Services for the following surcharge: up to 10 lb, $6.25; over 10 lb, $8.70 Pieces must be marked "Special Handling."

Delivery Confirmation

Applies to First-Class Mail parcels, Priority Mail, and Package services. Available for purchase at the time of mailing only. Provides mailer with the date and time an article was delivered and, if delivery was attempted but not successful, the date and time of the attempt. Electronic confirmation is available for barcoded matter.

Manual confirmation is available for retail purchasers on the Internet (www.usps.com) or toll-free by phone (800-222-1811).

Priority Mail fees: manual, 50¢; electronic, free. First-Class Mail parcels and Package Services fees: manual, 60¢; electronic, 14¢. Standard Mail fee: electronic, 14¢.

Registered Mail

Provides sender with mailing receipt, and a delivery record is maintained. Only matter prepaid with postage at First Class or priority mail rates may be registered. Stamps or meter stamps must be attached. The face of the article must be at least 5" long, 3½" high.

Declared Value	Fee
$0.00	$7.90
$0.01 to $100.00	8.45
$100.01 to $500.00	9.35
$500.01 to $1,000.00	10.25
$1,000.01 to $2,000.00	11.15
$2,000.01 to $3,000.00	12.05
$3,000.01 to $4,000.00	12.95
$4,000.01 to $5,000.00	13.85
$5,000.01 to $6,000.00	14.75
$6,000.01 to $7,000.00	15.65
$7,000.01 to $8,000.00	16.55
$8,000.01 to $9,000.00	17.45
$9,000.01 to $10,000.00	18.35
$10,000.01 to $25,000.00	8.35 plus $0.90 for each $1,000 or fraction thereof over $10,000
$25,000.01 to $1 million	31.85 plus $0.90 for each $1,000 or fraction thereof over $25,000
$1 million to $15 million	909.35 plus $0.90 for each $1,000 or fraction thereof over $1 million
Over $15 million	13,509.35 plus any additional amount determined by the Postal Service

Note: The mailer is required to declare the value of mail presented for registration. Fee for articles with declared value over $0.00 up to $25,000 includes insurance; fee is in addition to postage.

Collect on Delivery (C.O.D): Fee: $4.20 in addition to other C.O.D. charges; items must be sent as bona fide orders or be in conformity with agreements between senders and addressees. Maximum amount collectible is $1,000. For details, consult postmaster.

Certified mail: Available for any matter having no intrinsic value on which First Class or Priority Mail postage is paid. A receipt is furnished at the time of mailing, and evidence of delivery is obtained. Basic fee is $2.40 in addition to regular postage. Return receipt and restricted delivery available upon payment of additional fees. No indemnity.

Change of Address

The USPS will forward mail to another address provided a Change of Address (COA) card has been filed, either in person (free), on www.usps.com ($1 fee), or by phone at 1-800-ASK-USPS ($1). The COA card, which can be picked up at any post office or printed off the Internet, can also be dropped in any mailbox for filing.

International Mail Special Services

Registration: Available, for letter-post items only, to all countries except North Korea. Fee $7.90. The maximum indemnity payable is $44.86. Additional insurance may be purchased for most destinations.

Return Receipt: Shows to whom and when delivered; Fee: $1.85 (must be purchased at time of mailing).

Air Mail: Letter-post items weighing under 1 oz can be sent airmail for **84¢** to most countries daily.

Aerogrammes: Aerogrammes are letter sheets that can be folded into the form of an envelope and sealed. Intended for personal communication only and may not include enclosures. Fee: 75¢ from U.S. to all countries.

Air mail postcards (single): 55¢ to Canada and Mexico; 75¢ to all other countries.

International Reply Coupons (IRC): Provide foreign addressees with a prepaid means of responding to communications initiated by a U.S. sender. Each IRC is equivalent to the destination country's minimum postage rate for an unregistered airmail letter. Fee: $1.85 per coupon.

Restricted Delivery: Places restrictions on who receives an item. Available to many countries for registered mail; some limitations. Fee: $3.70.

Insurance: Available to many countries for loss of or damage to items paid at parcel post rate. Consult postmaster for indemnity limits for individual countries.

	Fees	
Limit of indemnity not over	Canada[1]	All other countries[1]
$50	$1.35	$1.95
100	2.30	2.75
200	3.35	3.80
300	4.40	4.85
400	5.45	5.90
500	6.50	6.95
600	7.55	8.00
675	8.60	9.05
700		9.05
800		10.10
900		11.15
1,000[2]		12.20

(1) Not all countries insure items up to the amounts listed in the table. Canada does not insure items for more than $675. (2) For amounts more than $1,000, add $1.00 for each $100 or fraction.

Post Office-Authorized 2-Letter State Abbreviations

The abbreviations below are approved by the U.S. Postal Service for use in addresses.

Alabama	AL	Hawaii	HI	Missouri	MO	Pennsylvania	PA
Alaska	AK	Idaho	ID	Montana	MT	Puerto Rico	PR
American Samoa	AS	Illinois	IL	Nebraska	NE	Rhode Island	RI
Arizona	AZ	Indiana	IN	Nevada	NV	South Carolina	SC
Arkansas	AR	Iowa	IA	New Hampshire	NH	South Dakota	SD
California	CA	Kansas	KS	New Jersey	NJ	Tennessee	TN
Colorado	CO	Kentucky	KY	New Mexico	NM	Texas	TX
Connecticut	CT	Louisiana	LA	New York	NY	Utah	UT
Delaware	DE	Maine	ME	North Carolina	NC	Vermont	VT
District of Columbia	DC	Marshall Islands[1]	MH	North Dakota	ND	Virgin Islands	VI
Federated States of Micronesia[1]	FM	Maryland	MD	Northern Mariana Is.	MP	Virginia	VA
Florida	FL	Massachusetts	MA	Ohio	OH	Washington	WA
Georgia	GA	Michigan	MI	Oklahoma	OK	West Virginia	WV
Guam	GU	Minnesota	MN	Oregon	OR	Wisconsin	WI
		Mississippi	MS	Palau[1]	PW	Wyoming	WY

(1) Although an independent nation, this country is currently subject to domestic rates and fees.

Canadian Province and Territory Postal Abbreviations

Source: Canada Post

Alberta	AB	Newfoundland and Labrador	NF	Nunavut	NU	Quebec	QC[1]
British Columbia	BC	Northwest Territories	NT	Ontario	ON	Saskatchewan	SK
Manitoba	MB	Nova Scotia	NS	Prince Edward Island	PE	Yukon Territory	YT
New Brunswick	NB						

(1) PQ is also acceptable.

Old-Age, Survivors, and Disability Insurance; Medicare; Supplemental Security Income; Temporary Assistance to Needy Families

Source: Social Security Administration; World Almanac research; provisions shown are as under current law, Sept. 2006

Social Security Benefits

Social Security benefits are based on a worker's **primary insurance amount (PIA)**, which is related by law to the average indexed monthly earnings (AIME) on which Social Security contributions have been paid. The full PIA is payable to a worker retiring at age 65 (plus a certain number of months after the 65th birthday, depending on birth year), and to an entitled disabled worker at any age. Spouses and children of retired or disabled workers and survivors of deceased workers receive set proportions of the PIA subject to a family maximum amount.

The PIA is calculated by applying varying percentages to succeeding parts of the AIME. The formula is adjusted annually to reflect changes in average annual wages.

Automatic increases in Social Security benefits are initiated for December of each year, assuming the Consumer Price Index (CPI) for the 3rd calendar quarter of the year increased relative to the base quarter, which is either the 3rd calendar quarter of the preceding year or the quarter in which an increase legislated by Congress became effective. The size of the benefit increase is determined by the percentage rise of the CPI between the quarters measured.

The **average monthly benefit** payable to all retired workers amounted to $1,002 in Dec. 2005. The average benefit for disabled workers in that month amounted to $938.

Minimum and maximum monthly retired-worker benefits payable to individuals who retired at age 65[1]

	Minimum benefit[2]		Maximum benefit[2]	
Year attaining age 65	Paid at retirement	Payable as of Dec. 2005	Payable at retirement (3)	Payable effective Dec. 2005 (4)
1970	$64.00	$360.90		
1980	133.90	360.90	$572.00	$1,546.90
1990	(5)	(5)	975.00	1,522.00
1995	(5)	(5)	1,199.10	1,576.80
1996	(5)	(5)	1,248.90	1,600.70
1997	(5)	(5)	1,326.60	1,652.60
1998	(5)	(5)	1,342.80	1,638.40
1999	(5)	(5)	1,373.10	1,653.90
2000	(5)	(5)	1,434.80	1,686.80
2001	(5)	(5)	1,536.70	1,746.58
2002	(5)	(5)	1,660.50	1,837.70
2003	(5)	(5)	1,741.10	1,879.20
2004	(5)	(5)	1,825.40	1,908.00
2005	(5)	(5)	1,874.30	1,951.10

(1) Assumes retirement at beginning of year. (2) The final benefit amount payable is rounded to next lower $1 (if not already a multiple of $1). (3) Benefits $196.40 for women and $189.80 for men. (4) Benefits $1,110.43 for women and $1,072.20 for men. (5) Minimum eliminated for workers who reached age 62 after 1981.

Amount of Work Required

To qualify for benefits, the worker generally must have worked a certain length of time in covered employment. Just how long depends on when the worker reaches age 62 or, if earlier, when he or she dies or becomes disabled. A person born after 1929 who dies, becomes disabled, or reaches age 62 after 1991 must have had at least 10 years work credit to qualify for full benefits.

A person is **fully insured** who has 1 quarter of coverage for every year after 1950 (or year age 21 is reached, if later) up to but not including the year the worker reaches 62, dies, or becomes disabled. In 2006, a person earns 1 quarter of coverage for each $970 of annual earnings in covered employment, up to 4 quarters per year.

To receive **disability benefits**, the worker, in addition to being fully insured, must generally have credit for 20 quarters of coverage out of the 40 calendar quarters before he or she became disabled. A disabled blind worker need meet only the fully insured requirement. Persons disabled before age 31 can qualify with a briefer period of coverage. Certain survivor benefits are payable if the deceased worker had 6 quarters of coverage in the 13 quarters preceding death.

Contribution and benefit base

Calendar year	OASDI[1]	Calendar year	OASDI[1]	Calendar year	OASDI[1]
1994	$60,600	1999 . . .	$72,600	2004 . . .	$87,900
1995	61,200	2000	76,200	2005 . . .	90,000
1996	62,700	2001 . . .	80,400	2006 . . .	94,200
1997	65,400	2002 . . .	84,900	2007 . . .	98,400[2]
1998	68,400	2003 . . .	87,000		

(1) Old-Age, Survivors, and Disability Ins. (2) Estimated **Note:** There is no base limit for Hospital Ins.

Tax-rate schedule
(percentage of covered earnings)

Year	Total (for employees and employers, each)	OASDI	HI
1979-80	6.13	5.08	1.05
1981	6.65	5.35	1.30
1982-83	6.70	5.40	1.30
1984	7.00	5.70	1.30
1985	7.05	5.70	1.35
1986-87	7.15	5.70	1.45
1988-89	7.51	6.06	1.45
1990 and after	7.65	6.20	1.45
(for self-employed)			
1979-80	8.10	7.05	1.05
1981	9.30	8.00	1.30
1982-83	9.35	8.05	1.30
1984	14.00	11.40	2.60
1985	14.10	11.40	2.70
1986-87	14.30	11.40	2.90
1988-89	15.02	12.12	2.90
1990 and after	15.30	12.40	2.90

What Aged Workers Receive

A person may receive monthly old-age benefits when he or she has enough work in covered employment and has reached retirement age—age 62 for reduced benefits, the age below for full benefits.

Full-Benefit Retirement Age (FRA) by Birth Year

Year of Birth	FRA	Year of Birth	FRA
1937 or earlier	65	1943-1954	66
1938	65 and 2 months	1955	66 and 2 months
1939	65 and 4 months	1956	66 and 4 months
1940	65 and 6 months	1957	66 and 6 months
1941	65 and 8 months	1958	66 and 8 months
1942	65 and 10 months	1959	66 and 10 months
		1960	67

Note: If born on Jan. 1, refer to the previous birth year.

In 2000, the retirement **earnings test** was eliminated beginning with the month when the beneficiary reaches **full-benefit retirement age (FRA)**. A person at and above FRA no longer has benefits reduced because of earnings. However, in the calendar year a beneficiary reaches FRA, benefits are reduced $1 for every $3 of earnings above the limit allowed by law ($33,240 in 2006) for the months prior to FRA. For years before the beneficiary attains FRA, the reduction is $1 for every $2 of earnings over the exempt amount ($12,480 for 2006).

For workers who reached age 65 between 1982 and 1989, Social Security benefits are raised by 3% for each year for which the worker between FRA and 70 (72 before 1984) failed to receive benefits, whether because of earnings from work, because the worker had not applied for benefits, or because the worker declined benefits after entitlement. The **delayed retirement credit** is 1% per year for workers who reached age 65 before 1982. The delayed retirement credit is scheduled to rise to 8% per year by 2008. The rate for workers who reached age 65 in 1998-99 is 5.5%; 2000-01, 6.0%; 2002-03, 6.5%; 2004-05, 7.0%. For 2006-07 it is 7.5%.

For workers retiring early, before full retirement age, benefits are **permanently reduced** 5/9 of 1% for each month before FRA, up to 36 months. If the number of months exceeds 36, then the benefit is further reduced 5/12 of 1% per month.

For example, when FRA reaches 67, for workers who retire at exactly age 62, there are a total of 60 months of reduction. The reduction for the first 36 months is 5/9 of 36%, or

20%. The reduction for the remaining 24 months is ⁵/₁₂ of 24%, or 10%. Thus, when the FRA reaches 67, the amount of reduction at age 62 will be 30%. The nearer to FRA the worker is when he or she begins collecting a benefit, the larger the benefit will be.

Benefits for Worker's Spouse

The spouse of a worker who is getting Social Security retirement or disability payments may become entitled to an insurance benefit of **one-half of the worker's PIA** if he or she claims benefits at full retirement age. Reduced spouse's benefits are available at age 62 and are permanently reduced ²⁵/₃₆ of 1% for each month before FRA, up to 36 months. If the number of months exceeds 36, then the benefit is further reduced ⁵/₁₂ of 1% per month. Benefits are also payable to the aged divorced spouse of an insured worker if he or she was married to the worker for at least 10 years. To qualify for divorced spouse benefits, the insured worker does not have to be receiving benefits. Benefits received as a spouse are reduced by the amount of one's own Social Security benefits.

Benefits for Children of Workers

If a retired or disabled worker has a child under age 18, the **child** will normally get a benefit equal to half of the worker's unreduced benefit. So will the worker's spouse, even if under age 62, if he or she is **caring for an entitled child** of the worker who is under 16 or became disabled before age 22. However, total benefits paid on a worker's earnings record are subject to a maximum. (Total monthly benefits paid to the family of a worker who retired in 2006 at FRA and always had the maximum earnings creditable under Social Security cannot exceed $3,594.)

When entitled children reach age 18, their benefits generally stop, but a child disabled before age 22 may get a benefit as long as the disability meets the definition in the law. Benefits will be paid until age 19 to a child attending elementary or secondary school full-time.

Benefits may also be paid to a grandchild or step-grandchild of a worker or of his or her spouse, in special circumstances.

OASDI Beneficiaries

Beneficiaries	May 2003	May 2004	May 2005	May 2006
total (in thousands)¹ ...	46,771	47,378	48,068	48,877
Aged 65 and over, total ..	33,179	33,400	33,811	34,232
Retired workers	26,680	27,014	27,413	27,898
Survivors/dependents .	6,498	6,386	6,286	6,192
Under age 65, total......	13,592	13,978	14,257	14,645
Retired workers	2,645	2,668	2,809	2,883
Disabled workers	5,702	6,035	6,239	6,465
Survivors and dependents	8,579	5,275	5,209	5,297
Total monthly benefits (in millions)	**$38,244**	**$39,960**	**$42,074**	**$44,956**

(1) Totals may not add because of rounding or incomplete enumeration.

What Disabled Workers Receive

A worker who becomes unable to work may be eligible for a monthly **disability benefit**. Benefits continue until it is determined that the individual is no longer disabled. When a disabled-worker beneficiary reaches FRA (65 years, 8 months in 2006), the disability benefit becomes a retired-worker benefit. In 2006, there were 143,100 disabled worker beneficiaries aged 65 and older who had not reached FRA.

Benefits generally like those for dependents of retired-worker beneficiaries may be paid to dependents of disabled beneficiaries. However, the maximum family benefit in disability cases is generally lower than in retirement cases.

Survivor Benefits

If an insured worker should die, one or more types of benefits may be payable to survivors, again subject to a maximum family benefit as described above.

1. If claiming benefits at FRA, the **surviving spouse** will receive a benefit equal to 100% of the deceased worker's PIA. Benefits claimed before FRA are reduced for age with a maximum reduction of 28.5 percent at age 60. However, for those whose spouses claimed their benefits before FRA, these are limited to the reduced amount the worker would be getting if alive, but not less than 82.5% of the worker's PIA. Remarriage

after the worker's death ends the surviving spouse's benefit rights. However, if the widow(er) marries and the marriage is ended, he or she regains benefit rights. (A marriage after age 60, age 50 if disabled, is deemed not to have occurred for benefit purposes.) Survivor benefits may also be paid to a divorced spouse if the marriage lasted for at least 10 years.

Disabled widows and widowers may under certain circumstances qualify for benefits after attaining age 50 at the rate of 71.5% of the deceased worker's PIA. The widow or widower must have become totally disabled before or within 7 years after the spouse's death or the last month in which he or she received mother's or father's insurance benefits.

2. There is a benefit for each **child under age 18**. The monthly benefit for each child of a deceased worker is ³/₄ of the amount the worker would have received if he or she had lived and drawn full retirement benefits. A child with a disability that began before age 22 may also receive benefits. Also, a child may receive benefits until reaching age 19 if he or she is in full-time attendance at an elementary or secondary school.

3. There is a **mother's or father's benefit** for the widow(er) if children of the worker under age 16 are in his or her care. The benefit is 75% of the PIA, and it continues until the youngest child reaches age 16, at which time payments stop even if the child's benefit continues. However, if the widow(er) has a disabled child beneficiary age 16 or over in care, benefits may continue.

4. **Dependent parents** may be eligible for benefits if they have been receiving at least half their support from the worker before his or her death, have reached age 62, and (except in certain circumstances) have not remarried since the worker's death. Each parent gets 75% of the worker's PIA; if only one parent survives, the benefit is 82%.

5. A **lump sum** cash payment of **$255** is made when there is a spouse who was living with the worker or a spouse or child eligible for immediate monthly survivor benefits.

Self-Employed Workers

A self-employed person who has **net earnings of $400** or more in a year must report such earnings for Social Security tax and credit purposes. The person reports net returns from the business. Income from real estate, savings, dividends, loans, pensions, or insurance policies are not included unless it is part of the business.

A self-employed person receives 1 quarter of coverage for each $970 (for 2006), up to a maximum of 4 quarters per year.

The nonfarm self-employed have the option of reporting their earnings as ²/₃ of their gross income from self-employment. This option can be used only if actual net earnings from self-employment income are less than $1,600 and less than ²/₃ of their gross income. The option may be used only 5 times. Also, the self-employed person must have actual net earnings of $400 or more in 2 of the 3 taxable years immediately preceding the year in which he or she uses the option.

When a person has both taxable wages and earnings from self-employment, wages are credited for Social Security purposes first; only as much self-employment income as brings total earnings up to the current taxable maximum becomes subject to the self-employment tax.

Farm Owners and Workers

Self-employed farmers whose gross annual earnings from farming are from **$600-$2,400** may report ²/₃ of their gross earnings instead of net earnings for Social Security purposes. (Farmers whose gross annual earnings are under $600 do not have to report.) Farmers whose gross income is over $2,400 and whose net earnings are less than $1,600 can report $1,600. Cash or crop shares received from a tenant or share farmer count if the owner participated materially in production or management. The self-employed farmer pays contributions at the same rate as other self-employed persons.

Agricultural employees. A worker's earnings from farm work count toward benefits (1) if the employer pays the worker $150 or more in cash during the year; or (2) if the employer spends $2,500 or more in the year for agricultural labor. Under these rules a person gets credit for 1 calendar quarter for each $970 in cash pay in 2006.

Foreign farm workers admitted to the U.S. on a temporary basis are not covered.

Household Workers

If an employer pays a household worker (e.g. maid, cook, laundry worker, nurse, babysitter, chauffeur, gardener, or other worker), who is age 18 or older, $1500 or more in wages in 2006, the wages are covered under Social Security. This includes transportation costs paid for in cash. The job need not be regular or full-time. The employee should get a Social Security card at the Social Security office and show it to the employer.

The employer deducts the amount of the employee's Social Security tax from the worker's pay, adds an identical amount as the employer's Social Security tax, and sends the total amount to the federal government.

Medicare Coverage

The Medicare health insurance program provides acute-care coverage for Social Security and Railroad Retirement beneficiaries age 65 and over, for persons entitled to 24 months to receive Social Security or Railroad Retirement disability benefits, and for certain persons with end-stage kidney disease. What follows is a basic description and may not cover all circumstances.

The **basic Medicare plan**, available nationwide, is a fee-for-service arrangement, where the beneficiary may use any provider accepting Medicare; some services are not covered and there are some out-of-pocket costs.

Under **Medicare Advantage** (formerly Medicare + Choice), persons eligible for Medicare may have the option of getting services through a health maintenance organization (HMO) or other **managed care** plan. Any such plan must provide at least the same benefits, except for hospice services, and may provide added benefits—such as lower or no deductibles and coverage for some prescription drugs—but is usually subject to restrictions in choice of health care providers. In some plans services by outside providers are still covered for an extra out-of-pocket cost. Also available as options in some areas are Medicare-approved private fee-for-service plans and Medicare medical savings accounts.

Hospital insurance (Part A). The basic hospital insurance program pays covered services for hospital and posthospital care including the following:

- All necessary inpatient hospital care for the first 60 days of each benefit period, except for a deductible ($952 in 2006). For days 61-90, Medicare pays for services over and above a coinsurance amount ($238 per day in 2006). After 90 days, the beneficiary has 60 lifetime reserve days for which Medicare helps pay. The coinsurance amount for reserve days was $476 in 2006.
- Up to 100 days of care in a skilled-nursing facility in each benefit period. Hospital insurance pays for all covered services for the first 20 days; for the 21-100th day, the beneficiary pays coinsurance ($119 per day in 2006).
- Part-time home health care provided by nurses or other health workers.
- Limited coverage of hospice care for individuals certified to be terminally ill.

There is a premium for this insurance in certain cases.

Medical insurance (Part B). Elderly persons can receive benefits under this supplementary program only if they sign up for them and agree to a monthly premium ($88.50 if you sign up upon becoming eligible in 2006). The federal government pays the covered costs of treatment. The Part B deductible was $124 in 2006; beginning in 2006, the deductible rises annually in proportion to the increase in average cost of Part B services to beneficiaries. After the deductible, the medical insurance program usually pays 80% of the approved amount for the following services:

- Covered services received from a doctor in his or her office, in a hospital, in a skilled-nursing facility, at home, or in other locations.
- Medical and surgical services, including anesthesia.
- Diagnostic tests and procedures that are part of the patient's treatment.
- Radiology and pathology services by doctors while the individual is a hospital inpatient or outpatient.
- Other services such as X rays, services of a doctor's office nurse, drugs and biologicals that cannot be self-administered, transfusions of blood and blood components, medical supplies, physical/occupational therapy and speech pathology services.

In addition to the above, certain other tests or preventive measures are now covered without an additional premium. These include a "Welcome to Medicare" physical exam and related services, mammograms, bone mass measurement, colo-rectal cancer screening, and flu shots. Routine physical exams, dental care, hearing aids, and routine eye care are generally not covered under the basic plan. There is limited coverage for nonhospital treatment of mental illness.

To get medical insurance (Part B), persons approaching age 65 may enroll in the **7-month period** that includes 3 months before the 65th birthday, the month of the birthday, and 3 months after the birthday, but if they want coverage to begin in the month they reach age 65, they must enroll in the 3 months before their birthday. Persons not enrolled within their first enrollment period may enroll later, but only during the first 3 months of each year (coverage begins July 1). Their premium may be 10% higher for each 12-month period elapsed since they first could have enrolled.

The monthly premium is deducted from the cash benefit for persons receiving Social Security, Railroad Retirement, or Civil Service retirement benefits. Income from the medical premiums and the federal matching payments are put in a Supplementary Medical Insurance Trust Fund, from which benefits and administrative expenses are paid.

Prescription Drug Coverage (Part D). Starting Jan. 1, 2006, a Medicare prescription drug plan provides insurance coverage for prescription drugs. Medicare recipients pay a monthly premium (averaging about $25 in 2006, depending on the provider) and a portion of drug costs. **Enrollment is scheduled to take place Nov. 15-Dec. 31 each year**, and is optional. Coverage varies depending on the drug plan selected.

Further details are available on the Internet at www.medicare.gov or by calling 1-800-MEDICARE (1-800-633-4227).

Medicare card. Persons qualifying for hospital insurance under Social Security receive a health insurance card similar to cards now used by Blue Cross and other health insurers. The card indicates whether the individual has taken out medical insurance protection. It is to be shown to the hospital, skilled-nursing facility, home health agency, doctor, or whoever provides the covered services.

Payments are generally made only in the 50 states, Puerto Rico, Virgin Islands, Guam, and American Samoa.

Social Security Financing

Social Security is paid for by a tax on certain earnings (for 2006, on earnings up to $94,200) for **Old Age, Survivors, and Disability Insurance** and on all earnings (no upper limit) for Hospital Insurance with the **Medicare** Program; the taxable earnings base for OASDI has been adjusted annually to reflect increases in average wages. The employed worker and his or her employer share Social Security taxes equally.

Employers remit amounts withheld from employee wages for Social Security and income taxes to the Internal Revenue Service; employer Social Security taxes are also payable at the same time. (Self-employed workers pay Social Security taxes when filing their regular income tax forms.) The Social Security taxes (along with revenues arising from partial taxation of the Social Security benefits of certain high-income people) are transferred to the Social Security Trust Funds—the Federal Old-Age and Survivors Insurance (OASI) Trust Fund, the Federal Disability Insurance (DI) Trust Fund, and the Federal Hospital Insurance (HI) Trust Fund; they can be used only to pay benefits, the cost of rehabilitation services, and administrative expenses. Money not immediately needed for these purposes is by law invested in obligations of the federal government, which must pay interest on the money borrowed and must repay the principal when the obligations are redeemed or mature.

Supplemental Security Income

On Jan. 1, 1974, the **Supplemental Security Income** (**SSI**) program established by the 1972 Social Security Act amendments replaced the former federal grants to states for aid to the needy aged, blind, and disabled in the 50 states and the District of Columbia. The program provides both for federal payments, based on uniform national standards and eligibility requirements, and for state supplementary payments varying from state to state. The Social Security Administration administers the federal payments financed from general funds of the Treasury—and the state supplements as well, if the state elects to have its supplementary program federally administered. States may supplement the federal payment for all recipients and must supplement it for persons otherwise adversely affected by the transition from the former public assistance programs. In May 2006, the number of persons receiving federally administered payments was 7,195,614 and the payments totaled $3.5 billion.

The **maximum** monthly federal SSI payment for individuals with no other countable income, living in their own household, was $603 in 2006. For couples the maximum payment was $904.

Social Security Statement

On Oct. 1, 1999, the Social Security Administration initiated regular mailings of an annual *Social Security Statement* to all workers age 25 and older not already receiving benefits. Workers will automatically receive statements about 3 months before their birth month. The statement provides estimates of potential monthly Social Security retirement, disability, and survivor benefits as well as a record of lifetime earnings. The statement also gives workers an easy way to determine whether their earnings are accurately posted in Social Security records.

For further information contact the Social Security Administration toll-free at 1-800-772-1213 or visit its website at www.socialsecurity.gov

Examples of Monthly Benefits Available

Description of benefit or beneficiary	For low earnings ($17,400 in 2006)[1,2]	For avg. earnings ($38,700 in 2006)[2]	For max. earnings ($94,200 in 2006)
Primary insurance amount (worker retiring at 65 years, 8 months....	$814.70	$1,341.90	$2,053.20
Maximum family benefit (worker retiring at 65 years, 8 months).....	1,222.10	2,451.50	3,594.00
Maximum family disability benefit (worker disabled at 55; in 2006)*..	1,226.80	2,043.70	3,154.20
Disabled worker (worker disabled at 55)			
Worker alone[3]	817.00	1,352.00	2,102.00
Worker, spouse, and 1 child...............................	1,225.00	2,042.00	3,152.00
Retired worker claiming benefits at age 62:			
Worker alone[3]	609.00	1,003.00	1,530.00
Worker with spouse claiming benefits at—			
Age 65 or over..	1,013.00	1,668.00	2,545.00
Age 62[3]	893.00	1,471.00	2,244.00
Widow or widower claiming benefits at—			
Age 65 and 8 months or over[4]..........................	814.00	1,341.00	2,053.00
Age 60[4]	582.00	959.00	1,468.00
Disabled widow or widower claiming benefits at age 50-59[5]........	582.00	959.00	1,539.00
1 surviving child[6]	611.00	1,006.00	1,454.00
Widow or widower age 65 or over and 1 child[6]	1,221.00	2,450.00	3,593.00
Widowed mother or father and 1 child[6]	1,221.00	2,012.00	3,078.00
Widowed mother or father and 2 children[6]....................	1,221.00	2,451.00	3,594.00

Effective Jan. 2006. *Assumes work beginning at age 22. (1) 45% of average. (2) Estimate. (3) Assumes maximum reduction. (4) Spouse died at age 65 without receiving reduced benefits. (5) Effective Jan. 1984, disabled widow(er)s claiming a benefit at ages 50-59 receive a benefit equal to 71.5% of the PIA. (6) Based on worker dying at age 65.

Social Security Trust Funds
Old-Age and Survivors Insurance Trust Fund, 1940-2005
(in millions)

		INCOME				DISBURSEMENTS					
Fiscal year[1]	Total	Net contributions[2]	Income from taxing benefits	Payments from the Treasury fund[3]	Net interest[4]	Total	Benefit payments[5]	Administrative expenses	Transfers to Railroad Retirement program	Net increase in fund[6]	Fund at end of period
1940..	$592	$550	—	—	$42	$28	$16	$12	—	$564	$1,745
1950..	2,367	2,106	—	$4	257	784	727	57	—	1,583	12,893
1960..	10,360	9,843	—	—	517	11,073	10,270	202	$600	−713	20,829
1970..	31,746	29,955	—	442	1,350	27,321	26,268	474	579	4,425	32,616
1980..	100,051	97,608	—	557	1,886	103,228	100,626	1,160	1,442	−3,177	24,566
1990..	278,607	261,506	2,924	34	14,143	223,481	218,948	1,564	2,969	55,126	203,445
1995	326,067	289,529	5,114	7	31,417	294,456	288,607	1,797	4,052	31,611	447,946
1997..	386,465	342,312	6,462	3	37,689	318,548	312,862	1,998	3,688	67,916	567,395
1999..	446,956	389,933	10,172	1	46,849	337,894	332,369	1,843	3,681	109,062	762,170
2000..	484,228	418,219	12,476	—	53,532	353,396	347,868	1,990	3,538	130,832	893,003
2001..	513,834	440,819	11,771	—	61,243	372,996	367,654	2,069	3,273	140,837	1,033,840
2002..	529,257	448,133	12,597	414	68,113	389,546	383,942	2,111	3,493	139,711	1,173,551
2003..	542,343	456,014	12,340	—	73,990	402,814	396,710	2,522	3,580	139,530	1,313,080
2004..	556,523	466,807	13,269	1	76,446	417,053	411,148	2,274	3,628	139,470	1,452,550
2005..	599,992	502,998	15,332	—	81,662	436,919	430,439	2,900	3,579	163,073	1,615,623

(1) Fiscal years 1980 and later consist of the 12 months ending on Sept. 30 of each year. Fiscal years prior to 1977 consisted of the 12 months ending on June 30 of each year. (2) Beginning in 1983, includes transfers from general fund of Treasury representing contributions that would have been paid on deemed wage credits for military service in 1957 and later, if such credits were considered covered wages. (3) Includes payments (a) in 1947-52 and in 1967 and later, for costs of noncontributory wage credits for military service performed before 1957; (b) in 1972-83, for costs of deemed wage credits for military service performed after 1956; and (c) in 1969 and later, for costs of benefits to certain uninsured persons who attained age 72 before 1968. (4) Net interest includes net profits or losses on marketable investments. Beginning in 1967, administrative expenses were charged currently to the trust fund on an estimated basis, with a final adjustment, including interest, made in the next fiscal year. The amounts of these interest adjustments are included in net interest. For years prior to 1967, the method of accounting for administrative expenses is described in the 1970 Annual Report. Beginning in Oct. 1973, the figures shown include relatively small amounts of gifts to the fund. During 1983-91, interest paid from the trust fund to the general fund on advance tax transfers is reflected. (5) Beginning in 1967, includes payments for vocational rehabilitation services furnished to disabled persons receiving benefits because of their disabilities. Beginning in 1983, amounts are reduced by amount of reimbursement for unnegotiated benefit checks. (6) Net change in assets during fiscal year, including amounts borrowed or repaid by other funds.

Disability Insurance Trust Fund, 1960-2005
(in millions)

Fiscal year[1]	Total	INCOME Net contributions[2]	Income from taxing benefits	Payments from the Treasury fund[3]	Net interest[4]	Total	DISBURSEMENTS Benefit payments[5]	Administrative expenses	Transfers to Railroad Retirement program	Net increase in fund[6]	Fund at end of period
1960...	$1,034	$987	—	—	$47	$533	$528	$32	$-27	$501	$2,167
1970...	4,380	4,141	—	$16	223	2,954	2,795	149	10	1,426	5,104
1980...	17,376	16,805	—	118	453	15,320	14,998	334	-12	2,056	7,680
1990...	28,215	27,291	$158	—	766	25,124	24,327	717	80	3,091	11,455
1995	70,209	67,987	335	—	1,888	41,374	40,234	1,072	68	28,835	35,206
2000...	77,023	70,001	756	—	6,266	56,008	54,244	1,608	159	21,014	113,752
2001...	82,079	74,611	732	-836	7,573	59,930	58,098	1,762	10	22,149	135,901
2002...	85,720	76,067	936	—	8,717	66,364	64,138	2,005	154	19,356	155,258
2003...	87,909	77,431	919	—	9,559	71,907	69,716	1,968	167	16,002	171,260
2004...	90,105	79,269	1,047	—	9,789	78,471	76,139	2,070	215	11,634	182,893
2005...	96,765	85,418	1,164	—	10,183	86,360	83,721	2,301	338	10,405	193,298

(1) Fiscal years 1977 and later consist of the 12 months ending Sept. 30 of each year. Fiscal years prior to 1977 consisted of the 12 months ending June 30 of each year. (2) Beginning in 1983, includes transfers from general fund of Treasury representing contributions that would have been paid on deemed wage credits for military service in 1957 and later, if such credits were considered to be covered wages. (3) Includes payments (a) for costs of noncontributory wage credits for military service performed before 1957; and (b) in 1972-83, for costs of deemed wage credits for military service performed after 1956. (4) Net interest includes net profits or losses on marketable investments. Administrative expenses are charged currently to the trust fund on an estimated basis, with a final adjustment, including interest, made in the following fiscal year. Figures shown include relatively small amounts of gifts to the fund. During the years 1983-91, interest paid from the trust fund to the general fund on advance tax transfers is reflected. (5) Includes payments for vocational rehabilitation services. Beginning in 1983, amounts are reduced by amount of reimbursement for unnegotiated benefit checks. (6) Net change in assets during fiscal year, including amounts borrowed or repaid by other funds. **NOTE:** Totals may not add because of rounding.

Supplementary Medical Insurance Trust Fund (Medicare SMI), 1975-2005
(in millions)

Fiscal year[1]	INCOME Premium from participants	Government contributions[2]	Interest and other income[3]	Total Income	DISBURSEMENTS Benefit payments[4]	Administrative expenses	Total disbursements	Net increase in fund	Balance in fund at end of year[5]
1975..	$1,887	$2,330	$106	$4,322	$3,765	$404	$4,170	$152	$1,424
1980..	2,928	6,932	416	10,275	10,144	593	10,737	-462	4,532
1990..	11,494[6]	33,210	1,434[6]	46,138[6]	41,498	1,524[6]	43,022[6]	3,115	14,527[6]
1995..	19,244	36,988	1,937	58,169	63,491	1,722	65,213	-7,045	13,874
2000..	20,515	65,561	3,164	89,239	87,212[7]	1,780	88,992	247	45,896
2001..	22,307	69,838	3,191	95,336	97,466[7]	1,986	99,452	-4,116	41,780
2002..	24,427	78,318	2,960	105,705	106,995[7]	1,830	108,825	-3,121	38,659
2003..	26,834	80,905	2,455	110,194	121,699[7]	2,356	124,055	-13,861	24,799
2004..	30,341	94,734	1,730	126,805	131,673	2,817	134,490	-7,684	17,114
2005..	35,939	115,200	1,366	152,505	149,820	2,914	152,735	-230	16,885

(1) Fiscal year 1975 consists of the 12 months ending on June 30, 1975; fiscal years 1980 and later consist of the 12 months ending on Sept. 30 of each year. (2) Includes Part B general fund matching payments, Part D subsidy transfers from the general fund (for the transitional assistance benefits in 2004 and 2005 and state expenses for making low-income eligibility determinations in 2005), and certain interest-adjustment items. (3) Other income includes recoveries of amounts reimbursed from the trust fund that are not obligations of the trust fund and other miscellaneous income. (4) Includes costs of Peer Review Organizations from 1983 to 2001, and costs of Quality Improvement Organizations beginning in 2002. Includes Part D costs for the transitional assistance benefits in 2004 and 2005 and for payments to states for making low-income eligibility determinations in 2005. (5) The financial status of SMI depends on both the assets and the liabilities of the trust fund. (6) Includes the impact of the Medicare Catastrophic Coverage Act of 1988. (7) Benefit payments less monies transferred from the HI trust fund for home health agency costs, as provided for by PL 105-33. **NOTE:** Totals do not necessarily equal sums of rounded components.

Hospital Insurance Trust Fund (Medicare HI), 1975-2005
(in millions)

Fisc. year[1]	Payroll taxes	Income from taxation of benefits	INCOME Transfers from railroad retirement acct.	Reimbursement for uninsured persons	Premiums from voluntary enrollees	Pymts. for military wage credits	Interest on investments and other income[2]	Total income	DISBURSEMENTS Benefit pymts.[3]	Administrative expenses[4]	Total disbursements	Net increase in fund	Fund at end of year
1975	$11,291	—	$132	$481	$6	$48	$609	$12,568	$10,353	$259	$10,612	$1,956	$9,870
1980	23,244	—	244	697	17	141	1,072	25,415	23,790	497	24,288	1,127	14,490
1990	70,655	—	367	413	113	107	7,908	79,563	65,912	774	66,687	12,876	95,631
1995	98,053	$3,913	396	462	998	61	10,963	114,847	113,583	1,300	114,883	-36	129,520
2000	137,738	8,787	465	470	1,392	2	10,827	159,681	127,934[6]	2,350	130,284	29,397	168,084
2001	151,931	4,903	470	453	1,440	-1,175[7]	12,993	171,014	139,356[6]	2,368	141,723	29,290	197,374
2002	151,575	10,946	425	442	1,525	0	14,850	179,762	145,566[6]	2,464	148,031	31,731	229,105
2003	149,839	8,318	426	393	1,598	0	15,239	175,813	151,250[6]	2,541	153,792	22,021	251,127
2004	153,448	8,577	419	365	1,799	173	16,034	180,815	164,079	2,920	166,998	13,816	264,943
2005	168,954	8,765	445	286	2,303	0	16,168	196,921	181,292	2,850	184,142	12,779	277,723

(1) Fiscal year 1975 consists of the 12 months ending on June 30, 1975; fiscal years 1980 and later consist of the 12 months ending Sept. 30 of each year. (2) Other income includes recoveries of amounts reimbursed from the trust fund that are not obligations of the trust fund, receipts from the fraud and abuse control program, and a small amount of miscellaneous income. (3) Includes costs of Peer Review Organizations from 1983 through 2001 (beginning with the implementation of the Prospective Payment System on Oct. 1, 1983), and costs of Quality Improvement Organizations beginning in 2002. (4) Includes costs of experiments and demonstration projects. Beginning in 1997, includes fraud and abuse control expenses, as provided for by PL 104-191. (5) Includes the lump-sum general revenue adjustment of -$2,366 mil, as provided for by PL 98-21. (6) Includes monies transferred to the SMI trust fund for home health agency costs, as provided for by PL 105-33. (7) Includes the lump-sum general review adjustment of -$1,117 million, as provided for by sec. 151 of PL 98-21. **NOTE:** Totals do not necessarily equal sums of rounded components.

Block Grants for Welfare (Temporary Assistance for Needy Families), Fiscal Year 2004

Source: Office of Family Assistance, Admin. for Children and Families, U.S. Dept. of Health and Human Services

State	Total Federal and State TANF Expenditures, 2004[1]	2004 Average Monthly Expenditure per Family	2004 Average Monthly Expenditure per Recipient	2004 Average Monthly Number of Families	2004 Average Monthly Number of Recipients	2004 Average Monthly Number of Children
Alabama	$114,195	$496.82	$209.72	19,154	45,377	35,526
Alaska	76,237	1,289.61	461.43	4,926	13,768	9,377
Arizona	305,055	512.94	221.11	49,559	114,970	84,342
Arkansas	41,521	345.23	154.75	10,023	22,360	16,756
California	6,177,941	1,127.36	466.69	456,666	1,103,152	899,753
Colorado	211,832	1,207.16	462.57	14,623	38,162	27,725
Connecticut	434,877	1,749.00	847.08	20,720	42,782	30,545
Delaware	53,521	790.37	350.54	5,643	12,723	9,669
Dist. of Columbia	168,634	818.11	322.24	17,177	43,610	32,605
Florida	877,066	1,272.06	628.95	57,457	116,208	94,661
Georgia	535,343	838.34	359.08	53,215	124,239	96,515
Hawaii	127,601	1,199.61	464.19	8,864	22,908	16,194
Idaho	41,470	1,869.60	1,014.92	1,848	3,405	2,714
Illinois	981,155	2,292.88	918.50	35,660	89,018	73,008
Indiana	313,987	517.22	199.55	50,589	131,125	100,649
Iowa	163,222	743.83	303.93	18,286	44,753	31,006
Kansas	156,063	776.57	298.01	16,747	43,640	29,954
Kentucky	196,430	459.43	209.39	35,629	78,174	57,932
Louisiana	252,078	1,118.72	461.62	18,777	45,506	37,274
Maine	102,409	878.67	320.22	9,713	26,651	18,191
Maryland	349,569	1,145.53	490.73	25,430	59,362	44,919
Massachusetts	681,214	1,141.00	527.44	49,753	107,630	75,134
Michigan	1,281,075	1,344.00	503.14	79,432	212,182	155,420
Minnesota	401,786	975.01	379.18	34,340	88,302	63,374
Mississippi	102,733	455.51	201.63	18,795	42,459	31,298
Missouri	300,308	610.69	251.23	40,979	99,613	70,646
Montana	44,888	711.65	261.88	5,256	14,284	9,578
Nebraska	88,945	679.97	277.10	10,901	26,749	19,255
Nevada	68,447	644.91	272.19	8,844	20,956	16,147
New Hampshire	60,054	827.40	356.66	6,049	14,032	9,673
New Jersey	888,893	1,655.70	687.77	44,739	107,703	80,282
New Mexico	132,567	628.03	240.54	17,590	45,926	32,479
New York	4,195,899	2,377.83	1,039.92	147,050	336,236	240,973
North Carolina	437,816	969.03	473.10	37,651	77,119	60,408
North Dakota	34,473	937.64	364.99	3,064	7,871	5,499
Ohio	833,955	821.72	373.09	84,574	186,272	139,988
Oklahoma	194,597	1,142.06	473.77	14,199	34,229	26,441
Oregon	242,993	1,093.12	478.01	18,525	42,362	31,476
Pennsylvania	1,191,955	1,127.11	429.52	88,128	231,260	165,972
Rhode Island	155,200	1,051.95	405.07	12,295	31,929	22,282
South Carolina	38,375	191.77	82.92	16,676	38,567	29,481
South Dakota	28,981	879.82	402.43	2,745	6,001	5,016
Tennessee	236,231	273.15	103.54	72,069	190,132	135,852
Texas	767,926	608.33	256.35	105,197	249,634	200,280
Utah	113,643	1,047.47	411.54	9,041	23,012	16,468
Vermont	68,524	1,182.12	465.89	4,831	12,257	7,850
Virginia	278,532	2,461.53	863.40	9,430	26,883	17,250
Washington	588,581	878.10	358.68	55,858	136,747	95,980
West Virginia	149,855	843.06	351.19	14,813	35,559	25,124
Wisconsin	492,734	1,825.50	756.00	22,493	54,314	42,676
Wyoming	39,845	9,439.68	5,249.66	352	633	555
2004 Totals	**25,821,230**	**1,082.66**	**449.78**	**1,987,476**	**4,784,042**	**3,617,569**
2003 Totals	**26,339,994**	**1,092.33**	**447.99**	**2,009,468**	**4,899,677**	**3,691,479**
2002 Totals	**25,414,383**	**1,039.38**	**418.01**	**2,037,618**	**5,066,574**	**3,790,207**
2001 Totals	**25,667,381**	**1,024.57**	**400.86**	**2,087,646**	**5,335,891**	**3,968,499**
2000 Totals	**24,780,711**	**926.32**	**353.72**	**2,229,315**	**5,838,043**	**4,303,943**
1999 Totals	**23,114,572**	**720.45**	**267.99**	**2,673,610**	**7,187,658**	**NA**
1998 Totals	**22,036,420**	**573.92**	**208.91**	**3,199,700**	**8,790,149**	**NA**
1997 Totals	**19,010,190**	**402.42**	**144.87**	**3,936,610**	**10,935,125**	**NA**

NOTE: Under 1996 legislation, the Aid to Families with Dependent Children (AFDC) program was converted to this state block-grant program. (1) In thousands. FY 2004 covers period from Oct. 2003 to Sept. 2004. NA = Not available.

Adults Receiving TANF[1] (Welfare) Funds, by Employment Status, Fiscal Year 2004

Source: Office of Family Assistance, Admin. for Children and Families, U.S. Dept. of Health and Human Services

STATE	Adults	Employed	STATE	Adults	Employed	STATE	Adults	Employed	STATE	Adults	Employed
AL	10,272	26.8%	IN	30,307	25.0%	NV	4,746	22.0%	SC	8,030	34.7%
AK	4,366	31.2	IA	13,491	46.4	NH	4,436	21.2	SD	977	22.1
AZ	30,895	19.0	KS	13,852	10.8	NJ	27,068	17.5	TN	54,614	19.0
AR	5,591	17.2	KY	20,407	20.3	NM	14,070	29.1	TX	49,394	34.5
CA	212,948	25.2	LA	8,568	29.5	NY	93,291	20.0	UT	6,574	24.4
CO	10,597	17.1	ME	7,498	28.5	NC	17,571	19.2	VT	4,382	22.9
CT	12,182	26.5	MD	15,507	8.6	ND	2,407	34.8	Virgin		
DE	3,021	24.3	MA	32,035	15.5	OH	46,359	23.7	Islands	402	3.5
DC	11,388	17.2	MI	57,909	26.5	OK	7,640	11.9	VA	9,611	62.5
FL	22,750	19.4	MN	25,110	29.3	OR	10,797	12.8	WA	40,883	18.6
GA	28,289	12.3	MS	10,970	15.4	PA	66,050	11.1	WV	9,998	13.5
Guam	N/A	N/A	MO	29,421	20.9	Puerto			WI	11,456	16.4
HI	6,701	30.3	MT	4,663	25.2	Rico	15,034	5.8	WY	76	9.7
ID	679	32.3	NE	7,154	16.5	RI	9,633	25.4	**U.S.**	**1,168,539**	**22.0**
IL	16,468	21.2									

NA=Not available. (1) TANF = the state block grant program known as Temporary Assistance for Needy Families.

TAXES

Federal Income Tax

Source: George W. Smith III, CPA, Managing Partner, George W. Smith & Company, P.C.

New 2006 Legislation

Pres. George W. Bush signed the Tax Increase Prevention and Reconciliation Act into law on May 18, 2006. The $70 bil tax-cut package includes a two year extension of the controversial dividend and capital gains tax rate cuts enacted in 2003 by the Jobs and Growth Tax Relief Act. Highlights include:

Dividend Income/Capital Gains. The 2003 tax cut reduced capital gains taxes from 20% to 15%. Taxes on dividends were also reduced to 15%, and 5% for taxpayers in the 15% and 10% brackets. The new law extends these cuts through December 31, 2010.

Roth IRAs. The $100,000 income ceiling for converting traditional IRAs to Roth IRAs is eliminated for tax years after December 31, 2009.

AMT. The Alternative Minimum Tax (AMT) exemptions are increased to $42,500 for single taxpayers and $62,500 for married couples filing jointly. These exemptions apply only for 2006 and are slightly higher than the 2005 exemptions. See Alternative Minimum Tax section on page 390.

Kiddie Tax. The "kiddie" tax was previously limited to children under 14 years of age. This legislation increases the age limit to children under age 18. Children in this age group with unearned income such as interest, dividends, and capital gains over $1,700, will be taxed at the parents' marginal rate, not the child's. Here's how it works: the first $850 of unearned income such as interest, dividends and capital gains, is tax free for children. The next $850 is taxed at no more than 10%. Unearned income over $1,700 is taxed at the parents' marginal rate.

Section 179. For 2006, taxpayers can expense up to $108,000 of the cost of qualifying business equipment and machinery. The new law extends this write-off for two more years through December 31, 2009.

Energy Policy Act of 2005

The Energy Policy Act was signed into law on August 8, 2005, and provides a number of important tax incentives for both individuals and businesses. Although these tax credits only started in 2006, most will run through 2007.

Hybrid Vehicles. Starting January 1, 2006, hybrid car buyers can claim a tax credit for certain vehicles including autos, pickups, and SUVs. Depending on their fuel economy, the tax credit can go as high as $3,400. This credit replaces the $2,000 clean-burning fuel deduction.

The credit will start to phase out once a manufacturer's line of hybrids sells its 60,000th vehicle. Thereafter, taxpayers can claim a partial credit for the remainder of the year.

Home Improvements. A 10% credit applies for the purchase of skylights, outside doors, windows, pigmented roofs and high-efficiency furnaces, water heaters, and central air conditioners. The maximum credit is $500 with no more than $200 allowed for window purchases.

Solar Energy. Homeowners can take a credit of 30% of the cost of solar units that are used to heat air or water. The maximum credit is $2,000 for each furnace or water heater installed. Swimming pools or hot tubs don't qualify.

Businesses receive a 30% credit on solar heating units and fuel cells. Builders can have a maximum credit of $2,000 for each energy efficient home sold in 2006.

2004 Legislation: Working Families Tax Relief Act and American Jobs Creation Act

Child Tax Credit. Congress keeps the child tax credit at $1,000. It will remain through 2010, canceling a provision that would have cut it to $700.

Filing Jointly. The standard deduction for married taxpayers filing jointly was increased to double the standard deduction amount for single taxpayers through 2010. The 15% tax bracket amount that applies to married taxpayers will be double the 15% tax bracket amount for single taxpayers through 2010.

Donated Vehicles. Individuals who donate their vehicles to charity can no longer deduct the "Blue Book" value. Taxpayers can deduct only the amount of gross proceeds received by the charity from the sale of the donor's vehicle if the claimed deduction is greater than $500.

Collections. Congress authorized the IRS to hire private contractors to collect unpaid taxes. According to IRS estimates, private collection agencies could recover up to $1.4 bil in unpaid taxes.

Citizenship. Congress closed a tax loophole that allowed wealthy individuals to relinquish their American citizenship and claim they were moving to a foreign tax haven, even though they still spent most of their time residing in the U.S. The law in effect states that if the individual is not really going to leave the country, the U.S. is going to tax the person.

Jobs and Growth Tax Relief Act of 2003

This 10-year, $350 bil package was the 3rd-largest tax cut in U.S. history.

Rate Reductions. This legislation reduced individual tax rates to 25%, 28%, 33%, and a maximum rate of 35%.

Dividend Income/Capital Gains. Congress reduces the tax rate for dividends and capital gains to a maximum of 15%. In 2006, Congress extends these rates for two more years.

Collectibles. Depending on the taxpayer's income there are additional capital gain rates for collectibles. Collectibles include works of art, antiques, gold and silver, gems, stamps, and coins. The rates are 5%, 15%, 25%, and 28%.

Tax Planning. Unless Congress decides otherwise, all the above rates after 2010 will revert back to previous higher tax rates.

Visiting Your Tax Preparer

Over 60% of all individual income tax returns are signed by paid tax professionals. Here are some things to keep in mind when visiting your tax preparer:

- Time spent with your preparer may affect your bill. If you bring in jumbled records and deductions, there may be an additional cost to have your tax preparer organize your records.
- Review last year's tax return. Make notes of any changes since then such as marriage, divorce, number of dependents, retirement, job changes, additional income, new deductions, etc.
- Organize your records with income items first, followed by itemized deductions in sequence (medical, taxes, interest, charitable, and other miscellaneous deductions), then questionable items.

- Prepare a list of questions in advance.
- Alert your preparer if you're waiting to receive additional information. He or she can start preparation of your tax return and include the missing data later.
- Don't hesitate to call the preparer if you receive additional information at a later time. However, if you call after the return is completed, changes may cost you additional fees.
- Review your tax return before signing it. Ask questions about any item you don't understand. Remember, even though your preparer is required to sign the return, **you** are responsible for its contents.

Additional Help: For more information about choosing tax preparers, call the IRS Tele-Tax information system at 800-829-4477. Follow the prompts and select Topic 254. This information is also available online at www.irs.gov/taxtopics/tc254.html.

IRS Rulings and Other Tax Matters

Dependent Care. The maximum expense eligible for the dependent care tax credit is $3,000 for one qualifying child or other dependent incapable of self-care, and $6,000 for 2 or more dependents.

Same Sex Marriage. The IRS ruled that it is unlawful for same-sex couples to file federal taxes under any married status, even if the jurisdiction in which the couple lives recognizes such marriages.

Weight Loss. The IRS allows a medical deduction for costs of certain weight-loss programs. Participation must be for treatment of a physician-diagnosed disease, including obesity. No deduction is allowed for purely cosmetic reasons or special diet foods.

Smoking. Taxpayers can deduct two types of aids for quitting cigarette smoking as a medical expense: (1) the cost of participation in a smoking-cessation program, and (2) prescription drugs to alleviate the effects of nicotine withdrawal. Over-the-counter products such as nicotine patches and chewing gum remain nondeductible.

Alimony. Payments to an individual under a written separation agreement constitute alimony for federal tax purposes even if the separation agreement is not enforceable under state law.

Penalties. Penalties and fines paid to a governmental agency or department are not deductible. This includes parking and speeding tickets as well as penalties for the late filing of a tax return.

Death Benefits. Qualified accelerated death benefits paid under a life insurance contract to terminally ill persons (certified as expected to die within 24 months) are excludable from gross income. A similar exclusion applies to the sale or assignment of insurance death benefits to another person.

Sale of Residence. Married couples filing jointly who have lived in their principal residence for at least 2 years out of the last 5-year period can exclude from their income tax up to $500,000 in gain from the sale of their residence. Single taxpayers can exclude a gain up to $250,000.

Domestic Workers. The annual threshold dollar amount for reporting and paying Social Security and federal unemployment taxes on domestic employees, including nannies and housekeepers, increased to $1,500 in 2006. Household workers under 18 are exempt unless household work is their principal occupation.

Exemptions. The overall limitation on personal exemption and Schedule A itemized deductions is reduced by 1/3 in 2006 and 2007, 2/3 for 2008 and 2009, and totally eliminated in 2010.

Student Loans. The 2006 income phase-out range for the interest deduction, up to $2,500 on student loans, is $50,000-$65,000 for single taxpayers and $105,000-$135,000 for married taxpayers filing jointly.

Mileage for Medical Treatment. The mileage allowance deduction for driving to obtain medical treatment, prescriptions, or dental care increased to 18 cents per mile starting in 2006. For cars used in volunteer work in charities, the rate remains at 14 cents per mile.

Adoption. The maximum adoption credit was increased and is adjusted annually for inflation. For 2006 the credit is $10,960 per child. The exclusion phases out for taxpayers between $164,410 and $204,410.

Day Camp. If both parents or legal guardians work, the cost of summer day camp for their children may qualify for the child care credit.

Investment Expenses. Investors can take a miscellaneous deduction on Schedule A for investment and custodial fees, trust administration fees, cost of investment advice, financial newspapers and reports, and other expenses incurred in managing their investment portfolio. However, investors cannot deduct expenses for attending a convention, seminar, or similar meeting.

Garage Sale. Revenues received from a garage sale usually do not result in taxable income. In most cases, the item that was sold cost more than the revenue received. Also, losses are considered personal and not deductible.

"Hands Off." In a unanimous 2005 decision, the U.S. Supreme Court held that individual retirement accounts (IRAs) are beyond the reach of creditors. This includes IRA assets of taxpayers who have filed for bankruptcy. Other retirement plan savings accounts are also protected.

Innocent Spouse. The IRS Reform Act provides a separate liability section for spouses who are divorced, legally separated or living apart for at least 12 months. In effect, this legislation prevents a former spouse from being held liable for the other spouse's tax liability and misdeeds.

Full-Time Student. A taxpayer may not claim a dependency exemption in 2006 for an individual who qualifies as a full-time student and is over age 23 at the end of the year, unless the student's gross income is less than $3,300.

Frivolous Returns. Taxpayers who file frivolous income tax returns face a $500 penalty and may be subject to civil penalties of 20-75% of the underpaid tax. Those who pursue frivolous tax cases in the courts may face a penalty of up to $25,000, in addition to the taxes, interest, and civil penalties they may owe.

Income Tax Filing and Payment Dates

Filing Dates. The due date for filing a 2006 Form 1040, 1040A, or 1040EZ U.S. Individual Income Tax Return including partnership tax returns is Mon., Apr. 16, 2007. (The 15th falls on a Sunday.) Calendar-year-ending corporate returns are due March 15, 2007.

Estimated Taxes. Due dates for filing individual quarterly federal estimated tax payments, Form 1040-ES, are: 1st quarter, Mon., Apr. 16, 2007; 2nd quarter, Fri., June 15; 3rd quarter, Mon., Sept. 17; and 4th quarter, Tue., Jan. 15, 2008. Different filing dates may apply for state and local tax payments.

Refunds. Individuals can call the IRS's toll-free number at 1-800-829-4477 for a recorded message or visit the IRS Web site at www.irs.gov to check on the status of their expected refund.

Filing Penalties. The IRS can levy 2 potential penalties when a return is filed after the due date with a balance owing: one penalty is for failing to file a timely tax return, the other is for failure to pay the tax when due. In addition, interest will be charged on any unpaid tax balance.

Installment Payments. Depending on the amount of tax owed, taxpayers may apply for monthly installment payments by attaching Form 9465 to their tax return. There is an IRS filing fee if the request is approved.

Need More Time? Individuals who cannot file their 2006 tax return by the due date may apply for an automatic 6-month extension to Oct. 15, 2007. Although the extension is automatic, Form 4868 must be filed no later than Apr. 16, 2007 to qualify. Approximately nine million extensions were filed by April 17, 2006, for 2005 tax returns.

Statute of Limitations. If you have not filed your 2003 federal tax return, you have until Apr. 15, 2007 (not April 16) to file and claim your refund. After that date any tax or withholding refund for the year 2003, including the refundable earned income tax credit, will be lost.

Electronic Filing. Seventy percent of all income tax returns filed through the middle of April, 2006 were e-filed. This represented a 6% increase over the previous year. Roughly 20 mil taxpayers e-filed from a home computer.

Tax Tip. According to an IRS spokesperson the better way to file all returns and extensions is electronically. For security purposes, taxpayers should request that tax refunds be deposited directly into their bank accounts.

IRS Services and Information

Tax Questions: Call 1-800-829-1040
Website: www.irs.gov   **Fax:** 1-703-368-9694
Forms/Publications: 1-800-829-3676
English And Spanish. The IRS provides videotaped instructions both in English and Spanish at participating libraries. Many IRS publications and tax forms, including instructions, are also printed in Spanish. For more information, call 1-800-TAX-FORM and ask for the free IRS Publication 1SP, Derechos del Contribuyente.

Hearing Impaired. The IRS telephone service for hearing impaired persons is available for taxpayers with access to TDD equipment. The toll-free number is 1-800-829-4059.

▶ **IT'S A FACT:** There are now over 67,000 pages of federal tax rules in the commonly used Standard Federal Tax Reporter. In 1913, when the federal income tax was first introduced, there were just 400 pages.

Individual Income Tax Rates and Tax Brackets

Taxable Income And Rates For 2006

Tax Rate	Single	Married Filing Separately	Married Filing Jointly or Qualifying Widow(er)	Head of Household	Estates and Trusts
10%	$1 to $7,550	$1 to $7,550	$1 to $15,100	$1 to $10,750	$0
15%	$7,551 to $30,650	$7,551 to $30,650	$15,101 to $61,300	$10,751 to $41,050	$1 to $2,050
25%	$30,651 to $74,200	$30,651 to $61,850	$61,301 to $123,700	$41,051 to $106,000	$2,051 to $4,850
28%	$74,201 to $154,800	$61,851 to $94,225	$123,701 to $188,450	$106,001 to $171,650	$4,851 to $7,400
33%	$154,801 to $336,550	$94,226 to $168,275	$188,451 to $336,550	$171,651 to $336,550	$7,401 to $10,050
35%	Over $336,550	Over $168,275	Over $336,500	Over $336,550	Over $10,050

Exemptions

Dollar Amounts. The personal exemption amount for each taxpayer, spouse, and dependent for 2006 is $3,300, a $100 increase over 2005. These exemption amounts are adjusted each year for the cost of living.

The Phase-Out. The exemption deduction for higher-income taxpayers begins to be phased out when their income exceeds certain threshold dollar amounts, adjusted annually for the cost of living. Each exemption is reduced by 2% for each $2,500 ($1,250 for married persons filing separately) or fraction thereof by which adjusted gross income for year 2006 exceeds the following:

Married filing jointly	$225,750
Qualifying widow(er)	$225,750
Head of household	$188,150
Single	$150,500
Married filing separately	$112,875

Standard Deductions

The standard deduction is a flat dollar amount that is subtracted from the adjusted gross income of taxpayers who do not itemize deductions.

2006 Standard Deduction Amount

Single	$5,150
Married filing jointly or qualifying widow(er)	$10,300
Married filing separately	$5,150
Head of household	$7,550

These figures are not applicable if an individual can be claimed as a dependent on another person's tax return.

Standard Deduction for Dependents. An individual reported as a dependent on another person's 2006 income tax return generally may claim on his or her own tax return only the greater of $850 or the sum of $300 plus earned income not to exceed the regular standard deduction.

Taxpayers in 2006 who are 65 or older and/or blind may claim an additional standard deduction:

Single or head of household, 65 or older OR blind	$1,250
Single or head of household, 65 or older AND blind	$2,500
Married filing jointly or qualifying widow(er), 65 or older OR blind (per person)	$1,000
Married filing jointly or qualifying widow(er), 65 or older AND blind (per person)	$2,000
Married filing separately, 65 or older OR blind	$1,000
Married filing separately, 65 or older AND blind	$2,000

Adjustments to Income

Traditional IRA. The maximum tax-deferred Individual Retirement Arrangement (IRA) deduction for a married couple filing jointly is $8,000 ($4,000 for singles) for 2006. Each spouse can contribute up to $4,000 annually even if one spouse has little or no income. Individuals age 50 or older can fund an additional "catch-up" amount of $1,000. However, there are income limitations and phase-outs.

Withdrawals. There is a 10% penalty for IRA distributions before age 59½. Distributions paid to the beneficiary due to a disability or death of the owner are not subject to this penalty, nor are payments for certain unreimbursed medical expenses, higher-education expenses, or first-time home buyer acquisition costs (up to $10,000).

Tax Tip. Withdrawals from a Roth IRA for "qualified higher education expenses" of the taxpayer, spouse, or any child or grandchild of the taxpayer or spouse are taxable but not subject to the early withdrawal penalty.

Roth IRA. Although contributions paid into a Roth IRA are not deductible, distributions of funds including investment earnings held in the account for 5 years or longer and distributed after age 59½ are free both of income tax and the 10%

early withdrawal penalty at the time of distribution. Withdrawals in less than 5 years can be subject both to income tax and the 10% withdrawal penalty regardless of age. There are income limitations on contributions.

Age 70½ Plus. The owner of a traditional IRA (or a SIMPLE plan, pension, or profit sharing plan account) must begin receiving distributions by Apr. 1 of the calendar year following the year in which he or she reaches age 70½. Any employee who works beyond age 70½ and is not a 5% or more owner of the business can continue to defer profit sharing and pension plan distributions.

IRA Publication. For more information on IRAs call the IRS at 1-800-829-3676 for a free copy of Publication 590, Individual Retirement Arrangements (IRA).

Itemized Deductions

If the total amount of itemized deductions is more than the standard deduction, taxpayers generally should itemize their deductions on Schedule A, Form 1040. The following examples are just a few of the deductions that may be itemized, some are subject to income limitations.

Medical expenses that exceed 7.5% of the taxpayer's adjusted gross income are deductible. Medicines, birth control pills, and insulin qualify if prescribed by a physician. Cosmetic surgery for congenital abnormality, for personal injury from an accident or trauma, or for a disfiguring disease also is allowed as a medical deduction. Long-term care insurance premiums, up to certain annual limits based on age, are deductible.

Tax Tip. A mother-to-be may deduct the cost of classes taken in Lamaze breathing and relaxation techniques, stages of labor, and delivery procedures.

Mortgage interest paid on a primary residence or a second home is deductible. However, there are limitations on mortgages in excess of $1 mil. Interest on home equity loans also is deductible, but only covering the first $100,000 of equity debt. Credit card interest is not deductible.

Taxes. State and local income taxes including real estate taxes are deductible. A tax based on the car value qualifies as a personal property tax.

Personal losses. Casualty and theft losses are deductible, but subject to the $100 and 10% limitation rule for each occurrence.

Charitable contributions. Taxpayers deducting individual contributions of $250 or more must obtain written substantiation from the charity.

Certain miscellaneous expenses are deductible, but only the amount that exceeds 2% of adjusted gross income. These include investment expenses, union and professional dues, cost of tax preparation, safe-deposit box rental fees, and certain expenses for a job search.

Employee Business Expenses. Miscellaneous expenses also include unreimbursed employee business expenses such as travel, automobile, telephone, and gifts. However, only 50% of the cost of customer meals and entertainment is deductible.

The 2006 standard mileage rate for business use of autos, including leased cars, is 44½ cents per mile.

Moving Expenses. Taxpayers who change jobs or are transferred, usually can deduct part of their moving expenses, including travel and the cost of the moving of household goods, but not meals. The mileage rate for automobiles used in the move increased to 18 cents per mile for 2006.

Gambling. Lottery, slots, Texas Hold 'em, or other gambling expenses are deductible if the taxpayer itemizes. However, expenses are limited to gambling winnings reported on page one. If no winnings, no deduction!

IT'S A FACT: Pres. George W. Bush and First Lady Laura Bush reported an adjusted gross income of $735,180 for 2005. Their taxable income after deductions was $618,694 with a tax liability of $187,769. Vice President and Mrs. Cheney paid $529,636 on taxable income of $1,961,157.

Tax Credits

A tax deduction reduces a taxpayer's taxable income. Tax credits reduce dollar-for-dollar the amount of tax owed.

Earned Income Credit. Lower-income workers who maintain a household may be eligible for an earned income credit. It is based on total earned income such as wages, commissions, and tips.

The phase-out range of the earned income credit for joint filers increases annually up to a maximum of $3,000 in 2008. Starting in 2009 the credit will be adjusted annually for the cost of living. After 2010 all these changes will expire.

The Hope Scholarship Credit applies to qualified tuition and expenses for the first 2 years of postsecondary education in a degree or certificate program at an eligible institution. However, it does not apply to room and board or cost of books. The credit can be as high as $1,650, up $150 from 2005.

The Lifetime Learning Credit is available for taxpayers whose postsecondary education expenses are not eligible for the Hope credit. The credit is 20% of tuition and other qualifying expenses paid for by the taxpayer, spouse, or dependents up to a total credit of $2,000 (20% of $10,000 in expenses) for all entitled students who are enrolled in an eligible educational institution. The credit begins to phase out for higher income levels.

Adoption Credit. The adoption credit for qualified expenses increased to $10,960 in 2006. The credit limit is per person, not per year, and is adjusted annually for inflation. There are income and phase out rules to contend with.

Taxable Social Security Benefits

Earnings Limitations. Social Security recipients who have not reached full retirement age lose $1 of their benefits for every $2 of earned income over $12,480, an increase of $480 over 2005.

Taxable Benefits. Up to 50% of Social Security benefits may be taxable if the person's total income is: over $25,000 but less than $34,000 for a single individual, head of household, qualifying widow(er), or a married person who is filing separately if spouses lived apart all year; or over $32,000 but less than $44,000 for married individuals filing jointly. For higher incomes, 85% of Social Security benefits may become taxable.

Good News. Social Security benefits are not taxable if they are the only income received during the year.

Alternative Minimum Tax

The Alternative Minimum Tax (AMT) was established in 1969 to prevent people with very high incomes from using special tax breaks to pay little or no tax. It was never indexed for inflation and is not adjusted each year for the cost of living. Because of changes in the tax law, this tax affects more and more middle-income taxpayers every year.

The instructions included with tax forms 1040 and 1040A provide help for individuals to determine whether they are subject to the AMT. Form 6251, Alternative Minimum Tax, is used to figure out how much additional tax is owed.

Estate and Gift Taxes

Exclusion. The Tax Relief Reconciliation Act of 2001 increased the estate tax exclusion from $675,000 in 2001 to $1 mil in 2002 and 2003, $1.5 mil in 2004 and 2005. Starting in 2006, the exclusion increases to $2 mil through 2008, and $3.5 mil in 2009.

Estate Tax Rates. For 2001, the maximum tax rate on the value of an estate was 55%, reduced to 50% in 2002, 47% in 2005 and 46% for 2006. The tax rate will continue to decrease once more in 2007 when the maximum will be 45%, and will remain at 45% until 2009.

Tax Planning. All estate taxes are repealed for the year 2010. Unless Congress passes new legislation prior to 2011, the estate laws revert to the higher 2001 tax rates and lower exclusion provisions.

Resident Alien. The estate of a resident alien is subject to the same rules as that of an American citizen. All property owned worldwide is subject to the U.S. estate tax rules and regulations.

Gifting. Citizens, resident and non-resident aliens can make tax-free gifts of up to $12,000 each year to as many individuals as he or she chooses; twice that amount with consent of the spouse even if only one spouse does the gifting.

Lifetime Gifting. A $1 mil gift tax exclusion is the limit an individual is allowed to give to other individuals (not charities) during his or her lifetime before having to pay gift taxes. The annual $12,000 gifts are not included in the gift tax exclusion.

Tax Tip. Generally, property received as a gift, bequest, or inheritance is not included as income for individual taxpayers.

IRS Tax Audits

The IRS conducted more than 1.2 mil audits of individual taxpayers in 2005, less than 1% of the returns filed. This was about 1 of every 108 tax returns, up from about 1 of every 128 in 2004.

The audit selection process is not random. It is based on a set of formulas that are designed to spot questionable returns.

If the IRS concludes that you owe more and you disagree with the findings, you can meet with a supervisor. If you still do not agree, you can appeal to a separate Appeals Office.

For more information about audits, call the IRS at 1-800-829-3676 for its free Publication 556, Examination of Returns, Appeal Rights, and Claims for Refund. Or visit www.irs.gov.

Retention Of Income Tax Records

How long to keep your records is a combination of judgment and statutes of limitations. Since federal tax returns generally can be audited for up to three years after filing, six years if the IRS suspects underreported income, it's wise to keep income tax records at least seven years after a return is filed.

Your Rights as a Taxpayer

Congress has enacted "taxpayer bill of rights" legislation and created an Office of the Taxpayer Advocate within the IRS, with authority to order IRS personnel to issue refund checks and meet deadlines for resolving disputes. Taxpayer advocates can be contacted at 1-877-777-4778 (1-800-829-4059 for TTY/TDD). The IRS must pay legal fees if the taxpayer wins the case and the IRS cannot show it was "substantially justified" in pursuing it.

To confidentially report misconduct, waste, fraud or abuse by an IRS employee, you can call 1-800-366-4484.

For more information ask for IRS Publication 1, Your Rights as a Taxpayer, by calling 1-800-TAX-FORM for a free copy.

U.S. Tax Court

The U.S. Tax Court is a Federal court where taxpayers can dispute tax deficiencies as determined by the Commissioner of Internal Revenue before payment of the disputed amounts. The Tax Court is composed of 19 presidentially appointed members. Trial sessions and other work are performed by these judges along with senior judges serving on recall, and by special trial judges. If you're not satisfied with the outcome of your tax audit, you can take it to the U.S. Tax Court, federal district court or the U.S. Court of Federal Claims. Many people choose the Tax Court because they are not required to pay the contested tax up front.

Federal Outlays to States Per Dollar of Tax Revenue Received

Source: The Tax Foundation

(figures for fiscal year 2004; ranked highest to lowest)

State	Outlay	State	Outlay	State	Outlay	State	Outlay	State	Outlay
District of Columbia	6.64	South Dakota	1.49	Idaho	1.28	Rhode Island	1.02	Colorado	0.79
New Mexico	2.00	Oklahoma	1.48	Utah	1.14	Ohio	1.01	New York	0.79
Alaska	1.87	Arkansas	1.47	Kansas	1.12	Indiana	0.97	California	0.79
West Virginia	1.83	Louisiana	1.45	Vermont	1.12	Oregon	0.97	Massachusetts	0.77
Mississippi	1.77	Kentucky	1.45	Iowa	1.11	Georgia	0.96	Nevada	0.73
North Dakota	1.73	Maryland	1.44	Wyoming	1.11	Texas	0.94	Illinois	0.73
Alabama	1.71	Maine	1.40	North Carolina	1.10	Washington	0.80	Minnesota	0.69
Virginia	1.66	South Carolina	1.38	Nebraska	1.07	Michigan	0.85	New Hampshire	0.67
Hawaii	1.60	Tennessee	1.30	Pennsylvania	1.06	Wisconsin	0.82	Connecticut	0.66
Montana	1.58	Arizona	1.30	Florida	1.02	Delaware	0.79	New Jersey	0.55
		Missouri	1.29						

State Government Personal Income Tax Rates, 2006

Source: Reproduced with permission from *CCH State Tax Guide*, published and copyrighted by CCH Inc., 2700 Lake Cook Road, Riverwoods, IL 60015
Alaska, Florida, Nevada, South Dakota, Texas, Washington, and Wyoming did not have state income taxes and are thus not listed. Tax rates apply in stages—for example, a single person in Arizona making $60,000 in taxable income would pay 2.73% on the first $10,000 of income, 3.04% on the next $15,000, etc. For further details, see notes at end of table.

Alabama
Single, Head of household, or
Married filing separately
$0 to $500	2%
$501 to $3,000	4%
$3,001 and over	5%

Married filing jointly
$0 to $1,000	2%
$1,001 to $6,000	4%
$6,001 and over	5%

Arizona[1]
Single or Married filing separately
$0 to $10,000	2.73%
$10,001 to $25,000	3.04%
$25,001 to $50,000	3.55%
$50,001 to $150,000	4.48%
$150,001 and over	4.79%

Married filing jointly, Head of household
$0 to $20,000	2.73%
$20,001 to $50,000	3.04%
$50,001 to $100,000	3.55%
$100,001 to $300,000	4.48%
$300,001 and over	4.79%

Arkansas[2,3]
Single, Head of household, Married filing jointly, or Married filing separately
$0 to $3,399	1%
$3,400 to $6,799	2%
$6,800 to $10,299	3.5%
$10,300 to $17,099	4.5%
$17,100 to $28,499	6%
$28,500 and over	7%

California[1,2]
Single or Married filing separately
$0 to $6,319	1%
$6,320 to $14,979	2%
$14,980 to $23,641	4%
$23,642 to $32,819	6%
$32,820 to $41,476	8%
$41,477 and over	9.3%

Head of household
$0 to $12,644	1%
$12,645 to $29,959	2%
$29,960 to $38,619	4%
$38,620 to $47,796	6%
$47,797 to $56,456	8%
$56,457 and over	9.3%

Married filing jointly or Surviving spouse
$0 to $12,638	1%
$12,639 to $29,958	2%
$29,959 to $47,282	4%
$47,282 to $65,638	6%
$65,639 to $82,952	8%
$82,953 and over	9.3%

Colorado
4.63% of federal taxable income

Connecticut
Single & Married filing separately
$0 to $10,000	3%
$10,001 and over	5%

Head of household
$0 to $16,000	3%
$16,001 and over	5%

Married filing jointly or Surviving spouse
$0 to $20,000	3%
$20,001 and over	5%

Delaware
Single, Head of household, Married filing jointly, or Married filing separately
$2,000 to $5,000	2.2%
$5,001 to $10,000	3.9%
$10,001 to $20,000	4.8%
$20,001 to $25,000	5.2%
$25,001 to $60,000	5.55%
$60,001 and over	5.95%

District of Columbia
Single, Head of household, Married filing jointly, or Married filing separately
$0 to $10,000	5%
$10,001 to $30,000	7.5%
$30,001 and over	9.0%

Georgia
Single
$0 to $750	1%
$751 to $2,250	2%
$2,251 to $3,750	3%
$3,751 to $5,250	4%
$5,251 to $7,000	5%
$7,001 and over	6%

Head of household, Married filing jointly, or Surviving spouse
$0 to $1,000	1%
$1,001 to $3,000	2%
$3,001 to $5,000	3%
$5,001 to $7,000	4%
$7,001 to $10,000	5%
$10,001 and over	6%

Married filing separately
$0 to $500	1%
$501 to $1,500	2%
$1,501 to $2,500	3%
$2,501 to $3,500	4%
$3,501 to $5,000	5%
$5,001 and over	6%

Hawaii
Single or Married filing separately
$0 to $2,000	1.4%
$2,001 to $4,000	3.2%
$4,001 to $8,000	5.5%
$8,001 to $12,000	6.4%
$12,001 to $16,000	6.8%
$16,001 to $20,000	7.2%
$20,001 to $30,000	7.6%
$30,001 to $40,000	7.9%
$40,001 and over	8.25%

Head of household
$0 to $3,000	1.4%
$3,001 to $6,000	3.2%
$6,001 to $12,000	5.5%
$12,001 to $18,000	6.4%
$18,001 to $24,000	6.8%
$24,001 to $30,000	7.2%
$30,001 to $45,000	7.6%
$45,001 to $60,000	7.9%
$60,001 and over	8.25%

Married filing jointly or Surviving spouse
$0 to $4,000	1.4%
$4,001 to $8,000	3.2%
$8,001 to $16,000	5.5%
$16,001 to $24,000	6.4%
$24,001 to $32,000	6.8%
$32,001 to $40,000	7.2%
$40,001 to $60,000	7.6%
$60,001 to $80,000	7.9%
$80,001 and over	8.25%

Idaho[1,2,3]
Single or Married filing separately
$0 to $1,128	1.6%
$1,129 to $2,257	3.6%
$2,258 to $3,386	4.1%
$3,387 to $4,514	5.1%
$4,515 to $5,643	6.1%
$5,644 to $8,465	7.1%
$8,466 to $22,576	7.4%
$22,577 and over	7.8%

Head of household, Married filing jointly, or Surviving spouse
$0 to $2,257	1.6%
$2,258 to $4,514	3.6%
$4,515 to $6,772	4.1%
$6,773 to $9,030	5.1%
$9,031 to $11,287	6.1%
$11,288 to $16,932	7.1%
$16,933 to $45,152	7.4%
$45,153 and over	7.8%

Illinois
3% of taxable net income

Indiana
3.4% of adjusted gross income

Iowa[2]
Single, Head of household, Married filing jointly, or Married filing separately
$0 to $1,269	0.36%
$1,270 to $2,538	0.72%
$2,539 to $5,076	2.43%
$5,077 to $11,421	4.5%
$11,422 to $19,035	6.12%
$19,036 to $25,380	6.48%
$25,381 to $38,070	6.8%
$38,071 to $57,105	7.92%
$57,106 and over	8.98%

Kansas
Single, Head of household, or Married filing separately
$0 to $15,000	3.5%
$15,001 to $30,000	6.25%
$30,001 and over	6.45%

Married filing jointly
$0 to $30,000	3.5%
$30,001 to $60,000	6.25%
$60,001 and over	6.45%

Kentucky
Single, Head of household, Married filing jointly, or Married filing separately
$0 to $3,000	2%
$3,001 to $4,000	3%
$4,001 to $5,000	4%
$5,001 to $8,000	5%
$8,001 to $75,000	5.8%
75,001 and over	6%

Louisiana[1]
Single, Head of household, or Married filing separately
$0 to $12,500	2%
$12,501 to $25,000	4%
$25,001 and over	6%

Married filing jointly
$0 to $25,000	2%
$25,001 to $50,000	4%
$50,001 and over	6%

Maine[2]
Single or Married filing separately
$0 to $4,449	2%
$4,450 to $8,849	4.5%
$8,850 to $17,699	7%
$17,770 and over	8.5%

Head of household
$0 to $6,649	2%
$6,650 to $13,249	4.5%
$13,250 to $26,599	7%
$26,600 and over	8.5%

Married filing jointly
$0 to $8,899	2%
$8,900 to $17,699	4.5%
$17,700 to $35,449	7%
$35,450 and over	8.5%

Maryland
Single, Head of household, Married filing jointly, or Married filing separately
$0 to $1,000	2%
$1,001 to $2,000	3%
$2,001 to $3,000	4%
$3,001 and over	4.75%

Massachusetts
Short-term capital gains	12%
All other income	5.3%

Michigan
3.9% of taxable income

Minnesota[2]
Single
$0 to $19,890	5.35%
$19,891 to $65,330	7.05%
$65,331 and over	7.85%

Head of household
$0 to $24,490	5.35%
$24,491 to $98,390	7.05%
$98,391 and over	7.85%

Married filing jointly
$0 to $29,070	5.35%
$29,071 to $115,510	7.05%
$115,511 and over	7.85%

Married filing separately
$0 to $14,540	5.35%
$14,541 to $57,760	7.05%
$57,761 and over	7.85%

Mississippi
Single, Head of household, Married filing jointly, or Married filing separately
$0 to $5,000	3%
$5,001 to $10,000	4%
$10,001 and over	5%

Missouri
Single, Head of household, Married filing jointly, or Married filing separately
$0 to $1,000	1.5%
$1,001 to $2,000	2%
$2,001 to $3,000	2.5%
$3,001 to $4,000	3%
$4,001 to $5,000	3.5%
$5,001 to $6,000	4%
$6,001 to $7,000	4.5%
$7,001 to $8,000	5%
$8,001 to $9,000	5.5%
$9,001 and over	6%

Montana[2,3]
Single, Head of household, Married filing jointly, or Married filing separately
$0 to $2,299	1%
$2,300 to $4,099	2%
$4,100 to $6,199	3%
$6,200to $8,399	4%
$8,400 to $10,799	5%
$10,800 to $13,899	6%
$13,900 and over	6.9%

Nebraska
Single
$0 to $2,400	2.56%
$2,401 to $17,000	3.57%
$17,001 to $26,500	5.12%
$26,501 and over	6.84%

Head of household
$0 to $3,800	2.56%
$3,801 to $24,000	3.57%
$24,001 to $35,000	5.12%
$35,001 and over	6.84%

Married filing jointly
$0 to $4,000	2.56%
$4,001 to $30,000	3.57%
$30,001 to $46,750	5.12%
$46,751 and over	6.84%

Married filing separately
$0 to $2,000	2.56%
$2,001 to $15,000	3.57%
$15,001 to $23,375	5.12%
$23,376 and over	6.84%

New Hampshire
5% on interest and dividends only

New Jersey
Single or Married filing separately
$0 to $20,000	1.4%
$20,001 to $35,000	1.75%
$35,001 to $40,000	3.5%
$40,001 to $75,000	5.525%
$75,001 to $500,000	6.37%
$500,001 and over	8.97%

Head of household, Married filing jointly, or Surviving spouse
$0 to $20,000	1.4%
$20,001 to $50,000	1.75%
$50,001 to $70,000	2.45%
$70,001 to $80,000	3.5%
$80,001 to $150,000	5.525%
$150,001 to $500,000	6.37%
$500,001 and over	8.97%

New Mexico[1]
Single
$0 to $5,500	1.7%
$5,501 to $11,000	3.2%
$11,001 to $16,000	4.7%
$16,001 and over	5.3%

Head of household
$0 to $8,000	1.7%
$8,001 to $16,000	3.2%
$16,001 to $24,000	4.7%
$24,001 and over	5.3%

Married filing jointly
$0 to $8,000	1.7%
$8,001 to $16,000	3.2%
$16,001 to $24,000	4.7%
$24,001 and over	5.3%

Married filing separately
$0 to $4,000	1.7%
$4,001 to $8,000	3.2%
$8,001 to $12,000	4.7%
$12,001 and over	5.3%

New York
Single & Married filing separately
$0 to $8,000	4%
$8,001 to $11,000	4.5%
$11,001 to $13,000	5.25%
$13,001 to $20,000	5.9%
$20,001 and over	6.85%

Head of household
$0 to $11,000	4%
$11,001 to $15,000	4.5%
$15,001 to $17,000	5.25%
$17,001 to $30,000	5.9%
$30,001 and over	6.85%

Married filing jointly
$0 to $16,000	4%
$16,001 to $22,000	4.5%
$22,001 to $26,000	5.25%
$26,001 to $40,000	5.9%
$40,001 and over	6.85%

North Carolina
Single
$0 to $12,750	6%
$12,751 to $60,000	7%
$60,001 to $120,000	7.75%
$120,001 and over	8.25%

Head of household
$0 to $17,000	6%
$17,001 to $80,000	7%
$80,001 to $160,000	7.75%
$160,001 and over	8.25%

Married filing jointly, or Surviving spouse
$0 to $21,250	6%
$21,251 to $100,000	7%
$100,001 to $200,000	7.75%
$200,001 and over	8.25%

Married filing separately
$0 to $10,625	6%
$10,626 to $50,000	7%
$50,001 to $100,000	7.75%
$100,001 and over	8.25%

North Dakota[2]
Single
$0 to $29,700	2.1%
$29,701 to $71,950	3.92%
$71,951 to $150,151	4.34%
$150,151 to $326,450	5.04%
$326,451 and over	5.54%

Head of household
$0 to $39,800	2.1%
$39,801 to $102,800	3.92%
$102,801 to $166,450	4.34%
$166,451 to $326,450	5.04%
$326,451 and over	5.54%

Married filing jointly, Surviving spouse
$0 to $49,600	2.1%
$49,601 to $119,950	3.92%

$119,951 to $182,800	4.34%
$182,801 to $326,450	5.04%
$326,451 and over	5.54%

Married filing separately
$0 to $24,800	2.1%
$24,801 to $59,975	3.92%
$59,976 to $91,400	4.34%
$91,401 to $163,225	5.04%
$163,226 and over	5.54%

Ohio
Single, Head of household, Married filing jointly, or Married filing separately
$0 to $5,000	0.712%
$5,001 to $10,000	1.424%
$10,001 to $15,000	2.847%
$15,001 to $20,000	3.559%
$20,001 to $40,000	4.27%
$40,001 to $80,000	4.983%
$80,001 to $100,000	5.693%
$100,001 to $200,000	6.61%
$200,001 and over	7.185%

Oklahoma
Single or Married filing separately
$0 to $1,000	0.5%
$1,001 to $2,500	1%
$2,501 to $3,750	2%
$3,751 to $4,900	3%
$4,901 to $7,200	4%
$7,201 to $8,700	5%
$8,701 to $10,500	6%
$10,501 and over	6.25%

Head of household or Married filing jointly
$0 to $2,000	0.5%
$2,001 to $5,000	1%
$5,001 to $7,500	2%
$7,501 to $9,800	3%
$9,801 to $12,200	4%
$12,201 to $15,000	5%
$15,001 to $21,000	6%
$21,001 and over	6.25%

Oregon[2]
Single or Married filing separately
$0 to $2,650	5%
$2,651 to $6,650	7%
$6,651 and over	9%

Married filing jointly or Head of household
$0 to $5,300	5%
$5,301 to $13,300	7%
$13,301 and over	9%

Pennsylvania
3.07% of taxable compensation, net profits, net gains from the sale of property, rent, royalties, patents or copyrights, income from estates or trusts, dividends, interest and winnings

Rhode Island
25% of the federal income tax rates, including capital gains rates and any other special rates for other types of income, that were in effect prior to enactment of the Economic Growth and Tax Relief Reconciliation Act of 2001. Effective for the 2006 tax year, taxpayers may elect to compute income tax liability based on the graduated rate schedule or an alternative flat rate equal to 8%.

South Carolina[2, 3]
Single, Head of household, Married filing jointly, or Married filing separately
$0 to $2,530	2.5%
$2,531 to $5,060	3%
$5,061 to $7,590	4%
$7,591 to $10,120	5%
$10,121 to $12,650	6%
$12,651 and over	7%

Tennessee
6% of interest and dividends

Utah
Single & Married filing separately
$0 to $863	2.3%
$864 to $1,726	3.3%
$1,727 to $2,588	4.2%
$2,589 to $3,450	5.2%
$3,451 to $4,313	6%
$4,314 and over	7%

Head of household or Married filing jointly
$0 to $1,726	2.3%
$1,727 to $3,450	3.3%
$3,451 to $5,176	4.2%
$5,177 to $6,900	5.2%
$6,901 to $8,626	6%
$8,627 and over	7%

Vermont[2, 3]
Single
$0 to $29,700	3.6%
$29,701 to $71,950	7.2%
$71,951 to $150,150	8.5%
$150,151 to $326,450	9.0%
$326,451 and over	9.5%

Head of household
$0 to $39,800	3.6%

$39,801 to $102,800	7.2%
$102,801 to $166,450	8.5%
$166,451 to $326,450	9.0%
$326,451 and over	9.5%

Married filing jointly, Surviving spouse, Civil Union filing jointly
$0 to $49,650	3.6%
$49,651 to $119,950	7.2%
$119,951 to $182,800	8.5%
$182,801 to $326,450	9.0%
$326,451 and over	9.5%

Married or Civil Union filing separately
$0 to $24,825	3.6%
$24,826 to $59,975	7.2%
$59,976 to $91,400	8.5%
$91,401 to $163,225	9.0%
$163,226 and over	9.5%

Virginia
Single, Head of household, Married filing jointly, or Married filing separately
$0 to $3,000	2%
$3,001 to $5,000	3%
$5,001 to $17,000	5%
$17,001 and over	5.75%

West Virginia
Single, Head of household, or Married filing jointly
$0 to $10,000	3%
$10,001 to $25,000	4%
$25,001 to $40,000	4.5%
$40,001 to $60,000	6%
$60,001 and over	6.5%

Married filing separately
$0 to $5,000	3%
$5,001 to $12,500	4%
$12,501 to $20,000	4.5%
$20,001 to $30,000	6%
$30,001 and over	6.5%

Wisconsin[1, 2]
Single or Head of household
$0 to $8,840	4.6%
$8,841 to $17,680	6.15%
$17,631 to $132,580	6.5%
$132,581 and over	6.75%

Married filing jointly
$0 to $11,780	4.6%
$11,781 to $23,570	6.15%
$23,571 to $176,770	6.5%
$176,771 and over	6.75%

Married filing separately
$0 to $5,890	4.6%
$5,891 to $11,780	6.15%
$11,781 to $88,390	6.5%
$88,391 and over	6.75%

(1) Community property state in which, in general, one-half of the community income is taxable to each spouse. (2) Brackets indexed for inflation annually. (3) 2006 adjusted brackets were not available. Bracketed rates listed are for 2005. **Arkansas:** Tax liability is associated with a 3% tax surcharge based on existing rates. Married filing separately combined-status couples calculate taxes separately and add the results. **California:** An additional 1% tax is imposed on taxable income in excess of $1 million. **Colorado:** Alternative minimum tax imposed. Individual taxpayers are subject to an alternative minimum tax equal to the amount by which 3.47% of their Colorado alternative minimum taxable income exceeds their Colorado normal tax. **Connecticut:** Resident estates and trusts are subject to the 5% income tax rate on all of their income. Additional state minimum tax imposed on resident individuals, trusts, and estates that are subject to the federal alternative minimum tax, equal to the amount by which the Connecticut minimum tax exceeds the Connecticut basic income tax (the lesser of [a] 19% of adjusted federal tentative minimum tax, or [b] 5.5% of adjusted federal alternative minimum taxable income). Separate provisions apply for non- and part-year resident individuals, trusts, and estates. **Illinois:** Additional personal property replacement tax of 1.5% of net income is imposed on partnerships, trusts, and S corporations. **Indiana:** Counties may impose an adjusted gross income tax on residents or on nonresidents, or a county option income tax. (Note: Rates have apparently changed.) **Iowa:** An alternative minimum tax of 6.7% of alternative minimum income is imposed if the minimum tax exceeds the taxpayer's regular income tax liability. The minimum tax is 75% of the maximum regular tax rate. **Maine:** Additional state minimum tax is imposed equal to the amount by which the tentative minimum tax exceeds regular income tax liability. **Massachusetts:** Part A income represents either interest and dividends or short-term capital gains. Part B income represents wages, salaries, tips, pensions, state bank interest, partnership income, business income, rents, alimony, winnings, and certain other items of income. Part C income represents gains from the sale of capital assets held for more than one year. **Michigan:** Persons with business activity allocated or apportioned to Michigan are also subject to a single business tax on an adjusted tax base. **Minnesota:** A 6.4% alternative minimum tax is imposed. **Montana:** Minimum tax, $1. **Nebraska:** The tax rates in the schedules are determined by multiplying the primary rate set by the legislature by the following factors for the brackets, from lowest to highest bracket. For tax years beginning on or after January 1, 2003, the respective factors are: 0.6932, 0.9646, 1.3846, and 1.848. For tax years beginning before January 1, 2003, the respective factors are: 0.6784, 0.9432, 1.3541, and 1.8054. The figure obtained for each bracket is rounded to the nearest hundredth of 1%. One rate schedule is to be established for each federal filing status (Sec. 77-2715.02). **New Mexico:** Qualified nonresident taxpayers may pay alternative tax of 0.75% of gross receipts from New Mexico sales. **New York:** A supplemental tax is imposed to recapture the tax table benefit. The supplemental tax is calculated in accordance with N.Y. Tax Law Sec. 601(d). **Oklahoma:** Rates given are for taxpayers not deducting federal income tax. Rates for married individuals filing jointly, surviving spouses and heads of households deducting federal income tax range from .50% of the first $2,000 to 10% of income over $24,000. For single individuals and married individuals filing separately that are deducting federal income tax, rates range from .50% of the first $1,000 to 10% of income over $16,000. **Vermont:** The tax amount in the schedules is increased by 24% of a taxpayer's federal tax liability for: additional taxes assessed due to early withdrawals from qualified retirement plans, individual retirement accounts, and medical savings accounts; recapture of the federal investment tax credit; or tax on qualified lump-sum distributions of pension income not included in federal taxable income. The amount of tax is decreased by 24% of the reduction in the taxpayer's federal liability due to farm income averaging. **West Virginia:** Minimum tax equal to the excess by which 25% of any federal minimum tax or alternative minimum tax for the taxable year exceeds the sum of the primary tax for West Virginia personal income tax purposes for the taxable year. **Wisconsin:** A permanent recycling surcharge is imposed on individuals, estates, trusts, and partnerships with at least $4 million in gross receipts at the rate of the greater of $25 or 0.2% of net business income as allocated or apportioned to Wisconsin. The maximum surcharge is $9,800. Farming is no longer treated preferentially.

ASSOCIATIONS AND SOCIETIES

Source: World Almanac research

Selected list, generally by first distinctive **key word** in each title; e.g., Retired Persons, American Association of. Listed by acronym when that is the official name. Founding year in parentheses; figure after ZIP code = membership as reported. Information, especially website addresses, subject to change. For other organizations, see Directory of Sports Organizations; Where to Get Help in Health chapter; Membership of Religious Groups in Religion chapter; Major International Organizations in Nations chapter.

AAA (American Automobile Assn.) (1902), 1000 AAA Dr., Box 28, Heathrow, FL 32746; www.aaa.com

AARP. See Retired Persons, American Assn. of

Abortion Federation, National (1977), 1755 Massachusetts Ave. NW, Ste. 600, Washington, DC 20036; 400 institutions; www.prochoice.org

Academies, Natl. (1863), 500 Fifth St. NW, Washington, DC 20001; approx. 6,000; www.nationalacademies.org

Accountants, American Institute of Certified Public (1887), 1211 Ave. of the Americas, New York, NY 10036; 336,000+; www.aicpa.org

Actuaries, Society of (1949), 475 N. Martingale Rd., Ste. 600, Schaumburg, IL 60173; 17,000; www.soa.org

Administrative Professionals, Intl. Assn. of (1942), 10502 NW Ambassador Dr., Kansas City, MO 64195-0404; 40,000; www.iaap-hq.org

Collegiate Schools of Business, Assn. to Advance (AACSB) (1916), 777 S. Harbour Island Blvd., Ste. 750, Tampa, FL 33602; 950+ institutions; www.aacsb.edu

Advancement and Support of Education, Council for (1974), 1307 New York Ave. NW, Ste. 1000, Washington, DC 20005; 3,000 schools; www.case.org

Aeronautic Assn., Natl. (1922), 1737 King St., Ste. 220, Alexandria, VA 22314; 3,000; www.naa-usa.org

Aerospace Industries Assn. of America Inc. (1919), 1000 Wilson Blvd., Ste. 1700, Arlington, VA 22209; 104 cos.; www.aia-aerospace.org

Aerospace Medical Assn. (1929), 320 S. Henry St., Alexandria, VA 22314; 3,100; www.asma.org

AFCEA (Armed Forces Communications and Electronics Assn.) (1946), 4400 Fair Lakes Ct., Fairfax, VA 22033; 20,000 indiv., 11,000 corp.; www.afcea.org

African-American Life and History, Assn. for the Study of (1915), CB Powell Building, 525 Bryant St., Ste. C142, Washington, DC 20059; 3,500; www.asalh.org

AFS Intercultural Programs USA (1947), 198 Madison Ave., 8th Fl., New York, NY 10016; www.afs.org/usa

Agricultural Engineers, American Soc. of (ASAE) (1907), 2950 Niles Road, St. Joseph, MI 49085; 9,000; www.asae.org

Air & Waste Management Assn. (1907), One Gateway Center, 3rd Fl., 420 Fort Duquesne Blvd., Pittsburgh, PA 15222; 9,000+; www.awma.org

Aircraft Owners and Pilots Assn. (1939), 421 Aviation Way, Frederick, MD 21701; 400,000+; www.aopa.org

Air Force Assn. (1946), 1501 Lee Hwy., Arlington, VA 22209; 230+ chapt.; www.afa.org

Al-Anon/Alateen (1951), 1600 Corporate Landing Pkwy., Virginia Beach, VA 23454; www.al-anon.alateen.org

Alcoholics Anonymous (AA) (1935), Box 459, Grand Central Station, New York, NY 10163; 2,000,000+; www.aa.org

Alcoholism and Drug Dependence Inc., Natl. Council on (1944), 22 Cortlandt St., Ste. 801, New York, NY 10007; 100 affil.; www.ncadd.org

Alexander Graham Bell Assn. for the Deaf & Hard of Hearing (1890), 3417 Volta Pl. NW, Washington, DC 20007; 5,000; www.agbell.org

Allergy, Asthma, and Immunology, American Academy of (1943), 555 E. Wells St., Ste. 2100, Milwaukee, WI 53202; 6,000; www.aaaai.org

Alpha Delta Kappa (1947), 1615 W. 92nd St., Kansas City, MO 64114; 46,563; www.alphadeltakappa.org

Alzheimer's Assn. (1980), 225 N. Michigan Ave., 17th Fl., Chicago, IL 60611; 81 chapt.; www.alz.org

AMBUCS, Inc., Natl. (1922), 4285 Regency Court, High Point, NC 27265; 6,000; www.ambucs.com

American. See also other entries under next major word in title.

American Federation of Labor & Congress of Industrial Oranizations (AFL-CIO) (1955), 815 16th St. NW, Washington, DC 20006; 9 mil+; www.aflcio.org

American Indians, Natl. Congress of (1944), 1301 Connecticut Ave. NW, Ste. 200, Washington, DC 20036; 262 member tribes; www.ncai.org

American-Islamic Relations, Council on (1994), 453 New Jersey Ave. SE, Washington, DC 20003; www.cair-net.org

American Legion (1919), P.O. Box 1055, 700 N. Pennsylvania St., Indianapolis, IN 46206; 3 mil.; www.legion.org

American Legion Auxiliary (1919), 777 N. Meridian St., 3rd Floor, Indianapolis, IN 46204; 1 mil; www.legion-aux.org

AmeriCares Foundation (1982), 88 Hamilton Ave., Stamford, CT 06902; www.americares.org

AMIDEAST (formerly American Mideast Educational & Training Services) (1951), 1730 M St. NW, Ste. 1100, Washington, DC 20036; www.amideast.org

Amnesty Intl. USA (1961), 5 Penn Plaza, 14th Fl., New York, NY 10001; 320,000+; www.amnestyusa.org

AMVETS (American Veterans) (1943); **AMVETS Natl. Auxiliary** (1946), 4647 Forbes Blvd., Lanham, MD 20706; 250,000; www.amvets.org

Amusement Parks and Attractions, Intl. Assn. of (IAAPA) (1918), 1448 Duke St., Alexandria, VA 22316; 4,000+; www.iaapa.org

Animals, American Society for Prevention of Cruelty to (ASPCA) (1866), 424 E. 92nd St., New York, NY 10128; 750,000; www.aspca.org

Animals, People for the Ethical Treatment of (PETA) (1980), 501 Front St., Norfolk, VA 23510; 850,000; www.peta.org

Animal Welfare Institute (1951), P.O. Box 3650, Washington, DC 20027; 22,000; www.awionline.org

Anthropological Assn., American (1902), 2200 Wilson Blvd., Ste. 600, Arlington, VA 22201; 11,500; www.aaanet.org

Antiquarian Society, American (1812), 185 Salisbury St., Worcester, MA 01609; 800; www.americanantiquarian.org

Anti-Vivisection Soc., Natl. (1929), 53 W. Jackson Blvd., Ste. 1552, Chicago, IL 60604; www.navs.org

APICS (Assn. for Operations Mgmt.) (1957), 5301 Shawnee Rd., Alexandria, VA 22312- 2317; 60,000; www.apics.org

Appalachian Mountain Club (1876), 5 Joy St., Boston, MA 02108; 90,000+; www.outdoors.org

Appalachian Trail Conference (1925), 799 Washington St., P.O. Box 807, Harpers Ferry, WV 25425; 125,000; www.appalachiantrail.org

Arbitration Assn., American (1926), 335 Madison Ave., 10th Fl., New York, NY 10017; 8,000; www.adr.org

Arc of the United States, The (1950), 1010 Wayne Avenue, Ste. 650, Silver Spring, MD 20910; 140,000; www.thearc.org

Archaeological Institute of America (1879), 656 Beacon St., 4th Fl., Boston, MA 02215; 9,000; www.archaeological.org

Architects, American Institute of (1857), 1735 New York Ave. NW, Washington, DC 20006; 74,000; www.aia.org

Army, Assn. of the United States (1950), 2425 Wilson Blvd., Arlington, VA 22201; 130 chapt.; www.ausa.org

Arthritis Foundation (1948), 1330 W. Peachtree St., Ste. 100, Atlanta, GA 30309; www.arthritis.org

Arts, Americans for the (1996), 1000 Vermont Ave. NW, 6th Fl., Washington, DC 20005; 1,500; www.artsusa.org

Arts and Sciences, American Academy of (1780), 136 Irving St., Cambridge, MA 02138; 4,600 fellows; www.amacad.org

ASPCA. See Animals, Amer. Soc. for Prev. of Cruelty to.

Associated Press (1848), 450 W. 33rd St., New York, NY 10001; 3,700 staff, 1,500+ newspapers, 5,000+ U.S. broadcast stations; www.ap.org

Astrologers, Inc., American Federation of (AFA, Inc.) (1938), 6535 South Rural Road, Tempe, AZ 85283; 4,000; www.astrologers.com

Astronautical Society, American (1954), 6352 Rolling Mill Pl., #102, Springfield, VA 22152; 1,500; www.astronautical.org

Astronomical Society, American (1899), 2000 Florida Ave. NW, Ste. 400, Washington, DC 20009; 6,400+; www.aas.org

Atheists, American (1963), P.O. Box 5733, Parsippany, NJ 07054; 2,300; www.atheists.org

Audubon Soc., Natl. (1905), 700 Broadway, New York, NY 10003; 600,000; www.audubon.org

Authors Guild, The (1912), 31 E. 32nd St., 7th Fl., New York, NY 10016; 8,200; www.authorsguild.org

Authors Registry, The (1995), 31 E. 32nd St., 7th Fl., New York, NY 10016; 30,000; www.authorsregistry.org

Autism Soc. of America (1965), 7910 Woodmont Ave., Ste. 300, Bethesda, MD 20814; 24,000; www.autism-society.org

Autograph Collectors Club, Universal (1965), P.O. Box 6181, Washington, DC 20044-6181; 1,300; www.uacc.org

Automobile, Aerospace, and Agricultural Implement Workers of America, United, The Intl. Union of (UAW) (1935), 8000 E. Jefferson Ave., Detroit, MI 48214; 710,000; www.uaw.org

Automobile Club of America, Antique (1935), 501 W. Governor Road, P.O. Box 417, Hershey, PA 17033; 60,000; www.aaca.org

Automobile License Plate Collectors Assn. (1954), 118 Quaker Rd. Hampton, VA 23669; ; 3,000; www.alpca.org

Badminton Assn., USA (1938), One Olympic Plaza, Colorado Springs, CO 80909; 3,000; www.usabadminton.com

Bald-Headed Men of America (1973), 102 Bald Dr., Morehead City, NC 28557; approx. 22,000; baldusa.org

Bankers of America, Independent Community (1930), One Thomas Circle NW, Ste. 400, Washington, DC 20005; 5,000; www.icba.org

Bar Assn., American (1878), 321 N. Clark St., Chicago, IL 60610; 400,000+; www.abanet.org

Bar Assn., Federal (1920), 2215 M Street NW, Washington, DC 20037; 16,000; www.fedbar.org

Barbershop Harmony Society (1938), 7930 Sheridan Rd., Kenosha, WI 53143; 30,000; www.spebsqsa.org

Baseball Congress, American Amateur (1935), 100 W. Broadway, Farmington, NM 87401; 14,500 teams; www.aabc.us

Baseball Congress, Natl. (1934), 300 S. Sycamore, Wichita, KS 67213; www.nbcbaseball.com

Baseball Research, Inc., Society for American (1971), 812 Huron Road E #719, Cleveland, OH 44115; 6,800; www.sabr.org

Battleship Assn., American (1964), P.O. Box 711247, San Diego, CA 92171; 1,025

Beer Can Collectors of America (1970), 747 Merus Ct., Fenton, MO 63026; 4,000; www.bcca.com

Beta Gamma Sigma Honor Society (1913), 125 Weldon Pkwy., Maryland Heights, MO 63043; 360,000; www.betagammasigma.org

Beta Sigma Phi (1931), 1800 W. 91st Pl., Kansas City, MO 64114; 200,000; www.betasigmaphi.org

Better Business Bureaus, Council of (1970), 4200 Wilson Blvd., Suite 800, Arlington, VA 22203; 120 bureaus; www.bbb.org

Bible Society, American (1816), 1865 Broadway, New York, NY 10023; 136 societies; www.americanbible.org

Biblical Literature, Society of (1880), 825 Houston Mill Rd., Ste. 350, Atlanta, GA 30329; 6,000; www.sbl-site.org

Big Brothers/Big Sisters of America (1904), 230 N. 13th St., Philadelphia, PA 19107; 470 agencies; bbbsa.org

Biochemistry and Molecular Biology, American Society for (1906), 9650 Rockville Pike, Bethesda, MD 20814; 11,900; www.asbmb.org

Biological Sciences, American Institute of (1947), 1444 I St. NW, Ste. 200, Washington, DC 20005; 240,000; www.aibs.org

Blind, American Council of the (1961), 1155 15th St. NW, Ste. 1004, Washington, DC 20005; 71 orgs.; www.acb.org

Blind, Natl. Federation of the (1940), 1800 Johnson St., Baltimore, MD 21230; 50,000+; www.nfb.org

Blinded Veterans Assn. (1958), 477 H St. NW, Washington, DC 20001; 10,035; www.bva.org

Blindness America, Prevent (1908), 211 W. Wacker Dr., Ste. 1700, Chicago, IL 60606; 50,000; www.preventblindness.org

B'nai B'rith Intl. (1843), 2020 K St. NW, 7th Fl., Washington, DC 20006; 180,000; www.bnaibrith.org

Boat Owners Assn. of the U.S. (1966), 880 S. Pickett St., Alexandria, VA 22304; 575,000; www.boatUS.com

Bookplate Collectors & Designers, Amer. Soc. of (1922), P.O. Box 380340, Cambridge, MA 02238; 250; www.bookplate.org

Boy Scouts of America (1910), P.O. Box 152079, Irving, TX 75015; 4 mil+; www.scouting.org

Boys & Girls Clubs of America (1906), 1275 Peachtree St. NE, Atlanta, GA 30309; 4.4 mil; www.bgca.org

Bread for the World (1974), 50 F St. NW, Ste. 500, Washington, DC 20001; 54,000; www.bread.org

Brewing Chemists, American Society of (1934), 3340 Pilot Knob Road, St. Paul, MN 55121; 800+; www.asbcnet.org

Broadcasters, Natl. Assn. of (1923), 1771 N St. NW, Washington, DC 20036; www.nab.org

Business Women's Assn., American (1949), 9100 Ward Pkwy., P.O. Box 8728, Kansas City, MO 64114; 55,000; www.abwa.org

Button Society, Natl. (1938), 2733 Juno Pl., Akron, OH 44333-4137; 3,500+

Camp Fire USA (formerly Camp Fire Boys & Girls) (1910), 1100 Walnut St., Ste. 1900, Kansas City, MO 64106; 750,000; www.campfireusa.org

Camping Assn., American (1910), 5000 State Rd. 67 N., Martinsville, IN 46151; 7,000+; www.acacamps.org

Cancer Society, American (1913), 1599 Clifton Rd. NE, Atlanta, GA 30329; 3,400 local offices; www.cancer.org

Cartoonists Society, Natl. (1948), 1133 West Morse Blvd., Ste. 201, Winter Park, FL 32789; 600; www.reuben.org

Cat Fanciers' Assn., The (1906), P.O. Box 1005, Manasquan, NJ 08736; 657 clubs; www.cfainc.org

Catholic Bishops, United States Conference of (1966), 3211 4th St. NE, Washington, DC 20017; 402 members, 350 staff; www.nccbuscc.org

Catholic Church Extension Society of the USA (1905), 150 S. Wacker Dr., 20th Fl., Chicago, IL 60606; www.catholic-extension.org

Catholic Daughters of the Americas (1903), 10 West 71st St., New York, NY 10023; 95,000; www.catholicdaughters.org

Catholic Educational Assn., Natl. (1904), 1077 30th St. NW, Ste. 100, Washington, DC 20007; 200,000; www.ncea.org

Catholic Historical Soc., American (1884), 263 S. Fourth St., Philadelphia, PA 19106-3819; 450; www.amchs.org

Catholic Library Association (1921), 100 North St., Ste. 224, Pittsfield, MA 01201-5109; 1,000; www.cathla.org

Catholic War Veterans, USA Inc. (1935), 441 N. Lee St., Alexandria, VA 22314-2301; 20,000; cwv.org

Ceramic Society, The American (1899), 735 Ceramic Pl., Ste. 100, Westerville, OH 43081; 7,500; www.ceramics.org

Cerebral Palsy, Inc., United (1949), 1660 L St. NW, Ste. 700, Washington, DC 20036; 100 affiliates; www.ucp.org

Chamber of Commerce of the U.S.A. (1912), 1615 H St. NW, Washington, DC 20062; 215,000; www.uschamber.com

Chamber Music Players, Inc., Amateur (1969), 1123 Broadway, Rm. 304, New York, NY 10010; 5,200; www.acmp.net

Chemical Society, American (1876), 1155 16th St. NW, Washington, DC 20036; 158,000; www.chemistry.org

Chemistry Council, American (1872), 1300 Wilson Blvd., Arlington, VA 22209; 170 cos.; www.americanchemistry.com

Chess Federation, U.S. (1939), P.O. Box 3967, Crossville, TN 38557; 90,000+; www.uschess.org

Chiefs of Police, Intl. Assn. of (1893), 515 N. Washington St., Alexandria, VA 22314; 20,000+; www.theiacp.org

Childhood Education Intl., Assn. for (1892), 17904 Georgia Ave., Ste. 215, Olney, MD 20832; 12,000; www.acei.org

Children's Aid Society (1912), 181 West Valley Ave., Ste. 300, Birmingham, AL 35209; www.childrensaid.org

Children's Book Council, The (1945), 12 W. 37th St., 2nd Fl., New York, NY 10018; 75 publishers; www.cbcbooks.org

Child Welfare League of America (1920), 440 First St. NW, 3rd Fl., Washington, DC 20001; 900 agencies; www.cwla.org

Chiropractic Assn., American (1963), 1701 Clarendon Blvd., Arlington, VA 22209; 18,000; www.amerchiro.org

Chris-Craft Antique Boat Club (1973), 112 14th St. SE, Cedar Rapids, IA 52403; 3,000; www.chris-craft.org

Christian Children's Fund (1938), 2821 Emerywood Pkwy., Richmond, VA 23294; 159 staff; www.christianchildrensfund.org

Cities, Natl. League of (1924), 1301 Pennsylvania Ave. NW, Ste. 550, Washington, DC 20004; 1,600+; www.nlc.org

Civil Air Patrol (1941), 105 S. Hansell St., Bldg. 714, Maxwell AFB, AL 36112; 58,000; www.cap.gov

Civil Engineers, American Society of (1852), 1801 Alexander Bell Dr., Reston, VA 20191; 123,000+; www.asce.org

Civil Liberties Union, American (ACLU) (1920), 125 Broad St., 18th Fl., New York, NY 10004; 400,000; www.aclu.org

Coaster Enthusiasts, American (1978), 3650 Annapolis Ln., Ste. 107, Minneapolis, MN 55447; 8,000; www.aceonline.org

Coast Guard Combat Veterans Assn. (1985), P.O. Box 544, Westfield Center, OH 44251; 1,800; www.aug.edu/~libwrw/cgcva/cgcva.htm

Collectors, Natl. Assn. of (1996), 18222 Flower Hill Way, #299, Gaithersburg, MD 20879; 30,000; collectors.org

Co-dependents Anonymous (1986), P.O. Box 33577; Phoenix, AZ 85067; www.codependents.org

College Admission Counseling, Natl. Assn. for (1937), 1631 Prince Street, Alexandria, VA 22314; 8,000; www.nacac.com

College Board, The (1900), 45 Columbus Ave., New York, NY 10023; 4,700 inst.; www.collegeboard.org

College Music Society, The (1958), 312 East Pine St., Missoula, MT 59802; 8,800; www.music.org

Colleges and Universities, Assn. of American (1915), 1818 R St. NW, Washington, DC 20009; 1,000+ institutions; www.aacu.org

Collegiate Schools of Business, Assn. to Advance (AACSB) (1916), 777 S. Harbour Island Blvd., Ste. 750, Tampa, FL 33602; www.aacsb.edu

Colonial Dames XVII Century, Natl. Soc. (1915), 1300 New Hampshire Ave. NW, Washington, DC 20036; 13,000+; www.colonialdames17c.net

Commercial Law League of America (1895), 70 E. Lake St., Ste. 630, Chicago, IL 60601; 4,000; www.clla.org

Common Cause (1970), 1133 19th St. NW, 9th Fl., Washington, DC 20036; 300,000+; www.commoncause.org

Communication Assn., Natl. (1914), 1765 N St. NW, Washington, DC, 20036; 7,700; www.natcom.org

Community & Justice, National Conference for (1927), 328 Flatbush Ave., Box 402, Brooklyn, NY 11217; 55 offices; www.nccj.org

Community Colleges, American Assn. of (1920), One Dupont Circle NW, Ste. 410, Washington, DC 20036; 1,100 inst; www.aacc.nche.edu

Composers, Authors & Publishers, American Soc. of (ASCAP) (1914), One Lincoln Plaza, New York, NY 10023; 200,000; www.ascap.com

Composers/USA, Natl. Assn. of (1933), P.O. Box 49256, Barrington Station, Los Angeles, CA 90049; 400+; www.music-usa.org/nacusa

Computing Machinery, Assn. for (1947), 1515 Broadway, 17th Fl., New York, NY 10036; 78,000+; www.acm.org

Computing Professionals, Institute for Certification of (1973), 2350 E. Devon Ave., Ste. 115, Des Plaines, IL 60018-4610; 50,000; www.iccp.org

Concerned Women for America (1979), 1015 Fifteenth St. NW, Ste. 1100, Washington, DC 20005; 500,000; www.cwfa.org

Congress of Racial Equality (CORE) (1942), 817 Broadway, 3rd Floor, New York, NY 10003; 82,000; www.core-online.org

Conscientious Objectors, Central Committee for (1948), 405 14th St., #205, Oakland, CA 94612; www.objector.org

Construction Inspectors, Assn. of (1974), 1224 N. Nokomis NE, Alexandria, MN 56308; 1,000; www.iami.org/aci

Construction Specifications Institute (1948), 99 Canal Center Plaza, Ste. 300, Alexandria, VA 22314; 17,000; www.csinet.org

Consumer Federation of America (1968), 1620 I St. NW, Washington, DC 20006; 300 member organizations; www.consumerfed.org

Consumer Interests, American Council on (ACCI) (1953), 415 S. Duff Ave. Ste. C, Ames, IA 50010-6600; 750; www.consumerinterests.org

Consumers Union of the U.S. (1936), 101 Truman Ave., Yonkers, NY 10703; 405,990; www.consumersunion.org

Contract Bridge League, American (1937), 2990 Airways Blvd., Memphis, TN 38116; 160,000; www.acbl.org

Co-op America (1982), 1612 K St. NW, Ste. 600, Washington, DC 20006; 50,000 indiv., 2,500 cos.; www.coopamerica.org

Correctional Assn., American (1870), 206 N. Washington St., Ste. 200, Alexandria, VA 22314; 20,000; www.aca.org

Cosmetology Assn., Natl. (1921), 401 N. Michigan Ave., Chicago, IL 60611; 25,000; www.ncacares.org

Counseling Assn., American (1952), 5999 Stevenson Ave., Alexandria, VA 22304; 52,000; www.counseling.org

Country Music Assn. (1958), One Music Circle S., Nashville, TN 37203; 5,500; www.CMAworld.com

Craft & Hobby Assn. (2004), 319 E. 54th St., Elmwood Park, NJ 07407; 4,900; www.hobby.org

Crime and Delinquency, Natl. Council on (1907), 1970 Broadway, Ste. 500, Oakland, CA 94612; 300+; www.nccdcrc.org

Croplife America (1933), 1156 15th St. NW, Ste. 400, Washington, DC 20005; 80 cos.; www.croplifeamerica.org

Cryogenic Soc. of America, Inc. (1964), 1033 South Blvd., Ste. 13, Oak Park, IL 60302; 500; www.cryogenicsociety.org

Customs Brokers and Forwarders Assn. of America, Inc., Natl. (1897), 1200 18th St. NW, Ste. 901, Washington, DC 20036; 700; www.ncbfaa.org

Cystic Fibrosis Foundation (1955), 6931 Arlington Rd., Bethesda, MD 20814; 30,000; www.cff.org

Dark-Sky Association, Intl. (1988), 3225 N. First Ave., Tucson, AZ 85719-2103; 10,629; www.darksky.org

Daughters of the American Revolution Natl. Society (1890), 1776 D Street NW, Washington, DC 20006; 168,000; www.dar.org

Daughters of the Confederacy, United (1894), 328 North Blvd., Richmond, VA 23220; 25,000; www.hqudc.org

Deaf, Natl. Assn. of the (1880), 8630 Fenton St., Ste. 820, Silver Spring, MD 20910; 16,500; www.nad.org

Defenders of Wildlife (1947), 1130 17th St. NW, Washington, DC 20036; 480,000; www.defenders.org

Delta Kappa Gamma Society Intl. (1929), P.O. Box 1589, Austin, TX 78767; 136,000; www.deltakappagamma.org

Democratic Natl. Committee (1848), 430 S. Capitol St. SE, Wash., DC 20003; 447 elected mem.; www.democrats.org

Dental Assn., American (1859), 211 E. Chicago Ave., Chicago, IL 60611; 152,000; www.ada.org

Diabetes Assn., American (1940), 1701 North Beauregard St., Alexandria, VA 22311; 416,967; www.diabetes.org

Dialect Society, American (1889), MMLA, 302 English Philosophy Bldg., Univ. of Iowa, Iowa City, IA 52242; 500; www.americandialect.org

Directors Guild of America (1936), 7920 Sunset Blvd., Los Angeles, CA 90046; 12,700+; www.dga.org

Disabled American Veterans (1932), 3725 Alexandria Pike, Cold Spring, KY 41076; 1,000,000; www.dav.org

Disabled Sports USA (1967), 451 Hungerford Dr., Ste. 100, Rockville, MD 20850; 60,000+; www.dsusa.org

Doctors Without Borders/Médecins Sans Frontières (1971), 333 Seventh Ave., 2nd Fl., New York, NY 10001; 3,400+ missions; www.doctorswithoutborders.org

Down Syndrome Society, Natl. (1979), 666 Broadway, 8th Fl., New York, NY 10012; 30,000; www.ndss.org

Ducks Unlimited (1937), One Waterfowl Way, Memphis, TN 38120; 620,000; www.ducks.org

Eagles, Fraternal Order of (1898), 1623 Gateway Circle South, Grove City, OH 43123; 700 chapt.; www.foe.com

Easter Seals (1919), 14 E. Jackson Blvd., Ste. 900, Chicago, IL 60606; www.easterseals.com

Eastern Star, General Grand Chapter, Order of the (1876), 1618 New Hampshire Ave. NW, Washington, DC 20009; 1 mil.; www.easternstar.org

Edsel Club (1967), 19296 Tuckaway Ct., N. Fort Myers, FL 33903; 300; www.edselworld.com

Education, American Council on (1918), One Dupont Circle NW, Ste. 800, Washington, DC 20036; 1,800 org.; www.acenet.edu

Education, Council for Advancement & Support of (1974), 1307 New York Ave. NW, Ste 1000, Washington, DC 20005; 3,000+ schools; www.case.org

Education of Young Children, Natl. Assn. for the (1926), 1313 L St. NW, Ste. 500, Washington, DC 20005; 100,000; www.naeyc.org

Educators for World Peace, Intl. Assn. of (1973), P.O. Box 3282, Mastin Lake Station, Huntsville, AL 35810; 35,000; www.iaewp.org

Egalitarian Communities, Federation of (1978), 1309 13th Ave. S., Seattle, WA 98144; 14 comm.; www.thefec.org

88th Infantry Division Assn. (1946), 11 Lovett Ave., Brockton, MA 02301-1750; 4,200; www.88infdiv.org

84th Infantry Div. Railsplitter Soc., (1945), P.O. Box 827, Sioux Falls, SD 57101-0827; 2,115

82nd Airborne Division Assn., Inc. (1946), P.O. Box 9308, Fayetteville, NC 28311; 27,000+; www.82ndassociation.org

Electrical and Electronics Engineers, Institute of (1963), 445 Hoes Lane, Piscataway, NJ 08854; 365,000; www.ieee.org

Electrical Manufacturers Assn., Natl. (1926), 1300 N. 17th St., Ste. 1752, Rosslyn, VA 22209; 400 cos.; www.nema.org

Electrochemical Society, Inc., The (ECS, Inc.) (1902), 65 South Main St., Bldg. D, Pennington, NJ 08534-2839; 8,000+; www.electrochem.org

Electronics Technicians, Intl. Soc. of Certified (1980), 3608 Pershing Ave., Ft. Worth, TX 76107; 46,000; www.iscet.org

Elks of the U.S.A., Benevolent and Protective Order of (1868), 2750 N. Lakeview Ave., Chicago, IL 60614; 2,100 chapt.; www.elks.org

Energy Engineers, Assn. of (1977), 4025 Pleasantdale Rd., Ste. 420, Atlanta, GA 30340; 9,000; www.aeecenter.org

Engineers, Natl. Society of Professional (1934), 1420 King St., Alexandria, VA 22314; 60,000; www.nspe.org

English Inc., U.S. (1983), 1747 Pennsylvania Ave. NW, Washington, DC 20006; 1.7 mil; www.usenglish.org

English-Speaking Union of the U.S. (1920), 144 E. 39th St., New York, NY 10016; 10,000; www.english-speakingunion.org

Entomological Society of America (1953), 10001 Derekwood Ln., Ste 100, Lanham, MD 20706-4876; 5,700; www.entsoc.org

Environmental Assessment Association (1972), 1224 North Nokomis NE, Alexandria, MN 56308; 5,000; www.iami.org/eaa

Environmental Health Assn., Natl. (1937), 720 S. Colorado Blvd., Ste. 970-S, Denver, CO 80246; approx. 5,000; www.neha.org

Esperanto League for North America Inc. (1953), P.O. Box 1129, El Cerrito, CA 94530; 700; www.esperanto-usa.org

Experimental Aircraft Assn. (1953), P.O. Box 3086, Oshkosh, WI 54903; 170,000+; www.eaa.org

Ex-Prisoners of War, American (1942), 3201 E. Pioneer Pkwy., #40, Arlington, TX 76010; 27,000; www.axpow.org

Fairs & Expositions, Intl. Assn. of (1885), P.O. Box 985, Springfield, MO 65801; 2,900; www.fairsandexpos.com

Family, Career and Com. Leaders of Am. (1945), 1910 Association Dr., Reston, VA 20191; 220,000; www.fcclainc.org

Family Physicians, American Academy of (1947), P.O. Box 11210, Shawnee Mission, KS 66207; 94,000; www.aafp.org

Family Relations, Natl. Council on (1938), 3989 Central Avenue NE, Suite 550, Minneapolis, MN 55421; 4,000; www.ncfr.org

Farm Bureau, American (1919), 600 Maryland Ave. SW, Ste. 800, Washington, DC 20024; 5 mil+ families; www.fb.org

Farmers of America Org., Natl. Future (1929), P.O. Box 68960, Indianapolis, IN 46268; 476,000+; www.ffa.org

Farmers Union, Natl. (1902), 5619 DTC Pkwy., Ste. 300, Greenwood Village, CO 80111; 250,000; www.nfu.org

Fat Acceptance, Inc., Natl. Assn. to Advance (NAAFA) (1969), P.O. Box 22510, Oakland, CA 94609; 50 chapt.; www.naafa.org

Feminists for Life of America (1972), P.O. Box 20685, Alexandria, VA 22320; c. 5,000; www.feministsforlife.org

Financial Professionals, Assn. for (formerly Treasury Management Assn.) (1979), 7315 Wisconsin Ave., Ste. 600W, Bethesda, MD 20814; 14,000; www.AFPonline.org

Financial Service Professionals, Soc. of (1928), 17 Campus Blvd, Newtown Square, PA 19073; 22,000; www.financialpro.org

Financial Women Intl. (1921 as Natl. Assoc. of Bank Women), 1027 W. Roselawn Ave., Roseville, MN 55113; 2,000+; www.fwi.org

Fire Chiefs, Intl. Assn. of (1873), 4025 Fair Ridge Dr., Ste. 300, Fairfax, VA 22033; 12,000; www.iafc.org

Fire Protection Assn., Natl. (NFPA) (1896), 1 Batterymarch Park, Quincy, MA 02169; 75,000; www.nfpa.org

Fire Protection Engineers, Soc. of (1950), 7315 Wisconsin Avenue, Ste. 620E, Bethesda, MD 20814; 3,500; www.sfpe.org

First Candle/SIDSAlliance (1987), 1314 Bedford Ave., Ste. 210, Baltimore, MD 21208; www.sidsalliance.org

Fisheries Soc., American (1870), 5410 Grosvenor Ln., Ste. 110, Bethesda, MD 20814; 100 chapt.; www.fisheries.org

Fleet Reserve Association (1924), 125 N. West St., Alexandria, VA 22314-2754; 122,000; www.fra.org

Food and Commercial Workers Intl. Union, United (UFCW) (1979), 1775 K St. NW, Washington, DC 2006; 1.4 mil; www. ufcw.org

Food Technologists, Institute of (1939), 525 W. Van Buren, Ste. 1000, Chicago, IL 60607; 27,000; www.ift.org

Foreign Study, The American Institute for (1964), River Plaza, 9 W. Broad St., Stamford, CT 06902; 1 mil+; www. aifs.com

Foreign Trade Council, Inc., Natl. (1914), 1625 K St. NW, Washington, DC 20006; 300 companies.; www.nftc.org

Forensic Sciences, American Academy of (1948), 410 N. 21st St., Colorado Springs, CO 90904; 5,600; www.aafs.org

Foresters, Society of American (1900), 5400 Grosvenor La., Bethesda, MD 20814; 17,500; www.safnet.org

Forest History Society (1946), 701 Wm. Vickers Ave., Durham, NC 27701-3162; 1,500; www.foresthistory.org

4-H Clubs (1914), CSREES/USDA, 1400 Independence Ave. SW, Washington, DC 20250; 7 mil; www.4h-usa.org

Freedom From Religion Foundation (1978), P.O. Box 750, Madison, WI 53701; 6,000; www.ffrf.org

Freedom of Information Center (1958), Missouri School of Journalism, 133 Neff Annex, Columbia, MO 65211-0012; foi. missouri.edu

Freemasonry, Scottish Rite of, Supreme Council Ancient and Accepted Scottish Rite of, Northern Masonic Jurisdiction (1872), P.O. Box 519, Lexington, MA 02420; 270,000; www.supremecouncil.org

Freemasonry, Scottish Rite of, Supreme Council Ancient and Accepted Scottish Rite of, Southern Jurisdiction (1802), 1733 16th St. NW, Washington, DC 20009-3103; 350,000; www.srmason-sj.org

Free Men, Natl. Coalition of (1977), P.O. Box 582023, Minneapolis, MN 55458; 2,000; www.ncfm.org

Free Press Readership Council, American (2001), 645 Pennsylvania Ave., S.E., Washington, DC 20003; 4,500; www.americanfreepress.net

French Institute/Alliance Française (1971), 22 E. 60th St., New York, NY 10022; 7,000; www.fiaf.org

Friends of the Earth (1969), 1717 Massachusetts Ave. NW, Ste. 600, Washington, DC 20036; 1 mil; www.foe.org

Frozen Food Institute, American (1942), 2000 Corporate Ridge, Suite 1000, McLean, VA 22102; 505; www.affi.com

Funeral Consumers Alliance (FAMSA) (1963), 33 Patchan Rd., S. Burlington, VT 05403; 120 soc.; www.funerals.org/famsa

Funeral Directors Assn., Natl. (1882), 13625 Bishop's Dr., Brookfield, WI 53005; 20,300; www.nfda.org

Future Business Leaders of America/Phi Beta Lambda, Inc. (1942), 1912 Association Dr., Reston, VA 20191; 233,000; www.fbla-pbl.org

Gamblers Anonymous (1957), P.O. Box 17173, Los Angeles, CA 90017; approx. 30,000; www.gamblersanonymous.org

Garden Club of America (1913), 14 E. 60th St., New York, NY 10022; 18,000; www.gcamerica.org

Garden Clubs, Inc., National Council of State (1929), 4401 Magnolia Ave., St. Louis, MO 63110; 217,233; www.garden club.org

Gay and Lesbian Alliance Against Defamation (1985), 248 W. 35th St., 8th Fl., New York, NY 10001; www.glaad.org

Gay and Lesbian Task Force, Natl. (1973), 1325 Massachusetts Ave. NW, Ste. 600, Washington, DC 20005; 20,000; www.thetaskforce.org

Genealogical Society, Natl. (1903), 3108 Columbia Pike, Ste. 300, Arlington, VA 22204; 11,000; www.ngsgenealogy.org

General Contractors of America, The Associated (1918), 2300 Wilson Blvd., Ste. 400, Arlington, VA 22201; 33,000+ cos.; www.agc.org

Genetic Association, American (1903), P.O. Box 257, Buckeystown, MD 21717; www.theaga.org

Geographers, Assn. of American (1904), 1710 16th St. NW, Washington, DC 20009; 7,500+; www.aag.org

Geographic Education, Natl. Council for (1915), 206-A Martin Hall, Jacksonville State Univ., Jacksonville, AL 36265; 2,500; www.ncge.org

Geographic Society, Natl. (1888), 1145 17th St. NW, Washington, DC 20036; 9.2 mil.; www.nationalgeographic.com

Geographical Society, The American (1851), 120 Wall St., Ste. 100, New York, NY 10005; 1,000; www.amergeog.org

Geological Society of America (1888), P.O. Box 9140, Boulder, CO 80301; 18,500; www.geosociety.org

Geriatrics Society, American (1942), 350 5th Ave., Ste. 801, New York, NY 10118; 6,800+; www.americangeriatrics.org

Gideons Intl. (1899), P.O. Box 140800, Nashville, TN 37214; 236,000+; www.gideons.org

Gifted Children, Natl. Assn. for (1954), 1707 L Street NW, Suite 550, Washington, DC 20036; 8,000; www.nagc.org

Girl Scouts of the U.S.A. (1912), 420 5th Ave., New York, NY 10018; 3.7 mil; www.girlscouts.org

Golf Assn., U.S. (1894), P.O. Box 708, Far Hills, NJ 07931; 750,000; www.usga.org

Gospel Music Assn. (1964), 1205 Division St., Nashville, TN 37203; 4,200; www.gospelmusic.org

Governors' Assn., Natl. (1908), Hall of the States, 444 N. Capitol, Ste. 267, Washington, DC 20001; 55 govs.; www.nga.org

Grange Patrons of Husbandry, Natl. (1867), 1616 H Street NW, Washington, DC 20006; 300,000; www.national grange.org

Graphic Arts, American Institute of (1914), 164 5th Ave., New York, NY 10010; 16,000; www.aiga.org

Gray Panthers (1970), 1612 K St. NW, Ste. 300, Washington, DC 20006; approx. 20,000; www.graypanthers.org

Green Mountain Club, The (1910), 4711 Waterbury-Stowe Rd., Waterbury Center, VT 05677; 9,000+; www.green mountain club.org

Green Party (1984), P.O. Box 408316, Chicago, IL 60640; www. greenparty.org

Greenpeace, Inc. (1971), 702 H St. NW, Suite 300, Washington, DC 20001; 2.8 mil; www.greenpeaceusa.org.

Ground Water Assn., Natl. (1948), 601 Dempsey Rd., Westerville, OH 43081; 15,000; www.ngwa.org

Guide Dog Foundation for the Blind, Inc. (1946), 371 E. Jericho Turnpike, Smithtown, NY 11787; www.guidedog.org

Hadassah, the Women's Zionist Organization of America (1912), 50 W. 58th St., New York, NY 10019; 300,000+; www.hadassah.org

Handball Assn., U.S. (1951), 2333 N. Tucson Blvd., Tucson, AZ 85716; 8,500; www.ushandball.org

Health Council, Natl. (1920), 1730 M St. NW,S Ste. 500, Washington, DC 20036; 115 org.; www.nationalhealthcouncil.org

Hearing Society, Intl. (1951), 16880 Middlebelt Rd., Ste. 4, Livonia, MI 48154; 54 chapt.; www.ihsinfo.org

Heart Assn., American (1924), 7272 Greenville Ave., Dallas, TX 75231; 22.5 mil.; www.americanheart.org

Heating, Refrigerating & Air-Conditioning Engineers, Inc., American Soc. of (1894), 1791 Tullie Cir. NE, Atlanta, GA 30329; 55,000; www.ashrae.org

Helicopter Society, American (1944), 271 N. Washington St., Alexandria, VA 22314, 6,000; www.vtol.org

Hemispheric Affairs, Council on (1975), 1250 Connecticut Ave. NW, Ste. 1C, Washington, DC 20036; 4,000; www.coha.org

Highpointers Club (1986), P.O. Box 1496, Golden, CO 80402; 2,600; www.highpointers.org

High School Band Directors Natl. Assn. (2005), P.O. Box 8892, Columbus, GA 31908; www.hsbdna.com

Hiking Society, American (1976), 1422 Fenwick Lane, Silver Spring, MD 20910; 170 clubs; www.americanhiking.org

Historic Preservation, Natl. Trust for (1949), 1785 Massachusetts Avenue NW, Washington, DC 20036; 270,000; www. nationaltrust.org

Historical Assn., American (1884), 400 A St. SE, Washington, DC 20003; 14,000; www.historians.org

Historical Society, United States (1971), 7433 Whitepine Rd., Richmond, VA 23237; 250,000; www.ushsdolls.com

Hockey, U.S.A. (1936), 1775 Bob Johnson Dr., Colorado Springs, CO 80906; 592,000; www.usahockey.com

Home Builders, Natl. Assn. of (1942), 1201 15th St. NW, Washington, DC 20005; 220,000; www.nahb.org

Homeless, Natl. Coalition for the (1984), 2201 P St. NW, Ste. 600, Washington, DC 20037; 2,500; www.nationalhomeless.org

Honor Society, Natl. (1921), 1904 Association Dr., Reston, VA 20191; 1 mil+; www.nhs.us

Horse Council, American (1969), 1616 H St. NW, 7th Fl., Washington, DC 20006; 195 org., 1,800 ind.; www.horse council.org

Hospital Assn., American (1898), 1 N. Franklin, Chicago, IL 60606; 5,000 hosp., 37,000 indiv. members; www.aha.org

Hostelling Intl. USA (1934), 8401 Colesville Rd, Ste. 600, Silver Spring, MD 20910; 100 affil.; www.hiayh.org

Hotel & Motel Assn., American (1910), 1201 New York Ave. NW, #600, Washington, DC 20005; 10,000+; www.ahma.com

Hot Rod Assn., Natl. (1951), 2035 Financial Way, Glendora, CA 91741; 80,000; www.nhra.com

Housing Inspection Foundation (1979), 1224 N. Nokomis NE, Alexandria, MN 56308; 1,800; www.iami.org/hif

Huguenot Society, Natl. (1951), 9033 Lyndale Ave. S, #108, Bloomington, MN 55420; 3,800; www.huguenot.netnation.com

> **IT'S A FACT:** The United States Lawn Mower Racing Association has been organizing and regulating riding mower races since 1992. The races attract crowds of up to 5,000 people, and its participants and fans are every bit as fervent as those who follow NASCAR. Among the regulations that U.S.L.M.R.A. has instituted: mowers can be souped up—some zooming along at speeds up to 60 mph—but blades must be removed and "kill switches" (which automatically cut off the mower's engine if the driver falls off) are installed to prevent injury to drivers or spectators. Unlike NASCAR racing, though, "paint-trading" in a lawn mower race is strictly forbidden.

Humane Society of the U.S. (1954), 2100 L St. NW, Washington, DC 20037; 650,000; www.hsus.org

Human Resource Management, Society for (SHRM) (1948), 1800 Duke St., Alexandria, VA 22314; 190,000; www.shrm.org

Human Rights Campaign (1980), 1640 Rhode Island Ave. NW, Washington, DC 20036; 600,000; www.hrc.org

Human Rights Watch (1978), 350 Fifth Ave. 34th Fl., New York, NY 10118; www.hrw.org

Illustrators, Inc., Society of (1901), 128 E. 63rd St., New York, NY 10021-7303; 900; www.societyillustrators.org

Industrial and Applied Mathematics, Society for (1952), 3600 Univ. City Science Center, Philadelphia, PA 19104; 10,000; www.siam.org

Industrial Designers Society of America (1965), 45195 Business Ct., Ste. 250, Dulles, VA 20166; 3,300; www.idsa.org

Industrial Security, American Soc. for (1955), 1625 Prince St., Alexandria, VA 22314; 33,000; www.asisonline.org

Insurance Assn., American (1866), 1130 Connecticut Avenue NW, Suite 1000, Washington, DC 20036; 450 companies; www.aiadc.org

Intellectual Property Owners Assn. (1972), 1255 23rd St. NW, Ste. 200, Washington, DC 20037; 350; www.ipo.org

Intelligence Officers, Assn. of Former (1975), 6723 Whittier Ave., Ste. 303A, McLean, VA 22101; 22 chapt.; www.afio.com

Intercollegiate Athletics, Natl. Assn. of (1937), 23500 W. 105th St., P.O. Box 1325, Olathe, KS 66061; 300 member coll./univ.; www.naia.org

Interfaith Alliance, The (1994), 1331 H St., 11th Floor, Washington, DC 20005-4706; 150,000; www.interfaithalliance.org

Interior Designers, American Society of (1975), 608 Massachusetts Avenue NE, Washington, DC 20002; 38,000; www.asid.org

International. See organizations under next major word in title.

Intl. Education, Institute of (1919), 809 United Nations Plaza, 7th Fl., New York, NY 10017; 800 coll./univ.; www.iie.org

Intl. Educational Exchange, Council on (1947), 7 Custom House St., 3rd Fl., Portland, ME 04101; 240 member groups; www.ciee.org

Intl. Educators, Assn. of (NAFSA) (1948), 1307 New York Ave. NW, 8th Fl., Washington, DC 20005; 9,000; www.nafsa.org

Intl. Law, American Society of (1906), 2223 Massachusetts Ave. NW, Washington, DC 20008; 4,000; www.asil.org

Inventors, American Soc. of (1953), P.O. Box 58426, Philadelphia, PA 19102; 150; www.asoi.org

Investigative Pathology, American Soc. for (1900), 9650 Rockville Pike, Bethesda, MD 20814; 1,718; www.asip.org

Investors Corp., Natl. Assn. of (1951), P.O. Box 220, Royal Oak, MI 48068; 220,000; www.better-investing.org

Irish American Cultural Inst. (1962), 1 Lackawanna Pl., Morristown, NJ 07960; 20 chapt.; www.irishaci.org

Jail Assn., American (1981), 1135 Professional Ct., Hagerstown, MD 21740; 4,500; www.corrections.com/aja

Japanese-American Citizens League (1929), 1765 Sutter St., San Francisco, CA 94115; 21,000; www.jacl.org

Jewish Committee, American (1906), P.O. Box 705, New York, NY 10150; 125,000; www.ajc.org

Jewish Community Centers Assn. of North America (1917), 15 E. 26th St., New York, NY 10010; 1,000,000+; www.jcca.org

Jewish Congress, American (1918), 825 Third Ave., Ste. 1800, New York, NY 10022; 50,000; www.ajcongress.org

Jewish War Veterans of the U.S.A. (1896), 1811 R St. NW, Washington, DC 20009; 37,000; jwv.org

Jewish Women, National Council of (1893), 53 W. 23rd St., 6th Fl., New York, NY 10010; 90,000; www.ncjw.org

John Birch Society (1958), P.O. Box 8040, Appleton, WI 54912; www.jbs.org

Joint Action in Community Service (JACS) (1967), 5225 Wisconsin Ave. NW, Ste. 404, Washington, DC 20015; www.jacs inc.org

Journalists, Society of Professional (1909), 3909 N. Meridian St., Indianapolis, IN 46208; 9,000; spj.org

Journalists and Authors, American Society of (1948), 1501 Broadway, Ste. 302, New York, NY 10036; 1,000+; www.asja.org

Judicature Society, American (1913), Opperman Ctr., 2700 University Ave., Des Moines, IA 50311; 5,500; www.ajs.org

Jugglers Assn., Intl. (1947), P.O. Box 112550, Carrollton, TX, 75001; 2,500; www.juggle.org

Junior Achievement, Inc. (1919), One Education Way, Colorado Springs, CO 80906; www.ja.org

Junior Auxiliaries, Natl. Assn. of (1941), 845 South Main St., Greenville, MS 38701; 12,876; www.najanet.org

Junior Chamber of Commerce, U.S. (1920), P.O. Box 7, Tulsa, OK 74102; 200,000; www.usjaycees.org

Junior College Athletic Assn., Natl. (1937), 1755 Telstar Dr., Ste. 103, Colorado Springs, CO 80920; 520; www.njcaa.org

Junior Honor Society, Natl. (1929), 1904 Association Dr., Reston, VA 20191; 1 mil+; www.njhs.us

Junior Leagues, Assn. of (1921), 90 Williams St., Ste. 200, New York, NY 10038; 294 leagues; www.ajli.org

Kidney Fund, The American (1971), 6110 Executive Blvd., Ste. 1010, Rockville, MD 20852; www.kidneyfund.org

Kiwanis International (1915), 3636 Woodview Trace, Indianapolis, IN 46268; 500,000+; www.kiwanis.org

Knights of Columbus (1882), One Columbus Plaza, New Haven, CT 06510-4000; 1.6 mil; www.kofc.org

Knights of Pythias, (1864), 59 Coddington Street, #202, Quincy, MA 02169; www.pythias.org

La Leche League Intl. (1957), 1400 N. Meacham Rd. Schaumburg, IL 60173; 26,000; www.lalecheleague.org

Lady Bird Johnson Wildflower Center (1982), 4801 La Crosse Avenue, Austin, TX 78739; 22,000; www.wild flower.org

Landscape Architects, American Society of (1899), 636 Eye St. NW, Washington, DC 20001; 15,200; www.asla.org

Law Libraries, American Assn. of (1906), 53 W. Jackson Blvd., #940, Chicago, IL 60604; 5,000; www.aallnet.org

Lawn Mower Racing Association, U.S. (1992), 1812 Glenview Rd., Glenview, IL 60025; www.letsmow.com

Learned Societies, American Council of (1919), 633 Third Ave., New York, NY 10017; 64 societies; www.acls.org

Legal Administrators, Assn. of (1971), 75 Tri-State Intl., Ste. 222, Lincolnshire, IL 60069-4435; 9,900; www.alanet.org

Legal Secretaries, Natl. Assn. of (NALS) (1929), 314 E 3rd St., Ste. 210, Tulsa, OK 74120; 8,500; www.nals.org

Legion of Valor Museum (1991), 2425 Fresno St., Fresno, CA 93721; 700+; www.legionofvalormuseum.org

Leprosy Missions, Inc., American (1906), One Alm Way, Greenville, SC 29601; www.leprosy.org

Leukemia and Lymphoma Society (1949), 1311 Mamaroneck Ave., White Plains, NY 10605; www.lls.org

Lewis and Clark Trail Heritage Foundation (1969), P.O. Box 3434, Great Falls, MT 59403; 3,600; www.lewisandclark.org

Libertarian Party (1971), 2600 Virginia Ave. NW, Ste. 200, Washington, DC 20037; 224,000; www.lp.org

Libraries Assn., Special (1909), 331 S. Patrick St., Alexandria, VA 22314; 12,000+; www.sla.org

Library Assn., American (1876), 50 E. Huron St., Chicago, IL 60611; 66,700+; www.ala.org

Lifesaving Assn., U.S. (1964), P.O. Box 366, Huntington Beach, CA 92648; 11,000; www.usla.org

Lighter-Than-Air Society (1952), 526 S. Main St., Akron, OH 44311; 1,000; www.blimpinfo.com

Linguistic Society of America (1924), 1325 18th St. NW, Ste. 211, Washington, DC 20036; 5,000 indiv.; www.lsadc.org

Lions Clubs, Intl., Assn. of (1917), 300 W. 22nd St., Oak Brook, IL 60523; 1,400,000; www.lionsclubs.org

Little League Baseball, Inc. (1939), 539 U.S. Rte. 15 Hwy., P.O. Box 3485, S. Williamsport, PA 17701; 4 mil, www.littleleague.org

Little People of America, Inc. (1961), 5289 NE Elam Young Pkwy, Ste. F100, Hillsboro, OR 97124; 8,000+; www.lpaon line.org

Logistics, Intl. Society of (SOLE) (1966), 8100 Professional Pl., Ste. 111, Hyattsville, MD 20785; 3,500; www.sole.org

Lung Assn., American (1904), 61 Broadway, 6th Fl., New York, NY 10006; www.lungusa.org

Magazine Publishers of America (1919), 810 Seventh Ave., 24th Fl., New York, NY 10019; 1,200 titles; www.magazine.org

Magicians, Intl. Brotherhood of (1922), 11155 S. Towne Sq., Ste. B, St. Louis, MO 63123; 15,000; www.magician.org

Magicians, Society of American (1902), P.O. Box 510260, St. Louis, MO 63151; www.magicsam.com

Management Accountants, Institute of (1919), 10 Paragon Dr., Montvale, NJ 07645; 75,000; www.imanet.org

Management Assn., American (1923), 1601 Broadway, New York, NY 10019; 700,000; www.amanet.org

Manufacturers, Natl. Assn. of (1895), 1331 Pennsylvania Ave. NW, Washington, DC 20004; 14,000 cos.; www.nam.org

> **IT'S A FACT:** Famed magician Harry Houdini was the president of the Society of American Magicians from 1917 until the time of his death in 1926. Upon his death, the S.A.M. instituted their 'Broken Wand' ceremony, breaking Houdini's wand at his gravesite to symbolize that it had lost its magic. The practice is now traditionally performed for all S.A.M. members in gravesite ceremonies.

March of Dimes Birth Defects Foundation (1938), 1275 Mamaroneck Avenue, White Plains, NY 10605; 3 mil; www.marchofdimes.com

Marine Corps League (1937), P.O. Box 3070, Merrifield, VA 22116-3070; 60,000+; www.mcleague.org

Marketing Assn., Am. (1915), 311 S. Wacker Dr., Ste. 5800, Chicago, IL 60606; 38,000; www.marketingpower.com

Masons. see Freemasonry

Master Brewers Association of the Americas (1887), 3340 Pilot Knob Rd., St. Paul, MN 55121; 3,500; www.mbaa.com

Materials and Process Engineering, Soc. for the Advancement of (1944), 1161 Park View Dr., Covina, CA 91724; 5,000; www.sampe.org

Mathematical Society, American (1888), 201 Charles St., Providence, RI 02904; 30,000; www.ams.org

Mayflower Descendants, General Society of (1897), P.O. Box 3297, Plymouth, MA 02361; 26,000; www.mayflower.org

Mayors, U.S. Conference of (1932), 1620 Eye St. NW, Washington, DC 20006; 1,183; www.usmayors.org

Mechanical Engineers, American Soc. of (1880), 3 Park Ave., New York, NY 10016; 120,000; www.asme.org

Medical Assn., American (1847), 515 N. State St., Chicago, IL 60601; 300,000; www.ama-assn.org

Medical Library Assn. (1898), 65 E. Wacker Pl., Ste. 1900, Chicago, IL 60602; 3,600; www.mlanet.org

MENC: The Natl. Assn. for Music Education (formerly Music Educators Natl. Conference) (1907), 1806 Robert Fulton Dr., Reston, VA 20191; 120,000; www.menc.org

Mended Hearts, Inc. (1950), 7272 Greenville Ave., Dallas, TX 75231; 460 hospitals; www.mendedhearts.org

Mensa, Ltd., American (1960), 1229 Corporate Dr. W, Arlington, TX 76006; 50,000; www.us.mensa.org

Mental Health Assn., Natl. (1909), 2001 N. Beauregard St., 12th Fl., Alexandria, VA 22311; 340 affiliates; www.nmha.org

Mentally Ill, Natl. Alliance for the (1979), Colonial Place Three, 2107 Wilson Blvd. Ste. 300, Arlington, VA 22201; 220,000; www.nami.org

Merrill's Marauders Assn. (1947), 11244 N. 33rd St., Phoenix, AZ 85028-2723; 1,698; www.marauder.org

Meteorological Society, American (1919), 45 Beacon St., Boston, MA 02108; 11,000+; www.ametsoc.org

Metric Assn., Inc., U.S. (1916), 10245 Andasol Ave., Northridge, CA 91325-1504; 1,200; www.metric.org

Microbiology, American Society for (1899), 1752 N. St. NW, Washington, DC 20036; 40,000; www.asm.org

Military Officers Assn. (1940), 201 N. Washington St., Alexandria, VA 22314; 370,000; www.moaa.org

Military Order of the Purple Heart of the USA (1958), 5413-B Backlick Road, Springfield, VA 22151; 36,765; www.purpleheart.org

Military Order of the World Wars (1919), 435 N. Lee St., Alexandria, VA 22314; 155 chapt.; www.militaryorder.net

Military Surgeons of the U.S., Assn. of (1898), 9320 Old Georgetown Road, Bethesda, MD 20814; 10,000+; www.amsus.org

Missing and Exploited Children, Natl. Center for (1984), The Charles B. Wang International Children's Building, 699 Prince St., Alexandria, VA 22314; www.missingkids.com

Model Railroad Assn., Natl. (1935), 4121 Cromwell Rd., Chattanooga, TN 37421-2119; 20,500; www.nmra.org

Modern Language Assn. of America (1883), 26 Broadway, 3rd Fl., New York, NY 10004; 30,000+; www.mla.org

Molecular Plant-Microbe Interactions, Intl. Soc. for (1990), 3340 Pilot Knob Rd., St. Paul, MN 55121; 450; www.ismpminet.org

Moose Intl., Inc. (1888), 155 S. International Dr., Mooseheart, IL 60539; 1.5 mil; www.mooseintl.org

Mothers of Twins Clubs, Natl. Organization of (1963), P.O. Box 700860, Plymouth, MI 48170; 23,000; www.nomotc.org

Motion Picture Arts & Sciences, Academy of (1927), 8949 Wilshire Blvd., Beverly Hills, CA 90211; 6,000; www.oscars.org

Motion Picture & Television Engineers, Soc. of (1916), 3 Barker Ave., White Plains, NY 10601; 10,000; www.smpte.org

Motorcyclist Assn., American (1924), 13515 Yarmouth Dr., Pickerington, OH 43147; 260,000+; www.amadirectlink.com

Motorists Association, Natl. (1982), 402 W. 2nd St., Waunakee, WI 53597; 6,000; www.motorists.org

Multiple Sclerosis Society, Natl. (1946), 733 3rd Ave,. 6th Fl., New York, NY 10017; 497,000; www.nationalmssociety.org

Muscular Dystrophy Assn., Inc. (1950), 3300 E. Sunrise Dr., Tucson, AZ 85718; 2 mil. volunteers; www.mdausa.org

Museums, American Assn. of (1906), 1575 Eye St. NW, Ste. 400, Washington, DC 20005; 16,000 indiv., 3,100 institutions; www.aam-us.org

Music Teachers Natl. Assn. (1876), 441 Vine St., Ste. 505, Cincinnati, OH 45202; 24,000; www.mtna.org

Musicological Society, American (1934), Bowdoin Coll. 6010 College Station, Brunswick, ME 04011; 3,300; www.ams-net.org

Muzzle Loading Rifle Assn., Natl. (1933), P.O. Box 67, Friendship, IN 47021; 18,000; www.nmlra.org

Myasthenia Gravis Foundation of America (1952), 1821 University Ave. W., Ste. S256, St. Paul, MN 55104; www.myasthenia.org

Mystery Writers of America, Inc. (1945), 17 E. 47th St., 6th Fl., New York, NY 10017; 2,235; www.mysterywriters.org

NA'AMAT USA (1921), 350 Fifth Ave., Ste. 4700, New York, NY 10118; 25,000; www.naamat.org

Name Society, American (1951), c/o Michael McGoff, Vice Provost, Provost's Office, SUNY Binghamton, Binghamton, NY 13902; 700; www.wtsn.binghamton.edu/ANS

Narcotics Anonymous World Services (1953), P.O Box 9999, Van Nuys, CA 94109; 20,000 groups; www.na.org

National. See other organizations under next major word in title.

Natl. Assn. for the Advancement of Colored People (NAACP) (1909), 4805 Mt. Hope Dr., Baltimore, MD 21215; www.naacp.org

National Guard Assn. of the U.S. (1878), One Massachusetts Ave. NW, Washington, DC 20001; 45,000; www.ngaus.org

Nature Conservancy, The (1951), 4245 N. Fairfax Drive, Ste. 100, Arlington, VA 22203; 1 mil; nature.org

Naval Institute, U.S. (1873), 291 Wood Rd., Annapolis, MD 21402; 70,000; www.usni.org

Naval Reserve Assn. (1954), 1619 King St., Alexandria, VA 22314; 23,000; www.navy-reserve.org

Navy League of the United States (1902), 2300 Wilson Blvd., Arlington, VA 22201-3308; 75,000; www.navyleague.org

Negro College Fund, United (1944), 8260 Willow Oaks Corporate Dr., Fairfax, VA 22031; 39 institutions; www.uncf.org

Neurofibromatosis Foundation, Natl. (1978), 95 Pine St., 16th Fl., New York, NY 10005; 24,000; www.nf.org

Newspaper Assn. of America (NAA) (1992), 1921 Gallows Rd., Ste. 600, Vienna, VA 22182-3900; 2,000+; www.naa.org

Ninety-Nines (Intl. Organization of Women Pilots) (1929), 4300 Amelia Earhart Rd., Oklahoma City, OK 73159; 6,000; www.ninety-nines.org

Non-Commissioned Officers Assn. (1960), 610 Madison St., Alexandria, VA 22314; 160,000; www.ncoausa.org

Notaries, American Society of (1965), P.O. Box 5707, Tallahassee, FL 32314; approx. 20,000; www.notaries.org

Nuclear Society, American (1954), 555 N. Kensington Ave., La Grange Park, IL 60526; 10,500; www.ans.org

Nude Recreation, American Assn. for (1931), 1703 N. Main St., Kissimmee, FL 34744; almost 50,000; www.aanr.com

Numismatic Assn., American (1891), 818 N. Cascade Ave., Colorado Springs, CO 80903; 30,000; www.money.org

Numismatic Society, American (1858), 96 Fulton St., New York, NY 10038; 2,127; www.amnumsoc.org

Nurses Assn., American (ANA) (1897), 8515 Georgia Ave., Ste. 400, Silver Spring, MD 20910; 2.7 mil; www.nursing world.org

Nursing, Natl. League for (1952), 61 Broadway, New York, NY 10006; 5,000; www.nln.org

Ocean Conservancy (1972), 2029 K St., Wash.,DC 20006; 500,000; www.oceanconservancy.org

Odd Fellows, Independent Order of (1819), 422 Trade St., Winston-Salem, NC 27101; 250,000; www.ioof.org

Optimist Intl. (1919), 4494 Lindell Blvd., St. Louis, MO 63108; 105,000; www.optimist.org

Optometric Assn., American (1918), 243 N. Lindbergh Blvd., St. Louis, MO 63141; 32,904; www.aoa.org

Organ Sharing, United Network for (1984), P.O. Box 2484, Richmond, VA 23218; 408; www.unos.org

Organists, American Guild of (1896), 475 Riverside Dr., Ste. 1260, New York, NY 10115; 20,000; www.agohq.org

Oriental Society, American (1842), Univ. of Michigan, Hatcher Graduate Library, 110D, Ann Arbor, MI 48109; 1,350; www.umich.edu/~aos

ORT Inc., American (Org. for Rehabilitation Through Training) (1922), 817 Broadway, 10th Fl., New York, NY 10003; 10,000; www.aort.org

Ornithologists' Union, American (1883), 1313 Dolley Madison Blvd., Ste. 402, McLean, VA 22101; 4,000; www.aou.org

Overeaters Anonymous (1960), P.O. Box 44020, Rio Rancho, NM 87174; www.oa.org

Oxfam America (1970), 26 West St., Boston, MA 02111; 150,000; www.oxfamamerica.org

Paralyzed Veterans of America (1946), 801 18th St. NW, Washington, DC 20006; 18,000; www.pva.org

Parapsychology Institute of America (1971), P.O. Box 5442, Babylon, NY, 11707; 400

Parents Without Partners, Inc. (1957), 1650 South Dixie Hwy, Ste. 510, Boca Raton, FL 33432; 200 chapt.; www.parents withoutpartners.org

Parkinson's Disease Foundation, Inc. (1957), 1359 Broadway, Ste. 1509, New York, NY 10018; 100,000; www.pdf.org

Parliamentarians, Natl. Assn. of (1930), 213 S. Main St., Independence, MO 64050; 4,000; www.parliamentarians.org

Peace Corps (1961), 1111 20th St., NW, Washington, DC 20526; 178,000; www.peacecorps.gov

Pearl Harbor History Associates, Inc. (1986), P.O. Box 1007, Stratford, CT 06615; 275; www.pearlharbor-history.org

PEN American Center, Inc. (1921), 588 Broadway, Ste. 303, New York, NY 10012; 2,900; www.pen.org

Pen Friends, Intl. (1967), 500 University Ave., #2415, Honolulu, HI 96826; 300,000; www.pen-pals.net

Pen Women, Natl. League of American (1897), 1300 17th St. NW, Washington, DC 20036; 3,569: www.americanpen women.org

People for the Ethical Treatment of Animals. See Animals.

Performance Improvement, Intl. Society for (1962), 1400 Spring St., Ste. 260, Silver Spring, MD 20910; 6,000; www.ispi.org

Petroleum Institute, American (1919), 1220 L St. NW, Washington, DC 20005; 400 companies; www.api.org

Pharmacists Assn., American (1852), 1100 15th St. NW, Ste. 400, Washington, DC 20005; 50,000; www.aphanet.org, www.pharmacist.com

Phi Beta Kappa Society (1776), 1606 New Hampshire Ave. NW, Washington, DC 20009; 270 inst.; www.pbk.org

Phi Kappa Phi, Honor Society of (1897), P.O. Box 16000, LSU Baton Rouge, Baton Rouge, LA 70893; 120,000+; www.phikappaphi.org

Phi Theta Kappa Int'l. Honor Society (1918), 1625 Eastover Drive, Jackson, MS 39211; 800,000; www.ptk.org

Philatelic Society, American (1886), 100 Match Factory Place, Bellefonte, PA 16823; 44,000+; www.stamps.org

Philological Association, American (1869), Univ. of Penn., 292 Logan Hall, 249 S. 36th St., Philadelphia, PA, 19104-6304; 3,100; www.apaclassics.org

Philosophical Assn., American (1900), 31 Amstel Ave., Univ. of Delaware, Newark, DE 19716; 11,097; www.apa.udel.edu/apa

Physical Therapy Assn., American (1921), 1111 N. Fairfax St., Alexandria, VA 22314; 66,000; www.apta.org

Physically Handicapped, Inc., Natl. Assn. of the (1958), Scarlet Oaks, 440 Lafayette Ave., #GA4, Cincinnati, OH 45220-1022; approx. 400; www.naph.net

Physics, American Inst. of (1931), One Physics Ellipse, College Park, MD 20740; 13 soc. and org.; www.aip.org

Physiological Society, American (1887), 9650 Rockville Pike, Bethesda, MD 20814-3991; 10,500; www.the-aps.org

Phytopathological Society, American (1908), 3340 Pilot Knob Rd., St. Paul, MN 55121; 5,000; www.apsnet.org

Pilgrims Natl. Soc., Sons and Daughters of (1909), 3917 Heritage Dr., #104, Bloomington, MN 55437-2633; 2,000; www.nssdp.com

Pilot Intl. & Pilot Intl. Foundation (1921), P.O. Box 4844, Macon, GA 31208; 25,000; www.pilotinternational.org

Planetary Society (1979), 65 N. Catalina Ave., Pasadena, CA 91106; approx. 70,000; www.planetary.org

Planned Parenthood Federation of America, Inc. (1916), 434 West 33rd Street, New York, NY 10001; www.planned parenthood.org

Plastics Engineers, Society of (1942), 14 Fairfield Dr., P.O. Box 403, Brookfield, CT 06804; 25,000+; www.4spe.org

Poetry Society of America (1910), 15 Gramercy Park, New York, NY 10003; approx. 3,000; www.poetrysociety.org

Poets, The Academy of American (1934), 504 Broadway, Ste. 604, New York, NY 10012; 8,000; www.poets.org

Police Assn., Intl. (1950 in UK, 1962 in U.S.), 100 Chase Ave., Yonkers, NY 10703; 291,000+; www.ipa-usa.org

Political Items Collectors, American (1945), P.O. Box 55, Avon, NY 14414; 3,000; apic.us

Political Science, Academy of (1886), 475 Riverside Drive, Ste. 1274, New York, NY 10115; 5,825; www.psqonline.org

Political & Social Science, American Academy of (1889), 3814 Walnut St., Univ. of Penn., Philadelphia, PA 19104; 400; www.aapss.org

Polo Assn., U.S. (1890), 771 Corporate Dr., Ste. 505, Lexington, KY 40503; 3,737; www.uspolo.org

Population Assn. of America (1931), 8630 Fenton St., Ste. 722, Silver Spring, MD 20910; 3,000; www.popassoc.org

Population Connection (formerly Zero Population Growth) (1968), 2120 L St. NW, Ste. 500, Washington, DC 20037; www.populationconnection.org

Postal Stationery Society, United (1945), P.O. Box 3982, Chester, VA 23831; 1,100; www.upss.org

Postcard Dealers, Inc., International Federation of (1979), P.O. Box 1765, Manassas, VA 20108; 202

Postmasters of the U.S., Natl. League of (1887), One Beltway Ctr., 5904 Richmond Hwy., Ste. 400, Alexandria, VA 22303; 95 clubs; www.post masters.org

Postmasters of the U.S., Natl. Assn. of (1898), 8 Herbert St., Arlington, VA 22305; 95 clubs, www.napus.org

Power Boat Assn., American (1903), 17640 Nine Mile Rd., Eastpointe, MI 48021; 6,000; www.apba-racing.com

Press Club, National (1908), 529 14th St., 13th Fl., NW, Washington, DC 20045; 4,000; www.press.org

Printing Industries of America, Inc. (1887), 200 Deer Run Rd., Sewickley, PA 15143; 12,000; www.gain.net

Procrastinators Club of America (1956), P.O. Box 712, Bryn Athyn, PA 19009; 14,500; www.geocities.com/procrastinators _club_of_america

Professional Ball Players of America, Assn. of (1924), 1820 W. Orangewood Ave., Ste. 206, Orange, CA 92868; 11,000; www.apbpa.org

ProLiteracy Worldwide (2002), 1320 Jamesville Ave., Syracuse, NY 13210; 1,200 affiliates; www.proliteracy.org

Psoriasis Foundation, Natl. (1968), 6600 SW 92nd Ave., Ste. 300, Portland, OR 97223; 33,000; www.psoriasis.org

Psychiatric Assn., American (1844), 1000 Wilson Blvd., Suite 1825, Arlington, VA 22209-3901; 37,000; www.psych.org

Psychical Research, American Society for (1885), 5 W. 73rd St., New York, NY 10023; www.aspr.com

Psychological Assn., American (1892), 750 1st St. NE, Washington, DC 20002; 150,000; www.apa.org

PTA, Natl. (1897), 541 N. Fairbanks Ct., Ste. 1300, Chicago, IL 60611; 5,896,672; www.pta.org

Public Administration, American Soc. for (1939), 1301 Pennsylvania Ave. NW, Ste. 840, Washington, DC 20004; 9,000+; www.aspanet.org

Public Health Assn., American (1872), 800 I St. NW, Washington, DC 20001; 50,000+; www.apha.org

Public Relations Soc. of America (1947), 33 Maiden Ln., 11th Fl., New York, NY 10038; 28,000; www.prsa.org

Publishers, Assn. of American (1970), 71 5th Ave., New York, NY 10003; 300+; www.publishers.org

Quill and Scroll Society (1926), School of Journalism, The University of Iowa, Iowa City, IA 52242; www.uiowa.edu/~quill-sc

Quota International, Inc. (1919), 1420 21st St. NW, Washington, DC 20036; 7,000+; www.quota.org

Rabbis, Central Conference of American (1889), 355 Lexington Ave., New York, NY 10017; 1,800; ccarnet.org

Radio and Television Society Foundation, Intl. (1939), 420 Lexington Ave., Ste. 1601, New York, NY 10170; 1,787; www.irts.org

Radio Relay League, American (1914), 225 Main St., Newington, CT 06111; 152,000; www.arrl.org

Railway Historical Society, Natl. (1935), 100 N. 17th St., Ste. 1203, Philadelphia, PA 19103; app. 17,000+; www.nrhs.com

Range Management, Society for (1948), 10030 W. 27th Ave., Wheat Ridge, CO 80215; 3,700; www.rangelands.org/srm.shtml

Reading Assn., Intl. (1956), 800 Barksdale Rd., P.O. Box 8139, Newark, DE 19714; 350,000; www.reading.org

Real Estate Appraisers, Natl. Assn. of (1966), 1224 N. Nokomis NE, Alexandria, MN 56308; 3,000; www.iami.org/narea

Real Estate Institute, Intl. (1975), 1224 N. Nokomis, Alexandria, MN 56308; 700; www.iami.org/irei

Recreation and Park Assn., Natl. (1965), 22377 Belmont Ridge Rd., Ashburn, VA 20148; 21,000; www.nrpa.org

Recycling Coalition, Natl. (1978), 1325 G St., NW, Washington, DC, 20005; 4,000; www.nrc-recycle.org

Red Cross, American Natl. (1881), 2025 E St. NW, Washington, DC 20006; 1.3 mil volunteers; www.redcross.org

Reform Party of the U.S.A. (1996), P.O. Box 126437, Ft. Worth, TX 76126; 500,000; www.reformparty.org

Refugee Committee, American (1978), 430 Oak Grove St., Ste. 204, Minneapolis, MN 55403; www.archq.org

Rehabilitation Assn., Natl. (1925), 633 S. Washington St., Alexandria, VA 22310-4109; approx. 11,000; www.national rehab.org

Religion, American Academy of (1909), 825 Houston Mill Rd., Suite 300, Atlanta, GA 30329; 9,000; www.aarweb.org

Renaissance Society of America (1954), (CUNY) 365 5th. Ave., Rm. 5400, New York, NY 10016; 3,000; www.rsa.org

Republican National Committee (1856), 310 1st St. SE, Washington, DC 20003; www.rnc.org

Reserve Officers Assn. of the U.S. (1922), One Constitution Ave. NE, Washington, DC 20002; 75,000; www.roa.org

Retail Federation, Natl. (1908), 325 7th St. NW, Ste. 1100, Washington, DC 20004; 50,000; www.nrf.com

Retired Persons, American Assn. of (1958), 601 E St. NW, Washington, DC 20049; 35 mil+; www.aarp.org

Reye's Syndrome Foundation, Natl. (1974), 426 N. Lewis St., Bryan, OH 43506-0829; 5,000+; www.reyessyndrome.org

Richard III Society, Inc. (1961), 11000 Anaheim Ave., Albuquerque, NM 87122; 4,000; www.r3.org

Rifle Assn., Natl. (1871), 11250 Waples Mill Rd., Fairfax, VA 22030; approx 3 mil; www.nra.org

Road & Transportation Builders Assn., American (1902), The ARTBA Building, 1219 28th St. NW, Washington, DC 20007; 5,000+; www.artba.org

Roller Sports, U.S.A. (1937), 4730 South St., Lincoln, NE 68506; 30,000; www.usarollersports.org

Rose Society, American (1892), P.O. Box 30000, Shreveport, LA 71130; 20,000; www.ars.org

Rotary Intl. (1905), One Rotary Center, 1560 Sherman Ave., Evanston, IL 60201; 1.2 mil; www.rotary.org

Running Assn., American (1968), 4405 East West Hwy, Ste. 405, Bethesda, MD 20814; 15,000; www.americanrunning.org

Safety Council, Natl. (1913), 1121 Spring Lake Dr., Itasca, IL 60143; 46,000 member facilities; www.nsc.org

Safety Engineers, American Soc. of (1911), 1800 E. Oakton St., Des Plaines, IL 60018; 32,000; www.asse.org

Save-the-Redwoods League (1918), 114 Sansome St., Ste. 1200, San Francisco, CA 94104; 40,000; www.savethered woods.org

School Administrators, American Assn. of (1865), 801 N. Quincy St., Ste 700, Arlington, VA 22203; 13,000+; www.aasa.org

Science, American Assn. for the Advancement of (1848), 1200 New York Ave. NW, Washington, DC 20005; approx. 10 mil.; www.aaas.org

Science Fiction Society, World (1939), P.O. Box 426159, Kendall Square Station, Cambridge, MA 02142; 10,000; www.wsfs.org

Sciences, Natl. Academy of (1863), 500 5th St. NW, Washington, DC 20001; 2,000+; www.nas.edu

Science Teachers Assn., Natl. (1944), 1840 Wilson Blvd., Arlington, VA 22201; 55,000; www.nsta.org

Science Writers, Natl. Assn. of (1955), P.O. Box 890, Hedgesville, WV 25427; 2,400; www.nasw.org

Scrabble® Assn., Natl. (1978), P.O. Box 700, 403 Front St., Greenport, NY 11944; 10,000+; www.scrabble-assoc.com

Screen Actors Guild (1933), 5757 Wilshire Blvd., Los Angeles, CA 90036; 120,000; www.sag.com

2nd Air Division Assn. of the 8th Air Force (1950), P.O. Box 484, Elkhorn, WI 53121-0484; 4,000

Secular Humanism, Council for (1980), P.O. Box 664, Amherst, NY 14226; 24,000; www.secularhumanism.org

Separation of Church & State, Americans United for (1947), 518 C St. NE, Washington, DC 20002; 75,000+; www.au.org

Sharkhunters Intl. (1983), P.O. Box 1539-WS, Hernando, FL 34442; 6,900; www.sharkhunters.com

Shipbuilders Council of America (1920), 1455 F St., NW, Ste. 225, Washington, DC 20005; 43 member cos; www.ship builders.org

Ships in Bottles Assn. of America (1982), P.O. Box 180550, Coronado, CA 92178; 250; www.shipsinbottles.org

Shriners of North America, The (1872), 2900 Rocky Point Dr., Tampa, FL 33607; approx 500,000+; www.shrinershq.org

Sierra Club (1892), 85 2nd St., 2nd Fl., San Francisco, CA 94105; 750,000+; www.sierraclub.org

Sigma Beta Delta (1994), P.O. Box 210570, St. Louis, MO 63121-0570; 20,000; www.sigmabetadelta.org

Skeet Shooting Assn., Natl. (1934), 5931 Roft Rd., San Antonio, TX 78253; 20,000; www.mynssa.com

Small Business United, Natl. (1937), 1156 15th St. NW, Ste. 1100, Washington, DC 20005; 150,000+; www.nsba.biz

Sociological Assn., American (1905), 1307 New York Avenue NW, Suite 700, Washington, DC 20005; 14,000; www.asa net.org

Softball Assn., Amateur (1933), 2801 NE 50th St., Oklahoma City, OK 73111; 245,000+ teams; www.softball.org

Software and Information Industry Assn. (1999), 1090 Vermont Ave. NW, 6th Fl., Wash. DC 20005; 750 cos.; www.siia.net

Soldiers', Sailors', Marines' and Airmen's Club (1919), 283 Lexington Ave., New York, NY 10016; www.ssmaclub.org

Songwriters Guild of America (1931), 209 10th Ave. S., Ste. 534, Nashville, TN 37203; 5,000+; www.songwritersguild.com

Sons of the American Colonists, Natl. Society of (1970), 5611 N. 15th St., Arlington, VA 22205-0482; 250

Sons of the American Legion (1932), P.O. Box 1055, Indianapolis, IN 46206; 287,000; www.sal.legion.org

Sons of the American Revolution, Natl. Society of (1889), 1000 S. 4th St., Louisville, KY 40203; 26,000; www.sar.org

Sons of Confederate Veterans (1896), P.O. Box 59, Columbia, TN 38402; 35,000; www.scv.org

Sons of Italy in America, Order (1905), 219 E St. NE, Washington, DC 20002; 600,000; www.osia.org

Sons of Norway (1895), 1455 W. Lake St., Minneapolis, MN 55408; 61,600; www.sofn.com

Southern Christian Leadership Conference (1957), P.O. Box 89128, Atlanta, GA 30312; 1 mil.; sclcnational.org

Space Society, Natl. (1974), 1620 Eye St. NW, Ste. 615, Washington, DC 20006; 22,000+; www.nss.org

Speech-Language-Hearing Assn., American (1925), 10801 Rockville Pike, Rockville, MD 20852; 118,000; www.asha.org

Speedskating, U.S. (1966), P.O. Box 450639, Westlake, OH 44145; 1,800; www.usspeedskating.org

Speleological Society, Natl. (1941), 2813 Cave Ave., Huntsville, AL 35810; 12,000; www.caves.org

Sports Car Club of America (1944), P.O. Box 19400, Topeka, KS 66619; 60,000; www.scca.org

Sportscasters Assn., The American (1980), 225 Broadway, Ste. 2030, New York, NY 10007; 500+; www.american sportscasters online.com

State, County, and Municipal Employees, American Federation of (AFSCME) (1936), 1625 L St. NW, Washington, DC 20036; 1.4 mil; www.afscme.org

State & Local History, American Assn. for (1940), 1717 Church St., Nashville, TN 37203; 6,100; www.aaslh.org

State Governments, Council of (1933), 2760 Research Park Drive, P.O. Box 11910, Lexington, KY 40578; 50 states, 4 territories; www.csg.org

Steamship Historical Society of America, Inc. (1935), 300 Ray Dr., Ste. 4, Providence, RI 02906; 3,400; www.sshsa.org

Steelworkers of America, United (USWA) (1942), 5 Gateway Center, Pittsburgh, PA 15222; 1.2 mil; www.uswa.org

Stock Exchange, American (1911), 86 Trinity Pl., New York, NY 10006; www.amex.com

Stock Exchange, New York (1792), 11 Wall St., New York, NY 10005; www.nyse.com

Stock Exchange, Philadelphia (1790), 1900 Market St., Philadelphia, PA 19103; www.phlx.com

Student Councils, Natl. Assn. of (1931), 1904 Association Dr., Reston, VA 20191; 17,000 councils; www.nasc.us

Stuttering Assn., Natl. (1977), 119 W. 40th St., 14th Fl, New York, NY 10018; 2,800; www.nsastutter.org

Supreme Court Historical Society (1974), Opperman House, 224 East Capitol St. NE, Washington, DC 20003; 5,700; www.supremecourthistory.org

Surgeons, American College of (1913), 633 N. Saint Clair St., Chicago, IL 60611; 64,000; www.facs.org

Symphony Orchestra League, American (1942), 33 W. 60th St., 5th Fl., New York, NY 10023; 900; www.symphony.org

Table Tennis Assn., U.S. (1933), One Olympic Plaza, Colorado Springs, CO 80909; 8,000+; www.usatt.org

Tall Buildings and Urban Habitat, Council on (1969), Illinois Inst. of Tech., S.R. Crown Hall, 3360 S. State St., Chicago, IL 60616; 1,400; www.ctbuh.org

Tau Beta Pi Association (1885), P.O. Box 2697, Knoxville, TN 37901; 477,318; www.tbp.org

Tax Administrators, Federation of (1937), 444 N. Capitol St. NW, Ste. 348, Washington, DC 20001; www.taxadmin.org

Tax Foundation (1937), 2001 L. St. NW, Ste. 1050, Washington, DC 20036; 50 U.S. states; www.taxfoundation.org

Taxpayers Union, Natl. (1969), 108 N. Alfred St., Alexandria, VA 22314; 335,000; www.ntu.org

Teachers, American Federation of (AFT) (1916), 555 New Jersey Ave. NW, Wash., DC 20001; 1.3 mil; www.aft.org

Teachers of English, Natl. Council of (1911), 1111 W. Kenyon Rd., Urbana, IL 61801; 60,000; www.ncte.org

Teachers of English to Speakers of Other Languages (1966), 700 S. Washington St., Ste. 200, Alexandria, VA 22314; 13,441; www.tesol.org

Teachers of French, American Assn. of (1927), Southern Illinois University, Mailcode 4510, Carbondale, IL 62901; 9,500; www.frenchteachers.org

Teachers of German, American Assn. of (1926), 112 Haddontowne Ct. #104, Cherry Hill, NJ 08034; 6,000; www.aatg.org

Teachers of Mathematics, Natl. Council of (1920), 1906 Association Dr., Reston, VA 20191; 100,000; www.nctm.org

Teachers of Singing, Natl. Assn. of (1944), 4745 Sutton Park Ct., Ste. 201, Jacksonville, FL 32224; 6,000; www.nats.org

Teachers of Spanish & Portuguese, American Assn. of (1917), 423 Exton Commons, Exton, PA, 19341; 11,522; www.aatsp.org

Teamsters, Intl. Brotherhood of (IBT) (1903), 25 Louisiana Ave. NW, Washington, DC 20001; 1.4 mil; www.teamster.org

TelecomPioneers (1911), P.O. Box 13888, Denver, CO 80201; 625,000; www.telecompioneers.com

Television Academy, Natl. (1957), 111 W. 57th St., Ste. 600, New York, NY 10019; www.emmyonline.org

Term Limits, U.S. (1992), 73 Spring St., Ste. 408, New York, NY 10012; www.termlimits.org

Theodore Roosevelt Assn. (1920), P.O. Box 719, Oyster Bay, NY 11771; 2,500; www.theodoreroosevelt.org

Theological Library Assn., American (1946), 250 S. Wacker Dr., Ste. 1600, Chicago, IL 60606; 1,000+; www.atla.com

Theological Schools in the U.S. and Canada, Assn. of (1918), 10 Summit Park Dr., Pittsburgh, PA 15275; 251; www.ats.edu

Theosophical Society in America (1875), P.O. Box 270, Wheaton, IL 60189; 5,000; www.theosophical.org

Therapy Dogs Intl., Inc. (1976), 88 Bartley Rd., Flanders, NJ 07836; 12,200; www.tdi-dog.org

Thoreau Society (1941), 55 Old Bedford Rd., Concord, MA 01742; 1,700+; www.thoreausociety.org

Thoroughbred Racing Assns. (1942), 420 Fair Hill Dr., Ste. 1, Elkton, MD 21921; 49 racing assoc.; www.tra-online.com

Tin Can Sailors (1976), P.O. Box 100, Somerset, MA 02726; 24,000; www.destroyers.org

Titanic Historical Society & Museum (1963), 208 Main St., Indian Orchard, MA 01151-0053; 4,328; www.titanichistorical society.org

Toastmasters Intl. (1924), P.O. Box 9052, Mission Viejo, CA 92690; 200,000+; www.toastmasters.org

Topical Assn., American (1949), P.O. Box 57, Arlington, TX, 76004-0057; 3,300; americantopicalassn.org

Toy Industry Assn., Inc. (1916), 1115 Broadway, Suite 400, New York, NY 10010; 400+ cos.; www.toy-tma.org

Transportation Alternatives (1973), 127 W. 26th St., Ste. 1002, New York, NY 10001; 5,000; www.transalt.org

Transportation Engineers, Inst. of (1930), 1099 14th St. NW, Suite 300-W, Washington, DC 20005; 16,000; www.ite.org

Trapshooting Assn. of America, Amateur (1900), 601 W. National Road, Vandalia, OH 45377; 54,208; www.shoot ata.com

Travel Agents, American Soc. of (1931), 1101 King St., Ste. 200, Alexandria, VA 22314; 20,000+; www.astanet.com

Travelers Protective Assn. of America (1890), 3755 Lindell Blvd., St. Louis, MO 63108; 91,008; www.tpahq.org

Truck Historical Soc., American (1971), P.O. Box 901611, Kansas City, MO 64190; 22,000+; www.aths.org

Tuberous Sclerosis Alliance (1974), 801 Roeder Rd., Ste. 750, Silver Spring, MD 20910; approx. 2,000; www.tsalliance.org

UFOs, Natl. Investigations Committee on (1967), 21601 Devonshire St., #217, Chatsworth, CA 91311; 250; www. nicufo.org

Underwriters (CPCU), Soc. of Chartered Property and Casualty (1944), 720 Providence Rd., Malvern, PA 19355; 24,800; www.cpcusociety.org

UNICEF, U.S. Fund for (1947), 333 E. 38th St., New York, NY 10016; www.unicefusa.org

United. See also other entries under next major word in title.

Uniformed Services, Natl. Assn. for (1968), 5535 Hempstead Way, Springfield, VA 22151; 202,780; www.naus.org

United Nations Assn. of the U.S.A. (1943), 801 2nd Ave., 2nd Fl., New York, NY 10017; 20,000; www.unausa.org

United Order True Sisters, Inc. (1846), Linton Intl. Plaza, 600 Linton Blvd, Ste. 6, Delray Beach, FL 33444; approx. 2,000; uots.org

United Press Intl. (1907), 1510 H St. NW, Washington, DC 20005; www.upi.com

United Way of America (1918), 701 N. Fairfax St., Alexandria, VA 22314; approx. 1,400 org.; national.unitedway.org

Universities, Assn. of American (1900), 1200 New York Ave., NW, Ste. 550, Washington, DC 20005; 62 coll/univ.; www. aau.edu

University Women, American Assn. of (1881), 1111 16th St. NW, Washington, DC 20036; 100,000+; www.aauw.org

Urban League, Natl. (1910), 120 Wall St., New York, NY 10005; 100 local affiliates; www.nul.org

USO World Headquarters (1941), 2111 Wilson Blvd., Ste. 1200, Arlington, VA 22201; www.uso.org

USS Forrestal CVA/CV/AVT-59 Assn., Inc. (1990), 300 Cassady Avenue, Virginia Beach, VA 23452; 2,600; www.ussforrestal.org

USS Idaho Assn. (1957), P.O. Box 711247, San Diego, CA 92171; 231

USS Los Angeles CA-135 Assn. (1977), c/o Jim Osborne, 1314 N. Alden Rd., Muncie, IN 47304; 365; www.uss-la-ca135.org

USS Missouri Memorial Assn., Inc. (1994), P.O. Box 879, Aiea, HI 96701; 1,500; www.ussmissouri.org

Ventriloquists' Assn., International (1944), P.O. Box 17153, Las Vegas, NV 89114; 1,450; www.inquista.com

Veterans of Foreign Wars of the U.S. (1899), 406 W. 34th St., Kansas City, MO 64111; 1.8 mil+.; www.vfw.org

Veterans of Foreign Wars of the U.S., Ladies Auxiliary to the (1914), 406 W. 34th St., Kansas City, MO 64111; 616,439; www.ladiesauxvfw.org

Veterans of the Vietnam War, Inc. (1978), 805 S. Township Blvd., Pittston, PA 18640-3327; 15,000; www.vvnw.org

Veterinary Medical Assn., American (1863), 1931 N. Meacham Rd., Schaumburg, IL 60173; 72,000; www.avma.org

Victorian Society in America (1966), 205 S Camac St., Philadelphia, PA 19107; 3,000; www.victoriansociety.org

Volleyball, USA (1928), 715 S. Circle Dr., Colorado Springs, CO 80910; 191,000; www.usavolleyball.org

Volunteers of America (1896), 1660 Duke St., Alexandria, VA 22314; 14,000 staff, 70,000 volunteers; www.voa.org

War Mothers, American (1917), 5415 Connecticut Ave., NW, Ste. L-30, Washington, DC 20015; 500

Watch & Clock Collectors, Inc., Natl. Assn. of (NAWCC) (1943), 514 Poplar St., Columbia, PA 17512; 27,000; www. nawcc.org

Watercolor Society, American (1866), 47 5th Ave., New York, NY 10003; 480; www.americanwatercolorsociety.com

Water Environment Federation (1928), 601 Wythe St., Alexandria, VA 22314; 76 assns.; www.wef.org

Water Works Assn., American (1881), 6666 W. Quincy Ave., Denver, CO 80235; 57,000; www.awwa.org

Wheelchair Sports, USA (1956), P.O. Box 5266, Kendall Park, NJ 08824; 4,000; www.wsusa.org

Wildlife Federation, Natl. (1936), 11100 Wildlife Center Dr., Reston, VA, 20190; 4 mil.; www.nwf.org

Wildlife Management Institute (1911), 1146 19th St. NW, Ste. 700, Washington, DC 20036; 300; www.wildlifemanagement institute.org

Wizard of Oz Club, Intl. (1957), P.O. Box 26249, San Francisco, CA 94126; 1,300+; www.ozclub.org

Women, Natl. Organization for (NOW) (1966), 1100 H St. NW, 3rd Fl., Washington, DC 20005; 500,000; www.now.org

Women and Families, Natl. Partnership for (1971), 1875 Connecticut Ave. NW, Ste. 650, Washington, DC 20009; 2,000; www.nationalpartnership.org

Women Artists, Inc., Natl. Assn. of (1889), 80 5th Ave., Ste. 1405, New York, NY 10011; 800+; www.nawanet.org

Women in Communications, The Association for (1909 as Theta Sigma Phi), 3337 Duke St., Alexandria, VA 22314; 4,000+; www.womcom.org

Women Engineers, Society of (1950), 230 E. Ohio St., Ste. 400, Chicago, IL 60611; 17,000; www.swe.org

Women in Radio and Television Inc., Amer. (1951), 8405 Greensboro Dr., Ste. 800, McLean, VA 22102; www.awrt.org

Women's Army Corps Veterans Assn. (1946), P.O. Box 5577, Ft. McClellan, AL 36205; 4,500; www.armywomen.org

Women's Christian Temperance Union, Natl. (1874), 1730 Chicago Ave., Evanston, IL 60201; www.wctu.org

Women's Clubs, General Federation of (1890), 1734 N St. NW, Washington, DC, 20036; 180,000 U.S.; www.gfwc.org

Women Voters of the U.S., League of (1920), 1730 M St. NW, Ste. 1000, Washington, DC 20036; 130,000; www.lwv.org

Woodmen of America, Modern (1883), 1701 1st Ave., Rock Island, IL 61201; 750,000; www.modern-woodmen.org

Workmen's Circle (1900), 45 E. 33rd St., New York, NY 10016; 35,000; www.circle.org

World Council of Churches, U.S. Office (1948), 475 Riverside Drive, Rm. 1371, New York, NY 10115; 330+ denominations, www.wcc-usa.org

World Federalist Assn. (1947), 418 7th St. SE, Washington, DC 20003; 11,000

World Future Society (1966), 7910 Woodmont Ave., Ste. 450, Bethesda, MD 20814; 25,000; www.wfs.org

World Learning (1954), Kipling Rd., P.O. Box 676, Brattleboro, VT 05302-0676; 100,000; www.worldlearning.org

World Wildlife Fund (1961), 1250 24th St. NW, Washington, DC 20037; 1.2 mil+; www.worldwildlife.org

Writers Guild of America, West (1933), 7000 W. Third St., Los Angeles, CA 90048; 10,500; www.wga.org

YMCA (Young Men's Christian Assn.) of the U.S.A. (1851) 101 N. Wacker Dr., Chicago, IL 60606; 18.9 mil.; www.ymca.net

YWCA (Young Women's Christian Assn.) of the U.S.A. (1858), 1015 18th St. NW, Ste. 1100, Washington, DC 20036; approx. 2 mil; www.ywca.org

Zionist Organization of America (1897), 4 E. 34th St., New York, NY 10016; 50,000; www.zoa.org

Zoo and Aquarium Assn., American (1924), 8403 Colesville Road, Suite 710, Silver Spring, MD 20910; 212 institutions, 5,500 individuals; www.aza.org

World Almanac Quick Quiz

Which of the following is not an actual organization listed in this directory?

(a) International Federation of Postcard Dealers (b) Toastmasters International

(c) Without a Net Society of Trapeze Artists (d) Bald-Headed Men of America

For the answer see page 1008.

EDUCATION

U.S. Public Schools: Students, Staff, Spending, 1899-2004
Source: National Center for Education Statistics, U.S. Dept. of Education

	1899-1900	1919-20	1939-40	1959-60	1969-70	1979-80	1989-90	1999-2000	2003-04
Population statistics (thousands)									
Total U.S. population[1]	75,995	104,514	131,028	177,830	201,385	224,567	246,819	279,040	290,850
Population 5-17 years of age	21,573	27,571	30,151	43,881	52,386	48,041	44,947	52,811	53,269
Percentage 5-17 years of age	28.4%	26.4%	23.0%	24.7%	26.0%	21.4%	18.2%	18.9%	18.3%
Enrollment (thousands)									
Elementary and secondary[2]	15,503	21,578	25,434	36,087	45,550	41,651	40,543	46,857	48,540
Kindergarten & grades 1-8	14,984	19,378	18,833	27,602	32,513	28,034	29,152	33,488	34,202
Grades 9-12	519	2,200	6,601	8,485	13,037	13,616	11,390	13,369	14,338
Percentage pop. 5-17 enrolled	71.9%	78.3%	84.4%	82.2%	87.0%	86.7%	90.2%	88.7%	91.1%
Percentage in high schools	3.3%	10.2%	26.0%	23.5%	28.6%	32.7%	28.1%	28.5%	29.5%
High school graduates (thousands)	62	231	1,143	1,627	2,589	2,748	2,320	2,554	2,762
Instructional staff									
Total instructional staff (thousands)	*	678	912	1,457	2,286	2,406	2,986	3,820	4,053
Teachers, librarians, and other non-supervisory instructional staff (thousands)	423	657	875	1,393	2,195	2,300	2,860	3,683	3,888
Revenue and expenditures (millions)									
Total revenue	$220	$970	$2,261	$14,747	$40,267	$96,881	$208,548	$372,944	$462,016
Total expenditures	215	1,036	2,344	15,613	40,683	95,962	212,770	381,838	473,863
Current expenditures[3,5]	180	861	1,942	12,329	34,218	86,984	188,229	323,889	403,376
Capital outlay	35	154	258	2,662	4,659	6,506	17,781	43,357	50,476
Interest on school debt	*	18	131	490	1,171	1,874	3,776	9,135	13,081
Others	*	3	13	133	636	598	2,983	5,457	6,930
Salaries and pupil cost									
Avg. annual salary of instruct. staff[4]	$325	$871	$1,441	$3,010	$8,626	$15,970	$31,367	$41,827	$46,752
Expenditure per capita total pop.	2.83	9.91	17.89	88	202	427	862	1,368	1,629
Current expenditure[5] per pupil ADA[6]	16.67	53.32	88.09	375	816	2,272	4,980	7,394	8,899

NOTE: Because of rounding, details may not add to totals. Prior to 1959-60, data do not include Alaska and Hawaii. * = Data not collected. (1) Population data for 1899-1900 are based on total population from the decennial census. From 1919-20 to 1959-60, population data are total population, including armed forces overseas, as of July 1 preceding the school year. Data for later years are for resident population that excludes armed forces overseas. (2) Data for 1899 through 1960 are school year enrollment; data for later years are fall enrollment. (3) In 1899-1900, includes interest on school debt. (4) Data prior to 1959-60 include supervisors, principals, teachers, and nonsupervisory instructional staff. (5) Because of changes in the definition of "current expenditures," data for 1959-60 and later years are not entirely comparable with prior years. (6) ADA means average daily attendance.

U.S. Public High School Graduation Rates, 2002-2003
Source: National Center for Education Statistics, U.S. Dept. of Education

	Rate (%)[1]	Rank		Rate (%)[1]	Rank		Rate (%)[1]	Rank		Rate (%)[1]	Rank
Alabama	60.1	43	Illinois	71.4	32	Montana	78.8	11	Rhode Island	74.3	20
Alaska	63.1	40	Indiana	71.4	30	Nebraska	81.1	6	South Carolina	51.7	50
Arizona	72.8	25	Iowa	84.2	3	Nevada	66.5	36	South Dakota	80.0	8
Arkansas	75.2	18	Kansas	75.5	16	New Hampshire	75.4	17	Tennessee	59.1	44
California	70.7	33	Kentucky	66.4	37	New Jersey	91.2	1	Texas	66.3	38
Colorado	72.2	28	Louisiana	58.9	45	New Mexico	57.7	46	Utah	82.1	5
Connecticut	76.6	14	Maine	76.0	15	New York	56.9	48	Vermont	79.7	9
Delaware	67.2	35	Maryland	73.7	23	North Carolina	62.5	41	Virginia	76.8	13
District of Columbia	51.5	51	Massachusetts	72.0	29	North Dakota	84.4	2	Washington	69.8	34
Florida	57.0	47	Michigan	73.8	22	Ohio	74.0	21	West Virginia	72.4	27
Georgia	53.3	49	Minnesota	83.4	4	Oklahoma	73.0	24	Wisconsin	80.1	7
Hawaii	64.1	39	Mississippi	60.4	42	Oregon	71.4	31	Wyoming	72.5	26
Idaho	79.1	10	Missouri	75.1	19	Pennsylvania	78.1	12	**TOTAL U.S.**	**69.1**	

NOTE: Data exclude ungraded pupils and have not been adjusted for interstate migration. (1) Graduates as percentage of fall 1999 9th-grade enrollment.

Technology in U.S. Public Schools*
Source: Quality Education Data, Inc., Denver, CO
Number and percentage of schools in each category that have the technology indicated.

	Total		Elementary[1]		Middle/ Jr. High[2]		Senior High[3]		K-12[4]		Special Ed./ Adult Ed.	
TOTAL SCHOOLS	93,189	100%	56,232	100%	14,475	100%	20,161	100%	2,530	100%	2,310	100%
Schools with computers	83,057	89	51,418	91	12,911	89	17,100	85	2,026	80	1,625	70
By number of computers:												
1-10	3,170	3	1,990	4	194	1	597	3	59	2	389	17
11-20	4,590	5	3,123	6	345	2	829	4	129	5	293	13
21-50	16,741	18	11,934	21	1,728	12	2,628	13	493	19	449	19
51-100	23,753	25	16,940	30	3,372	23	3,178	16	607	24	262	11
100+	34,803	37	17,431	31	7,272	50	9,868	49	738	29	232	10
Schools with LANs[5]	61,104	66	36,791	66	10,652	74	14,030	72	1,614	65	707	30
By enrollment:												
100-299	13,607	15	8,610	15	1,212	8	3,309	17	774	31	476	20
300-499	18,256	20	13,802	25	2,098	15	2,294	12	403	16	62	3
500+	29,241	32	14,379	26	7,342	51	8,427	43	437	18	169	7
Schools with WANs[6]	45,933	50	27,549	49	8,011	56	9,932	51	996	40	441	19
By enrollment:												
100-299	8,816	10	5,701	10	769	5	2,032	10	434	18	314	13
300-499	14,574	16	11,100	20	1,735	12	1,707	9	289	12	32	1
500+	22,543	24	10,748	19	5,507	38	6,193	32	273	11	95	4

*Data for schools with computers as of 2005. All other data from 2004. (1) Includes preschool and schools with grade spans of Preschool-3, K-6, K-8, and K-12. (2) Includes schools with grade spans of 4-8, 7-8, and 7-9. (3) Includes vocational, technical, and alternative high schools and schools with grade spans of 7-12, 9-12, and 10-12. (4) K-12 also included under Elementary schools. (5) LAN=Local area computer network. (6) WAN=Wide area computer network.

Overview of U.S. Public Schools, Fall 2004*

Source: National Center for Education Statistics, U.S. Dept. of Education; National Education Association

	Local school districts	Elementary schools[1]	Secondary schools[2]	Classroom teachers	Total enrollment	Pupils per teacher	Teacher's avg. pay[3]	Expend. per pupil[4]
Alabama	131	944	413	51,594	730,140	14.2	$38,863	$6,581
Alaska	54	188	84	7,756	132,970	17.1	52,424	10,116
Arizona	218	1,279	563	48,935	1,043,298	21.3	42,905	5,991
Arkansas	254	728	422	31,234	463,115	14.8	40,495	6,842
California	985	6,645	2,360	305,969	6,441,557	21.1	57,876	7,673
Colorado	178	1,208	409	45,165	765,976	17.0	44,161	7,478
Connecticut	166	820	244	38,808	577,390	14.9	58,688	11,436
Delaware	19	139	47	7,856	119,091	15.2	50,869	10,212
Dist. of Columbia	1	144	43	5,387	76,714	14.2	58,456	12,959
Florida	67	2,420	475	154,864	2,639,336	17.0	41,081	6,793
Georgia	180	1,665	365	104,987	1,553,437	14.8	46,526	7,742
Hawaii	1	207	55	11,146	183,185	16.4	44,273	8,533
Idaho	114	415	223	14,269	256,084	17.9	42,122	6,168
Illinois	880	3,157	1,001	131,047	2,097,503	16.0	55,629	8,606
Indiana	294	1,449	464	60,563	1,021,348	16.9	46,851	8,431
Iowa	367	1,034	455	34,697	478,319	13.8	40,347	7,626
Kansas	301	975	422	32,932	469,136	14.2	39,190	7,776
Kentucky	176	1,002	319	41,463	674,796	16.3	41,002	6,861
Louisiana	68	1,027	308	49,192	724,281	14.7	38,880	7,271
Maine	283	509	155	16,656	198,820	11.9	40,940	9,746
Maryland	24	1,083	265	55,101	865,561	15.7	52,331	9,433
Massachusetts	350	1,473	348	73,399	975,574	13.3	54,596	11,015
Michigan	552	2,727	848	100,634	1,750,919	17.4	55,693	9,094
Minnesota	343	1,263	850	52,152	838,503	16.1	46,906	8,405
Mississippi	152	600	326	31,321	495,376	15.8	36,590	6,199
Missouri	524	1,551	654	65,481	905,449	13.8	38,971	7,542
Montana	436	491	363	10,224	146,705	14.3	38,485	7,825
Nebraska	503	857	334	21,077	285,761	13.6	39,456	8,452
Nevada	17	412	136	20,950	400,083	19.1	43,394	6,410
New Hampshire	179	379	98	15,298	206,852	13.5	43,941	9,161
New Jersey	616	1,892	464	114,875	1,393,347	12.1	56,600	13,338
New Mexico	89	587	224	21,730	326,102	15.0	39,328	7,572
New York	733	3,223	1,034	218,612	2,836,337	13.0	56,200	12,638
North Carolina	115	1,786	412	92,550	1,385,754	15.0	43,313	6,613
North Dakota	210	319	198	8,070	100,513	12.5	36,449	7,297
Ohio	614	2,727	1,019	118,060	1,840,032	15.6	48,692	9,029
Oklahoma	540	1,201	581	40,416	629,476	15.6	37,141	6,154
Oregon	198	854	300	27,431	552,322	20.1	50,790	7,618
Pennsylvania	501	2,369	812	121,167	1,828,089	15.1	52,700	9,708
Rhode Island	32	265	72	11,898	156,498	13.2	53,473	11,078
South Carolina	85	847	277	46,914	703,736	15.0	42,207	7,177
South Dakota	168	434	263	9,064	122,798	13.5	34,040	7,068
Tennessee	136	1,257	361	60,022	941,091	15.7	41,527	6,466
Texas	1,038	5,312	2,095	294,547	4,405,215	15.0	41,009	7,151
Utah	40	552	327	22,287	503,607	22.6	39,965	4,991
Vermont	302	276	70	8,720	98,352	11.3	44,535	11,211
Virginia	134	1,485	403	93,732	1,204,739	12.9	44,763	8,219
Washington	296	1,424	586	53,125	1,020,005	19.2	45,712	7,391
West Virginia	55	583	185	19,958	280,129	14.0	38,360	8,588
Wisconsin	438	1,551	604	60,521	864,757	14.3	43,466	9,240
Wyoming	48	249	109	6,657	84,733	12.7	40,392	9,308
TOTAL U.S.	14,205	65,984	23,445	3,090,513	48,794,911	15.8	47,750	8,310

*Full-time elementary and secondary day schools only. (1) Includes schools with grade 6 and below and those with no grade higher than 8. (2) Includes schools with no grade lower than 7. (3) National Education Association estimate, Fall 2003. (4) Fall 2003, per total number of pupils.

Programs for the Disabled, 1993-2004

Source: Office of Special Education Programs, U.S. Dept. of Education

Number of children from 6 to 21 years old served annually in educational programs for the disabled; in thousands.

Type of Disability	1993	1994	1995	1996	1997	1998	1999	2000	2001	20002	2003	2004[1]
Learning disabilities	2,366	2,428	2,510	2,602	2,674	2,754	2,817	2,834	2,848	2,846	2,834	2,790
Speech impairments	998	1,018	1,020	1,027	1,049	1,064	1,075	1,081	1,085	1,084	1,102	1,138
Mental retardation	532	554	571	586	594	603	611	600	599	592	580	556
Emotional disturbance	402	415	428	439	446	454	463	469	472	476	480	483
Multiple disabilities	103	110	90	95	99	107	108	111	121	127	130	132
Hearing impairments	61	65	65	68	69	70	71	71	70	70	71	72
Orthopedic impairments	53	57	60	63	66	67	69	71	73	73	74	65
Other health impairments	66	83	107	134	161	191	221	253	290	337	390	508
Visual impairments	24	25	25	25	26	26	26	65	25	25	25	26
Autism	16	19	23	29	34	43	54	65	78	97	118	166
Deaf-blindness	1	1	1	1	1	1	2	2	1	2	2	2
Traumatic brain injury	4	5	7	10	10	12	13	14	15	21	21	23
Developmental delay[2]	—	—	—	—	—	—	—	—	—	45	58	74
ALL DISABILITIES	4,626	4,779	4,908	5,079	5,231	5,397	5,541	5,614	5,705	5,795	5,885	6,033

NOTE: Counts based on reports from states and District of Columbia. Details may not add to totals because of rounding and/or incomplete enumeration. — = not available or not reliable data. (1) Data for 2004 includes Bureau of Indian Affairs programs. (2) Applicable only to ages 3-9.

IT'S A FACT: In 1980, all workers aged 25-34 who graduated high school but not college earned an average salary of $32,400 (when measured in 2004 constant U.S. dollars). In 2004, they only earned $27,100. College graduates' salaries rose from $40,000 to $43,500 in the same period.

Trends in International Mathematics and Science Study (TIMSS), 2003

Source: National Center for Education Statistics

The TIMSS is an international assessment test that was administered to 4th and 8th graders in 1995, and again in 2003, to measure the degree to which students have learned concepts of mathematics and science that they studied in school. Listed below are the average scaled scores for each country. Only countries with data for 2003 are listed.

		Mathematics		Science				Mathematics		Science	
		2003	Change 1995-2003	2003	Change 1995-2003		2003	Change 1995-2003	2003	Change 1995-2003
4th Grade	**International Avg.**	**495**	**NA**	**489**	**NA**	Indonesia	411	NA	420	NA
	Australia	499	4	521	-1	Iran	411	-7	453	-9
	Cyprus	510	35	480	30	Israel*	496	NA	488	NA
	England	531	47	540	13	Italy*	484	NA	491	NA
	Hong Kong	575	18	542	35	Japan	570	-11	552	-2
	Hungary	529	7	530	22	Jordan	424	NA	475	NA
	Iran	389	2	414	34	Korea, Republic of	589	8	558	13
	Japan	565	-3	543	-10	Latvia	505	17	513	37
	Latvia	533	34	530	43	Lithuania	502	30	519	56
	Netherlands	540	-9	525	-5	Macedonia	435	NA	449	NA
	New Zealand	496	26	523	18	Malaysia	508	NA	510	NA
	Norway	451	-25	466	-38	Moldova	460	NA	472	NA
	Scotland	490	-3	502	-12	Netherlands	536	7	536	-6
	Singapore	594	4	565	42	New Zealand	494	-7	520	9
	Slovenia	479	17	490	26	Norway	461	-37	494	-21
	United States	518	0	536	-6	Philippines	378	NA	377	NA
						Romania	475	2	470	-1
8th Grade	**International Avg.**	**466**	**NA**	**473**	**NA**	Russian Federation	508	-16	514	-9
	Australia	505	-4	527	13	Scotland	498	4	512	10
	Belgium-Flemish	537	-13	516	-17	Singapore	605	-3	578	-3
	Bulgaria	476	-51	479	-66	Slovak Republic	508	-26	517	-15
	Chile	387	NA	413	NA	Slovenia	493	-2	520	7
	Chinese Taipei	585	NA	571	NA	South Africa	264	NA	244	NA
	Cyprus	459	-8	441	-11	Sweden	499	-41	524	-28
	Hong Kong	586	17	556	46	Tunisia	410	NA	404	NA
	Hungary	529	3	543	6	United States	504	12	527	15

* Because of changes in the population tested, 1995 data for Israel and Italy are not shown.

Mathematics, Reading, and Science Achievement of U.S. Students

Source: National Assessment of Educational Progress, National Center for Education Statistics, U.S. Dept. of Education

Percent of public school students who scored at or above basic level in national tests.*

	GRADE 4				GRADE 8					
	Math		Reading		Math		Reading		Science	
State	2000	2005	1998	2005	2000	2005	1998	2005	2000	2005
AL	55	66	56	53	52	53	67	63	53	48
AK	NA	77	NA	58	NA	69	NA	70	NA	NA
AZ	57	70	51	52	62	64	72	65	55	49
AR	55	78	54	63	52	64	68	69	53	56
CA	50	71	48	50	52	57	63	60	38	44
CO	NA	81	69	69	NA	70	77	75	NA	66
CT	76	84	76	71	72	70	81	74	64	63
DE	NA	84	53	73	NA	72	64	80	NA	63
DC	24	45	27	33	23	31	44	45	NA	NA
FL	NA	82	53	65	NA	65	67	66	NA	51
GA	57	76	54	58	55	62	68	67	52	53
HI	55	73	45	53	52	56	59	58	40	44
ID	68	86	NA	69	71	73	NA	76	71	71
IL	63	74	NA	62	68	68	NA	75	59	58
IN	77	84	NA	64	76	74	NA	73	66	62
IA	75	85	67	67	NA	75	NA	79	NA	NA
KS	76	88	70	66	77	77	81	78	NA	NA
KY	59	75	62	65	63	64	74	75	60	63
LA	57	74	44	53	48	59	63	64	44	47
ME	73	84	72	71	76	74	83	81	72	72
MD	60	79	58	65	65	66	70	69	57	54
MA	77	91	70	78	76	80	79	83	70	72
MI	71	79	62	63	70	68	NA	73	68	66
MN	76	88	69	71	80	79	78	80	72	71
MS	45	69	47	48	41	52	62	60	41	40
MO	71	79	61	67	67	68	75	76	66	66
MT	72	85	72	71	80	80	83	82	79	76
NE	65	80	NA	68	74	75	NA	80	52	48
NV	60	72	51	52	58	60	70	63	NA	NA
NH	NA	89	75	74	NA	77	NA	80	NA	76
NJ	NA	86	64	68	NA	74	NA	80	NA	65
NM	50	65	51	51	50	53	71	62	48	46
NY	66	81	62	69	68	70	76	75	NA	NA
NC	73	83	58	62	70	72	74	69	54	53
ND	73	89	NA	72	77	81	NA	83	72	77
OH	73	84	NA	69	75	74	NA	78	72	67
OK	67	79	66	60	64	63	80	72	60	57
OR	65	80	58	62	71	72	78	74	68	66
PA	NA	82	NA	69	NA	72	NA	77	NA	NA
RI	65	76	64	62	64	63	76	71	58	58
SC	59	81	53	57	55	71	66	67	48	54
SD	NA	86	NA	70	NA	80	NA	82	NA	76
TN	59	74	57	59	53	61	71	71	55	55
TX	76	87	59	64	68	72	74	69	52	53
UT	69	83	62	68	68	71	77	73	67	65
VT	73	87	NA	72	75	78	NA	79	71	76
VA	71	83	62	72	67	75	78	78	61	66
WA	NA	84	64	70	NA	75	76	75	NA	66
WV	65	75	60	61	62	60	75	67	57	57
WI	NA	84	72	67	NA	76	78	77	NA	70
WY	71	87	64	71	70	76	76	81	69	74
U.S.	**64**	**79**	**58**	**62**	**65**	**68**	**71**	**71**	**57**	**57**

NA = Not administered. * "Basic level" denotes a partial mastery of prerequisite knowledge and skills fundamental for proficient work at each grade.

Revenues[1] for Public Elementary and Secondary Schools, by State, 2004-2005

Source: National Education Association; in thousands

STATE	Total	Federal Amount	%	State Amount	%	Local and intermediate Amount	%
Alabama	$5,550,659	$631,427	11.4	$3,168,321	57.1	$1,750,911	31.5
Alaska	1,305,183*	163,525*	12.5*	829,259*	63.5*	312,399*	23.9*
Arizona	7,521,813*	582,344*	7.7*	3,854,582*	51.2*	3,084,887*	41.0*
Arkansas	3,703,559*	418,455*	11.3*	1,920,276*	51.8*	1,364,828*	36.9*
California	63,853,237	6,891,800	10.8	40,702,047	63.7	16,259,390	25.5
Colorado	6,625,435	434,443	6.6	2,855,490	43.1	3,335,502	50.3
Connecticut	7,664,500	460,000	6.0	3,008,000	39.2	4,196,500	54.8
Delaware	1,313,545*	87,679*	6.7*	842,341*	64.1*	383,525*	29.2*
District of Columbia	875,869*	129,447*	14.8*	0*	0.0*	746,422*	85.2*
Florida	22,927,896	2,465,995	10.8	9,784,197	42.7	10,677,704	46.6
Georgia	14,958,471*	1,314,698*	8.8*	6,753,646*	45.1*	6,890,127*	46.1*
Hawaii	2,137,479	175,526	8.2	1,929,936	90.3	32,017	1.5
Idaho	1,671,550*	160,050*	9.6*	1,004,000*	60.1*	507,500*	30.4*
Illinois	18,588,349	1,440,850	7.8	5,640,346	30.3	11,507,153	61.9
Indiana	10,184,727*	687,708*	6.8*	5,125,130*	50.3*	4,371,889*	42.9*
Iowa	4,339,853	318,811	7.3	2,005,990	46.2	2,015,052	46.4
Kansas	4,358,900	351,592	8.1	2,300,000	52.8	1,707,308	39.2
Kentucky	5,356,238	638,470	11.9	3,126,048	58.4	1,591,720	29.7
Louisiana	5,980,918	809,520	13.5	2,909,554	48.6	2,261,844	37.8
Maine	2,225,908	210,351	9.5	930,786	41.8	1,084,771	48.7
Maryland	9,487,269*	686,600*	7.2*	3,537,308*	37.3*	5,263,361*	55.5*
Massachusetts	12,804,417	846,351	6.6	4,923,947	38.5	7,034,119	54.9
Michigan	17,371,493*	985,343*	5.7*	11,619,892*	66.9*	4,766,258*	27.4*
Minnesota	8,724,560	592,019	6.8	6,067,078	69.5	2,065,463	23.7
Mississippi	3,599,875*	541,857*	15.1*	1,951,277*	54.2*	1,106,741*	30.7*
Missouri	8,312,309*	760,401*	9.1*	2,689,718*	32.4*	4,862,190*	58.5*
Montana	1,291,163*	157,041*	12.2*	608,383*	47.1*	525,739*	40.7*
Nebraska	2,291,379	163,052	7.1	925,648	40.4	1,202,679	52.5
Nevada	3,309,193	250,161	7.6	1,045,996	31.6	2,013,036	60.8
New Hampshire	2,163,230*	130,641*	6.0*	1,132,650*	52.4*	899,939*	41.6*
New Jersey	18,972,353*	526,068*	2.8*	7,266,110*	38.3*	11,180,175*	58.9*
New Mexico	2,852,262	440,125	15.4	2,068,787	72.5	343,350	12.0
New York	39,500,000	2,600,000	6.6	17,900,000	45.3	19,000,000	48.1
North Carolina	9,892,919	1,197,719	12.1	6,276,896	63.4	2,418,304	24.4
North Dakota	854,434	121,701	14.2	305,383	35.7	427,350	50.0
Ohio	19,712,163*	1,235,889*	6.3*	9,063,054*	46.0*	9,413,220*	47.8*
Oklahoma	4,548,154*	597,564*	13.1*	2,438,842*	53.6*	1,511,748*	33.2*
Oregon	4,607,424*	506,159*	11.0*	2,483,055*	53.9*	1,618,210*	35.1*
Pennsylvania	20,024,552*	1,659,858*	8.3*	7,126,038*	35.6*	11,238,656*	56.1*
Rhode Island	1,535,220*	52,905*	3.4*	563,222*	36.7*	919,094*	59.9*
South Carolina	6,367,184	733,208	11.5	2,851,967	44.8	2,782,009	43.7
South Dakota	1,043,458*	171,396*	16.4*	358,856*	34.4*	513,206*	49.2*
Tennessee	6,442,030	767,972	11.9	2,919,001	45.3	2,755,057	42.8
Texas	35,841,377	4,159,173	11.6	13,354,756	37.3	18,327,448	51.1
Utah	3,168,699*	299,909*	9.5*	1,827,701*	57.7*	1,041,089*	32.9*
Vermont	1,241,188	99,269	8.0	1,066,196	85.9	75,723	6.1
Virginia	12,169,967*	829,408*	6.8*	5,045,794*	41.5*	6,294,765*	51.7*
Washington	9,097,103	937,612	10.3	5,603,089	61.6	2,556,402	28.1
West Virginia	2,815,286	335,472	11.9	1,669,077	59.3	810,737	28.8
Wisconsin	9,822,445*	562,055*	5.7*	5,329,555*	54.3*	3,930,835*	40.0*
Wyoming	1,008,310	96,100	9.5	518,700	51.4	393,510	39.0
50 States and DC	472,015,505	41,415,719	8.8	229,227,924	48.6	201,371,862	42.7

*Indicates NEA estimate. (1) Included as revenue receipts are all appropriations from general funds of federal, state, county, and local governments; receipts from taxes levied for school purposes; income from permanent school funds and endowments; and income from leases of school lands and miscellaneous sources (interest on bank deposits, tuition, gifts, school lunch charges, etc.).

Enrollment in U.S. Public and Private Schools*, 1899-2016

Source: National Center for Education Statistics, U.S. Dept. of Education

School year[1]	Public school[2]	Private school[2]	% Private	School year[1]	Public school[2]	Private school[2]	% Private
1899-1900	15,503	1,352	8.7	1979-80	41,651	5,000[3]	12.0
1909-10	17,814	1,558	8.7	1989-90	40,543	5,198	11.4
1919-20	21,578	1,699	7.9	1999-2000	46,857	6,018	11.4
1929-30	25,678	2,651	10.3	2004-05[4]	48,560	6,404	11.7
1939-40	25,434	2,611	10.3	2005-06[4]	48,710	6,438	11.7
1949-50	25,111	3,380	13.5	2006-07[4]	48,948	6,512	11.7
1959-60	35,182	5,675	16.1	2007-08[4]	49,091	6,536	11.7
1969-70	45,550	5,500[3]	12.1	2015-16[4]	51,220	6,888	11.9

*Private includes all nonpublic schools. (1) Fall enrollment. (2) In thousands. (3) Estimated. (4) Projected.

Enrollment in U.S. Religious and Nonsectarian Private Schools, 2003-2004

Source: U.S. Department of Education, National Center for Education Statistics, *Private School Universe Survey, 2003–2004.*

Number and percentage distribution of private school students, by school level and religious or nonsectarian orientation of school. Religious groups listed only if at least some data met reporting standards.

	Total Number	Total Percent	Elementary Number	Elementary Percent	Secondary Number	Secondary Percent	Combined Number	Combined Percent
Total.................................	5,122,772	100.0%	2,694,494	100.0%	845,083	100.0%	1,583,194	100.0%
Nonsectarian.........................	921,993	18.0	301,318	11.2	118,497	14.0	502,179	31.7
Religious orientation	4,200,778	82.0	2,393,176	88.8	726,587	86.0	1,081,016	68.3
Roman Catholic......................	2,365,220	46.2	1,658,769	61.6	609,601	72.1	96,850	6.1
Amish............................	22,287	0.4	21,408	0.8	0	0.0	880	0.1
Assembly of God	62,360	1.2	23,780	0.9	(2)	(2)	37,948	2.4
Baptist	272,556	5.3	59,191	2.2	6,553	0.8	206,811	13.1
Brethren...........................	10,898	0.2	2,599	0.1	(2)	(2)	7,855	0.5
Calvinist...........................	41,809	0.8	19,452	0.7	7,065	0.8	15,292	1.0
Christian (unspecified).................	584,415	11.4	168,385	6.2	26,898	3.2	389,132	24.6
Church of Christ......................	40,515	0.8	6,661	0.2	(2)	(2)	33,557	2.1
Church of God.......................	10,576	0.2	4,197	0.2	(2)	(2)	6,167	0.4
Church of God in Christ	1,799	(1)	1,276	(1)	0	0.0	(2)	(2)
Episcopal...........................	99,675	1.9	43,163	1.6	10,845	1.3	45,667	2.9
Friends............................	17,970	0.4	5,658	0.2	(2)	(2)	11,331	0.7
Greek Orthodox......................	4,014	0.1	3,057	0.1	(2)	(2)	(2)	(2)
Islamic	22,958	0.4	10,080	0.4	(2)	(2)	12,830	0.8
Jewish	201,901	3.9	99,699	3.7	25,744	3.0	76,458	4.8
Lutheran Church—Missouri Synod	148,824	2.9	127,136	4.7	15,579	1.8	6,109	0.4
Evangelical Lutheran Church In America ..	17,415	0.3	15,722	0.6	0	0.0	(2)	(2)
Wisconsin Evangelical Lutheran Synod....	32,477	0.6	25,710	1.0	6,513	0.8	(2)	(2)
Other Lutheran.......................	9,626	0.2	5,719	0.2	(2)	(2)	(2)	(2)
Mennonite	25,977	0.5	12,211	0.5	(2)	(2)	12,618	0.8
Methodist..........................	18,613	0.4	8,304	0.3	(2)	(2)	9,068	0.6
Pentecostal	26,039	0.5	5,905	0.2	(2)	(2)	20,093	1.3
Presbyterian........................	40,177	0.8	18,362	0.7	(2)	(2)	19,717	1.2
Seventh-Day Adventist	57,891	1.1	26,096	1.0	8,769	1.0	23,027	1.5
Other	62,984	1 2	19,481	0.7	1,649	0.2	41,854	2.6

Note: Details may not add up to totals because of rounding and/or missing data. (1) Rounds to zero. (2) Reporting standards not met.

Homeschooled Students

A total of 1,096,000 U.S. students in grades K-12 were being homeschooled in 2003, 82% of them full-time, according to the latest available statistics from the U.S. Dept. of Education.

In a 2003 U.S. Dept. of Education survey of parents who homeschool their children the reasons given as *most important* included concern over the school environment, including such factors as safety, drugs, or negative peer pressure (31.2%); desire to provide religious or moral instruction (29.8%); dissatisfaction with academic instruction in schools (16.5%); and a physical or mental health problem or other special need (13.7%). In all, 85.4% cited concern over school environment as one of their reasons, while 72.3% cited religious or moral instruction and 68.2% cited dissatisfaction with academic instruction.

Below is a breakdown of homeschooled students by categories for 1999 and 2003.

Characteristic	1999 Number	1999 Percentage distribution	1999 Home-schooling rate[1]	2003 Number	2003 Percentage distribution	2003 Home-schooling rate[1]
Total	850,000	100.0	1.7	1,096,000	100.0	2.2
Homeschooled entirely	697,000	82.0	—	898,000	82.0	—
Homeschooled and enrolled in school part time ..	153,000	18.0	—	198,000	18.0	—
Race/ethnicity[2]						
Black.................................	84,000	9.9	1.0	103,000	9.4	1.3
White.................................	640,000	75.3	2.0	843,000	77.0	2.7
Other.................................	49,000	5.8	1.9	91,000	8.3	3.0
Hispanic	77,000	9.1	1.1	59,000	5.3	0.7
Number of children in the household						
One child.............................	120,000	14.1	1.5	110,000	10.1	1.4
Two children	207,000	24.4	1.0	306,000	28.0	1.5
Three or more children	523,000	61.6	2.4	679,000	62.0	3.1
Household income						
$25,000 or less.........................	262,000	30.9	1.6	283,000	25.8	2.3
$25,001–50,000	278,000	32.7	1.8	311,000	28.4	2.4
$50,001–75,000	162,000	19.1	1.9	264,000	24.1	2.4
$75,001 or more	148,000	17.4	1.5	238,000	21.7	1.7
Parents' education						
High school diploma or less	160,000	18.9	0.9	269,000	24.5	1.7
Some college or vocational/technical	287,000	33.7	1.9	338,000	30.8	2.1
Bachelor's degree	213,000	25.1	2.6	274,000	25.0	2.8
Graduate/professional degree...............	190,000	22.3	2.3	215,000	19.6	2.5

(1) The homeschooling rate is the percentage of the total group or subgroup that is homeschooled. For example, in 2003, 0.7% of all Hispanic students K-12 were homeschooled. (2) Race categories exclude Hispanic.

Teachers' Salaries in Upper Secondary Education, Selected Countries, 2003

Source: Organization for Economic Cooperation and Development

Annual statutory teachers' salaries in public institutions in upper secondary (senior high school) education, general programs, in equivalent U.S. dollars converted using PPPs[1]; ranked by starting salaries.

	Starting salary	Salary with 15 years' experience	Salary at top of scale		Starting salary	Salary with 15 years' experience	Salary at top of scale
Luxembourg....	$64,416	$80,520	$111,910	Tunisia........	$20,320	$20,511	$22,960
Switzerland	52,572	67,355	80,706	Portugal.......	20,150	33,815	53,085
Germany	42,881	52,570	54,928	New Zealand ...	18,132	35,078	35,078
Spain	34,614	40,231	49,712	India.........	17,313	22,977	27,381
Finland........	34,374	42,139	42,139	Czech Republic .	16,817	20,259	25,988
Belgium (Fl.) ...	33,588	48,485	58,279	Brazil[2]	15,494	17,669	17,908
Belgium (Fr.) ...	32,395	47,193	56,925	Malaysia[2]......	13,480	23,029	29,151
Denmark	32,331	45,425	45,425	Jamaica.......	13,354	16,520	16,520
Netherlands ..	31,492	57,647	63,586	Hungary.......	13,286	18,463	24,185
United States ..	**30,471**	**44,120**	**52,745**	Paraguay[2]	12,400	12,400	12,400
Norway	29,719	35,541	36,806	Israel	12,331	15,128	21,054
Australia.......	28,865	42,078	42,078	Turkey	11,952	13,630	15,900
England.......	28,608	41,807	41,807	Chile..........	11,709	14,306	19,302
Scotland.......	27,223	43,363	43,363	Philippines[2]	9,890	10,916	11,756
Korea	27,092	46,518	74,843	Argentina[2]	9,459	13,264	15,929
Sweden	26,278	30,934	35,610	Poland	6,257	9,462	10,354
France	26,035	34,010	48,957	Thailand.......	6,048	14,862	28,345
Austria	25,776	35,670	54,139	Slovak Republic.	5,771	7,309	9,570
Italy	25,602	32,186	40,058	Peru[2]	5,606	5,606	5,606
Ireland	25,295	40,514	45,910	Uruguay[2]	5,278	6,241	7,444
Japan.........	24,514	45,543	59,055	Sri Lanka	3,945	5,073	5,073
Iceland........	24,159	29,641	31,433	Indonesia......	1,042	1,910	3,022
Greece........	22,990	28,006	33,859				

NA = Not available. (1) Purchasing power parities (PPPs) are the rates of currency conversion that equalize the purchasing power of different currencies by eliminating the differences in price levels between countries. (2) Year of reference 2002.

Percent of Population with Upper Secondary Education, Selected Countries, 2003

Source: Organization for Economic Cooperation and Development

Percentage of the population ages 25-64 that have received at least some upper secondary (senior high school) education

Russian Federation .88%	Israel.............82%	United Kingdom....65%	Poland 48%	Uruguay[1].........33%
United States 88	Denmark 81	France...........65	Peru[1] 46	Brazil[1]............30
Norway 87	Austria 79	Australia 62	Italy[1]............44	Turkey 26
Slovak Republic....87	New Zealand 78	Belgium..........62	Spain 43	Indonesia.........24
Czech Republic ..86	Finland 76	Ireland 62	Malaysia[1] 42	Portugal 23
Japan...........84	Hungary 74	Luxembourg 59	Argentina[1] 42	Mexico...........21
Canada 84	Korea 73	Iceland[1] 59	Jordan 39	Paraguay[1] 21
Germany 83	Switzerland 70	Greece...........51	Philippines 36	Thailand 21
Sweden 82	Netherlands[1]......66	Chile............49		

(1) Year of reference 2002.

Charges at U.S. Institutions of Higher Education, 1969-70 to 2004-2005

Source: National Center for Education Statistics, U.S. Dept. of Education

Figures for 1969-70 are average charges for full-time resident degree-credit students; figures for later years are average charges per full-time equivalent student. Room and board are based on full-time students. These figures are enrollment-weighted, according to the number of full-time-equivalent undergraduates, and thus may vary from averages given elsewhere.

	TUITION AND FEES			BOARD RATES			DORMITORY CHARGES		
	All institutions	2-yr	4-yr	All institutions	2-yr	4-yr	All institutions	2-yr	4-yr
PUBLIC (in-state)									
1969-70	$323	$178	$427	$511	$465	$540	$369	$308	$395
1979-80	583	355	840	867	894	898	715	572	749
1989-90	1,356	756	2,035	1,635	1,581	1,728	1,513	962	1,561
1990-91	1,454	824	2,159	1,691	1,594	1,767	1,612	1,050	1,658
1995-96	2,179	1,239	2,848	2,020	1,681	2,045	2,057	1,297	2,121
1996-97	2,271	1,276	2,987	2,111	1,789	2,133	2,148	1,339	2,214
1997-98	2,360	1,314	3,110	2,228	1,795	2,263	2,225	1,401	2,301
1998-99	2,430	1,327	3,229	2,347	1,828	2,389	2,330	1,450	2,409
1999-2000	2,506	1,338	3,349	2,364	1,834	2,406	2,440	1,549	2,519
2000-2001	2,562	1,333	3,501	2,455	1,906	2,499	2,569	1,600	2,654
2001-2002	2,700	1,380	3,735	2,598	2,036	2,645	2,723	1,722	2,816
2002-2003	2,903	1,483	4,046	2,669	2,164	2,712	2,930	1,954	3,029
2003-2004	3,319	1,702	4,587	2,823	2,233	2,875	3,107	2,086	3,212
2004-2005[1]	3,638	1,847	5,038	2,935	2,333	2,985	3,304	2,154	3,418
PRIVATE									
1969-70	1,533	1,034	1,809	561	546	608	436	413	503
1979-80	3,130	2,062	3,811	955	924	1,078	827	769	999
1989-90	8,147	5,196	10,348	1,948	1,811	2,339	1,923	1,663	2,411
1990-91	8,772	5,570	11,379	2,074	1,989	2,470	2,063	1,744	2,654
1995-96	11,864	7,094	12,243	2,606	2,098	2,617	2,738	2,371	2,751
1996-97	12,498	7,236	12,881	2,663	2,181	2,672	2,878	2,537	2,889
1997-98	12,801	7,464	13,344	2,762	2,785	2,761	2,954	2,672	2,964
1998-99	13,428	7,854	13,973	2,865	2,884	2,865	3,075	2,581	3,091
1999-2000	14,081	8,235	14,588	2,882	2,922	2,881	3,224	2,808	3,237
2000-2001	15,000	9,067	15,470	2,993	3,000	2,993	3,374	2,722	3,392
2001-2002	15,742	10,076	16,211	3,104	2,633	3,109	3,567	3,116	3,576
2002-2003	16,383	10,651	16,826	3,206	3,870	3,197	3,752	3,232	3,764
2003-2004	17,327	11,546	17,777	3,364	4,432	3,354	3,945	3,581	3,952
2004-2005[1]	18,374	12,182	18,838	3,486	3,556	3,485	4,165	4,162	4,166

(1) Preliminary.

Top 20 Colleges and Universities in Endowment Assets, 2005[1]

Source: *2005 NACUBO Endowment Study*, National Association of College and University Business Officers (NACUBO)

College/University	Endowment assets[2]	College/University	Endowment assets[2]
1. Harvard University	$25,473,721	11. Emory University	$4,376,272
2. Yale University	15,224,900	12. University of Pennsylvania	4,369,782
3. Stanford University	12,205,000	13. Washington University	4,268,415
4. University of Texas System	11,610,997	14. Northwestern University	4,215,275
5. Princeton University	11,206,500	15. University of Chicago	4,137,494
6. Massachusetts Institute of Technology	6,712,436	16. Duke University	3,826,153
7. University of California	5,221,916	17. Cornell University	3,777,092
8. Columbia University	5,190,564	18. University of Notre Dame	3,650,224
9. The Texas A&M University System and Foundations	4,963,879	19. Rice University	3,611,127
10. University of Michigan	4,931,338	20. University of Virginia	3,219,098

NOTE: Market value of endowment assets, excluding pledges and working capital. (1) As of June 2005. (2) In thousands.

U.S. Higher Education Trends: Bachelor's Degrees Conferred

Source: National Center for Education Statistics, U.S. Dept. of Education
Figures for 2006-2007 and 2013-2014 are projected.

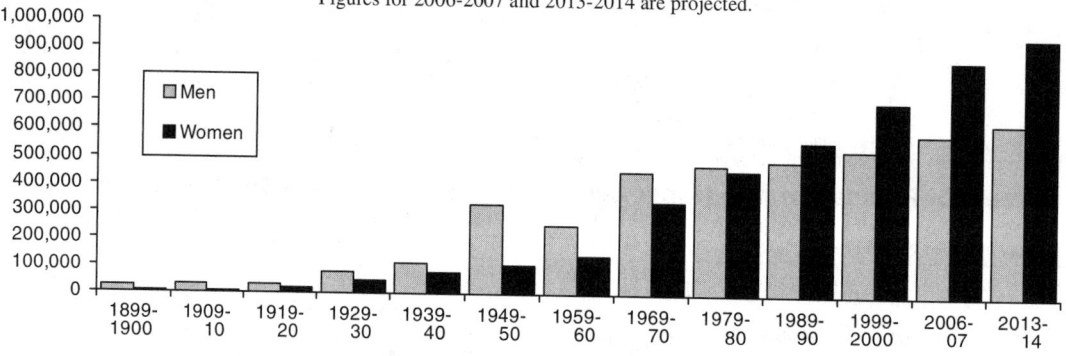

Financial Aid for College and Other Postsecondary Education

As of July 2006. Reviewed by National Assoc. of Student Financial Aid Administrators

The cost of postsecondary education in the U.S. has increased in recent years, but financial aid, which may be in the form of **grants** (no repayment needed), **loans**, and/or **work-study** programs, is widely available to help families meet these expenses. Most aid is limited to family financial need as determined by standard formulas. Students interested in receiving aid are advised to apply, without making prior assumptions. Financial aid personnel at each school can provide information about programs available to students, steps to apply for them, and deadlines, all of which may vary.

All applicants for federal aid must file a Free Application for Federal Student Aid (**FAFSA**), generally as soon as possible after Jan. 1 for the academic year starting the following September. Figures provided should agree with federal income tax forms filed for the previous year. Other possible sources of aid include state governments, employers and unions, civic organizations, and the institutions themselves. There are also special federal programs that pay for postsecondary education in return for service: AmeriCorps (phone: 1-800-942-2677) and ROTC (phone: 1-800-USA-ROTC). Additional forms and certain fees may be required if a student is to be considered for institutional aid. Aid must be reapplied for annually.

A **federal formula**, based on information provided on the FAFSA, takes into account such factors as family income in the preceding calendar year, parental and student assets (excluding the parents' home or farm), length of time to parents' retirement, and unusual expenses (such as very high medical expenses).

The resulting **Expected Family Contribution**, or EFC (which is divided among the family members—excluding parents—in college), is subtracted from the total cost of attendance for each person (including tuition and fee charges, room and board or allowance for living costs, books and supplies, transportation to and from school, and other miscellaneous costs) to determine financial need, and thus the maximum federal aid for which the family may be eligible. (Some institutions use a separate formula for need-based institutional aid.) Some schools guarantee to meet the full financial need of each admitted student; however, most others try to do so but may fall short, depending on the availability of funds. Outside scholarships (even if non-need-based) are taken into account in determining the amount of aid eligibility for federal, institutional, and state financial aid programs.

The **aid package** offered by each school may include one or more of the following resources: Federal Pell Grants, for those with greatest financial need; Federal Supplemental Educational Opportunity Grants, for those with great financial need who are also eligible for Pell Grants; grants from the school; Federal Work-Study or other work programs; low-interest Perkins loans; and subsidized and unsubsidized Stafford loans. Parents of undergraduates may also apply for a Federal PLUS loan. For unsubsidized Stafford loans and all PLUS loans to parents, need is not a requirement, but students and parents must still complete the FAFSA before eligibility for unsubsidized Stafford loans is determined.

Loans have varying interest rates and other requirements. Repayment of Perkins and Stafford loans does not begin until after graduation; deferments are available under certain circumstances. For PLUS loans, parents must pass a credit check and begin repayment of both principal and interest while the student is still in school.

Certain federal income **tax credits**—dollar for dollar reductions of the amount of tax due—are available to families who meet income and other requirements; see the chapter on Taxes.

Rules for financial aid are complex and changeable. *The Student Guide*, a comprehensive resource on financial aid from the U.S. Dept. of Education, can be found at the website www.studentaid.ed.gov/students/publications/student_guide/index.html

Further information and FAFSA forms are available from the school or from the Federal Student Aid Information Center, PO Box 84, Washington, DC 20044; phone: 1-800-4-FED-AID, Mon.-Fri., 8 AM - 12 midnight Eastern Time. The Information Center also has a free booklet called *The EFC Formula Book*. FAFSA forms can be obtained online at www.fafsa.ed.gov

Average Salaries of U.S. College Professors, 2005-2006

Source: American Association of University Professors. NA = Not available.

	MEN Type of institution			WOMEN Type of institution		
TEACHING LEVEL	Public	Private/ Independent	Church-related	Public	Private/ Independent	Church-related
Doctoral level.....Professor	103,441	133,483	116,281	93,980	121,929	104,945
Associate	72,839	86,652	79,515	67,652	80,288	73,992
Assistant.........	62,713	74,812	67,202	57,506	67,885	63,135
Master's level.....Professor	79,801	90,346	79,926	76,601	84,564	74,294
Associate	63,772	68,675	63,627	61,189	64,963	60,256
Assistant.........	54,006	56,135	52,718	51,671	53,833	50,211
General 4-year ....Professor	74,780	88,948	67,521	70,366	84,999	64,064
Associate	60,804	65,126	54,602	58,592	64,482	56,520
Assistant.........	50,711	53,930	46,324	48,281	52,224	45,440
2-year ....Professor	67,645	79,293	NA	64,177	70,039	NA
Associate	54,456	59,353	NA	52,346	52,807	NA
Assistant.........	47,750	47,371	NA	46,541	45,875	NA

ACT (formerly American College Testing) Mean Scores and Characteristics of College-Bound Students, 1990-2006

Source: ACT, Inc.

(for school year ending in year shown)

SCORES[1]	Unit[1]	1990	1995	2000	2001	2002	2003	2004	2005	2006
Composite Scores..	Points	20.6	20.8	21.0	21.0	20.8	20.8	20.9	20.9	21.1
Male	Points	21.0	21.0	21.2	21.1	20.9	21.0	21.0	21.1	21.2
Female	Points	20.3	20.7	20.9	20.9	20.7	20.8	20.9	20.9	21.0
English Score	Points	20.5	20.2	20.5	20.5	20.2	20.3	20.4	20.4	20.6
Male	Points	20.1	19.8	20.0	20.0	19.7	19.8	19.9	20.0	20.1
Female	Points	20.9	20.6	20.9	20.8	20.6	20.7	20.8	20.8	21.0
Math Score	Points	19.9	20.2	20.7	20.7	20.6	20.6	20.7	20.7	20.8
Male	Points	20.7	20.9	21.4	21.4	21.2	21.2	21.3	21.3	21.5
Female	Points	19.3	19.7	20.2	20.2	20.1	20.1	20.2	20.2	20.3
PARTICIPANTS										
Total Number	(1000s)	817	945	1,065	1,070	1,116	1,175	1,171	1,186	1,206
Male	Percent	46	44	43	43	44	44	43	44	44
White	Percent	79	80	72	71	69	68	67	66	63
Black...........	Percent	9	9	10	11	11	11	11	12	12
Hispanic	Percent	4	5	5	6	6	6	7	7	7
Composite Scores										
27 or above.......	Percent	12	13	14	14	13	14	14	14	14
18 or below.......	Percent	35	34	32	33	35	35	34	34	33

(1) Minimum point score, 1; maximum score, 36. Test scores and characteristics of college-bound students are based on the performance of all ACT-tested students who graduated in the spring of a given school year and took the ACT Assessment during junior or senior year of high school.

ACT Average Composite Scores by State, 2005-2006

Source: ACT, Inc.

STATE	Avg. Comp. Score	% Grads Taking ACT[1]	STATE	Avg. Comp. Score	% Grads Taking ACT[1]	STATE	Avg. Comp. Score	% Grads Taking ACT[1]
Alabama	20.2	79	Kentucky	20.6	76	Ohio	21.5	66
Alaska	21.1	25	Louisiana	20.1	74	Oklahoma........	20.5	72
Arizona	21.6	18	Maine...........	22.3	10	Oregon..........	22.4	13
Arkansas	20.6	75	Maryland	21.4	12	Pennsylvania	21.8	9
California	21.6	14	Masschusetts.....	23	13	Rhode Island	21.2	8
Colorado	20.3	100	Michigan	21.5	67	South Carolina	19.5	39
Connecticut	23.1	12	Minnesota	22.3	67	South Dakota	21.8	75
Delaware	21.4	5	Mississippi	18.8	93	Tennessee.......	20.7	93
District of Columbia......	18.4	30	Missouri	21.6	70	Texas...........	20.3	29
Florida	20.3	45	Montana.........	21.9	57	Utah	21.7	69
Georgia	20.2	30	Nebraska	21.9	76	Vermont.........	22.5	19
Hawaii	21.9	17	Nevada	21.5	27	Virginia	21.1	15
Idaho	21.4	57	New Hampshire ...	22.6	12	Washington	22.9	15
Illinois..........	20.5	100	New Jersey	21.8	8	West Virginia	20.6	64
Indiana..........	21.7	20	New Mexico......	20.1	60	Wisconsin........	22.2	68
Iowa............	22.1	65	New York	22.6	17	Wyoming	21.6	71
Kansas	21.8	75	North Carolina	20.5	14	U.S. AVG.	21.1	40
			North Dakota	21.4	80			

(1) Based on number of high school graduates in 2006, as projected by the Western Interstate Commission for Higher Education, and number of students in the class of 2006 who took the ACT.

The New SAT

The College Board administered a brand-new SAT in March 2005, to the graduating high school class of 2006. The new SAT, the first revision to the test since 1995, adds a new writing section in which test takers are asked to write an essay in 25 minutes, and changes other aspects of the two traditional sections: the critical reading section (formerly the verbal section) places more emphasis on reading comprehension, and the math section includes more concepts learned in Algebra II and Geometry. Each section is still scored on an 800 point scale, making a perfect score 2400. The new test has a time limit of three hours and 45 minutes, up from three hours for the old test.

Results for the graduating high school class of 2006 showed the sharpest drop in SAT scores in 31 years: composite reading and math scores fell by about 7 points. At the same time, the ACT reported its largest composite score increase on its competing test in 20 years. Some critics have charged that the drop in SAT scores may be attributed to the increased length, which leaves many test-takers feeling more tired. However, a College Board study of some 700,000 tests found no evidence to support this claim; College Board officials suggest that the drop may be due to a decrease in repeat test-taking.

SAT Mean Verbal and Math Scores of College-Bound Seniors, 1975-2006

Source: The College Board

(recentered scale; for school year ending in year shown)

	1975	1980	1985	1990	1995	1998	1999	2000	2001	2002	2003	2004	2005	2006
Critical Reading Scores	512	502	509	500	504	505	505	505	506	504	507	508	508	503
Male	515	506	514	505	505	509	509	507	509	507	512	512	513	505
Female	509	498	503	496	502	502	502	504	502	502	503	504	505	502
Math Scores	498	492	500	501	506	512	511	514	514	516	519	518	520	518
Male	518	515	522	521	525	531	531	533	533	534	537	537	538	536
Female	479	473	480	483	490	496	495	498	498	500	503	501	504	502
Writing Scores														
Male														497
Female														491
														502

NOTE: In 1995, the College Board recentered the scoring scale for the SAT by reestablishing the original mean score of 500 on the 200-800 scale. Earlier scores have been adjusted to account for this recentering. The Writing test was first given in March 2005, however, only the scores of the first graduating class to take them are given.

SAT Mean Scores by State, 1990, 2000, and 2003-2006

Source: The College Board

(recentered scale; for school year ending in year shown)

STATE	1990 V	1990 M	2000 V	2000 M	2003 V	2003 M	2004 V	2004 M	2005 V	2005 M	2006[1] CR	2006[1] M	2006[1] W	% Grads Taking SAT[2]
Alabama	545	534	559	555	559	552	560	553	567	559	565	561	565	9%
Alaska	514	501	519	515	518	518	518	514	523	519	517	517	493	51
Arizona	521	520	521	523	524	525	523	524	526	530	521	528	507	32
Arkansas	545	532	563	554	564	554	569	555	563	552	574	568	567	5
California	494	508	497	518	499	519	501	519	504	522	501	518	501	49
Colorado	533	534	534	537	551	553	554	553	560	560	558	564	548	26
Connecticut	506	496	508	509	512	514	515	515	517	517	512	516	511	84
Delaware	510	496	502	496	501	501	500	499	503	502	495	500	484	73
District of Columbia	483	467	494	486	484	474	489	476	490	478	487	472	482	78
Florida	495	493	498	500	498	498	499	499	498	498	496	497	480	65
Georgia	478	473	488	486	493	491	494	493	497	496	494	496	487	70
Hawaii	480	505	488	519	486	516	487	514	490	516	482	509	472	60
Idaho	542	524	540	541	540	540	540	539	544	542	543	545	525	19
Illinois	542	547	568	586	583	596	585	597	594	606	591	609	586	9
Indiana	486	486	498	501	500	504	501	506	504	508	498	509	486	62
Iowa	584	588	589	600	586	597	593	602	596	608	602	613	591	4
Kansas	566	563	574	580	578	582	584	585	585	588	582	590	566	8
Kentucky	548	541	548	550	554	552	559	557	561	559	562	562	555	11
Louisiana	551	537	562	558	563	559	564	561	565	562	570	571	571	6
Maine	501	490	504	500	503	501	505	501	509	505	501	501	491	73
Maryland	506	502	507	509	509	515	511	515	511	515	503	509	499	70
Massachusetts	503	498	511	513	516	522	518	523	520	527	513	524	510	85
Michigan	529	534	557	569	564	576	563	573	568	579	568	583	555	10
Minnesota	552	558	581	594	582	591	587	593	592	597	591	600	574	10
Mississippi	552	538	562	549	565	551	562	547	564	554	556	541	562	4
Missouri	548	541	572	577	582	583	587	585	588	588	587	591	582	7
Montana	540	542	543	546	538	543	537	539	540	540	538	545	524	28
Nebraska	559	562	560	571	573	578	569	576	574	579	576	583	566	7
Nevada	511	511	510	517	510	517	507	514	508	513	498	508	481	40
New Hampshire	518	510	520	519	522	521	522	521	525	525	520	524	509	82
New Jersey	495	498	498	513	501	515	501	514	503	517	496	515	496	82
New Mexico	554	546	549	543	548	540	554	543	558	547	557	549	543	13
New York	489	496	494	506	496	510	497	510	497	511	493	510	483	88
North Carolina	478	470	492	496	495	506	499	507	499	511	495	513	485	71
North Dakota	579	578	588	609	602	613	582	601	590	605	610	617	588	4
Ohio	526	522	533	539	536	541	538	542	539	543	535	544	521	28
Oklahoma	553	542	563	560	569	562	569	566	570	563	576	574	563	7
Oregon	515	509	527	527	526	527	527	528	526	528	523	529	503	55
Pennsylvania	497	490	498	497	500	502	501	502	501	503	493	500	483	74
Rhode Island	498	488	505	500	502	504	503	502	503	505	495	502	490	69
South Carolina	475	467	484	482	493	496	491	495	494	499	487	498	480	62
South Dakota	580	570	587	588	588	588	594	597	589	589	590	604	578	4
Tennessee	558	544	563	553	568	560	567	557	572	563	573	569	572	15
Texas	490	489	493	500	500	491	493	499	493	502	491	506	487	52
Utah	566	555	570	569	566	559	565	556	566	557	560	557	550	7
Vermont	507	493	513	508	515	512	516	512	521	517	513	519	502	67
Virginia	501	496	509	500	514	510	515	509	516	514	512	513	500	73
Washington	513	511	526	528	530	532	528	531	532	534	527	532	511	54

STATE	1990 V	M	2000 V	M	2003 V	M	2004 V	M	2005 V	M	2006[1] CR	M	W	% Grads Taking SAT[2]
West Virginia	520	514	526	511	522	510	524	514	523	511	519	510	515	20%
Wisconsin	552	559	584	597	585	594	587	596	592	599	588	600	577	6
Wyoming	534	538	545	545	548	549	551	546	544	543	548	555	537	10
NATIONAL AVG.	**500**	**501**	**505**	**514**	**507**	**519**	**508**	**518**	**508**	**520**	**503**	**518**	**497**	**48**

NOTE: In 1995, the College Board recentered the scoring scale for the SAT by reestablishing the original mean score of 500 on the 200-800 scale. The College Board states that comparing states or ranking them on the basis of SAT scores alone is invalid, and the College Board discourages doing so. (1) In 2005, the SAT was changed. The Verbal portion became Critical Reading, and a new Writing test was added. The 2006 graduating class was the first to take the new test. (2) Based on number of high school graduates in 2006, as projected by the Western Interstate Commission for Higher Education, and number of students in the class of 2006 who took the SAT.

Top 100 Libraries in U.S. by Volumes Held, 2003

Source: American Library Association, *ALA Library Fact Sheet 22*, August 2005

	Institution	Volumes Held*		Institution	Volumes Held*
1.	Library of Congress	29,550,914	51.	University of Southern California	3,800,702
2.	Harvard University	15,181,349	52.	Washington University - St. Louis	3,608,538
3.	Boston Public Library	14,933,349	53.	Johns Hopkins University	3,572,375
4.	Yale University	11,114,308	54.	Buffalo & Erie County Public Library	3,539,038
5.	Chicago Public Library	10,745,608	55.	Cuyahoga County Public Library	3,465,469
6.	University of Illinois - Urbana-Champaign	10,015,321	56.	University of South Carolina	3,374,496
7.	Public Library of Cincinnati & Hamilton County	9,885,359	57.	Brigham Young University	3,373,793
8.	Queens Borough Public Library	9,691,126	58.	University of California - Davis	3,365,689
9.	University of California - Berkeley	9,572,462	59.	St. Louis Public Library	3,360,942
10.	County of Los Angeles Public Library	9,185,321	60.	State University of New York - Buffalo	3,330,476
11.	University of Texas - Austin	8,322,944	61.	Wayne State University	3,323,580
12.	Stanford University	8,000,000	62.	University of Colorado	3,314,432
13.	University of Michigan	7,800,389	63.	University of Hawaii	3,294,184
14.	Columbia University	7,697,488	64.	Hawaii State Public Library System	3,281,117
15.	University of California - Los Angeles	7,576,790	65.	Brown University	3,257,242
16.	Detroit Public Library	7,265,306	66.	North Carolina State University	3,236,096
17.	University of Wisconsin - Madison	7,232,850	67.	Louisiana State University	3,213,314
18.	Cornell University	7,120,301	68.	University of Rochester	3,185,231
19.	University of Chicago	6,977,186	69.	San Diego Public Library	3,169,565
20.	New York Public Library	6,777,587	70.	University of Connecticut	3,168,617
21.	Indiana University	6,647,355	71.	University of Missouri - Columbia	3,149,211
22.	University of Washington	6,436,960	72.	University of Massachusetts	3,132,418
23.	Free Library of Philadelphia	6,388,077	73.	University of Utah	3,128,547
24.	Princeton University	6,224,270	74.	Mid-Continent Public Library	3,120,544
25.	University of Minnesota	6,200,669	75.	University of Notre Dame	3,054,075
26.	Dallas Public Library	5,916,549	76.	University of Kentucky	3,053,726
27.	Brooklyn Public Library	5,845,212	77.	University of Maryland	3,016,940
28.	Ohio State University	5,674,784	78.	Texas A&M University Libraries	3,016,358
29.	Los Angeles Public Library	5,554,904	79.	Milwaukee Public Library	2,989,081
30.	University of North Carolina - Chapel Hill	5,492,451	80.	University of Cincinnati Libraries	2,977,475
31.	Duke University	5,360,303	81.	Montgomery County Dept. of Public Libraries	2,959,184
32.	University of Pennsylvania	5,273,887	82.	Columbus Metropolitan Library	2,955,569
33.	University of Arizona	5,040,584	83.	University of California - San Diego	2,953,024
34.	University of Virginia	4,921,442	84.	Enoch Pratt Free Library	2,906,821
35.	Pennsylvania State University Libraries	4,779,165	85.	Temple University	2,900,832
36.	Michigan State University	4,582,004	86.	Syracuse University	2,900,448
37.	University of Oklahoma	4,427,670	87.	Vanderbilt University	2,882,057
38.	University of Pittsburgh	4,420,970	88.	University of Tennessee - Knoxville	2,880,949
39.	University of Iowa	4,380,734	89.	Broward County Libraries Division	2,825,077
40.	Houston Public Library	4,339,128	90.	Orange County Public Library	2,794,942
41.	Northwestern University Library	4,315,314	91.	Southern Illinois University - Carbondale	2,791,775
42.	King County Library System	4,213,810	92.	St. Louis County Library District	2,781,301
43.	New York University	4,176,065	93.	University of Nebraska - Lincoln	2,767,320
44.	Rutgers University	4,050,009	94.	University of California - Santa Barbara	2,765,756
45.	University of Florida	4,021,629	95.	Emory University	2,755,929
46.	Cleveland Public Library	3,999,771	96.	Auburn University	2,724,011
47.	Miami-Dade Public Library System	3,998,192	97.	Fairfax County Public Library	2,712,212
48.	University of Kansas	3,980,589	98.	Massachusetts Institute of Technology	2,707,849
49.	University of Georgia	3,955,004	99.	Toledo-Lucas County Public Library	2,689,922
50.	Arizona State University Libraries	3,856,561	100.	Kent State University Libraries	2,634,374

*Figures for public libraries include holdings by branches and include circulating books only.

Number of Public Libraries and Operating Income, by State, FY 2004

Source: Public Libraries Survey, National Center for Education Statistics, U.S. Dept. of Education

STATE	No.[1]	Income[2] (thous.)	STATE	No.[1]	Income[2] (thous.)	STATE	No.[1]	Income[2] (thous.)	STATE	No.[1]	Income[2] (thous.)
AL	284	$77,114	IL	789	$603,712	MT	108	$17,985	RI	72	$42,878
AK	105	25,198	IN	438	257,252	NE	292	41,146	SC	183	88,942
AZ	187	134,368	IA	564	81,006	NV	84	72,015	SD	144	17,170
AR	211	46,967	KS	374	91,025	NH	238	42,595	TN	286	93,020
CA	1,087	1,016,281	KY	190	102,947	NJ	454	378,385	TX	847	356,157
CO	241	193,005	LA	335	125,506	NM	120	36,724	UT	113	68,538
CT	244	157,124	ME	276	31,711	NY	1,081	970,962	VT	191	15,083
DE	33	20,752	MD	179	204,474	NC	381	163,353	VA	341	216,024
DC	27	28,952	MA	485	213,265	ND	91	9,937	WA	330	271,414
FL	498	474,698	MI	658	362,953	OH	717	650,503	WV	174	28,008
GA	369	165,056	MN	355	162,585	OK	206	70,931	WI	456	185,208
HI	51	26,430	MS	241	39,956	OR	210	133,658	WY	74	19,633
ID	143	31,407	MO	360	175,444	PA	632	290,127	U.S. Total	16,549	9,129,588

(1) Includes central libraries and branches. (2) Some totals may be underestimated because of nonresponse.

Four-Year Colleges and Universities

General Information for the 2005-2006 Academic Year

Source: © Thomson Peterson's, a part of The Thomson Corporation. All Rights Reserved.

Note: These listings **include only accredited degree-granting institutions** in the U.S. and the U.S. territories **with a total enrollment of 1,000 or more.** Only **four-year** colleges and universities (which award a bachelor's degree as their highest undergraduate degree) are included. Data reported **only for institutions that provided updated information** on Peterson's Annual Survey of Undergraduate Institutions for the 2005-2006 academic year.

All institutions are coeducational except those where the ZIP code is followed directly by a number in parentheses. (1) = men only, (2) = primarily men, (3) = women only, (4) = primarily women.

The **Tuition & Fees** column shows the annual tuition and required fees for full-time students, or, where indicated, the tuition and standard fees per unit for part-time students. Where tuition varies according to residence, the figure is given for the most local resident and is coded: (A) = area residents, (S) = state residents; all other figures apply to all students regardless of residence. Where annual expenses are expressed as a lump sum (including full-time tuition, mandatory fees, and room and board), the figure is entered under Tuition & Fees and coded: (C) = comprehensive fee. **Rm. & Board** is the average cost for one academic year. * indicates fee only.

Control: 1 = independent (nonprofit), 2 = independent-religious, 3 = proprietary (profit-making), 4 = federal, 5 = state, 6 = commonwealth (Puerto Rico), 7 = territory (U.S. territories), 8 = county, 9 = district, 10 = city, 11 = state and local, 12 = state-related, 13 = private (unspecified). **Degree** means the highest degree offered (B = bachelor's, M = master's, F = first professional, D = doctorate).

Enrollment is the total number of matriculated undergraduate and (if applicable) graduate students.

Faculty is the total number of faculty members teaching undergraduate courses and (if available) graduate courses.

NA or a **dash** indicates category is inapplicable or data not available.

Name, address	Year Founded	Tuition & Fees	Rm. & Board	Control, Degree	Enroll-ment	Faculty
Abilene Christian Univ, Abilene, TX 79699-9100	1906	$15,160	$5,670	2-D	4,685	359
Acad of Art Univ, San Francisco, CA 94105-3410	1929	$14,480	$12,000	3-M	8,270	675
Adams State Coll, Alamosa, CO 81102	1921	$2,854 (S)	$5,760	5-M	5,578	185
Adelphi Univ, Garden City, NY 11530-0701	1896	$19,720	$9,190	1-D	7,898	857
Adrian Coll, Adrian, MI 49221-2575	1859	$18,630	$6,270	2-B	1,013	104
Agnes Scott Coll, Decatur, GA 30030-3797	1889	$23,570	$8,500	2-M	1,016	110
Alabama Agr & Mech Univ, Huntsville, AL 35811	1875	$4,940 (S)	NA	5-D	6,323	384
Alabama State Univ, Montgomery, AL 36101-0271	1867	$4,008 (S)	$3,700	5-D	5,469	414
Albany Coll of Pharmacy of Union Univ, Albany, NY 12208-3425	1881	$18,770	$6,100	1-F	1,138	69
Albany State Univ, Albany, GA 31705-2717	1903	$2,896 (S)	$3,690	5-M	3,668	211
Albertus Magnus Coll, New Haven, CT 06511-1189	1925	$17,310	$7,550	2-M	2,230	167
Albion Coll, Albion, MI 49224-1831	1835	$24,296	$6,928	2-B	1,979	175
Albright Coll, Reading, PA 19612-5234	1856	$26,032	$7,888	2-M	2,180	155
Alcorn State Univ, Alcorn State, MS 39096-7500	1871	$4,726 (S)	$4,272	5-M	3,544	209
Alfred Univ, Alfred, NY 14802-1205	1836	$20,960	$9,746	1-D	2,235	205
Allegheny Coll, Meadville, PA 16335	1815	$28,300	$7,000	1-B	2,053	163
Alliant Intl Univ, San Diego, CA 92131-1799	1952	$14,370	$7,800	1-D	3,487	288
Alma Coll, Alma, MI 48801-1599	1886	$21,134	$7,410	2-B	1,284	119
Alvernia Coll, Reading, PA 19607-1799	1958	$19,089	$7,299	2-M	2,735	235
Alverno Coll, Milwaukee, WI 53234-3922	1887	$15,418	$6,210	2-M	2,372	225
Amberton Univ, Garland, TX 75041-5595	1971	$6,000	NA	2-M	1,648	39
American Coll of Computer & Information Sci, Birmingham, AL 35205 (2)	1988	$155/cr. hr.	NA	3-M	13,000	34
American InterContinental Univ, Los Angeles, CA 90066	1982	$16,190	$5,500	3-M	1,405	133
American InterContinental Univ, Weston, FL 33326	NA	$58,050	NA	3-M	1,318	79
American InterContinental Univ, Atlanta, GA 30326-1016	1977	$16,386	$5,400	3-M	1,732	111
American InterContinental Univ, Atlanta, GA 30328	1970	$17,945	NA	3-M	1,150	119
American Intl Coll, Springfield, MA 01109-3189	1885	$20,990	$9,270	1-D	1,815	159
American Public Univ System, Charles Town, WV 25414	1991	$6,000	NA	3-M	13,477	362
American Univ, Washington, DC 20016-8001	1893	$29,701	$11,342	2-D	11,279	941
American Univ of Puerto Rico, Bayamón, PR 00960-2037	1963	$4,590	NA	1-B	3,691	221
Amherst Coll, Amherst, MA 01002-5000	1821	$33,005	$8,585	1-B	1,623	218
Anderson Univ, Anderson, IN 46012-3495	1917	$19,990	$6,460	2-D	2,811	254
Anderson Univ, Anderson, SC 29621-4035	1911	$16,550	$6,400	2-M	1,644	150
Andrews Univ, Berrien Springs, MI 49104	1874	$16,506	$5,280	2-D	3,087	268
Angelo State Univ, San Angelo, TX 76909	1928	$4,290 (S)	$5,314	5-M	6,156	350
Anna Maria Coll, Paxton, MA 01612	1946	$21,880	$7,935	2-M	1,042	170
Appalachian State Univ, Boone, NC 28608	1899	$3,918 (S)	$4,960	5-D	14,653	998
Aquinas Coll, Grand Rapids, MI 49506-1799	1886	$17,926	$5,824	2-M	2,193	199
Arcadia Univ, Glenside, PA 19038-3295	1853	$25,990	$9,660	2-D	3,403	329
Argosy Univ/Schaumburg, Schaumburg, IL 60173	1979	NA	NA	3-D	NA	NA
Arizona State Univ, Tempe, AZ 85287	1885	$4,406 (S)	$6,768	5-D	51,612	2,282
Arizona State Univ at the Polytechnic Campus, Mesa, AZ 85212	1995	$4,346 (S)	$5,155	5-M	4,865	139
Arizona State Univ West, Phoenix, AZ 85069-7100	1984	$4,346 (S)	$5,836	5-M	7,734	388
Arkansas State Univ, State University, AR 72467	1909	$5,440 (S)	$4,190	5-D	10,414	606
Arkansas Tech Univ, Russellville, AR 72801	1909	$4,700 (S)	$4,290	5-M	6,842	398
Armstrong Atlantic State Univ, Savannah, GA 31419-1997	1935	$3,350 (S)	$4,980	5-M	6,710	424
Art Ctr Coll of Design, Pasadena, CA 91103-1999	1930	$28,000	NA	1-M	1,642	407
Art Inst of Atlanta, Atlanta, GA 30328	1949	$18,000	$7,311	3-B	2,651	165
Art Inst of Boston at Lesley Univ, Boston, MA 02215-2598	1912	$19,600	$9,950	1-M	6,521	185
Art Inst of California-Los Angeles, Santa Monica, CA 90405-3035	NA	$19,824	$7,920	3-B	2,102	129
Art Inst of California-Orange County, Santa Ana, CA 92704-9888	2000	$418/qtr. hr.	$9,800	3-B	1,757	114
Art Inst of California-San Diego, San Diego, CA 92121	1981	$20,128	$9,480	3-B	1,912	119
Art Inst of California-San Francisco, San Francisco, CA 94102-4908	1939	$18,486	NA	3-B	1,347	108
Art Inst of Colorado, Denver, CO 80203	1952	$25,088	$7,980	3-B	2,886	122
Art Inst of Dallas, Dallas, TX 75231-9959	1978	$17,542	$4,896	3-B	1,304	72
Art Inst of Fort Lauderdale, Fort Lauderdale, FL 33316-3000	1968	$16,425	$4,785	3-B	3,500	148
Art Inst of Houston, Houston, TX 77056-4115	1978	$23,580	$3,082	3-B	1,657	80
Art Inst of Las Vegas, Henderson, NV 89074	2002	$17,740	$4,725	3-B	1,046	79
Art Inst of Phoenix, Phoenix, AZ 85021-2859	1995	$18,144	$5,217	3-B	1,114	109
Art Inst of Pittsburgh, Pittsburgh, PA 15219	1921	$21,965	$6,900	3-B	4,872	136
Art Inst of Portland, Portland, OR 97209	1963	$17,460	$5,625	3-B	1,583	120
Art Inst of Seattle, Seattle, WA 98121-1642	1982	$17,550	$6,867	3-B	2,492	174
Art Inst of Washington, Arlington, VA 22209	2000	$385/qtr. hr.	$9,500	3-B	1,200	82
Art Institutes Intl Minnesota, Minneapolis, MN 55402-3137	1964	$17,904	NA	3-B	1,594	111
Asbury Coll, Wilmore, KY 40390-1198	1890	$18,956	$4,806	2-M	1,293	151
Ashland Univ, Ashland, OH 44805-3702	1878	$21,430	$7,790	2-D	6,472	593
Assumption Coll, Worcester, MA 01609-1296	1904	$26,310	$5,775	2-M	2,451	216
Athens State Univ, Athens, AL 35611	1822	$3,870 (S)	$900	5-B	2,643	177
Auburn Univ, Auburn University, AL 36849	1856	$5,516 (S)	$7,232	5-D	23,333	1,331

Name, address	Year Founded	Tuition & Fees	Rm. & Board	Control, Degree	Enroll-ment	Faculty
Auburn Univ Montgomery, Montgomery, AL 36124-4023	1967	$4,640 (S)	$4,890	5-D	5,128	305
Augsburg Coll, Minneapolis, MN 55454-1351	1869	$23,422	$6,604	2-M	3,508	370
Augustana Coll, Rock Island, IL 61201-2296	1860	$23,457	$6,405	2-B	2,386	235
Augustana Coll, Sioux Falls, SD 57197	1860	$19,986	$5,472	2-M	1,745	180
Augusta State Univ, Augusta, GA 30904-2200	1925	$2,920 (S)	$4,920	5-M	6,312	330
Aurora Univ, Aurora, IL 60506-4892	1893	$16,180	$6,590	1-D	3,556	271
Austin Coll, Sherman, TX 75090-4400	1849	$23,540	$7,741	2-M	1,327	131
Austin Peay State Univ, Clarksville, TN 37044-0001	1927	$4,635 (S)	$4,800	5-M	8,813	464
Averett Univ, Danville, VA 24541-3692	1859	$19,040	$6,560	2-M	1,487	102
Avila Univ, Kansas City, MO 64145-1698	1916	$16,700	$5,400	2-M	1,697	199
Azusa Pacific Univ, Azusa, CA 91702-7000	1899	$22,160	$6,366	2-D	8,162	356
Babson Coll, Babson Park, MA 02457-0310	1919	$32,256	$11,222	1-M	3,210	229
Baker Coll of Allen Park, Allen Park, MI 48101 (4)	2003	$6,480	NA	1-B	1,522	88
Baker Coll of Auburn Hills, Auburn Hills, MI 48326-1586	1911	$6,480	NA	1-B	3,517	155
Baker Coll of Cadillac, Cadillac, MI 49601	1986	$6,480	NA	1-B	1,559	105
Baker Coll of Clinton Township, Clinton Township, MI 48035-4701	1990	$6,480	NA	1-B	5,103	208
Baker Coll of Flint, Flint, MI 48507-5508	1911	$6,480	$2,600	1-B	6,065	315
Baker Coll of Jackson, Jackson, MI 49202	1994	$6,480	NA	1-B	1,625	85
Baker Coll of Muskegon, Muskegon, MI 49442-3497	1888	$6,480	$2,400	1-B	4,744	177
Baker Coll of Owosso, Owosso, MI 48867-4400	1984	$6,480	$2,400	1-B	2,823	144
Baker Coll of Port Huron, Port Huron, MI 48060-2597	1990	$6,480	NA	1-B	1,578	126
Baldwin-Wallace Coll, Berea, OH 44017-2088	1845	$21,236	$6,974	2-M	4,469	352
Ball State Univ, Muncie, IN 47306-1099	1918	$6,458 (S)	$6,680	5-D	20,351	1,149
Bard Coll, Annandale-on-Hudson, NY 12504	1860	$34,080	$9,850	1-D	1,858	230
Barnard Coll, New York, NY 10027-6598 (3)	1889	$30,676	$11,126	1-B	2,356	319
Barry Univ, Miami Shores, FL 33161-6695	1940	$22,430	$7,620	2-D	9,207	910
Barton Coll, Wilson, NC 27893-7000	1902	$16,670	$5,800	2-B	1,189	111
Bastyr Univ, Kenmore, WA 98028-4966	1978	$15,381	$2,460	1-F	1,098	148
Bates Coll, Lewiston, ME 04240-6028	1855	$42,100 (C)	NA	1-B	1,730	187
Bayamón Central Univ, Bayamón, PR 00960-1725	1970	$4,440	NA	2-M	3,311	218
Baylor Univ, Waco, TX 76798	1845	$22,814	$7,125	2-D	13,975	910
Bay Path Coll, Longmeadow, MA 01106-2292	1897	$20,606	$9,614	1-M	1,456	162
Becker Coll, Worcester, MA 01609	1784	$18,425	$8,000	1-B	1,660	103
Belhaven Coll, Jackson, MS 39202-1789	1883	$14,774	$5,704	2-M	2,580	225
Bellarmine Univ, Louisville, KY 40205-0671	1950	$24,150	$6,880	2-D	2,800	251
Bellevue Univ, Bellevue, NE 68005-3098	1965	$5,345	NA	1-M	5,929	398
Belmont Univ, Nashville, TN 37212-3757	1951	$17,260	$8,650	2-D	4,319	461
Beloit Coll, Beloit, WI 53511-5596	1846	$26,884	$5,924	1-B	1,385	127
Bemidji State Univ, Bemidji, MN 56601-2699	1919	$6,014 (S)	$5,014	5-M	4,893	362
Benedict Coll, Columbia, SC 29204	1870	$12,954	$5,958	2-B	3,005	168
Benedictine Coll, Atchison, KS 66002-1499	1859	$15,760	$7,208	2-M	1,508	114
Benedictine Univ, Lisle, IL 60532-0900	1887	$19,210	$6,600	2-D	3,400	353
Bentley Coll, Waltham, MA 02452-4705	1917	$28,614	$10,170	1-M	5,565	475
Berea Coll, Berea, KY 40404	1855	$516	$4,980	1-B	1,595	159
Berklee Coll of Music, Boston, MA 02215-3693	1945	$26,307	$11,690	1-B	4,037	484
Bernard M. Baruch Coll of the City Univ of New York, New York, NY 10010-5585	1919	$4,320 (S)	NA	11-D	15,756	925
Berry Coll, Mount Berry, GA 30149-0159	1902	$18,950	$7,164	2-M	1,970	196
Bethel Coll, Mishawaka, IN 46545-5591	1947	$17,450	$5,380	2-M	2,093	184
Bethel Coll, McKenzie, TN 38201	1842	$9,630	$5,384	2-F	1,297	74
Bethel Coll, St. Paul, MN 55112-6999	1871	$22,700	$7,140	2-M	3,857	306
Bethune-Cookman Coll, Daytona Beach, FL 32114-3099	1904	$11,230	$6,692	2-B	3,090	203
Biola Univ, La Mirada, CA 90639-0001	1908	$23,882	$7,116	2-D	5,455	395
Birmingham-Southern Coll, Birmingham, AL 35254	1856	$21,055	$7,080	2-M	1,411	137
Black Hills State Univ, Spearfish, SD 57799	1883	$5,072 (S)	$3,663	5-M	3,846	194
Bloomfield Coll, Bloomfield, NJ 07003-9981	1868	$15,100	$7,400	2-B	2,212	282
Bloomsburg Univ of Pennsylvania, Bloomsburg, PA 17815-1301	1839	$6,226 (S)	$5,376	5-D	8,570	400
Bluefield State Coll, Bluefield, WV 24701-2198	1895	$3,410 (S)	NA	5-B	1,708	143
Bluffton Univ, Bluffton, OH 45817	1899	$20,570	$7,082	2-M	1,211	114
Bob Jones Univ, Greenville, SC 29614	1927	$9,770	$4,980	2-D	4,099	302
Boise State Univ, Boise, ID 83725-0399	1932	$3,872 (S)	$5,566	5-D	18,586	1,127
Boricua Coll, New York, NY 10032-1560	1974	$9,050	NA	1-M	1,520	116
Boston Coll, Chestnut Hill, MA 02467-3800	1863	$31,438	$10,845	2-D	13,755	1,285
Boston Univ, Boston, MA 02215	1839	$31,966	$10,080	1-D	30,957	2,438
Bowdoin Coll, Brunswick, ME 04011	1794	$32,990	$8,670	1-B	1,666	194
Bowie State Univ, Bowie, MD 20715-9465	1865	$6,846 (S)	$5,219	5-D	5,415	351
Bowling Green State Univ, Bowling Green, OH 43403	1910	$8,560 (S)	$6,434	5-D	19,016	1,047
Bradley Univ, Peoria, IL 61625-0002	1897	$18,830	$6,450	1-F	6,154	550
Brandeis Univ, Waltham, MA 02454-9110	1948	$32,501	$9,050	1-D	5,189	472
Brewton-Parker Coll, Mt. Vernon, GA 30445-0197	1904	$12,684	$4,820	2-B	1,094	137
Briarcliffe Coll, Bethpage, NY 11714	1966	$15,792	$7,938	3-B	3,009	189
Briar Cliff Univ, Sioux City, IA 51104-0100	1930	$17,985	$5,565	2-M	1,122	98
Bridgewater Coll, Bridgewater, VA 22812-1599	1880	$20,190	$9,060	2-B	1,506	126
Bridgewater State Coll, Bridgewater, MA 02325-0001	1840	$5,506 (S)	$6,614	5-M	9,649	494
Brigham Young Univ-Hawaii, Laie, HI 96762-1294	1955	$2,760	$4,980	2-B	2,486	224
Brigham Young Univ, Provo, UT 84602-1001	1875	$5,116	$5,790	2-D	34,067	1,762
Brooklyn Coll of the City Univ of New York, Brooklyn, NY 11210-2889	1930	$4,375 (S)	NA	11-M	15,281	1,103
Brown Univ, Providence, RI 02912	1764	$33,224	$8,796	1-D	8,261	888
Bryant Univ, Smithfield, RI 02917-1284	1863	$24,762	$9,568	1-M	3,642	262
Bryn Mawr Coll, Bryn Mawr, PA 19010-2899	1885	$32,230	$10,550	1-D	1,799	185
Bucknell Univ, Lewisburg, PA 17837	1846	$36,002	$7,366	1-M	3,648	328
Buena Vista Univ, Storm Lake, IA 50588	1891	$21,688	$6,054	2-M	1,283	116
Buffalo State Coll, State Univ of New York, Buffalo, NY 14222-1095	1867	$5,231 (S)	$6,672	5-M	11,056	715
Butler Univ, Indianapolis, IN 46208-3485	1855	$23,774	$8,170	1-F	4,384	434
Cabrini Coll, Radnor, PA 19087-3698	1957	$24,000	$9,340	2-M	2,318	237
Caldwell Coll, Caldwell, NJ 07006-6195	1939	$19,000	$7,650	2-M	2,229	184
California Baptist Univ, Riverside, CA 92504-3206	1950	$17,470	$6,310	2-M	3,105	226
California Coll of the Arts, San Francisco, CA 94107	1907	$26,100	$8,430	1-M	1,616	370
California Inst of Integral Studies, San Francisco, CA 94103	1968	$610/unit	NA	1-D	1,005	61
California Inst of Tech, Pasadena, CA 91125-0001	1891	$27,309	$8,814	1-D	2,172	324
California Inst of the Arts, Valencia, CA 91355-2340	1961	$27,725	$7,697	1-M	1,327	287
California Lutheran Univ, Thousand Oaks, CA 91360-2787	1959	$23,370	$8,320	2-D	3,212	260
California Polytechnic State Univ, San Luis Obispo, San Luis Obispo, CA 93407	1901	$4,245 (S)	$8,145	5-M	18,475	1,246
California State Polytechnic Univ, Pomona, Pomona, CA 91768-2557	1938	$3,015 (S)	$7,908	5-M	19,885	1,281
California State Univ, Bakersfield, Bakersfield, CA 93311-1022	1970	$2,959 (S)	$5,946	5-M	7,549	515
California State Univ Channel Islands, Camarillo, CA 93012	2002	$2,980 (S)	$8,800	5-M	2,575	227

Name, address	Year Founded	Tuition & Fees	Rm. & Board	Control, Degree	Enroll-ment	Faculty
California State Univ, Chico, Chico, CA 95929-0722	1887	$3,370 (S)	$7,993	5-M	15,919	913
California State Univ, Dominguez Hills, Carson, CA 90747-0001	1960	$3,618 (S)	$5,850	5-M	12,357	678
California State Univ, East Bay, Hayward, CA 94542-3000	1957	$2,916 (S)	$6,759	5-M	12,535	741
California State Univ, Fresno, Fresno, CA 93740-8027	1911	$3,037 (S)	$7,344	5-D	20,371	1,267
California State Univ, Fullerton, Fullerton, CA 92834-9480	1957	$2,990 (S)	$4,504	5-M	35,040	1,935
California State Univ, Long Beach, Long Beach, CA 90840	1949	$2,864 (S)	$6,648	5-M	34,547	2,074
California State Univ, Los Angeles, Los Angeles, CA 90032-8530	1947	$3,035 (S)	$7,353	5-D	20,014	1,141
California State Univ, Monterey Bay, Seaside, CA 93955-8001	1994	$2,947 (S)	$6,900	5-M	3,020	280
California State Univ, Northridge, Northridge, CA 91330	1958	$3,036 (S)	$7,616	5-M	33,243	1,822
California State Univ, Sacramento, Sacramento, CA 95819-6048	1947	$3,624 (S)	$7,458	5-D	27,932	1,530
California State Univ, San Bernardino, San Bernardino, CA 92407-2397	1965	$3,398 (S)	$5,886	5-M	16,431	447
California State Univ, San Marcos, San Marcos, CA 92096-0001	1990	$3,062 (S)	$7,470	5-M	6,956	402
California State Univ, Stanislaus, Turlock, CA 95382	1957	$3,030 (S)	$8,253	5-M	8,137	495
California Univ of Pennsylvania, California, PA 15419-1394	1852	$6,491 (S)	$7,788	5-M	7,184	384
Calumet Coll of Saint Joseph, Whiting, IN 46394-2195	1951	$9,900	NA	2-M	1,265	131
Calvin Coll, Grand Rapids, MI 49546-4388	1876	$19,150	$6,585	2-M	4,177	398
Cambridge Coll, Cambridge, MA 02138-5304	1971	$8,190	NA	1-D	4,031	806
Cameron Univ, Lawton, OK 73505-6377	1908	$3,440 (S)	$3,014	5-M	5,873	297
Campbellsville Univ, Campbellsville, KY 42718-2799	1906	$16,340	$5,932	2-M	2,286	217
Campbell Univ, Buies Creek, NC 27506	1887	$17,027	$5,808	2-D	3,645	336
Canisius Coll, Buffalo, NY 14208-1098	1870	$23,297	$8,960	2-M	4,979	531
Capella Univ, Minneapolis, MN 55402	1993	NA	NA	3-D	12,000	372
Capital Univ, Columbus, OH 43209-2394	1830	$24,100	$6,344	2-M	3,901	460
Cardinal Stritch Univ, Milwaukee, WI 53217-3985	1937	$16,830	$5,430	2-D	6,785	880
Caribbean Univ, Bayamón, PR 00960-0493	1969	$3,630	NA	1-M	1,786	158
Carleton Coll, Northfield, MN 55057-4001	1866	$34,272	$8,592	1-B	1,959	216
Carlos Albizu Univ, Miami Campus, Miami, FL 33172-2209 (4)	1980	$11,109	NA	1-D	1,076	50
Carlow Univ, Pittsburgh, PA 15213-3165 (4)	1929	$18,498	$7,289	2-M	2,123	233
Carnegie Mellon Univ, Pittsburgh, PA 15213-3891	1900	$34,578	$9,280	1-D	10,017	995
Carroll Coll, Helena, MT 59625-0002	1909	$17,078	$6,406	2-B	1,452	134
Carroll Coll, Waukesha, WI 53186-5593	1846	$19,910	$6,070	2-M	3,123	243
Carson-Newman Coll, Jefferson City, TN 37760	1851	$16,060	$5,200	2-M	1,993	195
Carthage Coll, Kenosha, WI 53140	1847	$23,650	$6,800	2-M	2,699	210
Case Western Reserve Univ, Cleveland, OH 44106	1826	$31,688	$9,280	1-D	9,615	853
Castleton State Coll, Castleton, VT 05735	1787	$6,828 (S)	$6,942	5-M	2,392	201
Catawba Coll, Salisbury, NC 28144-2488	1851	$18,750	$6,250	2-M	1,288	98
Catholic Univ of America, Washington, DC 20064	1887	$26,000	$9,838	2-D	6,130	714
Cazenovia Coll, Cazenovia, NY 13035-1084	1824	$18,940	$7,510	1-B	1,124	139
Cedar Crest Coll, Allentown, PA 18104-6196 (3)	1867	$23,012	$7,953	2-M	1,856	145
Cedarville Univ, Cedarville, OH 45314-0601	1887	$17,120	$5,010	2-M	3,113	259
Centenary Coll, Hackettstown, NJ 07840-2100	1867	$20,870	$7,900	2-M	2,472	304
Centenary Coll of Louisiana, Shreveport, LA 71104	1825	$18,900	$6,780	2-M	1,044	122
Central Coll, Pella, IA 50219-1999	1853	$20,972	$7,224	2-B	1,635	139
Central Connecticut State Univ, New Britain, CT 06050-4010	1849	$6,164 (S)	$7,456	5-D	12,315	850
Central Michigan Univ, Mount Pleasant, MI 48859	1892	$5,868 (S)	$6,376	5-D	27,221	1,095
Central Missouri State Univ, Warrensburg, MO 64093	1871	$5,835 (S)	$5,109	5-M	10,604	705
Central State Univ, Wilberforce, OH 45384	1887	$4,994 (S)	$6,982	5-M	1,623	162
Central Washington Univ, Ellensburg, WA 98926	1891	$4,806 (S)	$6,924	5-M	10,190	535
Centre Coll, Danville, KY 40422-1394	1819	$23,110	$7,700	2-B	1,130	123
Chadron State Coll, Chadron, NE 69337	1911	$3,662 (S)	$4,074	5-M	2,636	110
Chaminade Univ of Honolulu, Honolulu, HI 96816-1578	1955	$14,960	$9,380	2-M	1,810	131
Champlain Coll, Burlington, VT 05402-0670	1878	$14,910	$9,695	1-M	2,529	258
Chapman Univ, Orange, CA 92866	1861	$30,748	$10,500	2-F	5,732	581
Charleston Southern Univ, Charleston, SC 29423-8087	1964	$16,780	$6,450	2-M	3,022	178
Charter Oak State Coll, New Britain, CT 06053-2142	1973	$165/credit(S)	NA	5-B	1,902	85
Chatham Coll, Pittsburgh, PA 15232-2826	1869	$24,179	$7,586	1-D	1,440	75
Chestnut Hill Coll, Philadelphia, PA 19118-2693 (4)	1924	$22,750	$7,950	2-D	1,719	255
Cheyney Univ of Pennsylvania, Cheyney, PA 19319-0200	1837	$5,818 (S)	$5,679	5-M	1,560	127
Chicago State Univ, Chicago, IL 60628	1867	$7,138 (S)	$6,492	5-D	7,131	462
Christian Brothers Univ, Memphis, TN 38104-5581	1871	$19,150	$5,500	2-M	1,778	154
Christopher Newport Univ, Newport News, VA 23606-2998	1960	$5,826 (S)	$7,500	5-M	4,699	239
Citadel, The Military Coll of South Carolina, Charleston, SC 29409 (2)	1842	$7,520 (S)	$4,840	5-M	3,386	232
City Coll of the City Univ of New York, New York, NY 10031-9198	1847	$4,080 (S)	NA	11-F	12,440	1,122
City Univ, Bellevue, WA 98005	1973	$8,160	NA	1-M	4,020	1,241
Claflin Univ, Orangeburg, SC 29115	1869	$10,890	$5,908	2-M	1,728	127
Claremont McKenna Coll, Claremont, CA 91711	1946	$32,650	$10,270	1-B	1,139	134
Clarion Univ of Pennsylvania, Clarion, PA 16214	1867	$6,467 (S)	$5,246	5-M	6,338	304
Clark Atlanta Univ, Atlanta, GA 30314	1865	$14,522	$6,816	2-D	4,598	264
Clarke Coll, Dubuque, IA 52001-3198	1843	$18,945	$6,445	2-M	1,246	130
Clarkson Univ, Potsdam, NY 13699	1896	$25,585	$9,345	1-D	3,045	192
Clark Univ, Worcester, MA 01610-1477	1887	$31,465	$5,900	1-D	3,118	263
Clayton State Univ, Morrow, GA 30260-0285	1969	$3,290 (S)	NA	5-B	6,152	367
Clemson Univ, Clemson, SC 29634	1889	$9,016 (S)	$5,780	5-D	17,165	1,143
Cleveland State Univ, Cleveland, OH 44115	1964	$6,792 (S)	$6,809	5-D	15,722	997
Coastal Carolina Univ, Conway, SC 29528-6054	1954	$6,860 (S)	$6,280	5-M	7,613	414
Coe Coll, Cedar Rapids, IA 52402-5092	1851	$25,120	$6,550	2-M	1,355	125
Colby Coll, Waterville, ME 04901-8840	1813	$41,770 (C)	NA	1-B	1,871	225
Colgate Univ, Hamilton, NY 13346-1386	1819	$33,105	$8,065	1-M	2,779	315
Coll for Creative Studies, Detroit, MI 48202-4034	1926	$24,635	$3,900	1-B	1,291	227
Coll Misericordia, Dallas, PA 18612-1098	1924	$19,700	$8,250	2-D	2,343	258
Coll of Biblical Studies-Houston, Houston, TX 77036	1979	$4,310	NA	2-B	1,492	50
Coll of Charleston, Charleston, SC 29424-0001	1770	$6,668 (S)	$6,948	5-M	11,332	858
Coll of Mount St. Joseph, Cincinnati, OH 45233-1670	1920	$18,790	$6,070	2-M	2,233	233
Coll of Mount Saint Vincent, Riverdale, NY 10471-1093	1911	$21,550	$8,500	1-M	1,855	161
Coll of New Jersey, Ewing, NJ 08628	1855	$9,707 (S)	$8,458	5-M	6,768	705
Coll of New Rochelle, New Rochelle, NY 10805-2308 (4)	1904	$20,596	$7,880	1-M	2,306	219
Coll of Notre Dame of Maryland, Baltimore, MD 21210-2476	1873	$21,600	$8,000	2-D	3,307	88
Coll of Saint Benedict, Saint Joseph, MN 56374 (4)	1887	$23,454	$6,637	2-B	2,045	170
Coll of St. Catherine-Minneapolis, Minneapolis, MN 55454-1494 (4)	1964	$14,750	$6,120	2	4,807	519
Coll of St. Catherine, St. Paul, MN 55105-1789	1905	$21,385	$6,120	2-D	4,907	483
Coll of Saint Elizabeth, Morristown, NJ 07960-6989	1899	$19,740	$8,975	2-M	1,858	178
Coll of Saint Mary, Omaha, NE 68124-2377 (3)	1923	$18,110	$5,900	2-M	1,015	54
Coll of Saint Rose, Albany, NY 12203-1419	1920	$17,954	$7,816	1-M	5,149	481
Coll of St. Scholastica, Duluth, MN 55811-4199	1912	$22,240	$6,216	2-F	3,238	252
Coll of Santa Fe, Santa Fe, NM 87505-7634	1947	$22,276	$6,702	1-M	1,661	275

Name, address	Year Founded	Tuition & Fees	Rm. & Board	Control, Degree	Enrollment	Faculty
Coll of Staten Island of the City Univ of New York, Staten Island, NY 10314-6600	1955	$4,328 (S)	NA	11-M	12,083	842
Coll of the Holy Cross, Worcester, MA 01610-2395	1843	$31,444	$9,220	2-B	2,816	297
Coll of the Ozarks, Point Lookout, MO 65726	1906	$280	$4,100	2-B	1,333	106
Coll of William & Mary, Williamsburg, VA 23187-8795	1693	$7,778 (S)	$6,417	5-D	7,544	763
Coll of Wooster, Wooster, OH 44691-2363	1866	$28,230	$7,060	2-B	1,846	191
Collins Coll: A School of Design & Tech, Tempe, AZ 85281-5206	1978	$13,875	$2,970	3-B	1,828	101
Colorado Christian Univ, Lakewood, CO 80226	1914	$16,740	$6,682	2-M	2,142	46
Colorado Coll, Colorado Springs, CO 80903-3294	1874	$30,048	$7,620	1-M	2,016	206
Colorado School of Mines, Golden, CO 80401-1887	1874	$8,143 (S)	$6,750	5-D	3,921	299
Colorado State Univ, Fort Collins, CO 80523-0015.	1870	$4,562 (S)	$6,316	5-D	27,133	881
Colorado State Univ-Pueblo, Pueblo, CO 81001-4901	1933	$3,866 (S)	$6,088	5-M	5,835	312
Colorado Tech Univ, Colorado Springs, CO 80907-3896	1965	NA	NA	3-D	1,684	137
Colorado Tech Univ Sioux Falls Campus, Sioux Falls, SD 57108	1965	$12,840	NA	3-M	1,036	61
Columbia Coll, Columbia, MO 65216-0002	1851	$11,995	$5,011	2-M	1,149	82
Columbia Coll, New York, NY 10027	1754	$33,246	$9,338	1-B	4,225	727
Columbia Coll, Columbia, SC 29203-5998	1854	$19,214	$5,818	2-M	1,493	154
Columbia Coll Chicago, Chicago, IL 60605-1996	1890	$16,788	$9,765	1-M	10,842	1,626
Columbia Intl Univ, Columbia, SC 29230-3122	1923	$14,880	$5,712	2-D	1,013	48
Columbia Southern Univ, Orange Beach, AL 36561	NA	$375/course	NA	3-M	2,200	45
Columbia Union Coll, Takoma Park, MD 20912-7796.	1904	$17,586	$5,950	2-M	1,047	56
Columbia Univ, School of General Studies, New York, NY 10027-6939	1754	$32,176	$8,540	1-B	1,579	727
Columbia Univ, The Fu Foundation School of Engineering & Applied Sci, New York, NY 10027	1864	$33,246	$9,338	1-D	1,436	137
Columbus Coll of Art & Design, Columbus, OH 43215-1758	1879	$20,278	$6,450	1-B	1,455	181
Columbus State Univ, Columbus, GA 31907-5645	1958	$2,944 (S)	$5,720	5-M	7,475	411
Concordia Coll, Moorhead, MN 56562	1891	$19,674	$4,990	2-M	2,764	252
Concordia Univ, Irvine, CA 92612-3299	1972	$21,130	$7,060	2-M	2,092	208
Concordia Univ, River Forest, IL 60305-1499	1864	$20,000	$6,300	2-D	2,783	NA
Concordia Univ, Seward, NE 68434-1599.	1894	$17,724	$4,710	2-M	1,317	120
Concordia Univ, Portland, OR 97211-6099	1905	$20,100	$5,900	2-M	1,506	137
Concordia Univ at Austin, Austin, TX 78705-2799	1926	$16,850	$6,900	2-M	1,219	135
Concordia Univ, St. Paul, St. Paul, MN 55104-5494	1893	$22,378	$6,596	2-M	2,069	438
Concordia Univ Wisconsin, Mequon, WI 53097-2402	1881	$17,280	$6,540	2-D	5,418	199
Concord Univ, Athens, WV 24712-1000	1872	$3,872 (S)	$5,796	5-M	3,015	185
Connecticut Coll, New London, CT 06320-4196	1911	$41,975 (C)	NA	1-M	1,898	242
Converse Coll, Spartanburg, SC 29302-0006	1889	$22,234	$6,848	1-M	2,176	173
Cooper Union for the Advancement of Sci & Art, New York, NY 10003-7120.	1859	$1,500	$13,360	1-B	1,003	215
Coppin State Univ, Baltimore, MD 21216-3698.	1900	$4,879 (S)	$6,239	5-M	4,003	202
Cornell Coll, Mount Vernon, IA 52314-1098	1853	$23,680	$6,430	2-B	1,179	112
Cornell Univ, Ithaca, NY 14853-0001	1865	$31,467	$10,250	1-D	19,447	1,844
Cornerstone Univ, Grand Rapids, MI 49525-5897	1941	$14,700	$5,800	2-F	2,515	140
Creighton Univ, Omaha, NE 68178-0001	1878	$22,378	$7,540	2-D	6,791	649
Crown Coll, St. Bonifacius, MN 55375-9001	1916	$17,054	$7,016	2-M	1,304	64
Culinary Inst of America, Hyde Park, NY 12538-1499.	1946	$20,160	$6,820	1-B	2,713	148
Cumberland Univ, Lebanon, TN 37087-3408	1842	$13,744	$4,820	1-M	1,508	98
Curry Coll, Milton, MA 02186-9984	1879	$24,300	$9,640	1-M	3,202	372
Daemen Coll, Amherst, NY 14226-3592	1947	$16,800	$7,780	1-F	2,315	259
Dakota State Univ, Madison, SD 57042-1799	1881	$5,699 (S)	$3,927	5-M	2,319	108
Dallas Baptist Univ, Dallas, TX 75211-9299	1965	$12,270	$4,770	2-M	4,988	456
Dalton State Coll, Dalton, GA 30720-3797	1963	$1,592 (S)	NA	5-B	4,267	187
Daniel Webster Coll, Nashua, NH 03063-1300	1965	$22,955	$8,450	1-B	1,109	61
Dartmouth Coll, Hanover, NH 03755.	1769	$32,046	$9,390	1-D	5,780	633
Davenport Univ, Dearborn, MI 48126-3799.	1985	$8,880	NA	1-M	12,822	1,096
David N. Myers Univ, Cleveland, OH 44115	1848	$9,840	NA	1-M	1,177	165
Davidson Coll, Davidson, NC 28035	1837	$28,667	$8,158	2-B	1,683	167
Delaware State Univ, Dover, DE 19901-2277.	1891	$5,850 (S)	$8,298	5-D	3,722	NA
Delaware Valley Coll, Doylestown, PA 18901-2697	1896	$21,814	$8,130	1-M	2,070	192
Delta State Univ, Cleveland, MS 38733-0001	1924	$4,252 (S)	$4,272	5-D	3,998	275
Denison Univ, Granville, OH 43023.	1831	$28,920	$8,120	1-B	2,329	198
DePaul Univ, Chicago, IL 60604-2287	1898	$21,040	$8,865	2-D	23,148	1,477
DePauw Univ, Greencastle, IN 46135-0037	1837	$27,780	$7,800	2-B	2,397	253
DeSales Univ, Center Valley, PA 18034-9568	1964	$20,700	$7,880	2-M	3,282	163
DeVry Inst of Tech, Long Island City, NY 11101	1998	$13,330	NA	3-M	1,376	89
DeVry Univ, Phoenix, AZ 85021-2995.	1967	$12,060	NA	3-M	1,380	87
DeVry Univ, Fremont, CA 94555	1998	$13,330	NA	3-M	1,580	78
DeVry Univ, Long Beach, CA 90806	1984	$12,720	NA	3-M	1,201	151
DeVry Univ, Pomona, CA 91768-2642	1983	$12,720	NA	3-M	1,899	80
DeVry Univ, Miramar, FL 33027-4150.	2002	$12,720	NA	3-M	1,068	56
DeVry Univ, Orlando, FL 32839	2000	$12,720	NA	3-M	1,181	91
DeVry Univ, Alpharetta, GA 30004	1997	$12,060	NA	3-M	1,044	76
DeVry Univ, Decatur, GA 30030-2198	1969	$12,060	NA	3-M	2,197	133
DeVry Univ, Addison, IL 60101-6106	1982	$12,160	NA	3-B	1,577	112
DeVry Univ, Chicago, IL 60618-5994	1931	$12,160	NA	3-B	2,166	113
DeVry Univ, Tinley Park, IL 60477	2000	$12,160	NA	3-M	1,285	74
DeVry Univ, Kansas City, MO 64131-3698	1931	$12,060	NA	3-M	1,233	88
DeVry Univ, North Brunswick, NJ 08902-3362	1969	$12,160	NA	3-B	1,503	154
DeVry Univ, Columbus, OH 43209-2705.	1952	$12,060	NA	3-M	2,643	116
DeVry Univ, Irving, TX 75063-2439.	1969	$12,060	NA	3-M	1,818	127
DeVry Univ Online, Oakbrook Terrace, IL 60181	2000	$13,090	NA	3-M	6,569	791
Dickinson Coll, Carlisle, PA 17013-2896.	1773	$32,120	$8,050	1-B	2,352	209
Dickinson State Univ, Dickinson, ND 58601-4896.	1918	$4,979 (S)	$3,694	5-B	2,516	205
Dillard Univ, New Orleans, LA 70122-3097.	1869	$11,550	$6,840	2-B	2,155	201
Doane Coll, Crete, NE 68333-2430.	1872	$17,536	$4,922	2-M	2,394	140
Dominican Coll, Orangeburg, NY 10962-1210	1952	$17,910	$8,720	1-D	1,530	163
Dominican Univ, River Forest, IL 60305-1099.	1901	$20,050	$6,320	2-M	3,250	309
Dominican Univ of California, San Rafael, CA 94901-2298	1890	$28,070	$11,300	2-M	1,631	287
Dordt Coll, Sioux Center, IA 51250-1697	1955	$17,640	$4,900	2-M	1,327	105
Dowling Coll, Oakdale, NY 11769-1999	1955	$13,800	$5,748	1-D	6,379	500
Drake Univ, Des Moines, IA 50311-4516	1881	$21,462	$6,170	1-D	5,277	388
Drew Univ, Madison, NJ 07940-1493	1867	$31,286	$8,412	2-D	2,627	233
Drexel Univ, Philadelphia, PA 19104-2875	1891	$24,280	$10,515	1-D	18,466	NA
Drury Univ, Springfield, MO 65802-3791.	1873	$15,512	$5,790	1-M	1,961	185
Duke Univ, Durham, NC 27708-0586	1838	$33,963	$9,152	2-D	14,075	NA
Duquesne Univ, Pittsburgh, PA 15282-0001.	1878	$21,480	$8,054	2-D	9,916	908
D'Youville Coll, Buffalo, NY 14201-1084	1908	$15,800	$7,800	1-D	2,906	216

Name, address	Year Founded	Tuition & Fees	Rm. & Board	Control, Degree	Enrollment	Faculty
Earlham Coll, Richmond, IN 47374-4095	1847	$27,684	$5,920	2-F	1,372	108
East Carolina Univ, Greenville, NC 27858-4353	1907	$3,627 (S)	$6,840	5-D	23,164	1,292
East Central Univ, Ada, OK 74820-6899	1909	$3,566 (S)	$3,000	5-M	4,571	255
Eastern Connecticut State Univ, Willimantic, CT 06226-2295	1889	$5,964 (S)	$7,300	5-M	5,113	397
Eastern Illinois Univ, Charleston, IL 61920-3099	1895	$6,373 (S)	$6,196	5-M	12,129	755
Eastern Kentucky Univ, Richmond, KY 40475-3102	1906	$5,120 (S)	$4,088	5-M	16,219	1,010
Eastern Mennonite Univ, Harrisonburg, VA 22802-2462	1917	$20,670	$6,550	2-F	1,301	163
Eastern Michigan Univ, Ypsilanti, MI 48197	1849	$6,541 (S)	$6,356	5-D	23,240	1,196
Eastern Nazarene Coll, Quincy, MA 02170-2999	1918	$18,310	$6,590	2-M	1,212	48
Eastern New Mexico Univ, Portales, NM 88130	1934	$2,784 (S)	$4,480	5-M	4,033	263
Eastern Oregon Univ, La Grande, OR 97850-2899	1929	$4,779 (S)	$7,300	5-M	3,533	128
Eastern Univ, St. Davids, PA 19087-3696	1952	$18,830	$7,840	2-M	3,253	343
Eastern Washington Univ, Cheney, WA 99004-2431	1882	$4,281 (S)	$5,733	5-D	10,908	575
East Stroudsburg Univ of Pennsylvania, East Stroudsburg, PA 18301-2999	1893	$6,462 (S)	$4,794	5-M	6,793	332
East Tennessee State Univ, Johnson City, TN 37614	1911	$4,487 (S)	$4,822	5-D	11,894	789
East Texas Baptist Univ, Marshall, TX 75670-1498	1912	$12,840	$3,873	2-B	1,326	108
East-West Univ, Chicago, IL 60605-2103	1978	$11,445	NA	1-B	1,040	70
Eckerd Coll, St. Petersburg, FL 33711	1958	$27,618	$7,868	2-B	1,779	160
Edgewood Coll, Madison, WI 53711-1997	1927	$17,000	$5,862	2-D	2,646	220
Edinboro Univ of Pennsylvania, Edinboro, PA 16444	1857	$6,290 (S)	$5,518	5-M	7,691	408
Elizabeth City State Univ, Elizabeth City, NC 27909-7806	1891	$3,223 (S)	$4,709	5-M	2,470	216
Elizabethtown Coll, Elizabethtown, PA 17022-2298	1899	$26,950	$7,300	2-M	2,248	207
Elmhurst Coll, Elmhurst, IL 60126-3296	1871	$21,600	$6,906	2-M	2,670	278
Elmira Coll, Elmira, NY 14901	1855	$30,050	$9,100	1-M	1,853	99
Elms Coll, Chicopee, MA 01013-2839 (4)	1928	$21,520	$8,400	2-M	1,234	146
Elon Univ, Elon, NC 27244-2010	1889	$18,949	$6,422	2-D	4,956	370
Embry-Riddle Aeronautical Univ, Prescott, AZ 86301-3720	1978	$23,490	$6,516	1-M	1,685	114
Embry-Riddle Aeronautical Univ, Daytona Beach, FL 32114-3900	1926	$23,500	$6,936	1-M	4,776	314
Embry-Riddle Aeronautical Univ, Extended Campus, Daytona Beach, FL 32114-3900	1970	$4,224	NA	1-M	16,255	2,104
Emerson Coll, Boston, MA 02116-4624	1880	$24,622	$10,420	1-D	4,326	381
Emmanuel Coll, Boston, MA 02115	1919	$22,300	$9,700	2-M	2,296	222
Emory & Henry Coll, Emory, VA 24327-0947	1836	$19,530	$7,040	2-M	1,101	95
Emory Univ, Atlanta, GA 30322-1100	1836	$30,794	$9,752	2-D	12,134	1,435
Emporia State Univ, Emporia, KS 66801-5087	1863	$3,306 (S)	$4,787	5-D	6,288	282
Endicott Coll, Beverly, MA 01915-2096	1939	$20,390	$9,766	1-M	3,326	146
Evangel Univ, Springfield, MO 65802-2191	1955	$12,750	$4,620	2-M	1,801	158
Evergreen State Coll, Olympia, WA 98505	1967	$4,337 (S)	$6,924	5-M	4,470	221
Excelsior Coll, Albany, NY 12203-5159	1970	$250/cr. hr.	NA	1-M	28,464	NA
Fairfield Univ, Fairfield, CT 06824-5195	1942	$30,255	$9,600	2-M	5,173	423
Fairleigh Dickinson Univ, Coll at Florham, Madison, NJ 07940-1099	1942	$24,904	$9,028	1-M	3,481	309
Fairleigh Dickinson Univ, Metro Campus, Teaneck, NJ 07666-1914	1942	$23,144	$9,502	1-D	7,937	561
Fairmont State Univ, Fairmont, WV 26554	1865	$4,412 (S)	$5,674	5-M	7,759	535
Farmingdale State Univ of New York, Farmingdale, NY 11735	1912	$5,257 (S)	$9,660	5-B	6,461	459
Fashion Inst of Tech, New York, NY 10001-5992 (4)	1944	$4,770 (S)	$8,409	11-M	10,381	918
Faulkner Univ, Montgomery, AL 36109-3398	1942	$11,425	$5,400	2-F	2,583	138
Fayetteville State Univ, Fayetteville, NC 28301-4298	1867	$3,205 (S)	$4,570	5-D	6,072	274
Felician Coll, Lodi, NJ 07644-2117	1942	$18,250	$7,950	2-M	1,806	148
Ferris State Univ, Big Rapids, MI 49307	1884	$6,882 (S)	$6,816	5-F	12,547	823
Fitchburg State Coll, Fitchburg, MA 01420-2697	1894	$5,002 (S)	$6,274	5-M	5,340	242
Five Towns Coll, Dix Hills, NY 11746-6055	1972	$14,100	$10,250	1-D	1,162	109
Flagler Coll, St. Augustine, FL 32085-1027	1968	$8,600	$5,190	1-B	2,157	165
Florida Agr & Mech Univ, Tallahassee, FL 32307-3200	1887	$3,318 (S)	$5,766	5-D	13,064	621
Florida Atlantic Univ, Boca Raton, FL 33431-0991	1961	$3,259 (S)	$7,962	5-D	25,704	1,386
Florida Gulf Coast Univ, Fort Myers, FL 33965-6565	1991	$3,420 (S)	$7,460	5-M	7,249	441
Florida Inst of Tech, Melbourne, FL 32901-6975	1958	$25,150	$6,800	1-D	4,745	408
Florida Intl Univ, Miami, FL 33199	1965	$3,314 (S)	$9,102	5-D	36,904	1,429
Florida Metro Univ-Brandon Campus, Tampa, FL 33619	1890	$13,440	NA	3-M	NA	68
Florida Metro Univ-North Orlando Campus, Orlando, FL 32810-5674	1953	$9,900	NA	3-M	1,498	96
Florida Metro Univ-Pinellas Campus, Clearwater, FL 33759	1890	$11,430	NA	3-M	1,201	44
Florida Metro Univ-South Orlando Campus, Orlando, FL 32819	NA	$9,900	NA	3-M	1,964	77
Florida Metro Univ-Tampa Campus, Tampa, FL 33614-5899	1890	$9,900	NA	3-M	1,390	83
Florida Southern Coll, Lakeland, FL 33801-5698	1885	$19,165	$6,800	2-M	1,921	166
Florida State Univ, Tallahassee, FL 32306	1851	$3,208 (S)	$6,778	5-D	39,146	1,592
Fontbonne Univ, St. Louis, MO 63105-3098	1917	$17,440	$6,988	2-M	2,836	372
Fordham Univ, New York, NY 10458	1841	$27,725	$10,895	2-D	14,664	1,326
Fort Hays State Univ, Hays, KS 67601-4099	1902	$2,442 (S)	$6,190	5-M	7,373	291
Fort Lewis Coll, Durango, CO 81301-3999	1911	$5,692 (S)	$6,160	5-B	3,946	241
Fort Valley State Univ, Fort Valley, GA 31030-4313	1895	$3,650 (S)	$4,496	5-D	2,174	121
Framingham State Coll, Framingham, MA 01701-9101	1839	$4,999 (S)	$6,157	5-M	5,874	234
Franciscan Univ of Steubenville, Steubenville, OH 43952-1763	1946	$16,450	$5,500	2-M	2,421	205
Francis Marion Univ, Florence, SC 29501-0547	1970	$6,512 (S)	$5,430	5-M	4,008	281
Franklin & Marshall Coll, Lancaster, PA 17604-3003	1787	$32,530	$8,060	1-B	2,025	210
Franklin Coll, Franklin, IN 46131-2623	1834	$19,275	$5,730	2-B	1,003	110
Franklin Pierce Coll, Rindge, NH 03461-0060	1962	$25,300	$8,200	1-B	1,635	150
Franklin Univ, Columbus, OH 43215-5399	1902	$7,320	NA	1-M	6,823	599
Freed-Hardeman Univ, Henderson, TN 38340-2399	1869	$13,092	$3,700	2-M	2,030	147
Fresno Pacific Univ, Fresno, CA 93702-4709	1944	$20,790	$5,990	2-M	2,371	198
Friends Univ, Wichita, KS 67213	1898	$14,600	NA	1-M	3,190	225
Frostburg State Univ, Frostburg, MD 21532-1099	1898	$6,616 (S)	$6,442	5-M	5,041	351
Furman Univ, Greenville, SC 29613	1826	$26,352	$6,912	1-M	3,221	272
Gallaudet Univ, Washington, DC 20002-3625	1864	$10,250	$8,500	1-D	1,834	230
Gannon Univ, Erie, PA 16541-0001	1925	$18,690	$7,410	2-D	3,590	299
Gardner-Webb Univ, Boiling Springs, NC 28017	1905	$16,310	$5,540	2-D	3,776	321
Geneva Coll, Beaver Falls, PA 15010-3599	1848	$17,475	$6,770	2-M	2,141	158
George Fox Univ, Newberg, OR 97132-2697	1891	$22,570	$7,210	2-D	3,193	260
George Mason Univ, Fairfax, VA 22030	1957	$5,880 (S)	$6,480	5-D	29,728	1,955
Georgetown Coll, Georgetown, KY 40324-1696	1829	$20,700	$6,070	2-M	1,904	167
Georgetown Univ, Washington, DC 20057	1789	$32,040	$11,159	2-D	13,652	1,258
George Washington Univ, Washington, DC 20052	1821	$37,820	$11,000	1-D	24,099	2,036
Georgia Coll & State Univ, Milledgeville, GA 31061	1889	$4,142 (S)	$6,878	5-M	5,659	402
Georgia Inst of Tech, Atlanta, GA 30332-0001	1885	$4,648 (S)	$6,802	5-D	17,135	837
Georgian Court Univ, Lakewood, NJ 08701-2697	1908	$19,100	$7,600	2-M	3,153	298
Georgia Southern Univ, Statesboro, GA 30460	1906	$3,462 (S)	$6,300	5-D	16,646	713
Georgia Southwestern State Univ, Americus, GA 31709-4693	1906	$3,034 (S)	$4,810	5-M	2,427	151

Name, address	Year Founded	Tuition & Fees	Rm. & Board	Control, Degree	Enrollment	Faculty
Georgia State Univ, Atlanta, GA 30303-3083	1913	$4,464 (S)	$6,980	5-D	25,945	1,430
Gettysburg Coll, Gettysburg, PA 17325-1483	1832	$32,070	$7,794	2-B	2,463	274
Glenville State Coll, Glenville, WV 26351-1200	1872	$3,628 (S)	$5,150	5-B	1,392	94
Global Univ of the Assemblies of God, Springfield, MO 65804	1948	$2,160	NA	2-F	6,665	618
Globe Inst of Tech, New York, NY 10007	NA	$9,086	$3,600	3-B	1,671	113
Golden Gate Univ, San Francisco, CA 94105-2968	1901	$11,520	NA	1-D	3,891	489
Goldey-Beacom Coll, Wilmington, DE 19808-1999	1886	$13,736	$4,240	1-M	1,324	49
Gonzaga Univ, Spokane, WA 99258	1887	$23,578	$6,700	2-D	6,377	335
Gordon Coll, Wenham, MA 01984-1899	1889	$22,924	$6,270	2-M	1,650	145
Goucher Coll, Baltimore, MD 21204-2794	1885	$27,525	$9,475	1-M	2,233	190
Governors State Univ, University Park, IL 60466-0975	1969	$4,300 (S)	NA	5-M	5,405	212
Grace Coll, Winona Lake, IN 46590-1294	1948	$16,020	$6,150	2-D	1,275	121
Graceland Univ, Lamoni, IA 50140	1895	$16,150	$5,400	2-M	2,351	114
Grambling State Univ, Grambling, LA 71245	1901	$3,506 (S)	$4,034	5-D	5,039	247
Grand Canyon Univ, Phoenix, AZ 85017-1097	1949	$4,875 (S)	$7,130	2-M	4,113	274
Grand Valley State Univ, Allendale, MI 49401-9403	1960	$6,220 (S)	$6,360	5-M	22,565	1,370
Grand View Coll, Des Moines, IA 50316-1599	1896	$16,110	$5,664	2-B	1,761	202
Granite State Coll, Concord, NH 03301	1972	$4,563 (S)	NA	11-B	1,827	223
Greensboro Coll, Greensboro, NC 27401-1875	1838	$18,120	$6,920	2-M	1,226	125
Greenville Coll, Greenville, IL 62246-0159	1892	$17,242	$5,904	2-M	1,350	124
Grinnell Coll, Grinnell, IA 50112-1690	1846	$27,504	$7,310	1-B	1,577	199
Grove City Coll, Grove City, PA 16127-2104	1876	$10,640	$5,344	2-B	2,341	184
Guilford Coll, Greensboro, NC 27410-4173	1837	$23,020	$6,690	2-B	2,682	202
Gustavus Adolphus Coll, St. Peter, MN 56082-1498	1862	$24,865	$6,065	2-B	2,603	250
Gwynedd-Mercy Coll, Gwynedd Valley, PA 19437-0901	1948	$19,220	$8,300	2-M	2,723	274
Hamilton Coll, Clinton, NY 13323-1296	1812	$33,350	$8,310	1-B	1,812	205
Hamline Univ, St. Paul, MN 55104-1284	1854	$23,157	$6,910	2-D	4,550	500
Hampden-Sydney Coll, Hampden-Sydney, VA 23943 (1)	1776	$26,170	$8,125	2-B	1,060	108
Hampshire Coll, Amherst, MA 01002	1965	$32,519	$8,519	1-B	1,376	137
Hampton Univ, Hampton, VA 23668	1868	$14,182	$6,746	1-D	6,209	447
Hannibal-LaGrange Coll, Hannibal, MO 63401-1999	1858	$11,780	$4,610	2-B	1,057	94
Hanover Coll, Hanover, IN 47243-0108	1827	$21,650	$6,500	2-B	1,008	103
Harding Univ, Searcy, AR 72149-0001	1924	$11,200	$5,312	2-M	5,744	332
Hardin-Simmons Univ, Abilene, TX 79698-0001	1891	$15,626	$4,580	2-D	2,435	179
Harrington Coll of Design, Chicago, IL 60606 (4)	1931	$7,510	$5,000	3-B	1,563	142
Harris-Stowe State Univ, St. Louis, MO 63103-2136	1857	$4,800 (S)	$5,400	5-B	1,662	133
Hartwick Coll, Oneonta, NY 13820-4020	1797	$27,010	$7,480	1-B	1,463	170
Harvard Univ, Cambridge, MA 02138	1636	$33,709	$9,946	1-D	19,376	2,035
Haskell Indian Nations Univ, Lawrence, KS 66046-4800	1884	$420 (S)	NA	4-B	1,028	48
Hastings Coll, Hastings, NE 68901-7696	1882	$17,268	$4,950	2-M	1,189	121
Haverford Coll, Haverford, PA 19041-1392	1833	$31,760	$9,840	1-B	1,168	116
Hawai`i Pacific Univ, Honolulu, HI 96813-2785	1965	$11,630	$9,450	1-M	8,046	612
Heidelberg Coll, Tiffin, OH 44883-2462	1850	$16,134	$7,108	2-M	1,435	140
Henderson State Univ, Arkadelphia, AR 71999-0001	1890	$4,625 (S)	$3,888	5-M	3,584	229
Hendrix Coll, Conway, AR 72032-3080	1876	$21,636	$6,310	2-M	1,031	107
Heritage Univ, Toppenish, WA 98948-9599	1982	$9,645	NA	1-M	1,311	187
High Point Univ, High Point, NC 27262-3598	1924	$18,410	$7,590	2-M	2,760	227
Hilbert Coll, Hamburg, NY 14075-1597	1957	$14,900	$5,580	1-B	1,109	101
Hillsdale Coll, Hillsdale, MI 49242-1298	1844	$17,410	$6,750	1-B	1,304	136
Hiram Coll, Hiram, OH 44234-0067	1850	$24,180	$7,610	2-M	1,111	103
Hobart & William Smith Colleges, Geneva, NY 14456-3397	1822	$32,737	$8,386	1-B	1,883	185
Hofstra Univ, Hempstead, NY 11549	1935	$21,530	$9,300	1-D	12,890	1,246
Hollins Univ, Roanoke, VA 24020-1603	1842	$22,945	$8,160	1-M	1,123	109
Holy Family Univ, Philadelphia, PA 19114-2094	1954	$17,740	$8,000	2-M	2,670	258
Holy Names Univ, Oakland, CA 94619-1699 (4)	1868	$22,710	NA	2-M	1,093	140
Hood Coll, Frederick, MD 21701-8575	1893	$22,335	$7,750	1-M	2,117	202
Hope Coll, Holland, MI 49422-9000	1866	$21,540	$6,668	2-B	3,141	332
Hope Intl Univ, Fullerton, CA 92831-3138	1928	$18,000	$6,000	2-M	1,136	211
Houghton Coll, Houghton, NY 14744	1883	$19,420	$6,560	2-M	1,411	103
Houston Baptist Univ, Houston, TX 77074-3298	1960	$16,500	$4,500	2-M	2,294	169
Howard Payne Univ, Brownwood, TX 76801-2715	1889	$12,000	$4,242	2-B	1,319	125
Howard Univ, Washington, DC 20059-0002	1867	$12,295	$6,186	1-D	10,623	1,576
Humboldt State Univ, Arcata, CA 95521-8299	1913	$2,866 (S)	$7,281	5-M	7,550	490
Hunter Coll of the City Univ of New York, New York, NY 10021-5085	1870	$4,349 (S)	$3,478	11-M	20,843	1,435
Huntington Univ, Huntington, IN 46750-1299	1897	$18,860	$6,530	2-M	1,019	122
Husson Coll, Bangor, ME 04401-2999	1898	$11,380	$6,030	1-M	2,245	54
Idaho State Univ, Pocatello, ID 83209	1901	NA	$5,030	5-D	13,977	908
Illinois Coll, Jacksonville, IL 62650-2299	1829	$17,100	$6,500	2-B	1,030	109
Illinois Inst of Art-Chicago, Chicago, IL 60654	1916	$19,020	$8,070	3-B	2,588	175
Illinois Inst of Art-Schaumburg, Schaumburg, IL 60173	NA	$16,605	NA	3-B	1,187	73
Illinois Inst of Tech, Chicago, IL 60616-3793	1890	$23,002	$7,518	1-D	6,378	580
Illinois State Univ, Normal, IL 61790-2200	1857	$7,091 (S)	$5,748	5-D	20,653	1,103
Illinois Wesleyan Univ, Bloomington, IL 61702-2900	1850	$29,076	$6,714	1-B	2,146	222
Immaculata Univ, Immaculata, PA 19345 (4)	1920	$20,575	$9,335	2-D	4,019	297
Indiana State Univ, Terre Haute, IN 47809-1401	1865	$5,864 (S)	$5,938	5-D	10,679	662
Indiana Tech, Fort Wayne, IN 46803-1297	1930	$17,850	$6,750	1-M	3,229	245
Indiana Univ-Purdue Univ Fort Wayne, Fort Wayne, IN 46805-1499	1917	$5,067 (S)	$4,750	5-M	11,795	766
Indiana Univ-Purdue Univ Indianapolis, Indianapolis, IN 46202-2896	1969	$6,219 (S)	$4,740	5-D	29,933	NA
Indiana Univ Bloomington, Bloomington, IN 47405-7000	1820	$7,112 (S)	$6,240	5-D	37,958	NA
Indiana Univ Northwest, Gary, IN 46408-1197	1959	$4,902 (S)	NA	5-M	4,987	NA
Indiana Univ of Pennsylvania, Indiana, PA 15705-1087	1875	$6,085 (S)	$4,866	5-D	14,081	711
Indiana Univ South Bend, South Bend, IN 46634-7111	1922	$4,989 (S)	NA	5-M	7,459	NA
Indiana Univ Southeast, New Albany, IN 47150-6405	1941	$4,880 (S)	NA	5-M	6,164	NA
Indiana Wesleyan Univ, Marion, IN 46953-4974	1920	$16,184	$5,890	2-D	11,020	148
Inter American Univ of Puerto Rico, Aguadilla Campus, Aguadilla, PR 00605	1957	$3,724	NA	1-M	4,129	254
Inter American Univ of Puerto Rico, Arecibo Campus, Arecibo, PR 00614-4050	1957	$3,664	NA	1-M	4,589	234
Inter American Univ of Puerto Rico, Barranquitas Campus, Barranquitas, PR 00794	1957	$4,770	$7,301	1-B	2,324	123
Inter American Univ of Puerto Rico, Bayamón Campus, Bayamón, PR 00957	1912	$3,764	NA	1-M	5,255	315
Inter American Univ of Puerto Rico, Fajardo Campus, Fajardo, PR 00738-7003	1965	$3,664	NA	1-M	2,245	118
Inter American Univ of Puerto Rico, Guayama Campus, Guayama, PR 00785	1958	$3,664	NA	1-M	2,273	139
Inter American Univ of Puerto Rico, Metro Campus, San Juan, PR 00919-1293	1960	$3,664	NA	1-D	10,451	599
Inter American Univ of Puerto Rico, Ponce Campus, Mercedita, PR 00715-1602	1962	$4,756	NA	1-M	5,327	257
Inter American Univ of Puerto Rico, San Germán Campus, San Germán, PR 00683-5008	1912	$4,616	$2,400	1-D	5,764	337
Intl Acad of Design & Tech, Tampa, FL 33634-7350	1984	$385/cr. hr.	NA	3	2,405	167

Name, address	Year Founded	Tuition & Fees	Rm. & Board	Control, Degree	Enroll-ment	Faculty
Intl Acad of Design & Tech, Chicago, IL 60602-9736	1977	$23,000	NA	3-B	2,768	184
Intl Coll, Naples, FL 34119	1990	$9,500	NA	1-M	1,544	109
Iona Coll, New Rochelle, NY 10801-1890	1940	$20,980	$9,898	2-M	4,184	373
Iowa State Univ of Sci & Tech, Ames, IA 50011	1858	$5,634 (S)	$6,197	5-D	25,741	1,636
Ithaca Coll, Ithaca, NY 14850-7020	1892	$25,194	$9,950	1-D	6,412	656
Jackson State Univ, Jackson, MS 39217	1877	$3,964 (S)	$5,044	5-D	8,351	465
Jacksonville State Univ, Jacksonville, AL 36265-1602	1883	$4,040 (S)	$3,258	5-M	9,110	434
Jacksonville Univ, Jacksonville, FL 32211-3394	1934	$19,970	$6,460	1-M	2,948	162
James Madison Univ, Harrisonburg, VA 22807	1908	$5,886 (S)	$6,372	5-D	16,938	1,164
Jamestown Coll, Jamestown, ND 58405	1883	$10,550	$4,340	2-B	1,026	78
John Brown Univ, Siloam Springs, AR 72761-2121	1919	$15,280	$5,630	2-M	1,904	148
John Carroll Univ, University Heights, OH 44118-4581	1886	$23,630	$7,526	2-M	4,101	409
John F. Kennedy Univ, Pleasant Hill, CA 94523-4817	1964	$14,436	NA	1-D	1,653	728
John Jay Coll of Criminal Justice of the City Univ of New York, New York, NY 10019-1093	1964	$4,259 (S)	NA	11-D	12,984	913
Johns Hopkins Univ, Baltimore, MD 21218-2699	1876	$34,400	$10,622	1-D	6,025	525
Johnson & Wales Univ, Denver, CO 80220	1993	$20,826	$8,500	1-B	1,544	82
Johnson & Wales Univ, North Miami, FL 33181	1992	$20,826	$9,300	1-B	2,452	76
Johnson & Wales Univ, Charlotte, NC 28202	2004	$20,826	$8,300	1-B	2,156	75
Johnson & Wales Univ, Providence, RI 02903-3703	1914	$20,826	$7,300	1-D	10,171	406
Johnson C. Smith Univ, Charlotte, NC 28216-5398	1867	$14,399	$5,563	1-B	1,404	121
Johnson State Coll, Johnson, VT 05656-9405	1828	$6,906 (S)	$6,910	5-M	1,866	143
Jones Intl Univ, Centennial, CO 80112	1995	$10,200	NA	3-M	1,411	60
Judson Coll, Elgin, IL 60123-1498	1963	$19,450	$6,900	2-M	1,241	111
Juniata Coll, Huntingdon, PA 16652-2119	1876	$27,540	$7,680	2-B	1,449	132
Kalamazoo Coll, Kalamazoo, MI 49006-3295	1833	$25,644	$6,709	2-B	1,263	114
Kansas State Univ, Manhattan, KS 66506	1863	$5,124 (S)	$5,772	5-D	23,182	792
Kean Univ, Union, NJ 07083	1855	$7,507 (S)	$8,374	5-M	12,958	1,160
Keene State Coll, Keene, NH 03435	1909	$7,818 (S)	$7,027	5-M	4,846	409
Kennesaw State Univ, Kennesaw, GA 30144-5591	1963	$3,044 (S)	$5,880	5-M	18,556	915
Kent State Univ, Kent, OH 44242-0001	1910	$7,954 (S)	$6,640	5-D	23,622	1,455
Kentucky State Univ, Frankfort, KY 40601	1886	$4,468 (S)	$5,620	12-M	2,386	160
Kenyon Coll, Gambier, OH 43022-9623	1824	$33,930	$5,570	1-B	1,661	186
Kettering Univ, Flint, MI 48504-4898	1919	$23,748	$5,440	1-M	2,935	157
Keuka Coll, Keuka Park, NY 14478-0098	1890	$18,070	$7,780	2-M	1,368	99
King's Coll, Wilkes-Barre, PA 18711-0801	1946	$21,220	$8,590	2-M	2,323	201
Knox Coll, Galesburg, IL 61401	1837	$26,100	$6,285	1-B	1,245	117
Kutztown Univ of Pennsylvania, Kutztown, PA 19530-0730	1866	$6,425 (S)	$5,480	5-M	9,864	461
Lafayette Coll, Easton, PA 18042-1798	1826	$31,669	$9,864	2-B	2,346	236
LaGrange Coll, LaGrange, GA 30240-2999	1831	$16,200	$6,674	2-M	1,046	118
Lake Forest Coll, Lake Forest, IL 60045-2399	1857	$27,334	$6,526	1-M	1,435	158
Lakeland Coll, Sheboygan, WI 53082-0359	1862	$16,796	$5,420	2-M	4,021	69
Lake Superior State Univ, Sault Sainte Marie, MI 49783	1946	$6,306 (S)	$6,536	5-M	2,888	211
Lamar Univ, Beaumont, TX 77710	1923	$2,880 (S)	$5,254	5-D	10,595	542
Lancaster Bible Coll, Lancaster, PA 17608-3403	1933	$12,360	$5,700	2-M	1,001	86
Lander Univ, Greenwood, SC 29649-2099	1872	$6,668 (S)	$5,468	5-M	2,703	190
Lane Coll, Jackson, TN 38301-4598	1882	$7,176	$4,534	2-B	1,045	52
La Roche Coll, Pittsburgh, PA 15237-5898	1963	$17,380	$7,344	2-M	1,707	225
La Salle Univ, Philadelphia, PA 19141-1199	1863	$27,810	$10,300	2-D	6,138	396
Lasell Coll, Newton, MA 02466-2709	1851	$20,900	$9,200	1-M	1,253	162
La Sierra Univ, Riverside, CA 92515	1922	$20,634	$5,873	2-M	1,941	164
Lawrence Tech Univ, Southfield, MI 48075-1058	1932	$19,443	$7,266	1-D	4,122	389
Lawrence Univ, Appleton, WI 54912-0599	1847	$29,598	$6,381	1-B	1,450	176
Lebanon Valley Coll, Annville, PA 17003-1400	1866	$24,860	$6,840	2-F	1,915	199
Lee Univ, Cleveland, TN 37320-3450	1918	$9,610	$5,170	2-M	3,930	312
Lehigh Univ, Bethlehem, PA 18015-3094	1865	$31,420	$8,560	1-D	6,748	621
Lehman Coll of the City Univ of New York, Bronx, NY 10468-1589	1931	$4,288 (S)	NA	11-M	10,615	NA
Le Moyne Coll, Syracuse, NY 13214	1946	$21,280	$8,290	2-M	3,580	324
Lenoir-Rhyne Coll, Hickory, NC 28603	1891	$18,920	$6,680	2-M	1,579	146
Lesley Univ, Cambridge, MA 02138-2790	1909	$24,450	$10,500	1-D	7,298	184
LeTourneau Univ, Longview, TX 75607-7001	1946	$15,890	$6,286	2-M	3,980	315
Lewis & Clark Coll, Portland, OR 97219-7899	1867	$27,710	$7,648	1-D	3,433	323
Lewis-Clark State Coll, Lewiston, ID 83501-2698	1893	$3,714 (S)	$4,500	5-B	3,451	229
Lewis Univ, Romeoville, IL 60446	1932	$19,200	$7,600	2-D	5,065	472
Liberty Univ, Lynchburg, VA 24502	1971	$15,350	$5,400	2-D	12,458	501
Life Univ, Marietta, GA 30060-2903	1974	$7,065	$10,980	1-F	1,473	108
Lincoln Memorial Univ, Harrogate, TN 37752-1901	1897	$13,750	$5,232	1-M	2,802	152
Lincoln Univ, Jefferson City, MO 65102	1866	$4,602 (S)	$3,790	5-M	3,180	174
Lincoln Univ, Lincoln University, PA 19352	1854	$7,618 (S)	$6,792	12-M	2,278	183
Lindenwood Univ, St. Charles, MO 63301-1695	1827	$12,240	$6,000	2-M	9,076	608
Lindsey Wilson Coll, Columbia, KY 42728-1298	1903	$14,438	$6,163	2-M	1,902	111
Linfield Coll, McMinnville, OR 97128-6894	1849	$23,022	$6,610	2-B	1,750	164
Lipscomb Univ, Nashville, TN 37204-3951	1891	$14,557	$6,410	2-F	2,518	196
Lock Haven Univ of Pennsylvania, Lock Haven, PA 17745-2390	1870	$6,258 (S)	$5,840	5-M	5,283	273
Logan Univ-Coll of Chiropractic, Chesterfield, MO 63006-1065	1935	$3,750	NA	1-F	1,076	87
Loma Linda Univ, Loma Linda, CA 92350	1905	$24,570	$2,370	2-D	3,906	150
Long Island Univ, Brentwood Campus, Brentwood, NY 11717	1959	$651/credit	NA	1-M	1,115	110
Long Island Univ, Brooklyn Campus, Brooklyn, NY 11201-8423	1926	$24,328	$7,810	1-D	8,144	954
Long Island Univ, C.W. Post Campus, Brookville, NY 11548-1300	1954	$23,230	$8,700	1-D	8,472	1,165
Longwood Univ, Farmville, VA 23909	1839	$7,020 (S)	$5,586	5-M	4,289	242
Loras Coll, Dubuque, IA 52004-0178	1839	$21,098	$6,095	2-M	1,683	142
Louisiana Coll, Pineville, LA 71359-0001	1906	$10,300	$3,886	2-B	1,085	92
Louisiana State Univ & Agr & Mech Coll, Baton Rouge, LA 70803	1860	$4,419 (S)	$6,330	5-D	31,264	1,467
Louisiana State Univ Health Sci Ctr, New Orleans, LA 70112-2223	1931	$4,392 (S)	$2,916	5-D	2,240	1,380
Louisiana State Univ in Shreveport, Shreveport, LA 71115-2399	1965	$3,815 (S)	$2,196	5-M	4,401	254
Louisiana Tech Univ, Ruston, LA 71272	1894	$4,375 (S)	$4,035	5-D	11,691	499
Lourdes Coll, Sylvania, OH 43560-2898	1958	$12,270	NA	2-M	1,460	150
Loyola Coll in Maryland, Baltimore, MD 21210-2699	1852	$29,683	$9,215	2-D	6,187	537
Loyola Marymount Univ, Los Angeles, CA 90045-2659	1911	$27,710	$10,502	2-D	8,855	868
Loyola Univ Chicago, Chicago, IL 60611-2196	1870	$26,906	$9,614	2-D	14,764	1,106
Loyola Univ New Orleans, New Orleans, LA 70118-6195	1912	$25,246	$8,312	2-F	5,423	483
Lubbock Christian Univ, Lubbock, TX 79407-2099	1957	$12,560	$4,250	2-F	2,076	154
Luther Coll, Decorah, IA 52101-1045	1861	$26,380	$4,290	2-B	2,545	239
Luther Rice Univ, Lithonia, GA 30038-2454	1962	$4,228	NA	2-D	1,600	33
Lycoming Coll, Williamsport, PA 17701-5192	1812	$24,080	$6,542	2-B	1,467	118

Name, address	Year Founded	Tuition & Fees	Rm. & Board	Control, Degree	Enrollment	Faculty
Lynchburg Coll, Lynchburg, VA 24501-3199	1903	$24,245	$6,400	2-M	2,428	237
Lyndon State Coll, Lyndonville, VT 05851-0919	1911	$6,484 (S)	$6,674	5-M	1,319	145
Lynn Univ, Boca Raton, FL 33431-5598	1962	$27,350	$9,650	1-D	2,747	271
Macalester Coll, St. Paul, MN 55105-1899	1874	$31,038	$7,982	2-B	1,869	223
Macon State Coll, Macon, GA 31206	1968	$1,730 (S)	NA	5-B	6,150	240
Madonna Univ, Livonia, MI 48150-1173	1947	$10,400	$5,768	2-M	4,308	400
Malone Coll, Canton, OH 44709-3897	1892	$17,790	$6,400	2-M	2,277	202
Manchester Coll, North Manchester, IN 46962-1225	1889	$20,500	$4,500	2-M	1,104	89
Manhattan Coll, Riverdale, NY 10471	1853	$20,350	$9,325	2-M	3,425	332
Manhattanville Coll, Purchase, NY 10577-2132	1841	$28,000	$11,550	1-M	2,806	298
Mansfield Univ of Pennsylvania, Mansfield, PA 16933	1857	$6,408 (S)	$5,868	5-M	3,390	223
Marian Coll, Indianapolis, IN 46222-1997	1851	$19,060	$6,300	2-M	1,685	145
Marian Coll of Fond du Lac, Fond du Lac, WI 54935-4699	1936	$16,705	$5,070	2-D	2,975	285
Marietta Coll, Marietta, OH 45750-4000	1835	$22,655	$6,445	1-M	1,461	140
Marist Coll, Poughkeepsie, NY 12601-1387	1929	$21,202	$9,364	1-M	5,744	596
Marquette Univ, Milwaukee, WI 53201-1881	1881	$25,074	$8,160	2-D	11,594	1,046
Marshall Univ, Huntington, WV 25755	1837	$3,932 (S)	$6,272	5-D	13,988	722
Mars Hill Coll, Mars Hill, NC 28754	1856	$17,950	$6,428	2-B	1,378	144
Mary Baldwin Coll, Staunton, VA 24401-3610 (4)	1842	$20,605	$5,860	1-M	1,740	134
Marygrove Coll, Detroit, MI 48221-2599 (4)	1905	$13,135	$6,200	2-M	3,591	71
Maryland Inst Coll of Art, Baltimore, MD 21217	1826	$26,920	$7,530	1-M	1,717	267
Marylhurst Univ, Marylhurst, OR 97036-0261	1893	$14,220	NA	2-M	1,268	209
Marymount Manhattan Coll, New York, NY 10021-4597	1936	$19,638	$12,090	1-B	2,007	315
Marymount Univ, Arlington, VA 22207-4299	1950	$18,114	$7,820	2-D	3,684	352
Maryville Coll, Maryville, TN 37804-5907	1819	$22,224	$7,000	2-B	1,146	110
Maryville Univ of Saint Louis, St. Louis, MO 63141-7299	1872	$17,320	$7,350	1-D	3,223	343
Marywood Univ, Scranton, PA 18509-1598	1915	$21,640	$9,100	2-D	3,127	313
Massachusetts Coll of Art, Boston, MA 02115-5882	1873	$6,850 (S)	$9,800	5-M	2,130	209
Massachusetts Coll of Liberal Arts, North Adams, MA 01247-4100	1894	NA	NA	5-M	1,811	122
Massachusetts Coll of Pharmacy & Health Sci, Boston, MA 02115-5896	1823	$21,050	$11,220	1-D	2,896	162
Massachusetts Inst of Tech, Cambridge, MA 02139-4307	1861	$32,300	$9,500	1-D	10,206	1,554
Massachusetts Maritime Acad, Buzzards Bay, MA 02532-1803 (2)	1891	$5,107 (A)	$6,464	5-M	1,008	70
Master's Coll & Seminary, Santa Clarita, CA 91321-1200	1927	$19,230	$6,620	2-D	1,537	159
McDaniel Coll, Westminster, MD 21157-4390	1867	$27,280	$5,900	1-M	3,524	190
McKendree Coll, Lebanon, IL 62254-1299	1828	$18,900	$7,380	2-M	2,585	214
McMurry Univ, Abilene, TX 79697	1923	$15,150	$5,852	2-B	1,430	128
McNeese State Univ, Lake Charles, LA 70609	1939	$3,159 (S)	$4,637	5-M	8,785	413
Medaille Coll, Buffalo, NY 14214-2695	1875	$15,030	$7,430	1-M	3,018	312
Medgar Evers Coll of the City Univ of New York, Brooklyn, NY 11225-2298	1969	$4,230 (S)	NA	11-B	5,212	339
Medical Coll of Georgia, Augusta, GA 30912	1828	$4,056 (S)	$2,334	5-D	2,115	764
Mercer Univ, Macon, GA 31207-0003	1833	$23,460	$7,413	2-D	7,154	614
Mercy Coll, Dobbs Ferry, NY 10522-1189	1951	$12,570	$8,678	1-M	9,539	830
Mercyhurst Coll, Erie, PA 16546	1926	$19,113	$7,074	2-M	4,120	248
Meredith Coll, Raleigh, NC 27607-5298	1891	$21,200	$5,940	1-M	2,168	250
Merrimack Coll, North Andover, MA 01845-5800	1947	$24,650	$9,730	2-M	2,188	223
Mesa State Coll, Grand Junction, CO 81501-3122	1925	$3,442 (S)	NA	5-M	6,062	396
Messiah Coll, Grantham, PA 17027	1909	$22,110	$6,800	2-B	2,916	297
Methodist Coll, Fayetteville, NC 28311-1498	1956	$17,850	$6,770	2-M	2,257	198
Metro Coll of New York, New York, NY 10013-1919 (4)	1964	$14,540	NA	1-M	1,555	297
Metro State Coll of Denver, Denver, CO 80217-3362	1963	$2,859 (S)	NA	5-B	20,761	1,141
Metro State Univ, St. Paul, MN 55106-5000	1971	$4,682 (S)	NA	5-M	6,516	422
Miami Intl Univ of Art & Design, Miami, FL 33132-1418	1965	$18,960	$6,150	3-M	1,406	110
Miami Univ, Oxford, OH 45056	1809	$21,487 (S)	$7,610	12-D	16,338	1,198
Michigan State Univ, East Lansing, MI 48824	1855	$7,587 (S)	$5,744	5-D	45,166	2,762
Michigan Tech Univ, Houghton, MI 49931-1295	1885	$8,194 (S)	$6,375	5-D	6,510	389
MidAmerica Nazarene Univ, Olathe, KS 66062-1899	1966	$15,968	$5,830	2-M	1,779	173
Middlebury Coll, Middlebury, VT 05753-6002	1800	$42,120 (C)	NA	1-D	2,455	300
Middle Tennessee State Univ, Murfreesboro, TN 37132	1911	$4,600 (S)	$5,626	5-D	22,554	NA
Midway Coll, Midway, KY 40347-1120 (3)	1847	$13,950	$6,200	2-B	1,279	149
Midwestern State Univ, Wichita Falls, TX 76308	1922	$4,566 (S)	$5,220	5-M	6,279	320
Miles Coll, Birmingham, AL 35208	1905	$5,826	$5,136	2-B	1,716	129
Millersville Univ of Pennsylvania, Millersville, PA 17551-0302	1855	$6,235 (S)	$5,878	5-M	7,998	468
Millikin Univ, Decatur, IL 62522-2084	1901	$21,121	$6,713	2-M	2,641	282
Millsaps Coll, Jackson, MS 39210-0001	1890	$20,690	$7,566	2-M	1,154	97
Mills Coll, Oakland, CA 94613-1000	1852	$29,990	$9,880	1-D	1,372	184
Milwaukee School of Engineering, Milwaukee, WI 53202-3109	1903	$24,960	$6,189	1-M	2,315	214
Minnesota State Univ Mankato, Mankato, MN 56001	1868	$5,846 (S)	$5,083	5-M	14,335	717
Minnesota State Univ Moorhead, Moorhead, MN 56563-0002	1885	$5,225 (S)	$4,974	5-M	7,652	303
Minot State Univ, Minot, ND 58707-0002	1913	$4,092 (S)	$4,460	5-M	3,797	273
Mississippi Coll, Clinton, MS 39058	1826	$12,288	$5,894	2-F	3,905	308
Mississippi State Univ, Mississippi State, MS 39762	1878	$4,312 (S)	$5,859	5-D	16,101	1,139
Mississippi Univ for Women, Columbus, MS 39701-9998 (4)	1884	$3,495 (S)	$3,778	5-M	2,328	214
Mississippi Valley State Univ, Itta Bena, MS 38941-1400	1946	$4,074 (S)	$3,946	5-M	3,165	183
Missouri Baptist Univ, St. Louis, MO 63141-8660	1964	$13,840	$5,800	2-M	4,460	191
Missouri Southern State Univ, Joplin, MO 64801-1595	1937	$3,916 (S)	$4,480	5-M	5,473	308
Missouri State Univ, Springfield, MO 65804-0094	1905	$5,454 (S)	$5,294	5-D	18,928	1,027
Missouri Valley Coll, Marshall, MO 65340-3197	1889	$14,500	$5,750	2-B	1,623	113
Missouri Western State Univ, St. Joseph, MO 64507-2294	1915	$4,778 (S)	$4,756	5-B	5,248	313
Molloy Coll, Rockville Centre, NY 11571-5002	1955	$16,460	NA	1-M	3,585	475
Monmouth Coll, Monmouth, IL 61462-1998	1853	$20,200	$5,750	2-B	1,345	155
Monmouth Univ, West Long Branch, NJ 07764-1898	1933	$20,686	$8,270	1-M	6,350	513
Monroe Coll, Bronx, NY 10468-5407	1933	$9,760	$6,900	3-M	4,285	237
Monroe Coll, New Rochelle, NY 10801-6410	1983	$9,760	$6,900	3-M	1,781	72
Montana State Univ-Billings, Billings, MT 59101-0298	1927	$4,856 (S)	$4,050	5-M	4,872	257
Montana State Univ-Northern, Havre, MT 59501-7751	1929	$4,519 (S)	$5,190	5-M	1,589	103
Montana State Univ, Bozeman, MT 59717	1893	$5,221 (S)	$6,150	5-D	12,166	828
Montana Tech of The Univ of Montana, Butte, MT 59701-8997	1895	$4,816 (S)	$5,106	5-M	2,230	149
Montclair State Univ, Montclair, NJ 07043-1624	1908	$7,709 (S)	$8,618	5-D	16,063	1,172
Montreat Coll, Montreat, NC 28757-1267	1916	$15,560	$5,008	2-M	1,035	120
Moody Bible Inst, Chicago, IL 60610-3284	1886	$1,400	$12,480	2-F	2,687	100
Moravian Coll, Bethlehem, PA 18018-6650	1742	$25,263	$7,530	2-F	2,030	190
Morehead State Univ, Morehead, KY 40351	1922	$4,320 (S)	$4,830	5-M	9,062	534
Morehouse Coll, Atlanta, GA 30314 (1)	1867	$16,830	$9,454	1-B	3,029	223
Morgan State Univ, Baltimore, MD 21251	1867	$6,110 (S)	$6,990	5-D	6,621	458
Morningside Coll, Sioux City, IA 51106	1894	$18,080	$5,624	2-M	1,440	132

Name, address	Year Founded	Tuition & Fees	Rm. & Board	Control, Degree	Enroll-ment	Faculty
Mountain State Univ, Beckley, WV 25802-9003	1933	$7,350	$5,526	1-M	4,404	316
Mount Aloysius Coll, Cresson, PA 16630-1999	1939	$14,650	$6,190	2-M	1,539	165
Mount Holyoke Coll, South Hadley, MA 01075 (3)	1837	$32,598	$9,550	1-M	2,127	241
Mount Ida Coll, Newton, MA 02459-3310	1899	$19,096	$9,830	1-B	1,297	214
Mount Marty Coll, Yankton, SD 57078-3724	1936	$15,730	$4,860	2-M	1,189	113
Mount Mary Coll, Milwaukee, WI 53222-4597	1913	$17,105	$5,790	2-M	1,722	198
Mount Mercy Coll, Cedar Rapids, IA 52402-4797	1928	$18,030	$5,680	2-B	1,490	151
Mount Olive Coll, Mount Olive, NC 28365	1951	$12,620	$4,952	2-B	2,830	241
Mount Saint Mary Coll, Newburgh, NY 12550-3494	1960	$16,930	$8,320	1-M	2,574	221
Mount St. Mary's Coll, Los Angeles, CA 90049-1599 (4)	1925	$24,150	$8,747	2-M	2,480	299
Mount St. Mary's Univ, Emmitsburg, MD 21727-7799	1808	$24,030	$8,690	2-F	2,176	205
Mt. Sierra Coll, Monrovia, CA 91016	1990	$16,200	NA	3-B	1,100	50
Mount Union Coll, Alliance, OH 44601-3993	1846	$19,850	$5,990	2-B	2,205	226
Mount Vernon Nazarene Univ, Mount Vernon, OH 43050-9500	1964	$16,726	$5,090	2-M	2,549	226
Muhlenberg Coll, Allentown, PA 18104-5586	1848	$30,260	$7,630	2-B	2,457	256
Murray State Univ, Murray, KY 42071-0009	1922	$4,428 (S)	$4,472	5-M	10,266	537
Muskingum Coll, New Concord, OH 43762	1837	$15,630	$6,200	2-M	2,142	129
Naropa Univ, Boulder, CO 80302-6697	1974	$18,500	$7,236	1-F	1,221	224
Natl-Louis Univ, Chicago, IL 60603	1886	$17,760	NA	1-D	7,345	284
Natl Univ, La Jolla, CA 92037-1011	1971	$8,352	NA	1-M	26,035	2,701
Nazareth Coll of Rochester, Rochester, NY 14618-3790	1924	$19,874	$8,360	1-D	3,120	301
Nebraska Wesleyan Univ, Lincoln, NE 68504-2796	1887	$18,410	$5,015	2-M	2,016	225
Neumann Coll, Aston, PA 19014-1298	1965	$17,920	$8,076	2-M	2,810	215
Newbury Coll, Brookline, MA 02445	1962	$16,100	$8,250	1-B	1,311	93
New Coll of California, San Francisco, CA 94102-5206	1971	$12,842	NA	1-M	1,133	192
New England Coll, Henniker, NH 03242-3293	1946	$23,010	$8,456	1-M	1,380	152
New England Inst of Art, Brookline, MA 02445	NA	$18,075	$9,978	3-B	1,293	115
New Jersey City Univ, Jersey City, NJ 07305-1597	1927	$7,040 (S)	$7,306	5-M	8,464	524
New Jersey Inst of Tech, Newark, NJ 07102	1881	$9,822 (S)	$8,572	5-D	8,058	654
Newman Univ, Wichita, KS 67213-2097	1933	$17,308	$5,372	2-M	2,103	153
New Mexico Highlands Univ, Las Vegas, NM 87701	1893	$2,300 (S)	$3,992	5-M	3,750	109
New Mexico Inst of Mining & Tech, Socorro, NM 87801	1889	$3,604 (S)	$4,866	5-D	1,891	147
New Mexico State Univ, Las Cruces, NM 88003-8001	1888	$3,918 (S)	$5,332	5-D	16,072	833
New School for General Studies, New York, NY 10011-8603	1919	$18,378	$11,750	1-D	1,650	506
New York Inst of Tech, Old Westbury, NY 11568-8000	1955	$19,236	$10,804	1-D	11,141	675
New York Univ, New York, NY 10012-1019	1831	$31,690	$11,480	1-D	40,004	4,073
Niagara Univ, Niagara University, NY 14109	1856	$19,800	$8,450	2-M	3,853	334
Nicholls State Univ, Thibodaux, LA 70310	1948	$3,389 (S)	$3,720	5-M	7,525	290
Nichols Coll, Dudley, MA 01571-5000	1815	$20,810	$8,052	1-M	1,792	65
Norfolk State Univ, Norfolk, VA 23504	1935	$4,670 (S)	$6,474	5-D	6,096	386
North Carolina Agr & Tech State Univ, Greensboro, NC 27411	1891	$3,124 (S)	$5,254	5-D	11,103	458
North Carolina Central Univ, Durham, NC 27707-3129	1910	$3,096 (S)	$4,526	5-F	8,219	560
North Carolina State Univ, Raleigh, NC 27695	1887	$4,784 (S)	$7,040	5-D	30,149	1,864
North Carolina Wesleyan Coll, Rocky Mount, NC 27804-8677	1956	$16,000	$6,670	2-B	1,752	164
North Central Coll, Naperville, IL 60566-7063	1861	$21,933	$6,993	2-M	2,472	203
Northcentral Univ, Prescott, AZ 86301-1747	NA	$9,000	NA	3-D	1,401	138
North Central Univ, Minneapolis, MN 55404-1322	1930	$12,166	$4,480	2-B	1,241	80
North Dakota State Univ, Fargo, ND 58105	1890	$5,264 (A)	$5,130	5-D	12,099	616
Northeastern Illinois Univ, Chicago, IL 60625-4699	1961	$5,646 (S)	NA	5-M	12,227	680
Northeastern State Univ, Tahlequah, OK 74464-2399	1846	$3,300 (S)	$3,312	5-F	9,562	480
Northeastern Univ, Boston, MA 02115-5096	1898	$28,792	$10,550	1-D	19,541	1,257
Northern Arizona Univ, Flagstaff, AZ 86011	1899	$4,393 (S)	$5,960	5-D	18,779	1,374
Northern Illinois Univ, De Kalb, IL 60115-2854	1895	$6,439 (S)	$5,950	5-D	25,208	1,193
Northern Kentucky Univ, Highland Heights, KY 41099	1968	$4,968 (S)	$4,660	5-F	13,908	788
Northern Michigan Univ, Marquette, MI 49855-5301	1899	$5,958 (S)	$6,013	5-M	9,379	422
Northern State Univ, Aberdeen, SD 57401-7198	1901	$4,699 (S)	$3,980	5-M	2,631	94
North Georgia Coll & State Univ, Dahlonega, GA 30597	1873	$3,068 (S)	$4,596	5-M	4,765	314
North Greenville Coll, Tigerville, SC 29688-1892	1892	$10,350	$5,950	2-B	1,766	132
North Park Univ, Chicago, IL 60625-4895	1891	$13,960	$7,280	2-D	2,181	121
Northwestern Coll, Orange City, IA 51041-1996	1882	$17,260	$4,914	2-B	1,273	128
Northwestern Coll, St. Paul, MN 55113-1598	1902	$19,100	$6,120	2-M	1,785	165
Northwestern Oklahoma State Univ, Alva, OK 73717-2799	1897	$3,270 (S)	$2,980	5-M	2,102	145
Northwestern State Univ of Louisiana, Natchitoches, LA 71497	1884	$3,393 (S)	$3,626	5-M	9,847	546
Northwestern Univ, Evanston, IL 60208	1851	$33,559	$10,266	1-D	17,004	1,145
Northwest Missouri State Univ, Maryville, MO 64468-6001	1905	$6,000 (S)	$5,492	5-M	6,249	259
Northwest Nazarene Univ, Nampa, ID 83686-5897	1913	$18,770	$5,010	2-M	1,625	100
Northwest Univ, Kirkland, WA 98033	1934	$18,144	$6,450	2-M	1,260	94
Northwood Univ, Midland, MI 48640-2398	1959	$15,533	$6,942	1-M	3,888	77
Northwood Univ, Texas Campus, Cedar Hill, TX 75104-1204	1966	$15,801	$6,636	1-B	1,061	30
Norwich Univ, Northfield, VT 05663	1819	$19,650	$7,090	1-M	2,707	272
Notre Dame Coll, South Euclid, OH 44121-4293	1922	$19,220	$6,648	2-M	1,299	87
Notre Dame de Namur Univ, Belmont, CA 94002-1908	1851	$23,850	$10,380	2-M	1,588	143
Nova Southeastern Univ, Fort Lauderdale, FL 33314-7796	1964	$17,800	$6,520	1-D	26,334	1,615
Nyack Coll, Nyack, NY 10960-3698	1882	$15,400	$7,600	2-F	3,000	288
Oakland City Univ, Oakland City, IN 47660-1099	1885	$14,220	$5,400	2-D	1,900	183
Oakland Univ, Rochester, MI 48309-4401	1957	$6,443 (S)	$6,080	5-D	17,339	890
Oakwood Coll, Huntsville, AL 35896	1896	$12,066	$6,828	2-B	1,751	170
Oberlin Coll, Oberlin, OH 44074	1833	$32,724	$8,180	1-M	2,864	288
Occidental Coll, Los Angeles, CA 90041-3314	1887	$33,644	$9,042	1-M	1,839	215
Oglethorpe Univ, Atlanta, GA 30319-2797	1835	$22,300	$8,000	1-M	1,083	115
Ohio Dominican Univ, Columbus, OH 43219-2099	1911	$19,450	$6,500	2-M	2,942	201
Ohio Northern Univ, Ada, OH 45810-1599	1871	$28,260	$7,080	2-F	3,542	282
Ohio State Univ-Mansfield Campus, Mansfield, OH 44906-1599	1958	$5,310 (S)	$6,264	5-M	1,610	89
Ohio State Univ-Newark Campus, Newark, OH 43055-1797	1957	$5,310 (S)	$6,264	5-M	2,183	135
Ohio State Univ, Columbus, OH 43210	1870	$8,082 (S)	$7,275	5-D	50,504	3,895
Ohio State Univ at Lima, Lima, OH 45804	1960	$5,310 (S)	$6,264	5-M	1,145	77
Ohio State Univ at Marion, Marion, OH 43302-5695	1958	$5,310 (S)	NA	5-M	1,485	108
Ohio Univ-Chillicothe, Chillicothe, OH 45601-0629	1946	$131/cr. hr. (S)	NA	5-M	2,000	106
Ohio Univ-Eastern, St. Clairsville, OH 43950-9724	1957	$131/cr. hr. (A)	NA	5-B	1,118	114
Ohio Univ-Lancaster, Lancaster, OH 43130-1097	1968	$144/cr. hr. (S)	NA	5-M	1,744	104
Ohio Univ-Southern Campus, Ironton, OH 45638-2214	1956	$136/cr. hr. (S)	NA	5-M	1,746	155
Ohio Univ-Zanesville, Zanesville, OH 43701-2695	1946	$4,596 (S)	NA	5-M	1,904	130
Ohio Univ, Athens, OH 45701-2979	1804	$8,235 (S)	$7,686	5-D	20,396	1,195
Ohio Wesleyan Univ, Delaware, OH 43015	1842	$28,280	$7,550	2-B	1,976	191
Oklahoma Baptist Univ, Shawnee, OK 74804	1910	$13,846	$4,140	2-M	1,883	119

Name, address	Year Founded	Tuition & Fees	Rm. & Board	Control, Degree	Enroll-ment	Faculty
Oklahoma Christian Univ, Oklahoma City, OK 73136-1100	1950	$14,976	$5,440	2-M	2,058	160
Oklahoma City Univ, Oklahoma City, OK 73106-1402	1904	$17,613	$6,250	2-F	3,688	285
Oklahoma Panhandle State Univ, Goodwell, OK 73939-0430	1909	$3,392 (S)	$4,270	5-B	1,144	89
Oklahoma State Univ, Stillwater, OK 74078	1890	$4,365 (S)	$5,848	5-D	23,461	1,237
Old Dominion Univ, Norfolk, VA 23529	1930	$5,611 (S)	$6,292	5-D	21,274	900
Olivet Coll, Olivet, MI 49076-9701	1844	$16,464	$5,480	2-M	1,069	67
Olivet Nazarene Univ, Bourbonnais, IL 60914-2271	1907	$16,490	$6,100	2-M	4,364	123
Oral Roberts Univ, Tulsa, OK 74171-0001	1963	$15,880	$6,770	2-D	4,086	235
Oregon Health & Sci Univ, Portland, OR 97239-3098	1974	$9,113 (S)	NA	12-D	2,511	836
Oregon Inst of Tech, Klamath Falls, OR 97601-8801	1947	$5,347 (S)	$6,037	5-M	3,373	130
Oregon State Univ, Corvallis, OR 97331	1868	$5,442 (S)	$6,930	5-D	19,236	1,215
Otis Coll of Art & Design, Los Angeles, CA 90045-9785	1918	$27,546	NA	1-M	1,098	277
Otterbein Coll, Westerville, OH 43081	1847	$22,518	$6,468	2-M	3,094	276
Ouachita Baptist Univ, Arkadelphia, AR 71998-0001	1886	$16,990	$5,000	2-B	1,499	142
Our Lady of Holy Cross Coll, New Orleans, LA 70131-7399	1916	$6,140	NA	2-M	1,446	123
Our Lady of the Lake Coll, Baton Rouge, LA 70808 (4)	1990	$7,280	NA	2-M	1,990	134
Our Lady of the Lake Univ of San Antonio, San Antonio, TX 78207-4689	1895	$17,546	$5,382	2-D	2,872	225
Pace Univ, New York, NY 10038	1906	$25,388	$8,940	1-D	14,177	1,238
Pacific Lutheran Univ, Tacoma, WA 98447	1890	$22,040	$6,765	2-M	3,680	260
Pacific Union Coll, Angwin, CA 94508-9707	1882	$19,125	$5,430	2-M	1,518	99
Pacific Univ, Forest Grove, OR 97116-1797	1849	$22,534	$6,468	1-D	2,563	128
Palm Beach Atlantic Univ, West Palm Beach, FL 33416-4708	1968	$17,350	$6,680	2-F	3,171	268
Palmer Coll of Chiropractic, Davenport, IA 52803-5287	1897	$6,030	NA	1-F	2,171	136
Park Univ, Parkville, MO 64152-3795	1875	$6,776	$5,180	1-M	13,253	889
Parsons The New School for Design, New York, NY 10011-8878	1896	$29,180	$11,750	1-M	3,502	951
Peirce Coll, Philadelphia, PA 19102-4699	1865	$12,760	NA	1-B	1,971	141
Pennsylvania Coll of Tech, Williamsport, PA 17701-5778	1965	$10,080 (S)	$6,900	12-B	6,537	491
Pennsylvania State Univ Abington Coll, Abington, PA 19001	1950	$10,190 (S)	NA	12-B	3,142	207
Pennsylvania State Univ Altoona Coll, Altoona, PA 16601-3760	1939	$10,626 (S)	$6,530	12-B	3,647	304
Pennsylvania State Univ at Erie, The Behrend Coll, Erie, PA 16563-0001	1948	$10,626 (S)	$6,530	12-M	3,542	261
Pennsylvania State Univ Berks Campus of the Berks-Lehigh Valley Coll, Reading, PA 19610-6009	1924	$10,626 (S)	$7,140	12-B	2,488	182
Pennsylvania State Univ Harrisburg Campus, Middletown, PA 17057-4898	1966	$10,616 (S)	$8,030	12-D	3,736	273
Pennsylvania State Univ Univ Park Campus, University Park, PA 16802-1503	1855	$11,508 (S)	$6,530	12-D	40,709	2,546
Pepperdine Univ, Malibu, CA 90263	1937	$32,740	$9,500	2-D	7,685	726
Peru State Coll, Peru, NE 68421	1867	$3,639 (S)	$4,486	5-M	1,959	130
Pfeiffer Univ, Misenheimer, NC 28109-0960	1885	$15,590	$6,310	2-M	2,150	143
Philadelphia Biblical Univ, Langhorne, PA 19047-2990	1913	$15,875	$6,550	2-F	1,439	156
Philadelphia Univ, Philadelphia, PA 19144-5497	1884	$22,140	$7,936	1-D	3,193	418
Piedmont Coll, Demorest, GA 30535-0010	1897	$15,500	$5,000	2-M	1,938	200
Pikeville Coll, Pikeville, KY 41501	1889	$11,500	$5,000	2-F	1,129	61
Pittsburg State Univ, Pittsburg, KS 66762	1903	$3,562 (S)	$4,550	5-M	6,628	373
Plymouth State Univ, Plymouth, NH 03264-1595	1871	$7,028 (S)	$6,780	5-M	5,264	452
Point Loma Nazarene Univ, San Diego, CA 92106-2899	1902	$22,150	$7,160	2-M	3,445	338
Point Park Univ, Pittsburgh, PA 15222-1984	1960	$16,740	$7,420	1-M	3,407	390
Polytechnic Univ, Brooklyn Campus, Brooklyn, NY 11201-2990	1854	$28,650	$8,500	1-D	2,801	266
Polytechnic Univ of Puerto Rico, Hato Rey, PR 00919	1966	$5,922	NA	1-M	5,771	300
Pomona Coll, Claremont, CA 91711	1887	$29,923	$10,851	1-B	1,532	206
Pontifical Catholic Univ of Puerto Rico, Ponce, PR 00717-0777	1948	$4,938	$3,140	2-D	7,474	352
Portland State Univ, Portland, OR 97207-0751	1946	$4,961 (S)	$8,445	5-D	24,120	1,234
Post Univ, Waterbury, CT 06723-2540	1890	$21,500	$8,400	1-B	1,101	122
Prairie View A&M Univ, Prairie View, TX 77446-0519	1878	$4,906 (S)	$6,204	5-D	7,912	485
Pratt Inst, Brooklyn, NY 11205-3899	1887	$29,230	$8,852	1-F	4,588	897
Presbyterian Coll, Clinton, SC 29325	1880	$23,244	$6,800	2-B	1,196	110
Prescott Coll, Prescott, AZ 86301	1966	$19,511	NA	1-D	1,044	87
Princeton Univ, Princeton, NJ 08544-1019	1746	$33,000	$9,200	1-D	6,916	1,060
Providence Coll, Providence, RI 02918	1917	$25,310	$9,270	2-M	4,832	369
Purchase Coll, State Univ of New York, Purchase, NY 10577-1400	1967	$5,608 (S)	$8,466	5-M	3,826	340
Purdue Univ, West Lafayette, IN 47907	1869	$7,096 (S)	NA	5-D	38,712	2,293
Purdue Univ Calumet, Hammond, IN 46323-2094	1951	$4,714 (S)	$3,990	5-M	9,302	471
Purdue Univ North Central, Westville, IN 46391-9542	1967	$5,583 (S)	NA	5-M	3,519	253
Queens Coll of the City Univ of New York, Flushing, NY 11367-1597	1937	$4,377 (S)	NA	11-M	17,638	1,271
Queens Univ of Charlotte, Charlotte, NC 28274-0002	1857	$19,450	$6,980	2-M	2,113	111
Quincy Univ, Quincy, IL 62301-2699	1860	$19,010	$6,960	2-M	1,359	127
Quinnipiac Univ, Hamden, CT 06518-1940	1929	$26,280	$10,700	1-D	7,293	780
Radford Univ, Radford, VA 24142	1910	$5,130 (S)	$6,120	5-M	9,552	570
Ramapo Coll of New Jersey, Mahwah, NJ 07430-1680	1969	$8,792 (S)	$9,464	5-M	5,538	433
Randolph-Macon Coll, Ashland, VA 23005-5505	1830	$23,945	$7,305	2-B	1,125	143
Reed Coll, Portland, OR 97202-8199	1908	$32,590	$8,516	1-M	1,340	131
Regent Univ, Virginia Beach, VA 23464-9800	1977	$11,850	NA	1-D	3,919	99
Regis Coll, Weston, MA 02493	1927	$21,525	$9,825	2-M	1,303	113
Regis Univ, Denver, CO 80221-1099	1877	$23,700	$8,190	2-D	16,335	2,379
Reinhardt Coll, Waleska, GA 30183-2981	1883	$13,220	$6,800	2-B	1,010	112
Rensselaer Polytechnic Inst, Troy, NY 12180-3590	1824	$31,857	$9,431	1-D	7,241	481
Rhode Island Coll, Providence, RI 02908-1991	1854	$4,676 (S)	$7,010	5-D	8,871	639
Rhode Island School of Design, Providence, RI 02903-2784	1877	$31,380	$9,360	1-F	2,258	494
Rhodes Coll, Memphis, TN 38112-1690	1848	$27,856	$6,904	2-M	1,692	184
Rice Univ, Houston, TX 77251-1892	1912	$23,746	$8,980	1-D	5,258	710
Richard Stockton Coll of New Jersey, Pomona, NJ 08240-0195	1969	$8,394 (S)	$7,902	5-M	7,034	426
Rider Univ, Lawrenceville, NJ 08648-3001	1865	$23,470	$8,840	1-M	5,552	501
Ringling School of Art & Design, Sarasota, FL 34234-5895	1931	$21,400	$9,165	1-B	1,088	119
Rivier Coll, Nashua, NH 03060-5086	1933	$20,580	$7,564	2-M	2,123	180
Roanoke Coll, Salem, VA 24153-3794	1842	$23,453	$7,295	2-B	1,936	174
Robert Morris Coll, Chicago, IL 60605	1913	$15,900	NA	1-M	5,418	368
Robert Morris Univ, Moon Township, PA 15108-1189	1921	$15,152	$7,670	1-D	5,095	384
Roberts Wesleyan Coll, Rochester, NY 14624-1997	1866	$20,286	$7,448	2-M	1,948	117
Rochester Coll, Rochester Hills, MI 48307-2764	1959	$12,356	$6,560	2-M	1,055	135
Rochester Inst of Tech, Rochester, NY 14623-5603	1829	$23,619	$8,451	1-D	15,200	1,204
Rockford Coll, Rockford, IL 61108-2393	1847	$22,460	$7,221	1-M	1,376	NA
Rockhurst Univ, Kansas City, MO 64110-2561	1910	$19,210	$5,900	2-D	2,944	217
Rocky Mountain Coll, Billings, MT 59102-1796	1878	$16,389	$6,624	2-M	1,009	113
Rogers State Univ, Claremore, OK 74017-3252	1909	$3,330 (S)	$6,210	5-B	3,300	151
Roger Williams Univ, Bristol, RI 02809	1956	$24,066	$10,693	1-F	5,214	398
Rollins Coll, Winter Park, FL 32789-4499	1885	$29,224	$9,142	1-M	2,493	217
Roosevelt Univ, Chicago, IL 60605-1394	1945	$14,430	$7,990	1-D	7,234	644

Name, address	Year Founded	Tuition & Fees	Rm. & Board	Control, Degree	Enroll-ment	Faculty
Rose-Hulman Inst of Tech, Terre Haute, IN 47803-3999 (2).	1874	$27,138	$7,419	1-M	1,887	157
Rosemont Coll, Rosemont, PA 19010-1699	1921	$20,550	$8,800	2-M	1,048	77
Rowan Univ, Glassboro, NJ 08028-1701	1923	$8,607 (S)	$8,242	5-D	9,762	886
Rush Univ, Chicago, IL 60612-3832	1969	$18,195	$5,715	1-D	1,362	796
Rust Coll, Holly Springs, MS 38635-2328	1866	$6,200	$2,750	2-B	1,001	50
Rutgers, The State Univ of New Jersey, Camden, Camden, NJ 08102-1401.	1927	$9,028 (S)	$8,088	5-F	5,321	401
Rutgers, The State Univ of New Jersey, Newark, Newark, NJ 07102.	1892	$8,812 (S)	$8,984	5-D	10,246	653
Rutgers, The State Univ of New Jersey, New Brunswick/Piscataway, New Brunswick, NJ 08901-1281.	1766	$9,221 (S)	$8,838	5-D	34,449	2,224
Sacred Heart Univ, Fairfield, CT 06825-1000	1963	$23,750	$9,654	2-D	5,560	472
Sage Coll of Albany, Albany, NY 12208-3425.	1957	$16,870	$7,540	1-B	1,031	88
Saginaw Valley State Univ, University Center, MI 48710	1963	$5,282 (S)	$6,150	5-M	9,569	560
St. Ambrose Univ, Davenport, IA 52803-2898	1882	$19,460	$7,240	2-D	3,623	290
Saint Anselm Coll, Manchester, NH 03102-1310	1889	$24,660	$9,070	2-B	1,986	177
St. Augustine Coll, Chicago, IL 60640-3501	1980	$7,128	NA	1-B	1,582	135
Saint Augustine's Coll, Raleigh, NC 27604-2298	1867	$11,428	$5,844	2-B	1,395	97
St. Bonaventure Univ, St. Bonaventure, NY 14778-2284	1858	$22,515	$7,760	2-M	2,614	207
St. Cloud State Univ, St. Cloud, MN 56301-4498	1869	$5,322 (S)	$4,688	5-M	15,964	861
St. Edward's Univ, Austin, TX 78704.	1885	$18,800	$6,900	2-M	4,947	440
St. Francis Coll, Brooklyn Heights, NY 11201-4398	1884	$12,710	$8,000	2-M	2,336	214
Saint Francis Univ, Loretto, PA 15940-0600	1847	$21,410	$7,568	2-M	2,065	164
St. John Fisher Coll, Rochester, NY 14618-3597	1948	$19,560	$8,300	2-M	3,528	305
Saint John's Univ, Collegeville, MN 56321 (2).	1857	$23,474	$6,275	2-F	1,996	176
St. John's Univ, Queens, NY 11439	1870	$24,970	$11,470	2-D	20,346	1,428
Saint Joseph Coll, West Hartford, CT 06117-2700	1932	$23,490	$9,760	2-M	1,858	88
Saint Joseph's Coll, Rensselaer, IN 47978	1889	$19,760	$6,480	2-M	1,003	77
St. Joseph's Coll, New York, Brooklyn, NY 11205-3688	1916	$12,236	NA	1-M	1,318	137
St. Joseph's Coll, Suffolk Campus, Patchogue, NY 11772-2399	1916	$12,766	NA	1-M	4,146	384
Saint Joseph's Univ, Philadelphia, PA 19131-1395.	1851	$27,455	$9,973	2-D	7,714	598
St. Lawrence Univ, Canton, NY 13617-1455.	1856	$32,150	$8,180	1-M	2,264	190
Saint Leo Univ, Saint Leo, FL 33574-6665	1889	$14,680	$7,460	2-M	2,263	122
St. Louis Coll of Pharmacy, St. Louis, MO 63110-1088	1864	$19,180	$7,510	1-F	1,093	105
Saint Louis Univ, St. Louis, MO 63103-2097.	1818	$26,448	$8,230	2-D	11,823	1,094
Saint Martin's Univ, Lacey, WA 98503-1297.	1895	$20,965	$6,400	2-M	1,463	162
Saint Mary-of-the-Woods Coll, Saint Mary-of-the-Woods, IN 47876.	1840	$18,660	$6,820	2-M	1,757	67
Saint Mary's Coll, Notre Dame, IN 46556 (3)	1844	$25,580	$8,425	2-B	1,397	198
Saint Mary's Coll of California, Moraga, CA 94575	1863	$27,280	$10,010	2-D	4,432	547
St. Mary's Coll of Maryland, St. Mary's City, MD 20686-3001.	1840	$11,710 (S)	$8,505	5-B	1,964	209
Saint Mary's Univ of Minnesota, Winona, MN 55987-1399	1912	$20,739	$5,900	2-D	5,222	561
St. Mary's Univ of San Antonio, San Antonio, TX 78228-8507	1852	$19,474	$6,688	2-D	3,963	333
Saint Michael's Coll, Colchester, VT 05439.	1904	$28,515	$6,990	2-M	2,474	217
St. Norbert Coll, De Pere, WI 54115-2099	1898	$22,509	$6,068	2-M	2,050	177
St. Olaf Coll, Northfield, MN 55057-1098	1874	$28,200	$7,400	2-B	3,058	332
Saint Peter's Coll, Jersey City, NJ 07306-5997.	1872	$19,750	$8,430	2-M	3,282	NA
St. Thomas Aquinas Coll, Sparkill, NY 10976	1952	$16,600	$8,850	1-M	2,194	139
St. Thomas Univ, Miami Gardens, FL 33054-6459	1961	$17,860	$5,630	2-F	2,692	250
Saint Vincent Coll, Latrobe, PA 15650-2690	1846	$21,679	$6,874	2-M	1,687	167
Saint Xavier Univ, Chicago, IL 60655-3105.	1847	$18,520	$7,078	2-M	5,705	426
Salem Coll, Winston-Salem, NC 27108-0548	1772	$17,190	$9,251	2-M	1,109	91
Salem State Coll, Salem, MA 01970-5353	1854	$5,284 (S)	$7,350	5-M	9,863	668
Salisbury Univ, Salisbury, MD 21801-6837.	1925	$6,376 (S)	$6,932	5-M	7,009	494
Salve Regina Univ, Newport, RI 02840-4192	1934	$23,950	$9,500	2-D	2,499	240
Samford Univ, Birmingham, AL 35229-0002.	1841	$14,642	$5,616	2-D	4,507	425
Sam Houston State Univ, Huntsville, TX 77341	1879	$3,822 (S)	$5,002	5-D	15,000	681
Samuel Merritt Coll, Oakland, CA 94609-3108 (4)	1909	$29,576	$5,903	1-D	1,080	157
San Diego State Univ, San Diego, CA 92182	1897	$3,155 (S)	$9,849	5-D	32,936	1,618
San Francisco State Univ, San Francisco, CA 94132-1722	1899	$3,370 (S)	$9,124	5-D	28,950	1,725
San Jose State Univ, San Jose, CA 95192-0001	1857	$3,292 (S)	$8,718	5-M	29,975	NA
Santa Clara Univ, Santa Clara, CA 95053	1851	$28,899	$10,032	2-D	8,097	746
Sarah Lawrence Coll, Bronxville, NY 10708-5999.	1926	$34,042	$11,464	1-M	1,662	222
Savannah Coll of Art & Design, Savannah, GA 31402-3146	1978	$23,450	$9,595	1-M	7,356	419
Savannah State Univ, Savannah, GA 31404	1890	$3,056 (S)	$4,716	5-M	3,055	167
School of the Art Inst of Chicago, Chicago, IL 60603-3103.	1866	$29,200	$8,600	1-M	2,679	468
School of Visual Arts, New York, NY 10010-3994.	1947	$21,080	$11,500	3-M	3,575	760
Seattle Pacific Univ, Seattle, WA 98119-1997	1891	$21,783	$7,572	2-D	3,873	333
Seattle Univ, Seattle, WA 98122-1090	1891	$22,905	$7,158	2-D	7,109	582
Seton Hall Univ, South Orange, NJ 07079-2697.	1856	$24,720	$10,466	2-D	9,637	926
Seton Hill Univ, Greensburg, PA 15601	1883	$21,990	$7,030	2-M	1,863	185
Sewanee: The Univ of the South, Sewanee, TN 37383-1000.	1857	$27,095	$7,550	2-D	1,528	174
Shawnee State Univ, Portsmouth, OH 45662-4344	1986	$5,508 (S)	$6,729	5-B	3,820	298
Shaw Univ, Raleigh, NC 27601-2399	1865	$10,020	$6,410	2-F	2,762	290
Shenandoah Univ, Winchester, VA 22601-5195.	1875	$20,050	$7,550	2-D	2,998	351
Shepherd Univ, Shepherdstown, WV 25443-3210	1871	$4,046 (S)	$6,020	5-M	3,901	253
Shippensburg Univ of Pennsylvania, Shippensburg, PA 17257-2299.	1871	$6,175 (S)	$5,710	5-M	7,485	371
Siena Coll, Loudonville, NY 12211-1462.	1937	$21,525	$8,475	2-B	3,336	312
Siena Heights Univ, Adrian, MI 49221-1796.	1919	$15,520	$5,460	2-M	2,153	NA
Simmons Coll, Boston, MA 02115.	1899	$25,440	$10,200	1-D	4,805	374
Simpson Coll, Indianola, IA 50125-1297	1860	$20,911	$5,922	2-B	2,035	170
Simpson Univ, Redding, CA 96003-8606	1921	$17,800	$6,200	2-M	1,087	107
Skidmore Coll, Saratoga Springs, NY 12866-1632	1903	$32,659	$9,120	1-M	2,828	321
Slippery Rock Univ of Pennsylvania, Slippery Rock, PA 16057-1383.	1889	$6,275 (S)	$4,796	5-M	8,105	401
Smith Coll, Northampton, MA 01063.	1871	$30,754	$10,720	1-D	3,093	316
Sojourner-Douglass Coll, Baltimore, MD 21205-1814 (4).	1980	$6,748	NA	1-M	1,124	136
Sonoma State Univ, Rohnert Park, CA 94928-3609	1960	$3,616 (S)	$8,890	5-M	7,749	542
South Carolina State Univ, Orangeburg, SC 29117-0001.	1896	$6,665 (S)	$6,028	5-D	4,294	267
South Dakota School of Mines & Tech, Rapid City, SD 57701-3995.	1885	$4,757 (S)	$2,867	5-D	2,313	140
South Dakota State Univ, Brookings, SD 57007	1881	$4,732 (S)	$4,769	5-D	10,938	584
Southeastern Louisiana Univ, Hammond, LA 70402.	1925	$3,341 (S)	$5,180	5-M	15,472	730
Southeastern Oklahoma State Univ, Durant, OK 74701-0609	1909	$3,372 (S)	$3,910	5-M	4,075	237
Southeastern Univ, Lakeland, FL 33801-6099	1935	$11,500	$5,678	2-B	1,964	116
Southeast Missouri State Univ, Cape Girardeau, MO 63701-4799.	1873	$5,145 (S)	$5,351	5-M	10,292	608
Southern Adventist Univ, Collegedale, TN 37315-0370	1892	$14,784	$4,604	2-M	2,522	217
Southern Arkansas Univ-Magnolia, Magnolia, AR 71753	1909	$4,290 (S)	$3,790	5-M	3,057	184
Southern Connecticut State Univ, New Haven, CT 06515-1355.	1893	$6,442 (S)	$8,031	5-D	12,158	958
Southern Illinois Univ Carbondale, Carbondale, IL 62901-4701	1869	$6,831 (S)	$5,560	5-D	21,441	1,081

Name, address	Year Founded	Tuition & Fees	Rm. & Board	Control, Degree	Enroll-ment	Faculty
Southern Illinois Univ Edwardsville, Edwardsville, IL 62026-0001	1957	$5,179 (S)	$5,819	5-F	13,460	819
Southern Methodist Univ, Dallas, TX 75275	1911	$28,630	$9,695	2-D	11,152	933
Southern Nazarene Univ, Bethany, OK 73008	1899	$15,024	$5,378	2-M	2,218	176
Southern New Hampshire Univ, Manchester, NH 03106-1045	1932	$21,714	$8,480	1-D	3,887	389
Southern Oregon Univ, Ashland, OR 97520	1926	$4,986 (S)	$6,468	5-M	4,977	289
Southern Polytechnic State Univ, Marietta, GA 30060-2896	1948	$3,174 (S)	$5,490	5-M	3,806	226
Southern Univ & Agr & Mech Coll, Baton Rouge, LA 70813	1880	$3,592 (S)	$4,646	5-D	9,941	573
Southern Univ at New Orleans, New Orleans, LA 70126-1009	1959	$2,990 (S)	NA	5-M	5,000	NA
Southern Utah Univ, Cedar City, UT 84720-2498	1897	$3,358 (S)	$5,400	5-M	6,859	274
Southern Wesleyan Univ, Central, SC 29630-1020	1906	$15,450	$5,450	2-M	2,632	228
South Univ, Savannah, GA 31406-4805	1899	$11,475	NA	3-D	1,037	91
Southwest Baptist Univ, Bolivar, MO 65613-2597	1878	$14,100	$4,200	2-D	3,440	246
Southwestern Adventist Univ, Keene, TX 76059	1894	$12,484	$5,806	2-M	1,191	92
Southwestern Coll, Winfield, KS 67156-2499	1885	$16,800	$5,438	2-M	1,416	144
Southwestern Oklahoma State Univ, Weatherford, OK 73096-3098	1901	$3,000 (S)	$3,090	5-F	4,841	NA
Southwestern Univ, Georgetown, TX 78626	1840	$21,900	$6,547	2-B	1,309	167
Southwest Minnesota State Univ, Marshall, MN 56258	1963	$5,294 (S)	$4,806	5-M	5,636	159
Spalding Univ, Louisville, KY 40203-2188	1814	$15,900	$3,672	2-D	1,641	174
Spelman Coll, Atlanta, GA 30314-4399 (3)	1881	$15,795	$8,455	1-B	2,318	245
Spring Arbor Univ, Spring Arbor, MI 49283-9799	1873	$16,666	$5,810	2-M	3,701	138
Springfield Coll, Springfield, MA 01109-3797	1885	$22,715	$8,130	1-D	3,155	342
Spring Hill Coll, Mobile, AL 36608-1791	1830	$20,948	$7,730	2-M	1,497	138
Stanford Univ, Stanford, CA 94305-9991	1891	$31,200	$9,932	1-D	19,042	1,031
State Univ of New York at Binghamton, Binghamton, NY 13902-6000	1946	$5,838 (S)	$8,150	5-D	14,018	769
State Univ of New York at Buffalo, Buffalo, NY 14260	1846	$6,068 (S)	$7,626	5-D	27,220	1,748
State Univ of New York at New Paltz, New Paltz, NY 12561	1828	$5,360 (S)	$7,230	5-M	7,825	706
State Univ of New York at Oswego, Oswego, NY 13126	1861	$5,322 (S)	$8,340	5-M	8,282	511
State Univ of New York at Plattsburgh, Plattsburgh, NY 12901-2681	1889	$5,296 (S)	$7,066	5-M	6,044	455
State Univ of New York Coll at Brockport, Brockport, NY 14420-2997	1867	$181/credit(S)	NA	5-M	8,484	615
State Univ of New York Coll at Cortland, Cortland, NY 13045	1868	$4,350 (S)	$7,850	5-M	7,260	555
State Univ of New York Coll at Geneseo, Geneseo, NY 14454-1401	1871	$5,520 (S)	$7,390	5-M	5,484	330
State Univ of New York Coll at Old Westbury, Old Westbury, NY 11568-0210	1965	$5,072 (S)	$8,083	5-M	3,398	253
State Univ of New York Coll at Oneonta, Oneonta, NY 13820-4015	1889	$5,367 (S)	$7,538	5-M	5,860	467
State Univ of New York Coll at Potsdam, Potsdam, NY 13676	1816	$5,289 (S)	$7,670	5-M	4,329	366
State Univ of New York Coll of Agriculture & Tech at Cobleskill, Cobleskill, NY 12043	1916	$5,345 (S)	$7,270	5-B	2,482	149
State Univ of New York Coll of Environmental Sci & Forestry, Syracuse, NY 13210-2779	1911	$5,032 (S)	$10,180	5-D	1,934	145
State Univ of New York Empire State Coll, Saratoga Springs, NY 12866-4391	1971	$4,575 (S)	NA	5-M	9,996	1,075
State Univ of New York, Fredonia, Fredonia, NY 14063-1136	1826	$5,441 (S)	$6,940	5-M	5,432	405
State Univ of New York Inst of Tech, Utica, NY 13504-3050	1966	$5,285 (S)	$7,290	5-M	2,590	162
State Univ of New York Maritime Coll, Throggs Neck, NY 10465-4198 (2)	1874	$7,405 (S)	$8,000	5-M	1,294	75
State Univ of New York Upstate Medical Univ, Syracuse, NY 13210-2334	1950	$9,166 (S)	$3,585	5-D	1,235	686
Stephen F. Austin State Univ, Nacogdoches, TX 75962	1923	$4,718 (S)	$5,459	5-D	11,435	582
Stetson Univ, DeLand, FL 32723	1883	$25,450	$7,275	1-F	3,665	268
Stevens Inst of Tech, Hoboken, NJ 07030	1870	$31,835	$9,500	1-D	4,689	331
Stonehill Coll, Easton, MA 02357-5510	1948	$25,540	$10,564	2-M	2,443	253
Stony Brook Univ, State Univ of New York, Stony Brook, NY 11794	1957	$5,575 (S)	$8,050	5-D	22,011	1,389
Strayer Univ, Washington, DC 20005-2603	1892	$10,368	NA	3-M	20,138	881
Suffolk Univ, Boston, MA 02108-2770	1906	$21,220	$11,940	1-D	8,474	779
Sullivan Univ, Louisville, KY 40205	1864	$13,335	$3,960	3-M	4,639	213
Sul Ross State Univ, Alpine, TX 79832	1920	$3,870 (S)	$4,050	5-M	1,954	133
Susquehanna Univ, Selinsgrove, PA 17870	1858	$26,265	$7,200	2-B	1,989	185
Swarthmore Coll, Swarthmore, PA 19081-1397	1864	$31,516	$9,764	1-B	1,479	195
Syracuse Univ, Syracuse, NY 13244	1870	$28,285	$10,370	1-D	17,266	1,391
Tarleton State Univ, Stephenville, TX 76402	1899	$4,170 (S)	$5,514	5-D	9,144	534
Taylor Univ, Upland, IN 46989-1001	1846	$20,746	$5,630	2-M	1,865	187
Temple Univ, Philadelphia, PA 19122-6096	1884	$9,640 (S)	$7,794	12-D	33,693	2,561
Tennessee State Univ, Nashville, TN 37209-1561	1912	$4,639 (S)	$4,270	5-D	8,880	604
Tennessee Tech Univ, Cookeville, TN 38505	1915	$4,660 (S)	$6,650	5-D	9,313	560
Texas A&M Intl Univ, Laredo, TX 78041-1900	1969	$4,218 (S)	$6,390	5-D	4,298	273
Texas A&M Univ-Commerce, Commerce, TX 75429-3011	1889	$4,824 (S)	$5,740	5-D	8,787	500
Texas A&M Univ-Corpus Christi, Corpus Christi, TX 78412-5503	1947	$4,516 (S)	$7,800	5-D	8,227	446
Texas A&M Univ-Kingsville, Kingsville, TX 78363	1925	$4,326 (S)	NA	5-D	7,126	438
Texas A&M Univ-Texarkana, Texarkana, TX 75505-5518	1971	$2,550 (S)	NA	5-M	1,653	100
Texas A&M Univ, College Station, TX 77843	1876	$6,399 (S)	$6,952	5-D	44,910	2,232
Texas A&M Univ at Galveston, Galveston, TX 77553-1675	1962	$5,118 (S)	$4,870	5-M	1,677	170
Texas Christian Univ, Fort Worth, TX 76129-0002	1873	$21,320	$6,980	2-D	8,749	810
Texas Lutheran Univ, Seguin, TX 78155-5999	1891	$18,840	$5,600	2-B	1,435	117
Texas Southern Univ, Houston, TX 77004-4584	1947	$3,772 (S)	$6,056	5-D	11,903	569
Texas State Univ-San Marcos, San Marcos, TX 78666	1899	$5,252 (S)	$5,610	5-D	27,129	1,297
Texas Tech Univ, Lubbock, TX 79409	1923	$6,152 (S)	$6,875	5-D	28,001	1,123
Texas Wesleyan Univ, Fort Worth, TX 76105-1536	1890	$14,000	$5,500	2-F	2,742	258
Texas Woman's Univ, Denton, TX 76201 (4)	1901	$5,010 (S)	$5,598	5-D	11,344	692
Thiel Coll, Greenville, PA 16125-2181	1866	$17,590	$6,990	2-B	1,320	122
Thomas Edison State Coll, Trenton, NJ 08608-1176	1972	$3,780/year (S)	NA	5-M	11,224	NA
Thomas Jefferson Univ, Philadelphia, PA 19107	1824	$21,975	NA	1-D	2,681	266
Thomas More Coll, Crestview Hills, KY 41017-3495	1921	$18,320	$6,150	2-M	1,434	134
Tiffin Univ, Tiffin, OH 44883-2161	1888	$15,870	$6,775	1-M	1,605	133
Touro Coll, New York, NY 10010	1971	NA	NA	1-D	11,447	999
Touro Univ Intl, Cypress, CA 90630	NA	$8,000	NA	1-D	2,507	194
Towson Univ, Towson, MD 21252-0001	1866	$7,096 (S)	$6,828	5-D	18,011	1,245
Transylvania Univ, Lexington, KY 40508-1797	1780	$19,650	$6,590	2-B	1,151	96
Trevecca Nazarene Univ, Nashville, TN 37210-2877	1901	$14,774	$6,470	2-D	2,196	217
Trinity Christian Coll, Palos Heights, IL 60463-0929	1959	$17,135	$6,600	2-B	1,280	127
Trinity Coll, Hartford, CT 06106-3100	1823	$33,630	$8,590	1-M	2,526	258
Trinity Intl Univ, Deerfield, IL 60015-1284	1897	$19,366	$6,320	2-D	2,836	360
Trinity Univ, San Antonio, TX 78212-7200	1869	$21,582	$8,725	2-M	2,756	280
Trinity (Washington) Univ, Washington, DC 20017-1094	1897	$17,360	$7,574	2-M	1,672	158
Tri-State Univ, Angola, IN 46703-1764	1884	$21,210	$6,240	1-M	1,172	99
Troy Univ, Troy, AL 36082	1887	$4,678 (S)	$4,964	5-M	26,880	1,405
Truman State Univ, Kirksville, MO 63501-4221	1867	$5,812 (S)	$5,380	5-M	5,803	378
Tufts Univ, Medford, MA 02155	1852	$32,621	$9,397	1-D	9,780	1,194
Tulane Univ, New Orleans, LA 70118-5669	1834	$32,946	$8,411	1-D	12,691	1,371
Tusculum Coll, Greeneville, TN 37743-9997	1794	$16,215	$6,500	2-M	2,656	150
Tuskegee Univ, Tuskegee, AL 36088	1881	$12,700	$7,887	1-D	2,880	265

Name, address	Year Founded	Tuition & Fees	Rm. & Board	Control, Degree	Enroll- ment	Faculty
Union Coll, Barbourville, KY 40906-1499	1879	$15,290	$4,600	2-M	1,224	71
Union Coll, Schenectady, NY 12308-2311	1795	$41,595 (C)	NA	1-B	2,252	209
Union Inst & Univ, Cincinnati, OH 45206-1925	1969	$8,910	NA	1-D	2,379	169
Union Univ, Jackson, TN 38305-3697	1823	$16,450	$5,470	2-D	2,866	278
United States Air Force Acad, USAF Academy, CO 80840-5025 (2)	1954	$0 (C)	NA	4-B	4,365	559
United States Coast Guard Acad, New London, CT 06320-8100	1876	$0 (C)	NA	4-B	1,012	118
United States Merchant Marine Acad, Kings Point, NY 11024-1699	1943	$0 (C)	NA	4-B	1,007	95
United States Military Acad, West Point, NY 10996 (2)	1802	$0 (C)	NA	4-B	4,231	604
United States Naval Acad, Annapolis, MD 21402-5000 (2)	1845	$0 (C)	NA	4-B	4,422	586
Universidad del Este, Carolina, PR 00983	1949	$3,872	NA	1-M	10,330	439
Universidad del Turabo, Gurabo, PR 00778-3030	1972	$3,872	NA	1-M	13,692	410
Universidad Metropolitana, San Juan, PR 00928-1150	1980	$3,872	NA	1-M	10,195	358
Univ at Albany, State Univ of New York, Albany, NY 12222-0001	1844	$5,887 (S)	$8,050	5-D	17,040	1,161
Univ of Advancing Tech, Tempe, AZ 85283-1042	1983	$14,600	NA	3-M	1,004	43
Univ of Akron, Akron, OH 44325	1870	$7,958 (S)	$7,208	5-D	21,049	1,474
Univ of Alabama, Tuscaloosa, AL 35487	1831	$4,864 (S)	$5,024	5-D	21,835	1,148
Univ of Alabama at Birmingham, Birmingham, AL 35294	1969	$4,792 (S)	$3,390	5-D	16,572	880
Univ of Alabama in Huntsville, Huntsville, AL 35899	1950	$4,688 (S)	$5,320	5-D	7,084	468
Univ of Alaska Anchorage, Anchorage, AK 99508-8060	1954	$3,465 (S)	$7,810	5-M	16,261	1,202
Univ of Alaska Fairbanks, Fairbanks, AK 99775-7520	1917	$4,518 (S)	$5,580	5-D	8,230	295
Univ of Alaska Southeast, Juneau, AK 99801	1972	$3,856 (S)	$6,714	5-M	3,126	229
Univ of Arizona, Tucson, AZ 85721	1885	$4,498 (S)	$7,460	5-D	37,036	1,424
Univ of Arkansas, Fayetteville, AR 72701-1201	1871	$5,494 (S)	$6,365	5-D	17,821	824
Univ of Arkansas at Fort Smith, Fort Smith, AR 72913-3649	1928	$2,830 (S)	$5,400	11-B	6,787	371
Univ of Arkansas at Little Rock, Little Rock, AR 72204-1099	1927	$5,213 (S)	$2,950	5-D	11,757	749
Univ of Arkansas at Monticello, Monticello, AR 71656	1909	$3,765 (S)	$3,150	5-M	2,875	247
Univ of Arkansas at Pine Bluff, Pine Bluff, AR 71601-2799	1873	$4,044 (S)	$5,436	5-M	3,303	236
Univ of Baltimore, Baltimore, MD 21201-5779	1925	$6,793 (S)	NA	5-D	4,987	331
Univ of Bridgeport, Bridgeport, CT 06604	1927	$20,595	$9,000	1-D	3,626	349
Univ of California, Berkeley, Berkeley, CA 94720-1500	1868	$6,558 (S)	$13,074	5-D	33,558	2,026
Univ of California, Davis, Davis, CA 95616	1905	$7,593 (S)	$11,239	5-D	28,815	1,883
Univ of California, Irvine, Irvine, CA 92697	1965	$6,141 (S)	$9,875	5-D	24,362	1,290
Univ of California, Los Angeles, Los Angeles, CA 90095	1919	$6,504 (S)	$11,928	5-D	37,221	2,460
Univ of California, Riverside, Riverside, CA 92521-0102	1954	$7,250 (S)	$10,200	5-D	16,622	849
Univ of California, San Diego, La Jolla, CA 92093	1959	$6,681 (S)	$9,421	5-D	24,645	1,149
Univ of California, Santa Barbara, Santa Barbara, CA 93106	1909	$6,993 (S)	$10,577	5-D	21,016	1,054
Univ of California, Santa Cruz, Santa Cruz, CA 95064	1965	$7,603 (S)	$11,571	5-D	15,012	742
Univ of Central Arkansas, Conway, AR 72035-0001	1907	$5,664 (S)	$4,320	5-D	11,375	607
Univ of Central Florida, Orlando, FL 32816	1963	$3,339 (S)	$7,400	5-D	44,953	1,637
Univ of Central Oklahoma, Edmond, OK 73034-5209	1890	$3,618 (S)	$4,476	5-M	15,953	812
Univ of Charleston, Charleston, WV 25304-1099	1888	$20,200	$7,400	1-M	1,006	99
Univ of Chicago, Chicago, IL 60637-1513	1891	$32,265	$10,104	1-D	14,150	1,587
Univ of Cincinnati, Cincinnati, OH 45221	1819	$8,883 (S)	$7,890	5-D	27,932	1,241
Univ of Colorado at Boulder, Boulder, CO 80309	1876	$5,372 (S)	$7,980	5-D	31,068	1,786
Univ of Colorado at Colorado Springs, Colorado Springs, CO 80933-7150	1965	$4,888 (S)	$6,418	5-D	8,437	556
Univ of Colorado at Denver & Health Sci Ctr - Downtown Denver Campus, Denver, CO 80217-3364	1912	$5,021 (S)	NA	5-D	19,755	1,362
Univ of Connecticut, Storrs, CT 06269	1881	$8,362 (S)	$8,266	5-D	23,185	1,265
Univ of Dallas, Irving, TX 75062-4736	1955	$21,805	$7,332	2-D	3,021	221
Univ of Dayton, Dayton, OH 45469-1300	1850	$22,846	$6,780	2-D	10,572	896
Univ of Delaware, Newark, DE 19716	1743	$7,318 (S)	$6,824	12-D	20,373	1,370
Univ of Denver, Denver, CO 80208	1864	$28,410	$8,749	1-D	10,374	1,050
Univ of Detroit Mercy, Detroit, MI 48219-0900	1877	$22,470	$7,328	2-D	5,521	708
Univ of Dubuque, Dubuque, IA 52001-5099	1852	$17,470	$5,950	2-D	1,441	158
Univ of Evansville, Evansville, IN 47722	1854	$21,660	$6,660	2-M	2,836	234
Univ of Findlay, Findlay, OH 45840-3653	1882	$21,746	$7,492	2-M	4,743	339
Univ of Florida, Gainesville, FL 32611	1853	$3,094 (S)	$6,260	5-D	49,693	2,311
Univ of Georgia, Athens, GA 30602	1785	$4,628 (S)	$6,376	5-D	33,660	2,111
Univ of Guam, Mangilao, GU 96923	1952	$4,350 (S)	$6,618	7-M	3,034	254
Univ of Hartford, West Hartford, CT 06117-1599	1877	$25,766	$9,922	1-D	7,260	753
Univ of Hawaii at Hilo, Hilo, HI 96720-4091	1970	$2,604 (S)	$5,374	5-M	3,288	264
Univ of Hawaii at Manoa, Honolulu, HI 96822	1907	$4,513 (S)	$6,690	5-D	20,644	1,169
Univ of Houston-Clear Lake, Houston, TX 77058-1098	1971	$4,653 (S)	NA	5-M	7,853	524
Univ of Houston-Downtown, Houston, TX 77002-1001	1974	$4,219 (S)	NA	5-M	11,484	573
Univ of Houston-Victoria, Victoria, TX 77901-4450	1973	$150/sem. hr.(S)	NA	5-M	2,491	130
Univ of Houston, Houston, TX 77204	1927	$6,486 (S)	$6,058	5-D	35,344	1,645
Univ of Idaho, Moscow, ID 83844-2282	1889	$3,968 (S)	$5,342	5-D	12,476	586
Univ of Illinois at Chicago, Chicago, IL 60607-7128	1946	$8,302 (S)	$7,954	5-D	24,812	1,456
Univ of Illinois at Springfield, Springfield, IL 62703-5407	1969	$5,335 (S)	$7,110	5-D	4,517	331
Univ of Illinois at Urbana-Champaign, Champaign, IL 61820	1867	$8,624 (S)	$7,176	5-D	41,938	2,701
Univ of Indianapolis, Indianapolis, IN 46227-3697	1902	$17,980	$7,010	2-D	4,462	416
Univ of Iowa, Iowa City, IA 52242-1316	1847	$5,935 (S)	$6,912	5-D	28,426	1,693
Univ of Kansas, Lawrence, KS 66045	1866	$5,413 (S)	$5,502	5-D	28,949	1,312
Univ of Kentucky, Lexington, KY 40506-0032	1865	$5,812 (S)	$5,129	5-D	25,672	1,724
Univ of La Verne, La Verne, CA 91750-4443	1891	$24,260	$9,210	1-D	4,000	398
Univ of Louisiana at Lafayette, Lafayette, LA 70504	1898	$3,324 (S)	$3,478	5-D	17,075	719
Univ of Louisiana at Monroe, Monroe, LA 71209-0001	1931	$3,402 (S)	$4,120	5-D	9,056	455
Univ of Louisville, Louisville, KY 40292-0001	1798	$5,532 (S)	$6,036	5-D	20,734	1,313
Univ of Maine, Orono, ME 04469	1865	$6,910 (S)	$6,732	5-D	11,435	823
Univ of Maine at Augusta, Augusta, ME 04330-9410	1965	$5,025 (S)	NA	5-B	5,494	324
Univ of Maine at Farmington, Farmington, ME 04938-1990	1863	$5,631 (S)	$5,984	5-B	2,452	175
Univ of Maine at Fort Kent, Fort Kent, ME 04743-1292	1878	$4,514 (S)	$5,600	5-B	1,076	72
Univ of Maine at Machias, Machias, ME 04654-1321	1909	$4,845 (S)	$5,678	5-B	1,149	88
Univ of Maine at Presque Isle, Presque Isle, ME 04769-2888	1903	$4,820 (S)	$5,246	5-B	1,548	116
Univ of Mary, Bismarck, ND 58504-9652	1959	$11,324	$4,050	2-D	2,758	349
Univ of Mary Hardin-Baylor, Belton, TX 76513	1845	$15,710	$4,200	2-M	2,727	227
Univ of Maryland, Baltimore County, Baltimore, MD 21250	1963	$8,520 (S)	$8,090	5-D	11,650	753
Univ of Maryland, Coll Park, College Park, MD 20742	1856	$7,821 (S)	$8,075	5-D	35,300	2,070
Univ of Maryland Eastern Shore, Princess Anne, MD 21853-1299	1886	$5,808 (S)	$6,130	5-D	3,762	234
Univ of Maryland Univ Coll, Adelphi, MD 20783	1947	$5,640 (S)	NA	5-D	28,374	1,341
Univ of Mary Washington, Fredericksburg, VA 22401-5358	1908	$5,634 (S)	$6,002	5-M	4,734	338
Univ of Massachusetts Amherst, Amherst, MA 01003	1863	$9,595 (S)	NA	5-D	25,093	1,338
Univ of Massachusetts Boston, Boston, MA 02125-3393	1964	$8,265 (S)	NA	5-D	11,862	813
Univ of Massachusetts Dartmouth, North Dartmouth, MA 02747-2300	1895	$8,036 (S)	$7,634	5-D	8,549	571
Univ of Massachusetts Lowell, Lowell, MA 01854-2881	1894	$8,166 (S)	$6,311	5-D	10,666	623

Name, address	Year Founded	Tuition & Fees	Rm. & Board	Control, Degree	Enroll- ment	Faculty
Univ of Memphis, Memphis, TN 38152	1912	$5,084 (S)	$6,069	5-D	20,465	1,285
Univ of Miami, Coral Gables, FL 33124	1925	$29,020	$8,906	1-D	15,674	1,275
Univ of Michigan-Dearborn, Dearborn, MI 48128-1491	1959	$6,841 (S)	NA	5-M	8,613	512
Univ of Michigan-Flint, Flint, MI 48502-1950	1956	$6,398 (S)	NA	5-F	6,423	420
Univ of Michigan, Ann Arbor, MI 48109	1817	$9,400 (S)	$7,374	5-D	39,993	2,936
Univ of Minnesota, Crookston, Crookston, MN 56716-5001	1966	$8,119 (S)	$5,038	5-B	2,134	104
Univ of Minnesota, Duluth, Duluth, MN 55812-2496	1947	$8,928 (S)	$5,546	5-F	10,496	506
Univ of Minnesota, Morris, Morris, MN 56267-2134	1959	$9,721 (S)	$5,750	5-B	1,678	176
Univ of Minnesota, Twin Cities Campus, Minneapolis, MN 55455-0213	1851	$8,622 (S)	$6,722	5-D	51,175	1,933
Univ of Mississippi, University, MS 38677	1844	$4,320 (S)	$5,762	5-D	14,901	NA
Univ of Mississippi Medical Ctr, Jackson, MS 39216-4505	1955	$3,519 (S)	$3,354	5-D	1,993	844
Univ of Missouri-Columbia, Columbia, MO 65211	1839	$7,745 (S)	$6,245	5-D	27,985	1,149
Univ of Missouri-Kansas City, Kansas City, MO 64110-2499	1929	$6,819 (S)	NA	5-D	14,310	1,055
Univ of Missouri-Rolla, Rolla, MO 65409-0910	1870	$7,492 (S)	$5,840	5-D	5,407	392
Univ of Missouri-St. Louis, St. Louis, MO 63121	1963	$7,618 (S)	$6,428	5-D	15,561	693
Univ of Mobile, Mobile, AL 36613	1961	$10,560	$6,390	2-M	1,758	156
Univ of Montana-Missoula, Missoula, MT 59812-0002	1893	$5,030 (S)	$5,860	5-D	13,602	734
Univ of Montana-Western, Dillon, MT 59725-3598	1893	$4,353 (S)	$4,920	5-B	1,159	72
Univ of Montevallo, Montevallo, AL 35115	1896	$5,664 (S)	$3,966	5-M	2,999	200
Univ of Nebraska-Lincoln, Lincoln, NE 68588	1869	$5,540 (S)	$6,008	5-D	21,675	1,058
Univ of Nebraska at Kearney, Kearney, NE 68849-0001	1903	$4,493 (S)	$5,326	5-M	6,445	380
Univ of Nebraska at Omaha, Omaha, NE 68182	1908	$4,825 (S)	$6,140	5-D	14,093	842
Univ of Nebraska Medical Ctr, Omaha, NE 68198	1869	$7,418 (S)	NA	5-D	2,995	1,007
Univ of Nevada, Las Vegas, Las Vegas, NV 89154-9900	1957	$3,818 (S)	$8,326	5-D	27,344	1,542
Univ of Nevada, Reno, Reno, NV 89557	1874	$3,270 (S)	$7,785	5-D	16,336	960
Univ of New England, Biddeford, ME 04005-9526	1831	$22,275	$8,730	1-F	3,312	241
Univ of New Hampshire, Durham, NH 03824	1866	$10,401 (S)	$7,584	5-D	14,564	962
Univ of New Hampshire at Manchester, Manchester, NH 03101-1113	1967	$7,163 (S)	NA	5-M	1,165	91
Univ of New Haven, West Haven, CT 06516-1916	1920	$22,982	$9,550	1-M	4,466	471
Univ of New Mexico, Albuquerque, NM 87131-2039	1889	$4,108 (S)	$6,518	5-D	26,172	1,411
Univ of New Orleans, New Orleans, LA 70148	1958	$3,810 (S)	$4,590	5-D	17,350	785
Univ of North Alabama, Florence, AL 35632-0001	1830	$4,366 (S)	$4,170	5-M	6,415	322
Univ of North Carolina at Asheville, Asheville, NC 28804-3299	1927	$3,525 (S)	$5,712	5-M	3,513	309
Univ of North Carolina at Chapel Hill, Chapel Hill, NC 27599	1789	$4,613 (S)	$6,516	5-D	27,276	1,497
Univ of North Carolina at Charlotte, Charlotte, NC 28223-0001	1946	$3,549 (S)	$5,550	5-D	20,772	1,245
Univ of North Carolina at Greensboro, Greensboro, NC 27412-5001	1891	$3,813 (S)	$5,706	5-D	16,060	989
Univ of North Carolina at Pembroke, Pembroke, NC 28372-1510	1887	$2,980 (S)	$4,890	5-M	5,732	328
Univ of North Carolina Wilmington, Wilmington, NC 28403-3297	1947	$3,695 (S)	$6,412	5-D	11,653	776
Univ of North Dakota, Grand Forks, ND 58202	1883	$5,327 (S)	$4,787	5-D	12,954	825
Univ of Northern Colorado, Greeley, CO 80639	1890	$3,837 (S)	$6,412	5-D	13,156	601
Univ of Northern Iowa, Cedar Falls, IA 50614	1876	$5,602 (S)	$5,531	5-D	12,622	829
Univ of North Florida, Jacksonville, FL 32224-2645	1965	$3,269 (S)	$6,640	5-D	15,234	700
Univ of North Texas, Denton, TX 76203	1890	$5,810 (S)	$5,364	5-D	32,047	1,413
Univ of Notre Dame, Notre Dame, IN 46556	1842	$33,442	$8,730	2-D	11,417	NA
Univ of Oklahoma, Norman, OK 73019-0390	1890	$4,408 (S)	$6,361	5-D	26,968	1,204
Univ of Oklahoma Health Sci Ctr, Oklahoma City, OK 73190	1890	$4,244 (S)	NA	5-D	3,538	403
Univ of Oregon, Eugene, OR 97403	1872	$5,613 (S)	$7,496	5-D	20,347	1,122
Univ of Pennsylvania, Philadelphia, PA 19104	1740	$32,364	$9,402	1-D	18,814	1,990
Univ of Phoenix-Atlanta Campus, Atlanta, GA 30350-4153	NA	$11,150	NA	3-M	2,495	217
Univ of Phoenix-Bay Area Campus, Pleasanton, CA 94588-3677	NA	$13,550	NA	3-M	3,681	747
Univ of Phoenix-Central Florida Campus, Maitland, FL 32751-7057	1996	$10,520	NA	3-M	2,267	243
Univ of Phoenix-Central Valley Campus, Fresno, CA 93720	2004	$12,335	NA	3-M	1,887	658
Univ of Phoenix-Charlotte Campus, Charlotte, NC 28273	2003	$10,730	NA	3-M	1,301	230
Univ of Phoenix-Chicago Campus, Schaumburg, IL 60173-4399	2002	$11,705	NA	3-M	1,602	207
Univ of Phoenix-Dallas Campus, Dallas, TX 75251	2001	$11,345	NA	3-M	2,972	243
Univ of Phoenix-Denver Campus, Lone Tree, CO 80124-5453	NA	$10,040	NA	3-M	3,420	378
Univ of Phoenix-Hawaii Campus, Honolulu, HI 96813-4317	NA	$12,110	NA	3-M	1,348	206
Univ of Phoenix-Houston Campus, Houston, TX 77079-2004	2001	$11,345	NA	3-M	4,808	442
Univ of Phoenix-Kansas City Campus, Kansas City, MO 64131-4517	2002	$11,705	NA	3-M	1,297	127
Univ of Phoenix-Louisiana Campus, Metairie, LA 70001-2082	1976	$9,680	NA	3-M	2,747	304
Univ of Phoenix-Maryland Campus, Columbia, MD 21045-5424	NA	$12,510	NA	3-M	2,028	218
Univ of Phoenix-Metro Detroit Campus, Troy, MI 48098-2623	NA	$11,900	NA	3-M	3,993	341
Univ of Phoenix-Nashville Campus, Nashville, TN 37214	2003	$10,730	NA	3-M	1,291	129
Univ of Phoenix-Nevada Campus, Las Vegas, NV 89128	1994	$10,310	NA	3-M	4,238	317
Univ of Phoenix-New Mexico Campus, Albuquerque, NM 87109-4645	NA	$9,950	NA	3-M	4,724	448
Univ of Phoenix-Northern Virginia Campus, Reston, VA 20190	NA	$12,365	NA	3-M	1,377	154
Univ of Phoenix-North Florida Campus, Jacksonville, FL 32216-0959	1976	$10,520	NA	3-M	2,380	255
Univ of Phoenix-Oklahoma City Campus, Oklahoma City, OK 73116-8244	1976	$9,920	NA	3-M	1,051	187
Univ of Phoenix-Oregon Campus, Portland, OR 97223-8368	1976	$10,970	NA	3-M	2,053	283
Univ of Phoenix-Philadelphia Campus, Wayne, PA 19087-2121	1999	$13,610	NA	3-M	1,694	187
Univ of Phoenix-Phoenix Campus, Phoenix, AZ 85040-1958	1976	$10,325	NA	3-M	9,408	784
Univ of Phoenix-Puerto Rico Campus, Guaynabo, PR 00968	1995	$6,200	NA	3-M	2,714	109
Univ of Phoenix-Sacramento Valley Campus, Sacramento, CA 95833-3632	1993	$12,785	NA	3-M	4,629	547
Univ of Phoenix-St. Louis Campus, St. Louis, MO 63043-4828	2000	$12,110	NA	3-M	1,026	167
Univ of Phoenix-San Diego Campus, San Diego, CA 92123	1988	$12,500	NA	3-M	4,563	476
Univ of Phoenix-Southern Arizona Campus, Tucson, AZ 85712-2732	1979	$10,235	NA	3-M	3,392	380
Univ of Phoenix-Southern California Campus, Costa Mesa, CA 92626	1980	$13,685	NA	3-M	16,134	1,297
Univ of Phoenix-Southern Colorado Campus, Colorado Springs, CO 80919-2335	1999	$10,049	NA	3-M	1,294	175
Univ of Phoenix-South Florida Campus, Fort Lauderdale, FL 33324-1393	NA	$10,520	NA	3-M	2,791	264
Univ of Phoenix-Tulsa Campus, Tulsa, OK 74146-3801	1998	$9,920	NA	3-M	1,302	161
Univ of Phoenix-Utah Campus, Salt Lake City, UT 84123-4617	1984	$10,580	NA	3-M	4,135	388
Univ of Phoenix-Washington Campus, Seattle, WA 98188-7500	1997	$11,615	NA	3-M	2,172	258
Univ of Phoenix-West Florida Campus, Temple Terrace, FL 33637]	NA	$10,520	NA	3-M	2,755	234
Univ of Phoenix-West Michigan Campus, Grand Rapids, MI 49544-1683	2000	$11,660	NA	3-M	1,156	203
Univ of Phoenix-Wisconsin Campus, Brookfield, WI 53045-6608	2001	$11,345	NA	3-M	1,357	217
Univ of Phoenix Online Campus, Phoenix, AZ 85034-7209	1989	$13,880	NA	3-D	117,259	5,974
Univ of Pittsburgh, Pittsburgh, PA 15260	1787	$11,436 (S)	$7,430	12-D	26,559	NA
Univ of Pittsburgh at Bradford, Bradford, PA 16701-2812	1963	$10,538 (S)	$6,470	12-B	1,301	122
Univ of Pittsburgh at Greensburg, Greensburg, PA 15601-5860	1963	$10,562 (S)	$7,210	12-B	1,796	138
Univ of Portland, Portland, OR 97203-5798	1901	$24,900	$7,400	2-M	3,413	279
Univ of Puerto Rico, Aguadilla Univ Coll, Aguadilla, PR 00604-0160	1972	$1,606 (S)	NA	6-B	3,393	133
Univ of Puerto Rico at Arecibo, Arecibo, PR 00613	1967	$1,245 (S)	NA	6-B	4,432	274
Univ of Puerto Rico at Bayamón, Bayamón, PR 00959	1971	$1,245 (S)	NA	6-B	4,852	247
Univ of Puerto Rico at Humacao, Humacao, PR 00791	1962	$1,245 (S)	NA	6-B	4,462	284
Univ of Puerto Rico at Ponce, Ponce, PR 00732-7186	1970	$2,174 (S)	NA	6-B	3,661	201

Name, address	Year Founded	Tuition & Fees	Rm. & Board	Control, Degree	Enroll- ment	Faculty
Univ of Puerto Rico at Utuado, Utuado, PR 00641-2500	1979	$1,245 (S)	NA	6-B	1,654	106
Univ of Puerto Rico, Cayey Univ Coll, Cayey, PR 00736	1967	$1,245 (A)	NA	6-B	3,987	219
Univ of Puerto Rico, Mayagüez Campus, Mayagüez, PR 00681-9000	1911	NA	NA	6-D	12,108	650
Univ of Puerto Rico, Río Piedras, San Juan, PR 00931-3300	1903	$790 (S)	$4,940	6-D	21,755	1,793
Univ of Puget Sound, Tacoma, WA 98416	1888	$28,460	$7,140	1-F	2,887	283
Univ of Redlands, Redlands, CA 92373-0999	1907	$27,164	$9,000	1-M	2,454	316
Univ of Rhode Island, Kingston, RI 02881	1892	$7,284 (S)	$8,114	5-D	15,095	691
Univ of Richmond, University of Richmond, VA 23173	1830	$36,550	$6,060	1-F	3,685	320
Univ of Rio Grande, Rio Grande, OH 45674	1876	$13,065 (A)	$6,404	1-M	2,376	265
Univ of Rochester, Rochester, NY 14627-0250	1850	$31,297	$10,188	1-D	8,588	768
Univ of St. Francis, Joliet, IL 60435-6169	1920	$19,150	$7,280	2-M	2,062	219
Univ of Saint Francis, Fort Wayne, IN 46808-3994	1890	$18,478	$5,834	2-M	2,003	229
Univ of St. Thomas, St. Paul, MN 55105-1096	1885	$30,380 (C)	NA	2-D	10,474	817
Univ of St. Thomas, Houston, TX 77006-4696	1947	$17,110	$6,700	2-D	3,776	272
Univ of San Diego, San Diego, CA 92110-2492	1949	$30,704	$10,960	2-D	7,548	722
Univ of San Francisco, San Francisco, CA 94117-1080	1855	$28,580	$10,580	2-D	8,457	861
Univ of Sci & Arts of Oklahoma, Chickasha, OK 73018	1908	$3,480 (S)	$4,170	5-B	1,430	84
Univ of Scranton, Scranton, PA 18510	1888	$24,030	$9,904	2-D	5,160	424
Univ of Sioux Falls, Sioux Falls, SD 57105-1699	1883	$16,720	$5,200	2-D	1,606	98
Univ of South Alabama, Mobile, AL 36688-0002	1963	$4,502 (S)	$4,428	5-D	13,122	970
Univ of South Carolina, Columbia, SC 29208	1801	$6,914 (S)	$6,080	5-D	27,065	1,567
Univ of South Carolina Aiken, Aiken, SC 29801-6309	1961	$6,158 (S)	$5,560	5-M	3,303	246
Univ of South Carolina Beaufort, Beaufort, SC 29902-4601	1959	$5,284 (S)	$6,900	5-B	1,319	85
Univ of South Carolina Upstate, Spartanburg, SC 29303-4999	1967	$6,762 (S)	$5,160	5-M	4,484	356
Univ of South Dakota, Vermillion, SD 57069-2390	1862	$4,829 (S)	$4,240	5-D	8,641	406
Univ of Southern California, Los Angeles, CA 90089	1880	$32,008	$9,610	1-D	32,836	2,479
Univ of Southern Indiana, Evansville, IN 47712-3590	1965	$4,304 (S)	$6,368	5-M	10,004	619
Univ of Southern Maine, Portland, ME 04104-9300	1878	$5,907 (S)	$6,755	5-D	10,944	704
Univ of Southern Mississippi, Hattiesburg, MS 39406-0001	1910	$4,342 (S)	$5,800	5-D	15,030	846
Univ of South Florida, Tampa, FL 33620-9951	1956	$3,384 (S)	$6,900	5-D	42,660	2,429
Univ of Tampa, Tampa, FL 33606-1490	1931	$18,848	$6,936	1-M	5,202	425
Univ of Tennessee, Knoxville, TN 37996	1794	$5,626 (S)	$5,560	5-D	31,157	1,386
Univ of Tennessee at Chattanooga, Chattanooga, TN 37403-2598	1886	$5,400 (S)	$6,238	5-D	8,656	623
Univ of Tennessee at Martin, Martin, TN 38238-1000	1900	$4,493 (S)	$4,220	5-M	6,484	416
Univ of Texas-Pan American, Edinburg, TX 78541-2999	1927	$4,160 (S)	$4,333	5-D	17,048	706
Univ of Texas at Arlington, Arlington, TX 76019	1895	$5,563 (S)	$5,345	5-D	25,432	1,113
Univ of Texas at Austin, Austin, TX 78712-1111	1883	$6,972 (S)	$7,638	5-D	49,696	2,734
Univ of Texas at Brownsville, Brownsville, TX 78520-4991	1973	$3,199 (S)	$2,300	5-M	13,316	659
Univ of Texas at Dallas, Richardson, TX 75083-0688	1969	$6,831 (S)	$6,244	5-D	14,480	696
Univ of Texas at El Paso, El Paso, TX 79968-0001	1913	$5,064 (S)	$4,095	5-D	19,268	1,059
Univ of Texas at San Antonio, San Antonio, TX 78249-0617	1969	$5,858 (S)	$7,190	5-D	27,337	1,083
Univ of Texas at Tyler, Tyler, TX 75799-0001	1971	$4,250 (S)	$7,010	5-M	5,748	360
Univ of Texas Health Sci Ctr at Houston, Houston, TX 77225-0036	1972	$5,602 (S)	NA	5-D	3,399	1,247
Univ of Texas Health Sci Ctr at San Antonio, San Antonio, TX 78229-3900	1976	$3,797 (S)	NA	5-D	2,754	1,372
Univ of Texas Medical Branch, Galveston, TX 77555	1891	$2,690 (S)	$2,322	5-D	2,198	102
Univ of Texas of the Permian Basin, Odessa, TX 79762-0001	1969	NA	NA	5-M	2,695	158
Univ of Texas Southwestern Medical Ctr at Dallas, Dallas, TX 75390	1943	$2,820 (S)	NA	5-D	2,393	103
Univ of the Arts, Philadelphia, PA 19102-4944	1870	$25,680	$6,300	1-M	2,277	472
Univ of the Cumberlands, Williamsburg, KY 40769-1372	1889	$13,658	$6,326	2-M	1,843	112
Univ of the District of Columbia, Washington, DC 20008-1175	1976	$2,070 (A)	NA	9-M	5,364	478
Univ of the Incarnate Word, San Antonio, TX 78209-6397	1881	$18,272	$6,475	2-D	5,217	444
Univ of the Pacific, Stockton, CA 95211-0197	1851	$26,088	$8,478	1-D	6,196	656
Univ of the Sacred Heart, San Juan, PR 00914-0383	1935	$4,810	$2,000	2-M	5,206	343
Univ of the Sci in Philadelphia, Philadelphia, PA 19104-4495	1821	$23,982	$9,380	1-D	2,808	249
Univ of the Virgin Islands, Saint Thomas, VI 00802-9990	1962	$3,726 (S)	$7,550	7-M	2,392	259
Univ of Toledo, Toledo, OH 43606-3390	1872	$7,494 (S)	$8,312	5-D	19,480	1,281
Univ of Tulsa, Tulsa, OK 74104-3189	1894	$20,738	$7,052	2-D	4,084	422
Univ of Utah, Salt Lake City, UT 84112-1107	1850	$4,342 (S)	$5,422	5-D	29,012	1,687
Univ of Vermont, Burlington, VT 05405	1791	$10,748 (S)	$7,332	5-D	11,597	723
Univ of Virginia, Charlottesville, VA 22903	1819	$7,370 (S)	$6,389	5-D	23,765	1,330
Univ of Virginia's Coll at Wise, Wise, VA 24293	1954	$5,081 (S)	$6,200	5-B	1,836	136
Univ of Washington, Seattle, WA 98195	1861	$5,532 (S)	NA	5-D	39,251	3,518
Univ of Washington, Bothell, Bothell, WA 98011-8246	NA	$5,496 (S)	NA	5-M	1,537	103
Univ of Washington, Tacoma, Tacoma, WA 98402-3100	1990	$5,622 (S)	$10,125	5-F	2,113	142
Univ of West Alabama, Livingston, AL 35470	1835	$4,326 (S)	$3,285	5-M	2,667	92
Univ of West Florida, Pensacola, FL 32514-5750	1963	$3,197 (S)	$6,600	5-D	9,632	527
Univ of West Georgia, Carrollton, GA 30118	1933	$3,270 (S)	$5,568	5-D	10,155	518
Univ of Wisconsin-Eau Claire, Eau Claire, WI 54702-4004	1916	$5,178 (S)	$4,737	5-M	10,566	508
Univ of Wisconsin-Green Bay, Green Bay, WI 54311-7001	1968	$5,425 (S)	$4,698	5-M	5,826	279
Univ of Wisconsin-La Crosse, La Crosse, WI 54601-3742	1909	$5,225 (S)	$4,820	5-M	9,397	448
Univ of Wisconsin-Madison, Madison, WI 53706-1380	1848	$6,617 (S)	$6,500	5-D	41,480	2,975
Univ of Wisconsin-Milwaukee, Milwaukee, WI 53201-0413	1956	$6,224 (S)	$4,922	5-D	27,502	NA
Univ of Wisconsin-Oshkosh, Oshkosh, WI 54901	1871	$4,981 (S)	$4,884	5-M	10,997	566
Univ of Wisconsin-Parkside, Kenosha, WI 53141-2000	1968	$5,001 (S)	$5,500	5-M	4,944	313
Univ of Wisconsin-Platteville, Platteville, WI 53818-3099	1866	$5,125 (S)	$4,654	5-M	6,431	348
Univ of Wisconsin-River Falls, River Falls, WI 54022-5001	1874	$4,968 (S)	NA	5-M	5,950	337
Univ of Wisconsin-Stevens Point, Stevens Point, WI 54481-3897	1894	$5,062 (S)	$4,322	5-M	8,577	437
Univ of Wisconsin-Stout, Menomonie, WI 54751	1891	$6,592 (S)	$4,572	5-M	7,891	394
Univ of Wisconsin-Superior, Superior, WI 54880-4500	1893	$5,188 (S)	$4,422	5-M	2,872	170
Univ of Wisconsin-Whitewater, Whitewater, WI 53190-1790	1868	$5,080 (S)	$4,210	5-M	10,750	497
Univ of Wyoming, Laramie, WY 82070	1886	$3,426 (S)	$6,240	5-D	13,126	704
Urbana Univ, Urbana, OH 43078-2091	1850	$16,254	$6,612	1-M	1,551	120
Ursinus Coll, Collegeville, PA 19426-1000	1869	$31,600	$7,350	1-B	1,571	165
Ursuline Coll, Pepper Pike, OH 44124-4398	1871	$19,090	$6,366	2-M	1,494	212
Utah State Univ, Logan, UT 84322	1888	$3,672 (S)	$4,330	5-D	14,458	764
Utah Valley State Coll, Orem, UT 84058-5999	1941	$3,022 (S)	NA	5-B	24,487	1,331
Utica Coll, Utica, NY 13502-4892	1946	$22,340	$9,056	1-F	2,888	286
Valdosta State Univ, Valdosta, GA 31698	1906	$3,278 (S)	$5,524	5-D	10,503	545
Valley City State Univ, Valley City, ND 58072	1890	$5,160 (S)	$4,694	5-B	1,035	77
Valparaiso Univ, Valparaiso, IN 46383	1859	$22,750	$6,220	2-F	3,864	362
Vanderbilt Univ, Nashville, TN 37240-1001	1873	$31,700	$10,286	1-D	11,481	NA
Vanguard Univ of Southern California, Costa Mesa, CA 92626-9601	1920	$20,315	$6,756	2-M	2,246	197
Vassar Coll, Poughkeepsie, NY 12604	1861	$33,800	$7,900	1-M	2,378	306
Vaughn Coll of Aeronautics & Tech, Flushing, NY 11369-1037 (2)	1932	$13,680	NA	1-B	1,126	113
Vermont Tech Coll, Randolph Center, VT 05061-0500	1866	$7,926 (A)	$6,674	5-B	1,356	139

Name, address	Year Founded	Tuition & Fees	Rm. & Board	Control, Degree	Enroll- ment	Faculty
Villa Julie Coll, Stevenson, MD 21153.	1952	$15,674	$9,548	1-M	2,956	349
Villanova Univ, Villanova, PA 19085-1699	1842	$29,435	$9,362	2-D	10,450	898
Virginia Coll at Birmingham, Birmingham, AL 35209.	1989	$10,950	NA	3-B	2,407	201
Virginia Commonwealth Univ, Richmond, VA 23284-9005	1838	$5,385 (S)	$7,042	5-D	29,349	2,813
Virginia Intermont Coll, Bristol, VA 24201-4298	1884	$16,450	$5,750	2-B	1,138	89
Virginia Military Inst, Lexington, VA 24450 (2).	1839	$6,988 (S)	$5,666	5-B	1,362	151
Virginia Polytechnic Inst & State Univ, Blacksburg, VA 24061	1872	$6,378 (S)	$4,400	5-D	27,979	1,532
Virginia State Univ, Petersburg, VA 23806-0001	1882	$4,892 (S)	$6,484	5-D	5,055	327
Virginia Union Univ, Richmond, VA 23220-1170.	1865	$12,770	$5,662	2-D	1,700	140
Virginia Wesleyan Coll, Norfolk, VA 23502-5599	1961	$23,136	$6,850	2-B	1,392	138
Viterbo Univ, La Crosse, WI 54601-4797	1890	$18,060	$5,640	2-M	2,534	224
Wagner Coll, Staten Island, NY 10301-4495.	1883	$25,350	$7,950	1-M	2,287	229
Wake Forest Univ, Winston-Salem, NC 27109	1834	$32,140	$8,800	1-D	6,716	548
Walden Univ, Minneapolis, MN 55401	1970	$8,280	NA	3-D	22,168	1,084
Walla Walla Coll, College Place, WA 99324-1198	1892	$19,917	$4,572	2-M	1,942	194
Walsh Coll of Accountancy & Business Administration, Troy, MI 48007-7006	1922	$9,230	NA	1-M	3,105	128
Walsh Univ, North Canton, OH 44720-3396	1958	$17,720	$7,130	2-M	2,183	189
Wartburg Coll, Waverly, IA 50677-0903	1852	$21,130	$5,765	2-B	1,811	179
Washburn Univ, Topeka, KS 66621	1865	$4,982 (S)	$4,752	10-F	7,261	510
Washington & Jefferson Coll, Washington, PA 15301	1781	$26,330	$7,160	1-B	1,418	130
Washington & Lee Univ, Lexington, VA 24450-0303	1749	$28,635	$7,225	1-F	2,179	217
Washington Coll, Chestertown, MD 21620-1197.	1782	$28,790	$6,200	1-M	1,412	144
Washington State Univ, Pullman, WA 99164	1890	$5,432 (S)	NA	5-D	23,544	1,449
Washington Univ in St. Louis, St. Louis, MO 63130-4899.	1853	$33,788	$10,452	1-D	13,383	1,081
Wayland Baptist Univ, Plainview, TX 79072-6998.	1908	$9,900	$3,584	2-M	1,124	102
Waynesburg Coll, Waynesburg, PA 15370-1222	1849	$14,810	$6,080	2-M	2,159	135
Wayne State Coll, Wayne, NE 68787	1910	$3,803 (S)	$4,300	5-M	3,322	205
Wayne State Univ, Detroit, MI 48202	1868	$6,439 (S)	$5,350	5-D	33,137	1,917
Weber State Univ, Ogden, UT 84408-1001.	1889	$3,138 (S)	$6,500	5-M	18,142	670
Webster Univ, St. Louis, MO 63119-3194.	1915	$17,210	$6,737	1-D	7,327	807
Wellesley Coll, Wellesley, MA 02481 (3).	1870	$31,348	$9,682	1-B	2,331	329
Wentworth Inst of Tech, Boston, MA 02115-5998.	1904	$18,500	$9,000	1-B	3,636	239
Wesleyan Univ, Middletown, CT 06459-0260 .	1831	$35,230	$9,540	1-D	3,207	368
Wesley Coll, Dover, DE 19901-3875.	1873	$14,600	$6,960	2-M	2,282	137
West Chester Univ of Pennsylvania, West Chester, PA 19383.	1871	$6,147 (S)	$6,208	5-M	12,988	797
Western Carolina Univ, Cullowhee, NC 28723	1889	$278/hr. (S)	NA	5-D	8,665	663
Western Connecticut State Univ, Danbury, CT 06810-6885 .	1903	$6,106 (S)	$7,784	5-D	5,907	485
Western Governors Univ, Salt Lake City, UT 84107	1998	$5,735	NA	1-M	2,821	51
Western Illinois Univ, Macomb, IL 61455-1390 .	1899	$6,899 (S)	$6,143	5-D	13,404	731
Western Intl Univ, Phoenix, AZ 85021-2718 .	1978	$9,760	NA	3-M	3,751	243
Western Kentucky Univ, Bowling Green, KY 42101-3576.	1906	$5,316 (S)	$4,876	5-M	18,634	1,107
Western Michigan Univ, Kalamazoo, MI 49008-5202 .	1903	$6,478 (S)	$6,651	5-D	26,239	1,460
Western New England Coll, Springfield, MA 01119 .	1919	$23,164	$8,890	1-F	3,729	320
Western New Mexico Univ, Silver City, NM 88062-0680.	1893	$2,818 (S)	NA	5-M	3,074	145
Western Oregon Univ, Monmouth, OR 97361-1394 .	1856	$4,332 (S)	$6,276	5-M	4,520	354
Western State Coll of Colorado, Gunnison, CO 81231 .	1901	$3,207 (S)	$6,976	5-B	2,177	135
Western Washington Univ, Bellingham, WA 98225-5996 .	1893	$4,738 (S)	$6,524	5-M	14,247	628
Westfield State Coll, Westfield, MA 01086 .	1838	$5,657 (S)	$6,470	5-M	5,345	344
West Liberty State Coll, West Liberty, WV 26074 .	1837	$3,736 (S)	$5,456	5-B	2,246	161
Westminster Coll, New Wilmington, PA 16172-0001.	1852	$24,325	$7,070	2-M	1,593	149
Westminster Coll, Salt Lake City, UT 84105-3697 .	1875	$19,724	$5,932	1-M	2,455	259
Westmont Coll, Santa Barbara, CA 93108-1099 .	1937	$27,806	$8,866	2-B	1,379	133
West Texas A&M Univ, Canyon, TX 79016-0001 .	1909	$3,756 (S)	$4,916	5-D	8,667	321
West Virginia State Univ, Institute, WV 25112-1000 .	1891	$3,528 (S)	$4,850	5-M	3,491	194
West Virginia Univ, Morgantown, WV 26506.	1867	$4,164 (S)	$6,342	5-D	26,051	1,120
West Virginia Univ Inst of Tech, Montgomery, WV 25136.	1895	$3,786 (S)	$4,970	5-M	2,468	176
West Virginia Wesleyan Coll, Buckhannon, WV 26201.	1890	$21,250	$5,550	2-M	1,408	160
Wheaton Coll, Wheaton, IL 60187-5593 .	1860	$21,100	$6,600	2-D	2,932	287
Wheaton Coll, Norton, MA 02766 .	1834	$32,350	$7,830	1-B	1,568	161
Wheeling Jesuit Univ, Wheeling, WV 26003-6295 .	1954	$21,350	$6,450	2-D	1,699	74
Wheelock Coll, Boston, MA 02215-4176 (4) .	1888	$23,625	$9,450	1-M	1,016	95
Whitman Coll, Walla Walla, WA 99362-2083 .	1859	$28,640	$7,470	1-B	1,512	187
Whittier Coll, Whittier, CA 90608-0634 .	1887	$26,138	$7,928	1-F	1,307	127
Whitworth Coll, Spokane, WA 99251-0001 .	1890	$24,154	$7,030	2-M	2,441	291
Wichita State Univ, Wichita, KS 67260 .	1895	$4,231 (S)	$5,070	5-D	14,076	515
Widener Univ, Chester, PA 19013-5792 .	1821	$24,970	$8,520	1-D	5,793	398
Wilkes Univ, Wilkes-Barre, PA 18766-0002 .	1933	$21,646	$9,240	1-F	4,480	217
Willamette Univ, Salem, OR 97301-3931 .	1842	$28,416	$7,000	2-F	2,642	301
William Carey Coll, Hattiesburg, MS 39401-5499 .	1906	$8,415	$3,465	2-M	2,758	185
William Jewell Coll, Liberty, MO 64068-1843 .	1849	$20,150	$5,510	2-B	1,331	155
William Paterson Univ of New Jersey, Wayne, NJ 07470-8420 .	1855	$8,740 (S)	$9,070	5-M	10,970	1,071
William Penn Univ, Oskaloosa, IA 52577-1799.	1873	$15,945	$4,982	2-B	1,892	52
Williams Coll, Williamstown, MA 01267.	1793	$31,760	$8,550	1-M	2,070	312
William Woods Univ, Fulton, MO 65251-1098.	1870	$15,120	$5,900	2-M	3,047	114
Wilmington Coll, New Castle, DE 19720-6491 .	1967	$7,670	NA	1-D	7,511	642
Wilmington Coll, Wilmington, OH 45177 .	1870	$19,962	$7,054	2-M	1,764	97
Wingate Univ, Wingate, NC 28174-0159.	1896	$16,850	$6,450	2-F	1,632	152
Winona State Univ, Winona, MN 55987-5838.	1858	$7,727 (S)	$5,000	5-M	8,236	357
Winston-Salem State Univ, Winston-Salem, NC 27110-0003.	1892	$2,805 (S)	$5,298	5-M	5,566	315
Winthrop Univ, Rock Hill, SC 29733 .	1886	$8,756 (S)	$5,352	5-M	6,480	542
Wittenberg Univ, Springfield, OH 45501-0720 .	1845	$29,280	$7,498	2-M	2,093	202
Wofford Coll, Spartanburg, SC 29303-3663 .	1854	$24,130	$6,805	2-B	1,173	122
Woodbury Univ, Burbank, CA 91504-1099 .	1884	$23,474	$8,198	1-M	1,436	230
Worcester Polytechnic Inst, Worcester, MA 01609-2280 .	1865	$33,270	$9,840	1-D	3,910	317
Worcester State Coll, Worcester, MA 01602-2597 .	1874	$5,079 (S)	$7,420	5-M	5,471	400
Wright State Univ, Dayton, OH 45435.	1964	$7,278 (S)	$7,180	5-D	16,207	835
Xavier Univ, Cincinnati, OH 45207 .	1831	$22,430	$8,640	2-D	6,665	598
Xavier Univ of Louisiana, New Orleans, LA 70125-1098.	1925	$13,100	$7,100	2-F	4,121	289
Yale Univ, New Haven, CT 06520.	1701	$31,460	$9,540	1-D	11,483	1,430
Yeshiva Univ, New York, NY 10033-3201.	1886	$23,650	$7,330	1-D	5,998	NA
York Coll of Pennsylvania, York, PA 17405-7199 .	1787	$10,050	$6,500	1-M	5,316	429
York Coll of the City Univ of New York, Jamaica, NY 11451-0001	1967	$4,000 (S)	NA	11-B	5,900	470
Youngstown State Univ, Youngstown, OH 44555-0001	1908	$6,333 (S)	$6,280	5-D	12,809	979

UNITED STATES GOVERNMENT

EXECUTIVE BRANCH	LEGISLATIVE BRANCH	JUDICIAL BRANCH
PRESIDENT	**CONGRESS**	**Supreme Court of the United States**
Vice President	**Senate**　　**House**	Courts of Appeals
Executive Office of the President	Architect of the Capitol	District Courts
White House Office*	U.S. Botanic Garden	Territorial Courts
Office of the Vice President	Government Accountability Office	Court of International Trade
Council of Economic Advisers	Government Printing Office	Bankruptcy Courts
Council on Environmental Quality	Library of Congress	Court of Federal Claims
National Security Council	Congressional Budget Office	Tax Court
Office of Administration	Medicare Payment Advisory Commission	Court of Appeals for the Armed Forces
Office of Management and Budget	Stennis Center for Public Service	Court of Appeals for Veterans Claims
Office of National Drug Control Policy		Administrative Office of the Courts
Office of Science and Technology Policy		Federal Judicial Center
Office of the U.S. Trade Representative		Sentencing Commission
		Judicial Panel on Multidistrict Litigation

*Includes Domestic Policy Council, Homeland Security Council, National Economic Council, Office of Faith-Based and Community Initiatives, Office of the First Lady, Office of National AIDS Policy, Privacy and Civil Liberties Oversight Board, USA Freedom Corps, White House Fellows Office, White House Military Office.

The Bush Administration

As of Sept. 19, 2006; mailing addresses are for Washington, DC, except for the Pentagon.
Terms of office of the president and vice president: Jan. 20, 2005 to Jan. 20, 2009.

President — By law, Pres. George W. Bush receives an annual salary of $400,000 (taxable) and an annual expense allowance of $50,000 (nontaxable) for costs resulting from official duties. In addition, up to $100,000 a year may be spent on travel expenses and $19,000 on official entertainment (both nontaxable). This does not include amounts available for expenditures within the Executive Office of the President, including $3,850,000 for necessary expenses for the White House and amounts for travel and entertainment.

Website: www.whitehouse.gov/president; **E-mail:** comments@whitehouse.gov

Vice President — By law, Vice Pres. Dick Cheney receives an annual salary of $212,100 (taxable), plus $90,000 for official entertainment expenses (nontaxable).

Website: www.whitehouse.gov/vicepresident; **E-mail:** vice_president@whitehouse.gov

The Cabinet Department Heads
(Salary: $183,500 per year)
Secretary of State — Condoleezza Rice
Secretary of the Treasury — Henry M. Paulson, Jr.
Secretary of Defense — Donald H. Rumsfeld
Attorney General — Alberto Gonzales
Secretary of the Interior — Dirk Kempthorne
Secretary of Agriculture — Mike Johanns
Secretary of Commerce — Carlos M. Gutierrez
Secretary of Labor — Elaine L. Chao
Secretary of Health and Human Services — Michael O. Leavitt
Secretary of Housing and Urban Development — Alphonso Jackson
Secretary of Transportation — Maria Cino, act.
Secretary of Energy — Samuel W. Bodman
Secretary of Education — Margaret Spellings
Secretary of Veterans Affairs — R. James Nicholson
Secretary of Homeland Security — Michael Chertoff

The White House Staff
1600 Pennsylvania Ave. NW 20500; www.whitehouse.gov
Counselor to the President — Dan Bartlett
Physician to the President — Richard Tubb
Assistants to the President:
　Chief of Staff — Joshua B. Bolten
　Deputy Chief of Staff and Senior Advisor — Karl Rove
　Deputy Chief of Staff — Joe Hagin
　Deputy Chief of Staff for Policy — Joel D. Kaplan
　Counsel to the President — Harriet Miers
　White House Press Secretary — Tony Snow
　Deputy National Security Advisor — Jack D. Crouch II
　Director, National Intelligence — John D. Negroponte
　Director, Office of Faith-Based and Community Initiatives — Jay Hein
　Staff Secretary — Raul Yanes
　Communications — Kevin Sullivan
　Domestic Policy — Karl Zinsmeister
　Economic Policy and Director of the National Economic Council — Allan Hubbard
　Homeland Security and Counterterrorism — Frances Fragos Townsend
　Legislative Affairs — Candida Wolff
　National Security Advisor — Stephen Hadley
　Presidential Personnel — Liza Wright
　Speechwriting — William McGurn

Chief of Staff to the Vice President —David Addington
Special Assistants to the President:
　Senior Director for Legislative Affairs — J. Michael Allen
　White House Social Secretary —Janet Lea Berman
Assistant to the President and Chief of Staff to the First Lady — Anita McBride
Press Secretary, Office of the First Lady — Susan Whitson

Executive Agencies
Council of Economic Advisers — Edward P. Lazear, chair; www.whitehouse.gov/cea
Office of Administration — John Straub, dir.; www.whitehouse.gov/oa
Office of Science & Technology Policy — John H. Marburger III; www.ostp.gov
Office of Natl. Drug Control Policy — John P. Walters, dir.; www.whitehousedrugpolicy.gov
Office of Management and Budget — Rob Portman, dir.; www.whitehouse.gov/omb
U.S. Trade Representative — Susan C. Schwab; www.ustr.gov
Council on Environ. Quality — James L. Connaughton, chair; www.whitehouse.gov/ceq

Department of State
2201 C St. NW 20520; www.state.gov
Secretary of State — Condoleezza Rice
Deputy Secretary — vacant
U.S. Permanent Rep. to the United Nations — John R. Bolton
U.S. Agency for Intl. Dev. (USAID) Admin. — Randall L. Tobias
Under Sec. for Political Affairs — R. Nicholas Burns
Under Sec. for Management — Henrietta H. Fore
Under Sec. for Democracy & Global Affairs — Paula J. Dobriansky
Under Sec. for Economic, Business, & Agricultural Affairs — Josette S. Shiner
Under Sec. for Arms Control & International Security Affairs — Robert Joseph
Under Sec. for Public Diplomacy & Public Affairs — Karen P. Hughes
Policy Planning Director — Stephen Krasner
Chief of Protocol — Donald B. Ensenat
Inspector General — Howard J. Krongard
Legal Adviser — John B. Bellinger III
Coord. for Counterterrorism — Henry A. Crumpton

▶ **IT'S A FACT:** Eight U.S. Presidents have traced their lineage to pilgrims who traveled to America on the *Mayflower* in 1620; John Adams, John Quincy Adams, Zachary Taylor, Ulysses S. Grant, James Garfield, Franklin D. Roosevelt, Richard Nixon, Gerald Ford, George H.W. Bush, and George W. Bush. George W. Bush is descended from Francis Cooke, John Howland, Henry Sampson, and Joan, John, and Elizabeth Tilley.

Director General of the Foreign Service & Director of Human Resources — George M. Staples
Assistant Secretaries for:
  Administration — Rajkumar Chellaraj
  African Affairs — Jendayi E. Frazer
  Bureau of International Security and Nonproliferation — John C. Rood
  Consular Affairs — Maura Harty
  Democracy, Human Rights, & Labor — Barry F. Lowenkron
  Diplomatic Security — Richard J. Griffin
  East Asian & Pacific Affairs — Christopher R. Hill
  Education & Cultural Affairs — Dina Powell
  European & Eurasian Affairs — Daniel Fried
  Intelligence & Research — Randall M. Fort
  International Narcotics & Law Enforcement Affairs — Anne W. Patterson
  International Organization Affairs — Kristen Silverberg
  Legislative Affairs — Dr. Jeffrey T. Bergner
  Near Eastern Affairs — C. David Welch
  Oceans, International Environmental, & Scientific Affairs — Claudia A. McMurray
  Political-Military Affairs — John Hillen
  Population, Refugees, & Migration — Ellen R. Sauerbrey
  Public Affairs — Sean McCormack
  Resource Management; Chief Financial Officer — Bradford R. Higgins
  South & Central Asian Affairs — Richard A. Boucher
  Verification, Compliance, & Implementation — Paula A. DeSutter
  Western Hemisphere Affairs — Thomas A. Shannon, Jr.

Department of the Treasury
1500 Pennsylvania Ave. NW 20220; www.ustreas.gov
Secretary of the Treasury — Henry M. Paulson, Jr.
Deputy Sec. of the Treasury — Robert M. Kimmitt
Chief of Staff — Jim Wilkinson
Executive Secretary — Jonathan R. Weinberger
White House Liaison — Janan Grissom
Under Sec. for Domestic Finance — Randal K. Quarles
Under Sec. for International Affairs — Timothy D. Adams
Under Sec. for Terrorism & Financial Intelligence (Terrorist Financing) — Stuart Levey
Financial Crimes Enforcement Network — Robert W. Werner, dir
General Counsel — Stephen Larson, act.
Inspector General — Harold Damelin
Inspector General for Tax Administration — J. Russell George
Treasurer of the U.S. — Anna Escobedo Cabral
Assistant Secretaries for:
  Economic Policy — vacant
  Financial Institutions — Emil Henry, Jr.
  Financial Markets — vacant
  Fiscal Affairs — Donald V. Hammond
  International Affairs — Clay Lowery
  Legislative Affairs — Kevin I. Fromer
  Management/CFO — Sandra Pack
  Public Affairs — Michele Davis
  Tax Policy — vacant
  Terrorism & Financial Intelligence (Terrorist Financing) — Patrick M. O'Brien
Bureaus:
  Alcohol and Tobacco Tax and Trade — John Manfreda, admin.
  Comptroller of the Currency — John Dugan
  Engraving & Printing — Larry R. Felix, dir.
  Financial Management Service — Kenneth Papaj, comm.
  Internal Revenue Service — Mark W. Everson, comm.
  U.S. Mint — Edmund C. Moy, act. dir.
  Office of Thrift Supervision — John Reich, dir.
  Public Debt — Van Zeck, comm.

Department of Defense
The Pentagon, Arlington, VA 20301; www.dod.gov
Secretary of Defense — Donald H. Rumsfeld
Deputy Sec. of Defense — Gordon England
Under Sec. Comptroller/CFO — Tina W. Jonas
Under Sec. for Acquis., Tech., & Logistics — Kenneth J. Krieg
Under Sec. for Intelligence — Dr. Stephen A. Cambone
Under Sec. for Personnel & Readiness — David S. C. Chu
Under Sec. for Policy — Eric S. Edelman
Assistant Secretaries for:
  Networks & Info Integration/CIO — Hon. John G. Grimes
  Health Affairs — William Winkenwerder Jr.
  Homeland Defense — Paul McHale

  International Security Affairs — Peter W. Rodman
  International Security Policy — Peter C. W. Flory
  Legislative Affairs — Hon. Robert Wilkie
  Nuclear and Chemical and Biological Defense Programs — Hon. Dale E. Klein
  Public Affairs — Dorrance J. Smith
  Reserve Affairs — Thomas F. Hall
  Special Operations & Low-Intensity Conflict — Thomas W. O'Connell
Inspector General — Thomas F. Gimble, act.
General Counsel — William J. Haynes II
Operational Test & Evaluation — Charles E. McQueary, dir.
Chairman, Joint Chiefs of Staff — Gen. Peter Pace
Secretary of the Army — Dr. Francis J. Harvey
Secretary of the Navy — Dr. Donald C. Winter
Commandant of the Marine Corps — Gen. Michael W. Hagee
Secretary of the Air Force — Michael W. Wynne

Department of Justice
950 Pennsylvania Avenue, NW 20530; www.usdoj.gov
Attorney General — Alberto Gonzales
Deputy Attorney General — Paul J. McNulty
Associate Attorney General — Wiliam Mercer, act.
Office of Dispute Resolution — Linda A. Cinciotta, dir.
Solicitor General — Paul D. Clement
Office of Inspector General — Glenn A. Fine
Assistants:
  Antitrust Division — Thomas O. Barnett
  Civil Division — Peter D. Keisler
  Civil Rights Division — Wan J. Kim
  Criminal Division — Alice S. Fisher
  Environ. & Nat. Resources Division — Sue Ellen Wooldridge
  Justice Programs — Regina B. Schofield
  Legal Counsel — Steven G. Bradbury, act.
  Legislative Affairs — William E. Moschella
  Legal Policy — Rachel L. Brand
  National Security Division — Kenneth Wainstein
  Tax Division — Eileen J. O'Connor
Office of Public Affairs — Tasia Scolinos, dir.
Office of Information & Privacy — Daniel J. Metcalfe
Community Oriented Policing Services — Carl R. Peed
Federal Bureau of Investigation — Robert S. Mueller III
Bureau of Alcohol, Tobacco, Firearms, & Explosives — Michael J. Sullivan, act.
Exec. Off. for Immigration Review — Kevin D. Rooney, dir.
Bureau of Prisons — Harley G. Lappin
Community Relations Service — Sharee M. Freeman, dir.
Drug Enforcement Admin. — Karen P. Tandy
Office of Intelligence Policy & Review — James A. Baker
Office of Professional Responsibility — H. Marshall Jarrett, counsel
Professional Responsibility Advisory Office — Barbara Kammerman, act.
Office of Tribal Justice — Tracy Toulou
Exec. Off. for U.S. Trustees — Cliff White III, act.
Foreign Claims Settlement Comm. — Mauricio J. Tamargo
Exec. Office for U.S. Attorneys — Michael Battle, dir.
Pardon Attorney — Roger C. Adams
U.S. Parole Commission — Edward F. Reilly Jr.
U.S. Marshals Service — John F. Clark
U.S. Natl. Central Bureau of INTERPOL — Martin Renkiewicz
Office of Intergovernmental and Public Liaison — Crystal Roberts Jezierski, dir.
Office of Violence Against Women — vacant
National Drug Intelligence Center — Michael F. Walther

Department of the Interior
1849 C St. NW 20240; www.doi.gov
Secretary of the Interior — Dirk Kempthorne
Deputy Secretary — P. Lynn Scarlett
Assistant Secretaries for:
  Fish, Wildlife, & Parks — David M. Verhey, act.
  Indian Affairs — vacant
  Land & Minerals Management — Johnnie Burton, act.
  Policy, Management, & Budget — R. Thomas Weimer
  Water & Science — Mark Limbaugh
Bureau of Land Management — Kathleen Clarke
Bureau of Reclamation — William E. Rinne, act.
Fish & Wildlife Service — Dale Hall
Geological Survey — Mark Myers, dir.
Inspector General — Earl E. Devaney
Minerals Management Service — R.M. "Johnnie" Burton, dir.
National Park Service — vacant
Chairman, National Indian Gaming Commission — Phil Hogen
Office of Surface Mining — Brent Wahlquist, act.

Special Trustee for American Indians — Ross Swimmer
Chief Information Officer — W. Hord Tipton
Congressional & Legislative Affairs — Matt Eames, dir.
Solicitor — David Bernhardt
External & Intergovernmental Affairs — Gary Smith, dir.

Department of Agriculture

1400 Independence Ave. SW 20250; www.usda.gov
Secretary of Agriculture — Mike Johanns
Deputy Secretary — Chuck Conner
Under Secretaries for:
  Farm & Foreign Agric. Services — vacant
  Food, Nutrition, & Consumer Services — Nancy Montanez-Johner
  Food Safety — Dr. Richard Raymond
  Marketing & Regulatory Progs. — Bruce I. Knight
  Natural Resources & Environment — Mark E. Rey
  Research, Education, & Economics — Joseph Jen
  Rural Development — Thomas C. Dorr
Assistant Secretaries for:
  Administration — Boyd K. Rutherford
  Civil Rights — Margo M. McKay
  Congressional Relations — Arlen Lancaster, act.
General Counsel — vacant
Inspector General — Phyllis K. Fong
Chief Financial Officer — Charles R. Christopherson, Jr.
Chief Information Officer — Dave Combs
Chief Economist — Keith Collins
Communications — Terri Teuber, dir.

Department of Commerce

1401 Constitution Ave. NW 20230; www.commerce.gov
Secretary of Commerce — Carlos M. Gutierrez
Deputy Secretary — David A. Sampson
Chief of Staff — Claire Buchan
General Counsel — John J. Sullivan
Inspector General — Johnnie E. Frazier
Under Sec. for Industry and Security — David H. McCormick
Under Sec. for Economic Affairs — vacant
Under Sec. for International Trade — Franklin L. Lavin
Under Sec. and Administrator for NOAA — Vice Admiral Conrad C. Lautenbacher Jr.
Under Sec. for Intellectual Property and Director USPTO — Jon W. Dudas
Under Sec. for Technology — Robert C. Cresanti
Assistant Secretaries:
  Administration and Chief Financial Officer — Otto J. Wolff
  Telecommunications and Information — John M.R. Kneuer, act.
  Economic Development Administration — Sandy K. Baruah
  Export Administration — vacant
  Export Enforcement — Darryl W. Jackson
  Import Administration — David Spooner
  Legislative and Intergovernmental Affairs — Nathaniel Wienecke
  Oceans and Atmosphere and Deputy Administrator — Dr. James Mahoney
  Manufacturing and Services — Albert Frink
  Market Access and Compliance — David Bohigian
  Technology Policy — Jo Gann, act.
Business Liaison — Dan McCardell
Policy and Strategic Planning — John Duncan
Public Affairs — E. Richard Mills
Bureau of the Census — Charles Louis Kincannon, dir.
Bureau of Economic Analysis — J. Steven Landefeld, dir.
Minority Business Development Agency — Ronald Langston
Natl. Institute of Standards and Technology — Dr. William A. Jeffrey

Department of Labor

200 Constitution Ave. NW 20210; www.dol.gov
Secretary of Labor — Elaine L. Chao
Deputy Secretary — Steven J. Law
Chief of Staff — Paul T. Conway
Assistant Secretaries for:
  Admin. & Management — Patrick Pizzella
  Congressional & Intergov. Affairs — Kristine Iverson
  Employee Benefits Security Admin. — Ann L. Combs
  Employment & Training — Emily Stover DeRocco
  Employment Standards — Victoria A. Lipnic
  Occupational Safety & Health — Edwin G. Foulke, Jr.

  Mine Safety & Health — vacant
  Policy — Veronica Vargas Stidvent
  Public Affairs — vacant
  Veterans Employment & Training — Charles S. Ciccollela
Solicitor — Howard M. Radzely
Bureau of International Labor Affairs — James Carter
Women's Bureau — Shinae Chun
Inspector General — Gordon S. Heddell
Bureau of Labor Statistics — Kathleen P. Utgoff

Department of Health and Human Services

200 Independence Ave. SW 20201; www.hhs.gov
Secretary of Health & Human Services — Michael O. Leavitt
Deputy Secretary — Alex M. Azar II
Chief of Staff — Rich McKeown
Centers for Disease Control and Prevention — Julie Louise Gerberding, dir.
Healthcare Research & Quality — Carolyn M. Clancy, dir.
National Institutes of Health — Elias A. Zerhouni, dir.
Assistant Secretaries for:
  Aging — Josefina G. Carbonell
  Children & Families — Wade F. Horn
  Health — John O. Agwunobi
  Legislation — Vincent J. Ventimiglia, Jr.
  Administration & Management — Joe Ellis
  Planning & Evaluation — Jerry Regier
  Public Affairs — Suzy DeFrancis
General Counsel — Daniel Meron
Inspector General — Daniel R. Levinson
Office for Civil Rights — Winston Wilkinson, dir.
Surgeon General — Kenneth Moritsugu, act.
Centers for Medicare and Medicaid Services — Mark B. McClellan
Faith-Based & Community Initiatives — Greg Morris, dir.

Department of Housing and Urban Development

451 7th St. SW 20410; www.hud.gov
Secretary of Housing & Urban Development — Alphonso Jackson
Deputy Secretary — Roy A. Bernardi
Chief of Staff — Camille T. Pierce
Assistant Secretaries for:
  Community Planning & Development — Pamela Patenaude
  Congressional & Intergov. Relations — vacant
  Fair Housing & Equal Opportunity — Kim Kendrick
  Administration — Keith Nelson
Housing/Federal Housing Comm. — Brian Montgomery
  Policy Development & Research — Darlene Williams
  Public & Indian Housing — Orlando J. Cabrera
  Public Affairs — vacant
General Counsel — Keith E. Gottfried
Inspector General — Kenneth M. Donohue Sr.
Chief Financial Officer — John W. Cox
Chief Executive Officer — Marcella E. Belt
Government National Mortgage Assn. — Robert M. Couch

Department of Transportation

400 7th St. SW 20590; www.dot.gov
Secretary of Transportation — Maria Cino, act.
Deputy Secretary — Maria Cino
Under Secretary for Policy — Jeffrey N. Shane
General Counsel — Rosalind A. Knapp, act.
Assistant Secretaries for:
  Administration — Linda J. Washington, act.
  Aviation & International Affairs — Michael W. Reynolds, act.
  Budget & Programs/CFO — Phyllis F. Scheinberg
  Governmental Affairs — Shane Karr
  Public Affairs — Robert Johnson
  Transportation Policy — Tyler Duvall
Bureau of Transportation Statistics — Terry Shelton, act.
Federal Aviation Admin. — Marion C. Blakey
Federal Highway Admin. — Richard Capka
Federal Motor Carrier Safety Admin. — John Hill
Federal Railroad Admin. — Joseph H. Boardman
Maritime Admin. — Sean T. Connaughton
Natl. Highway Traffic Safety Admin. — Nicole Nason
Federal Transit Admin. — James S. Simpson
Inspector General — Todd J. Zinser, act.
St. Lawrence Seaway Devel. Corp. — Albert S. Jacquez

Department of Energy
1000 Independence Ave. SW 20585; www.energy.gov
Secretary of Energy — Samuel W. Bodman
Deputy Secretary — Clay Sell
Under Sec. of Energy — David K. Garman
Under Sec. for Science — Dr. Raymond L. Orbach
Under Sec. & Admin. for Nuclear Security — Linton F. Brooks
General Counsel — David R. Hill
Inspector General — Gregory Friedman
Assistant Secretaries for:
  Congressional & Intergov. Affairs — Jill L. Sigal
  Energy Efficiency & Renewable Energy — Alexander Karsner
  Environment, Safety, & Health — vacant
  Environmental Management — James A. Rispoli
  Fossil Energy — Jeffrey Jarrett
  Policy & International Affairs — Karen A. Harbert
  Nuclear Energy — Dennis Spurgeon
Energy Information Admin. — Guy F. Caruso
Economic Impact & Diversity — Theresa Alvillar-Speake
Electricity Delivery & Energy Reliability — Kevin Kolevar
Hearings & Appeals — George B. Breznay
Civilian Radioactive Waste Management — vacant
Chief Financial Officer — James T. Campbell
Energy Advisory Board — Hon. M. Peter McPherson, chair
Office of Public Affairs — Anne Womack Kolton, dir.
Office of Legacy Management — Michael W. Owen, dir.
Chief Information Officer — Tom Pyke

Department of Education
400 Maryland Ave. SW 20202; www.ed.gov
Secretary of Education — Margaret Spellings
Deputy Secretary — Raymond J. Simon
Under Secretary — David Dunn, act.
Chief of Staff — David Dunn
Assistant Secretaries for:
  Special Education and Rehabilitative Services — John H. Hager
  Communications and Outreach — vacant
  Vocational and Adult Education — Troy Justesen
  Civil Rights — Stephanie Monroe
  Elementary and Secondary Education — Henry Johnson
  Postsecondary Education — Jim Manning
  Planning, Evaluation, & Policy Development — Tom Luce
  Legislation and Congressional Affairs — Terrell Halaska
  Management & CIO — Michell Clark
Chief Financial Officer — Lawrence A. Warder
Federal Student Aid — Theresa S. Shaw, chf. op. off.
Ctr for Faith-Based and Comm. Init. — Shayam K. Menon
Institute of Education Sciences — Grover J. Whitehurst, dir.
Inspector General — John P. Higgins, Jr.
Intergovernmental and Interagency Affairs — Rogers Johnson, dir.
General Counsel — Kent D. Talbert
Office of Educational Technology — Timothy J. Magner, dir.

Department of Veterans Affairs
810 Vermont Ave. NW 20420; www.va.gov
Secretary of Veterans Affairs — R. James Nicholson
Deputy Secretary — Gordon H. Mansfield
Chief of Staff — Thomas G. Bowman
Under Sec. for Health — Jonathan B. Perlin
Under Sec. for Benefits — Daniel L. Cooper
Under Sec. for Memorial Affairs — William F. Tuerk

Assistant Secretaries for:
  Policy, Planning, Preparedness — Paul J. Hutter, act.
  Management — Robert J. Henke
  Human Resource Administration — R. Allen Pittman
  Public and Intergovernmental Affairs — Lisette M. Mondello
  Information and Technology — vacant
  Congressional and Legislative Affairs — vacant
General Counsel — Tim S. McClain
Inspector General — George J. Opfer
Board of Veterans' Appeals — James P. Terry, chair.
Board of Contract Appeals — Gary J. Krump, chair.

Department of Homeland Security
20528 (no street address used); www.dhs.gov
Secretary of Homeland Security — Michael Chertoff
Deputy Secretary — Michael P. Jackson
Chief of Staff — John Wood
Executive Secretary — David Trulio
Under Sec. for Management — Scott Charbo, act.
Under Sec. for Preparedness — George W. Foresman
Under Sec. for Infrastructure Protection — Robert B. Stephan
Under Sec. for Federal Emergency Management Agency — R. David Paulison
Under Sec. for Science & Tech. — Rear Adm. Jay M. Cohen
Assistant Secretaries for:
  Grants and Training — Tracy Henke
  Infrastructure Protection — Robert B. Stephan
  International Affairs — Cris Arcos
  Immigration & Customs Enforcement — Julie L. Myers
  Policy — Stewart A. Baker
  Policy Development — Richard C. Barth, Ph.D.
  Private Sector Office — Alfonso Martinez-Fonts
  Public Affairs — vacant
  Strategic Plans — Randy Beardsworth
Transportation Security Administration — Kip Hawley, dir.
U.S. Coast Guard Commandant — Adm. Thad W. Allen
U.S. Secret Service — Mark J. Sullivan, dir.
Inspector General — Richard L. Skinner
General Counsel — Philip J. Perry
Chief Medical Officer — Dr. Jeffrey W. Runge
Citizenship & Immigration Services — Emilio T. Gonzalez, dir. / Prakash I. Khatri, ombudsman.
Office of Natl. Capital Region Coordination — Thomas J. Lockwood, dir.
  State & Local Govt Coordination — Chester Lunner,
Officer for Civil Rights & Civil Liberties — Daniel W. Sutherland
Office of Counternarcotics Enforcement — Uttam Dhillon
Office of Screening Coordination & Operations — Kathleen L. Kraninger, dir.
Chief Information Officer — Scott Charbo
Chief Intelligence Officer — Charles E. Allen
Chief Privacy Officer — Hugo Teufel III
Chief Procurement Officer — Elaine C. Duke
Chief Security Officer — Dwight M. Williams
Chief Financial Officer — David Norquist
Chief Human Capital Officer — Marta B. Pérez
Customs & Border Protection — W. Ralph Basham, comm.
Domestic Nuclear Detection Office — Vayl Oxford, dir.
Federal Law Enforcement Training — Connie L. Patrick, dir.
Homeland Security Advisory Council — William H. Webster, chair
Military Liaison — Rear Admiral Timothy S. Sullivan
U.S. Fire Administation — Charlie Dickinson, act.
Federal Coordinator of Gulf Coast Rebuilding — Donald E. Powell

Notable U.S. Government Agencies
Source: The U.S. Government Manual; National Archives and Records Administration; World Almanac research
All addresses are Washington, DC, unless otherwise noted; as of June 2006
* = independent agency

Bureau of Alcohol, Tobacco, Firearms and Explosives — Michael J. Sullivan, act. (Dept. of Justice, 650 Mass. Ave NW, 20226); www.atf.gov
Bureau of the Census — Charles Louis Kincannon, dir. (Dept. of Commerce, 4700 Silver Hill Rd., 20233); www.census.gov
Bureau of Citizenship & Immigration Services — Emilio T. Gonzalez, dir. (Dept. of Homeland Security, 20 Massachusetts Avenue NW, 20529); www.uscis.gov

Bureau of Economic Analysis — J. Steven Landefeld, dir. (Dept. of Commerce, 1441 L St. NW, 20005); www.bea.gov
Bureau of Prisons — Harley G. Lappin, dir. (Dept. of Justice, 320 First St. NW, 20534); www.bop.gov
Centers for Disease Control & Prevention — Julie Louise Gerberding, dir. (Dept. of HHS, 1600 Clifton Rd., Atlanta, GA 30333); www.cdc.gov
*Central Intelligence Agency — Gen. Michael V. Hayden, dir. (Wash., DC 20505); www.cia.gov

*Commission on Civil Rights — Gerald A. Reynolds, chair (624 9th St. NW, 20425); www.usccr.gov

*Commodity Futures Trading Commission — Reuben Jeffery III, chair (3 Lafayette Centre, 1155 21st St. NW, 20581); www.cftc.gov

*Consumer Product Safety Commission — Nancy Nord, chair (4330 East-West Hwy., Bethesda, MD 20814); www.cpsc.gov

*Environmental Protection Agency — Stephen L. Johnson, adm. (Ariel Rios Bldg., 1200 Pennsylvania Ave. NW, 20460); www.epa.gov

*Equal Employment Opportunity Commission — Naomi C. Earp, chair (1801 L St. NW, 20507); www.eeoc.gov

*Export-Import Bank of the United States — James H. Lambright, pres. and chair (811 Vermont Avenue NW, 20571); www.exim.gov

*Farm Credit Administration — Nancy C. Pellett, chair (1501 Farm Credit Drive, McLean, VA 22102); www.fca.gov

Federal Aviation Administration — Marion C. Blakey, adm. (Dept. of Trans., 800 Independence Ave. SW, 20591); www.faa.gov

Federal Bureau of Investigation — Robert S. Mueller III, dir. (Dept. of Justice, J. Edgar Hoover Building, 935 Pennsylvania Ave. NW, 20535); www.fbi.gov

*Federal Communications Commission — Kevin J. Martin, chair (445 12th St. SW, 20554); www.fcc.gov

*Federal Deposit Insurance Corporation — Sheila C. Bair, chair (550 17th St. NW, 20429); www.fdic.gov

*Federal Election Commission — Michael E. Toner, chair (999 E St. NW, 20463); www.fec.gov

Federal Emergency Management Agency — R. David Paulison, under sec. (Dept. of Homeland Security, 500 C St. SW, 20472); www.fema.gov

*Federal Energy Regulatory Commission — Joseph T. Kelliher, chair (888 1st St. NE, 20426); www.ferc.gov

Federal Highway Administration — J. Richard Capka, adm. (Dept. of Trans., 400 7th St. SW, 20590); www.fhwa.dot.gov

*Federal Maritime Commission — Steven R. Blust, chair (800 N. Capitol St. NW, 20573); www.fmc.gov

*Federal Mine Safety & Health Review Commission — Michael F. Duffy, chair (601 New Jersey Ave. NW, 20001); www.fmshrc.gov

*Federal Reserve System — Ben S. Bernanke, chair, Board of Governors (20th St. & Constitution Ave. NW, 20551); www.federalreserve.gov

*Federal Trade Commission — Deborah Platt Majoras, chair (600 Pennsylvania Ave. NW, 20580); www.ftc.gov

Fish & Wildlife Service — H. Dale Hall, dir. (Dept. of the Interior, 1849 C St. NW, 20240); www.fws.gov

Food and Drug Administration — Andrew C. von Eschenbach, act. comm. (Dept. of HHS, 5600 Fishers Lane, Rockville, MD 20857); www.fda.gov

Forest Service — Dale N. Bosworth, chief (Dept. of Agriculture, 1400 Independence Ave. SW, 20250); www.fs.fed.us

Government Accountability Office — (cong. agency) David M. Walker, comptroller gen. (441 G St. NW, 20548); www.gao.gov

*General Services Administration — Lurita A. Doan, admin. (1800 F St. NW, 20405); www.gsa.gov

Government Printing Office — (cong. agency) Judith C. Russell, Superintendent of Documents (732 N. Capitol St. NW, 20401); www.gpoaccess.gov

*Inter-American Foundation — Roger W. Wallace, pres. (901 N Stuart St., 10th floor, Arlington, VA 22203); www.iaf.gov

Internal Revenue Service — Mark W. Everson, comm. (Dept. of Treas., 1111 Constitution Ave. NW, 20224); www.irs.gov

Library of Congress — (cong. agency) James H. Billington, Librarian of Congress (101 Indep. Ave. SE, 20540); www.loc.gov

*National Aeronautics and Space Administration — Michael Griffin, adm. (300 E St. SW, 20546); www.nasa.gov

*National Archives & Records Administration — Allen Weinstein, archivist (8601 Adelphi Road, College Park, MD 20740-6001); www.archives.gov

*National Endowment for the Arts — Dana Gioia, chair (1100 Pennsylvania Ave. NW, 20506); www.arts.gov

*National Endowment for the Humanities — Bruce Cole, chair (1100 Pennsylvania Ave. NW, 20506); www.neh.gov

National Institutes of Health — Elias A. Zerhouni, dir. (Dept. of HHS, 9000 Rockville Pike, Bethesda, MD 20892); www.nih.gov

*National Labor Relations Board — Robert J. Battista, chair (1099 14th St. NW, 20570); www.nlrb.gov

National Oceanic and Atmospheric Administration — Vice Adm. Conrad C. Lautenbacher Jr., admin. (Dept. of Commerce, 14th & Constitution Ave. NW, 20230); www.noaa.gov

National Park Service — vacant (Dept. of the Interior, 1849 C St. NW, 20240); www.nps.gov

*National Railroad Passenger Corp. (Amtrak) — Alexander Kummant, pres. and CEO (60 Mass. Ave. NE, 20002); www.amtrak.com

*National Science Foundation — Dr. Arden L. Bement Jr., dir., National Science Foundation; Steven C. Beering, chair, National Science Board (4201 Wilson Blvd., Arlington, VA 22230); www.nsf.gov

*National Transportation Safety Board — Mark V. Rosenker, chair (490 L'Enfant Plaza SW, 20594); www.ntsb.gov

*Nuclear Regulatory Commission — Dale E. Klein, chair (U.S. Nuclear Regulatory Commission 20555); www.nrc.gov

Occupational Safety & Health Administration — Edwin G. Foulke, Jr. (Dept. of Labor, 200 Constitution Ave. NW, 20210); www.osha.gov

*Occupational Safety & Health Review Commission — Horace A. Thompson, chair (1120 20th St. NW, 9th Floor, 20036); www.oshrc.gov

*Office of Government Ethics — Robert I. Cusick, dir. (1201 New York Ave. NW, Suite 500, 20005); www.usoge.gov

*Office of Personnel Management — Linda M. Springer, dir. (1900 E St. NW, 20415-0001); www.opm.gov

*Office of Special Counsel — Scott J. Bloch, spec. counsel (1730 M St. NW, Suite 300, 20036); www.osc.gov

*Peace Corps — Ronald A. Tschetter, dir. (1111 20th St., NW, 20526); www.peacecorps.gov

*Postal Rate Commission — George A. Omas, chair (1901 New York Avenue, NW, Ste. 200, 20268); www.prc.gov

*Securities and Exchange Commission — Christopher Cox, chair (100 F Street NE, 20549); www.sec.gov

*Selective Service System — William A. Chatfield, dir. (National Headquarters, 1515 Wilson Blvd., Arlington, VA 22209-2425); www.sss.gov

*Small Business Administration — Steven C. Preston, adm. (409 Third St. SW, 20416); www.sba.gov

Smithsonian Institution — (quasi-official agency) Lawrence M. Small, sec. (PO Box 37012, SI Building, Rm. 153, MRC 010, 20013); www.si.edu

*Social Security Administration — Jo Anne B. Barnhart, comm. (6401 Security Blvd., Baltimore, MD 21235); www.ssa.gov

Surgeon General — Kenneth Moritsugu, act. (Dept. of HHS, 200 Independence Ave SW, 20201); www.surgeongeneral.gov

*Tennessee Valley Authority — Tom Kilgore, act. Chief Executive Officer, President, and Chief Operating Officer (400 W. Summit Hill Dr., Knoxville, TN 37902); www.tva.gov

*Trade and Development Agency — Thelma J. Askey, dir. (1000 Wilson Blvd. Ste. 1600, Arlington, VA 22209); www.tda.gov

United States Coast Guard — Adm. Thad W. Allen, commandant (Dept. of Homeland Security, 2100 2nd St. SW, 20593); www.uscg.mil

United States Customs and Border Protection — W. Ralph Basham, comm. (Dept. of Homeland Security, 1300 Pennsylvania Ave. NW, 20229); www.cbp.gov

United States Fire Administration — Charlie Dickinson, act. (Dept. of Homeland Security, 16825 S. Seton Ave., Emmitsburg, MD 21727) www.usfa.dhs.gov

United States Geological Survey — Mark Myers, dir. (Dept. of the Interior, 12201 Sunrise Valley Dr., Reston, VA 20192); www.usgs.gov

*United States International Trade Commission — Daniel R. Pearson, chair (Dept. of Commerce, 500 E St. SW, 20436); www.usitc.gov

United States Mint — Edmund C. Moy, dir. (Dept. of Treas., U.S. Mint Headquarters, 801 9th St., NW, 20002); www.usmint.gov

*United States Postal Service — John E. Potter, Postmaster General (475 L'Enfant Plaza SW, 20260); www.usps.com

United States Secret Service — Mark J. Sullivan, dir. (Dept. of Homeland Security, 245 Murray Dr., Bldg. 410, 20223); www.secretservice.gov

CABINETS OF THE U.S.

The U.S. Cabinet and Its Role

The heads of major executive departments of government constitute the Cabinet. This institution, not provided for in the U.S. Constitution, developed as an advisory body out of the desire of presidents to consult on policy matters. Aside from its advisory role, the Cabinet as a body has no formal function and wields no executive authority. Individual members exercise authority as heads of their departments, reporting to the president.

In addition to the heads of federal departments as listed below, the Cabinet commonly includes other officials designated by the president as of Cabinet rank.

The officials so designated by Pres. George W. Bush include: Vice Pres. Richard B. Cheney, Chief of Staff to the President Joshua B. Bolten, Environmental Protection Agency Administrator Dirk Kempthorne, Office of Management and Budget Director Robert Portman, Office of National Drug Control Policy Director John P. Walters, and United States Trade Representative Susan Schwab.

The Cabinet meets at times set by the president. Members of Pres. Bush's Cabinet listed in this chapter are as of June 2006.

Secretaries of State

The Department of Foreign Affairs was created by act of Congress on July 27, 1789, and the name changed to Department of State on Sept. 15, 1789.

President	Secretary	Home	Sworn In
Washington	Thomas Jefferson	VA	1789
	Edmund Randolph	VA	1794
	Timothy Pickering	PA	1795
Adams, J.	Timothy Pickering	PA	1797
	John Marshall	VA	1800
Jefferson	James Madison	VA	1801
Madison	Robert Smith	MD	1809
	James Monroe	VA	1811
Monroe	John Quincy Adams	MA	1817
Adams, J.Q.	Henry Clay	KY	1825
Jackson	Martin Van Buren	NY	1829
	Edward Livingston	LA	1831
	Louis McLane	DE	1833
	John Forsyth	GA	1834
Van Buren	John Forsyth	GA	1837
Harrison, W.H.	Daniel Webster	MA	1841
Tyler	Daniel Webster	MA	1841
	Abel P. Upshur	VA	1843
	John C. Calhoun	SC	1844
Polk	John C. Calhoun	SC	1845
	James Buchanan	PA	1845
Taylor	James Buchanan	PA	1849
	John M. Clayton	DE	1849
Fillmore	John M. Clayton	DE	1850
	Daniel Webster	MA	1850
	Edward Everett	MA	1852
Pierce	William L. Marcy	NY	1853
Buchanan	William L. Marcy	NY	1857
	Lewis Cass	MI	1857
	Jeremiah S. Black	PA	1860
Lincoln	Jeremiah S. Black	PA	1861
	William H. Seward	NY	1861
Johnson, A.	William H. Seward	NY	1865
Grant	Elihu B. Washburne	IL	1869
	Hamilton Fish	NY	1869
Hayes	Hamilton Fish	NY	1877
	William M. Evarts	NY	1877
Garfield	William M. Evarts	NY	1881
	James G. Blaine	ME	1881
Arthur	James G. Blaine	ME	1881
	F.T. Frelinghuysen	NJ	1881
Cleveland	F.T. Frelinghuysen	NJ	1885
	Thomas F. Bayard	DE	1885
Harrison, B.	Thomas F. Bayard	DE	1889
Harrison, B.	James G. Blaine	ME	1889
	John W. Foster	IN	1892
Cleveland	Walter Q. Gresham	IN	1893
	Richard Olney	MA	1895
McKinley	Richard Olney	MA	1897
	John Sherman	OH	1897
	William R. Day	OH	1898
	John Hay	DC	1898
Roosevelt, T.	John Hay	DC	1901
	Elihu Root	NY	1905
	Robert Bacon	NY	1909
Taft	Robert Bacon	NY	1909
	Philander C. Knox	PA	1909
Wilson	Philander C. Knox	PA	1913
	William J. Bryan	NE	1913
	Robert Lansing	NY	1915
	Bainbridge Colby	NY	1920
Harding	Charles E. Hughes	NY	1921
Coolidge	Charles E. Hughes	NY	1923
	Frank B. Kellogg	MN	1925
Hoover	Frank B. Kellogg	MN	1929
	Henry L. Stimson	NY	1929
Roosevelt, F.D.	Cordell Hull	TN	1933
	E.R. Stettinius Jr.	VA	1944
Truman	E.R. Stettinius Jr.	VA	1945
	James F. Byrnes	SC	1945
	George C. Marshall	PA	1947
	Dean G. Acheson	CT	1949
Eisenhower	John Foster Dulles	NY	1953
	Christian A. Herter	MA	1959
Kennedy	Dean Rusk	NY	1961
Johnson, L.B.	Dean Rusk	NY	1963
Nixon	William P. Rogers	NY	1969
	Henry A. Kissinger	DC	1973
Ford	Henry A. Kissinger	DC	1974
Carter	Cyrus R. Vance	NY	1977
	Edmund S. Muskie	ME	1980
Reagan	Alexander M. Haig Jr.	CT	1981
	George P. Shultz	CA	1982
Bush, G.H.W.	James A. Baker III	TX	1989
	Lawrence S. Eagleburger	MI	1992
Clinton	Warren M. Christopher	CA	1993
	Madeleine K. Albright	DC	1997
Bush, G.W.	Colin L. Powell	NY	2001
	Condoleezza Rice	AL	2005

Secretaries of the Treasury

The Treasury Department was organized by act of Congress on Sept. 2, 1789.

President	Secretary	Home	Sworn In
Washington	Alexander Hamilton	NY	1789
	Oliver Wolcott	CT	1795
Adams, J.	Oliver Wolcott	CT	1797
	Samuel Dexter	MA	1801
Jefferson	Samuel Dexter	MA	1801
	Albert Gallatin	PA	1801
Madison	Albert Gallatin	PA	1809
	George W. Campbell	TN	1814
	Alexander J. Dallas	PA	1814
	William H. Crawford	GA	1816
Monroe	William H. Crawford	GA	1817
Adams, J.Q.	Richard Rush	PA	1825
Jackson	Samuel D. Ingham	PA	1829
	Louis McLane	DE	1831
	William J. Duane	PA	1833
	Roger B. Taney	MD	1833
	Levi Woodbury	NH	1834
Van Buren	Levi Woodbury	NH	1837
Harrison, W.H.	Thomas Ewing	OH	1841
Tyler	Thomas Ewing	OH	1841
	Walter Forward	PA	1841
	John C. Spencer	NY	1843
	George M. Bibb	KY	1844
Polk	Robert J. Walker	MS	1845
Taylor	William M. Meredith	PA	1849
Fillmore	Thomas Corwin	OH	1850
Pierce	James Guthrie	KY	1853
Buchanan	Howell Cobb	GA	1857
	Phillip F. Thomas	MD	1860
	John A. Dix	NY	1861
Lincoln	Salmon P. Chase	OH	1861
	William P. Fessenden	ME	1864
	Hugh McCulloch	IN	1865
Johnson, A.	Hugh McCulloch	IN	1865

President	Secretary	Home	Sworn In
Grant	George S. Boutwell	MA	1869
	William A. Richardson	MA	1873
	Benjamin H. Bristow	KY	1874
	Lot M. Morrill	ME	1876
Hayes	John Sherman	OH	1877
Garfield	William Windom	MN	1881
Arthur	Charles J. Folger	NY	1881
	Walter Q. Gresham	IN	1884
	Hugh McCulloch	IN	1884
Cleveland	Daniel Manning	NY	1885
	Charles S. Fairchild	NY	1887
Harrison, B.	William Windom	MN	1889
	Charles Foster	OH	1891
Cleveland	John G. Carlisle	KY	1893
McKinley	Lyman J. Gage	IL	1897
Roosevelt, T.	Lyman J. Gage	IL	1901
	Leslie M. Shaw	IA	1902
	George B. Cortelyou	NY	1907
Taft	Franklin MacVeagh	IL	1909
Wilson	William G. McAdoo	NY	1913
	Carter Glass	VA	1918
	David F. Houston	MO	1920
Harding	Andrew W. Mellon	PA	1921
Coolidge	Andrew W. Mellon	PA	1923
Hoover	Andrew W. Mellon	PA	1929
	Ogden L. Mills	NY	1932
Roosevelt, F.D.	William H. Woodin	NY	1933
	Henry Morgenthau, Jr.	NY	1934
Truman	Fred M. Vinson	KY	1945
	John W. Snyder	MO	1946
Eisenhower	George M. Humphrey	OH	1953
	Robert B. Anderson	CT	1957
Kennedy	C. Douglas Dillon	NJ	1961
Johnson, L.B.	C. Douglas Dillon	NJ	1963
	Henry H. Fowler	VA	1965
	Joseph W. Barr	IN	1968
Nixon	David M. Kennedy	IL	1969
	John B. Connally	TX	1971
	George P. Shultz	IL	1972
	William E. Simon	NJ	1974
Ford	William E. Simon	NJ	1974
Carter	W. Michael Blumenthal	MI	1977
	G. William Miller	RI	1979
Reagan	Donald T. Regan	NY	1981
	James A. Baker III	TX	1985
	Nicholas F. Brady	NJ	1988
Bush, G.H.W.	Nicholas F. Brady	NJ	1989
Clinton	Lloyd Bentsen	TX	1993
	Robert E. Rubin	NY	1995
	Lawrence H. Summers	CT	1999
Bush, G.W.	Paul H. O'Neill	MO	2001
	John W. Snow	OH	2003
	Henry M. Paulson	FL	2006

Secretaries of Defense

The Department of Defense, originally designated the National Military Establishment, was created on Sept. 18, 1947. It is headed by the secretary of defense, who is a member of the president's Cabinet. The departments of the army, of the navy, and of the air force function within the Defense Department, and since 1947 the secretaries of these departments have not been members of the president's Cabinet.

President	Secretary	Home	Sworn In
Truman	James V. Forrestal	NY	1947
	Louis A. Johnson	WV	1949
	George C. Marshall	PA	1950
	Robert A. Lovett	NY	1951
Eisenhower	Charles E. Wilson	MI	1953
	Neil H. McElroy	OH	1957
	Thomas S. Gates Jr.	PA	1959
Kennedy	Robert S. McNamara	MI	1961
Johnson, L.B.	Robert S. McNamara	MI	1963
	Clark M. Clifford	MD	1968
Nixon	Melvin R. Laird	WI	1969
	Elliot L. Richardson	MA	1973
	James R. Schlesinger	VA	1973
Ford	James R. Schlesinger	VA	1974
	Donald H. Rumsfeld	IL	1975
Carter	Harold Brown	CA	1977

President	Secretary	Home	Sworn In
Reagan	Caspar W. Weinberger	CA	1981
	Frank C. Carlucci	PA	1987
Bush, G.H.W.	Richard B. Cheney	WY	1989
Clinton	Les Aspin	WI	1993
	William J. Perry	CA	1994
	William S. Cohen	ME	1997
Bush, G.W.	Donald H. Rumsfeld	IL	2001

Secretaries of War

The War Department (which included jurisdiction over the navy until 1798) was created by act of Congress on Aug. 7, 1789, and Gen. Henry Knox was commissioned secretary of war under that act on Sept. 12, 1789.

President	Secretary	Home	Sworn In
Washington	Henry Knox	MA	1789
	Timothy Pickering	PA	1795
	James McHenry	MD	1796
Adams, J.	James McHenry	MD	1797
	Samuel Dexter	MA	1800
Jefferson	Henry Dearborn	MA	1801
Madison	William Eustis	MA	1809
	John Armstrong	NY	1813
	James Monroe	VA	1814
	William H. Crawford	GA	1815
Monroe	John C. Calhoun	SC	1817
Adams, J.Q.	James Barbour	VA	1825
	Peter B. Porter	NY	1828
Jackson	John H. Eaton	TN	1829
	Lewis Cass	MI	1831
	Benjamin F. Butler	NY	1837
Van Buren	Joel R. Poinsett	SC	1837
Harrison, W.H.	John Bell	TN	1841
Tyler	John Bell	TN	1841
	John C. Spencer	NY	1841
	James M. Porter	PA	1843
	William Wilkins	PA	1844
Polk	William L. Marcy	NY	1845
Taylor	George W. Crawford	GA	1849
Fillmore	Charles M. Conrad	LA	1850
Pierce	Jefferson Davis	MS	1853
Buchanan	John B. Floyd	VA	1857
	Joseph Holt	KY	1861
Lincoln	Simon Cameron	PA	1861
	Edwin M. Stanton	PA	1862
Johnson, A.	Edwin M. Stanton	PA	1865
	John M. Schofield	IL	1868
Grant	John A. Rawlins	IL	1869
	William T. Sherman	OH	1869
	William W. Belknap	IA	1869
	Alphonso Taft	OH	1876
	James D. Cameron	PA	1876
Hayes	George W. McCrary	IA	1877
	Alexander Ramsey	MN	1879
Garfield	Robert T. Lincoln	IL	1881
Arthur	Robert T. Lincoln	IL	1881
Cleveland	William C. Endicott	MA	1885
Harrison, B.	Redfield Proctor	VT	1889
	Stephen B. Elkins	WV	1891
Cleveland	Daniel S. Lamont	NY	1893
McKinley	Russel A. Alger	MI	1897
	Elihu Root	NY	1899
Roosevelt, T.	Elihu Root	NY	1901
	William H. Taft	OH	1904
	Luke E. Wright	TN	1908
Taft	Jacob M. Dickinson	TN	1909
	Henry L. Stimson	NY	1911
Wilson	Lindley M. Garrison	NJ	1913
	Newton D. Baker	OH	1916
Harding	John W. Weeks	MA	1921
Coolidge	John W. Weeks	MA	1923
	Dwight F. Davis	MO	1925
Hoover	James W. Good	IL	1929
	Patrick J. Hurley	OK	1929
Roosevelt, F.D.	George H. Dern	UT	1933
	Harry H. Woodring	KS	1937
	Henry L. Stimson	NY	1940
Truman	Robert P. Patterson	NY	1945
	Kenneth C. Royall[1]	NC	1947

(1) Last member of the Cabinet with this title. The War Department became the Department of the Army and became a branch of the Department of Defense in 1947.

Secretaries of the Navy

The Navy Department was created by act of Congress on Apr. 30, 1798.

President	Secretary	Home	Sworn In
Adams, J.	Benjamin Stoddert	MD	1798
Jefferson	Benjamin Stoddert	MD	1801
	Robert Smith	MD	1801
Madison	Paul Hamilton	SC	1809
	William Jones	PA	1813
	Benjamin W. Crowninshield	MA	1814
Monroe	Benjamin W. Crowninshield	MA	1817
	Smith Thompson	NY	1818
	Samuel L. Southard	NJ	1823
Adams, J.Q.	Samuel L. Southard	NJ	1825
Jackson	John Branch	NC	1829
	Levi Woodbury	NH	1831
	Mahlon Dickerson	NJ	1834
Van Buren	Mahlon Dickerson	NJ	1837
	James K. Paulding	NY	1838
Harrison, W.H.	George E. Badger	NC	1841
Tyler	George E. Badger	NC	1841
	Abel P. Upshur	VA	1841
	David Henshaw	MA	1843
	Thomas W. Gilmer	VA	1844
	John Y. Mason	VA	1844
Polk	George Bancroft	MA	1845
	John Y. Mason	VA	1846
Taylor	William B. Preston	VA	1849
Fillmore	William A. Graham	NC	1850
	John P. Kennedy	MD	1852
Pierce	James C. Dobbin	NC	1853
Buchanan	Isaac Toucey	CT	1857
Lincoln	Gideon Welles	CT	1861
Johnson, A.	Gideon Welles	CT	1865
Grant	Adolph E. Borie	PA	1869
	George M. Robeson	NJ	1869
Hayes	Richard W. Thompson	IN	1877
	Nathan Goff Jr.	WV	1881
Garfield	William H. Hunt	LA	1881
Arthur	William E. Chandler	NH	1882
Cleveland	William C. Whitney	NY	1885
Harrison, B.	Benjamin F. Tracy	NY	1889
Cleveland	Hilary A. Herbert	AL	1893
McKinley	John D. Long	MA	1897
Roosevelt, T.	John D. Long	MA	1901
	William H. Moody	MA	1902
	Paul Morton	IL	1904
	Charles J. Bonaparte	MD	1905
	Victor H. Metcalf	CA	1906
	Truman H. Newberry	MI	1908
Taft	George von L. Meyer	MA	1909
Wilson	Josephus Daniels	NC	1913
Harding	Edwin Denby	MI	1921
Coolidge	Edwin Denby	MI	1923
	Curtis D. Wilbur	CA	1924
Hoover	Charles Francis Adams	MA	1929
Roosevelt, F.D.	Claude A. Swanson	VA	1933
	Charles Edison	NJ	1940
	Frank Knox	IL	1940
	James V. Forrestal	NY	1944
Truman	James V. Forrestal[1]	NY	1945

(1) Last member of Cabinet with this title. The Navy Department became a branch of the Department of Defense when the latter was created on Sept. 18, 1947.

Attorneys General

The Office of Attorney General was established by act of Congress on Sept. 24, 1789. It officially reached Cabinet rank in Mar. 1792, when the first attorney general, Edmund Randolph, attended his initial Cabinet meeting. The Department of Justice, headed by the attorney general, was created June 22, 1870.

President	Secretary	Home	Sworn In
Washington	Edmund Randolph	VA	1789
	William Bradford	PA	1794
	Charles Lee	VA	1795
Adams, J.	Charles Lee	VA	1797
Jefferson	Levi Lincoln	MA	1801
	John Breckenridge	KY	1805
	Caesar A. Rodney	DE	1807

President	Secretary	Home	Sworn In
Madison	Caesar A. Rodney	DE	1807
	William Pinkney	MD	1811
	Richard Rush	PA	1814
Monroe	Richard Rush	PA	1817
	William Wirt	VA	1817
Adams, J.Q.	William Wirt	VA	1825
Jackson	John M. Berrien	GA	1829
	Roger B. Taney	MD	1831
	Benjamin F. Butler	NY	1833
Van Buren	Benjamin F. Butler	NY	1837
	Felix Grundy	TN	1838
	Henry D. Gilpin	PA	1840
Harrison, W.H.	John J. Crittenden	KY	1841
Tyler	John J. Crittenden	KY	1841
	Hugh S. Legare	SC	1841
	John Nelson	MD	1843
Polk	John Y. Mason	VA	1845
	Nathan Clifford	ME	1846
	Isaac Toucey	CT	1848
Taylor	Reverdy Johnson	MD	1849
Fillmore	John J. Crittenden	KY	1850
Pierce	Caleb Cushing	MA	1853
Buchanan	Jeremiah S. Black	PA	1857
	Edwin M. Stanton	PA	1860
Lincoln	Edward Bates	MO	1861
	James Speed	KY	1864
Johnson, A.	James Speed	KY	1865
	Henry Stanbery	OH	1866
	William M. Evarts	NY	1868
Grant	Ebenezer R. Hoar	MA	1869
	Amos T. Akerman	GA	1870
	George H. Williams	OR	1871
	Edwards Pierrepont	NY	1875
	Alphonso Taft	OH	1876
Hayes	Charles Devens	MA	1877
Garfield	Wayne MacVeagh	PA	1881
Arthur	Benjamin H. Brewster	PA	1882
Cleveland	Augustus Garland	AR	1885
Harrison, B.	William H. H. Miller	IN	1889
Cleveland	Richard Olney	MA	1893
	Judson Harmon	OH	1895
McKinley	Joseph McKenna	CA	1897
	John W. Griggs	NJ	1898
	Philander C. Knox	PA	1901
Roosevelt, T.	Philander C. Knox	PA	1901
	William H. Moody	MA	1904
	Charles J. Bonaparte	MD	1906
Taft	George W. Wickersham	NY	1909
Wilson	J.C. McReynolds	TN	1913
	Thomas W. Gregory	TX	1914
	A. Mitchell Palmer	PA	1919
Harding	Harry M. Daugherty	OH	1921
Coolidge	Harry M. Daugherty	OH	1923
	Harlan F. Stone	NY	1924
	John G. Sargent	VT	1925
Hoover	William D. Mitchell	MN	1929
Roosevelt, F.D.	Homer S. Cummings	CT	1933
	Frank Murphy	MI	1939
	Robert H. Jackson	NY	1940
	Francis Biddle	PA	1941
Truman	Thomas C. Clark	TX	1945
	J. Howard McGrath	RI	1949
	J.P. McGranery	PA	1952
Eisenhower	Herbert Brownell Jr	NY	1953
	William P. Rogers	MD	1957
Kennedy	Robert F. Kennedy	MA	1961
Johnson, L.B.	Robert F. Kennedy	MA	1963
	N. de B. Katzenbach	IL	1964
	Ramsey Clark	TX	1967
Nixon	John N. Mitchell	NY	1969
	Richard G. Kleindienst	AZ	1972
	Elliot L. Richardson	MA	1973
	William B. Saxbe	OH	1974
Ford	William B. Saxbe	OH	1974
	Edward H. Levi	IL	1975
Carter	Griffin B. Bell	GA	1977
	Benjamin R. Civiletti	MD	1979
Reagan	William French Smith	CA	1981
	Edwin Meese III	CA	1985
	Richard Thornburgh	PA	1988

President	Secretary	Home	Sworn In
Bush, G.H.W.	Richard Thornburgh	PA	1989
	William P. Barr	NY	1991
Clinton	Janet Reno	FL	1993
Bush, G.W.	John Ashcroft	MO	2001
	Alberto Gonzales	TX	2005

Secretaries of the Interior

The Department of the Interior was created by act of Congress on Mar. 3, 1849.

President	Secretary	Home	Sworn In
Taylor	Thomas Ewing	OH	1849
Fillmore	Thomas M. T. McKennan	PA	1850
	Alex H. H. Stuart	VA	1850
Pierce	Robert McClelland	MI	1853
Buchanan	Jacob Thompson	MS	1857
Lincoln	Caleb B. Smith	IN	1861
	John P. Usher	IN	1863
Johnson, A.	John P. Usher	IN	1865
	James Harlan	IA	1865
	Orville H. Browning	IL	1866
Grant	Jacob D. Cox	OH	1869
	Columbus Delano	OH	1870
	Zachariah Chandler	MI	1875
Hayes	Carl Schurz	MO	1877
Garfield	Samuel J. Kirkwood	IA	1881
Arthur	Henry M. Teller	CO	1882
Cleveland	Lucius Q.C. Lamar	MS	1885
	William F. Vilas	WI	1888
Harrison, B.	John W. Noble	MO	1889
Cleveland	Hoke Smith	GA	1893
	David R. Francis	MO	1896
McKinley	Cornelius N. Bliss	NY	1897
	Ethan A. Hitchcock	MO	1898
Roosevelt, T.	Ethan A. Hitchcock	MO	1901
	James R. Garfield	OH	1907
Taft	Richard A. Ballinger	WA	1909
	Walter L. Fisher	IL	1911
Wilson	Franklin K. Lane	CA	1913
	John B. Payne	IL	1920
Harding	Albert B. Fall	NM	1921
	Hubert Work	CO	1923
Coolidge	Hubert Work	CO	1923
	Roy O. West	IL	1929
Hoover	Ray Lyman Wilbur	CA	1929
Roosevelt, F.D.	Harold L. Ickes	IL	1933
Truman	Harold L. Ickes	IL	1945
	Julius A. Krug	WI	1946
	Oscar L. Chapman	CO	1949
Eisenhower	Douglas McKay	OR	1953
	Fred A. Seaton	NE	1956
Kennedy	Stewart L. Udall	AZ	1961
Johnson, L.B.	Stewart L. Udall	AZ	1963
Nixon	Walter J. Hickel	AK	1969
	Rogers C.B. Morton	MD	1971
Ford	Rogers C.B. Morton	MD	1971
	Stanley K. Hathaway	WY	1975
	Thomas S. Kleppe	ND	1975
Carter	Cecil D. Andrus	ID	1977
Reagan	James G. Watt	CO	1981
	William P. Clark	CA	1983
	Donald P. Hodel	OR	1985
Bush, G.H.W.	Manuel Lujan	NM	1989
Clinton	Bruce Babbitt	AZ	1993
Bush, G.W.	Gale Norton	CO	2001
	Dirk Kempthorne	ID	2006

Secretaries of Agriculture

The Department of Agriculture was created by act of Congress on May 15, 1862. On Feb. 8, 1889, its commissioner was renamed secretary of agriculture and became a member of the Cabinet.

President	Secretary	Home	Sworn In
Cleveland	Norman J. Colman	MO	1889
Harrison, B.	Jeremiah M. Rusk	WI	1889
Cleveland	J. Sterling Morton	NE	1893
McKinley	James Wilson	IA	1897
Roosevelt, T.	James Wilson	IA	1901
Taft	James Wilson	IA	1909

President	Secretary	Home	Sworn In
Wilson	David F. Houston	MO	1913
	Edwin T. Meredith	IA	1920
Harding	Henry C. Wallace	IA	1921
Coolidge	Henry C. Wallace	IA	1923
	Howard M. Gore	WV	1924
	William M. Jardine	KS	1925
Hoover	Arthur M. Hyde	MO	1929
Roosevelt, F.D.	Henry A. Wallace	IA	1933
	Claude R. Wickard	IN	1940
Truman	Clinton P. Anderson	NM	1945
Truman	Charles F. Brannan	CO	1948
Eisenhower	Ezra Taft Benson	UT	1953
Kennedy	Orville L. Freeman	MN	1961
Johnson, L.B.	Orville L. Freeman	MN	1963
Nixon	Clifford M. Hardin	IN	1969
	Earl L. Butz	IN	1971
Ford	Earl L. Butz	IN	1974
	John A. Knebel	VA	1976
Carter	Bob Bergland	MN	1977
Reagan	John R. Block	IL	1981
	Richard E. Lyng	CA	1986
Bush, G.H.W.	Clayton K. Yeutter	NE	1989
	Edward Madigan	IL	1991
Clinton	Mike Espy	MS	1993
	Dan Glickman	KS	1995
Bush, G.W.	Ann M. Veneman	CA	2001
	Mike Johanns	NE	2005

Secretaries of Commerce and Labor

The Department of Commerce and Labor, created by Congress on Feb. 14, 1903, was divided by Congress Mar. 4, 1913, into separate departments of Commerce and Labor. The secretary of each was made a Cabinet member.

Secretaries of Commerce and Labor

President	Secretary	Home	Sworn In
Roosevelt, T.	George B. Cortelyou	NY	1903
	Victor H. Metcalf	CA	1904
	Oscar S. Straus	NY	1906
Taft	Charles Nagel	MO	1909

Secretaries of Labor

President	Secretary	Home	Sworn In
Wilson	William B. Wilson	PA	1913
Harding	James J. Davis	PA	1921
Coolidge	James J. Davis	PA	1923
Hoover	James J. Davis	PA	1929
	William N. Doak	VA	1930
Roosevelt, F.D.	Frances Perkins	NY	1933
Truman	L.B. Schwellenbach	WA	1945
	Maurice J. Tobin	MA	1949
Eisenhower	Martin P. Durkin	IL	1953
	James P. Mitchell	NJ	1953
Kennedy	Arthur J. Goldberg	IL	1961
	W. Willard Wirtz	IL	1962
Johnson, L.B.	W. Willard Wirtz	IL	1963
Nixon	George P. Shultz	IL	1969
	James D. Hodgson	CA	1970
	Peter J. Brennan	NY	1973
Ford	Peter J. Brennan	NY	1974
	John T. Dunlop	CA	1975
	W.J. Usery Jr.	GA	1976
Carter	F. Ray Marshall	TX	1977
Reagan	Raymond J. Donovan	NJ	1981
	William E. Brock	TN	1985
	Ann D. McLaughlin	DC	1987
Bush, G.H.W.	Elizabeth Hanford Dole	NC	1989
	Lynn Martin	IL	1991
Clinton	Robert B. Reich	MA	1993
	Alexis M. Herman	AL	1997
Bush, G.W.	Elaine L. Chao	KY	2001

Secretaries of Commerce

President	Secretary	Home	Sworn In
Wilson	William C. Redfield	NY	1913
	Joshua W. Alexander	MO	1919
Harding	Herbert C. Hoover	CA	1921

President	Secretary	Home	Sworn In
Coolidge	Herbert C. Hoover	CA	1923
	William F. Whiting	MA	1928
Hoover	Robert P. Lamont	IL	1929
	Roy D. Chapin	MI	1932
Roosevelt, F.D.	Daniel C. Roper	SC	1933
	Harry L. Hopkins	NY	1939
	Jesse Jones	TX	1940
	Henry A. Wallace	IA	1945
Truman	Henry A. Wallace	IA	1945
	W. Averell Harriman	NY	1947
	Charles Sawyer	OH	1948
Eisenhower	Sinclair Weeks	MA	1953
	Lewis L. Strauss	NY	1958
	Frederick H. Mueller	MI	1959
Kennedy	Luther H. Hodges	NC	1961
Johnson, L.B.	Luther H. Hodges	NC	1963
	John T. Connor	NJ	1965
	Alex B. Trowbridge	NJ	1967
	Cyrus R. Smith	NY	1968
Nixon	Maurice H. Stans	MN	1969
	Peter G. Peterson	IL	1972
	Frederick B. Dent	SC	1973
Ford	Frederick B. Dent	SC	1974
	Rogers C.B. Morton	MD	1975
	Elliot L. Richardson	MA	1975
Carter	Juanita M. Kreps	NC	1977
	Philip M. Klutznick	IL	1979
Reagan	Malcolm Baldrige	CT	1981
	C. William Verity Jr.	OH	1987
Bush, G.H.W.	Robert A. Mosbacher	TX	1989
	Barbara H. Franklin	PA	1992
Clinton	Ronald H. Brown	DC	1993
	Mickey Kantor	CA	1996
	William M. Daley	IL	1997
	Norman Y. Mineta	CA	2000
Bush, G.W.	Donald L. Evans	TX	2001
	Carlos Gutierrez	MI	2005

Secretaries of Housing and Urban Development

The Department of Housing and Urban Development was created by act of Congress on Sept. 9, 1965.

President	Secretary	Home	Sworn In
Johnson, L.B.	Robert C. Weaver	WA	1966
	Robert C. Wood	MA	1969
Nixon	George W. Romney	MI	1969
	James T. Lynn	OH	1973
Ford	James T. Lynn	OH	1974
	Carla Anderson Hills	CA	1975
Carter	Patricia Roberts Harris	DC	1977
	Moon Landrieu	LA	1979
Reagan	Samuel R. Pierce Jr.	NY	1981
Bush, G.H.W.	Jack F. Kemp	NY	1989
Clinton	Henry G. Cisneros	TX	1993
	Andrew M. Cuomo	NY	1997
Bush, G.W.	Mel Martinez	FL	2001
	Alphonso Jackson	TX	2004

Secretaries of Transportation

The Department of Transportation was created by act of Congress on Oct. 15, 1966.

President	Secretary	Home	Sworn In
Johnson, L.B.	Alan S. Boyd	FL	1966
Nixon	John A. Volpe	MA	1969
	Claude S. Brinegar	CA	1973
Ford	Claude S. Brinegar	CA	1974
	William T. Coleman Jr.	PA	1975
Carter	Brock Adams	WA	1977
	Neil E. Goldschmidt	OR	1979
Reagan	Andrew L. Lewis Jr.	PA	1981
	Elizabeth Hanford Dole	NC	1983
	James H. Burnley	NC	1987
Bush, G.H.W.	Samuel K. Skinner	IL	1989
	Andrew H. Card Jr.	MA	1992
Clinton	Federico F. Peña	CO	1993
	Rodney E. Slater	AR	1997
Bush, G.W.	Norman Y. Mineta	CA	2001

Secretaries of Energy

The Department of Energy was created by federal law on Aug. 4, 1977.

President	Secretary	Home	Sworn In
Carter	James R. Schlesinger	VA	1977
	Charles Duncan Jr.	WY	1979
Reagan	James B. Edwards	SC	1981
	Donald P. Hodel	OR	1982
	John S. Herrington	CA	1985
Bush, G.H.W.	James D. Watkins	CA	1989
Clinton	Hazel R. O'Leary	MN	1993
	Federico F. Peña	CO	1997
	Bill Richardson	NM	1998
Bush, G.W.	Spencer Abraham	MI	2001
	Samuel W. Bodman	MA	2005

Secretaries of Health, Education, and Welfare

The Department of Health, Education, and Welfare was created by Congress on Apr. 11, 1953. On Sept. 27, 1979, it was divided by Congress into the departments of Education and of Health and Human Services, with the secretary of each being a Cabinet member.

President	Secretary	Home	Sworn In
Eisenhower	Oveta Culp Hobby	TX	1953
	Marion B. Folsom	NY	1955
	Arthur S. Flemming	OH	1958
Kennedy	Abraham A. Ribicoff	CT	1961
	Anthony J. Celebrezze	OH	1962
Johnson, L.B.	Anthony J. Celebrezze	OH	1963
	John W. Gardner	NY	1965
	Wilbur J. Cohen	MI	1968
Nixon	Robert H. Finch	CA	1969
	Elliot L. Richardson	MA	1970
	Caspar W. Weinberger	CA	1973
Ford	Caspar W. Weinberger	CA	1974
	Forrest D. Mathews	AL	1975
Carter	Joseph A. Califano Jr.	DC	1977
	Patricia Roberts Harris	DC	1979

Secretaries of Health and Human Services

President	Secretary	Home	Sworn In
Carter	Patricia Roberts Harris	DC	1979
Reagan	Richard S. Schweiker	PA	1981
	Margaret M. Heckler	MA	1983
Reagan	Otis R. Bowen	IN	1985
Bush, G.H.W.	Louis W. Sullivan	GA	1989
Clinton	Donna E. Shalala	WI	1993
Bush, G.W.	Tommy Thompson	WI	2001
	Michael O. Leavitt	UT	2005

Secretaries of Education

President	Secretary	Home	Sworn In
Carter	Shirley Hufstedler	CA	1979
Reagan	Terrel Bell	UT	1981
	William J. Bennett	NY	1985
	Lauro F. Cavazos	TX	1988
Bush, G.H.W.	Lauro F. Cavazos	TX	1989
	Lamar Alexander	TN	1991
Clinton	Richard W. Riley	SC	1993
Bush, G.W.	Roderick R. Paige	TX	2001
	Margaret Spellings	TX	2005

Secretaries of Veterans Affairs

The Department of Veterans Affairs was created on Oct. 25, 1988, when Pres. Ronald Reagan signed a bill that made the Veterans Administration into a Cabinet department, effective Mar. 15, 1989.

President	Secretary	Home	Sworn In
Bush, G.H.W.	Edward J. Derwinski	IL	1989
Clinton	Jesse Brown	IL	1993
Clinton	Togo D. West Jr.	NC	1998
	Hershel W. Gober (acting)	AR	2000
Bush, G.W.	Anthony Principi	CA	2001
	Jim Nicholson	CO	2005

Secretaries of Homeland Security

The Department of Homeland Security was created by act of Congress on Nov. 25, 2002.

President	Secretary	Home	Sworn In
Bush, G.W.	Thomas Ridge	PA	2003
	Michael Chertoff	DC	2005

U.S. SUPREME COURT

(data as of Sept. 2006)

Justices of the U.S. Supreme Court

The Supreme Court comprises the chief justice of the U.S. and 8 associate justices, all appointed for life by the president with advice and consent of the Senate. Names of chief justices are in **boldface**. Terms of service begin with the year each justice took the Judicial oath. Service years are the number of complete years served by a justice. Current salaries: chief justice, $212,100; associate justice, $203,000. The U.S. Supreme Court Bldg. is at 1 First St. NE, Washington, DC 20543. The Court website is www.supremecourtus.gov

Members at start of 2006-2007 term (Oct. 2, 2006): Chief justice: John G. Roberts Jr; assoc. justices in seniority order: John Paul Stevens, Antonin Scalia, Anthony M. Kennedy, David H. Souter, Clarence Thomas, Ruth Bader Ginsburg, Stephen G. Breyer, Samuel A. Alito Jr.

Name, apptd. from	Service Term	Yrs	Born	Died	Name, apptd. from	Service Term	Yrs	Born	Died
John Jay, NY	1789-1795	5	1745	1829	Oliver W. Holmes, MA	1902-1932	29	1841	1935
John Rutledge, SC[1]	1790-1791	1	1739	1800	William R. Day, OH	1903-1922	19	1849	1923
William Cushing, MA	1790-1810*	20	1732	1810	William H. Moody, MA	1906-1910	3	1853	1917
James Wilson, PA	1789-1798	8	1742	1798	Horace H. Lurton, TN	1910-1914	4	1844	1914
John Blair, VA	1790-1795*	5	1732	1800	Charles E. Hughes, NY[1]	1910-1916	5	1862	1948
James Iredell, NC	1790-1799	9	1751	1799	Willis Van Devanter, WY	1911-1937	26	1859	1941
Thomas Johnson, MD	1792-1793	<1	1732	1819	Joseph R. Lamar, GA	1911-1916	5	1857	1916
William Paterson, NJ	1793-1806	13	1745	1806	**Edward D. White,** LA[2]	1910-1921	10	1845	1921
John Rutledge, SC[2,3]	1795	<1	1739	1800	Mahlon Pitney, NJ	1912-1922	10	1858	1924
Samuel Chase, MD	1796-1811	15	1741	1811	James C. McReynolds, TN	1914-1941	26	1862	1946
Oliver Ellsworth, CT	1796-1800	4	1745	1807	Louis D. Brandeis, MA	1916-1939	22	1856	1941
Bushrod Washington, VA	1799-1829*	30	1762	1829	John H. Clarke, OH	1916-1922	5	1857	1945
Alfred Moore, NC	1800-1804	3	1755	1810	**William H. Taft,** CT	1921-1930	8	1857	1930
John Marshall, VA	1801-1835	34	1755	1835	George Sutherland, UT	1922-1938	15	1862	1942
William Johnson, SC	1804-1834	30	1771	1834	Pierce Butler, MN	1923-1939	16	1866	1939
Henry B. Livingston, NY	1807-1823	16	1757	1823	Edward T. Sanford, TN	1923-1930	7	1865	1930
Thomas Todd, KY	1807-1826	18	1765	1826	Harlan F. Stone, NY[1]	1925-1941	16	1872	1946
Gabriel Duvall, MD	1811-1835	23	1752	1844	**Charles E. Hughes,** NY[2]	1930-1941	11	1862	1948
Joseph Story, MA	1812-1845*	33	1779	1845	Owen J. Roberts, PA	1930-1945	15	1875	1955
Smith Thompson, NY	1823-1843	20	1768	1843	Benjamin N. Cardozo, NY	1932-1938	6	1870	1938
Robert Trimble, KY	1826-1828	2	1777	1828	Hugo L. Black, AL	1937-1971	34	1886	1971
John McLean, OH	1830-1861*	31	1785	1861	Stanley F. Reed, KY	1938-1957	19	1884	1980
Henry Baldwin, PA	1830-1844	14	1780	1844	Felix Frankfurter, MA	1939-1962	23	1882	1965
James M. Wayne, GA	1835-1867	32	1790	1867	William O. Douglas, CT	1939-1975	36[4]	1898	1980
Roger B. Taney, MD	1836-1864	28	1777	1864	Frank Murphy, MI	1940-1949	9	1890	1949
Philip P. Barbour, VA	1836-1841	4	1783	1841	**Harlan F. Stone,** NY[2]	1941-1946	4	1872	1946
John Catron, TN	1837-1865	28	1786	1865	James F. Byrnes, SC	1941-1942	1	1879	1972
John McKinley, AL	1838-1852*	14	1780	1852	Robert H. Jackson, NY	1941-1954	13	1892	1954
Peter V. Daniel, VA	1842-1860*	18	1784	1860	Wiley B. Rutledge, IA	1943-1949	6	1894	1949
Samuel Nelson, NY	1845-1872	27	1792	1873	Harold H. Burton, OH	1945-1958	13	1888	1964
Levi Woodbury, NH	1845-1851	5	1789	1851	**Fred M. Vinson,** KY	1946-1953	7	1890	1953
Robert C. Grier, PA	1846-1870	23	1794	1870	Tom C. Clark, TX	1949-1967	17	1899	1977
Benjamin R. Curtis, MA	1851-1857	5	1809	1874	Sherman Minton, IN	1949-1956	7	1890	1965
John A. Campbell, AL	1853-1861*	8	1811	1889	**Earl Warren,** CA	1953-1969	15	1891	1974
Nathan Clifford, ME	1858-1881	23	1803	1881	John Marshall Harlan, NY	1955-1971	16	1899	1971
Noah H. Swayne, OH	1862-1881	18	1804	1884	William J. Brennan Jr., NJ	1956-1990	33	1906	1997
Samuel F. Miller, IA	1862-1890	28	1816	1890	Charles E. Whittaker, MO	1957-1962	5	1901	1973
David Davis, IL	1862-1877	14	1815	1886	Potter Stewart, OH	1958-1981	22	1915	1985
Stephen J. Field, CA	1863-1897	33	1816	1899	Byron R. White, CO	1962-1993	31	1917	2002
Salmon P. Chase, OH	1864-1873	8	1808	1873	Arthur J. Goldberg, IL	1962-1965	2	1908	1990
William Strong, PA	1870-1880	10	1808	1895	Abe Fortas, TN	1965-1969	3	1910	1982
Joseph P. Bradley, NJ	1870-1892	21	1813	1892	Thurgood Marshall, NY	1967-1991	24	1908	1993
Ward Hunt, NY	1873-1882	9	1810	1886	**Warren E. Burger,** VA	1969-1986	17	1907	1995
Morrison R. Waite, OH	1874-1888	14	1816	1888	Harry A. Blackmun, MN	1970-1994	24	1908	1999
John M. Harlan, KY	1877-1911	33	1833	1911	Lewis F. Powell Jr., VA	1972-1987	15	1907	1998
William B. Woods, GA	1881-1887	6	1824	1887	William H. Rehnquist, AZ[1]	1972-1986	14	1924	2005
Stanley Matthews, OH	1881-1889	7	1824	1889	John Paul Stevens, IL	1975-		1920	
Horace Gray, MA	1882-1902	20	1828	1902	Sandra Day O'Connor, AZ	1981-2006	24	1930	
Samuel Blatchford, NY	1882-1893	11	1820	1893	**William H. Rehnquist, VA**[2]	1986-2005	18	1924	2005
Lucius Q.C. Lamar, MS	1888-1893	5	1825	1893	Antonin Scalia, VA	1986-		1936	
Melville W. Fuller, IL	1888-1910	21	1833	1910	Anthony M. Kennedy, CA	1988-		1936	
David J. Brewer, KS	1890-1910	20	1837	1910	David H. Souter, NH	1990-		1939	
Henry B. Brown, MI	1891-1906	15	1836	1913	Clarence Thomas, GA	1991-		1948	
George Shiras Jr., PA	1892-1903	10	1832	1924	Ruth Bader Ginsburg, NY	1993-		1933	
Howell E. Jackson, TN	1893-1895	2	1832	1895	Stephen G. Breyer, MA	1994-		1938	
Edward D. White, LA[1]	1894-1910	16	1845	1921	**John G. Roberts Jr.,** MD	2005-		1955	
Rufus W. Peckham, NY	1896-1909	13	1838	1909	Samuel A. Alito Jr., NJ	2006-		1950	
Joseph McKenna, CA	1898-1925	26	1843	1926					

*Date oath taken from questionable source. (1) Later, chief justice, as listed. (2) Formerly assoc. justice. (3) Named as acting chief justice; confirmation rejected by the Senate. (4) Longest term of service.

CONGRESS

The One Hundred and Ninth Congress, With Official 2004 Election Results

The 109th Congress convened Jan. 3, 2005.

The Senate

Rep., 55; Dem., 44; Ind., 1; Total, 100. As of September 2006.

Senate officials as of September 2006 were: Pres. Pro Tempore, Ted Stevens (AK); Majority Leader, Bill Frist (TN); Majority Whip, Mitch McConnell (KY); Minority Leader, Harry Reid (NV); Minority Whip, Dick Durbin (IL). The Senate had 14 women (9 D, 5 R), same number as in the previous Senate; 1 Asian American (Daniel K. Akaka, D, HI), same number as in previous Senate; 3 Hispanics (Mel Martinez, R, FL, Ken Salazar, D, CO, and Robert Menendez, D, NJ) compared to none before; 1 African American (Barack Obama, D, IL), compared to none before; no Native Americans, compared to 1 before.

As of September 2006, 4 Senators (2 D, 1 R, 1 Ind) plan to retire from the Senate rather then seek reelection in 2006. Marked in list with *.

Terms are for 6 years and end Jan. 3 of the year preceding the senator's name in the following table. Annual salary, $165,200; President Pro Tempore, Majority Leader, and Minority Leader, $183,500. To be eligible for the Senate, one must be at least 30 years old, a U.S. citizen for at least 9 years, and a resident of the state from which chosen.

The address is U.S. Senate, Washington DC 20510; telephone, 202-224-3121; website, www.senate.gov

Term ends	Senator (Party); Service from[1]
Alabama	
2009	Jeff Sessions (R); 1/7/97
2011	Richard Shelby (R); 1/6/87
Alaska	
2009	Ted Stevens (R); 12/24/68
2011	Lisa Murkowski (R); 12/20/02
Arizona	
2007	Jon Kyl (R); 1/4/95
2011	John McCain (R); 1/6/87
Arkansas	
2009	Mark Pryor (D); 1/7/03
2011	Blanche L. Lincoln (D); 1/6/99
California	
2007	Dianne Feinstein (D); 11/10/92
2011	Barbara Boxer (D); 1993
Colorado	
2009	Wayne Allard (R); 1/7/97
2011	Ken Salazar (D); 2005
Connecticut	
2007	Joe Lieberman (D); 1989
2011	Christopher J. Dodd (D); 1981
Delaware	
2007	Thomas R. Carper (D); 2001
2007	Joseph Biden Jr. (D); 1973
Florida	
2007	Bill Nelson (D); 2001
2011	Mel Martinez (R); 2005
Georgia	
2009	Saxby Chambliss (R); 1/7/03
2011	Johnny Isakson (R); 2005
Hawaii	
2007	Daniel K. Akaka (D); 4/28/90
2011	Daniel K. Inouye (D); 1963
Idaho	
2009	Larry E. Craig (R); 1991
2011	Mike Crapo (R); 1/6/99
Illinois	
2009	Richard J. Durbin (D); 1/7/97
2011	Barack Obama (D); 2005
Indiana	
2007	Richard G. Lugar (R); 1977
2011	Evan Bayh (D); 1/6/99
Iowa	
2009	Tom Harkin (D); 1985
2011	Chuck Grassley (R); 1981
Kansas	
2009	Pat Roberts (R); 1/7/97
2011	Sam Brownback (R); 11/27/96
Kentucky	
2009	Mitch McConnell (R); 1985
2011	Jim Bunning (R); 1/6/99

Term ends	Senator (Party); Service from[1]
Louisiana	
2009	Mary L. Landrieu (D); 1/7/97
2011	David Vitter (R); 2005
Maine	
2007	Olympia J. Snowe (R); 1/4/95
2009	Susan M. Collins (R); 1/7/97
Maryland	
2007	Paul S. Sarbanes* (D); 1977
2011	Barbara Ann Mikulski (D); 1/6/87
Massachusetts	
2007	Edward M. Kennedy (D); 11/7/62
2009	John F. Kerry (D); 1/2/85
Michigan	
2007	Debbie Stabenow (D); 2001
2009	Carl Levin (D); 1979
Minnesota	
2007	Mark Dayton* (D); 2001
2009	Norm Coleman (R); 1/7/03
Mississippi	
2007	Trent Lott (R); 1989
2009	Thad Cochran (R); 12/27/78
Missouri	
2009	Jim Talent (R); 11/23/02
2011	Christopher (Kit) Bond (R); 1/6/87
Montana	
2007	Conrad Burns (R); 1989
2009	Max Baucus (D); 12/15/78
Nebraska	
2007	Ben Nelson (D); 2001
2009	Chuck Hagel (R); 1/7/97
Nevada	
2007	John Ensign (R); 2001
2011	Harry Reid (D); 1/6/87
New Hampshire	
2009	John Sununu (R); 1/7/03
2011	Judd Gregg (R); 1993
New Jersey	
2007	Robert Menendez (D); 1/18/06
2009	Frank Lautenberg (D); 1/7/03
New Mexico	
2007	Jeff Bingaman (D); 1983
2009	Pete V. Domenici (R); 1973
New York	
2007	Hillary Rodham Clinton (D); 2001
2011	Charles E. Schumer (D); 1/6/99
North Carolina	
2009	Elizabeth H. Dole (R); 1/7/03
2011	Richard Burr (R); 2005

Term ends	Senator (Party); Service from[1]
North Dakota	
2007	Kent Conrad (D); 1/6/87
2011	Byron L. Dorgan (D); 12/14/92
Ohio	
2007	Mike DeWine (R); 1/4/95
2011	George V. Voinovich (R); 1/6/99
Oklahoma	
2009	James M. Inhofe (R); 11/21/94
2011	Tom Coburn (R); 2005
Oregon	
2009	Gordon Smith (R); 1/7/97
2011	Ron Wyden (D); 2/6/96
Pennsylvania	
2007	Rick Santorum (R); 1/4/95
2011	Arlen Specter (R); 1981
Rhode Island	
2007	Lincoln D. Chafee (R); 11/2/99
2009	John F. Reed (D); 1/7/97
South Carolina	
2009	Lindsey Graham (R); 1/7/03
2011	Jim DeMint (R); 2005
South Dakota	
2009	Tim Johnson (D); 1/7/97
2011	John Thune (R); 2005
Tennessee	
2007	Bill Frist* (R); 1/4/95
2009	Lamar Alexander (R); 1/7/03
Texas	
2007	Kay Bailey Hutchison (R); 6/5/93
2009	John Cornyn (R); 12/2/02
Utah	
2007	Orrin G. Hatch (R); 1977
2011	Robert F. Bennett (R); 1993
Vermont	
2007	James M. Jeffords* (Ind.); 1989
2011	Patrick Leahy (D); 1975
Virginia	
2007	George F. Allen (R); 2001
2009	John W. Warner (R); 1/2/79
Washington	
2007	Maria Cantwell (D); 2001
2011	Patty Murray (D); 1993
West Virginia	
2007	Robert C. Byrd (D); 1959
2009	John D. Rockefeller IV (D); 1/15/85
Wisconsin	
2007	Herbert H. Kohl (D); 1989
2011	Russ Feingold (D); 1993
Wyoming	
2007	Craig Thomas (R); 1/4/95
2009	Michael B. Enzi (R); 1/7/97

(1) Jan. 3, unless otherwise noted.

The House of Representatives

Rep., 231; Dem., 201; Ind., 1; Vac., 2; Total, 435. As of September 2006.

House officials as of September 2006 were: Speaker of the House, J. Dennis Hastert (IL); Majority Leader, John Boehner (OH); Majority Whip, Roy Blunt (MO); Minority Leader, Nancy Pelosi (CA); Minority Whip, Steny Hoyer (MD). As of September 2006, there were 70 women in the House (46 D, 24 R), an increase of 7 from the 108th Congress. There were 42 African Americans (all D), up from 5 from before, and 23 Hispanics (18 D, 5 R), an increase of 1.

As of September 2006, 30 representatives (10 D, 19 R, 1 Ind) plan to retire from the House. Marked in list with *.

Terms are for 2 years ending Jan. 3, 2007. Annual salary, $165,200; Speaker of the House, $212,100; Majority Leader and Minority Leader, $183,500. To be eligible for membership, a person must be at least 25 years of age, a U.S. citizen for at least 7 years, and a resident of the state from which he or she is chosen.

The address is U.S. House of Representatives, Washington, DC 20515; telephone, 202-224-3121; website, www.house.gov

Dist.	Representative (Party)
Alabama	
1	Jo Bonner (R)
2	Terry Everett (R)
3	Mike Rogers (R)
4	Robert Aderholt (R)
5	Robert E. "Bud" Cramer Jr. (D)
6	Spencer Bachus (R)
7	Artur Davis (D)
Alaska	
	Don Young (R)
Arizona	
1	Rick Renzi (R)
2	Trent Franks (R)
3	John Shadegg (R)
4	Ed Pastor (D)
5	J.D. Hayworth (R)
6	Jeff Flake (R)
7	Raúl Grijalva (D)
8	Jim Kolbe* (R)
Arkansas	
1	Marion Berry (D)
2	Vic Snyder (D)
3	John Boozman (R)
4	Mike Ross (D)
California	
1	Mike Thompson (D)
2	Wally Herger (R)
3	Daniel E. Lungren (R)
4	John Doolittle (R)
5	Doris Matsui (D)#
6	Lynn Woolsey (D)
7	George Miller (D)
8	Nancy Pelosi (D)
9	Barbara Lee (D)
10	Ellen Tauscher (D)
11	Richard Pombo (R)
12	Tom Lantos (D)
13	Fortney Pete Stark (D)
14	Anna Eshoo (D)
15	Michael M. Honda (D)
16	Zoe Lofgren (D)
17	Sam Farr (D)
18	Dennis Cardoza (D)
19	George Radanovich (R)
20	Jim Costa (D)
21	Devin Nunes (R)
22	William M. Thomas* (R)
23	Lois Capps (D)
24	Elton Gallegly (R)
25	Howard "Buck" McKeon (R)

Dist.	Representative (Party)
26	David Dreier (R)
27	Brad Sherman (D)
28	Howard Berman (D)
29	Adam Schiff (D)
30	Henry Waxman (D)
31	Xavier Becerra (D)
32	Hilda Solis (D)
33	Diane Watson (D)
34	Lucille Roybal-Allard (D)
35	Maxine Waters (D)
36	Jane Harman (D)
37	Juanita Millender-McDonald (D)
38	Grace F. Napolitano (D)
39	Linda Sánchez (D)
40	Ed Royce (R)
41	Jerry Lewis (R)
42	Gary Miller (R)
43	Joe Baca (D)
44	Ken Calvert (R)
45	Mary Bono (R)
46	Dana Rohrabacher (R)
47	Loretta Sanchez (D)
48	John Campbell (R)##
49	Darrell Issa (R)
50	Brian P. Bilbray (R)###
51	Bob Filner (D)
52	Duncan Hunter (R)
53	Susan Davis (D)

Doris O. Matsui won a special election Mar. 8, 2005, to replace Robert T. Matsui (D), who died on Jan. 1, 2005. ##John Campbell won a special election Dec. 6, 2005, to replace Christopher Cox, who resigned Aug. 2, 2005. ###Brian Bilbray won a special election June 6, 2006, to replace Randy "Duke" Cunningham, who resigned Dec. 1, 2005.

Dist.	Representative (Party)
Colorado	
1	Diana DeGette (D)
2	Mark Udall (D)
3	John Salazar (D)
4	Marilyn Musgrave (R)
5	Joel Hefley* (R)
6	Tom Tancredo (R)
7	Bob Beauprez* (R)
Connecticut	
1	John Larson (D)
2	Rob Simmons (R)
3	Rosa DeLauro (D)
4	Christopher Shays (R)
5	Nancy Johnson (R)
Delaware	
	Mike Castle (R)

Dist.	Representative (Party)
Florida	
1	Jeff Miller (R)
2	Allen Boyd (D)
3	Corrine Brown (D)
4	Ander Crenshaw (R)
5	Ginny Brown-Waite (R)
6	Cliff Stearns (R)
7	John L. Mica (R)
8	Ric Keller (R)
9	Michael Bilirakis* (R)
10	C. W. Bill Young (R)
11	Jim Davis* (D)
12	Adam Putnam (R)
13	Katherine Harris* (R)
14	Connie Mack (R)
15	Dave Weldon (R)
16	Mark Foley (R)
17	Kendrick B. Meek (D)
18	Ileana Ros-Lehtinen (R)
19	Robert Wexler (D)
20	Debbie Wasserman Schultz (D)
21	Lincoln Diaz-Balart (R)
22	E. Clay Shaw Jr. (R)
23	Alcee L. Hastings (D)
24	Tom Feeney (R)
25	Mario Diaz-Balart (R)
Georgia	
1	Jack Kingston (R)
2	Sanford Bishop Jr. (D)
3	Jim Marshall (D)
4	Cynthia McKinney* (D)
5	John Lewis (D)
6	Tom Price (R)
7	John Linder (R)
8	Lynn Westmoreland (R)
9	Charlie Norwood (R)
10	Nathan Deal (R)
11	Phil Gingrey (R)
12	John Barrow (D)
13	David Scott (D)
Hawaii	
1	Neil Abercrombie (D)
2	Ed Case* (D)
Idaho	
1	C. L. "Butch" Otter* (R)
2	Mike Simpson (R)
Illinois	
1	Bobby Rush (D)
2	Jesse Jackson Jr. (D)
3	Daniel Lipinski (D)

Dist.	Representative (Party)
4	Luis Gutierrez (D)
5	Rahm Emanuel (D)
6	Henry Hyde* (R)
7	Danny Davis (D)
8	Melissa Bean (D)
9	Janice Schakowsky (D)
10	Mark Steven Kirk (R)
11	Jerry Weller (R)
12	Jerry Costello (D)
13	Judy Biggert (R)
14	J. Dennis Hastert (R)
15	Timothy Johnson (R)
16	Donald Manzullo (R)
17	Lane Evans* (D)
18	Ray LaHood (R)
19	John Shimkus (R)

Indiana

Dist.	Representative (Party)
1	Peter Visclosky (D)
2	Chris Chocola (R)
3	Mark Souder (R)
4	Steve Buyer (R)
5	Dan Burton (R)
6	Mike Pence (R)
7	Julia Carson (D)
8	John Hostettler (R)
9	Mike Sodrel (R)

Iowa

Dist.	Representative (Party)
1	Jim Nussle* (R)
2	Jim Leach (R)
3	Leonard Boswell (D)
4	Tom Latham (R)
5	Steve King (R)

Kansas

Dist.	Representative (Party)
1	Jerry Moran (R)
2	Jim Ryun (R)
3	Dennis Moore (D)
4	Todd Tiahrt (R)

Kentucky

Dist.	Representative (Party)
1	Ed Whitfield (R)
2	Ron Lewis (R)
3	Anne Northup (R)
4	Geoff Davis (R)
5	Harold "Hal" Rogers (R)
6	Ben Chandler (D)

Louisiana

Dist.	Representative (Party)
1	Bobby Jindal (R)
2	William Jefferson (D)
3	Charlie Melancon# (D)
4	Jim McCrery (R)
5	Rodney Alexander (R)
6	Richard H. Baker (R)
7	Charles Boustany Jr.# (R)

In Louisiana, all candidates of all parties ran against one another on Nov. 2, 2004, in a non-partisan primary. Candidates who received more than 50% of the vote in a district were declared elected. Because no candidate received a majority of the vote in Districts 3 or 7, runoffs were held in those districts, Dec. 4, 2004, between the top 2 vote-getters.

Dist.	Representative (Party)
	Maine
1	Tom Allen (D)
2	Michael Michaud (D)
	Maryland
1	Wayne Gilchrest (R)
2	C. A. Dutch Ruppersberger (D)
3	Ben Cardin* (D)
4	Albert Russell Wynn (D)
5	Steny Hoyer (D)
6	Roscoe Bartlett (R)
7	Elijah Cummings (D)
8	Chris Van Hollen (D)
	Massachusetts
1	John W. Olver (D)
2	Richard E. Neal (D)
3	Jim McGovern (D)
4	Barney Frank (D)
5	Marty Meehan (D)
6	John Tierney (D)
7	Ed Markey (D)
8	Michael E. Capuano (D)
9	Stephen F. Lynch (D)
10	Bill Delahunt (D)
	Michigan
1	Bart Stupak (D)
2	Peter Hoekstra (R)
3	Vernon Ehlers (R)
4	Dave Camp (R)
5	Dale Kildee (D)
6	Fred Upton (R)
7	John J. H. "Joe" Schwarz* (R)
8	Mike Rogers (R)
9	Joe Knollenberg (R)
10	Candice Miller (R)
11	Thad McCotter (R)
12	Sander Levin (D)
13	Carolyn C. Kilpatrick (D)
14	John Conyers Jr. (D)
15	John Dingell (D)
	Minnesota
1	Gil Gutknecht (R)
2	John Kline (R)
3	Jim Ramstad (R)
4	Betty McCollum (D)
5	Martin Olav Sabo* (D)
6	Mark Kennedy* (R)
7	Collin Peterson (D)
8	James Oberstar (D)
	Mississippi
1	Roger Wicker (R)
2	Bennie Thompson (D)
3	Charles "Chip" Pickering (R)
4	Gene Taylor (D)
	Missouri
1	William Lacy Clay (D)
2	W. Todd Akin (R)
3	Russ Carnahan (D)
4	Ike Skelton (D)
5	Emanuel Cleaver (D)
6	Sam Graves (R)

Dist.	Representative (Party)
7	Roy Blunt (R)
8	Jo Ann Emerson (R)
9	Kenny Hulshof (R)
	Montana
	Denny Rehberg (R)
	Nebraska
1	Jeff Fortenberry (R)
2	Lee Terry (R)
3	Tom Osborne* (R)
	Nevada
1	Shelley Berkley (D)
2	Jim Gibbons* (R)
3	Jon Porter (R)
	New Hampshire
1	Jeb Bradley (R)
2	Charles Bass (R)
	New Jersey
1	Rob Andrews (D)
2	Frank LoBiondo (R)
3	Jim Saxton (R)
4	Chris Smith (R)
5	Scott Garrett (R)
6	Frank Pallone Jr. (D)
7	Mike Ferguson (R)
8	Bill Pascrell Jr. (D)
9	Steve Rothman (D)
10	Donald Payne (D)
11	Rodney Frelinghuysen (R)
12	Rush Holt (D)
13	vacant#

Robert Menendez (D) resigned on Jan. 16, 2006 to become U.S. senator for NJ. A special election for his replacement was scheduled for Nov. 7, 2006.

Dist.	Representative (Party)
	New Mexico
1	Heather Wilson (R)
2	Stevan Pearce (R)
3	Tom Udall (D)
	New York
1	Timothy Bishop (D)
2	Steve Israel (D)
3	Peter King (R)
4	Carolyn McCarthy (D)
5	Gary Ackerman (D)
6	Gregory W. Meeks (D)
7	Joseph Crowley (D)
8	Jerrold Nadler (D)
9	Anthony Weiner (D)
10	Edolphus Towns (D)
11	Major Owens* (D)
12	Nydia Velázquez (D)
13	Vito Fossella (R)
14	Carolyn Maloney (D)
15	Charles Rangel (D)
16	José Serrano (D)
17	Eliot Engel (D)
18	Nita Lowey (D)
19	Sue Kelly (R)
20	John Sweeney (R)
21	Michael McNulty (D)
22	Maurice Hinchey (D)

Dist.	Representative (Party)
23	John McHugh (R)
24	Sherwood Boehlert* (R)
25	James Walsh (R)
26	Thomas Reynolds (R)
27	Brian Higgins (D)
28	Louise McIntosh Slaughter (D)
29	John "Randy" Kuhl Jr. (R)

North Carolina

Dist.	Representative (Party)
1	G.K. Butterfield (D)
2	Bob Etheridge (D)
3	Walter Jones (R)
4	David Price (D)
5	Virginia Foxx (R)
6	Howard Coble (R)
7	Mike McIntyre (D)
8	Robin Hayes (R)
9	Sue Wilkins Myrick (R)
10	Patrick McHenry (R)
11	Charles Taylor (R)
12	Mel Watt (D)
13	Brad Miller (D)

North Dakota

	Earl Pomeroy (D)

Ohio

Dist.	Representative (Party)
1	Steve Chabot (R)
2	Jean Schmidt (R)#
3	Mike Turner (R)
4	Michael Oxley* (R)
5	Paul Gillmor (R)
6	Ted Strickland* (D)
7	Dave Hobson (R)
8	John Boehner (R)
9	Marcy Kaptur (D)
10	Dennis Kucinich (D)
11	Stephanie Tubbs Jones (D)
12	Pat Tiberi (R)
13	Sherrod Brown* (D)
14	Steven LaTourette (R)
15	Deborah Pryce (R)
16	Ralph Regula (R)
17	Tim Ryan (D)
18	Bob Ney* (R)

#Rob Portman resigned on April 29, 2005 to become U.S. trade representative. Jean Schmidt was elected Aug. 2 to replace him.

Oklahoma

Dist.	Representative (Party)
1	John Sullivan (R)
2	Dan Boren (D)
3	Frank Lucas (R)
4	Tom Cole (R)
5	Ernest Istook Jr.* (R)

Oregon

Dist.	Representative (Party)
1	David Wu (D)
2	Greg Walden (R)
3	Earl Blumenauer (D)
4	Peter DeFazio (D)
5	Darlene Hooley (D)

Pennsylvania

Dist.	Representative (Party)
1	Robert Brady (D)
2	Chaka Fattah (D)
3	Phil English (R)
4	Melissa Hart (R)
5	John Peterson (R)
6	Jim Gerlach (R)
7	Curt Weldon (R)
8	Michael Fitzpatrick (R)
9	Bill Shuster (R)
10	Don Sherwood (R)
11	Paul Kanjorski (D)
12	John P. Murtha (D)
13	Allyson Schwartz (D)
14	Michael F. Doyle (D)
15	Charles Dent (R)
16	Joseph Pitts (R)
17	Tim Holden (D)
18	Tim Murphy (R)
19	Todd Russell Platts (R)

Rhode Island

Dist.	Representative (Party)
1	Patrick Kennedy (D)
2	Jim Langevin (D)

South Carolina

Dist.	Representative (Party)
1	Henry Brown Jr. (R)
2	Joe Wilson (R)
3	J. Gresham Barrett (R)
4	Bob Inglis (R)
5	John Spratt Jr. (D)
6	Jim Clyburn (D)

South Dakota

	Stephanie Herseth (D)

Tennessee

Dist.	Representative (Party)
1	Bill Jenkins* (R)
2	John Duncan Jr. (R)
3	Zach Wamp (R)
4	Lincoln Davis (D)
5	Jim Cooper (D)
6	Bart Gordon (D)
7	Marsha Blackburn (R)
8	John Tanner (D)
9	Harold Ford Jr.* (D)

Texas

Dist.	Representative (Party)
1	Louie Gohmert (R)
2	Ted Poe (R)
3	Sam Johnson (R)
4	Ralph Hall (R)
5	Jeb Hensarling (R)
6	Joe Barton (R)
7	John Abney Culberson (R)
8	Kevin Brady (R)
9	Al Green (D)
10	Michael McCaul (R)
11	K. Mike Conaway (R)
12	Kay Granger (R)
13	Mac Thornberry (R)
14	Ron Paul (R)
15	Rubén Hinojosa (D)
16	Silvestre Reyes (D)
17	Chet Edwards (D)
18	Sheila Jackson-Lee (D)
19	Randy Neugebauer (R)
20	Charlie Gonzalez (D)
21	Lamar Smith (R)
22	vacant#
23	Henry Bonilla (R)
24	Kenny Marchant (R)
25	Lloyd Doggett (D)
26	Michael Burgess (R)
27	Solomon Ortiz (D)
28	Henry Cuellar (D)
29	Gene Green (D)
30	Eddie Bernice Johnson (D)
31	John Carter (R)
32	Pete Sessions (R)

Tom Delay (R) won a primary election March 7, 2006. He resigned June 9, meaning no republican would be listed on the Nov. 7 ballot

Utah

Dist.	Representative (Party)
1	Rob Bishop (R)
2	Jim Matheson (D)
3	Chris Cannon (R)

Vermont

	Bernie Sanders (Ind.)*

Virginia

Dist.	Representative (Party)
1	Jo Ann Davis (R)
2	Thelma Drake (R)
3	Bobby Scott (D)
4	J. Randy Forbes (R)
5	Virgil Goode Jr. (R)
6	Bob Goodlatte (R)
7	Eric Cantor (R)
8	Jim Moran (D)
9	Rick Boucher (D)
10	Frank Wolf (R)
11	Tom Davis (R)

Washington

Dist.	Representative (Party)
1	Jay Inslee (D)
2	Rick Larsen (D)
3	Brian Baird (D)
4	Doc Hastings (R)
5	Cathy McMorris (R)
6	Norm Dicks (D)
7	Jim McDermott (D)
8	Dave Reichert (R)
9	Adam Smith (D)

West Virginia

Dist.	Representative (Party)
1	Alan Mollohan (D)
2	Shelley Moore Capito (R)
3	Nick Rahall II (D)

Wisconsin

Dist.	Representative (Party)
1	Paul Ryan (R)
2	Tammy Baldwin (D)
3	Ron Kind (D)
4	Gwen Moore (D)
5	F. James Sensenbrenner Jr. (R)
6	Tom Petri (R)
7	David Obey (D)
8	Mark Green* (R)

Wyoming

	Barbara Cubin (R)

The following members of Congress are nonvoting: Luis G. Fortuño (R) resident commissioner, Puerto Rico; Eleanor Holmes Norton (D), District of Columbia; Eni F. H. Faleomavaega (D), American Samoa; Donna M. Christian-Christiansen (D), Virgin Islands; Madeleine Bordallo (D), Guam.

IT'S A RECORD: Dennis Hastert (IL) became the longest serving Republican Speaker of the House on June 1, 2006, surpassing a 2,703-day record set by Joe Cannon (IL), who served from Nov. 9, 1903 until he was replaced on April 4, 1911.

Floor Leaders in the U.S. Senate Since the 1920s
(as of Aug. 2006)

Majority Leaders				Minority Leaders			
Name	Party	State	Tenure	Name	Party	State	Tenure
Charles Curtis[1]	Rep.	KS	1925-1929	Oscar W. Underwood[2]	Dem.	AL	1920-1923
James E. Watson	Rep.	IN	1929-1933	Joseph T. Robinson	Dem.	AR	1923-1933
Joseph T. Robinson	Dem.	AR	1933-1937	Charles L. McNary	Rep.	OR	1933-1944
Alben W. Barkley	Dem.	KY	1937-1947	Wallace H. White	Rep.	ME	1944-1947
Wallace H. White	Rep.	ME	1947-1949	Alben W. Barkley	Dem.	KY	1947-1949
Scott W. Lucas	Dem.	IL	1949-1951	Kenneth S. Wherry	Rep.	NE	1949-1951
Ernest W. McFarland	Dem.	AZ	1951-1953	Henry Styles Bridges	Rep.	NH	1952-1953
Robert A. Taft	Rep.	OH	1953	Lyndon B. Johnson	Dem.	TX	1953-1955
William F. Knowland	Rep.	CA	1953-1955	William F. Knowland	Rep.	CA	1955-1959
Lyndon B. Johnson	Dem.	TX	1955-1961	Everett M. Dirksen	Rep.	IL	1959-1969
Mike Mansfield	Dem.	MT	1961-1977	Hugh D. Scott	Rep.	PA	1969-1977
Robert C. Byrd	Dem.	WV	1977-1981	Howard H. Baker Jr.	Rep.	TN	1977-1981
Howard H. Baker Jr.	Rep.	TN	1981-1985	Robert C. Byrd	Dem.	WV	1981-1987
Robert J. Dole	Rep.	KS	1985-1987	Robert J. Dole	Rep.	KS	1987-1995
Robert C. Byrd	Dem.	WV	1987-1989	Thomas A. Daschle	Dem.	SD	1995-2001[3]
George J. Mitchell	Dem.	ME	1989-1995	Trent Lott	Rep.	MS	(3)
Robert J. Dole	Rep.	KS	1995-1996	Bill Frist	Rep.	TN	2002-2003[3]
Trent Lott	Rep.	MS	1996-2001[3]	Thomas A. Daschle	Dem.	SD	2003-2005[4]
Thomas A. Daschle	Dem.	SD	2001-2003[3]	Harry M. Reid	Dem.	NV	2005-
Bill Frist[5]	Rep.	TN	2003-				

Note: The offices of party (majority and minority) leaders in the Senate did not evolve until the 20th century. (1) First Republican to be designated floor leader. (2) First Democrat to be designated floor leader. (3) Starting Jan. 3, 2001, the Senate was split 50-50; with Al Gore (D) as outgoing vice pres. with the deciding vote, Thomas A. Daschle (D) briefly became majority leader and Trent Lott (R) was minority leader. From Jan. 20, 2001, with Dick Cheney (R) installed as vice pres., the positions were reversed. From June 6, 2001, the switch of Sen. James Jeffords (VT) from Republican to Independent meant the Democrats had a majority; Daschle resumed as majority leader, Lott as minority leader. Lott resigned as party leader Dec. 20, 2002, and Bill Frist was elected to replace him in the 108th Congress; since Republicans now had a majority, Frist became majority leader as of Jan. 7, 2003, with Daschle as minority leader. (4) Daschle was defeated in the 2004 election, and retired from the Senate Jan. 3, 2005; Democratic Whip Harry M. Reid was elected to the post for the 109th Congress. (5) Frist did not seek reelection in 2006.

Speakers of the House of Representatives
(as of Aug. 2006)

Name	Party	State	Tenure	Name	Party	State	Tenure
Frederick Muhlenberg	Federalist	PA	1789-1791	James G. Blaine	Rep.	ME	1869-1875
Jonathan Trumbull	Federalist	CT	1791-1793	Michael C. Kerr	Dem.	IN	1875-1876
Frederick Muhlenberg	Federalist	PA	1793-1795	Samuel J. Randall	Dem.	PA	1876-1881
Jonathan Dayton	Federalist	NJ	1795-1799	J. Warren Keifer	Rep.	OH	1881-1883
Theodore Sedgwick	Federalist	MA	1799-1801	John G. Carlisle	Dem.	KY	1883-1889
Nathaniel Macon	Dem.-Rep.	NC	1801-1807	Thomas B. Reed	Rep.	ME	1889-1891
Joseph B. Varnum	Dem.-Rep.	MA	1807-1811	Charles F. Crisp	Dem.	GA	1891-1895
Henry Clay	Dem.-Rep.	KY	1811-1814	Thomas B. Reed	Rep.	ME	1895-1899
Langdon Cheves	Dem.-Rep.	SC	1814-1815	David B. Henderson	Rep.	IA	1899-1903
Henry Clay	Dem.-Rep.	KY	1815-1820	Joseph G. Cannon	Rep.	IL	1903-1911
John W. Taylor	Dem.-Rep.	NY	1820-1821	Champ Clark	Dem.	MO	1911-1919
Philip P. Barbour	Dem.-Rep.	VA	1821-1823	Frederick H. Gillett	Rep.	MA	1919-1925
Henry Clay	Dem.-Rep.	KY	1823-1825	Nicholas Longworth	Rep.	OH	1925-1931
John W. Taylor	Dem.	NY	1825-1827	John N. Garner	Dem.	TX	1931-1933
Andrew Stevenson	Dem.	VA	1827-1834	Henry T. Rainey	Dem.	IL	1933-1934
John Bell	Dem.	TN	1834-1835	Joseph W. Byrns	Dem.	TN	1935-1936
James K. Polk	Dem.	TN	1835-1839	William B. Bankhead	Dem.	AL	1936-1940
Robert M. T. Hunter	Dem.	VA	1839-1841	Sam Rayburn	Dem.	TX	1940-1947
John White	Whig	KY	1841-1843	Joseph W. Martin Jr.	Rep.	MA	1947-1949
John W. Jones	Dem.	VA	1843-1845	Sam Rayburn	Dem.	TX	1949-1953
John W. Davis	Dem.	IN	1845-1847	Joseph W. Martin Jr.	Rep.	MA	1953-1955
Robert C. Winthrop	Whig	MA	1847-1849	Sam Rayburn	Dem.	TX	1955-1961
Howell Cobb	Dem.	GA	1849-1851	John W. McCormack	Dem.	MA	1962-1971
Linn Boyd	Dem.	KY	1851-1855	Carl Albert	Dem.	OK	1971-1977
Nathaniel P. Banks	American	MA	1856-1857	Thomas P. O'Neill Jr.	Dem.	MA	1977-1987
James L. Orr	Dem.	SC	1857-1859	James Wright	Dem.	TX	1987-1989
William Pennington	Rep.	NJ	1860-1861	Thomas S. Foley	Dem.	WA	1989-1995
Galusha A. Grow	Rep.	PA	1861-1863	Newt Gingrich	Rep.	GA	1995-1999
Schuyler Colfax	Rep.	IN	1863-1869	J. Dennis Hastert	Rep.	IL	1999-
Theodore M. Pomeroy	Rep.	NY	1869				

Political Divisions of the U.S. Senate and House of Representatives, 1901-2006
Source: Office of the Clerk; Congressional Research Service
Note: all figures reflect immediate post-election party breakdown; **boldface** denotes party in majority immediately after election.

		SENATE					HOUSE OF REPRESENTATIVES				
Congress	Years	Total Sens.	Demo-crats	Repub-licans	Other parties	Vacant	Total Members	Demo-crats	Repub-licans	Other parties	Vacant
57th	1901-03	90	32	**56**	2		357	151	**200**	6	
58th	1903-05	90	33	**57**			386	176	**207**	3	
59th	1905-07	90	32	**58**			386	135	**251**		
60th	1907-09	92	31	**61**			391	167	**223**	1	
61st	1909-11	92	32	**60**			391	172	**219**		
62nd	1911-13	96	44	**52**			394	**230**	162	2	
63rd	1913-15	96	**51**	44	1		435	**291**	134	10	
64th	1915-17	96	**56**	40			435	**230**	196	9	
65th	1917-19	96	**54**	42			435	214[1]	**215**	6	
66th	1919-21	96	47	**49**			435	192	**240**	2	1
67th	1921-23	96	37	**59**			435	131	**302**	2	

Congress	Years	Total Sens.	Demo- crats	Repub- licans	Other parties	Vacant	Total Members	Demo- crats	Repub- licans	Other parties	Vacant
68th	1923-25	96	42	53	1		435	207	225	3	
69th	1925-27	96	41	54	1		435	183	247	5	
70th	1927-29	96	46	48	1	1	435	194	238	3	
71st	1929-31	96	39	56	1		435	164	270	1	
72nd	1931-33	96	47	48	1		435	216[2]	218	1	
73rd	1933-35	96	59	36	1		435	313	117	5	
74th	1935-37	96	69	25	2		435	322	103	10	
75th	1937-39	96	76	16	4		435	334	88	13	
76th	1939-41	96	69	23	4		435	262	169	4	
77th	1941-43	96	66	28	2		435	267	162	6	
78th	1943-45	96	57	38	1		435	222	209	4	
79th	1945-47	96	57	38	1		435	242	191	2	
80th	1947-49	96	45	51			435	188	246	1	
81st	1949-51	96	54	42			435	263	171	1	
82nd	1951-53	96	49	47			435	235	199	1	
83rd	1953-55	96	47	48	1		435	213	221	1	
84th	1955-57	96	48	47	1		435	232	203		
85th	1957-59	96	49	47			435	234	201		
86th	1959-61	100	65	35			437[3]	283	153	1	
87th	1961-63	100	64	36			437[4]	263	174		
88th	1963-65	100	66	34			435	259	176		
89th	1965-67	100	68	32			435	295	140		
90th	1967-69	100	64	36			435	247	187		1
91st	1969-71	100	57	43			435	243	192		
92nd	1971-73	100	54	44	2		435	255	180		
93rd	1973-75	100	56	42	2		435	242	192	1	
94th	1975-77	100	60	38	2		435	291	144		
95th	1977-79	100	61	38	1		435	292	143		
96th	1979-81	100	58	41	1		435	277	158		
97th	1981-83	100	46	53	1		435	242	192	1	
98th	1983-85	100	46	54			435	269	166		
99th	1985-87	100	47	53			435	253	182		
100th	1987-89	100	55	45			435	258	177		
101st	1989-91	100	55	45			435	260	175		
102nd	1991-93	100	56	44			435	267	167	1	
103rd	1993-95	100	57	43			435	258	176	1	
104th	1995-97	100	48	52			435	204	230	1	
105th	1997-99	100	45	55			435	206	228	1	
106th	1999-2001	100	45	55			435	211	223	1	
107th	2001-03	100	50	50[5]			435	212	221	2	
108th	2003-05	100	48	51	1		435	204	229	1	1
109th	2005-07	100	44	55	1		435	202	232	1	

(1) Democrats organized the House with help of other parties. (2) Democrats organized House because of Republican deaths. (3) Proclamation declaring Alaska a state issued Jan. 3, 1959. (4) Proclamation declaring Hawaii a state issued Aug. 21, 1959. (5) While the Senate was split 50-50, control was held by whichever party had an incumbent vice president. Republican Sen. James M. Jeffords (VT) changed his party designation to Independent on June 6, 2001, switching control of the Senate to Democrats from Republicans.

Congressional Bills Vetoed, 1789-2006

Source: Senate Library

President	Regular vetoes	Pocket vetoes	Total vetoes	Vetoes overridden	President	Regular vetoes	Pocket vetoes	Total vetoes	Vetoes overridden
Washington	2	—	2	—	Benjamin Harrison	19	25	44	1
John Adams	—	—	—	—	Cleveland[2]	42	128	170	5
Jefferson	—	—	—	—	McKinley	6	36	42	—
Madison	5	2	7	—	Theodore Roosevelt	42	40	82	1
Monroe	1	—	1	—	Taft	30	9	39	1
John Q. Adams	—	—	—	—	Wilson	33	11	44	6
Jackson	5	7	12	—	Harding	5	1	6	—
Van Buren	—	1	1	—	Coolidge	20	30	50	4
William Harrison	—	—	—	—	Hoover	21	16	37	3
Tyler	6	4	10	1	Franklin Roosevelt	372	263	635	9
Polk	2	1	3	—	Truman	180	70	250	12
Taylor	—	—	—	—	Eisenhower	73	108	181	2
Fillmore	—	—	—	—	Kennedy	12	9	21	—
Pierce	9	—	9	5	Lyndon Johnson	16	14	30	—
Buchanan	4	3	7	—	Nixon	26	17	43	7
Lincoln	2	5	7	—	Ford	48	18	66	12
Andrew Johnson	21	8	29	15	Carter	13	18	31	2
Grant	45	48	93	4	Reagan	39	39	78	9
Hayes	12	1	13	1	George H. W. Bush[3]	29	15	44	1
Garfield	—	—	—	—	Clinton[4]	36	1	37	2
Arthur	4	8	12	1	George W. Bush[5]	1	—	1	—
Cleveland[1]	304	110	414	2	Total[3,4]	1,485	1,066	2,551	106

— = 0. (1) First term only. (2) Second term only. (3) Excluded from the figures are 2 additional bills, which Pres. George H. W. Bush claimed to be vetoed but Congress considered enacted into law because the president failed to return them to Congress during a recess period. (4) Does not include line-item vetoes, which were ruled unconstitutional by the Supreme Court on June 25, 1998. (5) As of Aug. 2006.

Librarians of Congress

Librarian	Served	Appointed by President	Librarian	Served	Appointed by President
John J. Beckley	1802-1807	Jefferson	Herbert Putnam	1899-1939	McKinley
Patrick Magruder	1807-1815	Jefferson	Archibald MacLeish	1939-1944	F. D. Roosevelt
George Watterston	1815-1829	Madison	Luther H. Evans	1945-1953	Truman
John Silva Meehan	1829-1861	Jackson	L. Quincy Mumford	1954-1974	Eisenhower
John G. Stephenson	1861-1864	Lincoln	Daniel J. Boorstin	1975-1987	Ford
Ainsworth Rand Spofford	1864-1897	Lincoln	James H. Billington	1987-	Reagan
John Russell Young	1897-1899	McKinley			

STATE GOVERNMENT

Governors of States and Puerto Rico

As of Sept. 2006. Of the 50 state governors, 29 are Republicans, 21 are Democrats.

State	Capital, ZIP Code	Governor	Party	Term years	Term expires	Annual salary
Alabama	Montgomery 36130	Bob Riley	Rep.	4	Jan. 2007	$96,361
Alaska	Juneau 99811	Frank Murkowski	Rep.	4	Dec. 2006	85,776
Arizona	Phoenix 85007	Janet Napolitano	Dem.	4	Jan. 2007	95,000
Arkansas	Little Rock 72201	Mike Huckabee	Rep.	4	Jan. 2007	77,028
California	Sacramento 95814	Arnold Schwarzenegger	Rep.	4	Jan. 2007	206,500
Colorado	Denver 80203	Bill Owens	Rep.	4	Jan. 2007	90,000
Connecticut	Hartford 06106	M. Jodi Rell	Rep.	4	Jan. 2007	150,000
Delaware	Dover 19901	Ruth Ann Minner	Dem.	4	Jan. 2007	132,500
Florida	Tallahassee 32399	Jeb Bush	Rep.	4	Jan. 2007	129,060
Georgia	Atlanta 30334	Sonny Perdue	Rep.	4	Jan. 2007	131,481
Hawaii	Honolulu 96813	Linda Lingle	Rep.	4	Dec. 2006	94,780
Idaho	Boise 83720	Jim Risch[1]	Rep.	4	Jan. 2007	101,500
Illinois	Springfield 62706	Rod R. Blagojevich	Dem.	4	Jan. 2007	150,691
Indiana	Indianapolis 46204	Mitch E. Daniels Jr.	Rep.	4	Jan. 2009	95,000
Iowa	Des Moines 50319	Tom Vilsack	Dem.	4	Jan. 2007	107,482
Kansas	Topeka 66612	Kathleen Sebelius	Dem.	4	Jan. 2007	105,889
Kentucky	Frankfort 40601	Ernie Fletcher	Rep.	4	Dec. 2007	116,520
Louisiana	Baton Rouge 70804	Kathleen Babineaux Blanco	Dem.	4	Jan. 2008	95,000
Maine	Augusta 04333	John E. Baldacci	Dem.	4	Jan. 2007	70,000
Maryland	Annapolis 21401	Robert L. Ehrlich Jr.	Rep.	4	Jan. 2007	145,000
Massachusetts	Boston 02133	Mitt Romney	Rep.	4	Jan. 2007	135,000
Michigan	Lansing 48909	Jennifer M. Granholm	Dem.	4	Jan. 2007	177,000
Minnesota	St. Paul 55155	Tim Pawlenty	Rep.	4	Jan. 2007	120,303
Mississippi	Jackson 39205	Haley Barbour	Rep.	4	Jan. 2008	122,160
Missouri	Jefferson City 65102	Matt Blunt	Rep.	4	Jan. 2009	120,087
Montana	Helena 59620	Brian Schweitzer	Dem.	4	Jan. 2009	96,462
Nebraska	Lincoln 68509	David Heineman	Rep.	4	Jan. 2007	85,000
Nevada	Carson City 89710	Kenny C. Guinn	Rep.	4	Jan. 2007	117,000
New Hampshire	Concord 03301	John H. Lynch	Dem.	2	Jan. 2007	108,990
New Jersey	Trenton 08625	Jon Corzine[1]	Dem.	4	Jan. 2010	175,000
New Mexico	Santa Fe 87503	Bill Richardson	Dem.	4	Jan. 2007	110,000
New York	Albany 12224	George E. Pataki	Rep.	4	Jan. 2007	179,000
North Carolina	Raleigh 27603	Mike Easley	Dem.	4	Jan. 2009	130,629
North Dakota	Bismarck 58505	John Hoeven	Rep.	4	Jan. 2007	92,483
Ohio	Columbus 43205	Bob Taft	Rep.	4	Jan. 2007	132,292
Oklahoma	Oklahoma City 73105	Brad Henry	Dem.	4	Jan. 2007	140,000
Oregon	Salem 97310	Ted Kulongoski	Dem.	4	Jan. 2007	93,600
Pennsylvania	Harrisburg 17120	Edward G. Rendell	Dem.	4	Jan. 2007	144,416
Rhode Island	Providence 02903	Donald L. Carcieri	Rep.	4	Jan. 2007	105,194
South Carolina	Columbia 29211	Mark Sanford	Rep.	4	Jan. 2007	106,078
South Dakota	Pierre 57501	Mike Rounds	Rep.	4	Jan. 2007	103,222
Tennessee	Nashville 37243	Phil Bredesen	Dem.	4	Jan. 2007	155,000
Texas	Austin 78711	Rick Perry	Rep.	4	Jan. 2007	115,345
Utah	Salt Lake City 84114	John M. Huntsman Jr.	Rep.	4	Jan. 2009	104,100
Vermont	Montpelier 05609	James H. Douglas	Rep.	2	Jan. 2007	168,466
Virginia	Richmond 23219	Timothy M. Kaine[1]	Dem.	4	Jan. 2010	175,000
Washington	Olympia 98504	Christine Gregoire	Dem.	4	Jan. 2009	148,035
West Virginia	Charleston 25305	Joe Manchin III	Dem.	4	Jan. 2009	95,000
Wisconsin	Madison 53707	Jim Doyle	Dem.	4	Jan. 2007	131,768
Wyoming	Cheyenne 82002	Dave Freudenthal	Dem.	4	Jan. 2007	105,000
Puerto Rico	San Juan 00936	Anibal Acevedo-Vila	PDP[2]	4	Jan. 2009	70,000

(1) New governor; began term in 2006. (2) Popular Democratic Party.

State Officials, Salaries, Party Membership

As of Sept. 2006, 19 legislatures were controlled by Democrats; 19 by Republicans; 11 were split; Nebraska is non-partisan. Some salaries may be rounded to the nearest dollar.

Alabama
Governor — Bob Riley, R, $96,361
Lt. Gov. — Lucy Baxley, D, $12 per day, plus $50 per day expenses, plus $3,780 per mo expenses
Atty. Gen. — Troy King, R, $155,828
Sec. of State — Nancy L. Worley, D, $71,500
Treasurer — Kay Ivey, R, $71,500
Auditor — Beth Chapman, R, $71,500
Legislature: meets annually at Montgomery 1st Tues. in Mar., 1st year of term of office; 1st Tues. in Feb., 2nd and 3rd yr; 2nd Tues. in Jan., 4th yr. Members receive $10 per day salary, plus $50 per day and $2,280 per month for expenses.
Senate — Dem., 25; Rep., 10. Total, 35
House — Dem., 63; Rep., 42. Total, 105

Alaska
Governor — Frank Murkowski, R, $85,776
Lt. Gov — Loren D. Leman, R, $80,040
Atty. General — David W. Márquez, R, $127,236
Legislature: meets annually in Jan. at Juneau for 120 days with a 10-day extension possible upon 2/3 vote. Members receive $24,012 annually, plus $163 or $218 session per diem, depending on season.

Arizona
Governor — Janet Napolitano, D, $95,000
Sec. of State — Jan Brewer, R, $70,000
Atty. Gen. — Terry Goddard, D, $90,000
Treasurer — David Petersen, R, $70,000
Legislature: meets annually in Jan. at Phoenix. Each member receives an annual salary of $24,000 plus a per diem.
Senate — Dem., 12; Rep., 18. Total, 30
House — Dem., 21; Rep., 39. Total, 60

Arkansas
Governor — Mike Huckabee, R, $77,028
Lt. Gov. — Winthrop P. Rockefeller, R, $37,229
Sec. of State — Charlie Daniels, D, $48,142
Atty. Gen. — Mike Beebe, D, $64,189
Treasurer — Gus Wingfield, D, $48,142
Auditor — Jim Wood, D, $48,142
General Assembly: meets odd years in Jan. at Little Rock. Members receive $14,067 annually.
Senate — Dem., 27; Rep., 8. Total, 35
House — Dem., 72; Rep., 28. Total, 100

California

Governor — Arnold Schwarzenegger, R, $206,500[1]
Lt. Gov. — Cruz Bustamante, D, $154,875
Sec. of State — Bruce McPherson, R, $154,875
Atty. Gen. — Bill Lockyer, D, $175,525
Controller — Steve Westly, D, $165,200
Treasurer — Phil Angelides, D, $165,200
Legislature: meets at Sacramento on the 1st Mon. in Dec. of even-numbered years; each session lasts 2 years. Members receive $113,098 annually, plus $121 per diem. High-ranking legislators earn an extra $16,964 or more, depending on post.
Senate — Dem., 25; Rep., 15. Total, 40
House — Dem., 48; Rep., 31; 1 vacant. Total, 80
(1) Does not accept salary.

Colorado

Governor — Bill Owens, R, $90,000
Lt. Gov. — Jane Norton, R, $68,500
Sec. of State — Gigi Dennis, R, $68,500
Atty. Gen. — John Suthers, D, $80,000
Treasurer — Mike Coffman, R, $68,500
General Assembly: meets annually in Jan. at Denver. Members receive $30,000 annually plus $99 per diem for attendance at interim committee meetings.
Senate — Dem., 18; Rep., 17. Total, 35
House — Dem., 35; Rep., 30. Total, 65

Connecticut

Governor — M. Jodi Rell, R, $150,000
Lt. Gov. — Kevin B. Sullivan, D, $110,000
Sec. of State — Susan Bysiewicz, D, $110,000
Treasurer — Denise Nappier, D, $110,000
Comptroller — Nancy S. Wyman, D, $110,000
Atty. Gen. — Richard Blumenthal, D, $110,000
General Assembly: meets annually odd years in Jan. and even years in Feb., at Hartford. Members receive $28,000 annually, plus $5,500 (senator), $4,500 (representative) per year for expenses.
Senate — Dem., 24; Rep., 12. Total, 36
House — Dem., 99; Rep., 52. Total, 151

Delaware

Governor — Ruth Ann Minner, D, $132,500
Lt. Gov. — John C. Carney Jr., D, $75,500
Sec. of State — Harriet Smith Windsor, D, $123,100
Atty. Gen. — Carl C. Danberg, D, $140,200
Treasurer — Jack A. Markell, D, $109,300
General Assembly: meets annually the 2nd Tues. in Jan. and continues each Tues., Wed., and Thurs. until June 30, at Dover. Members receive $42,000 annually.
Senate — Dem., 13; Rep., 8. Total, 21
House — Dem., 15; Rep., 25; 1 ind. Total, 41

Florida

Governor — Jeb Bush, R, $129,060
Lt. Gov. — Toni Jennings, R, $123,688
Chief Financial Officer — Tom Gallagher, R, $127,771
Atty. Gen. — Charlie Crist, R, $127,771
Comm. of Agriculture — Charles Bronson, R, $127,771
Legislature: meets annually at Tallahassee. Members receive $29,916 annually, plus expense allowance.
Senate — Dem., 14; Rep., 26. Total, 40
House — Dem., 35; Rep., 85. Total, 120

Georgia

Governor — Sonny Perdue, R, $131,481
Lt. Gov. — Mark Taylor, D, $86,443
Sec. of State — Cathy Cox, D, $116,664
Atty. Gen. — Thurbert Baker, D, $130,020
General Assembly: meets annually at Atlanta on 2nd Mon. in Jan. Members receive $16,524 annually ($128 per diem and $7,000 annual expense reimbursement).
Senate — Dem., 22; Rep., 34. Total, 56
House — Dem., 80; Rep., 99; 1 ind. Total, 180

Hawaii

Governor — Linda Lingle, R, $94,780
Lt. Gov. — James R. Aiona Jr., R, $90,041
Atty. Gen. — Mark J. Bennett, $109,242
Comptroller — Russ K. Saito, $104,040
Dir. of Budget & Finance — Georgina K. Kawamura, $104,040
Legislature: meets annually on 3rd Wed. in Jan. at Honolulu. Members receive $34,200 annually; presiding officers $41,700.
Senate — Dem., 20; Rep., 5. Total, 25
House — Dem., 41; Rep., 10. Total, 51

Idaho

Governor — Jim Risch, R, $101,500
Lt. Gov. — Mark Ricks, R, $26,750
Sec. of State — Ben Ysursa, R, $82,500
Treasurer — Ron Crane, R, $82,500
Atty. Gen. — Lawrence Wasden, R, $91,500
Legislature: meets annually the Mon. on or nearest Jan. 9 at Boise. Members receive $15,646 annually, plus $99 per day during session if required to maintain a 2nd residence; $38 if no 2nd residence; plus $1,700 unvouchered constituent service allowance.
Senate — Dem., 7, Rep., 28. Total, 35
House — Dem., 13; Rep., 57. Total, 70

Illinois

Governor — Rod R. Blagojevich, D, $150,691
Lt. Gov. — Patrick Quinn, D, $115,235
Sec. of State — Jesse White, D, $132,963
Comptroller — Daniel Hynes, D, $115,235
Atty. Gen. — Lisa Madigan, D, $132,963
Treasurer — Judy Baar Topinka, R, $115,235
General Assembly: meets annually in Nov. and Jan. at Springfield. Members receive $57,619 annually.
Senate — Dem., 31; Rep., 27; 1 ind. Total, 59
House — Dem., 65; Rep., 53. Total, 118

Indiana

Governor — Mitch E. Daniels Jr., R, $95,000
Lt. Gov. — Becky Skillman, R, $76,000
Sec. of State — Todd Rokita, R, $66,000
Atty. Gen. — Steve Carter, R, $79,400
Treasurer — Tim Berry, R, $66,000
Auditor — Connie Kay Nass, R, $66,000
Superintendent of Public Instruction — Dr. Suellen Reed, R, $79,400
General Assembly: meets annually on the Tues. after 2nd Mon. in Jan. at Indianapolis. Members receive $11,600 annually, plus $112 per day in session, $25 per day while not in session.
Senate — Dem., 17; Rep., 33. Total, 50
House — Dem., 48; Rep., 52. Total, 100

Iowa

Governor — Tom Vilsack, D, $107,482
Lt. Gov. — Sally Pederson, D, $76,698
Sec. of State — Chester J. Culver, D, $87,506
Atty. Gen. — Tom Miller, D, $123,669
Treasurer — Michael L. Fitzgerald, D, $103,212
Auditor — David A. Vaudt, R, $87,990
Sec. of Agriculture — Patty Judge, D, $87,990
General Assembly: meets annually in Jan. at Des Moines. Members receive $21,381 annually, plus expense allowance.
Senate — Dem., 25; Rep., 25. Total, 50
House — Dem., 49; Rep., 51. Total, 100

Kansas

Governor — Kathleen Sebelius, D, $105,889
Lt. Gov. — John Moore, D, $29,803
Sec. of State — Ron Thornburgh, R, $82,260
Atty. Gen. — Phill Kline, R, $94,597
Treasurer — Lynn Jenkins, R, $82,260
Insurance Commissioner — Sandy Praeger, R, $82,260
Legislature: meets annually on the 2nd Mon. of Jan. at Topeka, for a maximum of 90 days. Members receive $84.80 per day salary, plus $99 per diem in session, plus $6,775 total allowance.
Senate — Dem., 10; Rep., 30. Total, 40
House — Dem., 42; Rep., 83. Total, 125

Kentucky

Governor — Ernie Fletcher, R, $116,520
Lt. Gov. — Stephen Pence, R, $99,059
Sec. of State — Trey Grayson, R, $99,059
Atty. Gen. — Gregory Stumbo, D, $99,059
Treasurer — Jonathan Miller, D, $99,059
Auditor — Crit (Eugenia) Luallen, D, $99,059
Sec. of Economic Dev. — Gene Strong, $225,000
General Assembly: meets annually on the 1st Tues. after the 1st Mon. in Jan. at Frankfort. Members receive $166 per day, plus $100 per day expenses during session and $1,581 per month for expenses for interim.
Senate — Dem., 16; Rep., 21; 1 ind. Total, 38
House — Dem., 56; Rep., 44. Total, 100

Louisiana

Governor — Kathleen Babineaux Blanco, D, $95,000
Lt. Gov. — Mitch Landrieux, D, $85,000
Sec. of State — Al Ater, D, $85,000
Atty. Gen. — Charles C. Foti Jr., D, $85,000
Treasurer — John Kennedy, D, $85,000
Legislature: meets in even-numbered years at Baton Rouge starting last Mon. in Mar., for 60 legislative days of 85 calendar days; meets in odd-numbered years on last Mon. in Apr. for 45 days of 60 calendar days. Members receive $16,800 annually, plus $121 per day expenses while in session and $500 per month as an unvouchered expense allowance.
Senate — Dem., 24; Rep., 15. Total, 39
House — Dem., 65; Rep., 39; 1 ind. Total, 105

Maine

Governor — John E. Baldacci, D, $70,000
Sec. of State — Matthew Dunlap, D, $71,302
Atty. Gen. — G. Steven Rowe, D, $94,952
Treasurer — David G. Lemoine, D, $71,302
State Auditor — Neria R. Douglass, D, $83,949
Legislature: meets in odd-numbered years at Augusta on first Wed. in Dec.; meets in even-numbered years on Wed. after first Tues. in Jan. Members receive $11,384 for first regular session, $8,748 (est.) for 2nd, plus a daily expense allowance.
Senate — Dem., 19; Rep., 16. Total, 35
House — Dem., 74; Rep., 73; unenrolled, 3; Green Independent, 1. Total, 151

Maryland
Governor — Robert L. Ehrlich Jr., R, $150,000
Lt. Gov. — Michael S. Steele, R, $125,000
Comptroller — William Donald Schaefer, D, $125,000
Atty. Gen. — J. Joseph Curran Jr., D, $125,000
Sec. of State — Mary D. Kane, R, $87,500
Treasurer — Nancy Kopp, D, $125,000
General Assembly: meets 90 consecutive days annually beginning on 2nd Wed. in Jan. at Annapolis. Members receive $43,500 annually, plus expenses.
Senate — Dem., 33; Rep., 14. Total, 47
House — Dem., 98; Rep., 43. Total, 141

Massachusetts
Governor — Willard "Mitt" Romney, R, $135,000[1]
Lt. Gov. — Kerry Healey[1], R, $120,000
Sec. of the Commonwealth — William F. Galvin, D, $120,000
Atty. Gen. — Thomas F. Reilly, D, $122,500
Treasurer — Timothy P. Cahill, D, $120,000
State Auditor — A. Joseph DeNucci, D, $120,000
General Court (legislature): meets Jan. annually in Boston. Members receive $53,380 annually.
Senate — Dem., 34; Rep., 6. Total, 40
House — Dem., 137; Rep., 21; 2 vacancies. Total, 160
(1) Does not accept salary.

Michigan
Governor — Jennifer M. Granholm, D, $177,000
Lt. Gov. — John Cherry, D, $123,900
Sec. of State — Terri Lynn Land, R, $124,900
Atty. Gen. — Michael Cox, R, $124,900
Treasurer — Jay B. Rising, $174,204
Legislature: meets annually in Jan. at Lansing. Members receive $79,650 annually.
Senate — Dem., 16; Rep., 22. Total, 38
House — Dem., 49; Rep., 58; 3 vacancies. Total, 110

Minnesota
(DFL=Democratic-Farmer-Labor Party)
Governor — Tim Pawlenty, R, $120,303
Lt. Gov. — Carol Molnau, R, $78,197
Sec. of State — Mary Kiffmeyer, R, $90,227
Atty. Gen. — Michael Hatch, DFL, $114,288
Auditor — Patricia Anderson, R, $102,258
Legislature: meets for a total of 120 days within every 2 years, at St. Paul. Members receive $31,141 annually, plus expense allowance during session.
Senate — DFL, 38; Rep., 29; 1 ind. Total, 67
House — DFL, 66; Rep., 68. Total, 134

Mississippi
Governor — Haley Barbour, R, $122,160
Lt. Gov. — Amy Tuck, R, $60,000
Sec. of State — Eric Clark, D, $90,000
Atty. Gen. — Jim Hood, D, $108,960
Treasurer — Tate Reeves, R, $90,000
Auditor — Phil Bryant, R, $90,000
Legislature: meets annually in Jan. at Jackson. Members receive $10,000 per regular session, plus travel allowance, and $1,500 per month when not in session.
Senate — Dem., 27; Rep., 23; 2 vacancies. Total, 52
House — Dem., 76; Rep., 46; 2 vacancies. Total, 124

Missouri
Governor — Matt Blunt, R, $120,087
Lt. Gov. — Peter Kinder, R, $77,184
Sec. of State — Robin Carnahan, D, $96,455
Atty. Gen. — Jeremiah W. Nixon, D, $104,332
Treasurer — Sarah Steelman, R, $96,455
State Auditor — Claire McCaskill, D, $96,455
General Assembly: meets annually at Jefferson City beginning 1st Wed. after 1st Mon. in Jan. Members receive $31,351 annually.
Senate — Dem., 11; Rep., 23. Total, 34
House — Dem., 66; Rep., 95; 2 vacancies. Total, 163

Montana
Governor — Brian Schweitzer, D, $96,462
Lt. Gov. — John Bohlinger, R, $74,180
Sec. of State — Brad Johnson, R, $76,539
Atty. Gen. — Mike McGrath, D, $85,762
Legislative Assembly: meets odd years in Jan. at Helena. Members receive $76.80 per legislative day, plus $90.31 per diem while in session.
Senate — Dem., 27; Rep., 23. Total, 50
House — Dem., 50; Rep., 50. Total, 100

Nebraska
Governor — David Heineman, R, $85,000
Lt. Gov. — Rick Sheehy, R, $60,000
Sec. of State — John A. Gale, R, $65,000
Atty. Gen. — Jon Bruning, R, $75,000
Treasurer — Ron Ross, R, $60,000
State Auditor — Kate Witek, R, $60,000
Legislature: Unicameral body composed of 49 members who are elected on a nonpartisan ballot and are called senators; meets annually in Jan. at Lincoln. Members receive $12,000 annually, plus expenses.

Nevada
Governor — Kenny C. Guinn, R, $117,000
Lt. Gov. — Lorraine Hunt, R, $50,000
Sec. of State — Dean Heller, R, $80,000
Controller — Steve Martin, R, $80,000
Atty. Gen. — George Chanos, R, $110,000
Treasurer — Brian Krolicki, R, $80,000
Legislature: meets at Carson City odd years starting on 1st Mon. in Feb. for 120 days. Members receive $130 per day salary, plus a total of $10,000 in expenses and $2,860 in communications costs, while in session. Each legislator is allowed $1,200 in expenses during a special session, plus a $130 per diem for the first 20 days.
Senate — Dem., 9; Rep., 12. Total, 21
Assembly — Dem., 26; Rep., 16. Total, 42

New Hampshire
Governor — John H. Lynch, D, $108,990
Sec. of State — William M. Gardner, D, $94,584
Atty. Gen. — Kelly A. Ayotte, R, $105,396
Treasurer — Michael A. Ablowich, R, $94,584
General Court (Legis.): meets every year in Jan. at Concord. Members receive $200, presiding officers $250, biannually.
Senate — Dem., 8; Rep., 16. Total, 24
House —Dem., 150; Rep., 242; 8 vacancies. Total, 400

New Jersey
Governor — Jon Corzine, D, $175,000
Sec. of State — Nina Mitchell Wells, D, $141,000
Acting Atty. Gen. — Anne Milgram, D, $141,000
Acting Treasurer — Bradley Abelow, D, $141,000
Legislature: meets throughout the year at Trenton. Members receive $49,000 annually, except president of Senate and speaker of Assembly, who receive 1/3 more.
Senate — Dem., 22; Rep., 18. Total, 40
Assembly — Dem., 49; Rep., 31. Total, 80

New Mexico
Governor — Bill Richardson, D, $110,000
Lt. Gov. — Diane D. Denish, D, $85,000
Sec. of State — Rebecca Vigil-Giron, D, $85,000
Atty. Gen. — Patricia Madrid, D, $95,000
Treasurer — Douglas M. Brown, D, $85,000
Auditor — Domingo P. Martinez, D, $85,000
Commissioner of Public Lands — Patrick Lyons, R, $90,000
Legislature: meets starting on the 3rd Tues. in Jan. at Santa Fe; odd years for 60 days, even years for 30 days. Members receive $145 per day while in session.
Senate — Dem., 24; Rep., 18. Total, 42
House — Dem., 42; Rep., 28. Total, 70

New York
Governor — George E. Pataki, R, $179,000
Lt. Gov. — Mary O. Donohue, R, $151,500
Sec. of State — Christopher L. Jacobs, $120,800
Comptroller — Alan G. Hevesi, D, $151,500
Atty. Gen. — Eliot Spitzer, D, $151,500
Legislature: meets annually on the 1st Wed. after the 1st Mon. in Jan. at Albany. Members receive $79,500 annually, plus $138 per diem.
Senate — Dem., 27; Rep., 35. Total, 62
Assembly — Dem., 106; Rep., 44. Total, 150

North Carolina
Governor — Mike Easley, D, $130,624
Lt. Gov. — Beverly Perdue, D, $115,289
Sec. of State — Elaine F. Marshall, D, $115,289
Atty. Gen. — Roy Cooper, D, $115,289
Treasurer — Richard H. Moore, D, $115,289
General Assembly: meets odd years starting on the 3rd Wed. following the 2nd Mon. in Jan. at Raleigh. Members receive $13,951 annually and a $559 monthly expense allowance, plus travel and other allowances in session. Also meets in even years for a short session (about 6-8 weeks), usually in May.
Senate — Dem., 29; Rep., 21. Total, 50
House — Dem., 63; Rep., 57. Total, 120

North Dakota
Governor — John Hoeven, R, $92,483
Lt. Gov. — John S. Dalrymple III, R, $71,797
Sec. of State — Alvin A. Jaeger, R, $72,861
Atty. Gen. — Wayne Stenehjem, R, $79,984
Treasurer — Kelly Schmidt, R, $68,806
Legislative Assembly: meets odd years in Jan. at Bismarck. Members receive $350 per month salary, plus $125 per calendar day salary during session and $50 per day expenses, plus any additional state or local taxes on lodging, with a limit of $900 per month.
Senate — Dem., 15; Rep., 32. Total, 47
House — Dem., 27; Rep., 67. Total, 94

Ohio
Governor — Bob Taft, R, $132,292
Lt. Gov. — Bruce Johnson, R, $68,295
Sec. of State — J. Kenneth Blackwell, R, $107,279
Atty. Gen. — Jim Petro, R, $107,279
Treasurer — Jennette B. Bradley, R, $107,279
Auditor — Betty D. Montgomery, R, $107,279
General Assembly: meets odd years at Columbus starting on 1st Mon. in Jan. Members receive $57,595 annually.
Senate — Dem., 11; Rep., 22. Total, 33
House — Dem., 39; Rep., 60. Total, 99

Oklahoma

Governor — Brad Henry, D, $140,000
Lt. Gov. — Mary Fallin, R, $109,250
Sec. of State — M. Susan Savage, D, $90,000
Atty. Gen. — Drew Edmondson, D, $126,500
Treasurer — Scott Meacham, D, $109,250
Auditor — Jeff A. McMahan, D, $109,250
Legislature: meets annually the first Mon. in Feb. at Oklahoma City. In odd-numbered years, the session includes one day (1st Tues. after 1st Mon.) in Jan. Members receive $38,400 annually.
Senate — Dem., 26; Rep., 22. Total, 48
House — Dem., 44; Rep., 57. Total, 101

Oregon

Governor — Ted Kulongoski, D, $93,600
Sec. of State — Bill Bradbury, D, $72,000
Atty. Gen. — Hardy Myers, D, $77,200
Treasurer — Randall Edwards, D, $72,000
Legislative Assembly: meets odd years in Jan. at Salem. Members receive $1,484 monthly, $99 expenses per diem during session and when attending meetings during the interim, plus between $450 and $750 expense account during interim.
Senate — Dem., 17; Rep., 11; Ind., 2. Total, 30
House — Dem., 27; Rep., 33. Total, 60

Pennsylvania

Governor — Edward G. Rendell, D, $144,416
Lt. Gov. — Catherine Baker Knoll, D, $121,309
Sec. of the Commonwealth — Pedro A. Cortés, D, $103,890
Atty. Gen. — Tom Corbett, R, $120,154
Treasurer — Robert P. Casey, D, $120,154
General Assembly: convenes annually on the 1st Tues. in Jan. at Harrisburg. Members receive $72,187 annually, plus expenses.
Senate — Dem., 21; Rep., 29. Total, 50
House — Dem., 94; Rep., 109. Total, 203

Rhode Island

Governor — Donald L. Carcieri, R, $105,194
Lt. Gov. — Charles J. Fogarty, D, $88,584
Sec. of State — Matthew A. Brown, D, $88,584
Atty. Gen. — Patrick C. Lynch, D, $94,121
Treasurer — Paul J. Tavares, D, $88,584
General Assembly: meets annually in Jan. at Providence. Members receive $10,000 annually (plus mileage and cost-of-living increase).
Senate — Dem., 33; Rep., 5. Total, 38
House — Dem., 60; Rep., 15. Total, 75

South Carolina

Governor — Mark Sanford, R, $106,078
Lt. Gov. — R. André Bauer, R, $46,545
Sec. of State — Mark Hammond, R, $92,007
Comptroller — Richard A. Eckstrom, R, $92,007
Atty. Gen. — Henry McMaster, R, $92,007
Treasurer — Grady L. Patterson Jr., D, $92,007
General Assembly: meets annually on the 2nd Tues. in Jan. at Columbia. Members receive $10,400 annually, plus $130 per diem.
Senate — Dem., 20; Rep., 25; 1 vacancy. Total, 46
House — Dem., 50; Rep., 74. Total, 124

South Dakota

Governor — Mike Rounds, R, $103,222
Lt. Gov. — Dennis M. Daugaard, R, $14,083
Sec. of State — Chris Nelson, R, $70,135
Atty. Gen. — Larry Long, R, $87,646
Treasurer — Vernon L. Larson, R, $70,135
Auditor — Rich Sattgast, R, $70,135
Legislature: meets annually beginning the 2nd Tues. in Jan. at Pierre, for 40-day session in odd-numbered years, and 35-day session in even-numbered years. Members receive $12,000 per 2-year term plus $110 per diem for days in session.
Senate — Dem., 10; Rep., 25. Total, 35
House — Dem., 19; Rep., 51. Total, 70

Tennessee

Governor — Phil Bredesen, D, $155,000
Lt. Gov. — John S. Wilder, D, $54,363
Sec. of State — Riley C. Darnell, D, $143,289
Treasurer — Dale Sims, D, $143,289
Comptroller — John Morgan, D, $143,289
Atty. Gen. — Paul Summers, D, $134,364
General Assembly: meets annually on the 2nd Tues. in Jan. at Nashville. Members receive $16,500 annual salary, plus $150 per diem while in session.
Senate — Dem., 15; Rep., 18. Total, 33
House — Dem., 53; Rep., 46. Total, 99

Texas

Governor — Rick Perry, R, $115,345
Lt. Gov. — David Dewhurst, R, $7,200 (plus $128 per day during legislative sessions)
Sec. of State — Roger Williams, R, $117,516
Comptroller — Carole Keeton Strayhorn, R, $92,217
Atty. Gen. — Greg W. Abbott, R, $125,000

Railroad Commissioners — Elizabeth Jones, R, Chair; Michael L. Williams, R; Victor G. Carrillo, R; $125,000
Legislature: meets odd years in Jan. at Austin. Members receive $7,200 annually, plus $125 per diem while in session.
Senate — Dem., 12; Rep., 19. Total, 31
House — Dem., 61; Rep., 88; 1 vacancy. Total, 150

Utah

Governor — Jon M. Huntsman Jr., R, $104,100
Lt. Gov. — Gary R. Herbert, R, $98,900
Atty. Gen. — Mark Shurtleff, R, $98,900
Auditor — Auston G. Johnson, R, $83,500
Treasurer — Edward T. Alter, R, $81,000
Legislature: convenes for 45 days, starting on 3rd Mon. in Jan. each year at Salt Lake City. Members receive $130 per day, plus $39 a day expenses.
Senate — Dem., 8; Rep., 21. Total, 29
House — Dem., 19; Rep., 56. Total, 75

Vermont

Governor — Jim Douglas, R, $143,977
Lt. Gov. — Brian E. Dubie, R, $61,116
Sec. of State — Deborah L. Markowitz, D, $91,294
Atty. Gen. — William H. Sorrell, D, $109,292
Treasurer — Jeb (George B.) Spaulding, D, $91,294
Auditor — Randy Brock, R, $91,294
General Assembly: meets in Jan. at Montpelier (annual and biennial session). Members receive $589 per 4-day week while in session plus $105 per day for special session, plus expenses.
Senate — Dem., 21; Rep., 9. Total, 30
House — Dem., 83; Rep., 60; Progressive, 6; 1 ind. Total, 150

Virginia

Governor — Timothy M. Kaine, D, $175,000
Lt. Gov. — Bill Bolling, R, $36,321
Atty. Gen. — Bob McDonnell, R, $150,000
Sec. of the Commonwealth — Kate Hanley, D, $141,265
Treasurer — J. Braxton Powell, D, $123,864
General Assembly: meets annually in Jan. at Richmond. Members receive $18,000 (senate) or $17,640 (assembly) annually, plus expense and mileage allowances.
Senate — Dem., 17; Rep., 23. Total, 40
House — Dem., 40; Rep., 56; Ind., 3; 1 vacancy. Total, 100

Washington

Governor — Christine Gregoire, D, $148,035
Lt. Gov. — Brad Owen, D, $77,382
Sec. of State — Sam Reed, R, $103,736
Atty. Gen. — Rob McKenna, R, 134,577
Treasurer — Mike Murphy, D, $103,736
Auditor — Brian Sonntag, D, $103,736
Legislature: meets annually in Jan. at Olympia. Members receive $35,254 annually, plus $101 per diem while in session, and $101 per diem for attending meetings during interim.
Senate — Dem., 26; Rep., 23. Total, 49
House — Dem., 55; Rep., 43. Total, 98

West Virginia

Governor — Joe Manchin III, D, $95,000
Sec. of State — Betty Ireland, R, $75,000
Atty. Gen. — Darrell V. McGraw Jr., D, $80,000
Treasurer — John D. Perdue, D, $75,000
Comm. of Agric. — Gus R. Douglass, D, $75,000
Auditor — Glen B. Gainer III, D, $75,000
Legislature: meets annually in Jan. at Charleston, except after gubernatorial elections, when the legislature meets in Feb. Members receive $15,000 annually.
Senate — Dem., 21; Rep., 13. Total, 34
House — Dem., 68; Rep., 32. Total, 100

Wisconsin

Governor — Jim Doyle, D, $131,768
Lt. Gov. — Barbara Lawton, D, $65,579
Sec. of State — Douglas La Follette, D, $62,549
Treasurer — Jack Voight, R, $62,549
Atty. Gen. — Peggy A. Lautenschlager, D, $127,868
Legislature: meets in Jan. at Madison. Members receive $45,569 annually, plus $88 per day expenses.
Senate — Dem., 14; Rep., 19. Total, 33
Assembly — Dem., 39; Rep., 60. Total, 99

Wyoming

Governor — Dave Freudenthal, D, $105,000
Sec. of State — Joseph B. Meyer, R, $92,000
Atty. Gen. — Patrick J. Crank, R, $95,000
Treasurer — Cynthia Lummis, R, $92,000
State Auditor — Max Maxfield, R, $92,000
Legislature: meets odd years in Jan., even years in Feb., at Cheyenne. Members receive $150 per day while in session, plus $85 per diem.
Senate — Dem., 7; Rep., 23. Total, 30
House — Dem., 14; Rep., 46. Total, 60

UNITED STATES FACTS

Superlative U.S. Statistics[1]

Source: U.S. Geological Survey, Dept. of the Interior; U.S. Bureau of the Census, Dept. of Commerce; World Almanac research

Total Area for 50 states and Washington, DC (Land, 3,537,440 sq mi; Water, 256,648 sq mi)		3,794,085 sq mi[2]
Largest state	Alaska	663,267 sq mi
Smallest state	Rhode Island	1,545 sq mi
Largest county (excluding Alaska)	San Bernardino County, CA	20,105 sq mi
Smallest county	Arlington County, VA[3]	26 sq mi
Largest incorporated city	Sitka, AK	4,812 sq mi
Northernmost city	Barrow, AK	71°17′ N
Northernmost point	Point Barrow, AK	71°23′ N
Southernmost city	Hilo, HI	19°44′ N
Southernmost settlement	Naalehu, HI	19°03′ N
Southernmost point	Ka Lae (South Cape), Island of Hawaii	18° 55′ N (155°41′ W)
Easternmost city	Eastport, ME	66° 59′05′′ W
Easternmost settlement[4]	Amchitka Isl., AK	179°15′ E
Easternmost point[4]	Pochnoi Point, on Semisopochnoi Isl., AK	179°46′ E
Westernmost city	Atka, AK	174° 12′ W
Westernmost settlement	Adak Station, AK	176° 39′ W
Westernmost point	Amatignak Isl., AK	179° 06′ W
Lowest settlement	Calipatria, CA	−184 ft
Highest point on Atlantic coast	Cadillac Mountain, Mount Desert Isl., ME	1,530 ft
Oldest national park	Yellowstone National Park (1872), WY, MT, ID	2,219,791 acres
Largest national park	Wrangell-St. Elias, AK	8,323,148 acres
Highest waterfall	Yosemite Falls—Total in 3 sections	2,425 ft
	(Upper Yosemite Fall, 1,430 ft; Cascades, 675 ft; Lower Yosemite Fall, 320 ft)	
Longest river system	Mississippi-Missouri-Red Rock	3,710 mi
Highest mountain	Mount McKinley (Denali), AK	20,320 ft
Lowest point	Death Valley, CA	−282 ft
Deepest lake	Crater Lake, OR	1,932 ft
Rainiest spot	Mount Waialeale, HI	Annual avg rainfall 460 in
Largest gorge	Grand Canyon, Colorado River, AZ	277 mi long, 600 ft to 18 mi wide, 1 mi deep
Deepest gorge	Hells Canyon, Snake River, OR-ID	7,900 ft
Largest dam	New Cornelia Tailings, Ten Mile Wash, AZ[5]	274,026,000 cu yds material used
Tallest building	Sears Tower, Chicago, IL	1,450 ft
Largest building	Boeing Manufacturing Plant, Everett, WA	472,000,000 cu ft; covers 98 acres
Largest office building	Pentagon, Arlington, VA	77,025,000 cu ft; covers 29 acres
Tallest structure	TV tower, Blanchard, ND	2,063 ft
Longest bridge span	Verrazano-Narrows, NY	4,260 ft
Highest bridge	Royal Gorge, CO	1,053 ft above water
Deepest well	Gas well, Washita County, OK	31,441 ft

The 48 Contiguous States

Total Area for 48 states and Washington, DC (Land, 2,959,066 sq mi; Water, 160,824 sq mi)		3,119,887 sq mi[2]
Largest state	Texas	268,581 sq mi
Northernmost city	Bellingham, WA	48°46′ N
Northernmost settlement	Angle Inlet, MN	49°21′ N
Northernmost point	Northwest Angle, MN	49°23′ N
Southernmost city	Key West, FL	24°33′ N
Southernmost mainland city	Florida City, FL	25°27′ N
Southernmost point	Key West, FL	24°33′ N
Easternmost settlement	Lubec, ME	66°58′49″ W
Easternmost point	West Quoddy Head, ME	66°57′W
Westernmost town	La Push, WA	124°38′ W
Westernmost point	Cape Alava, WA	124°44′ W
Highest mountain	Mount Whitney, CA	14,494 ft

(1) All areas are total area, including water, unless otherwise noted. (2) Does not add, because of rounding. (3) Smallest county by land area is New York County (Manhattan) at 23 sq mi; its total area including water is 34 square miles. Superlative shown is for smallest total area. (4) Alaska's Aleutian Islands extend into the eastern hemisphere and thus technically contain the easternmost point and settlement in the U.S. (5) The New Cornelia Tailings Dam is a privately owned industrial dam composed of tailings, remnants of a mining process.

Geodetic Datum of North America

In July 1986, the National Oceanic and Atmospheric Administration's National Geodetic Survey (NGS), in cooperation with Canada and Mexico, completed readjustment and redefinition of the system of latitudes and longitudes. The resulting North American Datum of 1983 (NAD 83) replaces the North American Datum of 1927, as well as local reference systems for Hawaii and for Puerto Rico and the Virgin Islands. The change was prompted by Hawaii's increased need for accurate coordinate information. To facilitate use of satellite surveying and navigation systems, such as the Global Positioning System (GPS), the new datum was redefined using the Geodetic Reference System 1980 as the reference ellipsoid because this model more closely approximates the true size and shape of the earth. In addition, the origin of the coordinate system is referenced to the mass center of the earth to coincide with the orbital orientation of the GPS satellites. Positional changes resulting from the datum redefinition can reach 330 ft in the continental U.S., Canada, and Mexico. Changes that exceed 660 ft can be expected in Alaska, Puerto Rico, and the Virgin Islands. Hawaii's coordinates changed about 1,300 ft.

Additional Statistical Information About the U.S.

The annual *Statistical Abstract of the United States*, published by U.S. Dept. of Commerce, contains additional data. For information, write Supt. of Documents, Government Printing Office, P.O. Box 371954, Pittsburgh, PA 15250-7954, or call 1-866-512-1800. For electronic products, write Supt. of Documents, Government Printing Office, Attn: Electronic Products, P.O. Box 37082, Washington, DC 20013-7082. The *Statistical Abstract* can be viewed on the Internet at www.census.gov/compendia/statab

Highest and Lowest Altitudes in U.S. States and Territories

Source: U.S. Geological Survey, Dept. of the Interior

(Minus sign means below sea level)

State	HIGHEST POINT Name	County	Elev. (ft)	LOWEST POINT Name	County	Elev. (ft)
Alabama	Cheaha Mountain	Cleburne	2,407	Gulf of Mexico		Sea level
Alaska	Mount McKinley	Denali	20,320	Pacific Ocean		Sea level
Arizona	Humphreys Peak	Coconino	12,633	Colorado R.	Yuma	70
Arkansas	Magazine Mountain	Logan	2,753	Ouachita R.	Ashley-Union	55
California	Mount Whitney	Inyo-Tulare	14,494	Death Valley	Inyo	−282
Colorado	Mount Elbert	Lake	14,433	Arikaree R.	Yuma	3,315
Connecticut	S. slope of Mt. Frissell	Litchfield	2,380	Long Island Sound		Sea level
Delaware	Ebright Road	New Castle	448	Atlantic Ocean		Sea level
Dist. of Columbia	Tenleytown	NW part	410	Potomac R.		1
Florida	Britton Hill	Walton	345	Atlantic Ocean		Sea level
Georgia	Brasstown Bald	Towns-Union	4,784	Atlantic Ocean		Sea level
Guam	Mount Lamlam	Agat District	1,332	Pacific Ocean		Sea level
Hawaii	Mauna Kea	Hawaii	13,796	Pacific Ocean		Sea level
Idaho	Borah Peak	Custer	12,662	Snake R.	Nez Perce	710
Illinois	Charles Mound	Jo Daviess	1,235	Mississippi R.	Alexander	279
Indiana	Hoosier Hill	Wayne	1,257	Ohio R.	Posey	320
Iowa	Hawkeye Point	Osceola	1,670	Mississippi R.	Lee	480
Kansas	Mount Sunflower	Wallace	4,039	Verdigris R.	Montgomery	679
Kentucky	Black Mountain	Harlan	4,145	Mississippi R.	Fulton	257
Louisiana	Driskill Mountain	Bienville	535	New Orleans	Orleans	−8
Maine	Mount Katahdin	Piscataquis	5,268	Atlantic Ocean		Sea level
Maryland	Hoye Crest	Garrett	3,360	Atlantic Ocean		Sea level
Massachusetts	Mount Greylock	Berkshire	3,491	Atlantic Ocean		Sea level
Michigan	Mount Arvon	Baraga	1,979	Lake Erie		571
Minnesota	Eagle Mountain	Cook	2,301	Lake Superior		601
Mississippi	Woodall Mountain	Tishomingo	806	Gulf of Mexico		Sea level
Missouri	Taum Sauk Mt.	Iron	1,772	St. Francis R.	Dunklin	230
Montana	Granite Peak	Park	12,799	Kootenai R.	Lincoln	1,800
Nebraska	Panorama Point	Kimball	5,424	Missouri R.	Richardson	840
Nevada	Boundary Peak	Esmeralda	13,140	Colorado R.	Clark	479
New Hampshire	Mt. Washington	Coos	6,288	Atlantic Ocean		Sea level
New Jersey	High Point	Sussex	1,803	Atlantic Ocean		Sea level
New Mexico	Wheeler Peak	Taos	13,161	Red Bluff Res.	Eddy	2,842
New York	Mount Marcy	Essex	5,344	Atlantic Ocean		Sea level
North Carolina	Mount Mitchell	Yancey	6,684	Atlantic Ocean		Sea level
North Dakota	White Butte	Slope	3,506	Red R. of the North	Pembina	750
Ohio	Campbell Hill	Logan	1,550	Ohio R.	Hamilton	455
Oklahoma	Black Mesa	Cimarron	4,973	Little R.	McCurtain	289
Oregon	Mount Hood	Clackamas-Hood R.	11,239	Pacific Ocean		Sea level
Pennsylvania	Mt. Davis	Somerset	3,213	Delaware R.	Delaware	Sea level
Puerto Rico	Cerro de Punta	Ponce District	4,390	Atlantic Ocean		Sea level
Rhode Island	Jerimoth Hill	Providence	812	Atlantic Ocean		Sea level
Samoa	Lata Mountain	Tau Island	3,160	Pacific Ocean		Sea level
South Carolina	Sassafras Mountain	Pickens	3,560	Atlantic Ocean		Sea level
South Dakota	Harney Peak	Pennington	7,242	Big Stone Lake	Roberts	966
Tennessee	Clingmans Dome	Sevier	6,643	Mississippi R.	Shelby	178
Texas	Guadalupe Peak	Culberson	8,749	Gulf of Mexico		Sea level
Utah	Kings Peak	Duchesne	13,528	Beaver Dam Wash	Washington	2,000
Vermont	Mount Mansfield	Chittenden	4,393	Lake Champlain		95
Virginia	Mount Rogers	Grayson-Smyth	5,729	Atlantic Ocean		Sea level
Virgin Islands	Crown Mountain	St. Thomas Island	1,556	Atlantic Ocean		Sea level
Washington	Mount Rainier	Pierce	14,411	Pacific Ocean		Sea level
West Virginia	Spruce Knob	Pendleton	4,863	Potomac R.	Jefferson	240
Wisconsin	Timms Hill	Price	1,951	Lake Michigan		579
Wyoming	Gannett Peak	Fremont	13,804	Belle Fourche R.	Crook	3,099

U.S. Coastline by States

Source: National Oceanic and Atmospheric Administration, U.S. Dept. of Commerce

(in statute miles)

	Coastline[1]	Shoreline[2]
ATLANTIC COAST	2,069	28,673
Connecticut	0	618
Delaware	28	381
Florida	580	3,331
Georgia	100	2,344
Maine	228	3,478
Maryland	31	3,190
Massachusetts	192	1,519
New Hampshire	13	131
New Jersey	130	1,792
New York	127	1,850
North Carolina	301	3,375
Pennsylvania	0	89
Rhode Island	40	384
South Carolina	187	2,876
Virginia	112	3,315

	Coastline[1]	Shoreline[2]
GULF COAST	1,631	17,141
Alabama	53	607
Florida	770	5,095
Louisiana	397	7,721
Mississippi	44	359
Texas	367	3,359
PACIFIC COAST	7,623	40,298
Alaska	5,580	31,383
California	840	3,427
Hawaii	750	1,052
Oregon	296	1,410
Washington	157	3,026
ARCTIC COAST	1,060	2,521
UNITED STATES	12,383	88,633

(1) Figures are lengths of general outline of seacoast. Measurements were made with a unit measure of 30 minutes of latitude on charts as near the scale of 1:1,200,000 as possible. Coastline of sounds and bays is included to a point where they narrow to width of unit measure, and includes the distance across at such point. (2) Figures obtained in 1939-40 with a recording instrument on the largest-scale charts and maps then available. Shoreline of outer coast, offshore islands, sounds, bays, rivers, and creeks is included to the head of tidewater or to a point where tidal waters narrow to a width of 100 ft.

States: Capitals, Key Dates, Geographic Data

The 13 colonies that declared independence from Great Britain and fought the War of Independence (American Revolution) became the 13 original states. They were (in the order in which they ratified the Constitution): Delaware, Pennsylvania, New Jersey, Georgia, Connecticut, Massachusetts, Maryland, South Carolina, New Hampshire, Virginia, New York, North Carolina, and Rhode Island.

State	Settled[1]	Capital	Entered Union Date	Entered Union Order	Extent in miles Long (approx. mean)	Extent in miles Wide (approx. mean)	Area in sq mi Land	Area in sq mi Water	Area in sq mi Total	Rank in area[2]
AL	1702	Montgomery	Dec. 14, 1819	22	330	190	50,744	1,675	52,419	30
AK	1784	Juneau	Jan. 3, 1959	49	1,480[3]	810	571,951	91,316	663,267	1
AZ	1776	Phoenix	Feb. 14, 1912	48	400	310	113,635	364	113,998	6
AR	1686	Little Rock	June 15, 1836	25	260	240	52,068	1,110	53,179	29
CA	1769	Sacramento	Sept. 9, 1850	31	770	250	155,959	7,736	163,696	3
CO	1858	Denver	Aug. 1, 1876	38	380	280	103,718	376	104,094	8
CT	1634	Hartford	Jan. 9, 1788	5	110	70	4,845	699	5,543	48
DE	1638	Dover	Dec. 7, 1787	1	100	30	1,954	536	2,489	49
DC	NA	NA	NA	NA	...	...	61	7	68	51
FL	1565	Tallahassee	Mar. 3, 1845	27	500	160	53,927	11,828	65,755	22
GA	1733	Atlanta	Jan. 2, 1788	4	300	230	57,906	1,519	59,425	24
HI	1820	Honolulu	Aug. 21, 1959	50	...	...	6,423	4,508	10,931	43
ID	1842	Boise	July 3, 1890	43	570	300	82,747	823	83,570	14
IL	1720	Springfield	Dec. 3, 1818	21	390	210	55,584	2,331	57,914	25
IN	1733	Indianapolis	Dec. 11, 1816	19	270	140	35,867	551	36,418	38
IA	1788	Des Moines	Dec. 28, 1846	29	310	200	55,869	402	56,272	26
KS	1727	Topeka	Jan. 29, 1861	34	400	210	81,815	462	82,277	15
KY	1774	Frankfort	June 1, 1792	15	380	140	39,728	681	40,409	37
LA	1699	Baton Rouge	Apr. 30, 1812	18	380	130	43,562	8,278	51,840	31
ME	1624	Augusta	Mar. 15, 1820	23	320	190	30,862	4,523	35,385	39
MD	1634	Annapolis	Apr. 28, 1788	7	250	90	9,774	2,633	12,407	42
MA	1620	Boston	Feb. 6, 1788	6	190	50	7,840	2,715	10,555	44
MI	1668	Lansing	Jan. 26, 1837	26	490	240	56,804	39,912	96,716	11
MN	1805	St. Paul	May 11, 1858	32	400	250	79,610	7,329	86,939	12
MS	1699	Jackson	Dec. 10, 1817	20	340	170	46,907	1,523	48,430	32
MO	1735	Jefferson City	Aug. 10, 1821	24	300	240	68,886	818	69,704	21
MT	1809	Helena	Nov. 8, 1889	41	630	280	145,552	1,490	147,042	4
NE	1823	Lincoln	Mar. 1, 1867	37	430	210	76,872	481	77,354	16
NV	1849	Carson City	Oct. 31, 1864	36	490	320	109,826	735	110,561	7
NH	1623	Concord	June 21, 1788	9	190	70	8,968	382	9,350	46
NJ	1660	Trenton	Dec. 18, 1787	3	150	70	7,417	1,304	8,721	47
NM	1610	Santa Fe	Jan. 6, 1912	47	370	343	121,356	234	121,589	5
NY	1614	Albany	July 26, 1788	11	330	283	47,214	7,342	54,556	27
NC	1660	Raleigh	Nov. 21, 1789	12	500	150	48,711	5,108	53,819	28
ND	1812	Bismarck	Nov. 2, 1889	39	340	211	68,976	1,724	70,700	19
OH	1788	Columbus	Mar. 1, 1803	17	220	220	40,948	3,877	44,825	34
OK	1889	Oklahoma City	Nov. 16, 1907	46	400	220	68,667	1,231	69,898	20
OR	1811	Salem	Feb. 14, 1859	33	360	261	95,997	2,384	98,381	9
PA	1682	Harrisburg	Dec. 12, 1787	2	283	160	44,817	1,239	46,055	33
RI	1636	Providence	May 29, 1790	13	40	30	1,045	500	1,545	50
SC	1670	Columbia	May 23, 1788	8	260	200	30,109	911	32,020	40
SD	1859	Pierre	Nov. 2, 1889	40	380	210	75,885	1,232	77,116	17
TN	1769	Nashville	June 1, 1796	16	440	120	41,217	926	42,143	36
TX	1682	Austin	Dec. 29, 1845	28	790	660	261,797	6,784	268,581	2
UT	1847	Salt Lake City	Jan. 4, 1896	45	350	270	82,144	2,755	84,899	13
VT	1724	Montpelier	Mar. 4, 1791	14	160	80	9,250	365	9,614	45
VA	1607	Richmond	June 25, 1788	10	430	200	39,594	3,180	42,774	35
WA	1811	Olympia	Nov. 11, 1889	42	360	240	66,544	4,756	71,300	18
WV	1727	Charleston	June 20, 1863	35	240	130	24,078	152	24,230	41
WI	1766	Madison	May 29, 1848	30	310	260	54,310	11,188	65,498	23
WY	1834	Cheyenne	July 10, 1890	44	360	280	97,100	713	97,814	10

Note: Land and water areas may not add to totals because of rounding. NA = Not applicable.   (1) First permanent settlement by Europeans. (2) Rank is based on total area as shown. (3) Aleutian Islands and Alexander Archipelago not included.

The Continental Divide of the U.S.

The Continental Divide of the U.S., also known as the Great Divide, is located at the watershed created by the mountain ranges, or tablelands, of the Rocky Mountains. This watershed separates the waters that drain easterly into the Atlantic Ocean and its marginal seas, such as the Gulf of Mexico, from those waters that drain westerly into the Pacific Ocean. The majority of easterly flowing water in the U.S. drains into the Gulf of Mexico before reaching the Atlantic Ocean. The majority of westerly flowing water, before reaching the Pacific Ocean, drains either through the Columbia River or through the Colorado River, which flows into the Gulf of California before reaching the Pacific Ocean.

The location and route of the Continental Divide across the U.S. can briefly be described as follows:

Beginning at the U.S.-Mexican boundary, near long. 108° 45´ W, the Divide, in a northerly direction, crosses New Mexico along the W edge of the Rio Grande drainage basin, entering Colorado near long. 106° 41´ W.

From there by a very irregular route north across Colorado along the W summits of the Rio Grande and of the Ar-

kansas, the South Platte, and the North Platte river basins, and across Rocky Mountain National Park, entering Wyoming near long. 106° 52´ W.

From there in a northwesterly direction, forming the W rims of the North Platte, the Big Horn, and the Yellowstone river basins, crossing the SW portion of Yellowstone National Park.

From there in a westerly and then a northerly direction forming the common boundary of Idaho and Montana, to a point on said boundary near long. 114° 00´ W.

From there northeasterly and northwesterly through Montana and the Glacier National Park, entering Canada near long. 114° 04´ W.

World Almanac Quick Quiz

Which state originally requested admittance into the Union with the name, "Deseret," meaning "Land of Honeybees?"

(a) Nevada   (b) Oregon   (c) Colorado   (d) Utah

For the answer look in this chapter, or see page 1008

Chronological List of Territories, With State Admissions to Union

Source: National Archives and Records Service

Name of territory	Date of act creating territory	When act took effect	Admission as state	Yrs. terr.
Northwest Territory[1]	July 13, 1787	No fixed date	Mar. 1, 1803[2]	16
Territory southwest of River Ohio	May 26, 1790	No fixed date	June 1, 1796[3]	6
Mississippi	Apr. 7, 1798	When president acted	Dec. 10, 1817	19
Indiana	May 7, 1800	July 4, 1800	Dec. 11, 1816	16
Orleans	Mar. 26, 1804	Oct. 1, 1804	Apr. 30, 1812[4]	7
Michigan	Jan. 11, 1805	June 30, 1805	Jan. 26, 1837	31
Louisiana-Missouri[5]	Mar. 3, 1805	July 4, 1805	Aug. 10, 1821	16
Illinois	Feb. 3, 1809	Mar. 1, 1809	Dec. 3, 1818	9
Alabama	Mar. 3, 1817	When MS became a state	Dec. 14, 1819	2
Arkansas	Mar. 2, 1819	July 4, 1819	June 15, 1836	17
Florida	Mar. 30, 1822	No fixed date	Mar. 3, 1845	23
Wisconsin	Apr. 20, 1836	July 3, 1836	May 29, 1848	12
Iowa	June 12, 1838	July 3, 1838	Dec. 28, 1846	8
Oregon	Aug. 14, 1848	Date of act	Feb. 14, 1859	10
Minnesota	Mar. 3, 1849	Date of act	May 11, 1858	9
New Mexico	Sept. 9, 1850	On president's proclamation	Jan. 6, 1912	61
Utah	Sept. 9, 1850	Date of act	Jan. 4, 1896	46
Washington	Mar. 2, 1853	Date of act	Nov. 11, 1889	36
Nebraska	May 30, 1854	Date of act	Mar. 1, 1867	12
Kansas	May 30, 1854	Date of act	Jan. 29, 1861	6
Colorado	Feb. 28, 1861	Date of act	Aug. 1, 1876	15
Nevada	Mar. 2, 1861	Date of act	Oct. 31, 1864	3
Dakota	Mar. 2, 1861	Date of act	Nov. 2, 1889	28
Arizona	Feb. 24, 1863	Date of act	Feb. 14, 1912	49
Idaho	Mar. 3, 1863	Date of act	July 3, 1890	27
Montana	May 26, 1864	Date of act	Nov. 8, 1889	25
Wyoming	July 25, 1868	When officers were qualified	July 10, 1890	22
Alaska[6]	May 17, 1884	No fixed date	Jan. 3, 1959	75
Oklahoma	May 2, 1890	Date of act	Nov. 16, 1907	17
Hawaii	Apr. 30, 1900	June 14, 1900	Aug. 21, 1959	59

(1) Included what is now Ohio, Indiana, Illinois, Michigan, Wisconsin, E Minnesota. (2) Ohio was the first state of NW territory admitted. (3) Admitted as the state of Tennessee. (4) Admitted as the state of Louisiana. (5) The act creating Missouri Territory (June 4, 1812) became effective Dec. 7, 1812. (6) Although the May 17, 1884, act actually constituted Alaska as a district, it was often referred to as a territory, and administered as such. The Territory of Alaska was formally organized by an act of Aug. 24, 1912.

Geographic Centers, U.S. and Each State

Source: U.S. Geological Survey, Dept. of the Interior

There is no generally accepted definition of geographic center and no uniform method for determining it. Following the U.S. Geological Survey, the geographic center of an area is defined here as the center of gravity of the surface, or that point on which the surface would balance if it were a plane of uniform thickness. All locations in the following list are approximate.

No marked or monumented point has been officially established by any government agency as the geographic center of the 50 states, the conterminous U.S. (48 states), or the North American continent. A group of private citizens erected a monument in Lebanon, KS, marking it as geographic center of the conterminous U.S., and a cairn erected in Rugby, ND, asserts that location as the center of the North American continent.

Geographic centers as reported by the U.S. Geological Survey are indicated below:

United States, including Alaska and Hawaii—W of Castle Rock, Butte County, SD; lat. 44° 58′ N, long. 103° 46′ W
Conterminous U.S. (48 states)—Near Lebanon, Smith Co., Kansas, lat. 39° 50′ N, long. 98° 35′ W
North American continent—6 mi W of Balta, Pierce County, North Dakota; lat. 48° 10′ N, long. 100° 10′ W
Alabama—Chilton, 12 mi SW of Clanton
Alaska—lat. 63° 50′ N, long. 152° W; approx. 60 mi NW of Mt. McKinley
Arizona—Yavapai, 55 mi E-SE of Prescott
Arkansas—Pulaski, 12 mi NW of Little Rock
California—Madera, 38 mi E of Madera
Colorado—Park, 30 mi NW of Pikes Peak
Connecticut—Hartford, at East Berlin
Delaware—Kent, 11 mi S of Dover
District of Columbia—Near 4th and L Sts. NW
Florida—Hernando, 12 mi N-NW of Brooksville
Georgia—Twiggs, 18 mi SE of Macon
Hawaii—lat. 20° 15′ N, long. 156° 20′ W, off Maui
Idaho—Custer, SW of Challis
Illinois—Logan, 28 mi NE of Springfield
Indiana—Boone, 14 mi N-NW of Indianapolis
Iowa—Story, 5 mi NE of Ames
Kansas—Barton, 15 mi NE of Great Bend
Kentucky—Marion, 3 mi N-NW of Lebanon
Louisiana—Avoyelles, 3 mi SE of Marksville
Maine—Piscataquis, 18 mi N of Dover
Maryland—Prince George's, 4.5 mi NW of Davidsonville
Massachusetts—Worcester, N part of city

Michigan—Wexford, 5 mi N-NW of Cadillac
Minnesota—Crow Wing, 10 mi SW of Brainerd
Mississippi—Leake, 9 mi W-NW of Carthage
Missouri—Miller, 20 mi SW of Jefferson City
Montana—Fergus, 11 mi W of Lewistown
Nebraska—Custer, 10 mi NW of Broken Bow
Nevada—Lander, 26 mi SE of Austin
New Hampshire—Belknap, 3 mi E of Ashland
New Jersey—Mercer, 5 mi SE of Trenton
New Mexico—Torrance, 12 mi S-SW of Willard
New York—Madison, 12 mi S of Oneida and 26 mi SW of Utica
North Carolina—Chatham, 10 mi NW of Sanford
North Dakota—Sheridan, 5 mi SW of McClusky
Ohio—Delaware, 25 mi N-NE of Columbus
Oklahoma—Oklahoma, 8 mi N of Oklahoma City
Oregon—Crook, 25 mi S-SE of Prineville
Pennsylvania—Centre, 2.5 mi SW of Bellefonte
Rhode Island—Kent, 1 mi S-SW of Crompton
South Carolina—Richland, 13 mi SE of Columbia
South Dakota—Hughes, 8 mi NE of Pierre
Tennessee—Rutherford, 5 mi NE of Murfreesboro
Texas—McCulloch, 15 mi NE of Brady
Utah—Sanpete, 3 mi N of Manti
Vermont—Washington, 3 mi E of Roxbury
Virginia—Buckingham, 5 mi SW of Buckingham
Washington—Chelan, 10 mi W-SW of Wenatchee
West Virginia—Braxton, 4 mi E of Sutton
Wisconsin—Wood, 9 mi SW of Marshfield
Wyoming—Fremont, 58 mi E-NE of Lander

International Boundary Lines of the U.S.

The length of the N boundary of the conterminous U.S.—the U.S.-Canadian border, excluding Alaska—is 3,987 mi according to the U.S. Geological Survey, Dept. of the Interior. The length of the Alaskan-Canadian border is 1,538 mi. The U.S.-Mexican border, from the Gulf of Mexico to the Pacific Ocean, is about 1,933 mi (1963 boundary agreement).

Origins of the Names of U.S. States

Source: State officials, Smithsonian Institution, and Topographic Division, U.S. Geological Survey, Dept. of the Interior

Alabama—Indian for tribal town, later a tribe (Alabamas or Alibamons) of the Creek confederacy.

Alaska—Russian version of Aleutian (Eskimo) word, *alakshak,* for "peninsula," "great lands," or "land that is not an island."

Arizona—Spanish version of Pima Indian word for "little spring place," or Aztec *arizuma,* meaning "silver-bearing."

Arkansas—Algonquin name for the Quapaw Indians, meaning "south wind."

California—Bestowed by the Spanish conquistadors (possibly by Cortez). It was the name of an imaginary island, an earthly paradise, in *Las Serges de Esplandian,* a Spanish romance written by Montalvo in 1510. *Baja California* (Lower California, in Mexico) was first visited by Spanish in 1533. The present U.S. state was called *Alta* (Upper) *California.*

Colorado—From Spanish for "red," first applied to Colorado River.

Connecticut—From Mohican and other Algonquin words meaning "long river place."

Delaware—Named for Lord De La Warr, early governor of Virginia; first applied to river, then to Indian tribe (Lenni-Lenape), and the state.

District of Columbia—For Christopher Columbus, 1791.

Florida—Named by Ponce de Leon *Pascua Florida,* "Flowery Easter," on Easter Sunday, 1513.

Georgia—For King George II of England, by James Oglethorpe, colonial administrator, 1732.

Hawaii—Possibly derived from native word for homeland, *Hawaiki* or *Owhyhee.*

Idaho—Said to be a coined name with an invented meaning: "gem of the mountains"; originally suggested for the Pikes Peak mining territory (Colorado), then applied to the new mining territory of the Pacific Northwest. Another theory suggests *Idaho* may be a Kiowa Apache term for the Comanche.

Illinois—French for *Illini* or "land of *Illini,*" Algonquin word meaning "men" or "warriors."

Indiana—Means "land of the Indians."

Iowa—Indian word variously translated as "here I rest" or "beautiful land." Named for the Iowa R., which was named for the Iowa Indians.

Kansas—Sioux word for "south wind people."

Kentucky—Indian word that is variously translated as "dark and bloody ground," "meadowland," and "land of tomorrow."

Louisiana—Part of territory called Louisiana by Sieur de La Salle for French King Louis XIV.

Maine—From Maine, ancient French province. Also: descriptive, referring to the mainland as distinct from the many coastal islands.

Maryland—For Queen Henrietta Maria, wife of Charles I of England.

Massachusetts—From Indian tribe named after "large hill place" identified by Capt. John Smith as being near Milton, MA.

Michigan—From Chippewa words, *mici gama,* meaning "great water," after the lake of the same name.

Minnesota—From Dakota Sioux word meaning "cloudy water" or "sky-tinted water" of the Minnesota River.

Mississippi—Probably Chippewa; *mici zibi,* "great river" or "gathering-in of all the waters." Also: Algonquin word, *messipi.*

Missouri—An Algonquin Indian term meaning "river of the big canoes."

Montana—Latin or Spanish for "mountainous."

Nebraska—From Omaha or Otos Indian word meaning "broad water" or "flat river," describing the Platte River.

Nevada—Spanish, meaning "snow-clad."

New Hampshire—Named, 1629, by Capt. John Mason of Plymouth Council for his home county in England.

New Jersey—The Duke of York, 1664, gave a patent to John Berkeley and Sir George Carteret to be called Nova Caesaria, or New Jersey, after England's Isle of Jersey.

New Mexico—Spaniards in Mexico applied term to land north and west of Rio Grande in the 16th century.

New York—For Duke of York and Albany, who received patent to New Netherland from his brother Charles II and sent an expedition to capture it, 1664.

North Carolina—In 1619 Charles I gave a large patent to Sir Robert Heath to be called Province of Carolana, from *Carolus,* Latin name for Charles. A new patent was granted by Charles II to Earl of Clarendon and others. Divided into North and South Carolina, 1710.

North Dakota—*Dakota* is Sioux for "friend" or "ally."

Ohio—Iroquois word for "fine or good river."

Oklahoma—Choctaw word meaning "red man," proposed by Rev. Allen Wright, Choctaw-speaking Indian.

Oregon—Origin unknown. One theory holds that the name may have been derived from that of the Wisconsin River, shown on a 1715 French map as "Ouaricon-sint."

Pennsylvania—William Penn, the Quaker who was made full proprietor of this area by King Charles II in 1681, suggested "Sylvania," or "woodland," for his tract. The king's government owed Penn's father, Admiral William Penn, 16,000 pounds, and the land was granted as partial settlement. Charles II added the "Penn" to Sylvania, against the desires of the modest proprietor, in honor of the admiral.

Puerto Rico—Spanish for "rich port."

Rhode Island—Exact origin is unknown. One theory notes that Giovanni de Verrazano recorded an island about the size of Rhodes in the Mediterranean in 1524, but others believe the state was named *Roode Eylandt* by Adriaen Block, Dutch explorer, because of its red clay.

South Carolina—See North Carolina.

South Dakota—See North Dakota.

Tennessee—*Tanasi* was the name of Cherokee villages on the Little Tennessee River. From 1784 to 1788 this was the State of Franklin, or Frankland.

Texas—Variant of word used by Caddo and other Indians meaning "friends" or "allies," and applied to them by the Spanish in eastern Texas. Also written *Texias, Tejas, Teysas.*

Utah—From a Navajo word meaning "upper," or "higher up," as applied to a Shoshone tribe called Ute. Spanish form is *Yutta.* The English is *Uta* or *Utah.* Proposed name *Deseret,* "land of honeybees," from Book of Mormon, was rejected by Congress.

Vermont—From French words *vert* (green) and *mont* (mountain). The Green Mountains were said to have been named by Samuel de Champlain. When the state was formed, 1777, Dr. Thomas Young suggested combining *vert* and *mont* into Vermont.

Virginia—Named by Sir Walter Raleigh, who fitted out the expedition of 1584, in honor of Queen Elizabeth, the Virgin Queen of England.

Washington—Named after George Washington. When the bill creating the Territory of Columbia was introduced in the 32nd Congress, the name was changed to Washington because of the existence of the District of Columbia.

West Virginia—So named when western counties of Virginia refused to secede from the U.S. in 1863.

Wisconsin—An Indian name, spelled *Ouisconsin* and *Mesconsing* by early chroniclers. Believed to mean "grassy place" in Chippewa. Congress made it *Wisconsin.*

Wyoming—From the Algonquin words for "large prairie place," "at the big plains," or "on the great plain."

Territorial Sea of the U.S.

According to a Dec. 27, 1988, proclamation by Pres. Ronald Reagan: "The territorial sea of the United States henceforth extends to 12 nautical miles from the baselines of the United States determined in accordance with international law. In accordance with international law, as reflected in the applicable provisions of the 1982 United Nations Convention on the Law of the Sea, within the territorial sea of the United States, the ships of all countries enjoy the right of innocent passage and the ships and aircraft of all countries enjoy the right of transit passage through international straits."

Major Accessions of Territory by the U.S.

Source: U.S. Dept. of the Interior; Bureau of the Census, U.S. Dept. of Commerce

Not including territories such as Panama Canal Zone and the Philippines which are no longer under U.S. jurisdiction; area figures are for total area and may differ from figures for current areas given elsewhere.

	Acquisition date	Area (sq mi)		Acquisition date	Area (sq mi)		Acquisition date	Area (sq mi)
Territory in 1790[1]	NA	888,685	Oregon Territory	1846	285,580	Puerto Rico[2]	1899	3,435
Louisiana Purchase	1803	827,192	Mexican Cession	1848	529,017	Guam[3]	1899	212
Purchase of Florida	1819	58,560	Gadsden Purchase	1853	29,640	American Samoa[4]	1900	76
Other areas from Spain	1819	13,443	Alaska	1867	586,412	U.S. Virgin Islands	1917	133
Texas	1845	390,143	Hawaii	1898	6,450	Northern Marianas[5]	1986	179

NA = Not applicable. (1) Includes that part of a drainage basin of Red River of the North, S of 49th parallel, sometimes considered part of Louisiana Purchase. (2) Ceded by Spain in 1898, ratified in 1899, and became the Commonwealth of Puerto Rico by Act of Congress on July 25, 1952. (3) Acquired in 1898; ratified 1899. (4) Acquired in 1899; ratified 1900. (5) Formerly a part of the U.S. administered Trust Territory of the Pacific Islands; became a U.S. commonwealth, Nov. 3, 1986.

Federally Owned Land, by State

Source: Office of Governmentwide Policy, General Services Administration; as of Sept. 30, 2004

State	Total acreage[1]	Federal acreage[2]	% Federal acreage[2]	State	Total acreage[1]	Federal acreage[2]	% Federal acreage[2]
Alabama	32,678,400	513,913.0	1.57	Montana	93,271,040	27,910,151.8	29.92
Alaska	365,481,600	252,495,811.3	69.09	Nebraska	49,031,680	665,481.4	1.36
Arizona	72,688,000	34,933,236.1	48.06	Nevada	70,264,320	59,362,642.5	84.48
Arkansas	33,599,360	2,407,948.0	7.17	New Hampshire	5,768,960	775,665.1	13.45
California	100,206,720	45,393,237.5	45.30	New Jersey	4,813,440	148,440.8	3.08
Colorado	66,485,760	24,354,712.8	36.63	New Mexico	77,766,400	32,483,876.5	41.77
Connecticut	3,135,360	13,937.7	0.44	New York	30,680,960	233,533.4	0.76
Delaware	1,265,920	25,874.4	2.04	North Carolina	31,402,880	3,710,338.3	11.82
District of Columbia	39,040	9,630.6	24.67	North Dakota	44,452,480	1,185,776.9	2.67
Florida	34,721,280	2,858,781.8	8.23	Ohio	26,222,080	448,381.4	1.71
Georgia	37,295,360	1,409,406.3	3.78	Oklahoma	44,087,680	1,586,148.3	3.60
Hawaii	4,105,600	796,725.5	19.41	Oregon	61,598,720	32,715,514.1	53.11
Idaho	52,933,120	26,565,411.8	50.19	Pennsylvania	28,804,480	719,863.6	2.50
Illinois	35,795,200	641,959.0	1.79	Rhode Island	677,120	2,923.0	0.43
Indiana	23,158,400	463,244.6	2.00	South Carolina	19,374,080	560,955.9	2.90
Iowa	35,860,480	273,954.3	0.76	South Dakota	48,881,920	3,028,002.7	6.19
Kansas	52,510,720	631,351.2	1.20	Tennessee	26,727,680	865,836.9	3.24
Kentucky	25,512,320	1,378,677.1	5.40	Texas	168,217,600	3,130,345.0	1.8
Louisiana	28,867,840	1,474,788.4	5.11	Utah	52,696,960	30,271,905.2	57.45
Maine	19,847,680	208,421.8	1.05	Vermont	5,936,640	443,249.2	7.4
Maryland	6,319,360	178,526.9	2.83	Virginia	25,496,320	2,534,177.6	9.94
Massachusetts	5,034,880	93,950.1	1.87	Washington	42,693,760	12,949,661.7	30.33
Michigan	36,492,160	3,637,873.4	9.97	West Virginia	15,410,560	1,146,210.8	7.44
Minnesota	51,205,760	2,873,517.4	5.61	Wisconsin	35,011,200	1,971,901.8	5.63
Mississippi	30,222,720	2,196,940.3	7.27	Wyoming	62,343,040	26,391,487.2	42.33
Missouri	44,248,320	2,224,787.8	5.03	**Total**	**2,271,343,360**	**653,299,090.2**	**28.76**

Note: Totals do not include inland water. (1) Bureau of the Census, U.S. Dept. of Commerce figures. (2) Excludes trust properties.

Special Recreation Areas Administered by the U.S. Forest Service, 2006

Source: U.S. Forest Service, Dept. of Agriculture

NHL=National Historic Landmark; NS(A)=Nat. Scenic (Area); NM=National Monument; NP=National Preserve; NRA=National Recreation Area; NVM=Nat. Volcanic Monument; SRA=Scenic Recreation Area

Area name	Location	Estab.	Acres	Area name	Location	Estab.	Acres
Admiralty Island NM	AK	1980	978,881	Mount Pleasant NSA	VA	1994	7,580
Allegheny NRA	PA	1984	23,063	Mount Rogers NRA	VA	1966	114,520
Arapaho NRA	CO	1978	30,690	Mount St. Helens NVM	WA	1989	112,593
Beech Creek NS & Botanic Area	OK	1988	7,500	Newberry NVM	OR	1990	54,822
Cascade Head NS Research Area	OR	1974	6,630	North Cascades NSA	WA	1984	87,600
Columbia River Gorge NSA	OR-WA	1986	63,150	Opal Creek SRA	OR	1996	13,000
Coosa Bald NSA	GA	1991	7,100	Oregon Dunes NRA	OR	1972	27,212
Ed Jenkins NRA	GA	1991	23,166	Pine Ridge NRA	NE	1986	6,600
Flaming Gorge NRA	UT-WY	1968	189,825	Rattlesnake NRA	MT	1980	59,119
Giant Sequoia NM	CA	2000	327,769	Santa Rosa and			
Grand Island NRA	MI	1990	12,961	San Jacinto Mts. NM	CA	2000	272,000
Grey Towers NHL	PA	1963	102	Sawtooth NRA	ID	1972	729,322
Hells Canyon NRA	OR-ID	1975	536,648	Smith River NRA	CA	1990	305,169
Indian Nations NS & Wildlife Area	OK	1988	40,051	Spring Mt. NRA	NV	1993	316,000
Jemez NRA	NM	1993	57,000	Spruce Knob-Seneca Rocks NRA	WV	1965	57,237
Land Between the Lakes NRA	KY-TN	1998	170,000	Valles Caldera NP	NM	2000	88,900
Misty Fiords NM	AK	1980	2,293,428	Whiskeytown-Shasta-Trinity NRA	CA	1965	176,367
Mono Basin NSA	CA	1984	115,600	White Rocks NRA	VT	1984	36,400
Mount Baker NRA	WA	1984	8,473	Winding Stair Mt. NRA	OK	1988	25,890

20 Most-Visited Sites in the National Park System, 2005

Source: National Park Service, Dept. of the Interior

Attendance at all areas administered by the National Park Service in 2005 totaled 273,488,751 recreation visits.

Site (location)	Recreation visits	Site (location)	Recreation visits
Blue Ridge Parkway (NC-VA)	17,882,567	Statue of Liberty National Monument (NJ-NY)	4,235,595
Golden Gate National Recreation Area (CA)	13,602,629	San Francisco Maritime Natl. Historical Park (CA)	3,976,056
Great Smoky Mountains National Park (NC-TN)	9,192,477	Independence National Historical Park (PA)	3,951,073
Gateway National Recreation Area (NJ-NY)	8,294,353	Vietnam Veterans Memorial (DC)	3,799,968
Lake Mead National Recreation Area (AZ-NV)	7,692,438	Cape Cod National Seashore (MA)	3,712,812
George Washington Memorial Pkwy (VA-MD-DC)	7,284,165	Lincoln Memorial (DC)	3,638,806
Natchez Trace Parkway (MS-AL-TN)	5,482,282	Castle Clinton National Monument (NY)	3,487,301
Delaware Water Gap Natl. Recreation Area (NJ-PA)	5,052,264	Colonial National Historical Park (VA)	3,338,695
National World War II Memorial (DC)	4,410,379	Yosemite National Park (CA)	3,304,144
Grand Canyon National Park (AZ)	4,401,522	Korean War Veterans Memorial (DC)	3,214,467

National Parks, Other Areas Administered by National Park Service

Dates when sites were authorized for initial protection by Congress or by presidential proclamation are given in parentheses. If different, the date the area got its current designation, or was transferred to the National Park Service, follows. Gross area in acres, as of Sept. 30, 2005, follows date(s). Over 84 mil acres of federal land are now administered by the National Park Service.

NATIONAL PARKS

Acadia, ME (1916/1929): 47,390. Includes Mount Desert Isl., half of Isle au Haut, Schoodic Peninsula on mainland. Highest elevation on Eastern seaboard.

American Samoa, AS (1988): 9,000. Features a paleotropical rain forest and a coral reef.

Arches, UT (1929/1971): 76,519. Contains giant red sandstone arches and other products of erosion.

Badlands, SD (1929/1978): 242,756. Reformations and native prairie. Animal fossils 23-37 mil years old.

Big Bend, TX (1935): 801,163. Rio Grande, Chisos Mts.

Biscayne, FL (1968/1980): 172,971. Aquatic park encompassing chain of islands south of Miami.

Black Canyon of the Gunnison, CO (1933/1999): 30,750. Has a canyon 2,900 ft deep and 40 ft wide at its narrowest part.

Bryce Canyon, UT (1923/1928): 35,835. Spectacularly colorful and unusual display of erosion effects.

Canyonlands, UT (1964): 337,598. At junction of Colorado and Green rivers; extensive evidence of prehistoric Indians.

Capitol Reef, UT (1937/1971): 241,904. A 70-mi uplift of sandstone cliffs dissected by high-walled gorges.

Carlsbad Caverns, NM (1923/1930): 46,766. Largest known caverns; not yet fully explored.

Channel Islands, CA (1938/1980): 249,561. Sea lion breeding place, nesting sea birds, unique plants.

Crater Lake, OR (1902): 183,224. Extraordinary blue lake in the crater of Mt. Mazama, a volcano that erupted about 7,700 years ago; deepest U.S. lake.

Cuyahoga Valley, OH (1974/2000): 32,861. Rural landscape along Ohio and Erie Canal system between Akron and Cleveland.

Death Valley, CA-NV (1933/1994): 3,372,402. Large desert area. Includes the lowest point in the Western Hemisphere; also includes Scotty's Castle.

Denali, AK (1917/1980): 4,740,912. Name changed from Mt. McKinley National Park. Contains highest mountain in U.S.; wildlife.

Dry Tortugas, FL (1935/1992): 64,701. Formerly Ft. Jefferson National Monument.

Everglades, FL (1934): 1,508,539. Largest remaining subtropical wilderness in continental U.S.

Gates of the Arctic, AK (1978/1984): 7,523,898. Vast wilderness in north central region. Limited federal facilities.

Glacier, MT (1910): 1,013,572. Superb Rocky Mt. scenery, numerous glaciers and glacial lakes. Part of Waterton-Glacier Intl. Peace Park established by U.S. and Canada in 1932.

Glacier Bay, AK (1925/1986): 3,224,840. Great tidewater glaciers that move down mountainsides and break up into the sea; much wildlife.

Grand Canyon, AZ (1893/1919): 1,217,403. Most spectacular part of Colorado River's greatest canyon.

Grand Teton, WY (1929): 309,995. Most impressive part of the Teton Mts., winter feeding ground of largest American elk herd.

Great Basin, NV (1922/1986): 77,180. Includes Wheeler Pk., Lexington Arch, and Lehman Caves.

Great Smoky Mountains, NC-TN (1926/1934): 522,199. Largest Eastern mountain range, magnificent forests.

Guadalupe Mountains, TX (1966): 86,416. Extensive Permian limestone reef; tremendous earth fault.

Haleakala, HI (1916/1960): 29,111. Dormant volcano on Maui with large colorful craters.

Hawaii Volcanoes, HI (1916/1961): 323,431. Contains Kilauea and Mauna Loa, active volcanoes.

Hot Springs, AR (1832/1921): 5,550. Bathhouses are furnished with thermal waters from the park's 47 hot springs; these waters are used for bathing and drinking.

Isle Royale, MI (1931): 571,790. Largest island in Lake Superior, noted for its wilderness area and wildlife.

Joshua Tree, CA (1936/1994): 789,866. Desert region includes Joshua trees, other plant and animal life.

Katmai, AK (1918/1980): 3,674,530. "Valley of Ten Thousand Smokes," scene of 1912 volcanic eruption.

Kenai Fjords, AK (1978/1980): 669,983. Abundant marine mammals, birdlife; the Harding Icefield, one of the 4 major icecaps in U.S.

Kings Canyon, CA (1890/1940): 461,901. Mountain wilderness, dominated by Kings River Canyons and High Sierra; contains giant sequoias.

Kobuk Valley, AK (1978/1980): 1,750,717. Contains geological and recreational sites. Limited federal facilities.

Lake Clark, AK (1978/1980): 2,619,733. Across Cook Inlet from Anchorage. A scenic wilderness rich in fish and wildlife. Limited federal facilities.

Lassen Volcanic, CA (1907/1916): 106,372. Contains Lassen Peak, recently active volcano, and other volcanic phenomena.

Mammoth Cave, KY (1926/1941): 52,830. 144 mi of surveyed underground passages, beautiful natural formations, river 300 ft below surface.

Mesa Verde, CO (1906): 52,122. Most notable and best preserved prehistoric cliff dwellings in the U.S.

Mount Rainier, WA (1899): 235,625. Greatest single-peak glacial system in the U.S.

North Cascades, WA (1968): 504,781. Spectacular mountainous region with many glaciers, lakes.

Olympic, WA (1909/1938): 922,651. Mountain wilderness containing finest remnant of Pacific Northwest rain forest, active glaciers, Pacific shoreline, rare elk.

Petrified Forest, AZ (1906/1962): 221,540. Extensive petrified wood and Indian artifacts. Contains part of Painted Desert.

Redwood, CA (1968): 112,512. 40 mi of Pacific coastline, groves of ancient redwoods and world's tallest trees.

Rocky Mountain, CO (1915): 265,828. On the Continental Divide; includes peaks over 14,000 ft.

Saguaro, AZ (1933/1994): 91,440. Part of the Sonoran Desert; includes the giant saguaro cacti, unique to the region.

Sequoia, CA (1890): 404,051. Groves of giant sequoias, highest mountain in conterminous U.S.: Mt. Whitney (14,494 ft). World's largest tree.

Shenandoah, VA (1926): 199,074. Portion of the Blue Ridge Mts.; overlooks Shenandoah Valley; Skyline Drive.

Theodore Roosevelt, ND (1947/1978): 70,447. Contains part of T.R.'s ranch and scenic badlands.

Virgin Islands, VI (1956): 14,686. Authorized to cover 75% of St. John Isl. and Hassel Isl.; lush growth, lovely beaches, Carib Indian petroglyphs, evidence of colonial Danes.

Voyageurs, MN (1971): 218,200. Abundant lakes, forests, wildlife, canoeing, boating.

Wind Cave, SD (1903): 28,295. Limestone caverns in Black Hills. Extensive wildlife includes a herd of bison.

Wrangell-St. Elias, AK (1978/1980): 8,323,148. Largest area in park system, most peaks over 16,000 ft, abundant wildlife; day's drive east of Anchorage. Limited federal facilities.

Yellowstone, ID-MT-WY (1872): 2,219,791. World's first national park. World's greatest geyser area has about 10,000 geysers and hot springs; spectacular falls and impressive canyons of the Yellowstone River; grizzly bear, moose, and bison.

Yosemite, CA (1890): 761,266. Yosemite Valley, the nation's highest waterfall, grove of sequoias, and mountains.

Zion, UT (1909/1919): 146,598. Unusual shapes and landscapes resulting from erosion and faulting; evidence of past volcanic activity; Zion Canyon has sheer walls ranging up to 2,640 ft.

NATIONAL HISTORICAL PARKS

Adams, MA (1946/1998): 24. Home of Pres. John Adams, John Quincy Adams, and celebrated descendants.

Appomattox Court House, VA (1930/1954): 1,774. Where Lee surrendered to Grant.

Boston, MA (1974): 43. Includes Faneuil Hall, Old North Church, Bunker Hill, Paul Revere House.

Cane River Creole (and heritage area), LA (1994): 207. Preserves the Creole culture as it developed along the Cane R.

Cedar Creek and Belle Grove, VA (2002): 3,593. Civil War battle site and an antebellum plantation in the Shenandoah Valley.

Chaco Culture, NM (1907/1980): 33,960. Ruins of pueblos built by prehistoric Indians.

Chesapeake and Ohio Canal, MD-DC-WV (1938/1971): 19,586. 184-mi historic canal; DC to Cumberland, MD.

Colonial, VA (1930/1936): 8,677. Includes most of Jamestown Isl., site of first successful English colony; Yorktown, site of Cornwallis's surrender to George Washington; and the Colonial Parkway.

Cumberland Gap, KY-TN-VA (1940): 20,512. Mountain pass of the Wilderness Road, which carried the first great migration of pioneers into America's interior.

Dayton Aviation Heritage, OH (1992): 86. Commemorates the area's aviation heritage.

George Rogers Clark, Vincennes, IN (1966): 26. Commemorates American defeat of British in West during Revolution.

Harpers Ferry, MD-VA-WV (1944/1963): 3,646. At the confluence of the Shenandoah and Potomac rivers, the site of John Brown's 1859 raid on the Army arsenal.

Hopewell Culture, OH (1923/1992): 1,170. Formerly Mound City Group National Monument.

Independence, PA (1948): 44. Contains several properties associated with the American Revolution and the founding of the U.S. Includes Independence Hall.

Jean Laffite (and preserve), LA (1907/1978): 20,005. Includes Chalmette, site of 1815 Battle of New Orleans; French Quarter.

Kalaupapa, HI (1980): 10,779. Molokai's former leper colony site and other historic areas.

Kaloko-Honokohau, HI (1978): 1,161. Preserves the native culture of Hawaii.

> **IT'S A FACT:** The Antiquities Act, passed in 1906, allows presidents to bypass congressional hearings and designate sites for preservation. About one-quarter of the areas in the National Park System were first authorized under the Antiquities Act. In 2006, President George W. Bush used the century-old law to designate two new national monuments: the African Burial Ground National Monument in New York, NY (Feb. 2006), and Northwestern Hawaiian Islands Marine National Monument in the Pacific Ocean (June 2006). The Hawaiian monument has an area of about 140,000 sq mi, including 10 islands and atolls stretching about 1,400 mi, making it the largest protected marine area in the world. More than 4,500 sq mi of remote coral reef habitats and 7,000 marine species, many of which are threatened or endangered, are protected within its boundaries. The area is bigger than all other National Park Service sites combined, and bigger than all but 4 states.

Keweenaw, MI (1992): 1,869. Site of first significant copper mine in U.S.

Klondike Gold Rush, AK-WA (1976): 13,192. Alaskan Trails in 1898 Gold Rush. Museum in Seattle.

Lewis and Clark, OR-WA (1958/2004): 1,415. Lewis and Clark encampment, 1805-06. Incorporates former Fort Clatsop Natl. Mem. Park and OR-WA state parks.

Lowell, MA (1978): 141. Textile mills, canal, 19th-cent. structures; park shows planned city of Industrial Revolution.

Lyndon B. Johnson, TX (1969/1980): 1,570. President's birthplace, boyhood home, ranch.

Marsh-Billings-Rockefeller, VT (1992): 643. Boyhood home of conservationist George Perkins Marsh.

Minute Man, MA (1959): 961. Where the Minute Men battled the British, Apr. 19, 1775. Also contains Hawthorne's home.

Morristown, NJ (1933): 1,711. Sites of important military encampments during the American Revolution; Washington's headquarters, 1777, 1779-80.

Natchez, MS (1988): 105. Mansions, townhouses, and villas related to history of Natchez.

New Bedford Whaling, MA (1996): 34. Preserves structures and relics associated with the city's 19th-cent. whaling industry.

New Orleans Jazz, LA (1994): 5. Preserves, educates, and interprets jazz as it has evolved in New Orleans.

Nez Perce, ID (1965): 2,494. Illustrates the history and culture of the Nez Perce Indian country (38 separate sites).

Pecos, NM (1965/1990): 6,670. Ruins of ancient Pueblo of Pecos, archaeological sites, and 2 associated Spanish colonial missions from the 17th and 18th centuries.

Pu'uhonua o Honaunau, HI (1955/1978): 420. Until 1819, a sanctuary for Hawaiians vanquished in battle and for those guilty of crimes or breaking taboos.

Rosie the Riveter WWII Home Front, CA (2000): 145. Site of a shipyard that employed thousands of women in WWII; commemorates women who worked in war-time industries.

Salt River Bay (and ecological preserve), St. Croix, VI (1992): 978. The only known site where, in 1493, members of a Columbus party landed on what is now territory of the U.S.

San Antonio Missions, TX (1978): 826. Four of finest Spanish missions in U.S., 18th-cent. irrigation system.

San Francisco Maritime, CA (1988): 50. Artifacts, photographs, and historic vessels related to the development of the Pacific Coast.

San Juan Island, WA (1966): 1,752. Commemorates peaceful relations between the U.S., Canada, and Great Britain since the 1872 boundary disputes.

Saratoga, NY (1938): 3,394. Scene of a major 1777 battle that became a turning point in the American Revolution.

Sitka, AK (1910/1972): 112. Scene of last major resistance of the Tlingit Indians to the Russians, 1804.

Tumacacori, AZ (1908/1990): 360. Historic Spanish mission building stands near site first visited by Father Kino in 1691.

Valley Forge, PA (1976): 3,466. Continental Army campsite in 1777-78 winter.

War in the Pacific, GU (1978): 2,037. Seven distinct units illustrating the Pacific theater of WWII. Limited federal facilities.

Women's Rights, NY (1980): 7. Seneca Falls site where Lucretia Mott, Elizabeth Cady Stanton organized movement in 1848.

NATIONAL BATTLEFIELDS

Antietam, MD (1890/1978): 3,255. Battle here ended first Confederate invasion of North, Sept. 17, 1862.

Big Hole, MT (1910/1963): 1,011. Site of major battle with Nez Perce Indians, Aug. 9-10, 1877.

Cowpens, SC (1929/1972): 842. American Revolution battlefield, Jan. 17, 1781.

Fort Donelson, TN-KY (1928/1985): 552. Site of first major Union victory, Feb. 14-16, 1862.

Fort Necessity, PA (1931/1961): 903. Site of first battle of French and Indian War, July 3, 1754.

Monocacy, MD (1934/1976): 1,647. Civil War battle in defense of Washington, DC, fought here, July 9, 1864.

Moores Creek, NC (1926/1980): 88. 1776 battle between Patriots and Loyalists commemorated here.

Petersburg, VA (1926/1962): 2,739. Scene of 10-month Union campaigns, 1864-65.

Stones River, TN (1927/1960): 709. Scene of battle that began federal offensive to trisect the Confederacy, Dec. 31, 1862-Jan. 2, 1863.

Tupelo, MS (1929/1961): 1. Site of crucial battle over Sher-

man's supply line, July 15-15, 1865.

Wilson's Creek, MO (1960/1970): 2,365. Scene of Civil War battle for control of Missouri, Aug. 10, 1861.

NATIONAL BATTLEFIELD PARKS

Kennesaw Mountain, GA (1917/1935): 2,888. Site of two major battles of Atlanta campaign in Civil War.

Manassas, VA (1940): 5,073. Scene of two battles in Civil War, 1861 and 1862.

Richmond, VA (1936): 7,127. Site of battles defending Confederate capital.

NATIONAL BATTLEFIELD SITE

Brices Cross Roads, MS (1929): 1. Civil War battlefield.

NATIONAL MILITARY PARKS

Chickamauga and Chattanooga, GA-TN (1890): 9,036. Site of major Confederate victory, 1863.

Fredericksburg and Spotsylvania County, VA (1927/1933): 8,374. Sites of several major Civil War battles and campaigns.

Gettysburg, PA (1895/1933): 5,990. Site of decisive Confederate defeat in North, July 1863, and of Gettysburg Address.

Guilford Courthouse, NC (1917/1933): 230. American Revolution battle site.

Horseshoe Bend, AL (1956): 2,040. On Tallapoosa River, where Gen. Andrew Jackson's forces broke the power of the Upper Creek Indian Confederacy on March 27, 1814.

Kings Mountain, SC (1931/1933): 3,945. Site of American Revolution battle, fought on Oct. 7, 1780.

Pea Ridge, AR (1956): 4,300. Scene of Civil War battle.

Shiloh, TN (1894/1933): 5,065. Major Civil War battlesite; includes some well-preserved Indian burial mounds.

Vicksburg, MS (1899/1933): 1,795. Union victory gave North control of the Mississippi and split the Confederate forces.

NATIONAL MEMORIALS

Arkansas Post, AR (1960): 758. First permanent French settlement in the lower Mississippi River valley.

Arlington House, the Robert E. Lee Memorial, VA (1925/1972): 28. Lee's home overlooking the Potomac.

Chamizal, El Paso, TX (1966/1974): 55. Commemorates 1963 settlement of 99-year border dispute with Mexico.

Coronado, AZ (1941/1952): 4,750. Commemorates first European exploration of the Southwest.

DeSoto, FL (1948): 27. Commemorates 16th-cent. Spanish explorations.

Federal Hall, NY (1939/1955): 0.45. First seat of U.S. government under the Constitution.

Flight 93, Shanksville, PA (2002): 2,262. Commemorates the passengers and crew of Flight 93, who died thwarting an attack on Sept. 11, 2001. In planning stages; no federal facilities.

Fort Caroline, FL (1950): 138. On St. Johns River, overlooks site of a French Huguenot colony.

Franklin Delano Roosevelt, DC (1982): 8. Statues of Pres. Roosevelt and Eleanor Roosevelt; waterfalls and gardens.

General Grant, NY (1958): 0.76. Tomb of Grant and wife.

Hamilton Grange, NY (1962): 1. Home of Alexander Hamilton.

Jefferson National Expansion Memorial, St. Louis, MO (1935): 91. Commemorates westward expansion.

Johnstown Flood, PA (1964): 178. Commemorates tragic flood of 1889.

Korean War Veterans, DC (1986): 2. Dedicated in 1995; honors those who served in the Korean War.

Lincoln Boyhood, IN (1962): 200. Lincoln grew up here.

Lincoln Memorial, DC (1911/1933): 107. Marble statue of the 16th U.S. president.

Lyndon B. Johnson Memorial Grove on the Potomac, DC (1973): 17. Overlooks the Potomac R.; vista of the Capitol.

Mount Rushmore, SD (1925): 1,278. World-famous sculpture of 4 presidents.

Oklahoma City, OK (1997): 3.3. Commemorates site of April 19, 1995, bombing which killed 168.

Perry's Victory and International Peace Memorial, Put-in-Bay, OH (1936/1972): 25. The world's most massive Doric column, constructed 1912-15, promotes pursuit of peace through arbitration and disarmament.

Roger Williams, Providence, RI (1965): 5. Memorial to founder of Rhode Island.

Thaddeus Kosciuszko, PA (1972): 0.02. Memorial to Polish hero of American Revolution.

Theodore Roosevelt Island, DC (1932/1933): 89. Statue of Roosevelt in wooded island sanctuary.

Thomas Jefferson Memorial, DC (1934): 18. Statue of Jefferson in an inscribed circular, colonnaded structure.

USS *Arizona*, HI (1980): 11. Memorializes American losses at Pearl Harbor.

Vietnam Veterans, DC (1980): 2. Black granite wall inscribed with names of those missing or killed in action in Vietnam War.

Washington Monument, DC (1848/1933): 106. Obelisk honoring the first U.S. president.

Wright Brothers, NC (1927/1953): 428. Site of first powered flight.

NATIONAL HISTORIC SITES

Abraham Lincoln Birthplace, Hodgenville, KY (1916/1959): 345. Memorial building, sinking spring.

Allegheny Portage Railroad, PA (1964): 1,284. Linked the Pennsylvania Canal system and the West.

Andersonville, Andersonville, GA (1970): 515. Noted Civil War prisoner-of-war camp.

Andrew Johnson, Greeneville, TN (1935/1963): 17. Two homes and the tailor shop of the 17th U.S. president.

Bent's Old Fort, CO (1960): 799. Reconstruction of S Plains outpost.

Boston African-American, MA (1980): 0.59. Pre-Civil War black history structures.

Brown v. Board of Education, KS (1992): 2. Commemorates the landmark 1954 U.S. Supreme Court decision.

Carl Sandburg Home, Flat Rock, NC (1968): 264. Poet's home.

Carter G. Woodson Home, DC (2006): 0.05. Home of noted African American historian and educator

Charles Pinckney, SC (1988): 28. Statesman's farm.

Christiansted, St. Croix, VI (1952/1961): 27. Commemorates Danish colony.

Clara Barton, MD (1974): 9. Home of founder of American Red Cross.

Edgar Allan Poe, PA (1978/1980): 0.52. Writer's home.

Edison, West Orange, NJ (1955/1962): 21. Inventor's home and laboratory.

Eisenhower, Gettysburg, PA (1967): 690. Home of 34th president.

Eleanor Roosevelt, Hyde Park, NY (1977): 181. The former first lady's personal retreat.

Eugene O'Neill, Danville, CA (1976): 13. Playwright's home.

First Ladies, Canton, OH (2000): 0.33. Library devoted to America's first ladies.

Ford's Theatre, DC (1866/1970): 0.29. Includes theater, now restored, where Lincoln was assassinated, house where he died, and Lincoln Museum.

Fort Bowie, AZ (1964): 999. Focal point of operations against Geronimo and the Apaches.

Fort Davis, TX (1961): 474. Frontier outpost in West Texas.

Fort Laramie, WY (1938/1960): 833. Military post on Oregon Trail.

Fort Larned, KS (1964/1966): 718. Military post on Santa Fe Trail.

Fort Point, San Francisco, CA (1970): 29. West Coast fortification.

Fort Raleigh, NC (1941): 513. First attempted English settlement in North America.

Fort Scott, KS (1965/1978): 17. Commemorates U.S. frontier of 1840s and '50s.

Fort Smith, AR-OK (1961): 75. Active post during 1817-90.

Fort Union Trading Post, MT-ND (1966): 444. Principal fur-trading post on upper Missouri, 1829-67.

Fort Vancouver, WA (1948/1961): 210. Headquarters for Hudson's Bay Company in 1825. Early political seat.

Frederick Douglass, DC (1962/1988): 9. Home of famous black abolitionist, writer, and orator.

Frederick Law Olmsted, MA (1979): 7. Home of famous city planner.

Friendship Hill, PA (1978): 675. Home of Albert Gallatin, Jefferson's and Madison's secretary of treasury.

Golden Spike, UT (1957): 2,735. Commemorates completion of first transcontinental railroad in 1869.

Grant-Kohrs Ranch, MT (1972): 1,618. Ranch house and part of 19th-cent. ranch.

Hampton, MD (1948): 62. 18th-cent. Georgian mansion.

Harry S. Truman, MO (1983): 7. Home of Pres. Truman after 1919.

Herbert Hoover, West Branch, IA (1965): 187. Birthplace and boyhood home of 31st president.

Home of Franklin D. Roosevelt, Hyde Park, NY (1944): 800. FDR's birthplace, home, and "summer White House."

Hopewell Furnace, PA (1938/1985): 848. 19th-cent. ironmaking village.

Hubbell Trading Post, AZ (1965): 160. Still active today.

James A. Garfield, Mentor, OH (1980): 8. Home of 20th president.

Jimmy Carter, GA (1987): 72. Birthplace and home of 39th president.

John Fitzgerald Kennedy, Brookline, MA (1967): 0.09. Birthplace and childhood home of 35th president.

John Muir, Martinez, CA (1964): 345. Home of early conservationist and writer.

Knife River Indian Villages, ND (1974): 1,758. Remnants of villages last occupied by Hidatsa and Mandan Indians.

Lincoln Home, Springfield, IL (1971): 12. Lincoln's residence at the time he was elected 16th president, 1860.

Little Rock Central High School, AR (1998): 27. Commemorates 1957 desegregation during which federal troops had to be called in to protect 9 black students.

Longfellow, Cambridge, MA (1972): 2. Poet's home, 1837-82; Washington's headquarters during Boston siege, 1775-76.

Maggie L. Walker, VA (1978): 1. Richmond home of black leader and bank president, daughter of an ex-slave.

Manzanar, Lone Pine, CA (1992): 814. Commemorates Manzanar War Relocation Ctr., a Japanese-American internment camp during WWII.

Martin Luther King Jr., Atlanta, GA (1980): 39. Birthplace, grave, church of the civil rights leader.

Martin Van Buren, NY (1974): 40. Lindenwald, home of 8th president, near Kinderhook.

Mary McLeod Bethune Council House, DC (1982/1991): 0.07. Commemorates Bethune's leadership in the black women's movement.

Minuteman Missile, SD (1999): 15. Missile launch facilities dating back to the Cold War era.

Nicodemus, KS (1996): 161. Only remaining western town established by African Americans during Reconstruction.

Ninety Six, SC (1976): 1,022. Colonial trading village.

Palo Alto Battlefield, TX (1978): 3,407. Scene of first battle of the Mexican War.

Pennsylvania Avenue, DC (1965): Includes area next to the road between Capitol and White House, encompassing Ford's Theatre and other structures.

Puukohola Heiau, HI (1972): 86. Ruins of temple built by King Kamehameha.

Ronald Reagan Boyhood Home, Dixon, IL (2002): 1. Childhood home of 40th president.

Sagamore Hill, Oyster Bay, NY (1962): 83. Home of Pres. Theodore Roosevelt from 1885 until his death in 1919.

Saint-Gaudens, Cornish, NH (1964): 148. Home, studio, and gardens of American sculptor Augustus Saint-Gaudens.

Saint Paul's Church, NY, NY (1943): 6. Site associated with John Peter Zenger's "freedom of press" trial.

Salem Maritime, MA (1938): 9. Only port never seized from the patriots by the British. Major fishing and whaling port.

Sand Creek Massacre, Sand Creek, CO (2000): 12,583. Site where over 100 Cheyenne and Arapaho Indians were killed by U.S. soldiers in 1864.

San Juan, PR (1949): 75. 16th-cent. Span. fortifications.

Saugus Iron Works, MA (1974): 9. Reconstructed 17th-cent. colonial ironworks.

Springfield Armory, MA (1974): 55. Small-arms manufacturing center for nearly 200 years.

Steamtown, PA (1986): 62. Railyard, roadhouse, repair shops of former Delaware, Lackawanna & Western Railroad.

Theodore Roosevelt Birthplace, New York, NY (1962): 0.11. Reconstructed brownstone.

Theodore Roosevelt Inaugural, Buffalo, NY (1966): 1. Wilcox House where he took oath of office, 1901.

Thomas Stone, MD (1978): 328. Home of signer of Declaration of Independence, built in 1771.

Tuskegee Airmen, AL (1998): 90. Airfield where pilots of all-black air corps unit of WWII received flight training.

Tuskegee Institute, AL (1974): 58. College founded by Booker T. Washington in 1881 for blacks.

Ulysses S. Grant, St. Louis Co., MO (1989): 10. Home of Grant during pre-Civil War years.

Vanderbilt Mansion, Hyde Park, NY (1940): 212. Mansion of 19th-cent. financier.

Washita Battlefield, OK (1996): 315. Scene of Nov. 27, 1868, battle between Plains tribes and the U.S. army.

Weir Farm, Wilton, CT (1990): 74. Home and studio of American impressionist painter J. Alden Weir.

Whitman Mission, WA (1936/1963): 139. Mission site of Marcus and Narcissa Whitman.

William Howard Taft, Cincinnati, OH (1969): 3. Birthplace and early home of the 27th president.

NATIONAL MONUMENTS

Name	State	Year[1]	Acreage
African Burial Ground[4]	NY	2006	0.345
Agate Fossil Beds	NE	1965	3,055
Alibates Flint Quarries	TX	1965	1,371
Aniakchak[2]	AK	1978	137,176
Aztec Ruins	NM	1923	318
Bandelier	NM	1916	33,677
Booker T. Washington	VA	1956	239
Buck Island Reef	VI	1961	19,015
Cabrillo	CA	1913	160

Name	State	Year[1]	Acreage
Canyon de Chelly	AZ	1931	83,840
Cape Krusenstern[3]	AK	1978	649,085
Capulin Volcano	NM	1916	793
Casa Grande Ruins	AZ	1889	473
Castillo de San Marcos	FL	1924	18
Castle Clinton	NY	1946	1
Cedar Breaks	UT	1933	6,155
Chiricahua	AZ	1924	11,985
Colorado	CO	1911	20,534
Craters of the Moon National Monument and Preserve	ID	1924	714,727
Devils Postpile	CA	1911	798
Devils Tower	WY	1906	1,347
Dinosaur	CO-UT	1915	210,278
Effigy Mounds	IA	1949	2,526
El Malpais	NM	1987	114,277
El Morro	NM	1906	1,279
Florissant Fossil Beds	CO	1969	5,998
Fort Frederica	GA	1936	241
Fort Matanzas	FL	1924	300
Fort McHenry National Monument and Historic Shrine	MD	1925	43
Fort Pulaski	GA	1924	5,623
Fort Stanwix	NY	1935	16
Fort Sumter	SC	1948	200
Fort Union	NM	1954	721
Fossil Butte	WY	1972	8,198
George Washington Birthplace	VA	1930	662
George Washington Carver	MO	1943	210
Gila Cliff Dwellings	NM	1907	533
Governors Island	NY	2001	23
Grand Portage	MN	1951	710
Great Sand Dunes National Monument and Preserve	CO	2000	85,932
Hagerman Fossil Beds	ID	1988	4,351
Hohokam Pima[4]	AZ	1972	1,690
Homestead National Monument of America	NE	1936	211
Hovenweep	CO-UT	1923	785
Jewel Cave	SD	1908	1,274
John Day Fossil Beds	OR	1974	13,944
Lava Beds	CA	1925	46,560
Little Big Horn Battlefield	MT	1879	765
Minidoka Internment[2]	ID	2001	73
Montezuma Castle	AZ	1906	858
Muir Woods	CA	1908	554
Natural Bridges	UT	1908	7,636
Navajo	AZ	1909	360
Northwestern Hawaiian Islands Marine	HI	2006	NA[5]
Ocmulgee	GA	1934	702
Oregon Caves	OR	1909	488
Organ Pipe Cactus	AZ	1937	330,689
Petroglyph	NM	1990	7,232
Pinnacles	CA	1908	24,514
Pipe Spring	AZ	1923	40
Pipestone	MN	1937	282
Poverty Point[2]	LA	1988	911
Rainbow Bridge[3]	UT	1910	160
Russell Cave	AL	1961	310
Salinas Pueblo Missions	NM	1909	1,071
Scotts Bluff	NE	1919	3,005
Statue of Liberty	NJ-NY	1924	60
Sunset Crater Volcano	AZ	1930	3,040
Timpanogos Cave	UT	1922	250
Tonto	AZ	1907	1,120
Tuzigoot	AZ	1939	812
Virgin Islands Coral Reef	VI	2001	13,893
Walnut Canyon	AZ	1915	3,579
White Sands	NM	1933	143,733
Wupatki	AZ	1924	35,422
Yucca House[2]	CO	1919	34

NATIONAL PRESERVES

Name	State	Year[1]	Acreage
Aniakchak	AK	1978	464,118
Bering Land Bridge	AK	1978	2,697,393
Big Cypress	FL	1974	720,561
Big Thicket	TX	1974	97,609
Denali	AK	1917	1,334,118
Gates of the Arctic	AK	1978	948,608
Glacier Bay	AK	1925	58,406
Katmai	AK	1918	418,699
Lake Clark	AK	1978	1,410,292
Little River Canyon[3]	AL	1992	13,633
Mojave	CA	1994	1,529,927
Noatak	AK	1978	6,569,904
Tallgrass Prairie	KS	1996	10,894
Timucuan Ecological & Historic Preserve	FL	1988	46,295

Name	State	Year[1]	Acreage
Wrangell-St. Elias	AK	1978	4,852,753
Yukon-Charley Rivers[3]	AK	1978	2,526,512

NATIONAL SEASHORES

Name	State	Year[1]	Acreage
Assateague Island	MD-VA	1965	39,727
Canaveral	FL	1975	57,662
Cape Cod	MA	1961	43,609
Cape Hatteras	NC	1937	30,351
Cape Lookout	NC	1966	28,243
Cumberland Island	GA	1972	36,347
Fire Island	NY	1964	19,579
Gulf Islands	FL-MS	1971	137,991
Padre Island	TX	1962	130,434
Point Reyes	CA	1962	71,068

NATIONAL PARKWAYS

Name	State	Year[1]	Acreage
Blue Ridge	NC-VA	1933	93,735
George Washington Memorial	VA-MD-DC	1930	7,239
John D. Rockefeller Jr. Mem.	WY	1972	23,777
Natchez Trace	MS-AL-TN	1938	51,824

NATIONAL LAKESHORES

Name	State	Year[1]	Acreage
Apostle Islands	WI	1970	69,372
Indiana Dunes	IN	1966	15,067
Pictured Rocks	MI	1966	73,236
Sleeping Bear Dunes	MI	1970	71,290

NATIONAL RESERVES

Name	State	Year[1]	Acreage
City of Rocks	ID	1988	14,107
Ebey's Landing	WA	1978	19,324

NATIONAL RIVERS

Name	State	Year[1]	Acreage
Big South Fork Natl. R and Recreation Area	KY-TN	1976	125,310
Buffalo	AR	1972	94,293
Mississippi Natl. R and Recreation Area	MN	1988	53,775
New River Gorge	WV	1978	72,189
Ozark	MO	1964	80,785

NATIONAL WILD AND SCENIC RIVERS

Name	State	Year[1]	Acreage
Alagnak	AK	1980	30,665
Bluestone[2]	WV	1978	4,310
Delaware	NY-NJ-PA	1978	1,973
Great Egg Harbor	NJ	1992	43,311
Missouri	NE-SD	1991	34,159
Niobrara	NE	1991	23,074
Obed	TN	1976	5,073
Rio Grande[3]	TX	1978	9,600
Saint Croix	MN-WI	1968	67,469
Upper Delaware	NY-PA	1978	75,000

NATIONAL RECREATION AREAS

Name	State	Year[1]	Acreage
Amistad	TX	1965	58,500
Bighorn Canyon	MT-WY	1966	120,296
Boston Harbor Islands	MA	1996	1,482
Chattahoochee R.	GA	1978	9,359
Chickasaw	OK	1902	9,860
Curecanti	CO	1965	41,972
Delaware Water Gap	NJ-PA	1965	66,739
Gateway	NJ-NY	1972	26,607
Gauley R.[3]	WV	1988	11,507
Glen Canyon	AZ-UT	1958	1,254,429
Golden Gate	CA	1972	74,588
Lake Chelan	WA	1968	61,947
Lake Mead	AZ-NV	1936	1,495,664
Lake Meredith	TX	1965	44,978
Lake Roosevelt[6]	WA	1946	100,390
Ross Lake	WA	1968	117,575
Santa Monica Mts.[3]	CA	1978	154,109
Whiskeytown-Shasta-Trinity	CA	1965	42,503

NATIONAL SCENIC TRAIL

Name	State	Year[1]	Acreage
Appalachian	ME to GA	1968	227,001
Ice Age	WI	1980	NA
Natchez Trace	MS-TN	1983	10,995
North Country	NY to ND	1980	NA
Potomac Heritage	MD-DC-VA-PA	1983	NA

PARKS (no other classification)

Name	State	Year[1]	Acreage
Catoctin Mountain	MD	1954	5,810
Constitution Gardens	DC	1974	52
Fort Washington	MD	1930	341
Greenbelt	MD	1950	1,175
National Capital	DC	1933	6,693
National Mall	DC	1933	146
Piscataway	MD	1961	4,695
Prince William Forest	VA	1948	16,001
Rock Creek	DC	1890	1,755
White House	DC	1933	18
Wolf Trap Farm Park for the Performing Arts	VA	1966	130

INTERNATIONAL HISTORIC SITE

Name	State	Year[1]	Acreage
Saint Croix Island[3]	ME	1949	45

NA=Not available. (1) Year first designated. (2) No federal facilities. (3) Limited federal facilities. (4) Not open to the public. (5) Exact acreage to be determined; covers an estimated 140,000 sq mi. (6) Formerly Coulee Dam National Recreation Area.

UNITED STATES HISTORY

This chapter includes the following sections:

Chronology of Events

1492
Christopher Columbus and crew sighted land Oct. 12 in present-day Bahamas.

1497
John Cabot explored northeast coast to Delaware.

1513
Juan Ponce de León explored Florida coast.

1524
Giovanni da Verrazano led French expedition along coast from Carolina north to Nova Scotia; entered New York Harbor.

1526
San Miguel de Guadalupe, **first European settlement** in what became U.S. territory, was established in the summer off South Carolina coast; abandoned in October.

1539
Hernando de Soto landed in Florida May 28; crossed Mississippi River, **1541**.

1540
Francisco Vásquez de Coronado explored Southwest north of Rio Grande. **Hernando de Alarcón** reached Colorado River; **Don Garcia Lopez de Cardenas** reached Grand Canyon. Others explored California coast.

1562
First French colony in what became U.S. territory was founded on Parris Island off South Carolina coast; abandoned, **1564**.

1565
St. Augustine, FL, founded Sept. 8 by Pedro Menéndez. Razed by Francis Drake, **1586**.

1579
Francis Drake entered San Francisco Bay and claimed region for Britain.

1585

Sir Walter Raleigh

"**Lost colony**" sponsored by **Sir Walter Raleigh** was founded on **Roanoke Island**, off North Carolina coast; settlers found to have vanished, **1590**.

1587
Virginia Dare (on Roanoke Island) became **first infant born** in the 13 colonies of English parents.

1607
Capt. **John Smith** and 105 cavaliers in 3 ships landed on Virginia coast, started **first permanent English settlement** in New World at **Jamestown**.

1609
Henry Hudson, English explorer of Northwest Passage, employed by Dutch, sailed into New York Harbor in September and up Hudson to Albany. **Samuel de Champlain** explored Lake Champlain, to the north.
Spaniards settled **Santa Fe, NM**.

1619
House of Burgesses, first representative assembly in New World, elected July 30 at Jamestown, VA.
First black laborers—indentured servants—in English North American colonies, brought by Dutch to Jamestown in August. Chattel slavery legally recognized, **1650**.

1620
Pilgrims, Puritan separatists, left Plymouth, England, Sept. 16 on *Mayflower*; reached Cape Cod Nov. 19; 103 passengers landed, Dec. 26, at Plymouth. **Mayflower Compact**, signed Nov. 11, was agreement to form a self-government. Half of colony died during harsh winter.

1624
Dutch colonies started in Albany and in New York area, where **New Netherland** was established in May.

1626
Peter Minuit bought **Manhattan** for Dutch West India Co. from Manahatta Indians during summer for goods valued at $24; named island **New Amsterdam**.

1630
Settlement of **Boston** established by Massachusetts colonists led by **John Winthrop**; Winthrop began *The History of New England*.
William Bradford began his chronicle *History of the Plymouth Plantation*.

1634
Maryland founded as Catholic colony under charter to Lord Baltimore. Religious toleration granted **1649**.

1635
Boston Latin School, **oldest U.S. public school** in continuous existence, founded Apr. 23.

1636
Roger Williams founded Providence, RI, in June, as a democratically ruled colony with separation of church and state. Charter granted, **1644**.
Harvard College founded; **oldest institution of higher learning** in U.S.

1640
First book was printed in America, the so-called *Bay Psalm Book*.

1647
Liberal constitution drafted in Rhode Island.
First law in America providing for **free compulsory basic education** enacted in Massachusetts.

1660
British Parliament passed first **Navigation Act** Dec. 1, regulating colonial commerce to suit English needs.

1661
A version of the New Testament translated into Algonquian became the **first Bible** printed in the colonies.

1664
British troops Sept. 8 **seized New Netherland** from Dutch. Charles II granted New Netherland and city of New Amsterdam to brother, Duke of York; both renamed **New York**. Dutch recaptured colony **1673**, but ceded it to Britain Nov. 10, **1674**.

1670
Charles Town, South Carolina, was founded by English colonists in April.

1673
Regular **mail service** on horseback was instituted Jan. 1 between New York and Boston.
Jacques Marquette and **Louis Jolliet** reached the upper **Mississippi** and traveled down it.

1674

Future **Salem witch trial** judge Samuel Sewall began a renowned diary covering events through **1729**.

1676

Nathaniel Bacon led planters against autocratic British Gov. Sir William Berkeley, burned Jamestown, VA, Sept. 19. Rebellion collapsed when Bacon died; 23 followers executed.

Bloody **Indian war** in New England ended Aug. 12. **King Philip**, Wampanoag chief, and Narragansett Indians killed.

1678

A book of poetry by **Anne Bradstreet** was published posthumously in Massachusetts.

1679

A **fire** destroyed 150 houses in **Boston**. Bonston imported first fire engines from England.

1681

John Bunyan's *The Pilgrim's Progress* published in America; became a best seller.

1682

Robert Cavelier, Sieur de La Salle, claimed lower Mississippi River country for France and called it **Louisiana** Apr. 9. Had French outposts built in Illinois and Texas, **1684**. Killed during mutiny, **1687**.

Spanish colonists became the **first Europeans** to settle in **Texas**, at the site of present-day El Paso.

1683

William Penn signed treaty with Delaware Indians Apr. 23 and made payment for **Pennsylvania** lands. The **first German colonists** in America settled near Philadelphia.

1689

New York's English colonial governor, **Sir Edmund Andros**, resigned after an armed uprising in Boston on Apr. 18.

1690

The *New England Primer* came into use in elementary schools.

The **first colonial newspaper**, *Publick Occurrences*, was published by Benjamin Harris, but promptly shut down for lack of official permission.

Large-scale **whaling** operations began in Nantucket, MA.

1692

Witchcraft delusion at **Salem**, MA; 20 alleged witches executed by special court.

1696

Capt. **William Kidd** arrested and sent to England; hanged for piracy, **1701**.

1697

The Essays of Sir Francis Bacon, published in England in **1597**, was published in America; it became a bestseller.

1699

French settlements made in Mississippi, Louisiana.

1702

Legislation enacted making the **Church of England** the established church in Maryland.

1704

Indians attacked Deerfield, MA, Feb. 28-29; killed 40, carried off 100.

Boston News Letter, **first regular newspaper**, was started by postmaster John Campbell.

1709

British-colonial troops captured French fort, Port Royal, Nova Scotia, in **Queen Anne's War, 1701-13**. France yielded Nova Scotia by treaty, **1713**.

1712

Slaves revolted in New York Apr. 6; 21 were executed. Second uprising, **1741**; 13 slaves hanged, 13 burned, 71 deported.

1716

First theater in colonies opened in Williamsburg, VA.

1726

Poor people **rioted** in Philadelphia.

Great Awakening religious revival began.

1731

America's **first circulating library** founded in Philadelphia by Benjamin Franklin.

1732

Benjamin Franklin published the **first** *Poor Richard's Almanack*; published annually until **1757**.

Last of the 13 colonies, **Georgia**, chartered.

1733

Influenza epidemic swept through New York City and Philadelphia.

1735

Editor **John Peter Zenger** was acquitted of libel Aug. 5 in New York after criticizing the British governor's conduct in office.

1739

A series of **slave uprisings** put down in South Carolina.

1741

Famous sermon "Sinners in the Hands of an Angry God," delivered at Enfield, MA, July 8, by **Jonathan Edwards**, a major figure in the revivalist **Great Awakening**.

Capt. **Vitus Bering** reached Alaska.

1744

King George's War pitted British and colonials vs. French. Colonials captured Louisbourg, Cape Breton Is., Nova Scotia, June 17, **1745**. Returned to France **1748** by Treaty of Aix-la-Chapelle.

1752

Benjamin Franklin, flying kite in thunderstorm, proved lightning is electricity, June 15; invented lightning rod.

Liberty Bell, cast in England, was delivered to Pennsylvania.

1754

Delegates from 7 colonies to **Albany, NY, Congress**, July 19, approved a plan of union by Benjamin Franklin; plan was rejected by the colonies.

French and Indian War began when French occupied Ft. Duquesne (Pittsburgh). British moved Acadian French from Nova Scotia to Louisiana Oct. 8, **1755**. British captured Québec Sept. 18, **1759**, in battles in which French Gen. Joseph de Montcalm and British Gen. James Wolfe were killed. Peace pact signed Feb. 10, **1763**. French lost Canada and Midwest.

1757

The **first streetlights** appeared in Philadelphia.

1764

Sugar Act, Apr. 5, placed duties on lumber, foodstuffs, molasses, and rum in colonies, to pay French and Indian War debts.

1765

Stamp Act, enacted by Parliament Mar. 22, required revenue stamps to help fund royal troops. Nine colonies, at **Stamp Act Congress** in New York Oct. 7-25, adopted Declaration of Rights. Stamp Act **repealed** Mar. 17, **1766**.

Quartering Act, requiring colonists to house British troops, went into effect Mar. 24.

1767

Townshend Acts levied taxes on glass, painter's lead, paper, and tea. In **1770** all duties except on tea were repealed.

1770

British troops fired Mar. 5 into Boston mob, killed 5 including **Crispus Attucks**, a black man, reportedly leader of group; later called **Boston Massacre**.

1773

East India Co. tea ships turned back at Boston, New York, and Philadelphia in May. Cargo ship burned at Annapolis, Oct. 14; cargo thrown overboard at **Boston Tea Party**, Dec. 16, to protest the tea tax.

First museum in the colonies was officially established in Charleston, SC; later named the Charleston Museum.

World Almanac Quick Quiz

Can you match the event with the year?

(a) 1884   (b) 1894   (c) 1904   (d) 1914

(1) The U.S. hosted its first Olympics.
(2) The Panama Canal officially opened.
(3) The first roller coaster in the U.S. opened at New York's Coney Island.
(4) The Hershey Chocolate Company was started.

For the answer look in this chapter, or see page 1008.

1774

"Intolerable Acts" of Parliament curtailed Massachusetts self-rule; barred use of Boston Harbor till tea was paid for.

First Continental Congress held in Philadelphia Sept. 5-Oct. 26; called for civil disobedience against British.

Rhode Island abolished slavery.

1775

Patrick Henry addressed Virginia convention, Mar. 23, said, "Give me liberty or give me death!"

Paul Revere and **William Dawes**, Apr. 18, rode to alert Patriots that British were on their way to Concord to destroy arms. At **Lexington**, MA, Apr. 19, Minutemen lost 8. On return from **Concord**, British took 273 casualties.

Col. Ethan Allen (joined by Col. Benedict Arnold) captured **Ft. Ticonderoga, NY**, May 10, also Crown Point. Colonials headed for **Bunker Hill**, fortified Breed's Hill, Charlestown, MA. Repulsed British under Gen. William Howe twice before retreating, June 17.

Continental Congress June 15 named **George Washington** commander in chief. Established a postal system, July 26; Benjamin Franklin became the **first postmaster general**.

1776

Thomas Paine

Common Sense, famous pro-independence pamphlet by **Thomas Paine**, was published Jan. 10; quickly sold some 100,000 copies.

France and Spain each agreed May 2 to provide arms.

In Continental Congress June 7, Richard Henry Lee (VA) moved "that these united colonies are and of right ought to be free and independent states." Resolution adopted July 2. **Declaration of Independence** approved July 4.

Col. William Moultrie's batteries at **Charleston, SC**, repulsed British sea attack June 28. Washington lost **Battle of Long Island** Aug. 27, evacuated New York.

Nathan Hale executed as spy by British Sept. 22.

Brig. Gen. Arnold's **Lake Champlain** fleet was defeated at Valcour Oct. 11, but British returned to Canada. Howe failed to destroy Washington's army at White Plains, Oct. 28. Hessians captured Ft. Washington, Manhattan, and 3,000 men, Nov. 16; captured Ft. Lee, NJ, Nov. 18.

Washington, in Pennsylvania, recrossed **Delaware River** Dec. 25-26, defeated Hessians at Trenton, NJ, Dec. 26.

1777

Washington defeated Lord Cornwallis at **Princeton** Jan. 3.

Continental Congress, June 14, authorized an **American flag**, the Stars and Stripes.

Maj. Gen. John Burgoyne's force of 8,000 from Canada, captured **Ft. Ticonderoga**, July 6. Americans beat back Burgoyne at Bemis Heights, Oct. 7, cut off British escape route. Burgoyne surrendered 5,000 men at **Saratoga**, NY, Oct. 17.

Articles of Confederation adopted by Continental Congress, Nov. 15, took effect Mar. 1, **1781**.

1778

John Paul Jones

France signed treaty of aid with U.S. Feb. 6. Sent fleet; British evacuated Philadelphia in consequence, June 18.

1779

George Rogers Clark took Vincennes in February.

John Paul Jones on the *Bonhomme Richard* defeated *Serapis* in British North Sea waters, Sept. 23.

1780

Charleston, SC, fell to the British May 12, but a British force was defeated near **Kings Mountain, NC**, Oct. 7 by militiamen.

Benedict Arnold found to be a traitor Sept. 23. Arnold escaped, made brigadier general in British army.

1781

Bank of North America incorporated May 26.

Cornwallis retired to **Yorktown, VA**. Adm. Francois Joseph de Grasse landed 3,000 French and stopped British fleet in **Hampton Roads**. Washington and Jean Baptiste de Rocham-

beau joined forces, arrived near Williamsburg, Sept. 26. Siege of Cornwallis began, Oct. 6; **Cornwallis surrendered** Oct. 19.

1782

New **British** cabinet agreed in March to **recognize U.S. independence**. Preliminary agreement signed in Paris, Nov. 30.

Use of the **scarlet letter A**, sewn on clothing or branded on skin of adulterers, was discontinued in New England.

1783

Massachusetts Supreme Court declared **slavery** illegal in that state.

Britain, U.S. signed **Paris peace treaty**, Sept. 3, recognizing American independence. Congress ratified it Jan. 14, **1784**).

Washington ordered army disbanded Nov. 3, bade farewell to his officers at Fraunces Tavern, New York City, Dec. 4.

First regular daily newspaper, *Pennsylvania Evening Post*, went on sale in Philadelphia, May 30.

Noah Webster published *American Spelling Book*.

1784

Thomas Jefferson's proposal to **ban slavery** in new territory after 1802 was narrowly defeated, Mar. 1.

First successful daily newspaper, *Pennsylvania Packet & General Advertiser*, published Sept. 21.

1785

Regular **stagecoach routes** established between Albany, New York City, and Philadelphia.

1786

Delegates from 5 states at **Annapolis, MD**, Sept. 11-14 asked Congress to call a constitutional convention.

1787

Shays's Rebellion of debt-ridden farmers in Massachusetts failed, Jan. 25.

Northwest Ordinance adopted July 13 by Continental Congress for Northwest Territory, north of Ohio River, west of New York; made rules for statehood. Guaranteed freedom of religion, support for schools, no slavery.

Constitutional convention opened in Philadelphia, May 25, with Washington presiding. Constitution accepted by delegates, Sept. 17; **Delaware** became first state to ratify it, Dec. 7; **Pennsylvania** and **New Jersey** followed.

Federalist Papers first appeared in *NY Independent Journal*.

1788

A **large fire** in **New Orleans**, then a Spanish territory, destroyed much of the city, Mar. 21.

The **Constitution** was **adopted** June 21 after being ratified by the requisite ninth state (New Hampshire); also ratified by **Georgia, Connecticut, Massachusetts, Maryland, South Carolina, Virginia**, and **New York** throughout the year.

First U.S. senators elected Sept. 30, from Pennsylvania.

Settlers founded future cities **Cincinnati, OH; Dubuque, IA**; and **Charleston, WV**.

1789

George Washington chosen president by all electors voting (73 eligible, 69 voting, 4 absent); **John Adams**, vice president, got 34 votes. **First Congress** met at Federal Hall, New York City, and declared Constitution in effect, Mar. 4; Washington **inaugurated** there Apr. 30; **first inaugural ball** held May 7.

Tammany Hall founded as benevolent organization, May 12.

U.S. State Dept. established by Congress July 27. (**Thomas Jefferson** installed as first secretary of state Feb. **1790**.) **War Dept.** created, Aug. 7, with **Henry Knox** to be secretary; **Treasury Dept.** created Sept. 2, with **Alexander Hamilton** to be secretary.

Supreme Court created by Federal Judiciary Act, Sept. 24; **John Jay** confirmed by Congress as **first Supreme Court chief justice**, Sept. 26.

1790

Congress, Mar. 1, authorized decennial **U.S. census**.

Naturalization Act (2-year residency) passed Mar. 26.

John Carroll consecrated as **first American Catholic bishop**, Aug. 15.

Congress met in **Philadelphia**, new temporary capital, Dec. 6.

1791
Bill of Rights, submitted to states, Sept. 25, **1789**, went into effect Dec. 15.
First Bank of the U.S. chartered.

1792
Coinage Act established **U.S. Mint** in Philadelphia, Apr. 2.
Gen. **"Mad" Anthony Wayne** made commander in Ohio-Indiana area, trained American Legion, established string of forts. Routed Indians at Fallen Timbers on Maumee River, Aug. 20, **1794**, checked British at Fort Miami, OH, same year.
White House cornerstone laid Oct. 13.

1793

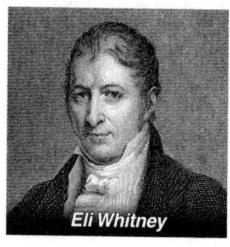

Eli Whitney

Washington inaugurated for second term, Mar. 4, having received 132 electoral votes; **John Adams** again became vice president, having received the second highest total, 77.

Washington declared **U.S. neutrality**, Apr. 22, in war between Britain and France.

Eli Whitney invented **cotton gin**, reviving Southern slavery.

1794
Whiskey Rebellion, western Pennsylvania farmers protesting liquor tax of **1791**, suppressed by federal militia in September.
John Jay's controversial **treaty** with Britain, signed Nov. 19, ratified June 24, **1795**. This treaty intended to settle long-standing differences between the U.S. and Britain.

1795
U.S. bought peace from **Algerian pirates** by paying $1 mil ransom for 115 seamen Sept. 5, followed by annual tributes.
Gen. Wayne signed peace with Indians at **Ft. Greenville**.
Univ. of North Carolina became **first operating state university**.

1796
Washington's farewell address as president delivered Sept. 17. Warned against permanent alliances with foreign powers, big public debt, large military establishment, and devices of "small, artful, enterprising minority."

1797
John Adams inaugurated as second president Mar. 4, having received 71 electoral votes; **Thomas Jefferson** became vice president, having received 68.
U.S. frigate *United States* launched at Philadelphia, July 10; *Constellation* at Baltimore, Sept. 7; *Constitution* (Old Ironsides) at Boston, Sept. 20.

1798
Alien & Sedition Acts passed by Federalists June-July; intended to silence political opposition.
War with France threatened over French raids on U.S. shipping and rejection of U.S. diplomats. Navy (45 ships) and 365 privateers captured 84 French ships. USS *Constellation* took French warship *Insurgente*, **1799**. Napoleon stopped French raids after becoming First Consul.

1799
Washington died at Mount Vernon Dec. 14.

1800
Federal government moved to **Washington, DC**.

1801
John Marshall named Supreme Court chief justice, Jan. 20.
Thomas Jefferson, who had received same number of electoral votes as Aaron Burr in **1800** election, won out over Burr in House vote reached Feb. 17; Burr named vice president.
Tripoli declared war June 10 against U.S., which refused added tribute to commerce-raiding Arab corsairs. Land and naval campaigns forced Tripoli to negotiate peace, June 4, **1805**.
Oldest U.S. art institution, Pennsylvania Academy of Fine Arts, founded.

1802
Congress established the U.S. Military Academy at **West Point**, NY.

1803
Supreme Court, in *Marbury v. Madison*, for the **first time overturned** a U.S. law, Feb. 24.
Napoleon sold all of Louisiana, stretching to Canadian border, to U.S. for $11,250,000 in bonds, plus $3,750,000 indemnities to American citizens with claims against France. U.S. took title Dec. 20. **Louisiana Purchase** doubled U.S. area.

Meriwether Lewis

William Clark

1804
Lewis and Clark expedition ordered by Pres. Thomas Jefferson to explore what is now northwest U.S. Started from St. Louis May 14; ended Sept. 23, **1806**.
Vice Pres. **Aaron Burr shot Alexander Hamilton** in a duel July 11 in Weehawken, NJ; Hamilton died next day.

1805
U.S. Marines aided by Arab mercenaries, Apr. 27, captured Tripolitan port of Derna, major victory in war against **Barbary pirates**; inspiration for "to the shores of Tripoli" in Marines Corps song.

1807
Robert Fulton made **first practical steamboat trip**; left New York City Aug. 17, reached Albany, 150 mi away, in 32 hrs.
Embargo Act banned all trade with foreign countries, forbidding ships to set sail for foreign ports Dec. 22.

1808
Slave importation outlawed. Some 250,000 slaves were illegally imported **1808-60**.

1810
Third U.S. Census found a population of 7,239,881. The black population was put at 1,378,110, of whom 186,746 were free citizens.

1811
William Henry Harrison, governor of Indiana, defeated Indians led by "the Prophet," in **Battle of Tippecanoe**, Nov. 7.
Construction began on **Cumberland Road** in Cumberland, MD; road became important route to West.
About 400 **slaves revolted** in Louisiana, killing the son of a plantation owner and marching on New Orleans. The insurrection was suppressed; some 75 slaves killed.

1812
War of 1812 had 3 main causes: Britain seized U.S. ships trading with France; Britain had seized 4,000 naturalized U.S. sailors by **1810**; Britain armed Indians, who raided western border. U.S. stopped trade with Europe **1807** and **1809**. Trade with Britain only was stopped **1810**.
Unaware that Britain had raised the blockade against France 2 days before, **Congress declared war** June 18.
British took Detroit Aug. 16.

1813
Oliver H. Perry defeated British fleet at **Battle of Lake Erie**, Sept. 10. U.S. won Battle of the Thames, Ontario, Oct. 5, but failed in Canadian invasion attempts. York (Toronto) and Buffalo were burned.

1814
British landed in Maryland in August, defeated U.S. force Aug. 24, **burned Capitol and White House**. Maryland militia stopped British advance, Sept. 12. Bombardment of Ft. McHenry, Baltimore, for 25 hours, Sept. 13-14, by British fleet failed, which inspired Francis Scott Key to write the words to **"The Star-Spangled Banner."**
Troops under Andrew Jackson defeated Creek Indians led by Chief Weatherford at **Battle of Horseshoe Bend** in Alabama, Mar. 29, ending Creek Indian War, begun a year earlier.
U.S. won naval **Battle of Lake Champlain** Sept. 11. Peace treaty with Great Britain signed at Ghent, Dec. 24.

1815

Some 5,300 British, unaware of peace treaty, attacked U.S. entrenchments near **New Orleans**, Jan. 8. British had more than 2,000 casualties; Americans lost 71.

U.S. flotilla finally ended attacks by priates from Ottoman states of **Algiers, Tunis, Tripoli**.

1816

Second Bank of the U.S. chartered Apr. 10.

The **American Colonization Society**, which sought to address slavery issue by transporting freed blacks to Africa, formed in Washington, DC, Dec. **1816**-Jan. **1817**.

1817

William Cullen Bryant's poem **"Thanatopsis"** published.

Thomas Hopkins Gallaudet established the **first free public school for the deaf** in Hartford, CT.

1818

Connecticut **expanded suffrage** among **white male voters**. Massachusetts followed suit in **1820**, and New York in **1821**, reducing or eliminating property qualifications.

1819

Spain ceded **Florida** to U.S. Feb. 22.

American steamship *Savannah* made **first part-steam-powered, part-sail-powered crossing** of **Atlantic**, traveling from Savannah, GA, to Liverpool, England, in 29 days.

Washington Irving's *Sketch Book* became a best seller.

1820

First organized immigration of blacks to Africa from U.S. began with 86 free blacks sailing to Sierra Leone, Feb.

Henry Clay's **Missouri Compromise** bill passed by Congress, Mar. 3. Slavery was allowed in Missouri, but not west of the Mississippi River north of 36° 30´ (the southern line of Missouri). Repealed **1854**.

1821

Emma Willard founded Troy Female Seminary, **first U.S. women's college**.

Stephen Austin established the **first American community in Texas**, San Felipe de Austin.

The Spy, a novel by **James Fenimore Cooper** set during the American Revolution, was published and became a best seller.

1822

Tension between sports and academics surfaced when Yale College Pres. Timothy Dwight **banned** a **primitive form of football**, setting fines for violators.

1823

Monroe Doctrine, opposing European intervention in the Americas, enunciated by Pres. James Monroe Dec. 2.

The **Hudson River School**, painters who focused on the beauties of nature, began to come to public attention.

1824

Pawtucket, RI, **weavers strike**, first such action by women.

Slavery abolished in the state of **Illinois** Aug. 2.

1825

After a deadlocked election, **John Quincy Adams** was elected president by the House, Feb. 9.

Erie Canal opened; first boat left Buffalo Oct. 26, reached New York City Nov. 4.

John Stevens, of Hoboken, NJ, built and operated **first experimental steam locomotive** in U.S.

1826

Thomas Jefferson and **John Adams** both died July 4.

James Fenimore Cooper's *The Last of the Mohicans* published.

1827

Massachusetts passed a law providing for **tax-supported public high schools**, the first state to do so.

1828

South Carolina Dec. 19 declared the right of **state nullification of federal laws**, opposing the "Tariff of Abominations."

Noah Webster published his *American Dictionary of the English Language*.

Baltimore & Ohio, the **first U.S. passenger railroad**, began operations July 4.

1829

Andrew Jackson inaugurated as president, Mar. 4.

1830

Famous **debate** Jan. 27 between Sen. **Daniel Webster** (MA) and Robert Hayne (SC), on state right to nullify federal law.

Mormon church organized by **Joseph Smith** in Fayette, NY, Apr. 6.

Pres. Jackson, May 28, signed **Indian Removal Act**, providing land and some pay to Indians who agree to resettle in West.

1831

William Lloyd Garrison began **abolitionist newspaper** *The Liberator* Jan. 1.

Nat Turner, black slave in Virginia, led local **slave rebellion**, starting Aug. 21; 57 whites killed. Troops called in, 100 slaves killed, Turner captured, tried, hanged Nov. 11.

1832

Black Hawk War in Illinois and Wisconsin Apr.-Sept. pushed Sauk and Fox Indians west across Mississippi.

1833

American Anti-Slavery Society founded in Philadelphia, Dec. 4.

Oberlin College became **first** in U.S. to adopt **coeducation**.

1835

Liberty Bell cracked July 8, tolling death of Chief Justice **John Marshall**.

Seminole Indians in Florida under **Osceola** began attacks Nov. 1, protesting forced removal. The unpopular war ended Aug. 14, **1842**; most of the Indians were sent to Oklahoma.

Texas proclaimed right to secede from Mexico; **Sam Houston** put in command of Texas army, Nov. 2-4.

Gold discovered on **Cherokee land** in Georgia. Indians forced to cede lands, Dec. 20, and to cross Mississippi.

1836

Texans besieged at **Alamo** in San Antonio by Mexicans under Santa Anna, Feb. 23-Mar. 6; entire garrison killed. Texas independence declared, Mar. 2. At San Jacinto Apr. 21, Sam Houston and Texans defeated Mexicans.

Ralph Waldo Emerson published his first work, *Nature,* espousing his philosophy of **transcendentalism**.

Marcus Whitman, H. H. Spaulding, and wives reached Fort Walla Walla on Columbia River, OR. **First white women to cross plains**.

1838

Cherokee Indians forced to walk the **"Trail of Tears"** from Georgia to Oklahoma starting in October.

1841

First emigrant **wagon train for California**, 47 persons, left Independence, MO, May 1, reached California Nov. 4.

Edgar Allan Poe published one of the **first** American **detective stories**, *The Murders in the Rue Morgue*.

New England transcendentalist intellectuals set up **Brook Farm commune**. Lasted until **1846**.

1842

Webster-Ashburton Treaty signed Aug. 9, fixing the U.S.-Canada border in Maine and Minnesota.

First use of **anesthetic** (sulfuric ether gas).

Settlement of Oregon began via **Oregon Trail**.

1843

More than 1,000 settlers left Independence, MO, for **Oregon** May 22, arriving in October.

1844

First message over **first telegraph line** sent May 24 by inventor **Samuel F.B. Morse** from Washington to Baltimore: "What hath God wrought!"

1845

Congress **overrode a presidential veto** for the first time, Mar. 3, after Pres. John Tyler vetoed a tariff bill.

Texas Congress **voted for annexation** by U.S., July 4. Texas admitted to Union, Dec. 29.

Edgar Allan Poe's poem "The Raven" published.

1846

Mexican War began after Pres. James K. Polk ordered Gen. Zachary Taylor to seize disputed Texan land settled by Mexicans. After border clash, U.S. declared war May 13; Mexico declared war May 23.

About 12,000 U.S. troops took Vera Cruz Mar. 27, **1847**, and Mexico City Sept. 14, **1847**. Treaty signed Feb. 2, **1848**, ended war, and Mexico ceded claims to Texas, California, and other territory.

Bear flag of **Republic of California** raised by American settlers at Sonoma, June 14.

Treaty with Britain June 15 set **Oregon territory boundary** at 49th parallel (extension of existing line). Expansionists had used slogan "54° 40´ or fight." The term **"manifest destiny,"** coined by a journalist in **1845**, also came into play.

Mormons, after violent clashes with settlers over polygamy, left Nauvoo, IL, for West under **Brigham Young**. They settled July **1847** at **Salt Lake City**, UT.

Elias Howe invented **sewing machine**.

1847

First adhesive U.S. postage stamps—Benjamin Franklin 5¢, Washington 10¢—were sold July 1.

Ralph Waldo Emerson published first book of poems. **Henry Wadsworth Longfellow** published *Evangeline*.

1848

Gold discovered Jan. 24 in California; 80,000 prospectors emigrated in **1849**.

Lucretia Mott and **Elizabeth Cady Stanton** led **Seneca Falls**, NY, **Women's Rights Convention**, July 19-20.

1850

Sen. Henry Clay's **Compromise of 1850** admitted California as 31st state Sept. 9, with slavery forbidden; made Utah and New Mexico territories; made **Fugitive Slave Law** more harsh; and ended District of Columbia slave trade.

Nathaniel Hawthorne's *The Scarlet Letter* published.

1851

Herman Melville's *Moby-Dick* published.

1852

Harriet Beecher Stowe's *Uncle Tom's Cabin* published.

Harriet Beecher Stowe

1853

Japan receives Comm. **Matthew C. Perry**, July 14. He negotiated a **treaty** to **open Japan** to U.S. ships.

New York City hosted **first World's Fair** in the U.S., beginning July 14.

Stephen Foster published "My Old Kentucky Home."

1854

Republican Party formed at Ripon, WI, Feb. 28. Opposed Kansas-Nebraska Act, which left issue of slavery to vote of settlers. Act became law May 30.

Henry David Thoreau published *Walden*.

Treaty ratified with Mexico Apr. 25, providing for **Gadsden Purchase** of a strip of land.

1855

Walt Whitman published *Leaves of Grass*.

First railroad train crossed Mississippi River on the river's **first bridge**, between Rock Island, IL, and Davenport, IA, Apr. 21.

1856

Republican Party's **first presidential nominee, John C. Fremont**, defeated. Abraham Lincoln

Walt Whitman

made 50 speeches for him.

Proslavery group sacked **Lawrence, KS**, May 21; abolitionist **John Brown** led antislavery contingent against Missourians at Osawatomie, KS, Aug. 30.

The **first U.S. kindergarten** was opened in Watertown, WI.

1857

Dred Scott decision by Supreme Court Mar. 6 held that slaves did not become free in a free state, Congress could not bar slavery from a territory, and blacks could not be citizens.

Currier & Ives issued their first print.

Dred Scott

1858

First Atlantic cable completed, by Cyrus W. Field Aug. 5.

Lincoln-Douglas debates in Illinois, Aug. 21-Oct. 15.

1859

Edwin L. Drake drilled the **first commercially productive oil well** near Titusville, PA, Aug. 27.

Abolitionist **John Brown**, with 21 men, seized U.S. Armory at **Harpers Ferry**, WV, Oct. 16. U.S. Marines captured raiders, killing several. Brown was hanged for treason Dec. 2.

1860

Approximately 20,000 **New England shoe workers** went on strike Feb. 22 and won higher wages.

First **Pony Express** between Sacramento, CA, and St. Joseph, MO, started Apr. 3.

Republican **Abraham Lincoln** was elected president Nov. 6 in a 4-way race.

1861

Seven southern states set up **Confederate States of America** Feb. 8, with **Jefferson Davis** as president. **Civil War** began as Confederates fired on **Ft. Sumter** in Charleston, SC, Apr. 12. They captured it Apr. 14.

Pres. **Lincoln** called for 75,000 volunteers Apr. 15. By May, 11 states had seceded. Lincoln blockaded Southern ports Apr. 19, cutting off vital exports and aid.

Confederates repelled Union forces at first **Battle of Bull Run**, July 21.

First transcontinental telegraph line was put in operation.

1862

Union forces were victorious in Western campaigns, took New Orleans May 1. Battles in East were largely inconclusive despite heavy casualties. The **Battle of Antietam**, in western Maryland Sept. 17, was the bloodiest one-day battle of the war; each side lost over 2,000 men.

Homestead Act, which granted free farms to settlers, was approved May 20.

Land Grant Act, which provided for public land sale to benefit agricultural education, was approved July 7. It eventually led to establishment of state university systems.

1863

Pres. Lincoln issued **Emancipation Proclamation** Jan. 1, freeing "all slaves in areas still in rebellion."

Entire Mississippi River was in Union hands by July 4. Union forces won a major victory at **Gettysburg** PA, July 1-3. Lincoln gave his **Gettysburg Address** Nov. 19.

Confederate forces under siege surrendered **Vicksburg**, MI, to Union forces under Gen. Ulysses S. Grant, July 4.

About 1,000 were killed or wounded in **draft riots** in New York City; some blacks were hanged by mobs July 13-16.

Pres. Lincoln declared **Thanksgiving** to be a national holiday.

1864

Sand Creek massacre of Cheyenne and Arapaho Indians Nov. 29. Soldiers drove Indians out of village; about 150 killed.

Gen. **William Tecumseh Sherman** marched through Georgia, taking Atlanta Sept. 1 and Savannah Dec. 22.

1865

Gen. **Robert E. Lee surrendered** 27,800 Confederate troops to Gen. Grant at **Appomattox Court House**, VA, Apr. 9. J. E. Johnston surrendered 31,200 to Sherman at Durham Station, NC, Apr. 18. Last rebel troops surrendered May 26.

Pres. **Lincoln was shot** Apr. 14 by **John Wilkes Booth** in Ford's Theater, Washington, DC. Lincoln died the following morning. Vice Pres. **Andrew Johnson** was sworn in as president. Booth was hunted down and fatally wounded, perhaps by his own hand, Apr. 26. Four co-conspirators were hanged July 7.

13th Amendment, abolishing slavery, ratified Dec. 6.

▶ **IT'S A FACT:** The territory of Wyoming, in 1869, became the first in the country to give women the right to vote. Although a constitutional amendment granting women voting rights was introduced in Congress in 1878, it did not become part of the Constitution until 1920, when Tennessee became the 36th state to ratify the 19th Amendment.

1866
Congress took control of Southern **Reconstruction**, backed freedmen's rights in legislation vetoed by Johnson; veto overridden by Congress, Apr. 9.

Ku Klux Klan formed secretly in South to terrorize blacks who voted. Disbanded **1869-71**. A second Klan was organized in **1915**.

1867
Alaska sold to U.S. by Russia for $7.2 mil Mar. 30, through efforts of Sec. of State William H. Seward.

The **Grange** was organized Dec. 4, to protect farmer interests.

Horatio Alger's *Ragged Dick* published.

1868

Pres. **Johnson** tried to remove secretary of war Edwin M. Stanton; he was impeached by the House Feb. 24 for violation of Tenure of Office Act. He was acquitted by the Senate March-May.

14th Amendment, providing for citizenship of all persons born or naturalized in U.S., ratified July 9.

Louisa May Alcott published *Little Women*.

The World Almanac, a publication of the *New York World*, appeared for the first time.

1869
Attempt to "corner" gold leads to financial **"Black Friday"** in New York Sept. 24.

Transcontinental railroad completed; golden spike driven at Promontory, UT, May 10, marking the junction of Central Pacific and Union Pacific lines.

Knights of Labor labor union formed in Philadelphia. By **1886**, it had 700,000 members nationally.

Woman suffrage law passed in Wyoming Territory Dec. 10.

1870
15th Amendment, making race no bar to voting rights, ratified Feb. 8.

First U.S. boardwalk completed, in Atlantic City, NJ.

U.S. Weather Bureau founded.

1871
Great fire destroyed **Chicago** Oct. 8-11.

National Rifle Association founded.

1872
Amnesty Act May 22 restored civil rights to citizens of the South, except for 500 Confederate leaders.

Congress established **first national park—Yellowstone**.

James McNeill Whistler painted famous portrait known informally as **"Whistler's Mother."**

1873
First U.S. postal card was issued May 1.

Jesse James and his gang robbed their first passenger train July 21.

Banks failed, panic began in September. Depression lasted 5 years.

"Boss" William Tweed of New York City was convicted Nov. 19 of stealing public funds. He died in jail in **1878**.

New York's Bellevue Hospital started **first nursing school**.

1874
Women's Christian Temperance Union was established in Cleveland.

The **first** U.S. **public zoo** was established in Philadelphia.

1875
Congress passed the **Civil Rights Act** Mar. 1, giving equal rights to blacks in public accommodations and jury duty. Act invalidated in **1883** by Supreme Court.

First **Jim Crow** segregation law enacted, in Tennessee.

First Kentucky Derby held May 17.

1876
Democrat **Samuel J. Tilden** received majority of popular votes for president over Republican **Rutherford B. Hayes**, but

22 electoral votes were in dispute. Congress agreed to certify Hayes as winner in Feb. **1877** after Republicans agreed to end federal Reconstruction of South.

Alexander Graham Bell patented the telephone Mar. 7

Col. **George A. Custer** and 264 soldiers of the 7th Cavalry were killed June 25 in "last stand," **Battle of the Little Bighorn**, MT, in Sioux Indian War.

1877
Molly Maguires, Irish terrorist society in Scranton, PA, mining areas was broken up by the hanging, June 21, of 11 leaders for murders of mine officials and police.

Pres. Rutherford B. Hayes sent federal troops to control violent national **railroad strike**.

1878
First commercial telephone exchange opened, New Haven, CT, Jan. 28.

Thomas A. Edison founded **Edison Electric Light Co.** on Oct. 15.

1879
F. W. Woolworth opened his **first five-and-ten** store, in Utica, NY, Feb. 22.

Henry George published *Progress & Poverty*, advocating single tax on land.

French actress **Sarah Bernhardt** made her U.S. debut Nov. 8 at New York City's Booth Theater.

1880
Chinese Exclusion Treaty was signed with China, Nov. 17, providing for restitution of Chinese nationals entering U.S.

Lew Wallace's *Ben Hur* published.

1881
Clara Barton founded the **American Red Cross** May 21.

Pres. **James A. Garfield shot** in Washington, DC, July 2; died Sept. 19.

Famous gun battle between the Earp brothers and outlaw rustlers Oct. 26 near the **OK Corral**, Tombstone, AZ.

Booker T. Washington founded Tuskegee Institute for blacks.

Clara Barton

Helen Hunt Jackson published *A Century of Dishonor*, about mistreatment of Indians.

1882
Chinese Exclusion Act, barring Chinese immigration, passed by Congress May 6.

1883
Pendleton Act passed Jan. 16, reformed civil service.

The **Brooklyn Bridge** opened May 24.

The **Northern Pacific Railroad** was completed Sept. 8.

Buffalo Bill Cody's Wild West Show began its 30-year touring run.

1884
First long-distance telephone call completed, Mar. 27, between Boston and New York.

First roller coaster in the U.S. opened at Coney Island in New York City.

Mark Twain's masterpiece, *The Adventures of Huckleberry Finn*, appeared.

1885
Washington Monument dedicated Feb. 21.

Postal rates lowered to 2¢ an ounce.

1886
Haymarket riot and bombing, May 4, followed labor battles for 8-hour day in Chicago; 7 police and 4 workers died. Eight anarchists found guilty Aug. 20; 4 hanged Nov. 11.

Coca-Cola first sold, May 8, at Jacob's Pharmacy in Atlanta.

Apache Indian **Geronimo** surrendered Sept. 4, ending last major Indian war.

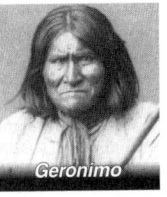

Geronimo

Statue of Liberty dedicated Oct. 28.

American Federation of Labor (AFL) formed Dec. 8 by 25 craft unions.

1887
Interstate Commerce Act enacted Feb. 4.

Pres. Grover Cleveland signed the **Hatch Act**, Mar. 2, establishing agriculture experiment stations across the U.S.

Eugene Field published poem **"Little Boy Blue."**

1888
Great blizzard struck Eastern U.S. Mar. 11-14, causing about 400 deaths.

Ernest Thayer's poem **"Casey at the Bat"** was recited for the first time in public, at a New York City theater in May.

1889
U.S. opened **Oklahoma** to white **settlement** Apr. 22; within 24 hours claims for 2 mil acres were staked by 50,000 "sooner" settlers.

Johnstown, PA, flood May 31; 2,200 lives lost.

Electric lights installed at the White House.

1890
Sherman Antitrust Act passed July 2, began federal effort to curb monopolies.

Massacre at **Wounded Knee**, SD, Dec. 29, the last major conflict between Indians and U.S. troops. About 200 Indian men, women, and children and 29 soldiers were killed.

Jacob Riis published *How the Other Half Lives*, about city slums.

Emily Dickinson's poems published, 4 years after her death.

1891
Forest Reserve Act, Mar. 3, let president close public forest land to settlement for establishment of national parks.

Carnegie Hall, in New York City, opened May 5.

1892
Ellis Island, in New York Bay, opened Jan. 1 to receive immigrants.

Homestead PA, **strike** at Carnegie steel mills; 7 guards and 11 strikers and spectators shot to death July 6.

James J. Corbett defeated John L. Sullivan Sept. 7 to become first world heavyweight champion under Marquess of Queensbury rules.

1893
Columbian Exposition world's fair held May-Oct. in Chicago.

Financial panic began, led to 4-year depression.

Mormon Temple dedicated in Salt Lake City, UT.

1894
Thomas A. Edison's **kinetoscope**, for motion pictures (invented **1887**), given first public showing Apr. 14.

Jacob S. Coxey led army of unemployed from the Midwest, reaching Washington, DC, Apr. 30. Coxey arrested May 1 for trespassing on Capitol grounds; his army disbanded.

Pullman strike began May 11 at a railroad car plant in Chicago.

Milton Hershey started **Hershey Chocolate Company**.

1895
"America the Beautiful" appeared for first time, in church publication, July 4.

Stephen Crane's *The Red Badge of Courage* published.

1896
William Jennings Bryan delivered "Cross of Gold" speech July 9; won Democratic Party nomination.

Supreme Court, in *Plessy v. Ferguson*, May 18, approved racial segregation under the **"separate but equal"** doctrine.

John Philip Sousa composed "Stars and Stripes Forever" on Dec. 25.

1897
Olney-Pauncefote Treaty with Britain, Jan. 11, gave wide scope to arbitration in settling disputes; never ratified by U.S.

John J. McDermott won **first Boston Marathon** Apr. 19.

First Klondike gold arrived in San Francisco July 14, helping set off **Klondike gold rush**.

Coal miners' strike settled Sept. 11, after more than 20 miners fired on and killed by officers of law.

1898
U.S. battleship *Maine* blown up Feb. 15 at Havana; 260 killed.

U.S. **blockaded Cuba** Apr. 22 in aid of independence forces. U.S. declared **war on Spain** Apr. 24; destroyed Spanish fleet in **Philippines** May 1; took **Guam** June 20.

U.S. took **Puerto Rico** July 25-Aug. 12. Spain agreed Dec. 10 to cede Philippines, Puerto Rico, and Guam, and approved independence for Cuba.

Annexation of **Hawaii** signed by Pres. William McKinley, July 7.

1899
Filipino insurgents, unable to get recognition of independence from U.S., started guerrilla war Feb. 4. Their leader, Emilio Aguinaldo, captured May 23, **1901**. **Philippine Insurrection** ended **1902**. Killed were 20,000 Filipino troops and some 200,000 civilians, mostly from disease and starvation.

Pres. McKinley signed treaty officially ending **Spanish-America War**, Feb. 10.

U.S. declared **Open Door Policy** Sept. 6, to make China an open international market.

John Dewey published *The School and Society*, advocating "progressive education."

Pianist **Scott Joplin**'s "Maple Leaf Rag" was published, popularizing **ragtime music**.

1900
International Ladies' Garment Workers Union was founded in New York City June 3.

Carry Nation, Kansas temperance leader, began raiding saloons with a hatchet.

U.S. helped suppress **"Boxer Rebellion"** in Beijing.

Eastman Kodak Co. introduced the **Brownie camera**, popularizing picture-taking.

1901
Texas had first significant **oil strike**, Jan. 10.

Pres. **McKinley shot** Sept. 6 in Buffalo, NY, by anarchist Leon Czolgosz; died Sept. 14. Vice Pres. **Theodore Roosevelt** sworn in as **youngest-ever president**, at age 42 years, 11 months.

Booker T. Washington published *Up from Slavery*.

1902
Permanent **Bureau of the Census** established Mar. 6.

U.S. withdrew troops from **Cuba** May 20, and Cuba became independent.

Helen Keller autobiography appeared in serial form.

First Flight, December 17, 1903

1903
Treaty between U.S. and Colombia to have U.S. dig **Panama Canal** signed Jan. 22, rejected by Colombia. Panama declared independence from Colombia with U.S. support Nov. 3; recognized by Pres. Theodore Roosevelt Nov. 6. U.S., Panama signed canal treaty Nov. 18.

Wisconsin set first **direct primary voting system**, May 23.

Henry Ford founded Ford Motor Co., June 16.

Boston defeated Pittsburgh, 5 games to 3, Oct. 13 in the **first modern World Series**.

First successful flight in **heavier-than-air mechanically propelled airplane** by **Orville Wright** Dec. 17 near Kitty Hawk, NC, 120 ft. in 12 secs. Later flight same day by **Wilbur Wright**, 852 ft. in 59 secs. Improved plane patented, **1906**.

Fire in **Iroquois Theater**, Chicago, killed about 600, Dec. 30.

Pioneering film *Great Train Robbery* produced.

1904
St. Louis hosted **first Olympics in U.S.**, July 1-Nov. 23.

First section of **New York subway** system opened, Oct. 27.

Ida Tarbell published muckraking *The History of the Standard Oil Company*.

Henry James's last great novel, *The Golden Bowl* appeared.

1905
Industrial Workers of the World (IWW) founded by radicals in Chicago, June 27.

First **Rotary Club** founded in Chicago.

1906
San Francisco earthquake and fire, Apr. 18-19, left 503 dead, $350 mil damages.

Pure Food and Drug Act and **Meat Inspection Act** both passed June 30.

Upton Sinclair published *The Jungle*.

1907
Financial panic and depression started Mar. 13.

Pres. Roosevelt sent **"Great White Fleet"** of 16 U.S. battleships around the world in show of power.

1908
Springfield, IL, torn by anti-black **rioting**, Aug. 14-15.

Henry Ford introduced **Model T** car, priced at $850, Oct. 1.

1909
Adm. **Robert E. Peary** claimed to have reached **North Pole** Apr. 6 on sixth attempt, accompanied by black explorer Matthew Henson and 4 Inuit; may have fallen short.

National Conference on the Negro convened May 30, leading to founding of **National Association for the Advancement of Colored People** (NAACP).

1910
Boy Scouts of America founded Feb. 8.

Former Pres. Roosevelt called for a **"new nationalism"** in a famous speech in Kansas, Aug. 10.

1911
Building holding New York City's **Triangle Shirtwaist Co. factory** caught fire Mar. 25; 146 died.

Supreme Court dissolved **Standard Oil Co.** May 15.

First transcontinental airplane flight (with numerous stops) by C. P. Rodgers, from New York to Pasadena, CA, Sept. 17-Nov. 5; time in air 82 hrs., 4 mins.

1912
American Girl Guides founded Mar. 12; name changed in **1913** to **Girl Scouts**.

U.S. Marines, Aug. 14, sent to **Nicaragua**, which was in default of loans to U.S. and Europe.

1913
16th Amendment, authorizing federal income tax, ratified Feb. 3.

The **Armory Show** in New York City brought modern art to U.S. for first time, Feb. 17.

17th Amendment, providing for direct popular election of U.S. senators, ratified Apr. 8.

Federal Reserve System was authorized Dec. 23, in a major reform of U.S. banking and finance.

Charles Beard published *Economic Interpretation of the Constitution*.

1914
Ford Motor Co. raised basic wage rates from $2.40 for 9-hr. day to $5 for 8-hr. day, Jan. 5.

When U.S. sailors were arrested at Tampico, Mexico, Apr. 9, Atlantic fleet was sent to **Veracruz**, occupied city.

Pres. Woodrow Wilson proclaimed **U.S. neutrality** in the European war, Aug. 4.

The **Panama Canal** was officially opened Aug. 15.

The **Clayton Antitrust Act** was passed Oct. 15, strengthening federal antimonopoly powers.

Lusitania

1915
First transcontinental telephone call, New York to San Francisco, was completed Jan. 25 by Alexander Graham Bell and Thomas A. Watson.

British ship *Lusitania* sunk May 7 by German submarine; 128 American passengers were lost. (Germany had warned passengers in advance.) As a result of U.S. campaign, Germany issued apology and promise of payments, Oct. 5. Pres. Wilson asked for a military fund increase, Dec. 7.

U.S. troops landed in **Haiti**, July 28. Haiti became a virtual U.S. protectorate under Sept. 16 treaty.

D. W. Griffith's film *The Birth of a Nation* released.

1916
Gen. **John J. Pershing** entered Mexico to pursue **Francisco (Pancho) Villa**, who had raided U.S. border areas. Forces withdrew Feb. 5, **1917**.

Rural Credits Acts passed July 17, followed by **Warehouse Act** Aug. 11; both provided financial aid to farmers.

Bomb exploded during **San Francisco** Preparedness Day parade July 22, killed 10. Thomas J. Mooney, labor organizer, and Warren K. Billings, shoe worker, were convicted **1917**; both later pardoned.

U.S. bought **Virgin Islands** from Denmark Aug. 4.

U.S. established military government in the **Dominican Republic** Nov. 29.

Jeannette Rankin (R-MT) elected as **first-ever female** member of U.S. **House**.

Trade and loans to **European allies** soared during the year.

1917
Germany, suffering from British blockade, declared almost unrestricted **submarine warfare** Jan. 31. U.S. cut diplomatic ties with Germany Feb. 3 and formally **declared war** Apr. 6.

Jones Act, passed Mar. 2, made **Puerto Rico a U.S. territory**, its inhabitants U.S. citizens.

Conscription law was passed May 18. First U.S. troops arrived in Europe June 26.

1918
Pres. Wilson set out his **14 Points** as basis for peace, Jan. 8.

More than 1 mil American troops were in Europe by July. Allied counteroffensive launched at Château-Thierry July 18. War ended with signing of **armistice** Nov. 11.

Influenza epidemic killed an estimated 20 mil worldwide, 548,000 in U.S.

1919
18th Amendment, providing for prohibition of manufacture, sale, or transportation of alcoholic beverages, ratified Jan. 16, to take effect on Jan. 16, **1920**.

First transatlantic flight, by U.S. Navy seaplane, left Rockaway, NY, May 8, stopped at Newfoundland, Azores, Lisbon May 27.

Boston police strike Sept. 9; National Guard breaks strike.

About 250 **alien radicals** were deported Dec. 22.

Sherwood Anderson published *Winesburg, Ohio*.

1920
In national **Red Scare**, some 2,700 Communists, anarchists, and other radicals were arrested Jan.-May.

League of Women Voters founded Feb. 14.

Senate refused Mar. 19 to ratify the **League of Nations Covenant**.

Nicola Sacco and **Bartolomeo Vanzetti** accused of killing 2 men in Massachusetts payroll holdup Apr. 15. Found guilty **1921**. A 6-year campaign for their release failed; both were executed Aug. 23, **1927**. Verdict repudiated **1977**, by proclamation of Gov. Michael Dukakis.

19th Amendment ratified Aug. 18, giving women the vote.

First regular **licensed radio broadcasting** began Aug. 20.

Bombing on New York City's **Wall St.** killed 30, injured 100, did $2 mil damage, Sept. 16.

Sinclair Lewis's *Main Street*, **F. Scott Fitzgerald**'s *This Side of Paradise*, **Edith Wharton**'s *The Age of Innocence* published.

1921
Congress sharply **curbed immigration**, set national quota system May 19.

Joint congressional resolution declaring **peace with Germany, Austria,** and **Hungary** signed July 2 by Pres. Warren G. Harding; treaties were signed in Aug.

In so-called **Black Sox scandal**, 8 Chicago White Sox players were banned from baseball Aug. 4 for conspiring with gamblers to throw the **1919 World Series**.

Limitation of Armaments Conference met in Washington, DC, Nov. 12-Feb. 6, **1922**. Major powers agreed to curtail naval construction, outlaw poison gas, restrict submarine attacks on merchant vessels, and respect China's integrity.

Ku Klux Klan began revival with violence against Catholics in North, South, and Midwest.

1922

Violence during **coal-mine strike** at Herrin, IL, June 22-23 cost 36 lives, including those of 21 nonunion miners.

Reader's Digest founded.

T. S. Eliot's *The Waste Land* published in London.

1923

First sound-on-film motion picture, *Phonofilm*, shown at Rivoli Theater, New York City, beginning in April.

Pres. Calvin Coolidge addressed Congress, Dec. 6; **first official broadcast** of a **presidential speech**.

1924

Law approved by Congress June 15 made all **Native Americans U.S. citizens**.

Nellie Tayloe Ross elected governor of Wyoming Nov. 9; inaugurated as nation's **first female governor** Jan. 5, **1925**. **Miriam (Ma) Ferguson** elected governor of Texas Nov. 9; installed Jan. 20, **1925**.

George Gershwin wrote *Rhapsody in Blue*.

1925

John T. Scopes found guilty of having taught **evolution** in Dayton, TN, high school, fined $100 and costs, July 24.

F. Scott Fitzgerald's *The Great Gatsby* published.

1926

Dr. **Robert H. Goddard** demonstrated practicality of rockets Mar. 16 in Auburn, MA, with **first liquid-fuel rocket**; rocket traveled 184 ft. in 2.5 secs.

Congress established **Army Air Corps** July 2.

Air Commerce Act passed Nov. 2, providing federal aid for airlines and airports.

Ernest Hemingway's *The Sun Also Rises* published.

1927

About 1,000 **Marines landed in China** Mar. 5 to protect property in civil war.

Capt. **Charles A. Lindbergh** left Roosevelt Field, NY, May 20 alone in *Spirit of St. Louis* on first New York-Paris nonstop flight. Reached Le Bourget airfield May 21, 3,610 mi. in 33½ hrs.

The Jazz Singer, with **Al Jolson**, demonstrated part-talking pictures in New York City Oct. 6.

Show Boat opened in New York Dec. 27.

Charles A. Lindbergh   Ameilia Earhart

1928

Amelia Earhart became first woman to fly across the Atlantic, June 17.

Herbert Hoover elected president Nov. 6, defeating New York Gov. **Alfred E. Smith**, a Catholic.

1929

Gangsters killed 7 rivals in Chicago **"St. Valentine's Day massacre"** Feb. 14.

Farm price stability aided by **Agricultural Marketing Act,** passed June 15.

Albert B. Fall, former secretary of the interior, was convicted of accepting $10,000 bribe in the leasing of the **Elk Hills (Teapot Dome)** naval oil reserve; sentenced Nov. 1 to a year in prison and fined.

Stock market crash Oct. 29 marked end of past prosperity as stock prices plummeted. Stock losses for **1929-31** estimated at $50 bil; beginning of **Great Depression**.

Thomas Wolfe published *Look Homeward, Angel*. **William Faulkner** published *The Sound and the Fury*.

1930

London **Naval Reduction Treaty** signed by U.S., Britain, Italy, France, and Japan Apr. 22; in effect Jan. 1, **1931**; expired Dec. 31, **1936.**

Hawley-Smoot Tariff signed; rate hikes slash world trade.

Sinclair Lewis became the **first American** to win a **Nobel Prize in literature**.

1931

Empire State Building opened in New York City May 1.

Al Capone was convicted of tax evasion Oct. 17.

Pearl Buck published *The Good Earth*.

1932

Reconstruction Finance Corp. established Jan. 22 to stimulate banking and business. Unemployment at 12 mil.

Nineteenth-month-old **Charles Lindbergh Jr.** was kidnapped Mar. 1; found dead May 12. Bruno Hauptmann found guilty in trial Jan.-Feb. **1935**; executed Apr. 3, **1936**.

World War I veterans demanding Congress pay their bonus in full launched **Bonus March** on Washington, DC, May 29.

Franklin D. Roosevelt elected president for the first time in Democratic landslide, Nov. 8.

Chicago Bears won **first NFL title game** Dec. 18, defeating the Portsmouth (OH) Spartans, 9-0.

1933

Pres. Roosevelt named **Frances Perkins** U.S. secretary of labor; **first woman** in **U.S. cabinet**.

Pres. Roosevelt ordered **all U.S. banks closed** Mar. 6.

In a "100 days" special session, Mar. 9-June 16, Congress passed **New Deal**, including measures to regulate banks, distribute funds to the jobless, create jobs, raise agricultural prices, and set wage and production standards for industry.

Tennessee Valley Authority created by act of Congress, May 18.

Gold standard dropped by U.S.; announced by Pres. Roosevelt Apr. 19, ratified by Congress June 5.

Prohibition ended in the U.S. as 36th state ratified **21st Amendment** Dec. 5.

Pres. Roosevelt foreswore armed intervention in **Western Hemisphere** nations, Dec. 26.

1934

Pres. Roosevelt signed law creating the **Securities and Exchange Commission**, June 6.

U.S. troops pulled out of **Haiti**, Aug. 6.

1935

Boulder Dam (later renamed **Hoover Dam**) completed, May 29.

Works Progress Administration (**WPA**) instituted May 6. Rural Electrification Administration created May 11. National Industrial Recovery Act struck down by Supreme Court May 27.

Comedian **Will Rogers** and aviator Wiley Post killed Aug. 15 in Alaska plane crash.

Social Security Act passed by Congress Aug. 14.

Huey Long, Louisiana senator and national political leader, shot Sept. 8; died Sept. 10.

George Gershwin's *Porgy and Bess* opened Oct. 10 in New York.

Committee for Industrial Organization (CIO; later Congress of Industrial Organizations) formed to expand industrial unionism Nov. 9.

1936

Jesse Owens won 4 gold medals at the **Berlin Olympics** in August.

Baseball Hall of Fame founded in Cooperstown, NY.

Margaret Mitchell published *Gone with the Wind*.

Jesse Owens

1937

Hindenburg exploded May 6 as it was landing in Lakehurst, NJ.

Golden Gate Bridge opened, May 27.

Joe Louis knocked out James J. Braddock to become world heavyweight champ June 22.

Aviator **Amelia Earhart** and copilot Fred Noonan disappeared July 2 near Howland Island, in the Pacific.

Pres. Roosevelt asked for 6 additional Supreme Court justices; **"packing" plan** defeated.

Auto, steel labor unions won first big contracts.

1938
Naval Expansion Act passed May 17.
National minimum wage enacted June 25.
Orson Welles radio dramatization of *War of the Worlds*, Oct. 30, caused Martian invasion scare.
Seabiscuit beat War Admiral in match race of the century, at Pimlico track, MD, Nov. 1.
Artist **"Grandma Moses"** discovered.
Thornton Wilder's *Our Town* produced on Broadway.

1939
New York World's Fair opened Apr. 30, closed Oct. 31; reopened May 11, **1940**, ended Oct. 21.
Lou Gehrig, seriously ill, said farewell to fans at Yankee Stadium, July 4.
Albert Einstein alerted Pres. Roosevelt to **A-bomb** possibilities in Aug. 2 letter.
U.S. declared its neutrality in European war Sept. 5.
Roosevelt proclaimed a limited **national emergency** Sept. 8, an unlimited emergency May 27, **1941**. Both ended by Pres. Harry Truman, Apr. 28, **1952**.
John Steinbeck published *The Grapes of Wrath*.
Pocket books appeared in U.S.
Film versions of *Gone with the Wind* and *The Wizard of Oz* released.

1940
U.S. OK'd sale of **surplus war material** to Britain June 3; announced transfer of 50 overaged destroyers Sept. 3.
First peacetime military draft in U.S. history approved, Sept. 14.
Forty-hour work week went into effect, Oct. 24.
Roosevelt elected Nov. 5 to third presidential term.
Richard Wright published *Native Son*.

1941
Four Freedoms—freedom of speech and religion, freedom from want and fear—termed essential by Pres. Roosevelt in speech to Congress Jan. 6.
Lend-Lease Act signed Mar. 11 provided $7 bil in military credits for Britain. Lend-lease for USSR approved in Nov.
The **Atlantic Charter**, 8-point declaration of principles, issued by Roosevelt and British Prime Min. Winston Churchill, Aug. 14.
Japan attacked **Pearl Harbor**, Hawaii, 7:55 AM Hawaiian time, Dec. 7; 19 ships sunk or damaged, 2,300 dead. Roosevelt called it "a date that will live in infamy." U.S. declared war on Japan Dec. 8, on Germany and Italy Dec. 11.
Japanese invaded Philippines, Dec. 22; Wake Island fell, Dec. 23.

1942
Japanese troops took **Bataan** peninsula Apr. 8, took **Corregidor** May 6.
Federal government forcibly moved 110,000 **Japanese-Americans** from West Coast to **detention camps**. Exclusion lasted 3 years.
Battle of Midway June 4-7 was Japan's first major defeat.
Marines landed on **Guadalcanal** Aug. 7; last Japanese not expelled until Feb. 9, **1943**.
U.S., Britain invaded **North Africa** Nov. 8.
First nuclear chain reaction (fission of uranium isotope U-235) produced at Univ. of Chicago under physicists Arthur Compton, Enrico Fermi, others, Dec. 2.

1943
Oklahoma! opened Mar. 31 on Broadway.
War contractors barred from **racial discrimination**, May 27.
Pres. Roosevelt signed June 10 pay-as-you-go income tax bill. Starting July 1, wage and salary earners were subject to a **paycheck withholding tax**.
Race riot in **Detroit** June 21; 34 dead, 700 injured. Six killed in riot in New York City's **Harlem** section Aug. 2.
U.S., Britain invaded **Sicily** July 9, Italian **mainland** Sept. 3.
Marines in Nov. recaptured the **Gilbert Islands**, captured by Japan in **1941** and **1942**.

1944
U.S., Allied forces invaded Europe at **Normandy**, France, on **"D Day,"** June 6, in greatest amphibious landing in history.
Battle of the Bulge, failed Nazi counteroffensive, waged Dec. 16 to Jan. 28, **1945**; 500,000 Americans fought.

GI Bill of Rights, providing benefits to veterans, signed by Pres. Roosevelt June 22.
Representatives of the U.S. and other major powers met at **Dumbarton Oaks**, Washington, DC, Aug. 21-Oct. 7, to work out formation of postwar world organization that became the **United Nations**.
U.S. forces landed on **Leyte**, Philippines, Oct. 20.
Roosevelt elected to fourth term as president Nov. 7.

Omaha Beach, June 6, 1944

1945
Yalta Conference met in the Crimea, USSR, Feb. 4-11. Roosevelt, Churchill, and Soviet leader Joseph Stalin agreed that their 3 countries, plus France, would occupy Germany and that the Soviet Union would enter war against Japan.
Marines landed on **Iwo Jima** Feb. 19, won control Mar. 16 after heavy casualties. U.S. forces invaded **Okinawa** Apr. 1, captured it June 21.
Pres. **Roosevelt** died in Warm Springs, GA, Apr. 12; Vice Pres. **Harry S. Truman** became president.
Germany surrendered May 7; May 8 proclaimed **V-E Day**.
First atomic bomb, produced at Los Alamos, NM, exploded at Alamogordo, NM, July 16. Bomb dropped on **Hiroshima** Aug. 6, killing about 75,000; bomb dropped on **Nagasaki** Aug. 9, killing about 40,000. Japan agreed to surrender Aug. 14; formally surrendered Sept. 2.
Empire State Building struck accidentally by Army B-25 bomber, July 28, killing 13.
At **Potsdam Conference**, July 17-Aug. 2, leaders of U.S., USSR, and Britain agreed on disarmament of Germany, occupation zones, war crimes trials.
U.S. forces entered **Korea** south of 38th parallel to displace Japanese Sept. 8.
Gen. **Douglas MacArthur** took over supervision of Japan Sept. 9.

1946
Steel strike by 750,000 started Jan. 21, settled in 4 weeks. Strike by 400,000 **mine workers** began Apr. 1 (settled May 29); other industries followed.
Winston Churchill employed the phrase **"iron curtain"** in Mar. 5 speech at Fulton, MO, college.
Atomic bomb tested off **Bikini Atoll** in Pacific, July 1.
Philippines given independence by U.S. July 4.
Mother Frances Xavier Cabrini first American to be canonized, July 7.
Dr. **Benjamin Spock**'s *Baby and Child Care* published as **baby boom** began.

1947
Pres. Truman asked Congress for financial and military aid for Greece and Turkey to help combat Communist subversion **(Truman Doctrine)**, Mar. 12. Approved May 15.
UN Security Council voted Apr. 2 to place under **U.S. trusteeship** the **Pacific islands** formerly mandated to Japan.
Jackie Robinson joined the Brooklyn Dodgers Apr. 11, breaking the color barrier in major league baseball.
The **Marshall Plan** for U.S. aid to European countries was proposed by Sec. of State George C. Marshall June 5. Congress authorized some $12 bil in next 4 years.
Taft-Hartley Labor Act restricting labor union power was vetoed by Truman June 20; Congress overrode the veto.
Air Force Capt. **Chuck Yeager** broke the sound barrier, Oct. 14, in X-1 rocket plane.

1948
USSR halted all surface traffic into **West Berlin** June 23; in response, U.S. and British troops launched an **airlift**. Soviet blockade halted May 12, **1949**; airlift ended Sept. 30.
Organization of American States founded Apr. 30.
Alger Hiss indicted Dec. 15 for perjury, after denying he had passed secret documents to Whittaker Chambers to go to a **Communist spy ring**. Convicted Jan. 21, **1950**.
Pres. **Truman** elected Nov. 2, defeating Gov. Thomas E. Dewey in a historic upset.
Kinsey Report on sexuality in the human male published.

1949

North Atlantic Treaty Organization (**NATO**) established Aug. 24 by U.S., Canada, and 10 Western European nations, agreeing that an armed attack against one would be considered an attack against all.

Eleven leaders of **U.S. Communist Party** convicted Oct. 14 of advocating violent overthrow of U.S. government; sentenced to prison. Supreme Court upheld convictions **1951**.

Pres. Truman Oct. 26 signed legislation raising **federal minimum wage** from 40¢ an hour to 75¢.

Arthur Miller's *Death of a Salesman* opened on Broadway.

1950

Masked bandits robbed **Brink's, Inc.**, Boston express office, Jan. 17 of $2.8 mil. Case solved **1956**; 8 sentenced to life.

Pres. Truman authorized production of the **H-bomb** Jan. 31.

North Korean forces **invaded South Korea** June 25. UN asked for troops to restore peace. Truman ordered Air Force and Navy to Korea June 27. Truman approved ground forces, air strikes against **North Korea** June 30.

U.S. sent 35 military advisers to **South Vietnam** June 27 and agreed to aid anti-Communist government.

Army seized all railroads Aug. 27 on Truman's order to prevent a general strike; returned to owners in **1952**.

U.S. forces landed at **Inchon**, South Korea, Sept. 15. UN forces took Pyongyang Oct. 20, reached China border Nov. 20; China sent troops across border Nov. 26.

Two members of **Puerto Rican nationalist movement** tried to kill Pres. Truman Nov. 1.

U.S. **banned shipments** Dec. 8 to Communist **China** and to Asiatic ports trading with it.

Your Show of Shows debuted on TV.

Peanuts comic strip appeared.

David Riesman's *The Lonely Crowd* published.

1951

Sen. **Estes Kefauver** led Senate probe into organized crime.

22nd Amendment, limiting presidential term of office, ratified Feb. 27.

Julius Rosenberg, his wife, **Ethel**, and Morton Sobell found guilty Mar. 29 of conspiracy to commit wartime **espionage**. Rosenbergs received death penalty. Sobell sentenced to 30 years; released **1969**.

Pres. Truman removed Gen. **Douglas MacArthur** from Korea command Apr. 11 for unauthorized policy statements.

Korea cease-fire talks began in July; lasted 2 years. Fighting ended July 27, **1953**.

The U.S., Australia, and New Zealand signed **ANZUS** mutual security pact Sept. 1.

Transcontinental TV began Sept. 4 with Pres. Truman's address at Japanese Peace Treaty Conference in San Francisco.

Japanese peace treaty signed in San Francisco Sept. 8 by U.S., Japan, and 47 other nations.

J. D. Salinger published *Catcher in the Rye*.

1952

Pres. Truman ordered the **seizure** of the **nation's steel mills** Apr. 8 to avert a strike. Ruled illegal by Supreme Court June 2.

Peace contract between West Germany, U.S., Great Britain, and France was signed May 26.

The last racial and ethnic barriers to naturalization removed, June 26-27, with passage of **Immigration and Naturalization Act** of **1952**.

Richard Nixon, as vice-pres. candidate, gave **"Checkers" speech**, Sept. 23.

Puerto Rico proclaimed **commonwealth** July 25, after referendum Mar. 3.

First hydrogen device explosion Nov. 1 in Pacific.

1953

Federal jury in New York convicted 13 **Communist** leaders on conspiracy charges, Jan. 20.

Julius and **Ethel Rosenberg** executed in the Sing Sing Prison electric chair, Ossining, NY, June 19, for relaying nuclear secrets to Soviet Union.

Korean War armistice signed July 27.

California Gov. **Earl Warren** was sworn in Oct. 5 as 14th **chief justice** of U.S. Supreme Court.

1954

Nautilus, **first atomic-powered submarine**, was launched at Groton, CT, Jan. 21.

Five **members of Congress** were **wounded** in the House Mar. 1 by 4 **Puerto Rican independence supporters** who fired at random from a spectators' gallery.

At televised **Army-McCarthy hearings**, Apr. 22-June 17, before a Senate subcommittee, Army officials accused Sen. **Joseph McCarthy** (R-WI) of seeking preferential treatment for a draftee, and McCarthy accused the Army of hindering probe of Communist infiltration into the Army. Senate voted to condemn Sen. McCarthy, 67-22, for abuse of the Senate during hearings and debates.

Racial segregation in public schools unanimously ruled unconstitutional by Supreme Court May 17, in *Brown v. Board of Education of Topeka*.

Southeast Asia Treaty Organization (SEATO) formed by defense pact signed in Manila Sept. 8 by U.S., Britain, Australia, New Zealand, Philippines, Pakistan, and Thailand.

Ernest Hemingway won Nobel Prize.

1955

U.S. agreed Feb. 12 to help train **South Vietnamese** army.

Supreme Court ordered **"all deliberate speed"** in **integration** of public schools, May 31.

A **summit meeting** of U.S., Britain, France, and USSR leaders took place July 18-23 in Geneva, Switzerland.

Rosa Parks refused Dec. 1 to give her seat to a white man on a bus in Montgomery, AL. Bus segregation ordinance declared unconstitutional by a federal court, in **1956**, following a**boycott** organized by Rev. **Martin Luther King Jr.**

Rosa Parks

America's 2 largest labor organizations merged Dec. 5, creating the **AFL-CIO**.

1956

Massive resistance to **Supreme Court desegregation rulings** was called for Mar. 12 by 101 Southern congressmen.

U.S. Supreme Court, Apr. 23, unanimously ruled against **racial segregation** on intrastate buses.

Federal-Aid Highway Act signed June 29, creating **interstate highway system**.

First transatlantic telephone cable activated Sept. 25.

On Oct. 8, in Game 5, Yankee right-hander Don Larsen pitched the **only World Series perfect game**.

My Fair Lady opened on Broadway in March. Eugene O'Neill's *Long Day's Journey into Night* opened in November.

1957

Congress approved **first civil rights bill** for blacks since Reconstruction, Apr. 29, to protect voting rights.

The U.S. surgeon general July 12 said studies showed a **"direct link"** between cigarette **smoking** and **lung cancer**.

Arkansas Gov. Orval Faubus called National Guardsmen Sept. 4 to bar 9 black students from entering all-white high school in **Little Rock**. Faubus complied Sept. 21 with federal court order to remove Guardsmen, but local authorities ordered black students to withdraw. Pres. Eisenhower sent troops Sept. 24 to enforce court order.

Jack Kerouac published *On the Road*.

1958

Army launched **first U.S. Earth-orbiting satellite**, *Explorer I*, Jan. 31 from Cape Canaveral, FL; discovered Van Allen radiation belt.

U.S. Marines sent to **Lebanon** to protect elected government from threatened overthrow July-Oct.

Nuclear sub *Nautilus* made **first undersea crossing** of the **North Pole** Aug. 5.

Presidential aide **Sherman Adams** resigned Sept. 22 over a scandal involving alleged improper gifts.

First domestic jet airline passenger service in U.S. opened by National Airlines Dec. 10 between New York and Miami.

1959

Alaska admitted as 49th state, Jan. 3; **Hawaii** admitted as 50th, Aug. 21.

St. Lawrence Seaway opened Apr. 25.

Vice Pres. **Richard Nixon**, on tour of USSR, held "kitchen debate," July 24, with Soviet Prem. **Nikita Khrushchev** at U.S. exhibit in Moscow.

Prem. **Khrushchev** paid unprecedented visit to U.S. Sept. 15-27; made transcontinental tour.

Pres. Eisenhower issued an injunction Oct. 12, upheld and made effective by the Supreme Court Nov. 7, ending a **record 116-day steel strike**.

In a **quiz show scandal**, Columbia Univ. Prof. Charles Van Doren admitted to a U.S. House subcommittee Nov. 2 that he had been coached before appearances on NBC-TV's *21* in **1956**; he had won $129,000.

1960

Sit-ins began Feb. 1 when 4 black college students in Greensboro, NC, refused to move from a Woolworth lunch counter after being denied service. By Sept. **1961** over 70,000 students, whites and blacks, had participated in sit-ins.

Congress approved a strong **voting rights act** Apr. 21.

A U.S. **U-2 reconnaissance plane** was shot down in the Soviet Union May 1; pilot Gary Powers captured. The incident led to cancellation of a Paris summit conference.

Vice Pres. **Richard Nixon** and Sen. **John F. Kennedy** faced each other Sept. 26 in the first in a series of televised debates. Kennedy defeated Nixon to win presidency, Nov. 8.

U.S. announced Dec. 15 its backing of rightist group in **Laos**, which took power the next day.

1961

U.S. severed diplomatic and consular relations with **Cuba** Jan. 3, after disputes over nationalizations of U.S. firms, U.S. military presence at Guantanamo base. U.S.-directed invasion of Cuba's **Bay of Pigs** Apr. 17 by Cuban exiles unsuccessfully attempted to overthrow the regime of Prem. **Fidel Castro**.

Peace Corps created by executive order, Mar. 1.

23rd Amendment, giving **DC** citizens the right to vote in presidential elections, ratified Mar. 29.

Comdr. **Alan B. Shepard Jr.** rocketed from Cape Canaveral, FL, in a Mercury capsule May 5, in **first U.S.-crewed suborbital space flight**.

"Freedom Rides" from Washington, DC, across Deep South were launched May 20 to protest segregation in interstate transportation.

Pres. Kennedy, May 27, signed bill creating **Alliance for Progress** for Latin America.

John Updike's *Rabbit, Run* published.

1962

Lt. Col. **John H. Glenn Jr.** became **first American in orbit** Feb. 20 when he circled the Earth 3 times in the Mercury capsule *Friendship 7*.

Pres. Kennedy said Feb. 14 that U.S. military advisers in **Vietnam** would fire if fired upon.

In *Baker v. Carr*, Mar. 26, Supreme Court backed **"one-man one-vote"** apportionment of seats in state legislatures.

James Meredith became first black student at Univ. of Mississippi Oct. 1 after 3,000 troops put down riots.

A Soviet **offensive missile buildup** in **Cuba** was revealed Oct. 22 by Pres. Kennedy, who ordered a naval and air quarantine on shipment of offensive military equipment to the island. He and Soviet Prem. Khrushchev agreed Oct. 28 on formula to end crisis. Kennedy announced Nov. 2 that missile bases in Cuba were being dismantled.

Rachel Carson's *Silent Spring* launched environmentalist movement.

1963

In *Gideon v. Wainwright*, Mar. 18, Supreme Court ruled that all **criminal defendants** must have counsel.

University of Alabama **desegregated** after Gov. **George Wallace** stepped aside when confronted by federally deployed National Guard troops June 11.

Civil rights leader **Medgar Evers** assassinated June 12.

Supreme Court ruled June 17 that laws requiring **recitation** of the **Lord's Prayer** or **Bible** verses in public schools were unconstitutional.

Pres. **Kennedy**, on Europe trip, addressed huge crowd in **West Berlin**, June 23.

A limited **nuclear test-ban treaty** was agreed upon July 25 by the U.S., the Soviet Union, and Britain.

March for civil rights begun May 2 in Birmingham, AL, led to desegregation accord, which in turn sparked rioting and violence.

On Aug. 28, 200,000 joined in **March on Washington** in support of black demands for **equal rights** led by Rev. **Martin Luther King Jr.**; highlight was King's "I have a dream" speech.

Four black girls killed in bombing of **16th St. Baptist Church** in Birmingham, AL, Sept. 15.

South Vietnam Pres. **Ngo Dinh Diem assassinated** Nov. 2; U.S. had earlier withdrawn support.

Pres. **Kennedy shot** and fatally wounded Nov. 22 as he rode in a motorcade through downtown Dallas, TX. Vice Pres. **Lyndon B. Johnson** sworn in as president. **Lee Harvey Oswald** was arrested and charged with the murder; Oswald was shot and fatally wounded Nov. 24. Nightclub owner **Jack Ruby** was convicted of Oswald's murder; he died in **1967** while awaiting retrial following reversal of his conviction.

Betty Friedan's *Feminine Mystique* was published.

The Beatles

1964

Panama suspended relations with U.S. Jan. 9 after riots. U.S. offered Dec. 18 to negotiate a new canal treaty.

The Beatles arrived in U.S. for first time, appeared Feb. 9 on the *Ed Sullivan Show*.

Supreme Court ordered Feb. 17 that **congressional districts** have equal populations.

U.S. reported May 27 it was sending military planes to **Laos**.

Three **civil rights workers** were reported missing in Mississippi June 22; bodies found Aug. 4. Twenty-one white men were arrested. On Oct. 20, **1967**, an all-white federal jury convicted 7 of conspiracy in the slayings.

Omnibus **civil rights bill** signed by Pres. Johnson July 2, banning discrimination in voting, jobs, public accommodations.

Congress Aug. 7 passed the **Tonkin Gulf Resolution**, authorizing presidential action in Vietnam, after North Vietnamese boats reportedly attacked 2 U.S. destroyers Aug. 2.

Congress approved **War on Poverty** bill Aug. 11, providing for a domestic Peace Corps (**VISTA**), a **Job Corps**, and antipoverty funding.

The **Warren Commission** released Sept. 27 a report concluding that Lee Harvey Oswald was solely responsible for the Kennedy assassination.

Pres. **Johnson** was elected to a full term, Nov. 3, defeating Sen. **Barry Goldwater** (R-AZ) in a landslide.

Verrazano-Narrows Bridge opened in New York City Nov. 21.

1965

In State of the Union address Jan. 4, Pres. Johnson outlined plans for his **"Great Society."**

Pres. Johnson in Feb. ordered continuous **bombing of North Vietnam** below 20th parallel.

Malcolm X assassinated Feb. 21 at New York City rally.

March from Selma to Montgomery, AL, began Mar. 21 by Rev. Martin Luther King Jr. to demand federal protection of **blacks' voting rights**. New **Voting Rights Act** signed Aug. 6.

Some 14,000 U.S. troops sent to **Dominican Republic** during civil war Apr. 28. All troops withdrawn by next year.

Bill establishing **Medicare**, government health insurance program for elderly, signed by Pres. Johnson July 30.

Riot by blacks living in **Watts** section of Los Angeles resulted in 34 deaths and $200 mil in property damage Aug. 11-16.

National **immigration quota system** abolished Oct. 3.

Electric power failure blacked out most of northeastern U.S., parts of 2 Canadian provinces the night of Nov. 9-10.

1966

U.S. forces began firing into **Cambodia** May 1.

Bombing of Hanoi area of North Vietnam by U.S. planes began June 29. By Dec. 31, 385,300 U.S. troops were stationed in South Vietnam, plus 60,000 offshore and 33,000 in Thailand.

Supreme Court ruled June 13, in *Miranda v. Arizona*, that suspects must be read their rights before police questioning.

Medicare began July 1.

Charles Whitman, killed 13 students from a tower at the Univ. of Texas, Austin, Aug. 1, before being shot dead by police.

Dept. of Transportation created, Oct. 15.

Edward Brooke (R-MA) elected Nov. 8 as **first black U.S. senator** in 85 years.

Robert C. Weaver named secretary of newly created Dept. of Housing and Urban Development (**HUD**), becoming **first black cabinet member**.

1967

Green Bay Packers beat Kansas City Chiefs, 35-10, in **first Super Bowl**, Jan. 15 in Los Angeles.

Black U.S. Rep. **Adam Clayton Powell** (D-NY) was denied his seat Mar. 1 because of charges he misused government funds. Reelected in **1968**, he was seated, but fined and stripped of his seniority.

Pres. **Johnson** and Soviet Prem. **Aleksei Kosygin** met June 23 and 25 at **Glassboro State College** in New Jersey; agreed not to let any crisis push them into war.

25th Amendment, providing for presidential succession, was ratified Feb. 10.

Riots by blacks in **Newark** NJ, July 12-17 killed 26, injured 1,500; more than 1,000 arrested. In **Detroit**, MI, July 23-30, 43 died, 2,000 injured, 5,000 left homeless by rioting, looting, and burning in city's black neighborhoods.

An **antiwar march** on Washington, DC, Oct. 21-22, drew 50,000 participants.

Thurgood Marshall was sworn in Oct. 2 as **first black** U.S. **Supreme Court justice**.

Carl B. Stokes (D, Cleveland) and **Richard G. Hatcher** (D, Gary, IN) were elected **first black mayors** of **major U.S. cities** Nov. 7.

Thurgood Marshall

Martin Luther King Jr.

1968

In **"Tet offensive,"** Communist troops attacked several provincial capitals and other major cities, including Saigon, Jan. 30, but suffered heavy casualties.

Pres. Johnson **curbed bombing** of North Vietnam Mar. 31. Peace talks began in Paris May 10. All bombing of North halted Oct. 31.

Rev. **Martin Luther King Jr. assassinated** Apr. 4 in Memphis, TN. **James Earl Ray**, an escaped convict, pleaded guilty to the slaying, was sentenced to 99 years.

Students at **Columbia Univ.**, Apr. 23-24, seized school buildings in protest demonstrations.

Sen. **Robert F. Kennedy** (D-NY) **shot** June 5 in Los Angeles after celebrating presidential primary victories. Died June 6. Sirhan Bishara Sirhan convicted of murder, **1969**; death sentence commuted to life in prison, **1972**.

Democrats nominated Vice Pres. **Hubert Humphrey** for president at **convention in Chicago**, marked by clash between police and **antiwar protesters**, Aug. 26-29. The Republican nominee, **Richard Nixon**, won the **presidency**, defeating Humphrey in a close race Nov. 5.

Apollo 8 **orbited moon** in 5-day mission, Dec. 21-27.

USS *Pueblo* and 83-man crew seized in Sea of Japan Jan. 23 by North Koreans; 82 men released Dec. 22.

1969

Expanded 4-party **Vietnam peace talks** began Jan. 18. U.S. force peaked at 543,400 in April. Withdrawal started July 8. Pres. Nixon set Vietnamization policy Nov. 3.

Earl Warren retired upon swearing in **Warren Burger**, June 23, as Supreme Court chief justice.

U.S. astronaut **Neil Armstrong**, commander of the *Apollo 11* mission, became the **first person** to **set foot on the moon**, July 20, followed by astronaut **Edwin "Buzz" Aldrin**. Astronaut **Michael Collins** remained aboard command module.

Woodstock music festival near Bethel, NY, drew 300,000-500,000 people, Aug. 15-18.

Anti-Vietnam War demonstrations held in cities across the U.S., marking Vietnam Moratorium day, Oct. 15; on Nov. 15, some 250,000 marched in Washington, DC.

Massacre of hundreds of civilians by U.S. troops at **My Lai**, South Vietnam, in **1968** reported Nov. 16.

Sesame Street launched on public TV.

1970

A federal jury Feb. 18 found the **"Chicago 7"** antiwar activists innocent of conspiring to incite riots during the **1968 Democratic National Convention**. However, 5 were convicted of crossing state lines with intent to incite riots.

Millions of Americans participated in antipollution demonstrations Apr. 22 to mark the **first Earth Day**.

U.S. and South Vietnamese forces crossed **Cambodian** borders Apr. 30 to get at enemy bases.

Four students were killed May 4 at **Kent State** Univ. in Ohio by National Guardsmen during a war protest. In protest at **Jackson State** Univ. in Mississippi, 2 were killed when police fired on protesters.

Two **female generals**, the **first** in U.S. history, were named by Pres. Nixon May 15.

A **postal reform** measure signed Aug. 12 created an independent U.S. Postal Service.

Pres. Nixon, Dec. 31, signed **clean air bill** calling for development of a cleaner auto engine and national air quality standards for 10 major pollutants.

Doonesbury comic strip launched in 30 papers.

1971

Charles Manson and 3 of his cult followers were found guilty Jan. 25 of first-degree murder in **1969** slaying of actress Sharon Tate and 6 others.

Pres. Nixon, Apr. 14, relaxed 20-year **trade embargo** with **China**.

26th Amendment, lowering the voting age to 18 in all elections, was ratified June 30.

A court-martial jury Mar. 29 convicted Lt. **William L. Calley Jr.** in murder of 22 South Vietnamese at **My Lai** on Mar. 16, **1968**. He was sentenced to life in prison Mar. 31, later reduced to 20 years.

New York Times began publishing June 13 classified **Pentagon papers** on U.S. involvement in Vietnam. Supreme Court June 30 upheld, 6-3, the right of the *Times* and *Washington Post* to publish the documents.

Pres. Nixon, Aug. 15, instituted a 90-day **wage and price freeze**.

U.S. bombers initiated massive 5-day strike Dec. 26 in North Vietnam in retaliation for alleged violations of agreements reached prior to the **1968** bombing halt.

1972

Pres. Nixon arrived in **Beijing** Feb. 21 for an 8-day visit to China, in a "journey for peace;" a joint communiqué released Feb. 27 called for increased Sino-U.S. contracts.

By a 84-8 vote, the Senate, Mar. 22, approved the **Equal Rights Amendment** banning discrimination on the basis of sex and sent the measure to the states for ratification.

North Vietnamese forces launched the biggest attacks in 4 years across the demilitarized zone Mar. 30. The U.S. responded Apr. 15 with resumption of bombing of Hanoi and Haiphong after a 4-year lull. Pres. Nixon announced May 8 the **mining** of **North Vietnam ports**. Last U.S. combat troops left Aug. 11.

Gov. **George C. Wallace** (AL), campaigning for president at a Laurel, MD, shopping center May 15, was **shot** and seriously wounded. **Arthur Bremer** convicted Aug. 4, sentenced to 63 years for shooting Wallace and 3 others.

In **first visit** of a **U.S. president to Moscow**, Pres. Nixon arrived May 22 for summit talks with Kremlin leaders that culminated in a landmark strategic arms pact (**SALT I**).

Five men were arrested June 17 for breaking into the Democratic National Committee offices in the **Watergate** office complex in Washington, DC.

Supreme Court in *Furman v. Georgia* June 29 ruled **capital punishment** as currently practiced was unconstitutional.

Mark Spitz won 7 gold medals in world record times at the Munich Olympics in September.

Pres. **Nixon** was reelected Nov. 7 in a landslide, carrying 49 states to defeat Sen. George McGovern (D-SD).

The **Dow Jones** Industrial Average closed above 1,000 for the first time, Nov. 14.

Full-scale **bombing of North Vietnam** resumed after Paris peace negotiations reached an impasse Dec. 18.

AFGHANISTAN	ALBANIA	ALGERIA	ANDORRA	ANGOLA

ANTIGUA AND BARBUDA	ARGENTINA	ARMENIA	AUSTRALIA	AUSTRIA

AZERBAIJAN	THE BAHAMAS	BAHRAIN	BANGLADESH	BARBADOS

BELARUS	BELGIUM	BELIZE	BENIN	BHUTAN

BOLIVIA	BOSNIA AND HERZEGOVINA	BOTSWANA	BRAZIL	BRUNEI

BULGARIA	BURKINA FASO	BURUNDI	CAMBODIA	CAMEROON

CANADA	CAPE VERDE	CENTRAL AFRICAN REPUBLIC	CHAD	CHILE

CHINA	COLOMBIA	COMOROS	CONGO, DEM. REP. OF THE	CONGO REPUBLIC

COSTA RICA	CÔTE D'IVOIRE	CROATIA	CUBA	CYPRUS

CZECH REPUBLIC	DENMARK	DJIBOUTI	DOMINICA	DOMINICAN REPUBLIC

ECUADOR	EGYPT	EL SALVADOR	EQUATORIAL GUINEA	ERITREA

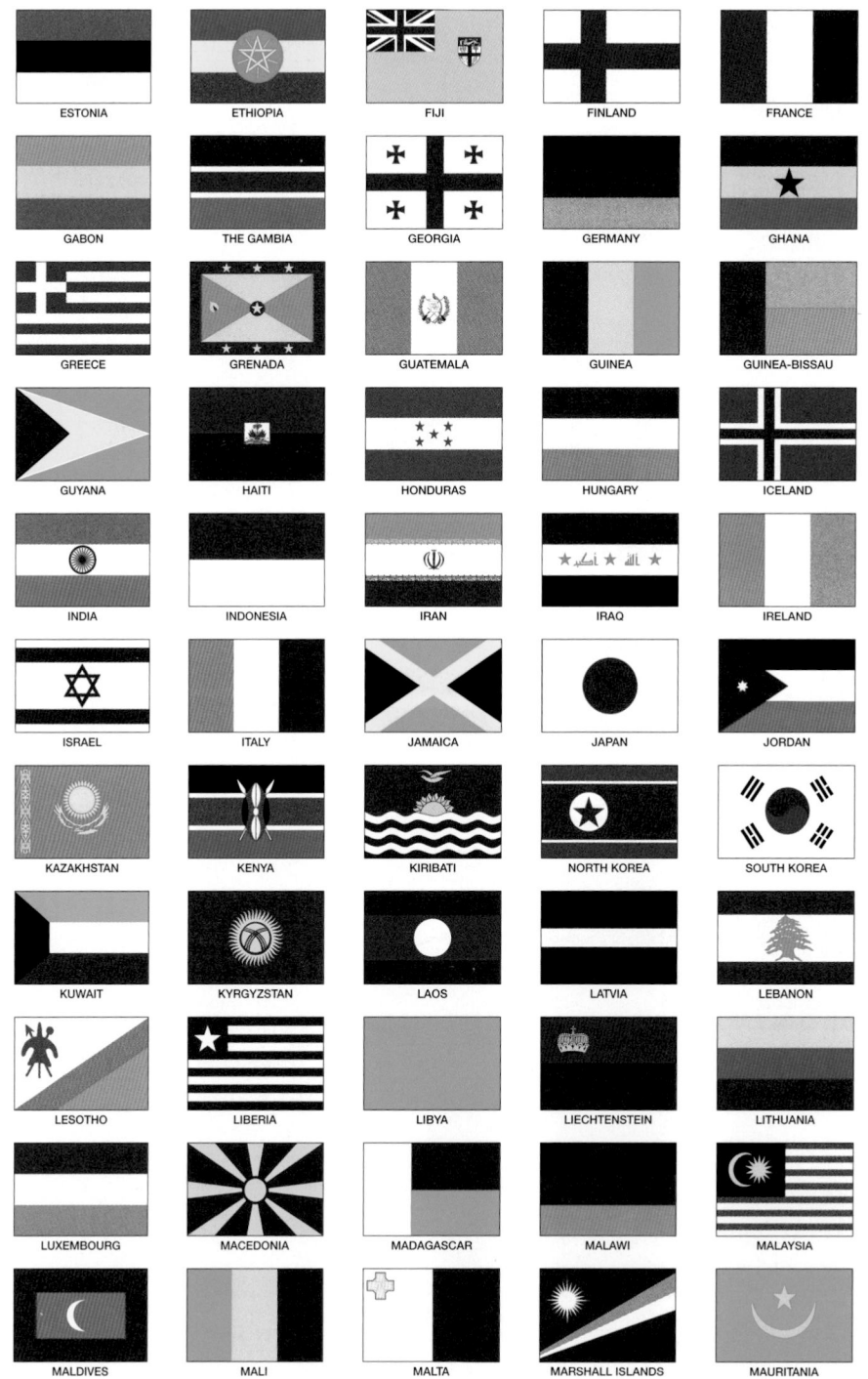

ESTONIA ETHIOPIA FIJI FINLAND FRANCE

GABON THE GAMBIA GEORGIA GERMANY GHANA

GREECE GRENADA GUATEMALA GUINEA GUINEA-BISSAU

GUYANA HAITI HONDURAS HUNGARY ICELAND

INDIA INDONESIA IRAN IRAQ IRELAND

ISRAEL ITALY JAMAICA JAPAN JORDAN

KAZAKHSTAN KENYA KIRIBATI NORTH KOREA SOUTH KOREA

KUWAIT KYRGYZSTAN LAOS LATVIA LEBANON

LESOTHO LIBERIA LIBYA LIECHTENSTEIN LITHUANIA

LUXEMBOURG MACEDONIA MADAGASCAR MALAWI MALAYSIA

MALDIVES MALI MALTA MARSHALL ISLANDS MAURITANIA

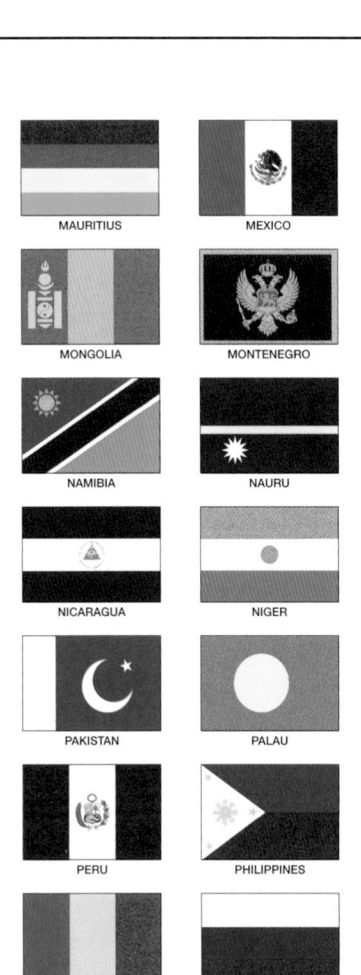

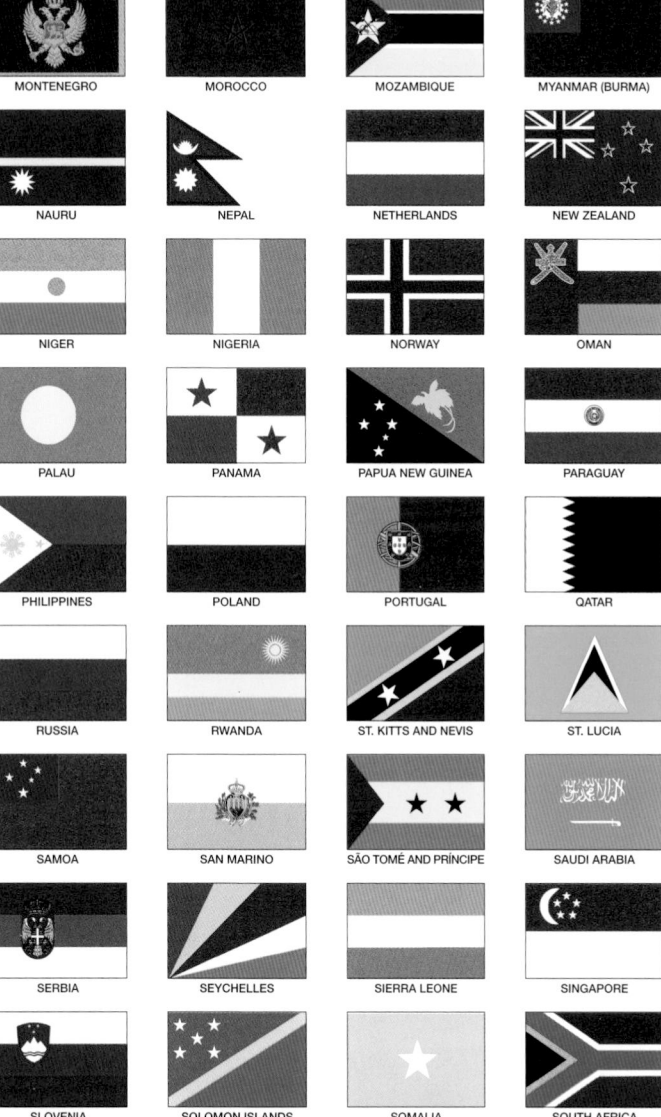

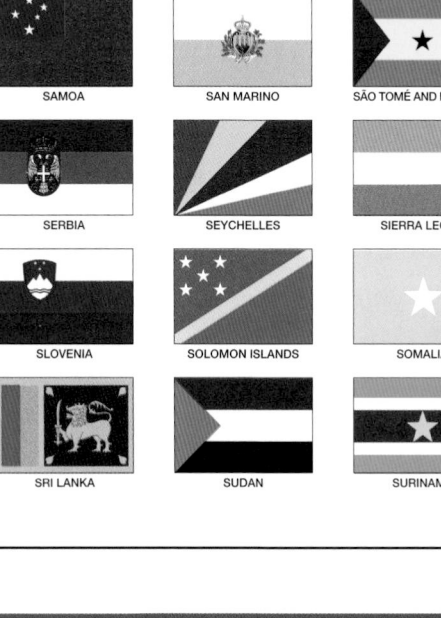

MAURITIUS	MEXICO	MICRONESIA	MOLDOVA	MONACO
MONGOLIA	MONTENEGRO	MOROCCO	MOZAMBIQUE	MYANMAR (BURMA)
NAMIBIA	NAURU	NEPAL	NETHERLANDS	NEW ZEALAND
NICARAGUA	NIGER	NIGERIA	NORWAY	OMAN
PAKISTAN	PALAU	PANAMA	PAPUA NEW GUINEA	PARAGUAY
PERU	PHILIPPINES	POLAND	PORTUGAL	QATAR
ROMANIA	RUSSIA	RWANDA	ST. KITTS AND NEVIS	ST. LUCIA
ST. VINCENT AND THE GRENADINES	SAMOA	SAN MARINO	SÃO TOMÉ AND PRÍNCIPE	SAUDI ARABIA
SENEGAL	SERBIA	SEYCHELLES	SIERRA LEONE	SINGAPORE
SLOVAKIA	SLOVENIA	SOLOMON ISLANDS	SOMALIA	SOUTH AFRICA
SPAIN	SRI LANKA	SUDAN	SURINAME	SWAZILAND

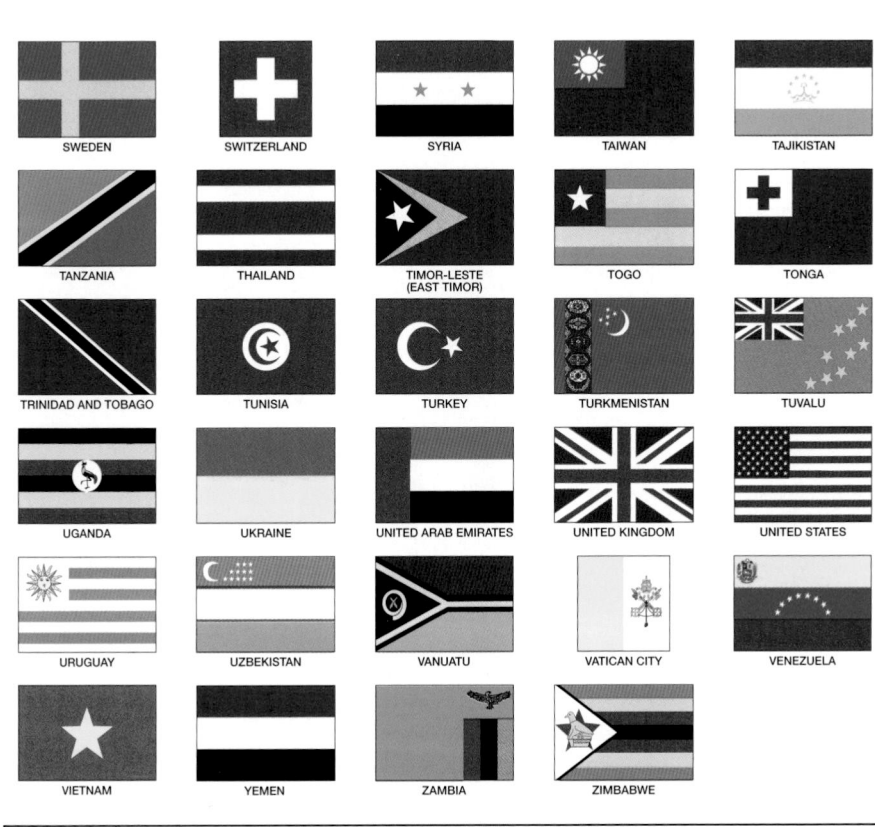

SWEDEN SWITZERLAND SYRIA TAIWAN TAJIKISTAN

TANZANIA THAILAND TIMOR-LESTE (EAST TIMOR) TOGO TONGA

TRINIDAD AND TOBAGO TUNISIA TURKEY TURKMENISTAN TUVALU

UGANDA UKRAINE UNITED ARAB EMIRATES UNITED KINGDOM UNITED STATES

URUGUAY UZBEKISTAN VANUATU VATICAN CITY VENEZUELA

VIETNAM YEMEN ZAMBIA ZIMBABWE

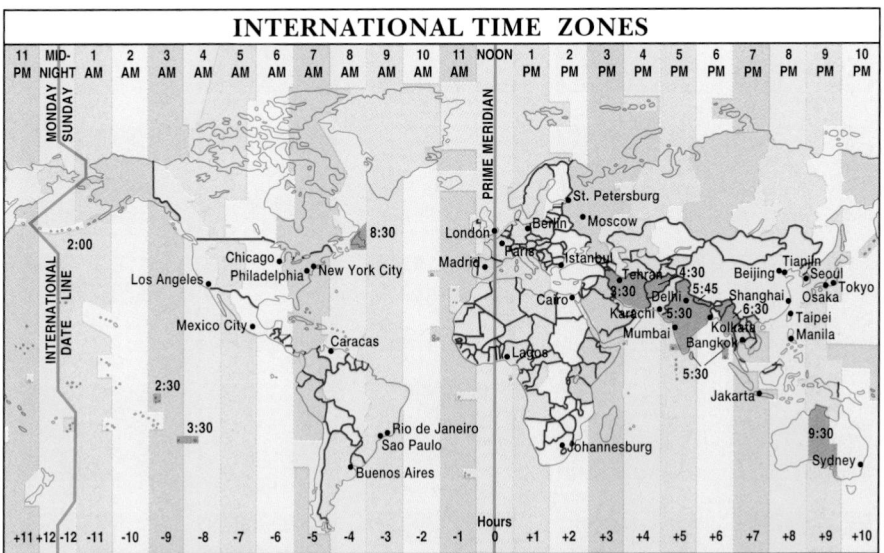

INTERNATIONAL TIME ZONES

The world is divided into 24 time zones, each 15° longitude wide. The longitudinal meridian passing through Greenwich, England, is the starting point, and is called the *prime meridian*. The 12th zone is divided by the 180th meridian (International Date Line). When the line is crossed going west, the date is advanced one day; when crossed going east, the date becomes a day earlier.

© MAPQUEST

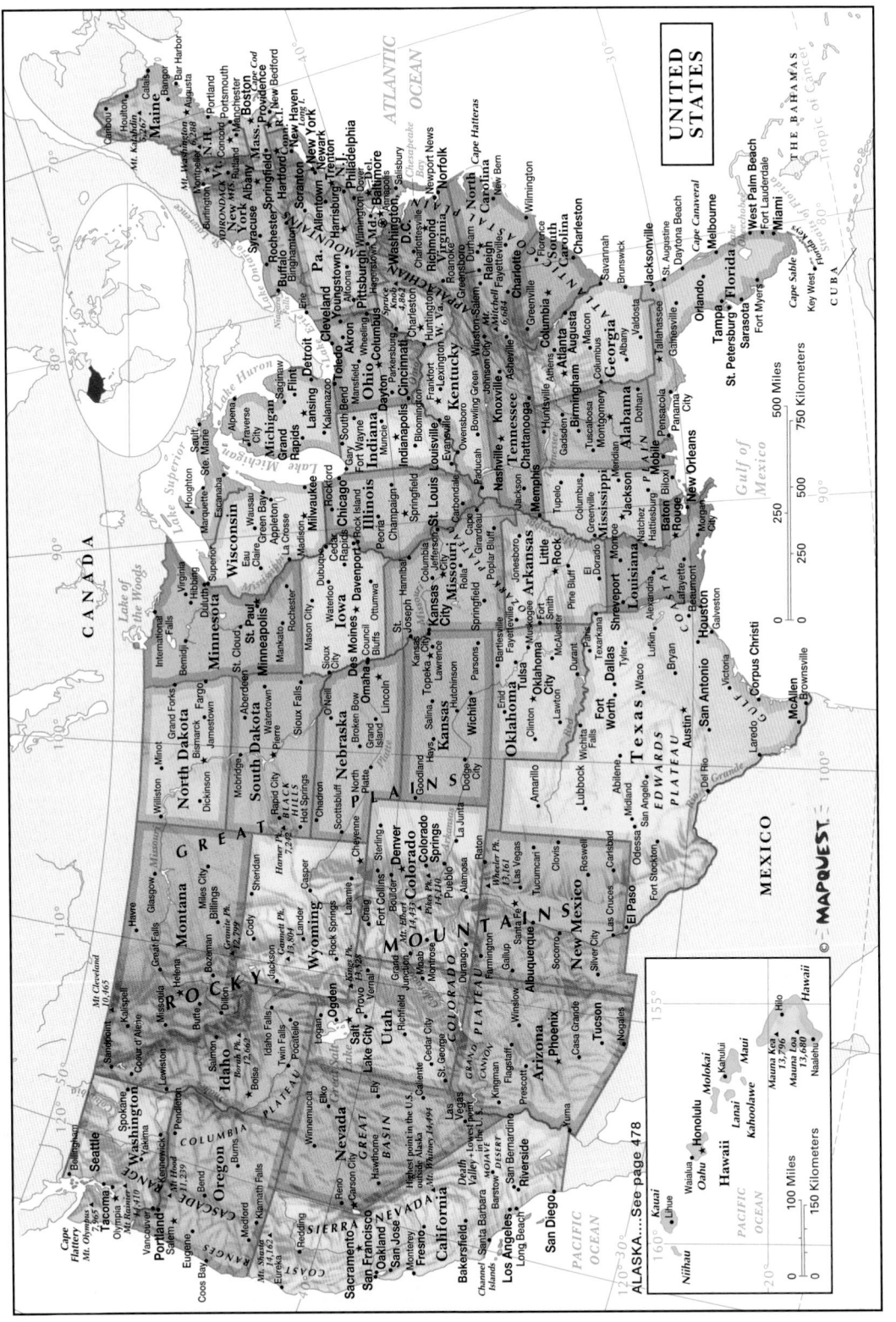

UNITED STATES

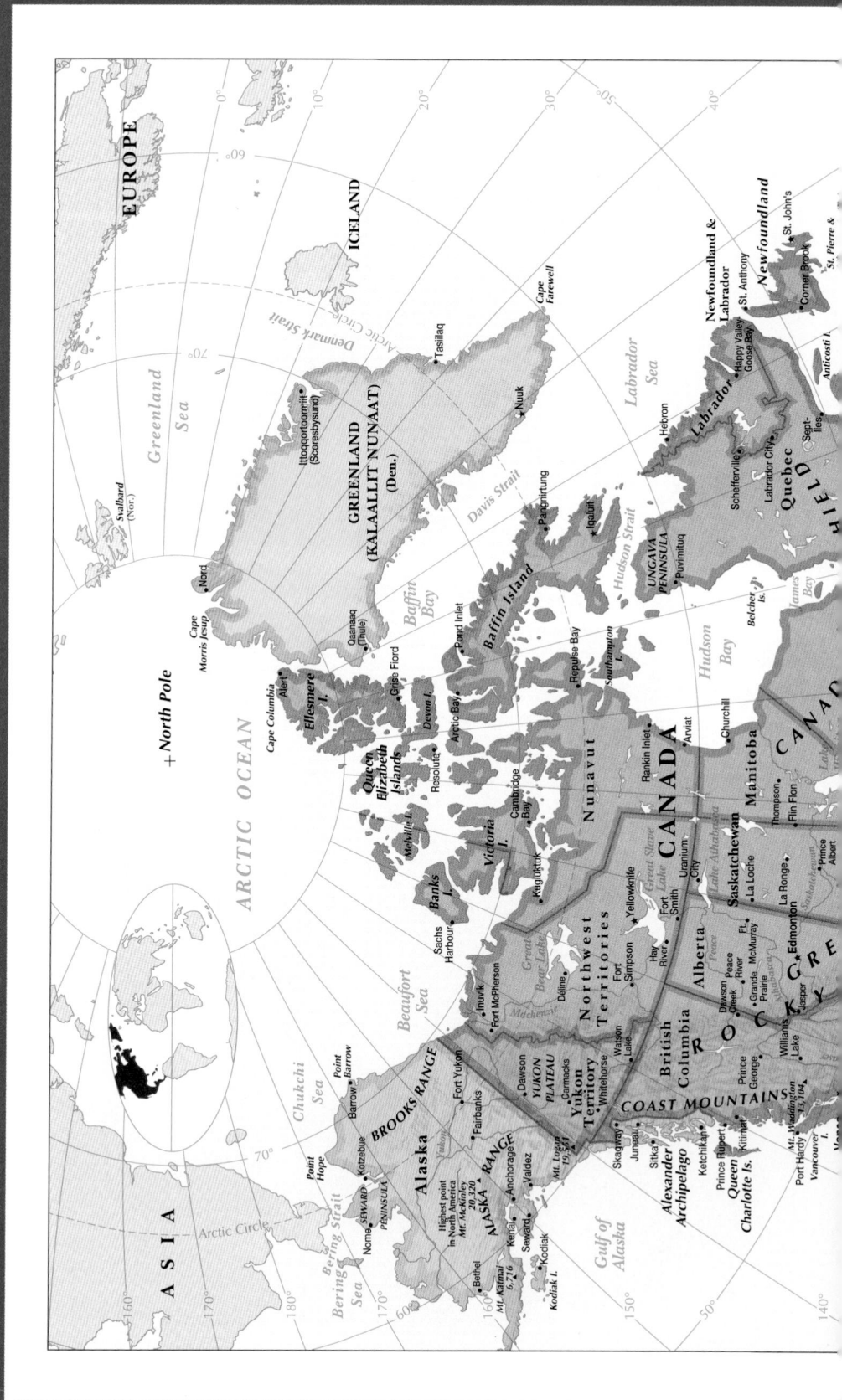

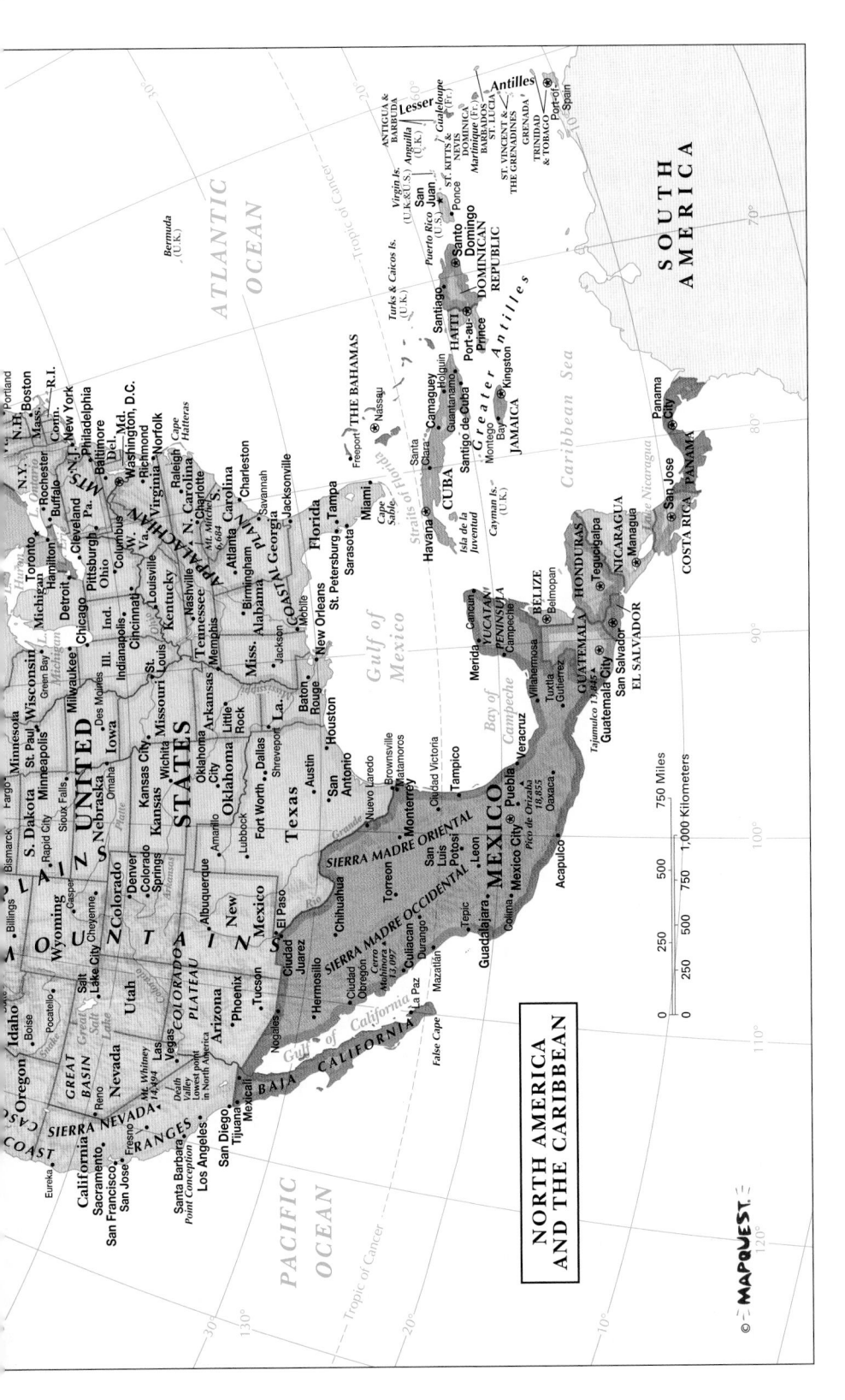

NORTH AMERICA
AND THE CARIBBEAN

© MAPQUEST

479

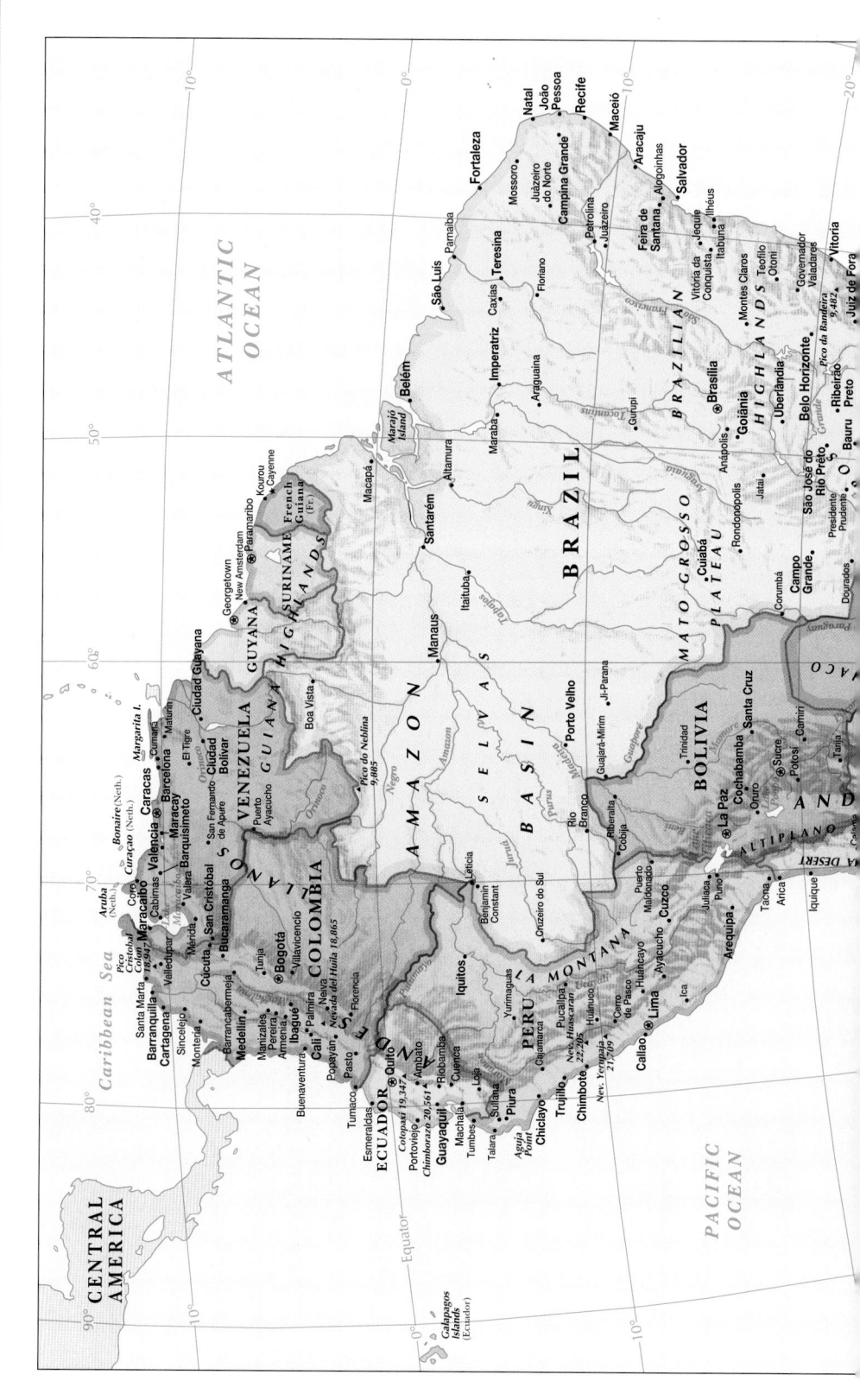

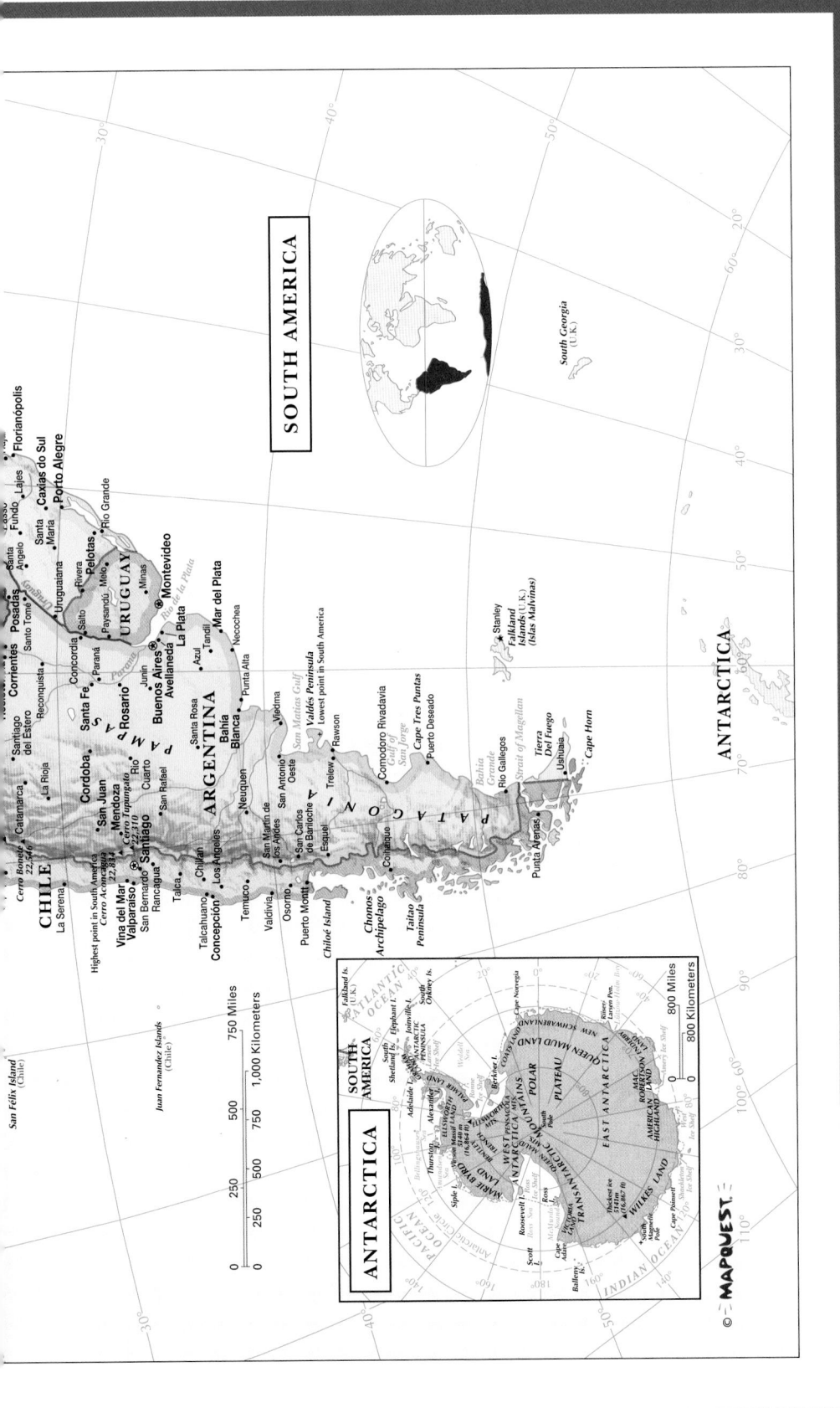

SOUTH AMERICA

ANTARCTICA

EUROPE

GREENLAND
(KALAALLIT NUNAAT)
(Denmark)

Isafjordhur

Keflavik •Akureyri
Reykjavik **ICELAND**
•Seydhisfjordhur

Norwegian Sea

Torshavn •*Faroe Islands* (Den.)

Namsos•

Trondheim•
Molde•
Alesund•

NORWAY SWE

Shetland Islands (U.K.)

Bergen•

•*Orkney Islands*
Thurso•
Inverness•

Haugesund• •Oslo
Stavanger• Drammen• Karlstad• Oret•
Skien• **Sto**
Kristiansand• Norrkopi•

Hebrides

Scotland •Aberdeen

Goteborg• Jonk•

Londonderry• •Aalborg Jutland• Arhus Halmstad• •Jonko
Northern Ireland
Galway• **Belfast** Esbjerg• **Copenhagen** •Helsingbor
IRELAND •**Dublin** **DENMARK** Odense• •Malmo
Limerick•
•Liverpool Kiel• Lubeck• •Rostock
Cork• Waterford •Manchester Lubeck•
Sheffield

•Namsos
Trondheim•
Molde•
Alesund•

ATLANTIC OCEAN

•Glasgow
Scotland •Dundee
•Ayr •Edinburgh
•Newcastle
North
•Leeds
•Kingston upon Hull
•Sheffield
Sea

•Groningen •Hamburg •Szcz
•Birmingham •Coventry
Wales• Swansea• **England** Norwich• **NETHERLANDS** •Bremen •Berlin •Byd
•Cardiff •Bristol •London •Amsterdam •Hannover **GERMANY** PO
Plymouth• The Hague• •Rotterdam •Bielefeld •Magdeburg
Land's End •Dover •Antwerp •Essen •Cologne •Leipzig •Dresden
Portsmouth• **BELGIUM** •Brussels •Bonn •Kassel •Erfurt •Liberec
English Channel •Lille •Liege •Wiesbaden •Chemnitz •Prague •Pizen
Channel Is. (U.K.) •Le Havre, •Frankfurt **CZECH R**
Brest• •Caen •Rouen **LUXEMBOURG** •Mannheim •Saarbrucken •Nurnberg
Luxembourg• •Nancy •Stuttgart •Regensburg
Rennes• •Paris •Strasbourg •Augsburg •Munich •Linz
•Le Mans •Orleans Dijon• **SWITZERLAND** •Salzburg •Vienna
Nantes• •Tours •Basel •Zurich •Innsbruck **AUSTRIA**
FRANCE •Bern *ALPS* Klagenfurt• •Graz
•Limoges •Geneva **LIECHTENSTEIN** **SLOVENIA**
•Clermont-Ferrand •Lyon *Mt. Blanc* •Matterhorn •Udine •Ljubljana •Z
A Coruña• •Gijon •Saint-Etienne 15,771 14,690 •Bergamo •Verona Trieste• **CRO**
Vigo• Santander• •Grenoble •Milan •Venice Rijeka•
Leon• •Bilbao Donostia– *PYRENEES* •Torino •Parma •Bologna *Adriatic*
Porto• •Braga Vitoria-Gasteiz• San Sebastian •Toulouse •Avignon •Genoa **SAN MARINO**
Coimbra• Pamplona• *Pico de* •Montpellier •Nice •Pisa •Ancona •Split
Valladolid• *Aneto* •Marseille •Florence •Perugia
IBERIAN Salamanca• 11,168 **ANDORRA** •Toulon **MONACO** *Corsica* Elba• •Du
PORTUGAL •Madrid (Fr.)
Lisbon• •Barcelona Ajaccio• **VATICAN CITY** •Rome *Adriatic*
•Setubal Toledo• Tarragona• **ITALY** •Foggi
Badajoz• **SPAIN** •Castellon de la Plana *Vesuvius*
PENINSULA •Valencia •Sassari •Naples• 4,202
Cape St. Vincent •Cordoba *Majorca* *Minorca* •Salerno
•Seville Palma de• •Mallorca *Sardinia*
Cadiz• •Alicante *Balearic* (It.) •Cagliari *Tyrrhenian*
Malaga• •Murcia Is. (Sp.)
Strait of Gibraltar **GIBRALTAR** •Cartagena *Sea*
(U.K.) •Almera *Mediterranean S*
Granada•

AFRICA

Palermo• Messina
Etna •Reggio
11,053▲ •Calabr
Sicily •Catania
(It.)

MALTA •Valletta

0	250		500 Miles
0	250	500	750 Kilometers

Barents Sea

North Cape
Vardo
*Murmansk
Apatity *KOLA
PENINSULA
LAPLAND
Ivalo

*Rovaniemi

FINLAND
Kuopio
Jyvaskyla
*Tampere
Lahti
Kotka
Helsinki
*Tallinn
ESTONIA
Tartu
Pskov

Riga
LATVIA
Daugavpils
LITHUANIA Vitsyebsk
Kaunas Vilnius
Orsha
Minsk Mahilyow
Hrodna Babruysk
BELARUS
Homyel
Brest Pinsk
Lublin Chernihiv
Sumy
Kiev
(Kyiv)
Zhytomyr Cherkasy
Lviv Poltava
UKRAINE
Vinnytsia
Chernivtsi Dnipropetrovsk Donetsk
Zaporizhzhia
Kryvyi Rih
MOLDOVA Mykolaiv
Iasi Chisinau
Odesa
CRIMEA
PENINSULA
Sevastopol Simferopol

ROMANIA Galati
Timisoara Brasov
Ploiesti
Bucharest Constanta
Craiova
Ruse
Pleven Varna
BULGARIA
Sofia Burgas
Stara
Zagora
Skopje Plovdiv
Istanbul
Kavala
PENINSULA
TURKEY
Thessaloniki
Olympos
9,570
Larisa
Ioannina Volos
Aegean
Sea
Dardanelles

GREECE
Corinth Athens
Peloponnese
Sparta
Cyclades

Sea of Crete
Hania Crete
(Gr.) Iraklion

Novaya
Zemlya
Naryan-Mar
Pechora

ASIA

URAL

Ukhta

Arkhangelsk
White Sea
Belomorsk
Dvina
Kotlas
Lake
Onega
Petrozavodsk
Lake
Ladoga
St.
Petersburg
Cherepovets Vologda
Rybinsk Kostroma
Velikiy Yaroslavl
Novgorod Ivanovo
Tver
Vladimir
Moscow
Kaluga Ryazan
Smolensk Tula

Bryansk Lipetsk
Kursk
Belgorod
Kharkiv
Luhansk
Horlivka
Mariupol
Sea of
Azov

RUSSIA

Syktyvkar
Berezniki
Perm
Kirov
Izhevsk
Naberezhnye
Chelny
Yoshkar Ola
Nizhniy Kazan
Novgorod Cheboksary
Ulyanovsk
Saransk
Penza
Tambov Saratov

MOUNTAINS

Ufa
Sterlitamak

Tolyatti
Samara
Orsk
Orenburg

Ural

Volga

KAZAKHSTAN

Voronezh

Volgograd

Astrakhan
Don

Rostov-na-Donu

Caspian

Krasnodar Stavropol
Nalchik Groznyy Makhachkala
Mt. Elbrus Vladikavkaz
18,510
Highest point
in Europe
CAUCASUS MTS.

Sea

Black Sea

ASIA

© MAPQUEST

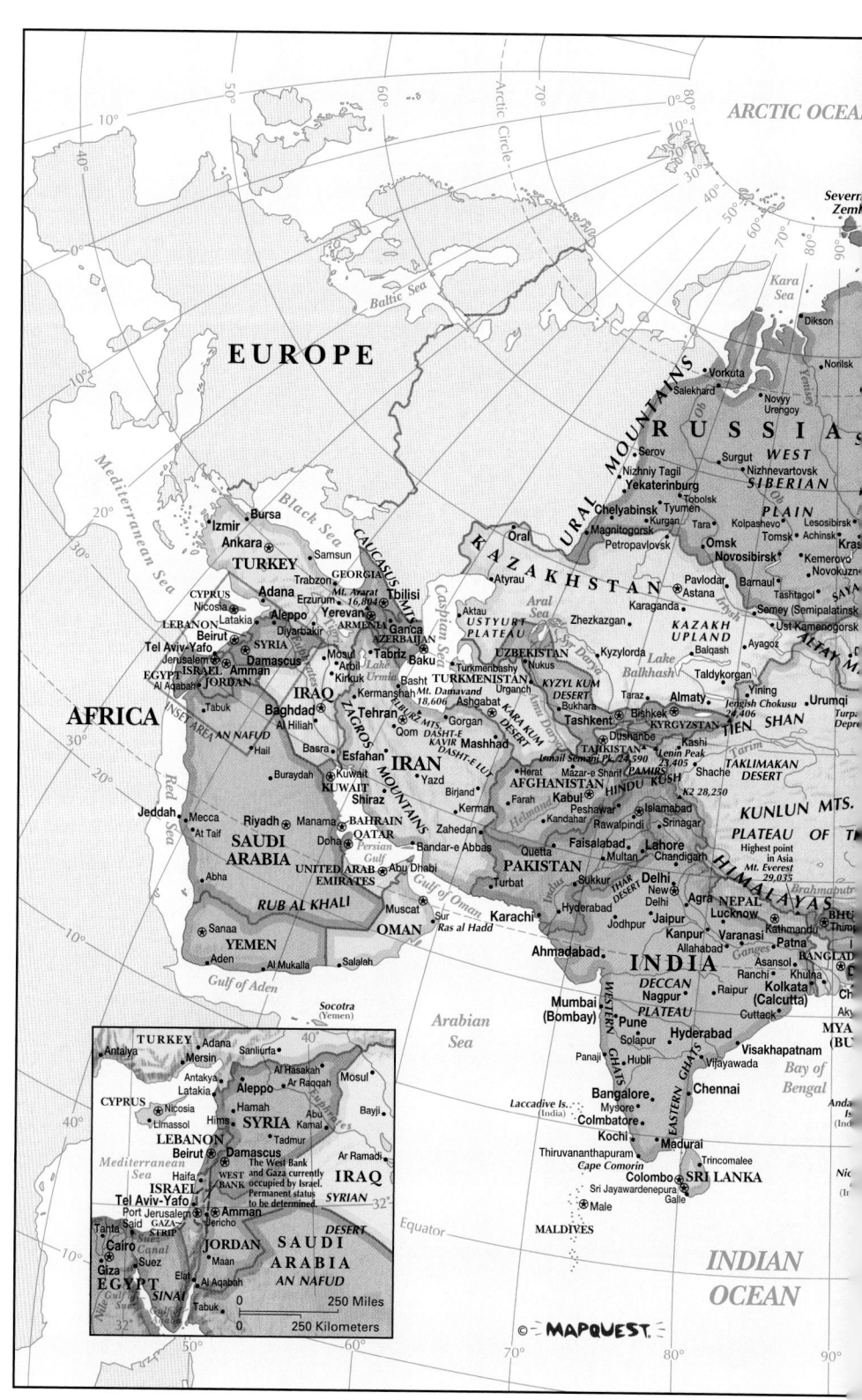

ARCTIC OCEAN

Severn
Zeml

Kara
Sea

Dikson

EUROPE

Vorkuta
Salekhard
Novyy
Urengoy

RUSSIA

Norilsk

Serov
Surgut
Nizhnevartovsk
WEST
SIBERIAN

URAL MOUNTAINS

Baltic Sea

Nizhniy Tagil
Yekaterinburg
Chelyabinsk
Tyumen
Tobolsk

PLAIN

Lesosibirsk

Bursa
Izmir
Ankara
TURKEY
Samsun
Trabzon
Adana
CYPRUS
Nicosia
Latakia
Aleppo
LEBANON
Beirut
Tel Aviv-Yafo
SYRIA
Jerusalem
ISRAEL
Damascus
Amman
EGYPT
JORDAN
Al Aqabah

GEORGIA
Tbilisi
Erzurum Mt. Ararat
16,804
Yerevan
ARMENIA Ganca
AZERBAIJAN
Diyarbakir
Baku
Mosul
Tabriz
Arbil
Kirkuk
Urmia
IRAQ

Black Sea

CAUCASUS MTS.

Oral
Atyrau

KAZAKHSTAN

Aktau

Tara
Omsk
Novosibirsk

Kemerovo
Novokuzn
Kras

Tomsk
Achinsk

Kolpashevo

SAYA

Kurgan
Petropavlovsk
Pavlodar
Astana

Magnitogorsk

Barnaul
Tashtagol
Semey (Semipalatinsk)
Ust-Kamenogorsk
ALTAI M

KAZAKH
UPLAND

Karaganda
Zhezkazgan
Balqash

Ayagoz

Aral
Sea

USTYURT
PLATEAU

Kyzylorda

Lake
Balkhash

Taldykorgan

Caspian Sea

Syr Darya

UZBEKISTAN
Nukus

Yining
Almaty
Jenish Chokusu
24,406
Urumqi
Turpa
Depre

Mt. Damavand
18,606

Urganch

KYZYL KUM
DESERT

Taraz
Bishkek
KYRGYZSTAN

Bukhara

Tashkent

Kashi

TIEN SHAN

TURKMENISTAN
Ashgabat

AFRICA

Tehran

Qom

Gorgan

Turkmenbashy

DASHT-E
KAVIR

Esfahan

IRAN

ZAGROS MOUNTAINS

Yazd

Baghdad
Al Hillah
Basra

KARA KUM
DESERT

Dushanbe
TAJIKISTAN
Ismail Semani Pk. 24,590
Lenin Peak
PAMIRS 23,405

Kandahar

Birjand

Kerman

Farah

HINDU KUSH
Kabul
AFGHANISTAN
Peshawar
Islamabad
Rawalpindi

Shache

K2 28,250

KUNLUN MTS.
PLATEAU OF TH

TAKLIMAKAN
DESERT

Tarim

Lenin Peak

Mazar-e Sharif
Herat

Kermanshah
Hamadan

DASHT-E LUT

Mashhad

Buraydah
Hail

AN NAFUD

Tabuk

Kuwait
KUWAIT
Shiraz
Zahedan
Bandar-e Abbas
BAHRAIN
Manama
QATAR
Doha

Jeddah
Mecca
At Taif

Riyadh

SAUDI
ARABIA

UNITED ARAB
EMIRATES

Abu Dhabi
Muscat

Srinagar

Quetta

Kandahar

THAR
DESERT

Multan

Faisalabad
Lahore

Chandigarh

HIMALAYAS

Highest point
in Asia
Mt. Everest
29,035

Brahmaputr

PAKISTAN

Sukkur

Hyderabad

Turbat

Sur
Ras al Hadd

OMAN

Gulf of Oman

Karachi

Delhi
New
Delhi
Agra

Jodhpur

Jaipur

Lucknow
Kanpur
Allahabad
Varanasi

Kathmandu
NEPAL

Ganges

BANGLAD

Abha

RUB AL KHALI

Ahmadabad.

Asansol

Ranchi
Khulna

Patna

BHU
Thimp

Sanaa
YEMEN
Aden
Al Mukalla
Salalah

Gulf of Aden

Socotra
(Yemen)

Arabian
Sea

Mumbai
(Bombay)
Pune

INDIA
DECCAN
Nagpur
PLATEAU

Hyderabad

Raipur
Kolkata
(Calcutta)
Cuttack

Ch

MYA
(BU

Solapur

WESTERN GHATS

Panaji

Hubli

Visakhapatnam

Bay of
Bengal

Anda
Is
(Ind

Vijayawada

Laccadive Is.
(India)

Bangalore
Mysore
Coimbatore

Kochi

Chennai

EASTERN GHATS

Nic
(Ir

Thiruvananthapuram
Cape Comorin

Madurai
Trincomalee
Colombo
SRI LANKA
Sri Jayawardenepura
Galle

MALDIVES
Male

Equator

INDIAN
OCEAN

TURKEY
Antalya
Mersin
Adana
Sanliurfa
Antakya
Latakia
Al Hasakah
Aleppo
Ar Raqqah
Mosul
CYPRUS
Nicosia
Hamah
Limassol
Hims
SYRIA
Abu
Kamal
Bayji
LEBANON
Tadmur
Beirut
Damascus
Mediterranean
Sea
Haifa
The West Bank
and Gaza currently
occupied by Israel.
Permanent status
to be determined.
WEST
BANK
Ar Ramadi
IRAQ
Tel Aviv-Yafo
Port Jerusalem
Said
GAZA
STRIP
Jericho
Amman
SYRIAN
Tanta
DESERT
Cairo
Canal
Suez
JORDAN
SAUDI
ARABIA
Giza
Maan
AN NAFUD
EGYPT
SINAI
Elat
Al Aqabah
Tabuk
Gulf of

0   250 Miles
0   250 Kilometers

© MAPQUEST

484

ASIA

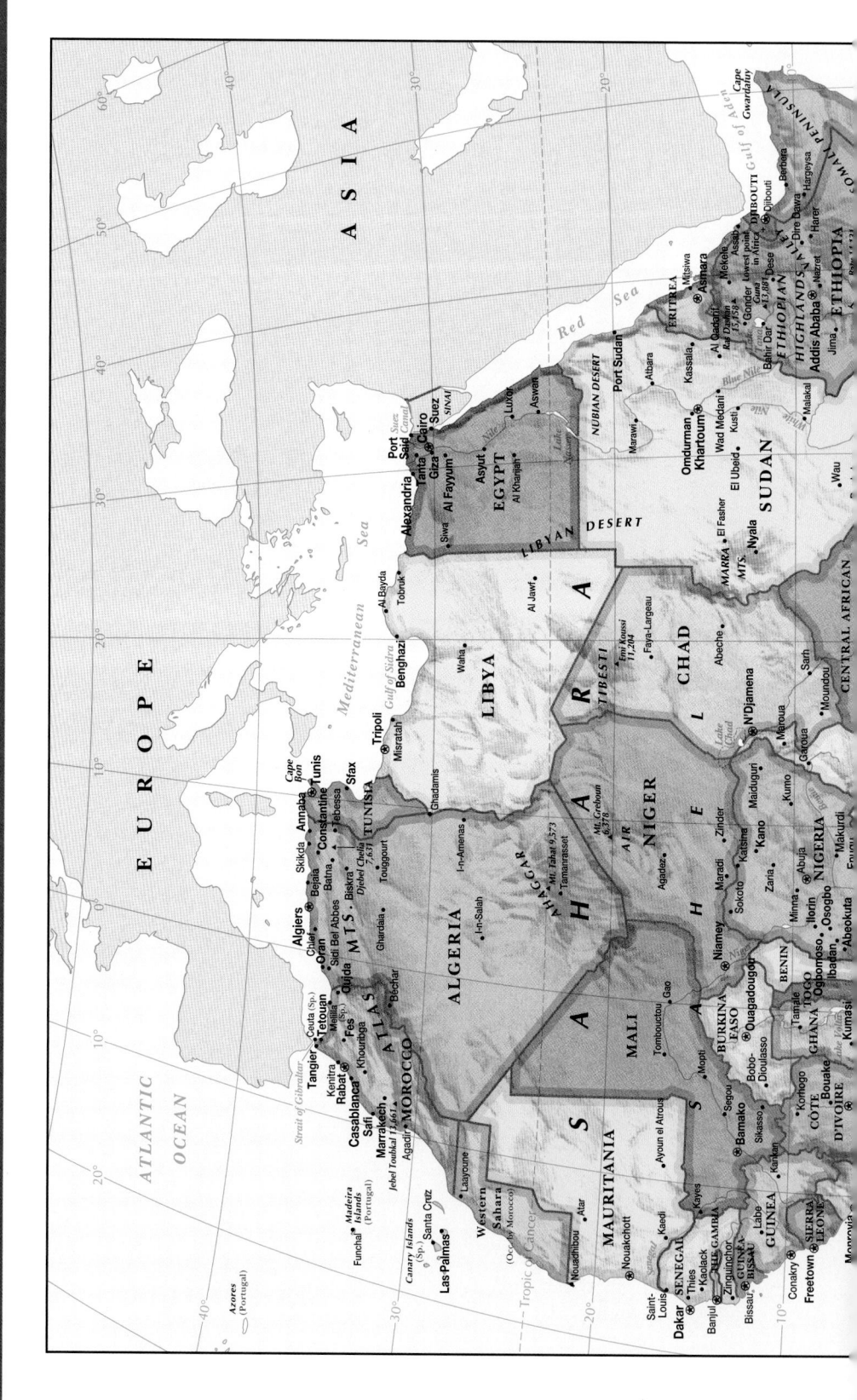

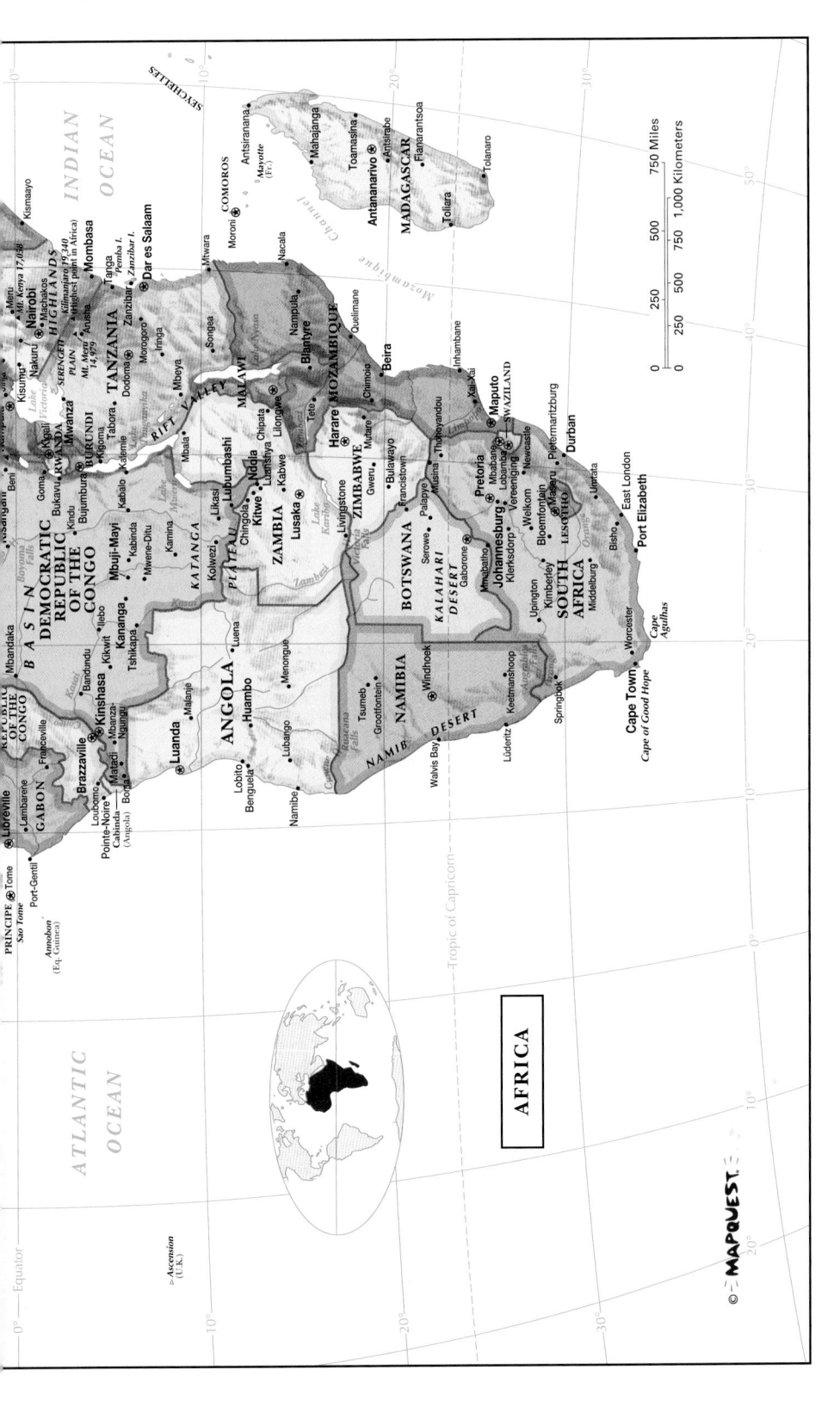

AFRICA

Equator

ATLANTIC
OCEAN

INDIAN
OCEAN

SEYCHELLES

COMOROS
Moroni ⊛
Mayotte
(Fr.)

MADAGASCAR
Antsiranana
Mahajanga
Toamasina
Antananarivo ⊛
Antsirabe
Fianarantsoa
Toliara
Tolanaro

Mozambique Channel

Kismaayo

Mt. Kenya 17,058
Meru ⊛ Nairobi
Machakos
KENYA
HIGHLANDS
Kilimanjaro 19,340
(highest point in Africa)
Arusha ⊛
Mombasa
Kisumu Nakuru
Tanga
Pemba I.
Zanzibar I.
Dar es Salaam
Mwanza
SERENGETI
PLAIN
RWANDA
Kigali ⊛
BURUNDI
Bujumbura
Mt. Meru
14,979
TANZANIA
Dodoma
Morogoro
Iringa
Tabora
Kigoma
Mbeya
Mtwara
Songea
Nampula
Nacala
Quelimane

Goma
Bukavu
Kindu
Kalabo
Kalemie
Kananga
Kamina
RIFT VALLEY
Lake
Malawi
Lake
Tanganyika
MALAWI
Lilongwe
Blantyre
MOZAMBIQUE
Beira
Chimoio

Bangui
Oubangui
Mbandaka
B A S I N
DEMOCRATIC
REPUBLIC
OF THE
CONGO
Ilebo
Mbuji-Mayi
Mwene-Ditu
KATANGA
Kolwezi
Likasi
Lubumbashi
Ndola
Kitwe
ZAMBIA
Lusaka
Lake
Kariba
ZIMBABWE
Harare
Mutare
Tete
Zambezi
Xai-Xai
Maputo
SWAZILAND
Mbabane
Lobamba
Pietermaritzburg
Durban

Boyoma
Falls
Beni
Kisangani
Goma

REPUBLIC
OF THE
CONGO
Brazzaville
GABON
Libreville ⊛
Lambaréné
Port-Gentil
Loubomo
Pointe-Noire
Cabinda
(Angola)
Matadi
Mbanza-
Ngungu
Boma
Kinshasa
Kikwit
Bandundu
Tshikapa
Kasai
Kwango

PRINCIPE ⊛ Tome
São Tomé
Annobón
(Eq. Guinea)

Luanda
ANGOLA
Malanje
Menongue
Lubango
Huambo
Benguela
Lobito
Luena
Namibe
PLATEAU
Chingola
Chipata
Lusitshya
Livingstone
Victoria
Falls
Kabwe
Gweru
Bulawayo
Francistown
Serowe
BOTSWANA
Gaborone ⊛
KALAHARI
DESERT
Mahalapye
Palapye
Musina
Tshoyandou
Pretoria ⊛
Johannesburg
Vereeniging
Klerksdorp
Welkom
Kimberley
SOUTH
AFRICA
Bloemfontein
LESOTHO
Maseru
Newcastle
Ladysmith
Umtata
East London
Port Elizabeth

Tsumeb
Grootfontein
NAMIBIA
Windhoek ⊛
Keetmanshoop
Lüderitz
Springbok
Walvis Bay
NAMIB
DESERT
KALAHARI
DESERT
Augrabies
Falls
Upington
Worcester
Cape Town
Cape of Good Hope
Cape
Agulhas
Middelburg
Bisho
Aliwal North

Okavango
Cunene
Orange

Ascension
(U.K.)

Tropic of Capricorn

0°   10°   20°   30°

0   250   500   750 Miles
0   250   500   750   1,000 Kilometers

© MAPQUEST.

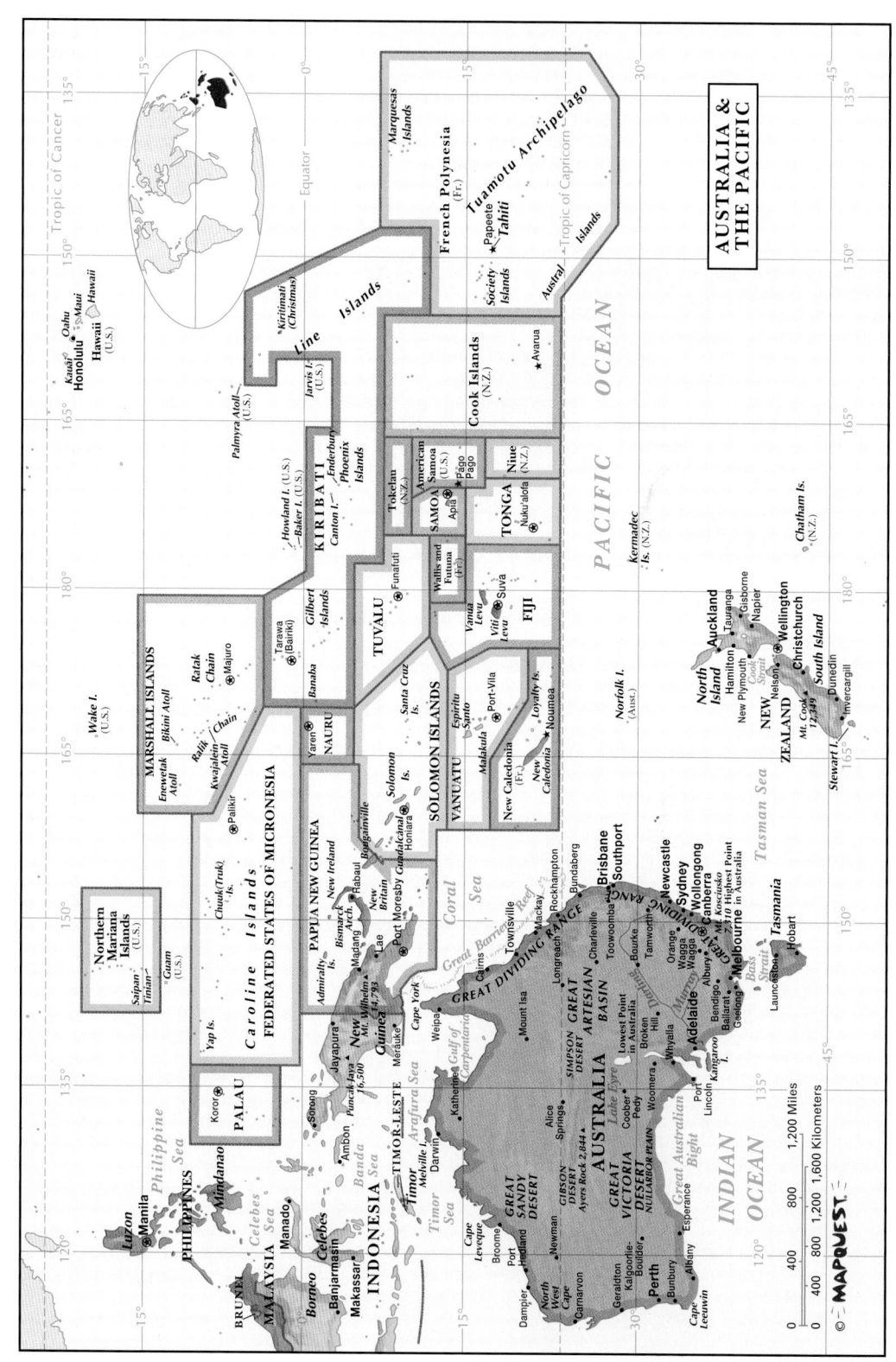

AUSTRALIA &
THE PACIFIC

1973

Five of 7 defendants in **Watergate** break-in trial pleaded guilty Jan. 11 and 15; the other 2 were convicted Jan. 30.

In *Roe v. Wade*, Supreme Court ruled, 7-2, Jan. 22, that states may not ban **abortions** during **first 3 months of pregnancy** and may regulate, but may not ban, abortions during 2nd trimester.

Four-party **Vietnam peace pacts** were signed in Paris Jan. 27, and North Vietnam released some 590 U.S. prisoners by Apr. 1. Last U.S. troops left Mar. 29.

American Indian Movement activists occupied Wounded Knee, SD, in protest Feb. 27.

End of the military **draft** announced Jan. 27.

Top **Nixon aides** H. R. Haldeman, John D. Ehrlichman, and John Dean and Attorney Gen. Richard Kleindienst **resigned** Apr. 30, amid charges of White House efforts to obstruct justice in the Watergate case.

Skylab, **first U.S. space station**, launched May 14.

Secretariat became first Triple Crown winner since Citation in 1948 by winning Belmont Stakes June 9 in record time.

John Dean, former Nixon counsel, told Senate hearings June 25 that Nixon, his staff and campaign aides, and the Justice Dept. had conspired to cover up **Watergate** facts.

The U.S. officially ceased bombing in **Cambodia** at midnight Aug. 14 in accord with a June congressional action.

Vice Pres. **Spiro Agnew**, Oct. 10, resigned and pleaded no contest to a charge of tax evasion on payments made to him by contractors when he was Maryland governor. **Gerald R. Ford**, Oct. 12, became **first appointed vice president** under the 25th Amendment; sworn in Dec. 6.

A total **ban** on **oil exports** to the U.S. was imposed by Arab oil-producing nations Oct. 19-21 after the outbreak of an Arab-Israeli war. The ban was lifted Mar. 18, **1974**.

The **"Saturday Night Massacre"** occurred Oct. 20, when Pres. Nixon ordered Attorney Gen. **Elliot Richardson** to fire Watergate special prosecutor **Archibald Cox**, who had sought the handover of Nixon's subpoenaed White House tapes. Richardson refused to comply and resigned; Dep. Attorney Gen. **William Ruckelshaus** refused and was fired. Solicitor Gen. **Robert Bork**, as acting attorney gen., then fired Cox. **Leon Jaworski** named Nov. 1 by the Nixon administration to succeed Cox.

Congress overrode Nov. 7 Pres. Nixon's veto of the **war powers bill**, which curbed president's power to commit forces to hostilities abroad without congressional approval.

1974

On Apr. 8, **Hank Aaron** of the Atlanta Braves hit his 715th career **home run** to break **Babe Ruth**'s record.

House Judiciary Committee opened **impeachment** hearings May 9 against Pres. Nixon.

John D. Ehrlichman and 3 **White House "plumbers"** found guilty July 12 of conspiring to violate the civil rights of the psychiatrist of Pentagon Papers leaker Daniel Ellsberg by breaking into his office.

Supreme Court ruled, 8-0, July 24 that Nixon had to turn over 64 **tapes** of **White House conversations**.

House Judiciary Committee, in televised hearings July 24-30, recommended 3 **articles of impeachment** against Pres. Nixon, involving conspiracy to obstruct justice in the Watergate cover-up, abuses of power, and defiance of committee subpoenas. The House voted Aug. 20, 412-3, to accept the committee report, which included the impeachment articles.

Pres. **Nixon** announced his **resignation**, Aug. 8, and stepped down the next day. His support in Congress had begun to collapse Aug. 5, after release of tapes appearing to implicate him in Watergate cover-up. Vice Pres. **Ford** was **sworn in** Aug. 9 as 38th U.S. president.

Ford, Aug. 20, nominated **Nelson Rockefeller** to be vice president; he was sworn in Dec. 10.

Pres. Ford, Sept. 8, issued a **pardon** to ex-Pres. Nixon for any federal crimes he committed while president.

1975

Former Atty. Gen. John Mitchell and ex-presidential advisers H. R. Haldeman and John Ehrlichman were found **guilty** Jan. 1 of **Watergate cover-up** charges. Mitchell was released **1979**, last of 25 jailed over scandal to leave prison.

U.S. launched **evacuation** of Americans and some South Vietnamese **from Saigon** Apr. 29 as Communist forces completed takeover of South Vietnam; **South Vietnamese** government officially **surrendered** Apr. 30.

U.S. merchant ship *Mayaguez* and its crew of 39 were seized by Cambodian forces in Gulf of Siam May 12. In rescue operation, U.S. Marines attacked Tang Island, planes bombed air base; Cambodia surrendered ship and crew.

Congress voted $405 mil for **South Vietnam refugees** May 16; 140,000 were flown to the U.S.

Illegal CIA operations described by panel headed by Vice Pres. Rockefeller June 10.

Publishing heiress **Patricia (Patty) Hearst**, kidnapped Feb. 5, **1974**, by Symbionese Liberation Army, captured in San Francisco Sept. 18 with other militants. She was convicted Mar. 20, **1976**, of bank robbery.

1976

In **"right to die"** case, New Jersey Supreme Court Mar. 31 allowed comatose **Karen Ann Quinlan** to be removed from respirator. She survived, dying in a nursing home in **1985**.

Supreme Court **reinstated death penalty**, July 2, subject to conditions.

U.S. celebrated **200th anniversary** of **independence** July 4, with festivals, parades, and New York City's Operation Sail, a gathering of tall ships from around the world.

"Legionnaire's disease" killed 29 people who attended an American Legion convention July 21-24 in Philadelphia.

Viking II set down on Utopia Plains of **Mars** Sept. 3, following the successful landing by *Viking I* July 20.

Two U.S. officers on routine mission near DMZ slain by **North Korean soldiers** Aug. 18; North Korea stated "regret," Aug. 21.

1977

Convicted murderer Gary Gilmore executed by a Utah firing squad Jan. 17; **first exercise** of **capital punishment** in the U.S. since **1967**.

Pres. Jimmy Carter Jan. 21 pardoned most Vietnam War **draft evaders.**

Natural gas shortage caused by severe winter weather led Congress Feb. 2 to approve emergency federal allocation program.

Pres. Carter signed an act Aug. 4 creating a new cabinet-level **energy department.**

FBI Dec. 7 released 40,000 pages of previously secret files relating to **Kennedy assassination**.

George Lucas's **first** *Star Wars* film produced.

1978

Crippling 110-day **coal miners strike** ended Mar. 25 with ratification of new contract.

Senate voted, 68-32, Apr. 18 to turn over **Panama Canal** to Panama on Dec. 31, **1999**; a Mar. 16 vote had given approval to a treaty guaranteeing the area's neutrality after the year **2000**.

Californians, June 6, approved **Proposition 13**, a state constitutional amendment slashing property taxes.

Supreme Court, June 28, ruled against **racial quotas** in *Bakke v. University of California*.

Egyptian Pres. **Anwar al-Sadat** and Israeli Prem. **Menachem Begin** reached accord on "framework for peace," Sept. 17, after Carter-mediated talks at **Camp David**.

New York's Chemical Bank Dec. 20 moved to raise **prime interest rate** to near-record 11.75%.

1979

Partial meltdown released radioactive material Mar. 28, at nuclear reactor on **Three Mile Island** near Middletown, PA.

American Airlines DC-10 **jetliner crashed** May 25 after takeoff from Chicago, killing 275 people.

In a speech July 15, Pres. Carter spoke of a national **"crisis of confidence"** and outlined a proposed 10-year $140 bil program to **reduce U.S. dependence** on **foreign oil**.

Federal government announced, Nov. 1, a $1.5 bil loan-guarantee plan to aid the ailing **Chrysler Corp.**

Militant followers of **Ayatollah Khomeini** took hostage some 90 people, including 63 Americans, Nov. 4 at **American embassy in Tehran**, Iran. Khomeini demanded return of former Shah Muhammad Reza Pahlavi, who was undergoing medical treatment in New York City.

1980

Pres. Carter announced, Jan. 4, economic sanctions against the USSR, in retaliation for Soviet invasion of Afghanistan. At Carter's request, U.S. Olympic Committee voted, Apr. 12, against U.S. participation in **Moscow Summer Olympics**.

Lake Placid, NY, hosted the **Winter Olympics** for the second time. The U.S. hockey team defeated the heavily favored Russian team Feb. 22 en route to winning the gold medal.

Eight Americans killed and 5 wounded, Apr. 24, in **ill-fated attempt to rescue hostages** held by Iranian militants.

Mt. St. Helens, in Washington state, **erupted** May 18. The blast, with others May 25 and June 12, left 57 dead.

In a sweeping victory, Nov. 4, **Ronald Reagan** (R) was elected 40th president, defeating incumbent Pres. Carter. Republicans gained control of the Senate.

Former Beatle **John Lennon** was shot and **killed**, Dec. 8, in New York City.

1981

Minutes after Reagan's inauguration Jan. 20, the 52 **Americans** held **hostage in Iran** for 444 days were **freed**.

Pres. **Reagan** was **shot** and **seriously wounded**, Mar. 30, in Washington, DC; also seriously wounded were a Secret Service agent, a policeman, and Press Sec. **James Brady**. **John W. Hinckley Jr.** arrested, found not guilty by reason of insanity in **1982**, committed to mental institution.

World's **first reusable spacecraft**, the **space shuttle *Columbia***, was sent into space, Apr. 12. It performed its first operational mission in **1982**.

Congress, July 29, passed Pres. Reagan's **tax-cut legislation**, expected to save taxpayers $750 bil over 5 years.

Federal air traffic controllers, Aug. 3, began an illegal **nationwide strike**. Most defied a back-to-work order and were dismissed by Pres. Reagan Aug. 5.

The Senate confirmed, Sept. 21, appointment of **Sandra Day O'Connor** as **first female Supreme Court justice**.

Sandra Day O'Connor

1982

The 13-year-old Justice Dept. lawsuit against **AT&T** was settled Jan. 8. AT&T agreed to give up the 22 Bell System companies and was allowed to expand.

The **Equal Rights Amendment** was **defeated** after a 10-year struggle, when the deadline for ratification expired June 30.

Centers for Disease Control, July 16, reported evidence of growing **AIDS epidemic**, responsible for 184 deaths in country since first reported in U.S. in June **1981**.

The economy showed signs of recovery from the **recession** that began in mid-**1981**, as the Dow Jones Industrial Average Oct. 13 hit 1016.93, its highest level in 18 months.

The **most expensive strike** in sports history ended Nov. 16 when **NFL** players and team owners settled.

Dr. **Barney B. Clark**, a retired dentist, became **first recipient** of a **permanent artificial heart**, Dec. 2; he died Mar. 23, **1983**, after 112 days.

The House, Dec. 16, cited **EPA administrator** Anne Gorsuch for **contempt** after refusing to produce certain documents concerning the **Superfund**.

1983

Pres. Reagan, Jan. 3, declared Times Beach, MO, a federal disaster area because of toxic **dioxin** in the soil.

The Commerce Dept. Jan 19 reported that average real **GNP** in the recessionary year **1982** fell 1.8% from **1981** levels, the **worst decline** since **1946**.

Harold Washington was elected Apr. 12 as the **first black mayor of Chicago**.

On Apr. 20, Pres. Reagan signed a compromise bipartisan bill designed to save **Social Security** from bankruptcy.

Sally Ride became the **first American woman** to travel in **space**, June 18, when space shuttle *Challenger* launched from Cape Canaveral, FL.

On Sept. 1, a **South Korean passenger jet** infringing on Soviet air space and apparently misidentified was **shot down**; 269 people, including 61 Americans, were killed.

On Oct. 23, 241 U.S. Marines and sailors were killed when a TNT-laden **suicide bomb** blew up Marine headquarters at **Beirut** International Airport in Lebanon.

U.S. troops, with a small force from 6 Caribbean nations, **invaded Grenada** Oct. 25. After a few days, Grenadian militia and Cuban "construction workers" were overcome, U.S. citizens were evacuated, and the **Marxist regime** was **deposed**.

1984

Seven **regional companies** took over **local telephone service** from AT&T, Jan. 1.

On space shuttle *Challenger*'s fourth trip, launched Feb. 3, two astronauts became **first humans** to **fly free of a spacecraft**.

On May 7, Vietnam War veterans reached an out-of-court settlement with 7 chemical companies in a **class-action suit** over the herbicide **Agent Orange**.

Former Vice Pres. **Walter Mondale** won the Democratic presidential nomination, June 6. He chose Rep. **Geraldine Ferraro** (D-NY) as candidate for vice president.

Pres. Reagan signed a bill July 17 cutting federal transportation aid to states that keep their **drinking age** under 21.

Pres. **Reagan** was **reelected** Nov. 6 in a Republican landslide, carrying 49 states for a record 525 electoral votes.

Bernhard Goetz shot and wounded 4 allegedly menacing teenage boys on a NYC subway train, Dec. 22; later was acquitted of major charges but was successfully sued.

1985

Visiting Germany, Pres. Reagan, May 5, laid wreath at concentration camp site and also at a **Bitburg** cemetery, where some Nazis were buried.

Philadelphia police bombed a rowhouse occupied by **MOVE** radical group, May 13; 11 were killed, and fire damaged 2 blocks of houses.

On June 14, **terrorists seized** a TWA jet after takeoff from Athens, Greece; 153 passengers and crew held hostage for 17 days; 1 U.S. serviceman killed.

Reversing an earlier decision to market "new" Coke, the **Coca-Cola Co.** said, July 10, it would resume marketing soda made under its original "Classic" formula.

Live Aid, a rock concert broadcast around the world July 13, raised $70 mil for starving peoples of Africa.

On Oct. 7, 4 **Palestinian hijackers** seized Italian cruise ship *Achille Lauro* in the Mediterranean for 2 days. One American, **Leon Klinghoffer**, was killed.

For first time in 6 years U.S. and Soviet leaders met at **summit in Geneva**, Nov. 19-20.

General Electric agreed Dec. 11 to buy RCA Corp. for $6.28 bil.

1986

The U.S. officially observed **Martin Luther King Jr. Day** for the first time Jan. 20.

Space shuttle *Challenger* **exploded** 73 seconds after liftoff, Jan. 28, killing 6 astronauts and Teacher in Space Project participant Christa McAuliffe.

In a 4-day extravaganza in July, the U.S. celebrated the 100th birthday of the **Statue of Liberty**.

Congress completed action Oct. 2

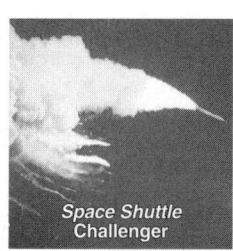

Space Shuttle Challenger

overriding a veto to place economic **sanctions** on **South Africa**.

The Senate confirmed, Sept. 17, Reagan's nomination of **William Rehnquist** as chief justice and **Antonin Scalia** as associate justice of the Supreme Court.

Press reports in early Nov. broke first news of the **Iran-Contra scandal**, involving secret U.S. sale of arms to Iran.

Ivan Boesky, accused of insider trading, agreed, Nov. 14, to plead guilty to an unspecified criminal count.

Robert Penn Warren was named by the Library of Congress as America's **first poet laureate**.

1987

Pres. Reagan produced the nation's **first trillion-dollar budget**, Jan. 5.

Dow Jones closed above 2,000 for first time, Jan. 8.

The FDA approved, Mar. 20, **AZT**, **first drug** shown to be effective in **fight against AIDS**.

Nearly 1.4 mil **illegal aliens** met May 4 deadline for applying for **amnesty** under a new federal policy.

An **Iraqi missile** killed 37 sailors on the frigate USS *Stark* in the Persian Gulf, May 17. Iraq called it an accident.

Public hearings by Senate and House committees investigating the **Iran-Contra affair** were held May-Aug. Lt. Col. **Oliver North**, former National Security Council staff member, said he had believed all his activities were authorized by his superiors. Pres. Reagan, Aug. 12, denied knowing of a diversion of funds to the contras.

The 200th anniversary of the **U.S. Constitution** signing was observed, Sept. 17, in Philadelphia and around the U.S.

Wall Street crashed, Oct. 19, with the Dow Jones plummeting a record 508 points to 1,738, ending a bull market that began in mid-**1982**.

Pres. **Reagan** and Soviet leader **Mikhail Gorbachev** Dec. 8, signed a **pact to dismantle** all 1,752 U.S. and 859 Soviet **missiles** with a 300- to 3,400-mi. range.

1988

In a report issued May 16, Surgeon Gen. C. Everett Koop declared that **cigarettes** were **addictive**.

Congress approved, in June, the greatest expansion yet of **Medicare** benefits, to protect the elderly and disabled against "catastrophic" medical costs. The act was repealed, however, in November **1989**.

Much of the U.S. suffered **worst drought** in over 50 years; by late June half the nation's agricultural counties had been declared disaster areas.

A missile, fired from U.S. Navy warship *Vincennes* in the Persian Gulf, mistakenly struck a commercial **Iranian airliner**, July 3, killing all 290 aboard.

George H. W. Bush (R) was elected 41st U.S. president, Nov. 8, decisively defeating Massachusetts Gov. **Michael Dukakis** (D).

Pan Am Flight 103 exploded and crashed, due to a terrorist bomb, into the town of **Lockerbie, Scotland**, Dec. 21, killing all 259 people aboard and 11 on the ground.

Drexel Burnham Lambert agreed, Dec. 21, to plead guilty to **insider trading** and other violations, and pay penalties of $650 mil, the largest such settlement ever.

1989

Major oil spill occurred when the *Exxon Valdez* struck Bligh Reef in Alaska's Prince William Sound, Mar. 24.

Oliver North was convicted, May 4, on charges related to **Iran-Contra scandal**. Conviction thrown out on appeal in **1991** because of his immunized testimony.

A measure to rescue the **savings and loan industry** was signed into law, Aug. 9, by Pres. Bush.

Army Gen. **Colin Powell** became **first black chairman** of the **Joint Chiefs of Staff** after being nominated Aug. 10 by Pres. Bush.

Baseball legend **Pete Rose** was banned from the game for life Aug. 24 for involvement with gamblers.

Hurricane Hugo swept through the Caribbean and the Carolinas Sept. 10-22, causing at least 40 deaths and $6 bil in damage in the Carolinas alone.

Just before a World Series game, Oct. 17, an **earthquake** struck the **San Francisco Bay area**, causing 62 deaths.

L. Douglas Wilder (D) elected governor of Virginia, the **first black governor** since Reconstruction.

U.S. troops **invaded Panama**, Dec. 20, overthrowing the government of **Manuel Noriega**. Noriega, wanted by U.S. authorities on drug charges, surrendered Jan. 3, **1990**.

1990

Junk bond financier **Michael Milken** pleaded guilty to fraud-related charges, Apr. 14; agreed to pay $500 mil in restitution; sentenced Nov. 21 to 10 years in prison.

Justice **William Brennan** announced, July 20, his resignation from the U.S. Supreme Court. His replacement, Judge **David Souter**, was confirmed Sept. 27.

Pres. Bush signed **Americans with Disabilities Act**, barring discrimination against the disabled, July 26.

Operation Desert Shield forces left for Saudi Arabia Aug. 7, to defend that country following the **invasion** of **Kuwait by Iraq**, Aug. 2.

Pres. Bush signed, Nov. 5, a bill to **reduce budget deficits** $500 bil over 5 years through spending curbs and tax hikes.

Pres. Bush Nov. 15 signed into law a strengthened version of the **1970 Clean Air Act**.

1991

The U.S. and its allies **defeated Iraq** in the **Persian Gulf War** and liberated Kuwait, which Iraq had invaded the previous year. On Jan. 17, the allies launched a devastating air attack. In a rapid ground war starting Feb. 24, which lasted just 100 hours, the U.S.-led forces killed or captured thousands of Iraqi soldiers and sent the rest into retreat before Pres. Bush ordered a cease-fire Feb. 27.

An 8-month **recession** showed signs of having ended in Mar. The **Dow Jones** Industrial Average closed above **3,000** for first time, Apr. 17.

U.S. **House bank** ordered closed Oct. 3 after revelations that House members had written 8,331 bad checks.

Justice **Thurgood Marshall**, first black to sit on U.S. Supreme Court announced, June 17, plans to retire. The Senate approved, Oct. 15, nomination of **Clarence Thomas** to replace Marshall, despite allegations of sexual harassment against him by former aide **Anita Hill**. Thomas became the second black person to serve on the Court.

Charles Keating convicted of securities fraud Dec. 4. The prosecution asserted that as chairman of an S&L he had induced investors to buy $250 mil in uninsured bonds.

1992

Retail giant **R.H. Macy & Co.** filed for bankruptcy, Jan. 27.

Major U.S. carrier **Trans World Airlines**, filed for bankruptcy Jan. 31.

Riots swept South Central **Los Angeles** Apr. 29, after jury acquitted 4 white police officers on all but one count in videotaped **1991** beating of black motorist **Rodney King**. Death toll in the L.A. violence was put at 52.

27th Amendment, regarding congressional pay raises, ratified May 7.

Hurricane Andrew ravaged South Florida and Louisiana Aug. 24-26, killing 23.

White supremacist and fugitive Randall Weaver surrendered Aug. 31 after an 11-day FBI **siege** at his **Ruby Ridge**, ID, cabin, during which his wife, son, and a deputy sheriff were killed in exchanges of gunfire.

Bill Clinton (D) was elected 42nd president, Nov. 3, defeating Pres. **Bush** (R) and independent **Ross Perot**.

A UN-sanctioned military force, led by U.S. troops, arrived in **Somalia** Dec. 9.

Presidents of U.S., Canada, and Mexico Dec. 17 signed **North American Free Trade Agreement** (NAFTA), which took effect Jan. 1, **1994**.

More than 1.1 mil votes were cast to choose a portrait of the late **Elvis Presley** for a **postage stamp**, the first in the U.S. to honor a rock performer.

1993

A **bomb** exploded in a parking garage beneath the **World Trade Center** in New York City, Feb. 26, killing 6 people. Two Islamic militants were convicted in the bombing, Nov. 12, **1997**. Four men were found guilty, Mar. 4, **1994**.

Janet Reno became the **first female** U.S. **attorney general** Mar. 12.

Four federal agents were killed Feb. 28 during an unsuccessful raid on the **Branch Davidian** compound near **Waco**, TX. A 51-day siege by agents ended Apr. 19, when the compound burned down, leaving more than 70 cult members dead. Eleven cult members were acquitted Feb. 26, **1994**, of charges in the deaths of the federal agents. U.S. agents were cleared of wrongdoing in **2000**.

A federal jury, Apr. 17, found 2 Los Angeles police officers guilty and 2 not guilty of violating the civil rights of motorist **Rodney King** in **1991** videotaped beating incident.

Defense Sec. Les Aspin, Apr. 28, removed restrictions on aerial **combat roles for women** in the armed forces.

In a May 14 plebiscite voters in **Puerto Rico** supported continuing **commonwealth status** with U.S.

A **"motor-voter" bill** was signed by Pres. Clinton, May 20, allowing citizens to register to vote by mail when applying for a driver's license or certain benefits.

"The Great Flood of 1993" inundated 8 mil acres in 9 Midwestern states in summer, leaving 50 dead.

Pres. Clinton July 2 approved recommendations that 33 major U.S. **military bases** be closed. On July 19 he announced a **"don't ask, don't tell, don't pursue"** policy for homosexuals in the military.

Judge **Ruth Bader Ginsburg** was sworn in, Aug. 10, as 107th justice of the Supreme Court.

Pres. Clinton, Aug. 10, signed a measure designed to **cut federal budget deficits** $496 bil over 5 years, through spending cuts and new taxes.

The **Brady Bill**, a major gun-control measure, was signed into law by Pres. Clinton Nov. 30.

1994

A predawn **earthquake** in the **Los Angeles** area, Jan. 17, claimed 61 lives and caused widespread devastation.

Pres. Clinton Feb. 3 lifted 19-year ban on U.S. **trade with Vietnam**.

Kenneth Starr named Aug. 5 as independent counsel to probe **Whitewater affair**; congressional committees, late July, began Whitewater hearings.

Byron De La Beckwith convicted Feb. 5 of the **1963** murder of civil rights leader **Medgar Evers**.

Longtime CIA officer **Aldrich Ames** and his wife were charged Feb. 21 with spying. Under a plea bargain, he received life in prison, while she drew 63 months.

U.S. troops, Mar. 25, officially ended peacekeeping and humanitarian aid mission in **Somalia** begun in **1992**.

Major league **baseball players** went on **strike** following Aug. 11 games; World Series canceled; strike ended Apr. 25, **1995**.

Senate Majority Leader George Mitchell (D-ME), Sept. 26, dropped efforts to pass Pres. Clinton's **health-care reform** package.

1995

Sen. **Bob Dole** (R-KS) became Senate majority leader and Rep. **Newt Gingrich** (R-GA) was elected House speaker when 104th Congress opened, Jan. 4. A bill to end Congress's exemption from federal labor laws, first in a series of measures in Republicans' "**Contract with America**," cleared Congress Jan. 17; signed into law Jan. 23.

Clinton invoked emergency powers, Jan. 31, to extend a **$20 bil loan** to help **Mexico** avert financial collapse.

The last UN peacekeeping troops withdrew from **Somalia** Feb. 28-Mar. 3, with the aid of U.S. Marines. In **Haiti**, peacekeeping responsibilities were transferred from U.S. to UN forces Mar. 31, with the U.S. providing 2,400 soldiers.

A truck **bomb** exploded outside a **federal office building** in **Oklahoma City** Apr. 19, killing 168 people in deadliest terrorist attack yet on U.S. soil; **Timothy McVeigh** was first and key suspect arrested, Apr. 21.

The U.S. space shuttle *Atlantis* made the first in a series of **dockings with** Russian space station *Mir*, June 29-July 4.

A U.S. **F-16 fighter jet** piloted by Air Force Capt. **Scott O'Grady** was shot down over Bosnia and Herzegovina June 2; O'Grady was rescued by U.S. Marines 6 days later.

The U.S. announced on July 11 that it was reestablishing diplomatic **relations with Vietnam**.

Former football star **O. J. Simpson** found not guilty Oct. 3 of the June **1994** murders of his former wife, Nicole Brown Simpson, and her friend Ron Goldman.

Ten Muslim militants convicted in New York, Oct. 1, in a failed plot to blow up **UN Headquarters** and other buildings and assassinate political leaders.

Shannon Faulkner won a legal fight to gain admission to the previously all-male cadet corps of **The Citadel** in South Carolina, Aug. 11, though she dropped out after a few days of training.

Hundreds of thousands of black men participated in **Million Man March** and rally in Washington, DC, Oct. 16, organized by Rev. **Louis Farrakhan**.

The federal **55-mph speed limit** was repealed by a measure signed Nov. 28.

After talks outside Dayton, OH, warring parties in **Bosnia and Herzegovina reached agreement** Nov. 21 to end their conflict; treaty was signed Dec. 14, after which first of some 20,000 U.S. peacekeeping troops arrived in Bosnia.

Five Americans were among 7 killed, Nov. 13, in **bombing** of a U.S. military post in **Riyadh**, Saudi Arabia.

A budget impasse between Congress and Pres. Clinton led to a **partial government shutdown** beginning Nov. 14. Operations resumed Nov. 20 under continuing resolutions.

1996

Senate, Jan. 26, approved, 87-4, the Second Strategic Arms Reduction Treaty (**START II**).

On Feb. 24 **Cuban jets** shot down 2 civilian planes owned by a Cuban exile group; 4 killed. Cuba claimed its territory was violated; U.S., Feb. 26, tightened embargo.

John Salvi found guilty, Mar. 18, in the **1994** murder of receptionists at 2 **abortion clinics** in Brookline, MA.

Congress, in March, approved a **line item veto** bill, but it was struck down by the Supreme Court, June 25, **1998**.

James and **Susan McDougal** were convicted May 28 of fraud and conspiracy in the **Whitewater** case. Arkansas Gov. **Jim Guy Tucker** was convicted of similar charges by the same jury.

The antitax **Freemen** surrendered to federal authorities June 13 after an 81-day standoff near Jordan, MT; 4 were convicted, July 8, **1998**, of conspiring to defraud banks.

Republicans June 12 chose Sen. **Trent Lott** (MS) as new majority leader to replace Sen. **Robert Dole**, who resigned, June 11, to focus on his presidential campaign.

A **bomb** exploded at a military complex near Dhahran, **Saudi Arabia**, June 25, killing 19 American service personnel.

On July 27 a **bomb** exploded in Atlanta, GA, near the **Summer Olympics**. One person was killed.

Major **welfare reform bill** was signed into law Aug. 22.

Shannon Lucid, Sept. 26, completed a **space voyage** of 188 days, a record for women and for U.S. astronauts.

Pres. **Clinton** was reelected to second term, Nov. 5.

1997

Bombs were detonated at **abortion clinics** in Tulsa, OK, Jan. 1, in Atlanta on Jan. 16, and again at the first site in Tulsa on Jan. 19; 6 people were injured.

Newt Gingrich (R-GA) was reelected Speaker of the U.S. House Jan. 7 but was fined and reprimanded by colleagues for alleged misuse of tax-exempt donations.

Madeleine Albright was sworn in as secretary of state Jan. 23, becoming the **first female head** of the **State Dept.**

Former CIA official **Harold Nicholson** pleaded guilty, Mar. 3, to spying for Russia.

Thirty-nine members of the **Heaven's Gate religious cult** found dead in Rancho Santa Fe, CA, house Mar. 26, in an apparent mass suicide.

Timothy McVeigh convicted of conspiracy and murder, June 2, in **1995** Oklahoma City bombing.

On Oct. 27, the **Dow Jones** fell 554.26 points, largest 1-day point decline yet. On Oct. 28, the Dow rebounded, surging 337.17 points, largest-yet single-day point advance.

Islamic militants **Ramzi Ahmed Yousef** and **Eyad Ismoil Yousef** convicted, Nov. 12, in the **1993** bombing of the New York City **World Trade Center**.

On Nov. 19, Bobbi McCaughey delivered the **first set** of **live septuplets** to survive more than a month.

Terry Nichols convicted Dec. 23 on charges related to the **1995** Oklahoma City bombing.

1998

It was reported Jan. 21 that Whitewater independent counsel **Kenneth Starr** had evidence of a **sexual relationship** between Pres. **Clinton** and onetime White House intern **Monica Lewinsky**. Clinton denied it.

Theodore Kaczynski, the "**Unabomber**," arrested in Montana in 1993, pleaded guilty Jan. 22 in California and New Jersey bombings that killed 3 people and injured 2.

The state of Texas, Feb. 3, **executed** its **first female convict** in 135 years—**Karla Faye Tucker**.

Two **youths aged 11 and 13** were arrested, Mar. 24, in the killing of 4 schoolgirls and a teacher outside a **Jonesboro, AR, school**; later committed to a juvenile detention center.

On Apr. 25, First Lady **Hillary Rodham Clinton** provided videotaped testimony at the White House for the Little Rock, AR, grand jury in the **Whitewater** case.

Lewinsky, Aug. 6, testified to having had a sexual relationship with Pres. **Clinton**, but said she was never asked to lie. In grand jury testimony and an address to the nation, Aug. 17, Clinton acknowledged an inappropriate relationship with Lewinsky. On Sept. 9, independent counsel Starr sent the House what he called "credible information that may constitute grounds" for impeachment.

Mark McGwire, Sept. 8, hit his 62nd **home run** of the season, breaking **Roger Maris**'s season record.

On Sept. 30, Pres. Clinton announced a **budget surplus** of $70 billion for fiscal year 1998, the first since 1969.

Terrorist **bombs** in **U.S. embassies** in Nairobi, Kenya, and Dar-es-Salaam, Tanzania, killed at least 257, Aug. 7. The U.S. launched **retaliatory strikes**, Aug. 20, against alleged terrorist-related targets in Afghanistan and Sudan.

The House Judiciary Committee, Oct. 5, voted 21-16 along party lines to recommend that the Clinton **impeachment** investigation proceed. The House concurred Oct. 8, voting 258-176; 31 Democrats voted yes.

John Glenn, first U.S. astronaut to orbit Earth, returned to space at age 77, Oct. 29-Nov. 7, aboard the shuttle *Discovery*.

Pres. **Clinton**, Nov. 13, settled a suit by agreeing to pay $850,000 to **Paula Corbin Jones**. She alleged that he had made an unwanted sexual advance on her in **1991**.

The country's 4 largest **tobacco companies**, in a settlement, Nov. 23, with 46 states, DC, and 4 territories, agreed to pay $206 bil over 25 years to cover public health costs related to smoking.

The House, Dec. 19, approved 2 articles of **impeachment** charging Pres. **Clinton** with grand jury perjury (228-206) and obstruction of justice (221-212) in a cover-up of his sexual relationship with **Lewinsky**; 2 other impeachment articles failed.

1999

J. Dennis Hastert (R-IL) was elected Speaker of the House for the 106th Congress, Jan. 6.

Pres. **Clinton's impeachment trial**—the second such trial in U.S. history—began in the GOP-controlled Senate Jan. 7. He was acquitted, Feb. 12. The perjury article failed, with 45 votes; the obstruction of justice article drew a 50-50 vote, with a two-thirds vote needed for conviction.

Dr. **Jack Kevorkian**, who claimed to have helped 130 people kill themselves, convicted of 2nd-degree murder Mar. 26 in one death; sentenced to 10-25 years in prison.

Two men were convicted in the **1998** beating death of **Matthew Shepard**, an openly homosexual student at the Univ. of Wyoming.

Eric Harris, 18, and **Dylan Klebold**, 17, killed 12 fellow students and a teacher Apr. 20 at **Columbine** High School in Littleton, CO, then fatally shot themselves.

One NYC police officer pleaded guilty to 6 charges, May 25, and another was convicted on an assault charge, June 8, in connection with the **1997** torture and sodomizing of Haitian immigrant **Abner Louima** in a police station.

John F. Kennedy Jr., son of the former president, died in a plane crash July 16, along with his wife and sister-in-law.

2000

Across the U.S., midnight celebrations marked the changeover to the **year 2000** on Jan. 1; the feared **Y2K** computer glitch caused only minor problems.

America Online Inc. announced Jan. 10 that it would buy **Time Warner Inc.**, in the largest merger to date. The FTC approved it Dec. 14.

Teams of scientists from the U.S. and Britain announced jointly, June 26, that they had determined the structure of the **human genome**.

Following a bitter legal controversy, 6-year-old Cuban **Elián González** was returned to Cuba June 28, 7 months after he was rescued from a boat wreck off the Florida coast.

The Justice Dept., July 21, cleared U.S. agents of any wrongdoing in a **1993** assault on the compound of the **Branch Davidian** religious sect in **Waco**, TX.

Tiger Woods became the youngest player, at age 24, to win all 4 of golf's majors with a record score in the British Open, July 23.

Seventeen U.S. sailors were killed Oct. 12 in terrorist bombing of the **USS Cole**, which was refueling in Aden, Yemen.

The U.S. Food and Drug Administration announced, Sept. 28, approval of **RU-486**, a pill that induces abortions.

On **election night**, Nov. 7, the winner of Florida's 25 deciding electoral votes remained uncertain. The Florida Supreme Court, Dec. 8, ordered a manual recount of all ballots that did not have a vote for president recorded by machine. On Dec. 12, the U.S. Supreme Court reversed that decision. Vice Pres. **Gore** conceded the presidential election to Texas Gov. **George W. Bush** in a televised address, Dec. 13.

2001

Congress, Jan. 6, certified **George W. Bush** as president by an electoral vote of 271-266 (1 Gore elector abstained). He was sworn in as the 43rd president Jan. 20.

AOL Time Warner merger completed, Jan. 11.

Outgoing Pres. Clinton issued 176 pardons and commutations, Jan. 20, including that of **Marc Rich**, a fugitive commodities trader whose ex-wife was a Clinton financial backer.

FBI agent **Robert Hanssen** was arrested Feb. 20 and charged 2 days later with spying for the Soviet Union and Russia.

A **U.S. Navy spy plane collided** with a Chinese fighter plane over the South China Sea Apr. 1, killing the fighter pilot. The 24 U.S. crew members were detained in Hainan until U.S. officials expressed apology, Apr. 12.

Sen. **James Jeffords** (R-VT) announced May 24 he was leaving his party, giving Democrats control of the Senate.

Congress approved, May 26, a $1.35 trillion **tax cut** spread over 10 years.

Oklahoma City bomber **Timothy McVeigh** was executed June 11 by lethal injection in Terre Haute, IN.

Rep. **Gary Condit** (D-CA), in a TV interview Aug. 23, denied involvement in the Apr. 30 disappearance of intern **Chandra Levy**, with whom he had had an affair. Levy's remains were later found in a DC park.

Bush announced Aug. 9 he would allow federal funding of limited **stem-cell research** using human embryos.

On the morning of **Sept. 11**, 2 hijacked commercial airliners struck the **twin towers** of the **World Trade Center** in New York City, in the **worst-ever terrorist attack** on American soil. A 3rd hijacked plane destroyed a portion of the **Pentagon**; a 4th crashed in a field in Somerset County, **Pennsylvania**. Some 3,000 people were killed, including about 2,800 at the World Trade Center. U.S. observed a national day of mourning, Sept. 14.

Congress, Sept. 21, approved a $15 bil **bailout package** for the **airline industry**.

Five people died, and 14 became ill from exposure to **anthrax** traveling through the U.S. mail, Oct. 5-Nov. 21.

The U.S. and Britain Oct. 7 launched a sustained air-strike campaign against Afghan-based terrorist organization **al-Qaeda** and the country's ruling **Taliban** militia.

On Oct. 7, San Francisco Giants outfielder **Barry Bonds** hit his 73rd **home run** for a single season record.

Pres. Bush created a new **Office of Homeland Security** Oct. 8 and signed a federal **antiterrorism bill** Oct. 26.

The **Taliban** surrendered Kabul, the Afghan capital, Nov. 13, and fled from Kandahar, their stronghold, Dec. 7.

Taliban member and U.S. citizen **John Walker Lindh** was captured Dec. 2 by U.S. forces in Afghanistan.

Leading energy-trading company **Enron** became the largest firm thus far to file for bankruptcy, Dec. 2.

The U.S. government, Dec. 11, indicted **Zacarias Moussaoui** as an alleged Sept. 11 co-conspirator.

Pres. Bush announced Dec. 13 that the U.S. would withdraw from the **1972 Antiballistic Missile Treaty**.

Pres. Bush, Dec. 28, formally granted **permanent normal trade status** to **China**, as of Jan. 1, **2002**.

2002

Taliban and al-Qaeda fighters captured in Afghanistan were flown to a U.S. naval base at **Guantanamo Bay** in Cuba, with the first 20 arriving Jan. 11.

A House committee Jan. 14 released parts of a letter from Sherron Watkins, an **Enron** employee, to CEO **Kenneth Lay**, warning him the company could "implode" in scandal. Lay resigned Jan. 23. Congress, Jan. 24, began public hearings into the Enron bankruptcy.

In his first State of the Union address, Jan. 29, Pres. Bush called Iran, Iraq, and North Korea part of an **"axis of evil."**

Eight U.S. troops were killed Mar. 2-4 in an assault against Taliban and al-Qaeda forces in eastern Afghanistan. By Mar. 6, 1,200 U.S. troops were involved in **Operation Anaconda**, which ended Mar. 12.

A final independent prosecutor's report Mar. 20 found **insufficient evidence** that Pres. Clinton or his wife had committed any crime in connection with **Whitewater**.

Pres. Bush Mar. 27 signed into law a major **campaign-finance reform** bill.

A ceremonial last girder was removed May 30 from the site of the **World Trade Center** towers in New York, signaling the **end** of a massive **clean-up and recovery** operation.

Coleen Rowley testified before a congressional committee June 6 that Washington FBI agents had stymied investigative efforts in Minneapolis prior to Sept. 11.

U.S. **Roman Catholic bishops**, meeting in Dallas, TX, June 13-15, approved stringent policies dealing with priests who sexually abuse minors; revised rules formulated with Vatican approval were adopted by the bishops Nov. 13.

A federal jury convicted the **Arthur Andersen** accounting firm of obstruction of justice June 15.

WorldCom announced June 25 that it had overstated its cash flow by billions; on July 21, it displaced Enron as the **largest U.S. company** to declare **bankruptcy**.

On July 4, an Egyptian-born gunman killed 2 people near a ticket counter for Israeli airline **El Al** at L.A. International Airport; he was shot dead by an El Al guard.

A **rescue** operation July 28 saved the lives of 9 miners trapped in a Pennsylvania **coal mine**.

Pres. Bush told the UN General Assembly Sept. 12 that he would work with the Security Council to deal with the threat posed by **Iraqi weapons of mass destruction**.

Richard Reid pleaded guilty Oct. 4 to all charges stemming from an incident aboard a Paris-to-Miami flight in Dec. **2001**, when he tried to ignite **explosives in his shoes**.

Four men were arrested in **Portland, OR**, Oct. 4, and charged with plotting to join **al-Qaeda** and **Taliban** forces; a fifth suspect was later arrested in Malaysia. On Oct. 9, the head of an Islamic charity, the Benevolence International Foundation, was charged with funneling money to al-Qaeda.

Former Pres. **Jimmy Carter** was named Oct. 10 as winner of a **Nobel Peace Prize**.

On Oct. 10-11 the House, 296-133, and Senate, 77-23, gave Bush backing to use **military force against Iraq**.

The Bush administration revealed Oct. 16 that **North Korea** had acknowledged it was developing **nuclear arms**.

John Muhammad and **Lee Malvo** were arrested Oct. 24 in connection with a series of random **sniper shootings** in the Washington, DC, area that left 10 dead.

Sen. **Paul Wellstone** (D-MN) died in a plane crash near Eveleth, MN, Oct. 25, with his wife, daughter, and 5 others.

Pres Bush, Oct. 29, signed a measure providing $3.9 bil to the states to fix shortcomings in their **election process**.

An **antitrust settlement** between **Microsoft Corp.** and Justice Dept. was approved Nov. 1 by a federal judge.

Republicans emerged from elections, Nov. 5, with a majority in the Senate and an increased margin in the House.

House Democrats elected Rep. **Nancy Pelosi** (CA) Nov. 14 to head their caucus in the new Congress, the **first woman** to **lead either party in the House**.

Pres. Bush Nov. 25 signed legislation creating a cabinet-level **Dept. of Homeland Security**.

Cardinal **Bernard Law**, Dec. 13, resigned as archbishop of Boston after being criticized for allegedly covering up instances of children being sexually abused by Catholic priests.

On Dec. 16, Pres. Bush named former New Jersey Gov. Thomas Kean to chair a national **commission** investigating the **Sept. 11 attacks**.

Bush, Dec. 17, ordered the Pentagon to proceed with construction of a limited **missile defense shield**.

Trent Lott (R-MS) bowed out as the new Senate majority leader Dec. 20 shortly after being chosen amid furor over a comment apparently supporting segregation; Sen. **Bill Frist** (R-TN) was elected as leader Dec. 23.

2003

On Jan. 10-11, shortly before leaving office, Gov. **George Ryan** (R-IL) **pardoned or commuted death sentences** of 171 Illinois death row convicts.

The Senate, Jan. 22, approved 94-0, Pres. Bush's nomination of **Tom Ridge** to be **secretary of homeland security**.

Space shuttle *Columbia* **broke apart** Feb. 1 over southwestern U.S. during its descent toward a planned landing; all 7 crew members were killed. An official report issued Aug. 26 found the immediate cause to be damage sustained during liftoff when a chunk of foam came loose and hit the left wing; it also cited a "broken safety culture" at NASA.

The Senate, Mar. 6, approved, 95-0, the **Strategic Offensive Reductions Treaty** signed in **2002** by U.S. and Russian leaders. It required the 2 countries to reduce their deployed nuclear warheads to 1,700-2,200 by **2012**.

A U.S.-led military offensive aimed at **ousting Saddam Hussein** got underway Mar. 19, when 40 Tomahawk cruise missiles hit targets in Baghdad; strikes continued in succeeding nights. U.S. forces Mar. 21 seized major **oil fields** near **Basra**. On Apr. 1, U.S. forces announced the rescue from an Iraqi hospital of injured Army Pfc. **Jessica Lynch**, one of a group of soldiers ambushed near Nasiriya.

On Apr. 3, U.S. Marines crossed the Tigris River and moved close to **Baghdad**. By Apr. 8, major government buildings had been occupied and **organized resistance** had **dropped**. With the collapse of the regime, services in major cities were disrupted, and looting became widespread. Pres. Bush, speaking from the aircraft carrier *Abraham Lincoln*, declared on May 1 the **end of major combat operations**. However, insurgents continued to mount attacks against both military and civilian targets.

The *New York Times*, May 11, published a long story documenting major deceptions and inaccuracies by reporter **Jayson Blair**.

Pres. Bush signed a measure May 28 providing $318 bil in **tax cuts** over 10 years.

Under a settlement in a private antitrust suit brought by Netscape (a unit of AOL), **Microsoft** agreed May 29 to pay **AOL Time Warner** $750 mil.

On June 23, the Supreme Court, voting 5-4, **upheld** an **affirmative action program** providing preference to minorities for admission to the Univ. of Michigan law school. But the Court, 6-3, rejected an undergraduate affirmative action program at the university that employed numerical formulas.

The Labor Dept. reported July 3 that June **unemployment** had climbed to a 9-year high of 6.4%. Since Feb. **2001**, the economy had lost almost 2.6 mil jobs.

U.S. soldiers killed 2 once-powerful **sons of Saddam Hussein**—**Uday and Qusay**—in a gun battle in Mosul, northern Iraq, July 22.

A **power failure** spread rapidly through Ohio, Michigan, and the Northeast, as well as eastern Canada, on Aug. 14. Some 50 mil people in 8 states and the province of Ontario were left without electricity for as long as 2 days.

Former priest **John Geoghan**, incarcerated for child sex abuse, was strangled in a state prison in Shirley, MA, Aug. 23, apparently by another inmate.

On Sept. 9, the Roman Catholic archdiocese of Boston and lawyers representing about 550 victims of **sexual abuse** by priests announced a **settlement** worth up to $85 mil.

Richard Grasso, chairman and CEO of the New York Stock Exchange, resigned under fire, Sept. 17.

California voters Oct. 7 voted to recall Democratic Gov. Gray Davis from office and replace him with Republican actor-turned-politician **Arnold Schwarzenegger**.

Forest fires in southern California in late October laid waste to over 700,000 acres and destroyed 3,000 homes.

The Rev. V. Gene Robinson was consecrated Nov. 2 as Episcopal bishop of New Hampshire, becoming the **first openly gay prelate** in the Episcopal Church U.S.A.

The Senate Nov. 3 approved by voice vote the **$87.5 bil** that Pres. Bush sought for **U.S. military forces** in **Iraq** and for helping to rebuild the country. The House had given its approval, 298-121, on Oct. 31.

A Virginia jury Nov. 17 found **John Muhammad** guilty in the **2002** Washington, DC, area **sniper attacks**; he was sentenced to death. Another VA jury found **Lee Malvo** guilty of 2 counts of murder in the attacks, Dec. 18; he was sentenced to life in prison without parole.

The **Massachusetts Supreme Judicial Court**, decided 4-3 Nov. 18, held that **gay couples** had a **right to marry** under the state constitution.

Saddam Hussein was **captured** by U.S. military forces Dec. 13, in an underground hideout southeast of Tikrit.

Pres. Bush signed a bill Dec. 8 overhauling **Medicare**. The program would offer in **2006** its first-ever prescription drug benefit, and private insurance companies would have a larger role in covering Medicare beneficiaries.

The Bush administration announced Dec. 23 that a Holstein in Washington State had tested positive for **mad-cow disease**; the animal, the first in the U.S. to be so identified, had already been slaughtered.

2004

Sen. **John Kerry** (MA) became the Democratic frontrunner in the candidacy for the presidency by winning the Jan. 19 Iowa caucus and the Jan. 27 New Hampshire primary.

During the Super Bowl XXXVIII **halftime show**, Feb. 1, Justin Timberlake tore Janet Jackson's top garment, exposing her breast in what was called a **"wardrobe malfunction."**

On Feb. 12, **San Francisco** began issuing **marriage licenses** to thousands of **same-sex couples**. On Mar. 11, the state supreme court issued a stay blocking the practice.

Media entrepreneur **Martha Stewart** was convicted Mar. 5 of conspiracy and obstruction of justice and sentenced to 5 months in prison.

The **National World War II Memorial** in Washington, DC, opened to the public April 29. It was dedicated May 29.

Photos showing humiliating **abuse** of **Abu Ghraib Prison inmates** in Iraq by American soldiers emerged Apr. 30, provoking outrage.

Ronald Reagan, 40th U.S. president, died at his home in Los Angeles June 5. He had been diagnosed with Alzheimer's disease in **1994**.

In one of the biggest upsets in NBA history, the **Detroit Pistons** defeated the Los Angeles Lakers to win the NBA championships, June 15.

The U.S.-led coalition formally **transferred power** to an **interim Iraqi government** on June 28.

Connecticut Gov. **John Rowland** (R), facing impeachment amid federal corruption charges, announced his resignation, effective July 1. He pleaded guilty Dec. 23 to one charge of corruption.

The **9/11 Commission Report**, released to the public July 22, summarized what was known about the events of that day and called for a restructuring of U.S. intelligence operations.

In Boston, July 26-29, **Democrats nominated** Sen. **John Kerry** for president and Sen. **John Edwards** (NC) for vice president.

The **Statue of Liberty reopened** Aug. 3, having been closed for nearly two years following the Sept. 11, **2001**, terrorist attacks. Extensive security and safety upgrades were completed to accommodate visitors.

Four hurricanes—Charley, Frances, Ivan, and Jeanne—hit Florida and surrounding states Aug. 13-Sept. 25. The storms were blamed for over 50 deaths and more than $20 bil in damage in the U.S. Flooding was severe in Alabama, Georgia, Louisiana, and South Carolina.

New Jersey Gov. **James McGreevey** (D) Aug. 12 announced his resignation, effective Nov. 15, citing an extramarital affair with another man.

Pres. **Bush** and Vice Pres. **Cheney** were renominated Sept. 1 on the **Republican ticket** at the party convention in New York.

The number of **U.S. soldiers killed** in the Iraqi conflict **reached 1,000** on Sept. 7, including 755 in combat.

CBS, Sept. 8, aired a *60 Minutes* story claiming it had obtained documents showing that Pres. **Bush** had failed to meet his responsibilities while in the **National Guard** in the 1970s. CBS Evening News managing editor and anchorman, **Dan Rather**, admitted on air Sept. 20, however, that the documents could not be authenticated.

The **Supreme Court** announced Oct. 25 that Chief Justice **William H. Rehnquist** was being treated for thyroid cancer. He did not attend oral arguments at the Court for the remainder of the year.

The **Boston Red Sox** swept their last 8 games to win the **World Series** Oct. 27, for the first time since **1918**.

Pres. **George W. Bush** was reelected Nov. 2, capturing 31 states with 286 electoral votes, just 16 more than the 270 needed. The Republicans gained 4 Senate seats for a new 55-44 majority. Republicans won a majority in the House for the sixth consecutive election. The newly elected House had 232 Republicans, 202 Democrats, and 1 independent.

After a weeklong campaign, U.S. forces took control of the Iraqi city of **Fallujah** from insurgents, Nov. 14.

In an episode broadcast Nov. 30, **Ken Jennings** ended his record-setting 75-game **winning streak** on *Jeopardy!*, having won over $2.5 mil.

Pres. Bush signed an intelligence reform bill Dec. 17, based on the 9/11 Commission's findings. The bill created a **director of national intelligence** to oversee the nation's intelligence agencies.

2005

Army Reserve Spec. **Charles Graner** was found guilty, Jan. 14, of assault and other charges in connection with the **Abu Ghraib** prisoner abuses in Iraq and sentenced to 10 years in prison. Pfc. **Lynndie England**, who had been photographed posing with prisoners, was convicted Sept. 26 and sentenced to 3 years in prison.

Pres. **Bush** inaugurated for a second term, Jan. 20.

Condoleezza Rice became **first black woman** to serve as **secretary of state**, Jan. 26.

Alberto Gonzalez became **first Hispanic U.S. attorney general**, Feb. 3.

The Supreme Court, Mar. 1, ruled 5-4 that **executing** convicts who committed their crimes **before age 18** violated the constitutional ban on cruel and unusual punishment.

Terri Schiavo, who had been in a persistent vegetative state since **1990**, died Mar. 31, 13 days after her feeding tube was removed. She had been at the center of a legal dispute between her husband, who was her legal guardian, and her parents.

Zacarias Moussaoui, a French citizen with Moroccan roots, pleaded guilty to 6 counts of conspiracy Apr. 22. He said Osama bin Laden had instructed him to fly a plane into the White House but denied he was to be one of the Sept. 11 hijackers.

A report in *Newsweek*, contending that Guantanamo Bay interrogators had **flushed** a copy of the **Koran down a toilet**, sparked riots in Afghanistan, May 10, and anti-American protests in several Muslim countries, May 27. *Newsweek* issued a retraction May 16, saying its source could no longer confirm the incident.

A bipartisan group of 14 Senators reached a compromise, May 23, averting a deadlock over judicial nominees. Democrats had threatened to filibuster to prevent an up or down vote on nominees they thought extreme. Majority Leader **Bill Frist** (R-TN) had said he was prepared to invoke the **"nuclear option"**—changing Senate rules to reduce from 60 to 51 the number of votes needed to cut off debate.

A *Vanity Fair* article revealed May 31 that former FBI official **W. Mark Felt** was **"Deep Throat"**—a source for *Washington Post* reporters Bob Woodward and Carl Bernstein when they investigated the **1972** Watergate break-in.

Supreme Court Justice **Sandra Day O'Connor** announced, July 1, that she would retire, effective when her replacement was confirmed.

Lance Armstrong won a record-setting seventh straight **Tour de France** July 24.

The **Teamsters** and the **Service Employees International Union** declared July 25 that they were pulling out of the **AFL-CIO** to form their own coalition. The **United Food and Commercial Workers** announced its secession July 29.

Discovery blasted off from Cape Canaveral, FL, July 26, in the first shuttle launch since the fleet was grounded following the **2003** *Columbia* disaster. **NASA** announced, July 27, however, that it was suspending future shuttle missions until continuing problems with foam insulation and the heat shield were resolved.

Pres. Bush Aug. 23 rejected calls from war protesters—including **Cindy Sheehan**, whose son was killed in Iraq—for the U.S. to **withdraw** its **troops from Iraq**.

After striking Florida's Atlantic coast, Aug. 26, **Hurricane Katrina** struck the Gulf Coast Aug. 29, causing devastation in Louisiana, Mississippi, and Alabama. A breech in a levee on Lake Pontchartrain Aug. 30 flooded **New Orleans**, forcing more than 10,000 refugees to crowd into the Superdome.

Chief Justice **William H. Rehnquist** died Sept. 3. Bush announced Sept. 5 that he would nominate as successor Judge **John G. Roberts Jr.**, who Bush had earlier nominated to replace Justice O'Connor. Roberts was sworn in as 17th chief justice Sept. 29. Roberts, at 50 years of age, became the **youngest chief justice** since **1801**.

House Majority Leader Rep. **Tom DeLay** (R-TX) was indicted in Texas Sept. 28 for allegedly conspiring to launder illegal contributions. He temporarily stepped down from his leadership post after his indictment. Majority Whip Rep. **Roy Blunt** (MO) was chosen interim leader.

Civil rights icon **Rosa Parks** died Oct. 24. On Oct. 30, she became the **first woman** to **lie in honor** in the **Capitol rotunda** and the 31st person overall.

The **Chicago White Sox** Oct. 26 defeated the Houston Astros to win their first **World Series** title since **1917**.

White House counsel **Harriet Miers**, nominated Oct. 3 to the Supreme Court, withdrew her name in a letter to the president Oct. 27. In her place, Pres. Bush, Oct. 31, named Judge **Samuel A. Alito Jr.**

A federal grand jury indicted **I. Lewis (Scooter) Libby**, chief of staff for Vice Pres. Cheney and an assistant to Pres. Bush, on 5 counts of obstruction of justice, false statements, and perjury, Oct. 28, in connection with the leaking of the identity of CIA agent **Valerie Plame Wilson**. Libby resigned the same day.

Judge John Jones III struck down, Dec. 20, a requirement by a Pennsylvania school district that 9th grade biology students be read a statement promoting **intelligent design** as an alternative to evolution.

The Senate, Dec. 21, passed a $453 bil **defense appropriations bill**, 93-0, after the inclusion of an **anti-torture amendment**. A provision that would have allowed oil drilling in Alaska's **Arctic National Wildlife Refuge** had been removed after Republican leaders realized they would not otherwise have enough votes to end debate.

Tropical Storm Zeta, Dec. 29, was the season's 28th tropical storm, ending the **most active hurricane season on record.**

Patrick Henry's Speech to the Virginia Convention

The following is an excerpt from Patrick Henry's speech to the Virginia Convention, which met at St. John's Church in Richmond, on Mar. 23, 1775, to react to British oppression.

Gentlemen may cry, peace, peace—but there is no peace. The war is actually begun! The next gale that sweeps from the north will bring to our ears the clash of resounding arms! Our brethren are already in the field! Why stand we here idle? What is it that gentlemen wish? What would they have? Is life so dear, or peace so sweet, as to be purchased at the price of chains and slavery? Forbid it, Almighty God! I know not what course others may take; but as for me, give me liberty, or give me death!

How the Declaration of Independence Was Adopted

On June 7, 1776, Richard Henry Lee, who had issued the first call for a congress of the colonies, introduced in the Continental Congress at Philadelphia a resolution declaring "that these United Colonies are, and of right ought to be, free and independent states, that they are absolved from all allegiance to the British Crown, and that all political connection between them and the state of Great Britain is, and ought to be, totally dissolved."

The resolution, seconded by John Adams on behalf of the Massachusetts delegation, came up again on June 11 when a committee of 5, headed by Thomas Jefferson, was appointed to express the purpose of the resolution in a declaration of independence. The other 4 were John Adams, Benjamin Franklin, Robert R. Livingston, and Roger Sherman.

Drafting the Declaration was assigned to Jefferson, who worked on a portable desk of his own construction in a room at Market and 7th St. The committee reported the result on June 28, 1776. The members of the Congress suggested a number of changes, which Jefferson called "deplorable." They didn't approve Jefferson's arraignment of the British people and King George III for encouraging and fostering the slave trade, which Jefferson called "an execrable commerce." They eliminated 630 words and added 146, leaving 1,322 words in the final draft. In its final form, capitalization was erratic. Jefferson had written that men were endowed with "inalienable" rights; in the final copy it came out as "unalienable" and has been thus ever since.

The Lee-Adams resolution of independence was adopted by 12 "yeas" on July 2—the actual date of the act of independence. The Declaration, which explains the act, was adopted July 4.

After the Declaration was adopted, July 4, 1776, it was turned over to John Dunlap, printer, to be printed on broadsides. The original copy was lost and one of his broadsides

was attached to a page in the journal of the Congress. It was read aloud July 8 in Philadelphia, PA, Easton, PA, and Trenton, NJ. On July 9, it was read by order of Gen. George Washington to the troops assembled on the Common in New York City (City Hall Park).

The Continental Congress of July 19, 1776, adopted the following resolution:

"Resolved, That the Declaration passed on the 4th, be fairly engrossed on parchment with the title and stile of 'The Unanimous Declaration of the thirteen United States of America' and that the same, when engrossed, be signed by every member of Congress."

Not all delegates who signed the engrossed Declaration were present on July 4. Robert Morris (PA), William Williams (CT), and Samuel Chase (MD) signed on Aug. 2; Oliver Wolcott (CT), George Wythe (VA), Richard Henry Lee (VA), and Elbridge Gerry (MA) signed in August and September; Matthew Thornton (NH) joined the Congress Nov. 4 and signed later. Thomas McKean (DE) rejoined Washington's army before signing and said later that he signed in 1781.

Charles Carroll of Carrollton was appointed a delegate by Maryland on July 4, 1776, presented his credentials July 18, and signed the engrossed Declaration on Aug. 2. Born Sept. 19, 1737, he was 95 years old and the last surviving signer when he died on Nov. 14, 1832.

Two Pennsylvania delegates who did not support the Declaration on July 4 were replaced. The 4 New York delegates did not have authority from their state to vote on July 4. On July 9, the New York state convention authorized its delegates to approve the Declaration, and the Congress was so notified on July 15, 1776. The 4 signed the Declaration on Aug. 2.

The original engrossed Declaration is preserved in the National Archives Building in Washington, DC.

Declaration of Independence

The Declaration of Independence was adopted by the Continental Congress in Philadelphia on July 4, 1776. John Hancock was president of the Congress, and Charles Thomson was secretary. A copy of the Declaration, engrossed on parchment, was signed by members of Congress on and after Aug. 2, 1776. On Jan. 18, 1777, Congress ordered that "an authenticated copy, with the names of the members of Congress subscribing the same, be sent to each of the United States, and that they be desired to have the same put on record." Authenticated copies were printed in broadside form in Baltimore, where the Continental Congress was then in session. The following text is that of the original printed by John Dunlap at Philadelphia for the Continental Congress. The original is on display at the National Archives in Washington, DC.

IN CONGRESS, July 4, 1776.
A DECLARATION
By the REPRESENTATIVES of the
UNITED STATES OF AMERICA,
In GENERAL CONGRESS assembled

When in the Course of human Events, it becomes necessary for one People to dissolve the Political Bands which have connected them with another, and to assume among the Powers of the Earth, the separate and equal Station to which the Laws of Nature and of Nature's God entitle them, a decent Respect to the Opinions of Mankind requires that they should declare the causes which impel them to the Separation.

We hold these Truths to be self-evident, that all Men are created equal, that they are endowed by their Creator with certain unalienable Rights, that among these are Life, Liberty, and the Pursuit of Happiness—That to secure these Rights, Governments are instituted among Men, deriving their just Powers from the Consent of the Governed, that whenever any Form of Government becomes destructive of these Ends, it is the Right of the People to alter or to abolish

it, and to institute new Government, laying its Foundation on such Principles, and organizing its Powers in such Form, as to them shall seem most likely to effect their Safety and Happiness. Prudence, indeed, will dictate that Governments long established should not be changed for light and transient Causes; and accordingly all Experience hath shewn, that Mankind are more disposed to suffer, while Evils are sufferable, than to right themselves by abolishing the Forms to which they are accustomed. But when a long Train of Abuses and Usurpations, pursuing invariably the same Object, evinces a Design to reduce them under absolute Despotism, it is their Right, it is their Duty, to throw off such Government, and to provide new Guards for their future Security. Such has been the patient Sufferance of these Colonies; and such is now the Necessity which constrains them to alter their former Systems of Government. The History of the present King of Great-Britain is a History of repeated Injuries and Usurpations, all having in direct Object the Establishment of an absolute Tyranny over these States. To prove this, let Facts be submitted to a candid World.

He has refused his Assent to Laws, the most wholesome and necessary for the public Good.

He has forbidden his Governors to pass Laws of immediate and pressing Importance, unless suspended in their Operation till his Assent should be obtained; and when so suspended, he has utterly neglected to attend to them.

He has refused to pass other Laws for the Accommodation of large Districts of People, unless those People would relinquish the Right of Representation in the Legislature, a Right inestimable to them, and formidable to Tyrants only.

He has called together Legislative Bodies at Places unusual, uncomfortable, and distant from the Depository of their Public Records, for the sole Purpose of fatiguing them into Compliance with his Measures.

He has dissolved Representative Houses repeatedly, for opposing with manly Firmness his Invasions on the Rights of the People.

He has refused for a long Time, after such Dissolutions, to cause others to be elected; whereby the Legislative Powers, incapable of Annihilation, have returned to the People at large for their exercise; the State remaining in the mean time exposed to all the Dangers of Invasion from without, and Convulsions within.

He has endeavoured to prevent the Population of these States; for that Purpose obstructing the Laws for Naturalization of Foreigners; refusing to pass others to encourage their Migrations hither, and raising the Conditions of new Appropriations of Lands.

He has obstructed the Administration of Justice, by refusing his Assent to Laws for establishing Judiciary Powers.

He has made Judges dependent on his Will alone, for the Tenure of their Offices, and the Amount and payment of their Salaries.

He has erected a Multitude of new Offices, and sent hither Swarms of Officers to harrass our People, and eat out their Substance.

He has kept among us, in Times of Peace, Standing Armies, without the consent of our Legislatures.

He has affected to render the Military independent of, and superior to the Civil Power.

He has combined with others to subject us to a Jurisdiction foreign to our Constitution, and unacknowledged by our Laws; giving his Assent to their Acts of pretended Legislation:

For quartering large Bodies of Armed Troops among us:

For protecting them, by a mock Trial, from Punishment for any Murders which they should commit on the Inhabitants of these States:

For cutting off our Trade with all Parts of the World:

For imposing Taxes on us without our Consent:

For depriving us, in many Cases, of the Benefits of Trial by Jury:

For transporting us beyond Seas to be tried for pretended Offences:

For abolishing the free System of English Laws in a neighbouring Province, establishing therein an arbitrary Government, and enlarging its Boundaries, so as to render it at once an Example and fit Instrument for introducing the same absolute Rule into these Colonies:

For taking away our Charters, abolishing our most valuable Laws, and altering fundamentally the Forms of our Governments:

For suspending our own Legislatures, and declaring themselves invested with Power to legislate for us in all Cases whatsoever.

He has abdicated Government here, by declaring us out of his Protection and waging War against us.

He has plundered our Seas, ravaged our Coasts, burnt our towns, and destroyed the Lives of our People.

He is, at this Time, transporting large Armies of foreign Mercenaries to complete the works of Death, Desolation, and Tyranny, already begun with circumstances of Cruelty and Perfidy, scarcely paralleled in the most barbarous Ages,

and totally unworthy the Head of a civilized Nation.

He has constrained our fellow Citizens taken Captive on the high Seas to bear Arms against their Country, to become the Executioners of their Friends and Brethren, or to fall themselves by their Hands.

He has excited domestic Insurrections amongst us, and has endeavoured to bring on the Inhabitants of our Frontiers, the merciless Indian Savages, whose known Rule of Warfare, is an undistinguished Destruction, of all Ages, Sexes and Conditions.

In every stage of these Oppressions we have Petitioned for Redress in the most humble Terms: Our repeated Petitions have been answered only by repeated Injury. A Prince, whose Character is thus marked by every act which may define a Tyrant, is unfit to be the Ruler of a free People.

Nor have we been wanting in Attentions to our British Brethren. We have warned them from Time to Time of Attempts by their Legislature to extend an unwarrantable Jurisdiction over us. We have reminded them of the Circumstances of our Emigration and Settlement here. We have appealed to their native Justice and Magnanimity, and we have conjured them by the Ties of our common Kindred to disavow these Usurpations, which, would inevitably interrupt our Connections and Correspondence. They too have been deaf to the Voice of Justice and of Consanguinity. We must, therefore, acquiesce in the Necessity, which denounces our Separation, and hold them, as we hold the rest of Mankind, Enemies in War, in Peace, Friends.

We, therefore, the Representatives of the UNITED STATES OF AMERICA, in General Congress, Assembled, appealing to the Supreme Judge of the World for the Rectitude of our Intentions, do, in the Name, and by Authority of the good People of these Colonies, solemnly Publish and Declare, That these United Colonies are, and of Right ought to be, Free and Independent States; that they are absolved from all Allegiance to the British Crown, and that all political Connection between them and the State of Great-Britain, is and ought to be totally dissolved; and that as Free and Independent States, they have full Power to levy War, conclude Peace, contract Alliances, establish Commerce, and to do all other Acts and Things which Independent States may of right do. And for the support of this declaration, with a firm Reliance on the Protection of Divine Providence, we mutually pledge to each other our lives, our Fortunes, and our sacred Honor.

JOHN HANCOCK, President

Attest.

CHARLES THOMSON, Secretary.

Signers of the Declaration of Independence

Delegate (state)	Occupation	Birthplace	Born	Died
Adams, John (MA)	Lawyer	Braintree (Quincy), MA	Oct. 30, 1735	July 4, 1826
Adams, Samuel (MA)	Political leader	Boston, MA	Sept. 27, 1722	Oct. 2, 1803
Bartlett, Josiah (NH)	Physician, judge	Amesbury, MA	Nov. 21, 1729	May 19, 1795
Braxton, Carter (VA)	Farmer	Newington Plantation, VA	Sept. 10, 1736	Oct. 10, 1797
Carroll, Charles of Carrollton (MD)	Merchant	Annapolis, MD	Sept. 19, 1737	Nov. 14, 1832
Chase, Samuel (MD)	Judge	Princess Anne, MD	Apr. 17, 1741	June 19, 1811
Clark, Abraham (NJ)	Surveyor	Elizabethtown, NJ	Feb. 15, 1726	Sept. 15, 1794
Clymer, George (PA)	Merchant	Philadelphia, PA	Mar. 16, 1739	Jan. 23, 1813
Ellery, William (RI)	Lawyer	Newport, RI	Dec. 22, 1727	Feb. 15, 1820
Floyd, William (NY)	Soldier	Brookhaven, NY	Dec. 17, 1734	Aug. 4, 1821
Franklin, Benjamin (PA)	Printer, publisher	Boston, MA	Jan. 17, 1706	Apr. 17, 1790
Gerry, Elbridge (MA)	Merchant	Marblehead, MA	July 17, 1744	Nov. 23, 1814
Gwinnett, Button (GA)	Merchant	Gloucester, England	c. 1735	May 19, 1777
Hall, Lyman (GA)	Physician	Wallingford, CT	Apr. 12, 1724	Oct. 19, 1790
Hancock, John (MA)	Merchant	Braintree (Quincy), MA	Jan. 12, 1737	Oct. 8, 1793
Harrison, Benjamin (VA)	Farmer	Charles City County, VA	Apr. 5, 1726	Apr. 24, 1791
Hart, John (NJ)	Farmer	Stonington, CT	c. 1711	May 11, 1779
Hewes, Joseph (NC)	Merchant	Kingston, NJ	Jan. 23, 1730	Nov. 10, 1779
Heyward, Thos. Jr. (SC)	Lawyer, farmer	St. Luke's Parish, SC	July 28, 1746	Mar. 6, 1809
Hooper, William (NC)	Lawyer	Boston, MA	June 17, 1742	Oct. 14, 1790
Hopkins, Stephen (RI)	Judge, educator	Providence, RI	Mar. 7, 1707	July 13, 1785
Hopkinson, Francis (NJ)	Judge, author	Philadelphia, PA	Oct. 2, 1737	May 9, 1791
Huntington, Samuel (CT)	Judge	Windham, CT	July 3, 1731	Jan. 5, 1796
Jefferson, Thomas (VA)	Lawyer	Shadwell, VA	Apr. 13, 1743	July 4, 1826
Lee, Francis Lightfoot (VA)	Farmer	Westmoreland County, VA	Oct. 14, 1734	Jan. 11, 1797
Lee, Richard Henry (VA)	Farmer	Westmoreland County, VA	Jan. 20, 1732	June 19, 1794
Lewis, Francis (NY)	Merchant	Llandaff, Wales	Mar. 21, 1713	Dec. 31, 1802
Livingston, Philip (NY)	Merchant	Albany, NY	Jan. 15, 1716	June 12, 1778
Lynch, Thomas Jr. (SC)	Farmer	Winyah, SC	Aug. 5, 1749	(at sea) 1779
McKean, Thomas (DE)	Lawyer	New London, PA	Mar. 19, 1734	June 24, 1817
Middleton, Arthur (SC)	Farmer	Charleston, SC	June 26, 1742	Jan. 1, 1787
Morris, Lewis (NY)	Farmer	Morrisania (Bronx County), NY	Apr. 8, 1726	Jan. 22, 1798
Morris, Robert (PA)	Merchant	Liverpool, England	Jan. 31, 1734	May 8, 1806
Morton, John (PA)	Judge	Ridley, PA	c. 1724	Apr. 1777
Nelson, Thos. Jr. (VA)	Farmer	Yorktown, VA	Dec. 26, 1738	Jan. 4, 1789
Paca, William (MD)	Judge	Abingdon, MD	Oct. 31, 1740	Oct. 23, 1799
Paine, Robert Treat (MA)	Judge	Boston, MA	Mar. 11, 1731	May 12, 1814
Penn, John (NC)	Lawyer	Caroline County, VA	May 17, 1741	Sept. 14, 1788
Read, George (DE)	Judge	Cecil County, MD	Sept. 18, 1733	Sept. 21, 1798
Rodney, Caesar (DE)	Judge	Dover, DE	Oct. 7, 1728	June 29, 1784
Ross, George (PA)	Judge	New Castle, DE	May 10, 1730	July 14, 1779
Rush, Benjamin (PA)	Physician	Byberry, PA (Philadelphia)	Jan. 4, 1746	Apr. 19, 1813
Rutledge, Edward (SC)	Lawyer	Charleston, SC	Nov. 23, 1749	Jan. 23, 1800
Sherman, Roger (CT)	Lawyer	Newton, MA	Apr. 19, 1721	July 23, 1793
Smith, James (PA)	Lawyer	Northern Ireland	c. 1719	July 11, 1806
Stockton, Richard (NJ)	Lawyer	Princeton, NJ	Oct. 1, 1730	Feb. 28, 1781
Stone, Thomas (MD)	Lawyer	Charles County, MD	c. 1743	Oct. 5, 1787
Taylor, George (PA)	Ironmaster	Ireland	c. 1716	Feb. 23, 1781
Thornton, Matthew (NH)	Physician	Ireland	c. 1714	June 24, 1803
Walton, George (GA)	Judge	Cumberland County, VA	c. 1741	Feb. 2, 1804
Whipple, William (NH)	Merchant, judge	Kittery, ME	Jan. 14, 1730	Nov. 28, 1785
Williams, William (CT)	Merchant	Lebanon, CT	Apr. 8, 1731	Aug. 2, 1811
Wilson, James (PA)	Judge	Carskerdo, Scotland	Sept. 14, 1742	Aug. 21, 1798
Witherspoon, John (NJ)	Clergyman, educator	Gifford, Scotland	Feb. 5, 1723	Nov. 15, 1794
Wolcott, Oliver (CT)	Judge	Windsor, CT	Nov. 20, 1726	Dec. 1, 1797
Wythe, George (VA)	Lawyer	Elizabeth City Co., VA	c. 1726	June 8, 1806

Origin of the Constitution

The War of Independence was conducted by delegates from the original 13 states, who comprised the Congress of the United States of America, known as the Continental Congress. In 1777 the Congress submitted to the legislatures of the states the Articles of Confederation and Perpetual Union, which were ratified by New Hampshire, Massachusetts, Rhode Island, Connecticut, New York, New Jersey, Pennsylvania, Delaware, Virginia, North Carolina, South Carolina, Georgia, and finally, in 1781, Maryland.

The first article read: "The stile of this confederacy shall be the United States of America." This did not signify a sovereign nation, because the states delegated only those powers they could not handle individually, such as to wage war, make treaties, and contract debts for general expenses (e.g., paying the army). Taxes for payment of such debts were levied by the individual states. The president signed himself "President of the United States in Congress assembled," but here the United States were considered in the plural, a cooperating group.

When the war was won, it became evident that a stronger federal union was needed. The Congress left the initiative to the legislatures. Virginia in Jan. 1786 appointed commissioners to meet with representatives of other states; delegates from Virginia, Delaware, New York, New Jersey, and Pennsylvania met at Annapolis. Alexander Hamilton prepared their call asking delegates from all states to meet in Philadelphia in May 1787 "to render the Constitution of the federal government adequate to the exigencies of the union." Congress endorsed the plan on Feb. 21, 1787. Delegates were appointed by all states except Rhode Island.

> **IT'S A FACT:** Jacob Shallus, an assistant clerk of the Pennsylvania State Assembly at the time of the Constitutional Convention, was paid $30 in 1787 to engross, or write down in final form, the copy of the Constitution that would later be signed by convention delegates.

The convention was called for May 14, 1787, but a quorum was not present until May 25. George Washington was chosen president (presiding officer). The states certified 65 delegates, but 10 did not attend. The work was done by 55, not all of whom were present at all sessions. Of the 55 attending delegates, 16 failed to sign, and 39 actually signed Sept. 17, 1787, some with reservations. Some historians have said 74 delegates (9 more than the 65 actually certified) were named and 19 failed to attend. These 9 additional persons refused the appointment, were never delegates, and were never counted as absentees. Washington sent the Constitution to Congress, and that body, Sept. 28, 1787, ordered it sent to the legislatures, "in order to be submitted to a convention of delegates chosen in each state by the people thereof."

The Constitution was ratified by votes of state conventions as follows: Delaware, Dec. 7, 1787, unanimous; Pennsylvania, Dec. 12, 1787, 46 to 23; New Jersey, Dec. 18, 1787, unanimous; Georgia, Jan. 2, 1788, unanimous; Connecticut, Jan. 9, 1788, 128 to 40; Massachusetts, Feb. 6, 1788, 187 to 168; Maryland, Apr. 28, 1788, 63 to 11; South Carolina, May 23, 1788, 149 to 73; New Hampshire, June 21, 1788, 57 to 46; Virginia, June 25, 1788, 89 to 79; New York, July 26, 1788, 30 to 27. Nine states were needed to establish the operation of the Constitution "between the states so ratifying the same," and New Hampshire was the 9th state. The government did not declare the Constitution in effect until the first Wednesday in Mar. 1789, which was Mar. 4. After that, North Carolina ratified it on Nov. 21, 1789, 194 to 77; and Rhode Island, May 29, 1790, 34 to 32. Vermont in convention ratified it on Jan. 10, 1791, and by act of Congress approved on Feb. 18, 1791, was admitted into the Union as the 14th state, Mar. 4, 1791.

Constitution of the United States
The Original 7 Articles

The text of the Constitution given here (except for Amendment XXVII) is from the pocket-size edition of the Constitution published by the U.S. Government Printing Office as a result of a congressional resolution to print the Constitution in its original form as amended through July 5, 1971. *Text in brackets* indicates that an item has been superseded or amended, or provides background information. **Boldface text preceding** an article, section, or amendment is a brief summary, added by *The World Almanac*.

PREAMBLE

We, the People of the United States, in Order to form a more perfect Union, establish Justice, insure domestic Tranquility, provide for the common defence, promote the general Welfare, and secure the Blessings of Liberty to ourselves and our Posterity, do ordain and establish this Constitution for the United States of America.

ARTICLE I.

Section 1—Legislative powers; in whom vested.

All legislative Powers herein granted shall be vested in a Congress of the United States, which shall consist of a Senate and House of Representatives.

Section 2—House of Representatives, how and by whom chosen. Qualifications of a Representative. Representatives and direct taxes, how apportioned. Enumeration. Vacancies to be filled. Power of choosing officers, and of impeachment.

The House of Representatives shall be composed of Members chosen every second Year by the People of the several States, and the Electors in each State shall have the Qualifications requisite for Electors of the most numerous Branch of the State Legislature.

No person shall be a Representative who shall not have attained to the Age of twenty-five Years, and been seven Years a Citizen of the United States, and who shall not, when elected, be an Inhabitant of that State in which he shall be chosen.

[Representatives and direct taxes shall be apportioned among the several States which may be included within this Union, according to their respective Numbers, which shall be determined by adding to the whole Number of free Persons, including those bound to Service for a Term of Years, and excluding Indians not taxed, three-fifths of all other persons.] [The previous sentence was superseded by Amendment XIV, section 2.] The actual Enumeration shall be made within three Years after the first Meeting of the Congress of the United States, and within every subsequent Term of ten Years, in such Manner as they shall by Law direct. The Number of Representatives shall not exceed one for every thirty Thousand, but each State shall have at Least one Representative; and until such enumeration shall be made, the State of New Hampshire shall be entitled to chuse three, Massachusetts eight, Rhode-Island and Providence Plantations one, Connecticut five, New-York six, New Jersey four, Pennsylvania eight, Delaware one, Maryland six, Virginia

ten, North Carolina five, South Carolina five, and Georgia three.

When vacancies happen in the Representation from any State, the Executive Authority thereof shall issue Writs of Election to fill such Vacancies.

The House of Representatives shall chuse their Speaker and other Officers; and shall have the sole Power of Impeachment.

Section 3—Senators, how and by whom chosen. How classified. Qualifications of a Senator. President of the Senate, his right to vote. President pro tem., and other officers of the Senate, how chosen. Power to try impeachments. When President is tried, Chief Justice to preside. Sentence.

The Senate of the United States shall be composed of two Senators from each State, *[chosen by the Legislature thereof]* *[The preceding five words were superseded by Amendment XVII.]* for six Years; and each Senator shall have one Vote.

Immediately after they shall be assembled in Consequence of the first Election, they shall be divided as equally as may be into three Classes. The Seats of the Senators of the first Class shall be vacated at the Expiration of the second Year, of the second Class at the Expiration of the fourth Year, and of the third Class at the Expiration of the Sixth year, so that one-third may be chosen every second Year; *[and if Vacancies happen by Resignation, or otherwise, during the Recess of the Legislature of any State, the Executive thereof may make temporary Appointments until the next Meeting of the Legislature, which shall then fill such Vacancies.]* *[The words in brackets were superseded by Amendment XVII.]*

No person shall be a Senator who shall not have attained to the Age of thirty Years, and been nine Years a Citizen of the United States, and who shall not, when elected, be an Inhabitant of that State for which he shall be chosen.

The Vice President of the United States shall be President of the Senate, but shall have no Vote, unless they be equally divided.

The Senate shall chuse their other Officers, and also a President pro tempore, in the absence of the Vice President, or when he shall exercise the Office of President of the United States.

The Senate shall have the sole Power to try all Impeachments. When sitting for that Purpose, they shall be on Oath or Affirmation. When the President of the United States is tried, the Chief Justice shall preside: And no Person shall be convicted without the Concurrence of two thirds of the Members present.

Judgment in Cases of Impeachment shall not extend further than to removal from Office, and disqualification to hold and enjoy any Office of honor, Trust or Profit under the United States: but the Party convicted shall nevertheless be liable and subject to Indictment, Trial, Judgment and Punishment, according to Law.

Section 4—Times, etc., of holding elections, how prescribed. One session each year.

The Times, Places and Manner of holding Elections for Senators and Representatives, shall be prescribed in each State by the Legislature thereof; but the Congress may at any time by Law make or alter such Regulations, except as to the Place of Chusing Senators.

The Congress shall assemble at least once in every Year, and such Meeting shall be *[on the first Monday in December,]* *[The words in brackets were superseded by Amendment XX, section 2.]* unless they shall by Law appoint a different Day.

Section 5—Membership, quorum, adjournments, rules. Power to punish or expel. Journal. Time of adjournments, how limited, etc.

Each House shall be the Judge of the Elections, Returns and Qualifications of its own Members, and a Majority of each shall constitute a Quorum to do Business; but a smaller number may adjourn from day to day, and may be authorized to compel the Attendance of absent Members, in such manner, and under such Penalties as each House may provide.

Each House may determine the Rules of its Proceedings, punish its members for disorderly Behavior, and, with the Concurrence of two thirds, expel a Member.

Each House shall keep a Journal of its Proceedings, and from time to time publish the same, excepting such Parts as may in their Judgment require Secrecy; and the Yeas and Nays of the Members of either House on any question shall, at the Desire of one fifth of those Present, be entered on the Journal.

Neither House, during the Session of Congress, shall, without the Consent of the other, adjourn for more than three days, nor to any other Place than that in which the two Houses shall be sitting.

Section 6—Compensation, privileges, disqualifications in certain cases.

The Senators and Representatives shall receive a Compensation for their Services, to be ascertained by Law, and paid out of the Treasury of the United States. They shall in all Cases, except Treason, Felony and Breach of the Peace, be privileged from Arrest during their Attendance at the Session of their respective Houses, and in going to and returning from the same; and for any Speech or Debate in either House, they shall not be questioned in any other Place.

No Senator or Representative shall, during the Time for which he was elected, be appointed to any civil Office under the Authority of the United States, which shall have been created, or the Emoluments whereof shall have been encreased during such time; and no Person holding any Office under the United States, shall be a Member of either House during his Continuance in Office.

Section 7—House to originate all revenue bills. Veto. Bill may be passed by two-thirds of each House, notwithstanding, etc. Bill, not returned in ten days, to become a law. Provisions as to orders, concurrent resolutions, etc.

All bills for raising Revenue shall originate in the House of Representatives; but the Senate may propose or concur with Amendments as on other Bills.

Every Bill which shall have passed the House of Representatives and the Senate, shall, before it become a Law, be presented to the President of the United States; If he approve he shall sign it, but if not he shall return it, with his Objections to that House in which it shall have originated, who shall enter the Objections at large on their Journal, and proceed to reconsider it. If after such Reconsideration two thirds of that House shall agree to pass the Bill, it shall be sent, together with the Objections, to the other House, by which it shall likewise be reconsidered, and if approved by two thirds of that House, it shall become a Law. But in all such Cases the Votes of both Houses shall be determined by Yeas and Nays, and the Names of the Persons voting for and against the Bill shall be entered on the Journal of each House respectively. If any Bill shall not be returned by the President within ten Days (Sundays excepted) after it shall have been presented to him, the Same shall be a Law, in like Manner as if he had signed it, unless the Congress by their Adjournment prevent its Return, in which Case it shall not be a Law.

Every order, Resolution, or Vote to which the Concurrence of the Senate and House of Representatives may be necessary (except on a question of Adjournment) shall be presented to the President of the United States; and before the Same shall take Effect, shall be approved by him, or being disapproved by him, shall be repassed by two thirds of the Senate and House of Representatives, according to the Rules and Limitations prescribed in the Case of a Bill.

Section 8—Powers of Congress.

The Congress shall have Power To lay and collect Taxes, Duties, Imposts and Excises, to pay the Debts and provide for the common Defence and general Welfare of the United States; but all Duties, Imposts and Excises shall be uniform throughout the United States;

To borrow money on the credit of the United States;

To regulate Commerce with foreign Nations, and among the several States, and with the Indian Tribes;

To establish an uniform Rule of Naturalization, and uniform Laws on the subject of Bankruptcies throughout the United States;

To coin Money, regulate the Value thereof, and of foreign Coin, and fix the Standard of Weights and Measures;

To provide for the Punishment of counterfeiting the Securities and current Coin of the United States;

To establish Post Offices and post Roads;

To promote the Progress of Science and useful Arts, by securing for limited Times to Authors and Inventors the exclusive Right to their respective Writings and Discoveries;

To constitute Tribunals inferior to the supreme Court;

To define and punish Piracies and Felonies committed on the high Seas, and Offenses against the Law of Nations;

To declare War, grant Letters of Marque and Reprisal, and make Rules concerning Captures on Land and Water;

To raise and support Armies, but no Appropriation of Money to that Use shall be for a longer Term than two Years;

To provide and maintain a Navy;

To make Rules for the Government and Regulation of the land and naval Forces;

To provide for calling forth the Militia to execute the Laws of the Union, suppress Insurrections and repel Invasions;

To provide for organizing, arming, and disciplining the Militia, and for governing such Part of them as may be employed in the Service of the United States, reserving to the States respectively, the Appointment of the Officers, and the Authority of training the Militia according to the discipline prescribed by Congress;

To exercise exclusive Legislation in all Cases whatsoever, over such District (not exceeding ten Miles square) as may, by Cession of particular States, and the acceptance of Congress, become the Seat of the Government of the United States, and to exercise like Authority over all Places purchased by the Consent of the Legislature of the State in which the Same shall be, for the Erection of Forts, Magazines, Arsenals, dock-Yards, and other needful Buildings;—And

To make all Laws which shall be necessary and proper for carrying into Execution the foregoing Powers, and all other Powers vested by this Constitution in the Government of the United States, or in any Department or Officer thereof.

Section 9—Provision as to migration or importation of certain persons. Habeas corpus, bills of attainder, etc. Taxes, how apportioned. No export duty. No commercial preference. Money, how drawn from Treasury, etc. No titular nobility. Officers not to receive presents, etc.

The Migration or Importation of such Persons as any of the States now existing shall think proper to admit, shall not be prohibited by the Congress prior to the Year one thousand eight hundred and eight, but a tax or duty may be imposed on such Importation, not exceeding ten dollars for each Person.

The privilege of the Writ of Habeas Corpus shall not be suspended, unless when in Cases of Rebellion or Invasion the public Safety may require it.

No Bill of Attainder or ex post facto Law shall be passed.

No capitation, or other direct, Tax shall be laid, unless in Proportion to the Census or Enumeration herein before directed to be taken. *[Modified by Amendment XVI.]*

No Tax or Duty shall be laid on Articles exported from any State.

No Preference shall be given by any Regulation of Commerce or Revenue to the Ports of one State over those of another: nor shall Vessels bound to, or from, one State, be obliged to enter, clear, or pay Duties in another.

No Money shall be drawn from the Treasury, but in Consequence of Appropriations made by Law; and a regular Statement and Account of the Receipts and Expenditures of all public Money shall be published from time to time.

No Title of Nobility shall be granted by the United States: and no Person holding any Office of Profit or Trust under them, shall, without the Consent of the Congress, accept of any present, Emolument, Office, or Title, of any kind whatever, from any King, Prince, or foreign State.

Section 10—States prohibited from the exercise of certain powers.

No State shall enter into any Treaty, Alliance, or Confederation; grant Letters of Marque and Reprisal; coin Money; emit Bills of Credit; make any Thing but gold and silver Coin a Tender in Payment of Debts; pass any Bill of Attainder, ex post facto Law, or Law impairing the Obligation of Contracts, or grant any Title of Nobility.

No State shall, without the Consent of the Congress, lay any Imposts or Duties on Imports or Exports, except what may be absolutely necessary for executing its inspection Laws: and the net Produce of all Duties and Imposts, laid by any State on Imports or Exports, shall be for the Use of the Treasury of the United States; and all such Laws shall be subject to the Revision and Control of the Congress.

No State shall, without the Consent of Congress, lay any duty of Tonnage, keep Troops, or Ships of War in time of Peace, enter into any Agreement or Compact with another State, or with a foreign Power, or engage in War, unless actually invaded, or in such imminent Danger as will not admit of delay.

ARTICLE II.

Section 1—President: his term of office. Electors of President; number and how appointed. Electors to vote on same day. Qualification of President. On whom his duties devolve in case of his removal, death, etc. President's compensation. His oath of office.

The executive Power shall be vested in a President of the United States of America. He shall hold his Office during the Term of four Years, and, together with the Vice President, chosen for the same Term, be elected, as follows.

Each State shall appoint, in such Manner as the Legislature thereof may direct, a Number of Electors, equal to the whole Number of Senators and Representatives to which the State may be entitled in the Congress: but no Senator or Representative, or Person holding an Office of Trust or Profit under the United States, shall be appointed an Elector.

[The Electors shall meet in their respective States, and vote by Ballot for two persons, of whom one at least shall not be an Inhabitant of the same State with themselves. And they shall make a List of all the Persons voted for, and of the Number of Votes for each; which List they shall sign and certify, and transmit sealed to the Seat of the Government of the United States, directed to the President of the Senate. The President of the Senate shall, in the Presence of the Sen-

ate and House of Representatives, open all the Certificates, and the Votes shall then be counted. The Person having the greatest Number of Votes shall be the President, if such Number be a Majority of the whole Number of Electors appointed; and if there be more than one who have such Majority, and have an equal Number of Votes, then the House of Representatives shall immediately chuse by Ballot one of them for President; and if no Person have a Majority, then from the five highest on the List the said House shall in like Manner chuse the President. But in chusing the President, the Votes shall be taken by States, the Representation from each State having one Vote; a quorum for this Purpose shall consist of a Member or Members from two thirds of the States, and a Majority of all the States shall be necessary to a Choice. In every Case, after the Choice of the President, the Person having the greatest Number of Votes of the Electors shall be the Vice President. But if there should remain two or more who have equal Votes, the Senate shall chuse from them by Ballot the Vice-President.] [This clause was superseded by Amendment XII.]

The Congress may detemine the Time of chusing the Electors, and the Day on which they shall give their Votes; which Day shall be the same throughout the United States.

No person except a natural born Citizen, or a Citizen of the United States, at the time of the Adoption of this Constitution, shall be eligible to the Office of President; neither shall any Person be eligible to that Office who shall not have attained to the Age of thirty-five Years, and been fourteen Years a Resident within the United States. [For qualification of the Vice President, see Amendment XII.]

[In Case of the Removal of the President from Office, or of his Death, Resignation, or Inability to discharge the Powers and Duties of the said Office, the same shall devolve on the Vice President, and the Congress may by Law, provide for the Case of Removal, Death, Resignation or Inability, both of the President and Vice President, declaring what Officer shall then act as President, and such Officer shall act accordingly, until the Disability be removed, or a President shall be elected. [This clause was superseded by Amendments XXV.]

The President shall, at stated Times, receive for his Services, a Compensation, which shall neither be encreased nor diminished during the Period for which he shall have been elected, and he shall not receive within that Period any other Emolument from the United States, or any of them.

Before he enter on the Execution of his Office, he shall take the following Oath or Affirmation:–"I do solemnly swear (or affirm) that I will faithfully execute the Office of President of the United States, and will to the best of my Ability, preserve, protect and defend the Constitution of the United States."

Section 2—President to be Commander-in-Chief. He may require opinions of cabinet officers, etc., may pardon. Treaty-making power. Nomination of certain officers. When President may fill vacancies.

The President shall be Commander in Chief of the Army and Navy of the United States, and of the Militia of the several States, when called into the actual Service of the United States; he may require the Opinion in writing, of the principal Officer in each of the executive Departments, upon any subject relating to the Duties of their respective Offices, and he shall have Power to Grant Reprieves and Pardons for Offenses against the United States, except in Cases of Impeachment.

He shall have Power, by and with the Advice and Consent of the Senate, to make Treaties, provided two-thirds of the Senators present concur; and he shall nominate, and by and with the Advice and Consent of the Senate, shall appoint Ambassadors, other public Ministers and Consuls, Judges of the supreme Court, and all other Officers of the United States, whose Appointments are not herein otherwise pro-

vided for, and which shall be established by Law: but the Congress may by Law vest the Appointment of such inferior Officers, as they think proper, in the President alone, in the Courts of Law, or in the Heads of Departments.

The President shall have Power to fill up all Vacancies that may happen during the Recess of the Senate, by granting Commissions which shall expire at the End of their next Session.

Section 3—President shall communicate to Congress. He may convene and adjourn Congress, in case of disagreement, etc. Shall receive ambassadors, execute laws, and commission officers.

He shall from time to time give to the Congress Information of the State of the Union, and recommend to their Consideration such Measures as he shall judge necessary and expedient; he may, on extraordinary Occasions, convene both Houses, or either of them, and in Case of Disagreement between them, with Respect to the Time of Adjournment, he may adjourn them to such Time as he shall think proper; he shall receive Ambassadors and other public Ministers; he shall take Care that the Laws be faithfully executed, and shall Commission all the Officers of the United States.

Section 4—All civil offices forfeited for certain crimes.

The President, Vice President and all civil Officers of the United States, shall be removed from Office on Impeachment for, and Conviction of, Treason, Bribery, or other high Crimes and Misdemeanors.

ARTICLE III.

Section 1—Judicial powers, tenure. Compensation.

The judicial Power of the United States, shall be vested in one supreme Court, and in such inferior Courts as the Congress may from time to time ordain and establish. The Judges, both of the supreme and inferior Courts, shall hold their Offices during good Behaviour, and shall, at stated Times, receive for their Services, a Compensation, which shall not be diminished during their Continuance in Office.

Section 2—Judicial power; to what cases it extends. Original jurisdiction of Supreme Court; appellate jurisdiction. Trial by jury, etc. Trial, where.

The judicial Power shall extend to all Cases, in Law and Equity, arising under this Constitution, the Laws of the United States, and Treaties made, or which shall be made, under their Authority;–to all Cases affecting Ambassadors, other public Ministers and Consuls;–to all Cases of admiralty and maritime Jurisdiction;–to Controversies to which the United States shall be a Party;–to Controversies between two or more States; [–between a State and Citizens of another State;–] between Citizens of different States; –between Citizens of the same State claiming Lands under Grants of different States, [and between a State, or the Citizens thereof, and foreign States, Citizens or Subjects.] [This section is modified by Amendment XI.]

In all Cases affecting Ambassadors, other public Ministers and Consuls, and those in which a State shall be Party, the supreme Court shall have original Jurisdiction. In all the other Cases before mentioned, the supreme Court shall have appellate Jurisdiction, both as to Law and Fact, with such Exceptions, and under such Regulations as the Congress shall make.

The trial of all Crimes, except in Cases of Impeachment, shall be by Jury; and such Trial shall be held in the State where the said Crimes shall have been committed; but when not committed within any State, the Trial shall be at such Place or Places as the Congress may by Law have directed.

Section 3—Treason Defined. Proof of. Punishment of.

Treason against the United States, shall consist only in levying War against them, or in adhering to their Enemies, giving them Aid and Comfort. No Person shall be convicted of Treason unless on the Testimony of two Witnesses to the same overt Act, or on Confession in open Court.

The Congress shall have Power to declare the Punishment of Treason, but no Attainder of Treason shall work Corruption of Blood, or Forfeiture except during the Life of the Person attainted.

ARTICLE IV.

Section 1—Each State to give credit to the public acts, etc., of every other State.

Full Faith and Credit shall be given in each State to the public Acts, Records, and judicial Proceedings of every other State. And the Congress may by general Laws prescribe the Manner in which such Acts, Records and Proceedings shall be proved, and the Effect thereof.

The judicial Power of the United States, shall be vested in one supreme Court, and in such inferior Courts as the Congress may from time to time ordain and establish. The Judges, both of the supreme and inferior Courts, shall hold their Offices during good Behaviour, and shall, at stated Times, receive for their Services, a Compensation, which shall not be diminished during their Continuance in Office.

Section 2—Privileges of citizens of each State. Fugitives from justice to be delivered up. Persons held to service having escaped, to be delivered up.

The Citizens of each State shall be entitled to all Privileges and Immunities of Citizens in the several States.

A Person charged in any State with Treason, Felony, or other Crime, who shall flee from Justice, and be found in another State, shall on demand of the executive Authority of the State from which he fled, be delivered up, to be removed to the State having Jurisdiction of the Crime.

[No Person held to Service or Labour in one State, under the Laws thereof, escaping into another, shall, in Consequence of any Law or Regulation therein, be discharged from such Service or Labour, but shall be delivered up on Claim of the Party to whom such Service or Labour may be due.] [This clause was superseded by Amendment XIII.]

Section 3—Admission of new States. Power of Congress over territory and other property.

New States may be admitted by the Congress into this Union; but no new State shall be formed or erected within the Jurisdiction of any other State; nor any State be formed by the Junction of two or more States, or parts of States, without the Consent of the Legislatures of the States concerned as well as of the Congress.

The Congress shall have Power to dispose of and make all needful Rules and Regulations respecting the Territory or other Property belonging to the United States; and nothing in this Constitution shall be so construed as to Prejudice any Claims of the United States, or of any particular State.

Section 4—Republican form of government guaranteed. Each State to be protected.

The United States shall guarantee to every State in this Union a Republican Form of Government, and shall protect each of them against Invasion; and on Application of the Legislature, or of the Executive (when the Legislature cannot be convened) against domestic Violence.

ARTICLE V.

Constitution: how amended; proviso.

The Congress, whenever two-thirds of both Houses shall deem it necessary, shall propose Amendments to this Constitution, or, on the Application of the Legislatures of two-thirds of the several States, shall call a Convention for proposing Amendments, which, in either Case, shall be valid to all Intents and Purposes, as part of this Constitution, when ratified by the Legislatures of three-fourths of the several States, or by Conventions in three-fourths thereof, as the one or the other Mode of Ratification may be proposed by the Congress: Provided that no Amendment which may be made prior to the Year One thousand eight hundred and eight shall in any Manner affect the first and fourth Clauses in the Ninth Section of the first Article; and that no State, without its Consent, shall be deprived of its equal Suffrage in the Senate.

ARTICLE VI.

Certain debts, etc., declared valid. Supremacy of Constitution, treaties, and laws of the United States. Oath to support Constitution, by whom taken. No religious test.

All Debts contracted and Engagements entered into, before the Adoption of this Constitution, shall be as valid against the United States under this Constitution, as under the Confederation.

This Constitution, and the Laws of the United States which shall be made in Pursuance thereof; and all Treaties made, or which shall be made, under the Authority of the United States, shall be the supreme Law of the Land; and the Judges in every State shall be bound thereby, any Thing in the Constitution or Laws of any State to the Contrary notwithstanding.

The Senators and Representatives before mentioned, and the Members of the several State Legislatures, and all executive and judicial Officers, both of the United States and of the several States, shall be bound by Oath or Affirmation, to support this Constitution; but no religious Test shall ever be required as a Qualification to any Office or public Trust under the United States.

ARTICLE VII.

What ratification shall establish Constitution.

The Ratification of the Conventions of nine States shall be sufficient for the Establishment of this Constitution between the States so ratifying the Same.

Done in Convention by the Unanimous Consent of the States present the Seventeenth Day of September in the Year of our Lord one thousand seven hundred and Eighty seven and of the Independence of the United States of America the Twelfth.

In Witness whereof We have hereunto subscribed our Names.

Go WASHINGTON, Presidt and deputy from Virginia

New Hampshire—John Langdon, Nicholas Gilman

Massachusetts—Nathaniel Gorham, Rufus King

Connecticut—Wm. Saml. Johnson, Roger Sherman

New York—Alexander Hamilton

New Jersey—Wil: Livingston, David Brearley, Wm. Paterson, Jona: Dayton

Pennsylvania—B Franklin, Thomas Mifflin, Robt Morris, Geo. Clymer, Thos. FitzSimons, Jared Ingersoll, James Wilson, Gouv Morris

Delaware—Geo: Read, Gunning Bedford jun, John Dickinson, Richard Bassett, Jaco: Broom

Maryland—James McHenry, Dan of St Thos. Jenifer, Danl Carroll

Virginia—John Blair, James Madison Jr.

North Carolina—Wm. Blount, Rich'd Dobbs Spaight, Hu Williamson

South Carolina—J. Rutledge, Charles Cotesworth Pinckney, Charles Pinckney, Pierce Butler

Georgia—William Few, Abr Baldwin

Attest: William Jackson, Secretary.

Ten Original Amendments: The Bill of Rights

In force Dec. 15, 1791

[The First Congress, at its first session in the City of New York, Sept. 25, 1789, submitted to the states 12 amendments to clarify certain individual and state rights not named in the Constitution. They are generally called the Bill of Rights.

Influential in framing these amendments was the Declaration of Rights of Virginia, written by George Mason (1725-92) in 1776. Mason, a Virginia delegate to the Constitutional Convention, did not sign the Constitution and opposed its ratification on the ground that it did not sufficiently oppose slavery or safeguard individual rights.

In the preamble to the resolution offering the proposed amendments, Congress said: "The conventions of a number of the States having at the time of their adopting the Constitution, expressed a desire, in order to prevent misconstruction or abuse of its powers, that further declaratory and restrictive clauses should be added, and as extending the ground of public confidence in the government will best insure the beneficent ends of its institution, be it resolved," etc.

Ten of these amendments, now commonly known as one to 10 inclusive, but originally 3 to 12 inclusive, were ratified by the states as follows: New Jersey, Nov. 20, 1789; Maryland, Dec. 19, 1789; North Carolina, Dec. 22, 1789; South Carolina, Jan. 19, 1790; New Hampshire, Jan. 25, 1790; Delaware, Jan. 28, 1790; New York, Feb. 27, 1790; Pennsylvania, Mar. 10, 1790; Rhode Island, June 7, 1790; Vermont, Nov. 3, 1791; Virginia, Dec. 15, 1791; Massachusetts, Mar. 2, 1939; Georgia, Mar. 18, 1939; Connecticut, Apr. 19, 1939. These original 10 ratified amendments follow as Amendments I to X inclusive.

Of the two original proposed amendments that were not ratified promptly by the necessary number of states, the first related to apportionment of Representatives; the second, relating to compensation of members of Congress, was ratified in 1992 and became Amendment 27.]

AMENDMENT I.
Religious establishment prohibited. Freedom of speech, of press, right to assemble and to petition.

Congress shall make no law respecting an establishment of religion, or prohibiting the free exercise thereof; or abridging the freedom of speech, or of the press; or the right of the people peaceably to assemble, and to petition the Government for a redress of grievances.

AMENDMENT II.
Right to keep and bear arms.

A well regulated Militia, being necessary to the security of a free State, the right of the people to keep and bear Arms, shall not be infringed.

AMENDMENT III.
Conditions for quarters for soldiers.

No Soldier shall, in time of peace be quartered in any house, without the consent of the Owner, nor in time of war, but in a manner to be prescribed by law.

AMENDMENT IV.
Protection from unreasonable search and seizure.

The right of the people to be secure in their persons, houses, papers, and effects, against unreasonable searches and seizures, shall not be violated, and no Warrants shall issue, but upon probable cause, supported by Oath or affirmation, and particularly describing the place to be searched, and the persons or things to be seized.

AMENDMENT V.
Provisions concerning prosecution and due process of law. Double jeopardy restriction. Private property not to be taken without compensation.

No person shall be held to answer for a capital, or otherwise infamous crime, unless on a presentment or indictment of a Grand Jury, except in cases arising in the land or naval forces, or in the Militia, when in actual service in time of War or public danger; nor shall any person be subject for the same offence to be twice put in jeopardy of life or limb; nor shall be compelled in any criminal case to be a witness against himself, nor be deprived of life, liberty, or property, without due process of law; nor shall private property be taken for public use, without just compensation.

AMENDMENT VI.
Right to speedy trial, witnesses, etc.

In all criminal prosecutions, the accused shall enjoy the right to a speedy and public trial, by an impartial jury of the State and district wherein the crime shall have been committed, which district shall have been previously ascertained by law, and to be informed of the nature and cause of the accusation; to be confronted with the witnesses against him; to have compulsory process for obtaining witnesses in his favor, and to have the Assistance of Counsel for his defence.

AMENDMENT VII.
Right of trial by jury.

In suits at common law, where the value in controversy shall exceed twenty dollars, the right of trial by jury shall be preserved, and no fact tried by a jury, shall be otherwise re-examined in any Court of the United States, than according to the rules of the common law.

AMENDMENT VIII.
Excessive bail or fines; cruel and unusual punishment.

Excessive bail shall not be required, nor excessive fines imposed, nor cruel and unusual punishments inflicted.

AMENDMENT IX.
Rule of construction of Constitution.

The enumeration in the Constitution, of certain rights, shall not be construed to deny or disparage others retained by the people.

AMENDMENT X.
Rights of States under Constitution.

The powers not delegated to the United States by the Constitution, nor prohibited by it to the States, are reserved to the States respectively, or to the people.

Amendments Since the Bill of Rights

AMENDMENT XI.
Judicial powers construed.

The Judicial power of the United States shall not be construed to extend to any suit in law or equity, commenced or prosecuted against one of the United States by Citizens of another State, or by Citizens or Subjects of any Foreign State.

[This amendment was proposed to the Legislatures of the several States by the Third Congress on March 4, 1794, and was declared to have been ratified in a message from the President to Congress, dated Jan. 8, 1798.

[It was on Jan. 5, 1798, that Secretary of State Pickering received from 12 of the States authenticated ratifications, and informed President John Adams of that fact.

[As a result of later research in the Department of State, it is now established that Amendment XI became part of the Constitution on Feb. 7, 1795, for on that date it had been ratified by 12 States as follows:

[1. New York, Mar. 27, 1794. 2. Rhode Island, Mar. 31, 1794. 3. Connecticut, May 8, 1794. 4. New Hampshire, June 16, 1794. 5. Massachusetts, June 26, 1794. 6. Vermont, between Oct. 9, 1794, and Nov. 9, 1794. 7. Virginia, Nov. 18, 1794. 8. Georgia, Nov. 29, 1794. 9. Kentucky, Dec. 7, 1794. 10. Maryland, Dec. 26, 1794. 11. Delaware, Jan. 23, 1795. 12. North Carolina, Feb. 7, 1795.]

[On June 1, 1796, more than a year after Amendment XI had become a part of the Constitution—but before anyone was officially aware of this—Tennessee had been admitted as a State; but not until Oct. 16, 1797, was a certified copy of the resolution of Congress proposing the amendment sent to the Governor of Tennessee, John Sevier, by Secretary of State Pickering, whose office was then at Trenton, New Jersey, because of the epidemic of yellow fever at Philadelphia; it seems, however, that the Legislature of Tennessee took no action on Amendment XI, owing doubtless to the fact that public announcement of its adoption was made soon thereafter.]

[Besides the necessary 12 States, one other, South Carolina, ratified Amendment XI, but this action was not taken until Dec. 4, 1797; the two remaining States, New Jersey and Pennsylvania, failed to ratify.]

AMENDMENT XII.

Manner of choosing President and Vice-President.

[Proposed by Congress Dec. 9, 1803; ratified June 15, 1804.]

The Electors shall meet in their respective states and vote by ballot for President and Vice-President, one of whom, at least, shall not be an inhabitant of the same state with themselves; they shall name in their ballots the person voted for as President, and in distinct ballots the person voted for as Vice-President, and they shall make distinct lists of all persons voted for as President, and of all persons voted for as Vice-President, and of the number of votes for each, which lists they shall sign and certify, and transmit sealed to the seat of the government of the United States, directed to the President of the Senate;–The President of the Senate shall, in presence of the Senate and House of Representatives, open all the certificates and the votes shall then be counted;—The person having the greatest number of votes for President, shall be the President, if such number be a majority of the whole number of Electors appointed; and if no person have such majority, then from the persons having the highest numbers not exceeding three on the list of those voted for as President, the House of Representatives shall choose immediately, by ballot, the President. But in choosing the President, the votes shall be taken by states, the representation from each state having one vote; a quorum for this purpose shall consist of a member or members from two-thirds of the states, and a majority of all the states shall be necessary to a choice. *[And if the House of Representatives shall not choose a President whenever the right of choice shall devolve upon them, before the fourth day of March next following, then the Vice-President shall act as President, as in the case of the death or other constitutional disability of the President.] [The words in brackets were superseded by Amendment XX, section 3.]* The person having the greatest number of votes as Vice-President, shall be the Vice-President, if such number be a majority of the whole number of Electors appointed, and if no person have a majority, then from the two highest numbers on the list, the Senate shall choose the Vice-President; a quorum for the purpose shall consist of two-thirds of the whole number of Senators, and a majority of the whole number shall be necessary to a choice. But no person constitutionally ineligible to the office of President shall be eligible to that of Vice-President of the United States.

THE RECONSTRUCTION AMENDMENTS

[Amendments XIII, XIV, and XV are commonly known as the Reconstruction Amendments, inasmuch as they followed the Civil War, and were drafted by Republicans who were bent on imposing their own policy of reconstruction on the South. Postbellum legislatures there—Mississippi, South Carolina, Georgia, for example—had set up laws which, it was charged, were contrived to perpetuate Negro slavery under other names.]

AMENDMENT XIII.

Slavery abolished.

[Proposed by Congress Jan. 31, 1865; ratified Dec. 6, 1865. The amendment, when first proposed by a resolution in Congress, was passed by the Senate, 38 to 6, on Apr. 8, 1864, but was defeated in the House, 95 to 66 on June 15, 1864. On reconsideration by the House, on Jan. 31, 1865, the resolution passed, 119 to 56. It was approved by President Lincoln on Feb. 1, 1865, although the Supreme Court had decided in 1798 that the President has nothing to do with the proposing of amendments to the Constitution, or their adoption.]

1. Neither slavery nor involuntary servitude, except as a punishment for crime whereof the party shall have been duly convicted, shall exist within the United States, or any place subject to their jurisdiction.

2. Congress shall have power to enforce this article by appropriate legislation.

AMENDMENT XIV.

Citizenship rights not to be abridged.

[The following amendment was proposed to the Legislatures of the several states by the 39th Congress, June 13, 1866, ratified July 9, 1868, and declared to have been ratified in a proclamation by the Secretary of State, July 28, 1868.]

[The 14th amendment was adopted only by virtue of ratification subsequent to earlier rejections. Newly constituted legislatures in both North Carolina and South Carolina (respectively July 4 and 9, 1868), ratified the proposed amendment, although earlier legislatures had rejected the proposal. The Secretary of State issued a proclamation, which, though doubtful as to the effect of attempted withdrawals by Ohio and New Jersey, entertained no doubt as to the validity of the ratification by North and South Carolina. The following day (July 21, 1868), Congress passed a resolution which declared the 14th Amendment to be a part of the Constitution and directed the Secretary of State so to promulgate it. The Secretary waited, however, until the newly constituted Legislature of Georgia had ratified the amendment, subsequent to an earlier rejection, before the promulgation of the ratification of the new amendment.]

1. All persons born or naturalized in the United States, and subject to the jurisdiction thereof, are citizens of the United States and of the State wherein they reside. No State shall make or enforce any law which shall abridge the privileges or immunities of citizens of the United States; nor shall any State deprive any person of life, liberty, or property, without due process of law; nor deny to any person within its jurisdiction the equal protection of the laws.

2. Representatives shall be apportioned among the several States according to their respective numbers, counting the whole number of persons in each State, excluding Indians not taxed. But when the right to vote at any election for the choice of electors for President and Vice-President of the United States, Representatives in Congress, the Executive and Judicial officers of a State, or the members of the Legislature thereof, is denied to any of the male inhabitants of such State, being twenty-one years of age, and citizens of the United States, or in any way abridged, except for partici-

pation in rebellion, or other crime, the basis of representation therein shall be reduced in the proportion which the number of such male citizens shall bear to the whole number of male citizens twenty-one years of age in such State.

3. No person shall be a Senator or Representative in Congress, or elector of President and Vice-President, or hold any office, civil or military, under the United States, or under any State, who, having previously taken an oath, as a member of Congress, or as an officer of the United States, or as a member of any State legislature, or as an executive or judicial officer of any State, to support the Constitution of the United States, shall have engaged in insurrection or rebellion against the same, or given aid or comfort to the enemies thereof. But Congress may by a vote of two-thirds of each House, remove such disability.

4. The validity of the public debt of the United States, authorized by law, including debts incurred for payment of pensions and bounties for services in suppressing insurrection or rebellion, shall not be questioned. But neither the United States nor any State shall assume or pay any debt or obligation incurred in aid of insurrection or rebellion against the United States, or any claim for the loss or emancipation of any slave; but all such debts, obligations and claims shall be held illegal and void.

The Congress shall have power to enforce, by appropriate legislation, the provisions of this article.

AMENDMENT XV.

Race no bar to voting rights.

[The following amendment was proposed to the legislatures of the several States by the 40th Congress, Feb. 26, 1869, and ratified Feb. 3, 1870.]

1. The right of citizens of the United States to vote shall not be denied or abridged by the United States or by any State on account of race, color, or previous condition of servitude–

2. The Congress shall have power to enforce this article by appropriate legislation.

AMENDMENT XVI.

Income taxes authorized.

[Proposed by Congress July 12, 1909; ratified Feb. 3, 1913.]

The Congress shall have power to lay and collect taxes on incomes, from whatever source derived, without apportionment among the several States, and without regard to any census or enumeration.

AMENDMENT XVII.

United States Senators to be elected by direct popular vote.

[Proposed by Congress May 13, 1912; ratified Apr. 8, 1913.]

The Senate of the United States shall be composed of two Senators from each State, elected by the people thereof, for six years; and each Senator shall have one vote. The electors in each State shall have the qualifications requisite for electors of the most numerous branch of the State legislatures.

When vacancies happen in the representation of any State in the Senate, the executive authority of such State shall issue writs of election to fill such vacancies: *Provided,* That the legislature of any State may empower the executive thereof to make temporary appointments until the people fill the vacancies by election as the legislature may direct.

This amendment shall not be so construed as to affect the election or term of any Senator chosen before it becomes valid as part of the Constitution.

AMENDMENT XVIII.

Liquor prohibition amendment.

[Proposed by Congress Dec. 18, 1917; ratified Jan. 16, 1919. Repealed by Amendment XXI, effective Dec. 5, 1933.]

1. After one year from the ratification of this article the manufacture, sale, or transportation of intoxicating liquors within, the importation thereof into, or the exportation thereof from the United States and all territory subject to the jurisdiction thereof for beverage purposes is hereby prohibited.

2. The Congress and the several States shall have concurrent power to enforce this article by appropriate legislation.

3. This article shall be inoperative unless it shall have been ratified as an amendment to the Constitution by the legislatures of the several States as provided in the Constitution, within seven years from the date of the submission hereof to the States by the Congress.

[The total vote in the Senates of the various States was 1,310 for, 237 against—84.6% dry. In the lower houses of the States the vote was 3,782 for, 1,035 against—78.5% dry.

[The amendment ultimately was adopted by all the States except Rhode Island.]

AMENDMENT XIX.

Giving nationwide suffrage to women.

[Proposed by Congress June 4, 1919; ratified Aug. 18, 1920.]

The right of citizens of the United States to vote shall not be denied or abridged by the United States or by any State on account of sex.

Congress shall have power to enforce this Article by appropriate legislation.

AMENDMENT XX.

Terms of President and Vice President to begin on Jan. 20; those of Senators, Representatives, Jan. 3.

[Proposed by Congress Mar. 2, 1932; ratified Jan. 23, 1933.]

1. The terms of the President and Vice President shall end at noon on the 20th day of January, and the terms of Senators and Representatives at noon on the 3d day of January, of the years in which such terms would have ended if this article had not been ratified; and the terms of their successors shall then begin.

2. The Congress shall assemble at least once in every year, and such meeting shall begin at noon on the 3d day of January, unless they shall by law appoint a different day.

3. If, at the time fixed for the beginning of the term of the President, the President elect shall have died, the Vice President elect shall become President. If a President shall not have been chosen before the time fixed for the beginning of his term, or if the President elect shall have failed to qualify, then the Vice President elect shall act as President until a President shall have qualified; and the Congress may by law provide for the case wherein neither a President elect nor a Vice President elect shall have qualified, declaring who shall then act as President, or the manner in which one who is to act shall be selected, and such person shall act accordingly until a President or Vice President shall have qualified.

4. The Congress may by law provide for the case of the death of any of the persons from whom the House of Representatives may choose a President whenever the right of choice shall have devolved upon them, and for the case of the death of any of the persons from whom the Senate may choose a Vice President whenever the right of choice shall have devolved upon them.

5. Sections 1 and 2 shall take effect on the 15th day of October following the ratification of this article (Oct. 1933).

6. This article shall be inoperative unless it shall have been ratified as an amendment to the Constitution by the

legislatures of three-fourths of the several States within seven years from the date of its submission.

AMENDMENT XXI.
Repeal of Amendment XVIII.

[Proposed by Congress Feb. 20, 1933; ratified Dec. 5, 1933.]

1. The eighteenth article of amendment to the Constitution of the United States is hereby repealed.

2. The transportation or importation into any State, Territory, or possession of the United States for delivery or use therein of intoxicating liquors, in violation of the laws thereof, is hereby prohibited.

3. This article shall be inoperative unless it shall have been ratified as an amendment to the Constitution by conventions in the several States, as provided in the Constitution, within seven years from the date of the submission hereof to the States by the Congress.

AMENDMENT XXII.
Limiting Presidential terms of office.

[Proposed by Congress Mar. 24, 1947; ratified Feb. 27, 1951.]

1. No person shall be elected to the office of the President more than twice, and no person who has held the office of President, or acted as President, for more than two years of a term to which some other person was elected President shall be elected to the office of the President more than once. But this Article shall not apply to any person holding the office of President when this Article was proposed by the Congress, and shall not prevent any person who may be holding the office of President, or acting as President, during the term within which this Article becomes operative from holding the office of President or acting as President during the remainder of such term.

2. This article shall be inoperative unless it shall have been ratified as an amendment to the Constitution by the legislatures of three-fourths of the several States within seven years from the date of its submission to the States by the Congress.

AMENDMENT XXIII.
Presidential vote for District of Columbia.

[Proposed by Congress June 16, 1960; ratified Mar. 29, 1961.]

1. The District constituting the seat of Government of the United States shall appoint in such manner as the Congress may direct:

A number of electors of President and Vice President equal to the whole number of Senators and Representatives in Congress to which the District would be entitled if it were a State, but in no event more than the least populous State; they shall be in addition to those appointed by the States, but they shall be considered, for the purposes of the election of President and Vice President, to be electors appointed by a State; and they shall meet in the District and perform such duties as provided by the twelfth article of amendment.

2. The Congress shall have power to enforce this article by appropriate legislation.

AMENDMENT XXIV.
Barring poll tax in federal elections.

[Proposed by Congress Sept. 14, 1962; ratified Jan. 23, 1964.]

1. The right of citizens of the United States to vote in any primary or other election for President or Vice President, for electors for President or Vice President, or for Senator or Representative in Congress, shall not be denied or abridged by the United States or any State by reason of failure to pay any poll tax or other tax.

2. The Congress shall have power to enforce this article by appropriate legislation.

AMENDMENT XXV.
Presidential disability and succession.

[Proposed by Congress July 6, 1965; ratified Feb. 10, 1967.]

1. In case of the removal of the President from office or of his death or resignation, the Vice President shall become President.

2. Whenever there is a vacancy in the office of the Vice President, the President shall nominate a Vice President who shall take office upon confirmation by a majority vote of both houses of Congress.

3. Whenever the President transmits to the President pro tempore of the Senate and the Speaker of the House of Representatives his written declaration that he is unable to discharge the powers and duties of his office, and until he transmits to them a written declaration to the contrary, such powers and duties shall be discharged by the Vice President as Acting President.

4. Whenever the Vice President and a majority of either the principal officers of the executive departments or of such other body as Congress may by law provide, transmit to the President pro tempore of the Senate and the Speaker of the House of Representatives their written declaration that the President is unable to discharge the powers and duties of his office, the Vice President shall immediately assume the powers and duties of the office as Acting President.

Thereafter, when the President transmits to the President pro tempore of the Senate and the Speaker of the House of Representatives his written declaration that no inability exists, he shall resume the powers and duties of his office unless the Vice President and a majority of either the principal officers of the executive department or of such other body as Congress may by law provide, transmit within four days to the President pro tempore of the Senate and the Speaker of the House of Representatives their written declaration that the President is unable to discharge the powers and duties of his office. Thereupon Congress shall decide the issue, assembling within forty-eight hours for that purpose if not in session. If the Congress, within twenty-one days after receipt of the latter written declaration, or, if Congress is not in session, within twenty-one days after Congress is required to assemble, determines by two-thirds vote of both Houses that the President is unable to discharge the powers and duties of his office, the Vice President shall continue to discharge the same as Acting President; otherwise, the President shall resume the powers and duties of his office.

AMENDMENT XXVI.
Lowering voting age to 18 years.

[Proposed by Congress Mar. 23, 1971; ratified July 1, 1971.]

1. The right of citizens of the United States, who are eighteen years of age or older, to vote shall not be denied or abridged by the United States or by any State on account of age.

2. The Congress shall have the power to enforce this article by appropriate legislation.

AMENDMENT XXVII.
Congressional pay.

[Proposed by Congress Sept. 25, 1789; ratified May 7, 1992.]

No law, varying the compensation for the services of the Senators and Representatives, shall take effect, until an election of Representatives shall have intervened.

How a Bill Becomes a Law

A senator or representative introduces a bill in Congress by sending it to the clerk of the House or the Senate, who assigns it a number and title. This procedure is termed the first reading. The clerk then refers the bill to the appropriate committee of the Senate or House.

If the committee opposes the bill, it will table, or kill, it. Otherwise, the committee holds hearings to listen to opinions and facts offered by members and other interested people. The committee then debates the bill and possibly offers amendments. A vote is taken, and if favorable, the bill is sent back to the clerk of the House or Senate.

The clerk reads the bill to the house—the second reading. Members may then debate the bill and suggest amendments.

After debate and possibly amendment, the bill is given a third reading, simply of the title, and put to a voice or roll-call vote.

If passed, the bill goes to the other house, where it may be defeated or passed, with or without amendments. If defeated, the bill dies. If passed with amendments, a conference committee made up of members of both houses works out the differences and arrives at a compromise.

After passage of the final version by both houses, the bill is sent to the president. If the president signs it, the bill becomes a law. The president may, however, veto the bill by refusing to sign it and sending it back to the house where it originated, with reasons for the veto.

The president's objections are then read and debated, and a roll-call vote is taken. If the bill receives less than a two-thirds majority, it is defeated. If it receives at least two-thirds, it is sent to the other house. If that house also passes it by at least a two-thirds majority, the 1 veto is overridden, and the bill becomes a law.

If the president neither signs nor vetoes the bill within 10 days—not including Sundays—it automatically becomes a law even without the president's signature. However, if Congress has adjourned within those 10 days, the bill is automatically killed; this indirect rejection is termed a pocket veto.

Note: Under the Line Item Veto Act, effective Jan. 1, 1997, the president was authorized, under certain circumstances, to veto a bill in part, but the legislation was found unconstitutional by the Supreme Court, June 25, 1998.

Confederate States and Secession

The American Civil War (1861-65) grew out of sectional disputes over the continued existence of slavery in the South and the contention of Southern legislators that the states retained many rights, including the right to secede.

The war was not fought by state against state but by one federal regime against another, the Confederate government in Richmond assuming control over the economic, political, and military life of the South, under protest from Georgia and South Carolina.

South Carolina voted an ordinance of secession from the Union, repealing its 1788 ratification of the U.S. Constitution on Dec. 20, 1860, to take effect on Dec. 24. Other states seceded in 1861. Their votes in conventions were: Mississippi, Jan. 9, 84-15; Florida, Jan. 10, 62-7; Alabama, Jan. 11, 61-39; Georgia, Jan. 19, 208-89; Louisiana, Jan. 26, 113-17; Texas, Feb. 1, 166-7, ratified by popular vote on Feb. 23 (for 34,794, against 11,325); Virginia, Apr. 17, 88-55, ratified by popular vote on May 23 (for 128,884; against 32,134); Arkansas, May 6, 69-1; Tennessee, May 7, ratified by popular

vote on June 8 (for 104,019, against 47,238); North Carolina, May 20.

Missouri Unionists stopped secession in conventions Feb. 28 and Mar. 9. The legislature condemned secession Mar. 7. Under the protection of Confederate troops, secessionist members of the legislature adopted a resolution of secession at Neosho, Oct. 31. The Confederate Congress seated the secessionists' representatives.

Kentucky did not secede, and its government remained Unionist. In a part of the state occupied by Confederate troops, Kentuckians approved secession, and the Confederate Congress admitted their representatives.

The Maryland legislature voted against secession Apr. 27, 53-13. Delaware did not secede. Western Virginia held conventions at Wheeling, named a pro-Union governor on June 11, 1861, and was admitted to the Union as West Virginia on June 20, 1863. Its constitution provided for gradual abolition of slavery.

Confederate Government

Forty-two delegates from South Carolina, Georgia, Alabama, Mississippi, Louisiana, and Florida met in convention at Montgomery, AL, on Feb. 4, 1861. They adopted a provisional constitution of the Confederate States of America and elected Jefferson Davis (MS) as provisional president and Alexander H. Stephens (GA) as provisional vice president.

A permanent constitution was adopted Mar. 11. It abolished the African slave trade, but it did not bar interstate

commerce in slaves. On July 20 the Congress moved to Richmond, VA. Davis was elected president in November and was inaugurated on Feb. 22, 1862.

The Congress adopted a flag, consisting of a red field with a white stripe, and a blue jack with a circle of white stars. Later the more popular flag was the red field with blue diagonal crossbars that held 13 white stars, for the 11 states in the Confederacy plus Kentucky and Missouri.

Lincoln's Address at Gettysburg, 1863

Fourscore and seven years ago our fathers brought forth on this continent a new nation, conceived in liberty and dedicated to the proposition that all men are created equal.

Now we are engaged in a great civil war, testing whether that nation or any nation so conceived and so dedicated can long endure. We are met on a great battle field of that war. We have come to dedicate a portion of that field, as a final resting-place for those who here gave their lives that that nation might live. It is altogether fitting and proper that we should do this.

But, in a larger sense, we can not dedicate—we can not consecrate—we can not hallow—this ground. The brave men, living and dead, who struggled here, have consecrated

it, far above our poor power to add or detract. The world will little note, nor long remember, what we say here, but it can never forget what they did here. It is for us the living, rather, to be dedicated here to the unfinished work which they who fought here have thus far so nobly advanced. It is rather for us to be here dedicated to the great task remaining before us—that from these honored dead we take increased devotion to that cause for which they gave the last full measure of devotion—that we here highly resolve that these dead shall not have died in vain—that this nation, under God, shall have a new birth of freedom—and that government of the people, by the people, for the people, shall not perish from the earth.

Selected Landmark Decisions of the U.S. Supreme Court, 1803-2006

See also Year in Review: Notable Supreme Court Decisions, 2005-06.

1803: *Marbury v. Madison.* The Court ruled that Congress exceeded its power in the Judiciary Act of 1789; the Court thus established its power to review acts of Congress and declare invalid those it found in conflict with the Constitution.

1819: *McCulloch v. Maryland.* The Court ruled that Congress had the authority to charter a national bank, under the Constitution's granting of the power to enact all laws "necessary and proper" to responsibilities of government.

1819: *Trustees of Dartmouth College v. Woodward.* The Court ruled that a state could not arbitrarily alter the terms of a college's contract. (The Court later used a similar principle to limit the states' ability to interfere with business contracts.)

1857: *Dred Scott v. Sanford.* The Court declared unconstitutional the already-repealed Missouri Compromise of 1820 because it deprived a person of his or her property—a slave—without due process of law. The Court also ruled that slaves were not citizens of any state nor of the U.S. (The latter part of the decision was overturned by ratification of the 14th Amendment in 1868.)

1896: *Plessy v. Ferguson.* The Court ruled that a state law requiring federal railroad trains to provide separate but equal facilities for black and white passengers neither infringed upon federal authority to regulate interstate commerce nor violated the 13th and 14th Amendments. (The "separate but equal" doctrine remained effective until the 1954 ***Brown v. Board of Education*** decision.)

1904: *Northern Securities Co. v. U.S.* The Court ruled that a holding company formed solely to eliminate competition between two railroad lines was a combination in restraint of trade, violating the federal antitrust act.

1908: *Muller v. Oregon.* The Court upheld a state law limiting the working hours of women. (Louis D. Brandeis, counsel for the state, cited evidence from social workers, physicians, and factory inspectors that the number of hours women worked affected their health and morals.)

1911: *Standard Oil Co. of New Jersey et al. v. U.S.* The Court ruled that the Standard Oil Trust must be dissolved because of its unreasonable restraint of trade.

1919: *Schenck v. U.S.* The Court sustained the Espionage Act of 1917, maintaining that freedom of speech and press could be constrained if "the words used . . . create a clear and present danger. . ."

1925: *Gitlow v. New York.* The Court ruled that the First Amendment prohibition against government abridgment of the freedom of speech applied to the states as well as to the federal government. The decision was the first of a number of rulings holding that the 14th Amendment extended the guarantees of the Bill of Rights to state action.

1935: *Schechter Poultry Corp. v. U.S.* The Court ruled that Congress exceeded its authority to delegate legislative powers and to regulate interstate commerce when it enacted the National Industrial Recovery Act, which afforded the U.S. president too much discretionary power.

1951: *Dennis et al. v. U.S.* The Court upheld convictions under the Smith Act of 1940 for invoking Communist theory advocating the forcible overthrow of the government. (In the 1957 *Yates v. U.S.* decision, the Court moderated this ruling by allowing such advocacy in the abstract, if not connected to action to achieve the goal.)

1954: *Brown v. Board of Education of Topeka.* The Court ruled that separate public schools for black and white students were inherently unequal, so that state-sanctioned segregation in public schools violated the equal protection guarantee of the 14th Amendment. And in *Bolling v. Sharpe* the same year, the Court ruled that the congressionally mandated segregated public school system in the District of Co-lumbia violated the 5th Amendment's due process guarantee of personal liberty. (The Brown ruling also led to abolition of state-sponsored segregation in other public facilities.)

1957: *Roth v. U.S., Alberts v. California.* The Court ruled obscene material was not protected by 1st Amendment guarantees of freedom of speech and press, defining obscene as "utterly without redeeming social value" and appealing to "prurient interests" in the view of the average person. This definition was modified in later decisions, and the "average person" standard was replaced by the "local community" standard in *Miller v. California* **(1973)**.

1961: *Mapp v. Ohio.* The Court ruled that evidence obtained in violation of the 4th Amendment guarantee against unreasonable search and seizure must be excluded from use at state as well as federal trials.

1962: *Engel v. Vitale.* The Court held that public schools could not require pupils to recite a state-composed prayer, even if nondenominational and voluntary, because this would be an unconstitutional attempt to establish religion.

1962: *Baker v. Carr.* The Court held that the constitutional challenges to the unequal distribution of voters among legislative districts could be resolved by federal courts.

1963: *Gideon v. Wainwright.* The Court ruled that state and federal defendants charged with serious crimes must have access to an attorney, at state expense if necessary.

1964: *New York Times Co. v. Sullivan.* The Court ruled that the 1st Amendment protected the press from libel suits for defamatory reports about public officials unless an injured party could prove that a defamatory report was made out of malice or "reckless disregard" for the truth.

1965: *Griswold v. Connecticut.* The Court ruled that a state unconstitutionally interfered with personal privacy in the marriage relationship when it prohibited anyone, including married couples, from using contraceptives.

1966: *Miranda v. Arizona.* The Court ruled that, under the guarantee of due process, suspects in custody, before being questioned, must be informed that they have the right to remain silent, that anything they say may be used against them, and that they have the right to counsel.

1973: *Roe v. Wade, Doe v. Bolton.* The Court ruled that the fetus was not a "person" with constitutional rights and that a right to privacy inherent in the 14th Amendment's due process guarantee of personal liberty protected a woman's decision to have an abortion. During the 1st trimester of pregnancy, the Court maintained, the decision should be left entirely to a woman and her physician. Some regulation of abortion procedures was allowed in the 2nd trimester, and some restriction of abortion in the 3rd.

1974: *U.S. v. Nixon.* The Court ruled that neither the separation of powers nor the need to preserve the confidentiality of presidential communications could alone justify an absolute executive privilege of immunity from judicial demands for evidence to be used in a criminal trial.

1976: *Gregg v. Georgia, Profitt v. Florida, Jurek v. Texas.* The Court held that death, as a punishment for persons convicted of first degree murder, was not in and of itself cruel and unusual punishment in violation of the 8th Amendment. But the Court ruled that the sentencing judge and jury must consider the individual character of the offender and the circumstances of the particular crime.

1978: *Regents of Univ. of Calif. v. Bakke.* The Court ruled that a special admissions program for a state medical school, under which a set number of places were reserved for minorities, violated the 1964 Civil Rights Act, which forbids excluding anyone, because of race, from a federally funded program. However, the Court ruled that race could be considered as one of a complex of factors.

1986: *Bowers v. Hardwick.* The Court refused to extend any constitutional right of privacy to homosexual activity, upholding a Georgia antisodomy law that in effect made such activity a crime. However, the law was struck down by the state supreme court in 1998, and in *Lawrence v. Texas* (2003), the U.S. Supreme Court struck down all state antisodomy laws, as violations of liberty prohibited in the 14th Amendment's due process clause. Also, in *Romer v. Evans* (1996), the Court struck down a Colorado constitutional provision that barred legislation protecting homosexuals from discrimination.

1990: *Cruzan v. Missouri.* The Court ruled that a person had the right to refuse life-sustaining medical treatment. However, the Court also ruled that, before treatment could be withheld from a comatose patient, a state could require "clear and convincing evidence" that the patient would not have wanted to live. And in 2 **1997** rulings, *Washington v. Glucksberg* and *Vacco v. Quill*, the Court ruled that states could ban doctor-assisted suicide.

1995: *Adarand Constructors, Inc., v. Peña.* The Court held that federal programs that classify people by race, unless "narrowly tailored" to accomplish a "compelling governmental interest," may violate the right to equal protection.

1995: *U.S. Term Limits Inc. v. Thornton.* The Court ruled that neither states nor Congress could limit terms of members of Congress, since the Constitution reserves to the people the right to choose federal lawmakers.

1997: *Clinton v. Jones.* Rejecting an appeal by Pres. Clinton in a sexual harassment suit, the Court ruled that a sitting president did not have temporary immunity from a lawsuit for actions outside the realm of official duties.

1997: *City of Boerne v. Flores.* The Court overturned a 1993 law banning enforcement of laws that "substantially burden" religious practice unless there is a "compelling need" to do so. The Court held that the act was an unwarranted intrusion by Congress on states' prerogatives and an infringement of the judiciary's role.

1997: *Reno v. ACLU.* Citing the right to free expression, the Court overturned a provision making it a crime to display or distribute "indecent" or "patently offensive" material on the Internet. In **1998**, however, the Court ruled in *NEA v. Finley* that "general standards of decency" may be used as a criterion in federal arts funding.

1998: *Clinton v. City of New York.* The Court struck down the Line-Item Veto Act (1996), holding that it unconstitutionally gave the president "the unilateral power to change the text of duly enacted statutes."

1998: *Faragher v. City of Boca Raton, Burlington Industries, Inc. v. Ellerth*. The Court issued new guidelines for workplace sexual harassment suits, holding employers responsible for misconduct by supervisory employees. And in *Oncale v. Sundowner Offshore Services*, the Court ruled that the law against sexual harassment applies regardless of whether harasser and victim are the same sex.

1999: *Dept. of Commerce v. U.S. House.* Upholding a challenge to plans for the 2000 census, the Court required an actual head count for apportioning the U.S. House of Representatives, but allowed statistical sampling for other purposes, such as the allocation of federal funds.

1999: *Alden v. Maine, Florida Prepaid v. College Savings Bank, College Savings Bank v. Florida.* In a series of rulings, the Court applied the principle of "sovereign immunity" to shield states in large part from being sued under federal law.

2000: *Troxel v. Granville.* The justices found that a Washington state law allowing grandparents visitation rights, as broadly applied, interfered with parents' right to determine the best care for their children.

2000: *Boy Scouts of America v. Dale.* The Court ruled that the Boy Scouts could dismiss a troop leader after learning he was gay, holding that the right to freedom of association outweighed a New Jersey antidiscrimination statute.

2000: *Stenberg v. Carhart.* The Court struck down a Nebraska law that banned so-called partial-birth abortion. It argued that the law could be interpreted as banning other abortion procedures and that it should have made exception for reasons of health. (*See* **1973: *Roe v. Wade.*)**

2000: *Bush v. Gore.* The Court ruled that manual recounts of presidential ballots in the Nov. 2000 election could not proceed because inconsistent evaluation standards in different counties violated the equal protection clause. In effect, the ruling meant existing official results leaving George W. Bush as narrow winner of the election would prevail.

2001: *Easley v. Cromartie.* The Court ruled that North Carolina's 12th Congressional District, whose irregular shape had been challenged as an unconstitutional racial gerrymander, was the permissible result of attempts to create a majority-Democrat district.

2001: *Good News Club v. Milford Central School.* The justices found that religious and secular organizations were entitled to equal access to public elementary school grounds for after-school meetings.

2002: *Atkins v. Virginia.* The Court ruled that the execution of mentally retarded felons violated the 8th Amendment ban on "cruel and unusual punishment."

2002: *Ring v. Arizona.* The Court found that only a jury, not a judge, could decide to impose the death penalty.

2002: *Zelman v. Simmons-Harris.* The Court ruled that publicly funded tuition vouchers could be used at religious schools without violating the separation of church and state.

2002: *Federal Maritime Commission v. South Carolina State Ports Authority.* The Court ruled that the 11th Amendment gave states immunity from private lawsuits involving federal agencies.

2003: *Grotter v. Bollinger, Gratz v. Bollinger.* The Court upheld affirmative action in admission policies at the University of Michigan Law School. However, in a second decision, the Court ruled against a strict point system based on racial and ethnic backgrounds, as used in the university's undergraduate admissions process.

2004: *Rasul v. Bush, Al Odah v. U.S.* The Court ruled that terrorism detainees held at the U.S. naval base at Guantanamo Bay, Cuba, could challenge their detentions in U.S. courts.

2004: *Tennessee v. Lane.* The Court ruled that disabled individuals could sue states under the Americans with Disabilities Act for failing to provide adequate access to state courthouses, despite states' usual immunity from private lawsuits in federal court.

2004: *Locke v. Davey.* The justices decided that a scholarship program provided by the state of Washington did not violate the right to free exercise of religion in denying aid to students preparing for the clergy.

2004: *Ashcroft v. ACLU et al.* The Court struck down the Child Online Protection Act, passed by Congress in 1998 to restrict access to online pornography by minors, on the basis that the law, as written, violated the 1st Amendment right of free speech.

2005: *Kelo v. City of New London.* The Court ruled that local governments could force property owners to sell their land in order to facilitate private development projects deemed to be economically beneficial to the community.

2005: *Roper v. Simmons.* The Court ruled that executions of convicts who committed their crimes before age 18 were prohibited under the Eighth Amendment ban on cruel and unusual punishment.

2006: *Garcetti v. Ceballos.* The Court ruled that the 1st Amendment guarantee of free speech did not protect statements made by public employees in the course of their official duties.

2006: *Hamdan v. Rumsfeld.* The Court ruled that Pres. George W. Bush's system for trying terrorism detainees at the U.S. military base in Guantanamo Bay, Cuba, was unauthorized under both federal law and the international Geneva Conventions.

> **IT'S A FACT:** Bill Clinton's second inauguration, in 1997, was the first presidential inauguration to be broadcast live on the Internet.

Presidential Oath of Office

The Constitution (Article II) directs that the president-elect shall take the following oath or affirmation to be inaugurated as president: "I do solemnly swear [affirm] that I will faithfully execute the office of President of the United States, and will, to the best of my ability, preserve, protect, and defend the Constitution of the United States." (Custom decrees the addition of the words "So help me God" at the end of the oath when taken by the president-elect, with the left hand on the Bible for the duration of the oath, and the right hand slightly raised.)

Law on Succession to the Presidency

If by reason of death, resignation, removal from office, inability, or failure to qualify there is neither a president nor vice president to discharge the powers and duties of the office of president, then the speaker of the House of Representatives shall upon his resignation as speaker and as representative, act as president. The same rule shall apply in the case of the death, resignation, removal from office, or inability of an individual acting as president.

If at the time when a speaker is to begin the discharge of the powers and duties of the office of president there is no speaker, or the speaker fails to qualify as acting president, then the president pro tempore of the Senate, upon his resignation as president pro tempore and as senator, shall act as president.

An individual acting as president shall continue to act until the expiration of the then current presidential term, except that (1) if his discharge of the powers and duties of the office is founded in whole or in part in the failure of both the president-elect and the vice president-elect to qualify, then he shall act only until a president or vice president qualifies, and (2) if his discharge of the powers and duties of the office is founded in whole or in part on the inability of the president or vice president, then he shall act only until the removal of the disability of one of such individuals.

If, by reason of death, resignation, removal from office, or failure to qualify, there is no president pro tempore to act as president, then the officer of the United States who is highest on the following list, and who is not under any disability to discharge the powers and duties of president shall act as president; the secretaries of state, treasury, defense, attorney general; secretaries of interior, agriculture, commerce, labor, health and human services, housing and urban development, transportation, energy, education, veterans affairs.

[Legislation approved July 18, 1947; amended Sept. 9, 1965, Oct. 15, 1966, Aug. 4, 1977, and Sept. 27, 1979. See also Constitutional Amendment XXV.]

Origin of the United States National Motto

In God We Trust, designated as the U.S. National Motto by Congress in 1956, originated during the Civil War as an inscription for U.S. coins, although it was used by Francis Scott Key in a slightly different form when he wrote "The Star-Spangled Banner" in 1814. On Nov. 13, 1861, when Union morale had been shaken by battlefield defeats, the Rev. M. R. Watkinson, of Ridleyville, PA, wrote to Secy. of the Treasury Salmon P. Chase. "From my heart I have felt our national shame in disowning God as not the least of our present national disasters," the minister wrote, suggesting "recognition of the Almighty God in some form on our coins." Secy. Chase ordered designs prepared with the inscription *In God We Trust* and backed coinage legislation that authorized use of this slogan. The motto first appeared on some U.S. coins in 1864, and disappeared and reappeared on various coins until 1955, when Congress ordered it placed on all paper money and all coins.

The Great Seal of the U.S.

On July 4, 1776, the Continental Congress appointed a committee consisting of Benjamin Franklin, John Adams, and Thomas Jefferson "to bring in a device for a seal of the United States of America." The designs submitted by this and a subsequent committee were considered unacceptable. After many delays, a third committee, appointed early in 1782, presented a design prepared by lawyer William Barton. Charles Thomson, the secretary of Congress, suggested certain changes, and Congress finally approved the design on June 20, 1782. The obverse side of the seal shows an American bald eagle. In its mouth is a ribbon bearing the motto *E Pluribus Unum* (out of many, one). In the eagle's talons are 13 arrows of war and an olive branch of peace. The reverse side shows an unfinished pyramid with an eye (the Eye of Providence) above it.

The Flag of the U.S.—The Stars and Stripes

The 50-star flag of the United States was raised for the first time officially at 12:01 AM on July 4, 1960, at Fort McHenry National Monument in Baltimore, MD. The 50th star had been added for Hawaii; a year earlier the 49th, for Alaska. Before that, no star had been added since 1912, when New Mexico and Arizona were admitted to the Union.

The true history of the Stars and Stripes has become so cluttered by myth and tradition that the facts are difficult, and in some cases impossible, to establish. For example, it is not certain who designed the Stars and Stripes, who made the first such flag, or even whether it ever flew in any sea fight or land battle of the American Revolution.

All agree, however, that the Stars and Stripes originated as the result of a resolution offered by the Marine Committee of the Second Continental Congress at Philadelphia and adopted on June 14, 1777. It read:

Resolved: that the flag of the United States be thirteen stripes, alternate red and white; that the union be thirteen stars, white in a blue field, representing a new constellation.

Congress gave no hint as to the designer of the flag, no instructions as to the arrangement of the stars, and no information on its appropriate uses. Historians have been unable to find the original flag law.

The resolution establishing the flag was not even published until Sept. 2, 1777. Despite repeated requests, Washington did not get the flags until 1783, after the American Revolution was over. And there is no certainty that they were the Stars and Stripes.

Early Flags

Many historians consider the first flag of the U.S. to have been the Grand Union (sometimes called Great Union) flag, although the Continental Congress never officially adopted it. This flag was a modification of the British Meteor flag, which had the red cross of St. George and the white cross of St. Andrew combined in the blue canton. For the Grand Union flag, 6 horizontal stripes were imposed on the red field, dividing it into 13 alternating red and white stripes. On Jan. 1, 1776, when the Continental Army came into formal existence, this flag was unfurled on Prospect Hill, Somerville, MA. Washington wrote that "we hoisted the Union Flag in compliment to the United Colonies."

One of several flags about which controversy has raged for years is at Easton, PA. Containing the devices of the national flag in reversed order, this flag has been in the public library at Easton for more than 150 years. Some contend that this flag was actually the first Stars and Stripes, first displayed on July 8, 1776. This flag has 13 red and white stripes in the canton, 13 white stars centered in a blue field.

A flag was hastily improvised from garments by the defenders of Fort Schuyler at Rome, NY, Aug. 3-22, 1777. Historians believe it was the Grand Union Flag.

The Sons of Liberty had a flag of 9 red and white stripes, to signify 9 colonies, when they met in New York in 1765 to oppose the Stamp Tax. By 1775, the flag had grown to 13 red and white stripes, with a rattlesnake on it.

At Concord, Apr. 19, 1775, the minutemen from Bedford, MA, are said to have carried a flag having a silver arm with sword on a red field. At Cambridge, MA, the Sons of Liberty used a plain red flag with a green pine tree on it.

In June 1775, Washington went from Philadelphia to Boston to take command of the army, escorted to New York by the Philadelphia Light Horse Troop. It carried a yellow flag that had an elaborate coat of arms—the shield charged with 13 knots, the motto "For These We Strive"—and a canton of 13 blue and silver stripes.

In Feb. 1776, Col. Christopher Gadsden, a member of the Continental Congress, gave the South Carolina Provincial Congress a flag "such as is to be used by the commander-in-chief of the American Navy." It had a yellow field, with a rattlesnake about to strike and the words "Don't Tread on Me."

At the Battle of Bennington, Aug. 16, 1777, patriots used a flag of 7 white and 6 red stripes with a blue canton extending down 9 stripes and showing an arch of 11 white stars over the figure 76 and a star in each of the upper corners. The stars are 7-pointed. This flag is preserved in the historical museum in Bennington, VT.

At the Battle of Cowpens, Jan. 17, 1781, the 3d Maryland Regiment is said to have carried a flag of 13 red and white stripes, with a blue canton containing 12 stars in a circle around one star.

Who Designed the Flag? No one knows for certain. Francis Hopkinson, designer of a naval flag, declared he also had designed the flag and in 1781 asked Congress to reimburse him for his services. Congress did not do so. Dumas Malone of Columbia University wrote: "This talented man . . . designed the American flag."

Who Called the Flag "Old Glory"? The flag is said to have been named Old Glory by William Driver, a sea captain of Salem, MA. One legend has it that when he raised the flag on his brig, the *Charles Doggett*, in 1824, he said: "I name thee Old Glory." But his daughter, who presented the flag to the Smithsonian Institution, said he named it at his 21st birthday celebration on Mar. 17, 1824, when his mother presented the homemade flag to him.

The Betsy Ross Legend. The widely publicized legend that Mrs. Betsy Ross made the first Stars and Stripes in June 1776, at the request of a committee composed of George Washington, Robert Morris, and George Ross, an uncle, was first made public in 1870, by a grandson of Mrs. Ross. Historians have been unable to find a historical record of such a meeting or committee.

Adding New Stars

The flag of 1777 was used until 1795. Then, on the admission of Vermont and Kentucky to the Union, Congress passed and Pres. Washington signed an act that after May 1, 1795, the flag should have 15 stripes, alternating red and white, and 15 white stars on a blue field.

When new states were admitted, it became evident that the flag would become burdened with stripes. Congress thereupon ordered that after July 4, 1818, the flag should have 13 stripes, symbolizing the 13 original states; that the union have 20 stars, and that whenever a new state was admitted a new star should be added on the July 4 following admission.

No law designates the permanent arrangement of the stars. However, since 1912, when a new state has been admitted, the new design has been announced by executive order. No star is specifically identified with any state.

Code of Etiquette for Display and Use of the U.S. Flag
Reviewed by National Flag Foundation

Although the Stars and Stripes originated in 1777, it was not until 146 years later that there was a serious attempt to establish a uniform code of etiquette for the U.S. flag. On Feb. 15, 1923, the War Department issued a circular on the rules of flag usage. These rules were adopted almost in their entirety June 14, 1923, by a conference of 68 patriotic organizations in Washington, DC. Finally, on June 22, 1942, a joint resolution of Congress, amended by Public Law 94-344, July 7, 1976, codified "existing rules and customs pertaining to the display and use of the flag."

When to Display the Flag—The flag should be displayed on all days, especially on legal holidays and other special occasions, on official buildings when in use, in or near polling places on election days, and in or near schools when in session. Citizens may fly the flag at any time. It is customary to display it only from sunrise to sunset on buildings and on stationary flagstaffs in the open. It may be displayed at night, however, on special occasions, preferably lighted. The flag now flies over the White House both day and night. It flies over the Senate wing of the Capitol when the Senate is in session and over the House wing when that body is in session. It flies day and night over the east and west fronts of the Capitol, without floodlights at night but receiving illumination from the Capitol Dome. It flies 24 hours a day at several other places, including the Fort McHenry National Monument in Baltimore, where it inspired Francis Scott Key to write "The Star Spangled Banner." The flag also flies 24 hours a day, properly illuminated, at U.S. Customs ports of entry.

Flying the Flag at Half-Staff—Flying the flag at half-staff, that is, halfway up the staff, is a signal of mourning. The flag should be hoisted to the top of the staff for an instant before being lowered to half-staff. It should be hoisted to the peak again before being lowered for the day or night.

As provided by presidential proclamation, the flag should fly at half-staff for 30 days from the day of death of a president or former president; for 10 days from the day of death of a vice president, chief justice or retired chief justice of the U.S., or speaker of the House of Representatives; from day of death until burial of an associate justice of the Supreme Court, cabinet member, former vice president, Senate president pro tempore, or majority or minority Senate or House leader; for a U.S. senator, representative, territorial delegate, or the resident commissioner of Puerto Rico, on day of death and the following day within the metropolitan area of the District of Columbia and from day of death until burial within the decedent's state, congressional district, territory or commonwealth; and for the death of the governor of a state, territory, or possession of the U.S., from day of death until burial.

On Memorial Day, the flag should fly at half-staff until noon and then be raised to the peak. The flag should also fly at half-staff on Korean War Veterans Armistice Day (July 27), National Pearl Harbor Remembrance Day (Dec. 7), and Peace Officers Memorial Day (May 15).

How to Fly the Flag—The flag should be hoisted briskly and lowered ceremoniously and should never be allowed to touch the ground or the floor. When the flag is hung over a sidewalk from a rope extending from a building to a pole, the union should be away from the building. When the flag is hung over the center of a street the union should be to the north in an east-west street and to the east in a north-south street. No other flag may be flown above or, if on the same level, to the right of the U.S. flag, except that at the United Nations Headquarters the UN flag may be placed above flags of all member nations and other national flags may be flown with equal prominence or honor with the flag of the U.S. At services by Navy chaplains at sea, the church pennant may be flown above the flag.

When 2 flags are placed against a wall with crossed staffs, the U.S. flag should be at right—its own right, and its staff should be in front of the staff of the other flag; when a number of flags are grouped and displayed from staffs, it should be at the center and highest point of the group.

Church and Platform Use—In an auditorium, the flag may be displayed flat, above and behind the speaker. When displayed from a staff in a church or in a public auditorium, the flag should hold the position of superior prominence, in advance of the audience, and in the position of honor at the speaker's right as she or he faces the audience. Any other flag so displayed should be placed on the left of the speaker or to the right of the audience.

When the flag is displayed horizontally or vertically against a wall, the stars should be uppermost and at the observer's left.

When used to cover a casket, the flag should be placed so that the union is at the head and over the left shoulder. It should not be lowered into the grave nor touch the ground.

How to Dispose of Worn Flags—When the flag is in such condition that it is no longer a fitting emblem for display, it should be destroyed in a dignified way, preferably by burning.

When to Salute the Flag—All persons present should face the flag, stand at attention, and salute on the following occasions: (1) when the flag is passing in a parade or in a review, (2) during the ceremony of hoisting or lowering, (3) when the national anthem is played, and (4) during the Pledge of Allegiance. Those present in uniform should render the military salute. Those not in uniform should place the right hand over the heart. A man wearing a hat should remove it with his right hand and hold it to his left shoulder during the salute.

Prohibited Uses of the Flag—The flag should not be dipped to any person or thing. (An exception—customarily, ships salute by dipping their colors.) It should never be displayed with the union down save as a distress signal. It should never be carried flat or horizontally, but always aloft and free.

It should not be displayed on a float, an automobile, or a boat except from a staff. It should never be used as a covering for a ceiling, nor have placed on it any word, design, or drawing. It should never be used as a receptacle for carrying anything. It should not be used to cover a statue or a monument.

The flag should never be used for advertising purposes, nor be embroidered on such articles as cushions or handkerchiefs, printed or otherwise impressed on boxes or anything that is designed for temporary use and discard; or used as a costume or athletic uniform. Advertising signs should not be fastened to its staff or halyard.

The flag should never be used as drapery of any sort, never festooned, drawn back, nor up, in folds, but always allowed to fall free. Bunting of blue, white, and red, always arranged with the blue above and the white in the middle, should be used for covering a speaker's desk, draping the front of a platform, and for decoration in general.

An act of Congress approved on Feb. 8, 1917, provided certain penalties for the desecration, mutilation, or improper use of the flag within the District of Columbia. A 1968 federal law provided penalties of as much as a year's imprisonment or a $1,000 fine or both for publicly burning or otherwise desecrating any U.S. flag. In addition, many states have laws against flag desecration. In 1989, the Supreme Court ruled that no laws could prohibit political protesters from burning the flag. The decision had the effect of declaring unconstitutional the flag desecration laws of 48 states, as well as a similar federal statute, in cases of peaceful political expression.

The Supreme Court, in June 1990, declared that a new federal law making it a crime to burn or deface the American flag violated the free-speech guarantee of the First Amendment. The 5-4 Court decision led to renewed calls in Congress for a constitutional amendment to make it possible to prosecute flag burners.

Pledge of Allegiance to the Flag

I pledge allegiance to the flag of the United States of America and to the republic for which it stands, one nation under God, indivisible, with liberty and justice for all.

This, the current official version of the Pledge of Allegiance, has developed from the original pledge, which was first published in the Sept. 8, 1892, issue of *Youth's Companion*, a weekly magazine then published in Boston. The original pledge contained the phrase "my flag," which was changed more than 30 years later to "flag of the United States of America." A 1954 act of Congress added the words "under God." (In 2002, the 9th Circuit U.S. Court of Appeals ruled that recitation of the pledge in public schools could not include that phrase. In 2004, however, the U.S. Supreme Court voted to decline to decide the case on a technicality. The lower court's decision was thus overturned.)

The authorship of the pledge was in dispute for many years. The *Youth's Companion* stated in 1917 that the original draft was written by James B. Upham, an executive of the magazine who died in 1910. A leaflet circulated by the magazine later named Upham as the originator of the draft "afterwards condensed and perfected by him and his associates of the Companion force."

Francis Bellamy, a former member of *Youth's Companion*

editorial staff, publicly claimed authorship of the pledge in 1923. In 1939, the United States Flag Association, acting on the advice of a committee named to study the controversy, upheld the claim of Bellamy, who had died 8 years earlier. In 1957 the Library of Congress issued a report attributing the authorship to Bellamy.

The History of the National Anthem

"The Star-Spangled Banner" was ordered played by the military and naval services by Pres. Woodrow Wilson in 1916. It was designated the national anthem by Act of Congress, Mar. 3, 1931. The words were written by Francis Scott Key, of Georgetown, MD, during the bombardment of Fort McHenry, Baltimore, Sept. 13-14, 1814. Key was a lawyer, a graduate of St. John's College, Annapolis, and a volunteer in a light artillery company. When a friend, Dr. Beanes, a Maryland physician, was taken aboard Admiral Cockburn's British squadron for interfering with ground troops, Key and J. S. Skinner, carrying a note from Pres. Madison, went to the fleet under a flag of truce on a cartel ship to ask Beanes's release. Cockburn consented, but as the fleet was about to sail up the Patapsco to bombard Fort McHenry, he detained them, first on HMS *Surprise* and then on a supply ship.

Key witnessed the bombardment from his own vessel. It began at 7 AM, Sept. 13, 1814, and lasted, with intermissions, for 25 hrs. The British fired more than 1,500 shells, each weighing as much as 220 lbs. They were unable to approach closely because the U.S. had sunk 22 vessels. Only 4 Americans were killed and 24 wounded. A British bombship was disabled.

During the event, Key wrote a stanza on the back of an envelope. Next day at Indian Queen Inn, Baltimore, he wrote out the poem and gave it to his brother-in-law, Judge J. H. Nicholson. Nicholson suggested use of the tune, "Anacreon in Heaven" (attributed to a British composer named John Stafford Smith), and had the poem printed on broadsides, of which 2 exist. On Sept. 20 it appeared in the *Baltimore American*. Later Key made 3 copies; one is in the Library of Congress, and one in the Pennsylvania Historical Society. The copy Key wrote on Sept. 14 remained in the Nicholson family for 93 years. In 1907 it was sold to Henry Walters of Baltimore. In 1934 it was bought at auction by the Walters Art Gallery, Baltimore, for $26,400. In 1953 it was sold to the Maryland Historical Society for the same price.

The flag that Key saw during the bombardment is preserved in the Smithsonian Institution, Washington, DC. It measures 30 by 42 ft and has 15 alternating red and white stripes and 15 stars, for the original 13 states plus Kentucky and Vermont. It was made by Mary Young Pickersgill. The Baltimore Flag House, a museum, occupies her premises, which were restored in 1953.

The Star-Spangled Banner

Note: The 2nd and 3rd stanzas are commonly omitted as a courtesy to the British.

I

Oh, say can you see by the dawn's early light
What so proudly we hailed at the twilight's last gleaming?
Whose broad stripes and bright stars thru the perilous fight,
O'er the ramparts we watched were so gallantly streaming?
And the rocket's red glare, the bombs bursting in air,
Gave proof through the night that our flag was still there.
Oh, say does that star-spangled banner yet wave
O'er the land of the free and the home of the brave?

II

On the shore, dimly seen through the mists of the deep,
Where the foe's haughty host in dread silence reposes,
What is that which the breeze, o'er the towering steep,
As it fitfully blows, half conceals, half discloses?
Now it catches the gleam of the morning's first beam,
In full glory reflected now shines in the stream:
'Tis the star-spangled banner! Oh long may it wave
O'er the land of the free and the home of the brave!

III

And where is that band who so vauntingly swore
That the havoc of war and the battle's confusion,
A home and a country should leave us no more!
Their blood has washed out their foul footsteps' pollution.
No refuge could save the hireling and slave
From the terror of flight, or the gloom of the grave:
And the star-spangled banner in triumph doth wave
O'er the land of the free and the home of the brave!

IV

Oh! thus be it ever, when freemen shall stand
Between their loved home and the war's desolation!
Blest with victory and peace, may the heav'n rescued land
Praise the Power that hath made and preserved us a nation.
Then conquer we must, when our cause it is just,
And this be our motto: "In God is our trust."
And the star-spangled banner in triumph shall wave
O'er the land of the free and the home of the brave!

America (My Country 'Tis of Thee)

First sung in public on July 4, 1831, at a service in the Park Street Church, Boston, the words were written by Rev. Samuel Francis Smith, a Baptist clergyman, who set them to a melody he found in a German songbook, unaware that it was the tune for the British anthem, "God Save the King/Queen."

My country, 'tis of thee,
Sweet land of liberty,
Of thee I sing.
Land where my fathers died!
Land of the Pilgrims' pride!
From ev'ry mountainside,
Let freedom ring!

My native country, thee,
Land of the noble free,
Thy name I love.
I love thy rocks and rills,
Thy woods and templed hills;
My heart with rapture thrills
Like that above.

Let music swell the breeze,
And ring from all the trees
Sweet freedom's song.
Let mortal tongues awake;
Let all that breathe partake;
Let rocks their silence break,
The sound prolong.

Our fathers' God, to Thee,
Author of liberty,
To Thee we sing.
Long may our land be bright
With freedom's holy light;
Protect us by Thy might,
Great God, our King!

IT'S A FACT: Fifteen-year-old Annie Moore from County Cork, Ireland, was the first immigrant to be processed when Ellis Island officially opened in 1892. In 1993, two statues of her were unveiled. One is on Ellis Island. The other is in Cobh (formerly Queenstown), Ireland, from where she departed with her two younger brothers, Anthony and Phillip, on Dec. 20, 1891.

America, the Beautiful

Words composed by Katharine Lee Bates, a Massachusetts educator and author, in 1893, inspired by the view she experienced atop Pikes Peak in Colorado. The final form was established in 1911, and it is set to the music of Samuel A. Ward's "Materna."

O beautiful for spacious skies.
For amber waves of grain,
For purple mountain majesties
Above the fruited plain.
America! America!
God shed His grace on thee,
And crown thy good with brotherhood
From sea to shining sea.

O beautiful for pilgrim feet
Whose stern impassion'd stress
A thorough-fare for freedom beat
Across the wilderness.
America! America!
God mend thine ev'ry flaw,
Confirm thy soul in self control,
Thy liberty in law.

O beautiful for heroes prov'd
In liberating strife,
Who more than self their country lov'd
And mercy more than life.
America! America!
May God thy gold refine
Till all success be nobleness,
And ev'ry gain divine.

O beautiful for patriot dream
That sees beyond the years,
Thine alabaster cities gleam,
Undimmed by human tears.
America! America!
God shed His grace on thee,
And crown thy good with brotherhood
From sea to shining sea.

The Liberty Bell: Its History and Significance

The Liberty Bell is housed in Independence National Historical Park in Philadelphia.

The original bell was ordered by Assembly Speaker and Chairman of the State House Superintendents Isaac Norris and was ordered from Thomas Lester, Whitechapel Foundry, London. It reached Philadelphia at the end of August 1752. It bore an inscription from Leviticus 25:10: "PROCLAIM LIBERTY THROUGHOUT ALL THE LAND UNTO ALL THE INHABITANTS THEREOF."

The bell was cracked by a stroke of its clapper in Sept. 1752 while it hung on a truss in the State House yard for testing. Pass & Stow, Philadelphia founders, recast the bell, adding 1½ ounces of copper to a pound of the original "Whitechapel" metal to reduce its high tone and brittleness. It was found that the bell contained too much copper, injuring its tone, so Pass & Stow recast it again, this time successfully.

In June 1753 the bell was hung in the old wooden steeple of the State House. In use while the Continental Congress was in session in the State House, it rang out in defiance of British tax and trade restrictions, and it proclaimed the Boston Tea Party and, on July 8, 1776, the first public reading of the Declaration of Independence.

On Sept. 18, 1777, when the British Army was about to occupy Philadelphia, the Liberty Bell was moved in a baggage train of the American Army to Allentown, PA, where it was hidden until June 27, 1778. The bell was moved back to Philadelphia after the British left the city.

In July 1781 the wooden steeple became insecure and had to be taken down. The bell was lowered into the brick section of the tower, where it remained until 1828. Between 1828 and 1844 the old State House bell continued to ring during special occasions. According to tradition, it cracked in 1835 as it tolled the death of Chief Justice John Marshall. It rang for the last time on Feb. 23, 1846. In 1852 it was placed on exhibition in the Declaration Chamber of Independence Hall.

In 1876, when thousands of Americans visited Philadelphia for the Centennial Exposition, the bell was placed in its old wooden support in the tower hallway. In 1877 it was hung from the ceiling of the tower by a chain of 13 links. It was returned again to the Declaration Chamber and in 1896 taken back to the tower hall, where it occupied a glass case. In 1915 the case was removed so that the public might touch it. On Jan. 1, 1976, just after midnight to mark the opening of the Bicentennial Year, the bell was moved to a new glass and steel pavilion behind Independence Hall for easier viewing.

The measurements of the bell are as follows: circumference around the lip, 12 ft ½ in; circumference around the crown, 6 ft 11¼ in; lip to the crown, 3 ft; height over the crown, 2 ft 3 in; thickness at lip, 3 in; thickness at crown, 1¼ in; weight, 2,080 lbs; length of clapper, 3 ft 2 in.

Statue of Liberty National Monument

Since 1886, the Statue of Liberty, formally known as "Liberty Enlightening the World," has stood as a symbol of freedom in New York harbor. It also commemorates French-American friendship, for it was given by the people of France and designed by French sculptor Frederic Auguste Bartholdi (1834-1904).

On Washington's Birthday, Feb. 22, 1877, Congress approved the use of a site on Bedloe's Island suggested by Bartholdi. This island of 12 acres had been owned in the 17th century by a Walloon named Isaac Bedloe. It was called Bedloe's until Aug. 3, 1956, when Pres. Dwight Eisenhower approved a measure changing the name to Liberty Island.

The statue was finished on May 21, 1884, and presented to the U.S. minister to France, Levi Parsons Morton, July 4, 1884, by Ferdinand de Lesseps, head of the Franco-American Union, promoter of the Panama Canal, and builder of the Suez Canal.

On Aug. 5, 1884, the Americans laid the cornerstone for the pedestal, to be built on the foundations of Fort Wood, erected by the government in 1811. The American committee had raised $125,000, but this was inadequate. Joseph Pulitzer, owner of the *New York World*, appealed on Mar. 16, 1885, for general donations. By Aug. 11, 1885, he had raised $100,000. The statue itself arrived dismantled, in 214 packing cases, from Rouen, France, in June 1885. The last rivet of the statue was driven on Oct. 28, 1886, when Pres. Grover Cleveland dedicated the monument.

The Statue of Liberty National Monument was designated as such in 1924. It is administered by the National Park Service. A $2.5 million building housing the American Museum of Immigration was opened by Pres. Richard Nixon on

Sept. 26, 1972, at the base of the statue. It houses a permanent exhibition tracing the history of American immigration.

Four years of restoration work funded and led by the Statue of Liberty-Ellis Island Foundation were completed before the statue's 1986 centennial. Among other repairs, the $87 million project included replacing the 1,600 wrought iron bands that hold the statue's copper skin to its frame, replacing its torch, and installing an elevator. A 4-day "Liberty Weekend" extravaganza of concerts, tall ships, ethnic festivals, and fireworks, July 3-6, 1986, celebrated the 100th anniversary. Chief Justice Warren E. Burger swore in 5,000 new citizens on Ellis Island, while 20,000 others across the country were sworn in through a satellite telecast. Other ceremonies followed on Oct. 28, 1986, the statue's exact 100th birthday.

Following the Sept. 11 terrorist attacks, Liberty Island was closed to visitors. On Dec. 20, 2001, the secretary of the interior reopened the island after installing airport-type screening facilities at passenger embarkation areas at Battery Park in Manhattan and Liberty State Park in New Jersey.

To open the statue, the federal government needed to increase security throughout the park. In addition to federally funded security upgrades, significant safety improvements were made to meet building codes. The National Park Service turned to the Statue of Liberty-Ellis Island Foundation, which began a fund-raising campaign to help finance safety renovations inside the statue, additional exits, improved handicapped access, and upgraded fire suppression and emergency warning systems. The federal investment in upgrades amounted to about $30 million, with the private sector contributing an additional $7 million. Access to the statue was finally restored on Aug. 3, 2004.

Two tours are now available (they must be reserved in advance). Reservations are available by visiting www.statuereservations.com or by calling 1-866-STATUE4. A limited number of "walk up" reservations are also available at ferry embarkation areas. The Promenade Tour goes along the promenade above the fort on which the statue and pedestal were built. The Observatory Tour incorporates the Promenade Tour and also goes up the pedestal by elevator to a panoramic observation deck; on that level is a view of the statue's interior. Both tours are ranger-guided and include a visit to the original torch, taken down during renovation in the 1980s, and the museum. The entire statue above the pedestal, including the crown, remains closed. (For more information, visit www.nps.gov/stli and www.statueofliberty.org)

Statue Statistics

The statue weighs 450,000 lbs., or 225 tons. The copper sheeting weighs 200,000 lbs. There are 167 steps from the land level to the top of the pedestal, 168 steps inside the statue to the head, and 54 rungs on the ladder leading to the arm that holds the torch.

	Ft	In		Ft	In
Height from base to torch tip	151	1	Nose, length	4	6
Foundation of pedestal to torch tip	305	1	Right arm, length	42	0
Heel to top of head	111	1	Right arm, max. thickness	12	0
Hand, length	16	5	Thickness of waist	35	0
Index finger, length	8	0	Mouth, width	3	0
Size of fingernail		13x10	Tablet, length	23	7
Head from chin to cranium	17	3	Tablet, width	13	7
Head thickness, ear to ear	10	0			

Emma Lazarus's Famous Poem

Engraved on pedestal below the statue.

The New Colossus

Not like the brazen giant of Greek fame,
With conquering limbs astride from land to land;
Here at our sea-washed, sunset gates shall stand
A mighty woman with a torch, whose flame
Is the imprisoned lightning, and her name
Mother of Exiles. From her beacon-hand
Glows world-wide welcome; her mild eyes command

The air-bridged harbor that twin cities frame.
"Keep ancient lands, your storied pomp!" cries she
With silent lips. "Give me your tired, your poor,
Your huddled masses yearning to breathe free,
The wretched refuse of your teeming shore.
Send these, the homeless, tempest-tost to me,
I lift my lamp beside the golden door!"

Ellis Island

Ellis Island was the gateway to America for over 12 mil immigrants between 1892 and 1924. In the late 18th century, Samuel Ellis, a New York City merchant, purchased the island and gave it his name. From Ellis, it passed to New York State, and the U.S. government bought it in 1808. On Jan. 1, 1892, the government opened the first federal immigration center in the U.S. there. The 27½-acre site eventually supported more than 35 buildings, including the Main Building with its Great Hall, in which as many as 5,000 people a day were processed.

Closed as an immigration station in 1954, Ellis Island was proclaimed part of the Statue of Liberty National Monument in 1965 by Pres. Lyndon B. Johnson. After a 6-year, $170 million restoration project funded by the Statue of Liberty-Ellis Island Foundation, Ellis Island was reopened as a museum in 1990. Artifacts, historic photographs and documents, oral histories, and ethnic music depicting 400 years of American immigration are housed in the museum. The museum also includes The American Immigrant Wall of Honor® (www.wallofhonor.com), which is inscribed with more than 600,000 names that have been placed in tribute. Registrations are still being accepted for inclusion in the memorial.

The American Family Immigration History Center® opened in April 2001. It contains an electronic database of ship passenger arrival information through the Port of New York and Ellis Island from 1892 to 1924. Data on over 25 million individuals are available, as well as an interactive database which features a Living Family Archive, multimedia presentations on various immigration groups and patterns, reproductions of original ships' passenger manifests, and pictures of over 800 immigrant ships (www.ellisisland.org).

In 1998, the Supreme Court ruled that nearly 90% of the island (the 24.2 acres which are landfill) lies in New Jersey, while the original 3.3 acres, on which the museum is located, are in New York.

PRESIDENTS OF THE UNITED STATES

U.S. Presidents

No.	Name	Politics	Born	in	Inaug.	at age	Died	at age
1.	George Washington	Fed.	1732, Feb. 22	VA	1789	57	1799, Dec. 14	67
2.	John Adams	Fed.	1735, Oct. 30	MA	1797	61	1826, July 4	90
3.	Thomas Jefferson	Dem.-Rep.	1743, Apr. 13	VA	1801	57	1826, July 4	83
4.	James Madison	Dem.-Rep.	1751, Mar. 16	VA	1809	57	1836, June 28	85
5.	James Monroe	Dem.-Rep.	1758, Apr. 28	VA	1817	58	1831, July 4	73
6.	John Quincy Adams	Dem.-Rep.	1767, July 11	MA	1825	57	1848, Feb. 23	80
7.	Andrew Jackson	Dem.	1767, Mar. 15	SC	1829	61	1845, June 8	78
8.	Martin Van Buren	Dem.	1782, Dec. 5	NY	1837	54	1862, July 24	79
9.	William Henry Harrison	Whig	1773, Feb. 9	VA	1841	68	1841, Apr. 4	68
10.	John Tyler	Whig	1790, Mar. 29	VA	1841	51	1862, Jan. 18	71
11.	James Knox Polk	Dem.	1795, Nov. 2	NC	1845	49	1849, June 15	53
12.	Zachary Taylor	Whig	1784, Nov. 24	VA	1849	64	1850, July 9	65
13.	Millard Fillmore	Whig	1800, Jan. 7	NY	1850	50	1874, Mar. 8	74
14.	Franklin Pierce	Dem.	1804, Nov. 23	NH	1853	48	1869, Oct. 8	64
15.	James Buchanan	Dem.	1791, Apr. 23	PA	1857	65	1868, June 1	77
16.	Abraham Lincoln	Rep.	1809, Feb. 12	KY	1861	52	1865, Apr. 15	56
17.	Andrew Johnson	(1)	1808, Dec. 29	NC	1865	56	1875, July 31	66
18.	Ulysses Simpson Grant	Rep.	1822, Apr. 27	OH	1869	46	1885, July 23	63
19.	Rutherford Birchard Hayes	Rep.	1822, Oct. 4	OH	1877	54	1893, Jan. 17	70
20.	James Abram Garfield	Rep.	1831, Nov. 19	OH	1881	49	1881, Sept. 19	49
21.	Chester Alan Arthur	Rep.	1829, Oct. 5	VT	1881	51	1886, Nov. 18	57
22.	Grover Cleveland	Dem.	1837, Mar. 18	NJ	1885	47	1908, June 24	71
23.	Benjamin Harrison	Rep.	1833, Aug. 20	OH	1889	55	1901, Mar. 13	67
24.	Grover Cleveland	Dem.	1837, Mar. 18	NJ	1893	55	1908, June 24	71
25.	William McKinley	Rep.	1843, Jan. 29	OH	1897	54	1901, Sept. 14	58
26.	Theodore Roosevelt	Rep.	1858, Oct. 27	NY	1901	42	1919, Jan. 6	60
27.	William Howard Taft	Rep.	1857, Sept. 15	OH	1909	51	1930, Mar. 8	72
28.	Woodrow Wilson	Dem.	1856, Dec. 28	VA	1913	56	1924, Feb. 3	67
29.	Warren Gamaliel Harding	Rep.	1865, Nov. 2	OH	1921	55	1923, Aug. 2	57
30.	Calvin Coolidge	Rep.	1872, July 4	VT	1923	51	1933, Jan. 5	60
31.	Herbert Clark Hoover	Rep.	1874, Aug. 10	IA	1929	54	1964, Oct. 20	90
32.	Franklin Delano Roosevelt	Dem.	1882, Jan. 30	NY	1933	51	1945, Apr. 12	63
33.	Harry S. Truman	Dem.	1884, May 8	MO	1945	60	1972, Dec. 26	88
34.	Dwight David Eisenhower	Rep.	1890, Oct. 14	TX	1953	62	1969, Mar. 28	78
35.	John Fitzgerald Kennedy	Dem.	1917, May 29	MA	1961	43	1963, Nov. 22	46
36.	Lyndon Baines Johnson	Dem.	1908, Aug. 27	TX	1963	55	1973, Jan. 22	64
37.	Richard Milhous Nixon (2)	Rep.	1913, Jan. 9	CA	1969	56	1994, Apr. 22	81
38.	Gerald Rudolph Ford	Rep.	1913, July 14	NE	1974	61		
39.	Jimmy (James Earl) Carter	Dem.	1924, Oct. 1	GA	1977	52		
40.	Ronald Reagan	Rep.	1911, Feb. 6	IL	1981	69	2004, June 5	93
41.	George H. W. Bush	Rep.	1924, June 12	MA	1989	64		
42.	Bill (Wm. Jefferson) Clinton	Dem.	1946, Aug. 19	AR	1993	46		
43.	George Walker Bush	Rep.	1946, July 6	CT	2001	54		

(1) Andrew Johnson, a Democrat, was nominated vice president by Republicans and elected with Lincoln on National Union ticket.
(2) Resigned Aug. 9, 1974.

U.S. Presidents, Vice Presidents, Congresses

	President	Service		Vice President	Congresses
1.	George Washington	Apr. 30, 1789—Mar. 3, 1797	1.	John Adams	1, 2, 3, 4
2.	John Adams	Mar. 4, 1797—Mar. 3, 1801	2.	Thomas Jefferson	5, 6
3.	Thomas Jefferson	Mar. 4, 1801—Mar. 3, 1805	3.	Aaron Burr	7, 8
		Mar. 4, 1805—Mar. 3, 1809	4.	George Clinton	9, 10
4.	James Madison	Mar. 4, 1809—Mar. 3, 1813		George Clinton (1)	11, 12
		Mar. 4, 1813—Mar. 3, 1817	5.	Elbridge Gerry (2)	13, 14
5.	James Monroe	Mar. 4, 1817—Mar. 3, 1825	6.	Daniel D. Tompkins	15, 16, 17, 18
6.	John Quincy Adams	Mar. 4, 1825—Mar. 3, 1829	7.	John C. Calhoun	19, 20
7.	Andrew Jackson	Mar. 4, 1829—Mar. 3, 1833		John C. Calhoun (3)	21, 22
		Mar. 4, 1833—Mar. 3, 1837	8.	Martin Van Buren	23, 24
8.	Martin Van Buren	Mar. 4, 1837—Mar. 3, 1841	9.	Richard M. Johnson	25, 26
9.	William Henry Harrison (4)	Mar. 4, 1841—Apr. 4, 1841	10.	John Tyler	27
10.	John Tyler	Apr. 6, 1841—Mar. 3, 1845		(none)	27, 28
11.	James K. Polk	Mar. 4, 1845—Mar. 3, 1849	11.	George M. Dallas	29, 30
12.	Zachary Taylor (4)	Mar. 5, 1849—July 9, 1850	12.	Millard Fillmore	31
13.	Millard Fillmore	July 10, 1850—Mar. 3, 1853		(none)	31, 32
14.	Franklin Pierce	Mar. 4, 1853—Mar. 3, 1857	13.	William R. King (5)	33, 34
15.	James Buchanan	Mar. 4, 1857—Mar. 3, 1861	14.	John C. Breckinridge	35, 36
16.	Abraham Lincoln	Mar. 4, 1861—Mar. 3, 1865	15.	Hannibal Hamlin	37, 38
	(4)	Mar. 4, 1865—Apr. 15, 1865	16.	Andrew Johnson	39
17.	Andrew Johnson	Apr. 15, 1865—Mar. 3, 1869		(none)	39, 40
18.	Ulysses S. Grant	Mar. 4, 1869—Mar. 3, 1873	17.	Schuyler Colfax	41, 42
		Mar. 4, 1873—Mar. 3, 1877	18.	Henry Wilson (6)	43, 44
19.	Rutherford B. Hayes	Mar. 4, 1877—Mar. 3, 1881	19.	William A. Wheeler	45, 46
20.	James A. Garfield (4)	Mar. 4, 1881—Sept. 19, 1881	20.	Chester A. Arthur	47
21.	Chester A. Arthur	Sept. 20, 1881—Mar. 3, 1885		(none)	47, 48
22.	Grover Cleveland (7)	Mar. 4, 1885—Mar. 3, 1889	21.	Thomas A. Hendricks (8)	49, 50
23.	Benjamin Harrison	Mar. 4, 1889—Mar. 3, 1893	22.	Levi P. Morton	51, 52
24.	Grover Cleveland (7)	Mar. 4, 1893—Mar. 3, 1897	23.	Adlai E. Stevenson	53, 54
25.	William McKinley	Mar. 4, 1897—Mar. 3, 1901	24.	Garret A. Hobart (9)	55, 56
	(4)	Mar. 4, 1901—Sept. 14, 1901	25.	Theodore Roosevelt	57
26.	Theodore Roosevelt	Sept. 14, 1901—Mar. 3, 1905		(none)	57, 58
		Mar. 4, 1905—Mar. 3, 1909	26.	Charles W. Fairbanks	59, 60
27.	William H. Taft	Mar. 4, 1909—Mar. 3, 1913	27.	James S. Sherman (10)	61, 62
28.	Woodrow Wilson	Mar. 4, 1913—Mar. 3, 1921	28.	Thomas R. Marshall	63, 64, 65, 66
29.	Warren G. Harding (4)	Mar. 4, 1921—Aug. 2, 1923	29.	Calvin Coolidge	67
30.	Calvin Coolidge	Aug. 3, 1923—Mar. 3, 1925		(none)	68
		Mar. 4, 1925—Mar. 3, 1929	30.	Charles G. Dawes	69, 70

	President	Service		Vice President	Congresses
31.	Herbert C. Hoover	Mar. 4, 1929—Mar. 3, 1933	31.	Charles Curtis	71, 72
32.	Franklin D. Roosevelt (11)	Mar. 4, 1933—Jan. 20, 1941	32.	John N. Garner	73, 74, 75, 76, 77
		Jan. 20, 1941—Jan. 20, 1945	33.	Henry A. Wallace	77, 78, 79
	(4)	Jan. 20, 1945—Apr. 12, 1945	34.	Harry S. Truman	79
33.	Harry S. Truman	Apr. 12, 1945—Jan. 20, 1949		(none)	79, 80, 81
		Jan. 20, 1949—Jan. 20, 1953	35.	Alben W. Barkley	81, 82, 83
34.	Dwight D. Eisenhower	Jan. 20, 1953—Jan. 20, 1961	36.	Richard M. Nixon	83, 84, 85, 86, 87
35.	John F. Kennedy (4)	Jan. 20, 1961—Nov. 22, 1963	37.	Lyndon B. Johnson	87, 88
36.	Lyndon B. Johnson	Nov. 22, 1963—Jan. 20, 1965		(none)	88, 89
		Jan. 20, 1965—Jan. 20, 1969	38.	Hubert H. Humphrey	89, 90, 91
37.	Richard M. Nixon	Jan. 20, 1969—Jan. 20, 1973	39.	Spiro T. Agnew (12)	91, 92, 93
	(13)	Jan. 20, 1973—Aug. 9, 1974	40.	Gerald R. Ford (14)	93
38.	Gerald R. Ford (15)	Aug. 9, 1974—Jan. 20, 1977	41.	Nelson A. Rockefeller (16)	93, 94, 95
39.	Jimmy Carter	Jan. 20, 1977—Jan. 20, 1981	42.	Walter F. Mondale	95, 96, 97
40.	Ronald Reagan	Jan. 20, 1981—Jan. 20, 1989	43.	George H. W. Bush	97, 98, 99, 100, 101
41.	George H. W. Bush	Jan. 20, 1989—Jan. 20, 1993	44.	Dan Quayle	101, 102, 103
42.	Bill Clinton	Jan. 20, 1993—Jan. 20, 2001	45.	Al Gore	103, 104, 105, 106, 107
43.	George W. Bush	Jan. 20, 2001—	46.	Dick Cheney	107, 108, 109, 110

(1) Died Apr. 20, 1812. (2) Died Nov. 23, 1814. (3) Resigned Dec. 28, 1832, to become U.S. senator. (4) Died in office. (5) Died Apr. 18, 1853. (6) Died Nov. 22, 1875. (7) Terms not consecutive. (8) Died Nov. 25, 1885. (9) Died Nov. 21, 1899. (10) Died Oct. 30, 1912. (11) First president to be inaugurated under 20th Amendment, Jan. 20, 1937. (12) Resigned Oct. 10, 1973. (13) Resigned Aug. 9, 1974. (14) First nonelected vice president, chosen under 25th Amendment procedure. (15) First president never elected president or vice president. (16) Second nonelected vice president, chosen under 25th Amendment. Confirmed Dec. 19, 1974.

Vice Presidents of the U.S.

The numerals given vice presidents do not coincide with those given presidents, because some presidents (Tyler, Fillmore, A. Johnson, Arthur) had none, and some had more than one.

	Name	Birthplace	Year	Home	Inaug.	Politics	Place of death	Year	Age
1.	John Adams	Quincy, MA	1735	MA	1789	Fed.	Quincy, MA	1826	90
2.	Thomas Jefferson	Shadwell, VA	1743	VA	1797	Dem.-Rep.	Monticello, VA	1826	83
3.	Aaron Burr	Newark, NJ	1756	NY	1801	Dem.-Rep.	Staten Island, NY	1836	80
4.	George Clinton	Ulster Co., NY	1739	NY	1805	Dem.-Rep.	Washington, DC	1812	73
5.	Elbridge Gerry	Marblehead, MA	1744	MA	1813	Dem.-Rep.	Washington, DC	1814	70
6.	Daniel D. Tompkins	Scarsdale, NY	1774	NY	1817	Dem.-Rep.	Staten Island, NY	1825	51
7.	John C. Calhoun (1)	Abbeville, SC	1782	SC	1825	Dem.-Rep.	Washington, DC	1850	68
8.	Martin Van Buren	Kinderhook, NY	1782	NY	1833	Dem.	Kinderhook, NY	1862	79
9.	Richard M. Johnson (2)	Louisville, KY	1780	KY	1837	Dem.	Frankfort, KY	1850	70
10.	John Tyler	Greenway, VA	1790	VA	1841	Whig	Richmond, VA	1862	71
11.	George M. Dallas	Philadelphia, PA	1792	PA	1845	Dem.	Philadelphia, PA	1864	72
12.	Millard Fillmore	Cayuga Co., NY	1800	NY	1849	Whig	Buffalo, NY	1874	74
13.	William R. King	Sampson Co., NC	1786	AL	1853	Dem.	Dallas Co., AL	1853	67
14.	John C. Breckinridge	Lexington, KY	1821	KY	1857	Dem.	Lexington, KY	1875	54
15.	Hannibal Hamlin	Paris, ME	1809	ME	1861	Rep.	Bangor, ME	1891	81
16.	Andrew Johnson	Raleigh, NC	1808	TN	1865	(3)	Carter Co., TN	1875	66
17.	Schuyler Colfax	New York, NY	1823	IN	1869	Rep.	Mankato, MN	1885	62
18.	Henry Wilson	Farmington, NH	1812	MA	1873	Rep.	Washington, DC	1875	63
19.	William A. Wheeler	Malone, NY	1819	NY	1877	Rep.	Malone, NY	1887	68
20.	Chester A. Arthur	Fairfield, VT	1829	NY	1881	Rep.	New York, NY	1886	57
21.	Thomas A. Hendricks	Zanesville, OH	1819	IN	1885	Dem.	Indianapolis, IN	1885	66
22.	Levi P. Morton	Shoreham, VT	1824	NY	1889	Rep.	Rhinebeck, NY	1920	96
23.	Adlai E. Stevenson (4)	Christian Co., KY	1835	IL	1893	Dem.	Chicago, IL	1914	78
24.	Garret A. Hobart	Long Branch, NJ	1844	NJ	1897	Rep.	Paterson, NJ	1899	55
25.	Theodore Roosevelt	New York, NY	1858	NY	1901	Rep.	Oyster Bay, NY	1919	60
26.	Charles W. Fairbanks	Unionville Centre, OH	1852	IN	1905	Rep.	Indianapolis, IN	1918	66
27.	James S. Sherman	Utica, NY	1855	NY	1909	Rep.	Utica, NY	1912	57
28.	Thomas R. Marshall	N. Manchester, IN	1854	IN	1913	Dem.	Washington, DC	1925	71
29.	Calvin Coolidge	Plymouth Notch, VT	1872	MA	1921	Rep.	Northampton, MA	1933	60
30.	Charles G. Dawes	Marietta, OH	1865	IL	1925	Rep.	Evanston, IL	1951	85
31.	Charles Curtis	Topeka, KS	1860	KS	1929	Rep.	Washington, DC	1936	76
32.	John Nance Garner	Red River Co., TX	1868	TX	1933	Dem.	Uvalde, TX	1967	98
33.	Henry A. Wallace	Adair County, IA	1888	IA	1941	Dem.	Danbury, CT	1965	77
34.	Harry S. Truman	Lamar, MO	1884	MO	1945	Dem.	Kansas City, MO	1972	88
35.	Alben W. Barkley	Graves County, KY	1877	KY	1949	Dem.	Lexington, VA	1956	78
36.	Richard M. Nixon	Yorba Linda, CA	1913	CA	1953	Rep.	New York, NY	1994	81
37.	Lyndon B. Johnson	Stonewall, TX	1908	TX	1961	Dem.	San Antonio, TX	1973	64
38.	Hubert H. Humphrey	Wallace, SD	1911	MN	1965	Dem.	Waverly, MN	1978	66
39.	Spiro T. Agnew (5)	Baltimore, MD	1918	MD	1969	Rep.	Berlin, MD	1996	77
40.	Gerald R. Ford (6)	Omaha, NE	1913	MI	1973	Rep.			
41.	Nelson A. Rockefeller (7)	Bar Harbor, ME	1908	NY	1974	Rep.	New York, NY	1979	70
42.	Walter F. Mondale	Ceylon, MN	1928	MN	1977	Dem.			
43.	George H. W. Bush	Milton, MA	1924	TX	1981	Rep.			
44.	J. Dan Quayle	Indianapolis, IN	1947	IN	1989	Rep.			
45.	Al Gore	Washington, DC	1948	TN	1993	Dem.			
46.	Dick Cheney	Lincoln, NE	1941	WY	2001	Rep.			

(1) Resigned Dec. 28, 1832, having been elected to the Senate to fill a vacancy. (2) Richard M. Johnson was the only vice president to be chosen by the Senate because of a tied vote in the Electoral College. (3) Andrew Johnson was a Democrat, nominated vice president by Republicans, and elected with Lincoln on the National Union Ticket. (4) Grandfather of Democratic candidate for president in 1952 and 1956. (5) Resigned Oct. 10, 1973. (6) First nonelected vice president, chosen under 25th Amendment procedure. (7) Second nonelected vice president, chosen under 25th Amendment.

> **IT'S A FACT:** Jimmy Carter is the only full-term president who did not get to nominate a Supreme Court justice. Three other presidents—William Henry Harrison, Zachary Taylor, and Andrew Johnson—also never had the opportunity to select a nominee.

Biographies of the Presidents

George Washington (1789-97), 1st president, Federalist, was born on Feb. 22, 1732, in Wakefield on Pope's Creek, Westmoreland Co., VA, the son of Augustine and Mary Ball Washington. He spent his early childhood on a farm near Fredericksburg. His father died when Washington was 11. He studied mathematics and surveying, and at 16, he went to live with his elder half brother, Lawrence, who built and named Mount Vernon. Washington surveyed the lands of Thomas Fairfax in the Shenandoah Valley, keeping a diary. He accompanied Lawrence to Barbados, West Indies, where he contracted smallpox and was deeply scarred. Lawrence died in 1752, and Washington inherited his property. He valued land, and when he died, he owned 70,000 acres in Virginia and 40,000 acres in what is now West Virginia.

Washington's military service began in 1753, when Lt. Gov. Robert Dinwiddie of Virginia sent him on missions deep into Ohio country. He clashed with the French and had to surrender Fort Necessity on July 3, 1754. He was an aide to the British general Edward Braddock and was at his side when the army was ambushed and defeated (July 9, 1755) on a march to Fort Duquesne. He helped take Fort Duquesne from the French in 1758.

After Washington's marriage to Martha Dandridge Custis, a widow, in 1759, he managed his family estate at Mount Vernon. Although not at first for independence, he opposed the repressive measures of the British crown and took charge of the Virginia troops before war broke out. He was made commander of the newly created Continental Army by the Continental Congress on June 15, 1775.

The American victory was due largely to Washington's leadership. He was resourceful, a stern disciplinarian, and the one strong, dependable force for unity. Washington favored a federal government. He became chairman of the Constitutional Convention of 1787 and helped get the Constitution ratified. Unanimously elected president by the Electoral College, he was inaugurated Apr. 30, 1789, on the balcony of New York's Federal Hall. He was reelected in 1792. Washington made an effort to avoid partisan politics as president.

Refusing to consider a 3rd term, Washington retired to Mount Vernon in March 1797. He suffered acute laryngitis after a ride in snow and rain around his estate, was bled profusely, and died Dec. 14, 1799.

John Adams (1797-1801), 2nd president, Federalist, was born on Oct. 30, 1735, in Braintree (now Quincy), MA, the son of John and Susanna Boylston Adams. He was a great-grandson of Henry Adams, who came from England in 1636. He graduated from Harvard in 1755 and then taught school and studied law. He married Abigail Smith in 1764. In 1765 he argued against taxation without representation before the royal governor. In 1770, he successfully defended in court the British soldiers who fired on civilians in the Boston Massacre. He was a delegate to the Continental Congress and a signer of the Declaration of Independence. In 1778, Congress sent Adams and John Jay to join Benjamin Franklin as diplomatic representatives in Europe. Because he ran second to Washington in Electoral College balloting in Feb. 1789, Adams became the nation's first vice president, a post he characterized as highly insignificant; he was reelected in 1792.

In 1796 Adams was chosen president by the electors. His administration was marked by growing conflict with fellow Federalist Alexander Hamilton and with others in his own cabinet who supported Hamilton's strongly anti-French position. Adams avoided full-scale war with France, but became unpopular, especially after securing passage of the Alien and Sedition Acts in 1798. His foreign policy contributed significantly to the election of Thomas Jefferson in 1800.

Adams lived for a quarter century after he left office, during which time he wrote extensively. He died July 4, 1826, on the same day as his rival Thomas Jefferson (the 50th anniversary of the Declaration of Independence).

Thomas Jefferson (1801-09), 3rd president, Democratic-Republican, was born on Apr. 13, 1743, in Shadwell in Goochland (now Albemarle) Co., VA, the son of Peter and Jane Randolph Jefferson. Peter died when Jefferson was 14, leaving him 2,750 acres and his slaves. Jefferson attended (1760-62) the College of William and Mary, read Greek and Latin classics, and played the violin. In 1769 he was elected to the Virginia House of Burgesses. In 1770 he began building his home, Monticello, and in 1772 he married Martha Wayles Skelton, a wealthy widow. Jefferson helped establish the Virginia Committee of Correspondence. As a member of the 2nd Continental Congress he drafted the Declaration of Independence. He also was a member of the Virginia House of Delegates (1776-79) and was elected governor of Virginia in 1779, succeeding Patrick Henry. He was reelected in 1780 but resigned in 1781 after British troops invaded Virginia. During his term he wrote the statute on religious freedom. After his wife's death in 1782, Jefferson again became a delegate to the Congress, and in 1784 he drafted the report that was the basis for the Ordinances of 1784, 1785, and 1787. He was minister to France from 1785 to 1789, when George Washington appointed him secretary of state.

Jefferson's strong faith in the consent of the governed conflicted with the emphasis on executive control, favored by Alexander Hamilton, secretary of the Treasury, and Jefferson resigned on Dec. 31, 1793. In the 1796 election Jefferson was the Democratic-Republican candidate for president; John Adams won the election, and Jefferson became vice president. In 1800, Jefferson and Aaron Burr received equal Electoral College votes; the House of Representatives elected Jefferson president. Jefferson was a strong advocate of westward expansion; major events of his first term were the Louisiana Purchase (1803) and the Lewis and Clark Expedition. An important development during his second term was passage of the Embargo Act, barring U.S. ships from setting sail to foreign ports. Jefferson established the University of Virginia and designed its buildings. He died July 4, 1826, on the same day as John Adams (the 50th anniversary of the Declaration of Independence).

Following analysis of DNA taken from descendants of Jefferson and Sally Hemings, one of his slaves, it has been widely acknowledged that Jefferson fathered at least one, perhaps all, of her six known children.

James Madison (1809-17), 4th president, Democratic-Republican, was born on Mar. 16, 1751, in Port Conway, King George Co., VA, the son of James and Eleanor Rose Conway Madison. Madison graduated from Princeton in 1771. He served in the Virginia Constitutional Convention (1776), and, in 1780, became a delegate to the 2nd Continental Congress. He was chief recorder at the Constitutional Convention in 1787 and supported ratification in the *Federalist Papers*, written with Alexander Hamilton and John Jay. In 1789, Madison was elected to the House of Representatives, where he helped frame the Bill of Rights and fought against passage of the Alien and Sedition Acts. In the 1790s, he helped found the Democratic-Republican Party, which ultimately became the Democratic Party. He became Jefferson's secretary of state in 1801.

Madison was elected president in 1808. His first term was marked by tensions with Great Britain, and his conduct of foreign policy was criticized by the Federalists and by his own party. Nevertheless, he was reelected in 1812, the year war was declared on Great Britain. The war that many considered a second American revolution ended with a treaty that settled none of the issues. Madison's most important action after the war was demilitarizing the U.S.-Canadian border.

In 1817, Madison retired to his estate, Montpelier, where he served as an elder statesman. He edited his famous papers on the Constitutional Convention and helped found the University of Virginia, of which he became rector in 1826. He died June 28, 1836.

James Monroe (1817-25), 5th president, Democratic-Republican, was born on Apr. 28, 1758, in Westmoreland Co., VA, the son of Spence and Eliza Jones Monroe. He entered the College of William and Mary in 1774 but left to serve in the 3rd Virginia Regiment during the American Revolution. After the war, he studied law with Thomas Jefferson. In 1782 he was elected to the Virginia House of Delegates, and he served (1783-86) as a delegate to the Continental Congress. He opposed ratification of the Constitution because it lacked a bill of rights. Monroe was elected to the U.S. Senate in 1790. In 1794, President Washington appointed Monroe minister to France. He served twice as governor of Virginia (1799-1802, 1811). President Jefferson also sent him to France as minister (1803), and from 1803 to 1807 he served as minister to Great Britain.

In 1816 Monroe was elected president; he was reelected in 1820 with all but one Electoral College vote. His administration became known as the Era of Good Feeling. He obtained Florida from Spain, settled boundary disputes with Britain over Canada, and eliminated border forts. He supported the antislavery position that led to the Missouri Compromise. His most significant contribution was the Monroe Doctrine, which opposed European intervention in the Western Hemisphere and became a cornerstone of U.S. foreign policy.

Although Monroe retired to Oak Hill, VA, financial problems forced him to sell his property and move to New York City. He died there on July 4, 1831.

John Quincy Adams (1825-29), 6th president, independent Federalist, later Democratic-Republican, was born on July 11, 1767, in Braintree (now Quincy), MA, the son of John and Abigail Adams. His father was the 2nd president. He studied abroad and at Harvard University, from which he graduated in 1787. In 1803, he was elected to the U.S. Senate. President Monroe chose him as his secretary of state in 1817. In this capacity he negotiated the cession of Florida from Spain, supported exclusion of slavery in the Missouri Compromise, and helped formulate the Monroe Doctrine. In 1824, Adams was elected president by the House of Representatives after he failed to win an Electoral College majority. His expansion of executive powers was strongly opposed, and in the 1828 election he lost to Andrew Jackson. In 1831 he entered the House of Representatives and served 17 years with distinction. He opposed slavery, the annexation of Texas, and the Mexican War. He helped establish the Smithsonian Institution.

Adams suffered a stroke in the House and died in the Speaker's Room on Feb. 23, 1848.

Andrew Jackson (1829-37), 7th president, Democratic-Republican, later a Democrat, was born on Mar. 15, 1767, in the Waxhaw district, on the border of North Carolina and South Carolina, the son of Andrew and Elizabeth Hutchinson Jackson. At the age of 13, he joined the militia to fight in the American Revolution and was captured. Orphaned at the age of 14, Jackson was brought up by a well-to-do uncle. By age 20, he was practicing law, and he later served as prosecuting attorney in Nashville, TN. In 1796 he helped draft the constitution of Tennessee, and for a year he occupied its one seat in the House of Representatives. The next year Jackson served in the U.S. Senate.

In the War of 1812, Jackson crushed the Creek Indians at Horseshoe Bend, AL (1814), and, with a greatly outnumbered army consisting chiefly of backwoodsmen, defeated General Edward Pakenham's British troops at the Battle of New Orleans (1815). Nicknamed "Old Hickory" for his toughness, he emerged a national hero.

In 1818 Jackson briefly invaded Spanish Florida to quell Seminoles and outlaws who harassed frontier settlements. He ran for president against John Quincy Adams in 1824,

but, although he won the most popular and electoral votes, he did not have a majority. The House of Representatives decided the election and chose Adams. In the 1828 election, however, Jackson defeated Adams, carrying the West and the South.

As president, Jackson introduced what became known as the spoils system—rewarding party members with government posts. Perhaps his most controversial act, however, was depositing federal funds in so-called pet banks, directed by Democratic bankers, rather than in the Bank of the United States. "Let the people rule" was his slogan. In 1832, Jackson killed the congressional caucus for nominating presidential candidates and substituted the national convention. When South Carolina refused to collect imports under his protective tariff, he ordered army and naval forces to Charleston. After leaving office in 1837, he retired to the Hermitage, outside Nashville, where he died on June 8, 1845.

Martin Van Buren (1837-41), 8th president, Democrat, was born on Dec. 5, 1782, in Kinderhook, NY, the son of Abraham and Maria Hoes Van Buren. After attending local schools, he studied law and became a lawyer at the age of 20. A consummate politician, Van Buren began his career in the New York state senate and then served as state attorney general from 1816 to 1819. He was elected to the U.S. Senate in 1821. He helped swing Eastern support to Andrew Jackson in the 1828 election and then served as Jackson's secretary of state from 1829 to 1831. In 1832 he was elected vice president. Known as the "Little Magician," Van Buren was extremely influential in Jackson's administration.

In 1836, Van Buren defeated William Henry Harrison for president and took office as the financial panic of 1837 initiated a nationwide depression. Although he instituted the independent treasury system, his refusal to spend land revenues led to his defeat by William Henry Harrison in 1840. In 1844 he lost the Democratic nomination to James Knox Polk. In 1848 he again ran for president on the Free Soil ticket but lost. He died in Kinderhook on July 24, 1862.

William Henry Harrison (1841), 9th president, Whig, who served only 31 days, was born on Feb. 9, 1773, in Berkeley, Charles City Co., VA, the son of Benjamin Harrison, a signer of the Declaration of Independence, and of Elizabeth Bassett Harrison. He attended Hampden-Sydney College. Harrison served as secretary of the Northwest Territory in 1798 and was its delegate to the House of Representatives in 1799. He was the first governor of the Indiana Territory and served as superintendent of Indian affairs. With 900 men he put down a Shawnee uprising at Tippecanoe, IN, on Nov. 7, 1811. A generation later, in 1840, he waged a rousing presidential campaign, using the slogan "Tippecanoe and Tyler Too." The Tyler of the slogan was his running mate, John Tyler.

Although born to one of the wealthiest, most prestigious, and most influential families in Virginia, Harrison was elected president with the slogan, "Log Cabin and Hard Cider." He caught pneumonia during the inauguration and died Apr. 4, 1841, after only one month in office.

John Tyler (1841-45), 10th president, independent Whig, was born on Mar. 29, 1790, in Greenway, Charles City Co., VA, the son of John and Mary Armistead Tyler. His father was governor of Virginia (1808-11). Tyler graduated from the College of William and Mary in 1807 and in 1811 was elected to the Virginia legislature. In 1816 he was chosen for the U.S. House of Representatives. He served in the Virginia legislature again from 1823 to 1825, when he was elected governor of Virginia. After a stint in the U.S. Senate (1827-36), he was elected vice president (1840).

When William Henry Harrison died only a month after taking office, Tyler succeeded him. Because he was the first person to occupy the presidency without having been elected to that office, he was referred to as "His Accidency." He gained passage of the Preemption Act of 1841, which gave squatters on government land the right to buy 160 acres at the minimum auction price. His last act as president was to sign a resolution annexing Texas. Tyler accepted renomination in 1844 from some Democrats but withdrew in favor of the official party candidate, James K. Polk. He died in Richmond, VA, on Jan. 18, 1862.

James Knox Polk (1845-49), 11th president, Democrat, was born on Nov. 2, 1795, in Mecklenburg Co., NC, the son of Samuel and Jane Knox Polk. He graduated from the University of North Carolina in 1818 and served in the Tennessee state legislature from 1823 to 1825. He served in the U.S. House of Representatives from 1825 to 1839, the last 4 years as Speaker. He was governor of Tennessee from 1839 to 1841. In 1844, after the Democratic National Convention became deadlocked, it nominated Polk, who became the first "dark horse" candidate for president. He was nominated primarily because he favored annexation of Texas.

As president, Polk reestablished the independent treasury system originated by Van Buren. He was so intent on acquiring California from Mexico that he sent troops to the Mexican border and, when Mexicans attacked, declared that a state of war existed. The Mexican War ended with the annexation of California and much of the Southwest as part of America's "manifest destiny." Polk compromised on the Oregon boundary ("54-40 or fight!") by accepting the 49th parallel and yielding Vancouver Island to the British. A few months after leaving office, Polk died in Nashville, TN, on June 15, 1849.

Zachary Taylor (1849-50), 12th president, Whig, who served only 16 months, was born on Nov. 24, 1784, in Orange Co., VA, the son of Richard and Sarah Strother Taylor. He grew up on his father's plantation near Louisville, KY, where he was educated by private tutors. In 1808 Taylor joined the regular army and was commissioned first lieutenant. He fought in the War of 1812, the Black Hawk War (1832), and the second Seminole War (beginning in 1837). He was called "Old Rough and Ready." In 1846 President Polk sent him with an army to the Rio Grande. When the Mexicans attacked him, Polk declared war. Outnumbered 4-1, Taylor defeated Santa Anna at Buena Vista (1847).

A national hero, Taylor received the Whig nomination in 1848 and was elected president, even though he had never bothered to vote. He resumed the spoils system and, though a slaveholder, worked to admit California as a free state. He fell ill and died in office on July 9, 1850.

Millard Fillmore (1850-53), 13th president, Whig, was born on Jan. 7, 1800, in Cayuga Co., NY, the son of Nathaniel and Phoebe Millard Fillmore. Although he had little schooling, he became a law clerk at the age of 22 and a year later was admitted to the bar. He was elected to the New York state assembly in 1828 and served until 1831. From 1833 until 1835 and again from 1837 to 1843, he represented his district in the U.S. House of Representatives. He opposed the entrance of Texas as a slave state and voted for a protective tariff. In 1844 he was defeated for governor of New York.

In 1848 he was elected vice president, and he succeeded as president after Taylor's death. Fillmore favored the Compromise of 1850 and signed the Fugitive Slave Law. His policies pleased neither expansionists nor slaveholders, and he was not renominated in 1852. In 1856 he was nominated by the American (Know-Nothing) Party, but despite the support of the Whigs, he was defeated by James Buchanan. He died in Buffalo, NY, on Mar. 8, 1874.

Franklin Pierce (1853-57), 14th president, Democrat, was born on Nov. 23, 1804, in Hillsboro, NH, the son of Benjamin Pierce, Revolutionary War general and governor of New Hampshire, and Anna Kendrick. He graduated from Bowdoin College in 1824 and was admitted to the bar in 1827. He was elected to the New Hampshire state legislature in 1829 and was chosen Speaker in 1831. He went to the U.S. House in 1833 and was elected a U.S. senator in 1837. He enlisted in the Mexican War and became brigadier general under Gen. Winfield Scott.

In 1852 Pierce was nominated as the Democratic presidential candidate on the 49th ballot. He decisively defeated Gen. Scott, his Whig opponent, in the election. Although against slavery, Pierce was influenced by proslavery Southerners. He supported the controversial Kansas-Nebraska Act, which left the question of slavery in the new territories of Kansas and Nebraska to popular vote. Pierce signed a reciprocity treaty with Canada and approved the Gadsden Purchase of a border area on a proposed railroad route, from Mexico. Denied renomination, he spent most of his remaining years in Concord, NH, where he died on Oct. 8, 1869.

James Buchanan (1857-61), 15th president, Federalist, later Democrat, was born on Apr. 23, 1791, near Mercersburg, PA, the son of James and Elizabeth Speer Buchanan. He graduated from Dickinson College in 1809 and was admitted to the bar in 1812. He fought in the War of 1812 as a volunteer. He was twice elected to the Pennsylvania general assembly, and in 1821 he entered the U.S. House of Representatives. After briefly serving (1832-33) as minister to Russia, he was elected U.S. senator from Pennsylvania. As Polk's secretary of state (1845-49), he ended the Oregon dispute with Britain and supported the Mexican War and annexation of Texas. As minister to Great Britain, he signed the Ostend Manifesto (1854), declaring a U.S. right to take Cuba by force should efforts to purchase it fail.

Nominated by Democrats, Buchanan was elected president in 1856. On slavery he favored popular sovereignty and choice by state constitutions but did not consistently uphold this position. He denied the right of states to secede but opposed coercion and attempted to keep peace by not provoking secessionists. Buchanan left office having failed to deal decisively with the situation. He died at Wheatland, his estate, near Lancaster, PA, on June 1, 1868.

Abraham Lincoln (1861-65), 16th president, Republican, was born on Feb. 12, 1809, in a log cabin on a farm in Hardin Co., KY, now known as Larue Co., the son of Thomas and Nancy Hanks Lincoln. The Lincolns moved to Spencer Co., IN, near Gentryville, when Lincoln was 7. After Lincoln's mother died, his father married Mrs. Sarah Bush Johnston in 1819. In 1830 the family moved to Macon Co., IL.

Defeated in 1832 in a race for the state legislature, Lincoln was elected on the Whig ticket 2 years later and served in the lower house from 1834 to 1842. In 1837 Lincoln was admitted to the bar and became partner in a Springfield, IL, law office. He soon won recognition as an effective and resourceful attorney. In 1846, he was elected to the House of Representatives, where he attracted attention during a single term for his opposition to the Mexican War and his position on slavery. In 1856 he campaigned for the newly founded Republican Party, and in 1858 he became its senatorial candidate against Stephen A. Douglas. Although he lost the election, Lincoln gained national recognition from his debates with Douglas.

In 1860, Lincoln was nominated for president by the Republican Party on a platform of restricting slavery. He ran against Douglas, a northern Democrat; John C. Breckinridge, a Southern proslavery Democrat; and John Bell, of the Constitutional Union Party. As a result of Lincoln's winning the election, South Carolina seceded from the Union on Dec. 20, 1860, followed in 1861 by 10 other Southern states.

The Civil War erupted when Fort Sumter, which Lincoln decided to resupply, was attacked by Confederate forces on Apr. 12, 1861. Lincoln called successfully for recruits from the North. On Sept. 22, 1862, 5 days after the Battle of Antietam, Lincoln announced that slaves in territory then in rebellion would be free Jan. 1, 1863, the date of the Emancipation Proclamation. His speeches, including his Gettysburg and inaugural addresses, are remembered for their eloquence.

Lincoln was reelected, in 1864, over Gen. George B. McClellan, Democrat. General Robert E. Lee surrendered on Apr. 9, 1865. On Apr. 14, Lincoln was shot by actor John Wilkes Booth in Ford's Theater, in Washington, DC. He died the next day.

Andrew Johnson (1865-69),

17th president, Democrat, was born on Dec. 29, 1808, in Raleigh, NC, the son of Jacob and Mary McDonough Johnson. He was apprenticed to a tailor as a youth, but ran away after two years and eventually settled in Greeneville, TN. He became popular with the townspeople and in 1829 was elected councilman and later mayor. In 1835 he was sent to the state general assembly. In 1843 he was elected to the U.S. House of Representatives, where he served for 10 years. Johnson was also governor of Tennessee from 1853 to 1857 when he was elected to the U.S. Senate. He supported John C. Breckinridge against Lincoln in the 1860 election. Although Johnson had held slaves, he opposed secession and tried to prevent Tennessee from seceding. In Mar. 1862, Lincoln appointed him military governor of occupied Tennessee.

In 1864, in order to balance Lincoln's ticket with a Southern Democrat, the Republicans nominated Johnson for vice president. He was elected vice president with Lincoln and then succeeded to the presidency upon Lincoln's death. Soon afterward, in a controversy with Congress over the president's power over the South, he proclaimed an amnesty to all Confederates, except certain leaders, if they would ratify the 13th Amendment abolishing slavery. States doing so added anti-Negro provisions that enraged Congress, which restored military control over the South. When Johnson removed Edwin M. Stanton, secretary of war, without notifying the Senate, the House impeached him in Feb. 1868. Charging him with thereby having violated the Tenure of Office Act, the House was actually responding to his opposition to harsh congressional Reconstruction, expressed in repeated vetoes. He was tried by the Senate, and in May, in two separate votes on different counts, Johnson was acquitted, both times by only one vote.

Johnson was denied renomination but remained politically active. He was reelected to the Senate in 1874. Johnson died July 31, 1875, at Carter Station, TN.

Ulysses Simpson Grant (1869-77),

18th president, Republican, was born on Apr. 27, 1822, in Point Pleasant, OH, the son of Jesse R. and Hannah Simpson Grant. The next year the family moved to Georgetown, OH. Grant was named Hiram Ulysses, but on entering West Point in 1839, his name was put down as Ulysses Simpson, and he adopted it. He graduated in 1843. During the Mexican War, Grant served under both Gen. Zachary Taylor and Gen. Winfield Scott. In 1854, he resigned his commission because of loneliness and drinking problems, and in the following years he engaged in generally unsuccessful farming and business ventures. With the start of the Civil War, he was named colonel and then brigadier general of the Illinois Volunteers. He took Forts Henry and Donelson and fought at Shiloh. His brilliant campaign against Vicksburg and his victory at Chattanooga made him so prominent that Lincoln placed him in command of all Union armies. Grant accepted Lee's surrender at Appomattox Court House on Apr. 9, 1865. President Johnson appointed Grant secretary of war when he suspended Stanton, but Grant was not confirmed.

Grant was nominated for president by the Republicans in 1868 and elected over Horatio Seymour, Democrat. The 15th Amendment, the amnesty bill, and peaceful settlement of disputes with Great Britain were events of his administration. The Liberal Republicans and Democrats opposed him with Horace Greeley in the 1872 election, but Grant was reelected. His second administration was marked by scandals, including widespread corruption in the Treasury Department and the Indian Service. An attempt by the Stalwarts (Old Guard Republicans) to nominate him in 1880 failed. In 1884 the collapse of an investment firm in which he was a partner left Grant penniless. He wrote his personal memoirs while ill with cancer and completed them shortly before his death at Mt. McGregor, NY, on July 23, 1885.

Rutherford Birchard Hayes (1877-81),

19th president, Republican, was born on Oct. 4, 1822, in Delaware, OH, the son of Rutherford and Sophia Birchard Hayes. He was reared by his uncle, Sardis Birchard. Hayes graduated from Kenyon College in 1842 and from Harvard Law School in 1845. He practiced law in Lower Sandusky (now Fremont), OH, and was city solicitor of Cincinnati from 1858 to 1861. During the Civil War, he was major of the 23rd Ohio Volunteers. He was wounded several times, and by the end of the war he had risen to the rank of brevet major general. While serving (1865-67) in the U.S. House of Representatives, Hayes supported Reconstruction and Johnson's impeachment. He was twice elected governor of Ohio (1867, 1869). After losing a race for the U.S. House in 1872, he was reelected governor of Ohio in 1875.

In 1876, Hayes was nominated for president and believed he had lost the election to Samuel J. Tilden, Democrat. But a few Southern states submitted 2 sets of electoral votes, and the result was in dispute. An electoral commission, consisting of 8 Republicans and 7 Democrats, awarded all disputed votes to Hayes, allowing him to become president by one electoral vote. Hayes, keeping a promise to Southerners, withdrew troops from areas still occupied in the South, ending the era of Reconstruction. He proposed civil service reforms, alienating those favoring the spoils system, and advocated repeal of the Tenure of Office Act restricting presidential power to dismiss officials. He supported sound money and specie payments.

Hayes died in Fremont, OH, on Jan. 17, 1893.

James Abram Garfield (1881),

20th president, Republican, was born on Nov. 19, 1831, in Orange, Cuyahoga Co., OH, the son of Abram and Eliza Ballou Garfield. His father died in 1833, and he was reared in poverty by his mother. He worked as a canal bargeman, a farmer, and a carpenter and managed to secure a college education. He taught at Hiram College and later became principal. In 1859 he was elected to the Ohio legislature. Antislavery and antisecession, he volunteered for military service in the Civil War, becoming colonel of the 42nd Ohio Infantry and brigadier in 1862. He fought at Shiloh, was chief of staff for Gen. William Starke Rosecrans, and was made major general for gallantry at Chickamauga. He entered Congress as a radical Republican in 1863, calling for execution or exile of Confederate leaders, but he moderated his views after the Civil War. On the electoral commission in 1877 he voted for Hayes against Tilden on strict party lines.

Garfield was a senator-elect in 1880 when he became the Republican nominee for president. He was chosen as a compromise over Gen. Grant, James G. Blaine, and John Sherman, and won election despite some bitterness among Grant's supporters. For much of his brief tenure as president, Garfield was concerned with a fight with New York Sen. Roscoe Conkling, who opposed two major appointments made by Garfield. On July 2, 1881, Garfield was shot and seriously wounded by a mentally disturbed officeseeker, Charles J. Guiteau, while entering a railroad station in Washington, DC. He died on Sept. 19, 1881, in Elberon, NJ.

Chester Alan Arthur (1881-85),

21st president, Republican, was born on Oct. 5, 1829, in Fairfield, VT, to William and Malvina Stone Arthur. He graduated from Union College in 1848, taught school in Vermont, then studied law and practiced in New York City. In 1853, he argued in a fugitive slave case that slaves transported through New York State were thereby freed. In 1871, he was appointed collector of the Port of New York. President Hayes, an opponent of the spoils system, forced him to resign in 1878. This made the New York machine enemies of Hayes. Arthur and the Stalwarts (Old Guard Republicans) tried to nominate Grant for a 3rd term as president in 1880. When Garfield was nominated, Arthur was nominated for vice president in the interests of harmony.

Upon Garfield's assassination, Arthur became president. Despite his past connections, he signed major civil service reform legislation. Arthur tried to dissuade Congress from enacting the high protective tariff of 1883. He was defeated for renomination in 1884 by James G. Blaine. He died in New York City on Nov. 18, 1886.

Grover Cleveland (1885-89; 1893-97)

(According to a ruling of the State Dept., Grover Cleveland should be counted as both the 22nd and the 24th president, because his 2 terms were not consecutive.)
Democrat, was born Stephen Grover Cleveland on Mar. 18, 1837, in Caldwell, NJ, the son of Richard F. and Ann Neal Cleveland. When he was a small boy, his family moved to New York. Prevented by his father's death from attending college, he studied by himself and was admitted to the bar in Buffalo, NY, in 1859. In succession he became assistant district attorney (1863), sheriff (1871), mayor (1881), and governor of New York (1882). He was an independent, honest administrator who hated corruption. Cleveland was nominated for president over Tammany Hall opposition in 1884 and defeated Republican James G. Blaine.

As president, he enlarged the civil service and vetoed many pension raids on the Treasury. In the 1888 election he was defeated by Benjamin Harrison, although his popular vote was larger. Reelected over Harrison in 1892, he faced a money crisis brought about by a lowered gold reserve, circulation of paper, and exorbitant silver purchases under the Sherman Silver Purchase Act. He obtained a repeal of the Sherman Act but was unable to secure effective tariff reform. A severe economic depression and labor troubles racked his administration, but he refused to interfere in business matters and rejected Jacob Coxey's demand for unemployment relief. In 1894, he broke the Pullman strike. Cleveland was not renominated in 1896.

He died in Princeton, NJ, on June 24, 1908.

Benjamin Harrison (1889-93),

23rd president, Republican, was born on Aug. 20, 1833, in North Bend, OH, the son of John Scott and Elizabeth Irwin Harrison. His great-grandfather, Benjamin Harrison, was a signer of the Declaration of Independence; his grandfather, William Henry Harrison, was 9th president; his father was a member of Congress. He attended school on his father's farm and graduated from Miami University in Oxford, OH, in 1852. He was admitted to the bar in 1854 and practiced in Indianapolis. During the Civil War, he rose to the rank of brevet brigadier general and fought at Kennesaw Mountain, Peachtree Creek, Nashville, and in the Atlanta campaign. He lost the 1876 gubernatorial election in Indiana but succeeded in becoming a U.S. senator in 1881.

In 1888 he defeated Cleveland for president despite receiving fewer popular votes. As president, he expanded the pension list and signed the McKinley high tariff bill, the Sherman Antitrust Act, and the Sherman Silver Purchase Act. During his administration, 6 states were admitted to the Union. He was defeated for reelection in 1892. He died in Indianapolis on Mar. 13, 1901.

William McKinley (1897-1901),

25th president, Republican, was born on Jan. 29, 1843, in Niles, OH, the son of William and Nancy Allison McKinley. McKinley briefly attended Allegheny College. When the Civil War broke out in 1861, he enlisted and served for the duration. He rose to captain and in 1865 was made brevet major. After studying law in Albany, NY, he opened a law office in Canton, OH (1867). He served twice in the U.S. House (1877-83; 1885-91) and led the fight there for the McKinley Tariff, passed in 1890; he was not reelected to the House as a result. He served two terms (1892-96) as governor of Ohio.

In 1896 he was elected president as a proponent of a protective tariff and sound money (gold standard), over William Jennings Bryan, the Democrat and a proponent of free silver. McKinley was reluctant to intervene in Cuba, but the loss of the battleship *Maine* at Havana crystallized opinion. He demanded Spain's withdrawal from Cuba; Spain made some concessions, but Congress announced a state of war as of Apr. 21, 1898. He was reelected in the 1900 campaign, defeating Bryan's anti-imperialist arguments with the promise of a "full dinner pail." McKinley was respected for his conciliatory nature and for his conservative stance on business issues. On Sept. 6, 1901, while welcoming citizens at the Pan-American Exposition, in Buffalo, NY, he was shot by Leon Czolgosz, an anarchist. He died Sept. 14.

Theodore Roosevelt (1901-09),

26th president, Republican, was born on Oct. 27, 1858, in New York City, the son of Theodore and Martha Bulloch Roosevelt. He was a 5th cousin of Franklin D. Roosevelt and an uncle of Eleanor Roosevelt. Roosevelt graduated from Harvard University in 1880. He attended Columbia Law School briefly but abandoned law to enter politics. He was elected to the New York State Assembly in 1881 and served until 1884. He spent the next 2 years ranching and hunting in the Dakota Territory. In 1886, he ran unsuccessfully for mayor of New York City. He was civil service commissioner in Washington, DC, from 1889 to 1895. From 1895 to 1897, he served as New York City's police commissioner. He was assistant secretary of the Navy under McKinley. The Spanish-American War made him nationally known. He organized the 1st U.S. Volunteer Cavalry (Rough Riders) and, as lieutenant colonel, led the charge up Kettle Hill in San Juan. Elected New York governor in 1898, he fought the spoils system and achieved taxation of corporation franchises.

Nominated for vice president in 1900, Roosevelt became the nation's youngest president when McKinley was assassinated. He was reelected in 1904. As president he fought corruption of politics by big business, dissolved the Northern Securities Co. and others for violating antitrust laws, intervened in the 1902 coal strike on behalf of the public, obtained the Elkins Law (1903) forbidding rebates to favored corporations, and helped pass the Hepburn Railway Rate Act of 1906 (extending jurisdiction of the Interstate Commerce Commission). He helped obtain passage of the Pure Food and Drug Act (1906) and of employers' liability laws. Roosevelt vigorously organized conservation efforts. He mediated the peace between Japan and Russia in 1905, for which he won the Nobel Peace Prize. He abetted the 1903 revolution in Panama that led to U.S. acquisition of territory for the Panama Canal.

In 1908 Roosevelt obtained the nomination of William H. Taft, who was elected. Feeling that Taft had abandoned his policies, he unsuccessfully sought the nomination in 1912. He then ran on the Progressive "Bull Moose" ticket against Taft and Woodrow Wilson, splitting the Republicans and ensuring Wilson's election. He was shot during the campaign but recovered. In 1916, after unsuccessfully seeking the presidential nomination, he supported the Republican candidate, Charles E. Hughes. A strong friend of Britain, he fought for U.S. intervention in World War I.

Roosevelt was a voracious reader and wrote some 40 books, including *The Winning of the West*. He died Jan. 6, 1919, at Sagamore Hill, Oyster Bay, NY.

William Howard Taft (1909-13), 27th president, Republican, and 10th chief justice of the U.S., was born on Sept. 15, 1857, in Cincinnati, OH, the son of Alphonso and Louisa Maria Torrey Taft. His father was secretary of war and attorney general in Grant's cabinet and minister to Austria and Russia under Arthur. Taft graduated from Yale in 1878 and from Cincinnati Law School in 1880. After working as a law reporter for Cincinnati newspapers, he served as assistant prosecuting attorney (1881-82), assistant county solicitor (1885), superior court judge (1887), U.S. solicitor-general (1890), and federal circuit judge (1892). In 1900 he became head of the U.S. Philippines Commission and was the first civil governor of the Philippines (1901-04). In 1904 he served as secretary of war, and in 1906 he was sent to Cuba to help avert a threatened revolution.

Taft was groomed for the presidency by Theodore Roosevelt and elected over William Jennings Bryan in 1908. Taft vigorously continued Roosevelt's trust-busting, instituted the Department of Labor, and drafted the amendments calling for direct election of senators and the income tax. However, his tariff and conservation policies angered progressives. Although renominated in 1912, he was opposed by Roosevelt, who ran on the Progressive Party ticket; the result was Democrat Woodrow Wilson's election.

Taft, with some reservations, supported the League of Nations. After leaving office, he was professor of constitutional law at Yale (1913-21) and chief justice of the U.S. (1921-30). Taft was the only person in U.S. history to have been both president and chief justice. He died in Washington, DC, on Mar. 8, 1930.

(Thomas) Woodrow Wilson (1913-21), 28th president, Democrat, was born on Dec. 28, 1856, in Staunton, VA, the son of Joseph Ruggles and Janet (Jessie) Woodrow Wilson. He grew up in Georgia and South Carolina. He attended Davidson College in North Carolina before graduating from Princeton University in 1879. He studied law at the University of Virginia and political science at Johns Hopkins University, where he received his PhD in 1886. He taught at Bryn Mawr (1885-88) and then at Wesleyan (1888-90) before joining the faculty at Princeton. He was president of Princeton from 1902 until 1910, when he was elected governor of New Jersey. In 1912 he was nominated for president with the aid of William Jennings Bryan, who sought to block James "Champ" Clark and Tammany Hall. Wilson won because the Republican vote for Taft was split by the Progressives.

As president, Wilson protected American interests in revolutionary Mexico and fought for American rights on the high seas. He oversaw the creation of the Federal Reserve system, cut the tariff, and developed a reputation as a reformer. His sharp warnings to Germany led to the resignation of his secretary of state, Bryan, a pacifist. In 1916 he was reelected by a slim margin with the slogan, "He kept us out of war," although his attempts to mediate in the war failed. After several American ships had been sunk by the Germans, he secured a declaration of war against Germany on Apr. 6, 1917.

Wilson outlined his peace program on Jan. 8, 1918, in the Fourteen Points, a state paper that had worldwide influence. He enunciated a doctrine of self-determination for the settlement of territorial disputes. The Germans accepted his terms and an armistice on Nov. 11, 1918.

Wilson went to Paris to help negotiate the peace treaty, the crux of which he considered the League of Nations. The Senate demanded reservations that would not make the U.S. subordinate to the votes of other nations in case of war. Wilson refused and toured the country to get support. He suffered a stroke in Oct. 1919. An invalid, he clung to his office while his wife and doctors effectively functioned as president.

Wilson was awarded the 1919 Nobel Peace Prize, but the treaty embodying the League of Nations was ultimately rejected by the Senate in 1920. He left the White House in Mar. 1921. He died in Washington, DC, on Feb. 3, 1924.

Warren Gamaliel Harding (1921-23), 29th president, Republican, was born on Nov. 2, 1865, near Corsica (now Blooming Grove), OH, the son of George Tyron and Phoebe Elizabeth Dickerson Harding. He attended Ohio Central College, studied law, and became editor and publisher of a county newspaper. He entered the political arena as state senator (1901-04) and then served as lieutenant governor (1904-06). In 1910 he ran unsuccessfully for governor of Ohio; then in 1914 he was elected to the U.S. Senate. In the Senate he voted for antistrike legislation, women's suffrage, and the Volstead Prohibition Enforcement Act over President Wilson's veto. He opposed the League of Nations.

In 1920 he was nominated for president and defeated James M. Cox in the election. The Republicans capitalized on war weariness and fear that Wilson's League of Nations would curtail U.S. sovereignty. Harding stressed a return to "normalcy" and worked for tariff revision and the repeal of excess profits law and high income taxes. His secretary of the interior, Albert B. Fall, became involved in the Teapot Dome scandal.

As rumors began to circulate about the corruption in his administration, Harding became ill while returning from a trip to Alaska, and he died in San Francisco on Aug. 2, 1923.

(John) Calvin Coolidge (1923-29), 30th president, Republican, was born on July 4, 1872, in Plymouth Notch, VT, the son of John Calvin and Victoria J. Moor Coolidge. Coolidge graduated from Amherst College in 1895. He entered Republican state politics and served as mayor of Northampton, MA, as state senator, as lieutenant governor, and, in 1919, as governor. In Sept. 1919, Coolidge attained national prominence by calling out the state guard in the Boston police strike. He declared: "There is no right to strike against the public safety by anybody, anywhere, anytime." This brought his name before the Republican convention of 1920, where he was nominated for vice president.

Coolidge succeeded to the presidency on Harding's death. As president, he opposed the League of Nations and the soldiers' bonus bill, which was passed over his veto. In 1924 he was elected to the presidency by a huge majority. He substantially reduced the national debt. He twice vetoed the McNary-Haugen farm bill, which would have provided relief to financially hard-pressed farmers.

With Republicans eager to renominate him, Coolidge simply announced, Aug. 2, 1927: "I do not choose to run for president in 1928." He died in Northampton, MA, on Jan. 5, 1933.

Herbert Clark Hoover (1929-33), 31st president, Republican, was born on Aug. 10, 1874, in West Branch, IA, the son of Jesse Clark and Hulda Randall Minthorn Hoover. Hoover grew up in Indian Territory (now Oklahoma) and Oregon and graduated from Stanford University with a degree in geology in 1895. He worked briefly with the U.S. Geological Survey and then managed mines in Australia, Asia, Europe, and Africa. While chief engineer of imperial mines in China, he directed food relief for victims of the Boxer Rebellion. He gained a reputation not only as an engineer but as a humanitarian as he directed the American Relief Committee, London (1914-15) and the U.S. Commission for Relief in Belgium (1915-19). He was U.S. Food Administrator (1917-19), American Relief Administrator (1918-23), and in charge of Russian Relief (1918-23). He served as secretary of commerce under both Harding and Coolidge. Some historians believe that he was the most effective secretary of commerce ever to hold that office.

In 1928 Hoover was elected president over Alfred E. Smith. In 1929 the stock market crashed, and the economy collapsed. During the Great Depression, Hoover inaugurated some government assistance programs, but he was opposed to administration of aid through a federal bureaucracy. As the effects of the depression continued, he was defeated in the 1932 election by Franklin D. Roosevelt. Hoover remained active after leaving office. President Truman named him coordinator of the European Food Program (1946) and chairman of the Commission on Organization of the Executive Branch (1947-49; 1953-55).

Hoover died in New York City on Oct. 20, 1964.

Franklin Delano Roosevelt (1933-45)

, 32nd president, Democrat, was born on Jan. 30, 1882, in Hyde Park, NY, the son of James and Sara Delano Roosevelt. He graduated from Harvard University in 1903. He attended Columbia University Law School without taking a degree and was admitted to the New York State bar in 1907. His political career began when he was elected to the New York State senate in 1910. In 1913 President Wilson appointed him assistant secretary of the navy, a post he held during World War I.

In 1920 Roosevelt ran for vice president with James Cox and was defeated. From 1921 to 1928 he worked in his New York law office and was also vice president of a bank. In Aug. 1921, he was stricken with poliomyelitis, which left his legs paralyzed. As a result of therapy he was able to stand, or walk a few steps, with the aid of leg braces.

Roosevelt served 2 terms as governor of New York (1929-33). In 1932, Democratic convention delegate W. G. McAdoo, pledged to nominee John N. Garner, threw his votes to Roosevelt, who was nominated for president. The Depression and the promise to repeal Prohibition ensured his election. He asked for emergency powers, proclaimed the New Deal, and put into effect a vast number of administrative changes. Foremost was the use of public funds for relief and public works, resulting in deficit financing. He greatly expanded the federal government's regulation of business and by an excess profits tax and progressive income taxes produced a redistribution of earnings on an unprecedented scale. He also promoted legislation establishing the Social Security system. He was the last president inaugurated on Mar. 4 (1933) and the first inaugurated on Jan. 20 (1937).

Roosevelt was the first president to use radio for "fireside chats." When the Supreme Court nullified some New Deal laws, he sought power to "pack" the Court with additional justices, but Congress refused to give him the authority. He was the first president to break the "no 3rd term" tradition (1940) and was elected to a 4th term in 1944, despite failing health.

Roosevelt was openly hostile to fascist governments before World War II and launched a lend-lease program on behalf of the Allies. With British Prime Min. Winston Churchill he wrote a declaration of principles to be followed after Nazi defeat (the Atlantic Charter of Aug. 14, 1941) and urged the Four Freedoms (freedom of speech, of worship, from want, from fear) Jan. 6, 1941. When Japan attacked Pearl Harbor on Dec. 7, 1941, the U.S. entered the war. Roosevelt guided the nation through the war and conferred with allied heads of state at Casablanca (Jan. 1943), Quebec (Aug. 1943), Tehran (Nov.-Dec. 1943), Cairo (Nov. and Dec. 1943), and Yalta (Feb. 1945).

Roosevelt did not, however, live to see the end of the war. He died of a cerebral hemorrhage in Warm Springs, GA, on Apr. 12, 1945.

Harry S. Truman (1945-53)

, 33rd president, Democrat, was born on May 8, 1884, in Lamar, MO, the son of John Anderson and Martha Ellen Young Truman. A family disagreement on whether his middle name should be Shipp or Solomon, after names of 2 grandfathers, resulted in his using only the middle initial S. After graduating from high school in Independence, MO, he worked for the *Kansas City Star*, (1901) as a railroad timekeeper, and as a clerk in Kansas City banks until about 1905. He ran his family's farm from 1906 to 1917, then served in France during World War I. After the war he opened a haberdashery shop, was a judge on the Jackson Co. Court (1922-24), and attended Kansas City School of Law (1923-25).

Truman was elected to the U.S. Senate in 1934 and reelected in 1940. In 1944, with Roosevelt's backing, he was nominated for vice president and elected. On Roosevelt's death in 1945, Truman became president. In 1948, in a famous upset victory, he defeated Republican Thomas E. Dewey to win election to a new term.

Truman authorized the first uses of the atomic bomb (Hiroshima and Nagasaki, Aug. 6 and 9, 1945), bringing World War II to a rapid end. He was responsible for what came to be called the Truman Doctrine (to aid nations such as Greece and Turkey, threatened by Communist takeover), and his strong commitment to NATO and to the Marshall Plan helped bring the two about. In 1948-49, he broke a Soviet blockade of West Berlin with a massive airlift. When Communist North Korea invaded South Korea (June 1950), he won UN approval for a "police action" and, boldly without prior congressional consent, sent in forces under Gen. Douglas MacArthur. When MacArthur opposed his policy of limited objectives, Truman removed him.

He died in Kansas City, MO, on Dec. 26, 1972.

Dwight David Eisenhower (1953-61)

, 34th president, Republican, was born on Oct. 14, 1890, in Denison, TX, the son of David Jacob and Ida Elizabeth Stover Eisenhower. He grew up on a small farm in Abilene, KS, and graduated from West Point in 1915. He was on the staff of Gen. Douglas MacArthur in the Philippines from 1935 to 1939. In 1942, he was made commander of Allied forces landing in North Africa; the next year he was made full general. He became supreme Allied commander in Europe that same year and as such led the Normandy invasion (June 6, 1944). He was given the rank of general of the Army on Dec. 20, 1944, which was made permanent in 1946.

On May 7, 1945, Eisenhower received the surrender of Germany at Rheims. He returned to the U.S. to serve as chief of staff (1945-48). His war memoir, *Crusade in Europe* (1948), was a best-seller. In 1948 he became president of Columbia University; in 1950 he became commander of NATO forces.

Eisenhower resigned from the army and was nominated for president by the Republicans in 1952. He defeated Adlai E. Stevenson in the 1952 election and again in 1956. Eisenhower called himself a moderate, favored the "free market system" versus government price and wage controls, kept government out of labor disputes, reorganized the defense establishment, and promoted missile programs. He continued foreign aid, sped the withdrawal of U.S. troops from Korea, endorsed Taiwan and SE Asia defense treaties, backed the UN in condemning the Anglo-French raid on Egypt, and advocated the "open skies" policy of mutual inspection with the USSR. He sent U.S. troops into Little Rock, AR, in Sept. 1957, during the segregation crisis.

Eisenhower died on Mar. 28, 1969, in Washington, DC.

John Fitzgerald Kennedy (1961-63)

, 35th president, Democrat, was born on May 29, 1917, in Brookline, MA, the son of Joseph P. and Rose Fitzgerald Kennedy. He graduated from Harvard University in 1940. While serving in the Navy (1941-45), he commanded a PT boat in the Solomons and won the Navy and Marine Corps Medal. In 1956, while recovering from spinal surgery, he wrote *Profiles in Courage*, which won a Pulitzer Prize in 1957. He served in the House of Representatives from 1947 to 1953 and was elected to the Senate in 1952 and 1958. In 1960, he won the Democratic nomination for president and narrowly defeated Republican Vice Pres. Richard M. Nixon. Kennedy was the youngest president ever elected to the office and the first Catholic.

Despite the image of youth and vigor he conveyed to the public, Kennedy suffered from serious medical problems, including Addison's disease and severe chronic back pain that required him to wear a back brace. The public was not aware of the extent of these problems, or of his extensive womanizing, including an affair with a young White House press aide that only became known in 2003. However, scholars have not generally claimed that these aspects of his life affected his performance in office.

In Apr. 1961, the new Kennedy administration suffered a severe setback when an invasion force of anti-Castro Cubans, trained and directed by the CIA, failed to establish a beachhead at the Bay of Pigs in Cuba. One of Kennedy's most important acts as president was his successful demand on Oct. 22, 1962, that the Soviet Union dismantle its missile bases in Cuba. Kennedy also defied Soviet attempts to force the Allies out of Berlin. He started the Peace Corps, backed civil rights, and expanded medical care for the aged. Space exploration was greatly developed during his administration.

On Nov. 22, 1963, President Kennedy was assassinated while riding in a motorcade in Dallas, TX. A commission chaired by Chief Justice Earl Warren concluded in Sept. 1964 that the sole assassin had been Lee Harvey Oswald, a former U.S. Marine and, at the time of the shooting, an ardent Marxist. Oswald was captured a short time after the assassination and charged with the crime, but was shot dead by nightclub owner Jack Ruby two days later while being moved to a county jail, before he could go to trial.

Lyndon Baines Johnson (1963-69),

36th president, Democrat, was born on Aug. 27, 1908, near Stonewall, TX, the son of Sam Ealy and Rebekah Baines Johnson. He graduated from Southwest Texas State Teachers College in 1930 and attended Georgetown University Law School. He taught public speaking in Houston (1930-31) and then served as secretary to Rep. R. M. Kleberg (1931-35). In 1937 Johnson won an election to fill the vacancy caused by the death of a U.S. representative and in 1938 was elected to the full term, after which he returned for 4 terms. During 1941 and 1942 he also served in the Navy in the Pacific, earning a Silver Star for bravery. He was elected U.S. senator in 1948 and reelected in 1954. He became Democratic leader of the Senate in 1953. Johnson had strong support for the Democratic presidential nomination at the 1960 convention, where the nominee, John F. Kennedy, asked him to run for vice president. His campaigning helped overcome religious bias against Kennedy in the South.

Johnson became president when Kennedy was assassinated. He was elected to a full term in 1964. Johnson's domestic program was of considerable importance. He won passage of major civil rights, anti-poverty, aid to education, and health-care (Medicare, Medicaid) legislation—the "Great Society" program. However, his escalation of the war in Vietnam came to overshadow the achievements of his administration. In the face of increasing division in the nation and in his own party over his handling of the war, Johnson declined to seek another term.

Johnson died on Jan. 22, 1973, in San Antonio, TX.

Richard Milhous Nixon (1969-74),

37th president, Republican, was born on Jan. 9, 1913, in Yorba Linda, CA, the son of Francis Anthony and Hannah Milhous Nixon. He graduated from Whittier College in 1934 and from Duke University Law School in 1937. After practicing law in Whittier and serving briefly in the Office of Price Administration in 1942, he entered the Navy and served in the South Pacific. Nixon was elected to the House of Representatives in 1946 and 1948. He achieved prominence as the House Un-American Activities Committee member who forced the showdown leading to the Alger Hiss perjury conviction. In 1950 he was elected to the Senate.

Nixon was elected vice president in the Eisenhower landslides of 1952 and 1956. He won the Republican nomination for president in 1960 but was narrowly defeated by John F. Kennedy. He ran unsuccessfully for governor of California in 1962. In 1968 he again won the GOP presidential nomination, then defeated Hubert Humphrey for the presidency.

As president, Nixon appointed 4 Supreme Court justices, including the chief justice, moving the court to the right, and as a "new federalist" sought to shift responsibility to state and local governments. He dramatically altered relations with China, which he visited in 1972—the first president to do so. With foreign affairs adviser Henry Kissinger he pursued détente with the Soviet Union, signing major arms limitation and other treaties and increasing trade. He began a gradual withdrawal from Vietnam, but U.S. troops remained there through his first term. He ordered an incursion into Cambodia (1970) and the bombing of Hanoi and mining of Haiphong Harbor (1972). Reelected by a large majority in Nov. 1972, he secured a Vietnam cease-fire in Jan. 1973.

Nixon's 2nd term was cut short by scandal, after disclosures relating to a June 1972 burglary of Democratic Party headquarters in the Watergate office complex. The courts and Congress sought tapes of Nixon's office conversations and called for criminal proceedings against former White House aides and for a House inquiry into possible impeachment. Nixon claimed executive privilege, but the Supreme Court ruled against him. In July, the House Judiciary Committee recommended adoption of 3 impeachment articles charging him with obstruction of justice, abuse of power, and contempt of Congress. On Aug. 5, he released transcripts of conversations that linked him to cover-up activities. He resigned on Aug. 9, becoming the first president ever to do so.

In later years, Nixon emerged as an elder statesman. He died Apr. 22, 1994, in New York City.

Gerald Rudolph Ford (1974-77),

38th president, Republican, was born on July 14, 1913, in Omaha, NE, the son of Leslie and Dorothy Gardner King, and was named Leslie Jr. When he was 2, his parents divorced, and he and his mother moved to Grand Rapids, MI. There she met and married Gerald R. Ford, who formally adopted him and gave him his own name. Ford graduated from the University of Michigan in 1935 and from Yale Law School in 1941. He began practicing law in Grand Rapids, but in 1942 joined the Navy and served in the Pacific, leaving the service in 1946 as a lieutenant commander. He entered the House of Representatives in 1949 and spent 25 years in the House, 8 of them as Republican leader.

On Oct. 12, 1973, after Vice President Spiro T. Agnew resigned, Ford was nominated by President Nixon to replace him. It was the first use of the procedures set out in the 25th Amendment. When Nixon resigned, Aug. 9, 1974, because of the Watergate scandal, Ford became president; he was the only president who was never elected either to the presidency or to the vice presidency.

President Ford was widely credited with having contributed to rebuilding morale after the Nixon presidency. But he was also criticized by many when, in a controversial move, he pardoned Nixon for any federal crimes he might have committed as president. Ford vetoed 48 bills in his first 21 months in office, mostly in the interest of fighting high inflation; he was less successful in curbing high unemployment. In foreign policy, Ford continued to pursue détente.

Ford was narrowly defeated in the 1976 election. In 1999, he received the Medal of Freedom, the country's highest civilian award, and the Congressional Gold Medal, in recognition of his public service.

James Earl (Jimmy) Carter (1977-81),

39th president, Democrat, was the first president from the Deep South since before the Civil War. He was born on Oct. 1, 1924, in Plains, GA, the son of James and Lillian Gordy Carter. Carter graduated from the U.S. Naval Academy in 1946 and in 1952 entered the Navy's nuclear submarine program as an aide to Capt. (later Adm.) Hyman Rickover. He studied nuclear physics at Union College.

Carter's father died in 1953, and he left the Navy to take over the family peanut farming businesses. He served in the Georgia state senate (1963-67) and as governor of Georgia (1971-75). In 1976, Carter won the Democratic nomination and defeated President Gerald R. Ford.

On his first full day in office, Carter pardoned all Vietnam draft evaders. He played a major role in the negotiations leading to the 1979 peace treaty between Israel and Egypt, and he won passage of new treaties with Panama providing for U.S. control of the Panama Canal to end in 2000. Carter was widely criticized, however, for the poor state of the economy and was viewed by some as weak in his handling of foreign policy. In Nov. 1979, Iranian student militants attacked the U.S. embassy in Tehran and held members of the embassy staff hostage. Efforts to obtain release of the hostages were a major preoccupation during the rest of his term. He reacted to the Soviet invasion of Afghanistan by imposing a grain embargo and boycotting the Moscow Olympic Games.

Carter was defeated by Ronald Reagan in the 1980 election. The American hostages were finally released on Inauguration Day, 1981, just after Reagan officially became president. In 1982, Carter established The Carter Center, which seeks to advance human rights and to mediate international disputes. In large part for his diplomatic efforts in office and subsequently, he was awarded the Nobel Peace Prize in 2002.

 **Ronald Wilson Reagan (1981-89),** 40th president, Republican, was born on Feb. 6, 1911, in Tampico, IL, the son of John Edward and Nellie Wilson Reagan. Reagan graduated from Eureka College in 1932, after which he worked as a sports announcer in Des Moines, IA. He began a successful career as an actor in 1937, starring in numerous movies, and later in television, until the 1960s. During World War II Reagan served in the Army Air Force, making training films. He was president of the Screen Actors Guild in 1947-52 and in 1959-60. Reagan was elected governor of California in 1966 and reelected in 1970.

In 1980, Reagan gained the Republican presidential nomination and won a landslide victory over Jimmy Carter. He was easily reelected in 1984. Reagan successfully forged a bipartisan coalition in Congress, which led to enactment of his program of large-scale tax cuts, cutbacks in many government programs, and a major defense buildup. He signed a Social Security reform bill designed to provide for the long-term solvency of the system. In 1986, he signed into law a major tax-reform bill. He was shot and seriously wounded in an assassination attempt in 1981.

In 1982, the U.S. joined France and Italy in maintaining a peacekeeping force in Beirut, Lebanon, and the next year Reagan sent a task force to invade Grenada after 2 Marxist coups on the island. Reagan's opposition to international terrorism led to the U.S. bombing of Libyan military installations in 1986. He strongly supported El Salvador, the Nicaraguan contras, and other anticommunist governments and forces throughout the world. He also held 4 summit meetings with Soviet leader Mikhail Gorbachev. At the 1987 meeting in Washington, DC, a historic treaty eliminating short- and medium-range missiles from Europe was signed.

Reagan faced a crisis in 1986-87, when it was revealed that the U.S. had sold weapons through Israeli brokers to Iran in exchange for release of U.S. hostages being held in Lebanon and that subsequently some of the money was diverted to the Nicaraguan contras (Congress had barred U.S. aid to the contras). The scandal led to the resignation of leading White House aides. As Reagan left office in Jan. 1989, the nation was experiencing its 6th consecutive year of economic prosperity. Over the same period, however, the federal government recorded large budget deficits.

In 1994, in a letter to the American people, Reagan revealed that he was suffering from Alzheimer's disease. He died on June 5, 2004, in Los Angeles, CA, from complications of the disease.

 **George Herbert Walker Bush (1989-93),** 41st president, Republican, was born on June 12, 1924, in Milton, MA, the son of Prescott and Dorothy Walker Bush. He served as a U.S. Navy pilot in World War II. After graduating from Yale University in 1948, he settled in Texas, where, in 1953, he helped found an oil company. After losing a bid for a U.S. Senate seat in Texas in 1964, he was elected to the House of Representatives in 1966 and 1968. He lost a 2nd U.S. Senate race in 1970. Subsequently he served as U.S. ambassador to the United Nations (1971-73), headed the U.S. Liaison Office in Beijing (1974-75), and was director of central intelligence (1976-77).

Following an unsuccessful bid for the 1980 Republican presidential nomination, Bush was chosen by Ronald Reagan as his vice presidential running mate. He served as U.S. vice president from 1981 to 1989.

In 1988, Bush gained the GOP presidential nomination and defeated Michael Dukakis in the November election. Bush took office faced with U.S. budget and trade deficits as well as the rescue of insolvent U.S. savings and loan institutions. He faced a severe budget deficit annually, struggled with military cutbacks in light of reduced Cold War tensions, and vetoed abortion-rights legislation. In 1990 he agreed to a budget deficit-reduction plan that included tax hikes.

Bush supported Soviet reforms, Eastern Europe democratization, and good relations with Beijing. In Dec. 1989, Bush sent troops to Panama; they overthrew the government and captured military dictator Gen. Manuel Noriega.

Bush reacted to Iraq's Aug. 1990 invasion of Kuwait by sending U.S. forces to the Persian Gulf area and assembling a UN-backed coalition, including NATO and Arab League members. After a month-long air war, in Feb. 1991, Allied forces retook Kuwait in a 4-day ground assault. The quick victory, with extremely light casualties on the U.S. side, gave Bush at the time one of the highest presidential approval ratings in history. His popularity plummeted by the end of 1991, however, as the economy slipped into recession. He was defeated by Bill Clinton in the 1992 election. His son George W. Bush became the 43rd president. In 2005, he led campaigns with former President Clinton to raise money for the victims of the Indian Ocean tsunami and Hurricane Katrina.

 **William Jefferson (Bill) Clinton (1993-2001),** 42nd president, Democrat, was born on Aug. 19, 1946, in Hope, AR, son of William Blythe and Virginia Cassidy Blythe, and was named William Jefferson Blythe IV. Blythe died in an automobile accident before his son was born. His widow married Roger Clinton, and at the age of 16, William Jefferson Blythe IV changed his last name to Clinton.

Clinton became interested in politics in high school and went on to Georgetown University in Washington, DC, where he graduated with high honors in 1968. He then attended Oxford University for 2 years as a Rhodes scholar. During that time he legally avoided the draft and possible service in Vietnam, according to some critics by misleading his draft board. He then earned a degree from Yale Law School in 1973.

Clinton worked on George McGovern's 1972 presidential campaign. He taught at the University of Arkansas from 1973 to 1976, when he was elected state attorney general. In 1978, he was elected governor, becoming the nation's youngest at the time. Defeated for reelection in 1980, he was returned to office several times thereafter. He married Hillary Rodham in 1975.

Despite some issues raised about his character, Clinton won most of the 1992 presidential primaries, moving his party toward the center as he tried to broaden his appeal; as the Democratic party's presidential nominee he defeated Pres. George H. W. Bush and Reform Party candidate Ross Perot in the November election. In 1993, Clinton won passage of a measure to reduce the federal budget deficit and won congressional approval of the North American Free Trade Agreement. His administration's plan for major health-care reform legislation died in Congress. After 1994 midterm elections, Clinton faced Republican majorities in both houses of Congress. He followed a centrist course at home, sent troops to Bosnia to help implement a peace settlement, and cultivated relations with Russia and China.

Though accused of improprieties in his involvement in an Arkansas real estate venture (Whitewater), Clinton easily won reelection in 1996, and an independent prosecutor found insufficient evidence of any criminality by Clinton or his wife. In 1997 he reached agreement with Congress on legislation to balance the federal budget by 2002. In 1998, Clinton became the 2nd U.S. president ever to be impeached by the House of Representatives. He was charged with perjury and obstruction of justice in connection with an attempted cover-up of a sexual relationship with a former White House intern, Monica Lewinsky. He was acquitted, however, by the Senate in 1999. He retained wide popularity, aided by a strong economy.

In 1999, the United States, under Clinton, joined other NATO nations in an aerial bombing campaign that induced Serbia to withdraw troops from the Kosovo region, where they had been terrorizing ethnic Albanians. In 2000, Clinton became the first president since the Vietnam war to visit Vietnam.

After leaving office, Clinton remained active in political affairs and encouraged the career of his wife, who was elected in 2000 to the U.S. Senate from New York. He established a foundation, which supports economic empowerment and the development of healthcare programs, in particular those targeting the global AIDS epidemic.

George Walker Bush (2001-)

, 43rd president, Republican, was born on July 6, 1946, in New Haven, CT. He was the first of six children born to George Herbert Walker Bush and his wife, the former Barbara Pierce, a descendant of Pres. Franklin Pierce. (His brother Jeb won the Florida governorship in 1998.) Bush was the first son of a former president to win the White House since John Quincy Adams took office in 1825.

Fun-loving, athletic, and popular, the young George Bush grew up in Midland and Houston, TX. In 1961 he was sent to the Phillips Academy in Andover, MA, the same prep school his father had attended. In 1964 he entered Yale University, his father's alma mater, where he majored in history. Eligible for the draft upon graduation during the Vietnam War, he signed on with the Texas Air National Guard. Bush received an honorable discharge. After earning a master's degree from Harvard Business School, he returned to Midland in 1975 and went into the oil business. Two years later he married Laura Welch, a schoolteacher and librarian; in 1981 she gave birth to twin daughters.

Bush, who had lost a race for Congress in 1978, returned to the oil business, but success proved elusive. Realizing that he had a drinking problem, he swore off alcohol and renewed his commitment to the Christian faith. After aiding in his father's successful 1988 presidential campaign, he joined a group of investors to buy the Texas Rangers baseball club and took a hands-on role as managing partner. Bush ran for governor in 1994, defeating a popular incumbent, Ann Richards. He won reelection by a landslide in 1998. As governor, he concentrated on building personal bonds with Democratic leaders and backed education reforms.

After defeating Sen. John McCain of Arizona and other rivals in the Republican party primaries, Bush chose Dick Cheney, a former U.S. representative and defense secretary, as his running mate. The Nov. 2000 presidential election was one of the closest in history. While Bush came out behind in the popular vote—by about 540,000 out of more than 100 million cast—the electoral vote total hinged on the outcome in Florida, where official totals, challenged by Demo-

crats, gave him a razor-thin lead. In December the Supreme Court in effect ended a Democratic-backed effort to recount the vote there, and Florida's 25 electoral votes decided the election in Bush's favor. Among the issues Bush had campaigned on was that of lowering federal taxes, and in May 2001 he won approval from Congress for a tax cut package projected to cost $1.35 trillion over the next decade.

On Sept. 11, 2001, Bush was faced with a crisis that would redefine his presidency. In a series of coordinated terrorist attacks, 2 hijacked jetliners crashed into the twin towers of the World Trade Center in New York City, which were destroyed; another jet struck the Pentagon near Washington, DC, with a 4th crashing in rural Pennsylvania. Some 3,000 people were killed in the attacks. The president vowed to punish those responsible. In a "war against terrorism," the U.S. military attacked and deposed Afghanistan's Taliban regime, which was sheltering elements of the al-Qaeda terrorist network, held responsible for the attacks. The Taliban and al-Qaeda, however, continued to function in parts of Afghanistan, and al-Qaeda was blamed for staging terrorist acts in a number of other countries. In 2002 Bush won congressional approval to create a cabinet-level department for homeland security.

Bush met in May 2002 with Russian Pres. Vladimir Putin in Moscow, where they signed a pact cutting nuclear armaments in each country. In July, with corporate scandals and a slumping stock market fueling demands for tighter regulation of business, Bush signed legislation aimed at curbing financial abuses.

In March 2003, the United States, aided mainly by forces from Great Britain, launched an air and ground war against Iraq and deposed the dictatorial regime of Pres. Saddam Hussein. The regime was accused of harboring weapons of mass destruction and of violating other UN resolutions. A Senate Intelligence Committee report issued in July 2004 concluded that pre-war intelligence on illicit weapons in Iraq had been seriously flawed, but Bush argued that the removal of Hussein had been a necessity to help safeguard the U.S., as well as a benefit in itself. Despite Hussein's capture in Iraq, Dec. 13, 2003, and the formation of a new Iraqi government in June 2004, insurgent violence continued into 2006.

The administration's Iraq policy and its conduct of the war and reconstruction efforts, along with domestic security, were major issues in the 2004 presidential campaign. Bush was elected to a 2nd term as president in Nov. 2004, winning about 59 million popular votes, or 3 million more than Sen. John Kerry (D-MA). In 2005, he presented an outline for winning the Iraq war but warned against "artificial timelines" for the withdrawal of U.S. troops. Bush also continued to press for Social Security reform, but his plans met with public and congressional resistance.

In Aug. 2005, Hurricane Katrina devastated the Gulf Coast. Hundreds of thousands of people were left homeless, and the flooded city of New Orleans was evacuated and shut down; as of July 2006, estimates of direct and indirect casualties from the storm stood at more than 1,800. Pres. Bush and the Federal Emergency Management Agency were severely criticized for what was widely perceived as a slow and ineffective response to the disaster. Bush and Congress quickly approved a $62 bil "down payment" on disaster relief efforts, but as of July 2006, funding and plans to rebuild New Orleans and other affected areas were still under debate.

In July 2005, Justice Sandra Day O'Connor resigned, creating the first Supreme Court vacancy in more than 11 years; in Sept., Chief Justice William H. Rehnquist died after a battle with thyroid cancer. Appeals court judge John G. Roberts, initially nominated to succeed O'Connor, was quickly confirmed as new chief justice, and judge Samuel A. Alito was appointed to fill O'Connor's seat after Bush's first nominee, Harriet Miers, withdrew because of disputes over her nomination.

In 2006, Bush called for Congress to create a temporary worker or guest-worker program that would grant legal status to some of the estimated 12 mil illegal immigrants in the U.S.. Bush exercised his veto power for the first time in July 2006, rejecting legislation that would have eased restrictions on federal funding for stem cell research.

Wives and Children of the Presidents

Name (Born-Died; Married)	State	Sons/ Daughters	Name (Born-Died; Married)	State	Sons/ Daughters
Martha Dandridge Custis Washington (1731-1802; 1759)	VA	None	Caroline Lavinia Scott Harrison (1832-92; 1853)	OH	1/1
Abigail Smith Adams (1744-1818; 1764)	MA	3/2	Mary Scott Lord Dimmick Harrison (1858-1948; 1896)	PA	0/1
Martha Wayles Skelton Jefferson (1748-82; 1772)	VA	1/5	Ida Saxton McKinley (1847-1907; 1871)	OH	0/2
Dolley Payne Todd Madison (1768-1849; 1794)	NC	None	Alice Hathaway Lee Roosevelt (1861-84; 1880)	MA	0/1
Elizabeth Kortright Monroe (1768-1830; 1786)	NY	1/2	Edith Kermit Carow Roosevelt (1861-1948; 1886)	CT	4/1
Louisa Catherine Johnson Adams (1775-1852; 1797)	MD (A)	3/1	Helen Herron Taft (1861-1943; 1886)	OH	2/1
Rachel Donelson Robards Jackson (1767-1828; 1791)	VA	None	Ellen Louise Axson Wilson (1860-1914; 1885)	GA	0/3
Hannah Hoes Van Buren (1783-1819; 1807)	NY	4/0	Edith Bolling Galt Wilson (1872-1961; 1915)	VA	None
Anna Tuthill Symmes Harrison (1775-1864; 1795)	NJ	6/4	Florence Kling De Wolfe Harding (1860-1924; 1891)	OH	None
Letitia Christian Tyler (1790-1842; 1813)	VA	3/5	Grace Anna Goodhue Coolidge (1879-1957; 1905)	VT	2/0
Julia Gardiner Tyler (1820-89; 1844)	NY	5/2	Lou Henry Hoover (1875-1944; 1899)	IA	2/0
Sarah Childress Polk (1803-91; 1824)	TN	None	Anna Eleanor Roosevelt (1884-1962; 1905)	NY	5/1
Margaret (Peggy) Mackall Smith Taylor (1788-1852; 1810)	MD	1/5	Elizabeth Virginia (Bess) Wallace Truman (1885-1982; 1919)	MO	0/1
Abigail Powers Fillmore (1798-1853; 1826)	NY	1/1	Mamie Geneva Doud Eisenhower (1896-1979; 1916)	IA	2/0
Caroline Carmichael McIntosh Fillmore (1813-81; 1858)	NJ	None	Jacqueline Lee Bouvier Kennedy (1929-94; 1953)	NY	2/1
Jane Means Appleton Pierce (1806-63; 1834)	NH	3/0	Claudia (Lady Bird) Alta Taylor Johnson (1912; 1934)	TX	0/2
Mary Todd Lincoln (1818-82; 1842)	KY	4/0	Thelma Catherine Patricia Ryan Nixon (1912-93; 1940)	NV	0/2
Eliza McCardle Johnson (1810-76; 1827)	TN	3/2	Elizabeth (Betty) Bloomer Warren Ford (1918; 1948)	IL	3/1
Julia Boggs Dent Grant (1826-1902; 1848)	MO	3/1	Rosalynn Smith Carter (1927; 1946)	GA	3/1
Lucy Ware Webb Hayes (1831-89; 1852)	OH	7/1	Anne Frances (Nancy) Robbins Davis Reagan (1921; 1952)	NY	1/1(B)
Lucretia Rudolph Garfield (1832-1918; 1858)	OH	5/2	Barbara Pierce Bush (1925; 1945)	NY	4/2
Ellen Lewis Herndon Arthur (1837-80; 1859)	VA	2/1	Hillary Rodham Clinton (1947; 1975)	IL	0/1
Frances Folsom Cleveland (1864-1947; 1886)	NY	2/3	Laura Welch Bush (1946; 1977)	TX	0/2

NOTE: Pres. Buchanan was unmarried. (A) Born in London, father a MD citizen. (B) Pres. Reagan's first wife, whom he later divorced, was Jane Wyman. They had a daughter who died in infancy, and a son and daughter who lived past infancy.

First Lady Laura Welch Bush

Laura Welch Bush was born in Midland, TX, Nov. 4, 1946. She graduated from Southern Methodist University, earned a master's in library science at the Univ. of Texas at Austin, and became a librarian and teacher in Texas public schools. She and George W. Bush were married in 1977; in 1981, their twin daughters, Jenna and Barbara, were born.

As First Lady of Texas (1995-2001), Laura Bush worked for educational reform and stressed literacy programs. She launched an early childhood development initiative and also worked to promote breast cancer awareness.

Laura Bush's first solo appearance as First Lady came at the launch of DC Teaching Fellows, a program encouraging professionals to become teachers. In Nov. 2001 she became the first First Lady to give a speech of her own in place of the president's weekly radio address. In 2005, she toured Afghanistan and the Middle East, seeking to promote women's rights and democracy in the region. She continues to be involved in such interests as early childhood education, the promotion of literacy and reading, and the preservation of the U.S.'s cultural and natural heritage.

Burial Places of the Presidents

President	Burial Place	President	Burial Place	President	Burial Place
Washington	Mt. Vernon, VA	Pierce	Concord, NH	Taft	Arlington Natl. Cemetery
J. Adams	Quincy, MA	Buchanan	Lancaster, PA	Wilson	Wash. Natl. Cathedral, DC
Jefferson	Charlottesville, VA	Lincoln	Springfield, IL	Harding	Marion, OH
Madison	Montpelier Station, VA	A. Johnson	Greeneville, TN	Coolidge	Plymouth Notch, VT
Monroe	Richmond, VA	Grant	New York, NY	Hoover	West Branch, IA
J. Q. Adams	Quincy, MA	Hayes	Fremont, OH	F. Roosevelt	Hyde Park, NY
Jackson	Nashville, TN	Garfield	Cleveland, OH	Truman	Independence, MO
Van Buren	Kinderhook, NY	Arthur	Albany, NY	Eisenhower	Abilene, KS
W. H. Harrison	North Bend, OH	Cleveland	Princeton, NJ	Kennedy	Arlington Natl. Cemetery
Tyler	Richmond, VA	B. Harrison	Indianapolis, IN	L. B. Johnson	Stonewall, TX
Polk	Nashville, TN	McKinley	Canton, OH	Nixon	Yorba Linda, CA
Taylor	Louisville, KY	T. Roosevelt	Oyster Bay, NY	Reagan	Simi Valley, CA
Fillmore	Buffalo, NY				

Presidential Facts

Oldest president: Ronald Reagan, who was 77 when he left office

Youngest president: Theodore Roosevelt, who was 42 when sworn in after McKinley's death

Youngest person elected president: John F. Kennedy, who was 43 when elected in 1960

Tallest president: Abraham Lincoln, who was 6 feet, 4 inches

Shortest president: James Madison, who was 5 feet, 4 inches

Heaviest president: William Howard Taft, who was 332 pounds in 1911

First president to live in the White House: John Adams, who moved there in 1800

First president inaugurated in Washington, DC: Thomas Jefferson, in 1801

First president whose parents were immigrants: Andrew Jackson; his parents immigrated from Ireland in 1765

First president born a U.S. citizen: Martin Van Buren, in Kinderhook, NY, 1782

First president born outside the original colonies: Abraham Lincoln, in Kentucky, 1809

Most common presidential home state: Virginia, with 8 presidents

First president of all 50 states: Dwight D. Eisenhower, first inaugurated in 1953

First president born in the 20th century: John F. Kennedy, in 1917

First president to be photographed while in office: James K. Polk, in 1849

First president to have a telephone in the White House: Rutherford B. Hayes, in 1879

First president to address the nation on radio: Warren G. Harding, in 1922

First president to appear on TV: Franklin D. Roosevelt, at opening ceremonies for the 1939 World's Fair

First president to give a live, televised news conference: John F. Kennedy, in 1961

First president to hold an Internet chat: Bill Clinton, in 1999

Only president elected unanimously: George Washington, by 63 electoral votes

Only presidents who lost the popular vote while winning election: John Quincy Adams, in 1824 (elected by the House after general election failed to produce a majority); Rutherford B. Hayes, in 1876; Benjamin Harrison, in 1888; George W. Bush, in 2000. Popular vote totals before 1824 are unknown.

Only presidents chosen by the House of Representatives: Thomas Jefferson (1st term) and John Quincy Adams

Most common Alma Mater (undergraduate): Harvard, with 5 presidents

Only left-handed presidents: James Garfield, Herbert Hoover, Harry Truman, Gerald Ford, Ronald Reagan, George H. W. Bush, and Bill Clinton

Only Catholic elected president: John F. Kennedy; the most common religious affiliations have been Episcopalian (11) and Presbyterian (7)

Only bachelor presidents: James Buchanan, who never married, and Grover Cleveland, who married Frances Folsom in the White House in 1886

Only divorced president: Ronald Reagan; divorced from actress Jane Wyman in 1948, married Nancy Davis in 1952

Presidents who died on July 4: John Adams and Thomas Jefferson (both 1826) and James Monroe (1831)

Only president buried in Washington, DC: Woodrow Wilson, who was interred at the Washington National Cathedral

Presidential Libraries

The libraries listed here, except for that of Richard Nixon (which is private), are coordinated by the National Archives and Records Administration (Website: www.archives.gov/presidential-libraries/index.html). NARA also has custody of the Nixon presidential historical materials and those of Bill Clinton. The William J. Clinton Library first made a selection of presidential papers publicly available in Feb. 2005. The Clinton presidential records became subject to the Freedom of Information Act on Jan. 20, 2006. Materials for presidents before Herbert Hoover are held by private institutions.

Herbert Hoover Library and Museum
210 Parkside Dr.
West Branch, IA 52358
PHONE: 319-643-5301
E-MAIL: hoover.library@nara.gov
WEBSITE: hoover.archives.gov

Franklin D. Roosevelt Library and Museum
4079 Albany Post Rd.
Hyde Park, NY 12538-1990
PHONE: 845-486-7770; 1-800-FDR-VISIT
E-MAIL: roosevelt.library@nara.gov
WEBSITE: www.fdrlibrary.marist.edu

Harry S. Truman Library and Museum
500 West U.S. Hwy. 24
Independence, MO 64050-2481
PHONE: 816-268-8200; 1-800-833-1225
E-MAIL: truman.library@nara.gov
WEBSITE: www.trumanlibrary.org

Dwight D. Eisenhower Library
200 S.E. 4th St.
Abilene, KS 67410-2900
PHONE: 785-263-6700; 1-877-RING-IKE
E-MAIL: eisenhower.library@nara.gov
WEBSITE: eisenhower.archives.gov

John F. Kennedy Library and Museum
Columbia Pt.
Boston, MA 02125-3312
PHONE: 617-514-1600; 1-866-JFK-1960
E-MAIL: kennedy.library@nara.gov
WEBSITE: www.jfklibrary.org

Lyndon Baines Johnson Library and Museum
2313 Red River St.
Austin, TX 78705-5737
PHONE: 512-721-0200
E-MAIL: johnson.library@nara.gov
WEBSITE: www.lbjlib.utexas.edu

Richard Nixon Library & Birthplace
18001 Yorba Linda Blvd.
Yorba Linda, CA 92886-3903
PHONE: 714-993-5075
E-MAIL: archives@nixonlibrary.org
WEBSITE: www.nixonlibrary.org

Gerald R. Ford Library and Museum
1000 Beal Ave.
Ann Arbor, MI 48109-2109
PHONE: 734-205-0555
E-MAIL: ford.library@nara.gov
WEBSITE: www.fordlibrarymuseum.gov

Jimmy Carter Library and Museum
441 Freedom Pkwy.
Atlanta, GA 30307-1496
PHONE: 404-865-7100
E-MAIL: carter.library@nara.gov
WEBSITE: www.jimmycarterlibrary.gov

Ronald Reagan Library and Museum
40 Presidential Dr.
Simi Valley, CA 93065-0600
PHONE: 800-410-8354
E-MAIL: reagan.library@nara.gov
WEBSITE: www.reagan.utexas.edu

George Bush Library and Museum
1000 George Bush Dr. West
College Station, TX 77845
PHONE: 979-691-4000
E-MAIL: bush.library@nara.gov
WEBSITE: bushlibrary.tamu.edu

William J. Clinton Library and Museum
1200 President Clinton Ave.
Little Rock, AR 72201
PHONE: 501-374-4242
E-MAIL: clinton.library@nara.gov
WEBSITE: www.clintonlibrary.gov

Presidential Impeachment in U.S. History

The U.S. Constitution provides for impeachment and removal from office of federal officials on grounds of "Treason, Bribery, or other high Crimes and Misdemeanors" (Article II, Sect. 4). Impeachment is the bringing of charges by the House of Representatives. It is followed by a Senate trial; a two-thirds majority vote of Senators present is needed for conviction and removal from office.

In 1868, **Andrew Johnson** became the first president impeached by the House. He was tried but not convicted. In 1974, impeachment articles against Pres. **Richard Nixon**, in connection with the Watergate scandal, were voted by the House Judiciary Committee. He resigned Aug. 9, and the House accepted the committee report without taking further action. In 1998, Pres. **Bill Clinton** was impeached by the House in connection with covering up a sexual relationship with former White House intern Monica Lewinsky. He was tried in the Senate in 1999 and acquitted.

IT'S A RECORD: The shortest inaugural speech was given by George Washington at his second inauguration, on Mar. 4, 1793. His speech, which contained 136 words, lasted only 90 seconds. The longest inaugural speech was given by William Henry Harrison, who spoke for nearly two hours at his inauguration on Mar. 4, 1841. After his inauguration, which was held outside on a cold day, Harrison caught a cold that developed into pneumonia. He died on Apr. 4, having served the shortest term of any U.S. president.

Electoral and Popular Vote, 2004 and 2000

Source: Federal Election Commission (2004); Voter News Service (2000).

State	2004 Electoral Vote Kerry	2004 Electoral Vote Bush	2004 Electoral Vote Nader	Democrat Kerry	Republican Bush	Indep[1] Nader	2000 Electoral Vote Gore	2000 Electoral Vote Bush	2000 Electoral Vote Nader	2000 Electoral Vote Buchanan	Democrat Gore	Republican Bush	Green[1] Nader	Reform[1] Buchanan
AL	0	9	0	693,933	1,176,394	6,701	0	9	0	0	692,611	941,173	18,323	6,303
AK	0	3	0	111,025	190,889	5,069	0	3	0	0	79,004	167,398	28,747	4,194
AZ	0	10	—	893,524	1,104,294	—	0	8	0	0	685,341	781,652	45,645	10,903
AR	0	6	0	469,953	572,898	6,171	0	6	0	0	422,768	472,940	13,421	10,936
CA	55	0	—	6,745,485	5,509,826	—	54	0	0	0	5,861,203	4,567,429	418,707	39,897
CO	0	9	0	1,001,732	1,101,255	12,718	0	8	0	0	738,227	883,748	91,434	10,282
CT	7	0	0	857,488	693,826	12,969	8	0	0	0	816,015	561,094	64,452	4,382
DE	3	0	0	200,152	171,660	2,153	3	0	0	0	180,068	137,288	8,307	775
DC	3	0	0	202,970	21,256	1,485	2[2]	0	0	0	171,923	18,073	10,576	—
FL	0	27	0	3,583,544	3,964,522	32,971	0	25	0	—	2,912,253	2,912,790	97,488	17,356
GA	0	15	—	1,366,149	1,914,254	—	0	13	—	0	1,116,230	1,419,720	—	10,868
HI	4	0	—	231,708	194,191	—	4	0	0	0	205,286	137,845	21,623	1,071
ID	0	4	—	181,098	409,235	—	0	4	—	0	138,637	336,937	—	7,687
IL	21	0	—	2,891,550	2,345,946	—	22	0	0	0	2,589,026	2,019,421	103,759	16,060
IN	0	11	—	969,011	1,479,438	—	0	12	0	0	901,980	1,245,836	—	17,173
IA	0	7	0	741,898	751,957	5,973	7	0	0	0	638,517	634,373	29,374	6,942
KS	0	6	0	434,993	736,456	9,348	0	6	0	0	399,276	622,332	36,086	7,239
KY	0	8	0	712,733	1,069,439	8,856	0	8	0	0	638,923	872,520	23,118	4,181
LA	0	9	0	820,299	1,102,169	7,032	0	9	0	0	792,344	927,871	20,473	14,478
ME	4	0	0	396,842	330,201	8,069	4	0	0	0	319,951	286,616	37,127	4,315
MD	10	0	0	1,334,493	1,024,703	11,854	10	0	0	0	1,144,008	813,827	53,768	4,067
MA	12	0	—	1,803,800	1,071,109	—	12	0	0	0	1,616,487	878,502	173,564	11,086
MI	17	0	0	2,479,183	2,313,746	24,035	18	0	0	—	2,170,418	1,953,139	84,165	—
MN	9[3]	0	0	1,445,014	1,346,695	18,683	10	0	0	0	1,168,266	1,109,659	126,696	22,256
MS	0	6	0	458,094	684,981	3,177	0	7	0	0	404,614	572,844	8,122	2,233
MO	0	11	—	1,259,171	1,455,713	—	0	11	0	0	1,111,138	1,189,924	38,515	9,806
MT	0	3	0	173,710	266,063	6,168	0	3	0	0	137,126	240,178	24,437	5,735
NE	0	5	0	254,328	512,814	5,698	0	5	0	0	231,780	433,862	24,540	3,431
NV	0	5	0	397,190	418,690	4,838	0	4	0	0	279,978	301,575	15,008	4,747
NH	4	0	0	340,511	331,237	4,479	0	4	0	0	266,348	273,559	22,198	2,603
NJ	15	0	0	1,911,430	1,670,003	19,418	15	0	0	0	1,788,850	1,284,173	94,554	6,868
NM	0	5	0	370,942	376,930	4,053	5	0	0	0	286,783	286,417	21,251	1,279
NY	31	0	0	4,314,280	2,962,567	99,873	33	0	0	0	4,112,965	2,405,570	244,360	33,202
NC	0	15	—	1,525,849	1,961,166	—	0	14	0	0	1,257,692	1,631,163	—	8,971
ND	0	3	0	111,052	196,651	3,756	0	3	0	0	95,284	174,852	9,486	7,330
OH	0	20	—	2,741,167	2,859,768	—	0	21	0	0	2,186,190	2,351,209	117,857	25,980
OK	0	7	—	503,966	959,792	—	0	8	—	0	474,276	744,337	—	9,014
OR	7	0	—	943,163	866,831	—	7	0	0	0	720,342	713,577	77,357	5,706
PA	21	0	—	2,938,095	2,793,847	—	23	0	0	0	2,485,967	2,281,127	103,392	16,879
RI	4	0	0	259,765	169,046	4,651	4	0	0	0	249,508	130,555	25,052	2,250
SC	0	8	0	661,699	937,974	5,520	0	8	0	0	566,039	786,892	20,279	3,540
SD	0	3	0	149,244	232,584	4,320	0	3	—	0	118,804	190,700	—	3,314
TN	0	11	0	1,036,477	1,384,375	8,992	0	11	0	0	981,720	1,061,949	19,781	4,218
TX	0	34	—	2,832,704	4,526,917	—	0	32	0	0	2,433,746	3,799,639	137,994	12,423
UT	0	5	0	241,199	663,742	11,305	0	5	0	0	203,053	515,096	35,850	9,277
VT	3	0	0	184,067	121,180	4,494	3	0	0	0	149,022	119,775	20,374	2,182
VA	0	13	—	1,454,742	1,716,959	—	0	13	0	0	1,217,290	1,437,490	59,398	5,578
WA	11	0	0	1,510,201	1,304,894	23,283	11	0	0	0	1,247,652	1,108,864	103,002	4,953
WV	0	5	0	326,541	423,778	4,063	0	5	0	0	295,497	336,475	10,680	3,101
WI	10	0	0	1,489,504	1,478,120	16,390	11	0	0	0	1,242,987	1,237,279	94,070	11,206
WY	0	3	0	70,776	167,629	2,741	0	3	—	0	60,481	147,947	—	2,724
Total	**251**	**286**	**0**	**59,028,444**	**62,040,610**	**411,306**	**266**	**271**	**0**	**0**	**51,003,894**	**50,459,211**	**2,834,410**	**441,001**

(—) = Not listed on state's ballot. (1) Listed on the ballot in some states as particular party. (2) One Washington, DC, elector abstained. (3) One Minnesota elector voted for Democratic vice-presidential candidate Sen. John Edwards (NC) for both president and vice president.

2004 Official Presidential General Election Results

Source: Federal Election Commission

Candidate (Party)	Popular Vote	Percent of Pop. Vote	Candidate (Party)	Popular Vote	Percent of Pop. Vote
George W. Bush (Republican)	62,040,610	50.73	Thomas J. Harens (Christian Freedom) . .	2,387	0.00
John Kerry (Democrat).	59,028,444	48.27	Gene Amondson (Concerns of People) . .	1,944	0.00
Ralph Nader (Independent)	465,650	0.38*	Bill Van Auken (Socialist Equality)	1,857	0.00
Michael Badnarik (Independent)	397,265	0.32	John Parker (Workers World).	1,646	0.00
Michael Anthony Peroutka (Independent)	143,630	0.12	Charles Jay (Personal Choice)	946	0.00
David Cobb (Green).	119,859	0.10	Stanford E. Andress (Unaffiliated)	804	0.00
Leonard Peltier (Peace and Freedom). .	27,607	0.02	Earl F. Dodge (Prohibition Party)	140	0.00
Walter F. Brown (Socialist).	10,837	0.01	Write-in (other).	37,240	0.03
James Harris (Socialist Workers)	7,102	0.01	None of These Candidates	3,688	0.00
Róger Calero (Socialist Workers)	3,689	0.00	**Total**	**122,295,645**	**100.00**

Note: Party designations may vary from one state to another. Percents do not add because of rounding. *Includes write-in votes in states where Nader was not on the ballot.

PRESIDENTIAL ELECTION RESULTS BY STATE SINCE 1948

Results for New England states are for selected cities or towns.

Source: Federal Election Commission. Not all write-ins are included.

Alabama

2004: Bush, R., 1,176,394; Kerry, D., 693,933; Nader, Ind., 6,701; Badnarik, Ind., 3,529; Peroutka, Ind., 1,994.

2000: Bush, R., 941,173; Gore, D., 692,611; Nader, Ind., 18,323; Buchanan, Ind., 6,351; Browne, Libertarian, 5,893; Phillips, Ind., 775 Hagelin, Ind., 447.

1996: Dole, R., 769,044; Clinton, D., 662,165; Perot, Ind. (Ref.), 92,149; Browne, Libertarian, 5,290; Phillips, Ind., 2,365; Hagelin, Natural Law, 1,697; Harris, Ind., 516.

1992: Bush, R., 804,283; Clinton, D., 690,080; Perot, Ind., 183,109; Marrou, Libertarian, 5,737; Fulani, New Alliance, 2,161.

1988: Bush, R., 815,576; Dukakis, D., 549,506; Paul, Lib., 8,460; Fulani, Ind., 3,311.

1984: Reagan, R., 872,849; Mondale, D., 551,899; Bergland, Libertarian, 9,504.

1980: Reagan, R., 654,192; Carter, D., 636,730; Anderson, Independent, 16,481; Rarick, Amer. Ind., 15,010; Clark, Libertarian, 13,318; Bubar, Statesman, 1,743; Hall, Com., 1,629; DeBerry, Soc. Workers, 1,303; McReynolds, Socialist, 1,006; Commoner, Citizens, 517.

1976: Carter, D., 659,170; Ford, R., 504,070; Maddox, Amer. Ind., 9,198; Bubar, Proh., 6,669; Hall, Com., 1,954; MacBride, Libertarian, 1,481.

1972: Nixon, R., 728,701; McGovern, D., 219,108 plus 37,815 Natl. Dem. Party of Alabama; Schmitz, Conservative, 11,918; Munn., Proh., 8,551.

1968: Wallace, 3rd Party, 691,425; Humphrey, D., 196,579; Nixon, R., 146,923; Munn, Proh., 4,022.

1964: Goldwater, R., 479,085; Dem. (electors unpledged), 209,848; scattered, 105.

1960: Kennedy, D., 324,050; Nixon, R., 237,981; Faubus, States' Rights, 4,367; Decker, Proh., 2,106; King, Afro-Americans, 1,485; scattered, 236.

1956: Stevenson, D., 290,844; Eisenhower, R., 195,694; Ind. electors, 20,323.

1952: Stevenson, D., 275,075; Eisenhower, R., 149,231; Hamblen, Proh., 1,814.

1948: Thurmond, States' Rights, 171,443; Dewey, R., 40,930; Wallace, Prog., 1,522; Watson, Proh., 1,085.

Alaska

2004: Bush, R., 190,889; Kerry, D., 111,025; Nader, Populist, 5,069; Peroutka, AK Ind., 2,092; Badnarik, Libertarian, 1,675; Cobb, Green, 1,058.

2000: Bush, R., 167,398; Gore, D., 79,004; Nader, Green, 28,747; Buchanan, Reform, 5,192; Browne, Libertarian, 2,636; Hagelin, Natural Law, 919; Phillips, Constitution, 596.

1996: Dole, R., 122,746; Clinton, D., 80,380; Perot, Ref., 26,333; Nader, Green, 7,597; Browne, Libertarian, 2,276; Phillips, Taxpayers, 925; Hagelin, Natural Law, 729.

1992: Bush, R., 102,000; Clinton, D., 78,294; Perot, Ind., 73,481; Gritz, Populist/America First, 1,379; Marrou, Libertarian, 1,378.

1988: Bush, R., 119,251; Dukakis, D., 72,584; Paul, Lib., 5,484; Fulani, New Alliance, 1,024.

1984: Reagan, R., 138,377; Mondale, D., 62,007; Bergland, Libertarian, 6,378.

1980: Reagan, R., 86,112; Carter, D., 41,842; Clark, Libertarian, 18,479; Anderson, Ind., 11,155; write-in, 857.

1976: Ford, R., 71,555; Carter, D., 44,058; MacBride, Libertarian, 6,785.

1972: Nixon, R., 55,349; McGovern, D., 32,967; Schmitz, Amer., 6,903.

1968: Nixon, R., 37,600; Humphrey, D., 35,411; Wallace, 3rd Party, 10,024.

1964: Johnson, D., 44,329; Goldwater, R., 22,930.

1960: Nixon, R., 30,953; Kennedy, D., 29,809.

Arizona

2004: Bush, R., 1,104,294; Kerry, D., 893,524; Badnarik, Libertarian, 11,856.

2000: Bush, R., 781,652; Gore, D., 685,341; Nader, Green, 45,645; Buchanan, R., 12,373; Smith, Libertarian, 5,775; Hagelin, Natural Law, 1,120.

1996: Clinton, D., 653,288; Dole, R., 622,073; Perot, Ref., 112,072; Browne, Libertarian, 14,358.

1992: Bush, R., 572,086; Clinton, D., 543,050; Perot, Ind., 353,741; Gritz, Populist/America First, 8,141; Marrou, Libertarian, 6,759; Hagelin, Natural Law, 2,267.

1988: Bush, R., 702,541; Dukakis, D., 454,029; Paul, Lib., 13,351; Fulani, New Alliance, 1,662.

1984: Reagan, R., 681,416; Mondale, D., 333,854; Bergland, Libertarian, 10,585.

1980: Reagan, R., 529,688; Carter, D., 246,843; Anderson, Ind., 76,952; Clark, Libertarian, 18,784; De Berry, Soc. Workers, 1,100; Commoner, Citizens, 551; Hall, Com., 25; Griswold, Workers World, 2.

1976: Ford, R., 418,642; Carter, D., 295,602; McCarthy, Ind., 19,229; MacBride, Libertarian, 7,647; Camejo, Soc. Workers, 928; Anderson, Amer., 564; Maddox, Amer. Ind., 85.

1972: Nixon, R., 402,812; McGovern, D., 198,540; Soc. Workers, 30,945; Schmitz, Amer., 21,208.

1968: Nixon, R., 266,721; Humphrey, D., 170,514; Wallace, 3rd Party, 46,573; McCarthy, New Party, 2,751; Cleaver, Peace and Freedom, 217; Halstead, Soc. Workers, 85; Blomen, Soc. Labor, 75.

1964: Goldwater, R., 242,535; Johnson, D., 237,753; Hass, Soc. Labor, 482.

1960: Nixon, R., 221,241; Kennedy, D., 176,781; Hass, Soc. Labor, 469.

1956: Eisenhower, R., 176,990; Stevenson, D., 112,880; Andrews, Ind. 303.

1952: Eisenhower, R., 152,042; Stevenson, D., 108,528.

1948: Truman, D., 95,251; Dewey, R., 77,597; Wallace, Prog., 3,310; Watson, Proh., 786; Teichert, Soc. Labor, 121.

Arkansas

2004: Bush, R., 572,898; Kerry, D., 469,953; Nader, Populist, 6,171; Badnarik, Libertarian, 2,352; Peroutka, Constitution, 2,083; Cobb, Green, 1,488.

2000: Bush, R., 472,940; Gore, D., 422,768; Nader, Green, 13,421; Buchanan, Reform, 7,358; Browne, Libertarian, 2,781; Phillips, Constitution, 1,415; Hagelin, Natural Law, 1,098.

1996: Clinton, D., 475,171; Dole, R., 325,416; Perot, Ref., 69,884; Nader, Ind., 3,649; Browne, Ind., 3,076; Phillips, Ind., 2,065; Forbes, Ind., 932; Collins, Ind., 823; Masters, Ind., 749; Moorehead, Ind., 747; Hagelin, Ind., 729; Hollis, Ind., 538; Dodge, Ind., 483.

1992: Clinton, D., 505,823; Bush, R., 337,324; Perot, Ind., 99,132; Phillips, U.S. Taxpayers, 1,437; Marrou, Libertarian, 1,261; Fulani, New Alliance, 1,022.

1988: Bush, R., 466,578; Dukakis, D., 349,237; Duke, Chr. Pop., 5,146; Paul, Lib., 3,297.

1984: Reagan, R., 534,774; Mondale, D., 338,646; Bergland, Libertarian, 2,220.

1980: Reagan, R., 403,164; Carter, D., 398,041; Anderson, Ind., 22,468; Clark, Libertarian, 8,970; Commoner, Citizens, 2,345; Bubar, Statesman, 1,350; Hall, Com., 1,244.

1976: Carter, D., 498,604; Ford, R., 267,903; McCarthy, Ind., 639; Anderson, Amer., 389.

1972: Nixon, R., 445,751; McGovern, D., 198,899; Schmitz, Amer., 3,016.

1968: Wallace, 3rd Party, 235,627; Nixon, R., 189,062; Humphrey, D., 184,901.

1964: Johnson, D., 314,197; Goldwater, R., 243,264; Kasper, Natl. States' Rights, 2,965.

1960: Kennedy, D., 215,049; Nixon, R., 184,508; Natl. States' Rights, 28,952.

1956: Stevenson, D., 213,277; Eisenhower, R., 186,287; Andrews, Ind., 7,008.

1952: Stevenson, D., 226,300; Eisenhower, R., 177,155; Hamblen, Proh., 886; MacArthur, Christian Nat., 458; Hass, Soc. Labor, 1.

1948: Truman, D., 149,659; Dewey, R., 50,959; Thurmond, States' Rights, 40,068; Thomas, Soc., 1,037; Wallace, Prog., 751; Watson, Proh., 1.

> **IT'S A FACT:** In the nine presidential elections since 1972, these states have a 100% record for voting for the winning candidate: Arkansas, Kentucky, Louisiana, Missouri, Ohio, and Tennessee.

California

2004: Kerry, D., 6,745,485; Bush, R., 5,509,826; Badnarik, Libertarian, 50,165; Cobb, Green, 40,771; Peltier, Peace & Freedom, 27,607; Peroutka, Amer. Ind., 26,645.

2000: Gore, D., 5,861,203; Bush, R., 4,567,429; Nader, Green, 418,707; Browne, Libertarian, 45,520; Buchanan, Reform, 44,987; Phillips, Amer. Ind., 17,042; Hagelin, Natural Law, 10,934.

1996: Clinton, D., 5,119,835; Dole, R., 3,828,380; Perot, Ref., 697,847; Nader, Green, 237,016; Browne, Libertarian, 73,600; Feinland, Peace & Freedom, 25,332; Phillips, Amer. Ind., 21,202; Hagelin, Natural Law, 15,403.

1992: Clinton, D., 5,121,325; Bush, R., 3,630,575; Perot, Ind., 2,296,006; Marrou, Libertarian, 48,139; Daniels, Ind., 18,597; Phillips, U.S. Taxpayers, 12,711.

1988: Bush, R., 5,054,917; Dukakis, D., 4,702,233; Paul, Lib., 70,105; Fulani, Ind., 31,181.

1984: Reagan, Rep. 5,305,410; Mondale, D., 3,815,947; Bergland, Libertarian, 48,400.

1980: Reagan, Rep. 4,524,858; Carter, Dem., 3,083,661; Anderson, Ind., 739,833; Clark, Libertarian, 148,434; Commoner, Ind., 61,063; Smith, Peace and Freedom, 18,116; Rarick, Amer. Ind., 9,856.

1976: Ford, R., 3,882,244; Carter, D., 3,742,284; write-in, McCarthy, 58,412; MacBride, Libertarian, 56,388; Maddox, Amer. Ind., 51,098; Wright, People's, 41,731; Camejo, Soc. Workers, 17,259; Hall, Com., 12,766; write-in, 4,935.

1972: Nixon, R., 4,602,096; McGovern, D., 3,475,847; Schmitz, Amer., 232,554; Spock, Peace and Freedom, 55,167; Hospers, Libertarian, 980; Jenness, Soc. Workers, 574; Hall, Com., 373; Fisher, Soc. Labor, 197; Munn, Proh., 53; Green, Universal, 21.

1968: Nixon, R., 3,467,664; Humphrey, D., 3,244,318; Wallace, 3rd Party, 487,270; Peace and Freedom, 27,707; McCarthy, Alternative, 20,721; Gregory, write-in, 3,230; Blomen, Soc. Labor, 341; Mitchell, Com., 260; Munn, Proh., 59; Soeters, Defense, 17.

1964: Johnson, D., 4,171,877; Goldwater, R., 2,879,108; Hass, Soc. Labor, 489; DeBerry, Soc. Workers, 378; Munn, Proh., 305; Hensley, Universal, 19.

1960: Nixon, R., 3,259,722; Kennedy, D., 3,224,099; Decker, Proh., 21,706; Hass, Soc. Labor, 1,051.

1956: Eisenhower, R., 3,027,668; Stevenson, D., 2,420,136; Holtwick, Proh., 11,119; Andrews, Constitution, 6,087; Hass, Soc. Labor, 300; Hoopes, Soc., 123; Dobbs, Soc. Workers, 96; Smith, Christian Natl., 8.

1952: Eisenhower, R., 2,897,310; Stevenson, D., 2,197,548; Hallinan, Prog., 24,106; Hamblen, Proh., 15,653; MacArthur, (Tenny Ticket), 3,326; Hass, Soc. Labor, 273; Hoopes, Soc., 206; (Kellems Ticket) 178; scattered, 3,249.

1948: Truman, D., 1,913,134; Dewey, R., 1,895,269; Wallace, Prog., 190,381; Watson, Proh., 16,926; Thomas, Soc., 3,459; Thurmond, States' Rights, 1,228; Teichert, Soc. Labor, 195; Dobbs, Soc. Workers, 133.

Colorado

2004: Bush, R., 1,101,255; Kerry, D., 1,001,732; Nader, Ref., 12,718; Badnarik, Libertarian, 7,664; Peroutka, Amer. Const., 2,562; Cobb, Green, 1,591; Andress, Ind., 804; Amondson, Concerns of People, 378; Van Auken, Soc. Equal., 329; Harris, Soc. Wkrs., 241; Brown, Soc., 216; Dodge, Prohib., 140.

2000: Bush, R., 883,748; Gore, Dem, 738,227; Nader, Green, 91,434; Browne, Libertarian, 12,799; Buchanan, Reform, 10,465; Hagelin, Reform, 2,240; Phillips, Amer. Constitution, 1,319; McReynolds, Soc., 712; Harris, Soc. Workers, 216; Dodge, Proh., 208.

1996: Dole, R., 691,848; Clinton, D., 671,152; Perot, Ref., 99,629; Nader, Green, 25,070; Browne, Libertarian, 12,392; Phillips, Amer. Constitution, 2,813; Collins, Ind., 2,809; Hagelin, Natural Law, 2,547; Hollis, Ind., 669; Moorehead, Workers World, 599; Templin, Amer., 557; Dodge, Proh., 375; Harris, Soc. Workers, 244.

1992: Clinton, D., 629,681; Bush, R., 562,850; Perot, Ind., 366,010; Marrou, Libertarian, 8,669; Fulani, New Alliance, 1,608.

1988: Bush, R., 728,177; Dukakis, D., 621,453; Paul, Lib., 15,482; Dodge, Proh., 4,604.

1984: Reagan, R., 821,817; Mondale, D., 454,975; Bergland, Libertarian, 11,257.

1980: Reagan, R., 652,264; Carter, D., 367,973; Anderson, Ind., 130,633; Clark, Libertarian, 25,744; Commoner, Citizens, 5,614; Bubar, Statesman, 1,180; Pulley, Socialist, 520; Hall, Com., 487.

1976: Ford, R., 584,367; Carter, D., 460,353; McCarthy, Ind., 26,107; MacBride, Libertarian, 5,330; Bubar, Proh., 2,882.

1972: Nixon, R., 597,189; McGovern, D., 329,980; Schmitz, Amer., 17,269; Fisher, Soc. Labor, 4,361; Spock, Peoples, 2,403; Hospers, Libertarian, 1,111; Jenness, Soc. Workers, 555; Munn, Proh., 467; Hall, Com., 432.

1968: Nixon, R., 409,345; Humphrey, D., 335,174; Wallace, 3rd Party, 60,813; Blomen, Soc. Labor, 3,016; Gregory, Newparty, 1,393; Munn, Proh., 275; Halstead, Soc. Workers, 235.

1964: Johnson, D., 476,024; Goldwater, R., 296,767; DeBerry, Soc. Workers, 2,537; Munn, Proh., 1,356; Hass, Soc. Labor, 302.

1960: Nixon, R., 402,242; Kennedy, D., 330,629; Hass, Soc. Labor, 2,803; Dobbs, Soc. Workers, 572.

1956: Eisenhower, R., 394,479; Stevenson, D., 263,997; Hass, Soc. Lab., 3,308; Andrews, Ind., 759; Hoopes, Soc., 531.

1952: Eisenhower, R., 379,782; Stevenson, D., 245,504; MacArthur, Constitution, 2,181; Hallinan, Prog., 1,919; Hoopes, Soc., 365; Hass, Soc. Labor, 352.

1948: Truman, D., 267,288; Dewey, R., 239,714; Wallace, Prog., 6,115; Thomas, Soc., 1,678; Dobbs, Soc. Workers, 228; Teichert, Soc. Labor, 214.

Connecticut

2004: Kerry, D., 857,488; Bush, R., 693,826; Nader, Petitioning Cand., 12,969; Cobb, Green, 9,564; Badnarik, Libertarian, 3,367; Peroutka, Concerned Citizens, 1,543.

2000: Gore, D., 816,015; Bush, R., 561,094; Nader, Green, 64,452; Phillips, Concerned Citizens, 9,695; Buchanan, Reform, 4,731; Browne, Libertarian, 3,484.

1996: Clinton, D., 735,740; Dole, R., 483,109; Perot, Ref., 139,523; Nader, Green, 24,321; Browne, Libertarian, 5,788; Phillips, Concerned Citizens, 2,425; Hagelin, Natural Law, 1,703.

1992: Clinton, D., 682,318; Bush, R., 578,313; Perot, Ind., 348,771; Marrou, Libertarian, 5,391; Fulani, New Alliance, 1,363.

1988: Bush, R., 750,241; Dukakis, D., 676,584; Paul, Lib., 14,071; Fulani, New Alliance, 2,491.

1984: Reagan, R., 890,877; Mondale, D., 569,597.

1980: Reagan, R., 677,210; Carter, D., 541,732; Anderson, Ind., 171,807; Clark, Libertarian, 8,570; Commoner, Citizens, 6,130; scattered, 836.

1976: Ford, R., 719,261; Carter, D., 647,895; Maddox, George Wallace Party, 7,101; LaRouche, U.S. Labor, 1,789.

1972: Nixon, R., 810,763; McGovern, D., 555,498; Schmitz, Amer., 17,239; scattered, 777.

1968: Humphrey, D., 621,561; Nixon, R., 556,721; Wallace, 3rd Party, 76,650; scattered, 1,300.

1964: Johnson, D., 826,269; Goldwater, R., 390,996; scattered, 1,313.

1960: Kennedy, D., 657,055; Nixon, R., 565,813.

1956: Eisenhower, R., 711,837; Stevenson, D., 405,079; scattered, 205.

1952: Eisenhower, R., 611,012; Stevenson, D., 481,649; Hoopes, Soc., 2,244; Hallinan, Peoples, 1,466; Hass, Soc. Labor, 535; write-in, 5.

1948: Dewey, R., 437,754; Truman, D., 423,297; Wallace, Prog., 13,713; Thomas, Soc., 6,964; Teichert, Soc. Labor, 1,184; Dobbs, Soc. Workers, 606.

Delaware

2004: Kerry, D., 200,152; Bush, R., 171,660; Nader, Ind., 2,153; Badnarik, Libertarian, 586; Peroutka, Constitution, 289; Cobb, Green, 250; Brown, Nat. Law, 100.

2000: Gore, D., 180,068; Bush, R., 137,288; Nader, Green, 8,307; Buchanan, Reform, 777; Browne, Libertarian, 774; Phillips, Constitution, 208; Hagelin, Natural Law, 107.

1996: Clinton, D., 140,355; Dole, R., 99,062; Perot, Ind. (Ref.), 28,719; Browne, Libertarian, 2,052; Phillips, Taxpayers, 348; Hagelin, Natural Law, 274.

1992: Clinton, D., 126,054; Bush, R., 102,313; Perot, Ind., 59,213; Fulani, New Alliance, 1,105.

1988: Bush, R., 139,639; Dukakis, D., 108,647; Paul, Lib., 1,162; Fulani, New Alliance, 443.

1984: Reagan, R., 152,190; Mondale, D., 101,656; Bergland, Libertarian, 268.

1980: Reagan, R., 111,252; Carter, D., 105,754; Anderson, Ind., 16,288; Clark, Libertarian, 1,974; Greaves, Amer., 400.

1976: Carter, D., 122,596; Ford, R., 109,831; McCarthy, non-partisan, 2,437; Anderson, Amer., 645; LaRouche, U.S. Labor, 136; Bubar, Proh., 103; Levin, Soc. Labor, 86.

1972: Nixon, R., 140,357; McGovern, D., 92,283; Schmitz, Amer., 2,638; Munn, Proh., 238.

1968: Nixon, R., 96,714; Humphrey, D., 89,194; Wallace, 3rd Party, 28,459.

1964: Johnson, D., 122,704; Goldwater, R., 78,078; Munn, Proh., 425; Hass, Soc. Labor, 113.

1960: Kennedy, D., 99,590; Nixon, R., 96,373; Faubus, States' Rights, 354; Decker, Proh., 284; Hass, Soc. Labor, 82.

1956: Eisenhower, R., 98,057; Stevenson, D., 79,421; Oltwick, Proh., 400; Hass, Soc. Labor, 110.

1952: Eisenhower, R., 90,059; Stevenson, D., 83,315; Hass, Soc. Lab., 242; Hamblen, Proh., 234; Hallinan, Prog., 155; Hoopes, Soc., 20.

1948: Dewey, R., 69,688; Truman, D., 67,813; Wallace, Prog., 1,050; Watson, Proh., 343; Thomas, Soc., 250; Teichert, Soc. Labor, 29.

District of Columbia

2004: Kerry, D., 202,970; Bush, R., 21,256; Nader, Ind., 1,485; Cobb, DC Statehd Green Pty., 737; Badnarik, Libertarian, 502; Harris, Soc. Wkrs., 130.

2000: Gore, D., 171,923; Bush, R., 18,073; Nader, Green, 10,576; Browne, Libertarian, 669; Harris, Soc. Workers, 114.

1996: Clinton, D., 158,220; Dole, R., 17,339; Nader, Green, 4,780; Perot, Ref., 3,611; Browne, Libertarian, 588; Hagelin, Natural Law, 283; Harris, Soc. Workers, 257.

1992: Clinton, D., 192,619; Bush, R., 20,698; Perot, Ind., 9,681; Fulani, New Alliance, 1,459; Daniels, Ind., 1,186.

1988: Dukakis, D., 159,407; Bush, R., 27,590; Fulani, New Alliance, 2,901; Paul, Lib., 554.

1984: Mondale, D., 180,408; Reagan, R., 29,009; Bergland, Libertarian, 279.

1980: Carter, D., 130,231; Reagan, R., 23,313; Anderson, Ind., 16,131; Commoner, Citizens, 1,826; Clark, Libertarian, 1,104; Hall, Com., 369; DeBerry, Soc. Workers, 173; Griswold, Workers World, 52; write-in, 690.

1976: Carter, D., 137,818; Ford, R., 27,873; Camejo, Soc. Workers, 545; MacBride, Libertarian, 274; Hall, Com., 219; LaRouche, U.S. Labor, 157.

1972: McGovern, D., 127,627; Nixon, R., 35,226; Reed, Soc. Workers, 316; Hall, Com., 252.

1968: Humphrey, D., 139, 566; Nixon, R., 31,012.

1964: Johnson, D., 169,796; Goldwater, R., 28,801.

Florida

2004: Bush, R., 3,964,522; Kerry, D., 3,583,544; Nader, Ref., 32,971; Badnarik, Libertarian, 11,996; Peroutka, Constitution, 6,626; Cobb, Green, 3,917; Brown, Soc., 3,502; Harris, Soc. Wkrs., 2,732.

2000: Bush, R., 2,912,790; Gore, D., 2,912,253; Nader, Green, 97,488; Buchanan, Reform, 17,484; Browne, Libertarian, 16,415; Hagelin, Nat. Law, 2,281; Moorehead, Wkrs. World, 1,804; Phillips, Constit., 1,371; McReynolds, Soc., 622; Harris, Soc. Wkrs., 562.

1996: Clinton, D., 2,545,968; Dole, R., 2,243,324; Perot, Ref., 483,776; Browne, Libertarian, 23,312.

1992: Bush, R., 2,171,781; Clinton, D., 2,071,651; Perot, Ind., 1,052,481; Marrou, Libertarian, 15,068.

1988: Bush, R., 2,616,597; Dukakis, D., 1,655,851; Paul, Lib., 19,796, Fulani, New Alliance, 6,655.

1984: Reagan, R., 2,728,775; Mondale, D., 1,448,344.

1980: Reagan, R., 2,046,951; Carter, D., 1,419,475; Anderson, Ind., 189,692; Clark, Libertarian, 30,524; write-in, 285.

1976: Carter, D., 1,636,000; Ford, R., 1,469,531; McCarthy, Ind., 23,643; Anderson, Amer., 21,325.

1972: Nixon, R., 1,857,759; McGovern, D., 718,117; scattered, 7,407.

1968: Nixon, R., 886,804; Humphrey, D., 676,794; Wallace, 3rd Party, 624,207.

1964: Johnson, D., 948,540; Goldwater, R., 905,941.

1960: Nixon, R., 795,476; Kennedy, D., 748,700.

1956: Eisenhower, R., 643,849; Stevenson, D., 480,371.

1952: Eisenhower, R., 544,036; Stevenson, D., 444,950; scattered, 351.

1948: Truman, D., 281,988; Dewey, R., 194,280; Thurmond, States' Rights, 89,755; Wallace, Prog., 11,620.

Georgia

2004: Bush, R., 1,914,254; Kerry, D., 1,366,149; Badnarik, Libertarian, 18,387.

2000: Bush, R., 1,419,720; Gore, D., 1,116,230; Browne, Libertarian, 36,332; Buchanan, Independent, 10,926.

1996: Dole, R., 1,080,843; Clinton, D., 1,053,849; Perot, Ref., 146,337; Browne, Libertarian, 17,870.

1992: Clinton, D., 1,008,966; Bush, R., 995,252; Perot, Ind., 309,657; Marrou, Libertarian, 7,110.

1988: Bush, R., 1,081,331; Dukakis, D., 714,792; Paul, Lib., 8,435; Fulani, New Alliance, 5,099.

1984: Reagan, R., 1,068,722; Mondale, D., 706,628.

1980: Carter, D., 890,955; Reagan, R., 654,168; Anderson, Ind., 36,055; Clark, Libertarian, 15,627.

1976: Carter, D., 979,409; Ford, R., 483,743; write-in, 4,306.

1972: Nixon, R., 881,496; McGovern, D., 289,529; Schmitz, Amer., 812; scattered, 2,935.

1968: Wallace, 3rd Party, 535,550; Nixon, R., 380,111; Humphrey, D., 334,440; write-in, 162.

1964: Goldwater, R., 616,600; Johnson, D., 522,557.

1960: Kennedy, D., 458,638; Nixon, R., 274,472; write-in, 239.

1956: Stevenson, D., 444,388; Eisenhower, R., 222,778; Andrews, Ind., write-in, 1,754.

1952: Stevenson, D., 456,823; Eisenhower, R., 198,979; Liberty Party, 1.

1948: Truman, D., 254,646; Thurmond, States' Rights, 85,055; Dewey, R., 76,691; Wallace, Prog., 1,636; Watson, Proh., 732.

Hawaii

2004: Kerry, D., 231,708; Bush, R., 194,191; Cobb, Green, 1,737; Badnarik, Libertarian, 1,377.

2000: Gore, D., 205,286; Bush, R., 137,845; Nader, Green, 21,623; Browne, Libertarian, 1,477; Buchanan, Reform, 1,071; Phillips, Constitution, 343; Hagelin, Natural Law, 306.

1996: Clinton, D., 205,012; Dole, R., 113,943; Perot, Ref., 27,358; Nader, Green, 10,386; Browne, Libertarian, 2,493; Hagelin, Natural Law, 570; Phillips, Taxpayers, 358.

1992: Clinton, D., 179,310; Bush, R., 136,822; Perot, Ind., 53,003; Gritz, Populist/America First, 1,452; Marrou, Libertarian, 1,119.

1988: Dukakis, D., 192,364; Bush, R., 158,625; Paul, Lib., 1,999; Fulani, New Alliance, 1,003.

1984: Reagan, R., 184,934; Mondale, D., 147,098; Bergland, Libertarian, 2,167.

1980: Carter, D., 135,879; Reagan, R., 130,112; Anderson, Ind., 32,021; Clark, Libertarian, 3,269; Commoner, Citizens, 1,548; Hall, Com., 458.

1976: Carter, D., 147,375; Ford, R., 140,003; MacBride, Libertarian, 3,923.

1972: Nixon, R., 168,865; McGovern, D., 101,409.

1968: Humphrey, D., 141,324; Nixon, R., 91,425; Wallace, 3rd Party, 3,469.

1964: Johnson, D., 163,249; Goldwater, R., 44,022.

1960: Kennedy, D., 92,410; Nixon, R., 92,295.

Idaho

2004: Bush, R., 409,235; Kerry, D., 181,098; Badnarik, Libertarian, 3,844; Peroutka, Constitution, 3,084.

2000: Bush, R., 336,937; Gore, D., 138,637; Buchanan, Reform, 7,615; Browne, Libertarian, 3,488; Phillips, Constitution, 1,469; Hagelin, Natural Law, 1,177.

1996: Dole, R., 256,595; Clinton, D., 165,443; Perot, Ref., 62,518; Browne, Libertarian, 3,325; Phillips, Taxpayers, 2,230; Hagelin, Natural Law, 1,600.

1992: Bush, R., 202,645; Clinton, D., 137,013; Perot, Ind., 130,395; Gritz, Populist/America First, 10,281; Marrou, Libertarian, 1,167.

1988: Bush, R., 253,881; Dukakis, D., 147,272; Paul, Lib., 5,313; Fulani, Ind., 2,502.

1984: Reagan, R., 297,523; Mondale, D., 108,510; Bergland, Libertarian, 2,823.

1980: Reagan, R., 290,699; Carter, D., 110,192; Anderson, Ind., 27,058; Clark, Libertarian, 8,425; Rarick, Amer., 1,057.

1976: Ford, R., 204,151; Carter, D., 126,549; Maddox, Amer., 5,935; MacBride, Libertarian, 3,558; LaRouche, U.S. Labor, 739.

1972: Nixon, R., 199,384; McGovern, D., 80,826; Schmitz, Amer., 28,869; Spock, Peoples, 903.

1968: Nixon, R., 165,369; Humphrey, D., 89,273; Wallace, 3rd Party, 36,541.

1964: Johnson, D., 148,920; Goldwater, Rep., 143,557.

1960: Nixon, R., 161,597; Kennedy, D., 138,853.

1956: Eisenhower, R., 166,979; Stevenson, D., 105,868; Andrews, Ind., 126; write-in, 16.

1952: Eisenhower, R., 180,707; Stevenson, D., 95,081; Hallinan, Prog., 443; write-in, 23.

1948: Truman, D., 107,370; Dewey, R., 101,514; Wallace, Prog., 4,972; Watson, Proh., 628; Thomas, Soc., 332.

Illinois

2004: Kerry, D., 2,891,550; Bush, R., 2,345,946; Badnarik, Libertarian, 32,442.

2000: Gore, D., 2,589,026; Bush, R., 2,019,421; Nader, Green, 103,759; Buchanan, Ind., 16,106; Browne, Libertarian, 11,623; Hagelin, Reform, 2,127.

1996: Clinton, D., 2,341,744; Dole, R., 1,587,021; Perot, Ref., 346,408; Browne, Libertarian, 22,548; Phillips, Taxpayers, 7,606; Hagelin, Natural Law, 4,606.

1992: Clinton, D., 2,453,350; Bush, R., 1,734,096; Perot, Ind., 840,515; Marrou, Libertarian, 9,218; Fulani, New Alliance, 5,267; Gritz, Populist/America First, 3,577; Hagelin, Natural Law, 2,751; Warren, Soc. Workers, 1,361.

1988: Bush, R., 2,310,939; Dukakis, D., 2,215,940; Paul, Lib., 14,944; Fulani, Solid., 10,276.

1984: Reagan, R., 2,707,103; Mondale, D., 2,086,499; Bergland, Libertarian, 10,086.

1980: Reagan, R., 2,358,049; Carter, D., 1,981,413; Anderson, Ind., 346,754; Clark, Libertarian, 38,939; Commoner, Citizens, 10,692; Hall, Com., 9,711; Griswold, Workers World, 2,257; DeBerry, Soc. Workers, 1,302; write-in, 604.

1976: Ford, R., 2,364,269; Carter, D., 2,271,295; McCarthy, Ind., 55,939; Hall, Com., 9,250; MacBride, Libertarian, 8,057; Camejo, Soc. Workers, 3,615; Levin, Soc. Labor, 2,422; LaRouche, U.S. Labor, 2,018; write-in, 1,968.

1972: Nixon, Rep. 2,788,179; McGovern, D., 1,913,472; Fisher, Soc. Labor, 12,344; Hall, Com., 4,541; Schmitz, Amer., 2,471; others, 2,229.

1968: Nixon, R., 2,174,774; Humphrey, D., 2,039,814; Wallace, 3rd Party, 390,958; Blomen, Soc. Labor, 13,878; write-in, 325.

1964: Johnson, D., 2,796,833; Goldwater, R., 1,905,946; write-in, 62.

1960: Kennedy, D., 2,377,846; Nixon, R., 2,368,988; Hass, Soc. Labor, 10,560; write-in, 15.

1956: Eisenhower, R., 2,623,327; Stevenson, D., 1,775,682; Hass, Soc. Labor, 8,342; write-in, 56.

1952: Eisenhower, R., 2,457,327; Stevenson, D., 2,013,920; Hass, Soc. Labor, 9,363; write-in, 448.

1948: Truman, D., 1,994,715; Dewey, R., 1,961,103; Watson, Proh., 11,959; Thomas, Soc., 11,522; Teichert, Soc. Labor, 3,118.

Indiana

2004: Bush, R., 1,479,438; Kerry, D., 969,011; Badnarik, Libertarian, 18,058.

2000: Bush, R., 1,245,836; Gore, D., 901,980; Buchanan, Ind., 16,959; Browne, Libertarian, 15,530.

1996: Dole, R., 1,006,693; Clinton, D., 887,424; Perot, Ref., 224,299; Browne, Libertarian, 15,632.

1992: Bush, R., 989,375; Clinton, D., 848,420; Perot, Ind., 455,934; Marrou, Libertarian, 7,936; Fulani, New Alliance, 2,583.

1988: Bush, R., 1,297,763; Dukakis, D., 860,643; Fulani, New Alliance, 10,215.

1984: Reagan, R., 1,377,230; Mondale, D., 841,481; Bergland, Libertarian, 6,741.

1980: Reagan, R., 1,255,656; Carter, D., 844,197; Anderson, Ind., 111,639; Clark, Libertarian, 19,627; Commoner, Citizens, 4,852; Greaves, Amer., 4,750; Hall, Com., 702; DeBerry, Soc., 610.

1976: Ford, R., 1,185,958; Carter, D., 1,014,714; Anderson, Amer., 14,048; Camejo, Soc. Workers, 5,695; LaRouche, U.S. Labor, 1,947.

1972: Nixon, R., 1,405,154; McGovern, D., 708,568; Reed, Soc. Workers, 5,575; Spock, Peace and Freedom, 4,544; Fisher, Soc. Labor, 1,688.

1968: Nixon, R., 1,067,885; Humphrey, D., 806,659; Wallace, 3rd Party, 243,108; Munn, Proh., 4,616; Halstead, Soc. Workers, 1,293; Gregory, write-in, 36.

1964: Johnson, D., 1,170,848; Goldwater, R., 911,118; Munn, Proh., 8,266; Hass, Soc. Labor, 1,374.

1960: Nixon, R., 1,175,120; Kennedy, D., 952,358; Decker, Proh., 6,746; Hass, Soc. Labor, 1,136.

1956: Eisenhower, R., 1,182,811; Stevenson, D., 783,908; Holtwick, Proh., 6,554; Hass, Soc. Labor, 1,334.

1952: Eisenhower, R., 1,136,259; Stevenson, D., 801,530; Hamblen, Proh., 15,335; Hallinan, Prog., 1,222; Hass, Soc. Labor, 979.

1948: Dewey, R., 821,079; Truman, D., 807,833; Watson, Proh., 14,711; Wallace, Prog., 9,649; Thomas, Soc., 2,179; Teichert, Soc. Labor, 763.

Iowa

2004: Bush, R., 751,957; Kerry, D., 741,898; Nader, Petitioning Cand., 5,973; Badnarik, Libertarian, 2,992; Peroutka, Constitution, 1,304; Cobb, Green, 1,141; Harris, Soc. Wkrs., 373; Van Auken, Petitioning Cand., 176.

2000: Gore, D., 638,517; Bush, R., 634,373; Nader, Green, 29,374; Buchanan, Reform, 5,731; Browne, Libertarian, 3,209; Hagelin, Ind., 2,281; Phillips, Constitution, 613; Harris, Soc. Workers, 190; McReynolds, Soc., 107.

1996: Clinton, D., 620,258; Dole, R., 492,644; Perot, Ref., 105,159; Nader, Green, 6,550; Hagelin, Natural Law, 3,349; Browne, Libertarian, 2,315; Phillips, Taxpayers, 2,229; Harris, Soc. Workers, 331.

1992: Clinton, D., 586,353; Bush, R., 504,891; Perot, Ind., 253,468; Hagelin, Natural Law, 3,079; Gritz, Populist/America First, 1,177; Marrou, Libertarian, 1,076.

1988: Dukakis, D., 670,557; Bush, R., 545,355; LaRouche, Ind., 3,526; Paul, Lib., 2,494.

1984: Reagan, R., 703,088; Mondale, D., 605,620; Bergland, Libertarian, 1,844.

1980: Reagan, R., 676,026; Carter, D., 508,672; Anderson, Ind., 115,633; Clark, Libertarian, 13,123; Commoner, Citizens, 2,273; McReynolds, Socialist, 534; Hall, Com., 298; DeBerry, Soc. Wrkrs., 244; Greaves, Amer., 189; Bubar, Statesman, 150; scattered, 519.

1976: Ford, R., 632,863; Carter, D., 619,931; McCarthy, Ind., 20,051; Anderson, Amer., 3,040; MacBride, Libertarian, 1,452.

1972: Nixon, R., 706,207; McGovern, D., 496,206; Schmitz, Amer., 22,056; Jenness, Soc. Workers, 488; Hall, Com., 272; Green, Universal, 199; Fisher, Soc. Labor, 195; scattered, 321.

1968: Nixon, R., 619,106; Humphrey, D., 476,699; Wallace, 3rd Party, 66,422; Halstead, Soc. Workers, 3,377; Cleaver, Peace and Freedom, 1,332; Munn, Proh., 362; Blomen, Soc. Labor, 241.

1964: Johnson, D., 733,030; Goldwater, R., 449,148; Munn, Proh., 1,902; Hass, Soc. Labor, 182; DeBerry, Soc. Workers, 159.

1960: Nixon, R., 722,381; Kennedy, D., 550,565; Hass, Soc. Labor, 230; write-in, 634.

1956: Eisenhower, R., 729,187; Stevenson, D., 501,858; Andrews (A.C.P. of Iowa), 3,202; Hoopes, Soc., 192; Hass, Soc. Labor, 125.

1952: Eisenhower, R., 808,906; Stevenson, D., 451,513; Hallinan, Prog., 5,085; Hamblen, Proh., 2,882; Hoopes, Soc., 219; Hass, Soc. Labor, 139; scattered, 29.

1948: Truman, D., 522,380; Dewey, R., 494,018; Wallace, Prog., 12,125; Teichert, Soc. Labor, 4,274; Watson, Proh., 3,382; Thomas, Soc., 1,829; Dobbs, Soc. Workers, 26.

Kansas

2004: Bush, R., 736,456; Kerry, D., 434,993; Nader, Ref., 9,348; Badnarik, Libertarian, 4,013; Peroutka, Ind., 2,899.

2000: Bush, R., 622,332; Gore, D., 399,276; Nader, Ind., 36,086; Buchanan, Reform, 7,370; Browne, Libertarian, 4,525; Hagelin, Ind., 1,373; Phillips, Constitution, 1,254.

1996: Dole, R., 583,245; Clinton, D., 387,659; Perot, Ref., 92,639; Browne, Libertarian, 4,557; Phillips, Ind., 3,519; Hagelin, Ind., 1,655.

1992: Bush, R., 449,951; Clinton, D., 390,434; Perot, Ind., 312,358; Marrou, Libertarian, 4,314.

1988: Bush, R., 554,049; Dukakis, D., 422,636; Paul, Ind., 12,553; Fulani, Ind., 3,806.

1984: Reagan, R., 674,646; Mondale, D., 332,471; Bergland, Libertarian, 3,585.

1980: Reagan, R., 566,812; Carter, D., 326,150; Anderson, Ind., 68,231; Clark, Libertarian, 14,470; Shelton, Amer., 1,555; Hall, Com., 967; Bubar, Statesman, 821; Rarick, Conservative, 789.

1976: Ford, R., 502,752; Carter, D., 430,421; McCarthy, Ind., 13,185; Anderson, Amer., 4,724; MacBride, Libertarian, 3,242; Maddox, Conservative, 2,118; Bubar, Proh., 1,403.

1972: Nixon, R., 619,812; McGovern, D., 270,287; Schmitz, Conservative, 21,808; Munn, Proh., 4,188.

1968: Nixon, R., 478,674; Humphrey, D., 302,996; Wallace, 3rd Party, 88,921; Munn, Proh., 2,192.

1964: Johnson, D., 464,028; Goldwater, R., 386,579; Munn, Proh., 5,393; Hass, Soc. Labor, 1,901.

1960: Nixon, R., 561,474; Kennedy, D., 363,213; Decker, Proh., 4,138.

1956: Eisenhower, R., 566,878; Stevenson, D., 296,317; Holtwick, Proh., 3,048.

1952: Eisenhower, R., 616,302; Stevenson, D., 273,296; Hamblen, Proh., 6,038; Hoopes, Soc., 530.

1948: Dewey, R., 423,039; Truman, D., 351,902; Watson, Proh., 6,468; Wallace, Prog., 4,603; Thomas, Soc., 2,807.

Kentucky

2004: Bush, R., 1,069,439; Kerry, D., 712,733; Nader, Ind., 8,856; Badnarik, Libertarian, 2,619; Peroutka, Constitution, 2,213.

2000: Bush, R., 872,520; Gore, D., 638,923; Nader, Green, 23,118; Buchanan, Reform, 4,152; Browne, Libertarian, 2,885; Hagelin, Natural Law, 1,513; Phillips, Constitution, 915.

1996: Clinton, D., 636,614; Dole, R., 623,283; Perot, Ref., 120,396; Browne, Libertarian, 4,009; Phillips, Taxpayers, 2,204; Hagelin, Natural Law, 1,493.

1992: Clinton, D., 665,104; Bush, R., 617,178; Perot, Ind., 203,944; Marrou, Libertarian, 4,513.

1988: Bush, R., 734,281; Dukakis, D., 580,368; Duke, Pop., 4,494; Paul, Lib., 2,118.

1984: Reagan, R., 815,345; Mondale, D., 536,756.

1980: Reagan, R., 635,274; Carter, D., 616,417; Anderson, Ind., 31,127; Clark, Libertarian, 5,531; McCormack, Respect For Life, 4,233; Commoner, Citizens, 1,304; Pulley, Socialist, 393; Hall, Com., 348.

1976: Carter, D., 615,717; Ford, R., 531,852; Anderson, Amer., 8,308; McCarthy, Ind., 6,837; Maddox, Amer. Ind., 2,328; MacBride, Libertarian, 814.

1972: Nixon, R., 676,446; McGovern, D., 371,159; Schmitz, Amer., 17,627; Spock, Peoples, 1,118; Jenness, Soc. Workers, 685; Hall, Com., 464.

1968: Nixon, R., 462,411; Humphrey, D., 397,547; Wallace, 3rd Party, 193,098; Halstead, Soc. Workers, 2,843.

1964: Johnson, D., 669,659; Goldwater, R., 372,977; Kasper, Natl. States Rights, 3,469.

1960: Nixon, R., 602,607; Kennedy, D., 521,855.

1956: Eisenhower, R., 572,192; Stevenson, D., 476,453; Byrd, States' Rights, 2,657; Holtwick, Proh., 2,145; Hass, Soc. Labor, 358.

1952: Stevenson, D., 495,729; Eisenhower, R., 495,029; Hamblen, Proh., 1,161; Hass, Soc. Labor, 893; Hallinan, Proh., 336.

1948: Truman, D., 466,756; Dewey, R., 341,210; Thurmond, States' Rights, 10,411; Wallace, Prog., 1,567; Thomas, Soc., 1,284; Watson, Proh., 1,245; Teichert, Soc. Labor, 185.

Louisiana

2004: Bush, R., 1,102,169; Kerry, D., 820,299; Nader, Better Life, 7,032; Peroutka, Constitution, 5,203; Badnarik, Libertarian, 2,781; Brown, Protect Wking Fam., 1,795; Amondson, Prohib., 1,566; Cobb, Green, 1,276; Harris, Soc. Wkrs., 985.

2000: Bush, R., 927,871; Gore, D., 792,344; Nader, Green, 20,473; Buchanan, Reform, 14,356; Phillips, Constitution, 5,483; Browne, Libertarian, 2,951; Harris, Soc. Workers, 1,103; Hagelin, Natural Law, 1,075.

1996: Clinton, D., 927,837; Dole, R., 712,586; Perot, Ref., 123,293; Browne, Libertarian, 7,499; Nader, Liberty, Ecology, Community, 4,719; Phillips, Taxpayers, 3,366; Hagelin, Natural Law, 2,981; Moorehead, Workers World, 1,678.

1992: Clinton, D., 815,971; Bush, R., 733,386; Perot, Ind., 211,478; Gritz, Populist/America First, 18,545; Marrou, Libertarian, 3,155; Daniels, Ind., 1,663; Phillips, U.S. Taxpayers, 1,552; Fulani, New Alliance, 1,434; LaRouche, Ind., 1,136.

1988: Bush, R., 883,702; Dukakis, D., 717,460; Duke, Pop., 18,612; Paul, Lib., 4,115.

1984: Reagan, R., 1,037,299; Mondale, D., 651,586; Bergland, Libertarian, 1,876.

1980: Reagan, R., 792,853; Carter, D., 708,453; Anderson, Ind., 26,345; Rarick, Amer. Ind., 10,333; Clark, Libertarian, 8,240; Commoner, Citizens, 1,584; DeBerry, Soc. Work., 783.

1976: Carter, D., 661,365; Ford, R., 587,446; Maddox, Amer., 10,058; Hall, Com., 7,417; McCarthy, Ind., 6,588; MacBride, Libertarian, 3,325.

1972: Nixon, R., 686,852; McGovern, D., 298,142; Schmitz, Amer., 52,099; Jenness, Soc. Workers, 14,398.

1968: Wallace, 3rd Party, 530,300; Humphrey, D., 309,615; Nixon, R., 257,535.

1964: Goldwater, R., 509,225; Johnson, D., 387,068.

1960: Kennedy, D., 407,339; Nixon, R., 230,890; States' Rights (unpledged), 169,572.

1956: Eisenhower, R., 329,047; Stevenson, D., 243,977; Andrews, States' Rights, 44,520.

1952: Stevenson, D., 345,027; Eisenhower, R., 306,925.

1948: Thurmond, States' Rights, 204,290; Truman, D., 136,344; Dewey, R., 72,657; Wallace, Prog., 3,035.

Maine

2004: Kerry, D., 396,842; Bush, R., 330,201; Nader, Better Life, 8,069; Cobb, Green, 2,936; Badnarik, Libertarian, 1,965; Peroutka, Constitution, 735.

2000: Gore, D., 319,951; Bush, R., 286,616; Nader, Green, 37,127; Buchanan, Reform, 4,443; Browne, Libertarian, 3,074; Phillips, Constitution, 579.

1996: Clinton, D., 312,788; Dole, R., 186,378; Perot, Ref., 85,970; Nader, Green, 15,279; Browne, Libertarian, 2,996; Phillips, Taxpayers, 1,517; Hagelin, Natural Law, 825.

1992: Clinton, D., 263,420; Perot, Ind., 206,820; Bush, R., 206,504; Marrou, Libertarian, 1,681.

1988: Bush, R., 307,131; Dukakis, D., 243,569; Paul, Lib., 2,700; Fulani, New Alliance, 1,405.

1984: Reagan, R., 336,500; Mondale, D., 214,515.

1980: Reagan, R., 238,522; Carter, D., 220,974; Anderson, Ind., 53,327; Clark, Libertarian, 5,119; Commoner, Citizens, 4,394; Hall, Com., 591; write-in, 84.

1976: Ford, R., 236,320; Carter, D., 232,279; McCarthy, Ind., 10,874; Bubar, Proh., 3,495.

1972: Nixon, R., 256,458; McGovern, D., 160,584; scattered, 229.

1968: Humphrey, D., 217,312; Nixon, R., 169,254; Wallace, 3rd Party, 6,370.

1964: Johnson, D., 262,264; Goldwater, R., 118,701.

1960: Nixon, R., 240,608; Kennedy, D., 181,159.

1956: Eisenhower, R., 249,238; Stevenson, D., 102,468.

1952: Eisenhower, R., 232,353; Stevenson, D., 118,806; Hallinan, Prog., 332; Hass, Soc. Labor, 156; Hoopes, Soc., 138; scattered, 1.

1948: Dewey, R., 150,234; Truman, D., 111,916; Wallace, Prog., 1,884; Thomas, Soc., 547; Teichert, Soc. Labor, 206.

Maryland

2004: Kerry, D., 1,334,493; Bush, R., 1,024,703; Nader, Populist, 11,854; Badnarik, Libertarian, 6,094; Cobb, Green, 3,632; Peroutka, Constitution, 3,421.

2000: Gore, D., 1,144,008; Bush, R., 813,827; Nader, Green, 53,768; Browne, Libertarian, 5,310; Buchanan, Reform., 4,248; Phillips, Constitution, 918.

1996: Clinton, D., 966,207; Dole, R., 681,530; Perot, Ref., 115,812; Browne, Libertarian, 8,765; Phillips, Taxpayers, 3,402; Hagelin, Natural Law, 2,517.

1992: Clinton, D., 988,571; Bush, R., 707,094; Perot, Ind., 281,414; Marrou, Libertarian, 4,715; Fulani, New Alliance, 2,786.

1988: Bush, R., 876,167; Dukakis, D., 826,304; Paul, Lib., 6,748; Fulani, New Alliance, 5,115.

1984: Reagan, R., 879,918; Mondale, D., 787,935; Bergland, Libertarian, 5,721.

1980: Carter, D., 726,161; Reagan, R., 680,606; Anderson, Ind., 119,537; Clark, Libertarian, 14,192.

1976: Carter, D., 759,612; Ford, R., 672,661.

1972: Nixon, R., 829,305; McGovern, D., 505,781; Schmitz, Amer., 18,726.

1968: Humphrey, D., 538,310; Nixon, R., 517,995; Wallace, 3rd Party, 178,734.

1964: Johnson, D., 730,912; Goldwater, R., 385,495; write-in, 50.

1960: Kennedy, D., 565,800; Nixon, R., 489,538.

1956: Eisenhower, R., 559,738; Stevenson, D., 372,613.

1952: Eisenhower, R., 499,424; Stevenson, D., 395,337; Hallinan, Prog., 7,313.

1948: Dewey, R., 294,814; Truman, D., 286,521; Wallace, Prog., 9,983; Thomas, Soc., 2,941; Thurmond, States' Rights, 2,476; Wright, write-in, 2,294.

Massachusetts

2004: Kerry, D., 1,803,800; Bush, R., 1,071,109; Badnarik, Libertarian, 15,022; Cobb, Green, 10,623.

2000: Gore, D., 1,616,487; Bush, R., 878,502; Nader, Green, 173,564; Browne, Libertarian, 16,366; Buchanan, Reform, 11,149; Hagelin, Natural Law, 2,884.

1996: Clinton, D., 1,571,509; Dole, R., 718,058; Perot, Ref., 227,206; Browne, Libertarian, 20,424; Hagelin, Natural Law, 5,183; Moorehead, Workers World, 3,276.

1992: Clinton, D., 1,318,639; Bush, R., 805,039; Perot, Ind., 630,731; Marrou, Libertarian, 9,021; Fulani, New Alliance, 3,172; Phillips, U.S. Taxpayers, 2,218; Hagelin, Natural Law, 1,812; LaRouche, Ind., 1,027.

1988: Dukakis, D., 1,401,415; Bush, R., 1,194,635; Paul, Lib., 24,251; Fulani, New Alliance, 9,561.

1984: Reagan, R., 1,310,936; Mondale, D., 1,239,606.

1980: Reagan, R., 1,057,631; Carter, D., 1,053,802; Anderson, Ind., 382,539; Clark, Libertarian, 22,038; DeBerry, Soc. Workers, 3,735; Commoner, Citizens, 2,056; McReynolds, Soc., 62; Bubar, Statesman, 34; Griswold, Workers World, 19; scattered, 2,382.

1976: Carter, D., 1,429,475; Ford, R., 1,030,276; McCarthy, Ind., 65,637; Camejo, Soc. Workers, 8,138; Anderson, Amer., 7,555; La Rouche, U.S. Labor, 4,922; MacBride, Libertarian, 135.

1972: McGovern, D., 1,332,540; Nixon, R., 1,112,078; Jenness, Soc. Workers, 10,600; Schmitz, Amer., 2,877; Fisher, Soc. Labor, 129; Spock, Peoples, 101; Hall, Com., 46; Hospers, Libertarian, 43; scattered, 342.

1968: Humphrey, D., 1,469,218; Nixon, R., 766,844; Wallace, 3rd Party, 87,088; Blomen, Soc. Labor, 6,180; Munn, Proh., 2,369; scattered, 53; blanks, 25,394.

1964: Johnson, D., 1,786,422; Goldwater, R., 549,727; Hass, Soc. Labor, 4,755; Munn, Proh., 3,735; scattered, 159; blank, 48,104.

1960: Kennedy, D., 1,487,174; Nixon, R., 976,750; Hass, Soc. Labor, 3,892; Decker, Proh., 1,633; others, 31; blank and void, 26,024.

1956: Eisenhower, R., 1,393,197; Stevenson, D., 948,190; Hass, Soc. Labor, 5,573; Holtwick, Proh., 1,205; others, 341.

1952: Eisenhower, R., 1,292,325; Stevenson, D., 1,083,525; Hallinan, Prog., 4,636; Hass, Soc. Labor, 1,957; Hamblen, Proh., 886; scattered, 69; blanks, 41,150.

1948: Truman, D., 1,151,788; Dewey, R., 909,370; Wallace, Prog., 38,157; Teichert, Soc. Labor, 5,535; Watson, Proh., 1,663.

Michigan

2004: Kerry, D., 2,479,183; Bush, R., 2,313,746; Nader, Ind., 24,035; Badnarik, Libertarian, 10,552; Cobb, Green, 5,325; Peroutka, U.S. Taxpayers, 4,980; Brown, Nat. Law, 1,431.

2000: Gore, D., 2,170,418; Bush, R., 1,953,139; Nader, Green, 84,165; Browne, Libertarian, 16,711; Phillips, U.S. Taxpayers, 3,791; Hagelin, Natural Law, 2,426.

1996: Clinton, D., 1,989,653; Dole, R., 1,481,212; Perot, Ref., 336,670; Browne, Libertarian, 27,670; Hagelin, Natural Law, 4,254; Moorehead, Workers World, 3,153; White, Soc. Equality, 1,554.

1992: Clinton, D., 1,871,182; Bush, R., 1,554,940; Perot, Ind., 824,813; Marrou, Libertarian, 10,175; Phillips, U.S. Taxpayers, 8,263; Hagelin, Natural Law, 2,954.

1988: Bush, R., 1,965,486; Dukakis, D., 1,675,783; Paul, Lib., 18,336; Fulani, Ind., 2,513.

1984: Reagan, R., 2,251,571; Mondale, D., 1,529,638; Bergland, Libertarian, 10,055.

1980: Reagan, R., 1,915,225; Carter, D., 1,661,532; Anderson, Ind., 275,223; Clark, Libertarian, 41,597; Commoner, Citizens, 11,930; Hall, Com., 3,262; Griswold, Workers World, 30; Greaves, Amer., 21; Bubar, Statesman, 9.

1976: Ford, R., 1,893,742; Carter, D., 1,696,714; McCarthy, Ind., 47,905; MacBride, Libertarian, 5,406; Wright, People's, 3,504; Camejo, Soc. Workers, 1,804; LaRouche, U.S. Labor, 1,366; Levin, Soc. Labor, 1,148; scattered, 2,160.

1972: Nixon, R., 1,961,721; McGovern, D., 1,459,435; Schmitz, Amer., 63,321; Fisher, Soc. Labor, 2,437; Jenness, Soc. Workers, 1,603; Hall, Com., 1,210.

1968: Humphrey, D., 1,593,082; Nixon, R., 1,370,665; Wallace, 3rd Party, 331,968; Halstead, Soc. Workers, 4,099; Blomen, Soc. Labor, 1,762; Cleaver, New Politics, 4,585; Munn, Proh., 60; scattered, 29.

1964: Johnson, D., 2,136,615; Goldwater, R., 1,060,152; DeBerry, Soc. Workers, 3,817; Hass, Soc. Labor, 1,704; Proh. (no candidate listed), 699; scattered, 145.

1960: Kennedy, D., 1,687,269; Nixon, R., 1,620,428; Dobbs, Soc. Workers, 4,347; Decker, Proh., 2,029; Daly, Tax Cut, 1,767; Hass, Soc. Labor, 1,718; Ind. Amer., 539.

1956: Eisenhower, R., 1,713,647; Stevenson, D., 1,359,898; Holtwick, Proh., 6,923.

1952: Eisenhower, R., 1,551,529; Stevenson, D., 1,230,657; Hamblen, Proh., 10,331; Hallinan, Prog., 3,922; Hass, Soc. Labor, 1,495; Dobbs, Soc. Workers, 655; scattered, 3.

1948: Dewey, R., 1,038,595; Truman, D., 1,003,448; Wallace, Prog., 46,515; Watson, Proh., 13,052; Thomas, Soc., 6,063; Teichert, Soc. Labor, 1,263; Dobbs, Soc. Workers, 672.

Minnesota

2004: Kerry, D., 1,445,014; Bush, R., 1,346,695; Nader, Better Life, 18,683; Badnarik, Libertarian, 4,639; Cobb, Green, 4,408; Peroutka, Constitution, 3,074; Harens, other, 2,387; Van Auken, Soc. Equal., 539; Calero, Soc. Wkrs., 416.

2000: Gore, D., 1,168,266; Bush, R., 1,109,659; Nader, Green, 126,696; Buchanan, Reform Minnesota, 22,166; Browne, Libertarian, 5,282; Phillips, Constitution, 3,272; Hagelin, Reform, 2,294; Harris, Soc. Workers, 1,022.

1996: Clinton, D., 1,120,438; Dole, R., 766,476; Perot, Ref., 257,704; Nader, Green, 24,908; Browne, Libertarian, 8,271; Peron, Grass Roots, 4,898; Phillips, Taxpayers, 3,416; Hagelin, Natural Law, 1,808; Birrenbach, Ind. Grass Roots, 787; Harris, Soc. Workers, 684; White, Soc. Equality, 347.

1992: Clinton, D., 1,020,997; Bush, R., 747,841; Perot, Ind., 562,506; Marrou, Libertarian, 3,373; Gritz, Populist/America First, 3,363; Hagelin, Natural Law, 1,406.

1988: Dukakis, D., 1,109,471; Bush, R., 962,337; McCarthy, Minn. Prog., 5,403; Paul, Lib., 5,109.

1984: Mondale, D., 1,036,364; Reagan, R., 1,032,603; Bergland, Libertarian, 2,996.

1980: Carter, D., 954,173; Reagan, R., 873,268; Anderson, Ind., 174,997; Clark, Libertarian, 31,593; Commoner, Citizens, 8,406; Hall, Com., 1,117; DeBerry, Soc. Workers, 711; Griswold, Workers World, 698; McReynolds, Soc., 536; write-in, 281.

1976: Carter, D., 1,070,440; Ford, R., 819,395; McCarthy, Ind., 35,490; Anderson, Amer., 13,592; Camejo, Soc. Workers, 4,149; MacBride, Libertarian, 3,529; Hall, Com., 1,092.

1972: Nixon, R., 898,269; McGovern, D., 802,346; Schmitz, Amer., 31,407; Fisher, Soc. Labor, 4,261; Spock, Peoples, 2,805; Jenness, Soc. Workers, 940; Hall, Com., 662; scattered, 962.

1968: Humphrey, D., 857,738; Nixon, R., 658,643; Wallace, 3rd Party, 68,931; Cleaver, Peace, 935; Halstead, Soc. Workers, 808; McCarthy, write-in, 585; Mitchell, Com., 415; Blomen, Ind. Gov't., 285; scattered, 2,613.

1964: Johnson, D., 991,117; Goldwater, R., 559,624; Hass, Industrial Gov., 2,544; DeBerry, Soc. Workers, 1,177.

1960: Kennedy, D., 779,933; Nixon, R., 757,915; Dobbs, Soc. Workers, 3,077; Industrial Gov., 962.

1956: Eisenhower, R., 719,302; Stevenson, D., 617,525; Hass, Soc. Labor (Ind. Gov.), 2,080; Dobbs, Soc. Workers, 1,098.

1952: Eisenhower, R., 763,211; Stevenson, D., 608,458; Hallinan, Prog., 2,666; Hass, Soc. Labor, 2,383; Hamblen, Proh., 2,147; Dobbs, Soc. Workers, 618.

1948: Truman, D., 692,966; Dewey, R., 483,617; Wallace, Prog., 27,866; Thomas, Soc., 4,646; Teichert, Soc. Labor, 2,525; Dobbs, Soc. Workers, 606.

Mississippi

2004: Bush, R., 684,981; Kerry, D., 458,094; Nader, Ref., 3,177; Badnarik, Libertarian, 1,793; Peroutka, Constitution, 1,759; Harris, Ind., 1,268; Cobb, Green, 1,073.

2000: Bush, R., 572,844; Gore, D., 404,614; Nader, Ind., 8,122; Phillips, Constitution, 3,267; Buchanan, Reform, 2,265; Browne, Libertarian, 2,009; Harris, Ind., 613; Hagelin, Natural Law, 450.

1996: Dole, R., 439,838; Clinton, D., 394,022; Perot, Ind. (Ref.), 52,222; Browne, Libertarian, 2,809; Phillips, Taxpayers, 2,314; Hagelin, Natural Law, 1,447; Collins, Ind., 1,205.

1992: Bush, R., 487,793; Clinton, D., 400,258; Perot, Ind., 85,626; Fulani, New Alliance, 2,625; Marrou, Libertarian, 2,154; Phillips, U.S. Taxpayers, 1,652; Hagelin, Natural Law, 1,140.

1988: Bush, R., 557,890; Dukakis, D., 363,921; Duke, Ind., 4,232; Paul, Lib., 3,329.

1984: Reagan, R., 582,377; Mondale, D., 352,192; Bergland, Libertarian, 2,336.

1980: Reagan, R., 441,089; Carter, D., 429,281; Anderson, Ind., 12,036; Clark, Libertarian, 5,465; Griswold, Workers World, 2,402; Pulley, Soc. Workers, 2,347.

1976: Carter, D., 381,309; Ford, R., 366,846; Anderson, Amer., 6,678; McCarthy, Ind., 4,074; Maddox, Ind., 4,049; Camejo, Soc. Workers, 2,805; MacBride, Libertarian, 2,609.

1972: Nixon, R., 505,125; McGovern, D., 126,782; Schmitz, Amer., 11,598; Jenness, Soc. Workers, 2,458.

1968: Wallace, 3rd Party, 415,349; Humphrey, D., 150,644; Nixon, R., 88,516.

1964: Goldwater, R., 356,528; Johnson, D., 52,618.

1960: Democratic unpledged electors, 116,248; Kennedy, D., 108,362; Nixon, R., 73,561. Mississippi's victorious slate of 8 unpledged Democratic electors cast their votes for Sen. Harry F. Byrd (D, VA).

1956: Stevenson, D., 144,498; Eisenhower, R., 56,372; Black and Tan Grand Old Party, 4,313; total, 60,685; Byrd, Ind., 42,966.

1952: Stevenson, D., 172,566; Eisenhower, Ind. vote pledged to Rep. candidate, 112,966.

1948: Thurmond, States' Rights, 167,538; Truman, D., 19,384; Dewey, R., 5,043; Wallace, Prog., 225.

Missouri

2004: Bush, R., 1,455,713; Kerry, D., 1,259,171; Badnarik, Libertarian, 9,831; Peroutka, Constitution, 5,355.

2000: Bush, R., 1,189,924; Gore, D., 1,111,138; Nader, Green, 38,515; Buchanan, Reform, 9,818; Browne, Libertarian, 7,436; Phillips, Constitution, 1,957; Hagelin, Natural Law, 1,104.

1996: Clinton, D., 1,025,935; Dole, R., 890,016; Perot, Ref., 217,188; Phillips, Taxpayers, 11,521; Browne, Libertarian, 10,522; Hagelin, Natural Law, 2,287.

1992: Clinton, D., 1,053,873; Bush, R., 811,159; Perot, Ind., 518,741; Marrou, Libertarian, 7,497.

1988: Bush, R., 1,084,953; Dukakis, D., 1,001,619; Fulani, New Alliance, 6,656; Paul, write-in, 434.

1984: Reagan, R., 1,274,188; Mondale, D., 848,583.

1980: Reagan, R., 1,074,181; Carter, D., 931,182; Anderson, Ind., 77,920; Clark, Libertarian, 14,422; DeBerry, Soc. Workers, 1,515; Commoner, Citizens, 573; write-in, 31.

1976: Carter, D., 999,163; Ford, R., 928,808; McCarthy, Ind., 24,329.

1972: Nixon, R., 1,154,058; McGovern, D., 698,531.

1968: Nixon, R., 811,932; Humphrey, D., 791,444; Wallace, 3rd Party, 206,126.

1964: Johnson, D., 1,164,344; Goldwater, R., 653,535.

1960: Kennedy, D., 972,201; Nixon, R., 962,221.

1956: Stevenson, D., 918,273; Eisenhower, R., 914,299.

1952: Eisenhower, R., 959,429; Stevenson, D., 929,830; Hallinan, Prog., 987; Hamblen, Proh., 885; MacArthur, Christian Nationalist, 302; America First, 233; Hoopes, Soc., 227; Hass, Soc. Labor, 169.

1948: Truman, D., 917,315; Dewey, R., 655,039; Wallace, Prog., 3,998; Thomas, Soc., 2,222.

Montana

2004: Bush, R., 266,063; Kerry, D., 173,710; Nader, Ind., 6,168; Peroutka, Constitution, 1,764; Badnarik, Libertarian, 1,733; Cobb, Green, 996.

2000: Bush, Rep, 240,178; Gore, D., 137,126; Nader, Green, 24,437; Buchanan, Reform, 5,697; Browne, Libertarian, 1,718; Phillips, Constitution, 1,155; Hagelin, Natural Law, 675.

1996: Dole, R., 179,652; Clinton, D., 167,922; Perot, Ref., 55,229; Browne, Libertarian, 2,526; Hagelin, Natural Law, 1,754.

1992: Clinton, D., 154,507; Bush, R., 144,207; Perot, Ind., 107,225; Gritz, Populist/America First, 3,658.

1988: Bush, R., 190,412; Dukakis, D., 168,936; Paul, Lib., 5,047; Fulani, New Alliance, 1,279.

1984: Reagan, R., 232,450; Mondale, D., 146,742; Bergland, Libertarian, 5,185.

1980: Reagan, R., 206,814; Carter, D., 118,032; Anderson, Ind., 29,281; Clark, Libertarian, 9,825.

1976: Ford, R., 173,703; Carter, D., 149,259; Anderson, Amer., 5,772.

1972: Nixon, R., 183,976; McGovern, D., 120,197; Schmitz, Amer., 13,430.

1968: Nixon, R., 138,835; Humphrey, D., 114,117; Wallace, 3rd Party, 20,015; Munn, Proh., 510; Caton, New Reform, 470; Halstead, Soc. Workers, 457.

1964: Johnson, D., 164,246; Goldwater, R., 113,032; Kasper, Natl. States' Rights, 519; Munn, Proh., 499; DeBerry, Soc. Workers, 332.

1960: Nixon, R., 141,841; Kennedy, D., 134,891; Decker, Proh., 456; Dobbs, Soc. Workers, 391.

1956: Eisenhower, R., 154,933; Stevenson, D., 116,238.

1952: Eisenhower, R., 157,394; Stevenson, D., 106,213; Hallinan, Prog., 723; Hamblen, Proh., 548; Hoopes, Soc., 159.

1948: Truman, D., 119,071; Dewey, R., 96,770; Wallace, Prog., 7,313; Thomas, Soc., 695; Watson, Proh., 429.

Nebraska

2004: Bush, R., 512,814; Kerry, D., 254,328; Nader, Petitioning Cand., 5,698; Badnarik, Libertarian, 2,041; Peroutka, Nebraska, 1,314; Cobb, Green, 978; Calero, Petitioning Cand., 82.

2000: Bush, R., 433,862; Gore, D., 231,780; Nader, Green, 24,540; Buchanan, Ind., 3,646; Browne, Libertarian, 2,245; Hagelin, Natural Law, 478; Phillips, Ind., 468.

1996: Dole, R., 363,467; Clinton, D., 236,761; Perot, Ref., 71,278; Browne, Libertarian, 2,792; Phillips, Ind., 1,928; Hagelin, Natural Law, 1,189.

1992: Bush, R., 343,678; Clinton, D., 216,864; Perot, Ind., 174,104; Marrou, Libertarian, 1,340.

1988: Bush, R., 397,956; Dukakis, D., 259,235; Paul, Lib., 2,534; Fulani, New Alliance, 1,740.

1984: Reagan, R., 459,135; Mondale, D., 187,475; Bergland, Libertarian, 2,075.

1980: Reagan, R., 419,214; Carter, D., 166,424; Anderson, Ind., 44,854; Clark, Libertarian, 9,041.

1976: Ford, R., 359,219; Carter, D., 233,287; McCarthy, Ind., 9,383; Maddox, Amer. Ind., 3,378; MacBride, Libertarian, 1,476.

1972: Nixon, R., 406,298; McGovern, D., 169,991; scattered, 817.

1968: Nixon, R., 321,163; Humphrey, D., 170,784; Wallace, 3rd Party, 44,904.

1964: Johnson, D., 307,307; Goldwater, R., 276,847.

1960: Nixon, R., 380,553; Kennedy, D., 232,542.

1956: Eisenhower, R., 378,108; Stevenson, D., 199,029.

1952: Eisenhower, R., 421,603; Stevenson, D., 188,057.

1948: Dewey, R., 264,774; Truman, D., 224,165.

Nevada

2004: Bush, R., 418,690; Kerry, D., 397,190; Nader, Ind., 4,838; "None of These Candidates," Ind., 3,688; Badnarik, Libertarian, 3,176; Peroutka, Indep. Amer., 1,152; Cobb, Green, 853.

2000: Bush, R., 301,575; Gore, D., 279,978; Nader, Green, 15,008; Buchanan, Citizens First, 4,747; "None of These Candidates," 3,315; Browne, Libertarian, 3,311; Phillips, Ind. Amer., 621; Hagelin, Natural Law, 415.

1996: Clinton, D., 203,974; Dole, R., 199,244; Perot, Ref., 43,986; "None of These Candidates," 5,608; Nader, Green, 4,730; Browne, Libertarian, 4,460; Phillips, Ind. Amer., 1,732; Hagelin, Natural Law, 545.

1992: Clinton, D., 189,148; Bush, R., 175,828; Perot, Ind., 132,580; Gritz, Populist/America First, 2,892; Marrou, Libertarian, 1,835.

1988: Bush, R., 206,040; Dukakis, D., 132,738; Paul, Lib., 3,520; Fulani, New Alliance, 835.

1984: Reagan, R., 188,770; Mondale, D., 91,655; Bergland, Libertarian, 2,292.

1980: Reagan, R., 155,017; Carter, D., 66,666; Anderson, Ind., 17,651; Clark, Libertarian, 4,358.

1976: Ford, R., 101,273; Carter, D., 92,479; MacBride, Libertarian, 1,519; Maddox, Amer. Ind., 1,497; scattered, 5,108.

1972: Nixon, R., 115,750; McGovern, D., 66,016.

1968: Nixon, R., 73,188; Humphrey, D., 60,598; Wallace, 3rd Party, 20,432.

1964: Johnson, D., 79,339; Goldwater, R., 56,094.

1960: Kennedy, D., 54,880; Nixon, R., 52,387.

1956: Eisenhower, R., 56,049; Stevenson, D., 40,640.

1952: Eisenhower, R., 50,502; Stevenson, D., 31,688.

1948: Truman, D., 31,291; Dewey, R., 29,357; Wallace, Prog., 1,469.

New Hampshire

2004: Kerry, D., 340,511; Bush, R., 331,237; Nader, Ind., 4,479.

2000: Bush, R., 273,559; Gore, D., 266,348; Nader, Green, 22,198; Browne, Libertarian, 2,757; Buchanan, Independence, 2,615; Phillips, Constitution, 328.

1996: Clinton, D., 246,166; Dole, R., 196,486; Perot, Ref., 48,387; Browne, Libertarian, 4,214; Phillips, Taxpayers, 1,344.

1992: Clinton, D., 209,040; Bush, R., 202,484; Perot, Ind., 121,337; Marrou, Libertarian, 3,548.

1988: Bush, R., 281,537; Dukakis, D., 163,696; Paul, Lib., 4,502; Fulani, New Alliance, 790.

1984: Reagan, R., 267,051; Mondale, D., 120,377; Bergland, Libertarian, 735.

1980: Reagan, R., 221,705; Carter, D., 108,864; Anderson, Ind., 49,693; Clark, Libertarian, 2,067; Commoner, Citizens, 1,325; Hall, Com., 129; Griswold, Workers World, 76; DeBerry, Soc. Workers, 72; scattered, 68.

1976: Ford, R., 185,935; Carter, D., 147,645; McCarthy, Ind., 4,095; MacBride, Libertarian, 936; Reagan, write-in, 388; La Rouche, U.S. Labor, 186; Camejo, Soc. Workers, 161; Levin, Soc. Labor, 66; scattered, 215.

1972: Nixon, R., 213,724; McGovern, D., 116,435; Schmitz, Amer., 3,386; Jenness, Soc. Workers, 368; scattered, 142.

1968: Nixon, R., 154,903; Humphrey, D., 130,589; Wallace, 3rd Party, 11,173; New Party, 421; Halstead, Soc. Workers, 104.

1964: Johnson, D., 182,065; Goldwater, R., 104,029.

1960: Nixon, R., 157,989; Kennedy, D., 137,772.

1956: Eisenhower, R., 176,519; Stevenson, D., 90,364; Andrews, Const., 111.

1952: Eisenhower, R., 166,287; Stevenson, D., 106,663.

1948: Dewey, R., 121,299; Truman, D., 107,995; Wallace, Prog., 1,970; Thomas, Soc., 86; Teichert, Soc. Labor, 83; Thurmond, States' Rights, 7.

New Jersey

2004: Kerry, D., 1,911,430; Bush, R., 1,670,003; Nader, Ind., 19,418; Badnarik, Ind., 4,514; Peroutka, Ind., 2,750; Cobb, Ind., 1,807; Brown, Ind., 664; Van Auken, Ind., 575; Calero, Ind., 530.

2000: Gore, D., 1,788,850; Bush, R., 1,284,173; Nader, Ind., 94,554; Buchanan, Ind., 6,989; Browne, Ind., 6,312; Hagelin, Ind., 2,215; McReynolds, Ind., 1,880; Phillips, Ind., 1,409; Harris, Ind., 844.

1996: Clinton, D., 1,652,361; Dole, R., 1,103,099; Perot, Ref., 262,134; Nader, Green, 32,465; Browne, Libertarian, 14,763; Hagelin, Natural Law, 3,887; Phillips, Taxpayers, 3,440; Harris, Soc. Workers, 1,837; Moorehead, Workers World, 1,337; White, Soc. Equality, 537.

1992: Clinton, D., 1,436,206; Bush, R., 1,356,865; Perot, Ind., 521,829; Marrou, Libertarian, 6,822; Fulani, New Alliance, 3,513; Phillips, U.S. Taxpayers, 2,670; LaRouche, Ind., 2,095; Warren, Soc. Workers, 2,011; Daniels, Ind., 1,996; Gritz, Populist/America First, 1,867; Hagelin, Natural Law, 1,353.

1988: Bush, R., 1,740,604; Dukakis, D., 1,317,541; Lewin, Peace and Freedom, 9,953; Paul, Lib., 8,421.

1984: Reagan, R., 1,933,630; Mondale, D., 1,261,323; Bergland, Libertarian, 6,416.

1980: Reagan, R., 1,546,557; Carter, D., 1,147,364; Anderson, Ind., 234,632; Clark, Libertarian, 20,652; Commoner, Citizens, 8,203; McCormack, Right to Life, 3,927; Lynen, Middle Class, 3,694; Hall, Com., 2,555; Pulley, Soc. Workers, 2,198; McReynolds, Soc., 1,973; Gahres, Down With Lawyers, 1,718; Griswold, Workers World, 1,288; Wendelken, Ind., 923.

1976: Ford, R., 1,509,688; Carter, D., 1,444,653; McCarthy, Ind., 32,717; MacBride, Libertarian, 9,449; Maddox, Amer., 7,716; Levin, Soc. Labor, 3,686; Hall, Com., 1,662; LaRouche, U.S. Labor, 1,650; Camejo, Soc. Workers, 1,184; Wright, People's, 1,044; Bubar, Proh., 554; Zeidler, Soc., 469.

1972: Nixon, R., 1,845,502; McGovern, D., 1,102,211; Schmitz, Amer., 34,378; Spock, Peoples, 5,355; Fisher, Soc. Labor, 4,544; Jenness, Soc. Workers, 2,233; Mahalchik, Amer. First, 1,743; Hall, Com., 1,263.

1968: Nixon, R., 1,325,467; Humphrey, D., 1,264,206; Wallace, 3rd Party, 262,187; Halstead, Soc. Workers, 8,667; Gregory, Peace and Freedom, 8,084; Blomen, Soc. Labor, 6,784.

1964: Johnson, D., 1,867,671; Goldwater, R., 963,843; DeBerry, Soc. Workers, 8,181; Hass, Soc. Labor, 7,075.

1960: Kennedy, D., 1,385,415; Nixon, R., 1,363,324; Dobbs, Soc. Workers, 11,402; Lee, Cons., 8,708; Hass, Soc. Labor, 4,262.

1956: Eisenhower, R., 1,606,942; Stevenson D., 850,337; Holtwick, Proh., 9,147; Hass, Soc. Labor, 6,736; Andrews, Cons., 5,317; Dobbs, Soc. Workers, 4,004; Krajewski, Amer. Third Party, 1,829.

1952: Eisenhower, R., 1,373,613; Stevenson, D., 1,015,902; Hoopes, Soc., 8,593; Hass, Soc. Labor, 5,815; Hallinan, Prog., 5,589; Krajewski, Poor Man's, 4,203; Dobbs, Soc. Workers, 3,850; Hamblen, Proh., 989.

1948: Dewey, R., 981,124; Truman, D., 895,455; Wallace, Prog., 42,683; Watson, Proh., 10,593; Thomas, Soc., 10,521; Dobbs, Soc. Workers, 5,825; Teichert, Soc. Labor, 3,354.

New Mexico

2004: Bush, R., 376,930; Kerry, D., 370,942; Nader, Ind., 4,053; Badnarik, Libert., 2,382; Cobb, Green, 1,226; Peroutka, Constitution, 771.

2000: Gore, D., 286,783; Bush, R., 286,417; Nader, Green, 21,251; Browne, Libertarian, 2,058; Buchanan, Reform, 1,392; Hagelin, Natural Law, 361; Phillips, Constitution, 343.

1996: Clinton, D., 273,495; Dole, R., 232,751; Perot, Ref., 32,257; Nader, Green, 13,218; Browne, Libertarian, 2,996; Phillips, Taxpayers, 713; Hagelin, Natural Law, 644.

1992: Clinton, D., 261,617; Bush, R., 212,824; Perot, Ind., 91,895; Marrou, Libertarian, 1,615.

1988: Bush, R., 270,341; Dukakis, D., 244,497; Paul, Lib., 3,268; Fulani, New Alliance, 2,237.

1984: Reagan, R., 307,101; Mondale, D., 201,769; Bergland, Libertarian, 4,459.

1980: Reagan, R., 250,779; Carter, D., 167,826; Anderson, Ind., 29,459; Clark, Libertarian, 4,365; Commoner, Citizens, 2,202; Bubar, Statesman, 1,281; Pulley, Soc. Workers, 325.

1976: Ford, R., 211,419; Carter, D., 201,148; Camejo, Soc. Wkrs., 2,462; MacBride, Libert., 1,110; Zeidler, Soc., 240; Bubar, Proh., 211.

1972: Nixon, R., 235,606; McGovern, D., 141,084; Schmitz, Amer., 8,767; Jenness, Soc. Workers, 474.

1968: Nixon, R., 169,692; Humphrey, D., 130,081; Wallace, 3rd Party, 25,737; Chavez, 1,519; Halstead, Soc. Workers, 252.

New York

1964: Johnson, D., 194,017; Goldwater, R., 131,838; Hass, Soc. Labor, 1,217; Munn, Proh., 543.

1960: Kennedy, D., 156,027; Nixon, R., 153,733; Decker, Proh., 777; Hass, Soc. Labor, 570.

1956: Eisenhower, R., 146,788; Stevenson, D., 106,098; Holtwick, Proh., 607; Andrews, Ind., 364; Hass, Soc. Labor, 69.

1952: Eisenhower, R., 132,170; Stevenson, D., 105,661; Hamblen, Proh., 297; Hallinan, Ind. Prog., 225; MacArthur, Christian National, 220; Hass, Soc. Labor, 35.

1948: Truman, D., 105,464; Dewey, R., 80,303; Wallace, Prog., 1,037; Watson, Proh., 127; Thomas, Soc., 83; Teichert, Soc. Lab., 49.

New York

2004: Kerry, D., 4,314,280; Bush, R., 2,962,567; Nader, Ind., 99,873; Badnarik, Libertarian, 11,607; Calero, Soc. Wkrs., 2,405.

2000: Gore, D., 4,112,965; Bush, R., 2,405,570; Nader, Green, 244,360; Buchanan, Reform, 31,554; Hagelin, Independence, 24,369; Browne, Libertarian, 7,664; Harris, Soc. Workers, 1,790; Phillips, Constitution, 1,503.

1996: Clinton, D., 3,756,177; Dole, R., 1,933,492; Perot, Ind. (Ref.), 503,458; Nader, Green, 75,956; Phillips, Right to Life, 23,580; Browne, Libertarian, 12,220; Hagelin, Natural Law, 5,011; Moorehead, Workers World, 3,473; Harris, Soc. Workers, 2,762.

1992: Clinton, D., 3,444,450; Bush, R., 2,346,649; Perot, Ind., 1,090,721; Warren, Soc. Workers, 15,472; Marrou, Libertarian, 13,451; Fulani, New Alliance, 11,318; Hagelin, Natural Law, 4,420.

1988: Dukakis, D., 3,347,882; Bush, R., 3,081,871; Marra, Right to Life, 20,497; Fulani, New Alliance, 15,845.

1984: Reagan, R., 3,664,763; Mondale, D., 3,119,609; Bergland, Libertarian, 11,949.

1980: Reagan, R., 2,893,831; Carter, D., 2,728,372; Anderson, Ind., 467,801; Clark, Libertarian, 52,648; McCormack, Right To Life, 24,159; Commoner, Citizens, 23,186; Hall, Com., 7,414; DeBerry, Soc. Wkrs., 2,068; Griswold, Wkrs. World, 1,416; scattered, 1,064.

1976: Carter, D., 3,389,558; Ford, R., 3,100,791; MacBride, Libertarian, 12,197; Hall, Com., 10,270; Camejo, Soc. Workers, 6,996; LaRouche, U.S. Labor, 5,413; blank, void, or scattered, 143,037.

1972: Nixon, R., 3,824,642; McGovern, D., 2,767,956; Lib., 183,128; total, 2,951,084; Reed, Cons., 368,136; Soc. Wkrs., 7,797; Fisher, Soc. Labor, 4,530; Hall, Com., 5,641; blank, void, or scattered, 161,641.

1968: Humphrey, D., 3,378,470; Nixon, R., 3,007,932; Wallace, 3rd Party, 358,864; Gregory, Freedom and Peace, 24,517; Halstead, Soc. Workers, 11,851; Blomen, Soc. Labor, 8,432; blank, void, and scattered, 171,624.

1964: Johnson, D., 4,913,156; Goldwater, R., 2,243,559; Hass, Soc. Labor, 6,085; DeBerry, Soc. Workers, 3,215; scattered, 188; blank and void, 151,383.

1960: Kennedy, D., 3,423,909; Liberal, 406,176; total, 3,830,085; Nixon, R., 3,446,419; Dobbs, Soc. Workers, 14,319; scattered, 256; blank and void, 88,896.

1956: Eisenhower, R., 4,340,340; Stevenson, D., 2,458,212, Liberal, 292,557, total, 2,750,769; write-in votes for Andrews, 1,027; Werdel, 492; Hass, 150; Hoopes, 82; others, 476.

1952: Eisenhower, R., 3,952,815; Stevenson, D., 2,687,890; Liberal, 416,711; total, 3,104,601; Hallinan, Amer. Lab., 64,211; Hoopes, Soc., 2,664; Dobbs, Soc. Workers, 2,212; Hass, Ind. Gov't., 1,560; scattered, 178; blank and void, 87,813.

1948: Dewey, R., 2,841,163; Truman, D., 2,557,642; Liberal, 222,562; total, 2,780,204; Wallace, Amer. Lab., 509,559; Thomas, Soc., 40,879; Teichert, Ind. Gov't., 2,729; Dobbs, Soc. Wkrs., 2,675.

North Carolina

2004: Bush, R., 1,961,166; Kerry, D., 1,525,849; Badnarik, Libertarian, 11,731.

2000: Bush, R., 1,631,163; Gore, D., 1,257,692; Browne, Libertarian, 13,891; Buchanan, Reform, 8,874.

1996: Dole, R., 1,225,938; Clinton, D., 1,107,849; Perot, Ref., 168,059; Browne, Libertarian, 8,740; Hagelin, Natural Law, 2,771.

1992: Bush, R., 1,134,661; Clinton, D., 1,114,042; Perot, Ind., 357,864; Marrou, Libertarian, 5,171.

1988: Bush, R., 1,237,258; Dukakis, D., 890,167; Fulani, New Alliance, 5,682; Paul, write-in, 1,263.

1984: Reagan, R., 1,346,481; Mondale, D., 824,287; Bergland, Libertarian, 3,794.

1980: Reagan, R., 915,018; Carter, D., 875,635; Anderson, Ind., 52,800; Clark, Libertarian, 9,677; Commoner, Citizens, 2,287; DeBerry, Soc. Workers, 416.

1976: Carter, D., 927,365; Ford, R., 741,960; Anderson, Amer., 5,607; MacBride, Libertarian, 2,219; LaRouche, U.S. Labor, 755.

1972: Nixon, R., 1,054,889; McGovern, D., 438,705; Schmitz, Amer., 25,018.

1968: Nixon, R., 627,192; Wallace, 3rd Party, 496,188; Humphrey, D., 464,113.

1964: Johnson, D., 800,139; Goldwater, R., 624,844.

1960: Kennedy, D., 713,136; Nixon, R., 655,420.

1956: Stevenson, D., 590,530; Eisenhower, R., 575,062.

1952: Stevenson, D., 652,803; Eisenhower, R., 558,107.

1948: Truman, D., 459,070; Dewey, R., 258,572; Thurmond, States' Rights, 69,652; Wallace, Prog., 3,915.

North Dakota

2004: Bush, R., 196,651; Kerry, D., 111,052; Nader, Ind., 3,756; Badnarik, Libertarian, 851; Peroutka, Constitution, 514.

2000: Bush, R., 174,852; Gore, D., 95,284; Nader, Ind., 9,486; Buchanan, Reform, 7,288; Browne, Ind., 660; Phillips, Constitution, 373; Hagelin, Ind., 313.

1996: Dole, R., 125,050; Clinton, D., 106,905; Perot, Ref., 32,515; Browne, Libertarian, 847; Phillips, Ind., 745; Hagelin, Natural Law, 349.

1992: Bush, R., 136,244; Clinton, D., 99,168; Perot, Ind., 71,084.

1988: Bush, R., 166,559; Dukakis, D., 127,739; Paul, Lib., 1,315; LaRouche, Natl. Econ. Recovery, 905.

1984: Reagan, R., 200,336; Mondale, D., 104,429; Bergland, Libertarian, 703.

1980: Reagan, R., 193,695; Carter, D., 79,189; Anderson, Ind., 23,640; Clark, Libertarian, 3,743; Commoner, Libertarian, 429; McLain, Natl. People's League, 296; Greaves, Amer., 235; Hall, Com., 93; DeBerry, Soc. Workers, 89; McReynolds, Soc., 82; Bubar, Statesman, 54.

1976: Ford, R., 153,470; Carter, D., 136,078; Anderson, Amer., 3,698; McCarthy, Ind., 2,952; Maddox, Amer. Ind., 269; MacBride, Libertarian, 256; scattered, 371.

1972: Nixon, R., 174,109; McGovern, D., 100,384; Schmitz, Amer., 5,646; Jenness, Soc. Workers, 288; Hall, Com., 87.

1968: Nixon, R., 138,669; Humphrey, D., 94,769; Wallace, 3rd Party, 14,244; Halstead, Soc. Workers, 128; Munn, Prohibition, 38; Troxell, Ind., 34.

1964: Johnson, D., 149,784; Goldwater, R., 108,207; DeBerry, Soc. Workers, 224; Munn, Proh., 174.

1960: Nixon, R., 154,310; Kennedy, D., 123,963; Dobbs, Soc. Workers, 158.

1956: Eisenhower, R., 156,766; Stevenson, D., 96,742; Andrews, Amer., 483.

1952: Eisenhower, R., 191,712; Stevenson, D., 76,694; MacArthur, Christian Nationalist, 1,075; Hallinan, Prog., 344; Hamblen, Proh., 302.

1948: Dewey, R., 115,139; Truman, D., 95,812; Wallace, Prog., 8,391; Thomas, Soc., 1,000; Thurmond, States' Rights, 374.

Ohio

2004: Bush, R., 2,859,768; Kerry, D., 2,741,167; Badnarik, nonpartisan, 14,676; Peroutka, nonpartisan, 939.

2000: Bush, R., 2,351,209; Gore, D., 2,186,190; Nader, Ind., 117,857; Buchanan, Ind., 26,724; Browne, Libertarian, 13,475; Hagelin, Natural Law, 6,169; Phillips, Ind., 3,823.

1996: Clinton, D., 2,148,222; Dole, R., 1,859,883; Perot, Ref., 483,207; Browne, Ind., 12,851; Moorehead, Ind., 10,813; Hagelin, Natural Law, 9,120; Phillips, Ind., 7,361.

1992: Clinton, D., 1,984,942; Bush, R., 1,894,310; Perot, Ind., 1,036,426; Marrou, Libertarian, 7,252; Fulani, New Alliance, 6,413; Gritz, Populist/America First, 4,699; Hagelin, Natural Law, 3,437; LaRouche, Ind., 2,446.

1988: Bush, R., 2,416,549; Dukakis, D., 1,939,629; Fulani, Ind., 12,017; Paul, Ind., 11,926.

1984: Reagan, R., 2,678,559; Mondale, D., 1,825,440; Bergland, Libertarian, 5,886.

1980: Reagan, R., 2,206,545; Carter, D., 1,752,414; Anderson, Ind., 254,472; Clark, Libertarian, 49,033; Commoner, Citizens, 8,564; Hall, Com., 4,729; Congress, Ind., 4,029; Griswold, Workers World, 3,790; Bubar, Statesman, 27.

1976: Carter, D., 2,011,621; Ford, R., 2,000,505; McCarthy, Ind., 58,258; Maddox, Amer. Ind., 15,529; MacBride, Libertarian, 8,961; Hall, Com., 7,817; Camejo, Soc. Workers, 4,717; LaRouche, U.S. Labor, 4,335; scattered, 130.

1972: Nixon, R., 2,441,827; McGovern, D., 1,558,889; Schmitz, Amer., 80,067; Fisher, Soc. Labor, 7,107; Hall, Com., 6,437; Wallace, Ind., 460.

1968: Nixon, R., 1,791,014; Humphrey, D., 1,700,586; Wallace, 3rd Party, 467,495; Gregory, 372; Blomen, Soc. Labor, 120; Halstead, Soc. Workers, 69; Mitchell, Com., 23; Munn, Proh., 19.

1964: Johnson, D., 2,498,331; Goldwater, R., 1,470,865.

1960: Nixon, R., 2,217,611; Kennedy, D., 1,944,248.

1956: Eisenhower, R., 2,262,610; Stevenson, D., 1,439,655.

1952: Eisenhower, R., 2,100,391; Stevenson, D., 1,600,367.

1948: Truman, D., 1,452,791; Dewey, R., 1,445,684; Wallace, Prog., 37,596.

Oklahoma

2004: Bush, R., 959,792; Kerry, D., 503,966.

2000: Bush, R., 744,337; Gore, D., 474,276; Buchanan, Reform, 9,014; Browne, Libertarian, 6,602.

1996: Dole, R., 582,315; Clinton, D., 488,105; Perot, Ref., 130,788; Browne, Libertarian, 5,505.

1992: Bush, R., 592,929; Clinton, D., 473,066; Perot, Ind., 319,878; Marrou, Libertarian, 4,486.

1988: Bush, R., 678,367; Dukakis, D., 483,423; Paul, Lib., 6,261; Fulani, New Alliance, 2,985.

1984: Reagan, R., 861,530; Mondale, D., 385,080; Bergland, Libertarian, 9,066.

1980: Reagan, R., 695,570; Carter, D., 402,026; Anderson, Ind., 38,284; Clark, Libertarian, 13,828.

1976: Ford, R., 545,708; Carter, D., 532,442; McCarthy, Ind., 14,101.

1972: Nixon, R., 759,025; McGovern, D., 247,147; Schmitz, Amer., 23,728.

1968: Nixon, R., 449,697; Humphrey, D., 301,658; Wallace, 3rd Party, 191,731.

1964: Johnson, D., 519,834; Goldwater, R., 412,665.

1960: Nixon, R., 533,039; Kennedy, D., 370,111.

1956: Eisenhower, R., 473,769; Stevenson, D., 385,581.

1952: Eisenhower, R., 518,045; Stevenson, D., 430,939.

1948: Truman, D., 452,782; Dewey, R., 268,817.

Oregon

2004: Kerry, D., 943,163; Bush, R., 866,831; Badnarik, Libertarian, 7,260; Cobb, Pac. Green, 5,315; Peroutka, Constitution, 5,257.

2000: Gore, D., 720,342; Bush, R., 713,577; Nader, Green, 77,357; Browne, Libertarian, 7,447; Buchanan, Ind., 7,063; Hagelin, Reform, 2,574; Phillips, Constitution, 2,189.

1996: Clinton, D., 649,641; Dole, R., 538,152; Perot, Ref., 121,221; Nader, Pacific, 49,415; Browne, Libertarian, 8,903; Phillips, Taxpayers, 3,379; Hagelin, Natural Law, 2,798; Hollis, Soc., 1,922.

1992: Clinton, D., 621,314; Bush, R., 475,757; Perot, Ind., 354,091; Marrou, Libertarian, 4,277; Fulani, New Alliance, 3,030.

1988: Dukakis, D., 616,206; Bush, R., 560,126; Paul, Lib., 14,811; Fulani, Ind., 6,487.

1984: Reagan, R., 658,700; Mondale, D., 536,479.

1980: Reagan, R., 571,044; Carter, D., 456,890; Anderson, Ind., 112,389; Clark, Libertarian, 25,838; Commoner, Citizens, 13,642; scattered, 1,713.

1976: Ford, R., 492,120; Carter, D., 490,407; McCarthy, Ind., 40,207; write-in, 7,142.

1972: Nixon, R., 486,686; McGovern, D., 392,760; Schmitz, Amer., 46,211; write-in, 2,289.

1968: Nixon, R., 408,433; Humphrey, D., 358,866; Wallace, 3rd Party, 49,683; write-in, McCarthy, 1,496; N. Rockefeller, 69; others, 1,075.

1964: Johnson, D., 501,017; Goldwater, R., 282,779; write-in, 2,509.

1960: Nixon, R., 408,060; Kennedy, D., 367,402.

1956: Eisenhower, R., 406,393; Stevenson, D., 329,204.

1952: Eisenhower, R., 420,815; Stevenson, D., 270,579; Hallinan, Ind., 3,665.

1948: Dewey, R., 260,904; Truman, D., 243,147; Wallace, Prog., 14,978; Thomas, Soc., 5,051.

Pennsylvania

2004: Kerry, D., 2,938,095; Bush, R., 2,793,847; Badnarik, Libertarian, 21,185; Cobb, Green, 6,319; Peroutka, Constitution, 6,318.

2000: Gore, D., 2,485,967; Bush, R., 2,281,127; Nader, Green, 103,392; Buchanan, Reform, 16,023; Phillips, Constitution, 14,428; Browne, Libertarian, 11,248.

1996: Clinton, D., 2,215,819; Dole, R., 1,801,169; Perot, Ref., 430,984; Browne, Libertarian, 28,000; Phillips, Constitutional, 19,552; Hagelin, Natural Law, 5,783.

1992: Clinton, D., 2,239,164; Bush, R., 1,791,841; Perot, Ind., 902,667; Marrou, Libertarian, 21,477; Fulani, New Alliance, 4,661.

1988: Bush, R., 2,300,087; Dukakis, D., 2,194,944; McCarthy, Consumer, 19,158; Paul, Lib., 12,051.

1984: Reagan, R., 2,584,323; Mondale, D., 2,228,131; Bergland, Libertarian, 6,982.

1980: Reagan, R., 2,261,872; Carter, D., 1,937,540; Anderson, Ind., 292,921; Clark, Libertarian, 33,263; DeBerry, Soc. Workers, 20,291; Commoner, Consumer, 10,430; Hall, Com., 5,184.

1976: Carter, D., 2,328,677; Ford, R., 2,205,604; McCarthy, Ind., 50,584; Maddox, Const., 25,344; Camejo, Soc. Workers, 3,009; LaRouche, U.S. Labor, 2,744; Hall, Com., 1,891; others, 2,934.

1972: Nixon, R., 2,714,521; McGovern, D., 1,796,951; Schmitz, Amer., 70,593; Jenness, Soc. Workers, 4,639; Hall, Com., 2,686; others, 2,715.

1968: Humphrey, D., 2,259,405; Nixon, R., 2,090,017; Wallace, 3rd Party, 378,582; Gregory, Peace and Freedom, 7,821; Blomen, Soc. Labor, 4,977; Halstead, Soc. Workers, 4,862; others, 2,264.

1964: Johnson, D., 3,130,954; Goldwater, R., 1,673,657; DeBerry, Soc. Workers, 10,456; Hass, Soc. Labor, 5,092; scattered, 2,531.

1960: Kennedy, D., 2,556,282; Nixon, R., 2,439,956; Hass, Soc. Labor, 7,185; Dobbs, Soc. Workers, 2,678; scattered, 440.

1956: Eisenhower, R., 2,585,252; Stevenson, D., 1,981,769; Hass, Soc. Labor, 7,447; Dobbs, Militant Workers, 2,035.

1952: Eisenhower, R., 2,415,789; Stevenson, D., 2,146,269; Hamblen, Proh., 8,771; Hallinan, Prog., 4,200; Hoopes, Soc., 2,684; Dobbs, Militant Workers, 1,502; Hass, Ind. Gov., 1,347; scattered, 155.

1948: Dewey, R., 1,902,197; Truman, D., 1,752,426; Wallace, Prog., 55,161; Thomas, Soc., 11,325; Watson, Proh., 10,338; Dobbs, Militant Workers, 2,133; Teichert, Ind. Gov., 1,461.

Rhode Island

2004: Kerry, D., 259,765; Bush, R., 169,046; Nader, Ref., 4,651; Cobb, Green, 1,333; Badnarik, Libertarian, 907; Peroutka, Constitution, 339; Parker, Workers World, 253.

2000: Gore, D., 249,508; Bush, R., 130,555; Nader, Ind., 25,052; Buchanan, Reform, 2,273; Browne, Ind., 742; Hagelin, Ind., 271; Moorehead, Ind., 199; Phillips, Ind., 97; McReynolds, Ind., 52; Harris, Ind., 34.

1996: Clinton, D., 233,050; Dole, R., 104,683; Perot, Ref., 43,723; Nader, Green, 6,040; Browne, Libertarian, 1,109; Phillips, Taxpayers, 1,021; Hagelin, Natural Law, 435; Moorehead, Workers World, 186.

1992: Clinton, D., 213,299; Bush, R., 131,601; Perot, Ind., 105,045; Fulani, New Alliance, 1,878.

1988: Dukakis, D., 225,123; Bush, R., 177,761; Paul, Lib., 825; Fulani, New Alliance, 280.

1984: Reagan, R., 212,080; Mondale, D., 197,106; Bergland, Libertarian, 277.

1980: Carter, D., 198,342; Reagan, R., 154,793; Anderson, Ind., 59,819; Clark, Libertarian, 2,458; Hall, Com., 218; McReynolds, Soc., 170; DeBerry, Soc. Workers, 90; Griswold, Workers World, 77.

1976: Carter, D., 227,636; Ford, R., 181,249; MacBride, Libertarian, 715; Camejo, Soc. Workers, 462; Hall, Com., 334; Levin, Soc. Labor, 188.

1972: Nixon, R., 220,383; McGovern, D., 194,645; Jenness, Soc. Workers, 729.

1968: Humphrey, D., 246,518; Nixon, R., 122,359; Wallace, 3rd Party, 15,678; Halstead, Soc. Workers, 383.

1964: Johnson, D., 315,463; Goldwater, R., 74,615.

1960: Kennedy, D., 258,032; Nixon, R., 147,502.

1956: Eisenhower, R., 225,819; Stevenson, D., 161,790.

1952: Eisenhower, R., 210,935; Stevenson, D., 203,293; Hallinan, Prog., 187; Hass, Soc. Labor, 83.

1948: Truman, D., 188,736; Dewey, R., 135,787; Wallace, Prog., 2,619; Thomas, Soc., 429; Teichert, Soc. Labor, 131.

South Carolina

2004: Bush, R., 937,974; Kerry, D., 661,699; Nader, Ind., 5,520; Peroutka, Constitution, 5,317; Badnarik, Libertarian, 3,608; Brown, United Citizen, 2,124; Cobb, Green, 1,488.

2000: Bush, R., 786,892; Gore, D., 566,039; Nader, United Citizens, 20,279; Browne, Libertarian, 4,898; Buchanan, Reform, 3,309; Phillips, Constitution, 1,682; Hagelin, Natural Law, 943.

1996: Dole, R., 573,458; Clinton, D., 506,283; Perot, Ref./Patriot, 64,386; Browne, Libertarian, 4,271; Phillips, Taxpayers, 2,043; Hagelin, Natural Law, 1,248.

1992: Bush, R., 577,507; Clinton, D., 479,514; Perot, Ind., 138,872; Marrou, Libertarian, 2,719; Phillips, U.S. Taxpayers, 2,680; Fulani, New Alliance, 1,235.

1988: Bush, R., 606,443; Dukakis, D., 370,554; Paul, Lib., 4,935; Fulani, United Citizens, 4,077.

1984: Reagan, R., 615,539; Mondale, D., 344,459; Bergland, Libertarian, 4,359.

1980: Reagan, R., 439,277; Carter, D., 428,220; Anderson, Ind., 13,868; Clark, Libertarian, 4,807; Rarick, Amer. Ind., 2,086.

1976: Carter, D., 450,807; Ford, R., 346,149; Anderson, Amer., 2,996; Maddox, Amer. Ind., 1,950; write-in, 681.

1972: Nixon, R., 477,044; McGovern, D., 184,559; Schmitz, Amer., 10,075; United Citizens, 2,265; write-in, 17.

1968: Nixon, R., 254,062; Wallace, 3rd Party, 215,430; Humphrey, D., 197,486.

1964: Goldwater, R., 309,048; Johnson, D., 215,700; write-in: Wallace, 5; Nixon, 1; Powell, 1; Thurmond, 1.

1960: Kennedy, D., 198,129; Nixon, R., 188,558; write-in, 1.

1956: Stevenson, D., 136,372; Byrd, Ind., 88,509; Eisenhower, R., 75,700; Andrews, Ind., 2.

1952: Stevenson, D., 173,004. Under state law votes cast for 2 Eisenhower slates of electors could not be combined. Eisenhower, Ind., 158,289; R., 9,793; total, 168,082. Hamblen, Proh., 1.

1948: Thurmond, States' Rights, 102,607; Truman, D., 34,423; Dewey, R., 5,386; Wallace, Prog., 154; Thomas, Soc., 1.

South Dakota

2004: Bush, R., 232,584; Kerry, D., 149,244; Nader, Ind., 4,320; Peroutka, Constitution, 1,103; Badnarik, Libertarian, 964.

2000: Bush, R., 190,700; Gore, D., 118,804; Buchanan, Reform, 3,322; Phillips, Ind., 1,781; Browne, Libertarian, 1,662.

1996: Dole, R., 150,543; Clinton, D., 139,333; Perot, Ref., 31,250; Browne, Libertarian, 1,472; Phillips, Taxpayers, 912; Hagelin, Natural Law, 316.

1992: Bush, R., 136,718; Clinton, D., 124,888; Perot, Ind., 73,295.

1988: Bush, R., 165,415; Dukakis, D., 145,560; Paul, Lib., 1,060; Fulani, New Alliance, 730.

1984: Reagan, R., 200,267; Mondale, D., 116,113.

1980: Reagan, R., 198,343; Carter, D., 103,855; Anderson, Ind., 21,431; Clark, Libertarian, 3,824; Pulley, Soc. Workers, 250.

1976: Ford, R., 151,505; Carter, D., 147,068; MacBride, Libertarian, 1,619; Hall, Com., 318; Camejo, Soc. Workers, 168.

1972: Nixon, R., 166,476; McGovern, D., 139,945; Jenness, Soc. Workers, 994.

1968: Nixon, R., 149,841; Humphrey, D., 118,023; Wallace, 3rd Party, 13,400.

1964: Johnson, D., 163,010; Goldwater, R., 130,108.

1960: Nixon, R., 178,417; Kennedy, D., 128,070.

1956: Eisenhower, R., 171,569; Stevenson, D., 122,288.

1952: Eisenhower, R., 203,857; Stevenson, D., 90,426.

1948: Dewey, R., 129,651; Truman, D., 117,653; Wallace, Prog., 2,801.

Tennessee

2004: Bush, R., 1,384,375; Kerry, D., 1,036,477; Nader, Ind., 8,992; Badnarik, Ind., 4,866; Peroutka, Ind., 2,570.

2000: Bush, R., 1,061,949; Gore, D., 981,720; Nader, Green, 19,781; Browne, Libertarian, 4,284; Buchanan, Reform, 4,250; Brown, Ind., 1,606; Phillips, Ind., 1,015; Hagelin, Reform, 613; Venson, Ind., 535.

1996: Clinton, D., 909,146; Dole, R., 863,530; Perot, Ind. (Ref.), 105,918; Nader, Ind., 6,427; Browne, Ind., 5,020; Phillips, Ind., 1,818; Collins, Ind., 688; Hagelin, Ind., 636; Michael, Ind., 408; Dodge, Ind., 324.

1992: Clinton, D., 933,521; Bush, R., 841,300; Perot, Ind., 199,968; Marrou, Libertarian, 1,847.

1988: Bush, R., 947,233; Dukakis, D., 679,794; Paul, Ind., 2,041; Duke, Ind., 1,807.

1984: Reagan, R., 990,212; Mondale, D., 711,714; Bergland, Libertarian, 3,072.

1980: Reagan, R., 787,761; Carter, D., 783,051; Anderson, Ind., 35,991; Clark, Libertarian, 7,116; Commoner, Citizens, 1,112; Bubar, Statesman, 521; McReynolds, Soc., 519; Hall, Com., 503; DeBerry, Soc. Workers, 490; Griswold, Workers World, 400; write-in, 152.

1976: Carter, D., 825,879; Ford, R., 633,969; Anderson, Amer., 5,769; McCarthy, Ind., 5,004; Maddox, Amer. Ind., 2,303; MacBride, Libertarian, 1,375; Hall, Com., 547; LaRouche, U.S. Labor, 512; Bubar, Proh., 442; Miller, Ind., 316; write-in, 230.

1972: Nixon, R., 813,147; McGovern, D., 357,293; Schmitz, Amer., 30,373; write-in, 369.

1968: Nixon, R., 472,592; Wallace, 3rd Party, 424,792; Humphrey, D., 351,233.

1964: Johnson, D., 635,047; Goldwater, R., 508,965; write-in, 34.

1960: Nixon, R., 556,577; Kennedy, D., 481,453; Faubus, States' Rights, 11,304; Decker, Proh., 2,458.

1956: Eisenhower, R., 462,288; Stevenson, D., 456,507; Andrews, Ind., 19,820; Holtwick, Proh., 789.

1952: Eisenhower, R., 446,147; Stevenson, D., 443,710; Hamblen, Proh., 1,432; Hallinan, Prog., 885; MacArthur, Christian Nationalist, 379.

1948: Truman, D., 270,402; Dewey, R., 202,914; Thurmond, States' Rights, 73,815; Wallace, Prog., 1,864; Thomas, Soc., 1,288.

IT'S A RECORD: The greatest majority ever won in the popular vote was by Richard Nixon in 1972. He defeated George McGovern by a record 17,994,460 votes (47,165,911 to 29,170,383) to win reelection.

Texas

2004: Bush, R., 4,526,917; Kerry, D., 2,832,704; Badnarik, Libertarian, 38,787.

2000: Bush, R., 3,799,639; Gore, D., 2,433,746; Nader, Green, 137,994; Browne, Libertarian, 23,160; Buchanan, Ind., 12,394.

1996: Dole, R., 2,736,167; Clinton, D., 2,459,683; Perot, Ind. (Ref.), 378,537; Browne, Libertarian, 20,256; Phillips, Taxpayers, 7,472; Hagelin, Natural Law, 4,422.

1992: Bush, R., 2,496,071; Clinton, D., 2,281,815; Perot, Ind., 1,354,781; Marrou, Libertarian, 19,699.

1988: Bush, R., 3,036,829; Dukakis, D., 2,352,748; Paul, Lib., 30,355; Fulani, New Alliance, 7,208.

1984: Reagan, R., 3,433,428; Mondale, D., 1,949,276.

1980: Reagan, R., 2,510,705; Carter, D., 1,881,147; Anderson, Ind., 111,613; Clark, Libertarian, 37,643; write-in, 528.

1976: Carter, D., 2,082,319; Ford, R., 1,953,300; McCarthy, Ind., 20,118; Anderson, Amer., 11,442; Camejo, Soc. Workers, 1,723; write-in, 2,982.

1972: Nixon, R., 2,298,896; McGovern, D., 1,154,289; Jenness, Soc. Workers, 8,664; Schmitz, Amer., 6,039; others, 3,393.

1968: Humphrey, D., 1,266,804; Nixon, R., 1,227,844; Wallace, 3rd Party, 584,269; write-in, 489.

1964: Johnson, D., 1,663,185; Goldwater, R., 958,566; Lightburn, Constitution, 5,060.

1960: Kennedy, D., 1,167,932; Nixon, R., 1,121,699; Sullivan, Constitution, 18,169; Decker, Proh., 3,870; write-in, 15.

1956: Eisenhower, R., 1,080,619; Stevenson, D., 859,958; Andrews, Ind., 14,591.

1952: Eisenhower, R., 1,102,878; Stevenson, D., 969,228; Hamblen, Proh., 1,983; MacArthur, Christian Nationalist, 833; MacArthur, Constitution, 730; Hallinan, Prog., 294.

1948: Truman, D., 750,700; Dewey, R., 282,240; Thurmond, States' Rights, 106,909; Wallace, Prog., 3,764; Watson, Proh., 2,758; Thomas, Soc., 874.

Utah

2004: Bush, R., 663,742; Kerry, D., 241,199; Nader, Ind., 11,305; Peroutka, Constitution, 6,841; Badnarik, Libertarian, 3,375; Jay, Pers. Choice, 946; Harris, Soc. Wkrs., 393.

2000: Bush, R., 515,096; Gore, D., 203,053; Nader, Green, 35,850; Buchanan, Reform, 9,319; Browne, Libertarian, 3,616; Phillips, Ind. Amer., 2,709; Hagelin, Natural Law, 763; Harris, Soc. Workers, 186; Youngkeit, Ind., 161.

1996: Dole, R., 361,911; Clinton, D., 221,633; Perot, Ref., 66,461; Nader, Green, 4,615; Browne, Libertarian, 4,129; Phillips, Taxpayers, 2,601; Templin, Ind. Amer., 1,290; Crane, Ind., 1,101; Hagelin, Natural Law, 1,085; Moorehead, Workers World, 298; Harris, Soc. Workers, 235; Dodge, Proh., 111.

1992: Bush, R., 322,632; Perot, Ind., 203,400; Clinton, D., 183,429; Gritz, Populist/America First, 28,602; Marrou, Libertarian, 1,900; Hagelin, Natural Law, 1,319; LaRouche, Ind., 1,089.

1988: Bush, R., 428,442; Dukakis, D., 207,352; Paul, Lib., 7,473; Dennis, Amer., 2,158.

1984: Reagan, R., 469,105; Mondale, D., 155,369; Bergland, Libertarian, 2,447.

1980: Reagan, R., 439,687; Carter, D., 124,266; Anderson, Ind., 30,284; Clark, Libertarian, 7,226; Commoner, Citizens, 1,009; Greaves, Amer., 965; Rarick, Amer. Ind., 522; Hall, Com., 139; DeBerry, Soc. Workers, 124.

1976: Ford, R., 337,908; Carter, D., 182,110; Anderson, Amer., 13,304; McCarthy, Ind., 3,907; MacBride, Libertarian, 2,438; Maddox, Amer. Ind., 1,162; Camejo, Soc. Workers, 268; Hall, Com., 121.

1972: Nixon, R., 323,643; McGovern, D., 126,284; Schmitz, Amer., 28,549.

1968: Nixon, R., 238,728; Humphrey, D., 156,665; Wallace, 3rd Party, 26,906; Peace and Freedom, 180; Halstead, Soc. Workers, 89.

1964: Johnson, D., 219,628; Goldwater, R., 181,785.

1960: Nixon, R., 205,361; Kennedy, D., 169,248; Dobbs, Soc. Workers, 100.

1956: Eisenhower, R., 215,631; Stevenson, D., 118,364.

1952: Eisenhower, R., 194,190; Stevenson, D., 135,364.

1948: Truman, D., 149,151; Dewey, R., 124,402; Wallace, Prog., 2,679; Dobbs, Soc. Workers, 73.

Vermont

2004: Kerry, D., 184,067; Bush, R., 121,180; Nader, Ind., 4,494; Badnarik, Libertarian, 1,102; Parker, Liberty Union, 265; Calero, Soc. Wkrs., 244.

2000: Gore, D., 149,022; Bush, R., 119,775; Nader, Green, 20,374; Buchanan, Reform, 2,192; Lane, Grass Roots, 1,044; Browne, Libertarian, 784; Hagelin, Natural Law, 219; McReynolds, Liberty Union, 161; Phillips, Constitution, 153; Harris, Soc. Workers, 70.

1996: Clinton, D., 137,894; Dole, R., 80,352; Perot, Ref., 31,024; Nader, Green, 5,585; Browne, Libertarian, 1,183; Hagelin, Natural Law, 498; Peron, Grass Roots, 480; Phillips, Taxpayers, 382; Hollis, Liberty Union, 292; Harris, Soc. Workers, 199.

1992: Clinton, D., 133,590; Bush, R., 88,122; Perot, Ind., 65,985.

1988: Bush, R., 124,331; Dukakis, D., 115,775; Paul, Lib., 1,000; LaRouche, Ind., 275.

1984: Reagan, R., 135,865; Mondale, D., 95,730; Bergland, Libertarian, 1,002.

1980: Reagan, R., 94,598; Carter, D., 81,891; Anderson, Ind., 31,760; Commoner, Citizens, 2,316; Clark, Libertarian, 1,900; McReynolds, Liberty Union, 136; Hall, Com., 118; DeBerry, Soc. Workers, 75; scattered, 413.

1976: Ford, R., 100,387; Carter, D., 77,798; Carter, Ind. Vermonter, 991; total, 79,789; McCarthy, Ind., 4,001; Camejo, Soc. Workers, 430; LaRouche, U.S. Labor, 196; scattered, 99.

1972: Nixon, R., 117,149; McGovern, D., 68,174; Spock, Liberty Union, 1,010; Jenness, Soc. Workers, 296; scattered, 318.

1968: Nixon, R., 85,142; Humphrey, D., 70,255; Wallace, 3rd Party, 5,104; Gregory, New Party, 579; Halstead, Soc. Workers, 295.

1964: Johnson, D., 107,674; Goldwater, R., 54,868.

1960: Nixon, R., 98,131; Kennedy, D., 69,186.

1956: Eisenhower, R., 110,390; Stevenson, D., 42,549; scattered, 39.

1952: Eisenhower, R., 109,717; Stevenson, D., 43,355; Hallinan, Prog., 282; Hoopes, Soc., 185.

1948: Dewey, R., 75,926; Truman, D., 45,557; Wallace, Prog., 1,279; Thomas, Soc., 585.

Virginia

2004: Bush, R., 1,716,959; Kerry, D., 1,454,742; Badnarik, Libertarian, 11,032; Peroutka, Constitution, 10,161.

2000: Bush, R., 1,437,490; Gore, D., 1,217,290; Nader, Green, 59,398; Browne, Libertarian, 15,198; Buchanan, Reform, 5,455; Phillips, Constitution, 1,809.

1996: Dole, R., 1,138,350; Clinton, D., 1,091,060; Perot, Ref., 159,861; Phillips, Taxpayers, 13,687; Browne, Libertarian, 9,174; Hagelin, Natural Law, 4,510.

1992: Bush, R., 1,150,517; Clinton, D., 1,038,650; Perot, Ind., 348,639; LaRouche, Ind., 11,937; Marrou, Libertarian, 5,730; Fulani, New Alliance, 3,192.

1988: Bush, R., 1,309,162; Dukakis, D., 859,799; Fulani, Ind., 14,312; Paul, Lib., 8,336.

1984: Reagan, R., 1,337,078; Mondale, D., 796,250.

1980: Reagan, R., 989,609; Carter, D., 752,174; Anderson, Ind., 95,418; Commoner, Citizens, 14,024; Clark, Libertarian, 12,821; DeBerry, Soc. Workers, 1,986.

1976: Ford, R., 836,554; Carter, D., 813,896; Camejo, Soc. Workers, 17,802; Anderson, Amer., 16,686; LaRouche, U.S. Labor, 7,508; MacBride, Libertarian, 4,648.

1972: Nixon, R., 988,493; McGovern, D., 438,887; Schmitz, Amer., 19,721; Fisher, Soc. Labor, 9,918.

1968: Nixon, R., 590,319; Humphrey, D., 442,387; Wallace, 3rd Party, *320,272; Blomen, Soc. Labor, 4,671; Gregory, Peace and Freedom, 1,680; Munn, Proh., 601. *10,561 votes for Wallace were omitted in the count.

1964: Johnson, D., 558,038; Goldwater, R., 481,334; Hass, Soc. Labor, 2,895.

1960: Nixon, R., 404,521; Kennedy, D., 362,327; Coiner, Cons., 4,204; Hass, Soc. Labor, 397.

1956: Eisenhower, R., 386,459; Stevenson, D., 267,760; Andrews, States' Rights, 42,964; Hoopes, Soc. D., 444; Hass, Soc. Labor, 351.

1952: Eisenhower, R., 349,037; Stevenson, D., 268,677; Hass, Soc. Labor, 1,160; Hoopes, Soc. D., 504; Hallinan, Prog., 311.

1948: Truman, D., 200,786; Dewey, R., 172,070; Thurmond, States' Rights, 43,393; Wallace, Prog., 2,047; Thomas, Soc., 726; Teichert, Soc. Labor, 234.

Washington

2004: Kerry, D., 1,510,201; Bush, R., 1,304,894; Nader, Ind., 23,283; Badnarik, Libertarian, 11,955; Peroutka, Constitution, 3,922; Cobb, Green, 2,974; Parker, Workers World, 1,077; Harris, Soc. Wkrs., 547; Van Auken, Soc. Equal., 231.

2000: Gore, D., 1,247,652; Bush, R., 1,108,864; Nader, Green, 103,002; Browne, Libertarian, 13,135; Buchanan, Freedom, 7,171; Hagelin, Natural Law, 2,927; ; Phillips, Constitution, 1,989; Moorehead, Wkrs. World, 1,729; McReynolds, Soc., 660; Harris, Soc. Wkrs., 304.

1996: Clinton, D., 1,123,323; Dole, R., 840,712; Perot, Ref., 201,003; Nader, Ind., 60,322; Browne, Libertarian, 12,522; Hagelin, Natural Law, 6,076; Phillips, Taxpayers, 4,578; Collins, Ind., 2,374; Moorehead, Workers World, 2,189; Harris, Soc. Workers, 738.

1992: Clinton, D., 993,037; Bush, R., 731,234; Perot, Ind., 541,780; Marrou, Libertarian, 7,533; Gritz, Populist/America First, 4,854; Hagelin, Natural Law, 2,456; Phillips, U.S. Taxpayers, 2,354; Fulani, New Alliance, 1,776; Daniels, Ind., 1,171.

1988: Dukakis, D., 933,516; Bush, R., 903,835; Paul, Lib., 17,240; LaRouche, Ind., 4,412.

1984: Reagan, R., 1,051,670; Mondale, D., 798,352; Bergland, Libertarian, 8,844.

1980: Reagan, R., 865,244; Carter, D., 650,193; Anderson, Ind., 185,073; Clark, Libertarian, 29,213; Commoner, Citizens, 9,403; DeBerry, Soc. Workers, 1,137; McReynolds, Soc., 956; Hall, Com., 834; Griswold, Workers World, 341.

1976: Ford, R., 777,732; Carter, D., 717,323; McCarthy, Ind., 36,986; Maddox, Amer. Ind., 8,585; Anderson, Amer., 5,046; MacBride, Libertarian, 5,042; Wright, People's, 1,124; Camejo, Soc. Workers, 905; LaRouche, U.S. Labor, 903; Hall, Com., 817; Levin, Soc. Labor, 713; Zeidler, Soc., 358.

1972: Nixon, R., 837,135; McGovern, D., 568,334; Schmitz, Amer., 58,906; Spock, Ind., 2,644; Hospers, Libertarian, 1,537; Fisher, Soc. Labor, 1,102; Jenness, Soc. Workers, 623; Hall, Com., 566.

1968: Humphrey, D., 616,037; Nixon, R., 588,510; Wallace, 3rd Party, 96,990; Cleaver, Peace and Freedom, 1,609; Blomen, Soc. Labor, 488; Mitchell, Free Ballot, 377; Halstead, Soc. Workers, 270.

1964: Johnson, D., 779,699; Goldwater, R., 470,366; Hass, Soc. Labor, 7,772; DeBerry, Freedom Soc., 537.

1960: Nixon, R., 629,273; Kennedy, D., 599,298; Hass, Soc. Labor, 10,895; Curtis, Constitution, 1,401; Dobbs, Soc. Workers, 705.

1956: Eisenhower, R., 620,430; Stevenson, D., 523,002; Hass, Soc. Labor, 7,457.

1952: Eisenhower, R., 599,107; Stevenson, D., 492,845; MacArthur, Christian Nationalist, 7,290; Hallinan, Prog., 2,460; Hass, Soc. Labor, 633; Hoopes, Soc., 254; Dobbs, Soc. Workers, 119.

1948: Truman, D., 476,165; Dewey, R., 386,315; Wallace, Prog., 31,692; Watson, Proh., 6,117; Thomas, Soc., 3,534; Teichert, Soc. Labor, 1,133; Dobbs, Soc. Workers, 103.

West Virginia

2004: Bush, R., 423,778; Kerry, D., 326,541; Nader, Ind., 4,063; Badnarik, Libertarian, 1,405.

2000: Bush, R., 336,475; Gore, D., 295,497; Nader, Green, 10,680; Buchanan, Reform, 3,169; Browne, Libertarian, 1,912; Hagelin, Natural Law, 367.

1996: Clinton, D., 327,812; Dole, R., 233,946; Perot, Ref., 71,639; Browne, Libertarian, 3,062.

1992: Clinton, D., 331,001; Bush, R., 241,974; Perot, Ind., 108,829; Marrou, Libertarian, 1,873.

1988: Dukakis, D., 341,016; Bush, R., 310,065; Fulani, New Alliance, 2,230.

1984: Reagan, R., 405,483; Mondale, D., 328,125.

1980: Carter, D., 367,462; Reagan, R., 334,206; Anderson, Ind., 31,691; Clark, Libertarian, 4,356.

1976: Carter, D., 435,864; Ford, R., 314,726.

1972: Nixon, R., 484,964; McGovern, D., 277,435.

1968: Humphrey, D., 374,091; Nixon, R., 307,555; Wallace, 3rd Party, 72,560.

1964: Johnson, D., 538,087; Goldwater, R., 253,953.

1960: Kennedy, D., 441,786; Nixon, R., 395,995.

1956: Eisenhower, R., 449,297; Stevenson, D., 381,534.

1952: Stevenson, D., 453,578; Eisenhower, R., 419,970.

1948: Truman, D., 429,188; Dewey, R., 316,251; Wallace, Prog., 3,311.

Wisconsin

2004: Kerry, D., 1,489,504; Bush, R., 1,478,120; Nader, Ind., 16,390; Badnarik, Libertarian, 6,464; Cobb, Green, 2,661; Brown, Ind., 471; Harris, Ind., 411.

2000: Gore, D., 1,242,987; Bush, R., 1,237,279; Nader, Green, 94,070; Buchanan, Reform, 11,446; Browne, Libertarian, 6,640; Phillips, Constitution, 2,042; Moorehead, Workers World, 1,063; Hagelin, Reform, 878; Harris, Soc. Workers, 306.

1996: Clinton, D., 1,071,971; Dole, R., 845,029; Perot, Ref., 227,339; Nader, Green, 28,723; Phillips, Taxpayers, 8,811; Browne, Libertarian, 7,929; Hagelin, Natural Law, 1,379; Moorehead, Workers World, 1,333; Hollis, Soc., 848; Harris, Soc. Workers, 483.

1992: Clinton, D., 1,041,066; Bush, R., 930,855; Perot, Ind., 544,479; Marrou, Libertarian, 2,877; Gritz, Populist/America First, 2,311; Daniels, Ind., 1,883; Phillips, U.S. Taxpayers, 1,772; Hagelin, Natural Law, 1,070.

1988: Dukakis, D., 1,126,794; Bush, R., 1,047,499; Paul, Lib., 5,157; Duke, Pop., 3,056.

1984: Reagan, R., 1,198,584; Mondale, D., 995,740; Bergland, Libertarian, 4,883.

1980: Reagan, R., 1,088,845; Carter, D., 981,584; Anderson, Ind., 160,657; Clark, Libertarian, 29,135; Commoner, Citizens, 7,767; Rarick, Constitution, 1,519; McReynolds, Soc., 808; Hall, Com., 772; Griswold, Workers World, 414; DeBerry, Soc. Workers, 383; scattered, 1,337.

1976: Carter, D., 1,040,232; Ford, R., 1,004,987; McCarthy, Ind., 34,943; Maddox, Amer. Ind., 8,552; Zeidler, Soc., 4,298; MacBride, Libertarian, 3,814; Camejo, Soc. Workers, 1,691; Wright, People's, 943; Hall, Com., 749; LaRouche, U.S. Lab., 738; Levin, Soc. Labor, 389; scattered, 2,839.

1972: Nixon, R., 989,430; McGovern, D., 810,174; Schmitz, Amer., 47,525; Spock, Ind., 2,701; Fisher, Soc. Labor 998; Hall, Com., 663; Reed, Ind., 506; scattered, 893.

1968: Nixon, R., 809,997; Humphrey, D., 748,804; Wallace, 3rd Party, 127,835; Blomen, Soc. Labor, 1,338; Halstead, Soc. Workers, 1,222; scattered, 2,342.

1964: Johnson, D., 1,050,424; Goldwater, R., 638,495; DeBerry, Soc. Workers, 1,692; Hass, Soc. Labor, 1,204.

1960: Nixon, R., 895,175; Kennedy, D., 830,805; Dobbs, Soc. Workers, 1,792; Hass, Soc. Labor, 1,310.

1956: Eisenhower, R., 954,844; Stevenson, D., 586,768; Andrews, Ind., 6,918; Hoopes, Soc., 754; Hass, Soc. Labor, 710; Dobbs, Soc. Workers, 564.

1952: Eisenhower, R., 979,744; Stevenson, D., 622,175; Hallinan, Ind., 2,174; Dobbs, Ind., 1,350; Hoopes, Ind., 1,157; Hass, Ind., 770.

1948: Truman, D., 647,310; Dewey, R., 590,959; Wallace, Prog., 25,282; Thomas, Soc., 12,547; Teichert, Soc. Labor, 399; Dobbs, Soc. Workers, 303.

Wyoming

2004: Bush, R., 167,629; Kerry, D., 70,776; Nader, Ind., 2,741; Badnarik, Libertarian, 1,171; Peroutka, Ind., 631.

2000: Bush, R., 147,947; Gore, D., 60,481; Buchanan, Reform, 2,724; Browne, Libertarian, 1,443; Phillips, Ind., 720; Hagelin, Natural Law, 411.

1996: Dole, R., 105,388; Clinton, D., 77,934; Perot, Ind. (Ref.), 25,928; Browne, Libertarian, 1,739; Hagelin, Natural Law, 582.

1992: Bush, R., 79,347; Clinton, D., 68,160; Perot, Ind., 51,263.

1988: Bush, R., 106,867; Dukakis, D., 67,113; Paul, Lib., 2,026; Fulani, New Alliance, 545.

1984: Reagan, R., 133,241; Mondale, D., 53,370; Bergland, Libertarian, 2,357.

1980: Reagan, R., 110,700; Carter, D., 49,427; Anderson, Ind., 12,072; Clark, Libertarian, 4,514.

1976: Ford, R., 92,717; Carter, D., 62,239; McCarthy, Ind., 624; Reagan, Ind., 307; Anderson, Amer., 290; MacBride, Libertarian, 89; Brown, Ind., 47; Maddox, Amer. Ind., 30.

1972: Nixon, R., 100,464; McGovern, D., 44,358; Schmitz, Amer., 748.

1968: Nixon, R., 70,927; Humphrey, D., 45,173; Wallace, 3rd Party, 11,105.

1964: Johnson, D., 80,718; Goldwater, R., 61,998.

1960: Nixon, R., 77,451; Kennedy, D., 63,331.

1956: Eisenhower, R., 74,573; Stevenson, D., 49,554.

1952: Eisenhower, R., 81,047; Stevenson, D., 47,934; Hamblen, Proh., 194; Hoopes, Soc., 40; Haas, Soc. Labor, 36.

1948: Truman, D., 52,354; Dewey, R., 47,947; Wallace, Prog., 931; Thomas, Soc., 137; Teichert, Soc. Labor, 56.

The Electoral College

The president and the vice president are the only elective federal officials not chosen by direct vote of the people. They are elected by the members of the Electoral College, an institution provided for in the U.S. Constitution.

On presidential election day, the first Tuesday after the first Monday in November of every 4th year, each state chooses as many electors as it has senators and representatives in Congress. In 1964, for the first time, as provided by the 23rd Amendment to the Constitution, the District of Columbia voted for 3 electors. Thus, with 100 senators and 435 representatives, there are 538 members of the Electoral College, with a majority of 270 electoral votes needed to elect the president and vice president.

Although political parties were not part of the original plan created by the Founding Fathers, today political parties customarily nominate their lists of electors at their respective state conventions. Some states print names of the candidates for president and vice president at the top of the Nov. ballot; others list only the electors' names. In either case, the electors of the party receiving the highest vote are elected. Two states, Maine and Nebraska, allow for proportional allocation.

The electors meet on the first Monday after the 2nd Wednesday in December in their respective state capitals or in some other place prescribed by state legislatures. By long-established custom, they vote for their party nominees, although this is not required by federal law; some states do require it.

The Constitution requires electors to cast a ballot for at least one person who is not an inhabitant of that elector's home state. This ensures that presidential and vice presidential candidates from the same party will not be from the same state. (In 2000, Republican vice presidential nominee Dick Cheney changed his voter registration to Wyoming from Gov. George W. Bush's home state of Texas.) Also, an elector cannot be a member of Congress or hold federal office.

Certified and sealed lists of the votes of the electors in each state are sent to the president of the U.S. Senate, who then opens them in the presence of the members of the Senate and House of Representatives in a joint session held in early Jan., and the electoral votes of all the states are then officially counted.

If no candidate for president has a majority, the House of Representatives chooses a president from the top 3 candidates, with all representatives from each state combining to cast one vote for that state. The House decided the outcome of the 1800 and 1824 presidential elections. If no candidate for vice president has a majority, the Senate chooses from the top 2, with the senators voting as individuals. The Senate chose the vice president following the 1836 election.

Under the electoral college system, a candidate who fails to be the top vote getter in the popular vote still may win a majority of electoral votes. This happened in the elections of 1876, 1888, and 2000.

Electoral Votes for President

Electoral votes based on the 2000 Census were in force beginning with the 2004 elections.

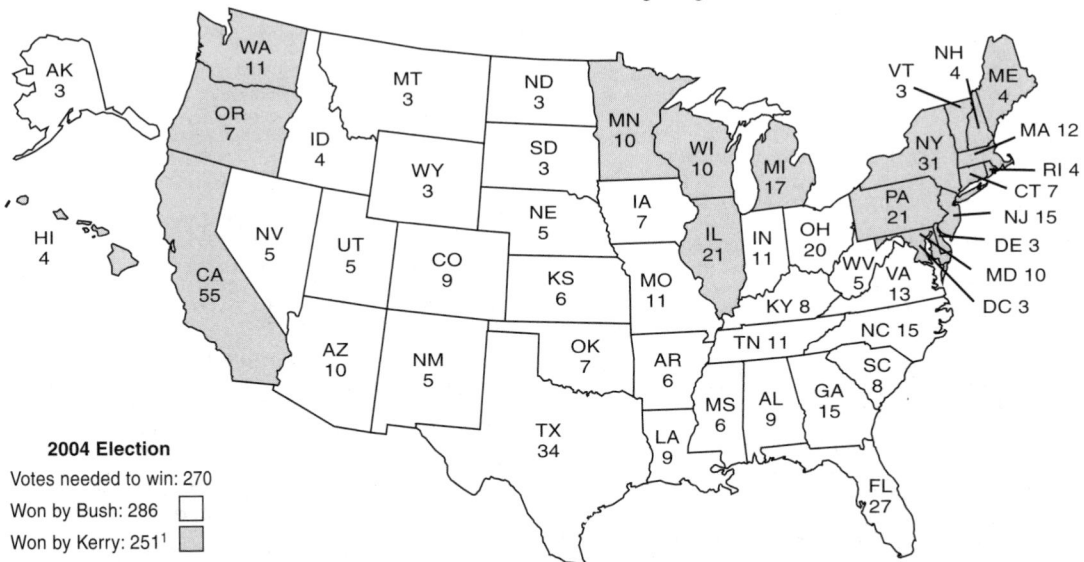

2004 Election

Votes needed to win: 270

Won by Bush: 286 ☐

Won by Kerry: 251[1] ▨

(1) A Minnesota elector pledged to Kerry voted for his running mate, Sen. John Edwards.

Voter Turnout in Presidential Elections, 1932-2004

Source: Federal Election Commission; Commission for Study of American Electorate; *Congressional Quarterly*

	Candidates	Voter Participation (% of voting-age population)		Candidates	Voter Participation (% of voting-age population)
1932	Roosevelt-Hoover	52.4	1972	Nixon-McGovern	55.2[1]
1936	Roosevelt-Landon	56.0	1976	Carter-Ford	53.5
1940	Roosevelt-Willkie	58.9	1980	Reagan-Carter	54.0
1944	Roosevelt-Dewey	56.0	1984	Reagan-Mondale	53.1
1948	Truman-Dewey	51.1	1988	Bush-Dukakis	50.2
1952	Eisenhower-Stevenson	61.6	1992	Clinton-Bush-Perot	55.9
1956	Eisenhower-Stevenson	59.3	1996	Clinton-Dole-Perot	49.0
1960	Kennedy-Nixon	62.8	2000	Bush-Gore	51.3
1964	Johnson-Goldwater	61.9	2004	Bush-Kerry	60.7
1968	Nixon-Humphrey	60.9			

(1) The sharp drop in 1972 followed the expansion of eligibility with the enfranchisement of 18- to 20-year-olds.

Major-Party Nominees for President and Vice President, 1856-2004

Asterisk (*) denotes winning ticket

Democratic			Republican		
Year	President	Vice President	Year	President	Vice President
1856	James Buchanan*	John Breckinridge	1856	John Frémont	William Dayton
1860	Stephen A. Douglas (1)	Herschel V. Johnson	1860	Abraham Lincoln*	Hannibal Hamlin
1864	George McClellan	G.H. Pendleton	1864	Abraham Lincoln*	Andrew Johnson
1868	Horatio Seymour	Francis Blair	1868	Ulysses S. Grant*	Schuyler Colfax
1872	Horace Greeley	B. Gratz Brown	1872	Ulysses S. Grant*	Henry Wilson
1876	Samuel J. Tilden	Thomas Hendricks	1876	Rutherford B. Hayes*	William Wheeler
1880	Winfield Hancock	William English	1880	James A. Garfield*	Chester A. Arthur
1884	Grover Cleveland*	Thomas Hendricks	1884	James Blaine	John Logan
1888	Grover Cleveland	A.G. Thurman	1888	Benjamin Harrison*	Levi Morton
1892	Grover Cleveland*	Adlai Stevenson	1892	Benjamin Harrison	Whitelaw Reid
1896	William J. Bryan	Arthur Sewall	1896	William McKinley*	Garret Hobart
1900	William J. Bryan	Adlai Stevenson	1900	William McKinley*	Theodore Roosevelt
1904	Alton Parker	Henry Davis	1904	Theodore Roosevelt*	Charles Fairbanks
1908	William J. Bryan	John Kern	1908	William H. Taft*	James Sherman
1912	Woodrow Wilson*	Thomas Marshall	1912	William H. Taft	James Sherman (2)
1916	Woodrow Wilson*	Thomas Marshall	1916	Charles Hughes	Charles Fairbanks
1920	James M. Cox	Franklin D. Roosevelt	1920	Warren G. Harding*	Calvin Coolidge
1924	John W. Davis	Charles W. Bryan	1924	Calvin Coolidge*	Charles G. Dawes
1928	Alfred E. Smith	Joseph T. Robinson	1928	Herbert Hoover*	Charles Curtis
1932	Franklin D. Roosevelt*	John N. Garner	1932	Herbert Hoover	Charles Curtis
1936	Franklin D. Roosevelt*	John N. Garner	1936	Alfred M. Landon	Frank Knox
1940	Franklin D. Roosevelt*	Henry A. Wallace	1940	Wendell L. Willkie	Charles McNary
1944	Franklin D. Roosevelt*	Harry S. Truman	1944	Thomas E. Dewey	John W. Bricker
1948	Harry S. Truman*	Alben W. Barkley	1948	Thomas E. Dewey	Earl Warren
1952	Adlai E. Stevenson	John J. Sparkman	1952	Dwight D. Eisenhower*	Richard M. Nixon
1956	Adlai E. Stevenson	Estes Kefauver	1956	Dwight D. Eisenhower*	Richard M. Nixon
1960	John F. Kennedy*	Lyndon B. Johnson	1960	Richard M. Nixon	Henry Cabot Lodge
1964	Lyndon B. Johnson*	Hubert H. Humphrey	1964	Barry M. Goldwater	William E. Miller
1968	Hubert H. Humphrey	Edmund S. Muskie	1968	Richard M. Nixon*	Spiro T. Agnew
1972	George S. McGovern	R. Sargent Shriver Jr. (3)	1972	Richard M. Nixon*	Spiro T. Agnew
1976	Jimmy Carter*	Walter F. Mondale	1976	Gerald R. Ford	Bob Dole
1980	Jimmy Carter	Walter F. Mondale	1980	Ronald Reagan*	George H. W. Bush
1984	Walter F. Mondale	Geraldine Ferraro	1984	Ronald Reagan*	George H. W. Bush
1988	Michael S. Dukakis	Lloyd Bentsen	1988	George H.W. Bush*	Dan Quayle
1992	Bill Clinton*	Al Gore	1992	George H.W. Bush	Dan Quayle
1996	Bill Clinton*	Al Gore	1996	Bob Dole	Jack Kemp
2000	Al Gore	Joseph Lieberman	2000	George W. Bush*	Richard Cheney
2004	John Kerry	John Edwards	2004	George W. Bush*	Richard Cheney

(1) Douglas and Johnson were nominated at the Baltimore convention. An earlier convention in Charleston, SC, failed to reach a consensus and resulted in a split in the party. The Southern faction of the Democrats nominated John Breckinridge for president and Joseph Lane for vice president. (2) Died Oct. 30; replaced on ballot by Nicholas Butler. (3) Chosen by Democratic National Committee after Thomas Eagleton withdrew because of controversy over past treatments for depression.

Third-Party and Independent Presidential Candidates

Although many "third party" candidates or independents have pursued the presidency, only 10 of these from 1832 to 2000 have polled more than a million votes. In most elections since 1860, fewer than one vote in 20 has been cast for a third-party candidate. Major vote getters among third-party and independent candidates include James B. Weaver (People's Party), 1892; former Pres. Theodore Roosevelt (Progressive Party), 1912; Robert M. La Follette (Progressive Party), 1924; George C. Wallace (American Independent Party), 1968; and H. Ross Perot, as an independent in 1992 and with the Reform Party in 1996. In these 6 elections non-major-party candidates combined polled at least 10% of the vote.

Roosevelt outpolled the Republican candidate, William Howard Taft, in 1912, capturing 28% of the popular vote

and 88 electoral votes. In 1948, Strom Thurmond was able to capture 39 electoral votes (from 5 Southern states); however, all third parties received only 5.75% of the popular vote in the election. Twenty years later, George Wallace's popularity in the same region allowed him to get 46 electoral votes and 13.5% of the popular vote.

In 1992 Perot captured 19% of the popular vote; however, he did not win a single state. In 1996, Perot won 8% of the popular vote; all third-party candidates combined won just over 10%. In 2000, Ralph Nader won about 3% of the vote.

Despite the difficulty in winning the presidency, independent and third-party candidates often bring attention to their most prominent issues. They can also affect the outcome between major-party candidates.

Notable Third Party and Independent Campaigns by Year

Party	Presidential nominee	Year	Issues	Strength in . . .
Anti-Masonic	William Wirt	1832	Against secret societies and oaths	PA, VT
Liberty	James G. Birney	1844	Anti-slavery	North
Free Soil	Martin Van Buren	1848	Anti-slavery	NY, OH
American (Know-Nothing)	Millard Fillmore	1856	Anti-immigrant	Northeast, South
Greenback	Peter Cooper	1876	For "cheap money," labor rights	National
Greenback	James B. Weaver	1880	For "cheap money," labor rights	National
Prohibition	John P. St. John	1884	Anti-liquor	National
People's (Populists)	James B. Weaver	1892	For "cheap money," end of national banks	South, West
Socialist	Eugene V. Debs	1900-12; 1902	For public ownership	National
Progressive (Bull Moose)	Theodore Roosevelt	1912	Against high tariffs	Midwest, West
Progressive	Robert M. La Follette	1924	Farmer and labor rights	Midwest, West
Socialist	Norman Thomas	1928-48	Liberal reforms	National
Union	William Lemke	1936	Anti-New Deal	National
States' Rights (Dixiecrats)	Strom Thurmond	1948	For states' rights	South
Progressive	Henry A. Wallace	1948	Anti-Cold War	NY, CA
American Independent	George C. Wallace	1968	For states' rights	South
American	John G. Schmitz	1972	For "law and order"	Far West, OH, LA
None (Independent)	John B. Anderson	1980	A 3rd choice	National
None (Independent)	H. Ross Perot	1992	Federal budget deficit	National
Reform	H. Ross Perot	1996	Deficit; campaign finance	National
Green, Independent	Ralph Nader	2000, 2004	Corporate power; domestic priorities	National

Popular and Electoral Vote for President, 1789-2004

(D) Democrat; (DR) Democratic Republican; (F) Federalist; (LR) Liberal Republican; (NR) National Republican;
(P) People's; (PR) Progressive; (R) Republican; (RF) Reform; (SR) States' Rights; (W) Whig; Asterisk (*)–See notes at bottom.

Year	President elected	Popular	Elec.	Major losing candidate(s)	Popular	Elec.
1789	George Washington (F)	Unknown	69	No opposition	—	—
1792	George Washington (F)	Unknown	132	No opposition	—	—
1796	John Adams (F)	Unknown	71	Thomas Jefferson (DR)	Unknown	68
1800*	Thomas Jefferson (DR)	Unknown	73	Aaron Burr (DR)	Unknown	73
1804	Thomas Jefferson (DR)	Unknown	162	Charles Pinckney (F)	Unknown	14
1808	James Madison (DR)	Unknown	122	Charles Pinckney (F)	Unknown	47
1812	James Madison (DR)	Unknown	128	DeWitt Clinton (F)	Unknown	89
1816	James Monroe (DR)	Unknown	183	Rufus King (F)	Unknown	34
1820	James Monroe (DR)	Unknown	231	John Quincy Adams (DR)	Unknown	1
1824*	John Quincy Adams (DR)	113,122	84	Andrew Jackson (DR)	151,271	99
				Henry Clay (DR)	46,587	37
				William H. Crawford (DR)	44,282	41
1828	Andrew Jackson (D)	642,553	178	John Quincy Adams (NR)	500,897	83
1832	Andrew Jackson (D)	701,780	219	Henry Clay (NR)	484,205	49
1836	Martin Van Buren (D)	764,176	170	William H. Harrison (W)	550,816	73
1840	William H. Harrison (W)	1,275,390	234	Martin Van Buren (D)	1,128,854	60
1844	James K. Polk (D)	1,339,494	170	Henry Clay (W)	1,300,004	105
1848	Zachary Taylor (W)	1,361,393	163	Lewis Cass (D)	1,223,460	127
				Martin Van Buren (Free Soil)	291,501	—
1852	Franklin Pierce (D)	1,607,510	254	Winfield Scott (W)	1,386,942	42
1856	James Buchanan (D)	1,836,072	174	John C. Fremont (R)	1,342,345	114
				Millard Fillmore (American)	873,053	8
1860	Abraham Lincoln (R)	1,865,908	180	Stephen A. Douglas (D)	848,019	12
				John C. Breckinridge (D)	845,763	72
				John Bell (Const. Union)	589,581	39
1864	Abraham Lincoln (R)	2,218,388	212	George McClellan (D)	1,812,807	21
1868	Ulysses S. Grant (R)	3,013,650	214	Horatio Seymour (D)	2,708,744	80
1872*	Ulysses S. Grant (R)	3,598,235	286	Horace Greeley (D-LR)*	2,834,671	—
1876*	Rutherford B. Hayes (R)	4,034,311	185	Samuel J. Tilden (D)	4,288,546	184
1880	James A. Garfield (R)	4,446,158	214	Winfield S. Hancock (D)	4,444,260	155
1884	Grover Cleveland (D)	4,874,621	219	James G. Blaine (R)	4,848,936	182
1888	Benjamin Harrison (R)	5,443,892	233	Grover Cleveland (D)	5,534,488	168
1892	Grover Cleveland (D)	5,551,883	277	Benjamin Harrison (R)	5,179,244	145
				James Weaver (P)	1,027,329	22
1896	William McKinley (R)	7,108,480	271	William J. Bryan (D-P)	6,511,495	176
1900	William McKinley (R)	7,218,039	292	William J. Bryan (D)	6,358,345	155
1904	Theodore Roosevelt (R)	7,626,593	336	Alton B. Parker (D)	5,082,898	140
1908	William H. Taft (R)	7,676,258	321	William J. Bryan (D)	6,406,801	162
1912	Woodrow Wilson (D)	6,293,152	435	Theodore Roosevelt (PR)	4,119,207	88
				William H. Taft (R)	3,483,922	8
1916	Woodrow Wilson (D)	9,126,300	277	Charles E. Hughes (R)	8,546,789	254
1920	Warren G. Harding (R)	16,153,115	404	James M. Cox (D)	9,133,092	127
1924	Calvin Coolidge (R)	15,719,921	382	John W. Davis (D)	8,386,704	136
				Robert M. La Follette (PR)	4,822,856	13
1928	Herbert Hoover (R)	21,437,277	444	Alfred E. Smith (D)	15,007,698	87
1932	Franklin D. Roosevelt (D)	22,829,501	472	Herbert Hoover (R)	15,760,684	59
1936	Franklin D. Roosevelt (D)	27,757,333	523	Alfred Landon (R)	16,684,231	8
1940	Franklin D. Roosevelt (D)	27,313,041	449	Wendell Willkie (R)	22,348,480	82
1944	Franklin D. Roosevelt (D)	25,612,610	432	Thomas E. Dewey (R)	22,117,617	99
1948	Harry S. Truman (D)	24,179,345	303	Thomas E. Dewey (R)	21,991,291	189
				Strom Thurmond (SR)	1,169,021	39
				Henry A. Wallace (PR)	1,157,172	—
1952	Dwight D. Eisenhower (R)	33,936,234	442	Adlai E. Stevenson (D)	27,314,992	89
1956*	Dwight D. Eisenhower (R)	35,590,472	457	Adlai E. Stevenson (D)	26,022,752	73
1960*	John F. Kennedy (D)	34,226,731	303	Richard M. Nixon (R)	34,108,157	219
1964	Lyndon B. Johnson (D)	43,129,566	486	Barry M. Goldwater (R)	27,178,188	52
1968	Richard M. Nixon (R)	31,785,480	301	Hubert H. Humphrey (D)	31,275,166	191
				George C. Wallace (3rd party)	9,906,473	46
1972*	Richard M. Nixon (R)	47,169,911	520	George S. McGovern (D)	29,170,383	17
1976*	Jimmy Carter (D)	40,830,763	297	Gerald R. Ford (R)	39,147,793	240
1980	Ronald Reagan (R)	43,904,153	489	Jimmy Carter (D)	35,483,883	49
				John B. Anderson (independent)	5,719,437	—
1984	Ronald Reagan (R)	54,455,075	525	Walter F. Mondale (D)	37,577,185	13
1988*	George H. W. Bush (R)	48,886,097	426	Michael S. Dukakis (D)	41,809,074	111
1992	Bill Clinton (D)	44,908,254	370	George H. W. Bush (R)	39,102,343	168
				H. Ross Perot (independent)	19,741,065	—
1996	Bill Clinton (D)	45,590,703	379	Bob Dole (R)	37,816,307	159
				H. Ross Perot (RF)	7,866,284	—
2000*	George W. Bush (R)	50,459,211	271	Al Gore (D)	51,003,894	266
				Ralph Nader (Green)	2,834,410	—
2004*	George W. Bush (R)	62,040,610	286	John Kerry (D)	59,028,444	251
				Ralph Nader (Independent)	411,306	—

*1800—Elected by House of Representatives because of tied electoral vote. 1824—Elected by House of Representatives because no candidate had polled a majority. By 1824, the Democratic Republicans had become a loose coalition of competing political groups. By 1828, the supporters of Jackson were known as Democrats, and the John Q. Adams and Henry Clay supporters as National Republicans. 1872—Greeley died Nov. 29, 1872. His electoral votes were split among 4 individuals. 1876—FL, LA, OR, and SC election returns were disputed. Congress in joint session (Mar. 2, 1877) declared Hayes and Wheeler elected president and vice president. 1956—Democrats elected 74 electors, but one from Alabama refused to vote for Stevenson. 1960—Sen. Harry F. Byrd (D, VA) received 15 electoral votes. 1972—John Hospers of California received one vote from an elector of Virginia. 1976—Ronald Reagan of CA received one vote from an elector of Washington. 1988—Sen. Lloyd Bentsen (D, TX) received 1 vote from an elector of West Virginia. 2000—One Gore elector from Washington, DC, abstained. Nader was listed as "Independent" on the ballot in some states, and was not on the ballot in all states. 2004—One Minnesota elector voted for VP candidate John Edwards for both president and vice president.

100 MOST POPULOUS U.S. CITIES

Source: Bureau of Labor Statistics: employment; Bureau of Econ. Analysis: per cap. income; other data U.S. Census Bureau.

Included here are the 100 most populous U.S. cities, using 2005 Census Bureau estimates. Population rank indicated by figure in parentheses. Most data are for the city proper. Some statistics, where noted, apply to the whole Metropolitan Statistical Area (MSA). Employment figures are for 2005 (exept for New Orleans, LA); per capita income figures for 2004. Mayors are as of Sept. 2006. Inc.=incorporated; est.=established. **Note:** Websites are as of Sept. 2006 and subject to change. For a listing of the 100 largest U.S. cities, ranked by population, *see* p. 479.

Akron, Ohio

Population (2005): 210,795 (89); **Pop. Density:** 3,394; **Pop. change (2000-2005):** –2.9%. **Area:** 62.1 sq. mi. **Employment (2005):** 100,172 employed; 6.6% unemployed. **Per capita income (MSA):** $32,462; increase (2003-2004): 4.5%.

Mayor: Donald L. Plusquellic, Democrat

History: settled 1825; inc. as city 1865; located on Ohio-Erie Canal and is a port of entry; polymer center of the Americas.

Transportation: 1 airport; major trucking industry; Conrail, Amtrak; metro transit system. **Communications:** 1 TV, 8 radio stations; 1 daily newspaper. **Medical facilities:** 4 hosp.; specialized children's treatment center. **Educational facilities:** 4 univ. and colleges; 68 pub. schools. **Further information:** Greater Akron Chamber, One Cascade Plaza, 17th Floor, Akron, OH 44308; www.ci.akron.oh.us; www.greaterakronchamber.org

Albuquerque, New Mexico

Population (2005): 494,236 (33); **Pop. Density:** 2,737; **Pop. change (2000-2005):** 10.2%. **Area:** 180.6 sq. mi. **Employment (2005):** 247,691 employed; 4.5% unemployed. **Per capita income (MSA):** $29,453; increase (2003-2004): 3.8%.

Mayor: Martin J. Chavez, Democrat

History: founded 1706 by the Spanish; inc. 1890.

Transportation: 1 intl. airport; 1 railroad; 11 bus service/charters. **Communications:** 13 TV, 32 radio stations. **Medical facilities:** 6 major hosp. **Educational facilities:** 1 univ., 25 colleges. **Further information:** Albuquerque Convention & Visitors Bureau, PO Box 26866, Albuquerque, NM 87125-6866; www.itsatrip.org; www.cabq.gov/a-z.org

Anaheim, California

Population (2005): 331,804 (55); **Pop. Density:** 6,785; **Pop. change (2000-2005):** 1.2%. **Area:** 48.9 sq. mi. **Employment (2005):** 164,830 employed; 4.9% unemployed. **Per capita income (MSA):** $35,188; increase (2003-2004): 5.3%.

Mayor: Curt Pringle, Republican

History: founded 1857; inc. 1870; home of Disneyland Resort, Mighty Ducks of Anaheim, and the Anaheim Angels.

Transportation: Amtrak, Metrolink (2 sta.), OCTA bus service, Greyhound. **Communications:** 2 TV, 2 radio stations (MSA). **Medical facilities:** 4 hosp.; 5 medical centers. **Educational facilities:** 13 univ. and colleges; 39 elem., 11 junior high, 10 high schools (MSA). **Further information:** City Hall, 200 South Anaheim Blvd., Ste. 733, Anaheim, CA 92805; www.anaheim.net

Anchorage, Alaska

Population (2005): 275,043 (68); **Pop. Density:** 162; **Pop. change (2000-2005):** 5.7%. **Area:** 1,697.2 sq. mi. **Employment (2005):** 139,888 employed; 5.4% unemployed. **Per capita income (MSA):** $37,058; increase (2003-2004): 3%.

Mayor: Mark Begich, Democrat

History: founded 1914 as a construction camp for railroad; HQ of Alaska Defense Command, WWII; severely damaged in earthquake 1964, now rebuilt; current population center of Alaska.

Transportation: 1 intl. airport; 1 railroad; transit system, 1 port. **Communications:** 9 TV, 28 radio stations. **Medical facilities:** 4 hosp. **Educational facilities:** 3 univ., 1 college, 91 pub. schools. **Further information:** Anchorage Chamber of Commerce, 441 W. 5th Ave., Ste. 300, Anchorage, AK 99501-2309; www.ci.anchorage.ak.us; www.anchoragechamber.org

Arlington, Texas

Population (2005): 362,805 (50); **Pop. Density:** 3,787; **Pop. change (2000-2005):** 9.0%. **Area:** 95.8 sq. mi. **Employment (2005):** 194,758 employed; 4.9% unemployed. **Per capita income (MSA):** $35,502; increase (2003-2004): 3.9%.

Mayor: Robert N. Cluck, Non-Partisan

History: settled in 1840s; inc. 1884.

Transportation: 1 intl. airport; 1 rail line, Union Pacific. **Communications:** 11 TV, 44 radio stations. **Medical facilities:** 2 hosp. **Educational facilities:** 1 univ., 1 junior college; 60 pub. schools. **Further information:** Arlington Chamber of Commerce, 505 East Border, Arlington, TX 76010; City of Arlington, 101 W. Abram, Arlington, TX 76010; www.ci.arlington.tx.us; www.arlingtontx.com

Atlanta, Georgia

Population (2005): 470,688 (35); **Pop. Density:** 3,574; **Pop. change (2000-2005):** 13.0%. **Area:** 131.7 sq. mi. **Employment (2005):** 187,783 employed; 6.6% unemployed. **Per capita income (MSA):** $33,838; increase (2003-2004): 3.2%.

Mayor: Shirley Franklin, Democrat

History: founded as "Terminus" 1837; renamed Atlanta 1845; inc. 1847; played major role in Civil War; became permanent state capital 1877; birthplace of civil rights movement; host to 1996 Centennial Olympic Games.

Transportation: 1 intl. airport; 3 railroad lines; MARTA bus and rapid rail service. **Communications:** 14 TV, 56 radio stations; 29 cable TV cos. **Medical facilities:** 61 hosp.; VA hosp.; U.S. Centers for Disease Control and Prevention; American Cancer Society. **Educational facilities:** 43 colleges, univ., seminaries, junior colleges; 85 pub. schools. **Further information:** Metro Atlanta Chamber of Commerce, 235 Andrew Young Intl. Blvd. NW, Atlanta, GA 30303; www.metroatlantachamber.com; www.atlantaga.gov

Aurora, Colorado

Population (2005): 297,235 (60); **Pop. Density:** 2,086; **Pop. change (2000-2005):** 7.5%. **Area:** 142.5 sq. mi. **Employment (2005):** 154,028 employed; 6.2% unemployed. **Per capita income (MSA):** $40,939; increase (2003-2004): 4.2%.

Mayor: Ed Tauer, Non-Partisan

History: founded in 1891 and originally called Fletcher; renamed Aurora in 1907; inc. 1929. Early growth stimulated by presence of military bases; fast-growing trade, technology, and medical science center.

Transportation: adjacent to Denver Intl. Airport; bus system. **Communications:** 1 TV station. **Medical facilities:** Major pub. univ. medical center; 2 pub. hosp. **Educational facilities:** 1 univ., 4 community and junior colleges, 2 technical colleges; 68 pub. schools, 4 private schools. **Further information:** Aurora Planning Dept., 15151 E. Alameda Pkwy., Aurora, CO 80012; www.auroragov.org; www.aurorachamber.org

Austin, Texas

Population (2005): 690,252 (16); **Pop. Density:** 2,745; **Pop. change (2000-2005):** 5.1%. **Area:** 251.5 sq. mi. **Employment (2005):** 386,776 employed; 4.4% unemployed. **Per capita income (MSA):** $32,494; increase (2003-2004): 3.5%.

Mayor: Will Wynn, Non-Partisan

History: first permanent settlement 1835; capital of Rep. of Texas 1839; named after Stephen Austin; inc. 1840.

Transportation: 1 intl. airport; 2 railroads. **Communications:** 8 TV, 29 radio stations. **Medical facilities:** 15 hosp. **Educational facilities:** 6 univ. and colleges. **Further information:** Greater Austin Chamber, 210 Barton Springs Rd., Ste. 400, Austin, TX 78704; www.ci.austin.tx.us; www.austinchamber.com

Bakersfield, California

Population (2005): 295,536 (61); **Pop. Density:** 2,613; **Pop. change (2000-2005):** 19.6%. **Area:** 113.1 sq. mi. **Employment (2005):** 132,276 employed; 5.7% unemployed. **Per capita income (MSA):** $24,335; increase (2003-2004): 4.6%.

Mayor: Harvey L. Hall, Non-Partisan

History: named after Col. Thomas Baker, an early settler; inc. 1898.

Transportation: 2 airports; 3 railroads; Amtrak; Greyhound buses; local bus system. **Communications:** 8 TV, 29 radio stations. **Medical facilities:** 9 major hosp.; 9 convalescent, 1 psychiatric, 3 physical rehab., 5 urgent care facilities; 3 clinics. **Educational facilities:** 9 univ., 1 community college, 14 vocational schools, 1 adult school, 15 elem. school districts, 14 high schools (Kern County). **Further information:** Greater Bakersfield Chamber of Commerce, 1725 Eye St., PO Box 1947, Bakersfield, CA 93303; www.bakersfieldchamber.org; www.bakersfieldcity.us

Baltimore, Maryland

Population (2005): 635,815 (18); **Pop. Density:** 7,869; **Pop. change (2000-2005):** –2.4%. **Area:** 80.8 sq. mi. **Employment (2005):** 256,000 employed; 7.1% unemployed. **Per capita income (MSA):** $38,813; increase (2003-2004): 5.3%.

Mayor: Martin O'Malley, Democrat

▶ IT'S A FACT: Anchorage, AK, is the largest city in the U.S in terms of land area. With an area of 1,697.2 sq. mi., Anchorage is actually larger than the entire state of Rhode Island, which has an area of 1,045 sq. mi.

History: founded by Maryland legislature 1729; inc. 1797; War of 1812 British artillery barrage of Ft. McHenry (1814) inspired Francis Scott Key to write "Star-Spangled Banner"; birthplace of America's railroads 1828; rebuilt after fire 1904; site of National Aquarium 1981.

Transportation: 1 major airport; 3 railroads; bus system; subway system; light rail system; Inner Harbor water taxi system; 2 underwater tunnels. **Communications:** 6 TV, 25 radio stations. **Medical facilities:** 31 hosp.; 2 major medical centers. **Educational facilities:** over 30 univ. and colleges; 186 pub. schools. **Further information:** Greater Baltimore Committee, 111 S. Calvert St., Ste. 1700, Baltimore, MD 21202-6180; www.ci.baltimore.md.us; www.baltimore.org

Baton Rouge, Louisiana

Population (2005): 222,064 (82); **Pop. Density:** 2,891; **Pop. change (2000-2005):** −2.5%. **Area:** 76.8 sq. mi. **Employment (2005):** 103,969 employed; 7.4% unemployed. **Per capita income (MSA):** $27,780; increase (2003-2004): 4.5%.

Mayor: Melvin "Kip" Holden, Democrat

History: claimed by Spain at time of Louisiana Purchase 1803; est. independence by rebellion 1810; inc. as town 1817; became state capital 1849; Union-held most of Civil War.

Transportation: 1 airport, 5 airlines; 1 bus line; 3 railroad trunk lines. **Communications:** 5 TV, 19 radio stations. **Medical facilities:** 5 hosp. **Educational facilities:** 107 pub., 52 nonpublic schools; 2 univ., 1 Community College, 1 Technical College. **Further information:** The Chamber of Greater Baton Rouge, PO Box 3217, Baton Rouge, LA 70821; www.brgov.com; www.brchamber.org

Birmingham, Alabama

Population (2005): 231,483 (79); **Pop. Density:** 1,544; **Pop. change (2000-2005):** −4.7%. **Area:** 149.9 sq. mi. **Employment (2005):** 98,895 employed; 5% unemployed. **Per capita income (MSA):** $33,067; increase (2003-2004): 5.2%.

Mayor: Bernard Kincaid, Democrat

History: settled 1871 at the intersection of 2 major railroads, within proximity of elements needed for iron and steel production.

Transportation: 1 intl. airport; 4 major rail freight lines, Amtrak; 1 bus line; 75 truck line terminals; 5 air cargo cos.; 7 barge lines; 5 interstate highways. **Communications:** 7 TV, 32 radio stations; 1 educational TV, 1 educational radio station. **Medical facilities:** 16, including the Univ. of Alabama at Birmingham Medical Center; VA hosp. **Educational facilities:** 1 pub., 2 private univ.; 4 private colleges, 3 private law schools. **Further information:** Birmingham Area Chamber of Commerce, 2027 First Ave. N, Birmingham, AL 35203; www.birminghamchamber.com; www.informationbirmingham.com

Boston, Massachusetts

Population (2005): 559,034 (24); **Pop. Density:** 11,550; **Pop. change (2000-2005):** −5.1%. **Area:** 48.4 sq. mi. **Employment (2005):** 274,327 employed; 5.2% unemployed. **Per capita income (MSA):** $46,060; increase (2003-2004): 5.9%.

Mayor: Thomas M. Menino, Democrat

History: settled 1630 by John Winthrop; capital of Mass. Bay Colony; figured prominently in Am. Revolution, earning distinction as the "Cradle of Liberty"; inc. 1822.

Transportation: 1 major airport; 2 railroads; city rail and subway system; 3 underwater tunnels; port. **Communications:** 12 TV, 21 radio stations. **Medical facilities:** 31 hosp.; 8 major medical research centers. **Educational facilities:** 31 univ. and colleges. **Further information:** Greater Boston Convention and Visitors Bureau, 2 Copley Pl., Suite 105, Boston, MA 02116; www.bostonusa.com

Buffalo, New York

Population (2005): 279,745 (66); **Pop. Density:** 6,890; **Pop. change (2000-2005):** −4.4%. **Area:** 40.6 sq. mi. **Employment (2005):** 116,523 employed; 6.6% unemployed. **Per capita income (MSA):** $31,006; increase (2003-2004): 4.9%.

Mayor: Byron W. Brown, Democrat

History: settled 1780 by Seneca Indians; raided twice by British, War of 1812; served as western terminus for Erie Canal, became a center for trade and manufacturing; inc. 1832; last stop on the Underground Railroad; key point for Canada-U.S. political, trade, and social relations.

Transportation: 1 intl. airport; 4 Class I railroads; Amtrak metro rail system; water service to Great Lakes-St. Lawrence Seaway system and Atlantic seaboard. **Communications:** 11 TV, 27 radio stations. **Medical facilities:** 16 hosp., 40 research centers. **Educational facilities:** 15 colleges and univ.; 500 pub. and private schools, 20 area colleges and universities. **Further information:** Buffalo Niagara Visitor Center, Market Arcade/Walden Galleria, 617 Main Street, Buffalo, NY 14203; www.ci.buffalo.ny.us; buffaloniagara.org

Chandler, Arizona

Population (2005): 234,939 (75); **Pop. Density:** 4,058; **Pop. change (2000-2005):** 33.0%. **Area:** 57.9 sq. mi. **Employment (2005):** 114,427 employed; 3.1% unemployed. **Per capita income (MSA):** $31,133; increase (2003-2004): 4.9%.

Mayor: Boyd W. Dunn, Non-Partisan

History: town formed 1912; population doubled in 1990s as "the high-tech oasis of the Silicon Desert."

Transportation: 1 municipal airport; mass transit system. **Communications:** 2 TV, 3 newspapers. **Medical facilities:** 1 medical center. **Educational facilities:** 2 univ., 1 community coll.; 25 elem., 6 junior high, 3 high schools; 13 charter schools **Further information:** Chandler Chamber, 25 South Arizona Pl., Suite 201, Chandler, AZ 85225; www.chandlerchamber.com; chandleraz.gov

Charlotte, North Carolina

Population (2005): 610,949 (20); **Pop. Density:** 2,521; **Pop. change (2000-2005):** 13.0%. **Area:** 242.3 sq. mi. **Employment (2005):** 313,295 employed; 4.8% unemployed. **Per capita income (MSA):** $34,816; increase (2003-2004): 6.1%.

Mayor: Patrick McCrory, Republican

History: settled by Scotch-Irish immigrants 1740s; inc. 1768 and named after Queen Charlotte, George III's wife; scene of first major U.S. gold discovery 1799.

Transportation: 1 airport; 2 major railway lines; 1 bus line; 605 trucking firms. **Communications:** 12 TV, 28 radio stations. **Medical facilities:** 10 hosp., 2 medical centers. **Educational facilities:** 9 univ., 9 colleges, 89 elem. schools, 31 middle schools, 17 high schools. **Further information:** Chamber of Commerce, PO Box 32785, Charlotte, NC 28232; www.charlottechamber.com

Chesapeake, Virginia

Population (2005): 218,968 (85); **Pop. Density:** 643; **Pop. change (2000-2005):** 9.9%. **Area:** 340.7 sq. mi. **Employment (2005):** 106,921 employed; 3.5% unemployed. **Per capita income (MSA):** $31,811; increase (2003-2004): 5.4%.

Mayor: Dalton S. Edge, Non-Partisan

History: region settled in 1620s with first English colonies on banks of Elizabeth River; home to Great Dismal Swamp Canal, first envisioned by George Washington in 1763; Battle of Great Bridge fought here Dec. 1775; inc. as a city 1963.

Transportation: Freight rail service; bus service; 2 regional airports. **Communications:** 9 TV, 48 radio stations (serving Hampton Roads community). **Medical facilities:** 1 hosp. **Educational facilities:** 9 colleges and univ.; 49 pub. schools and educational centers. **Further information:** City of Chesapeake, Public Communications Dept., 306 Cedar Rd., Chesapeake, VA 23322; www.cityofchesapeake.net

Chicago, Illinois

Population (2005): 2,842,518 (3); **Pop. Density:** 12,517; **Pop. change (2000-2005):** −1.8%. **Area:** 227.1 sq. mi. **Employment (2005):** 1,220,265 employed; 7% unemployed. **Per capita inc. (MSA):** $37,169; increase (2003-2004): 3.2%

Mayor: Richard M. Daley, Democrat

History: site acquired from Indians 1795; significant white settlement began with Erie Canal 1825; chartered as city 1837; boomed with arrival of railroads and canal to Mississippi R.; one-third of city destroyed by fire 1871; major grain and livestock market.

Transportation: 2 airports; major railroad system, trucking industry. **Communications:** 15 TV, 35 radio stations. **Medical facilities:** over 41 hosp. **Educational facilities:** 63 insts. of higher learning. **Further information:** Chicagoland Chamber of Commerce, 1 IBM Plaza, Ste. 2800, Chicago, IL 60611; www.cityofchicago.org; www.chicagolandchamber.com

Chula Vista, California

Population (2005): 210,497 (90); **Pop. Density:** 4,305; **Pop. change (2000-2005):** 21.3%. **Area:** 48.9 sq. mi. **Employment (2005):** 83,207 employed; 5.1% unemployed. **Per capita income (MSA):** $37,965; increase (2003-2004): 6%.

Mayor: Stephen C. Padilla, Non-Partisan

History: visited by Spanish in 1542; became part of Spanish land grant in 1795; came into the U.S. during the Mexican War in 1847; inc. 1911. WWII brought aircraft industry and growth.

Transportation: bus system; DART. **Communications:** See San Diego, CA. **Medical facilities:** 2 hosp. **Educational facilities:** 39 elementary, 7 middle, 3 junior high, 10 senior high, 5 colleges and univ. **Further Information:** Chula Vista Chamber of Commerce, 233 Fourth Ave., Chula Vista, CA 91910. www.chulavistachamber.org

Cincinnati, Ohio

Population (2005): 308,728 (58); **Pop. Density:** 3,958; **Pop. change (2000-2005):** −6.8%. **Area:** 78 sq. mi. **Employment (2005):** 147,116 employed; 6.4% unemployed. **Per capita income (MSA):** $34,368; increase (2003-2004): 1%.

Mayor: Mark Mallory, Democrat

▶ *IT'S A FACT:* Boston, MA, is a city of firsts: the first public school in North America was opened there in 1635; the Boston Public Library, opened in 1848, was the first public library to lend books for free, the first to have a branch library, and the first to have a dedicated children's room; the first subway in the U.S. was opened in Boston in 1897.

History: founded 1788 and named after the Society of Cincinnati, an organization of Revolutionary War officers; chartered as village 1802; inc. as city 1819. **Transportation:** 1 intl. airport; 3 railroads; 2 bus systems. **Communications:** 7 TV, 25 radio stations. **Medical facilities:** 28 hosp.; Cincinnati Children's Hosp. Medical Center; VA hosp. **Educational facilities:** 4 univ., 12 colleges, 8 technical & 2-year colleges. **Further information:** Chamber of Commerce, 300 Carew Tower, 441 Vine St., Cincinnati, OH 45202; www.cincinnatichamber.com; www.cincinnatiusa.org

Cleveland, Ohio

Population (2005): 452,208 (39); **Pop. Density:** 5,827; **Pop. change (2000-2005):** –5.5%. **Area:** 77.6 sq. mi. **Employment (2005):** 176,789 employed; 7.9% unemployed. **Per capita income (MSA):** $34,264; increase (2003-2004): 4.7%.
Mayor: Frank G. Jackson, Democrat
History: surveyed in 1796; given recognition as village 1815, inc. as city 1836; annexed Ohio City 1854. **Transportation:** 1 intl. airport; rail service; major port; rapid transit system. **Communications:** 9 TV, 21 radio stations. **Medical facilities:** 14 hosp. **Educational facilities:** 8 univ. and colleges; 127 pub. schools. **Further information:** Greater Cleveland Growth Assn., Tower City Center, 50 Pub. Square, Suite 200, Cleveland, OH 44113-2291; www.clevelandgrowth.com; www.city.cleveland.oh.us

Colorado Springs, Colorado

Population (2005): 369,815 (49); **Pop. Density:** 1,991; **Pop. change (2000-2005):** 2.5%. **Area:** 185.7 sq. mi. **Employment (2005):** 195,491 employed; 5.2% unemployed. **Per capita income (MSA):** $31,991; increase (2003-2004): 4.5%.
Mayor: Lionel Rivera, Non-Partisan
History: city founded in 1871 at the foot of Pike's Peak; inc. 1872. **Transportation:** 1 municipal airport; 1 bus line. **Communications:** 9 TV, 28 radio stations. **Medical facilities:** 5 hosp. **Educational facilities:** 11 univ., 5 colleges. **Further information:** Chamber of Commerce, 2 N. Cascade, Ste. 110, Colorado Springs, CO 80901; www.springsgov.com; www.coloradospringschamber.org

Columbus, Ohio

Population (2005): 730,657 (15); **Pop. Density:** 3,474; **Pop. change (2000-2005):** 2.7%. **Area:** 210.3 sq. mi. **Employment (2005):** 386,660 employed; 5.4% unemployed. **Per capita income (MSA):** $34,128; increase (2003-2004): 3.9%.
Mayor: Michael B. Coleman, Democrat
History: first settlement 1797; laid out as new capital 1812 with current name; became city 1834. **Transportation:** 6 airports; 2 railroads; 2 intercity bus lines. **Communications:** 8 TV, 32 radio stations. **Medical facilities:** 17 hosp. **Educational facilities:** 11 univ. and colleges; 8 technical/2-year schools; 150 pub. schools (95 elem., 26 middle, 19 high, 10 special-purpose). **Further information:** Greater Columbus Chamber of Commerce, 37 N. High St., Columbus, OH 43215. Experience Columbus, 90 N. High St., Columbus, OH 43215; www.columbus-chamber.org; www.experiencecolumbus.org

Corpus Christi, Texas

Population (2005): 283,474 (64); **Pop. Density:** 1,834; **Pop. change (2000-2005):** 2.2%. **Area:** 154.6 sq. mi. **Employment (2005):** 135,177 employed; 5.3% unemployed. **Per capita income (MSA):** $27,340; increase (2003-2004): 3.9%.
Mayor: Henry Garrett, Non-Partisan
History: settled 1839 and inc. 1852. **Transportation:** 1 intl. airport; 2 bus lines, metro bus system; 3 freight railroads. **Communications:** 6 TV, 17 radio stations. **Medical facilities:** 14 hosp. including a children's center. **Educational facilities:** 2 univ., 1 college. **Further information:** Corpus Christi Regional Economic Development Corp., PO Box 2724, Corpus Christi, TX 78403; www.ccredc.com; www.ci.corpuschristi.tx.us

Dallas, Texas

Population (2005): 1,213,825 (9); **Pop. Density:** 3,544; **Pop. change (2000-2005):** 2.1%. **Area:** 342.5 sq. mi. **Employment (2005):** 565,656 employed; 5.8% unemployed. **Per capita income (MSA):** $35,502; increase (2003-2004): 3.9%.
Mayor: Laura Miller, Non-Partisan
History: first settled 1841; platted 1846; inc. 1871; developed as the financial and commercial center of Southwest; headquarters of regional Federal Reserve Bank; major center for distribution and high-tech manufacturing. **Transportation:** 1 intl. airport, 1 regional airport; Amtrak; transit system. **Communications:** 17 TV, 52 radio stations. **Medical** facilities: 19 general hosp.; major medical center. **Educational facilities:** 218 pub. schools, 12 univ. and colleges, 3 community college campuses. **Further information:** Greater Dallas Chamber, Resource Center, 700 N. Pearl St., Ste. 1200, Dallas, TX 75201; www.dallaschamber.org; www.dallascityhall.com

Denver, Colorado

Population (2005): 557,917 (25); **Pop. Density:** 3,637; **Pop. change (2000-2005):** 0.6%. **Area:** 153.4 sq. mi. **Employment (2005):** 286,897 employed; 6% unemployed. **Per capita income (MSA):** $40,939; increase (2003-2004): 4.2%.
Mayor: John W. Hickenlooper, Democrat
History: settled 1858 by gold prospectors and miners; inc. 1861; became territorial capital 1867; growth spurred by gold and silver boom; became financial, industrial, cultural center of Rocky Mt. region. **Transportation:** 1 intl. airport, 3 corporate reliever airports; 5 rail freight lines, Amtrak; 1 bus line. **Communications:** 14 TV, 29 radio stations. **Medical facilities:** 20 hosp. **Educational facilities:** 15 four-yr. colleges and.univ.; 8 two-yr. and community colleges. **Further information:** Denver Metro Chamber of Commerce, 1445 Market St., Denver, CO 80202-1729; www.denverchamber.org

Detroit, Michigan

Population (2005): 886,671 (11); **Pop. Density:** 6,388; **Pop. change (2000-2005):** –6.8%. **Area:** 138.8 sq. mi. **Employment (2005):** 321,996 employed; 14.2% unemployed. **Per capita income (MSA):** $36,650; increase (2003-2004): 0.9%.
Mayor: Kwame M. Kilpatrick, Democrat
History: founded by French 1701; controlled by British 1760; acquired by U.S. 1796; destroyed by fire 1805; fought over during War of 1812; inc. as city 1815; capital of state 1837-47; auto manufacturing began 1890. **Transportation:** 1 intl. airport, 1 general aviation airport; 10 railroads (4 Class I); major intl. port; pub. transit system. **Communications:** 4 TV, 6 radio stations. **Medical facilities:** 13 hosp.; 3 major medical centers. **Educational facilities:** 2 univ., 3 colleges, 1 community college. **Further information:** Detroit Regional Chamber, One Woodward Ave., PO Box 33840, Detroit, MI 48232-0840; www.detroitchamber.com

Durham, North Carolina

Population (2005): 204,845 (94); **Pop. Density:** 2,165; **Pop. change (2000-2005):** 9.5%. **Area:** 94.6 sq. mi. **Employment (2005):** 104,020 employed; 4.2 % unemployed. **Per capita income (MSA):** $33,011; increase (2003-2004): 4.5%
Mayor: William V. Bell, Non-Partisan
History: Inc. 1869; Trinity College moved to Durham in 1892, renamed Duke Univ. in 1924. **Transportation:** 2 area bus systems; 1 airport; 1 train station. **Communications:** 34 radio stations; 6 TV stations. **Medical facilities:** 8 hosp. **Educational facilities:** 45 pub. schools, plus private and charter schools; 1 comm. coll.; school of nursing; 2 univ. **Further information:** Durham Convention and Visitors Bureau, 101 E. Morgan St., Durham, NC 2770-3333; www.durham-nc.com

El Paso, Texas

Population (2005): 598,590 (21); **Pop. Density:** 2,403; **Pop. change (2000-2005):** 6.2%. **Area:** 249.1 sq. mi. **Employment (2005):** 234,959 employed; 6.6% unemployed. **Per capita income (MSA):** $21,829; increase (2003-2004): 4.5%.
Mayor: John Cook, Non-Partisan
History: first settled 1598; inc. 1873; arrival of railroad 1881 boosted city's population and industries. **Transportation:** 1 intl. airport; 2 rail providers; 2 interstate highways; 4 intl. ports of entry. **Communications:** 12 TV, 21 radio stations. **Medical facilities:** 8 hosp.; 8 rehabilitation; 11 specialty centers. **Educational facilities:** 5 univ., 2 colleges; 2 grad. and doctoral programs. **Further information:** Greater El Paso Chamber of Commerce, 10 Civic Center Plaza, El Paso, TX 79901; www.elpaso.org

Fort Wayne, Indiana

Population (2005): 223,341 (81); **Pop. Density:** 2,827; **Pop. change (2000-2005):** 8.6%. **Area:** 79 sq. mi. **Employment (2005):** 105,916 employed; 5.7% unemployed. **Per capita income (MSA):** $30,214; increase (2003-2004): 3.3%.
Mayor: Graham A. Richard, Democrat
History: French fort 1680; U.S. fort 1794; settled by 1832; inc. 1840 prior to Wabash-Erie canal completion 1843. **Transportation:** 2 airports; 3 railroads; 6 bus lines. **Communications:** 6 TV, 25 radio stations, 11 newspapers. **Medical facilities:** 8 regional hosp.; VA hosp. **Educational facilities:** 5

univ., 4 colleges, 3 bus. schools; 92 pub. schools. **Further information:** Chamber of Commerce, 826 Ewing Street, Fort Wayne, IN 46802-2182; www.fwchamber.org

Fort Worth, Texas

Population (2005): 624,067 (19); **Pop. Density:** 2,134; **Pop. change (2000-2005):** 16.7%. **Area:** 292.5 sq. mi. **Employment (2005):** 278,363 employed; 5.3% unemployed. **Per capita income (MSA):** $35,502; increase (2003-2004): 3.9%.

Mayor: Mike J. Moncrief, Non-Partisan

History: established as military post 1849; inc. 1873; oil discovered 1917.

Transportation: 2 intl. airport, 1 industrial airport; 4 major railroads, Amtrak; local bus service; 1 transcontinental, 1 intrastate bus lines. **Communications:** 15 TV, 95 local radio stations. **Medical facilities:** 10 hosp.; 1 children's hosp.; 4 government hosp. **Educational facilities:** 5 univ. and colleges. **Further information:** Chamber of Commerce, 777 Taylor St. #900, Fort Worth, TX 76102; www.fortworthgov.org; www.fortworthchamber.com

Fremont, California

Population (2005): 200,468 (96); **Pop. Density:** 2,614; **Pop. change (2000-2005):** –1.4%. **Area:** 76.7 sq. mi. **Employment (2005):** 105,050 employed; 3.7% unemployed. **Per capita income (MSA):** $49,276; increase (2003-2004): 5.3%.

Mayor: Bob Wasserman, Non-Partisan

History: area first settled by Spanish 1769; inc. 1956 with consolidation of 5 communities.

Transportation: intracity bus line; Bay Area Rapid Transit System (southern terminal). **Communications:** 1 radio station. **Medical facilities:** 2 hosp.; 2 major medical facilities; 18 clinics. **Educational facilities:** 1 community college; 42 pub. schools. **Further information:** Chamber of Commerce, 39488 Stevenson Place, Suite 100, Fremont, CA 94539; www.fremontbusiness.com

Fresno, California

Population (2005): 461,116 (36); **Pop. Density:** 4,417; **Pop. change (2000-2005):** 7.8%. **Area:** 104.4 sq. mi. **Employment (2005):** 198,343 employed; 8.4% unemployed. **Per capita income (MSA):** $25,573; increase (2003-2004): 5.1%.

Mayor: Alan Autry, Non-Partisan

History: founded 1872; inc. as city 1885.

Transportation: 1 international airport; Amtrak; 1 bus line; intra-city bus system. **Communications:** 16 TV, 23 radio stations. **Medical facilities:** 17 general hosp. **Educational facilities:** 9 colleges; 102 pub. schools. **Further information:** Greater Fresno Area Chamber of Commerce, PO Box 1469, Fresno, CA 93716-1469; www.fresnochamber.com; fresno-online.com

Garland, Texas

Population (2005): 216,346 (86); **Pop. Density:** 3,789; **Pop. change (2000-2005):** 0.3%. **Area:** 57.1 sq. mi. **Employment (2005):** 108,164 employed; 5.6% unemployed. **Per capita income (MSA):** $35,502; increase (2003-2004): 3.9%.

Mayor: Bob Day, Democrat

History: settled 1850s; inc. 1891.

Transportation: 30 min. from Dallas/Ft. Worth Intl. Airport; 2 railroads. **Communications:** 14 local TV (Dallas/Ft. Worth), 25 radio stations. **Medical facilities:** 2 hosp.; 348 beds. **Educational facilities:** 3 univ., 2 community colleges; 64 pub. schools. **Further information:** Chamber of Commerce, 914 S. Garland Ave., Garland, TX 75040; www.garlandchamber.com

Glendale, Arizona

Population (2005): 239,435 (73); **Pop. Density:** 4,299; **Pop. change (2000-2005):** 9.4%. **Area:** 55.7 sq. mi. **Employment (2005):** 127,729 employed; 4.2% unemployed. **Per capita income (MSA):** $31,133; increase (2003-2004): 4.9%.

Mayor: Elaine M. Scruggs, Non-Partisan

History: est. 1892; inc. 1910.

Transportation: 1 municipal airport. **Communications:** 12 TV stations, 40 radio stations. **Medical facilities:** 3 hosp. **Educational facilities:** 12 institutes of higher education, 9 pub. school districts. **Further information:** City of Glendale Marketing/Communications Department, 5850 W. Glendale Ave, Glendale, AZ 85301; www.glendaleaz.com

Glendale, California

Population (2005): 200,065 (98); **Pop. Density:** 6,538; **Pop. change (2000-2005):** 2.6%. **Area:** 30.6 sq. mi. **Employment (2005):** 98,759 employed; 4.6% unemployed. **Per capita income (MSA):** $35,188; increase (2003-2004): 5.3%.

Mayor: Dave Weaver, Non-Partisan

History: became a town in 1887; inc. 1906.

Transportation: near Los Angeles Intl. airport; 1 local airport; commuter trains, Amtrak; bus system. **Communications:** 21 TV,

70 radio stations. **Medical facilities:** 3 hosp; other facilities. **Educational facilities:** 1 community college; 29 pub. schools. **Further information:** City of Glendale Public Information Officer, 613 E. Broadway, Glendale, CA 91206; www.ci.glendale.ca.us

Greensboro, North Carolina

Population (2005): 231,962 (77); **Pop. Density:** 2,215; **Pop. change (2000-2005):** 3.6%. **Area:** 104.7 sq. mi. **Employment (2005):** 120,055 employed; 5.1% unemployed. **Per capita income (MSA):** $29,999; increase (2003-2004): 4.6%.

Mayor: Keith Holliday, Non-Partisan

History: settled 1749; site of Revolutionary War conflict 1781 between Generals Nathanael Greene and Cornwallis; inc. 1807, origin of civil rights sit-in movement.

Transportation: 1 intl. airport; 2 railroads; Trailways/Greyhound bus service. **Communications:** all cable TV stations; 11 radio stations. **Medical facilities:** 4 hosp. **Educational facilities:** 3 univ., 4 colleges; 94 pub. schools. **Further information:** Chamber of Commerce, PO Box 3246, Greensboro, NC 27402; www.greensboro-nc.gov; www.greensboro.com

Henderson, Nevada

Population (2005): 232,146 (76); **Pop. Density:** 2,913; **Pop. change (2000-2005):** 32.4%. **Area:** 79.7 sq. mi. **Employment (2005):** 123,858 employed; 3% unemployed. **Per capita income (MSA):** $32,963; increase (2003-2004): 5.8%.

Mayor: James B. Gibson, Non-Partisan.

History: early growth spurred by World War II magnesium mining; inc. 1953.

Transportation: Henderson Executive Airport; Citizens Area Transit (CAT) public transportation. **Communications:** 9 TV stations; 38 radio stations. **Medical facilities:** 3 hosp.; medical center facilities. **Educational facilities:** 5 coll.; 2 vocational schools; 29 elem., 9 middle, 9 high schools. **Further information:** City of Henderson Public Information Office, 240 Water St., Henderson, NV 89015; www.cityofhenderson.gov; www.hendersonchamber.com

Hialeah, Florida

Population (2005): 220,485 (84); **Pop. Density:** 11,484; **Pop. change (2000-2005):** –2.6%. **Area:** 19.2 sq. mi. **Employment (2005):** 89,870 employed; 5.6% unemployed. **Per capita income (MSA):** $34,278; increase (2003-2004): 4.4%.

Mayor: Julio Robaina, Republican

History: founded 1917, inc. 1925; industrial and residential city NW of Miami; Hialeah Park Horse Racing Track.

Transportation: 5 mi from Miami Intl. Airport; access to Port of Miami; Amtrak; 2 rail freight lines; Metrorail, Metrobus systems. **Communications:** 5 TV, 7 radio stations. **Medical facilities:** 4 hosp. (30 more in the area). **Educational facilities:** 8 univ. and colleges, 25 pub., 39 private schools. **Further information:** Hialeah-Dade Development, Inc., 501 Palm Ave., Hialeah, FL 33010; www.ci.hialeah.fl.us; www.hddi.org

Honolulu, Hawaii

Population (2005): 377,379 (47); **Pop. Density:** 4,403; **Pop. change (2000-2005):** 1.5%. **Area:** 85.7 sq. mi. **Employment (2005):** 432,929 employed, 2.7% unemployed. **Per capita income (2004):** $34,911; increase (2003-2004): 6.7%.

Mayor: Mufi Hannemann, Non-Partisan

History: harbor entered by Europeans 1778; declared capital of kingdom by King Kamehameha III 1850; Pearl Harbor naval base attacked by Japanese Dec. 7, 1941.

Transportation: 1 major airport; 3 commercial harbors. **Communications:** 36 TV, 38 radio stations. **Medical facilities:** 10 acute, 26 long-term care facilities. **Educational facilities:** 7 univ., 7 community colleges; 169 pub. schools, 88 private schools, 9 charter schools. **Further information:** Hawaii Visitors and Convention Bureau, 2270 Kalakaua Ave., 8th Fl., Honolulu, HI 96815; www.co.honolulu.hi.us; www.gohawaii.com

Houston, Texas

Population (2005): 2,016,582 (4); **Pop. Density:** 3,480; **Pop. change (2000-2005):** 3.2%. **Area:** 579.4 sq. mi. **Employment (2005):** 933,057 employed; 6% unemployed. **Per capita income (MSA):** $36,852; increase (2003-2004): 4.2%.

Mayor: Bill White, Non-Partisan

History: founded 1836; inc. 1837; capital of Repub. of Texas 1837-39; developed rapidly after construction of channel to Gulf of Mexico 1914; world center of oil and natural gas technology.

Transportation: 2 commercial airports; 2 mainline railroads; major bus and rail transit system; major intl. port. **Communications:** 18 TV, 67 radio stations. **Medical facilities:** 75 hosp. (Harris Co.); major medical center. **Educational facilities:** 35 univ. and colleges (Harris Co.) **Further information:** Greater Houston Partnership, 1200 Smith St., Houston, TX 77002-4400; www.houston.org; www.cityofhouston.gov

Indianapolis, Indiana

Population (2005): 784,118 (12); **Pop. Density:** 2,169; **Pop. change (2000-2005):** 0.3%. **Area:** 361.5 sq. mi. **Employment (2005):** 403,578 employed; 5.6% unemployed. **Per capita income (MSA):** $35,266; increase (2003-2004): 4.6%.

Mayor: Bart Peterson, Democrat

History: settled 1820; became capital 1825.

Transportation: 1 intl. airport; 5 railroads; 3 interstate bus lines. **Communications:** 11 TV, 16 radio stations. **Medical facilities:** 21 hosp.; 1 major medical and research center. **Educational facilities:** 8 univ. and colleges; major pub. library system. **Further information:** Greater Indianapolis Chamber of Commerce, 111 Monument Circle, Ste. 1950, Indianapolis, IN 46204; www.ci.indianapolis.in.us; www.indychamber.com

Jacksonville, Florida

Population (2005): 782,623 (13); **Pop. Density:** 1,033; **Pop. change (2000-2005):** 6.4%. **Area:** 757.7 sq. mi. **Employment (2005):** 377,905 employed; 4% unemployed. **Per capita income (MSA):** $32,283; increase (2003-2004): 4.5%.

Mayor: John Peyton, Republican

History: settled 1816 as Cowford; renamed after Andrew Jackson 1822; inc. 1832; rechartered 1851; scene of conflicts in Seminole and Civil wars.

Transportation: 1 intl. airport, 2 small-craft airports; 3 railroads; 2 interstate bus lines; 2 seaports. **Communications:** 7 TV, 34 radio stations. **Medical facilities:** 11 hosp. **Educational facilities:** 7 univ., 5 colleges, 1 community college; 278 pub. schools, 114 private schools. **Further information:** Chamber of Commerce, 3 Independent Drive, Jacksonville, FL 32202; www.expandinjax.com; www.myjaxchamber.com; www.coj.net

Jersey City, New Jersey

Population (2005): 239,614 (72); **Pop. Density:** 16,081; **Pop. change (2000-2005):** –0.2%. **Area:** 14.9 sq. mi. **Employment (2005):** 104,529 employed; 5.9% unemployed. **Per capita income (MSA):** $43,277; increase (2003-2004): 6.0%.

Mayor: Jerramiah Healy, Democrat

History: site bought from Indians 1630; chartered as town by British 1668; scene of Revolutionary War conflict 1779; chartered under present name 1838; important station on Underground Railroad.

Transportation: Intercity bus and subway system; ferry service to Manhattan. **Communications:** see New York, NY. **Medical facilities:** 4 hosp. **Educational facilities:** 2 colleges, 1 univ. **Further information:** Hudson County Chamber of Commerce, 660 Newark Ave., Ste. 220, Jersey City, NJ 07306; www.jerseycityonline.com

Kansas City, Missouri

Population (2005): 444,965 (40); **Pop. Density:** 1,419; **Pop. change (2000-2005):** 0.8%. **Area:** 313.5 sq. mi. **Employment (2005):** 220,994 employed; 7% unemployed. **Per capita income (MSA):** $34,585; increase (2003-2004): 4.0%.

Mayor: Kay Barnes, Non-Partisan

History: settled by 1838 at confluence of the Missouri and Kansas rivers; inc. 1850.

Transportation: 1 intl. airport; a major rail center; more than 300 motor freight carriers; 7 barge lines. **Communications:** 9 TV, 43 radio stations. **Medical facilities:** 50 hosp.; 2 VA hosp. **Educational facilities:** 22 univ. and colleges. **Further information:** Greater Kansas City Chamber of Commerce, 911 Main St., Ste. 2600, Kansas City, MO 64105; www.kcchamber.com

Laredo, Texas

Population (2005): 208,754 (92); **Pop. Density:** 2,659; **Pop. change (2000-2005):** 18.2%. **Area:** 78.5 sq. mi. **Employment (2005):** 76,796 employed; 5.6% unemployed. **Per capita income (MSA):** $17,769; increase (2003-2004): 3.8%

Mayor: Raul G. Salinas, Non-Partisan

History: founded by Spanish colonists in 1755; part of U.S. from 1848; fast growth fueled by immigration; became principal port of entry into Mexico.

Transportation: 1 intl. airport; 2 railroads; 3 interstate bus lines, 2 local bus lines. **Communications:** 3 TV, 10 radio stations; 2 newspapers. **Medical facilities:** 3 hosp. **Educational facilities:** 1 univ., 1 community college; 62 public schools, 29 private schools; 7 vocational training centers. **Further information:** Laredo Chamber of Commerce, P.O. Box 790, Laredo, TX 78042; www.laredochamber.com

Las Vegas, Nevada

Population (2005): 545,147 (29); **Pop. Density:** 4,812; **Pop. change (2000-2005):** 13.9%. **Area:** 113.3 sq. mi. **Employment (2005):** 259,497 employed; 4.1% unemployed. **Per capita income (MSA):** $32,963; increase (2003-2004): 5.8%.

Mayor: Oscar B. Goodman, Democrat

History: occupied by Mormons 1855-57; bought by railroad 1903; city of Las Vegas inc. 1911; gambling legalized 1931.

Transportation: 1 intl. airport; 1 railroad; monorail; bus system. **Communications:** 21 TV, 44 radio stations. **Medical facilities:** 11 hosp. **Educational facilities:** 1 univ., 2 state colleges; 277 pub. schools in area. **Further information:** Las Vegas Chamber of Commerce, 3720 Howard Hughes Parkway, Las Vegas, NV 89109-0937; www.lvchamber.com; www.lasvegasnevada.gov

Lexington, Kentucky

Population (2005): 268,080 (69); **Pop. Density:** 942; **Pop. change (2000-2005):** 2.9%. **Area:** 284.5 sq. mi. **Employment (2005):** 140,498 employed; 4.6% unemployed. **Per capita income (MSA):** $32,722; increase (2003-2004): 4.3%.

Mayor: Teresa Ann Isaac, Non-Partisan

History: site was founded and named in 1775 by hunters after the site of the opening battle of the Revolutionary War at Lexington, Mass.; settled 1779; chartered 1782; inc. as a city 1832.

Transportation: 6 comm. airlines; 2 railroads; city buses. **Communications:** 5 TV, 20 radio stations. **Medical facilities:** 5 general, 5 specialized hosp. **Educational facilities:** 2 univ., 4 colleges, 53 public schools: 6 high schools, 10 middle schools, 35 elementary schools, 2 technology schools. **Further information:** Commerce Lexington, 330 E. Main St., Lexington, KY 40507; www.commercelexington.com

Lincoln, Nebraska

Population (2005): 239,213 (74); **Pop. Density:** 3,207; **Pop. change (2000-2005):** 6.0%. **Area:** 74.6 sq. mi. **Employment (2005):** 138,018 employed; 3.6% unemployed. **Per capita income (MSA):** $32,749; increase (2003-2004): 5.1%.

Mayor: Coleen J. Seng, Non-Partisan

History: originally called Lancaster; chosen state capital 1867, renamed after Abraham Lincoln; inc. 1869.

Transportation: 1 airport; Greyhound; Amtrak, 2 railroads. **Communications:** 3 TV, 15 radio stations. **Medical facilities:** 6 hosp. including VA, rehabilitation facilities. **Educational facilities:** 3 univ., 3 voc.-tech./business colleges; 55 pub., 30 private schools, 3 focus programs. **Further information:** Chamber of Commerce, PO Box 83006, Lincoln, NE 68501-3006; www.lincoln.org; www.lcoc.com

Long Beach, California

Population (2005): 474,014 (34); **Pop. Density:** 9,405; **Pop. change (2000-2005):** 2.7%. **Area:** 50.4 sq. mi. **Employment (2005):** 218,647 employed; 5.9% unemployed. **Per capita income (MSA):** $35,188; increase (2003-2004): 5.3%.

Mayor: Bob Foster, Democrat

History: settled as early as 1784 by Spanish; by 1884 present site developed on harbor; inc. 1888; oil discovered 1921.

Transportation: 1 airport; 3 railroads; major intl. port; 4 bus co. with 40 bus lines, light rail service. **Communications:** 1 radio station, 1 CATV franchise. **Medical facilities:** 5 hosp. **Educational facilities:** 1 univ., 1 community college (2 campuses); 87 pub. schools in district. **Further information:** Long Beach City Hall, 333 W. Ocean Blvd., Long Beach, CA 90802; www.ci.longbeach.ca.us; www.lbchamber.com

Los Angeles, California

Population (2005): 3,844,829 (2); **Pop. Density:** 8,196; **Pop. change (2000-2005):** 4.1%. **Area:** 469.1 sq. mi. **Employment (2005):** 1,764,781 employed; 5.9% unemployed. **Per capita income (MSA):** $35,188; increase (2003-2004): 5.3%.

Mayor: Antonio Villaraigosa, Democrat

History: founded by Spanish 1781; captured by U.S. 1846; inc. 1850; grew rapidly after coming of railroads, 1876 & 1885; Hollywood a district of L.A.

Transportation: 1 intl. airport; 3 railroads; major freeway system; intracity bus and rail system. **Communications:** 21 TV, 83 radio stations. **Medical facilities:** 822 hosp. and clinics in metro. area. **Educational facilities:** 158 univ. and colleges (incl. junior, community, and other); 1,858 pub. schools; 1,120 private schools. **Further information:** Los Angeles Area Chamber of Commerce, 350 S. Bixel St., PO Box 513696, Los Angeles, CA 90051-1696; www.ci.la.ca.us; www.lachamber.org

Louisville, Kentucky

Population (2005): 556,429 (26); **Pop. Density:** 1,442; **Pop. change (2000-2005):** 0.9%. **Area:** 386 sq. mi. **Employment (2005):** 332,856 employed; 6.2% unemployed. **Per capita income (MSA):** $33,058; increase (2003-2004): 4.5%.

Mayor: Jerry E. Abramson, Democrat

History: settled 1778; named for Louis XVI of France; inc. 1828; base for Union forces in Civil War.

Transportation: 1 municipal airport, 2 private-craft airport; 1 terminal, 4 trunk-line railroads; metro bus line, Greyhound station; 5 barge lines. **Communications:** 6 TV, 21 radio stations, 2 educational. **Medical facilities:** 23 hosp. **Educational facilities:** 10 univ. and colleges, 32 business and vocational schools. **Further information:** Greater Louisville, Inc. Metro Chamber of Commerce, 614 W. Main St., Louisville, KY 40202; www.greaterlouisville.com

Lubbock, Texas

Population (2005): 209,737 (91); **Pop. Density:** 1,827; **Pop. change (2000-2005):** 5.1%. **Area:** 114.8 sq. mi. **Employment (2005):** 110,975 employed; 3.9% unemployed. **Per capita income (MSA):** $26,867; increase (2003-2004): 5.5%.

Mayor: David Miller, Republican

History: settled 1879; laid out 1891; inc. 1909 through merger of two towns.

Transportation: 1 intl. airport; 2 railroads, bus line. **Communications:** 9 TV, 25 radio stations. **Medical facilities:** 7 hosp. **Educational facilities:** 3 univ., 1 junior college; 51 pub. schools. **Further information:** Chamber of Commerce, 1301 Broadway, Lubbock, TX 79401; www.ci.lubbock.tx.us; www. lubbockchamber.com

Madison, Wisconsin

Population (2005): 221,551 (83); **Pop. Density:** 3,225; **Pop. change (2000-2005):** 6.5%. **Area:** 68.7 sq. mi. **Employment (2005):** 137,029 employed; 3.1% unemployed. **Per capita income (MSA):** $37,447; increase (2003-2004): 5.1%.

Mayor: Dave Cieslewicz, Non-Partisan

History: first white settlement 1832; selected as site for state capital, named after James Madison, 1836; chartered 1856.

Transportation: 1 airport, 11 airlines; 1 intracity, 3 intercity bus systems; 3 freight rail lines. **Communications:** 10 TV, 26 radio stations, 3 cable providers. **Medical facilities:** 6 hosp., 92 clinics. **Educational facilities:** 7 colleges and univ., including main branch of Univ. of Wisconsin; 30 elem. schools, 11 middle schools, 5 high schools. **Further information:** Greater Madison Chamber of Commerce, PO Box 71, Madison, WI 53701-0071; www.cityofmadison.com; www.madisonchamber.com

Memphis, Tennessee

Population (2005): 672,277 (17); **Pop. Density:** 2,407; **Pop. change (2000-2005):** 3.4%. **Area:** 279.3 sq. mi. **Employment (2005):** 284,613 employed; 7.1% unemployed. **Per capita income (MSA):** $32,741; increase (2003-2004): 4.8%.

Mayor: Willie W. Herenton, Democrat

History: French, Spanish, and U.S. forts by 1797; settled by 1819; inc. as town 1826, as city 1840; surrendered charter to state 1879 after yellow fever epidemics; rechartered as city 1893.

Transportation: 1 intl. airport; 5 railroads; 1 bus system. **Communications:** 7 TV, 32 radio stns. **Medical facilities:** 20 hosp. **Educational facilities:** 17 univ. and colleges; 191 public schools. **Further information:** Memphis Regional Chamber, 22 N. Front St., 2nd Floor, Memphis, TN 38101; www.ci.memphis. tn.us; www.memphischamber.com

Mesa, Arizona

Population (2005): 442,780 (41); **Pop. Density:** 3,542; **Pop. change (2000-2005):** 11.7%. **Area:** 125 sq. mi. **Employment (2005):** 228,830 employed; 3.7% unemployed. **Per capita income (MSA):** $31,133; increase (2003-2004): 4.9%.

Mayor: Keno Hawker, Non-Partisan

History: founded by Mormons 1878; inc. 1883; population boomed fivefold 1960-80.

Transportation: 2 local airports; metro bus service. **Medical facilities:** 6 major hosp. **Educational facilities:** 5 univ., 7 colleges; 82 pub. schools. **Further information:** Convention and Visitor's Bureau and Mesa Chamber of Commerce, 120 N. Center, Mesa, AZ 85201; www.mesacvb.com; www.mesachamber.org; www.cityofmesa.org

Miami, Florida

Population (2005): 386,417 (45); **Pop. Density:** 10,824; **Pop. change (2000-2005):** 6.6%. **Area:** 35.7 sq. mi. **Employment (2005):** 150,038 employed; 4.7% unemployed. **Per capita income (MSA):** $34,278; increase (2003-2004): 4.4%.

Mayor: Manuel A. Diaz, Independent

History: site of fort 1836; settlement began 1870; inc. 1896; modern city developed into financial and recreation center; land speculation in 1920s added to city's growth, as did Cuban, Central and South American, and Haitian immigration since 1960.

Transportation: 1 intl. airport; seaport; Amtrak, transit rail system; 2 bus lines; 65 truck lines. **Communications:** 9 commercial, 2 educational TV stations; 48 radio stations. **Medical facilities:** 8 hosp.; VA hosp. **Educational facilities:** 6 univ. and colleges. **Further information:** Greater Miami Chamber of Commerce, Omni Intl. Complex, 1601 Biscayne Blvd., Miami, FL 33132; www.greatermiami.com; www.ci.miami.fl.us

Milwaukee, Wisconsin

Population (2005): 578,887 (22); **Pop. Density:** 6,024; **Pop. change (2000-2005):** -3.0%. **Area:** 96.1 sq. mi. **Employment (2005):** 249,095 employed; 7.3% unemployed. **Per capita income (MSA):** $36,488; increase (2003-2004): 4.2%.

Mayor: Tom Barrett, Democrat

History: Indian trading post by 1674; settlement began 1835; inc. as city 1848; famous beer industry.

Transportation: 1 intl. airport; 3 railroads; major port; 4 bus lines. **Communications:** 12 TV, 37 radio stations. **Medical facilities:** 7 hosp.; major medical center. **Educational facilities:** 7 univ. and colleges, 182 pub. schools. **Further information:** Visit Milwaukee, 648 N. Plankinton Ave, Milwaukee, WI 53703; www.visitmilwaukee.org

Minneapolis, Minnesota

Population (2005): 372,811 (48); **Pop. Density:** 6,791; **Pop. change (2000-2005):** -2.6%. **Area:** 54.9 sq. mi. **Employment (2005):** 212,872 employed; 4.2% unemployed. **Per capita income (MSA):** $40,915; increase (2003-2004): 5.1%.

Mayor: R.T. Rybak, Democrat

History: site visited by Hennepin 1680; included in area of military reservations 1819; inc. 1867.

Transportation: 1 intl. airport; 5 railroads. **Communications:** 10 TV, 30 radio stations. **Medical facilities:** 7 hosp., incl. leading heart hosp. at Univ. of Minnesota. **Educational facilities:** 10 univ. and colleges; 121 pub., 28 private schools. **Further information:** City of Minneapolis Office of Pub. Affairs, 323M City Hall, 350 S. 5th Street, Minneapolis, MN 55415; www.ci.minneapolis. mn.us

Modesto, California

Population (2005): 207,011 (93); **Pop. Density:** 5,782; **Pop. change (2000-2005):** 9.6%. **Area:** 35.8 sq. mi. **Employment (2005):** 92,770 employed; 7.1% unemployed. **Per capita income (MSA):** $25,885; increase (2003-2004): 6.0%.

Mayor: Jim Ridenour, Republican

History: founded 1870 after the Gold Rush of 1849 brought an influx of settlers to the region; recent growth boosted by agriculture and immigration.

Transportation: 1 airport. **Communications:** 8 TV, 15 radio stations. **Medical facilities:** 2 hosp. **Educational facilities:** 1 junior college, 5 public high schools. **Further information:** Modesto Convention & Visitor Bureau, 1150 Ninth St., Ste. C, Modesto, CA 95354; www.visitmodesto.com

Montgomery, Alabama

Population (2005): 200,127 (97); **Pop. Density:** 1,288; **Pop. change (2000-2005):** -0.7%. **Area:** 155.4 sq. mi. **Employment (2005):** 92,092 employed; 4.1% unemployed. **Per capita income (MSA):** $29,699; increase (2003-2004): 4.2%.

Mayor: Bobby N. Bright, Democrat

History: inc. as town 1819, as city 1837; became state capital 1846; first capital of Confederacy 1861.

Transportation: 3 airlines; 2 railroads; 2 bus lines; Alabama R. navigable to Gulf of Mexico. **Communications:** 4 TV, 2 CATV, 1 public TV, 16 radio stations. **Medical facilities:** 3 major hosp.; VA and 32 clinics. **Educational facilities:** 9 colleges and univ.; 35 pub., 35 private schools. **Further information:** Montgomery Area Chamber of Commerce, PO Box 79, Montgomery, AL 36101; www.montgomerychamber.com

Nashville, Tennessee

Population (2005): 549,110 (28); **Pop. Density:** 1,160; **Pop. change (2000-2005):** 0.7%. **Area:** 473.3 sq. mi. **Employment (2005):** 292,348 employed; 4.6% unemployed. **Per capita income (MSA):** $34,904; increase (2003-2004): 4.4%.

Mayor: Bill Purcell, Non-Partisan

History: settled 1779; first chartered 1806; became permanent state capital 1843; home of Grand Ole Opry.

Transportation: 1 airport; 1 railroad; bus line; transit system of buses and trolleys. **Communications:** 11 TV, 34 radio stations. **Medical facilities:** 14 hosp.; VA and speech-hearing center. **Educational facilities:** 17 universities and colleges, 129 pub. schools. **Further information:** Chamber of Commerce, 211 Commerce St., Ste 100, Nashville, TN 37201; www.nashville chamber.com

Newark, New Jersey

Population (2005): 280,666 (65); **Pop. Density:** 11,793; **Pop. change (2000-2005):** 2.6%. **Area:** 23.8 sq. mi. **Employment (2005):** 95,581 employed; 8.3% unemployed. **Per capita income (MSA):** $43,277; increase (2003-2004): 6.0%.

Mayor: Cory Booker, Democrat

History: settled by Puritans 1666; used as supply base by Washington 1776; inc. as town 1833, as city 1836.

Transportation: 1 intl. airport; 1 intl. seaport, 4 railroads; bus system; subways. **Communications:** 5 TV, 6 radio stations within city limits, 1 daily newspaper, 8 weekly newspapers. **Medical facilities:** 7 hosp. **Educational facilities:** 5 univ. and colleges; 58 pub. elementary schools, 13 junior and senior high schools, 10 special schools, 2 vocational schools, and 40 private schools. **Further information:** Newark Public Information Office, City of Newark, 920 Broad St., Newark, NJ 07102; www.ci.newark.nj.us; www.rbp.org

New Orleans, Louisiana

Hurricane Katrina struck New Orleans Aug. 29, 2005, causing widespread damage to the city's levee system, resulting in massive flooding. Many residents have since returned to the city. As a result of these events, updated 2005 employment and unemployment statistics are not available. The city of New Orleans Emergency Operations center conducted an unofficial population survey Jan. 28-29, 2006, to provide local, state, federal, and non-profit planners with accurate and reliable estimates during the post-Hurricane Katrina recovery period. According to that survey, the estimated population of New Orleans for the early spring of 2006 was 210,000. SInce then, many residents have returned to the city; however, no new formal surveys have been done.

Population (2005): 454,863 (38); **Pop. Density:** 2,519; **Pop. change (2000-2005):** −6.2%. **Area:** 180.6 sq. mi. **Employment (2004):** 189,726 employed; 5.2% unemployed. **Per capita income (MSA):** $31,024; increase (2003-2004): 5.4%.

Mayor: C. Ray Nagin, Democrat

History: founded by French 1718; became major seaport on Mississippi R.; acquired by U.S. as part of Louisiana Purchase 1803; inc. as city 1805; Americans defeated British forces at the Battle of New Orleans in 1815.

Transportation: 2 airports; major railroad center; street car and bus lines. **Communications:** 8 TV, 26 radio stations. **Medical facilities:** 22 hosp.; 2 major research centers. **Educational facilities:** 10 univ. and 9 colleges. **Further information:** New Orleans Metropolitan Convention & Visitors Bureau, Inc., 1520 Sugar Bowl Dr., New Orleans, LA 70112; www.neworleanscvb.com; www.city ofno.com

New York, New York

Population (2005): 8,143,197 (1); **Pop. Density:** 26,849; **Pop. change (2000-2005):** 1.7%. **Area:** 303.3 sq. mi. **Employment (2005):** 3,518,610 employed; 5.8% unemployed. **Per capita income (MSA):** $43,277; increase (2003-2004): 6.0%.

Mayor: Michael R. Bloomberg, Republican

History: trading post established 1624; British took control from Dutch 1664 and named city New York; briefly U.S. capital; Washington inaugurated as president 1789; under new charter, 1898, city expanded to include 5 boroughs: The Bronx, Brooklyn, Queens, and Staten Island, as well as Manhattan; Sept. 11, 2001, terrorist attack destroyed World Trade Center, killed about 2,800.

Transportation: 3 intl. airports serve area; 2 rail terminals; major subway network that includes 26 routes; 244 bus routes; ferry system; 4 underwater tunnels. **Communications:** 17 TV, 67 radio stations. **Medical facilities:** 79 hosp.; 6 academic medical centers. **Educational facilities:** 54 univ. and colleges; 1,198 pub. schools. **Further information:** Convention and Visitors Bureau, 810 Seventh Ave., New York, NY 10019; www.nyc.gov; www.nyc visit.com

Norfolk, Virginia

Population (2005): 231,954 (78); **Pop. Density:** 4,319; **Pop. change (2000-2005):** −1.0%. **Area:** 53.7 sq. mi. **Employment (2005):** 95,175 employed; 5.4% unemployed. **Per capita income (MSA):** $31,811; increase (2003-2004): 5.4%.

Mayor: Paul D. Fraim, Non-Partisan

History: founded 1682; burned by patriots to prevent capture by British during Revolutionary War; rebuilt and inc. as town 1805; as city 1845; site of world's largest naval base; major east coast commercial port and cruise terminal.

Transportation: 1 intl. airport; 2 railroads; Amtrak; bus system; free downtown shuttle. **Communications:** 13 TV, 27 radio stations. **Medical facilities:** 6 hosp. **Educational facilities:** 2 univ., 2 colleges, 1 medical school; 59 pub. schools. **Further information:** Norfolk Convention and Visitors Bureau, 232 E. Main St., Norfolk, VA 23510; www.norfolk. va.us; www.norfolkcvb.com

Oakland, California

Population (2005): 395,274 (44); **Pop. Density:** 7,046; **Pop. change (2000-2005):** −1.1%. **Area:** 56.1 sq. mi. **Employment (2005):** 178,591 employed; 8.1% unemployed. **Per capita income (MSA):** $49,276; increase (2003-2004): 5.3%.

Mayor: Jerry Brown, Non-Partisan

History: area settled by Spanish 1820; inc. as city under present name 1854.

Transportation: 1 intl. airport; western terminus for 2 railroads; underground, 75-mi underwater subway. **Communications:** 1 TV, 3 radio stations in city. **Medical facilities:** 10 hosp. in MSA. **Educational facilities:** 12 East Bay colleges and univ.; 81 pub. schools. **Further information:** Oakland Metropolitan Chamber of Commerce, 475 14th St., Oakland, CA 94612-1903; www.oaklandchamber.com; www.oaklandnet.com

Oklahoma City, Oklahoma

Population (2005): 531,324 (31); **Pop. Density:** 875; **Pop. change (2000-2005):** 5.0%. **Area:** 607 sq. mi. **Employment (2005):** 254,040 employed; 4.7% unemployed. **Per capita income (MSA):** $30,449; increase (2003-2004): 4.1%.

Mayor: Mick Cornett, Non-Partisan

History: settled during land rush in Midwest 1889; inc. 1890; became capital 1910; oil discovered 1928. Bomb in 1995 destroyed federal office bldg., killed 168 people.

Transportation: 1 intl. airport; 2 railroad; pub. transit system; 1 major bus line. **Communications:** 6 TV, 23 radio stations. **Medical facilities:** 26 hosp. **Educational facilities:** 20 univ. and colleges; 83 pub., 37 private schools. **Further information:** Chamber of Commerce, Economic Development Division, 123 Park Ave., Oklahoma City, OK 73102; www.okcchamber.com; www.okccvb.org; www.greateroklahomacity.com.

Omaha, Nebraska

Population (2005): 414,521 (43); **Pop. Density:** 3,583; **Pop. change (2000-2005):** 6.3%. **Area:** 115.7 sq. mi. **Employment (2005):** 216,540 employed; 5% unemployed. **Per capita income (MSA):** $36,124; increase (2003-2004): 4.9%.

Mayor: Mike Fahey, Democrat

History: founded 1854; inc. 1857; large food-processing, tele-communications, information-processing center.

Transportation: 10 major airlines; 3 major railroads; intercity bus line. **Communications:** 7 TV, 18 radio stations. **Medical facilities:** 11 hosp.; institute for cancer research. **Educational facilities:** 5 univ., 6 colleges; 243 pub., 78 private schools. **Further information:** Greater Omaha Chamber of Commerce, 1301 Harney St., Omaha, NE 68102; www.ci.omaha.ne.us; www.accessomaha.com

Orlando, Florida

Population (2005): 213,223 (87); **Pop. Density:** 2,280; **Pop. change (2000-2005):** 14.7%. **Area:** 93.5 sq. mi. **Employment (2005):** 115,440 employed; 3.4% unemployed. **Per capita income (MSA):** $29,576; increase (2003-2004): 4.6%.

Mayor: Buddy Dyer, Democrat.

History: Fort Gatlin built just south of present-day Orlando in 1838; name changed from Jernigan to Orlando, 1856; inc. 1875; Walt Disney World opened in 1971.

Transportation: 1 intl. airport; 2 bus lines. **Medical facilities:** 6 hosp. **Communications:** 7 TV, 20 radio stations. **Educational facilities:** 153 public schools; 4 tech schools; 5 colleges and univ. **Further Information:** Orlando/Orange County Convention and Visitors Bureau, 8723 International Dr., Suite 101, Orlando, FL 32819. www.orlandoinfo.com

Philadelphia, Pennsylvania

Population (2005): 1,463,281 (5); **Pop. Density:** 10,831; **Pop. change (2000-2005):** −3.6%. **Area:** 135.1 sq. mi. **Employment (2005):** 583,709 employed; 6.8% unemployed. **Per capita income (MSA):** $38,768; increase (2003-2004): 4.6%.

Mayor: John F. Street, Democrat

History: first settled by Swedes 1638; Swedes surrendered to Dutch 1654; settled by English and Scottish Quakers 1678; named Philadelphia 1682; chartered 1701; Continental Congresses convened 1774, 1775; Declaration of Independence signed here 1776; national capital 1790-1800; state capital 1683-1799.

Transportation: 1 major airport; 3 railroads; major freshwater port; subway, el, rail commuter bus, and streetcar system. **Communications:** 2 major daily newspapers, 14 TV, 102 radio stations. **Medical facilities:** 41 hosp. **Educational facilities:** 27 univ. and colleges. **Further information:** Greater Philadelphia Chamber of Commerce, Business Information Center, 200 South Broad St., Suite 700, Philadelphia PA 19102; www.phila.gov; www.philachamber.com

Phoenix, Arizona

Population (2005): 1,461,575 (6); **Pop. Density:** 3,078; **Pop. change (2000-2005):** 10.6%. **Area:** 474.9 sq. mi. **Employment (2005):** 753,099 employed; 4.8% unemployed. **Per capita income (MSA):** $31,133; increase (2003-2004): 4.9%.

Mayor: Phil Gordon, Democrat

History: founded 1867; inc. as city 1881; became territorial capital 1889.

Transportation: 1 intl. airport; 2 transcontinental and 10 intrastate railroads; transcontinental bus line; pub. transit system. **Communications:** 12 TV, 17 radio stations. **Medical facilities:** 8 hosp., 1 medical research center. **Educational facilities:** 36 institutions of higher learning; 380 pub. schools (247 elem. and junior high schools, 35 senior high schools, 98 charter schools). **Further information:** Greater Phoenix Chamber of Commerce, 201 N. Central Ave., 27th fl., Phoenix, AZ 85073; www.phoenix. gov; www.phoenix chamber.com

WORLD ALMANAC QUICK QUIZ

Rank these cities by per capita income from most to least.
(a) Cleveland, OH   (b) Washington, DC
(c) San Diego, CA   (d) Orlando, FL
For the answer look in this chapter, or see page 1008.

Pittsburgh, Pennsylvania

Population (2005): 316,718 (57); **Pop. Density:** 5,696; **Pop. change (2000-2005):** −5.3%. **Area:** 55.6 sq. mi. **Employment (2005):** 146,359 employed; 5.3% unemployed. **Per capita income (MSA):** $34,685; increase (2003-2004): 4.9%.

Mayor: Bob O'Connor, Democrat

History: settled around Ft. Pitt 1758; inc. as city 1816; became an inland port; by Civil War, already a center for iron production.

Transportation: 1 intl. airport; 20 railroads; 2 bus lines; trolley/subway system. **Communications:** 6 TV, 26 radio stations. **Medical facilities:** 35 hosp.; VA installation. **Educational facilities:** 3 univ., 6 colleges; 93 pub. schools. **Further information:** Greater Pittsburgh Convention & Visitors Bureau, Regional Enterprise Tower, 30th Floor, 425 Sixth Ave., Pittsburgh, PA 15219; Pittsburgh Regional Alliance, Regional Enterprise Tower, 36th Floor, 425 Sixth Ave., Pittsburgh, PA 15219; www.visitpittsburgh.com; www.pittsburghregion.org

Plano, Texas

Population (2005): 250,096 (70); **Pop. Density:** 3,493; **Pop. change (2000-2005):** 12.6%. **Area:** 71.6 sq. mi. **Employment (2005):** 135,298 employed; 4.5% unemployed. **Per capita income (MSA):** $35,502; increase (2003-2004): 3.9%.

Mayor: Pat Evans, Non-Partisan

History: settled 1846; inc. as city 1873.

Transportation: DART bus line; 2 DART (Dallas Area Rapid Transit) stations. **Communications:** 2 TV,1 radio station. **Medical facilities:** 2 full service hosp., 4 medical treatment centers. **Educational facilities:** 5 institutions of higher learning, 64 pub. schools. **Further information:** City of Plano Public Information Dept. 1520 K Ave., Suite 320, Plano, TX 75074; Plano Chamber of Commerce, PO Drawer 940287, Plano, TX 75094-0287; www.plano.gov; www.planochamber.org

Portland, Oregon

Population (2005): 533,427 (30); **Pop. Density:** 3,972; **Pop. change (2000-2005):** 0.8%. **Area:** 134.3 sq. mi. **Employment (2005):** 276,076 employed; 6.2% unemployed. **Per capita income (MSA):** $33,875; increase (2003-2004): 4.6%.

Mayor: Tom Potter, Non-Partisan

History: settled by pioneers 1845; developed as trading center, aided by California Gold Rush 1849; city chartered 1851.

Transportation: 1 intl. airport; 2 major rail freight lines, Amtrak; mass transit bus, light rail, and street car system; marine port. **Communications:** 9 TV, 27 radio stations. **Medical facilities:** 12 hosp.; VA hosp. **Educational facilities:** 25 univ. and colleges, 1 community college. **Further information:** Portland Business Alliance, 520 SW Yamhill St., Ste. 100, Portland, OR 97204; www.portlandalliance.com

Raleigh, North Carolina

Population (2005): 341,530 (53); **Pop. Density:** 2,980; **Pop. change (2000-2005):** 23.7%. **Area:** 114.6 sq. mi. **Employment (2005):** 179,904 employed; 3.8% unemployed. **Per capita income (MSA):** $34,498; increase (2003-2004): 4.0%.

Mayor: Charles Meeker, Democrat

History: named after Sir Walter Raleigh; site chosen for capital 1788; laid out 1792; inc. 1795; occupied by Gen. Sherman 1865.

Transportation: 1 intl. airport, 10 airlines, 6 commuter airlines; 3 railroads; 2 bus lines. **Communications:** 8 TV, 31 radio stations. **Medical facilities:** 3 hosp. **Educational facilities:** 6 univ. and colleges; 1 community college; 140 pub. schools (county). **Further information:** Chamber of Commerce, 800 S. Salisbury St., PO Box 2978, Raleigh, NC 27602; www.raleigh-wake.org; www.raleighchamber.org

Reno, Nevada

Population (2005): 203,550 (95); **Pop. Density:** 2,946; **Pop. change (2000-2005):** 12.8%. **Area:** 69.1 sq. mi. **Employment (2005):** 102,687 employed; 4% unemployed. **Per capita income (MSA):** $39,430; increase (2003-2004): 4.6%.

Mayor: Robert Cashell, Republican

History: Founded in 1857. Originally named Lakes Crossing. Name changed to Reno, after a Union Civil War general, in 1868 with the arrival of the transcontinental railroad.

Transportation: 2 airports; local and national bus lines; Amtrak, Union Pacific Railroad. **Communications:** 4 TV, 7 radio stations. **Medical Facilities:** 3 hosp. **Educational Facilities:** 58 public schools; 1 univ. **Further information:** City of Reno, NV PO Box 1900, Reno, NV 89505; www.cityofreno.com

Riverside, California

Population (2005: 290,086 (62); **Pop. density:** 3,693 per sq. mi; **Pop. change (2000–2005):** 13.7%. **Area:** 78.1 sq. mi. **Employment (2005):** 141,554 employed; 5.1% unemployed. **Per capita income (MSA):** $25,769; increase (2003-2004): 4.9%.

Mayor: Ronald O. Loveridge, Non-Partisan

History: founded 1870; inc. 1886; known for its citrus industry; home of the parent navel orange tree and the historic Mission Inn.

Transportation: municipal airport, intl. airport nearby; rail freight lines, commuter line; trolley/bus system; interstate freeways. **Communications:** 15 TV, 47 radio stations. **Medical facilities:** 3 hosp.; many clinics. **Educational facilities:** 3 univ., 1 community college. **Further information:** Chamber of Commerce, 3985 University Avenue, Riverside, CA 92501; www.ci.riverside.ca.us; www.riverside-chamber.com

Rochester, New York

Population (2005): 211,091 (88); **Pop. Density:** 5,896; **Pop. change (2000-2005):** −4.0%. **Area:** 35.8 sq. mi. **Employment (2005):** 90,549 employed; 6.1% unemployed. **Per capita income (MSA):** $32,303; increase (2003-2004): 4.6%.

Mayor: Robert Duffy, Democrat

History: first permanent settlement 1812; inc. as village 1817, as city 1834; developed as Erie Canal town.

Transportation: 1 intl. airport; Amtrak; 2 bus lines; intracity transit service; Port of Rochester. **Communications:** 6 TV, 19 radio stations. **Medical facilities:** 8 general hosp. **Educational facilities:** 11 colleges, 3 community colleges. **Further information:** Rochester Business Alliance, 150 State St., Rochester, NY 14614; www.rochesterbusinessalliance.com; www.ci.rochester.ny.us

Sacramento, California

Population (2005): 456,441 (37); **Pop. Density:** 4,696; **Pop. change (2000-2005):** 12.1%. **Area:** 97.2 sq. mi. **Employment (2005):** 199,019 employed; 5.7% unemployed. **Per capita income (MSA):** $33,338; increase (2003-2004): 4.5%.

Mayor: Heather Fargo, Non-Partisan

History: settled 1839; important trading center during California Gold Rush 1840s; became state capital 1854.

Transportation: international, executive, and cargo airports; 2 mainline transcontinental rail carriers; bus and light rail system; Port of Sacramento. **Communications:** 8 TV, 34 radio stations; 3 cable TV cos. **Medical facilities:** 15 major hosp. **Educational facilities:** 7 colleges and univ., 5 community colleges, 81 pub. schools. **Further information:** Sacramento Metropolitan Chamber of Commerce, 917 Seventh St., Sacramento, CA 95814; www.metrochamber.org; www.cityofsacramento.org

St. Louis, Missouri

Population (2005): 344,362 (52); **Pop. Density:** 5,563; **Pop. change (2000-2005):** −1.1%. **Area:** 61.9 sq. mi. **Employment (2005):** 147,825 employed; 8.1% unemployed. **Per capita income (MSA):** $34,735; increase (2003-2004): 3.1%.

Mayor: Francis Slay, Democrat

History: founded 1764 as a fur trading post by French; acquired by U.S. 1803; chartered as city 1822; became independent city 1876; lies on Mississippi R., near confluence with Missouri R.

Transportation: 2 intl. airports; 2d largest rail center, 7 trunkline railroads; 3d largest inland port; Amtrak; Greyhound; bus & light rail; 32 barge lines, 550 motor freight carriers. **Communications:** 8 TV, 19 radio stations. **Medical facilities:** 8 hosp., incl. 2 teaching hosp.; VA hosp., 2 pediatric hosp. **Educational facilities:** 8 univ., 13 colleges and seminaries; 63 public schools; 29 parochial schools; 5 magnet/charter high schools. **Further information:** St. Louis Planning & Urban Design Agency, 1015 Locust St., Ste. 1200, St. Louis, MO 63101; stlouis.missouri.org

St. Paul, Minnesota

Population (2005): 275,150 (67); **Pop. Density:** 5,211; **Pop. change (2000-2005):** −4.2%. **Area:** 52.8 sq. mi. **Employment (2005):** 143,172 employed; 4.4% unemployed. **Per capita income (MSA):** $40,915; increase (2003-2004): 5.1%.

Mayor: Chris Coleman, Democrat

History: founded in early 1840s as "Pig's Eye Landing"; became capital of the Minnesota territory 1849 and chartered as St. Paul 1854.

Transportation: 1 intl., 1 business airport; 6 major rail lines; 2 interstate bus lines; pub. transit system. **Communications:** 9 TV, 47 radio stations. **Medical facilities:** 6 hosp. **Educational facilities:** 5 univ., 5 colleges; 1 technical, 3 law schools, 1 art and design college; 65 public, 39 private schools. **Further information:** St. Paul Area Chamber of Commerce, 401 N. Robert St., Ste. 150, St. Paul, MN 55101; www.visitsaintpaul.com; www.stpaulcvb.org

St. Petersburg, Florida

Population (2005): 249,079 (71); **Pop. Density:** 4,179; **Pop. change (2000-2005):** 0.3%. **Area:** 59.6 sq. mi. **Employment (2005):** 126,837 employed; 3.7% unemployed. **Per capita income (MSA):** $31,677; increase (2003-2004): 4.2%.

Mayor: Rick Baker, Non-Partisan

History: founded 1888; inc. 1903.

Transportation: 1 municipal, 2 intl. airports; Amtrak bus connection; county-wide public bus system; downtown 'Looper' bus service; has largest municipal marina in Florida; 1 cruise port. **Communications:** 17 TV, 41 radio stations in area, 2 daily newspapers. **Medical facilities:** 4 major hosp.; VA hosp. **Educational facilities:** 1 univ., 1 college, 1 law school; 27 elem., 9 middle, 5 high schools; 3 alternative/vocational schools; 100 private schools. **Further information:** City of St. Petersburg , PO Box 2842, St. Petersburg, FL 33731; www.stpete.org

San Antonio, Texas

Population (2005): 1,256,509 (7); **Pop. Density:** 3,083; **Pop. change (2000-2005):** 9.8%. **Area:** 407.6 sq. mi. **Employment (2005):** 565,826 employed; 4.8% unemployed. **Per capita income (MSA):** $28,946; increase (2003-2004): 4.1%.

Mayor: Phil Hardberger, Democrat

History: first Spanish garrison 1718; Battle at the Alamo in 1836; city subsequently captured by Texans; inc. 1837; 1st town meeting in Texas took place here in 1845.

Transportation: 1 intl. airport; 2 railroads; 3 bus lines; pub. transit system. **Communications:** 14 TV, 49 radio stations. **Medical facilities:** 22 hosp.; major medical center. **Educational facilities:** 18 univ. and colleges; 16 pub. school districts. **Further information:** Chamber of Commerce, PO Box 1628, San Antonio, TX 78296; www.sachamber.org; www.sanantonio.gov

San Bernardino, California

Population (2005): 198,550 (100); **Pop. Density:** 3,377; **Pop. change (2000-2005):** 7.1%. **Area:** 58.8 sq. mi. **Employment (2005):** 76,979 employed; 6.9% unemployed. **Per capita income (MSA):** $25,769; increase (2003-2004): 4.9%.

Mayor: Patrick J. Morris, Democrat

History: Named by Spanish Franciscan missionaries in 1810. Major Mormon settlement in the 1850s, later recalled to Utah. Population grew in 1860s when gold was discovered nearby. Later became a transportation hub. Inc. 1854.

Transportation: 2 intl. airports; commuter rail; local bus lines.**Communications:** 1 TV, 21 radio stations. **Medical facilities:** 10 hosp. **Educational facilities:** 3 univ.; 66 public schools. **Further information:** San Bernardino Convention & Visitors Bureau 201 North "E" Street, Suite 103, San Bernardino, CA 92401; www.san-bernardino.com

San Diego, California

Population (2005): 1,255,540 (8); **Pop. Density:** 3,872; **Pop. change (2000-2005):** 2.6%. **Area:** 324.3 sq. mi. **Employment (2005):** 643,083 employed; 4.3% unemployed. **Per capita income (MSA):** $37,965; increase (2003-2004): 6%.

Mayor: Jerry Sanders, Republican

History: claimed by the Spanish 1542; first mission est. 1769; scene of conflict during Mexican-American War 1846; inc. 1850.

Transportation: 1 major airport; 1 railroad; major freeway system; bus system; trolley system. **Communications:** 9 TV, 25 radio stations, 2 cable providers. **Medical facilities:** 17 hosp. **Educational facilities:** 25 colleges and univ.; 177 pub. schools. **Further information:** San Diego Regional Chamber of Commerce, 402 W. Broadway, Ste. 1000, San Diego, CA 92101; www.sannet.gov; www.sdchamber.org

San Francisco, California

Population (2005): 739,426 (14); **Pop. Density:** 15,834; **Pop. change (2000-2005):** −4.8%. **Area:** 46.7 sq. mi. **Employment (2005):** 399,047; employed; 5.1% unemployed. **Per capita income (MSA):** $49,276; increase (2003-2004): 5.3%.

Mayor: Gavin Newsom, Non-Partisan

History: nearby Farallon Islands sighted by Spanish 1542; city settled by 1776; claimed by U.S. 1846; became a major city during California Gold Rush 1849; inc. as city 1850; earthquake devastated city 1906.

Transportation: 1 major airport; intracity railway system; 2 railway transit systems; bus and railroad service; ferry system; 1 underwater tunnel. **Communications:** 8 TV; 8 radio stations. **Medical facilities:** 16 hosp. **Educational facilities:** 18 univ. and colleges, 113 pub. schools, 5 charter schools. **Further information:** San Francisco Convention & Visitors Bureau, 201 3rd St., Ste. 900, San Francisco, CA 94103; www.ci.sf.ca.us; www.sfchamber.com; www.sfvisitor.org

San Jose, California

Population (2005): 912,332 (10); **Pop. Density:** 5,216; **Pop. change (2000-2005):** 1.9%. **Area:** 174.9 sq. mi. **Employment (2005):** 404,169 employed; 6.1% unemployed. **Per capita income (MSA):** $48,530; increase (2003-2004): 5.6%.

Mayor: Ron Gonzales, Democrat

History: founded by the Spanish 1777 between San Francisco and Monterey; state cap. 1849-51; inc. 1850.

Transportation: 1 intl. airport; 2 railroads; light rail system; bus system. **Communications:** 9 TV, 15 radio stations. **Medical facilities:** 6 hosp. **Educational facilities:** 6 univ. and colleges. **Further information:** San Jose Convention and Visitors Bureau, 408 Almaden Blvd., San Jose, CA 95110; www.sanjoseca.gov; www.sanjose.org

Santa Ana, California

Population (2005): 340,368 (54); **Pop. Density:** 12,560; **Pop. change (2000-2005):** 0.7%. **Area:** 27.1 sq. mi. **Employment (2005):** 147,234 employed; 6.1% unemployed. **Per capita income (MSA):** $35,188; increase (2003-2004): 5.3%.

Mayor: Miguel Pulido, Non-Partisan

History: founded 1769; inc. as city 1869.

Transportation: 1 airport; 5 major freeways including main Los Angeles-San Diego artery; Amtrak. **Communications:** 14 TV, 28 radio stations. **Medical facilities:** 4 hosp. **Educational facilities:** 1 community college. **Further information:** Santa Ana Chamber of Commerce, 2020 N. Broadway, 2nd floor, Santa Ana, CA 92706; www.santaanachamber.com

Scottsdale, Arizona

Population (2005): 226,013 (80); **Pop. Density:** 1,227; **Pop. change (2000-2005):** 11.5%. **Area:** 184.2 sq. mi. **Employment (2005):** 129,064 employed; 3% unemployed. **Per capita income (MSA):** $31,133; increase (2003-2004): 4.9%.

Mayor: Mary Manross, Democrat

History: founded 1888 by Army Chaplain Winfield Scott; inc. June 25, 1951; Frank Lloyd Wright built winter home here (Taliesin West); slogan "West's Most Western Town," by Mayor Malcolm White, adopted 1951.

Transportation: 1 intl. airport in area, 1 local airport; regional bus system; local bus system; taxi system. **Communications:** 12 TV, 45 radio stations. **Medical facilities:** 2 general hospitals; Mayo Clinic. **Educational facilities:** 1 univ. nearby, 1 community college; 3 unified school districts. **Further information:** Scottsdale Convention and Visitors Bureau, 4343 N. Scottsdale Rd., Ste. 170, Scottsdale, AZ 85251; www.scottsdaleaz.gov; www.scottsdalecvb.com

Seattle, Washington

Population (2005): 573,911 (23); **Pop. Density:** 6,840; **Pop. change (2000-2005):** 1.9%. **Area:** 83.9 sq. mi. **Employment (2005):** 332,234 employed; 4.6% unemployed. **Per capita income (MSA):** $41,634; increase (2003-2004): 7.6%.

Mayor: Greg Nickels, Democrat

History: settled 1851; inc. 1869; suffered severe fire 1889; played prominent role during Alaska Gold Rush 1897; growth followed opening of Panama Canal 1914; center of aircraft industry WWII.

Transportation: 2 intl. airport; 2 railroads; ferries serve Puget Sound, Alaska, Canada. **Communications:** 7 TV, 29 radio stations. **Medical facilities:** 40 hosp. **Educational facilities:** 7 univ., 6 colleges, 11 community colleges. **Further information:** Greater Seattle Chamber of Commerce, 1301 5th Ave., Ste. 2500, Seattle, WA 98101-2611; www.ci.seattle.wa.us; www.seattlechamber.com

Shreveport, Louisiana

Population (2005): 198,874 (99); **Pop. Density:** 1,929; **Pop. change (2000-2005):** −0.6%. **Area:** 103.1 sq. mi. **Employment (2005):** 87,746 employed; 6.1% unemployed. **Per capita income (MSA):** $28,990; increase (2003-2004): 6.1%.

Mayor: Keith Hightower, Democrat

History: founded 1836 near site of a 180-mi logjam cleared by Capt. Henry Shreve; inc. 1839; oil discovered 1905.

Transportation: 2 airports, over 40 flights daily; 3 bus lines. **Communications:** 6 TV, 20 radio stations. **Medical facilities:** 16 hosp. **Educational facilities:** 2 univ., 4 colleges; approx. 100 pub. schools. **Further information:** Chamber of Commerce, PO Box 20074, 400 Edwards St., Shreveport, LA 71120; www.shreveportchamber.org

Stockton, California

Population (2005): 286,926 (63); **Pop. Density:** 5,245; **Pop. change (2000-2005):** 17.7%. **Area:** 54.7 sq. mi. **Employment (2005):** 107,310 employed; 9.4% unemployed. **Per capita income (MSA):** $25,527; increase (2003-2004): 3.6%.

Mayor: Ed Chavez, Non-Partisan

History: site purchased 1842; settled 1849; inc. 1850; chief distributing point for agric. products of San Joaquin Valley.

Transportation: 1 airport; deepwater inland seaport; 4 railroads; 2 bus lines, county bus system. **Communications:** 5 TV stations. **Medical facilities:** 4 hosp.; regional burn, cancer, heart centers. **Educational facilities:** 9 univ. and colleges; 58 pub. schools. **Further information:** Chamber of Commerce, 445 W. Weber Ave., Ste. 220, Stockton, CA 95203; www.stocktongov.com; www.stocktonchamber.org

Tampa, Florida

Population (2005): 325,989 (56); **Pop. Density:** 2,908; **Pop. change (2000-2005):** 7.4%. **Area:** 112.1 sq. mi. **Employment (2005):** 154,968 employed; 3.7% unemployed. **Per capita income (MSA):** $31,677; increase (2003-2004): 4.2%.

Mayor: Pam Iorio, Non-Partisan

History: U.S. army fort on site 1824; inc. 1851; Ybor City National Historical Landmark district.

Transportation: 1 intl. airport; Port of Tampa; CSX rail, Amtrak Rail; bus system; downtown streetcar. **Communications:** 17 TV, 57 radio stations. **Medical facilities:** 21 hosp. **Educational facilities:** 5 univ. and colleges; 193 pub. schools. **Further information:** Greater Tampa Chamber of Commerce, 615 Channelside Drive, Ste. 108, P.O. Box 420, Tampa, FL 33602; www.tampachamber.com

Toledo, Ohio

Population (2005): 301,285 (59); **Pop. Density:** 3,738; **Pop. change (2000-2005):** –3.9%. **Area:** 80.6 sq. mi. **Employment (2005):** 135,478 employed; 7.5% unemployed. **Per capita income (MSA):** $30,599; increase (2003-2004): 2.2%.

Mayor: Carleton S. Finkbeiner, Democrat

History: site of Ft. Industry 1794; Battles of Ft. Meigs and Ft. Timbers 1812; figured in "Toledo War" 1835-36 between Ohio and Michigan over borders; inc. 1837.

Transportation: 7 major airlines; 4 railroads; 53 motor freight lines; 16 interstate bus lines. **Communications:** 6 TV, 22 radio stations. **Medical facilities:** 5 major hosp. complexes. **Educational facilities:** 6 univ. and colleges. **Further information:** Toledo Area Chamber of Commerce, 300 Madison Ave., Ste. 200, Toledo, OH 43604; www.toledochamber.com

Tucson, Arizona

Population (2005): 515,526 (32); **Pop. Density:** 2,648; **Pop. change (2000-2005):** 5.9%. **Area:** 194.7 sq. mi. **Employment (2005):** 240,699 employed; 5.1% unemployed. **Per capita income (MSA):** $27,244; increase (2003-2004): 5.4%.

Mayor: Robert E. Walkup, Republican

History: settled 1775 by Spanish as a presidio; acquired by U.S. in Gadsden Purchase 1853; inc. 1877.

Transportation: 1 intl. airport; 2 railroads; 1 bus system, 1 trolley. **Communications:** 10 TV, 34 radio stations. **Medical facilities:** 12 hosp. **Educational facilities:** 1 univ., 1 community college; 216 pub. schools. **Further information:** Tucson Metropolitan Chamber of Commerce, PO Box 991, Tucson, AZ 85702; www.ci.tucson.az.us; www.tucsonchamber.org

Tulsa, Oklahoma

Population (2005): 382,457 (46); **Pop. Density:** 2,095; **Pop. change (2000-2005):** –2.7%. **Area:** 182.6 sq. mi. **Employment (2005):** 199,474 employed; 4.6% unemployed. **Per capita income (MSA):** $32,150; increase (2003-2004): 5.1%.

Mayor: Kathryn L. Taylor, Democrat

History: settled in 1836 by Creek Indians; modern town founded 1882 and inc. 1898; oil discovered early 20th century; emerging as telecommunications hub.

Transportation: 1 intl. airport; 5 rail lines; 5 bus lines; transit bus system. **Communications:** 7 TV, 31 radio stations. **Medical facilities:** 10 hosp. **Educational facilities:** 8 univ. and colleges; 85 pub., 39 private schools. **Further information:** Tulsa Metro Chamber, 2 West 2nd Tower II, Ste. 150, Tulsa, OK 74103; www.tulsachamber.com; www.cityoftulsa.org

Virginia Beach, Virginia

Population (2005): 438,415 (42); **Pop. Density:** 1,766; **Pop. change (2000-2005):** 3.1%. **Area:** 248.3 sq. mi. **Employment (2005):** 216,447 employed; 3.4% unemployed. **Per capita income (MSA):** $31,811; increase (2003-2004): 5.4%.

Mayor: Meyera E. Oberndorf, Independent

History: area founded by Capt. John Smith 1607; formed by merger with Princess Anne Co. 1963.

Transportation: 1 airport; 2 railroads; 1 bus line; pub. transit system. **Communications:** 8 TV, 44 radio stations. **Medical facilities:** 2 hosp. **Educational facilities:** 1 univ., 2 colleges; 87 pub. schools. **Further information:** Virginia Beach Dept. of Economic Development, 222 Central Park Ave., Suite 1000, Virginia Beach, VA 23462; Virginia Beach Convention and Visitors Bureau, 2100 Parks Ave., Virginia Beach, VA 23451; www.yesvirginiabeach.com; www.vbfun.com

Washington, District of Columbia

Population (2005): 550,521 (27); **Pop. Density:** 8,966; **Pop. change (2000-2005):** –3.8%. **Area:** 61.4 sq. mi. **Employment (2005):** 276,972 employed; 6.5% unemployed. **Per capita income (MSA):** $46,782; increase (2003-2004): 6.1%.

Mayor: Anthony A. Williams, Democrat

History: U.S. capital; site at Potomac R. chosen by George Washington 1790 on land ceded from VA and MD (portion S of Potomac returned to VA 1846); Congress first met 1800; inc. 1802; sacked by British, War of 1812; 125 killed during Sept. 11, 2001 terrorist attack on the Pentagon.

Transportation: 3 intl. airports in area; Amtrak, 6 other passenger & cargo rail lines; Metrobus/Metrorail transit system; bus line. **Communications:** 5 TV, 61 radio stations. **Medical facilities:** 16 hosp. **Educational facilities:** 10 univ. and colleges. **Further information:** DC Chamber of Commerce, 1213 K Street NW, Washington, DC 20005; www.dc.gov; www.dcchamber.org

Wichita, Kansas

Population (2005): 354,865 (51); **Pop. Density:** 2,613; **Pop. change (2000-2005):** 3.1%. **Area:** 135.8 sq. mi. **Employment (2005):** 174,692 employed; 6.1% unemployed. **Per capita income (MSA):** $31,781; increase (2003-2004): 5.0%.

Mayor: Carlos Mayans, Non-Partisan

History: founded 1864; inc. 1871.

Transportation: 2 airports; 3 major rail freight lines; 2 bus lines. **Communications:** 80 TV, 34 radio stations. **Medical facilities:** 7 hosp., 2 psychiatric rehab. centers. **Educational facilities:** 3 univ., 1 medical school; 96 pub. schools. **Further information:** Chamber of Commerce, 350 W. Douglas Ave., Wichita, KS 67202; www.wichitakansas.org; www.wichita.gov; www.gwedc.org

Fastest-Growing Big Cities*

City	2005 population	2000 population	% change
1. Chandler, AZ	234,939	176,581	33.0%
2. Henderson, NV	232,146	175,381	32.4%
3. Raleigh, NC	341,530	276,093	23.7%
4. Chula Vista, CA	210,497	173,556	21.3%
5. Bakersfield, CA	295,536	247,057	19.6%
6. Laredo, TX	208,754	176,576	18.2%
7. Stockton, CA	286,926	243,771	17.7%
8. Fort Worth, TX	624,067	534,694	16.7%
9. Orlando, FL	213,223	185,951	14.7%
10. Las Vegas, NV	545,147	478,434	13.9%

Fastest-Shrinking Big Cities*

City	2005 population	2000 population	% change
1. Detroit, MI	886,671	951,270	–6.8%
2. Cincinnati, OH	308,728	331,285	–6.8%
3. New Orleans, LA	454,863	484,674	–6.2%
4. Cleveland, OH	452,208	478,403	–5.5%
5. Pittsburgh, PA	316,718	334,563	–5.3%
6. Boston, MA	559,034	589,141	–5.1%
7. San Francisco, CA	739,426	776,733	–4.8%
8. Birmingham, AL	231,483	242,820	–4.7%
9. Buffalo, NY	279,745	292,648	–4.4%
10. St. Paul, MN	275,150	287,151	–4.2%

*Among those with populations of 200,000 or more, based on 2005 U.S. Census Bureau estimates.

Percent of Population by Race and Hispanic Origin, 10 Largest Cities,[1] 2000

City	White	Black or African- Amer.	Amer. Indian, Alaska Native	Asian	Hawaiian & Other Pacific Isl.	Some other race[2]	Two or more races	Hispanic or Latino (of any race)
1. New York, NY	44.7	26.6	0.5	9.8	0.1	13.4	4.9	27.0
2. Los Angeles, CA	46.9	11.2	0.8	10.0	0.2	25.7	5.2	46.5
3. Chicago, IL	42.0	36.8	0.4	4.3	0.1	13.6	2.9	26.0
4. Houston, TX	49.3	25.3	0.4	5.3	0.1	16.5	3.1	37.4
5. Philadelphia, PA	45.0	43.2	0.3	4.5	0.0	4.8	2.2	8.5
6. Phoenix, AZ	71.1	5.1	2.0	2.0	0.1	16.4	3.3	34.1
7. San Antonio, TX	67.7	6.8	0.8	1.6	0.1	19.3	3.7	58.7
8. San Diego, CA	60.2	7.9	0.6	13.6	0.5	12.4	4.8	25.4
9. Dallas, TX	50.8	25.9	0.5	2.7	0.0	17.2	2.7	35.6
10. San Jose, CA	47.5	3.5	0.8	26.9	0.4	15.9	5.0	30.2

(1) Top 10 cities as determined by 2004 Census Bureau estimates. (2) Persons who, instead of checking off a race shown, filled in a designation under "some other race."

STATES AND OTHER AREAS OF THE U.S.

Sources: Population: U.S. Commerce Dept., Bureau of the Census—Census 2000: April 1, 2000, and July 2004 est. (including armed forces stationed in the state). Area: Bureau of the Census, Geography Division; forested land: Agriculture Dept., Forest Service. Lumber production: Bureau of the Census, Industry Division; mineral production: Dept. of Interior, Office of Mineral Information; commercial fishing: Commerce Dept., Natl. Marine Fisheries Service; new private housing: Bureau of the Census, Residential Construction Branch. Personal per capita income: Commerce Dept., Bureau of Economic Analysis; sales tax: CCH Inc.; unemployment: Labor Dept., Bureau of Labor Statistics. Lottery figures (not all states have a lottery): North American Assn. of State and Provincial Lotteries, for local fiscal year. Finance: Federal Deposit Insurance Corp. Federal employees: Labor Dept., Office of Personnel Management. Energy: Energy Dept., Energy Information Administration. Other information from sources in individual states. Some data on Outlying U.S. Areas & Other Islands provided by the CIA World Factbook. For information about tourism earnings, see p. 89.

NOTE: Population density is for land area only. Categories under racial distribution may not add to 100% due to rounding. "Nat. AK" (Native Alaskans) includes Eskimos and Aleuts. **Hispanic population may be any race** and is dispersed among racial categories, besides being listed separately. Nonfuel mineral values for some states exclude small amounts to avoid disclosing proprietary data. Categories under employment distribution are not all-inclusive. Commercial bank and savings institution figures are for FDIC-insured institutions only. Notable federal facilities marked with an asterisk (*) have been recommended for realignment or closure by the U.S. Dept. of Defense, which has until Sept. 15, 2007 to begin the process, to be completed by Sept. 15, 2011. **Famous Persons lists may include nonnatives** associated with the state as well as persons born there. Website addresses listed may not be official state sites and are not endorsed by *The World Almanac;* all website addresses are subject to change.

Alabama (AL)

Heart of Dixie, Camellia State

People. Population (2005 est.): 4,557,808; rank: 23; **net change** (2004-2005): 0.7%. **Pop. density:** 89.8 per sq mi. **Racial distribution** (2004): 71.4% white; 26.4% black; 0.8% Asian; 0.5% Native/Nat.AK; 0.04% Hawaiian/Pacific Islander; 2 or more races, 0.9%. **Hispanic pop.** (any race): 2.2%.

Geography. Total area: 52,419 sq mi; rank: 30. **Land area:** 50,744 sq mi; rank: 28. **Acres forested:** 23.0 mil. **Location:** East South Central state extending N-S from Tenn. to the Gulf of Mexico; E of the Mississippi River. **Climate:** long, hot summers; mild winters; generally abundant rainfall. **Topography:** coastal plains, including Prairie Black Belt, give way to hills, broken terrain; highest elevation, 2,407 ft. **Capital:** Montgomery. **Principal internat. airports at:** Birmingham, Huntsville.

Economy. Chief industries: pulp & paper, chemicals, electronics, apparel, textiles, primary metals, lumber and wood products, food processing, fabricated metals, automotive tires, oil and gas exploration. **Chief manuf. goods:** electronics, cast iron & plastic pipe, fabricated steel products, ships, paper products, chemicals, steel, mobile homes, fabrics, poultry processing, soft drinks, furniture, tires. **Chief crops:** cotton, greenhouse & nursery, peanuts, sweet potatoes, potatoes and other vegetables. **Livestock:** (Jan. 2006): 1.3 mil cattle/calves; (Dec. 2005): 160,000 hogs/pigs, 14.2 mil chickens (excl. broilers), 1.1 bil broilers. **Timber/lumber** (est. 2004): 2.7 bil bd. ft.; pine, hardwoods. **Nonfuel minerals** (est. 2005): $1.0 bil; cement (portland), stone (crushed), lime, sand and gravel (construction), cement (masonry). **Commercial fishing** (2004): $37.0 mil. **Chief port:** Mobile. **Gross state product** (2005): $149.8 bil. **Sales tax** (2006): 4.0%. **Employment distrib.** (May 2006): 18.5% govt; 19.4% trade/trans./util.; 15.2% mfg; 10.3% ed./health; 10.9% prof./bus. serv.; 8.7% leisure/hosp.; 5.0% finance; 5.6% constr.; 4.2% other serv.; 1.6% info. **Unemployment** (2005): 4.0%. **Per cap. pers. income** (2005): $29,136. **New private housing** (2005): 30,612 units/$4.1 bil. **Commercial banks** (2005): 165; **deposits:** $63.3 bil. **Savings institutions** (2005): 13; **deposits:** $2.0 bil.

Federal govt. Fed. civ. employees (Mar. 2005): 36,379; **avg. salary:** $62,376. **Notable fed. facilities:** Marshall Space Flight Ctr.; *Maxwell/Gunter AFB; Ft. Rucker; Intern'l. Fertilizer Development Ctr.; Navy Station & U.S. Corps of Engineers; Redstone Arsenal.

Energy. Electricity production (est. 2005, kWh by source): Coal: 77.8 bil; Gas: 6.6 bil; Hydroelectric: 9.8 bil; Nuclear: 31.7 bil; Petroleum: 108 mil.

State data. Motto: We dare defend our rights. **Flower:** Camellia. **Bird:** Yellowhammer. **Tree:** Southern Longleaf pine. **Song:** Alabama. **Entered union** Dec. 14, 1819; rank, 22nd. **State fair:** Regional and county fairs held in Sept. and Oct.; no state fair.

History. Alabama was inhabited by the Creek, Cherokee, Chickasaw, Alabama, and Choctaw peoples when Spanish explorers arrived in the early 1500s. The French made the first permanent settlement at Fort Louis, 1702, and founded Mobile, 1711. France later gave up the entire region to England under the Treaty of Paris, 1763. Spanish forces took control of the Mobile Bay area, 1780, and it remained under Spanish control until seized by U.S. troops, 1813. Most of present-day Alabama was held by the Creeks until Gen. Andrew Jackson broke their power, 1814, and they were removed to Oklahoma Territory. When Alabama became a state, 1819, black slaves made up about 1/3 of the population. The state seceded, 1861, and the Confederate states were organized Feb. 4, at Montgomery, the first capital; the state was readmitted, 1868. Birmingham, founded 1871, became a center for iron- and steelmaking. The Montgomery bus boycott, 1955, sparked by Rosa Parks, helped launch the civil rights movement; other confrontations came at Birmingham, 1963, and Selma, 1965. The leading political figure from the 1960s through the '80s, 4-term Gov. George Wallace, started as a segregationist but later won with black support. Growth in the auto industry boosted the state economy as the 21st cent. began.

Tourist attractions. First White House of the Confederacy, Civil Rights Memorial, Alabama Shakespeare Festival, Montgomery; Ivy Green, Helen Keller's birthplace, Tuscumbia; Civil Rights Museum, statue of Vulcan, Birmingham; Carver Museum, Tuskegee; W. C. Handy Home, Museum, & Library, Florence; Alabama Space and Rocket Center, Huntsville; Moundville State Monument, Moundville; Pike Pioneer Museum, Troy; USS *Alabama* Memorial Park, Mobile; Russell Cave Natl. Monument, near Bridgeport: a detailed record of occupancy by humans from about 10,000 BCE to 1650 CE.

Famous Alabamians. Hank Aaron, Tallulah Bankhead, Hugo L. Black, Paul "Bear" Bryant, George Washington Carver, Nat King Cole, William C. Handy, Bo Jackson, Helen Keller, Coretta Scott King, Harper Lee, Joe Louis, Willie Mays, John Hunt Morgan, Jim Nabors, Jesse Owens, Condoleezza Rice, George Wallace, Booker T. Washington, Hank Williams.

Tourist information. Bureau of Tourism and Travel, 401 Adams Avenue, Suite 126, Montgomery, AL 36103; (334) 242-4169 out of state. **Website:** www.touralabama.org

Website. www.alabama.gov

Alaska (AK)

The Last Frontier (unofficial)

People. Population (2005 est.): 663,661; rank: 47; **net change** (2004-2005): 0.9%. **Pop. density:** 1.2 per sq mi. Racial distribution (2004): 70.7% white; 3.6% black; 4.5% Asian; 15.8% Native/Nat.AK; 0.6% Hawaiian/Pacific Islander; 2 or more races, 4.7%. **Hispanic pop.** (any race): 4.9%.

Geography. Total area: 663,267 sq mi; rank: 1. **Land area:** 571,951 sq mi; rank: 1. **Acres forested:** 126.9 mil. **Location:** NW corner of North America, bordered on E by Canada. **Climate:** SE, SW, and central regions, moist and mild; far north extremely dry. Extended summer days, winter nights, throughout. **Topography:** includes Pacific and Arctic mountain systems, central plateau, and Arctic slope. Mt. McKinley, 20,320 ft, is the highest point in North America. **Capital:** Juneau. **Principal internat. airports at:** Anchorage, Fairbanks, Juneau.

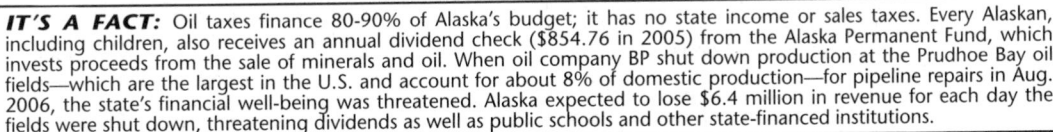

IT'S A FACT: Oil taxes finance 80-90% of Alaska's budget; it has no state income or sales taxes. Every Alaskan, including children, also receives an annual dividend check ($854.76 in 2005) from the Alaska Permanent Fund, which invests proceeds from the sale of minerals and oil. When oil company BP shut down production at the Prudhoe Bay oil fields—which are the largest in the U.S. and account for about 8% of domestic production—for pipeline repairs in Aug. 2006, the state's financial well-being was threatened. Alaska expected to lose $6.4 million in revenue for each day the fields were shut down, threatening dividends as well as public schools and other state-financed institutions.

Economy. Chief industries: petroleum, tourism, fishing, mining, forestry, transportation, aerospace. **Chief manuf. goods:** fish products, lumber & pulp, furs. **Chief crops:** greenhouse products, barley, oats, hay, potatoes, lettuce, aquaculture. **Livestock:** (Jan. 2006): 15,500 cattle/calves; (Dec. 2005): 1,600 hogs/pigs. **Timber/lumber:** figs. undisclosed; spruce, yellow cedar, hemlock. **Nonfuel minerals** (est. 2005): $4.7 bil; zinc, gold, lead, sand and gravel (construction), silver. **Commercial fishing** (2004): $1.2 bil. **Chief ports:** Anchorage, Dutch Harbor, Kodiak, Seward, Skagway, Juneau, Sitka, Valdez, Wrangell. **Gross state product** (2005): $39.9 bil. **Sales tax** (2006): none. **Employment distrib.** (May 2006): 26.4% govt; 20.8% trade/trans./util.; 3.2% mfg; 11.5% ed./health; 7.6% prof./bus. serv.; 10.3% leisure/hosp.; 4.7% finance; 6.0% constr.; 3.6% other serv.; 2.2% info. **Unemployment** (2005): 6.8%. **Per cap. pers. income** (2005): $35,612. **New private housing** (2005): 2,885 units/$525 mil. **Commercial banks** (2005): 7; **deposits:** $6.1 bil. **Savings institutions** (2005): 2; **deposits:** $328 mil.

Federal govt. Fed. civ. employees (Mar. 2005): 11,929; **avg. salary:** $55,362. **Notable fed. facilities:** *Ft. Richardson; Ft. Wainwright; *Elmendorf AFB; *Eilson AFB.

Energy. Electricity production (est. 2005, kWh by source): Coal: 219 mil; Gas: 3.9 bil; Hydroelectric: 1.4 bil; Petroleum: 669 mil.

State data. Motto: North to the future. **Flower:** Forget-Me-Not. **Bird:** Willow ptarmigan. **Tree:** Sitka spruce. **Song:** Alaska's Flag. **Entered union** Jan. 3, 1959; rank, 49th. **State fair** at Palmer; late Aug.-early Sept.

History. Early inhabitants included the Tlingit-Haida and Athabascan peoples. Ancestors of the Aleut and Inuit (Eskimo) probably arrived from Siberia between 10,000 and 6,000 years ago. Vitus Bering, a Dane sailing for Russia, was the first European to land in Alaska, 1741. Russians, pursuing the fur trade, established a permanent settlement on Kodiak Island, 1784. Sec. of State William H. Seward bought Alaska from Russia for $7.2 mil in 1867, a bargain some called "Seward's Folly." Discovery of gold in the Klondike region of Canada's Yukon Territory, 1896, triggered an Alaskan gold rush. Alaska became a territory, 1912, and a state, 1959. A huge oil find at Prudhoe Bay, 1968, led to construction of the Trans-Alaska Pipeline, 1974-77. The *Exxon Valdez* supertanker ran aground, 1989, spilling about 11 mil gallons of crude oil; the cleanup cost over $2.2 bil. A Bush administration plan to drill for oil in the Arctic National Wildlife Refuge has passed the U.S. House 12 times since 1995, most recently in 2006, but failed in the Senate.

Tourist attractions. Inside Passage; Portage Glacier; Mendenhall Glacier; Ketchikan Totems; Glacier Bay Natl. Park and Preserve; Denali Natl. Park, one of N. America's great wildlife sanctuaries, surrounding Mt. McKinley, N. America's highest peak; Mt. Roberts Tramway, Juneau; Pribilof Islands fur seal rookeries; restored St. Michael's Russian Orthodox Cathedral, Sitka; White Pass & Yukon Route railroad; Skagway; Katmai Natl. Park & Preserve.

Famous Alaskans. Tom Bodett, Susan Butcher, Ernest Gruening, Jewel (Kilcher), Gov. Tony Knowles, Sydney Laurence, Libby Riddles, Jefferson "Soapy" Smith.

Tourist information. Alaska Travel Industry Association, 2600 Cordova St., Ste. 201, Anchorage, AK 99503; (no official phone listed). **Website:** www.travelalaska.com **Website.** www.state.ak.us

Arizona (AZ)
Grand Canyon State

People. Population (2005 est.): 5,939,292; rank: 17; **net change** (2004-2005): 3.5%. **Pop. density:** 52.3 per sq mi. Racial distribution (2004): 87.6% white; 3.5% black; 2.1% Asian; 5.0% Native/Nat.AK; 0.2% Hawaiian/Pacific Islander; 2 or more races, 1.5%. **Hispanic pop.** (any race): 28%.

Geography. Total area: 113,998 sq mi; rank: 6. **Land area:** 113,635 sq mi; rank: 6. **Acres forested:** 19.4 mil. **Location:** in the southwestern U.S. **Climate:** clear and dry in the southern regions and northern plateau; high central areas have heavy winter snows. **Topography:** Colorado plateau in the N, containing the Grand Canyon; Mexican Highlands running diagonally NW to SE; Sonoran Desert in the SW. **Capital:** Phoenix. **Principal internat. airports at:** Phoenix, Tucson.

Economy. Chief industries: manufacturing, construction, tourism, mining, agriculture. **Chief manuf. goods:** electron-

ics, printing & publishing, foods, prim. & fabric. metals, aircraft and missiles, apparel. **Chief crops:** cotton, lettuce, cauliflower, broccoli, sorghum, barley, corn, wheat, citrus fruits. **Livestock:** (Jan. 2006): 940,000 cattle/calves, 105,000 sheep/lambs; (Dec. 2005): 142,000 hogs/pigs. **Timber/lumber** (est. 2004): 65 mil bd. ft.; pine, fir, spruce. **Nonfuel minerals** (est. 2005): $4.7 mil; copper, sand and gravel (construction), cement (portland), molybdenum concentrates, stone (crushed). **Gross state product** (2005): $215.8 bil. **Sales tax** (2005): 5.6%. **Employment distrib.** (May 2006): 15.9% govt; 19.2% trade/trans./util.; 7.0% mfg; 10.9% ed./health; 15.0% prof./bus. serv.; 10.4% leisure/hosp.; 6.9% finance; 9.1% constr.; 3.7% other serv.; 1.7% info. **Unemployment** (2005): 4.7%. **Per cap. pers. income** (2005): $30,267. **New private housing** (2005): 90,851 units/$14.5 bil. **Commercial banks** (2005): 64; **deposits:** $66.1 bil. **Savings institutions** (2005): 17; **deposits:** $6.7 bil. **Lottery** (2005): total sales: $397.6 mil; profit: $116.8 mil.

Federal govt. Fed. civ. employees (Mar. 2005): 33,363; **avg. salary:** $53,710. **Notable fed. facilities:** *Luke, Davis-Monthan AF bases; *Ft. Huachuca Army Base; Yuma Proving Grounds.

Energy. Electricity production (est. 2005, kWh by source): Coal: 39.8 bil; Gas: 10.7 bil; Hydroelectric: 6.4 bil; Nuclear: 25.8 bil; Petroleum: 42 mil

State data. Motto: Ditat Deus (God enriches). **Flower:** Blossom of the Saguaro cactus. **Bird:** Cactus wren. **Tree:** Paloverde. **Song:** Arizona. **Entered union** Feb. 14, 1912; rank, 48th. **State fair** at Phoenix; Oct.-early Nov.

History. Paleoindians hunted large game in the area at least 12,000 years ago. Anasazi, Mogollon, and Hohokam civilizations lived there c. 300 BCE-1300 CE; Navajo and Apache came c. 15th cent. Marcos de Niza, a Franciscan, and Estevanico, a black former slave, explored, 1539; Spanish explorer Francisco Vásquez de Coronado visited, 1540. Eusebio Francisco Kino, a Jesuit missionary, taught Indians 1692-1711, and left missions. Tubac, a Spanish fort, became the first European settlement, 1752. Spain ceded Arizona to Mexico, 1821. The U.S. took over, 1848, after the Mexican War. The area below the Gila River came from Mexico in the Gadsden Purchase, 1853. Arizona became a territory, 1863. Apache wars ended with Geronimo's surrender, 1886. Arizona became a state, 1912, and grew rapidly after 1960 with a fourfold rise in population over the next 4 decades. Barry Goldwater was a leading conservative voice in the U.S. Senate (1953-65, 1969-87). The border with Mexico is a major gateway for illegal immigration to the U.S.

Tourist attractions. The Grand Canyon; Painted Desert; Petrified Forest Natl. Park; Canyon de Chelly; Meteor Crater; London Bridge, Lake Havasu City; Biosphere 2, Oracle; Navajo Natl. Monument; Sedona.

Famous Arizonans. Bruce Babbitt, Cochise, Alice Cooper, Geronimo, Barry Goldwater, Zane Grey, Carl Hayden, George W. P. Hunt, Helen Jacobs, Bil Keane, Percival Lowell, John McCain, William H. Pickering, John J. Rhodes, Morris Udall, Stewart Udall, Frank Lloyd Wright.

Tourist information. Arizona Office of Tourism, 1110 W. Washington St., Ste. 155, Phoenix, AZ 85007; 1-866-275-5816. **Website:** www.arizonaguide.com **Website.** www.az.gov

Arkansas (AR)
The Natural State, The Razorback State

People. Population (2005 est.): 2,779,154; rank: 32; **net change** (2004-2005): 1.1%. **Pop. density:** 53.4 per sq mi. Racial distribution (2004): 81.3% white; 15.8% black; 0.9% Asian; 0.7% Native/Nat.AK; 0.08% Hawaiian/Pacific Islander; 2 or more races, 1.2%. **Hispanic pop.** (any race): 4.4%.

Geography. Total area: 53,179 sq mi; rank: 29. **Land area:** 52,068 sq mi; rank: 27. **Acres forested:** 18.8 mil. **Location:** in the west south-central U.S. **Climate:** long, hot summers, mild winters; generally abundant rainfall. **Topography:** eastern delta and prairie, southern lowland forests, and the northwestern highlands, which include the Ozark Plateaus. **Capital:** Little Rock. **Principal internat. airport at:** Blytheville.

Economy. Chief industries: manufacturing, agriculture, tourism, forestry. **Chief manuf. goods:** food products, chemicals, lumber, paper, plastics, electric motors, furniture, auto components, airplane parts, apparel, machinery, steel. **Chief crops:** rice, soybeans, cotton, tomatoes, grapes, apples, commercial vegetables, peaches, wheat. **Livestock:** (Jan.

2006): 1.8 mil cattle/calves; (Dec. 2005): 270,000 hogs/pigs, 24.2 mil chickens (excl. broilers), 1.2 bil broilers. **Timber/lumber** (est. 2004): 3.0 bil bd. ft.; oak, hickory, gum, cypress, pine. **Nonfuel minerals** (est. 2005): $523 mil; bromine, stone (crushed), cement (portland), sand and gravel (construction), lime. **Chief ports:** Little Rock, Pine Bluff, Osceola, Helena, Fort Smith, Van Buren, Camden, Dardanelle, North Little Rock, West Memphis, Crossett, McGehee, Morrilton. **Gross state product** (2005): $86.8 bil. **Sales tax** (2006): 6%. **Employment distrib.** (May 2006): 17.6% govt; 20.7% trade/trans./util.; 16.5% mfg; 12.5% ed./health; 9.4% prof./bus. serv.; 8.2% leisure/hosp.; 4.4% finance; 4.7% constr.; 3.6% other serv.; 1.7% info. **Unemployment** (2005): 4.9%. **Per cap. pers. income** (2005): $26,874. **New private housing** (2005): 17,932 units/$2.3 bil. **Commercial banks** (2005): 166; **deposits** (2005): $39.6 bil. **Savings institutions** (2005): 8; **deposits:** $1.4 bil.

Federal govt. Fed. civ. employees (Mar. 2005): 12,096; **avg. salary:** $52,704. **Notable fed. facilities:** Nat'l. Ctr. for Toxicological Research, Jefferson; Pine Bluff Arsenal, Little Rock AFB.

Energy. Electricity production (est. 2005, kWh by source): Coal: 22.9 bil; Gas: 276 mil; Hydroelectric: 3.2 bil; Nuclear: 13.7 bil; Petroleum: 437 mil.

State data. Motto: Regnat Populus (The people rule). **Flower:** Apple blossom. **Bird:** Mockingbird. **Tree:** Pine. **Song:** Arkansas. **Entered union** June 15, 1836; rank, 25th. **State fair** at Little Rock; late Sept.-early Oct.

History. Quapaw, Caddo, Osage, Cherokee, and Choctaw peoples lived in the area at the time of European contact. The first European explorers were de Soto, 1541; Marquette and Jolliet, 1673; and La Salle, 1682. French fur trader Henri de Tonty founded the first settlement, 1686, at Arkansas Post. In 1762, the area was ceded by France to Spain, then given back again, 1800, and was part of the Louisiana Purchase, 1803. It was made a territory, 1819, and entered the Union as a slave state, 1836. Arkansas seceded in 1861, after the Civil War began, and was readmitted, 1868. Pres. Eisenhower sent federal troops, 1957, to keep Gov. Orval Faubus from blocking racial integration at a Little Rock high school. Wal-Mart, now the world's leading retailer, opened its first store in Rogers, 1962. Elected 5 times as governor, Bill Clinton later served 2 terms in the White House (1993-2001); his presidential library opened, 2004, in Little Rock.

Tourist attractions. Hot Springs Natl. Park (water ranging from 95°F-147°F); Eureka Springs; Ozark Folk Center, Blanchard Caverns, both near Mountain View; Crater of Diamonds (only U.S. diamond mine) near Murfreesboro; Toltec Mounds Archeological State Park, Little Rock; Buffalo Natl. River; Mid-America Museum, Hot Springs; Pea Ridge National Military Park, Pead Ridge; Tanyard Springs, Morrilton; Wiederkehr Wine Village, Wiederkehr Village.

Famous Arkansans. Daisy Bates, Dee Brown, Paul "Bear" Bryant, Glen Campbell, Johnny Cash, Hattie Caraway, Wesley Clark, Bill Clinton, "Dizzy" Dean, Orval Faubus, James W. Fulbright, John Grisham, John H. Johnson, Douglas MacArthur, John L. McClellan, James S. McDonnell, Scottie Pippen, Dick Powell, Brooks Robinson, Billy Bob Thornton, Winthrop Rockefeller, Mary Steenburgen, Edward Durell Stone, Sam Walton, Archibald Yell.

Tourist Information. Arkansas Dept. of Parks & Tourism, 1 Capitol Mall, Little Rock, AR 72201; 1-800-NATURAL. **Website:** www.arkansas.com
Website. www.state.ar.us

California (CA)
Golden State

People. Population (2005 est.): 36,132,147; rank: 1; **net change** (2004-2005): 0.8%. **Pop. density:** 231.7 per sq mi. Racial distribution (2004): 77.2% white; 6.8% black; 12.1% Asian; 1.2% Native/Nat.AK; 0.4% Hawaiian/Pacific Islander; 2 or more races, 2.4%. **Hispanic pop.** (any race): 34.7%.

Geography. Total area: 163,696 sq mi; rank: 3. **Land area:** 155,959 sq mi; rank: 3. **Acres forested:** 40.2 mil. **Location:** on western coast of the U.S. **Climate:** moderate temperatures and rainfall along the coast; extremes in the interior. **Topography:** long mountainous coastline; central valley; Sierra Nevada on the east; desert basins of the southern interior; rugged mountains of the north. **Capital:** Sacramento. **Principal internat. airports at:** Fresno, Los Angeles, Oakland, Ontario, Sacramento, San Diego, San Francisco, San Jose.

Economy. Chief industries: agriculture, tourism, apparel, electronics, telecommunications, entertainment. **Chief manuf. goods:** electronic and electrical equip., computers, industrial machinery, transportation equip. and instruments, food. **Chief crops:** milk and cream, grapes, cotton, flowers, oranges, rice, nursery products, hay, tomatoes, lettuce, strawberries, almonds, asparagus. **Livestock:** (Jan. 2006): 5.5 mil cattle/calves, 650,000 sheep/lambs; (Dec. 2005): 145,000 hogs/pigs, 23.6 mil chickens (excl. broilers). **Timber/lumber** (est. 2004): 3.0 bil bd. ft.; fir, pine, redwood, oak. **Nonfuel minerals** (est. 2005): $3.5 bil; sand and gravel (construction), cement (portland), stone (crushed), boron minerals, soda ash. **Commercial fishing** (2004): $139.0 mil. **Chief ports:** Long Beach, Los Angeles, San Diego, Oakland, San Francisco, Sacramento, Stockton. **Gross state product** (2005): $1.6 trillion. **Sales tax** (2005): 7.25%. **Employment distrib.** (May 2006): 16.5% govt; 18.7% trade/trans./util.; 10.0% mfg; 10.8% ed./health; 14.6% prof./bus. serv.; 10.1% leisure/hosp.; 6.3% finance; 6.1% constr.; 3.5% other serv.; 3.1% info. **Unemployment** (2005): 5.4%. **Per cap. pers. income** (2005): $37,076. **New private housing** (2005): 205,020 units/$38.4 bil. **Commercial banks** (2005): 294; **deposits:** $514.7 bil. **Savings institutions** (2005): 38; **deposits:** $238.9 bil. **Lottery** (2005): total sales: $3.3 bil; profit: $1.8 bil.

Federal govt. Fed. civ. employees (Mar. 2005): 141,512; **avg. salary:** $63,908. **Notable fed. facilities:** Vandenberg, *Beale, Travis AF bases; San Diego Naval Sta.; Pt. Loma Naval Sub Base; *USMC Camp Pendleton; Lawrence Livermore Natl. Lab; Berkeley Natl. Lab; NASA Jet Propulsion Lab; Edwards AFB (NASA Dryden Flight Research Ctr., AF Flight Test Ctr.); San Francisco Mint.

Energy. Electricity production (est. 2005, kWh by source): Gas: 12.8 bil; Hydroelectric: 37.5 bil; Nuclear: 36.2 bil; Petroleum: 56 mil; Other: 1.2 bil.

State data. Motto: Eureka (I have found it). **Flower:** Golden poppy. **Bird:** California valley quail. **Tree:** California redwood. **Song:** I Love You, California. **Entered union** Sept. 9, 1850; rank, 31st. **State fair** at Sacramento; late Aug.-early Sept.

History. Early inhabitants included more than 100 different Native American tribes with multiple dialects. The first European explorers were Cabrillo, 1542, and Drake, 1579. The first settlement was the Spanish Alta California mission at San Diego, 1769, first in a string founded by Franciscan Father Junipero Serra. California became a province of independent Mexico, 1821. U.S. traders and settlers arrived in the 19th cent. and staged the Bear Flag revolt, 1846, in protest against Mexican rule; later that year U.S. forces occupied California. At the end of the Mexican War, Mexico ceded the territory to the U.S., 1848; that same year gold was discovered, and the famed gold rush began. California became a state, 1850. An economic downturn in the 1870s spurred riots against Chinese immigrants, who had come as laborers in the boom years. An earthquake and related fires devastated San Francisco, 1906. During World War II, Japanese Americans, many of them U.S. citizens, were held in detention camps, 1942-45. Ronald Reagan, a former movie actor, became state governor (1967-75) and U.S. president (1981-89). A budget crisis, 2003, resulted in the recall of Gov. Gray Davis and the election of another former actor, Arnold Schwarzenegger. Led by Hollywood in entertainment and Silicon Valley in high-tech, the state's economy dwarfs that of most nations.

Tourist attractions. The *Queen Mary*, Long Beach; Palomar Mountain; Disneyland, Anaheim; Getty Center, Los Angeles; Tournament of Roses and Rose Bowl, Pasadena; Universal Studios, Hollywood; Long Beach Aquarium of the Pacific; Golden State Museum, Sacramento; San Diego Zoo; Yosemite Valley; Lassen and Sequoia-Kings Canyon natl. parks; Lake Tahoe; Mojave and Colorado deserts; San Francisco Bay; Napa Valley; Monterey Peninsula; oldest living things on earth believed to be a stand of Bristlecone pines in the Inyo National Forest, est. 4,700 years old; world's tallest tree, 365-ft "National Geographic Society" coast redwood, in Humboldt Redwoods State Park.

Famous Californians. Edmund G. (Pat) Brown, Jerry Brown, Luther Burbank, Julia Child, Ted Danson, Cameron Diaz, Leonardo DiCaprio, Joe DiMaggio, Dianne Feinstein, John C. Fremont, Robert Frost, Tom Hanks, Bret Harte, William Randolph Hearst, Helen Hunt, Jack Kemp, Monica Lewinsky, Jack London, George Lucas, Mark McGwire, Marilyn Monroe, John Muir, Richard M. Nixon, George S. Patton Jr., Gregory Peck, Nancy Pelosi, Ronald Reagan, Sally K. Ride, William Saroyan, Father Junípero Serra, O.J. Simpson, Kevin Spacey, Leland Stanford, John Steinbeck, Arnold Schwarzenegger, Shirley Temple, Earl Warren, Ted Williams, Serena Williams, Venus Williams, Tiger Woods.

California Division of Tourism. P.O. Box 1499, Sacramento, CA 95812-1499;1-800-862-2543. **Website:** www.go calif.ca.gov

Website. www.state.ca.us

Colorado (CO)
Centennial State

People. Population (2005 est.): 4,665,177; rank: 22; **net change** (2004-2005): 1.4%. **Pop. density:** 45.0 per sq mi. Racial distribution (2004): 90.3% white; 4.1% black; 2.5% Asian; 1.1% Native/Nat.AK; 0.1% Hawaiian/Pacific Islander; 2 or more races, 1.8%. **Hispanic pop.** (any race): 19.1%.

Geography. Total area: 104,094 sq mi; rank: 8. **Land area:** 103,718 sq mi; rank: 8. **Acres forested:** 21.6 mil. **Location:** in W central U.S. **Climate:** low relative humidity, abundant sunshine, wide daily, seasonal temp. ranges; alpine conditions in the high mountains. **Topography:** eastern dry high plains; hilly to mountainous central plateau; western Rocky Mountains of high ranges, with broad valleys, deep, narrow canyons. **Capital:** Denver. **Principal internat. airport at:** Denver.

Economy. Chief industries: manufacturing, construction, government, tourism, agriculture, aerospace, electronics equipment. **Chief manuf. goods:** computer equip. & instruments, foods, machinery, aerospace products. **Chief crops:** corn, wheat, hay, sugar beets, barley, potatoes, apples, peaches, pears, dry edible beans, sorghum, onions, oats, sunflowers, vegetables. **Livestock:** (Jan. 2006): 2.7 mil cattle/calves, 390,000 sheep/lambs; (Dec. 2005): 840,000 hogs/pigs, 4.7 mil chickens (excl. broilers). **Timber/lumber** (est. 2004): 135 mil bd. ft.; oak, ponderosa pine, Douglas fir. **Nonfuel minerals** (est. 2005): $1.8 bil; sand and gravel (construction), cement (portland), molybdenum concentrates, gold, stone (crushed). **Gross state product** (2005): $216.1 bil. **Sales tax** (2006): 2.9%. **Employment distrib.** (May 2006): 16.6% govt; 18.4% trade/trans./util.; 6.6% mfg; 10.1% ed./health; 14.5% prof./bus. serv.; 11.2% leisure/hosp.; 7.1% finance; 7.4% constr.; 4.0% other serv.; 3.3% info. **Unemployment** (2005): 5.0%. **Per cap. pers. income** (2005): $37,946. **New private housing** (2005): 45,891 units/$8.8 bil. **Commercial banks** (2005): 189; **deposits:** $60.4 bil. **Savings institutions** (2005): 17; **deposits:** $10.0 bil. **Lottery** (2005): total sales: $417.0 mil; profit: $103.7 mil.

Federal govt. Fed. civ. employees (Mar. 2005): 33,845; **avg. salary:** $64,979. **Notable fed. facilities:** *U.S. Air Force Academy; U.S. Mint; Ft. Carson; Natl. Renewable Energy Labs; U.S. Rail Transportation Test Ctr.; Cheyenne Mtn. Operations Ctr. (NORAD, U.S. Space Comm.); Denver Federal Ctr.; Natl. Ctr. for Atmospheric Research; Natl. Instit. for Standards in Technology; Natl. Wildlife Res. Ctr.; NOAA Env. Technology Lab.

Energy. Electricity production (est. 2005, kWh by source): Coal: 35.5 bil; Gas: 4.5 bil; Hydroelectric: 1.1 bil; Petroleum: 16 mil; Other: 54 mil.

State data. Motto: Nil Sine Numine (Nothing Without Providence). **Flower:** Rocky Mountain columbine. **Bird:** Lark bunting. **Tree:** Colorado blue spruce. **Song:** Where the Columbines Grow. **Entered union:** Aug. 1, 1876; rank 38th. **State fair** at Pueblo; mid-Aug.–early Sept.

History. Paleoindians hunted big game in the area at least 11,000 years ago. Anasazi cliff dwellers flourished around Mesa Verde until about 1300 CE; other Native Americans were the Ute, Pueblo, Cheyenne, and Arapaho. The region was claimed by Spain, but passed to France, 1800. The U.S. acquired eastern Colorado in the Louisiana Purchase, 1803. Lt. Zebulon M. Pike explored the area, 1806, sighting the peak that bears his name. After the Mexican War, 1846-48, U.S. immigrants settled in the east, former Mexicans in the south. Gold was discovered in 1858, causing a population boom. Congress created Colorado Territory, 1861. Conflict between newcomers and displaced Native Americans led to the Sand Creek Massacre, 1864, in which U.S. soldiers and settlers killed some 150 Cheyenne and Arapaho. Most Native Americans were later removed to Oklahoma Territory. The 1870s brought statehood, 1876, and rich silver finds that

turned Leadville into a boomtown. Federal military and civilian employment in Colorado surged in the 1940s and '50s; since then, tourism and high-tech industries have fueled the economy. The state's Hispanic population grew from 5.8% in 1980 to 19.1% in 2005.

Tourist attractions. Rocky Mountain and Black Canyon of the Gunnison natl. parks; Aspen Ski Resort; Garden of the Gods, Colorado Springs; Great Sand Dunes, Dinosaur, and Colorado natl. monuments; Pikes Peak and Mt. Evans highways; Mesa Verde Natl. Park (ancient Anasazi Indian cliff dwellings); Grand Mesa Natl. Forest; mining towns of Central City, Silverton, Cripple Creek; Burlington's Old Town; Bent's Fort, outside La Junta; Georgetown Loop Historic Mining Railroad Park, Cumbres & Toltec Scenic Railroad; limited stakes gaming in Central City, Blackhawk, Cripple Creek, Ignacio, and Towaoe.

Famous Coloradans. Tim Allen, Frederick Bonfils, Henry Brown, Molly Brown, William N. Byers, M. Scott Carpenter, Lon Chaney, Jack Dempsey, Mamie Eisenhower, Douglas Fairbanks, Barney Ford, Scott Hamilton, John Kerry, Chief Ourey, "Baby Doe" Tabor, Lowell Thomas, Byron R. White, Paul Whiteman.

State Chamber of Commerce. 1776 Lincoln, Ste. 1200, Denver, CO 80203. Phone: 303-831-7411

Tourist information. Colorado Tourism Office, 1625 Broadway, Ste. 1700, Denver, CO 80202; 1-800-COLO-RADO. **Website:** www.colorado.com

Website. www.colorado.gov

Connecticut (CT)
Constitution State, Nutmeg State

People. Population (2005 est.): 3,510,297; rank: 29; **net change** (2004-2005): 0.3%. **Pop. density:** 724.5 per sq mi. Racial distribution (2004): 85.1% white; 10.1% black; 3.1% Asian; 0.3% Native/Nat.AK; 0.08% Hawaiian/Pacific Islander; 2 or more races, 1.3%. **Hispanic pop.** (any race): 10.6%.

Geography. Total area: 5,543 sq mi; rank: 48. **Land area:** 4,845 sq mi; rank: 48. **Acres forested:** 1.9 mil. **Location:** New England state in NE corner of the U.S. **Climate:** moderate; winters avg. slightly below freezing; warm, humid summers. **Topography:** western upland, the Berkshires, in the NW, highest elevations; narrow central lowland N-S; hilly eastern upland drained by rivers. **Capital:** Hartford. **Principal internat. airport at:** Windsor Locks.

Economy. Chief industries: manufacturing, retail trade, government, services, finances, insurance, real estate. **Chief manuf. goods:** aircraft engines and parts, submarines, helicopters, machinery and computer equipment, electronics and electrical equipment, medical instruments, pharmaceuticals. **Chief crops:** nursery stock, Christmas trees, mushrooms, vegetables, sweet corn, tobacco, apples. **Livestock:** (Jan. 2006): 52,000 cattle/calves; (Dec. 2005): 3,500 hogs/pigs, 3.7 mil chickens (excl. broilers) **Timber/lumber** (est. 2004): 48 mil bd. ft.; oak, birch, beech, maple. **Nonfuel minerals** (est. 2005): $140 mil; stone (crushed), sand and gravel (construction), stone (dimension), clays (common), gemstones. **Commercial fishing** (2004): $35.8 mil. Chief ports: New Haven, Bridgeport, New London. **Gross state product** (2005): $194.5 bil. **Sales tax** (2006): 6.0%. **Employment distrib.** (May 2006): 14.9% govt; 18.5% trade/trans./util.; 11.5% mfg; 16.5% ed./health; 12.1% prof./bus. serv.; 8.0% leisure/hosp.; 8.5% finance; 3.8% constr.; 3.8% other serv.; 2.2% info. **Unemployment** (2005): 4.9%. **Per cap. pers. income** (2005): $47,819. **New private housing** (2005): 11,885 units/$2.2 bil. **Commercial banks** (2005): 34; **deposits:** $44.1 bil. **Savings institutions** (2005): 37; **deposits:** $32.8 bil. **Lottery** (2005): total sales: $932.9 mil; profit: $268.5 mil.

Federal govt. Fed. civ. employees (Mar. 2005): 6,929; **avg. salary:** $64,143. **Notable fed. facilities:** U.S. Coast Guard Academy; *Navy Sub Base New London.

Energy. Electricity production (est. 2005, kWh, by source): Hydroelectric: 33 mil.

State data. Motto: Qui Transtulit Sustinet (He who transplanted still sustains). **Flower:** Mountain laurel. **Bird:** American robin. **Tree:** White oak. **Song:** Yankee Doodle. **Fifth** of the 13 original states to ratify the Constitution, Jan. 9, 1788. **State Fair:** largest fair at Durham, late Sept.; no state fair.

History. At the time of European contact, inhabitants of the area were Algonquian peoples, including the Mohegan and Pequot. Dutch explorer Adriaen Block was the first European visitor, 1614. By 1634, settlers from Plymouth Bay had started colonies along the Connecticut River; in 1637 they defeated the Pequots. The Colony of Connecticut was chartered by England, 1662, adding New Haven, 1665. A Patriot stronghold in the American Revolution, the state actively supported the antislavery movement and the Union cause in the Civil War. The state economy prospered in the 20th cent. from insurance- and defense-related industries. *Nautilus*, the first nuclear-powered submarine, was launched at Groton, 1954.

Tourist attractions. Mark Twain House, Hartford; Yale University's Art Gallery, Peabody Museum, both in New Haven; Mystic Seaport; Mystic Marine Life Aquarium; P. T. Barnum Museum, Bridgeport; Gillette Castle, Hadlyme; U.S.S. *Nautilus* Memorial, Groton (1st nuclear-powered submarine); Mashantucket Pequot Museum & Research Center, Foxwoods Resort & Casino, both in Ledyard; Mohegan Sun, Uncasville; Lake Compounce, Bristol.

Famous "Nutmeggers." Ethan Allen, Phineas T. Barnum, Samuel Colt, Jonathan Edwards, Nathan Hale, Katharine Hepburn, Isaac Hull, Robert Mitchum, J. Pierpont Morgan, Ralph Nader, Israel Putnam, Wallace Stevens, Harriet Beecher Stowe, Mark Twain, Noah Webster, Eli Whitney.

Tourist information. Connecticut Commission on Culture and Tourism, One Financial Plaza, 755 Main St., Hartford, CT 06103; (860) 256-2800. **Website:** www.ctbound.org

Website. www.ct.gov

Delaware (DE)
First State, Diamond State

People. Population (2005 est.): 843,524; rank: 45; **net change** (2004-2005): 1.6%. **Pop. density:** 431.8 per sq mi. Racial distribution (2004): 75.3% white; 20.4% black; 2.6% Asian; 0.4% Native/Nat.AK; 0.05% Hawaiian/Pacific Islander; 2 or more races, 1.3%. **Hispanic pop.** (any race): 5.8%.

Geography. Total area: 2,489 sq mi; rank: 49. **Land area:** 1,954 sq mi; rank: 49. **Acres forested:** 0.4 mil. **Location:** occupies the Delmarva Peninsula on the Atlantic coastal plain. **Climate:** moderate. **Topography:** Piedmont plateau to the N, sloping to a near sea-level plain. **Capital:** Dover. **Principal internat. airport at:** Philadelphia/Wilmington.

Economy. Chief industries: chemicals, agriculture, finance, poultry, shellfish, tourism, auto assembly, food processing, transportation equipment. **Chief manuf. goods:** nylon, apparel, luggage, foods, autos, processed meats and vegetables, railroad & aircraft equipment. **Chief crops:** soybeans, potatoes, corn, mushrooms, lima beans, green peas, barley, cucumbers, wheat, corn, grain sorghum, greenhouse & nursery. **Livestock:** (Jan. 2006): 23,000 cattle/calves; (Dec. 2005): 16,500 hogs/pigs, 282.3 mil broilers. **Timber/lumber:** figs. undisclosed; hardwoods and softwoods. **Nonfuel minerals** (est. 2005): $21.8 mil; sand and gravel (construction), magnesium compounds, gemstones. **Commercial fishing** (2004): $5.4 mil. **Chief ports:** Wilmington. **Gross state product** (2005): $54.4 bil. **Sales tax** (2006): none. **Employment distrib.** (May 2006): 14.0% govt; 18.9% trade/trans./util.; 7.3% mfg; 12.7% ed./health; 14.6% prof./bus. serv.; 9.6% leisure/hosp.; 10.2% finance; 6.6% constr.; 4.6% other serv.; 1.7% info. **Unemployment** (2005): 4.2%. **Per cap. pers. income** (2005): $37,065. **New private housing** (2005): 8,195 units/$988 mil. **Commercial banks** (2005): 34; **deposits:** $84.2 bil. **Savings institutions** (2005): 9; **deposits:** $54.6 bil. **Lottery** (2005): total sales: $689.3 mil; profit: $234.0 mil.

Federal govt. Fed. civ. employees (Mar. 2005): 2,716; **avg. salary:** $55,848. **Notable fed. facilities:** Dover AFB, Federal Wildlife Refuge, Bombay Hook.

Energy. Electricity production (est. 2004, kWh by source): Petroleum: 162 mil; Gas: 9 mil.

State data. Motto: Liberty and independence. **Flower:** Peach blossom. **Bird:** Blue hen chicken. **Tree:** American holly. **Song:** Our Delaware. **First** of original 13 states to ratify the Constitution, Dec. 7, 1787. **State fair** at Harrington; end of July.

History. The Lenni Lenape (Delaware) people lived in the region at the time of European contact. Henry Hudson located the Delaware R., 1609, and in 1610, English explorer Samuel Argall entered Delaware Bay, naming the area after Virginia's governor, Lord De La Warr. Dutch, Swedish, and Finnish settlers were followed by the British, who took control in 1664. After 1682, Delaware became part of Pennsylvania, and in 1704 it was granted its own assembly. It adopted a constitution as the state of Delaware, 1776, and was first to ratify the federal Constitution, 1787. Although it remained in the Union during the Civil War, Delaware retained slavery un-

til the 13th Amendment abolished it in1865. The Du Pont company, founded as a gunpowder mill in 1802, became an industrial giant in the 20th century, making nylon, Teflon, and other synthetics. Pro-business laws drew many out-of-state firms to incorporate in Delaware. In 2000, Ruth Ann Minner was elected Delaware's first woman governor.

Tourist attractions. Ft. Christina Monument, site of founding of New Sweden, Holy Trinity (Old Swedes) Church, erected 1698, the oldest Protestant church in the U.S. still in use, Wilmington; Hagley Museum, Winterthur Museum and Gardens, both near Wilmington; historic district, New Castle; John Dickinson "Penman of the Revolution" home, Dover; Rehoboth Beach, "nation's summer capital," Rehoboth; Dover Downs Intl. Speedway.

Famous Delawareans. Thomas F. Bayard, Joseph Biden, Henry Seidel Canby, E. I. du Pont, John P. Marquand, Howard Pyle, Caesar Rodney.

Tourist Information. Delaware Tourism Office, 99 Kings Highway, Dover, DE 19901. 1-866-2VISITDE. **Website:** www.visitdelaware.net

Website. www.delaware.gov

Florida (FL)
Sunshine State

People. Population (2005 est.): 17,789,864; rank: 4; **net change** (2004-2005): 2.3%. **Pop. density:** 329.9 per sq mi. Racial distribution (2004): 80.6% white; 15.7% black; 2.0% Asian; 0.4% Native/Nat.AK; 0.08% Hawaiian/Pacific Islander; 2 or more races, 1.2%. **Hispanic pop.** (any race): 19%.

Geography. Total area: 65,755 sq mi; rank: 22. **Land area:** 53,927 sq mi; rank: 26. **Acres forested:** 16.3 mil. **Location:** peninsula jutting southward 500 mi between the Atlantic and the Gulf of Mexico. **Climate:** subtropical N of Bradenton-Lake Okeechobee-Vero Beach line; tropical S of line. **Topography:** land is flat or rolling; highest point is 345 ft in the NW. **Capital:** Tallahassee. **Principal internat. airports at:** Daytona Beach, Ft. Lauderdale/Hollywood, Ft. Myers, Jacksonville, Key West, Miami, Orlando, St. Petersburg/Clearwater, Sarasota/Bradenton, Tampa, West Palm Beach.

Economy. Chief industries: tourism, agriculture, manufacturing, construction, services, international trade. **Chief manuf. goods:** electric & electronic equipment, transportation equipment, food, printing & publishing, chemicals, instruments, industrial machinery. **Chief crops:** citrus fruits, vegetables, melons, greenhouse and nursery products, potatoes, sugarcane, strawberries. **Livestock:** (Jan. 2006): 1.7 mil cattle/calves; (Dec. 2005): 20,000 hogs/pigs, 13.6 mil chickens (excl. broilers), 75.9 mil broilers. **Timber/lumber** (est. 2004): 1.1 bil bd. ft.; pine, cypress, cedar **Nonfuel minerals** (est. 2005): $2.6 bil; phosphate rock, stone (crushed), cement (portland), sand and gravel (construction), cement (masonry). **Commercial fishing** (2004): $190.6 mil. **Chief ports:** Pensacola, Tampa, Manatee, Miami, Port Everglades, Jacksonville, St. Petersburg, Canaveral. **Gross state product** (2005): $674.0 bil. **Sales tax** (2006): 6.0%. **Employment distrib.** (May 2006): 13.7% govt; 19.9% trade/trans./util.; 5.0% mfg; 12.0% ed./health; 17.1% prof./bus. serv.; 11.5% leisure/hosp.; 6.7% finance; 7.7% constr.; 4.2% other serv.; 2.1% info. **Unemployment** (2005): 3.8%. **Per cap. pers. income** (2005): $33,219. **New private housing** (2005): 287,250 units/$46.8 bil. **Commercial banks** (2005): 296; **deposits:** $282.8 bil. **Savings institutions** (2005): 53; **deposits:** $60.0 bil. **Lottery** (2005): total sales: $3.5 bil; profit: $1.1 bil.

Federal govt. Fed. civ. employees (Mar. 2005): 72,164; **avg. salary:** $58,420. **Notable fed. facilities:** John F. Kennedy Space Ctr., NASA-Kennedy Space Ctr.'s Spaceport USA; Eglin AFB, MacDill AFB; *Pensacola NAS; Jacksonville NAS; Mayport Naval Sta.

Energy. Electricity production (est. 2005, kWh by source): Coal: 57.7 bil; Gas: 73.9 bil; Hydroelectric: 244 mil; Nuclear: 28.8 bil; Petroleum: 28.1 bil; Other: 109 mil.

State data. Motto: In God we trust. **Flower:** Orange blossom. **Bird:** Mockingbird. **Tree:** Sabal palmetto palm. **Song:** Old Folks at Home. **Entered union** Mar. 3, 1845; rank, 27th. **State fair** at Tampa; early Feb.

History. Florida has been inhabited for at least 12,000 years. Timucua, Apalachee, and Calusa peoples were living in the region when the earliest Europeans came; later the Seminole migrated from Georgia to Florida, becoming dominant there in the early 18th cent. The first European to see Florida was Ponce de León, 1513. France established a colony, Fort Caroline, on the St. Johns River, 1564. Spain settled St. Augustine, 1565, and Spanish troops massacred most of the French. Britain's Sir Francis Drake burned St. Augustine, 1586. In 1763, Spain ceded Florida to Great Britain, which held the area 20 years before returning it to Spain. Florida was ceded to the U.S. in the Adams-Onís Treaty, 1819. The Seminole War, 1835-42, resulted in removal of most Native Americans to Oklahoma Territory. Florida joined the Union in 1845, seceded in 1861, and was readmitted in 1868. In the late 19th cent., hotel and railroad builder Henry M. Flagler laid the foundations of the tourism industry. The state experienced phenomenal population growth in the 20th cent., especially after 1950. The first U.S. astronaut was launched into space from Cape Canaveral, 1961. Walt Disney World opened near Orlando, 1971. Hurricane Andrew slammed S. Florida, 1992, causing at least $25 bil in property damage. A dispute over Florida's presidential vote in 2000 led to the U.S. Supreme Court decision awarding the White House to George W. Bush; his brother Jeb has been state governor since 1999. Cuban expatriates wield major political influence in the Miami area.

Tourist attractions. Miami Beach; St. Augustine, oldest permanent European settlement in U.S.; Castillo de San Marcos, St. Augustine; Walt Disney World's Magic Kingdom, EPCOT Center, Disney-MGM Studios, and Animal Kingdom, all near Orlando; Sea World, Universal Studios, near Orlando; Spaceport USA, Kennedy Space Center; Everglades Natl. Park; Ringling Museum of Art, Ringling Museum of the Circus, both in Sarasota; Cypress Gardens, Winter Haven; Busch Gardens, Tampa; U.S. Astronaut Hall of Fame, Mariana Caverns; Church St. Station, Orlando; Silver Springs, Ocala.

Famous Floridians. Edna Buchanan, Jeb Bush, Marjory Stoneman Douglas, Henry M. Flagler, Carl Hiaasen, Zora Neale Hurston, James Weldon Johnson, MacKinlay Kantor, John D. MacDonald, Chief Osceola, Claude Pepper, Henry B. Plant, A. Philip Randolph, Marjorie Kinnan Rawlings, Janet Reno, Joseph W. Stilwell, Charles P. Summerall, Ben Vereen.

Tourist information. Visit Florida, 661 E. Jefferson St., Tallahassee, FL 32301; (1-888-7FLA-USA). **Website:** www.visitflorida.com

Website. www.myflorida.com

Georgia (GA)
Empire State of the South, Peach State

People. Population (2005 est.): 9,072,576; rank: 9; **net change** (2004-2005): 1.7%. **Pop. density:** 156.7 per sq mi. Racial distribution (2004): 66.4% white; 29.6% black; 2.6% Asian; 0.3% Native/Nat.AK; 0.08% Hawaiian/Pacific Islander; 2 or more races, 1.0%. **Hispanic pop.** (any race): 6.8%.

Geography. Total area: 59,425 sq mi; rank: 24. **Land area:** 57,906 sq mi; rank: 21. **Acres forested:** 24.4 mil. **Location:** South Atlantic state. **Climate:** maritime tropical air masses dominate in summer; polar air masses in winter; E central area drier. **Topography:** most southerly of the Blue Ridge Mts. cover NE and N central; central Piedmont extends to the fall line of rivers; coastal plain levels to the coast flatlands. **Capital:** Atlanta. **Principal internat. airports at:** Atlanta, Savannah.

Economy. Chief industries: services, manufacturing, retail trade. **Chief manuf. goods:** textiles, apparel, food, and kindred products, pulp & paper products. **Chief crops:** peanuts, cotton, corn, tobacco, hay, soybeans. **Livestock:** (Jan. 2006): 1.2 mil cattle/calves; (Dec. 2005): 270,000 hogs/pigs, 27.8 mil chickens (excl. broilers), 1.3 bil broilers. **Timber/lumber** (est. 2004): 3.0 bil bd. ft.; pine, hardwood. **Nonfuel minerals** (est. 2005): $1.8 bil; clays (kaolin), stone (crushed), clays (fuller's earth), cement (portland), sand and gravel (construction). **Commercial fishing** (2004): $11.3 mil. **Chief ports:** Savannah, Brunswick. **Gross state product** (2005): $364.3 bil. **Sales tax** (2006): 4.0%. **Employment distrib.** (May 2006): 16.2% govt; 21.2% trade/trans./util.; 11.0% mfg; 10.6% ed./health; 13.4% prof./bus. serv.; 9.5% leisure/hosp.; 5.6% finance; 5.3% constr.; 3.9% other serv.; 2.9% info. **Unemployment** (2005): 5.3%. **Per cap. pers. income** (2005): $31,121. **New private housing** (2005): 109,336 units/$14.1 bil. **Commercial banks** (2005): 343; **deposits:** $143.2 bil. **Savings institutions** (2005): 24; **deposits:** $6.3 bil. **Lottery** (2005): total sales: $2.9 bil; profit: $802.2 mil.

Federal govt. Fed. civ. employees (Mar. 2005): 65,347; **avg. salary:** $59,283. **Notable fed. facilities:** Dobbins AFB; Ft. Benning; Ft. Gordon; *Ft. Gillem; Ft. Stewart; King's Bay Naval Base; Moody AFB; *Navy Supply Corps School; *Ft. McPherson; Fed. Law Enforcement Training Ctr., Glynco, Robins AFB; Centers for Disease Control.

Energy. Electricity production (est. 2005, kWh by source): Coal: 86.4 bil; Gas: 2.0 bil; Hydroelectric: 3.6 bil; Nuclear: 31.5 bil; Petroleum: 184 mil.

State data. Motto: Wisdom, justice and moderation. **Flower:** Cherokee rose. **Bird:** Brown thrasher. **Tree:** Live oak. **Song:** Georgia On My Mind. **Fourth** of the 13 original states to ratify the Constitution, Jan. 2, 1788. **State fair** at Macon, late Sept.-Oct.

History. Creek and Cherokee peoples were living in the region when Spaniards founded Santa Catalina mission, 1566, on Saint Catherines Island. Gen. James Oglethorpe established a colony at Savannah, 1733, for the poor and religiously persecuted. Oglethorpe defeated a Spanish army from Florida at Bloody Marsh, 1742. Georgia was a battleground in the American Revolution, with the British finally evacuating Savannah in 1782. When Georgia entered the Union, 1788, its plantation economy relied on slaves for rice and cotton growing. The Cherokee were removed to Oklahoma Territory, 1832-38, and thousands died on the long march, known as the Trail of Tears. By 1860 the number of slaves exceeded 462,000 (44% of the total population). Georgia seceded from the Union, 1861, and was invaded by Union forces, 1864, under Gen. William T. Sherman, who took Atlanta, Sept. 2, and proceeded on his famous "march to the sea," ending in Dec., in Savannah. Georgia was readmitted, 1870. Born 1929 in Atlanta, Martin Luther King Jr., made the city his home base during the civil rights struggles of the 1960s. Atlanta became the leading city of the "New South," world headquarters of Coca-Cola and CNN, and host of the 1996 Summer Olympic Games. Hispanics are a rapidly growing economic and political force in the state.

Tourist attractions. State Capitol, Stone Mt. Park, Six Flags Over Georgia, Kennesaw Mt. Natl. Battlefield Park, Martin Luther King Jr. Natl. Historic Site, Underground Atlanta, Jimmy Carter Library & Museum, all Atlanta; Chickamauga and Chattanooga Natl. Military Park, near Dalton; Chattahoochee Natl. Forest; alpine village of Helen; Dahlonega, site of America's first gold rush; Brasstown Bald Mt.; Lake Lanier; Franklin D. Roosevelt's Little White House, Warm Springs; Callaway Gardens, Pine Mt.; Andersonville Natl. Historic Site; Okefenokee Swamp, near Waycross; Jekyll Island; St. Simons Island; Cumberland Island Natl. Seashore; historic riverfront district, Savannah.

Famous Georgians. Kim Basinger, Griffin Bell, James Bowie, James Brown, Erskine Caldwell, Jimmy Carter, Ray Charles, Lucius D. Clay, Ty Cobb, James Dickey, John C. Fremont, Newt Gingrich, Joel Chandler Harris, "Doc" Holliday, Holly Hunter, Alan Jackson, Jasper Johns, Martin Luther King Jr., Gladys Knight, Sidney Lanier, Little Richard, Juliette Gordon Low, Margaret Mitchell, Sam Nunn, Flannery O'Connor, Otis Redding, Burt Reynolds, Julia Roberts, Jackie Robinson, Clarence Thomas, Travis Tritt, Ted Turner, Carl Vinson, Alice Walker, Herschel Walker, Joseph Wheeler, Joanne Woodward, Trisha Yearwood, Andrew Young.

Tourist Information. Dept. of Economic Development, 75 Fifth St., NW, Ste. 1200, Atlanta, GA 30308; 1-800-VISITGA. **Website:** www.georgia.org

Website. www.georgia.gov

Hawai'i (HI)
Aloha State

People. Population (2005 est.): 1,275,194; rank: 42; **net change** (2004-2005): 1.0%. **Pop. density:** 198.5 per sq mi. Racial distribution (2004): 26.5% white; 2.2% black; 41.8% Asian; 0.3% Native/Nat.AK; 9.1% Hawaiian/Pacific Islander; 2 or more races, 20.1%. **Hispanic pop.** (any race): 7.9%.

Geography. Total area: 10,931 sq mi; rank: 43. **Land area:** 6,423 sq mi; rank: 47. **Acres forested:** 1.7 mil. **Location:** Hawaiian Islands lie in the North Pacific, 2,397 mi SW from San Francisco. **Climate:** subtropical, with wide variations in rainfall; Waialeale, on Kaua'i, wettest spot in U.S. (annual rainfall 460 in.) **Topography:** islands are tops of a chain of submerged volcanic mountains; active volcanoes: Mauna Loa, Kilauea. **Capital:** Honolulu. **Principal internat. airports at:** Hilo, Honolulu, Kailua, Kahului.

Economy. Chief industries: tourism, defense, sugar, pineapples. **Chief manuf. goods:** processed sugar, canned pineapple, clothing, foods, printing & publishing. **Chief crops:** sugar, pineapples, macadamia nuts, fruits, coffee, vegetables, floriculture. **Livestock:** (Jan. 2006): 161,000 cattle/calves; (Dec. 2005): 19,000 hogs/pigs, 547,000 chickens (excl.broilers). **Timber/lumber:** figs. undisclosed. **Nonfuel minerals** (est. 2005): $71.1 mil; stone (crushed), sand and gravel (construction), gemstones. **Commercial fishing** (2004): $57.2 mil. **Chief ports:** Honolulu, Hilo, Kailua. **Gross state product** (2005): $53.7 bil. **Sales tax** (2006): 4.0%. **Employment distrib.** (May 2006): 20.0% govt; 19.6% trade/trans./util.; 2.5% mfg; 11.5% ed./health; 12.4% prof./bus. serv.; 17.4% leisure/hosp.; 4.8% finance; 5.8% constr.; 4.2% other serv.; 1.8% info. **Unemployment** (2005): 2.8%. **Per cap. pers. income** (2005): $34,539. **New private housing** (2005): 9,828 units/$2.1 bil. **Commercial banks** (2005): 7; **deposits** $19.1 bil. **Savings institutions** (2005): 3; **deposits** $5.7 bil.

Federal govt. Fed. civ. employees (Mar. 2005): 20,406; **avg. salary:** $54,163. **Notable fed. facilities:** Pearl Harbor Naval Shipyard; *Hickam AFB; Schofield Barracks; Ft. Shafter; Marine Corps Base-Kaneohe Bay; Barbers Point NAS; Wheeler AFB; Prince Kuhio Federal Bldg.

Energy. Electricity production (est. 2005, kWh by source): Petroleum: 6.7 bil; Other: 2 mil.

State data. Motto: The life of the land is perpetuated in righteousness. **Flower:** Yellow hibiscus. **Bird:** Hawaiian goose. **Tree:** Kukui (Candlenut). **Song:** Hawai'i Pono'i. **Entered union** Aug. 21, 1959; rank, 50th. **State fair:** at O'ahu, late July–early Aug.

History. Polynesians from islands 2,000 mi to the S settled the Hawaiian Islands, probably 300-600 CE. The first European visitor was British captain James Cook, 1778. King Kamehameha I united the islands by 1810. Christian missionaries arrived, 1819, bringing Western culture. Under the reign, 1825-54, of King Kamehameha III, a constitution, legislature, and public school system were instituted. Sugar production began, 1835, and it became the dominant industry. Queen Liliuokalani was deposed, 1893, and a republic was established, 1894, headed by Sanford B. Dole. Annexation by the U.S. came in 1898. The Japanese attack on Pearl Harbor, Dec. 7, 1941, brought the U.S. into World War II. Hawai'i attained statehood, 1959. Hurricane Iniki pounded Kauai, 1992, causing about $1 bil in damage. In 2006, Pres. George W. Bush designated the Northwestern Hawaiian Islands National Monument, a marine area of 140,000 sq mi.

Tourist attractions. Hawaii Volcanoes, Haleakala natl. parks; Natl. Memorial Cemetery of the Pacific, Waikiki Beach, Diamond Head, Honolulu; U.S.S. *Arizona* Memorial, Pearl Harbor; Hanauma Bay; Polynesian Cultural Center, Laie; Nu'uanu Pali; Waimea Canyon; Wailoa and Wailuku River state parks.

Famous Islanders. Bernice Pauahi Bishop, Tia Carrere, Father Damien de Veuster, Don Ho, Duke Kahanamoku, King Kamehameha, Brook Mahealani Lee, Daniel K. Inouye, Jason Scott Lee, Queen Liliuokalani, Bette Midler, Ellison Onizuka.

Tourist Information. Hawaii Visitors and Conventions Bureau, 2270 Kalakaua Ave., Ste. 801, Honolulu, HI 96815; 1-800-GOHAWAII. **Website:** www.gohawaii.com

Website. www.hawaii.gov

Idaho (ID)
Gem State

People. Population (2005 est.): 1,429,096; rank: 39; **net change** (2004-2005): 2.4%. **Pop. density:** 17.3 per sq mi. Racial distribution (2004): 95.5% white; 0.6% black; 1.0% Asian; 1.4% Native/Nat.AK; 0.1% Hawaiian/Pacific Islander; 2 or more races, 1.3%. **Hispanic pop.** (any race): 8.9%.

Geography. Total area: 83,570 sq mi; rank: 14. **Land area:** 82,747 sq mi; rank: 11. **Acres forested:** 21.6 mil. **Location:** northwestern Mountain state bordering on British Columbia. **Climate:** tempered by Pacific westerly winds; drier, colder, continental climate in SE; altitude an important factor. **Topography:** Snake R. plains in the S; central region of mountains, canyons, gorges (Hells Canyon, 7,900 ft, deepest in N. America); subalpine northern region. **Capital:** Boise.

Economy. Chief industries: manufacturing, agriculture, tourism, lumber, mining, electronics. **Chief manuf. goods:** electronic components, computer equipment, processed foods, lumber and wood products, chemical products, primary metals, fabricated metal products, machinery. **Chief crops:** potatoes, peas, dry beans, sugar beets, alfalfa seed,

lentils, wheat, hops, barley, plums and prunes, mint, onions, corn, cherries, apples, hay. **Livestock:** (Jan. 2006): 2.1 mil cattle/calves, 260,000 sheep/lambs; (Dec. 2005): 21,000 hogs/pigs, 1.2 mil chickens (excl. broilers). **Timber/lumber:** 1.7 bil. bd. ft; pine, fir, spruce. **Nonfuel minerals** (est. 2005): $893 mil; phosphate rock, sand and gravel (construction), molybdenum concentrates, silver, cement (portland). **Chief port:** Lewiston. **Gross state product** (2005): $47.2 bil. **Sales tax** (2006): 5.0%. **Employment distrib.** (May 2006): 18.7% govt; 19.7% trade/trans./util.; 9.9% mfg; 10.9% ed./health; 12.8% prof./bus. serv.; 9.5% leisure/hosp.; 5.0% finance; 8.2% constr.; 3.0% other serv.; 1.8% info. **Unemployment** (2005): 3.8%. **Per cap. pers. income** (2005): $28,158. **New private housing** (2005): 21,578 units/$3.5 bil. **Commercial banks** (2005): 25; **deposits** $12.6 bil. **Savings institutions** (2005): 8; **deposits:** $2.6 bil. **Lottery** (2005): total sales: $113.5 mil; profit: $26.0 mil.

Federal govt. Fed. civ. employees (Mar. 2005): 8,045; **avg. salary:** $56,012. **Notable fed. facilities:** Idaho Natl. Engineering Lab; *Mountain Home AFB.

Energy. Electricity production (est. 2005, kWh by source): Gas: 48 mil; Hydroelectric: 7.9 bil. .

State data. Motto: Esto Perpetua (It is perpetual). **Flower:** Syringa. **Bird:** Mountain bluebird. **Tree:** White pine. **Song:** Here We Have Idaho. **Entered union** July 3, 1890; rank, 43rd. **State fair** at Boise, late Aug.; at Blackfoot, early Sept.

History. Paleoindian hunters roamed the land over 13,000 years ago; later inhabitants included Shoshone, Northern Paiute, Bannock, and Nez Percé peoples. Lewis and Clark expedition explored, 1805-6. Next came fur traders, 1809-34, and missionaries, 1830s-50s. Mormons made their first permanent settlement at Franklin, 1860. Idaho's gold rush began the same year and brought thousands of permanent settlers. A series of Indian wars followed, including a remarkable campaign by Chief Joseph and the Nez Percé that ended with his surrender in Montana, 1877. Idaho became a territory, 1863, and a state, 1890. In the 20th cent., it emerged as a leader in potato, lumber, and silver output. The Sun Valley ski resort opened in 1936, boosting tourism. Startup of Lewiston's river port, 1975, opened Idaho to oceangoing trade. Fueled by high-tech job growth, the state's population jumped 10.4% in 2000-05.

Tourist attractions. Hells Canyon, deepest gorge in N. America; World Center for Birds of Prey; Craters of the Moon; Sun Valley, in Sawtooth Mts.; Crystal Falls Cave; Shoshone Falls; Lava Hot Springs; Lake Pend Oreille; Lake Coeur d'Alene; Sawtooth Natl. Recreation Area; River of No Return Wilderness Area; Redfish Lake.

Famous Idahoans. William E. Borah, Frank Church, Lou Dobbs, Fred T. Dubois, Chief Joseph, Harmon Killebrew, Ezra Pound, Sacagawea, Picabo Street, Lana Turner.

Tourist information. Division of Tourism Development, 700 W. State St., Boise, ID 83720; (208) 334-2470. **Website:** www.visitid.org

Website. www.state.id.us

Illinois (IL)
Prairie State

People. Population (2005 est.): 12,763,371; rank: 5; **net change** (2004-2005): 0.4%. **Pop. density:** 229.6 per sq mi. Racial distribution (2004): 79.5% white; 15.1% black; 4.0% Asian; 0.3% Native/Nat.AK; 0.06% Hawaiian/Pacific Islander; 2 or more races, 1.1%. **Hispanic pop.** (any race): 14%.

Geography. Total area: 57,914 sq mi; rank: 25. **Land area:** 55,584 sq mi; rank: 24. **Acres forested:** 4.3 mil. **Location:** East North Central state; western, southern, and eastern boundaries formed by Mississippi, Ohio, and Wabash rivers, respectively. **Climate:** temperate; typically cold, snowy winters, hot summers. **Topography:** prairie and fertile plains throughout; open hills in the southern region. **Capital:** Springfield. **Principal internat. airports at:** Chicago.

Economy. Chief industries: services, manufacturing, travel, wholesale and retail trade, finance, insurance, real estate, construction, health care, agriculture. **Chief manuf. goods:** machinery, electric and electronic equipment, prim. & fabric. metals, chemical products, printing & publishing, food and kindred products. **Chief crops:** corn, soybeans, wheat, sorghum, hay. **Livestock:** (Jan. 2006): 1.3 mil cattle/calves, 69,000 sheep/lambs; (Dec. 2005): 4.0 mil hogs/pigs, 4.7 mil chickens (excl. broilers). **Timber/lumber** (est. 2004): 123 mil bd. ft.; oak, hickory, maple, cottonwood. **Nonfuel minerals** (est. 2005): $1.1 bil; stone (crushed), cement (portland), sand

and gravel (construction), sand and gravel (industrial), lime. **Chief ports:** Chicago. **Gross state product** (2005): $560.2 bil. **Sales tax** (2006): 6.25%. **Employment distrib.** (May 2006): 14.4% govt; 20.0% trade/trans./util.; 11.4% mfg; 12.7% ed./health; 14.3% prof./bus. serv.; 9.1% leisure/hosp.; 6.9% finance; 4.7% constr.; 4.4% other serv.; 2.0% info. **Unemployment** (2005): 5.7%. **Per cap. pers. income** (2005): $36,120. **New private housing** (2005): 66,942 units/$11.0 bil. **Commercial banks** (2005): 654; **deposits:** $269.0 bil. **Savings institutions** (2005): 105; **deposits:** $34.5 bil. **Lottery** (2005): total sales: $1.8 bil; profit: $614.0 mil.

Federal govt. Fed. civ. employees (Mar. 2005):42,676; **avg. salary:** $65,022. **Notable fed. facilities:** Fermi Natl. Accelerator Lab; Argonne Natl. Lab; *Rock Island Arsenal; *Great Lakes Naval Station, Scott AFB.

Energy. Electricity production (est. 2005, kWh by source): Coal: 10.2 bil; Gas: 278 mil; Hydroelectric: 66 mil; Petroleum: 34 mil; Other: 4 mil.

State data. Motto: State sovereignty—national union. **Flower:** Native violet. **Bird:** Cardinal. **Tree:** White oak. **Song:** Illinois. **Entered union** Dec. 3, 1818; rank, 21st. **State fair** at Springfield, mid-Aug.; DuQuoin, late Aug.

History. The region has been inhabited for at least 10,000 years; seminomadic Algonquian peoples, including the Peoria, Illinois, Kaskaskia, and Tamaroa, lived there at the time of European contact. Fur traders were the first Europeans in Illinois, followed shortly by Jolliet and Marquette, 1673, and La Salle, 1680, who built a fort near present-day Peoria. French priests established the first permanent settlements, at Cahokia, near present-day St. Louis, 1699, and Kaskaskia, 1703. France ceded the area to Britain, 1763, and in 1778, American Gen. George Rogers Clark took Kaskaskia from the British without a shot. Illinois became a separate territory, 1809, and a state, 1818. Defeat of Native American tribes in the Black Hawk War, 1832, and canal, rail, and road construction brought rapid change. Mormon settlers at Nauvoo, 1839, met with hostility, and a Carthage mob killed Mormon leader Joseph Smith and his brother, 1844. The great Chicago Fire, 1871, destroyed the city's downtown. Illinois became a center for the labor movement, leading to bitter conflicts such as the Haymarket riot, 1886, and Pullman strike, 1894. Social reformer Jane Addams founded Hull House, 1889, to aid immigrants and the poor. During 1900-70, as manufacturing expanded, many African Americans arrived from the southern U.S. Chicago police violently suppressed antiwar protests at the1968 Democratic National Convention. Dennis Hastert (R, IL) has been Speaker of the House since 1999. Barack Obama (D, IL), elected in 2004, is the first male African American Democrat to serve in the U.S. Senate.

Tourist attractions. Chicago museums and parks; Lincoln shrines at Springfield, New Salem, Sangamon County; Cahokia Mounds, Collinsville; Starved Rock State Park; Crab Orchard Wildlife Refuge; Mormon settlement at Nauvoo; Fts. Kaskaskia, Chartres, Massac (parks); Shawnee Natl. Forest, Southern Illinois; Illinois State Museum, Springfield; Dickson Mounds Museum, between Havana and Lewistown.

Famous Illinoisans. Jane Addams, John Ashcroft, Saul Bellow, Jack Benny, Ray Bradbury, Gwendolyn Brooks, William Jennings Bryan, St. Frances Xavier Cabrini, Hillary Rodham Clinton, Clarence Darrow, John Deere, Stephen A. Douglas, James T. Farrell, George W. Ferris, Marshall Field, Betty Friedan, Benny Goodman, Ulysses S. Grant, Dennis Hastert, Ernest Hemingway, Charlton Heston, Wild Bill Hickok, Henry J. Hyde, Abraham Lincoln, Vachel Lindsay, Edgar Lee Masters, Oscar Mayer, Cyrus McCormick, Ronald Reagan, Donald Rumsfeld, Carl Sandburg, Adlai Stevenson, James Watson, Frank Lloyd Wright, Philip Wrigley.

Tourist information. Illinois Dept. of Commerce and Economic Opportunity, 620 E. Adams St., 4th fl., Springfield, IL 62701; 1-800-2-CONNECT. **Website:** www.enjoyillinois.com

Website. www.illinois.gov

Indiana (IN)

Hoosier State

People. Population (2005 est.): 6,271,973; rank: 15; **net change** (2004-2005): 0.7%. **Pop. density:** 174.9 per sq mi. Racial distribution (2004): 88.7% white; 8.8% black; 1.2% Asian; 0.3% Native/Nat.AK; 0.05% Hawaiian/Pacific Islander; 2 or more races, 1.1%. **Hispanic pop.** (any race): 4.3%.

Geography. Total area: 36,418 sq mi; rank: 38. **Land area:** 35,867 sq mi; rank: 38. **Acres forested:** 4.5 mil. **Location:** East North Central state; Lake Michigan on N border. **Climate:** 4 distinct seasons with a temperate climate. **Topography:** hilly southern region; fertile rolling plains of central region; flat, heavily glaciated north; dunes along Lake Michigan shore. **Capital:** Indianapolis. **Principal internat. airports at:** Indianapolis, Ft. Wayne.

Economy: Chief industries: manufacturing, services, agriculture, government, wholesale and retail trade, transportation and public utilities. **Chief manuf. goods:** primary metals, transportation equipment, motor vehicles & equip., industrial machinery & equipment, electronic & electric equipment. **Chief crops:** corn, soybeans, wheat, nursery and greenhouse products, vegetables, popcorn, fruit, hay, tobacco, mint. **Livestock:** (Jan. 2006): 900,000 cattle/calves, 50,000 sheep/lambs; (Dec. 2005): 3.2 mil hogs/pigs, 31.8 mil chickens (excl. broilers). **Timber/lumber** (est. 2004): 333 mil bd. ft.; oak, tulip, beech, sycamore. **Nonfuel minerals** (est. 2005): $789 mil; stone (crushed), cement (portland), sand and gravel (construction), lime, cement (masonry). **Chief ports:** Burns Harbor, Portage; Southwind Maritime, Mt. Vernon; Clark Maritime, Jeffersonville. **Gross state product** (2005): $238.6 bil. **Sales tax** (2006): 6.0%. **Employment distrib.** (May 2006): 14.6% govt; 19.5% trade/trans./util.; 19.1% mfg; 12.8% ed./health; 9.2% prof./bus. serv.; 9.6% leisure/hosp.; 4.7% finance; 5.1% constr.; 3.7% other serv.; 1.4% info. **Unemployment** (2005): 5.4%. **Per cap. pers. income** (2005): $31,276. **New private housing** (2005): 38,476 units/$5.8 bil. **Commercial banks** (2005): 164; **deposits:** $73.1 bil. **Savings institutions** (2005): 59; **deposits:** $11.5 bil. **Lottery** (2005): total sales: $739.6 mil; profit: $189.0 mil.

Federal govt. Fed. civ. employees (Mar. 2005): 18,459; **avg. salary:** $58,772. **Notable fed. facilities:** Nav. Surface Warfare Ctr., Crane Div.

Energy. Electricity production (est. 2005, kWh by source): Coal: 115.5 bil; Gas: 1.3 bil; Hydroelectric: 461 mil; Petroleum: 140 mil.

State data. Motto: Crossroads of America. **Flower:** Peony. **Bird:** Cardinal. **Tree:** Tulip poplar. **Song:** On the Banks of the Wabash, Far Away. **Entered union** Dec. 11, 1816; rank, 19th. **State fair** at Indianapolis; mid-Aug.

History. When the Europeans arrived, Miami, Potawatomi, Kickapoo, Piankashaw, Wea, and Shawnee peoples inhabited the region. La Salle visited the present South Bend area, 1679 and 1681. The first French fort was built near present-day Lafayette, 1717. A French trading post was established, 1731-32, at Vincennes. France ceded the area to Britain, 1763. During the American Revolution, American Gen. George Rogers Clark captured Vincennes, 1778, and defeated British forces, 1779. Indiana became a territory, 1800, and a state, 1816. The Miami were beaten, 1794, at Fallen Timbers, and Gen. William H. Harrison defeated Tecumseh's Indian confederation, 1811, at Tippecanoe. Manufacturing grew rapidly after the Civil War. U.S. Steel founded Gary, 1906. An automotive test track was the site of the first Indianapolis 500 race, 1911. The auto industry remains key to the state economy; in 2006, Honda announced it would build a $550-mil plant near Greensburg.

Tourist attractions. Lincoln Log Cabin Historic Site, near Charleston; George Rogers Clark Park, Vincennes; Wyandotte Cave; Tippecanoe Battlefield Memorial Park; Benjamin Harrison home; Indianapolis 500 raceway and museum, all Indianapolis; Indiana Dunes, near Chesterton; National College Football Hall of Fame, South Bend; Hoosier Nat'l. Forest, south-central Indiana.

Famous "Hoosiers." Larry Bird, Ambrose Burnside, Hoagy Carmichael, Jim Davis, James Dean, Eugene V. Debs, Theodore Dreiser, Paul Dresser, Jeff Gordon, Benjamin Harrison, Gil Hodges, Michael Jackson, David Letterman, Carole Lombard, John Mellencamp, Jane Pauley, Cole Porter, Gene Stratton Porter, Ernie Pyle, Dan Quayle, James Whitcomb Riley, Oscar Robertson, Red Skelton, Booth Tarkington, Kurt Vonnegut, Lew Wallace, Wendell L. Willkie, Wilbur Wright.

Tourist Information. Indiana Office of Tourism Development, 1 North Capital, Suite 100, Indianapolis, IN 46204; 800-677-9800. **Website:** www.in.gov/enjoyindiana

Website. www.in.gov

Iowa (IA)
Hawkeye State

People. Population (2005 est.): 2,966,334; rank: 30; **net change** (2004-2005): 0.5%. **Pop. density:** 53.1 per sq mi. Racial distribution (2004): 95.0% white; 2.3% black; 1.4% Asian; 0.3% Native/Nat.AK; 0.04% Hawaiian/Pacific Islander; 2 or more races, 0.9%. **Hispanic pop.** (any race): 3.5%.

Geography. Total area: 56,272 sq mi; rank: 26. **Land area:** 55,869 sq mi; rank: 23. **Acres forested:** 2.1 mil. **Location:** West North Central state bordered by Mississippi R. on the E and Missouri R. on the W. **Climate:** humid, continental. **Topography:** Watershed from NW to SE; soil especially rich and land level in the N central counties. **Capital:** Des Moines. **Principal internat. airport at:** Des Moines.

Economy. Chief industries: agriculture, communications, construction, finance, insurance, trade, services, manufacturing. **Chief manuf. goods:** processed food products, tires, farm machinery, electronic products, appliances, household furniture, chemicals, fertilizers, auto accessories. **Chief crops:** silage and grain corn, soybeans, oats, hay. **Livestock:** (Jan. 2006): 3.8 mil cattle/calves, 235,000 sheep/lambs; (Dec. 2005): 16.4 mil hogs/pigs, 58.5 mil chickens (excl. broilers). **Timber/lumber** (est. 2004): 78 mil bd. ft.; red cedar. **Nonfuel minerals** (est. 2005): $604 mil; cement (portland), stone (crushed), sand and gravel (construction), gypsum (crude), lime. **Gross state product** (2005): $114.3 bil. **Sales tax** (2006): 5.0%. **Employment distrib.** (May 2006): 16.8% govt; 20.4% trade/trans./util.; 15.4% mfg; 13.2% ed./health; 7.6% prof./bus. serv.; 8.9% leisure/hosp.; 6.6% finance; 5.1% constr.; 3.7% other serv.; 2.1% info. **Unemployment** (2005): 4.6%. **Per cap. pers. income** (2005): $32,315. **New private housing** (2005): 16,766 units/$2.4 bil. **Commercial banks** (2005): 408; **deposits:** $45.8 bil. **Savings institutions** (2005): 2; **deposits:** $5.2 bil. **Lottery** (2005): total sales: $210.7 mil; profit: $51.1 mil.

Federal govt. Fed. civ. employees (Mar. 2005): 7,442; **avg. salary:** $54,339. **Notable fed. facilities:** Ames Lab; Natl. Animal Disease Ctr.

Energy. Electricity production (est. 2005, kWh by source): Coal: 32.9 bil; Gas: 2.5 bil; Hydroelectric: 946 mil; Nuclear: 4.5 bil; Petroleum: 114 mil; Other: 536 mil.

State data. Motto: Our liberties we prize, and our rights we will maintain. **Flower:** Wild rose. **Bird:** Eastern goldfinch. **Tree:** Oak. **Rock:** Geode. **Entered union** Dec. 28, 1846; rank, 29th. **State fair** at Des Moines; mid-Aug.

History. Early inhabitants were Mound Builders who dwelt on Iowa's fertile plains. Later, Iowa and Yankton Sioux lived in the area. The first Europeans, Marquette and Jolliet, gave France its claim to the area, 1673. In 1762, France ceded the region to Spain, but Napoleon took it back, 1800. It became part of the U.S. through the Louisiana Purchase, 1803. Native American Sauk and Fox tribes moved into the area but relinquished their land in defeat, after the 1832 uprising led by the Sauk chieftain Black Hawk. Iowa became a territory in 1838, and entered as a free state, 1846, strongly supporting the Union. Fertile land lured farmers from eastern states, 1850-1900 and the population rose rapidly. Growth slowed in the 20th cent., as farming became mechanized. Surging demand for ethanol fuel from Iowa corn contributed more than $2.6 bil to the state economy in 2005. Every 4 years, the Iowa caucuses pose an early test for politicians hoping to win their party's presidential nomination.

Tourist attractions. Herbert Hoover birthplace and library, West Branch; Effigy Mounds Natl. Monument, prehistoric Indian burial site, Marquette; Amana Colonies; Grant Wood's paintings and memorabilia, Davenport Municipal Art Gallery; Living History Farms, Des Moines; Adventureland, Altoona; Boone & Scenic Valley Railroad, Boone; Greyhound Parks, in Dubuque and Council Bluffs; Prairie Meadows horse racing, Altoona; riverboat cruises and casino gambling, Mississippi and Missouri Rivers; Iowa Great Lakes, Okoboji.

Famous Iowans. Tom Arnold, Johnny Carson, Marquis Childs, Buffalo Bill Cody, Mamie Dowd Eisenhower, Bob Feller, George Gallup, Susan Glaspell, James Norman Hall, Harry Hansen, Herbert Hoover, Ann Landers, Glenn Miller, Lillian Russell, Billy Sunday, James A. Van Allen, Abigail Van Buren, Carl Van Vechten, Henry Wallace, John Wayne, Meredith Willson, Grant Wood.

Tourist information. Iowa Tourism Office, Iowa Dept. of Economic Development, 200 E. Grand Ave., Des Moines, IA 50309; (515) 242-4700. **Website:** www.traveliowa.com **Website.** www.iowa.gov

Kansas (KS)
Sunflower State

People. Population (2005 est.): 2,744,687; rank: 33; **net change** (2004-2005): 0.4%. **Pop. density:** 33.5 per sq mi. Racial distribution (2004): 89.4% white; 5.9% black; 2.1% Asian; 1.0% Native/Nat.AK; 0.07% Hawaiian/Pacific Islander; 2 or more races, 1.6%. **Hispanic pop.** (any race): 8.1%.

Geography. Total area: 82,277 sq mi; rank: 15. **Land area:** 81,815 sq mi; rank: 13. **Acres forested:** 1.5 mil. **Location:** West North Central state, with Missouri R. on E. **Climate:** temperate but continental, with great extremes between summer and winter. **Topography:** hilly Osage Plains in the E; central region level prairie and hills; high plains in the W. **Capital:** Topeka. **Principal internat. airport at:** Kansas City.

Economy. Chief industries: manufacturing, finance, insurance, real estate, services. **Chief manuf. goods:** transportation equipment, machinery & computer equipment, food and kindred products, printing & publishing. **Chief crops:** wheat, sorghum, corn, hay, soybeans, sunflowers. **Livestock:** (Jan. 2006): 6.7 mil cattle/calves, 95,000 sheep/lambs; (Dec. 2005): 1.8 mil hogs/pigs. **Timber/lumber:** figs. undisclosed; oak, walnut. **Nonfuel minerals** (est. 2005): $822 mil; cement (portland), helium (Grade-A), salt, stone (crushed), helium (crude). **Chief ports:** Kansas City. **Gross state product** (2005): $105.4 bil. **Sales tax** (2006): 5.3%. **Employment distrib.** (May 2006): 19.4% govt; 19.2% trade/trans./util.; 13.3% mfg; 12.3% ed./health; 9.8% prof./bus. serv.; 8.4% leisure/hosp.; 5.2% finance; 5.0% constr.; 4.0% other serv.; 2.8% info. **Unemployment** (2005): 5.1%. **Per cap. pers. income** (2005): $32,836. **New private housing** (2005): 14,048 units/$2.0 bil. **Commercial banks** (2005): 367; **deposits:** $39.8 bil. **Savings institutions** (2005): 21; **deposits:** $8.5 bil. **Lottery** (2005): total sales: $206.7 mil; profit: $62.3 mil.

Federal govt. Fed. civ. employees (Mar. 2005): 15,499; **avg. salary:** $55,968. **Notable fed. facilities:** Fts. Riley, Leavenworth; Leavenworth Fed. Pen.; McConnell AFB; Colmery-O'Neal Veterans Hospital.

Energy. Electricity production (est. 2005, kWh by source): Coal: 34.5 bil; Gas: 1.1 bil; Nuclear: 8.8 bil; Petroleum: 977 mil; Other: 1 mil.

State data. Motto: Ad Astra per Aspera (To the stars through difficulties). **Flower:** Native sunflower. **Bird:** Western meadowlark. **Tree:** Cottonwood. **Song:** Home on the Range. **Entered union** Jan. 29, 1861; rank, 34th. **State fair** at Hutchinson; begins Friday after Labor Day.

History. Wichita, Pawnee, Kansa, and Osage peoples lived in the area when Coronado explored it in 1541. These Native Americans—hunters who also farmed—were joined on the Plains by the nomadic Cheyenne, Arapaho, Comanche, and Kiowa about 1800. France claimed the region, 1682, ceded its claim to Spain, 1762, then regained control, 1800, before selling it to the U.S. in the Louisiana Purchase, 1803. After 1830, thousands of Native Americans were removed from more eastern states to Kansas. Organized as a territory, 1854, the area witnessed violent clashes between pro- and antislavery settlers and became known as "Bleeding Kansas." It entered the Union as a free state, 1861. After the Civil War, rail construction and huge cattle drives from Texas turned Abilene and Dodge City into cowboy capitals. Russian Mennonite immigrants brought a new strain of winter wheat, 1874, transforming Kansas agriculture. Carry Nation launched her antisaloon crusade in the 1890s. Part of the "Dust Bowl," the state experienced drought and depression in the 1930s. Topeka was the focus of the famous *Brown v. Board of Education* decision, 1954, that led to desegregation of U.S. public schools. Bob Dole represented Kansas in the U.S. Senate (1969-96) but failed in several efforts to win higher office.

Tourist attractions. Eisenhower Center, Abilene; Agricultural Hall of Fame and Natl. Center, Bonner Springs; Dodge City-Boot Hill & Frontier Town; Old Cowtown Museum, Wichita; Ft. Scott and Ft. Larned, restored 1800s cavalry forts; Kansas Cosmosphere and Space Center, Hutchinson; Woodlands Racetrack, Kansas City; U.S. Cavalry Museum, Ft. Riley; NCAA Visitors Center, Shawnee; Heartland Park Raceway, Topeka.

Famous Kansans. Kirstie Alley, Roscoe "Fatty" Arbuckle, Ed Asner, Gwendolyn Brooks, John Brown, George Washington Carver, Wilt Chamberlain, Walter P. Chrysler, Glenn Cunningham, John Stuart Curry, Robert Dole, Amelia Earhart, Wyatt Earp, Dwight D. Eisenhower, Ron Evans, Maurice Greene, Wild Bill Hickok, Cyrus Holliday, Dennis Hopper, William Inge, Don Johnson, Walter Johnson, Nancy Landon Kassebaum, Buster Keaton, Emmett Kelly, Alf Landon, Edgar Lee Masters, Hattie McDaniel, Oscar Micheaux, Carry Nation, Georgia Neese-Gray, Charlie Parker, Gordon Parks, Jim Ryun, Barry Sanders, Vivian Vance, William Allen White, Jess Willard.

Tourist information. Kansas Dept. of Commerce, Travel and Tourism Div., 1000 SW Jackson St., Ste. 100, Topeka, KS 66612; (785) 296-2009. **Website:** www.travelks.com

Website. www.accesskansas.org

Kentucky (KY)
Bluegrass State

People. Population (2005 est.): 4,173,405; rank: 26; **net change** (2004-2005): 0.8%. **Pop. density:** 105.0 per sq mi. Racial distribution (2004): 90.4% white; 7.5% black; 0.9% Asian; 0.2% Native/Nat.AK; 0.05% Hawaiian/Pacific Islander; 2 or more races, 1.0%. **Hispanic pop.** (any race): 1.9%.

Geography. Total area: 40,409 sq mi; rank: 37. **Land area:** 39,728 sq mi; rank: 36. **Acres forested:** 12.7 mil. **Location:** East South Central state, bordered on N by Illinois, Indiana, Ohio; on E by West Virginia and Virginia; on S by Tennessee; on W by Missouri. **Climate:** moderate, with plentiful rainfall. **Topography:** mountainous in E; rounded hills of the Knobs in the N; Bluegrass, heart of state; wooded rocky hillsides of the Pennyroyal; Western Coal Field; the fertile Purchase in the SW. **Capital:** Frankfort. **Principal internat. airports at:** Covington/Cincinnati, Louisville.

Economy. Chief industries: manufacturing, services, finance, insurance and real estate, retail trade, public utilities. **Chief manuf. goods:** transportation & industrial machinery, apparel, printing & publishing, food products, electric & electronic equipment. **Chief crops:** tobacco, corn, soybeans. **Livestock:** (Jan. 2006): 2.4 mil cattle/calves, 35,000 sheep/lambs; (Dec. 2005): 370,000 hogs/pigs, 6.6 mil chickens (excl. broilers), 297.8 mil broilers. **Timber/lumber** (est. 2004): 662 mil bd. ft.; hardwoods, pines. **Nonfuel minerals** (est. 2005): $645 mil; stone (crushed), lime, cement (portland), sand and gravel (construction), clays (ball). **Chief ports:** Paducah, Louisville, Covington, Owensboro, Ashland, Henderson County, Lyon County, Hickman-Fulton County. **Gross state product** (2005): $140.4 bil. **Sales tax** (2006): 6.0%. **Employment distrib.** (May 2006): 17.3% govt; 20.7% trade/trans./util.; 14.0% mfg; 12.9% ed./health; 9.3% prof./bus. serv.; 9.4% leisure/hosp.; 4.8% finance; 4.7% constr.; 4.1% other serv.; 1.6% info. **Unemployment** (2005): 6.1%. **Per cap. pers. income** (2005): $28,513. **New private housing** (2005): 21,159 units/$2.6 bil. **Commercial banks** (2005): 230; **deposits:** $55.1 bil. **Savings institutions** (2005): 27; **deposits:** $2.1 bil. **Lottery** (2004): total sales: $707.3 mil; profit: $158.2 mil.

Federal govt. Fed. civ. employees (Mar. 2005): 21,412; **avg. salary:** $51,287. **Notable fed. facilities:** U.S. Gold Bullion Depository, Ft. Knox; Ft. Campbell; Fed. Correctional Institution, Lexington.

Energy. Electricity production (est. 2005, kWh by source): Coal: 81.0 bil; Gas: 1.3 bil; Hydroelectric: 3.0 bil; Petroleum: 97 mil.

State data. Motto: United we stand, divided we fall. **Flower:** Goldenrod. **Bird:** Cardinal. **Tree:** Tulip Poplar. **Song:** My Old Kentucky Home. **Entered union** June 1, 1792; rank, 15th. **State fair** at Louisville, late Aug.

History. Paleoindians first arrived about 14,000 years ago. Much later, Shawnee, Wyandot, Delaware, and Cherokee peoples also used the area mostly for hunting. Explored by Thomas Walker and Christopher Gist, 1750-51, Kentucky was the first area W of the Alleghenies settled by American pioneers. The first permanent settlement was Harrodsburg, 1774. Daniel Boone blazed the Wilderness Trail through the Cumberland Gap and founded Ft. Boonesborough, 1775. Clashes with Native Americans were frequent, 1774-94. Virginia dropped its claims to the region, and Kentucky became a state, 1792. Tobacco growing, horse breeding, coal mining, and bourbon whiskey making were major industries in the 19th cent. A slave state, Kentucky tried to stay neutral in the

Civil War, but then opted for the Union; many Kentuckians sided with the Confederacy. The U.S. gold depository at Fort Knox opened, 1937. Led by Toyota, Ford, and GM, auto manufacturing has grown in recent decades; about 10% of cars and trucks built in the U.S. each year are made in Kentucky.

Tourist attractions. Kentucky Derby; Louisville; Land Between the Lakes Natl. Recreation Area, Kentucky Lake and Lake Barkley; Mammoth Cave Natl. Park; Echo River, 360 ft below ground; Lake Cumberland; Lincoln's birthplace, Hodgenville; My Old Kentucky Home State Park, Bardstown; Cumberland Gap Natl. Historical Park, Middlesboro; Kentucky Horse Park, Lexington; Shaker Village, Pleasant Hill.

Famous Kentuckians. Muhammad Ali, John James Audubon, Alben W. Barkley, Daniel Boone, Louis D. Brandeis, John C. Breckinridge, Kit Carson, Albert B. "Happy" Chandler, Henry Clay, Jefferson Davis, D. W. Griffith, "Casey" Jones, Abraham Lincoln, Mary Todd Lincoln, Thomas Hunt Morgan, Carry Nation, Col. Harland Sanders, Diane Sawyer, Adlai Stevenson, Jesse Stuart, Zachary Taylor, Hunter S. Thompson, Robert Penn Warren, Whitney Young Jr.

Tourist Information. Kentucky Dept. of Tourism, Capital Plaza Tower, 22nd fl., 500 Mero St., Frankfort, KY 40601; 1-800-225-8747. **Website:** www.kentuckytourism.com

Website. www.kentucky.gov

Louisiana (LA)
Pelican State

People. Population (2005 est.): 4,523,628; rank: 24; **net change** (2004-2005): 0.4%. **Pop. density:** 103.8 per sq mi. Racial distribution (2004): 64.1% white; 33.0% black; 1.4% Asian; 0.6% Native/Nat.AK; 0.03% Hawaiian/Pacific Islander; 2 or more races, 0.8%. **Hispanic pop.** (any race): 2.8%.

Geography. Total area: 51,840 sq mi; rank: 31. **Land area:** 43,562 sq mi; rank: 33. **Acres forested:** 13.8 mil. **Location:** West South Central state on the Gulf Coast. **Climate:** subtropical, affected by continental weather patterns. **Topography:** lowlands of marshes and Mississippi R. flood plain; Red R. Valley lowlands; upland hills in the Florida Parishes; average elevation, 100 ft. **Capital:** Baton Rouge. **Principal internat. airport at:** New Orleans.

Economy. Chief industries: wholesale and retail trade, tourism, manufacturing, construction, transportation, communication, public utilities, finance, insurance, real estate, mining. **Chief manuf. goods:** chemical products, foods, transportation equipment, electronic equipment, petroleum products, lumber, wood, and paper. **Chief crops:** soybeans, sugarcane, rice, corn, cotton, sweet potatoes, pecans, sorghum, aquaculture. **Livestock:** (Jan. 2006): 820,000 cattle/calves; (Dec. 2005): 14,000 hogs/pigs, 2.5 mil chickens (excl. broilers). **Timber/lumber** (est. 2004): 1.5 bil bd. ft.; pines, hardwoods, oak. **Nonfuel minerals** (est. 2005): $356 mil; salt, sand and gravel (construction), stone (crushed), sand and gravel (industrial), lime. **Commercial fishing** (2004): $274.4 mil. **Chief ports:** New Orleans, Baton Rouge, Lake Charles, Port of S. Louisiana (La Place), Shreveport, Plaquemine, St. Bernard, Alexandria. **Gross state product** (2005): $166.3 bil. **Sales tax** (2006): 4.0%. **Employment distrib.** (May 2006): 21.0% govt; 20.5% trade/trans./util.; 8.1% mfg; 12.0% ed./health; 9.6% prof./bus. serv.; 9.9% leisure/hosp.; 5.3% finance; 6.1% constr.; 3.3% other serv.; 1.6% info. **Unemployment** (2005): 7.1%. **Per cap. pers. income** (2005): $24,820. **New private housing** (2005): 22,811 units/$2.7 bil. **Commercial banks** (2005): 144; **deposits:** $53.5 bil. **Savings institutions** (2005): 28; **deposits:** $3.6 bil. **Lottery** (2005): total sales: $307.0 mil; profit: $108.9 mil.

Federal govt. Fed. civ. employees (Mar. 2005): 20,122; **avg. salary:** $55,286. **Notable federal facilities:** Strategic Petroleum Reserve, Michoud Assembly Plant, Southern Regional Research Ctr., U.S. Army Corps of Engineers, all New Orleans; Ft. Polk (Joint Readiness Training Ctr.); Barksdale AFB; New Orleans NAS.

Energy. Electricity production (est. 2005, kWh by source): Coal: 11.4 bil; Gas: 14.0 bil; Nuclear: 15.7 bil; Petroleum: 1.8 bil.

State data. Motto: Union, justice, and confidence. **Flower:** Magnolia. **Bird:** Eastern brown pelican. **Tree:** Cypress. **Song:** Give Me Louisiana. **Entered union** Apr. 30, 1812; rank, 18th. **State fair** at Shreveport; Oct.

History. Caddo, Tunica, Choctaw, Chitimacha, and Chawash peoples lived in the region at the time of European contact. Spanish explorers in the early 16th cent. reached the mouth of the Mississippi. La Salle, 1682, claimed the region for France. Early French and Spanish settlers were the ancestors of Louisiana Creoles. Cajuns descended from the Acadians, French settlers expelled by the British from Nova Scotia, Canada, in 1755. France ceded the Louisiana region to Spain, 1762, took it back, 1800, and sold it to the U.S., 1803, in the Louisiana Purchase. Admitted as a state in 1812, Louisiana witnessed the Battle of New Orleans, 1815. Cotton and sugar plantations relied on black slaves, who made up 47% of the population in 1860, on the eve of the Civil War. Louisiana seceded, 1861, and was readmitted, 1868. Jazz was born in New Orleans in the early 20th cent. As governor (1928-32), Huey Long pushed populist programs. The offshore oil and gas industry developed after World War II. Many tropical storms and floods have battered Louisiana, including Hurricane Katrina, 2005, which devastated New Orleans.

Tourist attractions. French Quarter and other New Orleans attractions. Battle of New Orleans site; Longfellow-Evangeline Memorial Park, St. Martinville; Kent House Museum, Alexandria; Hodges Gardens, Natchitoches; USS *Kidd* Memorial, Baton Rouge.

Famous Louisianans. Louis Armstrong, Pierre Beauregard, Judah P. Benjamin, Braxton Bragg, Kate Chopin, Johnnie Cochraw, Harry Connick Jr., Ellen DeGeneres, Fats Domino, Lillian Hellman, Grace King, Elmore Leonard, Bob Livingston, Huey Long, Eli & Peyton Manning, Wynton Marsalis, Leonidas K. Polk, Anne Rice, Henry Miller Shreve, Britney Spears, Edward D. White Jr.

Tourist information. Louisiana Office of Tourism, 1051 N. 3rd St., Baton Rouge, LA 70804-9291; (225) 342-8100. **Website:** www.louisianatravel.com
Website. www.louisiana.gov

Maine (ME)
Pine Tree State

People. Population (2005 est.): 1,321,505; rank: 40; **net change** (2004-2005): 0.5%. **Pop. density:** 42.8 per sq mi. Racial distribution (2004): 96.9% white; 0.7% black; 0.8% Asian; 0.6% Native/Nat.AK; 0.03% Hawaiian/Pacific Islander; 2 or more races, 0.9%. **Hispanic pop.** (any race): 1%.

Geography. Total area: 35,385 sq mi; rank: 39. **Land area:** 30,862 sq mi; rank: 39. **Acres forested:** 17.7 mil. **Location:** New England state at northeastern tip of U.S. **Climate:** Southern interior and coastal, influenced by air masses from the S and W; northern clime harsher, avg. over 100 in. snow in winter. **Topography:** Appalachian Mts. extend through state; western borders have rugged terrain; long sand beaches on southern coast; northern coast mainly rocky promontories, peninsulas, fjords. **Capital:** Augusta. **Principal internat. airports at:** Bangor, Portland.

Economy. Chief industries: manufacturing, agriculture, fishing, services, trade, government, finance, insurance, real estate, construction. **Chief manuf. goods:** paper & wood products, transportation equipment. **Chief crops:** potatoes, aquaculture products. **Livestock:** (Jan. 2006): 92,000 cattle/calves; (Dec. 2005): 5,000 hogs/pigs, 5.6 mil chickens (excl. broilers). **Timber/lumber** (est. 2004): 964 mil bd. ft.; pine, spruce, fir. **Nonfuel minerals** (est. 2005): $124 mil; sand and gravel (construction), cement (portland), stone (crushed), stone (dimension), peat. **Commercial fishing** (2004): $315.8 mil. **Chief ports:** Searsport, Portland, Eastport. **Gross state product** (2005): $45.1 bil. **Sales tax** (2005): 5.0%. **Employment distrib.** (May 2006): 17.7% govt; 20.0% trade/trans./util.; 9.6% mfg; 18.5% ed./health; 8.5% prof./bus. serv.; 9.7% leisure/hosp.; 5.5% finance; 5.2% constr.; 3.3% other serv.; 1.8% info. **Unemployment** (2005): 4.8%. **Per cap. pers. income** (2005): $31,252. **New private housing** (2005): 8,969 units/$1.4 bil. **Commercial banks** (2005): 18; **deposits:** $11.3 bil. **Savings institutions** (2005): 22; **deposits:** $6.8 bil. **Lottery** (2005): total sales: $209.3 mil; profit: $50.3 mil.

Federal govt. Fed. civ. employees (Mar. 2005): 9,198; **avg. salary:** $55,534. **Notable fed. facilities:** Kittery Naval Shipyard; *Brunswick NAS.

Energy. Electricity production (est. 2002, kWh, by source): Hydroelectric: 6 mil.

State data. Motto: Dirigo (I direct). **Flower:** White pine cone and tassel. **Bird:** Chickadee. **Tree:** Eastern white pine. **Song:** State of Maine Song. **Entered union** Mar. 15, 1820; rank, 23rd. **State fair:** at Bangor, late July; at Skowhegan, mid-Aug.

History. Paleoindians arrived about 11,500 years ago. Maine was inhabited by Algonquian peoples including the Abnaki, Penobscot, and Passamaquoddy at the time of European

contact. French settled, 1604, at the St. Croix River, English, c. 1607, on the Kennebec; both settlements failed. A royal charter, 1691, made Maine part of Massachusetts. Maine broke off, 1819, and became a separate state, 1820. Drawing on vast forest resources, the pulp and paper industry developed after the Civil War. Bath Iron Works began building U.S. Navy vessels and other ships in the 1890s. Mail-order and retail giant L.L. Bean was founded, 1912. Women have fared well in state politics: Margaret Chase Smith became the first woman to serve in both houses of Congress (House, 1940-49; Senate, 1949-73), and Olympia Snowe and Susan Collins have represented Maine in the Senate since the mid-1990s.

Tourist attractions. Acadia Natl. Park, Bar Harbor, on Mt. Desert Island; Old Orchard Beach; Portland's Old Port; Kennebunkport; Common Ground Country Fair; Portland Headlight; Baxter State Pk.; Freeport/L. L. Bean.

Famous "Down Easters." Leon Leonwood (L.L.) Bean, James G. Blaine, Cyrus H. K. Curtis, Hannibal Hamlin, Sarah Jewett, Stephen King, Henry Wadsworth Longfellow, Sir Hiram and Hudson Maxim, Edna St. Vincent Millay, George Mitchell, Edmund Muskie, Judd Nelson, Edwin Arlington Robinson, Joan Benoit Samuelson, Liv Tyler, Kate Douglas Wiggin, Ben Ames Williams.

Tourist Information. Maine Office of Tourism, 59 State House Station, Augusta, ME 04333; 1-888-624-6354 (from within the United States and Canada). **Website:** www.visitmaine.com

Website. www.state.me.us

Maryland (MD)
Old Line State, Free State

People. Population (2005 est.): 5,600,388; rank: 19; **net change** (2004-2005): 0.7%. **Pop. density:** 573.0 per sq mi. Racial distribution (2004): 64.5% white; 29.1% black; 4.6% Asian; 0.3% Native/Nat.AK; 0.06% Hawaiian/Pacific Islander; 2 or more races, 1.5%. **Hispanic pop.** (any race): 5.4%.

Geography. Total area: 12,407 sq mi; rank: 42. **Land area:** 9,774 sq mi; rank: 42. **Acres forested:** 2.6 mil. **Location:** South Atlantic state stretching from the Ocean to the Allegheny Mts. **Climate:** continental in the west; humid subtropical in the east. **Topography:** Eastern Shore of coastal plain and Maryland Main of coastal plain, piedmont plateau, and the Blue Ridge, separated by the Chesapeake Bay. **Capital:** Annapolis. **Principal internat. airport at:** Baltimore.

Economy. Chief industries: manufacturing, biotechnology and information technology, services, tourism. **Chief manuf. goods:** electric and electronic equipment; food and kindred products, chemicals and allied products, printed materials. **Chief crops:** greenhouse and nursery products, soybeans, corn. **Livestock:** (Jan. 2006): 230,000 cattle/calves, 22,000 sheep/lambs; (Dec. 2005): 35,000 hogs/pigs, 4.2 mil chickens (excl. broilers), 256.0 mil broilers. **Timber/lumber** (est. 2004): 272 mil bd. ft.; hardwoods. **Nonfuel minerals** (est. 2005): $507 mil; cement (portland), stone (crushed), sand and gravel (construction), cement (masonry), stone (dimension). **Commercial fishing** (2004): $49.2 mil. **Chief port:** Baltimore. **Gross state product** (2005): $244.9 bil. **Sales tax** (2006): 5.0%. **Employment distrib.** (May 2006): 18.3% govt; 18.2% trade/trans./util.; 5.3% mfg; 14.0% ed./health; 15.1% prof./bus. serv.; 9.2% leisure/hosp.; 6.2% finance; 7.2% constr.; 4.6% other serv.; 1.9% info. **Unemployment** (2005): 4.1%. **Per cap. pers. income** (2004): $41,760. **New private housing** (2005): 30,180 units/$4.7 bil. **Commercial banks** (2005): 90; **deposits:** $72.4 bil. **Savings institutions** (2005): 54; **deposits:** $16.5 bil. **Lottery** (2005): total sales: $1.5 bil; profit: $477.1 mil.

Federal govt. Fed. civ. employees (Mar. 2005): 103,799; **avg. salary:** $76,106. **Notable fed. facilities:** U.S. Naval Academy; Natl. Agriculture Res. Ctr.; Ft. Meade, Aberdeen Proving Ground; Goddard Space Flight Ctr.; Natl. Institutes of Health; Natl. Inst. of Standards & Technology; Food & Drug Administration; Bureau of the Census; Natl. Naval Med. Ctr., Bethesda; Natl. Marine Fisheries Serv.; Natl. Oceanic and Atmospheric Admin.

Energy. Electricity production (est. 2005, kWh, by source): Petroleum: 30 mil.

State data. Motto: Fatti Maschii, Parole Femine (Manly deeds, womanly words). **Flower:** Black-eyed Susan. **Bird:** Baltimore oriole. **Tree:** White oak. **Song:** Maryland, My Maryland. **Seventh** of the original 13 states to ratify the U.S. Constitution, Apr. 28, 1788. **State fair** held at Timonium; late Aug.-early Sept.

History. Europeans encountered Algonquian-speaking Nanticoke and Piscataway and Iroquois-speaking Susquehannock when they first visited the area. Italian navigator Verrazano reached the Chesapeake region in the early 16th cent. English Capt. John Smith explored and mapped the area, 1608. William Claiborne set up a trading post on Kent Island in Chesapeake Bay, 1631. King Charles I granted land to Cecilius Calvert, Lord Baltimore, 1632; Calvert's brother Leonard, with about 200 settlers, founded St. Marys, 1634. During the Revolutionary War, Baltimore (1776-77) and Annapolis (1783-84) served as temporary capitals of the U.S. In the War of 1812, when a British fleet tried to take Ft. McHenry, Marylander Francis Scott Key wrote "The Star-Spangled Banner," 1814. Born into slavery at Tuckahoe in 1818, Frederick Douglass became a leading abolitionist. Although a slaveholding state, Maryland stayed in the Union during the Civil War and was the site of the battle of Antietam, 1862. In 1973, U.S. Vice Pres. Spiro T. Agnew, a former Maryland governor, was charged with bribery and forced to resign. Israeli and Egyptian leaders reached a historic peace accord at the Camp David presidential retreat, 1978. A major effort is under way to clean up pollution in the Chesapeake Bay watershed.

Tourist attractions. The Preakness at Pimlico track, Baltimore; The Maryland Million at Laurel Race Course; Ocean City; restored Ft. McHenry, near which Francis Scott Key wrote "The Star-Spangled Banner"; Edgar Allan Poe house, Ravens Football at Memorial Stadium, Camden Yards, Natl. Aquarium, Harborplace, all Baltimore; Antietam Battlefield, near Hagerstown; South Mountain Battlefield; U.S. Naval Academy, Annapolis; Maryland State House, Annapolis, 1772, the oldest still in legislative use in the U.S.

Famous Marylanders. John Astin, Benjamin Banneker, Tom Clancy, Jonathan Demme, Francis Scott Key, H. L. Mencken, Kweisi Mfume, Ogden Nash, Charles Willson Peale, William Pinkney, Edgar Allan Poe, Cal Ripken Jr., Babe Ruth, Upton Sinclair, Roger B. Taney, John Waters, Montel Williams.

Tourist Information. Maryland Office of Tourism Development, 217 E. Redwood St., Baltimore, MD 21202; 1-866-MD-WELCOME. **Website:** www.mdwelcome.org

Website. www.maryland.gov

Massachusetts (MA)
Bay State, Old Colony

People. Population (2005 est.): 6,398,743; rank: 13; **net change** (2004-2005): -0.1%. **Pop. density:** 816.2 per sq mi. Racial distribution (2004): 87.0% white; 6.8% black; 4.6% Asian; 0.3% Native/Nat.AK; 0.08% Hawaiian/Pacific Islander; 2 or more races, 1.3%. **Hispanic pop.** (any race): 7.7%.

Geography. Total area: 10,555 sq mi; rank: 44. **Land area:** 7,840 sq mi; rank: 45. **Acres forested:** 3.1 mil. **Location:** New England state along Atlantic seaboard. **Climate:** temperate, with colder and drier clime in western region. **Topography:** jagged indented coast from Rhode Island around Cape Cod; flat land yields to stony upland pastures near central region and gentle hilly country in west; except in west, land is rocky, sandy, and not fertile. **Capital:** Boston. **Principal internat. airport at:** Boston.

Economy. Chief industries: services, trade, manufacturing. **Chief manuf. goods:** electric and electronic equipment, instruments, industrial machinery and equipment, printing and publishing, fabricated metal products. **Chief crops:** cranberries, greenhouse, nursery, vegetables. **Livestock:** (Jan. 2006): 47,000 cattle/calves; (Dec. 2005): 13,000 hogs/pigs, 296,000 chickens (excl.broilers). **Timber/lumber:** (2004 est.): 60 mil bd. ft.; white pine, oak, other hard woods. **Nonfuel minerals** (est. 2005): $208 mil; stone (crushed), sand and gravel (construction), lime, stone (dimension), clays (common). **Commercial fishing** (2004): $326.1 mil. **Chief ports:** Boston, Fall River, New Bedford, Salem, Gloucester, Plymouth. **Gross state product** (2005): $328.5 bil. **Sales tax** (2006): 5.0%. **Employment distrib.** (May 2006): 13.0% govt; 17.5% trade/trans./util.; 9.4% mfg; 18.4% ed./health; 14.5% prof./bus. serv.; 9.2% leisure/hosp.; 6.9% finance; 4.5% constr.; 3.7% other serv.; 2.7% info. **Unemployment** (2005): 4.8%. **Per cap. pers. income** (2005): $44,289. **New private housing** (2005): 24,549 units/$4.1 bil. **Commercial banks** (2005): 47; **deposits:** $107.9 bil. **Savings institutions** (2005): 161; **deposits:** $64.3 bil. **Lottery** (2005): total sales: $4.5 bil; profit: $936.1 mil.

Federal govt. Fed. civ. employees (Mar. 2005): 25,024; **avg. salary:** $64,499. **Notable fed. facilities:** Thomas P. O'Neill Jr. Fed. Bldg., J.W. McCormack Bldg., JFK Fed. Bldg., *Natick Army Soldier Systems Ctr.

Energy. Electricity production (est. 2005, kWh by source): Coal: 975 mil; Gas: 108 mil; Hydroelectric: 225 mil; Petroleum: 219 mil.

State data. Motto: Ense Petit Placidam Sub Libertate Quietem (By the sword we seek peace, but peace only under liberty). **Flower:** Mayflower. **Bird:** Chickadee. **Tree:** American elm. **Song:** All Hail to Massachusetts. **Sixth** of the original 13 states to ratify Constitution, Feb. 6, 1788. **State Fair** at Springfield, mid-Sept.–early Oct.

History. Early inhabitants were Algonquian peoples: Nauset, Wampanoag, Massachuset, Pennacook, Nipmuc, and Pocumtuc. Pilgrims settled in Plymouth, 1620, giving thanks for their survival with the first Thanksgiving Day, 1621. About 20,000 new settlers arrived, 1630-40. Colonist-Native American relations deteriorated, leading to King Philip's War, 1675-76, which the colonists won. Witch trials at Salem, 1692, led to the execution of about 20 people. Demonstrations against British restrictions set off the Boston Massacre, 1770, and the Boston Tea Party, 1773. The first bloodshed of American Revolution was at Lexington, 1775. After statehood, Massachusetts prospered from shipbuilding, seafaring, and the making of textiles, shoes, and metal goods, while artists, writers, and social reformers flourished. The controversial Sacco-Vanzetti case, 1920-27, ended with the execution of 2 Italian immigrants on murder and robbery charges. After World War II, old industries declined, knowledge-intensive enterprises thrived, and the Kennedys became a dominant political family. The state's highest court ruled, 2003, that same-sex couples could legally marry.

Famous "Bay Staters." John Adams, John Quincy Adams, Samuel Adams, Louisa May Alcott, Horatio Alger, Susan B. Anthony, Crispus Attucks, Clara Barton, Alexander Graham Bell, Stephen Breyer, George H. W. Bush, John Cheever, E. E. Cummings, Emily Dickinson, Charles Eliot, Ralph Waldo Emerson, William Lloyd Garrison, Edward Everett Hale, John Hancock, Nathaniel Hawthorne, Oliver Wendell Holmes, Winslow Homer, Elias Howe, John F. Kennedy, John Kerry, Jack Kerouac, Jack Lemmon, James Russell Lowell, Cotton Mather, Samuel F. B. Morse, Edgar Allan Poe, Paul Revere, Norman Rockwell, Dr. Seuss (Theodor Seuss Geisel), Henry David Thoreau, Barbara Walters, James McNeil Whistler, John Greenleaf Whittier.

Tourist information. Massachusetts Office of Travel & Tourism, 10 Park Plaza, Ste. 4510, Boston, MA 02116; 1-800-227-MASS. **Website:** www.massvacation.com

Website. www.mass.gov

Michigan (MI)
Great Lakes State, Wolverine State

People. Population (2005 est.): 10,120,860; rank: 8; **net change** (2004-2005): 0.2%. **Pop. density:** 178.2 per sq mi. Racial distribution (2004): 81.4% white; 14.3% black; 2.2% Asian; 0.6% Native/Nat.AK; 0.04% Hawaiian/Pacific Islander; 2 or more races, 1.4%. **Hispanic pop.** (any race): 3.7%.

Geography. Total area: 96,716 sq mi; rank: 11. **Land area:** 56,804 sq mi; rank: 22. **Acres forested:** 19.3 mil. **Location:** East North Central state bordering on 4 of the 5 Great Lakes, divided into an Upper and Lower Peninsula by the Straits of Mackinac, which link lakes Michigan and Huron. **Climate:** well-defined seasons tempered by the Great Lakes. **Topography:** low rolling hills give way to northern tableland of hilly belts in Lower Peninsula; Upper Peninsula is level in the east, with swampy areas; western region is higher and more rugged. **Capital:** Lansing. **Principal internat. airports at:** Detroit, Flint, Grand Rapids, Kalamazoo, Lansing, Saginaw.

Economy. Chief industries: manufacturing, services, tourism, agriculture, forestry/lumber. **Chief manuf. goods:** automobiles, transportation equipment, machinery, fabricated metals, food products, plastics, office furniture. **Chief crops:** corn, wheat, soybeans, dry beans, hay, potatoes, sweet corn, apples, cherries, sugar beets, blueberries, cucumbers, Niagra grapes. **Livestock:** (Jan. 2006): 1.0 mil cattle/calves, 88,000 sheep/lambs; (Dec. 2005): 950,000 hogs/pigs, 10.1 mil chickens (excl. broilers). **Timber/lumber** (est. 2004): 844 mil bd. ft.; maple, oak, aspen. **Nonfuel minerals** (est. 2005): $1.7 bil; cement (portland), sand and gravel (construction), iron ore (usable), stone (crushed), salt. **Commer-**

cial fishing (2004): $6.2 mil. **Chief ports:** Detroit, Saginaw River, Escanaba, Muskegon, Sault Ste. Marie, Port Huron, Marine City. **Gross state product** (2005): $377.9 bil. **Sales tax** (2006): 6.0%. **Employment distrib.** (May 2006): 15.6% govt; 18.0% trade/trans./util.; 15.0% mfg; 13.1% ed./health; 13.6% prof./bus. serv.; 9.5% leisure/hosp.; 5.0% finance; 4.4% constr.; 4.1% other serv.; 1.5% info. **Unemployment** (2005): 6.7%. **Per cap. pers. income** (2005): $33,116. **New private housing** (2005): 45,328 units/$6.6 bil. **Commercial banks** (2005): 173; **deposits:** $127.1 bil. **Savings institutions** (2005): 22; **deposits:** $12.2 bil. **Lottery** (2005): total sales: $2.1 bil; profit: $667.6 mil.

Federal govt. Fed. civ. employees (Mar. 2005): 23,706; **avg. salary:** $63,085. **Notable fed. facilities:** Isle Royal, Sleeping Bear Dunes national parks.

Energy. Electricity production (est. 2005, kWh by source): Coal: 68.8 bil; Gas: 2.1 bil; Hydroelectric: 1.3 bil; Nuclear: 32.9 bil; Petroleum: 791 mil; Other: 45 mil.

State data. Motto: Si Quaeris Peninsulam Amoenam, Circumspice (If you seek a pleasant peninsula, look about you). **Flower:** Apple blossom. **Bird:** Robin. **Tree:** White pine. **Song:** Michigan, My Michigan. **Entered union** Jan. 26, 1837; rank, 26th. **State fair** at Detroit, late Aug.–early Sept.; Upper Peninsula (Escanaba), mid-Aug.

History. Hunting and fishing peoples lived in the region as early as 11,000 years ago. Ojibwa, Ottawa, Miami, Potawatomi, and Huron inhabited the area at the time of European contact. French fur traders and missionaries arrived in the 17th cent. and established a settlement at Sault Ste. Marie, 1668. British took over, 1763, and crushed a Native American uprising led by Ottawa chieftain Pontiac. Treaty of Paris ceded the area to U.S., 1783, but British remained until 1796. Michigan was organized as a territory, 1805. The British seized Ft. Mackinac and Detroit, 1812, but the U.S. regained control, 1814. The opening of the Erie Canal, 1825, and new land laws and Native American cessions led the way for a flood of settlers. Strongly antislavery, Michigan became a state, 1837, and supplied 90,000 soldiers to the Union army in the Civil War. In the 20th cent., automobile manufacturing was the backbone of the economy. Henry Ford launched the Model T car, 1908; the United Auto Workers union was founded, 1935. Motown music flourished in Detroit in the 1960s, but riots in 1967 dealt the city a heavy blow. As the auto industry faltered, Michigan lost some 300,000 jobs in 2000-06.

Tourist attractions. Henry Ford Museum, Greenfield Village, both in Dearborn; Frederick Meijer Gardens and Sculpture Park, Grand Rapids; Michigan Space Center, Jackson; Tahquamenon (Hiawatha) Falls; DeZwaan windmill and Tulip Festival, Holland; "Soo Locks," St. Mary's Falls Ship Canal, Sault Ste. Marie; Kalamazoo Aviation History Museum; Mackinac Island; Kellogg's Cereal City USA, Battle Creek; Museum of African-American History, Motown Historical Museum, both Detroit.

Famous Michiganders. Ralph Bunche, Francis Ford Coppola, Paul de Kruif, Thomas Edison, Edna Ferber, Gerald R. Ford, Henry Ford, Aretha Franklin, Edgar Guest, Lee Iacocca, Robert Ingersoll, Magic Johnson, Casey Kasem, Will Kellogg, Ring Lardner, Elmore Leonard, Charles Lindbergh, Joe Louis, Madonna, Malcolm X, Terry McMillan, Michael Moore, Pontiac, Gilda Radner, Diana Ross, Glenn Seaborg, Tom Selleck, Sinbad (David Adkins), John Smoltz, Lily Tomlin, Stewart Edward White, Serena Williams.

Tourist Information. Michigan Economic Development Corp., 300 N. Washington Square, Lansing, MI 48913. Phone: 1-888-78GREAT. **Website:** travel.michigan.org

Website. www.michigan.gov

Minnesota (MN)

North Star State, Gopher State

People. Population (2005 est.): 5,132,799; rank: 21; **net change** (2004-2005): 0.7%. **Pop. density:** 64.5 per sq mi. Racial distribution (2004): 89.9% white; 4.1% black; 3.4% Asian; 1.2% Native/Nat.AK; 0.05% Hawaiian/Pacific Islander; 2 or more races, 1.4%. **Hispanic pop.** (any race): 3.5%.

Geography. Total area: 86,939 sq mi; rank: 12. **Land area:** 79,610 sq mi; rank: 14. **Acres forested:** 16.7 mil. **Location:** West North Central state bounded on the E by Wisconsin and Lake Superior, on the N by Canada, on the W by the Dakotas, and on the S by Iowa. **Climate:** northern part

of state lies in the moist Great Lakes storm belt; the western border lies at the edge of the semi-arid Great Plains. **Topography:** central hill and lake region covering approx. half the state; to the NE, rocky ridges and deep lakes; to the NW, flat plain; to the S, rolling plains and deep river valleys. **Capital:** St. Paul. **Principal internat. airport at:** Minneapolis-St. Paul.

Economy. Chief industries: agribusiness, forest products, mining, manufacturing, tourism. **Chief manuf. goods:** food, chemical and paper products, industrial machinery, electric and electronic equipment, computers, printing & publishing, scientific and medical instruments, fabricated metal products, forest products. **Chief crops:** corn, soybeans, wheat, sugar beets, hay, barley, potatoes, sunflowers. **Livestock:** (Jan. 2006): 2.4 mil cattle/calves, 155,000 sheep/lambs; (Dec. 2005): 6.6 mil hogs/pigs, 14.6 mil chickens (excl. broilers), 46.9 mil broilers. **Timber/lumber** (est. 2004): 265 mil bd. ft.; needle-leaves and hardwoods. **Nonfuel minerals** (est. 2005): $2.1 bil; iron ore (usable), sand and gravel (construction), stone (crushed), sand and gravel (industrial), stone (dimension). **Commercial fishing** (2004): $187,000. **Chief ports:** Duluth, St. Paul, Minneapolis. **Gross state product** (2005): $233.3 bil. **Sales tax** (2006): 6.5%. **Employment distrib.** (May 2006): 15.5% govt; 19.1% trade/trans./util.; 12.4% mfg; 14.3% ed./health; 11.4% prof./bus. serv.; 9.1% leisure/hosp.; 6.5% finance; 4.8% constr.; 4.3% other serv.; 2.2% info. **Unemployment** (2005): 4.0%. **Per cap. pers. income** (2005): $37,373. **New private housing** (2005): 36,509 units/$6.3 bil. **Commercial banks** (2005): 467; **deposits:** $92.9 bil. **Savings institutions** (2005): 29; **deposits:** $3.2 bil. **Lottery** (2005): total sales: $408.6 mil; profit: $106.2 mil.

Federal govt. Fed. civ. employees (Mar. 2005): 14,341; **avg. salary:** $60,868.

Energy. Electricity production (est. 2005, kWh by source): Coal: 30.6 bil; Gas: 1.6 bil; Hydroelectric: 509 bil; Nuclear: 12.8 bil; Petroleum: 118 mil.

State data. Motto: L'Etoile du Nord (The star of the north). **Flower:** Pink and white lady's-slipper. **Bird:** Common loon. **Tree:** Red pine. **Song:** Hail! Minnesota. **Entered union** May 11, 1858; rank, 32nd. **State fair** at St. Paul/Minneapolis; late Aug.-early Sept.

History. Inhabited for at least 10,000 years, the region was home to Dakota Sioux when Europeans arrived. French fur traders Pierre Esprit Radisson and Médard Chouart, sieur des Groseilliers, explored in the mid-17th cent. In 1679, Daniel Greysolon, sieur Duluth, claimed the entire region for France. Ojibwa arrived in the 18th cent. and warred with the Sioux for over 100 years. Britain took the area east of the Mississippi, 1763. The U.S. took over that portion after the American Revolution and gained the western area, 1803, in the Louisiana Purchase. The U.S. built Ft. St. Anthony (now Ft. Snelling), 1819, and bought Native American lands, 1837, spurring an influx of settlers from the east. Minnesota became a territory, 1849, and a state, 1858. Sioux staged a bloody uprising, the Battle of Wood Lake, 1862, and were driven from the state. Railroad construction after the Civil War spurred the growth of the grain, timber, and iron mining industries. Opening of the St. Lawrence Seaway, 1959, aided the port of Duluth. Elected as a reformer, colorful former wrestler Jesse Ventura served as governor, 1999-2003. Two-term Sen. Paul Wellstone, one of a long line of liberal Minnesota Democrats, died when his campaign plane crashed, 2002.

Tourist attractions. Minneapolis Institute of Arts, Walker Art Center, Minneapolis Sculpture Garden, Minnehaha Falls (inspiration for Longfellow's Hiawatha), Guthrie Theater, Minneapolis; Ordway Theater, St. Paul; Voyageurs Natl. Park; Mayo Clinic, Rochester; St. Paul Winter Carnival; North Shore (of Lake Superior).

Famous Minnesotans. Warren Burger, Ethan and Joel Coen, William O. Douglas, Bob Dylan, F. Scott Fitzgerald, Al Franken, Judy Garland, Cass Gilbert, Hubert Humphrey, Garrison Keillor, Sister Elizabeth Kenny, Jessica Lange, Sinclair Lewis, Paul Manship, Roger Maris, E. G. Marshall, William and Charles Mayo, Eugene McCarthy, Walter F. Mondale, Prince (Rodgers Nelson), Charles Schulz, Harold Stassen, Thorstein Veblen, Jesse Ventura, Paul Wellstone.

Tourist Information. Explore Minnesota Tourism, Metro Square, 121 7th Pl. E., Ste. 100, St. Paul, MN 55101. Phone: 1-888-TOURISM. **Website:** www.exploreminnesota.com

Website. www.state.mn.us

Mississippi (MS)

Magnolia State

People. Population (2005 est.): 2,921,088; rank: 31; **net change** (2004-2005): 0.7%. **Pop. density:** 62.3 per sq mi. Racial distribution (2004): 61.3% white; 36.8% black; 0.7% Asian; 0.5% Native/Nat.AK; 0.03% Hawaiian/Pacific Islander; 2 or more races, 0.6%. **Hispanic pop.** (any race): 1.7%.

Geography. Total area: 48,430 sq mi; rank: 32. **Land area:** 46,907 sq mi; rank: 31. **Acres forested:** 18.6 mil. **Location:** East South Central state bordered on the W by the Mississippi R. and on the S by the Gulf of Mexico. **Climate:** semi-tropical, with abundant rainfall, long growing season, and extreme temperatures unusual. **Topography:** low, fertile delta between the Yazoo and Mississippi rivers; loess bluffs stretching around delta border; sandy gulf coastal terraces followed by piney woods and prairie; rugged, high sandy hills in extreme NE followed by Black Prairie Belt, Pontotoc Ridge, and flatwoods into the north central highlands. **Capital:** Jackson. **Principal internat. airport at:** Jackson.

Economy. Chief industries: warehousing & distribution, services, manufacturing, government, wholesale and retail trade. **Chief manuf. goods:** chemicals & plastics, food & kindred products, furniture, lumber & wood products, electrical machinery, transportation equipment. **Chief crops:** cotton, rice, soybeans. **Livestock:** (Jan. 2006): 1.0 mil cattle/calves; (Dec. 2005): 375,000 hogs/pigs, 10.6 mil chickens (excl. broilers), 853.4 mil broilers. **Timber/lumber** (est. 2004): 2.7 bil bd. ft.; pine, oak, hardwoods. **Nonfuel minerals** (est. 2005): $202 mil; sand and gravel (construction), clays (fuller's earth), stone (crushed), cement (portland), sand and gravel (industrial). **Commercial fishing** (2004): $43.7 mil. **Chief ports:** Pascagoula, Vicksburg, Gulfport, Natchez, Greenville. **Gross state product** (2005): $80.2 bil. **Sales tax** (2006): 7.0%. **Employment distrib.** (May 2006): 21.4% govt; 19.9% trade/trans./util.; 15.5% mfg; 10.8% ed./health; 7.9% prof./bus. serv.; 10.3% leisure/hosp.; 4.0% finance; 4.9% constr.; 3.3% other serv.; 1.2% info. **Unemployment** (2005): 7.9%. **Per cap. pers. income** (2005): $25,318. **New private housing (2005):** 13,396 units/$1.6 bil. **Commercial banks (2005):** 103; **deposits:** $34.6 bil. **Savings institutions** (2005): 7; **deposits:** $483 mil.

Federal govt. Fed. civ. employees (Mar. 2005): 16,780; **avg. salary:** $55,434. **Notable fed. facilities:** Columbus AFB; *Keesler AFB; Meridian NAS; NASA Stennis Space Ctr.; Army Corps of Engineers Waterways Experiment Sta.; Naval Constr. Battalion Ctr., Gulfport.

Energy. Electricity production (est. 2005, kWh by source): Coal: 13.4 bil; Gas: 5.8 bil; Nuclear: 10.1 bil; Petroleum: 1.4 bil.

State data. Motto: Virtute et Armis (By valor and arms). **Flower:** Magnolia. **Bird:** Mockingbird. **Tree:** Magnolia. **Song:** Go, Mississippi! **Entered union** Dec. 10, 1817; rank, 20th. **State fair** at Jackson; early Oct.

History. Choctaw, Chickasaw, and Natchez peoples were living in the region at the time of European contact. The Spaniard Hernando de Soto explored the area, 1540-41. La Salle traced the Mississippi River from Illinois to its mouth and claimed the entire Mississippi Valley for France, 1682. The first settlement, was the French Ft. Maurepas, 1699, on Biloxi Bay. The region was ceded to Britain, 1763, and claimed by Spain, 1779-98, then became a U.S. territory, 1798, and a state, 1817. Slavery spread along with cotton plantations, and slaves made up 55% of the population, 1860. Mississippi seceded, 1861. In the Civil War, Union forces captured Vicksburg, 1863, and caused extensive damage elsewhere. Mississippi reentered the Union, 1870. For the next 100 years, resistance to desegregation and violence against blacks made the state a battleground for the African American civil rights movement. Hurricanes Camille, 1969, and Katrina, 2005, caused substantial damage to the Gulf Coast. Since the early 1990s, casino gambling has boosted the economy.

Tourist attractions. Vicksburg Natl. Military Park and Cemetery, other Civil War sites; Hattiesburg; Natchez Trace; Indian mounds; Antebellum homes; pilgrimages in Natchez and some 25 other cities; The Elvis Presley Birthplace & Museum, Tupelo; Smith Robertson Museum, Mynelle Gardens, both Jackson; Mardi Gras and Shrimp Festival, both in Biloxi; Gulf Islands Natl. Seashore.

Famous Mississippians. Margaret Walker Alexander, Dana Andrews, Jimmy Buffett, Hodding Carter III, Bo Diddley, William Faulkner, Brett Favre, Shelby Foote, Morgan Freeman, John Grisham, Fannie Lou Hamer, Jim Henson, Faith Hill, John Lee Hooker, Robert Johnson, James Earl Jones, B. B. King, L. Q. C. Lamar, Trent Lott, Gerald McRaney, Willie Morris, Walter Payton, Elvis Presley, Leontyne Price, Charley Pride, LeAnn Rimes, Muddy Waters, Eudora Welty, Tennessee Williams, Oprah Winfrey, Johnny Winter, Richard Wright, Tammy Wynette.

Tourist Information. Mississippi Division of Tourism. PO Box 849, Jackson, MS 39205-0849; 1-888-SEE-MISS. **Website:** www.visitmississippi.org

Website. www.ms.gov

Missouri (MO)

Show Me State

People. Population (2005 est.): 5,800,310; rank: 18; **net change** (2004-2005): 0.7%. **Pop. density:** 84.2 per sq mi. Racial distribution (2004): 85.4% white; 11.5% black; 1.3% Asian; 0.5% Native/Nat.AK; 0.07% Hawaiian/Pacific Islander; 2 or more races, 1.3%. **Hispanic pop.** (any race): 2.6%.

Geography. Total area: 69,704 sq mi; rank: 21. **Land area:** 68,886 sq mi; rank: 18. **Acres forested:** 14.0 mil. **Location:** West North Central state near the geographic center of the conterminous U.S.; bordered on the E by the Mississippi R., on the NW by the Missouri R. **Climate:** continental, susceptible to cold Canadian air, moist, warm gulf air, and drier SW air. **Topography:** rolling hills, open, fertile plains, and well-watered prairie N of the Missouri R.; south of the river land is rough and hilly with deep, narrow valleys; alluvial plain in the SE; low elevation in the west. **Capital:** Jefferson City. **Principal internat. airports at:** Kansas City, St. Louis.

Economy. Chief industries: agriculture, manufacturing, aerospace, tourism. **Chief manuf. goods:** transportation equipment, food and related products, electrical and electronic equipment, chemicals. **Chief crops:** soybeans, corn, wheat, hay. **Livestock:** (Jan. 2006): 4.6 mil cattle/calves, 75,000 sheep/lambs; (Dec. 2005): 2.8 mil hogs/pigs, 8.8 mil chickens (excl. broilers). **Timber/lumber** (est. 2004): 575 mil bd. ft.; oak, hickory. **Nonfuel minerals** (est. 2005): $1.7 bil; stone (crushed), cement (portland), lead, lime, sand and gravel (construction). **Gross state product** (2005): $216.1 bil. **Sales tax** (2006): 4.225%. **Employment distrib.** (May 2006): 16.0% govt; 19.7% trade/trans./util.; 11.0% mfg; 13.5% ed./health; 11.7% prof./bus. serv.; 10.3% leisure/hosp.; 6.0% finance; 5.2% constr.; 4.3% other serv.; 2.2% info. **Unemployment** (2005): 5.4%. **Per cap. pers. income** (2005): $31,899. **New private housing** (2005): 33,114 units/$4.7 bil. **Commercial banks** (2005): 364; **deposits:** $88.2 bil. **Savings institutions** (2005): 35; **deposits:** $4.5 bil. **Lottery** (2005): total sales: $785.0 mil; profit: $218.6 mil.

Federal govt. Fed. civ. employees (Mar. 2005): 33,109; **avg. salary:** $54,896. **Notable fed. facilities:** Federal Reserve banks; *Ft. Leonard Wood; Jefferson Barracks Natl. Cem.; Whiteman AFB.

Energy. Electricity production (est. 2005, kWh by source): Coal: 77.2 bil; Gas: 3.5 bil; Hydroelectric: 1.1 bil; Nuclear: 8.0 bil; Petroleum: 102 mil; Other: 66 mil.

State data. Motto: Salus Populi Suprema Lex Esto (The welfare of the people shall be the supreme law). **Flower:** Hawthorn. **Bird:** Bluebird. **Tree:** Dogwood. **Song:** Missouri Waltz. **Entered union** Aug. 10, 1821; rank, 24th. **State fair** at Sedalia; 3rd week in Aug.

World Almanac Quick Quiz

Which state was the first to be readmitted to the Union after the Civil War, in 1866?

(a) Tennessee   (b) Virginia

(c) Florida   (d) Missouri

For the answer look in this chapter, or see page 1008.

History. In the 17th cent., when French explorers arrived, Algonquian Sauk, Fox, and Illinois and Siouan Osage, Missouri, Iowa, and Kansa peoples were living in the region; few remained by the 1830s. French hunters and lead miners made the first settlement c. 1735, at Ste. Genevieve. The territory was ceded to Spain by the French, 1762, then returned to France, 1800, and acquired by the U.S. in the Louisiana Purchase, 1803. Powerful earthquakes rocked New Madrid, 1811-12. Missouri became a territory, 1812, and entered the Union as a slave state, 1821. St. Louis became the gateway for pioneers heading West. Though Missouri stayed with the Union, pro- and antislavery forces battled there during the Civil War. In the late 19th cent. railroad building and the cattle trade made Kansas City a boomtown. The most notable Missourian of the 20th cent., Harry S. Truman, was U.S. president, 1945-53. The state, a political bellwether, voted for the winner in every presidential election from 1960 to 2004.

Tourist attractions. Silver Dollar City, Branson; Mark Twain Area, Hannibal; Pony Express Museum, St. Joseph; Harry S. Truman Library, Independence; Gateway Arch, St. Louis; Worlds of Fun, Kansas City; Lake of the Ozarks; Churchill Mem., Fulton; State Capitol, Jefferson City.

Famous Missourians. Maya Angelou, Robert Altman, Burt Bacharach, Josephine Baker, Scott Bakula, Thomas Hart Benton, Tom Berenger, Yogi Berra, Chuck Berry, George Caleb Bingham, Daniel Boone, Omar Bradley, William Burroughs, Kate Capshaw, Dale Carnegie, George Washington Carver, Bob Costas, Walter Cronkite, Walt Disney, T. S. Eliot, Richard Gephardt, John Goodman, Betty Grable, Edwin Hubble, Jesse James, Rush Limbaugh, Marianne Moore, Reinhold Niebuhr, J. C. Penney, John J. Pershing, Brad Pitt, Joseph Pulitzer, Ginger Rogers, Bess Truman, Harry S. Truman, Kathleen Turner, Tina Turner, Mark Twain, Dick Van Dyke, Tennessee Williams, Lanford Wilson, Shelley Winters, Jane Wyman.

Tourist Information. Missouri Division of Tourism. P.O. Box 1055, Jefferson City, MO 65102; 1-800-519-2100. **Website.** www.visitmo.com

Website. www.state.mo.us

Montana (MT)
Treasure State

People. Population (2005 est.): 935,670; rank: 44; **net change** (2004-2005): 0.9%. **Pop. density:** 6.4 per sq mi. Racial distribution (2004): 91.1% white; 0.4% black; 0.5% Asian; 6.4% Native/Nat.AK; 0.06% Hawaiian/Pacific Islander; 2 or more races, 1.5%. **Hispanic pop.** (any race): 2.4%.

Geography. Total area: 147,042 sq mi; rank: 4. **Land area:** 145,552 sq mi; rank: 4. **Acres forested:** 23.3 mil. **Location:** Mountain state bounded on the E by the Dakotas, on the S by Wyoming, on the SSW by Idaho, and on the N by Canada. **Climate:** colder, continental climate with low humidity. **Topography:** Rocky Mts. in western third of the state; eastern two-thirds gently rolling northern Great Plains. **Capital:** Helena. **Principal internat. airports at:** Billings, Missoula.

Economy. Chief industries: agriculture, timber, mining, tourism, oil and gas. **Chief manuf. goods:** food products, wood & paper products, primary metals, printing & publishing, petroleum and coal products. **Chief crops:** wheat, barley, sugar beets, hay, oats. **Livestock:** (Jan. 2006): 2.4 mil cattle/calves, 295,000 sheep/lambs; (Dec. 2005): 175,000 hogs/pigs, 480,000 chickens (excl. broilers). **Timber/lumber** (est. 2004): 1.1 bil bd. ft.; Douglas fir, pines, larch. **Nonfuel minerals** (est. 2005): $866 mil; gold, molyblenym concentrates, palladium, platinum, sand and gravel (construction), cement (portland). **Gross state product** (2005): $29.9 bil. **Sales tax** (2006): none. **Employment distrib.** (May 2006): 20.8% govt; 20.7% trade/trans./util.; 4.5% mfg; 13.4% ed./health; 8.3% prof./bus. serv.; 12.8% leisure/hosp.; 5.1% finance; 7.0% constr.; 3.9% other serv.; 1.8% info. **Unemployment** (2005): 4.0%. **Per cap. pers. income** (2005): $29,387. **New private housing** (2005): 4,803 units/$691 mil. **Commercial banks** (2005): 82; **deposits:** $12.1 bil. **Savings institutions** (2005): 3; **deposits:** $442 mil. **Lottery** (2005): total sales: $33.8 mil; profit: $6.2 mil.

Federal govt. Fed. civ. employees (Mar. 2005): 8,988; **avg. salary:** $54,155. **Notable fed. facilities:** Malmstrom AFB; Ft. Peck, Hungry Horse, Libby, Yellowtail dams; numerous missile silos.

Energy. Electricity production (est. 2005, kWh by source): Coal: 380 mil; Gas: 22 mil; Hydroelectric: 6.3 bil.

State data. Motto: Oro y Plata (Gold and silver). **Flower:** Bitterroot. **Bird:** Western meadowlark. **Tree:** Ponderosa pine. **Song:** Montana. **Entered union** Nov. 8, 1889; rank, 41st. **State fair** at Great Falls; late July-early Aug.

History. Paleoindian hunters reached the area over 12,000 years ago. Cheyenne, Blackfoot, Crow, Assiniboin, Salish (Flatheads), Kootenai, and Kalispel peoples lived in the region before Europeans arrived. French explorers visited the region, 1742. The U.S. acquired the area partly through the Louisiana Purchase, 1803, partly through explorations of Lewis and Clark, 1805-6. Fur traders and missionaries established posts in the early 19th cent. Gold was discovered on Grasshopper Creek, 1862, and Montana Territory was established, 1864. Indian uprisings reached their peak with the defeat of Gen. George Custer at the Battle of Little Bighorn, 1876. Chief Joseph and the Nez Percé tribe surrendered here, 1877, after a long trek across the state. Mining activity and the coming of the Northern Pacific Railway, 1883, brought population growth. Montana became a state, 1889. Copper wealth from the Butte pits resulted in the turn of the century "War of Copper Kings" as feuding factions contended for "the richest hill on earth." During the first half of the 20th cent., the Anaconda Copper firm wielded enormous political influence. Jeannette Rankin, a suffragist and pacifist, was the first woman elected to Congress, 1916. Mike Mansfield served 34 years in Congress and was Senate Democratic leader, 1961-77. An 18-year hunt for notorious "Unabomber" Theodore Kaczynski ended with his arrest, 1996, at his cabin near Lincoln.

Tourist attractions. Glacier Natl. Park; Yellowstone Natl. Park; Museum of the Rockies, Bozeman; Museum of the Plains Indian, Blackfeet Reservation, near Browning; Little Bighorn Battlefield Natl. Monument and Custer Natl. Cemetery; Flathead Lake; Helena; Lewis and Clark Caverns State Park, near Whitehall; Lewis and Clark Interpretive Center, Great Falls.

Famous Montanans. Dana Carvey, Gary Cooper, Marcus Daly, Chet Huntley, Will James, Myrna Loy, David Lynch, Mike Mansfield, Brent Musburger, Jeannette Rankin, Charles M. Russell, Lester Thurow.

Tourist Information. Travel Montana, Dept. of Commerce, PO Box 200533, 301 S. Park, Helena, MT 59601; 1-800-VISITMT. **Website:** www.visitmt.org

Website. www.state.mt.us

Nebraska (NE)
Cornhusker State

People. Population (2005 est.): 1,758,787; rank: 38; **net change** (2004-2005): 0.6%. **Pop. density:** 22.9 per sq mi. Racial distribution (2004): 92.1% white; 4.3% black; 1.5% Asian; 0.9% Native/Nat.AK; 0.07% Hawaiian/Pacific Islander; 2 or more races, 1.1%. **Hispanic pop.** (any race): 6.9%.

Geography. Total area: 77,354 sq mi; rank: 16. **Land area:** 76,872 sq mi; rank: 15. **Acres forested:** 0.9 mil. **Location:** West North Central state with the Missouri R. for a NE and E border. **Climate:** continental semi-arid. **Topography:** till plains of the central lowland in the eastern third rising to the Great Plains and hill country of the north central and NW. **Capital:** Lincoln.

Economy. Chief industries: agriculture, manufacturing. **Chief manuf. goods:** processed foods, industrial machinery, printed materials, electric and electronic equipment, primary and fabricated metal products, transportation equipment. **Chief crops:** corn, sorghum, soybeans, hay, wheat, dry beans, oats, potatoes, sugar beets. **Livestock:** (Jan. 2006): 6.6 mil cattle/calves, 106,000 sheep/lambs; (Dec. 2005): 2.9 mil hogs/pigs, 13.8 mil chickens (excl. broilers), 4.8 mil broilers. **Timber/lumber** (est. 2004): 15 mil bd. ft.; oak, hickory, and elm. **Nonfuel minerals** (est. 2005): $116 mil; cement (portland), stone (crushed), sand and gravel (construction), cement (masonry), lime. **Chief ports:** Omaha, Sioux City, Brownville, Blair, Plattsmouth, Nebraska City. **Gross state product** (2005): $70.3 bil. **Sales tax** (2006): 5.5%. **Employment distrib.** (May 2006): 17.4% govt; 21.1% trade/trans./util.; 10.8% mfg; 13.8% ed./health; 10.4% prof./bus. serv.; 8.7% leisure/hosp.; 6.9% finance; 4.9% constr.; 3.8% other serv.; 2.1% info. **Unemployment** (2005): 3.8%. **Per cap. pers. income** (2005): $33,616. **New private housing** (2005): 9,929 units/$1.3 bil. **Commercial banks** (2005): 259; **deposits:** $29.3 bil. **Savings institutions** (2005): 16; **depos-**

its: $4.2 bil. **Lottery** (2005): total sales: $100.7 mil; profit: $23.9 mil.

Federal govt. Fed. civ. employees (Mar. 2005): 8,738; **avg. salary**: $55,575. **Notable fed. facilities:** *Offutt AFB.

Energy. Electricity production (est. 2005, kWh by source): Coal: 20.8 bil; Gas: 525 mil; Hydroelectric: 848 mil; Nuclear: 8.8 bil; Petroleum: 21 mil; Other: 120 mil.

State data. Motto: Equality before the law. **Flower:** Goldenrod. **Bird:** Western meadowlark. **Tree:** Cottonwood. **Song:** Beautiful Nebraska. **Entered union** Mar. 1, 1867; rank, 37th. **State fair** at Lincoln; Aug.-Sept.

History. When Europeans arrived, Pawnee, Ponca, Omaha, and Oto peoples lived in the region. Spanish and French explorers and fur traders visited the area prior to its acquisition in the Louisiana Purchase, 1803. Lewis and Clark passed through, 1804-6. The first permanent settlement was Bellevue, near Omaha, 1823. The 1834 Indian Intercourse Act declared Nebraska Indian country and excluded white settlement, but conflicts with settlers eventually forced Native Americans to move to reservations. Nebraska became a territory, 1854, and a state, 1867. Many Civil War veterans settled under free land terms of the 1862 Homestead Act; as agriculture grew, struggles followed between homesteaders and ranchers. Since the mid-1930s, Nebraska has been the only state with a unicameral legislature. A leader in agribusiness, Nebraska has also become a major telemarketing center. The "Oracle of Omaha," investor Warren Buffett, one of the world's wealthiest men, announced in 2006 he would give most of his $44 bil fortune to charity.

Tourist attractions. State Museum (Elephant Hall), State Capitol, both Lincoln; Stuhr Museum of the Prairie Pioneer, Grand Island; Museum of the Fur Trade, Chadron; Henry Doorly Zoo, Joslyn Art Museum, both Omaha; Ashfall Fossil Beds, Strategic Air Command Museum, Ashland; Boys Town, west of Omaha; Arbor Lodge State Park, Nebraska City; Buffalo Bill Ranch State Hist. Park, North Platte; Pioneer Village, Minden; Oregon Trail landmarks; Scotts Bluff Natl. Monument; Chimney Rock Natl. Historic Site; Ft. Robinson; Hastings Museum, Hastings.

Famous Nebraskans. Grover Cleveland Alexander, Fred Astaire, Marlon Brando, Charles W. Bryan, William Jennings Bryan, Warren Buffett, Johnny Carson, Willa Cather, Dick Cavett, Dick Cheney, William F. "Buffalo Bill" Cody, Loren Eiseley, Rev. Edward J. Flanagan, Henry Fonda, Gerald R. Ford, Bob Gibson, Rollin Kirby, Harold Lloyd, Malcolm X, J. Sterling Morton, John Neihardt, Nick Nolte, George Norris, Tom Osborne, John J. Pershing, Roscoe Pound, Chief Red Cloud, Mari Sandoz, Robert Taylor, Darryl F. Zanuck.

Tourist Infomation. Nebraska Division of Travel and Tourism, PO Box 98907, Lincoln, NE 68509-8907; 1-877-NE-BRASKA. **Website:** www.visitnebraska.org

Website. www.nebraska.gov

Nevada (NV)
Sagebrush State, Battle Born State, Silver State

People. Population (2005 est.): 2,414,807; rank: 35; **net change** (2004-2005): 3.5%. **Pop. density:** 22.0 per sq mi. Racial distribution (2004): 82.5% white; 7.5% black; 5.5% Asian; 1.4% Native/Nat.AK; 0.5% Hawaiian/Pacific Islander; 2 or more races, 2.5%. **Hispanic pop.** (any race): 22.8%.

Geography. Total area: 110,561 sq mi; rank: 7. **Land area:** 109,826 sq mi; rank: 7. **Acres forested:** 10.2 mil. **Location:** Mountain state bordered on N by Oregon and Idaho, on E by Utah and Arizona, on SE by Arizona, and on SW and W by California. **Climate:** semi-arid and arid. **Topography:** rugged N-S mountain ranges; highest elevation, Boundary Peak, 13,140 ft; southern area is within the Mojave Desert; lowest elevation, Colorado River at southern tip of state, 479 ft. **Capital:** Carson City. **Principal internat. airports at:** Las Vegas, Reno.

Economy. Chief industries: gaming, tourism, mining, manufacturing, government, retailing, warehousing, trucking. **Chief manuf. goods:** food products, plastics, chemicals, aerospace products, lawn and garden irrigation equipment, seismic and machinery-monitoring devices. **Chief crops:** hay, alfalfa seed, potatoes, onions, garlic, barley, wheat. **Livestock:** (Jan. 2006): 500,000 cattle/calves, 74,000 sheep/lambs; (Dec. 2005): 4,000 hogs/pigs. **Timber/lumber** (est. 2004): <0.5 mil bd. ft.; piñon, juniper, other pines. **Nonfuel minerals** (est. 2005): $3.6 bil; gold, sand and gravel (construction), lime, stone (crushed), diatomite. **Gross state product** (2005): $110.5 bil. **Sales tax** (2006): 6.5%. **Employ-**

ment distrib. (May 2006): 11.8% govt; 17.4% trade/trans./util.; 3.8% mfg; 6.8% ed./health; 12.2% prof./bus. serv.; 26.3% leisure/hosp.; 5.3% finance; 11.5% constr.; 2.9% other serv.; 1.2% info. **Unemployment** (2005): 4.1%. **Per cap. pers. income** (2005): $35,883. **New private housing** (2005): 47,728 units/$6.5 bil. **Commercial banks** (2005): 44; **deposits**: $43.8 bil. **Savings institutions** (2005): 10; **deposits:** $4.5 bil.

Federal govt. Fed. civ. employees (Mar. 2005) 9,275; **avg. salary:** $57,833. **Notable fed. facilities:** Nevada Test Site; *Hawthorne Army Depot; Nellis AFB and Range Complex; Fallon NAS; Natl. Wild Horse and Burro Ctr. at Palomino Valley.

Energy. Electricity production (est. 2005, kWh by source): Coal: 18.4 bil; Gas: 4.0 bil; Hydroelectric: 1.7 bil; Petroleum: 22 mil.

State data. Motto: All for our country. **Flower:** Sagebrush. **Bird:** Mountain bluebird. **Trees:** Single-leaf piñon and bristlecone pine. **Song:** Home Means Nevada. **Entered union** Oct. 31, 1864; rank, 36th. **State fair** at Reno; late Aug.

History. Shoshone, Paiute, Bannock, and Washoe peoples lived in the area at the time of European contact. Nevada was first explored by Spaniards, 1776. In the 1820s, fur traders Peter Skene Ogden and Jedediah Smith separately explored the area. It was acquired by the U.S., 1848, at the end of the Mexican War. A trading post at Mormon Station, now Genoa, was established, 1850. Discovery of the Comstock Lode, rich in gold and silver, 1859, spurred a population boom. Nevada became a territory, 1861, and a state, 1864. Hoover Dam was built, 1931-36. WIth gambling legal since 1931, a surge in resort casino construction after World War II turned Las Vegas into one of the nation's most popular tourist destinations. An influx of Hispanics and Asians, attracted by service-industry and construction jobs, helped make Nevada the fastest-growing state in the U.S. during 1990-2005.

Tourist attractions. Legalized gambling at: Lake Tahoe, Reno, Las Vegas, Laughlin, Elko County, and elsewhere. Hoover Dam; Lake Mead; Great Basin Natl. Park; Valley of Fire State Park; Virginia City; Red Rock Canyon Natl. Conservation Area; Liberace Museum, the Las Vegas Strip, Guinness World of Records Museum, Lost City Museum, Overton, Lamoille Canyon, Pyramid Lake, all Las Vegas. Skiing near Lake Tahoe.

Famous Nevadans. Andre Agassi, Walter Van Tilburg Clark, George Ferris, Sarah Winnemucca Hopkins, Paul Laxalt, Dat So La Lee, John William Mackay, Anne Martin, Pat McCarran, Key Pittman, William Morris Stewart.

Tourist information. Commission on Tourism, 401 N. Carson St., Carson City, NV 89701; 1-800-NEVADA8. **Website:** www.travelnevada.com

Website. www.nv.gov

New Hampshire (NH)
Granite State

People. Population (2005 est.): 1,309,940; rank: 41; **net change** (2004-2005): 0.8%. **Pop. density:** 146.1 per sq mi. Racial distribution (2004): 96.2% white; 0.9% black; 1.7% Asian; 0.2% Native/Nat.AK; 0.04% Hawaiian/Pacific Islander; 2 or more races, 0.9%. **Hispanic pop.** (any race): 2.1%.

Geography. Total area: 9,350 sq mi; rank: 46. **Land area:** 8,968 sq mi; rank: 44. **Acres forested:** 4.8 mil. **Location:** New England state bounded on S by Massachusetts, on W by Vermont, on N and NW by Canada, on E by Maine and the Atlantic Ocean. **Climate:** highly varied, due to its nearness to high mountains and ocean. **Topography:** low, rolling coast followed by countless hills and mountains rising out of a central plateau. **Capital:** Concord.

Economy. Chief industries: tourism, manufacturing, agriculture, trade, mining. **Chief manuf. goods:** machinery, electrical and electronic products, plastics, fabricated metal products. **Chief crops:** dairy products, nursery & greenhouse products, hay, vegetables, fruit, maple syrup & sugar products. **Livestock:** (Jan. 2006): 39,000 cattle/calves; (Dec. 2005): 3,200 hogs/pigs, 216,000 chickens (excl.broilers). **Timber/lumber** (est. 2004): 232 mil bd. ft.; white pine, hemlock, oak, birch. **Nonfuel minerals** (est. 2005): $75.1 mil; sand and gravel (construction), stone (crushed), stone (dimension), gemstones. **Commercial fishing** (2004): $8.8 mil. **Chief ports:** Portsmouth, Hampton, Rye. **Gross state product** (2005): $55.7 bil. **Sales tax** (2006): none. **Employment distrib.** (May 2006): 14.3% govt; 21.9% trade/trans./util.; 11.9% mfg; 15.7% ed./health; 9.5% prof./bus. serv.; 10.0%

leisure/hosp.; 6.3% finance; 5.0% constr.; 3.2% other serv.; 2.0% info. **Unemployment** (2005): 3.6%. **Per cap. pers. income** (2005): $38,408. **New private housing** (2005): 7,586 units/$1.4 bil. **Commercial banks** (2005): 20; **deposits:** $18.9 bil. **Savings institutions** (2005): 22; **deposits:** $10.8 bil. **Lottery** (2005): total sales: $227.9 mil; profit: $69.3 mil.

Federal govt. Fed. civ. employees (Mar. 2005): 3,367; avg. salary: $73,132. **Notable fed. facilities:** U.S. Army Cold Regions Res. & Engineering Lab.

Energy. Electricity production (est. 2005, kWh by source): Coal: 4.1 bil; Gas: 1 mil; Hydroelectric: 377 mil; Petroleum: 1.2 bil.

State data. Motto: Live free or die. **Flower:** Purple lilac. **Bird:** Purple finch. **Tree:** White birch. **Song:** Old New Hampshire. **Ninth** of the original 13 states to ratify the Constitution, June 21, 1788. **State Fair:** Many agricultural fairs statewide, July through Sept.; no State fair.

History. The area has been inhabited for about 10,000 years. Algonquian-speaking peoples, including the Pennacook, lived in the region when the Europeans arrived. The first explorers to visit the area were England's Martin Pring, 1603, and France's Champlain, 1605. The first settlement was Odiorne's Point (now port of Rye), 1623. Before the American Revolution, New Hampshire residents raided a British fort at Portsmouth, 1774, and drove the royal governor out, 1775. New Hampshire became the first colony to adopt its own constitution, 1776. After statehood, 1788, New Hampshire became a textile manufacturing center. The mill towns declined in the first half of the 20th cent., but tourism and high-technology industries, lured by low taxes, have revived the economy since the 1960s. Every 4 years, the first primary of the presidential campaign season is traditionally held here.

Tourist attractions. Mt. Washington, highest peak in Northeast; Lake Winnipesaukee; White Mt. National Forest; Crawford, Franconia—famous for the Old Man of the Mountain, described by Hawthorne as the Great Stone Face, Pinkham notches, all White Mt. region; the Flume, a spectacular gorge; the aerial tramway, Cannon Mt.; Strawbery Banke, Portsmouth; Shaker Village, Canterbury; Saint-Gaudens, Natl. Historic Site, Cornish; Mt. Monadnock.

Famous New Hampshirites. Salmon P. Chase, Ralph Adams Cram, Mary Baker Eddy, Daniel Chester French, Robert Frost, Horace Greeley, Sarah Buell Hale, Franklin Pierce, Augustus Saint-Gaudens, Adam Sandler, Alan Shepard, David H. Souter, Daniel Webster.

Tourist information. Division of Travel & Tourism Development, 172 Pembroke Rd., Concord, NH 03302-1856; PO Box 1856; 1-800-FUNINNH, ext. 169. **Website:** www.visitnh.gov **Website.** www.state.nh.us

New Jersey (NJ)
Garden State

People. Population (2005 est.): 8,717,925; rank: 10; **net change** (2004-2005): 0.4%. **Pop. density:** 1,175.3 per sq mi. Racial distribution (2004): 76.9% white; 14.5% black; 7.0% Asian; 0.3% Native/Nat.AK; 0.08% Hawaiian/Pacific Islander; 2 or more races, 1.2%. **Hispanic pop.** (any race): 14.9%.

Geography. Total area: 8,721 sq mi; rank: 47. **Land area:** 7,417 sq mi; rank: 46. **Acres forested:** 2.1 mil. **Location:** Middle Atlantic state bounded on N and E by New York and Atlantic Ocean, on S and W by Delaware and Pennsylvania. **Climate:** moderate, with marked difference bet. NW and SE extremities. **Topography:** Appalachian Valley in the NW also has highest elevation, High Pt., 1,801 ft; Appalachian Highlands, flat-topped NE-SW mountain ranges; Piedmont Plateau, low plains broken by high ridges (Palisades) rising 400-500 ft; Coastal Plain, covering three-fifths of state in SE, rises from sea level to gentle slopes. **Capital:** Trenton. **Principal internat. airports at:** Atlantic City, Newark.

Economy. Chief industries: pharmaceuticals/drugs, telecommunications, biotechnology, printing & publishing. **Chief manuf. goods:** chemicals, electronic equipment, food. **Chief crops:** nursery/greenhouse, tomatoes, blueberries, peaches, peppers, cranberries, soybeans. **Livestock:** (Jan. 2006): 42,000 cattle/calves; (Dec. 2005): 9,000 hogs/pigs, 2.0 mil chickens (excl. broilers). **Timber/lumber** (2004 est.): 24 mil bd. ft.; pine, cedar, mixed hardwoods. **Nonfuel minerals** (est. 2005): $365 mil; stone (crushed), sand and gravel (construction), sand and gravel (industrial), greensand marl, peat. **Commercial fishing** (2004): $139.4 mil. **Chief ports:** Newark, Elizabeth, Hoboken, Camden. **Gross state product** (2005): $430.8 bil. **Sales tax** (2006): 6.0%. **Employment distrib.** (May 2006): 16.0% govt; 21.5% trade/trans./util.; 7.8% mfg; 14.0% ed./health; 14.7% prof./bus. serv.; 8.5% leisure/hosp.; 6.9% finance; 4.2% constr.; 3.9% other serv.; 2.3% info. **Unemployment** (2005): 4.4%. **Per cap. pers. income** (2005): $43,771. **New private housing** (2005): 38,588 units/$5.0 bil. **Commercial banks** (2005): 94; **deposits:** $163.8 bil. **Savings institutions** (2005): 77; **deposits:** $58.8 bil. **Lottery** (2005): total sales: $2.3 bil; profit: $804.4 mil.

Federal govt. Fed. civ. employees (Mar. 2005): 26,916; **avg. salary:** $69,233. **Notable fed. facilities:** McGuire AFB; Ft. Dix; *Ft. Monmouth; Picatinny Arsenal; *Lakehurst Naval Air Engineering Ctr.; FAA William J. Hughes Technical Ctr.

Energy. Electricity production (est. 2005, kWh by source): Coal: 1.4 bil; Gas: 49 mil; Petroleum: 108 mil.

State data. Motto: Liberty and prosperity. **Flower:** Purple violet. **Bird:** Eastern goldfinch. **Tree:** Red oak. **Third** of the original 13 states to ratify the Constitution, Dec. 18, 1787. **State fair** at Augusta; late July-early Aug.

History. The Lenni Lenape (Delaware) peoples lived in the region and had mostly peaceful relations with European colonists, who arrived after the explorers Verrazano, 1524, and Hudson, 1609. The first permanent European settlement was Dutch, at Bergen (now Jersey City), 1660. When the British took New Netherland, 1664, the area between the Delaware and Hudson Rivers was given to Lord John Berkeley and Sir George Carteret. During the American Revolution, New Jersey was the scene of many major battles, including Trenton, 1776; Princeton, 1777; and Monmouth, 1778. New Jersey was the third state to ratify the Constitution, 1787, and the first to approve the Bill of Rights, 1789. In a duel at Weehawken, 1804, Vice Pres. Aaron Burr fatally shot Alexander Hamilton. Canal and railroad building stimulated the growth of cities and industries in the 19th cent. The 20th cent. arrival of large numbers of African Americans, Italians, Irish, European Jews, Puerto Ricans, Asian Indians, and other groups made New Jersey one of the most diverse states in the U.S. Construction of resort casinos in Atlantic City from the late 1970s revitalized tourism. Gov. James McGreevey resigned, 2004, after acknowledging an extramarital affair with a man later identified as his former homeland security adviser.

Tourist attractions. 127 mi of beaches; Atlantic City; Grover Cleveland birthplace, Caldwell; Cape May Historic District; Edison Natl. Historic Site, W. Orange; Six Flags Great Adventure, Jackson; Liberty State Park, Jersey City; Meadowlands Sports Complex, E. Rutherford; Pine Barrens wilderness area; Princeton University; numerous Revolutionary War historical sites; State Aquarium, Camden.

Famous New Jerseyans. Jason Alexander, Count Basie, Judy Blume, Jon Bon Jovi, Bill Bradley, Aaron Burr, Grover Cleveland, James Fenimore Cooper, Stephen Crane, Danny DeVito, Thomas Edison, Albert Einstein, James Gandolfini, Allen Ginsberg, Alexander Hamilton, Ed Harris, Whitney Houston, Buster Keaton, Joyce Kilmer, Norman Mailer, Jack Nicholson, Thomas Paine, Dorothy Parker, Joe Pesci, Molly Pitcher, Paul Robeson, Philip Roth, Antonin Scalia, Wally Schirra, H. Norman Schwarzkopf, Frank Sinatra, Bruce Springsteen, Martha Stewart, Meryl Streep, Dave Thomas, John Travolta, Walt Whitman, William Carlos Williams, Woodrow Wilson.

Tourist Information. New Jersey Commerce and Economic Growth Commission, PO Box 820, Trenton, NJ 08625-0820; 1-800-VISITNJ. **Website:** www.visitnj.org **Website.** www.state.nj.us

> ➤ **IT'S A FACT:** New Jersey chose a new tourism slogan in 2006 by turning to the public for help. The state had paid a marketing firm $260,000 for its suggestion, "New Jersey: We'll Win You Over," only to have it rejected by Gov. Richard Codey. People were invited to submit slogans and vote on finalists to replace the long-standing "New Jersey and You: Perfect Together." Of the nearly 8,000 submissions, those rejected early included "New Jersey: It's Not as Bad as it Smells," "New Jersey: Most of our Elected Officials Have Not Been Indicted," and "New Jersey: Got a Problem With That?" Around 11,000 people voted for one of five finalists, with the winner, "New Jersey: Come See for Yourself," earning about 3,400 votes.

New Mexico (NM)
Land of Enchantment

People. Population (2005 est.): 1,928,384; rank: 36; **net change** (2004-2005): 1.3%. **Pop. density:** 15.9 per sq mi. Racial distribution (2004): 84.7% white; 2.4% black; 1.3% Asian; 10.1% Native/Nat.AK; 0.1% Hawaiian/Pacific Islander; 2 or more races, 1.5%. **Hispanic pop.** (any race): 43.3%.

Geography. Total area: 121,589 sq mi; rank: 5. **Land area:** 121,356 sq mi; rank: 5. **Acres forested:** 16.7 mil. **Location:** southwestern state bounded by Colorado on the N, Oklahoma, Texas, and Mexico on the E and S, and Arizona on the W. **Climate:** dry, with temperatures rising or falling 5x F with every 1,000 ft elevation. **Topography:** eastern third, Great Plains; central third, Rocky Mts. (85% of the state is over 4,000-ft elevation); western third, high plateau. **Capital:** Santa Fe. **Principal internat. airport at:** Albuquerque.

Economy. Chief industries: government, services, trade. **Chief manuf. goods:** foods, machinery, apparel, lumber, printing, transportation equipment, electronics, semiconductors. **Chief crops:** hay, onions, chiles, greenhouse nursery, pecans, cotton. **Livestock:** (Jan. 2006): 1.6 mil cattle/calves, 155,000 sheep/lambs; (Dec. 2005): 2,000 hogs/pigs. **Timber/lumber:** figs. undisclosed; ponderosa pine, Douglas fir.

Nonfuel minerals (est. 2005): $1.1 bil; molyblenym concentrates, potash, copper, sand and gravel (construction), cement (portland), stone (crushed). **Gross state product** (2005): $69.3 bil. **Sales tax** (2006): 5.0%. **Employment distrib.** (May 2006): 24.9% govt; 17.0% trade/trans./util.; 4.4% mfg; 13.2% ed./health; 11.3% prof./bus. serv.; 10.3% leisure/hosp.; 4.3% finance; 7.0% constr.; 3.5% other serv.; 1.8% info. **Unemployment** (2005): 5.3%. **Per cap. pers. income** (2005): $27,644. **New private housing** (2005): 14,180 units/$2.2 bil. **Commercial banks** (2005): 56; **deposits:** $17.6 bil. **Savings institutions** (2005): 11; **deposits:** $2.1 bil. **Lottery** (2005): total sales: $139.3 mil; profit: $32.2 mil.

Federal govt. Fed. civ. employees (Mar. 2005): 21,855; **avg. salary:** $57,010. **Notable fed. facilities:** Kirtland, *Cannon, *Holloman AF bases; Los Alamos Natl. Lab; *White Sands Missile Range; Natl. Solar Observatory; Natl. Radio Astronomy Observatory, Sandia Natl. Labs.

Energy. Electricity production (est. 2005, kWh by source): Coal: 29.9 bil; Gas: 3.0 bil; Hydroelectric: 140 mil; Petroleum: 33 mil.

State data. Motto: Crescit Eundo (It grows as it goes). **Flower:** Yucca. **Bird:** Roadrunner. **Tree:** Piñon. **Song:** O, Fair New Mexico; Asi Es Nuevo Mexico. **Entered union** Jan. 6, 1912; rank, 47th. **State fair** at Albuquerque; mid-Sept.

History. Inhabited for more than 10,000 years, the region was home to Sandia, Clovis, Folsom, Mogollon, and Anasazi cultures, followed by the Pueblo people, Anasazi descendants; later, nomadic Navajo and Apache came. Franciscan Marcos de Niza and a former black slave, Estevanico, explored the area, 1539, seeking gold; Coronado followed, 1540. First settlements were near San Juan Pueblo, 1598, and at Santa Fe, 1610. Settlers alternately traded and fought with the Apache, Comanche, and Navajo. Trade on the Santa Fe Trail to Missouri started, 1821. After the Mexican War began, 1846, Gen. Stephen Kearny took Santa Fe without firing a shot, and declared New Mexico part of the U.S. All Hispanic New Mexicans and Pueblo became U.S. citizens by terms of the 1848 treaty ending the war. New Mexico became a territory, 1850, but did not attain statehood until 1912. Pancho Villa raided Columbus, 1916, and U.S. troops were sent to the area. The world's first atomic bomb was exploded at a test site near Alamogordo, 1945. An underground nuclear waste depository opened near Carlsbad, 1999. Construction on a $250 mil "spaceport" for space tourism, partially financed by the state, was to begin in 2007.

Tourist attractions. Carlsbad Caverns Natl. Park, with the largest natural underground chamber in the world; Santa Fe, oldest capital in U.S.; White Sands Natl. Monument, the largest gypsum deposit in the world; Chaco Culture National Historical Park; Acoma Pueblo, the "sky city," built atop a 357-ft mesa; Taos; Taos Art Colony; Taos Ski Valley; Ute Lake State Park; Shiprock.

Famous New Mexicans. Ben Abruzzo, Maxie Anderson, Jeff Bezos, Billy (the Kid) Bonney, Kit Carson, Bob Foster, Peter Hurd, Tony Hillerman, Archbishop Jean Baptiste Lamy, Nancy Lopez, Bill Mauldin, Georgia O'Keeffe, Bill Richardson, Kim Stanley, Al Unser, Bobby Unser, Lew Wallace.

Tourist information. New Mexico Dept. of Tourism, 491 Old Santa Fe Tr., Santa Fe, NM 87501; (800) 545-2070. **Website:** www.newmexico.org
Website. www.state.nm.us

New York (NY)
Empire State

People. Population (2005 est.): 19,254,630; rank: 3; **net change** (2004-2005): -0.1%. **Pop. density:** 407.8 per sq mi. Racial distribution (2004): 73.9% white; 17.5% black; 6.5% Asian; 0.5% Native/Nat.AK; 0.09% Hawaiian/Pacific Islander; 2 or more races, 1.5%. **Hispanic pop.** (any race): 16.0%.

Geography. Total area: 54,556 sq mi; rank: 27. **Land area:** 47,214 sq mi; rank: 30. **Acres forested:** 18.4 mil. **Location:** Middle Atlantic state, bordered by the New England states, Atlantic Ocean, New Jersey and Pennsylvania, Lakes Ontario and Erie, and Canada. **Climate:** variable; the SE region moderated by the ocean. **Topography:** highest and most rugged mountains in the NE Adirondack upland; St. Lawrence-Champlain lowlands extend from Lake Ontario NE along the Canadian border; Hudson-Mohawk lowland follows the flows of the rivers N and W, 10-30 mi wide; Atlantic coastal plain in the SE; Appalachian Highlands, covering half the state westward from the Hudson Valley, include the Catskill Mts., Finger Lakes; plateau of Erie-Ontario lowlands. **Capital:** Albany. **Principal internat. airports at:** Albany, Buffalo, New York, Newburgh, Rochester, Syracuse.

Economy. Chief industries: manufacturing, finance, communications, tourism, transportation, services. **Principal manuf. goods:** books & periodicals, clothing & apparel, pharmaceuticals, machinery, instruments, toys & sporting goods, electronic equipment, automotive & aircraft components. **Chief crops:** apples, grapes, strawberries, cherries, pears, onions, potatoes, cabbage, sweet corn, green beans, cauliflower, field corn, hay, wheat, oats, dry beans. **Chief farm prods.:** milk, cheese, maple syrup, wine. **Livestock:** (Jan. 2006): 1.4 mil cattle/calves, 70,000 sheep/lambs; (Dec. 2005): 83,000 hogs/pigs, 5.3 mil chickens (excl. broilers), 3.0 mil broilers. **Timber/lumber** (est. 2004): 480 mil bd. ft.; birch, sugar and red maple, basswood, hemlock, pine, oak, ash. **Nonfuel minerals** (est. 2005): $1.1 bil; stone (crushed), cement (portland), salt, sand and gravel (construction), wollastonite. **Commercial fishing** (2004): $46.4 mil. **Chief ports:** New York, Buffalo, Albany. **Gross state product** (2005): $963.5 bil. **Sales tax** (2006): 4.0%. **Employment distrib.** (May 2006): 17.5% govt; 17.4% trade/trans./util.; 6.5% mfg; 18.3% ed./health; 12.7% prof./bus. serv.; 8.0% leisure/hosp.; 8.4% finance; 3.9% constr.; 4.2% other serv.; 3.1% info. **Unemployment** (2005): 5.0%. **Per cap. pers. income** (2005): $40,507. **New private housing** (2005): 61,949 units/$7.8 bil. **Commercial banks** (2005): 157; **deposits:** $598.5 bil. **Savings institutions** (2005): 71; **deposits:** $91.3 bil. **Lottery** (2005): total sales: $6.3 bil; profit: $2.1 bil.

Federal govt. Fed. civ. employees (Mar. 2005): 58,613; **avg. salary:** $62,417. **Notable fed. facilities:** West Point Military Academy; Merchant Marine Academy; Ft. Drum; *Rome Labs.; Watervliet Arsenal; Brookhaven Natl. Lab.

Energy. Electricity production (est. 2005, kWh by source): Coal: 1.2 bil; Gas: 10.1 bil; Hydroelectric: 21.8 bil; Petroleum: 9.8 bil.

State data. Motto: Excelsior (Ever upward). **Flower:** Rose. **Bird:** Bluebird. **Tree:** Sugar maple. **Song:** I Love New York. **Eleventh** of the original 13 states to ratify the Constitution, July 26, 1788. **State fair** at Syracuse; late Aug.-early Sept.

History. When Europeans arrived, Algonquians including the Mahican, Wappinger, and Lenni Lenape inhabited the region, as did the Iroquoian Mohawk, Oneida, Onondaga, Cayuga, and Seneca tribes, who established the League of the Five Nations. Verrazano entered New York harbor, 1524. In 1609, Henry Hudson visited the river later named for him, and Champlain explored the lake that now bears his name. The first permanent settlement was Dutch, near present-day Albany, 1624. New Amsterdam was settled, 1626, at the S tip of Manhattan island. A British fleet seized New Netherland, 1664. Key battles of the American Revolution included Saratoga, 1777. In the 19th cent., New York City emerged as one of the world's great metropolitan areas, a center for trade, finance, and arts, and a haven for millions of immigrants. Completion of Erie Canal, 1825, established the state as a gateway to the West. The first women's rights convention was held in Seneca Falls, 1848. Although the state backed the Union in the Civil War, the military draft, 1863, triggered 3 days of riots in New York City. Industry declined in the 20th cent., and California and Texas passed New York in population. Attica was the scene of a bloody prison revolt, 1971. New Yorkers, 2000, elected former First Lady Hillary Rodham Clinton to the U.S. Senate. Two jet aircraft hijacked by terrorists on Sept. 11, 2001, destroyed the World Trade Center in lower Manhattan.

Tourist attractions. New York City; Adirondack and Catskill Mts.; Finger Lakes; Great Lakes; Thousand Islands; Niagara Falls; Saratoga Springs; Philipsburg Manor, Sunnyside (Washington Irving's home), the Dutch Church of Sleepy Hollow, all in Tarrytown area; Corning Glass Center and Steuben factory, Corning; Fenimore House, Natl. Baseball Hall of Fame and Museum, both in Cooperstown; Ft. Ticonderoga overlooking Lakes George and Champlain; Empire State Plaza, Albany; Lake Placid; Franklin D. Roosevelt Natl. Historic Site, including the Roosevelt Library, Hyde Park; Long Island beaches; Theodore Roosevelt estate, Sagamore Hill, Oyster Bay; Turning Stone Casino.

Famous New Yorkers. Woody Allen, Susan B. Anthony, James Baldwin, Lucille Ball, Ann Bancroft, L. Frank Baum, Milton Berle, Humphrey Bogart, Barbara Boxer, Mel Brooks, Benjamin Cardozo, De Witt Clinton, Peter Cooper, Aaron Copland, Tom Cruise, Robert De Niro, George Eastman, Millard Fillmore, Lou Gehrig, George and Ira Gershwin, Ruth Bader Ginsburg, Rudolph Giuliani, Jackie Gleason, Stephen Jay Gould, Julia Ward Howe, Charles Evans Hughes, Washington Irving, Henry and William James, John Jay, Michael Jordan, Edward Koch, Fiorello LaGuardia, Herman Melville, Arthur Miller, J. Pierpont Morgan Jr., Eddie Murphy, Joyce Carol Oates, Carroll O'Connor, Rosie O'Donnell, Eugene O'Neill, Jerry Orbach, George Pataki, Colin Powell, Nancy Reagan, John D. Rockefeller, Nelson Rockefeller, John Roberts, Richard Rodgers, Ray Romano, Eleanor Roosevelt, Franklin D. Roosevelt, Theodore Roosevelt, Tim Russert, J. D. Salinger, Caroline Kennedy Schlossberg, Jerry Seinfeld, Al Sharpton, Paul Simon, Alfred E. Smith, Elizabeth Cady Stanton, Barbra Streisand, Donald Trump, William (Boss) Tweed, Martin Van Buren, Luther Vandross, Gore Vidal, Denzel Washington, Edith Wharton, Walt Whitman.

Tourist information. Empire State Development, Travel Information Center, 1 Commerce Plaza, Albany, NY 12245; 1-800-CALLNYS from U.S. states and territories and Canada; 1-518-474-4116 from other areas. **Website:** www.il veny.com

Website. www.state.ny.us

North Carolina (NC)
Tar Heel State, Old North State

People. Population (2005 est.): 8,683,242; rank: 11; **net change** (2004-2005): 1.7%. **Pop. density:** 178.3 per sq mi. Racial distribution (2004): 74.1% white; 21.8% black; 1.7% Asian; 1.3% Native/Nat.AK; 0.07% Hawaiian/Pacific Islander; 2 or more races, 1.0%. **Hispanic pop.** (any race): 6.1%.

Geography. Total area: 53,819 sq mi; rank: 28. **Land area:** 48,711 sq mi; rank: 29. **Acres forested:** 19.3 mil. **Location:** South Atlantic state bounded by Virginia, South Carolina, Georgia, Tennessee, and the Atlantic Ocean. **Climate:** sub-tropical in SE, medium-continental in mountain region; tempered by the Gulf Stream and the mountains in W. **Topography:** coastal plain and tidewater, two-fifths of state, extending to the fall line of the rivers; piedmont plateau, another two-fifths, of gentle to rugged hills; southern Appalachian Mts. contains the Blue Ridge and Great Smoky Mts. **Capital:** Raleigh. **Principal internat. airports at:** Charlotte, Greensboro, Raleigh/Durham, Wilmington.

Economy. Chief industries: manufacturing, agriculture, tourism. **Chief manuf. goods:** food products, textiles, industrial machinery and equipment, electrical and electronic equipment, furniture, tobacco products, apparel. **Chief crops:** tobacco, cotton, soybeans, corn, food grains, wheat, peanuts, sweet potatoes. **Livestock:** (Jan. 2006): 860,000 cattle/calves, 18,000 sheep/lambs; (Dec. 2005): 9.8 mil hogs/pigs, 18.0 mil chickens (excl. broilers), 735.1 mil broilers. **Timber/lumber** (est. 2004): 2.6 bil bd. ft.; yellow pine, oak, hickory, poplar, maple. **Nonfuel minerals** (est. 2005): $846 mil; stone (crushed), phosphate rock, sand and gravel (construction), sand and gravel (industrial), feldspar. **Commercial fishing** (2004): $77.1 mil. **Chief ports:** Morehead City, Wilm-

ington. **Gross state product** (2005): $344.6 bil. **Sales tax** (2006): 4.5%. **Employment distrib.** (May 2006): 17.3% govt; 18.3% trade/trans./util.; 14.0% mfg; 12.0% ed./health; 11.3% prof./bus. serv.; 9.3% leisure/hosp.; 5.1% finance; 6.0% constr.; 4.5% other serv.; 1.9% info. **Unemployment** (2005): 5.2%. **Per cap. pers. income** (2005): $30,553. **New private housing** (2005): 97,910 units/$14.8 bil. **Commercial banks** (2005): 94; **deposits:** $178.9 bil. **Savings institutions** (2005): 39; **deposits:** $5.3 bil.

Federal govt. Fed. civ. employees (Mar. 2005): 33,206; **avg. salary:** $54,689. **Notable fed. facilities:** Ft. Bragg; *Camp LeJeune Marine Base; U.S. EPA R&D Labs, *Cherry Point Marine Corps Air Station; Natl. Humanities Ctr.; Natl. Inst. of Environmental Health Science; Natl. Ctr. for Health Statistics Lab, Research Triangle Park.

Energy. Electricity production (est. 2005, kWh by source): Coal: 74.9 bil; Gas: 2.7 bil; Hydroelectric: 3.7 bil; Nuclear: 40.0 bil; Petroleum: 244 mil.

State data. Motto: Esse Quam Videri (To be rather than to seem). **Flower:** Dogwood. **Bird:** Cardinal. **Tree:** Pine. **Song:** The Old North State. **Twelfth** of the original 13 states to ratify the Constitution, Nov. 21, 1789. **State fair** at Raleigh; mid-Oct.

History. Algonquian, Siouan, and Iroquoian peoples lived in the region at the time of European contact. Sir Walter Raleigh tried to found a colony, 1584-87; the "Lost Colony" on Roanoke Island, 1587, disappeared without a trace. Permanent settlers came from Virginia in the mid-17th cent. The province's congress was the first to vote for independence, 1776. In the Revolutionary War, Cornwallis's forces were defeated at Kings Mountain, 1780, and forced out after Guilford Courthouse, 1781. The state ratified the Constitution, 1789, only after Congress passed the Bill of Rights. North Carolina, with a slave population of 1/3, seceded from the Union,1861, and provided more troops to the Confederacy than any other state; it was readmitted, 1868. The Wright brothers made the first powered airplane flight at Kitty Hawk, 1903. Sit-ins at segregated Greensboro lunch counters, 1960, drew national attention to the civil rights movement. Long reliant on tobacco, textiles, and wood products, North Carolina has prospered since the 1960s from advanced technologies in the Raleigh-Durham-Chapel Hill area and banking in Charlotte. The hurricane-prone state was hit hard by Hazel, 1954, Fran, 1996, and Floyd, 1999.

Tourist attractions. Cape Hatteras and Cape Lookout natl. seashores; Great Smoky Mts.; Guilford Courthouse and Moore's Creek parks; 66 American Revolution battle sites; Bennett Place, near Durham, where Gen. Joseph Johnston surrendered the last Confederate army to Gen. William Sherman; Ft. Raleigh, Roanoke Island, where Virginia Dare, first child of English parents in the New World, was born Aug. 18, 1587; Wright Brothers Natl. Memorial, Kitty Hawk; Battleship *North Carolina*, Wilmington; NC Zoo, Asheboro; NC Symphony, NC Museum, Raleigh; Carl Sandburg Home, Hendersonville, Biltmore House & Gardens, Asheville.

Famous North Carolinians. David Brinkley, Shirley Caesar, John Coltrane, Rick Dees, Elizabeth Hanford Dole, John Edwards, Ava Gardner, Richard J. Gatling, Billy Graham, Andy Griffith, O. Henry, Andrew Jackson, Andrew Johnson, Michael Jordan, Wm. Rufus King, Charles Kuralt, Meadowlark Lemon, Dolley Madison, Thelonious Monk, Edward R. Murrow, Arnold Palmer, Richard Petty, James K. Polk, Charlie Rose, Carl Sandburg, Enos Slaughter, Dean Smith, James Taylor, Thomas Wolfe.

Tourist information. North Carolina Division of Tourism, Film & Sports Development, 301 N. Wilmington St., Raleigh, NC 27601; (919) 733-4151. **Website:** www.visitnc.com **Website.** www.nc.gov

North Dakota (ND)
Peace Garden State

People. Population (2005 est.): 636,677; rank: 48; **net change** (2004-2005): 0.1%. **Pop. density:** 9.2 per sq mi. Racial distribution (2004): 92.4% white; 0.7% black; 0.7% Asian; 5.2% Native/Nat.AK; 0.04% Hawaiian/Pacific Islander; 2 or more races, 0.9%. **Hispanic pop.** (any race): 1.5%.

Geography. Total area: 70,700 sq mi; rank: 19. **Land area:** 68,976 sq mi; rank: 17. **Acres forested:** 0.7 mil. **Location:** West North Central state, situated exactly in the middle of North America, bounded on the N by Canada, on the E by Minnesota, on the S by South Dakota, on the W by Montana. **Climate:** continental, with a wide range of temperature and moderate rainfall. **Topography:** Central Lowland in the E comprises the flat Red River Valley and the Rolling Drift Prairie; Missouri Plateau of the Great Plains on the W. **Capital:** Bismarck. **Principal internat. airport at:** Fargo.

Economy. Chief industries: agriculture, mining, tourism, manufacturing, telecommunications, energy, food processing. **Chief manuf. goods:** farm equipment, processed foods, fabricated metal, high-tech. electronics. **Chief crops:** spring wheat, durum, barley, flaxseed, oats, potatoes, dry edible beans, honey, soybeans, sugar beets, sunflowers, hay. **Livestock:** (Jan. 2006): 1.7 mil cattle/calves, 104,000 sheep/lambs; (Dec. 2005): 157,000 hogs/pigs. **Timber/lumber** (est. 2004): 1 mil bd. ft.; oak, ash, cottonwood, aspen. **Nonfuel minerals** (est. 2005): $51.3 mil; sand and gravel (construction), lime, stone (crushed), clays (common), sand and gravel (industrial). **Gross state product** (2005): $24.2 bil. **Sales tax** (2006): 5.0%. **Employment distrib.** (May 2006): 22.0% govt; 21.5% trade/trans./util.; 7.3% mfg; 13.9% ed./health; 7.7% prof./bus. serv.; 9.2% leisure/hosp.; 5.4% finance; 5.4% constr.; 4.3% other serv.; 2.1% info. **Unemployment** (2005): 3.4%. **Per cap. pers. income** (2005): $31,395. **New private housing** (2005): 4,038 units/$458 mil. **Commercial banks** (2005): 105; **deposits:** $11.5 bil. **Savings institutions** (2005): 2; **deposits:** $706 mil. **Lottery** (2005): total sales: $19.2 mil; profit: $6.5 mil.

Federal govt. Fed. civ. employees (Mar. 2005): 5,573; **avg. salary:** $52,416. **Notable fed. facilities:** Strategic Air Command Base; Northern Prairie Wildlife Res. Ctr.; Garrison Dam; Theodore Roosevelt Natl. Park; Grand Forks Energy Res. Ctr.; Ft. Union Natl. Historic Site.

Energy. Electricity production (est. 2005, kWh by source): Coal: 28.8 bil; Hydroelectric: 1.3 bil; Petroleum: 34 mil; Other: 4 mil.

State data. Motto: Liberty and union, now and forever, one and inseparable. **Flower:** Wild prairie rose. **Bird:** Western meadowlark. **Tree:** American elm. **Song:** North Dakota Hymn. **Entered union** Nov. 2, 1889; rank, 39th. **State fair** at Minot; July.

History. Paleoindian peoples hunted in the area at least 11,000 years ago. At the time of European contact, the Ojibwa, Yanktonai and Teton Sioux, Mandan, Arikara, and Hidatsa peoples lived in the region. Pierre de Varennes, sieur de La Vérendrye, was the first French fur trader in the area, 1738, followed by the English at the end of the 18th cent. Lewis and Clark built Ft. Mandan, near present-day Washburn, 1804-5, and wintered there. The first permanent settlement was at Pembina, 1812. Missouri River steamboats reached the area, 1832. Dakota Territory was organized, 1861. The first railroad arrived, 1872. The "bonanza farm" craze of the 1870s-80s led to statehood, 1889. The Nonpartisan League, a farmers' group favoring state ownership of industries, helped elect Lynn Frazier as governor, 1916, but he and others were ousted in a recall vote, 1921. The predominantly agricultural state had a 6.5% drop in population, 1930-2005.

Tourist attractions. North Dakota Heritage Center, Bismarck; Bonanzaville, Fargo; Ft. Union Trading Post Natl. Historic Site; Lake Sakakawea; Intl. Peace Garden; Theodore Roosevelt Natl. Park, including Elkhorn Ranch, Badlands; Ft. Abraham Lincoln State Park and Museum, near Mandan; Dakota Dinosaur Museum, Dickinson; Knife River Indian Villages-National Historic Site.

Famous North Dakotans. Maxwell Anderson, Angie Dickinson, John Bernard Flannagan, Phil Jackson, Louis L'Amour, Peggy Lee, Eric Sevareid, Ann Sothern, Vilhjalmur Stefansson, Lawrence Welk.

Tourist Information. North Dakota Tourism Division, Century Center, 1600 E. Century Ave., Ste 2, PO Box 2057, Bismarck, ND 58503; 1-800-435-5663. **Website:** www.ndtourism.com
Website. www.discovernd.com

Ohio (OH)
Buckeye State

People. Population (2005 est.): 11,464,042; rank: 7; **net change** (2004-2005): 0.1%. **Pop. density:** 280.0 per sq mi. Racial distribution (2004): 85.2% white; 11.9% black; 1.4% Asian; 0.2% Native/Nat.AK; 0.03% Hawaiian/Pacific Islander; 2 or more races, 1.2%. **Hispanic pop.** (any race): 2.2%.

Geography. Total area: 44,825 sq mi; rank: 34. **Land area:** 40,948 sq mi; rank: 35. **Acres forested:** 7.9 mil. **Location:** East North Central state bounded on the N by Michigan and Lake Erie; on the E and S by Pennsylvania, West Virginia, and Kentucky; on the W by Indiana. **Climate:** temperate but variable; weather subject to much precipitation. **Topography:** generally rolling plain; Allegheny plateau in E; Lake Erie plains extend southward; central plains in the W. **Capital:** Columbus. **Principal internat. airports at:** Akron, Cincinnati, Cleveland, Columbus, Dayton.

Economy. Chief industries: manufacturing, trade, services. **Chief manuf. goods:** transportation equipment, machinery, primary and fabricated metal products. **Chief crops:** corn, hay, winter wheat, oats, soybeans. **Livestock:** (Jan. 2006): 1.3 mil cattle/calves, 141,000 sheep/lambs; (Dec. 2005): 1.6 mil hogs/pigs, 36.4 mil chickens (excl. broilers), 43.1 mil broilers. **Timber/lumber** (est. 2004): 379 mil bd. ft.; oak, ash, maple, walnut, beech. **Nonfuel minerals** (est. 2005): $1.1 bil; stone (crushed), sand and gravel (construction), salt, lime, cement (portland). **Commercial fishing** (2004): $2.9 mil. **Chief ports:** Toledo, Conneaut, Cleveland, Ashtabula. **Gross state product** (2005): $442.4 bil. **Sales tax** (2006): 5.5%. **Employment distrib.** (May 2006): 14.9% govt; 18.9% trade/trans./util.; 14.7% mfg; 14.1% ed./health; 11.9% prof./bus. serv.; 9.6% leisure/hosp.; 5.7% finance; 4.4% constr.; 4.1% other serv.; 1.6% info. **Unemployment** (2005): 5.9%. **Per cap. pers. income** (2005): $32,478. **New private housing** (2005): 47,727 units/$7.9 bil. **Commercial banks** (2005): 191; **deposits:** $174.5 bil. **Savings institutions** (2005): 107; **deposits:** $26.7 bil. **Lottery** (2005): total sales: $2.2 bil; profit: $645.1 mil.

Federal govt. Fed. civ. employees (Mar. 2005): 41,648; **avg. salary:** $65,254. **Notable fed. facilities:** Wright Patterson AFB; Defense Supply Ctr., Columbus; *NASA John H. Glenn Res. Ctr.; Portsmouth Gaseous Diffusion Plant; Lima Army Tank Plant.

Energy. Electricity production (est. 2005, kWh by source): Coal: 131.8 bil; Gas: 820 mil; Hydroelectric: 769 mil; Nuclear: 15.5 bil; Petroleum: 308 mil.

State data. Motto: With God, all things are possible. **Flower:** Scarlet carnation. **Bird:** Cardinal. **Tree:** Buckeye. **Song:** Beautiful Ohio. **Entered union** Mar. 1, 1803; rank, 17th. **State fair** at Columbus; Aug.

History. Paleoindians hunted in the area about 11,000 years ago; the Adena and Hopewell cultures followed. Wyandot, Delaware, Miami, and Shawnee peoples sparsely occupied the area when the first Europeans arrived. La Salle visited the region, 1669. France claimed it, 1682, but ceded it to Britain, 1763. After the American Revolution, Ohio became part of the Northwest Territory, 1787. The first permanent settlement was at Marietta, 1788. Cincinnati was also founded, 1788; Cleveland, 1796. Indian warfare abated with the Treaty of Greenville, 1795. Ohio became a state, 1803. In the War of 1812, Oliver Hazard Perry's victory on Lake Erie and William Henry Harrison's invasion of Canada, 1813, ended British incursions. Columbus, founded 1812, became the state capital, 1816. Before the Civil War, Ohioans aided the Underground Railroad, helping runaway slaves. Agricultural for much of the 19th cent., the state became an industrial powerhouse in the 20th. Manufacturing jobs dropped by 21%, 1998-2006. No Republican has ever won the presidency without carrying Ohio, and the state's 20 electoral votes proved crucial to Pres. George W. Bush in 2004.

Tourist attractions. Mound City Group, a group of 24 prehistoric Indian burial mounds in Hopewell Culture Natl. Historical Park; Neil Armstrong Air and Space Museum, Wapakoneta; Air Force Museum, Dayton; Pro Football Hall of Fame, Canton; King's Island amusement park, Mason; Lake Erie Islands, Cedar Point amusement park, both Sandusky; birthplaces, homes of, and memorials to U.S. Pres. W. H. Harrison, Grant, Garfield, Hayes, McKinley, Harding, Taft, B. Harrison; Amish Region, Tuscarawas/Holmes counties; German Village, Columbus; Jack Nicklaus Sports Center, Mason; Bob Evans Farm, Rio Grande; Rock and Roll Hall of Fame and Museum, Cleveland.

Famous Ohioans. Sherwood Anderson, Neil Armstrong, George Bellows, Halle Berry, Ambrose Bierce, Erma Bombeck, Drew Carey, Hart Crane, George Custer, Clarence Darrow, Paul Laurence Dunbar, Thomas Edison, Clark Gable, John Glenn, Zane Grey, Bob Hope, William Dean Howells, Toni Morrison, Jack Nicklaus, Jesse Owens, Jack Paar, Pontiac, Eddie Rickenbacker, John D. Rockefeller Sr. and Jr., Roy Rogers, Pete Rose, Arthur Schlesinger Jr., Gen. William Sherman, Steven Spielberg, Gloria Steinem, Harriet Beecher Stowe, Charles Taft, Robert A. Taft, William H. Taft, Tecumseh, James Thurber, Ted Turner, Orville and Wilbur Wright.

Tourist Information. Division of Travel and Tourism, 77 S. High St., PO Box 1001, Columbus, OH 43216; 1-800-BUCK-EYE. **Website:** www.discoverohio.com
Website. www.ohio.gov

Oklahoma (OK)
Sooner State

People. Population (2005 est.): 3,547,884; rank: 28; **net change** (2004-2005): 0.7%. **Pop. density:** 51.7 per sq mi. Racial distribution (2004): 78.6% white; 7.7% black; 1.5% Asian; 8.1% Native/Nat.AK; 0.08% Hawaiian/Pacific Islander; 2 or more races, 4.0%. **Hispanic pop.** (any race): 6.3%.
Geography. Total area: 69,898 sq mi; rank: 20. **Land area:** 68,667 sq mi; rank: 19. **Acres forested:** 7.7 mil. **Location:** West South Central state bounded on the N by Colorado and Kansas; on the E by Missouri and Arkansas; on the S and W by Texas and New Mexico. **Climate:** temperate; southern humid belt merging with colder northern continental; humid eastern and dry western zones. **Topography:** high plains predominate in the W, hills and small mountains in the E; the east central region is dominated by the Arkansas R. Basin, and the Red R. Plains, in the S. **Capital:** Oklahoma City. **Principal internat. airports at:** Oklahoma City, Tulsa.
Economy. Chief industries: manufacturing, mineral and energy exploration and production, agriculture, services. **Chief manuf. goods:** nonelectrical machinery, transportation equipment, food products, fabricated metal products. **Chief crops:** wheat, cotton, hay, peanuts, grain sorghum, soybeans, corn, pecans. **Livestock:** (Jan. 2006): 5.5 mil cattle/calves, 80,000 sheep/lambs; (Dec. 2005): 2.4 mil hogs/pigs, 4.6 mil chickens (excl. broilers), 249.9 mil broilers. **Timber/lumber** (2004 est.): 355 mil bd. ft.; pine, oak, hickory. **Nonfuel minerals** (est. 2005): $555 mil; stone (crushed), cement (portland), sand and gravel (construction), sand and gravel (industrial), iodine (crude). **Chief ports:** Catoosa, Muskogee. **Gross state product** (2005): $120.5 bil. **Sales tax** (2006): 4.5%. **Employment distrib.** (May 2006): 20.9% govt; 18.3% trade/trans./util.; 9.5% mfg; 12.0% ed./health; 11.3% prof./bus. serv.; 8.9% leisure/hosp.; 5.4% finance; 4.5% constr.; 4.8% other serv.; 1.9% info. **Unemployment** (2005): 4.4%. **Per cap. pers. income** (2005): $29,330. **New private housing** (2005): 18,362 units/$2.5 bil. **Commercial banks** (2005): 278; **deposits**: $44.5 bil. **Savings institutions** (2005): 9; **deposits**: $3.9 bil.
Federal govt. Fed. civ. employees (Mar. 2005): 33,733; **avg. salary**: $54,950. **Notable fed. facilities:** FAA Mike Monroney Aeronautical Ctr.; *Altus AFB; Tinker AFB; Vance AFB; Ft. Sill; Natl. Inst. for Petroleum & Energy Res.; Natl. Severe Storms Lab.
Energy. Electricity production (est. 2005, kWh by source): Coal: 33.6 bil; Gas: 18.4 bil; Hydroelectric: 2.7 bil; Petroleum: 13 mil.
State data. Motto: Labor Omnia Vincit (Labor conquers all things). **Flower:** Mistletoe. **Bird:** Scissor-tailed flycatcher. **Tree:** Redbud. **Song:** Oklahoma! **Entered union** Nov. 16, 1907; rank, 46th. **State fair** at Oklahoma City; last 2 full weeks of Sept.
History. Few Native Americans inhabited the region when the Spanish explorer Coronado arrived, 1541; in the 16th and 17th cent., French traders visited. Part of the Louisiana Purchase, 1803, Oklahoma was known as Indian Country and, from 1834, Indian Territory. It became home to the "Five Civilized Tribes"—Cherokee, Choctaw, Chickasaw, Creek, and Seminole—after the forced removal of Indians from the eastern U.S., 1828-46. The land was also used by Comanche, Osage, and other Plains Indians. As white settlers pressed west, land was opened for homesteading by "runs" and lottery. The first run was in 1889; the most famous run, 1893, was to the Cherokee Outlet. Oklahoma became a state, 1907. In the early 20th cent., oil finds brought wealth to the Tulsa area; the Greenwood section of the city, then known as the "Negro Wall Street," was devastated by a white mob, 1921. Depression and drought drove many "Okies" from the Dust Bowl to California in the 1930s. A truck bomb in Oklahoma City, 1995, destroyed a federal office building, killing 168 people; Timothy McVeigh was executed for the crime, 2001.
Tourist attractions. Cherokee Heritage Center, Tahlequah; Oklahoma City Natl. Memorial; White Water Bay and Frontier City theme pks., both Oklahoma City; Will Rogers Memorial, Claremore; Natl. Cowboy Hall of Fame and Remington Park Race Track, both Oklahoma City; Ft. Gibson Stockade, near Muskogee; Ouachita Natl. Forest; Tulsa's art deco district; Wichita Mts. Wildlife Refuge, Lawton; Woolaroc Museum & Wildlife Preserve, Bartlesville; Sequoyah's Home Site, near Sallisaw; Philbrook Museum of Art and Gilcrease Museum, both Tulsa.
Famous Oklahomans. Troy Aikman, Carl Albert, Gene Autry, Johnny Bench, William "Hopalong Cassidy" Boyd, Garth Brooks, Lon Chaney, L. Gordon Cooper, Walter Cronkite, Jerome "Dizzy" Dean, Ralph Ellison, John Hope Franklin, James Garner, Geronimo, Woody Guthrie, Paul Harvey, Ron Howard, Gen. Patrick J. Hurley, Ben Johnson, Jeane Kirkpatrick, Louis L'Amour, Shannon Lucid, Mickey Mantle, Reba McEntire, Wiley Post, Tony Randall, Oral Roberts, Will Rogers, Sam Snead, Barry Switzer, Maria Tallchief, Jim Thorpe, J.C. Watts Jr.
Tourist Information. Travel and Tourism Division, 120 N. Robinson, 6th fl., PO Box 52002, Oklahoma City, OK 73152-2002; 1-800-652-6552. **Website:** www.travelok.com
Website. www.ok.gov

Oregon (OR)
Beaver State

People. Population (2005 est.): 3,641,056; rank: 27; **net change** (2004-2005): 1.4%. **Pop. density:** 37.9 per sq mi. Racial distribution (2004): 90.9% white; 1.8% black; 3.4% Asian; 1.4% Native/Nat.AK; 0.3% Hawaiian/Pacific Islander; 2 or more races, 2.3%. **Hispanic pop.** (any race): 9.5%.
Geography. Total area: 98,381 sq mi; rank: 9. **Land area:** 95,997 sq mi; rank: 10. **Acres forested:** 29.7 mil. **Location:** Pacific state, bounded on N by Washington; on E by Idaho; on S by Nevada and California; on W by the Pacific. **Climate:** coastal mild and humid climate; continental dryness and extreme temperatures in the interior. **Topography:** Coast Range of rugged mountains; fertile Willamette R. Valley to E and S; Cascade Mt. Range of volcanic peaks E of the valley; plateau E of Cascades, remaining two-thirds of state. **Capital:** Salem. **Principal internat. airports at:** Portland, Medford.
Economy. Chief industries: manufacturing, services, trade, finance, insurance, real estate, government, construction. **Chief manuf. goods:** electronics & semiconductors, lumber & wood products, metals, transportation equipment, processed food, paper. **Chief crops:** greenhouse, hay, wheat, grass seed, potatoes, onions, Christmas trees, pears, mint. **Livestock:** (Jan. 2006): 1.4 mil cattle/calves, 220,000 sheep/lambs; (Dec. 2005): 23,000 hogs/pigs, 3.8 mil chickens (excl. broilers), 147.3 mil broilers. **Timber/lumber** (est. 2004): 7.1 bil bd. ft.; Douglas fir, hemlock, ponderosa pine. **Nonfuel minerals** (est. 2005): $398 mil; sand and gravel (construction), stone (crushed), cement (portland), diatomite, lime. **Commercial fishing** (2004): $101.1 mil. **Chief ports:** Portland, Astoria, Coos Bay. **Gross state product** (2005): $145.4 bil. **Sales tax** (2006): none. **Employment distrib.** (May 2006): 17.2% govt; 19.5% trade/trans./util.; 12.2% mfg; 12.2% ed./health; 11.2% prof./bus. serv.; 9.7% leisure/hosp.; 6.2% finance; 5.8% constr.; 3.5% other serv.; 2.0% info. **Unemployment** (2005): 6.1%. **Per cap. pers. income** (2005): $32,103. **New private housing** (2005): 31,024 units/$5.5 bil. **Commercial banks** (2005): 49; **deposits**: $33.8 bil. **Savings institutions** (2005): 8; **deposits**: $8.4 bil. **Lottery** (2005): total sales: $943.1 mil; profit: $415.5 mil.
Federal govt. Fed. civ. employees (Mar. 2005): 18,297; **avg. salary**: $58,552. **Notable fed. facilities:** Bonneville Power Administration.
Energy. Electricity production (est. 2005, kWh by source): Coal: 3.5 bil; Gas: 3.1 bil; Hydroelectric: 31.0 bil; Petroleum: 47 mil.
State data. Motto: She flies with her own wings. **Flower:** Oregon grape. **Bird:** Western meadowlark. **Tree:** Douglas fir. **Song:** Oregon, My Oregon. **Entered union** Feb. 14, 1859; rank, 33rd. **State fair** at Salem; 12 days ending with Labor Day.
History. More than 100 Native American tribes inhabited the area at the time of European contact, including the Chinook, Yakima, Cayuse, Modoc, and Nez Percé. Capt. Robert Gray sighted and sailed into the Columbia River, 1792. Lewis and Clark, traveling overland, wintered at its mouth, 1805-6. Fur traders sent by John Jacob Astor established the Astoria trading post in the Columbia River region, 1811. Settlers arrived in the Williamette Valley, 1834. In 1843, the first large wave of settlers arrived via the Oregon Trail. Oregon became a territory, 1848, and a state, 1859. Early in the 20th cent., the "Oregon System"—political reforms that included initiative, referendum, recall, direct primary, and woman suffrage—was

adopted. Originally dominated by forest products, the economy diversified after World War II, with high-tech firms clustering in the "Silicon Forest" area around Portland. Oregonians were the first in the U.S. to pass measures allowing physician-assisted suicide for terminally ill patients, 1994, and establishing an all-mail voting system, 1998.

Tourist attractions. John Day Fossil Beds Natl. Monument; Columbia River Gorge; Timberline Lodge, Mt. Hood Natl. Forest; Crater Lake Natl. Park; Oregon Dunes Natl. Recreation Area; Ft. Clatsop Natl. Memorial; Oregon Caves Natl. Monument; Oregon Museum of Science and Industry, Portland; Shakespearean Festival, Ashland; High Desert Museum, Bend; Multnomah Falls; Diamond Lake; "Spruce Goose," Evergreen Aviation Museum, McMinnville.

Famous Oregonians. Ernest Bloch, Bill Bowerman, Ernest Haycox, Chief Joseph, Ken Kesey, Phil Knight, Ursula K. Le Guin, Edwin Markham, Tom McCall, Dr. John McLoughlin, Joaquin Miller, Bob Packwood, Linus Pauling, Steve Prefontaine, John Reed, Alberto Salazar, Mary Decker Slaney, William Simon U'Ren.

Tourist information. Oregon Tourism Commission, 670 Hawthorne SE, Ste. 240, Salem, OR 97301; 1-800-547-7842. **Website:** www.traveloregon.com

Website. www.oregon.gov

Pennsylvania (PA)
Keystone State

People. Population (2005 est.): 12,429,616; rank: 6; **net change** (2004-2005): 0.3%. **Pop. density:** 277.3 per sq mi. Racial distribution (2004): 86.2% white; 10.5% black; 2.2% Asian; 0.2% Native/Nat.AK; 0.04% Hawaiian/Pacific Islander; 2 or more races, 0.9%. **Hispanic pop.** (any race): 3.8%.

Geography. Total area: 46,055 sq mi; rank: 33. **Land area:** 44,817 sq mi; rank: 32. **Acres forested:** 16.9 mil. **Location:** Middle Atlantic state, bordered on the E by the Delaware R.; on the S by the Mason-Dixon Line; on the W by West Virginia and Ohio; on the N/NE by Lake Erie and New York. **Climate:** continental with wide fluctuations in seasonal temperatures. **Topography:** Allegheny Mts. run SW to NE, with Piedmont and Coast Plain in the SE triangle; Allegheny Front a diagonal spine across the state's center; N and W rugged plateau falls to Lake Erie Lowland. **Capital:** Harrisburg. **Principal internat. airports at:** Allentown, Harrisburg, Philadelphia, Pittsburgh, Wilkes-Barre/Scranton. **Principal internat. airports at:** Allentown, Harrisburg, Philadelphia, Pittsburgh, Wilkes-Barre/Scranton.

Economy. Chief industries: agribusiness, advanced manufacturing, health care, travel & tourism, depository institutions, biotechnology, printing & publishing, research & consulting, trucking & warehousing, transportation by air, engineering & management, legal services. **Chief manuf. goods:** fabricated metal products; industrial machinery & equipment, transportation equipment, rubber & plastics, electronic equipment, chemicals & pharmaceuticals, lumber & wood products, stone, clay, & glass products. **Chief crops:** corn, hay, mushrooms, apples, potatoes, winter wheat, oats, vegetables, tobacco, grapes, peaches. **Livestock:** (Jan. 2006): 1.6 mil cattle/calves, 110,000 sheep/lambs; (Dec. 2005): 1.1 mil hogs/pigs, 28.9 mil chickens (excl. broilers). **Timber/lumber** (est. 2004): 1.1 bil bd. ft.; pine, oak, maple. **Nonfuel minerals** (est. 2005): $1.4 bil; stone (crushed), cement (portland), sand and gravel (construction), lime, cement (masonry). **Commercial fishing** (2004): $65,000. **Chief ports:** Philadelphia, Pittsburgh, Erie. **Gross state product** (2005): $487.2 bil. **Sales tax** (2006): 6.0%. **Employment distrib.** (May 2006): 13.2% govt; 19.5% trade/trans./util.; 11.6% mfg; 18.2% ed./health; 11.6% prof./bus. serv.; 8.7% leisure/hosp.; 5.8% finance; 4.5% constr.; 4.6% other serv.; 1.9% info. **Unemployment** (2005): 5.0%. **Per cap. pers. income** (2005): $34,897. **New private housing** (2005): 44,525 units/$6.8 bil. **Commercial banks** (2005): 186; **deposits:** $161.5 bil. **Savings institutions** (2005): 97; **deposits:** $63.7 bil. **Lottery** (2005): total sales: $2.6 bil; profit: $852.6 mil.

Federal govt. Fed. civ. employees (Mar. 2005): 62,843; **avg. salary:** $57,161. **Notable fed. facilities:** Carlisle Barracks; Army War College; Naval Inventory Control Point, Phila. and Mechanicsbrg; Defense Personnel Support Ctr., Phila.; Defense Distribution Ctr., New Cumberland; Tobyhanna Army Depot; Letterkenny Army Depot; *NAS Willow Grove; 911th Air Wing, Pittsburgh; Naval Surface Warfare Ctr., Phila.; *Charles E. Kelly Support Facility.

Energy. Electricity production (est. 2005, kWh by source): Coal: 18.3 bil; Gas: 42 mil; Hydroelectric: 1.2 bil; Nuclear: 14.0 bil; Petroleum: 30 mil.

State data. Motto: Virtue, liberty and independence. **Flower:** Mountain laurel. **Bird:** Ruffed grouse. **Tree:** Hemlock. **Song:** Pennsylvania. **Second** of the original 13 states to ratify the Constitution, Dec. 12, 1787. **State fair** at Harrisburg; 2nd week in Jan. at State Farm Show Complex.

History. When Europeans came, Algonquian-speaking Lenni Lenape (Delaware) and Shawnee and the Iroquoian Susquehannocks, Erie, and Seneca occupied the region. Swedish explorers made the first permanent settlement, 1643, on Tinicum Island. The Dutch seized the settlement, 1655, but lost it to the British, 1664. The region was given by Charles II to William Penn, 1681. Philadelphia ("brotherly love") was the capital of the colonies during most of the American Revolution, and of the U.S., 1790-1800; the Declaration of Independence, 1776, and Constitution, 1787, were signed here. Philadelphia was taken by the British, 1777; Washington's troops encamped at Valley Forge in the bitter winter of 1777-78. Slavery was abolished, 1780. Union victory at the Battle of Gettysburg, July 1-3, 1863, marked a turning point in the Civil War. A dam collapse at Johnstown, 1889, killed at least 2,200 people. From the late 19th cent. to the mid-20th, Pittsburgh prospered from coal and steel; later, heavy industry declined, but the city revived as a hub of finance, health care, and research. The Three Mile Island nuclear plant near Harrisburg had a near-meltdown, 1979. One of 4 hijacked planes on Sept. 11, 2001, crashed near Shanksville; a national memorial was designated on the site in 2002.

Tourist attractions. Independence Natl. Historic Park; Franklin Institute Science Museum, Philadelphia Museum of Art, all in Philadelphia; Valley Forge Natl. Historic Park; Gettysburg Natl. Military Park; Pennsylvania Dutch Country; Hershey; Duquesne Incline, Carnegie Institute, Heinz Hall, all in Pittsburgh; Pocono Mts.; Pennsylvania's Grand Canyon, Tioga County; Allegheny Natl. Forest; Laurel Highlands; Presque Isle State Park; Fallingwater, Mill Run; Johnstown; SteamTown U.S.A., Scranton; State Flagship Niagara, Erie; Oil Heritage Region, Northwest PA.

Famous Pennsylvanians. Marian Anderson, Maxwell Anderson, George Blanda, James Buchanan, Andrew Carnegie, Rachel Carson, Perry Como, Bill Cosby, Thomas Eakins, Stephen Foster, Benjamin Franklin, Robert Fulton, Martha Graham, Milton Hershey, Gene Kelly, Grace Kelly (Princess Grace of Monaco), Dan Marino, George C. Marshall, Chris Matthews, John J. McCloy, Margaret Mead, Andrew W. Mellon, Joe Montana, Stan Musial, Joe Namath, John O'Hara, Arnold Palmer, Robert E. Peary, Mike Piazza, Tom Ridge, Mary Roberts Rinehart, Fred Rogers, Betsy Ross, Will Smith, Jimmy Stewart, Jim Thorpe, Johnny Unitas, John Updike, Honus Wagner, Andy Warhol, Benjamin West.

Tourist Information. Department of Community and Economic Development, Office of Tourism, 400 North St.,4th Fl., Harrisburg, PA 17120-0225; 1-800-VISITPA. **Website:** www.visitpa.com

Website. www.state.pa.us

Rhode Island (RI)
Little Rhody, Ocean State

People. Population (2005 est.): 1,076,189; rank: 43; **net change** (2004-2005): -0.3%. **Pop. density:** 1,029.9 per sq mi. Racial distribution (2004): 89.1% white; 6.1% black; 2.7% Asian; 0.6% Native/Nat.AK; 0.1% Hawaiian/Pacific Islander; 2 or more races, 1.5%. **Hispanic pop.** (any race): 10.3%.

Geography. Total area: 1,545 sq mi; rank: 50. **Land area:** 1,045 sq mi; rank: 50. **Acres forested:** 0.4 mil. **Location:** New England state. **Climate:** invigorating and changeable. **Topography:** eastern lowlands of Narragansett Basin; western uplands of flat and rolling hills. **Capital:** Providence.

Economy. Chief industries: services, manufacturing. **Chief manuf. goods:** costume jewelry, toys, machinery, textiles, electronics. **Chief crops:** nursery products, turf & vegetable production. **Livestock:** (Jan. 2006): 5,000 cattle/calves; (Dec. 2005): 1,800 hogs/pigs. **Timber/lumber** (est. 2004): 6 mil bd. ft. **Nonfuel minerals** (est. 2005): $37 mil; sand and gravel (construction), stone (crushed), sand and gravel (industrial), gemstones. **Commercial fishing** (2004): $71.1 mil. **Chief ports:** Providence, Quonset Point, Newport. **Gross state product** (2005): $43.8 bil. **Sales tax** (2006): 7.0%. **Employment distrib.** (May 2006): 13.3% govt; 16.0% trade/trans./util.; 10.7% mfg; 19.6% ed./health; 11.5% prof./bus.

serv.; 10.3% leisure/hosp.; 7.2% finance; 4.7% constr.; 4.5% other serv.; 2.1% info. **Unemployment** (2005): 5.0%. **Per cap. pers. income** (2005): $36,153. **New private housing** (2005): 2,836 units/$384 mil. **Commercial banks** (2005): 11; **deposits:** $18.1 bil. **Savings institutions** (2005): 14; **deposits:** $3.7 bil. **Lottery** (2005): total sales: $1.6 bil; profit: $313.5 mil.

Federal govt. Fed. civ. employees (Mar. 2005): 5,953; **avg. salary:** $70,454. **Notable fed. facilities:** Naval War College; Naval Underwater Warfare Ctr.; Natl. Marine Fisheries Lab; EPA Environmental Res. Lab.

Energy. Electricity production (est. 2005, kWh, by source): Petroleum: 12 mil.

State data. Motto: Hope. **Flower:** Violet. **Bird:** Rhode Island red. **Tree:** Red maple. **Song:** Rhode Island. **Thirteenth** of original 13 states to ratify the Constitution, May 29, 1790. **State fair** at Richmond; mid-Aug.

History. When Europeans arrived, Narragansett, Niantic, Nipmuc, and Wampanoag peoples lived in the region. Verrazano visited the area, 1524. The first permanent settlement was founded at Providence, 1636, by Roger Williams, who was exiled from the Massachusetts Bay Colony; Anne Hutchinson, also exiled, settled Portsmouth, 1638. Quaker and Jewish immigrants seeking freedom of worship began arriving, 1650s-60s. The colonists broke the power of the Narragansett in the Great Swamp Fight, 1675, the decisive battle in King Philip's War. The colony was the first to formally renounce all allegiance to King George III, May 4, 1776. Initially opposed to joining the Union, Rhode Island was the last of the 13 colonies to ratify the Constitution, 1790. Trade, textiles, and metal goods dominated the economy in the 19th cent., and Newport became a fashionable resort after the Civil War. Immigration from Ireland, Italy, Portugal, French Canada, and most recently Latin America have given Rhode Island the highest proportion of Roman Catholics of any state, 64% in 2006.

Tourist attractions. Newport mansions; yachting races including Newport to Bermuda; Block Island; Touro Synagogue, oldest in U.S.; first Baptist Church in America, Providence; Slater Mill Historic Site, Pawtucket; Gilbert Stuart birthplace, Saunderstown.

Famous Rhode Islanders. Ambrose Burnside, George M. Cohan, Nelson Eddy, Jabez Gorham, Nathanael Greene, Christopher and Oliver La Farge, John McLaughlin, Matthew C. and Oliver Hazard Perry, Gilbert Stuart.

Tourist Information. Rhode Island Tourism Division, 1 W. Exchange St., Providence, RI 02903; 1-800-556-2484. **Website:** www.visitrhodeisland.com
Website. www.state.ri.us

South Carolina (SC)
Palmetto State

People. Population (2005 est.): 4,255,083; rank: 25; **net change** (2004-2005): 1.4%. **Pop. density:** 141.3 per sq mi. Racial distribution (2004): 68.3% white; 29.4% black; 1.1% Asian; 0.4% Native/Nat.AK; 0.05% Hawaiian/Pacific Islander; 2 or more races, 0.8%. **Hispanic pop.** (any race): 3.1%.

Geography. Total area: 32,020 sq mi; rank: 40. **Land area:** 30,109 sq mi; rank: 40. **Acres forested:** 12.5 mil. **Location:** South Atlantic state, bordered by North Carolina on the N; Georgia on the SW and W; the Atlantic Ocean on the E, SE, and S. **Climate:** humid subtropical. **Topography:** Blue Ridge province in NW has highest peaks; piedmont lies between the mountains and the fall line; coastal plain covers two-thirds of the state. **Capital:** Columbia. **Principal internat. airports at:** Charleston, Greenville/Spartanburg, Myrtle Beach.

Economy. Chief industries: tourism, agriculture, manufacturing. **Chief manuf. goods:** textiles, chemicals and allied products, machinery and fabricated metal products, apparel and related products. **Chief crops:** tobacco, cotton, soybeans, corn, wheat, peaches, tomatoes. **Livestock:** (Jan. 2006): 415,000 cattle/calves; (Dec. 2005): 315,000 hogs/pigs, 6.5 mil chickens (excl. broilers), 213.3 mil broilers. **Timber/lumber** (est. 2004): 1.6 bil bd. ft.; pine, oak. **Nonfuel minerals** (est. 2005): $580 mil; cement (portland), stone (crushed), cement (masonry), sand and gravel (construction), clays (kaolin). **Commercial fishing** (2004): $18.5 mil. **Chief ports:** Charleston, Georgetown, Royal. **Gross state product** (2005): $139.8 bil. **Sales tax** (2005): 5.0%. **Employment distrib.** (May 2006): 17.7% govt; 19.3% trade/trans./util.; 13.5% mfg; 10.0% ed./health; 10.9% prof./bus. serv.; 11.0% leisure/

hosp.; 5.3% finance; 6.5% constr.; 4.1% other serv.; 1.5% info. **Unemployment** (2005): 6.8%. **Per cap. pers. income** (2005): $28,352. **New private housing** (2005): 54,157 units/$7.8 bil. **Commercial banks** (2005): 83; **deposits:** $48.6 bil. **Savings institutions** (2005): 23; **deposits:** $5.2 bil. **Lottery** (2005): total sales: $957 mil; profit: $277.5 mil.

Federal govt. Fed. civ. employees (Mar. 2005): 16,727; **avg. salary:** $55,766. **Notable fed. facilities:** Polaris Submarine Base; Barnwell Nuclear Power Plant; Ft. Jackson; Parris Island; Savannah River Plant.

Energy. Electricity production (est. 2005, kWh by source): Coal: 39.3 bil; Gas: 4.2 bil; Hydroelectric: 2.7 bil; Nuclear: 53.1 bil; Petroleum: 224 mil.

State data. Motto: Dum Spiro Spero (While I breathe, I hope). **Flower:** Yellow jessamine. **Bird:** Carolina wren. **Tree:** Palmetto. **Song:** Carolina. **Eighth** of the original 13 states to ratify the Constitution, May 23, 1788. **State fair** at Columbia; mid-Oct.

History. When Europeans arrived, Cherokee, Catawba, and Muskogean peoples lived in the area. Spanish and French came in the 16th cent. The first English colonists settled near the Ashley River, 1670, and moved to the site of present-day Charleston, 1680. The colonists seized the government, 1775, and the royal governor fled. The British took Charleston, 1780, but were defeated at Kings Mountain that same year, and at Cowpens, 1781. In the 1830s, South Carolinians, angered by federal protective tariffs, adopted the Nullification Doctrine, holding that a state can void an act of Congress. Plantation agriculture relied on slave labor to cultivate rice and cotton; slaves made up 57% of the population in 1860, when South Carolina was the first state to secede from the Union. Confederate troops fired on and forced the surrender of U.S. troops at Ft. Sumter, in Charleston Harbor, 1861, launching the Civil War. The state was readmitted to the Union,1868. Formerly dependent on textiles, the state has attracted new industries by courting foreign investment. Strom Thurmond, who ran for president as a segregationist in 1948, later served 48 years in the U.S. Senate (1955-2003).

Tourist attractions. Historic Charleston; Ft. Sumter Natl. Monument, in Charleston Harbor; Charleston Museum, est. 1773, oldest museum in U.S.; Middleton Place, Magnolia Plantation, Cypress Gardens, Drayton Hall, all near Charleston; other gardens at Brookgreen, Edisto, Glencairn; Myrtle Beach; Hilton Head Island; Revolutionary War battle sites; Andrew Jackson State Park & Museum; South Carolina State Museum, Columbia; Riverbanks Zoo, Columbia.

Famous South Carolinians. Charles Bolden, James F. Byrnes, John C. Calhoun, Joe Fraizer, DuBose Heyward, Ernest F. Hollings, Andrew Jackson, Jesse Jackson, "Shoeless" Joe Jackson, James Longstreet, Francis Marion, Andie McDowell, Ronald McNair, Charles Pinckney, John Rutledge, Thomas Sumter, Strom Thurmond, John B. Watson.

Tourist information. SC Dept. of Parks, Recreation, & Tourism, 1205 Pendleton St., Columbia, SC 29201; 803-734-0122; 1-800-346-3634. **Website:** www.discoversouthcarolina.com
Website. www.sc.gov

South Dakota (SD)
Coyote State, Mount Rushmore State

People. Population (2005 est.): 775,933; rank: 46; **net change** (2004-2005): 0.7%. **Pop. density:** 10.2 per sq mi. Racial distribution (2004): 88.7% white; 0.8% black; 0.7% Asian; 8.6% Native/Nat.AK; 0.04% Hawaiian/Pacific Islander; 2 or more races, 1.2%. **Hispanic pop.** (any race): 2.0%.

Geography. Total area: 77,116 sq mi; rank: 17. **Land area:** 75,885 sq mi; rank: 16. **Acres forested:** 1.6 mil. **Location:** West North Central state bounded on the N by North Dakota; on the E by Minnesota and Iowa; on the S by Nebraska; on the W by Wyoming and Montana. **Climate:** characterized by extremes of temperature, persistent winds, low precipitation and humidity. **Topography:** Prairie Plains in the E; rolling hills of the Great Plains in the W; the Black Hills, rising 3,500 ft, in the SW corner. **Capital:** Pierre.

Economy. Chief industries: agriculture, services, manufacturing. **Chief manuf. goods:** food and kindred products, machinery, electric and electronic equipment. **Chief crops:** corn, soybeans, oats, wheat, sunflowers, sorghum. **Livestock:** (Jan. 2006): 3.8 mil cattle/calves, 385,000 sheep/lambs; (Dec. 2005): 1.5 mil hogs/pigs, 3.7 mil chickens (excl. broilers). **Timber/lumber:** figs. undisclosed; ponderosa pine. **Nonfuel minerals** (est. 2005): $216 mil; cement (portland), sand and gravel (construction), stone (crushed), gold, stone (dimension). **Gross state product** (2005): $31.1 bil. **Sales tax** (2006): 4.0%. **Employment distrib.** (May 2006): 19.2% govt; 20.0% trade/trans./util.; 10.3% mfg; 14.6% ed./health; 6.3% prof./bus. serv.; 10.9% leisure/hosp.; 7.2% finance; 5.6% constr.; 3.9% other serv.; 1.8% info. **Unemployment** (2005): 3.9%. **Per cap. pers. income** (2005): $31,614. **New private housing** (2005): 5,685 units/$693 mil. **Commercial banks** (2005): 91; **deposits**: $41.1bil. **Savings institutions** (2005): 6; **deposits**: $1.0 bil. **Lottery** (2005): total sales: $675.6 mil; profit: $119.3 mil.

Federal govt. Fed. civ. employees (Mar. 2005): 7,210; **avg. salary**: $51,347. **Notable fed. facilities**: *Ellsworth AFB, Corp of Engineers, Nat'l Park Service.

Energy. Electricity production (est. 2005, kWh by source): Coal: 3.0 bil; Gas: 245 mil; Hydroelectric: 3.1 bil; Petroleum: 23 mil; Other: 4 mil.

State data. Motto: Under God, the people rule. **Flower:** Pasqueflower. **Bird:** Chinese ring-necked pheasant. **Tree:** Black Hills spruce. **Song:** Hail, South Dakota. **Entered union** Nov. 2, 1889; rank, 40th. **State fair** at Huron; early Sept.

History. Paleoindians hunted in the region at least 11,500 years ago. At the time of first European contact, Mandan, Hidatsa, Arikara, and Sioux lived in the area. The French Vérendrye brothers explored the region, 1742-43. The U.S. acquired the territory in the Louisiana Purchase, 1803, and Lewis and Clark passed through, 1804-6. In 1817 a trading post opened at what would become Fort Pierre. Dakota Territory was established, 1861. Gold was discovered, 1874, in the Black Hills on Sioux land; the "Great Dakota Boom" began in 1879. South Dakota became a state, 1889. The massacre of Native American families at Wounded Knee, 1890, ended Sioux resistance; 83 years later, armed supporters of the American Indian Movement, a Native American rights group, occupied the area, leading to a 70-day standoff. Major economic activities include agribusiness and, since the 1980s, credit card services. Republicans scored a key election victory, 2004, with the defeat of 3-term U.S. Sen. Tom Daschle, a national Democratic leader.

Tourist attractions. Black Hills; Mt. Rushmore; Needles Highway; Harney Peak, tallest E. of Rockies; Deadwood, 1876 Gold Rush town; Custer State Park; Jewel Cave Natl. Monument; Badlands Natl. Park "moonscape"; "Great Lakes of S. Dakota"; Ft. Sisseton; Great Plains Zoo & Museum, Sioux Falls; Corn Palace, Mitchell; Wind Cave Natl. Park; Crazy Horse Memorial, mountain carving in progress.

Famous South Dakotans. Sparky Anderson, Black Elk, Bob Barker, Tom Brokaw, Crazy Horse, Thomas Daschle, Myron Floren, Mary Hart, Cheryl Ladd, Dr. Ernest O. Lawrence, George McGovern, Billy Mills, Allen Neuharth, Pat O'Brien, Sitting Bull.

Tourist information. Department of Tourism and State Development, Capitol Lake Plaza, 711 E. Wells Ave., c/o 500 E. Capitol Ave., Pierre, SD 57501-5070; 1-800-SDAKOTA. **Website:** www.travelsd.com
Website. www.state.sd.us

Tennessee (TN)

Volunteer State

People. Population (2005 est.): 5,962,959; rank: 16; **net change** (2004-2005): 1.2%. **Pop. density:** 144.7 per sq mi. Racial distribution (2004): 80.7% white; 16.8% black; 1.2% Asian; 0.3% Native/Nat.AK; 0.05% Hawaiian/Pacific Islander; 2 or more races, 0.9%. **Hispanic pop.** (any race): 2.8%.

Geography. Total area: 42,143 sq mi; rank: 36. **Land area:** 41,217 sq mi; rank: 34. **Acres forested:** 14.4 mil. **Location:** East South Central state bounded on the N by Kentucky and Virginia; on the E by North Carolina; on the S by Georgia, Alabama, and Mississippi; on the W by Arkansas and Missouri. **Climate:** humid continental to the N; humid subtropical to the S. **Topography:** rugged country in the E; the Great Smoky Mts. of the Unakas; low ridges of the Appalachian Valley; the flat Cumberland Plateau; slightly rolling terrain and knobs of the Interior Low Plateau, the largest region; Eastern Gulf Coastal Plain to the W, laced with streams; Mississippi Alluvial Plain, a narrow strip of swamp and flood plain in the extreme W. **Capital:** Nashville. **Principal internat. airports at:** Memphis, Nashville.

Economy. Chief industries: manufacturing, trade, services, tourism, finance, insurance, real estate. **Chief manuf. goods:** chemicals, food, transportation equipment, industrial machinery & equipment, fabricated metal products, rubber/plastic products, paper & allied products, printing & publishing. **Chief crops:** tobacco, cotton, lint, soybeans, grain, corn. **Livestock:** (Jan. 2006): 2.2 mil cattle/calves, 27,000 sheep/lambs; (Dec. 2005): 190,000 hogs/pigs, 2.1 mil chickens (excl. broilers), 196.6 mil broilers. **Timber/lumber:** (est. 2004): 891 mil bd. ft.; red oak, white oak, yellow poplar, hickory. **Nonfuel minerals** (est. 2005): $696 mil; stone (crushed), cement (portland), sand and gravel (construction), zinc, clays (ball). **Chief ports:** Memphis, Nashville, Chattanooga, Knoxville. **Gross state product** (2005): $226.5 bil. **Sales tax** (2006): 7.0%. **Employment distrib.** (May 2006): 15.2% govt; 21.7% trade/trans./util.; 14.6% mfg; 12.1% ed./health; 11.2% prof./bus. serv.; 9.9% leisure/hosp.; 5.2% finance; 4.5% constr.; 3.7% other serv.; 1.8% info. **Unemployment** (2005): 5.6%. **Per cap. pers. income** (2004): $31,107. **New private housing** (2005): 46,615 units/$6.6 bil. **Commercial banks** (2005): 206; **deposits**: $91.8 bil. **Savings institutions** (2005): 19; **deposits**: $3.7 bil. **Lottery** (2005): total sales: $844.3 mil; profit: $227.4 mil.

Federal govt. Fed. civ. employees (Mar. 2005): 32,974; **avg. salary**: $58,025. **Notable fed. facilities:** Tennessee Valley Authority; Oak Ridge Nat'l. Lab; Arnold Engineering Development Ctr.; Ft. Campbell; Naval Support Activity, Mid-South.

Energy. Electricity production (est. 2005, kWh by source): Coal: 57.6 bil; Gas: 447 mil; Hydroelectric: 8.5 bil; Nuclear: 27.8 bil; Petroleum: 197 mil; Other: 3 mil.

State data. Motto: Agriculture and commerce. **Flower:** Iris. **Bird:** Mockingbird. **Tree:** Tulip poplar. **Songs:** My Homeland, Tennessee; When It's Iris Time in Tennessee; My Tennessee; Tennessee Waltz; Rocky Top. **Entered union** June 1, 1796; rank, 16th. **State fair** at Nashville; mid-Sept.

History. Inhabited for at least 20,000 years, the region was home to Creek and Yuchi peoples when the first Europeans arrived; the Cherokee moved into the region in the early 18th cent. Spanish explorers visited the area, 1540. English traders crossed the Great Smoky Mtns. from the east, while France's Marquette and Jolliet sailed down the Mississippi on the west, 1673. The first permanent settlement was of Virginians on the Watauga River, 1769. After the American Revolution, in which Tennesseans fought in eastern campaigns, the region became a territory, 1790, and a state, 1796. Slavery was widespread in western Tennessee, where cotton was the main crop, but much less common in the east. The state seceded, 1861, and saw many Civil War engagements; some 187,000 Tennesseans fought for the Confederacy and 51,000 for the Union. Tennessee was readmitted in 1866, the only former Confederate state not to have a postwar military government. The famous Scopes trial, 1925, questioned the teaching of evolution in public schools. In the 1930s, the Tennessee Valley Authority, a federal program, brought electric power to rural areas. Nashville became the capital of country music, while Memphis fostered the blues and, with Elvis Presley in the 1950s, rock 'n' roll. Martin Luther King Jr., was assassinated in Memphis, 1968. Since the 1970s, auto plants have become major employers, as has Federal Express. Al Gore Jr., U.S. vice pres. (1993-2001), lost his 2000 presidential bid partly because he failed to carry his home state of Tennessee.

Tourist attractions. Reelfoot Lake; Lookout Mountain, Chattanooga; Fall Creek Falls; Great Smoky Mountains Natl. Park; Lost Sea, Sweetwater; Cherokee Natl. Forest; Cumberland Gap Natl. Park; Andrew Jackson's home, the Hermitage, near Nashville; homes of Pres. Polk and Andrew Johnson; American Museum of Science and Energy, Oak Ridge; Parthenon, Grand Old Opry, Opryland USA, all Nashville; Dollywood theme park, Pigeon Forge; Tennessee Aquarium, Chattanooga; Graceland, home of Elvis Presley, Memphis; Alex Haley Home and Museum, Henning; Casey Jones Home and Museum, Jackson.

Famous Tennesseans. Roy Acuff, Davy Crockett, David Farragut, Ernie Ford, Aretha Franklin, Morgan Freeman, Bill Frist, Al Gore Jr., Alex Haley, William C. Handy, Sam Houston, Cordell Hull, Andrew Jackson, Andrew Johnson, Casey Jones, Estes Kefauver, Grace Moore, Dolly Parton, Minnie Pearl, James Polk, Elvis Presley, Dinah Shore, Bessie Smith, Fred Thompson, Hank Williams Jr., Alvin York.

Tourist information. Dept. of Tourist Development, Wm. Snodgrass/Tennessee Tower, 312 8th Ave., 25th Fl., Nashville, TN 37243; 1-615-741-2159. **Website:** www.tnvacation.com
Website. www.tn.gov

Texas (TX)
Lone Star State

People. Population (2005 est.): 22,859,968; rank: 2; **net change** (2004-2005): 1.7%. **Pop. density:** 87.3 per sq mi. Racial distribution (2004): 83.3% white; 11.7% black; 3.2% Asian; 0.7% Native/Nat.AK; 0.1% Hawaiian/Pacific Islander; 2 or more races, 1.0%. **Hispanic pop.** (any race): 34.6%.

Geography. Total area: 268,581 sq mi; rank: 2. **Land area:** 261,797 sq mi; rank: 2. **Acres forested:** 17.1 mil. **Location:** Southwestern state, bounded on the SE by the Gulf of Mexico; on the SW by Mexico, separated by the Rio Grande; surrounding states are Louisiana, Arkansas, Oklahoma, New Mexico. **Climate:** extremely varied; driest region is the Trans-Pecos; wettest is the NE. **Topography:** Gulf Coast Plain in the S and SE; North Central Plains slope upward with some hills; the Great Plains extend over the Panhandle, are broken by low mountains; the Trans-Pecos is the southern extension of the Rockies. **Capital:** Austin. **Principal internat. airports at:** Amarillo, Austin, Corpus Christi, Dallas/Ft. Worth, El Paso, Houston, San Antonio.

Economy. Chief industries: manufacturing, trade, oil and gas extraction, services. **Chief manuf. goods:** industrial machinery and equipment, foods, electrical and electronic products, chemicals and allied products, apparel. **Chief crops:** cotton, grains (wheat), sorghum grain, vegetables, citrus and other fruits, greenhouse/nursery, pecans, peanuts. **Chief farm products:** milk, eggs. **Livestock:** (Jan. 2006): 14.1 mil cattle/calves, 1.1 mil sheep/lambs; (Dec. 2005): 930,000 hogs/pigs, 24.7 mil chickens (excl. broilers), 627.9 mil broilers. **Timber/lumber** (est. 2004): 1.8 bil bd. ft.; pine, cypress. **Nonfuel minerals** (est. 2005): $2.6 bil; cement (portland), stone (crushed), sand and gravel (construction), lime, salt. **Commercial fishing** (2004): $166.2 mil. **Chief ports:** Houston, Galveston, Brownsville, Beaumont, Port Arthur, Corpus Christi. **Gross state product** (2005): $982.4 bil. **Sales tax** (2006): 6.25%. **Employment distrib.** (May 2006): 17.3% govt; 20.2% trade/trans./util.; 9.0% mfg; 12.2% ed./health; 12.1% prof./bus. serv.; 9.4% leisure/hosp.; 6.3% finance; 6.0% constr.; 3.5% other serv.; 2.2% info. **Unemployment** (2005): 5.3%. **Per cap. pers. income** (2005): $32,462. **New private housing** (2005): 210,611 units/$26.8 bil. **Commercial banks** (2005): 672; **deposits:** $312.6 bil. **Savings institutions** (2005): 49; **deposits:** $43.5 bil. **Lottery** (2005): total sales: $3.7 bil; profit: $1.1 bil.

Federal govt. Fed. civ. employees (Mar. 2005): 111,218; **avg. salary:** $57,764. **Notable fed. facilities:** *Ft. Hood, Kelly AFB; Ft. Sam Houston; NASA Johnson Space Ctr.; Naval Air Training School; Corpus Christi NAS; Kingsville NAS; Ft. Worth Western Currency Facility.

Energy. Electricity production (est. 2005, kWh by source): Coal: 61.3 bil; Gas: 31.6 bil; Hydroelectric: 1.1 bil; Petroleum: 55 mil; Other: 1 mil.

State data. Motto: Friendship. **Flower:** Bluebonnet. **Bird:** Mockingbird. **Tree:** Pecan. **Song:** Texas, Our Texas. **Entered union** Dec. 29, 1845; rank, 28th. **State fair** at Dallas; late Sept.-mid-Oct.

History. Humans have lived in the region for at least 12,000 years. Coahuiltecan, Karankawa, Caddo, Jumano, and Tonkawa peoples were in the area when the first Europeans came; later, Apache, Comanche, Cherokee, and Wichita arrived. Early Spanish explorers included Pineda, who sailed along the Texas coast, 1519; Cabeza de Vaca, shipwrecked near Galveston along with the former slave Estevanico, 1528; and Coronado, who crossed the Panhandle, 1541. Spaniards made the first settlement at Ysleta, near El Paso, 1682. Americans moved into the land early in the 19th cent. Mexico, of which Texas was a part, won independence from Spain, 1821.Texans rebelled, 1836, losing to Santa Anna at the Alamo, but winning decisively under Sam Houston at San Jacinto. With Houston as president, the Republic of Texas functioned as a nation, 1836-45, until admitted to the Union. With a slave population of 30%, Texas seceded, 1861; mostly unscathed by the Civil War, it was readmitted, 1870. In 1900 a powerful hurricane lashed Galveston, killing at least 8,000. Cotton and cattle were dominant until 1901, when the Spindletop gusher, near Beaumont, launched the petroleum and petrochemical industries. By 2000 the state population ranked 2nd in the U.S. With wealth and population came political power, notably in the presidencies of Lyndon B. Johnson, 1963-69, George H. W, Bush, 1989-93, and George W. Bush, since 2001.

Tourist attractions. Padre Island Natl. Seashore; Big Bend, Guadalupe Mts. natl. parks; The Alamo; Ft. Davis; Six Flags Amusement Park; Sea World and Fiesta Texas, both in San Antonio; San Antonio Missions Natl. Historical Park; Cowgirl Hall of Fame, Fort Worth; Lyndon B. Johnson Natl. Historical Park, marking his birthplace, boyhood home, and ranch, near Johnson City; Lyndon B. Johnson Library and Museum, Austin; Texas State Aquarium, Corpus Christi; Kimball Art Museum, Fort Worth; George Bush Library, College Station.

Famous Texans. Lance Armstrong, Stephen F. Austin, Lloyd Bentsen, James Bowie, Carol Burnett, George H. W. Bush, George W. Bush, Joan Crawford, J. Frank Dobie, Dwight D. Eisenhower, Morgan Fairchild, Farrah Fawcett, Sam Houston, Howard Hughes, Kay Bailey Hutchison, Molly Ivins, Lyndon B. Johnson, Tommy Lee Jones, Janis Joplin, Barbara Jordan, Mary Martin, Chester Nimitz, Sandra Day O'Connor, H. Ross Perot, Katherine Ann Porter, Dan Rather, Sam Rayburn, Ann Richards, Sissy Spacek, Kenneth Starr, George Strait.

Tourist Information. Texas Tourism, P.O. Box 12428, Austin, TX 78711; (512) 463-2000. **Website:** www.travel tex.com

Website. www.state.tx.us

Utah (UT)
Beehive State

People. Population (2005 est.): 2,469,585; rank: 34; **net change** (2004-2005): 2.0%. **Pop. density:** 30.1 per sq mi. Racial distribution (2004): 93.8% white; 0.9% black; 1.9% Asian; 1.3% Native/Nat.AK; 0.7% Hawaiian/Pacific Islander; 2 or more races, 1.3%. **Hispanic pop.** (any race): 10.6%.

Geography. Total area: 84,899 sq mi; rank: 13. **Land area:** 82,144 sq mi; rank: 12. **Acres forested:** 15.7 mil. **Location:** Middle Rocky Mountain state; its southeastern corner touches Colorado, New Mexico, and Arizona, and is the only spot in the U.S. where 4 states join. **Climate:** arid; ranging from warm desert in SW to alpine in NE. **Topography:** high Colorado plateau is cut by brilliantly colored canyons of the SE; broad, flat, desert-like Great Basin of the W; the Great Salt Lake and Bonneville Salt Flats to the NW; Middle Rockies in the NE run E-W; valleys and plateaus of the Wasatch Front. **Capital:** Salt Lake City. **Principal internat. airport at:** Salt Lake City.

Economy. Chief industries: services, trade, manufacturing, government, transportation, utilities. **Chief manuf. goods:** medical instruments, electronic components, food products, fabricated metals, transportation equipment, steel and copper. **Chief crops:** hay, corn, wheat, barley, apples, potatoes, cherries, onions, peaches, pears. **Livestock:** (Jan. 2006): 820,000 cattle/calves, 280,000 mil sheep/lambs; (Dec. 2005): 690,000 hogs/pigs, 4.2 mil chickens (excl. broilers). **Timber/lumber** (est. 2004): 57 mil bd. ft.; aspen, spruce, pine. **Nonfuel minerals** (est. 2005): $2.9 bil; copper, cement (portland), salt, gold, sand and gravel (construction). **Commercial fishing** (2004): $18.2 mil. **Gross state product** (2005): $89.8 bil. **Sales tax** (2006): 4.75%. **Employment distrib.** (May 2006): 17.4% govt; 19.3% trade/trans./util.; 10.1% mfg; 10.9% ed./health; 13.2% prof./bus. serv.; 8.9% leisure/hosp.; 5.9% finance; 7.8% constr.; 2.9% other serv.; 2.8% info. **Unemployment** (2005): 4.3%. **Per cap. pers. income** (2005): $28,061. **New private housing** (2005): 27,779 units/$4.6 bil. **Commercial banks** (2005): 70; **deposits:** $109.1 bil. **Savings institutions** (2005): 8; **deposits:** $9.0 bil.

Federal govt. Fed. civ. employees (Mar. 2005): 27,070; **avg. salary:** $52,717. **Notable fed. facilities:** *Hill AFB; Tooele Army Depot; Army Dugway Proving Ground.

Energy. Electricity production (est. 2005, kWh by source): Coal: 33.2 bil; Gas: 663 mil; Hydroelectric: 600 mil; Petroleum: 30 mil; Other: 168 mil.

State data. Motto: Industry. **Flower:** Sego lily. **Bird:** Seagull. **Tree:** Blue spruce. **Song:** Utah, This is the Place. **Entered union** Jan. 4, 1896; rank, 45th. **State fair** at Salt Lake City; Sept.

 IT'S A FACT: Utah has a higher proportion of families consisting of a married couple and their own children than any other state. About 32.4% of Utah households fit that description in 2005, beating the national average of 21.7% by a wide margin. Rounding out the top 5 are Idaho, Texas, Alaska, and California.

History. Ute, Gosiute, Southern Paiute, and Navajo peoples lived in the region at the time of European contact. Spanish Franciscans visited the area, 1776; American fur traders followed. Permanent settlement began with the arrival of the Latter-day Saints, or Mormons, 1847; they made the arid land bloom and created a prosperous economy. Organized in 1849, the State of Deseret asked admission to the Union; instead, Congress established Utah Territory, 1850, and Brigham Young was appointed governor. The Union Pacific and Central Pacific railroads met near Promontory Point, May 10, 1869, creating the first transcontinental railroad. Statehood was not achieved until 1896, after a long controversy over the Mormon practices of economic isolationism and polygamy, which the church renounced in 1890. The 20th cent. brought expansion in mining, defense-related industries, and, more recently, information technologies. More than 2/3 of Utahans are Mormons; the church has its world headquarters in Salt Lake City. Utah experienced 43% population growth, 1990-2005, and had the highest birthrate and lowest median age of any state in the U.S.

Tourist attractions. Temple Square, Mormon Church headquarters, Salt Lake City; Great Salt Lake; Zion, Canyonlands, Bryce Canyon, Arches, and Capitol Reef natl. parks; Dinosaur, Rainbow Bridge, Timpanogos Cave, and Natural Bridges natl. monuments; Lake Powell; Flaming Gorge Natl. Recreation Area.

Famous Utahans. Maude Adams, Ezra Taft Benson, John Moses Browning, Mariner Eccles, Philo Farnsworth, James Fletcher, David M. Kennedy, J. Willard Marriott, Merlin Olsen, Osmond family, Ivy Baker Priest, George Romney, Roseanne, Wallace Stegner, Brigham Young, Loretta Young.

Tourist information. Utah Travel Council, PO Box 147420, Salt Lake City, UT 84114; 1-800-200-1160 or 1-800-UTAH-FUN. **Website:** www.utah.com

Website. www.utah.gov

Vermont (VT)
Green Mountain State

People. Population (2005 est.): 623,050; rank: 49; **net change** (2004-2005): 0.3%. **Pop. density:** 67.4 per sq mi. Racial distribution (2004): 96.9% white; 0.6% black; 1.0% Asian; 0.4% Native/Nat.AK; 0.03% Hawaiian/Pacific Islander; 2 or more races, 1.1%. **Hispanic pop.** (any race): 1.0%.

Geography. Total area: 9,614 sq mi; rank: 45. **Land area:** 9,250 sq mi; rank: 43. **Acres forested:** 4.6 mil. **Location:** northern New England state. **Climate:** temperate, with considerable temperature extremes; heavy snowfall in mountains. **Topography:** Green Mts. N-S backbone 20-36 mi wide; avg. altitude 1,000 ft. **Capital:** Montpelier. **Principal internat. airport at:** Burlington.

Economy. Chief industries: manufacturing, tourism, agriculture, trade, finance, insurance, real estate, government. **Chief manuf. goods:** machine tools, furniture, scales, books, computer components, speciality foods. **Chief crops:** dairy products, apples, maple syrup, greenhouse/nursery, vegetables and small fruits. **Livestock:** (Jan. 2006): 280,000 cattle/calves; (Dec. 2005): 2,300 hogs/pigs, 238,000 chickens (excl.broilers). **Timber/lumber** (est. 2004): 183 mil bd. ft.; pine, spruce, fir, hemlock. **Nonfuel minerals** (est. 2005): $88.2 mil; stone (dimension), stone (crushed), sand and gravel (construction), talc (crude), gemstones. **Gross state product** (2005): $23.1 bil. **Sales tax** (2006): 6.0%. **Employment distrib.** (May 2006): 18.0% govt; 19.4% trade/trans./util.; 11.9% mfg; 18.0% ed./health; 7.3% prof./bus. serv.; 9.8% leisure/hosp.; 4.3% finance; 5.8% constr.; 3.3% other serv.; 2.1% info. **Unemployment** (2005): 3.5%. **Per cap. pers. income** (2005): $33,327. **New private housing** (2005): 2,917 units/$441 mil. **Commercial banks** (2005): 18; **deposits:** $8.3 bil. **Savings institutions** (2005): 7; **deposits:** $1.2 bil. **Lottery** (2005): total sales: $92.6 mil; profit: $20.4 mil.

Federal govt. Fed. civ. employees (Mar. 2005): 3,667; **avg. salary:** $54,744.

Energy. Electricity production (est. 2005, kWh by source): Gas: 2 mil; Hydroelectric: 369 mil; Petroleum: 15 mil; Other: 245 mil.

State data. Motto: Freedom and unity. **Flower:** Red clover. **Bird:** Hermit thrush. **Tree:** Sugar maple. **Song:** These Green Mountains. **Entered union** Mar. 4, 1791; rank, 14th. **State fair** at Rutland; early Sept.

History. Inhabited for 10,000 years or more, the region attracted Abenaki and Mahican peoples before Europeans arrived. Champlain explored the lake that now bears his name,

1609. The first European settlement was on Isle la Motte, in Lake Champlain, 1666. During the American Revolution, Ethan Allen and the Green Mountain Boys captured Ft. Ticonderoga (NY), 1775. Under a constitution that provided for public schools and abolished slavery, settlers declared a republic, 1777. Vermont joined the Union, 1791. Agriculture dominated in the 19th cent. Still mainly rural, the state expanded tourism and manufacturing after World War II, and IBM became the largest private employer. In 2000, with Howard Dean as governor (1991-2003), Vermont became the first state in the U.S. to legalize same-sex civil unions.

Tourist attractions. Shelburne Museum; Rock of Ages Quarry, Graniteville; Vermont Marble Exhibit, Proctor; Bennington Battle Monument; Pres. Calvin Coolidge homestead, Plymouth; Maple Grove Maple Museum, St. Johnsbury; Ben & Jerry's Factory, Waterbury.

Famous Vermonters. Ethan Allen, Chester A. Arthur, Calvin Coolidge, Howard Dean, John Deere, George Dewey, John Dewey, Stephen A. Douglas, Dorothy Canfield Fisher, James Fisk, James Jeffords, Rudy Vallee.

Chamber of Commerce. PO Box 37, Montpelier, VT 05601.

Tourist information. Vermont Dept. of Tourism and Marketing, Ntl. Life Building 6th Floor, Drawer 20, Montpelier, VT 05620; (802) 828-3676. **Website:** www.vermontvacation.com

Website. www.vermont.gov

Virginia (VA)
Old Dominion

People. Population (2005 est.): 7,567,465; rank: 12; **net change** (2004-2005): 1.2%. **Pop. density:** 191.1 per sq mi. Racial distribution (2004): 73.8% white; 19.9% black; 4.4% Asian; 0.3% Native/Nat.AK; 0.07% Hawaiian/Pacific Islander; 2 or more races, 1.5%. **Hispanic pop.** (any race): 5.7%.

Geography. Total area: 42,774 sq mi; rank: 35. **Land area:** 39,594 sq mi; rank: 37. **Acres forested:** 16.1 mil. **Location:** South Atlantic state bounded by the Atlantic Ocean on the E and surrounded by North Carolina, Tennessee, Kentucky, West Virginia, and Maryland. **Climate:** mild and equable. **Topography:** mountain and valley region in the W, including the Blue Ridge Mts.; rolling piedmont plateau; tidewater, or coastal plain, including the eastern shore. **Capital:** Richmond. **Principal internat. airports at:** Arlington, Norfolk, Loudon, Richmond, Newport News.

Economy. Chief industries: services, trade, government, manufacturing, tourism, agriculture. **Chief manuf. goods:** food processing, transportation equipment, printing, textiles, electronic & electrical equipment, industrial machinery & equipment, lumber & wood products, chemicals, rubber & plastics, furniture. **Chief crops:** tobacco, grain corn, soybeans, winter wheat, peanuts, lint & seed cotton. **Livestock:** (Jan. 2006): 1.7 mil cattle/calves, 67,000 mil sheep/lambs; (Dec. 2005): 490,000 hogs/pigs, 4.9 mil chickens (excl. broilers), 260.0 mil broilers. **Timber/lumber** (est. 2004): 1.5 bil bd. ft.; pine and hardwoods. **Nonfuel minerals** (est. 2005): $962 mil; stone (crushed), cement (portland), sand and gravel (construction), lime, clays (fuller's earth). **Commercial fishing** (2004): $160.3 mil. **Chief ports:** Hampton Roads, Richmond, Alexandria. **Gross state product** (2005): $352.7 bil. **Sales tax** (2006): 5.0%. **Employment distrib.** (May 2006): 18.0% govt; 17.6% trade/trans./util.; 8.0% mfg; 10.9% ed./health; 16.6% prof./bus. serv.; 9.1% leisure/hosp.; 5.2% finance; 7.0% constr.; 4.9% other serv.; 2.4% info. **Unemployment** (2005): 3.5%. **Per cap. pers. income** (2005): $38,390. **New private housing** (2005): 61,518 units/$9.0 bil. **Commercial banks** (2005): 151; **deposits:** $118.7 bil. **Savings institutions** (2005): 18; **deposits:** $36.6 bil. **Lottery** (2005): total sales: $1.3 bil; profit: $423.5 mil.

Federal govt. Fed. civ. employees (Mar. 2005): 120,062; **avg. salary:** $70,654. **Notable fed. facilities:** Pentagon; Norfolk Naval Sta., Shipyard; Marine Corps Base; Langley AFB; NASA Langley Res. Ctr.; CIA George Bush Ctr. for Intelligence, Langley; Quantico USMC Base; FBI Academy (Quantico); Dahlgren Nav. Surface Warfare Ctr. & Lab; USDA Food and Nutrition Serv.; U.S. Geological Survey Natl. Ctr.

Energy. Electricity production (est. 2005, kWh by source): Coal: 28.8 bil; Gas: 4.4 bil; Hydroelectric: 1.4 bil; Nuclear: 27.9 bil; Petroleum: 3.8 bil; Other: 540 mil.

State data. Motto: Sic Semper Tyrannis (Thus always to tyrants). **Flower:** Dogwood. **Bird:** Cardinal. **Tree:** Dogwood. **Song Emeritus:** Carry Me Back to Old Virginia. **Tenth** of the original 13 states to ratify the Constitution, June 25, 1788. **State fair** at Richmond; late Sept.-early Oct.

History. Cherokee and Susquehanna peoples and the Algonquians of the Powhatan Confederacy were in the region when Europeans arrived. English settlers founded Jamestown, 1607. Virginians were indispensable to the founding of the American republic, and 4 of the first 5 U.S. presidents—Washington, Jefferson, Madison, and Monroe—came from there. The conclusive battle of the American Revolution took place at Yorktown, 1781. The state profited from tobacco, cotton, and the slave trade; in 1860, slaves made up nearly 1/3 of the population. Virginia seceded from the Union, 1861, and Richmond became the capital of the Confederacy, but Western counties, loyal to the Union, split off to become West Virginia, 1863. The war ended with Lee's surrender to Grant at Appomattox, 1865, and Virginia was readmitted to the Union, 1870. In the 20th cent., expansion of federal civilian jobs and military facilities transformed the economy. State officials pledged "massive resistance" to racial integration in the mid-1950s, but eventually accommodated. In 1989, L. Douglas Wilder became the first elected black governor in U.S. history. On Sept. 11, 2001, terrorist hijackers crashed a jet into U.S. defense headquarters at the Pentagon, in Arlington.

Tourist attractions. Colonial Williamsburg; Busch Gardens, Williamsburg; Wolf Trap Farm, near Falls Church; Arlington Natl. Cemetery; Mt. Vernon, home of George Washington; Jamestown Festival Park; Yorktown; Jefferson's Monticello, Charlottesville; Robert E. Lee's birthplace, Stratford Hall, and grave, Lexington; Appomattox; Shenandoah Natl. Park; Blue Ridge Parkway; Virginia Beach; Paramount's King's Dominion, near Richmond.

Famous Virginians. Richard E. Byrd, James B. Cabell, Henry Clay, Katie Couric, Jubal Early, Jerry Falwell, William Henry Harrison, Patrick Henry, A.P. Hill, Thomas Jefferson, Joseph E. Johnston, Robert E. Lee, Meriwether Lewis and William Clark, James Madison, John Marshall, George Mason, James Monroe, George Pickett, Pocahontas, Edgar Allan Poe, John Randolph, Walter Reed, Rev. Pat Robertson, John Smith, J.E.B. Stuart, William Styron, Zachary Taylor, John Tyler, Maggie Walker, Booker T. Washington, George Washington, L. Douglas Wilder, Woodrow Wilson.

Tourist Information. Virginia Tourism Corp., 901 E. Byrd St., Richmond, VA 23219; (804) 545-5500. **Website:** www.virginia.org
Website. www.virginia.gov

Washington (WA)
Evergreen State

People. Population (2005 est.): 6,287,759; rank: **14; net change** (2004-2005): 1.3%. **Pop. density:** 94.5 per sq mi. Racial distribution (2004): 85.3% white; 3.5% black; 6.3% Asian; 1.6% Native/Nat.AK; 0.5% Hawaiian/Pacific Islander; 2 or more races, 2.9%. **Hispanic pop.** (any race): 8.5%.

Geography. Total area: 71,300 sq mi; rank: 18. **Land area:** 66,544 sq mi; rank: 20. **Acres forested:** 21.8 mil. **Location:** Pacific state bordered by Canada on the N; Idaho on the E; Oregon on the S; and the Pacific Ocean on the W. **Climate:** mild, dominated by the Pacific Ocean and protected by the Cascades. **Topography:** Olympic Mts. on NW peninsula; open land along coast to Columbia R.; flat terrain of Puget Sound Lowland; Cascade Mts. region's high peaks to the E; Columbia Basin in central portion; highlands to the NE; mountains to the SE. **Capital:** Olympia. **Principal internat. airports at:** Seattle/Tacoma, Spokane, Boeing Field.

Economy. Chief industries: advanced technology, aerospace, biotechnology, intl. trade, forestry, tourism, recycling, agriculture & food processing. **Chief manuf. goods:** computer software, aircraft, pulp & paper, lumber and plywood, aluminum, processed fruits and vegetables, machinery, electronics. **Chief crops:** apples, potatoes, hay, farm forest products. **Livestock:** (Jan. 2006): 1.1 mil cattle/calves, 50,000 mil sheep/lambs; (Dec. 2005): 30,000 hogs/pigs, 6.1 mil chickens (excl. broilers). **Timber/lumber** (est. 2004): 5.2 bil bd. ft.; Douglas fir, hemlock, cedar, pine. **Nonfuel minerals** (est. 2005): $562 mil; sand and gravel (construction), cement (portland), stone (crushed), diatomite, lime. **Commercial fishing** (2004): $175.1 mil. **Chief ports:** Seattle, Tacoma, Vancouver, Kelso-Longview. **Gross state product** (2005): $268.5 bil. **Sales tax** (2006): 6.5%. **Employment distrib.** (May 2006): 18.8% govt; 18.8% trade/trans./util.; 9.8% mfg; 11.9% ed./health; 11.6% prof./bus. serv.; 9.6% leisure/hosp.; 5.5% finance; 6.7% constr.; 3.7% other serv.; 3.4% info. **Unemployment** (2005): 5.5%. **Per cap. pers. income** (2005): $35,409. **New private housing** (2005): 52,988 units/$8.7 bil. **Commercial banks**

(2005): 101; **deposits:** $66.5 bil. **Savings institutions** (2005): 23; **deposits:** $25.0 bil. **Lottery** (2005): total sales: $457.6 mil; profit: $115.6 mil.

Federal govt. Fed. civ. employees (Mar. 2005): 45,673; **avg. salary:** $60,599. **Notable fed. facilities:** Bonneville Power Admin.; Ft. Lewis; *McChord AFB; Hanford Nuclear Reservation; Bremerton Naval Shipyards; *Naval Sub Base, Bangor; Naval Sta., Everett; Pacific Northwest Natl. Lab.

Energy. Electricity production (est. 2005, kWh by source): Gas: 2.5 bil; Hydroelectric: 72.5 bil; Nuclear: 8.2 bil; Other: 780 mil.

State data. Motto: Alki (By and by). **Flower:** Western rhododendron. **Bird:** Willow goldfinch. **Tree:** Western hemlock. **Song:** Washington, My Home. **Entered union** Nov. 11, 1889; rank, 42nd. **State fairs:** 5 area fairs, in Aug. and Sept.; no state fair.

History. People of the Clovis culture lived in the region 11,000 years ago. At the time of European contact, Native Americans in the area included Nez Percé, Spokane, Yakima, Cayuse, Okanogan, Walla Walla, and Colville peoples in the interior, and Nooksak, Chinook, Nisqually, Clallam, Makah, Quinault, and Puyallup peoples along the coast. Spain's Bruno Hezeta sailed the coast, 1775. In 1792, British naval officer George Vancouver mapped the Puget Sound area, and American Capt. Robert Gray sailed up the Columbia River. Fur traders and missionaries arrived in the first half of the 19th cent. Final agreement on the border of Washington and Canada was made with Britain, 1846. Completion in 1883 of a transcontinental rail link between Puget Sound and the eastern U.S. aided immigration, and Washington became a state in 1889. In the 20th cent., cheap hydroelectric power spurred growth in the aluminum and aircraft industries; founded in 1975, Microsoft became a computer software giant. Mt. St. Helens erupted, 1980. With grunge music, Starbucks coffee, and Amazon.com, Seattle became a national trendsetter in the 1990s; violent street protests disrupted a World Trade Organization meeting there in 1999. Gary Locke, in office 1997-2005, was the first U.S. governor of Chinese ancestry.

Tourist attractions. Seattle Waterfront, Seattle Center and Space Needle, Museum of Flight, Underground Tour, all Seattle; Mt. Rainier, Olympic, and North Cascades natl. parks; Mt. St. Helens; Puget Sound; San Juan Islands; Grand Coulee Dam; Columbia R. Gorge Natl. Scenic Area; Spokane's Riverfront Park.

Famous Washingtonians. Raymond Carver, Kurt Cobain, Bing Crosby, William O. Douglas, Bill Gates, Jimi Hendrix, Henry M. Jackson, Gary Larson, Mary McCarthy, Robert Motherwell, Edward R. Murrow, Theodore Roethke, Ann Rule, Hilary Swank, Julia Sweeney, Adam West, Marcus Whitman, Minoru Yamasaki.

Tourist information. WA State Tourism, 128 10th Ave. SW, PO Box 42500, Olympia, WA 98504; 1-800-544-1800. **Website:** www.experiencewashington.com
Website. www.access.wa.gov

West Virginia (WV)
Mountain State

People. Population (2005 est.): 1,816,856; rank: **37; net change** (2004-2005): 0.2%. **Pop. density:** 75.5 per sq mi. Racial distribution (2004): 95.2% white; 3.2% black; 0.6% Asian; 0.2% Native/Nat.AK; 0.02% Hawaiian/Pacific Islander; 2 or more races, 0.8%. **Hispanic pop.** (any race): 0.8%.

Geography. Total area: 24,230 sq mi; rank: 41. **Land area:** 24,078 sq mi; rank: 41. **Acres forested:** 12.1 mil. **Location:** South Atlantic state bounded on the N by Ohio, Pennsylvania, Maryland; on the S and W by Virginia, Kentucky, Ohio; on the E by Maryland and Virginia. **Climate:** humid continental climate except for marine modification in the lower panhandle. **Topography:** ranging from hilly to mountainous; Allegheny Plateau in the W, covers two-thirds of the state; mountains here are the highest in the state, over 4,000 ft. **Capital:** Charleston.

Economy. Chief industries: manufacturing, services, mining, tourism. **Chief manuf. goods:** machinery, plastic & hardwood prods., fabricated metals, chemicals, aluminum, automotive parts, steel. **Chief crops:** apples, peaches, hay, tobacco, corn, wheat, oats. **Chief farm products:** dairy products, eggs. **Livestock:** (Jan. 2006): 410,000 cattle/calves, 32,000 mil sheep/lambs; (Dec. 2005): 8,000 hogs/pigs, 1.9 mil chickens (excl. broilers), 88.5 mil broilers. **Timber/lumber** (est. 2004): 701 mil bd. ft.; oak, yellow poplar, hickory, walnut, cherry. **Nonfuel minerals** (est. 2005): $170 mil; stone (crushed), cement (portland), sand and gravel (industrial), lime, salt. **Chief port:** Huntington. **Gross state product** (2005): $53.8 bil. **Sales tax** (2006): 6.0%. **Employment distrib.** (May 2006): 19.1% govt; 18.5% trade/trans./util.; 8.1% mfg; 15.2% ed./health; 7.8% prof./bus. serv.; 9.4% leisure/hosp.; 4.0% finance; 5.3% constr.; 7.5% other serv.; 1.5% info. **Unemployment** (2005): 5.0%. **Per cap. pers. income** (2005): $27,215. **New private housing** (2005): 6,140 units/$996 mil. **Commercial banks** (2005): 82; **deposits:** $22.5 bil. **Savings institutions** (2005): 7; **deposits:** $820 mil. **Lottery** (2005): total sales: $1.4 bil; profit: $588.3 mil.

Federal govt. Fed. civ. employees (Mar. 2005): 13,020; **avg. salary:** $57,399. **Notable fed. facilities:** Natl. Radio Astronomy Observatory; Bureau of Public Debt Bldg.; Harpers Ferry Natl. Park; Correctional Institution for Women; FBI Identification Ctr.

Energy. Electricity production (est. 2005, kWh by source): Coal: 60.6 bil; Gas: 3 mil; Hydroelectric: 301 mil; Petroleum: 173 mil; Other: 12 mil.

State data. Motto: Montani Semper Liberi (Mountaineers are always free). **Flower:** Big rhododendron. **Bird:** Cardinal. **Tree:** Sugar maple. **Songs:** The West Virginia Hills; This Is My West Virginia; West Virginia, My Home, Sweet Home. **Entered union** June 20, 1863; rank, 35th. **State fair** at Lewisburg (Fairlea); late Aug.

History. Sparsely inhabited at the time of European contact, the area was primarily Native American hunting grounds. British explorers Thomas Batts and Robert Fallam reached the New River, 1671. Coal, discovered in 1742, was mined extensively by the mid-19th cent. White settlement led to conflicts with Native Americans, including a major battle in which frontiersmen defeated an Indian confederacy at Point Pleasant, 1774. The region joined the Union as part of Virginia, 1788. Longstanding tensions between the E and W parts of the state came to a head in 1861, when Virginia seceded. Delegates of W counties, meeting at Wheeling, repudiated the act and created a new state, Kanawha, later renamed West Virginia, which was admitted to the Union in 1863. Poverty has been a problem for much of the state's subsequent history. West Virginia continues to rank low in per capita personal income, despite billions of dollars in federal contracts brought to the state by 8-term U.S. Sen. Robert Byrd; in 2006 he became the longest-serving member in Senate history.

Tourist attractions. Harpers Ferry Natl. Historic Park; Science and Cultural Center, Charleston; White Sulphur (in Greenbrier) and Berkeley Springs mineral water spas; New River Gorge, Fayetteville; Winter Place, Exhibition Coal Mine, both Beckley; Monongahela Natl. Forest; Fenton Glass, Williamstown; Viking Glass, New Martinsville; Blenko Glass, Milton; Sternwheel Regatta, Charleston; Mountain State Forest Festival; Snowshoe Ski Resort, Slaty Fork; Canaan State Park, Davis; Mountain State Arts & Crafts Fair, Ripley; Ogle Bay, Wheeling; White water rafting, several locations.

Famous West Virginians. Newton D. Baker, Pearl Buck, Robert Byrd, John W. Davis, Thomas "Stonewall" Jackson, Don Knotts, Dwight Whitney Morrow, Michael Owens, Mary Lou Retton, Walter Reuther, Cyrus Vance, Jerry West, Charles "Chuck" Yeager.

Tourist information. West Virginia Division of Tourism, 90 MacCorkle Ave., SW, South Charleston, WV 25303; 1-800-CALLWVA. **Website:** www.wvtourism.com
Website. www.wv.gov

Wisconsin (WI)
Badger State

People. Population (2005 est.): 5,536,201; rank: 20; **net change** (2004-2005): 0.6%. **Pop. density:** 101.9 per sq mi. Racial distribution (2004): 90.2% white; 5.9% black; 1.9% Asian; 0.9% Native/Nat.AK; 0.04% Hawaiian/Pacific Islander; 2 or more races, 1.0%. **Hispanic pop.** (any race): 4.3%.

Geography. Total area: 65,498 sq mi; rank: 23. **Land area:** 54,310 sq mi; rank: 25. **Acres forested:** 16.0 mil. **Location:** East North Central state, bounded on the N by Lake Superior and Upper Michigan; on the E by Lake Michigan; on the S by Illinois; on the W by the St. Croix and Mississippi rivers. **Climate:** long, cold winters and short, warm summers tempered by the Great Lakes. **Topography:** narrow Lake Superior Lowland plain met by Northern Highland, which slopes gently to the sandy crescent Central Plain; Western Upland in the SW; 3 broad parallel limestone ridges running N-S are separated by wide and shallow lowlands in the SE. **Capital:** Madison. **Principal internat. airports at:** Green Bay, Milwaukee.

Economy. Chief industries: services, manufacturing, trade, government, agriculture, tourism. **Chief manuf. goods:** food products, motor vehicles & equip., paper products, medical instruments and supplies, printing, plastics. **Chief crops:** corn, hay, soybeans, potatoes, cranberries, sweet corn, peas, oats, snap beans. **Chief farm products:** milk, butter, cheese, canned and frozen vegetables. **Livestock:** (Jan. 2006): 3.4 mil cattle/calves, 89,000 mil sheep/lambs; (Dec. 2005): 430,000 hogs/pigs, 6.1 mil chickens (excl. broilers), 36.6 mil broilers. **Timber/lumber** (est. 2004): 539 mil bd. ft.; maple, birch, oak, evergreens. ft. **Nonfuel minerals** (est. 2005): $472 mil; stone (crushed), sand and gravel (construction), lime, sand and gravel (industrial), stone (dimension). **Commercial fishing** (2004): $3.1 mil. **Chief ports:** Superior, Ashland, Milwaukee, Green Bay, Kewaunee, Pt. Washington, Manitowoc, Sheboygan, Marinette, Kenosha. **Gross state product** (2005): $217.5 bil. **Sales tax** (2006): 5.0%. **Employment distrib.** (May 2006): 14.7% govt; 18.6% trade/trans./util.; 17.4% mfg; 13.9% ed./health; 9.2% prof./bus. serv.; 9.3% leisure/hosp.; 5.5% finance; 4.8% constr.; 4.8% other serv.; 1.7% info. **Unemployment** (2005): 4.7%. **Per cap. pers. income** (2005): $33,565. **New private housing** (2005): 35,334 units/$5.6 bil. **Commercial banks** (2005): 277; **deposits:** $85.6 bil. **Savings institutions** (2005): 41; **deposits:** $15.0 bil. **Lottery** (2005): total sales: $451.9 mil; profit: $128.5.

Federal govt. Fed. civ. employees (Mar. 2005): 11,748; **avg. salary:** $55,399. **Notable fed. facilities:** *Ft. McCoy.

Energy. Electricity production (est. 2005, kWh by source): Coal: 40.8 bil; Gas: 1.5 bil; Hydroelectric: 1.6 bil; Nuclear: 9.1 bil; Petroleum: 97 mil; Other: 287 mil.

State data. Motto: Forward. **Flower:** Wood violet. **Bird:** Robin. **Tree:** Sugar maple. **Song:** On, Wisconsin! **Entered union** May 29, 1848; rank, 30th. **State fair** at State Fair Park, West Allis; early Aug.

History. At the time of European contact, Ojibwa, Menominee, Winnebago, Kickapoo, Sauk, Fox, and Potawatomi peoples inhabited the area. French explorer Jean Nicolet reached Green Bay, 1634; French missionaries and fur traders followed. The British took over, 1763. The U.S. won the land after the American Revolution but did not wield control until forts were established at Green Bay and Prairie du Chien, 1816. Native Americans rebelled against the seizure of tribal lands in the Black Hawk War, 1832, but were defeated and relocated to reservations. Wisconsin became a territory, 1836, and a state, 1848. Some 96,000 soldiers served the Union cause during the Civil War. Many immigrants arrived from Germany, Poland, and Scandinavia. Wisconsin agriculture focused on dairy; Milwaukee became a manufacturing center. As gov., 1901-06, Robert La Follette pushed Progressive reforms such as direct primary voting and consumer protection laws. An era of "McCarthyism" ended when anti-Communist crusader Sen. Joseph McCarthy (R, WI) was censured by the U.S. Senate, 1954.

Tourist attractions. Old Wade House and Carriage Museum, Greenbush; Villa Louis, Prairie du Chien; Circus World Museum, Baraboo; Wisconsin Dells; Old World Wisconsin, Eagle; Door County peninsula; Chequamegon and Nicolet national forests; Lake Winnebago; House on the Rock, Dodgeville; Monona Terrace, Madison.

Famous Wisconsinites. Don Ameche, Carrie Chapman Catt, Willem Dafoe, Edna Ferber, Hamlin Garland, King Camp Gillette, Harry Houdini, Robert La Follette, Alfred Lunt, Pat O'Brien, Georgia O'Keeffe, William H. Rehnquist, John Ringling, Donald K. "Deke" Slayton, Spencer Tracy, Thorstein Veblen, Orson Welles, Laura Ingalls Wilder, Thornton Wilder, Frank Lloyd Wright.

Tourist information. Wisconsin Dept. of Tourism, 201 W. Washington Ave., PO Box 8690, Madison, WI 53708-8690; 1-800-432-TRIP. **Website:** www.travelwisconsin.com
Website. www.wisconsin.gov

Wyoming (WY)
Equality State, Cowboy State

People. Population (2005 est.): 509,294; rank: 51; **net change** (2004-2005): 0.7%. **Pop. density:** 5.2 per sq mi. Racial distribution (2004): 94.8% white; 0.9% black; 0.6% Asian; 2.4% Native/Nat.AK; 0.07% Hawaiian/Pacific Islander; 2 or more races, 1.2%. **Hispanic pop.** (any race): 6.7%.

Geography. Total area: 97,814 sq mi; rank: 10. **Land area:** 97,100 sq mi; rank: 9. **Acres forested:** 11.0 mil. **Location:** Mountain state lying in the high western plateaus of the

Great Plains. **Climate:** semi-desert conditions throughout; true desert in the Big Horn and Great Divide basins. **Topography:** the eastern Great Plains rise to the foothills of the Rocky Mts.; the Continental Divide crosses the state from the NW to the SE. **Capital:** Cheyenne. **Principal internat. airport at:** Casper.

Economy. Chief industries: mineral extraction, oil, natural gas, tourism and recreation, agriculture. **Chief manuf. goods:** refined petroleum, wood, stone, clay products, foods, electronic devices, sporting apparel, and aircraft. **Chief crops:** wheat, beans, barley, oats, sugar beets, hay. **Livestock:** (Jan. 2006): 1.4 mil cattle/calves; 450,000 mil sheep/lambs; (Dec. 2005): 113,000 hogs/pigs, 16,000 chickens (excl.broilers). **Timber/lumber** (est. 2004): 165 mil bd. ft.; ponderosa & lodgepole pine, Douglas fir, Engelmann spruce. **Nonfuel minerals** (est. 2005): $1.2 bil; soda ash, clays (bentonite), helium (Grade-A), cement (portland), sand and gravel (construction). **Gross state product** (2005): $27.4 bil. **Sales tax** (2006): 4.0%. **Employment distrib.** (May 2006): 24.7% govt; 18.9% trade/trans./util.; 3.6% mfg; 8.2% ed./health; 6.1% prof./bus. serv.; 11.7% leisure/hosp.; 4.0% finance; 8.2% constr.; 3.7% other serv.; 1.6% info. **Unemployment** (2005): 3.6%. **Per cap. pers. income** (2005): $36,778. **New private housing** (2005): 3,997 units/$657 mil. **Commercial banks** (2005): 47; **deposits:** $8.2 bil. **Savings institutions** (2004): 4; **deposits** $340 mil.

Federal govt. Fed. civ. employees (Mar. 2005): 4,952; **avg. salary:** $53,039. **Notable fed. facilities:** Warren AFB.

Energy. Electricity production (est. 2005, kWh by source): Coal: 40.0 bil; Gas: 43 mil; Hydroelectric: 782 bil; Petroleum: 38 mil; Other: 15 mil.

State data. Motto: Equal Rights. **Flower:** Indian Paintbrush. **Bird:** Western Meadowlark. **Tree:** Plains Cottonwood. **Song:** Wyoming. **Entered union** July 10, 1890; rank, 44th. **State fair** at Douglas; late Aug.

History. Inhabited for at least 12,000 years. the region supported Shoshone, Crow, Cheyenne, Oglala Sioux, and Arapaho peoples when Europeans arrived. France's Vérendrye brothers were the first Europeans to see the region, 1742-43. John Colter, an American, traversed the Yellowstone area, 1807-8. Trappers and fur traders followed in the 1820s. Forts Laramie and Bridger became important stops on trails to the West Coast. Population grew after the Union Pacific crossed the state, 1867-68. Wyoming became a territory, 1868, and the first to extend full voting rights to women, 1869. Statehood was attained, 1890. Disputes between large landowners and small ranchers culminated in the Johnson County Cattle War, 1892; federal troops were called in to restore order. Nellie Tayloe Ross was the first woman governor to take office in the U.S., 1925. Wyoming, the least populous state, has relied on the energy, tourism, and ranching industries in recent decades. Dick Cheney, Wyoming's representative in the U.S. House, 1979-89, became U.S. vice pres., 2001.

Tourist attractions. Yellowstone Natl. Park, the first U.S. national park, est. 1872; Grand Teton Natl. Park; Natl. Elk Refuge; Devils Tower Natl. Monument; Fort Laramie Natl. Historic Site and nearby pioneer trail ruts; Buffalo Bill Historical Center, Cody; Cheyenne Frontier Days, Cheyenne.

Famous Wyomingites. James Bridger, William F. "Buffalo Bill" Cody, Curt Gowdy, Esther Hobart Morris, Jackson Pollock, Nellie Tayloe Ross.

Tourist information. Wyoming Travel and Tourism, I-25 at College Dr., Cheyenne, WY 82002; 1-800-225-5996. **Website:** www.wyomingtourism.org

Website. www.state.wy.us

District of Columbia (DC)

People. Population (2005 est.): 550,521; rank: 50; **net change** (2004-2005): -0.7%. **Pop. density:** 8,966.1 per sq mi. Racial distribution (2004): 37.4% white; 57.7% black; 3.0% Asian; 0.3% Native/Nat.AK; 0.07% Hawaiian/Pacific Islander; 2 or more races, 1.5%. **Hispanic pop.** (any race): 8.5%.

Geography. Total area: 68 sq mi; rank: 50. **Land area:** 61 sq mi; rank: 51. **Location:** at the confluence of the Potomac and Anacostia rivers, flanked by Maryland on the N, E, and SE and by Virginia on the SW. **Climate:** hot humid summers, mild winters. **Topography:** low hills rise toward the N away from the Potomac R. and slope to the S; highest elevation, 410 ft, lowest Potomac R., 1 ft. **Principal internat. airports at:** Arlington (VA), Dulles (VA).

Economy. Chief industries: government, service, tourism. **Gross product** (2005): $82.8 bil. **Sales tax** (2006): 5.75%. **Employment distrib.** (May 2006): 33.3% govt; 4.1% trade/trans./util.; 0.3% mfg; 13.7% ed./health; 21.9% prof./bus. serv.; 8.4% leisure/hosp.; 4.4% finance; 1.9% constr.; 8.6% other serv.; 3.4% info. **Unemployment** (2005): 6.5%. **Per cap. pers. income** (2005): $54,985. **New private housing** (2005): 2,860 units/$228 mil. **Commercial banks** (2005): 22; **deposits:** $19.8 bil. **Savings institutions** (2005): 7; **deposits:** $2.8 bil. **Lottery** (2005): total sales: $233.4 mil; profit: $71.1 mil.

Federal govt. Fed. civ. employees (Mar. 2005): 150,451; **avg. salary:** $83,243.

Energy. Electricity production (2000, kWh, by source): Petroleum: 95 mil; Other: 28 mil.

District data. Motto: Justitia omnibus (Justice for all). **Flower:** American beauty rose. **Tree:** Scarlet oak. **Bird:** Wood thrush.

History. The District of Columbia, coextensive with the city of Washington, is the seat of the U.S. federal government. It lies on the west central edge of Maryland on the Potomac River, opposite Virginia. The Piscataway, an Algonquian-speaking people, were living in the region when Europeans arrived in the 17th cent. Proposals for a "federal town" for the deliberations of the Continental Congress were made in 1783. Authorized by Congress, 1790, Pres. George Washington chose the Potomac site and persuaded landowners to sell their holdings to the government. Its area was originally 100 sq mi taken from the sovereignty of Maryland and Virginia. Virginia's portion south of the Potomac was given back to that state in 1846.

Pres. Washington chose Pierre Charles L'Enfant, a Frenchman, to plan the capital. Surveyor Andrew Ellicott finished the official map and design of the city, assisted by Benjamin Banneker, a black architect and astronomer. Pres. Washington laid the cornerstone of the north wing of the Capitol building, 1793, and Pres. John Adams moved to the new national capital, 1800. The City of Washington was incorporated, 1802. British troops invaded, 1814, setting fire to the Capitol, the President's House (as the White House was then called), and other buildings. Pres. Lincoln ended slavery in the district, 1862. Many African Americans arrived after the Civil War, but racial segregation remained legal until the mid-20th cent. After federal government expansion spurred population growth, 1930-50, an exodus to the suburbs shrank city's population, 1950-2005.

The 23rd Amendment (1961) granted residents the right to vote for president and vice president. Congress, which has legislative authority over the District under the Constitution, approved legislation in 1970 giving the District one delegate to the House of Representatives, who could vote in committee but not on the floor. Voters approved, 1974, a congressionally drafted charter giving them the right to elect their own mayor and city council. The district won the right to levy taxes, but Congress retained power to veto council actions and approve the city budget. Security measures were dramatically increased after terrorists attacked the U.S. on Sept. 11, 2001. After a 34-year absence, major league baseball returned to the city in 2005.

Tourist attractions: *See* Washington, DC, Capital of the U.S., page 455.

Famous Washingtonians: Edward Albee, Frederick Douglass, John Foster Dulles, Duke Ellington, Al Gore, Katherine Grahm, Goldie Hawn, J. Edgar Hoover, Pete Sampras, John Philip Sousa.

Tourist information. Washington, DC Convention and Tourism Corp., 901 7th St NW, 4th Fl., Washington, D.C., 20001-3719; 202-789-7000. **Website:** www.washington.org

Website. www.dc.gov

World Almanac Quick Quiz

Which state had the lowest unemployment rate of any state in 2005, at 2.8%?

(a) Colorado

(b) New Hampshire

(c) South Carolina

(d) Hawaii

For the answer look in this chapter, or see page 1008.

OUTLYING U.S. AREAS

American Samoa (AS)

People. Population (July 2006 est.): 57,794. **Population growth rate** (2005-06 est.): –0.2%. **Pop. density** (2006): 751 per sq mi. **Ethnic distrib.** (2000): 92.9% Pacific Islander; 2.9% Asian; 1.2% white; 2.8% 2 or more races. **Languages:** Samoan, English.

Geography. Total area: 77 sq mi. **Land area:** 77 sq. mi. **Location:** American Samoa is the most southerly of all lands under U.S. sovereignt, about 2,300 mi. SW of Honolulu. It is an unincorporated territory consisting of 7 small islands of the Samoan group: **Tutuila, Aunu'u, Manu'a Group (Ta'u, Olosega, Ofu),** and **Rose** and **Swains Island.** Climate: Marine tropical: avg. temp 82°F with little seasonal variation; avg. annual rainfall about 36 in. **Topography:** volcanic islands, rugged peaks, and limited coastal plains.**Capital:** Pago Pago, Tuuila.

Economy. Chief industries: tuna fishing and processing, trade, services, tourism. **Chief crops:** giant taro, taro, yams, copra, coconuts, breadfruits, bananas. **Livestock** (2005): 103 cattle; 38,000 chickens; 10,500 hogs/pigs. **Fed. employees** (2005): 70. **Commercial fishing** (2000): $2 mil. **Gross domestic product** (2000 est.): $500 mil. **Commercial banks** (2005): 2; **deposits:** $152 mil. **Principal airport at:** Pago Pago.

Energy. Electricity production (2001): 130 mil. kWh

Misc. data: Motto: Samoa Muamua le Atua (In Samoa, God Is First). **Song:** Amerika Samoa. **Flower:** Paogo (Ula-fa-la). **Plant:** Ava.

History. American Samoans are of Polynesian origin. They are nationals of the U.S.; approximately 20,000 live in Hawaii, 65,000 in California and Washington.

A tripartite agreement between Great Britain, Germany, and the U.S. in 1899 gave the U.S. sovereignty over the eastern islands of the Samoan group; these islands became American Samoa. Local chiefs ceded Tutuila and Aunu'u to the U.S. in 1900, and the Manu'a group and Rose Island in 1904; Swains Island was annexed in 1925. Samoa (Western), comprising the larger islands of the Samoan group, was a New Zealand mandate and UN Trusteeship until it became independent Jan. 1, 1962 (now called Samoa).

Tutuila and Aunu'u have an area of 53 sq mi. Ta'u has an area of 17 sq mi, and the islets of Ofu and Olosega, 5 sq mi with a population of a few thousand. Swains Island has nearly 2 sq mi and a population of about 100.

About 70% of the land is bush and mountains. Chief exports are fish products, especially tuna. Taro, breadfruit, yams, coconuts, pineapples, oranges, and bananas are also produced.

From 1900 to 1951, American Samoa was under the jurisdiction of the U.S. Navy. Since 1951, it has been under the Interior Dept. On Jan. 3, 1978, the first popularly elected Samoan governor and lieutenant governor were inaugurated. Previously, the governor was appointed by the Secretary of the Interior. American Samoa has a bicameral legislature and elects a delegate to the House of Representatives, with no vote except in committees.

Hurricane Val, 1991, caused $80 mil in damages. Scientists discovered a rapidly growing volcano nearby, 2005.

American Samoans are of Polynesian origin. They are nationals of the U.S.; approximately 20,000 live in Hawaii, 65,000 in California and Washington.

Tourist information. Office of Tourism, Dept. of Commerce, American Samoa Govt., P.O. Box 1147, Pago Pago, AS 96799; 684-699-9411. **Website:** www.washington.org

Website. www.amsamoa.com

Guam (GU)
Where America's Day Begins

People. Population (July 2006 est.): 171,019. **Population growth rate** (2005-06 est.): 1.4%. **Pop. density** (2006): 807 per sq mi. **Ethnic distrib.** (2000): 37.1% Chamorro, 26.3% Filipino, 11.3% other Pacific Islander, 6.9% white, 6.3% Asian, 2.3% other, 9.8% two or more race/ethnicities. **Languages:** English, Chamorro, Philippine/other Pacific Island languages.

Geography. Total area: 212 sq mi. **Land area:** 212 sq. mi. **Location:** largest and southernmost of the Mariana Islands in the West Pacific, 3,700 mi W of Hawaii. **Climate:** tropical, with temperatures from 70° to 90° F; avg. annual rainfall, about 70 in. **Topography:** coralline limestone plateau in the N; southern chain of low volcanic mountains sloping gently to the W, more steeply to coastal cliffs on the E; general elevation, 500 ft; highest point, Mt. Lamlam, 1,334 ft. **Capital:** Hagatna.

Economy. Chief industries: U.S. military, tourism, construction, shipping, concrete products, printing & publishing. **Chief manuf. goods:** textiles, foods. **Chief crops:** cabbages, eggplants, cucumber, long beans, tomatoes, bananas, coconuts, watermelon, yams, cantaloupe, papayas, maize, sweet potatoes. **Livestock** (2005): 130 cattle; 200,000 chickens; 5,100 hogs/pigs. **Commercial fishing** (2005): $1.3 mil. **Chief port:** Apra Harbor. **Gross domestic product** (2005 est.): $2.5 bil. **Employment distrib.** (2000 est.): 26% govt.; 24% trade; 40% serv.; 10% indust. **Fed. employees** (2005): 2,170. **Unemployment** (2002 est.): 11.4%. **Per capita income** (2000 est.): $21,000. **Commercial banks** (2005): 6; **deposits:** $1.6 bil. **Savings institutions** (2005): 1; **deposits:** $49 mil. **Principal internat. airport at:** Hagatna.

Energy. Electricity production (2002): 835 mil. kWh

Federal govt. Federal employees (1990): 7,200. **Notable fed. facilities:** Anderson AFB; naval, air, and port bases.

Misc. data. Flower: Puti Tai Nobio (Bougainvillea). **Bird:** Toto (Fruit dove). **Tree:** Ifit (Intsiabijuga). **Song:** Stand Ye Guamanians.

History. Guam was probably settled by voyagers from the Indonesian-Philippine archipelago by 3rd cent. BCE. Pottery, rice cultivation, and megalithic technology show strong East Asian cultural influence. Centralized, village clan-based communities engaged in agriculture and offshore fishing. The estimated population by the early 16th cent. was 50,000-75,000. Magellan arrived in the Marianas Mar. 6, 1521. They were colonized in 1668 by Spanish missionaries, who named them the Mariana Islands in honor of Maria Anna, queen of Spain. When Spain ceded Guam to the U.S., it sold the other Marianas to Germany. Japan obtained a League of Nations mandate over the German islands in 1919; in Dec. 1941 it seized Guam, which was retaken by the U.S. in July-August 1944.

Guam is a self-governing organized unincorporated U.S. territory. The Organic Act of 1950 provided for a governor, elected to a 4-year term, and a 21-member unicameral legislature, elected biennially by the residents, who are American citizens. In 1970, the first governor was elected. In 1972, a U.S. law gave Guam one delegate to the U.S. House of Representatives who has a voice but no vote, except in committees.

Guam's quest to change its status to a U.S. Commonwealth began in the late 1970s. The Guam Commission on Self-Determination, created in 1984, developed a draft Commonwealth Act. In 1993, legislation proposing a change of status was submitted to the U.S. Congress. In 1994, the U.S. Congress passed legislation transferring 3,200 acres of land on Guam from federal to local control.

Typhoon Omar damaged 75-90% of the island's buildings, 1992. A Korean Air jetliner crashed and burned near Agana, 1997, killing 228 of 254 aboard.

Tourist attractions. Tropical climate, oceanic marine environment; annual mid-Aug. Merizo Water Festival; Tarzan Falls; beaches; water sports; duty-free port shopping.

Website: www.ns.gov.gu

Tourism website. www.ns.gov.gu/visiting.html

Commonwealth of the Northern Mariana Islands (MP)

People. Population (July 2006 est.): 82,459. **Population growth rate** (2005-06 est.): 2.5%. **Pop. density** (2006): 448 per sq mi. **Ethnic distrib.** (2000): 56.3% Asian, 36.3% Pacific Islander, 1.8% white, 0.8% other, 4.8% two or more races/ethnicities. **Languages:** Philippine languages, Chinese, English, Chamorro.

Geography. Total area: 184.2 sq mi. **Land area:** 184.2 sq mi. **Location:** Between Guam and the Tropic of Cancer, the 14 islands of the Northern Marianas form a 300-mi. long archipelago. The indigenous population is concentrated on the 3 largest of the 6 inhabited islands: **Saipan,** the seat of government and commerce, **Rota,** and **Tinian. Climate.** Tropical, with avg. temperature around 82°F, moderated by northeast trade winds; avg. annual rainfall, 80-100 in. **Topography:** Limestone S islands with even terraces and coral reefs; volcanic N isles. **Capital:** Saipan.

Economy. Chief industries: tourism, manufacturing, construction, apparel, handicrafts. **Chief manuf. goods:** apparel, stone, clay and glass products. **Chief crops:** coconuts, fruits, and vegetables. **Livestock:** (1998): 1,789 cattle; 831 hogs/pigs, 29,409 chickens. **Commercial fishing** (2000): $938,365. **Chief ports:** Saipan, Tinian. **Gross domestic**

product (2000 est., incl. U.S. subsidy): $900 mil. **Employment distrib.** (1999 est.): 35% manuf.; 18% managerial; 16% serv. **Fed. employees** (2005): 124. **Unemployment** (1999): 4.3%. **Commercial banks** (2005): 3; **deposits**: $505 mil. **Savings institutions** (2005): 1; **deposits**: $9 mil.

History. The people of the Northern Marianas are predominantly of Chamorro cultural extraction, although Carolinians and immigrants from other areas of E. Asia and Micronesia have also settled in the islands. English is among the several languages commonly spoken.

The German-controlled Northern Marianas were placed under Japanese control by a League of Nations mandate after World War I. The U.S. captured the islands during World War II. From July 18, 1947, the U.S. had administered the Northern Marianas under a trusteeship agreement with the UN Security Council. In 1975, the residents voted to become a U.S. commonwealth.

The Northern Mariana Islands has been self-governing since 1978, when a constitution drafted and adopted by the people became effective and a popularly elected bicameral legislature (2-year term), with offices of governor (4-year term) and lieut. governor, was inaugurated. Pres. Ronald Reagan proclaimed the Northern Marianas a commonwealth, 1986, and the UN formally ended its trusteeship, 1990.

Under the 1976 Commonweath Covenant with the U.S., the islands are exempt from federal immigration and import laws, and minimum wage is lower than on the mainland. The garment making industry, which has since boomed, has drawn accusations of sweatshop conditions from some critics.

Website: www.gov.mp
Tourism website. www.mymarianas.com

Commonwealth of Puerto Rico (PR)
(Estado Libre Asociado de Puerto Rico)

People. Population (2005 est.): 3,912,054 (about 3.4 mil. more Puerto Ricans reside in the mainland U.S.). **Population growth rate:** (2003-2004): 0.4%. **Pop. density:** 1,131 per sq mi. **Racial distribution** (2000): 80.5% white; 8.0% black; 0.2% Asian; 0.4% Native American/Nat. AK; 6.8% other; 2 or more races, 4.2%. **Hispanic pop.** (any race): 98.8%. **Languages:** Spanish and English are joint official languages.

Geography. Total area: 3,515 sq mi. **Land area:** 3,459 sq mi. **Location:** island lying between the Atlantic to the N and the Caribbean to the S; it is easternmost of the West Indies group called the Greater Antilles, of which Cuba, Hispaniola, and Jamaica are the larger islands. **Climate:** mild, with a mean temperature of 77°F. **Topography:** mountainous throughout three-fourths of its rectangular area, surrounded by a broken coastal plain; highest peak, Cerro de Punto, 4,390 ft. **Capital:** San Juan.

Economy. Chief industries: manufacturing, service, tourism. **Chief manuf. goods:** pharmaceuticals, apparel, electronics, food products. **Chief crops:** coffee, plantains, pineapples, sugarcane, bananas. **Livestock** (2005): 420,000 cattle;11.2 mil. chickens; 100,000 hogs/pigs; 16,000 sheep. **Nonfuel minerals** (est. 2000): $159 mil; mostly portland cement, crushed stone. **Commercial fishing** (2000): $6.4 mil. **Chief ports:** San Juan, Ponce, Mayagüez. **Gross domestic product:** (2004 est.) $69.0 bil. **Employment distrib.** (May 2006): 28.6% govt; 17.7% trade/trans./util.; 10.4% mfg; 10.0% ed./health; 10.1% prof./bus. serv.; 7.1% leisure/hosp.; 4.8% finance; 6.6% constr.; 2.3% other serv.; 2.2% info. **Unemployment** (2005): 11.3%. **Per capita pers. income** (2004): $12,031. **Commercial banks** (2005): 12; **deposits:** $53.8 bil. **Lottery** (2005): total sales: $317.9 mil; profit: $79.0 mil. **Principal airports at:** San Juan, Ponce, Mayagüez, Aguadilla.

Federal govt. Fed. civ. employees (2005): 11,308. **Notable fed. facilities:** U.S. Naval Station at Roosevelt Roads; P.R. Natl. Guard Training Area at Camp Santiago, and at Ft. Allen, Juana Diaz; Sabana SECA Communications Ctr. (U.S. Navy); *U.S. Army Station at Ft. Buchanan.

Energy. Electricity production (2002): 22.1 bil kWh

Misc. data. Motto: Joannes Est Nomen Eius (John is his name). **Flower:** Maga. **Bird:** Reinita. **Tree:** Ceiba. **National anthem:** La Borinqueña.

History. Puerto Rico (or Borinquen, after the original Arawak Indian name, Boriquen) was visited by Columbus on his second voyage, Nov. 19, 1493. In 1508, the Spanish arrived.

Sugarcane was introduced, 1515, and slaves were imported 3 years later. Gold mining petered out, 1570. Spaniards

fought off a series of British and Dutch attacks; slavery was abolished, 1873. Under the treaty of Paris, Puerto Rico was ceded to the U.S. after the Spanish-American War, 1898. In 1952 the people voted in favor of Commonwealth status.

The Commonwealth of Puerto Rico is a self-governing part of the U.S. with a primarily Hispanic culture. The island's citizens have virtually the same control over their internal affairs as do the 50 states of the U.S. However, they do not vote in national general elections, only in national primaries.

Puerto Rico is represented in the U.S. House of Representatives by a Resident Commissioner who has a voice but no vote, except in committees.

No federal income tax is collected from residents on income earned from local sources in Puerto Rico. Nevertheless, as part of the U.S. legal system, Puerto Rico is subject to the provisions of the U.S. Constitution; most federal laws apply as they do in the 50 states.

Puerto Rico's famous "Operation Bootstrap," begun in the late 1940s, succeeded in changing the island from "The Poorhouse of the Caribbean" to an area with the highest per capita income in Latin America. This program encouraged manufacturing and development of the tourist trade by selective tax exemption, low-interest loans, and other incentives. Despite the marked success of Puerto Rico's development efforts over an extended period of time, per capita income in Puerto Rico is low in comparison to that of the 50 states.

In plebiscites held in 1967, 1993, and 1998, voters chose to retain Commonwealth status. Protests mounted in the late-1990s over the U.S. Navy's use of Vieques Island for live ammunition training; offficial military exercises there were terminated, 2003.

Tourist attractions. Ponce Museum of Art; Forts El Morro and San Cristobal; Old Walled City of San Juan; Arecibo Observatory; Cordillera Central and state parks; El Yunque Rain Forest; San Juan Cathedral; Porta Coeli Chapel and Museum of Religious Art, Interamerican Univ., San Germán; Condado Convention Center; Casa Blanca, Ponce de León family home, Puerto Rican Family Museum of 16th and 17th centuries, and Fine Arts Center all in San Juan.

Cultural facilities and events. Festival Casals classical music concerts, mid-June; Puerto Rico Symphony Orchestra at Music Conservatory; Botanical Garden and Museum of Anthropology, Art, and History at the University of Puerto Rico; Institute of Puerto Rican Culture, at the Dominican Convent; and many popular festivals.

Famous Puerto Ricans. Julia de Burgos, Marta Casals Istomin, Pablo Casals, José Celso Barbosa, Orlando Cepeda, Roberto Clemente, José de Diego, José Feliciano, Doña Felisa Rincón de Gautier, Luis A. Ferré, José Ferrer, Commodore Diégo E. Hernández, Miguel Hernández Agosto, Rafael Hernández (El Jibarito), Rafael Hernández Colón, Raúl Juliá, René Marqués, Ricky Martin, Concha Meléndez, Rita Moreno, Luis Muñoz Marín, Luis Palés Matos, Adm. Horacio Rivero.

Chamber of Commerce. La Princesa Bldg., #2 Paseo la Princesa, Old San Juan, PR 00902; 800-866-7827. **Website:** www.gobierno.pr (site is in Spanish).

Tourism Website. www.gotopuertorico.com

Virgin Islands (VI)
St. John, St. Croix, St. Thomas

People. Population (July 2006 est.): 108,605. **Population growth rate** (2005-06 est.): –0.1%. **Pop. density** (2005): 804 per sq mi. **Ethnic distrib.** (2000): 76.2% black, 13.1% white, 1.1% Asian, 6.1% other races, 3.5% two or more races. **Languages:** English (official), Spanish, Creole.

Geography. Total area: 136 sq mi. **Land area:** 135 sq mi. **Location:** 3 larger and 50 smaller islands and cays in the S and W of the V.I. group (British V.I. colony to the N and E), which is situated 70 mi E of Puerto Rico, located W of the Anegada Passage, a major channel connecting the Atlantic Ocean and the Caribbean Sea. **Climate:** subtropical; the sun tempered by gentle trade winds; humidity is low; average temperature, 78° F. **Topography:** St. Thomas is mainly a ridge of hills running E and W, and has little tillable land; St. Croix rises abruptly in the N but slopes to the S to flatlands and lagoons; St. John has steep, lofty hills and valleys with little level tillable land. **Capital:** Charlotte Amalie, St.Thomas.

Economy. Chief industries: tourism, rum distilling, alumina, petroleum refining, watch assembly, textiles, electronics, printing & publishing. **Chief manuf. goods:** rum, textiles, pharmaceuticals, perfumes, stone, glass & clay products. **Chief crops:** vegetables, horticulture, fruits and nuts. **Live-**

stock (2005): 8,000 cattle; 35,000 chickens; 2,600 hogs/pigs; 3,200 sheep. **Minerals:** sand, gravel. **Chief ports:** Cruz Bay, St. John; Frederiksted and Christiansted, St. Croix; Charlotte Amalie, St. Thomas. **Principal internat. airports on:** St. Thomas, St. Croix. **Gross domestic product** (2004 est.): $1.6 bil. **Fed. employees** (2005): 690. **Unemployment** (2004 est.): 6.2%. **Per capita income** (2001 est.): $19,000. **Commercial banks** (2005): 4; **deposits:** $1.8 bil.

Energy. Electricity production (2002): 1.0 bil. kWh

Misc. data. Flower: Yellow elder or yellow trumpet, local designation Ginger Thomas. **Bird:** Yellow breast. **Song:** Virgin Islands March.

History. The islands were visited by Columbus in 1493. Spanish forces, 1555, defeated the Caribes and claimed the territory; by 1596 the native population was annihilated. First permanent settlement in the U.S. territory, 1672, by the Danes; U.S. purchased the islands, 1917, for defense purposes.

The Virgin Islands has a republican form of government, headed by a governor and lieut. governor elected, since 1970, by popular vote for 4-year terms. There is a 15-member unicameral legislature, elected by popular vote for a 2-year term. Residents of the V.I. have been U.S. citizens since 1927. Since 1973 they have elected a delegate to the U.S. House of Representatives, who has a voice but no vote, except in committees.

Hurricane Hugo, 1989, caused $500 mil in damages; U.S. troops were deployed to suppress looting and unrest.

Tourist attractions. Magens Bay, St. Thomas; duty-free shopping; Virgin Islands Natl. Park, beaches, Indian relics, and evidence of colonial Danes.

Tourist information. Dept. of Economic Development & Agriculture: St. Thomas, P.O. Box 6400, St. Thomas, VI 00804; St. Croix, P.O. Box 4535, Christiansted, St. Croix 00820. **Website.** www.usvitourism.vi
Website. www.usvi.net

Other Islands

Navassa lies between Jamaica and Haiti, 100 mi south of Guantanamo Bay, Cuba, in the Caribbean; it covers about 2 sq mi, is reserved by the U.S. for a lighthouse, and is uninhabited. It is administered by the U.S. Coast Guard.

Wake Atoll, and its neighboring atolls, **Wilkes** and **Peale,** lie in the Pacific Ocean on the direct route from Hawaii to Hong Kong, about 2,300 mi W of Honolulu and 1,290 mi E of Guam. The group is 4.5 mi long, 1.5 mi wide, and totals less than 3 sq mi in land area. The U.S. flag was hoisted over Wake Atoll, July 4, 1898; formal possession taken Jan. 17, 1899. Wake was administered by the U.S. Air Force, 1972-94. The population consists of about 200 persons.

Midway Atoll, acquired in 1867, consists of 2 atolls, **Sand** and **Eastern,** in N Pacific 1,150 mi. NW of Honolulu, with an area of about 2 sq mi, administered by the U.S. Navy. There is no indigenous population; total pop. is about 450. **Johnston Atoll,** 717 mi WSW of Honolulu, area 1 sq mi, is operated by the Defense Nuclear Agency, and the Fish and Wildlife Service, U.S. Dept. of the Interior; its population is about 396. **Kingman Reef,** 920 mi S of Hawaii, is under Navy control. **Howland, Jarvis,** and **Baker Islands,** 1,400-1,650 mi SW of Honolulu, uninhabited since World War II, are under the Interior Dept. **Palmyra** is an atoll about 1,000 mi S of Hawaii, area, 5 sq mi. Privately owned, it is under the Interior Dept.

WASHINGTON, DC, CAPITAL OF THE U.S.

Most attractions are free. All times are subject to change. For more details call the Washington, DC, Convention and Visitors Association at 1-800-422-8644, or check out the website at: www.washington.org

Bureau of Engraving and Printing

The **Bureau of Engraving and Printing** of the U.S. Treasury Dept. is the headquarters for the making of U.S. paper money. Public tours are offered Mon.-Fri., 9-10:45 AM, 12:30-2 PM, except on federal holidays. 14th and C Sts. SW. Phone: 866-874-2330. **Website.** www.moneyfactory.com

Capitol

The **United States Capitol** was originally designed by Dr. William Thornton, an amateur architect, who submitted a plan in 1793 that won him $500 and a city lot. Three other architects designed or supervised the construction of the Capitol before its completion.

The present cast iron dome at its greatest exterior height measures 135 ft 5 in. and is topped by the bronze Statue of Freedom, which stands 19½ ft and weighs 14,985 lb. On its base are the words *E Pluribus Unum* ("Out of Many, One").

The Capitol is open to the public, for guided tours only, from 9 AM to 4:30 PM. It is closed Jan. 1, Thanksgiving Day, and Dec. 25.

To observe debate while Congress is in session, those living in the U.S. may obtain tickets from their U.S. representative or senator. Visitors from other countries may obtain passes at the Capitol. Between Constitution & Independence Aves., at Pennsylvania Ave. Phone: 202-225-6827. **Website.** www.aoc.gov

Federal Bureau of Investigation

The **Federal Bureau of Investigation** offers guided one-hour tours of its headquarters. Visitors learn about the history of the FBI and see weapons confiscated from famous gangsters, photos of most-wanted fugitives, the DNA laboratory, goods forfeited/seized in narcotics operations, and a sharpshooting demonstration.

Tours have been suspended for building renovation. J. Edgar Hoover Bldg., Pennsylvania Ave., between 9th and 10th Sts. NW. Phone: 202-324-3447. **Website.** www.fbi.gov

Folger Shakespeare Library

The **Folger Shakespeare Library,** on Capitol Hill, is a research institution holding rare books and manuscripts of the Renaissance period and the largest collection of Shakespearean materials in the world. Exhibit may be visited Mon.-Sat., 10 AM-4 PM, 201 E. Capitol St., SE , Phone: 202-544-4600. **Website.** www.folger.edu

Holocaust Memorial Museum

The **U.S. Holocaust Memorial Museum** opened on Apr. 21, 1993. The museum documents the events of the Holocaust through permanent and temporary displays, interactive videos, and special lectures. The permanent exhibition is not recommended for children under age 11.

The museum is open daily, 10 AM-5:30 PM, except Yom Kippur and Dec. 25, and extended hours Tues. and Thurs. (10 AM-7:50 PM) from Apr.-June. A limited number of free tickets are available at the door; advance tickets may be ordered for a small fee at 800-400-9373. 100 Raoul Wallenberg Pl. SW. Phone: 202-488-0400. **Website.** www.ushmm.org

Jefferson Memorial

Dedicated in 1943, the **Thomas Jefferson Memorial** stands on the south shore of the Tidal Basin in West Potomac Park. It is a circular stone structure that combines architectural elements of the dome of the Pantheon in Rome and the rotunda designed by Jefferson for the Univ. of Virginia.

The memorial is open daily, 8 AM-midnight; closed Dec. 25. Has elevator and curb ramps for handicapped. Phone: 202-426-6841. **Website.** www.nps.gov/thje

John F. Kennedy Center

The **John F. Kennedy Center for the Performing Arts** opened Sept. 8, 1971. Designed by Edward Durell Stone, it includes an opera house, a concert hall, several theaters, 2 restaurants, and a library. Free tours are available Mon.-Fri., 10 AM-5 PM and Sat. & Sun., 10 AM-1 PM. 2700 F St. NW. Phone: 202-467-4600, or 1-800-444-1324. **Website.** www.kennedy-center.org

Korean War Veterans Memorial

Dedicated on July 27, 1995, the **Korean War Veterans Memorial** honors Americans who served in the Korean War. Situated at the west end of the Mall, the triangular-shaped stone and steel memorial features a multiservice formation of 19 combat-ready troops clad in ponchos with the wind at their back. A granite wall, with images of men and women who served, juts into a pool of water, the Pool of Remembrance.

The memorial is open 8 AM-11:45 pm; closed Dec. 25. French Dr., SW across from Lincoln Memorial. Phone: 202-426-6841. **Website.** www.nps.gov/kwvm

Library of Congress

Established by and for Congress in 1800, the **Library of Congress** extends its services to other government agencies and libraries, scholars, and the general public, and now serves as the national library. It contains over 80 mil. items in 470 languages.

Exhibit halls are open to the public Mon.-Fri., 8:30 AM-9:30 PM; Sat., 8:30 AM-6:30 PM. The Library is closed all federal holidays. 101 Independence Ave., SE. Phone: 202-707-8000. **Website.** www.loc.gov

Lincoln Memorial

Designed by Henry Bacon, the **Lincoln Memorial** in West Potomac Park is a large marble hall enclosing a statue of Abraham Lincoln seated on an armchair. The memorial was dedicated May 30, 1922. The statue was designed by Daniel Chester French and sculpted by French and the Piccirilli brothers. The text of the Gettysburg Address is in the south chamber; that of Lincoln's Second Inaugural speech is in the north chamber. Each is engraved on a stone tablet.

The memorial is open daily 8 AM-midnight, and is wheel-chair-accessible. W. Potomac Park at 23rd St. NW. Phone: 202-426-6841. **Website**. www.nps.gov/linc

National Archives and Records

Original copies of the Declaration of Independence, the Constitution, and the Bill of Rights are on display in the **National Archives** Exhibition Hall. The National Archives also holds other valuable U.S. government records and historic maps, photographs, and manuscripts. Central Research and Microfilm Research Rooms are also available to the public for genealogical research.

Exhibition Hall open daily 10 AM-5:30PM (later in spring and summer). 7th & Pennsylvania Ave. NW. Phone: 866-325-7208. **Website**. www.archives.gov

National Gallery of Art

The **National Gallery of Art** was established by Congress, Mar. 24, 1937, and opened Mar. 17, 1941. The original West building was designed by John Russell Pope. The East building, opened in 1978, was designed by I. M. Pei. Open daily, Mon.-Sat. 10 AM-5 PM, Sunday 11 AM-6 PM. Closed Jan. 1 and Dec. 25. 4th & Constitution Ave NW. Phone: 202-737-4215. **Website**. www.nga.gov

Franklin Delano Roosevelt Memorial

Opened May 2, 1997, the **FDR Memorial** features 9 bronze sculptural ensembles depicting FDR, Eleanor Roosevelt, and events from the Great Depression and World War II. This 7.5-acre memorial is located near the Tidal Basin in a park-like setting and is wheelchair accessible.

Grounds, staffed daily, 8 AM-midnight, except Dec. 25. 1850 W. Basin Dr. SW. Phone: 202-426-6841. **Website**. www.nps.gov/fdrm

Smithsonian Institution

The **Smithsonian Institution**, established in 1846, is the world's largest museum complex and consists of 14 museums and the National Zoo. It holds some 100 mil artifacts and specimens in its trust. The **Smithsonian Information Center** is located in "the Castle" on the Mall. Also on the Mall are the **National Museum of American History**, the **National Museum of Natural History**, the **National Air and Space Museum**, the **Hirshhorn Museum and Sculpture Garden**, the **Arthur M. Sackler Gallery**, the **National Museum of African Art**, the **Freer Gallery of Art**, and the **Arts and Industries Building**. Near the Sackler Gallery is the **Enid A. Haupt Garden**. Located nearby are the **National Postal Museum**, the **National Museum of American Art**, the **National Portrait Gallery**, and the **Renwick Gallery**. Farther away, at 1901 Fort Place SE, is the **Anacostia Museum.**

Most museums are open daily, except Dec. 25, 10 AM-5:30 PM. Phone: 202-357-2020. **Website**. www.si.edu

Vietnam Veterans Memorial

Originally dedicated on Nov. 13, 1982, the **Vietnam Veterans Memorial** recognizes the men and women who served in the armed forces in the Vietnam War. The names of more than 58,000 Americans who lost their lives or remain missing are inscribed on a V-shaped black-granite wall, designed by Maya Ying Lin.

Since 1982, 2 additions have been made to the Memorial. The 1st, dedicated on Nov. 11, 1984, is the Frederick Hart sculpture *Three Servicemen*. On Nov. 11, 1993, the Vietnam Women's Memorial, designed by Glenna Goodacre, was dedicated, honoring the more than 11,500 women who served in Vietnam.

The memorial is open 8 AM-midnight daily. Constitution Ave. & Bacon Dr. NW. Phone: 202-426-6841. **Website**. www.nps.gov/vive

Washington Monument

The **Washington Monument**, dedicated in 1885, is a tapering shaft, or obelisk, of white marble, 555 ft, 5 $^1/_8$ inches in height and 55 ft, 1½ in. square at base. Eight small windows, 2 on each side, are located at the 500-ft level.

Open daily (except Dec. 25), 9 AM-4:45 PM. Free timed passes are available; passes are available in advance for a small fee. 15th & Constitution Ave. NW. Phone: 202-426-6841. **Website**. www.nps.gov/wash

White House

The **White House,** the President's residence, stands on 18 acres on the south side of Pennsylvania Ave., between the Treasury and the old Executive Office Building. The walls are of sandstone, quarried at Aquia Creek, VA. On Aug. 24, 1814, during Madison's administration, the house was burned by the British, but it was rebuilt by Oct. 1817 and painted white, giving rise to the name "White House.

The White House is normally open for free self-guided tours Tues.-Sat., 7:30 AM-12:30 pm. (Tour requests must be made at least one month in advance through your member of Congress.) Only the public rooms on the ground floor and state floor may be visited. 1600 Pennsylvania Ave. The White House Visitor Center at 1450 Pennsylvania Ave. is open daily 7:30 AM - 4 PM. Phone: 202-456-7041. **Website**. www.whitehouse.gov

National World War II Memorial

The **National WWII Memorial** is dedicated to the approx. 16 mil. veterans who served and the more than 400,000 who died in the war. It rests on 7.4 acres of land at the east end of the reflecting pool on the Mall. The memorial opened on April 29, 2004, and was dedicated on May 29.

At the north and south entrances are 43-ft. archways, representing the Atlantic and Pacific theaters. Inside the grounds is a large, oval plaza with a wall of 4,000 gold stars; each represents 100 American deaths. Fifty-six pillars ringing the center represent the states, territories, and District of Columbia. There is also a garden enclosed by a stone wall (called the "Circle of Remembrance").

The memorial is wheelchair-accessible and open daily, 24 hours a day, except Dec. 25. Located on 17th St. between Constitution and Independence Aves. Phone: 202-619-7222. **Website**. www.nps.gov/nwwm

Attractions Near Washington, DC

Arlington National Cemetery

Arlington National Cemetery, on the former Custis-Lee estate in Arlington, VA, is the site of the **Tomb of the Unknowns** and is the final resting place of Pres. John F. Kennedy and his wife, Jacqueline Bouvier Kennedy Onassis. An eternal flame burns over the grave site. Many other famous Americans are buried at Arlington, as well as more than 200,000 U.S. military personnel, from every major war.

North of the National Cemetery stands the **U.S. Marine Corps War Memorial**, also known as Iwo Jima. The memorial is a bronze statue of the raising of the U.S. flag on Mt. Suribachi, Feb. 23, 1945, during World War II, executed by Felix de Weldon from the photograph by Joe Rosenthal.

On the southern side of the Memorial Bridge, near the cemetery entrance, a memorial honoring the women in the military was dedicated, Oct. 18, 1997. The **Women in Military Service for America Memorial** is a granite monument, 30 ft. high and 226 ft. in diameter, with the Great Seal of the U.S. in the center.

Open daily, 8 AM-5 PM (8 AM-7 PM., Apr.-Sept.), Arlington, VA. Phone: 703-607-8000. **Website**. www.arlingtoncemetery.org

Mount Vernon

Mount Vernon, George Washington's estate, is on the south bank of the Potomac R., 16 mi from Washington, DC, in northern Virginia. The present house is an enlargement of one apparently built on the site by Augustine Washington, who lived there 1735-38. His son Lawrence came there in 1743; he died in 1752 and was succeeded as proprietor by his half-brother, George Washington. The estate has been restored to its 18th-century appearance and includes many original furnishings. Washington and his wife, Martha, are buried on the grounds.

Open 365 days, 8 AM-5 PM, Apr.-Aug., 9 AM-5 PM, Sept., Oct., Mar.; 9 AM-4 PM, Nov.-Feb. Phone: 703-780-2000, or 1-800-429-1520. Admission: adults $11, seniors (62+) $10.50, children (6-11) $5, age 5 and under free. **Website**. www.mountvernon.org

The Pentagon

The **Pentagon,** headquarters of the Dept. of Defense, is the largest office building in the U.S. Situated in Arlington, VA, it houses more than 23,000 employees in offices occupying 3,705,793 sq ft. The building was severely damaged when struck by a plane Sept. 11, 2001.

Tours available to schools, educational organizations, and other select groups by reservation only. Arlington, VA (I-395 South to Boundary Channel Drive exit). Pentagon tour office: 703-697-1776. **Website**. www.defenselink.mil/pubs/pentagon

UNITED STATES POPULATION

Census Bureau Profile of a Nation of 300 Million

by Charles Louis Kincannon, Director, U.S. Census Bureau

In late 2006, our nation achieved a historic milestone: a population of 300 million. Since our population topped 100 million (in 1915)—and even since it grew to 200 million (in 1967)—our country has been completely transformed. For instance, when the population reached 100 million, we were barely out of the "horse and buggy" era and the milk carton and the "Model T" represented the latest in technological innovation. When the 200 million population mark was reached, color TV was the rage and the space race was soon to culminate with man reaching the moon. Today, we live in an era of cell phones, DVD players and GPS technology. We saw the number of motor vehicle registrations jump from less than 3 million in 1915, to about 99 million in 1967 and to more than 237 million today. Life expectancy has climbed from 54.5 years (1915), to 70.5 years (1967) and to 77.8 years (2005). And Phoenix, a hot, dusty, desert town of only 11,000 people in 1915 is now the sixth most populous city in the United States with 1.5 million residents. Following is a look at life in our great nation of 300 million people.

Responding to Natural Disasters

The damage from hurricanes Katrina and Rita last year served as poignant reminders of how increasingly vulnerable our nation is to natural disasters. As of July 1, 2005, nearly 35 million of us, or 12% of the U.S. population, resided in the area most threatened by Atlantic hurricanes—the coastal portion of the states stretching from North Carolina to Texas. In 1950, 10 million people, or 7%, lived in these areas.

Through the American Community Survey (ACS), the Census Bureau is now able to provide up-to-date information to aid local officials in emergency preparedness and planning. Recently released ACS data, along with a special set of population estimates, enabled us to shed some light on the effects of the devastating hurricanes that impacted the Gulf Coast last year. We were able to provide information on population characteristics in the 117 counties in Alabama, Mississippi, Louisiana and Texas initially designated by the Federal Emergency Management Agency as eligible for individual or public assistance. These data revealed, for instance, that the population of New Orleans, about 437,000 on July 1, 2005—less than two months before Hurricane Katrina—dropped to 158,000 on Jan. 1, 2006. Demographically, the black population of the entire metro area declined from 37% before the hurricane to 22% afterward; the median age rose from 38 to 42; and the average household income changed from $55,326 to $64,122.

An Increasingly Diverse Nation

Mid-decade numbers provide further evidence of the increasing diversity of our nation's population. About 1 in every 3 U.S. residents, or 98 million, is a minority; that is, they are part of a group other than single-race non-Hispanic white. Hispanics continue to be the largest minority group at 42.7 million. With a 3.3% increase in population from July 1, 2004, to July 1, 2005, they are also the fastest-growing group. Blacks were the second largest minority group (39.7 million), followed by Asians (14.4 million), American Indians and Alaska Natives (4.5 million) and Native Hawaiians and other Pacific Islanders (990,000). The population of non-Hispanic whites who indicated no other race totaled 198.4 million in 2005. The nation's population of preschoolers—children under age 5—was 45% minority.

Texas recently joined Hawaii, New Mexico and California as a majority-minority state, along with the District of Columbia. Five states—Maryland, Georgia, Mississippi, Nevada and Arizona—are in the next tier with minority populations of about 40%. According to July 1, 2005, population estimates, Texas had a minority population of 11.6 million, comprising 50.8% of its 22.9 million population. In comparison, 77% of Hawaii's population was minority. In New Mexico and California, the proportions were 57% and 56%, respectively, while the District of Columbia was 69% minority.

A Rapidly Aging Population

The U.S. population age 65 and older is expected to double in size within the next 25 years. By 2030, almost 1 out of 5 Americans—some 72 million people—will be in this age group.

The financial condition of older people has improved dramatically, although there are still wide variations in income and wealth. The proportion of people age 65 and older in poverty decreased from 35% in 1959 to 10% in 2003.

Migration Continues South and West

Nevada's population increased by 3.5% between July 1, 2004, and July 1, 2005, marking its 19th consecutive year as the fastest-growing state. Neighboring Arizona was a close second with a growth rate just under 3.5%. The South and West again dominated the list of the fastest-growing states: Idaho, Florida, Utah, Georgia, Texas, North Carolina, Delaware, and Oregon rounded out the top 10. The South now accounts for 36% of the nation's total population, with the West comprising 23%, the Midwest 22% and the Northeast 18%.

The nation's counties and cities displayed a similar pattern. Flagler County in Florida, located along the Atlantic Coast between Daytona Beach and Jacksonville, was the fastest-growing county for the second year in a row with a 10.7% population increase over the one-year period. All but one of the top-10 fastest-growing counties between 2004 and 2005 were located in either the South or the West.

Located south of Sacramento, Elk Grove, Calif., had the nation's fastest growth rate (12%) among large cities (100,000 or more population) between July 1, 2004, and July 1, 2005.

More Foreign-Born and Second Generation Americans

The nation's foreign-born population numbered 34.2 million in 2004, accounting for 12% of the total U.S. population. In 1920, when arrivals at Ellis Island were nearing their peak, there were only 13.9 million foreign-born; however, the foreign-born population made up 13% of the nation's population.

In 2004, 53% of our foreign-born population was born in Latin America, 25% in Asia, 14% in Europe and the remaining 8% in other regions of the world, such as Africa and Oceania (Australia, New Zealand and island nations in the Pacific).

Second-generation Americans, individuals with one or both parents born in a foreign country, numbered 30.4 million, or 11% of the total U.S. population.

IT'S A FACT: According to the U.S. Census Bureau, the cost of a gallon of milk was 36¢ ($7.22 in 2006 dollars) in 1915, when the U.S. population reached 100 mil. A gallon of regular gas was 25¢ ($5.01 in 2006 dollars) while a new home cost $3,200 ($64,158 in 2006 dollars). Compare those figures to the prices of things in 2006, when the U.S. population reached 300 mil: about $3 for a gallon of milk, $3.04 for a gallon of regular gas, and $290,600 for a new home.

The Census: Looking Back and Looking Ahead

The U.S. census is conducted every 10 years as mandated by the Constitution, Article 1, Section 2. The primary purpose is to apportion seats in the House of Representatives and determine state legislative district boundaries. The data are also critical for a vast array of government programs at every level and for providing demographic information to individuals and businesses.

The first U.S. census, which counted 3.9 million people, was conducted in 1790, shortly after George Washington became president. It counted the number of free white males age 16 and over, the number under 16 (to measure how many men might be available for military service), the number of free white females, all other free persons (including any American Indians who paid taxes), and slaves. It took 18 months to collect the data, often on unofficial sheets of paper supplied by U.S. marshals. In contrast to today's pledge of confidentiality, the 1790 census results were publicly displayed. The 1790 census resulted in an increase of 41 seats (65 to 106) in the House of Representatives.

As the nation expanded, so did the scope of the census data. The first inquiry on manufactures was made in 1810. Questions on agriculture, mining, and fisheries were added in 1840. In 1850, the census included inquiries on social issues—taxation, churches, pauperism, and crime.

The 1880 census had so many questions that it took the full 10 years between censuses to publish all the results. Because of this delay, Congress limited the 1900 census to questions on population, manufactures, agriculture, and mortality. (Many of the dropped topics reappeared in later censuses.)

For many years, the undertaking of each census had to be authorized by a specific act of Congress. In 1954, Congress specified the laws under which the Census Bureau operates in Title 13 of the U.S. Code. This title delineates the basic scope of the census, the requirements for the public to provide information as well as for the Bureau to keep information confidential, and the penalties for violating any of these obligations.

Today, the secretary of commerce (and through that individual, the Census Bureau) is directed by law to take censuses of population, housing, agriculture, irrigation, manufactures, mineral industries, other businesses (wholesale trade, retail trade, services), construction, transportation, and governments at stated intervals, and may take surveys related to any of these subjects.

U.S. marshals supervised their assistants' enumeration of the first 9 censuses and reported to the president (1790), the secretary of state (1800-40), or the secretary of the interior (1850-70). There was no continuity of personnel from one census to the next. However, in 1902, Congress authorized the president to set up a permanent Census Office in the Interior Dept. In 1903, the agency was transferred to the new Dept. of Commerce and Labor, and when the department split in 1913, the Bureau of the Census was placed in the Commerce Dept.

The Census Bureau began using statistical sampling techniques in the 1940s, computers in the 1950s, and mail enumeration in the 1960s, all as part of an effort to publish more data sooner and at a lower cost, and with less burden on the public. For the 2010 Census, the Census Bureau plans to continue mailing questionnaires to most housing units in the country, but to use handheld computers, rather than paper and pencil, in doing follow-up interviews at nonresponding households.

In addition, unlike previous censuses, the 2010 Census will consist of a short-form questionnaire only. To gather other informative data about America's people, we will look to the American Community Survey (ACS). The ACS—first implemented nationwide in 2005—replaces the need for a long-form questionnaire in 2010. With responses from our nation's residents, the ACS can provide current demographic, economic and housing information about America's communities every year—information previously available only once every 10 years from the decennial censuses.

10 Largest Counties, by Population, 2000, 2005

Source: 2000 Census, 2005 Population Estimates, U.S. Census Bureau, U.S. Dept of Commerce

County	2005 Population	2000 Population	Percent change	County	2005 Population	2000 Population	Percent change
Los Angeles County, CA	9,935,475	9,519,330	4.4	San Diego County, CA	2,933,462	2,813,833	4.3
Cook County, IL	5,303,683	5,376,822	−1.4	Kings County, NY	2,486,235	2,465,525	0.8
Harris County, TX	3,693,050	3,400,580	8.6	Miami-Dade County, FL	2,376,014	2,253,779	5.4
Maricopa County, AZ	3,635,528	3,072,335	18.3	Dallas County, TX	2,305,454	2,218,842	3.9
Orange County, CA	2,988,072	2,846,289	5.0	Queens County, NY	2,241,600	2,229,379	0.5

Note on least populated counties: The following are the 10 smallest counties by 2005 population: Loving County, TX (62); Kalawao County, HI (111); King County, TX (307); Arthur County, NE (378); Kenedy County, TX (417); Petroleum County, MT (470); Blaine County, NE (484); McPherson County, NE (507); San Juan County, CO (577); and Thomas County, NE (623).

Population by State, 2000, 2005

Source: 2000 Census, 2005 Population Estimates, U.S. Census Bureau, U.S. Dept. of Commerce

Rank	State	2005 population	2000 population	Percent change 2000-2005	Rank	State	2005 population	2000 population	Percent change 2000-2005
1.	California	36,132,147	33,871,653	6.7	27.	Oregon	3,641,056	3,421,436	6.4
2.	Texas	22,859,968	20,851,792	9.6	28.	Oklahoma	3,547,884	3,450,652	2.8
3.	New York	19,254,630	18,976,821	1.5	29.	Connecticut	3,510,297	3,405,602	3.1
4.	Florida	17,789,864	15,982,824	11.3	30.	Iowa	2,966,334	2,926,382	1.4
5.	Illinois	12,763,371	12,419,647	2.8	31.	Mississippi	2,921,088	2,844,656	2.7
6.	Pennsylvania	12,429,616	12,281,054	1.2	32.	Arkansas	2,779,154	2,673,398	4.0
7.	Ohio	11,464,042	11,353,145	1.0	33.	Kansas	2,744,687	2,688,824	2.1
8.	Michigan	10,120,860	9,938,480	1.8	34.	Utah	2,469,585	2,233,198	10.6
9.	Georgia	9,072,576	8,186,816	10.8	35.	Nevada	2,414,807	1,998,257	20.8
10.	New Jersey	8,717,925	8,414,347	3.6	36.	New Mexico	1,928,384	1,819,046	6.0
11.	North Carolina	8,683,242	8,046,491	7.9	37.	West Virginia	1,816,856	1,808,350	0.5
12.	Virginia	7,567,465	7,079,030	6.9	38.	Nebraska	1,758,787	1,711,265	2.8
13.	Massachusetts	6,398,743	6,349,105	0.8	39.	Idaho	1,429,096	1,293,956	10.4
14.	Washington	6,287,759	5,894,140	6.7	40.	Maine	1,321,505	1,274,923	3.7
15.	Indiana	6,271,973	6,080,517	3.1	41.	New Hampshire	1,309,940	1,235,786	6.0
16.	Tennessee	5,962,959	5,689,262	4.8	42.	Hawaii	1,275,194	1,211,537	5.3
17.	Arizona	5,939,292	5,130,632	15.8	43.	Rhode Island	1,076,189	1,048,319	2.7
18.	Missouri	5,800,310	5,596,683	3.6	44.	Montana	935,670	902,195	3.7
19.	Maryland	5,600,388	5,296,506	5.7	45.	Delaware	843,524	783,600	7.6
20.	Wisconsin	5,536,201	5,363,715	3.2	46.	South Dakota	775,933	754,840	2.8
21.	Minnesota	5,132,799	4,919,492	4.3	47.	Alaska	663,661	626,931	5.9
22.	Colorado	4,665,177	4,302,015	8.4	48.	North Dakota	636,677	642,204	-0.9
23.	Alabama	4,557,808	4,447,351	2.5	49.	Vermont	623,050	608,827	2.3
24.	Louisiana	4,523,628	4,468,958	1.2	50.	District of Columbia	550,521	572,059	-3.8
25.	South Carolina	4,255,083	4,011,816	6.1	51.	Wyoming	509,294	493,782	3.1
26.	Kentucky	4,173,405	4,042,285	3.2		**Total Resident Pop.[1]**	**296,410,404**	**281,424,602**	**5.3**

(1) Resident population excludes military personnel and others living abroad and allocated to the state in total population count.

IT'S A RECORD: New York County, New York, which consists mainly of Manhattan, is the smallest county in the U.S. by land area, at 23 square miles. With approximately 1.5 mil residents in 2000, New York County also ranked as the country's most densely populated, with about 66,834 residents per square mile.

Density of Population by State, 1930-2000

Source: U.S. Census Bureau, U.S. Dept. of Commerce
(per square mile, land area only)

STATE	1930	1960	1980	1990	2000	STATE	1930	1960	1980	1990	2000
AL......	51.8	64.2	76.6	79.6	87.6	MT......	3.7	4.6	5.4	5.5	6.2
AK*......	.1	0.4	0.7	1.0	1.1	NE......	18.0	18.4	20.5	20.5	22.3
AZ......	3.8	11.5	23.9	32.3	45.2	NV......	.8	2.6	7.3	10.9	18.2
AR......	35.2	34.2	43.9	45.1	51.3	NH......	51.6	67.2	102.4	123.7	137.8
CA......	36.2	100.4	151.4	190.8	217.2	NJ......	537.3	805.5	986.2	1,042.0	1,134.5
CO......	10.0	16.9	27.9	31.8	41.5	NM......	3.5	7.8	10.7	12.5	15.0
CT......	328.0	520.6	637.8	678.4	702.9	NY......	262.6	350.6	370.6	381.0	401.9
DE......	120.5	225.2	307.6	340.8	401.0	NC......	64.5	93.2	120.4	136.1	165.2
DC......	7,981.5	12,523.9	10,132.3	9,882.8	9,378.0	ND......	9.7	9.1	9.4	9.3	9.3
FL......	27.1	91.5	180.0	239.6	296.4	OH......	161.6	236.6	263.3	264.9	277.3
GA......	49.7	67.8	94.1	111.9	141.4	OK......	34.6	33.8	44.1	45.8	50.3
HI*......	57.5	98.5	150.1	172.5	188.6	OR......	9.9	18.4	27.4	29.6	35.6
ID......	5.4	8.1	11.5	12.2	15.6	PA......	213.8	251.4	264.3	265.1	274.0
IL......	136.4	180.4	205.3	205.6	223.4	RI......	649.8	819.3	897.8	960.3	1,003.2
IN......	89.4	128.8	152.8	154.6	169.5	SC......	56.8	78.7	103.4	115.8	133.2
IA......	44.1	49.2	52.1	49.7	52.4	SD......	9.1	9.0	9.1	9.2	9.9
KS......	22.9	26.6	28.9	30.3	32.9	TN......	62.4	86.2	111.6	118.3	138.0
KY......	65.2	76.2	92.3	92.8	101.7	TX......	22.1	36.4	54.3	64.9	79.6
LA......	46.5	72.2	94.5	96.9	102.6	UT......	6.2	10.8	17.8	21.0	27.2
ME......	25.7	31.3	36.3	39.8	41.3	VT......	38.8	42.0	55.2	60.8	65.8
MD......	165.0	313.5	428.7	489.2	541.9	VA......	60.7	99.6	134.7	156.3	178.8
MA......	537.4	657.3	733.3	767.6	809.8	WA......	23.3	42.8	62.1	73.1	88.6
MI......	84.9	137.7	162.6	163.6	175.0	WV......	71.8	77.2	80.8	74.5	75.1
MN......	32.0	43.1	51.2	55.0	61.8	WI......	53.7	72.6	86.5	90.1	98.8
MS......	42.4	46.0	53.4	54.9	60.6	WY......	2.3	3.4	4.9	4.7	5.1
MO......	52.4	62.6	71.3	74.3	81.2	**U.S......**	**41.2**	**50.6**	**64.0**	**70.3**	**79.6**

* For purposes of comparison, Alaska and Hawaii are included in above tabulation for 1930, even though not states then.

U.S. Area and Population, 1790-2000

Source: Decennial Censuses, U.S. Census Bureau, U.S. Dept. of Commerce

Census date	AREA (square miles) Gross Area	Land Area	Water Area	POPULATION Number	Per sq mi of land	Increase over preceding census Number	%
1790 (Aug. 2)	891,364	864,746	24,065	3,929,214	4.5	—	—
1800 (Aug. 4)	891,364	864,746	24,065	5,308,483	6.1	1,379,269	35.1
1810 (Aug. 6)	1,722,685	1,681,828	34,175	7,239,881	4.3	1,931,398	36.4
1820 (Aug. 7)	1,792,552	1,749,462	38,544	9,638,453	5.5	2,398,572	33.1
1830 (June 1)	1,792,552	1,749,462	38,544	12,866,020[2]	7.4	3,227,567	33.5
1840 (June 1)	1,792,552	1,749,462	38,544	17,069,453[2]	9.8	4,203,433	32.7
1850 (June 1)	2,991,655	2,940,042	52,705	23,191,876	7.9	6,122,423	35.9
1860 (June 1)	3,021,295	2,969,640	52,747	31,443,321	10.6	8,251,445	35.6
1870 (June 1)	3,612,299	3,540,705	52,747	39,818,449[3]	11.2	8,375,128	26.6
1880 (June 1)	3,612,299	3,540,705	52,747	50,189,209	14.2	10,370,760	26.0
1890 (June 1)	3,612,299	3,540,705	52,747	62,979,766	17.8	12,790,557	25.5
1900 (June 1)	3,618,770	3,547,314	52,553	76,212,168	21.5	13,232,402	21.0
1910 (Apr. 15)	3,618,770	3,547,045	52,822	92,228,496	26.0	16,016,328	21.0
1920 (Jan. 1)	3,618,770	3,546,931	52,936	106,021,537	29.9	13,793,041	15.0
1930 (Apr. 1)	3,618,770	3,551,608	45,259	123,202,624	34.7	17,181,087	16.2
1940 (Apr. 1)	3,618,770	3,551,608	45,259	132,164,569	37.2	8,961,945	7.3
1950 (Apr. 1)	3,618,770	3,552,206	63,005	151,325,798	42.6	19,161,229	14.5
1960 (Apr. 1)	3,618,770	3,540,911	74,212	179,323,175	50.6	27,997,377	18.5
1970 (Apr. 1)	3,618,770	3,536,855	78,444	203,302,031	57.5	23,978,856	13.4
1980 (Apr. 1)	3,618,770	3,539,289	79,481	226,542,199[4]	64.0	23,240,168	11.4
1990 (Apr. 1)	3,717,796[1]	3,536,278	181,518[1]	248,718,302[5]	70.3	22,176,103	9.8
2000 (Apr. 1)	3,794,083[1]	3,537,438	256,645[1]	281,424,602[6]	79.6	32,706,300	13.1

(1) Figure for 1990 includes inland, coastal, and Great Lakes water. Figure for 2000 includes additional territorial water as determined by presidential decree in Dec. 1998. Figures for 1790 to 1980 cover inland water only. (2) The U.S. total includes persons (5,318 in 1830 and 6,100 in 1840) on public ships in the service of the U.S. not credited to any region, division, or state. (3) Revised to include adjustments for underenumeration in southern states; unrevised number is 38,558,371. (4) Total population count has been revised since the 1980 census publications. Numbers by age, race, Hispanic origin, and sex have not been corrected. (5) Census count includes count question resolution corrections processed through Dec. 1997 and does not include adjustments for census coverage errors. (6) Reflects modifications to the Census 2000 population as documented in the Count Question Resolution program.
NOTE: Percent changes are computed on the basis of change in population since the preceding census date, so the period covered is not always exactly 10 years. Population density figures given for various years represent the area within the boundaries of the U.S. that was under the jurisdiction on the date in question—including, in some cases, considerable areas not organized or settled and not actually covered by the census. In 1870, for example, Alaska was not covered by the census, but its area is included in density calculations. Population figures shown here may reflect corrections made to the initial tabulated census counts.

Congressional Apportionment

Source: Decennial Censuses, U.S. Census Bureau, U.S. Dept. of Commerce

The Constitution, in Article 1, Section 2, provided for a census of the population every 10 years to serve as a basis for apportionment of representatives among the states. This apportionment largely determines the number of electoral votes allotted to each state.

The number of representatives of each state in Congress is determined by the state's population, though each state is entitled to one representative regardless of population size. A congressional apportionment has been made after each decennial census except that of 1920. (The year given above is the year of the census on which apportionment for the next election year is based.) Prior to 1870, $^3/_5$ the number of slaves were added to the total free population. Indians "not taxed" were excluded until 1940.

Under provisions of a law that became effective Nov. 15, 1941, representatives are apportioned by the method of equal proportions. In the application of this method, the apportionment is made so that the average population per representative has the least possible variation between one state and any other.

The first House of Representatives, in 1789, had 65 members, as provided by the Constitution. Of these, the largest numbers were from Virginia (19), Massachusetts (14), and Pennsylvania (13).

As the nation's population grew, the number of representatives was increased, but the total membership of the House has been fixed at 435 since the apportionment based on the 1910 census.

	2000	1990	1980	1970	1950	1900	1850		2000	1990	1980	1970	1950	1900	1850
AL....	7	7	7	7	9	9	7	NE.....	3	3	3	3	4	6	NA
AK....	1	1	1	1	1	NA	NA	NV.....	3	2	2	1	1	1	NA
AZ....	8	6	5	4	2	NA	NA	NH.....	2	2	2	2	2	2	3
AR....	4	4	4	4	6	7	2	NJ.....	13	13	14	15	14	10	5
CA....	53	52	45	43	30	8	2	NM.....	3	3	3	2	2	NA	NA
CO....	7	6	6	5	4	3	NA	NY.....	29	31	34	39	43	37	33
CT....	5	6	6	6	6	5	4	NC.....	13	12	11	11	12	10	8
DE....	1	1	1	1	1	1	1	ND.....	1	1	1	1	2	2	NA
FL.....	25	23	19	15	8	3	1	OH.....	18	19	21	23	23	21	21
GA....	13	11	10	10	10	11	8	OK.....	5	6	6	6	6	5	NA
HI.....	2	2	2	2	1	NA	NA	OR.....	5	5	5	4	4	2	1
ID.....	2	2	2	2	2	1	NA	PA.....	19	21	23	25	30	32	25
IL.....	19	20	22	24	25	25	9	RI......	2	2	2	2	2	2	2
IN.....	9	10	10	11	11	13	11	SC.....	6	6	6	6	6	7	6
IA.....	5	5	6	6	8	11	2	SD.....	1	1	1	2	2	2	NA
KS....	4	4	5	5	6	8	NA	TN.....	9	9	9	8	9	10	10
KY....	6	6	7	7	8	11	10	TX.....	32	30	27	24	22	16	2
LA....	7	7	8	8	8	7	4	UT.....	3	3	3	2	2	1	NA
ME....	2	2	2	2	3	4	6	VT.....	1	1	1	1	1	2	3
MD....	8	8	8	8	7	6	6	VA.....	11	11	10	10	10	10	13
MA....	10	10	11	12	14	14	11	WA.....	9	9	8	7	7	3	NA
MI.....	15	16	18	19	18	12	4	WV.....	3	3	4	4	6	5	NA
MN....	8	8	8	8	9	9	2	WI.....	8	9	9	9	10	11	3
MS....	4	5	5	5	6	8	5	WY.....	1	1	1	1	1	1	NA
MO....	9	9	9	10	11	16	7	**TOTAL**	**435**	**435**	**435**	**435**	**435**	**391**	**237**
MT....	1	1	2	2	2	1	NA								

Note: NA = Not applicable.

U.S. Slave and "Free Colored" Population, 1790, 1820, 1860[1]

Source: Decennial Censuses, U.S. Census Bureau, U.S. Dept. of Commerce

	1790 CENSUS			1820 CENSUS			1860 CENSUS		
	Slaves	% Slaves	Free Colored	Slaves	% Slaves	Free Colored	Slaves	% Slaves	Free Colored
Northern States[2]........	40,370	2.1	33,016	18,001	0.3	92,351	18	0.0	225,224
Connecticut..........	2,759	1.2	2,801	97	0.0	7,844	0	0.0	8,627
New Jersey..........	11,423	6.2	2,762	7,557	2.7	12,460	18	0.0	25,318
New York...........	21,324	6.3	4,654	10,088	0.7	29,279	0	0.0	49,005
Pennsylvania........	3,737	0.9	6,537	211	0.0	30,202	0	0.0	56,949
Border/Disputed States..	123,753	27.4	12,056	248,860	22.4	55,794	429,403	20.6	118,652
Delaware............	8,887	15.0	3,899	4,509	6.2	12,958	1,798	1.6	19,829
Kansas	....	....	....	....	....	....	2	0.0	625
Kentucky............	11,830	16.2	114	126,732	22.5	2,759	225,483	19.5	10,684
Maryland............	103,036	32.2	8,043	107,397	26.4	39,730	87,189	12.7	83,942
Missouri.............	....	....	....	10,222	15.4	347	114,931	9.7	3,572
Southern States	533,774	35.4	20,301	1,263,780	37.8	74,381	3,521,110	34.3	132,760
Alabama	....	....	....	41,879	32.7	571	435,080	45.1	2,690
Arkansas	....	....	....	1,617	11.3	59	111,115	25.5	144
Florida..............	....	....	....	....	....	....	61,745	44.0	932
Georgia.............	29,264	35.5	398	149,654	43.9	1,763	462,198	43.7	3,500
Louisiana...........	....	....	....	69,064	45.2	10,476	331,726	46.9	18,647
Mississippi..........	....	....	....	32,814	43.5	458	436,631	55.2	773
North Carolina........	100,572	25.5	4,975	205,017	32.1	14,612	331,059	33.4	30,463
South Carolina........	107,094	43.0	1,801	258,475	51.4	6,826	402,406	57.2	9,914
Tennessee..........	3,417	9.5	361	80,107	18.9	2,727	275,719	24.8	7,300
Texas..............	....	....	....	....	....	....	182,566	30.2	355
Virginia	293,427	39.2	12,766	425,153	39.9	36,889	490,865	30.7	58,042
Total Territories[3]........	....	....	....	6,377	19.3	4,048	3,229	1.1	11,434
Total States and Territories	697,897	17.8	59,466	1,538,125	16.0	233,504	3,953,760	12.6	488,070

(1) "Free colored" was an official Census Bureau designation in these decades. All pop. figures for slaves and free colored include both blacks and those of mixed-race background. (2) Some states had negligible slave populations that are not listed separately but are included in regional totals (relevant census years in parentheses): California (1860), Illinois (1820, 1860), Indiana (1820, 1860), Iowa (1860), Maine (1820, 1860), Massachusetts (1790, 1820, 1860), Michigan (1860), Minnesota (1860), New Hampshire (1790, 1820, 1860), Ohio (1820, 1860), Oregon (1860), Rhode Island (1790, 1820, 1860), Vermont (1820, 1860), and Wisconsin (1860). (3) Inc. Colorado (1860), Dakota (1860), the District of Columbia (1820, 1860), Nebraska (1860), Nevada (1860), New Mexico (1860), Utah (1860), and Washington (1860).

U.S. Population by Official

Source: Decennial Censuses, U.S. Census Bureau

STATE	1790[1]	1800[1]	1810[1]	1820[1]	1830[1]	1840	1850	1860	1870	1880	1890	1900
AL..	....	1	9	128	310	590,756	771,623	964,201	996,992	1,262,505	1,513,401	1,828,697
AK..	....	....	....	....	....	....	....	....	....	33,426	32,052	63,592
AZ..	....	....	....	....	....	....	....	....	9,658	40,440	88,243	122,931
AR..	....	....	1	14	30	97,574	209,897	435,450	484,471	802,525	1,128,211	1,311,564
CA..	....	....	....	....	....	....	92,597	379,994	560,247	864,694	1,213,398	1,485,053
CO..	....	....	....	....	....	....	....	34,277	39,864	194,327	413,249	539,700
CT..	238	251	262	275	298	309,978	370,792	460,147	537,454	622,700	746,258	908,420
DE..	59	64	73	73	77	78,085	91,532	112,216	125,015	146,608	168,493	184,735
DC..	....	8	16	23	30	33,745	51,687	75,080	131,700	177,624	230,392	278,718
FL..	....	....	....	....	35	54,477	87,445	140,424	187,748	269,493	391,422	528,542
GA..	83	163	252	341	517	691,392	906,185	1,057,286	1,184,109	1,542,180	1,837,353	2,216,331
HI..	....	....	....	....	....	....	....	....	....	....	....	154,001
ID..	....	....	....	....	....	....	....	....	14,999	32,610	88,548	161,772
IL..	....	....	12	55	157	476,183	851,470	1,711,951	2,539,891	3,077,871	3,826,352	4,821,550
IN..	....	6	25	147	343	685,866	988,416	1,350,428	1,680,637	1,978,301	2,192,404	2,516,462
IA..	....	....	....	....	....	43,112	192,214	674,913	1,194,020	1,624,615	1,912,297	2,231,853
KS..	....	....	....	....	....	....	....	107,206	364,399	996,096	1,428,108	1,470,495
KY..	74	221	407	564	688	779,828	982,405	1,155,684	1,321,011	1,648,690	1,858,635	2,147,174
LA..	....	....	77	153	216	352,411	517,762	708,002	726,915	939,946	1,118,588	1,381,625
ME..	97	152	229	298	399	501,793	583,169	628,279	626,915	648,936	661,086	694,466
MD..	320	342	381	407	447	470,019	583,034	687,049	780,894	934,943	1,042,390	1,188,044
MA..	379	423	472	523	610	737,699	994,514	1,231,066	1,457,351	1,783,085	2,238,947	2,805,346
MI..	....	....	5	9	32	212,267	397,654	749,113	1,184,059	1,636,937	2,093,890	2,420,982
MN..	....	....	....	....	....	....	6,077	172,023	439,706	780,773	1,310,283	1,751,394
MS..	....	8	31	75	137	375,651	606,526	791,305	827,922	1,131,597	1,289,600	1,551,270
MO..	....	....	20	67	140	383,702	682,044	1,182,012	1,721,295	2,168,380	2,679,185	3,106,665
MT..	....	....	....	....	....	....	....	....	20,595	39,159	142,924	243,329
NE..	....	....	....	....	....	....	....	28,841	122,993	452,402	1,062,656	1,066,300
NV..	....	....	....	....	....	....	....	6,857	42,491	62,266	47,355	42,335
NH..	142	184	214	244	269	284,574	317,976	326,073	318,300	346,991	376,530	411,588
NJ..	184	211	246	278	321	373,306	489,555	672,035	906,096	1,131,116	1,444,933	1,883,669
NM..	....	....	....	....	....	....	61,547	93,516	91,874	119,565	160,282	195,310
NY..	340	589	959	1,373	1,919	2,428,921	3,097,394	3,880,735	4,382,759	5,082,871	6,003,174	7,268,894
NC..	394	478	556	639	736	753,419	869,039	992,622	1,071,361	1,399,750	1,617,949	1,893,810
ND..	....	....	....	....	....	....	....	....	2,405[2]	36,909	190,983	319,146
OH..	....	45	231	581	938	1,519,467	1,980,329	2,339,511	2,665,260	3,198,062	3,672,329	4,157,545
OK..	....	....	....	....	....	....	....	....	....	....	258,657	790,391
OR..	....	....	....	....	....	....	12,093	52,465	90,923	174,768	317,704	413,536
PA..	434	602	810	1,049	1,348	1,724,033	2,311,786	2,906,215	3,521,951	4,282,891	5,258,113	6,302,115
RI..	69	69	77	83	97	108,830	147,545	174,620	217,353	276,531	345,506	428,556
SC..	249	346	415	503	581	594,398	668,507	703,708	705,606	995,577	1,151,149	1,340,316
SD..	....	....	....	....	....	....	....	4,837[2]	11,776[2]	98,268	348,600	401,570
TN..	36	106	262	423	682	829,210	1,002,717	1,109,801	1,258,520	1,542,359	1,767,518	2,020,616
TX..	....	....	....	....	....	....	212,592	604,215	818,579	1,591,749	2,235,527	3,048,710
UT..	....	....	....	....	....	....	11,380	40,273	86,786	143,963	210,779	276,749
VT..	85	154	218	236	281	291,948	314,120	315,098	330,551	332,286	332,422	343,641
VA..	692	808	878	938	1,044	1,025,227	1,119,348	1,219,630	1,225,163	1,512,565	1,655,980	1,854,184
WA..	....	....	....	....	....	....	1,201	11,594	23,955	75,116	357,232	518,103
WV..	56	79	105	137	177	224,537	302,313	376,688	442,014	618,457	762,794	958,800
WI..	....	....	....	....	....	30,945	305,391	775,881	1,054,670	1,315,497	1,693,330	2,069,042
WY..	....	....	....	....	....	....	....	....	9,118	20,789	62,555	92,531
U.S..	3,929	5,308	7,240	9,638	12,866[3]	17,063,353[3]	23,191,876	31,443,321	38,558,371	50,189,209	62,979,766	76,212,168

Note: Where possible, population shown is that of the 2000 area of the state. Members of the Armed Forces overseas or other U.S. nationals abroad are not included. Totals revised to include corrections of initial tabulated counts. (1) Totals for 1790 through 1830 are in thousands. (2) 1860 figure is for Dakota Territory; 1870 figures are for parts of Dakota Territory. (3) Includes persons (5,318 in 1830 and 6,100 in 1840) on public ships in the service of the U.S. not credited to any region, division, or state.

Estimated Population of American Colonies, 1630-1780

Source: U.S. Census Bureau, U.S. Dept. of Commerce

(numbers in thousands)

Colony	1630	1650	1670	1690	1700	1720	1740	1750	1770	1780
TOTAL....................	4.6	50.4	111.9	210.4	250.9	466.2	905.6	1,170.8	2,148.1	2,780.4
Maine (counties)[1].................	0.4	1.0	...	...	...	...	...	...	31.3	49.1
New Hampshire[2].................	0.5	1.3	1.8	4.2	5.0	9.4	23.3	27.5	62.4	87.8
Vermont[3]......................	...	...	...	...	...	...	...	...	10.0	47.6
Plymouth and Massachusetts[1,2,4]....	0.9	15.6	35.3	56.9	55.9	91.0	151.6	188.0	235.3	268.6
Rhode Island[2].................	...	0.8	2.2	4.2	5.9	11.7	25.3	33.2	58.2	52.9
Connecticut[2]...................	...	4.1	12.6	21.6	26.0	58.8	89.6	111.3	183.9	206.7
New York[2]....................	0.4	4.1	5.8	13.9	19.1	36.9	63.7	76.7	162.9	210.5
New Jersey[2]...................	...	...	1.0	8.0	14.0	29.8	51.4	71.4	117.4	139.6
Pennsylvania[2].................	...	...	...	11.4	18.0	31.0	85.6	119.7	240.1	327.3
Delaware[2]....................	...	0.2	0.7	1.5	2.5	5.4	19.9	28.7	35.5	45.4
Maryland[2].....................	...	4.5	13.2	24.0	29.6	66.1	116.1	141.1	202.6	245.5
Virginia[2]....................	2.5	18.7	35.3	53.0	58.6	87.8	180.4	231.0	447.0	538.0
North Carolina[2]..............	...	...	3.9	7.6	10.7	21.3	51.8	73.0	197.2	270.1
South Carolina[2]..............	...	...	0.2	3.9	5.7	17.0	45.0	64.0	124.2	180.0
Georgia[2]....................	...	...	...	...	...	...	2.0	5.2	23.4	56.1
Kentucky[5]....................	...	...	...	...	...	...	...	...	15.7	45.0
Tennessee[6]...................	...	...	...	...	...	...	...	...	1.0	10.0

(1) For 1660–1750, Maine counties are included with Massachusetts. Maine was part of Massachusetts until it became a separate state in 1820. (2) One of the original 13 states. (3) Admitted to statehood in 1791. (4) Plymouth became a part of the Province of Massachusetts in 1691. (5) Admitted to statehood in 1792. (6) Admitted to statehood in 1796.

Census, 1790-2000
U.S. Dept. of Commerce

1910	1920	1930	1940	1950	1960	1970	1980	1990	2000
2,138,093	2,348,174	2,646,248	2,832,961	3,061,743	3,266,740	3,444,165	3,893,888	4,040,587	4,447,100
64,356	55,036	59,278	72,524	128,643	226,167	300,382	401,851	550,043	626,932
204,354	334,162	435,573	499,261	749,587	1,302,161	1,770,900	2,718,215	3,665,228	5,130,632
1,574,449	1,752,204	1,854,482	1,949,387	1,909,511	1,786,272	1,923,295	2,286,435	2,350,725	2,673,400
2,377,549	3,426,861	5,677,251	6,907,387	10,586,223	15,717,204	19,953,134	23,667,902	29,760,021	33,871,648
799,024	939,629	1,035,791	1,123,296	1,325,089	1,753,947	2,207,259	2,889,964	3,294,394	4,301,261
1,114,756	1,380,631	1,606,903	1,709,242	2,007,280	2,535,234	3,031,709	3,107,576	3,287,116	3,405,565
202,322	223,003	238,380	266,505	318,085	446,292	548,104	594,338	666,168	783,600
331,069	437,571	486,869	663,091	802,178	763,956	756,510	638,333	606,900	572,059
752,619	968,470	1,468,211	1,897,414	2,771,305	4,951,560	6,789,443	9,746,324	12,937,926	15,982,378
2,609,121	2,895,832	2,908,506	3,123,723	3,444,578	3,943,116	4,589,575	5,463,105	6,478,216	8,186,453
191,909	255,912	368,336	422,330	499,794	632,772	768,561	964,691	1,108,229	1,211,537
325,594	431,866	445,032	524,873	588,637	667,191	712,567	943,935	1,006,749	1,293,953
5,638,591	6,485,280	7,630,654	7,897,241	8,712,176	10,081,158	11,113,976	11,426,518	11,430,602	12,419,293
2,700,876	2,930,390	3,238,503	3,427,796	3,934,224	4,662,498	5,193,669	5,490,224	5,544,159	6,080,485
2,224,771	2,404,021	2,470,939	2,538,268	2,621,073	2,757,537	2,824,376	2,913,808	2,776,755	2,926,324
1,690,949	1,769,257	1,880,999	1,801,028	1,905,299	2,178,611	2,246,578	2,363,679	2,477,574	2,688,418
2,289,905	2,416,630	2,614,589	2,845,627	2,944,806	3,038,156	3,218,706	3,660,777	3,685,296	4,041,769
1,656,388	1,798,509	2,101,593	2,363,880	2,683,516	3,257,022	3,641,306	4,205,900	4,219,973	4,468,976
742,371	768,014	797,423	847,226	913,774	969,265	992,048	1,124,660	1,227,928	1,274,923
1,295,346	1,449,661	1,631,526	1,821,244	2,343,001	3,100,689	3,922,399	4,216,975	4,781,468	5,296,486
3,366,416	3,852,356	4,249,614	4,316,721	4,690,514	5,148,578	5,689,170	5,737,037	6,016,425	6,349,097
2,810,173	3,668,412	4,842,325	5,256,106	6,371,766	7,823,194	8,875,083	9,262,078	9,295,297	9,938,444
2,075,708	2,387,125	2,563,953	2,792,300	2,982,483	3,413,864	3,804,971	4,075,970	4,375,099	4,919,479
1,797,114	1,790,618	2,009,821	2,183,796	2,178,914	2,178,141	2,216,912	2,520,638	2,573,216	2,844,658
3,293,335	3,404,055	3,629,367	3,784,664	3,954,653	4,319,813	4,676,501	4,916,686	5,117,073	5,595,211
376,053	548,889	537,606	559,456	591,024	674,767	694,409	786,690	799,065	902,195
1,192,214	1,296,372	1,377,963	1,315,834	1,325,510	1,411,330	1,483,493	1,569,825	1,578,385	1,711,263
81,875	77,407	91,058	110,247	160,083	285,278	488,738	800,493	1,201,833	1,998,257
430,572	443,083	465,293	491,524	533,242	606,921	737,681	920,610	1,109,252	1,235,786
2,537,167	3,155,900	4,041,334	4,160,165	4,835,329	6,066,782	7,168,164	7,364,823	7,730,188	8,414,350
327,301	360,350	423,317	531,818	681,187	951,023	1,016,000	1,302,894	1,515,069	1,819,046
9,113,614	10,385,227	12,588,066	13,479,142	14,830,192	16,782,304	18,236,967	17,558,072	17,990,455	18,976,457
2,206,287	2,559,123	3,170,276	3,571,623	4,061,929	4,556,155	5,082,059	5,881,766	6,628,637	8,049,313
577,056	646,872	680,845	641,935	619,636	632,446	617,761	652,717	638,800	642,200
4,767,121	5,759,394	6,646,697	6,907,612	7,946,627	9,706,397	10,652,017	10,797,630	10,847,115	11,353,140
1,657,155	2,028,283	2,396,040	2,336,434	2,233,351	2,328,284	2,559,229	3,025,290	3,145,585	3,450,654
672,765	783,389	953,786	1,089,684	1,521,341	1,768,687	2,091,385	2,633,105	2,842,321	3,421,399
7,665,111	8,720,017	9,631,350	9,900,180	10,498,012	11,319,366	11,793,909	11,863,895	11,881,643	12,281,054
542,610	604,397	687,497	713,346	791,896	859,488	946,725	947,154	1,003,464	1,048,319
1,515,400	1,683,724	1,738,765	1,899,804	2,117,027	2,382,594	2,590,516	3,121,820	3,486,703	4,012,012
583,888	636,547	692,849	642,961	652,740	680,514	665,507	690,768	696,004	754,844
2,184,789	2,337,885	2,616,556	2,915,841	3,291,718	3,567,089	3,923,687	4,591,120	4,877,185	5,689,283
3,896,542	4,663,228	5,824,715	6,414,824	7,711,194	9,579,677	11,196,730	14,229,191	16,986,510	20,851,820
373,351	449,396	507,847	550,310	688,862	890,627	1,059,273	1,461,037	1,722,850	2,233,169
355,956	352,428	359,611	359,231	377,747	389,881	444,330	511,456	562,758	608,827
2,061,612	2,309,187	2,421,851	2,677,773	3,318,680	3,966,949	4,648,494	5,346,818	6,187,358	7,078,515
1,141,990	1,356,621	1,563,396	1,736,191	2,378,963	2,853,214	3,409,169	4,132,156	4,866,692	5,894,121
1,221,119	1,463,701	1,729,205	1,901,974	2,005,552	1,860,421	1,744,237	1,949,644	1,793,477	1,808,344
2,333,860	2,632,067	2,939,006	3,137,587	3,434,575	3,951,777	4,417,731	4,705,767	4,891,769	5,363,675
145,965	194,402	225,565	250,742	290,529	330,066	332,416	469,557	453,588	493,782
92,228,531	106,021,568	123,202,660	132,164,569	151,325,798	179,323,175	203,211,926	226,545,805	248,709,873	281,421,906

U.S. Center of Population, 1790-2000
Source: Decennial Censuses, U.S. Census Bureau, U.S. Dept. of Commerce

The **U.S. center of population (mean)** is considered here to be the center of population gravity, or that point upon which the U.S. would balance if it were a rigid plane without weight and the population distributed thereon, with each individual assumed to have equal weight and to exert an influence on a central point proportional to his or her distance from that point.

CENSUS YEAR	N Lat °	′	″	W Long °	′	″	APPROXIMATE LOCATION
1790	39	16	30	76	11	12	Kent Co., MD, 23 miles east of Baltimore
1800	39	16	6	76	56	30	Howard Co., MD, 18 miles west of Baltimore
1810	39	11	30	77	37	12	Loudoun Co., VA, 40 miles northwest by west of Washington, D.C.
1820	39	5	42	78	33	0	Hardy Co., WV, 16 miles east of Moorefield[1]
1830	38	57	54	79	16	54	Grant Co., WV, 19 miles west-southwest of Moorefield[1]
1840	39	2	0	80	18	0	Upshur Co., WV, 16 miles south of Clarksburg[1]
1850	38	59	0	81	19	0	Wirt Co., WV, 23 miles southeast of Parkersburg[1]
1860	39	0	24	82	48	48	Pike Co., OH, 20 miles south by east of Chillicothe
1870	39	12	0	83	35	42	Highland Co., OH, 48 miles east by north of Cincinnati
1880	39	4	8	84	39	40	Boone Co., KY, 8 miles west by south of Cincinnati, OH
1890	39	11	56	85	32	53	Decatur Co., IN, 20 miles east of Columbus
1900	39	9	36	85	48	54	Bartholomew Co., IN, 6 miles southeast of Columbus
1910	39	10	12	86	32	20	Monroe Co., IN, in the city of Bloomington
1920	39	10	21	86	43	15	Owen Co., IN, 8 miles south-southeast of Spencer
1930	39	3	45	87	8	6	Greene Co., IN, 3 miles northeast of Linton
1940	38	56	54	87	22	35	Sullivan Co., IN, 2 miles southeast by east of Carlisle
1950 (incl. Alaska & Hawaii)	38	48	15	88	22	8	Clay Co., IL, 3 miles northeast of Louisville
1960	38	35	58	89	12	35	Clinton Co., IL, 6½ miles northwest of Centralia
1970	38	27	47	89	42	22	St. Clair Co., IL, 5 miles east-southeast of Mascoutah
1980	38	8	13	90	34	26	Jefferson Co., MO, ¼ mile west of DeSoto
1990	37	52	20	91	12	55	Crawford Co., MO, 9.7 miles southeast of Steelville
2000	37	41	49	91	48	34	Phelps Co., MO, 2.8 miles east of Edgar Springs

(1) West Virginia was set off from Virginia on Dec. 31, 1862, and was admitted as a state on June 20, 1863.

Metropolitan Area Populations, 1990-2000

Source: Decennial Censuses, U.S. Census Bureau, U.S. Dept. of Commerce
(MSAs ranked by Census 2000 population counts)

Metropolitan Statistical Areas (MSAs) are defined for federal statistical use by the Office of Management and Budget (OMB), with technical assistance from the U.S. Census Bureau. These definitions have been revised periodically and were last modified in 2000. The list below was released in Dec. 2003. MSAs must have at least one urbanized area of 50,000 or more inhabitants, plus an adjacent area closely integrated socially and economically with the core as measured by commuting ties. A new category, Micropolitan Statistical Areas (not listed here) must in general have at least one urban cluster with a population of at least 10,000 but no more than 50,000. Some metropolitan areas with a population of 2.5 mil or more may, under certain circumstances, be subdivided into smaller groupings of counties referred to as Metropolitan Divisions.

The OMB has designated 361 MSAs in the U.S. and 8 MSAs in Puerto Rico.

Applying the 2003 OMB revisions to 2000 Census figures showed that the nation in that year had 49 metropolitan areas of at least 1 mil people, including 6 that had reached that size in the decade since 1990. The 49 areas had 149.2 mil people, or 53% of the U.S. population, in 2000. In all, about 236.2 mil people, or 83.9% of the total U.S. population, resided in MSAs in 2000. This number was an increase of 28.9 mil (13.9%) since 1990.

Rank	Metropolitan Statistical Area (MSA)	Population 2000	Population 1990	Percent Change 1990-2000
1.	New York–Northern New Jersey–Long Island, NY–NJ–PA	18,323,002	16,846,046	8.8
2.	Los Angeles–Long Beach–Santa Ana, CA	12,365,627	11,273,720	9.7
3.	Chicago–Naperville–Joliet, IL–IN–WI	9,098,316	8,182,076	11.2
4.	Philadelphia–Camden–Wilmington, PA–NJ–DE	5,687,147	5,435,468	4.6
5.	Dallas–Fort Worth–Arlington, TX	5,161,544	3,989,294	29.4
6.	Miami–Fort Lauderdale–Miami Beach, FL	5,007,564	4,056,100	23.5
7.	Washington–Arlington–Alexandria, DC–VA–MD	4,796,183	4,122,914	16.3
8.	Houston–Baytown–Sugar Land, TX	4,715,407	3,767,335	25.2
9.	Detroit–Warren–Livonia, MI	4,452,557	4,248,699	4.8
10.	Boston–Cambridge–Quincy, MA–NH	4,391,344	4,133,895	6.2
11.	Atlanta–Sandy Springs–Marietta, GA	4,247,981	3,069,425	38.4
12.	San Francisco–Oakland–Fremont, CA	4,123,740	3,686,592	11.9
13.	Riverside–San Bernardino–Ontario, CA	3,254,821	2,588,793	25.7
14.	Phoenix–Mesa–Scottsdale, AZ	3,251,876	2,238,480	45.3
15.	Seattle–Tacoma–Bellevue, WA	3,043,878	2,559,164	18.9
16.	Minneapolis–St. Paul–Bloomington, MN–WI	2,968,806	2,538,834	16.9
17.	San Diego–Carlsbad–San Marcos, CA	2,813,833	2,498,016	12.6
18.	St. Louis, MO–IL	2,698,687	2,580,897	4.6
19.	Baltimore–Towson, MD	2,552,994	2,382,172	7.2
20.	Pittsburgh, PA	2,431,087	2,468,289	–1.5
21.	Tampa–St. Petersburg–Clearwater, FL	2,395,997	2,067,959	15.9
22.	Denver–Aurora, CO	2,179,240	1,666,883	30.7
23.	Cleveland–Elyria–Mentor, OH	2,148,143	2,102,248	2.2
24.	Cincinnati–Middletown, OH–KY–IN	2,009,632	1,844,917	8.9
25.	Portland–Vancouver–Beaverton, OR–WA	1,927,881	1,523,741	26.5
26.	Kansas City, MO–KS	1,836,038	1,636,528	12.2
27.	Sacramento–Arden-Arcade–Roseville, CA	1,796,857	1,481,102	21.3
28.	San Jose–Sunnyvale–Santa Clara, CA	1,735,819	1,534,274	13.1
29.	San Antonio, TX	1,711,703	1,407,745	21.6
30.	Orlando, FL	1,644,561	1,224,852	34.3
31.	Columbus, OH	1,612,694	1,405,168	14.8
32.	Providence–New Bedford–Fall River, RI–MA	1,582,997	1,509,789	4.8
33.	Virginia Beach–Norfolk–Newport News, VA–NC	1,576,370	1,449,389	8.8
34.	Indianapolis, IN	1,525,104	1,294,217	17.8
35.	Milwaukee–Waukesha–West Allis, WI	1,500,741	1,432,149	4.8
36.	Las Vegas–Paradise, NV	1,375,765	741,459	85.5
37.	Charlotte–Gastonia–Concord, NC–SC	1,330,448	1,024,643	29.8
38.	New Orleans–Metairie–Kenner, LA	1,316,510	1,264,391	4.1
39.	Nashville-Davidson–Murfreesboro, TN	1,311,789	1,048,216	25.1
40.	Austin–Round Rock, TX	1,249,763	846,227	47.7
41.	Memphis, TN–MS–AR	1,205,204	1,067,263	12.9
42.	Buffalo–Niagara Falls, NY	1,170,111	1,189,288	–1.6
43.	Louisville, KY–IN	1,161,975	1,055,973	10.0
44.	Hartford–West Hartford–East Hartford, CT	1,148,618	1,123,678	2.2
45.	Jacksonville, FL	1,122,750	925,213	21.4
46.	Richmond, VA	1,096,957	949,244	15.6
47.	Oklahoma City, OK	1,095,421	971,042	12.8
48.	Birmingham–Hoover, AL	1,052,238	956,844	10.0
49.	Rochester, NY	1,037,831	1,002,410	3.5
50.	Salt Lake City, UT	968,858	768,075	26.1
51.	Bridgeport–Stamford–Norwalk, CT	882,567	827,645	6.6
52.	Honolulu, HI	876,156	836,231	4.8
53.	Tulsa, OK	859,532	761,019	12.9
54.	Dayton, OH	848,153	843,835	0.5
55.	Tucson, AZ	843,746	666,880	26.5
56.	Albany–Schenectady–Troy, NY	825,875	809,443	2.0
57.	New Haven–Milford, CT	824,008	804,219	2.5
58.	Fresno, CA	799,407	667,490	19.8
59.	Raleigh–Cary, NC	797,071	541,100	47.3
60.	Omaha–Council Bluffs, NE–IA	767,041	685,797	11.8
61.	Oxnard–Thousand Oaks–Ventura, CA	753,197	669,016	12.6
62.	Worcester, MA	750,963	709,705	5.8
63.	Grand Rapids–Wyoming, MI	740,482	645,914	14.6
64.	Allentown–Bethlehem–Easton, PA–NJ	740,395	686,688	7.8
65.	Albuquerque, NM	729,649	599,416	21.7
66.	Baton Rouge, LA	705,973	623,853	13.2
67.	Akron, OH	694,960	657,575	5.7
68.	Springfield, MA	680,014	672,970	1.0
69.	El Paso, TX	679,622	591,610	14.9
70.	Bakersfield, CA	661,645	543,477	21.7

Population of 100 Largest U.S. Cities, 1850-2005

Source: 2005 Population Estimates, U.S. Census Bureau, U.S. Dept. of Commerce

Rank	City	2005	2000	1990	1980	1970	1950	1900	1850
1.	New York, NY	8,143,197	8,008,654	7,322,564	7,071,639	7,895,563	7,891,957	3,437,202	696,115
2.	Los Angeles, CA	3,844,829	3,694,742	3,485,398	2,968,528	2,811,801	1,970,358	102,479	1,610
3.	Chicago, IL	2,842,518	2,896,047	2,783,726	3,005,072	3,369,357	3,620,962	1,698,575	29,963
4.	Houston, TX	2,016,582	1,953,633	1,630,553	1,595,138	1,233,535	596,163	44,633	2,396
5.	Philadelphia, PA	1,463,281	1,517,550	1,585,577	1,688,210	1,949,996	2,071,605	1,293,697	121,376
6.	Phoenix, AZ	1,461,575	1,321,190	983,403	789,704	584,303	106,818	5,544	...
7.	San Antonio, TX	1,256,509	1,151,305	935,933	785,940	654,153	408,442	53,321	3,488
8.	San Diego, CA	1,255,540	1,223,400	1,110,549	875,538	697,471	334,387	17,700	...
9.	Dallas, TX	1,213,825	1,188,580	1,006,877	904,599	844,401	434,462	42,638	...
10.	San Jose, CA	912,332	894,943	782,248	629,400	459,913	95,280	21,500	...
11.	Detroit, MI	886,671	951,270	1,027,974	1,203,368	1,514,063	1,849,568	285,704	21,019
12.	Indianapolis, IN[1]	784,118	781,870	741,952	700,807	736,856	427,173	169,164	8,091
13.	Jacksonville, FL[1]	782,623	735,617	635,230	540,920	504,265	204,517	28,429	1,045
14.	San Francisco, CA	739,426	776,733	723,959	678,974	715,674	775,357	342,782	34,776
15.	Columbus, OH	730,657	711,470	632,910	565,021	540,025	375,901	125,560	17,882
16.	Austin, TX	690,252	656,562	465,622	345,890	253,539	132,459	22,258	629
17.	Memphis, TN	672,277	650,100	610,337	646,174	623,988	396,000	102,320	8,841
18.	Baltimore, MD	635,815	651,154	736,014	786,741	905,787	949,708	508,957	169,054
19.	Fort Worth, TX	624,067	541,099	447,619	385,164	393,455	278,778	26,688	...
20.	Charlotte, NC	610,949	540,828	395,934	315,474	241,420	134,042	18,091	1,065
21.	El Paso, TX	598,590	563,662	515,342	425,259	322,261	130,485	15,906	...
22.	Milwaukee, WI	578,887	596,974	628,088	636,297	717,372	637,392	285,315	20,061
23.	Seattle, WA	573,911	563,374	516,259	493,846	530,831	467,591	80,671	...
24.	Boston, MA	559,034	589,141	574,283	562,994	641,071	801,444	560,892	136,881
25.	Denver, CO	557,917	554,636	467,610	492,686	514,678	415,786	133,859	...
26.	Louisville, KY[1]	556,429	256,207	269,063	298,694	361,706	369,129	204,731	43,194
27.	Washington, DC	550,521	572,059	606,900	638,432	756,668	802,178	278,718	40,001
28.	Nashville, TN[1]	549,110	545,524	510,784	455,651	426,029	174,307	80,865	10,165
29.	Las Vegas, NV	545,147	478,434	258,295	164,674	125,787	24,624	...	...
30.	Portland, OR	533,427	529,121	437,319	368,148	379,967	373,628	90,426	...
31.	Oklahoma City, OK	531,324	506,132	444,719	404,014	368,164	243,504	10,037	...
32.	Tucson, AZ	515,526	486,699	405,390	330,537	262,933	45,454	7,531	...
33.	Albuquerque, NM	494,236	448,607	384,736	332,920	244,501	96,815	6,238	...
34.	Long Beach, CA	474,014	461,522	429,433	361,498	358,879	250,767	2,252	...
35.	Atlanta, GA	470,688	416,474	394,017	425,022	495,039	331,314	89,872	2,572
36.	Fresno, CA	461,116	427,652	354,202	217,491	165,655	91,669	12,470	...
37.	Sacramento, CA	456,441	407,018	369,365	275,741	257,105	137,572	29,282	6,820
38.	New Orleans, LA	454,863	484,674	496,938	557,927	593,471	570,445	287,104	116,375
39.	Cleveland, OH	452,208	478,403	505,616	573,822	750,879	914,808	381,768	17,034
40.	Kansas City, MO	444,965	441,545	435,146	448,028	507,330	456,622	163,752	...
41.	Mesa, AZ	442,780	396,375	288,091	152,404	63,049	16,790	722	...
42.	Virginia Beach, VA	438,415	425,257	393,069	262,199	172,106	5,390	...	...
43.	Omaha, NE	414,521	390,007	335,795	313,939	346,929	251,117	102,555	...
44.	Oakland, CA	395,274	399,484	372,242	339,337	361,561	384,575	66,960	...
45.	Miami, FL	386,417	362,470	358,548	346,681	334,859	249,276	1,681	...
46.	Tulsa, OK	382,457	393,049	367,302	360,919	330,350	182,740	1,390	...
47.	Honolulu, HI[2]	377,379	371,657	365,272	365,048	324,871	248,034	39,306	...
48.	Minneapolis, MN	372,811	382,618	368,383	370,951	434,400	521,718	202,718	...
49.	Colorado Springs, CO	369,815	360,890	281,140	215,105	135,517	45,472	21,085	...
50.	Arlington, TX	362,805	332,969	261,721	160,113	90,229	7,692	1,079	...
51.	Wichita, KS	354,865	344,284	304,011	279,838	276,554	168,279	24,671	...
52.	St. Louis, MO	344,362	348,189	396,685	452,801	622,236	856,796	575,238	77,860
53.	Raleigh, NC	341,530	282,093	207,951	150,255	122,830	65,679	13,643	4,518
54.	Santa Ana, CA	340,368	337,977	293,742	204,023	155,710	45,533	4,933	...
55.	Anaheim, CA	331,804	328,014	266,406	219,494	166,408	14,556	1,456	...
56.	Tampa, FL	325,989	303,447	280,015	271,577	277,714	124,681	15,839	...
57.	Pittsburgh, PA	316,718	334,563	369,879	423,959	520,089	676,806	321,616	46,601
58.	Cincinnati, OH	308,728	331,285	364,040	385,409	453,514	503,998	325,902	115,435
59.	Toledo, OH	301,285	313,619	332,943	354,635	383,062	303,616	131,822	3,829
60.	Aurora, CO	297,235	276,393	222,103	158,588	74,974	11,421	202	...
61.	Bakersfield, CA	295,536	247,057	174,820	105,611	69,515	34,784	4,836	...
62.	Riverside, CA	290,086	255,166	226,505	170,591	140,089	46,764	7,973	...
63.	Stockton, CA	286,926	243,771	210,943	148,283	109,963	70,853	17,506	...
64.	Corpus Christi, TX	283,474	277,454	257,453	232,134	204,525	108,287	4,703	...
65.	Newark, NJ	280,666	273,546	275,221	329,248	381,930	438,776	246,070	38,894
66.	Buffalo, NY	279,745	292,648	328,123	357,870	462,768	580,132	352,387	42,261
67.	St. Paul, MN	275,150	287,151	272,235	270,230	309,866	311,349	163,065	1,112
68.	Anchorage, AK	275,043	260,283	226,338	174,431	48,081	11,254	...	...
69.	Lexington, KY	268,080	260,512	225,366	204,165	108,137	55,534	26,369	8,159
70.	Plano, TX	250,096	222,030	128,713	72,331	17,872	2,126	1,304	...
71.	St. Petersburg, FL	249,079	248,232	238,629	238,647	216,159	96,738	1,575	...
72.	Jersey City, NJ	239,614	240,055	228,537	223,532	260,350	299,017	206,433	6,856
73.	Glendale, AZ	239,435	218,812	148,134	96,988	36,228	8,179	...	...
74.	Lincoln, NE	239,213	225,581	191,972	171,932	149,518	98,884	40,169	...
75.	Chandler, AZ	234,939	176,381	89,862	29,673	13,763	3,799	...	...
76.	Henderson, NV	232,146	175,406	64,942	23,376	16,400	5,717	...	...
77.	Greensboro, NC	231,962	223,891	183,521	155,642	144,076	74,389	10,035	...
78.	Norfolk, VA	231,954	234,403	261,229	266,979	307,951	213,513	46,624	14,326
79.	Birmingham, AL	231,483	242,820	265,968	284,413	300,910	326,037	38,415	...
80.	Scottsdale, AZ	226,013	202,705	130,069	88,364	67,823	2,032	...	...
81.	Fort Wayne, IN	223,341	205,727	173,072	172,391	178,269	133,607	45,115	4,282

Rank	City	2005	2000	1990	1980	1970	1950	1900	1850
82.	Baton Rouge, LA	222,064	227,818	219,531	220,394	165,921	125,629	11,269	3,905
83.	Madison, WI	221,551	208,903	191,262	170,616	171,809	96,056	19,164	1,525
84.	Hialeah, FL	220,485	226,419	188,004	145,254	102,452	19,676	...	...
85.	Chesapeake, VA	218,968	199,184	151,976	114,486	89,580	...	...	...
86.	Garland, TX	216,346	215,768	180,650	138,857	81,437	10,571	819	...
87.	Orlando, FL	213,223	185,951	164,693	128,394	99,006	52,367	2,481	...
88.	Rochester, NY	211,091	219,773	231,636	241,741	295,011	332,488	162,608	36,403
89.	Akron, OH	210,795	217,074	223,019	237,177	275,425	274,605	42,728	3,266
90.	Chula Vista, CA	210,497	173,556	135,163	83,927	67,901	31,339	...	...
91.	Lubbock, TX	209,737	199,564	186,206	174,361	149,101	71,747	...	...
92.	Laredo, TX	208,754	176,576	122,899	91,449	69,024	51,910	13,429	...
93.	Modesto, CA	207,011	188,856	164,730	106,963	61,712	17,389	2,024[3]	...
94.	Durham, NC	204,845	187,035	136,611	100,831	95,438	71,311	6,679	...
95.	Reno, NV	203,550	180,480	134,230	100,756	72,863	32,497	4,500	—
96.	Fremont, CA	200,468	203,413	173,339	131,945	100,869	...	...	...
97.	Montgomery, AL	200,127	201,568	187,106	177,857	133,386	106,525	30,346	8,728
98.	Glendale, CA	200,065	194,973	180,038	139,060	133,000	96,000	...	...
99.	Shreveport, LA	198,874	200,145	198,525	206,989	182,064	127,206	16,013	1,728
100.	San Bernardino, CA	198,550	185,401	170,036	118,794	106,869	63,058	6,150	NA[4]

(1) Indianapolis, IN; Jacksonville, FL; Louisville, KY; and Nashville, TN, are parts of consolidated city–county governments. Populations of other incorporated places in the county have been excluded from the population totals shown here. For years that predate the establishment of a consolidated city–county government, city population is shown. (2) Locations in Hawaii are called "census designated places (CDPs)." Although these areas are not incorporated, they are recognized for census purposes as large urban places. Honolulu CDP is coextensive with Honolulu Judicial District within the city and county of Honolulu. (3) Estimated. (4) The earliest census figure for San Bernardino is 940, in 1860.

Mobility, by Selected Characteristics, 2003-04

Source: 2004 Annual Social and Economic Supplement to Current Population Survey, U.S. Census Bureau, U.S. Dept. of Commerce
(numbers in thousands)

	Total no. of movers[1]	MOVED TO:					Total no. of movers[1]	MOVED TO:			
		Same county	Diff. county, same state	Diff. state	Abroad			Same county	Diff. county, same state	Diff. state	Abroad
Marital status						**Income[3]**					
Married, spouse present	11,499	6,156	2,499	2,399	445	Under $5,000	3,343	1,793	679	723	149
Married, spouse absent	721	372	119	128	102	$5,000–$9,999	3,208	1,949	569	580	110
Widowed	926	535	179	189	23	$10,000–$19,999	6,225	3,770	1,099	1,225	131
Divorced	3,303	2,001	658	610	34	$20,000–$29,999	4,631	2,650	1,037	849	97
Separated	1,089	733	190	143	23	$30,000–$39,999	3,164	1,753	760	600	51
Never married	12,364	7,118	2,463	2,347	436	$40,000–$49,999	1,956	1,040	472	391	53
						$50,000–$59,999	1,144	638	278	219	10
Educational attainment[2]						$60,000–$74,999	1,111	611	266	214	20
Less than 9th grade	1,214	732	188	159	135	$75,000–$99,999	769	423	153	180	12
Grades 9-12, no diploma	2,008	1,311	305	324	68	$100,000 and over	849	457	142	210	40
High school grad	6,289	3,762	1,270	1,109	148	**Ownership status**					
Some college or AA degree	5,610	3,147	1,209	1,163	91	Owner	14,841	8,303	3,398	2,824	316
Bachelor's degree	4,229	2,165	943	955	166	Renter	24,154	14,248	4,443	4,505	957
Prof. or graduate degree	2,035	943	367	576	149	**ALL MOVERS[4]**	38,995	22,551	7,842	7,330	1,272

(1) People who moved to a new residence in the 12 months preceding the survey, made in Feb.-Apr. 2004. (2) People 25 years and older. (3) People 15 years and older. (4) People 1 year and older.

U.S. Population, by Age, Sex, and Household, 2000

Source: 2000 Census, U.S. Census Bureau, U.S. Dept. of Commerce

	Number	%
Total population	**281,421,906**	**100**
AGE		
Under 5 years	19,175,798	6.8
5 to 9 years	20,549,505	7.3
10 to 14 years	20,528,072	7.3
15 to 19 years	20,219,890	7.2
20 to 24 years	18,964,001	6.7
25 to 34 years	39,891,724	14.2
35 to 44 years	45,148,527	16.0
45 to 54 years	37,677,952	13.4
55 to 59 years	13,469,237	4.8
60 to 64 years	10,805,447	3.8
65 to 74 years	18,390,986	6.5
75 to 84 years	12,361,180	4.4
85 years and over	4,239,587	1.5
18 years and over	209,128,094	74.3
Male	100,994,367	35.9
Female	108,133,727	38.4
21 years and over	196,899,193	70.0
NA = Not applicable.		

	Number	%
62 years and over	41,256,029	14.7
65 years and over	34,991,753	12.4
SEX		
Male	138,053,563	49.1
Female	143,368,343	50.9
HOUSEHOLDS BY TYPES		
Total Households (or Householders)	105,480,101	100.0
Family households (families)	71,787,347	68.1
Married-couple families	54,493,232	51.7
Female householder, no husband present	12,900,103	12.2
Nonfamily households	33,692,754	31.9
Householder living alone	27,230,075	25.8
Householder 65 years and over	9,722,857	9.2
Persons living in households	273,643,273	97.2
Persons per household	2.59	NA
Persons living in group quarters	7,778,633	2.8
Institutionalized persons	4,059,039	1.4
Other persons in group quarters	3,719,594	1.3

▶ IT'S A FACT: Of the nearly 43 mil Hispanics in the U.S., about 64% are of Mexican origin. Puerto Rico (10% of U.S. Hispanics) and Cuba (3%) are the next two most common places of origin.

U.S. Foreign-Born Population

Source: Current Population Surveys, U.S. Census Bureau, U.S. Dept. of Commerce

Percentage of Population That Is Foreign-Born, 1900-2005

	1900	1910	1920	1930	1940	1950	1960	1970	1980	1990	2000	2005
%	13.6	14.7	13.2	11.6	8.8	6.9	5.4	4.7	6.2	8.0	10.4	11.7

U.S. Foreign-Born Population by Regional Origin, 1995-2005

Source: U.S. Census Bureau, U.S. Dept. of Commerce
(numbers in thousands)

Region	2005	%	2000	1995
Europe.........	4,519	12.9	4,355	3,937
Under 18	311	9.6	250	232
Asia	8,970	25.5	7,246	6,121
Under 18	704	21.7	657	767
Latin America	15,688	44.6	14,477	11,777
Under 18	1,684	51.9	1,684	1,481
Other	5,979	17.0	2,301	2,658
Under 18	543	16.8	245	275
ALL REGIONS ...	35,157	100.0	28,379	24,493
Under 18	3,242	100.0	2,837	2,726

Foreign-Born Population: Top Countries of Origin, 1880-2000

Source: Decennial Censuses, U.S. Census Bureau, U.S. Dept. of Commerce
(numbers in thousands; % is percent of all foreign-born)

	1880			1920			1960			1980			2000	
Country	No.	%	Country	No.	%	Country	No.	%	Country	No.	%	Country	No.	%
Germany	1,967	29.4	Germany	1,686	12.1	Italy	1,257	12.9	Mexico	2,199	15.6	Mexico	9,177	29.5
Ireland	1,855	27.8	Italy	1,610	11.6	Germany	990	10.2	Germany	849	6.0	China[2]	1,519	4.9
Gr. Britain	918	13.7	U.S.S.R.	1,400	10.1	Canada	953	9.8	Canada	843	6.0	Philippines	1,369	4.4
Canada	717	10.7	Poland	1,140	8.2	Gr. Britain	765	7.9	Italy	832	5.9	India	1,023	3.3
Sweden	194	2.9	Canada	1,138	8.2	Poland	748	7.7	Gr. Britain	649	4.6	Vietnam	988	3.2
Norway	182	2.7	Gr. Britain	1,135	8.2	U.S.S.R.	691	7.1	Cuba	608	4.3	Cuba	873	2.8
France	107	1.6	Ireland	1,037	7.5	Mexico	576	5.9	Philippines	501	3.6	Korea[3]	864	2.8
China[1]	104	1.6	Sweden	626	4.5	Ireland	339	3.5	Poland	418	3.0	Canada	821	2.6
Switzerland	89	1.3	Austria	576	4.1	Austria	305	3.1	U.S.S.R.	406	2.9	El Salvador	817	2.6
Czech.	85	1.3	Mexico	486	3.5	Hungary	245	2.5	Korea[3]	290	2.1	Germany	707	2.3
Total	6,680	100.0	Total	13,921	100.0	Total	9,738	100.0	Total	14,080	100.0	Total	31,108	100.0

(1) Includes Taiwan. (2) Includes Hong Kong and Taiwan. (3) Includes N. and S. Korea.

Languages Spoken at Home by the U.S. Population[1], 2000

Source: 2000 Census, U.S. Census Bureau, U.S. Dept. of Commerce
(numbers in thousands)

Language	Speakers	Language	Speakers	Language	Speakers
Total U.S. pop. 5		Italian	1,008	Urdu	263
years and older.........	262,375	Korean	894	Gujarathi.................	236
Speak only English.........	215,424	Russian	706	Serbo-Croatian............	234
Speak other language	46,952	Polish	667	Armenian	203
Spanish or Spanish Creole ...	28,101	Arabic	615	Hebrew..................	195
Chinese	2,022	Portuguese or		Mon-Khmer, Cambodian	182
French		Portuguese Creole	565	Navajo	178
(inc. Patois, Cajun)........	1,644	Japanese	478	Miao, Hmong	168
German	1,383	Greek	365	Laotian..................	149
Tagalog	1,224	Hindi....................	317	Thai	120
Vietnamese	1,010	Persian..................	312	Hungarian................	118

(1) 5 years and older

Immigrants Admitted, by State of Intended Residence, 2005

Source: Office of Immigration Statistics, U.S. Dept. of Homeland Security
(fiscal year 2005)

State	Immigrants	State	Immigrants	State	Immigrants
Alabama................	4,200	Maine	1,908	Pennsylvania	28,908
Alaska	1,525	Maryland	22,870	Rhode Island	3,852
Arizona................	18,988	Massachusetts..........	34,236	South Carolina	5,029
Arkansas..............	2,698	Michigan...............	23,597	South Dakota............	881
California	232,023	Minnesota.............	15,456	Tennessee	8,962
Colorado..............	11,977	Mississippi	1,831	Texas..................	95,958
Connecticut	15,335	Missouri	8,744	Utah...................	5,082
Delaware	2,992	Montana...............	589	Vermont	1,042
Dist. of Columbia	2,457	Nebraska	2,997	Virginia................	27,100
Florida	122,918	Nevada................	9,823	Washington	26,482
Georgia	31,535	New Hampshire	3,298	West Virginia	847
Hawaii	6,480	New Jersey	56,180	Wisconsin...............	7,909
Idaho	2,768	New Mexico	3,513	Wyoming	321
Illinois................	52,419	New York	136,828	U.S. Armed Services posts .	128
Indiana...............	6,915	North Carolina	16,715	U.S. possessions	5,868
Iowa.................	4,536	North Dakota	864	Other or unknown.........	9
Kansas...............	4,514	Ohio..................	16,897	Total.................	1,122,373
Kentucky	5,267	Oklahoma..............	4,702		
Louisiana.............	3,777	Oregon	9,623		

Immigrants Admitted, by Top 50 Metropolitan Areas of Intended Residence, 2004

Source: Office of Immigration Statistics, U.S. Dept. of Homeland Security
(fiscal year 2004)

Metropolitan Statistical Area (MSA)	Number	Percentage	Metropolitan Statistical Area (MSA)	Number	Percentage
Total immigrants admitted to U.S.	946,142	100%	Jersey City, NJ	7,236	0.8%
Los Angeles-Long Beach, CA	88,366	9.3	Portland-Vancouver, OR-WA	7,228	0.8
New York, NY......................	83,633	8.8	Las Vegas, NV-AZ..................	7,205	0.8
Chicago, IL.......................	42,455	4.5	Tampa-St. Petersburg-Clearwater, FL .	7,140	0.8
Houston, TX.......................	32,926	3.5	Denver, CO........................	6,962	0.7
Washington, DC-MD-VA-WV	31,925	3.4	West Palm Beach-Boca Raton, FL	6,540	0.7
Miami, FL.........................	29,688	3.1	Orlando, FL.......................	5,921	0.6
Orange County, CA	22,179	2.3	Baltimore, MD.....................	5,718	0.6
San Jose, CA.....................	20,562	2.2	Fort Worth-Arlington, TX	5,604	0.6
Oakland, CA......................	20,285	2.1	Fresno, CA	5,474	0.6
San Diego, CA	19,859	2.1	McAllen-Edinburg-Mission, TX	5,375	0.6
Dallas, TX........................	19,430	2.1	Honolulu, HI......................	4,862	0.5
Boston, MA-NH	18,558	2.0	Ventura, CA.......................	4,492	0.5
Riverside-San Bernardino, CA	17,401	1.8	Austin-San Marcos, TX	4,194	0.4
San Francisco, CA	17,145	1.8	El Paso, TX	4,156	0.4
Fort Lauderdale, FL	13,443	1.4	Hartford, CT......................	4,075	0.4
Philadelphia, PA-NJ...............	13,069	1.4	San Juan-Bayamon, PR	4,051	0.4
Atlanta, GA.......................	12,654	1.3	St. Louis, MO-IL	4,019	0.4
Newark, NJ.......................	12,573	1.3	Providence-Fall River-Warwick, RI-MA .	3,929	0.4
Phoenix-Mesa, AZ	12,504	1.3	Columbus, OH.....................	3,600	0.4
Detroit, MI........................	12,438	1.3	Raleigh-Durham-Chapel Hill, NC	3,559	0.4
Seattle-Bellevue-Everett, WA......	12,152	1.3	San Antonio, TX	3,526	0.4
Bergen-Passaic, NJ	11,531	1.2	Tucson, AZ	3,519	0.4
Nassau-Suffolk, NY	10,312	1.1	Kansas City, MO-KS	3,348	0.4
Middlesex-Somerset-Hunterdon, NJ ...	10,132	1.1	Non-MSA.........................	45,903	4.9
Minneapolis-St. Paul, MN-WI........	9,814	1.0	Other & Unknown	175,304	18.5
Sacramento, CA...................	8,168	0.9			

U.S. Population by Reported Ancestry, 2005[1]

Source: 2005 American Community Survey, U.S. Census Bureau, U.S. Dept. of Commerce
(Numbers in thousands)

	Pop.	%		Pop.	%		Pop.	%
German	49,179	17.1	Scottish	5,859	2.0	West Indian[2] (except		
Irish	34,669	12.0	Scotch-Irish	5,289	1.8	Hispanic groups)	2,233	0.8
English	27,762	9.6	Dutch	5,079	1.8	Czech...............	1,556	0.5
Unclassified or not			Norwegian	4,601	1.6	Hungarian...........	1,522	0.5
reported	25,581	8.9	Swedish	4,260	1.5	Danish	1,434	0.5
American	20,536	7.1	Russian	3,010	1.0	Arab	1,400	0.5
Italian	17,235	6.0	European	2,527	0.9	Portuguese..........	1,379	0.5
Polish...............	9,771	3.4	French Canadian	2,266	0.8	**Total**...............	**288,378**	**100.0**
French (except Basque) .	9,530	3.3						

(1) Ancestry listed in this table refers to the total number of people who claimed a particular ancestry on the American Community Survey. Race and Hispanic origin groups are not included because official data for those groups are tracked elsewhere by the Census Bureau. Data exclude population living in institutions, college dormitories, and other group quarters. (2) Inc. Bahamian, Barbadian, Belizean, Bermudan, British West Indian, Dutch West Indian, Haitian, Jamaican, Trinidadian and Tobagonian, U.S. Virgin Islander, West Indian, and Other West Indian.

Disability Status of the Elderly (65 and Over)[1], 2000

Source: 2000 Census, U.S. Census Bureau, U.S. Dept. of Commerce
(numbers in thousands)

	Number	%		Number	%
Population 65 years and over	**33,347**	**100.0**	Mental disability[2]...............	3,593	10.8
With one or more disabilities	13,978	41.9	Self-care disability[3]	3,184	9.5
Sensory disability...............	4,738	14.2	Go-outside-home disability[4]	6,796	20.4
Physical disability...............	9,546	28.6	With no disability	19,369	58.1

(1) Noninstitutionalized population. (2) Learning, remembering, or concentrating. (3) Dressing, bathing, or getting around inside the home. (4) Going outside the home alone to shop or visit a doctor's office.

The Elderly U.S. Population, 1900-2050

Source: Decennial Censuses, 2005 Population Estimates, U.S. Interim Projections, U.S. Census Bureau, U.S. Dept. of Commerce

	65 AND OVER		85 AND OVER			65 AND OVER		85 AND OVER	
Year	Number[1]	Percent	Number[1]	Percent	Year	Number[1]	Percent	Number[1]	Percent
1900	3,080	4.1	122	0.2	2000	34,992	12.4	4,240	1.5
1910	3,950	4.3	167	0.2	2001[2]........	35,330	12.4	4,418	1.5
1920	4,933	4.7	210	0.2	2002[2]........	35,589	12.4	4,547	1.6
1930	6,634	5.4	272	0.2	2003[2]........	35,952	12.4	4,716	1.6
1940	9,019	6.8	365	0.3	2004[2]........	36,333	12.4	4,867	1.7
1950	12,270	8.1	577	0.4	2005[2]........	36,790	12.4	5,096	1.7
1960	16,560	9.2	929	0.5	2010[3]........	40,244	13.0	6,123	2.0
1970	20,066	9.9	1,511	0.7	2020[3]........	54,632	16.3	7,269	2.2
1980	25,549	11.3	2,240	1.0	2030[3]........	71,453	19.7	9,603	2.6
1990	31,242	12.6	3,080	1.2	2040[3]........	80,049	19.1	15,409	3.9
1995[2]	33,619	12.8	3,685	1.4	2050[3]........	86,705	22.1	20,861	5.0

NOTE: Figures for 1900 to 1950 exclude Alaska and Hawaii. (1) Resident population, in thousands. (2) Estimates for July 1 of year indicated. (3) Projected.

Projections of Total U.S. Population, by Age, 2010-50

Source: U.S. Interim Projections, U.S. Census Bureau, U.S. Dept. of Commerce

Age	2010 Pop.[1]	2010 % Distrib.	2020 Pop.[1]	2020 % Distrib.	2030 Pop.[1]	2030 % Distrib.	2040 Pop.[1]	2040 % Distrib.	2050 Pop.[1]	2050 % Distrib.
TOTAL............	308,936	100	335,805	100	363,584	100	391,946	100	419,854	100
Under 5 years......	21,426	6.9	22,932	6.8	24,272	6.7	26,299	6.7	28,080	6.7
5–14 years........	40,473	13.1	44,478	13.2	47,329	13.0	50,503	12.9	54,495	13.0
15–24 years.......	43,012	13.9	42,229	12.6	46,639	12.8	49,721	12.7	52,869	12.6
25–34 years.......	41,646	13.5	45,065	13.4	44,935	12.4	49,755	12.7	52,804	12.6
35–44 years.......	41,121	13.3	42,816	12.8	46,676	12.8	47,008	12.0	51,796	12.3
45–54 years.......	44,827	14.5	40,921	12.2	42,902	11.8	46,981	12.0	47,383	11.3
55–64 years.......	36,186	11.7	42,732	12.7	39,378	10.8	41,629	10.6	45,721	10.9
65 years and over ..	40,244	13.0	54,632	16.3	71,453	19.7	80,050	20.4	86,706	20.7
85 years and over ..	6,123	2.0	7,269	2.2	9,603	2.6	15,409	3.9	20,861	5.0

NOTE: Estimates of U.S. population consistent with Census 2000, as enumerated. All figures shown are for July 1 of the given year, exclude Armed Forces and U.S. citizens residing outside of the U.S., and are based on middle series projections for births, deaths, and net migration. Percentage distribution may not equal 100, because of overlapping categories shown and rounding. (1) In thousands.

Young Adults Living at Home or Dormitory in the U.S., 1960-2005

Source: Decennial Censuses, Current Population Surveys, U.S. Census Bureau, U.S. Dept. of Commerce
(numbers in thousands)

	18-24 years old Male Total	Male At home[1]	%	Female Total	Female At home[1]	%		25-34 years old Male Total	Male At home[1]	%	Female Total	Female At home[1]	%
YEAR							YEAR						
1960....	6,842	3,583	52	7,876	2,750	35	1960 ...	10,896	1,185	11	11,587	853	7
1970....	10,398	5,641	54	11,959	4,941	41	1970 ...	11,929	1,129	10	12,637	829	7
1980....	14,278	7,755	54	14,844	6,336	43	1980 ...	18,107	1,894	11	18,689	1,300	7
1985....	13,695	8,172	60	14,149	6,758	48	1985 ...	20,184	2,685	13	20,673	1,661	8
1990....	12,450	7,232	58	12,860	6,135	48	1990 ...	21,462	3,213	15	21,779	1,774	8
1995....	12,545	7,328	58	12,613	5,896	47	1995 ...	20,589	3,166	15	20,800	1,759	9
1996....	12,402	7,327	59	12,441	5,955	48	1996 ...	20,390	3,213	16	20,528	1,810	9
1997....	12,534	7,501	60	12,452	6,006	48	1997 ...	20,039	2,909	15	20,217	1,745	9
1998....	12,633	7,399	59	12,568	5,974	48	1998 ...	19,526	2,845	15	19,828	1,680	9
1999....	12,936	7,440	58	13,031	6,389	49	1999 ...	18,924	2,636	14	19,551	1,699	9
2000....	13,291	7,593	57	13,242	6,232	47	2000 ...	18,563	2,387	13	19,222	1,602	8
2001[2] ...	13,412	7,385	55	13,361	6,068	45	2001[2]...	19,308	2,520	13	19,527	1,583	8
2002[2] ...	13,696	7,575	55	13,602	6,252	46	2002[2]...	19,220	2,610	14	19,428	1,618	8
2003[2] ...	13,811	7,569	55	13,592	6,215	46	2003[2]...	19,543	2,631	14	19,659	1,375	7
2004[2] ...	14,165	8,010	57	13,611	6,327	47	2004[2]...	19,553	2,720	14	19,587	1,559	8
2005[2] ...	14,042	7,482	53	13,915	6,422	46	2005[2]...	19,654	2,686	14	19,630	1,601	8

(1) Includes young adults living in their parent(s)' home and unmarried college students living in dormitories. (2) Data for 2001 and later use population controls based on Census 2000 and an expanded sample of households.

Living Arrangements of Children, 1970-2005

Source: Current Population Surveys, U.S. Census Bureau, U.S. Dept. of Commerce
(excludes persons under 18 years of age who maintained households or resided in group quarters)

Race, Hispanic origin, and year	Number (1,000)	BOTH PARENTS	MOTHER ONLY Total	MOTHER ONLY Divorced	MOTHER ONLY Married Spouse absent	MOTHER ONLY Single[1]	MOTHER ONLY Widowed	FATHER ONLY	NEITHER PARENT
White									
1970	58,790	90	8	3	3	Z	2	1	2
1980	52,242	83	14	7	4	1	2	2	2
1990	51,390	79	16	8	4	3	1	3	2
1999	56,265	74	18	NA	NA	NA	NA	4	3
2000	56,455	75	17	NA	NA	NA	NA	4	3
2001	56,135	75	18	8	1	5	1	4	3
2002	58,276	75	18	8	1	5	1	5	3
2003	55,920	74	18	8	1	5	1	5	3
2004	55,902	74	18	8	1	6	1	4	3
2005	56,259	74	18	8	1	6	1	5	3
Black									
1970	9,422	59	30	5	16	4	4	2	10
1980	9,375	42	44	11	16	13	4	2	12
1990	10,018	38	51	10	12	27	2	4	8
1999	11,425	35	51	NA	NA	NA	NA	4	10
2000	11,412	38	49	NA	NA	NA	NA	4	9
2001	11,578	38	48	8	2	30	2	5	10
2002	11,646	39	48	9	2	31	1	5	8
2003	11,340	36	51	11	2	30	1	5	9
2004	11,424	35	50	9	2	31	2	6	9
2005	11,295	35	50	9	2	32	1	5	10
Hispanic[2]									
1970	4,006[3]	78	NA	NA	NA	NA	NA	NA	NA
1980	5,459	75	20	6	8	4	2	2	4
1990	7,174	67	27	7	10	8	2	3	3
1999	11,236	63	27	NA	NA	NA	NA	5	5
2000	11,613	65	25	NA	NA	NA	NA	4	5
2001	12,446	65	25	6	2	11	1	5	6
2002	12,817	65	25	6	2	11	1	5	5
2003	13,284	65	25	5	2	11	1	6	5
2004	13,752	65	25	6	1	11	1	5	5
2005	14,248	65	25	6	2	11	1	5	5

NA = Not available. Z = Less than 0.5%. (1) Never married. (2) Hispanic persons may be of any race. (3) All persons under 18 years old.

Grandchildren Living in the Home of Their Grandparents, 1970-2005

Source: Current Population Surveys, U.S. Census Bureau, U.S. Dept. of Commerce (numbers in thousands)

YEAR	Total children under 18	Total	Both parents present	Mother only present	Father only present	Without parent(s) present
			Grandchildren living with grandparents			
			WITH PARENT(S) PRESENT			
1970	69,276	2,214	363	817	78	
1980	63,369	2,306	310	922	86	957
1990	64,137	3,155	467	1,563	191	988
1995	70,254	3,965	427	1,876	195	935
1996	70,908	4,060	467	1,943	220	1,466
1997	70,983	3,894	554	1,785	247	1,431
1998	71,377	3,989	503	1,827	241	1,309
1999	71,703	3,919	535	1,803	250	1,417
2000	72,012	3,842	531	1,732	220	1,331
2001[1]	72,006	3,844	510	1,755	231	1,359
2002[1]	72,321	3,681	477	1,658	275	1,348
2003[1]	73,001	3,767	547	1,576	227	1,274
2004[1]	73,205	4,050	526	1,765	259	1,416
2005[1]	73,523	4,136	486	1,817	239	1,501
						1,592

(1) Data for 2001-2005 are based on Census 2000 figures and an expanded sample of households.

Children by Relationship to Householder, 2000

Source: 2000 Census, U.S. Census Bureau, U.S. Dept. of Commerce
(numbers in thousands; totals may not add due to rounding)

	All Ages		Under 6		6-17 yrs		18 yrs +	
	Total	%	Total	%	Total	%	Total	%
Children of householder	83,714	100	20,120	100	44,532	100	19,062	100
Adopted children	2,059	2.5	389	1.9	1,197	2.7	473	2.5
Stepchildren................	4,385	5.2	328	1.6	2,964	6.7	1,092	5.7
Biological children	77,271	92.3	19,402	96.4	40,371	90.7	17,497	91.8

Marital Status of the U.S. Population, 1990-2005

Source: Current Population Surveys, U.S. Census Bureau, U.S. Dept. of Commerce
(numbers in millions)

Marital status	Total				Male				Female			
	1990	1995	2000	2005	1990	1995	2000	2005	1990	1995	2000	2005
Total pop.[1]..........	191.8	202.7	213.8	230.3	92.0	97.7	103.1	111.6	99.8	105.0	110.7	118.7
Never married	50.2	55.0	60.0	66.8	27.5	30.3	32.3	36.3	22.7	24.7	27.8	30.6
Married...............	112.6	116.6	120.2	127.4	55.8	57.6	59.7	63.4	56.8	59.0	60.5	64.0
Widowed	13.8	13.4	13.7	13.8	2.3	2.3	2.6	2.7	11.5	11.1	11.1	11.1
Divorced.............	15.1	17.7	19.9	22.2	6.3	7.4	8.6	9.2	8.8	10.3	11.3	13.0
Percent of total pop.[1]												
Never married	26.2	27.1	28.1	29.0	29.9	31.0	31.3	32.5	22.8	23.5	25.1	25.8
Married...............	58.7	57.5	56.2	55.3	60.7	58.9	57.9	56.8	56.9	56.2	54.7	54.0
Widowed	7.2	6.6	6.4	6.0	2.5	2.3	2.5	2.4	11.5	10.6	10.0	9.4
Divorced.............	7.9	8.7	9.3	9.6	6.8	7.6	8.3	8.3	8.9	9.8	10.2	10.9

(1) Aged 15 and older. Totals may not add because of rounding.

U.S. Households Headed by Couples, 1960-2005

Source: Current Population Surveys, U.S. Census Bureau, U.S. Dept. of Commerce
(numbers in thousands[1])

YEAR	Total	Married-couple households	% of Total	Unmarried-couple households[2]	% of Total	YEAR	Total	Married-couple households	% of Total	Unmarried-couple households[2]	% of Total
1960	52,799	39,254	74	439	0.8	1992	95,669	52,457	55	3,308	3.5
1970	63,401	44,728	71	523	0.8	1993	96,426	53,090	55	3,510	3.6
1980	80,776	49,112	61	1,589	2.0	1994	97,107	53,171	55	3,661	3.8
1981	82,368	49,294	60	1,808	2.2	1995	98,990	53,858	54	3,668	3.7
1982	83,527	49,630	59	1,863	2.2	1996	99,627	53,567	54	3,958	4.0
1983	83,918	49,908	59	1,891	2.3	1997	101,018	53,604	53	4,130	4.1
1984	85,407	50,090	59	1,988	2.3	1998	102,528	54,317	53	4,236	4.1
1985	86,789	50,350	58	1,983	2.3	1999	103,874	54,770	53	4,486	4.3
1986	88,458	50,933	58	2,220	2.5	2000	104,705	55,311	53	4,736	4.5
1987	89,479	51,537	58	2,334	2.6	2001	108,209	56,592	52	4,893	4.5
1988	91,124	51,675	57	2,588	2.8	2002	109,297	56,747	52	4,898	4.5
1989	92,830	52,100	56	2,764	3.0	2003	111,278	57,320	52	5,054	4.5
1990	93,347	52,317	56	2,856	3.1	2004	112,000	57,719	52	5,080	4.5
1991	94,312	52,147	55	3,039	3.2	2005	113,146	58,109	51	4,855	4.3

(1) Data may differ from Census figures. (2) Does not include same-sex couples or families living in U.S. military barracks or emergency/homeless shelters.

Unmarried-Partner Households by Sex of Partners, 2000

Source: 2000 Census, U.S. Census Bureau, U.S. Dept. of Commerce

Household	Number	Household	Number
Total U.S. households	105,480,101	Female householder and female partner	293,365
Unmarried-partner households	5,475,768	Female householder and male partner	2,266,258
Male householder and male partner	301,026	All other households	100,004,333
Male householder and female partner	2,615,119		

Note: Does not include families living in institutions, college dormitories, and other group quarters.

Population, by Sex, Race, Residence, and Median Age, 1790-2005

Source: Decennial Censuses, Population Estimates, U.S. Census Bureau, U.S. Dept. of Commerce
(numbers in thousands, except as indicated)

| | SEX | | RACE | | | | RESIDENCE | | MEDIAN AGE (years) | | |
	Male	Female	White	Black Number	Black Percent	Other[5]	Urban	Rural	All races	White	Black
Conterminous U.S.[1]											
1790 (Aug. 2)	NA	NA	3,172	757	19.3	NA	202	3,728	NA	NA	NA
1810 (Aug. 6)	NA	NA	5,862	1,378	19.0	NA	525	6,714	NA	16.0	NA
1820 (Aug. 7)	4,897	4,742	7,867	1,772	18.4	NA	693	8,945	16.7	16.6	17.2
1840 (June 1)	8,689	8,381	14,196	2,874	16.8	NA	1,845	15,218	17.8	17.9	17.6
1860 (June 1)	16,085	15,358	26,923	4,442	14.1	79	6,217	25,227	19.4	19.7	17.5
1870 (June 1)	19,494	19,065	33,589	4,880	12.7	89	9,902	28,656	20.2	20.4	18.5
1880 (June 1)	25,519	24,637	43,403	6,581	13.1	172	14,130	36,059	20.9	21.4	18.0
1890 (June 1)	32,237	30,711	55,101	7,489	11.9	358	22,106	40,874	22.0	22.5	17.8
1900 (June 1)	38,816	37,178	66,809	8,834	11.6	351	30,215	45,997	22.9	23.4	19.4
1920 (Jan. 1)	53,900	51,810	94,821	10,463	9.9	427	54,158	51,553	25.3	25.5	22.3
1930 (Apr. 1)	62,137	60,638	110,287	11,891	9.7	597	69,161	53,820	26.5	26.9	23.5
1940 (Apr. 1)	66,062	65,608	118,215	12,866	9.8	589	74,705	57,246	29.0	29.5	25.3
United States											
1950 (Apr. 1)	74,833	75,864	135,150	15,042	9.9	1,131	90,128	54,230	30.2	30.7	26.2
1960 (Apr. 1)	88,331	90,992	158,832	18,872	10.5	1,620	125,269	54,054	29.5	30.3	23.5
1970 (Apr. 1)[2]	98,912	104,300	177,749	22,580	11.1	2,883	149,647	53,565	28.1	28.9	22.4
1980 (Apr. 1)[3]	110,053	116,493	194,713	26,683	11.8	5,150	167,051	59,495	30.0	30.9	24.9
1985 (July 1, est.) . . .	115,730	122,194	202,031	28,569	12.0	7,324	NA	NA	31.4	32.3	26.6
1990 (Apr. 1)	121,239	127,470	199,686	29,986	12.1	9,233	187,053	61,656	32.9	34.4	28.1
1991 (July 1, est.) . . .	122,984	129,122	210,979	31,107	12.3	10,020	NA	NA	33.1	34.1	28.1
1992 (July 1, est.) . . .	124,506	130,496	212,885	31,670	12.4	10,446	NA	NA	33.4	34.4	28.5
1993 (July 1, est.) . . .	125,938	131,858	214,760	32,168	12.5	10,867	NA	NA	33.7	34.7	28.7
1994 (July 1, est.) . . .	127,216	133,076	216,413	32,653	12.5	11,227	NA	NA	34.0	35.0	29.0
1995 (July 1, est.) . . .	128,565	134,321	218,149	33,095	12.6	11,646	NA	NA	34.3	35.3	29.2
1996 (July 1, est.) . . .	129,746	135,434	219,686	33,514	12.6	11,979	NA	NA	34.6	35.7	29.5
1997 (July 1, est.) . . .	131,018	136,618	221,334	33,947	12.7	12,355	NA	NA	34.9	36.0	29.7
1998 (July 1, est.) . . .	132,263	137,766	222,932	34,370	12.7	12,727	NA	NA	35.3	36.3	29.9
1999 (July 1, est.) . . .	133,352	139,526	224,692	34,903	12.8	13,283	NA	NA	35.5	36.6	30.1
2000 (Apr. 1)[4]	138,054	143,368	228,104	35,704	12.7	13,716	222,361	59,061	35.3	36.6	30.0
2001 (July 1, est.)[4] . . .	140,016	145,092	230,509	36,250	12.7	14,291	NA	NA	35.6	36.9	30.2
2002 (July 1, est.)[4] . . .	141,542	146,442	232,375	36,671	12.7	14,749	NA	NA	35.7	37.1	30.4
2003 (July 1, est.)[4] . . .	143,058	147,792	234,241	37,082	12.7	15,207	NA	NA	35.9	37.3	30.6
2004 (July 1, est.)[4] . . .	144,535	149,121	236,064	37,496	12.8	15,657	NA	NA	36.0	37.5	30.8
2005 (July 1, est.)[4] . . .	146,000	150,411	237,855	37,909	12.8	16,067	NA	NA	36.2	37.6	30.9

NA = Not available. **NOTE:** For 2000 "urban" includes residents of Urban Areas (densely settled areas with 50,000 or more inhabitants); or Urban Clusters (densely settled areas with at least 2,500 but fewer than 50,000). These definitions differ from previous Census years. (1) Excludes Alaska and Hawaii. (2) The revised 1970 resident population count is 203,302,031, which incorporates changes due to errors found after tabulations were completed. The race and sex data shown here reflect the official 1970 census count; the residence data come from the tabulated count. (3) The race data shown for Apr. 1, 1980, have been modified. (4) Race data for 2000-2005 are for one race alone. (5) "Other" consists of American Indians, Alaska Natives, Asians, Native Hawaiians and other Pacific Islanders.

U.S. Population by Race and Hispanic Origin, 1990-2000

Source: Decennial Censuses, U.S. Census Bureau, U.S. Dept. of Commerce

| | 2000 Census | | 1990 Census | | % change, 1990-2000[4] | |
	One race only	One race or more[3]	Number	% of total pop.	Using one race only for 2000 Census	Using one race only or in combination for 2000 Census
RACE[1]						
Total population[2]	281,421,906	281,421,906	248,709,873	100.0	13.2	13.2
White	211,460,626	216,930,975	199,686,070	80.3	5.9	8.6
Black or African American	34,658,190	36,419,434	29,986,060	12.1	15.6	21.5
American Indian and Alaska Native . . .	2,475,956	4,119,301	1,959,234	0.8	26.4	110.3
Asian	10,242,998	11,898,828	6,908,638	2.8	48.3	72.2
Native Hawaiian and Other Pac. Isl. . .	398,835	874,414	365,024	0.1	9.3	139.5
Some other race.	15,359,073	18,521,486	9,804,847	3.9	56.6	88.9
HISPANIC ORIGIN AND RACE						
Total population[2]	281,421,906	281,421,906	248,709,873	100.0	13.2	13.2
Hispanic or Latino (of any race)[2]	35,305,818	35,305,818	22,354,059	9.0	57.9	57.9
Not Hispanic or Latino[2]	246,116,088	246,116,088	226,355,814	91.0	8.7	8.7
White	194,552,774	198,177,900	188,128,296	75.6	3.4	5.3
Black or African American	33,947,837	35,383,751	29,216,293	11.7	16.2	21.1
American Indian and Alaska Native .	2,068,883	3,444,700	1,793,773	0.7	15.3	92.0
Asian	10,123,169	11,579,494	6,642,481	2.7	52.4	74.3
Native Hawaiian and Other Pac. Isl.	353,509	748,149	325,878	0.1	8.5	129.6
Some other race.	467,770	1,770,645	249,093	0.1	87.8	610.8

(1) Because individuals could report only one race in 1990 and could report more than one race in 2000, and because of other changes in the census questionnaire, the race data for 1990 and 2000 are not directly comparable. (2) The differences in data for the total population, Hispanic or Latino population, and total Not Hispanic or Latino population are not affected by the changes cited in (1). Hispanic or Latino persons may be of any race. (3) Alone or in combination with one or more of the other five races listed. (4) Columns 5 and 6 provide, respectively, a "minimum–maximum" range for the percent change in population of each race between 1990 and 2000.

The Undocumented Population

Source: Pew Hispanic Center

The number of unauthorized migrants as of early 2006 was between 11.5 and 12 mil, according to the Pew Hispanic Center, with more unauthorized migrants than new legal immigrants arriving each year since the mid-1990s. Most of the unauthorized population lives in families, with 1.8 mil children representing 16% of the unauthorized population. About 7.2 mil unauthorized workers were employed as of March 2005, making up 4.9% of the work force, though it has been illegal for employers to hire undocumented workers since 1986. The top occupations for this illegal labor force were service (31% of all unauthorized workers, compared to 16% of all native workers); construction and extractive industries (19%); production, installation, and repair (15%); sales and administrative support (12%); management, business, and professional (10%); and transportation and material moving (8%). While 4% of the total work in agriculture, unauthorized workers account for 24% of all farm workers.

Hispanic Voting Power

Source: 2004 Current Population Survey, U.S. Census Bureau, U.S. Dept. of Commerce. More information is available from the Census Bureau's Annual Population Estimates Program, at www.census.gov/popest/estimates.php

Data compiled by the Tomás Rivera Policy Institute show that Latino voter turnout in presidential elections increased from 2,453,000 in 1980 to 5,934,000 by 2000. In the Nov. 2004 U.S. election, the Latino turnout rose to 7,587,000. Two candidates, Mel Martinez of Florida and Ken Salazar of Colorado, were elected as, respectively, the fourth and fifth Latino senators in U.S. history.

Two states—California and Texas—account for more than half of all Hispanic registered voters. In Florida, a hotly contested state in recent presidential elections, the proportion of registered Hispanics to all registered voters is approaching 1 in 8. Except for Cubans, most Hispanic-Americans are Democrats or independents.

According to the National Association of Latino Elected and Appointed Officials (NALEO), the number of elected Hispanic officeholders at all levels of government rose from 3,128 in 1984 to 5,132 as of Jan. 1, 2006; during the same period, the number of Hispanics in Congress increased from 9 to 22, including 3 in the U.S. Senate.

Top 10 States in Hispanic Percent of All Registered Voters, 2004

Source: Univision

Rank	State (electoral votes)	Hispanics Registered	% of Elig. Hispanic Reg.	Hispanic % of All Reg. Voters
1.	New Mexico (5)	259,000	56.1	32.5
2.	Texas (34)	2,035,000	60.0	21.7
3.	Arizona (10)	331,000	49.3	16.4
4.	California (55)	2,032,000	55.0	14.6
5.	Florida (27)	857,000	63.4	12.0
6.	Colorado (9)	213,000	57.0	10.7
7.	New York (31)	606,000	56.0	7.3
8.	Nevada (5)	59,000	47.2	7.1
9.	New Jersey (15)	218,000	61.4	5.4
10.	Illinois (21)	267,000	65.5	4.6

Party Affiliation of Latino Voters by Origin, 2004

Source: Pew Hispanic Center/Kaiser Family Foundation

Democrats ■ Republicans ■ Independents ☐ Other ☐ Don't Know

	Democrats	Republicans	Independents	Other	Don't Know
All Registered Latinos	45%	19%	21%	8%	5%
Puerto Ricans	50%	17%	15%	12%	5%
Mexicans	47%	18%	22%	7%	5%
Cubans	17%	52%	9%	8%	7%

Race and Minority Group Populations by Age, 2005

Source: 2005 American Community Survey, U.S. Census Bureau, U.S. Dept. of Commerce; resident population

Hispanic Americans were the youngest of the population groups below, with a median age of 27.2 in 2005. The median age for blacks was 31.3; for Asians, 35.1; and for whites, 40.4.

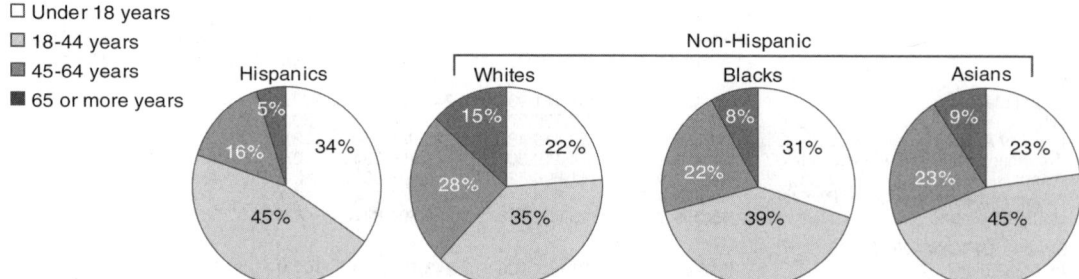

☐ Under 18 years
☐ 18-44 years
■ 45-64 years
■ 65 or more years

Hispanics: 5%, 16%, 34%, 45%
Non-Hispanic Whites: 15%, 22%, 28%, 35%
Non-Hispanic Blacks: 8%, 31%, 22%, 39%
Non-Hispanic Asians: 9%, 23%, 23%, 45%

Educational Attainment of the U.S. Population 25 Years of Age and Over, 2005

Source: 2005 American Community Survey; U.S. Census Bureau, U.S. Dept. of Commerce

Group	Pop. (in thousands)	High school grad. or more	Some college or more	Bachelor's degree or more
Hispanics (of any race)	22,663	59.3%	32.3%	12.2%
Non-Hispanic whites	134,106	89.0%	58.7%	30.0%
Blacks	20,518	79.9%	47.0%	17.3%
Asians	8,520	85.6%	68.8%	49.1%
U.S. Total	**188,951**	**84.2%**	**54.7%**	**27.2%**

U.S. Population Growth by Race and Hispanic Origin, 1970-2020[1]

Source: Decennial Censuses, 2005 American Community Survey, U.S. Interim Projecitons, U.S. Census Bureau, U.S. Dept. of Commerce

(figures in millions)

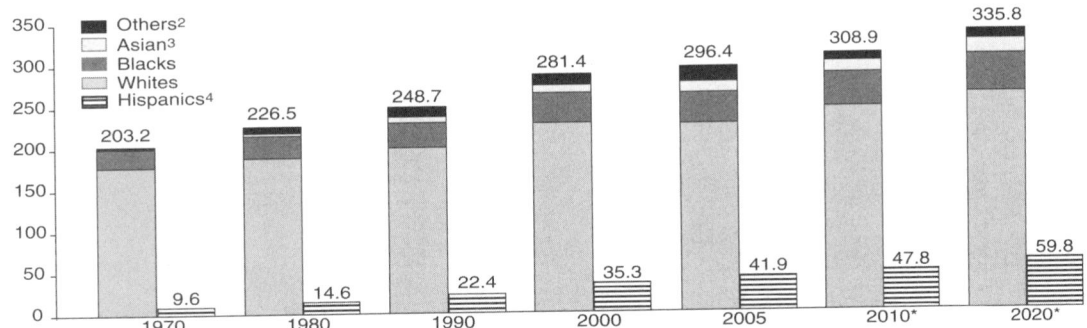

*Projected. (1) Because of changes in census questions and methods, data on race and Hispanic origin may not be wholly comparable over time. (2) Includes American Indians, Alaska Natives, and other races. From 2000 on, this category also includes Native Hawaiians, other Pacific Islanders, and persons reporting 2 or more races. (3) Figures for 1970-90 include Pacific Islanders. (4) May be of any race.

Race and Minority Groups, Percentage by State

Source: 2005 American Community Survey, except where noted; U.S. Census Bureau, U.S. Dept. of Commerce

Non-Hispanic White Population Percentage by State, 2005

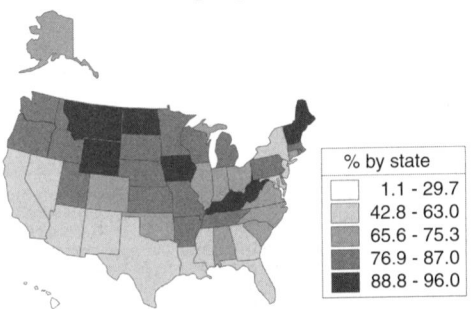

Black Population Percentage by State, 2005

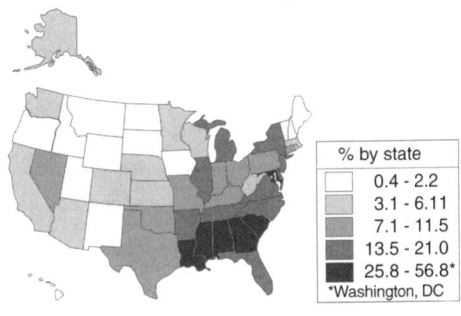

Hispanic Population Percentage by State, 2000
Source: 2000 Census

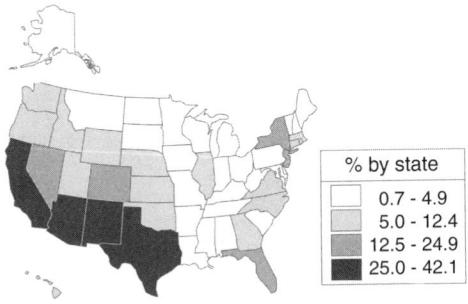

Asian Population Percentage by State, 2005

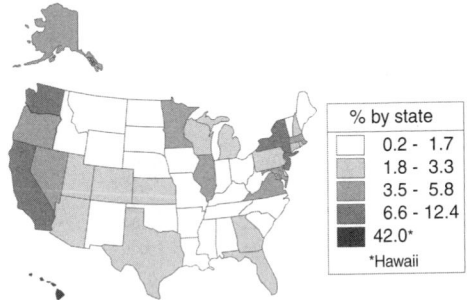

American Indian and Alaska Native Population Percentage by State, 2005

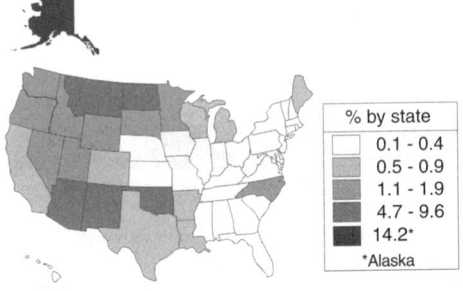

Two or More Races Population Percentage by State, 2005

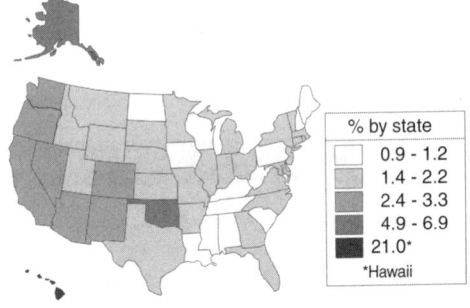

U.S. States Ranked by American Indian and Alaska Native Population, 2000

Source: 2000 Census, U.S. Census Bureau, U.S. Dept. of Commerce

Rank	State	One race only[1]	More than one race[2]	Rank	State	One race only[1]	More than one race[2]
1.	California.........	333,346	294,216	27.	Georgia	21,737	31,460
2.	Oklahoma	273,230	118,719	28.	Virginia............	21,172	31,692
3.	Arizona	255,879	36,673	29.	New Jersey	19,492	29,612
4.	New Mexico	173,483	17,992	30.	Pennsylvania.......	18,348	34,302
5.	Texas	118,362	97,237	31.	Arkansas	17,808	19,194
6.	North Carolina......	99,551	32,185	32.	Idaho	17,645	9,592
7.	Alaska............	98,043	21,198	33.	Indiana............	15,815	23,448
8.	Washington........	93,301	65,639	34.	Maryland	15,423	24,014
9.	New York	82,461	89,120	35.	Tennessee.........	15,152	24,036
10.	South Dakota	62,283	5,998	36.	Massachusetts......	15,015	23,035
11.	Michigan	58,479	65,933	37.	Nebraska	14,896	7,308
12.	Montana	56,068	10,252	38.	South Carolina	13,718	13,738
13.	Minnesota.........	54,967	26,107	39.	Mississippi	11,652	7,903
14.	Florida............	53,541	64,339	40.	Wyoming	11,133	3,879
15.	Wisconsin	47,228	22,158	41.	Connecticut	9,639	14,849
16.	Oregon	45,211	40,456	42.	Iowa..............	8,989	9,257
17.	Colorado	44,241	35,448	43.	Kentucky	8,616	15,936
18.	North Dakota.......	31,329	3,899	44.	Maine	7,098	6,058
19.	Illinois	31,006	42,155	45.	Rhode Island	5,121	5,604
20.	Utah	29,684	10,761	46.	West Virginia	3,606	7,038
21.	Nevada	26,420	15,802	47.	Hawaii	3,535	21,347
22.	Louisiana..........	25,477	17,401	48.	New Hampshire	2,964	4,921
23.	Missouri...........	25,076	35,023	49.	Delaware	2,731	3,338
24.	Kansas	24,936	22,247	50.	Vermont	2,420	3,976
25.	Ohio	24,486	51,589	51.	Washington, D.C.....	1,713	3,062
26.	Alabama	22,430	22,019		**UNITED STATES....**	**2,475,956**	**1,643,345**

(1) Respondents classified themselves only under the category "American Indian and Alaska Native" on Census 2000. (2) Respondents classified themselves as "American Indian and Alaska Native" in combination with one or more other races.

Largest American Indian and Alaska Native Tribal Groupings, 2000

Source: 2000 Census, U.S. Census Bureau, U.S. Dept. of Commerce

Based on self-identification in Census 2000. Some respondents reported themselves as being American Indian or an Alaska Native in combination with one or more races and/or as members of more than one tribal grouping. The last column is the sum of preceding columns.

Tribal grouping[1]	American Indian and Alaska Native alone		American Indian and Alaska Native in combination with one or more races		American Indian and Alaska Native tribal grouping alone or in any combination
	One tribal grouping reported	More than one tribal grouping reported	One tribal grouping reported	More than one tribal grouping reported	
ALL AMERICAN INDIANS[2]	2,423,531	52,425	1,585,396	57,949	4,119,301
Cherokee	281,069	18,793	390,902	38,769	729,533
Navajo	269,202	6,789	19,491	2,715	298,197
Sioux	108,272	4,794	35,179	5,115	153,360
Chippewa...................	105,907	2,730	38,635	2,397	149,669
Latin American..............	104,354	1,850	73,042	1,694	180,940
Choctaw....................	87,349	9,552	50,123	11,750	158,774
Pueblo	59,533	3,527	9,943	1,082	74,085
Apache.....................	57,060	7,917	24,947	6,909	96,833
Lumbee	51,913	642	4,934	379	57,868
Eskimo	45,919	1,418	6,919	505	54,761
Iroquois	45,212	2,318	29,763	3,529	80,822
Creek	40,223	5,495	21,652	3,940	71,310
Blackfeet	27,104	4,358	41,389	12,899	85,750
Chickasaw	20,887	3,014	12,025	2,425	38,351
Tohono O'odham	17,466	714	1,748	159	20,087
Inupiat Eskimo	16,047	845	2,282	191	19,365
Potawatomi	15,817	592	8,602	584	25,595
Yaqui	15,224	1,245	5,184	759	22,412
Tlingit-Haida................	14,825	1,059	6,047	434	22,365
Alaskan Athabascan	14,520	815	3,218	285	18,838
Seminole	12,431	2,982	9,505	2,513	27,431
Aleut.......................	11,941	832	3,850	355	16,978
Cheyenne...................	11,191	1,365	4,655	993	18,204
Puget Sound Salish	11,034	226	3,212	159	14,631
Comanche	10,120	1,568	6,120	1,568	19,376
Paiute......................	9,705	1,163	2,315	349	13,532

(1) Ranked by totals shown in first column. (2) Totals include tribal groupings not listed separately.

World Almanac Quick Quiz

Which of the following states did not have any cities that ranked among the 100 largest cities in the U.S.? (Its largest city had an estimated population of 117,088 in 2005.)

(a) Kansas (b) Minnesota (c) Hawaii (d) South Carolina

For the answer look in this chapter, or see page 1008.

U.S. Places of 5,000 or More Population–With ZIP and Area Codes

Source: U.S. Bureau of the Census, Dept. of Commerce; NeuStar Inc.

The following is a list of places of 5,000 or more inhabitants recognized by the Bureau of the Census, U.S. Dept. of Commerce, based on July 1, 2005 Census Bureau estimates. Also given are 1990 census populations. This list includes **places that are incorporated** under the laws of their respective states as cities, boroughs, towns, and villages, as well as boroughs in Alaska and towns in the 6 New England states, New York, and Wisconsin. Townships are not included.

Places that the Census Bureau designates as **"census designated places"** (CDPs) are also included; these are marked (c). The Census Bureau does not calculate estimates for CDPs; for these places, the 2000 Census figure is given, in *italics*, in place of the 2005 estimate. CDP boundaries can change from one census to another.

This list also includes, in *italics*, **minor civil divisions** (MCDs), for Connecticut, Maine, Massachusetts, New Hampshire, Rhode Island, and Vermont. MCDs are not incorporated and not recognized as CDPs, but are often the primary political or administrative divisions of a county.

An **asterisk** (*) denotes that the ZIP code given is for general delivery; named streets and/or P.O. boxes within the community may differ; consult www.usps.com. Telephone **area codes** are given in parentheses. Some regions have 2 or more area codes intermixed (where new customers receive the newer area code); these are known as **overlays**. States where this occurs are noted. When 2 or more area codes are listed for one place, consult local operators for assistance. Area codes based on latest information as of Aug. 2006. For a listing in numerical order of specific area codes in the U.S., Canada, and the Caribbean, see Computers and Telecommunications chapter, page 382. For some places listed, no area code and/or ZIP code is available. — = Not available.

Alabama

ZIP	Place	Area Code	2005	1990
*35007	Alabaster	(205)	27,517	14,619
*35950	Albertville	(256)	18,615	14,507
*35010	Alexander City	(256)	14,957	14,917
*36420	Andalusia	(334)	8,691	9,269
*36201	Anniston	(256)	23,741	26,638
35016	Arab	(256)	7,498	6,321
*35611	Athens	(256)	20,972	16,901
*36502	Atmore	(251)	7,530	8,046
35954	Attalla	(256)	6,474	6,859
*36830	Auburn	(334)	49,928	33,830
36507	Bay Minette	(251)	7,808	7,168
*35020	Bessemer	(205)	28,641	33,581
*35201	Birmingham	(205)	231,483	265,347
*35956	Boaz	(256)	7,893	6,928
*36426	Brewton	(251)	5,373	5,885
35040	Calera	(205)	6,707	2,136
35243	Cahaba Heights (c)	(205)	*5,203*	4,778
*35215	Center Point	(205)	*15,368*	22,658
36611	Chickasaw	(251)	6,000	6,651
35044	Childersburg	(256)	5,000	4,756
*35045	Clanton	(205)	8,336	7,669
*35055	Cullman	(256)	14,735	13,367
36526	Daphne	(251)	18,581	11,291
*35601	Decatur	(256)	54,909	49,917
36732	Demopolis	(334)	7,555	7,512
*36301	Dothan	(334)	62,713	54,131
*36330	Enterprise	(334)	22,892	20,119
*36027	Eufaula	(334)	13,463	13,220
35064	Fairfield	(205)	11,696	12,200
*36532	Fairhope	(251)	15,391	9,189
*35630	Florence	(256)	36,480	36,426
*36535	Foley	(251)	11,419	4,937
35214	Forestdale (c)	(205)	*10,509*	10,395
*35967	Fort Payne	(256)	13,573	11,838
36362	Fort Rucker (c)	(334)	*6,052*	7,593
35068	Fultondale	(205)	6,853	6,400
*35901	Gadsden	(256)	37,405	42,523
35071	Gardendale	(205)	12,830	9,251
35905	Glencoe	(256)	5,265	4,687
35235	Grayson Valley (c)	(205)	*5,447*	—
36037	Greenville	(334)	7,104	7,847
*36542	Gulf Shores	(251)	7,263	3,261
35976	Guntersville	(256)	7,721	7,038
35570	Hamilton	(205)	6,496	6,171
35640	Hartselle	(256)	13,080	11,114
35080	Helena	(205)	13,237	4,303
*35209	Homewood	(205)	23,963	23,644
*35244	Hoover	(205)	67,469	39,988
*35023	Hueytown	(205)	15,192	15,280
*35801	Huntsville	(256)	166,313	159,880
35210	Irondale	(205)	9,531	9,458
36545	Jackson	(251)	5,285	5,819
36265	Jacksonville	(256)	8,862	10,283
*35501	Jasper	(205)	14,088	13,553
35242	Lake Purdy (c)	(205)	*5,799*	1,840
36863	Lanett	(334)	7,590	8,985
35094	Leeds	(205)	11,053	10,009
*35758	Madison	(256)	35,893	14,792
35228	Midfield	(205)	5,319	5,559
36054	Millbrook	(334)	14,805	6,046
*36601	Mobile	(251)	191,544	199,973
*36460	Monroeville	(251)	6,690	6,993
35115	Montevallo	(205)	5,092	4,239
*36104	Montgomery	(334)	200,127	190,350
35004	Moody	(205)	10,764	4,921
35811	Moores Mill (c)	(256)	*5,178*	3,362
*35223	Mountain Brook	(205)	20,821	19,810
*35661	Muscle Shoals	(256)	12,523	9,611
*35476	Northport	(205)	21,216	17,297
35121	Oneonta	(205)	6,537	4,844
*36801	Opelika	(334)	23,804	22,122
36467	Opp	(334)	6,658	7,011
—	Orange Beach	(251)	5,055	2,253
36203	Oxford	(256)	19,981	9,537
*36360	Ozark	(334)	14,833	13,030
35124	Pelham	(205)	19,450	9,356
*35125	Pell City	(205)	11,010	7,945
*36867	Phenix City	(334)	29,460	25,311
35126	Pinson (c)	(205)	*5,033*	10,987
35127	Pleasant Grove	(205)	10,312	8,458
*36067	Prattville	(334)	30,043	19,816
36610	Prichard	(251)	27,963	34,320
*35906	Rainbow City	(256)	8,880	7,667
36274	Roanoke	(334)	6,650	6,362
*35653	Russellville	(256)	8,793	7,812
36206	Saks (c)	(256)	*10,698*	11,138
36571	Saraland	(251)	12,683	11,784
36572	Satsuma	(251)	5,951	5,194
*35768	Scottsboro	(256)	14,840	13,786
*36701	Selma	(334)	19,401	23,755
35660	Sheffield	(256)	9,228	10,380
35907	Southside	(256)	7,838	5,580
*36527	Spanish Fort	(251)	5,642	3,732
*35150	Sylacauga	(256)	12,956	12,520
*35160	Talladega	(256)	17,149	18,175
36078	Tallassee	(334)	5,032	5,112
35217	Tarrant	(205)	6,691	8,046
*36081	Troy	(334)	13,935	13,051
35173	Trussville	(205)	16,760	8,283
*35401	Tuscaloosa	(205)	81,358	77,866
35674	Tuscumbia	(256)	8,170	8,413
36083	Tuskegee	(334)	11,590	12,257
*36854	Valley	(334)	9,000	9,556
*35216	Vestavia Hills	(205)	31,022	19,550
*36092	Wetumpka	(334)	6,905	4,670

Alaska (907)

ZIP	Place	2005	1990
*99501	Anchorage	275,043	226,338
*99559	Bethel	6,262	4,674
*99708	College (c)	*11,402*	11,249
99702	Eielson AFB (c)	*5,400*	5,251
*99701	Fairbanks	31,324	30,843
99603	Homer	5,364	3,660
*99801	Juneau	30,987	26,751
*99611	Kenai	7,464	6,327
*99901	Ketchikan	7,410	8,263
99654	Knik-Fairview (c)	*7,049*	272
*99615	Kodiak	6,273	6,365
99654	Lakes (c)	*6,706*	—
99645	Palmer	6,920	2,901
*99835	Sitka	8,986	8,588
*99654	Wasilla	8,471	4,028

Arizona

ZIP	Place	Area Code	2005	1990
*85220	Apache Junction	(480)	32,297	18,092
85323	Avondale	(623)	66,706	17,595
85653	Avra Valley (c)	(520)	*5,038*	3,403
86351	Big Park (c)	(928)	*5,245*	3,024
85603	Bisbee	(520)	6,177	6,288
*85326	Buckeye	(623)	9,619	4,436
*86442	Bullhead City	(928)	39,101	21,951
86322	Camp Verde	(928)	10,155	6,243
85704	Casas Adobes (c)	(520)	*54,011*	—
*85738	Catalina (c)	(520)	*7,025*	4,864
85718	Catalina Foothills (c)	(520)	*53,794*	—
*85222	Casa Grande	(520)	32,855	19,076
*85225	Chandler	(480)	234,939	89,862
86323	Chino Valley	(928)	9,710	4,837
85228	Coolidge	(520)	8,154	6,934
86326	Cottonwood	(928)	10,894	5,918
86326	Cottonwood-Verde Village (c)	(928)	*10,610*	7,037
86327	Dewey-Humboldt (c)	(928)	*6,295*	3,640
*85607	Douglas	(520)	16,791	13,908
85746	Drexel Heights (c)	(520)	*23,849*	14,013
85335	El Mirage	(623)	22,171	5,001
85231	Eloy	(520)	10,855	7,211
*86004	Flagstaff	(928)	57,391	45,857
*85232	Florence	(520)	17,053	7,321
85705	Flowing Wells (c)	(520)	*15,050*	14,013
85367	Fortuna Foothills (c)	(928)	*20,478*	7,737
*85268	Fountain Hills	(480)	23,217	10,030

ZIP	Place	Area Code	2005	1990
*85234	Gilbert	(480)	173,989	29,149
*85301	Glendale	(623)	239,435	147,070
*85501	Globe	(928)	7,187	6,062
85219	Gold Camp (c)	(480)	6,029	—
85338	Goodyear	(623)	43,941	6,258
*85614	Green Valley (c)	(520)	17,283	13,231
85283	Guadalupe	(480)	5,258	5,458
86025	Holbrook	(928)	5,126	4,770
*86401	Kingman	(928)	25,547	13,208
*86403	Lake Havasu City	(928)	55,338	24,363
85653	Marana	(520)	26,098	2,565
*85201	Mesa	(480)	442,780	289,199
*86440	Mohave Valley (c)	(928)	13,694	6,962
86401	New Kingman-Butler (c)	(928)	14,810	11,627
*85087	New River (c)	(623)	10,740	—
*85621	Nogales	(520)	20,833	19,489
*85737	Oro Valley	(520)	38,438	9,024
*86040	Page	(928)	6,794	6,598
85253	Paradise Valley	(480)	14,558	11,903
*85541	Payson	(928)	14,729	8,377
*85345	Peoria	(623)	138,200	51,080
*85034	Phoenix	(602)	1,461,575	988,015
85743	Picture Rocks (c)	(520)	8,139	4,026
*86301	Prescott	(928)	40,360	26,592
*86314	Prescott Valley	(928)	33,068	8,904
85242	Queen Creek	(480)	16,628	2,639
85629	Sahuarita	(520)	9,007	—
85349	San Luis	(928)	21,646	4,212
*85251	Scottsdale	(480)	226,013	130,099
*86336	Sedona	(928)	11,220	7,720
*85901	Show Low	(928)	10,000	5,020
*85635	Sierra Vista	(520)	41,908	32,983
*85650	Sierra Vista Southeast (c)	(520)	9,042	9,237
85350	Somerton	(928)	10,071	5,293
85713	South Tucson	(520)	5,562	5,171
*85351	Sun City (c)	(623)	38,309	38,126
*85375	Sun City West (c)	(623)	26,344	15,997
85248	Sun Lakes (c)	(480)	11,936	6,578
*85374	Surprise	(623)	74,411	7,122
*85749	Tanque Verde (c)	(520)	16,195	—
*85282	Tempe	(480)	161,143	141,993
85736	Three Points (c)	(520)	5,273	2,175
85353	Tolleson	(623)	5,974	4,483
86045	Tuba City (c)	(928)	8,225	7,323
*85726	Tucson	(520)	515,526	415,444
85735	Tucson Estates (c)	(520)	9,755	2,662
85941	Whiteriver (c)	(928)	5,220	3,775
*85390	Wickenburg	(928)	6,224	4,515
86047	Winslow	(928)	9,931	9,279
*85364	Yuma	(928)	84,688	56,966

Arkansas

ZIP	Place	Area Code	2005	1990
*71923	Arkadelphia	(870)	10,548	10,014
*72501	Batesville	(870)	9,556	9,187
72012	Beebe	(501)	5,623	4,809
*72714	Bella Vista (c)	(479)	16,582	9,083
*72015	Benton	(501)	25,673	18,177
72712	Bentonville	(479)	29,538	11,257
*72315	Blytheville	(870)	16,638	22,523
*72022	Bryant	(501)	13,185	5,940
72023	Cabot	(501)	21,039	8,319
*71701	Camden	(870)	12,204	14,701
72719	Centerton	(479)	5,477	491
72830	Clarksville	(479)	8,311	5,833
*72032	Conway	(501)	51,999	26,481
71635	Crossett	(870)	5,802	6,282
71832	De Queen	(870)	5,953	4,633
72065	East End (c)	(501)	5,623	—
*71730	El Dorado	(870)	20,467	23,146
*72701	Fayetteville	(479)	66,655	42,247
*72335	Forrest City	(870)	14,078	13,364
*72901	Fort Smith	(479)	82,481	72,798
72936	Greenwood	(479)	7,914	3,984
*72601	Harrison	(870)	12,764	9,936
*72543	Heber Springs	(501)	7,016	5,628
72342	Helena	(870)	5,687	7,491
*71801	Hope	(870)	10,467	9,768
*71901	Hot Springs	(501)	37,847	33,095
*71909	Hot Springs Village (c)	(501)	8,397	6,361
*72076	Jacksonville	(501)	30,367	29,101
*72401	Jonesboro	(870)	59,358	46,535
*72201	Little Rock	(501)	184,564	175,727
72745	Lowell	(479)	7,042	1,224
*71753	Magnolia	(870)	10,478	11,151
*72104	Malvern	(501)	9,068	9,236
72364	Marion	(870)	9,792	4,405
*72113	Maumelle	(501)	14,318	6,714
71953	Mena	(479)	5,608	5,475
*71655	Monticello	(870)	9,327	8,119
72110	Morrilton	(501)	6,607	6,551
*72653	Mountain Home	(870)	11,896	9,027
72112	Newport	(870)	7,281	7,459
*72114	North Little Rock	(501)	58,803	61,829
72370	Osceola	(870)	8,128	9,165
*72450	Paragould	(870)	23,775	18,540
*71601	Pine Bluff	(870)	52,693	57,140
72455	Pocahontas	(870)	6,765	6,151

ZIP	Place	Area Code	2005	1990
*72756	Rogers	(479)	48,353	24,692
*72801	Russellville	(479)	25,520	21,260
*72143	Searcy	(501)	20,663	15,180
*72120	Sherwood	(501)	23,149	18,890
72761	Siloam Springs	(479)	13,604	8,151
*72764	Springdale	(479)	60,096	29,945
72160	Stuttgart	(870)	9,376	10,420
71854	Texarkana	(870)	30,006	22,631
72472	Trumann	(870)	6,922	6,346
*72956	Van Buren	(479)	21,249	14,899
71671	Warren	(870)	6,263	6,455
72390	West Helena	(870)	7,876	10,137
*72301	West Memphis	(870)	28,181	28,259
*71602	White Hall	(870)	5,114	3,849
72396	Wynne	(870)	8,569	8,187

California

ZIP	Place	Area Code	2005	1990
92301	Adelanto	(760)	24,360	6,815
*91376	Agoura Hills	(818)	22,765	20,396
*94501	Alameda	(510)	70,576	73,979
94507	Alamo (c)	(925)	15,626	12,277
94706	Albany	(510)	15,994	16,327
*91802	Alhambra	(626)	87,410	82,087
92656	Aliso Viejo	(949)	41,541	7,612
90249	Alondra Park (c)	(310)	8,622	12,215
*91901	Alpine (San Diego Co.) (c)	(619)	13,143	9,695
*91003	Altadena (c)	(626)	42,610	42,658
95945	Alta Sierra (c)	(530)	6,522	5,709
95127	Alum Rock (c)	(408)	13,479	—
94589	American Canyon	(707)	15,331	7,734
*92803	Anaheim	(714)	331,804	266,406
96007	Anderson	(530)	10,528	8,299
*94509	Antioch	(925)	100,631	62,195
*92307	Apple Valley	(760)	65,156	46,079
*95003	Aptos (c)	(831)	9,396	9,061
*91006	Arcadia	(626)	56,153	48,284
*95521	Arcata	(707)	16,914	15,211
95825	Arden-Arcade (c)	(916)	96,025	92,040
*93420	Arroyo Grande	(805)	16,315	14,432
*90701	Artesia	(562)	16,672	15,464
93203	Arvin	(661)	14,724	9,286
94577	Ashland (c)	(510)	20,793	16,590
*93422	Atascadero	(805)	27,130	23,138
94027	Atherton	(650)	7,177	7,163
95301	Atwater	(209)	27,107	22,282
*95603	Auburn	(530)	12,912	10,653
95202	August (c)	(209)	7,808	6,376
93204	Avenal	(559)	16,631	9,770
91746	Avocado Heights (c)	(626)	15,148	14,232
91702	Azusa	(626)	47,120	41,203
*93302	Bakersfield	(661)	295,536	176,264
91706	Baldwin Park	(626)	78,861	69,330
92220	Banning	(951)	29,308	20,572
*92312	Barstow	(760)	23,737	21,472
94565	Bay Point (c)	(925)	21,534	17,453
—	Bayview-Montalvin (c)	(510)	5,004	3,988
93402	Baywood-Los Osos (c)	(805)	14,351	14,377
95903	Beale AFB (c)	(530)	5,115	6,912
92223	Beaumont	(951)	20,530	9,685
*90201	Bell	(323)	37,521	34,365
*90202	Bell Gardens	(213)/(323)/(562)	45,135	42,315
*90706	Bellflower	(562)	74,570	61,815
94002	Belmont	(650)	24,522	24,165
94510	Benicia	(707)	26,489	24,437
*94704	Berkeley	(510)	100,744	102,724
92203	Bermuda Dunes (c)	(760)	6,229	4,571
*90210	Beverly Hills	(213)/(310)/(323)	35,078	31,971
92314	Big Bear City (c)	(909)	5,779	4,920
92315	Big Bear Lake	(909)	6,158	5,351
94526	Blackhawk-Camino Tassajara (c)	(925)	10,048	6,199
92316	Bloomington (c)	(951)	19,318	15,116
*92225	Blythe	(760)	22,130	10,835
93637	Bonadelle Ranchos-Madera Ranchos (c)	(559)	7,300	5,705
*91902	Bonita (c)	(619)	12,401	12,542
92021	Bostonia (c)	(619)	15,169	13,670
95416	Boyes Hot Springs (c)	(707)	6,665	5,973
92227	Brawley	(760)	22,433	18,923
*92822	Brea	(562)/(714)	38,465	32,873
*94513	Brentwood	(925)	43,794	7,563
—	Bret Harte (c)	(209)	5,161	—
*90622	Buena Park	(714)	79,174	68,784
*91510	Burbank (Los Angeles Co.)	(818)	104,108	93,649
—	Burbank (Santa Clara Co.) (c)	(408)	5,239	4,902
*94010	Burlingame	(650)	27,380	26,666
*91372	Calabasas	(818)	21,908	16,577
*92231	Calexico	(760)	36,005	18,633
*93504	California City	(760)	11,790	5,955
92320	Calimesa	(909)	7,491	6,654
92233	Calipatria	(760)	7,725	2,701
94515	Calistoga	(707)	5,190	4,468
*93010	Camarillo	(805)	61,576	52,297
93428	Cambria (c)	(805)	6,232	5,382
95682	Cameron Park (c)	(530)	14,549	11,897
*95008	Campbell	(408)	37,042	36,088
92054	Camp Pendleton North (c)	(760)	8,197	10,373
92055	Camp Pendleton South (c)	(760)	8,854	11,299

ZIP	Place	Area Code	2005	1990
92587	Canyon Lake	(951)	11,287	9,991
95010	Capitola	(831)	9,553	10,171
*92008	Carlsbad	(760)	90,773	63,292
*95608	Carmichael (c)	(916)	49,742	48,702
*93013	Carpinteria	(805)	13,549	13,747
*90745	Carson	(310)	93,955	83,995
92077	Casa de Oro-Mt. Helix (c)	(619)	18,874	30,727
*94546	Castro Valley (c)	(510)	57,292	48,619
95012	Castroville (c)	(831)	6,724	95012
*92235	Cathedral City	(760)	51,713	30,085
95307	Ceres	(209)	40,571	26,413
90703	Cerritos	(562)	52,561	53,244
91724	Charter Oak (c)	(626)	9,027	8,858
94541	Cherryland (c)	(510)	13,837	11,088
*95926	Chico	(530)	71,427	39,970
*91708	Chino	(909)	77,578	59,682
91709	Chino Hills	(909)	75,722	37,868
93610	Chowchilla	(559)	16,525	5,930
*91910	Chula Vista	(619)	210,497	135,160
91702	Citrus (c)	(626)	10,581	9,481
*95621	Citrus Heights	(916)	86,272	107,439
91711	Claremont	(909)	35,182	32,610
94517	Clayton	(925)	11,142	7,317
95422	Clearlake	(707)	14,728	11,804
95425	Cloverdale	(707)	8,016	4,924
*93612	Clovis	(559)	86,527	50,323
92236	Coachella	(760)	32,432	16,896
93210	Coalinga	(559)	17,350	8,212
*92324	Colton	(909)	51,350	40,213
95932	Colusa	(530)	5,826	4,934
90040	Commerce	(323)	13,455	12,135
*90221	Compton	(310)	95,659	90,454
*94520	Concord	(925)	123,252	111,308
*93212	Corcoran	(559)	22,456	13,360
*96021	Corning	(530)	7,140	5,870
92877	Corona	(951)	149,387	75,943
*92118	Coronado	(619)	26,424	26,540
*94925	Corte Madera	(415)	9,120	8,272
*92628	Costa Mesa	(714)/(949)	109,830	96,357
94931	Cotati	(707)	7,138	5,714
92679	Coto de Caza (c)	(949)	13,057	2,853
94556	Country Club (c)	(209)	9,462	9,325
*91722	Covina	(626)	47,850	43,332
92325	Crestline (c)	(909)	7,825	8,594
90201	Cudahy	(323)	25,004	22,817
*90230	Culver City	(310)	39,603	38,793
*95014	Cupertino	(408)	52,171	39,967
90630	Cypress	(714)	47,383	42,655
*94015	Daly City	(415)/(650)	100,339	92,088
*92629	Dana Point	(949)	35,867	31,896
*94526	Danville	(925)	41,852	31,306
*95616	Davis	(530)	60,709	46,322
90250	Del Aire (c)	(310)	9,012	8,040
*93215	Delano	(661)	45,531	22,762
95315	Delhi (c)	(209)	8,022	3,280
*92240	Desert Hot Springs	(760)	20,492	11,668
91765	Diamond Bar	(909)	57,975	53,672
93618	Dinuba	(559)	19,308	12,743
95620	Dixon	(707)	17,330	10,417
93620	Dos Palos	(209)	5,036	4,196
90239	Downey	(562)	109,718	91,444
94514	Discovery Bay (c)	(925)	8,981	5,351
*91009	Duarte	(626)	22,194	20,716
94568	Dublin	(925)	39,328	23,229
*95938	Durham (c)	(530)	5,220	4,784
93219	Earlimart (c)	(661)	6,583	5,881
90220	East Compton (c)	(310)	9,286	7,967
—	East Foothills (c)	(408)	8,133	14,898
92343	East Hemet (c)	(951)	14,823	17,611
90638	East La Mirada (c)	(562)	9,538	9,367
90022	East Los Angeles (c)	(323)	124,283	126,379
94303	East Palo Alto	(650)	32,242	23,451
91107	East Pasadena (c)	(626)	6,045	5,910
93257	East Porterville (c)	(559)	6,730	5,790
91775	East San Gabriel (c)	(626)	14,512	12,736
*93524	Edwards AFB (c)	(661)	5,909	7,423
*92020	El Cajon	(619)	92,487	88,918
*92244	El Centro	(760)	39,636	31,405
94530	El Cerrito	(510)	22,868	22,869
95762	El Dorado Hills (c)	(916)	18,016	6,395
94018	El Granada (c)	(650)	5,724	4,426
*91734	El Monte	(626)	122,513	106,162
*93446	El Paso de Robles	(805)	27,477	18,583
93030	El Rio (c)	(805)	6,193	6,419
90245	El Segundo	(310)	16,517	15,223
*94803	El Sobrante	(510)	12,260	9,852
*95624	Elk Grove	(916)	112,338	17,483
*94608	Emeryville	(510)	8,528	5,740
*92024	Encinitas	(760)	59,525	55,406
95320	Escalon	(209)	7,171	4,437
*92025	Escondido	(760)	134,085	108,648
*95501	Eureka	(707)	25,579	27,025
93221	Exeter	(559)	9,974	7,276
*94930	Fairfax	(415)	7,106	6,931
94533	Fairfield	(707)	104,476	78,650
95628	Fair Oaks (c)	(916)	28,000	26,867
94541	Fairview (c)	(510)	9,470	9,045
*92028	Fallbrook (c)	(760)	29,100	22,095
93223	Farmersville	(559)	9,918	6,235
*93015	Fillmore	(805)	14,895	11,992
93622	Firebaugh	(559)	7,001	4,429
90001	Florence-Graham (c)	(323)	60,197	57,147
95828	Florin (c)	(916)	27,653	24,330
*95630	Folsom	(916)	65,611	29,802
*92334	Fontana	(909)	163,860	87,535
95841	Foothill Farms (c)	(916)	17,426	17,135
92610	Foothill Ranch (c)	(949)	10,899	—
95437	Fort Bragg	(707)	6,814	6,078
95540	Fortuna	(707)	11,155	8,788
94404	Foster City	(650)	28,756	28,176
*92728	Fountain Valley	(714)	55,942	53,691
95019	Freedom (c)	(831)	6,000	8,361
*94537	Fremont	(510)	200,468	173,339
*93706	Fresno	(559)	461,116	354,091
*92834	Fullerton	(714)	132,787	114,144
95632	Galt	(209)	23,173	8,889
95205	Garden Acres (c)	(209)	9,747	8,547
*92842	Garden Grove	(714)	166,075	142,965
*90247	Gardena	(310)	59,891	51,481
*95020	Gilroy	(408)	45,718	31,487
92509	Glen Avon (c)	(951)	14,853	12,663
*91209	Glendale	(818)	200,065	180,038
*91741	Glendora	(626)	50,540	47,832
93561	Golden Hills (c)	(661)	7,434	5,423
95670	Gold River (c)	(916)	8,023	—
*93116	Goleta	(805)	29,367	—
93926	Gonzales	(831)	8,498	4,660
92324	Grand Terrace	(951)	12,342	10,946
95746	Granite Bay (c)	(916)	19,388	—
*95945	Grass Valley	(530)	12,449	9,048
93927	Greenfield	(831)	13,330	7,464
95948	Gridley	(530)	5,588	4,631
93433	Grover Beach	(805)	12,887	11,602
93434	Guadalupe	(805)	6,346	5,479
95322	Gustine	(209)	5,324	4,137
91745	Hacienda Heights (c)	(626)	53,122	52,354
94019	Half Moon Bay	(650)	12,203	8,886
*93230	Hanford	(559)	47,485	30,463
90716	Hawaiian Gardens	(562)	15,398	13,639
*90250	Hawthorne	(310)/(323)	85,697	71,349
*94544	Hayward	(510)	140,293	114,705
95448	Healdsburg	(707)	11,051	9,469
92546	Hemet	(951)	68,063	43,366
94547	Hercules	(510)	24,109	16,829
90254	Hermosa Beach	(310)	19,500	18,219
*92340	Hesperia	(760)	77,984	50,418
92346	Highland	(909)	50,892	34,439
94010	Hillsborough	(650)	10,615	10,667
*95023	Hollister	(831)	35,941	19,318
92250	Holtville	(760)	5,470	4,820
91720	Home Gardens (c)	(951)	9,461	7,780
95326	Hughson	(209)	5,705	2,918
*92647	Huntington Beach	(714)	194,457	181,519
90255	Huntington Park	(323)	62,491	56,129
93234	Huron	(559)	7,187	4,766
92251	Imperial	(760)	9,707	4,113
*91932	Imperial Beach	(619)	26,374	26,512
*92201	Indio	(760)	70,542	36,850
*90301	Inglewood	(310)/(323)	114,467	109,602
—	Interlaken (c)	(831)	7,328	6,404
95640	Ione	(209)	7,607	6,516
*92619	Irvine	(714)/(949)	186,852	110,330
93117	Isla Vista (c)	(805)	18,344	20,395
91935	Jamul (c)	(619)	5,920	2,258
94914	Kentfield (c)	(415)	6,351	6,030
93630	Kerman	(559)	11,223	5,448
93930	King City	(831)	11,004	7,634
93631	Kingsburg	(559)	11,148	7,245
*91011	La Canada Flintridge	(818)	20,998	19,378
90045	Ladera Heights (c)	(310)	6,568	6,316
94549	Lafayette	(925)	24,767	23,366
—	Laguna (c)	(916)	34,309	9,828
*92652	Laguna Beach	(949)	24,127	23,170
*92654	Laguna Hills	(949)	32,198	22,719
*92607	Laguna Niguel	(949)	64,664	44,723
—	Laguna West-Lakeside (c)	—	8,414	—
*92654	Laguna Woods	(949)	18,293	—
*90631	La Habra	(562)/(949)	59,326	51,263
90631	La Habra Heights	(562)	5,970	6,226
92352	Lake Arrowhead (c)	(909)	8,934	6,539
*92531	Lake Elsinore	(951)	39,258	19,733
92630	Lake Forest	(949)	76,412	56,036
92530	Lakeland Village (c)	(909)	5,626	5,159
*93535	Lake Los Angeles (c)	(661)	11,523	7,977
95453	Lakeport	(707)	5,241	4,567
92040	Lakeside(c)	(619)	19,560	39,412
*90714	Lakewood	(562)	80,467	73,553
*91941	La Mesa	(619)	53,081	52,911
*90638	La Mirada	(562)/(714)	49,640	40,452
93241	Lamont (c)	(661)	13,296	11,517
*93539	Lancaster	(661)	134,032	97,300
90623	La Palma	(562)/(714)	15,805	15,392
—	La Presa (c)	(619)	32,721	—
*91747	La Puente	(626)	41,762	36,955
*92253	La Quinta	(760)	38,232	11,215
95401	La Riviera (c)	(916)	10,273	10,986
95403	Larkfield-Wikiup (c)	(707)	7,479	6,779
*94939	Larkspur	(415)	11,724	11,068
92688	Las Flores (c)	(949)	5,625	—
95330	Lathrop	(209)	13,116	6,841

ZIP	Place	Area Code	2005	1990
91750	La Verne	(909)	33,185	30,843
*90260	Lawndale	(310)	32,193	27,331
*91945	Lemon Grove	(619)	24,124	23,984
93245	Lemoore	(559)	22,699	13,622
90304	Lennox (c)	(310)	22,950	22,757
95648	Lincoln	(916)	32,804	7,248
95901	Linda (c)	(530)	13,474	13,033
93247	Lindsay	(559)	10,767	8,338
95062	Live Oak (Santa Cruz Co.) (c)	(831)	16,628	15,212
95953	Live Oak (Sutter Co.)	(530)	7,128	4,320
*94550	Livermore	(925)	78,409	56,741
95334	Livingston	(209)	12,585	7,317
*95240	Lodi	(209)	62,133	51,874
92354	Loma Linda	(951)	20,901	18,470
90717	Lomita	(310)	20,515	19,442
*93436	Lompoc	(805)	39,985	37,649
*90801	Long Beach	(310)/(562)	474,014	429,321
95650	Loomis	(916)	6,577	5,705
*90720	Los Alamitos	(562)/(949)	11,657	11,788
*94022	Los Altos	(650)	27,096	26,599
94022	Los Altos Hills	(650)	8,164	7,514
*90086	Los Angeles	(213)/(310)/(323)/(818)	3,844,829	3,485,557
93635	Los Banos	(209)	33,506	14,519
*95030	Los Gatos	(408)	28,029	27,357
94903	Lucas Valley-Marinwood (c)	(415)	6,357	5,982
90262	Lynwood	(213)/(310)/(323)	71,208	61,945
93250	Mc Farland	(661)	11,875	7,005
95521	McKinleyville (c)	(707)	13,599	10,749
*93638	Madera	(559)	52,147	29,283
93637	Madera Acres (c)	(559)	7,741	5,245
95954	Magalia (c)	(530)	10,569	8,987
*90265	Malibu	(310)	13,208	11,730
93546	Mammoth Lakes	(760)	7,156	4,785
*90266	Manhattan Beach	(310)	36,481	32,063
*95336	Manteca	(209)	62,651	40,773
93933	Marina	(831)	19,006	26,512
*90291	Marina del Rey (c)	(310)	8,176	7,431
94553	Martinez	(925)	35,916	31,800
95901	Marysville	(530)	12,131	12,324
—	Mayflower Village (c)	—	5,081	4,978
90270	Maywood	(323)	28,600	27,893
93640	Mendota	(559)	8,942	6,821
*94025	Menlo Park	(650)	29,661	28,403
92359	Mentone (c)	(909)	7,803	5,675
*95340	Merced	(209)	73,767	56,155
94030	Millbrae	(650)	20,342	20,414
*94941	Mill Valley	(415)	13,286	13,029
*95035	Milpitas	(408)	63,383	50,690
91752	Mira Loma (c)	(951)	17,617	15,786
*93641	Miramonte (c)	(805)	7,177	7,744
*92690	Mission Viejo	(949)	94,982	79,464
*95350	Modesto	(209)	207,011	164,746
*91017	Monrovia	(626)	37,954	35,733
91763	Montclair	(909)	35,474	28,434
90640	Montebello	(323)	63,290	59,564
*93940	Monterey	(831)	29,217	31,954
*91754	Monterey Park	(323)/(626)/(818)	62,065	60,738
*93021	Moorpark	(805)	35,844	25,494
*94556	Moraga	(925)	16,869	15,987
*92552	Moreno Valley	(951)	178,367	118,779
*95037	Morgan Hill	(408)	34,852	23,928
*93442	Morro Bay	(805)	10,208	9,664
*94041	Mountain View	(650)	69,276	67,365
*92564	Murrieta	(951)	82,778	18,557
92407	Muscoy (c)	(714)	8,919	7,541
*94558	Napa	(707)	74,782	61,865
*91950	National City	(619)	61,419	54,249
92363	Needles	(760)	5,348	5,475
94560	Newark	(510)	41,956	37,861
95360	Newman	(209)	9,623	4,158
*92658	Newport Beach	(949)	79,834	66,643
93444	Nipomo (c)	(805)	12,626	7,109
91760	Norco	(951)	26,960	23,302
*90650	Norwalk	(562)	105,834	94,279
95603	North Auburn (c)	(530)	11,847	10,301
94025	North Fair Oaks (c)	(650)	15,440	13,912
95660	North Highlands (c)	(916)	44,187	42,105
*94947	Novato	(415)	50,335	47,585
95361	Oakdale	(209)	18,561	11,978
*94617	Oakland	(510)	395,274	372,242
94561	Oakley	(925)	27,177	18,374
93445	Oceano (c)	(805)	7,260	6,169
*92056	Oceanside	(760)	166,108	128,090
93308	Oildale (c)	(661)	27,885	26,553
*93023	Ojai	(805)	7,945	7,613
95961	Olivehurst (c)	(530)	11,061	9,738
*91761	Ontario	(909)	172,679	133,179
95060	Opal Cliffs (c)	(831)	6,458	5,940
*92863	Orange	(714)	134,950	110,658
93646	Orange Cove	(559)	9,578	5,604
95662	Orangevale (c)	(916)	26,705	26,266
*93457	Orcutt (c)	(805)	28,830	—
94563	Orinda	(925)	18,259	16,642
95963	Orland	(530)	6,757	5,052
93647	Orosi (c)	(559)	7,318	5,486
*95965	Oroville	(530)	13,468	11,885
*93030	Oxnard	(805)	183,628	142,560
94044	Pacifica	(650)	37,092	37,670
93950	Pacific Grove	(831)	15,091	16,117
95968	Palermo (c)	(530)	5,720	5,260
*93590	Palmdale	(661)	134,570	73,314
*92260	Palm Desert	(760)	47,058	23,252
*92262	Palm Springs	(760)	47,082	40,144
*94303	Palo Alto	(650)	56,982	55,900
*90274	Palos Verdes Estates	(310)	13,812	13,512
*95969	Paradise	(530)	26,517	25,401
90723	Paramount	(562)	56,540	47,669
95823	Parkway-So. Sacramento (c)	(916)	36,468	31,903
93648	Parlier	(559)	13,025	7,938
*91109	Pasadena	(323)/(626)/(818)	143,731	131,586
	Paso Robles. See El Paso de Robles			
95363	Patterson	(209)	15,500	8,626
92509	Pedley (c)	(951)	11,207	8,869
*92572	Perris	(951)	45,671	21,500
*94952	Petaluma	(707)	54,846	43,166
—	Phoenix Lake-Cedar Ridge (c)	—	5,123	3,569
*90660	Pico Rivera	(562)	64,679	59,177
*94611	Piedmont	(510)	10,559	10,602
94564	Pinole	(510)	19,061	17,460
*93449	Pismo Beach	(805)	8,419	7,669
94565	Pittsburg	(925)	62,547	47,607
94523	Pleasant Hill	(925)	33,153	31,583
*94566	Pleasanton	(925)	65,950	50,570
*91769	Pomona	(909)	153,787	131,700
*93257	Porterville	(559)	44,959	29,521
*93041	Port Hueneme	(805)	22,032	20,322
92679	Portola Hills (c)	(949)	6,391	2,677
*92064	Poway	(858)	48,476	43,396
93907	Prunedale (c)	(831)	16,432	7,393
*93551	Quartz Hill (c)	(661)	9,890	9,626
92065	Ramona (c)	(760)	15,691	13,040
*95670	Rancho Cordova	(916)	57,164	48,731
*91729	Rancho Cucamonga	(909)	169,353	101,409
92270	Rancho Mirage	(760)	16,514	9,778
90275	Rancho Palos Verdes	(310)	41,949	41,667
91941	Rancho San Diego (c)	(619)	20,155	6,977
92688	Rancho Santa Margarita	(949)	50,682	11,390
96080	Red Bluff	(530)	14,059	12,363
*96049	Redding	(530)	89,641	66,176
*92373	Redlands	(909)	69,995	62,667
*90277	Redondo Beach	(310)	66,824	60,167
*94063	Redwood City	(650)	73,114	66,072
93654	Reedley	(559)	22,368	15,791
*92377	Rialto	(909)	99,513	72,395
*94802	Richmond	(510)	102,186	86,019
*93556	Ridgecrest	(760)	25,974	28,295
95003	Rio del Mar (c)	(831)	9,198	8,919
95673	Rio Linda (c)	(916)	10,466	9,481
94571	Rio Vista	(707)	7,077	3,488
95366	Ripon	(209)	13,658	7,455
95367	Riverbank	(209)	19,727	8,591
*92502	Riverside	(951)	290,086	226,546
*95677	Rocklin	(916)	49,626	18,806
*94572	Rodeo (c)	(510)	8,717	7,589
*94928	Rohnert Park	(707)	41,101	36,326
*90274	Rolling Hills Estates	(310)	8,105	7,789
93560	Rosamond (c)	(661)	14,349	7,430
—	Rosedale (c)	(805)	8,445	4,673
95407	Roseland (c)	(707)	6,369	8,779
*91770	Rosemead	(626)	55,119	51,638
95826	Rosemont (c)	(916)	22,904	22,851
*95678	Roseville	(916)	105,940	44,685
90720	Rossmoor (c)	(714)	10,298	9,893
91748	Rowland Heights (c)	(626)	48,553	42,647
*92519	Rubidoux (c)	(951)	29,180	24,367
92382	Running Springs (c)	(909)	5,125	4,195
*95814	Sacramento	(916)	456,441	369,365
94574	Saint Helena	(707)	5,938	4,990
95368	Salida (c)	(209)	12,560	4,499
*93907	Salinas	(831)	146,431	108,777
*94960	San Anselmo	(415)	12,018	11,735
*92401	San Bernardino	(909)	198,550	170,036
*94066	San Bruno	(650)	39,752	38,961
*93001	San Buenaventura (Ventura)	(805)	104,017	92,557
*94070	San Carlos	(650)	26,821	26,382
*92674	San Clemente	(949)	60,235	41,100
*92138	San Diego	(619)/(858)	1,255,540	1,110,623
*92065	San Diego Country Estates (c)	(760)	9,262	6,874
91773	San Dimas	(909)	35,850	32,398
*91341	San Fernando	(818)	24,207	22,580
*94142	San Francisco	(415)	739,426	723,959
*91778	San Gabriel	(626)	41,056	37,120
93657	Sanger	(559)	22,041	16,839
*92581	San Jacinto	(951)	30,253	17,614
*95113	San Jose	(408)	912,332	782,224
*92690	San Juan Capistrano	(949)	34,673	26,183
*94577	San Leandro	(510)	78,178	68,223
*93401	San Luis Obispo	(805)	43,509	41,958
*92069	San Marcos	(760)	73,487	38,974
*91108	San Marino	(626)	13,165	12,959
*94402	San Mateo	(650)	91,081	85,619
94806	San Pablo	(510)	31,004	25,158
*94915	San Rafael	(415)	55,716	48,410
94583	San Ramon	(925)	49,999	35,303
*92711	Santa Ana	(714)/(949)	340,368	293,827
*93102	Santa Barbara	(805)	85,899	85,571
*95050	Santa Clara	(408)	105,402	93,613
*91380	Santa Clarita	(661)	168,253	120,050

ZIP	Place	Area Code	2005	1990
*95060	Santa Cruz	(831)	54,760	49,711
90670	Santa Fe Springs	(562)	17,058	15,520
*93454	Santa Maria	(805)	84,346	61,552
*90401	Santa Monica	(310)	87,800	86,905
*93060	Santa Paula	(805)	28,478	25,062
*95402	Santa Rosa	(707)	153,158	113,261
*92071	Santee	(619)	52,306	52,902
*95070	Saratoga	(408)	29,663	28,061
*94965	Sausalito	(415)	7,184	7,152
*95066	Scotts Valley	(831)	11,154	8,667
90740	Seal Beach	(562)	24,295	25,098
93955	Seaside	(831)	34,214	38,826
*95472	Sebastopol	(707)	7,598	7,008
93662	Selma	(559)	22,261	14,757
—	Shackelford (c)	—	5,170	
*93263	Shafter	(661)	14,569	9,404
*96019	Shasta Lake	(916)	10,233	8,821
*91025	Sierra Madre	(626)	10,988	10,762
*90806	Signal Hill	(562)	10,851	8,371
*93065	Simi Valley	(805)	118,687	100,218
92075	Solana Beach	(858)	12,716	12,956
93960	Soledad	(831)	27,210	13,426
*93463	Solvang	(805)	5,141	4,741
95476	Sonoma	(707)	9,885	8,168
95073	Soquel (c)	(831)	5,081	9,188
91733	South El Monte	(626)	21,666	20,850
90280	South Gate	(323)/(562)	98,897	86,284
*96151	South Lake Tahoe	(530)	24,016	21,586
95965	South Oroville (c)	(530)	7,695	7,463
*91030	So. Pasadena	(213)/(323)/626)/(818)	24,889	23,936
*94080	South San Francisco	(650)	60,735	54,312
91770	South San Gabriel (c)	(626)	7,595	7,700
91744	South San Jose Hills (c)	(626)	20,218	17,814
90605	South Whittier (c)	(562)	55,193	49,514
95991	South Yuba City (c)	(530)	12,651	8,816
*91977	Spring Valley (c)	(619)	26,663	55,331
*94309	Stanford (c)	(650)	13,315	18,097
90680	Stanton	(714)	37,661	30,491
*95208	Stockton	(209)	286,926	210,943
95375	Strawberry (c)	(209)	5,302	4,377
*94585	Suisun City	(707)	26,762	22,704
*92586	Sun City (c)	(951)	17,773	14,930
*94086	Sunnyvale	(408)	128,902	117,324
*96130	Susanville	(530)	18,101	12,130
93268	Taft	(661)	9,106	5,902
94941	Tamalpais-Homestead Val. (c)	(415)	10,691	9,601
94806	Tara Hills (c)	(510)	5,332	4,998
*93581	Tehachapi	(661)	11,752	6,182
*92589	Temecula	(951)	85,799	27,177
91780	Temple City	(626)	37,363	31,153
95965	Thermalito (c)	(530)	6,045	5,646
*91359	Thousand Oaks	(805)	124,359	104,381
92276	Thousand Palms (c)	(760)	5,120	4,122
94920	Tiburon	(415)	8,671	7,554
*90503	Torrance	(310)	142,384	133,107
95376	Tracy	(209)	79,964	33,558
*96161	Truckee	(916)	15,737	8,848
*93274	Tulare	(559)	50,127	33,249
*95380	Turlock	(209)	67,669	42,224
*92781	Tustin	(714)/(949)	69,096	50,689
92705	Tustin Foothills (c)	(714)	24,044	24,358
*92277	Twentynine Palms	(760)	28,409	11,821
92278	Twentynine Palms Base (c)	(760)	8,413	10,606
95060	Twin Lakes (c)	(831)	5,533	5,379
*95482	Ukiah	(707)	15,463	14,632
94587	Union City	(510)	69,176	53,762
*91785	Upland	(909)	73,589	63,374
*95687	Vacaville	(707)	92,985	71,476
91744	Valinda (c)	(626)	21,776	18,735
*94590	Vallejo	(707)	117,483	109,199
92343	Valle Vista (c)	(951)	10,488	8,751
92082	Valley Center (c)	(760)	7,323	1,711
93437	Vandenberg AFB (c)	(805)	6,151	9,846
93436	Vandenberg Village (c)	(805)	5,802	5,971
*92393	Victorville	(760)	91,264	50,103
90043	View Park-Windsor Hills (c)	(310)	10,958	11,769
92861	Villa Park	(714)	6,026	6,299
—	Vincent (c)	—	15,097	13,713
—	Vineyard (c)	—	10,109	—
*93291	Visalia	(559)	108,669	75,659
*92083	Vista	(760)	90,402	71,861
—	Waldon (c)	—	5,133	—
*91788	Walnut	(626)	31,424	29,105
*94596	Walnut Creek	(925)	64,196	60,569
90255	Walnut Park (c)	(213)	16,180	14,722
93280	Wasco	(661)	23,874	12,412
95386	Waterford	(209)	8,161	4,771
*95076	Watsonville	(831)	47,927	31,099
90044	West Athens (c)	(310)	9,101	8,859
90502	West Carson (c)	(310)	21,138	20,143
90247	West Compton (c)	(310)	5,435	5,451
*91790	West Covina	(626)	108,185	96,226
90069	West Hollywood	(310)/(323)	36,732	36,118
*91359	Westlake Village	(805)	41,744	7,455
*92685	Westminster	(714)	8,585	78,293
—	West Modesto (c)	—	6,096	
90047	Westmont (c)	(323)	31,623	31,044
91746	West Puente Valley (c)	(626)	22,589	20,254
*95691	West Sacramento	(916)	41,744	28,898
*90606	West Whittier-Los Nietos (c)	(562)	25,129	24,164

ZIP	Place	Area Code	2005	1990
*90605	Whittier	(562)	84,473	77,671
92595	Wildomar (c)	(951)	14,064	10,411
*95490	Willits	(707)	5,066	5,027
90022	Willowbrook (c)	(323)	34,138	32,772
95988	Willows	(530)	6,296	5,988
95492	Windsor	(707)	24,968	12,002
—	Winter Gardens (c)	—	19,771	
95694	Winters	(530)	6,764	4,639
95388	Winton (c)	(209)	8,832	7,559
92504	Woodcrest (c)	(951)	8,342	7,796
93286	Woodlake	(559)	7,215	5,678
*95695	Woodland	(530)	51,020	40,230
94061	Woodside	(650)	5,463	5,034
*92885	Yorba Linda	(714)	64,476	52,422
96097	Yreka	(530)	7,295	6,948
*95991	Yuba City	(530)	58,628	27,385
92399	Yucaipa	(909)	49,100	32,819
*92286	Yucca Valley	(760)	19,696	16,539

Colorado

Area code (720) overlays area code (303). See introductory note.

ZIP	Place	Area Code	2005	1990
*80840	Air Force Academy (c)	(719)	7,526	9,062
*81101	Alamosa	(719)	8,682	7,579
80401	Applewood (c)	(303)	7,123	11,069
*80004	Arvada	(303)	103,966	89,261
*81611	Aspen	(970)	5,804	5,049
*80017	Aurora	(303)	297,235	222,103
81620	Avon	(970)	6,349	1,798
80221	Berkley (c)	(970)	10,743	
80513	Berthoud	(970)	5,055	3,087
*80908	Black Forest (c)	(719)	13,247	8,143
*80302	Boulder	(303)	91,685	85,127
*80601	Brighton	(303)	28,013	14,203
*80020	Broomfield	(303)	43,478	24,638
80723	Brush	(970)	5,186	4,165
*81212	Canon City	(719)	16,000	12,687
81623	Carbondale	(970)	5,825	3,004
80104	Castle Pines (c)	(303)	5,958	—
*80104	Castle Rock	(303)	35,745	8,710
80120	Castlewood (c)	(303)	25,567	24,392
*80015	Centennial	(303)	98,243	
*80110	Cherry Hills Village	(303)	6,138	5,245
81222	Cimarron Hills (c)	(719)	15,194	11,160
81520	Clifton (c)	(970)	17,345	12,671
*80903	Colorado Springs	(719)	369,815	280,430
80120	Columbine (c)	(303)	24,095	23,969
*80022	Commerce City	(303)	34,189	16,466
81321	Cortez	(970)	8,244	7,284
*81625	Craig	(970)	9,143	8,091
81416	Delta	(970)	8,135	3,789
*80202	Denver	(303)	557,917	467,610
80022	Derby (c)	(303)	6,423	6,043
*81301	Durango	(970)	15,501	12,439
80214	Edgewater	(303)	5,211	4,613
81632	Edwards (c)	(970)	8,257	
*80110	Englewood	(303)	32,350	29,396
80516	Erie	(303)	12,351	1,258
*80517	Estes Park	(970)	5,812	3,184
80620	Evans	(970)	17,470	5,876
*80439	Evergreen (c)	(303)	9,216	7,582
80221	Federal Heights	(303)	11,706	9,342
*80504	Firestone	(303)	6,410	1,358
80913	Fort Carson (c)	(719)	10,566	11,309
*80525	Fort Collins	(970)	128,026	87,491
80621	Fort Lupton	(303)	7,121	5,159
*80701	Fort Morgan	(970)	10,844	9,068
80817	Fountain	(719)	19,081	10,754
*80530	Frederick	(303)	6,620	988
81521	Fruita	(970)	6,878	4,045
81504	Fruitvale (c)	(303)	6,936	5,222
*81601	Glenwood Springs	(970)	8,564	6,561
*80401	Golden	(303)	17,366	13,127
*81501	Grand Junction	(970)	45,299	32,893
*80631	Greeley	(970)	87,596	60,454
*80111	Greenwood Village	(303)	12,817	7,589
80501	Gunbarrel (c)	(303)	9,435	9,388
*81230	Gunnison	(970)	5,298	4,636
80163	Highlands Ranch (c)	(303)	70,931	10,181
80534	Johnstown	(970)	7,250	1,579
80127	Ken Caryl (c)	(303)	30,887	24,391
*80026	Lafayette	(303)	23,884	14,708
81050	La Junta	(719)	7,260	7,678
*80226	Lakewood	(303)	140,671	126,475
81052	Lamar	(719)	8,414	8,343
*80126	Littleton	(303)	40,396	33,711
*80124	Lone Tree	(303)	8,554	1,261
*80501	Longmont	(303)	81,818	51,976
80027	Louisville	(303)	18,358	12,363
*80538	Loveland	(970)	59,563	37,357
80829	Manitou Springs	(719)	5,039	4,540
80543	Milliken	(970)	5,593	1,605
*81401	Montrose	(970)	15,479	8,854
*80233	Northglenn	(303)	32,906	27,195
80649	Orchard Mesa (c)	(303)	6,456	5,977
*80134	Parker	(303)	38,428	5,450
*81003	Pueblo	(719)	103,495	98,640
81007	Pueblo West (c)	(719)	16,899	4,386
81503	Redlands (c)	(970)	8,043	9,355

ZIP	Place	Area Code	2005	1990
81650	Rifle	(970)	8,038	4,858
*81201	Salida	(719)	5,476	4,737
80911	Security-Widefield (c)	(719)	29,845	23,822
80110	Sheridan	(303)	5,483	4,976
80221	Sherrelwood (c)	(303)	17,657	16,636
80122	Southglenn (c)	(303)	43,520	43,087
*80477	Steamboat Springs	(970)	9,354	6,695
80751	Sterling	(970)	12,589	10,362
80134	Stonegate (c)	(719)	6,284	—
80906	Stratmoor (c)	(719)	6,650	5,854
80027	Superior	(303)	10,308	255
80134	The Pinery (c)	(303)	7,253	4,885
*80229	Thornton	(303)	105,182	55,031
81082	Trinidad	(719)	9,077	8,580
81251	Twin Lakes (c)	(719)	6,301	—
80229	Welby (c)	(303)	12,973	10,218
*80030	Westminster	(303)	105,084	74,619
*80033	Wheat Ridge	(303)	31,242	29,419
*80550	Windsor	(970)	14,874	5,062
*80863	Woodland Park	(719)	6,660	4,610
*80132	Woodmoor (c)	(719)	7,177	3,858

Connecticut
See introductory note.

ZIP	Place	Area Code	2005	1990
06401	Ansonia	(203)	18,744	18,403
06001	Avon	(860)	17,209	13,937
06403	Beacon Falls	(203)	5,596	5,083
06037	Berlin	(860)	19,590	16,787
06524	Bethany	(203)	5,473	—
06801	Bethel	(203)	18,760	17,541
06002	Bloomfield	(860)	20,581	19,483
06043	Bolton	(860)	5,170	—
06405	Branford	(203)	29,089	27,603
06405	Branford Center (c)	(203)	5,735	5,688
*06602	Bridgeport	(203)	139,008	141,686
*06010	Bristol	(860)	61,353	60,640
06804	Brookfield	(203)	16,354	14,113
06234	Brooklyn	(860)	7,711	6,681
*06013	Burlington	(860)	9,097	7,026
06331	Canterbury	(860)	5,060	—
06019	Canton	(860)	9,932	8,268
06040	Central Manchester (c)	(860)	30,595	30,934
*06410	Cheshire	(203)	29,097	25,684
06410	Cheshire Village (c)	(203)	5,789	5,759
06413	Clinton	(860)	13,612	12,767
*06415	Colchester	(860)	15,389	10,980
06237	Columbia	(860)	5,336	4,510
06340	Conning Towers-Nautilus Pk. (c)	(860)	10,241	10,013
06238	Coventry	(860)	12,190	10,063
06416	Cromwell	(860)	13,594	12,286
*06810	Danbury	(203)	78,736	65,585
06820	Darien	(203)	20,452	18,196
06418	Derby	(203)	12,536	12,199
06422	Durham	(860)	7,266	5,732
06026	East Granby	(860)	5,058	4,302
06423	East Haddam	(860)	8,808	6,676
*06424	East Hampton	(860)	12,194	10,428
*06108	East Hartford	(860)	49,173	50,452
*06512	East Haven	(203)	28,755	26,144
06333	East Lyme	(860)	18,459	15,340
06612	Easton	(203)	7,488	6,303
*06088	East Windsor	(860)	10,447	10,081
06029	Ellington	(860)	14,217	11,197
*06082	Enfield	(860)	45,441	45,532
06426	Essex	(860)	6,783	5,904
*06825	Fairfield	(203)	57,813	53,418
*06032	Farmington	(860)	24,941	20,608
06033	Glastonbury	(860)	33,089	27,901
06033	Glastonbury Center (c)	(860)	7,157	7,082
*06035	Granby	(860)	11,088	9,369
*06830	Greenwich	(203)	62,236	58,441
06351	Griswold	(860)	11,254	10,384
*06340	Groton Naval Base	(860)	9,493	9,837
06340	Groton	(860)	41,366	45,144
06437	Guilford	(203)	22,307	19,848
06438	Haddam	(860)	7,635	6,769
*06514	Hamden	(203)	58,180	52,434
*06101	Hartford	(860)	124,397	139,739
06791	Harwinton	(860)	5,571	5,228
06248	Hebron	(860)	9,198	7,079
06037	Kensington (c)	(860)	8,541	8,306
*06239	Killingly	(860)	17,386	15,889
06419	Killingworth	(860)	6,403	4,814
06249	Lebanon	(860)	7,334	6,041
06339	Ledyard	(860)	15,172	14,913
*06759	Litchfield	(860)	8,684	8,365
06443	Madison	(203)	18,812	15,485
*06040	Manchester	(860)	55,752	51,618
*06250	Mansfield	(860)	24,558	21,103
06447	Marlborough	(860)	6,267	5,535
*06450	Meriden	(203)	59,653	59,479
*06762	Middlebury	(203)	6,974	6,145
06457	Middletown	(860)	47,438	42,762
*06460	Milford	(203)	54,802	48,168
06468	Monroe	(203)	19,650	16,896
06353	Montville	(860)	19,612	16,673
06770	Naugatuck	(203)	31,864	30,625

ZIP	Place	Area Code	2005	1990
*06050	New Britain	(860)	71,254	75,491
*06840	New Canaan	(203)	19,984	17,864
06812	New Fairfield	(203)	14,261	12,911
06057	New Hartford	(860)	6,746	5,769
*06511	New Haven	(203)	124,791	130,474
*06101	Newington	(860)	29,676	29,208
06320	New London	(860)	26,174	28,540
06776	New Milford	(860)	28,667	23,629
06470	Newtown	(203)	26,996	20,779
06471	North Branford	(203)	14,398	12,996
06473	North Haven	(203)	23,908	22,247
06359	North Stonington	(860)	5,218	4,907
*06856	Norwalk	(203)	84,437	78,331
06360	Norwich	(860)	36,598	37,391
06779	Oakville (c)	(860)	8,618	8,741
06371	Old Lyme	(860)	7,488	6,535
06475	Old Saybrook	(860)	10,512	9,552
06477	Orange	(203)	13,970	12,830
06478	Oxford	(203)	11,709	8,685
06379	Pawcatuck (c)	(860)	5,474	5,289
06374	Plainfield	(860)	15,443	14,363
06062	Plainville	(860)	17,382	17,392
06782	Plymouth	(860)	12,183	11,822
06480	Portland	(860)	9,543	8,418
06712	Prospect	(203)	9,234	7,775
*06260	Putnam	(860)	9,288	9,031
06260	Putnam District (c)	(860)	6,746	6,835
06896	Redding	(203)	8,646	7,927
*06877	Ridgefield (c)	(203)	7,212	6,363
06877	Ridgefield	(203)	24,210	20,919
06066	Rockville (c)	(860)	7,708	—
06067	Rocky Hill	(860)	18,760	16,554
*06483	Seymour	(203)	16,144	14,288
06484	Shelton	(203)	39,477	35,418
06082	Sherwood Manor (c)	(860)	5,689	6,357
*06070	Simsbury	(860)	23,656	22,023
06070	Simsbury Center (c)	(860)	5,603	5,577
06071	Somers	(860)	10,877	9,108
06488	Southbury	(203)	19,677	15,818
06489	Southington	(860)	42,077	38,518
*06074	South Windsor	(860)	25,985	22,090
06082	Southwood Acres (c)	(860)	8,067	8,963
*06075	Stafford	(860)	11,857	11,091
*06904	Stamford	(203)	120,045	108,056
06378	Stonington	(860)	18,336	16,919
*06268	Storrs (c)	(860)	10,996	12,198
*06602	Stratford	(203)	49,943	49,389
*06078	Suffield	(860)	14,704	11,427
*06786	Terryville (c)	(860)	5,360	5,426
*06787	Thomaston	(860)	7,938	6,947
06277	Thompson	(860)	9,345	8,668
06082	Thompsonville (c)	(860)	8,125	8,458
06084	Tolland	(860)	14,571	11,001
*06790	Torrington	(860)	35,995	33,687
06611	Trumbull	(203)	35,299	32,016
06066	Vernon	(860)	29,491	29,841
*06492	Wallingford	(203)	44,736	40,822
06492	Wallingford Center (c)	(203)	17,509	17,827
*06702	Waterbury	(203)	107,902	108,961
*06385	Waterford	(860)	18,940	17,930
06795	Watertown	(860)	22,330	20,456
06498	Westbrook	(860)	6,599	5,414
*06101	West Hartford	(860)	61,173	60,110
06516	West Haven	(203)	52,923	54,021
06883	Weston	(203)	10,276	8,648
*06880	Westport	(203)	26,615	24,410
*06101	Wethersfield	(860)	26,220	25,651
06226	Willimantic (c)	(860)	15,823	14,746
06279	Willington	(860)	6,216	5,979
06897	Wilton	(203)	17,960	15,989
*06094	Winchester	(860)	10,857	11,524
*06280	Windham	(860)	23,503	22,039
*06095	Windsor	(860)	28,778	27,817
06096	Windsor Locks	(860)	12,411	12,358
*06098	Winsted (c)	(860)	7,321	8,254
*06716	Wolcott	(203)	16,228	13,700
06525	Woodbridge	(203)	9,264	7,924
06798	Woodbury	(203)	9,734	8,131
06281	Woodstock	(860)	8,047	6,008

Delaware (302)

ZIP	Place	2005	1990
19701	Bear (c)	17,593	—
19713	Brookside (c)	14,806	15,307
19703	Claymont (c)	9,220	9,800
*19901	Dover	34,288	27,630
*19809	Edgemoor (c)	5,992	5,853
19805	Elsmere	5,722	5,935
19702	Glasgow (c)	12,840	—
19707	Hockessin (c)	12,902	—
19709	Middletown	9,121	3,834
19963	Milford	7,201	6,032
*19711	Newark	30,060	26,463
19800	Pike Creek (c)	19,751	10,163
19973	Seaford	6,997	5,689
19977	Smyrna	7,413	5,231
*19899	Wilmington	72,786	71,529
19720	Wilmington Manor (c)	8,262	8,568

District of Columbia (202)

ZIP	Place	2005	1990
*20090	Washington	550,521	606,900

Florida

Area code (321) overlays area code (407). Area code (754) overlays (954). Area code (786) overlays (305). See introductory note.

ZIP	Place	Area Code	2005	1990
*32615	Alachua	(386)	7,557	4,667
*32714	Altamonte Springs	(407)	41,057	35,167
33169	Andover (c)	(305)	8,489	6,251
33572	Apollo Beach (c)	(813)	7,444	6,025
*32712	Apopka	(407)	34,728	13,611
*34266	Arcadia	(863)	7,151	6,488
*32233	Atlantic Beach	(904)	13,436	11,636
33823	Auburndale	(863)	12,381	8,846
*33160	Aventura	(305)	29,391	14,914
*33825	Avon Park	(863)	8,872	8,078
32807	Azalea Park (c)	(407)	11,073	8,926
*33830	Bartow	(863)	16,278	14,716
33154	Bay Harbor Islands	(305)	5,093	4,703
32819	Bay Hill (c)	(407)	5,177	5,346
34667	Bayonet Point (c)	(727)	23,577	21,860
33507	Bayshore Gardens (c)	(941)	17,350	17,062
33589	Beacon Square (c)	(727)	7,263	6,265
34233	Bee Ridge (c)	(941)	8,744	6,406
*33756	Bellair-Meadowbrook Terrace (c)	(904)	16,539	15,606
33430	Belle Glade	(561)	15,423	16,177
*32802	Belle Isle	(407)	6,431	5,272
*34420	Belleview	(352)	21,201	19,386
*34465	Beverly Hills (c)	(352)	8,317	6,163
33043	Big Pine Key (c)	(305)	5,032	4,206
*33509	Bloomingdale (c)	(813)	19,839	13,912
33433	Boca Del Mar (c)	(561)	21,832	17,754
*33431	Boca Raton	(561)	86,632	61,486
*34135	Bonita Springs	(239)	37,992	13,600
33547	Boyette (c)	(813)	64,775	5,895
*33436	Boynton Beach	(561)	66,885	46,284
*34206	Bradenton	(941)	53,917	43,769
*33509	Brandon (c)	(813)	77,895	57,985
32503	Brent (c)	(850)	22,257	21,624
33317	Broadview Park (c)	(954)	6,798	6,109
33313	Broadview-Pompano Park (c)	(954)	5,314	5,230
*34601	Brooksville	(352)	7,637	7,589
33142	Brownsville (c)	(305)	14,393	15,607
32404	Callaway	(850)	14,437	12,253
32920	Cape Canaveral	(321)	10,523	8,014
*33920	Cape Coral	(239)	140,010	74,991
*33055	Carol City (c)	(305)	59,443	53,331
*32707	Casselberry	(407)	24,298	20,736
32404	Cedar Grove	(850)	5,226	1,479
33401	Century Village (c)	(305)	7,616	8,363
33549	Cheval (c)	(813)	7,602	—
33624	Citrus Park (c)	(813)	20,226	—
*32966	Citrus Ridge (c)	(772)	12,015	—
*33758	Clearwater	(727)	108,687	98,669
*34711	Clermont	(352)	11,617	6,910
33440	Clewiston	(863)	7,173	6,085
*32922	Cocoa	(321)	16,898	17,710
*32931	Cocoa Beach	(321)	12,435	12,123
*32922	Cocoa West (c)	(321)	5,921	6,160
*33097	Coconut Creek	(954)	49,017	27,269
33064	Collier Manor-Cresthaven (c)	(954)	7,741	7,322
33801	Combee Settlement (c)	(863)	5,436	5,463
32809	Conway (c)	(407)	14,394	13,159
*33328	Cooper City	(954)	30,022	21,335
*33114	Coral Gables	(305)	42,871	40,091
*33075	Coral Springs	(954)	128,804	78,864
33157	Coral Terrace (c)	(305)	24,380	23,255
33015	Country Club (c)	(305)	36,310	3,408
33196	Country Walk (c)	(305)	10,653	—
*32536	Crestview	(850)	17,707	9,886
33803	Crystal Lake (c)	(863)	5,341	5,300
*33157	Cutler (c)	(305)	17,390	16,201
*33157	Cutler Ridge (c)	(305)	24,781	21,268
33884	Cypress Gardens (c)	(863)	8,844	9,188
33919	Cypress Lake (c)	(239)	12,072	10,491
*33525	Dade City	(352)	6,823	5,633
*33004	Dania Beach	(954)	28,782	—
*33329	Davie	(954)	84,204	47,143
*32114	Daytona Beach	(386)	64,421	61,991
*32713	DeBary	(386)	16,413	9,327
*33441	Deerfield Beach	(954)	76,348	46,997
*32433	DeFuniak Springs	(850)	5,038	5,200
*32720	De Land	(386)	24,375	16,622
*33444	Delray Beach	(561)	64,757	47,184
*32783	Deltona	(407)	82,788	49,429
*32541	Destin	(850)	12,423	8,090
32819	Doctor Phillips (c)	(407)	9,548	7,963
*33178	Doral	(305)	21,895	3,126
*34698	Dunedin	(727)	36,690	34,427
33610	East Lake (c)	(813)	29,394	—
33610	East Lake-Orient Park (c)	(813)	5,703	6,171
33157	East Perrine (c)	(305)	7,079	—
*32132	Edgewater	(386)	21,132	15,351
32542	Eglin AFB (c)	(850)	8,082	8,347
33614	Egypt Lake-Leto (c)	(813)	32,782	—
34680	Elfers (c)	(727)	13,161	12,356
*34295	Englewood (c)	(941)	16,196	15,025
32534	Ensley (c)	(850)	18,752	16,362
33928	Estero (c)	(239)	9,503	3,177
*32726	Eustis	(352)	17,683	12,856
32804	Fairview Shores (c)	(305)	13,898	13,192
*32034	Fernandina Beach	(904)	11,264	8,765
32730	Fern Park (c)	(407)	8,318	8,294
32514	Ferry Pass (c)	(850)	27,176	26,301
*33034	Florida City	(305)	8,913	5,978
32960	Florida Ridge (c)	(772)	15,217	12,218
32714	Forest City (c)	(407)	12,612	10,638
*33310	Fort Lauderdale	(954)	167,380	149,238
33841	Fort Meade	(863)	5,742	5,151
*33902	Fort Myers	(239)	58,428	44,947
*33931	Fort Myers Beach	(239)	6,834	9,284
*33922	Fort Myers Shores (c)	(239)	5,793	5,460
*34981	Fort Pierce	(772)	38,552	36,830
*33452	Fort Pierce North (c)	(772)	7,386	5,833
*34982	Fort Pierce South (c)	(772)	5,672	5,320
*32548	Fort Walton Beach	(850)	19,817	21,407
33172	Fountainbleau (c)	(305)	59,549	—
*32259	Fruit Cove (c)	(904)	16,077	5,904
34232	Fruitville (c)	(941)	12,741	9,808
33823	Fussels Corner (c)	(863)	5,313	3,840
*32602	Gainesville	(352)	108,184	91,482
33534	Gibsonton (c)	(813)	8,752	7,706
32960	Gifford (c)	(772)	7,599	6,278
33138	Gladeview (c)	(954)	14,468	15,637
33143	Glenvar Heights (c)	(305)	16,243	14,823
34116	Golden Gate (c)	(239)	20,951	14,148
33055	Golden Glades (c)	(305)	32,623	25,474
33411	Golden Lakes (c)	(561)	6,694	3,867
32733	Goldenrod (c)	(407)	12,871	12,362
32560	Gonzalez (c)	(850)	11,365	7,669
33170	Goulds (c)	(305)	7,453	7,284
33624	Greater Carrollwood (c)	(813)	33,519	—
33624	Greater Northdale (c)	(813)	20,461	16,318
33573	Greater Sun Center (c)	(813)	16,321	—
*33454	Greenacres	(561)	32,525	18,683
34736	Groveland	—	5,205	—
32043	Green Cove Springs	(904)	6,085	4,497
*32561	Gulf Breeze	(850)	6,455	5,530
33581	Gulf Gate Estates (c)	(941)	11,647	11,622
*33737	Gulfport	(727)	12,661	11,709
*33844	Haines City	(863)	16,371	11,683
*33009	Hallandale Beach	(305)/(954)	37,083	30,997
33434	Hamptons at Boca Raton (c)	(561)	11,306	11,686
34442	Hernando (c)	(352)	8,253	2,103
*33010	Hialeah	(305)	220,485	188,000
33016	Hialeah Gardens	(305)	19,930	7,727
*33455	Hobe Sound (c)	(772)	11,376	11,507
*34690	Holiday (c)	(727)	21,904	19,360
*32125	Holly Hill	(386)	12,630	11,141
*33022	Hollywood	(954)	145,629	121,720
*34218	Holmes Beach	(941)	5,100	4,826
*33030	Homestead	(305)	44,494	26,694
34447	Homosassa Springs (c)	(352)	12,458	6,271
*34667	Hudson (c)	(727)	12,765	7,344
32837	Hunters Creek (c)	(407)	9,369	—
*34142	Immokalee (c)	(239)	19,763	14,120
32937	Indian Harbour Beach	(321)	8,441	6,933
32963	Indian River Estates (c)	(772)	5,793	4,858
33785	Indian Rocks Beach	(727)	5,265	3,963
34956	Indiantown (c)	(772)	5,588	4,794
*34450	Inverness	(352)	7,295	5,797
34452	Inverness Highlands South (c)	(352)	5,781	—
33880	Inwood (c)	(863)	6,925	6,824
33908	Iona (c)	(239)	11,756	9,565
*33036	Islamorada, Village of Islands	(305)	6,606	1,220
33162	Ives Estates (c)	(305)	17,586	13,531
*32203	Jacksonville	(904)	782,623	635,230
*32250	Jacksonville Beach	(904)	21,770	17,839
33880	Jan Phyl Village (c)	(863)	5,633	5,308
33568	Jasmine Estates (c)	(727)	18,213	17,136
*34957	Jensen Beach (c)	(772)	11,100	9,884
*33458	Jupiter	(561)	47,909	26,753
33183	Kendale Lakes (c)	(305)	56,901	48,524
*33256	Kendall (c)	(305)	75,226	87,271
33193	Kendall West (c)	(305)	38,034	—
33149	Key Biscayne	(305)	10,158	8,854
33037	Key Largo (c)	(305)	11,886	11,336
33556	Keystone (c)	(813)	14,627	—
*33040	Key West	(305)	23,935	24,832
*33573	Kings Point (c)	(305)	12,207	12,422
*34744	Kissimmee	(407)	59,364	30,337
*32159	Lady Lake	(352)	13,244	8,071
34786	Lake Butter (c)	—	7,062	—
*32055	Lake City	(386)	10,970	9,626
*33804	Lakeland	(863)	88,713	70,576
33801	Lakeland Highlands (c)	(863)	12,557	9,972
32569	Lake Lorraine (c)	(850)	7,106	6,779
33054	Lake Lucerne (c)	(305)	9,132	9,478
33612	Lake Magdalene (c)	(813)	28,755	15,973
*32746	Lake Mary	(407)	14,638	5,929
*33403	Lake Park	(561)	9,039	6,704
33189	Lakes by the Bay (c)	(305)	9,055	5,615
32073	Lakeside (c)	(904)	30,927	29,137
*33853	Lake Wales	(863)	12,964	9,670
34951	Lakewood Park (c)	(772)	10,458	7,211
*33461	Lake Worth	(561)	36,342	28,564
*33461	Lake Worth Corridor (c)	—	18,663	—
*34639	Land O'Lakes (c)	(813)	20,971	7,892

ZIP	Place	Area Code	2005	1990
*33465	Lantana	(561)	10,498	8,392
*33770	Largo	(727)	74,473	65,910
*33062	Lauderdale-by-the-Sea	(954)	5,990	4,014
*33313	Lauderdale Lakes	(954)	31,826	27,341
*33313	Lauderhill	(954)	59,621	49,015
34272	Laurel (c)	(941)	8,393	8,245
*34461	Lecanto (c)	(352)	5,161	1,243
*34748	Leesburg	(352)	19,086	14,783
*33936	Lehigh Acres (c)	(239)	33,430	13,611
*33033	Leisure City (c)	(305)	22,152	19,379
*33074	Lighthouse Point	(954)	11,262	10,378
*32060	Live Oak	(386)	6,922	6,332
32810	Lockhart (c)	(407)	12,944	11,636
34228	Longboat Key	(941)	7,583	5,937
*32750	Longwood	(407)	13,580	13,316
*33549	Lutz (c)	(813)	17,081	10,552
32444	Lynn Haven	(850)	15,677	9,270
33919	McGregor (c)	(904)	7,136	6,504
32063	Macclenny	(904)	5,186	3,966
*32751	Maitland	(407)	14,125	8,932
33550	Mango (c)	(813)	8,842	8,700
33050	Marathon	(305)	9,822	8,857
*34145	Marco Island	(239)	16,109	—
*33093	Margate	(954)	56,002	42,985
*32446	Marianna	(850)	6,275	6,292
32824	Meadow Woods (c)	(407)	11,286	4,876
33811	Medulla (c)	(863)	6,637	3,977
*32901	Melbourne	(321)	76,646	60,034
32666	Melrose Park (c)	(954)	7,114	6,477
33561	Memphis (c)	(941)	7,264	6,760
*32953	Merritt Island (c)	(321)	36,090	32,886
*33101	Miami	(305)	386,417	358,648
*33152	Miami Beach	(305)	87,925	92,639
33023	Miami Gardens	(305)	99,438	—
*33014	Miami Lakes	(305)	22,321	12,750
*33153	Miami Shores	(305)	10,040	10,084
*33266	Miami Springs	(305)	13,170	13,268
32976	Micco (c)	(772)	9,498	8,757
*32068	Middleburg (c)	(904)	10,338	6,223
*32570	Milton	(850)	8,131	7,216
32754	Mims (c)	(321)	9,147	9,412
*34755	Minneola	(352)	8,665	1,515
33023	Miramar	(954)	106,623	40,663
*32757	Mount Dora	(352)	11,474	7,294
32526	Myrtle Grove (c)	(850)	17,211	17,402
*34102	Naples	(239)	21,709	19,505
34113	Naples Manor (c)	(239)	5,186	4,574
34102	Naples Park (c)	(239)	6,741	8,002
32266	Neptune Beach	(904)	7,018	6,816
*34653	New Port Richey	(727)	16,928	14,044
33552	New Port Richey East (c)	(727)	9,916	9,683
*32168	New Smyrna Beach	(386)	22,356	16,549
*32578	Niceville	(850)	12,582	10,509
33269	Norland (c)	(305)	22,995	22,109
33308	North Andrews Gardens (c)	(954)	9,656	9,002
33141	North Bay Village	(305)	7,615	5,383
*33918	North Fort Myers (c)	(239)	40,214	30,027
*33068	North Lauderdale	(954)	42,262	26,473
*33261	North Miami	(305)	57,654	50,001
*33160	North Miami Beach	(305)	39,442	35,361
*33408	North Palm Beach	(561)	12,663	11,538
*34287	North Port	(941)	42,253	11,973
34234	North Sarasota (c)	(941)	6,738	6,702
33307	Oakland Park	(305)	31,713	26,326
33860	Oak Ridge (c)	(407)	22,349	15,388
*34478	Ocala	(352)	49,745	42,045
32548	Ocean City (c)	(850)	5,594	5,422
34761	Ocoee	(407)	29,849	12,778
*33163	Ojus (c)	(305)	16,642	15,519
*34972	Okeechobee	(863)	5,900	4,943
34677	Oldsmar	(813)	13,552	8,361
*33265	Olympia Heights (c)	(305)	13,452	37,792
*33054	Opa-Locka	(305)	15,763	15,283
*33054	Opa-Locka North (c)	(305)	6,224	6,568
*32763	Orange City	(386)	7,862	5,372
*32073	Orange Park	(904)	9,205	9,488
*32802	Orlando	(407)	213,223	164,674
32811	Orlo Vista (c)	(407)	6,047	5,990
*32174	Ormond Beach	(386)	38,613	29,721
32074	Ormond By-The-Sea (c)	(386)	8,430	8,157
*32765	Oviedo	(407)	29,848	11,114
32571	Pace (c)	(850)	7,393	6,277
33476	Pahokee	(561)	6,554	6,822
*32177	Palatka	(386)	10,942	10,447
*32905	Palm Bay	(321)	92,833	62,543
33480	Palm Beach	(561)	9,852	9,814
*33408	Palm Beach Gardens	(561)	48,989	24,139
*34990	Palm City (c)	(772)	20,097	3,925
*32135	Palm Coast	(386)	60,952	14,287
*34221	Palmetto	(941)	13,510	9,268
33157	Palmetto Bay	(305)/(786)	23,590	—
33157	Palmetto Estates (c)	(305)	13,675	12,293
*34683	Palm Harbor (c)	(727)	59,248	50,256
*33601	Palm River-Clair Mel (c)	(813)	17,589	13,691
*33406	Palm Springs	(561)	15,267	9,763
33012	Palm Springs North (c)	(305)	5,460	5,300
32082	Palm Valley (c)	(904)	19,860	9,960
*32401	Panama City	(850)	37,188	34,396
*32417	Panama City Beach	(850)	11,477	4,051
*33067	Parkland	(954)	22,145	3,773
34108	Pelican Bay (c)	(239)	5,686	—
*33021	Pembroke Park	(954)	5,487	4,933
*33029	Pembroke Pines	(954)	150,380	65,566
*32502	Pensacola	(850)	54,055	59,198
*32347	Perry	(850)	6,734	7,151
32839	Pine Castle (c)	(407)	8,803	8,276
33156	Pinecrest	(305)	19,204	—
32858	Pine Hills (c)	(407)	41,764	35,322
33324	Pine Island Ridge (c)	(954)	5,199	5,244
*33781	Pinellas Park	(727)	47,352	43,571
*34465	Pine Ridge (c)	(352)	5,490	—
33168	Pinewood (c)	(305)	16,523	15,518
*33318	Plantation	(954)	85,989	66,814
*33566	Plant City	(813)	31,450	22,754
*34758	Poinciana (c)	(407)	13,647	—
*33060	Pompano Beach	(954)	104,179	72,411
33064	Pompano Beach Highlands (c)	(954)	6,505	17,915
*33952	Port Charlotte (c)	(941)	46,451	41,535
*32129	Port Orange	(904)	53,746	35,399
32927	Port St. John (c)	(321)	12,112	8,933
*34981	Port St. Lucie	(772)	131,692	55,761
*34983	Port St. Lucie-River Park (c)	(772)	5,175	4,874
*34992	Port Salerno (c)	(772)	10,141	7,786
*33032	Princeton (c)	(305)	10,090	7,073
*33950	Punta Gorda	(941)	17,111	10,637
*32351	Quincy	(850)	6,993	7,452
*33156	Richmond Heights (c)	(305)	8,479	8,583
*33177	Richmond West (c)	(305)	28,082	—
34231	Ridge Wood Heights (c)	(941)	5,028	4,851
*33569	Riverview (c)	(813)	12,035	6,478
*33419	Riviera Beach	(561)	33,772	27,646
*32955	Rockledge	(321)	24,245	16,023
*33947	Rotonda (c)	(941)	6,574	3,576
*33411	Royal Palm Beach	(561)	30,886	15,532
*33570	Ruskin (c)	(813)	8,321	6,046
*34695	Safety Harbor	(727)	17,517	15,120
*32084	Saint Augustine	(904)	12,263	11,695
32080	Saint Augustine Beach	(904)	5,753	3,830
32086	Saint Augustine South (c)	(904)	5,035	4,218
*34769	Saint Cloud	(407)	22,508	12,684
*33706	Saint Pete Beach	(727)	10,173	9,200
*33733	Saint Petersburg	(727)	249,079	240,318
33912	San Carlos Park (c)	(239)	16,317	11,785
33432	Sandalfoot Cove (c)	(305)	16,582	14,214
*32771	Sanford	(407)	47,257	32,387
33957	Sanibel	(239)	6,072	5,468
*34230	Sarasota	(941)	53,711	50,897
33577	Sarasota Springs (c)	(941)	15,875	16,088
32937	Satellite Beach	(321)	9,811	9,889
33055	Scott Lake (c)	(305)	14,401	14,588
*32958	Sebastian	(772)	19,643	10,248
*33870	Sebring	(863)	10,431	8,841
*33584	Seffner (c)	(813)	5,467	5,371
*33770	Seminole	(813)	18,505	9,251
34610	Shady Hills (c)	(727)	7,798	—
*34242	Siesta Key (c)	(941)	7,150	7,772
34472	Silver Springs Shores (c)	(352)	6,690	6,421
32809	Sky Lake (c)	(407)	5,651	6,202
32703	South Apopka (c)	(407)	5,800	6,360
33505	South Bradenton (c)	(941)	21,587	20,398
32121	South Daytona	(386)	13,733	12,488
34266	Southeast Arcadia (c)	(863)	6,064	4,145
34277	Southgate (c)	(941)	7,455	7,324
34233	South Gate Ridge (c)	(941)	5,655	5,924
33760	South Highpoint (c)	(727)	8,839	—
*33243	South Miami	(305)	11,147	10,404
33157	South Miami Heights (c)	(305)	33,522	30,030
33707	South Pasadena	(727)	5,715	5,644
32937	South Patrick Shores (c)	(321)	8,913	10,249
34230	South Sarasota (c)	(941)	5,314	5,298
33595	South Venice (c)	(941)	13,539	11,951
*33331	Southwest Ranches	(954)	7,388	—
32206	Springfield	(850)	9,043	8,719
*34604	Spring Hill (c)	(352)	69,078	31,117
32091	Starke	(904)	5,844	5,226
*34994	Stuart	(772)	15,764	11,936
34446	Sugarmill Woods (c)	(352)	6,409	4,073
33160	Sunny Isles Beach	(305)	15,424	—
*33325	Sunrise	(954)	90,589	65,683
*33283	Sunset (c)	(305)	17,150	15,810
33144	Sweetwater	(305)	13,741	13,909
*32301	Tallahassee	(850)	158,500	124,773
*33320	Tamarac	(954)	59,923	44,822
33144	Tamiami (c)	(305)	54,788	33,845
*33601	Tampa	(813)	325,989	280,015
*34689	Tarpon Springs	(727)	22,651	17,874
32778	Tavares	(352)	11,621	7,488
*33687	Temple Terrace	(813)	21,978	16,444
33469	Tequesta	(561)	5,989	4,499
33186	The Crossings (c)	(305)	23,557	—
33196	The Hammocks (c)	(305)	47,379	—
*32159	The Villages (c)	(352)	8,333	—
33592	Thonotosassa (c)	(813)	6,091	—
33186	Three Lakes (c)	(305)	6,955	—
33025	Timber Pines (c)	(352)	5,840	3,182
*32780	Titusville	(321)	43,767	39,394
32615	Town 'n' Country (c)	(813)	72,523	60,946
*33706	Treasure Island	(727)	7,542	7,266
32817	Union Park (c)	(407)	10,191	6,890
33024	University (c)	(813)	30,736	—

ZIP	Place	Area Code	2005	1990
33165	University Park (c)	(305)	26,538	—
32401	Upper Grand Lagoon (c)	(850)	10,889	7,855
32580	Valparaiso	(850)	6,365	6,316
*33594	Valrico	(813)	6,582	—
34231	Vamo (c)	(941)	5,285	3,325
*34285	Venice	(941)	20,974	17,052
33595	Venice Gardens (c)	(941)	7,466	7,701
*32960	Vero Beach	(772)	17,078	17,350
32960	Vero Beach South (c)	(772)	20,362	16,973
33901	Villas (c)	(239)	11,346	9,898
32507	Warrington (c)	(850)	15,207	16,040
32791	Wekiva Springs (c)	(407)	23,169	23,026
*33414	Wellington	(561)	53,583	20,670
33543	Wesley Chapel (c)	(813)	5,691	—
33714	West and East Lealman (c)	(727)	21,753	—
33626	Westchase (c)	(813)	11,116	—
33165	Westchester (c)	(305)	30,271	29,883
33409	Westgate-Belvedere Homes (c)	(561)	8,134	6,880
33138	West Little River (c)	(305)	32,498	33,575
*32912	West Melbourne	(321)	15,054	8,398
*33144	West Miami	(305)	5,829	5,727
*33326	Weston	(954)	65,679	—
*33416	West Palm Beach	(561)	97,498	67,764
32505	West Pensacola (c)	(850)	21,939	22,107
33157	West Perrine (c)	(305)	8,600	—
34208	West Samoset (c)	(941)	5,507	3,819
32966	West Vero Corridor (c)	(772)	7,695	—
33168	Westview (c)	(305)	9,692	9,668
33165	Westwood Lakes (c)	(305)	12,005	11,522
33496	Whisper Walk (c)	(561)	5,135	3,037
32821	Williamsburg (c)	(407)	6,736	3,093
*33305	Wilton Manors	(954)	12,858	11,804
33803	Winston (c)	(813)	9,024	9,118
*34787	Winter Garden	(407)	25,500	9,863
*33880	Winter Haven	(863)	29,501	24,725
*32789	Winter Park	(407)	28,179	24,260
*32707	Winter Springs	(407)	32,583	22,151
32547	Wright (c)	(850)	21,697	18,945
34972	Yeehaw Junction (c)	(407)	21,778	—
*32097	Yulee (c)	(904)	8,392	6,915
*33540	Zephyrhills	(813)	12,258	8,220
33541	Zephyrhills West (c)	(813)	5,242	4,249

Georgia

Area code (678) overlays (770). Area code (762) overlays (706).
See introductory note.

ZIP	Place	Area Code	2005	1990
*30101	Acworth	(770)	18,428	4,519
31620	Adel	(229)	5,434	5,093
*31706	Albany	(229)	75,394	78,804
*30004	Alpharetta	(770)	40,128	13,002
*31709	Americus	(229)	16,873	16,516
*30603	Athens-Clarke County[1]	(706)	103,238	86,522
*30301	Atlanta	(404)	470,688	393,929
30011	Auburn	(770)	7,134	3,139
*30903	Augusta-Richmond County[2]	(706)	190,782	186,616
*30168	Austell	(770)	6,566	4,173
*39818	Bainbridge	(229)	11,874	10,803
30204	Barnesville	(770)	5,808	4,747
30032	Belvedere Park (c)	(404)	18,945	18,089
31723	Blakely	(229)	5,476	5,595
30110	Bremen	(770)	5,350	4,353
*31520	Brunswick	(912)	15,956	16,433
*30518	Buford	(404)	10,972	8,771
*39827	Cairo	(229)	9,389	9,035
*30701	Calhoun	(706)	13,570	7,135
31730	Camilla	(229)	5,616	5,124
30032	Candler-McAfee (c)	(404)	28,294	29,491
*30114	Canton	(770)	17,685	4,817
*30117	Carrollton	(770)	21,837	16,029
*30120	Cartersville	(770)	17,653	12,037
30125	Cedartown	(770)	9,771	7,976
31028	Centerville	(478)	6,624	3,509
30366	Chamblee	(404)	9,763	7,668
30021	Clarkston	(404)	7,078	5,385
30337	College Park	(404)	20,181	20,645
*31908	Columbus	(706)	185,271	178,683
*30529	Commerce	(770)	5,856	4,108
30288	Conley (c)	(404)	6,188	5,528
*30013	Conyers	(404)	12,205	7,380
*31015	Cordele	(229)	11,493	10,833
31525	Country Club Estates (c)	(912)	7,594	7,500
*30014	Covington	(770)	13,856	9,860
*30040	Cumming	(770)	5,802	2,798
31805	Cusseta-Chattahoochee County	(706)	9,805	1,107
*30132	Dallas	(770)	8,667	2,810
*30720	Dalton	(706)	32,140	22,218
*30030	Decatur	(404)	17,884	17,304
31520	Dock Junction (c)	(912)	6,951	7,094
*30362	Doraville	(404)	9,872	7,626
*31533	Douglas	(912)	10,978	10,464
*30134	Douglasville	(404)	27,568	11,635
30333	Druid Hills (c)	(404)	12,741	12,174
*31021	Dublin	(478)	16,924	16,312
*30096	Duluth	(404)	24,482	9,821
*30356	Dunwoody (c)	(404)	32,808	26,302
31023	Eastman	(478)	5,441	5,153
30364	East Point	(404)	40,680	34,595
*31024	Eatonton	(706)	6,758	6,479

ZIP	Place	Area Code	2005	1990
30809	Evans (c)	(706)	17,727	13,713
30213	Fairburn	(770)	8,564	4,013
30060	Fair Oaks (c)	(404)	8,443	6,996
30535	Fairview (c)	(706)	6,601	6,444
*30214	Fayetteville	(404)	14,363	5,827
31750	Fitzgerald	(229)	8,920	8,901
*30297	Forest Park	(404)	22,201	16,958
31905	Fort Benning South (c)	(706)	11,737	14,617
30742	Fort Oglethorpe	(706)	8,964	5,880
*31313	Fort Stewart (c)	(912)	11,205	13,774
31030	Fort Valley	(478)	8,197	8,198
*30501	Gainesville	(770)	32,444	17,885
*31418	Garden City	(912)	9,550	7,410
31754	Georgetown (c)	(912)	10,599	5,554
30427	Glennville	(912)	5,031	3,676
30316	Gresham Park (c)	(404)	9,215	9,000
*30223	Griffin	(770)	23,286	21,325
30813	Grovetown	(706)	7,483	3,596
30354	Hapeville	(404)	6,085	5,483
*31313	Hinesville	(912)	28,615	21,596
30142	Holly Springs	—	5,328	2,406
30238	Irondale (c)	—	7,727	3,352
30549	Jefferson	(706)	5,599	2,763
*31546	Jesup	(912)	9,851	8,958
*30144	Kennesaw	(404)	30,522	8,936
31548	Kingsland	(912)	12,063	6,089
30728	La Fayette	(706)	6,753	6,655
*30240	LaGrange	(706)	27,362	25,574
*30045	Lawrenceville	(404)	28,393	17,250
*30047	Lilburn	(404)	11,416	9,295
30052	Loganville	(770)	8,881	3,180
30126	Mableton (c)	(404)	29,733	25,725
30253	McDonough	(770)	15,523	2,929
*31201	Macon	(478)	94,316	107,365
*30060	Marietta	(404)	61,261	44,129
30907	Martinez (c)	(706)	27,749	33,731
31061	Midway-Hardwick (c)	—	5,135	4,910
*31061	Milledgeville	(478)	19,397	17,727
*30655	Monroe	(770)	12,329	9,759
*30260	Morrow	(770)	5,283	5,074
*31768	Moultrie	(229)	14,913	14,865
30087	Mountain Park (c)	(404)	11,753	11,025
*30263	Newnan	(770)	24,654	12,497
*30071	Norcross	(404)	9,887	5,947
30319	North Atlanta (c)	(404)	38,579	27,812
30033	North Decatur (c)	(404)	15,270	13,936
30033	North Druid Hills (c)	(404)	18,852	14,170
30032	Panthersville (c)	(404)	11,791	9,874
*30269	Peachtree City	(404)	34,524	19,027
31069	Perry	(478)	11,018	9,452
31322	Pooler	(912)	10,019	4,649
30127	Powder Springs	(404)	14,507	6,862
30074	Redan (c)	(404)	33,841	24,376
31324	Richmond Hill	(912)	9,187	2,934
31326	Rincon	(912)	6,349	2,992
*30274	Riverdale	(404)	15,475	9,495
*30161	Rome	(706)	35,816	30,425
*30077	Roswell	(404)	85,920	47,986
31558	Saint Marys	(912)	16,404	8,204
31522	Saint Simons (c)	(912)	13,381	12,026
31082	Sandersville	(478)	6,031	6,290
30358	Sandy Springs (c)	(404)	85,781	67,842
*31402	Savannah	(912)	128,453	137,812
30079	Scottdale (c)	(404)	9,803	8,636
31411	Skidaway Island (c)	(912)	6,914	4,495
*30080	Smyrna	(404)	47,643	32,453
*30078	Snellville	(404)	19,238	12,084
*30458	Statesboro	(912)	24,612	20,770
30281	Stockbridge	(404)	13,140	3,359
*30086	Stone Mountain	(404)	7,080	6,544
30518	Sugar Hill	(404)	15,696	4,519
30024	Suwanee	(770)	12,553	2,412
30401	Swainsboro	(478)	7,162	7,361
31791	Sylvester	(229)	5,924	6,023
30286	Thomaston	(706)	9,265	9,127
*31792	Thomasville	(229)	18,725	17,554
30824	Thomson	(706)	6,866	6,862
*31794	Tifton	(229)	16,327	14,215
*30577	Toccoa	(706)	9,103	8,720
*30084	Tucker (c)	(404)	26,532	25,781
30290	Tyrone	(770)	5,789	2,724
30291	Union City	(404)	15,382	9,347
*31603	Valdosta	(229)	45,205	40,038
*30474	Vidalia	(912)	11,037	11,118
30180	Villa Rica	(770)	9,897	3,916
30339	Vinings (c)	(404)	9,677	7,417
*31088	Warner Robins	(478)	57,907	43,861
*31501	Waycross	(912)	15,112	16,410
30830	Waynesboro	(706)	5,999	5,669
31410	Whitemarsh Island (c)	(912)	5,824	2,824
31410	Wilmington Island (c)	(912)	14,213	11,230
30680	Winder	(770)	12,451	7,373
*30188	Woodstock	(770)	19,602	4,361

(1) Athens merged with Clarke County in 1991. The 2005 and 1990 populations are for all of Clarke County except Winterville and Bogart, which are part of the county but are also separate incorporated places.
(2) Augusta merged with Richmond County in 1996. The 2005 and 1990 populations are for all of Richmond County except Blythe and Hephzibah, which are part of the county but are also separate incorporated places.

Hawaii (808)

ZIP	Place	2005	1990
96744	Ahuimanu (c)	8,506	8,387
96701	Aiea (c)	9,019	8,906
96706	Ewa Beach(c)	14,650	14,315
96708	Haiku-Pauwela (c)	6,578	4,509
96701	Halawa (c)	13,891	13,408
96778	Hawaiian Paradise Park (c)	7,051	3,389
96853	Hickam Housing (c)	5,471	6,553
*96720	Hilo (c)	40,759	37,808
96725	Holualoa (c)	6,107	3,834
*96820	Honolulu (c)	377,379	377,059
*96732	Kahului (c)	20,146	16,889
96734	Kailua (Hawaii Co.) (c)	9,870	9,126
96863	Kailua (Honolulu Co.) (c)	36,513	36,818
96740	Kalaoa (c)	6,794	4,490
96744	Kaneohe (c)	34,970	35,448
96863	Kaneohe Station (c)	11,827	11,662
96746	Kapaa (c)	9,472	8,149
96753	Kihei (c)	16,749	11,107
*96761	Lahaina (c)	9,118	9,073
96766	Lihue (c)	5,674	5,536
96792	Maili (c)	5,943	6,059
96792	Makaha (c)	7,753	7,990
96706	Makakilo (c)	13,156	9,828
96768	Makawao (c)	6,327	5,405
96789	Mililani Town (c)	28,608	29,359
96792	Nanakuli (c)	10,814	9,575
96761	Napili-Honokowai (c)	6,788	4,332
96782	Pearl City (c)	30,976	30,993
96788	Pukalani (c)	7,380	5,879
96857	Schofield Barracks (c)	14,428	19,597
96797	Village Park (c)	9,625	7,407
*96786	Wahiawa (c)	16,151	17,386
96792	Waianae (c)	10,506	8,758
96793	Waihee-Waiehu (c)	7,310	4,004
96753	Wailea-Makena (c)	5,671	3,799
96793	Wailuku (c)	12,296	10,688
96701	Waimalu (c)	29,371	29,967
96796	Waimea (c)	7,028	5,972
96797	Waipahu (c)	33,108	31,435
96797	Waipio (c)	11,672	11,812
*96786	Waipio Acres (c)	5,298	5,304

Idaho (208)

ZIP	Place	2005	1990
*83401	Ammon	10,925	5,002
83221	Blackfoot	10,828	9,646
*83707	Boise	193,161	126,685
83318	Burley	9,131	8,702
*83605	Caldwell	34,433	18,586
83202	Chubbuck	10,707	7,794
*83814	Coeur d'Alene	40,059	24,561
83616	Eagle	17,338	3,327
83617	Emmett	6,124	4,601
*83714	Garden City	11,424	6,369
83333	Hailey	7,583	3,575
83835	Hayden	11,906	4,888
*83402	Idaho Falls	52,338	43,973
83338	Jerome	8,503	6,529
*83634	Kuna	10,153	1,955
83501	Lewiston	31,081	28,082
*83642	Meridian	52,240	9,596
83843	Moscow	21,862	18,398
*83647	Mountain Home	11,565	7,913
83648	Mountain Home AFB (c)	8,894	5,936
*83653	Nampa	71,713	28,365
83661	Payette	7,560	5,672
*83201	Pocatello	53,372	46,117
*83854	Post Falls	23,162	7,349
83263	Preston	5,019	3,710
83858	Rathdrum	5,740	2,014
*83440	Rexburg	26,265	14,298
*83350	Rupert	5,225	5,455
*83864	Sandpoint	8,105	5,561
*83301	Twin Falls	38,630	27,634
83672	Weiser	5,420	4,571

Illinois

Area code (224) overlays area code (847). See introductory note.

ZIP	Place	Area Code	2005	1990
60101	Addison	(630)	36,811	32,053
*60102	Algonquin	(847)	29,022	11,764
60803	Alsip	(708)	19,072	18,227
62002	Alton	(618)	29,433	33,060
62906	Anna	(618)	5,070	4,805
60002	Antioch	(847)	12,353	6,105
*60005	Arlington Heights	(847)	74,620	75,463
*60505	Aurora	(630)	168,181	99,672
*60010	Barrington	(847)	10,179	9,538
*60103	Bartlett	(630)	38,479	19,395
61607	Bartonville	(309)	6,146	6,555
*60510	Batavia	(630)	27,172	17,076
*60083	Beach Park	(847)	12,486	9,492
62618	Beardstown	(217)	5,876	5,270
*62220	Belleville	(618)	41,143	42,806
60104	Bellwood	(708)	19,517	20,241
61008	Belvidere	(815)	24,593	16,059

ZIP	Place	Area Code	2005	1990
*60106	Bensenville	(630)	20,514	17,767
62812	Benton	(618)	6,930	7,216
60163	Berkeley	(708)	5,006	5,137
60402	Berwyn	(708)	51,409	45,426
62010	Bethalto	(618)	9,660	9,507
*60108	Bloomingdale	(630)	21,924	16,614
*61701	Bloomington	(309)	69,749	51,889
*60406	Blue Island	(708)	22,788	21,203
*60440	Bolingbrook	(630)	68,365	40,843
60538	Boulder Hill (c)	(630)	8,169	8,894
60914	Bourbonnais	(815)	16,875	13,929
60915	Bradley	(815)	13,812	10,954
60408	Braidwood	(815)	6,320	3,584
60455	Bridgeview	(708)	14,933	14,402
*60153	Broadview	(708)	7,856	8,538
60513	Brookfield	(708)	18,462	18,876
60089	Buffalo Grove	(847)	43,115	36,417
60459	Burbank	(708)	27,634	27,600
60527	Burr Ridge	(630)	10,949	8,247
62206	Cahokia	(618)	15,608	17,550
60409	Calumet City	(708)	37,795	37,840
*60643	Calumet Park	(708)	8,124	8,418
61520	Canton	(309)	14,938	13,959
*62901	Carbondale	(618)	24,806	27,033
62626	Carlinville	(217)	5,768	5,416
62821	Carmi	(618)	5,414	5,735
*60188	Carol Stream	(630)	40,040	31,759
60110	Carpentersville	(847)	37,204	23,049
62918	Carterville	(618)	5,099	3,630
60013	Cary	(847)	19,115	10,025
62801	Centralia	(618)	13,600	14,476
62207	Centreville	(618)	5,837	7,489
*61821	Champaign	(217)	71,568	63,502
60410	Channahon	(815)	12,218	4,266
61920	Charleston	(217)	20,189	20,398
62629	Chatham	(217)	9,787	6,074
62233	Chester	(618)	7,872	8,204
*60607	Chicago	(312)/(773)	2,842,518	2,783,726
*60411	Chicago Heights	(708)	31,373	32,966
60415	Chicago Ridge	(708)	13,668	13,643
61523	Chillicothe	(309)	5,781	5,959
60804	Cicero	(708)	82,741	67,436
60514	Clarendon Hills	(630)	8,397	6,994
61727	Clinton	(217)	7,261	7,437
60416	Coal City	(815)	5,170	3,907
62234	Collinsville	(618)	25,487	22,424
61241	Colona	(309)	5,275	2,237
62236	Columbia	(618)	8,902	5,524
60478	Country Club Hills	(708)	16,534	15,431
60525	Countryside	(708)	5,831	5,961
60435	Crest Hill	(815)	19,438	10,999
60445	Crestwood	(708)	11,207	10,823
60417	Crete	(708)	8,772	6,773
61610	Creve Coeur	(309)	5,261	5,938
*60014	Crystal Lake	(815)	40,922	24,692
*61832	Danville	(217)	32,920	33,828
60561	Darien	(630)	22,730	20,556
*62525	Decatur	(217)	77,836	83,900
60015	Deerfield	(847)	19,471	17,327
60115	DeKalb	(815)	42,085	35,076
*60018	Des Plaines	(847)	56,551	53,414
61021	Dixon	(815)	15,372	15,134
60419	Dolton	(708)	24,504	23,956
*60515	Downers Grove	(630)	49,094	47,464
62832	Du Quoin	(618)	6,412	6,697
62024	East Alton	(618)	6,609	7,063
61244	East Moline	(309)	21,250	20,147
*61611	East Peoria	(309)	22,536	21,378
*62201	East St. Louis	(618)	29,843	40,944
*62025	Edwardsville	(618)	24,047	14,582
62401	Effingham	(217)	12,440	11,927
*60120	Elgin	(847)	98,645	77,014
*60009	Elk Grove Village	(847)	34,025	33,429
60126	Elmhurst	(630)	44,976	42,029
60707	Elmwood Park	(708)	24,499	23,206
61530	Eureka	(309)	5,084	—
*60201	Evanston	(847)	75,236	73,233
60805	Evergreen Park	(708)	19,876	20,874
*62837	Fairfield	(618)	5,230	5,439
*62208	Fairview Heights	(618)	16,471	14,768
60422	Flossmoor	(708)	9,390	8,651
*60130	Forest Park	(708)	15,197	14,918
60020	Fox Lake	(847)	10,736	7,539
60021	Fox River Grove	(847)	5,084	3,629
60423	Frankfort	(815)	15,819	7,180
60423	Frankfort Square (c)	(815)	7,766	6,227
*60131	Franklin Park	(847)	18,490	18,485
61032	Freeport	(815)	25,612	25,840
60030	Gages Lake (c)	(847)	10,415	8,349
*61401	Galesburg	(309)	32,017	33,530
61254	Geneseo	(309)	6,524	5,990
60134	Geneva	(630)	23,424	12,625
62034	Glen Carbon	(618)	11,932	7,774
60022	Glencoe	(847)	8,979	8,499
*60139	Glendale Heights	(630)	32,465	27,915
*60137	Glen Ellyn	(630)	27,193	24,919
*60025	Glenview	(847)	45,989	38,436
60425	Glenwood	(708)	8,663	9,289
62035	Godfrey	(618)	16,996	15,675
60441	Goodings Grove (c)	(815)	17,084	14,054

ZIP	Place	Area Code	2005	1990
62040	Granite City	(618)	30,796	32,766
60030	Grayslake	(847)	21,099	7,388
62246	Greenville	(618)	7,067	5,108
60031	Gurnee	(847)	30,772	13,715
60133	Hanover Park	(630)	37,229	32,918
62946	Harrisburg	(618)	9,628	9,318
60033	Harvard	(815)	9,104	5,975
*60426	Harvey	(708)	28,771	29,771
*60656	Harwood Heights	(708)	8,188	7,680
60047	Hawthorn Woods	(847)	7,176	4,423
60429	Hazel Crest	(708)	14,415	13,334
62948	Herrin	(618)	11,688	10,857
*60457	Hickory Hills	(708)	13,542	13,021
62249	Highland	(618)	9,200	7,546
*60035	Highland Park	(847)	31,380	30,575
60040	Highwood	(847)	5,468	5,358
*60162	Hillside	(708)	7,771	7,672
*60521	Hinsdale	(630)	17,898	16,029
*60195	Hoffman Estates	(847)	52,046	46,363
60491	Homer Glen	(708)	24,736	—
*60430	Homewood	(708)	18,917	19,278
60942	Hoopeston	(217)	5,753	5,871
60142	Huntley	(847)	17,674	2453
*60067	Inverness	(847)	7,343	6,516
60042	Island Lake	(847)	8,419	4,449
60143	Itasca	(630)	8,444	6,947
*62650	Jacksonville	(217)	19,470	19,327
62052	Jerseyville	(618)	8,187	7,382
*60050	Johnsburg	(815)	6,277	—
*60436	Joliet	(815)	136,208	77,217
60458	Justice	(708)	12,692	11,137
60901	Kankakee	(815)	26,642	27,541
61443	Kewanee	(309)	12,655	12,969
60525	La Grange	(708)	15,482	15,362
60526	La Grange Park	(708)	12,726	12,861
*60010	Lake Barrington	(847)	5,033	3,855
60044	Lake Bluff	(847)	6,251	5,486
60045	Lake Forest	(847)	21,123	17,836
*60102	Lake in the Hills	(847)	28,786	5,882
60050	Lakemoor	(815)	5,085	1,332
60046	Lake Villa	(847)	8,492	2,857
*60047	Lake Zurich	(847)	20,045	14,927
60438	Lansing	(708)	27,324	28,131
61301	La Salle	(815)	9,510	9,717
*60439	Lemont	(630)	15,146	7,359
*60048	Libertyville	(847)	21,760	19,174
62656	Lincoln	(217)	14,971	15,418
60069	Lincolnshire	(847)	6,841	4,928
*60645	Lincolnwood	(847)	12,026	11,365
60046	Lindenhurst	(847)	14,403	8,044
60532	Lisle	(630)	23,376	19,584
62056	Litchfield	(217)	6,771	6,883
*60441	Lockport	(815)	22,161	9,401
60148	Lombard	(630)	42,816	39,408
*60047	Long Grove	(847)	7,833	4,747
*61130	Loves Park	(815)	22,983	15,457
60411	Lynwood	(708)	7,655	6,535
60534	Lyons	(708)	10,466	9,828
*60050	McHenry	(815)	24,863	16,343
*61115	Machesney Park	(815)	21,846	19,042
61455	Macomb	(309)	18,587	19,952
61853	Mahomet	(217)	5,714	3,499
60442	Manhattan	(815)	5,169	2,059
60950	Manteno	(815)	7,955	3,709
60152	Marengo	(815)	7,381	4,768
62959	Marion	(618)	17,104	14,597
*60426	Markham	(708)	12,304	13,136
62062	Maryville	(618)	6,629	2,576
*62258	Mascoutah	(618)	5,824	5,511
*60443	Matteson	(708)	15,675	11,378
61938	Mattoon	(217)	17,385	18,441
*60153	Maywood	(708)	25,777	27,139
*60160	Melrose Park	(708)	22,512	20,859
61342	Mendota	(815)	7,077	7,017
62960	Metropolis	(618)	6,468	6,734
60445	Midlothian	(708)	13,949	14,372
61264	Milan	(309)	5,237	5,753
60447	Minooka	(815)	8,403	2,561
60448	Mokena	(708)	17,396	6,128
*61265	Moline	(309)	42,892	43,080
61462	Monmouth	(309)	9,198	9,489
60538	Montgomery	(630)	11,959	4,487
61856	Monticello	(217)	5,275	4,775
60450	Morris	(815)	12,939	10,274
61550	Morton Village	(309)	15,761	13,799
60053	Morton Grove	(847)	22,202	22,373
62863	Mount Carmel	(618)	7,690	8,287
60056	Mount Prospect	(847)	54,482	53,168
62864	Mount Vernon	(618)	16,344	17,082
62549	Mount Zion	(217)	5,032	4,522
60060	Mundelein	(847)	32,774	21,224
62966	Murphysboro	(618)	8,288	9,176
*60540	Naperville	(630)	141,579	85,806
60451	New Lenox	(815)	23,197	9,698
60714	Niles	(847)	29,330	28,375
*61761	Normal	(309)	49,927	40,023
*60634	Norridge	(708)	14,054	14,459
60542	North Aurora	(630)	14,394	6,010
*60062	Northbrook	(708)	34,190	32,565
*60064	North Chicago	(847)	33,376	34,978
60093	Northfield	(847)	5,543	4,924
60164	Northlake	(708)	11,358	12,505
60546	North Riverside	(708)	6,382	6,180
*60521	Oak Brook	(630)	8,835	9,087
60452	Oak Forest	(708)	28,116	26,202
*60303	Oak Lawn	(708)	53,991	56,182
*60303	Oak Park	(708)	50,757	53,648
62269	O'Fallon	(618)	25,155	16,064
62450	Olney	(618)	8,470	8,873
60477	Orland Hills	(708)	7,273	5,510
*60462	Orland Park	(708)	55,461	35,720
60543	Oswego	(630)	23,330	3,949
61350	Ottawa	(815)	18,824	17,574
*60067	Palatine	(847)	67,232	41,554
60463	Palos Heights	(708)	12,561	11,478
60465	Palos Hills	(708)	17,258	17,803
62557	Pana	(217)	5,529	5,796
61944	Paris	(217)	8,834	9,105
60085	Park City	(847)	6,775	4,677
60466	Park Forest	(708)	23,036	24,656
60068	Park Ridge	(847)	36,983	37,075
*61554	Pekin	(309)	33,331	32,254
*61601	Peoria	(309)	112,685	113,508
61616	Peoria Heights	(309)	6,298	6,930
61354	Peru	(815)	9,815	9,302
62274	Pinckneyville	(618)	5,452	3,372
*60544	Plainfield	(815)	28,162	4,557
60545	Plano	(630)	7,338	5,104
61764	Pontiac	(815)	11,457	11,428
62040	Pontoon Beach	(618)	6,046	4,013
61356	Princeton	(815)	7,554	7,197
60070	Prospect Heights	(847)	16,387	15,236
*62301	Quincy	(217)	39,841	39,682
61866	Rantoul	(217)	12,483	17,212
60471	Richton Park	(708)	12,998	10,523
60827	Riverdale	(708)	14,588	13,671
60305	River Forest	(708)	11,289	11,669
60171	River Grove	(708)	10,216	9,961
60546	Riverside	(708)	8,485	8,774
60472	Robbins	(708)	6,375	7,498
62454	Robinson	(618)	6,471	6,740
61068	Rochelle	(815)	9,712	8,769
61071	Rock Falls	(815)	9,470	9,669
*61125	Rockford	(815)	152,916	142,815
*61201	Rock Island	(309)	38,702	40,630
61072	Rockton	(815)	5,348	2,928
60008	Rolling Meadows	(847)	23,909	22,598
*60446	Romeoville	(815)	36,396	14,101
61073	Roscoe	(815)	6,355	2,079
60172	Roselle	(630)	23,240	20,803
60073	Round Lake	(847)	14,803	3,550
60073	Round Lake Beach	(847)	28,253	16,406
60073	Round Lake Park	(847)	6,224	4,045
*60174	Saint Charles	(630)	32,332	22,636
62881	Salem	(618)	7,574	7,470
60548	Sandwich	(815)	7,018	5,607
60411	Sauk Village	(708)	10,486	10,734
*60194	Schaumburg	(847)	72,805	68,586
*60176	Schiller Park	(847)	11,597	11,189
*62269	Shiloh	(618)	10,367	2,655
*60436	Shorewood	(815)	12,114	6,264
61282	Silvis	(309)	7,489	6,926
*60077	Skokie	(847)	64,678	59,432
61080	South Beloit	(815)	5,421	4,072
60177	South Elgin	(847)	20,758	7,474
60473	South Holland	(708)	21,552	22,105
*62703	Springfield	(217)	115,668	105,412
60081	Spring Grove	(815)	5,303	1,066
61362	Spring Valley	(815)	5,380	5,246
62088	Staunton	(618)	5,109	4,806
60475	Steger	(708)	10,409	9,251
61081	Sterling	(815)	15,381	15,142
*60402	Stickney	(708)	5,899	5,678
60107	Streamwood	(630)	37,312	31,197
61364	Streator	(815)	13,899	14,121
60554	Sugar Grove	(630)	8,416	2,123
60501	Summit	(708)	10,348	9,971
*62221	Swansea	(618)	12,274	8,201
60178	Sycamore	(815)	14,831	9,896
62568	Taylorville	(217)	11,240	11,133
60477	Tinley Park	(708)	57,477	37,115
62294	Troy	(618)	9,374	6,194
60466	University Park	(708)	8,102	6,204
*61801	Urbana	(217)	38,463	36,383
62471	Vandalia	(618)	6,811	6,114
60061	Vernon Hills	(847)	23,957	15,319
60181	Villa Park	(630)	22,616	22,279
60555	Warrenville	(630)	13,217	11,389
61571	Washington	(309)	12,759	10,136
*62204	Washington Park	(618)	5,740	7,431
62298	Waterloo	(618)	9,225	5,030
60970	Watseka	(815)	5,547	5,424
60084	Wauconda	(847)	10,903	6,294
*60085	Waukegan	(847)	91,396	69,481
60154	Westchester	(708)	16,177	17,301
*60185	West Chicago	(630)	26,554	14,808
60118	West Dundee	(847)	7,875	3,728
60558	Western Springs	(708)	12,530	11,956
62896	West Frankfort	(618)	8,285	8,526
60559	Westmont	(630)	24,863	21,402

ZIP	Place	Area Code	2005	1990
*60187	Wheaton	(630)	54,700	51,441
60090	Wheeling	(847)	36,641	29,911
60527	Willowbrook	(630)	8,893	8,651
60480	Willow Springs	(708)	6,011	4,509
60091	Wilmette	(847)	26,922	26,694
60481	Wilmington	(815)	5,957	4,743
60190	Winfield	(630)	9,844	7,096
60093	Winnetka	(847)	12,452	12,210
60096	Winthrop Harbor	(847)	7,090	6,240
60097	Wonder Lake (c)	(815)	7,463	6,664
*60191	Wood Dale	(630)	13,419	12,394
60517	Woodridge	(630)	34,058	26,359
62095	Wood River	(618)	10,985	11,490
60098	Woodstock	(815)	21,985	14,368
60482	Worth	(708)	10,652	11,208
60560	Yorkville	(630)	10,791	3,974
60099	Zion	(847)	24,303	19,783

Indiana

ZIP	Place	Area Code	2005	1990
46001	Alexandria	(765)	5,868	5,709
*46011	Anderson	(765)	57,500	59,518
46703	Angola	(260)	7,890	5,851
46706	Auburn	(260)	12,687	9,386
46123	Avon	(317)	8,918	—
47006	Batesville	(812)	6,407	4,720
47421	Bedford	(812)	13,551	13,817
46107	Beech Grove	(317)	14,069	13,383
*47408	Bloomington	(812)	69,017	62,735
46714	Bluffton	(260)	9,460	9,104
47601	Boonville	(812)	6,782	6,686
47834	Brazil	(812)	8,214	7,640
47025	Bright (c)	(812)	5,405	3,945
46112	Brownsburg	(317)	18,290	7,751
*46032	Carmel	(317)	59,243	25,380
46303	Cedar Lake	(219)	9,901	8,885
47111	Charlestown	(812)	8,052	5,889
46304	Chesterton	(219)	12,032	9,118
*47129	Clarksville	(812)	21,060	19,838
46725	Columbia City	(260)	8,024	5,883
*47201	Columbus	(812)	39,380	33,948
47331	Connersville	(765)	14,368	15,550
*47933	Crawfordsville	(765)	15,155	13,584
*46307	Crown Point	(219)	22,697	17,728
46229	Cumberland	(317)	5,319	4,557
46122	Danville	(317)	7,425	4,345
46733	Decatur	(260)	9,547	8,642
46517	Dunlap (c)	(574)	5,887	5,705
*46311	Dyer	(219)	15,071	10,923
46312	East Chicago	(219)	30,946	33,892
*46515	Elkhart	(574)	52,270	44,661
47429	Ellettsville	(812)	5,294	3,275
46036	Elwood	(765)	9,167	9,494
*47708	Evansville	(812)	115,918	126,272
*46038	Fishers	(317)	57,220	7,189
*46802	Fort Wayne	(260)	223,341	195,680
*46041	Frankfort	(765)	16,432	14,754
46131	Franklin	(317)	21,747	12,932
46738	Garrett	(260)	5,760	5,349
*46401	Gary	(219)	98,715	116,646
46933	Gas City	(765)	5,819	6,311
*46526	Goshen	(574)	31,269	23,794
46530	Granger (c)	(574)	28,284	20,241
46135	Greencastle	(765)	10,065	8,984
46140	Greenfield	(317)	16,654	11,657
47240	Greensburg	(812)	10,536	9,286
*46142	Greenwood	(317)	42,236	26,507
46319	Griffith	(219)	16,666	17,914
*46320	Hammond	(219)	79,217	84,236
47348	Hartford City	(765)	6,684	6,960
*46322	Highland	(219)	23,172	23,696
46342	Hobart	(219)	27,768	24,440
47542	Huntingburg	(812)	5,929	5,236
46750	Huntington	(260)	17,011	16,389
*46206	Indianapolis	(317)	784,118	731,278
*47546	Jasper	(812)	13,767	10,030
*47130	Jeffersonville	(812)	28,621	24,016
46755	Kendallville	(260)	10,018	7,984
*46902	Kokomo	(765)	46,178	44,996
*47901	Lafayette	(765)	60,459	45,933
46307	Lakes of the Four Seasons (c)	(219)	7,291	6,556
46405	Lake Station	(219)	13,565	13,899
*46350	La Porte	(219)	21,092	21,507
46226	Lawrence	(317)	40,959	26,849
46052	Lebanon	(765)	14,633	12,059
47441	Linton	(812)	5,808	5,814
46947	Logansport	(574)	19,211	16,865
46356	Lowell	(219)	8,039	6,430
47250	Madison	(812)	12,443	12,006
*46952	Marion	(765)	30,644	32,607
46151	Martinsville	(765)	11,657	11,677
*46401	Merrillville	(219)	31,525	27,257
*46360	Michigan City	(219)	32,205	33,822
*46544	Mishawaka	(574)	48,497	42,635
47960	Monticello	(574)	5,462	5,237
46158	Mooresville	(317)	11,111	5,779
47620	Mount Vernon	(812)	7,238	7,217
*47302	Muncie	(765)	66,164	71,170
46321	Munster	(219)	22,347	19,949

ZIP	Place	Area Code	2005	1990
46550	Nappanee	(574)	6,955	5,474
*47150	New Albany	(812)	36,772	36,322
47362	New Castle	(765)	18,718	17,753
46774	New Haven	(260)	13,676	11,234
*46060	Noblesville	(317)	38,825	17,655
46962	North Manchester	(260)	5,980	6,383
47265	North Vernon	(812)	6,433	5,129
47130	Oak Park (c)	(812)	5,379	5,630
*46970	Peru	(765)	12,732	12,843
46168	Plainfield	(317)	23,532	14,953
46563	Plymouth	(574)	10,876	8,291
46368	Portage	(219)	35,687	29,062
46304	Porter	(219)	5,217	3,242
47371	Portland	(260)	6,191	6,483
47670	Princeton	(812)	8,652	8,127
47978	Rensselaer	(219)	6,234	5,045
*47374	Richmond	(765)	37,560	38,705
46975	Rochester	(574)	6,451	5,969
46173	Rushville	(765)	5,679	5,533
46373	Saint John	(219)	10,783	4,921
47167	Salem	(812)	6,453	5,619
46375	Schererville	(219)	28,394	20,155
47170	Scottsburg	(812)	6,060	5,334
47172	Sellersburg	(812)	6,028	5,936
47274	Seymour	(812)	18,890	15,605
46176	Shelbyville	(765)	18,063	15,347
*46624	South Bend	(574)	105,262	105,511
46383	South Haven (c)	(219)	5,619	6,112
46224	Speedway	(317)	12,408	13,092
47586	Tell City	(812)	7,690	8,088
*47808	Terre Haute	(812)	56,893	57,475
46072	Tipton	(765)	5,254	4,751
*46383	Valparaiso	(219)	29,102	24,414
47591	Vincennes	(812)	18,077	19,867
46992	Wabash	(260)	11,209	12,127
*46580	Warsaw	(574)	12,735	10,968
47501	Washington	(812)	11,357	10,864
46074	Westfield	(317)	12,322	3,304
*46580	West Lafayette	(765)	28,599	26,144
46391	Westville	(219)	5,219	5,234
46077	Zionsville	(317)	11,853	6,207

Iowa

ZIP	Place	Area Code	2005	1990
50511	Algona	(515)	5,505	6,015
50009	Altoona	(515)	12,938	7,242
*50010	Ames	(515)	52,263	47,198
52205	Anamosa	(319)	5,616	5,100
*50021	Ankeny	(515)	36,681	18,482
50022	Atlantic	(712)	6,959	7,432
52722	Bettendorf	(563)	31,890	28,139
*50036	Boone	(515)	12,831	12,392
52601	Burlington	(319)	25,436	27,208
51401	Carroll	(712)	10,047	9,579
*52401	Cedar Rapids	(319)	123,119	108,772
52544	Centerville	(641)	5,788	5,936
*50616	Charles City	(641)	7,606	7,878
51012	Cherokee	(712)	5,027	6,026
51632	Clarinda	(712)	5,523	5,104
50428	Clear Lake	(641)	7,913	8,183
*52732	Clinton	(563)	27,086	29,201
50325	Clive	(515)	13,851	7,446
52241	Coralville	(319)	17,811	10,347
*51501	Council Bluffs	(712)	59,568	54,315
50801	Creston	(641)	7,359	7,911
*52802	Davenport	(563)	98,845	95,333
52101	Decorah	(563)	8,084	8,063
51442	Denison	(712)	7,374	6,604
*50318	Des Moines	(515)	194,163	193,189
50742	De Witt	(563)	5,204	4,514
*52001	Dubuque	(563)	57,798	57,538
51334	Estherville	(712)	6,347	6,720
*52556	Fairfield	(641)	9,404	9,955
50501	Fort Dodge	(515)	25,493	26,057
52627	Fort Madison	(319)	11,048	11,614
51534	Glenwood	(712)	5,650	4,960
50111	Grimes	(515)	6,037	2,653
*50112	Grinnell	(641)	9,332	8,902
*51537	Harlan	(712)	5,170	5,148
52233	Hiawatha	(319)	6,596	5,354
50644	Independence	(319)	6,054	5,972
50125	Indianola	(515)	13,944	11,340
*52240	Iowa City	(319)	62,887	59,735
50126	Iowa Falls	(641)	5,112	5,435
50131	Johnston	(515)	12,931	4,702
52632	Keokuk	(319)	10,762	12,451
*50138	Knoxville	(641)	7,512	8,232
51031	Le Mars	(712)	9,349	8,454
52057	Manchester	(563)	5,074	5,137
52060	Maquoketa	(563)	6,054	6,130
52302	Marion	(319)	30,233	20,422
50158	Marshalltown	(641)	25,977	25,178
*50401	Mason City	(641)	27,909	29,040
52641	Mount Pleasant	(319)	8,767	7,959
52761	Muscatine	(563)	22,757	22,881
50201	Nevada	(515)	6,129	6,009
50208	Newton	(641)	15,607	14,799
52317	North Liberty	(319)	8,808	2,926

ZIP	Place	Area Code	2005	1990
50211	Norwalk	(515)	7,877	5,726
50662	Oelwein	(319)	6,371	6,691
51041	Orange City	(712)	5,775	4,940
52577	Oskaloosa	(641)	11,026	10,600
52501	Ottumwa	(641)	24,798	24,488
50219	Pella	(641)	10,291	9,270
50220	Perry	(515)	8,865	6,652
*50317	Pleasant Hill	(515)	6,229	3,671
*51566	Red Oak	(712)	5,919	6,264
*51601	Shenandoah	(712)	5,239	5,572
51250	Sioux Center	(712)	6,513	5,074
*51101	Sioux City	(712)	83,148	80,505
51301	Spencer	(712)	11,117	11,066
50588	Storm Lake	(712)	9,963	8,769
*50322	Urbandale	(515)	34,696	23,775
52349	Vinton	(319)	5,219	5,103
52353	Washington	(319)	7,207	7,074
*50701	Waterloo	(319)	66,483	66,467
50263	Waukee	(515)	9,213	2,512
50677	Waverly	(319)	9,298	8,539
50595	Webster City	(515)	8,077	7,894
*50265	West Des Moines	(515)	52,768	31,702

Kansas

ZIP	Place	Area Code	2005	1990
67410	Abilene	(785)	6,409	6,242
67002	Andover	(316)	9,114	4,204
67005	Arkansas City	(620)	11,581	12,762
66002	Atchison	(913)	10,169	10,656
67010	Augusta	(316)	8,608	7,848
*66952	Bel Aire	(316)	6,557	3,695
66012	Bonner Springs	(913)	6,942	6,413
66720	Chanute	(620)	9,006	9,488
67337	Coffeyville	(620)	10,359	12,917
67701	Colby	(785)	5,030	5,510
66901	Concordia	(785)	5,371	6,152
67037	Derby	(316)	20,543	14,691
66018	De Soto	(913)	5,170	2,291
*67801	Dodge City	(620)	26,104	21,129
67042	El Dorado	(316)	12,659	11,495
66801	Emporia	(620)	26,456	25,512
66025	Eudora	(785)	5,284	3,006
66442	Fort Riley North (c)	(785)	8,114	12,848
66701	Fort Scott	(620)	7,990	8,362
*67846	Garden City	(620)	27,098	24,097
*66030	Gardner	(913)	14,317	4,277
67530	Great Bend	(620)	15,440	15,427
*67601	Hays	(785)	19,632	18,632
67060	Haysville	(316)	9,817	8,364
*67501	Hutchinson	(620)	40,961	39,308
67301	Independence	(620)	9,284	10,030
66749	Iola	(620)	6,008	6,351
*66441	Junction City	(785)	16,402	20,642
*66102	Kansas City	(913)	144,210	151,521
66043	Lansing	(913)	10,214	7,120
*66044	Lawrence	(785)	81,816	65,608
*66048	Leavenworth	(913)	35,213	38,495
*66209	Leawood	(913)	30,145	19,693
*66214	Lenexa	(913)	43,434	34,110
*67901	Liberal	(620)	20,257	16,573
67460	McPherson	(620)	13,695	12,422
*66502	Manhattan	(785)	48,668	43,081
*66202	Merriam	(913)	10,769	11,819
*66201	Mission	(913)	9,751	9,504
67110	Mulvane	(316)	5,628	4,683
*67114	Newton	(316)	18,229	16,700
*66061	Olathe	(913)	111,334	63,402
66067	Ottawa	(785)	12,597	10,667
*66204	Overland Park	(913)	164,811	111,790
66071	Paola	(913)	5,292	4,698
*67219	Park City	(316)	7,173	5,081
67357	Parsons	(620)	11,212	11,919
*66762	Pittsburg	(620)	19,214	17,789
*66208	Prairie Village	(913)	21,454	23,186
67124	Pratt	(620)	6,447	6,687
66205	Roeland Park	(913)	6,975	7,706
*67401	Salina	(785)	45,956	42,299
*66203	Shawnee	(913)	57,628	37,962
*66601	Topeka	(785)	121,946	119,883
67880	Ulysses	(620)	5,650	5,474
67147	Valley Center	(316)	5,508	4,272
67152	Wellington	(620)	8,098	8,517
*67202	Wichita	(316)	354,865	304,017
67156	Winfield	(620)	11,861	11,931

Kentucky

ZIP	Place	Area Code	2005	1990
41001	Alexandria	(859)	7,996	5,592
*41101	Ashland	(606)	21,510	23,622
40004	Bardstown	(502)	10,984	6,712
*41073	Bellevue	(859)	6,022	6,997
*40403	Berea	(859)	13,230	9,129
42101	Bowling Green	(270)	52,272	41,688
40218	Buechel (c)	(502)	7,272	7,081
41005	Burlington (c)	(859)	10,779	6,070
42718	Campbellsville	(270)	10,906	9,592
*42330	Central City	(270)	5,785	4,979
41076	Cold Spring	(859)	5,255	2,880
40701	Corbin	(606)	8,230	7,644

ZIP	Place	Area Code	2005	1990
41011	Covington	(859)	42,811	43,646
41031	Cynthiana	(859)	6,311	6,497
40422	Danville	(859)	15,409	14,454
*41074	Dayton	(859)	5,556	6,576
40243	Douglass Hills	(502)	5,597	5,431
*41017	Edgewood	(859)	8,913	8,143
*42701	Elizabethtown	(270)	23,450	18,167
41018	Elsmere	(859)	7,948	6,847
*41018	Erlanger	(859)	16,852	15,979
40118	Fairdale (c)	(502)	7,658	6,563
40291	Fern Creek (c)	(502)	17,870	16,406
41139	Flatwoods	(606)	7,621	7,799
*41042	Florence	(859)	26,349	18,586
42223	Fort Campbell North (c)	(270)	14,338	18,861
40121	Fort Knox (c)	(270)	12,377	21,495
41017	Fort Mitchell	(859)	7,605	7,438
41075	Fort Thomas	(859)	15,592	16,032
41011	Fort Wright	(859)	5,438	6,404
*40601	Frankfort	(502)	27,210	26,535
*42134	Franklin	(270)	8,079	7,607
40324	Georgetown	(502)	19,988	11,414
*42141	Glasgow	(270)	14,062	12,777
40330	Harrodsburg	(859)	8,126	7,335
*42420	Henderson	(270)	27,666	25,945
*41076	Highland Heights	(859)	5,791	4,223
40228	Highview (c)	(502)	15,161	14,814
40129	Hillview	(502)	7,349	6,119
*42240	Hopkinsville	(270)	28,821	29,809
41051	Independence	(859)	19,065	10,444
*40269	Jeffersontown	(502)	26,100	23,223
*40031	La Grange	(502)	6,046	3,901
40342	Lawrenceburg	(502)	9,403	5,911
40033	Lebanon	(270)	5,959	5,695
*42754	Leitchfield	(270)	6,462	4,965
*40507	Lexington	(859)	268,080	225,366
*40741	London	(606)	7,787	5,757
*40232	Louisville	(502)	556,429	269,555
*40252	Lyndon	(502)	10,248	8,037
42431	Madisonville	(270)	19,273	18,693
42066	Mayfield	(270)	10,288	9,935
41056	Maysville	(606)	9,136	8,113
40965	Middlesborough	(606)	10,164	11,328
*40253	Middletown	(502)	6,072	5,016
42633	Monticello	(606)	6,062	5,357
40351	Morehead	(606)	7,592	8,357
40353	Mount Sterling	(859)	6,317	5,362
40047	Mount Washington	(502)	8,624	5,256
42071	Murray	(270)	15,538	14,442
40219	Newburg (c)	(502)	20,636	21,647
*41071	Newport	(859)	15,911	18,871
*40356	Nicholasville	(859)	23,897	13,603
41042	Oakbrook (c)	(859)	7,726	4,113
42262	Oak Grove	(502)	7,570	2,863
*40259	Okolona (c)	(502)	17,807	18,902
*42301	Owensboro	(270)	55,459	53,577
*42003	Paducah	(270)	25,575	27,256
*40361	Paris	(859)	9,334	8,730
*41501	Pikeville	(606)	6,312	6,324
*40268	Pleasure Ridge Park (c)	(502)	25,776	25,131
42445	Princeton	(270)	6,447	6,940
*40160	Radcliff	(502)	21,471	19,778
*40475	Richmond	(859)	30,893	21,183
42276	Russellville	(270)	7,271	7,454
40216	Saint Dennis (c)	(502)	9,177	10,326
*40207	Saint Matthews	(502)	17,309	15,691
*40066	Shelbyville	(502)	10,730	6,155
40165	Shepherdsville	(502)	8,874	4,805
40256	Shively	(502)	15,212	15,535
*42501	Somerset	(606)	12,136	10,735
41015	Taylor Mill	(859)	6,733	5,530
*40272	Valley Station (c)	(502)	22,946	22,840
*40383	Versailles	(859)	7,728	7,269
41017	Villa Hills	(859)	7,749	7,370
40769	Williamsburg	(606)	5,162	5,493
40390	Wilmore	(859)	5,826	4,215
*40391	Winchester	(859)	16,494	15,799

Louisiana

ZIP	Place	Area Code	2005	1990
*70510	Abbeville	(337)	11,664	11,769
*71301	Alexandria	(318)	45,693	49,049
70032	Arabi (c)	(504)	8,093	8,787
70094	Avondale (c)	(504)	5,441	5,813
70714	Baker	(225)	13,250	13,087
71220	Bastrop	(318)	12,403	13,916
*70821	Baton Rouge	(225)	222,064	219,531
*70364	Bayou Cane (c)	(985)	17,046	15,876
*70037	Belle Chasse (c)	(504)	9,848	8,512
*70427	Bogalusa	(985)	12,964	14,280
*71111	Bossier City	(318)	60,505	52,721
70517	Breaux Bridge	(337)	7,902	6,694
70094	Bridge City (c)	(504)	8,323	8,327
70518	Broussard	(337)	6,754	3,213
70811	Brownfields (c)	(225)	5,222	5,229
71292	Brownsville-Bawcomville (c)	(318)	7,616	7,397
70520	Carencro	(337)	6,097	5,518
*70043	Chalmette (c)	(504)	32,069	31,860
70443	Claiborne (c)	(318)	9,830	8,300
*70433	Covington	(985)	9,347	7,691

ZIP	Place	Area Code	2005	1990
*70526	Crowley	(337)	13,861	13,983
70345	Cut Off (c)	(985)	5,635	5,325
*70726	Denham Springs	(225)	10,206	8,381
70634	De Ridder	(337)	9,976	10,475
70047	Destrehan (c)	(985)	11,260	8,031
70346	Donaldsonville	(225)	7,535	7,949
70458	Eden Isle (c)	(985)	6,261	3,768
70072	Estelle (c)	(504)	15,880	14,091
70535	Eunice	(337)	11,527	11,162
71459	Fort Polk South (c)	(337)	11,000	10,911
70538	Franklin	(337)	7,822	9,004
70354	Galliano (c)	(985)	7,356	4,294
70810	Gardere (c)	(225)	8,992	7,209
*70737	Gonzales	(225)	8,499	7,208
*70053	Gretna	(504)	17,161	17,208
*70401	Hammond	(985)	18,096	15,871
70123	Harahan	(504)	9,716	9,927
*70058	Harvey (c)	(504)	22,226	21,222
*70360	Houma	(985)	32,105	30,495
70544	Jeanerette	(337)	5,945	6,205
70121	Jefferson (c)	(504)	11,843	14,521
70546	Jennings	(337)	10,652	11,305
70548	Kaplan	(337)	5,131	4,535
*70062	Kenner	(504)	69,911	72,033
*70501	Lafayette	(337)	112,030	101,865
*70601	Lake Charles	(337)	70,555	70,580
71254	Lake Providence (c)	(318)	5,104	5,380
*70068	Laplace (c)	(985)	27,684	24,194
*70373	Larose (c)	(985)	7,306	5,772
*71446	Leesville	(337)	6,160	7,638
70070	Luling (c)	(985)	11,512	2,803
*70471	Mandeville	(985)	11,632	7,474
71052	Mansfield	(318)	5,504	5,389
71351	Marksville	(318)	5,707	5,526
*70072	Marrero (c)	(504)	36,165	36,671
70075	Meraux (c)	(504)	10,192	8,849
70812	Merrydale (c)	(225)	10,427	10,395
*70009	Metairie (c)	(504)	146,136	149,428
*71055	Minden	(318)	13,281	13,661
*71201	Monroe	(318)	51,914	54,909
*70380	Morgan City	(985)	11,930	14,531
70611	Moss Bluff (c)	(337)	10,535	8,039
*71457	Natchitoches	(318)	17,701	16,609
*70560	New Iberia	(337)	32,495	31,828
*70140	New Orleans	(504)	454,863	496,938
71463	Oakdale	(318)	7,981	6,837
70810	Oak Hills Place (c)	(225)	7,996	5,479
70817	Old Jefferson (c)	(225)	5,631	4,531
*70570	Opelousas	(337)	22,897	19,091
70392	Patterson	(985)	5,152	5,166
*71360	Pineville	(318)	14,083	15,308
*70764	Plaquemine	(225)	6,717	7,101
70454	Ponchatoula	(985)	5,784	5,499
70767	Port Allen	(225)	5,062	6,277
70605	Prien (c)	(337)	7,215	6,448
70394	Raceland (c)	(985)	10,224	5,564
70578	Rayne	(337)	8,516	8,502
71037	Red Chute (c)	(318)	5,984	5,431
70084	Reserve (c)	(985)	9,111	8,847
70123	River Ridge (c)	(504)	14,588	14,800
*71270	Ruston	(318)	20,667	20,071
70776	Saint Gabriel	(225)	5,471	3,854
70582	Saint Martinville	(337)	6,947	7,226
70087	Saint Rose (c)	(504)	6,540	6,259
70395	Schriever (c)	(985)	5,880	4,958
70583	Scott	(337)	8,120	4,912
70817	Shenandoah (c)	(318)	17,070	13,429
*71102	Shreveport	(318)	198,874	198,518
*70458	Slidell	(985)	26,840	24,124
71075	Springhill	(318)	5,237	5,668
*70663	Sulphur	(337)	19,608	20,125
*71282	Tallulah	(318)	8,152	8,526
70056	Terrytown (c)	(504)	25,430	23,787
*70301	Thibodaux	(985)	14,408	14,125
70056	Timberlane (c)	(504)	11,405	12,614
70810	Village Saint George (c)	(225)	6,993	6,242
70586	Ville Platte	(337)	8,250	9,037
70092	Violet (c)	(504)	8,555	8,574
70094	Waggaman (c)	(504)	9,435	9,405
70785	Walker	(225)	5,751	3,846
*71291	West Monroe	(318)	13,038	14,096
*70094	Westwego	(504)	10,489	11,218
71483	Winnfield	(318)	5,307	6,138
70592	Youngsville	(337)	5,289	1,195
70791	Zachary	(225)	12,258	9,036

Maine (207)

See introductory note.

ZIP	Place	2005	1990
*04210	Auburn	23,602	24,309
*04330	Augusta	18,626	21,325
*04401	Bangor	31,074	33,181
04609	Bar Harbor	5,118	4,443
04530	Bath	9,257	9,799
04915	Belfast	6,872	6,355
03901	Berwick	7,348	5,995
*04005	Biddeford	22,072	20,710
04412	Brewer	9,138	9,021
04011	Brunswick (c)	14,816	14,683

ZIP	Place	2005	1990
04011	Brunswick	21,820	20,906
04093	Buxton	8,163	6,494
*04843	Camden	5,341	5,060
04107	Cape Elizabeth	8,922	8,854
04736	Caribou	8,308	9,415
04021	Cumberland	7,656	5,836
03903	Eliot	6,413	5,329
04605	Ellsworth	7,021	5,975
04937	Fairfield	6,702	6,718
04105	Falmouth	10,601	7,610
04938	Farmington	7,504	7,436
*04032	Freeport	8,066	6,905
04345	Gardiner	6,237	6,746
04038	Gorham	15,300	11,856
04039	Gray	7,376	5,904
04444	Hampden	6,773	5,974
04079	Harpswell	5,242	5,012
*04730	Houlton (c)	5,270	5,627
04730	Houlton	6,317	6,613
04043	Kennebunk	11,510	8,004
03904	Kittery	10,453	9,372
04027	Lebanon	5,561	—
*04240	Lewiston	36,050	39,757
04457	Lincoln	5,258	5,587
*04250	Lisbon	9,444	9,457
04462	Millinocket	5,034	6,956
04462	Millinocket (c)	5,190	6,922
04260	New Gloucester	5,291	3,878
04963	Oakland	6,190	5,595
04064	Old Orchard Beach	9,350	7,789
04064	Old Orchard Beach (c)	8,856	7,789
04468	Old Town	7,792	8,317
04473	Orono	9,463	10,573
04473	Orono (c)	8,253	9,789
*04101	Portland	63,889	64,157
04769	Presque Isle	9,377	10,550
04841	Rockland	7,658	7,972
04276	Rumford	6,429	7,078
04072	Saco	18,230	15,181
04073	Sanford (c)	10,133	10,296
04073	Sanford	21,734	20,463
*04074	Scarborough	18,897	12,518
04976	Skowhegan (c)	6,696	6,990
04976	Skowhegan	8,833	8,725
03908	South Berwick	7,304	5,877
*04106	South Portland	23,742	23,163
04084	Standish	9,915	7,678
04086	Topsham (c)	6,271	6,147
04086	Topsham	9,939	8,746
04282	Turner	5,469	4,293
04572	Waldoboro	5,114	4,601
04087	Waterboro	7,233	4,510
*04901	Waterville	15,621	17,173
04090	Wells	10,088	7,778
*04092	Westbrook	16,108	16,121
*04062	Windham	16,371	13,020
04901	Winslow (c)	7,743	5,436
04901	Winslow	7,968	7,997
04364	Winthrop	6,480	5,968
04096	Yarmouth	8,257	7,862
03909	York	13,490	9,818

Maryland

Area code (240) overlays area code (301). Area code (443) overlays (410). See introductory note.

ZIP	Place	Area Code	2005	1990
21001	Aberdeen	(410)	14,305	13,087
20607	Accokeek (c)	(301)	7,349	4,477
*20783	Adelphi (c)	(301)	14,998	13,524
20762	Andrews AFB (c)	(410)	7,925	10,228
*21401	Annapolis	(410)	36,300	33,195
21227	Arbutus (c)	(410)	20,116	19,750
*21012	Arnold (c)	(410)	23,422	20,261
*20916	Aspen Hill (c)	(301)	50,228	45,494
21220	Ballenger Creek (c)	(410)	13,518	5,546
*21203	Baltimore	(410)	635,815	736,014
*21014	Bel Air	(410)	10,014	8,942
21050	Bel Air North (c)	(410)	25,798	14,880
21015	Bel Air South (c)	(410)	39,711	26,421
*20705	Beltsville (c)	(301)	15,690	14,476
20603	Bennsville (c)	(301)	7,325	—
*20814	Bethesda (c)	(301)	55,277	62,936
20710	Bladensburg	(301)	7,918	8,064
*20715	Bowie	(301)	53,878	37,642
21220	Bowleys Quarters (c)	(410)	6,314	5,595
21225	Brooklyn Park (c)	(410)	10,938	10,987
*21716	Brunswick	(301)	5,242	5,091
*20866	Burtonsville (c)	(301)	7,305	5,853
20619	California (c)	(410)	9,307	7,626
20705	Calverton (c)	(301)	12,610	12,046
21613	Cambridge	(410)	11,089	11,514
*20748	Camp Springs (c)	(301)	17,968	16,392
21401	Cape St. Clair (c)	(410)	8,022	7,878
21234	Carney (c)	(410)	28,264	25,578
*21228	Catonsville (c)	(410)	39,820	35,233
20657	Chesapeake Ranch Estates-Drum Point (c)	(301)	11,503	5,423
*20784	Cheverly	(301)	6,668	6,023
*20815	Chevy Chase (c)	(301)	9,381	8,559

ZIP	Place	Area Code	2005	1990
20782	Chillum (c)	(301)	34,252	31,309
20735	Clinton (c)	(301)	26,064	19,987
20904	Cloverly (c)	(301)	7,835	7,904
21030	Cockeysville (c)	(410)	19,388	18,668
*20914	Colesville (c)	(301)	19,810	18,819
*20740	College Park	(301)	25,171	23,714
*21045	Columbia (c)	(410)/(301)	88,254	75,883
20743	Coral Hills (c)	(410)	10,720	11,032
21502	Cresaptown-Bel Air (c)	(301)	5,884	4,586
21114	Crofton (c)	(410)	20,091	12,781
*21502	Cumberland	(301)	20,915	23,712
20872	Damascus (c)	(301)	11,430	9,817
*20874	Darnestown (c)	(301)	6,378	—
*20747	District Heights	(301)	6,296	6,711
21222	Dundalk (c)	(410)	62,306	65,800
*21601	Easton	(410)	13,447	9,372
20737	East Riverdale (c)	(301)	14,961	14,187
21219	Edgemere (c)	(410)	9,248	9,226
21040	Edgewood (c)	(410)	23,378	23,903
21784	Eldersburg (c)	(410)	27,741	9,720
21075	Elkridge (c)	(410)	22,042	12,953
*21921	Elkton	(410)	14,466	9,073
*21043	Ellicott City (c)	(410)	56,397	41,396
21221	Essex (c)	(410)	39,078	40,872
20904	Fairland (c)	(301)	21,738	19,828
21047	Fallston (c)	(410)	8,427	5,730
21061	Ferndale (c)	(410)	16,056	16,355
20902	Forest Glen (c)	(301)	7,344	—
*20747	Forestville (c)	(301)	12,707	16,731
20755	Fort Meade (c)	(301)	9,882	12,509
*20744	Fort Washington (c)	(301)	23,845	24,032
*21701	Frederick	(301)	57,907	40,186
20744	Friendly (c)	(301)	10,938	9,028
21532	Frostburg	(301)	7,958	8,069
*20877	Gaithersburg	(301)	57,698	39,676
21117	Garrison (c)	(410)	7,969	5,045
*20874	Germantown (c)	(301)	55,419	41,145
*20706	Glenarden (c)	(301)	6,380	5,025
*21061	Glen Burnie (c)	(410)	38,922	37,305
20769	Glenn Dale (c)	(301)	12,609	9,689
20706	Goddard (c)	(301)	5,554	4,576
20785	Greater Landover (c)	(301)	22,900	—
20772	Greater Upper Marlboro (c)	(301)	18,720	11,528
*20770	Greenbelt	(301)	22,242	20,561
21122	Green Haven (c)	(410)	17,415	14,416
20771	Green Valley (c)	(301)	12,262	9,424
*21740	Hagerstown	(301)	38,326	35,306
21740	Halfway (c)	(301)	10,065	8,873
21074	Hampstead	(410)	5,451	2,608
21211	Hampton (c)	(410)	5,004	4,926
21078	Havre de Grace	(410)	11,884	8,952
20748	Hillcrest Heights (c)	(301)	16,359	17,136
*20780	Hyattsville	(301)	16,677	13,864
20794	Jessup (c)	(410)	7,865	6,537
21085	Joppatowne (c)	(410)	11,391	11,084
20901	Kemp Mill (c)	(301)	9,956	—
*20772	Kettering (c)	(301)	11,008	9,901
20721	Lake Arbor (c)	(301)	8,533	—
*21122	Lake Shore (c)	(410)	13,065	13,269
21122	Langley Park (c)	(301)	16,214	17,474
20706	Lanham-Seabrook (c)	(301)	18,190	16,792
21227	Lansdowne-Baltimore Highlands (c)	(410)	15,724	15,509
20646	La Plata (c)	(301)	8,442	5,841
20772	Largo (c)	(301)	8,408	9,475
*20707	Laurel	(301)	22,125	19,086
20653	Lexington Park (c)	(410)	11,021	9,943
21701	Linganore-Bartonsville (c)	(301)	12,529	4,079
21090	Linthicum (c)	(410)	7,539	7,547
21207	Lochearn (c)	(410)	25,269	25,240
21037	Londontowne (c)	(410)	7,595	6,992
*21093	Lutherville-Timonium (c)	(410)	15,814	16,442
*20748	Marlow Heights (c)	(301)	6,059	5,885
20772	Marlton (c)	(301)	7,798	5,523
20724	Maryland City (c)	(301)	6,814	6,813
21093	Mays Chapel (c)	(410)	11,427	10,132
21220	Middle River (c)	(410)	23,958	24,616
21207	Milford Mill (c)	(410)	26,527	22,547
*20717	Mitchellville (c)	(301)	9,611	12,593
*20886	Montgomery Village (c)	(301)	38,051	32,315
21771	Mount Airy	(301)/(410)	8,375	3,730
20712	Mount Rainier	(301)	8,751	7,954
20784	New Carrollton	(301)	12,818	12,002
*20815	North Bethesda (c)	(301)	38,610	29,656
20895	North Kensington (c)	(301)	8,940	8,607
20707	North Laurel (c)	(301)	20,468	15,008
20878	North Potomac (c)	(301)	23,044	18,456
*21842	Ocean City	(410)	7,049	5,146
21811	Ocean Pines (c)	(410)	10,496	4,251
21113	Odenton (c)	(410)	20,534	12,833
*20832	Olney (c)	(301)	31,438	23,019
21206	Overlea (c)	(410)	12,148	12,137
21117	Owings Mills (c)	(410)	20,193	9,474
*20750	Oxon Hill-Glassmanor (c)	(301)	35,355	35,794
21234	Parkville (c)	(410)	31,118	31,617
21401	Parole (c)	(410)	14,031	10,054
*21122	Pasadena (c)	(410)	12,093	10,012
21128	Perry Hall (c)	(410)	28,705	22,723
*21282	Pikesville (c)	(410)	29,123	24,815
20837	Poolesville	(301)	5,498	3,796
*20850	Potomac (c)	(301)	44,822	45,634
21227	Pumphrey (c)	(410)	5,317	5,483
21133	Randallstown (c)	(301)	30,870	26,277
20855	Redland (c)	(301)	16,998	16,145
*21136	Reisterstown (c)	(410)	22,438	19,314
*20737	Riverdale Park	(301)	6,630	4,843
21017	Riverside (c)	(410)	6,128	—
*21122	Riviera Beach (c)	(410)	12,695	11,376
*20850	Rockville (c)	(301)	57,402	44,830
20772	Rosaryville (c)	(301)	12,322	8,976
21237	Rosedale (c)	(410)	19,199	18,703
20906	Rossmoor (c)	(301)	7,569	6,182
21221	Rossville (c)	(410)	11,515	9,492
*20602	Saint Charles (c)	(301)	33,379	28,717
*21801	Salisbury	(410)	26,295	20,592
*20763	Savage-Guilford (c)	(410)	12,918	9,669
20743	Seat Pleasant	(301)	5,063	5,354
21144	Severn (c)	(410)	35,076	24,499
21146	Severna Park (c)	(410)	28,507	25,879
20764	Shady Side (c)	(410)	5,559	4,107
*20907	Silver Spring (c)	(301)	76,540	76,046
21061	South Gate (c)	(410)	28,672	27,564
20895	South Kensington (c)	(301)	7,887	8,777
20707	South Laurel (c)	(301)	20,479	18,591
21666	Stevensville (c)	(410)	5,880	1,862
*20752	Suitland-Silver Hills (c)	(301)	33,515	35,111
*20913	Takoma Park	(301)	18,540	16,724
21787	Taneytown	(410)	5,453	3,695
*20748	Temple Hills (c)	(301)	7,792	6,865
21788	Thurmont	(301)	6,036	3,398
*21204	Towson (c)	(410)	51,793	49,445
20854	Travilah (c)	(301)	7,442	—
*20602	Waldorf (c)	(301)	22,312	15,058
20743	Walker Mill (c)	(301)	11,104	10,920
21793	Walkersville	(301)	5,593	4,145
*21157	Westminster	(410)	17,761	13,060
*20902	Wheaton-Glenmont (c)	(301)	57,694	53,720
21162	White Marsh (c)	(410)	8,485	8,183
20903	White Oak (c)	(301)	20,973	18,671
21207	Woodlawn (c) (Baltimore Co.)	(410)	36,079	32,907
21284	Woodlawn (c) (Pr. George's Co.)	(410)	6,251	5,329
20721	Woodmore (c)	(240)/(301)	6,077	2,874

Massachusetts

Area code (339) overlays area code (781). Area code (351) overlays (978). Area code (774) overlays (508). Area code (857) overlays (617). See introductory note.

ZIP	Place	Area Code	2005	1990
02351	Abington	(781)	16,351	13,817
*01720	Acton	(978)	20,562	17,872
*02743	Acushnet	(508)	10,544	9,554
01220	Adams	(413)	8,455	9,445
01220	Adams (c)	(413)	5,784	6,356
01001	Agawam	(413)	28,599	27,323
01913	Amesbury	(978)	16,643	14,997
01913	Amesbury (c)	(978)	12,327	12,109
*01002	Amherst	(413)	34,047	35,228
*01002	Amherst Center (c)	(413)	17,050	17,824
*01810	Andover (c)	(978)	7,900	8,242
*01810	Andover	(978)	33,042	29,151
*02205	Arlington	(781)	41,224	44,630
01430	Ashburnham	(978)	5,981	5,433
01721	Ashland	(508)	15,551	12,066
*01331	Athol	(978)	11,697	11,451
*01331	Athol (c)	(978)	8,370	8,732
02703	Attleboro	(508)	43,382	38,383
01501	Auburn	(508)	16,400	15,005
*01432	Ayer	(978)	7,228	6,871
*02630	Barnstable	(508)	47,826	40,949
01005	Barre	(508)	5,380	1,094
*01730	Bedford	(781)	12,462	12,996
01007	Belchertown	(413)	13,958	10,579
02019	Bellingham	(508)	15,784	14,877
*02478	Belmont	(781)	23,371	24,720
02779	Berkley	(508)	6,375	4,237
01915	Beverly	(978)	39,876	38,195
*01821	Billerica	(978)	39,963	37,609
01504	Blackstone	(508)	9,057	8,023
02748	Bliss Corner (c)	(508)	5,466	4,908
*02205	Boston	(617)	559,034	574,283
*02532	Bourne	(508)	19,356	16,064
01921	Boxford	(978)	8,177	6,266
*02185	Braintree	(781)	33,681	33,836
02631	Brewster	(508)	10,242	8,440
*02324	Bridgewater (c)	(508)	6,664	7,242
*02324	Bridgewater	(508)	25,720	21,249
*02303	Brockton	(508)	94,632	92,788
*02446	Brookline	(617)	55,590	54,718
*01803	Burlington	(781)	23,299	23,302
*02139	Cambridge	(617)	100,135	95,802
02021	Canton	(781)	21,571	18,530
*02330	Carver	(508)	11,562	10,590
01507	Charlton	(508)	12,475	9,576
02633	Chatham	(508)	6,832	6,579
01824	Chelmsford	(978)	33,759	32,383
02150	Chelsea	(617)	32,518	28,710
*01020	Chicopee	(413)	54,680	56,632
01510	Clinton	(978)	13,995	13,222
01510	Clinton (c)	(978)	7,884	7,943

ZIP	Place	Area Code	2005	1990
01778	Cochituate (c)	(508)	6,768	6,046
02025	Cohasset	(781)	7,222	7,075
01742	Concord	(978)	16,833	17,076
*01226	Dalton	(413)	6,700	7,155
01923	Danvers	(978)	26,045	24,174
*02714	Dartmouth	(508)	31,389	27,244
*02026	Dedham	(781)	23,736	23,782
02638	Dennis	(508)	15,891	13,864
02715	Dighton	(508)	6,665	5,631
01516	Douglas	(508)	7,885	5,438
02030	Dover	(508)	5,641	4,915
01826	Dracut	(978)	28,892	25,594
01571	Dudley	(508)	10,812	9,540
*02332	Duxbury	(781)	14,660	13,895
02333	East Bridgewater	(508)	13,859	11,104
02536	East Falmouth (c)	(508)	6,615	5,577
02642	Eastham	(508)	5,551	4,462
01027	Easthampton	(413)	16,004	15,537
*01028	East Longmeadow	(413)	14,886	13,367
*02334	Easton	(508)	23,028	19,807
02149	Everett	(617)	36,837	35,701
02719	Fairhaven	(508)	16,222	16,132
*02722	Fall River	(508)	91,802	92,703
*02540	Falmouth	(508)	33,644	27,960
01420	Fitchburg	(978)	40,045	41,194
02035	Foxborough	(508)	16,313	14,637
02035	Foxborough (c)	(508)	5,509	5,706
*01701	Framingham	(508)	65,060	64,989
02038	Franklin	(508)	30,893	22,095
02702	Freetown	(508)	8,979	8,522
*01440	Gardner	(978)	20,908	20,125
01833	Georgetown	(978)	8,041	6,384
*01930	Gloucester	(978)	30,713	28,716
01519	Grafton	(508)	16,890	13,035
01033	Granby	(413)	6,344	5,565
01230	Great Barrington	(413)	7,441	7,725
*01301	Greenfield	(413)	17,834	18,666
*01301	Greenfield (c)	(413)	13,716	14,016
*01450	Groton	(978)	10,437	7,511
01834	Groveland	(978)	6,608	5,214
02338	Halifax	(781)	7,809	6,526
*01936	Hamilton	(978)	8,349	7,280
01036	Hampden	(413)	5,318	—
*02339	Hanover	(781)	14,101	11,912
*02341	Hanson	(781)	9,926	9,028
01451	Harvard	(978)	6,074	12,329
02645	Harwich	(508)	12,675	10,275
*01830	Haverhill	(978)	60,242	51,418
*02018	Hingham (c)	(781)	5,352	5,454
*02043	Hingham	(781)	21,507	19,821
02343	Holbrook	(781)	10,775	11,041
01520	Holden	(508)	16,592	14,628
01746	Holliston	(508)	13,847	12,926
*01040	Holyoke	(413)	39,958	43,704
01747	Hopedale	(508)	6,243	5,666
01748	Hopkinton	(508)	14,112	9,191
01749	Hudson	(978)	18,943	17,233
01749	Hudson (c)	(978)	14,388	14,267
02045	Hull	(781)	11,280	10,466
02601	Hyannis (c)	(508)	11,050	14,120
01938	Ipswich	(978)	13,302	11,873
02364	Kingston (c)	(781)	5,380	4,774
02364	Kingston	(781)	12,457	9,045
02347	Lakeville	(508)	10,569	7,785
01523	Lancaster	(978)	6,845	6,661
*01842	Lawrence	(978)	71,314	70,207
*01238	Lee	(413)	5,885	5,849
01524	Leicester	(508)	10,967	10,191
01240	Lenox	(413)	5,156	5,069
01453	Leominster	(978)	41,804	38,145
*02420	Lexington	(781)	30,266	28,974
01773	Lincoln	(781)	7,931	7,666
01460	Littleton	(978)	8,589	7,051
*01028	Longmeadow	(413)	15,569	15,467
*01853	Lowell	(978)	103,111	103,439
01056	Ludlow	(413)	21,946	18,820
01462	Lunenburg	(978)	10,024	9,117
*01901	Lynn	(781)	88,792	81,245
01940	Lynnfield	(781)	11,546	11,049
02148	Malden	(781)	55,871	53,884
01944	Manchester-by-the-Sea	(978)	5,335	5,286
*02048	Mansfield	(508)	22,977	16,568
02048	Mansfield Center (c)	(508)	7,320	7,170
01945	Marblehead	(781)	20,297	19,971
02738	Marion	(508)	5,319	4,496
01752	Marlborough	(508)	37,444	31,813
*02050	Marshfield	(781)	24,890	21,531
02649	Mashpee	(508)	14,280	7,884
02739	Mattapoisett	(508)	6,479	5,850
01754	Maynard	(978)	10,230	10,325
02052	Medfield (c)	(508)	6,670	5,985
02052	Medfield	(508)	12,343	10,531
*02155	Medford	(781)	53,523	57,407
02053	Medway	(508)	12,812	9,931
02176	Melrose	(781)	26,365	28,150
01756	Mendon	(508)	5,754	—
01860	Merrimac	(978)	6,360	5,166
01844	Methuen	(978)	44,609	39,990
*02346	Middleborough	(508)	21,198	17,867
02346	Middleborough Center (c)	(508)	6,913	6,837

ZIP	Place	Area Code	2005	1990
01949	Middleton	(978)	9,273	4,921
01757	Milford	(508)	27,519	25,355
01757	Milford (c)	(508)	24,230	23,339
*01527	Millbury	(508)	13,459	12,228
02054	Millis	(508)	7,964	7,613
02186	Milton	(617)	26,034	25,725
01057	Monson	(413)	8,763	7,776
01351	Montague	(413)	8,408	8,316
*02584	Nantucket	(508)	10,168	6,012
01760	Natick	(508)	31,943	30,510
*02494	Needham	(781)	28,418	27,557
*02740	New Bedford	(508)	93,102	99,922
01951	Newbury	(978)	7,002	5,623
01950	Newburyport	(978)	17,414	16,317
*02456	Newton	(617)	83,158	82,585
02056	Norfolk	(508)	10,490	9,259
01247	North Adams	(413)	14,010	16,797
01059	North Amherst (c)	(413)	6,019	6,239
*01060	Northampton	(413)	28,715	11,929
01845	North Andover	(978)	27,155	29,289
*02760	North Attleborough	(508)	28,133	22,792
02760	North Attleborough Center (c)	(508)	16,796	16,178
01532	Northborough (c)	(508)	6,257	5,761
01532	Northborough	(508)	14,675	13,371
01534	Northbridge	(508)	14,216	12,002
*01864	North Reading	(978)	13,949	25,038
02060	North Scituate (c)	(781)	5,065	4,891
*02766	Norton	(508)	19,169	14,265
02061	Norwell	(781)	10,396	9,279
02062	Norwood	(781)	28,478	28,700
02065	Ocean Bluff-Brant Rock (c)	(781)	5,100	4,541
*01364	Orange	(978)	7,667	7,312
02653	Orleans	(508)	6,458	5,838
01540	Oxford (c)	(508)	5,899	5,969
01540	Oxford	(508)	13,718	12,588
01069	Palmer	(413)	12,925	12,054
*01960	Peabody	(978)	51,239	47,264
*02359	Pembroke	(781)	18,095	14,544
01463	Pepperell	(978)	11,408	10,098
01866	Pinehurst (c)	(978)	6,941	6,614
*01201	Pittsfield	(413)	43,860	48,622
02762	Plainville	(508)	8,022	6,871
*02360	Plymouth (c)	(508)	7,658	7,258
*02360	Plymouth	(508)	54,923	45,608
*02169	Quincy	(617)	90,250	84,985
02368	Randolph	(781)	30,468	30,093
*02767	Raynham	(508)	13,498	9,867
01867	Reading	(781)	23,164	22,539
02769	Rehoboth	(508)	11,256	8,656
02151	Revere	(781)	45,807	42,786
02370	Rockland	(781)	17,839	16,123
01966	Rockport (c)	(978)	5,606	5,448
01966	Rockport	(978)	7,763	7,482
01969	Rowley	(978)	5,845	4,452
01543	Rutland	(508)	7,446	4,936
*01970	Salem	(978)	41,756	38,091
01952	Salisbury	(978)	8,284	6,882
*02563	Sandwich	(508)	20,726	15,489
01906	Saugus	(781)	26,915	25,549
02066	Scituate (c)	(781)	5,069	5,180
*02066	Scituate	(781)	18,120	16,786
02771	Seekonk	(508)	13,668	13,046
02067	Sharon	(781)	17,207	15,517
02067	Sharon (c)	(781)	5,941	5,893
01464	Shirley	(978)	7,612	6,118
*01545	Shrewsbury	(508)	33,174	24,146
*02725	Somerset	(508)	18,570	17,655
*02143	Somerville	(617)	74,963	76,210
01002	South Amherst (c)	(413)	5,039	5,053
01073	Southampton	(413)	5,841	4,478
*01772	Southborough	(508)	9,559	6,628
01550	Southbridge	(508)	17,234	17,816
01550	Southbridge (c)	(508)	12,878	13,631
01075	South Hadley	(413)	17,063	16,685
01077	Southwick	(413)	9,548	7,667
01562	Spencer (c)	(508)	6,032	6,306
01562	Spencer	(508)	12,092	11,645
*01101	Springfield	(413)	151,732	156,983
01564	Sterling	(978)	7,770	6,481
02180	Stoneham	(781)	21,582	22,203
02072	Stoughton	(781)	26,692	26,777
01775	Stow	(978)	6,179	5,328
*01566	Sturbridge	(508)	8,860	7,775
01776	Sudbury	(978)	17,066	14,358
01590	Sutton	(508)	8,989	6,824
01907	Swampscott	(781)	14,288	13,650
02777	Swansea	(508)	16,250	15,411
*02780	Taunton	(508)	56,251	49,832
01468	Templeton	(978)	7,491	6,438
01876	Tewksbury	(978)	29,043	27,266
01983	Topsfield	(978)	6,183	5,754
01469	Townsend	(978)	9,285	8,496
01879	Tyngsborough	(978)	11,338	8,642
01568	Upton	(508)	6,397	4,677
01569	Uxbridge	(508)	12,409	10,415
01880	Wakefield	(781)	24,575	24,825
*02081	Walpole (c)	(508)	5,867	5,495
02081	Walpole	(508)	23,112	20,223
*02451	Waltham	(781)	59,556	57,878
01082	Ware (c)	(413)	6,174	6,533

ZIP	Place	Area Code	2005	1990
01082	Ware	(413)	10,005	9,808
02571	Wareham	(508)	21,296	19,232
*02471	Watertown	(781)	32,303	33,284
01778	Wayland	(508)	13,002	11,874
01570	Webster	(508)	16,851	16,196
01570	Webster (c)	(508)	11,600	11,849
*02457	Wellesley	(781)	26,978	26,615
*01581	Westborough	(508)	18,732	14,133
01583	West Boylston	(508)	7,699	6,611
02379	West Bridgewater	(508)	6,821	6,389
01742	West Concord (c)	(978)	5,632	5,761
*01085	Westfield	(413)	40,525	38,372
01886	Westford	(978)	21,461	16,392
*01473	Westminster	(978)	7,370	6,191
02493	Weston	(781)	11,581	10,200
02790	Westport	(508)	15,071	13,852
*01089	West Springfield	(413)	27,989	27,537
02090	Westwood	(781)	13,900	12,557
02673	West Yarmouth (c)	(508)	6,460	5,409
*02188	Weymouth	(781)	53,788	54,063
01588	Whitinsville (c)	(508)	6,340	5,639
02382	Whitman	(781)	14,439	13,240
01095	Wilbraham	(413)	14,003	12,635
01267	Williamstown	(413)	8,238	8,220
01887	Wilmington	(978)	21,472	17,651
01475	Winchendon	(978)	10,104	8,805
01890	Winchester	(781)	21,181	20,267
02152	Winthrop	(617)	17,069	18,127
*01801	Woburn	(781)	37,147	35,943
*01613	Worcester	(508)	175,898	169,759
*02093	Wrentham	(508)	11,093	9,006
*02675	Yarmouth	(508)	24,621	21,174
02675	Yarmouth Port (c)	(508)	5,395	4,271

Michigan

Area code (947) overlays area code (248). See introductory note.

ZIP	Place	Area Code	2005	1990
49221	Adrian	(517)	21,784	22,097
49224	Albion	(517)	9,348	10,066
49401	Allendale (c)	(616)	11,555	6,950
*48101	Allen Park	(313)	28,083	31,092
*48801	Alma	(989)	9,260	9,034
49707	Alpena	(989)	10,792	11,354
*48106	Ann Arbor	(734)	113,271	109,608
*48321	Auburn Hills	(248)	21,011	17,076
*49016	Battle Creek	(269)	53,202	53,516
*48707	Bay City	(989)	34,879	38,936
48505	Beecher (c)	(810)	12,793	14,465
*48809	Belding	(616)	5,895	5,969
*49022	Benton Harbor	(269)	10,749	12,818
49022	Benton Heights (c)	(269)	5,458	5,465
48072	Berkley	(248)	15,089	16,960
48025	Beverly Hills	(248)	10,086	10,610
49307	Big Rapids	(231)	10,704	12,603
*48012	Birmingham	(248)	19,081	19,997
*48301	Bloomfield (c)	(248)	43,021	42,137
48722	Bridgeport (c)	(989)	7,849	8,569
*48116	Brighton	(810)	7,139	5,686
48601	Buena Vista (c)	(989)	7,845	8,196
*48509	Burton	(810)	30,916	27,437
49601	Cadillac	(231)	10,167	10,104
*48184	Canton (c)	(734)	76,366	57,047
48724	Carrollton (c)	(989)	6,602	6,521
48015	Center Line	(586)	8,308	9,026
48813	Charlotte	(517)	9,069	8,083
49721	Cheboygan	(231)	5,191	4,997
*48017	Clawson	(248)	12,337	13,874
*48046	Clinton (c)	(517)	95,648	85,866
49036	Coldwater	(517)	10,783	9,607
49321	Comstock Park (c)	(616)	10,674	6,530
49508	Cutlerville (c)	(616)	15,114	11,228
48423	Davison	(810)	5,372	5,693
*48120	Dearborn	(313)	94,090	89,286
*48127	Dearborn Heights	(313)	56,176	60,838
*48231	Detroit	(313)	886,671	1,027,974
49047	Dowagiac	(269)	5,955	6,418
*49506	East Grand Rapids	(616)	10,384	10,807
*48826	East Lansing	(517)	46,419	50,677
48021	Eastpointe	(586)	33,180	35,283
49001	Eastwood (c)	(269)	6,265	6,340
48827	Eaton Rapids	(517)	5,266	4,695
48229	Ecorse	(313)	10,757	12,180
49829	Escanaba	(906)	12,679	13,659
49022	Fair Plain (c)	(269)	7,828	8,051
*48333	Farmington	(248)	10,035	10,170
*48333	Farmington Hills	(248)	80,223	74,614
48430	Fenton	(810)	11,946	8,434
48220	Ferndale	(248)	21,460	25,084
48134	Flat Rock	(734)	9,560	7,290
*48501	Flint	(810)	118,551	140,925
48433	Flushing	(810)	8,110	8,542
49506	Forest Hills (c)	(616)	20,942	16,690
48026	Fraser	(586)	15,095	13,899
48623	Freeland (c)	(989)	5,147	1,421
*48135	Garden City	(734)	28,960	31,846
48173	Gibraltar	(734)	5,191	4,297
49837	Gladstone	(906)	5,255	4,565
48439	Grand Blanc	(810)	7,898	7,760
49417	Grand Haven	(616)	10,586	11,951

ZIP	Place	Area Code	2005	1990
48837	Grand Ledge	(517)	7,768	7,562
*49501	Grand Rapids	(616)	193,780	189,126
*49418	Grandville	(616)	16,711	15,624
48838	Greenville	(616)	8,306	8,101
48138	Grosse Ile (c)	(734)	10,894	9,781
*48230	Grosse Pointe	(313)	5,426	5,681
48230	Grosse Pointe Farms	(313)	9,325	10,092
48230	Grosse Pointe Park	(313)	11,905	12,857
48230	Grosse Pointe Woods	(313)	16,317	17,715
*48212	Hamtramck	(313)	21,994	18,372
48225	Harper Woods	(313)	13,621	14,903
48625	Harrison (c)	(989)	24,461	24,685
48840	Haslett (c)	(517)	11,283	10,230
49058	Hastings	(269)	7,166	6,549
48030	Hazel Park	(248)	18,391	20,051
48203	Highland Park	(313)	15,430	20,121
49242	Hillsdale	(517)	7,904	8,175
*49423	Holland	(616)	34,429	30,745
48442	Holly	(248)	6,375	5,595
48842	Holt (c)	(517)	11,315	11,744
*49931	Houghton	(906)	7,076	7,498
*48844	Howell	(517)	9,757	8,147
49426	Hudsonville	(616)	7,052	6,170
48070	Huntington Woods	(248)	5,928	6,419
48141	Inkster	(313)/(734)	28,870	30,772
48846	Ionia	(616)	12,336	10,349
*49801	Iron Mountain	(906)	8,173	8,525
49938	Ironwood	(906)	5,728	6,849
*49849	Ishpeming	(906)	6,507	7,200
*49204	Jackson	(517)	34,879	37,425
*49428	Jenison (c)	(616)	17,211	17,882
49001	Kalamazoo	(269)	72,700	80,277
*49518	Kentwood	(616)	46,491	37,826
49802	Kingsford	(906)	5,565	5,480
48144	Lambertville (c)	(734)	9,299	7,860
*48901	Lansing	(517)	115,518	127,321
48446	Lapeer	(810)	9,370	7,759
48146	Lincoln Park	(313)	38,237	41,832
*48150	Livonia	(734)	97,977	100,850
49431	Ludington	(231)	8,292	8,507
48071	Madison Heights	(248)	30,251	32,196
49660	Manistee	(231)	6,656	6,734
49855	Marquette	(906)	20,581	21,977
*49068	Marshall	(269)	7,363	6,941
48040	Marysville	(810)	10,042	8,515
48854	Mason	(517)	7,985	6,768
48122	Melvindale	(313)	10,612	11,216
49858	Menominee	(906)	8,753	9,398
*48640	Midland	(989)	41,760	38,053
48160	Milan	(734)	5,376	4,040
*48381	Milford	(248)	6,587	5,500
*48161	Monroe	(734)	21,791	22,902
*48046	Mount Clemens	(586)	17,053	18,405
*48804	Mount Pleasant	(989)	26,253	23,299
*49440	Muskegon	(231)	39,919	39,809
49444	Muskegon Heights	(231)	11,821	13,176
*48047	New Baltimore	(586)	11,165	5,798
*49120	Niles	(269)	11,738	12,458
49505	Northview (c)	(616)	14,730	13,712
*48167	Northville	(248)	6,311	6,226
*49441	Norton Shores	(231)	23,479	21,755
*48376	Novi	(248)	53,115	32,998
48237	Oak Park	(248)	31,194	30,468
*48805	Okemos (c)	(517)	22,805	20,216
*48867	Owosso	(989)	15,422	16,322
49770	Petoskey	(231)	6,198	6,056
48170	Plymouth	(734)	9,100	9,560
48170	Plymouth Township (c)	(734)	27,798	23,646
*48343	Pontiac	(248)	67,331	71,136
*49081	Portage	(269)	45,277	41,042
*48061	Port Huron	(810)	31,501	33,694
*48239	Redford (c)	(313)	51,622	54,387
48062	Richmond	(586)	5,607	4,028
48218	River Rouge	(313)	9,202	11,314
*48192	Riverview	(734)	12,744	13,894
*48308	Rochester	(248)	11,209	7,130
*48306	Rochester Hills	(248)	69,995	61,766
49341	Rockford	(616)	5,062	3,750
48174	Romulus	(313)/(734)	23,853	22,897
48066	Roseville	(586)	47,708	51,412
*48068	Royal Oak	(248)	58,299	65,410
*48605	Saginaw	(989)	58,361	69,512
48604	Saginaw Township North (c)	(989)	24,994	23,018
48603	Saginaw Township South (c)	(989)	13,801	13,987
48079	Saint Clair	(810)	5,933	5,116
*48080	Saint Clair Shores	(313)	61,561	68,107
48879	Saint Johns	(989)	7,436	7,392
49085	Saint Joseph	(269)	8,675	9,214
48880	Saint Louis	(989)	6,513	3,828
48176	Saline	(734)	8,826	6,663
*49783	Sault Sainte Marie	(906)	14,318	14,689
49455	Shelby (c)	(231)	65,159	48,655
48609	Shields (c)	(989)	6,590	6,634
*48037	Southfield	(248)	76,818	75,727
48195	Southgate	(734)	29,572	30,771
49090	South Haven	(269)	5,157	5,563
48178	South Lyon	(248)	11,040	6,479
48161	South Monroe (c)	(734)	6,370	5,266
49015	Springfield	(269)	5,203	5,582
*48311	Sterling Heights	(586)	128,034	117,810

ZIP	Place	Area Code	2005	1990
49091	Sturgis	(269)	11,134	10,130
48473	Swartz Creek	(810)	5,341	4,851
48180	Taylor	(313)/(734)	64,962	70,811
49286	Tecumseh	(517)	8,863	7,462
48182	Temperance (c)	(734)	7,757	6,542
49093	Three Rivers	(269)	7,342	7,464
*49684	Traverse City	(231)	14,513	15,155
48183	Trenton	(734)	19,311	20,586
*48099	Troy	(248)	81,168	72,884
49534	Walker	(616)	23,420	17,279
*48390	Walled Lake	(248)	6,919	6,278
*48090	Warren	(586)	135,311	144,864
*48329	Waterford (c)	(248)	73,150	66,692
48917	Waverly (c)	(517)	16,194	15,614
48184	Wayne	(734)	18,589	19,899
*48323	West Bloomfield Township (c)	(248)	64,862	54,843
*48185	Westland	(313)/(734)	85,623	84,724
49009	Westwood (c)	(269)	9,122	8,957
48189	Whitmore Lake (c)	(734)	6,574	3,251
48393	Wixom	(248)	13,384	8,550
48183	Woodhaven	(734)	13,354	11,631
*48192	Wyandotte	(734)	26,940	30,938
*49509	Wyoming	(616)	70,122	63,891
*48197	Ypsilanti	(734)	21,832	24,846
49464	Zeeland	(616)	5,532	5,417

Minnesota

ZIP	Place	Area Code	2005	1990
56007	Albert Lea	(507)	17,915	18,310
55301	Albertville	(763)	5,733	1,252
56308	Alexandria	(320)	10,603	8,029
*55304	Andover	(763)	29,745	15,216
*55303	Anoka	(612)/(763)	17,608	17,192
55124	Apple Valley	(952)	49,856	34,598
*55112	Arden Hills	(651)	9,780	9,199
55912	Austin	(507)	23,469	21,926
*56425	Baxter	(218)	7,400	3,695
*56601	Bemidji	(218)	13,296	11,165
55309	Big Lake	(763)	8,804	3,113
*55014	Blaine	(651)/(763)	54,084	38,975
*55420	Bloomington	(952)	81,164	86,335
*56401	Brainerd	(218)	13,684	12,353
*55429	Brooklyn Center	(763)	27,551	28,887
*55443	Brooklyn Park	(763)	68,550	56,381
55313	Buffalo	(763)	13,290	7,302
*55337	Burnsville	(651)/(952)	59,159	51,288
55008	Cambridge	(763)	7,198	5,094
55316	Champlin	(763)	23,302	16,849
55317	Chanhassen	(952)	23,229	11,736
55318	Chaska	(952)	22,820	11,339
55014	Circle Pines	(763)/(651)	5,356	4,704
55720	Cloquet	(218)	11,476	10,885
55421	Columbia Heights	(612)/(763)	18,110	18,910
*55433	Coon Rapids	(763)	62,417	52,978
*55340	Corcoran	(763)	5,683	5,199
55016	Cottage Grove	(651)	32,553	22,935
56716	Crookston	(218)	7,929	8,119
*55428	Crystal	(763)	21,645	23,788
*56501	Detroit Lakes	(218)	7,914	7,141
*55806	Duluth	(218)	84,896	85,493
*55121	Eagan	(651)/(952)	63,665	47,409
*55005	East Bethel	(763)	12,013	8,050
56721	East Grand Forks	(218)	7,734	8,658
*55344	Eden Prairie	(612)/(952)	60,649	39,311
*55424	Edina	(952)	45,567	46,075
55330	Elk River	(763)	21,329	11,143
*56031	Fairmont	(507)	10,505	11,265
*55113	Falcon Heights	(651)	5,469	5,380
55021	Faribault	(507)	22,047	17,085
55024	Farmington	(651)/(952)	17,740	5,940
*56537	Fergus Falls	(218)	13,722	12,362
55025	Forest Lake	(651)	17,353	5,833
*55432	Fridley	(763)	26,515	28,335
55336	Glencoe	(320)	5,553	4,648
*55427	Golden Valley	(763)	20,003	20,971
*55744	Grand Rapids	(218)	8,277	7,976
*55304	Ham Lake	(763)	14,774	8,924
55033	Hastings	(651)	20,910	15,478
*55810	Hermantown	(218)	8,861	6,761
*55746	Hibbing	(218)	16,509	18,046
*55343	Hopkins	(952)	16,825	16,529
55038	Hugo	(651)	9,683	4,417
55350	Hutchinson	(320)	13,721	11,459
56649	International Falls	(218)	6,332	8,325
*55076	Inver Grove Heights	(651)	33,182	22,477
55040	Isanti	(763)	5,167	1,128
55352	Jordan	(952)	5,120	3,514
55944	Kasson	(507)	5,333	3,514
55947	La Crescent	(507)	5,095	4,311
55041	Lake City	(651)	5,282	4,490
55042	Lake Elmo	(651)	7,615	5,900
*55044	Lakeville	(952)	51,484	24,854
*55014	Lino Lakes	(651)	19,424	8,807
55355	Litchfield	(320)	6,658	6,041
*55117	Little Canada	(651)	9,543	8,971
56345	Little Falls	(320)	8,139	7,371
55115	Mahtomedi	(651)	8,017	5,633
*56001	Mankato	(507)	34,976	31,459
*55311	Maple Grove	(763)	59,756	38,736

ZIP	Place	Area Code	2005	1990
*55109	Maplewood	(651)	35,085	30,954
56258	Marshall	(507)	12,291	12,023
*55118	Mendota Heights	(651)	11,338	9,388
*55440	Minneapolis	(612)/(763)/(952)	372,811	368,383
*55345	Minnetonka	(952)	50,045	48,370
55359	Minnetrista	(952)	5,501	3,439
56265	Montevideo	(320)	5,365	5,499
*55362	Monticello	(763)	10,882	5,045
*56560	Moorhead	(218)	34,081	32,295
56267	Morris	(320)	5,091	5,613
55364	Mound	(952)	9,416	9,634
55112	Mounds View	(763)	12,106	12,541
55112	New Brighton	(651)	20,738	22,207
*54427	New Hope	(763)	20,296	21,853
56071	New Prague	(952)	6,439	3,575
56073	New Ulm	(507)	13,619	13,132
55056	North Branch	(651)/(763)	10,234	4,267
55057	Northfield	(507)	18,671	14,684
*56002	North Mankato	(507)	12,078	10,662
55109	North Saint Paul	(651)	11,355	12,376
*55128	Oakdale	(651)	27,389	18,377
55011	Oak Grove	(763)	7,944	5,488
*55323	Orono	(952)	7,756	7,285
*55330	Otsego	(763)	10,800	5,219
55060	Owatonna	(507)	24,133	19,386
*55446	Plymouth	(763)	69,701	50,889
55372	Prior Lake	(952)	22,168	11,482
55303	Ramsey	(763)	22,074	12,408
55066	Red Wing	(651)	15,799	15,134
56283	Redwood Falls	(507)	5,272	4,859
55423	Richfield	(612)	33,497	35,710
55422	Robbinsdale	(763)	13,331	14,396
*55901	Rochester	(507)	94,950	70,729
55374	Rogers	(763)	6,042	722
55068	Rosemount	(651)/(952)	19,311	8,622
*55113	Roseville	(651)	32,079	33,485
*55418	Saint Anthony	(612)	7,560	7,727
*56301	Saint Cloud	(320)	65,792	48,812
55070	Saint Francis	(763)	7,101	2,479
*56374	Saint Joseph	(320)	5,437	3,294
*55426	Saint Louis Park	(952)	43,296	43,787
55376	Saint Michael	(763)	14,319	2,506
*55101	Saint Paul	(651)	275,150	272,235
55071	Saint Paul Park	(651)	5,193	4,965
56082	Saint Peter	(507)	10,529	9,481
56377	Sartell	(320)	12,668	5,409
56379	Sauk Rapids	(320)	11,523	7,823
55378	Savage	(952)	26,581	9,906
*55379	Shakopee	(612)	31,233	11,739
55126	Shoreview	(651)	26,855	24,587
*55331	Shorewood	(952)	7,452	5,913
*55075	South Saint Paul	(651)	19,362	20,197
55432	Spring Lake Park	(763)	6,699	6,532
55976	Stewartville	(507)	5,494	4,520
*55082	Stillwater	(651)	17,378	13,882
*56701	Thief River Falls	(218)	8,377	8,010
*55127	Vadnais Heights	(651)	12,586	11,041
55386	Victoria	(952)	5,702	2,354
*55792	Virginia	(218)	8,666	9,432
55387	Waconia	(952)	8,692	3,498
*56387	Waite Park	(320)	6,832	5,020
56093	Waseca	(507)	9,445	8,385
*55118	West Saint Paul	(651)	18,955	19,248
*55110	White Bear Lake	(651)	23,733	24,622
56201	Willmar	(320)	18,183	17,531
*55987	Winona	(507)	26,587	25,435
*55125	Woodbury	(651)	52,479	20,075
56187	Worthington	(507)	11,092	9,977

Mississippi

Area code (769) overlays area code (601). See introductory note.

ZIP	Place	Area Code	2005	1990
39730	Aberdeen	(662)	6,227	6,837
38821	Amory	(662)	7,415	7,093
38606	Batesville	(662)	7,708	6,403
*39520	Bay Saint Louis	(228)	8,317	8,063
*39530	Biloxi	(228)	50,209	46,319
38829	Booneville	(662)	8,585	7,955
*39042	Brandon	(601)	19,390	11,089
*39601	Brookhaven	(601)	9,907	10,243
39272	Byram (c)	(601)	7,386	—
39046	Canton	(601)	12,507	11,723
*38614	Clarksdale	(662)	19,297	21,180
*38732	Cleveland	(662)	12,818	15,384
*39056	Clinton	(601)	26,017	21,847
39429	Columbia	(601)	6,408	6,815
*39701	Columbus	(662)	24,425	23,799
*38834	Corinth	(662)	14,256	11,820
39059	Crystal Springs	(601)	5,913	5,643
39525	Diamondhead (c)	(228)	5,912	2,661
39540	D'Iberville	(228)	7,900	6,566
39232	Flowood	(601)	6,762	2,770
39074	Forest	(601)	6,029	5,062
39553	Gautier	(228)	16,846	10,088
*38701	Greenville	(662)	38,724	45,226
*38930	Greenwood	(662)	17,344	18,906
*38901	Grenada	(662)	14,569	10,864
39564	Gulf Hills (c)	(228)	5,900	5,004
*39501	Gulfport	(228)	72,464	64,045

ZIP	Place	Area Code	2005	1990
*39401	Hattiesburg	(601)	47,176	45,325
38632	Hernando	(662)	9,890	3,125
*38635	Holly Springs	(662)	8,014	7,261
38637	Horn Lake	(662)	22,151	9,069
*38751	Indianola	(662)	11,321	11,809
*39205	Jackson	(601)	177,977	202,062
39090	Kosciusko	(662)	7,334	6,986
*39440	Laurel	(601)	18,298	18,827
38756	Leland	(662)	5,157	6,366
39560	Long Beach	(228)	17,283	15,804
39339	Louisville	(662)	6,797	7,165
*39648	McComb	(601)	13,244	11,797
*39110	Madison	(601)	16,737	7,471
*39302	Meridian	(601)	38,605	41,036
*39563	Moss Point	(228)	15,125	17,837
*39120	Natchez	(601)	16,966	19,460
38652	New Albany	(662)	8,009	6,775
*39564	Ocean Springs	(228)	17,783	15,221
38654	Olive Branch	(662)	27,964	3,567
38655	Oxford	(662)	13,618	10,026
*39567	Pascagoula	(228)	25,173	25,899
*39571	Pass Christian	(228)	6,851	5,557
*39288	Pearl	(601)	23,111	19,588
39465	Petal	(601)	10,088	7,883
39350	Philadelphia	(601)	7,618	6,758
39466	Picayune	(601)	10,830	10,633
38863	Pontotoc	(662)	5,784	4,570
39218	Richland	(601)	7,051	4,014
*39157	Ridgeland	(601)	21,236	11,714
38663	Ripley	(662)	5,633	5,371
39532	Saint Martin (c)	(228)	*6,676*	6,349
38668	Senatobia	(601)	6,869	4,772
*38671	Southaven	(662)	38,840	18,705
*39759	Starkville	(662)	22,131	18,458
*38801	Tupelo	(662)	35,673	30,685
*39180	Vicksburg	(601)	25,752	26,886
39576	Waveland	(228)	7,227	5,369
39367	Waynesboro	(601)	5,719	5,143
39402	West Hattiesburg (c)	(601)	*6,305*	5,450
39773	West Point	(662)	11,582	8,489
39194	Yazoo City	(662)	11,879	12,427

Missouri

ZIP	Place	Area Code	2005	1990
63123	Affton (c)	(314)	*20,535*	21,106
63010	Arnold	(636)	20,413	18,828
65605	Aurora	(417)	7,307	6,459
*63011	Ballwin	(636)	30,481	27,054
63012	Barnhart (c)	(314)	*6,108*	4,911
63137	Bellefontaine Neighbors	(314)	10,616	10,918
64012	Belton	(816)	24,140	18,145
*63134	Berkeley	(314)	9,631	12,250
63033	Black Jack	(314)	6,920	6,131
*64015	Blue Springs	(816)	53,099	40,103
*65613	Bolivar	(417)	10,179	6,845
63628	Bonne Terre	(573)	6,520	3,871
65233	Boonville	(660)	8,669	7,095
63334	Bowling Green	(573)	5,185	3,046
*65615	Branson	(417)	7,010	3,706
63144	Brentwood	(314)	7,365	8,150
*63044	Bridgeton	(314)	15,259	17,732
64429	Cameron	(816)	9,141	6,782
*63701	Cape Girardeau	(573)	36,204	34,475
64834	Carl Junction	(417)	6,483	4,123
64836	Carthage	(417)	13,096	10,747
*63830	Caruthersville	(573)	6,450	7,389
63834	Charleston	(573)	5,129	5,131
*63017	Chesterfield	(636)	47,020	42,325
64601	Chillicothe	(660)	8,686	8,799
*63105	Clayton	(314)	16,061	13,926
64735	Clinton	(660)	9,414	8,703
*65201	Columbia	(573)	91,814	69,133
*63128	Concord (c)	(314)	*16,689*	19,859
63126	Crestwood	(314)	11,691	11,229
63141	Creve Coeur	(314)	16,975	12,289
*63366	Dardenne Prairie	(636)	6,984	1,769
*63135	Dellwood	(314)	5,027	5,245
63020	De Soto	(636)	6,552	5,993
*63131	Des Peres	(636)	8,619	8,395
63601	Desloge	(573)	5,143	4,150
63841	Dexter	(573)	7,596	7,506
*63011	Ellisville	(636)	9,353	7,183
63025	Eureka	(636)	8,957	4,683
64024	Excelsior Springs	(816)	11,472	10,373
63640	Farmington	(573)	15,176	11,596
*63135	Ferguson	(314)	21,458	22,290
63028	Festus	(636)	10,905	8,105
*63033	Florissant	(314)	51,812	51,038
65473	Fort Leonard Wood (c)	(573)	*13,666*	15,863
65251	Fulton	(573)	12,101	10,033
*64118	Gladstone	(816)	27,306	26,243
63137	Glasgow Village (c)	(573)	*5,234*	5,199
63122	Glendale	(314)	5,595	5,945
64029	Grain Valley	(816)	8,644	1,898
64030	Grandview	(816)	24,549	24,973
63401	Hannibal	(573)	17,649	18,004
64701	Harrisonville	(816)	9,790	7,696
*63042	Hazelwood	(314)	25,535	15,512
*64050	Independence	(816)	110,208	112,301
63755	Jackson	(573)	12,982	9,256
*65101	Jefferson City	(573)	39,062	35,517
63136	Jennings	(314)	14,926	15,841
*64801	Joplin	(417)	47,183	41,175
*64108	Kansas City	(816)	444,965	434,829
64060	Kearney	(816)	7,399	1,790
63857	Kennett	(573)	11,028	10,941
63501	Kirksville	(660)	16,986	17,152
63122	Kirkwood	(314)	27,038	28,318
63124	Ladue (St. Louis Co.)	(314)	8,269	8,795
63367	Lake Saint Louis	(636)	13,281	7,536
65536	Lebanon	(417)	13,336	9,983
*64063	Lee's Summit	(816)	80,338	46,418
63125	Lemay (c)	(314)	*17,215*	18,005
*64068	Liberty	(816)	29,042	20,459
63552	Macon	(660)	5,428	5,571
*63011	Manchester	(636)	18,970	6,506
63143	Maplewood	(314)	8,808	9,962
65340	Marshall	(660)	12,403	12,711
65706	Marshfield	(417)	6,763	4,374
63043	Maryland Heights	(314)	26,544	25,440
64468	Maryville	(816)	10,567	10,663
63129	Mehlville (c)	(314)	*28,822*	27,557
65265	Mexico	(573)	11,018	11,290
65270	Moberly	(660)	13,921	12,839
65708	Monett	(417)	8,349	6,529
63026	Murphy (c)	(636)	*9,048*	9,342
*64850	Neosho	(417)	11,130	9,254
64772	Nevada	(417)	8,457	8,597
65714	Nixa	(417)	15,925	4,893
63121	Normandy	(314)	5,032	4,480
64116	North Kansas	(816)	5,388	4,130
64075	Oak Grove	(816)	6,763	4,565
63129	Oakville (c)	(314)	*35,309*	31,750
63366	O'Fallon	(636)	69,694	17,427
63132	Olivette	(314)	7,455	7,573
63114	Overland	(314)	16,082	17,987
65721	Ozark	(417)	15,265	4,401
*63069	Pacific	(636)	7,098	4,350
*63601	Park Hills	(573)	8,525	7,866
64152	Parkville	(816)	5,116	2,402
*63775	Perryville	(573)	7,935	6,933
64080	Pleasant Hill	(816)	6,747	3,827
*63901	Poplar Bluff	(573)	16,912	16,841
64083	Raymore	(816)	15,530	5,592
*64133	Raytown	(816)	28,923	30,601
65738	Republic	(417)	10,637	6,290
64085	Richmond	(816)	6,075	5,738
63117	Richmond Heights	(314)	9,309	10,448
*65401	Rolla	(573)	17,717	14,090
63074	Saint Ann	(314)	13,092	14,449
*63301	Saint Charles	(636)	62,304	50,634
63114	Saint John	(314)	6,558	7,502
*64501	Saint Joseph	(816)	72,661	71,852
*63166	Saint Louis	(314)	344,362	396,685
*63376	Saint Peters	(636)	54,209	40,660
*63126	Sappington (c)	(314)	*7,287*	10,917
*65301	Sedalia	(660)	20,430	19,800
63119	Shrewsbury	(314)	6,393	6,416
63801	Sikeston	(573)	17,180	17,641
64089	Smithville	(816)	7,118	2,525
63138	Spanish Lake (c)	(314)	*21,337*	20,322
*65801	Springfield	(417)	150,298	140,494
63080	Sullivan	(573)	6,613	5,661
63127	Sunset Hills	(314)	8,374	4,915
63011	Town and Country	(314)	10,807	10,944
64683	Trenton	(660)	6,121	6,129
63379	Troy	(314)	9,862	3,811
63084	Union	(636)	8,897	6,196
63130	University City	(314)	37,170	40,087
63088	Valley Park	(636)	6,405	4,165
64093	Warrensburg	(660)	17,769	15,244
63383	Warrenton	(636)	6,612	3,564
63090	Washington	(636)	14,136	11,367
64870	Webb City	(417)	10,764	7,538
63119	Webster Groves	(314)	22,896	22,992
*63304	Weldon Spring	(636)	5,361	1,470
63385	Wentzville	(636)	17,988	4,640
*65775	West Plains	(417)	11,348	9,214
*63011	Wildwood	(314)	34,831	16,742

Montana (406)

ZIP	Place	2005	1990
59711	Anaconda-Deer Lodge County	8,948	10,356
59714	Belgrade	7,033	3,422
*59101	Billings	98,721	81,125
*59718	Bozeman	33,535	22,660
*59701	Butte	32,282	33,336
59901	Evergreen (c)	*6,215*	4,109
*59401	Great Falls	56,338	55,125
59501	Havre	9,390	10,201
*59601	Helena	27,383	24,609
59635	Helena Valley Southeast (c)	*7,141*	4,601
59602	Helena Valley West Central (c)	6,983	6,327
*59901	Kalispell	18,480	11,917
59044	Laurel	6,342	5,686
59457	Lewistown	6,099	6,097
59047	Livingston	7,146	6,701
59301	Miles City	8,162	8,461

ZIP	Place	2005	1990
*59801	Missoula	62,923	42,918
59801	Orchard Homes (c)	5,199	10,317
59937	Whitefish	7,067	4,368

Nebraska

ZIP	Place	Area Code	2005	1990
69301	Alliance	(308)	8,331	9,765
68310	Beatrice	(402)	12,890	12,352
*68108	Bellevue	(402)	47,334	39,240
*68008	Blair	(402)	7,765	6,860
*69337	Chadron	(308)	5,320	5,588
68108	Chalco (c)	(402)	10,736	7,337
*68601	Columbus	(402)	20,909	19,480
68333	Crete	(402)	6,308	4,841
68022	Elkhorn	(402)	8,192	1,398
*68025	Fremont	(402)	25,314	23,680
69341	Gering	(308)	7,767	7,946
*68802	Grand Island	(308)	44,546	39,487
*68901	Hastings	(402)	25,437	22,837
*68949	Holdrege	(308)	5,349	5,671
*68847	Kearney	(308)	28,958	24,396
68128	La Vista	(402)	15,692	9,992
68850	Lexington	(308)	10,085	6,600
*68501	Lincoln	(402)	239,213	191,972
69001	McCook	(308)	7,680	8,112
68410	Nebraska City	(402)	7,035	6,547
*68701	Norfolk	(402)	23,946	21,476
*69101	North Platte	(308)	24,324	22,605
68113	Offutt AFB (c)	(402)	8,901	—
*68005	Omaha	(402)	414,521	344,463
*68046	Papillion	(402)	20,431	13,892
68048	Plattsmouth	(402)	7,023	6,415
68127	Ralston	(402)	6,193	6,236
68661	Schuyler	(402)	5,327	4,052
*69361	Scottsbluff	(308)	14,814	13,711
68434	Seward	(402)	6,776	5,641
*69162	Sidney	(308)	6,442	5,959
68776	South Sioux City	(402)	11,979	9,677
68787	Wayne	(402)	5,163	5,142
68467	York	(402)	7,888	7,940

Nevada

ZIP	Place	Area Code	2005	1990
*89005	Boulder City	(702)	15,177	12,567
*89701	Carson City	(775)	56,062	40,443
89403	Dayton (c)	(775)	5,907	2,217
*89801	Elko	(775)	16,685	14,836
89139	Enterprise (c)	(702)	14,676	6,412
*89406	Fallon	(775)	8,103	6,430
89408	Fernley	(775)	11,342	5,164
89410	Gardnerville Ranchos (c)	(775)	11,054	7,455
*89015	Henderson	(702)	232,146	64,948
*89450	Incline Village-Crystal Bay (c)	(775)	9,952	7,119
*89125	Las Vegas	(702)	545,147	258,877
*89028	Laughlin (c)	(702)	7,076	4,791
89506	Lemmon Valley-Golden Valley(c)	(702)	6,855	—
*89024	Mesquite	(702)	13,523	1,871
89040	Moapa Valley (c)	(702)	5,784	3,444
89191	Nellis AFB (c)	(702)	8,896	8,377
*89030	North Las Vegas	(702)	176,635	47,849
*89041	Pahrump (c)	(775)	24,631	7,424
89109	Paradise (c)	(702)	186,070	124,682
*89501	Reno	(775)	203,550	134,230
89436	Spanish Springs (c)	(775)	9,018	—
*89431	Sparks	(775)	82,051	53,367
89815	Spring Creek (c)	(702)	10,548	5,866
89147	Spring Valley (c)	(702)	117,390	51,726
89110	Sunrise Manor (c)	(702)	156,120	95,362
89433	Sun Valley (c)	(775)	19,461	11,391
89101	Winchester (c)	(702)	26,958	23,365
89445	Winnemucca City	(775)	7,726	6,134

New Hampshire (603)
See introductory note.

ZIP	Place	2005	1990
03031	Amherst	11,614	9,068
03811	Atkinson	6,613	5,188
03825	Barrington	8,162	6,164
03110	Bedford	20,732	12,563
03220	Belmont	7,322	5,796
03570	Berlin	10,097	11,824
03304	Bow	8,020	5,500
03743	Claremont	13,388	13,902
*03301	Concord	42,336	36,006
03818	Conway	9,208	7,940
03038	Derry (c)	22,661	20,446
03038	Derry	34,290	29,603
*03820	Dover	28,486	25,042
03824	Durham (c)	12,904	9,236
03824	Durham	13,040	11,818
03042	Epping	6,087	5,162
03833	Exeter (c)	9,759	9,556
03833	Exeter	14,704	12,481
03835	Farmington	6,439	5,739
03235	Franklin	8,763	8,304
03246	Gilford	7,510	5,867
03045	Goffstown	17,687	14,621
03841	Hampstead	8,739	6,732
*03842	Hampton (c)	9,126	7,989
*03842	Hampton	15,450	12,278
03755	Hanover Compact (c)	8,162	6,538
03755	Hanover	11,156	9,212
03244	Hillsborough	5,402	4,698
03049	Hollis	7,740	5,705
03106	Hooksett	13,279	9,002
03229	Hopkinton	5,620	4,806
03051	Hudson (c)	7,814	7,626
03051	Hudson	24,568	19,530
03452	Jaffrey	5,711	5,361
*03431	Keene	22,778	22,430
03848	Kingston	6,240	5,591
*03246	Laconia	17,060	15,743
*03766	Lebanon	12,606	12,183
03052	Litchfield	8,277	5,516
03561	Littleton	6,139	5,827
03053	Londonderry (c)	11,417	10,114
03053	Londonderry	24,837	19,781
*03103	Manchester	109,691	99,332
03253	Meredith	6,615	4,837
03054	Merrimack	26,652	22,156
03055	Milford (c)	8,293	8,015
03055	Milford	14,862	11,795
*03060	Nashua	87,321	79,662
03857	Newmarket (c)	5,124	4,917
03857	Newmarket	9,175	7,157
03773	Newport	6,561	6,110
03076	Pelham	12,474	9,408
03275	Pembroke	7,366	6,561
03458	Peterborough	6,073	5,239
03102	Pinardville (c)	5,779	4,654
03865	Plaistow	7,769	7,316
03264	Plymouth	6,204	5,811
*03801	Portsmouth	20,674	25,925
03077	Raymond	10,122	8,713
03461	Rindge	6,302	4,941
*03867	Rochester	30,004	26,630
03870	Rye	5,241	—
03079	Salem	29,558	25,746
03873	Sandown	5,725	—
03874	Seabrook	8,434	6,503
03878	Somersworth	11,720	11,249
03106	South Hooksett (c)	5,282	3,638
03885	Stratham	6,892	4,955
03275	Suncook (c)	5,362	5,214
03446	Swanzey	7,313	6,236
03281	Weare	8,730	6,193
03087	Windham	12,721	9,000
03894	Wolfeboro	6,660	4,807

New Jersey
Area code (551) overlays area code (201). Area code (848) overlays (732). Area code (862) overlays (973). See introductory note.

ZIP	Place	Area Code	2005	1990
*08201	Absecon	(609)	7,989	7,298
07401	Allendale	(201)	6,754	5,900
07712	Asbury Park	(732)	16,624	16,799
08034	Ashland (c)	(856)	8,375	
*08401	Atlantic City	(609)	40,368	37,986
08106	Audubon	(856)	9,047	9,205
07001	Avenel (c)	(732)	17,552	15,504
08034	Barclay-Kingston (c)	(856)	10,728	
08007	Barrington	(856)	7,050	6,792
07002	Bayonne	(201)	59,987	61,464
08722	Beachwood	(732)	10,738	9,324
07109	Belleville (c)	(973)	35,928	34,213
*08031	Bellmawr	(856)	11,159	12,603
*07719	Belmar	(732)	5,962	5,877
07621	Bergenfield	(201)	26,056	24,458
07922	Berkeley Heights (c)	(908)	13,407	11,980
08009	Berlin	(856)	7,844	5,672
07924	Bernardsville	(908)	7,612	6,597
07403	Bloomingdale	(973)	7,654	7,530
07603	Bogota	(201)	8,150	7,824
07005	Boonton	(973)	8,555	8,343
08805	Bound Brook	(732)	10,168	9,487
08302	Bridgeton	(856)	23,959	18,942
08203	Brigantine	(609)	12,861	11,354
08015	Browns Mills (c)	(609)	11,257	11,429
07828	Budd Lake (c)	(973)	8,100	7,272
08016	Burlington	(609)	9,791	9,835
07405	Butler	(973)	8,091	7,392
*07006	Caldwell	(973)	7,489	7,542
*08101	Camden	(856)	80,010	87,492
07072	Carlstadt	(201)	6,018	5,510
08069	Carney's Point (c)	(856)	6,914	8,443
07008	Carteret	(732)	21,460	19,025
07009	Cedar Grove (c)	(973)	12,300	12,053
07928	Chatham	(973)	8,439	8,007
08002	Cherry Hill Mall (c)	(856)	13,238	—
07066	Clark (c)	(732)/(908)	14,597	14,629
08312	Clayton	(856)	7,447	6,155
07010	Cliffside Park	(201)	23,035	20,393
*07015	Clifton	(973)	79,922	71,984
07624	Closter	(201)	8,669	8,094
08108	Collingswood	(856)	14,083	15,289
07067	Colonia (c)	(732)	17,811	18,238

ZIP	Place	Area Code	2005	1990
07016	Cranford (c)	(908)	22,578	22,633
07626	Cresskill	(201)	8,449	7,558
08759	Crestwood Village (c)	(732)	8,392	8,030
08810	Dayton (c)	(732)	6,235	4,321
*07627	Demarest	(201)	5,005	4,800
*07801	Dover	(973)	18,441	15,115
07628	Dumont	(201)	17,474	17,187
08812	Dunellen	(732)	6,994	6,528
08816	East Brunswick (c)	(732)	46,756	43,548
*07019	East Orange	(973)	68,190	73,552
07073	East Rutherford	(201)/(973)	8,960	7,902
*07724	Eatontown	(732)	14,088	13,800
08043	Echelon (c)	(856)	10,440	—
07020	Edgewater	(201)	9,646	5,001
*08818	Edison (c)	(732)/(908)	97,687	88,680
*07207	Elizabeth	(908)	125,809	110,002
*07407	Elmwood Park	(201)	18,905	17,623
07630	Emerson	(201)	7,334	6,930
*07631	Englewood	(201)	26,207	24,850
07632	Englewood Cliffs	(201)	5,738	5,634
08002	Erlton-Ellisburg (c)	(856)	8,168	—
08618	Ewing (c)	(609)	35,707	34,185
07004	Fairfield (Essex Co.) (c)	(973)	7,063	7,615
07704	Fair Haven	(732)	5,899	5,270
07410	Fair Lawn	(201)/(973)	31,408	30,548
07022	Fairview (Bergen Co.)	(201)	13,565	10,733
07023	Fanwood	(908)	7,228	7,115
08518	Florence-Roebling (c)	(609)	8,200	8,564
07932	Florham Park	(973)	12,626	8,521
08863	Fords (c)	(732)	15,032	14,392
08640	Fort Dix (c)	(609)	7,464	10,205
07024	Fort Lee	(201)	37,175	31,997
07416	Franklin (Sussex Co.)	(973)	5,233	4,977
07417	Franklin Lakes	(201)	11,302	9,873
07728	Freehold	(732)	11,439	10,742
07026	Garfield	(862)/(973)	29,772	26,727
08028	Glassboro	(856)	19,290	15,614
07028	Glen Ridge	(973)	7,020	7,076
07452	Glen Rock	(201)	11,457	10,883
*08030	Gloucester City	(856)	11,582	12,649
08053	Greentree (c)	(856)	11,536	—
07093	Guttenberg	(201)	10,885	8,268
*07602	Hackensack	(201)	43,735	37,049
07840	Hackettstown	(908)	9,375	8,120
08033	Haddonfield	(856)	11,591	11,633
08035	Haddon Heights	(856)	7,427	7,860
*07508	Haledon	(973)	8,398	6,951
08037	Hammonton	(609)	13,585	12,208
07029	Harrison	(973)	14,060	13,425
07604	Hasbrouck Heights	(201)	11,643	11,488
*07506	Hawthorne	(973)	18,268	17,084
07422	Highland Lake (c)	(973)	5,051	4,550
08904	Highland Park	(732)	14,268	13,279
08520	Hightstown	(609)	5,293	5,126
07642	Hillsdale	(201)	10,089	9,750
07205	Hillside (c)	(908)/(973)	21,747	21,044
07030	Hoboken	(201)	39,900	33,397
08753	Holiday City-Berkeley (c)	(732)	13,884	14,293
07843	Hopatcong	(973)	16,001	15,586
07111	Irvington (c)	(973)	60,695	59,774
08830	Iselin (c)	(732)	16,698	16,141
08831	Jamesburg	(732)	6,521	5,294
*07303	Jersey City	(201)	239,614	228,517
07734	Keansburg	(732)	10,619	11,069
*07032	Kearny	(201)/(973)	38,771	34,874
08824	Kendall Park (c)	(908)	9,006	7,127
07033	Kenilworth	(908)	7,743	7,574
07735	Keyport	(732)	7,505	7,586
07405	Kinnelon	(973)	9,631	8,470
07871	Lake Mohawk (c)	(973)	9,755	8,930
08701	Lakewood (c)	(732)	36,065	26,095
08879	Laurence Harbor (c)	(732)	6,227	6,361
*08733	Leisure Village West-Pine Lake Park (c)	(732)	11,085	10,139
07605	Leonia	(201)	8,853	8,365
07035	Lincoln Park	(973)	10,899	10,978
07738	Lincroft (c)	(732)	6,255	6,193
07036	Linden	(732)/(908)	40,014	36,701
08021	Lindenwold	(856)	17,265	18,734
08221	Linwood	(609)	7,398	6,866
07424	Little Falls (c)	(973)	10,855	11,294
07643	Little Ferry	(201)	10,775	9,989
07739	Little Silver	(732)	6,137	5,721
07039	Livingston (c)	(973)	27,391	26,609
07644	Lodi	(201)/(973)	24,310	22,355
07740	Long Branch	(732)	32,091	28,658
07071	Lyndhurst (c)	(201)	19,383	18,262
08641	McGuire AFB (c)	(609)	6,478	7,580
07940	Madison	(973)	15,918	15,850
08859	Madison Park (c)	(732)	6,929	7,490
08736	Manasquan	(732)	6,201	5,369
08835	Manville	(908)	10,404	10,567
07040	Maplewood (c)	(973)	23,868	21,756
08402	Margate City	(609)	8,666	8,431
08053	Marlton (c)	(856)	10,260	10,228
07747	Matawan	(732)	8,819	9,239
07607	Maywood	(201)	9,442	9,536
07945	Mendham	(973)	5,172	4,890
08619	Mercerville-Hamilton Sq. (c)	(609)	26,419	26,873
08840	Metuchen	(732)	13,383	12,804
08846	Middlesex	(732)	13,938	13,055
07432	Midland Park	(201)	6,952	7,047
07041	Millburn (c)	(973)	19,765	18,630
08850	Milltown	(732)	7,130	6,968
08332	Millville	(856)	27,886	25,992
*07042	Montclair (c)	(973)	38,977	37,729
07645	Montvale	(201)	7,306	6,946
08057	Moorestown-Lenola (c)	(856)	13,860	13,242
07751	Morganville (c)	(732)	11,255	—
07950	Morris Plains	(973)	5,629	5,219
*07960	Morristown	(973)	18,851	16,189
07092	Mountainside	(908)	6,635	6,657
07856	Mount Arlington	(973)	5,332	3,630
08087	Mystic Islands (c)	(609)	8,694	7,400
07753	Neptune City	(732)	5,176	4,997
*07102	Newark	(973)	280,666	275,221
*08901	New Brunswick	(732)	50,156	41,711
07646	New Milford	(201)	16,318	15,990
07974	New Providence	(908)	11,905	11,439
07860	Newton	(973)	8,416	7,521
07031	North Arlington	(201)	15,179	13,790
08902	North Brunswick Twp. (c)	(732)	36,287	31,287
07006	North Caldwell	(973)	7,284	6,706
08225	Northfield	(609)	8,025	7,305
*07508	North Haledon	(973)	9,073	7,987
*07060	North Plainfield	(908)	21,608	18,820
07648	Norwood	(201)	6,249	4,858
07110	Nutley (c)	(973)	27,362	27,099
07436	Oakland	(201)	13,645	11,997
*08050	Ocean Acres (c)	(609)	13,155	5,587
08226	Ocean City	(609)	15,330	15,512
07757	Oceanport	(732)	5,780	6,146
08857	Old Bridge (c)	(732)	22,833	22,151
07675	Old Tappan	(201)	5,903	4,254
07649	Oradell	(201)	8,005	8,024
*07051	Orange (c)	(973)	32,868	29,925
07650	Palisades Park	(201)	18,857	14,536
08065	Palmyra	(856)	7,641	7,056
*07652	Paramus	(201)	26,545	25,004
07656	Park Ridge	(201)	8,959	8,102
07055	Passaic	(973)	68,338	58,041
*07510	Paterson	(973)	149,843	140,891
08066	Paulsboro	(856)	6,096	6,577
*08110	Pennsauken (c)	(856)	35,737	34,738
08070	Pennsville (c)	(856)	11,657	12,218
*08861	Perth Amboy	(732)	48,797	41,967
08865	Phillipsburg	(908)	14,920	15,757
08021	Pine Hill	(856)	11,305	9,854
08071	Pitman	(856)	9,251	9,365
*07061	Plainfield	(908)	47,642	46,577
*08232	Pleasantville	(609)	19,032	16,027
08742	Point Pleasant	(732)	19,861	18,177
08742	Point Pleasant Beach	(732)	5,397	5,112
07442	Pompton Lakes	(973)	11,313	10,539
*08540	Princeton	(609)	13,495	12,016
08536	Princeton Meadows (c)	(609)	13,436	—
*07508	Prospect Park	(973)	5,760	5,053
07065	Rahway	(732)	27,563	25,325
08057	Ramblewood (c)	(856)	6,003	6,181
07446	Ramsey	(201)	14,558	13,228
*08869	Raritan	(908)	6,391	5,798
*07701	Red Bank	(732)	11,876	10,636
07657	Ridgefield	(201)	11,014	9,996
07660	Ridgefield Park	(201)	12,746	12,454
*07451	Ridgewood	(201)/(973)	24,790	24,152
07456	Ringwood	(973)	12,809	12,623
07661	River Edge	(201)	10,911	10,603
07866	Rockaway	(973)	6,419	6,243
07068	Roseland	(973)	5,402	4,847
07203	Roselle	(908)	21,265	20,314
07204	Roselle Park	(908)	13,189	12,805
07760	Rumson	(732)	7,233	6,701
08078	Runnemede	(856)	8,520	9,042
07070	Rutherford	(201)	17,967	17,790
08079	Salem	(856)	5,812	6,883
*08872	Sayreville	(732)	43,017	34,998
*07094	Secaucus	(201)	15,623	14,061
08083	Somerdale	(856)	5,155	5,440
08244	Somers Point	(609)	11,701	11,216
08876	Somerville	(908)	12,478	11,632
08879	South Amboy	(732)	7,975	7,851
07080	South Plainfield	(732)/(908)	23,064	20,489
*08882	South River	(732)	16,000	13,692
08884	Spotswood	(732)	8,237	7,983
07762	Spring Lake Heights	(732)	5,135	5,341
08084	Stratford	(856)	7,184	7,614
*07901	Summit	(908)	21,200	19,757
07670	Tenafly	(201)	14,362	13,326
*07724	Tinton Falls	(732)	17,274	12,361
*07512	Totowa	(973)	10,592	10,177
*08650	Trenton	(609)	84,639	88,675
07083	Union (Union Co.) (c)	(908)	66,167	50,024
07735	Union Beach	(732)	6,659	6,156
*07087	Union City	(201)	65,128	58,012
07458	Upper Saddle River	(201)	8,509	7,198
08406	Ventnor City	(609)	12,737	11,005
*08360	Vineland	(856)	58,164	54,780
07463	Waldwick	(201)	9,650	9,757
07057	Wallington	(201)/(973)	11,491	10,828

ZIP	Place	Area Code	2005	1990
07465	Wanaque	(201)/(973)	10,616	9,711
07882	Washington	(908)	6,876	6,474
07069	Watchung	(908)	6,170	5,110
*07091	Westfield	(732)/(908)	29,918	28,870
07764	West Long Branch	(732)	8,286	7,690
07093	West New York	(201)	46,667	38,125
07424	West Paterson	(973)	11,245	10,982
*07675	Westwood	(201)	10,994	10,446
07885	Wharton	(973)	6,222	5,405
08260	Wildwood	(609)	5,291	4,484
*08096	Woodbury	(856)	10,435	10,904
07677	Woodcliff Lake	(201)	5,887	5,303
07075	Wood-Ridge	(201)/(973)	7,634	7,506

New Mexico (505)

ZIP	Place	2005	1990
*88310	Alamogordo	36,245	27,596
*87101	Albuquerque	494,236	384,915
88021	Anthony (c)	7,904	5,160
*88210	Artesia	10,481	10,610
87410	Aztec	7,084	5,480
87002	Belen	7,121	6,547
87004	Bernalillo	6,938	5,864
87413	Bloomfield	7,442	5,214
*88220	Carlsbad	25,300	24,952
88021	Chaparral (c)	6,117	2,962
*88101	Clovis	33,357	30,954
87048	Corrales	7,638	5,453
*88030	Deming	14,876	11,422
87031	El Cerro-Monterey Park (c)	5,483	—
87505	Eldorado at Santa Fe (c)	5,799	2,260
*87532	Espanola	9,655	8,389
*87401	Farmington	43,161	33,997
*87301	Gallup	19,378	19,157
87020	Grants	9,043	8,626
*88240	Hobbs	29,006	29,121
87417	Kirtland (c)	6,190	3,552
*88001	Las Cruces	82,671	62,360
*87701	Las Vegas	14,020	14,753
87544	Los Alamos (c)	11,909	11,455
87002	Los Chaves (c)	5,033	3,872
87031	Los Lunas	11,338	6,013
*87107	Los Ranchos de Albuquerque	5,396	5,075
88260	Lovington	9,603	9,322
87107	North Valley (c)	11,923	12,507
*88130	Portales	11,295	10,690
87740	Raton	6,944	7,372
*87124	Rio Rancho	66,599	32,512
*88201	Roswell	45,199	44,260
*88345	Ruidoso	8,812	4,600
*87501	Santa Fe	70,631	56,537
87420	Shiprock (c)	8,156	7,687
*88061	Silver City	9,999	10,683
87801	Socorro	8,621	8,159
87105	South Valley (c)	39,060	35,701
*88063	Sunland Park	14,089	8,179
87571	Taos	5,126	4,065
87901	Truth or Consequences	7,071	6,221
*88401	Tucumcari	5,335	6,827
87544	White Rock (c)	6,045	6,192
87327	Zuni Pueblo (c)	6,367	5,857

New York

Area code (347) overlays area code (718). Area codes (646) and (917) overlay (212). See introductory note.

ZIP	Place	Area Code	2005	1990
*10901	Airmont	(845)	8,600	7,674
*12201	Albany	(518)	93,523	100,031
11507	Albertson (c)	(516)	5,200	5,166
14411	Albion	(585)	5,766	5,863
14802	Alfred	(607)	5,009	4,559
*11701	Amityville	(516)/(631)	9,477	9,286
12010	Amsterdam	(518)	17,749	20,714
12603	Arlington (c)	(845)	12,481	11,948
*13021	Auburn	(315)	27,941	31,258
11702	Babylon	(631)	12,659	12,249
11510	Baldwin (c)	(516)	23,455	22,719
11510	Baldwin Harbor (c)	(516)	8,147	7,899
13027	Baldwinsville	(315)	7,149	6,591
12020	Ballston Spa	(518)	5,574	5,194
*14020	Batavia	(585)	15,661	16,310
14810	Bath	(607)	5,589	5,801
11705	Bayport (c)	(631)	8,662	7,702
11706	Bay Shore (c)	(631)	23,852	21,279
11709	Bayville	(516)	7,123	7,193
12508	Beacon	(845)	14,836	13,243
11710	Bellmore (c)	(516)	16,441	16,438
11714	Bethpage (c)	(516)	16,543	15,761
*13902	Binghamton	(607)	45,492	53,008
10913	Blauvelt (c)	(845)	5,207	4,838
11716	Bohemia (c)	(631)	9,871	9,556
11717	Brentwood (c)	(631)	53,917	45,218
10510	Briarcliff Manor	(914)	7,938	7,070
14610	Brighton (c)	(585)	35,584	34,455
14420	Brockport	(585)	8,134	8,749
10708	Bronxville	(914)	6,455	6,028
*14240	Buffalo	(716)	279,745	328,175
11933	Calverton (c)	(631)	5,704	4,759
*14424	Canandaigua	(585)	11,391	10,725

ZIP	Place	Area Code	2005	1990
13617	Canton	(315)	6,060	6,379
11514	Carle Place (c)	(516)	5,247	5,107
10512	Carmel Hamlet (c)	(845)	5,650	4,800
11516	Cedarhurst	(516)	6,082	5,716
11720	Centereach (c)	(631)	27,285	26,720
11934	Center Moriches (c)	(631)	6,655	5,987
11721	Centerport (c)	(631)	5,446	5,333
11722	Central Islip (c)	(516)	31,950	26,028
10514	Chappaqua (c)	(914)	9,468	—
14225	Cheektowaga (c)	(716)	79,988	84,387
*10977	Chestnut Ridge	(845)	7,843	7,517
12047	Cohoes	(518)	15,085	16,825
12205	Colonie	(518)	8,236	8,019
11725	Commack (c)	(631)	36,367	36,124
10920	Congers (c)	(845)	8,303	8,003
11726	Copiague (c)	(631)	21,922	20,769
11727	Coram (c)	(631)	34,923	30,111
*14830	Corning	(607)	10,551	11,938
13045	Cortland	(607)	18,522	19,801
*10520	Croton-on-Hudson	(914)	7,803	7,018
11729	Deer Park (c)	(631)	28,316	28,840
12054	Delmar (c)	(518)	8,292	8,360
14043	Depew	(716)	15,798	17,673
11746	Dix Hills (c)	(631)	26,024	25,849
10522	Dobbs Ferry	(914)	11,070	9,940
*14048	Dunkirk	(716)	12,493	13,989
14052	East Aurora	(585)/(716)	6,418	6,647
10709	Eastchester (c)	(914)	18,564	18,537
12302	East Glenville (c)	(518)	6,064	6,518
*11576	East Hills	(516)	6,745	6,746
11730	East Islip (c)	(631)	14,078	14,325
11758	East Massapequa (c)	(516)	19,565	19,550
11554	East Meadow (c)	(516)	37,461	36,909
11731	East Northport (c)	(631)	20,845	20,411
11772	East Patchogue (c)	(631)	20,824	20,195
14445	East Rochester	(585)	6,366	6,932
11518	East Rockaway	(516)	10,263	10,152
11786	East Shoreham (c)	(631)	5,809	5,461
*14901	Elmira	(607)	29,928	33,724
11003	Elmont (c)	(516)	32,657	28,612
11731	Elwood (c)	(631)	10,916	10,916
*13760	Endicott	(607)	12,639	13,531
13762	Endwell (c)	(607)	11,706	12,602
13219	Fairmount (c)	(315)	10,795	12,266
14450	Fairport	(585)	5,576	5,943
12601	Fairview (c)	(845)	5,421	4,811
*11735	Farmingdale	(516)	8,668	8,022
*11001	Floral Park	(516)	15,737	15,947
13603	Fort Drum(c)	(315)	12,123	11,578
11768	Fort Salonga (c)	(631)	9,634	9,176
11010	Franklin Square (c)	(516)	29,342	28,205
14063	Fredonia	(716)	10,735	10,436
11520	Freeport	(516)	43,519	39,894
13069	Fulton	(315)	11,525	12,929
*11530	Garden City	(516)	21,697	21,675
11040	Garden City Park (c)	(516)	7,554	7,437
14624	Gates-North Gates (c)	(585)	15,138	14,995
14454	Geneseo	(585)	7,809	7,187
14456	Geneva	(315)	13,509	14,143
11542	Glen Cove	(516)	26,633	24,149
12801	Glens Falls	(518)	14,108	15,023
12801	Glens Falls North (c)	(518)	8,061	7,978
12078	Gloversville	(518)	15,283	16,656
10924	Goshen	(845)	5,437	5,255
*11021	Great Neck	(516)	9,605	8,745
11020	Great Neck Plaza	(516)	6,929	5,897
14616	Greece (c)	(585)	14,614	15,632
11740	Greenlawn (c)	(631)	13,286	13,208
*10583	Greenville (Westchester Co.) (c)	(914)	8,648	9,528
14075	Hamburg	(716)	9,637	10,442
11946	Hampton Bays (c)	(631)	12,236	7,893
10528	Harrison	(914)	25,827	23,308
10530	Hartsdale (c)	(914)	9,830	9,587
10706	Hastings-on-Hudson	(914)	7,702	8,000
*11788	Hauppauge (c)	(631)	20,100	19,750
10927	Haverstraw	(845)	10,487	9,438
10532	Hawthorne (c)	(845)	5,083	4,764
*11551	Hempstead	(516)	52,829	45,982
13350	Herkimer	(315)	7,264	7,945
11557	Hewlett (c)	(516)	7,060	6,620
*11802	Hicksville (c)	(516)	41,260	40,174
12528	Highland (c)	(845)	5,060	4,492
10977	Hillcrest (c)	(845)	7,106	6,447
14468	Hilton	(585)	5,957	5,216
14843	Hornell	(607)	8,762	9,877
*14845	Horseheads	(607)	6,366	6,802
12534	Hudson	(518)	7,145	8,034
12839	Hudson Falls	(518)	6,864	7,651
11743	Huntington (c)	(631)	18,403	18,243
11746	Huntington Station (c)	(631)	29,910	28,247
13357	Ilion	(315)	8,330	8,888
11096	Inwood (c)	(516)	9,325	7,767
14617	Irondequoit (c)	(585)	52,354	52,322
10533	Irvington	(914)	6,615	6,348
11751	Islip (c)	(631)	20,575	18,924
11752	Islip Terrace (c)	(631)	5,641	5,530
*14850	Ithaca	(607)	29,766	29,541
*14702	Jamestown	(716)	30,381	34,681
10535	Jefferson Valley-Yorktown (c)	(914)	14,891	14,118
11753	Jericho (c)	(516)	13,045	13,141

ZIP	Place	Area Code	2005	1990
13790	Johnson City	(607)	14,955	16,578
12095	Johnstown	(518)	8,572	9,058
*14217	Kenmore	(716)	15,555	17,180
11754	Kings Park (c)	(631)	16,146	17,773
11024	Kings Point	(516)	5,257	4,843
*12401	Kingston	(845)	23,067	23,095
10950	Kiryas Joel	(845)	18,300	7,437
14218	Lackawanna	(716)	18,175	20,585
10512	Lake Carmel (c)	(845)	8,663	8,489
11755	Lake Grove	(631)	10,670	9,612
10547	Lake Mohegan (c)	(914)	5,979	—
11779	Lake Ronkonkoma (c)	(631)	19,701	18,997
11552	Lakeview (c)	(516)	5,607	5,476
*14086	Lancaster	(716)	11,490	11,940
10538	Larchmont	(914)	6,487	6,181
11559	Lawrence	(516)	6,501	6,513
11756	Levittown (c)	(516)	53,067	53,286
11757	Lindenhurst	(631)	28,248	26,879
13365	Little Falls	(315)	5,026	5,829
*14094	Lockport	(716)	21,271	24,426
11561	Long Beach	(516)	35,336	33,510
11563	Lynbrook	(516)	19,640	19,208
12953	Malone	(518)	5,929	6,777
11565	Malverne	(516)	8,832	9,054
10543	Mamaroneck	(914)	18,350	17,325
11030	Manhasset (c)	(516)	8,362	7,718
11050	Manorhaven	(516)	6,328	5,672
11949	Manorville (c)	(631)	11,131	6,198
11758	Massapequa (c)	(516)	22,652	22,018
11762	Massapequa Park	(516)	17,220	18,044
13662	Massena	(315)	10,859	11,716
11950	Mastic (c)	(631)	15,436	13,778
11951	Mastic Beach (c)	(631)	11,543	10,293
13211	Mattydale (c)	(315)	6,367	6,418
10940	Mechanicstown (c)	(845)	6,061	—
11763	Medford (c)	(631)	21,985	21,274
14103	Medina	(585)/(716)	6,235	6,686
11747	Melville (c)	(631)	14,533	12,586
11566	Merrick (c)	(516)	22,764	23,042
11953	Middle Island (c)	(631)	9,702	7,848
*10940	Middletown	(845)	26,067	24,160
11764	Miller Place (c)	(631)	10,580	9,315
11501	Mineola	(516)	18,978	19,005
*10950	Monroe	(845)	8,127	6,672
10952	Monsey (c)	(845)	14,504	13,986
*12701	Monticello	(845)	6,649	6,597
10970	Mount Ivy (c)	(845)	6,536	6,013
10549	Mount Kisco	(914)	10,331	9,108
11766	Mount Sinai (c)	(631)	8,734	8,023
*10551	Mount Vernon	(914)	67,924	67,153
12590	Myers Corner (c)	(845)	5,546	5,599
10954	Nanuet (c)	(845)	16,707	14,065
11767	Nesconset (c)	(631)	11,992	10,712
14513	Newark	(315)	9,411	9,849
*12550	Newburgh	(845)	28,548	26,454
11590	New Cassel (c)	(516)	13,298	10,257
10956	New City (c)	(845)	34,038	33,673
*11040	New Hyde Park	(516)	9,472	9,728
12561	New Paltz	(845)	6,765	5,470
*10802	New Rochelle	(914)	72,967	67,265
10977	New Square	(845)	6,332	2,623
*12550	New Windsor (c)	(845)	9,077	8,898
*10001	New York	(212)/(718)	8,143,197	7,322,564
*14302	Niagara Falls	(716)	52,866	61,840
11701	North Amityville (c)	(631)	16,572	13,849
11703	North Babylon (c)	(631)	17,877	18,081
11706	North Bay Shore (c)	(631)	14,992	12,799
11710	North Bellmore (c)	(516)	20,079	19,707
11713	North Bellport (c)	(631)	9,007	8,182
11757	North Lindenhurst (c)	(631)	11,767	10,563
11758	North Massapequa (c)	(516)	19,152	19,365
11566	North Merrick (c)	(516)	11,844	12,113
11040	North New Hyde Park	(516)	14,542	14,359
11772	North Patchogue (c)	(631)	7,825	7,374
11768	Northport	(631)	7,587	7,572
13212	North Syracuse	(315)	6,726	7,363
14120	North Tonawanda	(716)	32,072	34,989
11580	North Valley Stream (c)	(516)	15,789	14,574
11793	North Wantagh (c)	(516)	12,156	12,276
13815	Norwich	(607)	7,233	7,613
10960	Nyack	(845)	6,676	6,558
11769	Oakdale (c)	(631)	8,075	7,875
11572	Oceanside (c)	(516)	32,733	32,423
13669	Ogdensburg	(315)	11,422	13,521
11804	Old Bethpage (c)	(516)	5,400	5,610
11568	Old Westbury	(516)	5,035	3,897
14760	Olean	(585)/(716)	14,799	16,946
13421	Oneida	(315)	10,923	10,850
13820	Oneonta	(607)	13,206	13,954
12550	Orange Lake (c)	(845)	6,085	5,196
10562	Ossining	(914)	23,547	22,582
13126	Oswego	(315)	17,705	19,195
11771	Oyster Bay (c)	(516)	6,826	6,687
11772	Patchogue	(631)	11,901	11,060
10965	Pearl River (c)	(845)	15,553	15,314
10566	Peekskill	(914)	24,044	19,536
10803	Pelham	(914)	6,364	5,443
10803	Pelham Manor	(914)	5,395	6,413
14527	Penn Yan	(315)	5,170	5,248
11714	Plainedge (c)	(516)	9,195	8,739
11803	Plainview (c)	(516)	25,637	26,207
*12901	Plattsburgh	(518)	19,181	21,255
*10570	Pleasantville	(914)	7,130	6,592
10573	Port Chester	(914)	27,886	24,728
11777	Port Jefferson	(631)	7,935	7,455
11776	Port Jefferson Station (c)	(631)	7,527	7,232
*12771	Port Jervis	(845)	9,202	9,060
11050	Port Washington (c)	(516)	15,215	15,387
*13676	Potsdam	(315)	9,705	10,251
*12601	Poughkeepsie	(845)	30,355	28,844
12144	Rensselaer	(518)	7,859	8,255
11961	Ridge (c)	(631)	13,380	11,734
11901	Riverhead (c)	(631)	10,513	8,814
*14692	Rochester	(585)	211,091	230,356
*11571	Rockville Centre	(516)	24,237	24,727
11778	Rocky Point (c)	(631)	10,185	8,596
*13440	Rome	(315)	34,344	44,350
11779	Ronkonkoma (c)	(631)	20,029	20,391
11575	Roosevelt (c)	(516)	15,854	15,030
11577	Roslyn Heights (c)	(516)	6,295	6,405
12303	Rotterdam (c)	(518)	20,536	21,228
10580	Rye	(914)	14,992	14,936
10573	Rye Brook	(914)	9,471	7,765
11780	Saint James (c)	(631)	13,268	12,703
14779	Salamanca	(716)	5,851	6,566
13454	Salisbury (c)	(315)	12,341	12,226
12866	Saratoga Springs	(518)	28,036	25,001
11782	Sayville (c)	(631)	16,735	16,550
10583	Scarsdale	(914)	17,763	16,987
*12301	Schenectady	(518)	61,280	65,566
10940	Scotchtown (c)	(845)	8,954	8,765
12302	Scotia	(518)	7,958	7,359
11783	Seaford (c)	(516)	15,791	15,597
11507	Searingtown (c)	(516)	5,034	5,020
11784	Selden (c)	(631)	21,861	20,608
13148	Seneca Falls	(315)	6,837	7,370
10591	Sleepy Hollow[1]	(914)	9,977	8,152
11787	Smithtown (c)	(631)	26,901	25,638
13209	Solvay	(315)	6,606	6,717
11789	Sound Beach (c)	(631)	9,807	9,102
11735	South Farmingdale (c)	(516)	15,061	15,377
14850	South Hill (c)	(607)	6,003	5,423
11746	South Huntington (c)	(631)	9,465	9,624
14094	South Lockport (c)	(716)	8,552	7,112
11971	Southold (c)	(631)	5,465	5,192
14904	Southport (c)	(607)	7,396	7,753
11581	South Valley Stream (c)	(516)	5,638	5,328
10977	Spring Valley	(845)	25,355	21,802
*11790	Stony Brook (c)	(631)	13,727	13,726
10980	Stony Point (c)	(845)	11,744	10,587
*10901	Suffern	(845)	10,897	11,055
11791	Syosset (c)	(516)	18,544	18,967
*13220	Syracuse	(315)	141,683	163,860
10983	Tappan (c)	(845)	6,757	6,867
10591	Tarrytown	(914)	11,346	10,739
11776	Terryville (c)	(631)	10,589	10,275
10594	Thornwood (c)	(914)	5,980	7,025
*14150	Tonawanda	(716)	15,335	17,284
*12180	Troy	(518)	48,310	54,269
10707	Tuckahoe	(914)	6,256	6,302
11553	Uniondale (c)	(516)	23,011	20,328
*13504	Utica	(315)	59,336	68,637
10595	Valhalla (c)	(914)	5,379	—
10989	Valley Cottage (c)	(845)	9,269	9,007
*11582	Valley Stream	(516)	35,799	33,946
10952	Viola (c)	—	5,931	4,504
11792	Wading River (c)	(631)	6,668	5,317
12586	Walden	(845)	6,755	5,836
12590	Wappingers Falls	(845)	5,085	4,605
11793	Wantagh (c)	(516)	18,971	18,567
10990	Warwick	(845)	6,571	5,984
10992	Washingtonville	(845)	6,236	4,906
13165	Waterloo	(315)	5,134	5,116
*13601	Watertown	(315)	27,220	29,429
12189	Watervliet	(518)	9,889	11,061
14580	Webster	(585)	5,089	5,464
10952	Wesley Hills	(845)	5,051	4,308
*11704	West Babylon (c)	(631)	43,452	42,410
*11590	Westbury	(516)	14,691	13,060
14905	West Elmira (c)	(607)	5,136	5,218
12801	West Glens Falls (c)	(518)	6,721	5,964
10993	West Haverstraw	(845)	10,259	9,183
11743	West Hills (c)	(631)	5,607	5,849
11795	West Islip (c)	(631)	28,907	28,419
12203	Westmere (c)	(518)	7,188	6,750
*10996	West Point (c)	(845)	7,138	8,024
11796	West Sayville (c)	(631)	5,003	4,680
14224	West Seneca (c)	(716)	45,943	47,866
13219	Westvale (c)	(315)	5,166	5,952
11798	Wheatley Heights (c)	(631)	5,013	5,027
*10602	White Plains	(914)	56,733	48,718
*14231	Williamsville	(716)	5,315	5,583
11596	Williston Park	(516)	7,113	7,516
11797	Woodbury (c)	(516)	9,010	8,008
11598	Woodmere (c)	(516)	16,447	15,578
11798	Wyandach (c)	(631)	10,546	8,950
11980	Yaphank (c)	(631)	5,025	4,637
*10702	Yonkers	(914)	196,425	188,082
10598	Yorktown Heights (c)	(914)	7,972	7,690

(1) North Tarrytown changed its name to Sleepy Hollow on Dec. 12, 1996.

North Carolina
Area code (980) overlays area code (704). See introductory note.

ZIP	Place	Area Code	2005	1990
*28001	Albemarle	(704)	15,325	14,940
*27502	Apex	(919)	28,551	4,789
27263	Archdale	(336)	9,428	6,975
*27203	Asheboro	(336)	23,639	16,362
*28802	Asheville	(828)	72,231	63,379
28012	Belmont	(704)	8,779	8,434
28016	Bessemer City	(704)	5,319	4,698
28711	Black Mountain	(828)	7,650	7,156
*28607	Boone	(828)	13,192	12,949
28712	Brevard	(828)	6,643	5,452
*27215	Burlington	(336)	47,592	39,498
27509	Butner (c)	(919)	5,192	4,679
28428	Carolina Beach	(910)	5,388	4,002
27510	Carrboro	(919)	16,425	12,134
*27511	Cary	(919)	106,439	44,394
*27514	Chapel Hill	(919)	49,543	38,719
*28204	Charlotte	(704)	610,949	419,558
28021	Cherryville	(704)	5,455	4,756
*27520	Clayton	(919)	12,943	4,756
27012	Clemmons	(336)	16,430	5,982
*28328	Clinton	(910)	8,768	8,385
*28025	Concord	(704)	61,092	29,591
28613	Conover	(828)	7,093	5,311
28031	Cornelius	(704)	18,870	2,581
*28036	Davidson	(704)	8,581	4,046
*28334	Dunn	(910)	9,889	9,258
*27701	Durham	(919)	204,845	138,894
*27288	Eden	(336)	15,679	15,238
27932	Edenton	(252)	5,001	5,268
*27909	Elizabeth City	(252)	18,456	16,087
27244	Elon	(336)	7,100	4,394
*28302	Fayetteville	(910)	129,928	75,850
28043	Forest City	(828)	7,273	7,475
*28307	Fort Bragg (c)	(910)	29,183	34,744
27526	Fuquay-Varina	(919)	12,200	4,447
27529	Garner	(919)	22,364	14,716
*28052	Gastonia	(704)	68,964	54,725
*27530	Goldsboro	(919)	38,670	40,736
27253	Graham	(336)	13,952	10,368
*27420	Greensboro	(336)	231,962	185,125
*27834	Greenville	(252)	69,517	46,274
*28540	Half Moon (c)	(910)	6,645	6,306
28345	Hamlet	(910)	5,824	6,722
28075	Harrisburg	(704)	5,145	1,625
*28532	Havelock	(252)	21,827	20,300
*27536	Henderson	(252)	16,213	15,655
*28739	Hendersonville	(828)	11,396	7,284
*28603	Hickory	(828)	40,232	28,474
*27260	High Point	(336)	95,086	69,428
27278	Hillsborough	(919)	5,382	4,263
27540	Holly Springs	(919)	15,228	1,203
28348	Hope Mills	(910)	12,782	8,272
*28070	Huntersville	(704)	36,377	3,014
28079	Indian Trail	(704)	16,473	1,942
*28540	Jacksonville	(910)	62,668	78,031
28560	James City (c)	(252)	5,420	4,279
*28081	Kannapolis	(704)	39,041	31,592
*27284	Kernersville	(336)	21,361	11,860
27948	Kill Devil Hills	(252)	6,550	4,238
27021	King	(336)	6,353	4,059
28405	Kings Grant (c)	(910)	7,738	—
28086	Kings Mountain	(704)	10,862	8,768
*28502	Kinston	(252)	22,851	25,295
27545	Knightdale	(919)	6,319	1,884
*28352	Laurinburg	(910)	15,810	16,131
*28645	Lenoir	(828)	17,912	16,337
27023	Lewisville	(336)	9,547	6,433
*27292	Lexington	(336)	20,398	16,583
*28092	Lincolnton	(704)	10,393	6,955
*28358	Lumberton	(910)	21,591	18,656
28752	Marion	(828)	5,013	4,765
28403	Masonboro (c)	(910)	11,812	7,010
*28105	Matthews	(704)	25,306	13,756
27302	Mebane	(919)	8,945	4,754
28759	Mills River	(828)	5,979	—
28227	Mint Hill	(704)	17,871	13,637
*28110	Monroe	(704)	29,987	18,623
*28115	Mooresville	(704)	20,488	9,563
28557	Morehead City	(252)	8,847	6,473
*28655	Morganton	(828)	17,041	15,085
27560	Morrisville	(919)	12,192	1,022
*27030	Mount Airy	(336)	8,454	7,156
28120	Mount Holly	(704)	9,676	7,710
28411	Murraysville (c)	(910)	7,279	—
28409	Myrtle Grove (c)	(910)	7,125	4,275
*28562	New Bern	(252)	24,106	20,728
28658	Newton	(828)	13,016	11,134
*28465	Oak Island	(910)	7,679	—
28411	Ogden (c)	(910)	5,481	3,228
27565	Oxford	(919)	8,530	7,965
*28374	Pinehurst	(910)	11,437	5,825
28399	Piney Green (c)	(910)	11,658	8,999
*27611	Raleigh	(919)	341,530	218,859
*27320	Reidsville	(336)	14,778	14,085
27870	Roanoke Rapids	(252)	16,458	15,722
*28379	Rockingham	(910)	9,220	9,399
*27801	Rocky Mount	(252)	56,626	53,078
*27573	Roxboro	(336)	8,755	7,332
28704	Royal Pines (c)	(828)	5,334	4,418
28601	Saint Stephens (c)	(828)	9,439	8,734
*28144	Salisbury	(704)	27,563	23,626
*27330	Sanford	(919)	26,710	18,881
27576	Selma	(919)	6,646	4,600
*28150	Shelby	(704)	21,263	15,460
27344	Siler City	(919)	8,079	4,808
28412	Silver Lake (c)	(910)	5,788	4,071
27577	Smithfield	(919)	11,970	10,180
*28387	Southern Pines	(910)	11,881	9,213
28052	South Gastonia (c)	(704)	5,433	5,487
28390	Spring Lake	(910)	8,197	7,552
*28677	Statesville	(704)	24,875	20,647
27358	Summerfield	(336)	7,228	2,051
27886	Tarboro	(252)	10,600	11,037
*27360	Thomasville	(336)	25,872	15,915
27370	Trinity	(336)	6,915	5,469
28110	Unionville	(704)	6,477	
28170	Wadesboro	(704)	5,263	—
*27587	Wake Forest	(919)	20,126	5,832
27889	Washington	(252)	9,841	9,160
*28786	Waynesville	(828)	9,386	7,282
28104	Weddington	(704)	8,465	3,803
28472	Whiteville	(910)	5,212	5,340
27892	Williamston	(252)	5,650	5,870
*28402	Wilmington	(910)	95,476	55,530
*27893	Wilson	(252)	46,967	38,400
*27102	Winston-Salem	(336)	193,755	162,292

North Dakota (701)

ZIP	Place	2005	1990
*58501	Bismarck	57,377	49,272
58301	Devils Lake	6,816	7,782
*58601	Dickinson	15,666	16,097
*58102	Fargo	90,672	74,084
*58201	Grand Forks	49,792	49,417
*58401	Jamestown	14,826	15,571
58554	Mandan	17,225	15,177
*58701	Minot	34,984	34,544
*58701	Minot AFB (c)	7,599	9,095
58072	Valley City	6,439	7,163
*58075	Wahpeton	8,220	8,751
58078	West Fargo	19,487	12,287
*58801	Williston	12,193	13,136

Ohio
Area code (234) overlays area code (330). Area code (567) overlays (419). See introductory note.

ZIP	Place	Area Code	2005	1990
45810	Ada	(419)	5,847	5,428
*44309	Akron	(330)	210,795	223,019
44601	Alliance	(330)	22,801	23,376
44001	Amherst	(440)	11,872	10,332
44805	Ashland	(419)	21,550	20,079
*44004	Ashtabula	(440)	20,321	21,633
45701	Athens	(740)	20,918	21,265
44202	Aurora	(330)	14,353	9,192
44515	Austintown (c)	(330)	31,627	32,371
44011	Avon	(440)	15,741	7,337
44012	Avon Lake	(440)	20,608	15,066
44203	Barberton	(330)	27,192	27,623
44140	Bay Village	(440)	15,236	17,000
44122	Beachwood	(216)	11,535	10,644
45434	Beavercreek	(937)	39,655	33,626
45069	Beckett Ridge (c)	(513)	8,663	4,505
44146	Bedford	(216)/(440)	13,571	14,822
*44146	Bedford Heights	(216)/(440)	10,855	12,131
45305	Bellbrook	(937)	6,960	6,511
43311	Bellefontaine	(937)	13,009	12,126
44811	Bellevue	(419)	8,029	8,157
45714	Belpre	(740)	6,560	6,796
44017	Berea	(440)	18,242	19,051
43209	Bexley	(614)	12,322	13,088
43004	Blacklick Estates (c)	(614)	9,518	10,080
*45242	Blue Ash	(513)	11,747	11,923
44513	Boardman (c)	(330)	37,215	38,596
*43402	Bowling Green	(419)	29,793	28,303
44141	Brecksville	(440)	13,250	11,818
45211	Bridgetown North (c)	(513)	12,569	11,748
44147	Broadview Heights	(440)	17,505	12,219
44144	Brooklyn	(216)	10,901	11,706
44142	Brook Park	(216)/(440)	20,059	22,865
45309	Brookville	(937)	5,317	4,621
44212	Brunswick	(330)	35,159	28,218
43506	Bryan	(419)	8,360	8,348
44820	Bucyrus	(419)	12,885	13,496
*43725	Cambridge	(740)	11,562	11,748
44405	Campbell	(330)	8,888	10,038
44614	Canal Fulton	(330)	5,054	4,157
43110	Canal Winchester	(614)	5,652	2,652
44406	Canfield	(330)	7,153	5,409
*44711	Canton	(330)	79,478	84,161
45005	Carlisle	(937)	5,688	4,872
*45822	Celina	(419)	10,348	9,945
*45458	Centerville (Montgomery Co.)	(937)	23,162	21,082
44024	Chardon	(440)	5,280	4,446
45211	Cheviot	(513)	8,235	9,616
45601	Chillicothe	(740)	22,081	21,923

ZIP	Place	Area Code	2005	1990
*45202	Cincinnati	(513)	308,728	364,114
43113	Circleville	(740)	13,559	11,666
45315	Clayton	(937)	13,194	713
*44101	Cleveland	(216)	452,208	505,616
*44118	Cleveland Heights	(216)	48,029	54,052
43410	Clyde	(419)	6,143	6,087
44408	Columbiana	(330)	5,807	4,961
*43216	Columbus	(614)	730,657	632,945
44030	Conneaut	(440)	12,648	13,241
44410	Cortland	(330)	6,640	5,652
43812	Coshocton	(740)	11,632	12,193
45238	Covedale (c)	(513)	6,360	6,669
*44222	Cuyahoga Falls	(330)	50,494	48,950
*45401	Dayton	(937)	158,873	182,011
45236	Deer Park	(513)	5,615	6,181
43512	Defiance	(419)	16,150	16,787
43015	Delaware	(740)	31,322	19,966
45833	Delphos	(419)	6,820	7,093
*45247	Dent (c)	(513)	7,612	6,416
44622	Dover	(330)	12,516	11,329
45663	Dry Run (c)	(614)	6,553	5,389
*43016	Dublin	(614)/(740)	34,964	16,366
*44112	East Cleveland	(216)	25,708	33,096
*44095	Eastlake	(440)	19,795	21,161
43920	East Liverpool	(330)	12,396	13,654
45320	Eaton	(937)	8,242	7,396
*44035	Elyria	(440)	56,061	56,746
*45322	Englewood	(937)	12,727	11,402
*44117	Euclid	(216)	49,619	54,875
45324	Fairborn	(937)	31,650	31,300
*45011	Fairfield	(513)	42,294	39,709
*44334	Fairlawn	(330)	7,202	5,779
44126	Fairview Park	(440)	16,528	18,028
*45839	Findlay	(419)	39,118	35,703
45224	Finneytown (c)	(513)	13,492	13,096
45240	Forest Park	(513)	18,069	18,621
45230	Forestville (c)	(513)	10,978	9,185
44830	Fostoria	(419)	13,395	14,971
45005	Franklin	(513)	12,410	11,026
43420	Fremont	(419)	17,049	17,619
43230	Gahanna	(614)	33,077	23,898
44833	Galion	(419)	11,449	11,859
*44125	Garfield Heights	(216)	29,042	31,739
44041	Geneva	(440)	6,478	6,597
*45325	Germantown	(937)	5,157	4,916
44420	Girard	(330)	10,490	11,304
44044	Grafton	(440)	5,855	3,423
43212	Grandview Heights	(614)	6,273	7,010
43023	Granville	(740)	5,281	4,315
44232	Green	(330)	23,463	19,179
*45123	Greenfield	(937)	5,146	5,172
45331	Greenville	(937)	13,166	12,863
45253	Groesbeck (c)	(513)	7,202	6,684
43123	Grove City	(614)	30,892	19,661
*45011	Hamilton	(513)	61,943	61,438
45030	Harrison	(513)	7,821	7,520
43056	Heath	(740)	8,888	7,231
44134	Highland Heights	(440)	8,621	6,249
43026	Hilliard	(614)/(740)	26,656	11,794
45133	Hillsboro	(937)	6,677	6,235
44484	Howland Center (c)	(330)	6,481	6,732
44425	Hubbard	(330)	8,006	8,248
45424	Huber Heights	(937)	38,089	38,696
*44236	Hudson	(330)	23,084	5,159
44839	Huron	(419)	7,581	7,067
44131	Independence	(216)/(440)	6,869	6,500
45638	Ironton	(740)	11,417	12,751
45640	Jackson	(740)	6,240	6,167
*44240	Kent	(330)	28,135	28,835
43326	Kenton	(419)	8,169	8,356
43606	Kenwood (c)	(513)	7,423	7,469
*45429	Kettering	(937)	55,481	60,569
*44094	Kirtland	(440)	7,251	5,881
44107	Lakewood	(216)	53,244	59,718
43130	Lancaster	(740)	36,063	34,507
45039	Landen (c)	(513)	12,766	9,263
45036	Lebanon	(513)	19,978	10,461
*45802	Lima	(419)	38,608	45,553
43228	Lincoln Village (c)	(614)	9,482	9,958
43138	Logan	(740)	7,090	6,725
43140	London	(614)/(740)	9,396	7,807
*44052	Lorain	(440)	67,820	71,245
44641	Louisville	(330)	9,367	8,087
*45140	Loveland	(513)	11,219	10,122
44124	Lyndhurst	(216)/(440)	14,450	15,982
*44056	Macedonia	(330)	10,314	7,509
45233	Mack South (c)	—	5,837	5,767
45243	Madeira	(513)	8,330	9,141
*44901	Mansfield	(419)	50,615	50,627
44137	Maple Heights	(216)	24,739	27,089
45750	Marietta	(740)	14,270	15,026
*43302	Marion	(740)	36,494	34,075
43935	Martins Ferry	(740)	6,860	8,003
*43040	Marysville	(937)	17,483	10,362
45040	Mason	(513)	28,847	11,450
*44646	Massillon	(330)	32,150	30,969
43537	Maumee	(419)	14,285	15,561
44124	Mayfield Heights	(440)	18,380	19,847
*44256	Medina	(330)	26,461	19,231
*44060	Mentor	(440)	51,485	47,491
44060	Mentor-on-the-Lake	(216)	8,293	8,271
*45343	Miamisburg	(937)	19,796	17,834
44130	Middleburg Heights	(216)/(440)	15,437	14,702
*45042	Middletown	(513)	51,472	46,758
45150	Milford	(513)	6,325	5,660
*45050	Monroe	(513)	10,410	5,380
45242	Montgomery	(513)	10,015	9,733
—	Montrose-Ghent (c)	—	5,261	4,906
45439	Moraine	(937)	6,702	5,989
45231	Mount Healthy	(513)	6,600	7,580
43050	Mount Vernon	(740)	16,000	14,550
44262	Munroe Falls	(330)	5,300	5,359
*43545	Napoleon	(419)	9,169	8,884
45764	Nelsonville	(740)	5,444	4,563
43054	New Albany	(614)	5,827	1,621
*43055	Newark	(740)	47,301	44,396
45344	New Carlisle	(937)	5,639	6,049
44663	New Philadelphia	(330)	17,430	15,698
44446	Niles	(330)	20,016	21,128
45239	Northbrook (c)	(513)	11,076	11,471
*44720	North Canton	(330)	16,780	14,904
45239	North College Hill	(513)	9,359	11,002
45251	Northgate (c)	(513)	8,016	7,864
44057	North Madison (c)	(440)	8,451	8,699
44070	North Olmsted	(440)	32,653	34,204
45502	Northridge (c) (Clark Co.)	(937)	6,853	5,939
45414	Northridge (c) (Montgomery Co.)	(937)	8,487	9,448
*44039	North Ridgeville	(440)	26,108	21,564
44133	North Royalton	(440)	29,538	23,197
*43619	Northwood	(419)	5,499	5,506
44203	Norton	(330)	11,563	11,477
44857	Norwalk	(419)	16,505	14,731
*45212	Norwood	(513)	19,997	23,674
*45873	Oakwood	(973)	8,749	8,957
44074	Oberlin	(440)	8,280	8,191
44138	Olmsted Falls	(440)	8,437	6,741
44862	Ontario	(419)	5,350	4,026
*43616	Oregon	(419)	19,175	18,334
44667	Orrville	(330)	8,485	7,955
45056	Oxford	(513)	22,123	19,013
44077	Painesville	(440)	17,789	15,769
*44129	Parma	(216)/(440)	81,469	87,876
44130	Parma Heights	(216)/(440)	20,657	21,448
43062	Pataskala	(740)	12,624	3,046
*44124	Pepper Pike	(216)/(440)	5,794	6,185
44646	Perry Heights (c)	(330)	8,900	9,055
*43551	Perrysburg	(419)	16,980	12,551
43147	Pickerington	(614)/(740)	15,878	5,668
45356	Piqua	(937)	20,883	20,612
45231	Pleasant Run (c)	(513)	5,267	4,964
44319	Portage Lakes (c)	(330)	9,870	13,373
*43452	Port Clinton	(419)	6,336	7,106
*45662	Portsmouth	(740)	20,101	22,676
43065	Powell	(614)	10,504	2,154
44266	Ravenna	(330)	11,510	12,069
*45215	Reading	(513)	10,320	12,038
43068	Reynoldsburg	(614)/(740)	33,059	25,748
*44143	Richmond Heights	(216)/(440)	10,521	9,611
44270	Rittman	(330)	6,311	6,147
45431	Riverside	(937)	22,733	1,471
44116	Rocky River	(440)	19,681	20,410
43460	Rossford	(419)	6,387	5,861
43950	Saint Clairsville	(740)	5,075	5,136
45885	Saint Marys	(419)	8,238	8,441
44460	Salem	(330)	12,005	12,233
*44870	Sandusky	(419)	26,666	29,764
44870	Sandusky South (c)	(419)	6,599	6,336
44131	Seven Hills	(216)/(440)	12,041	12,339
*44122	Shaker Heights	(216)	27,723	30,955
*45241	Sharonville	(513)	13,079	13,121
44054	Sheffield Lake	(440)	9,157	9,825
44875	Shelby	(419)	9,471	9,610
44878	Shiloh (c)	(419)	11,272	11,607
*45365	Sidney	(937)	20,188	18,710
44139	Solon	(440)	22,335	18,548
*44121	South Euclid	(216)	22,210	23,866
45066	Springboro	(513)	16,403	6,574
45246	Springdale	(513)	9,809	10,621
*45501	Springfield	(937)	63,302	70,487
*43952	Steubenville	(740)	19,314	22,125
44224	Stow	(330)	34,404	27,998
44241	Streetsboro	(330)	14,210	9,932
*44136	Strongsville	(440)	43,949	35,308
44471	Struthers	(330)	11,240	12,284
45244	Summerside (c)	(513)	5,523	4,573
43560	Sylvania	(419)	19,069	17,489
44278	Tallmadge	(330)	17,408	14,870
45243	The Village of Indian Hill	(513)	5,661	5,383
44883	Tiffin	(419)	17,438	18,604
45371	Tipp City	(937)	9,357	6,483
*43601	Toledo	(419)	301,285	332,943
43964	Toronto	(740)	5,402	6,127
45067	Trenton	(513)	10,488	6,189
*45426	Trotwood	(937)	26,608	29,358
*45373	Troy	(937)	22,343	19,478
44087	Twinsburg	(330)	17,380	9,606
44683	Uhrichsville	(740)	5,647	5,604
45322	Union	(937)	5,920	5,531
*44122	University Heights	(216)	13,242	14,787
*43221	Upper Arlington	(614)	31,550	34,128

ZIP	Place	Area Code	2005	1990
43351	Upper Sandusky	(419)	6,455	5,906
43078	Urbana	(937)	11,561	11,353
45377	Vandalia	(937)	14,298	13,872
45891	Van Wert	(419)	10,435	10,922
*44089	Vermilion	(440)	11,000	11,127
*44281	Wadsworth	(330)	19,951	15,718
*45895	Wapakoneta	(419)	9,602	9,214
*44481	Warren	(330)	45,796	50,793
*44122	Warrensville Heights	(216)	14,223	15,884
*43160	Washington	(740)	13,466	13,080
43566	Waterville	(419)	5,189	4,594
43567	Wauseon	(419)	7,311	6,322
45692	Wellston	(740)	6,025	6,049
*45449	West Carrollton City	(937)	13,198	14,403
*43081	Westerville	(614)	34,722	30,269
44145	Westlake	(440)	31,331	27,018
45694	Wheelersburg (c)	(740)	*6,471*	5,113
43213	Whitehall	(614)	18,052	20,572
45239	White Oak (c)	(513)	*13,277*	12,430
44092	Wickliffe	(440)	13,205	14,558
*44890	Willard	(419)	6,818	6,210
*44094	Willoughby	(440)	22,336	20,510
*44094	Willoughby Hills	(440)	8,459	8,427
*44095	Willowick	(440)	14,004	15,269
45177	Wilmington	(937)	12,474	11,199
45459	Woodbourne-Hyde Park (c)	(937)	*7,910*	7,837
*43085	Worthington	(614)	13,202	14,869
45433	Wright-Patterson AFB (c)	(937)	*6,656*	8,579
*45215	Wyoming	(513)	7,719	8,128
45385	Xenia	(937)	23,600	24,836
*44501	Youngstown	(330)	82,837	95,732
*43701	Zanesville	(740)	25,253	26,778

Oklahoma

ZIP	Place	Area Code	2005	1990
*74820	Ada	(580)	15,999	15,765
*73521	Altus	(580)	19,899	21,910
73005	Anadarko	(405)	6,584	6,586
*73401	Ardmore	(580)	24,280	23,079
*74003	Bartlesville	(918)	34,734	34,256
73008	Bethany	(405)	19,786	20,075
74008	Bixby	(918)	18,600	9,502
74631	Blackwell	(580)	7,297	7,538
*74012	Broken Arrow	(918)	86,228	58,082
74015	Catoosa	(918)	6,440	2,954
*73018	Chickasha	(405)	16,849	14,988
73020	Choctaw	(405)	10,529	8,545
*74017	Claremore	(918)	17,161	13,280
73601	Clinton	(580)	8,363	9,298
74429	Coweta	(918)	8,352	6,159
74023	Cushing	(918)	8,267	7,218
*73115	Del City	(405)	21,945	23,928
*73533	Duncan	(580)	22,306	21,732
*74701	Durant	(580)	14,795	12,929
*73034	Edmond	(405)	74,881	52,310
*73644	Elk City	(580)	10,743	10,428
73036	El Reno	(405)	16,097	15,414
*73701	Enid	(580)	46,416	45,309
74033	Glenpool	(918)	8,960	6,688
*74344	Grove	(918)	5,752	4,020
73044	Guthrie	(405)	10,800	10,440
73942	Guymon	(580)	10,643	7,803
74437	Henryetta	(918)	6,110	5,872
74848	Holdenville	(405)	5,538	4,893
74743	Hugo	(580)	5,521	5,978
74745	Idabel	(580)	6,916	6,957
74037	Jenks	(918)	13,095	7,484
*73501	Lawton	(580)	90,234	80,561
73443	Lone Grove	(—)	5,075	4,114
*74501	McAlester	(918)	18,105	16,739
*74354	Miami	(918)	13,565	13,142
*73140	Midwest City	(405)	54,890	52,267
*73153	Moore	(405)	47,697	40,318
*74401	Muskogee	(918)	39,766	37,708
73064	Mustang	(405)	15,887	10,434
73065	Newcastle	(405)	6,303	4,214
73068	Noble	(405)	5,518	4,710
*73069	Norman	(405)	101,719	80,071
*73125	Oklahoma City	(405)	531,324	444,724
74447	Okmulgee	(918)	12,854	13,441
*74055	Owasso	(918)	23,771	11,151
73075	Pauls Valley	(405)	6,178	6,150
73077	Perry	(580)	5,105	4,978
*74601	Ponca City	(580)	25,070	26,359
74953	Poteau	(918)	8,152	7,210
*74361	Pryor Creek	(918)	9,227	8,327
73080	Purcell	(405)	5,858	4,784
74955	Sallisaw	(918)	8,621	7,122
74063	Sand Springs	(918)	17,667	15,339
*74066	Sapulpa	(918)	20,619	18,074
*74868	Seminole	(405)	6,913	7,071
*74801	Shawnee	(405)	29,824	26,017
74070	Skiatook	(918)	6,290	4,910
*74074	Stillwater	(405)	40,906	36,676
*74464	Tahlequah	(918)	16,075	10,586
74873	Tecumseh	(405)	6,516	5,750
73120	The Village	(405)	9,827	10,353
*74103	Tulsa	(918)	382,457	367,302

ZIP	Place	Area Code	2005	1990
73089	Tuttle	(405)	5,365	2,807
74301	Vinita	(918)	6,017	5,804
*74467	Wagoner	(918)	7,877	6,894
*73123	Warr Acres	(405)	9,475	9,288
73772	Watonga	(580)	5,588	3,408
73096	Weatherford	(580)	9,738	10,124
*73801	Woodward	(580)	11,931	12,340
*73099	Yukon	(405)	22,032	20,935

Oregon

Area code (971) overlays area code (503). See introductory note.

ZIP	Place	Area Code	2005	1990
*97321	Albany	(541)	44,797	33,523
*97006	Aloha (c)	(503)	*41,741*	34,284
97601	Altamont (c)	(541)	*19,603*	18,591
97520	Ashland	(541)	20,829	16,252
97103	Astoria	(503)	9,784	10,069
97814	Baker City	(541)	9,703	9,140
*97005	Beaverton	(503)	85,775	53,307
*97701	Bend	(541)	67,152	23,740
97415	Brookings	(541)	6,297	4,400
97013	Canby	(503)	14,989	8,990
97225	Cedar Hills (c)	(503)	*8,949*	9,294
97291	Cedar Mill (c)	(503)	*12,597*	9,697
97502	Central Point	(541)	15,672	7,512
97058	City of the Dalles	(541)	11,894	11,021
97015	Clackamas (c)	(503)	*5,177*	2,578
97420	Coos Bay	(541)	15,823	15,076
97113	Cornelius	(503)	10,820	6,148
*97333	Corvallis	(541)	49,553	44,757
*97424	Cottage Grove	(541)	8,724	7,403
97338	Dallas	(503)	14,001	9,422
97009	Damascus	(—)	9,454	—
97524	Eagle Point	(541)	7,496	3,026
*97440	Eugene	(541)	144,515	112,733
97024	Fairview	(503)	9,327	2,588
97439	Florence	(541)	7,841	5,171
97116	Forest Grove	(503)	19,689	13,559
97301	Four Corners (c)	(503)	*13,922*	12,156
97223	Garden Home-Whitford (c)	(503)	*6,931*	6,652
97027	Gladstone	(503)	12,117	10,152
*97526	Grants Pass	(541)	28,882	17,503
97470	Green (c)	(541)	*6,174*	5,076
*97030	Gresham	(503)	96,072	68,285
*97015	Happy Valley	(503)	8,282	1,552
97303	Hayesville (c)	(503)	*18,222*	14,318
97838	Hermiston	(541)	14,657	10,047
*97123	Hillsboro	(503)	84,533	37,598
97031	Hood River	(541)	6,480	4,632
97351	Independence	(503)	8,193	4,425
97222	Jennings Lodge (c)	(503)	*7,036*	6,530
97448	Junction City	(541)	5,369	3,961
97307	Keizer	(503)	34,644	21,884
*97601	Klamath Falls	(541)	19,882	17,737
97850	La Grande	(541)	12,440	11,766
*97034	Lake Oswego	(503)	36,502	30,576
97739	La Pine (c)	(541)	*5,799*	—
97355	Lebanon	(541)	13,834	10,950
97367	Lincoln City	(541)	7,849	5,903
97128	McMinnville	(503)	29,646	17,894
97741	Madras	(541)	5,300	3,443
*97501	Medford	(541)	70,147	47,021
97862	Milton-Freewater	(541)	6,445	5,533
*97269	Milwaukie	(503)	20,810	18,670
97038	Molalla	(503)	6,737	3,651
97361	Monmouth	(503)	8,987	6,288
97132	Newberg	(503)	20,681	13,086
*97365	Newport	(541)	9,833	8,437
97459	North Bend	(541)	9,843	9,614
97268	Oak Grove (c)	(503)	*12,808*	12,576
97006	Oak Hills (c)	(—)	*9,050*	6,450
97267	Oatfield (c)	(—)	*15,750*	15,348
97914	Ontario	(541)	11,125	9,394
97045	Oregon City	(503)	30,221	14,698
97801	Pendleton	(541)	16,636	15,142
*97208	Portland	(503)	533,427	485,975
97754	Prineville	(541)	8,908	5,355
97225	Raleigh Hills (c)	(503)	*5,865*	6,066
97756	Redmond	(541)	19,771	7,165
97527	Redwood (c)	(—)	*5,844*	3,702
97229	Rockcreek (c)	(—)	*9,404*	8,282
97470	Roseburg	(541)	20,727	18,389
97470	Roseburg North (c)	(541)	*5,473*	6,831
97051	Saint Helens	(503)	11,874	7,535
*97309	Salem	(503)	148,751	107,793
97055	Sandy	(503)	7,871	4,154
97056	Scappoose	(503)	5,913	3,550
97138	Seaside	(503)	6,116	5,359
97378	Sheridan	(503)	5,570	3,950
97140	Sherwood	(503)	15,398	3,093
97381	Silverton	(503)	8,233	5,635
*97477	Springfield	(541)	55,641	44,664
97383	Stayton	(503)	7,184	5,011
97015	Sunnyside (c)	(503)	*6,791*	4,423
97479	Sutherlin	(541)	7,281	5,020
97386	Sweet Home	(541)	8,389	6,850
97540	Talent	(541)	6,018	3,274
*97281	Tigard	(503)	47,968	29,435
97060	Troutdale	(503)	14,898	7,852

ZIP	Place	Area Code	2005	1990
97062	Tualatin	(503)	25,881	14,664
97882	Umatilla	(541)	6,306	3,058
97225	West Haven-Sylvan (c)	(503)	7,147	6,009
97068	West Linn	(503)	25,094	16,389
*97225	West Slope (c)	(503)	6,442	7,959
97503	White City (c)	(541)	5,466	5,891
97070	Wilsonville	(503)	16,075	7,510
97071	Woodburn	(503)	21,736	13,404

Pennsylvania

Area code (267) overlays area code (215). Area code (484) overlays (610). Area code (878) overlays (412). See introductory note.

ZIP	Place	Area Code	2005	1990
15001	Aliquippa	(724)	11,105	13,374
*18105	Allentown	(610)	106,992	105,301
*16603	Altoona	(814)	47,176	51,881
19002	Ambler	(215)	6,349	6,609
15003	Ambridge	(724)	7,329	8,133
18403	Archbald	(570)	6,290	6,291
19003	Ardmore (c)	(610)	12,616	12,646
15210	Arlington Heights (c)	(412)	5,132	4,768
15068	Arnold	(724)	5,401	6,113
19407	Audubon (c)	(610)	6,549	6,328
18612	Back Mountain (c)	—	26,690	—
15234	Baldwin	(412)	18,842	21,923
*18013	Bangor	(610)	5,305	5,383
15010	Beaver Falls	(724)	9,402	10,687
16823	Bellefonte	(814)	6,161	6,358
15202	Bellevue	(412)	8,231	9,126
18603	Berwick	(570)	10,352	10,976
15102	Bethel Park	(412)	32,313	33,823
*18016	Bethlehem	(610)	72,895	71,427
19508	Birdsboro	(610)	5,191	4,222
18447	Blakely	(570)	6,817	7,222
*17815	Bloomsburg	(570)	12,915	12,439
19422	Blue Bell (c)	(215)/(610)	6,395	6,091
19061	Boothwyn (c)	(610)	5,206	5,069
16701	Bradford	(814)	8,651	9,625
15227	Brentwood	(412)	9,811	10,823
15017	Bridgeville	(412)	5,022	5,445
19007	Bristol	(215)	9,810	10,405
19015	Brookhaven	(610)	7,849	8,570
19008	Broomall (c)	(610)	11,046	10,930
*16001	Butler	(724)	14,521	15,714
15419	California	(724)	5,072	5,748
*17011	Camp Hill	(717)	7,424	7,831
15317	Canonsburg	(724)	8,810	9,200
18407	Carbondale	(570)	9,348	10,664
17201	Chambersburg	(717)	17,961	16,647
*17013	Carlisle	(717)	18,108	18,419
15106	Carnegie	(412)	8,149	9,278
15108	Carnot-Moon (c)	(412)	10,637	10,187
15234	Castle Shannon	(412)	8,269	9,135
18032	Catasauqua	(610)	6,553	6,662
17201	Chambersburg	(717)	17,961	16,647
*19013	Chester	(610)	37,058	41,856
15025	Clairton	(412)	8,081	9,656
16214	Clarion	(814)	5,507	6,457
18411	Clarks Summit	(570)	5,010	5,433
16830	Clearfield	(814)	6,339	6,633
19018	Clifton Heights	(610)	6,626	7,111
19320	Coatesville	(610)	11,495	11,038
19426	Collegeville	—	5,055	—
19023	Collingdale	(610)	8,501	9,175
17109	Colonial Park (c)	(717)	13,259	13,777
17512	Columbia	(717)	10,092	10,701
15425	Connellsville	(724)	8,644	9,229
*19428	Conshohocken	(610)	7,711	8,064
15108	Coraopolis	(412)	5,754	6,747
16407	Corry	(814)	6,548	7,216
15205	Crafton	(412)	6,289	7,188
19021	Croydon (c)	(215)	9,993	9,967
19023	Darby	(610)	10,046	11,140
19036	Darby Twp. (c)	(610)	9,622	10,955
19333	Devon-Berwyn (c)	(610)	5,067	5,019
18519	Dickson City	(570)	5,967	6,276
15033	Donora	(724)	5,420	5,928
15216	Dormont	(412)	8,696	9,772
*19335	Downingtown	(610)	7,858	7,749
18901	Doylestown	(215)	8,225	8,575
19026	Drexel Hill (c)	(610)	29,364	29,744
15801	Du Bois	(814)	7,838	8,286
*18512	Dunmore	(570)	13,968	15,403
15110	Duquesne	(412)	6,875	8,525
19401	East Norriton (c)	(610)	13,211	13,324
*18042	Easton	(610)	26,267	26,276
18301	East Stroudsburg	(570)	10,621	8,781
17402	East York (c)	(717)	8,782	8,487
—	Economy	(724)	9,291	9,305
*16412	Edinboro	(814)	6,737	7,736
17022	Elizabethtown	(717)	11,892	9,952
16117	Ellwood City	(724)	8,262	8,894
*18049	Emmaus	(610)	11,351	11,157
17025	Enola (c)	(717)	5,627	5,961
17522	Ephrata	(717)	13,092	12,133
*16501	Erie	(814)	102,612	108,718
18643	Exeter	(570)	6,007	5,691
19030	Fairless Hills (c)	(215)	8,365	9,026
16121	Farrell	(724)	5,999	6,835
19053	Feasterville-Trevose (c)	(215)	6,525	6,696

ZIP	Place	Area Code	2005	1990
16063	Fernway (c)	(724)	12,188	9,072
19032	Folcroft	(610)	6,906	7,506
19033	Folsom (c)	(610)	8,072	8,173
15221	Forest Hills	(412)	6,424	7,335
15238	Fox Chapel	(412)	5,238	5,319
16323	Franklin	(814)	6,879	7,329
—	Franklin Park	(412)	11,765	10,109
18052	Fullerton (c)	(610)	14,268	13,127
*17325	Gettysburg	(717)	8,014	7,025
19036	Glenolden	(610)	7,309	7,260
19038	Glenside (c)	(215)	7,914	8,704
*15601	Greensburg	(724)	15,569	16,318
16125	Greenville	(724)	6,355	6,734
16127	Grove City	(412)	7,764	8,240
15101	Hampton Twp. (c) (Allegheny Co.)	(412)	17,526	15,568
*17331	Hanover	(717)	14,990	14,399
19438	Harleysville (c)	(215)	8,795	7,405
*17105	Harrisburg	(717)	47,472	52,376
15065	Harrison Twp. (c) (Allegheny Co.)	(412)	10,934	11,763
19040	Hatboro	(215)	7,288	7,382
*18201	Hazleton	(570)	22,125	24,730
18055	Hellertown	(610)	5,615	5,662
16148	Hermitage	(724)	16,571	15,260
17033	Hershey (c)	(717)	12,771	11,860
16648	Hollidaysburg	(814)	5,519	5,624
16001	Homeacre-Lyndora (c)	(724)	6,685	7,511
19044	Horsham (c)	(215)	14,779	15,051
*16652	Huntingdon	(814)	6,876	6,843
*15701	Indiana	(724)	15,016	15,174
15644	Jeannette	(724)	10,196	11,221
15025	Jefferson Hills	(412)	9,642	—
*15907	Johnstown	(814)	22,539	28,124
15108	Kennedy Twp. (c)	(412)	7,504	7,152
19348	Kennett Square	(610)	5,292	5,218
19406	King of Prussia (c)	(610)	18,511	18,406
18704	Kingston	(570)	13,176	14,507
19443	Kulpsville (c)	(215)	8,005	5,183
*17604	Lancaster	(717)	54,757	55,551
19446	Lansdale	(215)	15,913	16,362
19050	Lansdowne	(610)	10,789	11,712
15650	Latrobe	(724)	8,654	9,265
17540	Leacock-Leola-Bareville (c)	(717)	6,625	5,685
*17042	Lebanon	(717)	23,986	24,800
18235	Lehighton	(610)	5,523	5,914
*19055	Levittown (c)	(215)	53,966	55,362
*17837	Lewisburg	(570)	5,562	5,785
17044	Lewistown	(717)	8,649	9,341
17112	Linglestown (c)	(717)	6,414	5,862
19353	Lionville-Marchwood (c)	(610)	6,298	6,468
17543	Lititz	(717)	9,008	8,280
17745	Lock Haven	(570)	8,784	9,230
17011	Lower Allen (c)	(717)	6,619	6,329
15068	Lower Burrell	(724)	12,444	12,251
15237	McCandless Twp. (c)	(412)	29,022	28,781
*15134	McKeesport	(412)	22,701	26,016
15136	McKees Rocks	(412)	6,201	7,691
19002	Maple Glen (c)	(215)	7,042	5,881
*16335	Meadville	(814)	13,368	14,318
*17055	Mechanicsburg	(717)	8,818	9,452
*19063	Media	(610)	5,451	5,957
17057	Middletown (Dauphin Co.)	(717)	8,944	9,254
18017	Middletown (c) (Northampton Co.)	(610)	7,378	6,866
17551	Millersville	(717)	7,583	8,099
17847	Milton	(570)	6,484	6,746
15061	Monaca	(724)	5,973	6,739
15062	Monessen	(724)	8,307	9,901
18936	Montgomeryville (c)	(215)	12,031	9,114
18507	Moosic	(570)	5,738	5,397
19067	Morrisville (Bucks Co.)	(215)	9,810	9,765
18707	Mountain Top (c)	(570)	15,269	—
17851	Mount Carmel	(570)	6,053	7,196
17552	Mount Joy	(717)	6,944	6,398
15228	Mount Lebanon (c)	(412)	33,017	34,414
15120	Munhall	(412)	11,513	13,158
*15146	Municipality of Monroeville	(412)	28,175	29,169
15668	Municipality of Murrysville	(724)	19,441	17,240
18634	Nanticoke	(570)	10,382	12,267
18064	Nazareth	(610)	6,023	5,713
19086	Nether Providence Twp. (c)	(610)	13,456	12,730
15066	New Brighton	(724)	6,275	6,854
*16108	New Castle	(724)	25,030	28,334
17070	New Cumberland	(717)	7,127	7,665
17557	New Holland	(717)	5,140	4,484
*15068	New Kensington	(724)	14,085	15,894
*19403	Norristown	(610)	30,689	30,754
18067	Northampton	(610)	9,699	8,717
15104	North Braddock	(412)	5,996	7,036
15137	North Versailles (c)	(412)	11,125	13,294
16421	Northwest Harborcreek (c)	(814)	8,658	7,485
19074	Norwood	(610)	5,852	6,162
15139	Oakmont	(412)	6,587	6,961
15238	O'Hara Twp. (c)	(412)	8,856	9,096
16301	Oil City	(814)	10,942	11,949
18518	Old Forge	(570)	8,558	8,834
19075	Oreland (c)	(215)	5,509	5,695
18071	Palmerton	(610)	5,279	5,394
17078	Palmyra	(717)	6,957	6,910
19301	Paoli (c)	(610)	5,425	5,277
16801	Park Forest Village (c)	(814)	8,830	6,703
17331	Parkville (c)	(717)	6,593	5,009

ZIP	Place	Area Code	2005	1990
17112	Paxtonia (c)	(570)	5,254	4,862
15235	Penn Hills (c)	(412)	46,809	57,632
19096	Penn Wynne (c)	(610)	5,382	5,807
18944	Perkasie	(215)	8,736	7,878
*19104	Philadelphia	(215)	1,463,281	1,585,577
*19460	Phoenixville	(610)	15,420	15,066
*15233	Pittsburgh	(412)	316,718	369,879
*18640	Pittston	(570)	7,689	9,389
15236	Pleasant Hills	(412)	7,940	8,884
15239	Plum	(412)	26,452	25,609
18651	Plymouth	(570)	6,161	7,134
19462	Plymouth Meeting (c)	(610)	5,593	6,241
*19464	Pottstown	(610)	21,551	21,831
17901	Pottsville	(570)	14,764	16,603
17109	Progress (c)	(717)	9,647	9,654
19076	Prospect Park	(610)	6,449	6,764
15767	Punxsutawney	(814)	6,036	6,782
18951	Quakertown	(215)	8,823	8,982
19087	Radnor Twp. (c)	(610)	30,878	27,676
*19612	Reading	(610)	80,855	78,380
17356	Red Lion	(717)	6,084	6,130
18954	Richboro (c)	(215)	6,678	5,141
19078	Ridley Park	(610)	7,062	7,592
15237	Ross Twp. (c)	(412)	32,551	35,102
15857	Saint Marys	(814)	13,873	14,020
19464	Sanatoga (c)	(610)	7,734	3,723
18840	Sayre	(570)	5,606	5,791
17972	Schuylkill Haven	(570)	5,283	5,610
15106	Scott Twp. (c)	(412)	17,288	20,413
*18505	Scranton	(570)	73,120	81,805
17870	Selinsgrove	(570)	5,417	5,384
15116	Shaler Twp. (c)	(412)	29,757	33,694
17872	Shamokin	(570)	7,581	9,184
*16146	Sharon	(724)	15,504	17,533
19079	Sharon Hill	(610)	5,357	5,771
17976	Shenandoah	(570)	5,296	6,221
19607	Shillington	(610)	5,031	5,062
17404	Shiloh (c)	(717)	10,192	5,315
17257	Shippensburg	(717)	5,605	5,331
*15501	Somerset	(814)	6,500	6,454
18964	Souderton	(215)	6,691	5,957
15129	South Park Twp. (c)	(814)	14,340	14,292
17702	South Williamsport	(570)	6,189	6,496
19064	Springfield (c) (Delaware Co.)	(610)	23,677	25,326
*16804	State College	(814)	38,720	38,981
17113	Steelton	(717)	5,667	5,152
15136	Stowe Twp. (c)	(412)	6,706	9,202
18360	Stroudsburg	(570)	6,264	5,312
—	Sugarcreek	(814)	5,115	5,532
*17801	Sunbury	(570)	10,086	11,591
19081	Swarthmore	(610)	6,146	6,157
15218	Swissvale	(412)	9,043	10,637
18252	Tamaqua	(570)	6,754	7,943
18517	Taylor	(570)	6,227	6,941
16354	Titusville	(814)	5,862	6,434
19401	Trooper (c)	(610)	6,061	7,370
15145	Turtle Creek	(412)	5,704	6,556
16686	Tyrone	(814)	5,324	5,743
15401	Uniontown	(724)	11,935	12,034
19063	Upper Providence Twp. (c)	(610)	10,509	9,477
15241	Upper Saint Clair (c)	(412)	20,053	19,023
15690	Vandergrift	(724)	5,190	5,904
19013	Village Green-Green Ridge (c)	(610)	8,279	9,026
*16365	Warren	(814)	9,648	11,122
15301	Washington (Wash. Co.)	(724)	15,136	15,864
17268	Waynesboro	(717)	9,700	9,578
17315	Weigelstown (c)	(717)	10,117	8,665
*19380	West Chester	(610)	18,047	18,041
19380	West Goshen (c)	(610)	8,472	8,948
*15122	West Mifflin	(412)	21,236	23,644
—	Westmont	(814)	5,234	5,789
19401	West Norriton (c)	(610)	14,901	15,209
15229	West View	(412)	6,863	7,734
18052	Whitehall (Allegheny Co.)	(412)	13,744	14,451
15131	White Oak	(412)	8,185	8,761
*18703	Wilkes-Barre	(570)	41,331	47,523
15221	Wilkinsburg	(412)	18,008	21,080
15145	Wilkins Twp. (c)	(412)	6,917	7,487
*17701	Williamsport	(570)	30,111	31,933
19090	Willow Grove (c)	(215)	16,234	16,325
17584	Willow Street (c)	(717)	7,258	5,817
15025	Wilson	(412)	7,753	7,830
19094	Woodlyn (c)	(610)	10,036	10,151
19038	Wyndmoor (c)	(215)	5,601	5,682
19610	Wyomissing	(610)	10,434	7,332
19050	Yeadon	(610)	11,506	11,980
*17405	York	(717)	40,418	42,192

Rhode Island (401)

See introductory note.

ZIP	Place	2005	1990
02806	Barrington	16,757	15,849
02809	Bristol	24,658	21,625
02830	Burrillville	16,563	16,230
02863	Central Falls	19,159	17,637
02813	Charlestown	8,269	6,478
02816	Coventry	35,080	31,083
02864	Cumberland	81,614	29,038
02864	Cumberland Hill (c)	7,738	6,379

ZIP	Place	2005	1990
*02905	Cranston	81,614	76,060
02818	East Greenwich	13,616	11,865
02914	East Providence	49,515	50,380
02822	Exeter	6,298	5,461
02814	Glocester	10,603	9,227
02828	Greenville (c)	8,626	8,303
02833	Hopkinton	8,121	6,873
02835	Jamestown	5,611	4,999
02919	Johnston	29,163	26,542
02881	Kingston (c)	5,446	6,504
02865	Lincoln	22,106	18,045
02842	Middletown	16,737	19,460
02882	Narragansett	16,906	15,004
02840	Newport	25,340	28,227
02843	Newport East (c)	11,463	11,080
02852	North Kingstown	27,093	23,786
02908	North Providence	33,165	32,090
02896	North Smithfield	11,191	10,497
*02860	Pawtucket	73,742	72,644
02871	Portsmouth	17,129	16,857
*02904	Providence	176,862	160,728
02812	Richmond	7,769	5,351
02857	Scituate	10,971	9,796
02917	Smithfield	21,806	19,163
02879	South Kingstown	29,327	24,612
02878	Tiverton (c)	7,282	7,259
02878	Tiverton	15,336	14,312
02864	Valley Falls (c)	11,599	11,175
*02879	Wakefield-Peacedale (c)	8,468	7,134
02885	Warren	11,328	11,385
*02886	Warwick	87,233	85,427
02891	Westerly (c)	17,682	16,477
02891	Westerly	23,635	21,605
02817	West Greenwich	5,677	—
02893	West Warwick	29,984	29,268
02895	Woonsocket	44,328	43,877

South Carolina

ZIP	Place	Area Code	2005	1990
29620	Abbeville	(864)	5,732	5,778
*29801	Aiken	(803)	27,490	20,386
*29621	Anderson	(864)	25,899	26,385
*29070	Batesburg-Leesville	(803)	5,575	6,107
29920/				
29906	Beaufort	(843)	12,058	9,576
29841	Belvedere (c)	(803)	5,631	6,133
29512	Bennettsville	(843)	9,351	10,095
29611	Berea (c)	(864)	14,158	13,535
29902	Burton (c)	(843)	7,180	6,917
29020	Camden	(803)	7,000	6,696
29033	Cayce	(803)	12,432	10,824
29625	Centerville (c)	(573)	5,181	4,866
*29402	Charleston	(843)	106,712	88,256
29520	Cheraw	(843)	5,474	5,553
29706	Chester	(803)	6,199	7,158
*29631	Clemson	(864)	12,364	11,145
29325	Clinton	(864)	9,071	9,603
*29201	Columbia	(803)	117,088	110,734
*29526	Conway	(843)	13,442	9,819
*29532	Darlington	(843)	6,525	7,310
29204	Dentsville (c)	(803)	13,009	11,839
29536	Dillon	(843)	6,366	6,829
*29640	Easley	(864)	18,852	15,179
29681	Five Forks (c)	(864)	8,064	—
*29501	Florence	(843)	31,269	29,913
29206	Forest Acres	(803)	9,991	7,181
*29715	Fort Mill	(803)	8,257	4,930
29644	Fountain Inn	(864)	6,729	4,388
*29341	Gaffney	(864)	12,934	13,149
29605	Gantt (c)	(864)	13,962	13,891
29576	Garden City (c)	(843)	9,357	6,305
*29442	Georgetown	(843)	8,941	9,517
29445	Goose Creek	(843)	32,516	24,692
*29602	Greenville	(864)	56,676	58,256
*29646	Greenwood	(864)	22,378	20,807
*29650	Greer	(864)	21,421	10,322
*29406	Hanahan	(843)	13,818	13,176
*29550	Hartsville	(843)	7,414	8,372
*29928	Hilton Head Island	(843)	34,497	23,694
29621	Homeland Park (c)	(864)	6,337	6,569
29063	Irmo	(803)	11,223	11,284
29456	Ladson (c)	(843)	13,264	13,540
29560	Lake City	(843)	6,690	7,153
*29720	Lancaster	(803)	8,371	8,914
29902	Laurel Bay (c)	(843)	6,625	4,972
29360	Laurens	(864)	9,824	9,694
*29072	Lexington	(803)	13,586	4,046
29566	Little River (c)	(843)	7,027	3,470
29078	Lugoff (c)	(803)	6,278	3,211
29571	Marion	(843)	6,997	7,658
29662	Mauldin	(864)	19,343	11,662
*29461	Moncks Corner	(843)	6,525	5,599
*29465	Mount Pleasant	(843)	57,932	30,108
29576	Murrells Inlet (c)	(843)	5,519	3,334
*29575	Myrtle Beach	(803)	26,593	24,848
29108	Newberry	(803)	10,659	10,543
*29841	North Augusta	(803)	19,467	15,684
*29410	North Charleston	(843)	86,313	70,304
*29582	North Myrtle Beach	(843)	14,096	8,731

ZIP	Place	Area Code	2005	1990
29565	Oak Grove (c)	(803)	8,183	7,173
*29115	Orangeburg	(803)	14,460	13,772
29935	Port Royal	(843)	9,347	2,985
29611	Parker (c)	(864)	10,760	11,072
29642	Powderville (c)	—	5,362	—
29072	Red Bank (c)	(803)	8,811	5,950
29020	Red Hill (c)	(843)	10,509	6,112
*29730	Rock Hill	(803)	59,554	42,112
*29417	Saint Andrews (c)	(843)	21,814	25,692
29609	Sans Souci (c)	(864)	7,836	7,612
*29678	Seneca	(864)	7,962	7,726
29210	Seven Oaks (c)	(803)	15,755	15,722
*29681	Simpsonville	(864)	15,135	11,744
29577	Socastee (c)	(843)	14,295	10,426
*29306	Spartanburg	(864)	38,379	43,479
*29483	Summerville	(843)	37,714	22,519
*29150	Sumter	(803)	39,679	40,977
29687	Taylors (c)	(864)	20,125	19,619
29379	Union	(864)	8,321	9,840
29607	Wade Hampton (c)	(864)	20,458	20,014
29488	Walterboro	(843)	5,548	5,595
29611	Welcome (c)	(864)	6,390	6,560
*29169	West Columbia	(803)	13,413	10,974
29206	Woodfield (c)	(803)	9,238	8,862
29745	York	(803)	7,233	6,709

South Dakota (605)

ZIP	Place	2005	1990
*57401	Aberdeen	24,098	24,995
57005	Brandon	7,176	3,545
*57006	Brookings	18,715	16,270
*57350	Huron	11,086	12,448
57042	Madison	6,223	6,257
57301	Mitchell	14,696	13,798
57501	Pierre	14,052	12,906
*57701	Rapid City	62,167	54,523
*57701	Rapid Valley (c)	61,459	5,968
*57101	Sioux Falls	139,517	100,836
*57783	Spearfish	9,355	6,966
57785	Sturgis	6,260	5,537
57069	Vermillion	9,964	10,034
57201	Watertown	20,265	17,623
*57078	Yankton	13,716	12,703

Tennessee

ZIP	Place	Area Code	2005	1990
37701	Alcoa	(865)	8,388	6,400
*37303	Athens	(423)	13,878	12,054
38004	Atoka	(901)	5,676	659
*38184	Bartlett	(901)	43,263	27,038
37660	Bloomingdale (c)	(423)	10,350	10,953
38008	Bolivar	(731)	5,652	5,969
*37027	Brentwood	(615)	32,426	16,392
*37621	Bristol	(423)	24,994	23,421
38012	Brownsville	(731)	10,720	10,017
*37401	Chattanooga	(423)	154,762	152,393
*37642	Church Hill	(423)	6,370	5,208
*37040	Clarksville	(931)	112,878	75,542
*37311	Cleveland	(423)	38,186	32,236
*37716	Clinton	(865)	9,381	8,960
37315	Collegedale	(423)	7,215	5,048
*38017	Collierville	(901)	37,564	14,501
37663	Colonial Heights (c)	(423)	7,067	6,716
*38401	Columbia	(931)	33,777	28,583
*38501	Cookeville	(931)	27,743	21,744
38019	Covington	(901)	9,018	7,487
*38555	Crossville	(931)	10,424	6,930
37321	Dayton	(423)	6,443	5,671
*37055	Dickson	(615)	12,873	10,487
*38024	Dyersburg	(731)	17,466	16,321
37411	East Brainerd (c)	(423)	14,132	11,594
37412	East Ridge	(423)	19,821	21,101
*37643	Elizabethton	(423)	13,944	13,087
37650	Erwin	(423)	5,786	5,318
37062	Fairview	(615)	7,190	4,210
*37922	Farragut	(865)	19,054	12,802
37334	Fayetteville	(931)	7,034	7,158
37215	Forest Hills (c)	(615)	5,168	—
*37064	Franklin	(615)	53,311	20,098
37066	Gallatin	(615)	26,720	18,794
*38138	Germantown	(901)	37,480	33,159
*37072	Goodlettsville	(615)	15,320	11,219
37073	Greenbrier	(615)	6,054	3,062
*37743	Greeneville	(423)	15,383	13,532
37215	Green Hill (c)	(615)	7,068	6,763
37748	Harriman	(865)	6,725	7,119
37341	Harrison (c)	(423)	7,630	7,191
37074	Hartsville-Trousdale	(615)	7,677	2,222
38340	Henderson	(731)	6,061	4,760
*37075	Hendersonville	(615)	44,876	32,188
38343	Humboldt	(731)	9,269	9,651
*38301	Jackson	(731)	62,099	49,145
37760	Jefferson City	(865)	7,931	5,875
*37601	Johnson City	(423)	58,718	50,354
*37662	Kingsport	(423)	44,130	40,457
37763	Kingston	(423)	5,472	4,552
*37950	Knoxville	(865)	180,130	169,761
*37766	La Follette	(423)	8,166	7,201
*37086	La Vergne	(615)	25,885	7,496

ZIP	Place	Area Code	2005	1990
38002	Lakeland	(901)	7,388	1,204
38464	Lawrenceburg	(931)	10,911	10,397
*37087	Lebanon	(615)	23,043	15,208
*37771	Lenoir City	(865)	7,675	6,147
37091	Lewisburg	(931)	10,790	9,879
38351	Lexington	(731)	7,667	5,810
*37352	Lynchburg	(931)	6,024	4,721
38201	McKenzie	(731)	5,434	5,168
*37110	McMinnville	(931)	13,242	11,194
37355	Manchester	(931)	9,497	7,709
38237	Martin	(731)	10,151	8,600
37801	Maryville	(865)	25,851	19,208
*38101	Memphis	(901)	672,277	618,652
37343	Middle Valley (c)	(423)	11,854	12,255
38358	Milan	(731)	7,823	7,512
37072	Millersville	(615)	6,114	2,575
*38053	Millington	(901)	10,306	17,866
*37813	Morristown	(423)	26,187	22,513
*37645	Mount Carmel	(423)	5,270	4,268
*37122	Mount Juliet	(615)	18,099	5,389
38058	Munford	(901)	5,652	2,944
*37130	Murfreesboro	(615)	86,793	44,922
*37202	Nashville	(615)	549,110	488,366
*37821	Newport	(423)	7,299	7,123
*37830	Oak Ridge	(865)	27,297	27,310
37363	Ooltewah (c)	(423)	5,681	4,903
38242	Paris	(731)	9,874	9,332
*37862	Pigeon Forge	(865)	5,784	3,027
37148	Portland	(615)	10,342	5,539
38478	Pulaski	(931)	7,917	7,916
37415	Red Bank	(423)	11,726	12,320
38063	Ripley	(731)	7,772	6,634
37854	Rockwood	(865)	5,426	5,348
38372	Savannah	(731)	7,200	6,547
*37862	Sevierville	(865)	14,788	7,178
37865	Seymour (c)	(865)	8,850	7,026
*37160	Shelbyville	(931)	18,648	14,042
37377	Signal Mountain	(423)	7,146	7,034
37167	Smyrna	(615)	33,497	14,720
*37379	Soddy-Daisy	(423)	11,985	8,240
37311	South Cleveland (c)	(423)	6,216	5,372
37172	Springfield	(615)	15,916	11,227
37174	Spring Hill	(931)	17,148	1,464
37874	Sweetwater	(423)	6,117	5,066
*37388	Tullahoma	(931)	18,909	16,761
*38261	Union City	(731)	10,788	10,513
37188	White House	(615)	8,723	2,987
37398	Winchester	(931)	7,752	6,305

Texas

Area codes (281) and (832) overlay area code (713). Area code (430) overlays (903). Area code (682) overlays (817). Area codes (972) and (469) overlay (214). See introductory note.

ZIP	Place	Area Code	2005	1990
*79604	Abilene	(325)	114,757	106,707
—	Abram-Perezville (c)	—	5,444	3,999
75001	Addison	(214)	13,667	8,783
78516	Alamo	(956)	15,976	8,352
78209	Alamo Heights	(210)	7,113	6,502
77039	Aldine (c)	(713)	13,979	11,133
*78332	Alice	(361)	19,519	19,788
*75002	Allen	(214)	69,222	19,315
*79830	Alpine	(432)	6,065	5,622
78574	Alton	(956)	7,057	3,048
78572	Alton North (c)	(956)	5,051	—
*77511	Alvin	(713)	22,171	19,220
*79105	Amarillo	(806)	183,021	157,571
78750	Anderson Mill (c)	—	8,953	9,468
79714	Andrews	(432)	9,391	10,678
*77515	Angleton	(979)	18,761	17,140
*78336	Aransas Pass	(361)	8,877	7,180
*76004	Arlington	(817)	362,805	261,717
77346	Atascocita (c)	(281)	35,757	—
*75751	Athens	(903)	12,559	10,982
75551	Atlanta	(214)	5,677	6,118
*78712	Austin	(512)	690,252	472,020
*76020	Azle	(817)	10,350	8,868
77518	Bacliff (c)	(409)	19,343	5,549
75180	Balch Springs	(214)	19,475	17,406
78602	Bastrop	(512)	7,297	4,044
*77414	Bay City	(979)	18,323	18,170
*77520	Baytown	(713)	68,371	63,843
*77707	Beaumont	(409)	111,799	114,323
*76021	Bedford	(817)	48,390	43,762
*78102	Beeville	(361)	13,560	13,547
*77401	Bellaire	(713)	17,206	13,844
*76715	Bellmead	(254)	9,555	8,336
76513	Belton	(254)	15,530	12,463
*76126	Benbrook	(817)	21,922	19,564
*79720	Big Spring	(432)	24,253	23,093
*78006	Boerne	(830)	8,054	4,361
75418	Bonham	(903)	10,556	6,688
*79007	Borger	(806)	13,305	15,675
76230	Bowie	(940)	5,543	4,990
76825	Brady	(325)	5,345	5,946
76424	Breckenridge	(254)	5,649	5,665
*76020	Briar (c)	(817)	5,350	3,899
*77833	Brenham	(979)	14,161	11,952
77611	Bridge City	(409)	8,800	8,010

ZIP	Place	Area Code	2005	1990
76426	Bridgeport	(940)	5,659	3,581
79316	Brownfield	(806)	9,173	9,560
*78520	Brownsville	(956)	167,493	107,027
*76801	Brownwood	(325)	19,566	18,387
78717	Brushy Creek (c)	(903)	15,371	5,833
*77801	Bryan	(979)	66,306	55,002
76354	Burkburnett	(940)	10,378	10,145
*76028	Burleson	(817)	29,613	16,113
78611	Burnet	(512)	5,562	3,423
76520	Cameron	(254)	5,900	5,635
78526	Cameron Park (c)	(956)	5,961	5,802
79835	Canutillo (c)	(915)	5,129	4,442
*79015	Canyon	(806)	13,353	11,365
78130	Canyon Lake (c)	(830)	16,870	9,975
78834	Carrizo Springs	(830)	5,681	5,745
*75006	Carrollton	(214)	118,870	82,169
75633	Carthage	(903)	6,611	6,496
*75104	Cedar Hill	(214)	41,582	19,988
*78613	Cedar Park	(512)	48,139	5,161
75935	Center	(936)	5,781	4,950
77530	Channelview (c)	(713)	29,685	25,564
79201	Childress	(940)	6,606	5,055
78108	Cibolo	(210)	7,804	1,757
77450	Cinco Ranch (c)	(281)	11,196	—
*76031	Cleburne	(817)	29,184	22,205
*77327	Cleveland	(713)	8,032	7,124
77015	Cloverleaf (c)	(713)	23,508	18,230
77531	Clute	(979)	10,731	9,467
*77840	College Station	(979)	72,388	52,443
76034	Colleyville	(817)	22,394	12,724
*75428	Commerce	(903)	8,971	6,825
*77301	Conroe	(936)	47,042	27,675
78109	Converse	(210)	12,650	8,887
*75019	Coppell	(214)	38,704	16,881
76522	Copperas Cove	(254)	30,643	24,079
*76205	Corinth	(940)	17,980	3,944
*78469	Corpus Christi	(361)	283,474	257,428
*75110	Corsicana	(903)	26,052	22,911
75835	Crockett	(936)	7,039	7,024
76036	Crowley	(817)	9,691	6,974
78839	Crystal City	(830)	7,224	8,263
77954	Cuero	(361)	6,770	6,700
79022	Dalhart	(806)	7,146	6,246
*75221	Dallas	(214)	1,213,825	1,007,618
77535	Dayton	(936)	6,622	5,042
76234	Decatur	(214)	6,031	4,245
77536	Deer Park	(713)	28,993	27,424
*78840	Del Rio	(830)	36,020	30,705
*75020	Denison	(903)	23,648	21,505
*76201	Denton	(940)	104,153	66,270
*75115	De Soto	(214)	44,653	30,544
75941	Diboll	(936)	5,441	4,341
77539	Dickinson	(281)	17,898	11,692
78537	Donna	(956)	15,846	12,652
79029	Dumas	(806)	13,887	12,871
*75138	Duncanville	(214)	35,150	35,008
76135	Eagle Mountain (c)	(817)	6,599	5,847
*78852	Eagle Pass	(830)	25,571	20,651
*78539	Edinburg	(956)	62,735	31,091
77957	Edna	(361)	5,870	5,436
78852	Eidson Road (c)	(830)	9,348	—
77437	El Campo	(979)	10,884	10,511
78621	Elgin	(512)	8,689	4,846
*79910	El Paso	(915)	598,590	515,342
78543	Elsa	(956)	6,458	5,242
*75119	Ennis	(214)	18,735	13,869
*76039	Euless	(817)	51,226	38,149
76140	Everman	(817)	5,733	5,672
79838	Fabens (c)	(915)	8,043	5,599
*78015	Fair Oaks Ranch	(210)	5,715	1,886
75069	Fairview	—	5,201	—
78355	Falfurrias	(361)	5,050	5,788
*75381	Farmers Branch	(214)	26,487	24,250
78114	Floresville	(830)	7,024	5,247
*75022	Flower Mound	(214)	63,526	15,527
76119	Forest Hill	(817)	13,227	11,482
75126	Forney	(214)	10,579	4,070
79906	Fort Bliss (c)	(915)	8,264	13,915
76544	Fort Hood (c)	(254)	33,711	35,580
79735	Fort Stockton	(432)	7,268	8,524
*76161	Fort Worth	(817)	624,067	447,619
78624	Fredericksburg	(830)	10,432	6,934
*77541	Freeport	(979)	12,605	11,389
*77546	Friendswood	(281)	33,094	22,814
*75034	Frisco	(214)	70,793	6,138
*76240	Gainesville	(940)	16,569	14,256
77547	Galena Park	(713)	10,221	10,033
*77550	Galveston	(409)	57,466	59,067
*75040	Garland	(214)	216,346	180,635
*76528	Gatesville	(254)	15,651	11,492
*78626	Georgetown	(512)	39,015	14,840
78942	Giddings	(979)	5,442	4,093
*75644	Gilmer	(903)	5,141	4,822
75647	Gladewater	(903)	6,295	6,027
75154	Glenn Heights	(214)	9,324	4,564

ZIP	Place	Area Code	2005	1990
78629	Gonzales	(830)	7,514	6,527
77479	Greatwood (c)	—	6,640	—
76450	Graham	(940)	8,715	8,986
*76048	Granbury	(817)	7,360	4,045
*75051	Grand Prairie	(214)	144,337	99,606
*76051	Grapevine	(817)	47,460	29,407
*75401	Greenville	(903)	25,637	23,071
77619	Groves	(409)	15,006	16,744
*75147	Gun Barrel City	(903)	5,962	3,526
*76117	Haltom City	(817)	39,875	32,856
*76548	Harker Heights	(254)	21,337	12,932
*78550	Harlingen	(956)	62,318	48,746
75032	Heath	(214)	6,418	2,128
78023	Helotes	(210)	6,187	1,556
77445	Hempstead	(979)	6,546	3,598
*75652	Henderson	(903)	11,496	11,139
79045	Hereford	(806)	14,472	14,745
76643	Hewitt	(254)	12,987	8,983
78557	Hidalgo	(956)	10,889	3,292
*75205	Highland Park	(214)	8,793	8,739
77562	Highlands (c)	(713)	7,089	6,632
75067	Highland Village	(214)	15,105	7,027
76645	Hillsboro	(254)	9,000	7,072
77563	Hitchcock	(409)	7,193	5,868
79938	Homestead Meadows South (c)	—	6,807	—
78861	Hondo	(830)	8,779	6,018
*79927	Horizon City	(915)	8,695	2,308
*77052	Houston	(281)/(713)/(832)	2,016,582	1,654,348
*77338	Humble	(713)	14,803	12,060
*77340	Huntsville	(936)	36,699	30,628
*76053	Hurst	(817)	37,967	33,574
78634	Hutto	(512)	7,401	
78362	Ingleside	(361)	9,531	5,696
76367	Iowa Park	(940)	6,175	6,072
*75015	Irving	(214)	193,649	155,037
77029	Jacinto City	(713)	9,945	9,343
75766	Jacksonville	(903)	14,395	12,765
75951	Jasper	(409)	7,531	7,160
*77040	Jersey Village	(713)	7,087	4,826
78729	Jollyville (c)	(512)	15,813	15,206
76058	Joshua	(817)	5,500	3,634
*77449	Katy	(713)	13,255	8,004
75142	Kaufman	(214)	7,872	5,251
76059	Keene	(817)	5,952	3,944
*76248	Keller	(817)	35,706	13,683
76060	Kennedale	(817)	6,547	4,096
79745	Kermit	(432)	5,281	6,875
*78028	Kerrville	(830)	22,010	17,384
*75662	Kilgore	(903)	11,858	11,066
*76540	Killeen	(254)	100,233	63,535
*78363	Kingsville	(361)	24,740	25,276
78219	Kirby	(210)	8,612	8,326
78640	Kyle	(512)	17,770	2,225
78236	Lackland AFB (c)	(210)	7,123	9,352
78705	Lacy-Lakeview	(254)	5,804	3,617
78559	La Feria	(956)	6,815	4,360
78645	Lago Vista	(512)	5,573	2,199
78572	La Homa (c)	—	10,433	1,403
75065	Lake Dallas	(940)	7,000	3,656
77566	Lake Jackson	(979)	27,386	22,771
*78734	Lakeway	(512)	8,852	4,044
77568	La Marque	(409)	13,860	14,120
79331	Lamesa	(806)	9,321	10,809
76550	Lampasas	(512)	7,465	6,382
*75146	Lancaster	(214)	32,233	22,117
*75571	La Porte	(713)	33,136	27,923
*78041	Laredo	(956)	208,754	122,893
*77573	League City	(281)	61,490	30,159
*78641	Leander	(512)	17,851	3,354
*78268	Leon Valley	(210)	9,650	9,581
*79336	Levelland	(806)	12,777	13,986
*75067	Lewisville	(214)	90,348	46,521
77575	Liberty	(936)	8,433	7,690
75068	Little Elm	(214)	18,012	1,242
79339	Littlefield	(806)	6,329	6,489
*78233	Live Oak	(210)	10,942	10,023
*77351	Livingston	(936)	6,401	5,019
78644	Lockhart	(512)	13,567	9,205
*75606	Longview	(903)	75,609	70,311
78566	Los Fresnos	(956)	5,192	2,473
*79408	Lubbock	(806)	209,737	186,206
*75901	Lufkin	(936)	33,522	30,210
78648	Luling	(830)	5,386	4,661
77657	Lumberton	(409)	9,637	6,640
*78501	McAllen	(956)	123,622	84,021
*75070	McKinney	(214)	96,581	21,283
76063	Mansfield	(817)	37,976	15,615
*78654	Marble Falls	(830)	6,745	4,017
76661	Marlin	(254)	6,206	6,386
*75670	Marshall	(903)	24,006	23,682
78368	Mathis	(361)	5,462	5,423
77477	Meadows Place	(281)/(713)	6,442	4,663
78570	Mercedes	(956)	14,185	12,694
*75149	Mesquite	(214)	129,902	101,484
76667	Mexia	(254)	6,742	6,933

ZIP	Place	Area Code	2005	1990
*79701	Midland	(432)	99,227	89,343
76065	Midlothian	(214)	13,188	5,040
*76067	Mineral Wells	(940)	16,919	14,935
*78572	Mission	(956)	60,146	28,653
77083	Mission Bend (c)	—	30,831	24,945
*77489	Missouri City	(713)	69,941	36,143
79756	Monahans	(432)	6,325	8,101
*75455	Mount Pleasant	(903)	14,760	12,291
75094	Murphy	(214)	11,026	1,603
*75961	Nacogdoches	(936)	30,806	30,872
*77868	Navasota	(936)	7,253	6,296
77627	Nederland	(409)	16,751	16,192
*78130	New Braunfels	(830)	47,168	27,334
77479	New Territory (c)	(281)	13,861	—
*76161	North Richland Hills	(817)	61,115	45,895
78539	Nurillo (c)	(956)	5,056	—
*79761	Odessa	(432)	93,546	89,699
*77630	Orange	(409)	18,052	19,370
77465	Palacios	(361)	5,166	4,418
*75801	Palestine	(903)	17,912	18,042
78572	Palmview South (c)	(956)	6,219	—
*79065	Pampa	(806)	16,744	19,959
*75460	Paris	(903)	26,539	24,799
*77501	Pasadena	(713)	143,852	119,604
*77581	Pearland	(713)	56,790	18,927
78061	Pearsall	(830)	7,772	6,924
78721	Pecan Grove (c)	—	13,551	9,502
*79772	Pecos	(432)	8,251	12,069
79070	Perryton	(806)	8,096	7,619
*78660	Pflugerville	(512)	27,531	4,444
78577	Pharr	(956)	58,986	32,921
*79072	Plainview	(806)	21,991	21,698
*75074	Plano	(214)	250,096	127,885
78064	Pleasanton	(830)	9,375	7,678
*77640	Port Arthur	(409)	56,684	58,551
78578	Port Isabel	(956)	5,373	4,740
78374	Portland	(361)	16,219	12,224
77979	Port Lavaca	(361)	11,696	10,886
77651	Port Neches	(409)	13,131	12,908
78579	Progreso	(956)	5,082	2,808
*78580	Raymondville	(956)	9,483	8,880
75154	Red Oak	(214)	7,171	3,660
76028	Rendon (c)	(817)	9,022	7,658
*75080	Richardson	(214)	99,187	74,840
*76118	Richland Hills	(817)	8,047	7,978
*77469	Richmond	(713)	13,262	10,042
78043	Rio Bravo	(956)	5,724	—
78582	Rio Grande City	(956)	13,651	10,725
76114	River Oaks	(817)	6,910	6,580
76701	Robinson	(254)	9,062	7,111
78380	Robstown	(361)	12,484	12,849
76567	Rockdale	(512)	6,048	5,235
*78382	Rockport	(361)	9,041	5,619
*75087	Rockwall	(214)	29,354	10,486
78584	Roma	(956)	10,900	8,059
77471	Rosenberg	(713)	30,322	20,183
*78681	Round Rock	(512)	86,316	30,923
*75088	Rowlett	(214)	53,664	23,260
75189	Royse	(649)/(214)/(972)	5,589	2,206
75785	Rusk	(903)	5,234	4,366
75048	Sachse	(214)	17,009	5,346
*76179	Saginaw	(817)	17,701	8,551
*76902	San Angelo	(325)	88,014	84,462
*78265	San Antonio	(210)	1,256,509	976,514
78586	San Benito	(956)	24,699	20,125
79849	San Elizario (c)	(915)	11,046	4,385
76266	Sanger	(940)	6,354	3,602
78589	San Juan	(956)	30,773	12,561
*78666	San Marcos	(512)	46,111	28,738
*77510	Santa Fe	(409)	10,498	8,429
*78154	Schertz	(210)	26,668	10,597
77586	Seabrook	(281)	10,907	6,685
75159	Seagoville	(214)	11,112	8,969
77474	Sealy	(979)	6,038	4,541
*78155	Seguin	(830)	24,230	18,692
79360	Seminole	(432)	5,954	6,342
78739	Shady Hollow (c)	—	5,140	—
*75090	Sherman	(903)	36,790	31,584
77656	Silsbee	(409)	6,722	6,368
78387	Sinton	(361)	5,509	5,549
79364	Slaton	(806)	5,727	6,078
*79549	Snyder	(325)	10,580	12,195
79927	Socorro	(915)	29,685	22,995
77587	South Houston	(713)	16,219	14,207
76092	Southlake	(817)	24,902	7,082
*77373	Spring (c)	(713)	36,385	33,111
*77477	Stafford	(713)	19,227	8,395
*76401	Stephenville	(254)	15,948	13,502
*77478	Sugar Land	(713)	75,754	33,712
*75482	Sulphur Springs	(903)	15,228	14,062
79556	Sweetwater	(325)	10,694	11,967
76574	Taylor	(512)	15,014	11,472
*76501	Temple	(254)	55,447	46,150
*75160	Terrell	(214)	17,665	12,490
78209	Terrell Hills	(210)	5,108	4,592

ZIP	Place	Area Code	2005	1990
*75501	Texarkana	(903)	35,746	32,294
*77590	Texas City	(409)	44,274	40,822
*75056	The Colony	(214)	37,972	22,113
77387	The Woodlands (c)	(713)	55,649	29,205
78258	Timberwood Park (c)	(210)	5,889	2,578
*77375	Tomball	(713)	9,938	6,370
76262	Trophy Club	(817)	7,334	3,922
*75702	Tyler	(903)	91,936	75,450
*78148	Universal City	(830)	16,653	13,057
75205	University Park	(214)	23,806	22,259
*78801	Uvalde	(830)	16,441	14,729
*76384	Vernon	(940)	11,077	12,001
*77901	Victoria	(361)	61,790	55,076
*77662	Vidor	(409)	11,290	10,935
*76702	Waco	(254)	120,465	103,590
75501	Wake Village	(903)	5,226	4,761
76148	Watauga	(817)	23,548	20,009
*75165	Waxahachie	(214)	25,454	17,984
*76086	Weatherford	(817)	23,315	14,804
77598	Webster	(281)	8,852	4,678
78728	Wells Branch (c)	—	11,271	7,094
*78596	Weslaco	(956)	31,442	22,739
77351	West Livingston (c)	—	6,612	—
79764	West Odessa (c)	(432)	17,799	16,568
77005	West University Place	(713)	14,886	12,920
77488	Wharton	(979)	9,374	9,011
77591	Whitehouse	(903)	7,122	4,018
75693	White Oak	(903)	6,130	5,136
76108	White Settlement	(817)	15,736	15,472
*76307	Wichita Falls	(940)	99,846	96,259
78239	Windcrest	(210)	5,090	5,331
*78660	Windemere (c)	—	6,868	3,207
76712	Woodway	(254)	8,689	8,695
75098	Wylie	(214)	29,061	8,716
77995	Yoakum	(361)	5,720	5,611

Utah

ZIP	Place	Area Code	2005	1990
84004	Alpine	(801)	9,063	3,492
84003	American Fork	(801)	21,372	15,722
84065	Bluffdale	(801)	6,569	2,142
*84010	Bountiful	(801)	41,085	37,544
84302	Brigham City	(435)	18,355	15,644
84109	Canyon Rim (c)	(801)	10,428	10,527
*84720	Cedar City	(435)	23,983	13,443
84062	Cedar Hills	(801)	7,790	708
84014	Centerville	(801)	14,898	11,500
*84015	Clearfield	(801)	27,413	21,435
84015	Clinton	(801)	17,735	7,945
84121	Cottonwood Heights (c)	(801)	27,569	28,766
84121	Cottonwood West (c)	(801)	18,727	17,476
84020	Draper	(801)	35,119	7,143
84043	Eagle Mountain	(801)	10,343	30
84109	East Millcreek (c)	(801)	21,385	21,184
84025	Farmington	(801)	14,357	9,049
84029	Grantsville	(435)	7,494	4,500
84404	Harrisville	(801)	5,020	3,004
84032	Heber	(435)	9,147	4,782
84065	Herriman	(801)	11,226	—
84003	Highland	(801)	13,350	5,007
*84117	Holladay	(801)	19,319	14,095
84737	Hurricane	(435)	10,989	3,915
84319	Hyrum	(435)	6,061	4,829
84738	Ivins	(435)	6,738	1,639
84037	Kaysville	(801)	22,510	13,961
84118	Kearns (c)	(801)	33,659	28,374
*84041	Layton	(801)	61,782	41,784
84043	Lehi	(801)	31,730	8,475
84042	Lindon	(801)	9,679	3,818
84093	Little Cottonwood Creek Valley (c)	(801)	7,221	5,042
*84321	Logan	(435)	47,357	32,771
84044	Magna (c)	(801)	22,770	17,829
84664	Mapleton	(801)	5,972	3,572
84047	Midvale	(801)	27,170	11,886
84109	Millcreek (c)	(801)	30,377	32,230
84117	Mount Olympus (c)	(801)	7,103	7,413
*84157	Murray	(801)	44,555	31,274
84648	Nephi	(435)	5,045	3,515
84341	North Logan	(435)	6,730	3,775
*84404	North Ogden	(801)	16,542	11,593
84054	North Salt Lake	(801)	10,538	6,464
*84401	Ogden	(801)	78,309	63,943
84084	Oquirrh (c)	(801)	10,390	7,593
*84057	Orem	(801)	89,713	67,561
*84060	Park City	(435)	8,066	4,468
84651	Payson	(801)	16,442	9,510
84062	Pleasant Grove	(801)	29,376	13,476
*84404	Pleasant View	(801)	6,151	3,597
84501	Price	(435)	8,081	8,712
84332	Providence	(435)	5,516	3,344
*84601	Provo	(801)	113,459	86,835
84701	Richfield	(435)	7,044	5,593
84405	Riverdale	(801)	7,934	6,419
*84065	Riverton	(801)	32,089	11,261
*84067	Roy	(801)	35,229	24,560

ZIP	Place	Area Code	2005	1990
*84770	Saint George	(435)	64,201	28,572
*84101	Salt Lake City	(801)	178,097	159,928
*84070	Sandy	(801)	89,664	75,240
84765	Santa Clara	(435)	5,864	2,323
84655	Santaquin	(801)	6,901	2,522
84043	Saratoga Springs	(801)	6,502	—
84335	Smithfield	(435)	7,589	5,566
84095	South Jordan	(801)	40,209	12,215
84403	South Ogden	(801)	15,195	12,105
84165	South Salt Lake	(801)	21,411	10,129
*84403	South Weber	(801)	5,593	2,853
84660	Spanish Fork	(801)	26,606	11,272
84663	Springville	(801)	25,309	13,950
84098	Summit Park (c)	—	6,597	—
84075	Syracuse	(801)	17,938	4,658
84118	Taylorsville	(801)	58,009	51,550
84074	Tooele	(435)	28,369	13,887
84337	Tremonton	(435)	6,286	4,262
*84078	Vernal	(435)	7,960	6,640
84780	Washington	(435)	13,669	4,198
84405	Washington Terrace	(801)	8,352	8,189
84401	West Haven	(801)	5,558	—
*84084	West Jordan	(801)	91,444	42,915
84015	West Point	(801)	7,650	4,258
*84170	West Valley City	(801)	113,300	86,969
84070	White City (c)	(801)	5,988	6,506
*84087	Woods Cross	(801)	8,019	5,384

Vermont (802)

See introductory note.

ZIP	Place	2005	1990
05641	Barre	9,128	9,482
05641	Barre	8,002	7,411
05201	Bennington (c)	9,168	9,532
05201	Bennington	15,375	16,451
*05301	Brattleboro	11,849	12,241
*05301	Brattleboro (c)	8,289	8,612
*05401	Burlington	38,531	39,127
05446	Colchester	17,165	14,731
*05451	Essex Junction	19,146	16,498
05047	Hartford	10,822	9,404
05465	Jericho	5,068	1,405
05849	Lyndon	5,602	5,371
05753	Middlebury (c)	6,252	6,007
*05753	Middlebury Town	8,152	8,034
05468	Milton	10,169	8,404
*05602	Montpelier	8,003	8,247
05661	Morristown	5,522	4,733
05855	Newport	5,207	4,434
05663	Northfield	5,816	5,610
*05701	Rutland	17,046	18,230
*05478	Saint Albans	7,476	7,339
05478	Saint Albans City	7,548	4,606
05819	Saint Johnsbury (c)	6,319	6,424
05819	Saint Johnsbury	7,495	7,608
05482	Shelburne	6,995	5,871
*05403	South Burlington	16,993	12,809
05156	Springfield	8,891	9,579
05488	Swanton	6,454	5,636
05676	Waterbury	5,211	4,614
05495	Williston	8,243	4,887
05404	Winooski	6,353	6,649

Virginia

Area code (571) overlays area code (703). See introductory note.

ZIP	Place	Area Code	2005	1990
*24210	Abingdon	(276)	7,925	7,003
*22313	Alexandria	(703)	135,337	111,182
22003	Ananndale (c)	(703)	54,994	50,975
22554	Aquia Harbour (c)	(703)	7,856	6,308
*22210	Arlington	(703)	195,965	170,897
23005	Ashland	(804)	6,996	5,864
*22041	Bailey's Crossroads (c)	(703)	23,166	19,507
24523	Bedford	(540)	6,211	6,177
22306	Belle Haven (c)	(757)	6,269	6,427
24219	Big Stone Gap	(276)	5,854	4,847
*24060	Blacksburg	(540)	39,130	34,590
23235	Bon Air (c)	(804)	16,213	16,413
22812	Bridgewater	(540)	5,413	3,918
*24203	Bristol	(276)	17,335	18,426
24416	Buena Vista	(540)	6,437	6,406
20109	Bull Run (c)	(703)	11,337	5,525
*22150	Burke (c)	(703)	57,737	57,734
24018	Cave Spring (c)	(540)	24,941	24,053
*20120	Centreville (c)	(703)	48,661	26,585
*20151	Chantilly (c)	(703)	41,041	29,337
*22906	Charlottesville	(434)	40,437	40,475
*23320	Chesapeake	(757)	218,968	151,982
*23831	Chester (c)	(804)	17,890	14,986
*24073	Christiansburg	(540)	17,926	15,004
24078	Collinsville (c)	(276)	7,777	7,280
23834	Colonial Heights	(804)	17,567	16,064
24426	Covington	(540)	6,205	7,198
*22701	Culpeper	(540)	12,047	8,581
22193	Dale City (c)	(703)	55,971	47,170
*24541	Danville	(434)	46,143	53,056
23228	Dumbarton (c)	(804)	6,674	8,526
22027	Dunn Loring (c)	(703)	7,861	6,509
23222	East Highland Park (c)	(804)	12,488	11,850
23847	Emporia	(434)	5,587	5,479
23803	Ettrick (c)	(804)	5,627	5,290
*22030	Fairfax	(703)	21,963	19,894
*22046	Falls Church	(703)	10,781	9,522
*23901	Farmville	(434)	6,876	6,505
24551	Forest (c)	(434)	8,006	5,624
22060	Fort Belvoir (c)	(703)	7,176	8,590
22308	Fort Hunt (c)	(703)	12,923	12,989
23801	Fort Lee (c)	(804)	7,269	6,895
22310	Franconia (c)	(703)	31,907	19,882
23851	Franklin	(757)	8,594	7,864
*22404	Fredericksburg	(540)	20,732	19,027
22630	Front Royal	(540)	14,499	11,880
24333	Galax	(276)	6,676	6,699
*23060	Glen Allen (c)	(804)	12,562	9,010
23062	Gloucester Point (c)	(804)	9,429	8,509
22066	Great Falls (c)	(703)	8,549	6,945
22306	Groveton (c)	(703)	21,296	19,997
*23670	Hampton	(757)	145,579	133,811
*22801	Harrisonburg	(540)	40,438	30,707
*20170	Herndon	(703)	21,965	16,139
23075	Highland Springs (c)	(804)	15,137	13,823
24019	Hollins (c)	(540)	14,309	13,305
23860	Hopewell	(804)	22,690	23,101
22303	Huntington (c)	(703)	8,325	7,489
22306	Hybla Valley (c)	(703)	16,721	15,491
22043	Idylwood (c)	(703)	16,005	14,710
22042	Jefferson (c)	(703)	27,422	25,782
22041	Lake Barcroft (c)	(703)	8,906	8,686
22963	Lake Monticello (c)	(434)	6,852	2,331
22191	Lake Ridge (c)	(540)	30,404	23,862
23228	Lakeside (c)	(804)	11,157	12,081
23060	Laurel (c)	(804)	14,875	13,011
*20175	Leesburg	(703)	36,269	16,202
24450	Lexington	(540)	6,776	6,959
22312	Lincolnia (c)	(703)	15,788	13,041
20136	Linton Hall (c)	(703)	8,620	
*22079	Lorton (c)	(703)	17,786	15,385
*24506	Lynchburg	(434)	66,973	66,049
*22101	McLean (c)	(703)	38,929	38,168
24572	Madison Heights (c)	(434)	11,584	11,700
*20110	Manassas	(703)	37,569	27,957
20113	Manassas Park	(703)	11,622	6,734
22030	Mantua (c)	(703)	7,485	6,804
24354	Marion	(276)	6,164	6,630
*24112	Martinsville	(276)	14,925	16,162
*23111	Mechanicsville (c)	(804)	30,464	22,027
*22116	Merrifield (c)	(703)	11,170	8,399
22026	Montclair (c)		15,728	11,399
23231	Montrose (c)	(804)	7,018	6,405
22121	Mount Vernon (c)	(703)	28,582	27,485
22122	Newington (c)	(703)	19,784	17,965
*23607	Newport News	(757)	179,899	171,439
*23501	Norfolk	(757)	231,954	261,250
22151	North Springfield (c)	(703)	9,173	8,996
22124	Oakton (c)	(703)	29,348	24,610
*23804	Petersburg	(804)	32,604	37,027
22043	Pimmit Hills (c)	(703)	6,152	6,019
23662	Poquoson	(757)	11,811	11,005
*23707	Portsmouth	(757)	100,169	103,910
24301	Pulaski	(540)	9,088	9,985
22134	Quantico Station (c)	(703)	6,571	7,425
*24141	Radford	(540)	14,575	15,940
*20190	Reston (c)	(703)	56,407	48,556
*23232	Richmond	(804)	193,777	202,798
*24022	Roanoke	(540)	92,631	96,509
24281	Rose Hill (c)	(276)	15,058	12,675
*24153	Salem	(540)	24,654	23,797
22044	Seven Corners (c)	(703)	8,701	7,280
*23430	Smithfield	(757)	6,840	4,686
24592	South Boston	(434)	8,115	6,997
*22150	Springfield (c)	(703)	30,417	23,706
*24402	Staunton	(540)	23,337	24,461
24477	Stuarts Draft (c)	(540)	8,367	5,087
23162	Sudley (c)	(540)	7,719	7,321
*23434	Suffolk	(757)	78,994	52,143
24502	Timberlake (c)	(434)	10,683	10,314
22172	Triangle (c)	(703)	5,500	4,740
23229	Tuckahoe (c)	(804)	43,242	42,629
22101	Tysons Corner (c)	(703)	18,540	13,124
*22180	Vienna	(703)	14,842	14,852
24179	Vinton	(540)	7,734	7,643
*23450	Virginia Beach	(757)	438,415	393,089
*20186	Warrenton	(540)	8,635	4,882
22980	Waynesboro	(540)	21,269	18,549
22110	West Gate (c)	(703)	7,493	6,565
22152	West Springfield (c)	(703)	28,378	28,126
*23185	Williamsburg	(757)	11,751	11,409

ZIP	Place	Area Code	2005	1990
*22601	Winchester	(540)	25,119	21,947
24592	Wolf Trap (c)	(703)	14,001	13,133
*22191	Woodbridge (c)	(703)	31,941	26,401
23059	Wyndham (c)	—	6,176	
24382	Wytheville	(276)	8,038	8,036
22110	Yorkshire (c)	(703)	6,732	5,699

Washington

ZIP	Place	Area Code	2005	1990
98520	Aberdeen	(360)	16,358	16,565
98036	Alderwood Manor (c)	(425)	15,329	22,945
*98221	Anacortes	(360)	16,083	11,451
98223	Arlington	(360)	15,277	4,037
98335	Artondale (c)	(253)	8,630	7,141
*98002	Auburn	(253)	47,086	33,650
98110	Bainbridge Island	(206)	21,951	
98315	Bangor Trident Base (c)	(360)	7,253	3,702
98604	Battle Ground	(360)	13,237	3,758
*98009	Bellevue	(425)	117,137	95,213
*98225	Bellingham	(360)	74,547	52,179
*98390	Bonney Lake	(360)	14,611	7,494
*98011	Bothell	(425)	30,916	12,575
*98337	Bremerton	(360)	37,828	38,142
98036	Brier	(425)	6,344	5,633
98178	Bryn Mawr-Skyway (c)	(206)	13,977	12,514
*98166	Burien	(206)	30,737	27,507
98233	Burlington	(360)	8,247	4,349
98292	Camano (c)	—	13,347	
98607	Camas	(360)	16,671	6,762
98055	Cascade-Fairwood (c)	(425)	34,580	30,107
98531	Centralia	(360)	15,404	12,101
98532	Chehalis	(360)	7,205	6,527
99004	Cheney	(509)	10,356	7,723
99403	Clarkston	(509)	7,304	6,753
99403	Clarkston Heights-Vineland (c)	(509)	6,117	2,832
99324	College Place	(509)	8,945	6,308
99114	Colville	(509)	5,029	4,360
98072	Cottage Lake (c)	(206)	24,330	
99218	Country Homes (c)	(509)	5,203	5,126
98042	Covington	(253)	16,610	
*98198	Des Moines	(206)	28,767	20,830
99213	Dishman (c)	(509)	10,031	9,671
98327	DuPont	—	5,374	592
98019	Duvall	(425)	5,710	2,640
98031	East Hill-Meridian (c)	—	29,308	42,696
98366	East Port Orchard (c)	(360)	5,116	5,409
98056	East Renton Highlands (c)	(425)	13,264	13,218
98802	East Wenatchee	(509)	8,819	3,886
98801	East Wenatchee Bench (c)	(509)	13,658	12,539
*98371	Edgewood	(253)	9,718	8,702
*98020	Edmonds	(425)	39,937	30,743
98387	Elk Plain (c)	—	15,697	12,197
*98926	Ellensburg	(509)	16,914	12,360
98022	Enumclaw	(360)	10,896	7,243
98823	Ephrata	(509)	7,178	5,349
*98201	Everett	(425)	96,604	70,997
99218	Fairwood (c)	(509)	6,764	5,807
*98002	Federal Way	(253)	83,088	67,535
98685	Felida (c)	(360)	5,683	3,109
98248	Ferndale	(360)	9,977	5,398
98424	Fife	—	5,567	3,864
99336	Finley (c)	(509)	5,770	4,897
98466	Fircrest	(253)	6,086	5,270
98597	Five Corners (c)	—	12,207	6,776
98433	Fort Lewis (c)	(253)	19,089	22,224
98373	Frederickson (c)	(206)	5,758	3,502
*98329	Gig Harbor	(253)	6,620	3,236
98338	Graham (c)	(253)	8,739	
98930	Grandview	(509)	8,908	7,169
99016	Green Acres (c)	(509)	5,158	4,626
98660	Hazel Dell North (c)	(360)	9,261	6,924
98665	Hazel Dell South (c)	(360)	6,605	5,796
98025	Hobart (c)	—	6,251	
98606	Hockinson (c)	(360)	5,136	
98550	Hoquiam	(360)	9,030	8,972
98011	Inglewood-Finn Hill (c)	(425)	22,661	29,132
*98027	Issaquah	(425)	17,059	7,786
98626	Kelso	(360)	11,854	11,767
98028	Kenmore	(425)	19,564	8,917
*99336	Kennewick	(509)	60,997	42,148
*98031	Kent	(253)/(425)	81,800	37,960
98033	Kingsgate (c)	(425)	12,222	14,259
*98033	Kirkland	(425)	45,814	40,059
*98509	Lacey	(360)	33,368	19,279
98155	Lake Forest Park	(206)	12,476	4,031
98002	Lakeland North (c)	(253)	15,085	14,402
98002	Lakeland South (c)	(253)	11,436	9,027
98042	Lake Morton-Berrydale (c)	(425)	9,659	
98665	Lake Shore (c)	(360)	6,670	6,268
98258	Lake Stevens	(425)	7,558	3,435
*98498	Lakewood	(253)	57,671	55,937
98092	Lea Hill (c)	(253)	10,871	6,876
99019	Liberty Lake	(509)	5,613	2,015
98632	Longview	(360)	36,137	31,499
98264	Lynden	(360)	10,697	5,709
*98046	Lynnwood	(425)	33,504	28,637
98290	Maltby (c)	(360)	8,267	
98038	Maple Valley	(425)	15,153	1,211
98012	Martha Lake (c)	(425)	12,633	10,155
*98270	Marysville	(360)	29,889	12,248
98040	Mercer Island	(206)	22,862	20,816
98444	Midland (c)	(253)	7,414	5,587
*98082	Mill Creek	(425)	13,501	7,180
*98682	Mill Plain (c)	(360)	7,400	
98354	Milton	(253)	6,468	4,995
98661	Minnehaha (c)	(360)	7,689	9,661
98272	Monroe	(360)	15,653	4,275
98837	Moses Lake	(509)	16,793	11,235
98043	Mountlake Terrace	(425)	20,251	19,320
*98273	Mount Vernon	(360)	29,271	17,647
98686	Mount Vista (c)	—	5,770	
98275	Mukilteo	(425)	19,857	11,575
*98059	Newcastle	(425)	9,287	4,649
*98166	Normandy Park	(206)	6,178	6,794
98012	North Creek (c)	(425)	25,742	23,236
98270	North Marysville (c)	(425)	21,161	18,711
*98277	Oak Harbor	(360)	22,327	17,176
*98501	Olympia	(360)	44,114	33,729
99214	Opportunity (c)	(509)	25,065	22,326
98662	Orchards (c)	(360)	17,852	
*99327	Othello	(509)	6,221	4,638
99027	Otis Orchards-East Farms (c)	(360)	6,318	5,811
98047	Pacific	(253)	5,722	4,622
98204	Paine Field-Lake Stickney (c)	—	24,383	18,670
98444	Parkland (c)	(253)	24,053	20,882
98366	Parkwood (c)	(360)	7,213	6,853
*98301	Pasco	(509)	46,444	20,337
98037	Picnic Point-North Lynnwood (c)	—	22,953	
*98362	Port Angeles	(360)	18,927	17,710
*98366	Port Orchard	(360)	7,986	4,984
98368	Port Townsend	(360)	9,001	7,001
98370	Poulsbo	(360)	7,593	4,848
98390	Prairie Ridge (c)	—	11,688	8,278
98350	Prosser	(509)	5,140	4,492
*99163	Pullman	(509)	25,262	23,478
*98371	Puyallup	(253)	35,861	23,878
98848	Quincy	(509)	5,568	3,738
*98052	Redmond	(425)	47,579	35,800
*98058	Renton	(425)	55,817	41,688
*99352	Richland	(509)	44,317	32,315
98188	Riverton-Boulevard Park (c)	(206)	11,188	15,337
98686	Salmon Creek (c)	(360)	16,767	11,989
*98074	Sammamish	(425)	34,364	
*98148	SeaTac	(206)	25,081	22,760
*98101	Seattle	(206)/(425)	573,911	516,259
98208	Seattle Hill-Silver Firs (c)	—	35,311	
98284	Sedro-Woolley	(360)	10,045	6,333
98942	Selah	(509)	6,875	5,113
98382	Sequim	—	5,162	
98584	Shelton	(360)	9,065	7,241
*98133	Shoreline	(206)	52,024	46,979
*98315	Silverdale (c)	(360)	15,816	7,660
*98290	Snohomish	(360)	8,720	6,499
*98065	Snoqualmie	(425)	6,082	1,546
98373	South Hill (c)	—	31,623	12,963
98387	Spanaway (c)	(253)	21,588	15,001
*99210	Spokane	(509)	196,818	177,165
*99211	Spokane Valley	(509)	81,380	
98292	Stanwood	—	5,068	1,961
98388	Steilacoom	(253)	6,140	5,728
*98371	Summit (c)	(253)	8,041	6,312
*98390	Sumner	(253)	9,298	7,535
*98944	Sunnyside	(509)	14,426	11,238
*98402	Tacoma	(253)	195,898	176,664
98501	Tanglewilde-Thompson Place (c)	(360)	5,670	6,061
98901	Terrace Heights (c)	(509)	6,447	4,223
98948	Toppenish	(509)	9,207	7,419
*98138	Tukwila	(206)	16,969	14,506
*98501	Tumwater	(360)	13,331	9,976
98901	Union Gap	(509)	5,707	3,120
98053	Union Hill-Novelty Hill (c)	—	11,265	
98467	University Place	(253)	30,425	26,724
*98661	Vancouver	(360)	157,493	62,065
*98013	Vashon (c)	(206)	10,123	
99037	Veradale (c)	(509)	9,387	7,836
98362	Walla Walla	(509)	30,989	26,482
98443	Waller (c)	(253)	9,200	6,415
98661	Walnut Grove (c)	(360)	7,164	3,906
98671	Washougal	(360)	10,732	4,764
*98801	Wenatchee	(509)	29,374	21,746
98027	West Lake Sammamish (c)	(425)	5,937	6,087
98258	West Lake Stevens (c)	(425)	18,071	12,453
*99353	West Richland	(509)	9,907	3,962
99181	West Valley (c)	(509)	10,433	6,594
98166	White Center (c)	(206)	20,975	20,531
*98072	Woodinville	(425)	9,889	7,628
*98903	Yakima	(509)	81,214	58,427

West Virginia (304)

ZIP	Place	2005	1990
*25801	Beckley	16,936	18,274
24701	Bluefield	11,119	12,756
26330	Bridgeport	7,486	6,837
26201	Buckhannon	5,687	5,909
*25301	Charleston	51,176	57,287
*26507	Cheat Lake (c)	6,396	3,992
*26301	Clarksburg	16,439	17,970
25301	Cross Lanes (c)	10,353	10,878
25064	Dunbar	7,740	8,697
26241	Elkins	7,109	7,494
*26554	Fairmont	19,049	20,210
26354	Grafton	5,407	5,524
*25704	Huntington	49,198	54,844
25526	Hurricane	5,968	4,461
26726	Keyser	5,410	5,870
*25401	Martinsburg	15,996	14,073
*26505	Morgantown	28,292	25,879
26041	Moundsville	9,567	10,753
26155	New Martinsville	5,791	6,705
25143	Nitro	6,750	6,851
*25901	Oak Hill	7,312	6,812
*26101	Parkersburg	32,020	33,862
25705	Pea Ridge (c)	6,363	6,535
24740	Princeton	6,222	7,043
25177	Saint Albans	11,105	12,241
*25303	South Charleston	12,700	13,645
25569	Teays Valley (c)	12,704	8,436
*26105	Vienna	10,770	10,862
26062	Weirton	19,544	22,124
26003	Wheeling	29,639	34,882

Wisconsin

ZIP	Place	Area Code	2005	1990
54301	Allouez	(920)	14,875	14,431
54720	Altoona	(715)	6,448	5,889
54409	Antigo	(715)	8,282	8,284
*54911	Appleton	(920)	70,217	65,695
54806	Ashland	(715)	8,306	8,695
*54304	Ashwaubenon	(920)	16,911	16,376
53913	Baraboo	(608)	10,927	9,203
53916	Beaver Dam	(920)	15,153	14,196
54311	Bellevue Town	(920)	14,467	7,541
*53511	Beloit	(608)	35,621	35,571
54923	Berlin	(920)	5,213	5,371
*53045	Brookfield	(262)	39,656	35,184
*53209	Brown Deer	(414)	11,611	12,236
53105	Burlington	(262)	11,148	8,851
53012	Cedarburg	(262)	11,298	10,086
*54729	Chippewa Falls	(715)	13,374	12,749
53925	Columbus	(920)	5,101	4,093
53527	Cottage Grove	(608)	5,271	1,131
53110	Cudahy	(414)	18,316	18,659
53532	De Forest	(608)	8,438	4,882
53018	Delafield	(262)	6,767	5,347
53115	Delavan	(262)	8,370	6,073
54115	De Pere	(920)	23,375	16,594
*54703	Eau Claire	(715)	62,570	56,806
53534	Edgerton	(608)	5,102	4,254
53121	Elkhorn	(262)	9,021	5,337
53122	Elm Grove	(262)	6,182	6,261
*53711	Fitchburg	(608)	22,040	15,648
*54935	Fond du Lac	(920)	42,435	37,755
53538	Fort Atkinson	(920)	11,949	10,213
53217	Fox Point	(414)	6,741	7,238
53132	Franklin	(414)	33,263	21,855
53022	Germantown	(262)	19,245	13,658
*53209	Glendale	(414)	12,880	14,088
53024	Grafton	(262)	11,625	9,340
*54303	Green Bay	(920)	101,203	96,466
53129	Greendale	(414)	13,860	15,128
*53220	Greenfield	(414)	35,753	33,403
*53130	Hales Corners	(414)	7,535	7,623
53027	Hartford	(262)	13,017	8,188
53029	Hartland	(262)	8,672	6,906
54313	Hobart	—	5,795	4,284
54636	Holmen	(608)	7,446	3,220
*54303	Howard	(920)	15,912	9,874
*54016	Hudson	(715)	11,367	6,378
53037	Jackson	(262)	6,036	2,603
*53545	Janesville	(608)	61,962	52,210
53549	Jefferson	(920)	7,592	6,078
54130	Kaukauna	(920)	14,656	11,982
*53140	Kenosha	(262)	95,240	80,426
54136	Kimberly	(920)	6,230	5,406
54455	Kronenwetter	—	6,228	4,850
*54601	La Crosse	(608)	50,287	51,140
53147	Lake Geneva	(262)	8,223	5,979
53551	Lake Mills	(920)	5,241	4,143
54140	Little Chute	(920)	10,870	9,207
53558	McFarland	(608)	7,383	5,232
*53714	Madison	(608)	221,551	190,766
*54220	Manitowoc	(920)	33,917	32,521
54143	Marinette	(715)	11,275	11,843
*54449	Marshfield	(715)	18,796	19,293

ZIP	Place	Area Code	2005	1990
53050	Mayville	(920)	5,055	4,374
54952	Menasha	(920)	16,306	14,711
*53051	Menomonee Falls	(262)	34,125	26,840
54751	Menomonie	(715)	15,244	13,547
*53097	Mequon	(262)	23,820	18,885
54452	Merrill	(715)	10,145	9,860
53562	Middleton	(608)	15,816	13,785
53563	Milton	(608)	5,464	4,574
*53201	Milwaukee	(414)	578,887	628,088
*53716	Monona	(608)	7,716	8,637
53566	Monroe	(608)	10,563	10,241
53572	Mount Horeb	(608)	6,188	4,182
53406	Mount Pleasant	(262)	25,999	20,884
53149	Mukwonago	(262)	6,857	4,495
53150	Muskego	(414)	22,872	16,813
*54956	Neenah	(920)	24,596	23,219
*53186	New Berlin	(262)	38,547	33,592
54961	New London	(920)	6,926	6,658
54017	New Richmond	(715)	7,726	5,106
54937	North Fond du Lac	(920)	5,024	4,292
53154	Oak Creek	(414)	32,312	19,513
53066	Oconomowoc	(262)	13,711	10,993
54650	Onalaska	(608)	15,701	12,201
53575	Oregon	(608)	8,493	4,519
*54901	Oshkosh	(920)	63,485	55,006
53072	Pewaukee (city)	(262)	12,769	—
53072	Pewaukee (village)	(262)	8,918	5,287
53818	Platteville	(608)	9,854	9,862
*53158	Pleasant Prairie	(262)	18,551	12,037
54467	Plover	(715)	11,256	8,176
53073	Plymouth	(920)	8,217	6,769
53901	Portage	(608)	10,035	8,640
53074	Port Washington	(262)	10,892	9,338
53821	Prairie du Chien	(608)	5,880	5,657
*53401	Racine	(262)	79,392	84,298
*53959	Reedsburg	(608)	8,497	5,834
54501	Rhinelander	(715)	7,889	7,382
54401	Rib Mountain (c)	(715)	6,059	4,634
54868	Rice Lake	(715)	8,361	7,998
53581	Richland Center	(608)	5,177	5,018
54971	Ripon	(920)	7,268	7,241
54022	River Falls	(715)	13,254	10,610
54474	Rothschild	(715)	5,096	3,310
*53235	Saint Francis	(414)	9,382	9,245
54166	Shawano	(715)	8,441	7,598
*53081	Sheboygan	(920)	48,872	49,587
53085	Sheboygan Falls	(920)	7,527	5,823
53211	Shorewood	(414)	13,192	14,116
53172	South Milwaukee	(414)	20,849	20,958
54656	Sparta	(608)	8,827	7,788
*54481	Stevens Point	(715)	24,298	23,002
53589	Stoughton	(608)	12,646	8,786
54235	Sturgeon Bay	(920)	9,180	9,176
53177	Sturtevant	(262)	6,190	3,803
*54173	Suamico	(920)	10,221	5,214
*53590	Sun Prairie	(608)	25,392	15,352
54880	Superior	(715)	26,779	27,134
53089	Sussex	(262)	9,812	5,039
54660	Tomah	(608)	8,620	7,572
53181	Twin Lakes	(262)	5,513	3,989
*54241	Two Rivers	(920)	12,144	13,030
53593	Verona	(608)	10,166	5,374
*53094	Watertown	(920)	22,816	19,142
*53186	Waukesha	(262)	67,658	56,894
53597	Waunakee	(608)	10,360	5,897
54981	Waupaca	(715)	5,877	4,946
53963	Waupun	(920)	10,558	8,844
*54403	Wausau	(715)	37,292	37,060
*53213	Wauwatosa	(414)	45,014	49,366
*53214	West Allis	(414)	58,798	63,221
*53095	West Bend	(262)	29,549	24,470
*54476	Weston	(715)	12,921	9,714
*53217	Whitefish Bay	(414)	13,508	14,272
53190	Whitewater	(262)	14,311	12,636
53185	Wind Lake (c)	(262)	5,202	3,748
*54494	Wisconsin Rapids	(715)	17,621	18,245

Wyoming (307)

ZIP	Place	2005	1990
*82609	Casper	51,738	46,765
*82009	Cheyenne	55,731	50,008
82414	Cody	9,100	7,897
82633	Douglas	5,581	5,076
*82930	Evanston	11,459	10,904
*82716	Gillette	22,685	17,545
*82935	Green River	11,787	12,711
*83002	Jackson	9,038	4,708
82520	Lander	6,898	7,023
*82072	Laramie	26,050	26,687
82435	Powell	5,288	5,292
*82301	Rawlins	8,658	9,380
82501	Riverton	9,430	9,202
*82901	Rock Springs	18,772	19,050
82801	Sheridan	16,333	13,904
82240	Torrington	5,533	5,651

Populations and Areas of Counties and States

Source: U.S. Bureau of the Census, Dept. of Commerce; World Almanac research

Counties are the primary legal divisions of most states and generally are functioning governmental units. In **Alaska**, however, the chief units of local government are boroughs; outside the boroughs there are "census areas," delineated for statistical purposes. In **Louisiana**, the primary legal divisions are known as parishes.

State population figures are estimates for July 1, 2005. **For counties,** July 1, 2005, population estimates and Apr. 1, 1990, decennial census figures are given. **Land areas** are from 2000 census. County areas may not add to state areas because of rounding.

Alabama
(67 counties, 50,744 sq. mi. land; pop. 4,557,808)

County	County seat or courthouse	2005 Pop.	1990 Pop.	Land area sq. mi.
Autauga	Prattville	48,612	34,222	596
Baldwin	Bay Minette	162,586	98,280	1,596
Barbour	Clayton	28,414	25,417	885
Bibb	Centreville	21,516	16,598	623
Blount	Oneonta	55,725	39,248	646
Bullock	Union Springs	11,055	11,042	625
Butler	Greenville	20,766	21,892	777
Calhoun	Anniston	112,141	116,032	608
Chambers	Lafayette	35,460	36,876	597
Cherokee	Centre	24,522	19,543	553
Chilton	Clanton	41,744	32,458	694
Choctaw	Butler	14,807	16,018	914
Clarke	Grove Hill	27,269	27,240	1,238
Clay	Ashland	13,964	13,252	605
Cleburne	Heflin	14,460	12,730	553
Coffee	Elba	45,567	40,240	679
Colbert	Tuscumbia	54,660	51,666	595
Conecuh	Evergreen	13,257	14,054	851
Coosa	Rockford	11,162	11,063	652
Covington	Andalusia	37,003	36,478	1,034
Crenshaw	Luverne	13,727	13,635	610
Cullman	Cullman	79,886	67,613	738
Dale	Ozark	48,748	49,633	561
Dallas	Selma	44,366	48,130	981
De Kalb	Fort Payne	67,271	54,651	778
Elmore	Wetumpka	73,937	49,210	621
Escambia	Brewton	38,082	35,518	947
Etowah	Gadsden	103,189	99,840	535
Fayette	Fayette	18,228	17,962	628
Franklin	Russellville	30,737	27,814	636
Geneva	Geneva	25,735	23,647	576
Greene	Eutaw	9,661	10,153	646
Hale	Greensboro	18,316	15,498	644
Henry	Abbeville	16,610	15,374	562
Houston	Dothan	94,249	81,331	580
Jackson	Scottsboro	53,650	47,796	1,079
Jefferson	Birmingham	657,221	651,520	1,113
Lamar	Vernon	14,962	15,715	605
Lauderdale	Florence	87,691	79,661	669
Lawrence	Moulton	34,605	31,513	693
Lee	Opelika	123,254	87,146	609
Limestone	Athens	70,469	54,135	568
Lowndes	Hayneville	13,076	12,658	718
Macon	Tuskegee	22,810	24,928	611
Madison	Huntsville	298,192	238,912	805
Marengo	Linden	21,879	23,084	977
Marion	Hamilton	30,154	29,830	741
Marshall	Guntersville	85,634	70,832	567
Mobile	Mobile	401,427	378,643	1,233
Monroe	Monroeville	23,733	23,968	1,026
Montgomery	Montgomery	221,619	209,085	790
Morgan	Decatur	113,740	100,043	582
Perry	Marion	11,371	12,759	719
Pickens	Carrollton	20,178	20,699	881
Pike	Troy	29,639	27,595	671
Randolph	Wedowee	22,717	19,881	581
Russell	Phenix City	49,326	46,860	641
Saint Clair	Ashville & Pell City	72,330	49,811	634
Shelby	Columbiana	171,465	99,363	795
Sumter	Livingston	13,819	16,174	905
Talladega	Talladega	80,457	74,109	740
Tallapoosa	Dadeville	40,717	38,826	718
Tuscaloosa	Tuscaloosa	168,908	150,500	1,324
Walker	Jasper	70,117	67,670	794
Washington	Chatom	17,773	16,694	1,081
Wilcox	Camden	12,937	13,568	889
Winston	Double Springs	24,498	22,053	614

Alaska
(27 divisions, 571,951 sq. mi. land; pop. 663,661)

Borough or Census Division	2005 Pop.	1990 Pop.	Land area sq. mi.
Aleutians East Borough	2,713	2,464	6,988
Aleutians West Census Area	5,382	9,478	4,397
Anchorage Municipality	275,043	226,338	1,697
Bethel Census Area	17,127	13,660	40,633
Bristol Bay Borough	1,112	1,410	505
Denali Borough	1,881	1,682	12,750
Dillingham Census Area	4,926	4,010	18,675
Fairbanks North Star Borough	87,560	77,720	7,366
Haines Borough	2,272	2,117	2,344
Juneau Borough	30,987	26,752	2,717
Kenai Peninsula Borough	51,960	40,802	16,013
Ketchikan Gateway Borough	13,262	13,828	1,233
Kodiak Island Borough	13,051	13,309	6,560
Lake and Peninsula Borough	1,570	1,666	23,782
Matanuska-Susitna Borough	76,006	39,683	24,682
Nome Census Area	9,328	8,288	23,001
North Slope Borough	6,924	5,986	88,817
Northwest Arctic Borough	7,621	6,106	35,898
Prince of Wales-Outer Ketchikan Census Area	5,660	6,278	7,411
Sitka Borough	8,986	8,588	2,874
Skagway-Hoonah-Angoon Census Area	3,126	3,679	7,896
Southeast Fairbanks Census Area	6,614	5,925	24,815
Valdez-Cordova Census Area	9,899	9,920	34,319
Wade Hampton Census Area	7,541	5,789	17,194
Wrangell-Petersburg Census Area	6,245	7,042	5,835
Yakutat Borough	722	725	7,650
Yukon-Koyukuk Census Area	6,143	6,798	145,900

Arizona
(15 counties, 113,635 sq. mi. land; pop. 5,939,292)

County	County seat or courthouse	2005 Pop.	1990 Pop.	Land area sq. mi.
Apache	Saint Johns	69,343	61,591	11,205
Cochise	Bisbee	126,106	97,624	6,169
Coconino	Flagstaff	123,866	96,591	18,617
Gila	Globe	51,663	40,216	4,768
Graham	Safford	33,073	26,554	4,629
Greenlee	Clifton	7,521	8,008	1,847
La Paz	Parker	20,238	13,844	4,500
Maricopa	Phoenix	3,635,528	2,122,101	9,203
Mohave	Kingman	187,200	93,497	13,312
Navajo	Holbrook	108,432	77,674	9,953
Pima	Tucson	924,786	666,957	9,186
Pinal	Florence	229,549	116,397	5,370
Santa Cruz	Nogales	42,009	29,676	1,238
Yavapai	Prescott	198,701	107,714	8,123
Yuma	Yuma	181,277	106,895	5,514

Arkansas
(75 counties, 52,068 sq. mi. land; pop. 2,779,154)

County	County seat or courthouse	2005 Pop.	1990 Pop.	Land area sq. mi.
Arkansas	DeWitt & Stuttgart	20,073	21,653	988
Ashley	Hamburg	23,178	24,319	921
Baxter	Mountain Home	40,330	31,186	554
Benton	Bentonville	186,938	97,530	846
Boone	Harrison	35,793	28,297	591
Bradley	Warren	12,192	11,793	651
Calhoun	Hampton	5,589	5,826	628
Carroll	Berryville & Eureka Springs	26,999	18,623	630
Chicot	Lake Village	13,027	15,713	644
Clark	Arkadelphia	22,916	21,437	865
Clay	Corning & Piggott	16,578	18,107	639
Cleburne	Heber Springs	25,391	19,411	553
Cleveland	Rison	8,903	7,781	595
Columbia	Magnolia	24,695	25,691	766
Conway	Morrilton	20,739	19,151	556
Craighead	Jonesboro & Lake City	86,735	68,956	711
Crawford	Van Buren	57,630	42,493	595
Crittenden	Marion	51,882	49,939	610
Cross	Wynne	19,237	19,225	616
Dallas	Fordyce	8,524	9,614	667
Desha	Arkansas City	14,358	16,798	765
Drew	Monticello	18,693	17,369	828
Faulkner	Conway	97,147	60,006	647
Franklin	Charleston & Ozark	18,218	14,897	610
Fulton	Salem	11,934	10,037	618
Garland	Hot Springs	93,551	73,397	677
Grant	Sheridan	17,348	13,948	632
Greene	Paragould	39,401	31,804	578
Hempstead	Hope	23,383	21,621	729
Hot Spring	Malvern	31,264	26,115	615
Howard	Nashville	14,552	13,569	587
Independence	Batesville	34,737	31,192	764
Izard	Melbourne	13,430	11,364	581
Jackson	Newport	17,601	18,944	634
Jefferson	Pine Bluff	81,700	85,487	885
Johnson	Clarksville	24,042	18,221	662
Lafayette	Lewisville	8,027	9,643	527
Lawrence	Walnut Ridge	17,153	17,455	587
Lee	Marianna	11,545	13,053	602
Lincoln	Star City	14,262	13,690	561
Little River	Ashdown	13,227	13,966	532
Logan	Booneville & Paris	22,944	20,557	710
Lonoke	Lonoke	60,658	39,268	766
Madison	Huntsville	14,962	11,618	837
Marion	Yellville	16,735	12,001	598
Miller	Texarkana	43,162	38,467	624

County	County seat or courthouse	2005 Pop.	1990 Pop.	Land area sq. mi.
Mississippi	Blytheville & Osceola	47,911	57,525	898
Monroe	Clarendon	9,302	11,333	607
Montgomery	Mount Ida	9,274	7,841	781
Nevada	Prescott	9,550	10,101	620
Newton	Jasper	8,452	7,666	823
Ouachita	Camden	27,102	30,574	732
Perry	Perryville	10,468	7,969	551
Phillips	Helena	24,107	28,830	693
Pike	Murfreesboro	11,038	10,086	603
Poinsett	Harrisburg	25,349	24,664	758
Polk	Mena	20,176	17,347	859
Pope	Russellville	56,580	45,883	812
Prairie	Des Arc & De Valls Bluff	9,113	9,518	646
Pulaski	Little Rock	366,463	349,773	771
Randolph	Pocahontas	18,465	16,558	652
Saint Francis	Forrest City	27,902	28,497	634
Saline	Benton	91,188	64,183	723
Scott	Waldron	11,150	10,205	894
Searcy	Marshall	7,969	7,841	667
Sebastian	Fort Smith & Greenwood	118,750	99,590	536
Sevier	De Queen	16,456	13,637	564
Sharp	Ash Flat	17,397	14,109	604
Stone	Mountain View	11,716	9,775	607
Union	El Dorado	44,186	46,719	1,039
Van Buren	Clinton	16,529	14,008	712
Washington	Fayetteville	180,357	113,409	950
White	Searcy	71,332	54,676	1,034
Woodruff	Augusta	8,098	9,520	587
Yell	Danville & Dardanelle	21,391	17,759	928

California
(58 counties, 155,959 sq. mi. land; pop. 36,132,147)

County	County seat or courthouse	2005 Pop.	1990 Pop.	Land area sq. mi.
Alameda	Oakland	1,448,905	1,304,347	738
Alpine	Markleeville	1,159	1,113	739
Amador	Jackson	38,471	30,039	593
Butte	Oroville	214,185	182,120	1,639
Calaveras	San Andreas	46,871	31,998	1,020
Colusa	Colusa	21,095	16,275	1,151
Contra Costa	Martinez	1,017,787	803,731	720
Del Norte	Crescent City	28,705	23,460	1,008
El Dorado	Placerville	176,841	125,995	1,711
Fresno	Fresno	877,584	667,479	5,963
Glenn	Willows	27,759	24,798	1,315
Humboldt	Eureka	128,376	119,118	3,572
Imperial	El Centro	155,823	109,303	4,175
Inyo	Independence	18,156	18,281	10,203
Kern	Bakersfield	756,825	544,981	8,141
Kings	Hanford	143,420	101,469	1,391
Lake	Lakeport	65,147	50,631	1,258
Lassen	Susanville	34,751	27,598	4,557
Los Angeles	Los Angeles	9,935,475	8,863,052	4,061
Madera	Madera	142,788	88,090	2,136
Marin	San Rafael	246,960	230,096	520
Mariposa	Mariposa	18,069	14,302	1,451
Mendocino	Ukiah	88,161	80,345	3,509
Merced	Merced	241,706	178,403	1,929
Modoc	Alturas	9,524	9,678	3,944
Mono	Bridgeport	12,509	9,956	3,044
Monterey	Salinas	412,104	355,660	3,322
Napa	Napa	132,764	110,765	754
Nevada	Nevada City	98,394	78,510	958
Orange	Santa Ana	2,988,072	2,410,668	789
Placer	Auburn	317,028	172,796	1,404
Plumas	Quincy	21,477	19,739	2,554
Riverside	Riverside	1,946,419	1,170,413	7,207
Sacramento	Sacramento	1,363,482	1,066,789	966
San Benito	Hollister	55,936	36,697	1,389
San Bernardino	San Bernardino	1,963,535	1,418,380	20,053
San Diego	San Diego	2,933,462	2,498,016	4,200
San Francisco	San Francisco	739,426	723,959	47
San Joaquin	Stockton	664,116	480,628	1,399
San Luis Obispo	San Luis Obispo	255,487	217,162	3,304
San Mateo	Redwood City	699,610	649,623	449
Santa Barbara	Santa Barbara	400,762	369,608	2,737
Santa Clara	San Jose	1,699,052	1,497,577	1,291
Santa Cruz	Santa Cruz	249,666	229,734	445
Shasta	Redding	179,904	147,036	3,785
Sierra	Downieville	3,434	3,318	953
Siskiyou	Yreka	45,259	43,531	6,287
Solano	Fairfield	411,593	339,469	829
Sonoma	Santa Rosa	466,477	388,222	1,576
Stanislaus	Modesto	505,505	370,522	1,494
Sutter	Yuba City	88,876	64,409	603
Tehama	Red Bluff	61,197	49,625	2,951
Trinity	Weaverville	13,622	13,063	3,179
Tulare	Visalia	410,874	311,932	4,824
Tuolumne	Sonora	59,380	48,456	2,235
Ventura	Ventura	796,106	669,016	1,845
Yolo	Woodland	184,932	141,212	1,013
Yuba	Marysville	67,153	58,234	631

Colorado
(64 counties, 103,718 sq. mi. land; pop. 4,665,177)

County	County seat or courthouse	2005 Pop.	1990 Pop.	Land area sq. mi.
Adams[1]	Brighton	399,426	265,038	1,192
Alamosa	Alamosa	15,282	13,617	723
Arapahoe	Littleton	529,090	391,572	803
Archuleta	Pagosa Springs	11,886	5,345	1,350
Baca	Springfield	4,069	4,556	2,556
Bent	Las Animas	5,558	5,048	1,514
Boulder[1]	Boulder	280,440	225,339	742
Broomfield[2]	Broomfield	43,478	NA	27
Chaffee	Salida	16,968	12,684	1,013
Cheyenne	Cheyenne Wells	1,953	2,397	1,781
Clear Creek	Georgetown	9,197	7,619	395
Conejos	Conejos	8,512	7,453	1,287
Costilla	San Luis	3,424	3,190	1,227
Crowley	Ordway	5,401	3,946	789
Custer	Westcliffe	3,860	1,926	739
Delta	Delta	29,947	20,980	1,142
Denver	Denver	557,917	467,549	153
Dolores	Dove Creek	1,827	1,504	1,067
Douglas	Castle Rock	249,416	60,391	840
Eagle	Eagle	47,530	21,928	1,688
Elbert	Kiowa	22,788	9,646	1,851
El Paso	Colorado Springs	565,582	397,014	2,126
Fremont	Canon City	47,766	32,273	1,533
Garfield	Glenwood Springs	49,810	29,974	2,947
Gilpin	Central City	4,932	3,070	150
Grand	Hot Sulphur Springs	13,211	7,966	1,847
Gunnison	Gunnison	14,226	10,273	3,239
Hinsdale	Lake City	765	467	1,118
Huerfano	Walsenburg	7,771	6,009	1,591
Jackson	Walden	1,448	1,605	1,613
Jefferson[1]	Golden	526,801	438,430	772
Kiowa	Eads	1,422	1,688	1,771
Kit Carson	Burlington	7,642	7,140	2,161
Lake	Leadville	7,738	6,007	377
La Plata	Durango	47,452	32,284	1,692
Larimer	Fort Collins	271,927	186,136	2,601
Las Animas	Trinidad	15,446	13,765	4,772
Lincoln	Hugo	5,618	4,529	2,586
Logan	Sterling	20,719	17,567	1,839
Mesa	Grand Junction	129,872	93,145	3,328
Mineral	Creede	932	558	876
Moffat	Craig	13,417	11,357	4,742
Montezuma	Cortez	24,778	18,672	2,037
Montrose	Montrose	37,482	24,423	2,241
Morgan	Fort Morgan	27,995	21,939	1,285
Otero	La Junta	19,495	20,185	1,263
Ouray	Ouray	4,260	2,295	540
Park	Fairplay	16,949	7,174	2,201
Phillips	Holyoke	4,586	4,189	688
Pitkin	Aspen	14,914	12,661	970
Prowers	Lamar	13,892	13,347	1,640
Pueblo	Pueblo	151,322	123,051	2,389
Rio Blanco	Meeker	5,973	6,051	3,221
Rio Grande	Del Norte	12,227	10,770	912
Routt	Steamboat Springs	21,313	14,088	2,362
Saguache	Saguache	7,031	4,619	3,168
San Juan	Silverton	577	745	387
San Miguel	Telluride	7,213	3,653	1,287
Sedgwick	Julesburg	2,529	2,690	548
Summit	Breckenridge	24,892	12,881	608
Teller	Cripple Creek	21,918	12,468	557
Washington	Akron	4,633	4,812	2,521
Weld[1]	Greeley	228,943	131,821	3,992
Yuma	Wray	9,789	8,954	2,366

NA = Not available. (1) Parts of these counties were taken to create Broomfield County in 2001. (2) Created in 2001.

Connecticut
(8 counties, 4,845 sq. mi. land; pop. 3,510,297)

County	County seat or courthouse	2005 Pop.	1990 Pop.	Land area sq. mi.
Fairfield	Bridgeport	902,775	827,645	626
Hartford	Hartford	877,393	851,783	735
Litchfield	Litchfield	190,071	174,092	920
Middlesex	Middletown	163,214	143,196	369
New Haven	New Haven	846,766	804,219	606
New London	New London	266,618	254,957	666
Tolland	Rockville	147,634	128,699	410
Windham	Putnam	115,826	102,525	513

Delaware
(3 counties, 1,954 sq. mi. land; pop. 843,524)

County	County seat or courthouse	2005 Pop.	1990 Pop.	Land area sq. mi.
Kent	Dover	143,968	110,993	590
New Castle	Wilmington	523,008	441,946	426
Sussex	Georgetown	176,548	113,229	938

District of Columbia
(61 sq. mi. land; pop. 550,521)
Has no counties; coextensive with city of Washington.

Florida
(67 counties, 53,927 sq. mi. land; pop. 17,789,864)

County	County seat or courthouse	2005 Pop.	1990 Pop.	Land area sq. mi.
Alachua	Gainesville	223,852	181,596	874
Baker	Macclenny	24,569	18,486	585
Bay	Panama City	161,558	126,994	764
Bradford	Starke	28,118	22,515	293
Brevard	Titusville	531,250	398,978	1,018
Broward	Fort Lauderdale	1,777,638	1,255,531	1,205
Calhoun	Blountstown	13,290	11,011	567
Charlotte	Punta Gorda	157,536	110,975	694
Citrus	Inverness	134,370	93,513	584
Clay	Green Cove Springs	171,095	105,986	601
Collier	Naples	307,242	152,099	2,025
Columbia	Lake City	64,040	42,613	797
De Soto	Arcadia	35,406	23,865	637
Dixie	Cross City	14,647	10,585	704
Duval	Jacksonville	826,436	672,971	774
Escambia	Pensacola	296,772	262,445	662
Flagler	Bunnell	76,410	28,701	485
Franklin	Apalachicola	10,177	8,967	544
Gadsden	Quincy	46,428	41,116	516
Gilchrist	Trenton	16,402	9,667	349
Glades	Moore Haven	11,252	7,591	774
Gulf	Port Saint Joe	13,975	11,504	555
Hamilton	Jasper	13,983	10,930	515
Hardee	Wauchula	28,286	19,499	637
Hendry	La Belle	39,561	25,773	1,153
Hernando	Brooksville	158,409	101,115	478
Highlands	Sebring	95,496	68,432	1,028
Hillsborough	Tampa	1,132,152	834,054	1,051
Holmes	Bonifay	19,264	15,778	482
Indian River	Vero Beach	128,594	90,208	503
Jackson	Marianna	48,985	41,375	916
Jefferson	Monticello	14,490	11,296	598
Lafayette	Mayo	7,953	5,578	543
Lake	Tavares	277,035	152,104	953
Lee	Fort Myers	544,758	335,113	804
Leon	Tallahassee	245,756	192,493	667
Levy	Bronson	37,998	25,912	1,118
Liberty	Bristol	7,773	5,569	836
Madison	Madison	19,092	16,569	692
Manatee	Bradenton	306,779	211,707	741
Marion	Ocala	303,442	194,835	1,579
Martin	Stuart	139,728	100,900	556
Miami-Dade	Miami	2,376,014	1,937,194	1,946
Monroe	Key West	76,329	78,024	997
Nassau	Fernandina Beach	64,746	43,941	652
Okaloosa	Crestview	182,172	143,777	936
Okeechobee	Okeechobee	39,836	29,627	774
Orange	Orlando	1,023,023	677,491	907
Osceola	Kissimmee	231,578	107,728	1,322
Palm Beach	West Palm Beach	1,268,548	863,503	1,974
Pasco	Dade City	429,065	281,131	745
Pinellas	Clearwater	928,032	851,659	280
Polk	Bartow	542,912	405,382	1,874
Putnam	Palatka	73,568	65,070	722
Saint Johns	Saint Augustine	161,525	83,829	609
Saint Lucie	Fort Pierce	241,305	150,171	572
Santa Rosa	Milton	143,105	81,961	1,017
Sarasota	Sarasota	366,256	277,776	572
Seminole	Sanford	401,619	287,521	308
Sumter	Bushnell	64,182	31,577	546
Suwannee	Live Oak	38,624	26,780	688
Taylor	Perry	19,622	17,111	1,042
Union	Lake Butler	14,916	10,252	240
Volusia	De Land	490,055	370,737	1,103
Wakulla	Crawfordville	28,212	14,202	607
Walton	De Funiak Springs	50,324	27,759	1,058
Washington	Chipley	22,299	16,919	580

Georgia
(159 counties, 57,906 sq. mi. land; pop. 9,072,576)

County	County seat or courthouse	2005 Pop.	1990 Pop.	Land area sq. mi.
Appling	Baxley	17,954	15,744	509
Atkinson	Pearson	8,030	6,213	338
Bacon	Alma	10,379	9,566	285
Baker	Newton	4,154	3,615	343
Baldwin	Milledgeville	45,230	39,530	258
Banks	Homer	16,055	10,308	234
Barrow	Winder	59,954	29,721	162
Bartow	Cartersville	89,229	55,915	459
Ben Hill	Fitzgerald	17,316	16,245	252
Berrien	Nashville	16,708	14,153	452
Bibb	Macon	154,918	150,137	250
Bleckley	Cochran	12,141	10,430	217
Brantley	Nahunta	15,491	11,077	444
Brooks	Quitman	16,327	15,398	494
Bryan	Pembroke	28,549	15,438	442
Bulloch	Statesboro	61,454	43,125	682
Burke	Waynesboro	23,299	20,579	830
Butts	Jackson	21,045	15,326	187
Calhoun	Morgan	5,972	5,013	280
Camden	Woodbine	45,759	30,167	630
Candler	Metter	10,321	7,744	247
Carroll	Carrollton	105,453	71,422	499
Catoosa	Ringgold	60,813	42,464	162
Charlton	Folkston	10,790	8,496	781
Chatham	Savannah	238,410	216,774	438
Chattahoochee	Cusseta	14,679	16,934	249
Chattooga	Summerville	26,570	22,236	313
Cherokee	Canton	184,211	90,204	424
Clarke	Athens	104,439	87,594	121
Clay	Fort Gaines	3,242	3,364	195
Clayton	Jonesboro	267,966	181,436	143
Clinch	Homerville	6,996	6,160	809
Cobb	Marietta	663,818	447,745	340
Coffee	Douglas	39,674	29,592	599
Colquitt	Moultrie	43,915	36,645	552
Columbia	Appling	103,812	66,031	290
Cook	Adel	16,366	13,456	229
Coweta	Newnan	109,903	53,853	443
Crawford	Knoxville	12,874	8,991	325
Crisp	Cordele	22,017	20,011	274
Dade	Trenton	16,040	13,183	174
Dawson	Dawsonville	19,731	9,429	211
Decatur	Bainbridge	28,618	25,517	597
DeKalb	Decatur	677,959	546,174	268
Dodge	Eastman	19,574	17,607	500
Dooly	Vienna	11,749	9,901	393
Dougherty	Albany	94,882	96,321	330
Douglas	Douglasville	112,760	71,120	199
Early	Blakely	12,056	11,854	511
Echols	Statenville	4,253	2,334	404
Effingham	Springfield	46,924	25,687	479
Elbert	Elberton	20,799	18,949	369
Emanuel	Swainsboro	22,108	20,546	686
Evans	Claxton	11,443	8,724	185
Fannin	Blue Ridge	21,887	15,992	386
Fayette	Fayetteville	104,248	62,415	197
Floyd	Rome	94,198	81,251	513
Forsyth	Cumming	140,393	44,083	226
Franklin	Carnesville	21,590	16,650	263
Fulton	Atlanta	915,623	648,776	529
Gilmer	Ellijay	27,335	13,368	427
Glascock	Gibson	2,705	2,357	144
Glynn	Brunswick	71,874	62,496	422
Gordon	Calhoun	50,279	35,067	356
Grady	Cairo	24,466	20,279	458
Greene	Greensboro	15,693	11,793	388
Gwinnett	Lawrenceville	726,273	352,910	433
Habersham	Clarkesville	39,603	27,622	278
Hall	Gainesville	165,771	95,434	394
Hancock	Sparta	9,643	8,908	473
Haralson	Buchanan	28,338	21,966	282
Harris	Hamilton	27,779	17,788	464
Hart	Hartwell	24,036	19,712	232
Heard	Franklin	11,346	8,628	296
Henry	McDonough	167,848	58,741	323
Houston	Perry	126,163	89,208	377
Irwin	Ocilla	10,093	8,649	357
Jackson	Jefferson	52,292	30,005	342
Jasper	Monticello	13,147	8,453	370
Jeff Davis	Hazlehurst	13,083	12,032	333
Jefferson	Louisville	16,926	17,408	528
Jenkins	Millen	8,729	8,247	350
Johnson	Wrightsville	9,538	8,329	304
Jones	Gray	26,836	20,739	394
Lamar	Barnesville	16,378	13,038	185
Lanier	Lakeland	7,553	5,531	187
Laurens	Dublin	46,896	39,988	812
Lee	Leesburg	31,099	16,250	356
Liberty	Hinesville	57,544	52,745	519
Lincoln	Lincolnton	8,207	7,442	211
Long	Ludowici	11,083	6,202	401
Lowndes	Valdosta	96,705	75,981	504
Lumpkin	Dahlonega	24,324	14,573	284
McDuffie	Thomson	21,743	20,119	260
McIntosh	Darien	11,068	8,634	433
Macon	Oglethorpe	13,745	13,114	403
Madison	Danielsville	27,289	21,050	284
Marion	Buena Vista	7,244	5,590	367
Meriwether	Greenville	22,919	22,411	503
Miller	Colquitt	6,228	6,280	283
Mitchell	Camilla	23,791	20,275	512
Monroe	Forsyth	23,785	17,113	396
Montgomery	Mount Vernon	8,909	7,379	245
Morgan	Madison	17,492	12,883	350
Murray	Chatsworth	40,812	26,147	344
Muscogee	Columbus	185,271	179,280	216
Newton	Covington	86,713	41,808	276
Oconee	Watkinsville	29,748	17,618	186
Oglethorpe	Lexington	13,609	9,763	441
Paulding	Dallas	112,411	41,611	313
Peach	Fort Valley	24,794	21,189	151
Pickens	Jasper	28,442	14,432	232
Pierce	Blackshear	17,119	13,328	343
Pike	Zebulon	16,128	10,224	218
Polk	Cedartown	40,479	33,815	311

County	County seat or courthouse	2005 Pop.	1990 Pop.	Land area sq. mi.
Pulaski	Hawkinsville	9,737	8,108	247
Putnam	Eatonton	19,829	14,137	345
Quitman	Georgetown	2,467	2,210	152
Rabun	Clayton	16,087	11,648	371
Randolph	Cuthbert	7,310	8,023	429
Richmond	Augusta	195,769	189,719	324
Rockdale	Conyers	78,545	54,091	131
Schley	Ellaville	4,122	3,590	168
Screven	Sylvania	15,430	13,842	648
Seminole	Donalsonville	9,226	9,010	238
Spalding	Griffin	61,289	54,457	198
Stephens	Toccoa	25,060	23,436	179
Stewart	Lumpkin	4,882	5,654	459
Sumter	Americus	32,912	30,232	485
Talbot	Talbotton	6,709	6,524	393
Taliaferro	Crawfordville	1,826	1,915	195
Tattnall	Reidsville	23,211	17,722	484
Taylor	Butler	8,887	7,642	377
Telfair	McRae	13,205	11,000	441
Terrell	Dawson	10,711	10,653	335
Thomas	Thomasville	44,692	38,943	548
Tift	Tifton	40,793	34,998	265
Toombs	Lyons	27,274	24,072	367
Towns	Hiawassee	10,315	6,754	167
Treutlen	Soperton	6,753	5,994	201
Troup	La Grange	62,015	55,532	414
Turner	Ashburn	9,474	8,703	286
Twiggs	Jeffersonville	10,299	9,806	360
Union	Blairsville	19,782	11,993	323
Upson	Thomaston	27,679	26,300	325
Walker	La Fayette	63,890	58,310	447
Walton	Monroe	75,647	38,586	329
Ware	Waycross	34,492	35,471	902
Warren	Warrenton	6,101	6,078	286
Washington	Sandersville	20,118	19,112	680
Wayne	Jesup	28,390	22,356	645
Webster	Preston	2,289	2,263	210
Wheeler	Alamo	6,706	4,903	298
White	Cleveland	24,055	13,006	242
Whitfield	Dalton	90,889	72,462	290
Wilcox	Abbeville	8,721	7,008	380
Wilkes	Washington	10,457	10,597	471
Wilkinson	Irwinton	10,143	10,228	447
Worth	Sylvester	21,996	19,744	570

Hawaii

(5 counties, 6,423 sq. mi. land; pop. 1,275,194)

County	County seat or courthouse	2005 Pop.	1990 Pop.	Land area sq. mi.
Hawaii	Hilo	167,293	120,317	4,028
Honolulu	Honolulu	905,266	836,231	600
Kalawao[1]		111	130	13
Kauai	Lihue	62,640	51,177	622
Maui	Wailuku	139,884	100,374	1,159

(1) Administered by state government.

Idaho

(44 counties, 82,747 sq. mi. land; pop. 1,429,096)

County	County seat or courthouse	2005 Pop.	1990 Pop.	Land area sq. mi.
Ada	Boise	344,727	205,775	1,055
Adams	Council	3,591	3,254	1,365
Bannock	Pocatello	78,155	66,026	1,113
Bear Lake	Paris	6,176	6,084	971
Benewah	Saint Maries	9,218	7,937	776
Bingham	Blackfoot	43,739	37,583	2,095
Blaine	Hailey	21,166	13,552	2,645
Boise	Idaho City	7,535	3,509	1,902
Bonner	Sandpoint	40,908	26,622	1,738
Bonneville	Idaho Falls	91,856	72,207	1,868
Boundary	Bonners Ferry	10,619	8,332	1,269
Butte	Arco	2,808	2,918	2,233
Camas	Fairfield	1,050	727	1,075
Canyon	Caldwell	164,593	90,076	590
Caribou	Soda Springs	7,131	6,963	1,766
Cassia	Burley	21,324	19,532	2,566
Clark	Dubois	943	762	1,765
Clearwater	Orofino	8,373	8,505	2,461
Custer	Challis	4,077	4,133	4,925
Elmore	Mountain Home	28,634	21,205	3,078
Franklin	Preston	12,371	9,232	665
Fremont	Saint Anthony	12,242	10,937	1,867
Gem	Emmett	16,273	11,844	563
Gooding	Gooding	14,461	11,633	731
Idaho	Grangeville	15,697	13,768	8,485
Jefferson	Rigby	21,580	16,543	1,095
Jerome	Jerome	19,638	15,138	600
Kootenai	Coeur d'Alene	127,668	69,795	1,245
Latah	Moscow	34,714	30,617	1,077
Lemhi	Salmon	7,909	6,899	4,564
Lewis	Nez Perce	3,750	3,516	479
Lincoln	Shoshone	4,545	3,308	1,206
Madison	Rexberg	30,975	23,674	472
Minidoka	Rupert	19,014	19,361	760

County	County seat or courthouse	2005 Pop.	1990 Pop.	Land area sq. mi.
Nez Perce	Lewiston	37,931	33,754	849
Oneida	Malad City	4,209	3,492	1,200
Owyhee	Murphy	11,073	8,392	7,678
Payette	Payette	22,197	16,434	408
Power	American Falls	7,753	7,086	1,406
Shoshone	Wallace	13,157	13,931	2,634
Teton	Driggs	7,467	3,439	450
Twin Falls	Twin Falls	69,419	53,580	1,925
Valley	Cascade	8,332	6,109	3,678
Washington	Weiser	10,098	8,550	1,456

Illinois

(102 counties, 55,584 sq. mi. land; pop. 12,763,371)

County	County seat or courthouse	2005 Pop.	1990 Pop.	Land area sq. mi.
Adams	Quincy	67,040	66,090	857
Alexander	Cairo	8,927	10,626	236
Bond	Greenville	18,027	14,991	380
Boone	Belvidere	50,483	30,806	281
Brown	Mount Sterling	6,835	5,836	306
Bureau	Princeton	35,330	35,688	869
Calhoun	Hardin	5,163	5,322	254
Carroll	Mount Carroll	16,086	16,805	444
Cass	Virginia	13,898	13,437	376
Champaign	Urbana	184,905	173,025	997
Christian	Taylorville	35,176	34,418	709
Clark	Marshall	16,976	15,921	502
Clay	Louisville	14,122	14,460	469
Clinton	Carlyle	36,095	33,944	474
Coles	Charleston	51,065	51,644	508
Cook	Chicago	5,303,683	5,105,044	946
Crawford	Robinson	19,898	19,464	444
Cumberland	Toledo	10,973	10,670	346
DeKalb	Sycamore	97,665	77,932	634
De Witt	Clinton	16,617	16,516	398
Douglas	Tuscola	19,950	19,464	417
DuPage	Wheaton	929,113	781,689	334
Edgar	Paris	19,157	19,595	624
Edwards	Albion	6,784	7,440	222
Effingham	Effingham	34,581	31,704	479
Fayette	Vandalia	21,713	20,893	716
Ford	Paxton	14,157	14,275	486
Franklin	Benton	39,723	40,319	412
Fulton	Lewistown	37,708	38,080	866
Gallatin	Shawneetown	6,152	6,909	324
Greene	Carrollton	14,581	15,317	543
Grundy	Morris	43,838	32,337	420
Hamilton	McLeansboro	8,301	8,499	435
Hancock	Carthage	19,153	21,373	795
Hardin	Elizabethtown	4,718	5,189	178
Henderson	Oquawka	7,972	8,096	379
Henry	Cambridge	50,591	51,159	823
Iroquois	Watseka	30,677	30,787	1,116
Jackson	Murphysboro	57,954	61,067	588
Jasper	Newton	10,020	10,609	494
Jefferson	Mount Vernon	40,434	37,020	571
Jersey	Jerseyville	22,456	20,539	369
Jo Daviess	Galena	22,580	21,821	601
Johnson	Vienna	13,169	11,347	345
Kane	Geneva	482,113	317,471	520
Kankakee	Kankakee	107,972	96,255	677
Kendall	Yorkville	79,514	39,413	321
Knox	Galesburg	53,309	56,393	716
Lake	Waukegan	702,682	516,418	448
La Salle	Ottawa	112,604	106,913	1,135
Lawrence	Lawrenceville	15,930	15,972	372
Lee	Dixon	35,669	34,392	725
Livingston	Pontiac	39,186	39,301	1,044
Logan	Lincoln	30,603	30,798	618
McDonough	Macomb	31,966	35,244	589
McHenry	Woodstock	303,990	183,241	604
McLean	Bloomington	159,013	129,180	1,184
Macon	Decatur	110,167	117,206	581
Macoupin	Carlinville	49,111	47,679	864
Madison	Edwardsville	264,309	249,238	725
Marion	Salem	40,144	41,561	572
Marshall	Lacon	13,217	12,846	386
Mason	Havana	15,741	16,269	539
Massac	Metropolis	15,348	14,752	239
Menard	Petersburg	12,738	11,164	314
Mercer	Aledo	16,912	17,290	561
Monroe	Waterloo	31,040	22,422	388
Montgomery	Hillsboro	30,396	30,728	704
Morgan	Jacksonville	35,722	36,397	569
Moultrie	Sullivan	14,510	13,930	336
Ogle	Oregon	54,290	45,957	759
Peoria	Peoria	182,328	182,827	620
Perry	Pinckneyville	22,851	21,412	441
Piatt	Monticello	16,680	15,548	440
Pike	Pittsfield	17,099	17,577	830
Pope	Golconda	4,211	4,373	371
Pulaski	Mound City	6,794	7,523	201
Putnam	Hennepin	6,094	5,730	160
Randolph	Chester	33,122	34,583	578
Richland	Olney	15,798	16,545	360
Rock Island	Rock Island	147,808	148,723	427

County	County seat or courthouse	2005 Pop.	1990 Pop.	Land area sq. mi.
Saint Clair	Belleville	260,067	262,852	664
Saline	Harrisburg	26,072	26,551	383
Sangamon	Springfield	192,789	178,386	868
Schuyler	Rushville	7,073	7,498	437
Scott	Winchester	5,412	5,644	251
Shelby	Shelbyville	22,322	22,261	759
Stark	Toulon	6,169	6,534	288
Stephenson	Freeport	47,965	48,052	564
Tazewell	Pekin	129,999	123,692	649
Union	Jonesboro	18,202	17,619	416
Vermilion	Danville	82,344	88,257	899
Wabash	Mount Carmel	12,570	13,111	223
Warren	Monmouth	17,558	19,181	543
Washington	Nashville	14,922	14,965	563
Wayne	Fairfield	16,796	17,241	714
White	Carmi	15,284	16,522	495
Whiteside	Morrison	59,863	60,186	685
Will	Joliet	642,813	357,313	837
Williamson	Marion	63,617	57,733	423
Winnebago	Rockford	288,695	252,913	514
Woodford	Eureka	37,448	32,653	528

Indiana
(92 counties, 35,867 sq. mi. land; pop. 6,271,973)

County	County seat or courthouse	2005 Pop.	1990 Pop.	Land area sq. mi.
Adams	Decatur	33,849	31,095	339
Allen	Fort Wayne	344,006	300,836	657
Bartholomew	Columbus	73,540	63,657	407
Benton	Fowler	9,039	9,441	406
Blackford	Hartford City	13,849	14,067	165
Boone	Lebanon	52,061	38,147	423
Brown	Nashville	15,154	14,080	312
Carroll	Delphi	20,426	18,809	372
Cass	Logansport	40,130	38,413	413
Clark	Jeffersonville	101,592	87,774	375
Clay	Brazil	27,142	24,705	358
Clinton	Frankfort	34,091	30,974	405
Crawford	English	11,216	9,914	306
Daviess	Washington	30,466	27,533	431
Dearborn	Lawrenceburg	49,082	38,835	305
Decatur	Greensburg	25,184	23,645	373
De Kalb	Auburn	41,659	35,324	363
Delaware	Muncie	116,362	119,659	393
Dubois	Jasper	40,858	36,616	430
Elkhart	Goshen	195,362	156,198	464
Fayette	Connersville	24,885	26,015	215
Floyd	New Albany	71,997	64,404	148
Fountain	Covington	17,462	17,808	396
Franklin	Brookville	23,085	19,580	386
Fulton	Rochester	20,665	18,840	369
Gibson	Princeton	33,408	31,913	489
Grant	Marion	70,557	74,169	414
Greene	Bloomfield	33,479	30,410	542
Hamilton	Noblesville	240,685	108,936	398
Hancock	Greenfield	63,138	45,527	306
Harrison	Corydon	36,827	29,890	485
Hendricks	Danville	127,483	75,717	408
Henry	New Castle	47,244	48,139	393
Howard	Kokomo	84,977	80,827	293
Huntington	Huntington	38,236	35,427	383
Jackson	Brownstown	42,237	37,730	509
Jasper	Rensselaer	31,876	24,823	560
Jay	Portland	21,606	21,512	384
Jefferson	Madison	32,430	29,797	361
Jennings	Vernon	28,427	23,661	377
Johnson	Franklin	128,436	88,109	320
Knox	Vincennes	38,366	39,884	516
Kosciusko	Warsaw	76,072	65,294	538
Lagrange	Lagrange	36,875	29,477	380
Lake	Crown Point	493,297	475,594	497
La Porte	La Porte	110,512	107,066	598
Lawrence	Bedford	46,403	42,836	449
Madison	Anderson	130,412	130,669	452
Marion	Indianapolis	863,133	797,159	396
Marshall	Plymouth	46,945	42,182	444
Martin	Shoals	10,386	10,369	336
Miami	Peru	35,620	36,897	376
Monroe	Bloomington	121,407	108,978	394
Montgomery	Crawfordsville	38,239	34,436	505
Morgan	Martinsville	69,778	55,920	406
Newton	Kentland	14,456	13,551	402
Noble	Albion	47,448	37,877	411
Ohio	Rising Sun	5,874	5,315	87
Orange	Paoli	19,770	18,409	400
Owen	Spencer	22,823	17,281	385
Parke	Rockville	17,362	15,410	445
Perry	Tell City	19,032	19,107	381
Pike	Petersburg	12,766	12,509	336
Porter	Valparaiso	157,772	128,932	418
Posey	Mount Vernon	26,852	25,968	409
Pulaski	Winamac	13,783	12,780	434
Putnam	Greencastle	36,957	30,315	480
Randolph	Winchester	26,684	27,148	453
Ripley	Versailles	27,710	24,616	446
Rush	Rushville	17,823	18,129	408

County	County seat or courthouse	2005 Pop.	1990 Pop.	Land area sq. mi.
Saint Joseph	South Bend	266,160	247,052	457
Scott	Scottsburg	23,820	20,991	190
Shelby	Shelbyville	43,766	40,307	413
Spencer	Rockport	20,528	19,490	399
Starke	Knox	22,933	22,747	309
Steuben	Angola	33,773	27,446	309
Sullivan	Sullivan	21,763	18,993	447
Switzerland	Vevay	9,718	7,738	221
Tippecanoe	Lafayette	153,875	130,598	500
Tipton	Tipton	16,385	16,119	260
Union	Liberty	7,208	6,976	162
Vanderburgh	Evansville	173,187	165,058	235
Vermillion	Newport	16,562	16,773	257
Vigo	Terre Haute	102,592	106,107	403
Wabash	Wabash	33,843	35,069	413
Warren	Williamsport	8,785	8,176	365
Warrick	Boonville	56,362	44,920	384
Washington	Salem	27,885	23,717	514
Wayne	Richmond	69,192	71,951	404
Wells	Bluffton	28,085	25,948	370
White	Monticello	24,463	23,265	505
Whitley	Columbia City	32,323	27,651	336

Iowa
(99 counties, 55,869 sq. mi. land; pop. 2,966,334)

County	County seat or courthouse	2005 Pop.	1990 Pop.	Land area sq. mi.
Adair	Greenfield	7,859	8,409	569
Adams	Corning	4,264	4,866	424
Allamakee	Waukon	14,709	13,855	640
Appanoose	Centerville	13,666	13,743	496
Audubon	Audubon	6,457	7,334	443
Benton	Vinton	27,000	22,429	716
Black Hawk	Waterloo	125,891	123,798	567
Boone	Boone	26,602	25,186	571
Bremer	Waverly	23,677	22,813	438
Buchanan	Independence	21,019	20,844	571
Buena Vista	Storm Lake	20,151	19,965	575
Butler	Allison	15,072	15,731	580
Calhoun	Rockwell City	10,443	11,508	570
Carroll	Carroll	21,034	21,423	569
Cass	Atlantic	14,219	15,128	564
Cedar	Tipton	18,254	17,444	580
Cerro Gordo	Mason City	44,645	46,733	568
Cherokee	Cherokee	12,237	14,098	577
Chickasaw	New Hampton	12,563	13,295	505
Clarke	Osceola	9,161	8,287	431
Clay	Spencer	16,897	17,585	569
Clayton	Elkader	18,337	19,054	779
Clinton	Clinton	49,717	51,040	695
Crawford	Denison	16,889	16,775	714
Dallas	Adel	51,762	29,755	586
Davis	Bloomfield	8,659	8,312	503
Decatur	Leon	8,605	8,338	532
Delaware	Manchester	18,025	18,035	578
Des Moines	Burlington	40,810	42,614	416
Dickinson	Spirit Lake	16,687	14,909	381
Dubuque	Dubuque	91,631	86,403	608
Emmet	Estherville	10,534	11,569	396
Fayette	West Union	21,298	21,843	731
Floyd	Charles City	16,443	17,058	501
Franklin	Hampton	10,732	11,364	582
Fremont	Sidney	7,759	8,226	511
Greene	Jefferson	9,963	10,045	568
Grundy	Grundy Center	12,329	12,029	503
Guthrie	Guthrie Center	11,547	10,935	591
Hamilton	Webster City	16,209	16,071	577
Hancock	Garner	11,786	12,638	571
Hardin	Eldora	18,003	19,094	569
Harrison	Logan	15,884	14,730	697
Henry	Mount Pleasant	20,246	19,226	434
Howard	Cresco	9,700	9,809	473
Humboldt	Dakota City	9,973	10,756	434
Ida	Ida Grove	7,379	8,365	432
Iowa	Marengo	16,055	14,630	586
Jackson	Maquoketa	20,335	19,950	636
Jasper	Newton	37,674	34,795	730
Jefferson	Fairfield	15,972	16,310	435
Johnson	Iowa City	117,067	96,119	614
Jones	Anamosa	20,509	19,444	575
Keokuk	Sigourney	11,157	11,624	579
Kossuth	Algona	16,142	18,591	973
Lee	Fort Madison & Keokuk	36,705	38,687	517
Linn	Cedar Rapids	198,903	168,767	717
Louisa	Wapello	11,842	11,592	402
Lucas	Chariton	9,672	9,070	431
Lyon	Rock Rapids	11,750	11,952	588
Madison	Winterset	15,158	12,483	561
Mahaska	Oskaloosa	22,364	21,532	571
Marion	Knoxville	32,984	30,001	554
Marshall	Marshalltown	39,418	38,276	572
Mills	Glenwood	15,284	13,202	437
Mitchell	Osage	10,919	10,928	469
Monona	Onawa	9,520	10,034	693
Monroe	Albia	7,835	8,114	433

County	County seat or courthouse	2005 Pop.	1990 Pop.	Land area sq. mi.
Montgomery	Red Oak	11,313	12,076	424
Muscatine	Muscatine	42,756	39,907	439
O'Brien	Primghar	14,414	15,444	573
Osceola	Sibley	6,694	7,267	399
Page	Clarinda	16,253	16,870	535
Palo Alto	Emmetsburg	9,697	10,669	564
Plymouth	Le Mars	24,958	23,388	864
Pocahontas	Pocahontas	7,930	9,525	578
Polk	Des Moines	401,006	327,140	569
Pottawattamie	Council Bluffs	89,738	82,628	954
Poweshiek	Montezuma	18,925	19,033	585
Ringgold	Mount Ayr	5,273	5,420	538
Sac	Sac City	10,621	12,324	576
Scott	Davenport	160,998	150,973	458
Shelby	Harlan	12,634	13,230	591
Sioux	Orange City	32,277	29,903	768
Story	Nevada	79,952	74,252	573
Tama	Toledo	17,919	17,419	721
Taylor	Bedford	6,614	7,114	534
Union	Creston	11,972	12,750	424
Van Buren	Keosauqua	7,786	7,676	485
Wapello	Ottumwa	35,965	35,696	432
Warren	Indianola	42,981	36,033	572
Washington	Washington	21,457	19,612	569
Wayne	Corydon	6,601	7,067	526
Webster	Fort Dodge	39,003	40,342	715
Winnebago	Forest City	11,351	12,122	400
Winneshiek	Decorah	21,234	20,847	690
Woodbury	Sioux City	102,605	98,276	873
Worth	Northwood	7,768	7,991	400
Wright	Clarion	13,647	14,269	581

Kansas

(105 counties, 81,815 sq. mi. land; pop. 2,744,687)

County	County seat or courthouse	2005 Pop.	1990 Pop.	Land area sq. mi.
Allen	Iola	13,787	14,638	503
Anderson	Garnett	8,182	7,803	583
Atchison	Atchison	16,804	16,932	432
Barber	Medicine Lodge	4,958	5,874	1,134
Barton	Great Bend	28,105	29,382	894
Bourbon	Fort Scott	14,997	14,966	637
Brown	Hiawatha	10,239	11,128	571
Butler	El Dorado	62,354	50,580	1,428
Chase	Cottonwood Falls	3,081	3,021	776
Chautauqua	Sedan	4,109	4,407	642
Cherokee	Columbus	21,555	21,374	587
Cheyenne	Saint Francis	2,946	3,243	1,020
Clark	Ashland	2,283	2,418	975
Clay	Clay Center	8,629	9,158	644
Cloud	Concordia	9,759	11,023	716
Coffey	Burlington	8,683	8,404	630
Comanche	Coldwater	1,935	2,313	788
Cowley	Winfield	35,298	36,915	1,126
Crawford	Girard	38,222	35,582	593
Decatur	Oberlin	3,191	4,021	894
Dickinson	Abilene	19,209	18,958	848
Doniphan	Troy	7,816	8,134	392
Douglas	Lawrence	102,914	81,798	457
Edwards	Kinsley	3,292	3,787	622
Elk	Howard	3,075	3,327	647
Ellis	Hays	26,767	26,004	900
Ellsworth	Ellsworth	6,343	6,586	716
Finney	Garden City	38,988	33,070	1,302
Ford	Dodge City	33,751	27,463	1,099
Franklin	Ottawa	26,247	21,994	574
Geary	Junction City	24,585	30,453	385
Gove	Gove	2,763	3,231	1,071
Graham	Hill City	2,721	3,543	898
Grant	Ulysses	7,530	7,159	575
Gray	Cimarron	5,861	5,396	869
Greeley	Tribune	1,349	1,774	778
Greenwood	Eureka	7,338	7,847	1,140
Hamilton	Syracuse	2,604	2,388	996
Harper	Anthony	6,081	7,124	801
Harvey	Newton	33,843	31,028	539
Haskell	Sublette	4,232	3,886	577
Hodgeman	Jetmore	2,110	2,177	860
Jackson	Holton	13,535	11,525	656
Jefferson	Oskaloosa	19,106	15,905	536
Jewell	Mankato	3,352	4,251	909
Johnson	Olathe	506,562	355,021	477
Kearny	Lakin	4,516	4,027	871
Kingman	Kingman	8,165	8,292	863
Kiowa	Greensburg	2,984	3,660	722
Labette	Oswego	22,169	23,693	649
Lane	Dighton	1,894	2,375	717
Leavenworth	Leavenworth	73,111	64,371	463
Lincoln	Lincoln	3,411	3,653	719
Linn	Mound City	9,914	8,254	599
Logan	Oakley	2,794	3,081	1,073
Lyon	Emporia	35,609	34,732	851
McPherson	McPherson	29,523	27,268	900
Marion	Marion	12,952	12,888	943
Marshall	Marysville	10,405	11,705	903
Meade	Meade	4,625	4,247	978
Miami	Paola	30,496	23,466	577
Mitchell	Beloit	6,420	7,203	700
Montgomery	Independence	34,570	38,816	645
Morris	Council Grove	6,049	6,198	697
Morton	Elkhart	3,196	3,480	730
Nemaha	Seneca	10,443	10,446	718
Neosho	Erie	16,529	17,035	572
Ness	Ness City	3,009	4,033	1,075
Norton	Norton	5,664	5,947	878
Osage	Lyndon	17,150	15,248	704
Osborne	Osborne	4,050	4,867	892
Ottawa	Minneapolis	6,123	5,634	721
Pawnee	Larned	6,739	7,555	754
Phillips	Phillipsburg	5,504	6,590	886
Pottawatomie	Westmoreland	19,129	16,128	844
Pratt	Pratt	9,496	9,702	735
Rawlins	Atwood	2,672	3,404	1,070
Reno	Hutchinson	63,558	62,389	1,254
Republic	Belleville	5,164	6,482	716
Rice	Lyons	10,452	10,610	727
Riley	Manhattan	62,826	67,139	610
Rooks	Stockton	5,351	6,039	888
Rush	LaCrosse	3,406	3,842	718
Russell	Russell	6,845	7,835	885
Saline	Salina	53,919	49,301	720
Scott	Scott City	4,600	5,289	718
Sedgwick	Wichita	466,061	403,662	999
Seward	Liberal	23,274	18,743	640
Shawnee	Topeka	172,365	160,976	550
Sheridan	Hoxie	2,591	3,043	895
Sherman	Goodland	6,153	6,926	1,056
Smith	Smith Center	4,121	5,078	895
Stafford	Saint John	4,488	5,365	792
Stanton	Johnson	2,245	2,333	680
Stevens	Hugoton	5,412	5,048	728
Sumner	Wellington	24,797	25,841	1,182
Thomas	Colby	7,639	8,258	1,075
Trego	WaKeeney	3,050	3,694	888
Wabaunsee	Alma	6,919	6,603	797
Wallace	Sharon Springs	1,573	1,821	914
Washington	Washington	6,009	7,073	898
Wichita	Leoti	2,309	2,758	719
Wilson	Fredonia	9,834	10,289	574
Woodson	Yates Center	3,572	4,116	501
Wyandotte	Kansas City	155,750	162,026	151

Kentucky

(120 counties, 39,728 sq. mi. land; pop. 4,173,405)

County	County seat or courthouse	2005 Pop.	1990 Pop.	Land area sq. mi.
Adair	Columbia	17,573	15,360	407
Allen	Scottsville	18,706	14,628	346
Anderson	Lawrenceburg	20,394	14,571	203
Ballard	Wickliffe	8,277	7,902	251
Barren	Glasgow	40,073	34,001	491
Bath	Owingsville	11,626	9,692	279
Bell	Pineville	29,665	31,506	361
Boone	Burlington	106,272	57,589	246
Bourbon	Paris	19,833	19,236	291
Boyd	Catlettsburg	49,594	51,096	160
Boyle	Danville	28,363	25,590	182
Bracken	Brooksville	8,670	7,766	203
Breathitt	Jackson	15,957	15,703	495
Breckinridge	Hardinsburg	19,293	16,312	572
Bullitt	Shepherdsville	68,474	47,567	299
Butler	Morgantown	13,414	11,245	428
Caldwell	Princeton	12,973	13,232	347
Calloway	Murray	35,122	30,735	386
Campbell	Newport	87,251	83,866	152
Carlisle	Bardwell	5,329	5,238	192
Carroll	Carrollton	10,454	9,292	130
Carter	Grayson	27,306	24,340	411
Casey	Liberty	16,290	14,211	446
Christian	Hopkinsville	70,145	68,941	721
Clark	Winchester	34,887	29,496	254
Clay	Manchester	24,146	21,746	471
Clinton	Albany	9,559	9,135	197
Crittenden	Marion	8,984	9,196	362
Cumberland	Burkesville	7,147	6,784	306
Daviess	Owensboro	93,060	87,189	462
Edmonson	Brownsville	12,030	10,357	303
Elliott	Sandy Hook	6,902	6,455	234
Estill	Irvine	15,089	14,614	254
Fayette	Lexington	268,080	225,366	285
Fleming	Flemingsburg	14,610	12,292	351
Floyd	Prestonsburg	42,218	43,586	394
Franklin	Frankfort	48,207	44,143	210
Fulton	Hickman	7,217	8,271	209
Gallatin	Warsaw	8,134	5,393	99
Garrard	Lancaster	16,579	11,579	231
Grant	Williamstown	24,610	15,737	260
Graves	Mayfield	37,625	33,550	556
Grayson	Leitchfield	25,189	21,050	504
Green	Greensburg	11,588	10,371	289
Greenup	Greenup	37,184	36,796	346
Hancock	Hawesville	8,613	7,864	189
Hardin	Elizabethtown	96,947	89,240	628
Harlan	Harlan	31,614	36,574	467

County	County seat or courthouse	2005 Pop.	1990 Pop.	Land area sq. mi.
Harrison	Cynthiana	18,527	16,248	310
Hart	Munfordville	18,319	14,890	416
Henderson	Henderson	45,573	43,044	440
Henry	New Castle	15,903	12,823	289
Hickman	Clinton	5,075	5,566	244
Hopkins	Madisonville	46,705	46,126	551
Jackson	McKee	13,618	11,955	346
Jefferson	Louisville	699,827	665,123	385
Jessamine	Nicholasville	43,463	30,508	173
Johnson	Paintsville	24,001	23,248	262
Kenton	Covington	153,665	142,005	162
Knott	Hindman	17,561	17,906	352
Knox	Barbourville	32,069	29,676	388
Larue	Hodgenville	13,699	11,679	263
Laurel	London	56,338	43,438	436
Lawrence	Louisa	16,166	13,998	419
Lee	Beattyville	7,709	7,422	210
Leslie	Hyden	11,994	13,642	404
Letcher	Whitesburg	24,434	27,000	339
Lewis	Vanceburg	13,872	13,029	484
Lincoln	Stanford	25,122	20,096	336
Livingston	Smithland	9,760	9,062	316
Logan	Russellville	27,169	24,416	556
Lyon	Eddyville	8,160	6,624	216
McCracken	Paducah	64,698	62,879	251
McCreary	Whitley City	17,233	15,603	428
McLean	Calhoun	9,926	9,628	254
Madison	Richmond	77,749	57,508	441
Magoffin	Salyersville	13,472	13,077	309
Marion	Lebanon	18,939	16,499	346
Marshall	Benton	30,967	27,205	305
Martin	Inez	12,215	12,526	231
Mason	Maysville	17,140	16,666	241
Meade	Brandenburg	28,447	24,170	309
Menifee	Frenchburg	6,809	5,092	204
Mercer	Harrodsburg	21,610	19,148	251
Metcalfe	Edmonton	10,197	8,963	291
Monroe	Tompkinsville	11,660	11,401	331
Montgomery	Mount Sterling	24,256	19,561	199
Morgan	West Liberty	14,334	11,648	381
Muhlenberg	Greenville	31,548	31,318	475
Nelson	Bardstown	41,088	29,710	423
Nicholas	Carlisle	7,027	6,725	197
Ohio	Hartford	23,676	21,105	594
Oldham	La Grange	53,533	33,263	189
Owen	Owenton	11,374	9,035	352
Owsley	Booneville	4,746	5,036	198
Pendleton	Falmouth	15,125	12,062	281
Perry	Hazard	29,452	30,283	342
Pike	Pikeville	66,922	72,584	788
Powell	Stanton	13,687	11,686	180
Pulaski	Somerset	59,200	49,489	662
Robertson	Mount Olivet	2,279	2,124	100
Rockcastle	Mount Vernon	16,712	14,803	318
Rowan	Morehead	22,226	20,353	281
Russell	Jamestown	17,020	14,716	254
Scott	Georgetown	39,380	23,867	285
Shelby	Shelbyville	38,205	24,824	384
Simpson	Franklin	17,021	15,145	236
Spencer	Taylorsville	15,651	6,801	186
Taylor	Campbellsville	23,754	21,146	270
Todd	Elkton	11,944	10,940	376
Trigg	Cadiz	13,349	10,361	443
Trimble	Bedford	9,023	6,090	149
Union	Morganfield	15,592	16,557	345
Warren	Bowling Green	98,960	77,720	545
Washington	Springfield	11,399	10,441	301
Wayne	Monticello	20,352	17,468	459
Webster	Dixon	14,161	13,955	335
Whitley	Williamsburg	38,029	33,326	440
Wolfe	Campton	7,070	6,503	223
Woodford	Versailles	24,246	19,955	191

Louisiana
(64 parishes, 43,562 sq. mi. land; pop. 4,523,628)

Parish	Parish seat or courthouse	2005 Pop.	1990 Pop.	Land area sq. mi.
Acadia	Crowley	59,552	55,882	655
Allen	Oberlin	25,270	21,226	765
Ascension	Donaldsonville	90,501	58,214	292
Assumption	Napoleonville	23,196	22,753	339
Avoyelles	Marksville	42,098	39,159	832
Beauregard	De Ridder	34,562	30,083	1,160
Bienville	Arcadia	15,176	16,232	811
Bossier	Benton	105,541	86,088	839
Caddo	Shreveport	251,309	248,253	882
Calcasieu	Lake Charles	185,419	168,134	1,071
Caldwell	Columbia	10,563	9,806	529
Cameron	Cameron	9,558	9,260	1,313
Catahoula	Harrisonburg	10,447	11,065	704
Claiborne	Homer	16,309	17,405	755
Concordia	Vidalia	19,273	20,828	696
De Soto	Mansfield	26,383	25,668	877
East Baton Rouge*	Baton Rouge	411,417	380,105	455
East Carroll	Lake Providence	8,756	9,709	421
East Feliciana	Clinton	20,823	19,211	453
Evangeline	Ville Platte	35,540	33,274	664
Franklin	Winnsboro	20,380	22,387	624
Grant	Colfax	19,503	17,526	645
Iberia	New Iberia	74,388	68,297	575

Parish	Parish seat or courthouse	2005 Pop.	1990 Pop.	Land area sq. mi.
Iberville	Plaquemine	32,386	31,049	619
Jackson	Jonesboro	15,135	15,859	570
Jefferson*	Gretna	452,824	448,306	307
Jefferson Davis	Jennings	31,272	30,722	652
Lafayette	Lafayette	197,390	164,762	270
Lafourche	Thibodaux	92,179	85,860	1,085
La Salle	Jena	14,040	13,662	624
Lincoln	Ruston	42,108	41,745	471
Livingston	Livingston	109,206	70,523	648
Madison	Tallulah	12,457	12,463	624
Morehouse	Bastrop	29,989	31,938	794
Natchitoches	Natchitoches	38,541	37,254	1,255
Orleans*	New Orleans	454,863	496,938	181
Ouachita	Monroe	148,237	142,191	611
Plaquemines	Pointe a la Hache	28,995	25,575	845
Pointe Coupee	New Roads	22,377	22,540	557
Rapides	Alexandria	128,462	131,556	1,323
Red River	Coushatta	9,465	9,526	389
Richland	Rayville	20,526	20,629	558
Sabine	Many	23,786	22,646	865
Saint Bernard*	Chalmette	65,364	66,631	465
Saint Charles	Hahnville	50,633	42,437	284
Saint Helena	Greensburg	10,259	9,874	408
Saint James	Convent	21,150	20,879	246
Saint John the Baptist	Edgard	46,393	39,996	219
Saint Landry	Opelousas	89,937	80,312	929
Saint Martin	Saint Martinville	50,434	44,097	740
Saint Mary	Franklin	51,416	58,086	613
Saint Tammany	Covington	220,295	144,500	854
Tangipahoa	Amite	106,502	85,709	790
Tensas	Saint Joseph	6,125	7,103	602
Terrebonne	Houma	107,491	96,982	1,255
Union	Farmerville	22,901	20,796	878
Vermilion	Abbeville	55,195	50,055	1,174
Vernon	Leesville	48,745	61,961	1,328
Washington	Franklinton	44,623	43,185	670
Webster	Minden	41,356	41,989	595
West Baton Rouge	Port Allen	21,634	19,419	191
West Carroll	Oak Grove	11,806	12,093	359
West Feliciana	Saint Francisville	15,199	12,915	406
Winn	Winnfield	15,968	16,498	950

*Due primarily to the effects of Hurricane Katrina, Census estimates as of Jan. 1, 2006 were: East Baton Rouge, 413,700; Jefferson, 411,305; Orleans, 158,353; St. Bernard, 3,361.

Maine
(16 counties, 30,862 sq. mi. land; pop. 1,321,505)

County	County seat or courthouse	2005 Pop.	1990 Pop.	Land area sq. mi.
Androscoggin	Auburn	108,039	105,259	470
Aroostook	Houlton	73,240	86,936	6,672
Cumberland	Portland	274,950	243,135	836
Franklin	Farmington	29,704	29,008	1,698
Hancock	Ellsworth	53,660	46,948	1,588
Kennebec	Augusta	120,986	115,904	868
Knox	Rockland	41,219	36,310	366
Lincoln	Wiscasset	35,240	30,357	456
Oxford	South Paris	56,628	52,602	2,078
Penobscot	Bangor	147,068	146,601	3,396
Piscataquis	Dover-Foxcroft	17,674	18,653	3,966
Sagadahoc	Bath	36,962	33,535	254
Somerset	Skowhegan	51,667	49,767	3,927
Waldo	Belfast	38,705	33,018	730
Washington	Machias	33,448	35,308	2,568
York	Alfred	202,315	164,587	991

Maryland
(23 counties, 1 ind. city, 9,774 sq. mi. land; pop. 5,600,388)

County	County seat or courthouse	2005 Pop.	1990 Pop.	Land area sq. mi.
Allegany	Cumberland	73,639	74,946	425
Anne Arundel	Annapolis	510,878	427,239	416
Baltimore	Towson	786,113	692,134	599
Calvert	Prince Frederick	87,925	51,372	215
Caroline	Denton	31,822	27,035	320
Carroll	Westminster	168,541	123,372	449
Cecil	Elkton	97,796	71,347	348
Charles	La Plata	138,822	101,154	461
Dorchester	Cambridge	31,410	30,236	558
Frederick	Frederick	220,701	150,208	663
Garrett	Oakland	29,900	28,138	648
Harford	Bel Air	239,259	182,132	440
Howard	Ellicott City	269,457	187,328	252
Kent	Chestertown	19,989	17,842	279
Montgomery	Rockville	927,583	762,875	496
Prince George's	Upper Marlboro	846,123	722,705	485
Queen Anne's	Centreville	45,612	33,953	372
Saint Mary's	Leonardtown	96,518	75,974	361
Somerset	Princess Anne	25,845	23,440	327
Talbot	Easton	35,683	30,549	269
Washington	Hagerstown	141,985	121,393	458
Wicomico	Salisbury	90,402	74,339	377
Worcester	Snow Hill	48,750	35,028	473
Independent City				
Baltimore		635,815	736,014	81

Massachusetts
(14 counties, 7,840 sq. mi. land; pop. 6,398,743)

County	County seat or courthouse	2005 Pop.	1990 Pop.	Land area sq. mi.
Barnstable	Barnstable	226,514	186,605	396
Berkshire	Pittsfield	131,868	139,352	931
Bristol	Taunton	546,331	506,325	556
Dukes	Edgartown	15,592	11,639	104
Essex	Salem	738,301	670,080	501
Franklin	Greenfield	72,334	70,086	702
Hampden	Springfield	461,591	456,310	618
Hampshire	Northampton	153,339	146,568	529
Middlesex	East Cambridge	1,459,011	1,398,468	823
Nantucket	Nantucket	10,168	6,012	48
Norfolk	Dedham	653,595	616,087	400
Plymouth	Plymouth	492,409	435,276	661
Suffolk	Boston	654,428	663,906	59
Worcester	Worcester	783,262	709,711	1,513

Michigan
(83 counties, 56,804 sq. mi. land; pop. 10,120,860)

County	County seat or courthouse	2005 Pop.	1990 Pop.	Land area sq. mi.
Alcona	Harrisville	11,653	10,145	674
Alger	Munising	9,662	8,972	918
Allegan	Allegan	113,174	90,509	827
Alpena	Alpena	30,428	30,605	574
Antrim	Bellaire	24,422	18,185	477
Arenac	Standish	17,154	14,906	367
Baraga	L'Anse	8,746	7,954	904
Barry	Hastings	59,892	50,057	556
Bay	Bay City	109,029	111,723	444
Benzie	Beulah	17,644	12,200	321
Berrien	Saint Joseph	162,611	161,378	571
Branch	Coldwater	46,460	41,502	507
Calhoun	Marshall	139,191	135,982	709
Cass	Cassopolis	51,996	49,477	492
Charlevoix	Charlevoix	26,722	21,468	417
Cheboygan	Cheboygan	27,463	21,398	716
Chippewa	Sault Sainte Marie	38,780	34,604	1,561
Clare	Harrison	31,653	24,952	567
Clinton	Saint Johns	69,329	57,893	571
Crawford	Grayling	15,074	12,260	558
Delta	Escanaba	38,347	37,780	1,170
Dickinson	Iron Mountain	28,032	26,831	766
Eaton	Charlotte	107,394	92,879	576
Emmet	Petoskey	33,580	25,040	468
Genesee	Flint	443,883	430,459	640
Gladwin	Gladwin	27,209	21,896	507
Gogebic	Bessemer	16,861	18,052	1,102
Grand Traverse	Traverse City	83,971	64,273	465
Gratiot	Ithaca	42,345	38,982	570
Hillsdale	Hillsdale	47,066	43,431	599
Houghton	Houghton	35,705	35,446	1,012
Huron	Bad Axe	34,640	34,951	837
Ingham	Mason	278,592	281,912	559
Ionia	Ionia	64,608	57,024	573
Iosco	Tawas City	26,992	30,209	549
Iron	Crystal Falls	12,299	13,175	1,166
Isabella	Mount Pleasant	65,618	54,624	574
Jackson	Jackson	163,629	149,756	707
Kalamazoo	Kalamazoo	240,536	223,411	562
Kalkaska	Kalkaska	17,239	13,497	561
Kent	Grand Rapids	596,666	500,631	856
Keweenaw	Eagle River	2,195	1,701	541
Lake	Baldwin	12,069	8,583	567
Lapeer	Lapeer	93,361	74,768	654
Leelanau	Leland	22,157	16,527	348
Lenawee	Adrian	102,033	91,476	751
Livingston	Howell	181,517	115,645	568
Luce	Newberry	6,789	5,763	903
Mackinac	Saint Ignace	11,331	10,674	1,022
Macomb	Mount Clemens	829,453	717,400	480
Manistee	Manistee	25,226	21,265	544
Marquette	Marquette	64,760	70,887	1,821
Mason	Ludington	28,986	25,537	495
Mecosta	Big Rapids	42,391	37,308	556
Menominee	Menominee	24,996	24,920	1,044
Midland	Midland	84,064	75,651	521
Missaukee	Lake City	15,299	12,147	567
Monroe	Monroe	153,935	133,600	551
Montcalm	Stanton	63,893	53,059	708
Montmorency	Atlanta	10,445	8,936	548
Muskegon	Muskegon	175,554	158,983	509
Newaygo	White Cloud	50,019	38,206	842
Oakland	Pontiac	1,214,361	1,083,592	873
Oceana	Hart	28,473	22,455	540
Ogemaw	West Branch	21,905	18,681	564
Ontonagon	Ontonagon	7,363	8,854	1,312
Osceola	Reed City	23,750	20,146	566
Oscoda	Mio	9,298	7,842	565
Otsego	Gaylord	24,665	17,957	515
Ottawa	Grand Haven	255,406	187,768	566
Presque Isle	Rogers City	14,330	13,743	660
Roscommon	Roscommon	26,079	19,776	521
Saginaw	Saginaw	208,356	211,946	809
Saint Clair	Port Huron	171,426	145,607	724
Saint Joseph	Centreville	62,984	58,913	504
Sanilac	Sandusky	44,752	39,928	964
Schoolcraft	Manistique	8,819	8,302	1,178
Shiawassee	Corunna	72,945	69,770	539
Tuscola	Caro	58,428	55,498	812
Van Buren	Paw Paw	78,812	70,060	611
Washtenaw	Ann Arbor	341,847	282,937	710
Wayne	Detroit	1,998,217	2,111,687	614
Wexford	Cadillac	31,876	26,360	565

Minnesota
(87 counties, 79,610 sq. mi. land; pop. 5,132,799)

County	County seat or courthouse	2005 Pop.	1990 Pop.	Land area sq. mi.
Aitkin	Aitkin	16,174	12,425	1,819
Anoka	Anoka	323,996	243,641	424
Becker	Detroit Lakes	31,868	27,881	1,310
Beltrami	Bemidji	42,871	34,384	2,505
Benton	Foley	38,505	30,185	408
Big Stone	Ortonville	5,481	6,285	497
Blue Earth	Mankato	58,030	54,044	752
Brown	New Ulm	26,534	26,984	611
Carlton	Carlton	34,026	29,259	860
Carver	Chaska	84,864	47,915	357
Cass	Walker	28,910	21,791	2,018
Chippewa	Montevideo	12,802	13,228	583
Chisago	Center City	49,400	30,521	418
Clay	Moorhead	53,838	50,422	1,045
Clearwater	Bagley	8,476	8,309	995
Cook	Grand Marais	5,367	3,868	1,451
Cottonwood	Windom	11,834	12,694	640
Crow Wing	Brainerd	59,917	44,249	997
Dakota	Hastings	383,592	275,210	570
Dodge	Mantorville	19,595	15,731	440
Douglas	Alexandria	35,138	28,674	634
Faribault	Blue Earth	15,506	16,937	714
Fillmore	Preston	21,368	20,777	861
Freeborn	Albert Lea	31,946	33,060	708
Goodhue	Red Wing	45,585	40,690	758
Grant	Elbow Lake	6,114	6,246	546
Hennepin	Minneapolis	1,119,364	1,032,431	557
Houston	Caledonia	19,941	18,497	558
Hubbard	Park Rapids	18,861	14,939	922
Isanti	Cambridge	37,664	25,921	439
Itasca	Grand Rapids	44,384	40,863	2,665
Jackson	Jackson	11,182	11,677	702
Kanabec	Mora	16,215	12,802	525
Kandiyohi	Willmar	41,199	38,761	796
Kittson	Hallock	4,792	5,767	1,097
Koochiching	International Falls	13,907	16,299	3,102
Lac qui Parle	Madison	7,604	8,924	765
Lake	Two Harbors	11,156	10,415	2,099
Lake of the Woods	Baudette	4,421	4,076	1,297
Le Sueur	Le Center	27,490	23,239	449
Lincoln	Ivanhoe	6,050	6,890	537
Lyon	Marshall	24,472	24,789	714
McLeod	Glencoe	36,636	32,030	492
Mahnomen	Mahnomen	5,113	5,044	556
Marshall	Warren	9,965	10,993	1,772
Martin	Fairmont	21,002	22,914	709
Meeker	Litchfield	23,371	20,846	609
Mille Lacs	Milaca	25,680	18,670	574
Morrison	Little Falls	32,788	29,604	1,125
Mower	Austin	38,799	37,385	712
Murray	Slayton	8,852	9,660	704
Nicollet	Saint Peter	30,848	28,076	452
Nobles	Worthington	20,508	20,098	715
Norman	Ada	7,003	7,975	876
Olmsted	Rochester	135,189	106,470	653
Otter Tail	Fergus Falls	57,658	50,714	1,980
Pennington	Thief River Falls	13,608	13,306	617
Pine	Pine City	28,485	21,264	1,411
Pipestone	Pipestone	9,421	10,491	466
Polk	Crookston	31,133	32,589	1,970
Pope	Glenwood	11,252	10,745	670
Ramsey	Saint Paul	494,920	485,760	156
Red Lake	Red Lake Falls	4,317	4,525	432
Redwood	Redwood Falls	16,022	17,254	880
Renville	Olivia	16,764	17,673	983
Rice	Faribault	60,949	49,183	498
Rock	Luverne	9,520	9,806	483
Roseau	Roseau	16,495	15,026	1,663
Saint Louis	Duluth	197,179	198,232	6,225
Scott	Shakopee	119,825	57,846	357
Sherburne	Elk River	81,752	41,945	436
Sibley	Gaylord	15,237	14,366	589
Stearns	Saint Cloud	142,654	119,324	1,345
Steele	Owatonna	35,755	30,729	430
Stevens	Morris	9,826	10,634	562
Swift	Benson	11,324	10,724	744
Todd	Long Prairie	24,603	23,363	942
Traverse	Wheaton	3,810	4,463	574
Wabasha	Wabasha	22,200	19,744	525
Wadena	Wadena	13,650	13,154	535
Waseca	Waseca	19,330	18,079	423
Washington	Stillwater	220,426	145,860	392
Watonwan	Saint James	11,234	11,682	435
Wilkin	Breckenridge	6,802	7,516	751
Winona	Winona	49,276	47,828	626
Wright	Buffalo	110,730	68,710	661
Yellow Medicine	Granite Falls	10,449	11,684	758

World Almanac Quick Quiz

Which one of the following is not a real county?

(a) Colorado, TX   (b) Texas, LA
(c) Dakota, NE   (d) Wyoming, NY

For the answer look in this chapter, or see page 1008.

Mississippi

(82 counties, 46,907 sq. mi. land; pop. 2,921,088)

County	County seat or courthouse	2005 Pop.	1990 Pop.	Land area sq. mi.
Adams	Natchez	32,099	35,356	460
Alcorn	Corinth	35,306	31,722	400
Amite	Liberty	13,435	13,328	730
Attala	Kosciusko	19,552	18,481	735
Benton	Ashland	7,852	8,046	407
Bolivar	Cleveland & Rosedale	38,641	41,875	876
Calhoun	Pittsboro	14,652	14,908	587
Carroll	Carrollton & Vaiden	10,397	9,237	628
Chickasaw	Houston & Okolona	19,184	18,085	502
Choctaw	Ackerman	9,572	9,071	419
Claiborne	Port Gibson	11,492	11,370	487
Clarke	Quitman	17,670	17,313	691
Clay	West Point	21,223	21,120	409
Coahoma	Clarksdale	29,002	31,665	554
Copiah	Hazlehurst	29,164	27,592	777
Covington	Collins	20,273	16,527	414
De Soto	Hernando	137,004	67,910	478
Forrest	Hattiesburg	75,095	68,314	467
Franklin	Meadville	8,411	8,377	565
George	Lucedale	21,259	16,673	478
Greene	Leakesville	13,183	10,220	713
Grenada	Grenada	22,861	21,555	422
Hancock*	Bay Saint Louis	46,711	31,760	477
Harrison*	Gulfport	193,810	165,365	581
Hinds	Jackson & Raymond	249,345	254,441	869
Holmes	Lexington	21,099	21,604	756
Humphreys	Belzoni	10,527	12,134	418
Issaquena	Mayersville	1,909	1,909	413
Itawamba	Fulton	23,359	20,017	532
Jackson	Pascagoula	135,940	115,243	727
Jasper	Bay Springs & Paulding	18,162	17,114	676
Jefferson	Fayette	9,432	8,653	519
Jefferson Davis	Prentiss	13,158	14,051	408
Jones	Ellisville & Laurel	66,160	62,031	694
Kemper	De Kalb	10,246	10,356	766
Lafayette	Oxford	44,616	31,826	631
Lamar	Purvis	77,218	30,424	497
Lauderdale	Meridian	13,502	75,555	704
Lawrence	Monticello	22,453	12,458	431
Leake	Carthage	44,616	18,436	583
Lee	Tupelo	78,793	65,579	450
Leflore	Greenwood	36,431	37,341	592
Lincoln	Brookhaven	33,906	30,278	586
Lowndes	Columbus	59,895	59,308	502
Madison	Canton	84,286	53,794	717
Marion	Columbia	25,235	25,544	542
Marshall	Holly Springs	35,659	30,361	706
Monroe	Aberdeen	37,704	36,582	764
Montgomery	Winona	11,829	12,387	407
Neshoba	Philadelphia	29,905	24,800	570
Newton	Decatur	22,366	20,291	578
Noxubee	Macon	12,202	12,604	695
Oktibbeha	Starkville	41,247	38,375	458
Panola	Batesville & Sardis	35,331	29,996	684
Pearl River	Poplarville	52,659	38,714	811
Perry	New Augusta	12,160	10,865	647
Pike	Magnolia	39,426	36,882	409
Pontotoc	Pontotoc	28,208	22,237	497
Prentiss	Booneville	25,593	23,278	415
Quitman	Marks	9,512	10,490	405
Rankin	Brandon	131,841	87,161	775
Scott	Forest	28,739	24,137	609
Sharkey	Rolling Fork	5,967	7,066	428
Simpson	Mendenhall	27,944	23,953	589
Smith	Raleigh	16,058	14,798	636
Stone	Wiggins	14,862	10,750	445
Sunflower	Indianola	32,311	35,129	694
Tallahatchie	Charleston & Sumner	14,191	15,210	644
Tate	Senatobia	26,548	21,432	404
Tippah	Ripley	21,212	19,523	458
Tishomingo	Iuka	19,202	17,683	424
Tunica	Tunica	10,321	8,164	455
Union	New Albany	26,784	22,085	415
Walthall	Tylertown	15,460	14,352	404
Warren	Vicksburg	49,131	47,880	587
Washington	Greenville	59,220	67,935	724
Wayne	Waynesboro	21,291	19,517	810
Webster	Walthall	10,092	10,222	422
Wilkinson	Woodville	10,269	9,678	677
Winston	Louisville	19,870	19,433	607
Yalobusha	Coffeeville & Water Valley	13,417	12,033	467
Yazoo	Yazoo City	28,195	25,506	919

*Due primarily to the effects of Hurricane Katrina, Census estimates as of Jan. 1, 2006 were: Hancock, 35,129; Harrison, 155,817.

Missouri

(114 counties, 1 ind. city, 68,886 sq. mi. land; pop. 5,800,310)

County	County seat or courthouse	2005 Pop.	1990 Pop.	Land area sq. mi.
Adair	Kirksville	24,509	24,577	567
Andrew	Savannah	16,899	14,632	435
Atchison	Rockport	6,246	7,457	545
Audrain	Mexico	25,759	23,599	693
Barry	Cassville	35,599	27,547	779
Barton	Lamar	13,057	11,312	594
Bates	Butler	17,027	15,025	848
Benton	Warsaw	18,854	13,859	706
Bollinger	Marble Hill	12,325	10,619	621
Boone	Columbia	143,326	112,379	685
Buchanan	Saint Joseph	84,904	83,083	410
Butler	Poplar Buff	41,338	38,765	698
Caldwell	Kingston	9,307	8,380	429
Callaway	Fulton	42,541	32,809	839
Camden	Camdenton	39,432	27,495	655
Cape Girardeau	Jackson	71,161	61,633	579
Carroll	Carrollton	10,193	10,748	695
Carter	Van Buren	5,910	5,515	508
Cass	Harrisonville	94,232	63,808	699
Cedar	Stockton	14,160	12,093	476
Chariton	Keytesville	8,124	9,202	756
Christian	Ozark	67,266	32,644	563
Clark	Kahoka	7,323	7,547	507
Clay	Liberty	202,078	153,411	396
Clinton	Plattsburg	20,715	16,595	419
Cole	Jefferson City	72,757	63,579	391
Cooper	Boonville	17,294	14,835	565
Crawford	Steelville	23,932	19,173	743
Dade	Greenfield	7,830	7,449	490
Dallas	Buffalo	16,437	12,646	542
Daviess	Gallatin	8,121	7,865	567
De Kalb	Maysville	12,342	9,967	424
Dent	Salem	15,083	13,702	754
Douglas	Ava	13,594	11,876	815
Dunklin	Kennett	32,545	33,112	546
Franklin	Union	99,000	80,603	923
Gasconade	Hermann	15,745	14,006	521
Gentry	Albany	6,555	6,854	492
Greene	Springfield	250,784	207,949	675
Grundy	Trenton	10,327	10,536	436
Harrison	Bethany	8,876	8,469	725
Henry	Clinton	22,577	20,044	702
Hickory	Hermitage	9,271	7,335	399
Holt	Oregon	5,081	6,034	462
Howard	Fayette	9,957	9,631	466
Howell	West Plains	38,400	31,447	928
Iron	Ironton	10,273	10,726	551
Jackson	Independence	662,959	633,234	605
Jasper	Carthage	110,624	90,465	640
Jefferson	Hillsboro	213,669	171,380	657
Johnson	Warrensburg	50,784	42,514	830
Knox	Edina	4,171	4,482	506
Laclede	Lebanon	34,492	27,158	766
Lafayette	Lexington	33,108	31,107	629
Lawrence	Mount Vernon	37,127	30,236	613
Lewis	Monticello	10,186	10,233	505
Lincoln	Troy	47,727	28,892	630
Linn	Linneus	13,133	13,885	620
Livingston	Chillicothe	14,291	14,592	535
McDonald	Pineville	22,844	16,938	540
Macon	Macon	15,600	15,345	804
Madison	Fredericktown	12,151	11,127	497
Maries	Vienna	8,989	7,976	528
Marion	Palmyra	28,375	27,682	438
Mercer	Princeton	3,595	3,723	454
Miller	Tuscumbia	24,712	20,700	592
Mississippi	Charleston	13,599	14,442	413
Moniteau	California	15,084	12,298	417
Monroe	Paris	9,379	9,104	646
Montgomery	Montgomery City	12,166	11,355	537
Morgan	Versailles	20,436	15,574	597
New Madrid	New Madrid	18,566	20,928	678
Newton	Neosho	55,554	44,445	626
Nodaway	Maryville	21,710	21,709	877
Oregon	Alton	10,403	9,470	791
Osage	Linn	13,485	12,018	606
Ozark	Gainesville	9,490	8,598	742
Pemiscot	Caruthersville	19,412	21,921	493
Perry	Perryville	18,571	16,648	475
Pettis	Sedalia	40,121	35,437	685
Phelps	Rolla	42,125	35,248	673
Pike	Bowling Green	18,762	15,969	673
Platte	Platte City	82,085	57,867	420
Polk	Bolivar	28,892	21,826	637
Pulaski	Waynesville	44,187	41,307	547
Putnam	Unionville	5,168	5,079	518
Ralls	New London	9,761	8,476	471
Randolph	Huntsville	25,336	24,370	482
Ray	Richmond	24,101	21,968	569

County	County seat or courthouse	2005 Pop.	1990 Pop.	Land area sq. mi.
Reynolds	Centerville	6,585	6,661	811
Ripley	Doniphan	13,851	12,303	629
Saint Charles	Saint Charles	329,940	212,751	560
Saint Clair	Osceola	9,686	8,457	677
Sainte Genevieve	Sainte Genevieve	18,198	16,037	502
Saint Francois	Farmington	61,661	48,904	449
Saint Louis	Clayton	1,004,666	993,508	508
Saline	Marshall	23,075	23,523	756
Schuyler	Lancaster	4,308	4,236	308
Scotland	Memphis	4,928	4,822	438
Scott	Benton	41,143	39,376	421
Shannon	Eminence	8,367	7,613	1,004
Shelby	Shelbyville	6,744	6,942	501
Stoddard	Bloomfield	29,714	28,895	827
Stone	Galena	30,931	19,078	463
Sullivan	Milan	6,907	6,326	651
Taney	Forsyth	42,985	25,561	632
Texas	Houston	24,614	21,476	1,179
Vernon	Nevada	20,441	19,041	834
Warren	Warrenton	28,764	19,534	431
Washington	Potosi	24,032	20,380	760
Wayne	Greenville	13,097	11,543	761
Webster	Marshfield	34,745	23,753	593
Worth	Grant City	2,174	2,440	267
Wright	Hartville	18,306	16,758	682

Independent City

County	County seat or courthouse	2005 Pop.	1990 Pop.	Land area sq. mi.
Saint Louis		344,362	396,685	62

Montana
(56 counties, 145,552 sq. mi. land; pop. 935,670)

County	County seat or courthouse	2005 Pop.	1990 Pop.	Land area sq. mi.
Beaverhead	Dillon	8,773	8,424	5,542
Big Horn	Hardin	13,149	11,337	4,995
Blaine	Chinook	6,629	6,728	4,226
Broadwater	Townsend	4,517	3,318	1,191
Carbon	Red Lodge	9,902	8,0080	2,048
Carter	Ekalaka	1,320	1,503	3,340
Cascade	Great Falls	79,569	77,691	2,698
Chouteau	Fort Benton	5,463	5,452	3,973
Custer	Miles City	11,267	11,697	3,783
Daniels	Scobey	1,836	2,266	1,426
Dawson	Glendive	8,688	9,505	2,373
Deer Lodge	Anaconda	8,948	10,356	737
Fallon	Baker	2,717	3,103	1,620
Fergus	Lewistown	11,551	12,083	4,339
Flathead	Kalispell	83,172	59,218	5,098
Gallatin	Bozeman	78,210	50,484	2,606
Garfield	Jordan	1,199	1,589	4,668
Glacier	Cut Bank	13,552	12,121	2,995
Golden Valley	Ryegate	1,159	912	1,175
Granite	Philipsburg	2,965	2,548	1,727
Hill	Havre	16,304	17,654	2,896
Jefferson	Boulder	11,170	7,939	1,657
Judith Basin	Stanford	2,198	2,282	1,870
Lake	Polson	28,297	21,041	1,494
Lewis & Clark	Helena	58,441	47,495	3,461
Liberty	Chester	2,003	2,295	1,430
Lincoln	Libby	19,193	17,481	3,613
McCone	Circle	1,805	2,276	2,643
Madison	Virginia City	7,274	5,989	3,587
Meagher	White Sulphur Springs	1,999	1,819	2,392
Mineral	Superior	4,014	3,315	1,220
Missoula	Missoula	100,086	78,687	2,598
Musselshell	Roundup	4,497	4,106	1,867
Park	Livingston	15,968	14,515	2,802
Petroleum	Winnett	470	519	1,654
Phillips	Malta	4,179	5,163	5,140
Pondera	Conrad	6,087	6,433	1,625
Powder River	Broadus	1,705	2,090	3,297
Powell	Deer Lodge	6,999	6,620	2,326
Prairie	Terry	1,105	1,383	1,737
Ravalli	Hamilton	39,940	25,010	2,394
Richland	Sidney	9,096	10,716	2,084
Roosevelt	Wolf Point	10,524	10,999	2,356
Rosebud	Forsyth	9,212	10,505	5,012
Sanders	Thompson Falls	11,057	8,669	2,762
Sheridan	Plentywood	3,524	4,732	1,677
Silver Bow	Butte	32,982	33,941	718
Stillwater	Columbus	8,493	6,536	1,795
Sweet Grass	Big Timber	3,672	3,154	1,855
Teton	Choteau	6,240	6,271	2,273
Toole	Shelby	5,031	5,046	1,911
Treasure	Hysham	689	874	979
Valley	Glasgow	7,143	8,239	4,921
Wheatland	Harlowton	2,037	2,246	1,423
Wibaux	Wibaux	951	1,191	889
Yellowstone	Billings	136,691	113,419	2,635

Nebraska
(93 counties, 76,872 sq. mi. land; pop. 1,758,787)

County	County seat or courthouse	2005 Pop.	1990 Pop.	Land area sq. mi.
Adams	Hastings	33,070	29,625	563
Antelope	Neligh	7,004	7,965	857
Arthur	Arthur	378	462	715
Banner	Harrisburg	733	852	746
Blaine	Brewster	484	675	711
Boone	Albion	5,772	6,667	687
Box Butte	Alliance	11,374	13,130	1,075
Boyd	Butte	2,261	2,835	540
Brown	Ainsworth	3,328	3,657	1,221
Buffalo	Kearney	43,572	37,447	968
Burt	Tekamah	7,455	7,868	493
Butler	David City	8,720	8,601	584
Cass	Plattsmouth	25,734	21,318	559
Cedar	Hartington	9,066	10,131	740
Chase	Imperial	3,866	4,381	895
Cherry	Valentine	6,098	6,307	5,961
Cheyenne	Sidney	9,993	9,494	1,196
Clay	Clay Center	6,733	7,123	573
Colfax	Schuyler	10,433	9,139	413
Cuming	West Point	9,688	10,117	572
Custer	Broken Bow	11,410	12,270	2,576
Dakota	Dakota City	20,349	16,742	264
Dawes	Chadron	8,636	9,021	1,396
Dawson	Lexington	24,617	19,940	1,013
Deuel	Chappell	2,004	2,237	440
Dixon	Ponca	6,155	6,143	476
Dodge	Fremont	36,078	34,500	534
Douglas	Omaha	486,929	416,444	331
Dundy	Benkelman	2,133	2,582	920
Fillmore	Geneva	6,385	7,103	576
Franklin	Franklin	3,421	3,938	575
Frontier	Stockville	2,795	3,101	975
Furnas	Beaver City	5,019	5,553	718
Gage	Beatrice	23,306	22,794	855
Garden	Oshkosh	1,997	2,460	1,704
Garfield	Burwell	1,816	2,141	570
Gosper	Elwood	2,020	1,928	458
Grant	Hyannis	670	769	776
Greeley	Greeley	2,512	3,006	569
Hall	Grand Island	55,104	48,925	546
Hamilton	Aurora	9,568	8,862	544
Harlan	Alma	3,462	3,810	553
Hayes	Hayes Center	1,027	1,222	713
Hitchcock	Trenton	2,970	3,750	710
Holt	O'Neill	10,784	12,599	2,413
Hooker	Mullen	744	793	721
Howard	Saint Paul	6,708	6,057	569
Jefferson	Fairbury	7,925	8,759	573
Johnson	Tecumseh	4,695	4,673	376
Kearney	Minden	6,774	6,629	516
Keith	Ogallala	8,330	8,584	1,061
Keya Paha	Springview	902	1,029	773
Kimball	Kimball	3,782	4,108	952
Knox	Center	8,916	9,564	1,108
Lancaster	Lincoln	264,814	213,641	839
Lincoln	North Platte	35,636	32,508	2,564
Logan	Stapleton	740	878	571
Loup	Taylor	686	683	570
McPherson	Tryon	507	546	859
Madison	Madison	35,488	32,655	573
Merrick	Central City	8,066	8,062	485
Morrill	Bridgeport	5,165	5,423	1,424
Nance	Fullerton	3,666	4,275	441
Nemaha	Auburn	6,965	7,980	409
Nuckolls	Nelson	4,739	5,786	575
Otoe	Nebraska City	15,509	14,252	616
Pawnee	Pawnee City	2,878	3,317	432
Perkins	Grant	3,057	3,367	883
Phelps	Holdrege	9,449	9,715	540
Pierce	Pierce	7,600	7,827	574
Platte	Columbus	31,262	29,820	678
Polk	Osceola	5,421	5,655	439
Red Willow	McCook	11,060	11,705	717
Richardson	Falls City	8,732	9,937	553
Rock	Bassett	1,567	2,019	1,008
Saline	Wilber	14,195	12,715	575
Sarpy	Papillion	139,371	102,583	241
Saunders	Wahoo	20,458	18,285	754
Scotts Bluff	Gering	36,752	36,025	739
Seward	Seward	16,739	15,450	575
Sheridan	Rushville	5,668	6,750	2,441
Sherman	Loup City	3,112	3,718	566
Sioux	Harrison	1,458	1,549	2,067
Stanton	Stanton	6,534	6,244	430
Thayer	Hebron	5,436	6,635	575
Thomas	Thedford	623	851	713
Thurston	Pender	7,365	6,936	394
Valley	Ord	4,402	5,169	568
Washington	Blair	19,772	16,607	390
Wayne	Wayne	9,211	9,364	443
Webster	Red Cloud	3,762	4,279	575
Wheeler	Bartlett	820	948	575
York	York	14,397	14,428	576

Nevada
(16 counties, 1 ind. city, 109,826 sq. mi. land; pop. 2,414,807)

County	County seat or courthouse	2005 Pop.	1990 Pop.	Land area sq. mi.
Churchill	Fallon	24,556	17,938	4,929
Clark	Las Vegas	1,710,551	741,368	7,910
Douglas	Minden	47,017	27,637	710
Elko	Elko	45,570	33,463	17,179
Esmeralda	Goldfield	787	1,344	3,589
Eureka	Eureka	1,428	1,547	4,176
Humboldt	Winnemucca	17,129	12,844	9,648
Lander	Battle Mountain	5,114	6,266	5,494
Lincoln	Pioche	4,391	3,775	10,634
Lyon	Yerington	47,515	20,001	1,994
Mineral	Hawthorne	4,910	6,475	3,756
Nye	Tonopah	40,477	17,781	18,147
Pershing	Lovelock	6,360	4,336	6,037
Storey	Virginia City	4,074	2,526	263
Washoe	Reno	389,872	254,667	6,342
White Pine	Ely	8,994	9,264	8,876
Independent City				
Carson City		56,062	40,443	143

New Hampshire
(10 counties, 8,968 sq. mi. land; pop. 1,309,940)

County	County seat or courthouse	2005 Pop.	1990 Pop.	Land area sq. mi.
Belknap	Laconia	61,547	49,216	401
Carroll	Ossipee	47,439	35,410	934
Cheshire	Keene	77,287	70,121	707
Coos	Lancaster	33,655	34,828	1,800
Grafton	Woodsville	84,708	74,929	1,713
Hillsborough	Nashua	401,291	335,838	876
Merrimack	Concord	146,881	120,240	934
Rockingham	Brentwood	295,076	245,845	695
Strafford	Dover	119,015	104,233	369
Sullivan	Newport	43,041	38,592	537

New Jersey
(21 counties, 7,417 sq. mi. land; pop. 8,717,925)

County	County seat or courthouse	2005 Pop.	1990 Pop.	Land area sq. mi.
Atlantic	Mays Landing	271,015	224,327	561
Bergen	Hackensack	902,561	825,380	234
Burlington	Mount Holly	450,743	395,066	805
Camden	Camden	518,249	502,824	222
Cape May	Cape May Court House	99,286	95,089	255
Cumberland	Bridgeton	153,252	138,053	489
Essex	Newark	791,057	777,964	126
Gloucester	Woodbury	276,910	230,082	325
Hudson	Jersey City	603,521	553,099	47
Hunterdon	Flemington	130,404	107,852	430
Mercer	Trenton	366,256	325,759	226
Middlesex	New Brunswick	789,516	671,712	310
Monmouth	Freehold	635,952	553,192	472
Morris	Morristown	490,593	421,330	469
Ocean	Toms River	558,341	433,203	636
Passaic	Paterson	499,060	470,872	185
Salem	Salem	66,346	65,294	338
Somerset	Somerville	319,900	240,222	305
Sussex	Newton	153,130	130,936	521
Union	Elizabeth	531,457	493,819	103
Warren	Belvidere	110,376	91,675	358

New Mexico
(33 counties, 121,356 sq. mi. land; pop. 1,928,384)

County	County seat or courthouse	2005 Pop.	1990 Pop.	Land area sq. mi.
Bernalillo	Albuquerque	603,562	480,577	1,166
Catron	Reserve	3,409	2,563	6,928
Chaves	Roswell	61,860	57,849	6,071
Cibola	Grants	27,620	23,794	4,539
Colfax	Raton	13,755	12,925	3,757
Curry	Clovis	45,846	42,207	1,406
DeBaca	Fort Sumner	2,016	2,252	2,325
Dona Ana	Las Cruces	189,444	135,510	3,807
Eddy	Carlsbad	51,437	48,605	4,182
Grant	Silver City	29,747	27,676	3,966
Guadalupe	Santa Rosa	4,369	4,156	3,030
Harding	Mosquero	740	987	2,125
Hidalgo	Lordsburg	5,139	5,958	3,446
Lea	Lovington	56,719	55,765	4,393
Lincoln	Carrizozo	21,007	12,219	4,831
Los Alamos	Los Alamos	18,822	18,115	109
Luna	Deming	26,498	18,110	2,965
McKinley	Gallup	71,918	60,686	5,449
Mora	Mora	5,107	4,264	1,931
Otero	Alamogordo	63,538	51,928	6,627
Quay	Tucumcari	9,259	10,823	2,875
Rio Arriba	Tierra Amarilla	40,828	34,365	5,858
Roosevelt	Portales	18,238	16,702	2,449
Sandoval	Bernalillo	107,460	63,319	3,709

County	County seat or courthouse	2005 Pop.	1990 Pop.	Land area sq. mi.
San Juan	Aztec	126,208	91,605	5,514
San Miguel	Las Vegas	29,530	25,743	4,717
Santa Fe	Santa Fe	140,855	98,928	1,909
Sierra	Truth or Consequences	12,815	9,912	4,180
Socorro	Socorro	18,148	14,764	6,646
Taos	Taos	31,722	23,118	2,203
Torrance	Estancia	17,501	10,285	3,345
Union	Clayton	3,850	4,124	3,830
Valencia	Los Lunas	69,417	45,235	1,068

New York
(62 counties, 47,214 sq. mi. land; pop. 19,254,630)

County	County seat or courthouse	2005 Pop.	1990 Pop.	Land area sq. mi.
Albany	Albany	297,414	292,812	523
Allegany	Belmont	50,602	50,470	1,030
Bronx[1]	Bronx	1,357,589	1,203,789	42
Broome	Binghamton	196,947	212,160	707
Cattaraugus	Little Valley	82,502	84,234	1,310
Cayuga	Auburn	81,454	82,313	693
Chautauqua	Mayville	136,409	141,895	1,062
Chemung	Elmira	89,512	95,195	408
Chenango	Norwich	51,755	51,768	894
Clinton	Plattsburgh	82,047	85,969	1,039
Columbia	Hudson	63,622	62,982	636
Cortland	Cortland	48,622	48,963	500
Delaware	Delhi	47,534	47,352	1,446
Dutchess	Poughkeepsie	294,849	259,462	802
Erie	Buffalo	930,703	968,584	1,044
Essex	Elizabethtown	38,676	37,152	1,797
Franklin	Malone	51,033	46,540	1,631
Fulton	Johnstown	55,625	54,191	496
Genesee	Batavia	59,257	60,060	494
Greene	Catskill	49,682	44,739	648
Hamilton	Lake Pleasant	5,228	5,279	1,720
Herkimer	Herkimer	63,780	65,809	1,411
Jefferson	Watertown	116,384	110,943	1,272
Kings[1]	Brooklyn	2,486,235	2,300,664	71
Lewis	Lowville	26,571	26,796	1,275
Livingston	Geneseo	64,205	62,372	632
Madison	Wampsville	70,337	69,166	656
Monroe	Rochester	733,366	713,968	659
Montgomery	Fonda	48,968	51,981	405
Nassau	Mineola	1,333,137	1,287,873	287
New York[1]	New York	1,593,200	1,487,536	23
Niagara	Lockport	217,008	220,756	523
Oneida	Utica	234,105	250,836	1,213
Onondaga	Syracuse	458,053	468,973	780
Ontario	Canandaigua	104,461	95,101	644
Orange	Goshen	372,893	307,571	816
Orleans	Albion	43,387	41,846	391
Oswego	Oswego	123,373	121,785	953
Otsego	Cooperstown	62,746	60,390	1,003
Putnam	Carmel	100,507	83,941	231
Queens[1]	Jamaica	2,241,600	1,951,598	109
Rensselaer	Troy	155,251	154,429	654
Richmond[1]	Saint George	464,573	378,977	58
Rockland	New City	292,916	265,475	174
Saint Lawrence	Canton	111,380	111,974	2,686
Saratoga	Ballston Spa	214,859	181,276	812
Schenectady	Schenectady	149,078	149,285	206
Schoharie	Schoharie	32,277	31,840	622
Schuyler	Watkins Glen	19,342	18,662	329
Seneca	Waterloo	34,855	33,683	325
Steuben	Bath	98,632	99,088	1,393
Suffolk	Riverhead	1,474,927	1,321,339	912
Sullivan	Monticello	76,539	69,277	970
Tioga	Owego	51,475	52,337	519
Tompkins	Ithaca	100,018	94,097	476
Ulster	Kingston	182,693	165,380	1,126
Warren	Lake George	65,548	59,209	869
Washington	Hudson Falls	63,024	59,330	835
Wayne	Lyons	93,609	89,123	604
Westchester	White Plains	940,807	874,866	433
Wyoming	Warsaw	42,693	42,507	593
Yates	Penn Yan	24,756	22,810	338

(1) New York City comprises 5 counties: Bronx, Kings (Brooklyn), New York (Manhattan), Queens, and Richmond (Staten Island).

North Carolina
(100 counties, 48,711 sq. mi. land; pop. 8,683,242)

County	County seat or courthouse	2005 Pop.	1990 Pop.	Land area sq. mi.
Alamance	Graham	140,533	108,213	430
Alexander	Taylorsville	35,492	27,544	260
Alleghany	Sparta	10,900	9,590	235
Anson	Wadesboro	25,499	23,474	532
Ashe	Jefferson	25,347	22,209	426
Avery	Newland	17,641	14,867	247
Beaufort	Washington	46,018	42,283	828
Bertie	Windsor	19,480	20,388	699

County	County seat or courthouse	2005 Pop.	1990 Pop.	Land area sq. mi.
Bladen	Elizabethtown	32,938	28,663	875
Brunswick	Bolivia	89,162	50,985	855
Buncombe	Asheville	218,876	174,357	656
Burke	Morganton	89,399	75,740	507
Cabarrus	Concord	150,244	98,935	364
Caldwell	Lenoir	79,122	70,709	472
Camden	Camden	8,967	5,904	241
Carteret	Beaufort	62,525	52,407	520
Caswell	Yanceyville	23,608	20,662	425
Catawba	Newton	151,641	118,412	400
Chatham	Pittsboro	58,002	38,979	683
Cherokee	Murphy	25,796	20,170	455
Chowan	Edenton	14,528	13,506	173
Clay	Hayesville	9,765	7,155	215
Cleveland	Shelby	98,288	84,958	465
Columbus	Whiteville	54,746	49,587	935
Craven	New Bern	90,795	81,812	708
Cumberland	Fayetteville	304,520	274,713	653
Currituck	Currituck	23,112	13,736	262
Dare	Manteo	33,903	22,746	384
Davidson	Lexington	154,623	126,688	552
Davie	Mocksville	39,136	27,859	265
Duplin	Kenansville	51,985	39,995	818
Durham	Durham	242,582	181,844	290
Edgecombe	Tarboro	54,129	56,692	505
Forsyth	Winston-Salem	325,967	265,855	410
Franklin	Louisburg	54,429	36,414	492
Gaston	Gastonia	196,137	174,769	356
Gates	Gatesville	11,224	9,305	341
Graham	Robbinsville	8,085	7,196	292
Granville	Oxford	53,674	38,341	531
Greene	Snow Hill	20,026	15,384	265
Guilford	Greensboro	443,519	347,431	649
Halifax	Halifax	56,023	55,516	725
Harnett	Lillington	103,692	67,833	595
Haywood	Waynesville	56,482	46,948	554
Henderson	Hendersonville	97,217	69,747	374
Hertford	Winton	23,574	22,317	353
Hoke	Raeford	41,016	22,856	391
Hyde	Swan Quarter	5,413	5,411	613
Iredell	Statesville	140,924	93,205	576
Jackson	Sylva	35,368	26,835	491
Johnston	Smithfield	146,437	81,306	792
Jones	Trenton	10,311	9,361	472
Lee	Sanford	55,704	41,370	257
Lenoir	Kinston	57,961	57,274	400
Lincoln	Lincolnton	69,851	50,319	299
McDowell	Marion	43,201	35,681	442
Macon	Franklin	32,148	23,504	516
Madison	Marshall	20,256	16,953	449
Martin	Williamston	24,643	25,078	461
Mecklenburg	Charlotte	796,372	511,211	526
Mitchell	Bakersville	15,784	14,433	221
Montgomery	Troy	27,322	23,359	492
Moore	Carthage	81,685	59,000	698
Nash	Nashville	91,378	76,677	540
New Hanover	Wilmington	179,553	120,284	199
Northampton	Jackson	21,483	21,004	536
Onslow	Jacksonville	152,440	149,838	767
Orange	Hillsborough	118,386	93,662	400
Pamlico	Bayboro	12,735	11,368	337
Pasquotank	Elizabeth City	38,270	31,298	227
Pender	Burgaw	46,429	28,855	871
Perquimans	Hertford	12,080	10,447	247
Person	Roxboro	37,217	30,180	392
Pitt	Greenville	142,570	108,480	652
Polk	Columbus	19,134	14,458	238
Randolph	Asheboro	138,367	106,546	787
Richmond	Rockingham	46,781	44,511	474
Robeson	Lumberton	127,586	105,170	949
Rockingham	Wentworth	92,614	86,064	566
Rowan	Salisbury	135,099	110,605	511
Rutherford	Rutherfordton	63,771	56,956	564
Sampson	Clinton	63,063	47,297	945
Scotland	Laurinburg	37,180	33,763	319
Stanly	Albemarle	58,964	51,765	395
Stokes	Danbury	45,858	37,224	452
Surry	Dobson	72,601	61,704	537
Swain	Bryson City	13,167	11,268	528
Transylvania	Brevard	29,626	25,520	378
Tyrrell	Columbia	4,157	3,856	390
Union	Monroe	162,929	84,210	637
Vance	Henderson	43,771	38,892	254
Wake	Raleigh	748,815	426,311	832
Warren	Warrenton	19,729	17,265	429
Washington	Plymouth	13,282	13,997	348
Watauga	Boone	42,472	36,952	313
Wayne	Goldsboro	114,448	104,666	553
Wilkes	Wilkesboro	67,390	59,393	757
Wilson	Wilson	76,281	66,061	371
Yadkin	Yadkinville	37,668	30,488	336
Yancey	Burnsville	18,201	15,419	312

North Dakota
(53 counties, 68,976 sq. mi. land; pop. 636,677)

County	County seat or courthouse	2005 Pop.	1990 Pop.	Land area sq. mi.
Adams	Hettinger	2,433	3,174	988
Barnes	Valley City	11,075	12,545	1,492
Benson	Minnewaukan	6,999	7,198	1,381
Billings	Medora	813	1,108	1,151
Bottineau	Bottineau	6,741	8,011	1,669
Bowman	Bowman	3,048	3,596	1,162
Burke	Bowbells	2,032	3,002	1,104
Burleigh	Bismarck	73,818	60,131	1,633
Cass	Fargo	131,019	102,874	1,765
Cavalier	Langdon	4,330	6,064	1,488
Dickey	Ellendale	5,487	6,107	1,131
Divide	Crosby	2,149	2,899	1,260
Dunn	Manning	3,442	4,005	2,010
Eddy	New Rockford	2,626	2,951	630
Emmons	Linton	3,845	4,830	1,510
Foster	Carrington	3,580	3,983	635
Golden Valley	Beach	1,739	2,108	1,002
Grand Forks	Grand Forks	65,940	70,683	1,438
Grant	Carson	2,615	3,549	1,659
Griggs	Cooperstown	2,497	3,303	709
Hettinger	Mott	2,486	3,445	1,132
Kidder	Steele	2,481	3,332	1,351
La Moure	La Moure	4,384	5,383	1,147
Logan	Napoleon	2,059	2,847	993
McHenry	Towner	5,511	6,528	1,874
McIntosh	Ashley	3,013	4,021	975
McKenzie	Watford City	5,594	6,383	2,742
McLean	Washburn	8,604	10,457	2,110
Mercer	Stanton	8,364	9,808	1,045
Morton	Mandan	25,528	23,700	1,926
Mountrail	Stanley	6,513	7,021	1,824
Nelson	Lakota	3,424	4,410	982
Oliver	Center	1,813	2,381	724
Pembina	Cavalier	8,038	9,238	1,119
Pierce	Rugby	4,291	5,052	1,018
Ramsey	Devils Lake	11,429	12,681	1,185
Ransom	Lisbon	5,810	5,921	863
Renville	Mohall	2,422	3,160	875
Richland	Wahpeton	17,340	18,148	1,437
Rolette	Rolla	13,864	12,772	902
Sargent	Forman	4,150	4,549	859
Sheridan	McClusky	1,430	2,148	972
Sioux	Fort Yates	4,182	3,761	1,094
Slope	Amidon	709	907	1,218
Stark	Dickinson	22,073	22,832	1,338
Steele	Finley	2,007	2,420	712
Stutsman	Jamestown	20,835	22,241	2,221
Towner	Cando	2,544	3,627	1,025
Traill	Hillsboro	8,321	8,752	862
Walsh	Grafton	11,607	13,840	1,282
Ward	Minot	55,767	57,921	2,013
Wells	Fessenden	4,574	5,864	1,271
Williams	Williston	19,282	21,129	2,070

Ohio
(88 counties, 40,048 sq. mi. land; pop. 11,464,042)

County	County seat or courthouse	2005 Pop.	1990 Pop.	Land area sq. mi.
Adams	West Union	28,454	25,371	584
Allen	Lima	106,234	109,755	404
Ashland	Ashland	54,123	47,507	424
Ashtabula	Jefferson	103,221	99,880	702
Athens	Athens	62,062	59,549	507
Auglaize	Wapakoneta	47,242	44,585	401
Belmont	Saint Clairsville	69,228	71,074	537
Brown	Georgetown	44,398	34,966	492
Butler	Hamilton	350,412	291,479	467
Carroll	Carrollton	29,388	26,521	395
Champaign	Urbana	39,698	36,019	429
Clark	Springfield	142,376	147,538	400
Clermont	Batavia	190,589	150,094	452
Clinton	Wilmington	42,570	35,444	411
Columbiana	Lisbon	110,928	108,276	532
Coshocton	Coshocton	36,945	35,427	564
Crawford	Bucyrus	45,774	47,870	402
Cuyahoga	Cleveland	1,335,317	1,412,140	458
Darke	Greenville	52,983	53,617	600
Defiance	Defiance	39,112	39,350	411
Delaware	Delaware	150,268	66,929	442
Erie	Sandusky	78,665	76,781	255
Fairfield	Lancaster	138,423	103,468	505
Fayette	Washington Court House	28,199	27,466	407
Franklin	Columbus	1,090,771	961,437	540
Fulton	Wauseon	42,955	38,498	407
Gallia	Gallipolis	31,362	30,954	469
Geauga	Chardon	95,218	81,087	404
Greene	Xenia	151,996	136,731	415

County	County seat or courthouse	2005 Pop.	1990 Pop.	Land area sq. mi.
Guernsey	Cambridge	41,123	39,024	522
Hamilton	Cincinnati	806,652	866,228	407
Hancock	Findlay	73,503	65,536	531
Hardin	Kenton	32,032	31,111	470
Harrison	Cadiz	15,920	16,085	404
Henry	Napoleon	29,453	29,108	417
Highland	Hillsboro	42,818	35,728	553
Hocking	Logan	29,009	25,533	423
Holmes	Millersburg	41,567	32,849	423
Huron	Norwalk	60,385	56,238	493
Jackson	Jackson	33,526	30,230	420
Jefferson	Steubenville	70,599	80,298	410
Knox	Mount Vernon	58,398	47,473	527
Lake	Painesville	232,466	215,500	228
Lawrence	Ironton	63,112	61,834	455
Licking	Newark	154,806	128,300	687
Logan	Bellefontaine	46,580	42,310	458
Lorain	Elyria	296,307	271,126	493
Lucas	Toledo	448,229	462,361	340
Madison	London	41,295	37,078	465
Mahoning	Youngstown	254,274	264,806	415
Marion	Marion	65,932	64,274	404
Medina	Medina	167,010	122,354	422
Meigs	Pomeroy	23,232	22,987	429
Mercer	Celina	41,202	39,443	463
Miami	Troy	101,619	93,184	407
Monroe	Woodsfield	14,698	15,497	456
Montgomery	Dayton	547,435	573,809	462
Morgan	McConnelsville	14,958	14,194	418
Morrow	Mount Gilead	34,322	27,749	406
Muskingum	Zanesville	85,579	82,068	665
Noble	Caldwell	14,156	11,336	399
Ottawa	Port Clinton	41,583	40,029	255
Paulding	Paulding	19,537	20,488	416
Perry	New Lexington	35,246	31,557	410
Pickaway	Circleville	52,989	48,248	502
Pike	Waverly	28,146	24,249	441
Portage	Ravenna	155,631	142,585	492
Preble	Eaton	42,527	40,113	425
Putnam	Ottawa	34,928	33,819	484
Richland	Mansfield	127,949	126,137	497
Ross	Chillicothe	75,197	69,330	688
Sandusky	Fremont	61,676	61,963	409
Scioto	Portsmouth	76,561	80,327	612
Seneca	Tiffin	57,483	59,733	551
Shelby	Sidney	48,736	44,915	409
Stark	Canton	380,608	367,585	576
Summit	Akron	546,604	514,990	413
Trumbull	Warren	219,296	227,795	616
Tuscarawas	New Philadelphia	91,944	84,090	568
Union	Marysville	45,751	31,969	437
Van Wert	Van Wert	29,154	30,464	410
Vinton	McArthur	13,429	11,098	414
Warren	Lebanon	196,622	113,993	400
Washington	Marietta	62,210	62,254	635
Wayne	Wooster	113,697	101,461	555
Williams	Bryan	38,688	36,956	422
Wood	Bowling Green	123,929	113,269	617
Wyandot	Upper Sandusky	22,813	22,254	406

Oklahoma
(77 counties, 68,667 sq. mi. land; pop. 3,547,884)

County	County seat or courthouse	2005 Pop.	1990 Pop.	Land area sq. mi.
Adair	Stilwell	21,988	18,421	576
Alfalfa	Cherokee	5,725	6,416	867
Atoka	Atoka	14,456	12,778	978
Beaver	Beaver	5,379	6,023	1,814
Beckham	Sayre	18,880	18,812	902
Blaine	Watonga	12,859	11,470	928
Bryan	Durant	37,815	32,089	909
Caddo	Anadarko	30,229	29,550	1,278
Canadian	El Reno	98,701	74,409	900
Carter	Ardmore	47,125	42,919	824
Cherokee	Tahlequah	44,671	34,049	751
Choctaw	Hugo	15,297	15,302	774
Cimarron	Boise City	2,833	3,301	1,835
Cleveland	Norman	224,898	174,253	536
Coal	Coalgate	5,743	5,780	518
Comanche	Lawton	112,429	111,486	1,069
Cotton	Walters	6,589	6,651	637
Craig	Vinita	15,078	14,104	761
Creek	Sapulpa	68,708	60,915	956
Custer	Arapaho	25,208	26,897	987
Delaware	Jay	39,146	28,070	741
Dewey	Taloga	4,568	5,551	1,000
Ellis	Arnett	3,963	4,497	1,229
Garfield	Enid	56,958	56,735	1,058
Garvin	Pauls Valley	27,228	26,605	807
Grady	Chickasha	49,369	41,747	1,101
Grant	Medford	4,779	5,689	1,001

County	County seat or courthouse	2005 Pop.	1990 Pop.	Land area sq. mi.
Greer	Mangum	5,901	6,559	639
Harmon	Hollis	3,030	3,793	538
Harper	Buffalo	3,313	4,063	1,039
Haskell	Stigler	12,183	10,940	577
Hughes	Holdenville	13,885	13,014	807
Jackson	Altus	26,518	28,764	803
Jefferson	Waurika	6,461	7,010	759
Johnston	Tishomingo	10,259	10,032	645
Kay	Newkirk	46,480	48,056	919
Kingfisher	Kingfisher	14,302	13,212	903
Kiowa	Hobart	9,848	11,347	1,015
Latimer	Wilburton	10,635	10,333	722
Le Flore	Poteau	49,528	43,270	1,586
Lincoln	Chandler	32,311	29,216	958
Logan	Guthrie	36,894	29,011	744
Love	Marietta	9,126	7,788	515
McClain	Purcell	30,096	22,795	570
McCurtain	Idabel	33,992	33,433	1,852
McIntosh	Eufaula	19,965	16,779	620
Major	Fairview	7,364	8,055	957
Marshall	Madill	14,461	10,829	371
Mayes	Pryor	39,471	33,366	656
Murray	Sulphur	12,880	12,042	418
Muskogee	Muskogee	70,607	68,078	814
Noble	Perry	11,211	11,045	732
Nowata	Nowata	10,864	9,992	565
Okfuskee	Okemah	11,434	11,551	625
Oklahoma	Oklahoma City	684,543	599,611	709
Okmulgee	Okmulgee	39,732	36,490	697
Osage	Pawhuska	45,416	41,645	2,251
Ottawa	Miami	32,866	30,561	471
Pawnee	Pawnee	16,860	15,575	569
Payne	Stillwater	69,151	61,507	686
Pittsburg	McAlester	44,641	40,950	1,306
Pontotoc	Ada	35,346	34,119	720
Pottawatomie	Shawnee	68,272	58,760	788
Pushmataha	Antlers	11,693	10,997	1,397
Roger Mills	Cheyenne	3,311	4,147	1,142
Rogers	Claremore	80,757	55,170	675
Seminole	Wewoka	24,770	25,412	633
Sequoyah	Sallisaw	40,868	33,828	674
Stephens	Duncan	42,946	42,299	874
Texas	Guymon	20,112	16,419	2,037
Tillman	Frederick	8,513	10,384	872
Tulsa	Tulsa	572,059	503,341	570
Wagoner	Wagoner	64,183	47,883	563
Washington	Bartlesville	49,149	48,066	417
Washita	Cordell	11,471	11,441	1,003
Woods	Alva	8,546	9,103	1,287
Woodward	Woodward	19,088	18,976	1,242

Oregon
(36 counties, 95,997 sq. mi. land; pop. 3,641,056)

County	County seat or courthouse	2005 Pop.	1990 Pop.	Land area sq. mi.
Baker	Baker City	16,287	15,317	3,068
Benton	Corvallis	78,640	70,811	676
Clackamas	Oregon City	368,470	278,850	1,868
Clatsop	Astoria	36,798	33,301	827
Columbia	Saint Helens	48,065	37,557	657
Coos	Coquille	64,711	60,273	1,600
Crook	Prineville	22,067	14,111	2,979
Curry	Gold Beach	22,427	19,327	1,627
Deschutes	Bend	141,382	74,976	3,018
Douglas	Roseburg	104,202	94,649	5,037
Gilliam	Condon	1,794	1,717	1,204
Grant	Canyon City	7,297	7,853	4,529
Harney	Burns	6,898	7,060	10,134
Hood River	Hood River	21,284	16,903	522
Jackson	Medford	195,322	146,387	2,785
Jefferson	Madras	20,100	13,676	1,781
Josephine	Grants Pass	80,761	62,649	1,640
Klamath	Klamath Falls	66,192	57,702	5,944
Lake	Lakeview	7,313	7,186	8,136
Lane	Eugene	335,180	282,912	4,554
Lincoln	Newport	45,994	38,889	980
Linn	Albany	108,914	91,227	2,292
Malheur	Vale	31,330	26,038	9,887
Marion	Salem	305,265	228,483	1,184
Morrow	Heppner	11,666	7,625	2,032
Multnomah	Portland	672,906	583,887	435
Polk	Dallas	70,295	49,541	741
Sherman	Moro	1,749	1,918	823
Tillamook	Tillamook	25,277	21,570	1,102
Umatilla	Pendleton	73,878	59,249	3,215
Union	La Grande	24,540	23,598	2,037
Wallowa	Enterprise	7,014	6,911	3,145
Wasco	The Dalles	23,593	21,683	2,381
Washington	Hillsboro	499,794	311,554	724
Wheeler	Fossil	1,455	1,396	1,715
Yamhill	McMinnville	92,196	65,551	716

Pennsylvania
(67 counties, 44,817 sq. mi. land; pop. 12,429,616)

County	County seat or courthouse	2005 Pop.	1990 Pop.	Land area sq. mi.
Adams	Gettysburg	99,749	78,274	520
Allegheny	Pittsburgh	1,235,841	1,336,449	730
Armstrong	Kittanning	70,586	73,478	654
Beaver	Beaver	177,377	186,093	434
Bedford	Bedford	50,091	47,919	1,015
Berks	Reading	396,314	336,523	859
Blair	Hollidaysburg	126,795	130,542	526
Bradford	Towanda	62,537	60,967	1,151
Bucks	Doylestown	621,342	541,174	607
Butler	Butler	182,087	152,013	789
Cambria	Ebensburg	148,073	163,062	688
Cameron	Emporium	5,639	5,913	397
Carbon	Jim Thorpe	61,959	56,803	381
Centre	Bellefonte	140,561	124,812	1,108
Chester	West Chester	474,027	376,389	756
Clarion	Clarion	40,589	41,699	602
Clearfield	Clearfield	82,783	78,097	1,147
Clinton	Lock Haven	37,439	37,182	891
Columbia	Bloomsburg	64,939	63,202	486
Crawford	Meadville	89,442	86,166	1,013
Cumberland	Carlisle	223,089	195,257	550
Dauphin	Harrisburg	253,995	237,813	525
Delaware	Media	555,648	547,658	184
Elk	Ridgway	33,577	34,878	829
Erie	Erie	280,446	275,575	802
Fayette	Uniontown	146,142	145,351	790
Forest	Tionesta	5,739	4,802	428
Franklin	Chambersburg	137,409	121,082	772
Fulton	McConnellsburg	14,673	13,837	438
Greene	Waynesburg	39,808	39,550	576
Huntingdon	Huntingdon	45,947	44,164	874
Indiana	Indiana	88,703	89,994	829
Jefferson	Brookville	45,759	46,083	655
Juniata	Mifflintown	23,507	20,625	392
Lackawanna	Scranton	209,525	219,097	459
Lancaster	Lancaster	490,562	422,822	949
Lawrence	New Castle	92,809	96,246	360
Lebanon	Lebanon	125,578	113,744	362
Lehigh	Allentown	330,433	291,130	347
Luzerne	Wilkes-Barre	312,861	328,149	891
Lycoming	Williamsport	118,395	118,710	1,235
McKean	Smethport	44,370	47,131	982
Mercer	Mercer	119,598	121,003	672
Mifflin	Lewistown	46,235	46,197	412
Monroe	Stroudsburg	163,234	95,681	609
Montgomery	Norristown	775,883	678,193	483
Montour	Danville	18,032	17,735	131
Northampton	Easton	287,767	247,110	374
Northumberland	Sunbury	92,610	96,771	460
Perry	New Bloomfield	44,728	41,172	554
Philadelphia	Philadelphia	1,463,281	1,585,577	135
Pike	Milford	56,337	28,032	547
Potter	Coudersport	17,384	16,717	1,081
Schuylkill	Pottsville	147,447	152,585	778
Snyder	Middleburg	38,207	36,680	331
Somerset	Somerset	78,907	78,218	1,075
Sullivan	Laporte	6,391	6,104	450
Susquehanna	Montrose	42,124	40,380	823
Tioga	Wellsboro	41,649	41,126	1,134
Union	Lewisburg	43,131	36,176	317
Venango	Franklin	55,928	59,381	675
Warren	Warren	42,033	45,050	883
Washington	Washington	206,406	204,584	857
Wayne	Honesdale	50,113	39,944	729
Westmoreland	Greensburg	367,635	370,321	1,025
Wyoming	Tunkhannock	28,160	28,076	397
York	York	408,801	339,574	904

Rhode Island
(5 counties, 1,045 sq. mi. land; pop. 1,076,189)

County	County seat or courthouse	2005 Pop.	1990 Pop.	Land area sq. mi.
Bristol	Bristol	52,743	48,859	25
Kent	East Greenwich	171,590	161,143	170
Newport	Newport	83,740	87,194	104
Providence	Providence	639,653	596,270	413
Washington	West Kingston	128,463	109,998	333

South Carolina
(46 counties, 30,110 sq. mi. land; pop. 4,255,083)

County	County seat or courthouse	2005 Pop.	1990 Pop.	Land area sq. mi.
Abbeville	Abbeville	26,133	23,862	508
Aiken	Aiken	150,181	120,991	1,073
Allendale	Allendale	10,917	11,727	408
Anderson	Anderson	175,514	145,177	718
Bamberg	Bamberg	15,880	16,902	393
Barnwell	Barnwell	23,345	20,293	548
Beaufort	Beaufort	137,849	86,425	587
Berkeley	Moncks Corner	151,673	128,658	1,098
Calhoun	Saint Matthews	15,100	12,753	380
Charleston	Charleston	330,368	295,159	919
Cherokee	Gaffney	53,844	44,506	393
Chester	Chester	33,228	32,170	581
Chesterfield	Chesterfield	43,435	38,575	799
Clarendon	Manning	33,363	28,450	607
Colleton	Walterboro	39,605	34,377	1,056
Darlington	Darlington	67,346	61,851	561
Dillon	Dillon	30,974	29,114	405
Dorchester	Saint George	112,858	83,060	575
Edgefield	Edgefield	25,528	18,360	502
Fairfield	Winnsboro	24,047	22,295	687
Florence	Florence	131,097	114,344	800
Georgetown	Georgetown	60,983	46,302	815
Greenville	Greenville	407,383	320,127	790
Greenwood	Greenwood	67,979	59,567	456
Hampton	Hampton	21,329	18,186	560
Horry	Conway	226,992	144,053	1,134
Jasper	Ridgeland	21,398	15,487	656
Kershaw	Camden	56,486	43,599	726
Lancaster	Lancaster	63,113	54,516	549
Laurens	Laurens	70,293	58,132	715
Lee	Bishopville	20,638	18,437	410
Lexington	Lexington	235,272	167,526	699
McCormick	McCormick	10,108	8,868	360
Marion	Marion	34,904	33,899	489
Marlboro	Bennettsville	28,021	29,716	480
Newberry	Newberry	37,250	33,172	631
Oconee	Walhalla	69,577	57,494	625
Orangeburg	Orangeburg	92,167	84,804	1,106
Pickens	Pickens	113,575	93,896	497
Richland	Columbia	340,078	286,321	756
Saluda	Saluda	18,895	16,441	452
Spartanburg	Spartanburg	266,809	226,793	811
Sumter	Sumter	105,517	101,276	665
Union	Union	28,539	30,337	514
Williamsburg	Kingstree	35,395	36,815	934
York	York	190,097	131,497	682

South Dakota
(66 counties, 75,885 sq. mi. land; pop. 775,933)

County	County seat or courthouse	2005 Pop.	1990 Pop.	Land area sq. mi.
Aurora	Plankinton	2,901	3,135	708
Beadle	Huron	15,896	18,253	1,259
Bennett	Martin	3,585	3,206	1,185
Bon Homme	Tyndall	7,087	7,089	563
Brookings	Brookings	28,121	25,207	794
Brown	Aberdeen	34,706	35,580	1,713
Brule	Chamberlain	5,187	5,485	819
Buffalo	Gannvalley	2,100	1,759	471
Butte	Belle Fourche	9,326	7,914	2,249
Campbell	Mound City	1,565	1,965	736
Charles Mix	Lake Andes	9,194	9,131	1,098
Clark	Clark	3,799	4,403	958
Clay	Vermillion	12,995	13,186	412
Codington	Watertown	26,010	22,698	688
Corson	McIntosh	4,366	4,195	2,473
Custer	Custer	7,904	6,179	1,558
Davison	Mitchell	18,777	17,503	435
Day	Webster	5,757	6,978	1,029
Deuel	Clear Lake	4,296	4,522	624
Dewey	Timber Lake	6,161	5,523	2,303
Douglas	Armour	3,309	3,746	434
Edmunds	Ipswich	4,112	4,356	1,146
Fall River	Hot Springs	7,355	7,353	1,740
Faulk	Faulkton	2,386	2,744	1,000
Grant	Milbank	7,384	8,372	683
Gregory	Burke	4,290	5,359	1,016
Haakon	Philip	1,912	2,624	1,813
Hamlin	Hayti	5,707	4,974	507
Hand	Miller	3,307	4,272	1,437
Hanson	Alexandria	3,747	2,994	435
Harding	Buffalo	1,218	1,669	2,671
Hughes	Pierre	16,875	14,817	741
Hutchinson	Olivet	7,581	8,262	813
Hyde	Highmore	1,614	1,696	861
Jackson	Kadoka	2,858	2,811	1,869
Jerauld	Wessington Springs	2,136	2,425	530
Jones	Murdo	1,033	1,324	971
Kingsbury	De Smet	5,532	5,925	838
Lake	Madison	11,039	10,550	563
Lawrence	Deadwood	22,395	20,655	800
Lincoln	Canton	33,381	15,427	578
Lyman	Kennebec	3,919	3,638	1,640
McCook	Salem	5,930	5,688	575
McPherson	Leola	2,617	3,228	1,137
Marshall	Britton	4,418	4,844	838
Meade	Sturgis	24,623	21,878	3,471
Mellette	White River	2,088	2,137	1,306
Miner	Howard	2,584	3,272	570
Minnehaha	Sioux Falls	160,087	123,809	810
Moody	Flandreau	6,637	6,507	520
Pennington	Rapid City	93,580	81,343	2,776
Perkins	Bison	3,023	3,932	2,872
Potter	Gettysburg	2,351	3,190	866

County	County seat or courthouse	2005 Pop.	1990 Pop.	Land area sq. mi.
Roberts	Sisseton	10,044	9,914	1,101
Sanborn	Woonsocket	2,541	2,833	569
Shannon	(Attached to Fall River)	13,657	9,902	2,094
Spink	Redfield	6,899	7,981	1,504
Stanley	Fort Pierre	2,829	2,453	1,443
Sully	Onida	1,430	1,589	1,007
Todd	(Attached to Tripp)	9,882	8,352	1,388
Tripp	Winner	6,065	6,924	1,614
Turner	Parker	8,520	8,576	617
Union	Elk Point	13,462	10,189	460
Walworth	Selby	5,494	6,087	708
Yankton	Yankton	21,718	19,252	522
Ziebach	Dupree	2,631	2,220	1,962

Tennessee
(95 counties, 41,217 sq. mi. land; pop. 5,962,959)

County	County seat or courthouse	2005 Pop.	1990 Pop.	Land area sq. mi.
Anderson	Clinton	72,430	68,250	338
Bedford	Shelbyville	42,204	30,411	474
Benton	Camden	16,467	14,524	395
Bledsoe	Pikeville	12,928	9,669	406
Blount	Maryville	115,535	85,962	559
Bradley	Cleveland	92,092	73,712	329
Campbell	Jacksboro	40,686	35,079	480
Cannon	Woodbury	13,337	10,467	266
Carroll	Huntingdon	29,121	27,514	599
Carter	Elizabethton	58,865	51,505	341
Cheatham	Ashland City	38,603	27,140	303
Chester	Henderson	15,941	12,819	289
Claiborne	Tazewell	31,033	26,137	434
Clay	Celina	7,992	7,238	236
Cocke	Newport	34,929	29,141	434
Coffee	Manchester	50,869	40,343	429
Crockett	Alamo	14,595	13,378	265
Cumberland	Crossville	51,346	34,736	682
Davidson	Nashville	575,261	510,786	502
Decatur	Decaturville	11,686	10,472	334
De Kalb	Smithville	18,254	14,360	305
Dickson	Charlotte	45,894	35,061	490
Dyer	Dyersburg	37,829	34,854	511
Fayette	Somerville	34,458	25,559	705
Fentress	Jamestown	17,159	14,669	499
Franklin	Winchester	41,003	34,923	555
Gibson	Trenton	48,148	46,315	603
Giles	Pulaski	29,297	25,741	611
Grainger	Rutledge	22,283	17,095	280
Greene	Greeneville	65,318	55,832	622
Grundy	Altamont	14,608	13,362	361
Hamblen	Morristown	59,898	50,480	161
Hamilton	Chattanooga	310,935	285,536	542
Hancock	Sneedville	6,704	6,739	222
Hardeman	Bolivar	28,170	23,377	668
Hardin	Savannah	25,930	22,633	578
Hawkins	Rogersville	56,196	44,565	487
Haywood	Brownsville	19,656	19,437	533
Henderson	Lexington	26,425	21,844	520
Henry	Paris	31,511	27,888	562
Hickman	Centerville	23,793	16,754	613
Houston	Erin	7,988	7,018	200
Humphreys	Waverly	18,212	15,813	532
Jackson	Gainesboro	11,072	9,297	309
Jefferson	Dandridge	48,394	33,016	274
Johnson	Mountain City	18,116	13,766	298
Knox	Knoxville	404,972	335,749	508
Lake	Tiptonville	7,583	7,129	163
Lauderdale	Ripley	26,795	23,491	470
Lawrence	Lawrenceburg	41,101	35,303	617
Lewis	Hohenwald	11,445	9,247	282
Lincoln	Fayetteville	32,392	28,157	570
Loudon	Loudon	43,387	31,255	229
McMinn	Athens	51,327	42,383	430
McNairy	Selmer	25,285	22,422	560
Macon	Lafayette	21,549	15,906	307
Madison	Jackson	94,916	77,982	557
Marion	Jasper	27,757	24,683	498
Marshall	Lewisburg	28,372	21,539	375
Maury	Columbia	76,292	54,812	613
Meigs	Decatur	11,657	8,033	195
Monroe	Madisonville	43,185	30,541	635
Montgomery	Clarksville	147,202	100,498	539
Moore	Lynchburg	6,024	4,696	129
Morgan	Wartburg	20,157	17,300	522
Obion	Union City	32,213	31,717	545
Overton	Livingston	20,523	17,636	433
Perry	Linden	7,574	6,612	415
Pickett	Byrdstown	4,821	4,548	163
Polk	Benton	15,944	13,643	435
Putnam	Cookeville	66,580	51,373	401
Rhea	Dayton	29,918	24,344	316
Roane	Kingston	52,889	47,227	361
Robertson	Springfield	60,379	41,492	476
Rutherford	Murfreesboro	218,292	118,570	619
Scott	Huntsville	21,868	18,358	532
Sequatchie	Dunlap	12,691	8,863	266

County	County seat or courthouse	2005 Pop.	1990 Pop.	Land area sq. mi.
Sevier	Sevierville	79,282	51,050	592
Shelby	Memphis	909,035	826,330	755
Smith	Carthage	18,647	14,143	314
Stewart	Dover	12,969	9,479	458
Sullivan	Blountville	152,716	143,596	413
Sumner	Gallatin	145,009	103,281	529
Tipton	Covington	55,998	37,568	459
Trousdale	Hartsville	7,677	5,920	114
Unicoi	Erwin	17,572	16,549	186
Union	Maynardville	19,076	13,694	224
Van Buren	Spencer	5,470	4,846	273
Warren	McMinnville	39,753	32,992	433
Washington	Jonesborough	112,507	92,336	326
Wayne	Waynesboro	16,909	13,935	734
Weakley	Dresden	33,732	31,972	580
White	Sparta	24,253	20,090	377
Williamson	Franklin	153,595	81,021	583
Wilson	Lebanon	100,508	67,675	571

Texas
(254 counties, 261,797 sq. mi. land; pop. 22,859,968)

County	County seat or courthouse	2005 Pop.	1990 Pop.	Land area sq. mi.
Anderson	Palestine	56,408	48,024	1,071
Andrews	Andrews	12,748	14,338	1,501
Angelina	Lufkin	81,557	69,884	802
Aransas	Rockport	24,640	17,892	252
Archer	Archer City	9,095	7,973	910
Armstrong	Claude	2,173	2,021	914
Atascosa	Jourdanton	43,226	30,533	1,232
Austin	Bellville	26,123	19,832	653
Bailey	Muleshoe	6,726	7,064	827
Bandera	Bandera	19,988	10,562	792
Bastrop	Bastrop	69,932	38,263	888
Baylor	Seymour	3,843	4,385	871
Bee	Beeville	32,873	25,135	880
Bell	Belton	256,057	191,073	1,060
Bexar	San Antonio	1,518,370	1,185,394	1,247
Blanco	Johnson City	9,110	5,972	711
Borden	Gail	648	799	899
Bosque	Meridian	18,053	15,125	989
Bowie	Boston	90,643	81,665	888
Brazoria	Angleton	278,484	191,707	1,386
Brazos	Bryan	156,305	121,862	586
Brewster	Alpine	9,079	8,653	6,193
Briscoe	Silverton	1,644	1,971	900
Brooks	Falfurrias	7,687	8,204	943
Brown	Brownwood	38,664	34,371	944
Burleson	Caldwell	17,238	13,625	666
Burnet	Burnet	41,676	22,677	996
Caldwell	Lockhart	36,523	26,392	546
Calhoun	Port Lavaca	20,606	19,053	512
Callahan	Baird	13,516	11,859	899
Cameron	Brownsville	378,311	260,120	906
Camp	Pittsburg	12,238	9,904	198
Carson	Panhandle	6,586	6,576	923
Cass	Linden	30,155	29,982	937
Castro	Dimmitt	7,640	9,070	898
Chambers	Anahuac	28,411	20,088	599
Cherokee	Rusk	48,464	41,049	1,052
Childress	Childress	7,676	5,953	710
Clay	Henrietta	11,287	10,024	1,098
Cochran	Morton	3,289	4,377	775
Coke	Robert Lee	3,612	3,424	899
Coleman	Coleman	8,665	9,710	1,260
Collin	McKinney	659,457	264,036	848
Collingsworth	Wellington	2,968	3,573	919
Colorado	Columbus	20,736	18,383	963
Comal	New Braunfels	96,018	51,832	561
Comanche	Comanche	13,709	13,381	938
Concho	Paint Rock	3,735	3,044	991
Cooke	Gainesville	38,847	30,777	874
Coryell	Gatesville	75,802	64,226	1,052
Cottle	Paducah	1,746	2,247	901
Crane	Crane	3,837	4,652	786
Crockett	Ozona	3,934	4,078	2,807
Crosby	Crosbyton	6,686	7,304	900
Culberson	Van Horn	2,627	3,407	3,812
Dallam	Dalhart	6,174	5,461	1,505
Dallas	Dallas	2,305,454	1,852,691	880
Dawson	Lamesa	14,256	14,349	902
Deaf Smith	Hereford	18,538	19,153	1,497
Delta	Cooper	5,480	4,857	277
Denton	Denton	554,642	273,644	889
DeWitt	Cuero	20,507	18,840	909
Dickens	Dickens	2,646	2,571	904
Dimmit	Carrizo Springs	10,395	10,433	1,331
Donley	Clarendon	3,889	3,696	930
Duval	San Diego	12,578	12,918	1,793
Eastland	Eastland	18,393	18,488	926
Ector	Odessa	125,339	118,934	901
Edwards	Rocksprings	1,987	2,266	2,120
Ellis	Waxahachie	133,474	85,167	940

County	County seat or courthouse	2005 Pop.	1990 Pop.	Land area sq. mi.
El Paso	El Paso	721,598	591,610	1,013
Erath	Stephenville	34,076	27,991	1,086
Falls	Marlin	17,646	17,712	769
Fannin	Bonham	33,142	24,804	891
Fayette	La Grange	22,537	20,095	950
Fisher	Roby	4,089	4,842	901
Floyd	Floydada	7,174	8,497	992
Foard	Crowell	1,518	1,794	707
Fort Bend*	Richmond	463,650	225,421	875
Franklin	Mount Vernon	10,200	7,802	286
Freestone	Fairfield	18,800	15,818	877
Frio	Pearsall	16,387	13,472	1,133
Gaines	Seminole	14,712	14,123	1,502
Galveston	Galveston	277,563	217,396	398
Garza	Post	5,002	5,143	896
Gillespie	Fredericksburg	23,088	17,204	1,061
Glasscock	Garden City	1,327	1,447	901
Goliad	Goliad	7,102	5,980	854
Gonzales	Gonzales	19,587	17,205	1,068
Gray	Pampa	21,479	23,967	928
Grayson	Sherman	116,834	95,019	934
Gregg	Longview	115,649	104,948	274
Grimes	Anderson	25,192	18,843	794
Guadalupe	Seguin	103,032	64,873	711
Hale	Plainview	36,233	34,671	1,005
Hall	Memphis	3,700	3,905	903
Hamilton	Hamilton	8,105	7,733	836
Hansford	Spearman	5,230	5,848	920
Hardeman	Quanah	4,291	5,283	695
Hardin	Kountze	50,976	41,320	894
Harris*	Houston	3,693,050	2,818,101	1,729
Harrison	Marshall	63,459	57,483	899
Hartley	Channing	5,450	3,634	1,462
Haskell	Haskell	5,541	6,820	903
Hays	San Marcos	124,432	65,614	678
Hemphill	Canadian	3,422	3,720	910
Henderson	Athens	80,017	58,543	874
Hidalgo	Edinburg	678,275	383,545	1,570
Hill	Hillsboro	35,424	27,146	962
Hockley	Levelland	22,787	24,199	908
Hood	Granbury	47,930	28,981	422
Hopkins	Sulphur Springs	33,381	28,833	782
Houston	Crockett	23,218	21,375	1,231
Howard	Big Spring	32,522	32,343	903
Hudspeth	Sierra Blanca	3,295	2,915	4,571
Hunt	Greenville	82,543	64,343	841
Hutchinson	Stinnett	22,484	25,689	887
Irion	Mertzon	1,756	1,629	1,051
Jack	Jacksboro	9,064	6,981	917
Jackson	Edna	14,339	13,039	829
Jasper	Jasper	35,587	31,102	937
Jeff Davis	Fort Davis	2,306	1,946	2,264
Jefferson	Beaumont	247,571	239,389	904
Jim Hogg	Hebbronville	5,029	5,109	1,136
Jim Wells	Alice	40,951	37,679	865
Johnson	Cleburne	146,376	97,165	729
Jones	Anson	19,736	16,490	931
Karnes	Karnes City	15,351	12,455	750
Kaufman	Kaufman	89,129	52,220	786
Kendall	Boerne	28,607	14,589	662
Kenedy	Sarita	417	460	1,457
Kent	Jayton	782	1,010	902
Kerr	Kerrville	46,496	36,304	1,106
Kimble	Junction	4,591	4,122	1,251
King	Guthrie	307	354	912
Kinney	Brackettville	3,327	3,119	1,363
Kleberg	Kingsville	30,757	30,274	871
Knox	Benjamin	3,781	4,837	849
Lamar	Paris	49,644	43,949	917
Lamb	Littlefield	14,467	15,072	1,016
Lampasas	Lampasas	19,669	13,521	712
La Salle	Cotulla	6,016	5,254	1,489
Lavaca	Hallettsville	18,925	18,690	970
Lee	Giddings	16,526	12,854	629
Leon	Centerville	16,344	12,665	1,072
Liberty	Liberty	75,141	52,726	1,160
Limestone	Groesbeck	22,763	20,946	909
Lipscomb	Lipscomb	3,101	3,143	932
Live Oak	George West	11,717	9,556	1,036
Llano	Llano	18,236	11,631	935
Loving	Mentone	62	107	673
Lubbock	Lubbock	252,284	222,636	899
Lynn	Tahoka	6,237	6,758	892
McCulloch	Brady	7,956	8,778	1,069
McLennan	Waco	224,668	189,123	1,042
McMullen	Tilden	883	817	1,113
Madison	Madisonville	13,167	10,931	470
Marion	Jefferson	10,952	9,984	381
Martin	Stanton	4,391	4,956	915
Mason	Mason	3,880	3,423	932
Matagorda	Bay City	37,849	36,928	1,114
Maverick	Eagle Pass	51,181	36,378	1,280
Medina	Hondo	43,027	27,312	1,328
Menard	Menard	2,201	2,252	902
Midland	Midland	121,371	106,611	900
Milam	Cameron	25,354	22,946	1,017
Mills	Goldthwaite	5,237	4,531	748
Mitchell	Colorado City	9,413	8,016	910
Montague	Montague	19,677	17,274	931
Montgomery*	Conroe	378,033	182,201	1,044
Moore	Dumas	20,348	17,865	900
Morris	Daingerfield	12,936	13,200	255
Motley	Matador	1,299	1,532	989
Nacogdoches	Nacogdoches	60,468	54,753	947
Navarro	Corsicana	48,687	39,926	1,008
Newton	Newton	14,309	13,569	933
Nolan	Sweetwater	14,878	16,594	912
Nueces	Corpus Christi	319,704	291,145	836
Ochiltree	Perryton	9,385	9,128	918
Oldham	Vega	2,118	2,278	1,501
Orange	Orange	84,983	80,509	356
Palo Pinto	Palo Pinto	27,478	25,055	953
Panola	Carthage	22,997	22,035	801
Parker	Weatherford	102,801	64,785	904
Parmer	Farwell	9,754	9,863	882
Pecos	Fort Stockton	15,859	14,675	4,764
Polk	Livingston	46,640	30,687	1,057
Potter	Amarillo	119,852	97,841	909
Presidio	Marfa	7,722	6,637	3,856
Rains	Emory	11,305	6,715	232
Randall	Canyon	110,053	89,673	914
Reagan	Big Lake	2,995	4,514	1,175
Real	Leakey	3,031	2,412	700
Red River	Clarksville	13,575	14,317	1,050
Reeves	Pecos	11,638	15,852	2,636
Refugio	Refugio	7,639	7,976	770
Roberts	Miami	820	1,025	924
Robertson	Franklin	16,192	15,511	855
Rockwall	Rockwall	62,944	25,604	129
Runnels	Ballinger	10,974	11,294	1,051
Rusk	Henderson	47,971	43,735	924
Sabine	Hemphill	10,416	9,586	490
San Augustine	San Augustine	8,907	7,999	528
San Jacinto	Coldspring	24,801	16,372	571
San Patricio	Sinton	69,209	58,749	692
San Saba	San Saba	6,076	5,401	1,134
Schleicher	Eldorado	2,742	2,990	1,311
Scurry	Snyder	16,217	18,634	903
Shackelford	Albany	3,167	3,316	914
Shelby	Center	26,346	22,034	794
Sherman	Stratford	3,002	2,858	923
Smith	Tyler	190,594	151,309	928
Somervell	Glen Rose	7,578	5,360	187
Starr	Rio Grande City	60,941	40,518	1,223
Stephens	Breckenridge	9,561	9,010	895
Sterling	Sterling City	1,303	1,438	923
Stonewall	Aspermont	1,372	2,013	919
Sutton	Sonora	4,212	4,135	1,454
Swisher	Tulia	7,828	8,133	900
Tarrant	Fort Worth	1,620,479	1,170,103	863
Taylor	Abilene	125,039	119,655	916
Terrell	Sanderson	996	1,410	2,358
Terry	Brownfield	12,419	13,218	890
Throckmorton	Throckmorton	1,618	1,880	912
Titus	Mount Pleasant	29,445	24,009	411
Tom Green	San Angelo	103,611	98,458	1,522
Travis	Austin	888,185	576,407	989
Trinity	Groveton	14,363	11,445	693
Tyler	Woodville	20,617	16,646	923
Upshur	Gilmer	37,881	31,370	588
Upton	Rankin	3,056	4,447	1,242
Uvalde	Uvalde	26,955	23,340	1,557
Val Verde	Del Rio	47,596	38,721	3,170
Van Zandt	Canton	52,491	37,944	849
Victoria	Victoria	85,648	74,361	883
Walker	Huntsville	62,735	50,917	787
Waller	Hempstead	34,821	23,374	514
Ward	Monahans	10,237	13,115	835
Washington	Brenham	31,521	26,154	609
Webb	Laredo	224,695	133,239	3,357
Wharton	Wharton	41,554	39,955	1,090
Wheeler	Wheeler	4,799	5,879	914
Wichita	Wichita Falls	125,894	122,378	628
Wilbarger	Vernon	13,896	15,121	971
Willacy	Raymondville	20,382	17,705	597
Williamson	Georgetown	333,457	139,551	1,123
Wilson	Floresville	37,529	22,650	807
Winkler	Kermit	6,690	8,626	841
Wise	Decatur	56,696	34,679	905
Wood	Quitman	40,855	29,380	650
Yoakum	Plains	7,408	8,786	800
Young	Graham	18,000	18,126	922
Zapata	Zapata	13,373	9,279	997
Zavala	Crystal City	11,796	12,162	1,298

*Due primarily to the effects of Hurricane Katrina, Census estimates as of Jan. 1, 2006 were: Fort Bend, 472,635; Harris country, 3,740,480; Montgomery 387,278.

Utah
(29 counties, 82,144 sq. mi. land; pop. 2,469,585)

County	County seat or courthouse	2005 Pop.	1990 Pop.	Land area sq. mi.
Beaver	Beaver	6,204	4,765	2,590
Box Elder	Brigham City	46,440	36,485	5,723
Cache	Logan	98,055	70,183	1,165
Carbon	Price	19,437	20,228	1,478
Daggett	Manila	943	690	698
Davis	Farmington	268,187	187,941	304
Duchesne	Duchesne	15,354	12,645	3,238
Emery	Castle Dale	10,711	10,332	4,452
Garfield	Panguitch	4,470	3,980	5,174
Grand	Moab	8,743	6,620	3,682
Iron	Parowan	38,311	20,789	3,298
Juab	Nephi	9,113	5,817	3,392
Kane	Kanab	6,202	5,169	3,992
Millard	Fillmore	12,284	11,333	6,589
Morgan	Morgan	7,906	5,528	609
Piute	Junction	1,365	1,277	758
Rich	Randolph	2,051	1,725	1,029
Salt Lake	Salt Lake City	948,172	725,956	737
San Juan	Monticello	14,104	12,621	7,820
Sanpete	Manti	24,044	16,259	1,588
Sevier	Richfield	19,386	15,431	1,910
Summit	Coalville	35,001	15,518	1,871
Tooele	Tooele	51,311	26,601	6,930
Uintah	Vernal	26,995	22,211	4,477
Utah	Provo	443,738	263,590	1,998
Wasatch	Heber City	18,974	10,089	1,177
Washington	Saint George	118,885	48,560	2,427
Wayne	Loa	2,450	2,177	2,460
Weber	Ogden	210,749	158,330	576

Vermont
(14 counties, 9,250 sq. mi. land; pop. 623,050)

County	County seat or courthouse	2005 Pop.	1990 Pop.	Land area sq. mi.
Addison	Middlebury	36,965	32,953	770
Bennington	Bennington	36,999	35,845	676
Caledonia	Saint Johnsbury	30,440	27,846	651
Chittenden	Burlington	149,613	131,761	539
Essex	Guildhall	6,602	6,405	665
Franklin	Saint Albans	47,914	39,980	637
Grand Isle	North Hero	7,703	5,318	83
Lamoille	Hyde Park	24,495	19,735	461
Orange	Chelsea	29,287	26,149	689
Orleans	Newport	27,640	24,053	698
Rutland	Rutland	63,743	62,142	933
Washington	Montpelier	59,478	54,928	689
Windham	Newfane	44,143	41,588	789
Windsor	Woodstock	58,028	54,055	971

Virginia
(95 counties, 39 ind. cities, 39,594 sq. mi. land; pop. 7,567,465)

County	County seat or courthouse	2005 Pop.	1990 Pop.	Land area sq. mi.
Accomack	Accomac	39,424	31,703	455
Albemarle	Charlottesville	90,717	68,177	723
Alleghany[1]	Covington	16,715	12,815	445
Amelia	Amelia Court House	12,273	8,787	357
Amherst	Amherst	32,134	28,578	475
Appomattox	Appomattox	13,967	12,300	334
Arlington	Arlington	195,965	170,895	26
Augusta	Staunton	69,725	54,557	970
Bath	Warm Springs	4,937	4,799	532
Bedford	Bedford	65,286	45,553	755
Bland	Bland	6,943	6,514	359
Botetourt	Fincastle	32,027	24,992	543
Brunswick	Lawrenceville	17,920	15,987	566
Buchanan	Grundy	24,755	31,333	504
Buckingham	Buckingham	16,058	12,873	581
Campbell	Rustburg	52,339	47,499	504
Caroline	Bowling Green	25,563	19,217	533
Carroll	Hillsville	29,438	26,519	476
Charles City	Charles City	7,119	6,282	183
Charlotte	Charlotte Court	12,404	11,688	475
Chesterfield	Chesterfield	288,876	209,599	426
Clarke	Berryville	14,205	12,101	177
Craig	New Castle	5,154	4,372	331
Culpeper	Culpeper	42,530	27,791	381
Cumberland	Cumberland	9,378	7,825	298
Dickenson	Clintwood	16,243	17,620	332
Dinwiddie	Dinwiddie	25,391	22,279	504
Essex	Tappahannock	10,492	8,689	258
Fairfax	Fairfax	1,006,529	818,310	395
Fauquier	Warrenton	64,997	48,700	650
Floyd	Floyd	14,649	11,965	381
Fluvanna	Palmyra	24,751	12,429	287
Franklin	Rocky Mount	50,345	39,549	692
Frederick	Winchester	69,123	45,723	415
Giles	Pearisburg	17,098	16,366	357
Gloucester	Gloucester	37,787	30,131	217
Goochland	Goochland	19,360	14,163	284
Grayson	Independence	16,366	16,278	443
Greene	Stanardsville	17,418	10,297	157
Greensville	Emporia	11,088	8,553	295
Halifax	Halifax	36,284	36,030	819

County	County seat or courthouse	2005 Pop.	1990 Pop.	Land area sq. mi.
Hanover	Hanover	97,426	63,306	473
Henrico	Richmond	280,581	217,878	238
Henry	Collinsville	56,501	56,942	382
Highland	Monterey	2,475	2,635	416
Isle of Wight	Isle of Wight	33,417	25,053	316
James City	Williamsburg	57,525	34,779	143
King and Queen	King and Queen Court House	6,796	6,289	316
King George	King George	20,637	13,527	180
King William	King William	14,732	10,913	275
Lancaster	Lancaster	11,593	10,896	133
Lee	Jonesville	23,686	24,496	437
Loudoun	Leesburg	255,518	86,185	520
Louisa	Louisa	30,020	20,325	497
Lunenburg	Lunenburg	13,194	11,419	432
Madison	Madison	13,398	11,949	321
Mathews	Mathews	9,194	8,348	86
Mecklenburg	Boydton	32,529	29,241	624
Middlesex	Saluda	10,493	8,653	130
Montgomery	Christiansburg	84,303	73,913	388
Nelson	Lovingston	15,101	12,778	472
New Kent	New Kent	16,107	10,466	210
Northampton	Eastville	13,548	13,061	207
Northumberland	Heathsville	12,874	10,524	192
Nottoway	Nottoway	15,560	14,993	315
Orange	Orange	30,246	21,421	342
Page	Luray	23,831	21,690	311
Patrick	Stuart	19,209	17,473	483
Pittsylvania	Chatham	61,854	55,672	971
Powhatan	Powhatan	26,598	15,328	261
Prince Edward	Farmville	20,455	17,320	353
Prince George	Prince George	36,725	27,390	266
Prince William	Manassas	348,588	214,954	338
Pulaski	Pulaski	35,081	34,496	321
Rappahannock	Washington	7,271	6,622	267
Richmond	Warsaw	9,114	7,273	191
Roanoke	Salem	88,172	79,278	251
Rockbridge	Lexington	21,242	18,350	600
Rockingham	Harrisonburg	71,251	57,482	851
Russell	Lebanon	28,949	28,667	475
Scott	Gate City	22,962	23,204	537
Shenandoah	Woodstock	39,184	31,636	512
Smyth	Marion	32,640	32,370	452
Southampton	Courtland	17,585	17,022	600
Spotsylvania	Spotsylvania	116,549	57,397	401
Stafford	Stafford	117,874	62,255	270
Surry	Surry	7,013	6,145	279
Sussex	Sussex	12,071	10,248	491
Tazewell	Tazewell	44,795	45,960	520
Warren	Front Royal	35,556	26,142	214
Washington	Abingdon	52,085	45,887	563
Westmoreland	Montross	17,227	15,480	229
Wise	Wise	41,997	39,573	404
Wythe	Wytheville	28,421	25,471	463
York	Yorktown	61,758	42,434	106
Independent Cities				
Alexandria		135,337	111,183	15
Bedford		6,211	6,176	7
Bristol		17,335	18,426	13
Buena Vista		6,437	6,406	7
Charlottesville		40,437	40,470	10
Chesapeake		218,968	151,982	341
Colonial Heights		17,567	16,064	7
Covington		6,205	7,352	6
Danville		46,143	53,056	43
Emporia		5,587	5,556	7
Fairfax		21,963	19,945	6
Falls Church		10,781	9,464	2
Franklin		8,594	8,392	8
Fredericksburg		20,732	19,033	11
Galax		6,676	6,745	8
Hampton		145,579	133,773	52
Harrisonburg		40,438	30,707	18
Hopewell		22,690	23,101	10
Lexington		6,776	6,959	2
Lynchburg		66,973	66,120	49
Manassas		37,569	27,757	10
Manassas Park		11,622	6,798	2
Martinsville		14,925	16,162	11
Newport News		179,899	171,477	68
Norfolk		231,954	261,250	54
Norton		3,677	4,247	8
Petersburg		32,604	37,071	23
Poquoson		11,811	11,005	16
Portsmouth		100,169	103,910	33
Radford		14,575	15,940	10
Richmond		193,777	202,713	60
Roanoke		92,631	96,487	43
Salem		24,654	23,835	15
Staunton		23,337	24,581	20
Suffolk		78,994	52,143	400
Virginia Beach		438,415	393,089	248
Waynesboro		21,269	18,549	15
Williamsburg		11,751	11,600	9
Winchester		25,119	21,947	9

(1) The independent city of Clifton Forge became part of Alleghany County in 2001.

Washington
(39 counties, 66,544 sq. mi. land; pop. 6,287,759)

County	County seat or courthouse	2005 Pop.	1990 Pop.	Land area sq. mi.
Adams	Ritzville	16,803	13,603	1,925
Asotin	Asotin	21,178	17,605	635
Benton	Prosser	157,950	112,560	1,703
Chelan	Wenatchee	69,791	52,250	2,921
Clallam	Port Angeles	69,689	56,210	1,739
Clark	Vancouver	403,766	238,053	628
Columbia	Dayton	4,129	4,024	869
Cowlitz	Kelso	97,325	82,119	1,139
Douglas	Waterville	34,977	26,205	1,821
Ferry	Republic	7,542	6,295	2,204
Franklin	Pasco	63,011	37,473	1,242
Garfield	Pomeroy	2,344	2,248	711
Grant	Ephrata	81,229	54,798	2,681
Grays Harbor	Montesano	70,900	64,175	1,917
Island	Coupeville	79,252	60,195	208
Jefferson	Port Townsend	28,666	20,406	1,814
King	Seattle	1,793,583	1,507,305	2,126
Kitsap	Port Orchard	240,661	189,731	396
Kittitas	Ellensburg	36,841	26,725	2,297
Klickitat	Goldendale	19,839	16,616	1,872
Lewis	Chehalis	72,449	59,358	2,408
Lincoln	Davenport	10,381	8,864	2,311
Mason	Shelton	54,359	38,341	961
Okanogan	Okanogan	39,782	33,350	5,268
Pacific	South Bend	21,579	18,882	933
Pend Oreille	Newport	12,673	8,915	1,400
Pierce	Tacoma	753,787	586,203	1,679
San Juan	Friday Harbor	15,274	10,035	175
Skagit	Mount Vernon	113,171	79,545	1,735
Skamania	Stevenson	10,664	8,289	1,656
Snohomish	Everett	655,944	465,628	2,089
Spokane	Spokane	440,706	361,333	1,764
Stevens	Colville	42,013	30,948	2,478
Thurston	Olympia	228,867	161,238	727
Wahkiakum	Cathlamet	3,849	3,327	264
Walla Walla	Walla Walla	57,558	48,439	1,271
Whatcom	Bellingham	183,471	127,780	2,120
Whitman	Colfax	40,170	38,775	2,159
Yakima	Yakima	231,586	188,823	4,296

West Virginia
(55 counties, 24,078 sq. mi. land; pop. 1,816,856)

County	County seat or courthouse	2005 Pop.	1990 Pop.	Land area sq. mi.
Barbour	Philippi	15,689	15,699	341
Berkeley	Martinsburg	93,394	59,253	321
Boone	Madison	25,703	25,870	503
Braxton	Sutton	14,851	12,998	513
Brooke	Wellsburg	24,515	26,992	89
Cabell	Huntington	94,031	96,827	282
Calhoun	Grantsville	7,387	7,885	281
Clay	Clay	10,356	9,983	342
Doddridge	West Union	7,476	6,994	320
Fayette	Fayetteville	46,823	47,952	664
Gilmer	Glenville	6,950	7,669	340
Grant	Petersburg	11,673	10,428	477
Greenbrier	Lewisburg	35,027	34,693	1,021
Hampshire	Romney	22,025	16,498	642
Hancock	New Cumberland	31,350	35,233	83
Hardy	Moorefield	13,287	10,977	583
Harrison	Clarksburg	68,369	69,371	416
Jackson	Ripley	28,403	25,938	466
Jefferson	Charles Town	49,206	35,926	210
Kanawha	Charleston	193,559	207,619	903
Lewis	Weston	17,199	17,223	382
Lincoln	Hamlin	22,374	21,382	437
Logan	Logan	36,237	43,032	454
McDowell	Welch	24,273	35,233	535
Marion	Fairmont	56,509	57,249	310
Marshall	Moundsville	34,337	37,356	307
Mason	Point Pleasant	25,761	25,178	432
Mercer	Princeton	61,589	64,980	420
Mineral	Keyser	27,028	26,697	328
Mingo	Williamson	27,210	33,739	423
Monongalia	Morgantown	84,386	75,509	361
Monroe	Union	13,507	12,406	473
Morgan	Berkeley Springs	16,022	12,128	229
Nicholas	Summersville	26,464	26,775	649
Ohio	Wheeling	45,112	50,871	106
Pendleton	Franklin	7,844	8,054	698
Pleasants	St. Marys	7,376	7,546	131
Pocahontas	Marlinton	8,851	9,008	940
Preston	Kingwood	30,115	29,037	648
Putnam	Winfield	54,443	42,835	346
Raleigh	Beckley	79,167	76,819	607
Randolph	Elkins	28,571	27,803	1,040
Ritchie	Harrisville	10,540	10,233	454

County	County seat or courthouse	2005 Pop.	1990 Pop.	Land area sq. mi.
Roane	Spencer	15,407	15,120	484
Summers	Hinton	13,740	14,204	361
Taylor	Grafton	16,291	15,144	173
Tucker	Parsons	6,943	7,728	419
Tyler	Middlebourne	9,340	9,796	258
Upshur	Buckhannon	23,712	22,867	355
Wayne	Wayne	42,091	41,636	506
Webster	Webster Springs	9,804	10,729	556
Wetzel	New Martinsville	17,117	19,258	359
Wirt	Elizabeth	5,896	5,192	233
Wood	Parkersburg	87,047	86,915	367
Wyoming	Pineville	24,479	28,990	501

Wisconsin
(72 counties, 54,310 sq. mi. land; pop. 5,536,201)

County	County seat or courthouse	2005 Pop.	1990 Pop.	Land area sq. mi.
Adams	Friendship	20,828	15,682	648
Ashland	Ashland	16,627	16,307	1,044
Barron	Barron	45,834	40,750	863
Bayfield	Washburn	15,145	14,008	1,476
Brown	Green Bay	238,987	194,594	529
Buffalo	Alma	13,968	13,584	684
Burnett	Siren	16,528	13,084	822
Calumet	Chilton	44,137	34,291	320
Chippewa	Chippewa Falls	59,950	52,360	1,010
Clark	Neillsville	34,098	31,647	1,216
Columbia	Portage	55,364	45,088	774
Crawford	Prairie du Chien	17,134	15,940	573
Dane	Madison	458,106	367,085	1,202
Dodge	Juneau	88,103	76,559	882
Door	Sturgeon Bay	28,349	25,690	483
Douglas	Superior	44,208	41,758	1,309
Dunn	Menomonie	41,708	35,909	852
Eau Claire	Eau Claire	94,089	85,183	638
Florence	Florence	4,974	4,590	488
Fond du Lac	Fond du Lac	99,337	90,083	723
Forest	Crandon	9,961	8,776	1,014
Grant	Lancaster	49,671	49,266	1,148
Green	Monroe	35,165	30,339	584
Green Lake	Green Lake	19,168	18,651	354
Iowa	Dodgeville	23,569	20,150	763
Iron	Hurley	6,649	6,153	757
Jackson	Black River Falls	19,758	16,588	987
Jefferson	Jefferson	79,328	67,783	557
Juneau	Mauston	26,725	21,650	768
Kenosha	Kenosha	160,544	128,181	273
Kewaunee	Kewaunee	20,840	18,878	343
La Crosse	La Crosse	108,958	97,904	453
Lafayette	Darlington	16,310	16,074	634
Langlade	Antigo	20,735	19,505	873
Lincoln	Merrill	30,319	26,993	883
Manitowoc	Manitowoc	81,949	80,421	592
Marathon	Wausau	128,941	115,400	1,545
Marinette	Marinette	43,406	40,548	1,402
Marquette	Montello	15,237	12,321	455
Menominee	Keshena	4,580	4,075	358
Milwaukee	Milwaukee	921,654	959,212	242
Monroe	Sparta	42,644	36,633	901
Oconto	Oconto	37,666	30,226	998
Oneida	Rhinelander	36,994	31,679	1,125
Outagamie	Appleton	171,006	140,510	640
Ozaukee	Port Washington	86,072	72,894	232
Pepin	Durand	7,380	7,107	232
Pierce	Ellsworth	39,102	32,765	576
Polk	Balsam Lake	44,329	34,773	917
Portage	Stevens Point	67,585	61,405	806
Price	Phillips	15,220	15,600	1,253
Racine	Racine	195,708	175,034	333
Richland	Richland Center	18,403	17,521	586
Rock	Janesville	157,538	139,510	720
Rusk	Ladysmith	15,198	15,079	913
Saint Croix	Hudson	77,144	50,251	722
Sauk	Baraboo	57,746	46,975	838
Sawyer	Hayward	16,975	14,181	1,256
Shawano	Shawano	41,335	37,157	893
Sheboygan	Sheboygan	114,610	103,877	514
Taylor	Medford	19,766	18,901	975
Trempealeau	Whitehall	27,812	25,263	734
Vernon	Viroqua	29,055	25,617	795
Vilas	Eagle River	22,330	17,707	874
Walworth	Elkhorn	99,884	75,000	555
Washburn	Shell Lake	16,601	13,772	810
Washington	West Bend	126,158	95,328	431
Waukesha	Waukesha	378,971	304,715	556
Waupaca	Waupaca	52,563	46,104	751
Waushara	Wautoma	24,789	19,385	626
Winnebago	Oshkosh	159,482	140,320	439
Wood	Wisconsin Rapids	75,234	73,605	793

Wyoming

(23 counties, 97,100 sq. mi. land; pop. 509,294)

County	County seat or courthouse	2005 Pop.	1990 Pop.	Land area sq. mi.
Albany	Laramie	30,890	30,797	4,273
Big Horn	Basin	11,333	10,525	3,137
Campbell	Gillette	37,405	29,370	4,797
Carbon	Rawlins	15,331	16,659	7,896
Converse	Douglas	12,766	11,128	4,255
Crook	Sundance	6,182	5,294	2,859
Fremont	Lander	36,491	33,662	9,182
Goshen	Torrington	12,243	12,373	2,225
Hot Springs	Thermopolis	4,537	4,809	2,004
Johnson	Buffalo	7,721	6,145	4,166

County	County seat or courthouse	2005 Pop.	1990 Pop.	Land area sq. mi.
Laramie	Cheyenne	85,163	73,142	2,686
Lincoln	Kemmerer	15,999	12,625	4,069
Natrona	Casper	69,799	61,226	5,340
Niobrara	Lusk	2,286	2,499	2,626
Park	Cody	26,664	23,178	6,942
Platte	Wheatland	8,619	8,145	2,085
Sheridan	Sheridan	27,389	23,562	2,523
Sublette	Pinedale	6,926	4,843	4,883
Sweetwater	Green River	37,975	38,823	10,425
Teton	Jackson	19,032	11,173	4,008
Unita	Evanston	19,939	18,705	2,082
Washakie	Worland	7,933	8,388	2,240
Weston	Newcastle	6,671	6,518	2,398

Population of Outlying Areas

Source: Bureau of the Census, U.S. Dept. of Commerce; World Almanac research

Population estimates for July 1, 2005, are given for Puerto Rican municipios (a municipio is the governmental unit that is the primary legal subdivision of Puerto Rico; the Census Bureau treats the municipio as the statistical equivalent of a county). All other population counts and all land area figures are from the 2000 census. Because only selected areas are shown, the population and land area figures may not equal the total reported.

ZIP codes with an asterisk (*) are general delivery ZIP codes. Consult the local postmaster or www.usps.com for more specific delivery information. Wake Atoll, Johnston Atoll, and Midway Atoll receive mail through APO and FPO addresses.

Commonwealth of Puerto Rico

ZIP code	Municipio	2005 Pop.	Land area sq. mi.	ZIP code	Municipio	2005 Pop.	Land area sq. mi.	ZIP code	Municipio	2005 Pop.	Land area sq. mi.
*00601	Adjuntas	18,566	67	00650	Florida	14,678	15	00720	Orocovis	24,648	63
00602	Aguada	44,653	31	00653	Guánica	22,514	37	00723	Patillas	20,120	47
*00605	Aguadilla	66,536	37	*00785	Guayama	45,100	65	00624	Peñuelas	28,692	44
00703	Aguas Buenas	30,705	31	00656	Guayanilla	23,552	42	*00732	Ponce	182,387	115
00705	Aibonito	26,942	31	*00970	Guaynabo	102,287	27	00678	Quebradillas	27,316	23
00610	Añasco	29,644	39	00778	Gurabo	41,177	28	00677	Rincón	15,996	14
*00613	Arecibo	101,920	126	00659	Hatillo	41,952	42	00745	Río Grande	55,453	61
00714	Arroyo	18,960	15	00660	Hormigueros	17,265	11	00637	Sabana Grande	27,238	36
00617	Barceloneta	22,829	19	*00791	Humacao	60,345	45	00751	Salinas	31,969	69
00794	Barranquitas	29,971	34	00662	Isabela	46,824	55	00683	San Germán	37,544	55
*00958	Bayamón	222,195	44	00664	Jayuya	18,010	45	*00936	San Juan	428,591	48
00623	Cabo Rojo	51,238	70	00795	Juana Díaz	52,409	60	00754	San Lorenzo	43,566	53
*00726	Caguas	142,378	59	00777	Juncos	39,647	27	00685	San Sebastián	46,684	70
00627	Camuy	38,180	46	00667	Lajas	27,409	60	00757	Santa Isabel	22,641	34
00729	Canóvanas	46,108	33	00669	Lares	36,868	61	*00954	Toa Alta	75,395	27
*00984	Carolina	187,472	45	00670	Las Marías	11,854	46	*00950	Toa Baja	95,007	23
*00963	Cataño	27,488	5	00771	Las Piedras	38,018	34	*00976	Trujillo Alto	83,184	21
*00737	Cayey	47,279	52	00772	Loíza	33,557	19	00641	Utuado	34,972	113
00735	Ceiba	17,961	29	00773	Luquillo	20,448	26	00692	Vega Alta	39,315	28
00638	Ciales	20,378	67	00674	Manatí	48,545	45	*00694	Vega Baja	64,115	46
00739	Cidra	46,404	36	00606	Maricao	6,405	37	00765	Vieques	9,220	51
00769	Coamo	38,934	78	00707	Maunabo	12,776	21	00766	Villalba	29,637	35
00782	Comerío	19,524	28	*00681	Mayagüez	95,280	78	00767	Yabucoa	40,237	55
00783	Corozal	38,332	43	00676	Moca	43,086	50	00698	Yauco	47,894	68
00775	Culebra	2,016	12	00687	Morovis	32,012	39				
00646	Dorado	35,687	23	00718	Naguabo	24,167	52	**TOTAL**		**3,912,054**	**3,425**
00738	Fajardo	41,729	30	00719	Naranjito	30,019	27				

Commonwealth of the Northern Mariana Islands

ZIP code	Municipality	2000 Pop.	Land area sq. mi.	ZIP code	Municipality	2000 Pop.	Land area sq. mi.	ZIP code	Municipality	2000 Pop.	Land area sq. mi.
96950	Northern Islands	6	60	96950	Saipan	62,392	45				
96951	Rota	3,283	33	96952	Tinian	3,540	42	**TOTAL**		**69,221**	**179**

Other U.S. External Territories

ZIP code	Location	2000 Pop.	Land area sq. mi.	ZIP code	Location	2000 Pop.	Land area sq. mi.	ZIP code	Location	2000 Pop.	Land area sq. mi.
American Samoa				**Guam**				*96910	Mongmong-Toto-Maite	5,845	2
96799	American Samoa	57,291	77	*96910	Agaña Hts.	3,940	1	96915	Piti	1,666	7
				96928	Agat	5,656	10	96915	Santa Rita	7,500	16
Virgin Islands				*96910	Asan	2,090	6	96910	Sinajana	2,853	1
00820	Saint Croix	53,234	83	*96913	Barrigada	8,652	8	96915	Talofofo	3,215	18
*00820	Christiansted	2,637		96924	Chalan Pago-Ordot	5,923	6	*96913	Tamuning	18,012	6
*00841	Frederiksted	732		96929	Dededo	42,980	31	96915	Umatac	887	6
*00830	Saint John	4,197	20	*96910	Hagåtña	1,100	1	96929	Yigo	19,474	35
*00804	Saint Thomas	51,181	31	96915	Inarajan	3,052	19	96915	Yona	6,484	20
*00802	Charlotte Amalie	11,004		96913	Mangilao	13,313	10				
				96915	Merizo	2,163	6				
TOTAL		**108,612**	**134**					**TOTAL**		**154,805**	**210**

World Almanac Quick Quiz

These are the five most common county names in the United States. Which is the most common of all, with 31 counties across the country with this name?

(a) Franklin   (b) Washington   (c) Jefferson   (d) Jackson   (3) Lincoln

For the answer look in this chapter, or see page 1008.

WORLD HISTORY

Chronology of World History
Reviewed by Helen A. Gaudette, Ph.D.

Note: In this section, the notation BCE (before the common era) is applied to years dating to the traditional BC (before Christ) era, and CE (common era) is applied to AD (anno domini) dates. This notation is now preferred in scientific and academic publications. The traditional Gregorian Calendar system and its dates and years are unaltered except by these labels.

Prehistory: Our Ancestors Emerge
Revised by Susan Skomal, Ph.D.

Evidence of the origins of *Homo sapiens sapiens,* the species to which all humans belong, comes from a small, but increasing, number of fossils, from genetic and anatomical studies, and from interpretation of the geological record. The latest evidence suggests that humans evolved from apelike primate ancestors that lived in central Africa 5-7 mil years ago (MYA). Although all humans living today are members of a single subspecies, the fossil record confirms that our ancestors coexisted with a number of similar species throughout evolution. Current theories trace the first hominid (upright walking, humanlike primate) to Africa, where several distinct species appeared 4-6 mil years ago. These species lived in a variety of environments throughout the continent, including swampy forests, woodlands, and open savannas. In addition to *Australopithecus*—best known from "Lucy," a 3.2-MYA-Ethiopian specimen found in 1974—these early hominid species include such recent discoveries as *Sahelanthropus*, *Ardipithecus*, *Kenyanthropus*, and *Orrorin*.

Our own human ancestry arose 2-3 MYA, when hominid species began to produce elaborate stone tools. The oldest tools are dated to 2.5-2.6 MYA from Ethiopia, and were made by systematically removing sharp flakes from a core. This produced tools for scraping meat and sinew, as well as a sharp chopping implement useful for obtaining marrow from long bones. Although we cannot determine whether these early hominids had the ability to speak, they were social animals, lived in semi-permanent camps, and had a food-gathering economy. A closer ancestor, *Homo erectus,* appeared in Africa 1.9 MYA and was the first to leave the continent, spreading into Asia by 1.8 MYA, and Europe by 800,000 BP. These individuals had skeletal structures similar to modern humans, hunted, learned to control fire, and may have had primitive language skills.

Europe has provided a particularly rich set of fossil evidence. Human-like in many important respects, Neanderthals appeared c. 200,000 BP (years before the present), had sophisticated tools and a developed social culture, and was well adapted to the harsh climate of Ice Age Europe. Recent genetic evidence supports the theory that Neanderthals were a distinct species that in some places coexisted with, but did not interbreed with, early modern humans (also called Crô-Magnons). A similar situation may have occurred in Asia, where more primitive species of *Homo* coexisted with early modern humans 100,000-150,000 BP. Further study of *Homo antecessor,* a new species identified in Spain, may clarify the relationship between anatomically modern *Homo sapiens* and Neanderthals in Europe.

The 1st *Homo sapiens sapiens* originated in E Africa 100,000-200,000 BP. The oldest modern human fossils are dated to 195,000 BP, and were found at the Ethiopian site of Omo. Our species quickly spread. Humans were living in Israel by 100,000 BP, and in Romania by 35,000 BP. Migration from Asia to Australia via the Timor Straits took place as early as 100,000 BP. First confirmation for the crossing from Asia to the Americas by land bridge dates to the end of the last Ice Age, at 14,000 BP; however, genetic data suggest that small, isolated groups of people arrived in the Americas 18,000 to 14,000 years ago, settling in both continents.

A variety of cultural modes—in toolmaking, diet, shelter, social arrangements, and spiritual expression—arose as humans adapted to different geographic and climatic zones and the knowledge base grew. Sites from all over the world show seasonal migration patterns and efficient exploitation of a wide range of plant and animal foods.

Fire-making probably began 1 MYA in Africa and spread to Asia and Europe. Hearths were used in N Israel by c. 750,000 BP, and by 465,000 BP in W France. Fire-hardened wooden spears, weighted and set with small stone blades, were fashioned by big-game hunters 400,000 BP in Germany. Scraping tools, dated 30,000-200,000 BP in Europe, N Africa, the Middle East, and Central Asia, suggest the treatment of skins for clothing. The oldest evidence of personal adornment, perforated snail shell beads, was found c. 100,000-135,000 BP at Skhul Cave in Israel. Impressions in clay artifacts from the Czech Republic document the ability to weave cloth baskets and nets by 28,000 BP. By the time Australia was settled, human ancestors had learned to navigate in boats over open water. The earliest bone tools found so far were fashioned 80,000 BP in the Congo basin by fishermen, who created sophisticated fishing tackle to catch giant catfish.

About 60,000 BP the earliest immigrants to Australia carved and painted designs on rocks. Painting and decoration flourished, along with stone and ivory sculpture, from 35,000 BP in Europe, where more than 200 caves show remarkable examples of naturalistic wall painting. A variety of musical instruments, including bone flutes with precisely bored holes, have been found in sites dated to 40,000-80,000 BP. Around 30,000 BP, the number of people surviving long enough to become grandparents dramatically increased. There were now 2 adults over 30 for every adult under 30. With more adults available to provide child care, humans began to develop more complex social systems.

Shortly after 10,000 BCE, among widely separated communities, a series of dramatic technological and social changes occurred, marking the Neolithic, or New Stone, Age. As the world climate became drier and warmer, humans learned to cultivate plants and domesticate animals. This encouraged growth of permanent settlements. Manufacture of pottery and cloth began at this time. These techniques precipitated a dramatic increase in world population and social complexity. Growing genetic research suggests that mutations related to traits currently found in human populations, such as unusually light skin pigmentation in Europeans and the ability to process lactose amongst Europeans and alcohol amongst East Asians, occurred at this time.

Sites in the Americas, SE Europe, and the Middle East show roughly contemporaneous (8000-10,000 BCE) evidence of Neolithic traits. Dates near 5000-8000 BCE have been given for E and S Asian, W European, and sub-Saharan African Neolithic remains. Farming spread rapidly throughout the Mediterranean, perhaps in 100-200 years. The variety of crops—field grains, rice, maize, squash, and roots—and a mix of other characteristics suggest that this adaptation occurred independently in each region. Evidence for fermented beverages likewise coincides with the early Neolithic settled farming lifestyle. Northern Chinese farmers concocted a wine-like drink from rice, honey, and fruit between 6000 and 7000 BCE; in the Middle East, Iranian vintners were fermenting grapes by 5400 BCE.

▶ **IT'S A FACT:** Ancient Egyptian medical treatments are documented in the Edwin Smith Surgical Papyrus, which dates to about 1600 BCE, but was displayed publicly for the first time in 2005. The papyrus describes treating traumatic injuries and rudimentary surgeries, including procedures for cyst removal and closing wounds with stitches. Egyptians also demonstrated an understanding of pharmacology, recommending treating patients' pains with a willow bark concoction, which contains a painkiller similar to aspirin, and applying honey, a natural antibiotic, to open wounds.

Major Gods & Goddesses of Ancient Egypt

Name	Relations	Sphere or Position	Emblem/Attribute
Ra (Re)/Atum/Amon	Self-created	The sun, creation	Hawk
Thoth (Djeheuty)	Son of Ra	The moon, wisdom, writing	Ibis/baboon
Ptah	Creator of Atum	Creation, craftsmen	—
Osiris	Brother of Set(h) & Isis	The underworld (dead), fertility, resurrection, vegetation	Bull
Isis	Sister/consort of Osiris	The underworld (dead)	—
Set(h)	Brother of Osiris	Evil, trickery, chaos	Boar, pig
Horus (several)	Sons of Osiris & Isis and Ra & Hathor	The earth	Falcon
Hathor	Consort of Ra	Motherhood, love	Cow
Anubis	Son of Osiris	Embalmer & judge of the dead	Jackal/dog

Earliest Civilizations: 4000-1000 BCE

Mesopotamia. If history began with writing, the first chapter opened in Mesopotamia, the Tigris-Euphrates river valley. The Sumerians used clay tablets with pictographs to keep records after 4000 BCE. A **cuneiform** (wedge-shaped) script evolved by 3000 BCE as a full syllabic alphabet. Neighboring peoples adapted the script for their own use.

Sumerian life centered, from 4000 BCE, on large cities (Eridu, Ur, Uruk, Nippur, Kish, and Lagash) organized around temples and priestly bureaucracies, with surrounding plains watered by vast irrigation works and worked with traction plows. Sailboats, wheeled vehicles, potter's wheels, and kilns were used. Copper was smelted and tempered from c. 4000 BCE; bronze was produced not long after. Ores, as well as precious stones and metals, were obtained through long-distance ship and caravan trade. Iron was used from c. 2000 BCE. Improved ironworking, developed partly by the Hittites, became widespread by 1200 BCE.

Sumerian political primacy passed among cities and their kingly dynasties. Semitic-speaking peoples, with cultures derived from the Sumerian, founded a succession of dynasties that ruled in Mesopotamia and neighboring areas for most of 1,800 years; among them were the **Akkadians** (first under Sargon I, c. 2350 BCE), the Amorites (whose laws, codified by **Hammurabi,** c. 1792-1750 BCE, have biblical parallels), and the Assyrians, with interludes of rule by the Hittites, Kassites, and Mitanni.

Mesopotamian learning, maintained by scribes and preserved in vast libraries, was practically oriented. Lists of astronomical phenomena, plants, animals, and stones were maintained; medical texts listed ailments and herbal cures. The Sumerians worshiped anthropomorphic gods representing natural forces. Sacrifices were made at **ziggurats**—huge stepped temples.

The Syria-Palestine area, site of some of the earliest urban remains (Jericho, 7000 BCE), and of the recently uncovered **Ebla** civilization (fl. 2500 BCE), experienced Egyptian cultural and political influence along with Mesopotamian. The **Phoenician** coast was an active commercial center. A phonetic alphabet was invented here before 1600 BCE. It became the ancestor of many other alphabets.

Egypt. Agricultural villages along the Nile River were united by around 3300 BCE into 2 kingdoms, Upper and Lower Egypt, unified (c. 3100 BCE) under the pharaoh Menes. A bureaucracy supervised construction of canals and monuments (**pyramids** starting 2700 BCE). Control over Nubia to the S was asserted from 2600 BCE. Brilliant **Old Kingdom** Period achievements in architecture, sculpture, and painting reached their height during the 3rd and 4th Dynasties. **Hieroglyphic writing** appeared by 3200 BCE, recording a sophisticated literature that included religious writings, philosophy, history, and science. An ordered hierarchy of gods, including totemistic animal elements, was served by a powerful

Egyptian hieroglyphics

priesthood in Memphis. The pharaoh was identified with the falcon god Horus. Other trends included belief in an afterlife and short-lived quasi-monotheistic reforms introduced by the pharaoh **Akhenaton** (c. 1379-1362 BCE), also the husband of Nefertiti.

After a period of dominance by Semitic Hyksos from Asia (c. 1700-1550 BCE), the **New Kingdom** established an empire in Syria. Egypt became increasingly embroiled in Asiatic wars and diplomacy. Conquered by Persia in 525 BCE, it eventually faded away as an independent culture.

India. An urban civilization with a so-far-undeciphered writing system stretched across the Indus Valley and along the Arabian Sea c. 3000-1500 BCE. Major sites are Harappa and **Mohenjo-Daro** in Pakistan, well-planned geometric cities with underground sewers and vast granaries. The entire region may have been ruled as a single state. Bronze was used, and arts and crafts were well developed. Religious life apparently took the form of fertility cults. Indus civilization was probably in decline when it was destroyed by **Aryans** who arrived from the NW, speaking an Indo-European language. Led by a warrior aristocracy whose legendary deeds are in the **Rig Veda**, the Aryans spread E and S, bringing their sky gods, priestly (Brahman) ritual, and the beginnings of the caste system; local customs and beliefs were assimilated by the conquerors.

Europe. On Crete, the Bronze Age **Minoan civilization** emerged c. 2500 BCE. A prosperous economy and richly decorative art was supported by seaborne commerce. Mycenae and other cities in mainland Greece and Asia Minor (e.g., **Troy**) preserved elements of the culture until c. 1200 BCE. Cretan Linear A script (c. 2000-1700 BCE) remains undeciphered; Linear B script (c. 1300-1200 BCE) records an early Greek dialect. The possible connection between Mycenaean monumental stonework and the megalithic monuments of W Europe, Iberia, and Malta (c. 4000-1500 BCE) is unclear.

China. Proto-Chinese neolithic cultures had long covered N and SE China when the first large political state was organized in the N by the **Shang dynasty** (c. 1523 BCE). Shang kings called themselves Sons of Heaven, and they presided over a cult of human and animal sacrifice to ancestors and nature gods. The Chou dynasty, starting c. 1027 BCE, expanded the area of the Son of Heaven's dominion, but feudal states exercised most temporal power. A writing system with 2,000 characters was already in use under the Shang, with **pictographs** later supplemented by phonetic characters. Many of its principles and symbols, despite changes in spoken Chinese, were preserved in later writing systems. Technical advances allowed urban specialists to create fine ceramic and jade products, and bronze casting after 1500 BCE was the most advanced in the world. Bronze artifacts discovered in N Thailand date from 3600 BCE, hundreds of years before similar Middle Eastern finds.

Americas. Olmecs settled (1500 BCE) on the Gulf coast of Mexico and developed the first known civilization in the western hemisphere. Temple cities and huge stone sculpture date from 1200 BCE. A rudimentary calendar and writing system existed. Olmec religion, centering on a jaguar god, and Olmec art forms influenced later Meso-American cultures.

Formation of Classical Societies: 1000 BCE-400 BCE

Greece. After a period of decline during the Dorian Greek invasions (1200-1000 BCE), the Aegean area developed a unique civilization. Drawing on Mycenaean traditions, Mesopotamian learning (weights and measures, lunisolar calendar, astronomy, musical scales), the Phoenician alphabet (modified for Greek), and Egyptian art, **Greek city-states** saw a rich elaboration of intellectual life. The two great epic poems attributed to **Homer**, the *Iliad* and the *Odyssey,* were probably composed around the 8th cent. BCE. Long-range commerce was aided by metal coinage (introduced by the Lydians in Asia Minor before 700 BCE; colonies were founded around the Mediterranean (Cumae in Italy in 760 BCE; Massalia in France c. 600 BCE) and Black Sea shores.

Philosophy, starting with Ionian speculation on the nature of matter (Thales, c. 634-546 BCE), continued by other "Pre-Socratics" (e.g., Heraclitus, c. 535-415 BCE; Parmenides, b. c. 515 BCE), reached a high point in Athens in the rationalist idealism of **Plato** (c. 428-347 BCE), a disciple of **Socrates** (c. 469-399 BCE; executed for alleged impiety), and in **Aristotle** (384-322 BCE), a pioneer in many fields, from natural sciences to logic, ethics, and metaphysics. The **arts** were highly valued. Architecture culminated in the **Parthenon** (438 BCE) by Phidias (fl. 490-430 BCE). Poetry (Sappho, c. 610-580 BCE; Pindar, c. 518-438 BCE) and **drama** (Aeschylus, 525-456 BCE; Sophocles, c. 496-406 BCE; Euripides, c. 484-406 BCE) thrived. Male beauty and strength, a chief artistic theme, were celebrated at the national games at Olympia.

Ruled by local tyrants or **oligarchies**, the Greeks were not politically united, but managed to resist inclusion in the Persian Empire—Persian king Darius was defeated at Marathon (490 BCE), his son Xerxes at Salamis (480 BCE), and the Persian army at Plataea (479 BCE). Democracy sprouted in Athens as statesman Pericles (495-429 BCE) sought participation in government from all citizens. Local warfare was common; the **Peloponnesian Wars** (431-404 BCE) ended in Sparta's victory over Athens. Greek political power subsequently waned, but Greek cultural forms spread far and wide.

Hebrews. Nomadic Hebrew tribes entered Canaan before 1200 BCE, settling among other Semitic peoples speaking the same language. They brought from the desert a **monotheistic** faith said to have been revealed to Abraham in Canaan c. 1800 BCE and Moses at Mt. Sinai c. 1250 BCE, after the Hebrews' escape from bondage in Egypt. David (r. 1000-961 BCE) and Solomon (r. 961-922 BCE) united them in a kingdom that briefly dominated the area. **Phoenicians** to the N founded Mediterranean colonies (Carthage, c. 814 BCE) and sailed into the Atlantic.

A temple in Jerusalem became the national religious center, with sacrifices performed by a hereditary priesthood. Polytheistic influences, especially of the fertility cult of Baal, were opposed by **prophets** (Elijah, Amos, Isaiah).

Divided into **two kingdoms** after Solomon, the Hebrews were unable to resist the revived Assyrian empire, which conquered Israel, the N kingdom, in 722 BCE. Judah, the S kingdom, was conquered in 586 BCE by the Babylonians under Nebuchadnezzar II. With the fixing of most of the biblical canon by the mid-4th cent. BCE and the emergence of rabbis, Judaism successfully survived the loss of Hebrew autonomy. A Jewish kingdom was revived under the Hasmoneans (168-42 BCE).

China. During the **Eastern Chou** dynasty (770-256 BCE), Chinese culture spread E to the sea and S to the Yangtze R. Large feudal states on the periphery of the empire contended for preeminence, but continued to recognize the Son of Heaven (king), who retained a purely ritual role enriched with courtly music and dance. In the Age of Warring States (403-221 BCE), when the first sections of the **Great Wall** were built, the Ch'in state in the W gained supremacy and finally united all of China.

Iron tools entered China c. 500 BCE, and casting techniques were advanced, aiding agriculture. Peasants owned their land and owed civil and military service to nobles. China's cities grew in number and size; barter remained the chief trade medium.

Intellectual ferment among noble scribes and officials produced the Classical Age of Chinese literature and philosophy. **Confucius** (551-479 BCE) urged a restoration of a supposedly harmonious social order of the past through proper conduct in accordance with one's station and through filial and ceremonial piety. The *Analects* attributed to him are revered throughout E Asia.

Among other thinkers, **Mencius** (d. 289 BCE) added the view that the Mandate of Heaven can be removed from an unjust dynasty. The Legalists sought to curb the supposed natural wickedness of people through new institutions and harsh laws. The Naturalists emphasized the balance of opposites—yin, yang—in the world. **Taoists** sought mystical knowledge through meditation and disengagement.

The Seven Wonders of the Ancient World

These ancient works of art and architecture were considered awe-inspiring by the Greek and Roman world of the first few centuries BCE. Later classical writers disagreed as to which works belonged, but the following were usually included:

The Pyramids of Egypt: The only surviving ancient Wonder, these monumental structures of masonry, located at Giza on the W bank of the Nile R above Cairo, were built from c. 2700 to 2500 BCE as royal tombs. Three—Khufu (Cheops), Khafra (Chephren), and Menkaura (Mycerimus)—were often grouped as the first Wonder of the World. The largest, the Great Pyramid of Khufu covers 13 acres. It is estimated to contain 2.3 million blocks of stone, the stones themselves averaging 2½ tons and some weighing 30 tons. Its construction reputedly took 100,000 laborers 20 years.

The Hanging Gardens of Babylon: These gardens were laid out on a brick terrace 400 ft square and 75 ft above the ground. To irrigate the plants, screws were turned to lift water from the Euphrates R. The gardens were probably built by King Nebuchadnezzar II about 600 BCE. The Walls of Babylon, long, thick, and made of colorfully glazed brick, were also considered by some among the Seven Wonders.

The Pharos (Lighthouse) of Alexandria: This structure was designed about 270 BCE, during the reign of Ptolemy II, by the Greek architect Sostratos. Estimates of its height range from 200 to 600 ft.

The Colossus of Rhodes: A bronze statue of the sun god Helios, the Colossus was worked on for 12 years in the third cent. BCE by the sculptor Chares. It was probably 120 ft high. A symbol of the city of Rhodes at its height, the statue stood on a promontory overlooking the harbor.

The Temple of Artemis (Diana) at Ephesus: This largest and most complex temple of ancient times was built about 550 BCE and was made of marble except for its tile-covered wooden roof. It was begun in honor of a non-Hellenic goddess who later became identified with the Greek goddess of the same name. Ephesus was one of the greatest of the Ionian cities.

The Mausoleum at Halicarnassus: The source of our word *mausoleum*, this marble tomb was built in what is now SE Turkey by Artemisia for her husband Mausolus, king of Caria in Asia Minor, who died in 353 BCE. About 135 ft high, the tomb was adorned with the works of 4 sculptors.

The Statue of Zeus (Jupiter) at Olympia: This statue showed Zeus seated on a throne. His flesh was made of ivory, his robe and ornaments of gold. Reputedly 40 ft high, the statue was made by Phidias and was placed in the great temple of Zeus in the sacred grove of Olympia about 457 BCE.

India. The political and cultural center of India shifted from the Indus to the Ganges River Valley. Buddhism, Jainism, and mystical revisions of orthodox Vedism all developed c. 500-300 BCE. The *Upanishads,* last part of the *Veda,* urged escape from the cycle of rebirth into the physical world. Vedism remained the preserve of the Brahman caste.

Buddha

In contrast, **Buddhism**, founded by Siddhartha Gautama (c. 563-c. 483 BCE)—Buddha ("Enlightened One")—appealed to merchants in the urban centers and took hold at first (and most lastingly) on the geographic fringes of Indian civilization. The classic Indian epics were composed in this era: the **Ramayana** perhaps c. 300 BCE, the **Mahabharata** over a period starting around 400 BCE.

N India was divided into a large number of monarchies and aristocratic republics, probably derived from tribal groupings, when the Magadha kingdom was formed in Bihar c. 542 BCE. It soon became the dominant power. The **Maurya dynasty**, founded by Chandragupta c. 321 BCE, expanded the kingdom, uniting most of N India in a centralized bureaucratic empire. The third Mauryan king, **Asoka** (reigned c. 274-236 BCE), conquered most of the subcontinent. He converted to Buddhism and inscribed its tenets on pillars throughout India. He downplayed the caste system.

Before its final decline in India, Buddhism developed into a popular worship of heavenly Bodhisattvas ("enlightened beings"), and it produced a refined architecture (the Great Stupa [shrine] at Sanchi, 100 CE) and sculpture (Gandhara reliefs, 1-400) CE.

Persia. Aryan peoples (Persians, Medes) dominated the area of present Iran by the beginning of the 1st millennium BCE. The prophet **Zoroaster** (born c. 628 BCE) introduced a dualistic religion in which the forces of good (Ahura Mazda, "Lord of Wisdom") and evil (Ahriman) battle for dominance; individuals are judged by their actions and earn damnation or salvation. Zoroaster's hymns (*Gathas*) are included in the *Avesta,* the Zoroastrian scriptures. A version of this faith became the established religion of the Persian Empire.

Africa. Nubia, periodically occupied by Egypt since about 2600 BCE, ruled Egypt c. 750-661 BCE and survived as an independent Egyptianized kingdom (**Kush;** capital Meroe) for 1,000 years. The Iron Age Nok culture flourished c. 500 BCE- 200 CE on the Benue Plateau of **Nigeria**.

Americas. The Chavin culture controlled N Peru c. 900 BCE to 200 BCE. Its ceremonial centers, featuring the jaguar god, survived long after. Its architecture, ceramics, and textiles had influenced other Peruvian cultures. **Mayan civilization** began to develop in Central America as early as 1500 BCE.

Great Empires Unite the Classical World: 400 BCE-400 CE

Alexander the Great

Persia and Alexander the Great. Cyrus, ruler of a small kingdom in Persia from 559 BCE, united the Persians and Medes within 10 years and conquered Asia Minor and Babylonia in another 10. His son Cambyses, followed by **Darius** (r. 522-486 BCE), added vast lands to the E and N as far as the Indus Valley and Central Asia, as well as Egypt and Thrace. The whole empire was ruled by an international bureaucracy and army, with Persians holding the chief positions. The resources and styles of all the subject civilizations were exploited to create a rich syncretic art.

The kingdom of Macedon, which under Philip II dominated the Greek world and Egypt, was passed on to his son **Alexander** in 336 BCE. Within 13 years, Alexander had conquered all the Persian dominions. Imbued by his tutor Aristotle with Greek ideals, Alexander encouraged colonization, and Greek-style cities were founded. After his death in 323 BCE, wars of succession divided the empire into 3 significant dynasties—the Antigonids in Asia Minor and **Macedon,** the Ptolemies in Egypt, and the **Seleucids** in Mesopotamia. In the ensuing 300 years (the **Hellenistic Era**), a cosmopolitan Greek-oriented culture permeated the ancient world from W Europe to the borders of India, absorbing native elites everywhere.

Hellenistic philosophy stressed the private individual's search for happiness. The Cynics followed Diogenes (c. 372-287 BCE), who stressed self-sufficiency and restriction of desires and expressed contempt for luxury and social convention. Zeno (c. 335-c.263 BCE) and the **Stoics** exalted reason, identified it with virtue, and counseled an ascetic disregard for misfortune. The **Epicureans** tried to build lives of moderate pleasure without political or emotional involvement. Hellenistic arts imitated life realistically, especially in sculpture and literature (comedies of Menander, 342-292 BCE).

The sciences thrived, especially at Alexandria, where the Ptolemies financed a great library and museum. Fields of study included mathematics (**Euclid's** geometry, c. 300 BCE); astronomy (heliocentric theory of Aristarchus, 310-230 BCE; Julian calendar, 45 BCE; **Ptolemy's** *Almagest,* c. 150 CE); geography (world map of Eratosthenes, 276-194 BCE); hydraulics (**Archimedes,** 287-212 BCE); medicine (Galen, 130-200 CE); and chemistry. Inventors refined uses for siphons, valves, gears, springs, screws, levers, cams, and pulleys.

A restored Persian empire under the **Parthians** (northern Iranian tribesmen) controlled the eastern Hellenistic world from 250 BCE to 229 CE. The Parthians and the succeeding Sassanian dynasty (c. 224-651 CE) fought with Rome periodically. The **Sassanians** revived Zoroastrianism as a state religion and patronized a nationalistic artistic and scholarly renaissance.

Rome. The city of Rome was founded, according to legend, by Romulus in 753 BCE. Through military expansion and colonization, and by granting citizenship to conquered tribes, the city annexed all of Italy S of the Po in the 100-year period before 268 BCE. The Latin and other Italic tribes were annexed first, followed by the **Etruscans** (founders of a great civilization, N of Rome) and the Greek colonies in the S. With a large standing army and reserve forces of several hundred thousand, Rome was able to defeat **Carthage** in the 3 **Punic Wars** (264-241, 218-201, 149-146 BCE), despite the invasion of Italy by **Hannibal** (218 BCE), thus gaining Sicily and territory in Spain and N Africa.

Rome exploited local disputes to conquer Greece and Asia Minor in the 2nd cent. BCE, and Egypt in the 1st (after the defeat and suicide of **Antony and Cleopatra**, 30 BCE). The Mediterranean civilized world, up to the disputed Parthian border, was now Roman and remained so for 500 years. Less civilized regions were added to the Empire: Gaul (conquered by **Julius Caesar**, 58-51 BCE), Britain (43 CE), and Dacia NE of the Danube (107 CE).

The original aristocratic republican government, with democratic features added in the 5th and 4th cent. BCE, deteriorated under the pressures of empire and class conflict (**Gracchus** brothers, social reformers, murdered in 133 BCE and 121 BCE; slave revolts in 135 BCE and 73 BCE). After a series of civil wars (Marius vs. Sulla 88-82 BCE, Caesar vs. **Pompey** 49-45 BCE, triumvirate vs. Caesar's assassins 44-43 BCE, Antony vs. Octavian 32-30 BCE), the empire came under the rule of a deified monarch (first emperor, **Augustus**, 27 BCE-14 CE).

Provincials (nearly all granted citizenship by Caracalla, 212 CE) came to dominate the army and civil service. Traditional **Roman law,** systematized and interpreted by independent jurists, and local self-rule in provincial cities were supplanted by a vast tax-collecting bureaucracy in the 3rd and 4th cent. The legal rights of women, children, and slaves were strengthened.

Roman innovations in **civil engineering** included water mills, windmills, and rotary mills and use of cement that hardened under water. Monumental architecture (baths, theaters, temples) relied on the arch and the dome. The network of roads (some still standing) stretched 53,000 mi, passing through mountain tunnels as long as 3.5 mi. Aqueducts brought water to cities; underground sewers removed waste.

Roman art and literature were to a large extent derivative of Greek models. Innovations were made in sculpture (naturalistic busts, equestrian statues), decorative wall painting (as at Pompeii), satire (**Juvenal,** 60-127 CE), history (**Tacitus,** 56-120 CE), prose romance (Petronius, d. 66 CE). Gladiatorial contests dominated public amusements, which were supported by the state.

India. The **Gupta** monarchs reunited N India c. 320 CE. Their peaceful and prosperous reign saw a revival of Hindu religious thought and Brahman power. The old Vedic traditions were combined with devotion to many indigenous deities (who were seen as manifestations of Vedic gods). Caste lines were reinforced, and Buddhist practices gradually disappeared or were integrated with Hindu traditions. The art (often erotic), architecture, and literature of the period, patronized by the Gupta court, are considered among India's finest achievements (Kalidasa, poet and dramatist, fl. c. 400 CE). Mathematical innovations included use of the zero and decimal numbers. Invasions by White Huns from the NW destroyed the empire c. 550 CE.

Rich cultures also developed in S India during this period. Emotional Tamil religious poetry contributed to the Hindu revival. The Pallava kingdom controlled much of S India c. 350-880 CE and helped to spread Indian civilization to SE Asia.

China. The Ch'in ruler Shih Huang Ti (r. 221-210 BCE), known as the First Emperor, centralized political authority. standardized the written language, laws, weights, measures, and coinage, and conducted a census, but tried to destroy most philosophical texts. The **Han dynasty** (202 BCE-220 CE) instituted the Mandarin bureaucracy, which lasted 2,000 years. Local officials were selected by examination in Confucian classics and trained at the imperial university and provincial schools.

The invention of **paper** facilitated this bureaucratic system. Agriculture was promoted, but peasants bore most of the tax burden. Irrigation was improved, water clocks and sundials were used, astronomy and mathematics thrived, and landscape painting was perfected.

With the expansion S and W (to nearly the present borders of today's China), trade was opened with India, SE Asia, and the Middle East, over sea and caravan routes. Indian missionaries brought Mahayana Buddhism to China by the 1st cent. CE and spawned a variety of sects. Taoism was revived and merged with popular superstitions. **Taoist and Buddhist monasteries** and convents multiplied in the turbulent centuries after the collapse of the Han dynasty.

Monotheism Spreads: 1-750 CE

Roman Empire. Polytheism was practiced in the Roman Empire, and religions indigenous to particular Middle Eastern nations became international. Roman citizens worshiped **Isis** of Egypt, **Mithras** of Persia, **Demeter** of Greece, and the great mother **Cybele** of Phrygia. Their cults centered on mysteries (secret ceremonies) and the promise of an afterlife, symbolized by the death and rebirth of the god. The Jews of the empire preserved their monotheistic religion, Judaism, the world's oldest (c. 1300 BCE) continuous religion. Its teachings are contained in the Bible (the Old Testament). 1st-cent. Judaism embraced several sects, including the **Sadducees,** mostly drawn from the Temple priesthood, who were culturally Hellenized; the **Pharisees,** who upheld the full range of traditional customs and practices as of equal weight to literal scriptural law and elaborated synagogue worship; and the **Essenes,** an ascetic, millennarian sect. Messianic fervor led to repeated, unsuccessful rebellions against Rome (66-70, 135). As a result, the Temple in Jerusalem was destroyed and the population decimated; this event marked the beginning of the Diaspora (living in exile). To preserve the faith, a program of codification of law was begun at the academy of Yavneh. The work continued for some 500 years in Palestine and in Babylonia, ending in the final redaction (c. 600) of the **Talmud,** a huge collection of legal and moral debates, rulings, liturgy, biblical exegesis, and legendary materials.

Christianity, which emerged as a distinct sect by the 2nd half of the 1st cent., is based on the teachings of **Jesus,** whom believers considered the Savior (Messiah or Christ) and son of God. Missionary activities of the Apostles and such early leaders as **Paul of Tarsus** spread the faith. Intermittent persecution, as in Rome under Nero in 64 CE, on grounds of suspected disloyalty, failed to disrupt the Christian communities. Each congregation, generally urban and of plebeian character, was tightly organized under a leader (bishop), elders (presbyters or priests), and assistants (deacons). The four **Gospels** (accounts of the life and teachings of Jesus) and the Acts of the Apostles were written down in the late 1st and early 2nd cent. and circulated along with letters of Paul and other Christian leaders. An authoritative canon of these writings was not fixed until the 4th cent.

A school for priests was established at Alexandria in the 2nd cent. Its teachers (**Origen** c. 182-251) helped define doctrine and promote the faith in Greek-style philosophical works. Neoplatonism underwent Christian coloration in the writings of Church Fathers such as **Augustine** (354-430). Christian hermits began to associate in monasteries, first in Egypt (St. Pachomius c. 290-345), then in other eastern lands, then in the W (**St. Benedict's rule,** 529). Devotion to saints, especially Mary, mother of Jesus, spread. Under **Constantine** (r. 306-37), Christianity became in effect the established religion of the Empire. Pagan temples were expropriated, state funds were used to build churches and support the hierarchy, and laws were adjusted in accordance with Christian ideas. Pagan worship was banned by the end of the 4th cent., and severe restrictions were placed on Judaism.

The newly established church was rocked by doctrinal disputes, often exacerbated by regional rivalries. Chief heresies (as defined by church councils, backed by imperial authority) were **Arianism,** which denied the divinity of Jesus; **Monophysitism,** denying the human nature of Christ; **Donatism,** which regarded as invalid any sacraments administered by sinful clergy; and **Pelagianism,** which denied the necessity of unmerited divine aid (grace) for salvation.

Islam. The earliest Arab civilization emerged by the end of the 2nd millennium BCE in the watered highlands of Yemen. Seaborne and caravan trade in frankincense and myrrh connected the area with the Nile and Fertile Crescent. The Minaean, Sabean (Sheba), and Himyarite states successively held sway. By Muhammad's time (7th cent. CE), the region was a province of Sassanian Persia. In the N, the Nabataean kingdom at Petra and the kingdom of Palmyra were Aramaicized, Romanized, and finally absorbed, as neighboring Judea had been, into the Roman Empire. Nomads shared the central region with a few trading towns and oases. Wars between tribes and raids on communities were common and were celebrated in a poetic tradition that by the 6th cent. helped establish a classic literary Arabic.

Major Gods & Goddesses of the Classical World

Greek	Roman	Relations	Sphere or Position
Aphrodite	Venus	Daughter of Zeus & Dione	Love
Apollo	——	Son of Zeus & Leto	Healing, poetry, light
Ares	Mars	Son of Zeus & Hera	War
Artemis	Diana	Daughter of Zeus & Leto	Hunting, chastity
Athena	Minerva	Daughter of Zeus & Metis	Wisdom, crafts, war
Cronus	Saturn	Father of Zeus	Titans' ruler
Demeter	Ceres	Sister of Zeus	Agriculture, fertility
Dionysus	Bacchus	Son of Zeus & Semele	Wine, fertility, ecstasy
Eros	Cupid	Son of Ares & Aphrodite	Love
Hades	Pluto	Brother of Zeus	The underworld, death
Hephaestus	Vulcan	Son of Zeus & Hera	Fire
Hera	Juno	Wife & sister of Zeus	Earth
Hermes	Mercury	Son of Zeus & Maia	Travel, commerce, gods' messenger
Hestia	Vesta	Sister of Zeus	The hearth
Pan	——	Son of Hermes & a wood nymph	Forests, flocks, shepherds
Persephone	Proserpina	Daughter of Zeus & Demeter	Grain
Poseidon	Neptune	Brother of Zeus	The sea
Rhea	Ops	Mother of Zeus	The earth
Uranus	Uranus	Father of Titans (elder gods)	The heavens
Zeus	Jupiter	Son of Cronus & Rhea	Ruler of the gods

About 610, **Muhammad**, a 40-year-old Arab of Mecca, emerged as a prophet. He proclaimed a revelation from the one true God, calling on contemporaries to abandon idolatry and restore the faith of Abraham. He introduced his religion as "**Islam**," meaning "submission" to the one God, Allah, as a continuation of the biblical faith of Abraham, Moses, and Jesus, all respected as prophets in his system. His teachings, recorded in the **Koran** (*al-Qur'an* in Arabic), in many ways were inclusive of Abrahamic monotheistic ideas known to the Jews and Christians in Arabia. A key aspect of the Abrahamic connection was insistence on justice in society, which led to severe opposition among the aristocrats in Mecca. As conditions worsened for Muhammad and his followers, he decided in 622 to make a *hegira* ("flight") to Medina, 200 mi to the N. This event marks the beginning of the Muslim lunar calendar. Hostilities between Mecca and Medina increased, and in 629 Muhammad conquered Mecca. By the time he died in 632, nearly all the Arabian peninsula accepted his political and religious leadership.

After his death the majority of Muslims (later known as **Sunni** Muslims) recognized the leadership of the **caliph** ("successor") Abu Bakr (632-34), followed by Umar (634-44), Uthman (644-56), and Ali (656-60). A minority, the **Shiites**, insisted instead on the leadership of Ali, Muhammad's cousin and son-in-law. By 644, **Muslim rule** over Arabia was confirmed. Muslim armies had threatened the Byzantine and Persian empires, which were weakened by wars and disaffection among subject peoples (including Coptic and Syriac Christians opposed to the Byzantine Orthodox establishment).

Syria, Palestine, Egypt, Iraq, and Persia fell to Muslim armies. The new administration assimilated existing systems in the region; hence the conquered peoples participated in running of the empire. The Koran recognized the so-called Peoples of the Book, i.e., Christians, Jews, and Zoroastrians, as tolerated monotheists, and Muslim policy was relatively tolerant to minorities living as "protected" peoples. An expanded tax system, based on conquests of the Persian and Byzantine empires, provided revenue to organize campaigns against neighboring non-Muslim regions.

Under the **Umayyads** (661-750) and **Abbasids** (750-1256), territorial expansion led Muslim armies across N Africa and into Spain (711). Muslim armies in the W were stopped at Tours (France) in 732 by the Frankish ruler **Charles Martel**. Asia Minor, the Indus Valley, and Transoxiana were conquered in the E. The conversion of conquered peoples to Islam was gradual. In many places the official Arabic language supplanted the local tongues. But in the eastern regions the Arab rulers and their armies adopted Persian cultures and language as part of their Muslim identity.

Disputes over succession, and pious opposition to injustices in society, led to a number of oppositional movements, which also led to the factionalization of Muslim community. The **Shiites** supported leadership candidates descended from Muhammad, believing them to be carriers of some kind of divine authority. The **Kharijites** supported an egalitarian system derived from the Koran, opposing and even engaging in battle against those who did not agree with them.

New Peoples Enter World History: 400-900 CE

Barbarian invasions. Germanic tribes infiltrated S and E from their Baltic homeland during the 1st millennium BCE, reaching S Germany by 100 BCE and the Black Sea by 214 CE. Organized into large federated tribes under elected kings, most resisted Roman domination and raided the empire in time of civil war (Goths took Dacia in 214, raided Thrace in 251-69). Germanic troops and commanders dominated the Roman armies by the end of the 4th cent. **Huns**, invaders from Asia, entered Europe in 372, driving more Germans into the W empire. Emperor Valens allowed Visigoths to cross the Danube in 376. Huns under Attila (d. 453) raided Gaul, Italy, and the Balkans.

The W empire, weakened by overtaxation and social stagnation, was overrun in the 5th cent. Gaul was effectively lost in 406-7, Spain in 409, Britain in 410, Africa in 429-39. Rome was sacked in 410 by Visigoths under Alaric and in

455 by Vandals. **The last western emperor**, Romulus Augustulus, was deposed in 476 by the Germanic chief Odovacar.

Celts. Celtic cultures, which in pre-Roman times covered most of W Europe, were confined almost entirely to the British Isles after the Germanic invasions. **St. Patrick** completed (c. 457-92) the conversion of Ireland and a strong monastic tradition took hold. Irish monastic missionaries in Scotland, England, and the continent (Columba c. 521-97; Columbanus c. 543-615) helped restore Christianity after the Germanic invasions. **Monasteries** became centers of classic and Christian learning and presided over the recording of a Christianized Celtic mythology, elaborated by secular writers and bards. An intricate decorative art style developed, especially in book illumination (Lindisfarne Gospels, c. 700; Book of Kells, 8th cent.).

► **IT'S A FACT:** The Maya on Central America's Yucatan peninsula were the first to regularly eat and drink cocoa as early as 600 BCE. Cocoa beans were regarded so highly that temples were engraved with their images, and Mayan royalty drank *cacahuatl*—a bitter drink of cocoa, water, and (frequently) corn and chili peppers—at sacred ceremonies. Cocoa was also important in Aztec culture, which dominated the Yucatan peninsula after the 1300s. One 16th century Spanish explorer noted that it was possible to exchange 10 cocoa beans for a rabbit, or 100 beans for a slave. Spanish explorers were the first to add sugar to cocoa drinks, which the Aztecs named *chocolatl* to distinguish it from their bitter cocoa beverages.

Successor states. The Visigothic kingdom in Spain (from 419) and much of France (to 507) saw continuation of Roman administration, language, and law (Breviary of Alaric, 506) until its destruction by the Muslims (711). The Vandal kingdom in Africa (from 429) was conquered by the Byzantines in 533. Italy was ruled successively by an Ostrogothic kingdom under Byzantine suzerainty (489-554), direct Byzantine government, and German Lombards (568-774). The Lombards divided the peninsula with the Byzantines and papacy under the dynamic reformer **Pope Gregory the Great** (590-604) and successors.

King Clovis (r. 481-511) united the Franks on both sides of the Rhine and, after his conversion to Christianity, defeated the Arian heretics, Burgundians (after 500), and Visigoths (507) with the support of native clergy and the papacy. Under the **Merovingian** kings, a feudal system emerged: Power was fragmented among hierarchies of military landowners. Social stratification, which in late Roman times had acquired legal, hereditary sanction, was reinforced. The Carolingians (747-987) expanded the kingdom and restored central power. **Charlemagne** (r. 768-814) conquered nearly all the Germanic lands, including Lombard Italy, and was crowned Emperor by Pope Leo III in Rome in 800. A centuries-long decline in commerce and arts was reversed under Charlemagne's patronage. He welcomed Jews to his kingdom, which became a center of Jewish learning (Rashi, 1040-1105). He sponsored the Carolingian Renaissance of learning under the Anglo-Latin scholar Alcuin (c. 732-804), who reformed church liturgy.

Byzantine Empire. Under **Diocletian** (r. 284-305) the Roman empire had been divided into 2 parts to facilitate administration and defense. **Constantine** founded (330) **Constantinople** (at old Byzantium) as a fully Christian city. Commerce and taxation financed a sumptuous, orientalized court, a class of hereditary bureaucratic families, and magnificent urban construction (Hagia Sophia, 532-37). The city's fortifications and naval innovations repelled assaults by Goths, Huns, Slavs, Bulgars, Avars, Arabs, and Scandinavians. Greek replaced Latin as the official language by c. 700. **Byzantine art**, a solemn, sacral, and stylized variation of late classical styles (mosaics at the Church of San Vitale, Ravenna, Italy 526-48), was a starting point for medieval art in E and W Europe.

Justinian (r. 527-65) reconquered parts of Spain, N Africa, and Italy, codified **Roman law** (Codex Justinianus [529] was medieval Europe's chief legal text), closed the Platonic Academy at Athens, and ordered all pagans to convert. Lombards in Italy and Arabs in Africa retook most of his conquests. The Isaurian dynasty from Anatolia (from 717) and the Macedonian dynasty (867-1054) restored military and commercial power. The Iconoclast controversy (726-843) over the permissibility of images helped alienate the Eastern Church from the papacy.

Abbasid Empire. Baghdad (est. 762), became seat of the **Abbasid dynasty** (est. 750), while Ummayads continued to rule in Spain. A brilliant cosmopolitan civilization emerged, inaugurating a Muslim-Arab golden age. Arabic was the lingua franca of the empire; intellectual sources from Persian, Sanskrit, Greek, and Syriac were rendered into Arabic. Christians and Jews equally participated in this translation movement, which also involved interaction between Jewish legal thought and Islamic law, as much as between Christian theology and Muslim scholasticism. Persian-style court life, with art and music, flourished at the court of **Harun al-Rashid** (786-809), celebrated in the masterpiece known to English readers as *The Arabian Nights*. The sciences, medi-

cine, and mathematics were pursued at Baghdad, Cordova, and Cairo (est. 969). The culmination of this intellectual synthesis in Islamic civilization came with the scientific and philosophical works of **Avicenna** (Ibn Sina, 980-1037), **Averroes** (Ibn Rushd, 1126-98), and **Maimonides** (1135-1204), a Jew who wrote in Arabic. This intellectual tradition was translated into Latin and opened a new period in Christian thought.

The decentralization of the **Abbasid** empire, from 874, led to establishment of various Muslim dynasties under different ethnic groups. Persians, Berbers, and Turks ruled different regions, retaining connection with the Abbasid caliph at the religious level. The Abbasid period also saw various religious movements against the orthodox position held by governing authorities. This situation in Muslim religion led to the establishment of different legal, theological, and mystical schools of thought. The most influential mass movement was **Sufism**, which aimed at the reaching out of the average individual in quest of a spiritual path. Al-Ghazali (1058-1111) is credited with reconciling personal Sufism with orthodox Sunni tradition.

Africa. Immigrants from Saba in S Arabia helped set up the **Axum** kingdom in Ethiopia in the 1st cent. (their language, Ge'ez, is preserved by the Ethiopian Church). In the 3rd cent., when the kingdom became Christianized, it defeated Kushite Meroe and expanded its influence into Yemen. Axum was the center of a vast ivory trade and controlled the Red Sea coast until c. 1100. Arab conquest in Egypt cut Axum's political and economic ties with Byzantium.

The Iron Age entered W Africa by the end of the 1st millennium BCE. **Ghana**, the first known sub-Saharan state, ruled in the upper Senegal-Niger region c. 400-1240, controlling the trade of gold from mines in the S to trans-Sahara caravan routes to the N. The **Bantu** peoples, probably of W African origin, began to spread E and S perhaps 2,000 years ago, displacing the Pygmies and Bushmen of central and S Africa during a 1,500-year period.

Japan. The advanced Neolithic Yayoi period, when irrigation, rice farming, and iron and bronze casting techniques were introduced from China or Korea, persisted to c. 400 CE. The myriad Japanese states were then united by the **Yamato** clan, under an emperor who acted as chief priest of the animistic Shinto cult. Japanese political and military intervention by the 6th cent. in Korea, then under strong Chinese influence, quickened a Chinese cultural invasion of Japan, bringing Buddhism, the Chinese language (which long remained a literary and governmental medium), Chinese ideographs, and Buddhist styles in painting, sculpture, literature, and architecture (7th cent., Horyu-ji temple at Nara). The Taika Reforms (646) tried unsuccessfully to centralize Japan according to Chinese bureaucratic and Buddhist philosophical values.

A nativist reaction against the Buddhist **Nara period** (710-94) ushered in the **Heian period** (794-1185) centered at the new capital, Kyoto. Japanese elegance and simplicity modified Chinese styles in architecture, scroll painting, and literature; the writing system was also simplified. The courtly novel *Tale of Genji* (1010-20) testifies to the enhanced role of women in medieval Japanese literature and culture.

Southeast Asia. The historic peoples of SE Asia began arriving some 2,500 years ago from China and Tibet, displacing scattered aborigines. Their agriculture relied on rice and yams. Indian cultural influences were strongest; literacy and Hindu and Buddhist ideas followed the S India-China trade route. From the S tip of Indochina, the kingdom of **Funan** (1st-7th cent.) traded as far W as Persia. It was absorbed by Chenla, itself conquered by the **Khmer Empire** (600-1300). The Khmers, under Hindu god-kings (Suryavarman II, 1113-c. 1150), built the monumental Angkor Wat temple center for the royal phallic cult. The **Nam-Viet** kingdom in Annam, dominated by China and Chinese culture for 1,000 years, emerged in the 10th cent., growing at the expense of the Khmers, who also lost ground in the NW to the new, highly organized **Thai** kingdom. On Sumatra, the **Srivijaya** Empire controlled vital sea lanes (7th to 10th cent.). A Buddhist dynasty, the Sailendras, ruled central **Java** (8th-9th cent.), building at Borobudur one of the largest stupas in the world.

China. The Sui dynasty (581-618) ushered in a period of commercial, artistic, and scientific achievement in China, continuing under the **Tang** dynasty (618-906). Inventions like the magnetic compass, gunpowder, the abacus, and printing were introduced or perfected. Medical innovations included cataract surgery. The state, from its cosmopolitan capital, Chang-an, supervised foreign trade, which exchanged Chinese silks, porcelains, and art for spices, ivory, etc., over Central Asian caravan routes and sea routes reaching Africa. A golden age of poetry bequeathed valu-

able works to later generations (Tu Fu, 712-70; Li Po, 701-62). Landscape painting flourished.

Commercial and industrial expansion continued under the **Northern Sung** dynasty (960-1126), facilitated by paper money and credit notes. But commerce never achieved respectability; government monopolies expropriated successful merchants. The population, long stable at 50 million, doubled in 200 years with the introduction of early-ripening rice and the double harvest. In art, native Chinese styles were revived.

Americas. From 300 to 600 a Native American empire stretched from the Valley of Mexico to Guatemala, centering on the huge city **Teotihuacán** (founded 100 BCE). To the S, in Guatemala, a high **Mayan** civilization developed

Mayan temple

(150-900) around hundreds of rural ceremonial centers. The Mayans improved on Olmec writing and the calendar and pursued astronomy and mathematics. In South America, a widespread pre-Inca culture grew from **Tiahuanacu,** Bolivia, near Lake Titicaca (Gateway of the Sun, c. 700).

Christian Europe Regroups and Expands: 900-1300

Scandinavians. Pagan Danish and Norse (Viking) adventurers, traders, and pirates raided the coasts of the British Isles (Dublin, est. c. 831), France, and even the Mediterranean for over 200 years beginning in the late 8th cent. Inland settlement in the W was limited to Great Britain (King Canute, 994-1035) and Normandy, settled (911) under Rollo, as a fief of France. Vikings also reached Iceland (874), Greenland (c. 986), and North America (**Leif Ericson** and others, c. 1000). Norse traders (**Varangians**) developed Russian river commerce from the 8th to the 11th cent. and helped set up a state at Kiev in the late 9th cent. Conversion to Christianity occurred in the 10th cent., reaching Sweden 100 years later. In the 11th cent. Norman bands conquered S Italy and Sicily, and Duke **William of Normandy** conquered (1066) England, bringing feudal government and the French language, essential elements in later English civilization.

Central and East Europe. Slavs began to expand from about 150 CE in all directions in Europe, and by the 7th cent. they reached as far S as the Adriatic and Aegean seas. In the Balkan Peninsula they dislocated Romanized local populations or assimilated newcomers (Bulgarians, a Turkic people). The first **Slavic states** were Moravia (628) in Central Europe and the Bulgarian state (680) in the Balkans. Missions of St. Methodius and Cyril (whose Greek-based cyrillic alphabet is still used by some S and E Slavs) converted (863) Moravia.

The Eastern Slavs, part-civilized under the overlordship of the Turkish-Jewish **Khazar** trading empire (7th-10th cent.), gravitated toward Constantinople by the 9th cent. The **Kievan state** adopted (989) Eastern Christianity under Prince Vladimir. King Boleslav I (992-1025) began **Poland's** long history of eastern conquest. The Magyars (**Hungarians**), in present-day Hungary since 896, accepted (1001) Latin Christianity.

Germany. The German kingdom that emerged after the breakup of Charlemagne's W Empire remained a confederation of largely autonomous states. Otto I, a Saxon who was king from 936, established the **Holy Roman Empire**—a union of Germany and N Italy—in alliance with Pope John XII, who crowned (962) him emperor; he defeated (955) the Magyars. Imperial power was greatest under the **Hohenstaufens** (1138-1254), despite the growing opposition of the papacy, which ruled central Italy, and the Lombard League cities. Frederick II (1194-1250) improved administration and patronized the arts; after his death, German influence was removed from Italy.

Christian Spain. From its N mountain redoubts, Christian rule slowly migrated S through the 11th cent., when Muslim unity collapsed. After the capture (1085) of **Toledo,** the kingdoms of Portugal, Castile, and Aragon undertook repeated crusades of reconquest, finally completed in 1492. Elements of Islamic civilization persisted in recaptured areas, influencing all Western Europe.

Major Norse Gods & Goddesses

Name	Relations	Sphere or Position	Emblem/Attribute
Odin	Father of the Aesir (gods)	War and death, poetry, wisdom, magic	Spear, mead, ring/One-eyed
Thor	Son of Odin	Thunder, lightning, rain; champion of the gods	Hammer, belt
Njord	Father of Freyja & Freyr	Wind and sea, wealth and prosperity	——
Frigg	Wife of Odin	Marriage and motherhood, home	——
Freyja (Freya)	Daughter of Njord	Fertility, birth, crops	Necklace
Freyr	Son of Njord	Agriculture, sun, rain	Magic ship, golden boar
Tyr	Son of Odin[1]	Justice, war	Spear/One-handed
Heimdall	Son of nine giantesses	Watchman of the gods; keen sight & hearing	Horn
Balder (Baldur)	Son of Odin	Light, purity	——
Loki	Son of giants; father of Hel (goddess of death), Jormungand (serpent encompassing the world), Fenrir (the wolf).	Malicious trickster	——

(1) Referred to as the son of Hymir in some mythologies.

Chartres Cathedral

Crusades. Pope Urban II called for a crusade (1095) to restore Asia Minor to Byzantium and the Holy Land to Christendom, respectively. This first crusade captured Jerusalem and led to the foundation of 4 Frankish states in the Levant. The defeat inflicted upon crusaders at the Battle of Hattin (1187) by **Saladin** (c. 1137-93), the Kurdish ruler of Egypt and Syria, effectively negated territorial gains. Many crusades followed until 1291. The 4th crusade sacked Constantinople (1204). Other crusades were launched against Christian heretics (Albigensian Crusade, 1229), pagans, and enemies of the papacy.

Economy. The agricultural base of European life benefited from improvements in **plow design** (c. 1000) and by draining of lowlands and clearing of forests, leading to a rural population increase. Towns grew in N Italy, Flanders, and N Germany (Hanseatic League). Improvements in **loom design** permitted factory textile production. **Guilds** dominated urban trades from the 12th cent. Banking (centered in Italy, 12th-15th cent.) facilitated long-distance trade.

The Church. The split between the Eastern and Western churches was formalized in 1054. Western and Central Europe was divided into 500 bishoprics under one united hierarchy, but conflicts between secular and church authorities were frequent (German **Investiture Controversy**, 1075-1122). Clerical power was first strengthened through the international monastic reform begun at Cluny in 910. Popular religious enthusiasm often expressed itself in heretical movements (Waldensians from 1173), but was channeled by the **Dominican** (1215) and **Franciscan** (1223) friars into the religious mainstream.

Arts. Romanesque architecture (9th-mid-12th cent.) expanded on late Roman models, using the rounded arch and massed stone to support enlarged basilicas. Painting and sculpture followed Byzantine models. The literature of **chivalry** was exemplified by the epic (*Chanson de Roland*, c. 1100) and by courtly love poems of the troubadours of Provence and minnesingers of Germany. **Gothic** architecture emerged in France (choir of St. Denis, c. 1140) and spread along with French cultural influence. Rib vaulting and pointed arches were used to combine soaring heights with delicacy, and they freed walls for display of stained glass. Exteriors were covered with painted relief sculpture and embellished with elaborate architectural detail.

Learning. Law, medicine, and philosophy were advanced at independent **universities** (Bologna, Paris, 12th cent.), originally corporations of students and masters. Twelfth-cent. translations of Greek classics, especially Aristotle, encouraged an analytic approach. Scholastic philosophy, from Anselm (1033-1109) to **Aquinas** (1225-74), attempted to understand revelation through reason.

Apogee of Central Asian Power and the Spread of Islam: 1250-1500

Turks. Turkic peoples, of Central Asian ancestry, were a military threat to the Byzantine and Persian Empires from the 6th cent. After several waves of invasions, during which most of the Turks adopted Islam, the **Seljuk Turks** took (1055) Baghdad. They ruled Persia, Iraq and, after 1071, Asia Minor, where massive numbers of Turks settled. The empire was divided in the 12th cent. into smaller states ruled by Seljuks, Kurds, and Mamluks (a military caste of former Turk, Kurd, and Circassian slaves), which governed Egypt and the Middle East until the Ottoman era (c. 1290-1922).

Osman I (r. c. 1290-1326) and succeeding sultans united Anatolian Turkish warriors in a militaristic state that waged holy war against Byzantium and Balkan Christians. Most of the Balkans had been subdued, and Anatolia united, when Constantinople fell (1453). By the mid-16th cent., Hungary, the Middle East, and N Africa had been conquered. The Turkish advance was stopped at Vienna (1529) and at the naval battle of Lepanto (1571) by Spain, Venice, and the papacy.

The Ottoman state was governed in accordance with orthodox Muslim law. Greek, Armenian, and Jewish communities were segregated and were ruled by religious leaders responsible for taxation; they dominated trade. State offices and most army ranks were filled by slaves through a system of child conscription among Christians.

India. Mahmud of Ghazni (971-1030) led repeated Turkish raids into N India. Turkish power was consolidated in 1206 with the start of the **Sultanate at Delhi**. Centralization of state power under the early Delhi sultans went far beyond traditional Indian practice. Muslim rule of most of the subcontinent lasted until the British conquest 600 years later.

Mongols. Genghis Khan (c. 1167-1227) first united the feuding Mongol tribes, and built their armies into an effective offensive force around a core of highly mobile cavalry. He and his immediate successors created the largest land empire in history; by 1279 it stretched from the E coast of Asia to the Danube, from the Siberian steppes to the Arabian Sea. East-West trade and contacts were facilitated (Marco Polo, c. 1254-1324).

The western Mongols were Islamized by 1295; successor states soon lost their Mongol character by assimilation. They were briefly reunited under the Turk Tamerlane (1336-1405).

Kublai Khan ruled China from his new capital Beijing (est. c. 1264). Naval campaigns against Japan (1274, 1281) and Java (1293) were defeated, the latter by the Hindu-Buddhist maritime kingdom of Majapahit. The **Yuan** dynasty used Mongols and other foreigners (including Europeans) in official posts and tolerated the return of Nestorian Christianity (suppressed 841-45) and the spread of Islam in the S and W. A native reaction expelled the Mongols in 1367-68.

Russia. The Kievan state in Russia, weakened by the decline of Byzantium and the rise of the Catholic Polish-Lithuanian state, was overrun (1238-40) by the Mongols. Only the northern trading republic of Novgorod remained independent. The grand dukes of Moscow emerged as leaders of a coalition of princes that eventually (by 1481) defeated the Mongols. After the fall of Constantinople in 1453, the **Tsars** (Caesars) at Moscow (from Ivan III, r. 1462-1505) set up an independent Russian Orthodox Church. Commerce failed to revive. The isolated Russian state remained agrarian, with the peasant class falling into serfdom.

Persia. A revival of Persian literature, making use of the Arab alphabet and literary forms, began in the 10th cent. (epic of Firdausi, 935-1020). An art revival, influenced by Chinese styles introduced after the Mongols came to power in Iran, began in the 13th cent. Persian cultural and political forms, and often the Persian language, were used for centuries by Turkish and Mongol elites from the Balkans to India. Persian mystics from Rumi (1207-73) to Jami (1414-92) promoted **Sufism** in their poetry.

Africa. Two militant Islamic Berber dynasties emerged from the Sahara to carve out empires from the Sahel to central Spain—the **Almoravids** (c. 1050-1140) and the fanatical **Almohads** (c. 1125-1269). The Ghanaian empire was replaced in the upper Niger by Mali (c. 1230-1340), whose Muslim rulers imported Egyptians to help make **Timbuktu** a center of commerce (in gold, leather, and slaves) and learning. The Songhay empire (to 1590) replaced Mali. To the S, forest kingdoms produced refined artworks (Ife terra cotta, **Benin** bronzes).

Other **Muslim states** in Nigeria (Hausas) and Chad originated in the 11th cent. and continued in some form until the 19th-cent. European conquest. Less-developed Bantu kingdoms existed across central Africa.

Some 40 Muslim Arab-Persian trading colonies and city-states were established all along the E African coast from the 10th cent. (Kilwa, Mogadishu). The interchange with Bantu peoples produced the **Swahili** language and culture. Gold, palm oil, and slaves were brought from the interior, stimulating the growth of the Monamatapa kingdom of the Zambezi (15th cent.). The Christian Ethiopian empire (from 13th cent.) continued the traditions of Axum.

Southeast Asia. Islam was introduced into Malaya and the Indonesian islands by Arab, Persian, and Indian traders. Coastal Muslim cities and states (starting before 1300) soon dominated the interior. Chief among these was the **Malacca** state (c. 1400-1511), on the Malay peninsula.

Arts and Statecraft Thrive in Europe: 1350-1600

Italy. Distinctive Italian achievements in literature and fine arts during the late Middle Ages (**Dante,** 1265-1321; Giotto, 1276-1337) led to the vigorous new styles of the Renaissance (14th-16th cent.). Patronized by the rulers of the quarreling petty states of Italy (**Medicis** in Florence and the papacy, c. 1400-1737), the plastic arts perfected realistic techniques, including **perspective** (Masaccio, 1401-28, **Leonardo da Vinci,** 1452-1519). Classical motifs were used in architecture, and increased talent and expense were put into secular buildings. The Florentine dialect was refined as a national literary language (**Petrarch,** 1304-74). Greek refugees from the E strengthened the respect of humanist scholars for the classic sources. Soon an international movement aided by the spread of **printing** (Gutenberg, c. 1397(?)-1468), **humanism** was optimistic about the power of human reason (Erasmus of Rotterdam, 1466-1536, **More's** *Utopia,* 1516) and valued individual effort in the arts and in politics (**Machiavelli,** 1469-1527).

France. The French monarchy, strengthened in its repeated struggles with powerful nobles (Burgundy, Flanders, Aquitaine) by alliances with the growing commercial towns, consolidated bureaucratic control under Philip IV (r. 1285-1314) and extended French influence into Germany and Italy (popes at Avignon, France, 1309-1417). The **Hundred Years War** (1337-1453) ended English dynastic claims in France (battles of Crécy, 1346, and Poitiers, 1356; Joan of Arc executed, 1431). A French Renaissance, dating from royal invasions (1494, 1499) of Italy, was encouraged at the court of Francis I (r. 1515-47), who centralized taxation and law. French vernacular literature consciously asserted its independence (La Pléiade, 1549).

Henry VIII

England. The evolution of England's unique political institutions began with the **Magna Carta** (1215), by which King John guaranteed the privileges of nobles and church against the monarchy and assured jury trial. After the **Wars of the Roses** (1455-85), the **Tudor dynasty** reasserted royal prerogatives (Henry VIII, r. 1509-47), but the trend toward independent departments and ministerial government also continued. English trade (wool exports from c. 1340) was protected by the nation's growing maritime power (**Spanish Armada** destroyed, 1588).

English replaced French and Latin in the late 14th cent. in law and literature (**Chaucer,** c. 1340-1400) and English translation of the Bible began (Wycliffe, 1380s). **Elizabeth I** (r. 1558-1603) presided over a confident flowering of poetry (Spenser, 1552-99), drama (**Shakespeare,** 1564-1616), and music.

German Empire. From among a welter of minor feudal states, church lands, and independent cities, the **Habsburgs** assembled a far-flung territorial domain, based in Austria from 1276. Family members held the title of Holy Roman Emperor from 1438 to the Empire's dissolution in 1806, but failed to centralize its domains, leaving Germany disunited for centuries. Resistance to Turkish expansion brought Hungary under Austrian control from the 16th cent. The Netherlands, Luxembourg, and Burgundy were added in 1477, curbing French expansion.

The Flemish painting tradition of naturalism, technical proficiency, and bourgeois subject matter began in the 15th cent. (**Jan Van Eyck,** c. 1390-1441), the earliest northern manifestation of the Renaissance. Albrecht **Dürer** (1471-1528) typified the merging of late Gothic and Italian trends in 16th-cent. German art. Imposing civic architecture flourished in the prosperous commercial cities.

Spain. Despite the unification of Castile and Aragon in 1479, the 2 countries retained separate governments, and the nobility, especially in Aragon and Catalonia, retained many privileges. Spanish lands in Italy (Naples, Sicily) and the Netherlands entangled the country in European wars through the mid-17th cent., while explorers, traders, and conquerors built up a Spanish empire in the Americas and the Philippines.

From the late 15th cent., a **golden age** of literature and art produced works of social satire (plays of Lope de Vega, 1562-1635; **Cervantes,** 1547-1616), as well as spiritual intensity (**El Greco,** 1541-1614; **Velazquez,** 1599-1660).

Black Death. The bubonic plague reached Europe from the E in 1348, killing up to half the population by 1350 (and recurring periodically in most areas until the early 18th cent. Labor scarcity forced wages to rise and brought greater freedom to the peasantry, making possible **peasant uprisings** (Jacquerie in France, 1358; Wat Tyler's rebellion in England, 1381).

Explorations. Organized European maritime exploration began, seeking to evade the Venice-Ottoman monopoly of E trade and to promote Christianity. Beginning in 1418, expeditions from Portugal explored the W coast of Africa, until Vasco da Gama rounded the Cape of Good Hope in 1497 and reached India. A Portuguese trading empire was consolidated by the seizure of Goa (1510) and Malacca (1551). Japan was reached in 1542. The voyages of Christopher **Columbus** (1492-1504) uncovered a world new to Europeans, which Spain hastened to subdue. Navigation schools in Spain and Portugal, the development of large sailing ships (carracks) mounted with cannons, and the invention (c. 1475) of the rifle aided European penetration.

Christopher Columbus

Mughals and Safavids. E of the Ottoman Empire, 2 Muslim dynasties ruled unchallenged in the 16th and 17th cent. The Mughal dynasty of India, founded by Persianized Turkish invaders from the NW under Babur, dates from their 1526 conquest of the Delhi Sultanate. The dynasty ruled most of India for more than 200 years, surviving nominally until 1857. **Akbar** (r. 1556-1605) consolidated administration at his glorious court, where the Urdu language (Persian-influenced Hindi) developed. Trade relations with Europe increased. Under Shah Jahan (1629-58), a secularized art fusing Hindu and Muslim elements flourished in miniature painting and in architecture (**Taj Mahal**). **Sikhism** (founded c. 1519) combined elements of both faiths. Suppression of Hindus and Shi'ite Muslims in S India in the late 17th cent. weakened the empire.

Taj Mahal

Fanatical devotion to the Shi'ite sect characterized the Safavids (1502-1736) of Persia and led to hostilities with the Sunni Ottomans for more than a century. The prosperity and the strength of the empire are evidenced by the mosques at its capital city, **Isfahan.** The Safavids enhanced Iranian national consciousness.

China. The **Ming** emperors (1368-1644), the last native dynasty in China, wielded unprecedented personal power, while the Confucian bureaucracy began to suffer from inertia. European trade (Portuguese monopoly through **Macao** from 1557) was strictly controlled. Jesuit scholars and scientists (Matteo Ricci, 1552-1610) introduced some Western science; their writings familiarized the West with China. Chinese technological inventiveness declined from

this era, but the arts thrived, especially in the areas of painting and ceramics.

Japan. After the decline of the first hereditary shogunate (chief generalship) at **Kamakura** (1185-1333), fragmentation of power accelerated, as did the consequent social mobility. Under Kamakura and the Ashikaga shogunate (1338-1573), the daimyos (lords) and samurai (warriors) grew more powerful and promoted a martial ideology. Japanese pirates and traders plied the China coast. Popular Buddhist movements included the nationalist Nichiren sect (from c. 1250) and **Zen** (brought from China, 1191), which stressed meditation and a disciplined esthetic (tea ceremony, gardening, martial arts, *No* drama).

Reformed Europe Expands Overseas: 1500-1700

Reformation. Theological debate and protests against real and perceived clerical corruption existed in the medieval Christian world, expressed by such dissenters as John **Wycliffe** (c. 1320-84) and his followers (the Lollards) in England, and **Huss** (burned as a heretic, 1415) in Bohemia.

Martin Luther

Martin **Luther** (1483-1546) preached that faith alone leads to salvation, without the mediation of clergy or good works. He attacked the authority of the pope, rejected priestly celibacy, and recommended individual study of the Bible (which he translated into German c. 1525). His 95 Theses (1517) led to his excommunication (1521). John **Calvin** (1509-64) said that God's elect were predestined for salvation and all others for damnation; good conduct and success were signs of election. Calvin in Geneva and John **Knox** (1505-72) in Scotland established theocratic states.

Henry VIII asserted English national authority and secular power by breaking away (1534) from the Catholic Church, creating what would become the Anglican Church. Monastic property was confiscated, and some Protestant doctrines given official sanction.

Religious wars. A century and a half of religious wars began with a S German peasant uprising (1524), repressed with Luther's support. Radical sects—democratic, pacifist, millennarian—arose (Anabaptists ruled Münster in 1534-35) and were suppressed violently. Civil war in France from 1562 between **Huguenots** (Protestant nobles and merchants) and Catholics ended with the 1598 **Edict of Nantes,** tolerating Protestants (revoked 1685). Habsburg attempts to restore Catholicism in Germany were resisted in 25 years of fighting; the 1555 Peace of Augsburg guarantee of religious independence to local princes and cities was confirmed only after the **Thirty Years War** (1618-48), when much of Germany was devastated by local and foreign armies (Sweden, France).

A Catholic Reformation, or **Counter Reformation**, met the Protestant challenge, defining an official theology at the Council of Trent (1545-63). The **Jesuit** order (Society of Jesus), founded in 1534 by Ignatius Loyola (1491-1556), helped reconvert large areas of Poland, Hungary, and S Germany and sent missionaries to the New World, India, and China, while the **Inquisition** suppressed heresy in Catholic countries. A revival of religious fervor appeared in the devotional literature (Teresa of Avila, 1515-82) and in grandiose **Baroque** art (Bernini, 1598-1680).

Scientific Revolution. The late nominalist thinkers (Ockham, c. 1300-49) of Paris and Oxford challenged Aristotelian orthodoxy, allowing for a freer scientific approach. At the same time, metaphysical values, such as the Neoplatonic faith in an orderly, mathematical cosmos, still motivated and directed inquiry. Nicolaus **Copernicus** (1473-1543) promoted the heliocentric theory, which was

confirmed when Johannes **Kepler** (1571-1630) discovered the mathematical laws describing the elliptical orbits of the planets. The traditional Christian-Aristotelian belief that the heavens and the earth were fundamentally different collapsed when **Galileo** (1564-1642) discovered moving sunspots, irregular moon topography, and moons around Jupiter, though he

Copernicus

did face religious opposition (Galileo's retraction, 1633). He and Sir Isaac **Newton** (1642-1727) developed a mechanics that unified cosmic and earthly phenomena. Newton and Gottfried von **Leibniz** (1646-1716) invented calculus. René **Descartes** (1596-1650), best known for his influential philosophy, also invented analytic geometry.

An explosion of **observational science** included the discovery of blood circulation (Harvey, 1578-1657) and microscopic life (Leeuwenhoek, 1632-1723) and advances in anatomy (Vesalius, 1514-64, dissected corpses) and chemistry (Boyle, 1627-91). Scientific research institutes were founded: Florence (1657), London (**Royal Society**, 1660), Paris (1666). Inventions proliferated (Savery's steam engine, 1696).

Arts. Mannerist trends of the High Renaissance (**Michelangelo**, 1475-1564) exploited virtuosity, grace, novelty, and exotic subjects and poses. The notion of artistic genius was promoted. Private connoisseurs entered the art market. These trends were elaborated in the 17th cent. **Baroque** era on a grander scale. Dynamic movement in painting and sculpture was emphasized by sharp lighting effects, rich materials (colored marble, gilt), and realistic details. Curved facades, broken lines, rich detail, and ceiling decoration characterized Baroque architecture. Monarchs, princes, and prelates, usually Catholic, used Baroque art to enhance and embellish their authority, as in royal portraits (Velazquez, 1599-1660; Van Dyck, 1599-1641).

National styles emerged. In France, a taste for rectilinear order and serenity (Poussin, 1594-1665), linked to the new rational philosophy, was expressed in classical forms. The influence of **classical values** in French literature (tragedies of **Racine**, 1639-99) gave rise to the "battle of the Ancients and Moderns." New forms included the essay (**Montaigne**, 1533-92) and novel (*Princesse de Cleves*, La Fayette, 1678).

Dutch painting of the 17th cent. was unique in its wide social distribution. The Flemish tradition of undemonstrative realism reached its peak in **Rembrandt** (1606-69) and Jan Vermeer (1632-75).

Economy. European economic expansion, known as the **commercial revolution**, was stimulated by the new trade with the East, by New World gold and silver, and by a doubling of population (50 million in 1450, 100 million in 1600). **New business and financial techniques** were developed and refined, such as joint-stock companies, insurance, and letters of credit and exchange. The Bank of Amsterdam (1609) and the Bank of England (1694) broke the old monopoly of private banking families. The rise of a business mentality was typified by the spread of clock towers in cities in the 14th cent. By the mid-15th cent., portable clocks were available; the first watch was invented in 1502.

By 1650, most governments had adopted the **mercantile system**, in which they sought to amass metallic wealth by protecting merchants' foreign and colonial trade monopolies. The rise in prices and the new coin-based economy undermined craft guild and feudal manorial systems. Expanding industries (clothweaving, mining) benefited from technical advances. Coal replaced wood as the chief fuel; it was used to fuel new 16th-cent. blast furnaces making cast iron.

New World. The **Aztecs** united much of the Meso-American area in a militarist empire by 1519, from their capital, Tenochtitlán (pop. 300,000), which was the center of a cult requiring ritual human sacrifice. Most of the civilized areas of South America were ruled by the centralized Inca Empire (1476-1534), stretching 2,000 mi from Ecuador to NW Argentina. Lavish and sophisticated traditions in pottery, weaving, sculpture, and architecture were maintained in both regions.

These empires, beset by revolts, fell in 2 short campaigns to gold-seeking Spanish forces based in the Antilles and Panama. Hernan **Cortes** took Mexico (1519-21); Francisco **Pizarro,** Peru (1532-35). From these centers, land and sea expeditions claimed most of North and South America for Spain. The indigenous high cultures did not survive the impact of **Christian missionaries** and the new upper class of whites and mestizos. Although the Spanish administration intermittently concerned itself with their welfare, the population was reduced by European diseases and remained impoverished at most levels. New World silver and such native products as potatoes, tobacco, corn, peanuts, chocolate, and rubber exercised a major economic influence on Europe.

Brazil, which the Portuguese reached in 1500 and settled after 1530, and the Caribbean colonies of several European nations developed a plantation economy where sugarcane, tobacco, cotton, coffee, rice, indigo, and lumber were grown by slaves. From the early 16th to late 19th cent., 10 million Africans were transported to **slavery** in the New World.

Netherlands. The urban, Calvinist N provinces of the Netherlands rebelled (1568) against Habsburg Spain and founded an oligarchic mercantile republic. Their control of the Baltic grain market enabled them to exploit Mediterranean food shortages. Religious refugees—French and Belgian Protestants, Iberian Jews—added to the commercial talent pool. After Spain absorbed Portugal (1580), the Dutch seized Portuguese possessions and created a vast but short-lived commercial empire in Brazil, the Antilles, Africa, India, Ceylon, Malacca, Indonesia, and Taiwan. The Dutch also challenged or supplanted Portuguese traders in China and Japan. Revolution in 1640 restored Portuguese independence.

England. Anglicanism became firmly established under **Elizabeth I** after a brief Catholic interlude under "Bloody

Mary" (1553-58). But religious and political conflicts led to a rebellion (1642) by Parliament. Forces of the Roundheads (Puritans) defeated the Cavaliers (Royalists); Charles I was beheaded (1649). The new Commonwealth was ruled as a military dictatorship by Oliver **Cromwell,** who also brutally crushed (1649-51) an Irish rebellion. Conflicts within the Puritan camp (democratic Levelers defeated, 1649) aided the Stuart restoration (1660), but Parliament was strengthened and the peaceful **"Glorious Revolution"** (1688) advanced political and religious liberties (writings of **Locke,** 1632-1704). British privateers (Drake, 1540-96) challenged Spanish control of the New World and penetrated Asian trade routes (Madras taken, 1639). North American colonies (Jamestown, 1607; Plymouth, 1620) provided an outlet for religious dissenters from Europe.

Elizabeth I

France. Emerging from the religious civil wars in 1628, France regained military and commercial great power status (under the ministries of **Richelieu,** Mazarin, and Colbert). Under **Louis XIV** (reigned 1643-1715), royal absolutism triumphed over nobles and local *parlements* (defeat of Fronde, 1648-53). Permanent colonies were founded in Canada (1608), the Caribbean (1626), and India (1674).

Sweden. Sweden seceded from the Scandinavian Union in 1523. The thinly populated agrarian state (with copper, iron, and timber exports) was united by the Vasa kings, whose conquests by the mid-17th cent. made Sweden the dominant Baltic power. The empire collapsed in the Great Northern War (1700-21).

Poland. After the union with Lithuania in 1447, Poland ruled vast territories from the Baltic to the Black Sea, resisting German and Turkish incursions. Catholic nobles failed to gain the loyalty of their Orthodox Christian subjects in the E; commerce and trades were practiced by German and Jewish immigrants. The bloody 1648-49 Cossack uprising began the kingdom's dismemberment.

China. A new dynasty, the **Manchus,** invaded from the NE, seized power in 1644, and expanded Chinese control to its greatest extent in Central and SE Asia. Trade and diplomatic contact with Europe grew, carefully controlled by China. New crops (sweet potato, maize, peanut) allowed an economic and population growth (pop. 300 million, in 1800). Traditional arts and literature were pursued with increased sophistication (*Dream of the Red Chamber*, novel, mid-18th cent.).

Japan. Tokugawa Ieyasu, shogun from 1603, finally unified and pacified feudal Japan. Hereditary daimyos and samurai monopolized government office and the professions. An urban merchant class grew, literacy spread, and a cultural renaissance occurred (**haiku,** a verse innovation of the poet Basho, 1644-94). Fear of European domination led to persecution of Christian converts from 1597 and to stringent isolation from outside contact from 1640.

Philosophy, Industry, and Revolution: 1700-1800

Science and Reason. Greater faith in reason and empirical observation, instead of tradition and religious beliefs, espoused since the Renaissance (Francis Bacon, 1561-1626), was bolstered by scientific discoveries. René **Descartes** (1596-1650) used a rationalistic approach modeled on geometry and introspection to discover "self-evident" truths as a foundation of knowledge. Sir Isaac **Newton** emphasized induction from experimental observation. Baruch de **Spinoza** (1632-77), who called for political and intellectual freedom, developed a systematic rationalistic philosophy in his classic work *Ethics*.

French philosophers assumed leadership of the **Enlightenment** in the 18th cent. Montesquieu (1689-1755) used British history to support his notions of limited government. **Voltaire's** (1694-1778) diaries and novels of exotic travel illustrated the intellectual trends toward secular ethics and relativism. Jean-Jacques **Rousseau's** (1712-1778) radical concepts of the **social contract** and of the inherent goodness of the common man gave impetus to antimonarchical republicanism. The *Encyclopedia* (1751-72, edited by Diderot and d'Alembert), designed as a monument to reason, was largely devoted to practical technology.

In England, ideals of liberty were connected with empiricist philosophy and science in the followers of John **Locke**. But British empiricism, especially as developed by the skeptical David **Hume** (1711-76), radically reduced the role of reason in philosophy, as did the evolutionary approach to law and politics of Edmund Burke (1729-97) and the utilitarian ethics of Jeremy Bentham (1748-1832). Adam Smith (1723-90) and other **physiocrats** called for a rationalization of economic activity by removing artificial barriers to a supposedly natural free exchange of goods known as **laissez-faire**.

German writers participated in the new philosophical trends popularized by Christian von Wolff (1679-1754). Immanuel Kant's (1724-1804) transcendental idealism, unifying an empirical epistemology with a priori moral and

Benjamin Franklin

logical concepts, directed German thought away from skepticism. Italian contributions included work on electricity (Galvani, 1737-98; Volta, 1745-1827), the pioneer historiography of Vico (1668-1744), and writings on penal reform (Beccaria, 1738-94). Benjamin Franklin (1706-90) was celebrated in Europe for his varied achievements.

The growth of the **press** (*Spectator*, 1711-12) and the wide distribution of realistic but sentimental **novels** attested to the increase of a large bourgeois public.

Arts. Rococo art, characterized by extravagant decorative effects, asymmetries copied from organic models, and artificial pastoral subjects, was favored by the continental aristocracy for most of the cent. (Watteau, 1684-1721) and had musical analogies in the ornamentalized polyphony of late Baroque. The **Neoclassical** art after 1750, associated with the new scientific archaeology, was more streamlined and was infused with the supposed moral and geometric rectitude of the Roman Republic (David, 1748-1825). In England, **town planning** on a grand scale began.

Industrial Revolution in England. Agricultural improvements, such as the sowing drill (1701) and livestock breeding, were implemented on the large fields provided by enclosure of common lands by private owners. Profits from agriculture and from colonial and foreign trade (1800 volume, £54 million) were channeled through hundreds of banks and the **Stock Exchange** (est. 1773) into new industrial processes.

The Newcomen steam pump (1712) aided coal mining. Coal fueled the new efficient steam engines patented by James Watt in 1769, and coke-smelting produced cheap, sturdy iron for machinery by the 1730s. The **flying shuttle** (1733) and **spinning jenny** (c. 1764) were used in the large new cotton textile factories, where women and children were much of the work force. Goods were transported cheaply over **canals** (2,000 mi; built 1760-1800).

American Revolution. The British colonies in North America attracted a mass immigration of religious dissenters and poor people throughout the 17th and 18th cent., coming from the British Isles, Germany, the Netherlands, and other countries. The population reached 3 million non-natives by the 1770s. The small native population was greatly reduced by European diseases and by wars with the various colonies. British attempts to control colonial trade and to tax the colonists to pay for the costs of colonial administration and defense clashed with notions of local self-government and eventually provoked the colonies to rebellion.

Central and East Europe. The monarchs of the three states that dominated E Europe—Austria, Prussia, and Russia—accepted the advice and legitimation of philosophes in creating modern, centralized institutions in their kingdoms, which were enlarged by the division (1772-95) of Poland.

Under **Frederick II** (called the Great) (r. 1740-86) Prussia, with its efficient modern army, doubled in size. State monopolies and tariff protection fostered industry, and some legal reforms were introduced. Austria's heterogeneous realms were unified under **Maria Theresa** (r. 1740-80) and **Joseph II** (r. 1780-90). Reforms in education, law, and religion were enacted, and the Austrian serfs were freed (1781). With its defeat in the Seven Years' War in 1763, Austria failed to regain Silesia, which had been seized by Prussia, but it was compensated by expansion to the E and S (Hungary, Slavonia, 1699; Galicia, 1772).

Russia, whose borders continued to expand, adopted some Western bureaucratic and economic policies under **Peter I** (r. 1682-1725) and **Catherine II** (r. 1762-96). Trade and cultural contacts with the West multiplied from the new Baltic Sea capital, **St. Petersburg** (est. 1703).

French Revolution. The growing French middle class lacked political power and resented aristocratic tax privileges, especially in light of the successful American Revolution. Peasants lacked adequate land and were burdened with feudal obligations to nobles. War with Britain led to the loss of French Canada and drained the treasury, finally forcing the king to call the **Estates-General** in 1789 (first time since 1614), in an atmosphere of food riots (poor crop in 1788).

Aristocratic resistance to absolutism was soon overshadowed by the reformist Third Estate (middle class), which proclaimed itself the **National Constituent Assembly** June 17 and took the "Tennis Court oath" on June 20 to secure a constitution. The storming of the **Bastille** on July 14, 1789, by Parisian artisans was followed by looting and seizure of aristocratic property throughout France. Assembly reforms included abolition of class and regional privileges, a Declaration of Rights, suffrage by taxpayers (75% of males), and the **Civil Constitution of the Clergy** providing for election and loyalty oaths for priests. A republic was declared Sept. 22, 1792, in spite of royalist pressure from Austria and Prussia, which had declared war in April (joined by Britain the next year). Louis XVI was beheaded Jan. 21, 1793, and Queen Marie Antoinette was beheaded Oct. 16, 1793.

Royalist uprisings in La Vendée and military reverses led to institution of a **reign of terror** in which tens of thousands of opponents of the Revolution and criminals were executed. Radical reforms in the **Convention** period (Sept. 1793-Oct. 1795) included the abolition of colonial slavery, economic measures to aid the poor, support of public education, and a short-lived de-Christianization.

Napoleon Bonaparte

Division among radicals (execution of Hebert, Danton, and Robespierre, 1794) aided the ascendancy of a moderate **Directory**, which consolidated military victories. **Napoleon Bonaparte** (1769-1821), a popular young general, exploited political divisions and participated in a coup Nov. 9, 1799, making himself first consul (dictator).

India. Sikh and Hindu rebels (Rajputs, Marathas) and Afghans destroyed the power of the Mughals during the 18th cent. After France's defeat (1763) in the Seven Years' War, Britain was the primary European trade power in India. Its control of inland **Bengal and Bihar** was recognized (1765) by the Mughal shah, who granted the **British East India Co.** (under Clive, 1725-74) the right to collect land revenue there. Despite objections from Parliament (1784 India Act), the company's involvement in local wars and politics led to repeated acquisitions of new territory. The company exported Indian textiles, sugar, and indigo.

Nationalism Gathers Momentum: 1800-40

French ideals and empire spread. Inspired by the ideals of the French Revolution, and supported by the expanding French armies, new republican regimes arose near France: the **Batavian** Republic in the Netherlands (1795-1806), the **Helvetic** Republic in Switzerland (1798-1803), the **Cisalpine** Republic in N Italy (1797-1805), the **Ligurian** Republic in Genoa (1797-1805), and the **Parthenopean** Republic in S Italy (1799). A Roman Republic existed briefly in 1798 after Pope Pius VI was arrested by French troops. In Italy and Germany, new nationalist sentiments were stimulated both in imitation of and in reaction to developments in France (anti-French and anti-Jacobin peasant uprisings in Italy, 1796-99).

From 1804, when Napoleon declared himself emperor, to 1812, a succession of military victories (Austerlitz, 1805; Jena, 1806) extended his control over most of Europe, through puppet states (**Confederation of the Rhine** united W German states for the first time and **Grand Duchy of Warsaw** revived Polish national hopes), expansion of the empire, and alliances.

Among the lasting reforms initiated under Napoleon's absolutist reign were: establishment of the Bank of France, centralization of tax collection, codification of law along Roman models (Code Napoléon), and reform and extension of secondary and university education. In an 1801 concordat, the papacy recognized the effective autonomy of the French Catholic Church.

Napoleon's continental successes were offset by British victory under Adm. Horatio Nelson in the **Battle of Trafalgar** (1805).

In all, some 400,000 French soldiers were killed in the Napoleonic Wars, along with about 600,000 foreign troops.

Last gasp of old regime. The disastrous 1812 invasion of Russia exposed Napoleon's overextension. After Napoleon's 1814 exile at Elba, his armies were defeated (1815) at **Waterloo**, by British and Prussian troops.

At the **Congress of Vienna**, the monarchs and princes of Europe redrew their boundaries, to the advantage of Prussia (in Saxony and the Ruhr), Austria (in Illyria and Venetia), and Russia (in Poland and Finland). British conquest of Dutch and French colonies (S Africa, Ceylon, Mauritius) was recognized, and France, under the restored Bourbons, retained its expanded 1792 borders. The settlement brought 50 years of international peace to Europe.

But the Congress was unable to check the advance of liberal ideals and of nationalism among the smaller European nations. The 1825 **Decembrist uprising** by liberal officers in Russia was easily suppressed. But an independence movement in **Greece**, stirred by commercial prosperity and a cultural revival, succeeded in expelling Ottoman rule by 1831, with the aid of Britain, France, and Russia.

A constitutional monarchy was secured in France by the **1830 Revolution**; Louis Philippe became king. The revolutionary contagion spread to **Belgium**, which gained its independence (1830) from the Dutch monarchy, to **Poland**, whose rebellion was defeated (1830-31) by Russia, and to Germany.

Romanticism. A new style in intellectual and artistic life replaced Neoclassicism and Rococo after the mid-18th cent. By the early 19th cent., Romanticism prevailed in Europe.

Rousseau had begun the reaction against rationalism; in education (*Émile*, 1762) he stressed subjective spontaneity

over regularized instruction. German writers (Lessing, 1729-81; Herder, 1744-1803) favorably compared the German folk song to classical forms and began a cult of Shakespeare, whose passion and "natural" wisdom was a model for the romantic *Sturm und Drang* (Storm and Stress) movement. **Goethe's** *Sorrows of Young Werther* (1774) set the model for the tragic, passionate genius.

A new interest in **Gothic architecture** in England after 1760 (Walpole, 1717-97) spread through Europe, associated with an aesthetic Christian and mystic revival (**Blake,** 1757-1827). Celtic, Norse, and German mythology and folk tales were revived or imitated (Macpherson's Ossian translation, 1762; Grimm's Fairy Tales, 1812-22). The medieval revival (Scott's *Ivanhoe*, 1819) led to a new interest in history, stressing national differences and organic growth (**Carlyle,** 1795-1881; Michelet, 1798-1874), corresponding to theories of natural evolution (Lamarck's *Philosophie Zoologique*, 1809; Lyell's *Geology*, 1830-33). A reaction against classicism characterized the English **romantic poets** (beginning with **Wordsworth,** 1770-1850). Revolution and war fed an emphasis on freedom and conflict, expressed by both poets (**Byron,** 1788-1824; **Hugo,** 1802-85) and philosophers (**Hegel,** 1770-1831).

Wild gardens replaced the formal French variety, and painters favored rural, stormy, and mountainous landscapes (**Turner,** 1775-1851; **Constable,** 1776-1837). Clothing became freer, with wigs, hoops, and ruffles discarded. Originality and genius were expected in the life as well as the work of inspired artists (Murger's *Scenes from Bohemian Life*, 1847-49). Exotic locales and themes (as in Gothic horror stories) were used in art and literature (Delacroix, 1798-1863; **Poe,** 1809-49).

Music exhibited the new dramatic style and a breakdown of classical forms (**Beethoven,** 1770-1827). The use of folk melodies and modes aided the growth of distinct national traditions (Glinka in Russia, 1804-57).

Latin America. Francois **Toussaint L'Ouverture** led a successful slave revolt in Haiti, which subsequently became the first Latin American state to achieve independence (1804). The mainland Spanish colonies won their independence (1810-24), under such leaders as Simon **Bolivar** (1783-1830). Brazil became an independent empire (1822) under the Portuguese prince regent. A new class of military officers divided power with large landholders and the church.

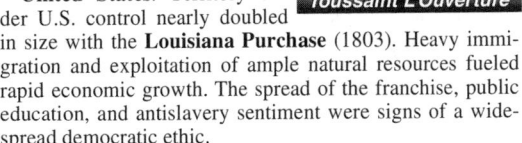

United States. Territory under U.S. control nearly doubled

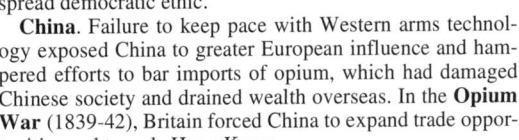

Francois Toussaint L'Ouverture

in size with the **Louisiana Purchase** (1803). Heavy immigration and exploitation of ample natural resources fueled rapid economic growth. The spread of the franchise, public education, and antislavery sentiment were signs of a widespread democratic ethic.

China. Failure to keep pace with Western arms technology exposed China to greater European influence and hampered efforts to bar imports of opium, which had damaged Chinese society and drained wealth overseas. In the **Opium War** (1839-42), Britain forced China to expand trade opportunities and to cede Hong Kong.

World Almanac Quick Quiz

Can you put these events in chronological order?

(a) Soviet Union launches *Sputnik*

(b) East Germany builds the Berlin Wall

(c) Fidel Castro comes to power in Cuba

(d) U.S. develops the H-bomb

For the answer look in this chapter, or see page 1008.

Triumph of Progress: 1840-80

Charles Darwin

Idea of Progress. As a result of the cumulative scientific, economic, and political changes of the preceding eras, the idea took hold among literate people in the West that continuing growth and improvement was the usual state of human and natural life.

Charles **Darwin's** statement of the **theory of evolution** and survival of the fittest (*Origin of Species*, 1859), defended by intellectuals and scientists against theological objections, was taken as confirmation that progress was the natural direction of life. The controversy helped define popular ideas of the dedicated scientist and of science's increasing control over the world (Foucault's demonstration of earth's rotation, 1851; **Pasteur's** germ theory, 1861).

Liberals following Ricardo (1772-1823) in their faith that unrestrained competition would bring continuous economic expansion sought to adjust political life to new social realities and believed that unregulated competition of ideas would yield truth (**Mill**, 1806-73). In England, successive reform bills (1832, 1867, 1884) gave representation to the new industrial towns and extended the franchise to the middle and lower classes and to Catholics, Dissenters, and Jews. On both sides of the Atlantic, reformists tried to improve conditions for the mentally ill (**Dix**, 1802-87), women (Anthony, 1820-1906), and prisoners. Slavery was barred in the British Empire (1833), the U.S. (1865), and Brazil (1888).

Karl Marx

Socialist theories based on ideas of human perfectibility or progress were widely disseminated. Utopian socialists such as Saint-Simon (1760-1825) envisaged an orderly, just society directed by a technocratic elite. A model factory town, New Lanark, Scotland, was set up by utopian Robert Owen (1771-1858), and communal experiments were tried in the U.S. (Brook Farm, Mass., 1841-47). Bakunin's (1814-76) anarchism represented the opposite extreme of total freedom. Karl **Marx** (1818-83) posited the inevitable triumph of socialism in industrial countries through a dialectical process of class conflict.

Spread of industry. The technical processes and managerial innovations of the English industrial revolution spread to Europe (especially Germany) and the U.S., causing an explosion of industrial production, demand for raw materials, and competition for markets. Inventors, both trained and self-taught, provided means for larger-scale production (Bessemer steel, 1856; sewing machine, 1846). Many inventions were shown at the universal prosperity-themed 1851 London Great Exhibition at the **Crystal Palace**.

Local specialization and long-distance trade were aided by a revolution in transportation and communication. Railroads were first introduced in the 1820s in England and the U.S. Over 150,000 mi of track had been laid worldwide by 1880, with another 100,000 mi laid in the next decade. Steamships were improved (*Savannah* crossed Atlantic, 1819). The **telegraph**, perfected by 1844 (Morse), connected the Old and New Worlds by cable in 1866 and quickened the pace of international commerce and politics. The first commercial **telephone** exchange went into operation in the U.S. in 1878.

The new class of industrial workers, uprooted from their rural homes, lacked job security and suffered from dangerous overcrowding at work and at home. Many responded by organizing **trade unions** (legalized in England, 1824; France, 1884). The U.S. Knights of Labor had 700,000 members by 1886. The First International (1864-76) tried to unite workers worldwide around a Marxist program. The quasi-Socialist Paris Commune uprising (1871) was violently suppressed. Acts to reduce child labor and regulate conditions were passed (1833-50 in England). Social security measures were introduced by the Bismarck regime (1883-89) in Germany.

Revolutions of 1848. Among the causes of the continent-wide revolutions were an international collapse of credit and resulting unemployment, bad harvests in 1845-47, and a cholera epidemic. The new urban proletariat and expanding bourgeoisie demanded greater political roles. Republics were proclaimed in France, Rome, and Venice. Nationalist feelings reached fever pitch in the Habsburg empire, as Hungary declared independence under Kossuth, as a Slav Congress demanded equality, and as Piedmont tried to drive Austria from Lombardy. A national liberal assembly at Frankfurt called for German unification.

But riots fueled bourgeois fear of socialism (**Marx and Engels**, *Communist Manifesto*, 1848), and peasants remained conservative. The old establishment—the Papacy, the Habsburgs with the help of the Czarist Russian army— was able to rout the revolutionaries by 1849. The French Republic succumbed to a renewed monarchy by 1852 (Emperor Napoleon III).

Great nations unified. Using the "blood and iron" tactics of Bismarck from 1862, Prussia controlled N Germany by 1867 (war with Denmark, 1864; Austria, 1866). After defeating France in 1870 (annexation of Alsace-Lorraine), it won the allegiance of S German states. A new **German Empire** was proclaimed (1871). **Italy**, inspired by Giuseppe Mazzini (1805-72) and Giuseppe Garibaldi (1807-82), was unified by the reformed Piedmont kingdom through uprisings, plebiscites, and war.

The **U.S.**, its area expanded after the 1846-48 Mexican War, defeated (1861-65) a secession attempt by southern states in the **Civil War**. Canadian provinces were united in an autonomous **Dominion of Canada** (1867). Control in **India** was removed from the East India Co. and centralized under British administration after the 1857-58 Sepoy rebellion, laying the groundwork for the modern Indian State. Queen Victoria was named Empress of India (1876).

Europe dominates Asia. The Ottoman Empire began to collapse in the face of Balkan nationalisms and European imperial incursions in N Africa (**Suez Canal**, 1869). The Turks had lost control of most of both regions by 1882. Russia completed its expansion S by 1884 (despite the temporary setback of the **Crimean War** with Turkey, Britain, and France, 1853-56), taking Turkestan, all the Caucasus, and Chinese areas in the E and sponsoring Balkan Slavs against the Turks. A succession of reformist and reactionary regimes presided over a slow modernization (serfs freed, 1861). Persian independence suffered as Russia and British India competed for influence.

China was forced to sign a series of unequal treaties with European powers and Japan. Overpopulation and an inefficient dynasty brought misery and caused rebellions (Taiping, Muslims) leaving tens of millions dead. **Japan** was forced by the U.S. (Commodore Perry's visits, 1853-54) and Europe to end its isolation. The Meiji restoration (1868) gave power to a Westernizing oligarchy. Intensified empire-building gave Burma to Britain (1824-85) and Indochina to France (1862-95). Christian missionary activity followed imperial and trade expansion in Asia.

Respectability. Fine arts were expected to reflect and encourage the good morals and manners among the Victorians. Prudery, exaggerated delicacy, and familial piety were heralded by **Bowdler's** expurgated Shakespeare edition (1818). Government-supported mass education sought to inculcate a work ethic as a means to escape poverty (**Horatio Alger**, 1832-99).

The official **Beaux Arts** school in Paris set an international style of imposing public buildings (Paris Opera, 1861-

74; Vienna Opera, 1861-69) and uplifting statues (Bartholdi's Statue of Liberty, 1884). Realist painting, influenced by photography (Daguerre, 1837), appealed to a new mass audience with social or historical narrative (Wilkie, 1785-1841; Poynter, 1836-1919) or with serious religious, moral, or social messages (pre-Raphaelites, Millet's *Angelus*, 1858) often drawn from ordinary life. The **Impressionists** (Monet, 1840-1926; Pissarro, 1830-1903; Renoir, 1841-1919) rejected the formalism, sentimentality, and precise techniques of academic art in favor of a spontaneous, undetailed rendering of the world through careful representation of the effect of natural light on objects.

Realistic **novelists** presented the full panorama of social classes and personalities, but retained sentimentality and moral judgment (**Dickens,** 1812-70; **Eliot,** 1819-80; **Tolstoy,** 1828-1910; **Balzac,** 1799-1850).

Veneer of Stability: 1880-1900

Imperialism triumphant. The vast **African** interior, visited by European explorers (Barth, 1821-65; Livingstone, 1813-73), was conquered by the European powers in rapid, competitive thrusts from their coastal bases after 1880, mostly for domestic political and international strategic reasons. W African Muslim kingdoms (Fulani), Arab slave traders (Zanzibar), and Bantu military confederations (Zulu) were alike subdued. Only Christian Ethiopia (defeat of Italy, 1896) and Liberia resisted successfully. France (W Africa) and Britain ("Cape to Cairo," **Boer War,** 1899-1902) were the major beneficiaries. The ideology of "the white man's burden" (Kipling, *Barrack Room Ballads*, 1892) or of a "civilizing mission" (France) justified the conquests.

W European foreign capital investment soared to nearly $40 billion by 1914, but most was in E Europe (France, Germany), the Americas (Britain), and Europe's colonies. The foundation of the modern interdependent world economy was laid, with cartels dominating raw material trade.

An industrious world. Industrial and technological proficiency characterized the 2 new great powers—Germany and the U.S. Coal and iron deposits enabled Germany to reach 2nd or 3rd place status in iron, steel, and shipbuilding by the 1900s. German electrical and chemical industries were world leaders. The U.S. post-Civil War boom (interrupted by "panics"—1884, 1893, 1896) was shaped by massive immigration from S and E Europe from 1880, government subsidy of railroads, and huge private monopolies (Standard Oil, 1870; U.S. Steel, 1901). The **Spanish-American War,** 1898 (Philippine Insurrection, 1899-1902), and the **Open Door policy** in China (1899) made the U.S. a world power.

Hyde Park, London

England led in **urbanization**, with **London** the world capital of finance, insurance, and shipping. Sewer systems (Paris, 1850s), electric subways (London, 1890), parks, and bargain department stores helped improve living standards for most of the urban population of the industrial world.

Westernization of Asia. Asian reaction to European economic, military, and religious incursions took the form of imitation of Western techniques and adoption of Western ideas of progress and freedom. The Chinese "self-strengthening" movement of the 1860s and 1870s included rail, port, and arsenal improvements and metal and textile mills. Reformers such as **K'ang Yu-wei** (1858-1927) won liberalizing reforms in 1898, right after the European and Japanese "scramble for concessions."

A universal education system in Japan and importation of foreign industrial, scientific, and military experts aided Japan's rapid modernization after 1868, under the authoritarian Meiji regime. Japan's victory in the **Sino-Japanese War** (1894-95) put Formosa and Korea in its power.

In India, the British alliance with the remaining princely states masked reform sentiment among the Westernized urban elite; higher education had been conducted largely in English for 50 years. The **Indian National Congress,** founded in 1885, demanded a larger government role for Indians.

Fin-de-siècle **sophistication. Naturalist** writers pushed realism to its extreme limits, adopting a quasi-scientific attitude and writing about formerly taboo subjects such as sex, crime, extreme poverty, and corruption (Flaubert, 1821-80; Zola, 1840-1902; Hardy, 1840-1928). Unseen or repressed psychological motivations were explored in the clinical and theoretical works of Sigmund **Freud** (1856-1939) and in works of fiction (**Dostoyevsky,** 1821-81; James, 1843-1916; Schnitzler, 1862-1931; others).

A contempt for bourgeois life or a desire to shock a complacent audience was shared by the French **symbolist** poets (Verlaine, 1844-96; Rimbaud, 1854-91), by neopagan English writers (Swinburne, 1837-1909), by continental dramatists (**Ibsen,** 1828-1906), and by satirists (**Wilde,** 1854-1900). The German philosopher Friedrich **Nietzsche** (1844-1900) was influential in his elitism and pessimism.

Postimpressionist art neglected long-cherished conventions of representation (Cézanne, 1839-1906) and showed a willingness to learn from primitive and non-European art (Gauguin, 1848-1903; Japanese prints).

Racism. Gobineau (1816-82) gave a pseudobiological foundation to modern racist theories, which spread in Europe in the latter 19th cent., along with **Social Darwinism,** the belief that societies are and should be organized as a struggle for survival of the fittest. The medieval period was interpreted as an era of natural Germanic rule (Chamberlain, 1855-1927), and notions of racial superiority were associated with German national aspirations (Treitschke, 1834-96). **Anti-Semitism,** with a new racist rationale, became a significant political force in Germany (Anti-Semitic Petition, 1880), Austria (Lueger, 1844-1910), and France (**Dreyfus affair,** 1894-1906).

Last Respite: 1900-9

Alliances. While the peace of Europe (and its dependencies) continued to hold (1907 **Hague Conference** extended the rules of war and international arbitration procedures), imperial rivalries, protectionist trade practices (in Germany and France), and the escalating arms race (British *Dreadnought* battleship launched; Germany widens Kiel canal, 1906) exacerbated minor disputes (German-French Moroccan "crises," 1905, 1911).

Security was sought through balance-of-power alliances: **Triple Alliance** (Germany, Austria-Hungary, Italy; renewed in 1902 and 1907); Anglo-Japanese Alliance (1902), Franco-Russian Alliance (1899), **Entente Cordiale** (Britain, France, 1904), Anglo-Russian Treaty (1907), German-Ottoman friendship.

Ottomans decline. The inefficient, corrupt Ottoman government was unable to resist further loss of territory. Nearly all European lands were lost in 1912 to Serbia, Greece, Montenegro, and Bulgaria. Italy took Libya and the Dodecanese islands the same year, and Britain took Kuwait (1899) and the Sinai (1906). The **Young Turk** revolution in 1908 forced the sultan to restore a constitution, and it introduced some social reform, industrialization, and secularization.

British Empire. British trade and cultural influence remained dominant in the empire, but constitutional reforms presaged its eventual dissolution: The colonies of **Australia** were united in 1901 under a self-governing commonwealth. **New Zealand** acquired dominion status in 1907. The old

Boer republics joined Cape Colony and Natal in the self-governing **Union of South Africa** in 1910.

The 1909 Indian Councils Act enhanced the role of elected province legislatures in **India**. The Muslim League (founded 1906) sought separate communal representation.

East Asia. Japan exploited its growing industrial power to expand its empire. Victory in the 1904-5 war against Russia (naval battle of Tsushima, 1905) assured Japan's domination of **Korea** (annexed 1910) and Manchuria (Port Arthur taken, 1905).

In China, central authority began to crumble (empress died, 1908). Reforms (Confucian exam system ended 1905, modernization of the army, building of railroads) were inadequate, and secret societies of reformers and nationalists, inspired by the Westernized **Sun Yat-sen** (1866-1925) fomented periodic uprisings in the S.

Sun Yat-sen

Siam, whose independence had been guaranteed by Britain and France in 1896, was split into spheres of influence by those countries in 1907.

Russia. The population of the Russian Empire approached 150 million in 1900. Reforms in education, in law, and in local institutions (*zemstvos*) and an industrial boom starting in the 1880s (oil, railroads) created the beginnings of a modern state, despite the autocratic tsarist regime. Liberals (1903 Union of Liberation), Socialists (Social Democrats founded 1898, Bolsheviks split off 1903), and populists (Social Revolutionaries founded 1901) were periodically repressed, and national minorities were persecuted (anti-Jewish pogroms, 1903, 1905-6).

An industrial crisis after 1900 and harvest failures aggravated poverty among urban workers, and the 1904-5 defeat by Japan (which checked Russia's Asian expansion) sparked **the Revolution of 1905-6**. A **Duma** (parliament) was created, and an agricultural reform (under Stolypin, prime minister 1906-11) created a large class of land-owning peasants (kulaks).

The world shrinks. Developments in transportation and communication and mass population movements helped create an awareness of an interdependent world. Early **automobiles** (Daimler, Benz, 1885) were experimental or were designed as luxuries. Assembly-line mass production (Ford Motor Co., 1903) made the invention practicable, and by 1910 nearly 500,000 motor vehicles were registered in the U.S. alone. **Heavier-than-air flights** began in 1903 in the U.S. (Wright brothers' *Flyer*), preceded by glider, balloon, and model plane advances in several countries. Trade was advanced by improvements in **ship design** (gyrocompass, 1910), speed (*Lusitania* crossed Atlantic in 5 days, 1907), and reach (Panama Canal begun, 1904).

The first transatlantic **radio** telegraphic transmission occurred in 1901, 6 years after Marconi discovered radio. Radio transmission of human speech had been made in 1900.

Telegraphic transmission of photos was achieved in 1904, lending immediacy to news reports. **Phonographs**, popularized by Caruso's recordings (starting 1902), made for quick international spread of musical styles (ragtime). **Motion pictures**, perfected in the 1890s (Dickson, Lumière brothers), became a popular and artistic medium after 1900; newsreels appeared in 1909.

Emigration from crowded European centers soared in the decade: 9 million migrated to the U.S., and millions more went to Siberia, Canada, Argentina, Australia, South Africa, and Algeria. Some 70 million Europeans emigrated in the cent. before 1914. Several million Chinese, Indians, and Japanese migrated to SE Asia, where their urban skills often enabled them to take a predominant economic role.

Social reform. The social and economic problems of the poor were kept in the public eye by realist fiction writers (Dreiser's *Sister Carrie*, 1900; Gorky's *Lower Depths*, 1902; Sinclair's *The Jungle*, 1906), journalists (U.S. **muckrakers**—Steffens, Tarbell), and artists (Ashcan school). Frequent labor strikes and occasional assassinations by anarchists or radicals (Empress Elizabeth of Austria, 1898; King Umberto I of Italy, 1900; U.S. Pres. McKinley, 1901; Russian Interior Minister Plehve, 1904; Portugal's King Carlos, 1908) added to social tension and fear of revolution.

But democratic reformism prevailed. In Germany, Bernstein's (1850-1932) **revisionist Marxism**, downgrading revolution, was accepted by the powerful Social Democrats and trade unions. The British Fabian Society (the Webbs, Shaw) and the Labour Party (founded 1906) worked for reforms such as Social Security and union rights (1906), while woman suffragists grew more militant. U.S. **progressives** fought big business (Pure Food and Drug Act, 1906). In France, the 10-hour work day (1904) and separation of church and state (1905) were reform victories, as was universal suffrage in Austria (1907).

Arts. An unprecedented period of experimentation, centered in France, produced several new **painting** styles: Fauvism exploited bold color areas (Matisse, *Woman With Hat*, 1905); expressionism reflected powerful inner emotions (the Brücke group, 1905); cubism combined several views of an object on one flat surface (Picasso's *Demoiselles*, 1906-7); futurism tried to depict speed and motion (Italian Futurist Manifesto, 1910). **Architects** explored new uses of steel structures, with facades either neoclassical (Adler and Sullivan in U.S.); curvilinear Art Nouveau (Gaudi's Casa Mila, 1905-10); or functionally streamlined (Wright's Robie House, 1909).

Music and dance shared the experimental spirit. Ruth St. Denis (1877-1968) and Isadora Duncan (1878-1927) pioneered modern dance, while Sergei Diaghilev in Paris revitalized classic ballet from 1909. Composers explored atonal music (Debussy, 1862-1918) and dissonance (Schoenberg, 1874-1951) or revolutionized classical forms (Stravinsky, 1882-1971), often showing jazz or folk music influences.

War and Revolution: 1910-19

War threatens. Germany under Wilhelm II sought a political and imperial role consonant with its industrial strength, challenging Britain's world supremacy and threatening France, which was still resenting the loss (1871) of Alsace-Lorraine. Austria wanted to curb an expanded Serbia (after 1912) and the threat it posed to its own Slav lands. Russia feared Austrian and German political and economic aims in the Balkans and Turkey.

An accelerated arms race resulted from these circumstances. The German standing army rose to more than 2 million men by 1914. Russia and France had more than a million each, and Austria and the British Empire nearly a million each. Dozens of enormous battleships were built by the powers after 1906.

The **assassination of Austrian Archduke Franz Ferdinand** by a Serbian, June 28, 1914, was the pretext for war.

The system of alliances made the conflict Europe-wide; Germany's invasion of Belgium to outflank France forced Britain to enter the war. Patriotic fervor was nearly unanimous among all classes in most countries.

World War I. German forces were stopped in France in one month. The rival armies dug **trench networks**. Artillery and improved machine guns prevented either side from any lasting advance despite repeated assaults (600,000 dead at **Verdun**, Feb.-July 1916). Poison gas, used by Germany in 1915, proved ineffective. The entrance of more than 1 million U.S. troops tipped the balance after mid-1917, forcing Germany to sue for peace the next year. The formal armistice was signed on Nov. 11, 1918.

In the E, the Russian armies were thrown back (battle of **Tannenberg**, Aug. 20, 1914), and the war grew unpopular in Russia. An allied attempt to relieve Russia through Turkey failed (**Gallipoli,** 1915). The **Russian Revolution** (1917) abolished the monarchy. The new Bolshevik regime signed the capitulatory Brest-Litovsk peace in March 1918. Italy entered the war on the allied side in May 1915 but was pushed back by Oct. 1917. A renewed offensive with Allied aid in Oct.-Nov. 1918 forced Austria to surrender.

The British Navy successfully blockaded Germany, which responded with submarine U-boat attacks; **unrestricted submarine warfare** against neutrals after Jan. 1917 helped bring the U.S. into the war. Other battlefields included Palestine and Mesopotamia, both of which Britain wrested from the Turks in 1917, and the African and Pacific colonies of Germany, most of which fell to Britain, France, Australia, Japan, and South Africa.

Settlement. At the **Paris Peace Conference** (Jan.-June 1919), concluded by the **Treaty of Versailles**, and in subsequent negotiations and local wars (Russian-Polish War, 1920), the **map of Europe** was **redrawn** with a nod to U.S. Pres. Woodrow Wilson's principle of self-determination. Austria and Hungary were separated, and much of their land was given to Yugoslavia (formerly Serbia), Romania, Italy, and the newly independent Poland and Czechoslovakia. Germany lost territory in the W, N, and E, while Finland and the Baltic states were detached from Russia. Turkey lost nearly all its Arab lands to British-sponsored Arab states or to direct French and British rule. Belgium's sovereignty was recognized.

From 1916, the civilian populations and economies of both sides were mobilized to an unprecedented degree. Hardships intensified among fighting nations in 1917 (French mutiny crushed in May). More than 10 million soldiers died in the war.

A huge **reparations** burden and partial demilitarization were imposed on Germany. Pres. Wilson obtained approval for a League of Nations, but the U.S. Senate refused to allow the U.S. to join.

Russian revolution. Military defeats and high casualties caused a contagious lack of confidence in Tsar Nicholas, who was forced to abdicate Mar. 1917. A liberal provisional government failed to end the war, and massive desertions, riots, and fighting between factions followed. A moderate socialist government under Aleksandr Kerensky was overthrown (Nov. 1917) in a violent coup by the **Bolsheviks** in Petrograd under **Lenin,** who later disbanded the elected Constituent Assembly.

The Bolsheviks brutally suppressed all opposition and ended the war with Germany in Mar. 1918. **Civil war** broke out in the summer between the Red Army (the Bolsheviks and their supporters), and monarchists, anarchists, nationalities (Ukrainians, Georgians, Poles), and others. Small U.S., British, French, and Japanese units also opposed the Bolsheviks (1918-19; Japan in Vladivostok to 1922). The civil war,

anarchy, and pogroms devastated the country until the 1920 Red Army victory. The **Communist Party** leadership retained absolute power.

Other European revolutions. An unpopular monarchy in **Portugal** was overthrown in 1910. The new republic took severe anticlerical measures in 1911.

After a century of Home Rule agitation, during which **Ireland** was devastated by famine (1 million dead, 1846-47) and emigration, republican militants staged an unsuccessful uprising in Dublin during **Easter 1916**. The execution of the leaders and mass arrests by the British won popular support for the rebels. The **Irish Free State,** comprising all but the 6 N counties, achieved dominion status in 1922.

In the aftermath of the world war, radical revolutions were attempted in Germany (**Spartacist** uprising, Jan. 1919), **Hungary** (Kun regime, 1919), and elsewhere. All were suppressed or failed for lack of support.

Chinese revolution. The Manchu Dynasty was overthrown and a republic proclaimed in Oct. 1911. First Pres. Sun Yat-sen resigned in favor of strongman Yuan Shih-k'ai. Sun organized the parliamentarian **Kuomintang** party.

Students launched protests on May 4, 1919, against League of Nations concessions in China to Japan. Nationalist, liberal, and socialist ideas and political groups spread. The **Communist Party** was founded in 1921. A Communist regime took power in Mongolia with Soviet support in 1921.

India restive. Indian objections to British rule erupted in nationalist riots as well as in the nonviolent tactics of Mahatma **Gandhi** (1869-1948). Nearly 400 unarmed demonstrators were shot at **Amritsar** in Apr. 1919. Britain approved limited self-rule that year.

Mexican revolution. Under the long Diaz dictatorship (1877-1911) the economy advanced, but Indian and mestizo lands were confiscated, and concessions to foreigners (mostly U.S.) damaged the middle class. A **revolution in 1910** led to civil wars and U.S. intervention (1914, 1916-17). Land reform and a more democratic constitution (1917) were achieved.

Sciences. Scientific specialization prevailed by the 20th cent. Advances in knowledge and technological aptitude increased with the geometric rise in the number of practitioners. Physicists challenged common-sense views of causality, observation, and a mechanistic universe, putting science further beyond popular grasp (**Einstein's** general theory of relativity, 1916; Bohr's quantum mechanics, 1913; Heisenberg's uncertainty principle, 1927).

Albert Einstein

The Aftermath of War: 1920-29

U.S. Easy credit, technological ingenuity, and war-related industrial decline in Europe caused a long economic boom,

New York City

in which ownership of the new products—**autos, phones, radios**—became more democratized. **Prosperity.** An increase in women workers, women's suffrage (19th Amendment ratified, 1920), and drastic change in fashion (flappers, mannish bob for women, clean-shaven men) created a wide perception of social change, despite prohibition of alcoholic beverages (1919-33). Union membership and strikes increased. Fear of radicals led to Palmer raids (1919-20) and the Sacco/Vanzetti case (1921-27).

Europe sorts itself out. Germany's liberal **Weimar constitution** (1919) could not guarantee a stable government in

the face of rightist violence (Rathenau assassinated, 1922) and Communist refusal to cooperate with Socialists. Reparations and Allied occupation of the Rhineland caused staggering inflation that destroyed middle-class savings, but economic expansion resumed after mid-decade, aided by U.S. loans. A sophisticated, **innovative culture** developed in architecture and design (Bauhaus, 1919-28), film (Lang, *M*, 1931), painting (Grosz), music (Weill, *Threepenny Opera*, 1928), theater (Brecht, *A Man's a Man*, 1926), criticism (Benjamin), philosophy (Jung), and fashion. This culture was considered decadent and socially disruptive by rightists.

England elected its first Labour governments (Jan. 1924, June 1929). A 10-day general strike in support of coal miners failed in May 1926. In **Italy**, strikes, political chaos, and violence by small Fascist bands culminated in the Oct. 1922 Fascist March on Rome, which established **Mussolini's** dictatorship. Strikes were outlawed (1926), and Italian influence was pressed in the Balkans (Albania a protectorate, 1926). A conservative dictatorship was also established in **Portugal** in a 1926 military coup.

Czechoslovakia, the only stable democracy to emerge from the war in Central or E Europe, faced opposition from Germans (in the Sudetenland), Ruthenians, and some Slovaks. As the industrial heartland of the old Habsburg empire, it remained fairly prosperous. With French backing, it formed the Little Entente with Yugoslavia (1920) and **Romania** (1921) to block Austrian or Hungarian irredentism. Croats and Slovenes in **Yugoslavia** demanded a federal state until King Alexander I proclaimed (1929) a royal dictatorship. Poland faced nationality problems as well (Germans, Ukrainians, Jews); Pilsudski ruled as dictator from 1926. The Baltic states were threatened by traditionally dominant ethnic Germans and by Soviet-supported Communists.

An economic collapse and famine in **Russia** (1921-22) claimed 5 million lives. The New Economic Policy (1921) allowed land ownership by peasants and some private commerce and industry. **Stalin** was absolute ruler within 4 years of Lenin's death (1924). He inaugurated a brutal collectivization program (1929-32) and used foreign Communist parties for Soviet state advantage.

Internationalism. Revulsion against World War I led to pacifist agitation, to the Kellogg-Briand Pact renouncing aggressive war (1928), and to **naval disarmament** pacts (Washington, 1922; London, 1930). But the League of Nations was able to arbitrate only minor disputes (Greece-Bulgaria, 1925).

Middle East. Mustafa Kemal (**Ataturk**) led **Turkish** nationalists in resisting Italian, French, and Greek military advances (1919-23). The sultanate was abolished (1922), and elaborate reforms were passed, including secularization of law and adoption of the Latin alphabet. Ethnic conflict led to persecution of **Armenians** (more than 1 million dead in 1915, 1 million expelled), Greeks (forced Greek-Turk population exchange, 1923), and Kurds (1925 uprising).

With evacuation of the Turks from **Arab** lands, the puritanical Wahabi dynasty of E Arabia conquered (1919-25) what is now Saudi Arabia. British, French, and Arab dynas-

tic and nationalist maneuvering resulted in the creation of 2 more Arab monarchies in 1921—Iraq and Transjordan (both under British control)—and 2 French mandates—Syria and Lebanon. Jewish immigration into British-mandated **Palestine**, inspired by the Zionist movement, was resisted by Arabs, at times violently (1921, 1929 massacres).

Reza Khan ruled **Persia** after his 1921 coup (shah from 1925), centralized control, and created the trappings of a modern secular state.

In 1922, English archaeologist Howard Carter discovered the **tomb** of the boy pharaoh **Tutankhamen** in the Valley of the Kings in Egypt.

China. The Kuomintang under **Chiang Kai-shek** (1887-1975) subdued the warlords by 1928. The Communists were brutally suppressed after their alliance with the Kuomintang was broken in 1927. Relative peace thereafter allowed for industrial and financial improvements, with some Russian, British, and U.S. cooperation.

Arts. Nearly all bounds of subject matter, style, and attitude were broken in the arts of the period. **Abstract** art first took inspiration from natural forms or narrative themes (Kandinsky from 1911) and then worked free of any representational aims (Malevich's suprematism, 1915-19; Mondrian's geometric style from 1917). The **Dada** movement (from 1916) mocked artistic pretension with absurd collages and constructions. Paradox, illusion, and psychological taboos were exploited by **surrealists** by the late 1920s (Dali, Magritte). Architectural schools celebrated industrial values, whether vigorous abstract constructivism (Tatlin, *Monument to 3rd International*, 1919) or the machined, streamlined **Bauhaus** style, which was extended to many design fields (Helvetica typeface).

Prose writers explored revolutionary narrative modes related to dreams (Kafka's *Trial*, 1925), internal monologue (Joyce's **Ulysses**, 1922), and word play (Stein's *Making of Americans*, 1925). Poets and novelists wrote of modern alienation (Eliot's **Waste Land**, 1922) and aimlessness (Lost Generation).

Rise of Totalitarians: 1930-39

Depression. A worldwide financial panic and economic depression began with the Oct. 1929 U.S. stock market crash and the May 1931 failure of the Austrian Credit-Anstalt. A credit crunch caused international bankruptcies and **unemployment**: 12 million jobless by 1932 in the U.S., 5.6 million in Germany, 2.7 million in England. Governments responded with **tariff restrictions** (Smoot-Hawley Act, 1930; Ottawa Imperial Conference, 1932), which dried up world trade. Government public works programs were vitiated by deflationary budget balancing.

Mussolini & Hitler

Germany. Years of agitation by violent extremists were brought to a head by the Depression. Nazi leader Adolf Hitler was named chancellor in Jan. 1933 and given dictatorial power by the Reichstag in March. Opposition parties were disbanded, strikes banned, and all aspects of economic, cultural, and religious life were brought under central government and Nazi party control and manipulated by sophisticated propaganda. Severe persecution of Jews began (**Nuremberg Laws**, Sept. 1935). Many Jews, political opponents, and others were sent to concentration camps (Dachau, 1933), where thousands died or were killed. Public works, renewed conscription (1935), arms production, and a 4-year plan (1936) all but ended unemployment.

Hitler's expansionism started with reincorporation of the Saar (1935), occupation of the **Rhineland** (Mar. 1936),

and annexation of Austria (Mar. 1938). At **Munich** (Sept. 1938) an indecisive Britain and France sanctioned German dismemberment of Czechoslovakia.

Russia. Rapid industrialization was achieved through successive **5-year plans** starting in 1928, using severe labor discipline and mass forced labor. Industry was financed by a decline in living standards and exploitation of agriculture, which was almost totally collectivized by the early 1930s (*kolkhoz*, collective farm; *sovkhoz*, state farm, often in newly worked lands). Successive **purges** increased the role of professionals and management at the expense of workers. Millions perished in a series of manufactured disasters: extermination (1929-34) of kulaks (peasant landowners), severe famine (1932-33), party purges and show trials (Great Purge, 1936-38), suppression of nationalities, and poor conditions in labor camps.

Spain. An industrial revolution during World War I created an urban proletariat, which was attracted to socialism and anarchism; Catalan nationalists challenged central authority. The 5 years after King Alfonso left Spain in Apr. 1931 were dominated by tension between intermittent leftist and anticlerical governments and clericals, monarchists, and other rightists. Anarchist and Communist rebellions were crushed, but a July 1936 extreme right rebellion led by Gen. Francisco **Franco** and aided by Nazi Germany and Fascist Italy succeeded, after a 3-year **civil war** (more than 1 million dead in battles and atrocities). The war polarized international public opinion.

Italy. Despite propaganda for the ideal of the Corporate State, few domestic reforms were attempted. An entente with Hungary and Austria (Mar. 1934), a pact with Germany and Japan (Nov. 1937), and intervention by 50,000-75,000 troops in Spain (1936-39) sealed Italy's identification with the fascist bloc (anti-Semitic laws after Mar. 1938). Ethiopia was conquered (1935-36), and Albania annexed (Jan. 1939) in conscious imitation of ancient Rome.

East Europe. Repressive regimes fought for power against an active opposition (liberals, socialists, Communists, peasants, Nazis). Minority groups and Jews were restricted within national boundaries that did not coincide with ethnic population patterns. In the destruction of **Czechoslovakia**, Hungary occupied S Slovakia (Nov. 1938) and Ruthenia (Mar. 1939), and a pro-Nazi regime took power in the rest of Slovakia. Other boundary disputes (e.g., Poland-Lithuania, Yugoslavia-Bulgaria, and Romania-Hungary) doomed attempts to build joint fronts against Germany or Russia. Economic depression was severe.

East Asia. After a period of liberalism in **Japan**, nativist militarists dominated the government with peasant support. Manchuria was seized (Sept. 1931-Feb. 1932), and a puppet state was set up (Manchukuo). Adjacent Jehol (Inner Mongolia) was occupied in 1933. China proper was invaded in July 1937; large areas were conquered by Oct. 1938. Hundreds of thousands of rapes, murders, and other atrocities were attributed to the Japanese.

In **China** Communist forces left Kuomintang-besieged strongholds in the S in a Long March (1934-35) to the N. The Kuomintang-Communist civil war was suspended in Jan. 1937 in the face of threatening Japan.

The democracies. The Roosevelt Administration, in office Mar. 1933, embarked on an extensive program of **New Deal** social reform and economic stimulation, including protection for labor unions (heavy industries organized), Social Security, public works, wage-and-hour laws, and assistance to farmers. Isolationist sentiment (1937 Neutrality Act) prevented U.S. intervention in Europe, but military expenditures were increased in 1939.

French political instability and polarization prevented resolution of economic and international security questions. The **Popular Front** government under Leon Blum (June 1936-Apr. 1938) passed social reforms (40-hr week) and raised arms spending. National coalition governments, which ruled Britain from Aug. 1931, brought economic recovery but failed to define a consistent international policy until Chamberlain's government (from May 1937), which practiced **appeasement** of Germany and Italy.

India. Twenty years of agitation for autonomy and then for independence (Gandhi's **salt march**, 1930) achieved some constitutional reform (extended provincial powers, 1935) despite Muslim-Hindu strife. Social issues assumed prominence with peasant uprisings (1921), strikes (1928), Gandhi's efforts for untouchables (1932 "fast unto death"), and social and agrarian reform by the provinces after 1937.

War, Hot and Cold: 1940-49

Arts. The streamlined, geometric design motifs of Art Deco (from 1925) prevailed through the 1930s. **Abstract art** flourished (Moore sculptures from 1931) alongside a new **realism** related to social and political concerns (Socialist Realism, the official Soviet style from 1934; Mexican muralist Rivera, 1886-1957; and Orozco, 1883-1949), which were also expressed in fiction and poetry (Steinbeck's *Grapes of Wrath*, 1939; Sandburg's *The People, Yes*, 1936). Modern architecture (International Style, 1932) was unchallenged in its use of artificial materials (concrete, glass), lack of decoration, and monumentality (Rockefeller Center, 1929-40). Larger-than-life U.S.-made films captured a worldwide audience *(Gone With the Wind, The Wizard of Oz,* both 1939).

Pearl Harbor

War in Asia-Pacific. Japan occupied Indochina in Sept. 1940, dominated Thailand in Dec. 1941, and attacked Hawaii (**Pearl Harbor**), the Philippines, Hong Kong, and Malaya on Dec. 7, 1941 (precipitating U.S. entrance into the war). Indonesia was attacked in Jan. 1942, and Burma was conquered in Mar. 1942. The Battle of **Midway** (June 1942) turned back the Japanese advance. "Island-hopping" battles (**Guadalcanal**, Aug. 1942-Jan. 1943; **Leyte Gulf**, Oct. 1944; **Iwo Jima**, Feb.-Mar. 1945; **Okinawa**, Apr. 1945) and massive bombing raids on Japan from June 1944 wore out Japanese defenses. U.S. atom bombs, dropped Aug. 6 and 9 on **Hiroshima** and Nagasaki, forced Japan to agree, on Aug. 14, to surrender; formal surrender was on Sept. 2, 1945.

War in Europe. The Nazi-Soviet nonaggression pact (Aug. 1939) freed Germany to attack Poland (Sept.). Britain and France, which had guaranteed Polish independence, declared war on Germany. Russia seized E Poland (Sept.), attacked Finland (Nov.), and took the Baltic states (July 1940). Mobile German forces staged *blitzkrieg* attacks during Apr.-June 1940, conquering neutral Denmark, Norway, and the Low Countries and defeating France; 350,000 British and French troops were evacuated at

Dunkirk (May). The **Battle of Britain** (June-Dec. 1940) denied Germany air superiority. German-Italian campaigns won the Balkans by Apr. 1941. Three million Axis troops **invaded Russia** in June 1941, marching through Ukraine to the Caucasus, and through White Russia and the Baltic republics to Moscow and Leningrad.

Russian winter counter-thrusts (1941-42 and 1942-43) stopped the German advance (**Stalingrad**, Sept. 1942-Feb. 1943). Sustaining great casualties, the Russians drove the Axis from all E Europe and the Balkans in the next 2 years. Invasions of N Africa (Nov. 1942), Italy (Sept. 1943), and **Normandy**

Stalin, Roosevelt & Churchill

(launched on D-Day, June 6, 1944) brought U.S., British, Free French, and allied troops to Germany by spring 1945. In Feb. 1945, the 3 Allied leaders, Winston **Churchill** (Britain), Joseph **Stalin** (USSR), and Franklin D. Roosevelt (U.S.), met in Yalta to discuss strategy and resolve political issues, including the postwar Allied occupation of Germany. Germany surrendered May 7, 1945.

Atrocities. The war brought 20th-cent. cruelty to its peak. The Nazi regime systematically killed an estimated 5-6 million Jews, including some 3 million who died in death camps (e.g., **Auschwitz**). Gypsies, political opponents, sick and retarded people, and others deemed undesirable were also murdered by the Nazis, as were vast numbers of Slavs.

Civilian deaths. German bombs killed 70,000 British civilians. More than 100,000 Chinese civilians were killed by Japanese forces in the capture and occupation of Nanking. Severe retaliation by the Soviet army, E European partisans, Free French, and others took a heavy toll. U.S. and British bombing of Germany killed hundreds of thousands, as did U.S. bombing of Japan (80,000-200,000 at Hiroshima alone). Some 45 million people lost their lives in the war.

Settlement. The **United Nations** charter was signed in San Francisco on June 26, 1945, by 50 nations. The International Tribunal at **Nuremberg** convicted 22 German leaders for war crimes in Sept. 1946; 23 Japanese leaders were convicted in Nov. 1948. Postwar border changes included large gains in territory for the USSR, losses for Germany, a shift to the W in Polish borders, and minor losses for Italy. Communist regimes, supported by Soviet troops, took power in most of E Europe, including Soviet-occupied Germany (GDR proclaimed Oct. 1949). Japan lost all overseas lands.

Recovery. Basic political and social changes were imposed on Japan and W Germany by the western allies (Japan constitution adopted, Nov. 1946; W German basic law, May 1949). U.S. **Marshall Plan** aid ($12 billion, 1947-51) spurred W European economic recovery after a period of severe inflation and strikes in Europe and the U.S. The British Labour Party introduced a national health service and nationalized basic industries in 1946.

Cold War. Western fears of further Soviet advances (Cominform formed in Oct. 1947; Czechoslovakia coup, Feb. 1948; Berlin blockade, Apr. 1948-Sept. 1949) led to the formation of **NATO**. Civil War in Greece and Soviet pressure on Turkey led to U.S. aid under the **Truman Doctrine** (Mar. 1947). Other anti-Communist security pacts were the Organization of American States (Apr. 1948) and the SE Asia Treaty Organization (Sept. 1954). A new wave of **Soviet purges** and repression intensified in the last years of Stalin's rule, extending to E Europe (Slansky trial in Czechoslovakia, 1951). Only Yugoslavia resisted Soviet control (expelled by Cominform, June 1948; U.S. aid, June 1949).

China, Korea. Communist forces emerged from World War II strengthened by the Soviet takeover of industrial Manchuria. In 4 years of fighting, the Kuomintang was driven from the mainland; the People's Republic was proclaimed Oct. 1, 1949. Korea was divided by USSR and U.S. occupation forces. Separate republics were proclaimed in the 2 zones in Aug.-Sept. 1948.

India. India and Pakistan became independent dominions on Aug. 15, 1947. Millions of Hindu and Muslim refugees

were created by the partition; riots (1946-47) took hundreds of thousands of lives; Mahatma **Gandhi** was assassinated in Jan. 1948. Burma became completely independent in Jan. 1948; Ceylon took dominion status in Feb.

Mahatma Gandhi

Middle East. The UN approved partition of Palestine into Jewish and Arab states. **Israel** was proclaimed a state, May 14, 1948. Arabs rejected partition, but failed to defeat Israel in war (May 1948-July 1949). Immigration from Europe and the Middle East swelled Israel's Jewish population. British and French forces left Lebanon and Syria in 1946. Transjordan occupied most of Arab Palestine.

Southeast Asia. Communists and others fought against restoration of French rule in **Indochina** from 1946; a non-Communist government was recognized by France in Mar. 1949, but fighting continued. Both Indonesia and the Philippines became independent; the former in 1949 after 4 years of war with Netherlands, the latter in 1946. Philippine economic and military ties with the U.S. remained strong; a Communist-led peasant rising was checked in 1948.

Arts. New York became the center of the world art market; **abstract expressionism** was the chief mode (Pollock from 1943, de Kooning from 1947). Literature and philosophy explored **existentialism** (Camus's *The Stranger*, 1942; Sartre's *Being and Nothingness*, 1943). Non-Western attempts to revive or create regional styles (Senghor's Négritude, Mishima's novels) only confirmed the emergence of a universal culture. Radio and phonograph records spread American popular music (swing, bebop) around the world.

The American Decade: 1950-59

Polite decolonization. The peaceful decline of European political and military power in Asia and Africa accelerated in the 1950s. Nearly all of **N Africa** was freed by 1956, but France fought a bitter war to retain Algeria, with its large European minority, until 1962. **Ghana**, independent in 1957, led a parade of new black African nations (more than 2 dozen by 1962), which altered the political character of the UN. Ethnic disputes often exploded in the new nations after decolonization (UN troops in Cyprus, 1964; **Nigerian civil war**, 1967-70). Leaders of the new states, mostly sharing socialist ideologies, tried to create an Afro-Asian bloc (Bandung Conference, 1955), but Western economic influence and U.S. political ties remained strong (Baghdad Pact, 1955).

Trade. World trade volume soared, in an atmosphere of monetary stability assured by international accords (**Bretton Woods**, 1944). In Europe, economic integration advanced (**European Economic Community**, 1957; European Free Trade Association, 1960). Comecon (1949) coordinated the economies of Soviet-bloc countries.

U.S. Economic growth produced an abundance of consumer goods (9.3 million motor vehicles sold, 1955). Suburban housing changed life patterns for middle and working classes (Levittown, 1947-51). Pres. Dwight **Eisenhower's** landslide election victories (1952, 1956) reflected consensus politics. A system of alliances and military bases bolstered U.S. influence on all continents. Trade and payments surpluses were balanced by overseas investments and foreign aid ($50 billion, 1950-59).

USSR. In the "thaw" after Stalin's death in 1953, relations with the West improved (evacuation of Vienna, Geneva summit conference, both 1955). Repression of scientific and cultural life eased, and many prisoners were freed culminating in **de-Stalinization** (1956). **Nikita Khrushchev's** leadership aimed at consumer sector growth,

but farm production lagged, despite the virgin lands program (from 1954). Soviet crushing of the 1956 Hungarian revolution, the 1960 U-2 spy plane episode, and other incidents renewed East-West tension and domestic curbs.

Eastern Europe. Resentment of Russian domination and Stalinist repression combined with nationalist, economic, and religious factors to produce periodic violence. E Berlin workers rioted (1953), Polish workers rioted in Poznan (June 1956), and a broad-based **revolution** broke out in **Hungary** (Oct. 1956). All were suppressed by Soviet force or threats (at least 7,000 dead in Hungary), but Poland was allowed to restore private ownership of farms, and a degree of personal and economic freedom returned to Hungary. Yugoslavia experimented with worker self-management and a market economy.

Korea. The 1945 division of Korea along the 38th parallel left industry in the N, which was organized into a militant regime and armed by the USSR. The S was politically disunited. More than 60,000 N Korean troops invaded the S on June 25, 1950. The U.S., backed by the UN Security Council, sent troops. **UN troops** reached the Chinese border in Nov. Some 200,000 Chinese troops crossed the Yalu R. and drove back UN forces. By spring 1951 battle lines had become stabilized near the original 38th parallel border, but heavy fighting continued. Finally, an armistice was signed on July 27, 1953. U.S. troops remained in the S, and U.S. economic and military aid continued. The war stimulated rapid economic recovery in Japan.

China. Starting in 1952, industry, agriculture, and social institutions were forcibly collectivized. In a massive purge, as many as several million people were executed as Kuomintang supporters or as class and political enemies. The **Great Leap Forward** (1958-60) unsuccessfully tried to force the pace of development by substituting labor for investment.

Indochina. Ho Chi Minh's forces, aided by the USSR and the new Chinese Communist government, fought French and pro-French Vietnamese forces to a standstill and captured the strategic **Dienbienphu** camp in May 1954. The Geneva Agreements divided Vietnam in half pending elections (never held) and recognized Laos and Cambodia as independent. The U.S. aided the anti-Communist Republic of Vietnam in the S.

Middle East. Arab revolutions placed leftist, militantly nationalist regimes in power in Egypt (1952) and Iraq (1958). But Arab unity attempts failed (United Arab Republic joined Egypt, Syria, Yemen, 1958-61). Arab refusal to recognize Israel (Arab League economic blockade began Sept. 1951) led to a permanent **state of war**, with repeated incidents (Gaza, 1955). Israel occupied Sinai, and Britain and France took (Oct. 1956) the Suez Canal, but were replaced by the UN Emergency Force. The Mossadegh government in Iran nationalized (May 1951) the British-owned oil industry in May, but was overthrown (Aug. 1953) in a U.S.-aided coup.

Latin America. Argentinian dictator Juan **Perón,** in office 1946, crushed opposition and enforced land reform, some nationalization, welfare state measures, and curbs on the Roman Catholic Church. A Sept. 1955 coup deposed Perón. The 1952 revolution in Bolivia brought land reform, nationalization of tin mines, and improvement in the status of Native Americans, who nevertheless remained poor. The Batista regime in Cuba was overthrown (Jan. 1959) by Fidel **Castro,** who imposed a Communist dictatorship, aligned Cuba with the USSR, but improved education and health care. A U.S.-backed anti-Castro invasion (**Bay of Pigs**, Apr. 1961) was crushed. Self-government advanced in the British Caribbean.

Technology. Large outlays on research and development in the U.S. and the USSR focused on military applications (H-bomb in U.S., 1952; USSR, 1953; Britain, 1957; intercontinental missiles, late 1950s). Soviet launching of the **Sputnik** satellite (Oct. 4, 1957) spurred increases in U.S. science education funds (National Defense Education Act).

Literature and film. Alienation from social and literary conventions reached an extreme in the theater of the absurd (Beckett's *Waiting for Godot,* 1952), the "new novel" (Robbe-Grillet's *Voyeur,* 1955), and avant-garde film (Antonioni's *L'Avventura,* 1960). U.S. beatniks (Kerouac's *On the Road,* 1957) and others rejected the supposed conformism of Americans (Riesman's *The Lonely Crowd,* 1950).

Rising Expectations: 1960-69

Economic boom. The longest sustained economic boom on record spanned almost the entire decade in the capitalist world; the closely watched GNP figure doubled (1960-70) in the U.S., fueled by Vietnam War-related budget deficits. The **General Agreement on Tariffs and Trade** (1967) stimulated W European prosperity, which spread to peripheral areas (Spain, Italy, E Germany). Japan became a top economic power. Foreign investment aided the industrialization of Brazil. There were limited Soviet economic reform attempts.

Reform and radicalization. Pres. John F. **Kennedy**, inaugurated 1961, emphasized youthful idealism and vigor; his assassination Nov. 22, 1963, was a national trauma. A series of political and social reform movements took root in the U.S. and other countries. Blacks demonstrated nonviolently and with partial success against segregation and poverty (1963 March on Washington; 1964 **Civil Rights Act**), but some urban areas erupted in extensive riots (Watts, 1965; Detroit, 1967; **Martin Luther King** assassination, Apr. 4, 1968). New concern for the poor (Harrington's *Other America*, 1963) helped lead to Pres. Lyndon Johnson's **"Great Society"** programs (Medicare, Water Quality Act, Higher Education Act, all 1965). Concern for the **environment** surged (Carson's *Silent Spring*, 1962).

Feminism revived as a cultural and political movement (Friedan's *Feminine Mystique*, 1963; National Organization for Women founded 1966), and a movement for homosexual rights emerged (Stonewall riot in NYC, 1969). Pope John XXIII called the **Second Vatican Council** (1962-65), which liberalized Roman Catholic liturgy and some other aspects of Catholicism.

Opposition to U.S. involvement in Vietnam, especially among university students (**Moratorium** protest, Nov. 1969), turned violent (Weatherman Chicago riots, Oct. 1969). **New Left** and Marxist theories became popular, and membership in radical groups (Students for a Democratic Society, Black Panthers) increased. Maoist groups, especially in Europe, called for total transformation of society. In France, students sparked a nationwide strike affecting 10 million workers in May-June 1968, but an electoral reaction barred revolutionary change.

China. China's revolutionary militancy under **Mao** Zedong caused disputes with the USSR under "revisionist" Khrushchev, starting in 1960. The 2 powers exchanged fire in 1969 border disputes. China used force to capture (1962) areas disputed with India. The **"Great Proletarian Cul-** tural Revolution"** tried to impose a utopian egalitarian program in China and spread revolution abroad; political struggle, often violent, convulsed China in 1965-68.

Indochina. Communist-led guerrillas aided by N Vietnam fought from 1960 against the S Vietnam government of Ngo Dinh Diem (killed 1963). The U.S. military role increased after the 1964 **Tonkin Gulf** incident. U.S. forces peaked at 543,400 in Apr. 1969. Massive numbers of N Vietnamese troops also fought. Laotian and Cambodian neutrality were threatened by Communist insurgencies, with N Vietnamese aid, and U.S. intrigues.

Mao Zedong

Developing World. A bloc of authoritarian leftist regimes among the newly independent nations emerged in political opposition to the U.S.-led Western alliance and came to dominate the conference of nonaligned nations (Belgrade, 1961; Cairo, 1964; Lusaka, 1970). Soviet political ties and military bases were established in Cuba, Egypt, Algeria, Guinea, and other countries whose leaders were regarded as revolutionary heroes by opposition groups in pro-Western or colonial countries. Some leaders were ousted in coups by pro-Western groups—Zaire's Patrice Lumumba (killed 1961), Ghana's Kwame Nkrumah (exiled 1966), and Indonesia's Sukarno (effectively ousted in 1965 after a Communist coup failed).

Middle East. Arab-Israeli tension erupted into a brief war June 1967. Israel emerged from the war as a major regional power. Military shipments before and after the war brought much of the Arab world into the Soviet political sphere. Most Arab states broke U.S. diplomatic ties, while Communist countries cut their ties to Israel. Intra-Arab disputes continued: Egypt and Saudi Arabia supported rival factions in a bloody Yemen civil war 1962-70; Lebanese troops fought Palestinian commandos 1969.

East Europe. To stop the large-scale exodus of citizens, E German authorities built (Aug. 1961) a **fortified wall across Berlin.** Soviet sway in the Balkans was weakened by Albania's support of China (USSR broke ties in Dec. 1961) and Romania's assertion (1964) of industrial and foreign policy autonomy. Liberalization (spring 1968) in Czechoslovakia was crushed with massive force by troops of 5 Warsaw Pact countries. W German treaties (1970) with the

Buzz Aldrin on Moon, 1969

USSR and Poland facilitated the transfer of German technology and confirmed postwar boundaries.

Arts and styles. The boundary between fine and popular arts was blurred to some extent by Pop Art (Warhol) and rock musicals (*Hair*, 1968). Informality and exaggeration prevailed in fashion (beards, miniskirts). A nonpolitical "counterculture" developed, rejecting traditional bourgeois life goals and personal habits, and use of marijuana and hallucinogens spread (**Woodstock** festival, Aug. 1969). Indian influence was felt in religion (Ram Dass) and fashion, and The **Beatles,** who brought unprecedented sophistication to rock music, became for many a symbol of the decade.

Science. Achievements in space (**humans on the moon,** July 1969) and electronics (lasers, integrated circuits) encouraged a faith in scientific solutions to problems in agriculture ("green revolution"), medicine (heart transplants, 1967), and other areas. Harmful technology, it was believed, could be controlled (1963 nuclear weapon test ban treaty, 1968 nonproliferation treaty).

Disillusionment: 1970-79

U.S.: Caution and neoconservatism. A relatively sluggish economy, energy shortages, and environmental problems contributed to a **"limits of growth"** philosophy. Suspicion of science and technology killed or delayed major projects (supersonic transport dropped, 1971; Seabrook nuclear power plant protests, 1977-78) and was fed by the Three Mile Island nuclear reactor accident (Mar. 1979).

There were signs of growing mistrust of big government and less support for new social policies. School busing and racial quotas were opposed (Bakke decision, June 1978); the proposed Equal Rights Amendment for women languished; civil rights legislation aimed at protecting homosexuals was opposed (Dade County referendum, June 1977).

Completion of Communist forces' takeover of **South Vietnam** (evacuation of U.S. civilians, Apr. 1975), revelations of Central Intelligence Agency misdeeds (Rockefeller Commission report, June 1975), and **Watergate** scandals (Nixon resigned in Aug. 1974) reduced faith in U.S. moral and material capacity to influence world affairs. Revelations of Soviet crimes (Solzhenitsyn's *Gulag Archipelago,* 1974) and Soviet intervention in Africa helped foster a revival of anti-Communist sentiment.

Economy sluggish. The 1960s boom faltered in the 1970s; a severe recession in the U.S. and Europe (1974-75) followed a huge oil price hike (Dec. 1973). Monetary instability (U.S. cut ties to gold in Aug. 1971), the decline of the dollar, and protectionist moves by industrial countries (1977-78) threatened trade. Business investment and spending for research declined. Severe inflation plagued many countries (25% in Britain, 1975; 18% in U.S., 1979).

China picks up pieces. After the 1976 deaths of Mao Zedong and Zhou Enlai, struggle for the leadership succession was won by pragmatists. A nationwide purge of orthodox Maoists was carried out, and the **Gang of Four,** led by Mao's widow, Chiang Ching, arrested. The new leaders freed more than 100,000 political prisoners and reduced public adulation of Mao. Political and trade ties were expanded with Japan, Europe, and the U.S. in the late 1970s, as relations worsened with the USSR, Cuba, and Vietnam (4-week invasion by China, 1979). Ideological guidelines in industry, science, education, and the armed forces, which the ruling faction said had caused chaos and decline, were reversed (bonuses to workers, Dec. 1977; exams for college entrance, Oct. 1977). Severe restrictions on cultural expression were eased.

Europe. European unity moves (EEC-EFTA trade accord, 1972) faltered as economic problems appeared (Britain floated pound, 1972; France floated franc, 1974). Germany and Switzerland curbed guest workers from southern Europe. Greece and Turkey quarreled over Cyprus and Aegean oil rights.

All non-Communist Europe was under democratic rule after free elections were held (June 1976) in **Spain** 7 months after the death of Franco. The conservative, colonialist regime in **Portugal** was overthrown in Apr. 1974. In **Greece** the 7-year-old military dictatorship yielded power in 1974. Northern Europe, though ruled mostly by Socialists (**Swedish** Socialists unseated in 1976 after 44 years in power), turned more conservative. The **British** Labour government imposed (1975) wage curbs and suspended nationalization schemes. Terrorism in **Germany** (1972 Munich Olympics killings) led to laws curbing some civil liberties. **French** "new philosophers" rejected leftist ideologies, and the shaky Socialist-Communist coalition lost a 1978 election bid.

Religion and politics. The improvement in **Muslim** countries' political fortunes by the 1950s (with the exception of Central Asia under Soviet and Chinese rule) and the growth of Arab oil wealth were followed by a resurgence of traditional religious fervor. Libyan dictator Muammar al-Qaddafi mixed Islamic laws with socialism and called for Muslim return to Spain and Sicily. The illegal Muslim Brotherhood in **Egypt** was accused of violence, while extreme groups bombed (1977) theaters to protest Western and secular values.

In **Turkey**, the National Salvation Party was the first Islamic group to share (1974) power since secularization in the 1920s. In **Iran, Ayatollah Ruhollah Khomeini,** led a revolution that deposed the secular shah (Jan. 1979) and created an Islamic republic there. Religiously motivated Muslims took part in an insurrection in Saudi Arabia that briefly seized (1979) the Grand Mosque in Mecca. Muslim puritan opposition to **Pakistan** Pres. Zulfikar Ali-Bhutto helped lead to his overthrow in July 1977. Muslim solidarity, however, could not prevent Pakistan's eastern province (**Bangladesh**) from declaring (Dec. 1971) independence after a bloody civil war.

Muslim and Hindu resentment of coerced sterilization in **India** helped defeat the Gandhi government, which was replaced (Mar. 1977) by a coalition including religious Hindu parties. Muslims in the S **Philippines**, aided by Libya, rebelled against central rule from 1973.

The Buddhist Soka Gakkai movement launched (1964) the Komeito party in **Japan,** which became a major opposition party in 1972 and 1976 elections.

Evangelical Protestant groups grew in the U.S. A revival of interest in Orthodox Christianity occurred among **Russian** intellectuals (Solzhenitsyn). The secularist **Israeli** Labor party, after decades of rule, was ousted in 1977 by conservatives led by Menachem Begin; religious militants founded settlements on the disputed West Bank, part of biblically promised Israel. U.S. Reform Judaism revived many previously discarded traditional practices.

Old-fashioned religious wars raged intermittently in **Northern Ireland** (Catholic vs. Protestant, 1969-) and **Lebanon** (Christian vs. Muslim, 1975-), while religious militancy complicated the Israel-Arab dispute (1973 Israel-Arab war). The Camp David Accords in 1978, negotiated by Egyptian Pres. Anwar al-Sadat,

Sadat, Carter, Begin

Israeli Prime Min. Menachem Begin, and U.S. Pres. Jimmy Carter, facilitated the landmark 1979 **Egypt-Israel peace treaty**, but increased militancy on the West Bank impeded further progress.

Latin America. Repressive conservative regimes strengthened their hold on most of the continent, with a violent coup against the elected (Sept. 1973) Allende government in **Chile**, a 1976 military coup in **Argentina**, and coups against reformist regimes in **Bolivia** (1971, 1979) and **Peru** (1976). In Central America increasing liberal and leftist militancy led to the ouster (1979) of the Somoza regime of **Nicaragua** and to civil conflict in **El Salvador**.

Indochina. Communist victories in Vietnam, Cambodia, and Laos by May 1975 led to new turmoil. The **Pol Pot regime** ordered millions of city-dwellers to resettle in rural areas, in a program of forced labor, combined with terrorism, that cost more than 1 million lives (1975-79) and caused hundreds of thousands of ethnic Chinese and others to flee Vietnam ("boat people," 1979). The Vietnamese invasion of Cambodia swelled the refugee population and contributed to widespread starvation in that devastated country.

Russian expansion. Soviet influence, checked in some countries (troops ousted by Egypt, 1972), was projected farther afield, often with the use of Cuban troops (Angola, 1975-89; Ethiopia, 1977-88) and aided by a growing navy, a merchant fleet, and international banking ability. **Détente** with the West—1972 Berlin pact, 1972 strategic arms pact (**SALT**)—gave way to a more antagonistic relationship in the late 1970s, exacerbated by the Soviet invasion (1979) of **Afghanistan**.

Africa. The last remaining European colonies were granted independence (**Spanish Sahara**, 1976; **Djibouti**, 1977) and, after 10 years of civil war and many negotiation sessions, a black government took over (1979) in Zimbabwe (Rhodesia); white domination remained in **South Africa**. Great power involvement in local wars (Russia in **Angola, Ethiopia**; France in **Chad, Zaire, Mauritania**) and the use of tens of thousands of Cuban troops were denounced by some African leaders. Ethnic or tribal clashes made Africa a locus of sustained warfare during the late 1970s.

Arts. Traditional modes of painting, architecture, and music received increased popular and critical attention in the 1970s. These more conservative styles coexisted with modernist works in an atmosphere of increased variety and tolerance.

Revitalization of Capitalism, Demand for Democracy: 1980-89

USSR, Eastern Europe. A troublesome 1980-85 for the USSR was followed by 5 years of astonishing change: the surrender of the Communist monopoly, the remaking of the Soviet state, and the beginning of the disintegration of the Soviet empire. After the deaths of Leonid **Brezhnev** (1982) and 2 successors (Andropov in 1984 and Chernenko in 1985), the harsh treatment of dissent and restriction of emigration, and the Soviet invasion (Dec. 1979) of Afghanistan, Gen. Sec. Mikhail **Gorbachev** (in office 1985-1991) promoted *glasnost* and *perestroika*—eco-

Reagan and Gorbachev

nomic, political, and social reform. Supported by the Communist Party (July 1988), he signed (Dec. 1987) the INF disarmament treaty, and he pledged (1988) to cut the military budget. Military withdrawal from Afghanistan was completed in Feb. 1989, the process of democratization went ahead unhindered in Poland and Hungary, and the Soviet people chose (Mar. 1989) part of the new Congress of People's Deputies from competing candidates. By decade's end the **Cold War** appeared to be fading away.

In **Poland, Solidarity**, the labor union founded (1980) by Lech **Walesa**, was outlawed in 1982 and then legalized in 1988, after years of unrest. Poland's first free election since the Communist takeover brought Solidarity victory (June 1989); Tadeusz Mazowiecki, a Walesa adviser, became (Aug. 1989) prime minister in a government with the Communists. In the fall of 1989 the failure of Marxist economies in **Hungary, East Germany, Czechoslovakia, Bulgaria,** and **Romania** brought the collapse of the Communist monopoly and a demand for democracy. In a historic step, the **Berlin Wall** was opened in Nov. 1989.

U.S. "The Reagan Years" (1981-88) brought the **longest economic boom** yet in U.S. history via budget and tax cuts, deregulation, "junk bond" financing, leveraged buyouts, and mergers and takeovers. However, there was a stock market crash (Oct. 1987), and federal budget deficits and the trade deficit increased. Foreign policy showed a **strong anti-Communist stance**, via increased defense spending, aid to anti-Communists in Central America, invasion of Cuba-threatened Grenada, and championing of the MX missile system and "Star Wars" missile defense program. Four Reagan-Gorbachev summits (1985-88) climaxed in the INF treaty (1987), as the Cold War began to wind down. The Iran-contra affair (North's TV testimony, July 1987) was a major political scandal. Homelessness and drug abuse (espe-

cially "crack" cocaine) were growing social problems. In 1988, Vice Pres. George Bush was elected to succeed Ronald Reagan as president.

Middle East. The Middle East remained militarily unstable, with sharp divisions along economic, political, racial, and religious lines. In **Iran**, the Islamic revolution of 1979 created a strong anti-U.S. stance (hostage crisis, Nov. 1979-Jan. 1981). In Sept. 1980, **Iraq** repudiated its border agreement with Iran and began major hostilities that led to an 8-year war in which millions were killed.

Libya's support for international terrorism induced the U.S. to close (May 1981) its diplomatic mission there and embargo (Mar. 1982) Libyan oil. The U.S. accused Libyan leader Muammar al-Qaddafi of aiding (Dec. 1985) terrorists in Rome and of Vienna airport attacks, and retaliated by bombing Libya (Apr. 1986).

Israel affirmed (July 1980) all Jerusalem as its capital, destroyed (1981) an Iraqi atomic reactor, and invaded (1982) Lebanon, forcing the PLO to agree to withdraw. A **Palestinian uprising**, including women and children hurling rocks and bottles at troops, began (Dec. 1987) in Israeli-occupied Gaza and spread to the West Bank; troops responded with force, killing 300 by the end of 1988, with 6,000 more in detention camps.

Israeli withdrawal from **Lebanon** began in Feb. 1985 and ended in June 1985, as Lebanon continued torn by military and political conflict. Artillery duels (Mar.-Apr. 1989) between Christian East Beirut and Muslim West Beirut left 200 dead and 700 wounded. At decade's end, violence still dominated.

Latin America. In **Nicaragua**, the leftist Sandinista National Liberation Front, in power after the 1979 civil war, faced problems as a result of Nicaragua's military aid to leftist guerrillas in El Salvador and U.S. backing of antigovernment contras. The U.S. CIA admitted (1984) having directed the mining of Nicaraguan ports, and the U.S. sent humanitarian (1985) and military (1986) aid. Profits from secret arms sales to Iran were found (1987) diverted to contras. Cease-fire talks between the Sandinista government and contras came in 1988, and elections were held in Nicaragua in Feb. 1990.

In **El Salvador**, a military coup (Oct. 1979) failed to halt extreme right-wing violence and left-wing terrorism. Archbishop Oscar Romero was assassinated in Mar. 1980; from Jan. to June some 4,000 civilians were killed in the civil unrest. In 1984, newly elected Pres. José Napoleon Duarte worked to stem human rights abuses, but violence continued.

In **Chile**, Gen. Augusto Pinochet yielded the presidency after a democratic election (Dec. 1989), but remained as head of the army. He had ruled the country since 1973, imposing harsh measures against leftists and dissidents; at the same time he introduced economic programs that restored prosperity to Chile.

Africa. 1980-85 marked a rapid decline in the economies of virtually all African countries, a result of accelerating desertification, the world economic recession, heavy indebtedness to overseas creditors, rapid population growth, and political instability. Some 60 million Africans faced prolonged hunger in 1981; much of Africa had one of the worst droughts ever in 1983, and by year's end **150 million faced near-famine**. "Live Aid," a marathon rock concert, was presented in July 1985, and the U.S. and Western nations sent aid in Sept. 1985. Economic hardship fueled political unrest and coups. Wars in Ethiopia and Sudan and military strife in several other nations continued. AIDS took a heavy toll.

South Africa. Anti-apartheid sentiment gathered force in South Africa as demonstrations and violent police response grew. White voters approved (Nov. 1983) the first constitution to give Coloureds and Asians a voice, while still excluding blacks (70% of the population). The U.S. imposed economic sanctions in Aug. 1985, and 11 Western nations followed in September. P. W. **Botha**, 1980s president, was succeeded by F. W. **de Klerk**, in Sept. 1989, who promised "evolutionary" change via negotiation with the black population.

China. During the 1980s the Communist government and paramount leader **Deng Xiaoping** pursued **far-reaching changes**, expanding commercial and technical ties to the industrialized world and increasing the role of market forces in stimulating urban development. Apr. 1989 brought new demands for political reforms; student demonstrators camped out in Tiananmen Square, Beijing, in a massive peaceful protest. Some 100,000 students and workers marched, and at least 20 other cities saw protests. In response, martial law was imposed; army troops crushed the demonstration in and around Tiananmen Square on June 3-4, with death toll estimates at 500-7,000, up to 10,000 dissidents arrested, 31 people tried and executed. The conciliatory Communist Party chief was ousted; the Politburo adopted (July) reforms against official corruption.

Japan. Japan's relations with other nations, especially the U.S., were dominated by **trade imbalances favoring Japan**. In 1985 the U.S. trade deficit with Japan was $49.7 billion, one-third of the total U.S. trade deficit. After Japan was found (Apr. 1986) to sell semiconductors and computer memory chips below cost, the U.S. was assured a "fair share" of the market, but charged (Mar. 1987) Japan with failing to live up to the agreement.

European Community. With the addition of Greece, Portugal, and Spain, the EC became a common market of more than **300 million people**, the West's largest trading entity. Margaret **Thatcher** became the first British prime minister in the 20th century to win a 3rd consecutive term (1987). France elected (1981) its first socialist president, François **Mitterrand**, who was reelected in 1988. Italy elected (1983) its first socialist premier, Bettino **Craxi**.

Margaret Thatcher

International terrorism. With the 1979 overthrow of the shah of Iran, terrorism became a prominent tactic. It increased through the 1980s, but with fewer high-profile attacks after 1985. In 1979-81, Iranian militants held 52 U.S. hostages in Iran for 444 days; in 1983 a TNT-laden suicide terrorist blew up U.S. Marine headquarters in Beirut, killing 241 Americans, and a truck bomb blew up a French paratroop barracks, killing 58. The *Achille Lauro* cruise ship was hijacked in 1986, and an American passenger killed; the U.S. subsequently intercepted the Egyptian plane flying the terrorists to safety. Incidents rose to 700 in 1985, and to 1,000 in 1988. **Assassinated leaders** included Egypt's Pres. Anwar al-**Sadat** (1981), India's Prime Min. Indira **Gandhi** (1984), and Lebanese Premier Rashid **Karami** (1987).

Post–Cold War World: 1990-99

Soviet Empire breakup. The world community witnessed the extraordinary disintegration of the **Soviet Union** into 15 independent states. The 1980s had already seen internal reforms and a decline of Communist power both within the Soviet Union and in Eastern Europe. The Soviet breakup began in earnest with the declarations of independence adopted by the Baltic republics of **Lithuania, Latvia**, and **Estonia** during an abortive coup against reformist leader Mikhail Gorbachev (Aug. 1991). The other republics soon took the same step. In Dec. 1991, **Russia, Ukraine**, and **Belarus** declared the Soviet Union dead; Gorbachev resigned, and the Soviet Parliament went out of existence. The Warsaw Pact and the Council for Mutual Economic Assistance (Comecon) were disbanded. Most of the former Soviet republics joined in a loose confederation called the **Commonwealth of Independent States**. Russia remained the predominant country after the breakup, but its people soon suffered severe economic hardship as the nation, under Pres. Boris **Yeltsin**, moved to revamp the economy and adopt a free market system. In Oct. 1993, **anti-Yeltsin forces** occupied the Parliament building and were ousted by the army; about 140 people died in the fighting.

The Muslim republic of **Chechnya** declared independence from the rest of Russia, but this was met with an invasion by Russian troops (Dec. 1994). After almost 21 months of vicious fighting, a cease-fire took hold in 1996, and the Russians withdrew. In 1999 Russia forcibly suppressed Muslim insurgents in Dagestan and entered neighboring Chechnya, again fighting to gain control over separatist rebels there. Yeltsin resigned office Dec. 31, 1999, to be replaced by Vladimir **Putin** (elected in his own right, Mar. 2000).

Europe. Yugoslavia broke apart, and hostilities ensued among the republics along ethnic and religious lines. **Croatia, Slovenia**, and **Macedonia** declared independence (1991), followed by **Bosnia-Herzegovina** (1992). **Serbia** and **Montenegro** remained as the republic of Yugoslavia.

Bitter fighting followed, especially in Bosnia, where Serbs reportedly engaged in **"ethnic cleansing"** of the Muslim population; a peace plan (Dayton accord), brokered by the United States, was signed by **Bosnia, Serbia**, and **Croatia** (Dec. 1995), with **NATO** responsible for policing its implementation. In spring 1999, NATO conducted a bombing campaign aimed at stopping Yugoslavia from its campaign to drive out ethnic Albanians from the Kosovo region; a peace accord was reached in June under which NATO peacekeeping troops entered Kosovo.

The two **Germanys** were reunited after 45 years (Oct. 1990). The union was greeted with jubilation, but stresses became apparent when free market principles were applied to the aging East German industries, resulting in many plant closings and rising unemployment. West German chancellor Helmut **Kohl**, a Christian Democrat, lost power after 16 years, in Sept. 1998 elections; Gerhard **Schroeder**, a Social Democrat, took over. Czechoslovakia broke apart peacefully (Jan. 1993), becoming the **Czech Republic** and **Slovakia.** In **Poland**, Lech **Walesa** was elected president (Dec. 1991) but was defeated in his bid for a 2nd term (Nov. 1995).

NATO approved the **Partnership for Peace** Program (Jan. 1994) coordinating the defense of **Eastern** and **Central European** countries; Russia joined the program later that year. NATO signed a pact with **Russia** (1997) providing for NATO expansion into the former Soviet-bloc countries; a similar treaty was set up with **Ukraine**. The **Czech Republic, Hungary**, and **Poland** became members in Jan. 1999; in that year **NATO** celebrated its 50th anniversary. Efforts toward European unity continued with adoption of a single market (Jan. 1993) and conversion of the European Community to the **European Union** as the Maestricht Treaty took effect (Nov. 1993). Agreement was reached for 11 EU members to participate in Economic and Monetary Union, adopting a common currency (**euro**) for some purposes in Jan. 1999.

An intraparty revolt forced Margaret **Thatcher** out as prime minister of **Great Britain**, to be succeeded by John **Major** (Nov. 1990); 7 years later, Major suffered an overwhelming defeat at the hands of the new Labour Party leader, Tony **Blair** (May 1997). The divorce of Prince **Charles and** Princess **Diana**, followed by the death of Diana in a car accident (Aug. 1997), made headlines around the world. Talks on **peace** in **Northern Ireland** that included participation of Sinn Fein, political arm of the IRA, led to a ground-breaking peace plan, approved in an all-Ireland vote (May 1998). In Dec. 1999, Northern Ireland was granted home rule under a power-sharing cabinet. In **Scotland** voters overwhelmingly approved establishment of a regional legislature (1997), and in **Wales** voters narrowly approved establishment of a local assembly (1997). In a historic innovation, the Church of England **ordained 32 women** as priests (Mar. 1994).

Middle East. In Aug. 1990, **Iraq's Saddam Hussein** ordered his troops to invade **Kuwait**. The UN approved military action in response (Nov. 1990), and an international military force, led by the U.S., bombed Iraq (Jan. 1991) and launched a land attack, crushing the invasion (Feb. 1991). After Iraq accepted a cease-fire (Apr. 1991), U.S. troops withdrew, but "no-fly" zones were set up over northern Iraq to protect the Kurds and over southern Iraq to protect Shiite Muslims. The UN imposed **sanctions** on Iraq for failure to abide by the cease-fire. Iraq's reported failure to cooperate with UN arms inspectors seeking to eliminate "weapons of mass destruction" led to repeated air strikes by the U.S. and Britain.

The last Western hostages were freed in **Lebanon,** June 1992. **Israel** and the **Palestine Liberation Organization** signed a peace accord (Sept. 1993) providing for Palestinian self-government in the West Bank and Gaza Strip. Prime Min. Yitzhak **Rabin** and Foreign Min. Shimon **Peres** of Israel and Yasir **Arafat** of the PLO received the Nobel Peace Prize for their efforts (1994). Six Arab nations relaxed their boycott against Israel (1994), and Israel and **Jordan** signed a peace treaty (Oct. 1994). **Rabin was assassinated** (Nov. 1995) by an Israeli opponent of the peace process. After new elections (May 1996), Benjamin Netanyahu as prime minister adopted a harder line in peace negotiations. **Arafat** was elected to the presidency of the Palestinian Authority (Jan. 1996). A long-delayed interim agreement (the Wye Memorandum) on Israel military withdrawal from part of the West Bank was reached Oct. 1998. A Labour government under Ehud **Barak** took power after May 1999 elections, but further progress in peace negotiations proved elusive.

King **Hussein** of Jordan died (Feb. 1999), to be succeeded by his son Abdullah.

Asia and the Pacific. Hong Kong was returned to **China** (July 1997) after 156 years as a British colony, and **Macao** reverted to Chinese sovereignty (Dec. 1999) after over 400 years of Portuguese rule. Both were to retain their legal and capitalist economic systems for 50 years. **Jiang Zemin**, general secretary of the Chinese Communist Party, assumed the additional post of president of China (Mar. 1993) and emerged as the key leader after the death of leader **Deng Xiaoping** (Feb. 1997). China released from prison—and exiled—some well-known dissidents but continued to be criticized for detentions and other alleged widespread **human rights abuses**. In Nov. 1999 the U.S. and China signed a landmark pact normalizing trade relations.

After years of prosperity, **Thailand, Indonesia**, and **South Korea** in 1997 began to suffer economic reverses that had a worldwide ripple effect. These countries received billion-dollar IMF bailout packages. In **Indonesia**, protests over mismanagement led to the resignation of Pres. **Suharto** (May 1998) after 32 years of nearly autocratic rule. Abdurraham Wahid was elected (Oct. 1999) in the country's first fully democratic elections. In a referendum (Aug. 1999), **East Timor** voted overwhelmingly for independence from Indonesia; pro-Indonesian militias then rampaged through the territory, but a multinational peacekeeping force was allowed in (Sept. 1999) to help restore order. In **South Korea**, former dissident **Kim Dae Jung** was elected president (Dec. 1997). Two previous presidents, Roh Tae Woo and Chun Doo Hwan, were convicted of crimes committed in office but were given amnesty by the new president.

In **Japan** members of a religious cult, released the nerve gas sarin on 5 Tokyo subway cars, killing 12 people and injuring more than 5,500 (Mar. 1995). Tamil rebels continued their armed conflict in **Sri Lanka**. In **Afghanistan** the **Taliban**, an extreme Islamic fundamentalist group, gained control of Kabul (Sept. 1996) and, eventually, most of the country. In **North Korea**, longtime dictator **Kim Il Sung** died (July 1994), to be succeeded by his son, **Kim Jong Il**. In the same year the country signed an agreement with the U.S. setting a timetable for North Korea to eliminate its nuclear program. The country also suffered a severe drought, and widespread starvation was feared.

India was beset by riots following destruction of a mosque by Hindu militants (Dec. 1992); Indian army troops repeatedly clashed with pro-independence demonstrators in the disputed Muslim region of **Kashmir**, exacerbating relations with **Pakistan**. Uneasy relations between India and Pakistan reached a new level when both nations conducted nuclear tests in 1998. Conflict in Pakistan between government and the military led to a bloodless coup (Oct. 1999).

Africa. South Africa was transformed as the white-dominated government abandoned **apartheid** and the country made the transition to a nonracial democratic government. Pres. F. W. **de Klerk** released Nelson **Mandela** from prison (Feb. 1990), after he had been held by the government for 27 years, and lifted a ban on the African National Congress. The white government repealed its apartheid laws (1990, 1991). **Mandela** was elected **president** (Apr. 1994), and a new constitution became law (Dec. 1996). Thabo **Mbeki**, the ANC's candidate to succeed Mandela, was overwhelmingly elected president in June 1999. I n **Nigeria**, Gen. Olusegun **Obasanjo** was elected president (Feb. 1999), to become the country's first civilian leader in 15 years.

The decades-long rule of **Mobutu** Sese Seko in **Zaire** came to an end (May 1997) at the hands of rebel forces led by Laurent **Kabila**; an ailing Mobutu fled the country and soon after died. Kabila changed the country's name back to **Democratic Republic of the Congo**; conditions remained unstable.

After the presidents of **Burundi** and **Rwanda** were killed in an airplane crash (Apr. 1994), violence erupted in Rwanda between Hutu and Tutsi factions; hundreds of thousands were slain. The conflict spread to refugee camps in neighboring Zaire and Burundi. Factional fighting also erupted in **Somalia** after Pres. Muhammad Siad Barre was ousted (Jan. 1991). The UN sent a U.S.-led **peacekeeping force**, but it was unsuccessful in restoring order. Some soldiers of the peacekeeping force were killed, including 23 Pakistanis (June 1993) and 18 U.S. Rangers (Oct. 1993). The UN ended its mission (Mar. 1995) with no durable government in place. **Liberia** endured factional fighting that lasted almost 5 years and claimed over 150,000 lives; a cease-fire was concluded in Aug. 1995. The World Health Organization reported (1995) that Africa accounted for 70% of **AIDS** cases worldwide.

A 16-year civil war appeared to end in **Angola** (May 1991) when the government signed a peace accord with the rebel UNITA faction. But despite the inauguration of a national unity government (Apr. 1997), insurgents continued to fight and gain territory. **Namibia** officially became independent in Mar. 1990. Claimed by South Africa since 1919 and placed under UN authority in 1971, it had long been a focus of colonial rivalries. In **Algeria,** the army cancelled a 2nd round of parliamentary elections (Jan. 1992) after the Islamic party won a first round. Islamic fundamentalists then began a terrorist campaign that, along with killings by pro-government squads, eventually claimed thousands of lives. A peace plan was worked out with the militants in 1999.

North America. The **North American Free Trade Agreement** (NAFTA), liberalizing trade between the United

States, Canada, and Mexico, went into effect Jan. 1, 1994. In **Canada**, the Progressive Conservative Party suffered a crushing defeat in general elections (Oct. 1993), and liberal Jean **Chrétien** became prime minister. The map of Canada was altered in Apr. 1999 to create a new territory, **Nunavut,** out of an area that had been part of Northwest Territories.

In the **United States'** 1992 presidential election, Democrat Bill **Clinton** defeated Pres. George Bush, but in 1994 congressional elections Republicans gained control of Congress. Clinton reached agreement with Congress on measures to eliminate the federal budget deficit. Clinton won reelection in 1996; the new administration was plagued by scandals but remained popular amid continued economic prosperity. In Dec. 1998 **Clinton** was **impeached** by the U.S. House on charges related to the Monica Lewinsky scandal; he was **acquitted** by the Senate in Feb. 1999.

The U.S. Army and Navy were torn by sexual scandals involving abuse of women personnel. The **United States** suffered embarrassment with the discovery of espionage by CIA agents (Aldrich Ames, Harold Nicholson).

In **Mexico,** Ernesto **Zedillo** of the ruling PRI party was elected president (July 1994) after the party's first candidate was assassinated. The country soon faced a crisis affecting the value of the peso, but recovered with the help of a bailout package from the U.S. A peasant revolt spearheaded by the **Zapatista National Liberation Army** erupted in the state of Chiapas (Jan. 1994) and was suppressed.

Central America and the Caribbean. In **Haiti**, Jean-Bertrand **Aristide** was elected president (Dec. 1990) but was ousted in a military coup after 9 months in office. The UN approved a U.S.-led invasion to restore the elected leader; shortly before troops arrived, a delegation headed by former U.S. Pres. Jimmy Carter arranged (Sept. 1994) for the junta to step aside for Aristide, who served until 1996. In **Nicaragua**, Violetta Chamarro defeated Daniel **Ortega** in the presidential election (Feb. 1990), thus ousting the Sandinistas. In **Panama**, U.S. troops invaded and overthrew the government of Manuel **Noriega** (Dec. 1989), who was wanted on drug charges; Noriega was captured Jan. 1990. On Dec. 31, 1999, Panama assumed full control of the **Panama Canal**, in accord with a treaty with the U.S. In **El Salvador** (1992) and **Guatemala** (1996) the governments signed agreements with rebel factions aimed at ending long-running civil conflicts.

South America. Alberto **Fujimori** was elected president of **Peru** in June 1990 and, despite his suppression of the constitution (1992), was reelected in 1995. Peru succeeded in capturing (Sept. 1992) the leader of the **Shining Path** guerrilla movement. Leftist guerrillas took hostages at an ambassador's residence in Lima (Dec. 1996); one hostage was killed during a government assault rescuing the rest (Apr. 1997). Peronist Pres. Carlos Saúl **Menem** served as

Argentina's president for much of the decade (elected 1989, reelected 1995), imposing stringent economic measures; he was succeeded in 1999 by Fernando de la **Rúa**.

Former Chilean Pres. Gen. Augusto **Pinochet** continued to head the army until Mar. 1998; he was arrested in London (Oct. 1998) on human rights charges but was judged medically unfit for trial and returned to Chile (Mar. 2000).

In **Brazil**, Fernando Henrique **Cardoso** was elected president (Oct. 1994) and reelected in 1998 amid a growing economic slump; the IMF announced a $42 billion aid package (Nov. 1998). The first UN Conference on Environment and Development, or **Earth Summit**, was held (June 1992) in **Rio de Janeiro**, with delegates from 178 nations.

Terrorism and Crime. Terrorism, often linked to Mideastern sources continued to target the U.S. and Europe. A terrorist bomb exploded in a garage beneath New York City's **World Trade Center**, killing 6 people (Feb. 1993). Bombings of a U.S. military training center (Nov. 1995) and a barracks holding U.S. airmen (June 1996), both in **Saudi Arabia**, killed 7 and 19, respectively. Bombs exploded outside **U.S. embassies** in Kenya and Tanzania, Aug. 1998, killing over 220 people; the U.S. retaliated with missiles fired at alleged terrorist-linked sites in Afghanistan and Sudan. The Alfred P. Murrah Federal Building in **Oklahoma City**, OK, was destroyed by a bomb that killed 168 people (Apr. 1995).

Science and Technology. The powerful **Hubble Space Telescope** was launched in Apr. 1990; flaws in its mirrors and solar panels were repaired by space-walking astronauts (Dec. 1993). U.S. space shuttle **Atlantis** docked with the orbiting Russian space station **Mir** (June 1995) in first of several joint missions in a spirit of post-Cold-War cooperation. In Nov. 1998 first component for a new **International Space Station** was launched into space from Kazakhstan.

Mir and Shuttle Atlantis

Scottish scientist Ian Wilmut announced (Feb. 1997) the **cloning** of a sheep, nicknamed Dolly—the first mammal successfully cloned from a cell from an adult animal.

Tim Berners-Lee launched the first World Wide Web server (1990) from the European Center for Nuclear Research (CERN) in Switzerland; CERN announced (1993) that the technology could be used for free. User-friendly graphical browsers (Mosaic, 1993; Netscape, 1994) and affordable Internet service providers (America Online for Macs, 1989, and Windows, 1993) rapidly expanded the reach of the Internet.

Opening a New Century: 2000-2005

Terrorism. In Oct. 2000, 17 American sailors were killed aboard the **USS Cole** in Aden, **Yemen**, when a small boat exploded alongside it in a terrorist attack. On **Sept. 11, 2001**, hijackers crashed 2 jetliners into the twin towers of the **World Trade Center** in New York City and another into the **Pentagon** outside Washington, DC; a 4th crashed in a field in **Pennsylvania**. The attacks, which destroyed both towers and damaged the Pentagon, killed about 3,000 people, including all 265 aboard the planes. Saudi exile Osama bin Laden and his **al-Qaeda terrorist network**, based in **Afghanistan** and backed by the Taliban government there, emerged as responsible for the attacks. A U.S.-led military campaign launched in Oct. 2001 **ousted the Taliban**, and a transitional government was installed (Dec. 2001), although al-Qaeda remained active in some areas of Afghanistan and elsewhere, and Bin Laden remained at large.

Among incidents elsewhere, a bomb exploded in a truck outside a synagogue in **Tunisia** (Apr. 2002), killing 17 (including the driver). A car bomb on the Indonesian island of

Bali (Oct. 2002) killed about 200, mostly foreign tourists; Muslim extremists were arrested. Chechen guerrillas seized a **Moscow movie theater** (Oct. 2002); more than 100 hostages were killed in a subsequent raid by Russian troops. A terrorist explosion in **Moscow subways** killed 39 (Feb. 2004), and 89 died when 2 Russian planes were destroyed apparently by bombs (Aug. 2004). Chechen guerrillas took over a **Beslan, Russia, school**; 330 hostages, many students, and 31 guerrillas were killed in the standoff (Sept. 2004). The bombing of an Israeli-owned **hotel in Kenya** (Nov. 2002) killed 13 (including the 3 bombers). Suicide attacks against Western targets in **Riyadh**, Saudi Arabia (May 2003), killed 34 people (including 9 attackers). Suicide bombings in **Istanbul**, Turkey (Nov. 2003), hit two Jewish synagogues and British targets, killing about 60 people in all. Four **commuter trains were bombed** in Madrid, Spain, killing 202 (Mar. 2004); elections held a week later ousted Spain's premier. Three subway trains and a bus were **bombed in London** during rush hour (June 2005); 52 people were killed, including 4 bombers. Three suicide bombers killed 20 others on Indonesian resort island **Bali** (Oct. 2005). Al-Qaeda in Iraq claimed responsibility (Nov. 2005) for a **hotel bombings** in Jordan that killed 59, excluding the suicide bombers.

War in Iraq. The U.S., with Great Britain, launched an **invasion of Iraq** (Mar. 2003), aimed at ousting the dictatorial regime of **Saddam Hussein**. Troops took control of Baghdad and other cities, and Pres. Bush declared major combat ended, May 1, but **insurgents** caused continuing casualties among troops and civilians. Searches for **weapons of mass destruction**, cited as major grounds for the invasion, yielded no evidence. **Saddam Hussein** was eventually **captured** (Dec. 2003), as well as other regime leaders, to be put on trial by Iraqis. An interim government was installed (June 2004). Evidence that U.S. soldiers at **Abu Ghraib** prison in Iraq abused detainees arose in Apr. 2004. U.S. military deaths topped 2,000 (Oct. 2005) as attacks by insurgents continued. Despite threats by insurgents, Iraqis turned out in large numbers to vote in national elections (Jan. 2005); the transitional national assembly appointed a Kurdish president and Shiite premier (Apr. 2005). In a referendum, **Iraqis approved a constitution** (Oct. 2005), and voted again in parliamentary elections (Dec. 2005).

Middle East. Violence between Israelis and Palestinians escalated, with **suicide bombings** by Palestinians and retaliation by Israeli armed forces, the peace process languished. Likud leader Ariel **Sharon** was **elected** prime minister of Israel (Feb. 2001). In reponse to Palestinian suicide attacks that killed 26, Israeli forces stormed the compound of Palestinian leader Yasir Arafat (Mar. 2002), keeping him confined there until early May. **Arafat died** in a Paris hospital (Nov. 2004) and was succeeded by Mahmoud Abbas following elections. The U.S., Russia, UN, and European Union (EU) formally initiated (Apr. 2003) a **"road map"** plan for Israeli-Palestinian **peace negotiations**, but little progress was made. Israel completed (Aug. 2005) evacuation of 25 Jewish settlements in the **West Bank** and **Gaza Strip**.

Syrian Pres. Hafez al-**Assad died** (June 2000); succeeded by his son. Iran was censured (Dec. 2003) by the UN Intl. Atomic Energy Agency for covering up aspects of its nuclear weapons program.

Europe. In Oct. 2000, Yugoslav strongman Slobodan **Milosevic yielded** power to Vojislav Kostunica, who had declared himself president in the face of anti-Milosevic protests after a disputed election. Milosevic surrendered to Serbian authorities; in Feb. 2002 he went on trial for **war crimes** allegedly committed during 1990s ethnic conflicts in the Balkans. The first-ever **Concorde jet crash**, near Paris, killed 113 people (July 2000). The Russian nuclear sub *Kursk* sank in the Barents Sea, killing 118 crew members.

By early 2002 the **euro** was the common currency in 12 European Union nations. The EU admitted 10 Eastern European nations (May 2004). The deadline to ratify the EU constitution was extended (June 2005) after voters defeated referenda in France and the Netherlands.

Some 35,000 people across Europe, including over 11,000 in France, reportedly died in 2003 **summer heat waves**.

Pope **John Paul II**, the leader of the world's Roman Catholics, died (Apr. 2005); German cardinal Joseph Ratzinger elected his successor: Pope Benedict XVI.

Rioting shook France's immigrant communities in 300 major cities and towns (Nov. 2005); over 3,000 arrests were made.

Russia. The Russian nuclear sub *Kursk* sank in the Barents Sea (Aug. 2000) killing 118 crew members. Vladimir Putin, reelected in Mar. 2004, signed legislation ending popular election of governors (Dec. 2004).

Asia. South Korean Pres. **Kim Dae Jung** and **North Korean** ruler **Kim Jong Il** held a **summit** meeting and agreed to seek peace and reunification (June 2000), but tensions rose after North Korea admitted conducting a covert nuclear weapons development program (Oct. 2002). **Nepal**'s King

Birendra and other Nepalese royals were shot to death inside the palace, apparently by Crown Prince Dipendra, who then killed himself (June 2001). **Chinese** Pres. Jiang Zemin and **Russian** Pres. Vladimir Putin signed a **friendship treaty** (July 2001). With Jiang's retirement **Hu Jintao** was named as China's new Communist party chief (Nov. 2002) and president (Mar. 2003).

North Korea **withdrew** (Jan. 2003) from the Nuclear Nonproliferation Treaty; multi-nation talks were held in Beijing (Aug. 2003) about the status of its **nuclear program**. Pakistan and India **restored diplomatic ties** (May 2003) and declared a **cease-fire** in disputed territory (Nov. 2003). Pakistani Pres. Gen. Pervez Musharraf twice **escaped assassination** by Islamic militants (Dec. 2003). Afghanistan held its first presidential elections and selected Hamid Karzai (Oct.-Nov 2004).

A massive **tsunami** in the Indian Ocean (Dec. 2004) devastated parts of Indonesia, Thailand, India, Sri Lanka, and other Asian and African nations and left some 200,000 dead. An **earthquake** struck the disputed territory of Kashmir and parts of N. Pakistan and India (Oct. 2005); nearly 80,000 were killed.

Africa. The 13th International **AIDS Conference**, held in Durban, South Africa (July 2000), focused on ways of controlling surging AIDS rates in developing countries. **Ethiopia** and **Eritrea** signed a **peace treaty** (Dec. 2000). Laurent **Kabila**, president of the Democratic Republic of the **Congo**, was **shot to death** by a bodyguard (Jan. 2001). Liberian Pres. Charles Taylor went into voluntary exile (Aug. 2003) as part of a deal to end a 14-year-old civil war; other accords were reached at **ending civil wars** in Angola (Apr. 2002) and Côte d'Ivoire (Jan. 2003).

A peace agreement in the Dem. Rep. of **Congo** (Apr. 2003) did not end violence there. Civil war between the Muslim-led government and rebels from Christian areas in **Sudan** continued, with massive casualties. Sudanese government-backed militias (janjaweed) in the Darfur region were accused of displacing 2 mil. people in acts bordering on genocide; the U.N. appointed the International Criminal Court to prosecute **Sudanese war crimes** (estimated to have left 180,000 dead) in Mar. 2005. Zimbabwean Pres. Robert Mugabe pulled his country out of the **Commonwealth** (Dec. 2003) after the group reaffirmed suspension of **Zimbabwe** for alleged fraud in the 2002 election. **Libya** agreed (Dec. 2003) to abandon programs pursuing weapons of mass destruction.

Americas and the Caribbean. Vicente **Fox** of the center-right National Action Party (PAN) was elected **president of Mexico** (July 2000), in a historic defeat for the long-supreme Institutional Revolutionary Party (PRI). Peruvian Pres. Alberto **Fujimori stepped down** during his 3rd term (Nov. 2000), amid scandal, and did not seek reelection. In Jan. 2001, George W. **Bush** was inaugurated as U.S. president, after one of the tightest and most controversial elections in U.S. history; he was reelected in Nov. 2004. Venezuelan Pres. Hugo Chavez regained power after 48-hr. coup (Dec. 2002). Argentina's **record default** on International Monetary Fund loans resulted (Sept. 2003) in a **$12.5 billion debt-refinancing** agreement. **Haiti** was wracked by anti-government protests, leading to the resignation of Jean-Bertrand **Aristide** in Feb. 2004.

Hurricanes and subsequent flooding and landslides in 2005 killed thousands in the U.S. and abroad: Katrina, U.S. Gulf Coast (Aug.); Stan, S. Mexico and N. Central America (Oct.).

Paul Martin succeeded Jean Chrétien as **Canadian prime minister** (Dec. 2003) after he was elected to lead the ruling Liberal Party.

Space. The U.S. space shuttle *Columbia* broke up on re-entering Earth's atmosphere Feb. 1, 2003, killing all 7 crew members.

International. Negotiators from 178 countries agreed to adopt the **Kyoto Protocol** July 2001, calling for a reduction of greenhouse gases in developed nations; 141 nations had ratified the treaty when it took effect (Feb. 2005).

HISTORICAL FIGURES

Ancient Greeks and Romans

Greeks

Aeschines, orator, 389-314 BCE
Aeschylus, dramatist, 525-456 BCE
Aesop, fableist, c. 620-c. 560 BCE
Alcibiades, politician, 450-404 BCE
Anacreon, poet, c. 582-c. 485 BCE
Anaxagoras, philosopher, c. 500-428 BCE
Anaximander, philosopher, 611-546 BCE
Anaximenes, philosopher, c. 570-500 BCE
Antiphon, speechwriter, c. 480-411 BCE
Apollonius, mathematician, c. 265-170 BCE
Archimedes, mathematician, 287-212 BCE
Aristophanes, dramatist, c. 448-380 BCE
Aristotle, philosopher, 384-322 BCE
Athenaeus, scholar, fl. c. 200
Callicrates, architect, fl. 5th cent. BCE
Callimachus, poet, c. 305-240 BCE
Cratinus, comic dramatist, 520-421 BCE
Democritus, philosopher, c. 460-370 BCE
Demosthenes, orator, 384-322 BCE
Diodorus, historian, fl. 20 BCE
Diogenes, philosopher, 372-c. 287 BCE
Dionysius, historian, d. c. 7 BCE
Empedocles, philosopher, c. 490-430 BCE
Epicharmus, dramatist, c. 530-440 BCE
Epictetus, philosopher, c. 55-c. 135
Epicurus, philosopher, 341-270 BCE
Eratosthenes, scientist, 276-194 BCE
Euclid, mathematician, fl. c. 300 BCE
Euripides, dramatist, c. 484-406 BCE
Galen, physician, 130-200 BCE
Heraclitus, philosopher, c. 540-c. 475 BCE

Herodotus, historian, c. 484-420 BCE
Hesiod, poet, 8th cent. BCE
Hippocrates, physician, c. 460-377 BCE
Homer, poet, fl. c. 700 BCE(?)
Isocrates, orator, 436-338 BCE
Menander, dramatist, 342-292 BCE
Parmenides, philosopher, b. c. 515 BCE
Pericles, statesman, c. 495-429 BCE
Phidias, sculptor, c. 500-435 BCE
Pindar, poet, c. 518-c. 438 BCE
Plato, philosopher, c. 428-347 BCE
Plutarch, biographer, c. 46-120
Polybius, historian, c. 200-c. 118 BCE
Praxiteles, sculptor, 400-330 BCE
Pythagoras, phil., math., c. 580-c. 500 BCE
Sappho, poet, c. 610-c. 580 BCE
Simonides, poet, 556-c. 468 BCE
Socrates, philosopher, 469-399 BCE
Solon, statesman, 640-560 BCE
Sophocles, dramatist, c. 496-406 BCE
Strabo, geographer, c. 63 BCE-24 CE
Thales, philosopher, c. 634-546 BCE
Themistocles, politician, c. 524-c. 460 BCE
Theocritus, poet, c. 310-250 BCE
Theophrastus, phil., c. 372-c. 287 BCE
Thucydides, historian, fl. 5th cent. BCE
Timon, philosopher, c. 320-c. 230 BCE
Xenophon, historian, c. 434-c. 355 BCE
Zeno, philosopher, c. 335-c. 263 BCE

Romans

Ammianus, historian, c. 330-395
Apuleius, satirist, c. 124-c. 170

Boethius, scholar, c. 480-524
Caesar, Julius, leader, 100-44 BCE
Catiline, politician, c. 108-62 BCE
Cato (Elder), statesman, 234-149 BCE
Catullus, poet, c. 84-54 BCE
Cicero, orator, 106-43 BCE
Claudian, poet, c. 370-c. 404
Ennius, poet, 239-170 BCE
Gellius, author, c. 130-c. 165
Horace, poet, 65-8 BCE
Juvenal, satirist, 60-127
Livy, historian, 59 BCE-17 CE
Lucan, poet, 39-65
Lucilius, poet, c. 180-c.102 BCE
Lucretius, poet, c. 99-c. 55 BCE
Martial, epigrammatist, c. 38-c. 103
Nepos, historian, c. 100-c. 25 BCE
Ovid, poet, 43 BCE-17 CE
Persius, satirist, 34-62
Plautus, dramatist, c. 254-c. 184 BCE
Pliny the Elder, scholar, 23-79
Pliny the Younger, author, 62-113
Quintilian, rhetorician, c. 35-c. 97
Sallust, historian, 86-34 BCE
Seneca, philosopher, 4 BCE-65 CE
Silius, poet, c. 25-101
Statius, poet, c. 45-c. 96
Suetonius, biographer, c. 69-c. 122
Tacitus, historian, 56-120
Terence, dramatist, 185-c. 159 BCE
Tibullus, poet, c. 55-c. 19 BCE
Vergil, poet, 70-19 BCE
Vitruvius, architect, fl. 1st cent. BCE

Roman Rulers

From Romulus to the end of the Empire in the West. Rulers in the East sat in Constantinople and, for a brief period, in Nicaea, until the capture of Constantinople by the Turks in 1453, when Byzantium was succeeded by the Ottoman Empire.

The Kingdom

BCE
753 Romulus (Quirinus)
716 Numa Pompilius
673 Tullus Hostilius
640 Ancus Marcius
616 L. Tarquinius Priscus
578 Servius Tullius
534 L. Tarquinius Superbus

The Republic

509 Consulate established
509 Quaestorship instituted
498 Dictatorship introduced
494 Plebeian Tribunate created
494 Plebeian Aedileship created
444 Consular Tribunate organized
435 Censorship instituted
366 Praetorship established
366 Curule Aedileship created
362 Military Tribunate elected
326 Proconsulate introduced
311 Naval Duumvirate elected
217 Dictatorship of Fabius Maximus
133 Tribunate of Tiberius Gracchus
123 Tribunate of Gaius Gracchus
82 Dictatorship of Sulla
60 First Triumvirate formed (Caesar, Pompeius, Crassus)
46 Dictatorship of Caesar
43 Second Triumvirate formed (Octavianus, Antonius, Lepidus)

The Empire

27 Augustus (Octavian)
CE
14 Tiberius I
37 Caligula
41 Claudius I
54 Nero
68 Galba
69 Galba; Otho, Vitellius
69 Vespasianus
79 Titus
81 Domitianus

96 Nerva
98 Trajanus
117 Hadrianus
138 Antoninus Pius
161 Marcus Aurelius and Lucius Verus
169 Marcus Aurelius (alone)
180 Commodus
193 Pertinax; Julianus I
193 Septimius Severus
211 Caracalla and Geta
212 Caracalla (alone)
217 Macrinus
218 Elagabalus (Heliogabalus)
222 Alexander Severus
235 Maximinus I (the Thracian)
238 Gordianus I and Gordianus II; Pupienus and Balbinus
238 Gordianus III
244 Philippus (the Arabian)
249 Decius
251 Gallus and Volusianus
253 Aemilianus
253 Valerianus and Gallienus
258 Gallienus (alone)
268 Claudius Gothicus
270 Quintillus
270 Aurelianus
275 Tacitus
276 Florianus
276 Probus
282 Carus
283 Carinus and Numerianus
286 Diocletianus and Maximianus
305 Galerius and Constantius I
306 Galerius, Maximinus II, Severus I
307 Galerius, Maximinus II, Constantinus I, Licinius, Maxentius
311 Maximinus II, Constantinus I, Licinius, Maxentius
314 Maximinus II, Constantinus I, Licinius

314 Constantinus I and Licinius
324 Constantinus I (the Great)
337 Constantinus II, Constans I, Constantius II
340 Constantinus II and Constans I
350 Constantius II
361 Julianus II (the Apostate)
363 Jovianus

West (Rome) and East (Constantinople)
364 Valentinianus I (West) and Valens (East)
367 Valentinianus I with Gratianus (West) and Valens (East)
375 Gratianus with Valentinianus II (West) and Valens (East)
378 Gratianus with Valentinianus II (West),Theodosius I (East)
383 Valentinianus II (West) and Theodosius I (East)
394 Theodosius I (the Great)
395 Honorius (West) and Arcadius (East)
408 Honorius (West) and Theodosius II (East)
423 Valentinianus III (West) and Theodosius II (East)
450 Valentinianus III (West) and Marcianus (East)
455 Maximus (West), Avitus (West); Marcianus (East)
456 Avitus (West), Marcianus (East)
457 Majorianus (West), Leo I (East)
461 Severus II (West), Leo I (East)
467 Anthemius (West), Leo I (East)
472 Olybrius (West), Leo I (East)
473 Glycerius (West), Leo I (East)
474 Julius Nepos (West), Leo II (East)
475 Romulus Augustulus (West) and Zeno (East)
476 End of Empire in West; Odovacar, King, drops title of Emperor; murdered by King Theodoric of Ostrogoths, 493

Rulers of England and Great Britain

ENGLAND

Name	Saxons and Danes	Reign Began	Died	Death Age	Years Reigned
Egbert	King of Wessex, won allegiance of all English	829	839	NA	10
Ethelwulf	Son, King of Wessex, Sussex, Kent, Essex	839	858	NA	19
Ethelbald	Son of Ethelwulf, displaced father in Wessex	858	860	NA	2
Ethelbert	2nd son of Ethelwulf, united Kent and Wessex	860	866	NA	6
Ethelred I	3rd son, King of Wessex, fought Danes	866	871	NA	5
Alfred	The Great, 4th son of Ethelwulf, defeated Danes, fortified London	871	899	52	28
Edward	The Elder, Alfred's son, united English, claimed Scotland	899	924	55	25
Athelstan	The Glorious, Edward's son, King of Mercia, Wessex	924	940	45	16
Edmund	3rd son of Edward, King of Wessex, Mercia	940	946	25	6
Edred	4th son of Edward	946	955	32	9
Edwy	The Fair, eldest son of Edmund, King of Wessex	955	959	18	3
Edgar	The Peaceful, 2nd son of Edmund, ruled all English	959	975	32	17
Edward	The Martyr, eldest son of Edgar, murdered by stepmother	975	978	17	4
Ethelred II	The Unready, 2nd son of Edgar, married Emma of Normandy	978	1016	48	37
Edmund II	Ironside, son of Ethelred II, King of London	1016	1016	27	0
Canute	The Dane, gave Wessex to Edmund, married Emma, Ethelred II's widow	1016	1035	40	19
Harold I	Harefoot, illegitimate son of Canute	1035	1040	NA	5
Hardecanute	Son of Canute by Emma, Danish King	1040	1042	24	2
Edward	The Confessor, son of Ethelred II (canonized 1161)	1042	1066	62	24
Harold II	Edward's brother-in-law, last Saxon King	1066	1066	44	0
	House of Normandy				
William I	The Conqueror, defeated Harold at Hastings	1066	1087	60	21
William II	Rufus, 3rd son of William I, killed by arrow	1087	1100	43	13
Henry I	Beauclerc, youngest son of William I	1100	1135	67	35
	House of Blois				
Stephen	Son of Adela, daughter of William I, and Count of Blois	1135	1154	50	19
	House of Plantagenet				
Henry II	Son of Geoffrey Plantagenet (Angevin) by Matilda, daughter of Henry I	1154	1189	56	35
Richard I	Coeur de Lion, son of Henry II, crusader	1189	1199	42	10
John	Lackland, son of Henry II, approved Magna Carta, 1215	1199	1216	50	17
Henry III	Son of John, acceded at 9, under regency until 1227	1216	1272	65	56
Edward I	Son of Henry III	1272	1307	68	35
Edward II	Son of Edward I, deposed by Parliament, 1327	1307	1327	43	20
Edward III	Of Windsor, son of Edward II	1327	1377	65	50
Richard II	Grandson of Edward III, minor until 1389, deposed 1399	1377	1400	33	22
	House of Lancaster				
Henry IV	Son of John of Gaunt, Duke of Lancaster, son of Edward III	1399	1413	47	13
Henry V	Son of Henry IV, victor of Agincourt	1413	1422	34	9
Henry VI	Son of Henry V, deposed 1461, died in Tower of London	1422	1471	49	39
	House of York				
Edward IV	Great-great-grandson of Edward III, son of Duke of York	1461	1483	40	22
Edward V	Son of Edward IV, murdered in Tower of London	1483	1483	13	0
Richard III	Brother of Edward IV, fell at Bosworth Field	1483	1485	32	2
	House of Tudor				
Henry VII	Son of Edmund Tudor, Earl of Richmond, whose father had married the widow of Henry V; descended from Edward III through his mother, Margaret Beaufort, via John of Gaunt. By marrying daughter of Edward IV, united Lancaster and York	1485	1509	53	24
Henry VIII	Son of Henry VII, by Elizabeth, daughter of Edward IV	1509	1547	56	38
Edward VI	Son of Henry VIII, by Jane Seymour, Henry VIII's 3rd queen. Ruled under regents. Was forced to name Lady Jane Grey his successor. Council of State proclaimed her queen July 10, 1553. Mary Tudor won Council, was proclaimed queen July 19, 1553. Mary had Lady Jane Grey beheaded for treason, Feb. 1554.	1547	1553	16	6
Mary I	Daughter of Henry VIII, by Catherine of Aragon	1553	1558	43	5
Elizabeth I	Daughter of Henry VIII, by Anne Boleyn	1558	1603	69	44

GREAT BRITAIN

Name	House of Stuart	Reign Began	Died	Death Age	Years Reigned
James I	James VI of Scotland, son of Mary, Queen of Scots. First to call self King of Great Britain; this became official with the Act of Union, 1707.	1603	1625	59	22
Charles I	Only surviving son of James I, beheaded Jan. 30, 1649	1625	1649	48	24
	Commonwealth, 1649-60				
	Council of State, 1649; Protectorate, 1653[1]				
The Cromwells	Oliver Cromwell, Lord Protector	1653	1658	59	5
	Richard Cromwell, son, Lord Protector, resigned May 25, 1659.	1658	1712	86	1
	House of Stuart (Restored)				
Charles II	Eldest son of Charles I, died without issue	1660	1685	55	25
James II	2nd son of Charles I, deposed 1688. Interregnum 1688-89	1685	1701	68	3
William III	Son of William, Prince of Orange, by Mary, daughter of Charles I	1689	1702	51	13
and Mary II	Eldest daughter of James II and wife of William III	1689	1694	33	6
Anne	2nd daughter of James II	1702	1714	49	12
	House of Hanover				
George I	Son of Elector of Hanover, by Sophia, granddaughter of James I	1714	1727	67	13
George II	Only son of George I, married Caroline of Brandenburg	1727	1760	77	33
George III	Grandson of George II, married Charlotte of Mecklenburg	1760	1820	81	59
George IV	Eldest son of George III, Prince Regent, from Feb. 1811	1820	1830	67	10
William IV	3rd son of George III, married Adelaide of Saxe-Meiningen	1830	1837	71	7
Victoria	Daughter of Edward, 4th son of George III; married (1840) Prince Albert of Saxe-Coburg and Gotha, who became Prince Consort	1837	1901	81	63

Name	Reign Began	Died	Death Age	Years Reigned
House of Saxe-Coburg and Gotha				
Edward VII . . . . . Eldest son of Victoria, married Alexandra, Princess of Denmark	1901	1910	68	9
House of Windsor[2]				
George V . . . . 2nd son of Edward VII, married Princess Mary of Teck	1910	1936	70	25
Edward VIII . . . . Eldest son of George V, acceded Jan. 20, 1936, abdicated Dec. 11, 1936	1936	1936	70	1
George VI . . . . . . 2nd son of George V, married Lady Elizabeth Bowes-Lyon	1936	1972	77	15
Elizabeth II . . . . . Elder daughter of George VI, acceded Feb. 6, 1952	1952	1952	56	

NA = age/birth date not certain. (1) The Cromwells ruled Britain following overthow of the monarchy in 1649. (2) Name adopted by proclamation of George V, July 17, 1917.

Rulers of Scotland

Kenneth I MacAlpin was the first Scot to rule both Scots and Picts, 846 CE.

Duncan I was the first general ruler, 1034. Macbeth seized the kingdom, 1040, was slain by Duncan's son, Malcolm III MacDuncan (Canmore), 1057.

Malcolm married Margaret, Saxon princess who had fled from the Normans. Queen Margaret introduced English language and monastic customs. She was canonized, 1250. Her son Edgar, 1097, moved the court to Edinburgh. His brothers Alexander I and David I succeeded. Malcolm IV the Maiden, 1153, grandson of David I, was followed by his brother, William the Lion, 1165, whose son was Alexander II, 1214. The latter's son, Alexander III, 1249, defeated the Norse and regained the Hebrides. When he died, 1286, his granddaughter, Margaret, child of Eric of Norway and grandniece of Edward I of England, known as the Maid of Norway, was chosen ruler, but died 1290, aged 8.

John Baliol, 1292-96. (Interregnum, 10 years.)

Robert Bruce (The Bruce), 1306-29, victor at Bannockburn, 1314. David II, his only son, 1329-71.

Robert II, 1371-90, grandson of Robert Bruce, son of Walter, the Steward of Scotland, was called The Steward, first of the so-called Stuart line.

Robert III, son, 1390-1406.

James I, son, 1406-37.

James II, son, 1437-60.

James III, eldest son, 1460-88.

James IV, eldest son, 1488-1513.

James V, eldest son, 1513-42.

Mary, daughter of James V, became queen before she was 1 week old; crowned 1543. Married 1558, Francis, son of Henry II of France, who became king 1559, d. 1560. Mary ruled Scots, 1561, until abdication, 1567. She also married Henry Stewart, Lord Darnley (1565), and James, Earl of Bothwell (1567). Imprisoned by Elizabeth I; beheaded 1587.

James VI, 1567-1625, son of Mary and Lord Darnley, became King of England on death of Elizabeth in 1603. Although the thrones were thus united, the legislative union of Scotland and England was not effected until the Act of Union, May 1, 1707.

Prime Ministers of Great Britain

Designations in parentheses describe each government;
W=Whig; T=Tory; Cl=Coalition; P=Peelite; Li=Liberal; C=Conservative[1]; La=Labour

Sir Robert Walpole (W)[2] 1721-42	Benjamin Disraeli (C) 1868
Earl of Wilmington (W) 1742-43	William E. Gladstone (Li) 1868-74
Henry Pelham (W) 1743-54	Benjamin Disraeli (C) 1874-80
Duke of Newcastle (W) 1754-56	William E. Gladstone (Li) 1880-85
Duke of Devonshire (W) 1756-57	Marquess of Salisbury (C) 1885-86
Duke of Newcastle (W) 1757-62	William E. Gladstone (Li) 1886
Earl of Bute (T) 1762-63	Marquess of Salisbury (C) 1886-92
George Grenville (W) 1763-65	William E. Gladstone (Li) 1892-94
Marquess of Rockingham (W) 1765-66	Earl of Rosebery (Li) 1894-95
William Pitt the Elder (Earl of Chatham) (W) 1766-68	Marquess of Salisbury (C) 1895-1902
Duke of Grafton (W) 1768-70	Arthur J. Balfour (C) 1902-05
Frederick North (Lord North) (T) 1770-82	Sir Henry Campbell Bannerman (Li) 1905-08
Marquess of Rockingham (W) 1782	Herbert H. Asquith (Li) 1908-15
Earl of Shelburne (W) 1782-83	Herbert H. Asquith (Cl) 1915-16
Duke of Portland (Cl) 1783	David Lloyd George (Cl) 1916-22
William Pitt the Younger (T) 1783-1801	Andrew Bonar Law (C) 1922-23
Henry Addington (T) 1801-04	Stanley Baldwin (C) 1923-24
William Pitt the Younger (T) 1804-06	James Ramsay MacDonald (La) 1924
William Wyndham Grenville, Baron Grenville (W) . . .1806-07	Stanley Baldwin (C) 1924-29
Duke of Portland (T) 1807-09	James Ramsay MacDonald (La) 1929-31
Spencer Perceval (T) 1809-12	James Ramsay MacDonald (Cl) 1931-35
Earl of Liverpool (T) 1812-27	Stanley Baldwin (Cl) 1935-37
George Canning (T) 1827	Neville Chamberlain (Cl) 1937-40
Viscount Goderich (T) 1827-28	Winston Churchill (Cl) 1940-45
Duke of Wellington (T) 1828-30	Winston Churchill (C) 1945
Earl Grey (W) 1830-34	Clement Attlee (La) 1945-51
Viscount Melbourne (W) 1834	Sir Winston Churchill (C) 1951-55
Sir Robert Peel (C) 1834-35	Sir Anthony Eden (C) 1955-57
Viscount Melbourne (W) 1835-41	Harold Macmillan (C) 1957-63
Sir Robert Peel (C) 1841-46	Sir Alec Douglas-Home (C) 1963-64
Lord (later Earl) John Russell (W) 1846-52	Harold Wilson (La) 1964-70
Earl of Derby (C) 1852	Edward Heath (C) 1970-74
Earl of Aberdeen (P) 1852-55	Harold Wilson (La) 1974-76
Viscount Palmerston (Li) 1855-58	James Callaghan (La) 1976-79
Earl of Derby (C) 1858-59	Margaret Thatcher (C) 1979-90
Viscount Palmerston (Li) 1859-65	John Major (C) 1990-97
Earl Russell (Li) 1865-66	Tony Blair (La) 1997-
Earl of Derby (C) 1866-68	

(1) The Conservative Party was formed in 1834, an outgrowth of the Tory party. (2) Walpole is commonly regarded as the first prime minister of Britain, though the title was not commonly used then and did not become official until 1905.

Rulers of France: Kings, Queens, Presidents

Caesar to Charlemagne

Julius Caesar subdued the Gauls, native tribes of Gaul (France), 58 to 51 BCE. The Romans ruled 500 years. The Franks, a Teutonic tribe, reached the Somme from the East c. 250 CE. By the 5th century the Merovingian Franks ousted the Romans. In 451, with the help of Visigoths, Burgundians, and others, they defeated Attila and the Huns at Chalons-sur-Marne.

Childeric I became leader of the Merovingians, 458. His son Clovis I (Chlodwig, Ludwig, Louis), crowned 481, founded the dynasty. After defeating the Alemanni (Germans), 496, he was baptized a Christian and made Paris his capital. His line ruled until Childeric III was deposed, 751.

The West Merovingians were called Neustrians, the eastern Austrasians. Pepin of Herstal (687-714), major domus, or head of the palace, of Austrasia, took over Neustria as dux (leader) of the Franks. Pepin's son, Charles, called Martel (the Hammer), defeated the Saracens at Tours-Poitiers, 732; was succeeded by his son, Pepin the Short, 741, who deposed Childeric III and ruled as king until 768.

His son, Charlemagne, or Charles the Great (742-814), became king of the Franks, 768, with his brother Carloman, who died 771. Charlemagne ruled France, Germany, parts of Italy, Spain, and Austria, and enforced Christianity. Crowned Emperor of the Romans by Pope Leo III in St. Peter's, Rome, Dec. 25, 800. Succeeded by son, Louis I the Pious, 814. At death, 840, Louis left empire to sons, Lothair (Roman emperor); Pepin I (king of Aquitaine); Louis II (of Germany); Charles the Bald (France). They quarreled and, by the Treaty of Verdun, 843, divided the empire.

The date preceding each entry is year of accession.

The Carolingians

843 Charles I (the Bald), Roman Emperor, 875
877 Louis II (the Stammerer), son
879 Louis III (d. 882) and Carloman, brothers
885 Charles II (the Fat), Roman Emperor, 881
888 Eudes (Odo), elected by nobles
898 Charles III (the Simple), son of Louis II, defeated by
922 Robert, brother of Eudes, killed in war
923 Rudolph (Raoul), Duke of Burgundy
936 Louis IV, son of Charles III
954 Lothair, son, aged 13, defeated by Capet
986 Louis V (the Sluggard), left no heirs

The Capets

987 Hugh Capet, son of Hugh the Great
996 Robert II (the Pious), his son
1031 Henry I, son
1060 Philip I (the Fair), son
1108 Louis VI (the Fat), son
1137 Louis VII (the Younger), son
1180 Philip II (Augustus), son, crowned at Reims
1223 Louis VIII (the Lion), son
1226 Louis IX, son, crusader; Louis IX (1214-1270) reigned 44 years, arbitrated disputes with English King Henry III, led crusades, 1248 (captured in Egypt, 1250) and 1270, when he died of plague in Tunis. Canonized 1297 as St. Louis.
1270 Philip III (the Hardy), son
1285 Philip IV (the Fair), son, king at 17
1314 Louis X (the Headstrong), son. His posthumous son, John I, lived only 7 days.
1316 Philip V (the Tall), brother of Louis X
1322 Charles IV (the Fair), brother of Louis X

House of Valois

1328 Philip VI (of Valois), grandson of Philip III
1350 John II (the Good), his son, retired to England
1364 Charles V (the Wise), son
1380 Charles VI (the Beloved), son
1422 Charles VII (the Victorious), son. In 1429 Joan of Arc (Jeanne d'Arc) promised Charles to oust the English, who occupied northern France. Joan won at Orleans and Patay and had Charles crowned at Reims, July 17, 1429. Joan was captured May 24, 1430, and executed May 30, 1431, at Rouen for heresy. Charles ordered her rehabilitation, effected 1455.
1461 Louis XI (the Cruel), son, civil reformer
1483 Charles VIII (the Affable), son
1498 Louis XII, great-grandson of Charles V
1515 Francis I, of Angouleme, nephew, son-in-law. Francis I (1494-1547) reigned 32 years, fought 4 big wars, was

patron of the arts, aided Cellini, del Sarto, Leonardo da Vinci, Rabelais, embellished Fontainebleau.
1547 Henry II, son, killed at a joust in a tournament. He was the husband of Catherine de Medicis (1519-89) and the lover of Diane de Poitiers (1499-1566). Catherine was born in Florence, daughter of Lorenzo de Medici. By her marriage to Henry II she became the mother of Francis II, Charles IX, Henry III, and Queen Margaret (Reine Margot), wife of Henry IV. She persuaded Charles IX to order the massacre of Huguenots on the Feast of St. Bartholomew, Aug. 24, 1572, six days after her daughter was married to Henry of Navarre.
1559 Francis II, son. Betrothed in 1548 at age 4 to Mary, Queen of Scots, aged 6. They were married 1558. Francis died 1560, aged 16; Mary ruled Scotland, abdicated 1567.
1560 Charles IX, brother
1574 Henry III, brother, assassinated

House of Bourbon

1589 Henry IV, of Navarre, assassinated. Henry IV made enemies when he gave tolerance to Protestants by Edict of Nantes, 1598. He was grandson of Queen Margaret of Navarre, literary patron. He married Margaret of Valois, daughter of Henry II and Catherine de Medicis; was divorced; in 1600 married Marie de Medicis, who became Regent of France, 1610-17, for her son, Louis XIII, but was exiled by Richelieu, 1631.
1610 Louis XIII (the Just), son. Louis XIII (1601-43) married Anne of Austria. He came to be dominated by his chief minister (1622-42), Cardinal Richelieu.
1643 Louis XIV (the "Sun King"), son. Louis XIV was king 72 years. Until 1661, Anne of Austria was regent, with Cardinal Mazarin as chief minister; after that, Louis ruled absolutely. Known for his lavish court and patronage of the arts, he exhausted a prosperous country in wars for thrones and territory.
1715 Louis XV, great-grandson. Louis XV married a Polish princess, lost Canada to the English. His favorites, Mme. Pompadour and Mme. Du Barry, influenced policies. Noted for saying, "After me, the deluge."
1774 Louis XVI, grandson; married Marie Antoinette, daughter of Empress Maria Therese of Austria. King and queen beheaded by Revolution, 1793. Their son, called Louis XVII, died in prison, never ruled.

First Republic

1792 National Convention of the French Revolution
1795 Directory, under Barras and others
1799 Consulate, Napoleon Bonaparte, first consul. Elected consul for life, 1802.

First Empire

1804 Napoleon I (Napoleon Bonaparte), emperor. Josephine (de Beauharnais), empress, 1804-09; Marie Louise, empress, 1810-14. Her son, Francois (1811-32), titular King of Rome, later Duke de Reichstadt and "Napoleon II," never ruled. Napoleon abdicated 1814, died 1821.

Bourbons Restored

1814 Louis XVIII, king, brother of Louis XVI
1824 Charles X, brother, reactionary, deposed by the July Revolution, 1830

House of Orleans

1830 Louis-Philippe, the "Citizen King"

Second Republic

1848 Louis Napoleon Bonaparte, president, nephew of Napoleon I

Second Empire

1852 Napoleon III (Louis Napoleon Bonaparte), emperor, Eugenie (de Montijo), empress. Lost Franco-Prussian war, deposed 1870. Son, Prince Imperial (1856-79), died in Zulu War. Eugenie died 1920.

Third Republic—Presidents

1871 Thiers, Louis Adolphe (1797-1877)
1873 MacMahon, Marshal Patrice M. de (1808-93)
1879 Grevy, Paul J. (1807-91)
1887 Sadi-Carnot, M. (1837-94), assassinated
1894 Casimir-Perier, Jean P. P. (1847-1907)
1895 Faure, François Felix (1841-99)
1899 Loubet, Emile (1838-1929)
1906 Fallieres, C. Armand (1841-1931)
1913 Poincare, Raymond (1860-1934)
1920 Deschanel, Paul (1856-1922)
1920 Millerand, Alexandre (1859-1943)
1924 Doumergue, Gaston (1863-1937)

1931 Doumer, Paul (1857-1932), assassinated
1932 Lebrun, Albert (1871-1950), resigned 1940
1940 Vichy govt. under German armistice: Henri Philippe Petain (1856-1951), Chief of State, 1940-44.
Provisional govt. after liberation: Charles de Gaulle (1890-1970), Oct. 1944-Jan. 21, 1946; Felix Gouin (1884-1977), Jan. 23, 1946; Georges Bidault (1899-1983), June 24, 1946.

Fourth Republic—Presidents
1947 Auriol, Vincent (1884-1966)
1954 Coty, Rene (1882-1962)

Fifth Republic—Presidents
1959 De Gaulle, Charles Andre J. M. (1890-1970)
1969 Pompidou, Georges (1911-74)
1974 Giscard d'Estaing, Valery (1926-   )
1981 Mitterrand, François (1916-96)
1995 Chirac, Jacques (1932-   )

Rulers of Middle Europe; Rise and Fall of Dynasties; Rulers of Germany

Carolingian Dynasty

Charles the Great, or Charlemagne, ruled France, Italy, and Middle Europe; established Ostmark (later Austria); crowned Roman emperor by pope in Rome, 800 CE; died 814.

Louis I (Ludwig) the Pious, son, crowned by Charlemagne 814; died 840.

Louis II, the German, son, succeeded to East Francia (Germany) 843-76.

Charles the Fat, son, inherited East Francia and West Francia (France) 876, reunited empire, crowned emperor by pope, 881; deposed 887.

Arnulf, nephew, 887-99, partition of empire.

Louis the Child, 899-911, last direct descendant of Charlemagne.

Conrad I, duke of Franconia, first elected German king, 911-18, founded House of Franconia.

Saxon Dynasty; First Reich

Henry I, the Fowler, duke of Saxony, 919-36.

Otto I, the Great, 936-73, son; crowned Holy Roman Emperor by pope, 962.

Otto II, 973-83, son; failed to oust Greeks and Arabs from Sicily.

Otto III, 983-1002, son; crowned emperor at 16.

Henry II, the Saint, duke of Bavaria, 1002-24, great-grandson of Otto the Great.

House of Franconia

Conrad II, 1024-39, elected king of Germany.

Henry III, the Black, 1039-56, son; deposed 3 popes, annexed Burgundy.

Henry IV, 1056-1106, son; regency by his mother, Agnes of Poitou. Banned by Pope Gregory VII, he did penance at Canossa.

Henry V, 1106-25, son; last of Salian Dynasty.

Lothair, duke of Saxony, 1125-37. Crowned emperor in Rome, 1134.

House of Hohenstaufen

Conrad III, duke of Swabia, 1138-52, in 2nd Crusade.

Frederick I, Barbarossa, 1152-90; Conrad's nephew.

Henry VI, 1190-96, took lower Italy from Normans. Son became king of Sicily.

Philip of Swabia, 1197-1208, brother.

Otto IV, of House of Welf, 1198-1215, deposed.

Frederick II, 1215-50, son of Henry VI; king of Sicily; crowned king of Jerusalem in 5th Crusade.

Conrad IV, 1250-54, son; lost lower Italy to Charles of Anjou.

Conradin, 1252-68, son, king of Jerusalem and Sicily, beheaded. Last Hohenstaufen.

Interregnum, 1254-73. Rise of the Electors.

Transition

Rudolph I, of Hapsburg, 1273-91, defeated King Ottocar II of Bohemia. Bequeathed duchy of Austria to eldest son, Albert.

Adolph of Nassau, 1292-98, killed in war with Albert of Austria.

Albert I, king of Germany, 1298-1308, son of Rudolph.

Henry VII, of Luxemburg, 1308-13, crowned emperor in Rome; seized Bohemia, 1310.

Louis IV, of Bavaria (Wittelsbach), 1314-47. Also elected was Frederick of Austria, 1314-30 (Hapsburg). Abolition of papal sanction for election of Holy Roman Emperor.

Charles IV, of Luxemburg, 1347-78, grandson of Henry VII, German emperor and king of Bohemia, Lombardy, Burgundy, took Mark of Brandenburg.

Wenceslaus, 1378-1400, deposed.

Rupert, Duke of Palatine, 1400-10.

Sigismund, 1411-37.

Hungary

Stephen I, House of Arpad, 997-1038. Crowned king, 1000; converted Magyars; canonized 1083. After several centuries of feuds Charles Robert of Anjou became Charles I, 1308-42.

Louis I, the Great, son, 1342-82, joint ruler of Poland with Casimir III, 1370. Defeated Turks.

Mary, daughter, 1382-95, ruled with husband, Sigismund of Luxemburg, 1387-1437, also king of Bohemia. As brother of Wenceslaus he succeeded Rupert as Holy Roman Emperor, 1410.

Albert, 1438-39, son-in-law of Sigismund, also Roman emperor as Albert II *(see under Hapsburg)*.

Ulaszlo I of Poland, 1440-44.

Ladislaus V, posthumous son of Albert II, 1444-57. John Hunyadi (Janos Hunyadi), governor (1446-52), fought Turks, Czechs; died 1456.

Matthias I (Corvinus), son of Hunyadi, 1458-90. Shared rule of Bohemia, captured Vienna, 1485, annexed Austria, Styria, Carinthia.

Ulaszlo II (king of Bohemia), 1490-1516.

Louis II, son, aged 10, 1516-26. Wars with Suleiman, Turk. In 1527, Hungary split between Ferdinand I, Archduke of Austria, brother-in-law of Louis II, and John Zapolya of Transylvania. After Turkish invasion, 1547, Hungary split between Ferdinand, Prince John Sigismund (Transylvania), and the Turks.

House of Hapsburg

Albert V, of Austria, Hapsburg, crowned king of Hungary, Jan. 1438; Roman emperor, March 1438, as Albert II; died 1439.

Frederick III, cousin, 1440-93, fought Turks.

Maximilian I, son, 1493-1519, assumed title of Holy Roman Emperor (German), 1493.

Charles V, grandson, 1519-56. King of Spain with mother co-regent, crowned Roman emperor at Aix, 1520. Confronted Luther at Worms; attempted church reform and religious conciliation; abdicated 1556.

Ferdinand I, king of Bohemia, 1526; of Hungary, 1527; disputed. German king, 1531. Crowned Roman emperor on abdication of brother Charles V, 1556.

Maximilian II, son, 1564-76.

Rudolph II, son, 1576-1612.

Matthias, brother, 1612-19, king of Bohemia and Hungary.

Ferdinand II, of Styria, king of Bohemia, 1617; of Hungary, 1618; Roman emperor, 1619. Bohemian Protestants deposed him, elected Frederick V of Palatine, starting Thirty Years War.

Ferdinand III, son, king of Hungary, 1625, Bohemia, 1627; Roman emperor, 1637. Peace of Westphalia, 1648, ended war. Leopold I, 1658-1705; Joseph I, 1705-11; Charles VI, 1711-40.

Maria Theresa, daughter, 1740-80, Archduchess of Austria, queen of Hungary; ousted pretender, Charles VII, crowned 1742; in 1745 obtained election of her husband Francis I as Roman emperor and co-regent (d. 1765). Fought Seven Years' War with Frederick II of Prussia. Mother of Marie Antoinette.

Joseph II, son, 1765-90, Roman emperor, reformer; powers restricted by Empress Maria Theresa until her death, 1780. First partition of Poland. Leopold II, 1790-92.

Francis II, son, 1792-1835. Fought Napoleon. Proclaimed first hereditary emperor of Austria, 1804. Forced to abdicate as Roman, 1806; last use of title. Ferdinand I, son, 1835-48, abdicated during revolution.

Austro-Hungarian Monarchy

Francis Joseph I, nephew, 1848-1916, emperor of Austria, king of Hungary. Dual monarchy of Austria-Hungary formed, 1867. After assassination of heir, Archduke Francis Ferdinand, June 28, 1914, Austrian diplomacy precipitated World War I.

Charles I, grand-nephew, 1916-18, last emperor of Austria and king of Hungary. Abdicated Nov. 11-13, 1918, died 1922.

Rulers of Prussia

Nucleus of Prussia was the Mark of Brandenburg. First margrave Albert the Bear (Albrecht), 1134-70. First Hohenzollern margrave was Frederick, burgrave of Nuremberg, 1417-40.

Frederick William, 1640-88, the Great Elector. Son, Frederick III, 1688-1713, crowned King Frederick of Prussia, 1701.

Frederick William I, son, 1713-40.

Frederick II, the Great, son, 1740-86, annexed Silesia, part of Austria.

Frederick William II, nephew, 1786-97.

Frederick William III, son, 1797-1840, Napoleonic wars.

Frederick William IV, son, 1840-61. Uprising of 1848 and first parliament and constitution.

Second and Third Reich

William I, 1861-88, brother. Annexation of Schleswig and Hanover; Franco-Prussian war, 1870-71; proclamation of German Reich, Jan. 18, 1871, at Versailles; William, German emperor (Deutscher Kaiser); Bismarck, chancellor.

Frederick III, son, 1888.

William II, son, 1888-1918, led Germany in World War I, abdicated as German emperor and king of Prussia, Nov. 9, 1918. Died in exile in Netherlands, June 4, 1941. Minor rulers of Bavaria, Saxony, Wurttemberg also abdicated.

Germany proclaimed republic at Weimar, July 1, 1919. Presidents included Frederick Ebert, 1919-25; Paul von Hindenburg-Beneckendorff, 1925, reelected 1932, died Aug. 2, 1934. Adolf Hitler, chancellor, chosen successor as Leader-Chancellor (Fuehrer-Reichskanzler) of Third Reich. Annexed Austria, Mar. 1938. Precipitated World War II, 1939-45. Suicide Apr. 30, 1945.

Germany After 1945

Following World War II, Germany was split between democratic West and Soviet-dominated East. West German chancellors: Konrad Adenauer, 1949-63; Ludwig Erhard, 1963-66; Kurt Georg Kiesinger, 1966-69; Willy Brandt, 1969-74; Helmut Schmidt, 1974-82; Helmut Kohl, 1982-90. East German Communist party leaders: Walter Ulbricht, 1946-71; Erich Honecker, 1971-89; Egon Krenz, 1989-90.

Germany reunited Oct. 3, 1990. Post-reunification chancellors: Helmut Kohl, 1990-98; Gerhard Schröder, 1998-2005; Angela Merkel, 2005- .

Rulers of Poland

House of Piasts

Miesko I, 962?-92; Poland Christianized 966. Expansion under 3 Boleslavs: I, 992-1025, son, crowned king 1024; II, 1058-79, great-grandson, exiled after killing bishop Stanislav, who became chief patron saint of Poland; III, 1106-38, nephew, divided Poland among 4 sons, eldest suzerain.

1138-06, feudal division. 1226 founding in Prussia of military order Teutonic Knights. 1226 invasion by Tartars/Mongols.

Vladislav I, 1306-33, reunited most Polish territories, crowned king 1320. Casimir III the Great, 1333-70, son, developed economic, cultural life, foreign policy.

House of Anjou

Louis I, 1370-82, nephew, was also Louis I of Hungary.

Jadwiga, 1384-99, daughter, married Jagiello, Grand Duke of Lithuania, 1386.

House of Jagiellonians

Vladislav II, 1386-1434, Christianized Lithuania, founded personal union between Poland and Lithuania. Defeated 1410 Teutonic Knights at Grunwald.

Vladislav III, 1434-44, son, simultaneously king of Hungary. Fought Turks, killed 1444 in battle of Varna.

Casimir IV, 1446-92, brother, competed with Hapsburgs, put son Vladislav on throne of Bohemia, later also of Hungary (Ulaszlo II).

Sigismund I, 1506-48, son, patronized science and arts, his and son's reign "Golden Age."

Sigismund II, 1548-72, son, established 1569 real union of Poland and Lithuania (lasted until 1795).

Elective Kings

Polish nobles in 1572 proclaimed Poland a republic headed by king to be elected by whole nobility.

Stephen Batory, 1576-86, duke of Transylvania, married Ann, sister of Sigismund II August. Fought Russians.

Sigismund III Vasa, 1587-1632, newphew of Sigismund II. 1592-98 also king of Sweden. His generals fought Russians, Turks.

Vladislav II Vasa, 1632-48, son. Fought Russians.

John II Casimir Vasa, 1648-68, brother. Fought Cossacks, Swedes, Russians, Turks, Tatars (the "Deluge"). Abdicated 1668.

John III Sobieski, 1674-96. Won Vienna from besieging Turks, 1683.

Stanislav II, 1764-95, last king. Encouraged reforms; 1791 first modern constitution in Europe. 1772, 1793, 1795 Poland partitioned among Russia, Prussia, Austria. Unsuccessful insurrection against foreign invasion, 1794, under Kosciusko, American-Polish general.

1795-1918: Poland Under Foreign Rule

1807-15 Grand Duchy of Warsaw created by Napoleon I, Frederick August of Saxony grand duke.

1815 Congress of Vienna proclaimed part of Poland "Kingdom" in personal union with Russia.

Polish uprisings: 1830 against Russia; 1846, 1848 against Austria; 1863 against Russia—all repressed.

1918-39: Second Republic

1918-22 Head of State Jozef Pilsudski. Presidents: Gabriel Narutowicz, 1922, assassinated; Stanislav Wojciechowski, 1922-26, had to abdicate after Pilsudski's coup d'état; Ignacy Moscicki, 1926-39, ruled (with Pilsudski until his death, 1935) as virtual dictator.

1939-45: Poland Under Foreign Occupation

Nazi and Soviet invasion, Sept. 1939. Polish government-in-exile, first in France, then in England. Vladislav Raczkiewicz, president; Gen. Vladislav Sikorski, then Stanislav Mikolajczyk, prime ministers. Soviet-sponsored Polish Committee of National Liberation proclaimed at Lublin, July 1944, transformed into government Jan. 1, 1945.

Poland After 1945

In the late 1940s, Poland came increasingly under Soviet control. Communist party ruled in Poland until Aug. 1989, when democratic Solidarity party, led by Lech Walesa, gained control of government. Walesa was elected president in 1990, but lost the office to former communist Aleksander Kwasniewski in 1995. The government remained democratic, and Kwasniewski was reelected in Oct. 2000. He was succeeded by Lech Kaczynski, 2005.

Rulers of Denmark, Sweden, Norway

Denmark

Earliest rulers invaded Britain. King Canute, who ruled in London 1016-35, was most famous. The Valdemars furnished kings until the 15th century. In 1282 the Danes won the first national assembly, Danehof, from King Erik V.

Most redoubtable medieval character was Margaret, daughter of Valdemar IV, born 1353, married at 10 to King Haakon VI of Norway. In 1376 she had her first infant son, Olaf, made king of Denmark. After his death, 1387, she was regent of Denmark and Norway. In 1388, Sweden accepted her as sovereign. In 1389, she made her grand-nephew, Duke Erik of Pomerania, titular king of Denmark, Sweden, and Norway, with herself as regent. In 1397, she effected the Union of Kalmar of the three kingdoms and had Erik VII crowned. In 1439, the three kingdoms deposed him and elected, 1440, Christopher of Bavaria king (Christopher III). On his death, 1448, the union broke up.

Succeeding rulers were unable to enforce their claims as rulers of Sweden until 1520, when Christian II conquered Sweden. He was thrown out 1522, and in 1523, Gustavus Vasa united Sweden. Denmark continued to dominate Norway until the Napoleonic wars, when Frederick VI, 1808-39, joined the Napoleonic cause after Britain destroyed the Danish fleet, 1807. In 1814, he was forced to cede Norway to Sweden and Helgoland to Britain, receiving Lauenburg. Successors Christian VIII, 1839; Frederick VII, 1848; Christian IX, 1863; Frederick VIII, 1906; Christian X, 1912; Frederick IX, 1947; Margrethe II, 1972.

Sweden

Early kings ruled at Uppsala, but did not dominate the country. Sverker, c. 1130-c. 1156, united the Swedes and Goths. In 1435 Sweden obtained the Riksdag, or parliament. After the Union of Kalmar, 1397, the Danes either ruled or harried the country until Christian II of Denmark conquered it anew, 1520. This led to a rising under Gustavus Vasa, who ruled Sweden 1523-60, and established an independent kingdom. Charles IX, 1599-1611, crowned 1604, conquered Moscow. Gustavus II Adolphus, 1611-32, was called the Lion of the North. Later rulers: Christina, 1632; Charles X Gustavus, 1654; Charles XI, 1660; Charles XII (invader of Russia and Poland, defeated at Poltava, June 28, 1709), 1697; Ulrika Eleanora, sister, elected queen, 1718; Frederick I (of Hesse), her husband, 1720; Adolphus Frederick, 1751; Gustavus III, 1771; Gustavus IV Adolphus, 1792; Charles XIII, 1809. (Union with Norway began 1814.) Charles XIV John, 1818 (he was Jean Bernadotte, Napoleon's Prince of Ponte Corvo, elected 1810 to succeed Charles XIII). He founded the present dynasty: Oscar I, 1844; Charles XV, 1859; Oscar II, 1872; Gustavus V, 1907; Gustav VI Adolf, 1950; Carl XVI Gustaf, 1973.

Norway

Overcoming many rivals, Harald Haarfager, 872-930, conquered Norway, Orkneys, and Shetlands. Olaf I, great-grandson, 995-1000, brought Christianity into Norway, Iceland, and Greenland. In 1035 Magnus the Good also became king of Denmark. Haakon V, 1299-1319, had married his daughter to Erik of Sweden. Their son, Magnus, became ruler of Norway and Sweden at 6. His son, Haakon VI, married Margaret of Denmark; their son Olaf IV became king of Norway and Denmark, followed by Margaret's regency and the Union of Kalmar, 1397.

In 1450, Norway became subservient to Denmark. Christian IV, 1588-1648, founded Christiania, now Oslo. After Napoleonic wars, when Denmark ceded Norway to Sweden, a strong nationalist movement forced recognition of Norway as an independent kingdom united with Sweden under the Swedish kings, 1814-1905. In 1905, the union was dissolved, and Prince Charles of Denmark became Haakon VII. He died Sept. 21, 1957; succeeded by son, Olav V. Olav V died Jan. 17, 1991; succeeded by son, Harald V.

Rulers of the Netherlands and Belgium

The Netherlands (Holland)

William Frederick, Prince of Orange, led a revolt against French rule, 1813; crowned king, 1815. Belgium seceded Oct. 4, 1830, after a revolt. The secession was ratified by the two kingdoms by treaty, Apr. 19, 1839.

Succession: William II, son, 1840; William III, son, 1849; Wilhelmina, daughter of William III and his 2nd wife, Princess Emma of Waldeck, 1890; Wilhelmina abdicated, Sept. 4, 1948, in favor of daughter, Juliana. Juliana abdicated, Apr. 30, 1980, in favor of daughter, Beatrix.

Belgium

A national congress elected Prince Leopold of Saxe-Coburg as king; he took the throne July 21, 1831, as Leopold I.

Succession: Leopold II, son, 1865; Albert I, nephew of Leopold II, 1909; Leopold III, son of Albert, 1934; Prince Charles, Regent 1944; Leopold returned 1950, yielded powers to son Baudouin, Prince Royal, Aug. 6, 1950, abdicated July 16, 1951. Baudouin I took throne July 17, 1951, died July 31, 1993; succeeded by brother, Albert II.

Rulers of Modern Italy

After the fall of Napoleon in 1814, the Congress of Vienna, 1815, restored Italy as a political patchwork, comprising the Kingdom of Naples and Sicily, the Papal States, and smaller units. Piedmont and Genoa were awarded to Sardinia, ruled by King Victor Emmanuel I of Savoy.

United Italy emerged under the leadership of Camillo, Count di Cavour (1810-61), Sardinian prime minister. Agitation was led by Giuseppe Mazzini (1805-72) and Giuseppe Garibaldi (1807-82), soldier; Victor Emmanuel I abdicated 1821. After a brief regency for a brother, Charles Albert was king 1831-49, abdicating when defeated by the Austrians at Novara. Succeeded by Victor Emmanuel II, 1849-61.

In 1859 France forced Austria to cede Lombardy to Sardinia, which gave rights to Savoy and Nice to France. In 1860, Garibaldi led 1,000 volunteers in a campaign, took Sicily and expelled the King of Naples. In 1860 the House of Savoy annexed Tuscany, Parma, Modena, Romagna, the Two Sicilys, the Marches, and Umbria. Victor Emmanuel assumed the title of King of Italy at Turin Mar. 17, 1861.

In 1866, Victor Emmanuel allied with Prussia in the Austro-Prussian War, and with Prussia's victory, received Venetia. On Sept. 20, 1870, his troops under Gen. Raffaele Cadorna entered Rome and took over the Papal States, ending the temporal power of the Roman Catholic Church.

Succession: Umberto I, 1878, assassinated 1900; Victor Emmanuel III, 1900, abdicated 1946, died 1947; Humbert II, 1946, ruled a month. In 1921 Benito Mussolini (1883-1945) formed the Fascist party; he became prime minister Oct. 31, 1922. He entered World War II as an ally of Hitler. He was deposed July 25, 1943.

At a plebiscite June 2, 1946, Italy voted for a republic; Premier Alcide de Gasperi became chief of state June 13, 1946. On June 28, 1946, the Constituent Assembly elected Enrico de Nicola, Liberal, provisional president. Successive presidents: Luigi Einaudi, elected May 11, 1948; Giovanni Gronchi, Apr. 29, 1955; Antonio Segni, May 6, 1962; Giuseppe Saragat, Dec. 28, 1964; Giovanni Leone, Dec. 29, 1971; Alessandro Pertini, July 9, 1978; Francesco Cossiga, July 9, 1985; Oscar Luigi Scalfaro, May 28, 1992; Carlo Azeglio Ciampi, May 18, 1999; Giorgio Napolitano, May 10, 2006.

World Almanac Quick Quiz

Which French monarch supposedly said, "After me, the deluge" ("Après moi le deluge"), possibly meaning that he did not care if the situation in France deteriorated after his death?

(a) Charles VII   (b) Francis II   (c) Louis XV   (d) Napoleon Bonaparte

For the answer look in this chapter, or see page 1008.

Rulers of Spain

From 8th to 11th centuries Spain was dominated by the Moors (Arabs and Berbers). The Christian reconquest established small kingdoms (Asturias, Aragon, Castile, Catalonia, Leon, Navarre, and Valencia). In 1474 Isabella, b. 1451, became Queen of Castile and Leon. Her husband, Ferdinand, b. 1452, inherited Aragon, 1479, with Catalonia, Valencia, and the Balearic Islands, became Ferdinand V of Castile. By Isabella's request Pope Sixtus IV established the Inquisition, 1478. Last Moorish kingdom, Granada, fell 1492. Columbus opened New World of colonies, 1492. Isabella died 1504, succeeded by her daughter, Juana "the Mad," but Ferdinand ruled until his death 1516.

Charles I, b. 1500, son of Juana, grandson of Ferdinand and Isabella, and of Maximilian I of Hapsburg, succeeded later as Holy Roman Emperor, Charles V, 1520; abdicated 1556. Philip II, son, 1556-98, inherited only Spanish throne; conquered Portugal, fought Turks, sent Armada vs. England. Married to Mary I of England, 1554-58. Succession: Philip III, 1598-1621; Philip IV, 1621-65; Charles II, 1665-1700, left Spain to Philip of Anjou, grandson of Louis XIV, who as Philip V, 1700-46, founded Bourbon dynasty; Ferdinand VI, 1746-59; Charles III, 1759-88; Charles IV, 1788-1808, abdicated.

Napoleon now dominated politics and made his brother Joseph King of Spain, 1808, but the Spanish ousted him in 1813. Ferdinand VII, 1808, 1814-33, lost American colonies (except Cuba, Puerto Rico); succeeded by daughter Isabella II, aged 3, with wife Maria Christina of Naples regent until 1843. Isabella deposed by revolution, 1868. Elected king by the Cortes (parliament), Amadeo of Savoy, 1870, abdicated 1873. First republic, 1873-74. Alfonso XII, son of Isabella, 1875-85. His posthumous son was Alfonso XIII, with his mother, Queen Maria Christina regent. Spanish-American War, 1898, Spain lost Cuba, gave up Puerto Rico, Philippines, Sulu Is., Marianas. Alfonso took throne, 1902, aged 16, married British Princess Victoria Eugenia of Battenberg, 1906. Dictatorship of Primo de Rivera, 1923-30, precipitated revolution of 1931. Alfonso agreed to leave without formal abdication. Monarchy abolished; the second republic established, with socialist backing. Niceto Alcala Zamora was president until 1936, when Manuel Azaña was chosen.

In July 1936, the army in Morocco revolted against the government and General Francisco Franco led the troops into Spain. The revolution succeeded by Feb. 1939, when Azaña resigned. Franco became chief of state, with provisions that if he was incapacitated, the Regency Council by two-thirds vote could propose a king to the Cortes, which needed to have a two-thirds majority to elect him.

Alfonso XIII died in Rome Feb. 28, 1941, aged 54. His property and citizenship had been restored.

A law restoring the monarchy was approved in a 1947 referendum. Prince Juan Carlos, b. 1938, grandson of Alfonso XIII, was designated by Franco and the Cortes in 1969 as future king and chief of state. Franco died in office, Nov. 20, 1975; Juan Carlos proclaimed king, Nov. 22.

Rulers of Russia; Leaders of the USSR and Russian Federation

First ruler to consolidate Slavic tribes was Rurik, leader of the Russians who established himself at Novgorod, 862 CE. He and his immediate successors had Scandinavian affiliations. They moved to Kiev after 972 and ruled as Dukes of Kiev. In 988, Vladimir was converted and adopted the Byzantine Greek Orthodox service, later modified by Slav influences. Important as organizer and lawgiver was Yaroslav, 1019-54, whose daughters married kings of Norway, Hungary, and France. His grandson, Vladimir II (Monomakh), 1113-25, was progenitor of several rulers, but in 1169, Andrew Bogolubski overthrew Kiev and began the line known as Grand Dukes of Vladimir.

Of the Grand Dukes of Vladimir, Alexander Nevsky, 1246-63, had a son, Daniel, first to be called Duke of Muscovy (Moscow), who ruled 1263-1303. His successors became Grand Dukes of Muscovy. After Dmitri III Donskoi defeated the Tatars in 1380, they also became Grand Dukes of all Russia. Tatar independence and considerable territorial expansion were achieved under Ivan III, 1462-1505.

Tsars of Muscovy: Ivan III was referred to in church ritual as Tsar. He married Sofia, niece of the last Byzantine emperor. His successor, Basil III, died in 1533 when Basil's son Ivan was only 3. He became Ivan IV, "the Terrible," crowned 1547 as Tsar of all the Russias, ruled until 1584. Under the weak rule of his son, Feodor I, 1584-98, Boris Godunov had control. The dynasty died, and after years of tribal strife and intervention by Polish and Swedish armies, the Russians united under 17-year-old Michael Romanov, distantly related to Ivan IV's first wife. He ruled 1613-45, established the Romanov line. Fourth ruler after Michael was Peter I.

Tsars, or Emperors, of Russia (Romanovs): Peter I, 1682-1725, known as Peter the Great, took title of Emperor in 1721. His successors and dates of accession were Catherine, his widow, 1725; Peter II, his grandson, 1727; Anne, Duchess of Courland, 1730, daughter of Peter the Great's brother, Tsar Ivan V; Ivan VI, 1740, great-grandson of Ivan V, while still a child, kept in prison and murdered, 1764; Elizabeth, daughter of Peter I, 1741; Peter III, grandson of Peter I, 1761, deposed 1762 for his consort, Catherine II, former princess of Anhalt Zerbst (Germany), who is known as Catherine the Great; Paul I, her son, 1796, killed 1801; Alexander I, son of Paul, 1801, defeated Napoleon; Nicholas I, his brother, 1825; Alexander II, son of Nicholas, 1855, assassinated 1881 by terrorists; Alexander III, son, 1881. Nicholas II, son, 1894-1917, last Tsar of Russia, was forced to abdicate by the March 1917 Revolution that followed losses to Germany in WWI. The Tsar, Empress, Tsarevich (Crown Prince), and Tsar's 4 daughters were murdered by the Bolsheviks in Yekaterinburg, July 16, 1918.

Provisional Government: premiers, Prince Georgi Lvov, followed by Alexander Kerensky, 1917.

Union of Soviet Socialist Republics

Bolshevik Revolution, Nov. 7, 1917, removed Kerensky from power; council of People's Commissars formed; Lenin (Vladimir Ilyich Ulyanov) became premier. Lenin died Jan. 21, 1924. Aleksei Rykov (executed 1938) and V. M. Molotov held the office, but actual ruler was Joseph Stalin (Joseph Vissarionovich Djugashvili), general secretary of the Central Committee of the Communist Party. Stalin became president of the Council of Ministers (premier) May 7, 1941; died Mar. 5, 1953. Succeeded by Georgi M. Malenkov, as head of the Council and premier, and Nikita S. Khrushchev, first secretary of the Central Committee. Malenkov resigned Feb. 8, 1955, became deputy premier, was dropped July 3, 1957. Marshal Nikolai A. Bulganin became premier Feb. 8, 1955, was demoted, and Khrushchev became premier Mar. 27, 1958.

Khrushchev was ousted Oct. 14-15, 1964, replaced by Leonid I. Brezhnev as first secretary of the party and by Aleksei N. Kosygin as premier. On June 16, 1977, Brezhnev also took office as president. He died Nov. 10, 1982; 2 days later the Central Committee elected former KGB head Yuri V. Andropov president. Andropov died Feb. 9, 1984; on Feb. 13, Konstantin U. Chernenko chosen by Central Committee as its general secretary. Chernenko died Mar. 10, 1985; Mar. 11, he was succeeded as general secretary by Mikhail Gorbachev, who replaced Andrei Gromyko as president on Oct. 1, 1988. Gorbachev resigned Dec. 25, 1991, and the Soviet Union officially disbanded the next day. Each of the 15 former Soviet constituent republics became independent.

Post-Soviet Russia

After adopting a degree of sovereignty, the Russian Republic held elections in June 1991. Boris Yeltsin was sworn in July 10, 1991, as Russia's first elected president. With the Dec. 1991 dissolution of the Soviet Union, Russia (officially Russian Federation) became a founding member of the Commonwealth of Independent States. On Dec. 31, 1999, Yeltsin stepped down as president; he named Vladimir Putin his interim successor. Putin won a presidential election Mar. 26, 2000, and was reelected Mar. 14, 2004.

Leaders in the South American Wars of Liberation

Francisco Antonio Gabriel Miranda (1750-1816), Jose Francisco de San Martin (1778-1850), and Simon Bolivar (1783-1830) led early 19th-century struggles of South American nations to free themselves from Spain. All three, and their contemporaries, operated in periods of factional strife, during which soldiers and civilians suffered.

Miranda, a Venezuelan, had served with the French in the American Revolution and commanded parts of the French Revolutionary armies in the Netherlands, attempted to start a revolt in Venezuela in 1806 and failed. In 1810, with British and American backing, he returned and was briefly dictator, until the British withdrew their support. In 1812 he was overcome by the royalists in Venezuela and taken prisoner, dying in a Spanish prison in 1816.

San Martin was born in Argentina and during 1789-1811, served in campaigns of the Spanish armies in Europe and Africa. He first joined the independence movement in Argentina in 1812 and in 1817 invaded Chile with 4,000 men over the mountain passes. Here he and Gen. Bernardo O'Higgins (1778-1842) defeated the Spaniards at Chacabuco, 1817; O'Higgins was named Liberator and became first director of Chile, 1817-23. In 1821 San Martin occupied Lima and Callao, Peru, and became protector of Peru.

Bolivar was born in Venezuela, the son of an aristocratic family. He first served under Miranda in 1812 and in 1813 captured Caracas, where he was named Liberator. Forced out next year by civil strife, he led a campaign that captured Bogota in 1814. In 1817 he was again in control of Venezuela and was named dictator. He organized Nueva Granada with the help of General Francisco de Paula Santander (1792-1840). By joining Nueva Granada, Venezuela, and the area that is now Panama and Ecuador, the republic of Colombia was formed, with Bolivar president. After numerous setbacks he decisively defeated the Spaniards in the second battle of Carabobo, Venezuela, June 24, 1821.

In May 1822, Gen. Antonio Jose de Sucre, Bolivar's lieutenant, took Quito. Bolivar went to Guayaquil to confer with San Martin, who resigned as protector of Peru and withdrew from politics. With a new army of Colombians and Peruvians, Bolivar defeated the Spaniards in a battle at Junin in 1824 and cleared Peru.

De Sucre organized Charcas (Upper Peru) as Republica Bolivar (now Bolivia) and acted as president in place of Bolivar, who wrote its constitution. De Sucre defeated the Spanish faction of Peru at Ayacucho, Dec. 19, 1824.

Continued civil strife finally caused the Colombian federation to break apart. Santander turned against Bolivar, but the latter defeated him and banished him. In 1828 Bolivar gave up the presidency he had held precariously for 14 years. He became ill from tuberculosis and died Dec. 17, 1830. He is buried in the national pantheon in Caracas.

Governments of China

(Until 221 BCE and frequently thereafter, China was not a unified state. Where dynastic dates overlap, the rulers or events referred to appeared in different areas of China.)

Hsia	1994-c. 1523 BCE
Shang	c. 1523-c. 1028 BCE
Western Chou	c. 1027-770 BCE
Eastern Chou	770-256 BCE
Period of the Warring States	403-222 BCE
Ch'in (first unified empire)	221-206 BCE
Western Han (expanded Chinese state beyond the Yellow and Yangtze River valleys)	202 BCE-9 CE
Hsin (Wang Mang, usurper, deposed infant emperor)	9-23 CE
Eastern Han (expanded Chinese state into Indochina and Turkestan)	25-220
Three Kingdoms (Wei, Shu, Wu)	220-265
Chin (western)	265-317
(eastern)	317-420
Southern Dynasties (capital at Nanjing)	420-589
Sui (reunified China)	581-618
Tang (a golden age of Chinese culture; capital at Xian)	618-906
Five Dynasties (Yellow River basin)	902-960
Liao (Khitan Mongols; capital at site of Beijing)	947-1125
Northern Sung (reunified central and southern China)	960-1126
Western Hsai (non-Chinese rulers in northwest)	990-1227
Chin (Tatars; drove Sung out of central China)	1115-1234
Yuan (Mongols; Kublai Khan est. capital at site of Beijing, c. 1264)	1271-1368
Ming (China reunified under Chinese rule; capital at Nanjing, then Beijing in 1420)	1368-1644
Ch'ing (Manchus, descendents of Tatar)	1644-1912
Republic (disunity, provincial rulers, warlords)	1912-1949
People's Republic of China	1949-

Leaders of China Since 1949

Mao Zedong . . . . Chairman, 1949-59, Central People's Administrative Council, Chinese Communist Party (CPC) Chairman, 1949-76

Zhou Enlai . . . . . Premier, 1949-76; foreign minister, 1949-76

Deng Xiaoping . . Deputy Premier, 1952-66, 1973-76; "paramount leader," 1977-97

Liu Shaoqi . . . . . Chairman, 1959-68

Hua Guofeng . . . Premier, 1976-80; CPC Chairman, 1976-81

Zhao Ziyang . . . . Premier, 1980-87; CPC General Secretary, 1987-89

Hu Yaobang . . . .CPC General Secretary, 1980-87

Li Xiannian . . . . .President, 1983-88

Yang Shangkun . . .President, 1988-93

Li Peng . . . . .Premier, 1988-98

Jiang Zemin . . . .CPC General Secretary, 1989-2002; President, 1993-2003

Zhu Rongji . . . . .Premier, 1998-2003

Hu Jintao . . . . . .CPC General Secretary, 2002- ; President, 2003-

Wen Jiabao . . . .Premier, 2003-

Historical Periods of Japan

Yamato	c. 300-592	Conquest of Yamato plain c. 300 CE
Asuka	592-710	Accession of Empress Suiko, 592
Nara	710-794	Completion of Heijo (Nara), 710; the capital moved to Nagaoka, 784
Heian	794-1185	Completion of Heian (Kyoto), 794
Fujiwara	858-1160	Fujiwara-no-Yoshifusa became regent, 858
Taira	1160-1185	Taira-no-Kiyomori assumed control, 1160; Minamoto-no-Yoritomo victor over Taira, 1185
Kamakura	1192-1333	Yoritomo became shogun, 1192
Namboku	1334-1392	Restoration of Emperor Godaigo, 1334; Godaigo established Southern Court at Yoshino, 1336
Ashikaga	1338-1573	Ashikaga Takauji became shogun, 1338
Muromachi	1392-1573	Unification of Southern and Northern Courts, 1392
Sengoku	1467-1600	Beginning of the Onin war, 1467
Momoyama	1573-1603	Oda Nobunaga entered Kyoto, 1568; Nobunaga deposed last Ashikaga shogun, 1573; Tokugawa Ieyasu victor at Sekigahara, 1600
Edo	1603-1867	Ieyasu became shogun, 1603
Meiji	1868-1912	Enthronement of Emperor Mutsuhito (Meiji), 1867; Meiji Restoration and Charter Oath, 1868
Taisho	1912-1926	Accession of Emperor Yoshihito, 1912
Showa	1926-1989	Accession of Emperor Hirohito, 1926
Heisei	1989-	Accession of Emperor Akihito, 1989

WORLD EXPLORATION AND GEOGRAPHY

Early Explorers of the Western Hemisphere

Reviewed by Susan Skomal, Ph.D.

In the light of recent discoveries, theories about how and when the first people arrived in the western hemisphere are being reconsidered. Genetic evidence suggests that beginning 14,000 years before the present (BP), the earliest immigrants crossed a "land bridge" from Siberia to Alaska in small groups and spread south through the Americas. Kennewick Man, found in Washington state (9,200-9,600 BP), and "Luzia" from Brazil (11,500 BP) are examples of these early arrivals. Modern Native Americans, who exhibit markedly different physical characteristics from Kennewick and Luzia, appear to be descended from peoples from N and Central Asia who arrived in subsequent waves of migration. A growing body of genetic, skeletal, and linguistic evidence documents their migration throughout the Americas.

Archaeologists have confirmed evidence of habitation by at least 12,900 BP at sites located on the shores of ancient lakes 2 miles high in the Atacama Desert of Chile. There is also growing support for the settlement of the lowland jungles of Chile 2,000 years earlier. Because a glacier covered most of N America from 20,000 to 13,000 years ago, those who settled in S America may have traveled in vessels along the west coast, sailed directly from Australia or S Asia, or spread from N to S America before the ice came. Evidence from a burial site at Santana do Riacho 1 in Brazil (8,000-11,000 BP) suggests that some of the early immigrants who came via the land bridge from Siberia may have originated in Africa. Long before Europeans arrived, the Americas were densely populated by complex societies. Irrigation canals dating to 4700 BP provide evidence for the origins of large-scale agriculture along the western slopes of Peru's Andes mountains. The earliest known civilization occupied a 700-square-mile area in 4 river valleys of coastal Peru between 500 and 3500 BP.

Norsemen (Norwegian Vikings sailing out of Iceland and Greenland), led by Leif Ericson, are credited with having been the first Europeans to reach America, with at least 5 voyages occurring about 1000 CE to areas they called Helluland, Markland, and Vinland—possibly what are known today as Baffin Island, Labrador, and either Newfoundland or further south in New England. L'Anse aux Meadows, on the N tip of Newfoundland, is the only documented settlement, with evidence of occupation dating to 1000 CE.

Sustained contact between the hemispheres began with the first voyage of Christopher Columbus (born Cristoforo Colombo, c. 1451, near Genoa, Italy). Columbus made trips to the New World while sailing for the Spanish. He left Palos, Spain, Aug. 3, 1492, with 88 men and landed at San Salvador (Watling Islands, Bahamas), Oct. 12, 1492. His fleet included 3 vessels, the *Niña*, *Pinta*, and *Santa María*, and also stopped on Cuba and Hispaniola. A 2nd expedition left Cadiz, Spain, Sept. 25, 1493, with 17 ships and 1,500 men, reaching the Lesser Antilles Nov. 3. His 3rd voyage brought him from Sanlucar, Spain (May 30, 1498, with 6 ships), to the N coast of S America. A 4th voyage reached the mainland of Central America, after leaving Cadiz, Spain, May 9, 1502. Columbus died May 20, 1506, convinced he had reached Asia by sailing west.

In N America, John and Sebastian Cabot, Italian explorers sailing for the English, reached Newfoundland and possibly Nova Scotia in 1497. John's 2nd voyage (1498), seeking a new trade route to Asia, resulted in the loss of his entire fleet. During this period exploration was dominated by Spain and Portugal.

In 1497 and 1499 Amerigo Vespucci (for whom the Americas are named), an Italian explorer sailing for Spain, passed along the N and E coasts of S America. He was the first to argue that the newly discovered lands were a continent other than Asia.

Other early explorations are listed below.

Year	Explorer	Nationality (sponsor, if different)	Area reached or explored
1497-98	Vasco da Gama	Portuguese	Cape of Good Hope (Africa), India
1499	Alonso de Ojeda	Spanish	N South American coast, Venezuela
1500, Feb.	Vicente Yañez Pinzon	Spanish	S. American coast, Amazon R.
1500, Apr.	Pedro Álvarez Cabral	Portuguese	Brazil
1501	Rodrigo de Bastidas	Spanish	Central America
1513	Vasco Núñez de Balboa	Spanish	Panama, Pacific Ocean
1513	Juan Ponce de León	Spanish	Florida, Yucatán Peninsula
1515	Juan de Solis	Spanish	Río de la Plata
1519	Alonso de Pineda	Spanish	Mouth of Mississippi R.
1519	Hernando Cortes	Spanish	Mexico
1519-20	Ferdinand Magellan	Portuguese (Spanish)	Straits of Magellan, Tierra del Fuego
1524	Giovanni da Verrazano	Italian (French)	Atlantic coast, incl. New York harbor
1528	Cabeza de Vaca	Spanish	Texas coast and interior
1532	Francisco Pizarro	Spanish	Peru
1534	Jacques Cartier	French	Canada, Gulf of St. Lawrence
1536	Pedro de Mendoza	Spanish	Buenos Aires
1539	Francisco de Ulloa	Spanish	California coast
1539-41	Hernando de Soto	Spanish	Mississippi R., near Memphis
1539	Marcos de Niza	Italian (Spanish)	SW United States
1540	Francisco de Coronado	Spanish	SW United States
1540	Hernando Alarcon	Spanish	Colorado R.
1540	Garcia de Lopez Cardenas	Spanish	Colorado, Grand Canyon
1541	Francisco de Orellana	Spanish	Amazon R.
1542	Juan Rodriguez Cabrillo	Portuguese (Spanish)	W Mexico, San Diego harbor
1565	Pedro Menéndez de Aviles	Spanish	St. Augustine, FL
1576	Sir Martin Frobisher	English	Frobisher Bay, Canada
1577-80	Sir Francis Drake	English	California coast
1582	Antonio de Espejo	Spanish	Southwest U.S. (New Mexico)
1584	Amadas & Barlow (for Raleigh)	English	Virginia
1585-87	Sir Walter Raleigh's men	English	Roanoke Isl., NC
1595	Sir Walter Raleigh	English	Orinoco R.
1603-09	Samuel de Champlain	French	Canadian interior, Lake Champlain
1607	Capt. John Smith	English	Atlantic coast
1609-10	Henry Hudson	English (Dutch)	Hudson R., Hudson Bay
1634	Jean Nicolet	French	Lake Michigan, Wisconsin
1673	Jacques Marquette, Louis Jolliet	French	Mississippi R., S to Arkansas
1682	Robert Cavelier, sieur de La Salle	French	Mississippi R., S to Gulf of Mexico
1727-29	Vitus Bering	Danish (Russian)	Bering Strait and Alaska
1789	Sir Alexander Mackenzie	Canadian	NW Canada
1804-06	Meriwether Lewis and William Clark	American	Missouri R., Rocky Mts., Columbia R.

Arctic Exploration

Early Explorers

1587 — John Davis (Eng.). Davis Strait to Sanderson's Hope, 72°12′N.

1596 — Willem Barents and Jacob van Heemskerck (Holland). Discovered Bear Isl., touched NW tip of Spitsbergen, 79°49′N, rounded Novaya Zemlya, wintered at Ice Haven.

1607 — Henry Hudson (Eng.). North along Greenland's E coast to Cape Hold-with-Hope, 73°30′, then N of Spitsbergen to 80°23′. Explored Hudson's Touches (Jan Mayen).

1616 — William Baffin and Robert Bylot (Eng.). Baffin Bay to Smith Sound.

1728 — Vitus Bering (Russ.). Sailed through strait (Bering) proving Asia and America are separate.

1733-40 — Great Northern Expedition (Russ.). Surveyed Siberian Arctic coast.

1741 — Vitus Bering (Russ.). Sighted Alaska, named Mount St. Elias. His lieutenant, Chirikof, explored coast.

1771 — Samuel Hearne (Hudson's Bay Co.). Overland from Prince of Wales Fort (Churchill) on Hudson Bay to mouth of Coppermine R.

1778 — James Cook (Brit.). Through Bering Strait to Icy Cape, AK, and North Cape, Siberia.

1789 — Alexander Mackenzie (North West Co., Brit.). Montreal to mouth of Mackenzie River.

1806 — William Scoresby (Brit.). N of Spitsbergen to 81°30′.

1820-23 — Ferdinand von Wrangel (Russ.). Surveyed Siberian Arctic coast. His exploration joined James Cook's at North Cape, confirming separation of the continents.

1878-79 — (Nils) Adolf Erik Nordenskjöld (Swed.). The 1st to navigate the Northeast Passage—an ocean route connecting Europe's North Sea, along the Arctic coast of Asia and through the Bering Sea, to the Pacific Ocean.

1881 — The U.S. steamer *Jeannette*, led by Lt. Cmdr. George W. DeLong, was trapped in ice and crushed, June 1881. DeLong and 11 others died; 12 survived.

1888 — Fridtjof Nansen (Nor.) crossed Greenland icecap.

1893-96 — Nansen in *Fram* drifted from New Siberian Isls. to Spitsbergen; tried polar dash in 1895, reached Franz Josef Land, 86°14′N.

1897 — Salomon A. Andrée (Sweden) and 2 others started in balloon from Spitsbergen, July 11, to drift across pole to U.S., and disappeared. Aug. 6, 1930, their bodies were found on White Isl., 82°57′N, 29°52′E.

1903-6 — Roald Amundsen (Nor.) 1st sailed the Northwest Passage—an ocean route linking the Atlantic Ocean to the Pacific via Canada's marine waterways.

North Pole Exploration

Robert E. Peary explored Greenland's coast, 1891-92; tried for North Pole, 1893. In 1900 he reached N limit of Greenland and 83°50′N; in 1902 he reached 84°17′N; in 1906 he went from Ellesmere Isl. to 87° 06′N. He sailed in the *Roosevelt*, July 1908, to winter off Cape Sheridan, Grant Land. The dash for the North Pole began Mar. 1 from Cape Columbia, Ellesmere Isl. Peary reportedly reached the pole, 90°N, Apr. 6, **1909**; however, later research suggests he may have fallen short of his goal by c. 30-60 mi. The first surface expedition independently confirmed to have reached the N Pole was that of Ralph Plaisted in 1968 (see below).

Peary had several support groups carrying supplies until the last group turned back at 87°47′ N. Peary, Matthew

Henson, and 4 Eskimos proceeded with dog teams and sleds. They were said to have crossed the pole several times, then built an igloo there and remained 36 hours. Started south, Apr. 7 at 4 PM, for Cape Columbia.

1914 — Donald MacMillan (U.S.). Northwest, 200 mi, from Axel Heiberg Isl. to seek Peary's Crocker Land.

1915-17 — Vihjalmur Stefansson (Can.). Discovered Borden, Brock, Meighen, and Lougheed Isls.

1918-20 — Roald Amundsen (Nor.) sailed the Northeast Passage.

1925 — Amundsen and Lincoln Ellsworth (U.S.) reached 87°44′N in attempt to fly to N Pole from Spitsbergen.

1926 — Richard E. Byrd and Floyd Bennett (U.S.) reputedly flew over North Pole, May 9. (Claim to have reached the pole is in dispute, however.)

1926 — Amundsen, Ellsworth, and Umberto Nobile (It.) flew from Spitsbergen over N Pole May 12, to Teller, AK, in dirigible *Norge*.

1928 — Nobile crossed N Pole in airship, May 24; crashed, May 25. Amundsen died attempting a rescue.

North Pole Exploration Records

On Aug. 3, 1958, submarine *Nautilus,* under Comdr. William R. Anderson, crossed the N Pole beneath the ice.

In Aug. 1960, the nuclear-powered U.S. submarine *Seadragon* (Comdr. George P. Steele 2nd) made the 1st E-W underwater transit through the Northwest Passage. Traveling submerged for the most part, it took 6 days to make the 850-mi trek from Baffin Bay to the Beaufort Sea.

On Apr. 19, 1968, Ralph Plaisted (U.S.) and 3 amateur explorers on snowmobiles became the first independently confirmed surface expedition to reach the N. Pole.

On Aug. 16, 1977, the Soviet nuclear icebreaker *Arktika* became the 1st surface ship to reach the N Pole.

On Apr. 30, 1978, Naomi Uemura (Jap.) became the 1st person to reach the N Pole alone, traveling by dog sled in a 54-day, 600-mi trek over the frozen Arctic.

In Apr. 1982, Sir Ranulph Fiennes and Charles Burton, Brit. explorers, reached the N Pole and became the 1st to circle the earth from pole to pole. They had reached the S Pole 16 months earlier. The 52,000-mi trek took 3 years, involved 23 people, and cost an estimated $18 mil.

On May 2, 1986, 6 explorers reached the N Pole assisted only by dogs. They became the 1st to reach the pole without aerial logistics support since at least 1909. The explorers, Amer. Will Steger, Paul Schurke, Ann Bancroft, and Geoff Carroll, and Can. Brent Boddy and Richard Weber, completed the 500-mi journey in 56 days.

On June 15, 1995, Weber and Russ. Mikhail Malakhov became the 1st pair to make it to the N pole and back without any mechanical assistance. The 940-mi trip, made entirely on skis, took 121 days.

On May 20, 2003, Pen Hadow (U.K.) became the 1st to reach the N pole from Canada, solo and without resupply. The 377-mile journey across the ice took 64 days.

On April 16, 2006, Prince Albert II of Monaco became the first royal to reach the N Pole.

Antarctic Exploration

Antarctica has been approached since 1773-75, when Capt. James Cook (Brit.) reached 71°10′S. Many sea and landmarks bear names of early explorers. Fabian von Bellingshausen (Russ.) discovered Peter I and Alexander I Isls., 1819-21. Nathaniel Palmer (U.S.) traveled throughout Palmer Peninsula, 60°W, 1820, without realizing that this was a continent. Capt. John Davis (U.S.) made the 1st known landing on the continent on Feb. 7, 1821. Later, in 1823, James Weddell (Brit.) found Weddell Sea, 74°15′S, the southernmost point that had been reached.

First to announce existence of the continent of Antarctica was Charles Wilkes (U.S.), who followed the coast for 1,500 mi, 1840. Adelie Coast, 140° E, was found by Dumont d'Urville (Fr.), 1840. Ross Ice Shelf was found by James Clark Ross (Brit.), 1841-42.

1895 — Leonard Kristensen (Nor.) landed a party on the coast of Victoria Land. They were the 1st ashore on the main continental mass. C. E. Borchgrevink, a member of that party, returned in 1899 with a Brit. expedition, 1st to winter on Antarctica.

1902-4 — Robert Falcon Scott (Brit.) explored Edward VII Peninsula to 82°17′S, 146°33′E from McMurdo Sound.

1908-9 — Ernest Shackleton (Brit.) 1st to use Manchurian ponies in Antarctic sledging. He reached 88°23′S, discovering a route on to the plateau by way of the Beardmore Glacier and pioneering the way to the pole.

1911 — Roald Amundsen (Nor.) with 4 men and dog teams reached the S Pole, Dec. 14.

1912 — Scott reached the pole from Ross Isl., Jan. 18, with 4 companions. None of Scott's party survived. Their bodies and expedition notes were found, Nov. 12.

1928 — 1st person to use an airplane over Antarctica was Sir George Hubert Wilkins (Austral.).

1929 — Richard E. Byrd (U.S.) established Little America on Bay of Whales. On 1,600-mi airplane flight begun Nov. 28, he crossed S Pole, Nov. 29, with 3 others.

1934-35 — Byrd led 2nd expedition to Little America, explored 450,000 sq mi, wintered alone at 80°08′S.

1934-37 — John Rymill led British Graham Land expedition; discovered Palmer Penin. is part of mainland.

1935 — Lincoln Ellsworth (U.S.) flew S along E Coast of Palmer Penin., then crossed continent to Little America, making 4 landings.

1939-41 — U.S. Navy plane flights discovered about 150,000 sq mi of new land.

1940 — Byrd charted most of coast between Ross Sea and Palmer Penin.

1946-47 — U.S. Navy undertook Operation Highjump, commanded by Byrd, included 13 ships and 4,000 men. Airplanes photomapped coastline and penetrated beyond pole.

1946-48 — Ronne Antarctic Research Expedition Comdr., Finn Ronne, USNR, determined the Antarctic to be one continent with no strait between Weddell Sea and Ross Sea; explored 250,000 sq mi of land by flights to 79ºS.

1955-57 — U.S. Navy's Operation Deep Freeze led by Adm. Byrd. Supporting U.S. scientific efforts for the International Geophysical Year (IGY), the operation established 5 coastal stations fronting the Indian, Pacific, and Atlantic oceans and also 3 interior stations; explored more than 1,000,000 sq mi in Wilkes Land.

1957-58 — During the IGY, July 1957 through Dec. 1958, scientists from 12 countries conducted Antarctic research at a network of some 60 stations on Antarctica.
Dr. Vivian E. Fuchs led a 12-person Trans-Antarctic Expedition on the 1st land crossing of Antarctica. Starting from the Weddell Sea, they reached Scott Station, Mar. 2, 1958, after traveling 2,158 mi in 98 days.

1958 — A group of 5 U.S. scientists led by Edward C. Thiel, seismologist, moving by tractor from Ellsworth Station on Weddell Sea, identified a huge mountain range, 5,000 ft above the ice sheet and 9,000 ft above sea level. The range,

originally seen by a Navy plane, was named the Dufek Massif, for Rear Adm. George Dufek.

1959 — Argentina, Australia, Belgium, Chile, France, Japan, New Zealand, Norway, South Africa, USSR, U.K., and U.S. signed a treaty suspending territorial claims for 30 yrs. and reserving the continent, S of 60°S, for research.

1961-62 — Scientists discovered the Bentley Trench, running from Ross Ice Shelf into Marie Byrd Land, near the end of the Ellsworth Mts., toward the Weddell Sea.

1962 — Nuclear power plant online at McMurdo Sound.

1963 — On Feb. 22, a U.S. plane made the region's longest nonstop flight from McMurdo Station S past the pole to Shackleton Mts., SE to the "Area of Inaccessibility," and back to McMurdo Station covering 3,600 mi in 10 hrs.

1964 — New Zealanders mapped the mountain area from from Cape Adare W some 400 mi to Pennell Glacier.

1985 — Igor A. Zotikov, a Russian researcher, discovered sediments in the Ross Ice Shelf that seem to support the continental drift theory. Ocean Drilling Project finds that the ice sheets of E Antarctica are 37 million yrs. old.

1989 — Victoria Murden and Shirley Metz became both the 1st women and the 1st Americans to reach the S Pole overland when they arrived with 9 others on Jan. 17, 1989.

1991 — 24 nations approved a protocol to the 1959 Antarctica Treaty, Oct. 4. New conservation provisions, including banning oil and other mineral exploration for 50 yrs.

1994 — On Dec. 25, after 50-day trek, Liv Arnesen (Nor.) became 1st woman to ski alone and unaided to the S Pole.

1995 — On Dec. 22, a Norwegian, Borge Ousland, reached the S Pole in the fastest time on skis: 44 days.

1996-97 — Ousland became 1st person to traverse Antarctica alone; reached S Pole Dec. 19, 1996; traveled 1,675 mi in 64 days, ending Jan. 18, 1997.

2000-2001 — On Feb. 11, Ann Bancroft and Liv Arnesen (Nor.) became 1st women to ski unaided across Antarctica. The 1,717-mile journey took 94 days.

Volcanoes

Sources: *Volcanoes of the World*, Geoscience Press; Global Volcanism Network, Smithsonian Institution

Roughly 540 volcanoes are known to have erupted during historical times. Nearly 75% of these historically active volcanoes lie along the so-called **Ring of Fire**, running along the W coast of the Americas from the southern tip of Chile to Alaska, down the E coast of Asia from Kamchatka to Indonesia, and continuing from New Guinea to New Zealand. The Ring of Fire marks the boundary between the mobile tectonic plates underlying the Pacific Ocean and those of the surrounding continents. Other active regions occur along rift zones, where plates pull apart, as in Iceland, or where molten material moves up from the mantle over local "hot spots," as in Hawaii. The vast majority of the earth's volcanism occurs at submarine rift zones. For more information on volcanoes, see the Smithsonian Institution's global volcanism website at www.volcano.si.edu

Notable Volcanic Eruptions

Approximately 7,000 years ago, Mazama, a 9,900-ft volcano in southern Oregon, erupted violently, ejecting large amounts of ash and pumice and voluminous pyroclastic flows. The ash spread over the entire northwestern U.S. and as far away as Saskatchewan, Can. During the eruption, the top of the mountain collapsed, leaving a caldera 6 mi across and about a half mile deep, which filled with rainwater to form what is now called Crater Lake.

In AD 79, Vesuvio, or Vesuvius, a 4,190-ft volcano overlooking Naples Bay, became active after several centuries of apparent inactivity. On Aug. 24 of that year, a heated mud and ash flow swept down the mountain, engulfing the cities of Pompeii, Herculaneum, and Stabiae with debris more than 60 ft deep. About 10% of the population of the 3 towns were killed.

In 1883, an eruption similar to the Mazama eruption occurred on the island of Krakatau. At least 2,000 people died in pyroclastic flows on Aug. 26. The next day, the 2,640-ft peak of the volcano collapsed to 1,000 ft below sea level, sinking most of the island and killing over 3,000. A tsunami (tidal wave) generated by the collapse killed more than 31,000 people in Java and Sumatra, and eventually reached England. Ash from the eruption colored sunsets around the world for 2 years. A similar, even more powerful eruption had taken place 68 years earlier at Mt. Tambora on the Indonesian island of Sumbawa.

Date	Volcano	Deaths (est.)	Date	Volcano	Deaths (est.)
Aug. 24, AD 79	Mt. Vesuvius, Italy	16,000	May 8, 1902	Mt. Pelée, Martinique	28,000
1586	Kelut, Java, Indon.	10,000	Jan. 30, 1911	Mt. Taal, Phil.	1,400
Dec. 15, 1631	Mt. Vesuvius, Italy	4,000	May 19, 1919	Mt. Kelut, Java, Indon.	5,000
Aug. 12, 1772	Mt. Papandayan, Java, Indon.	3,000	Jan. 17-21, 1951	Mt. Lamington, New Guinea	3,000
June 8, 1783	Laki, Iceland	9,350	May 18, 1980	Mt. St. Helens, U.S.	57
May 21, 1792	Mt. Unzen, Japan	14,500	Mar. 28, 1982	El Chichon, Mex.	1,880
Apr. 10-12, 1815	Mt. Tambora, Sumbawa, Indon.	92,000[1]	Nov. 13, 1985	Nevado del Ruiz, Colombia	23,000
Aug. 26-28, 1883	Krakatau, Indon.	36,000	Aug. 21, 1986	Lake Nyos, Cameroon	1,700
Apr. 24, 1902	Santa María, Guatemala	1,000[2]	June 15, 1991	Mt. Pinatubo, Luzon, Phil.	800

(1) Of these, 10,000 were directly related to the eruption; an additional 82,000 were the result of starvation and disease brought on by the event. (2) An additional 3,000 deaths due to a malaria outbreak are sometimes attributed to the eruption.

▶ ***IT'S A FACT:*** The fallout from the 1815 eruption of Mt. Tambora, in Sumbawa, Indonesia, was global and is said to have caused a "year without a summer" in 1816. Global average temperatures plummeted and large-scale crop failures and other weather-related disturbances were recorded halfway around the world, in areas as distant as Europe and northeast North America.

Notable Active Volcanoes

Active volcanoes display a wide range of activity. In this table, years are given for last display of eruptive activity, as of mid-2006 the list does not include submarine volcanoes. An eruption may involve explosive ejection of new or old fragmental material, escape of liquid lava, or both. Volcanoes are listed by height, which does not reflect eruptive magnitude.

Name (latest eruption)		Height (ft)
Africa		
Mt. Cameroon (2000)	Cameroon	13,435
Nyiragongo (2006)	Congo	11,384
Nyamuragira (2004)	Congo	10,033
Mt. Oku [Lake Nyos] (1986)	Cameroon	9,878
Ol Doinyo Lengai (2006)	Tanzania	9,718
Fogo (1995)	Cape Verde Isls.	9,281
Piton de la Fournaise (2006)	Réunion Isl., Indian O.	8,635
Karthala (2005)	Comoros	7,746
Erta Ale (2006)	Ethiopia	2,011
Antarctica		
Erebus (2006)	Ross Isl.	12,447
Deception Island (1970)	S. Shetland Isl.	1,890
Asia-Oceania		
Kliuchevskoi (2005)	Kamchatka, Russia	15,863
Kerinci (2004)	Sumatra, Indon.	12,467
Fuji (1708)	Honshu, Japan.	12,388
Tolbachik (1976)	Kamchatka, Russia	12,080
Semeru (2006)	Java, Indon.	12,060
Slamet (1999)	Java, Indon.	11,247
Raung (2002)	Java, Indon.	10,932
Shiveluch (2006)	Kamchatka, Russia	10,771
On-take (1980)	Honshu, Japan.	10,049
Merapi (2002)	Java, Indon.	9,737
Bezymianny (2005)	Kamchatka, Russia	9,455
Peuet Sague (2000)	Sumatra, Indon.	9,190
Ruapehu (1997)	New Zealand	9,176
Heard (2004)	Indian Ocean	9,006
Baitoushan (1702)	China/Korea.	9,003
Asama (2004)	Honshu, Japan.	8,425
Mayon (2005)	Luzon, Phil.	8,077
Canlaon (2005)	Negros Isls., Phil.	7,989
Niigata Yake-yama (1998)	Honshu, Japan.	7,874
Alaid (1996)	Kuril Isl., Russia.	7,674
Ulawun (2005)	Papua New Guinea	7,657
Chokai (1974)	Honshu, Japan.	7,326
Galunggung (1984)	Java, Indon.	7,113
Azuma (1977)	Honshu, Japan.	6,676
Tongariro (Ngauruhoe) (1977)	New Zealand	6,489
Sangeang Api (1988)	Lesser Sunda Isl., Indon.	6,394
Nasu (1963)	Honshu, Japan.	6,283
Karkar (1979)	Papua New Guinea	6,033
Tiatia (1981)	Kuril Isl., Russia.	5,968
Bandai (1888)	Honshu, Japan.	5,968
Manam (2006)	Papua New Guinea	5,928
Kuju (1996)	Kyushu, Japan.	5,876
Karangetang (Api Siau) (2005)	Sangihe Isls., Indon.	5,853
Soputan (2006)	Sulawesi, Indon.	5,853
Bagana (2006)	Papua New Guinea	5,741
Kelut (1990)	Java, Indon.	5,679
Adatara (1996)	Honshu, Japan.	5,636
Gamalama (2003)	Halmahera, Indon.	5,627
Kirishima (1992)	Kyushu, Japan.	5,577
Gamkonora (1987)	Halmahera, Indon.	5,364
Aso (2004)	Kyushu, Japan.	5,223
Lokon-Empung (2003)	Sulawesi, Indon.	5,184
Bulusan (1995)	Luzon, Phil.	5,134
Karymsky (2006)	Kamchatka, Russia	5,039
Unzen (1996)	Kyushu, Japan.	4,921
Akan (1998)	Hokkaido, Japan.	4,918
Sarychev Peak (1989)	Kuril Isl., Russia.	4,908
Pinatubo (1993)	Luzon, Phil.	4,875
Lopevi (2006)	Vanuatu	4,636
Akita-Yake-yama (1997)	Honshu, Japan.	4,482
Dukono (2006)	Halmahera, Indon.	4,380
Ambrym (2005)	Vanuatu	4,377
Langila (2006)	Papua New Guinea	4,363
Awu (2004)	Sangihe Isl., Indon.	4,331
Akademia Nauk (1996)	Kamchatka, Russia	3,871
Komaga-take (2000)	Hokkaido, Japan	3,711
Sakura-jima (2006)	Kyushu, Japan.	3,665
Miyake-jima (2005)	Izu Isls., Japan.	2,674
Krakatau (2001)	Indonesia	2,667
Suwanose-jima (2006)	Ryukyu Isls., Japan	2,621
Gaua (1982)	Vanuatu	2,615
Oshima (1990)	Izu Isls., Japan.	2,507
Usu (2001)	Hokkaido, Japan.	2,418
Rabaul (2006)	Papua New Guinea	2,257
Pagan (1993)	N. Mariana Isl.	1,870
Taal (1977)	Luzon, Phil.	1,312

Name (latest eruption)		Height (ft)
Yasur (2006)	Tanna Island, Vanuatu	1,184
White Island (2001)	Bay of Plenty, New Zealand	1,053
McDonald Islands (2005)	Indian Ocn., Australia	755
Central America—Caribbean		
Tacaná (1986)	Guatemala	13,320
Acatenango (1972)	Guatemala	13,044
Santa María (2006)	Guatemala	12,375
Fuego (2006)	Guatemala	12,346
Irazú (1994)	Costa Rica	11,260
Turrialba (1866)	Costa Rica	10,958
Póas (1996)	Costa Rica	8,884
Pacaya (2005)	Guatemala	8,373
San Miguel (2002)	El Salvador	6,988
Rincón de la Vieja (1998)	Costa Rica	6,286
San Cristóbal (2005)	Nicaragua	5,725
Concepción (2005)	Nicaragua	5,577
Arenal (2006)	Costa Rica	5,479
Soufrière Guadeloupe (1977)	Guadeloupe	4,813
Pelée (1932)	Martinique	4,583
Momotombo (1905)	Nicaragua	4,255
Soufrière St. Vincent (1979)	St. Vincent.	4,003
Soufrière Hills (2006)	Montserrat.	3,002
Masaya (2003)	Nicaragua	2,083
South America		
Llullaillaco (1877)	Argentina-Chile	22,109
Guallatiri (1960)	Chile	19,918
Tupungatito (1987)	Argentia-Chile	19,685
Cotopaxi (1940)	Ecuador.	19,393
El Misti (1784)	Peru	19,101
Láscar (2005)	Chile	18,346
Nevado del Ruiz (1991)	Colombia	17,457
Sangay (2006)	Ecuador.	17,159
Irruputuncu (1995)	Chile	16,939
Tungurahua (2006)	Ecuador.	16,479
Guagua Pichincha (2004)	Ecuador.	15,695
Puracé (1977)	Colombia	15,256
Galeras (2006)	Colombia	14,029
Llaima (2003)	Chile	10,253
Villarrica (2006)	Chile	9,340
Cerro Hudson (1991)	Chile	6,250
Fernandina (2005)	Galapagos Isls., Ecuad.	4,842
Mid-Pacific		
Mauna Loa (1984)	Hawaii, HI	13,681
Kilauea (2006)	Hawaii, HI	4,009
Mid-Atlantic Ridge		
Jan Mayen (1985)	N. Atlantic Ocn., Norway	7,470
Grímsvötn (2004)	Iceland	5,659
Hekla (2000)	Iceland	4,892
Krafla (1984)	Iceland	2,133
Europe		
Etna (2005)	Italy	10,991
Vesuvius (1944)	Italy	4,203
Stromboli (2006)	Italy	3,031
Santorini (1950)	Greece	1,204
North America		
Pico de Orizaba (1846)	Mexico.	18,619
Popocatépetl (2006)	Mexico.	17,802
Rainier (1825?)	Washington	14,409
Wrangell (1999)	Alaska.	14,163
Shasta (1786)	California.	14,163
Colima (2006)	Mexico.	12,631
Lassen Peak (1917)	California.	10,456
Redoubt (1990)	Alaska.	10,197
Iliamna (1876)	Alaska.	10,016
Shishaldin (2004)	Aleutian Isl., AK.	9,373
St. Helens (2006)	Washington.	8,363
Pavlof (1997)	Alaska.	8,264
Veniaminof (2005)	Alaska.	8,225
Katmai [Novarupta] (1912)	Alaska.	6,716
Makushin (1995)	Aleutian Isl., AK.	5,905
Great Sitkin (1974)	Aleutian Isl., AK.	5,709
Cleveland (2005)	Aleutian Isl., AK.	5,676
Gareloi (1989)	Aleutian Isl., AK.	5,161
Korovin [Atka complex] (1998)	Aleutian Isl., AK.	5,029
Akutan (1992)	Aleutian Isl., AK.	4,275
Augustine (2006)	Alaska.	4,108
Kiska (1990)	Aleutian Isl., AK.	4,003
El Chichón (1982)	Mexico.	3,773
Okmok (1997)	Aleutian Isl., AK.	3,520
Seguam (1993)	Aleutian Isl., AK.	3,458

Mountains

United States, Canada, Mexico

Peak, state/country	Height (ft)	Peak, state/country	Height (ft)	Peak, state/country	Height (ft)
McKinley, Alaska	20,320	Alverstone, Alaska-Yukon	14,565	Shavano, Colorado	14,229
Logan, Yukon	19,551	Browne Tower, Alaska	14,530	Belford, Colorado	14,197
Pico de Orizaba, Mexico	18,619	Whitney, California	14,494	Princeton, Colorado	14,197
St. Elias, Alaska-Yukon	18,008	Elbert, Colorado	14,433	Crestone Needle, Colorado	14,197
Popocatépetl, Mexico	17,930	Massive, Colorado	14,421	Yale, Colorado	14,196
Foraker, Alaska	17,400	Harvard, Colorado	14,420	Bross, Colorado	14,172
Iztaccihuatl, Mexico	17,343	Rainier, Washington	14,410	Kit Carson, Colorado	14,165
Lucania, Yukon	17,147	University Peak, Alaska	14,410	Wrangell, Alaska	14,163
King, Yukon	16,971	Williamson, California	14,375	Shasta, California	14,162
Steele, Yukon	16,644	La Plata Peak, Colorado	14,361	El Diente Peak, Colorado	14,159
Bona, Alaska	16,550	Blanca Peak, Colorado	14,345	Point Success, Washington	14,158
Blackburn, Alaska	16,390	Uncompahgre Peak, Colorado	14,309	Maroon Peak, Colorado	14,156
Kennedy, Alaska	16,286	Crestone Peak, Colorado	14,294	Tabeguache, Colorado	14,155
Sanford, Alaska	16,237	Lincoln, Colorado	14,286	Oxford, Colorado	14,153
Vancouver, Alaska-Yukon	15,979	Grays Peak, Colorado	14,270	Sill, California	14,153
South Buttress, Alaska	15,885	Antero, Colorado	14,269	Sneffels, Colorado	14,150
Wood, Yukon	15,885	Torreys Peak, Colorado	14,267	Democrat, Colorado	14,148
Churchill, Alaska	15,638	Castle Peak, Colorado	14,265	Capitol Peak, Colorado	14,130
Fairweather, Alaska-BC	15,300	Quandary Peak, Colorado	14,265	Liberty Cap, Washington	14,112
Zinantecatl (Toluca), Mexico	15,016	Evans, Colorado	14,264	Pikes Peak, Colorado	14,110
Hubbard, Alaska-Yukon	15,015	Longs Peak, Colorado	14,255	Snowmass, Colorado	14,092
Bear, Alaska	14,831	McArthur, Yukon	14,253	Russell, California	14,088
Walsh, Yukon	14,780	Wilson, Colorado	14,246	Eolus, Colorado	14,083
East Buttress, Alaska	14,730	White Mt. Peak, California	14,246	Windom, Colorado	14,082
Matlalcueyetl, Mexico	14,636	North Palisade, California	14,242	Columbia, Colorado	14,073
Hunter, Alaska	14,753	Cameron, Colorado	14,238	Augusta, Alaska	14,070

The highest point in the West Indies is in the Dominican Republic, Pico Duarte (10,417 ft).

South America

Peak, country	Height (ft)	Peak, country	Height (ft)	Peak, country	Height (ft)
Aconcagua, Argentina	22,834	Coropuna, Peru	21,083	Solo, Argentina	20,492
Ojos del Salado, Arg.-Chile	22,572	Laudo, Argentina	20,997	Polleras, Argentina	20,456
Bonete, Argentina	22,546	Ancohuma, Bolivia	20,958	Pular, Chile	20,423
Tupungato, Argentina-Chile	22,310	Ausangate, Peru	20,945	Chani, Argentina	20,341
Pissis, Argentina	22,241	Toro, Argentina-Chile	20,932	Aucanquilcha, Chile	20,295
Mercedario, Argentina	22,211	Illampu, Bolivia	20,873	Juncal, Argentina-Chile	20,276
Huascaran, Peru	22,205	Tres Cruces, Argentina-Chile	20,853	Negro, Argentina	20,184
Llullaillaco, Argentina-Chile	22,109	Huandoy, Peru	20,852	Quela, Argentina	20,128
El Libertador, Argentina	22,047	Parinacota, Bolivia-Chile	20,768	Condoriri, Bolivia	20,095
Cachi, Argentina	22,047	Tortolas, Argentina-Chile	20,745	Palermo, Argentina	20,079
Incahuasi, Argentina-Chile	21,720	Ampato, Peru	20,702	Solimana, Peru	20,068
Yerupaja, Peru	21,709	El Condor, Argentina	20,669	San Juan, Argentina-Chile	20,049
Galan, Argentina	21,654	Salcantay, Peru	20,574	Sierra Nevada, Argentina-Chile	20,023
El Muerto, Argentina-Chile	21,457	Chimborazo, Ecuador	20,561	Antofalla, Argentina	20,013
Sajama, Bolivia	21,391	Huancarhuas, Peru	20,531	Marmolejo, Argentina-Chile	20,013
Nacimiento, Argentina	21,302	Famatina, Argentina	20,505	Chachani, Peru	19,931
Illimani, Bolivia	21,201	Pumasillo, Peru	20,492		

Africa

Peak, country	Height (ft)	Peak, country	Height (ft)	Peak, country	Height (ft)
Kilimanjaro, Tanzania	19,340	Meru, Tanzania	14,979	Guna, Ethiopia	13,881
Kenya, Kenya	17,058	Karisimbi, Congo-Rwanda	14,787	Gughe, Ethiopia	13,780
Margherita Pk., Uganda-Congo	16,763	Elgon, Kenya-Uganda	14,178	Toubkal, Morocco	13,661
Ras Dashan, Ethiopia	15,158	Batu, Ethiopia	14,131	Cameroon, Cameroon	13,435

Australia, New Zealand, SE Asian Islands

Peak, country	Height (ft)	Peak, country	Height (ft)	Peak, country	Height (ft)
Jaya, New Guinea	16,500	Wilhelm, New Guinea	14,793	Cook, New Zealand	12,349
Trikora, New Guinea	15,585	Kinabalu, Malaysia	13,455	Semeru, Java, Indonesia	12,060
Mandala, New Guinea	15,420	Kerinci, Sumatra, Indon.	12,467	Kosciusko, Australia	7,310

Other Notable U.S. Mountains

Peak, state	Height (ft)	Peak, state	Height (ft)	Peak, state	Height (ft)
Gannett Peak, WY	13,804	Adams, WA	12,277	Clingmans Dome, NC-TN	6,643
Grand Teton, WY	13,766	San Gorgonio, CA	11,502	Washington, NH	6,288
Kings, UT	13,528	Hood, OR	11,239	Rogers, VA	5,729
Cloud, WY	13,175	Lassen, CA	10,457	Marcy, NY	5,344
Wheeler, NM	13,161	Granite, CA	10,321	Katahdin, ME	5,268
Boundary, NV	13,140	Guadalupe, TX	8,749	Spruce Knob, WV	4,861
Granite, MT	12,799	Olympus, WA	7,965	Mansfield, VT	4,393
Borah, ID	12,662	Harney, SD	7,242	Black Mountain, KY	4,145
Humphreys, AZ	12,633	Mitchell, NC	6,684		

Height of Mount Everest

Mt. Everest, the world's highest mountain, was considered 29,002 ft when Edmund Hillary and Tenzing Norgay became the 1st climbers to scale it, in 1953. This triangulation figure had been accepted since 1850. In 1954 the Surveyor General of the Republic of India set the height at 29,028 ft, plus or minus 10 ft because of snow; this figure was also accepted by the National Geographic Society.

In 1999, a team of climbers sponsored by Boston's Museum of Science and the National Geographic Society measured the height at the summit using sophisticated satellite-based technology. This new measurement, of 29,035 ft, was accepted by the National Geographic Society and other authorities, including the U.S. National Imagery and Mapping Agency.

By May 31, 2006, over 50 years after the 1st climbers had reached the summit, some 2,250 more had followed, and about 186 had died in the attempt.

Europe

Peak, country	Height (ft)	Peak, country	Height (ft)	Peak, country	Height (ft)
Alps		Dent D'Herens, Switzerland	13,686	Gletscherhorn, Switzerland	13,068
Mont Blanc, France-Italy	15,771	Breithorn, It., Switzerland	13,665	Schalihorn, Switzerland	13,040
Monte Rosa (highest peak		Bishorn, Switzerland	13,645	Scerscen, Switzerland	13,028
of group), Switzerland	15,203	Jungfrau, Switzerland	13,642	Eiger, Switzerland	13,025
Dom, Switzerland	14,911	Ecrins, France	13,461	Jagerhorn, Switzerland	13,024
Liskamm, It., Switzerland	14,852	Monch, Switzerland	13,448	Rottalhorn, Switzerland	13,022
Weisshorn, Switzerland	14,780	Pollux, Switzerland	13,422	**Pyrenees**	
Taschhorn, Switzerland	14,733	Schreckhorn, Switzerland	13,379	Aneto, Spain	11,168
Matterhorn, It., Switzerland	14,690	Ober Gabelhorn, Switzerland	13,330	Posets, Spain	11,073
Dent Blanche, Switzerland	14,293	Gran Paradiso, Italy	13,323	Perdido, Spain	11,007
Nadelhorn, Switzerland	14,196	Bernina, It., Switzerland	13,284	Vignemale, France-Spain	10,820
Grand Combin, Switzerland	14,154	Fiescherhorn, Switzerland	13,283	Long, Spain	10,479
Lenzpitze, Switzerland	14,088	Grunhorn, Switzerland	13,266	Estats, Spain	10,304
Finsteraarhorn, Switzerland	14,022	Lauteraarhorn, Switzerland	13,261	Montcalm, Spain	10,105
Castor, Switzerland	13,865	Durrenhorn, Switzerland	13,238	**Caucasus (Europe-Asia)**	
Zinalrothorn, Switzerland	13,849	Allalinhorn, Switzerland	13,213	Elbrus, Russia	18,510
Hohberghom, Switzerland	13,842	Weissmies, Switzerland	13,199	Shkhara, Georgia	17,064
Alphubel, Switzerland	13,799	Lagginhorn, Switzerland	13,156	Dykh Tau, Russia	17,054
Rimpfischhom, Switzerland	13,776	Zupo, Switzerland	13,120	Kashtan Tau, Russia	16,877
Aletschorn, Switzerland	13,763	Fletschhorn, Switzerland	13,110	Janqi, Georgia	16,565
Strahlhorn, Switzerland	13,747	Adlerhorn, Switzerland	13,081	Kazbek, Georgia	16,558

Asia (Mainland)

Peak, country	Height (ft)	Peak, country	Height (ft)	Peak, country	Height (ft)
Everest, Nepal-Tibet	29,035	Tirich Mir, Pakistan	25,230	Badrinath, India	23,420
K2 (Godwin Austen), Kashmir	28,250	Makalu II, Nepal-Tibet	25,120	Nunkun, Kashmir	23,410
Kanchenjunga, India-Nepal	28,208	Minya Konka, China	24,900	Lenin Peak, Tajikistan	23,405
Lhotse I (Everest), Nepal-Tibet	27,923	Kula Gangri, Bhutan-Tibet	24,784	Pyramid, India-Nepal	23,400
Makalu I, Nepal-Tibet	27,824	Changtzu (Everest), Nepal- Tibet.	24,780	Api, Nepal	23,399
Lhotse II (Everest), Nepal-Tibet	27,560	Muz Tagh Ata, Xinjiang	24,757	Pauhunri, India-Tibet	23,385
Dhaulagiri, Nepal	26,810	Skyang Kangri, Kashmir	24,750	Trisul, India	23,360
Manaslu I, Nepal	26,760	Ismail Semani Peak,Tajikistan	24,590	Kangto, India-Tibet	23,260
Cho Oyu, Nepal-Tibet	26,750	Jongsang Peak, India-Nepal	24,472	Nyenchhe Thanglha, Tibet	23,255
Nanga Parbat, Kashmir	26,660	Jengish Chokusu, Xinjiang-		Trisuli, India	23,210
Annapurna I, Nepal	26,504	Kyrgyzstan	24,406	Pumori, Nepal-Tibet	23,190
Gasherbrum, Kashmir	26,470	Sia Kangri, Kashmir	24,350	Dunagiri, India	23,184
Broad, Kashmir	26,400	Haramosh Peak, Pakistan	24,270	Lombo Kangra, Tibet	23,165
Gosainthan Nepal-Tibet	26,287	Istoro Nal, Pakistan	24,240	Saipal, Nepal	23,100
Annapurna II, Nepal	26,041	Tent Peak, India-Nepal	24,165	Macha Pucchare, Nepal	22,958
Gyachung Kang, Nepal-Tibet	25,910	Chomo Lhari, Bhutan-Tibet	24,040	Numbar, Nepal	22,817
Disteghil Sar, Kashmir	25,868	Chamlang, Nepal	24,012	Kanjiroba, Nepal	22,580
Himalchuli, Nepal	25,801	Kabru, India-Nepal	24,002	Ama Dablam, Nepal	22,350
Nuptse (Everest), Nepal-Tibet	25,726	Alung Gangri, Tibet	24,000	Cho Polu, Nepal	22,093
Masherbrum, Kashmir	25,660	Baltoro Kangri, Kashmir	23,990	Lingtren, Nepal-Tibet	21,972
Nanda Devi, India	25,645	Mussu Shan, Xinjiang	23,890	Khumbutse, Nepal-Tibet	21,785
Rakaposhi, Kashmir	25,550	Mana, India	23,860	Hlako Gangri, Tibet	21,266
Kamet, India-Tibet	25,447	Baruntse, Nepal	23,688	Mt. Grosvenor, China	21,190
Namcha Barwa, Tibet	25,445	Nepal Peak, India-Nepal	23,500	Thagchhab Gangri, Tibet	20,970
Gurla Mandhata, Tibet	25,355	Amne Machin, China	23,490	Damavand, Iran	18,606
Ulugh Muz Tagh, Xinjiang-Tibet	25,340	Gauri Sankar, Nepal-Tibet	23,440	Ararat, Turkey	16,804
Kungur, Xinjiang	25,325				

Antarctica

Peak	Height (ft)	Peak	Height (ft)	Peak	Height (ft)
Vinson Massif	16,864	Miller	13,650	Falla	12,549
Tyree	16,290	Long Gables	13,620	Rucker	12,520
Shinn	15,750	Dickerson	13,517	Goldthwait	12,510
Gardner	15,375	Giovinetto	13,412	Morris	12,500
Epperly	15,100	Wade	13,400	Erebus	12,450
Kirkpatrick	14,855	Fisher	13,386	Campbell	12,434
Elizabeth	14,698	Fridtjof Nansen	13,350	Don Pedro Christophersen	12,355
Markham	14,290	Wexler	13,202	Lysaght	12,326
Bell	14,117	Lister	13,200	Huggins	12,247
Mackellar	14,098	Shear	13,100	Sabine	12,200
Anderson	13,957	Odishaw	13,008	Astor	12,175
Bentley	13,934	Donaldson	12,894	Mohl	12,172
Kaplan	13,878	Ray	12,808	Frankes	12,064
Andrew Jackson	13,750	Sellery	12,779	Jones	12,040
Sidley	13,720	Waterman	12,730	Gjelsvik	12,008
Ostenso	13,710	Anne	12,703	Coman	12,000
Minto	13,668	Press	12,566		

Important Islands and Their Areas

Figures are for total areas in square miles. Boldface figure in parentheses shows rank among the world's 10 largest individual islands. Because some islands have not been surveyed accurately, some areas shown are estimates. Some "islands" listed are island groups. Only the largest islands in a group are listed individually. Only islands over 10 sq. miles in area are listed.

Antarctica

Adelaide	1,400
Alexander	16,700
Berkner	18,500
Roosevelt	2,900

Arctic Ocean

Akimiski, Nunavut	1,159
Amund Ringnes, Nun.	2,029
Axel Heiberg, Nun.	16,671
Baffin, Nun. (5)	195,928
Banks, Northwest Territories	27,038
Bathurst, Nun.	6,194
Bolshevik, Russia	4,368
Bolshoy Lyakhovsky, Russia	1,776
Borden, NWT., Nun.	1,079
Bylot, Nun.	4,273
Coats, Nun.	2,123
Cornwallis, Nun.	2,701
Devon, Nun.	21,331
Disko, Greenland	3,312
Ellef Ringnes, Nun.	4,361
Ellesmere, Nun. (10)	75,767
Faddayevskiy, Russia	1,930
Franz Josef Land, Russia	8,000
Iturup (Etorofu), Russia	2,596
King William, Nun.	5,062
Komsomolets, Russia	3,477
Mackenzie King, NWT	1,949
Mansel, Nun.	1,228
Melville, NWT, Nun.	16,274
Milne Land, Greenland	1,400
New Siberian Islands, Russia	14,500
Kotelnyy, Russia	4,504
Novaya Zemlya, Russia (2 isls.)	31,730
Oktyabrskoy, Russia	5,471
Prince Charles, NWT	3,676
Prince of Wales, Nun.	12,872
Prince Patrick, NWT	6,119
Somerset, Nun.	9,570
Southampton, Nun.	15,913
Svalbard (tot. group)	23,957
Nordaustlandet	5,410
Spitsbergen	15,060
Traill, Greenland	1,300
Victoria, NWT, Nun. (9)	83,897
Wrangel, Russia	2,800

Atlantic Ocean

Anticosti, Canada	3,068
Ascension, UK	34
Azores, Portugal (tot. group)	868
Faial	67
San Miguel	291
Bahama Isls. (tot. group)	5,382
Andros, Bahamas	2,300
Bermuda Islands, UK	21
Bioko Isl., Equatorial Guinea	785
Block Islands, RI, U.S.	21
Canary Islands, Spain (tot. group)	2,807
Fuerteventura	688
Gran Canaria	592
Tenerife	795
Cape Breton, Canada	3,981
Cape Verde Islands	1,557
Caviana, Para, Brazil	1,918
Channel Islands, UK (tot. group)	75
Guernsey	24
Jersey	45
Faroe Islands, Denmark	540
Falkland Islands, UK (tot. group)	4,700
East Falkland	2,550
West Falkland	1,750
Great Britain, UK (8)	84,200
Greenland, Denmark (1)	840,000
Gurupa, Para, Brazil	1,878
Hebrides, Scotland	2,744
Iceland	39,699
Ireland (tot. group)	32,589
Irish Republic	27,137
Northern Ireland (UK)	5,452
Isle of Man, UK	227
Isle of Wight, England	147
Long Island, NY, U.S.	1,320

Atlantic Ocean

Madeira Islands, Portugal	306
Marajo, Brazil	15,444
Martha's Vineyard, MA, U.S.	89
Mount Desert, ME, U.S.	104
Nantucket, MA, U.S.	45
Newfoundland, Canada	42,031
Orkney Islands, Scotland	390
Prince Edward, Canada	2,185
St. Helena, UK	47
Shetland Islands, Scotland	587
Skye, Scotland	670
South Georgia, UK	1,450
Tierra del Fuego, Chile, Arg.	18,800
Tristan da Cunha, UK	40

Baltic Sea

Aland Islands, Finland	590
Bornholm, Denmark	227
Gotland, Sweden	1,159

Caribbean Sea

Antigua	108
Aruba, Netherlands	75
Barbados	166
Cuba	42,804
Isle of Youth	926
Cayman Islands	100
Curacao, Netherlands	171
Dominica	290
Guadeloupe, France	687
Hispaniola (Haiti and Dominican Rep)	29,389
Jamaica	4,244
Martinique, France	436
Puerto Rico, U.S.	3,339
Tobago	116
Trinidad	1,864
Virgin Islands, UK	59
Virgin Islands, U.S.	134

East Indies

Bali, Indonesia	2,171
Bangka, Indonesia	4,375
Borneo, Indonesia-Malaysia-Brunei (3)	280,100
Bougainville, Papua New Guinea	3,880
Buru, Indonesia	3,670
Celebes, Indonesia	69,000
Flores, Indonesia	5,500
Halmahera, Indonesia	6,865
Java (Jawa), Indonesia	48,900
Madura, Indonesia	2,113
Moluccas, Indonesia	32,307
New Britain, Papua New Guinea	14,093
New Guinea, Indon.-PNG (2)	306,000
New Ireland, PNG	3,707
Seram, Indonesia	6,621
Sumba, Indonesia	4,306
Sumbawa, Indonesia	5,965
Sumatra, Indonesia (6)	165,000
Timor, Indonesia	13,094
Yos Sudarsa, Indonesia	4,500

Indian Ocean

Andaman Isls., India	2,500
Kerguelen	2,247
Madagascar (4)	226,658
Mauritius	720
Pemba, Tanzania	380
Reunion, France	970
Seychelles	176
Sri Lanka	25,332
Zanzibar, Tanzania	640

Mediterranean Sea

Balearic Isls., Spain	1,927
Corfu, Greece	229
Corsica, France	3,369
Crete, Greece	3,189
Cyprus	3,572
Elba, Italy	86
Euboea, Greece	1,411
Malta	95
Rhodes, Greece	540
Sardinia, Italy	9,301
Sicily, Italy	9,926

Pacific Ocean

Admiralty, AK, U.S.	1,709
Aleutian Isls., AK, U.S. (tot. group)	6,912
Adak	275
Amchitka	116
Attu	350
Kanaga	142
Kiska	106
Tanaga	195
Umnak	686
Unalaska	1,051
Unimak	1,571
Baranof, AK, U.S.	1,636
Chichagof, AK, U.S.	2,062
Chiloe, Chile	3,241
Christmas, Kiribati	94
Diomede, Big, Russia	11
Easter Isl., Chile	69
Fiji (tot. group)	7,056
Vanua Levu	2,242
Viti Levu	4,109
Galapagos Isls., Ecuador	3,043
Graham Isl., British Columbia	2,456
Guadalcanal, Solomon Isls.	2,180
Guam, U.S.	210
Hainan, China	13,000
Hawaiian Isls., HI, U.S. (tot. group)	6,428
Hawaii	4,028
Oahu	600
Hong Kong, China	31
Hoste, Chile	1,590
Japan (tot. group)	145,850
Hokkaido	30,144
Honshu (7)	87,805
Kyushu	14,114
Okinawa	459
Shikoku	7,049
Kangaroo, South Australia	1,680
Kodiak, AK, U.S.	3,485
Kupreanof, AK, U.S.	1,084
Marquesas Isls., France	492
Marshall Isls.	70
Melville, N Terr., Australia	2,240
Micronesia	271
New Caledonia, France	6,530
New Zealand (tot. group)	104,454
Chatham Isls.	372
North	44,204
South	58,384
Stewart	674
North Mariana Isls., U.S.	179
Nunivak, AK, U.S.	1,600
Palau	188
Philippines (tot. group)	115,860
Leyte	2,787
Luzon	40,680
Mindanao	36,775
Mindoro	3,690
Negros	4,907
Palawan	4,554
Panay	4,446
Samar	5,050
Prince of Wales, AK, U.S.	2,770
Revillagedo, AK, U.S.	1,134
Riesco, Chile	1,973
St. Lawrence, AK, U.S.	1,780
Sakhalin, Russia	29,500
Samoa Isls. (tot. group)	1,177
American Samoa, U.S.	77
Tutuila, U.S.	55
Savail, Samoa	659
Upolu, Samoa	432
Santa Catalina, CA, U.S.	75
Santa Ines, Chile	1,407
Tahiti, France	402
Taiwan, China (tot. group)	13,969
Jinmen Dao (Quemoy)	56
Tasmania, Australia	26,178
Tonga Isls.	290
Vancouver Isl., Brit. Columbia	12,079
Vanuatu	4,707
Wellington, Chile	2,549

Persian Gulf

Bahrain	217

Notable Deserts of the World

Deserts are defined as regions of the Earth receiving less than 10 in. of precipitation annually, usually in combination with an evaporation rate exceeding precipitation.

In addition to areas listed below, the continent of Antarctica, with an area of about 5.4 mil square miles (roughly doubled by ice in winter), is generally considered a desert. Annual precipitation averages 8 in. along the coast and far less in the deep interior; however, there is little evaporation.

Arabian (Eastern), 70,000 sq mi in Egypt between the Nile R. and Red Sea, extending southward into Sudan

Atacama, 600-mi-long area rich in nitrate and copper deposits in N Chile

Chihuahuan, 140,000 sq mi in TX, NM, AZ, and Mexico

Dasht-e Kauir, approx. 300 mi long by approx. 100 mi wide in N central Iran

Dasht-e Lut, 20,000 sq mi in E Iran

Death Valley, 3,300 sq mi in CA and NV

Gibson, 120,000 sq mi in the interior of W Australia

Gobi, 500,000 sq mi in Mongolia and China

Great Sandy, 150,000 sq mi in W Australia

Great Victoria, 150,000 sq mi in SW Australia

Kalahari, 225,000 sq mi in S Africa

Kara Kum, 120,000 sq mi in Turkmenistan

Kyzyl Kum, 100,000 sq mi in Kazakhstan and Uzbekistan

Libyan, 450,000 sq mi in the Sahara, extending from Libya through SW Egypt into Sudan

Mojave, 15,000 sq mi in southern CA

Namib, long narrow area (varies from 30-100 mi wide) extending 800 mi along SW coast of Africa

Nubian, 100,000 sq mi in the Sahara in NE Sudan

Painted Desert, section of high plateau in northern AZ extending 150 mi

Patagonia, 300,000 sq mi in S Argentina

Rub al-Khali (Empty Quarter), 250,000 sq mi in the S Arabian Peninsula

Sahara, 3,500,000 sq mi in N Africa, extending westward to the Atlantic. Largest desert in the world

Sonoran, 70,000 sq mi in southwestern AZ and southeastern CA extending into NW Mexico

Syrian, 100,000-sq-mi arid wasteland extending over much of N Saudi Arabia, E Jordan, S Syria, and W Iraq

Taklimakan, 140,000 sq mi in Xinjiang Prov., China

Thar (Great Indian), 100,000-sq-mi arid area extending 400 mi along India-Pakistan border

Areas and Average Depths of Oceans, Seas, and Gulfs[1]

Geographers and mapmakers recognize at least 4 major bodies of water: the Pacific, the Atlantic, the Indian, and the Arctic oceans. The Atlantic and Pacific oceans are considered divided at the equator into the N and S Atlantic and the N and S Pacific. The Arctic Ocean is the name for waters N of the continental landmasses in the region of the Arctic Circle.

	Area (sq mi)	Avg. depth (ft)		Area (sq mi)	Avg. depth (ft)
Pacific Ocean	64,186,300	12,925	Hudson Bay	281,900	305
Atlantic Ocean	33,420,000	11,730	East China Sea	256,600	620
Indian Ocean	28,350,500	12,598	Andaman Sea	218,100	3,667
Arctic Ocean	5,105,700	3,407	Black Sea	196,100	3,906
South China Sea	1,148,500	4,802	Red Sea	174,900	1,764
Caribbean Sea	971,400	8,448	North Sea	164,900	308
Mediterranean Sea	969,100	4,926	Baltic Sea	147,500	180
Bering Sea	873,000	4,893	Yellow Sea	113,500	121
Gulf of Mexico	582,100	5,297	Persian Gulf	88,800	328
Sea of Okhotsk	537,500	3,192	Gulf of California	59,100	2,375
Sea of Japan	391,100	5,468			

(1) The International Hydrographic Organization delimited a fifth world ocean in 2000. The Southern Ocean as defined extends from the coast of Antarctica north to 60° south latitude, covering portions of the Atlantic, Indian, and Pacific oceans, an area of 7,848,400 square miles.

Principal Ocean Depths

Source: National Imagery and Mapping Agency, U.S. Dept. of Defense

	Location		Depth		
Name of area	(lat.)	(long.)	(meters)	(fathoms)	(ft)
Pacific Ocean					
Marianas Trench	11°22′ N	142°36′ E	10,924	5,973	35,840
Tonga Trench	23°16′ S	174°44′ W	10,800	5,906	35,433
Philippine Trench	10°38′ N	126°36′ E	10,057	5,499	32,995
Kermadec Trench	31°53′ S	177°21′ W	10,047	5,494	32,963
Bonin Trench	24°30′ N	143°24′ E	9,994	5,464	32,788
Kuril Trench	44°15′ N	150°34′ E	9,750	5,331	31,988
Izu Trench	31°05′ N	142°10′ E	9,695	5,301	31,808
New Britain Trench	06°19′ S	153°45′ E	8,940	4,888	29,331
Yap Trench	08°33′ N	138°02′ E	8,527	4,663	27,976
Japan Trench	36°08′ N	142°43′ E	8,412	4,600	27,599
Peru-Chile Trench	23°18′ S	71°14′ W	8,064	4,409	26,457
Palau Trench	07°52′ N	134°56′ E	8,054	4,404	26,424
Aleutian Trench	50°51′ N	177°11′ E	7,679	4,199	25,194
New Hebrides Trench	20°36′ S	168°37′ E	7,570	4,139	24,836
North Ryukyu Trench	24°00′ N	126°48′ E	7,181	3,927	23,560
Mid. America Trench	14°02′ N	93°39′ W	6,662	3,643	21,857
Atlantic Ocean					
Puerto Rico Trench	19°55′ N	65°27′ W	8,605	4,705	28,232
S Sandwich Trench	55°42′ S	25°56′ W	8,325	4,552	27,313
Romanche Gap	0°13′ S	18°26′ W	7,728	4,226	25,354
Cayman Trench	19°12′ N	80°00′ W	7,535	4,120	24,721
Brazil Basin	09°10′ S	23°02′ W	6,119	3,346	20,076
Indian Ocean					
Java Trench	10°19′ S	109°58′ E	7,125	3,896	23,376
Ob′ Trench	09°45′ S	67°18′ E	6,874	3,759	22,553
Diamantina Trench	35°50′ S	105°14′ E	6,602	3,610	21,660
Vema Trench	09°08′ S	67°15′ E	6,402	3,501	21,004
Agulhas Basin	45°20′ S	26°50′ E	6,195	3,387	20,325
Arctic Ocean					
Eurasia Basin	82°23′ N	19°31′ E	5,450	2,980	17,881
Mediterranean Sea					
Ionian Basin	36°32′ N	21°06′ E	5,150	2,816	16,896

Note: Greater depths have been reported in some areas but are not officially confirmed by research vessels.

Principal World Rivers

For N American rivers, see separate table.

River	Outflow	Length (mi)
Africa		
Chari	Lake Chad	500
Congo	Atlantic Ocean	2,900
Gambia	Atlantic Ocean	700
Kasai	Congo River	1,000
Limpopo	Indian Ocean	1,100
Lualaba	Congo River	1,100
Niger	Gulf of Guinea	2,590
Nile	Mediterranean	4,160
Okavango	Okavango Delta	1,000
Orange	Atlantic Ocean	1,300
Senegal	Atlantic Ocean	1,020
Ubangi	Congo River	660
Zambezi	Indian Ocean	1,700
Asia		
Amu Darya	Aral Sea	1,550
Amur	Tatar Strait	1,780
Angara	Yenisey River	1,151
Brahmaputra	Bay of Bengal	1,800
Chang	East China Sea	3,964
Euphrates	Shatt al-Arab	1,700
Ganges	Bay of Bengal	1,560
Godavari	Bay of Bengal	900
Hsi (see Xi)		
Huang	Yellow Sea	3,395
Indus	Arabian Sea	1,800
Irrawaddy	Andaman Sea	1,337
Jordan	Dead Sea	200
Kolyma	Arctic Ocean	1,323
Krishna	Bay of Bengal	800
Kura	Caspian Sea	848
Lena	Laptev Sea	2,734
Mekong	South China Sea	2,700
Narbada (see Narmada)		
Narmada	Arabian Sea	800
Ob	Gulf of Ob	2,268
Ob-Irtysh	Gulf of Ob	3,362
Salween	Gulf of Martaban	1,500
Songhua	Amur River	1,150
Sungari	Amur River	1,197
Sutlej	Indus River	900
Syr	Aral Sea	1,370
Tarim	Lop Nor Basin	1,261
Tigris	Shatt al-Arab	1,180
Xi	South China Sea	1,200
Yamuna	Ganges River	855
Yangtze (see Chang)		
Yellow (see Huang)		
Yenisey	Kara Sea	2,543
Australia		
Murray-Darling	Indian Ocean	2,310
Murrumbidgee	Murray River	981
Europe		
Bug, Northern	Wisla	481
Bug, Southern	Dnieper River	532
Danube	Black Sea	1,776
Don	Sea of Azov	1,224
Dnieper	Black Sea	1,420
Dniester	Black Sea	877
Drava	Danube River	447
Dvina, North	White Sea	824
Dvina, West	Gulf of Riga	634
Ebro	Mediterranean	565
Elbe	North Sea	724
Garonne	Bay of Biscay	357
Kama	Volga River	1,122
Loire	Bay of Biscay	634
Mame	Seine River	326
Meuse	North Sea	580
Oder	Baltic Sea	567
Oka	Volga River	932
Pechora	Barents Sea	1,124
Po	Adriatic Sea	405
Rhine	North Sea	820
Rhone	Gulf of Lions	505
Seine	English Channel	496
Shannon	Atlantic Ocean	230
Tagus	Atlantic Ocean	626
Thames	North Sea	210
Tiber	Tyrrhenian Sea	252
Tisza	Danube River	600
Ural	Caspian Sea	1,575
Volga	Caspian Sea	2,290
Weser	North Sea	454
Wisla	Gulf of Gdansk	675
South America		
Amazon	Atlantic Ocean	4,000
Araguaia	Tocantins River	1,100
Iça (see Putumayo)		
Iguaça	Parana River	808
Japura	Amazon River	1,750
Madeira	Amazon River	2,013
Magdalena	Caribbean Sea	956
Negro	Amazon River	1,400
Orinoco	Atlantic Ocean	1,600
Paraguay	Parana River	1,584
Parana	Rio de la Plata	2,485
Pilcomayo	Paraguay River	1,000
Purus	Amazon River	2,100
Putumayo	Amazon River	1,000
Rio de la Plata	Atlantic Ocean	150
Rio Roosevelt	Aripuana	400
Sao Francisco	Atlantic Ocean	1,988
Tocantins	Para River	1,677
Ucayali	Marañón River	910
Uruguay	Rio de la Plata	1,000
Xingu	Amazon River	1,300

Major Rivers in North America

River	Source or upper limit of length	Outflow	Length (mi)
Alabama	Gilmer County, GA	Mobile River	729
Albany	Lake St. Joseph, Ontario	James Bay	610
Allegheny	Potter County, PA.	Ohio River	325
Altamaha-Ocmulgee	Junction of Yellow and South Rivers, Newton County, GA	Atlantic Ocean	392
Apalachicola-Chattahoochee	Towns County, GA	Gulf of Mexico	524
Arkansas	Lake County, CO	Mississippi River	1,459
Assiniboine	Eastern Saskatchewan	Red River	450
Attawapiskat	Attawapiskat, Ontario	James Bay	465
Back (NWT)	Contwoyto Lake	Chantrey Inlet, Arctic Ocean	605
Big Black (MS)	Webster County, MS	Mississippi River	330
Brazos	Junction of Salt and Double Mountain Forks, Stonewall County, TX	Gulf of Mexico	950
Canadian	Las Animas County, CO	Arkansas River	906
Cedar (IA)	Dodge County, MN	Iowa River	329
Cheyenne	Junction of Antelope Creek and Dry Fork, Converse County, WY	Missouri River	290
Churchill, Lab.	Lake Ashuanipi, Labrador	Atlantic Ocean	532
Churchill, Man.	Methy Lake, Saskatchewan	Hudson Bay	1,000
Cimarron	Colfax County, NM	Arkansas River	600
Colorado (AZ)	Rocky Mountain Natl. Park, CO (90 mi in Mexico)	Gulf of California	1,450
Colorado (TX)	West Texas	Matagorda Bay	862
Columbia	Columbia Lake, British Columbia	Pacific Ocean, bet. OR and WA	1,243
Columbia, Upper	Columbia Lake, British Columbia	To mouth of Snake River	890
Connecticut	Third Connecticut Lake, NH	Long Island Sound, CT	407
Coppermine (NWT)	Lac de Gras	Coronation Gulf, Arctic Ocean	525
Cumberland	Letcher County, KY	Ohio River	720
Delaware	Schoharie County, NY	Liston Point, Delaware Bay	390
Fraser	Near Mount Robson (on Continental Divide)	Strait of Georgia	850
Gila	Catron County, NM.	Colorado River	649
Green (UT-WY)	Junction of Wells and Trail Creeks, Sublette County, WY	Colorado River	730
Hudson	Henderson Lake, Essex County, NY	Upper NY Bay	306
Illinois	St. Joseph County, IN	Mississippi River	420
James (ND-SD)	Wells County, ND	Missouri River	710
James (VA)	Junction of Jackson and Cowpasture Rivers, Botetourt County, VA	Hampton Roads	340
Kanawha-New	Junction of North and South Forks of New River, NC	Ohio River	352
Kentucky	Junction of North and Middle Forks, Lee County, KY	Ohio River	259
Klamath	Lake Ewauna, Klamath Falls, OR	Pacific Ocean	250
Kootenay	Kootenay Lake, British Columbia	Columbia River	485
Koyukuk	Endicott Mountains, AK	Yukon River	470
Kuskokwim	Alaska Range	Kuskokwim Bay	724

River	Source or upper limit of length	Outflow	Length (mi)
Liard	Southern Yukon, AK	Mackenzie River	693
Little Missouri	Crook County, WY	Missouri River	560
Mackenzie	Great Slave Lake, N.W.T.	Arctic Ocean	1,060
Milk	Junction of North and South Forks, Alberta	Missouri River	625
Minnesota	Big Stone Lake, MN	Mississippi River	332
Mississippi	Lake Itasca, MN	Gulf of Mexico	2,340
Mississippi-Missouri-Red Rock	Source of Red Rock, Beaverhead Co., MT	Gulf of Mexico	3,710
Missouri	Junction of Jefferson, Madison, and Gallatin Rivers, Gallatin County, MT	Mississippi River	2,315
Missouri-Red Rock	Source of Red Rock, Beaverhead Co., MT	Mississippi River	2,540
Mobile-Alabama-Coosa	Gilmer County, GA	Mobile Bay	774
Nelson (Man.)	Lake Winnipeg	Hudson Bay	410
Neosho	Morris County, KS	Arkansas River, OK	460
Niobrara	Niobrara County, WY	Missouri River, NE	431
North Canadian	Union County, NM	Canadian River, OK	800
North Platte	Junction of Grizzly and Little Grizzly Creeks, Jackson County, CO	Platte River, NE	618
Ohio	Junction of Allegheny and Monongahela Rivers, Pittsburgh, PA	Mississippi River	981
Ohio-Allegheny	Potter County, PA.	Mississippi River	1,310
Osage	East-central Kansas	Missouri River	500
Ottawa	Lake Capimitchigama	St. Lawrence River	790
Ouachita	Polk County, AR	Black River	605
Peace	Stikine Mountains, B.C.	Slave River	1,210
Pearl	Neshoba County, MS	Gulf of Mexico	411
Pecos	Mora County, NM	Rio Grande	926
Pee Dee-Yadkin	Watauga County, NC	Winyah Bay	435
Pend Oreille-Clark Fork	Near Butte, MT.	Columbia River	531
Platte	Junction of North and South Platte Rivers, NE	Missouri River	310
Porcupine	Ogilvie Mountains, AK	Yukon River, AK	569
Potomac	Garrett County, MD	Chesapeake Bay	383
Powder	Junction of South and Middle Forks, WY	Yellowstone River	375
Red (OK-TX-LA)	Curry County, NM.	Mississippi River	1,290
Red River of the North	Junction of Otter Tail and Bois de Sioux Rivers, Wilkin County, MN.	Lake Winnipeg	545
Republican	Junction of North Fork and Arikaree River, NE	Kansas River	445
Rio Grande	San Juan County, CO	Gulf of Mexico	1,900
Roanoke	Junction of N and S Forks, Montgomery Co., VA.	Albemarle Sound	380
Rock (IL-WI)	Dodge County, WI	Mississippi River	300
Sabine	Junction of S and Caddo Forks, Hunt County, TX	Sabine Lake	380
Sacramento	Siskiyou County, CA.	Suisun Bay	377
St. Francis	Iron County, MO.	Mississippi River	425
St. John	Northwestern Maine	Bay of Fundy	418
St. Lawrence	Lake Ontario	Gulf of St. Lawrence, Atlantic Ocean	800
Saguenay	Lake St. John, Quebec.	St. Lawrence River.	434
Salmon (ID)	Custer County, ID.	Snake River	420
San Joaquin	Junction of S and Middle Forks, Madera Co., CA	Suisun Bay	350
San Juan	Silver Lake, Archuleta County, CO.	Colorado River	360
Santee-Wateree-Catawba	McDowell County, NC	Atlantic Ocean	538
Saskatchewan, North	Rocky Mountains	Saskatchewan R.	800
Saskatchewan, South	Rocky Mountains	Saskatchewan R.	865
Savannah	Junction of Seneca and Tugaloo Rivers, Anderson County, SC	Atlantic Ocean, GA-SC	314
Severn (Ont.)	Sandy Lake	Hudson Bay	610
Smoky Hill	Cheyenne County, CO	Kansas River, KS	540
Snake	Teton County, WY	Columbia River, WA.	1,038
South Platte	Junction of S and Middle Forks, Park County, CO.	Platte River	424
Susitna	Alaska Range	Cook Inlet	313
Susquehanna	Huyden Creek, Otsego County, NY	Chesapeake Bay	447
Tallahatchie	Tippah County, MS.	Yazoo River	301
Tanana	Wrangell Mountains, AK.	Yukon River	659
Tennessee	Junction of French Broad and Holston Rivers	Ohio River	652
Tennessee-French Broad	Courthouse Creek, Transylvania County, NC	Ohio River	886
Tombigbee	Prentiss County, MS.	Mobile River	525
Trinity	North of Dallas, TX.	Galveston Bay	360
Wabash	Darke County, OH	Ohio River	512
Washita	Hemphill County, TX	Red River, OK	500
White (AR-MO)	Madison County, AR	Mississippi River	722
Willamette	Douglas County, OR	Columbia River	309
Wind-Bighorn	Junction of Wind and Little Wind Rivers, Fremont Co., WY (Source of Wind R. is Togwotee Pass, Teton Co., WY)	Yellowstone River	338
Wisconsin	Lac Vieux Desert, Vilas County, WI	Mississippi River	430
Yellowstone	Park County, WY	Missouri River	682
Yukon	McNeil R., Yukon Territory	Bering Sea	1,979

World Almanac Quick Quiz

Which of these cities is closest to the Equator?

(a) Honolulu, HI   (b) Santiago, Chile   (c) Manila, Philippines   (d) Mumbai (Bombay), India

For the answer look in this chapter, or see page 1008.

Major Natural Lakes of the World

Source: Geological Survey, U.S. Dept. of the Interior; GeoAccess Division, Natural Resources Canada

A lake is generally defined as a body of water surrounded by land. By this definition some bodies of water that are called seas, such as the Caspian Sea and the Aral Sea, are really lakes. In the following table, the word *lake* is omitted when it is part of the name.

Name	Continent	Area (sq mi)	Length (mi)	Maximum depth (ft)	Elevation (ft)
Caspian Sea[1]	Asia-Europe	143,244	760	3,363	−92
Superior	North America	31,700	350	1,330	600
Victoria	Africa	26,828	250	270	3,720
Huron	North America	23,000	206	750	579
Michigan	North America	22,300	307	923	579
Aral Sea[1]	Asia	13,000[2]	260	220	125
Tanganyika	Africa	12,700	420	4,823	2,534
Baykal	Asia	12,162	395	5,315	1,493
Great Bear	North America	12,096	192	1,463	512
Nyasa (Malawi)	Africa	11,150	360	2,280	1,550
Great Slave	North America	11,031	298	2,015	513
Erie	North America	9,910	241	210	570
Winnipeg	North America	9,417	266	200	713
Ontario	North America	7,340	193	802	245
Balkhash[1]	Asia	7,115	376	85	1,115
Ladoga	Europe	6,835	124	738	13
Maracaibo	South America	5,217	133	115	sea level
Onega	Europe	3,710	145	328	108
Eyre[1]	Australia	3,600[3]	90	4	−52
Titicaca	South America	3,200	122	922	12,500
Nicaragua	North America	3,100	102	230	102
Athabasca	North America	3,064	208	407	700
Reindeer	North America	2,568	143	720	1,106
Tonle Sap	Asia	2,500[3]	...	45	...
Turkana (Rudolf)	Africa	2,473	154	240	1,230
Issyk Kul[1]	Asia	2,355	115	2,303	5,279
Torrens[1]	Australia	2,230[3]	130	...	92
Vanern	Europe	2,156	91	328	144
Nettilling	North America	2,140	67	...	95
Winnipegosis	North America	2,075	141	38	830
Albert	Africa	2,075	100	168	2,030
Nipigon	North America	1,872	72	540	1,050
Gairdner[1]	Australia	1,840[3]	90	...	112
Urmia[1]	Asia	1,815	90	49	4,180
Manitoba	North America	1,799	140	21	813
Chad	Africa	839[4]	175	24	787

(1) Salt lake. (2) Approximate figure, could be less. The diversion of feeder rivers since the 1960s has devastated the Aral—once the world's 4th-largest lake (26,000 sq. miles). By 2000, the Aral had effectively become three lakes, with the total area shown. (3) Approximate figure, subject to great seasonal variation. (4) Once 4th-largest lake in Africa (about 10,000 sq. mi in the 1960s), Chad had shrunk more than 90% by 2001 as a result of irrigation and long-term drought.

The Great Lakes

Source: National Ocean Service, U.S. Dept. of Commerce

The Great Lakes form the world's **largest body of fresh water** (in surface area), and with their connecting waterways are the largest inland water transportation unit. Draining the great North Central basin of the U.S., they enable shipping to reach the Atlantic via their outlet, the St. Lawrence R., and to reach the Gulf of Mexico via the Illinois Waterway, from Lake Michigan to the Mississippi R. A 3rd outlet connects with the Hudson R. and then the Atlantic via the New York State Barge Canal System. Traffic on the Illinois Waterway and the N.Y. State Barge Canal System is limited to recreational boating and small shipping vessels.

Only one of the lakes, Lake Michigan, is wholly in the U.S.; the others are shared with Canada. Ships move from the shores of Lake Superior to Whitefish Bay at the E end of the lake, then through the Soo (Sault Ste. Marie) locks, through the St. Mary's R. and into Lake Huron. To reach Gary and the Port of Indiana and South Chicago, IL, ships move W from Lake Huron to Lake Michigan through the Straits of Mackinac. Lake Superior is 601 ft above low water datum at Rimouski, Quebec, on the International Great Lakes Datum (1985). From Duluth, MN, to the E end of Lake Ontario is 1,156 mi.

	Superior	Michigan	Huron	Erie	Ontario
Length in mi	350	307	206	241	193
Breadth in mi	160	118	183	57	53
Deepest soundings in ft	1,333	923	750	210	802
Volume of water in cu mi	2,935	1,180	850	116	393
Area (sq mi) water surface—U.S.	20,600	22,300	9,100	4,980	3,460
Canada	11,100	.....	13,900	4,930	3,880
Area (sq mi) entire drainage basin—U.S.	16,900	45,600	16,200	18,000	15,200
Canada	32,400	.....	35,500	4,720	12,100
TOTAL AREA (sq mi) U.S. and Canada	**81,000**	**67,900**	**74,700**	**32,630**	**34,850**
Low water datum above mean water level at Rimouski, Quebec, avg. level in ft (1985)	601.10	577.50	577.50	569.20	243.30
Latitude, N	46°25′	41°37′	43°00′	41°23′	43°11′
	49°00′	46°06′	46°17′	42°52′	44°15′
Longitude, W	84°22′	84°45′	79°43′	78°51′	76° 03′
	92°06′	88°02′	84°45′	83°29′	79°53′
National boundary line in mi	282.8	None	260.8	251.5	174.6
United States shoreline (mainland only) mi	863	1,400	580	431	300

Famous Waterfalls

Source: National Geographic Society

The earth has thousands of waterfalls, some of considerable magnitude. Their magnitude is determined not only by height but also by volume of flow, steadiness of flow, crest width, whether the water drops sheerly or over a sloping surface, and whether it descends in one leap or in a succession of leaps. A series of low falls flowing over a considerable distance is known as a **cascade**.

Estimated mean annual flow, in cubic feet per second, of major waterfalls is as follows: Niagara, 212,200; Paulo Afonso, 100,000; Urubupunga, 97,000; Iguazu, 61,000; Patos-Maribondo, 53,000; Victoria, 35,400; and Kaieteur, 23,400.

Height = total drop in feet in one or more leaps. # = falls of more than one leap; * = falls that diminish greatly seasonally; ** = falls that reduce to a trickle or are dry for part of each year. If the river names are not shown, they are same as the falls. R. = river; (C) = cascade.

Name and location	Height (ft)
Africa	
Angola	
Ruacana, Cunene R.	406
Ethiopia	
Fincha	508
Lesotho	
Maletsunyane*	630
Zimbabwe-Zambia	
Victoria, Zambezi R.*	343
South Africa	
Augrabies, Orange R.*	480
Tugela#	2,014
Tanzania-Zambia	
Kalambo*	726
Asia	
India	
Cauvery*	330
Jog (Gersoppa), Sharavathi R.*	830
Japan	
Kegon, Daiya R.*	330
Australia	
New South Wales	
Wentworth	614
Wollomombi	1,100
Queensland	
Tully	885
Wallaman, Stony Cr.#	1,137
New Zealand	
Helena	890
Sutherland, Arthur R.#	1,904
Europe	
Austria	
Gastein#	492
Krimml#	1,312
France	
Gavarnie*	1,385
Great Britain	
Scotland	
Glomach	370
Wales	
Rhaiadr	240
Italy	
Frua, Toce R. (C)	470

Name and location	Height (ft)
Norway	
Mardalsfossen (Northern)	1,535
Mardalsfossen (Southern)#	2,149
Skjeggedal, Nybuai R.#**	1,378
Skykje**	984
Vetti, Morka-Koldedola R.	900
Sweden	
Handol#	427
Switzerland	
Giessbach (C)	984
Reichenbach#	656
Simmen#	459
Staubbach	984
Trummelbach#	1,312
North America	
Canada	
Alberta	
Panther, Nigel Cr.	600
British Columbia	
Della#	1,443
Takakkaw, Daly Glacier#	1,200
Quebec	
Montmorency	274
Canada—United States	
Niagara: American	182
Horseshoe	173
United States	
Alabama	
Noccalula Falls	90
California	
Feather, Fall R.*	640
Yosemite National Park	
Bridalveil*	620
Illilouette*	370
Nevada, Merced R.*	594
Ribbon**	1,612
Silver Strand, Meadow Br.**	1,170
Vernal, Merced R. *	317
Yosemite#**	2,425
Colorado	
Seven, South Cheyenne Cr.#.	300
Hawaii	
Akaka, Kolekole Str.	442
Idaho	
Shoshone, Snake R.**	212
Kentucky	
Cumberland	68

Name and location	Height (ft)
Maryland	
Great, Potomac R. (C) *	71
Minnesota	
Minnehaha**	53
New Jersey	
Passaic	70
New York	
Taughannock*	215
Oregon	
Multnomah#	620
Tennessee	
Fall Creek	256
Washington	
Mt. Rainier Natl. Park	
Sluiskin, Paradise R.	300
Snoqualmie**	268
Wisconsin	
Big Manitou, Black R. (C)*	165
Wyoming	
Yellowstone Natl. Pk. Tower.	132
Yellowstone (upper)*	109
Yellowstone (lower)*	308
Mexico	
El Salo	218
South America	
Argentina-Brazil	
Iguazu	230
Brazil	
Glass	1,325
Patos-Maribondo, Grande R.	115
Paulo Afonso, Sao Francisco R.	275
Urubupunga, Parana R.	39
Colombia	
Catarvata de Candelas, Cusiana R.	984
Tequendama, Bogota R.*	427
Ecuador	
Agoyan, Pastaza R.*	200
Guyana	
Kaieteur, Potaro R.	741
Great, Kamarang R.	1,600
Marina, Ipobe R.#	500
Venezuela	
Angel#*	3,212
Cuquenan	2,000

Latitude, Longitude, and Altitude of U.S. and Canadian Cities

Source: U.S. geographic positions, U.S. altitudes provided by Geological Survey, U.S. Dept. of the Interior. Canadian geographic positions and altitudes provided by Natural Resources Canada.

City	Lat. N °	'	''	Long. W °	'	''	Elev. (ft)	City	Lat. N °	'	''	Long. W °	'	''	Elev. (ft)
Abilene, TX	32	26	55	99	43	58	1,718	Belleville, Ont.	44	14	0	77	21	0	320
Akron, OH	41	4	53	81	31	9	1,050	Bellingham, WA	48	45	35	122	29	13	100
Albany, NY	42	39	9	73	45	24	20	Berkeley, CA	37	52	18	122	16	18	150
Albuquerque, NM	35	5	4	106	39	2	4,955	Billings, MT	45	47	0	108	30	0	3,124
Alert, N.W.T.	82	30	0	62	22	0	100	Biloxi, MS	30	23	45	88	53	7	25
Allentown, PA	40	36	30	75	29	26	350	Binghamton, NY	42	5	55	75	55	6	865
Amarillo, TX	35	13	19	101	49	51	3,685	Birmingham, AL	33	31	14	86	48	9	600
Anchorage, AK	61	13	5	149	54	1	101	Bismarck, ND	46	48	30	100	47	0	1,700
Ann Arbor, MI	42	16	15	83	43	35	880	Bloomington, IL	40	29	3	88	59	37	829
Asheville, NC	35	36	3	82	33	15	2,134	Boise, ID	43	36	49	116	12	9	2,730
Ashland, KY	38	28	42	82	38	17	558	Boston, MA	42	21	30	71	3	37	20
Atlanta, GA	33	44	56	84	23	17	1,050	Bowling Green, KY	36	59	25	86	26	37	510
Atlantic City, NJ	39	21	51	74	25	24	8	Brandon, Man.	49	54	35	99	57	03	1,343
Augusta, GA	33	28	15	81	58	30	414	Brantford, Ont.	43	08	0	80	16	0	815
Augusta, ME	44	18	38	69	46	48	45	Brattleboro, VT	42	51	3	72	33	30	240
Austin, TX	30	16	1	97	44	34	501	Bridgeport, CT	41	10	1	73	12	19	10
Bakersfield, CA	35	22	24	119	1	4	408	Brockton, MA	42	5	6	71	1	8	112
Baltimore, MD	39	17	25	76	36	45	100	Buffalo, NY	42	53	11	78	52	43	585
Bangor, ME	44	48	4	68	46	42	158	Burlington, Ont.	43	23	10	79	50	15	640
Baton Rouge, LA	30	27	2	91	9	16	53	Burlington, VT	44	28	33	73	12	45	113
Battle Creek, MI	42	19	16	85	10	47	820	Butte, MT	46	0	14	112	32	2	5,549
Bay City, MI	43	35	40	83	53	20	595	Calgary, Alta.	51	03	0	114	5	0	3,557
Beaumont, TX	30	5	9	94	6	6	20	Cambridge, MA	42	22	30	71	6	22	30

City	Lat. N °	′	″	Long. W °	′	″	Elev. (ft)	City	Lat. N °	′	″	Long. W °	′	″	Elev. (ft)
Canton, OH	40	47	56	81	22	43	1,100	Juneau, AK	58	18	7	134	25	11	50
Carson City, NV	39	9	50	119	45	59	4,730	Kalamazoo, MI	42	17	30	85	35	14	755
Cedar Rapids, IA	42	0	30	91	38	38	730	Kansas City, KS	39	6	51	94	37	38	750
Central Islip, NY	40	47	26	73	12	8	88	Kansas City, MO	39	5	59	94	34	42	740
Champaign, IL	40	6	59	88	14	36	740	Kenosha, WI	42	35	5	87	49	16	610
Charleston, SC	32	46	35	79	55	52	118	Key West, FL	24	33	19	81	46	58	8
Charleston, WV	38	20	59	81	37	58	606	Kingston, Ont.	44	18	0	76	28	0	305
Charlotte, NC	35	13	37	80	50	36	850	Kitchener, Ont.	43	27	0	80	29	0	1,040
Charlottetown, P.E.I.	46	14	25	63	08	05	160	Knoxville, TN	35	57	38	83	55	15	889
Chattanooga, TN	35	2	44	85	18	35	685	Lafayette, IN	40	25	0	86	52	31	567
Cheyenne, WY	41	8	24	104	49	11	6,067	Lancaster, PA	40	2	16	76	18	21	368
Chicago, IL	41	51	0	87	39	0	596	Lansing, MI	42	43	57	84	33	20	830
Churchill, Man.	58	43	30	94	07	0	94	Laredo, TX	27	30	22	99	30	26	414
Cincinnati, OH	39	9	43	84	27	25	683	Las Vegas, NV	36	10	30	115	8	11	2,000
Cleveland, OH	41	29	58	81	41	44	690	Lawrence, MA	42	42	25	71	9	49	50
Colorado Springs, CO	38	50	2	104	49	15	6,008	Lethbridge, Alta.	49	42	0	112	49	0	3,047
Columbia, MO	38	57	6	92	20	2	758	Lexington, KY	37	59	19	84	28	40	955
Columbia, SC	34	0	2	81	2	6	314	Lihue, HI	21	58	52	159	22	16	206
Columbus, GA	32	27	39	84	59	16	300	Lima, OH	40	44	33	84	6	19	875
Columbus, OH	39	57	40	82	59	56	800	Lincoln, NE	40	48	0	96	40	0	1,150
Concord, NH	43	12	29	71	32	17	288	Little Rock, AR.	34	44	47	92	17	22	350
Corpus Christi, TX	27	48	1	97	23	46	35	London, Ont.	42	59	0	81	14	0	875
Dallas, TX.	32	47	0	96	48	0	463	Los Angeles, CA	34	3	8	118	14	34	330
Dawson, Yukon	64	03	45	139	25	50	1,214	Louisville, KY	38	15	15	85	45	34	462
Dayton, OH	39	45	32	84	11	30	750	Lowell, MA.	42	38	0	71	19	0	102
Daytona Beach, FL	29	12	38	81	1	23	10	Lubbock, TX	33	34	40	101	51	17	3,195
Decatur, IL	39	50	25	88	57	17	670	Macon, GA	32	50	26	83	37	57	400
Denver, CO	39	44	21	104	59	3	5,260	Madison, WI	43	4	23	89	24	4	863
Des Moines, IA.	41	36	2	93	36	32	803	Manchester, NH	42	59	44	71	27	19	175
Detroit, MI.	42	19	53	83	2	45	585	Marshall, TX	32	32	41	94	22	2	410
Dodge City, KS.	37	45	10	100	1	0	2,550	Medicine Hat, Alta.	50	03	0	110	40	0	2,352
Dubuque, IA	42	30	2	90	39	52	620	Memphis, TN.	35	8	58	90	2	56	254
Duluth, MN.	46	47	0	92	6	23	610	Meriden, CT.	41	32	17	72	48	27	190
Durham, NC	35	59	38	78	53	56	394	Miami, FL.	25	46	26	80	11	38	11
Eau Claire, WI	44	48	41	91	29	54	850	Milwaukee, WI.	43	2	20	87	54	23	634
Edmonton, Alta.	53	33	0	113	28	0	2,200	Minneapolis, MN	44	58	48	93	15	49	815
Elizabeth, NJ	40	39	50	74	12	40	38	Minot, ND	48	13	57	101	17	45	1,555
El Paso, TX	31	45	31	106	29	11	3,695	Mobile, AL	30	41	39	88	2	35	16
Enid, OK.	36	23	44	97	52	41	1,246	Moncton, N.B.	46	06	57	64	48	11	232
Erie, PA	42	7	45	80	5	7	650	Montgomery, AL	32	22	0	86	18	0	250
Eugene, OR	44	3	8	123	5	8	419	Montpelier, VT	44	15	36	72	34	33	525
Eureka, CA.	40	48	8	124	9	45	44	Montréal, Que.	45	31	0	73	39	0	221
Evansville, IN	37	58	29	87	33	21	388	Moose Jaw, Sask.	50	24	0	105	32	0	1,892
Fairbanks, AK.	64	50	16	147	42	59	440	Muncie, IN	40	11	36	85	23	11	952
Fall River, MA.	41	42	5	71	9	20	200	Nashville, TN	36	9	57	86	47	4	440
Fargo, ND.	46	52	38	96	47	22	900	Natchez, MS	31	33	37	91	24	11	230
Flagstaff, AZ.	35	11	53	111	39	2	6,900	Newark, NJ	40	44	8	74	10	22	95
Flint, MI	43	0	45	83	41	15	750	New Britain, CT	41	39	40	72	46	48	200
Ft. Smith, AR	35	23	9	94	23	54	446	New Haven, CT.	41	18	29	72	55	43	40
Ft. Wayne, IN	41	7	50	85	7	44	781	New Orleans, LA	29	57	16	90	4	30	11
Ft. Worth, TX	32	43	31	97	19	14	670	New York, NY	40	42	51	74	0	23	55
Fredericton, N.B.	45	56	43	66	40	0	67	Niagara Falls, Ont.	43	06	0	79	04	0	589
Fresno, CA.	36	44	52	119	46	17	296	Nome, AK	64	30	4	165	24	23	25
Gadsden, AL	34	0	51	86	0	24	554	Norfolk, VA	36	50	48	76	17	8	10
Gainesville, FL	29	39	5	82	19	30	183	North Bay, Ont.	46	19	0	79	28	0	1,200
Gallup, NM	35	31	41	108	44	31	6,508	Oakland, CA	37	48	16	122	16	11	42
Galveston, TX	29	18	4	94	47	51	10	Ogden, UT.	41	13	23	111	58	23	4,299
Gary, IN	41	35	36	87	20	47	600	Oklahoma City, OK	35	28	3	97	30	58	1,195
Grand Junction, CO	39	3	50	108	33	0	4,597	Omaha, NE	41	15	31	95	56	15	1,040
Grand Rapids, MI.	42	57	48	85	40	5	610	Orlando, FL	28	32	17	81	22	46	106
Great Falls, MT	47	30	1	111	18	0	3,334	Ottawa, Ont.	45	16	0	75	45	0	382
Green Bay, WI	44	31	9	88	1	11	594	Paducah, KY	37	5	0	88	36	0	345
Greensboro, NC	36	4	21	79	47	32	770	Pasadena, CA	34	8	52	118	8	37	865
Greenville, SC	34	51	9	82	23	39	966	Paterson, NJ	40	55	0	74	10	20	70
Guelph, Ont.	43	33	0	80	15	0	1,100	Pensacola, FL	30	25	16	87	13	1	32
Gulfport, MS.	30	22	2	89	5	34	25	Peoria, IL	40	41	37	89	35	20	470
Halifax, N.S.	44	52	0	63	43	0	477	Peterborough, Ont.	44	18	0	78	19	0	628
Hamilton, OH	39	23	58	84	33	41	600	Philadelphia, PA	39	57	8	75	9	51	40
Hamilton, Ont.	43	14	0	79	57	0	780	Phoenix, AZ.	33	26	54	112	4	24	1,090
Harrisburg, PA	40	16	25	76	53	5	320	Pierre, SD	44	22	6	100	21	2	1,484
Hartford, CT.	41	45	49	72	41	8	40	Pittsburgh, PA	40	26	26	79	59	46	770
Helena, MT.	46	35	34	112	2	7	4,090	Pittsfield, MA	42	27	0	73	14	45	1,039
Hilo, HI	19	43	47	155	5	24	38	Pocatello, ID	42	52	17	112	26	41	4,464
Honolulu, HI	21	18	25	157	51	30	18	Pt. Arthur, TX.	29	53	55	93	55	43	10
Houston, TX	29	45	47	95	21	47	40	Portland, ME	43	39	41	70	15	21	25
Huntsville, AL.	34	43	49	86	35	10	641	Portland, OR	45	31	25	122	40	30	50
Indianapolis, IN	39	46	6	86	9	29	717	Portsmouth, NH.	43	4	18	70	45	47	21
Iowa City, IA.	41	39	40	91	31	48	685	Portsmouth, VA.	36	50	7	76	17	55	10
Jackson, MI	42	14	45	84	24	5	940	Prince Rupert, B.C.	54	19	0	130	19	0	116
Jackson, MS.	32	17	55	90	11	5	294	Providence, RI.	41	49	26	71	24	48	80
Jacksonville, FL	30	19	55	81	39	21	12	Provo, UT	40	14	2	111	39	28	4,549
Jersey City, NJ.	40	43	41	74	4	41	83	Pueblo, CO	38	15	16	104	36	31	4,662
Johnstown, PA.	40	19	36	78	55	20	1200	Québec City, Que.	46	49	0	71	13	0	244
Joplin, MO	37	5	3	94	30	47	990	Racine, WI.	42	43	34	87	46	58	630

City	Lat. N °	'	''	Long. W °	'	''	Elev. (ft)
Raleigh, NC	35	46	19	78	38	20	350
Rapid City, SD	44	4	50	103	13	50	3,247
Reading, PA	40	20	8	75	55	38	266
Regina, Sask.	50	27	0	104	37	0	1,894
Reno, NV	39	31	47	119	48	46	4,498
Richmond, VA	37	33	13	77	27	38	190
Roanoke, VA	37	16	15	79	56	30	940
Rochester, MN	44	1	18	92	28	11	990
Rochester, NY	43	9	17	77	36	57	515
Rockford, IL	42	16	16	89	5	38	715
Sacramento, CA	38	34	54	121	29	36	20
Saginaw, MI	43	25	10	83	57	3	595
St. Catharines, Ont.	43	10	0	79	15	0	321
St. Cloud, MN	45	33	39	94	9	44	1,040
St. John, N.B.	45	15	33	66	02	20	357
St. John's, Nfld.	47	34	0	52	44	0	461
St. Joseph, MO	39	46	7	94	50	47	850
St. Louis, MO	38	37	38	90	11	52	455
St. Paul, MN	44	56	40	93	5	35	780
St. Petersburg, FL	27	46	14	82	40	46	44
Salem, OR	44	56	35	123	2	2	154
Salina, KS	38	50	25	97	36	40	1,225
Salt Lake City, UT	40	45	39	111	53	25	4,266
San Antonio, TX	29	25	26	98	29	36	650
San Bernardino, CA	34	6	30	117	17	20	1,200
San Diego, CA	32	42	55	117	9	23	40
San Francisco, CA	37	46	30	122	25	6	63
San Jose, CA	37	20	22	121	53	38	87
San Juan, P.R.	18	28	6	66	6	22	8
Santa Barbara, CA	34	25	15	119	41	50	50
Santa Cruz, CA	36	58	27	122	1	47	20
Santa Fe, NM	35	41	13	105	56	14	6,989
Sarasota, FL	27	20	10	82	31	51	27
Saskatoon, Sask.	52	07	0	106	38	0	1,653
Sault Ste. Marie, Ont.	46	31	0	84	20	0	630
Savannah, GA	32	5	0	81	6	0	42
Schenectady, NY	42	48	51	73	56	24	245
Seattle, WA	47	36	23	122	19	51	350
Sheboygan, WI	43	45	3	87	42	52	630
Sherbrooke, Que.	45	24	0	71	54	0	792
Sheridan, WY	44	47	50	106	57	20	3,742
Shreveport, LA	32	31	30	93	45	0	209
Sioux City, IA	42	30	0	96	24	0	1,117
Sioux Falls, SD	43	32	48	96	43	48	1,442
South Bend, IN	41	41	0	86	15	0	725
Spartanburg, SC	34	56	58	81	55	56	816
Spokane, WA	47	39	32	117	25	30	2,000
Springfield, IL	39	48	6	89	38	37	610
Springfield, MA	42	6	5	72	35	25	70
Springfield, MO	37	12	55	93	17	53	1,300
Springfield, OH	39	55	27	83	48	32	1,000
Stamford, CT	41	3	12	73	32	21	35
Steubenville, OH	40	22	11	80	38	3	1,060
Stockton, CA	37	57	28	121	17	23	15
Sudbury, Ont.	46	31	0	80	54	0	1,140
Superior, WI	46	43	15	92	6	14	642
Sydney, N.S.	46	09	0	60	11	0	203
Syracuse, NY	43	2	53	76	8	52	400
Tacoma, WA	47	15	11	122	26	35	380
Tallahassee, FL	30	26	17	84	16	51	188
Tampa, FL	27	56	50	82	27	31	48
Terre Haute, IN	39	28	0	87	24	50	501
Texarkana, TX	33	25	30	94	2	51	324
Thunder Bay, Ont.	48	24	0	89	19	0	653
Timmins, Ont.	48	28	0	81	20	0	967
Toledo, OH	41	39	50	83	33	19	615
Topeka, KS	39	2	54	95	40	40	1,000
Toronto, Ont.	43	37	39	79	23	46	251
Trenton, NJ	40	13	1	74	44	36	54
Trois-Rivières, Que.	46	21	0	72	33	0	198
Troy, NY	42	43	42	73	41	32	35
Tucson, AZ	32	13	18	110	55	33	2,390
Tulsa, OK	36	9	14	95	59	33	804
Urbana, IL	40	6	38	88	12	26	725
Utica, NY	43	6	3	75	13	59	415
Vancouver, B.C.	49	15	0	123	7	0	14
Victoria, B.C.	48	26	0	123	22	0	63
Waco, TX	31	32	57	97	8	47	405
Walla Walla, WA	46	3	53	118	20	31	1,000
Washington, DC	38	53	42	77	2	12	25
Waterloo, IA	42	29	34	92	20	34	850
West Palm Beach, FL	26	42	54	80	3	13	21
Wheeling, WV	40	3	50	80	43	16	672
Whitehorse, Yukon	60	43	0	135	03	0	2,305
White Plains, NY	41	2	2	73	45	48	220
Wichita, KS	37	41	32	97	20	14	1,305
Wilkes-Barre, PA	41	14	45	75	52	54	550
Wilmington, DE	39	44	45	75	32	49	100
Wilmington, NC	34	13	32	77	56	42	50
Windsor, Ont.	42	18	0	83	01	0	622
Winnipeg, Man.	49	54	39	97	14	36	783
Winston-Salem, NC	36	5	59	80	14	40	912
Worcester, MA	42	15	45	71	48	10	480
Yakima, WA	46	36	8	120	30	17	1,066
Yellowknife, N.W.T.	62	27	20	114	21	0	675
Youngstown, OH	41	5	59	80	38	59	861
Yuma, AZ	32	43	31	114	37	25	160
Zanesville, OH	39	56	25	82	0	48	710

Latitude and Longitude of World Cities

Source: National Imagery Mapping Agency, U.S. Dept. of Defense

City	Lat. °	'	Long. °	'
Athens, Greece	37	59 N	23	44 E
Bangkok, Thailand	13	45 N	100	31 E
Beijing, China	39	56 N	116	24 E
Berlin, Germany	52	31 N	13	25 E
Bogotá, Colombia	04	36 N	74	05 W
Buenos Aires, Argentina	34	36 S	58	28 W
Cairo, Egypt	30	03 N	31	15 E
Jakarta, Indonesia	06	10 S	106	48 E
Jerusalem, Israel	31	46 N	35	14 E
Johannesburg, South Africa	26	12 S	28	05 E
Kathmandu, Nepal	27	43 N	85	19 E
Kiev, Ukraine	50	26 N	30	31 E
London, UK (Greenwich)	51	30 N	00	00
Manila, Philippines	14	35 N	121	00 E
Mexico City, Mexico	19	24 N	99	09 W
Moscow, Russia	55	45 N	37	35 E
Mumbai (Bombay), India	18	58 N	72	50 E
New Delhi, India	28	36 N	77	12 E
Panama City, Panama	08	58 N	79	32 W
Paris, France	48	52 N	02	20 E
Quito, Ecuador	00	13 S	78	30 W
Rio de Janeiro, Brazil	22	43 S	43	13 W
Rome, Italy	41	53 N	12	30 E
Santiago, Chile	33	27 S	70	40 W
Seoul, South Korea	37	34 N	127	00 E
Sydney, Australia	33	53 S	151	12 E
Tehran, Iran	35	40 N	51	26 E
Tokyo, Japan	35	42 N	139	46 E
Warsaw, Poland	52	15 N	21	00 E
Wellington, New Zealand	41	18 S	174	47 E

Highest and Lowest Continental Altitudes

Source: National Geographic Society

Continent	Highest point	Elev. (ft)	Lowest point	ft below sea level
Asia	Mount Everest, Nepal-Tibet	29,035	Dead Sea, Israel-Jordan	1,348
South America	Mount Aconcagua, Argentina	22,834	Valdes Peninsula, Argentina	131
North America	Mount McKinley, Alaska	20,320	Death Valley, California	282
Africa	Kilimanjaro, Tanzania	19,340	Lake Assal, Djibouti	512
Europe	Mount Elbrus, Russia	18,510	Caspian Sea, Russia, Azerbaijan	92
Antarctica	Vinson Massif	16,864	Bentley Subglacial Trench	8,327[1]
Australia	Mount Kosciusko, New South Wales	7,310	Lake Eyre, South Australia	52

(1) Estimated level of the continental floor. Lower points that have yet to be discovered may exist further beneath the ice.

RELIGION

Membership of Religious Groups in the U.S.

Sources: *2006 Yearbook of American & Canadian Churches,* © National Council of the Churches of Christ in the USA; World Christian Database; *World Almanac* research

These membership figures are the latest available and generally are based on reports made by officials of each group, and not on any religious census. Figures from other sources may vary. Many groups keep careful records; others only estimate. Not all groups report annually. Church membership figures vary from one denomination to another, but generally the figures reported in this table are inclusive and do not refer simply to full communicants or confirmed members.

The number of houses of worship appears in parentheses. * Indicates that the group declines to make membership figures public. Groups reporting fewer than 5,000 members are not included; where membership numbers are not available, only those groups with 50 or more houses of worship are listed.

Religious Group	Members
Adventist churches:	
Advent Christian Ch. (292)	24,800
Seventh-day Adventist Ch. (4,619)	935,428
American Catholic Church (100)	25,000
Apostolic Christian Churches of America (86)	12,880
Apostolic Episcopal Church (250)	18,000
Bahá'í Faith (1,127 assemblies)	829,260
Baptist churches:	
American Baptist Assn. (1,760)	275,000
American Baptist Chs. in the U.S.A. (5,793)	1,429,840
Baptist Bible Fellowship Intl. (4,500)	1,200,000
Baptist General Conference (902)	145,148
Baptist Missionary Assn. of America (1,334)	234,732
Conservative Baptist Assn. of America (1,200)	200,000
Free Will Baptists, Natl. Assn. of (2,461)	204,353
General Assn. of General Baptists (700)	81,502
General Assn. of Regular Baptist Chs. (1,415)	129,407
Natl. Baptist Convention, U.S.A., Inc. (9,000)	5,000,000
Natl. Missionary Baptist Convention of America (NA)	2,500,000
North American Baptist Conference (270)	47,692
Progressive National Baptist Convention (2,000)	2,500,000
Separate Baptists in Christ (100)	8,000
Southern Baptist Convention (43,465)	16,267,494
Brethren in Christ (232)	20,739
Brethren (German Baptists):	
Brethren Ch. (Ashland, OH) (115)	10,240
Church of the Brethren (1,068)	131,201
Grace Brethren Chs., Fellowship of (260)	30,371
Old German Baptist Brethren (54)	6,420
Buddhists (NA)	2,721,335[1]
Christian Brethren (Plymouth Brethren) (1,150)	86,000
Christian Church (Disciples of Christ) (3,737)	744,397
Christian Congregation, Inc. (1,496)	122,181
Christian and Missionary Alliance (1,974)	419,100
Christian Union (114)	9,800
Christian Union, Churches of Christ in (288)	11,504
Church of Christ (Holiness) U.S.A. (154)	10,460
Church of Christ, Scientist (2,250)	862,000[1]
Church of the United Brethren in Christ (215)	23,000
Churches of Christ (15,000)	1,500,000
Churches of God:	
Chs. of God, General Conference (336)	32,880
Ch. of God (Anderson, IN) (2,290)	297,007
Ch. of God (Seventh Day), Denver, CO (200)	11,000
Ch. of God by Faith, Inc. (148)	30,000
Ch. of God, Mountain Assembly, Inc. (118)	8,000
Church of the Nazarene (4,868)	631,258
Community Churches, Intl. Council of (137)	108,806
Congreg. Christian Chs., Nat'l Assoc. of (432)	65,392
Conservative Congregational Christian Conference (272)	42,725
Eastern Catholic Churches:	
Armenian Catholic Church (U.S. and Canada) (9)	36,000
Chaldean Catholic Church (14)	120,200
Maronite Catholic Church (59)	75,232
Melkite Greek Catholic Church (35)	27,207
Romanian Greek Catholic Church (15)	5,000
Ruthenian Byzantine Catholic Church (223)	99,288
Syrian Catholic Church (12)	13,270
Syro-Malabar Catholic Church (8)	100,000
Ukranian Greek Catholic Church (200)	102,632
Eastern Orthodox churches:	
American Carpatho-Russian Orthodox Greek Catholic Ch. (80)	13,590
Antiochian Orthodox Christian Archdiocese of N.A. (226)	390,000

Religious Group	Members
Apostolic Catholic Assyrian Ch. of the East, N.A. Dioceses (22)	120,000
Armenian Apostolic Ch. of America (24)	337,000
Armenian Apostolic Church, Dioceses of America (72)	414,000
Coptic Orthodox Ch. (100)	300,000
Greek Orthodox Archdiocese of America (563)	1,500,000
Mar Thoma Syrian Church of India (73)	40,000
Orthodox Ch. in America (737)	1,064,000
Patriarchal Parishes of the Russian Orthodox Ch. in the USA (31)	17,000
Russian Orthodox Church Outside of Russia (180)	480,000
Serbian Orthodox Ch. of the U.S. and Can. (68)	67,000
Syrian Orthodox Ch. of Antioch (31)	32,500
Ukrainian Orthodox Ch. of the USA (115)	13,000
Episcopal Church (7,220)	2,284,233
Evangelical Church (133)	12,475
Evangelical Congregational Church (146)	20,743
Evangelical Covenant Church (757)	115,620
Evangelical Free Church of America (1,420)	350,000
Friends:	
Evangelical Friends Intl.-N.A. Region (288)	25,423
Friends General Conference (650)	34,000
Friends United Meeting (427)	42,680
Religious Society of Friends (Conservative) (1,200)	104,000
Full Gospel Fellowship of Churches and Ministers Intl. (902)	414,100
General Church of the New Jerusalem (36)	6,618
Grace Gospel Fellowship (128)	60,000
Hindus	1,143,864[1]
Independent Fundamental Churches of America Int'l., Inc. (IFCA) (616)	80,600
Jehovah's Witnesses (12,317)	1,029,902
Jews	5,764,208[2]
Jewish organizations:[3]	
Union for Reform Judaism (900+)	1,500,000
Union of Orthodox Jewish Congregations of America (1,000)	*
United Synagogue of Conservative Judaism, The (760)	1,500,000+
Jewish Reconstructionist Federation (103)	180,000
Latter-day Saints:	
Ch. of Jesus Christ of Latter-day Saints (Mormon) (12,463)	5,599,177
Reorganized Ch. of Jesus Christ of Latter-day Saints (1,353)	247,000
Liberal Catholic Church—Province of the U.S.A. (21)	5,800
Lutheran churches:	
Apostolic Lutheran Ch. of America (57)	6,800
Ch. of the Lutheran Brethren of America (108)	13,763
Ch. of the Lutheran Confession (77)	8,390
Evangelical Lutheran Ch. in America (10,585)	4,930,429
Evangelical Lutheran Synod (140)	20,981
Free Lutheran Congregations, Assn. of (289)	45,200
Latvian Evangelical Lutheran Church in America (60)	12,586
Lutheran Ch.—Missouri Synod (6,151)	2,463,747
Lutheran Chs., American Assn. of (84)	25,908
Wisconsin Evangelical Lutheran Synod (1,261)	400,858
Mennonite churches:	
Beachy Amish Mennonite Chs. (207)	11,487
Church of God in Christ (Mennonite) (127)	13,570
Hutterian Brethren (444)	43,000
Mennonite Brethren Chs., Gen. Conf. (368)	82,130
Mennonite Church USA (959)	111,375
Old Order Amish Ch. (898)	80,820

Religious Group	Members
Methodist churches:	
African Methodist Episcopal Ch. (4,174)	2,500,000
African Methodist Episcopal Zion Ch. (3,236)	1,432,795
Evangelical Methodist Ch. (123)	8,615
Free Methodist Ch. of North America (1,008)	63,272
Southern Methodist Ch. (105)	6,493
United Methodist Ch. (34,892)	8,251,175
The Wesleyan Church (1,714)	125,127
Messianic Jews	c. 75,000
Metropolitan Community Churches, Universal Fellowship of (300)	44,000
Missionary Church (391)	36,162
Moravian Ch. in America, Northern Province (92)	23,834
Muslims	4,657,005[1]
Natl. Organization of the New Apostolic Ch. of North America (338)	37,736
Pentecostal churches:	
Apostolic Faith Mission Ch. of God (23)	10,340
Assemblies of God (12,277)	2,779,095
Bible Church of Christ, Inc. (6)	6,850
Bible Fellowship Church (58)	7,546
Church of God (Cleveland, TN) (6,511)	989,965
Church of God in Christ (15,300)	5,499,875
Church of God of Prophecy (1,901)	114,476
Elim Fellowship (262)	44,600
Intl. Ch. of the Foursquare Gospel (1,888)	326,614
Intl. Pentecostal Church of Christ (67)	4,961
Intl. Pentecostal Holiness Church (1,964)	291,846
Open Bible Standard Chs. (314)	38,000

Religious Group	Members
Pentecostal Assemblies of the World Inc. (1,750)	1,500,000
Pentecostal Church of God (1,158)	117,000
Pentecostal Free Will Baptist Ch. (204)	20,000
United Pentecostal Ch. Intl. (4,259)	860,000
Presbyterian churches:	
Associate Reformed Presbyterian Ch. (General Synod) (256)	41,019
Cumberland Presbyterian Ch. (763)	83,007
Cumberland Presbyterian Ch. in America (152)	15,142
Evangelical Presbyterian Ch. (181)	73,941
Genl. Assembly of the Korean Presbyterian Church in America (458)	52,606
Orthodox Presbyterian Ch. (241)	27,582
Presbyterian Ch. in America (1,534)	325,791
Presbyterian Ch. (U.S.A.) (11,019)	3,189,573
Reformed Presbyterian Ch. of N. America (80)	6,347
Reformed churches:	
Christian Reformed Ch. in N. America (761)	190,587
Hungarian Reformed Ch. in America (27)	6,000
Netherlands Reformed Congregations (27)	9,524
Protestant Reformed Churches in America (28)	7,157
Reformed Ch. in America (895)	276,304
United Church of Christ (5,682)	1,265,786
Reformed Episcopal Church (142)	11,281
Roman Catholic Church (23,003)	65,900,000
Salvation Army (1,316)	427,027
Sikhs	270,034[1]
Unitarian Universalist Assn. of Congregations (1,010)	214,738

(1) Source: World Christian Database. (2) From American Jewish Committee. (3) As reported by organizations.

Adherents of All Religions by Six Continental Areas[1], Mid-2004

Source: *2006 Encyclopædia Britannica Book of the Year; figures rounded*

	Africa	Asia	Europe	Latin America	Northern America	Oceania	World
Baha'is	1,929,000	3,639,000	146,000	813,000	847,000	122,000	7,496,000
Buddhists	148,000	369,394,000	1,634,000	699,000	3,063,000	493,000	375,440,000
Chinese Universists	35,400	400,718,000	266,000	200,000	713,000	133,000	402,065,000
Christians	401,717,000	341,337,000	553,689,000	510,131,000	273,941,000	26,147,000	2,106,962,000
Roman Catholics	143,065,000	121,618,000	276,739,000	476,699,000	79,217,000	8,470,000	1,105,880,000
Protestants	115,276,000	56,512,000	70,908,000	53,572,000	65,881,000	7,699,000	369,848,000
Orthodox	37,989,000	13,240,000	158,974,000	848,000	6,620,000	756,000	218,427,000
Anglicans	43,404,000	733,000	25,727,000	909,000	2,986,000	4,986,000	78,745,000
Independents	87,913,000	176,516,000	24,445,000	44,810,000	81,138,000	1,719,000	416,541,000
Confucianists	300	6,379,000	16,600	800	0	50,600	6,447,000
Ethnic religionists	105,251,000	141,589,000	1,238,000	3,109,000	1,263,000	319,000	252,769,000
Hindus	2,604,000	844,593,000	1,467,000	766,000	1,444,000	417,000	851,291,000
Jains	74,900	4,436,000	0	0	7,500	700	4,519,000
Jews	224,000	5,317,000	1,985,000	1,206,000	6,154,000	104,000	14,990,000
Muslims	350,453,000	892,440,000	33,290,000	1,724,000	5,109,000	408,000	1,283,424,000
New-Religionists	112,000	104,352,000	381,000	764,000	1,561,000	84,800	107,255,000
Shintoists	0	2,717,000	0	0	7,200	60,000	0	2,784,000
Sikhs	58,400	24,085,000	238,000	0	583,000	24,800	24,989,000
Spiritists	3,100	2,000	135,000	12,575,000	160,000	7,300	12,882,000
Taoists	0	2,702,000	0	0	11,900	0	2,714,000
Zoroastrians	900	2,429,000	89,900	0	81,600	3,200	2,605,000
Other religionists	75,000	68,000	257,500	105,000	650,000	10,000	1,166,000
Nonreligious	5,912,000	601,478,000	108,674,000	15,939,000	31,286,000	3,894,600	767,184,000
Atheists	585,000	122,870,000	22,048,000	2,756,000	1,997,000	400,000	150,656,000

(1) **Continental Areas.** Following current UN demographic terminology, which divides the world into the 6 major areas shown above. Note that "Asia" includes the former Soviet Central Asian states and "Europe" includes all of Russia, extending eastward to Vladivostok, the East Sea/Sea of Japan, and the Bering Strait.

Adherents. As defined in the 1948 Universal Declaration of Human Rights, a person's religion is what he or she says it is. Totals are enumerated following the methodology of the World Christian Encyclopedia, 2nd ed. (2001) and World Christian Trends (2001), using recent censuses, polls, literature, and other data. Totals may conflict with some estimates for total populations. **Buddhists.** 56% Mahayana, 38% Theravada (Hinayana), 6% Tantrayana (Lamaism). **Chinese Universists (folk religionists).** Followers of traditional Chinese religion (local deities, ancestor veneration, Confucian ethics, universism, divination, some Buddhist elements). **Christians.** Total Christians include those affiliated with churches not shown, plus other persons professing in censuses or polls to be Christians but not affiliated with any church. Figures for the subgroups of Christians do not add up to the totals because all subgroups are not shown and some Christians adhere to more than one denomination. **Independents.** Members of churches and networks that regard themselves as postdenominationalist and neo-apostolic and thus independent of historic, organized, institutionalized denominationalist Christianity. **Confucianists.** Non-Chinese followers of Confucius and Confucianism, mostly Koreans in Korea. **Ethnic religionists.** Followers of local, tribal, animistic, or shamanistic religions, with members restricted to one ethnic group. **Hindus.** 70% Vaishnavites, 25% Shaivites, 2% neo-Hindus and reform Hindus. **Jews.** Adherents of Judaism. **Muslims.** 83% Sunni Muslims, 16% Shia Muslims (Shi'ites), 1% other schools. **New-Religionists.** Followers of Asian 20th-cent. New Religions, New Religious movements, radical new crisis religions, and non-Christian syncretistic mass religions, all founded since 1800 and most since 1945. **Other religionists.** Including a handful of religions, quasi-religions, pseudoreligions, parareligions, religious or mystic systems, and religious and semireligious brotherhoods of numerous varieties. **Nonreligious.** Persons professing no religion, nonbelievers, agnostics, freethinkers, uninterested, dereligionized secularists indifferent to all religion. **Atheists.** Persons professing atheism, skepticism, disbelief, or irreligion, including antireligious (opposed to all religion).

Episcopal Church Liturgical Colors and Calendar, 2006-2010

Source: The Rt. Rev. Barry E. Yingling, Editor, the *Churchman's Ordo Kalendar*

The most common liturgical colors in the Episcopal Church are: **White**—Christmas Day through First Sunday after Epiphany; Maundy Thursday (as an alternative to crimson at the Eucharist); from the Vigil of Easter to the Day of Pentecost (Whitsunday); Trinity Sunday; Feasts of the Lord (except Holy Cross Day); the Confession of St. Peter; the Conversion of St. Paul; St. Joseph; St. Mary Magdalene; St. Mary the Virgin; St. Michael and All Angels; All Saints' Day; St. John the Evangelist; memorials of other saints who were not martyred; Independence Day and Thanksgiving Day; weddings and funerals. **Red**—the Day of Pentecost; Holy Cross Day; feasts of apostles and evangelists (except those listed above); feasts and memorials of martyrs (including Holy Innocents' Day). **Violet**—Advent and Lent. **Crimson** or oxblood (dark red)—Holy Week. **Green**—the seasons after Epiphany and after Pentecost. **Black**—optional alternative for funerals and Good Friday.

The days of fasting are Ash Wednesday and Good Friday. Other days of special devotion (penitence) include the 40 days of Lent. Ember Days are days of prayer for the church's ministry. They fall on the Wednesday, Friday, and Saturday after the first Sunday in Lent, the Day of Pentecost, Holy Cross Day, and December 13. Rogation Days, the 3 days before Ascension Day, are days of prayer for God's blessing on the crops, on commerce and industry, and for conservation of the earth's resources.

Days, etc.	2006	2007	2008	2009	2010
Golden Number	12	13	14	15	16
Sunday Letter	A	G	F	D	C
Sundays after Epiphany	8	7	4	7	6
Ash Wednesday	Mar. 1	Feb. 21	Feb. 6	Feb. 25	Feb. 17
First Sunday in Lent	Mar. 5	Feb. 25	Feb. 10	Mar. 1	Feb. 21
Passion/Palm Sunday	Apr. 9	Apr. 1	Mar. 16	Apr. 5	Mar. 28
Good Friday	Apr. 14	Apr. 6	Mar. 21	Apr. 10	Apr. 2
Easter Day	Apr. 16	Apr. 8	Mar. 23	Apr. 12	Apr. 4
Ascension Day	May 25	May 17	May 1	May 21	May 13
The Day of Pentecost	June 4	May 27	May 11	May 31	May 23
Trinity Sunday	June 11	June 3	May 18	June 7	May 30
Numbered Proper of 2 Pentecost	#6	#5	#3	#6	#5
First Sunday of Advent	Dec. 3	Dec. 2	Nov. 30	Nov. 29	Nov. 28

Greek Orthodox Movable Ecclesiastical Dates, 2006-2010

Feast days and fasting days are determined annually on the basis of the date of Holy Pascha (Easter). This ecclesiastical cycle begins with the first day of the Triodion and ends with the Sunday of All Saints, a total of 18 weeks.

	2006	2007	2008	2009	2010
Triodion begins	Feb. 12	Jan. 28	Feb. 17	Feb. 8	Jan. 24
1st Sat. of Souls	Feb. 25	Feb. 10	Mar. 1	Feb. 21	Feb. 6
Meat Fare	Feb. 26	Feb. 11	Mar. 2	Feb. 22	Feb. 7
2nd Sat. of Souls	Mar. 4	Feb. 17	Mar. 8	Feb. 28	Feb. 13
Lent Begins	Mar. 6	Feb. 19	Mar. 10	Mar. 2	Feb. 15
St. Theodore—3rd Sat. of Souls	Mar. 11	Feb. 24	Mar. 15	Mar. 7	Feb. 20
Sunday of Orthodoxy	Mar. 12	Feb. 25	Mar. 16	Mar. 8	Feb. 21
Sat. of Lazarus	Apr. 15	Mar. 31	Apr. 19	April 11	Mar. 27
Palm Sunday	Apr. 16	Apr. 1	Apr. 20	April 12	Mar. 28
Holy (Good) Friday	Apr. 21	Apr. 6	Apr. 25	April 17	April 2
Western Easter	Apr. 16	Apr. 8	Mar. 23	April 12	April 4
Orthodox Easter	Apr. 23	Apr. 8	Apr. 27	April 19	April 4
Ascension	June 1	May 17	June 5	May 28	May 13
Sat. of Souls	June 10	May 26	June 14	June 6	May 22
Pentecost	June 11	May 27	June 15	June 7	May 23
All Saints	June 18	June 3	June 22	June 14	May 30
Fast of Holy Apostles (First day)	June 19	June 4	June 23	June 15	May 31

Important Islamic Dates, 1427-1431 AH (2006-2010)

Source: Imad-ad-Dean, Inc., Bethesda, MD 20814

The Islamic calendar is a strict lunar calendar reckoned from the year of the Hijra (Anno Hegirae, or AH)—Muhammad's flight from Mecca to Medina, in 622 CE. Each year consists of 12 lunar months of 29 or 30 days beginning and ending with each new moon's visible crescent. Common years have 354 days; leap years have 355 days. Some Muslim countries employ a conventionalized calendar with the leap day added to the last month, Dhûl Hijah, but for religious purposes the leap date is taken into account by tracking each new moon sighting. The dates given below are based on the convention that the first new moon must be seen before the following dawn on the East Coast of the Americas. Actual (local) Western Hemisphere sightings may occur a day later, but never a day earlier, than these dates reflect. Holy days begin at sunset on the previous day.

	(1427) 2006	(1428) 2007	(1429) 2008	(1430) 2008-09	(1431) 2009-2010
New Year's Day (Muharram 1)	Jan. 30, 2006	Jan. 20, 2007	Jan. 9, 2008	Dec. 28, 2008	Dec. 17, 2009
Ashura (Muharram 10)	Feb. 8, 2006	Jan. 29, 2007	Jan. 18, 2008	Jan. 6, 2009	Dec. 26, 2009
Mawlid (Rabi'l 12)	Apr. 10, 2006	Mar. 31, 2007	Mar. 20, 2008	Mar. 9, 2009	Feb. 26, 2010
Ramadan 1	Sept. 23, 2006	Sept. 12, 2007	Sept. 1, 2008	Aug. 21, 2009	Aug. 11, 2010
Eid al-Fitr (Shawwal 1)	Oct. 23, 2006	Oct. 12, 2007	Sept. 30, 2008	Sept. 20, 2009	Sept. 9, 2010
Eid al-Adha (Dhûl-Hijjah 10)	Dec. 30, 2006	Dec. 20, 2007	Dec. 8, 2008	Nov. 27, 2009	Nov. 16, 2010

Jewish Holy Days, Festivals, and Fasts, 5767-5771 (2006-2011)

The Jewish calendar consists of 12 lunar months, alternating between 29 and 30 days. It is lunisolar, and adjusts for the solar cycle by adding an extra month (Adar II) in the 3rd, 6th, 8th, 11th, 14th, 17th, and 19th years of a 19-year cycle. The calendar started on the day of Creation, reckoned in the 2nd-3rd cent. BCE as Tishrei 1, 3,761 years before the common era.

The religious calendar begins with the month Nisan, from which all other months are counted, and the civil calendar with Tishrei. The months are 1) Nisan; 2) Iyar; 3) Sivan; 4) Tammuz; 5) Av (also Abh); 6) Elul; 7) Tishrei; 8) Cheshvan (also Marcheshvan); 9) Kislev; 10) Tevet (also Tebeth); 11) Shevat (also Shebhat); 12) Adar; 12a) Adar Sheni (II), added in leap years. The names are Aramaic versions of the Babylonian months, adopted during the Jews' exile in Babylon in the 4th century BCE. Rosh Hashanah, the New Year, begins on Tishrei 1 (Sept.-Oct.). Yom Kippur is the holiest day of the year. All holidays listed below begin at sunset on the previous day, except where noted.

Holiday	Date on Jewish Cal.	(5767) 2006-07	(5768) 2007-08	(5769) 2008-09	(5770) 2009-10	(5771) 2010-11
Rosh Hashanah (New Year)	Tishrei 1	Sept. 23 Sat.	Sept. 13 Thu.	Sept. 30 Tue.	Sept. 19 Sat.	Sept. 9 Thu.
	Tishrei 2	Sept. 24 Sun.	Sept. 14 Fri.	Oct. 1 Wed.	Sept. 20 Sun.	Sept. 10 Fri.
Fast of Gedalya[1]	Tishrei 3	Sept. 25 Mon.	Sept. 16 Sun.*	Oct. 2 Thu.	Sept. 21 Mon.	Sept. 12 Sun.
Yom Kippur (Day of Atonement)	Tishrei 10	Oct. 2 Mon.	Sept. 22 Sat.	Oct. 9 Thu.	Sept. 28 Mon.	Sept. 18 Sat.
Sukkot	Tishrei 15	Oct. 7 Sat.	Sept. 27 Thu.	Oct. 14 Tue.	Oct. 3 Sat.	Sept. 23 Thu.
	Tishrei 21	Oct. 13 Fri.	Oct. 3 Wed.	Oct. 20 Mon.	Oct. 9 Fri.	Sept. 29 Wed.
Shemini Atzeret	Tishrei 22	Oct. 14 Sat.	Oct. 4 Thu.	Oct. 21 Tue.	Oct. 10 Sat.	Sept. 30 Thu.
Simchat Torah	Tishrei 23	Oct. 15 Sun.	Oct. 5 Fri.	Oct. 22 Wed.	Oct. 11 Sun.	Oct. 1 Fri.
Hanukkah	Kislev 25	Dec. 16 Sat.	Dec. 5 Wed.	Dec. 22 Mon.	Dec. 11 Sat.	Dec. 1 Wed.
	Tevet 2	Dec. 23 Sat.	Dec. 12 Wed.	Dec. 29 Mon.	Dec. 19 Sat.	Dec. 9 Thu.
Fast of the 10th of Tevet[1]	Tevet 10	Dec. 31 Sun.	Dec. 19 Wed.	Jan. 6 Tue.	Dec. 27 Sun.	Dec. 16 Thu.
Tu B'Shevat	Shevat 15	Feb. 3 Sat.	Jan. 22 Tue.	Feb. 9 Mon.	Jan. 30 Sat.	Jan. 20 Thu.
Ta'anis Esther (Fast of Esther)[1]	Adar 13	Mar. 1 Thu.*	Mar. 20 Thu.	Mar. 9 Mon.	Feb. 25 Thu.	Mar. 17 Thu.
Purim	Adar 14	Mar. 4 Sun.	Mar. 21 Fri.	Mar. 10 Tue.	Feb. 28 Sun.	Mar. 20 Sun.
Pesach (Passover)	Nisan 15	Apr. 3 Tue.	Apr. 20 Sun.	Apr. 9 Thu.	Mar. 30 Tue.	Apr. 19 Tue.
	Nisan 22	Apr. 10 Tue.	Apr. 27 Sun.	Apr. 16 Thu.	Apr. 6 Tue.	Apr. 26 Tue.
Lag B'Omer	Iyar 18	May 6 Sun.	May 23 Fri.	May 12 Tue.	May 2 Sun.	May 22 Sun.
Shavuot (Pentecost)	Sivan 6	May 23 Wed.	June 9 Mon.	May 29 Fri.	May 19 Wed.	June 8 Wed.
	Sivan 7	May 24 Thu.	June 10 Tue.	May 30 Sat.	May 20 Thu.	June 9 Thu.
Fast of the 17th Day of Tammuz[1]	Tammuz 17	July 3 Tue.	July 20 Sun.	July 9 Thu.	June 29 Tue.	July 19 Tue.
Fast of the 9th Day of Av	Av 9	July 24 Tue.	Aug.10 Sun.	July 30 Thu.	July 20 Tue.	Aug. 9 Tue.

*Date changed to avoid Sabbath. (1) "Minor fasts" begin at sunrise.

Ash Wednesday and Easter Sunday (Western churches), 1901-2100

Year	Ash Wed.	Easter Sunday	Year	Ash Wed.	Easter Sunday	Year	Ash Wed.	Easter Sunday	Year	Ash Wed.	Easter Sunday	Year	Ash Wed.	Easter Sunday	Year	Ash Wed.	Easter Sunday
1901	Feb. 20	Apr. 7	1941	Feb. 26	Apr. 13	1981	Mar. 4	Apr. 19	2021	Feb. 17	Apr. 4	2061	Feb. 23	Apr. 10
1902	Feb. 12	Mar. 30	1942	Feb. 18	Apr. 5	1982	Feb. 24	Apr. 11	2022	Mar. 2	Apr. 17	2062	Feb. 8	Mar. 26
1903	Feb. 25	Apr. 12	1943	Mar. 10	Apr. 25	1983	Feb. 16	Apr. 3	2023	Feb. 22	Apr. 9	2063	Feb. 28	Apr. 15
1904	Feb. 17	Apr. 3	1944	Feb. 23	Apr. 9	1984	Mar. 7	Apr. 22	2024	Feb. 14	Mar. 31	2064	Feb. 20	Apr. 6
1905	Mar. 8	Apr. 23	1945	Feb. 14	Apr. 1	1985	Feb. 20	Apr. 7	2025	Mar. 5	Apr. 20	2065	Feb. 11	Mar. 29
1906	Feb. 28	Apr. 15	1946	Mar. 6	Apr. 21	1986	Feb. 12	Mar. 30	2026	Feb. 18	Apr. 5	2066	Feb. 24	Apr. 11
1907	Feb. 13	Mar. 31	1947	Feb. 19	Apr. 6	1987	Mar. 4	Apr. 19	2027	Feb. 10	Mar. 28	2067	Feb. 16	Apr. 3
1908	Mar. 4	Apr. 19	1948	Feb. 11	Mar. 28	1988	Feb. 17	Apr. 3	2028	Mar. 1	Apr. 16	2068	Mar. 7	Apr. 22
1909	Feb. 24	Apr. 11	1949	Mar. 2	Apr. 17	1989	Feb. 8	Mar. 26	2029	Feb. 14	Apr. 1	2069	Feb. 27	Apr. 14
1910	Feb. 9	Mar. 27	1950	Feb. 22	Apr. 9	1990	Feb. 28	Apr. 15	2030	Mar. 6	Apr. 21	2070	Feb. 12	Mar. 30
1911	Mar. 1	Apr. 16	1951	Feb. 7	Mar. 25	1991	Feb. 13	Mar. 31	2031	Feb. 26	Apr. 13	2071	Mar. 4	Apr. 19
1912	Feb. 21	Apr. 7	1952	Feb. 27	Apr. 13	1992	Mar. 4	Apr. 19	2032	Feb. 11	Mar. 28	2072	Feb. 24	Apr. 10
1913	Feb. 5	Mar. 23	1953	Feb. 18	Apr. 5	1993	Feb. 24	Apr. 11	2033	Mar. 2	Apr. 17	2073	Feb. 8	Mar. 26
1914	Feb. 25	Apr. 12	1954	Mar. 3	Apr. 18	1994	Feb. 16	Apr. 3	2034	Feb. 22	Apr. 9	2074	Feb. 28	Apr. 15
1915	Feb. 17	Apr. 4	1955	Feb. 23	Apr. 10	1995	Mar. 1	Apr. 16	2035	Feb. 7	Mar. 25	2075	Feb. 20	Apr. 7
1916	Mar. 8	Apr. 23	1956	Feb. 15	Apr. 1	1996	Feb. 21	Apr. 7	2036	Feb. 27	Apr. 13	2076	Mar. 4	Apr. 19
1917	Feb. 21	Apr. 8	1957	Mar. 6	Apr. 21	1997	Feb. 12	Mar. 30	2037	Feb. 18	Apr. 5	2077	Feb. 24	Apr. 11
1918	Feb. 13	Mar. 31	1958	Feb. 19	Apr. 6	1998	Feb. 25	Apr. 12	2038	Mar. 10	Apr. 25	2078	Feb. 16	Apr. 3
1919	Mar. 5	Apr. 20	1959	Feb. 11	Mar. 29	1999	Feb. 17	Apr. 4	2039	Feb. 23	Apr. 10	2079	Mar. 8	Apr. 23
1920	Feb. 18	Apr. 4	1960	Mar. 2	Apr. 17	2000	Mar. 8	Apr. 23	2040	Feb. 15	Apr. 1	2080	Feb. 21	Apr. 7
1921	Feb. 9	Mar. 27	1961	Feb. 15	Apr. 2	2001	Feb. 28	Apr. 15	2041	Mar. 6	Apr. 21	2081	Feb. 12	Mar. 30
1922	Mar. 1	Apr. 16	1962	Mar. 7	Apr. 22	2002	Feb. 13	Mar. 31	2042	Feb. 19	Apr. 6	2082	Mar. 4	Apr. 19
1923	Feb. 14	Apr. 1	1963	Feb. 27	Apr. 14	2003	Mar. 5	Apr. 20	2043	Feb. 11	Mar. 29	2083	Feb. 17	Apr. 4
1924	Mar. 5	Apr. 20	1964	Feb. 12	Mar. 29	2004	Feb. 25	Apr. 11	2044	Mar. 2	Apr. 17	2084	Feb. 9	Mar. 26
1925	Feb. 25	Apr. 12	1965	Mar. 3	Apr. 18	2005	Feb. 9	Mar. 27	2045	Feb. 22	Apr. 9	2085	Feb. 28	Apr. 15
1926	Feb. 17	Apr. 4	1966	Feb. 23	Apr. 10	2006	Mar. 1	Apr. 16	2046	Feb. 7	Mar. 25	2086	Feb. 13	Mar. 31
1927	Mar. 2	Apr. 17	1967	Feb. 8	Mar. 26	2007	Feb. 21	Apr. 8	2047	Feb. 27	Apr. 14	2087	Mar. 5	Apr. 20
1928	Feb. 22	Apr. 8	1968	Feb. 28	Apr. 14	2008	Feb. 6	Mar. 23	2048	Feb. 19	Apr. 5	2088	Feb. 25	Apr. 11
1929	Feb. 13	Mar. 31	1969	Feb. 19	Apr. 6	2009	Feb. 25	Apr. 12	2049	Mar. 3	Apr. 18	2089	Feb. 16	Apr. 3
1930	Mar. 5	Apr. 20	1970	Feb. 11	Mar. 29	2010	Feb. 17	Apr. 4	2050	Feb. 23	Apr. 10	2090	Mar. 1	Apr. 16
1931	Feb. 18	Apr. 5	1971	Feb. 24	Apr. 11	2011	Mar. 9	Apr. 24	2051	Feb. 15	Apr. 2	2091	Feb. 21	Apr. 8
1932	Feb. 10	Mar. 27	1972	Feb. 16	Apr. 2	2012	Feb. 22	Apr. 8	2052	Mar. 6	Apr. 21	2092	Feb. 13	Mar. 30
1933	Mar. 1	Apr. 16	1973	Mar. 7	Apr. 22	2013	Feb. 13	Mar. 31	2053	Feb. 19	Apr. 6	2093	Feb. 25	Apr. 12
1934	Feb. 14	Apr. 1	1974	Feb. 27	Apr. 14	2014	Mar. 5	Apr. 20	2054	Feb. 11	Mar. 29	2094	Feb. 17	Apr. 4
1935	Mar. 6	Apr. 21	1975	Feb. 12	Mar. 30	2015	Feb. 18	Apr. 5	2055	Mar. 3	Apr. 18	2095	Mar. 9	Apr. 24
1936	Feb. 26	Apr. 12	1976	Mar. 3	Apr. 18	2016	Feb. 10	Mar. 27	2056	Feb. 16	Apr. 2	2096	Feb. 29	Apr. 15
1937	Feb. 10	Mar. 28	1977	Feb. 23	Apr. 10	2017	Mar. 1	Apr. 16	2057	Mar. 7	Apr. 22	2097	Feb. 13	Mar. 31
1938	Mar. 2	Apr. 17	1978	Feb. 8	Mar. 26	2018	Feb. 14	Apr. 1	2058	Feb. 27	Apr. 14	2098	Mar. 5	Apr. 20
1939	Feb. 22	Apr. 9	1979	Feb. 28	Apr. 15	2019	Mar. 6	Apr. 21	2059	Feb. 12	Mar. 30	2099	Feb. 25	Apr. 12
1940	Feb. 7	Mar. 24	1980	Feb. 20	Apr. 6	2020	Feb. 26	Apr. 12	2060	Mar. 3	Apr. 18	2100	Feb. 10	Mar. 28

Roman Catholic Hierarchy
Source: U.S. Catholic Conference; Holy See Press

Supreme Pontiff

At the head of the Roman Catholic Church is the supreme pontiff, Pope Benedict XVI, Joseph Ratzinger, born in Marktl am Inn, in Bavaria, Germany, on April 16, 1927; ordained priest on June 29, 1951, named archbishop of Munich and Feising in March 1977 and elevated to Cardinal three months later. In 1981, he was appointed prefect of the Congregation for the Doctrine of the Faith, and confirmed as dean of the College of Cardinals on November 30, 2002. He was elected pope by the College of Cardinals on April 19, 2005.

Chronological List of Popes
Source: Annuario Pontificio. Table lists year of accession of each pope.

The Roman Catholic Church named the Apostle Peter as founder of the church in Rome and the first pope. He arrived there c. 42, was martyred there c. 67, and was ultimately canonized as a saint. **The pope's temporal title is:** Sovereign of the State of Vatican City. **The pope's spiritual titles are:** Bishop of Rome, Vicar of Jesus Christ, Successor of St. Peter, Prince of the Apostles, Supreme Pontiff of the Universal Church, Patriarch of the West, Primate of Italy, Archbishop and Metropolitan of the Roman Province.

The names of antipopes are *in italics* and followed by an *. Antipopes were illegitimate claimants to the papal throne.

Year	Pope	Year	Pope	Year	Pope	Year	Pope	Year	Pope
	St. Peter	526	St. Felix IV (III)	872	John VIII	1100	*Theodoric**	1417	Martin V
67	St. Linus	530	Boniface II	882	Marinus I	1102	*Albert**	1431	Eugene IV
76	St. Anacletus	530	*Dioscorus**	884	St. Adrian III	1105	*Sylvester IV**	1439	*Felix V**
	or Cletus	533	John II	885	Stephen V (VI)	1118	Gelasius II	1447	Nicholas V
88	St. Clement I	535	St. Agapitus I	891	Formosus	1118	*Gregory VIII**	1455	Callistus III
97	St. Evaristus	536	St. Silverius, Martyr	896	Boniface VI	1119	Callistus II	1458	Pius II
105	St. Alexander I	537	Vigilius	896	Stephen VI (VII)	1124	Honorius II	1464	Paul II
115	St. Sixtus I	556	Pelagius I	897	Romanus	1124	*Celestine II**	1471	Sixtus IV
125	St. Telesphorus	561	John III	897	Theodore II	1130	Innocent II	1484	Innocent VIII
136	St. Hyginus	575	Benedict I	898	John IX	1130	*Anacletus II**	1492	Alexander VI
140	St. Pius I	579	Pelagius II	900	Benedict IV	1138	*Victor IV**	1503	Pius III
155	St. Anicetus	590	St. Gregory I	903	Leo V	1143	Celestine II	1503	Julius II
166	St. Soter	604	Sabinian	903	*Christopher**	1144	Lucius II	1513	Leo X
175	St. Eleutherius	607	Boniface III	904	Sergius III	1145	Bl. Eugene III	1522	Adrian VI
189	St. Victor I	608	St. Boniface IV	911	Anastasius III	1153	Anastasius IV	1523	Clement VII
199	St. Zephyrinus	615	St. Deusdedit or	913	Landus	1154	Adrian IV	1534	Paul III
217	St. Callistus I		Adeodatus	914	John X	1159	Alexander III	1550	Julius III
217	*St. Hippolytus**	619	Boniface V	928	Leo VI	1159	*Victor IV**	1555	Marcellus II
222	St. Urban I	625	Honorius I	928	Stephen VII(VIII)	1164	*Paschal III**	1555	Paul IV
230	St. Pontian	640	Severinus	931	John XI	1168	*Callistus III**	1559	Pius IV
235	St. Anterus	640	John IV	936	Leo VII	1179	*Innocent III**	1566	St. Pius V
236	St. Fabian	642	Theodore I	939	Stephen VIII(IX)	1181	Lucius III	1572	Gregory XIII
251	St. Cornelius	649	St. Martin I, Martyr	942	Marinus II	1185	Urban III	1585	Sixtus V
251	*Novatian**	654	St. Eugene I	946	Agapitus II	1187	Clement III	1590	Urban VII
253	St. Lucius I	657	St. Vitalian	955	John XII	1187	Gregory VIII	1590	Gregory XIV
254	St. Stephen I	672	Adeodatus II	963	Leo VIII	1191	Celestine III	1591	Innocent IX
257	St. Sixtus II	676	Donus	964	Benedict V	1198	Innocent III	1592	Clement VIII
259	St. Dionysius	678	St. Agatho	965	John XIII	1216	Honorius III	1605	Leo XI
269	St. Felix I	682	St. Leo II	973	Benedict VI	1227	Gregory IX	1605	Paul V
275	St. Eutychian	684	St. Benedict II	974	*Boniface VII**	1241	Celestine IV	1621	Gregory XV
283	St. Caius	685	John V	974	Benedict VII	1243	Innocent IV	1623	Urban VIII
296	St. Marcellinus	686	Conon	983	John XIV	1254	Alexander IV	1644	Innocent X
308	St. Marcellus I	687	*Theodore**	985	John XV	1261	Urban IV	1655	Alexander VII
309	St. Eusebius	687	*Paschal**	996	Gregory V	1265	Clement IV	1667	Clement IX
311	St. Melchiades	687	St. Sergius I	997	*John XVI**	1271	Bl. Gregory X	1670	Clement X
314	St. Sylvester I	701	John VI	999	Sylvester II	1276	Bl. Innocent V	1676	Bl. Innocent XI
336	St. Marcus	705	John VII	1003	John XVII	1276	Adrian V	1689	Alexander VIII
337	St. Julius I	708	Sisinnius	1004	John XVIII	1276	John XXI	1691	Innocent XII
352	Liberius	708	Constantine	1009	Sergius IV	1277	Nicholas III	1700	Clement XI
355	*Felix II**	715	St. Gregory II	1012	Benedict VIII	1281	Martin IV	1721	Innocent XIII
366	St. Damasus I	731	St. Gregory III	1012	*Gregory**	1285	Honorius IV	1724	Benedict XIII
366	*Ursinus**	741	St. Zachary	1024	John XIX	1288	Nicholas IV	1730	Clement XII
384	St. Siricius	752	Stephen II (III)[1]	1032	Benedict IX	1294	St. Celestine V	1740	Benedict XIV
399	St. Anastasius I	757	St. Paul I	1045	Sylvester III	1294	Boniface VIII	1758	Clement XIII
401	St. Innocent I	767	*Constantine**	1045	Benedict IX	1303	Bl. Benedict XI	1769	Clement XIV
417	St. Zosimus	768	*Philip**	1045	Gregory VI	1305	Clement V	1775	Pius VI
418	St. Boniface I	768	Stephen III (IV)	1046	Clement II	1316	John XXII	1800	Pius VII
418	*Eulalius**	772	Adrian I	1047	Benedict IX	1328	*Nicholas V**	1823	Leo XII
422	St. Celestine I	795	St. Leo III	1048	Damasus II	1334	Benedict XII	1829	Pius VIII
432	St. Sixtus III	816	Stephen IV (V)	1049	St. Leo IX	1342	Clement VI	1831	Gregory XVI
440	St. Leo I	817	St. Paschal I	1055	Victor II	1352	Innocent VI	1846	Pius IX
461	St. Hilary	824	Eugene II	1057	Stephen IX (X)	1362	Bl. Urban V	1878	Leo XIII
468	St. Simplicius	827	Valentine	1058	*Benedict X**	1370	Gregory XI	1903	St. Pius X
483	St. Felix III (II)	827	Gregory IV	1059	Nicholas II	1378	Urban VI	1914	Benedict XV
492	St. Gelasius I	844	*John**	1061	Alexander II	1378	*Clement VII**	1922	Pius XI
496	Anastasius II	844	Sergius II	1061	*Honorius II**	1389	Boniface IX	1939	Pius XII
498	St. Symmachus	847	St. Leo IV	1073	St. Gregory VII	1394	*Benedict XIII**	1958	John XXIII
498	*Lawrence** (501-	855	Benedict III	1080	*Clement III**	1404	Innocent VII	1963	Paul VI
	505)	855	*Anastasius**	1086	Bl. Victor III	1406	Gregory XII	1978	John Paul I
514	St. Hormisdas	858	St. Nicholas I	1088	Bl. Urban II	1409	*Alexander V**	1978	John Paul II
523	St. John I, Martyr	867	Adrian II	1099	Paschal II	1410	*John XXIII**	2005	Benedict XVI

(1) After St. Zachary, a Roman priest named Stephen was elected, but died before assuming the papacy. Another Stephen was then elected to succeed Zachary as Stephen II. He is sometimes listed as Stephen III.

College of Cardinals

Source: U.S. Catholic Conference

Members of the Sacred College of Cardinals are chosen by the pope to be his chief assistants and advisers in the administration of the church. Among their duties is the election of the pope.

In its present form, the College of Cardinals dates from the 12th century. The first cardinals, from about the 6th century, were deacons and priests of the leading churches of Rome and were bishops of neighboring dioceses. The title of cardinal was limited to members of the college in 1567. The number of cardinals was set at 70 in 1586 by Pope Sixtus V. From 1959 Pope John XXIII began to increase the number; however, the number eligible to participate in papal elections was limited to 120. Previous limitations were set aside by Pope John Paul II when he created new cardinals. In 1918 the Code of Canon Law specified that all cardinals must be priests. Pope John XXIII in 1962 established that all cardinals must be bishops, but this can be dispensed with, as in the case of Cardinal Avery Dulles. In 1971, Pope Paul VI decreed that at age 80 cardinals must retire from curial departments and offices and from participation in papal elections.

As of Aug. 2006, there were 192 members of the College, of whom 120 remained eligible to vote.

North American Cardinals

Name	Office	Born	Named Cardinal
Aloysius M. Ambrozic	Archbishop of Toronto	1930	1998
William W. Baum[1]	Archbishop emeritus of Washington, DC	1926	1976
Anthony J. Bevilacqua[1]	Archbishop emeritus of Philadelphia	1923	1991
Ernesto Corripio Ahumada[1]	Archbishop emeritus of Mexico City	1919	1979
Avery Robert Dulles[1]	Professor, Fordham University, NYC	1918	2001
Edward M. Egan	Archbishop of New York	1932	2001
Edouard Gagnon[1]	Pres. emeritus of the Commission of Intl. Eucharistic Congresses	1918	1985
Francis E. George	Archbishop of Chicago	1937	1998
William Henry Keeler	Archbishop of Baltimore	1931	1994
Bernard F. Law	Archbishop emeritus of Boston	1931	1985
William Levada	Prefect of the Congregation for the Doctrine of the Faith	1936	2006
Roger Mahony	Archbishop of Los Angeles	1936	1991
Javier Lozano Barragan	Pres. Pontifical Council for Health Care Workers, Mexico	1933	2003
Adam Joseph Maida	Archbishop of Detroit	1930	1994
Luis Aponte Martinez[1]	Archibishop emeritus of San Juan	1922	1973
Sean O'Malley	Archbishop of Boston	1944	2006
Marc Ouellet	Archbishop of Quebec	1944	2003
Justin F. Rigali	Archbishop of Philadelphia	1935	2003
Norberto Rivera Carrera	Archbishop of Mexico City	1942	1998
Juan Sandoval Iniguez	Archbishop of Guadalajara	1933	1994
James F. Stafford	President of the Pontifical Council for the Laity	1932	1998
Adolfo Antonio Suarez Rivera	Archbishop emeritus of Monterrey	1927	1994
Jean-Claude Turcotte	Archbishop of Montreal	1936	1994
Louis-Albert Vachon[1]	Archbishop emeritus of Quebec	1912	1985

(1) Ineligible to take part in papal elections (as of Sept. 2006).

The Ten Commandments

In the Hebrew Bible (Old Testament) the Ten Commandments (also called the Decalogue, from the Greek meaning "ten words") were revealed by God to Moses on Mt. Sinai. They form the covenant between God and the Israelites and the moral code that is the basis for the Jewish and Christian religions. The Ten Commandments appear in 2 places in the Old Testament—Exodus 20:1-17 and Deuteronomy 5:6-21.

Most Protestant, Anglican, and Orthodox Christians follow Jewish tradition, as here, which considers the introduction ("I am the Lord . . .") the first commandment and makes the prohibition against idolatry the second. Roman Catholic and Lutheran traditions combine I and II and split the last commandment into 2 that separately prohibit coveting of a neighbor's wife and a neighbor's goods. This arrangement alters the numbering of the other commandments by one.

Following is the text of the Ten Commandments as it appears in Exodus 20:1-17, in the King James version of the Bible [Roman numerals added]:

And God spake all these words, saying,

I. I *am* the LORD thy God, which have brought thee out of the land of Egypt, out of the house of bondage. Thou shalt have no other gods before me.

II. Thou shalt not make unto thee any graven image, or any likeness of *any thing* that *is* in heaven above, or that *is* in the earth beneath, or that *is* in the water under the earth. Thou shalt not bow down thyself to them, nor serve them: for I the LORD thy God *am* a jealous God, visiting the iniquity of the fathers upon the children unto the third and fourth *generation* of them that hate me; and shewing mercy unto thousands of them that love me, and keep my commandments.

III. Thou shalt not take the name of the LORD thy God in vain: for the LORD will not hold him guiltless that taketh his name in vain.

IV. Remember the sabbath day, to keep it holy. Six days shalt thou labour, and do all thy work: but the seventh day *is* the sabbath of the LORD thy God: *in it* thou shalt not do any work, thou, nor thy son, nor thy daughter, thy manservant, nor thy maidservant, nor thy cattle, nor thy stranger that *is* within thy gates: for *in* six days the LORD made heaven and earth, the sea, and all that in them *is*, and rested the seventh day: wherefore the LORD blessed the sabbath day, and hallowed it.

V. Honour thy father and thy mother: that thy days may be long upon the land which the LORD thy God giveth thee.

VI. Thou shalt not kill.

VII. Thou shalt not commit adultery.

VIII. Thou shalt not steal.

IX. Thou shalt not bear false witness against thy neighbour.

X. Thou shalt not covet thy neighbour's house, thou shalt not covet thy neighbour's wife, nor his manservant, nor his maidservant, nor his ox, nor his ass, nor any thing that *is* thy neighbour's.

Books of the Bible

Old Testament—Standard Protestant List				New Testament List		
Genesis	I Kings	Ecclesiastes	Obadiah	Matthew	Ephesians	Hebrews
Exodus	II Kings	Song of Solomon	Jonah	Mark	Phillippians	James
Leviticus	I Chronicles	Isaiah	Micah	Luke	Colossians	I Peter
Numbers	II Chronicles	Jeremiah	Nahum	John	I Thessalonians	II Peter
Deuteronomy	Ezra	Lamentations	Habakkuk	Acts	II Thessalonians	I John
Joshua	Nehemiah	Ezekiel	Zephaniah	Romans	I Timothy	II John
Judges	Esther	Daniel	Haggai	I Corinthians	II Timothy	III John
Ruth	Job	Hosea	Zechariah	II Corinthians	Titus	Jude
I Samuel	Psalms	Joel	Malachi	Galatians	Philemon	Revelation
II Samuel	Proverbs	Amos				

The standard Protestant Old Testament consists of the same 39 books as in the Bible of Judaism, but the latter is organized differently. The Old Testament used by Roman Catholics has 7 additional "deuterocanonical" books, plus some additional parts of books. The 7 are: **Tobit, Judith, Wisdom, Sirach (Ecclesiasticus), Baruch, I Maccabees**, and **II Maccabees**. Both Catholic and Protestant versions of the New Testament have 27 books, with the same names.

Figures in the Hebrew Bible (Old Testament)

Aaron: First of Hebrew high priests; brother of Moses and Miriam.
Abel: Second son of Adam and Eve; slain by Cain.
Abraham: Founder of monotheism; patriarch; also called Abram.
Adam: First human according to Genesis.
Amos: Herdsman; prophesized against social injustice and oppression of the poor.
Bathsheba: Seduced by King David; mother of King Solomon.
Cain: Tiller of the soil; son of Adam and Eve; killed his brother Abel.
Cyrus: Persian ruler; sent Jews home from exile.
Daniel: Cast into lion's den by Nebuchadnezzer; saved.
David: Israel's greatest king; shepherd, warrior, musician, psalmist.
Deborah: Prophet and judge; ruled over Israel.
Elijah: Great prophet; was victorious over the priests of the Phoenician god, Baal.
Elisha: Prophet; successor to Elijah.
Esther: Jewish wife of the king of Persia; saved Jews from annihilation.
Eve: First woman according to Genesis.
Ezekiel: Visionary; prophesized hope to exiled Jews in Babylon.
Ezra: Great Jewish leader; rededicated worship and Torah law after exile.
Goliath: Giant Philistine warrior; slain by David.
Hannah: Childless; promised child to God; mother to the prophet Samuel.
Hosea: Enacted prophecy; asked God's forgiveness for Israel's unfaithfulness.
Isaac: Son of Abraham and Sarah; saved from sacrificial altar.
Isaiah: Highly educated prophet; avoided war with Assyria. Israel destroyed. Jerusalem survived.
Jacob: Son of Isaac; father of the Twelve Tribes; renamed "Israel" by angel.
Jeremiah: Confronted leaders; urged surrender to Babylon.
Jezebel: Phoenician queen of King Ahab; had Israelite prophets killed.

Job: "Blameless" man; lost family and possessions but not his faith.
Jonah: Swallowed by a great fish; prophesized repentance in Nineveh.
Jonathan: Son of King Saul; friend of David.
Joseph: Favorite of Jacob; interprets Pharaoh's dreams; brings Hebrews to Egypt.
Josiah: Reformist king; repaired Temple; restored worship; reintroduced Passover.
Joshua: Successor of Moses; led Hebrews into land of Israel.
Leah: Matriarch; older sister of Rachel; Jacob's wife.
Micah: Prophet; predicted the end of war and beginning of peace.
Miriam: Prophet and great leader of the Hebrews; sister to Moses and Aaron.
Moses: Most important Hebrew prophet; leader of the Israelites; received the Torah.
Nathan: Prophet; confronted King David over his seduction of Bathsheba.
Nebuchadnezzer: Babylonian king; destroyed Jerusalem.
Nehemiah: Led Jews back to Jerusalem from Babylonian exile.
Noah: A man of great faith who, according to *Genesis*, saved the world from a great flood.
Rachel: Matriarch; younger sister of Leah; Jacob's wife; Joseph's mother.
Rebecca: Matriarch; wife of Isaac; mother of Jacob.
Ruth: Moabite convert; ancestor of David and all the kings of Israel.
Samuel: Prophet; anointed Saul king of Israel and later anointed David to succeed him.
Samson: Judge and military leader of Israel, possessed super-human strength .
Sarah: First matriarch of Israel; wife of Abraham; mother of Isaac.
Saul: First king of Israel; father of Jonathan.
Solomon: King of Israel at its zenith; known for great wisdom.
Zachariah: Prophet; encouraged rebuilding of Temple destroyed by Babylonians.

Figures in the New Testament

Andrew: One of the Twelve Apostles; brother of Peter and former fisherman; one of the earlier disciples.
Barabbas: Imprisoned with Jesus; set free by Pilate on Passover.
Barnabas: Disciple of Jesus; closely connected with Paul.
Bartholomew: A lesser known member of the Twelve Apostles; cheerful and prayed often.
Cornelius: A Roman convert defended by Peter, allowing Gentiles to become Christians.
Elizabeth: Mother of John the Baptist; relation of the Virgin Mary.
Gabriel: Archangel; appeared to the Virgin Mary to announce that she was to give birth to the messiah.
Herod: Two Herods appear in the New Testament: Herod the Great ordered the death of children around the time of Jesus's birth; his son, Herod, imprisoned John the Baptist, leading to his beheading.
James: One of the Twelve; brother of John the apostle.
Jesus: Central figure of the Gospels; believed to be the messiah and son of God; crucified by the Romans.
John (Baptist): Known as "John the Baptist"; important prophet and forerunner to Jesus; relation of the Virgin Mary.
John (Apostle): Beloved disciple of Jesus; one of the Twelve; possible author of 4th Gospel; brother of James.
Joseph: Husband of the Virgin Mary; descendant of King David.
Judas Iscariot: Betrayer of Jesus; prominent member of the apostles; committed suicide.
Judas Thaddeus: One of the Twelve; also called "Jude" to distinguish him from Judas Iscariot.
Lazarus: Brother of the disciples Martha and Mary of Bethany; raised from the dead at their request; possibly the same Lazarus who appears in Jesus's parable of the rich man.
Luke: Traditional author of the Gospel of Luke; possibly a follower of Paul.

Mark: Traditional author of the Gospel of Mark; possibly the same Mark who is a companion of Peter.
Matthew: One of the Twelve; possible author of the Gospel of Matthew; a former tax collector.
Mary Magdalene: Important female disciple of Jesus; witness to his death and resurrection.
Mary, the mother of Jesus: traditionally believed to be a virgin and conceived without sin; wife of Joseph.
Matthias: Often included on lists of the Twelve Apostles as the apostle who replaced Judas Iscariot after his betrayal.
Paul (Saul): Writer of nearly a quarter of the New Testament; a former persecutor of Christians, converted after a vision; played a significant role in spreading Christianity.
Peter: Considered to be the foremost of the Twelve Apostles; traditionally the first pope and "rock" of the Christian church; author of epistles; also called Simon and Simon Peter.
Philip: One of the Twelve; considered pragmatic and sensible.
Pilate, Pontius: A Roman prefect; played large role in the trial and crucifixion of Jesus.
Simon: One of the Twelve; known as "the Zealot" to distinguish from Simon Peter.
Stephen: Fervently preached that Jesus was the Messiah; stoned to death by angry mob, including Saul; important figure in Saul's conversion.
Thomas: One of the Twelve; known as "Doubting Thomas" because he did not believe Jesus was risen until he could touch him.
Timothy: A disciple closely connected with Paul; author of epistles.
Zechariah: Father of John the Baptist; husband of Elizabeth; struck dumb when he doubted his barren wife could become pregnant.

Major Christian Denominations:

Brackets indicate some features that tend to

Denomination	Origins	Organization	Authority	Special rites
Baptists	In radical Reformation, objections to infant baptism, demands for church and state separation; John Smyth, English Separatist, in 1609; Roger Williams, 1638, Providence, RI.	Congregational; each local church is autonomous.	Scripture; some Baptists, particularly in the South, interpret the Bible literally.	[Baptism, usually early teen years and after, by total immersion;] Lord's Supper.
Church of Christ (Disciples)	Among evangelical Presbyterians in KY (1804) and PA (1809), in distress over Protestant factionalism and decline of fervor; organized in 1832.	Congregational.	["Where the Scriptures speak, we speak; where the Scriptures are silent, we are silent."]	Adult baptism; Lord's Supper (weekly).
Episcopalians	Henry VIII separated English Catholic Church from Rome, 1534, for political reasons; Protestant Episcopal Church in U.S. founded in 1789.	[Diocesan bishops, in apostolic succession, are elected by parish representatives; the national Church is headed by General Convention and Presiding Bishop; part of the Anglican Communion.]	Scripture as interpreted by tradition, especially 39 Articles (1563); tri-annual convention of bishops, priests, and lay people.	Infant baptism, Eucharist, and other sacraments; sacrament taken to be symbolic, but as having real spiritual effect.
Jehovah's Witnesses	Founded in 1870 in PA by Charles Taze Russell; incorporated as Watch Tower Bible and Tract Society of PA, 1884; name Jehovah's Witnesses adopted in 1931.	A governing body located in NY coordinates worldwide activities; each congregation cared for by a body of elders; each Witness considered a minister.	The Bible.	Baptism by immersion; annual Lord's Meal ceremony.
Latter-day Saints (Mormons)	In a vision of the Father and the Son reported by Joseph Smith (1820s) in NY. Smith also reported receiving new scripture on golden tablets: The Book of Mormon.	Theocratic; 1st Presidency (church president, 2 counselors), 12 Apostles preside over international church. Local congregations headed by lay priesthood leaders.	Revelation to living prophet (church president). The Bible, Book of Mormon, and other revelations to Smith and his successors.	Baptism, at age 8; laying on of hands (which confers the gift of the Holy Ghost); Lord's Supper; temple rites: baptism for the dead, marriage for eternity, others.
Lutherans	Begun by Martin Luther in Wittenberg, Germany, in 1517; objection to Catholic doctrine of salvation and sale of indulgences; break complete, 1519.	Varies from congregational to episcopal; in U.S., a combination of regional synods and congregational polities is most common.	Scripture alone. The Book of Concord (1580), which includes the three Ecumenical Creeds, is subscribed to as a correct exposition of Scripture.	Infant baptism; Lord's Supper; Christ's true body and blood present "in, with, and under the bread and wine."
Methodists	Rev. John Wesley began movement in 1738, within Church of England; first U.S. denomination, Baltimore (1784).	Conference and superintendent system; [in United Methodist Church, general superintendents are bishops—not a priestly order, only an office— who are elected for life.]	Scripture as interpreted by tradition, reason, and experience.	Baptism of infants or adults; Lord's Supper commanded; other rites: marriage, ordination, solemnization of personal commitments.
Orthodox	Developed in original Christian proselytizing; broke with Rome in 1054, after centuries of doctrinal disputes and diverging traditions.	Synods of bishops in autonomous, usually national, churches elect a patriarch, archbishop, or metropolitan; these men, as a group, are the heads of the church.	Scripture, tradition, and the first 7 church councils up to Nicaea II in 787; bishops in council have authority in doctrine and policy.	Seven sacraments: infant baptism and anointing, Eucharist, ordination, penance, marriage, and anointing of the sick.
Pentecostal	In Topeka, KS (1901) and Los Angeles (1906), in reaction to perceived loss of evangelical fervor among Methodists and others.	Originally a movement, not a formal organization. Pentecostalism now has a variety of organized forms and continues also as a movement.	Scripture; individual charismatic leaders, the teachings of the Holy Spirit.	[Spirit baptism, especially as shown in "speaking in tongues"; healing and sometimes exorcism;] adult baptism; Lord's Supper.
Presbyterians	In 16th-cent. Calvinist reformation; differed with Lutherans over sacraments, church government; John Knox founded Scotch Presbyerian church about 1560.	[Highly structured representational system of ministers and lay persons (presbyters) in local, regional, and national bodies (synods).]	Scripture.	Infant baptism; Lord's Supper; bread and wine symbolize Christ's spiritual presence.
Roman Catholics	Traditionally, founded by Jesus who named St. Peter the 1st vicar; developed in early Christian proselytizing, especially after the conversion of imperial Rome in the 4th cent.	[Hierarchy with supreme power vested in pope elected by cardinals;] councils of bishops advise on matters of doctrine and policy.	[The pope, when speaking for the whole church in matters of faith and morals; and tradition (which is expressed in church councils and in part contained in Scripture).]	Mass; 7 sacraments: baptism, reconciliation, Eucharist, confirmation, marriage, ordination, and anointing of the sick (unction).
United Church of Christ	[By ecumenical union, in 1957, of Congregationalists and Evangelical & Reformed, representing both Calvinist and Lutheran traditions.]	Congregational; a General Synod, representative of all congregations, sets general policy.	Scripture.	Infant baptism; Lord's Supper.

How Do They Differ?

distinguish a denomination sharply from others.

Practice	Ethics	Doctrine	Other	Denomination
Worship style varies from staid to evangelistic; extensive missionary activity.	Usually opposed to alcohol and tobacco; some tendency toward a perfectionist ethical standard.	*[No creed; true church is of believers only, who are all equal.]*	Believing no authority can stand between the believer and God, the Baptists are strong supporters of church and state separation.	**Baptists**
Tries to avoid any rite not considered part of the 1st-century church; some congregations may reject instrumental music.	Some tendency toward perfectionism; increasing interest in social action programs.	Simple New Testament faith; avoids any elaboration not firmly based on Scripture.	Highly tolerant in doctrinal and religious matters; strongly supportive of scholarly education.	**Church of Christ (Disciples)**
Formal, based on "Book of Common Prayer," updated 1979; services range from austerely simple to highly liturgical.	Tolerant, sometimes permissive; some social action programs.	Scripture; the "historic creeds," which include the Apostles, Nicene, and Athanasian, and the "Book of Common Prayer"; ranges from Anglo-Catholic to low church, with Calvinist influences.	Strongly ecumenical, holding talks with many branches of Christendom.	**Episcopalians**
Meetings are held in Kingdom Halls and members' homes for study and worship; *[extensive door-to-door visitations.]*	High moral code; stress on marital fidelity and family values; avoidance of tobacco and blood transfusions.	*[God, by his first creation, Christ, will soon destroy all wickedness; 144,000 faithful ones will rule in heaven with Christ over others on a paradise earth.]*	Total allegiance proclaimed only to God's kingdom or heavenly government by Christ; main periodical, The Watchtower, is printed in 115 languages.	**Jehovah's Witnesses**
Simple service with prayers, hymns, sermon; private temple ceremonies may be more elaborate.	Temperance; strict moral code; *[tithing]*; a strong work ethic with communal self-reliance; *[strong missionary activity]*; family emphasis.	Jesus Christ is the Son of God, the Eternal Father. Jesus' atonement saves all humans; those who are obedient to God's laws may become joint-heirs with Christ in God's kingdom.	Mormons believe theirs is the true church of Jesus Christ, restored by God through Joseph Smith. Official name: The Church of Jesus Christ of Latter-day Saints.	**Latter-day Saints (Mormons)**
Relatively simple, formal liturgy with emphasis on the sermon.	Generally conservative in personal and social ethics; doctrine of "2 kingdoms" (worldly and holy) supports conservatism in secular affairs.	Salvation by grace alone through faith; Lutheranism has made major contributions to Protestant theology.	Though still somewhat divided along ethnic lines (German, Swedish, etc.), main divisions are between fundamentalists and liberals.	**Lutherans**
Worship style varies widely by denomination, local church, geography.	Originally pietist and perfectionist; always strong social activist elements.	No distinctive theological development; 25 Articles abridged from Church of England's 39, not binding.	In 1968, The United Methodist Church was formed by the union of The Methodist Church and The Evangelical United Brethren Church.	**Methodists**
Elaborate liturgy, usually in the vernacular, though extremely traditional; the liturgy is the essence of Orthodoxy; veneration of icons.	Tolerant; little stress on social action; divorce, remarriage permitted in some cases; bishops are celibate; priests need not be.	Emphasis on Christ's resurrection, rather than crucifixion; the Holy Spirit proceeds from God the Father only.	Orthodox Church in America originally under Patriarch of Moscow, was granted autonomy in 1970; Greek Orthodox do not recognize this autonomy.	**Orthodox**
Loosely structured service with rousing hymns and sermons, culminating in spirit baptism.	Usually, emphasis on perfectionism, with varying degrees of tolerance.	Simple traditional beliefs, usually Protestant, with emphasis on the immediate presence of God in the Holy Spirit.	Once confined to lower-class "holy rollers," Pentecostalism now appears in mainline churches and has established middle-class congregations.	**Pentecostal**
A simple, sober service in which the sermon is central.	Traditionally, a tendency toward strictness, with firm church- and self-discipline; otherwise tolerant.	Emphasizes the sovereignty and justice of God; no longer dogmatic.	Although traces of belief in predestination (that God has foreordained salvation for the "elect") remain, this idea is no longer a central element in Presbyterianism.	**Presbyterians**
Relatively elaborate ritual centered on the Mass; also rosary recitation, novenas, etc.	Traditionally strict, but increasingly tolerant in practice; divorce and remarriage not accepted, but annulments sometimes granted; celibate clergy, except in Eastern rite.	Highly elaborated; salvation by merit gained through grace; dogmatic; special veneration of Mary, the mother of Jesus.	Relatively rapid change followed Vatican Council II; Mass now in vernacular; more stress on social action, tolerance, ecumenism.	**Roman Catholics**
Usually simple services with emphasis on the sermon.	Tolerant; some social action emphasis.	Standard Protestant; "Statement of Faith" (1959) is not binding.	The 2 main churches in the 1957 union represented earlier unions with small groups of almost every Protestant denomination.	**United Church of Christ**

Major Non-Christian World Religions

Sources: Hinduism and Judaism reviewed by Anthony Padovano, PhD, STD, Prof. of Literature & Relig. Studies, Ramapo College, NJ, Adj. Prof. of Theol., Fordham U., NYC; Bahai reviewed by the Bahai Community Relations Center; Sikhism reviewed by The Sikh Coalition of New York, NY; Islam reviewed by Natana Delong-Bas, Lecturer in Islamic Studies, Boston College.

Islam

Founded: Muhammad received his first revelation in 610 CE.

Founder: Muhammad (c. 570-632), the Prophet.

Sacred texts: Two texts constitute the Muslim sacred canon, the *Qur'an* and the *Hadith*. The **Qur'an** provides the foundation for Islamic religion and culture. Regarded as the final, perfect, and complete word of God as revealed to Muhammad over the course of his life. Received by Muhammad in the Arabic language, it is memorized in Arabic by adherents regardless of their native language. It is divided into 114 chapters of unequal length, the shortest containing only three verses, and the longest containing 306 verses. The Qur'an is the ultimate source of everything Islamic, from metaphysics to theology to sacred history, to ethics and law, to art. The **Hadith**, which describes Muhammad's actions, attitudes and teachings, complements the Qur'an. Due to its long history of oral transmission, the Hadith's lessons are seen as somewhat vulnerable to human error; it does not contain God's unadulterated voice as does the Qur'an, but functions as a powerful spiritual and behavioral code nonetheless.

Divisions: There are 2 major groups: the majority Sunni (85% of the worldwide Muslim population) and the minority Shiites (15%). Sects first appeared in Islam at the time of Muhammad's death. The group that came to be known as **Sunni** accepted Abu Bakr, an early convert, as his successor (caliph), while a smaller number, which became the **Shi'a**, believed that Ali ibn Abi Talib, the son-in-law and first cousin of the prophet, should have become his successor (Imam). The Sunni successor is called a *Caliph*, while the Shiite successor is an *Imam*. Imams are believed to interpret the Qur'an infallibly. **Shiites** fall into 3 major branches: Fivers, Seveners, and Twelvers, reflecting the number of Imams they recognize. Twelvers believe that the 12th Imam has lived an invisible existence since 874, and will return as the *Mahdi* (a messiah figure) who will usher in a 1,000-year reign of peace and justice. **Sufism** (mystical dimension of Islam) emphasizes personal relation to God and obedience informed by love of God; it is prevalent among both Sunni and Shiites.

Organization: Muhammad was both the last prophet and a statesman. Muslim leaders have often assumed both civil and moral functions within Islamic states. Within the larger community, there are cultural and national groups, held together by a common religious law, the *Shari'a*. Muslims believe that God is the ultimate law giver and that human beings cannot devise laws that oppose divine laws; still the Shari'a is approached differently in different parts of the Islamic world. Over the centuries, **Sunnis** have developed 4 major schools of law: the Hanafi, the Shafi'i, the Hanbali, and the Maliki schools. The Ja'fari school is the most important and well-known Shiite school. Before the 20th century, religious scholars known as the *ulama* held much legal power. Judges (*qadis*) and law-interpreters (*muftis*) are people learned in religious law who lead congregational prayers in mosques and perform other religious duties.

Practice: Five duties (of both men and women), known as the "Pillars of Islam," are regarded as cardinal in Islam and as central to the life of the Islamic community. In accordance with Islam's absolute commitment to monotheism, the first duty is the profession of faith (the *Shahadah*): "There is no God but Allah and Muhammad is his Prophet."

A Muslim must profess this belief publicly at least once in his or her lifetime; it defines the membership of an individual in the Islamic community. The second duty is that of five daily prayers organized in intervals throughout the day: sunrise, early afternoon, late afternoon, immediately after sunset, and before midnight. During prayer, Muslims face the *Kaaba*, a small, cube-shaped structure in the courtyard toward *al-Haram* (the "inviolate place"), at the great mosque of Mecca. All five prayers in Islam are congregational and are to be offered in a mosque, but they may be offered individually if one cannot be present with a congregation. Congregational prayer is required only at the early afternoon prayer on Friday for men. The third cardinal duty of a Muslim is to pay alms, or *zakat*, which should be 2.5% of one's total wealth. This was originally the tax levied by Muhammad on the wealthy members of the community, primarily to help the poor. Only when zakat has been paid is the rest of a Muslim's property considered purified and legitimate. The fourth duty is the fast of the lunar month of Ramadan. During the fasting month, one must abstain from eating, drinking, smoking, impure thoughts, and sexual intercourse from dawn until sunset, and feed at least one poor person, if able. The fifth duty is the pilgrimage to the Kaaba in the Grand Mosque at Mecca, which a Muslim must undertake, with exceptions for poverty and ill health, at least once during his or her lifetime.

Location: W Africa to Philippines, across a band including E Africa, Central Asia and W China, India, Malaysia, Indonesia. Islam has several million adherents in North America and about 30 mil in Europe.

Beliefs: Strictly monotheistic. God is creator of the universe, omnipotent, omniscient, just, forgiving, and merciful. God revealed the Qur'an to Muhammad to guide humanity to truth and justice. Those who sincerely "submit" (literal meaning of "islam") to God attain salvation.

World's Largest Muslim Populations, estimated, mid-2005

Source: Government sources; World Christian Database, www.worldchristiandatabase.org

Rank	Country	Muslim population	% of total pop.
1.	Pakistan	154,563,023	95.9
2.	India	134,149,817	12.2
3.	Bangladesh	132,868,312	87.1
4.	Indonesia	121,606,358	54.0*
5.	Turkey	71,322,513	97.3
6.	Iran	67,724,004	95.8
7.	Egypt	63,503,397	84.8
8.	Nigeria	54,665,801	42.0
9.	Algeria	31,858,555	96.9
10.	Morocco	31,000,895	98.6
11.	Iraq	25,624,902	96.5
12.	Afghanistan	25,420,191	97.9
13.	Ethiopia	25,278,158	34.1
14.	Sudan	25,029,295	71.4
15.	Saudi Arabia	23,636,269	92.2
16.	Yemen	21,256,139	99.0
17.	Uzbekistan	20,527,687	76.4
18.	China	19,842,064	1.5
19.	Syria	17,182,303	92.1
20.	Malaysia	11,663,835	45.9

*Includes about 50 million persons classified as Muslim by the Indonesian government, but sometimes classified as New Religionists.

World Almanac Quick Quiz

Which group of Biblical figures were NOT siblings?

(a) Moses, Aaron, and Miriam   (b) Martha, Mary of Bethany, and Lazarus   (c) Elisha and Elijah   (d) Rachel and Leah

For the answer look in this chapter, or see page 1008.

Baha'i

Founded: Mid-19th century

Founder: Mirza Husayn-Ali Nuri (1817-1892), later known as Baha'u'llah (Arabic for "Glory of God")

Sacred Texts: The writings of Baha'u'llah and of his herald the Bab (Siyyid Ali-Muhammad, 1819-1850). The primary text is *Kitab-i-Aqdas* (the Most Holy Book).

Organization: The Baha'i administrative system consists of elected nine-member councils at the local, national, and international levels. There are also more than 180 National Spiritual Assemblies and an elected, international governing body known as the Universal House of Justice.

Practice: Prayer, meditation, and fasting are key components of Baha'i faith. Work performed in a spirit of service to humanity is considered an important form of worship. The Baha'i Faith has no clergy and minimal ritual and congregational worship.

Divisions: In a religion in which unity is perhaps the central spiritual value, the Baha'i Faith has avoided separating into sects with differentiated theologies and practices.

Location: Worldwide, with practitioners in 236 countries.

Beliefs: God has progressively revealed His will and purpose through a series of Divine manifestations including Jesus, Buddha, Muhammad, Zoroaster, and Baha'u'llah. Baha'u'llah's teachings include the oneness of humanity, the equality of men and women, the harmony of science and religion, the abandonment of all forms of prejudice, and the elimination of extremes of poverty and wealth.

Buddhism

Founded: About 525 BCE, reportedly near Benares, India.

Founder: Gautama Siddhartha (c. 563-483 BCE), the Buddha, who achieved enlightenment through intense meditation.

Sacred Texts: The *Tripitaka*, a collection of the Buddha's teachings, rules of monastic life, and philosophical commentaries on the teachings; also a vast body of Buddhist teachings and commentaries, many of which are called *sutras.*

Organization: The basic institution is the *sangha*, or monastic order, through which traditions are passed down. Monastic life tends to be democratic and anti-authoritarian.

Practice: Varies widely according to the sect, and ranges from austere meditation to magical chanting and elaborate temple rites. Many practices, such as exorcism of devils, reflect pre-Buddhist beliefs.

Divisions: A variety of sects grouped into 3 primary branches: Theravada, which emphasizes the importance of pure thought and deed; Mahayana (includes Zen and Soka-gakkai), which ranges from philosophical schools to belief in the saving grace of higher beings or ritual practices and to practical meditative disciplines; and Vajrayana, or Tantrism, a combination of belief in ritual magic and sophisticated philosophy.

Location: Mainly in Asia, from Sri Lanka to Japan.

Beliefs: Life is suffering, and there is no ultimate reality behind it. The cycle of birth and rebirth continues because of desire and attachment to the unreal "self." Meditation and deeds will end the cycle and achieve Nirvana (nothingness, enlightenment).

Hinduism

Founded: About 1500 BCE by Aryans who migrated to India, where their Vedic religion intermixed with the practices and beliefs of the natives.

Sacred texts: The *Veda,* including the *Upanishads,* a collection of rituals and commentaries; a vast number of epic stories about gods, heroes, and saints, including the *Bhagavadgita,* a part of the *Mahabharata,* and the *Ramayana.*

Organization: None, strictly speaking. Generally, rituals should be performed or assisted by Brahmins, the priestly caste, but in practice, simpler rituals can be performed by anyone. Brahmins are the final judges of ritual purity, the vital element in Hindu life. Temples and religious organizations are usually presided over by Brahmins.

Practice: Primarily passage rites (e.g., initiation, marriage, death, etc.) and daily devotions. Of the public rites, the *puja,* a ceremonial dinner for a god, is the most common.

Divisions: There is no concept of orthodoxy in Hinduism, which presents a variety of sects. The 3 major living traditions are those devoted to the gods Vishnu and Shiva and to

the goddess Shakti. Numerous folk beliefs and practices, often in amalgamation with the above groups, exist side by side with philosophical schools.

Location: Mainly India, Nepal, Malaysia, Guyana, Suriname, and Sri Lanka.

Beliefs: There is only one divine principle; the many gods are only aspects of that unity. Life in all its forms is an aspect of the divine, but it appears as a separation from the divine, a meaningless cycle of birth and rebirth (*samsara*) determined by the purity or impurity of past deeds (*karma*). To improve one's *karma* or escape *samsara* by pure acts, thought, and/or devotion is the aim of every Hindu.

Judaism

Founded: About 2000 BCE.

Founder: Abraham is regarded as the founding patriarch, The Torah of Moses is the basic source of the teachings.

Sacred Texts: The 5 books of Moses (the Torah).

Organization: Originally theocratic, Judaism has evolved into a congregational polity. The basic institution is the local synagogue or temple, operated by the congregation and led by a rabbi of their choice. Chief rabbis in France and Great Britain have authority only over those who accept it; in Israel, the 2 chief rabbis have civil authority in family law.

Practice: Among traditional practicioners, almost all areas of life are governed by strict discipline. Sabbath and holidays are marked by observances, and attendance at public worship is considered especially important. Chief annual observances are Passover, celebrating liberation of the Israelites from Egypt and marked by the Seder meal in homes, and the 10 days from Rosh Hashanah (New Year) to Yom Kippur (Day of Atonement), a period of penitence.

Divisions: Judaism is an unbroken spectrum from ultraconservative to ultraliberal, largely reflecting different points of view regarding the binding character of the prohibitions and duties—particularly the dietary and Sabbath observations—traditionally prescribed for the daily life of the Jew.

Location: Mainly in Israel and the U.S.

Beliefs: Strictly monotheistic. God is the creator and ruler of the universe. God established a particular relationship with the Hebrew people: by obeying a divine law God gave them, they would be a special witness to God's mercy and justice. Judaism stresses ethical behavior (and, among the traditional, careful ritual obedience) as true worship of God.

Sikhism

Founded: Late 15th century in South Asia.

Founder: Guru Nanak Dev ji, Sikhism's first Guru.

Sacred Texts: The *Guru Granth Sahib* was compiled by the Sikh Gurus and contains their experiences of the Divine. It also contains writing by other saintly figures of different faiths.

Organization: Each Sikh must make her or his own spiritual journey and not depend on clergy. Congregational prayer led by both men and women takes place in local *Gurudwaras.* Harmandir Sahib in Amritsar, Punjab (Northern India) is the central place of worship.

Practice: Prayers are required in the morning, evening, and before sleeping. The most important mode of congregational prayer is the singing of hymns from the *Guru Granth Sahib.* The "Five Ks" are five articles of faith required of all Sikhs: *Kes* (uncut hair), *Kangha* (comb), *Kara* (steel bracelet), *Kirpan* (sword), and *Kaccha* (short pants).

Divisions: The last living Guru, Guru Gobind Singh (1666-1708) crystallized the practices and beliefs of the faith and determined that no future living Guru was needed. Today the religion is guided by joint sovereignty of Guru Granth and Guru Panth. Guru Granth is the Sikh scripture, as the spiritual manifestation of the Guru, while the Guru Panth is the collectivity of all initiated Sikhs worldwide, as the physical manifestation of the Guru.

Location: Many Sikhs are from Punjabi backgrounds. Punjab is divided between India and Pakistan.

Beliefs: Sikhism preaches a message of devotion, remembrance of God at all times, truthful living, equality between all human beings, and social justice, while emphatically denouncing superstitions and blind rituals. Sikhism is a monotheistic religion based on revelation.

Headquarters of Selected Religious Groups in the U.S.

Sources: *2006 Yearbook of American & Canadian Churches,* © National Council of the Churches of Christ in the USA; *World Almanac* research

(Year organized in parentheses)

African Methodist Episcopal Church (1787), 3801 Market St., Suite 300, Philadelphia, PA 29204; Senior Bishop, Bishop Philip Robert Cousin

African Methodist Episcopal Zion Church (1796), 3225 West Sugar Creek Rd., Charlotte, NC 28269; Pres. Warren M. Brown.

American Baptist Churches in the U.S.A. (1907), PO Box 851, Valley Forge, PA 19482; www.abc-usa.org; Pres., Margaret Johnson

Antiochian Orthodox Christian Archdiocese of North America (1895), 358 Mountain Rd., Englewood, NJ 07631; www.antiochian.org; Primate, Metropolitan Philip Saliba

Armenian Apostolic Church of America (1887), **Eastern Prelacy**: 138 E. 39th St., New York, NY 10016; www.armprelacy.org; Prelate, Archbishop Oshagan Choloyan; **Western Prelacy**: 6252 Honolulu Ave., La Crecsenta, CA 91214; Prelate, Bishop Moushegh Mardirossian

Assemblies of God (1914), 1445 N. Boonville Ave., Springfield, MO 65802; www.ag.org; Gen. Supt., Thomas E. Trask

Bahá'í Faith, National Spiritual Assembly of the Bahá'í's of the U.S., 1233 Central St., Evanston, IL 60201; www.us.bahai.org; Secy. Gen., Dr. Robert C. Henderson

Baptist Bible Fellowship Intl. (1950), Baptist Bible Fellowship Missions Bldg., 720 E. Kearney St., Springfield, MO 65803; www.bbfi.org; Pres., Rev. Bill Monroe

Baptist Convention, Southern (1845), 901 Commerce St., Nashville, TN 37203; www.sbc.net; Pres. Bobby Welch,

Baptist Convention, U.S.A., Inc., National (1895), 1700 Baptist World Center Dr., Nashville, TN 37207; www.nationalbaptist.com; Pres., Dr. William J. Shaw

Baptist Convention of America, Inc., National (1880), 777 S. R.L. Thornton Freeway, Ste. 205, Dallas, TX 75203; Pres., Dr. E. Edward Jones

Baptist Convention of America, Natl. Missionary (1988), 1404 E. Firestone, Los Angeles, CA 90001; www.nmbca.com; Pres., Dr. W. T. Snead Sr.

Baptist General Conference (1852), 2002 S. Arlington Heights Rd., Arlington Heights, IL 60005; www.bgcworld.org; Pres. and CEO, Dr. Gerald Sheveland

Brethren in Christ Church (1778), PO Box A, Grantham, PA 17027; www.bic-church.org; Moderator, Dr. Warren L. Hoffman

Buddhist Churches of America (1899), 1710 Octavia St., San Francisco, CA 94109; www.buddhistchurchesofamerica.com; Presiding Bishop, Hakubun Watanabe

Christian Church (Disciples of Christ) (1832), Disciples Center, 130 E. Washington St., PO Box 1986, Indianapolis, IN 46206; www.disciples.org; Gen. Minister and Pres., William Chris Hobgood

Christian Churches and Churches of Christ, 4210 Bridgetown Rd., Box 11326, Cincinnati, OH 45211

Christian Methodist Episcopal Church (1870), 4466 Elvis Presley Blvd., Memphis, TN 38116; Executive Secretary, Attorney Juanita Bryant

Church of the Brethren (1708), General Offices, 1451 Dundee Ave., Elgin, IL 60120; www.brethren.org; Moderator, Christopher D. Bowman

Church of Christ (1830), Temple Lot, 200 S. River St., PO Box 472, Independence, MO 64051; http://church-of-christ.com; Council of Apostles, Secy., Apostle Smith N. Brickhouse

Church of God (Anderson, IN) (1881), Box 2420, Anderson, IN 46018; www.chog.org; Gen. Dir., Pres. J. Perry Grubbs

Church of God (Cleveland, TN) (1886), 2490 Keith St. NW, Cleveland, TN 37320; www.churchofgod.cc; Gen. Overseer, R. Lamar Vest

Church of God in Christ (1907), Mason Temple, 938 Mason St., Memphis, TN 38126; www.netministries.org/see/churches/ch00833; Presiding Bishop, Bishop Chandler D. Owens

Church of Jesus Christ (Bickertonites) (1862), 6th & Lincoln Sts., Monongahela, PA 15063; www.thechurchofjesuschrist.com; Pres., Dominic Thomas.

Church of Jesus Christ of Latter-day Saints (Mormon), The (1830), 47 E. South Temple St., Salt Lake City, UT 84150; www.lds.org; Pres., Gordon B. Hinckley

Church of the Nazarene (1907), 6401 The Paseo, Kansas City, MO 64131; www.nazarene.org; Gen. Secy., Dr. Jack Stone

Community of Christ (Reorganized Church of Jesus Christ of Latter-Day Saints) (1830), Int'l. Headquarters, 1001 W. Walnut, Independence, MO 54050; www.CofChrist.org; Pres. W. Grant McMurray

Community Churches, International Council of (1950), 21116 Washington Pkwy., Frankfort, IL 60423; www.icccusa.com; Pres., Grace O'Neal

Conservative Judaism, United Synagogue of, 155 5th Ave., New York, NY 10010; www.uscj.org; Pres., Judy Yudof

Cumberland Presbyterian Church (1810), 1978 Union Ave., Memphis, TN 38104; www.cumberland.org; Moderator, Rev. E. G. Sims

Episcopal Church (1789), 815 Second Ave., New York, NY 10017; www.ecusa.anglican.org; Presiding Bishop and Primate, Most Rev. Frank Tracy Griswold

Evangelical Lutheran Church in America (1987), 8765 W. Higgins Rd., Chicago, IL 60631; www.elca.org; Presiding Bishop, Rev. Mark S. Hanson

First Church of Christ, Scientist, The (1879), Christian Science Plaza, 175 Huntington Ave., Boston, MA 02115; www.spirituality.com; Pres., Cynthia Neely

Free Methodist Church of North America (1860), World Ministries Center, 770 N. High School Rd., Indianapolis, IN 46214; www.freemethodistchurch.org

Friends General Conference (1900), 1216 Arch St., 2B, Philadelphia, PA 19107; www.fgcquaker.org; Gen. Secy., Bruce Birchard

Greek Orthodox Archdiocese of America (1922), 8-10 E. 79th St., New York, NY 10021; www.goarch.org; Primate, Archbishop Demetrios

Islamic Society of North America, P.O. Box 38, Plainfield, IN 46168; www.isna.net; Genl. Secy., Dr. Sayyid M. Syeed

Jehovah's Witnesses (1884), 25 Columbia Heights, Brooklyn, NY 11201; www.watchtower.org; Pres., Don Adams

Jewish Reconstructionist Federation (1935), Beit Devora, 7804 Montgomery Ave., Suite 9, Elkins Park, PA 19027; www.jrf.org; Dir., Chayim Herzig-Moss

Lutheran Church—Missouri Synod (1847), 1333 S. Kirkwood Rd., St. Louis, MO 63122; www.lcms.org; Pres., Dr. Gerald B. Kieschnick

Mennonite Brethren Churches, General Conference of (1860), 4812 E. Butler Ave., Fresno CA 93727; Moderator, Ed Boschman

Mennonite Church USA (2001), 722 Main St., PO Box 347, Newton, KS 67114. www.MennoniteChurchUSA.org; Moderator, Duane Oswald

Moravian Church in America (1735), **Northern Prov.:** 1021 Center St., PO Box 1245, Bethlehem, PA 18016; www.moravian.org; Pres., David L. Wickmann; **Southern Prov.:** 459 S. Church St., Winston-Salem, NC 27101; Pres., Rev. Dr. Robert E. Sawyer; **Alaska Prov.:** PO Box 545, 361 3rd Ave., Bethel, AK 99559; Pres., Rev. Peter Green

North American Shi'a Muslim Communities Organization (NASIMCO), P.O. Box 29691, Minneapolis, MN 55429; www.nasimco.org; Pres., Hussein Walji

Orthodox Jewish Congregations in America, Union of (1898), 11 Broadway, New York, NY 10004; www.ou.org; Pres., Harvey Blitz

Pentecostal Assemblies of the World, Inc., 3939 Meadows Dr., Indianapolis, IN 46205; www.pawinc.org; Presiding Bishop, Norman L. Wagner

Presbyterian Church (U.S.A.), (1983), 100 Witherspoon St., Louisville, KY 40202; www.pcusa.org; Moderator, Rich Ufford-Chase

Progressive National Baptist Convention, Inc. (1961), 601 50th St., NE, Washington, DC 20019; www.pribc.org; Pres., Dr. Bennett W. Smith Sr.

Reform Judaism, Union for, 633 3rd Ave., New York, NY 10017; www.urj.org; Pres., Rabbi Eric Yoffie

Roman Catholic Church (1634), U.S. Conference of Catholic Bishops, 3211 Fourth St. NE, Washington, DC 20017; www.usccb.org; Pres., Bishop William S. Skylstad

Seventh-day Adventist Church (1863), 12501 Old Columbia Pike, Silver Spring, MD 20904; www.adventist.org; Pres., Jan Paulsen

Unitarian Universalist Association of Congregations (1961), 25 Beacon St., Boston, MA 02108; www.uua.org; Pres., The Rev. William Sinkford

United Church of Christ (1957), 700 Prospect Ave., Cleveland, OH 44115; www.ucc.org; Pres., Rev. John H. Thomas

United Methodist Church (1968), www.umc.org; Pres. Council of Bishops, Bishop Sharon Brown Christopher

United Pentecostal Church Intl. (1925), 8855 Dunn Rd., Hazelwood, MO 63042; www.upci.org; Gen. Supt., Rev. Kenneth F. Haney

Wesleyan Church (1968), PO Box 50434, Indianapolis, IN 46250; www.wesleyan.org; Gen. Supts., Dr. Earle L. Wilson, Dr. David H. Holdren, Dr. Thomas E. Armiger

LANGUAGE

New Words in English

The following words and definitions were provided by Merriam-Webster Inc., publishers of *Merriam-Webster's Collegiate Dictionary, Eleventh Edition*, released in 2003. The words or meanings are among those that the Merriam-Webster editors decided had achieved enough currency in English to be added to the 2006 printing of the dictionary.

agritourism: the practice of touring agricultural areas to see farms and often to participate in farm activities

arm candy: a young attractive person who accompanies a usually older person at social events

biodiesel: a fuel that is similar to diesel fuel and is derived from usually vegetable sources

bling-bling or **bling:** flashy jewelry worn especially as an indication of wealth

bodyboard: a short surfboard on which the rider rides prone

cybersecurity: measures taken to protect a computer or computer system against unauthorized access or attack

degenderize: to eliminate any reference to a specific gender in (as a word, text, or act)

drama queen: a person given to often excessively emotional performances or reactions

dreamscape: a dreamlike usually surrealistic scene

empty suit: an ineffectual executive

gastric bypass: a surgical bypass operation that involves reducing the size of the stomach and reconnecting the smaller stomach to bypass the first portion of the small intestine so as to restrict food intake

google: to use the Google search engine to obtain information about (as a person) on the World Wide Web

himbo: an attractive but vacuous man

infotech: the technology involving the development, maintenance, and use of computer systems, software, and networks for the processing and distribution of data

intelligent design: the theory that matter, the various forms of life, and the world were created by a designing intelligence

manga: a Japanese comic book or graphic novel

metrosexual: a usually urban heterosexual male given to enhancing his personal appearance by fastidious grooming, beauty treatments, and fashionable clothes

micropolitan: of, relating to, or being a population area that includes a city with 10,000 to 50,000 residents and its surrounding communities

mouse potato: a person who spends a great deal of time using a computer

phishing: a scam in which an e-mail user is duped into revealing personal or confidential information which the scammer can use illicitly

ponzu: a tangy sauce made with citrus juice, rice wine vinegar, and soy sauce and used especially on seafood

ringtone: the sound made by a cell phone to signal an incoming call

senioritis: an ebbing of effort by school seniors as evidenced by tardiness, absences, and lower grades

slurb: a suburb of wearisomely uniform and usually poorly constructed houses

soul patch: a small growth of beard under a man's lower lip

spyware: software that is installed in a computer without the user's knowledge and transmits information about the user's computer activities over the Internet

supersize: to increase considerably the size, amount, or extent of

technopreneur: an entrepreneur whose business involves high technology

text messaging: the sending of short text messages electronically especially from one cell phone to another

unibrow: a single continuous brow resulting from the growing together of eyebrows

Words About Words

allegory: extended use of symbols, in the form of characters, animals, or events, that represent ideas or themes. Ex: John Bunyan, *Pilgrim's Progress*

alliteration: repetition of same, initial consonant sounds of two or more words in sequence or in short intervals. Ex: "I have stood still and stopped the sound of feet." —Robert Frost

anagram: a word or phrase made by rearranging letters from another word or phrase. Ex: Clint Eastwood=Old West Action

antithesis: an expression in which contrasting ideas are intentionally juxtaposed, usually in parallel structure. Ex: "The world will little note, nor long remember, what we say here, but it can never forget what they did here." —Abraham Lincoln, Gettysburg Address

assonance: repetition of same or similar vowel sounds in words located near each other. Ex: "Green as a dream, and deep as death." —Rupert Brooke

cliché: a saying or expression that has been used so often it has lost its effect. Ex: work like a dog

euphemism: a mild, indirect expression used instead of a plainer one that might be harsh, unpleasant, or offensive. Ex: restroom, pass away

hyperbole: exaggeration for emphasis or effect. Ex: "And fired the shot heard round the world." —Ralph Waldo Emerson, "Concord Hymn"

irony: an expression in which the intended meaning is contrary to its literal meaning; the words say one thing but mean another. Ex: "Yet Brutus says he was ambitious; / And Brutus is an honorable man." —Shakespeare, *Julius Caesar*

litotes: intentional understatement made by negating the opposite of what is meant. Ex: This was no small matter.

metaphor: implied comparison of two dissimilar things, without using "as" or "like." Ex: "Dawn's rosy fingers" —Homer

metonymy: substitution of one word for another which it suggests. Ex: The pen is mightier than the sword.

onomatopoeia: words that imitate the sounds they describe. Ex: buzz, murmur

oxymoron: juxtaposition of contradictory words. Ex: deafening silence

palindrome: a type of anagram in which a word, phrase, or sentence reads the same backward and forward. Ex: Ma is a nun as I am.

paradox: a statement that is seemingly contradictory, odd, or opposed to common sense or expectation and yet is presented as true. Ex: "What a pity that youth must be wasted on the young." —George Bernard Shaw

personification: treating ideas or objects as though they were persons. Ex: "Because I could not stop for Death— / He kindly stopped for me." —Emily Dickinson

simile: a comparison between two dissimilar things using "like" or "as." Ex: "My love is like a red, red rose" —Robert Burns

spoonerism: play on words in which the initial sounds of two or more words are transposed, creating different phrases whose meanins, whern compared can be humorous. Ex: a blushing crow, a crushing blow

synecdoche: (a form of metonymy) the use of a part for the whole, or the whole for the part. Ex: All hands on deck!

tautology: unnecessary repetition of an idea in different words, phrases, or sentences. Ex: close proximity

National Spelling Bee

The Scripps National Spelling Bee, conducted by The E.W. Scripps Company and other newspapers since 1941, was instituted by *The Courier-Journal* of Louisville, KY, in 1925. Students under 16 who are not beyond the 8th grade are eligible to compete for cash prizes at the finals, held annually in Washington, DC (The experiences of 8 contestants in the 1999 Spelling Bee were highlighted in a 2002 documentary, *Spellbound*.) The 2006 winners were Katharine Close (1st place), of Spring Lake, NJ; Finola Hackett (2nd place), of Tofield, Alberta, Canada; and Saryn Hooks (3rd place), of Taylorsville, NC.

Here are the last words given, and spelled correctly, in each of the years from 1981 to 2006 at the National Spelling Bee.

1981	sarcophagus	1987	staphylococci	1992	lyceum	1997	euonym	2002	prospicience
1982	psoriasis	1988	elegiacal	1993	kamikaze	1998	chiaroscurist	2003	pococurante
1983	Purim	1989	spoliator	1994	antediluvian	1999	logorrhea	2004	autochthonous
1984	luge	1990	fibranne	1995	xanthosis	2000	demarche	2005	appoggiatura
1985	milieu	1991	antipyretic	1996	vivisepulture	2001	succedaneum	2006	ursprache
1986	odontalgia							

▶ **IT'S A FACT:** The word "English" is derived from the name of the Angles who, along with the Saxons and Jutes, migrated from Germany to England in the fifth century. The oldest written Old English document in existence is the 42-word poem *Caedmon's Hymn* (Hymn of Creation), written around 670 CE.

Names of the Days

ENGLISH	RUSSIAN	HEBREW	FRENCH	ITALIAN	SPANISH	GERMAN	JAPANESE
Sunday	voskresenye	yom rishon	dimanche	domenica	domingo	Sonntag	nichiyoubi
Monday	ponedelnik	yom sheni	lundi	lunedì	lunes	Montag	getsuyoubi
Tuesday	vtornik	yom shlishi	mardi	martedì	martes	Dienstag	kayoubi
Wednesday	sreda	yom ravii	mercredi	mercoledì	miércoles	Mittwoch	suiyoubi
Thursday	chetverg	yom hamishi	jeudi	giovedì	jueves	Donnerstag	mokuyoubi
Friday	pyatnitsa	yom shishi	vendredi	venerdì	viernes	Freitag	kinyoubi
Saturday	subbota	shabbat	samedi	sabato	sábado	Samstag	doyoubi

Foreign Words and Phrases

(A=Arabic; F=French; Ger=German; Gk=Greek; I=Italian; L=Latin; S=Spanish; Y=Yiddish)

à bientôt (F; ah bee-en-TOE): so long; see you soon

ad hoc (L; ad HOK): for the end or purpose at hand; impromptu

ad hominem (L; ad HOH-mee-nem): emotional rather than intellectual; in a dispute, using slander to obscure issues

al fresco (I; ahl FRAYS-koh): outdoors

antebellum (L; AHN-teh-BEL-lum): pre-war

apercu(s) (F; ah-per-SOO): first perception or insight; outline

auf Wiedersehen (Ger; owf-VEE-duh-zehn): Good-bye

belles lettres (F; bel-LET-truh): writing aspiring to artistic merit

bête noire (F; BET NWAHR): a thing or person viewed with particular dislike or fear

bijou (F; BEE-zhoo): gem, jewel

Bildungsroman (Ger; BIL-doongs-roh-mahn): novel embodying coming-of-age story

bodega (S; boh-DAY-gah): grocery store

bonhomie (F; boh-noh-MEE): friendliness

bon vivant (F; bon-vee-VAHN): a person with refined tastes, especially for food and drink

bourgeois (F; boo-ZHWAH): middle-class; conventional; materialistic

carte blanche (F; kahrt BLANSH): full discretionary power

casus belli (L; KAH-soos BEL-lee): reason for going to war.

cause célèbre (F; kawz suh-LEB-ruh): a notorious incident

cognoscenti (I; koh-nyoh-SHEN-tee): experts; connoisseurs

contretemps (F; kon-truh-tahm): awkward situation

coup de grâce (F; kooh duh GRAHS): the final blow

cum laude/magna cum laude/summa cum laude (L; kuhm LOUD-ay; MAGN-a ...; SOO-ma ...): with praise or honor/with great praise or honor/with the highest praise or honor

de facto (L; day FAK-toh): in fact, if not by law

de jure (L; dee JOOR-ee, day YOOR-ay): in accordance with right or law; officially

deo gratias (L; dey oh GROT-SEE-us): thanks be to God

de rigueur (F; duh ree-GUR): necessary according to convention or etiquette

détente (F; day-TAHNT): an easing of strained relations

deus ex machina (L; DAY-us eks MAH-keh-nah): a person/event that provides a solution unexpectedly or suddenly, espec. (in literature) a contrived solution to a plot

dictum (L; DIK-tahm): an official or formal pronouncement

double entendre (F; DOO-blahn-TAHN-druh): expression with a double meaning, one meaning of which is often risqué

éminence grise (F; ay-meh-nahns-GREEZ): one who wields power behind the scenes

enfant terrible (F; ahn-FAHN te-REE-bluh): one who is noteworthy for embarrassing or unconventional behavior

ennui (F; ah-NOOEE): boredom; world-weariness; annoyance

e pluribus unum (L; eh-PLOO-ree-boos-OO-noom): out of many, one (U.S. motto)

ersatz (Ger; EHR-zats): artificial; being a (usually inferior) substitute

eureka (Gk; yoor-EE-kuh): I have found it!; hurrah!

ex post facto (L; eks pohst FAK-toh): retroactive(ly)

fait accompli (F; fayt uh-kom-PLEE): an accomplished fact

fatwa (A; FAHT-wah): in Islam, a legal or religious decree

faux pas (F; foh PAH): as false step; a social blunder or breach of etiquette

habeas corpus (L; HAY-bee-ahs KOR-pus): an order for an accused person to be brought to court

hoi polloi (Gk; hoy puh-LOY): the masses

impresario (I; im-prah-SAH-ri-oh): manager, promoter, or sponsor of a musical or theatrical program or company

imprimatur (L; im-prah-MAH-toor): approval or official permission to print, espec. by the Roman Catholic church

in loco parentis (L; in LOH-koh puh-REN-tis): in place of parent

in medias res (L; in MAY-dee-oos rays): into the middle of things

in omnibus (L; in OHM-nee-bus): in all things; in all ways

je ne sais quoi (F; zhuh nuh say KWAH): I don't know what; the little something that eludes description

joie de vivre (F; zhwah duh VEEV-ruh): zest for life

leitmotif (Ger; lyt-moh-TEEF): the central theme or idea, particularly in art and literature

mano a mano (S; MAH-noh ah MAH-noh): hand to hand; in direct combat

mea culpa (L; MAY-uh CUL-puh): through my fault

mensch (Y; mentsh): an upright, noble, admirable person

modus operandi (L; MOH-duhs op-uh-RAN-dee): method of operation

mujahadeen (A; moo-jah-ha-DEEN): Islamic holy fighters

noblesse oblige (F; noh-BLES oh-BLEEZH): the obligation of nobility to help the less fortunate

nolo contendere (L; NOH-loh-kohn-TEN-deh-reh): "I will not contest," a plea of no defense, equivalent to a plea of guilty

non compos mentis (L; non KOM-puhs MEN-tis): not of sound mind

non sequitur (L; non SEH-kwi-tour): a conclusion that does not logically follow from what preceded it

nouveau riche (F; noo-voh REESH): a person newly rich, espec. one who spends money conspicuously

par excellence (F; par ek-seh-LANS): best of all; incomparable

parvenu (F; par-vuh-NOO): upstart

persona non grata (L; per-SOH-nah non GRAH-tah): unwelcome person

pièce de résistance (F; pee-es duh ray-ZEES-tonz): the outstanding item in a series or group

pro bono (L; proh BOH-noh): (legal work) donated for the public good

qué será será (S; keh sair-AH sair-AH): what will be will be

quid pro quo (L; kwid proh KWOH): something given or received for something else

raison d'être (F; RAY-zohn DET-ruh): reason for being

sans souci (F; SAHNN sooh-SEE): without worry

savoir faire (F; sav-wahr-FAIR): dexterity in social affairs

Schadenfreude (Ger; SHAH-d'n-froy-deh): joy at another's misfortune

schlemiel (Y; shleh-MEEL): an unlucky, bungling person

schlepp (Y; shlep): move slowly, tediously, drag oneself along

semper fidelis (L; SEM-puhr fee-DAY-lis): always faithful

sobriquet (F; soh-bree-KAY): nickname

terra firma (L; TER-uh FUR-muh): solid ground

vis-à-vis (F; vee-zuh-VEE): compared with; with regard to

voir dire (F; vwar-DEER): examination by lawyers or judge to determine the suitability of a witness or a prospective juror

zeitgeist (Ger; ZITE-gyste): the general intellectual, moral, and cultural climate of an era

wadi (A; WAH-dee): a stream bed or valley that fills with water only during seasonal rains; gully

Names for Animal Young

calf: cattle, elephant, rhino, hippo, others
cheeper: grouse, partridge, quail
chick, chicken: fowl
cockerel: rooster
codling, sprag: codfish
colt: horse (male)
cria: llama, alpaca
cub: lion, bear, shark, fox, others
cygnet: swan
duckling: duck
elver: eel
ephyra: jellyfish
eyas: hawk, others
fawn: deer
filly: horse (female)

fingerling, fry: fish generally
fledgling, nestling: birds generally
foal: horse, zebra, others
gosling: goose
heifer: cow
hoglet: hedgehog
joey: kangaroo, opossum, wombat, others
kid: goat
kit: fox, beaver, rabbit, cat
kitten, kitty, catling: cat, other small mammals
lamb, lambkin, cosset, hog: sheep
larva: frog, sea urchin, insects generally
leveret: hare

nestling: birds generally
nymph: insects
parr, smolt, grilse: salmon
peachick: peafowl
piglet, shoat, farrow, suckling: pig
polliwog, froglet, tadpole: frog
poult: turkey
pullet: hen
pup: dog, fox, seal, sea lion
spat: oyster
spike, blinker, tinker: mackerel
squab: pigeon
squeaker: pigeon, others
whelp: dog, tiger, beasts of prey
yearling: cattle, sheep, horse, others

IT'S A FACT: "The quick brown fox jumps over the lazy dog" is one of the more well-known English pangrams, or sentences that use every letter of the alphabet at least once. A lipogram, on the other hand, is a piece of writing that omits one or more letters of the alphabet. French author Georges Perec wrote *La Disparition* (*A Void*) entirely without the letter e. Gilbert Adair's English translation of Perec's lipogrammatic novel also avoids all use of the letter e.

Names for Animal Collectives

alligators: congregation
ants: army, colony, or swarm
apes: shrewdness or troop
badgers: cete
bats: colony
bears: sleuth or sloth
bees: grist or swarm
birds: flight or volery
boars/swine: singular or sounder
buffalo: gang or obstinacy
butterflies: flutter
buzzards: wake
camels: caravan, flock, or train
cats: clowder, cluster, glaring, or pounce
cattle: drove
cheetahs: coalition
clams/oysters: bed
cockroaches: intrusion

cormorants: gulp
cranes: sedge or siege
crocodiles: bask, nest, or float
crows: murder
dolphins: pod
doves: dule or pitying
ducks: brace or team
eagles: convocation or aerie
ferrets: business
finches: charm
fish: school or shoal
flamingos: stand
foxes: skulk
geese: flock, gaggle, or skein
giraffes: corps, herd, or tower
gnats: cloud or horde
goats: tribe or trip
gorillas: band or whoop
grasshoppers: cloud
hares: down, husk, or trip

hedgehogs: array
hawks: cast
hippopotami: bloat
horses: pair or team
hounds: cry, mute, or pack
hyenas: cackle
iguanas: mess
jellyfish: smack
kangaroos: mob or troop
larks: exaltation
leopards: leap
lions: pride
locusts: plague or swarm
monkeys: troop
mules: barren or span
nightingales: watch
otters: romp
owls: parliament
oxen: yoke
peacocks: muster

pheasants: nest or nide
ponies: string
raccoons: gaze
ravens: unkindness
rhinoceroses: crash
seals: pod
sheep: flock, drove, or hurtle
snakes: nest
squirrels: dray or scurry
swans: bevy
tigers: streak
toads: knot
turkeys: rafter
turtles: bale
vultures: committee
whales: gam, herd, or pod
wolves: pack
woodchucks: fall
woodpeckers: descent
zebras: herd or zeal

Some Common Abbreviations and Acronyms

Acronyms are pronounceable words formed from first letters (or syllables) of other words. Some **abbreviations** below (e.g., AIDS, NATO) are thus acronyms. Some acronyms are words coined as abbreviations and written in lower case (e.g., "sonar," "yuppie"). Acronyms do not have periods; usage for other abbreviations varies, but periods have become less common. Capitalization usage may vary from what is shown here. Italicized words preceding parenthetical definitions below are Latin unless otherwise noted. See also other chapters, including Computers and Telecommunications; Weights and Measures.

AA=Alcoholics Anonymous; Associate in Arts; administrative assistant
AAA=American Automobile Association
AARP=American Association of Retired Persons
ABA=American Bar Association
abr.=abridged
AC=alternating current
ad=*anno Domini* (in the year of the Lord)
ADD=Attention Deficit Disorder
AFL-CIO=American Federation of Labor and Congress of Industrial Organizations
AI=artificial intelligence
AIDS=acquired immune deficiency syndrome
am=*ante meridiem* (before noon)
anon=anonymous
APO=army post office
APR=annual percentage rate
ARM=adjustable rate mortgage
ASCAP=American Society of Composers, Authors, and Publishers
ASCII=American Standard Code for Information Interchange
ASPCA=American Society for Prevention of Cruelty to Animals
ATM=automated teller machine
AWOL=absent without leave
BA=Bachelor of Arts
bbl=barrel(s)
bc=before Christ
bce=before the Common Era
bpd=barrels per day
BS=Bachelor of Science
Btu=British thermal unit(s)
bu=bushel(s)
byob=bring your own bottle
C= Celsius, centigrade
c=*circa* (about); copyright
CAFTA=Central American Free Trade Agreement
CAT=computerized axial tomography
CBD=Central Business District
CDC=Centers for Disease Control and Prevention, Community Development Corporation
ce=Common Era
CEO=chief executive officer
cf.=*confer* (compare)

CFO=chief financial officer
CIA=Central Intelligence Agency
CIF=cost, insurance, and freight
CIO=chief information officer
COD=cash (or collect) on delivery
Col.=Colonel
COLA=cost of living adjustment
colloq.=colloquial
COO=chief operating officer
CPA=certified public accountant
CPI=Consumer Price Index
Cpl.=Corporal
CPR=cardiopulmonary resuscitation
CPU=central processing unit
CST=Central Standard Time
CWO=Chief Warrant Officer
DA=district attorney
DC=direct current
DD=Doctor of Divinity
DDS=Doctor of Dental Science (or Surgery)
DHS=Dept. of Homeland Security
DMD=Doctor of Dental Medicine
DMZ=demilitarized zone
DNA=deoxyribonucleic acid
DNR=do not resuscitate
DOA=dead on arrival
DOB=date of birth
dpi=dots per inch
DPT=diphtheria, pertussis, tetanus
DUI=driving under the influence
DVD=digital video disc
DVM=Doctor of Veterinary Medicine
DWI=driving while intoxicated
ed.=edited, edition, editor
EEG=electroencephalogram
e.g.=*exempli gratia* (for example)
EKG=electrocardiogram
EOE=equal opportunity employer
EP=extended play
EPA=Environmental Protection Agency
ERA=Equal Rights Amendment; earned run average
ESL=English as a second language
ESP=extrasensory perception
Esq.=esquire
EST=Eastern standard time
et al.=*et alii* (and others)
etc.=*et cetera* (and so forth)
EU=European Union

F=Fahrenheit
FBI=Federal Bureau of Investigation
FDA=Food and Drug Administration
FDIC=Federal Deposit Insurance Corp.
FEMA=Federal Emergency Management Agency
ff.=and those following
FICA=Federal Insurance Contributions Act (Social Security)
fl.=*floruit* (flourished), used for hist. figures when life dates uncertain
FY=fiscal year
FYI=for your information
GATT=General Agreement on Tariffs and Trade
GB=gigabyte(s)
GDP=gross domestic product
GED=general equivalency diploma (for high school)
GMT=Greenwich mean time
GOP=Grand Old Party (Republican Party)
GPS=Global Positioning System
GUI=graphical user interface
Hazmat=hazardous material
HMS=His/Her Majesty's Ship (UK)
Hon.=the Honorable
HOV=high-occupancy vehicle
HRH=her (his) royal highness (UK)
HTML=hypertext markup language
HTTP=hypertext transfer protocol
HVAC=heating, ventilating, and air-conditioning
Hz=hertz
ibid=*ibidem* (in the same place)
i.e.=*id est* (that is)
IMF=International Monetary Fund
IOC=International Olympic Committee
IPO=initial public offering
IQ=intelligence quotient
IRA=individual retirement account; Irish Republican Army
IRS=Internal Revenue Service
ISBN=International Standard Book Number
JCS=Joint Chiefs of Staff
JD=*Juris Doctor* (Doctor of Laws)
K=Kelvin
k=karat

KCB=Knight Commander of the Bath (UK)
kWh=kilowatt-hour(s)
laser=Light Amplification by Stimulated Emission of Radiation
Lieut. or Lt.=Lieutenant
LLB=*Legum Baccalaurens* (Bachelor of Laws)
LLP=limited licensed partners
loc. cit.=*loco citato* (in the place cited)
LSAT=Law School Admission Test
MA=Master of Arts
MB=megabyte(s)
MBA=Master of Business Administration
MCAT=Medical College Admission Test
MD=*Medicinae Doctor* (doctor of medicine)
MIA=missing in action
modem=MOdulator-DEModulator
MP=Member of Parliament (UK)
mph=miles per hour
MRI=magnetic resonance imaging
ms, mss=manuscript(s)
MS=Master of Science; multiple sclerosis
MSG=monosodium glutamate
MST=mountain standard time
MVP=most valuable player
NA=not applicable; not available
NAACP=National Association for the Advancement of Colored People
NAFTA=North American Free Trade Agreement
NASA=National Aeronautics and Space Administration
NATO=North Atlantic Treaty Org.
NB=*nota bene* (note carefully)
NCAA=National Collegiate Athletic Assn.
NIH=National Institutes of Health
NOW=National Organization for Women

NPR=National Public Radio
NRA=National Rifle Association
OED=Oxford English Dictionary
op=*opus* (work)
OPEC=Organization of Petroleum Exporting Countries
OTC=over the counter
p, pp=page(s)
PA=Public Address
PC=personal computer; political correctness
pd.=paid, per diem
PAC=political action committee
PDA=Personal Digital Assistant
Ph.D.=*Philosophiae Doctor* (doctor of philosophy)
PIN=Personal Identification Number
pm=*post meridiem* (afternoon)
PS=*post scriptum* (postscript)
PST=Pacific Standard Time
pt=part(s), pint(s), point(s)
Pvt.=Private
QC=Queen's Counsel (UK)
QED=*quod erat demonstrandum* (which was to be demonstrated)
q.v.=*quod vide* (which see)
radar=radio detecting and ranging
RCMP=Royal Canadian Mounted Police
REM=rapid eye movement
Rev.=Reverend
rev.=revised
RICE=rest, ice, compression, elevation
RIP=*requiescat in pace* (May he/she rest in peace)
RN=registered nurse
RNA=ribonucleic acid
ROTC=Reserve Officers' Training Corps
rpm=revolutions per minute

RSVP=*répondez s'il vous plaît* (Fr.) (Please reply)
SARS=severe acute respiratory syndrome
SASE=self-addressed stamped envelope
SETI=Search for Extraterrestrial Intelligence
Sgt.=Sergeant
SIDS=suddent infant death syndrome
S.J.=Society of Jesus (Jesuits)
sonar=sound navigation and ranging
SOP=Standard Operating Procedure
SSI=Supplementary Security Income
SUV=sport utility vehicle
TBA=to be announced
TBD=to be determined
TEFL=teaching English as a foreign language
UFO=unidentified flying object
UPC=Universal Product Code
URL=Univeral Resource Locator
USCG=U.S. Coast Guard
USS=United States ship
UTC=coordinated universal time
var.=variant
VCR=videocassette recorder
viz=*videlicet* (namely)
VP=vice president
W=watt(s)
WHO=World Health Organization
WMD=weapons of mass destruction
WPM=words per minute
YMCA=Young Men's Christian Association
YTD=year to date
yuppie=young urban professional
ZIP=zone improvement plan (U.S. Postal Service)

Eponyms

(words named for people)

bobbies—in Great Britain, police officers; after Sir Robert Peel, who organized the London police force in 1850

boycott—to avoid trade or dealings with, as a protest; after Charles C. Boycott, an English land agent in County Mayo, Ireland, ostracized in 1880 for refusing to reduce rents

chauvinist—excessively patriotic; after Nicolas Chauvin, a character in a 19th-cent. play who is devoted to Napoleon

derby—a stiff felt hat with a dome-shaped crown and rather narrow rolled brim; after Edward Stanley, 12th earl of Derby, who in 1780 founded the Derby horse race, to which these hats are worn

derrick—a type of crane consisting of a boom connected to the base of an upright mast; after Derrick, an early 17th cent. English hangman who used a gallows that operated via cables and pulleys

draconian—harsh or severe; after Draco, a statesman who codified the laws in Athens in 621 BCE

galvanize—to shock with an electric current, to energize or spur; from Luigi Galvano, Italian physicist who invented a process to cover metals with electrons for protection against rust

gerrymander—to draw an election district in such a way as to favor a political party; after Elbridge Gerry, who created (1812) just such an election district (shaped like a salamander) during his governorship of Massachusetts

guillotine—a machine for beheading; after Joseph Guillotin, a French physician who proposed its use in 1789 as more humane than hanging

leotard—a close-fitting garment, worn by dancers, acrobats, and the like; after Julius Leotard, a 19th-cent. French aerial gymnast

Luddite—one who opposes new technology; from Ned Ludd, leader of a group of textile workers in England who destroyed machinery in the early 1800s

maudlin—excessively sentimental, from Mary Magdalene, a Scriptural figure whose portraits often showed her weeping

mesmerize—to hypnotize or enthrall; from Franz Mesmer, an 18th-cent. German physicist who developed therapy using magnetism that led to hypnosis

milquetoast—a timid, unassertive person; after Caspar Milquetoast, comic strip character created by Harold Tucker Webster in 1924

philippic—a tirade or heated denunciation; from 4th cent. BCE Greek orator Demosthenes' speeches against the rise of Philip II of Macedonia

pollyanna—an overly optimistic person; based on the title character in a novel (1913) by American writer Eleanor Porter

sandwich—2 or more slices of bread with a filling in between; after John Montagu, 4th earl of Sandwich (1718-92), who supposedly ate these at the gaming table

shrapnel—originally, a projectile with lead balls designed to inflict maximum damage in explosions, later pieces of shell casings; from Henry Shrapnel (1761-1842), British artillery officer who designed the projectile

silhouette—an outline image; from Étienne de Silhouette (1709-67), a stingy French finance minister

Contranyms

Words that can have opposite meanings depending on their usage are known as **contranyms** or self-antonyms. They are also called Janus words, after the Roman god of doors and gates, who is often depicted with two faces looking in opposite directions. Contranyms are produced in various ways: For example, two words with different origins and contradictory meanings might acquire the same spelling, or a word's archaic meaning might be the opposite of the word's meaning in current usage. Here are a few examples of contranyms:

cleave:	to split apart	*or*	to stick together
clip:	to cut	*or*	to fasten
sanction:	approval	*or*	punishment
screen:	to shield	*or*	to present
trim:	to cut away	*or*	to ornament

Contranyms may also have similar sounds but different spellings (e.g., *raise* and *raze*).

IT'S A FACT: The top ten U.S. baby names in 2005, according to the Social Security Administration, were **boys:** Jacob, Michael, Joshua, Matthew, Ethan, Andrew, Daniel, Anthony, Christopher, Joseph; **girls:** Emily, Emma, Madison, Abigail, Olivia, Isabella, Hannah, Samantha, Ava, Ashley. Anthony and Ava joined the top 10, displacing William and Elizabeth.

Top 10 First Names of Americans by Decade of Birth

Source: Compiled by Dr. Cleveland Kent Evans, Bellevue Univ., Bellevue, NE, based on U.S. Social Security Admin. records

BOYS

1880-1889 . . . . .John, William, Charles, George, James, Frank, Joseph, Harry, Henry, Edward
1890-1899 . . . . .John, William, George, James, Charles, Joseph, Frank, Robert, Harry, Henry
1900-1909 . . . . .John, William, James, George, Joseph, Charles, Robert, Frank, Edward, Henry
1910-1919 . . . . .John, William, James, Robert, Joseph, Charles, George, Edward, Frank, Walter
1920-1929 . . . . .John, Robert, James, William, Charles, George, Joseph, Richard, Edward, Donald
1930-1939 . . . . .Robert, James, John, William, Richard, Charles, Donald, George, Thomas, Joseph
1940-1949 . . . . .James, Robert, John, William, Richard, David, Charles, Thomas, Michael, Ronald
1950-1959 . . . . .Michael, James, Robert, John, David, William, Steven, Richard, Thomas, Mark
1960-1969 . . . . .Michael, John, David, James, Robert, Mark, Steven, William, Jeffrey, Richard
1970-1979 . . . . .Michael, Christopher, Jason, David, James, John, Brian, Robert, Steven, William
1980-1989 . . . . .Michael, Christopher, Matthew, Joshua, David, Daniel, James, John, Robert, Brian
1990-1999 . . . . .Michael, Christopher, Matthew, Joshua, Nicholas, Jacob, Andrew, Daniel, Brandon, Tyler

GIRLS

1880-1889 . . . . .Mary, Anna, Elizabeth, Catherine, Margaret, Emma, Bertha, Minnie, Florence, Clara
1890-1899 . . . . .Mary, Anna, Margaret, Helen, Catherine, Elizabeth, Florence, Ruth, Rose, Ethel
1900-1909 . . . . .Mary, Helen, Margaret, Anna, Ruth, Catherine, Elizabeth, Dorothy, Marie, Mildred
1910-1919 . . . . .Mary, Helen, Dorothy, Margaret, Ruth, Catherine, Mildred, Anna, Elizabeth, Frances
1920-1929 . . . . .Mary, Dorothy, Betty, Helen, Margaret, Ruth, Virginia, Catherine, Doris, Frances
1930-1939 . . . . .Mary, Betty, Barbara, Shirley, Patricia, Dorothy, Joan, Margaret, Carol, Nancy
1940-1949 . . . . .Mary, Linda, Barbara, Patricia, Carol, Sandra, Nancy, Sharon, Judith, Susan
1950-1959 . . . . .Deborah, Mary, Linda, Patricia, Susan, Barbara, Karen, Nancy, Donna, Catherine
1960-1969 . . . . .Lisa, Deborah, Mary, Karen, Michelle, Susan, Kimberly, Lori, Teresa, Linda
1970-1979 . . . . .Jennifer, Michelle, Amy, Melissa, Kimberly, Lisa, Angela, Heather, Kelly, Sarah
1980-1989 . . . . .Jessica, Jennifer, Ashley, Sarah, Amanda, Stephanie, Nicole, Melissa, Katherine, Megan
1990-1999 . . . . .Ashley, Jessica, Sarah, Brittany, Emily, Kaitlyn, Samantha, Megan, Brianna, Katherine

Origins of Popular American Given Names

Source: Dr. Cleveland Kent Evans, Bellevue University, Bellevue, NE

Boys

Andrew: Gr. *andreios*, "man, manly"
Anthony: Roman *Antonius*, pos. from Gr. *anthos*, "flower"
Brandon: Eng. place name, "gorse-covered hill"
Brian: Irish, perhaps Celtic *Brigonos*, "high, noble"
Charles: Ger. *ceorl*, "free man"
Christopher: Gr. *Khristophoros*, "bearing Christ [in one's heart]"
Daniel: Heb. "God is my judge"
David: Heb. *Dodavehu*, perhaps "darling"
Donald: Scots Gaelic *Domhnall*, "world rule"
Edward: Old Eng. *Eadweard*, "wealth-guard"

Ethan: Heb. "solid," "firm"
Frank: Ger. "Frenchman"
George: Gr. *georgos*, "soil tiller, farmer"
Harry: Middle Eng. form of Henry
Henry: Ger. *Haimric*, "home-power"
Jacob: Heb. *Yaakov*, "God protects" or "supplanter"
James: Late Lat. *Iacomus*, form of Jacob
Jason: Gr. *Iason*, "healer"
Jeffrey: Norman Fr., from Ger. *Gaufrid*, "land-peace," or *Gisfrid*, "pledge-peace"
John: Heb. *Yohanan*, "God is gracious"
Joseph: Heb. *Yosef*, "[God] shall add"
Joshua: Heb. *Yoshua*, "God saves"
Mark: Lat. *Marcus*, perhaps from Mars, the war god

Matthew: Heb. *Mattathia*, "gift of God"
Michael: Heb. "Who could ever be like God?"
Nicholas: Gr. *Nikolaos*, "victory-people"
Patrick: Lat. *Patricius*, "belonging to the noble class"
Richard: Ger. "power-hardy"
Robert: Ger. *Hrodberht*, "fame-bright"
Sean: Gaelic form of John
Steven: Gr. *stephanos*, "crown, garland"
Theodore: Gr. *Theodoros,* "gift of God"
Thomas: Aramaic "twin"
Tyler: Old Eng. *tigeler*, "tile layer"
Walter: Ger. *Waldheri*, "rule-army"
William: Ger. *Wilhelm*, "will-helmet"

Girls

Abigail: Heb. "My father is joy"
Alexis: Gr. "helper" or "defender"
Amanda: 17th-cent. invention from Lat., "lovable"
Amy: Old Fr. *Amee*, "beloved"
Angela: Gr. *angelos*, "messenger [of God]"
Ann (Eng. form), **Anne** (Eng., Fr., Ger. form) of Hannah
Anna: Lat. and Gr. form of Hannah
Ashley: Eng. place name, "ash grove"
Ava: prob. modern form of Eva, Lat. form of Heb. Eve, "to breathe"
Barbara: Gr. *barbarus*, "foreign"
Bertha: Ger. *behrt*, "bright"
Betty 18th-cent. pet form of Elizabeth
Brianna: modern fem. form of Brian
Brittany: place name, Fr. province settled by Britons
Carol: form of Charles
Clara: Lat. *clarus*, "famous"
Deborah: Heb. "bee"
Donna: Ital. "lady"
Doris: Gr. "woman of the Dorian tribe," name of a sea nymph
Dorothy: Gr. *Dorothea*, "gift of God"
Elizabeth: Heb. *Elisheba*, perhaps "God is my oath" or "God is good fortune"
Emily: Roman *Aemilia*, possibly from Lat. *aemulus*, "rival"
Emma: Ger. *ermen*, "whole, entire"
Ethel: Old Eng. *aethel*, "noble"
Florence: Lat. *florens*, "flourishing"

Frances: fem. form of Francis, "a Frenchman"
Haley: Eng. place name, "hay clearing"
Hannah: Heb. "He has favored me"
Heather: Middle Eng. *hathir*, "heather"
Helen: Gr. *Helene*, possibly "sunbeam"
Isabella, Isabel: Lat., Sp. variant of Elizabeth
Jennifer: Cornish form of Welsh *Gwenhwyfar*, "fair-smooth"
Jessica: Shakesp. invention, prob. fem. form of Jesse, Heb. "God exists"
Joan: Middle Eng. fem. form of John
Judith: Heb. "Jewish woman"
Kaitlyn: American spelling of Caitlin, the Irish form of Katherine
Karen: Danish form of Katherine
Katherine: from *Aikaterine*, Egyptian name later modified to resemble Gr. *katharos*, "pure"
Kelly: Irish Gaelic *Ceallagh*, perhaps "churchgoer" or "bright-headed"
Kimberly: Eng. place name, "Cyneburgh's clearing"
Linda: Sp. "pretty" or Ger. "tender"
Lisa: pet form of Elizabeth
Lori: pet form of either Lorraine (Fr. "land of Lothar's people") or Laura (Lat. "laurel")
Madison: Middle Eng. surname, "son of Madeline or Maud"
Margaret: Gr. *margaron*, "pearl"
Maria: Lat. form of Mary
Marie: Fr. form of Mary

Mary: Eng. form of Heb. *Maryam*, perhaps "seeress" or "wished-for child"
Megan: Welsh form of Margaret
Melissa: Gr. "bee"
Michelle: Fr. fem. form of Michael
Mildred: Old Eng. *Mildthryth*, "mild-strength"
Minnie: Pet form of Wilhelmina, fem. form of William
Nancy: medieval Eng. pet form of Agnes, Gr. *hagnos*, "holy"; later also pet form for Ann
Nicole: Fr. fem. form of Nicholas
Olivia: Lat. *oliva*, "olive tree"
Patricia: Lat. fem. form of Patrick
Rose: Ger. *hros*, "horse," or Lat. *rosa*, "rose"
Ruth: Heb., perhaps "companion"
Samantha: colonial American invention, probably combining Sam from Samuel (Heb. "name of God") with -antha from Gr. *anthos*, "flower"
Sandra: short form of Alessandra, Ital. fem. of Alexander, Gr. "defend-man"
Sarah: Heb. "princess"
Sharon: Biblical place name, Heb. "plain"
Shirley: Eng. place name, "bright clearing" or "shire meadow"
Stephanie: Fr. fem. form of Steven
Susan: Eng. form of Heb. *Shoshana*, "lily"
Teresa: Spanish, perhaps "woman from Therasia"
Virginia: Lat. "virgin-like"

30 Most Common Last Names in the U.S. Population

Source: 1990 Census, U.S. Census Bureau, U.S. Dept. of Commerce

Rank	Name	Frequency[1] (%)	Rank	Name	Frequency[1] (%)	Rank	Name	Frequency[1] (%)
1.	Smith	1.006	11.	Anderson	0.311	21.	Clark	0.231
2.	Johnson	0.810	12.	Thomas	0.311	22.	Rodriguez	0.229
3.	Williams	0.699	13.	Jackson	0.310	23.	Lewis	0.226
4.	Jones	0.621	14.	White	0.279	24.	Lee	0.220
5.	Brown	0.621	15.	Harris	0.275	25.	Walker	0.219
6.	Davis	0.480	16.	Martin	0.273	26.	Hall	0.200
7.	Miller	0.424	17.	Thompson	0.269	27.	Allen	0.199
8.	Wilson	0.339	18.	Garcia	0.254	28.	Young	0.193
9.	Moore	0.312	19.	Martinez	0.234	29.	Hernandez	0.192
10.	Taylor	0.311	20.	Robinson	0.233	30.	King	0.190

(1) Percent of people in the population sample with the name shown.

Pen Names

Shalom Aleichem	Solomon J. Rabinowitz
Woody Allen	Allen Stewart Konigsberg
Maya Angelou	Marguerite Johnson
Nellie Bly	Elizabeth Jane Cochrane Seaman
John le Carré	David John Moore Cornwell
Lewis Carroll	Charles Lutwidge Dodgson
Colette	Sidonie Gabrielle Colette
Amanda Cross	Carolyn Heilbrun
Isak Dinesen	Karen Blixen
George Eliot	Mary Ann or Marian Evans
Maksim Gorky	Aleksey Maksimovich Peshkov
O. Henry	William Sydney Porter
James Herriot	James Alfred Wight
P. D. James	Phyllis Dorothy James White
Ann Landers	Esther Pauline Lederer
André Maurois	Émile Herzog
Molière	Jean Baptiste Poquelin
Toni Morrison	Chloe Anthony Wofford
Pablo Neruda	Neftalí Ricardo Reyes Basoalto
Frank O'Connor	Michael Donovan
George Orwell	Eric Arthur Blair
Ellery Queen	Frederic Dannay and Manfred B. Lee
Mary Renault	Mary Challans
Anne Rice	Howard Allen O'Brien
Saki	Hector Hugh Munro
George Sand	Amandine Lucie Aurore Dupin
Ouida	Marie Louise de la Ramée
Dr. Seuss	Theodor Seuss Geisel
Lemony Snicket	Daniel Handler
Stendhal	Marie Henri Beyle
Mark Twain	Samuel Clemens
Voltaire	François Marie Arouet

Commonly Misspelled English Words

accidentally
accommodate
accumulate
acknowledgment
acquainted
acquire
all right
already
amateur
appearance
appropriate
assimilate
bellwether
bureau
business
calendar
canceled
Caribbean
cemetery
changeable

Cincinnati
collectible
commitment
committee
connoisseur
conscience
conscientious
conscious
convenience
corduroy
deceive
defendant
definitely
desirable
desperate
deterrent
eligible
eliminate
embarrass
environment

existence
fascinating
February
fluorine
forty
gauge
government
grammar
grateful
harass
humorous
incidentally
independent
indispensable
inoculate
irresistible
jewelry
judgment
laboratory
liaison

leisure
library
license
lieutenant
lightning
liquefy
maintenance
marriage
medieval
millennium
miniature
miscellaneous
Mississippi
misspelled
mnemonic
mysterious
necessary
noticeable
occasionally
occurrence

omitted
opportunity
optimistic
parallel
patience
performance
permanent
permissible
perseverance
personnel
possess
prescient
privilege
propaganda
questionnaire
receipt
receive
recommend
rhythm
ridiculous

sacrilegious
sergeant
separate
seize
sheriff
sincerely
stubbornness
supersede
temperament
temperature
transferred
truly
twelfth
vacillate
vaccinate
vacuum
Wednesday
weird
wholly

American Manual Alphabet

In the American Manual Alphabet, each letter of the alphabet is represented by a position of the fingers. This system was originally developed in France by Charles Michel de l'Epee in the 1700s. Laurent Clerc and Thomas Gallaudet further refined it into the American Manual Alphabet.

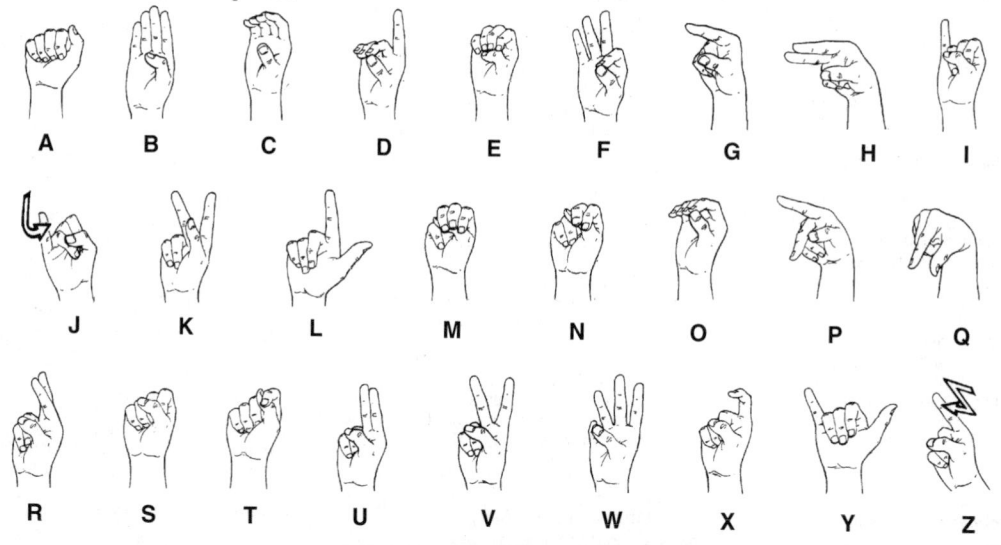

The Principal Languages of the World

Source: Database of *Ethnologue: Languages of the World*, 15th Edition, www.ethnologue.com. Raymond G. Gordon, Editor. Copyright © 2005, SIL International. Used by permission.

The following tables count only "first language" speakers. All figures are estimates.

Languages Spoken by the Most People

Speakers	(millions)	Speakers	(millions)	Speakers	(millions)
Chinese, Mandarin	873	Bengali	171	Javanese	75
Spanish	322	Russian	145	Telugu	69
English	309	Japanese	122	Marathi	68
Hindi	180	German, standard	95	Vietnamese	67
Portuguese	177	Chinese, Wu	77	Korean	67

Languages Spoken by at Least 2 Million People

A "Hub" country is the country of origin, not necessarily the country where the most speakers reside (e.g., Portugal is the "hub" country of Portuguese, although more Portuguese speakers live in Brazil). Number of speakers listed is worldwide total for each language.

Hub	Language	Countries	Speakers (millions)	Hub	Language	Countries	Speakers (millions)
Afghanistan	Farsi, Eastern	3	7	Georgia	Georgian	13	4
	Hazaragi	4	2	Germany	German, standard	41	95
Albania	Albanian, Tosk	9	2		Saxon, Upper	1	2
Algeria	Arabic, Algerian spoken	5	21	Ghana	Akan	1	8
	Kabyle	3	3		Éwé	2	3
Angola	Mbundu	1	3	Greece	Greek	35	12
	Umbundu	2	4	Guinea	Maninkakan, Eastern	3	2
Armenia	Armenian	30	6		Pular	6	2
Austria	Bavarian	5	7	Haiti	Haitian Creole French	9	7
Azerbaijan	Azerbaijani, North	9	7	Hungary	Hungarian	11	13
Bangladesh	Bengali	9	171	India	Assamese	3	15
	Chittagonian	2	14		Awadhi	2	20
	Sylheti	10	10		Bagri	2	2
Belarus	Belarusan	16	10		Bhojpuri	3	26
Bolivia	Aymara, Central	4	2		Chhattisgarhi	1	11
	Quechua, South Bolivian	2	3		Deccan	1	10
Bosnia and Herzegovina	Bosnian	1	4		Dhundari	1	9
					Dogri	1	2
Botswana	Tswana	4	4		Garhwali	1	2
Bulgaria	Bulgarian	11	8		Gujarati	17	46
Burkina Faso	Mòoré	6	5		Haryanvi	1	13
Burundi	Rundi	4	4		Hindi	17	180
Cambodia	Khmer, Central	7	7		Kanauji	1	6
Cameroon	Beti	1	2		Kannada	1	35
China	Bouyei	4	2		Kashmiri	3	4
	Chinese, Gan	1	20		Konkani	1	4
	Chinese, Hakka	16	29		Konkani, Goanese	3	3
	Chinese, Jinyu	1	45		Kumauni	2	2
	Chinese, Mandarin	16	873		Kurux	2	2
	Chinese, Min Bei	2	10		Lambadi	1	2
	Chinese, Min Dong	6	9		Magahi	1	13
	Chinese, Min Nan	9	46		Maithili	2	24
	Chinese, Pu-Xian	3	2		Malayalam	9	35
	Chinese, Wu	1	77		Marathi	3	68
	Chinese, Xiang	1	36		Marwari	3	13
	Chinese, Yue	20	54		Mewati	1	5
	Mongolian, Peripheral	2	3		Mundari	3	2
	Uyghur	16	7		Oriya	2	31
	Zhuang, Northern	1	10		Panjabi, Eastern	11	27
	Zhuang, Southern	1	4		Rajbanshi	3	2
Côte d'Ivoire	Baoulé	1	2		Sadri	2	2
Croatia	Croatian	8	6		Santali	4	6
Czech Republic	Czech	10	11		Shekhawati	1	3
Dem. Rep. of Congo	Kituba	1	4		Tamil	15	66
	Lingala	3	2		Telugu	7	69
	Luba-Kasai	1	6	Indonesia	Aceh	1	3
Denmark	Danish	8	5		Bali	1	3
Egypt	Arabic, Egyptian spoken	9	46		Banjar	2	3
	Arabic, Sa'idi spoken	1	18		Batak Toba	1	2
Ethiopia	Amharic	4	17		Betawi	1	3
	Oromo, Borana-Arsi-Guji	3	3		Bugis	2	3
	Oromo, Eastern	1	4		Indonesian	6	23
	Oromo, West Central	2	8		Javanese	4	75
	Tigrigna	4	5		Madura	2	13
Finland	Finnish	7	5		Malay, Balinese	1	3
France	French	56	64		Minangkabau	1	6
					Sasak	1	2
					Sunda	1	27

Hub	Language	Countries	Speakers (millions)
Iran	Azerbaijani, South	8	24
	Farsi, Western	26	24
	Gilaki	1	3
	Kurdish, Southern	2	5
	Mazanderani	1	3
Iraq	Arabic, Gulf spoken	9	2
	Arabic, Mesopotamian spoken	5	15
	Arabic, North Mesopotamian spoken	4	6
	Kurdish, Central	2	3
Israel	Hebrew	8	5
	Yiddish, Eastern	21	3
Italy	Emiliano-Romagnolo	2	2
	Italian	30	61
	Lombard	3	9
	Napoletano-Calabrese	1	7
	Piemontese	3	3
	Sicilian	1	4
	Venetian	3	2
Jamaica	Jamaican Creole English	7	3
Japan	Japanese	25	122
Jordan	Arabic, South Levantine spoken	8	6
Kazakhstan	Kazakh	13	8
Kenya	Gikuyu	1	5
	Kalenjin	1	2
	Kamba	1	2
	Luo	2	3
	Luyia	2	3
Korea, South	Korean	31	67
Kyrgyzstan	Kirghiz	7	3
Laos	Lao	7	3
Lesotho	Sotho, Southern	3	4
Libya	Arabic, Libyan spoken	3	4
Lithuania	Lithuanian	19	3
Madagascar	Malagasy, Plateau	3	5
Malawi	Nyanja	5	5
Malaysia	Malay	8	17
Mali	Bamanankan	7	2
Mauritania	Hassaniyya	6	2
Mongolia	Mongolian, Halh	4	2
Morocco	Arabic, Moroccan spoken	8	19
	Tachelhit	3	3
	Tamazight, Central Atlas	3	3
Mozambique	Makhuwa	1	2
	Ndau	2	2
Myanmar	Arakanese	3	2
	Burmese	5	32
	Shan	3	2
Nepal	Nepali	4	17
Netherlands	Dutch	8	17
Niger	Zarma	4	2
Nigeria	Hausa	13	24
	Igbo	1	18
	Kanuri, Central	6	3
	Tiv	2	2
	Yoruba	5	19
Pakistan	Balochi, Southern	4	3
	Brahui	4	2
	Panjabi, Western	7	60
	Pashto, Central	1	7
	Pashto, Northern	5	9
	Pashto, Southern	6	2
	Seraiki	3	13
	Sindhi	7	19
	Urdu	21	60
Paraguay	Guaraní, Paraguayan	2	4
Philippines	Bicolano, Central	1	2
	Cebuano	2	20
	Hiligaynon	2	7
	Ilocano	2	8
	Tagalog	7	15
	Waray-Waray	1	2
Poland	Polish	21	42
Portugal	Portuguese	33	177
Romania	Romanian	17	23
Russia	Russian	31	145
Rwanda	Rwanda	4	7
Saudi Arabia	Arabic, Hijazi spoken	2	6
	Arabic, Najdi spoken	7	9
Senegal	Pulaar	6	3
	Wolof	6	3
Serbia and Montenegro*	Albanian, Gheg	7	2
	Serbian	16	11
Slovakia	Slovak	8	5
Somalia	Somali	12	12
South Africa	Afrikaans	10	5
	Sotho, Northern	2	3
	Tsonga	4	3
	Xhosa	3	7
	Zulu	6	9
Spain	Catalan-Valencian-Balear	18	6
	Galician	2	3
	Spanish	43	322
Sri Lanka	Sinhala	6	13
Sudan	Arabic, Sudanese spoken	5	18
Sweden	Swedish	7	8
Switzerland	Schwyzerdütsch	5	6
Syria	Arabic, North Levantine spoken	15	14
Tajikistan	Tajiki	8	4
Tanzania	Sukuma	1	5
Thailand	Malay, Pattani	1	3
	Thai	4	20
	Thai, Northeastern	1	15
	Thai, Northern	2	6
	Thai, Southern	1	5
Tunisia	Arabic, Tunisian spoken	4	9
Turkey	Kurdish, Northern	31	9
	Turkish	35	50
Turkmenistan	Turkmen	13	6
Uganda	Ganda	1	3
Ukraine	Ukrainian	25	39
United Kingdom	English	107	309
Uzbekistan	Uzbek, Northern	12	18
Vietnam	Vietnamese	20	67
Yemen	Arabic, Sanaani spoken	1	7
	Arabic, Ta'izzi-Adeni spoken	5	6
Zambia	Bemba	4	2
Zimbabwe	Shona	4	10

*As of 2006, Montenegro is an independent nation.

World Almanac Quick Quiz

Which of the following names consistently made the list of top 10 first names of American boys for every decade from the 1880s through the 1980s?

(a) Edward   (b) James

(c) Charles   (d) William

For the answer look in this chapter, or see page 1008.

BUILDINGS, BRIDGES, AND TUNNELS

Tallest Buildings in the World

Source: Council on Tall Buildings and Urban Habitat, Illinois Inst. of Technology, www.ctbuh.com; Emporis.com, www.emporis.com
Structures under construction as of mid-2006 and due for completion by the end of 2007 are denoted by asterisk *. Year in parentheses is date of completion or projected completion.

Building	Ht. (ft.)	Stories
Taipei 101, Taipei, Taiwan (2004)	1,667	101
Petronas Tower I, Kuala Lumpur, Malaysia (1998)	1,483	88
Petronas Tower II, Kuala Lumpur, Malaysia (1998)	1,483	88
Sears Tower, Chicago, IL, U.S. (1974)	1,451	110
Jin Mao Bldg., Shanghai, China (1999)	1,381	88
Two International Finance Centre, Hong Kong, China (2003)	1,362	88
CITIC Plaza, Guangzhou, China (1996)	1,283	80
Shun Hing Square, Shenzhen, China (1996)	1,260	69
Empire State Building, New York, NY, U.S. (1931)	1,250	102
Central Plaza, Hong Kong, China (1992)	1,227	78
Bank of China, Hong Kong, China (1989)	1,205	70
Emirates Tower One, Dubai, UAE (1999)	1,165	54
Tuntex Sky Tower, Kaohsiung, China (1997)	1,140	85
Aon Centre, Chicago, IL, U.S. (1973)	1,136	83
The Center, Hong Kong, China (1998)	1,135	73
John Hancock Center, Chicago, IL, U.S. (1969)	1,127	100
*Shimao International Plaza, Shanghai, China (2006)	1,093	60
*Minsheng Bank Building, Wuhan, China (2006)	1,087	68
Ryugyong Hotel, Pyongyang, North Korea (1995)	1,083	105
Q1, Gold Coast, Australia (2005)	1,058	78
Burj al Arab Hotel, Dubai, UAE (1999)	1,053	60
*Nina Tower I, Hong Kong, China (2006)	1,046	80
Chrysler Building, New York, NY, U.S. (1930)	1,046	77
Bank of America Plaza, Atlanta, GA, U.S. (1993)	1,039	55
U.S. Bank Tower, Los Angeles, CA, U.S. (1990)	1,018	73
Menara Telekom Headquarters, Kuala Lumpur, Malaysia (1999)	1,017	55

Building	Ht. (ft.)	Stories
Emirates Tower Two, Dubai, UAE (2000)	1,014	56
AT&T Corporate Center, Chicago, IL, U.S. (1989)	1,007	60
JP Morgan Chase Tower, Houston, TX, U.S. (1982)	1,002	75
Baiyoke Tower II, Bangkok, Thailand (1997)	997	85
Two Prudential Plaza, Chicago, IL, U.S. (1990)	995	64
Wells Fargo Plaza, Houston, TX, U.S. (1983)	992	71
Kingdom Centre, Riyadh, Saudi Arabia (2002)	992	41
First Canadian Place, Toronto, Canada (1975)	978	72
*Eureka Tower, Melbourne, Australia (2006)	975	91
Landmark Tower, Yokohama, Japan (1993)	971	70
311 South Wacker Drive, Chicago, IL, U.S. (1990)	961	65
SEG Plaza, Shenzhen, China (2000)	957	71
American International Building, New York, NY, U.S. (1932)	952	67
Key Tower, Cleveland, OH, U.S. (1991)	947	57
Plaza 66, Shanghai, China (2001)	945	66
One Liberty Place, Philadelphia, PA, U.S. (1987)	945	61
Sunjoy Tomorrow Square, Shanghai, China (2003)	934	55
Columbia Center, Seattle, WA, U.S. (1984)	933	76
Cheung Kong Centre, Hong Kong, China (1999)	929	63
Chongqing World Trade Center, Chongqing, China (2005)	929	60
The Trump Building, New York, NY, U.S. (1930)	927	71
Bank of America Plaza, Dallas, TX, U.S. (1985)	921	72
United Overseas Bank Plaza, Singapore (1992)	919	66
Republic Plaza, Singapore (1995)	919	66
Overseas Union Bank Centre, Singapore (1986)	919	63
*Bright Start Tower, Dubai, UAE (2007)	919	59

World's 10 Tallest Free-Standing Towers

Structures under construction as of mid-2006 are denoted by asterisk *. Year is date of completion or projected completion.

Name	City	Country	Ht. (ft.)	Year
*Guangzhou TV Tower	Guangzhou	China	2,001	2009
*Jakarta Tower	Jakarta	Indonesia	1,831	2009
CN Tower	Toronto	Canada	1,815	1976
Ostankino Tower	Moscow	Russia	1,772	1967
*Xi'an Broadcasting, Telephone and TV Tower	Xi'an	China	1,542	NA
Oriental Pearl TV Tower	Shanghai	China	1,535	1995
*Milad Tower	Tehran	Iran	1,427	2007
Menara Kuala Lumpur	Kuala Lumpur	Malaysia	1,379	1996
Tianjin TV & Radio Tower	Tianjin	China	1,362	1991
Central Radio & TV Tower	Beijing	China	1,268	1992

Tall Buildings in Selected North American Cities

Source: Marshall Gerometta and Rick Bronson, Emporis.com, www.emporis.com;
Council on Tall Buildings and Urban Habitat, Illinois Inst. of Technology, www.ctbuh.org

Lists include freestanding towers and other structures that do not have stories and are not technically considered buildings. Structures still under construction as of mid-2006 and due for completion by the end of 2007 are denoted by asterisk *. Year in parentheses is date of completion or projected completion. Height is generally measured from sidewalk to roof, including penthouse and tower if enclosed as integral part of structure; stories generally counted from street level. NA = not available or not applicable.

Atlanta, GA

Building	Ht. (ft.)	Stories
Bank of America Plaza (incl. spire), 600 Peachtree St. NE (1992)	1,039	55
SunTrust Plaza, 303 Peachtree St. NE (1992)[1]	867	60
One Atlantic Center, 1201 W. Peachtree St. (1987)	820	50
191 Peachtree Tower (1991)	770	50
Westin Peachtree Plaza, 210 Peachtree St. NW (1976)[2]	723	73
Georgia Pacific Tower, 133 Peachtree St. NE (1981)	697	51
Promenade II, 1230 Peachtree St. NE (1989)	691	40
Bellsouth, 675 W. Peachtree St. (1980)	677	47
1180 Peachtree (2006)	672	41
*Sovereign, 3344 Peachtree (2007)	660	48
GLG Grand/Four Seasons Hotel, 75 14th St. NE (1992)	609	53
Wachovia Bank of Georgia, 2 Peachtree St. NW (1967)	556	44
Marriott Marquis, 265 Peachtree Center Ave. NE (1985)	554	52
Park Avenue Condominiums., 750 Park Ave. NE (2000)	486	42
*Terminus, 3280 Peachtree Rd. NE, Buckhead (2007)	485	27
Paramount at Buckhead, 3445 Stratford Rd. NE (2004)	478	40
Centennial Tower, 101 Marietta St. (1976)	459	36
Equitable Bldg., 100 Peachtree St. NW (1967)	453	34
Spire, 860 Peachtree St. (2006)	453	28
Buckhead Grand, 3338 Peachtree Rd. NE (2004)	451	38
One Park Tower, 34 Peachtree St. (1961)	439	32
1100 Peachtree St. NE (1990)	428	28
Atlanta Plaza I, 950 E. Paces Ferry Rd. (1986)	425	32
Park Place, 2660 Peachtree NW (1986)	420	40
2828 Peachtree Luxury Condominiums (2002)	420	33

(1) 902 ft. with antenna. (2) 883 ft. with antenna.

Baltimore, MD

Building	Ht. (ft.)	Stories
Legg Mason Bldg., 100 Light St. (1973)	529	40
Bank of America, 10 Light St. (1924)	509	37
William Donald Schaefer Tower, 6 St. Paul Pl. (1992)	493	29
Commerce Place, 1 South St. (1992)	454	31
Marriott Baltimore Inner Harbor East, 700 Aliceanna St. (2001)	430	32
100 E. Pratt St. (1992)	418	28
World Trade Center, 401 E. Pratt St. (1977)	405	32

Boston, MA

Building	Ht. (ft.)	Stories
John Hancock Tower, 200 Clarendon St. (1976)	790	62
Prudential Tower, 800 Boylston St. (1964)[1]	750	52
Federal Reserve Bldg., 600 Atlantic Ave. (1978)	604	32
Boston Company Bldg., 1 Boston Place (1970)	601	41
One International Place, 100 Oliver St. (1987)	600	46
First National Bank of Boston, 100 Federal St. (1971)	591	37
One Financial Center, 10 Dewey Square (1984)	590	46
111 Huntington Ave. (2002)	564	36
Two International Place (1993)	538	35
One Post Office Square (1981)	525	40
1 Federal St. (1975)	520	38
Exchange Place, 53 State St. (1984)	510	39
Sixty State St. (1977)	509	38
1 Beacon St. (1972)	507	36
1 Lincoln Place (2003)	503	36
28 State St. (1970)	500	40
Marriott's Custom House, 3 Mckinley Square (1915)	496	32
John Hancock Bldg., 175 Berkeley St. (1949)	495	26
33 Arch St. (2003)	489	31
State St. Bank, 225 Franklin St. (1966)	477	33
Millennium Place 1-Ritz Carlton Hotel (2001)	475	38
125 High St. (1990)	452	30
100 Summer St. (1975)	450	33
Millennium Place 2, 3 Avery St. (2001)	445	36
McCormack Bldg., I Ashburton Pl. (1975)	401	22
Harbor Towers I, 85 E. India (1971)	400	40
Keystone Bldg., 99 High St. (1971)	400	32

(1) 836 ft. with antenna.

Calgary, Alberta

Building	Ht. (ft.)	Stories
Petro Canada Centre West Tower, 150 6th Ave. SW (1984)	705	53
Bankers Hall East Tower, 855 2nd St. SW (1989)	645	50
Bankers Hall West Tower, 888 3rd St. SW (2000)	645	50
Calgary Tower, 101 9th Ave. SW (1967)	626	NA
TransCanada Tower, 450 1st St. SW (2001)	581	38
Canterra Tower, 400 3rd Ave. SW (1988)	580	46
First Canadian Centre, 350 7th Ave. SW (1982)	547	41
Western Canadian Place-N. Tower, 707 6th St. SW (1983)	538	41

Building	Ht. (ft.)	Stories
Canada Trust, Calgary Eatons Centre, 421 7th Ave. SW (1991)	530	40
Scotia Square, 700 2nd St. SW (1976)	509	41
Nexen Bldg., 801 7th Ave. SW (1982)	500	37
Two Bow Valley Square, 205 5th Ave. SW (1974)	468	39
Dome Tower, 333 7th Ave. SW (1976)	463	34
5th & 5th Bldg., 605 5th Ave. SW (1980)	460	35
Shell Centre, 400 4th Ave. SW (1977)	460	34
Home Oil Tower, 324 8th Ave. SW (1976)	449	33
Four Bow Valley Square, 250 6th Ave. SW (1982)	441	37
Fifth Avenue Place East Tower, 425 1st St. SW (1981)	435	35
Fifth Avenue Place West Tower, 237 4th Ave. SW (1981)	435	35
Petro-Canada Tower, E Tower, 111 5th Ave. SW (1983)	427	33
*Calgary Courts Centre-North Tower (2007)	423	24
Western Canadian Place-S. Tower, 801 6th St. SW (1983)	420	32
*arriVa Tower 1, 411 11th Ave. SE (NA)	418	34
Altius Centre, 500 4th Ave. SW (1972)	415	32
EnCana Place, 150 9th Ave. SW (1982)	410	28
Hewlett Packard Tower, 715 5th Ave. SW (1975)	408	31
Alberta Stock Exchange, 300 5th Ave. (1979)	407	33

Charlotte, NC

Building	Ht. (ft.)	Stories
Bank of America Corporate Ctr., 100 N. Tryon St. (1992)	871	60
Hearst Tower, 214 N. Tryon St. (2002)	659	50
*EpiCentre, 210 Trade St. (2007)	601	53
One Wachovia Center, 301 S. College St. (1988)	588	42
Bank of America Plaza, 101 S. Tryon St. (1974)	503	40
Interstate Tower, 121 W. Trade St. (1990)	462	32
IJL Financial Center, 201 N. Tryon St. (1997)	447	30
Three Wachovia Center, 401 S. Tryon St. (2000)	440	29
Two Wachovia Plaza, 301 S. Tryon St. (1971)	433	32
Wachovia Center, 400 S. Tryon St. (1974)	420	32

Chicago, IL

Building	Ht. (ft.)	Stories
Sears Tower, 233 S. Wacker Dr. (1974)[1]	1,451	108
Aon Center, 200 E. Randolph St. (1973)	1,136	83
John Hancock Center, 875 N. Michigan Ave. (1969)[2]	1,127	100
AT&T Corporate Center (incl. spires), 227 W. Monroe St. (1989)	1,007	60
Two Prudential Plaza (incl. spire), 180 N. Stetson Ave. (1990)	995	64
311 S. Wacker Drive (1990)	961	65
900 N. Michigan Ave. (1989)	871	66
Water Tower Place, 845 N. Michigan Ave. (1976)	859	74
Chase Tower, 21 S. Clark St. (1969)	850	60
Park Tower, 800 N. Michigan Ave. (2000)	844	67
3 First National Plaza, 70 W. Madison St. (1981)	767	57
Chicago Title & Trust Center, 161 N. Clark St. (1992)	756	50
*One Museum Park, 1215 S. Prairie Ave. (2007)	734	62
Olympia Centre, 737 N. Michigan Ave. (1986)	725	63
IBM Bldg., 330 N. Wabash Ave. (1973)	695	52
111 S. Wacker Dr. (2005)	681	51
181 W. Madison St. (1990)	680	50
Hyatt Center, 71 S. Wacker (2005)	679	48
One Magnificent Mile, 980 N. Michigan Ave. (1983)	673	57
*340 on the Park, 340 W. Randolph St. (2007)	672	64
R.R. Donnelley Center, 77 W. Wacker Dr. (1992)	668	49
UBS Tower, 1 N. Wacker Dr. (2001)	652	50
Daley Center, 55 W. Washington St. (1965)	648	32
55 E. Erie St. (2004)	647	56
Lake Point Tower, 505 N. Lake Shore Dr. (1968)	645	70
River East Center, 350 E. Illinois St. (2001)	644	58
Grand Plaza I (incl. spire), 540 N. State St. (2003)	641	57
Leo Burnett Bldg., 35 W. Wacker Dr. (1989)	635	46
The Heritage at Millenium Park, 125 N. Wabash Ave. (2005)	631	57
NBC Tower (incl. spire), 455 N. Cityfront Plaza Dr. (1989)	627	37
Millennium Centre, 33 W. Ontario St. (2003)	610	58
Chicago Place, 700 N. Michigan Ave. (1990)	608	49
Board of Trade (incl. statue), 141 W. Jackson Blvd. (1930)	605	44
CNA Plaza, 325 S. Wabash St. (1972)	601	44
Heller International Tower, 500 W. Monroe St. (1992)	600	45
One Madison Plaza, 200 W. Madison St. (1982)	599	44
*The Clare at Water Tower, 55 East Pearson St. (2007)	595	50
1000 Lake Shore Plaza (1964)	590	55
Marina City Apts. 1, 300 N. State St. (1964)	588	61
Marina City Apts. 2, 300 N. State St. (1964)	588	61
Citicorp Center, 500 W. Madison St. (1987)	588	42
Mid Continental Plaza, 55 E. Monroe St. (1972)	582	50
Prudential Bldg., 130 E. Randolph St. (1955)[3]	601	41
Smurfit-Stone Bldg., 150 N. Michigan Ave. (1983)	582	41
North Pier Tower, 474 N. Lake Shore Dr. (1990)	581	61
Chase Center, 131 S. Dearborn St. (2003)	580	39
The Fordham, 25 E. Superior St. (2003)	574	52
190 S. LaSalle St. (1987)	573	40
One S. Dearborn (2005)	571	39
Onterie Center, 446 E. Ontario St. (1986)	570	58
Chicago Temple, 77 W. Washington St. (1924)	568	23
Palmolive Bldg. (incl. beacon), 919 N. Michigan Ave. (1929)	565	37
Huron Plaza Apts., 30 E. Huron St. (1983)	560	56
Boeing International HQ., 100 N. Riverside Plaza (1990)	560	36
The Parkshore, 195 N. Harbor Dr. (1991)	556	56
North Harbor Tower, 175 N. Harbor Dr. (1988)	556	55
Civic Opera Bldg., 20 N. Wacker Dr. (1929)	555	45
Newberry Plaza, 1000 N. State St. (1974)	553	53
Michigan Plaza South, 205 N. Michigan Ave. (1985)	553	46

Building	Ht. (ft.)	Stories
30 N. LaSalle St. (1975)	553	44
Pittsfield Bldg., 55 E. Washington St. (1927)	551	38
Harbor Point, 155 N. Harbor Dr. (1975)	550	54
One S. Wacker Dr. (1982)	550	40
Kluczynski Federal Bldg., 230 S. Dearborn St. (1975)	545	45
Park Millennium, 222 N. Columbus Dr. (2002)	544	57
USG Bldg., 125 S. Franklin St. (1992)	538	35
The Pinnacle, 21 E. Huron St. (2004)	535	48
LaSalle National Bank, 135 S. LaSalle St. (1934)	535	45
Park Place Tower, 655 W. Irving Park Rd. (1971)	531	56
One N. LaSalle St. (1930)	530	48
The Elysees, 111 E. Chestnut St. (1973)	529	56
Morrison Hotel (Demolished) (1925)	526	45
River Plaza, 405 N. Wabash St. (1977)	524	56
35 E. Wacker Drive (1927)	523	40
Unitrin Bldg., 1 E. Wacker Dr. (1962)	522	41
Mather Tower, 75 E. Wacker St. (1928)	521	41
Chicago Mercantile Exchange, 10 S. Wacker Dr. (1987)	520	40
Chicago Mercantile Exchange, 30 S. Wacker Dr. (1983)	520	40
*The Columbian, 1180 S. Michigan Ave. (2007)	517	47
191 N. Wacker Drive (2002)	516	37
401 E. Ontario St. (1990)	515	51
One Financial Place, 440 S. LaSalle St. (1985)	515	39
*The Streeter, 345 E. Ohio St. (2006)	514	50
5415 N. Sheridan Rd. (1973)	513	54
LaSalle-Wacker Bldg., 221 N. LaSalle St. (1930)[4]	512	41
Harris Bank III, 115 S. LaSalle St. (1974)	510	38
321 N. Clark St. (1987)	510	35
400 E. Ohio St. (1982)	505	50
Carbide & Carbon Bldg., 230 N. Michigan Ave. (1929)	503	37
1 Superior Place, 1 W. Superior St. (1999)	502	52
120 N. LaSalle St. (1992)	501	39
Chase Plaza, 10 S. LaSalle St. (1986)	501	37
200 S. Wacker Drive (1981)	500	41
*The Tides, 360 E. South Water St. (2007)	498	51
Ontario Place, 10 E. Ontario St. (1983)	495	49
Xerox Centre, 55 W. Monroe St. (1980)	495	41
*50 E. Chestnut St. (2007)	495	40
1 N. Franklin St. (1992)	494	36
The Bristol, 57 E. Delaware Pl. (2000)	488	42
333 W. Wacker Dr. (1983)	487	36
AT&T, 10 S. Canal St. (1971)	485	28
Plaza 440, 440 N. Wabash Ave. (1991)	480	49
33 N. LaSalle St. (1930)	479	38
Bankers Bldg., 105 W. Adams St. (1927)	476	41
Cook County Admin. Bldg., 69 W. Washington St. (1964)	475	35
Metropolitan Tower, 310 S. Michigan Ave. (1924)	475	37
American Furniture Mart, 680 N. Lake Shore Dr. (1926)	474	29
Intercontinental Hotel, 505 N. Michigan Ave. (1929)	471	42
City Place, 676 N. Michigan Ave. (1990)	470	40
Columbus Plaza, 233 E. Wacker Dr. (1980)	468	47
The Sterling, 345 N. LaSalle St. (2001)	466	50
*The Regatta, Lakeshore East (2006)	466	45
200 N. Dearborn St. (1989)	463	47
Randolph Tower, 188 W. Randolph St. (1929)	463	45
Tribune Tower, 435 N. Michigan Ave. (1925)	463	34
The New York, 3660 N. Lake Shore Drive (1986)	461	49
Presidential Towers, 555 W. Madison St. (1985)	461	49
Presidential Towers, 575 W. Madison St. (1985)	461	49
Presidential Towers, 605 W. Madison St. (1985)	461	49
Presidential Towers, 625 W. Madison St. (1985)	461	49
Chicago Marriott, 540 N. Michigan Ave. (1978)	460	46
Grand Plaza II, 545 Dearborn St. (2003)	458	39
Swissotel, 323 E. Wacker Dr. (1989)	457	45
Equitable Bldg., 401 N. Michigan Ave. (1965)	457	35
*The Grand Kingsbury, 520 N. Kingsbury St. (2007)	456	47
400 N. LaSalle St. (2003)	454	45
*622 N. Lake Shore Dr. (2007)	453	41
ABN-AMRO Plaza I, 550 W. Madison St. (2003)	453	29
Roanoke Bldg., 11 S. LaSalle St. (1925)	452	37
*600 N. Fairbanks (2007)	451	41
Riverbend, 323 N. Canal St. (2002)	451	38
The Shoreham, Lakeshore East (2005)	450	47
Eugenie Terrace on the Park, 1730 N. Clark St. (1987)	450	44
Gateway Center III, 222 S. Riverside Plaza (1971)	450	35

(1) 1,729 ft. with antenna. (2) 1,499 ft. with antenna. (3) 912 ft. with antenna. (4) 543 ft. with antenna.

Cincinnati, OH

Building	Ht. (ft.)	Stories
Carew Tower, 441 Vine St. (1931)[1]	574	49
PNC Tower, 1 W. 4th St. (1913)	495	31
Scripps Center, 312 Walnut St. (1990)	468	36
Fifth Third Center, 511 Walnut St. (1969)	423	32
Chemed Center, 255 5th St. (1990)	410	32
Convergys Center, 600 Vine St. (1984)	402	29

(1) 623 ft. with antenna.

Cleveland, OH

Building	Ht. (ft.)	Stories
Key Tower (incl. spire), 127 Public Square (1991)	947	57
Terminal Tower, 50 Public Square (1930)[1]	708	52
BP America, 200 Public Square (1985)	658	46
100 Erieview, 1801 E. 9th St. (1964)	529	40
One Cleveland Center, 1375 E. 9th St. (1983)	450	31
Fifth Third Center, 600 Superior Ave. (1991)	446	28
Federal Courthouse, 801 W. Superior Ave. (2002)	430	24
Justice Center, 1250 Ontario St. (1976)	420	26
Federal Bldg., 1240 E. 9th St. (1967)	419	32
National City Center, 1900 E. 9th St. (1980)	410	35

(1) 771 ft. with flagpole.

Columbus, OH

Building	Ht. (ft.)	Stories
James A. Rhodes State Office Tower, 30 E. Broad St. (1973)	624	41
Leveque-Lincoln Tower, 50 W. Broad St. (1927)	555	47
William Green Bldg., 30 W. Spring St. (1990)	530	33
Huntington Center, 41 S. High St. (1983)	512	37
Vern Riffe State Office Tower, 77 S. High St. (1988)	503	33
One Nationwide Plaza (1976)	485	40
Franklin County Courthouse, 373 S. High St. (1991)	464	27
AEP Bldg., One Riverside Plaza (1983)	456	31
Borden Bldg., 180 E. Broad St. (1974)	438	34
Three Nationwide Plaza (1989)	408	27

Dallas, TX

Building	Ht. (ft.)	Stories
Bank of America Plaza, 901 Main St. (1985)	921	72
Renaissance Tower (incl. spire), 1201 Elm St. (1974)	886	56
Chase Center, 1717 Main St. (1987)	787	60
JP Morgan Chase Tower, 2200 Ross Ave. (1987)	738	55
Fountain Place, 1445 Ross Ave. (1986)	720	58
Trammel Crow Tower, 2001 Ross Ave. (1984)	686	50
1700 Pacific Ave. (1983)	655	50
Thanksgiving Tower, 1600 Pacific Ave. (1982)	645	50
Energy Plaza, 1601 Bryan St. (1983)	629	49
Elm Place, 1401 Elm St. (1965)	625	52
Republic Center Tower I (incl. spire), 300 N. Ervay (1954)	602	36
Republic Center Tower II, 325 N. St. Paul (1964)	598	50
One SBC Plaza, 208 S. Akard St. (1984)	580	37
One Lincoln Plaza, 500 Akard St. (1984)	579	45
Cityplace Center East, 2711 N. Haskell Ave. (1989)	560	42
Reunion Tower, 300 Reunion Blvd. (1976)	560	NA
Adams Mark Hotel Center Tower, 400 Olive St. (1959)	550	42
Mercantile Bldg., 1700 Main St. (1943)	523	31
2001 Bryan St. (1973)	512	40
Harwood Center, 1999 Bryan St. (1982)	483	36
KMPG Centre, 717 N. Harwood St. (1980)	481	34
San Jacinto Tower, 2121 San Jacinto St. (1982)	456	33
Renaissance Hotel, 2222 Stemmons Fwy. (1983)	451	29
Adam's Mark Hotel North Tower (1980)	448	31
One Dallas Centre, 350 N. Paul St. (1979)	448	30
One Main Place, 1201 Main St. (1968)	445	34
*W Dallas Victory Hotel & Residences, 2425 Houston St. (2006)	439	32
1600 Pacific Bldg. (1964)	434	31
Mosaic I, 1507 Pacific Ave. (1959)	400	33

Denver, CO

Building	Ht. (ft.)	Stories
Republic Plaza, 330 17th St. (1984)	714	56
1801 California Street (1982)	709	52
Wells Fargo Center, 1700 Lincoln Ave. (1983)	698	50
1999 Broadway (1985)	544	43
707 17th St. (1981)	522	42
555 17th St. (1978)	507	40
1670 Broadway (1980)	448	36
Hyatt Regency Denver at the Colorado Convention Center, 650 15th St. (2005)	439	37
17th St. Plaza, 1225 17th St. (1982)	438	32
First Interstate Tower North, 633 17th St. (1974)	434	32
Brooks Towers, 1020 15th St. (1968)	420	42
Denver Place South Tower, 999 18th St. (1981)	416	34
One Tabor Center, 1200 17th St. (1984)	408	32
Johns Manville Plaza, 717 17th St. (1989)	404	29

Detroit, MI

Building	Ht. (ft.)	Stories
Marriott Hotel, Renaissance Center I (1977)[1]	727	70
Comerica Tower, 500 Woodward Ave. (1991)[2]	619	45
Penobscot Bldg., 633 Griswold Ave. (1928)	566	46
Renaissance Center 100 Tower (1976)	508	39
Renaissance Center 200 Tower (1976)	508	39
Renaissance Center 300 Tower (1976)	508	39
Renaissance Center 400 Tower (1976)	508	39
Guardian Bldg., 500 Griswold Ave. (1929)	489	36
Book Tower, 1249 Washington Blvd. (1925)	472	35
150 W. Jefferson Ave. (1988)	470	29
Fisher Bldg., 3011 W. Grand Blvd. (1928)	444	28
Cadillac Tower, 65 Cadillac Sq. (1928)	437	40
David Stott Bldg., 1150 Griswold St. (1928)	436	38
One Woodward Ave. (1962)	430	30
(1) 755 ft. with antenna. (2) 665 ft. with antenna.

Edmonton, Alberta

Building	Ht. (ft.)	Stories
Manulife Place, 10170-101 St. (1983)	480	36
Telus Plaza South, 10020-100 St. (1971)	441	34
Bell Tower, 10104-103 Ave. (1982)	426	34
Commerce Place, 10155-102 St. (1990)	404	27

Fort Worth, TX

Building	Ht. (ft.)	Stories
Burnett Plaza, 801 Cherry St. (1983)	567	40
D.R. Horton Tower, 301 Commerce St. (1984)	547	38
Carter Burgess Plaza, 777 Main St. (1982)	525	40
The Tower, 400 Throckmorton St. (1974)	488	36
Wells Fargo Tower, 201 Main St. (1982)	477	33

Hartford, CT

Building	Ht. (ft.)	Stories
City Place I, 185 Asylum St. (1980)	535	38
Travelers Tower, 26 Grove St. (1919)	527	34
Goodwin Square, 225 Asylum St. (1990)	522	30
*Hartford 21 (2006)	440	36

Honolulu, HI

Building	Ht. (ft.)	Stories
First Hawaiian Center, 999 Bishop St. (1996)	429	30
Nauru Tower, 1330 Ala Moana Blvd. (1991)	418	44
Hokua Tower, 1288 Ala Moana Blvd. (2006)	418	40
Ko'olani (2006)	400	47
One Waterfront Tower-Makai, 425 South King St. (1990)	400	45

Building	Ht. (ft.)	Stories
One Waterfront Tower-Mauka, 415 South King St. (1990)	400	45
Hawaiki Tower, 88 Piikoi St. (1999)	400	45
One Archer Lane, 801 S. King St. (1998)	400	41
Imperial Plaza, 725 Kapiolani Blvd. (1992)	400	40

Houston, TX

Building	Ht. (ft.)	Stories
JPMorganChase Tower, 600 Travis St. (1982)	1,002	75
Wells Fargo Plaza, 1000 Louisiana St. (1983)	992	71
Williams Tower, 2800 Post Oak Blvd. (1983)	901	64
Bank of America Center, 700 Louisiana St. (1983)	780	56
Texaco Heritage Plaza, 1111 Bagby St. (1987)	762	53
1100 Louisiana Building (1980)	748	55
Centerpoint Energy Plaza, 1111 Louisiana St. (1974)	741	47
Continental Airlines Center, 1600 Smith St. (1984)	732	55
Fullright Tower, 1301 McKinney St. (1982)	725	52
One Shell Plaza, 900 Louisiana St. (1970)[1]	714	50
1400 Smith St. (1983)	691	50
3 Allen Center, 333 Clay St. (1980)	685	50
One Houston Center, 1221 McKinney St. (1978)	678	47
First City Tower, 1001 Fannin St. (1984)	662	47
San Felipe Plaza, 5847 San Felipe Blvd. (1984)	625	45
Exxon Bldg., 800 Bell Ave. (1962)	606	44
1500 Louisiana St. (2002)	600	40
America General Center, 2929 Allen Pkwy. (1983)	590	42
Two Houston Center, 909 Fannin St. (1974)	579	40
San Jacinto Column (1939)	570	NA
Marathon Oil Tower, 5555 San Felipe Blvd. (1983)	562	41
Wedge International Tower, 1415 Louisiana St. (1983)	550	44
KBR Tower, 601 Jefferson St. (1973)	550	40
Pennzoil Place I, 700 Milam St. (1976)	523	36
Pennzoil Place II, 700 Milam St. (1976)	523	36
Devon Energy Center, 1200 Smith St. (1978)	521	36
Reliant Energy Plaza, 1000 Main St. (2003)	518	36
Louisiana Plaza, 1201 Louisiana St. (1971)	518	35
The Huntington, 2121 Kirby Dr. (1982)	503	34
El Paso Energy Bldg, 1010 Milam St. (1962)	502	33
*Orion Tower 1, 8 Asbury Pl. (NA)	494	37
5 Greenway Plaza (1973)	465	31
Calpine Center, 717 Texas Ave. (2003)	453	34
One Allen Center, 500 Dallas St. (1974)	452	34
Four Leafs Towers I, 5100 San Felipe Blvd. (1982)	444	40
Four Leafs Towers II, 5110 San Felipe Blvd. (1982)	444	40
9 Greenway Plaza (1978)	441	31
11 Greenway Plaza (1979)	441	31
Phoenix Tower, 3200 Southwest Fwy. (1984)	434	34
*Memorial Hermann Medical Plaza, 6400 Fannin St. (2007)	430	30
Chase Bank Bldg., 712 Main St. (1929)	428	37
The Spires, 2001 Holcomb Blvd. (1984)	426	41
Aon Tower, 4 Oaks Place, 1330 Post Oak Blvd. (1983)	420	30
One City Center, 1001 Main St. (1960)	410	32
Bob Lanier Public Works Bldg., 611 Walker Ave. (1968)	410	27
Neils Esperson Bldg., 802 Travis St. (1927)	410	31
Hyatt Regency, 1200 Louisiana St. (1972)	401	30
The Mercer West Tower, 3288 Sage Rd. (2003)	401	30
(1) 999 ft. with antenna.

Indianapolis, IN

Building	Ht. (ft.)	Stories
Chase Tower (incl. spires), 111 Monument Circle (1990)	811	49
One America Tower, 200 N. Illinois St. (1982)	533	38
One Indiana Square, 200 N. Delaware St. (1970)	504	36
Market Tower, 10 W. Market St. (1988)	421	32
300 N. Meridian Bldg. (1988)	408	28
First Indiana Plaza, 135 N. Pennsylvania St. (1988)	401	29

Jacksonville, FL

Building	Ht. (ft.)	Stories
Bank of America Tower, 50 N. Laura St. (1990)	617	42
Modis Tower, 1 Independent Dr. (1975)	535	37
*The Peninsula at St. John's Center (2006)	437	38
BellSouth Tower, 424 N. Pearl St. (1983)	435	27
Riverplace Tower, 1301 Riverplace Blvd. (1967)	433	28

Jersey City, NJ

Building	Ht. (ft.)	Stories
30 Hudson St. (2004)	781	42
101 Hudson St. (1992)	548	42
Newport Tower, 525 Washington Blvd. (1990)	528	37
Exchange Place Center, 10 Exchange Pl. (1990)	516	32
Harborside Financial Plaza V, 160 Greene St. (2002)	480	34
Marbella Apts., 425 Washington Blvd. (2003)	427	40

Kansas City, MO

Building	Ht. (ft.)	Stories
One Kansas City Place, 1200 Main St. (1988)	632	42
Town Pavilion, 1111 Main St. (1986)	591	38
Hyatt Regency Crown Center, 2345 McGee St. (1980)	504	45
Power & Light Bldg., 1330 Baltimore Ave. (1931)	481	34
Fidelity Bank & Trust Bldg. Apts., 909 Walnut St. (1931)	454	35
City Hall, 414 E. 12th St. (1937)	443	29
1201 Walnut St. (1991)	427	30
Commerce Tower, 911 Main St. (1965)	407	32
City Center Square, 1100 Main St. (1977)	404	30

Las Vegas, NV

Building	Ht. (ft.)	Stories
Stratosphere Tower, 2000 Las Vegas Blvd. S (1996)	1,149	NA
*The Palazzo (2007)	642	53
*Trump International Hotel and Tower 1, 3128 Las Vegas Blvd. S (2007)	622	64
Wynn Las Vegas, 3145 Las Vegas Blvd. S (2005)	613	45
*Planet Hollywood Towers (2007)	600	50
Eiffel Tower, Paris Hotel and Casino, 3645 Las Vegas Blvd. S (1998)	540	NA
New York, New York Hotel & Casino, 3790 Las Vegas Blvd. S (1997)	529	48
*Palms Place, 4321 W. Flamingo Rd. (NA)	520	50

Building	Ht. (ft.)	Stories
Bellagio Hotel & Casino, 3600 Las Vegas Blvd. S (1998)	508	37
*Sky Las Vegas, 2780 Las Vegas Blvd. S (2006)	500	45
THEhotel, Mandalay Bay, 3950 Las Vegas Blvd. S (2003)	485	43
*Panorama Tower III, 4631 Industrial Blvd. (2007)	483	43
Mandalay Bay Hotel & Casino, 3950 Las Vegas Blvd. S (1999)	480	43
Turnberry Place I, 2777 Paradise Rd. (2001)	477	38
Turnberry Place II, 2777 Paradise Rd. (2002)	477	38
Turnberry Place III, 2777 Paradise Rd. (2004)	477	38
*Turnberry Place IV, 2777 Paradise Rd.	477	38
*The Signature at MGM Grand Tower I, 155 E. Harmon Ave. (2006)	475	38
*The Signature at MGM Grand Tower II, 155 E. Harmon Ave. (2006)	475	38
*The Signature at MGM Grand Tower III, 155 E. Harmon Ave. (2007)	475	38
Venetian Resort-Hotel-Casino 1, 3355 Las Vegas Blvd. S (1999)	475	35
*Allure Condominiums I (2007)	466	41
*Palms Resort-Fantasy Tower, 4321 W. Flamingo Rd. (2006)	457	40
*Turnberry Towers I, 222 Karen Ave. (2007)	453	45
Caesars Palace Tower, 3570 Las Vegas Blvd. S (1998)	435	29
Rio Masquerade Tower, 3700 W. Flamingo Rd. (1997)	423	42
*Panorama Tower I, 4631 Industrial Blvd. (2006)	420	32
*Panorama Tower II, 4631 Industrial Blvd. (2006)	420	32
Palms Casino Hotel, 4321 W. Flamingo Rd. (2001)	413	42
*Hilton Grand Vacations Club II, 2650 Las Vegas Blvd. S (2006)	405	41
Fitzgeralds Hotel & Casino, 301 Fremont St. (1980)	400	33

Los Angeles, CA

Building	Ht. (ft.)	Stories
US Bank Tower, 633 W. 5th St. (1990)	1,018	73
Aon Center, 707 Wilshire Blvd. (1974)	858	62
Two California Plaza, 350 S Grand Ave. (1992)	750	52
Gas Company Tower, 555 W. 5th St. (1991)	749	52
Bank of America Plaza, 333 South Hope St. (1975)	735	55
777 Tower, 777 S. Figueroa St. (1991)	725	53
Wells Fargo Tower, 333 S. Grand Ave. (1983)	723	54
Figueroa at Wilshire, 601 S. Figueroa St. (1989)	717	52
Paul Hastings Tower, 515 S. Flower St. (1971)	699	52
City National Tower, 555 S. Flower St. (1971)	699	52
Citigroup Center, 444 S. Flower St. (1979)	625	48
611 Place, 611 W. 6th St. (1969)	620	42
One California Plaza, 300 S. Grand Ave. (1985)	578	42
Century Plaza Tower 1, 2029 Century Park East (1973)	571	44
Century Plaza Tower 2, 2049 Century Park East (1973)	571	44
KPMG Tower, 355 S. Grand Ave. (1984)	560	45
Ernst & Young, LLP Plaza, 725 S. Figueroa St. (1986)	534	41
SunAmerica Center, 1999 Ave. of the Stars (1989)	533	39
TCW Tower, 865 S. Figueroa St. (1990)	517	37
Union Bank Plaza, 445 S. Figueroa St. (1968)	516	40
10 Universal City Plaza (1984)	506	36
1100 Wilshire (1987)	496	36
Fox Plaza, 2121 Ave. of Stars (1987)	492	34
Constellation Place, 10250 Constellation Blvd. (2003)	491	35
1055 W. 7th St. (1988)	462	33
Equitable Life, 3435 Wilshire Blvd. (1969)	454	34
City Hall, 200 N. Spring St. (1927)	454	28
SBC Tower, 1150 Olive St. (1965)	452	32
Madison Complex/Pacific Bell Switching Station, 420 S. Grand Ave. (1961)	448	17
5900 Wilshire Blvd. (1971)	435	32
Warner Center Plaza III, 21650 Oxnard St., Woodland Hills (1991)	415	25
MCI Plaza, 700 S. Flower St. (1973)	414	33

Louisville, KY

Building	Ht. (ft.)	Stories
AEGON Center, 400 W. Market St. (1992)	549	35
National City Tower, 101 S. 5th St. (1972)	512	40
PNC Plaza, 5th & Jefferson (1971)	420	30
Humana Center, 500 W. Main St. (1985)	417	27

Mexico City, Mexico

Building	Ht. (ft.)	Stories
Torre Mayor, Paseo de la Reforma 505 (2003)	738	55
Torre de Pemex, Marina Nacional 329 Col. Huasteca (1984)	702	52
Torre Altus, Paseo de los Laureles 416 (1999)	640	42
Torre Latino Americana (incl. spire), Eje Central Lazaro Cardenas 2 (1956)	597	45
World Trade Center, Montecito 38 Col. Napoles (1972)	565	50
Los Arcos Bosques I, Paeo de los Tamarindos 400 (1997)	529	35
Santa Fe Flats, Av. Sante Fe 443 (2005)	492	37
Torre Lomas, Paseo de las Palmas 800 (1988)	481	36
Torre Impulso (2005)	461	37
Hotel Nikko Mexico, Campos Eliseos 24 (1987)	446	38
Torre del Caballito, Paseo de la Reforma 10 (1988)	443	34
Torre Mural, Insurgentes Sur 1605 (1995)	440	33
Edificio Mexicana de Aviacion, Av. Xola 535 (1984)	433	30
Torre Reforma El Angel, Paseo de la Reforma 347 (2005)	430	31
Presidente Inter-Continental Hotel, Campos Eliseos 218 (1976)	427	42
Torre Libertad, Paseo de la Reforma 439 (2004)	427	30
Torre HSBC (2005)	427	32
Torre Insignia (1962)	417	25
Punta Poniente, Av. Santa Fe 596 (2005)	410	32
Corporativo Santa Fe 505 (2003)	410	29
Torre Reforma, Andres Bello 45 (NA)	410	28

Miami, FL

Building	Ht. (ft.)	Stories
Four Seasons Hotel & Tower, 1441 Brickell Ave (2003)	789	64
Wachovia Financial Center, 200 S. Biscayne Blvd. (1983)	764	55
*Infinity at Brickell, 60 W. 13th St. (2006)	630	52
Bank of America Tower, 100 S.E. Second St. (1987)	625	47
*Marinablue, 888 Biscayne Blvd. (2007)	615	57
*Plaza on Brickell Tower I, 901 Brickell Ave. (2007)	610	56
*Ten Museum Park, 1040 Biscayne Blvd. (2006)	585	50
*50 Biscayne Blvd. (2007)	554	55
*Quantum on the Bay South Tower, 1900 N. Bayshore Dr. (2007)	554	52
*Element Miami, 620 NE 31st St. (2007)	545	54
*Opera Tower, 1750 N. Bayshore Dr. (2006)	543	56
*Onyx 2 on the Bay, 421 NE 28th St. (2007)	543	49
*Everglades on the Bay North Tower, 244 Biscayne Blvd. (2007)	538	49
*Everglades on the Bay South Tower, 244 Biscayne Blvd. (2006)	538	49
*Quantum on the Bay North Tower, 1900 N. Bayshore Dr. (2006)	536	48
Jade at Brickell Bay, 1331 Brickell Bay Dr. (2005)	528	49
*Plaza on Brickell Tower II, 901 Brickell Ave. (2006)	525	48
Santa Maria, 1643 Brickell Ave. (1997)	520	51
*Soleil, 3100 Biscayne Blvd. (2007)	514	43
*The Ivy, 90-95 SW 3rd St. (2007)	512	45
Stephen P. Clark Center, 111 NW 1 St. (1985)	510	28
*Wind, 330 S. Miami Ave. (2007)	501	41
*Epic Hotel & Residences (2007)	500	48
One Biscayne Tower, 2 S. Biscayne Blvd. (1973)	492	39
Espirito Santo Plaza, 1301 Brickell Ave. (2004)	487	36
Citicorp Tower at Miami Centre, 201 S. Biscayne Blvd. (1986)	484	35
*Asia, 900 Brickell Key Blvd. (2007)	483	36
Brickell on the River North, 27 SE 5th St. (2005)	482	42
*Avenue Brickell Tower, 1060 Brickell Ave. (2007)	480	47
Three Tequesta Point, 848 Brickell Key Dr. (2001)	480	46
*Latitude on the River, 615 SW 2nd Ave. (2007)	476	44
One Miami East Tower, 205 S. Brickell Ave. (2005)	460	44
701 Brickell Ave. (1986)	450	33
One Miami West Tower, 205 S. Brickell Ave. (2005)	449	45
*Met 1, 300 SE 3rd St. (2006)	440	40
One Broadway, 1440 Brickell Ave. (2005)	439	36
Mellon Financial Center, 1111 Brickell Ave. (2001)	435	31
*The Loft 2, 133 NE 2nd Ave. (2007)	433	35
*500 Brickell East Tower, 550 Brickell Ave. (2007)	426	42
*500 Brickell West Tower, 550 Brickell Ave. (2007)	426	42
Blue on the Bay, 510 NE 36th St. (2005)	425	36
*Brickell on the River South, 31 SE 5th St. (2006)	423	42
*1800 Club, 1800 N. Bayshore Dr. (2006)	423	40
Vue at Brickell, 1200 S. Miami Ave. (2004)	423	36
Mark on Brickell, 1155 Brickell Bay Dr. (2001)	420	36
*Axis at Brickell Village I, 1111 SW 1st Ave. (2007)	418	37
*Axis at Brickell Village II, 1111 SW 1st Ave. (2007)	418	37
The Club at Brickell Bay, 1200 Brickell Ave. (2004)	411	42
Two Tequesta Point, 808 Brickell Key Dr. (1999)	410	40
Courthouse Center, 175 NW First Ave. (1986)	405	30
The Palace, 1541 Brickell Ave. (1982)	400	42

Miami Beach, FL

Building	Ht. (ft.)	Stories
Blue Diamond Tower, 4779 Collins Ave. (2000)	559	44
Green Diamond Tower, 4775 Collins Ave. (2000)	559	44
Akoya Condominiums, 6365 Collins Ave. (2004)	492	47
Portofino Tower, 300 South Pointe Dr. (1997)	484	44
The Continuum on South Beach, South Tower, 1 South Pointe Dr. (2002)	474	40
ICON at South Beach, 450 Alton Rd. (2004)	423	43
*The Continuum on South Beach, North Tower, 200 South Pointe Dr. (2007)	415	37
Murano Grande at Portofino, 400 Alton Rd. (2003)	407	37
Murano at Portofino, 1000 South Pointe Dr. (2001)	402	38

Milwaukee, WI

Building	Ht. (ft.)	Stories
U.S. Bank Center, 777 E. Wisconsin Ave. (1973)	601	42
100 E. Wisconsin Ave. (1989)	549	37
*University Club Tower, 825 N. Prospect Ave. (2006)	446	36
Milwaukee Center. 111 E. Kilbourn Ave. (1987)	426	29
411 Bldg., 411 E. Wisconsin Ave. (1983)	408	30

Minneapolis, MN

Building	Ht. (ft.)	Stories
IDS Tower, 80 8th St. South (1973)[1]	792	57
225 South Sixth (1992)	776	56
Wells Fargo Center, 90 7th St. South (1988)	774	57
33 South 6th St. (1983)	668	52
Campbell Mithun Tower, 222 9th St. South (1984)	582	42
US Bank Plaza I, 200 6th St. South (1982)	561	41
Dain Rauscher Plaza, 60 6th St. South (1992)	539	40
Fifth Street Towers II, 150 5th St. South (1988)	503	36
American Express Finance Ctr., 707 2nd Ave. S (2000)	498	31
Target Plaza South, 1020 Nicollet Mall (2001)	492	33
Plaza VII, 45 7th St. South (1987)	475	36
*The Carlyle, 220 2nd St. South (2007)	469	41
US Bancorp Center, 800 Nicollet Mall (2000)	468	32
AT&T Tower, 901 Marquette Ave. (1991)	464	34
Accenture Tower, 333 7th St. South (1987)	455	33
Foshay Tower, 821 Marquette Ave. (1929)[1]	448	32
Qwest Bldg., 224 5th St. South (1931)	416	26
Fifty South Sixth (2001)	404	30
Hennepin Co. Government Ctr., 300 6th St. S (1977)	403	24

(1) 910 ft. with antenna.

Montreal, Quebec

Building	Ht. (ft.)	Stories
1250 Boulevard Rene Levesque (incl. spire) (1992)	743	47
1000 Rue de la Gauchetiere (1992)	673	51
Tour de la Bourse, 800 Place Victoria (1963)	624	47
1 Place Villa Marie (1962)	616	42
La Tour CIBC, 1155 Rene Levesque Blvd. (1962)	604	43
Montreal Tower (1987)	574	NA
Tour McGill College, 1501 McGill College (1992)	519	38
Le Complexe Desjardins Sud (1975)	498	40
Tour KMPG, 600 Maisonneuve (1987)	479	34
Place Montreal Trust, 1800 McGill College (1988)	440	30
500 Place d'Armes (1968)	435	32
Tour TELUS, 630 Rene Levesque Blvd. (1962)	429	32
Le Complexe Desjardins Est (1975)	428	32
Port Royal Apts., 1455 Sherbrooke Quest (1964)	424	33
Marriott Hotel, 1 Place du Canada (1967)	420	38
Tour de la Banque Nationale, 600 Rue de la Gauchetiere (1983)	420	28
Tour Bell, 700 Rue de la Gauchetiere (1983)	420	28
Centre Mount Royal, 1000 Sherbrooke Quest (1974)	420	28
Tour Terminal, 800 Rene Levesque Blvd. Quest (1966)	400	30

Nashville, TN

Building	Ht. (ft.)	Stories
BellSouth Tower (incl. spires) 333 Commerce St. (1994)	617	33
Financial Center, 424 Church St. (1986)	490	31
William R. Snodgrass Tennessee Tower, 311 7th Ave. North (1970)	452	31
Nashville Life & Casualty Tower, 401 Church St. (1957)	409	30
City Center, 511 Union St. (1987)	402	27

New Orleans, LA

Building	Ht. (ft.)	Stories
One Shell Square, 701 Poydras St. (1972)	697	51
Bank One Center, 201 St. Charles Ave. (1985)	645	53
Plaza Tower, 1001 Howard Ave. (1969)	531	45
Energy Centre, 1100 Poydras St. (1984)	530	39
LL&E Tower, 901 Poydras St. (1987)	481	36
Sheraton Hotel, 500 Canal St. (1985)	478	47
Marriott Hotel, 555 Canal St. (1972)	450	42
Texaco Center, 400 Poydras St. (1983)	442	33
Canal Place One, 365 Canal St. (1979)	439	32
Bank of New Orleans, 1010 Common St. (1971)	438	31
World Trade Center, 2 Canal St. (1965)	407	33
CNG Tower, 1450 Poydras St. (1989)	406	26

New York, NY

Building	Ht. (ft.)	Stories
Empire State Building, 350 5th Ave. (1931)[1]	1,250	102
Chrysler Building. (incl. spire), 405 Lexington Ave. (1930)	1,046	77
*New York Times Tower (incl. spire), 620 8th Ave. (2007)	1,046	52
American International Bldg. (incl. spire), 70 Pine St. (1932)	952	67
The Trump Bldg., 40 Wall St. (1930)	927	71
Citigroup Center, 153 E. 53th St. (1977)	915	59
Trump World Tower, 845 UN Plaza (2001)	861	72
G. E. Bldg., 30 Rockefeller Center (1933)	850	70
Cityspire Center, 150 W. 56th St. (1989)	814	75
One Chase Manhattan Plaza (1960)	813	60
Conde Nast Bldg., 4 Times Square (1999)[2]	809	48
MetLife Bldg., 200 Park Ave. (1963)	808	59
Bloomberg Tower, 731 Lexington Ave. (2005)[3]	806	54
Woolworth Building, 233 Broadway (1913)	792	57
1 Worldwide Plaza, 935 8th Ave. (1989)	778	47
Carnegie Hall Tower, 152 W. 57th St. (1991)	757	60
Bear Stearns World HQ, 383 Madison Ave. (2001)	755	47
7 World Trade Center (2006)	752	52
AXA Center, 787 7th Ave. (1985)	752	51
One Penn Plaza, 250 W. 34th St. (1972)	750	57
Time Warner Center S Tower, 10 Columbus Circle (2004)	750	55
Time Warner Center N Tower, 10 Columbus Circle (2004)	750	55
1251 Ave. of the Americas (1971)	750	54
JP Morgan HQ, 60 Wall St. (1989)	745	55
One Astor Plaza, 1515 Broadway (1970)	745	54
1 Liberty Plaza, 165 Broadway (1973)	743	54
20 Exchange Place (1931)	741	57
Three World Financial Center, 200 Vesey St. (1986)	739	51
Bertelsmann Building (incl. spire), 1540 Broadway (1990)	732	42
Times Square Tower (2004)	726	47
Metropolitan Tower, 142 W. 57th St. (1985)	716	68
JPMorganChase World HQ, 270 Park Ave. (1960)	707	52
General Motors Bldg., 767 5th Ave. (1968)	705	50
Metropolitan Life Tower, 1 Madison Ave. (1909)	700	50
500 5th Ave. (1931)	697	60
Americas Tower, 1177 Ave. of the Americas (1992)	692	48
Solow Bldg. 9 W. 57th St. (1974)	689	49
HSBC Bank Bldg., 140 Broadway (1967)	688	52
55 Water St. (1972)	687	53
277 Park Ave. (1963)	687	50
1585 Broadway (1989)	685	42
Random House/Park Imperial, 1739 Broadway (2003)	684	52
Four Seasons Hotel, 57 E. 57th St. (1993)	682	52
McGraw Hill, 1221 Ave. of the Americas (1972)	674	51
Lincoln Bldg., 60 E. 42nd St. (1930)	673	53
Paramount Plaza, 1633 Broadway (1970)	670	48
Trump Tower, 725 5th Ave. (1982)	664	58
Citicorp, Queens	658	50
Bank of New York Bldg., 1 Wall St. (1932)	654	50
599 Lexington Ave. (1986)	653	51
712 5th Ave. (1990)	650	53
Chanin Bldg., 122 E. 42nd St. (1929)	649	56
245 Park Ave. (1967)	648	47
Sony Bldg., 550 Madison Ave. (1983)	647	37
Two World Financial Center, 225 Liberty St. (1986)	645	44
RCA Victor Bldg., 570 Lexington Ave. (1930)	642	50

Building	Ht. (ft.)	Stories
1 New York Plaza, 1 Water St. (1969)	640	50
1 Dag Hammarskjold Plaza, 885 2nd Ave. (1972)	637	48
345 Park Ave. (1968)	634	44
10 E. 40th St. (1929)	632	48
*123 Washington St. (2007)	630	53
Grace Plaza, 1114 Ave. of the Americas (1972)	630	50
Home Insurance Co., 59 Maiden Ln. (1966)	630	44
Verizon Bldg., 1095 Ave. of Amer. (1970)	630	40
101 Park Ave. (1982)	629	49
Central Park Place, 301 W. 57th St. (1988)	628	56
888 7th Ave. (1971)	628	45
Alliance Capital Bldg., 1345 Ave. of the Americas (1969)	625	50
Waldorf-Astoria, 301 Park Ave. (1931)	625	47
Trump Palace, 200 E. 69th St. (1991)	623	55
Olympic Tower, 645 5th Ave. (1976)	620	51
425 Fifth Avenue (2003)	618	55
*The Epic, 125 W. 31st St. (2007)	615	58
919 3rd Ave. (1970)	615	47
750 7th Ave. (incl. spire) (1989)	615	35
New York Life, 51 Madison Ave. (1928)	615	33
Tower 49, 12 E. 49th St. (1985)	614	44
Credit Lyonnais Bldg., 1301 Ave. of the Americas (1964)	609	46
The Orion, 350 W. 42nd St. (2006)	604	58
590 Madison Ave. (1983)	603	41
Hearst Magazine Tower, 959 8th Ave. (2006)	597	46
3 Lincoln Center, 160 W. 66th St. (1993)	595	60
Celanese Bldg., 1211 Ave. of the Americas (1973)	592	45
Rihga Royal Hotel, 151 W. 54th St. (1990)	590	54
Thurgood Marshall U. S. Court House, 505 Pearl St. (1927)	590	37
The Millennium Hilton Hotel, 55 Church St. (1992)	588	58
*Sky House, 11 E. 29th St. (2007)	588	55
The Museum Tower Apts. 21 W. 53rd St. (1985)	588	52
Time & Life, 1271 Ave. of the Americas (1959)	587	48
Jacob K. Javits Federal Bldg., 26 Federal Plaza (1967)	587	41
*10 Barclay St. (2007)	584	56
W Times Square, 1567 Broadway (2000)	584	53
Trump International Hotel & Tower, 15 Columbus Circle (1970)	583	44
Stevens Tower, 1185 Ave. of the Americas (1971)	580	42
Municipal Bldg., 1 Centre St. (1914)	580	34
520 Madison Ave. (1981)	577	43
One World Financial Center, 200 Liberty St. (1985)	577	37
Merchandise Mart, 41 Madison Ave. (1973)	576	42
Park Ave. Plaza, 55 E. 52nd St. (1981)	575	44
Lehman Bldg., 745 7th Ave. (2001)	575	38
One Financial Square, 33 Old Slip (1987)	575	37
Marriot Marquis Times Square, 1531 Broadway (1985)	574	50
Westvaco Bldg., 299 Park Ave. (1967)	574	42
Ernst & Young Tower, 5 Times Sq., 590 7th Ave. (2002)	574	40
Marsh & McLennan HQ, 1166 Ave. of the Americas (1974)	572	44
Socony Mobil, 150 E. 42nd St. (1956)	572	42
AXA Finance Center, 1290 Ave. of the Americas (1963)	571	43
Wang Bldg., 780 3rd Ave. (1983)	570	49
600 3rd Ave. (1971)	570	42
450 Lexington Ave. (1991)	568	38
Paramount Tower, 240 E. 39th St. (1998)	567	51
Helmsley Bldg., 230 Park Ave. (1928)	566	35
New York Palace Hotel, 455 Madison Ave. (1980)	563	51
Continental Bank Bldg., 30 Broad St. (1932)	562	48
Park Ave. Tower, 65 E. 55th St. (1986)	561	36
Nelson Tower, 450 7th Ave. (1931)	560	46
Sherry-Netherland, 781 5th Ave. (1927)	560	40
Swiss Bank Tower, 10 E. 50th St. (1990)	560	36
100 UN Plaza, 327 E. 48th St. (1986)	557	52
Continental Can, 633 3rd Ave. (1962)	557	39
3 Park Ave. (1975)	556	42
Continental Corp., 180 Maiden Ln. (1983)	555	41
Sperry & Hutchinson, 330 Madison Ave. (1964)	555	41
Reuters Bldg., 3 Times Square (2001)[4]	555	30
Madison Belvedere, 14 E. 29th St. (1999)	554	48
Inmont Bldg., 1133 Ave. of the Americas (1970)	552	45
Equitable Trust Co. Bldg., 15 Broad St. (1927)	551	42
Biltmore Tower, 267 W. 47th St. (2003)	550	51
Burroughs Bldg., 605 3rd Ave. (1963)	550	44
2 Grand Central Tower, 140 E. 45th St. (1982)	550	43
*The Tower at 15 Central Park West (2007)	550	35
Bell Atlantic, 33 Thomas St. (1974)	550	29
Bankers Trust, 33 E. 48th St. (1971)	547	41
The Corinthian, 330 E. 38th St. (1988)	546	55
Transportation Bldg., 225 Broadway (1928)	546	44
Millennium Tower, 101 W. 67th St. (1995)	545	54
Equitable, 120 Broadway (1915)	545	36
Galleria, 117 E. 57th St. (1975)	544	56
2 Gold St. (2005)	543	51
220 Riverside Blvd. at Trump Place (2003)	542	49
17 State St. (1988)	542	41
Grand Central Plaza, 622 3rd Ave. (1973)	542	38
New York Telephone, 375 Pearl St. (1976)	540	42
Paine Webber Bldg., 1285 Ave. of the Americas (1959)	540	42
Ritz Tower, 109 E. 57th St. (1925)	540	41
Bankers Trust, 16 Wall St. (1912)	540	39
Tribeca Tower, 105 Duane St. (1990)	537	53
Lefcourt Colonial Bldg., 295 Madison Ave. (1929)	537	45
300 Madison Ave. (2003)	535	35
1700 Broadway (1969)	533	41
Westin Hotel New York, 43rd and 8th Ave. (2002)	532	45
515 Park Ave. (1999)	532	43
The Metropolis, 150 E. 44th St. (2001)	528	50
North American Plywood, 800 3rd Ave. (1972)	526	41
Hotel Pierre, 2 E. 61st. St. (1928)	525	44

Building	Ht. (ft.)	Stories
767 3rd Ave. (1980)	525	39
Citibank, 399 Park Ave. (1961)	524	41
Random House, 825 3rd Ave. (1969)	522	40
Du Mont Bldg., 515 Madison Ave. (1931)	520	42
26 Broadway (1922)	520	31
Newsweek Bldg., 444 Madison Ave. (1931)	518	42
Downtown Athletic Club, 19 West St. (1930)	518	39
Architect's and Designer's Bldg., 964 Third Ave. (1969)	518	39
House of Seagram, 375 Park Ave. (1958)	518	38
South Park Tower, 124 W. 60th St. (1986)	516	51
High Point Condominium, 250 E. 40th St. (1988)	516	49
Sterling Drug Bldg., 90 Park Ave. (1964)	515	41
Navarre, 512 7th Ave. (1930)[5]	513	44
Bank Of New York, 48 Wall St. (1927)	513	31
The Belaire, 524 E. 72nd St. (1988)	512	50
Republic National Bank, Brooklyn, 1 Hansen Pl. (1929)	512	42
1407 Broadway Realty Corp. (1950)	512	41
International, Rockefeller Center, 630 5th Ave. (1935)	512	41
ITT-American, 437 Madison Ave. (1967)	512	40
Continental, 1450 Broadway (1931)	511	42
1155 Ave. of the Americas (1984)	511	40
10 Liberty St. (2004)	510	45
810 7th Ave. (1970)	506	41
The Sheffield Apts., 325 W. 56th St. (1978)	505	50
United Nations Secretariat Bldg., 405 E. 42nd St. (1950)	505	39
1 UN Plaza (1975)	505	39
2 UN Plaza (1981)	505	39
2 New York Plaza, 125 Broad St. (1970)	504	40
Johns-Manville Bldg., 22 E. 40th St. (1931)	503	43
60 Broad St. (1962)	503	39
Lefcourt National Bldg., 521 5th Ave. (1928)	503	37
1325 Ave. of the Americas (1989)	502	35
Sheraton Centre, 811 7th Ave. (1962)	501	51
World Apparel Center, 1411 Broadway (1969)	501	39
Bristol Plaza, 200 E. 65th St. (1987)	500	50
Pennmark Towers, 315 W. 33rd St. (2001)	500	35
Four World Financial Center, 250 Vesey St. (1986)	500	34

(1) 1,455 ft. with antenna. (2) 1,118 ft. with antenna. (3) 941 ft. with antenna. (4) 659 ft. with antenna. (5) Site of World Almanac offices.

Oklahoma City, OK

Chase Tower, 100 N. Broadway Ave. (1971)	500	36
First National Center (incl. spire), 120 N. Robinson St. (1931)	493	33
City Place, 204 N. Robinson St. (1931)	440	32
Oklahoma City, 210 Park Ave. (1982)	434	31

Orlando, FL

SunTrust Center Tower, 200 S. Orange Ave. (1988)	441	31
*Vue at Lake Eola, 136 E. Robinson St. (2006)	426	35
Orange County Courthouse, 425 N. Orange Ave. (1997)	416	24
Bank of America Center, 390 N. Orange Ave. (1988)	409	28

Philadelphia, PA

*Comcast Center, 1701 JFK Blvd. (2007)	975	57
One Liberty Place (incl. spire), 1650 Market St. (1987)	945	61
Two Liberty Place (incl. spire), 1601 Chestnut St. (1989)	848	58
Mellon Bank Center, 1735 Market St. (1990)	792	54
Bell-Atlantic Tower, 1717 Arch St. (1991)	725	53
G. Fred DiBona Jr. Bldg., 1901 Market St. (1990)	625	45
Commerce Square #1, 2005 Market St. (1990)	572	40
Commerce Square #2, 2001 Market St. (1992)	572	40
City Hall (incl. statue) (1901)	548	7
1818 Market St. (1974)	500	40
The St. James, 700 Walnut St. (2004)	498	45
Loews Philadelphia Hotel, 12 S. 12th St. (1932)	492	39
PNC Bank Bldg., 1600 Market St. (1983)	491	40
Centre Square II, 1542 Market St. (1973)	490	38
5 Penn Center, 1601 Market St. (1970)	488	36
1700 Market St. (1969)	482	32
1 South Broad St. (1930)	472	28
Cira Centre, 2929 Arch St. (2005)	437	28
Two Logan Square, 100 N. 18th St. (1988)	435	34
1835 Market St. (1985)	430	29
Aramark Tower, 1101 Market St. (1984)	417	31
Centre Square I, 1500 Market St. (1973)	416	32
Wachovia Bldg., 123 S. Broad St. (1927)	405	30
Ritz Carlton Hotel, 28 S. Broad St. (1930)	404	30
One Logan Square, 130 N. 18th St. (1982)	400	32

Phoenix, AZ

Chase Tower, 201 N. Central Ave. (1972)	486	40
*44 Monroe (2007)	411	34
101 N. Second Ave. (1976)	407	31

Pittsburgh, PA

US Steel Tower, 600 Grant St. (1970)	841	64
One Mellon Bank Center, 500 Grant St. (1983)	725	54
One PPG Place (1984)	635	40
Fifth Ave. Place, 120 5th Ave. (1987)	616	32
One Oxford Centre, 301 Grant St. (1982)	615	46
Gulf Tower, 707 Grant St. (1932)	582	44
University of Pittsburgh Cathedral of Learning, 4200 5th Ave. (1936)	535	42
3 Mellon Bank Center, 525 Wm. Penn Way (1951)	520	41
Freemarkets Center, 210 6th Ave. (1968)	511	39
Grant Bldg., 330 Grant St. (1928)	485	40
Koppers Bldg., 436 7th Ave. (1929)	475	34
Two PNC Plaza, 620 Liberty Ave. (1975)	445	34
Dominion Tower, 625 Liberty Ave. (1987)	430	32
One PNC Plaza, 249 5th Ave. (1972)	424	30
Regional Enterprise Tower, 425 6th Ave. (1953)	410	30

Portland, OR

Building	Ht. (ft.)	Stories
Wells Fargo Center, 1300 SW 5th Ave. (1973)	546	40
U. S. Bancorp Tower, 111 SW 5th Ave. (1983)	536	42
Koin Plaza, 222 SW Columbia St. (1984)	509	31
Pacwest Center, 1211 SW 5th Ave. (1984)	418	30

Providence, RI

*One Ten Westminster (incl. spire) (2007)	520	35
Bank of America Bldg., 55 Exchange Pl. (1927)	428	26
One Financial Plaza (1973)	410	28

St. Louis, MO

Gateway Arch (1965)	630	NA
Metropolitan Square Tower, 211 N. Broadway (1988)	593	42
AT&T Center, 900 Pine St. (1984)	588	44
Thomas F. Eagleton Federal Courthouse, 111 S. 10th St (2000)	557	29
One U.S. Bank Plaza, 505 N. 7th St. (1976)	484	35
Laclede Gas Bldg., 720 Olive St. (1969)	400	31

St. Paul, MN

Wells Fargo Place, 30 E. 7th St. (1987)	471	36
Galtier Plaza Jackson Tower, 168 E. 6th St. (1986)	443	46
First National Bank, 332 Minnesota St. (1930)	417	32

San Antonio, TX

Tower of the Americas, 600 Hemisphere Way (1968)	622	NA
Marriott Rivercenter (incl. spires), 101 Bowie St. (1988)	546	38
Weston Centre, 112 Pecan St. (1988)	444	32
Tower Life, 310 S. St. Mary's St. (1929)[1]	404	30

(1) 541 ft. with antenna.

San Diego, CA

One American Plaza, 600 W. Broadway (1991)	500	34
Symphony Tower, 759 B St. (1989)	499	34
Manchester Grand Hyatt, One Market Pl. (1992)	497	40
*Electra, 701 W. Broadway (2007)	475	43
Pinnacle Museum Tower, 500 Front St. (2005)	455	35
Emerald Plaza, 400 W. Broadway (1990)	450	30
Manchester Grand Hyatt Tower 2, One Market Pl. (2003)	446	32
One Harbor Drive, 100 Harbor Dr. (1992)	424	41
Two Harbor Drive, 100 Harbor Dr. (1992)	424	41
*Vantage Point (2007)	420	41
The Grande North at Sante Fe Place (2005)	420	39
The Grande South at Sante Fe Place, 1199 Pacific Hwy. (2004)	420	39
Broadway 655 (2005)	412	23

San Francisco, CA

Sutro Tower (1972)	977	NA
Transamerica Pyramid, 600 Montgomery St. (1972)	853	48
555 California St. (1969)	779	52
345 California Center (incl. spires) (1986)	695	48
101 California St. (1986)	600	48
50 Fremont (1983)	600	43
Chevron Tower, 575 Market St. (1975)	573	40
Four Embarcadero Center, 55 Clay St. (1984)	570	45
One Embarcadero Center, 355 Clay St. (1970)	569	45
44 Montgomery St. (1967)	565	43
Spear Tower, 1 Market St. (1976)	565	42
Citicorp Center, 1 Sansome St. (1984)	550	39
Shaklee Terrace Bldg., 444 Market St. (1982)	537	38
One Post Plaza, 1 Post St. (1969)	529	38
525 Market St. (1972)	529	38
One Metro Plaza, 425 Market St. (1973)	524	38
Telsis Tower, 1 Montgomery St. (1982)	500	38
333 Bush St. (1986)	495	43
Hilton Hotel, 201 Mason St. (1971)	493	46
Pacific Gas & Electric, 77 Beale St. (1971)	492	34
50 California St. (1972)	487	37
St. Regis San Francisco, 25 3rd St. (2005)	484	42
100 Pine Center (1972)	476	34
Bechtel Bldg., 45 Fremont St. (1979)	475	34
333 Market Bldg. (1979)	474	33
Hartford Bldg., 650 California St. (1965)	465	33
*The Infinity I, 300 Spear St. (2007)	450	40
100 First Plaza (1988)	447	27
One California St. (1969)	438	32
Marriott Hotel, 777 Market St. (1989)	436	39
Russ Bldg., 235 Montgomery St. (1927)	435	32
Pacific Bell Headquarters, 140 Montgomery St. (1925)	435	26
JPMorganChase Bldg., 560 Mission St. (2002)	421	31
Paramount, 680 Mission St. (2002)	418	41
Providian Financial Bldg., 201 Mission St. (1983)	416	30
Three Embarcadero Center, 255 Clay St. (1974)	412	31
Three Embarcadero Center, 155 Clay St. (1976)	412	31
595 Market Bldg. (1977)	410	31
123 Mission Bldg. (1986)	406	29
Embarcadero Center West, 275 Battery St. (1988)	405	33
101 Montgomery St. (1983)	405	29

Seattle, WA

Columbia Center, 701 5th Ave. (1985)[1]	933	76
Washington Mutual Tower, 1201 3rd Ave. (1988)	772	55
Two Union Square, 601 Union St. (1989)	740	56
Seattle Municipal Tower, 700 5th Ave. (1990)	722	57
1001 Fourth Avenue Plaza (1969)	609	50
Space Needle, 203 6th Ave. (1962)	605	NA
WaMu Center, 1301 2nd Ave. (2006)	598	42
U.S. Bank Centre, 1420 5th Ave. (1989)	580	44
Wells Fargo Center, 999 3rd Ave. (1983)	574	47
Bank of America Fifth Avenue Plaza, 800 Fifth Ave. (1981)	543	42

Building	Ht. (ft.)	Stories
Union Bank of California Center, 900 4th Ave. (1973)	536	41
Rainier Tower, 1301 5th Ave. (1977)	514	31
IDX Tower at Fourth & Madison, 915 4th Ave. (2003)	512	40
1000 2nd Ave. (1986)	493	40
Henry M. Jackson Bldg., 915 2nd Ave. (1974)	487	37
Qwest Plaza, 1600 7th Ave. (1976)	466	33
Smith Tower, 506 2nd Ave. (1914)	465	38
One Union Square, 600 University Ave. (1981)	456	36
1111 3rd Ave. (1980)	454	34
Westin Hotel North Tower, 1900 5th Ave. (1982)	448	44
Westin Bldg., 2001 6th Ave. (1981)	409	34
(1) 997 ft. with antenna.		

Sunny Isles Beach, FL

Building	Ht. (ft.)	Stories
Trump Palace, 18101 Collins Ave. (2005)	551	43
*Trump Royale, 18201 Collins Ave. (2007)	551	43
*Jade on the Beach Condominiums, 17001 Collins Ave. (2006)	550	52
Aqualina Ocean Residences, 17875 Collins Ave. (2004)	550	51
The Pinnacle, 17555 Collins Ave. (1999)	476	40
*La Perla Ocean Residences, 16701 Collins Ave. (2006)	447	42
Ocean Two Condominiums I, 19111 Collins Ave. (2001)	426	40
Ocean Two Condominiums II, 19111 Collins Ave. (2001)	426	40
Ocean Three Condominiums, 18911 Collins Ave. (2003)	405	37

Tampa, FL

Building	Ht. (ft.)	Stories
*Trump Tower Tampa, 111 S. Ashley Dr. (2007)	593	52
AmSouth Bldg, 100 N. Tampa St. (1992)	579	42
Bank of America Plaza, 101 E. Kennedy Blvd. (1986)	577	42
One Tampa City Center, 201 N. Franklin St. (1981)	537	39
Suntrust Financial Center, 401 E. Jackson St. (1992)	525	36
Park Tower, 400 N. Tampa St. (1973)	458	36
Rivergate Tower, 400 N. Ashley Dr. (1988)	454	33

Toronto, Ontario

Building	Ht. (ft.)	Stories
CN Tower, 310 Front St. West (1976)	1,815	NA
First Canadian Place, 100 King St. West (1975)[1]	978	72
Scotia Plaza, 40 King's St. West (1989)	902	68
BCE Place, Canada Trust Tower (incl. spire), 161 Bay St. (1990)	856	53
Commerce Court West, 199 Bay St. (1973)[2]	784	57
TD Centre, Toronto Dominion Bank Tower, 66 Wellington St. West (1967)	730	56
BCE Place, Bay-Wellington Tower, 181 Bay St. (1991)	679	49
TD Centre-Royal Trust Tower, 77 King St. West (1969)	600	46
1 King West (2005)	578	51
Royal Bank Plaza-South Tower, 200 Bay St. (1976)	567	41
44 Charles St. West (1974)	545	51
*Residences of College Park I, Bay St. & College St. (2006)	505	51
TD Centre-79 Wellington St. West (1985)	504	39
The 250, 250 Yonge St. (1991)	494	35
Harbourview Estates Phase 2 (2005)	491	49
Two Bloor West (1974)	488	34
Simcoe Place, 200 Front St. West (1995)	486	33

Building	Ht. (ft.)	Stories
*West One (2007)	484	49
Exchange Tower, 130 King St. West (1983)	480	30
CIBC-Commerce Court North, 25 King St. West (1931)	477	34
*Spire (2006)	476	45
Simpson Tower, 401 Bay St. (1968)	473	33
Cadillac-Fairview Tower, 20 Queen St. West (1982)	465	36
*Murano Tower, 825 Bay St. (NA)	459	41
Pantages Tower (2002)	458	45
One Palace Pier Court, Etobicoke (1991)	455	46
Three Palace Pier Court, Etobicoke (1978)	453	46
Continental Bank of Canada, 130 Adelaide St. West (1980)	450	35
*The Residences of College Park II, 763 Bay St. (2007)	446	45
Sheraton Centre, 123 Queen St. West (1972)	443	43
Two Bloor East (1974)	439	35
Royal York Hotel, 200 Front St. West (1929)	439	26
TD Centre-Ernst & Young Tower, 222 Bay St. (1990)	437	31
Empire Tower, 17 Barberry Pl., North York (2005)	427	28
One Financial Place, 1 Adelaide St. East (1991)	424	31
Leaside Towers I, 85 Thorncliffe Park Dr., East York (1970)	423	44
Leaside Towers II, 95 Thorneclliffe Park Dr., East York (1970)	423	44
TD Centre-Canadian Pacific Tower, 100 Wellington St. West (1974)	420	32
Metro Hall West, 55 John St. (1991)	420	27
Marriott Hotel/Plaza 2 Apartments, 90 Bloor St. East (1973)	415	41
*N1/N2, Spadina Ave. & Bremmer Blvd. (2007)	410	41
Sun Life Financial Centre East Tower, 150 King St. West (1981)	410	27
Young-Eglinton Centre I, 2300 Yonge St. (1974)	408	30
(1) 1,116 ft. with antenna. (2) 942 ft. with antenna.		

Tulsa, OK

Building	Ht. (ft.)	Stories
One Williams Center, 1 W. 2nd St. (1975)	667	52
Cityplex Central Tower, 2448 E. 81st St. (1979)	648	60
First Place Tower, 15 E. 5th St. (1973)	516	40
Mid-Continent Tower, 401 S. Boston St. (1984)	513	36
Bank of America Center, 15 W. 6th St. (1967)	412	32
320 S. Boston St. (1928)	400	22

Vancouver, British Columbia

Building	Ht. (ft.)	Stories
One Wall Centre, 1000 Burrard St. (2001)	491	45
Shaw Tower, 298 Thurlow St. (2004)	489	40
Harbour Centre, 555 W. Hastings St. (1977)	481	30
200 Granville Square (1973)	466	32
*The Melville, 1189 Melville St. (2006)	464	43
Royal Centre, 1055 W. Georgia St. (1973)	461	37
Park Place, 666 Burrard St. (1984)	459	35
Bentall IV, 1055 Dunsmir St. (1981)	454	36
Scotia Tower, 650 W. Georgia St. (1977)	452	36
T-D Bank Tower, 700 W. Georgia St. (1970)	417	30
Bentall III, 595 Burrard St. (1974)	400	31

Other Tall Buildings in North American Cities

Lists include freestanding towers and other structures that do not have stories and are not technically considered "buildings." Also included are some structures still under construction as of mid-2006 and due for completion by the end of 2007 (denoted by asterisk *). Year in parentheses is date of completion or projected completion. Height is generally measured from sidewalk to roof, including penthouse and tower if enclosed as integral part of structure; stories generally counted from street level. NA = not available or not applicable.

Building		Ht. (ft.)	Stories
*RSA Battlehouse Tower (2006)	Mobile, AL	745	35
The Tower at First National Center (2002)	Omaha, NE	634	45
801 Grand (1991)	Des Moines, IA	630	44
Dataflux Tower (2000)	Monterrey, Mexico	597	43
Erastus Corning II Tower (1973)	Albany, NY	589	44
*360 Nueces St. (incl. spire) (2007)	Austin, TX	581	44
Concourse Corporate Center V (1988)	Sandy Springs, GA	570	34
Washington Monument (1884)	Washington, DC	555	NA
Concourse Corporate Center VI (1991)	Sandy Springs, GA	553	34
Metropolitan Tower (1986)	Little Rock, AK	546	40
One HSBC Center (1970)	Buffalo, NY	529	40
Vehicle Assembly Bldg. (1965)	Cape Canaveral, FL	525	40
Skylon (1965)	Niagara Falls, Ont.	520	NA
Frost Bank Tower (2004)	Austin, TX	516	33
*Town Center Westin Hotel and Residences (2007)	Virginia Beach, VA	508	37
Mohegan Sun Hotel (2002)	Uncasville, CT	487	34
Woodmen Tower (1969)	Omaha, NE	478	30
National Newark Bldg. (1931)	Newark, NJ	465	36
*Granby Tower (2007)	Norfolk, VA	461	31
State Capitol (1932)	Baton Rouge, LA	460	34
Wachovia Center (1995)	Winston-Salem, NC	460	34
The Tower (1988)	Burbank, CA	460	32
Ruan Center (1974)	Des Moines, IA	457	36
Southtrust Tower (1986)	Birmingham, AL	454	34
Regions Center (1975)	Little Rock, AK	454	30
Lincoln Tower One (2005)	Bellevue, WA	450	42
James Monroe Bldg. (1981)	Richmond, VA	449	29
1180 Raymond Blvd. (1930)	Newark, NJ	448	34
Prudential (1975)	Southfield, MI	448	32
The Westin Diplomat (2002)	Hollywood, FL	444	39
Ravinia #3 (1991)	Dunwoody, GA	444	33
Xerox Tower (1967)	Rochester, NY	443	30
One Summit Square (1981)	Fort Wayne, IN	442	27
Anadarko Tower (2002)	The Woodlands, TX	439	32
AmSouth/Harbert Plaza (1989)	Birmingham, AL	437	32
*Trump Plaza (2007)	New Rochelle, NY	435	32
The Palisades (2001)	Fort Lee, NJ	434	41
2 Hanover Square (1991)	Raleigh, NC	431	29
Torre Commercial America (1994)	Monterrey, Mexico	427	35
AmSouth Bank Bldg. (1969)	Mobile, AL	424	33
Wells Fargo Center (1991)	Sacramento, CA	423	30
Wells Fargo Center (1998)	Salt Lake City, UT	422	24
CanWest Global Place (1990)	Winnipeg, Man.	420	33
L.D.S. Church Office Bldg. (1972)	Salt Lake City, UT	420	28
Century 21 (1974)	Hamilton, Ont.	418	43
Hidden Bay 1 (2000)	Aventura, FL	417	40
Edifice Marie-Guyart (1972)	Quebec City, Que.	415	31
AmSouth Bank Bldg. (1996)	Montgomery, AL	415	24
*Eddie Bauer at Lincoln Square (2006)	Bellevue, WA	412	27
One Seagate (1982)	Toledo, OH	411	32
One Shoreline Plaza, South Tower (1988)	Corpus Christi, TX	411	28
Silver Legacy (1995)	Reno, NV	410	38
Lexington Financial Center (1987)	Lexington, KY	410	30
Winston Tower (1965)	Winston-Salem, NC	410	26
The Plaza in Clayton Residential Tower (2002)	Clayton, MO	409	30
Kettering Tower (1970)	Dayton, OH	408	30
Richardson Bldg. (1969)	Winnipeg, Man.	406	34
1000 Town Center (1988)	Southfield, MI	405	32
Ordway Bldg. (1985)	Oakland, CA	404	28
Three Lakeway Center (1987)	Metairie, LA	403	34
Bausch and Lomb Place (1995)	Rochester, NY	401	20
*Ocean Palms Phase I (2006)	Hollywood, Fl	400	38
Fiberglass Tower (1970)	Toledo, OH	400	30
Monarch Place (1987)	Springfield, MA	400	26
SunTrust Plaza (1984)	Richmond, VA	400	24

World Almanac Quick Quiz

Rank the following North American cities by the height of their tallest building.

(a) Mexico City, Mex.   (b) Indianapolis, IN   (c) Las Vegas, NV   (d) Atlanta, GA

For the answer look in this chapter, or see page 1008.

Notable Bridges in North America

Source: Federal Highway Administration, Office of Bridge Tech., U.S. Dept. of Transportation; World Almanac Research
Asterisk (*) designates railroad bridge. Year is date of completion or expected completion. Span of a bridge is the distance between its supports.

Suspension

Year	Bridge	Location	Main span (ft.)
1964	Verrazano-Narrows	New York, NY	4,260
1937	Golden Gate	San Fran. Bay, CA.	4,200
1957	Mackinac	Straits of Mackinac, MI	3,800
1931	George Washington	Hudson R., NY–NJ	3,500
2007	Tacoma Narrows (New)	Tacoma, WA	2,800
1950	Tacoma Narrows (Current)	Tacoma, WA	2,800
2003	Carquinez (Al Zampa Memorial)	Carquinez Strait, CA	2,388
1936	San Fran.-Oakland Bay (West)[1]	San Fran. Bay, CA.	2,310
1939	Bronx-Whitestone	East R., NY	2,300
1970	Pierre Laporte	Quebec City, Quebec	2,190
1951	Del. Memorial[2]	Pennsville, NJ–New Castle, DE.	2,150
1957	Walt Whitman	Philadelphia, PA	2,000
1929	Ambassador	Detroit, MI–Can.	1,850
1961	Throgs Neck	Long Is. Sound., NY	1,801
1926	Benjamin Franklin	Philadelphia, PA	1,750
1924	Bear Mtn.	Hudson R., NY.	1,632
1903	Williamsburg	East R., NY.	1,600
1952	William Preston Lane Jr Mem.[3]	Sandy Point, MD	1,600
1969	Newport/Pell.	Narragansett Bay, RI.	1,600
1883	Brooklyn	East R., NY.	1,596
1938	Lions' Gate	Vancouver, BC	1,550
1963	Vincent Thomas	L.A. Harbor, CA	1,500
1930	Mid-Hudson	Poughkeepsie, NY.	1,495
1909	Manhattan	East R., NY.	1,470
1955	Angus L. Macdonald	Halifax, Nova Scotia	1,447
1970	A. Murray MacKay	Halifax, Nova Scotia	1,400
1936	Triborough (Hrlm. River Lift/Brnx. Crossing/ East R. Suspension)	East R., NY	1,380
2013	San. Fran-Oakland Bay (East)	San Fran. Bay, CA.	1,263
1931	St. Johns	Portland, OR	1,207
1929	Mount Hope	Portsmouth–Bristol, RI.	1,200
1960	Ogdensburg-Prescott	Ogdensburg, NY–Can.	1,150
1965	Bidwell Bar	Oroville, CA	1,108
1964	Middle Fork Feather	Butte Co., CA.	1,105
1939	Deer Isle	Deer Isle, ME.	1,080
1931	Simon Kenton Memorial	Ohio R., Maysville, KY.	1,060
1935	Ile d'Orleans	St. Lawrence R., Quebec	1,059
1867	John A. Roebling	Ohio R., KY–Cincinnati, OH	1,057
1971	Dent	Orofino, ID	1,050
1900	Ojuela	Mapimi, Mexico	1,030
1849	Wheeling	Ohio R., WV.	1,010

Cantilever

Year	Bridge	Location	Main span (ft.)
1917	Québec	St. Lawrence R., Quebec	1,801
1974	Commodore Barry	Chester, PA–Bridgeport, NJ	1,644
1988	Greater New Orleans No. 2	Mississippi R., LA	1,594
1958	Greater New Orleans No. 1	Mississippi R., LA	1,575
1995	Gramercy	Mississippi R., Gramercy, LA	1,460
1936	East Bay[4]	San Fran. Bay, CA.	1,400
1968	Baton Rouge	Mississippi R., LA	1,235
1955	Tappan Zee	Hudson R., NY.	1,212
1930	Lewis and Clark	Longview, WA–OR	1,200
1909	Queensboro	East R., NY	1,182
1927	Carquinez Strait (west)[5]	San Fran. Bay, CA.	1,100
1958	Carquinez Strait (east)	San Fran. Bay, CA.	1,100
1930	Jacques Cartier	Montreal, Quebec	1,097
1968	Isaiah D. Hart	Jacksonville, FL.	1,088
1956	Richmond-San Rafael[6]	San Fran. Bay, CA.	1,070
1963	Newburgh-Beacon (north)	Hudson R., NY.	1,000
1980	Newburgh-Beacon (south)	Hudson R., NY.	1,000
1950	Martin Luther King	St. Louis, MO.	963
1975	Caruthersville	Mississippi R., MO–TN	920
1969	Silver Memorial	Pt. Pleasant, WV–OH	900
1977	Saint Marys	Saint Marys, WV–OH	900
1981	William S. Ritchie	Ohio R., Ravenswood, WV	900
1987	Carl Perkins	Ohio R., OH–KY	900
1941	Mississippi R.	Natchez, MS	875
1988	Mississippi R.	Natchez, MS	875
1938	Blue Water	Pt. Huron, MI–Ont.	871
1972	Mississippi R.	Vicksburg, MS.	870
1972	N. Fork American R.	Auburn, CA	862
1940	*Baton Rouge	Mississippi R., LA	848
1899	*Cornwall	St. Lawrence R., LA.	843
1940	Rte. 82	Mississippi R., AR.	840
1961	Mississippi R.	Greenville, MS.	840
1963	Brent Spence	KY–Cincinnati, OH	830
1940	Mississippi R.	Vicksburg, MS	825
1963	Mississippi R.	Donaldsonville, LA.	825
1931	Mississippi R.	Vicksburg, MS	824
1929	Clark Memorial	Ohio R., KY	820

Year	Bridge	Location	Main span (ft.)
1961	Campbellton-Cross Pt.	New Brunswick, Can.	815
1932	Washington Mem.	Seattle, WA	800
1935	Rip Van Winkle	Catskill, NY	800
1938	Cairo	Ohio R., IL–KY	800
1936	McCullough	Coos Bay, OR	793
1949	Memphis	Mississippi R., TN	790
1935	Huey P. Long[7]	New Orleans, LA	790
1949	Rte. 55	Mississippi R., AR–TN	790
1910	*P&LE RR	Ohio R., PA	750
1930	Ashland-Coal Grove	Ohio R., OH.	739
1922	Ironton-Russell[7]	Ohio R., OH–Ky	725
1932	Bi-State Vietnam Gold Star	Henderson, KY	720
1979	I-275	Ohio R., Fort Thomas, KY	720
1962	Champlain	Montreal, Quebec	707
1926	Columbia R.	Cascade Locks, OR	706
1964	John F. Kennedy (I-65)	Ohio R., Louisville, KY	700
1928	Ohio River, B&O RR, HV RR	Pomeroy-Mason, OH	657
1941	*Pit River	Redding, CA	630
1941	Columbia R.	Kettle Falls, WA	600
1954	Columbia R.	Umatilla, OR	600
1965	Bi-State Vietnam Gold Star	Henderson, KY	600
1954	Columbia R.	The Dalles, OR	576
1968	W. 17th St.	Huntington, WV	562

Simple Truss

Year	Bridge	Location	Main span (ft.)
1977	Chester	Chester, WV–OH	745
1929	Irvin S. Cobb	Ohio R., IL–KY	716
1923	*Tanana R.	Nenana, AK.	700
1967	WIlliamstown-Marietta (I-77)	Ohio R., WV–OH.	650
1917	MacArthur7	St. Louis, MO	647
1992	Discovery	Missouri R, MO	625
1958	*Castleton	Hudson R., NY	598
1938	Easton-Phillipsburg	Delaware R., PA	550
1930	Swindell	Pittsburgh, PA	545
1951	Penn. Tpk. Allegheny	Pittsburgh, PA	534
1951	Rankin	Pittsburgh, PA	525
1906	Donora-Webster	Donora-Webster, PA	515
1908	Hulton	Allegheny R., Harmar, PA.	505
1967	Alaska Native Veterans' Honor.	Nenana R., AK	500

Steel Truss

Year	Bridge	Location	Main span (ft.)
1990	Glade Creek	Raleigh Co., WV	785
1973	Atchafalaya R. (U.S. 190)	Krotz Springs, LA	780
1971	Piscataqua R.	Portsmouth, NH–ME	756
1972	Atchafalaya R.	Simmesport, LA.	720
1957	Robert O. Norris	Middlesex Co., VA.	648
1978	Atchafalaya R.	Morgan City, LA	607
1960	Summit	Summit, DE.	600
1968	Reedy Point	Delaware City, DE.	600
1955	Interstate (I-5)	Columbia R., OR–WA	531
1910	McKinley[8]	Mississippi R., MO–IL	517
1972	Mississippi R.	Muscatine, IA	512
1896	Newport	Ohio R., KY	511
1931	Lucy Jefferson Lewis	Cumberland R., KY	500
1958	Lake Oahe	Gettysburg, SD	500
1958	Lake Oahe	Mobridge, SD	500
1970	Lake Koocanusa	Lincoln Co., MT	500

Continuous Truss

Year	Bridge	Location	Main span (ft.)
1966	Astoria	Columbia R., OR–WA	1,232
1976	Francis Scott Key	Baltimore, MD	1,200
1981	Ravenswood	Ohio R., Ravenswood, WV	902
1995	Taylor-Southgate	Ohio R., KY–OH	850
1943	Julien Dubuque	Mississippi R., IA–IL	845
1966	Charles Braga	Fall River, MA	840
1956	Earle C. Clements[9]	Ohio R., IL–KY	825
1929	George Rogers Clark	Ohio R., IN–KY	820
1953	John E. Mathews	Jacksonville, FL.	810
1950	Maurice J. Tobin	Boston, MA	800
1940	Gov. Nice Memorial	Potomac R., MD–VA	800
1957	Kingston-Rhinecliff	Hudson R., NY	800
1992	Cooper River	Charleston, SC	800
1986	Rochester-Monaca	Rochester-Monaca, PA	780
1917	Sciotoville[10]	Sciotoville, OH.	775
1940	U.S. 231	Ohio R., IN	750
1974	I-275 Carroll C. Cropper	Ohio R., IN–KY	750
1981	Sewickley	Sewickley, PA	750
1984	13th St. Bridge	Ohio R., PA–OH	740
1959	Monaca-E. Rochester	Monaca-E. Rochester, PA.	730
1976	Betsy Ross	Philadelphia, PA	729
1929	Milton-Madison	Ohio R., IN–KY	727
1967	Matthew E. Welsh[11]	Mauckport, IN	725
1962	U.S. 41	Ohio R., IN–KY	720
1994	Robert C. Byrd	Huntington, WV	720
1970	Vanport	Vanport, PA.	715
1962	Champlain	Montreal, Que.	707
1962	John F. Kennedy (I-65)[12]	Ohio R., Louisville, KY–IN.	701
1973	Girard Point	Philadelphia, PA	700

Year	Bridge	Location	Main span (ft.)
1956	DE R.-PA Turnpike	Delaware R., NJ–PA	682
1938	Rainbow	Port Arthur-Orange, TX	680
1949	George C. Platt	Philadelphia, PA	680
1946	Chester	Mississippi R., IL–MO	670
1994	Williamstown-Marietta	Ohio R., WV–OH	650
1955	Jefferson City	Missouri R., MO	640
2000	Mark Twain Mem.	Mississippi R., Hannibal, MO–IL	640
1930	Quincy Memorial	Mississippi R., IL	628
1959	Harbor	Corpus Christi, TX	620
1961	Shippingport	Shippingport, PA	620
1935	Bourne and Sagamore (twin)	Cape Cod Canal, MA	616
1965	I-80, Clarion R.	Clarion, PA	612
1975	Donora-Monessen	Donora-Monessen, PA	608
1961	John A. Blatnik	Superior, WI–Duluth, MN	600
1965	Rio Grande Gorge	Taos, NM	600
1991	Hoffstadt Creek	Mt. St. Helens, WA	600
1991	Jefferson City	Missouri R., MO	596
1962	W. Branch Feather R.	Oroville, CA	576
1966	Glenwood	Pittsburgh, PA	557
1932	Pulaski Skyway[13]	Newark, NJ	550
1966	Emlenton	Emlenton, PA	540
1943	Gold Star Memorial	New London, CT	540
1936	Homestead Grays	Pittsburgh, PA	534
1962	Benicia-Martinez	Benicia-Martinez, CA	528
1914	Brownsville	Brownsville, PA	518
1971	Grandad	Elk River, ID	504

Continuous Box and Plate Girder

Year	Bridge	Location	Main span (ft.)
1967	San Mateo-Hayward #2	San Fran. Bay, CA	750
1976	Intracoastal Canal	Forked Is., LA	750
1977	Intracoastal Canal	Gibbstown, LA	750
1969	San Diego-Coronado[14]	San Diego Bay, CA	660
1992/1994	Acosta (twin)	Jacksonville, FL	630
1981	Douglas	Juneau, AK	620
1976	Wax L. Outlet	Calumet, LA	618
1963	Poplar St.	St. Louis, MO	600
1981	Glenn Jackson (I-205)	Columbia R., OR–WA	600
1976	Archie Stevenot	Stanislaus R., Sonora, CA	550
1982	Illinois R.	Pekin, IL	550
1982	I-440	Arkansas R., AR	540
1980	Harrison-McGarity, Tenn. R.	Savannah, TN	525
1965	MacDonald-Cartier	Ottawa, Ont.	520
1988	Mon City	Monongahela, PA	520
1984	I-182, Columbia R.	Richland, WA.	450
1986	Veterans	Pittsburgh, PA	440
1987	SR 76, Cumberland R.	Dover, TN	440
1987	SR 20, Tennessee R.	Perryville, TN	440
1970	Abernathy (I-205)	Willamette R., OR	430
1974	I-430, Arkansas R.	Little Rock, AR	430
1965	I-24, Tennessee R.	Marion Co., TN	420
1974	Dunbar-S. Charleston	S. Charleston, WV	420
1975	36th St.	Charleston, WV	420
1978	Lewiston-Clarkston	Snake R., Clarkston, WA.	420
1984	FAU 3456, Tenn. R.	Chattanooga, TN	420

Continuous Plate

Year	Bridge	Location	Main span (ft.)
1973	Sidney Sherman (I-610)	Houston, TX	630
1971	Atchafalaya Basin (I-10)	Henderson, LA	573
1992	SR 76, Tennessee R.	Paris, TN	525
1997	SR 114, Tennessee R.	Clifton, TN	525
1981	Illinois 23	Illinois R., IL	510
1968	IH-45, Trinity R.	Dallas, TX	480
1978	Antioch	San Joaquin R., CA	460
1977	Thomas Johnson Mem.	Solomons, MD	451
1967	I-90, Mississippi R.	La Crosse, WI	450
1975	I-129	Missouri R., IA–NE	450
1979	Lewis (U.S. 67)	Missouri R., St. Louis, MO	450
1992	Cuba Landing	Tennessee R., TN	450
1966	I-480	Missouri R., IA–NE	425
1972	Whiskey Bay Pilot	Ramah, LA	425
1972	I-80	Missouri R., IA–NE	425
1972	I-635, Missouri R.	Kansas City, KS–MO	425
1983	US-36	Missouri R., KS–MO	425
1987	I-435	Missouri R., KS–MO	425
1978	I-24	Cumberland R., KY	420
1993	Bob Michel (SR 40)	Peoria, IL	360
1999	SR 53, Clear Fork R.	Fentress/Morgan Co., TN	350

Cable-Stayed

Year	Bridge	Location	Main span (ft.)
2005	Arthur Ravenel Jr.	Charleston, SC	1,546
1986	Alex Fraser	Vancouver, BC	1,526
1994	Clark Bridge	Alton, IL	1,360
1988	Dames Point	Jacksonville, FL	1,300
1995	Fred Hartman	Houston Ship Channel, Baytown, TX	1,250
2003	Sidney Lanier	Brunswick, GA	1,250
1983	Hale Boggs Memorial	Luling, LA	1,222
1987	Sunshine Skyway	Tampa Bay, FL	1,200
2002	William Natcher	Ohio R., KY–IN	1,200
1988	Tampico	Panuco R., Mexico	1,181
1988	Skybridge (ALRT)[15]	Fraser R., Vancouver, BC	1,115
1991	Talmadge Mem.	Savannah, GA	1,100
1993	Mezcala	Mex. City/Acapulco Hwy.	1,024
1978	Pasco-Kennewick	Columbia R., WA.	981
1984	Coatzacoalcos	Coatzacoalcos R., Mexico	945
1985	E. Huntington	Huntington, WV–OH	900
1987	Bayview	Quincy, IL	900
1970	Burton	New Brunswick, Canada	850

Year	Bridge	Location	Main span (ft.)
1990	Weirton-Steubenville	Ohio R., WV–OH	820
1969	Papineau-Leblanc	Montreal, Que.	790
1991	Cochrane	Mobile, AL	780
1995	Chesapeake & Delaware Canal	C&D Canal, St. Georges, DE	750
2003	Leonard Zakim Bunker Hill	Boston, MA	745
1966	Kelly's Creek	New Brunswick, Canada	713
1967	Hawkshaw	New Brunswick, Canada	713
1993	Quetzalapa	Quetzalapa, Mexico	699
1996	Burlington	Burlington, IA	660
1991	Veterans Memorial	Neches R., Port Arthur-Bridge City, TX	640
1990	Varina-Enon	Richmond, VA	630

I-Beam Girder

Year	Bridge	Location	Main span (ft.)
1980	I-20	Shreveport, LA	438
2001	Moore Haven	Caloosahachee Canal, FL	320
1988	Route 18	Weston's Mill Pond, NJ	276

Steel Arch

Year	Bridge	Location	Main span (ft.)
1977	New River Gorge	Fayetteville, WV	1,700
1931	Bayonne (Kill Van Kull)	Bayonne, NJ	1,675
1973	Fremont	Portland, OR	1,255
1964	Port Mann	Vancouver, BC	1,200
1967	Laviolette	Trois-Rivières, Quebec	1,100
1990	Roosevelt Lake	Roosevelt Lake, AZ	1,080
1917	'Hell Gate	East R., NY	978
1959	Glen Canyon	Page, AZ	1,028
1962	Lewiston-Queenston	Niagara R., NY–Ont.	1,001
1976	Perrine	Twin Falls, ID	993
1941	Rainbow	Niagara Falls, NY–Ont.	984
1997	Blue Water	Port Huron, MI–Ont.	922
1977	Moundsville	Ohio R., WV	912
1992	Jefferson Barracks (I-255)	Mississippi R., St. Louis, MO	909
1972	Hernando de Soto (I-40)[16]	Mississippi R., AR–TN	900
1936	Henry Hudson	Harlem R., NY	840
1966	Bob Cummings-Lincoln Trail	Ohio R., IN–KY	825
1978	I-57 Miss. R. Crossing	Cairo, IL	821
1961	Sherman Minton, I-64	IN–Louisville, KY	800
1980	I-65, Mobile R.	Mobile, AL	800
1932	West End	Pittsburgh, PA	780
1978	I-470, Ohio R.	Wheeling, WV	780
1997	Navajo	Marble Canyon, AZ	726
1959	Theodore Kosciusko	Mohawk R., NY	600
1917	Detroit-Superior High Level	Cuyahoga R., Cleveland, OH	591
2000	Paper Mill Road	Baltimore, MD	500

Concrete Arch

Year	Bridge	Location	Main span (ft.)
1995	Natchez Trace Pkwy.	Franklin, TN.	582
1993	Lake Street	Minneapolis, St. Paul, MN.	556
1971	Fred Redmon (twin)	Selah, WA	549
1968	Cowlitz R.	Mossyrock, WA	520
1931	Westinghouse	Pittsburgh, PA	460
1923	Cappelen Memorial	Minneapolis, MN	435
2000	Crooked River	Terrebonne, OR	410
1930	Jack's Run	Pittsburgh, PA	400
1932	Isaac Lee Patterson	Rogue R. Gold Beach, OR	230

Segmental Concrete

Year	Bridge	Location	Main span (ft.)
1997	Confederation	Prince Edward Is., NB	820
1978	Shubenacadie R.	S. Maitland, Nova Scotia	790
1982	Jesse H. Jones Memorial	Houston, TX	750
1992	Jamestown-Verrazano	Narragansett Bay, RI.	674
2002	Vietnam Veterans Memorial	James R., Richmond, VA	672
1986	Umatilla	Columbia R., OR-WA	660
1978	Stanislaus R.	Parrets Ferry. CA	640
1981	Juneau-Douglas	Gastineau Channel, AK.	620
1991	Veterans Memorial Centennial Bridge	Coeur d'Alene, ID	520
2001	Smart Road	Blacksburg, VA	472
1974	Pine Valley Creek	Pine Valley, CA	450
1988	Zilwaukee (twin)	Zilwaukee, MI	392
1985	Red River	Boyce, LA	370

Twin Concrete Trestle[17]

Year	Bridge	Location	Main span (ft.)
1979	I-55/I-10	Manchac, LA	181,157
1969	L. Pontchartrain Cswy.	near New Orleans, LA	126,720
1972	Atchafalaya Swamp Frwy.	Baton Rouge, LA	93,984
1983	*Interstate 310	Kenner, LA	25,925

Concrete Slab Dam[17]

Year	Bridge	Location	Main span (ft.)
1927	Conowingo Dam	Susquehanna R., MD	4,611
1952	John H. Kerr	Mecklenburg Co., VA	2,785
1936	Hoover Dam	Lake Mead, NV	1,324

Miscellaneous Bridges

Year	Bridge	Type	Loc.	Main span (ft.)
1962	International	Arch Truss	Sault Ste. Marie, MI–Ont.	430
1997	Second Blue Water	Continuous Tied Arch.	Pt. Huron, MI–Ont.	922
1982	SR 193	Seg. Box Girder	Dauphin Is., AL	400
1939	O'Neal (U.S. 43)	Through Truss	Tenn. R., Florence, AL	420
1958	John Snodgrass	Through Truss	Tenn. R., Stevenson, AL	500
1936	Yaquina Bay	Steel Braced and Concrete Tied Arches	Newport, OR	600
1958	Tombigbee R.	Steel Girder	Choctow Co., AL	400
1916	C&O RR	Steel Girder	Portsmouth, OH	775
1987	Powder Point[17]	Tropical Hardwood	Duxbury, MA	2,200
2002	Croatan Sound[17]	Continuous Postension Girder	Manteo, NC	5.2 mi

Drawbridges
Vertical Lift

Year	Bridge	Location	Main span (ft.)
1959	*Arthur Kill	NY–NJ	558
1965	Pennsylvania Railroad	Kirkwood-Mt. Pleas., DE	548
1935	*Cape Cod Canal	Cape Cod, MA	544
1961	*Delair	Delaware R., NJ	542
1931	Burlington-Bristol	Delaware R., NJ–PA	540
1937	Marine Parkway Gil Hodges Mem.	Jamaica Bay, NY	540
1908	*Willamette R.	Portland, OR.	521
1968	Second Narrows	Vancouver, B.C.	493
1911	*Armour-Swift-Burlington	Kansas City, MO	428
1945	*Harry S Truman	Kansas City, MO	427
1955	Roosevelt Island	East R., NY.	418
1980	US-17, James R.	Isle of Wight Co., VA	415
1932	*M-K-T RR	Missouri R., MO	414
1969	Cape Fear Mem.	Wilmington, NC	408
1930	Aerial Lift	Duluth, MN	386
1962	Burlington	Ontario, Can.	370
1941	Main Street	Jacksonville, FL	365
1967	SR-156, James R.	Prince George Co., VA.	364
1950	Red R.	Moncla, LA	360
1957	Industrial Canal	New Orleans, LA	360
1936	Triborough	Harlem R., NY	344
1939	U.S. 1&9, Passaic R.	Newark, NJ	333
1930	*Martinez	Martinez, CA	328
1960	St. Andrews Bay	Panama City, FL.	327
1929	*Penn-Lehigh	Newark Bay, PA	322
1987	Industrial Canal	New Orleans, LA	320
1920	*Chattanooga	Tennessee R., TN	310
1960	Broadway	Harlem R., NY	304
1910	Hawthorne	Willamette R., Portland, OR	244

Steel Suspension

Year	Bridge	Location	Main span (ft.)
1931	Maumee R.	Toledo, OH	785

Bascule

Year	Bridge	Location	Main span (ft.)
1917	Market Street	Tenn. R., Chattanooga, TN	306
2003	*SW 2nd Avenue	Miami, FL	302
1956	Duwamish R.	Seattle, WA	300
1955	Chehalis R.	Aberdeen, WA	288
1968	Elizabeth R.	Chesapeake, VA	280
1913	Broadway	Portland, OR	278
1936	Siuslaw River	Florence, OR	154

Swing Bridges

Year	Bridge	Location	Main span (ft.)
1927	Fort Madison[7]	Mississippi R., IA	545
1991	SW Spokane St.	Seattle, WA	480
1930	Rigolets Pass	New Orleans, LA	400
1950	Douglass Memorial	Washington, DC	386
1945	Lord Delaware	Mattaponi R., VA	252

Swing Span

Year	Bridge	Location	Main span (ft.)
1897	*Duluth	St. Louis Bay, MN	486
1899	*C.M.&N. RR.	Chicago, IL	474
1913	Rt. 82, Conn. R.	E. Haddam, CT	465
1914	*Coos Bay RR	Coos Bay, OR	458
1936	Umpqua River	Reedsport, OR	430

Floating Pontoon

Year	Bridge	Location	Main span (ft.)
1963	Evergreen Pt.	Seattle, WA	7,578
1961	Hood Canal	Hood Canal, WA	6,521
1993	Lacey V. Murrow[18]	Seattle, WA	6,620
1989	Third Lake Washington	Seattle, WA	5,811

(1) Swing span bridge with 2 spans of 2,310 ft. each. (2) A second parallel bridge was completed in 1968. (3) A second parallel bridge was completed in 1978. (4) Currently scheduled for demolition in 2014 upon completion of the new East Span, a suspension bridge. (5) Under demolition, to be completed in 2007. (6) The Richmond Bridge has twin spans of 1,070 ft. each. (7) Railroad and vehicular bridge. (8) Railroad and vehicular bridge. McKinley Bridge has been out of service since 2001. It is currently being renovated and is scheduled to be reopened in 2007. (9) Two spans each 825 ft. (10) Two spans each 707 ft. (11) Two spans each 700 ft. (12) Two spans each 775 ft. (13) Two spans each 550 ft. (14) Two spans each 660 ft. (15) ALRT = Automated Light Rail Transit. Transit-only bridge. (16) Two spans each 900 ft. (17) Length listed is total length of bridge. (18) Replaces the original Lacey V. Murrow bridge, which opened in 1940 and sank in 1990.

Oldest U.S. Bridges in Continuous Use

Built in 1697, the stone-arch Frankford Ave. Bridge crosses Pennypack Creek in Philadelphia, PA. A 3-span bridge with a total length of 75 ft., it was constructed as part of the King's Road, which eventually connected Philadelphia to New York.

The oldest covered bridge, completed in 1827, is the double-span, 278-ft. Haverhill Bath Bridge, which spans the Ammonoosuc River, between the towns of Bath and Haverhill, NH.

Some Notable International Bridges

Span of bridge is the distance between its supports. Asterisk (*) designates under construction.

Suspension

Year	Bridge	Location	Main span (ft.)
2012	*Strait of Messina	Italy	10,827
1998	Akashi Kaikyo	Japan	6,532
NA	*Izmit Bay.	Turkey	5,538
1998	Storebælt (East Bridge)	Denmark	5,328
2005	Runyang	China	4,888
1981	Humber	England	4,626
1999	Jiangyin Yangtze	China	4,544
1997	Tsing Ma[1]	China	4,518
1997	Höga Kusten	Sweden	3,970
1988	Minami Bisan-Seto	Japan	3,609
1988	Fatih Sultan Mehmet (Second Bosphorus)	Turkey	3,576
1973	Bosphorus	Turkey	3,524
1999	Kurushima III	Japan	3,379
1999	Kurushima II.	Japan	3,346
1966	Tagus River[2]	Portugal	3,323
1964	Forth Road.	Scotland	3,300
1988	Kita Bisan-Seto	Japan	3,248
1966	Severn	England	3,241
2001	Yichang	China	3,150
1988	Shimotsui Strait	Japan	3,084

NA = not available. (1) Double-decked road and rail bridge. (2) Railroad and highway bridge.

Steel Arch

Year	Bridge	Location	Main span (ft.)
2003	Lupu Bridge	China	1,804
1932	Sydney Harbour	Australia	1,650
2005	Wuhan Yangtze River	China	1,614
2007	*Chenab	India	1,513
2007	*Numata River Gorge	Japan	1,247
2000	Yajisha	China	1,181
1962	Bridge of the Americas	Panama	1,128
1967	Zdakov	China	1,083
1961	Runcorn-Widnes	England	1,082
1935	Birchenough	Zimbabwe	1,080

Concrete Arch

Year	Bridge	Location	Main span (ft.)
1997	Wanxian	China	1,378
1980	Krk I	Croatia	1,280
1995	Jiangjiehe	China	1,083
1998	Yijiang	China	1,024
1964	Gladesville	Australia	1,000
1965	Amizade	Brazil	951

Year	Bridge	Location	Main span (ft.)
1984	Bloukrans	South Africa	892
1963	Arrabida	Portugal	886
1943	Sandö	Sweden	866

Cantilever

Year	Bridge	Location	Main span (ft.)
1890	Forth[1] (rail)	Scotland	1,709
1974	Minato	Japan	1,673
1943	Howrah	India	1,500

(1) Two spans of 1,709 ft. each.

Steel Plate and Box Girder

Year	Bridge	Location	Main span (ft.)
1974	Rio-Niteroi	Brazil	984
1956	Sava I	Serbia	856
1966	Zoobrücke	Germany	850

Cable-Stayed

Year	Bridge	Location	Main span (ft.)
2009	*Sutong	China	3,570
2008	*Stonecutters	China	3,340
1999	Tatara	Japan	2,920
1995	Pont de Normandie	France	2,808
2009	*Second Incheon	South Korea	2,625
2001	Nanjing Second Yangtze River	China	2,060
2000	Wuhan Baishazhou Yangtze River	China	2,028
1996	Quingzhou Minjang	China	1,985
1993	Yangpu	China	1,975
1997	Xupu	China	1,936
1998	Meiko Chuo	Japan	1,936
2004	Rion-Antirion	Greece	1,837
1991	Skarnsundet	Norway	1,739
1999	Queshi	China	1,699
1995	Tsurumi Tsubasa	Japan	1,673
2002	Jingsha	China	1,640
2000	Oresund	Denmark–Sweden	1,614
1991	Ikuchi	Japan	1,608
1994	Higashi Kobe	Japan	1,591
1998	Zhanjiang	China	1,575
1997	Ting Kau	China	1,558
1992	Arade	Portugal	1,542
1999	Seo Hae Grand	South Korea	1,542
1989	Yokohama Bay	Japan	1,509
1993	Second Hooghly River	India	1,499
1995	Second Severn Crossing	England/Wales	1,496

World's Longest Railway Tunnels

Source: World Almanac Research

(* = under construction)

Tunnel	Date	Miles	Operating railway	Country
*Gotthard Base Tunnel	2015	35.	Swiss Federal Railways	Switzerland-Italy
*Brenner Base Tunnel	2015	34.	Austrian Federal Railways	Austria-Italy
Seikan	1988	33.5	Japan Railways	Japan
*Mont d'Ambin Base Tunnel	2015	33.0	RFF & RFI	France-Italy
English Channel Tunnel	1994	31.1	Eurotunnel	UK-France
*Loetschberg	2007	21.0	BLS Lötschbergbahn AG	Switzerland
*Guadarrama	2007	17.6	Renfe	Spain
*Hakkoda	2010	16.4	Japan Railways	Japan
Iwate-Ichinohe	2002	16.0	Japan Railways	Japan
Daishimizu	1982	13.8	Japan Railways	Japan
Wushaoling	2006	12.5	Chinese state	China
Simplon No. 1 and 2	1906, 1922	12.3	BLS Lötschbergbahn AG	Switzerland-Italy
Vereina	1999	11.8	Rhätische Bahn (RhB)	Switzerland
*London Tunnels (Channel Tunnel Link)	2007	11.8	LCR	UK
Shin-Kanmon	1975	11.6	Japan Railways	Japan
Vaglia	2006	11.5	Ferrovie dello Stato (FS)	Italy
Appennino	1934	11.5	Ferrovie dello Stato (FS)	Italy
Qinling	2002	11.5	Chinese state	China
Rokko	1972	10.1	Japan Railways	Japan
Furka Base Tunnel	1982	9.6	Matterhorn Gotthard Railway	Switzerland
Haruna	1982	9.6	Japan Railways	Japan
Severomuyskiy	2003	9.5	Russian Railways	Russia
Gorigamine	1997	9.4	Japan Railways	Japan
*Firenzuola	2008	9.4	Ferrovie dello Stato (FS)	Italy
Monte Santomarco	1987	9.3	Ferrovie dello Stato (FS)	Italy

Underwater Vehicular Tunnels in North America

Source: World Almanac Research

(more than 5,000 ft. in length; year in parentheses is year of completion)

Name	Location	Waterway	Feet
Brooklyn-Battery Tunnel (1950) (twin)	New York, NY	East River	9,117
Holland Tunnel (1927) (twin)	New York, NY–Jersey City, NJ	Hudson River	8,558/8,371
Ted Williams Tunnel (1995)	Boston, MA	Boston Harbor	8,448
Lincoln Tunnel (1937, 1945, 1957) (3 tubes)	New York, NY–Weehawken, NJ	Hudson River	8,216/7,482/8,006
Thimble Shoal Channel (1964)	Northampton Co., VA	Chesapeake Bay	5,734
Chesapeake Channel (1964)	Northampton Co., VA	Chesapeake Bay	5,423
Fort McHenry Tunnel (1985) (twin)	Baltimore, MD	Patapsco River	7,920
Hampton Roads (1957, 1976) (twin)	Hampton, VA	Hampton Roads	7,479
Baltimore Harbor Tunnel (1957) (twin)	Baltimore, MD	Baltimore Harbor	7,392
Queens Midtown Tunnel (1940) (twin)	New York, NY	East River	6,414
Sumner Tunnel (1934)	Boston, MA	Boston Harbor	5,653
Louis-Hippolyte Lafontaine Tunnel (1967)	Montreal, Que.	St. Lawrence River	4,921
Detroit-Windsor Tunnel (1930)	Detroit, MI–Windsor, Ont.	Detroit River	5,160
Callahan Tunnel (1961)	Boston, MA	Boston Harbor	5,070

Land Vehicular Tunnels in the U.S.

Source: Federal Highway Administration, U.S. Dept. of Transportation; World Almanac Research

(more than 3,000 ft. in length)

Name	Location	Feet	Name	Location	Feet
Anton Anderson Memorial[1]	Whittier, AK	13,300	Lehigh (twin)	PA Turnpike	4,380
Edwin Johnson Memorial	I-70, CO	8,960	Wawona	Yosemite Natl. Pk., CA	4,233
Eisenhower Memorial	I-70, CO	8,939	Big Walker Mt. (twin)	Bland Co., VA	4,229
Allegheny (twin)	PA Turnpike	6,070	Squirrel Hill	Pittsburgh, PA	4,225
Liberty Tunnel (twin)	Pittsburgh, PA	5,920	Hanging Lake (twin)	Glenwood Canyon, CO	4,000
Zion-Mt. Carmel	Zion Natl. Park, UT	5,808	Caldecott (3 tubes)	Oakland, CA	3,610/3,771
East River Mt. (twin)	VA–WV	5,412			
Tuscarora Mt. (twin)	PA Turnpike	5,326	Fort Pitt (twin)	Pittsburgh, PA	3,614
Tetsuo Harano (twin)	H-3 Freeway, HI	5,165	Mount Baker	Seattle, WA	3,456
Kittatinny Mt. (twin)	PA Turnpike	4,727	Dingess Tunnel	Mingo Co., WV	3,400
Cumberland Gap (twin)	KY–TN	4,600	Mall Tunnel	Dist. of Columbia	3,400
Blue Mountain (twin)	PA Turnpike	4,339	Cody	U.S. 14, 16, 20, WY	3,202

(1) Tunnel is used for vehicular and railroad traffic.

Major U.S. Dams and Reservoirs

Source: 2005 National Inventory of Dams; U.S. Army Corps of Engineers

Highest U.S. Dams

Rank Order	Dam name	River	State	Type	Height Feet	Height Meters	Year completed
1.	Oroville	Feather	California	E	770	230	1968
2.	Hoover	Colorado	Nevada-Arizona	A	730	221	1936
3.	Dworshak	N. Fork Clearwater	Idaho	G	717	219	1973
4.	Glen Canyon	Colorado	Arizona	A	710	216	1964
5.	New Bullards Bar	North Yuba	California	A	645	194	1969
6.	New Melones	Stanislaus	California	R	625	191	1979
7.	Mossyrock	Cowlitz	Washington	A	606	185	1968
8.	Shasta	Sacramento	California	G	602	183	1945
9.	Don Pedro	Tuolumne	California	G	585	178	1971
10.	Hungry Horse	S. Fork Flathead	Montana	A	564	172	1952

E = Embankment, Earthfill; R = Embankment, Rockfill; G = Gravity; A = Arch.

Largest U.S. Embankment Dams*

Rank Order	Dam name	River	State	Volume Cubic yards × 1000	Volume Cubic meters × 1000	Year completed
1.	Fort Peck	Missouri	Montana	125,624	96,050	1957
2.	Diamond Valley Lake	Domenigion Valley	California	110,551	84,522	2000
3.	Oahe	Missouri	South Dakota	91,996	70,339	1958
4.	Oroville	Feather	California	77,997	59,635	1968
5.	B.F. Sisk	San Luis Creek	California	77,897	59,559	1967
6.	Garrison	Missouri	North Dakota	66,498	50,843	1953
7.	Cochiti	Rio Grande	New Mexico	65,693	50,228	1975
8.	Fort Randall	Missouri	South Dakota	49,962	38,200	1952
9.	Castaic	Castaic Creek	California	43,998	33,640	1973
10.	Seven Oaks	Santa Ana	California	38,373	29,338	1999

* All earthfill.

Largest U.S. Reservoirs

Rank Order	Dam name	Reservoir name	State	Reservoir capacity Cubic meters × 1000	Year completed
1.	Hoover	Lake Mead	Nevada-Arizona	34,850,000	1936
2.	Glen Canyon	Lake Powell	Arizona	33,300,000	1964
3.	Garrison	Lake Sakakawea	North Dakota	27,920,000	1953
4.	Oahe	Lake Oahe	South Dakota	27,430,000	1966
5.	Fort Peck	Fort Peck Lake	Montana	22,120,000	1957
6.	Grand Coulee	F. D. Roosevelt Lake	Washington	11,790,000	1942
7.	Libby	Lake Koocanusa	Montana	7,170,000	1973
8.	Fort Randall	Lake Francis Case	South Dakota	6,300,000	1954
9.	Wolf Creek	Lake Cumberland	Kentucky	6,089,222	1951
10.	Shasta	Lake Shasta	California	5,610,000	1945

Major Dams of the World

Source: Intl. Commission on Large Dams, *World Register of Dams*

World's Highest Dams

Rank order	Name	Country	Height above lowest formation (m)
1.	Rogun*	Tajikistan	335
2.	Nurek	Tajikistan	300
3.	Xiaowan (Yunnan Gorge)*	China	292
4.	Grand Dixence	Switzerland	285
5.	Inguri	Georgia	272
6.	Vaiont	Italy	262
7.	Manuel M. Torres	Mexico	261
8.	Tehri*	India	261
9.	Alvaro Obregon	Mexico	260
10.	Mauvoisin	Switzerland	250
11.	Mica	Canada	243
12.	Alberto Lleras C.	Colombia	243
13.	Sayano-Shushenskskaya	Russia	242
14.	Ertan*	China	240
15.	La Esmeralda	Colombia	237
16.	Kishau*	India	236
17.	Oroville	U.S.	235
18.	El Cajón	Honduras	234
19.	Chirkey	Russia	233
20.	Shuibuya*	China	233

*Under construction.

World's Largest-Volume Embankment Dams

Rank order	Name	Country	Volume cubic meters × 1000
1.	Tarbela	Pakistan	148,500
2.	Fort Peck Gorge	U.S.	96,050
3.	Tucurui	Brazil	85,200
4.	Ataturk	Turkey	85,000
5.	Yacyreta	Argentina	81,000
6.	Rogun*	Tajikistan	75,500
7.	Oahe	U.S.	70,339
8.	Guri	Venezuela	70,000
9.	Parambikulam	India	69,165
10.	High Island West	China	67,000
11.	Gardiner	Canada	65,000
12.	Afsluitdijk	Netherlands	63,400
13.	Mangla	Pakistan	63,379
14.	Oroville	U.S.	59,635
15.	San Luis	U.S.	59,559
16.	Nurek	Tajikistan	58,000
17.	Tanda	Pakistan	57,250
18.	Garrison	U.S.	50,843
19.	Cochiti	U.S.	50,228
20.	Oosterschelde	Netherlands	50,000

*Under construction.

World's Largest-Capacity Hydro Plants

Source: Intl. Commission on Large Dams, *World Register of Dams*

Rank[1]	Name	Country	Rated capacity planned (MW)
1.	Sanxia (Three Gorges Dam)[2]	China	18,200
2.	Itaipu	Brazil-Paraguay	14,000
3.	Guri (Raúl Leoni)	Venezuela	10,000
4.	Tucuruí	Brazil	8,370
5.	Sayano-Shushenskaya	Russia	6,400
6.	Itaipu	Paraguay	6,300
7.	Krasnoyarsk	Russia	6,000
8.	Bratsk	Russia	4,500
9.	Longtan (Guangxi, Tian'e)	China	4,200
10.	Xiaowan (Yunnan)	China	4,200
11.	Ust-Ilim	Russia	3,840
12.	Ilha Solteira	Brazil	3,230
13.	Ertan	China	3,300
14.	Yacyreta	Argentina/Paraguay	3,100
15.	Xingo	Brazil	3,000
16.	Macagua II	Venezuela	2,940
17.	Gezhouba	China	2,715
18.	Minamiaiki	Japan	2,700
19.	Volgograd	Russia	2,541
20.	Chief Joseph Dam	U.S.	2,512

(1) Ranked by rated capacity planned. (2) Construction completed May 2006. Power generation planned to begin in 2008. *Planned or under construction.

World's Largest-Capacity Reservoirs

Source: Intl. Commission on Large Dams, *World Register of Dams*

Rank Order	Name	Country	Capacity cubic meters × 1,000,000
1.	Kariba Gorges	Zimbabwe/Zambia	180,600
2.	Bratsk	Russia	169,000
3.	High Aswan	Egypt	162,000
4.	Akosombo	Ghana	147,960
5.	Daniel Johnson	Canada	141,851
6.	Guri	Venezuela	135,000
7.	W.A.C. Bennett	Canada	74,300
8.	Krasnoyarsk	Russia	73,300
9.	Zeya	Russia	68,400
10.	La Grande 2	Canada	61,715
11.	La Grande 3	Canada	60,020
12.	Ust-Ilim	Russia	59,300
13.	Boguchany	Russia	58,200
14.	Kuibyshev	Russia	58,000
15.	Serra da Mesa	Brazil	54,400

> **IT'S A FACT:** The steel arch Perrine Bridge (main span 993 ft.), in Twin Falls, ID, is the only U.S. structure where BASE jumping is legal year-round without a permit. In BASE jumping ("BASE" stands for buildings, antennae, spans, and earth), participants leap off fixed locations with a parachute.

Timeline of Selected Architectural Styles and Structures

*Denotes part of World Heritage Site

Style and Period	Location; Characteristics; Significant Examples

Mesopotamian
c.3500-539 BCE
	City-states of Sumer, Akkad, Babylon, Assyria (modern-day Iraq). Mud brick rectangular temples on oval platforms with simple corbel vaults, later ziggurats. Painted terra-cotta mosaics and murals; carved reliefs on columns and walls.
	    Ziggurat of Nanna, Ur (Muqayyar, Iraq), ordered by Ur-Nammu, c. 2100 BCE
	    Anu Ziggurat and White Temple, Uruk (Warka, Iraq), c. 3000 BCE

Egyptian
c.3000-30 BCE
	Along Nile R. Mud brick and limestone tombs and massive, geometric pyramids, post-and-lintel construction. Highly decorative with colorful hieroglyphics, carvings, columns, obelisks, paintings, and sculpture.
	    *Stepped Pyramid of Pharaoh Zoser, Saqqara, by Imhotep, c. 2737-2717 BCE
	    *Great Pyramid of Khufu (Giza), c. 2250 BCE
	    *Great Temple of Amon-Ra (Karnak), c.1530-300 BCE
	    *Mortuary Temple of Queen Hatshepsut, Deir el Bahari (Thebes), by Senenmut, c.1479-1458 BCE

Three Dynasties c.2100-221 BCE	China. Single-level mudbrick or mud-smeared timber structures on earthen platforms with thatched roofs. Later, bracketed wooden-framed structures with brick-tiled floors, roofs with overhanging eaves. City of Erlitou (Yanshi, China), c.1900-1500 BCE
Minoan c.1800-1450 BCE	Crete. Palaces, tombs in monumental style adapted from Mesopotamia and Egypt. Multi-level stone palaces with large central court, no fortifications. *Polythyron* walls made of doors; stone porticoes and lintels; wooden ceilings and columns; beehive-shaped tombs (*tholi*). Palace at Knossos (Heraklion, Crete), c.1700 BCE
Mycenaean c.1600-1100 BCE	Greece. Adapted Minoan style, with large stone masonry, huge walls, and fortified citadels with complex palaces (*megaron*). *Treasury of Atreus (Mycenae, Greece), c.1250 BCE
Olmec c.1200-400 BCE	Mexican Gulf Coast. Many religious structures, including stone temple-pyramids centered in cities; also large stone sculptures and mosaic pavement with natural and animistic themes. **Great Pyramid** (La Venta, Mexico), c. 800-400 BCE

Mayan
c.900 BCE-900 CE
	Central America. Religious structures with plaster-surfaced stone temple-pyramids with stairs, containing tombs. Decorative animistic and geometric relief sculptures, lintels, and stone monuments with hieroglyphics.
	    *Pyramid of the Magician (Uxmal, Mexico), c. 700-910 CE
	    North Acropolis (Tikal, Guatemala), c. 200 CE

Greek
c.750-323 BCE
	Greek peninsula, Asia Minor, north Africa, western Mediterranean. Religious, civic buildings in monumental style, inspired by Egypt, based on strict rules of form and human proportion; many ornamental details. Marble and limestone structures (including rectangular temples) with pediment, colonnaded porticos in diverse regional styles, defined by "orders of architecture" like Ionic, Doric, Corinthian. Most early buildings with timber supports; solid stone in later temples.
	    *Parthenon, Acropolis (Athens, Greece), by Ictinus and Callicrates, 447-436 BCE
	    *Temple of Zeus (Olympia, Greece), by Libon of Elis, (mid-5th cent. BCE)
	    Mausoleum of Halicarnassus (Bodrum, Turkey) by Pythis, c.353 BCE (destroyed)
	    *Temple of Apollo Epicurius (Bassae, Greece), by Ictinus, c.420 BCE

Achaemenid
c.550-334 BCE
	Persian empire (Eastern Mediterranean to Indus River). Palatial complexes influenced by cultures absorbed by the empire; limestone and mud brick complexes on raised stone terraces, with ornamental stairways, rectangular pillared audience halls with porticoes and corner towers; pleasure gardens (*bâgh*) as focal point of architecture.
	    *Pasargadae (Iran), founded by Cyrus II after 547 BCE
	    *Persepolis (Iran), founded by Darius I around 518 BCE

Roman
c.500 BCE-400 CE
	Roman Empire. Civic and religious structures with grandiose limestone brick and concrete construction in systematic, practical layout. Adapted Greek orders in many structures, including circular temples and large covered halls (basilica), but emphasized movement with rounded arches and domes, geometric vaults.
	    *Pantheon (Rome, Italy), ordered by Emperor Hadrian, 118-28 CE
	    *Colosseum (Rome, Italy), ordered by Emperor Vespasian, 70-82 CE
	    *Roman Forum (Rome, Italy), 500s BCE -608 CE

Qin & Han
c.221 BCE-220 CE
	China. Massive public works, palaces, tombs, and planned cities; systematic layout and design determined by divination techniques (geomancy). Multi-storied timber palace complexes with gardens, courtyards laid along a long hall with a south-north axis for weather; decorative roof with overhanging eaves.
	    *The Great Wall (China), ordered by Qin Shi Huang, 220-c.1600 CE
	    *Mausoleum of the First Qin Emperor (Xianyang [Xi'an]), c.210 BCE

Sassanian
226-651 CE
	Iran. Mud brick, mortared rubble, and stone palaces on platforms. Tall, vaulted entry chambers with one open side (iwans). Three-aisled hall chambers covered with rudimentary barrel vaults. Parabolic domes abandoned for square courtyards in later Sassanian period.
	    Palace of Ardashir I (Firuzabad, Iran), c.224
	    Taq-i Kisra [Arch of Khosrau] (Ctesiphon, Iraq), c.260 or c.550

Byzantine
330-1453
	Byzantine Empire, Italy, Russia. Religious structures with masonry construction based on Roman architecture, many salvaged pieces of old structures. Centralized cross-in-square layout, with large central dome supported by vaults. Highly decorative, with iconographic frescoes, glass mosaics.
	    *Hagia Sophia (Istanbul, Turkey), by Anthemius and Isidorous, 532-37
	    *St. Mark's Basilica (Venice, Italy), ordered by Domenico Contarini, 1063-94

Sui-Tang Dynasties
581-906
	China. Includes influences from other cultures; geomancy used to enhance "harmony" and social status. Rectangular, multi-story modular timber structures with interlinking corridors; single-eaved roofs with exposed beams.
	    Daming Palace (Xi'an, China), 634 (destroyed)
	    Hall of the Great Buddha at Foguang Temple (Wutai Mountain), ordered rebuilt by Xuan Zhong, 857

Early Islamic (Umayyad)
692-c.1000
	Syria, Middle East, northern Africa, southern Spain. Mosques in adapted Sassanian style. Austere exteriors; simple columned halls with minarets and mihrab, walled courtyards and gardens, onion domes. Highly decorative interiors with patterned marble, mosaics.
	    Dome of the Rock [Qubbat al-Sakhra] (Jerusalem), ordered by Abd al-Malik, 692
	    Great Mosque of Córdoba (Spain), order by Abd al-Rahman I, 784-86

Khmer c.880-1200s	Indochina. Hindu or Buddhist temple complexes, including brick, later sandstone beehive-shaped shrines with arches atop terraced temple "mountains" symbolizing Mount Meru, Hindu and Buddhist "Mountain of the Gods." Concentric layout of structures mimics the cosmos, relating religious narrative in carved reliefs. *Angkor Wat (Cambodia), ordered by Suryavarman II, 12th cent.

Romanesque (Norman)
c.900s-1100s
	Western Europe. Churches and monasteries in localized Roman style; many reused material from Roman structures. Austere, heavy, simple, masonry construction with thick walls, concealed buttresses, small windows, barrel arches & vaults. Churches like Roman basilica with arched central nave, lower side aisles, apse, transept formed Latin cross. Monumental art and ornaments with Christian narrative throughout, especially on façade and portals.
	    *Durham Cathedral (England), ordered by Bishop William de Saint-Calais, 1093-1133
	    *Cathedral, Baptistery, and "Leaning" Tower (Pisa, Italy), by various architects, begun in 1063, tower not completed until 1372

Style and Period	Location; Characteristics; Significant Examples

Gothic
c.1100s-1500s
	France, Europe. Cathedrals meant to inspire spirituality with design like Roman basilica: pointed arches and spires that reach towards heaven, skeletal masonry, revealed structure like flying buttresses, ribbed vaults (to allow better lighting), large stained-glass windows.
	    Abbey Church of Saint-Denis (France), ordered by Abbot Suger, 1136-47
	    *Cathedral of Notre-Dame (Paris, France), ordered by Bishop Maurice de Sully, 1163-1351
	    *Chartres Cathedral (France), 1194-1260
	    *Cologne Cathedral (Cologne, Germany), ordered by Archbishop Konrad von Hochstaden, 1248-1880
	    *St. Vitus Cathedral (Prague, Czech Republic), by Matthias of Arras, later Peter Parler, 1344-1929

Yüan & Ming 1279-1644	China. Mongol-influenced timber and some brick structures, influenced by geomancy. Emphasized monumental mass in sprawling yet low-lying structures with simple rectangular pavilions, great halls, elaborate wooden latticework, carved and painted details. ***Forbidden City** (Beijing, China), ordered by Emperor Yung Lo, 1406-20

Renaissance
1420s-1520s
	Italy. The "rebirth" or rediscovery of ancient Roman design, grounded in a scholarly approach to architecture. Followed rules of proportion in perspective and symmetry, classical orders, and simple but perfected geometric forms; emphasis on human scale.
	    *Pazzi Chapel (Florence, Italy), by Filippo Brunelleschi, 1429-61
	    *Palazzo Medici-Riccardi (Florence, Italy), by Michelozzo di Bartolomeo, 1444-60
	    *Tempietto San Pietro (Rome, Italy), by Donato Bramante, 1502-10
	    Villa Almerico Capra "La Rotonda" (near Vicenza, Italy), by Andrea Palladio, later Vincenzo Scamozzi, 1566-1610

Mughal
1526-1858
	India. Monumental palaces and mosques, blending Hindu and Islamic architecture. Sandstone with marble inlay; highly decorative, with semi-precious stones, vegetal and Koranic motifs. Formulaic four-part pleasure gardens (*charbâgh*), exemplified by grounds of Taj Mahal.
	    *Humayun Tomb (Delhi, India), by Sayyid Muhammad, 1562-72
	    *Taj Mahal (Agra, India), ordered by Emperor Shah Jahan, 1631-48

Baroque
1630s-1700s
	Italy, later Western Europe. Elaborate and theatrical religious and civic structures, focused on dramatic overall effect. Complex geometric shapes and elaborate sculptures meant to be viewed from many angles.
	    St. Carlo alle Quattro Fontane, Rome, by Francesco Borromini, 1638-41
	    *Palace of Versailles (Versailles, France), royal hunting lodge (built 1631-34) expanded under Louis XIV, 1661-1710
	    Church of San Lorenzo (Turin, Italy), by Guarino Guarini, 1666-79
	    Church of St. John of Nepomuk "Asamkirche" (Munich, Germany), by Cosmas Damian & Egid Quirin Asam, 1733-46

Rococo 1690s-1700s	Europe. Mostly interior, simplified but still fanciful Baroque designs; ornate with natural motifs, gold trim, light and creamy colors, asymmetrical designs and unusual materials. *Sanssouci Palace (Potsdam, Germany), by Georg Wenzeslaus von Knobelsdorff, 1745-47

Neoclassicism
1750-1830
	Europe, Americas. Civic, commercial, and religious structures; chaste, non-decorative designs in reaction to Baroque excess. Grounded in enlightenment-era principles and simple, strict adherence to classic (Greek, Roman, Renaissance) forms and details. Palladian style in England, Federal style in U.S.
	    Chiswick House (Chiswick, England), by Richard Boyle, 1725-29
	    *Monticello (Charlottesville, VA), by Thomas Jefferson, 1768-1809

Neogothic
1837-1900s
	Britain and U.S. Civic, commercial, and religious structures utilizing Gothic forms in new commercial enterprises like railway stations and hotels. Traditional masonry façade disguised modern structural material like iron and glass.
	    *Westminster Palace (London, England), by Charles Barry & A.W.N. Pugin, 1840-47
	    Hotel fronting St. Pancras Railway Station (London, England), by George Gilbert Scott, 1865-71

Arts and Crafts
1850s-1930s
	England and U.S. Residential structures made of brick and other indigenous materials with pastoral and traditional elements like gabled roofs. Conceived as a reaction against homogenization of style following the industrial revolution.
	    Red House (Bexley Heath, England) by Philip Webb, 1859
	    Tigbourne Court (Surrey, England) by Edwin Lutyens, 1898

Beaux-Arts
1870s-1930s
	France, U.S. Grandiose, highly decorative style, using a mix of classical forms taught at the Ecole des Beaux-Arts in Paris: columns, wall projections, elaborate rooftops, high-relief decoration.
	    Boston Public Library (Boston, MA), by McKim, Mead, and White, 1888-95
	    Grand Central Terminal (New York, NY), Reed & Stem and Warren & Wetmore, 1903-13

Art Noveau
1884-1905
	Europe (esp. Brussels, Belgium, France). Civic and residential structures using industrial products like metal and glass to mimic natural forms; airy, fluid, and ornate.
	    Hôtel Tassel (Brussels, Belgium), by Victor Horta, 1892-93
	    Entrances to Metro (Paris, France), by Hector Guimard, 1900

Prairie
1893-1917
	U.S. Mostly residences, some civic buildings in adapted Arts and Crafts style. Inspired by American midwest and small-town values. Frank Lloyd Wright most notable architect of the style. Buildings centered on chimney, with overhanging eaves and horizontal emphasis, long bands of windows.
	    Robie House (Chicago, IL), by Frank Lloyd Wright, 1908-10
	    National Farmer's Bank (Owatonna, MN), by Louis Sullivan, 1906-08

Futurism 1913-14	Italy. Purely theoretical style that produced no actual structures; emphasized concrete, glass, and steel construction, pure geometric forms and straight lines, and exposed structure and utilities. La Citta Nuova (sketches), by Antonio Sant'Elia, 1913
Constructivism 1914-20s	Russia, Europe. Public buildings based on socialist philosophies. Purely utilitarian industrial design, modern materials. Rusakov Club (Moscow), by Konstantin Melnikov, 1927–28
De Stijl 1917-31	Netherlands. Building and fixtures designed as a complete, sculpture-like piece of art; emphasis on primary colors, simple but asymmetrical geometry. Name is Dutch for "The Style." Schröder House (Utrecht, Netherlands), by Gerrit Thomas Rietveld, 1923-24
Bauhaus 1919-33	Weimar Republic Germany. Art and design school founded by Walter Gropius with philosophy that the machine is the modern medium. Concrete, glass, and steel construction that united industrial crafts and fine arts with simple geometric forms and colors. Bauhaus (Dessau, Germany), by Walter Gropius, 1925-26

International Style
1920s-70s
	Asia, Europe, N. America. Reinforced concrete and steel structures, mostly commercial buildings with some residences and civic structures. Post-and-slab construction meant walls no longer support weight so façades could be continuous strip (ribbon) glass "curtain-walls" with modular interiors. Emphasis on simple forms; glass, marble, and stainless steel; minimal decoration.
	    Philadelphia Savings Fund Society Building (Philadelphia, PA), by George Howe & William Lescaze, 1926-32
	    Villa Savoye (Poissy, France), by Le Corbusier, 1928-31
	    Seagram Building (New York, NY), by Ludwig Mies Van Der Rohe with Philip Johnson, 1954-58

Art Deco
1925-30s
	Europe, U.S. Traditional, symmetric, elegant construction (like Beaux-Arts) whimsically mixed with modern styles like geometric forms and steel or chrome features.
	    Chrysler Building (New York, NY), by William van Alen, 1928-30
	    Empire State Building (New York, NY), by Shreve, Lamb, & Harmon, 1930-31

Postmodernism
1970s-present
	Asia, Europe, N. America. Playful reaction against generic, mainstream "orthodox modern architecture" (not all modern architecture). Token references to traditional architectural elements like pediments or gables on houses; aim to present "old clichés in new settings."
	    Vanna Venturi House (Philadelphia, PA), by Robert Venturi, 1962
	    Public Service Building (Portland, OR), by Michael Graves, 1980-83

As of mid-2006, there were **194 nations** in the world. This number includes 2 nations that are not members of the United Nations—Taiwan and Vatican City (the Holy See). The 194 nations are profiled below, in alphabetical order. Certain regions and territories that are not independent nations can be found under the entry for the governing nation. Following the nation profiles are comparative statistics, information on international organizations, and other information about nations.

Sources: U.S. Census Bureau; Intl. Data Base; U.S. Central Intelligence Agency: *The World Factbook*; U.S. Dept. of Energy; U.S. Dept. of State; United Nations Education, Scientific, and Cultural Org. (UNESCO); UN Food and Agriculture Org.: FAO Statistical Database and Yearbook of Fishery Statistics; UNAIDS and World Health Organization; Intl. Monetary Fund; Intl. Telecommunication Union ; UN Population Division: *World Population Prospects* and *World Urbanization Prospects*; UN Statistics Division: *Statistical Yearbook*; World Tourism Organization; Intl. Institute for Strategic Studies: *The Military Balance*.

Note: Because of rounding or incomplete enumeration, some percentages may not add to 100%. FY = fiscal year. **National population** and **health** figures are mid-2006 estimates, unless otherwise noted. **Percentage of urban population** is for mid-2003. **City populations** and **capital** populations are 2005 estimates for **urban agglomerations**, i.e., whole metropolitan areas. Where indicated, the latest available population of the city proper is also given. **Defense budget** and **active troops** figures are from mid-2005, unless otherwise noted. **GDP** estimates are based on purchasing power parity calculations, which involve use of intl. dollar price weights applied to quantities of goods and services produced. **Tourism** figures are latest available and represent receipts from international tourism. **Budget** figures are for expenditures, unless otherwise noted. Figures for **gold reserves**, **international reserves less gold**, and changes in **consumer prices** are from 2005, unless otherwise noted. **Railroad, motor vehicle**, and **civil aviation** statistics are latest available; comm. (commercial) vehicles include trucks and buses. Airport figures include total number with paved runways as of mid-2006. **TV, radio**, and **daily newspaper circ.** figures are latest available. **Telephone** and **Internet** data are for 2005, unless otherwise noted. **Life expect.** is at birth for persons born in 2006. **AIDS rate** is the est. number of adults, aged 15-49, living with HIV at year-end 2005, divided by the total 2005 population aged 15-49. **Education** figures are for the 2003-04 school year unless otherwise noted. **Literacy rates** generally measure the percent of population able to read and write on a lower elementary school level, not the (smaller) percent able to read instructions necessary for a job or license. **Embassy addresses** are for Wash., DC, area code (202), unless otherwise noted.

For further details and later information on developments around the world, see the Chronology of the Year's Events. See pages 457-472 for full-color maps and flags of all nations.

Afghanistan
Islamic Republic of Afghanistan
People: Population: 31,056,997. **Age distrib.** (%) <15: 44.6; 65+: 2.4. **Pop. density:** 124 per sq mi, 47 per sq km. **Urban:** 23.3%. **Ethnic groups:** Pashtun 44%, Tajik 25%, Hazara 10%, Uzbek 8%. **Principal languages:** Dari (Afghan Persian), Pashtu (both official); Turkic (incl. Uzbek, Turkmen); Balochi, Pashai, many others. **Chief religion:** Muslim (official; Sunni 80%, Shi'a 19%).

Geography: Total area: 250,001 sq mi, 647,500 sq km; **Land area:** 250,001 sq mi, 647,500 sq km. **Location:** In SW Asia, NW of the Indian subcontinent. **Neighbors:** Pakistan on E, S; Iran on W; Turkmenistan, Tajikistan, Uzbekistan on N. The NE tip touches China. **Topography:** The country is landlocked and mountainous, much of it over 4,000 ft. above sea level. The Hindu Kush Mts. tower 16,000 ft. above Kabul and reach a height of 25,000 ft. to the E. Trade with Pakistan flows through the 35-mile-long Khyber Pass. The climate is dry, with extreme temperatures, and there are large desert regions. **Capital:** Kabul, 2,994,000.

Government: Type: Islamic republic. **Head of state and gov.:** Pres. Hamid Karzai; b. Dec. 24, 1957; in office: June 19, 2002. **Local divisions:** 32 provinces. **Defense budget** (2005): NA. **Active troops:** 27,000.

Economy: Industries: textiles, soap, furniture, shoes. **Chief crops:** wheat, fruits, nuts, wool. **Natural resources:** nat. gas, oil, coal, copper, chromite, talc, barite, sulfur, lead, zinc, iron ore, salt, gems. **Arable land:** 12%. **Livestock** (2002): chickens: 6.50 mil; goats: 5 mil; sheep: 11 mil. **Fish catch** (2004): 1,000 metric tons. **Electricity prod.** (2004): 0.73 bil kWh. **Labor force** (2004 est.): agriculture 80%, industry 10%, services 10%.

Finance: Monetary unit: Afghani (AFN) (Sept. 2006: 50.30 = $1 U.S.). **GDP** (2004 est.): $21.5 bil; **per capita GDP:** $800; **GDP growth:** 8%. **Imports** (2005 est.): $3.87 bil; partners (2004): Pakistan 25.2%, U.S. 8.7%, South Korea 7.1%, India 7.6%, Germany 6.5%, Turkmenistan 4.5%, Turkey 4.1%. **Exports** (2005 est.): $471.0 mil.; partners (2004): India 23.1%, Pakistan 20.5%, U.S. 12.9%, Germany 6%. **Tourism** (1998) $1 mil. **Budget** (2005 est.): $561 mil.

Transport: Railroad: Length: 15 mi. **Motor vehicles:** 8,600 pass. cars, 4,500 comm. vehicles. **Civil aviation:** 88.9 mil pass.-mi; 11 airports.

Communications: TV sets: 14 per 1,000 pop. **Radios:** 132 per 1,000 pop. **Telephone lines:** 100,000 main lines. **Daily newspaper circ.:** NA. **Internet:** 25,000 users.

Health: Life expect.: 43.2 male; 43.5 female. **Births** (per 1,000 pop.): 46.6. **Deaths** (per 1,000 pop.): 20.3. **Natural inc.:** 2.63%. **Infant mortality** (per 1,000 live births): 160.2. **AIDS rate:** <0.1%.

Education: Compulsory: ages 6-15. **Literacy:** 28.1%.

Major Intl. Organizations: UN (FAO, IBRD, ILO, IMF, WHO). **Embassy:** 2341 Wyoming Ave. NW 20008; 483.6410. **Website:** www.embassyofafghanistan.org

Afghanistan, occupying a favored invasion route since antiquity, has been variously known as Ariana or Bactria (in ancient times) and Khorasan (in the Middle Ages). Foreign empires alternated rule with local emirs and kings until the 18th cent., when a unified kingdom was established. In 1973, a military coup ushered in a republic.

Pro-Soviet leftists took power in a bloody 1978 coup and concluded an economic and military treaty with the USSR. In Dec. 1979 the USSR began a massive airlift into Kabul and backed a new coup, leading to installation of a more pro-Soviet leader. Soviet troops fanned out over Afghanistan and waged a protracted guerrilla war with Muslim rebels, in which some 15,000 Soviet troops reportedly died.

A UN-mediated agreement was signed Apr. 14, 1988, providing for withdrawal of Soviet troops, a neutral Afghan state, and repatriation of refugees. Afghan rebels rejected the pact. The Soviets completed their troop withdrawal Feb. 15, 1989; fighting between Afghan rebels and government forces ensued. Communist Pres. Najibullah resigned Apr. 16, 1992, as competing guerrilla forces advanced on Kabul. The rebels achieved power Apr. 28, ending 14 years of Soviet-backed regimes. More than 2 mil Afghans had been killed and 6 mil had left the country since 1979.

Following the rebel victory there were clashes between moderates and Islamic fundamentalist forces. Burhanuddin Rabbani, a guerrilla leader, became president June 28, 1992, but fierce fighting continued around Kabul and elsewhere. The Taliban, an insurgent Islamic radical faction, gained increasing control and in Sept. 1996 captured Kabul and set up a government. The Taliban executed former President Najibullah and empowered Islamic religious police to enforce codes of dress and behavior that were especially restrictive to women. Rabbani and other ousted leaders fled to the north.

Victories in the northern cities of Mazar-e Sharif, Aug. 8, 1998, and Taloqan, Aug. 8-11, 1998, gave the Taliban control over more than 90% of the country. On Aug. 20, U.S. cruise missiles struck southeast of Kabul, hitting facilities the U.S. said were terrorist training camps run by a wealthy Saudi, Osama bin Laden. The UN imposed sanctions Nov. 14, 1999, when Afghanistan refused to turn over bin Laden to the U.S. for prosecution; a UN ban on all military aid to the Taliban took effect Jan. 19, 2001.

Ahmed Shah Massoud, leader of the anti-Taliban resistance, died of wounds sustained in a suicide bombing, Sept. 9, 2001, by assassins posing as journalists. After the Sept. 11 attacks on the World Trade Center and Pentagon, the U.S., blaming bin Laden, demanded that the Taliban surrender him and shut down his al-Qaeda terrorist network. When the Taliban refused, the U.S., with British assistance, began bombing Afghanistan Oct. 7. Supported by the U.S., the opposition Northern Alliance recaptured Mazar-e Sharif Nov. 9 and took Kabul 4 days later; the Taliban forces abandoned Kandahar, their last stronghold, to southern tribesmen Dec. 7. A power-sharing agreement signed in Bonn, Germany, Dec. 5 by 4 anti-Taliban factions, including the Northern Alliance, provided for an interim government headed by Hamid Karzai, a Pashtun tribal leader. The UN authorized Dec. 20 a multinational security force. Meanwhile, U.S. and allied forces continued to hunt for bin Laden and other top al-Qaeda and Taliban officials.

In Mar. 2002, the U.S. launched Operation Anaconda to hunt down Taliban in the mountains of the southeast. Meeting June 13 in Kabul, a traditional council (*loya jirga*) chose Karzai to head a new transitional government. An errant U.S. air strike on the night of June 30-July 1 apparently killed 48 people at Kakarak, north of Kandahar. Gunmen July 6 assassinated Vice Pres. Haji Abdul Qadir, a Pashtun. A car bomb in Kabul killed 30 people Sept. 5; the same day Karzai, guarded by U.S. troops, survived an assassination attempt. Continued lawlessness allowed for a dramatic increase in opium production.

The U.S. announced the end of major combat operations in Afghanistan, May 1, 2003, but resistance continued, with relief and reconstruction workers targeted. NATO officially assumed control of peacekeeping forces (ISAF) Aug. 11.

A new constitution took effect Jan. 26, 2004. Pres. Karzai won reelection Oct. 9 with 55.4% of the vote. During the campaign, insurgents attempted to kill Pres. Karzai, Sept. 16; Vice Pres. Nematullah Shahrani, Sept. 20; and Karzai's vice pres. running mate, Ahmed Zia Massoud (brother of the slain anti-Taliban leader), Oct. 6. U.S.

troops launched a new offensive, Dec. 11, but were unable to suppress the insurgency.

A prominent anti-Taliban Muslim cleric, Mawlavi Abdullah Fayaz, was assassinated in Kandahar, May 29, 2005; a suicide bomb at his funeral, June 1, killed at least 20 people in a Kandahar mosque, including the police chief of Kabul. Violence continued to rise in the run-up to elections Sept. 18, 2005, for a 249-seat national assembly. Millions defied threats of violence to vote; at least 14 people were killed in more than 20 attacks by insurgents. The new assembly convened Dec. 19, with U.S. Vice Pres. Dick Cheney present. Meeting in London, Jan. 31-Feb.1, 2006, international donors pledged more than $10 bil in aid; prior assistance, 2001-06, had included $10.3 bil in funding from the U.S. and pledges of $9.5 bil from other countries, of which about half had been delivered.

The most intense fighting in more than 4 years erupted Mar. 2006 with a new wave of suicide bombings, rocket and mortar attacks, and other strikes by Taliban insurgents against military and civilian targets. Coalition forces responded in southeastern and eastern regions with Operation Mountain Thrust, beginning mid-May. A suicide bombing near the U.S. embassy in Kabul, Sept. 8, killed at least 16 people, including 5 U.S. soldiers. Erosion of government authority led to an increase in opium growing, with a record poppy crop in 2006.

Between Oct. 2001 and Sept. 2006, at least 330 U.S. military personnel died in Afghanistan. Current U.S. troop strength is 20,000. In Sept., the Pentagon dropped plans for further troop reductions. NATO's ISAF troop strength increased from 11,000 to 18,000. NATO took command of military operations in southern Afghanistan, July 31.

Albania
Republic of Albania

People: Population: 3,581,655. **Age distrib.** (%) <15: 24.8; 65+: 8.9. **Pop. density:** 338 per sq mi, 130 per sq km. **Urban:** 23.3%. **Ethnic groups:** Albanian 95%, Greek 3%. **Principal languages:** Albanian (Tosk is the official dialect), Greek. **Chief religions:** Muslim 70%, Albanian Orthodox 20%, Roman Catholic 10%.

Geography: Total area: 11,100 sq mi, 28,748 sq km; **Land area:** 10,578 sq mi, 27,398 sq km. **Location:** SE Europe, on SE coast of Adriatic Sea. **Neighbors:** Greece on S, Yugoslavia on N, Macedonia on E. **Topography:** Apart from a narrow coastal plain, Albania consists of hills and mountains covered with scrub forest, cut by small E-W rivers. **Capital:** Tirana, 388,000.

Government: Type: Republic. **Head of state:** Pres. Alfred Moisiu; b. Dec. 1, 1929; in office: July 24, 2002. **Head of gov.:** Prime Min. Sali Berisha; b. Oct. 15, 1944; in office: Sept. 11, 2005. **Local divisions:** 12 counties divided into 36 districts. **Defense budget** (2005): $116 mil. **Active troops:** 21,500.

Economy: Industries: food proc., textiles, clothing, lumber. **Chief crops:** wheat, corn, potatoes, sugar beets, grapes. **Natural resources:** oil, nat. gas, coal, chromium, copper, timber, nickel, hydropower. **Crude oil reserves** (2005): 165 mil bbls. **Arable land:** 21%. **Livestock** (2005): cattle: 700,000; chickens: 4.4 mil; goats: 1 mil; pigs: 109,000; sheep: 1.8 mil. **Fish catch** (2004): 5,132 metric tons. **Electricity prod.** (2004): 5.4 bil kWh. **Labor force** (2004 est.): agriculture 58%, industry 19%, services 23%.

Finance: Monetary unit: Lek (ALL) (Sept. 2006: 96.47 = $1 U.S.). **GDP** (2005 est.): $19 bil; **per capita GDP:** $4,900; **GDP growth:** 5.5%. **Imports** (2005 est.): $2.5 bil; partners (2004): Italy 36%, Greece 20.4%, Turkey 8.1%, Germany 5.5%. **Exports** (2005 est.): $650.1 mil; partners (2004): Italy 71.9%, Greece 6.3%, Canada 4.4%. **Tourism:** $735 mil. **Budget** (2005 est.): $2.4 bil. **Intl. reserves less gold:** $982 mil. **Gold:** 70,000 oz t. **Consumer prices:** 2.37%.

Transport: Railroad: Length: 278 mi. **Motor vehicles** 174,400 pass. cars, 88,800 comm. vehicles. **Civil aviation:** 59.7 mil pass.-mi; 3 airports. **Chief ports:** Durres, Sarande, Vlore.

Communications: TV sets: 146 per 1,000 pop. **Radios:** 259 per 1,000 pop. **Telephone lines:** 255,000. **Daily newspaper circ.:** NA. **Internet:** 75,000 users.

Health: Life expect.: 74.8 male; 80.3 female. **Births** (per 1,000 pop.): 15.1. **Deaths** (per 1,000 pop.): 5.2. **Natural inc.:** 0.99%. **Infant mortality** (per 1,000 live births): 20.8. **AIDS rate:** NA.

Major Intl. Organiz.: UN (IBRD, ILO, FAO, IMF, IMO, WHO, WTO), OSCE.

Education: Compulsory: ages 6-13. **Literacy:** 98.7%.

Embassy: 2100 S St. NW 20008; 223-4942.

Website: www.keshilliministrave.al/english/

Ancient Illyria was conquered by Romans, Slavs, and Turks (15th cent.); the latter Islamized the population. Independent Albania was proclaimed in 1912; the republic was formed in 1920. King Zog I ruled 1925-39, until Italy invaded.

Communist partisans took over in 1944, allied Albania with USSR, then broke with USSR in 1960 over de-Stalinization. Strong political alliance with China followed, leading to several billion dollars in aid, which was curtailed after 1974. China cut off aid in 1978 when Albania attacked its policies after the death of Chinese ruler Mao Zedong. Large-scale purges of officials occurred during the 1970s.

Enver Hoxha, the nation's ruler for 4 decades, died Apr. 11, 1985. Eventually the new regime introduced some liberalization, including measures in 1990 providing for freedom to travel abroad. Efforts were begun to improve ties with the outside world. Mar. 1991 elections left the former Communists in power, but a general strike and urban opposition led to the formation of a coalition cabinet including non-Communists.

Albania's former Communists were routed in elections Mar. 1992, amid economic collapse and social unrest. Sali Berisha was elected as the first non-Communist president since WWII. Berisha's party claimed a landslide victory in disputed parliamentary elections, May 26 and June 2, 1996. Public protests over the collapse of fraudulent investment schemes in Jan. 1997 led to armed rebellion and anarchy. The UN Security Council, Mar. 28, authorized a 7,000-member force to restore order. Socialists and their allies won parliamentary elections, June 29 and July 6, and international peacekeepers completed their pullout by Aug. 11.

During NATO's air war against Yugoslavia, Mar.-June 1999, Albania hosted some 465,000 Kosovar refugees. Victory by a coalition backing Berisha in parliamentary voting, July 3, 2005, ended 8 years of Socialist rule.

Algeria
People's Democratic Republic of Algeria

People: Population: 32,930,091. **Age distrib.** (%) <15: 28.1; 65+: 4.8. **Pop. density:** 35 per sq mi, 13 per sq km. **Urban:** 58.8%. **Ethnic groups:** Arab-Berber 99%. **Principal languages:** Arabic (official), French, Berber dialects. **Chief religion:** Sunni Muslim (official) 99%.

Geography: Total area: 919,595 sq mi, 2,381,740 sq km; **Land area:** 919,595 sq mi, 2,381,740 sq km. **Location:** In NW Africa, from Mediterranean Sea into Sahara Desert. **Neighbors:** Morocco on W; Mauritania, Mali, Niger on S; Libya, Tunisia on E. **Topography:** The Tell, located on the coast, comprises fertile plains 50-100 miles wide, with a moderate climate and adequate rain. Two major chains of the Atlas Mts., running roughly E-W and reaching 7,000 ft., enclose a dry plateau region. Below lies the Sahara, mostly desert with major mineral resources. **Capital:** Algiers (El Djazair), 3,200,000.

Government: Type: Republic. **Head of state:** Pres. Abdelaziz Bouteflika; b. Mar. 2, 1937; in office: Apr. 27, 1999. **Head of gov.:** Prime Min. Abdelaziz Belkhadem; b. Nov. 8, 1945; in office: May 24, 2006. **Local divisions:** 48 provinces. **Defense budget** (2004): $2.9 bil. **Active troops:** 137,500.

Economy: Industries: oil, nat. gas, light industries, mining, petrochemical, food proc. **Chief crops:** wheat, barley, oats, grapes, olives, citrus. **Natural resources:** oil, nat. gas, iron ore, phosphates, uranium, lead, zinc. **Crude oil reserves** (2005): 11.8 bil bbls. **Arable land:** 3%. **Livestock** (2005): cattle: 1.6 mil; chickens: 125 mil; goats: 3.2 mil; pigs: 5,700; sheep: 18.7 mil. **Fish catch** (2004): 140,586 metric tons. **Electricity prod.** (2004): 29.4 bil kWh. **Labor force** (2003 est.): agriculture 14%, industry 13.4%, construction and public works 10%, trade 14.6%, government 32%, other 16%.

Finance: Monetary unit: Dinar (DZD) (Sept. 2006: 70.88 = $1 U.S.). **GDP** (2005 est.): $233.2 bil; **per capita GDP:** $7,200; **GDP growth:** 6%. **Imports** (2005 est.): $22.5 bil; partners (2004): France 31.6%, Italy 8.5%, Germany 6.3%, Spain 5.6%, China 5.3%, U.S. 4.9%, Turkey 4.5%. **Exports** (2005 est.): $49.6 bil; partners (2004): U.S. 22.5%, Italy 17.8%, France 11.8%, Spain 10.2%, Canada 7.8%, Belgium 4.8%. **Tourism** (2003): $161 mil. **Budget** (2005 est.): $30.8 bil. **Intl. reserves less gold:** $39.39 bil. **Gold:** 5.58 mil oz t. **Consumer prices:** 1.64%.

Transport: Railroad: Length: 2,469 mi. **Motor vehicles** 1.74 mil pass. cars, 1 mil. comm. vehicles. **Civil aviation:** 2 bil pass.-mi; 52 airports **Chief ports:** Algiers, Annaba, Oran.

Communications: TV sets: 107 per 1,000 pop. **Radios:** 242 per 1,000 pop. **Telephone lines:** 3.2 mil. **Daily newspaper circ.:** 27.2 per 1,000 pop. **Internet:** 845,000 users.

Health: Life expect.: 71.7 male; 74.9 female. **Births** (per 1,000 pop.): 17.1. **Deaths** (per 1,000 pop.): 4.6. **Natural inc.:** 1.25%. **Infant mortality** (per 1,000 live births): 29.9. **AIDS rate:** 0.1%.

Education: Compulsory: ages 6-14. **Literacy:** 69.9%.

Major Intl. Organizations: UN (FAO, IBRD, ILO, IMF, IMO, WHO), AL, AU, OPEC.

Embassy: 2118 Kalorama Rd. NW 20008; 265-2800.

Website: www.algeria-us.org

Earliest known inhabitants were ancestors of Berbers, followed by Phoenicians, Romans, Vandals, and, finally, Arabs. Turkey ruled 1518 to 1830, when France took control. Large-scale European immigration followed. Arab nationalists launched a guerrilla war, 1954, that more than 400,000 French troops were unable to supress. After French Pres. Charles de Gaulle came to power, 1958, colonial rule ended, nearly all Europeans left, and Algeria declared independence July 5, 1962. Ahmed Ben Bella ruled until 1965, when an army coup installed Col. Houari Boumedienne, a former guerrilla leader who held power until his death in 1978.

Hundreds died in antigovernment riots protesting economic hardship in Oct. 1988. In 1989, voters approved a new constitution, which cleared the way for a multiparty system. The government canceled the Jan. 1992 elections that Islamic fundamentalists were expected to win, and banned all nonreligious activities at Algeria's 10,000 mosques. Pres. Mohammed Boudiaf was assassinated June 29, 1992. Over the next 7 years, Muslim fundamentalists carried out attacks on high-ranking officials, security forces, foreigners, and others; pro-government death squads also were active.

Liamine Zeroual won the presidential election of Nov. 16, 1995. A new constitution banning Islamic political parties and increasing the president's powers passed in a referendum on Nov. 28, 1996. Abdelaziz Bouteflika, who became president after a flawed election on Apr. 15, 1999, made peace with rebels and won approval for an amnesty plan in a referendum on Sept. 16. Some 100 people died and thousands were injured in violent protests Apr.-June 2001, chiefly by Algeria's Berber minority. Bouteflika was reelected Apr. 8, 2004, in a landslide; opponents charged fraud.

An earthquake in northern Algeria, May 21, 2003, claimed over 2,200 lives and left 200,000 people homeless. The army launched a campaign against the militant Islamic group GSPC after its members killed 12 soldiers in June. GSPC leader Nabil Sahraoui was killed by Algerian forces, June 20, 2004. Under a reconciliation plan approved by referendum Sept. 29, 2005, the government in Mar. 2006 began freeing Islamists jailed for their role in the 1990s civil war, in which up to 200,000 people were killed, and 8,000 "disappeared."

Andorra
Principality of Andorra

People: Population: 71,201. **Age distrib.** (%) <15: 14.7; 65+: 14. **Pop. density:** 393 per sq mi, 152 per sq km. **Urban:** 91.7%. **Ethnic groups:** Spanish 43%, Andorran 33%, Portuguese 11%, French 7%. **Principal languages:** Catalan (official), Castilian Spanish, French. **Chief religion:** Predominantly Roman Catholic.

Geography: Total area: 181 sq mi, 468 sq km; **Land area:** 181 sq mi, 468 sq km. **Location:** SW Europe, in Pyrenees Mts. **Neighbors:** Spain on S, France on N. **Topography:** High mountains and narrow valleys cover the country. **Capital** (2002): Andorra la Vella, 20,787.

Government: Type: Parliamentary co-principality. **Heads of state:** President of France & Bishop of Urgel (Spain), as co-princes. **Head of gov.:** Albert Pintat Santolària; b. June 23, 1943; in office: May 27, 2005. **Local divisions:** 7 parishes. **Defense budget:** Responsibility of France and Spain.

Economy: Industries: tourism, cattle raising, timber, tobacco, banking. **Chief crops:** tobacco, rye, wheat, barley, oats. **Natural resources:** hydropower, mineral water, timber, iron ore, lead. **Arable land:** 2%. **Labor force** (2004 est.): agriculture .34%, industry 19.6%, services 80%.

Finance: Monetary unit: Euro (EUR) (Sept. 2006: 0.78 = $1 U.S.). **GDP** (2004): $1.8 bil; **per capita GDP:** $24,000; **GDP growth:** 4%. **Imports** (1998 est.): $1.1 bil; partners (2000): Spain 48%, France 35%, U.S. 2.3%. **Exports** (2004): $145 mil; partners (2000): Spain 58%, France 34%. **Tourism:** NA. **Budget** (2004): $373.5 mil.

Transport: Motor vehicles: 35,358 pass. cars, 4,238 comm. vehicles.

Communications: TV sets: 440 per 1,000 pop. **Radios:** 229 per 1,000 pop. **Telephone lines:** 35,400. **Daily newspaper circ.:** NA. **Internet** (2004): 11,000 users.

Health: Life expect.: 80.6 male; 86.6 female. **Births** (per 1,000 pop.): 8.7. **Deaths** (per 1,000 pop.): 6.2. **Natural inc.:** 0.25%. **Infant mortality** (per 1,000 live births): 4. **AIDS rate:** NA.

Education: Compulsory: ages 6-16. **Literacy:** 100%.

Major Intl. Organizations: UN (WHO), OSCE.

Embassy: 2 UN Plaza, 25th floor, New York, NY 10017; 750-8064.

Website: www.andorra.ad

Andorra was a co-principality, with joint sovereignty by France and the bishop of Urgel, from 1278 to 1993. Voters chose to adopt a parliamentary system Mar. 14, 1993.

Tourism, especially skiing, is the economic mainstay. A free port, Andorra attracted more than 11 mil tourists in 2005.

Angola
Republic of Angola

People: Population: 11,992,807. **Age distrib.** (%) <15: 43.8; 65+: 2.8. **Pop. density:** 24 per sq mi, 9 per sq km. **Urban:** 35.7%. **Ethnic groups:** Ovimbundu 37%, Kimbundu 25%, Bakongo 13%. **Principal languages:** Portuguese (official), Bantu and other African languages. **Chief religions:** Roman Catholic 62%, other Christian 32%.

Geography: Total area: 481,354 sq mi, 1,246,700 sq km; **Land area:** 481,354 sq mi, 1,246,700 sq km. **Location:** In SW Africa on Atlantic coast. **Neighbors:** Namibia on S, Zambia on E, Congo-Kinshasa (formerly Zaire) on N; Cabinda, an enclave separated from rest of country by short Atlantic coast of Congo-Kinshasa, borders Congo-Brazzaville. **Topography:** Most of Angola consists of a plateau elevated 3,000 to 5,000 feet above sea level, rising from a narrow coastal strip. There is also a temperate highland area in the west-central region, a desert in the S, and a tropical rainforest covering Cabinda. **Capital:** Luanda, 2,766,000.

Government: Type: Republic. **Head of state:** Pres. José Eduardo dos Santos; b. Aug. 28, 1942; in office: Sept. 20, 1979. **Head of gov.:** Prime Min. Fernando da Piedade Dias dos Santos; b. Mar. 5, 1952; in office: Dec. 6, 2002. **Local divisions:** 18 provinces. **Defense budget:** $1.2 bil. **Active troops:** 108,400.

Economy: Industries: oil, mining, cement, metals, fish & food proc. **Chief crops:** bananas, sugarcane, coffee, sisal. **Natural resources:** oil, diamonds, iron ore, phosphates, copper, feldspar, gold, bauxite, uranium. **Crude oil reserves** (2005): 5.4 bil bbls. **Arable land:** 2%. **Livestock** (2005): cattle: 4.2 mil; chickens: 6.8 mil; goats: 2.1 mil; pigs: 780,000; sheep: 340,000. **Fish catch** (2004): 240,005 metric tons. **Electricity prod.** (2004): 2.2 bil kWh. **Labor force** (2003 est.): agriculture 85%, industry and services 15%.

Finance: Monetary unit: Kwanza (AOA) (Sept. 2006: 80.17 = $1 U.S.). **GDP** (2005 est.): $45.9 bil; **per capita GDP:** $3,200; **GDP growth:** 19.1%. **Imports** (2005 est.): $8.2 bil; partners (2004): Por-

tugal 18.4%, U.S. 13.1%, South Africa 10.7%, Japan 6.9%, France 6.3%, Brazil 5.6%, UK 4.9%, China 4.5%. **Exports** (2005 est.): $26.8 bil; partners (2004): U.S. 39.8%, China 30.3%, Taiwan 8.1%, France 7.1%. **Tourism:** $66 mil. **Budget** (2005 est.): $10 bil. **Intl. reserves less gold:** $2.24 bil. **Consumer prices:** 22.4%.

Transport: Railroad: Length: 1,716 mi. **Motor vehicles** 117,200 pass. cars, 118,300 comm. vehicles. **Civil aviation:** 292 mil pass.-mi; 31 airports. **Chief ports:** Cabinda, Lobito, Luanda.

Communications: TV sets: 15 per 1,000 pop. **Radios:** 67 per 1,000 pop. **Telephone lines:** 94,300. **Daily newspaper circ.:** 11.3 per 1,000 pop. **Internet:** 172,000 users.

Health: Life expect.: 36.5 male; 38.2 female. **Births** (per 1,000 pop.): 45. **Deaths** (per 1,000 pop.): 25.2. **Natural inc.:** 1.97%. **Infant mortality** (per 1,000 live births): 186.6. **AIDS rate:** 3.7%.

Education: Compulsory: ages 6-9. **Literacy:** 67.4%.

Major Intl. Organizations: UN (FAO, IBRD, ILO, IMF, IMO, WHO, WTO), AU.

Embassy: 2100-2108 16th St. NW 20009; 785-1156.

Website: www.angola.org

From the early centuries CE to 1500, Bantu tribes penetrated most of the region. Portuguese came in 1583, allied with the Bakongo kingdom in the north, and developed the slave trade. Large-scale colonization did not begin until the 20th cent, when 400,000 Portuguese immigrated.

A guerrilla war begun in 1961 lasted until 1975, when Portugal granted independence. Fighting then erupted between three rival rebel groups—the National Front, based in Zaire (now Congo), the Soviet-backed Popular Movement for the Liberation of Angola (MPLA), and the National Union for the Total Independence of Angola (UNITA), aided by the U.S. and South Africa.

Cuban troops and Soviet aid helped the MPLA win control of most of the country by 1976, although fighting continued through the 1980s. A peace accord between the MPLA government and UNITA was signed May 1, 1991.

Elections were held in Sept. 1992, but fighting again broke out, as UNITA rejected the results. UNITA signed a new peace treaty with the government, Nov. 20, 1994, but the rebels were slow to demobilize. The UN Security Council voted, Aug. 28, 1997, to impose sanctions on UNITA. In Aug. 1998, Angola sent thousands of troops into Congo-Kinshasa (formerly Zaire) to support Laurent Kabila's regime. The UN ended its mission in Angola in Mar. 1999, as the civil war continued.

As of 2001, the UN estimated that the war with UNITA had claimed some 1 mil lives and left another 2.5 mil people homeless. More than 250 died when UNITA rebels ambushed a train Aug. 10. Rebel leader Jonas Savimbi was killed by government troops Feb. 22, 2002. UNITA agreed to a truce Apr. 4 of that year, ending the 27-year-long civil war. Fighting continued, however, between government forces and separatist guerrillas in oil-rich Cabinda; rebels there agreed to a cease-fire July 2006.

Mismanagement and corruption led to the diversion of up to $4.2 bil in oil revenues during 1997-2002, according to a Human Rights Watch report. In Apr. 2004, the govt. arrested nearly 3,000 illegal diamond diggers, many of them foreigners. An outbreak of Marburg hemorrhagic fever, caused by a rare Ebola-like virus, claimed more than 300 lives in 2005. A cholera epidemic beginning Feb. 2006 killed at least 1,600 people.

Antigua and Barbuda

People: Population: 69,108. **Age distrib.** (%) <15: 27.6; 65+: 3.9. **Pop. density:** 404 per sq mi, 156 per sq km. **Urban:** 37.7%. **Ethnic groups:** Black, British, Portuguese, Lebanese, Syrian. **Principal languages:** English (official), local dialects. **Chief religions:** Predominantly Protestant; some Roman Catholic.

Geography: Total area: 171 sq mi, 443 sq km; **Land area:** 171 sq mi, 443 sq km. **Location:** Eastern Caribbean. **Neighbors:** St. Kitts & Nevis to W, Guadeloupe (Fr.) to S. **Topography:** These are mostly low-lying and limestone coral islands. Antigua is mostly hilly with an indented coast; Barbuda is a flat island with a large lagoon on the W. **Capital** (2004): Saint John's, 23,600.

Government: Type: Constitutional monarchy with British-style parliament. **Head of state:** Queen Elizabeth II; represented by Gov.-Gen. James Carlisle; b. Aug. 5, 1937; in office: June 10, 1993. **Head of gov.:** Prime Min. Baldwin Spencer; b. Oct. 8, 1948; in office: Mar. 24, 2004. **Local divisions:** 6 parishes, 2 dependencies. **Defense budget** (2005): $4.8 mil. **Active troops:** 170.

Economy: Industries: tourism, constr., light mfg. **Chief crops:** cotton, fruits, vegetables. **Arable land:** 18%. **Livestock** (2005): cattle: 14,300; chickens: 105,000; goats: 36,000; pigs: 2,800; sheep: 19,000. **Fish catch** (2004): 2,527 metric tons. **Electricity prod.** (2004): 110 mil kWh. **Labor force** (1983): agriculture 7%, industry 11%, services 82%.

Finance: Monetary unit: East Caribbean Dollar (XCD) (Sept. 2006: 2.67 = $1 U.S.). **GDP** (2002 est.): $750 mil; **per capita GDP:** $11,000; **GDP growth:** 3%. **Imports** (2004 est.): $735 mil; partners (2004): U.S. 21.8%, Singapore 18.8%, China 10.7%, Poland 6.7%, Trinidad and Tobago 4.6%, UK 4.4%. **Exports** (2004 est.): $214 mil; partners (2004): Germany 49.5%, UK 29.7%, France 3.5%. **Tourism:** $337 mil. **Budget** (2000 est.): $145.9 mil. **Intl. reserves less gold:** $89 mil.

Transport: Railroad: Length: 48 mi. **Motor vehicles** 24,000 pass. cars and comm. vehicles. **Civil aviation:** 187 mil. pass.-mi; 2 airports.

Communications: TV sets: 493 per 1,000 pop. **Radios:** 545 per 1,000 pop. **Telephone lines:** 38,000. **Daily newspaper circ.:** NA. **Internet:** 20,000 users.

Health: Life expect.: 69.8 male; 74.7 female. **Births** (per 1,000 pop.): 16.9. **Deaths** (per 1,000 pop.): 5.4. **Natural inc.:** 1.16%. **Infant mortality** (per 1,000 live births): 18.9. **AIDS rate:** NA.

Education: Compulsory: ages 5-16. **Literacy:** 89%.

Major Intl. Organizations: UN (FAO, IBRD, ILO, IMF, IMO, WHO, WTO), the Commonwealth, OAS, CARICOM.

Embassy: 3216 New Mexico Ave. NW 20016; 362-5122.

Website: www.antigua-barbuda.com

Columbus landed on Antigua in 1493. The British colonized it in 1632.

The British associated state of Antigua achieved independence as Antigua and Barbuda on Nov. 1, 1981. The government maintains close relations with the U.S., the UK, and Venezuela. The country was hit hard by Hurricane Luis, Sept. 1995. About 3,000 refugees from the nearby island of Montserrat settled in Antigua following volcanic eruptions there in 1995-97.

Argentina
Argentine Republic

People: Population: 39,921,833. **Age distrib.** (%) <15: 25.2; 65+: 10.6. **Pop. density:** 37 per sq mi, 14 per sq km. **Urban:** 90.1%. **Ethnic groups:** European 97%, Amerindian 3%. **Principal languages:** Spanish (official), English, Italian, German, French. **Chief religion:** Roman Catholic 92% (official).

Geography: Total area: 1,068,302 sq mi, 2,766,890 sq km; **Land area:** 1,056,642 sq mi, 2,736,690 sq km. **Location:** Occupies most of southern South America. **Neighbors:** Chile on W; Bolivia, Paraguay on N; Brazil, Uruguay on NE. **Topography:** Mountains in the W are: the Andean, Central, Misiones, and Southern ranges. Aconcagua is the highest peak in the western hemisphere, alt. 22,834 ft. E of the Andes are heavily wooded plains, called the Gran Chaco in the N, and the fertile, treeless Pampas in the central region. Patagonia, in the S, is bleak and arid. Rio de la Plata, an estuary in the NE, 170 by 140 mi., is mostly fresh water, from 2,485-mi Parana and 1,000-mi Uruguay rivers. **Capital:** Buenos Aires, 12,550,000 (the Senate has approved moving the capital to the Patagonia Region). **Cities (urban aggr.):** Córdoba, 1,423,000; Rosario, 1,186,000.

Government: Type: Republic. **Head of state and gov.:** Pres. Néstor Kirchner; b. Feb. 25, 1950; in office: May 25, 2003. **Local divisions:** 23 provinces, 1 federal district. **Defense budget** (2005): $1.8 bil. **Active troops:** 71,400.

Economy: Industries: food proc., vehicles, consumer durables, textiles, chemicals. **Chief crops:** sunflower seeds, lemons, soybeans, grapes, corn. **Natural resources:** lead, zinc, tin, copper, iron ore, mang., oil, uranium. **Crude oil reserves** (2005): 2.7 bil bbls. **Arable land:** 9%. **Livestock** (2005): cattle: 50.8 mil; chickens: 95 mil; goats: 4.2 mil; pigs: 1.5 mil; sheep: 12.5 mil. **Fish catch** (2004): 953,260 metric tons. **Electricity prod.** (2004): 93.9 bil kWh.

Finance: Monetary unit: Peso (ARS) (Sept. 2006: 3.10 = $1 U.S.). **GDP** (2005 est.): $518.1 bil; **per capita GDP:** $13,100; **GDP growth:** 8.7%. **Imports** (2005 est.): $28.8 bil; partners (2004): Brazil 27%, U.S. 20%, Germany 6.6%, China 4.6%, France 4.2%, Italy 4.1%. **Exports** (2005 est.): $40 bil; partners (2004): Brazil 16.5%, Chile 10.9%, U.S. 10.2%, China 8.5%, Spain 4.5%. **Tourism:** $2.2 bil. **Budget** (2005 est.): $40 bil. **Intl. reserves less gold:** $19.02 bil. **Gold:** 1.76 mil oz t. **Consumer prices:** 9.64%.

Transport: Railroad: Length: 21,183 mi. **Motor vehicles** 5.3867 mil pass. cars, 1 mil comm. vehicles. **Civil aviation:** 6.1 bil pass.-mi; 154 airports. **Chief ports:** Buenos Aires, Bahia Blanca, La Plata.

Communications: TV sets: 293 per 1,000 pop. **Radios:** 681 per 1,000 pop. **Telephone lines:** 8.8 mil. **Daily newspaper circ.:** 40.5 per 1,000 pop. **Internet:** 10 mil users.

Health: Life expect.: 72.4 male; 80 female. **Births** (per 1,000 pop.): 16.7. **Deaths** (per 1,000 pop.): 7.5. **Natural inc.:** 0.92%. **Infant mortality** (per 1,000 live births): 14.7. **AIDS rate:** 0.6%.

Education: Compulsory: ages 5-14. **Literacy:** 97.2%.

Major Intl. Organizations: UN (FAO, IBRD, ILO, IMF, IMO, WHO, WTO), OAS.

Embassy: 1600 New Hampshire Ave. NW 20009; 238-6400.

Website: www.turismo.gov.ar/eng/menu.htm

Nomadic Indians roamed the Pampas when Spaniards arrived, 1515-16, led by Juan Diaz de Solis. Nearly all the Indians were killed by the late 19th cent. The colonists won independence, 1816, and a long period of disorder ended in a strong centralized government.

Large-scale Italian, German, and Spanish immigration in the decades after 1880 spurred modernization. Social reforms were enacted in the 1920s, but military coups prevailed 1930-46 until the election of Gen. Juan Perón as president.

Perón, with his wife, Eva Duarte (d. 1952), effected labor reforms but also suppressed speech and press freedoms, closed religious schools, and ran the country into debt. A 1955 coup exiled Perón, who was followed by a series of military and civilian regimes. Perón returned in 1973 and was once more elected president. He died 10 months later, succeeded by his wife Isabel, who had been elected vice president, and who became the first woman head of state in the Western Hemisphere.

A military junta ousted Mrs. Perón in 1976 amid charges of corruption. Under a continuing state of siege, the army conducted a "dirty war" against guerrillas and leftists in which an estimated 30,000 people "disappeared." On Dec. 9, 1985, after a trial of 5

months and nearly 1,000 witnesses, 5 former junta members were found guilty of murder and human rights abuses.

Argentine troops seized control of the British-held Falkland Islands (Islas Malvinas) on Apr. 2, 1982. The British imposed an air and sea blockade around the Falklands. Fighting began May 1. British troops landed on East Falkland May 21 and eventually surrounded Stanley, the capital city. Argentine troops surrendered, June 14; Argentine Pres. Leopoldo Galtieri resigned June 17.

Democratic rule returned in 1983 with a victory by Raul Alfonsín's Radical Civic Union party. By 1989 the nation was plagued by severe financial and political problems, as hyperinflation sparked looting and rioting in several cities. The government of Peronist Pres. Carlos Saúl Menem, installed 1989, introduced harsh economic measures to curtail inflation, control government spending, and restructure the foreign debt.

About 85 people were killed and nearly 300 injured in the terrorist bombing of a Jewish cultural center in Buenos Aires, July 18, 1994. Following passage of a new constitution in Aug. 1994, Menem was reelected president on May 14, 1995.

Buenos Aires Mayor Fernando de la Rúa won the presidential election Oct. 24, 1999. A prolonged recession and a debt of more than $130 bil left Argentina facing an economic crisis in 2001, which austerity measures and IMF aid failed to remedy. After widespread rioting and looting Dec. 19, de la Rúa resigned.

A 2-week period of protests and political upheavals abated when Congress, Jan. 1, 2002, chose a Peronist, Eduardo Alberto Duhalde, to finish de la Rúa's term. Duhalde devalued the peso by cutting its ties with the U.S. dollar. Further economic decline and renewed protests led Duhalde July 2 to schedule an early presidential election for Mar. 2003; another Peronist, Néstor Kirchner, took office May 25, 2003, after Menem pulled out of a runoff election. Kirchner moved to end corruption and human rights abuses among the military and police. A new IMF aid deal, approved Sept. 10, 2003, rescued Argentina from default.

Fire at a Buenos Aires nightclub, Dec. 30, 2004, killed 194 people. The supreme court, June 14, 2005, overturned amnesty laws that had barred prosecution for "dirty war" crimes committed while the military ruled Argentina. Robust economic growth, 2004-05, allowed Argentina to repay its $9.57 bil debt to the IMF, Jan. 3, 2006.

Armenia
Republic of Armenia

People: Population: 2,976,372. **Age distrib.** (%) <15: 20.5; 65+: 11.1. **Pop. density:** 271 per sq mi, 104 per sq km. **Urban:** 64.4%. **Ethnic groups:** Armenian 93%, Russian 2%. **Principal languages:** Armenian (official), Russian. **Chief religions:** Armenian Apostolic 95%, other Christian 4%, Yezidi 2%.

Geography: Total area: 11,506 sq mi, 29,800 sq km; **Land area:** 10,965 sq mi, 28,400 sq km. **Location:** SW Asia. **Neighbors:** Georgia on N, Azerbaijan on E, Iran on S, Turkey on W. **Topography:** Mountainous with many peaks above 10,000 ft. **Capital:** Yerevan, 1,103,000.

Government: Type: Republic. **Head of state:** Pres. Robert Kocharian; b. Aug. 31, 1954; in office: Apr. 9, 1998. **Head of gov.:** Prime Min. Andranik Markarian; b. June 12, 1951; in office: May 12, 2000. **Local divisions:** 10 provinces, 1 city. **Defense budget** (2005): $135 mil. **Active troops:** 48,160.

Economy: Industries: machine tools & machines, electric motors, tires, knitted wear. **Chief crops:** grapes, vegetables. **Natural resources:** gold, copper, molybd., zinc, alumina. **Arable land:** 17%. **Livestock** (2005): cattle: 573,300; chickens: 3.5 mil; goats: 45,000; pigs: 89,100; sheep: 558,300. **Fish catch** (2004): 1,031 metric tons. **Electricity prod.** (2004): 5.7 bil kWh. **Labor force** (2002 est.): agriculture 45%, industry 25%, services 30%.

Finance: Monetary unit: Dram (AMD) (Sept. 2006: 439.50 = $1 U.S.). **GDP** (2005 est.): $13.5 bil; **per capita GDP:** $4,500; **GDP growth:** 13.9%. **Imports** (2005 est.): $1.5 bil; partners (2004): Belgium 10.3%, Iran 10.2%, Russia 9.8%, Israel 8.6%, U.S. 7.7%, UAE 6.2%, Italy 5.4%, Germany 5%, France 4.6%, Ukraine 4.5%. **Exports** (2005 est.): $800 mil; partners (2004): Belgium 16.8%, Israel 14.3%, Russia 14.2%, Germany 11.4%, Iran 9.9%, U.S. 7.8%, Netherlands 5.8%. **Tourism:** $86 mil. **Budget** (2005 est.): $930.7 mil. **Intl. reserves less gold:** $528 mil. **Consumer prices:** 0.64%.

Transport: Railroad: Length: 525 mi. **Civil aviation:** 464.2 mil pass.-mi; 11 airports.

Communications: TV sets: 241 per 1,000 pop. **Radios:** 239 per 1,000 pop. **Telephone lines:** 582,500. **Daily newspaper circ.:** NA. **Internet:** 150,000 users.

Health: Life expect.: 68.2 male; 76 female. **Births** (per 1,000 pop.): 12.1. **Deaths** (per 1,000 pop.): 8.2. **Natural inc.:** 0.38%. **Infant mortality** (per 1,000 live births): 22.5. **AIDS rate:** 0.1%.

Education: Compulsory: ages 6-17. **Literacy:** 99.4%.

Major Intl. Organizations: UN (FAO, IBRD, ILO, IMF, WHO, WTO), CIS, OSCE.

Embassy: 2225 R St. NW 20008; 319-1976.

Website: www.armeniaemb.org

Ancient Armenia extended into parts of what are now Turkey and Iran. Present-day Armenia was set up as a Soviet republic Apr. 2, 1921. It joined Georgian and Azerbaijan SSRs Mar. 12, 1922, to form the Transcaucasian SFSR, which became part of the USSR Dec. 30, 1922. Armenia became a constituent republic of the USSR Dec. 5, 1936. An earthquake struck Armenia Dec. 7, 1988; approximately 55,000 were killed and several cities and towns were left in ruins.

Armenia declared independence Sept. 23, 1991, and became an independent state when the USSR disbanded Dec. 26, 1991.

Fighting between mostly Christian Armenia and mostly Muslim Azerbaijan escalated in 1992. Each country claimed Nagorno-Karabakh, an enclave in Azerbaijan that has a majority population of ethnic Armenians. A temporary cease-fire was announced in May 1994, with Armenian forces in control of the enclave.

Voters approved, July 5, 1995, a new constitution increasing presidential powers. Pres. Levon Ter-Petrosian won reelection on Sept. 22, 1996, amid claims of fraud; he resigned Feb. 3, 1998, in a conflict over Nagorno-Karabakh. Robert Kocharian, a nationalist born in the disputed region, won the presidency on Mar. 30, 1998. Gunmen stormed Parliament Oct. 27, 1999, killing Prime Min. Vazgen Sarkissian and 7 others. Kocharian won a second term Mar. 5, 2003, in a runoff vote viewed as flawed by opposition groups and Western observers.

An Armenian airliner crashed into the Black Sea, May 3, 2006, killing all 113 people on board.

Australia
Commonwealth of Australia

People: Population: 20,264,082. **Age distrib.** (%) <15: 19.6; 65+: 13.1. **Pop. density:** 6 per sq mi, 2 per sq km. **Urban:** 92.0%. **Ethnic groups:** White 92%, Asian 7%, Aborigine and other 1%. **Principal languages:** English (official), Aboriginal languages. **Chief religions:** Roman Catholic 26%, Anglican 21%, other Christian 21%.

Geography: Total area: 2,967,909 sq mi, 7,686,850 sq km; **Land area:** 2,941,299 sq mi, 7,617,930 sq km. **Location:** SE of Asia, Indian O. is W and S, Pacific O. (Coral, Tasman seas) is E; they meet N of Australia in Timor and Arafura seas. Tasmania lies 150 mi. S of Victoria state, across Bass Strait. **Neighbors:** Nearest are Indonesia, Papua New Guinea on N; Solomons, Fiji, and New Zealand on E. **Topography:** An island continent. The Great Dividing Range along the E coast has Mt. Kosciusko, 7,310 ft. The W plateau rises to 2,000 ft., with arid areas in the Great Sandy and Great Victoria deserts. The NW part of Western Australia and Northern Terr. are arid and hot. The NE has heavy rainfall and Cape York Peninsula has jungles. **Capital:** Canberra, 381,000. **Cities (urban aggr.):** Sydney, 4,331,000; Melbourne, 3,626,000; Brisbane, 1,758,000; Perth, 1,474,000; Adelaide, 1,134,000.

Government: Type: Democratic, federal state system. **Head of state:** Queen Elizabeth II, represented by Gov.-Gen. Michael Jeffery; b. Dec. 12, 1937; in office: Aug. 11, 2003. **Head of gov.:** Prime Min. John Howard; b. July 26, 1939; in office: Mar. 11, 1996. **Local divisions:** 6 states, 2 territories. **Defense budget** (2005): $13.2 bil. **Active troops:** 52,872.

Economy: Industries: mining, industrial & transp. equip., food proc., chemicals, steel. **Chief crops:** wheat, barley, sugarcane, fruits. **Natural resources:** bauxite, coal, iron ore, copper, tin, silver, uranium, nickel, tungsten, mineral sands, lead, zinc, diamonds, nat. gas, oil. **Crude oil reserves** (2005): 1.5 bil bbls. **Other resources:** Wool (world's leading producer), beef. **Arable land:** 6%. **Livestock** (2005): cattle: 27.9 mil; chickens: 85 mil; goats: 400,000; pigs: 2.6 mil; sheep: 106 mil. **Fish catch** (2004): 267,369 metric tons. **Electricity prod.** (2004): 225.3 bil kWh. **Labor force** (2004 est.): agriculture 3.6%, industry 21.2%, services 75.2%.

Finance: Monetary unit: Dollar (AUD) (Sept. 2006: 1.33 = $1 U.S.). **GDP** (2005 est.): $640.1 bil; **per capita GDP:** $31,900; **GDP growth:** 2.5%. **Imports** (2005 est.): $119.6 bil; partners (2004): U.S. 14.8%, China 12.7%, Japan 11.8%, Germany 5.8%, Singapore 4.4%, UK 4.1%. **Exports** (2005 est.): $103 bil; partners (2004): Japan 18.6%, China 9.2%, U.S. 8.1%, South Korea 7.7%, New Zealand 7.4%, India 4.6%, UK 4.2%. **Tourism:** $12.7 bil. **Budget** (2005 est.): $240.2 bil. **Intl. reserves less gold:** $29.35 bil. **Gold:** 2.57 mil oz t. **Consumer prices:** 2.67%.

Transport: Railroad: Length: 33,959 mi. **Motor vehicles** 10.1 mil pass. cars, 2.35 mil comm. vehicles. **Civil aviation:** 53.5 bil pass.-mi; 311 airports. **Chief ports:** Sydney, Melbourne, Brisbane, Adelaide, Fremantle, Geelong.

Communications: TV sets: 716 per 1,000 pop. **Radios:** 1,391 per 1,000 pop. **Telephone lines:** 11.5 mil. **Daily newspaper circ.:** 161 per 1,000 pop. **Internet:** 14.2 mil users.

Health: Life expect.: 77.6 male; 83.5 female. **Births** (per 1,000 pop.): 12.1. **Deaths** (per 1,000 pop.): 7.5. **Natural inc.:** 0.46%. **Infant mortality** (per 1,000 live births): 4.6. **AIDS rate:** 0.1%.

Education: Compulsory: ages 5-15. **Literacy:** 100%.

Major Intl. Organizations: UN and all of its specialized agencies, APEC, the Commonwealth, OECD.

Embassy: 1601 Massachusetts Ave. NW 20036; 797-3000.

Website: www.australia.gov.au

Australia harbors many plant and animal species not found elsewhere, including kangaroos, koalas, platypuses, dingos (wild dogs), Tasmanian devils (raccoon-like marsupials), wombats (bear-like marsupials), and barking and frilled lizards.

Capt. James Cook explored the eastern coast in 1770, when the continent was inhabited by a variety of indigenous peoples. The first European settlers, beginning in 1788, were mostly convicts, soldiers, and government officials. By 1830, Britain had claimed the entire continent, and the immigration of free settlers began to accelerate. The Commonwealth was proclaimed Jan. 1, 1901. Northern Terr. was granted limited self-rule July 1, 1978.

State/Territory, Capital	Area (sq mi)	Population (2005 est.)
New South Wales, Sydney	309,500	6,803,000
Victoria, Melbourne	87,900	5,052,400
Queensland, Brisbane	666,990	4,001,000
Western Australia, Perth	975,100	2,028,700
South Australia, Adelaide	379,900	1,546,300
Tasmania, Hobart	26,200	487,200
Australian Capital Terr., Canberra	900	326,700
Northern Terr., Darwin	519,800	204,500

Racially discriminatory immigration policies were abandoned in 1973, after 3 mil Europeans (half British) had entered since 1945. The 50,000 aborigines and 150,000 part-aborigines are mostly detribalized, but there are several preserves in the Northern Territory. They remain economically disadvantaged.

Australia's agricultural success makes the country among the top exporters of beef, lamb, wool, and wheat. Major mineral deposits have been developed, largely for export. Industrialization has been completed. The nation endured a deep recession 1990-93 but has rebounded strongly.

The Labor Party won a majority in Feb. 1983 general elections and was reelected in 1984, 1987, 1990, and 1993. After an election that focused mainly on economic issues, conservatives swept into power in elections Mar. 2, 1996. Incumbent Prime Min. John Howard retained power in the 1998,2001, and 2004 elections.

Australia led an international peacekeeping force into East Timor in Sept. 1999. In a referendum Nov. 6, voters rejected a proposal that would have made Australia a republic. Sydney hosted the Olympics Sept. 15-Oct. 1, 2000.

Australian troops fought in U.S.-led military operations in Afghanistan (2001) and Iraq (2003). Some 2,000 Australian peacekeepers began arriving in the Solomon Is., July 24, 2003; nearly all had been withdrawn by mid-2005. In race riots in Sydney suburbs, Dec. 11-12, 2005, thousands of white youths assaulted people of Middle Eastern ancestry, who then retaliated against whites. Australian troops were dispatched, 2006, to suppress disorders in the Solomon Is. in April and Timor in May.

Australian External Territories

Norfolk Isl., area 13 sq mi, pop. (2006 est.) 1,828, was taken over, 1914. The soil is very fertile, suitable for citrus, bananas, and coffee. Many of the inhabitants are descendants of the *Bounty* mutineers, moved to Norfolk 1856 from Pitcairn Isl. Australia offered the island limited home rule in 1978.

Coral Sea Isls. Territory, area 1 sq mi, is administered from Norfolk Isl.

Territory of Ashmore and Cartier Isls., area 2 sq mi, in the Indian O., came under Australian authority 1934 and are administered as part of Northern Territory. **Heard Isl. and McDonald Isls.,** area 159 sq mi, are administered by the Dept. of Science.

Cocos (Keeling) Isls., 27 small coral islands in the Indian O. 1,750 mi. NW of Australia. Pop. (2006 est.) 574; area 5 sq mi. The residents voted to become part of Australia, Apr. 1984.

Christmas Isl., area 52 sq mi. (2006 est.) 1,493; 230 mi S of Java, was transferred by Britain in 1958. It has phosphate deposits.

Australian Antarctic Territory was claimed by Australia in 1933, including 2,362,000 sq mi of territory S of 60th parallel S Lat. and between 160th-45th meridians E Long. It does not include Adelie Coast.

Austria
Republic of Austria

People: Population: 8,192,880. **Age distrib.** (%) <15: 15.4; 65+: 17.1. **Pop. density:** 257 per sq mi, 99 per sq km. **Urban:** 65.8%. **Ethnic groups:** German 88%. **Principal languages:** German (official), Serbo-Croatian, Slovenian. **Chief religions:** Roman Catholic 74%, Protestant 5%.

Geography: Total area: 32,382 sq mi, 83,870 sq km; **Land area:** 31,832 sq mi, 82,444 sq km. **Location:** In S Central Europe. **Neighbors:** Switzerland, Liechtenstein on W; Germany, Czech Rep. on N; Slovakia, Hungary on E; Slovenia, Italy on S. **Topography:** Austria is primarily mountainous, with the Alps and foothills covering the western and southern provinces. The eastern provinces and Vienna are located in the Danube River Basin. **Capital:** Vienna, 2,260,000.

Government: Type: Federal republic. **Head of state:** Pres. Heinz Fischer; b. Oct. 9, 1938; in office: July 8, 2004. **Head of gov.:** Chancellor Wolfgang Schüssel; b. June 7, 1945; in office: Feb. 4, 2000. **Local divisions:** 9 bundeslaender (states). **Defense budget** (2005): $2.3 bil. **Active troops:** 39,900.

Economy: Industries: constr., machinery, vehicles & parts, food, chemicals. **Chief crops:** grains, potatoes, sugar beets, grapes. **Natural resources:** iron ore, oil, timber, magnesite, lead, coal, lignite, copper, hydropower. **Crude oil reserves** (2005): 62 mil bbls. **Arable land:** 17%. **Livestock** (2005): cattle: 2 mil; chickens: 11.7 mil; goats: 58,000; pigs: 3.1 mil; sheep: 327,000. **Fish catch** (2004): 2,667 metric tons. **Electricity prod.** (2004): 65.6 bil kWh. **Labor force** (2005 est.): agriculture 3%, industry 27%, services 70%.

Finance: Monetary unit: Euro (EUR) (Sept. 2006: 0.78 = $1 U.S.). **GDP** (2005 est.): $267.6 bil; **per capita GDP:** $32,700; **GDP growth:** 1.9%. **Imports** (2005 est.): $118.8 bil; partners (2004): Germany 45.9%, Italy 6.7%, Switzerland 4.3%. **Exports** (2005 est.): $122.5 bil; partners (2004): Germany 31.4%, Italy 9%, U.S. 6%,

Switzerland 4.8%, UK 4.4%, France 4.2%. **Tourism:** $15.3 bil. **Budget** (2005 est.): $154.5 bil. **Intl. reserves less gold:** $4.79 bil. **Gold:** 9.73 mil oz t. **Consumer prices:** 2.3%.

Transport: Railroad: Length: 3,741 mi. **Motor vehicles:** 4.05 mil pass. cars, 765,700 comm. vehicles. **Civil aviation:** 8.6 bil pass.-mi; 25 airports. **Chief ports:** Linz, Vienna, Enns, Krems.

Communications: TV sets: 526 per 1,000 pop. **Radios:** 751 per 1,000 pop. **Telephone lines:** 3.7 mil. **Daily newspaper circ.:** 309 per 1,000 pop. **Internet:** 4.65 mil users.

Health: Life expect.: 76.2 male; 82.1 female. **Births** (per 1,000 pop.): 8.7. **Deaths** (per 1,000 pop.): 9.8. **Natural inc.:** −0.10%. **Infant mortality** (per 1,000 live births): 4.6. **AIDS rate:** 0.3%.

Education: Compulsory: ages 6-14. **Literacy:** 98%.

Major Intl. Organizations: UN and all of its specialized agencies, EU, OECD, OSCE.

Embassy: 3524 International Ct. NW 20008; 895-6700.

Website: www.austria.gv.at

Rome conquered Austrian lands from Celtic tribes around 15 BC. In 788 the territory was incorporated into Charlemagne's empire. By 1300, the House of Hapsburg had gained control; they added vast territories in all parts of Europe to their realm in the next few hundred years.

Austrian dominance of Germany was undermined in the 18th century and ended by Prussia by 1866. But the Congress of Vienna, 1815, confirmed Austrian control of a large empire in southeast Europe consisting of Germans, Hungarians, Slavs, Italians, and others. The dual Austro-Hungarian monarchy was established in 1867, giving autonomy to Hungary and almost 50 years of peace.

World War I, started after the June 28, 1914, assassination of Archduke Franz Ferdinand, the Hapsburg heir, by a Serbian nationalist, destroyed the empire. By 1918 Austria was reduced to a small republic, with the borders it has today.

Nazi Germany, ruled by the Austrian born Adolf Hitler, annexed Austria Mar. 13, 1938. The republic was reestablished in 1945, under Allied occupation. Full independence and neutrality were restored in 1955. Austria joined the European Union Jan. 1, 1995.

The rise of the right-wing, anti-immigrant Austrian Freedom Party challenged the dominance of the Austrian Social Democratic Party in the late 1990s. When Freedom Party members joined the cabinet, Feb. 4, 2000, the EU imposed political sanctions on Austria, Feb. 4-Sept. 12, 2000. Party support plummeted in elections Nov. 24, 2002. Pres. Thomas Klestil died July 6, 2004, 2 days before his term expired; he was succeeded by Heinz Fischer, a Social Democrat.

Azerbaijan
Republic of Azerbaijan

People: Population: 8,066,157. **Age distrib.** (%) <15: 26.3; 65+: 7. **Pop. density:** 242 per sq mi, 93 per sq km. **Urban:** 50.0%. **Ethnic groups:** Azeri 90%, Dagestani 3%, Russian 3%, Armenian 2%. **Principal languages:** Azeri (official), Russian, Armenian. **Chief religions:** Muslim 93%, Russian Orthodox 3%, Armenian Orthodox 2%.

Geography: Total area: 33,436 sq mi, 86,600 sq km; **Land area:** 33,243 sq mi, 86,100 sq km. **Location:** SW Asia. **Neighbors:** Russia, Georgia on N; Iran on S; Armenia on W; Caspian Sea on E. **Topography:** The Great Caucasus Mts. in N, Karabakh Upland in W border the Kur-Abas lowland; climate is arid except in the subtropical SE. **Capital:** Baku, 1,856,000.

Government: Type: Republic. **Head of state:** Pres. Ilham Aliyev; b. Dec. 24, 1961; in office: Oct. 31, 2003. **Head of gov.:** Prime Min. Artur Rasizade; b. Feb. 26, 1935; in office: Nov. 4, 2003. **Local division:** 59 rayons, 11 cities, 1 autonomous republic. **Defense budget** (2005): $310 mil. **Active troops:** 66,490.

Economy: Industries: oil products, oil field equip., steel, iron ore, cement. **Chief crops:** cotton, grain, rice, grapes. **Natural resources:** oil, nat. gas, iron ore, nonferrous metals, alumina. **Crude oil reserves** (2005): 7 bil bbls. **Arable land:** 18%. **Livestock** (2005): cattle: 2 mil; chickens: 17.6 mil; goats: 601,387; pigs: 22,932; sheep: 6.9 mil. **Fish catch** (2004): 9,296 metric tons. **Electricity prod.** (2004): 20.4 bil kWh. **Labor force** (2001): agriculture 41%, industry 7%, services 52%.

Finance: Monetary unit: New Manat (AZN) (Sept. 2006: 0.92 = $1 U.S.). **GDP** (2005 est.): $37.9 bil; **per capita GDP:** $4,800; **GDP growth:** 26.4%. **Imports** (2005 est.): $4.7 bil; partners (2004): UK 13.9%, Russia 13.1%, Turkey 11.5%, Germany 8%, Netherlands 5.3%, China 5%, U.S. 4.7%, Italy 4.5%, Ukraine 4.3%. **Exports** (2005 est.): $6.1 bil; partners (2004): Italy 31.1%, Czech Republic 14.5%, Germany 9.4%, Turkey 6.1%, Russia 6%, Georgia 5.3%, France 4.9%. **Tourism:** $65 mil. **Budget** (2005 est.): $3 bil. **Intl. reserves less gold:** $824 mil. **Consumer prices:** 9.48%.

Transport: Railroad: Length: 1,834 mi. **Motor vehicles:** 370,400 pass. cars, 129,300 comm. vehicles. **Civil aviation:** 359.8 mil pass.-mi; 27 airports. **Chief port:** Baku.

Communications: TV sets: 257 per 1,000 pop. **Radios:** 23 per 1,000 pop. **Telephone lines:** 1.1 mil. **Daily newspaper circ.:** 9.9 per 1,000 pop. **Internet:** 408,000 users.

Health: Life expect.: 61.5 male; 70.3 female. **Births** (per 1,000 pop.): 17.4. **Deaths** (per 1,000 pop.): 8.4. **Natural inc.:** 0.9%. **Infant mortality** (per 1,000 live births): 60.2. **AIDS rate:** 0.1%.

Education: Compulsory: ages 6-17. **Literacy:** 98.8%.

Major Intl. Organizations: UN (FAO, IBRD, ILO, IMF, IMO, WHO), CIS, OSCE.

Embassy: 2741 34th St NW 20008 337-3500.

Website: www.azembassy.com

Azerbaijan was the home of Scythian tribes and part of the Roman Empire. Overrun by Turks in the 11th century and conquered by Russia in 1806 and 1813, it joined the USSR Dec. 30, 1922, and became a constituent republic in 1936. Azerbaijan declared independence Aug. 30, 1991, and became an independent state when the Soviet Union disbanded Dec. 26, 1991.

Fighting between mostly Muslim Azerbaijan and mostly Christian Armenia escalated in 1992 and continued in 1993 and 1994. Each country claimed Nagorno-Karabakh, an enclave in Azerbaijan with a majority population of ethnic Armenians. A temporary cease-fire was announced in May 1994, with Armenian forces in control of the enclave.

A National Council ousted Communist Pres. Mutaibov and took power May 19, 1992. Abulfaz Elchibey became the nation's first democratically elected president June 7 but was ousted from office by Surat Huseynov, commander of a private militia, June 30, 1993. Huseynov became prime minister, and Haydar Aliyev, a pro-Russian former Communist, became president. Huseynov fled the country after his supporters staged an unsuccessful coup attempt Oct. 1994. Voters approved a new constitution expanding presidential powers, Nov. 12, 1995. Pres. Aliyev was reelected Oct. 11, 1998, but international monitors called the vote seriously flawed.

The dying Pres. Aliyev named his son Ilham prime minister Aug. 4, 2003. The younger Aliyev won the presidential election of Oct. 15, in a vote considered fraudulent by international observers; he responded to violent protests Oct. 16 by arresting hundreds of opposition leaders and their supporters. Serious abuses also marred the parliamentary elections of Nov. 6, 2005, won by parties loyal to Aliyev. The opening May 25, 2005, of the Baku-Tbilisi-Ceyhan pipeline, providing an outlet for Azerbaijan's vast Caspian oil reserves, is expected to transform the nation's economy.

The Bahamas
Commonwealth of The Bahamas

People: Population: 303,770. **Age distrib.** (%) <15: 27.5; 65+: 6.4. **Pop. density:** 78 per sq mi, 30 per sq km. **Urban:** 89.5%. **Ethnic groups:** Black 85%, White 12%. **Principal languages:** English, Creole (among Haitian immigrants). **Chief religions:** Baptist 35%, Anglican 15%, Roman Catholic 14%, other Christian 15%.

Geography: Total area: 5,382 sq mi, 13,940 sq km; **Land area:** 3,888 sq mi, 10,070 sq km. **Location:** In Atlantic O., E of Florida. **Neighbors:** Nearest are U.S. on W, Cuba on S. **Topography:** Nearly 700 islands (29 inhabited) and over 2,000 islets in the W Atlantic O. extend 760 mi. NW to SE. **Capital:** Nassau, 233,000.

Government: Type: Independent commonwealth. **Head of state:** Queen Elizabeth II, represented by Gov.-Gen. Arthur Dion Hanna; b. Mar. 7, 1928; in office: Feb. 1, 2006. **Head of gov.:** Prime Min. Perry Christie; b. Aug. 21,1943; in office: May 3, 2002. **Local divisions:** 21 districts. **Defense budget** (2005): $32 mil. **Active troops:** 860.

Economy: Industries: tourism, banking, cement, oil refining & shipment, salt, rum. **Chief crops:** citrus, vegetables. **Natural resources:** salt, aragonite, timber. **Arable land:** 1%. **Livestock** (2005): cattle: 750; chickens: 3 mil; goats: 14,500; pigs: 5,000; sheep: 6,500. **Fish catch** (2004): 11,357 metric tons. **Electricity prod.** (2004): 1.8 bil kWh. **Labor force** (2005 est.): agriculture 5%, industry 5%, tourism 50%, other services 40%.

Finance: Monetary unit: Dollar (BSD) (Sept. 2006: 1.00 = $1 U.S.). **GDP** (2005 est.): $6.1 bil; **per capita GDP:** $20,200; **GDP growth:** 3.5%. **Imports** (2004 est.): $1.82 bil; partners (2004): U.S. 22.3%, South Korea 19%, Japan 8.2%, Brazil 8.2%, Italy 8.1%, Venezuela 6.8%. **Exports** (2004 est.): $469.3 mil; partners (2004): U.S. 42.1%, Spain 10.3%, Poland 6.1%, Germany 6.1%, Switzerland 4.9%, Paraguay 4.8%, France 4.5%, Mexico 4.5%. **Tourism:** $1.9 bil. **Budget** (2005 est.): $1 bil. **Intl. reserves less gold:** $410 mil. **Consumer prices:** 1.56%.

Transport: Motor vehicles: 80,000 pass. cars, 25,000 comm. vehicles. **Civil aviation:** 229.3 mil pass.-mi; 29 airports. **Chief ports:** Nassau, Freeport.

Communications: TV sets: 243 per 1,000 pop. **Radios:** 739 per 1,000 pop. **Telephone lines:** 139,900. **Daily newspaper circ.:** NA. **Internet:** 93,000 users.

Health: Life expect.: 62.2 male; 69 female. **Births** (per 1,000 pop.): 17.6. **Deaths** (per 1,000 pop.): 9.1. **Natural inc.:** 0.85%. **Infant mortality** (per 1,000 live births): 24.7. **AIDS rate:** 3.3%.

Education: Compulsory: ages 5-16. **Literacy:** 95.6%.

Major Intl. Organizations: UN (FAO, IBRD, ILO, IMF, IMO, WHO), Caricom, the Commonwealth, OAS.

Embassy: 2220 Massachusetts Ave. NW 20008; 319-2660.

Website: www.bahamas.gov.bs

Christopher Columbus first set foot in the New World on San Salvador (Watling Isl.) in 1492, when Arawak Indians inhabited the islands. British settlement began in 1647; the islands became a British colony in 1783. Internal self-government was granted in 1964; full independence within the Commonwealth was attained July 10, 1973. International banking and investment management have become major industries alongside tourism.

Bahrain
Kingdom of Bahrain

People: Population: 698,585. **Age distrib.** (%) <15: 27.4; 65+: 3.5. **Pop. density:** 2,718 per sq mi, 1,050 per sq km. **Urban:** 90.0%. **Ethnic groups:** Arab 73%, Asian 19%, Iranian 8%. **Principal languages:** Arabic (official), English, Farsi, Urdu. **Chief religion:** Muslim (Shi'a 70% and Sunni) 81%.

Geography: Total area: 257 sq mi, 665 sq km; **Land area:** 257 sq mi, 665 sq km. **Location:** SW Asia, in Persian Gulf. **Neighbors:** Nearest are Saudi Arabia on W, Qatar on E. **Topography:** Bahrain Island, and several adjacent, smaller islands, are flat, hot, and humid, with little rain. **Capital:** Manama, 162,000.

Government: Type: Constitutional monarchy. **Head of state:** King Hamad bin Isa al-Khalifa; b. Jan. 28, 1950; in office: as emir Mar. 6, 1999; as king Feb. 14, 2002. **Head of gov.:** Prime Min. Khalifa bin Sulman al-Khalifa; b. 1936; in office: Jan. 19, 1970. **Local divisions:** 12 municipalities. **Defense budget** (2005): $526 mil. **Active troops:** 11,200.

Economy: Industries: oil proc. & refining, aluminum smelting, offshore banking, ship repair. **Chief crops:** fruit, vegetables. **Natural resources:** oil, nat. gas, fish, pearls. **Crude oil reserves** (2005): 125.6 mil bbls. **Arable land:** 1%. **Livestock** (2005): cattle: 9,000; chickens: 470,000; goats: 26,000; sheep: 40,000. **Fish catch** (2004): 14,267 metric tons. **Electricity prod.** (2004): 7.8 bil kWh. **Labor force** (1997 est.): agriculture 1%, industry 79%, services 20%.

Finance: Monetary unit: Dinar (BHD) (Sept. 2006: 0.38 = $1 U.S.). **GDP** (2005 est.): $15.8 bil; **per capita GDP:** $23,000; **GDP growth:** 5.9%. **Imports** (2005 est.): $7.8 bil; partners (2004): Saudi Arabia 33.1%, Japan 7.6%, Germany 6.1%, U.S. 5.7%, UK 5.6%, France 4.9%. **Exports** (2005 est.): $11.2 bil; partners (2004): U.S. 3.1%, South Korea 2.3%, Japan 2%. **Tourism:** $864 mil. **Budget** (2005 est.): $3.4 bil. **Intl. reserves less gold** (2004): $1.25 bil. **Gold:** 150,000 oz t. **Consumer prices:** 2.6%.

Transport: Motor vehicles: 187,000 pass. cars, 38,400 comm. vehicles. **Civil aviation:** 1.8 bil pass.-mi; 3 airports. **Chief ports:** Manama, Sitrah.

Communications: TV sets: 446 per 1,000 pop. **Radios:** 64 per 1,000 pop. **Telephone lines:** 196,500. **Daily newspaper circ.:** NA. **Internet:** 152,700 users.

Health: Life expect.: 72 male; 77 female. **Births** (per 1,000 pop.): 17.8. **Deaths** (per 1,000 pop.): 4.1. **Natural inc.:** 1.37%. **Infant mortality** (per 1,000 live births): 16.8. **AIDS rate:** NA.

Education: Non-Compulsory: ages 6-17. **Literacy:** 86.5%.

Major Intl. Organizations: UN (FAO, IBRD, ILO, IMF, IMO, WHO, WTO), AL.

Embassy: 3502 International Dr. NW 20008; 342-0741.

Website: www.bahrainembassy.org

Long ruled by the Khalifa family, Bahrain was a British protectorate from 1861 to Aug. 15, 1971, when it regained independence.

Pearls, shrimp, fruits, and vegetables were the mainstays of the economy until oil was discovered in 1932. By the 1970s, oil reserves were depleted; international banking thrived.

Bahrain took part in the 1973-74 Arab oil embargo against the U.S. and other nations. The government bought controlling interest in the oil industry in 1975. Shiite dissidents have clashed with the Sunni-led government since 1996.

Emir Hamad bin Isa al-Khalifa proclaimed himself king Feb. 14, 2002. Local elections in May marked the first time Bahraini women were allowed to vote and run for office. The first female judge was appointed June 6, 2006.

Bangladesh
People's Republic of Bangladesh

People: Population: 147,365,352. **Age distrib.** (%) <15: 32.9; 65+: 3.5. **Pop. density:** 2,850 per sq mi, 1,100 per sq km. **Urban:** 24.2%. **Ethnic groups:** Bengali 98%. **Principal languages:** Bangla (official, also known as Bengali), English. **Chief religions:** Muslim 83% (official), Hindu 16%.

Geography: Total area: 55,599 sq mi, 144,000 sq km; **Land area:** 51,703 sq mi, 133,910 sq km. **Location:** In S Asia, on N bend of Bay of Bengal. **Neighbors:** India nearly surrounds country on W, N, E; Myanmar on SE. **Topography:** The country is mostly a low plain cut by the Ganges and Brahmaputra rivers and their delta. The land is alluvial and marshy along the coast, with hills only in the extreme SE and NE. A tropical monsoon climate prevails, among the rainiest in the world. **Capital:** Dhaka, 12,430,000. **Cities (urban aggr.):** Chittagong, 4,114,000; Khulna, 1,494,000.

Government: Type: Parliamentary democracy. **Head of state:** Pres. Iajuddin Ahmed; b. Feb. 1,1931; in office: Sept. 6, 2002. **Head of gov.:** Prime Min. Khaleda Zia; b. Aug. 15,1945; in office: Oct. 10, 2001. **Local divisions:** 6 divisions. **Defense budget** (2005): $785 mil. **Active troops:** 125,500.

Economy: Industries: cotton textiles, jute, garments, tea processing, newsprint, cement, chemical fertilizer, light engineering, sugar. **Chief crops:** rice, jute, tea, wheat, sugarcane, potatoes, tobacco. **Natural resources:** nat. gas, timber, coal. **Crude oil reserves** (2005): 56 mil bbls. **Arable land:** 73%. **Livestock** (2005): cattle: 24.5 mil; chickens: 142 mil; goats: 36.9 mil; sheep: 1.3 mil. **Fish catch** (2004): 2,102,026 metric tons. **Electricity prod.** (2004): 18.1 bil kWh. **Labor force** (1995-96): agriculture 63%, industry 11%, services 26%.

Finance: Monetary unit: Taka (BDT) (Sept. 2006: 64.45 = $1 U.S.). **GDP** (2005 est.): $304.3 bil; **per capita GDP:** $2,100; **GDP growth:** 5.7%. **Imports** (2005 est.): $13 bil; partners (2004): India 14.6%, China 11.7%, Singapore 7.8%, Japan 5.8%, Hong Kong 4.8%. **Exports** (2005 est.): $9.4 bil; partners (2004): U.S. 22.7%, Germany 14.5%, UK 10.8%, France 6.7%. **Tourism:** $67 mil. **Budget** (2005 est.): $8.6 bil. **Intl. reserves less gold:** $1.94 bil. **Gold:** 110,000 oz t. **Consumer prices** (2004): 3.16%.

Transport: Railroad: Length: 1,681 mi. **Motor vehicles:** 65,000 pass. cars, 145,900 comm. vehicles. **Civil aviation:** 2.8 bil pass.-mi; 15 airports. **Chief ports:** Chittagong, Dhaka, Mongla Port.

Communications: TV sets: 7 per 1,000 pop. **Radios:** 50 per 1,000 pop. **Telephone lines:** 831,000. **Daily newspaper circ.:** NA. **Internet:** 300,000 users.

Health: Life expect.: 62.5 male; 62.5 female. **Births** (per 1,000 pop.): 29.8. **Deaths** (per 1,000 pop.): 8.3. **Natural inc.:** 2.15%. **Infant mortality** (per 1,000 live births): 60.8. **AIDS rate:** <0.1%.

Education: Compulsory: ages 6-10. **Literacy:** 43.1%.

Major Intl. Organizations: UN (FAO, IBRD, ILO, IMF, IMO, WHO, WTO), the Commonwealth.

Embassy: 3510 International Dr. NW 20007; 244-0183.

Website: www.bangladeshgov.org

Muslim invaders conquered the formerly Hindu area in the 12th century. British rule lasted from the 18th century to 1947, when East Bengal became part of Pakistan.

Charging West Pakistani domination, the Awami League, based in the East, won National Assembly control in 1971. Assembly sessions were postponed; riots broke out. Pakistani troops attacked Mar. 25; Bangladesh independence was proclaimed the next day. In the ensuing civil war, 1 mil died and 10 mil fled to India.

War between India and Pakistan broke out Dec. 3, 1971. Pakistan surrendered in the East on Dec. 16. Mujibur Rahman, known as Sheikh Mujib, became prime minister; he was killed in a coup Aug. 15, 1975. During the 1970s the country moved into the Indian and Soviet orbits in response to U.S. support of Pakistan, and much of the economy was nationalized.

On May 30, 1981, Pres. Ziaur Rahman was killed in an unsuccessful coup attempt by army rivals. Vice Pres. Abdus Sattar assumed the presidency but was ousted in a coup led by army chief of staff Gen. H. M. Ershad, Mar. 1982. Ershad declared Bangladesh an Islamic Republic in 1988; a parliamentary system of government was adopted in 1991.

Bangladesh is subject to devastating storms and floods that kill thousands. A cyclone struck Apr. 1991, killing over 131,000 people and causing $2.7 bil in damages. Chronic destitution in the densely crowded population has been worsened by the decline of jute as a world commodity. Pollution of surface water and naturally occurring contamination of groundwater by arsenic have caused widespread health problems.

Political turmoil led to the resignation, Mar. 30, 1996, of Prime Min. Khaleda Zia, the widow of Ziaur Rahman. Sheikh Mujib's daughter, Hasina (known as Sheikh Hasina), led the country after the June 12, 1996 election. Bangladesh and India signed a treaty, Dec. 12, resolving their long-standing dispute over the use of water from the Ganges River. A cyclone in May 1997 left an estimated 800,000 people homeless. Floods in July-Sept. 1998 inundated most of the country, killed over 1,400 people (many through disease), and stranded at least 30 mil.

Khaleda Zia returned to power following the parliamentary elections of Oct. 1, 2001. Floods July-Aug. 2004 caused at least 950 deaths and $7 bil in property damage. Militant Islamists set off more than 400 small bombs in over 50 cities and towns, Aug. 17, 2005, killing 3 people. Another wave of jihadist bombings, Nov. 29-Dec. 8, killed 22.

Barbados

People: Population: 279,912. **Age distrib.** (%) <15: 20.1; 65+: 8.8. **Pop. density:** 1,686 per sq mi, 649 per sq km. **Urban:** 51.7%. **Ethnic groups:** Black 90%, White 4%. **Principal languages:** English. **Chief religions:** Protestant 67%, Roman Catholic 4%.

Geography: Total area: 166 sq mi, 431 sq km; **Land area:** 166 sq mi, 431 sq km. **Location:** In Atlantic O., farthest E of West Indies. **Neighbors:** Nearest are St. Lucia and St. Vincent & the Grenadines to the W. **Topography:** The island lies alone in the Atlantic almost completely surrounded by coral reefs. Highest point is Mt. Hillaby, 1,115 ft. **Capital:** Bridgetown, 142,000.

Government: Type: Parliamentary democracy. **Head of state:** Queen Elizabeth II, represented by Gov.-Gen. Sir Clifford Husbands; b. Aug. 5, 1926; in office: June 1, 1996. **Head of gov.:** Prime Min. Owen Arthur; b. Oct. 17, 1949; in office: Sept. 7, 1994. **Local divisions:** 11 parishes and Bridgetown. **Defense budget** (2005): $14 mil. **Active troops:** 610.

Economy: Industries: tourism, sugar, light mfg., component assembly. **Chief crops:** sugarcane, vegetables, cotton. **Natural resources:** oil, fish, nat. gas. **Crude oil reserves** (2005): 3 mil bbls. **Other resources:** Fish. **Arable land:** 37%. **Livestock** (2005): cattle: 10,300; chickens: 3.4 mil; goats: 5,100; pigs: 19,000; sheep: 10,800. **Fish catch** (2004): 2,500 metric tons. **Electricity prod.** (2004): 900 mil kWh. **Labor force** (1996 est.): agriculture 10%, industry 15%, services 75%.

Finance: Monetary unit: Dollar (BBD) (Sept. 2006: 2.00 = $1 U.S.). **GDP** (2005 est.): $4.7 bil; **per capita GDP:** $17,000; **GDP growth:** 4.1%. **Imports** (2004 est.): $1.5 bil; partners (2004): U.S. 31.6%, Trinidad and Tobago 21.6%, UK 7.9%, Japan 5.3%. **Exports** (2004 est.): $209 mil; partners (2004): Trinidad and Tobago 14.2%, U.S. 13.9%, UK 13%, Jamaica 7.7%, Saint Lucia 5.8%,

Spain 5.8%, Saint Vincent and the Grenadines 4.6%. **Tourism:** $776 mil. **Budget** (2000 est.): $886 mil. **Intl. reserves less gold:** $422 mil. **Consumer prices:** 6.06%.

Transport: Motor vehicles: 62,100 pass. cars, 9,400 comm. vehicles. **Civil aviation:** NA; 1 airport. **Chief port:** Bridgetown.

Communications: TV sets: 290 per 1,000 pop. **Radios:** 651 per 1,000 pop. **Telephone lines:** 135,700. **Daily newspaper circ.:** 155 per 1,000 pop. **Internet:** 150,000 users.

Health: Life expect.: 70.8 male; 74.8 female. **Births** (per 1,000 pop.): 12.7. **Deaths** (per 1,000 pop.): 8.7. **Natural inc.:** 0.4%. **Infant mortality** (per 1,000 live births): 11.8. **AIDS rate:** 1.5%.

Education: Compulsory: ages 5-15. **Literacy:** 97.4%.

Major Intl. Organizations: UN (FAO, IBRD, ILO, IMF, IMO, WHO, WTO), Caricom, the Commonwealth, OAS.

Embassy: 2144 Wyoming Ave. NW 20008; 939-9200.

Website: www.barbados.gov.bb

Barbados was probably named by Portuguese sailors in reference to bearded fig trees. An English ship visited in 1605, and British settlers arrived on the uninhabited island in 1627. Slaves worked the sugar plantations until slavery was abolished in 1834. Self-rule came gradually, with full independence proclaimed Nov. 30, 1966. British traditions have remained.

Belarus
Republic of Belarus

People: Population: 9,765,736. **Age distrib.** (%) <15: 15; 65+: 15. **Pop. density:** 121 per sq mi, 47 per sq km. **Urban:** 70.9%. **Ethnic groups:** Belarusian 81%, Russian 11%. **Principal languages:** Belarusian, Russian. **Chief religions:** Eastern Orthodox 80%, other 20%.

Geography: Total area: 80,155 sq mi, 207,600 sq km; **Land area:** 80,155 sq mi, 207,600 sq km. **Location:** E Europe. **Neighbors:** Poland on W; Latvia, Lithuania on N; Russia on E; Ukraine on S. **Topography:** Belarus is a landlocked country consisting mostly of hilly lowland with significant marsh areas in S. **Capital:** Minsk, 1,778,000.

Government: Type: Republic. **Head of state:** Pres. Aleksandr Lukashenko; b. Aug. 30, 1954; in office: July 20,1994. **Head of gov.:** Prime Min. Syarhey Sidorski; b. Mar. 13, 1954; in office: Dec. 19, 2003 (acting from July 10, 2003). **Local divisions:** 6 oblasts and 1 municipality. **Defense budget** (2005): $251 mil. **Active troops:** 72,940.

Economy: Industries: machine tools, tractors, trucks, earthmovers, motorcycles. **Chief crops:** grain, potatoes, vegetables, sugar beets, flax. **Natural resources:** timber, peat, oil, nat. gas, granite, dolomitic limestone, marl, chalk, sand, gravel, clay. **Crude oil reserves** (2005): 198 mil bbls. **Arable land:** 29%. **Livestock** (2005): cattle: 4 mil; chickens: 24.6 mil; goats: 66,000; pigs: 3.4 mil; sheep: 59,000. **Fish catch** (2004): 5,040 metric tons. **Electricity prod.** (2004): 29.3 bil kWh. **Labor force** (2003 est.): agriculture 14%, industry 34.7%, services 51.3%.

Finance: Monetary unit: Rubel (BYR) (Sept. 2006: 2,143.76 = $1 U.S.). **GDP** (2005 est.): $70.7 bil; **per capita GDP:** $6,900; **GDP growth:** 8%. **Imports** (2005 est.): $16.94 bil; partners (2004): Russia 50%, Germany 13.3%, Ukraine 4.3%, Poland 4.2%. **Exports** (2005 est.): $16.1 bil; partners (2004): Russia 38.7%, Poland 6.5%, Latvia 5.1%, Germany 5.1%, Ukraine 5.1%. **Tourism:** $270 mil. **Budget** (2005 est.): $6.3 bil. **Intl. reserves less gold:** $795 mil. **Consumer prices:** 10.34%.

Transport: Railroad: Length: 3,432 mi. **Motor vehicles** 1.66 mil pass. cars. **Civil aviation:** 191.4 mil pass.-mi; 41 airports. **Chief port:** Mazyr.

Communications: TV sets: 331 per 1,000 pop. **Radios:** 292 per 1,000 pop. **Telephone lines:** 3.3 mil. **Daily newspaper circ.:** 153.9 per 1,000 pop. **Internet:** 1.6 mil. users.

Health: Life expect.: 64 male; 75.9 female. **Births** (per 1,000 pop.): 9.4. **Deaths** (per 1,000 pop.): 14.1. **Natural inc.:** –0.47%. **Infant mortality** (per 1,000 live births): 6.7. **AIDS rate:** 0.3%.

Education: Compulsory: ages 6-16. **Literacy:** 99.6%.

Major Intl. Organizations: UN (FAO, IBRD, ILO, IMF, WHO), CIS, OSCE.

Embassy: 1619 New Hampshire Ave. NW 20009; 986-1604.

Website: www.belarusembassy.org

The region was subject to Lithuanians and Poles in medieval times, and was a prize of war between Russia and Poland beginning in 1503. It became part of the USSR in 1922, although the western part of the region was controlled by Poland. Belarus was overrun by German armies in 1941; recovered by Soviet troops in 1944. Following WWII, Belarus increased in area through Soviet annexation of part of NE Poland. Belarus declared independence Aug. 25, 1991. It became an independent state when the Soviet Union disbanded Dec. 26, 1991.

A new constitution was adopted, Mar. 15, 1994, and a new president was chosen in elections concluding July 1. Russia and Belarus signed a pact Apr. 2, 1996, linking their political and economic systems. An authoritarian constitution enacted in Nov. gave Pres. Aleksandr Lukashenko vast new powers. Opponents charged harassment and fraud in the presidential election of Sept. 9, 2001, won by Lukashenko. In elections on Oct. 17, 2004, considered flawed by foreign observers, nearly all winning candidates were Lukashenko supporters, and a constitutional provision limiting the president to 2 terms was repealed. Lukashenko won a 3rd term, Mar. 19, 2006, in elections criticized by the U.S., EU, and OSCE observers; police in Minsk suppressed postelection protests.

Belgium
Kingdom of Belgium

People: Population: 10,379,067. **Age distrib.** (%) <15: 16.7; 65+: 17.4. **Pop. density:** 887 per sq mi, 342 per sq km. **Urban:** 97.2%. **Ethnic groups:** Fleming 58%, Walloon 31%. **Principal languages:** Dutch, French, German (all official); Flemish, Luxembourgish. **Chief religions:** Roman Catholic 75%, Protestant, other 25%.

Geography: Total area: 11,787 sq mi, 30,528 sq km; **Land area:** 11,690 sq mi, 30,278 sq km. **Location:** In W Europe, on North Sea. **Neighbors:** France on W and S, Luxembourg on SE, Germany on E, Netherlands on N. **Topography:** Mostly flat, the country is trisected by the Scheldt and Meuse, major commercial rivers. The land becomes hilly and forested in the SE (Ardennes) region. **Capital:** Brussels, 1,012,000.

Government: Type: Parliamentary democracy under a constitutional monarch. **Head of state:** King Albert II; b. June 6, 1934; in office: Aug. 9, 1993. **Head of gov.:** Premier Guy Verhofstadt; b. Apr. 11, 1953; in office: July 12, 1999. **Local divisions:** 10 provinces and Brussels. **Defense budget** (2005): $3.4 bil. **Active troops:** 36,900.

Economy: Industries: engineering & metal products, motor vehicle assembly, proc. food & beverages, chemicals, textiles, glass, oil, coal. **Chief crops:** sugar beets, vegetables, fruits, grain, tobacco. **Natural resources:** coal, nat. gas. **Arable land:** 24%. **Livestock** (2005): cattle: 2.7 mil; chickens: 34.2 mil; goats: 26,455; pigs: 6.3 mil; sheep: 155,333. **Fish catch** (2004): 27,775 metric tons. **Electricity prod.** (2004): 80.2 bil kWh. **Labor force** (2003 est.): agriculture 1.3%, industry 24.5%, services 74.2%.

Finance: Monetary unit: Euro (EUR) (Sept. 2006: 0.78 = $1 U.S.). **GDP** (2005 est.): $325 bil; **per capita GDP:** $31,400; **GDP growth:** 1.5%. **Imports** (2005 est.): $264.5 bil; partners (2004): Germany 18.4%, Netherlands 17%, France 12.5%, UK 6.8%, Ireland 6.3%, U.S. 5.5%. **Exports** (2005 est.): $269.6 bil; partners (2004): Germany 19.9%, France 17.2%, Netherlands 11.8%, UK 8.6%, U.S. 6.5%, Italy 5.2%. **Tourism:** $9.2 bil. **Budget** (2005 est.): $180.5 bil. **Intl. reserves less gold:** $5.77 bil. **Gold:** 7.32 mil oz t. **Consumer prices:** 2.78%.

Transport: Railroad: Length: 2,188 mi. **Motor vehicles** 4.78 mil pass. cars, 602,100 comm. vehicles. **Civil aviation:** 1.6 bil pass.-mi; 25 airports. **Chief ports:** Antwerp (one of the world's busiest), Zeebrugge, Ghent.

Communications: TV sets: 532 per 1,000 pop. **Radios:** 797 per 1,000 pop. **Telephone lines:** 4.8 mil. **Daily newspaper circ.:** 153 per 1,000 pop. **Internet:** 5.1 mil users.

Health: Life expect.: 75.6 male; 82.1 female. **Births** (per 1,000 pop.): 10.4. **Deaths** (per 1,000 pop.): 10.3. **Natural inc.:** 0.01%. **Infant mortality** (per 1,000 live births): 4.6. **AIDS rate:** 0.3%.

Education: Compulsory: ages 6-18. **Literacy:** 98%.

Major Intl. Organizations: UN and all of its specialized agencies, EU, NATO, OECD, OSCE.

Embassy: 3330 Garfield St. NW 20008; 333-6900.

Website: belgium.fgov.be

Belgium derives its name from the Belgae, the first recorded inhabitants, probably Celts. The land was conquered by Julius Caesar and was ruled for 1800 years by conquerors, including Rome, the Franks, Burgundy, Spain, Austria, and France. After 1815, Belgium was made a part of the Netherlands, but it became an independent constitutional monarchy in 1830.

Belgian neutrality was violated by Germany in both world wars. King Leopold III surrendered to Germany, May 28, 1940. After the war, he was forced by political pressure to abdicate in favor of his son, King Baudouin. Baudouin was succeeded by his brother, Albert II, Aug. 9, 1993.

The Flemings of northern Belgium speak Dutch, while French is the language of the Walloons in the south. The language difference has been a perennial source of controversy and led to antagonism between the 2 groups. Parliament has passed measures aimed at transferring power from the central government to 3 regions—Wallonia, Flanders, and Brussels. Constitutional changes in 1993 made Belgium a federal state. Sabena, the national airline, went bankrupt Nov. 6, 2001.

Belize

People: Population: 287,730. **Age distrib.** (%) <15: 39.5; 65+: 3.5. **Pop. density:** 32 per sq mi, 12 per sq km. **Urban:** 48.3%. **Ethnic groups:** Mestizo 49%, Creole 25%, Maya 11%, Garifuna 6%. **Principal languages:** English (official), Spanish, Mayan, Garifuna (Carib), Creole. **Chief religions:** Roman Catholic 50%, Protestant 27%.

Geography: Total area: 8,867 sq mi, 22,966 sq km; **Land area:** 8,805 sq mi, 22,806 sq km. **Location:** Eastern coast of Central America. **Neighbors:** Mexico on N, Guatemala on W and S. **Topography:** Belize has swampy lowlands in N, Maya Mts. in S, coral reefs and cays near coast. Climate is tropical. **Capital:** Belmopan, 14,000.

Government: Type: Parliamentary democracy. **Head of state:** Queen Elizabeth II, represented by Gov.-Gen. Sir Colville Young; b. Nov. 20, 1932; in office: Nov. 17, 1993. **Head of gov.:** Prime Min. Said Musa; b. Mar. 19, 1944; in office: Aug. 28, 1998. **Local divisions:** 6 districts. **Defense budget** (2005): $16 mil. **Active troops (est.):** 1,050.

Economy: Industries: clothing, food proc., tourism, constr. **Chief crops:** bananas, coca, citrus, sugarcane. **Natural resourc-**

es: timber, fish, hydropower. **Arable land:** 2%. **Livestock** (2005): cattle: 57,800; chickens: 1.6 mil; goats: 165; pigs: 21,224; sheep: 6,265. **Fish catch** (2004): 14,335 metric tons. **Electricity prod.** (2004): 180 mil kWh. **Labor force** (2001 est.): agriculture 27%, industry 18%, services 55%.

Finance: Monetary unit: Dollar (BZD) (Sept. 2006: 1.99 = $1 U.S.). **GDP** (2004 est.): $1.8 bil; **per capita GDP:** $6,800; **GDP growth:** 3.8%. **Imports** (2005 est.): $622.4 mil; partners (2004): U.S. 32.7%, Mexico 14.4%, Cuba 6.5%, Japan 4.7%. **Exports** (2005 est.): $349.9 mil; partners (2004): U.S. 36.8%, UK 28.5%, Thailand 3.6%. **Tourism:** $133 mil. **Budget** (2005 est.): $329 mil. **Intl. reserves less gold:** $50 mil. **Consumer prices:** 3.64%.

Transport: Motor vehicles: 32,600 pass. cars, 7,800 comm. vehicles; **Civil aviation:** NA; 5 airports. **Chief ports:** Belize City, Big Creek.

Communications: TV sets: 183 per 1,000 pop. **Radios:** 594 per 1,000 pop. **Telephone lines:** 33,300. **Internet:** 35,000 users.

Health: Life expect.: 66.4 male; 70.3 female. **Births** (per 1,000 pop.): 28.8. **Deaths** (per 1,000 pop.): 5.7. **Natural inc.:** 2.31%. **Infant mortality** (per 1,000 live births): 24.9. **AIDS rate:** 2.5%.

Education: Compulsory: ages 5-14. **Literacy:** 94.1%.

Major Intl. Organizations: UN (FAO, IBRD, ILO, IMF, IMO, WHO, WTO), Caricom, the Commonwealth, OAS.

Embassy: 2535 Massachusetts Ave. NW 20008; 332-9636.

Website: www.belize.gov.bz

Belize (formerly British Honduras) was Britain's last colony on the American mainland; independence was achieved Sept. 21, 1981. Relations with neighboring Guatemala, initially tense, have improved in recent years. Belize has become a center for drug trafficking between Colombia and the U.S.

Benin
Republic of Benin

People: Population: 7,862,944. **Age distrib.** (%) <15: 44.1; 65+: 2.4. **Pop. density:** 184 per sq mi, 71 per sq km. **Urban:** 44.6%. **Ethnic groups:** 42 groups, incl. Fon, Adja, Yoruba, and Bariba. **Principal languages:** French (official), Fon, Yoruba, various tribal languages. **Chief religions:** Indigenous beliefs 50%, Christian 30%, Muslim 20%.

Geography: Total area: 43,483 sq mi, 112,620 sq km; **Land area:** 42,711 sq mi, 110,690 sq km. **Location:** In W Africa on Gulf of Guinea. **Neighbors:** Togo on W; Burkina Faso, Niger on N; Nigeria on E. **Topography:** Most of Benin is flat and covered with dense vegetation. The coast is hot, humid, and rainy. **Capitals** (2004):Porto-Novo (official), 242,000; Cotonou (administrative), 818,100.

Government: Type: Republic. **Head of state and gov.:** Pres. Yayi Boni; b. 1952; in office: Apr. 6, 2006. **Local divisions:** 12 departments. **Defense budget** (2005): $71 mil. **Active troops:** 4,550.

Economy: Industries: textiles, food proc., chemical prod., constr. materials. **Chief crops:** cotton, corn, cassava, yams, beans. **Natural resources:** oil, limestone, marble, timber. **Crude oil reserves** (2005): 8.2 mil bbls. **Arable land:** 13%. **Livestock** (2005): cattle: 1.8 mil; chickens: 13 mil; goats: 1.4 mil; pigs: 322,000; sheep: 750,000. **Fish catch** (2004): 39,995 metric tons. **Electricity prod.** (2004): 80 mil kWh.

Finance: Monetary unit: CFA Franc BCEAO (XOF) (Sept. 2006: 512.27 = $1 U.S.). **GDP** (2005 est.): $8.6 bil; **per capita GDP:** $1,100; **GDP growth:** 3.5%. **Imports** (2005 est.): $1.043 bil; partners (2004): China 29.7%, France 13.8%, Thailand 7.2%, Côte d'Ivoire 4.6%. **Exports** (2005 est.): $826.9 mil; partners (2004): China 30.2%, India 15.6%, Thailand 6%, Ghana 5.9%, Niger 4.5%. **Tourism** (2003): $106 mil. **Budget** (2005 est.): $1 bil. **Intl. reserves less gold:** $460 mil. **Consumer prices:** 5.36%.

Transport: Railroad: Length: 359 mi. **Motor vehicles:** 103,400 pass. cars, 96,000 comm. vehicles. **Civil aviation:** 80.8 mil pass.-mi; 1 airport. **Chief port:** Cotonou.

Communications: TV sets: 44 per 1,000 pop. **Radios:** 448 per 1,000 pop. **Telephone lines:** 76,300. **Daily newspaper circ.:** 5.4 per 1,000 pop. **Internet:** 100,000 users.

Health: Life expect.: 51.9 male; 54.2 female. **Births** (per 1,000 pop.): 38.9. **Deaths** (per 1,000 pop.): 12.2. **Natural inc.:** 2.66%. **Infant mortality** (per 1,000 live births): 79.6. **AIDS rate:** 1.8%.

Education: Compulsory: ages 6-11. **Literacy:** 34.7%.

Major Intl. Organizations: UN (FAO, IBRD, ILO, IMF, IMO, WHO, WTO), AU.

Embassy: 2124 Kalorama Rd. NW 20008; 232-6656.

Website: www.gouv.bj/en/index.php

The Kingdom of Abomey, rising to power in wars with neighboring kingdoms in the 17th cent., came under French domination in the late 19th century and was incorporated into French West Africa by 1904. Under the name Dahomey, the country gained independence Aug. 1, 1960; it became Benin in 1975. In the fifth coup since independence Col. Ahmed Kerekou took power in 1972; two years later he declared a socialist state with a "Marxist-Leninist" philosophy. In Dec. 1989, Kerekou announced Marxism-Leninism would no longer be the state ideology.

In Mar. 1991, Kerekou lost to Nicéphore Soglo in Benin's first free presidential election in 30 years. Kerekou defeated Soglo in Mar. 1996 to reclaim the presidency. He won reelection in a runoff Mar. 22, 2001. A plane bound for Beirut, Lebanon, crashed on takeoff from Cotonou, Dec. 25, 2003, killing 140 people. Yayi Boni, an economist, won a presidential runoff vote, Mar. 19, 2006.

Bhutan
Kingdom of Bhutan

People: Population: 2,279,723. **Age distrib.** (%) <15: 38.9; 65+: 4. **Pop. density:** 125 per sq mi, 48 per sq km. **Urban:** 8.5%. **Ethnic groups:** Bhote 50%, Nepalese 35%, indigenous tribes 15%. **Principal languages:** Dzongkha (official); Tibetan, Nepalese dialects. **Chief religions:** Lamaistic Buddhist 75% (official), Hindu 25%.

Geography: Total area: 18,147 sq mi, 47,000 sq km; **Land area:** 18,147 sq mi, 47,000 sq km. **Location:** S Asia, in eastern Himalayan Mts. **Neighbors:** India on W (Sikkim) and S, China on N. **Topography:** Bhutan is comprised of very high mountains in the N, fertile valleys in the center, and thick forests in the Duar Plain in the S. **Capital:** Thimphu, 85,000.

Government: Type: Monarchy. **Head of state:** King Jigme Singye Wangchuk; b. Nov. 11, 1955; in office: July 21, 1972. **Head of gov.:** Prime Min. Lyonpo Khandu Wangchuk; b. 1950; in office Sept. 4, 2006. **Local divisions:** 18 districts. **Defense budget** (2002): $19 mil. **Active troops:** NA.

Economy: Industries: cement, wood products, proc. fruits, alcoholic beverages, calcium carbide. **Chief crops:** rice, corn, root crops, citrus, grains. **Natural resources:** timber, hydropower, gypsum, calcium carbide. **Arable land:** 2%. **Livestock** (2005): cattle: 372,000; chickens: 230,000; goats: 30,000; pigs: 41,000; sheep: 20,000. **Fish catch** (2004): 300 metric tons. **Electricity prod.** (2004): 2.1 bil kWh. **Labor force:** agriculture 93%, industry 2%, services 5%.

Finance: Monetary unit: Ngultrum (BTN) (Sept. 2006: 45.82 = $1 U.S.). **GDP** (2003 est.): $2.9 bil; **per capita GDP:** $1,400; **GDP growth:** 5.3%. **Imports** (2000 est.): $196 mil; partners (2004): India 71.3%, Japan 7.8%, Austria 3%. **Exports** (2000 est.): $154 mil; partners (2004): India 87.9%, Bangladesh 4.6%, Philippines 2%. **Tourism:** $12 mil. **Budget:** $152 mil. **Intl. reserves less gold:** $327 mil. **Consumer prices:** 5.29%.

Transport: Civil aviation: 37.9 mil pass.-mi; 1 airport.

Communications: TV sets: 6 per 1,000 pop. **Radios:** 19 per 1,000 pop. **Telephone lines:** 32,700. **Internet:** 20,000 users.

Health: Life expect.: 55 male; 54.5 female. **Births** (per 1,000 pop.): 33.6. **Deaths** (per 1,000 pop.): 12.7. **Natural inc.:** 2.1%. **Infant mortality** (per 1,000 live births): 98.4. **AIDS rate:** <0.1%.

Education: Compulsory: ages 6-16. **Literacy:** 42.2%.

Major Intl. Organizations: UN (FAO, IBRD, IMF, WHO).

Embassy: 2 UN Plaza, 27th Fl., New York, NY 10017; 212-826-1919.

Website: www.bhutan.gov.bt

The region came under Tibetan rule in the 16th cent. British influence grew in the 19th cent. A Buddhist monarchy was set up in 1907. According to a 1910 treaty, Britain guided Bhutan's external affairs, while the country remained internally self-governing. Upon independence, India assumed Britain's role in a 1949 revision of the treaty. Isolated for much of its history, Bhutan has taken steps toward modernization. The king proposed, Mar. 27, 2005, a constitution creating a multiparty system, with an elected parliament empowered to impeach the sovereign. He said Dec. 12 that he would yield the throne to Crown Prince Jigme Khesar Namgyel Wangchuk in 2008, when national elections would be held.

Bolivia
Republic of Bolivia

People: Population: 8,989,046. **Age distrib.** (%) <15: 35; 65+: 4.6. **Pop. density:** 21 per sq mi, 8 per sq km. **Urban:** 63.4%. **Ethnic groups:** Quechua 30%, Mestizo 30%, Aymara 25%, white 15%. **Principal languages:** Spanish, Quechua, Aymara (all official) **Chief religion:** Roman Catholic 95% (official).

Geography: Total area: 424,164 sq mi, 1,098,580 sq km; **Land area:** 418,685 sq mi, 1,084,390 sq km. **Location:** In W central South America, in the Andes Mts. (one of 2 landlocked countries in South America). **Neighbors:** Peru and Chile on W, Argentina and Paraguay on S, Brazil on E and N. **Topography:** The great central plateau, at an altitude of 12,000 ft., over 500 mi. long, lies between two great cordilleras having 3 of the highest peaks in South America. Lake Titicaca, on Peruvian border, is highest lake in world on which steamboats ply (12,506 ft.). The E central region has semitropical forests; the llanos, or Amazon-Chaco lowlands are in E. **Capitals:** La Paz (administrative), 1,527,000; Sucre (judicial), 227,000. **Cities (urban aggr.):** Santa Cruz, 1,320,000.

Government: Type: Republic. **Head of state and gov.:** Pres. Juan Evo Morales Aima; b. Oct. 26, 1959; in office: Jan. 22, 2006. **Local divisions:** 9 departments. **Defense budget** (2005): $146 mil. **Active troops:** 31,500.

Economy: Industries: mining, smelting, oil, food & beverages, tobacco, handicrafts, clothing. **Chief crops:** soybeans, coffee, coca, cotton, corn, sugarcane, rice, potatoes, timber. **Natural resources:** tin, nat. gas, oil, zinc, tungsten, antimony, silver, iron, lead, gold, timber, hydropower. **Crude oil reserves** (2005): 441 mil bbls. **Other resources:** Timber. **Arable land:** 2%. **Livestock** (2005): cattle: 6.8 mil; chickens: 75 mil; goats: 1.5 mil; pigs: 3 mil; sheep: 8.6 mil. **Fish catch** (2004): 7,196 metric tons. **Electricity prod.** (2004): 4.5 bil kWh.

Finance: Monetary unit: Boliviano (BOB) (Sept. 2006: 8.02 = $1 U.S.). **GDP** (2005 est.): $26 bil; **per capita GDP:** $2,900; **GDP growth:** 4%. **Imports** (2005 est.): $1.8 bil; partners (2004): Brazil 25.3%, Argentina 17%, U.S. 13.1%, Chile 9.2%, Peru 7.2%. **Ex-**

ports (2005 est.): $2.4 bil; partners (2004): Brazil 33.9%, U.S. 12.7%, Colombia 11.8%, Venezuela 11.6%, Peru 5.1%, Japan 4.2%. **Tourism:** $177 mil. **Budget** (2005 est.): $3.2 bil. **Intl. reserves less gold:** $929 mil. **Gold:** 910,000 oz t. **Consumer prices:** 5.4%.

Transport: Railroad: Length: 2,187 mi. **Motor vehicles** 292,800 pass. cars, 172,700 comm. vehicles. **Civil aviation:** 889.8 mil pass.-mi; 16 airports.

Communications: TV sets: 118 per 1,000 pop. **Radios:** 675 per 1,000 pop. **Telephone lines:** 646,300. **Daily newspaper circ.:** 98.8 per 1,000 pop. **Internet:** 350,000 users.

Health: Life expect.: 63.2 male; 68.6 female. **Births** (per 1,000 pop.): 23.3. **Deaths** (per 1,000 pop.): 7.5. **Natural inc.:** 1.58%. **Infant mortality** (per 1,000 live births): 51.8. **AIDS rate:** 0.1%.

Education: Compulsory: ages 6-13. **Literacy:** 86.7%.

Major Intl. Organizations: UN (FAO, IBRD, ILO, IMF, IMO, WHO, WTO), OAS.

Embassy: 3014 Massachusetts Ave. NW 20008; 483-4410.

Website: www.bolivia.gov.bo

The Incas conquered the region's earlier Indian inhabitants in the 13th century. Spanish rule began in the 1530s and lasted until Aug. 6, 1825. The country is named after Simon Bolivar, independence fighter.

In a series of wars, Bolivia lost its Pacific coast to Chile, the oil-bearing Chaco to Paraguay, and rubber-growing areas to Brazil, 1879-1935.

Economic unrest, especially among militant mine workers, has contributed to continuing political instability. A reformist government under Victor Paz Estenssoro, 1951-64, nationalized tin mines and attempted to improve conditions for Indian majority but was overthrown by a military junta. A long series of coups and countercoups continued until constitutional government was restored in 1982.

U.S. pressure on the government to reduce the country's coca output, the raw material for cocaine, has led to clashes between police and coca growers and increased anti-U.S. feeling among Bolivians. Gen. Hugo Banzer Suárez, who ruled as a dictator, 1971-78, later governed as president, 1997-2001.

After an inconclusive presidential election June 30, 2002, Congress Aug. 4 chose Gonzalo Sánchez de Lozada, a U.S.-educated mining executive, as head of state. He quit Oct. 17, 2003, after a month of antigovernment protests, led by Bolivian Indians, in which over 70 people died. His successor, Vice Pres. Carlos D. Mesa Gisbert, a former historian and TV reporter, won a referendum July 18, 2004, on his plan to boost exports of Bolivia's huge natural gas reserves. Further protests, mainly over energy issues, forced Mesa to step down.

Juan Evo Morales Aima, a leftist and coca-farmer advocate, won the presidential election, Dec. 18, 2005, and was inaugurated Jan. 22, 2006. In his first year in office, he launched an initiative to nationalize the hydrocarbon sector, a land-redistribution program to benefit poor farmers, and tightened ties with Venezuela and Cuba.

Bosnia and Herzegovina

People: Population: 4,498,976. **Age distrib.** (%) <15: 15.5; 65+: 14.4. **Pop. density:** 227 per sq mi, 87 per sq km. **Urban:** 44.3%. **Ethnic groups:** Bosniak 48%, Serbian 37%, Croatian 14%. **Principal languages:** Bosnian (official), Croatian, Serbian. **Chief religions:** Muslim 40%, Orthodox 31%, Roman Catholic 15%, other 14%.

Geography: Total area: 19,741 sq mi, 51,129 sq km; **Land area:** 19,741 sq mi, 51,129 sq km. **Location:** On Balkan Peninsula in SE Europe. **Neighbors:** Yugoslavia on E and SE, Croatia on N and W. **Topography:** Hilly with some mountains. About 36% of the land is forested. **Capital:** Sarajevo, 380,000.

Government: Type: Federal republic. **Heads of state:** Collective presidency with rotating leadership. **Head of gov.:** Chrm. of Council Ministers Adnan Terzic; b. 1960; in office: Dec. 23, 2002. **Local divisions:** Muslim-Croat Federation, divided into 10 cantons; Serbian-led region (Republika Srpska); internationally supervised Brcko district. **Defense budget** (2005): $143 mil. **Active troops:** 24,672 (16,400 Muslim-Croat; 8,200 Serbian).

Economy: Industries: steel, mining, vehicle assembly, textiles, tobacco products, wooden furniture, tank & aircraft assembly, domestic appliances. **Chief crops:** wheat, corn, fruits, vegetables. **Natural resources:** coal, iron, bauxite, mang., timber, copper, chromium, lead, zinc, hydropower. **Arable land:** 14%. **Livestock** (2005): cattle: 440,000; chickens: 4.7 mil; pigs: 600,000; sheep: 900,000. **Fish catch** (2004): 8,394 metric tons. **Electricity prod.** (2004): 13 bil kWh.

Finance: Monetary unit: Convertible Marka (BAM) (Sept. 2006: 0.65 = $1 U.S.). **GDP** (2005 est.): $22.9 bil; **per capita GDP:** $6,800; **GDP growth:** 5.3%. **Imports** (2005 est.): $6.8 bil; partners (2004): Croatia 26.4%, Germany 14.9%, Slovenia 13.4%, Italy 12%, Austria 6.9%, Hungary 6.4%. **Exports** (2005 est.): $2.7 bil; partners (2004): Italy 22.9%, Croatia 22.1%, Germany 20.3%, Austria 7.5%, Slovenia 6.9%, Hungary 4.9%. **Tourism:** $488 mil. **Budget** (2005 est.): $4.4 bil. **Intl. reserves less gold:** $1.77 bil.

Transport: Railroad: Length: 634 mi. **Chief port:** Bosanski Brod. **Civil aviation:** 26.7 mil pass.-mi; 8 airports.

Communications: TV sets: 112 per 1,000 pop. **Radios:** 245 per 1,000 pop. **Telephone lines:** 968,900. **Daily newspaper circ.:** NA. **Internet:** 225,000 users.

Health: Life expect.: 74.4 male; 81.9 female. **Births** (per 1,000 pop.): 8.8. **Deaths** (per 1,000 pop.): 8.3. **Natural inc.:** 0.05%. **Infant mortality** (per 1,000 live births): 9.8. **AIDS rate:** <0.1%.

Education: Compulsory: ages 6-15. **Literacy:** 96.7%.

Major Intl. Organizations: UN (FAO, IBRD, ILO, IMF, IMO, WHO), OSCE.

Embassy: 2109 E St. NW 20037; 337-1500.

Website: www.bhembassy.org

Bosnia was ruled by Croatian kings c. 958 CE, and by Hungary 1000-1200. It became organized c. 1200 and later took control of Herzegovina. The kingdom disintegrated from 1391, with the southern part becoming the independent duchy Herzegovina. It was conquered by Turks in 1463 and made a Turkish province. The area was placed under control of Austria-Hungary in 1878 and made part of the province of **Bosnia and Herzegovina**, which was formally annexed to Austria-Hungary 1908; Bosnia became a province of Yugoslavia in 1918. It was reunited with Herzegovina as a federated republic in the 1946 Yugoslavian constitution.

Bosnia and Herzegovina declared sovereignty Oct. 15, 1991. A referendum for independence was passed Feb. 29, 1992. Ethnic Serbs' opposition to the referendum spurred violent clashes and bombings. The U.S. and EU recognized the republic Apr. 7. Fierce three-way fighting continued between Bosnia's Serbs, Muslims, and Croats. Serb forces massacred thousands of Bosnian Muslims and engaged in "ethnic cleansing" (the expulsion of Muslims and other non-Serbs from areas under Bosnian Serb control). The capital, Sarajevo, was surrounded and besieged by Bosnian Serb forces. Muslims and Croats in Bosnia reached a cease fire Feb. 23, 1994, and signed an accord, Mar. 18, to create a Muslim-Croat confederation in Bosnia. However, by mid-1994, Bosnian Serbs controlled over 70% of the country.

As fighting continued in 1995, the balance of power began to shift toward the Muslim-Croat alliance. Massive NATO air strikes at Bosnian Serb targets beginning Aug. 30 triggered a new round of peace talks, and the siege of Sarajevo was lifted Sept. 15. The new talks produced an agreement in principle to create autonomous regions within Bosnia, with the Serb region (Republika Srpska) constituting 49% of the country. A Croat-Muslim offensive in Sept. recaptured significant territory, leaving Bosnian Serbs in control of approximately half that percentage.

A peace agreement initialed in Dayton, Ohio, Nov. 21, 1995, was signed in Paris, Dec. 14, by leaders of Bosnia, Croatia, and Serbia. Some 60,000 NATO troops (about 20,000 from the U.S.) moved in to police the accord. Meanwhile, a UN tribunal began bringing charges against suspected war criminals. Elections were held Sept. 14, 1996, for a 3-person collective presidency, for seats in a federal parliament, and for regional offices. In Dec. a revamped NATO "stabilization force" (SFOR) of over 30,000 members (more than 8,000 from the U.S.) received an 18-month mandate, which was later extended.

In a landmark verdict Aug. 2, 2001, the UN tribunal found Radislav Krstic, a Bosnian Serb general, guilty in connection with the genocide of thousands of Muslims at Srebrenica in 1995. A European Union peacekeeping force (EUFOR), with 7,000 members, assumed responsibility from SFOR, Dec. 2, 2004. On Sept. 27, 2006, the UN tribunal sentenced former Bosnian Serb leader Momcilo Krajisnik to 27 years for crimes against humanity, but acquitted him of two counts of genocide.

Botswana
Republic of Botswana

People: Population: 1,639,833. **Age distrib.** (%) <15: 38.3; 65+: 3.8. **Pop. density:** 7 per sq mi, 2 per sq km. **Urban:** 51.6%. **Ethnic groups:** Tswana 79%, Kalanga 11%, Basarwa 3%. **Principal languages:** English (official), Setswana. **Chief religions:** Christian 72%, none 20.6.

Geography: Total area: 231,804 sq mi, 600,370 sq km; **Land area:** 226,013 sq mi, 585,370 sq km. **Location:** In southern Africa. **Neighbors:** Namibia on N and W, South Africa on S, Zimbabwe on NE; Botswana claims border with Zambia on N. **Topography:** The Kalahari Desert, supporting nomadic Bushmen and wildlife, spreads over SW; there are swamplands and farming areas in N, and rolling plains in E where livestock are grazed. **Capital:** Gaborone, 210,000.

Government: Type: Parliamentary republic. **Head of state and gov.:** Pres. Festus Mogae; b. Aug. 21, 1939; in office: Apr. 1, 1998. **Local divisions:** 10 districts, 4 town councils. **Defense budget** (2005): $359 mil. **Active troops:** 9,000.

Economy: Industries: diamonds, copper, nickel, salt, soda ash, potash, proc., textiles. **Chief crops:** sorghum, maize, millet, beans, sunflowers. **Natural resources:** diamonds, copper, nickel, salt, soda ash, potash, coal, iron ore, silver. **Arable land:** 1%. **Livestock** (2005): cattle: 1.7 mil; chickens: 4 mil; goats: 2.3 mil; pigs: 8,000; sheep: 400,000. **Fish catch** (2004): 161 metric tons. **Electricity prod.** (2004): 820 mil kWh.

Finance: Monetary unit: Pula (BWP) (Sept. 2006: 6.23 = $1 U.S.). **GDP** (2005 est.): $17.2 bil; **per capita GDP:** $10,500; **GDP growth:** 4.5%. **Imports** (2005 est.): $3.4 bil; partners Southern African Customs Union (SACU) 74%, European Free Trade Assn. (EFTA) 17%, Zimbabwe 4%. **Exports** (2005 est.): $3.7 bil; partners (2000): EFTA 87%, SACU 7%, Zimbabwe 4%. **Tourism:** $549 mil. **Budget** (2005 est.): $3.8 bil. **Intl. reserves less gold:** $4.41 bil. **Consumer prices:** 8.65%.

Transport: Railroad: Length: 552 mi. **Motor vehicles** 44,500 pass. cars, 67,900 comm. vehicles. **Civil aviation:** 49.7 mil pass.-mi; 10 airports.

Communications: TV sets: 21 per 1,000 pop. **Radios:** 154 per 1,000 pop. **Telephone lines:** 132,000. **Daily newspaper circ.:** 24.7 per 1,000 pop. **Internet** (2002): 60,000 users.

Health: Life expect.: 33.9 male; 33.6 female. **Births** (per 1,000 pop.): 23.1. **Deaths** (per 1,000 pop.): 29.5. **Natural inc.:** −0.64%. **Infant mortality** (per 1,000 live births): 53.7. **AIDS rate:** 24.1%.

Education: Compulsory: ages 6-15. **Literacy:** 81.2%.

Major Intl. Organizations: UN (FAO, IBRD, ILO, IMF, WHO, WTO), the Commonwealth, AU.

Embassy: 1531-3 New Hampshire Ave. NW 20036; 244-4990.

Website: www.gov.bw

First inhabited by bushmen, then Bantus, the region became the British protectorate of Bechuanaland in 1886, halting encroachment by Boers and Germans from the south and southwest. The country became fully independent Sept. 30, 1966, as Botswana. Cattle raising and mining (diamonds, copper, nickel) have contributed to economic growth; its economy is closely tied to South Africa's. According to the UN, about 15% of the population has HIV/AIDS.

Brazil
Federative Republic of Brazil

People: Population: 188,078,227. **Age distrib.** (%) <15: 25.8; 65+: 6.1. **Pop. density:** 57 per sq mi, 22 per sq km. **Urban:** 83.1%. **Ethnic groups:** European 55%, Creole 38%, African 6%. **Principal languages:** Portuguese (official), Spanish, English, French. **Chief religion:** Roman Catholic (nominal) 74%, Protestant 15%.

Geography: Total area: 3,286,488 sq mi, 8,511,965 sq km; **Land area:** 3,265,077 sq mi, 8,456,510 sq km. **Location:** Occupies E half of South America. **Neighbors:** French Guiana, Suriname, Guyana, Venezuela on N; Colombia, Peru, Bolivia, Paraguay, on W; Uruguay on S. **Topography:** Brazil's Atlantic coastline stretches 4,603 miles. In N is the heavily wooded Amazon basin covering half the country. Its network of rivers is navigable for 15,814 mi. The Amazon itself flows 2,093 miles in Brazil, all navigable. The NE region is semiarid scrubland, heavily settled and poor. The S central region, favored by climate and resources, has almost half of the population, produces 75% of farm goods and 80% of industrial output. The narrow coastal belt includes most of the major cities. Almost the entire country has a tropical or semitropical climate. **Capital:** Brasília, 3,341,000. **Cities (urban aggr.):** São Paulo, 18,333,000; Rio de Janeiro, 11,469,000; Belo Horizonte, 5,304,000.

Government: Type: Federal republic. **Head of state and gov.:** Luiz Inacio Lula da Silva; b. Oct. 27, 1945; in office: Jan. 1, 2003. **Local divisions:** 26 states, 1 federal district (Brasília). **Defense budget** (2005): $13.1 bil. **Active troops:** 302,909.

Economy: Industries: textiles, shoes, chemicals, cement, lumber, iron ore, steel, aircraft, motor vehicles & parts. **Chief crops:** coffee, soybeans, wheat, rice, corn, sugarcane, cocoa, citrus. **Natural resources:** bauxite, gold, iron ore, mang., nickel, phosphates, platinum, tin, uranium, oil, hydropower, timber. **Crude oil reserves** (2005): 10.6 bil bbls. **Arable land:** 5%. **Livestock** (2005): cattle: 192 mil; chickens: 1.1 bil; goats: 9.1 mil; pigs: 33 mil; sheep: 14.2 mil. **Fish catch** (2004): 1,015,916 metric tons. **Electricity prod.** (2004): 380.9 bil kWh. **Labor force** (2003 est.): agriculture 20%, industry 14%, services 66%.

Finance: Monetary unit: Real (BRL) (Sept. 2006: 2.21 = $1 U.S.). **GDP** (2005 est.): $1.6 tril; **per capita GDP:** $8,400; **GDP growth:** 2.4%. **Imports** (2005 est.): $78 bil; partners (2004): U.S. 22.4%, Germany 9.2%, Argentina 8.1%, China 5.5%. **Exports** (2005 est.): $115.1 bil; partners (2004): U.S. 21.2%, China 7.8%, Argentina 6%, Germany 5.1%, Netherlands 4.8%. **Tourism:** $3.2 bil. **Budget** (2004): $172.4 bil. **Intl. reserves less gold:** $37.48 bil. **Gold:** 440,000 oz t. **Consumer prices:** 6.88%.

Transport: Railroad: Length: 18,276 mi. **Motor vehicles** 15.21 mil pass. cars, 4.26 mil comm. vehicles. **Civil aviation:** 28.6 bil pass.-mi; 714 airports. **Chief ports:** Santos, Rio de Janeiro, Vitoria, Salvador, Rio Grande, Recife.

Communications: TV sets: 333 per 1,000 pop. **Radios:** 434 per 1,000 pop. **Telephone lines:** 42.4 mil. **Daily newspaper circ.:** 45.9 per 1,000 pop. **Internet:** 25.9 mil users.

Health: Life expect.: 68 male; 76.1 female. **Births** (per 1,000 pop.): 16.6. **Deaths** (per 1,000 pop.): 6.2. **Natural inc.:** 1.04%. **Infant mortality** (per 1,000 live births): 28.6. **AIDS rate:** 0.5%.

Education: Compulsory: ages 7-14. **Literacy:** 88.6%.

Major Intl. Organizations: UN and most of its specialized agencies, OAS.

Embassy: 3006 Massachusetts Ave. NW 20008; 238-2700.

Website: www.brasilemb.org

Pedro Alvares Cabral, a Portuguese navigator, is generally credited as the first European to reach Brazil, in 1500. The country was thinly settled by various Indian tribes. Only a few have survived to the present, mostly in the Amazon basin.

In the next centuries, Portuguese colonists gradually pushed inland, bringing along large numbers of African slaves. (Slavery was not abolished until 1888.) The King of Portugal, fleeing before Napoleon's army, moved the seat of government to Brazil in 1808. Brazil thereupon became a kingdom under Dom Joao VI. After his return to Portugal, his son Pedro proclaimed the independence of Brazil, Sept. 7, 1822, and was crowned emperor. The second emperor, Dom Pedro II, was deposed in 1889, and a republic proclaimed, called the United States of Brazil. In 1967 the country was renamed the Federative Republic of Brazil.

A military junta took control in 1930; dictatorial power was assumed by Getulio Vargas, until finally forced out by the military in 1945. A democratic regime prevailed 1945-64, during which time

the capital was moved from Rio de Janeiro to Brasília. In 1964, Pres. Joao Belchoir Marques Goulart instituted economic policies that aggravated Brazil's inflation; he was overthrown by an army revolt. The next 5 presidents were all military leaders. Censorship was imposed, and much of the opposition was suppressed amid charges of torture.

Since 1930, successive governments have pursued industrial and agricultural growth and interior area development. Exploiting vast natural resources and a huge labor force, Brazil became the leading industrial power of Latin America by the 1970s, while agricultural output soared. By the 1990s, Brazil had one of the world's largest economies; income was poorly distributed, however, and more than one out of four Brazilians continued to survive on less than $1 a day. Despite protective environmental legislation, development has destroyed much of the Amazon ecosystem. Brazil hosted delegates from 178 countries at the Earth Summit, June 3-14, 1992.

Democratic presidential elections were held in 1985 as the nation returned to civilian rule. Fernando Collor de Mello was elected president in Dec. 1989. In Sept. 1992, Collor was impeached for corruption. He resigned on Dec. 29 as his trial was beginning, and Itamar Franco, who had been acting president, was sworn in as president. In elections held on Oct. 3, 1994, Fernando Henrique Cardoso was elected president. Reelected Oct. 4, 1998, he guided Brazil through a series of financial crises.

A new civil code guaranteeing legal equality for women was enacted Aug. 15, 2001. The IMF approved a $30 bil loan to Brazil Aug. 7, 2002; by then, Brazil's debt already exceeded $260 bil. Luiz Inacio Lula da Silva, a union leader and reformer, won a presidential runoff Oct. 27 with 61% of the vote. Brazil's space program suffered a setback when a rocket exploded on its launchpad Aug. 22, 2003, killing 21 people; the country successfully launched its first rocket into space Oct. 23, 2004.

A top aide to Pres. Lula resigned June 16, 2005, amid allegations the ruling party bribed legislators in exchange for votes. Gang violence in São Paulo, May-July 2006, claimed more than 150 lives.

Brunei
State of Brunei Darussalam

People: Population: 379,444. **Age distrib.** (%) <15: 28.1; 65+: 3.1. **Pop. density:** 186 per sq mi, 72 per sq km. **Urban:** 76.2%. **Ethnic groups:** Malay 67%, Chinese 15%, indigenous 6%. **Principal languages:** Malay (official), English, Chinese. **Chief religions:** Muslim (official) 67%, Buddhist 13%, Christian 10%; indigenous beliefs, other 10%.

Geography: Total area: 2,228 sq mi, 5,770 sq km; **Land area:** 2,035 sq mi, 5,270 sq km. **Location:** In SE Asia, on the N coast of the island of Borneo; it is surrounded on its landward side by the Malaysian state of Sarawak. Topography: Brunei has a narrow coastal plain, with mountains in E, hilly lowlands in W. There are swamps in W and NE. Climate is tropical. **Capital:** Bandar Seri Begawan, 64,000.

Government: Type: Independent sultanate. **Head of state and gov.:** Sultan Sir Muda Hassanal Bolkiah Mu'izzadin Waddaulah; b. July 15, 1946; in office: Jan. 1, 1984 (sultan since Oct. 5, 1967). **Local divisions:** 4 districts. **Defense budget** (2004): $357 mil. **Active troops:** 7,000.

Economy: Industries: oil, oil refining, nat. gas liquefaction, constr. **Chief crops:** rice, vegetables, fruits. **Natural resources:** oil, nat. gas, timber. **Crude oil reserves** (2005): 1.4 bil bbls. **Arable land:** 1%. **Livestock** (2005): cattle: 1,300; chickens: 13 mil; goats: 3,000; pigs: 1,800; sheep: 3,000. **Fish catch** (2004): 3,136 metric tons. **Electricity prod.** (2004): 2.8 bil kWh. **Labor force** (2003 est.): agriculture 2.9%, industry 61.1%, services 36%.

Finance: Monetary unit: Dollar (BND) (Sept. 2006: 1.58 = $1 U.S.). **GDP** (2003 est.): $6.8 bil; **per capita GDP:** $23,600; **GDP growth:** 1.7%. **Imports** (2004 est.): $1.6 bil; partners (2004): Singapore 33.1%, Malaysia 21.5%, Japan 7.3%, UK 6.8%. **Exports** (2004 est.): $4.5 bil; partners (2004): Japan 37.8%, South Korea 13.6%, Australia 11.1%, U.S. 9%, Thailand 7.9%, China 5.9%. **Tourism** (1998): $37 mil. **Budget** (2004 est.): $4.8 bil. **Intl. reserves less gold:** $346 mil.

Transport: Railroad: Length: 8 mi. **Motor vehicles:** 211,800 pass. cars, 20,800 comm. vehicles. **Civil aviation:** 2.3 bil pass.-mi; 1 airport.

Communications: TV sets: 637 per 1,000 pop. **Radios:** 302 per 1,000 pop. **Telephone lines** 90,000. **Daily newspaper circ.:** NA. **Internet:** 56,000 users.

Health: Life expect.: 72.6 male; 77.6 female. **Births** (per 1,000 pop.): 18.8. **Deaths** (per 1,000 pop.): 3.5. **Natural inc.:** 1.53%. **Infant mortality** (per 1,000 live births): 12.2. **AIDS rate:** <0.1%.

Education: Compulsory: ages 5-16. **Literacy:** 92.7%.

Major Intl. Organizations: UN and some of its specialized agencies, APEC, ASEAN, the Commonwealth.

Embassy: 3520 International Court NW 20008; 237-1838.

Website: www.brunei.gov.bn/index.htm

The Sultanate of Brunei was a powerful state in the early 16th cent., with authority over all of the island of Borneo as well as parts of the Sulu Islands and the Philippines. In 1888, a treaty placed the state under the protection of Great Britain.

Brunei became a fully sovereign and independent state on Jan. 1, 1984. Much of the country's oil wealth has been squandered in recent years by members of the royal family.

Bulgaria
Republic of Bulgaria

People: Population: 7,385,367. **Age distrib.** (%) <15: 13.9; 65+: 17.3. **Pop. density:** 173 per sq mi, 66 per sq km. **Urban:** 69.8%. **Ethnic groups:** Bulgarian 84%, Turk 10%, Roma 5%. **Principal languages:** Bulgarian (official), Turkish. **Chief religions:** Bulgarian Orthodox 83%, Muslim 12%.

Geography: Total area: 42,823 sq mi, 110,910 sq km; **Land area:** 42,684 sq mi, 110,550 sq km. **Location:** SE Europe, in E Balkan Peninsula on Black Sea. **Neighbors:** Romania on N; Yugoslavia, Macedonia on W; Greece, Turkey on S. **Topography:** The Stara Planina (Balkan) Mts. stretch E-W across the center of the country, with the Danubian plain on N, the Rhodope Mts. on SW, and Thracian Plain on SE. **Capital:** Sofia, 1,093,000.

Government: Type: Republic. **Head of state:** Pres. Georgi Parvanov; b. June 28, 1957; in office: Jan. 22, 2002. **Head of gov.:** Prime Min. Sergei Stanishev; b. May 5, 1966; in office: Aug. 16, 2005. **Local divisions:** 28 provinces. **Defense budget** (2005): $630 mil. **Active troops:** 51,000.

Economy: Industries: utilities, food, beverages, tobacco, machinery, metals, chemicals. **Chief crops:** vegetables, fruits, tobacco, wine, wheat, barley, sunflowers, sugar beets. **Natural resources:** bauxite, copper, lead, zinc, coal, timber. **Crude oil reserves** (2005): 15 mil bbls. **Arable land:** 37%. **Livestock** (2005): cattle: 671,579; chickens: 18 mil; goats: 718,117; pigs: 931,402; sheep: 1.7 mil. **Fish catch** (2004): 10,739 metric tons. **Electricity prod.** (2004): 42 bil kWh. **Labor force** (3rd quarter 2004 est.): agriculture 11%, industry 32.7%, services 56.3%.

Finance: Monetary unit: Lev (BGN) (Sept. 2006: 1.53 = $1 U.S.). **GDP** (2005 est.): $71.5 bil; **per capita GDP:** $9,600; **GDP growth:** 5.5%. **Imports** (2005 est.): $15.9 bil; partners (2004): Germany 15.7%, Italy 10.9%, Russia 9%, Greece 8%, Turkey 7.5%, France 4.7%, Austria 4%. **Exports** (2005 est.): $11.7 bil; partners (2004): Italy 13.2%, Germany 11.5%, Turkey 9.7%, Belgium 6.4%, Greece 6.1%, U.S. 5.6%, France 5.1%. **Tourism:** $2.1 bil. **Budget** (2005 est.): $10.9 bil. **Intl. reserves less gold:** $5.63 bil. **Gold:** 1.28 mil oz t. **Consumer prices:** 5.04%.

Transport: Railroad: Length: 2,668 mi. **Motor vehicles:** 2.3 mil pass. cars, 337,200 comm. vehicles. **Civil aviation:** 35.4 mil pass.-mi; 132 airports. **Chief ports:** Burgas, Varna.

Communications: TV sets: 429 per 1,000 pop. **Radios:** 537 per 1,000 pop. **Telephone lines:** 2.5 mil. **Daily newspaper circ.:** 172.9. **Internet:** (2002): 630,000 users.

Health: Life expect.: 68.7 male; 76.1 female. **Births** (per 1,000 pop.): 9.7. **Deaths** (per 1,000 pop.): 14.3. **Natural inc.:** −0.46%. **Infant mortality** (per 1,000 live births): 19.9. **AIDS rate:** <0.1%.

Education: Compulsory: ages 7-14. **Literacy:** 98.2%.

Major Intl. Organizations: UN (FAO, IBRD, ILO, IMF, IMO, WHO, WTO), NATO, OSCE.

Embassy: 1621 22d St. NW 20008; 387-0174.

Website: www.government.bg

Bulgaria was settled by Slavs in the 6th cent. Turkic Bulgars arrived in the 7th cent., merged with the Slavs, became Christians by the 9th cent., and set up powerful empires in the 10th and 12th centuries. The Ottomans prevailed in 1396 and remained for 500 years.

An 1876 revolt led to an independent kingdom in 1908. Bulgaria expanded after the first Balkan War but lost its Aegean coastline in WWI, when it sided with Germany. Bulgaria joined the Axis in WWII but withdrew in 1944. Communists took power with Soviet aid; monarchy was abolished Sept. 8, 1946.

On Nov. 10, 1989, Communist Party leader and head of state Todor Zhivkov, who had held power for 35 years, resigned. Zhivkov was imprisoned, Jan. 1990, and convicted, Sept. 1992, of corruption and abuse of power. In Jan. 1990, Parliament voted to revoke the constitutionally guaranteed dominant role of the Communist Party. A new constitution took effect July 13, 1991. An economic austerity program was launched in May 1996. Former Prime Min. Andrei Lukanov, a longtime Communist leader, was assassinated Oct. 2 in Sofia. Petar Stoyanov won a presidential runoff election Nov. 3.

Bulgaria's deteriorating economy provoked nationwide strikes and demonstrations in Jan. 1997. The Union of Democratic Forces, an anti-Communist group, won national elections on Apr. 19, 1997. The UDF lost the elections of June 17, 2001, to a party headed by the former king, Simeon II. Socialist opposition leader Georgi Parvanov won a presidential runoff vote Nov. 18.

Bulgaria became a full member of NATO, Apr. 2, 2004, and was expected to enter the European Union by 2007. Following parliamentary elections, June 25, 2005, Socialist leader Sergei Stanishev formed a broad coalition government. Parliament approved, June 29, 2006, a law that would abolish the military draft by 2008.

Burkina Faso

People: Population: 13,902,972. **Age distrib.** (%) <15: 46.8; 65+: 2.5. **Pop. density:** 131 per sq mi, 50 per sq km. **Urban:** 17.8%. **Ethnic groups:** Mossi (approx. 40%), Gurunsi, Senufo, Lobi, Bobo, Mande, Fulani. **Principal languages:** French (official), Sudanic languages. **Chief religions:** Muslim 50%, indigenous beliefs 40%, Christian (mainly Roman Catholic) 10%.

Geography: Total area: 105,869 sq mi, 274,200 sq km; **Land area:** 105,715 sq mi, 273,800 km. **Location:** In W Africa, S of the Sahara. **Neighbors:** Mali on NW; Niger on NE; Benin, Togo, Ghana, Côte d'Ivoire on S. **Topography:** Landlocked Burkina Faso is in

the savanna region of W Africa. The N is arid, hot, and thinly populated. **Capital:** Ouagadougou, 926,000.

Government: Type: Republic. **Head of state:** Pres. Blaise Compaoré; b. Feb. 3, 1951; in office: Oct. 15, 1987. **Head of gov.:** Prime Min. Paramanga Ernest Yonli; b. 1956; in office: Nov. 7, 2000. **Local divisions:** 45 provinces. **Defense budget** (2005): $72.7 mil. **Active troops:** 10,800.

Economy: Industries: cotton, beverages, agric. proc., soap, cigarettes, textiles, gold. **Chief crops:** peanuts, shea nuts, sesame, cotton, sorghum, millet. **Natural resources:** mang., limestone, marble, gold, antimony, copper, nickel, bauxite, lead, phosphates, zinc, silver. **Arable land:** 13%. **Livestock** (2005): cattle: 8 mil; chickens: 25.7 mil; goats: 10.7 mil; pigs: 2.3 mil; sheep: 7 mil.. **Fish catch** (2004): 9,005 metric tons. **Electricity prod.** (2004): 400 mil kWh. **Labor force** (2000 est.): agriculture 90%, industry and services 10%.

Finance: Monetary unit: CFA BCEAO Franc (XOF) (Sept. 2006: 512.27 = $1 U.S.). **GDP** (2005 est.): $17 bil; **per capita GDP:** $1,300; **GDP growth:** 4.5%. **Imports** (2005 est.): $992 mil; partners (2004): France 31.5%, Côte d'Ivoire 13.9%, Togo 8.5%. **Exports** (2005 est.): $395 mil; partners (2004): China 32.3%, Singapore 10.7%, Bangladesh 4.5%, Ghana 4.4%, Colombia 4.4%. **Tourism** (2001): $20 mil. **Budget** (2005 est.): $1.4 bil. **Intl. reserves less gold:** $307 mil. **Consumer prices:** 6.42%.

Transport: Railroad: Length: 386 mi. **Motor vehicles:** 26,500 pass. cars, 22,600 comm. vehicles. **Civil aviation:** 18 mil pass.-mi; 2 airports.

Communications: TV sets: 11 per 1,000 pop. **Radios:** 34 per 1,000 pop. **Telephone lines:** 97,400. **Daily newspaper circ.:** 1.3 per 1,000 pop. **Internet:** 53,200 users.

Health: Life expect.: 47.3 male; 50.4 female. **Births** (per 1,000 pop.): 45.6. **Deaths** (per 1,000 pop.): 15.6. **Natural inc.:** 3%. **Infant mortality** (per 1,000 live births): 91.3. **AIDS rate:** 2%.

Education: Compulsory: ages 7-16. **Literacy:** 21.8%.

Major Intl. Organizations: UN and many of its specialized agencies, AU.

Embassy: 2340 Massachusetts Ave. NW 20008; 332-5577.

Website: www.burkinaembassy-usa.org

The Mossi people entered the area in the 11th to 13th centuries. Their kingdoms ruled until they were defeated by the Mali and Songhai empires.

French control came by 1896, but Upper Volta (renamed Burkina Faso on Aug. 4, 1984) was not established as a separate territory until 1947. Full independence came Aug. 5, 1960, and a pro-French government was elected. The military seized power in 1980. A 1987 coup established the current regime, which instituted a multiparty system in the early 1990s. Pres. Blaise Compaoré won reelection, Nov. 13, 2005, with 80% of the vote. The country, one of the world's poorest, depends heavily on foreign aid.

Burma
(See Myanmar)

Burundi
Republic of Burundi

People: Population: 8,090,068. **Age distrib.** (%) <15: 46.3; 65+: 2.6. **Pop. density:** 816 per sq mi, 315 per sq km. **Urban:** 9.9%. **Ethnic groups:** Hutu 85%, Tutsi 14%, Twa (Pygmy) 1%. **Principal languages:** Kirundi, French (both official); Swahili. **Chief religions:** Roman Catholic 62%, indigenous beliefs 23%, Muslim 10%, Protestant 5%.

Geography: Total area: 10,745 sq mi, 27,830 sq km; **Land area:** 9,904 sq mi, 25,650 sq km. **Location:** In central Africa. **Neighbors:** Rwanda on N, Dem. Rep. of the Congo (formerly Zaire) on W, Tanzania on E and S. **Topography:** Much of the country is grassy highland, with mountains reaching 8,900 ft. The southernmost source of the White Nile is located in Burundi. Lake Tanganyika is the second deepest lake in the world. **Capital:** Bujumbura, 447,000.

Government: Type: In transition. **Head of state and gov.:** Pres. Pierre Nkurunziza; b. 1964; in office: Aug. 26, 2005. **Local divisions:** 16 provinces. **Defense budget** (2005): $46 mil. **Active troops:** 50,500.

Economy: Industries: light consumer goods, component assembly, constr., food proc. **Chief crops:** coffee, cotton, tea, corn, sorghum, sweet potatoes, bananas. **Natural resources:** nickel, uranium, rare earth oxides, peat, cobalt, copper, platinum, vanadium, hydropower. **Arable land:** 44%. **Livestock** (2005): cattle: 325,000; chickens: 4.3 mil; goats: 750,000; pigs: 70,000; sheep: 230,000. **Fish catch** (2004): 13,631 metric tons. **Electricity prod.** (2004): 140 mil kWh. **Labor force** (2002 est.): agriculture 93.6%, industry 2.3%, services 4.1%.

Finance: Monetary unit: Franc (BIF) (Sept. 2006: 1,059.30 = $1 U.S.). **GDP** (2005 est.): $5.7 bil; **per capita GDP:** $700; **GDP growth:** 1.1%. **Imports** (2005 est.): $200 mil; partners (2004): Kenya 11.7%, Tanzania 9.6%, U.S. 9.1%, Belgium 9%, France 8.8%, Italy 5.4%, Japan 4.8%, Uganda 4.8%, Zambia 4.2%. **Exports** (2005 est.): $52 mil; partners (2004): Switzerland 25.8%, Germany 12.2%, Belgium 7.9%, U.S. 5.5%, Thailand 5.3%, Rwanda 5.2%. **Tourism:** $1.2 mil. **Budget** (2005 est.): $278 mil. **Intl. reserves less gold:** $70 mil. **Consumer prices:** 13.52%.

Transport: Motor vehicles: 7,000 pass. cars, 9,300 comm. vehicles. **Civil aviation:** NA; 1 airport. **Chief port:** Bujumbura.

Communications: TV sets: 15 per 1,000 pop. **Radios:** 152 per 1,000 pop. **Telephone lines:** 27,700. **Daily newspaper circ.:** NA. **Internet:** 25,000 users.

Health: Life expect.: 50.1 male; 51.6 female. **Births** (per 1,000 pop.): 42.2. **Deaths** (per 1,000 pop.): 13.5. **Natural inc.:** 2.88%. **Infant mortality** (per 1,000 live births): 63.1. **AIDS rate:** 3.3%.

Education: Compulsory: ages 7-12. **Literacy:** 59.3%.

Major Intl. Organizations: UN (FAO, IBRD, ILO, IMF, WHO, WTO), AU.

Embassy: 2233 Wisconsin Ave. NW, Suite 212, 20007; 342-2574.

Website: www.burundiembassy-usa.org

The pygmy Twa were the first inhabitants, followed by Bantu Hutus, who were conquered in the 16th cent. by the Tutsi (Watusi), probably from Ethiopia. Under German control in 1899, the area fell to Belgium in 1916, which exercised successively a League of Nations mandate and UN trusteeship over Ruanda-Urundi (now the two countries of Rwanda and Burundi). Burundi became independent July 1, 1962.

An unsuccessful Hutu rebellion in 1972-73 left 10,000 Tutsi and 150,000 Hutu dead. Over 100,000 Hutu fled to Tanzania and Zaire (now Congo). In the 1980s, Burundi's Tutsi-dominated regime pledged itself to ethnic reconciliation and democratic reform. In the nation's first democratic presidential election, in June 1993, a Hutu, Melchior Ndadaye, was elected. He was killed in an attempted coup, Oct. 21, 1993. At least 150,000 Burundians died as a result of ethnic conflict during the next three years. Pres. Cyprien Ntaryamira, elected Jan. 1994, was killed with the president of Rwanda in a mysterious plane crash, Apr. 6. The incident sparked massive carnage in Rwanda; violence in Burundi, initially far more limited, intensified in 1995. Ethnic strife continued after a military coup, July 25, 1996. Former South African Pres. Nelson Mandela mediated peace talks from Dec. 1999; most warring groups signed a draft peace treaty in Arusha, Tanzania, Aug. 28, 2000. Coup attempts were suppressed Apr. 18 and July 23, 2001. A power-sharing government headed by Buyoya was sworn in Nov. 1, but clashes with rebels continued.

Domitien Ndayizeye, a Hutu, became president Apr. 30, 2003. The UN Security Council authorized, May 21, 2004, a 5,650-member peacekeeping force for Burundi. Hutu rebels Aug. 13 attacked a UN camp for Congolese Tutsi refugees in western Burundi, killing more than 160 people, many of them women and children. Approval of a power-sharing constitution by referendum, Feb. 28, 2005, paved the way for local and parliamentary elections. Pierre Nkurunziza, the former leader of a Hutu rebel group, became president Aug. 26.

Cambodia
Kingdom of Cambodia

People: Population: 13,881,427. **Age distrib.** (%) <15: 35.6; 65+: 3.4. **Pop. density:** 203 per sq mi, 78 per sq km. **Urban:** 18.6%. **Ethnic groups:** Khmer 90%, Vietnamese 5%, Chinese 1%. **Principal languages:** Khmer (official), French, English. **Chief religion:** Theravada Buddhist 95% (official).

Geography: Total area: 69,900 sq mi, 181,040 sq km; **Land area:** 68,155 sq mi, 176,520 sq km. **Location:** SE Asia, on Indochina Peninsula. **Neighbors:** Thailand on W and N, Laos on NE, Vietnam on E. **Topography:** The central area, formed by the Mekong R. basin and Tonle Sap lake, is level. Hills and mountains are in SE, a long escarpment separates the country from Thailand on NW. 76% of the area is forested. **Capital:** Phnom Penh, 1,364,000.

Government: Type: Constitutional monarchy. **Head of state:** King Norodom Sihamoni; b. May 14, 1953; in office: Oct. 14, 2004. **Head of gov.:** Prime Min. Samdech Hun Sen; b. Aug. 5, 1952; in office: Nov. 30, 1998. **Local divisions:** 20 provinces and 4 municipalities. **Defense budget** (2005): $74 mil. **Active troops:** 124,300.

Economy: Industries: tourism, garments, rice milling, fishing, wood & wood products, rubber, cement, gem mining, textiles. **Chief crops:** rice, rubber, corn, vegetables. **Natural resources:** timber, gems, iron ore, mang., phosphates. **Arable land:** 13%. **Livestock** (2005): cattle: 3.1 mil; chickens: 15 mil; pigs: 2.5 mil. **Fish catch** (2004): 326,652 metric tons. **Electricity prod.** (2004): 130 mil kWh. **Labor force** (2004 est.): agriculture 75%.

Finance: Monetary unit: Riel (KHR) (Sept. 2006: 4,131.80 = $1 U.S.). **GDP** (2005 est.): $30.7 bil; **per capita GDP:** $2,200; **GDP growth:** 6%. **Imports** (2005 est.): $3.5 bil; partners (2004): Thailand 23.9%, Hong Kong 15%, China 13.5%, Singapore 11.5%, Vietnam 7.6%, Taiwan 7.3%. **Exports** (2005 est.): $2.7 bil; partners (2004): U.S. 56.2%, Germany 11.5%, UK 7%, Canada 4.3%. **Tourism:** $604 mil. **Budget** (2005 est.): $772 mil. **Intl. reserves less gold:** $667 mil. **Gold:** 400,000 oz t. **Consumer prices:** 5.65%.

Transport: Railroad: Length: 374 mi. **Motor vehicles:** 8,300 pass. cars, 3,100 comm. vehicles **Civil aviation:** 37.9 mil pass.-mi; 6 airports. **Chief port:** Kampong Saom (Sihanoukville).

Communications: TV sets: 9 per 1,000 pop. **Radios:** 128 per 1,000 pop. **Telephone lines:** 36,400. **Daily newspaper circ.:** NA. **Internet:** 41,000 users.

Health: Life expect.: 57.4 male; 61.3 female. **Births** (per 1,000 pop.): 26.9. **Deaths** (per 1,000 pop.): 9.1. **Natural inc.:** 1.78%. **Infant mortality** (per 1,000 live births): 68.8. **AIDS rate:** 1.6%.

Education: Compulsory: ages 6-12. **Literacy:** 73.6%.

Major Intl. Organizations: UN (FAO, IBRD, ILO, IMF, IMO, WHO, WTO), ASEAN.

Embassy: 4530 16th St. NW 20011; 726-7742.

Website: www.cambodia.gov.kh

Early kingdoms dating from that of Funan in the 1st cent. CE culminated in the great Khmer empire that flourished from the 9th cent. to the 13th, encompassing present-day Thailand, Cambodia, Laos, and southern Vietnam. The peripheral areas were lost to invading Siamese and Vietnamese, and France established a protectorate in 1863. Independence came in 1953.

Prince Norodom Sihanouk, king 1941-55 and head of state from 1960, tried to maintain neutrality. Relations with the U.S. were broken in 1965, after South Vietnam planes attacked Vietcong forces within Cambodia. Relations were restored in 1969, after Sihanouk charged Viet Communists with arming Cambodian insurgents.

In 1970, pro-U.S. Prem. Lon Nol seized power, demanding removal of 40,000 North Viet troops; the monarchy was abolished. Sihanouk formed a government-in-exile in Beijing, and open war began between the government and Communist Khmer Rouge guerrillas. The U.S. provided heavy military and economic aid.

Khmer Rouge forces captured Phnom Penh Apr. 17, 1975. Cities were depopulated and their residents executed or condemned to forced labor. An estimated 1.7 mil people died in "killing fields" or from other hardships under Khmer Rouge rule, 1975-79.

Severe border fighting broke out with Vietnam in 1978 and developed into a full-fledged Vietnamese invasion. Formation of a Vietnamese-backed government was announced, Jan. 8, 1979, one day after the capture of Phnom Penh. Thousands of refugees fled to Thailand, and widespread starvation was reported. Vietnamese troops remained in Cambodia during the 1980s, meeting resistance from Khmer Rouge guerrillas, especially along the Thai border. Vietnam withdrew nearly all its troops by Sept. 1989.

Following UN-sponsored elections in Cambodia that ended May 28, 1993, the 2 leading parties agreed to share power in an interim government until a new constitution was adopted. On Sept. 21, a constitution reestablishing a monarchy was adopted by the National Assembly. It took effect Sept. 24, with Sihanouk as king. The Khmer Rouge, which had boycotted the elections, opposed the new government, and armed violence continued in the mid-1990s. Ieng Sary, a Khmer Rouge leader, broke with the guerrillas, formed a rival group, and announced his support for the monarchy in Aug. 1996, as Khmer Rouge strength rapidly diminished.

Co-Prime Min. Hun Sen staged a coup July 5, 1997, ousting his rival, Prince Norodom Ranariddh. Pol Pot, the Khmer Rouge leader who held power during the late 1970s, was denounced by his former comrades at a show trial, July 25, and sentenced to house arrest; he died Apr. 15, 1998. Hun Sen's party won parliamentary elections on July 26. He retained power in elections July 27, 2003, but without a parliamentary majority. Sihanouk abdicated because of poor health and was succeeded, Oct. 14, 2004, by his son Norodom Sihamoni. Charged with defaming Hun Sen and other members of the ruling coalition, opposition leader Sam Rainsy fled Feb. 3, 2005, after he was stripped of legal immunity; granted a royal pardon, he returned a year later. Arrested in 1999, former Khmer Rouge military chief Ta Mok died July 21, 2006, before he could stand trial for genocide and crimes against humanity.

Cameroon
Republic of Cameroon

People: Population: 17,657,856. **Age distrib.** (%) <15: 41.5; 65+: 3.2. **Pop. density:** 97 per sq mi, 37 per sq km. **Urban:** 51.4%. **Ethnic groups:** Highlanders 31%, Equatorial Bantu 19%, Kirdi 11%, Fulani 10%, NW Bantu 8%, E Nigritic 7%. **Principal languages:** English, French (both official); 24 African language groups. **Chief religions:** Indigenous beliefs 40%, Christian 40%, Muslim 20%.

Geography: Total area: 183,568 sq mi, 475,440 sq km; **Land area:** 181,252 sq mi, 469,440 sq km. **Location:** Between W and central Africa. **Neighbors:** Nigeria on NW; Chad, Central African Republic on E; Congo, Gabon, Equatorial Guinea on S. **Topography:** A low coastal plain with rain forests in S; plateaus in center lead to forested mountains in W, including Mt. Cameroon, 13,435 ft.; grasslands in N lead to marshes around Lake Chad. **Capital:** Yaoundé, 1,485,000. **Cities** (urban ag.): Douala, 1,761,000.

Government: Type: Republic. **Head of state:** Pres. Paul Biya; b. Feb. 13, 1933; in office: Nov. 6, 1982. **Head of gov.:** Prime Min. Ephraïm Inoni; b. Aug. 16, 1947; in office: Dec. 8, 2004. **Local divisions:** 10 provinces. **Defense budget** (2005): $306 mil. **Active troops:** 23,100.

Economy: Industries: oil prod. & refining, food proc., light consumer goods, textiles, lumber. **Chief crops:** coffee, cocoa, cotton, rubber, bananas, oilseed, grains. **Natural resources:** oil, bauxite, iron ore, timber, hydropower. **Crude oil reserves** (2005): 400 mil bbls. **Arable land:** 13%. **Livestock** (2005): cattle: 5.6 mil; chickens: 31 mil; goats: 4.4 mil; pigs: 1.4 mil; sheep: 3.8 mil. **Fish catch** (2004): 108,330 metric tons. **Electricity prod.** (2004): 3.9 bil kWh. **Labor force:** agriculture 70%, industry 13%, services 17%.

Finance: Monetary unit: CFA BEAC Franc (XAF) (Sept. 2006: 512.27 = $1 U.S.). **GDP** (2005 est.): $40.8 bil; **per capita GDP:** $2,400; **GDP growth:** 2.8%. **Imports** (2005 est.): $2.5 bil; partners (2004): France 28.2%, Nigeria 9.4%, Belgium 7.6%, U.S. 4.8%, Germany 4.6%, China 4.4%, Italy 4%. **Exports** (2005 est.): $3.2 bil; partners (2004): Spain 16.2%, Italy 14.1%, France 10.2%, UK 9.9%, U.S. 9.6%, Netherlands 5.1%. **Tourism** (1995): $36 mil. **Budget**

(2005 est.): $2.7 bil. **Intl. reserves less gold:** $664 mil. **Gold:** 30,000 oz t. **Consumer prices:** 2.01%.

Transport: Railroad: Length: 626 mi. **Motor vehicles:** 173,100 pass. cars, 57,400 comm. vehicles. **Civil aviation:** 401.4 mil pass.-mi; 11 airports. **Chief ports:** Douala, Kribi.

Communications: TV sets: 34 per 1,000 pop. **Radios:** 163 per 1,000 pop. **Telephone lines:** 99,400. **Daily newspaper circ.:** 6.3 per 1,000 pop. **Internet:** 167,000 users.

Health: Life expect.: 51.7 male; 53 female. **Births** (per 1,000 pop.): 35.6. **Deaths** (per 1,000 pop.): 13. **Natural inc.:** 2.27%. **Infant mortality** (per 1,000 live births): 67.2. **AIDS rate:** 5.4%.

Education: Compulsory: ages 6-11. **Literacy:** 67.9%.

Major Intl. Organizations: UN (FAO, IBRD, ILO, IMF, IMO, WHO, WTO), the Commonwealth, AU.

Embassy: 2349 Massachusetts Ave. NW 20008; 265-8790.

Website: www.spm.gov.cm

Portuguese sailors were the first Europeans to reach Cameroon, in the 15th cent. The European and American slave trade was very active in the area. German control lasted from 1884 to 1916, when France and Britain divided the territory, later receiving League of Nations mandates and UN trusteeships. French Cameroon became independent Jan. 1, 1960; one part of British Cameroon joined Nigeria in 1961, the other part joined Cameroon. Stability has allowed for development of roads, railways, agriculture, and petroleum production.

Pres. Paul Biya has retained power in a series of elections that were boycotted by opposition parties or disputed as fraudulent.

Canada

People: Population: 33,098,932. **Age distrib.:** (%) <15: 17.6; 65+: 13.3. **Pop. density:** 9 per sq mi, 3 per sq km. **Urban:** 80.4%. **Ethnic groups:** British 28%, French 23%, other European 15%, Amerindian 2%. **Principal languages:** English, French (both official). **Chief religions:** Roman Catholic 43%, Protestant 23%, none 16%.

Geography: Total area: 3,855,103 sq mi, 9,984,670 sq km; **Land area:** 3,511,023 sq mi, 9,093,507 sq km. the largest country in land size in the western hemisphere. **Topography:** Canada stretches 3,426 miles from east to west and extends southward from the North Pole to the U.S. border. Its seacoast includes 36,356 miles of mainland and 115,133 miles of islands, including the Arctic islands almost from Greenland to near the Alaskan border. **Climate:** While generally temperate, varies from freezing winter cold to blistering summer heat. **Capital:** Ottawa, 1,156,000. **Cities (urban aggr.):** Toronto, 5,312,000; Montreal, 3,640,000; Vancouver, 2,188,000; Edmonton, 1,015,000; Calgary, 1,058,000.

Government: Type: Confederation with parliamentary democracy. **Head of state:** Queen Elizabeth II, represented by Gov.-Gen. Michaëlle Jean; b. Sept. 6, 1957; in office: Sept. 27, 2005. **Head of gov.:** Prime Min. Stephen Harper; b. Apr. 30, 1959; in office: Feb. 6, 2006. **Local divisions:** 10 provinces, 3 territories. **Defense budget** (2005): $10.9 bil. **Active troops:** 62,000.

Economy: Industries: transp. equipment, chemicals, minerals, food & fish products, wood & paper products, oil & natural gas. **Chief crops:** wheat, barley, oilseed, tobacco, fruits, vegetables. **Natural resources:** iron ore, nickel, zinc, copper, gold, lead, molybd., potash, silver, fish, timber, wildlife, coal, oil, nat. gas, hydropower. **Crude oil reserves** (2005): 178.8 bil bbls. **Arable land:** 5%. **Livestock** (2005): cattle: 15.1 mil; chickens: 160 mil; goats: 30,000; pigs: 14.7 mil; sheep: 1 mil. **Fish catch** (2004): 1,318,845 metric tons. **Electricity prod.** (2004): 573.0 bil kWh. **Labor force** (2004): agriculture 2%, manufacturing 14%, construction 5%, services 75%, other 3%.

Finance: Monetary unit: Dollar (CAD) (Sept. 2006: 1.12 = $1 U.S.). **GDP** (2005 est.): $1.1 tril; **per capita GDP:** $34,000; **GDP growth:** 2.9%. **Imports** (2005 est.): $317.7 bil; partners (2004): U.S. 58.9%, China 6.8%, Mexico 3.8%. **Exports** (2005 est.): $364.8 bil; partners (2004): U.S. 85.2%, Japan 2.1%, UK 1.6%. **Tourism:** $12.8 bil. **Budget** (2004): $152.6 bil. **Intl. reserves less gold:** $23.06 bil. **Gold:** 110,000 oz t. **Consumer prices:** 2.23%.

Transport: Railroad: Length: 30,250 mi. **Motor vehicles:** 17.76 mil pass. cars, 660,400 comm. vehicles. **Civil aviation:** 50 bil pass.-mi; 509 airports. **Chief ports:** Halifax, Montreal, Quebec, Saint John, Toronto, Vancouver.

Communications: TV sets: 709 per 1,000 pop. **Radios:** 1,038 per 1,000 pop. **Telephone lines:** 18.3 mil. **Daily newspaper circ.:** 167.9 per 1,000 pop. **Internet:** 20.9 mil users.

Health: Life expect.: 76.9 male; 83.7 female. **Births** (per 1,000 pop.): 10.8. **Deaths** (per 1,000 pop.): 7.8. **Natural inc.:** 0.3%. **Infant mortality** (per 1,000 live births): 4.7. **AIDS rate:** 0.3%.

Education: Compulsory: ages 6-16. **Literacy:** 97%.

Major Intl. Organizations: UN and all of its specialized agencies, APEC, the Commonwealth, NATO, OAS, OECD, OSCE.

Embassy: 501 Pennsylvania Ave. NW 20001; 682-1740.

Website: www.canada.gc.ca

French explorer Jacques Cartier, who reached the Gulf of St. Lawrence in 1534, is generally regarded as Canada's founder. But English seaman John Cabot sighted Newfoundland in 1497, and Vikings are believed to have reached the Atlantic coast centuries before either explorer. Canadian settlement was pioneered by the French who established Quebec City (1608) and Montreal (1642) and declared New France a colony in 1663.

Britain acquired Acadia (later Nova Scotia) in 1717 and, through military victory over French forces in Canada, captured Quebec (1759) and obtained control of the rest of New France in 1763. The French, through the Quebec Act of 1774, retained the rights to their own language, religion, and civil law. The British presence in Canada increased during the American Revolution when many colonials, proudly calling themselves United Empire Loyalists, moved north to Canada. Fur traders and explorers led Canadians westward across the continent. Sir Alexander Mackenzie reached the Pacific in 1793 and scrawled on a rock, "From Canada by land."

In Upper and Lower Canada (later called Ontario and Quebec) and in the Maritimes, legislative assemblies appeared in the 18th cent. and reformers called for responsible government. But the War of 1812 intervened. The war, a conflict between Great Britain and the U.S. fought mainly in Upper Canada, ended in a stalemate in 1814.

In 1837 political agitation for more democratic government culminated in rebellions in Upper and Lower Canada. Britain sent Lord Durham to investigate; in a famous report (1839), he recommended union of the 2 parts into one colony called Canada. The union lasted until Confederation, July 1, 1867, when proclamation of the British North America (BNA) Act (now known as the Constitution Act, 1867) launched the Dominion of Canada, consisting of Ontario, Quebec, and the former colonies of Nova Scotia and New Brunswick.

Since 1840 the Canadian colonies had held the right to internal self-government. The BNA Act, which was the basis for the country's written constitution, established a federal system of government on the model of a British parliament and cabinet structure under the crown. Canada was proclaimed a self-governing Dominion within the British Empire in 1931. With the ratification of the Constitution Act, 1982, Canada severed its last formal legislative link with Britain by obtaining the right to amend its constitution.

The so-called Meech Lake Agreement, 1987, which would have assured constitutional protection for Quebec's efforts to preserve its French language and culture, sparked a separatist revival in Quebec. Subsequently, the Charlottetown agreement, which called for constitutional changes, such as recognition of Quebec as a "distinct society" within the Canadian confederation. It was defeated by a national referendum Oct. 26, 1992.

Canada became the first nation to ratify the North American Free Trade Agreement between Canada, Mexico, and the U.S. June 23, 1993. It went into effect Jan. 1, 1994.

On Feb. 24, 1993, Brian Mulroney resigned as prime minister after more than 8 years in office; he was succeeded by Kim Campbell. In elections Oct. 25, 1993, the ruling Conservatives were defeated in a landslide that left them only 2 of the 295 seats in the House of Commons. Jean Chrétien became prime minister. In a Quebec referendum held Oct. 30, 1995, proponents of secession lost by a razor-thin margin. The elections of June 2, 1997, left the Liberals with a slim majority.

On Jan. 7, 1998, the government apologized to indigenous peoples for 150 years of mistreatment and pledged to set up a "healing fund." Canada's highest court ruled, Aug. 20, that Quebec cannot secede unilaterally, even if a majority of the province approves. Nunavut ("Our Land"), carved from Northwest Territories as a homeland for the Inuit, was established Apr. 1, 1999. Victory by the Liberals in national elections Nov. 27, 2000, made Chrétien the first Canadian prime minister in over 50 years to head a third successive majority government.

Canada sent 5 warships in Oct. 2001 and 850 troops in Feb. 2002, to join U.S. counterterrorism operations in Afghanistan. Four Canadian soldiers conducting a training exercise near Kandahar were accidentally killed Apr. 17 by U.S. forces, Canada's first war casualties since its participation in the Korean War. Relations between Canada and the U.S. cooled after Prime Min. Chrétien refused to contribute troops to the U.S.-led invasion of Iraq in Mar. 2003.

A SARS outbreak killed more than 40 people in the Toronto area in 2003 and cost the city and national economy millions of dollars in lost revenues. Chrétien retired Dec. 12, and Paul Martin became prime minister. Weakened by a scandal involving improper payments to Quebec firms for advertising and sponsorship of cultural and sporting events, the Liberals won only 135 of 308 seats in parliamentary elections June 28, 2004; the Conservatives finished second with 99. Martin stayed in office as head of a minority government.

Parliament gave final approval July 19, 2005, to a bill making same-sex marriage (already permitted in 8 of 10 provinces) legal throughout the country. Michaëlle Jean, a Haitian-born TV journalist, was installed Sept. 27 as Canada's first black governor general.

Twelve years of Liberal party rule ended when Conservatives won 124 seats to the Liberals' 103 in parliamentary elections, Jan. 23, 2006. Conservative leader Stephen Harper took office Feb. 6 as head of a minority government. Police and intelligence officials in the Toronto area, June 2-3, arrested and charged 17 people with plotting terrorist attacks in Canada; their targets were said to include the House of Commons and the prime minister.

Canada's Provinces and Territories

Provinces/Territories	Joined Confed.	Area (sq mi)	Population (2004 est.)	Capital	Premier	Party	In office
Alberta	1905	255,287	3,332,225	Edmonton	Ralph Klein	Prog. Cons.	1992
British Columbia	1871	365,948	4,292,166	Victoria	Gordon Campbell	Liberal	2001
Manitoba	1870	250,947	1,179,681	Winnipeg	Gary Doer	New Democratic	1999
New Brunswick	1867	28,355	750,504	Fredericton	Bernard Lord	Prog. Cons.	1999
Newfoundland & Labrador	1949	156,649	512,509	St. John's	Danny Williams	Prog. Cons.	2003
Nova Scotia	1867	21,425	935,824	Halifax	Rodney MacDonald	Prog. Cons.	2006
Ontario	1867	412,581	12,630,547	Toronto	Dalton McGuinty	Liberal	2003
Prince Edward Island	1873	2,185	138,307	Charlottetown	Pat Binns	Prog. Cons.	1996
Quebec	1867	594,860	7,636,710	Québec	Jean Charest	Liberal	2003
Saskatchewan	1905	251,866	988,980	Regina	Lorne Calvert	New Democratic	2001
Northwest Territories[1]	1871	503,951	42,179	Yellowknife	Joe Handley	non-partisan	2003
Nunavut[1]	(2)	818,959	30,446	Iqaluit	Paul Okalik	non-partisan	1999
Yukon Territory[1]	1898	186,661	31,069	Whitehorse	Dennis Fentie	Yukon	2002

(1) Territories also have federally appointed commissioners to represent federal interests. (2) Territory created in 1999 from eastern portion of Northwest Territories.

Prime Ministers of Canada

Canada is a constitutional monarchy with a parliamentary system of government. It is also a federal state. Canada's official head of state, Queen Elizabeth II, is represented by a resident Governor-General. However, in practice the nation is governed by the Prime Minister, leader of the party that commands the support of a majority of the House of Commons, dominant chamber of Canada's bicameral Parliament.

Name	Party	Term
Sir John A. Macdonald	Conservative	1867-1873
Alexander Mackenzie	Liberal	1873-1878
Sir John A. Macdonald	Conservative	1878-1891
Sir John J. C. Abbott	Conservative	1891-1892
Sir John S. D. Thompson	Conservative	1892-1894
Sir Mackenzie Bowell	Conservative	1894-1896
Sir Charles Tupper	Conservative	1896[1]
Sir Wilfrid Laurier	Liberal	1896-1911
Sir Robert Laird Borden	Cons./Union.[2]	1911-1920
Arthur Meighen	Unionist	1920-1921
W. L. Mackenzie King	Liberal	1921-1926
Arthur Meighen	Conservative	1926[3]
W. L. Mackenzie King	Liberal	1926-1930
Richard Bedford Bennett	Conservative	1930-1935
W. L. Mackenzie King	Liberal	1935-1948
Louis St. Laurent	Liberal	1948-1957
John G. Diefenbaker	Prog. Cons.	1957-1963
Lester Bowles Pearson	Liberal	1963-1968
Pierre Elliott Trudeau	Liberal	1968-1979
Joe Clark	Prog. Cons.	1979-1980
Pierre Elliott Trudeau	Liberal	1980-1984
John Napier Turner	Liberal	1984[4]
Brian Mulroney	Prog. Cons.	1984-1993
Kim Campbell	Prog. Cons.	1993[5]
Jean Chrétien	Liberal	1993-2003
Paul Martin	Liberal	2003-2006
Stephen Harper	Conservative	2006-

(1) May-July. (2) Conservative 1911-17, Unionist 1917-20. (3) June-Sept. (4) June-Sept. (5) June-Oct.

Cape Verde
Republic of Cape Verde

People: Population: 420,979. **Age distrib.** (%) <15: 37.9; 65+: 6.7. **Pop. density:** 270 per sq mi, 104 per sq km. **Urban:** 55.9%. **Ethnic groups:** Creole 71%, African 28%, European 1%. **Principal languages:** Portuguese (official), Crioulo. **Chief religions:** Roman Catholic (infused with indigenous beliefs); Protestant (mostly Church of the Nazarene).

Geography: Total area: 1,557 sq mi, 4,033 sq km; **Land area:** 1,557 sq mi, 4,033 sq km. **Location:** In Atlantic O., off W tip of Africa. **Neighbors:** Nearest are Mauritania, Senegal to E. **Topography:** Cape Verde Islands are 15 in number, volcanic in origin (active crater on Fogo). The landscape is eroded and stark, with vegetation mostly in interior valleys. **Capital:** Praia, 117,000.

Government: Type: Republic. **Head of state:** Pres. Pedro Pires; b. Apr. 29, 1934; in office: Mar. 22, 2001. **Head of gov.:** Prime Min. José Maria Neves; b. Mar. 28, 1960; in office: Feb. 1, 2001. **Local divisions:** 17 districts. **Defense budget** (2005): $7 mil. **Active troops:** 1,200.

Economy: Industries: food & beverages, fish proc., shoes & garments, salt mining, ship repair. **Chief crops:** bananas, corn, beans, sweet potatoes, sugarcane, coffee, peanuts. **Natural resources:** salt, basalt rock, limestone, kaolin, fish. **Arable land:** 11%. **Livestock** (2005): cattle: 23,000; chickens: 460,000; goats: 112,750; pigs: 205,000; sheep: 10,000. **Fish catch** (2004): 8,446 metric tons. **Electricity prod.** (2004): 40 mil kWh.

Finance: Monetary unit: Escudo (CVE) (Sept. 2006: 86.90 = $1 U.S.). **GDP** (2005 est.): $3 bil. **per capita GDP:** $6,200; **GDP growth:** 5.5%. **Imports** (2005 est.): $500 mil; partners (2004): Portugal 43.2%, U.S. 12.5%, Netherlands 8.7%. **Exports** (2005 est.): $73.4 mil; partners (2004): Portugal 62.5%, U.S. 15.8%, UK 11.3%.

Tourism $125 mil. **Budget** (2005 est.): $393.1 mil. **Intl. reserves less gold:** $122 mil. **Consumer prices:** 0.42%

Transport: Motor vehicles (1999): 13,500 pass. cars, 3,100 comm. vehicles. **Civil aviation:** 173.4 mil pass.-mi; 7 airports. **Chief ports:** Mindelo, Praia.

Communications: TV sets: 5 per 1,000 pop. **Radios:** NA. **Telephone lines:** 71,400. **Internet:** 25,000 users.

Health: Life expect.: 67.4 male; 74.2 female. **Births** (per 1,000 pop.): 24.9. **Deaths** (per 1,000 pop.): 6.5. **Natural inc.:** 1.83%. **Infant mortality** (per 1,000 live births): 46.5. **AIDS rate** (2001): 0.04%.

Education: Compulsory: ages 6-11. **Literacy:** 76.6%.

Major Intl. Organizations: UN (FAO, IBRD, ILO, IMF, IMO, WHO), AU.

Embassy: 3415 Massachusetts Ave. NW 20007; 965-6820.

Website: virtualcapeverde.net

The first Portuguese colonists landed in 1462; African slaves were brought soon after, and most Cape Verdeans descend from both groups. Cape Verde independence came July 5, 1975. Antonio Mascarenhas Monteiro won the nation's first free presidential election Feb. 17, 1991; he was reelected without opposition five years later. Pedro Pires won a presidential runoff election Feb. 25, 2001, and was reelected Feb. 12, 2006. Remittances from Cape Verdean emigrants are a major source of income.

Central African Republic

People: Population: 4,303,356. **Age distrib.** (%) <15: 41.9; 65+: 4.2. **Pop. density:** 17 per sq mi, 6 per sq km. **Urban:** 42.7%. **Ethnic groups:** Baya 33%, Banda 27%, Mandjia 13%, Sara 10%, Mboum 7%, M'Baka 4%, Yakoma 4%. **Principal languages:** French (official), Sangho (national), tribal languages. **Chief religions:** Indigenous beliefs 35%, Protestant 25%, Roman Catholic 25%, Muslim 15%.

Geography: Total area: 240,535 sq mi, 622,984 sq km; **Land area:** 240,535 sq mi, 622,984 sq km. **Location:** In central Africa. **Neighbors:** Chad on N, Cameroon on W, Congo-Brazzaville and Congo-Kinshasa (formerly Zaire) on S, Sudan on E. **Topography:** Mostly rolling plateau, average altitude 2,000 ft., with rivers draining S to the Congo and N to Lake Chad. Open, well-watered savanna covers most of the area, with an arid area in NE, and tropical rain forest in SW. **Capital:** Bangui, 541,000.

Government: Type: Republic. **Head of state:** Pres. François Bozizé; b. Oct. 14, 1946; in office: Mar. 15, 2003. **Head of gov.:** Prime Min. Élie Doté; in office: June 13, 2005. **Local divisions:** 14 prefectures, 2 economic prefectures, 1 commune. **Defense budget** (2005): $15 mil. **Active troops:** 2,550.

Economy: Industries: diamond mining, sawmills, breweries, textiles, footwear, bicycle & motorcycle assembly. **Chief crops:** cotton, coffee, tobacco, cassava, yams, millet, corn, bananas. **Natural resources:** diamonds, uranium, timber, gold, oil, hydropower. **Arable land:** 3%. **Livestock** (2005): cattle: 3.4 mil; chickens: 4.8 mil; goats: 3.1 mil; pigs: 805,000; sheep: 259,000. **Fish catch** (2004): 15,000 metric tons. **Electricity prod.** (2004): 110 mil kWh.

Finance: Monetary unit: CFA BEAC Franc (XAF) (Sept. 2006: 512.27 = $1 U.S.). **GDP** (2005 est.): $4.8 bil; **per capita GDP:** $1,100; **GDP growth:** 2.2%. **Imports** (2004 est.): $203 mil; partners (2004): France 19.4%, U.S. 16.3%, Cameroon 8.3%, Belgium 5.6%. **Exports** (2004 est.): $131 mil; partners (2004): Belgium 41%, Italy 8.9%, Spain 8.5%, Indonesia 7.6%, France 6.3%, U.S. 5.3%. **Tourism** (2002): $3 mil. **Intl. reserves less gold:** $97 mil. **Gold:** 10,000 oz t. **Consumer prices:** 2.88%.

Transport: Motor vehicles: 5,300 pass. cars, 6,300 comm. vehicles. **Civil aviation:** 80.8 mil pass.-mi; 3 airports. **Chief port:** Bangui.

Communications: TV sets: 6 per 1,000 pop. **Radios:** 83 per 1,000 pop. **Telephone lines:** 10,000. **Daily newspaper circ.:** 1.7 per 1,000 pop. **Internet:** 9,000 users.

Health: Life expect.: 43.5 male; 43.6 female. **Births** (per 1,000 pop.): 33.9. **Deaths** (per 1,000 pop.): 18.6. **Natural inc.:** 1.53%. **Infant mortality** (per 1,000 live births): 85.6. **AIDS rate:** 10.7%.

Education: Compulsory: ages 6-15. **Literacy:** 48.6%.

Major Intl. Organizations: UN (FAO, IBRD, ILO, IMF, WHO, WTO), AU.

Embassy: 1618 22d St. NW 20008; 483-7800.

Website: www.state.gov/p/af/ci/ct

Various Bantu peoples migrated through the region for centuries before French control was asserted in the late 19th cent., when the region was named Ubangi-Shari. Complete independence was attained Aug. 13, 1960. All political parties were dissolved in 1960, and the country became a center for Chinese political influence in Africa. Relations with China were severed after 1965.

Pres. Jean-Bedel Bokassa, who seized power in a 1965 military coup, proclaimed himself constitutional emperor of the renamed Central African Empire Dec. 1976. Bokassa's rule was characterized by ruthless authoritarianism and human rights violations. He was ousted in a bloodless coup aided by the French government, Sept. 20, 1979. In 1981, Gen. André Kolingba became head of state in another bloodless coup. Multiparty legislative and presidential elections were held in Oct. 1992 but were canceled by the government when Kolingba was losing. New elections, held in Aug. and Sept. 1993, led to the replacement of Kolingba with a civilian government under Pres. Ange-Félix Patassé.

France sent in troops to suppress army mutinies in 1996 and 1997. Patassé loyalists won a narrow majority in legislative elections on Nov. 22 and Dec. 13, 1998, and he was reelected to a 2nd 6-year term on Sept. 19, 1999. After thwarting several coup attempts, Patassé was ousted Mar. 15, 2003, by rebels under former army chief François Bozizé. Bozizé won a presidential runoff election May 8, 2005. As of mid-2006, at least 48,000 refugees from fighting in the northern region were living in southern Chad.

Chad
Republic of Chad

People: Population: 9,944,201. **Age distrib.** (%) <15: 47.9; 65+: 2.7. **Pop. density:** 20 per sq mi, 7 per sq km. **Urban:** 24.9%. **Ethnic groups:** About 200 groups; largest are Arabs in N and Sara in S. **Principal languages:** French, Arabic (both official), Sara, more than 120 different languages and dialects. **Chief religions:** Muslim 51%, Christian 35%, animist 7%, other 7%.

Geography: Total area: 495,755 sq mi, 1,284,000 sq km; **Land area:** 486,180 sq mi, 1,259,200 sq km. **Location:** In central N Africa. **Neighbors:** Libya on N; Niger, Nigeria, Cameroon on W; Central African Republic on S; Sudan on E. **Topography:** Wooded savanna, steppe, and desert in the S; part of the Sahara in the N. Southern rivers flow N to Lake Chad, surrounded by marshland. **Capital:** N'Djamena, 888,000.

Government: Type: Republic. **Head of state:** Pres. Idriss Déby; b. 1952; in office: Dec. 4, 1990. **Head of gov.:** Prime Min. Pascal Yoadimnadji; in office: Feb. 3, 2005. **Local divisions:** 14 prefectures. **Defense budget** (2005): $57 mil. **Active troops:** 30,350.

Economy: Industries: cotton textiles, meatpacking, beer brewing, sodium carbonate, soap, cigarettes, constr. materials. **Chief crops:** cotton, sorghum, millet, peanuts, rice, potatoes, cassava. **Natural resources:** oil, uranium, natron, kaolin, fish. **Arable land:** 3%. **Livestock** (2005): cattle: 6.5 mil; chickens: 5.2 mil; goats: 5.8 mil; pigs: 25,000; sheep: 2.6 mil. **Fish catch** (2004): 70,000 metric tons. **Electricity prod.** (2004): 90 mil kWh. **Labor force:** agriculture 80% (subsistence farming, herding, and fishing), industry and services 20%.

Finance: Monetary unit: CFA BEAC Franc (XAF) (Sept. 2006: 512.27 = $1 U.S.). **GDP** (2005 est.): $14.8 bil; **per capita GDP:** $1,500; **GDP growth:** 6%. **Imports** (2005 est.): $749.1 mil; partners (2004): France 22.9%, Cameroon 13.7%, U.S. 11.8%, Portugal 10.9%, Germany 7.7%, Belgium 4.8%. **Exports** (2005 est.): $3 bil; partners (2004): U.S. 74.2%, China 14.8%, Portugal 5.2%. **Tourism** (2002): $25 mil. **Budget** (2005 est.): $653.3 mil. **Intl. reserves less gold:** $158 mil. **Gold:** 10,000 oz t. **Consumer prices:** 7%.

Transport: Motor vehicles: 8,700 pass. cars, 12,400 comm. vehicles. **Civil aviation:** 80.8 mil pass.-mi; 7 airports

Communications: TV sets: 1 per 1,000 pop. **Radios:** 236 per 1,000 pop. **Telephone lines** 13,000. **Daily newspaper circ.:** 0.2 per 1,000 pop. **Internet:** 60,000 users.

Health: Life expect.: 45.9 male; 49.2 female. **Births** (per 1,000 pop.): 45.7. **Deaths** (per 1,000 pop.): 16.4. **Natural inc.:** 2.94%. **Infant mortality** (per 1,000 live births): 91.5. **AIDS rate:** 3.5%.

Education: Compulsory: ages 6-11. **Literacy:** 25.7%.

Major Intl. Organizations: UN (FAO, IBRD, ILO, IMF, WHO, WTO), AU.

Embassy: 2002 R St. NW 20009; 462-4009.

Website: www.chadembassy.org

Chad was the site of paleolithic and neolithic cultures before the Sahara Desert formed. A succession of kingdoms and Arab slave traders dominated Chad until France took control around 1900. Independence came Aug. 11, 1960. Northern Muslim rebels have fought animist and Christian southern government and French troops from 1966, despite numerous cease-fires and peace pacts.

Rebel forces, led by Hissène Habré, captured the capital and forced Pres. Goukouni Oueddei to flee the country in June 1982. In 1983, France sent some 3,000 troops to Chad to assist Pres. Habré in opposing Libyan-backed rebels. France and Libya agreed to a simultaneous withdrawal of troops from Chad in Sept. 1984, but Libyan forces remained in the north until Mar. 1987, when Chad forces drove them out. In Dec. 1990, Habré was overthrown by a Libyan-supported insurgent group, the Patriotic Salvation Movement.

On Feb. 3, 1994, the World Court dismissed a long-standing territorial claim by Libya to the mineral-rich Aozou Strip, on the Libyan border. Libyan troops reportedly withdrew at the end of May. Following approval of a new constitution in March 1996, Chad's first multiparty presidential election was held in June and July. The U.S.

Peace Corps withdrew from Chad in Apr. 1998 because of continuing clashes between rebels and Chad government forces.

Oil began flowing July 15, 2003, through a 665-mi pipeline that allows landlocked Chad to export via Cameroon. Pres. Idriss Déby won a 3rd term, May 3, 2006, in an election boycotted by major opposition groups. Violence along the Sudan border escalated during the year, as Sudanese *janjaweed* militias and Chadian rebels attacked civilians, and Darfur rebels preyed on refugee camps.

Chile
Republic of Chile

People: Population: 16,134,219. **Age distrib.** (%) <15: 24.7; 65+: 8.2. **Pop. density:** 55 per sq mi, 21 per sq km. **Urban:** 87.0%. **Ethnic groups:** European and Mestizo 95%, Amerindian 3%. **Principal languages:** Spanish (official), Araucanian. **Chief religions:** Roman Catholic 89%, Protestant 11%.

Geography: Total area: 292,260 sq mi, 756,950 sq km; **Land area:** 289,113 sq mi, 748,800 sq km. **Location:** Occupies western coast of S South America. **Neighbors:** Peru on N, Bolivia on NE, on E. **Topography:** Andes Mts. on E border incl. some of the world's highest peaks; on W is 2,650-mile Pacific coast. Width varies between 100 and 250 miles. In N is Atacama Desert, in center are agricultural regions, in S, forests and grazing lands. **Capital:** Santiago, 5,683,000.

Government: Type: Republic. **Head of state and gov.:** Pres. Verónica Michelle Bachelet Jeria; b. Sept. 29, 1951; in office: Mar. 11, 2006. **Local divisions:** 13 regions. **Defense budget** (2005): $1.7 bil. **Active troops:** 78,098.

Economy: Industries: copper, other minerals, foodstuffs, fish proc., iron, steel, wood & wood products, transp. equip., cement, textiles. **Chief crops:** wheat, corn, grapes, beans, sugar beets, potatoes, fruit. **Natural resources:** copper, timber, iron ore, nitrates, prec. metals, molybd., hydropower. **Crude oil reserves** (2005): 150 mil bbls. **Arable land:** 5%. **Livestock** (2005): cattle: 4.5 mil; chickens: 95 mil; goats: 735,000; pigs: 3.5 mil; sheep: 3.4 mil. **Fish catch** (2004): 5,610,355 metric tons. **Electricity prod.** (2004): 50.9 bil kWh. **Labor force** (2003): agriculture 13.6%, industry 23.4%, services 63%.

Finance: Monetary unit: Peso (CLP) (Sept. 2006: 540.15 = $1 U.S.). **GDP** (2005 est.): $187.1 bil; **per capita GDP:** $11,300; **GDP growth:** 6%. **Imports** (2005 est.): $30.1 bil; partners (2004): Argentina 17%, U.S. 14.1%, Brazil 11.1%, China 7.1%. **Exports** (2005 est.): $38 bil; partners (2004): U.S. 14%, Japan 11.4%, China 9.9%, South Korea 5.5%, Netherlands 5.1%, Brazil 4.3%, Italy 4.1%, Mexico 4%. **Tourism** (2003): $1.1 bil. **Budget** (2005 est.): $24.8 bil. **Intl. reserves less gold:** $11.85 bil. **Gold:** 10,000 oz t. **Consumer prices:** 3.05%.

Transport: Railroad: Length: 4,092 mi. **Motor vehicles:** 1.4 mil pass. cars, 737,600 comm. vehicles. **Civil aviation:** 6.9 bil pass.-mi; 73 airports. **Chief ports:** Valparaiso, Arica, Antofagasta.

Communications: TV sets: 240 per 1,000 pop. **Radios:** 354 per 1,000 pop. **Telephone lines:** 3.4 mil. **Daily newspaper circ.:** NA. **Internet** (2004): 5.6 mil users.

Health: Life expect.: 73.5 male; 80.2 female. **Births** (per 1,000 pop.): 15.2. **Deaths** (per 1,000 pop.): 5.8. **Natural inc.:** 0.94%. **Infant mortality** (per 1,000 live births): 8.6. **AIDS rate:** 0.3%.

Education: Compulsory: ages 6-13. **Literacy:** 95.7%.

Major Intl. Organizations: UN and all of its specialized agencies, APEC, OAS.

Embassy: 1732 Massachusetts Ave. NW 20036; 785-1746.

Website: www.chileangovernment.cl/

Northern Chile was under Inca rule before the Spanish conquest, 1536-40. The southern Araucanian Indians resisted until the late 19th cent. Independence was gained 1810-18, under José de San Martin and Bernardo O'Higgins; the latter, as supreme director 1817-23, sought social and economic reforms until deposed. Chile defeated Peru and Bolivia in 1836-39 and 1879-84, gaining mineral-rich northern land.

In 1970, Salvador Allende Gossens, a Marxist, became president with a narrow plurality of the popular vote. His government improved conditions for the poor, but property seizures by left-wing extremists, poorly planned socialist economic programs, and a destabilization campaign backed by the U.S. led to political and financial chaos.

A military junta seized power Sept. 11, 1973. With the presidential palace under attack, Allende refused to surrender; police said he killed himself. The junta, headed by Gen. Augusto Pinochet Ugarte, named a mostly military cabinet and announced plans to "exterminate Marxism." Repression continued through most of the 1980s.

In Dec. 1989 voters elected a civilian president, although Pinochet continued to head the army until Mar. 10, 1998. In Mar. 1994 a Chilean human rights group estimated that human rights violations had claimed more than 3,100 lives during Pinochet's rule. Initial attempts to prosecute him failed when he was declared mentally unfit to stand trial by courts in Britain and Chile.

Ricardo Lagos Escobar, Chile's first Socialist president since the 1973 coup, took office Mar. 11, 2000. Chile and the U.S. signed a free trade accord June 6, 2003. In Aug. 2004, Chile's Supreme Court voted to strip Pinochet of immunity from prosecution, allowing for the possibility of a future trial. Verónica Michelle Bachelet Jeria, a Socialist, won a runoff election Jan. 15, 2006, and took office Mar. 11 as Chile's first woman president.

Tierra del Fuego is the largest (18,800 sq mi) island in the archipelago of the same name at the southern tip of S. America, an area of majestic mountains, tortuous channels, and high winds. It was visited 1520 by Magellan and named Land of Fire because of its many Indian bonfires. Part of the island is in Chile, part in Argentina. Punta Arenas, on a mainland peninsula, is a center of sheep raising and the world's southernmost city (pop. [2002 census] 116,005); Puerto Williams is the southernmost settlement.

China
People's Republic of China
(Statistical data do not include Hong Kong or Macao.)

People: Population: 1,313,973,713. **Age distrib.** (%) <15: 20.8; 65+: 7.7. **Pop. density:** 364 per sq mi, 140 per sq km. **Urban:** 38.6%. **Ethnic groups:** 56 groups; Han 92%. Also Zhuang, Manchu, Hui, Miao, Uygur, Yi, Tujia, Tong, Tibetan, Mongol, et al. **Principal languages:** Mandarin (official), Yue (Cantonese), Wu (Shanghaiese), Minbei (Fuzhou), Minnan (Hokkien-Taiwanese), Xiang, Gan, Hakka, minority languages. **Chief religions:** Officially atheist; Buddhism, Taoism, some Muslims, Christians.

Geography: Total area: 3,705,407 sq mi, 9,596,960 sq km; **Land area:** 3,600,947 sq mi, 9,326,410 sq km. **Location:** Occupies most of the habitable mainland of E Asia. **Neighbors:** Mongolia on N; Russia on NE and NW; Afghanistan, Pakistan, Tajikistan, Kyrgystan, Kazakhstan on W; India, Nepal, Bhutan, Myanmar, Laos, Vietnam on S; North Korea on NE. **Topography:** Two-thirds of the vast territory is mountainous or desert; only one-tenth is cultivated. Rolling topography rises to high elevations in the N in the Daxinganlingshanmai separating Manchuria and Mongolia; the Tien Shan in Xinjiang; the Himalayan and Kunlunshanmai in the SW and in Tibet. Length is 1,860 mi. from N to S, width E to W is more than 2,000 mi. The eastern half of China is one of the world's best-watered lands. Three great river systems, the Chang (Yangtze), Huang (Yellow), and Xi, provide water for vast farmlands. **Capital:** Beijing, 10,717,000. **Cities (urban aggr.):** Guangzhou, Guangdong 8,425,000; Shanghai 14,503,000; Shenzhen 7,233,000; Tianjin 7,040,000; Wuhan 7,093,000.

Government: Type: Communist Party-led state. **Head of state:** Pres. Hu Jintao; b. Dec. 1942; in office: Mar. 15, 2003 (also gen. secy of Communist Party since Nov. 15, 2002). **Head of gov.:** Premier Wen Jiabao; b. Sept. 1942; in office: Mar. 16, 2003. **Local divisions:** 22 provinces (not including Taiwan), 5 autonomous regions, and 4 municipalities, plus the special administrative regions of Hong Kong (as of July 1, 1997) and Macao (as of Dec. 20, 1999). **Defense budget** (2005): $29.5 bil. **Active troops:** 2,255,000.

Economy: Industries: iron, steel, coal, machine building, armaments, textiles & apparel, oil, cement, chemical fertilizers. **Chief crops:** rice, wheat, potatoes, sorghum, peanuts, tea. **Natural resources:** coal, iron ore, oil, nat. gas, mercury, tin, tungsten, antimony, mang., molybd., vanadium, magnetite, aluminum, lead, zinc, uranium, hydropower. **Crude oil reserves** (2005): 18.3 bil bbls. **Arable land:** 10%. **Livestock** (2005): cattle: 115.2 mil; chickens: 4.4 bil; goats: 195.8 mil; pigs: 488.8 mil; sheep: 170.9 mil. **Fish catch** (2004): 47,507,761 metric tons. **Electricity prod.** (2004): 2079.7 bil kWh. **Labor force** (2003 est.): agriculture 49%, industry 22%, services 29%.

Finance: Monetary unit: Yuan Renminbi (CNY) (Sept. 2006: 7.92 = $1 U.S.). (2005 est.): $8.9 tril; **per capita GDP:** $6,800; **GDP growth:** 9.9%. **Imports** (2005 est.): $631.8 bil; partners (2004): Japan 16.1%, Taiwan 10.9%, South Korea 10.4%, U.S. 7.7%, Hong Kong 7.4%, Germany 5.4%. **Exports** (2005 est.): $752.2 bil; partners (2004): U.S. 22.8%, Hong Kong 16.2%, Japan 12.4%, South Korea 4.4%, Germany 4%. **Tourism:** $25.7 bil. **Budget** (2005 est.): $424.3 bil. **Intl. reserves less gold:** $574.78 bil. **Gold:** 19.29 mil oz t. **Consumer prices:** 1.82%.

Transport: Railroad: Length: 44,675 mi. **Motor vehicles** 12.02 mil pass. cars, 8.12 mil comm. vehicles. **Civil aviation:** 77 bil pass.-mi; 403 airports. **Chief ports:** Shanghai, Qinhuangdao, Dalian, Guangzhou (Canton).

Communications: TV sets: 291 per 1,000 pop. **Radios:** 342 per 1,000 pop. **Telephone lines:** 350.4 mil. **Daily newspaper circ.:** 59.3 per 1,000 pop. **Internet:** 111 mil users.

Health: Life expect.: 70.9 male; 74.5 female. **Births** (per 1,000 pop.): 13.2. **Deaths** (per 1,000 pop.): 7. **Natural inc.:** 0.63%. **Infant mortality** (per 1,000 live births): 23.1. **AIDS rate:** 0.1%.

Education: Compulsory: ages 6-14. **Literacy:** 90.9%.

Major Intl. Organizations: UN (FAO, IBRD, ILO, IMF, IMO, WHO, WTO), APEC.

Embassy: 2300 Conn. Ave. NW 20008; 328-2500.

Website: english.gov.cn

Remains of various humanlike creatures who lived as early as several hundred thousand years ago have been found in many parts of China. Neolithic agricultural settlements dotted the Huang (Yellow) R. basin from about 5000 BCE. Their language, religion, and art were the sources of later Chinese civilization.

Bronze metallurgy reached a peak and Chinese pictographic writing, similar to today's, was in use in the more developed culture of the Shang Dynasty (c. 1500 BCE-c. 1000 BCE), which ruled much of North China.

A succession of dynasties and interdynastic warring kingdoms ruled China for the next 3,000 years. They expanded Chinese political and cultural domination to the south and west, and developed a brilliant technologically and a culturally advanced society. Rule by foreigners (Mongols in the Yuan Dynasty, 1271-1368, and Manchus in the Ch'ing Dynasty, 1644-1911) did not alter the underlying culture.

A period of relative stagnation left China vulnerable to internal and external pressures in the 19th cent. Rebellions left tens of millions dead, and Russia, Japan, Britain, and other powers exercised political and economic control in large parts of the country. China became a republic Jan. 1, 1912, following the Wuchang Uprising inspired by Dr. Sun Yat-sen, founder of the Kuomintang (Nationalist) party. By 1928, the Kuomintang, led by Chiang Kai-shek, succeeded in nominal reunification of China. About the same time, a bloody purge of Communists from the ranks of the Kuomintang fomented hostilities between the two groups that would continue for decades.

For over 50 years, 1894-1945, China was involved in conflicts with Japan. In 1895, China ceded Korea, Taiwan, and other areas. On Sept. 18, 1931, Japan seized the Northeastern Provinces (Manchuria) and set up a puppet state called Manchukuo. The border province of Jehol was cut off as a buffer state in 1933. Taking advantage of Chinese dissension, Japan invaded China proper July 7, 1937. On Nov. 20 the retreating Nationalist government moved its capital to Chongqing (Chungking) from Nanking (Nanjing), which Japanese troops then ravaged Dec. 13.

From 1939 the Sino-Japanese War (1937-45) became part of the broader world conflict. After its defeat in World War II, Japan gave up all seized land, and internal conflicts involving the Kuomintang, Communists, and other factions resumed. China came under the domination of Communist armies, 1949-1950. The Kuomintang government moved to Taiwan, Dec. 8, 1949.

The Chinese People's Political Consultative Conference convened Sept. 21, 1949; The People's Republic of China was proclaimed in Beijing (Peking) Oct. 1, 1949, under Mao Zedong. China and the USSR signed a 30-year treaty of "friendship, alliance, and mutual assistance," Feb. 15, 1950. The U.S. refused recognition of the new regime. On Nov. 26, 1950, the People's Republic sent armies into Korea against U.S. troops and forced a stalemate in the Korean War.

After an initial period of consolidation, 1949-52, industry, agriculture, and social and economic institutions were forcibly molded according to Maoist ideals. However, frequent drastic changes in policy and violent factionalism interfered with economic development. In 1957, Mao admitted an estimated 800,000 people had been executed 1949-54; opponents claimed much higher figures.

The Great Leap Forward, 1958-60, tried to force the pace of economic development through intensive labor on huge new rural communes, and through emphasis on ideological purity. The program caused resistance and was largely abandoned.

By the 1960s, relations with the USSR deteriorated, with disagreements on borders, ideology, and leadership of world Communism. The USSR canceled aid accords, and China, with Albania, launched anti-Soviet propaganda drives.

The Great Proletarian Cultural Revolution, 1965, was an attempt to oppose pragmatism and bureaucratic power and instruct a new generation in revolutionary principles. Massive purges took place. A program of forcibly relocating millions of urban teenagers into the countryside was launched. By 1968 the movement had run its course; many purged officials returned to office in subsequent years, and reforms that had placed ideology above expertise were gradually weakened.

On Oct. 25, 1971, the UN General Assembly ousted the Taiwan government from the UN and seated the People's Republic in its place. The U.S. had supported the mainland's admission but opposed Taiwan's expulsion.

U.S. Pres. Richard Nixon visited China Feb. 21-28, 1972, on invitation from Premier Zhou Enlai, ending years of antipathy between the 2 nations. China and the U.S. opened liaison offices in each other's capitals, May-June 1973. The U.S., Dec. 15, 1978, formally recognized the People's Republic of China as the sole legal government of China; diplomatic relations between the 2 nations were established, Jan. 1, 1979.

Mao died Sept. 9, 1976. By 1978, Vice Premier Deng Xiaoping had consolidated his power, succeeding Mao as "paramount leader" of China. The new ruling group modified Maoist policies in education, culture, and industry, and sought better ties with non-Communist countries. During this "reassessment" of Mao's policies his widow, Jiang Qing, and other "Gang of Four" leftists were convicted of "committing crimes during the 'Cultural Revolution,'" Jan. 25, 1981.

By the mid-1980s, China had enacted far-reaching economic reforms, deemphasizing centralized planning and incorporating market-oriented incentives. Some 100,000 students and workers staged a march in Beijing to demand political reforms, May 4, 1989. As the unrest spread, martial law was imposed, May 20. Troops entered Beijing, June 3-4, and crushed the pro-democracy protests, as tanks and armored personnel carriers rolled through Tiananmen Square. It is estimated that 5,000 died, 10,000 were injured, and hundreds of students and workers were arrested.

Deng Xiaoping died Feb. 19, 1997, leaving Jiang Zemin in control as president. By agreement with the UK, Hong Kong reverted to Chinese sovereignty July 1 (see below). NATO bombs hit the Chinese embassy in Belgrade, Yugoslavia, on May 7, 1999, killing 3 people and wounding 27, for which the U.S. paid compensation. The government banned a popular religious sect, the Falun Gong, July 22, after it staged the largest unauthorized demonstrations in Beijing since 1989. The U.S. and China signed a major trade agreement Nov. 15. Portugal returned Macao to China Dec. 20, 1999.

Beijing was chosen, July 13, 2001, to host the 2008 Summer Olympics. Admission to the WTO Dec. 11 marked an economic milestone, though protested by many human rights and labor organizations. Hu Jintao was named Communist Party general secretary at the 16th party congress, Nov. 15, 2002, and elected president by the 10th National People's Congress, Mar. 15, 2003. A SARS epidemic beginning in late 2002 killed 349 people in mainland China by mid-2003.

In Aug. 2003, China assumed an unprecedented diplomatic role when it hosted multinational talks on N. Korea's nuclear weapons program. With the successful launch and recovery, Oct. 15-16, of the *Shenzhou 5* spacecraft, China became the third nation (after the U.S. and USSR) to send a man into space. Floods in summer 2004 killed more than 1,000 people and caused $8 bil in damage. Pres. Hu Jintao expanded his power when he became China's military chief Sept. 19 after Jiang Zemin's resignation.

A UN-China survey found that 650,000 Chinese had HIV/AIDS in 2005, less than previously estimated. Floods and mudslides from Tropical Storm Bilis, which hit China July 14, 2006, killed at least 612 people and caused $3.3 bil in damage. China's industries, exports, and demand for oil have all increased rapidly since the 1980s.

Manchuria. Home of the Manchus, rulers of China 1644-1911, Manchuria has accommodated millions of Chinese settlers in the 20th century. Under Japanese rule 1931-45, the area became industrialized. The region is divided into the 3 northeastern provinces of Heilongjiang, Jilin, and Liaoning.

Autonomous Regions

Guangxi Zhuang is in SE China, bounded on the N by Guizhou and Hunan provinces, E and S by Guangdong, on the SW by Vietnam, and on the W by Yunnan. It produces rice in the river valleys and has valuable forest products. Pop. (2000): 44.89 mil.

Inner Mongolia was organized by the People's Republic in 1947. Its boundaries have undergone frequent changes, reaching its greatest extent in 1956 (and restored in 1979), with an area of 454,600 sq mi, allegedly in order to dilute the minority Mongol population. Chinese settlers outnumber the Mongols more than 10 to 1. Pop. (2000): 23.76 mil. Capital: Hohhot.

Ningxia Hui, in north central China, is about 60,000 sq mi. Pop. (2000): 5.62 mil. Capital: Yinchuan. Situated mainly of the semiarid Inner Mongolian plateau region with desert areas in the N. The Huang He (Yellow R.) flows across the N furnishes water for irrigation. Coal is mined in the E. Modern industry is relatively undeveloped, and only one railroad crosses the region. The majority of the population is Han, and the Hui (Chinese Muslims) constitute about one-third of the population. The region experienced a significant population boom from 1950-80, which has now stabilized.

Xinjiang Uygur, in Central Asia, is 635,900 sq mi, pop. (2000): 19.25 mil (75% Uygurs, a Turkic Muslim group, with a heavy Chinese increase in recent years). Capital: Urumqi. It is China's richest region in strategic minerals. China has moved to crack down on Uygur separatists, whom Beijing regards as terrorists.

Tibet, 471,700 sq mi, is a thinly populated region of high plateaus and massive mountains, the Himalayas on the S, the Kunluns on the N. High passes connect with India and Nepal; roads lead into China proper. Capital: Lhasa. Average altitude is 15,000 ft. Jiachan, 15,870 ft, is believed to be the highest inhabited town on earth. Agriculture is primitive. Pop. (2000): 2.62 mil (of whom about 500,000 are Chinese). Another 4 mil Tibetans form the majority of the population of vast adjacent areas that have long been incorporated into China.

China ruled all of Tibet from the 18th cent. Independence came in 1911, but China reasserted control in 1951, and a Communist government was installed in 1953, revising the theocratic Lamaist Buddhist rule. Serfdom was abolished, but all land remained collectivized.

A Tibetan uprising within China in 1956 spread to Lhasa in 1959. The rebellion was crushed by Chinese troops, and Buddhism was almost totally suppressed. The Dalai Lama and 100,000 Tibetans fled to India.

Rail service from Beijing to Lhasa began July 1, 2006, with completion of the 710-mi Qinghai-Tibet line, the world's highest railway, an ambitious engineering project that cost more than $4 bil.

Hong Kong

Hong Kong (Xianggang), located at the mouth of the Zhu Jiang (Pearl R.) in SE China, 90 mi S of Canton (Guangzhou), was a British dependency from 1842 until July 1, 1997, when it became a Special Administrative Region of China. Its nucleus is Hong Kong Is., 31 sq mi, occupied by the British in 1841 and formally ceded to them in 1842, on which is located the seat of government. Opposite is Kowloon Peninsula, 3 sq mi, and Stonecutters Is., added to the territory in 1860. An additional 355 sq mi known as the New Territories, a mainland area and islands, were leased from China, 1898, for 99 years. Area 422 sq mi (total); 402 sq mi (land); pop. (2006 est.) 6,940,432, including fewer than 20,000 British.

Hong Kong is a major center for trade and banking. Per capita GDP, $32,900 (2005 est.), is among the highest in the world. Principal industries are textiles and apparel; also tourism ($11.9 bil expenditures in 2004), electronics, shipbuilding, iron and steel, fishing, cement, and small manufactures. Hong Kong's spinning mills are among the best in the world.

Hong Kong harbor was long an important British naval station and one of the world's great transshipment ports. The colony was often a place of refuge for exiles from mainland China. It was occupied by Japan during WWII.

From 1949 to 1962 Hong Kong absorbed more than a million refugees fleeing Communist China. Starting in the 1950s, cheap labor led to a boom in light manufacturing, while liberal tax policies attracted foreign investment; Hong Kong became one of the wealthiest,

most productive areas in the Far East. Poor living and working conditions and low wages for many led to political unrest in the 1960s, but legislation and public works programs raised the standard of living by the 1970s.

With the end of the 99-year lease on the New Territories drawing near, Britain and China signed an agreement, Dec. 19, 1984, under which all of Hong Kong was to be returned to China in 1997; under this agreement Hong Kong was to be allowed to keep its capitalist system for 50 years. In Dec. 1996, an electoral college appointed by China chose a shipping magnate, Tung Chee-hwa, to be Hong Kong's chief executive when it reverted to Chinese control.

Following the transfer of government on July 1, Hong Kong retained its street names and its currency, the Hong Kong dollar (HK$7.78 = $1 U.S.), but without the queen's picture. Official languages remained Chinese (Cantonese dialect) and English. Pro-democracy candidates did well in May 24, 1998, elections, despite having been excluded from the provisional government. in 1997. A SARS outbreak in 2003 claimed almost 300 lives and damaged the economy.

Hundreds of thousands of Hong Kong residents turned out July 1, 2003, to protest a proposed anti-subversion law; the bill was withdrawn Sept. 5. Another mass march, July 1, 2004, protested Beijing's refusal to allow greater freedom. Pro-democracy candidates won a majority of the popular vote in elections, Sept. 12, but failed to gain control of the Legislative Council. After Tung Chee-hwa resigned Mar. 10, 2005, Donald Tsang was chosen to serve the remaining 2 years of Tung's term as chief executive.

Macao

Macao, area of 10 sq mi, is an enclave, a peninsula and 2 small islands, at the mouth of the Xi (Pearl) R. in China. It was established as a Portuguese trading colony in 1557. In 1849, Portugal claimed sovereignty over the territory; this claim was accepted by China in an 1887 treaty. Portugal granted broad autonomy in 1976. Under a 1987 agreement, Macao reverted to China Dec. 20, 1999. As in the case of Hong Kong, the Chinese government guaranteed Macao it would not interfere in its way of life and capitalist system for a period of 50 years. Pop. (2006 est.): 453,125.

Colombia
Republic of Colombia

People: Population: 43,593,035. **Age distrib.** (%) <15: 30.3; 65+: 5.2. **Pop. density:** 108 per sq mi, 41 per sq km. **Urban:** 76.5%. **Ethnic groups:** Mestizo 58%, European 20%, Creole 14%, Black 4%, Black-Amerindian 1%, Amerindian 3%. **Principal languages:** Spanish (official). **Chief religion:** Roman Catholic 90%.

Geography: Total area: 439,736 sq mi, 1,138,910 sq km; **Land area:** 401,044 sq mi, 1,038,700 sq km. **Location:** At the NW corner of South America. **Neighbors:** Panama on NW, Ecuador and Peru on S, Brazil and Venezuela on E. **Topography:** Three ranges of Andes—Western, Central, and Eastern Cordilleras—run through the country from N to S. The eastern range consists mostly of high tablelands, densely populated. The Magdalena R. rises in the Andes, flows N to Caribbean, through a rich alluvial plain. Sparsely settled plains in E are drained by Orinoco and Amazon systems. **Capital:** Bogotá (Full name: Santa Fe de Bogotá.), 7,747,000. **Cities (urban aggr.):** Medellin, 3,058,000; Cali, 2,514,000; Barranquilla, 1,857,000.

Government: Type: Republic. **Head of state and gov.:** Pres. Álvaro Uribe Vélez; b. July 4, 1952; in office: Aug. 7, 2002. **Local divisions:** 32 departments, capital district of Bogota. **Defense budget** (2005): $3.5 bil. **Active troops:** 207,000.

Economy: Industries: textiles, food proc., oil, clothing & footwear, beverages, chemicals, cement, mining. **Chief crops:** coffee, cut flowers, bananas, rice, tobacco, corn, sugarcane, cocoa. **Natural resources:** oil, nat. gas, coal, iron ore, nickel, gold, copper, emeralds, hydropower. **Crude oil reserves** (2005): 1.5 bil bbls. **Arable land:** 4%. **Livestock** (2005): cattle: 25 mil; chickens: 125 mil; goats: 1.2 mil; pigs: 1.2 mil; sheep: 2.2 mil. **Fish catch** (2004): 211,385 metric tons. **Electricity prod.** (2004): 46.9 bil kWh. **Labor force** (2000): agriculture 22.7%, industry 18.7%, services 58.5%.

Finance: Monetary unit: Peso (COP) (Sept. 2006: 2,410.00 = $1 U.S.). **GDP** (2005 est.): $337.5 bil; **per capita GDP:** $7,900; **GDP growth:** 5.1%. **Imports** (2005 est.): $18 bil; partners (2004): U.S. 30.6%, Venezuela 6.3%, Brazil 5.2%, Japan 5.2%, Germany 5.1%, Mexico 5%, China 4.2%. **Exports** (2005 est.): $19.3 bil; partners (2004): U.S. 40.9%, Ecuador 5.8%, Venezuela 4.8%. **Tourism:** $1 bil. **Budget** (2005 est.): $48.8 bil. **Intl. reserves less gold:** $10.35 bil. **Gold:** 330,000 oz t. **Consumer prices:** 5.05%.

Transport: Railroad: Length: 2,053 mi. **Motor vehicles** 812,100 pass. cars, 402,900 comm. vehicles. **Civil aviation:** 5.1 bil pass.-mi; 101 airports. **Chief ports:** Buenaventura, Barranquilla, Cartagena.

Communications: TV sets: 279 per 1,000 pop. **Radios:** 539 per 1,000 pop. **Telephone lines:** 7.8 mil. **Daily newspaper circ.:** 26.4 per 1,000 pop. **Internet** (2004): 3.6 mil users.

Health: Life expect.: 68.2 male; 76 female. **Births** (per 1,000 pop.): 20.5. **Deaths** (per 1,000 pop.): 5.6. **Natural inc.:** 1.49%. **Infant mortality** (per 1,000 live births): 20.4. **AIDS rate:** 0.6%.

Education: Compulsory: ages 5-14. **Literacy:** 92.8%.

Major Intl. Organizations: UN (FAO, IBRD, ILO, IMF, IMO, WHO, WTO), OAS.

Embassy: 2118 Leroy Pl. NW 20008; 387-8338.

Website: www.colombiaemb.org

Spain subdued the local Indian kingdoms (Funza, Tunja) by the 1530s and ruled Colombia and neighboring areas as New Granada for 300 years. Independence was won by 1819. Venezuela and Ecuador broke away in 1829-30, and Panama withdrew in 1903.

Colombia is plagued by rural and urban violence. "La Violencia" of 1948-58 claimed 200,000 lives; since 1989, political killings, kidnappings, and "disappearances" have victimized many thousands of civilians, and the internally displaced population has grown to over 3 mil. Attempts at land and social reform and progress in industrialization have not reduced massive social problems.

The government's increased activity against local drug traffickers sparked a series of retaliation killings. On Aug. 18, 1989, Luis Carlos Galán, the ruling party's presidential hopeful for the 1990 election, was assassinated. In 1990, 2 other presidential candidates were assassinated, as drug traffickers carried on a campaign of intimidation.

Right-wing paramilitaries launched a campaign Dec. 22, 2000, against suspected left-wing guerrillas. Legislation expanding the powers of the military was signed Aug. 13, 2001. The collapse of talks with the rebels in Feb. 2002 brought an upsurge of fighting. A hardliner, Álvaro Uribe Vélez, whose father had been killed by leftist rebels in 1983, won a presidential election May 26. A wave of guerrilla violence as he took office led Uribe to declare a "state of unrest" Aug. 12. Police powers were increased Sept. 10 as part of a new government offensive. The constitution was amended, Nov. 30, 2004, to allow the president to seek a second consecutive term; he easily won reelection May 28, 2006.

Colombia produces an estimated 90% of the cocaine reaching the U.S. Since 2000, the U.S. has provided more than $4 bil to Colombia, much of it to combat the drug trade.

Comoros
Union of Comoros

People: Population: 690,948. **Age distrib.** (%) <15: 42.7; 65+: 3. **Pop. density:** 824 per sq mi, 318 per sq km. **Urban:** 35.0%. **Ethnic groups:** Antalote, Cafre, Makoa, Oimatsaha, Sakalava (all are mostly an African-Arab mix). **Principal languages:** Arabic, French (both official), Shikomoro (a blend of Swahili and Arabic). **Chief religion:** Muslim 98% (official).

Geography: Total area: 838 sq mi, 2,170 sq km; **Land area:** 838 sq mi, 2,170 sq km. **Location:** 3 islands—Grande Comore (Njazidja), Anjouan (Nzwani), and Moheli (Mwali)—in the Mozambique Channel between NW Madagascar and SE Africa. **Neighbors:** Nearest are Mozambique on W, Madagascar on E. **Topography:** The islands are of volcanic origin, with an active volcano on Grande Comore. **Capital:** Moroni, 44,000.

Government: Type: Republic. **Head of state and gov.:** Pres. Ahmed Abdallah Mohamed Sambi; b. June 5, 1958; in office: May 26, 2006. **Local divisions:** 3 main islands with 4 municipalities.

Economy: Industries: tourism, perfume distillation. **Chief crops:** vanilla, cloves, perfume essences, copra, coconuts, bananas, cassava. **Arable land:** 35%. **Livestock** (2005): cattle: 45,000; chickens: 510,000; goats: 115,000; sheep: 21,000. **Fish catch** (2004): 14,935 metric tons. **Electricity prod.** (2004): 20 mil kWh. **Labor force:** agriculture 80%, industry and services 20%.

Finance: Monetary unit: Franc (KMF) (Sept. 2006: 384.22 = $1 U.S.). **GDP** (2002 est.): $441 mil; **per capita GDP:** $600; **GDP growth:** 3%. **Imports** (2004 est.): $115 mil; partners (2004): France 24.4%, South Africa 11.5%, UAE 7.3%, Kenya 6.1%, Italy 5.1%, Mauritius 4.8%, Singapore 4.2%. **Exports** (2004 est.): $34 mil; partners (2004): U.S. 42.2%, France 18%, Singapore 16%, Turkey 4.7%. **Tourism** (1995): $21 mil. **Budget:** NA. **Intl. reserves less gold:** $60 mil.

Transport: Civil aviation: NA; 4 airports. **Chief ports:** Fomboni, Moroni, Moutsamoudou.

Communications: TV sets: 4 per 1,000 pop. **Radios:** 141 per 1,000 pop. **Telephone lines:** 16,900. **Internet:** 8,000 users.

Health: Life expect.: 60 male; 64.7 female. **Births** (per 1,000 pop.): 36.9. **Deaths** (per 1,000 pop.): 8.2. **Natural inc.:** 2.87%. **Infant mortality** (per 1,000 live births): 72.8. **AIDS rate:** <0.1%.

Education: Compulsory: ages 6-13. **Literacy:** 56.5%.

Major Intl. Organizations: UN (FAO, IBRD, ILO, IMF, WHO), AL, AU.

Embassy: 336 E. 45th St., 2d floor, New York, NY 10017 212-750-1637.

Website: www.state.gov/p/af/ci/cn

The islands were controlled by Muslim sultans until the French acquired them 1841-1909. They became a French overseas territory in 1947. A 1974 referendum favored independence, with only the Christian island of Mayotte preferring association with France. The French National Assembly decided to allow each of the islands to decide its own fate. The Comore Chamber of Deputies declared independence July 6, 1975, with Ahmed Abdallah as president. In a referendum in 1976, Mayotte voted to remain French.

A leftist regime that seized power from Abdallah in 1975 was deposed in a pro-French 1978 coup in which he regained the presidency. In Nov. 1989, Pres. Abdallah was assassinated; soon after, a multiparty system was instituted. A Sept. 1995 military coup, assisted by French mercenaries, ousted Pres. Said Mohamed Djohar. French troops invaded, Oct. 4, and forced coup leaders to surrender. Djohar returned from exile in Jan. 1996, and in March a new presidential election was held. A hijacked Ethiopian Airlines Boeing 767 crashed offshore on Nov. 23, killing 123 of the 175 people on board.

Attempts to work out a new constitutional relationship between Grande Comore, Anjouan, and Moheli have been ongoing since Anjouan and Moheli seceded from the Comoros in 1997. Unrest on Grande Comore culminated in a military coup, Apr. 30, 1999. Anjouans endorsed secession in a disputed vote Jan. 23, 2000. Irregularities marred the presidential runoff election of Apr. 14, 2002, won by Azali Assoumani, who led the 1999 coup; each of the 3 islands also elected its own president in 2002. Elections for national and island assemblies took place Mar.-Apr. 2004. Ahmed Abdallah Mohamed Sambi won a presidential runoff vote, May 14, 2006.

Congo (formerly Zaire)
Democratic Republic of the Congo

(Congo, officially Democratic Republic of the Congo, is also known as Congo-Kinshasa. It should not be confused with Republic of the Congo, commonly called Congo Republic, and also known as Congo-Brazzaville.)

People: Population: 62,660,551. **Age distrib.** (%) <15: 47.4; 65+: 2.5. **Pop. density:** 71 per sq mi, 27 per sq km. **Urban:** 53.5%. **Ethnic groups:** Over 200 groups. Four largest, the Mongo, Luba, Kongo (all Bantu), and Mangbetu-Azande (Hamitic), make up 45% of pop. **Principal languages:** French (official), Lingala, Kingswana (a swahili dialect), Tshiluba. **Chief religions:** Roman Catholic 50%, Protestant 20%, Kimbanguist 10%, Muslim 10%.

Geography: Total area: 905,568 sq mi, 2,345,410 sq km; **Land area:** 875,525 sq mi, 2,267,600 sq km. **Location:** In central Africa. **Neighbors:** Congo-Brazzaville on W; Central African Republic, Sudan on N; Uganda, Rwanda, Burundi, Tanzania on E; Zambia, Angola on S. **Topography:** Congo includes the bulk of the Congo R. basin. The vast central region is a low-lying plateau covered by rain forest. Mountainous terraces in the W, savannas in the S and SE, grasslands toward the N, and the high Ruwenzori Mts. on the E surround the central region. A short strip of territory borders the Atlantic O. **Capital:** Kinshasa, 6,049,000. **Cities (urban aggr.):** Lubumbashi, 906,000.

Government: Type: In transition. **Head of state and gov.:** Pres. Joseph Kabila; b. June 24, 1971; in office: Jan. 26, 2001. **Local divisions:** 10 provinces, 1 city. **Defense budget** (2005): NA. **Active troops:** 64,800.

Economy: Industries: mining, mineral proc., textiles, footwear, cigarettes, proc. foods & beverages, cement. **Chief crops:** coffee, sugar, rubber, tea, quinine, cassava, bananas, root crops, corn, fruits, wood products. **Natural resources:** cobalt, copper, cadmium, oil, diamonds, gold, silver, zinc, mang., tin, germanium, uranium, radium, bauxite, iron ore, coal, hydropower, timber. **Crude oil reserves** (2005): 187 mil bbls. **Arable land:** 3%. **Livestock** (2005): cattle: 756,940; chickens: 19.8 mil; goats: 4 mil; pigs: 959,080; sheep: 899,570. **Fish catch** (2004): 222,965 metric tons. **Electricity prod.** (2004): 6.8 bil kWh.

Finance: Monetary unit: Franc (CDF) (Sept. 2006: 432.00 = $1 U.S.). **GDP** (2005 est.): $40.7 bil; **per capita GDP:** $700; **GDP growth:** 6.5%. **Imports** (2004 est.): $1.3 bil; partners (2004): South Africa 18.5%, Belgium 15.6%, France 10.9%, U.S. 6.2%, Germany 5.9%, Kenya 4.9%. **Exports** (2004 est.): $1.1 bil; partners (2004): Belgium 42.5%, Finland 17.8%, Zimbabwe 12.2%, U.S. 9.2%, China 6.5%. **Tourism** (2003): $20 mil. **Budget** (2004 est.): $750 mil. **Consumer prices:** 21%.

Transport: Railroad: Length: 3,192 mi. **Motor vehicles:** 172,600 pass. cars, 34,600 comm. vehicles. **Civil aviation:** NA; 25 airports. **Chief ports:** Matadi, Boma, Kinshasa.

Communications: TV sets: 2 per 1,000 pop. **Radios:** 376 per 1,000 pop. **Telephone lines:** 10,000. **Daily newspaper circ.:** 2.8 per 1,000 pop. **Internet** (2002): 50,000 users.

Health: Life expect.: 50 male; 52.9 female. **Births** (per 1,000 pop.): 43.7. **Deaths** (per 1,000 pop.): 13.3. **Natural inc.:** 3.04%. **Infant mortality** (per 1,000 live births): 88.6. **AIDS rate:** 3.2%.

Education: Compulsory: ages 6-13. **Literacy:** 67.2%.

Major Intl. Organizations: UN and most of its specialized agencies, AU.

Embassy: 1800 New Hampshire Ave. NW 20009; 234-7690.

Website: www.un.int/drcongo

The earliest inhabitants of Congo may have been the pygmies, followed by Bantus from the east and Nilotic tribes from the north. The large Bantu Bakongo kingdom ruled much of Congo and Angola when Portuguese explorers visited in the 15th cent.

Leopold II, king of the Belgians, formed an international group to exploit the Congo region in 1876. In 1877 Henry M. Stanley explored the Congo, and in 1878 the king's agent sent him back to organize the region and win over the native chiefs. The Conference of Berlin, 1884-85, established the Congo Free State with Leopold as king and chief owner. Exploitation of native laborers on the rubber plantations caused international criticism and led to granting of a colonial charter, 1908; the colony became known as the Belgian Congo. Millions of Congolese are believed to have died between 1880 and 1920 as a result of slave labor and other causes under European rule.

Belgian and Congolese leaders agreed Jan. 27, 1960, that Congo would become independent in June. In the first general elections, May 31, the National Congolese movement of Patrice Lumumba won a plurality in the National Assembly. The Republic of the Congo was proclaimed June 30. Widespread violence caused Europeans and others to flee. The UN Security Council, Aug. 9, called on Belgium to withdraw its troops and sent a UN contingent. Pres. Joseph Kasavubu removed Lumumba as premier in Sept.; Lumumba was murdered Jan. 17, 1961. The last UN troops left the Congo June 30, 1964, and Moise Tshombe became president.

On Sept. 7, 1964, leftist rebels set up a "People's Republic" in Stanleyville (now Kisangani). Tshombe hired foreign mercenaries and sought to rebuild the Congolese Army. In Nov. and Dec. 1964 rebels killed scores of white hostages and thousands of Congolese; Belgian paratroopers, dropped from U.S. transport planes, rescued hundreds. By July 1965 the rebels had lost their effectiveness.

In late 1965 Gen. Joseph D. Mobutu was named president. He later changed his name to Mobutu Sese Seko and ruled as a dictator. The country became the Democratic Republic of the Congo (1966) and the Republic of Zaire (1971). Under Mobutu, economic decline and government corruption plagued Zaire. In 1990, Pres. Mobutu announced an end to a 20-year ban on multiparty politics. He sought to retain power despite mounting international pressure and internal opposition.

During 1994, Zaire was inundated with refugees from the massive ethnic bloodshed in Rwanda. Ethnic violence spread to E Zaire in 1996. In Oct. militant Hutus, who dominated in the refugee camps, fought against rebels (mostly Tutsis) in Zaire, precipitating intervention by government troops. As a result of the fighting, Rwandan refugees abandoned the camps; hundreds of thousands returned to Rwanda, while hundreds of thousands more were dispersed throughout eastern Zaire. The rebels, led by Gen. Laurent Kabila—a former Marxist and longtime opponent of Mobutu—gained momentum and began to move west across Zaire. As turmoil engulfed his nation, Mobutu stayed in Western Europe during the latter part of 1996. With Mobutu out of the country, the Zairean army put up little resistance; rebels were aided by several of Mobutu's enemies, notably Rwanda and Uganda. Mobutu returned to Zaire in March 1997, but attempts to negotiate with Kabila were ineffectual. On May 17, Kabila's troops entered Kinshasa and Mobutu went into exile. The country again assumed the name Democratic Republic of the Congo. Mobutu died Sept. 7 in Rabat, Morocco.

Kabila, who ruled by decree, alienated UN officials, international aid donors, and former allies. Rebels assisted by Rwanda and Uganda threatened Kinshasa in Aug. 1998, but the assault was turned back with help from Angola, Namibia, and Zimbabwe. Rebel groups agreed to a cease-fire on Aug. 31, 1999, but the truce was widely violated. Kabila was assassinated Jan. 16, 2001, apparently by one of his bodyguards, and was succeeded by his son Joseph.

The overall death toll from the civil war and related causes was estimated at 3.3 mil through Nov. 2002. By then the war had apparently begun to wind down, with agreements by Rwanda and Uganda to pull out their remaining troops. A power-sharing accord signed Apr. 2, 2003, led to the installation of a new Congolese government in July. A new constitution won legislative approval May 13, 2005. A 17,600-member UN peacekeeping force (MONUC), established in 1999, remained in the country to oversee multiparty elections, held July 30-31, 2006, in which an estimated 20 million voters went to the polls in the first multi-party election since 1960. A presidential runoff between Kabila and former rebel leader Jean-Pierre Bemba was set for October.

Congo Republic
Republic of the Congo

(Congo Republic, officially Republic of the Congo, is also known as Congo-Brazzaville. It should not be confused with Democratic Republic of the Congo [formerly Zaire], now commonly called Congo, and also known as Congo-Kinshasa.)

People: Population: 3,702,314. **Age distrib.** (%) <15: 46.4; 65+: 2.9. **Pop. density:** 28 per sq mi, 10 per sq km. **Urban:** 31.6%. **Ethnic groups:** Kongo 48%, Sangha 20%, M'Bochi 12%, Teke 17%. **Principal languages:** French (official), Lingala, Monokutuba, Kikongo, many local languages and dialects. **Chief religions:** Christian 50%, animist 48%, Muslim 2%.

Geography: Total area: 132,047 sq mi, 342,000 sq km; **Land area:** 131,854 sq mi, 341,500 sq km. **Location:** In W central Africa. **Neighbors:** Gabon and Cameroon on W, Central African Republic on N, Congo-Kinshasa (formerly Zaire) on E, Angola on SW. **Topography:** Much of the Congo is covered by thick forests. A coastal plain leads to the fertile Niari Valley. The center is a plateau; the Congo R. basin consists of flood plains in the lower and savanna in the upper portion. **Capital:** Brazzaville, 1,173,000.

Government: Type: Republic. **Head of state and gov.:** Pres. Denis Sassou-Nguesso; b. 1943; in office: Oct. 25, 1997. **Local divisions:** 10 regions, 6 communes. **Defense budget** (2005): $57 mil. **Active troops:** 10,000.

Economy: Industries: oil, cement, lumber, brewing, sugar, palm oil. **Chief crops:** cassava, sugar, rice, corn, peanuts, vegetables, coffee, cocoa. **Natural resources:** oil, timber, potash, lead, zinc, uranium, copper, phosphates, nat. gas, hydropower. **Crude oil reserves** (2005): 1.5 bil bbls. **Livestock** (2005): cattle: 115,000; chickens: 2.4 mil; goats: 295,000; pigs: 46,500; sheep: 99,000. **Fish catch** (2004): 43,527 metric tons. **Electricity prod.** (2004): 350 mil kWh.

Finance: Monetary unit: CFA BEAC Franc (XAF) (Sept. 2006: 512.47 = $1 U.S.). **GDP** (2005 est.): $4.6 bil; **per capita GDP:** $1,300; **GDP growth:** 8%. **Imports** (2005 est.): $806.5 mil; partners (2004): France 20.2%, China 6.6%, Italy 6.5%, India 4.8%, Belgium 4.7%, U.S. 4.6%. **Exports** (2005 est.): $2.2 bil; partners (2004): China 30.8%, U.S. 18.2%, Taiwan 16.8%, South Korea 11.2%, Trinidad and Tobago 5.6%. **Tourism:** $20 mil. **Budget** (2005 est.): $1.1 bil. **Intl. reserves less gold:** $512 mil. **Gold:** 10,000 oz t.

Transport: Railroad: Length: 556 mi. **Motor vehicles:** 29,700 pass. cars, 23,100 comm. vehicles. **Civil aviation:** 16.8 mil pass.-mi; 4 airports. **Chief ports:** Pointe-Noire, Brazzaville.

Communications: TV sets: 13 per 1,000 pop. **Radios:** 126 per 1,000 pop. **Telephone lines:** 13,800. **Daily newspaper circ.:** 6.4 per 1,000 pop. **Internet:** 36,000 users.

Health: Life expect.: 51.6 male; 54 female. **Births** (per 1,000 pop.): 42.6. **Deaths** (per 1,000 pop.): 12.9. **Natural inc.:** 2.96%. **Infant mortality** (per 1,000 live births): 85.3. **AIDS rate:** 5.3%.

Education: Compulsory: ages 6-16. **Literacy:** 83.8%.

Major Intl. Organizations: UN (FAO, IBRD, ILO, IMF, IMO, WHO, WTO), AU.

Embassy: 4891 Colorado Ave. NW 20011; 726-5500.

Website: www.state.gov/p/af/ci/cf

The Loango Kingdom flourished in the 15th cent., as did the Anzico Kingdom of the Batekes; by the late 17th cent. they had become weakened. By 1885, France established control of the region, then called the Middle Congo. Republic of the Congo gained independence Aug. 15, 1960.

After a 1963 coup sparked by trade unions, the country adopted a Marxist-Leninist stance, with the USSR and China vying for influence. France remained a dominant trade partner and source of technical assistance, however, and French-owned private enterprise retained a major economic role. In 1970, the country was renamed People's Republic of the Congo.

In 1990, Marxism was renounced and opposition parties were legalized. In 1991 the country's name was changed back to Republic of the Congo, and a new constitution was approved. A democratically elected government came into office in 1992. Factional fighting broke out in Brazzaville, June 5, 1997, and intensified during the summer, devastating the capital. Troops loyal to former Marxist dictator Denis Sassou-Nguesso took control of the city Oct. 15. He claimed a lopsided victory in the presidential election of Mar. 10, 2002. The government and "Ninja" rebels in the Pool Region agreed to a cease-fire Mar. 17, 2003.

Costa Rica
Republic of Costa Rica

People: Population: 4,075,261. **Age distrib.** (%) <15: 28.3; 65+: 5.7. **Pop. density:** 208 per sq mi, 80 per sq km. **Urban:** 60.6%. **Ethnic groups:** European and Mestizo 94%, black 3%, Amerindian 1%, Chinese 1%. **Principal languages:** Spanish (official), English spoken around Puerto Limon. **Chief religions:** Roman Catholic 76% (official), Protestant 14%.

Geography: Total area: 19,730 sq mi, 51,100 sq km; **Land area:** 19,560 sq mi, 50,660 sq km. **Location:** In Central America. **Neighbors:** Nicaragua on N, Panama on S. **Topography:** Lowlands on the Caribbean are tropical. The interior plateau, with an altitude of about 4,000 ft., is temperate. **Capital:** San José, 1,217,000.

Government: Type: Republic. **Head of state and gov.:** Pres. Óscar Arias Sánchez; b. Sept. 13, 1940; in office: May 8, 2006. **Local divisions:** 7 provinces. **Defense budget** (2005): $101 mil. **Active troops:** 0.

Economy: Industries: microprocessors, food proc., textiles and clothing, constr. materials, fertilizer, plastics. **Chief crops:** coffee, pineapples, bananas, sugar, corn, rice, beans, potatoes, timber. **Natural resources:** hydropower. **Arable land:** 6%. **Livestock** (2005): cattle: 1.1 mil; chickens: 19.5 mil; goats: 4,700; pigs: 550,000; sheep: 2,700. **Fish catch** (2004): 45,525 metric tons. **Electricity prod.** (2004): 8.4 bil kWh. **Labor force** (1999 est.): agriculture 20%, industry 22%, services 58%.

Finance: Monetary unit: Colon (CRC) (Sept. 2006: 522.01 = $1 U.S.). **GDP** (2005 est.): $44.7 bil; **per capita GDP:** $11,100; **GDP growth:** 4%. **Imports** (2005 est.): $9.7 bil; partners (2004): U.S. 35.5%, Japan 4.8%, Mexico 3.7%. **Exports** (2005 est.): $7 bil; partners (2004): U.S. 23.7%, Netherlands 7.7%, UK 6.6%. **Tourism:** $1.6 bil. **Budget** (2005 est.): $3.2 bil. **Intl. reserves less gold:** $1.62 bil. **Consumer prices:** 13.8%.

Transport: Railroad: Length: 172 mi. **Motor vehicles:** 367,800 pass. cars, 191,300 comm. vehicles. **Civil aviation:** 1.1 bil pass.-mi; 32 airports. **Chief ports:** Limon, Puntarenas, Golfito.

Communications: TV sets: 229 per 1,000 pop. **Radios:** 774 per 1,000 pop. **Telephone lines:** 1.4 mil. **Daily newspaper circ.:** 70 per 1,000 pop. **Internet:** 1 mil users.

Health: Life expect.: 74.4 male; 79.7 female. **Births** (per 1,000 pop.): 18.3. **Deaths** (per 1,000 pop.): 4.4. **Natural inc.:** 1.4%. **Infant mortality** (per 1,000 live births): 9.7. **AIDS rate:** 0.3%.

Education: Compulsory: ages 6-15. **Literacy:** 94.9%.

Major Intl. Organizations: UN (FAO, IBRD, ILO, IMF, IMO, WHO, WTO), OAS.

Embassy: 2114 S St. NW 20008; 234-2945.

Website: www.costarica-embassy.org

Guaymi Indians inhabited the area when Spaniards arrived, 1502. Independence came in 1821. Costa Rica seceded from the Central American Federation in 1838. Since the civil war of 1948-49, there has been little violent social conflict, and free political institutions have been preserved.

Costa Rica, though still a largely agricultural country, has achieved a relatively high standard of living, and land ownership is widespread. Tourism is growing rapidly. Nobel Peace Prize-winner Óscar Arias Sánchez, president 1986-90, won a 2nd term in a close election, Feb. 5, 2006.

Côte d'Ivoire
Republic of Côte d'Ivoire
People: Population: 17,654,843. **Age distrib.** (%) <15: 40.8; 65+: 2.8. **Pop. density:** 143 per sq mi, 55 per sq km. **Urban:** 44.9%. **Ethnic groups:** Akan 42%, Voltaiques (Gur) 18%, N Mandes 17%, Krous 11%, S Mandes 10%. **Principal languages:** French (official), Dioula, many native dialects. **Chief religions:** Muslim 35-40%, Christian 20-30%, indigenous beliefs 25-40%.

Geography: Total area: 124,503 sq mi, 322,460 sq km; **Land area:** 122,780 sq mi, 318,000 sq km. **Location:** On S coast of W Africa. **Neighbors:** Liberia, Guinea on W; Mali, Burkina Faso on N; Ghana on E. **Topography:** Forests cover the W half of the country, and range from a coastal strip to halfway to the N on the E. A sparse inland plain leads to low mountains in NW. **Capital** (2003): Yamoussoukro (official), 185,600; Abidjan (de facto), 3,577,000.

Government: Type: In transition. **Head of state:** Pres. Laurent Gbagbo; b. May 31, 1945; in office: Oct. 26, 2000. **Head of gov.:** Prime Min. Charles Konan Banny; b. Nov. 11, 1942; in office: Dec. 7, 2005. **Local divisions:** 58 departments. **Defense budget** (2005) $191 mil. **Active troops:** 17,050.

Economy: Industries: foodstuffs, beverages, wood products, oil refining, truck & bus assembly, textiles, fertilizer, building materials, electricity. **Chief crops:** coffee, cocoa beans, bananas, palm kernels. **Natural resources:** oil, nat. gas, diamonds, mang., iron ore, cobalt, bauxite, copper, hydropower. **Crude oil reserves** (2005): 100 mil bbls. **Arable land:** 8%. **Livestock** (2005): cattle: 1.5 mil; chickens: 33 mil; goats: 1.2 mil; pigs: 345,000; sheep: 1.5 mil. **Fish catch** (2004): 55,264 metric tons. **Electricity prod.** (2004): 4.6 bil kWh. **Labor force:** agric. 51%; manuf. & mining 12%.

Finance: Monetary unit: CFA BCEAO Franc (XOF) (Sept. 2006: 512.27 = $1 U.S.). **GDP** (2005 est.): $28.5 bil; **per capita GDP:** $1,600; **GDP growth:** 1%. **Imports** (2005 est.): $4.8 bil; partners (2004): France 24.7%, Nigeria 18.5%, Italy 4%. **Exports** (2005 est.): $6.5 bil; partners (2004): U.S. 11.3%, Netherlands 10.1%, France 9.4%, Italy 5.3%, Belgium 4.7%, Germany 4.3%. **Tourism** (2003): $76 mil. **Budget** (2005 est.): $2.8 bil. **Intl. reserves less gold:** $925 mil. **Consumer prices:** 3.89%.

Transport: Railroad: Length: 410 mi. **Motor vehicles:** 113,900 pass. cars, 54,900 comm. vehicles. **Civil aviation:** 80.8 mil pass.-mi; 7 airports. **Chief ports:** Abidjan, Dabou, San-Pédro. **Communications: TV sets:** 65 per 1,000 pop. **Radios:** 161 per 1,000 pop. **Telephone lines:** 238,000. **Daily newspaper circ.:** 15.6 per 1,000 pop. **Internet:** 300,000 users.

Health: Life expect.: 46.2 male; 51.5 female. **Births** (per 1,000 pop.): 35.1. **Deaths** (per 1,000 pop.): 14.8. **Natural inc.:** 2.03%. **Infant mortality** (per 1,000 live births): 89.1. **AIDS rate:** 7.1%. **Education:** Compulsory: ages 6-15. **Literacy:** 48.7%. **Major Intl. Organizations:** UN and all of its specialized agencies, AU.

Embassy: 2424 Massachusetts Ave. NW 20008; 797-0300. **Website:** cotedivoire.usembassy.gov

A French protectorate from 1842, Côte d'Ivoire became independent in 1960. The name was officially changed from Ivory Coast, Oct. 1985. The country is a leading producer of coffee and cocoa beans.

Students and workers protested, Feb. 1990, demanding the ouster of longtime Pres. Félix Houphouët-Boigny. Côte d'Ivoire held its first multiparty presidential election Oct. 1990, and Houphouët-Boigny retained his office. He died Dec. 7, 1993. The National Assembly named a successor, Henri Konan Bédié, who was reelected Oct. 22, 1995; he was ousted in a military coup Dec. 24, 1999. The coup leader, Robert Guéi, apparently lost a presidential vote Oct. 22, 2000, but claimed victory anyway. After mass protests, he fled, and Laurent Gbagbo became president. Guéi was killed in Abidjan Sept. 19, 2002, after a mutiny broke out there and in Bouaké and Korhogo.

Agreement on power sharing was reached in Mar. 2003, and Gbagbo and former rebel leaders held a ceremony July 5, declaring that the war was over. The country remained divided, however, with rebels holding the north and government forces controlling the south. In Feb. 2004, the UN approved a peacekeeping force (UNOCI); by mid-2006, the country had about 7,600 UNOCI and 4,000 French peacekeepers. In Nov. 2004, while carrying out an air campaign against rebels, a government aircraft hit a French military installation, killing 9 French troops and one American. The French responded with attacks on the Ivorian air force and anti-French riots ensued. Presidential elections, originally scheduled for Oct. 30, 2005, have been postponed. Toxic waste dumped in Abidjan Aug.-Sept. 2006 killed at least 7 people and sickened 30,000 more.

Croatia
Republic of Croatia
People: Population: 4,494,749. **Age distrib.** (%) <15: 16.2; 65+: 16.8. **Pop. density:** 206 per sq mi, 79 per sq km. **Urban:** 59.0%. **Ethnic groups:** Croat 78%, Serb 12%, Bosniak 1%. **Principal languages:** Croatian (official), Serbian. **Chief religions:** Roman Catholic 88%, Orthodox 5%.

Geography: Total area: 21,831 sq mi, 56,542 sq km; **Land area:** 21,782 sq mi, 56,414 sq km. **Location:** SE Europe, on the Balkan Peninsula. **Neighbors:** Slovenia, Hungary on N; Bosnia and Herzegovina, Yugoslavia on E. **Topography:** Flat plains in NE; highlands, low mtns. along Adriatic coast. **Capital:** Zagreb, 689,000.

Government: Type: Parliamentary democracy. **Head of state:** Pres. Stipe Mesic; b. Dec. 24, 1934; in office: Feb. 18, 2000. **Head of gov.:** Prime Min. Ivo Sanader; b. June 8, 1953; in office: Dec. 23,

2003. **Local divisions:** 20 counties and Zagreb. **Defense budget** (2005): $626 mil. **Active troops:** 20,800.

Economy: Industries: chemicals, plastics, machine tools, fabricated metal, electronics. **Chief crops:** wheat, corn, sugar beets, sunflower seeds, barley. **Natural resources:** oil, coal, bauxite, iron ore, calcium, natural asphalt, silica, mica, clays, salt, hydropower. **Crude oil reserves** (2005): 75 mil bbls. **Arable land:** 21%. **Livestock** (2005): cattle: 471,025; chickens: 10.6 mil; goats: 120,000; pigs: 1.2 mil; sheep: 796,480. **Fish catch** (2004): 40,311 metric tons. **Electricity prod.** (2004): 13 bil kWh. **Labor force** (2004): agriculture 2.7%, industry 32.8%, services 64.5%.

Finance: Monetary unit: Kuna (HRK) (Sept. 2006: 5.81 = $1 U.S.). **GDP** (2005 est.): $55.8 bil; **per capita GDP:** $11,600; **GDP growth:** 4%. **Imports** (2005 est.): $18.9 bil; partners (2004): Italy 17.3%, Germany 15.7%, Slovenia 7.1%, Austria 7.1%, Russia 7%, France 4.3%. **Exports** (2005 est.): $10.3 bil; partners (2004): Italy 23.1%, Bosnia and Herzegovina 14.7%, Germany 11.5%, Austria 9.6%, Slovenia 7.7%. **Tourism:** $6.9 bil. **Budget** (2005 est.): $19.4 bil. **Intl. reserves less gold:** $6.16 bil. **Consumer prices:** 3.34%.

Transport: Railroad: Length: 1,694 mi. **Motor vehicles:** 1.29 mil pass. cars, 153,100 comm. vehicles. **Civil aviation:** 486.5 mil pass.-mi. 23 airports. **Chief ports:** Rijeka, Split, Dubrovnik. **Communications: TV sets:** 286 per 1,000 pop. **Radios:** 337 per 1,000 pop. **Telephone lines:** 1.9 mil. **Daily newspaper circ.:** 133.8 per 1,000 pop. **Internet** (2003): 1 mil users.

Health: Life expect.: 71 male; 78.5 female. **Births** (per 1,000 pop.): 9.6. **Deaths** (per 1,000 pop.): 11.5. **Natural inc.:** –0.19%. **Infant mortality** (per 1,000 live births): 6.7. **AIDS rate:** <0.1%. **Education:** Compulsory: ages 7-14. **Literacy:** 98.1%. **Major Intl. Organizations:** UN (FAO, IBRD, ILO, IMF, IMO, WHO, WTO), OSCE.

Embassy: 2343 Massachusetts Ave. NW 20008; 588-5899. **Website:** www.vlada.hr/default.asp?ru=2

From the 7th cent. the area was inhabited by Croats, a south Slavic people. It was formed into a kingdom under Tomislav in 924, and joined with Hungary in 1102. The Croats became westernized and separated from Slavs under Austro-Hungarian influence. The Croats retained autonomy under the Hungarian crown. Slavonia was taken by Turks in the 16th cent.; the northern part was restored by the Treaty of Karlowitz in 1699. Croatia helped Austria put down the Hungarian revolution 1848-49 and as a result was set up with Slavonia as the separate Austrian crownland of Croatia and Slavonia, which was reunited to Hungary as part of Ausgleich in 1867. It united with other Yugoslav areas to proclaim the Kingdom of Serbs, Croats, and Slovenes in 1918. At the reorganization of Yugoslavia in 1929, Croatia and Slavonia became Savska county, which in 1939 was united with Primorje county to form the county of Croatia. A nominally independent state between 1941 and 1945, it became a federal republic in the 1946 constitution.

On June 25, 1991, Croatia declared independence from Yugoslavia. Fighting began between ethnic Serbs and Croats, with the former gaining control of about 30% of Croatian territory. A ceasefire was declared in Jan. 1992, but new hostilities broke out in 1993. A cease-fire with Serb rebels forming a self-declared republic of Krajina was agreed to Mar. 30, 1994. Croatian government troops recaptured most of the Serb-held territory Aug. 1995. Pres. Franjo Tudjman signed a peace accord with leaders of Bosnia and Serbia in Paris, Dec. 14. Tudjman won reelection June 15, 1997; international monitors called the vote "free but not fair." The last Serb-held enclave, E Slavonia, returned to Croatian control Jan. 15, 1998.

Tudjman died Dec. 10, 1999. Stipe Mesic, a moderate, won a presidential runoff election Feb. 7, 2000, and was reelected Jan. 16, 2005. EU membership talks, scheduled to start Mar. 17, 2005, were postponed because of Croatia's failure to hand over a suspected war criminal, Gen. Ante Gotovina; he was arrested Dec. 7, 2005, in Spain's Canary Islands.

Cuba
Republic of Cuba
People: Population: 11,382,820. **Age distrib.** (%) <15: 19.1; 65+: 10.6. **Pop. density:** 265 per sq mi, 102 per sq km. **Urban:** 75.6%. **Ethnic groups:** Creole 51%, White 37%, Black 11%, Chinese 1%. **Principal language:** Spanish (official). **Chief religions:** Roman Catholic, Santeria.

Geography: Total area: 42,803 sq mi, 110,860 sq km; **Land area:** 42,803 sq mi, 110,860 sq km. **Location:** In the Caribbean, westernmost of West Indies. **Neighbors:** Bahamas and U.S. to N, Mexico to W, Jamaica to S, Haiti to E. **Topography:** The coastline is about 2,500 miles. The N coast is steep and rocky, the S coast low and marshy. Low hills and fertile valleys cover more than half the country. Sierra Maestra, in the E, is the highest of 3 mountain ranges. **Capital:** Havana 2,189,000.

Government: Type: Communist state. **Head of state and gov.:** Pres. Fidel Castro Ruz; b. Aug. 13, 1926; in office: Dec. 3, 1976 (formerly prime min. since Feb. 16, 1959). **Local divisions:** 14 provinces, 1 special municipality. **Defense budget:** NA. **Active troops:** 49,000.

Economy: Industries: sugar, oil, tobacco, chemicals, constr., services. **Chief crops:** sugar, tobacco, citrus, coffee, rice. **Natural resources:** cobalt, nickel, iron ore, copper, mang., salt, timber, silica, oil. **Crude oil reserves** (2005): 750 mil bbls. **Arable land:** 24%. **Livestock** (2005): cattle: 4.1 mil; chickens: 26 mil; goats: 1.1 mil; pigs: 1.7 mil; sheep: 2.6 mil. **Fish catch** (2004): 64,836 metric tons.

Electricity prod. (2004): 15.2 bil kWh. **Labor force** (2004): agriculture 21.2%, industry 14.4%, services 64.4%.

Finance: Monetary unit: Peso (CUP) (Sept. 2006: 26.50 = $1 U.S.) **GDP** (2005 est.): $39.2 bil; **per capita GDP:** $3,500; **GDP growth:** 8%. **Imports** (2005 est.): $6.9 bil; partners (2004): Spain 15.4%, Venezuela 13.7%, U.S. 11.5%, China 8%, Canada 6.6%, Italy 6.5%, Mexico 4.9%, Germany 4.2%. **Exports** (2005 est.): $2.4 bil; partners (2004): Netherlands 23.5%, Canada 21.9%, China 8.3%, Russia 7.8%, Spain 6.6%. **Tourism:** $1.9 bil. **Budget** (2005 est.): $23.7 bil.

Transport: Railroad: Length: 2,626 mi. **Motor vehicles:** 10,100 comm. vehicles. **Civil aviation:** 1.2 bil pass.-mi; 78 airports **Chief ports:** Havana, Matanzas, Cienfuegos, Santiago de Cuba.

Communications: TV sets: 248 per 1,000 pop. **Radios:** 352 per 1,000 pop. **Telephone lines:** 849,900. **Daily newspaper circ.:** 53.6 per 1,000 pop. **Internet:** 150,000.

Education: Compulsory: ages 6-14. **Literacy:** 99.8%.

Health: Life expect.: 75.1 male; 79.8 female. **Births** (per 1,000 pop.): 11.9. **Deaths** (per 1,000 pop.): 7.2. **Natural inc.:** 0.47%. **Infant mortality** (per 1,000 live births): 6.2. **AIDS rate:** 0.1%.

Major Intl. Organizations: UN (FAO, ILO, IMO, WHO, WTO). Cuba is an OAS member state, but its current govt. has been excluded from OAS participation since 1962.

Cuba Interests Section: 2630 and 2639 16th St. NW 20009; 797-8518.

Website: www.cubagob.cu/ingles/default.htm

Some 50,000 Indians lived in Cuba when it was reached by Columbus in 1492. Its name derives from the Indian Cubanacan. Except for British occupation of Havana, 1762-63, Cuba remained Spanish until 1898. A slave-based sugar plantation economy developed from the 18th cent., aided by early mechanization of milling. Sugar remains the chief product and main export.

A 10-year uprising ended in 1878 with guarantees of rights by Spain, which Spain failed to carry out. A full-scale liberation movement under Jose Martí began Feb. 24, 1895.

The Spanish-American War began Apr. 1898, after the sinking of the USS *Maine* in Havana harbor. Spain, which lost the war, gave up all claims to Cuba. U.S. troops withdrew in 1902, but under 1903 and 1934 agreements, the U.S. continued to lease a site at Guantánamo Bay in the southeast as a naval base. U.S. and other foreign investments acquired a dominant role in the economy. In 1952, former Pres. Fulgencio Batista seized control and established a dictatorship, which grew increasingly harsh and corrupt. Fidel Castro assembled a rebel band in 1956; guerrilla fighting intensified in 1958. Batista fled Jan. 1, 1959, and in the resulting political vacuum Castro took power, becoming premier Feb. 16.

The government began a program of sweeping economic and social changes, without restoring promised liberties. Opponents were imprisoned, and some were executed. Some 700,000 Cubans emigrated in the first years after the Castro takeover, mostly to the U.S. By 1960 all banks and industrial companies had been nationalized, including over $1 bil worth of U.S.-owned properties, mostly without compensation.

In 1961, some 1,400 Cubans, trained and backed by the U.S. Central Intelligence Agency, unsuccessfully tried to invade and overthrow the regime. In the fall of 1962, the U.S. learned the USSR had brought nuclear missiles to Cuba. After an Oct. 22 warning from Pres. John F. Kennedy, the missiles were removed.

In 1977, Cuba and the U.S. signed agreements to exchange diplomats, without restoring full ties, and to regulate offshore fishing. In 1978 and 1980, the U.S. agreed to accept political prisoners released by Cuba, some of whom were criminals and mental patients. A 1987 agreement provided for 20,000 Cubans to emigrate to the U.S. each year; Cuba agreed to take back some 2,500 jailed in the U.S. since 1980. Cuba's support for left-wing regimes and liberation movements in Central America, Africa, and the Caribbean contributed to poor relations with the U.S.

Cuba's economy, hobbled by U.S. sanctions and dependent on aid from other Communist countries, was severely shaken by the collapse of the Communist bloc in the late 1980s. Stiffer trade sanctions enacted by the U.S. in 1992 made things worse. Antigovernment demonstrations in Aug. 1994 prompted Castro to loosen emigration restrictions. A new U.S.-Cuba accord in Sept. ended the exodus of "boat people" after more than 30,000 had left Cuba. In another policy shift, the U.S. announced May 2, 1995, it would admit 20,000 Cuban refugees held at the Guantánamo base but would send further boat people back to Cuba.

The U.S. imposed additional sanctions after Cuba, Feb. 24, 1996, shot down 2 aircraft operated by an anti-Castro exile group based in Miami. Cuba blamed exile groups for bombings at Havana tourist hotels, July-Sept. 1997. Pope John Paul II visited Cuba, Jan. 21-25, 1998. U.S. restrictions on contact were eased in 1999.

In one of its largest crackdowns in recent years, Cuba arrested about 78 dissidents in Mar. 2003. On Apr. 11, the government executed 3 men who had hijacked a ferry in Havana bay in a failed attempt to escape to the U.S. Both the crackdown and executions were denounced worldwide. New U.S. sanctions in May 2004 limited Cuban exiles' visits and remittances to the island, provided funds for U.S. govt. TV and radio broadcasts while Cuban dissidents. On July 31, 2006, the ailing Fidel Castro temporarily yielded power to his 75-year-old brother Raúl.

The U.S., Jan. 11, 2002, began using its naval base at Guantánamo Bay to detain prisoners captured in Afghanistan; in mid-2006,

about 450 detainees were still being held at the base. The indefinite detention and aggressive interrogation of Afghan prisoners and others at Guantánamo were criticized by human rights groups. The U.S. Supreme Court ruled, June 29, 2006, that the Bush administration's treatment of detainees and its plan to try them before military commissions violated U.S. law and the Geneva Conventions governing prisoners of war.

Cyprus
Republic of Cyprus

People: Population: 784,301. **Age distrib.** (%) <15: 20.4; 65+: 11.6. **Pop. density:** 219 per sq mi, 84 per sq km. **Urban:** 69.2%. **Ethnic groups:** Greek 85%, Turkish 12%. **Principal languages:** Greek, Turkish (both official), English. **Chief religions:** Greek Orthodox 78%, Muslim 18%.

Geography: Total area: 3,571 sq mi, 9,250 sq km; **Land area:** 3,568 sq mi, 9,240 sq km. **Location:** In eastern Mediterranean Sea, off Turkish coast. **Neighbors:** Nearest are Turkey on N, Syria and Lebanon on E. **Topography:** Two mountain ranges run E-W, separated by a wide, fertile plain. **Capital:** Nicosia, 211,000.

Government: Type: Republic. **Head of state and gov.:** Pres. Tassos Papadopoulos; b. Jan. 7, 1934; in office: Feb. 28, 2003. **Local divisions:** 6 districts. **Defense budget** (2005): $280 mil. **Active troops:** 10,000.

Economy: Industries: food, beverages, textiles, chemicals, metal products, tourism. **Chief crops:** potatoes, citrus, vegetables, barley, grapes, olives. **Natural resources:** copper, pyrites, asbestos, gypsum, timber, salt, marble, clay earth pigment. **Arable land:** 12%. **Livestock** (2005): cattle: 57,000; chickens: 3.6 mil; goats: 460,000; pigs: 498,000; sheep: 295,000. **Fish catch** (2004): 3,992 metric tons. **Electricity prod.** (2004): 3.9 bil kWh. **Labor force** (2004 est.): Republic of Cyprus: agriculture 7.4%, industry 38.2%, services 54.4%. North Cyprus: agriculture 14.5%, industry 29%, services 56.5%.

Finance: Monetary unit: Pound (CYP) (Sept. 2006: 0.45 = $1 U.S.). **GDP** (2005 est.): Greek area: $16.9 bil; Turkish area: $4.5 bil; **per capita GDP:** Greek area: $21,600; Turkish area (2004 est.): $7,135; **GDP growth:** Greek area: 3.7%; Turkish area: 10.6%. **Imports** (2005 est.): Greek area: $5.6 bil; Turkish area: 415.2 mil; partners (2004): Russia 30.2%, Italy 8%, Greece 7.5%, Germany 6.4%, UK 6.1%, Japan 5.8%, France 4.2%. **Exports** (2005 est.): Greek area: $1.2 bil; Turkish area: $69 mil; partners (2004): UK 20.2%, Greece 13.1%, Israel 7.4%, Germany 7%, Belgium 4.6%. **Tourism:** $2.6 bil. **Budget** (2005 est.): $7.1 bil. **Intl. reserves less gold:** $2.93 bil. **Gold:** 470,000 oz t. **Consumer prices:** 2.56%.

Transport: Motor vehicles 302,500 pass. cars, 125,700 comm. vehicles. **Civil aviation:** 2.1 bil pass.-mi; 13 airports. **Chief ports:** Famagusta, Limassol.

Communications: Television sets: 154 per 1000 pop. **Radios:** 406 per 1,000 pop. **Telephone lines:** 420,000. **Daily newspaper circ.:** 69.5 per 1,000 pop. **Internet:** 298,000 users.

Health: Life expect.: 75.4 male; 80.3 female. **Births** (per 1,000 pop.): 12.6. **Deaths** (per 1,000 pop.): 7.7. **Natural inc.:** 0.49%. **Infant mortality** (per 1,000 live births): 7. **AIDS rate:** NA.

Education: Compulsory: ages 6-14. **Literacy:** 96.8%.

Major Intl. Organizations: UN (FAO, IBRD, ILO, IMF, IMO, WHO, WTO), the Commonwealth, EU, OSCE.

Embassy: 2211 R St. NW 20008; 462-5772.

Website: www.moi.gov.cy

The Ottoman Empire held Cyprus, 1571-1878, until it yielded control over the island to Britain. Agitation for enosis (union) with Greece increased after WWII, with the Turkish minority opposed, and broke into violence in 1955-56. In 1959, Britain, Greece, Turkey, and Cypriot leaders approved a plan for an independent republic, with constitutional guarantees for the Turkish minority and permanent division of offices on an ethnic basis. Greek and Turkish Communal Chambers dealt with religion, education, and other matters.

Archbishop Makarios III, formerly the leader of the enosis movement, was elected president, and full independence became final Aug. 16, 1960. Further communal strife led the United Nations to send a peacekeeping force in 1964; its mandate has been repeatedly renewed.

The Cypriot National Guard, led by officers from the army of Greece, seized the government July 15, 1974. On July 20, Turkey invaded the island; Greece mobilized its forces but did not intervene. A cease-fire was arranged but collapsed. By Aug. 16, Turkish forces had occupied the northeastern 40% of the island, despite the presence of UN peacekeeping forces.

Face-to-face talks between the Greek and Turkish Cypriot leaders resumed Dec. 4, 2001, for the first time in 4 years. Turkish Cyprus opened its border with Greek Cyprus Apr. 23, 2003, for the first time since partition. In separate referendums Apr. 24, 2004, 65% of Turkish Cypriot voters accepted a UN-sponsored reunification plan, but 76% of Greek Cypriots rejected it. Still divided, Cyprus became a full member of the EU on May 1. Beginning July 2006, thousands of refugees were evacuated to Cyprus from war-torn Lebanon.

Turkish Republic of Northern Cyprus

A declaration of independence was announced by Turkish-Cypriot leader Rauf Denktash, Nov. 15, 1983. The state is not internationally recognized, although it does have trade relations with some countries. Area of TRNC: 1,295 sq mi; pop. (2001 est.): 208,886, 99% Turkish. Capital: Lefkosa (Nicosia).

Czech Republic

People: Population: 10,235,455. **Age distrib.** (%) <15: 14.4; 65+: 14.5. **Pop. density:** 343 per sq mi, 132 per sq km. **Urban:** 74.3%. **Ethnic groups:** Czech 81%, Moravian 13%, Slovak 3%. **Principal languages:** Czech (official), German, Polish, Romani. **Chief religions:** Roman Catholic 27%, Unaffiliated 59%, Protestant 5%, Orthodox 3%.

Geography: Total area: 30,450 sq mi, 78,866 sq km; **Land area:** 29,836 sq mi, 77,276 sq km. **Location:** In E central Europe. **Neighbors:** Poland on N, Germany on N and W, Austria on S, Slovakia on E and SE. **Topography:** Bohemia, in W, is a plateau surrounded by mountains; Moravia is hilly. **Capital:** Prague, 1,171,000.

Government: Type: Republic. **Head of state:** Vaclav Klaus; b. June 19, 1941; in office: Mar. 7, 2003. **Head of gov.:** Prime Min. Mirek Topolanek; b. May 15, 1956; in office: Sept. 4, 2006. **Local divisions:** 13 regions and Prague. **Defense budget** (2005): $2.2 bil. **Active troops:** 22,272.

Economy: Industries: metallurgy, machinery, motor vehicles, glass, armaments. **Chief crops:** wheat, potatoes, sugar beets, hops, fruit. **Natural resources:** coal, kaolin, clay, graphite, timber. **Arable land:** 41%. **Crude oil reserves** (2005): 15 mil bbls. **Livestock** (2005): cattle: 1.4 mil; chickens: 12.4 mil; goats: 12,623; pigs: 2.9 mil; sheep: 140,197. **Fish catch** (2004): 23,912 metric tons. **Electricity prod.** (2004): 79.1 bil kWh. **Labor force** (2002 est.): agriculture 4%, industry 38%, services 58%.

Finance: Monetary unit: Koruna (CZK) (Sept. 2006: 22.23 = $1 U.S.). **GDP** (2005 est.): $199.4 bil; **per capita GDP:** $19,500; **GDP growth:** 6%. **Imports** (2005 est.): $76.6 bil; partners (2004): Germany 36.2%, Austria 5.6%, Italy 5.4%, France 4.8%, Netherlands 4.7%, Slovakia 4.7%. **Exports** (2005 est.): $78.4 bil; partners (2004): Germany 36.2%, Slovakia 9.1%, Austria 6.1%, Poland 5.5%. **Tourism:** $4.9 bil. **Budget** (2005 est.): $53 bil. **Intl. reserves less gold:** $20.52 bil. **Gold:** 440,000 oz t. **Consumer prices:** 1.85%.

Transport: Railroad: Length: 5,929 mi. **Motor vehicles** 3.7 mil pass. cars, 414,000 comm. vehicles. **Civil aviation:** 2.4 bil pass.-mi; 46 airports. **Chief ports:** Decin, Prague, Ustinad Labem.

Communications: TV sets: 487 per 1,000 pop. **Radios:** 803 per 1,000 pop. **Telephone lines:** 3.2 mil. **Daily newspaper circ.:** NA. **Internet:** 4.8 mil users.

Health: Life expect.: 72.9 male; 79.7 female. **Births** (per 1,000 pop.): 9. **Deaths** (per 1,000 pop.): 10.6. **Natural inc.:** −0.16%. **Infant mortality** (per 1,000 live births): 3.9. **AIDS rate:** 0.1%.

Education: Compulsory: ages 6-15. **Literacy:** 99.9%.

Major Intl. Organizations: UN (FAO, IBRD, ILO, IMF, IMO, WHO, WTO), EU, NATO, OECD, OSCE.

Embassy: 3900 Spring of Freedom St. NW 20008; 274-9100. **Website:** www.czech.cz

Bohemia and Moravia were part of the Great Moravian Empire in the 9th cent. and later became part of the Holy Roman Empire. Under the kings of Bohemia, Prague in the 14th cent. was the cultural center of Central Europe. Bohemia and Hungary became part of Austria-Hungary.

In 1914-18 Thomas G. Masaryk and Eduard Benes formed a provisional government with the support of Slovak leaders including Milan Stefanik. They proclaimed the Republic of Czechoslovakia Oct. 28, 1918.

Czechoslovakia

By 1938 Nazi Germany had worked up disaffection among German-speaking citizens in Sudetenland and demanded its cession. British Prime Min. Neville Chamberlain, with the acquiescence of France, signed with Hitler at Munich, Sept. 30, 1938, an agreement to the cession, with a guarantee of peace by Hitler and Mussolini. Germany occupied Sudetenland Oct. 1-2.

Hitler on Mar. 15, 1939, dissolved Czechoslovakia, made protectorates of Bohemia and Moravia, and supported the autonomy of Slovakia, proclaimed independent Mar. 14, 1939.

Soviet troops with some Czechoslovak contingents entered eastern Czechoslovakia in 1944 and reached Prague in May 1945; Benes returned as president. In May 1946 elections, the Communist Party won 38% of the votes, and Benes accepted Klement Gottwald, a Communist, as prime minister.

In Feb. 1948, the Communists seized power in advance of scheduled elections. In May 1948 a new constitution was approved. Benes refused to sign it. On May 30 the voters were offered a one-slate ballot and the Communists won full control. Benes resigned June 7 and Gottwald became president. The country was renamed the Czechoslovakia Socialist Republic. A harsh Stalinist period followed, with complete and violent suppression of all opposition.

In Jan. 1968 a liberalization movement spread through Czechoslovakia. Antonin Novotny, long the Stalinist ruler, was deposed as party leader and succeeded by Alexander Dubcek, a Slovak, who supported democratic reforms. On Mar. 22 Novotny resigned as president and was succeeded by Gen. Ludvik Svoboda. On Apr. 6, Prem. Joseph Lenart resigned and was succeeded by Oldrich Cernik, a reformer.

In July 1968, the USSR and 4 Warsaw Pact nations demanded an end to liberalization. On Aug. 20, the Soviet, Polish, East German, Hungarian, and Bulgarian armies invaded Czechoslovakia. Despite demonstrations and riots by students and workers, press censorship was imposed, liberal leaders were ousted from office and promises of loyalty to Soviet policies were made by some old-line Communist Party leaders.

On Apr. 17, 1969, Dubcek resigned as leader of the Communist Party and was succeeded by Gustav Husak. In Jan. 1970, Cernik was ousted. Censorship was tightened, and the Communist Party expelled a third of its members. In 1973, amnesty was offered to some of the 40,000 who fled the country after the 1968 invasion, but repressive policies continued.

More than 700 leading Czechoslovak intellectuals and former party leaders signed a human rights manifesto in 1977, called Charter 77, prompting a renewed crackdown by the regime.

The police crushed the largest antigovernment protests since 1968, when tens of thousands of demonstrators took to the streets of Prague, Nov. 17, 1989. As protesters demanded free elections, the Communist Party leadership resigned Nov. 24; millions went on strike Nov. 27.

On Dec. 10, 1989, the first cabinet in 41 years without a Communist majority took power; Vaclav Havel, playwright and human rights campaigner, was chosen president, Dec. 29. In Mar. 1990 the country was officially renamed the Czech and Slovak Federal Republic. Havel failed to win reelection July 3, 1992; his bid was blocked by a Slovak-led coalition.

Slovakia declared sovereignty, July 17. Czech and Slovak leaders agreed, July 23, on a basic plan for a peaceful division of Czechoslovakia into 2 independent states.

Czech Republic

Czechoslovakia split into 2 separate states—the Czech Republic and Slovakia—on Jan. 1, 1993. Havel was elected president of the Czech Republic on Jan. 26. Record floods in July 1997 caused more than $1.7 bil in damage. The country became a full member of NATO on Mar. 12, 1999. Floods Aug. 2002 damaged cultural treasures in Prague.

Vaclav Klaus was chosen Feb. 28, 2003, to replace the retiring Havel. After Czech voters June 13-14, 2003, endorsed joining the EU, the nation became a full EU member May 1, 2004. When his Social Democratic Party fared poorly in EU elections June 11-12, Prime Min. Vladimir Spidla resigned; his successor, Stanislav Gross, 34, was Europe's youngest head of government. A scandal surrounding his 1999 purchase of a luxury apartment in Prague forced Gross to resign Apr. 25, 2005. Inconclusive parliamentary elections, June 2-3, 2006, led to a prolonged political deadlock, after which a minority center-right government took office Sept. 4.

Denmark
Kingdom of Denmark

People: Population: 5,450,661. **Age distrib.** (%) <15: 18.7; 65+: 15.2. **Pop. density:** 333 per sq mi, 128 per sq km. **Urban:** 85.3%. **Ethnic groups:** Mainly Danish; German minority in S. **Principal languages:** Danish (official), Faroese, Greenlandic (an Inuit dialect), German. **Chief religion: Chief religions:** Evangelical Lutheran 95% (official), other Christian 3%, Muslim 2%.

Geography: Total area: 16,639 sq mi, 43,094 sq km; **Land area:** 16,368 sq mi, 42,394 sq km. **Location:** In N Europe, separating the North and Baltic seas. **Neighbors:** Germany on S, Norway on NW, Sweden on NE. **Topography:** Denmark consists of the Jutland Peninsula and about 500 islands, 100 inhabited. The land is flat or gently rolling and is almost all in productive use. **Capital:** Copenhagen, 1,088,000.

Government: Type: Constitutional monarchy. **Head of state:** Queen Margrethe II; b. Apr. 16, 1940; in office: Jan. 14, 1972. **Head of gov.:** Prime Min. Anders Fogh Rasmussen; b. Jan. 26, 1953; in office: Nov. 27, 2001. **Local divisions:** 14 counties, 2 kommunes. **Defense budget** (2005): $3.2 bil. **Active troops:** 21,180.

Economy: Industries: food proc., machinery, textiles & clothing, chemicals, electronics, constr., furniture. **Chief crops:** barley, wheat, potatoes, sugar beets. **Natural resources:** oil, nat. gas, fish, salt, limestone, stone, gravel, sand. **Crude oil reserves** (2005): 1.3 bil bbls. **Arable land:** 60%. **Livestock** (2005): cattle: 1.6 mil; chickens: 16 mil; pigs: 13.3 mil; sheep: 141,000. **Fish catch** (2004): 1,132,238 metric tons. **Electricity prod.** (2004): 38 bil kWh. **Labor force** (2004 est.): agriculture 3%, industry 21%, services 76%.

Finance: Monetary unit: Krone (DKK) (Sept. 2006: 5.82 = $1 U.S.). **GDP** (2005 est.): $188.1 bil; **per capita GDP:** $34,600; **GDP growth:** 3.4%. **Imports** (2005 est.): $74.7 bil; partners (2004): Germany 22.9%, Sweden 12.4%, Netherlands 7.6%, France 5.6%, UK 5.4%, Norway 5%, Italy 4.3%. **Exports** (2005 est.): $85 bil; partners (2004): Germany 16.9%, Sweden 14%, UK 6.9%, U.S. 5.4%, France 5.2%, Netherlands 5.1%, Norway 4.8%. **Tourism:** $5,265 mil. **Budget** (2005 est.): $135 bil. **Intl. reserves less gold:** $23.04 bil. **Gold:** 2.14 mil oz t. **Consumer prices:** 1.81%.

Transport: Railroad: Length: 1,632 mi. **Motor vehicles** 1.89 mil pass. cars, 426,900 comm. vehicles. **Civil aviation:** 4.6 bil pass.-mi; 28 airports. **Chief ports:** Copenhagen, Alborg, Arhus, Odense.

Communications: TV sets: 776 per 1,000 pop. **Radios:** 1,325 per 1,000 pop. **Telephone lines:** 3.4 mil. **Daily newspaper circ.:** 283.2 per 1,000 pop. **Internet:** 3.8 mil users.

Health: Life expect.: 75.5 male; 80.2 female. **Births** (per 1,000 pop.): 11.1. **Deaths** (per 1,000 pop.): 10.4. **Natural inc.:** 0.08%. **Infant mortality** (per 1,000 live births): 4.5. **AIDS rate:** 0.2%.

Education: Compulsory: ages 7-16. **Literacy:** 100%.

Major Intl. Organizations: UN and all of its specialized agencies, EU, NATO, OECD, OSCE.

Embassy: 3200 Whitehaven St. NW 20008; 234-4300. **Website:** denmark.dk

The origin of Copenhagen dates back to ancient times, when the fishing and trading place named Havn (port) grew up on a cluster of islets, but Bishop Absalon (1128-1201) is regarded as the actual founder of the city.

Danes formed a large component of the Viking raiders in the early Middle Ages. The Danish kingdom was a major power until the 17th cent., when it lost its land in southern Sweden. Norway was separated in 1815, and Schleswig-Holstein in 1864. Northern Schleswig was returned in 1920.

Voters ratified the Maastricht Treaty, the basic document of the European Union, in May 1993, after rejecting it in 1992. On Sept. 28, 2000, Danes voted not to join the euro currency zone. The Danish newspaper *Jyllands-Posten* published, Sept. 30, 2005, cartoon images of the prophet Muhammad, offensive to Muslims; the caricatures, republished elsewhere, triggered violent protests and a boycott of Danish products in Islamic countries in early 2006.

The **Faroe Islands** in the North Atlantic, about 300 mi NW of the Shetlands, and 850 mi from Denmark proper, 18 inhabited, have an area of 540 sq mi and pop. (2006 est.) of 47,246. They are an administrative division of Denmark, self-governing in most matters. Torshavn is the capital. Fish is a primary export (641,265 metric tons in 2004).

Greenland (Kalaallit Nunaat)

Greenland, a huge island between the North Atlantic and the Polar Sea, is separated from the North American continent by Davis Strait and Baffin Bay. Its total area is 836,330 sq mi, 84% of which is ice-capped. Most of the island is a lofty plateau 9,000 to 10,000 ft in altitude. The average thickness of the cap is 1,000 ft. Scientists point to accelerated melting of Greenland's ice sheet in recent years as evidence of global warming. The population (2006 est.) is 56,361. Under the 1953 Danish constitution the colony became an integral part of the realm with representatives in the Folketing (Danish legislature). The Danish parliament, 1978, approved home rule for Greenland, effective May 1, 1979. With home rule, Greenlandic place names came into official use. The technically correct name for Greenland is now Kalaallit Nunaat; the official name for its capital is Nuuk, rather than Godthab. Fish is the principal export (261,302 metric tons in 2004).

Djibouti
Republic of Djibouti

People: Population: 486,530. **Age distrib.** (%) <15: 43.3; 65+: 3.3. **Pop. density:** 54 per sq mi, 21 per sq km. **Urban:** 83.7%. **Ethnic groups:** Somali 60%, Afar 35%. **Principal languages:** French, Arabic (both official); Somali, Afar. **Chief religions:** Muslim 94%, Christian 6%.

Geography: Total area: 8,880 sq mi, 23,000 sq km; **Land area:** 8,873 sq mi, 22,980 sq km. **Location:** On E coast of Africa, separated from Arabian Peninsula by the strategically vital strait of Bab el-Mandeb. **Neighbors:** Ethiopia on W and SW, Eritrea on NW, Somalia on SE. **Topography:** The territory, divided into a low coastal plain, mountains behind, and an interior plateau, is arid, sandy, and desolate. The climate is generally hot and dry. **Capital:** Djibouti, 555,000.

Government: Type: Republic. **Head of state:** Pres. Ismail Omar Guelleh; b. Nov. 27, 1947; in office: May 8, 1999. **Head of gov.:** Prime Min. Dileita Mohamed Dileita; b. Mar. 12, 1958; in office: Mar. 7, 2001. **Local divisions:** 5 districts. **Defense budget** (2005): $26 mil. **Active troops:** 9,850.

Economy: Industries: constr., agricult. proc. **Chief crops:** fruits, vegetables. **Natural resources:** geothermal areas. **Livestock** (2005): cattle: 297,000; goats: 512,000; sheep: 466,000. **Fish catch** (2004): 260 metric tons. **Electricity prod.** (2004): 200 mil kWh.

Finance: Monetary unit: Franc (DJF) (Sept. 2006: 175.16 = $1 U.S.). **GDP** (2002 est.): $619 mil; **per capita GDP:** $1,300; **GDP growth:** 3.5%. **Imports** (2004 est.): $987 mil; partners (2004): Saudi Arabia 21%, Ethiopia 9.9%, India 8.2%, China 7.8%, U.S. 6.1%, France 6%. **Exports** (2004 est.): $250 mil; partners (2004): Somalia 63.9%, Yemen 22.6%, Ethiopia 5%. **Tourism** (1995): $4 mil. **Budget** (1999 est.): $182 mil. **Intl. reserves less gold:** $62 mil.

Transport: Railroad: Length: 62 mi. **Motor vehicles:** 13,500 pass. cars, 3,000 comm. vehicles. **Civil Aviation:** NA; 3 airports. **Chief port:** Djibouti.

Communications: TV sets: 48 per 1,000 pop. **Radios:** 86 per 1,000 pop. **Telephone lines:** 11,100. **Daily newspaper circ.:** NA. **Internet:** 9,000 users.

Health: Life expect.: 41.9 male; 44.5 female. **Births** (per 1,000 pop.): 39.5. **Deaths** (per 1,000 pop.): 19.3. **Natural inc.:** 2.02%. **Infant mortality** (per 1,000 live births): 102.4. **AIDS rate:** 3.1%.

Education: Compulsory: ages 6-15. **Literacy:** 67.9%.

Major Intl. Organizations: UN (FAO, IBRD, ILO, IMF, IMO, WHO, WTO), AL, AU.

Embassy: 1156 15th St. NW, Ste. 515, 20005; 331-0270.

Website: djibouti.usembassy.gov

France gained control of the territory in stages between 1862 and 1900. As French Somaliland it became an overseas territory of France in 1945; in 1967 it was renamed the French Territory of the Afars and the Issas.

Ethiopia and Somalia have renounced their claims to the area, but each has accused the other of trying to gain control. There were clashes between Afars (ethnically related to Ethiopians) and Issas (related to Somalis) in 1976. Immigrants from both countries contin-

ued to enter the country up to independence, which came June 27, 1977.

French aid is the mainstay of the economy, as well as assistance from Arab countries. A peace accord Dec. 1994 ended a 3-year-long uprising by Afar rebels. As of early 2006, at least 2,600 French and 1,800 U.S. troops were based in Djibouti.

Dominica
Commonwealth of Dominica

People: Population: 68,910. **Age distrib.** (%) <15: 26.1; 65+: 7.9. **Pop. density:** 236 per sq mi, 91 per sq km. **Urban:** 72.0%. **Ethnic groups:** Black, Creole, White, Carib Amerindian. **Principal languages:** English (official), French patois. **Chief religions:** Roman Catholic 77%, Protestant 15%.

Geography: Total area: 291 sq mi, 754 sq km; **Land area:** 291 sq mi, 754 sq km. **Location:** In Eastern Caribbean, most northerly Windward Isl. **Neighbors:** Guadeloupe to N, Martinique to S. **Topography:** Mountainous, a central ridge running from N to S, terminating in cliffs; volcanic in origin, with numerous thermal springs; rich deep topsoil on leeward side, red tropical clay on windward coast. **Capital** (2004): Roseau, 20,200.

Government: Type: Parliamentary democracy. **Head of state:** Pres. Nicholas Liverpool; b. 1934; in office: Oct. 2, 2003. **Head of gov.:** Prime Min. Roosevelt Skerrit; b. June 8, 1972; in office: Jan. 8, 2004. **Local divisions:** 10 parishes.

Economy: Industries: soap, coconut oil, tourism, copra, furniture, cement blocks, shoes. **Chief crops:** bananas, citrus, mangoes, coconuts, cocoa. **Natural resources:** timber, hydropower. **Arable land:** 9%. **Livestock** (2005): cattle: 13,400; chickens: 190,000; goats: 9,700; pigs: 5,000; sheep: 7,600. **Fish catch** (2004): 1,023 metric tons. **Electricity prod.** (2004): 80 mil kWh. **Labor force:** agriculture 40%, industry and commerce 32%, services 28%.

Finance: Monetary unit: East Caribbean Dollar (XCD) (Sept. 2006: 2.67 = $1 U.S.). **GDP** (2003 est.): $384 mil; **per capita GDP:** $5,500; **GDP growth:** -1%. **Imports** (2004 est.): $234 mil; partners (2004): China 20.1%, U.S. 18.7%, Trinidad and Tobago 10.2%, UK 7.2%, South Korea 5.3%, Japan 4.5%. **Exports** (2004 est.): $74 mil; partners (2004): UK 21.5%, Jamaica 20%, Antigua and Barbuda 8.3%, Guyana 7%, Japan 5.3%, U.S. 4.6%, Trinidad and Tobago 4.5%, Poland 4%. **Tourism:** $51 mil. **Budget** (2001): $84.4 mil. **Intl. reserves less gold:** $34 mil. **Consumer prices:** 1.74%.

Transport: Motor vehicles: 8,700 pass. cars, 3,400 comm. vehicles. **Civil Aviation:** NA; 2 airports. **Chief port:** Roseau.

Communications: TV sets: 232 per 1,000 pop. **Radios:** 648 per 1,000 pop. **Telephone lines:** 21,000. **Internet:** 18,500 users.

Health: Life expect.: 72 male; 77.9 female. **Births** (per 1,000 pop.): 15.3. **Deaths** (per 1,000 pop.): 6.7. **Natural inc.:** 0.85%. **Infant mortality** (per 1,000 live births): 13.7. **AIDS rate:** NA.

Education: Compulsory: ages 5-16. **Literacy:** 94%.

Major Intl. Organizations: UN (FAO, IBRD, ILO, IMF, IMO, WHO, WTO), Caricom, the Commonwealth, OAS, OECS.

Embassy: 3216 New Mexico Ave. NW 20016; 364-6781.

Website: www.dominica.dm

A British colony since 1805, Dominica was granted self-government in 1967. Independence was achieved Nov. 3, 1978.

Hurricane David struck, Aug. 30, 1979, devastating the island and destroying the banana plantations, Dominica's economic mainstay. Coups were attempted in 1980 and 1981.

Dominica participated in the 1983 U.S.-led invasion of nearby Grenada. Prime Min. Pierre Charles, 49, died of a heart attack Jan. 6, 2004, and was succeeded by Roosevelt Skerrit.

Dominican Republic

People: Population: 9,226,157. **Age distrib.** (%) <15: 32.5; 65+: 5.6. **Pop. density:** 493 per sq mi, 190 per sq km. **Urban:** 59.3%. **Ethnic groups:** Creole 73%, White 16%, Black 11%. **Principal languages:** Spanish (official). **Chief religion:** Roman Catholic 95%.

Geography: Total area: 18,815 sq mi, 48,730 sq km; **Land area:** 18,680 sq mi, 48,380 sq km. **Location:** In West Indies, sharing isl. of Hispaniola with Haiti. **Neighbors:** Haiti on W, Puerto Rico (U.S.) to E. **Topography:** The Cordillera Central range crosses the center of the country, rising to over 10,000 ft., highest in the Caribbean. The Cibao Valley to the N is major agricultural area. **Capital:** Santo Domingo, 2,022,000.

Government: Type: Republic. **Head of state and gov.:** Pres. Leonel Fernández Reyna; b. Dec. 26, 1953; in office: Aug. 16, 2004. **Local divisions:** 29 provinces and national district. **Defense budget** (2005): $190 mil. **Active troops:** 24,500.

Economy: Industries: tourism, sugar proc., mining, textiles, cement, tobacco. **Chief crops:** sugarcane, coffee, cotton, cocoa, tobacco, rice, beans. **Natural resources:** nickel, bauxite, gold, silver. **Arable land:** 21%. **Livestock** (2005): cattle: 2.2 mil; chickens: 47.5 mil; goats: 190,000; pigs: 580,000; sheep: 123,000. **Fish catch** (2004): 16,223 metric tons. **Electricity prod.** (2004): 150 mil kWh. **Labor force** (1998 est.): agriculture 17%, industry 24.3%, services 58.7%.

Finance: Monetary unit: Peso (DOP) (Sept. 2006: 33.14 = $1 U.S.). **GDP** (2005 est.): $63.7 bil; **per capita GDP:** $7,000; **GDP growth:** 9.3%. **Imports** (2005 est.): $9.7 bil; partners (2004): U.S. 49%, Venezuela 13.8%, Mexico 4.6%, Colombia 4.2%. **Exports** (2005 est.): $5.8 bil; partners (2004): U.S. 79.7%, Canada 1.8%,

Haiti 1.7%. **Tourism:** $3,110 mil. **Budget** (2005): $5.5 bil. **Intl. reserves less gold:** $1.29 bil. **Gold:** 20,000 oz t. **Consumer prices:** 4.19%.

Transport: Railroad: Length: 321 mi. **Motor vehicles** 561,300 pass. cars, 284,700 comm. vehicles. **Civil aviation:** 3.1 mil pass.-mi; 14 airports. **Chief ports:** Santo Domingo, San Pedro de Macoris, Puerto Plata.

Communications: TV sets: 96 per 1,000 pop. **Radios:** 178 per 1,000 pop. **Telephone lines:** 894,500. **Daily newspaper circ.:** NA. **Internet:** 800,000 users.

Health: Life expect.: 71 male; 74.5 female. **Births** (per 1,000 pop.): 23.2. **Deaths** (per 1,000 pop.): 5.4. **Natural inc.:** 1.78%. **Infant mortality** (per 1,000 live births): 29. **AIDS rate:** 1.1%.

Education: Compulsory: ages 5-13. **Literacy:** 87%.

Major Intl. Organizations: UN (FAO, IBRD, ILO, IMF, IMO, WHO, WTO), OAS.

Embassy: 1715 22d St. NW 20008; 332-6280.

Website: www.domrep.org

Carib and Arawak Indians inhabited the island of Hispaniola when Columbus landed in 1492. The city of Santo Domingo, founded 1496, is the oldest settlement by Europeans in the hemisphere and has the supposed ashes of Columbus in an elaborate tomb in its ancient cathedral.

The western third of the island was ceded to France in 1697. Santo Domingo itself was ceded to France in 1795. Haitian leader Toussaint L'Ouverture seized it, 1801. Spain returned intermittently 1803-21, as several native republics came and went. Haiti ruled again, 1822-44; Spanish occupation occurred 1861-63.

The country was occupied by U.S. Marines from 1916 to 1924, when a constitutionally elected government was installed.

In 1930, Gen. Rafael Leonidas Trujillo Molina was elected president. Trujillo ruled brutally until his assassination in 1961. Pres. Joaquín Balaguer, appointed by Trujillo in 1960, resigned under pressure in 1962.

Juan Bosch, elected president in the first free elections in 38 years, was overthrown in 1963. On Apr. 24, 1965, a revolt was launched by followers of Bosch and others, including a few Communists. Four days later U.S. Marines intervened against pro-Bosch forces. Token units were later sent by 5 South American countries as a peacekeeping force. A provisional government supervised a June 1966 election, in which Balaguer defeated Bosch. Balaguer remained in office for most of the next 28 years, but his May 1994 reelection was widely denounced as fraudulent. He cut short his term and on June 30, 1996, Leonel Fernández Reyna was elected.

Hurricane Georges struck Sept. 22, 1998, causing extensive property damage and claiming more than 200 lives. The leftist candidate, Hipólito Mejía, won a presidential vote May 16, 2000. With the nation reeling from a banking scandal and soaring inflation, Fernández defeated Mejía in the election of May 16, 2004. Floods and mudslides in late May killed about 395 people. A fight between rival prison gangs led to a fire, Mar. 7, 2005, in which 136 inmates died.

East Timor
(*See* Timor-Leste)

Ecuador
Republic of Ecuador

People: Population: 13,547,510. **Age distrib.** (%) <15: 33; 65+: 5. **Pop. density:** 126 per sq mi, 48 per sq km. **Urban:** 61.8%. **Ethnic groups:** Mestizo 65%, Amerindian 25%, Black 3%. **Principal languages:** Spanish (official), Amerindian languages (especially Quechua). **Chief religion:** Roman Catholic 95%.

Geography: Total area: 109,483 sq mi, 283,560 sq km; **Land area:** 106,889 sq mi, 276,840 sq km. **Location:** In NW South America, on Pacific coast, astride the Equator. **Neighbors:** Colombia on N, Peru on E and S. **Topography:** Two ranges of Andes run N and S, splitting the country into 3 zones: hot, humid lowlands on the coast; temperate highlands between the ranges; and rainy, tropical lowlands to the E. **Capital:** Quito, 1,514,000. **Cities (urban aggr.):** Guayaquil, 2,387,000.

Government: Type: Republic. **Head of state and gov.:** Pres. Alfredo Palacio González; b. Jan. 22, 1939; in office: Apr. 20, 2005. **Local divisions:** 22 provinces. **Defense budget** (2005): $593 mil. **Active troops:** 46,500.

Economy: Industries: oil, food proc., textiles, metal work, paper & wood products. **Chief crops:** bananas, coffee, cocoa, rice, potatoes, cassava, plantains, sugarcane. **Natural resources:** oil, fish, timber, hydropower. **Crude oil reserves** (2005): 4.6 bil bbls. **Arable land:** 6%. **Livestock** (2005): cattle: 5 mil; chickens: 104.2 mil; goats: 250,000; pigs: 1.9 mil; sheep: 2.6 mil. **Fish catch** (2004): 399,390 metric tons. **Electricity prod.** (2004): 12.2 bil kWh. **Labor force** (2001): agriculture 8%, industry 24%, services 68%.

Finance: Monetary unit: U.S. Dollar (USD) (Sept. 2006: 1.00 = $1 U.S.). **GDP** (2005 est.): $56.9 bil; **per capita GDP:** $4,300; **GDP growth:** 3.9%. **Imports** (2005 est.): $8.4 bil; partners (2004): U.S. 24.5%, Colombia 12.7%, Venezuela 8.3%, Brazil 5.8%, Chile 4.9%, China 4.8%, Japan 4.3%. **Exports** (2005 est.): $9.2 bil; partners (2004): U.S. 48.3%, Colombia 5.5%, Germany 4.8%. **Tourism:** $462 mil. **Budget** (2005 est.): $8.2 bil. **Intl. reserves less gold:** $1.2 bil. **Gold:** 850,000 oz t. **Consumer prices:** 2.41%.

Transport: Railroad: Length: 600 mi. **Motor vehicles:** 343,800 pass. cars, 296,500 comm. vehicles. **Civil aviation:** 389 mil pass.-

mi; 98 airports. **Chief ports:** Guayaquil, Manta, Esmeraldas, Puerto Bolivar.

Communications: TV sets: 213 per 1,000 pop. **Radios:** 406 per 1,000 pop. **Telephone lines:** 1.7 mil. **Daily newspaper circ.:** 98.2 per 1,000 pop. **Internet:** 624,600 users.

Health: Life expect.: 73.5 male; 79.4 female. **Births** (per 1,000 pop.): 22.3. **Deaths** (per 1,000 pop.): 4.2. **Natural inc.:** 1.81%. **Infant mortality** (per 1,000 live births): 22.9. **AIDS rate:** 0.3%.

Education: Compulsory: ages 5-14. **Literacy:** 91%.

Major Intl. Organizations: UN (FAO, IBRD, ILO, IMF, IMO, WHO, WTO), OAS.

Embassy: 2535 15th St. NW 20009; 234-7200.

Website: www.ecuador.org/main.htm

The region, which was the northern Inca empire, was conquered by Spain in 1533. Liberation forces defeated the Spanish May 24, 1822, near Quito. Ecuador became part of the Great Colombia Republic but seceded, May 13, 1830.

Ecuadoran Indians staged protests in the 1990s to demand greater rights. A border war with Peru flared from Jan. 26, 1995, until a truce took effect Mar. 1. Vice Pres. Alberto Dahik resigned and fled Ecuador, Oct. 11, 1995, to avoid arrest on corruption charges. Elected president in a runoff, July 7, 1996, Abdalá Bucaram—a populist known as El Loco, or "The Crazy One"—imposed stiff price increases and other austerity measures. His rising unpopularity and erratic behavior led the National Congress, Feb. 6, 1997, to dismiss him for "mental incapacity."

Jamil Mahuad Witt, mayor of Quito, won a presidential runoff election July 12, 1998. In Sept. 1998 and Mar. 1999 he imposed emergency measures to cope with a continuing economic crisis. Opposed by Indian groups and military leaders, he was ousted Jan. 21, 2000, and succeeded by Vice Pres. Gustavo Noboa Bejarano. Noboa went ahead with a plan introduced by Mahuad to replace the sucre with the U.S. dollar as Ecuador's currency. Lucio Gutiérrez Borbúa, a leader in the 2000 coup, won a presidential runoff Nov. 24, 2002. Noboa, under investigation for financial mismanagement, went into exile Aug. 23, 2003.

Gutiérrez imposed economic austerity measures, purged opponents from the supreme court, Dec. 2004, and then dissolved the court, Apr. 15, 2005. With street protests rising, the military withdrew support of Gutiérrez. Congress ousted him Apr. 20, and Vice Pres. Alfredo Palacio González became president. The U.S. suspended free-trade talks after Ecuador, May 15, 2006, took over oil assets belonging to U.S.-based Occidental Pretroleum.

The **Galápagos Islands**, pop. (2001 est.) 16,000, about 600 mi to the W, are the home of huge tortoises and other unusual animals. The oil tanker *Jessica* ran aground Jan. 16, 2001, off San Cristóbal Is., spilling some 185,000 gallons of fuel.

Egypt
Arab Republic of Egypt

People: Population: 78,887,007. **Age distrib.** (%) <15: 32.6; 65+: 4.5. **Pop. density:** 205 per sq mi, 79 per sq km. **Urban:** 42.1%. **Ethnic groups:** Egyptian Arab 99%. **Principal languages:** Arabic (official); English, French. **Chief religions:** Muslim (official; mostly Sunni) 94%, Coptic Christian and other 6%.

Geography: Total area: 386,662 sq mi, 1,001,450 sq km; **Land area:** 384,345 sq mi, 995,450 sq km. **Location:** Northeast corner of Africa. **Neighbors:** Libya on W, Sudan on S, Israel and Gaza Strip on E. **Topography:** Almost entirely desolate and barren, with hills and mountains in E and along Nile. The Nile Valley, where most of the people live, stretches 550 miles. **Capital:** Cairo, 11,128,000. **Cities (urban aggr.):** Alexandria, 3,770,000.

Government: Type: Republic. **Head of state:** Pres. Hosni Mubarak; b. May 4, 1928; in office: Oct. 14, 1981. **Head of gov.:** Prime Min. Ahmed Nazif; b. July 8, 1952; in office: July 14, 2004. **Local divisions:** 26 governorates. **Defense budget** (2005): $2.5 bil. **Active troops:** 468,500.

Economy: Industries: textiles, food proc., tourism, chemicals, hydrocarbons, constr., cement, metals. **Chief crops:** cotton, rice, corn, wheat, beans, fruits, vegetables. **Natural resources:** oil, nat. gas, iron ore, phosphates, mang., limestone, gypsum, talc, asbestos, lead, zinc. **Crude oil reserves** (2005): 3.7 bil bbls. **Arable land:** 2%. **Livestock** (2005): cattle: 4.5 mil; chickens: 95 mil; goats: 4 mil; pigs: 30,000; sheep: 5.2 mil. **Fish catch** (2004): 865,029 metric tons. **Electricity prod.** (2004): 91.7 bil kWh. **Labor force** (2001 est.): agriculture 32%, industry 17%, services 51%.

Finance: Monetary unit: Pound (EGP) (Sept. 2006: 5.75 = $1 U.S.). **GDP** (2005 est.): $303.5 bil; **per capita GDP:** $3,900; **GDP growth:** 4.9%. **Imports** (2005 est.): $24.1 bil; partners (2004): U.S. 13.2%, Germany 7.2%, Italy 7.1%, France 6.1%, China 5.5%, UK 4.9%, Saudi Arabia 4.4%. **Exports** (2005 est.): $14.3 bil; partners (2004): Italy 13.1%, U.S. 11.6%, UK 7.5%, Germany 5.1%, Spain 4.5%, France 4.2%. **Tourism:** $6.1 bil. **Budget** (2005 est.): $27.7 bil. **Intl. reserves less gold:** $14.42 bil. **Gold:** 2.43 mil oz t. **Consumer prices:** 4.87%.

Transport: Railroad: Length: 3,146 mi. **Motor vehicles** 1.88 mil pass. cars, 686,000 comm. vehicles. **Civil aviation:** 5.6 bil pass.-mi; 72 airports. **Chief ports:** Alexandria, Port Said, Suez, Damietta.

Communications: TV sets: 170 per 1,000 pop. **Radios:** 317 per 1,000 pop. **Telephone lines:** 10.4 mil. **Daily newspaper circ.:** 31.3 per 1,000 pop. **Internet:** 5 mil users.

Health: Life expect.: 68.8 male; 73.9 female. **Births** (per 1,000 pop.): 22.9. **Deaths** (per 1,000 pop.): 5.2. **Natural inc.:** 1.77%. **Infant mortality** (per 1,000 live births): 31.3. **AIDS rate:** <0.1%.

Education: Compulsory: ages 6-13. **Literacy:** 71.4%.

Major Intl. Organizations: UN (FAO, IBRD, ILO, IMF, IMO, WHO, WTO), AL, AU.

Embassy: 3521 International Ct. NW 20008; 895-5400.

Website: www.sis.gov.eg

Archaeological records of ancient Egyptian civilization date back to 4000 BCE. A unified kingdom arose around 3200 BCE and extended its way south into Nubia and as far north as Syria. A high culture of rulers and priests was built on an economic base of serfdom, fertile soil, and annual flooding of the Nile.

Imperial decline facilitated conquest by Asian invaders (Hyksos, Assyrians). The last native dynasty fell in 341 BCE to the Persians, who were in turn replaced by Greeks (Alexander and the Ptolemies), Romans, Byzantines, and Arabs, who introduced Islam and the Arabic language. The ancient Egyptian language is preserved only in Coptic Christian liturgy.

Egypt was ruled as part of larger Islamic empires for many centuries. Britain intervened in Egypt in 1882 and ruled the country as a protectorate, 1914-22. A 1936 treaty strengthened Egyptian autonomy, but Britain retained bases in Egypt and a condominium over the Sudan. When the state of Israel was proclaimed in 1948, Egypt joined other Arab nations invading Israel and was defeated. In 1951 Egypt abrogated the 1936 treaty; the Sudan became independent in 1956.

An uprising on July 23, 1952, overthrew King Farouk and established a republic. Lt. Col. Gamal Abdel Nasser rose to power, becoming premier in 1954 and president in 1956. Nasser emerged as the most influential leader in the Arab world at the time; within Egypt, he pushed construction of the Aswan High Dam, completed in 1970.

After guerrilla raids across its border, Israel invaded Egypt's Sinai Peninsula, Oct. 29, 1956. Egypt rejected a cease-fire demand by Britain and France; on Oct. 31 the 2 nations dropped bombs and on Nov. 5-6 landed forces. Egypt and Israel accepted a UN cease-fire; fighting ended Nov. 7. Subsequently, a UN Emergency Force guarded the border. Full-scale war with Israel broke out again, June 5, 1967; before it ended under a UN cease-fire June 10, Israel had captured Gaza and the Sinai Peninsula and taken control of the E bank of the Suez Canal.

Nasser died Sept. 28,1970, and was replaced by Vice Pres. Anwar Sadat. In a surprise attack Oct. 6, 1973, Egyptian forces crossed the Suez Canal into the Sinai. (At the same time, Syrian forces attacked Israelis on the Golan Heights.) Egypt was supplied by a USSR military airlift; the U.S. responded with an airlift to Israel. Israel counterattacked, crossed the canal, and surrounded Suez City. A UN cease-fire took effect Oct. 24. Under an agreement signed Jan. 18, 1974, Israeli forces withdrew from the canal's W bank; limited numbers of Egyptian forces occupied a strip along the E bank. A second accord was signed in 1975, with Israel yielding Sinai oil fields.

Pres. Sadat's surprise visit to Jerusalem, Nov. 1977, opened the prospect of peace with Israel. On Mar. 26, 1979, Egypt and Israel signed a formal peace treaty, ending 30 years of war, and establishing diplomatic relations. On Oct. 6, 1981, Pres. Sadat was assassinated by Muslim extremists within the army; he was succeeded by Hosni Mubarak. Israel returned control of the Sinai to Egypt in Apr. 1982.

Egypt saw a rising tide of Islamic fundamentalist violence in the 1990s. U.S. aid to Egypt, totaling more than $50 bil since 1979, helped to keep Mubarak in power. Egypt supported the U.S.-led coalition against Iraq in the Persian Gulf War, 1991. Egyptian security forces conducted raids against Islamic militants, some of whom were executed for terrorism. Naguib Mahfouz, winner of the 1988 Nobel Prize for literature, was stabbed by Islamic militants Oct. 14, 1994. Pres. Mubarak escaped assassination in Ethiopia, June 26, 1995; Egypt blamed Sudan for the attack. On Nov. 17, 1997, near Luxor, Muslim extremists killed 58 foreign tourists and 4 Egyptians.

Mubarak, who was grazed by a knife-wielding assailant Sept. 6, 1999, was confirmed by popular vote Sept. 26 for a 4th presidential term. An EgyptAir jetliner bound from New York to Cairo plunged into the Atlantic near Nantucket Is., Oct. 31, 1999, killing all 217 people on board. Fire on a train bound from Cairo to Luxor, Feb. 20, 2002, left more than 360 people dead. An Egyptian charter plane plunged into the Red Sea shortly after takeoff Jan. 3, 2004, killing 148 people, including 133 French tourists.

Terrorists stepped up their campaign against the economically important tourism industry. Bombs Oct. 7, 2004, in and near Taba (a Sinai tourist site popular with Israelis) killed at least 35 people. Another 88 people were killed in bombings July 23, 2005, at Sharm el Sheikh, a Red Sea resort city. Pressured by the U.S., Mubarak agreed to allow opposition candidates in the Sept. 7 presidential election, which he won with an 88.5% majority; turnout was only 23%. Suicide bombings at the Sinai resort town of Dhab, Apr. 24, 2006, killed at least 18 people and injured 85; security forces May 9 killed Nasser Khamis al-Mallahi, leader of the group blamed for the Taba, Sharm el Sheikh, and Dahab sttacks.

The **Suez Canal**, 103 mi long, links the Mediterranean and Red seas. It was built by a French corporation 1859-69, but Britain obtained controlling interest in 1875. The last British troops were removed June 13, 1956. On July 26, Egypt nationalized the canal.

El Salvador
Republic of El Salvador

People: Population: 6,822,378. **Age distrib.** (%) <15: 36.3; 65+: 5.2. **Pop. density:** 852 per sq mi, 329 per sq km. **Urban:** 59.6%. **Ethnic groups:** Mestizo 90%, White 9%, Amerindian 1%. **Principal languages:** Spanish (official), Nahua. **Chief religions:** Roman Catholic 83%, many Protestant groups.

Geography: Total area: 8,124 sq mi, 21,040 sq km; **Land area:** 8,000 sq mi, 20,720 sq km. **Location:** In Central America. **Neighbors:** Guatemala on W, Honduras on N. **Topography:** A hot Pacific coastal plain in the south rises to a cooler plateau and valley region, densely populated. The N is mountainous, including many volcanoes. **Capital:** San Salvador, 1,517,000.

Government: Type: Republic. **Head of state and gov.:** Pres. Antonio Elías Saca González; b. Mar. 9, 1965; in office: June 1, 2004. **Local divisions:** 14 departments. **Defense budget** (2004): $106 mil. **Active troops:** 15,500.

Economy: Industries: food proc., beverages, oil, chemicals, fertilizer, textiles, furniture, light metals. **Chief crops:** coffee, sugar, corn, rice, beans, oilseed, cotton, sorghum. **Natural resources:** hydropower, geothermal power, oil. **Arable land:** 27%. **Livestock** (2005): cattle: 1.3 mil; chickens: 13.2 mil; goats: 10,750; pigs: 188,025; sheep: 5,100. **Fish catch** (2004): 44,634 metric tons. **Electricity prod.** (2004): 4.2 bil kWh. **Labor force** (2003 est.): agriculture 17.1%, industry 17.1%, services 65.8%.

Finance: Monetary unit: Colon (SVC) (Sept. 2006: 8.75 = $1 U.S.). **GDP** (2005 est.): $31.2 bil; **per capita GDP:** $4,700; **GDP growth:** 2.8%. **Imports** (2005 est.): $6.678 bil; partners (2004): U.S. 37.3%, Guatemala 9%, Mexico 6.1%. **Exports** (2005 est.): $3.6 bil; partners (2004): U.S. 57.9%, Guatemala 13.6%, Honduras 7%. **Tourism:** $337 mil. **Budget** (2006 est.): $3.2 bil. **Intl. reserves less gold:** $1.21 bil. **Gold:** 330,000 oz t. **Consumer prices:** 4.69%.

Transport: Railroad: Length: 176 mi. **Motor vehicles** 148,000 pass. cars, 250,800 comm. vehicles. **Civil aviation:** 2.1 bil pass.-mi; 4 airports. **Chief ports:** La Union, Acajutla, La Libertad.

Communications: TV sets: 191 per 1,000 pop. **Radios:** 478 per 1,000 pop. **Telephone lines:** 971,500. **Daily newspaper circ.:** 28.5 per 1,000 pop. **Internet:** 587,500 users.

Health: Life expect.: 67.9 male; 75.3 female. **Births** (per 1,000 pop.): 26.6. **Deaths** (per 1,000 pop.): 5.8. **Natural inc.:** 2.08%. **Infant mortality** (per 1,000 live births): 24.4. **AIDS rate:** 0.9%.

Education: Compulsory: ages 7-15. **Literacy:** 80.2%.

Major Intl. Organizations: UN (FAO, IBRD, ILO, IMF, IMO, WHO, WTO), OAS.

Embassy: 2308 California St. NW 20008; 265-9671.

Website: www.elsalvador.org

El Salvador became independent of Spain in 1821, and of the Central American Federation in 1839.

A fight with Honduras in 1969 over the presence of 300,000 Salvadoran workers left 2,000 dead.

A military coup overthrew the government of Pres. Carlos Humberto Romero in 1979, but the ruling military-civilian junta failed to quell a rebellion by leftist insurgents, armed by Cuba and Nicaragua. Extreme right-wing death squads organized to eliminate suspected leftists were blamed for thousands of deaths in the 1980s. The Reagan administration staunchly supported the government with military aid. The 12-year civil war ended Jan. 16, 1992, as the government and leftist rebels signed a formal peace treaty. The civil war had taken the lives of some 75,000 people. The treaty provided for military and political reforms.

Nine soldiers, including 3 officers, were indicted Jan. 1990 in the Nov. 1989 slaying of 6 Jesuit priests in San Salvador. Two of the officers received maximum 30-year jail sentences. They were released Mar. 20, 1993, when the National Assembly passed a sweeping amnesty.

Francisco Flores, candidate of the right-wing ARENA party, won the presidential election of Mar. 7, 1999. Another ARENA nominee, Antonio Saca, a businessman and former sportscaster, won the presidential election of Mar. 21, 2004. Remittances from Salvadorans working in the U.S. are a major source of income.

Equatorial Guinea
Republic of Equatorial Guinea

People: Population: 540,109. **Age distrib.** (%) <15: 41.7; 65+: 3.8. **Pop. density:** 49 per sq mi, 19 per sq km. **Urban:** 48.1%. **Ethnic groups:** Fang 83%, Bubi 10%. **Principal languages:** Spanish, French (both official), Fang, Bubi, pidgin English, Portuguese Creole, Ibo. **Chief religions:** nominally Christian and predominantly Roman Catholic, pagan practices.

Geography: Total area: 10,831 sq mi, 28,051 sq km; **Land area:** 10,831 sq mi, 28,051 sq km. **Location:** Bioko Isl. off W Africa coast in Gulf of Guinea, and Rio Muni, mainland enclave. **Neighbors:** Gabon on S, Cameroon on E and N. **Topography:** Bioko Isl. consists of 2 volcanic mountains and a connecting valley. Rio Muni, with over 90% of the area, has a coastal plain and low hills beyond. **Capital:** Malabo, 96,000.

Government: Type: Republic. **Head of state:** Pres. Teodoro Obiang Nguema Mbasogo; b. June 5, 1942; in office: Aug. 3, 1979. **Head of gov.:** Prime Min. Ricardo Mangue Obama Nfubea; in office: Aug. 14, 2006. **Local divisions:** 7 provinces. **Defense budget** (2005): $7 mil. **Active troops:** 1,320.

Economy: Industries: oil, fishing, sawmilling, nat. gas. **Chief crops:** coffee, cocoa, rice, yams, cassava, bananas. **Natural re-**

sources: oil, timber, gold, mang., uranium. **Crude oil reserves** (2005): 12 mil bbls. **Arable land:** 5%. **Livestock** (2005): cattle: 5,050; chickens: 320,000; goats: 9,000; pigs: 6,100; sheep: 37,600. **Fish catch** (2004): 3,500 metric tons. **Electricity prod.** (2004): 30 bil kWh.

Finance: Monetary unit: CFA BEAC Franc (XAF) (Sept. 2006: 512.47 = $1 U.S.). **GDP** (2005 est.): $25.7 bil; **per capita GDP:** $50,200; **GDP growth:** 18.6%. **Imports** (2005 est.): $1 bil; partners (2004): U.S. 32.1%, Côte d'Ivoire 16.9%, Spain 13.7%, France 8.6%, UK 7.4%. **Exports** (2005 est.): $6.7 bil; partners (2004): U.S. 34%, China 23.7%, Spain 21.1%, Canada 8.6%. **Tourism** (2001): $14 mil. **Budget** (2005 est.): $711.5 mil. **Intl. reserves less gold:** $1.47 bil.

Transport: Motor vehicles: 4,000 pass. cars, 3,600 comm. vehicles. **Civil aviation:** NA; 3 airports. **Chief ports:** Malabo, Bata.

Communications: TV sets: 116 per 1,000 pop. **Radios:** 429 per 1,000 pop. **Telephone lines:** 10,000. **Daily newspaper circ.:** 4.6 per 1,000 pop. **Internet:** 5,000 users.

Health: Life expect.: 48 male; 51.1 female. **Births** (per 1,000 pop.): 35.6. **Deaths** (per 1,000 pop.): 15.1. **Natural inc.:** 2.05%. **Infant mortality** (per 1,000 live births): 89.2. **AIDS rate:** 3.2%.

Education: Compulsory: ages 7-11. **Literacy:** 87%.

Major Intl. Organizations: UN (FAO, IBRD, ILO, IMF, IMO, WHO), AU.

Embassy: 2020 16th St. NW 20009; 202-518-5700.

Website: www.state.gov/p/af/ci/ek

Fernando Po (now Bioko) Island was reached by Portugal in the late 15th century and ceded to Spain in 1778. Independence came Oct. 12, 1968. Riots occurred in 1969 over disputes between the island and the more backward Rio Muni province on the mainland. Masie Nguema Biyogo, a mainlander, became pres. for life in 1972.

Masie's reign was one of the most brutal in Africa, resulting in a bankrupted nation; most of the nation's 7,000 Europeans emigrated. He was ousted in a military coup, Aug. 1979. Teodoro Obiang Nguema Mbasogo, leader of the coup, became president and installed his family members in key government posts. His regime eventually agreed to elections, held Nov. 21, 1993. These were nominally won by the ruling party, but boycotted by opposition parties that maintained the rules were rigged. Elections for president, Feb. 25, 1996, and Dec. 15, 2002, were similarly condemned.

Oil sales, especially to the U.S., have boomed in recent years. Authorities in Zimbabwe and Equatorial Guinea arrested 85 people in Mar. 2004 on charges of plotting to overthrow the Obiang regime. Mark Thatcher, son of the former British prime min., was arrested in South Africa Aug. 25 for alleged involvement; in a plea bargain Jan. 13, 2005, he agreed to pay a $500,000 fine. Pres. Obiang revamped his entire cabinet in Aug. 2006.

Eritrea
State of Eritrea

People: Population:4,786,994. **Age distrib.** (%) <15: 44; 65+: 3.5. **Pop. density:** 102 per sq mi, 39 per sq km. **Urban:** 19.9%. **Ethnic groups:** Tigrinya 50%, Tigre and Kunama 40%, Afar 4%, Saho 3%. **Principal languages:** Arabic, Tigrinya (both official); Afar, Amharic, Tigre, Kunama, other Cushitic languages. **Chief religions:** Muslim, Coptic Christian, Roman Catholic, Protestant.

Geography: Total area: 46,842 sq mi, 121,320 sq km; **Land area:** 46,842 sq mi, 121,320 sq km. **Location:** In E Africa, on SW coast of Red Sea. **Neighbors:** Ethiopia on S, Djibouti on SE, Sudan on W. **Topography:** Includes many islands of the Dahlak Archipelago, low coastal plains in S, mountain range with peaks to 9,000 ft. in N. **Capital:** Asmara, 551,000.

Government: Type: In transition. **Head of state and gov.:** Isaias Afwerki; b. Feb. 2, 1946; in office: May 24, 1993. **Local divisions:** 8 provinces. **Defense budget** (2005): $74 mil. **Active troops:** 201,750.

Economy: Industries: food proc., beverages, clothing, textiles. **Chief crops:** sorghum, lentils, vegetables, corn, cotton, tobacco, coffee, sisal. **Natural resources:** gold, potash, zinc, copper, salt, fish. **Arable land:** 12%. **Livestock** (2005): cattle: 2 mil; chickens: 1.4 mil; goats: 1.7 mil; sheep: 2.1 mil **Fish catch** (2004): 7,404 metric tons. **Electricity prod.** (2004): 280 mil kWh. **Labor force:** agriculture 80%, industry and services 20%.

Finance: Monetary unit: Nakfa (ERN) (Sept. 2006: 15.00 = $1 U.S.). **GDP** (2005 est.): $4.5 bil; **per capita GDP:** $1,000; **GDP growth:** 2%. **Imports** (2005 est.): $676.5 mil; partners (2004): U.S. 32.3%, Italy 15.5%, Turkey 5.5%, UK 4.6%, Russia 4.4%, Italy 6.4%. **Exports** (2005 est.): $33.6 mil; partners (2004): Malaysia 54.7%, Italy 8.8%, France 3.7%. **Tourism** (2002): $73 mil. **Budget** (2005 est.): $409.4 mil. **Intl. reserves less gold:** $20 mil.

Transport: Railroad: Length: 190 mi. **Civil aviation:** NA; 4 airports. **Chief ports:** Mitsiwa, Aseb.

Communications: TV sets: 16 per 1,000 pop. **Radios:** 484 per 1,000 pop. **Telephone lines:** 37,700. **Internet:** 50,000 users.

Health: Life expect.: 57.4 male; 60.7 female. **Births** (per 1,000 pop.): 34.3. **Deaths** (per 1,000 pop.): 9.6. **Natural inc.:** 2.47%. **Infant mortality** (per 1,000 live births): 46.3. **AIDS rate:** 2.4%.

Education: Compulsory: ages 7-14. **Literacy:** 58.6%.

Major Intl. Organizations: UN (FAO, IBRD, ILO, IMF, IMO, WHO), AU.

Embassy: 1708 New Hampshire Ave. NW 20009; 319-1991.

Website: www.shabait.com

Eritrea was part of the Ethiopian kingdom of Aksum. It was an Italian colony from 1890 to 1941, when it was captured by the British. Following a period of British and UN supervision, Eritrea was awarded to Ethiopia as part of a federation in 1952. Ethiopia annexed Eritrea as a province in 1962. This led to a 31-year struggle for independence, which ended when Eritrea formally declared itself an independent nation May 24, 1993. A constitution was ratified in 1997 but not implemented.

A border war with Ethiopia that erupted in June 1998 intensified in May 2000, as Ethiopian troops plunged into western Eritrea; a cease-fire signed June 18 provided for a UN peacekeeping force (UNMEE) to patrol a buffer zone on Eritrean territory. A peace treaty was signed Dec. 12, 2000. An international tribunal adjudicated the boundary dispute in Apr. 2002; the ruling was rejected by Ethiopia, Sept. 2003, but accepted "in principle," Nov. 2004. Maximum authorized UNMEE strength was 2,300 personnel in mid-2006.

Estonia
Republic of Estonia

People: Population: 1,324,333. **Age distrib.** (%) <15: 15.2; 65+: 17.2. **Pop. density:** 79 per sq mi, 30 per sq km. **Urban:** 69.4%. **Ethnic groups:** Estonian 65%, Russian 28%. **Principal languages:** Estonian (official), Russian, Ukrainian, Finnish. **Chief religions:** Unaffiliated 34%, others 32%, Evangelical Lutheran 14%, Russian Orthodox 13%.

Geography: Total area: 17,462 sq mi, 45,226 sq km; **Land area:** 16,684 sq mi, 43,211 sq km. **Location:** E Europe, bordering the Baltic Sea and Gulf of Finland. **Neighbors:** Russia on E, Latvia on S. **Topography:** Estonia is a marshy lowland with numerous lakes and swamps; about 40% forested. Elongated hills show evidence of former glaciation. More than 800 islands on Baltic coast. **Capital:** Tallinn, 392,000.

Government: Type: Republic. **Head of state:** Pres. Toomas Hendrik Ilves; b. Dec. 26, 1953; in office: Oct. 9, 2006. **Head of gov.:** Prime Min. Andrus Ansip; b. Oct. 1, 1956; in office: Apr. 13, 2005. **Local divisions:** 15 counties. **Defense budget** (2005): $207 mil. **Active troops:** 4,934.

Economy: Industries: engineering, electronics, timber, wood products, textiles, telecom. **Chief crops:** potatoes, vegetables. **Natural resources:** oil shale, peat, phosphorite, clay, limestone, sand, dolomite, sea mud. **Arable land:** 25%. **Livestock** (2005): cattle: 249,800; chickens: 2.2 mil; goats: 2,900; pigs: 340,100; sheep: 38,800. **Fish catch** (2004): 88,158 metric tons. **Electricity prod.** (2004): 9.3 bil kWh. **Labor force** (1999 est.): agriculture 11%, industry 20%, services 69%.

Finance: Monetary unit: Kroon (EEK) (Sept. 2006: 12.22 = $1 U.S.). **GDP** (2005 est.): $22.3 bil; **per capita GDP:** $16,700; **GDP growth:** 9.6%. **Imports** (2005 est.): $9.2 bil; partners (2004): Finland 19.9%, Russia 13.2%, Germany 11.6%, Sweden 7.9%. **Exports** (2005 est.): $7.4 bil; partners (2004): Finland 16.6%, Sweden 11.1%, UK 8.6%, Latvia 7.4%, Germany 7.2%, Russia 6.9%, U.S. 5.5%, Lithuania 4%. **Tourism:** $887 mil.. **Budget** (2005 est.): $5 bil. **Intl. reserves less gold:** $1.36 bil. **Gold:** 10,000 oz t. **Consumer prices:** 4.09%.

Transport: Railroad: Length: 595 mi. **Motor vehicles:** 434,000 pass. cars, 83,400 comm. vehicles. **Civil aviation:** 175.8 mil pass.-mi; 12 airports. **Chief port:** Tallinn.

Communications: TV sets: 567 per 1,000 pop. **Radios:** 191.6 per 1,000 pop. **Telephone lines:** 442,000. **Daily newspaper circ.:** 191.6 per 1,000 pop. **Internet:** 670,000 users.

Health: Life expect.: 66.6 male; 77.8 female. **Births** (per 1,000 pop.): 10. **Deaths** (per 1,000 pop.): 13.2. **Natural inc.:** −0.32%. **Infant mortality** (per 1,000 live births): 7.7. **AIDS rate:** 1.3%.

Education: Compulsory: ages 7-15. **Literacy:** 99.8%.

Major Intl. Organizations: UN (FAO, IBRD, ILO, IMF, IMO, WHO, WTO), EU, NATO, OSCE.

Embassy: 2131 Massachusetts Av., NW 20008 588 0101

Website: www.riik.ee/en

Estonia was a province of imperial Russia before World War I, and was independent between World Wars I and II. It was conquered by the USSR in 1940 and incorporated as the Estonian SSR. Estonia declared itself an "occupied territory," and proclaimed itself a free nation Mar. 1990. During an abortive Soviet coup, Estonia declared immediate full independence, Aug. 20, 1991; the Soviet Union recognized its independence in Sept. 1991. The first free elections in over 50 years were held Sept. 20, 1992. The last occupying Russian troops were withdrawn by Aug. 31, 1994. Estonia became a full member of the EU and NATO in 2004.

Ethiopia
Federal Democratic Republic of Ethiopia

People: Population: 74,777,981. **Age distrib.** (%) <15: 43.7; 65+: 2.7. **Pop. density:** 172 per sq mi, 66 per sq km. **Urban:** 15.6%. **Ethnic groups:** Oromo 40%, Amhara and Tigre 32%, Sidamo 9%, Shankella 6%, Somali 6%, Afar 4%, Gurage 2%. **Principal languages:** Amharic, Tigrinya, Oromigna, Guaragigna, Somali, Arabic, over 200 other languages. **Chief religions:** Muslim 45%-50%, Ethiopian Orthodox 35%-40%, animist 12%.

Geography: Total area: 435,186 sq mi, 1,127,127 sq km; **Land area:** 432,312 sq mi, 1,119,683 sq km. **Location:** In East Africa. **Neighbors:** Sudan on W, Kenya on S, Somalia and Djibouti on E, Eritrea on N. **Topography:** A high central plateau, between 6,000 and 10,000 ft. high, rises to higher mountains near the Great Rift Valley, cutting in from the SW. The Blue Nile and other rivers cross the plateau, which descends to plains on both W and SE. **Capital:** Addis Ababa, 2,893,000.

Government: Type: Federal republic. **Head of state:** Pres. Girma Wolde Giorgis; b. Dec. 1924; in office: Oct. 8, 2001. **Head of gov.:** Prime Min. Meles Zenawi; b. May 8, 1955; in office: Aug. 23, 1995. **Local divisions:** 9 states, 2 charted cities. **Defense budget** (2005): $229 mil. **Active troops:** 182,500.

Economy: Industries: food proc., beverages, textiles, chemicals, metals proc., cement. **Chief crops:** cereals, coffee, oilseed, sugarcane, potatoes. **Natural resources:** gold, platinum, copper, potash, nat. gas, hydr'opower. **Crude oil reserves** (2005): 400,000 bbls. **Arable land:** 12%. **Livestock** (2005): cattle: 38.5 mil; chickens: 39 mil; goats: 9.6 mil; pigs: 29,000; sheep: 17 mil. **Fish catch** (2004): 10,005 metric tons. **Electricity prod.** (2004): 2.3 bil kWh. **Labor force** (1985): agriculture 80%, industry 8%, government 12%.

Finance: Monetary unit: Birr (ETB) (Sept. 2006: 8.77 = $1 U.S.). **GDP** (2005 est.): $62.9 bil; **per capita GDP:** $900; **GDP growth:** 8.9%. **Imports** (2005 est.): $2.7 bil; partners (2004): Saudi Arabia 25%, U.S. 15.9%, China 6.7%. **Exports** (2005 est.): $612 mil; partners (2004): Djibouti 13.6%, Germany 9.7%, Japan 9%, Saudi Arabia 6.5%, U.S. 5.4%, Italy 4.9%, UK 4.3%. **Tourism:** $173 mil. **Budget** (2005 est.): $2.9 bil. **Intl. reserves less gold:** $785 mil. **Consumer prices:** 11.61%.

Transport: Railroad: Length: 423 mi. **Motor vehicles:** 81,200 pass. cars, 44,500 comm. vehicles. **Civil aviation:** 2 bil pass.-mi; 14 airports

Communications: TV sets: 5 per 1,000 pop. **Radios:** 185 per 1,000 pop. **Telephone lines:** 435,000. **Daily newspaper circ.:** 0.4 per 1,000 pop. **Internet:** 113,000 users.

Health: Life expect.: 47.9 male; 50.2 female. **Births** (per 1,000 pop.): 38. **Deaths** (per 1,000 pop.): 14.9. **Natural inc.:** 2.31%. **Infant mortality** (per 1,000 live births): 93.6. **AIDS rate:** 1.6%.

Education: Compulsory: ages 7-12. **Literacy:** 42.7%.

Major Intl. Organizations: UN (FAO, IBRD, ILO, IMF, IMO, WHO), AU.

Embassy: 3506 International Dr. NW 20008; 364-1200.

Website: www.moinfo.gov.et

Ethiopian culture was influenced by Egypt and Greece. The ancient monarchy was invaded by Italy in 1880 but maintained its independence until another Italian invasion in 1936. British forces freed the country in 1941.

A series of droughts in the 1970s killed hundreds of thousands. An army mutiny, strikes, and student demonstrations led to the dethronement, Sept. 12, 1974, of Ethiopia's last emperor, Haile Selassie I, ending his 58-year reign; he died Aug. 1975, while being held by the ruling junta, known as the Dergue. The junta dissolved parliament, abolished the monarchy, established a socialist state, redistributed land, and violently suppressed opposition. The influence of the Coptic Church, embraced in 330 CE.

The regime, torn by bloody coups, faced uprisings by tribal and political groups aided in part by Sudan and Somalia. Ties with the U.S., once a major ally, deteriorated, while cooperation accords were signed with the USSR in 1977. In 1978, Soviet advisers and Cuban troops helped defeat Somali forces. Ethiopia and Somalia signed a peace agreement in 1988.

A worldwide relief effort began in 1984, as an extended drought threatened the country with famine; up to 1 mil people may have died as a result of starvation and disease.

The Ethiopian People's Revolutionary Democratic Front (EPRDF), an umbrella group of 6 rebel armies, launched a major push against government forces, Feb. 1991. In May, Pres. Mengistu Haile Mariam resigned and left the country. The EPRDF took over and set up a transitional government. Ethiopia's first multiparty general elections were held in 1995.

Eritrea, a province on the Red Sea, declared its independence May 24, 1993. Fighting along the border with Eritrea, which erupted in June 1998, intensified in May 2000, as Ethiopian forces plunged into Eritrean territory; a cease-fire was signed June 18 and a peace treaty Dec. 12. The war displaced 350,000 Ethiopians and is estimated to have cost the country nearly $3 bil. A collapse of crop prices in 2001, followed by drought in 2002-03, led to severe food shortages. Ethnic clashes Dec. 2003-Jan. 2004 in western Ethiopia, left more than 250 people dead; thousands fled to Sudan.

The ruling EPRDF won parliamentary elections May 15, 2005, but opposition parties made big gains. Police opened fire on anti-government protesters in Addis Ababa, June 8, killing at least 36; the government arrested some 3,000 dissidents. Police suppression of further protests in the capital, Nov. 1-4, left at least 46 dead. As part of a crackdown on Oromo Liberation Front rebels, the government rounded up thousands of Oromo, Nov. 2005-Jan. 2006. In July 2006, Ethiopia sent troops into Somalia in response to advances by Islamist militias there.

Fiji
Republic of the Fiji Islands

People: Population: 905,949. **Age distrib.** (%) <15: 31.1; 65+: 4.3. **Pop. density:** 128 per sq mi, 49 per sq km. **Urban:** 51.7%. **Ethnic groups:** Fijian 51%, Indian 44%. **Principal languages:** English (official), Fijian, Hindustani. **Chief religions:** Christian 52%, Hindu 38%, Muslim 8%.

Geography: Total area: 7,054 sq mi, 18,270 sq km; **Land area:** 7,054 sq mi, 18,270 sq km. **Location:** In western South Pacific O. **Neighbors:** Nearest are Vanuatu to W, Tonga to E. **Topography:** 322 islands (106 inhabited), many mountainous, with tropical forests and large fertile areas. Viti Levu, the largest island, has over half the total land area. **Capital:** Suva, 219,000.

Government: Type: Republic. **Head of state:** Pres. Ratu Josefa Iloilo; b. Dec. 29, 1920; in office: July 18, 2000. **Head of gov.:** Prime Min. Laisenia Qarase; b. Feb. 4, 1941; in office: Mar. 16, 2001. **Local divisions:** 4 divisions comprising 14 provinces and 1 dependency. **Defense budget** (2005): $39 mil. **Active troops:** 3,500.

Economy: Industries: tourism, sugar, clothing, copra, gold & silver prod. **Chief crops:** sugarcane, coconuts, cassava, rice, sweet potatoes, bananas. **Natural resources:** timber, fish, gold, copper, oil, hydropower. **Arable land:** 10%. **Livestock** (2005): cattle: 310,000; chickens: 4.3 mil; goats: 260,000; pigs: 140,000; sheep: 5,000. **Fish catch** (2004): 46,734 metric tons. **Electricity prod.** (2004): 820 mil kWh. **Labor force** (2001 est.): agriculture 70%, industry and services 30%.

Finance: Monetary unit: Dollar (FJD) (Sept. 2006: 1.73 = $1 U.S.). **GDP** (2005 est.): $5.4 bil; **per capita GDP:** $6,000; **GDP growth:** 1.7%. **Imports** (2004 est.): $1.2 bil; partners (2004): Australia 27.7%, Singapore 24.8%, New Zealand 17.8%, Japan 4.2%. **Exports** (2004 est.): $862 mil; partners (2004): U.S. 23.6%, Australia 19.2%, UK 12.8%, Samoa 6.2%, Japan 4.1%. **Tourism:** $414 mil. **Budget** (2000 est.): $531.4 mil. **Intl. reserves less gold:** $220 mil. **Gold:** 10,000 oz t. **Consumer prices:** 2.37%.

Transport: Railroad: Length: 371 mi. **Motor vehicles:** 51,700 pass. cars, 48,600 comm. vehicles. **Civil aviation:** 1.8 bil pass.-mi; 3 airports. **Chief ports:** Suva, Lautoka.

Communications: TV sets: 110 per 1,000 pop. **Radios:** 677 per 1,000 pop. **Telephone lines:** 102,000. **Daily newspaper circ.:** NA. **Internet** (2004): 61,000 users.

Health: Life expect.: 67.3 male; 72.5 female. **Births** (per 1,000 pop.): 22.6. **Deaths** (per 1,000 pop.): 5.7. **Natural inc.:** 1.69%. **Infant mortality** (per 1,000 live births): 12.3. **AIDS rate:** 0.1%.

Education: Compulsory: ages 6-15. **Literacy:** 93.7%.

Major Intl. Organizations: UN (FAO, IBRD, ILO, IMF, IMO, WHO, WTO), the Commonwealth.

Embassy: 2233 Wisconsin Ave. NW, Suite 240, 20007; 337-8320.

Website: www.fiji.gov.fj

A British colony since 1874, Fiji became independent Oct. 10, 1970. Cultural differences between the Indian community (descendants of contract laborers brought to the islands in the 19th cent.) and indigenous Fijians have led to political polarization. More than 100,000 Indians have left Fiji since the mid-1980s.

In 1987, a military coup ousted the government; order was restored May 21 under a compromise granting Lt. Col. Sitiveni Rabuka, the coup's leader, increased power. Rabuka staged a second coup Sept. 25 and declared Fiji a republic. Civilian government was restored in Dec. A new constitution favoring indigenous Fijians was issued July 25, 1990; amendments enacted in July 1997 made the constitution more equitable.

Fiji's first Indian prime minister, Mahendra Chaudhry, took office May 19, 1999. He and other government officials were taken captive May 19, 2000, by indigenous Fijian gunmen led by George Speight. The hostage crisis led to a military takeover, May 29. Release of the last remaining hostages in July 2000 coincided with the installation of an interim military-backed government. Speight was charged with treason (sentenced to life in prison Feb. 18, 2002). The government was reconstituted in Mar. 2001 after an appellate court ruled it illegal. Voting ending Sept. 1, 2001, returning caretaker Prime Min. Laisenia Qarase to office. Fiji's High Court, Aug. 5, 2004, convicted Vice Pres. Jope Seniloli of aiding the 2000 coup plot; he resigned Nov. 29 after winning early release from prison for medical reasons. Qarase retained his office in parliamentary elections, May 6-13, 2006.

Finland
Republic of Finland

People: Population: 5,231,372. **Age distrib.** (%) <15: 17.1; 65+: 16.2. **Pop. density:** 44 per sq mi, 17 per sq km. **Urban:** 60.9%. **Ethnic groups:** Finnish 93%, Swedish 6%. **Principal languages:** Finnish, Swedish (both official); Russian, Sami. **Chief religion:** Lutheran National Church 85%.

Geography: Total area: 130,559 sq mi, 338,145 sq km; **Land area:** 117,558 sq mi, 304,473 sq km. **Location:** In northern Europe. **Neighbors:** Norway on N, Sweden on W, Russia on E. **Topography:** South and central Finland are generally flat areas with low hills and many lakes. The N has mountainous areas, 3,000-4,000 ft. above sea level. **Capital:** Helsinki, 1,091,000.

Government: Type: Constitutional republic. **Head of state:** Pres. Tarja Halonen; b. Dec. 24, 1943; in office: Mar. 1, 2000. **Head of gov.:** Prim Min. Matti Vanhanen, b. Nov. 4, 1955; in office: June 24, 2003. **Local divisions:** 6 laanit (provinces). **Defense budget** (2005): $2.7 bil. **Active troops:** 28,300.

Economy: Industries: metal products, electronics, shipbuilding, paper, copper refining, foodstuffs, chemicals, textiles, clothing. **Chief crops:** barley, wheat, sugar beets, potatoes. **Natural resources:** timber, copper, zinc, iron ore, silver. **Arable land:** 8%. **Livestock** (2005): cattle: 950,000; chickens: 6 mil; goats: 4,800; pigs: 1.4 mil; sheep: 115,000. **Fish catch** (2004): 148,700 metric tons. **Electricity prod.** (2004): 81.6 bil kWh. **Labor force:** agriculture and forestry 8%, industry 22%, construction 6%, commerce 14%, finance, insurance, and business services 10%, transport and communications 8%, public services 32%.

Finance: Monetary unit: Euro (EUR) (Sept. 2006: 0.78 = $1 U.S.). **GDP** (2005 est.): $161.5 bil; **per capita GDP:** $30,900; **GDP growth:** 2.2%. **Imports** (2005 est.): $56.5 bil; partners (2004): Germany 16.2%, Sweden 14.1%, Russia 12.8%, Netherlands 6.3%,

Denmark 5.3%, UK 4.6%, France 4.3%. **Exports** (2005 est.): $67.9 bil; partners (2004): Sweden 11%, Germany 10.6%, Russia 8.9%, UK 7%, U.S. 6.4%, Netherlands 5.2%, China 4.1%. **Tourism:** $2.1 bil. **Budget** (2005 est.): $97.1 bil. **Intl. reserves less gold:** $7.41 bil. **Gold:** 1.58 mil oz t. **Consumer prices:** 0.86%.

Transport: Railroad: Length: 3,635 mi. **Motor vehicles:** 2.27 mil pass. cars, 337,500 comm. vehicles. **Civil aviation:** 5.5 bil pass.-mi; 76 airports. **Chief ports:** Helsinki, Turku, Rauma, Kotka.

Communications: TV sets: 643 per 1,000 pop. **Radios:** 1,564 per 1,000 pop. **Telephone lines:** 2.1 mil. **Daily newspaper circ.:** 445 per 1,000 pop. **Internet:** 3.3 mil users.

Health: Life expect.: 75 male; 82.2 female. **Births** (per 1,000 pop.): 10.4. **Deaths** (per 1,000 pop.): 9.9. **Natural inc.:** 0.06%. **Infant mortality** (per 1,000 live births): 3.5. **AIDS rate:** 0.1%.

Education: Compulsory: ages 7-16. **Literacy:** 100%.

Major Intl. Organizations: UN (FAO, IBRD, ILO, IMF, IMO, WHO, WTO), EU, OECD, OSCE.

Embassy: 3301 Massachusetts Ave. NW 20008; 298-5800. **Website:** www.finland.fi

The early Finns probably migrated from the Ural area at about the beginning of the Christian era. Swedish settlers brought the country into Sweden, 1154 to 1809, when Finland became an autonomous grand duchy of the Russian Empire. Russian exactions created a strong national spirit; on Dec. 6, 1917, Finland declared its independence and in 1919 became a republic.

On Nov. 30, 1939, the Soviet Union invaded, and the Finns were forced to cede 16,173 sq mi of territory. After World War II, further cessions were exacted. In 1948, Finland signed a treaty of mutual assistance with the USSR; Finland and Russia nullified this treaty with a new pact in Jan. 1992.

Following approval by Finnish voters in an advisory referendum Oct. 16, 1994, Finland joined the EU effective Jan. 1, 1995. Pres. Tarja Halonen won a 2nd 6-year term, Jan. 29, 2006.

Åland or **Ahvenanmaa,** constituting an autonomous province, is a group of small islands, 590 sq mi, in the Gulf of Bothnia, 25 mi from Sweden, 15 mi from Finland. Mariehamn is the chief port.

France
French Republic

People: Population: 60,876,136. **Age distrib.** (%) <15: 18.3; 65+: 16.4. **Pop. density:** 288 per sq mi, 111 per sq km. **Urban:** 76.3%. **Ethnic groups:** French, with Slavic, N African, Indochinese, Basque minorities. **Principal languages:** French (official), Italian, Breton, Alsatian (German), Corsican, Gascon, Portuguese, Provençal, Dutch, Flemish, Catalan, Basque, Romani. **Chief religions:** Roman Catholic 83%-88%, Muslim 5%-10%.

Geography: Total area: 211,209 sq mi, 547,030 sq km; **Land area:** 210,669 sq mi, 545,630 sq km. **Location:** In western Europe, between Atlantic O. and Mediterranean Sea. **Neighbors:** Spain on S; Italy, Switzerland, Germany on E; Luxembourg, Belgium on N. **Topography:** A wide plain covers more than half of the country, in N and W, drained to W by Seine, Loire, Garonne rivers. The Massif Central is a mountainous plateau in center. In E are Alps (Mt. Blanc is tallest in W Europe, 15,771 ft.), the lower Jura range, and the forested Vosges. The Rhone flows from Lake Geneva to Mediterranean. Pyrenees are in SW, on border with Spain. **Capital:** Paris, 9,820,000. **Cities (urban aggr.):** Lyon, 1,403,000; Marseilles, 1,382,000; Lille, 1,029,000.

Government: Type: Republic. **Head of state:** Pres. Jacques Chirac; b. Nov. 29, 1932; in office: May 17, 1995. **Head of gov.:** Prime Min. Dominique de Villepin; b. Nov. 14, 1953; in office: May 31, 2005. **Local divisions:** 22 administrative regions containing 96 departments. **Defense budget** (2005): $41.6 bil. **Active troops:** 254,895.

Economy: Industries: machinery, chemicals, automobiles, metallurgy, aircraft, electronics, textiles, food proc. tourism. **Chief crops:** wheat, cereals, sugar beets, potatoes, wine grapes. **Natural resources:** coal, iron ore, bauxite, zinc, potash, timber, fish. **Crude oil reserves** (2005): 146 mil bbls. **Other resources:** Timber, dairy. **Arable land:** 33%. **Livestock** (2005): cattle: 19.4 mil; chickens: 215 mil; goats: 1.2 mil; pigs: 15 mil; sheep: 9.1 mil. **Fish catch** (2004): 840,888 metric tons. **Electricity prod.** (2004): 540.6 bil kWh. **Labor force** (1999): agriculture 4.1%, industry 24.4%, services 71.5%.

Finance: Monetary unit: Euro (EUR) (Sept. 2006: 0.78 = $1 U.S.). **GDP**(2005 est.): $1.8 tril; **per capita GDP:** $29,900; **GDP growth:** 1.4%. **Imports** (2005 est.): $473.3 bil; partners (2004): Germany 19.2%, Belgium 9.8%, Italy 8.8%, Spain 7.3%, UK 7%, Netherlands 6.7%, U.S. 5.1%. **Exports** (2005 est.): $443.4 bil; partners (2004): Germany 15%, Spain 9.4%, UK 9.3%, Italy 9%, Belgium 7.2%, U.S. 6.7%. **Tourism:** $40.7 bil. **Budget** (2005 est.): $1.1 tril. **Intl. reserves less gold:** $19.42 bil. **Gold:** 90.58 mil oz t. **Consumer prices:** 1.77%.

Transport: Railroad: Length: 18,342 mi. **Motor vehicles:** 29.56 mil pass. cars, 6.4 mil comm. vehicles. **Civil aviation:** 71.3 bil pass.-mi; 292 airports. **Chief ports:** Marseille, Le Havre, Bordeaux, Rouen.

Communications: TV sets: 620 per 1,000 pop. **Radios:** 946 per 1,000 pop. **Telephone lines:** 35.7 mil. **Daily newspaper circ.:** 142.1 per 1,000 pop. **Internet:** 26.2 mil users.

Health: Life expect.: 76.1 male; 83.5 female. **Births** (per 1,000 pop.): 12. **Deaths** (per 1,000 pop.): 9.1. **Natural inc.:** 0.28%. **Infant mortality** (per 1,000 live births): 4.2. **AIDS rate:** 0.4%.

Education: Compulsory: ages 6-16. **Literacy:** 99%.

Major Intl. Organizations: UN and most of its specialized agencies, EU, NATO, OECD, OSCE.

Embassy: 4101 Reservoir Rd. NW 20007; 944-6000. **Website:** www.diplomatie.gouv.fr

Celtic Gaul was conquered by Julius Caesar 58-51 BCE; Romans ruled for 500 years. Under Charlemagne, Frankish rule extended over much of Europe. After his death France emerged as one of the successor kingdoms.

The monarchy was overthrown by the French Revolution (1789-93) and succeeded by the First Republic, followed by the First Empire under Napoleon (1804-15), a monarchy (1814-48), the Second Republic (1848-52), the Second Empire (1852-70), the Third Republic (1871-1946), the Fourth Republic (1946-58), and the Fifth Republic (1958 to present).

France suffered severe losses in manpower and wealth in WWI, when it was invaded by Germany. By the Treaty of Versailles, France exacted return of Alsace and Lorraine, provinces seized by Germany in 1871. Germany invaded France again in May 1940, and signed an armistice with a government based in Vichy. After France was liberated by the Allies in Sept. 1944, Gen: Charles de Gaulle became head of the provisional government, serving until 1946. De Gaulle again became premier in 1958, during a crisis over Algeria, and obtained voter approval for a new constitution, ushering in the Fifth Republic. He then became president.

France had withdrawn from Indochina in 1954, and from Morocco and Tunisia in 1956. Most of its remaining African territories, including Algeria, were freed 1958-62. In 1966, France withdrew all its troops from the integrated military command of NATO, though 60,000 remained stationed in Germany.

In May 1968 rebellious students in Paris and other centers rioted, battled police, and were joined by workers who launched nationwide strikes. The government awarded pay increases to the strikers May 26. De Gaulle resigned from office in Apr. 1969, after losing a nationwide referendum on constitutional reform. Georges Pompidou, who was elected to succeed him, continued De Gaulle's emphasis on French independence from the U.S. and Soviet Union. After Pompidou's death, in 1974, Valery Giscard d'Estaing was elected president; he continued the basically conservative policies of his predecessors.

On May 10, 1981, France elected François Mitterrand, a Socialist, president. Under Mitterrand the government nationalized 5 major industries and most private banks. After 1986, however, when rightists won a narrow victory in the National Assembly, Mitterrand chose conservative Jacques Chirac as premier. A 2-year period of "cohabitation" ensued, and France began to pursue a privatization program in which many state-owned companies were sold. After Mitterrand was elected to a 2nd 7-year term in 1988, he appointed a Socialist as premier. The center-right won a large majority in 1993 legislative elections, ushering in another period of "cohabitation" with a conservative premier.

Former conservative Prime Min. Jacques Chirac won the presidency in a runoff May 7, 1995. A series of terrorist bombings and bombing attempts began in summer 1995; Islamic extremists, opposed to France's support of the Algerian government and its struggle with Islamic fundamentalists, were believed responsible. France stirred widespread protests by resuming nuclear tests in the South Pacific, 1995-96, after a 3-year moratorium.

Chirac cut government spending to help the French economy meet the budgetary goals set for the introduction of a common European currency. With unemployment at nearly 13%, legislative elections completed June 1, 1997, produced a decisive victory for the leftist parties. The result was a new period of "cohabitation," this time between a conservative president and a Socialist prime minister, Lionel Jospin. France contributed 7,000 troops to the NATO-led security force (KFOR) that entered Kosovo in June 1999.

French voters, disaffected by government scandals, shocked the political establishment in the first round of presidential voting Apr. 21, 2002, by giving Jean-Marie Le Pen, leader of the far-right National Front, a second place finish with 16.9% of the vote; Chirac won only 19.9%, and Jospin was 3rd, with 16.2%. Chirac easily won the May 5 runoff, with 82%, and his center-right allies won parliamentary elections June 9 and 16.

In Mar. 2003, Parliament approved constitutional amendments strengthening regional governments. Parliament gave final approval Mar. 3, 2004, to a law barring the wearing of Islamic head scarves and other religious symbols in public schools.

Displeased with sluggish economic growth, high unemployment, and budget cuts in entitlement programs, voters boosted left-wing parties in 2004 elections for regional offices, Mar. 21 and 28 and for the European Parliament, June 13. Voters again showed their discontent by rejecting, May 29, 2005, a proposed EU constitution strongly supported by the Chirac government. Prime Min. Jean-Pierre Raffarin resigned May 31 and was replaced by Dominique de Villepin. A state of emergency was declared Nov. 8 after 12 days of riots that began in Paris and spread to some 300 French cities and towns; rioters were mainly young North and West African immigrants. After a wave of mass protests and strikes, Chirac agreed, Apr. 10, 2006, to rescind a new law that made it easier for employers to fire inexperienced young workers.

The island of **Corsica**, in the Mediterranean W of Italy and N of Sardinia, is a territorial collectivity and region of France comprising 2 departments. It elects a total of 2 senators and 3 deputies to the French Parliament. Area: 3,369 sq mi; pop. (2001 census): 260,149. The capital is Ajaccio, birthplace of Napoleon I. Violence by Corsican separatist groups has hurt tourism, a leading industry on the island. Corsicans rejected, 51-49%, a limited autonomy plan in a referendum July 6, 2003.

Overseas Departments

French Guiana is on the NE coast of South America with Suriname on the W and Brazil on the E and S. Its area is 35,135 sq mi (total); 34,421 sq mi (land).; pop. (2006 est.) 199,509. Guiana sends one senator and 2 deputies to the French Parliament. Guiana is administered by a prefect and has a Council General of 16 elected members; capital is Cayenne.

The famous penal colony, Devil's Island, was phased out between 1938 and 1951. The European Space Agency maintains a satellite-launching center (established by France in 1964) in the city of Kourou.

Immense forests of rich timber cover 88% of the land. Fishing (especially shrimp), forestry, and gold mining are the most important industries.

Guadeloupe, in the West Indies' Leeward Islands, consists of 2 large islands, Basse-Terre and Grande-Terre, separated by the Salt River, plus Marie Galante and the Saintes group to the S and, to the N, Desirade, St. Barthelemy, and over half of St. Martin (the Netherlands' portion is called St. Maarten). A French possession since 1635, the department is represented in the French Parliament by 2 senators and 4 deputies; administration consists of a prefect (governor) as well as an elected general and regional councils.

Area of the islands is 687 sq mi (total); 659 sq mi (land); pop. (2006 est.) 452,776, mainly descendants of slaves; capital is Basse-Terre on Basse-Terre Island. The land is fertile; sugar, rum, and bananas are exported. Tourism is an important industry.

Martinique, the northernmost of the Windward Islands, in the West Indies, has been a possession since 1635, and a department since Mar. 1946. It is represented in the French Parliament by 2 senators and 4 deputies. The island was the birthplace of Napoleon's Empress Josephine.

It has an area of 425 sq mi (total); 409 sq mi (land); pop. (2006 est.) 436,131, mostly descendants of slaves. The capital is Fort-de-France, pop. (1991) is 101,000. It is a popular tourist stop. The chief exports are rum, bananas, and petroleum products.

Réunion is a volcanic island in the Indian O. about 420 mi E of Madagascar, and has belonged to France since 1665. Area, 972 sq mi (total); 968 sq mi (land); pop. (2006 est.) 787,584, 30% of French extraction. Capital: Saint-Denis. The chief export is sugar. It elects 5 deputies, 3 senators to the French Parliament.

Overseas Territorial Collectivities

Mayotte, claimed by Comoros and administered by France, voted in 1976 to become a territorial collectivity of France. An island NW of Madagascar, area is 144 sq mi, pop. (2006 est.) 201,234. The capital is Mamoutzou.

St. Pierre and Miquelon, formerly an overseas territory (1816-1976) and department (1976-85), made the transition to territorial collectivity in 1985. It consists of 2 groups of rocky islands near the SW coast of Newfoundland, inhabited by fishermen. The exports are chiefly fish products. The St. Pierre group has an area of 10 sq mi; Miquelon, 83 sq mi. Total pop. (2006 est.) 7,026. Capital: St. Pierre.

Both Mayotte and St. Pierre and Miquelon elect a deputy and a senator to the French Parliament.

Overseas Territories

Territory of **French Polynesia** comprises 130 islands widely scattered among 5 archipelagos in the South Pacific; administered by a Council of Ministers (headed by a president). Territorial Assembly and the Council have headquarters at Papeete, on Tahiti, one of the **Society Islands** (which include the **Windward** and **Leeward** islands). Two deputies and a senator are elected to the French Parliament.

Other groups are the **Marquesas Islands**, the **Tuamotu Archipelago**, including the **Gambier Islands**, and the **Austral Islands**.

Total area of the islands administered from Tahiti is 1,609 sq. mi. (total); 1,413 sq mi (land); pop. (2006 est.) 274,578, more than half on Tahiti. Tahiti is picturesque and mountainous with a productive coastline bearing coconuts, citrus, pineapples, and vanilla. Cultured pearls are also produced.

Tahiti was visited by Capt. James Cook in 1769 and by Capt. Bligh in the *Bounty*, 1788-89. Its beauty impressed Herman Melville, Paul Gauguin, and Charles Darwin. A coalition favoring independence for French Polynesia within 20 years gained control of the territorial assembly after elections May 23, 2004.

Territory of the **French Southern and Antarctic Lands** comprises **Adelie Land**, on Antarctica, and 4 island groups in the Indian O. **Area:** 3,023 sq mi (total); 3,023 sq mi (land).

Adelie, reached 1,840, has a research station, a coastline of 185 mi, and tapers 1,240 mi inland to the South Pole. The U.S. does not recognize national claims in Antarctica. There are 2 huge glaciers, Ninnis, 22 mi wide, 99 mi long, and Mentz, 11 mi wide, 140 mi long. The Indian O. groups are:

Kerguelen Archipelago, visited 1772, consists of one large and 300 small islands. The chief is 87 mi long, 74 mi wide, and has Mt. Ross, 6,429 ft tall. Principal research station is Port-aux-Français. Seals often weigh 2 tons; there are blue whales, coal, peat, semiprecious stones. **Crozet Archipelago**, reached 1772, covers 195 sq mi. Eastern Island rises to 6,560 ft. **Saint Paul**, in southern Indian O., has warm springs with earth at places heating to 120° to 390° F. **Amsterdam** is nearby; both produce cod and rock lobster.

Territory of **New Caledonia** and Dependencies is a group of islands in the Pacific O. about 1,115 mi E of Australia and approx. the same distance NW of New Zealand. Dependencies are the **Loyalty Islands, Isle of Pines, Belep Archipelago**, and **Huon Islands**.

The largest island, New Caledonia, is 6,530 sq mi. Total area of the territory is 7,359 sq mi (total); 7,172 sq mi (land); pop. (2006 est.) 219,246. The group was acquired by France in 1853.

The territory is administered by a High Commissioner. There is a popularly elected Territorial Congress. Two deputies and a senator are elected to the French Parliament. Capital: Noumea.

Mining is the chief industry. New Caledonia is one of the world's largest nickel producers. Other minerals found are chrome, iron, cobalt, manganese, silver, gold, lead, and copper. Agricultural products include yams, sweet potatoes, potatoes, manioc (cassava), corn, and coconuts.

In 1987, New Caledonian voters chose by referendum to remain within the French Republic. There were clashes between French and Melanesians (Kanaks) in 1988. An agreement Apr. 21, 1998, between France and rival New Caledonian factions specified a 15- to 20-year period of "shared sovereignty." The French constitution was amended, July 6, to allow the territory a gradual increase in autonomy, and New Caledonian voters approved the plan Nov. 8, 1998, by a 72% majority.

Territory of the **Wallis and Futuna Islands** comprises 2 island groups in the SW Pacific S of Tuvalu, N of Fiji, and W of Western Samoa; became an overseas territory July 29, 1961. The islands have a total area of 106 sq mi and population (2006 est.) of 16,025. **Alofi**, attached to Futuna, is uninhabited. Capital: Mata-Utu. Chief products are copra, yams, taro roots, bananas, and coconuts. A senator and a deputy are elected to the French Parliament.

Gabon
Gabonese Republic

People: Population: 1,424,906. **Age distrib.** (%) <15: 42.1; 65+: 4. **Pop. density:** 14 per sq mi, 5 per sq km. **Urban:** 83.8%. **Ethnic groups:** Fang, Bapounou, Nzebi, Obamba, European. **Principal languages:** French (official), Fang, Myene, Nzebi, Bapounou/Eschira, Bandjabi. **Chief religion:** Christian 55%-75%.

Geography: Total area: 103,347 sq mi, 267,667 sq km; **Land area:** 99,486 sq mi, 257,667 sq km. **Location:** On Atlantic coast of W central Africa. **Neighbors:** Equatorial Guinea and Cameroon on N, Congo on E and S. **Topography:** Heavily forested, the country consists of coastal lowlands; plateaus in N, E, and S; mountains in N, SE, and center. The Ogooue R. system covers most of Gabon. **Capital:** Libreville, 556,000.

Government: Type: Republic. **Head of state:** Pres. Omar Bongo Ondimba; b. Dec. 30, 1935; in office: Dec. 2, 1967. **Head of gov.:** Prime Min. Jean Eyeghe Ndong; b. Feb. 12, 1946; in office: Jan. 20, 2006. **Local divisions:** 9 provinces. **Defense budget** (2005): $19 mil. **Active troops:** 4,700.

Economy: Industries: food & beverages, textiles, lumber, cement, oil, mining, chemicals, ship repair. **Chief crops:** cocoa, coffee, sugar, palm oil, rubber. **Natural resources:** oil, mang., uranium, gold, timber, iron, hydropower. **Crude oil reserves** (2005): 2.5 bil bbls. **Arable land:** 1%. **Livestock** (2005): cattle: 35,000; chickens: 3.1 mil; goats: 90,000; pigs: 212,000; sheep: 195,000. **Fish catch** (2004): 46,040 metric tons. **Electricity prod.** (2004): 1.5 bil kWh. **Labor force:** agriculture 60%, industry 15%, services 25%.

Finance: Monetary unit: CFA BEAC Franc (XAF) (Sept. 2006: 512.47 = $1 U.S.). **GDP** (2005 est.): $9.5 bil; **per capita GDP:** $6,800; **GDP growth:** 2.1%. **Imports** (2005 est.): $1.5 bil; partners (2004): France 46.1%, U.S. 6.8%, U.K. 6.0%. **Exports** (2005 est.): $5.8 bil; partners (2004): France 46.1%, U.S. 6.8%, UK 6%. **Exports** (2005 est.): $5.8 bil; partners (2004): U.S. 51.9%, China 9.1%, France 7.7%. **Tourism** (2003): $15 mil. **Budget** (2005 est.): $1.6 bil. **Intl. reserves less gold:** $468 mil. **Gold:** 10,000 oz t. **Consumer prices:** 0.07%.

Transport: Railroad: Length: 506 mi. **Motor vehicles** 23,000 pass. cars, 10,000 comm. vehicles. **Civil aviation:** 399.5 mil pass.mi; 11 airports. **Chief ports:** Port-Gentil, Owendo, Libreville.

Communications: TV sets: 251 per 1,000 pop. **Radios:** 501 per 1,000 pop. **Telephone lines:** 39,100. **Daily newspaper circ.:** 29 per 1,000 pop. **Internet:** 40,000 users.

Health: Life expect.: 53.2 male; 55.8 female. **Births** (per 1,000 pop.): 36.2. **Deaths** (per 1,000 pop.): 12.2. **Natural inc.:** 2.39%. **Infant mortality** (per 1,000 live births): 54.5. **AIDS rate:** 7.9%.

Education: Compulsory: ages 6-16. **Literacy:** 63.2%.

Major Intl. Organizations: UN (FAO, IBRD, ILO, IMF, IMO, WHO, WTO), AU.

Embassy: 2034 20th St. NW, Ste. 200, 20009; 797-1000.

Website: www.legabon.org

France established control over the region in the second half of the 19th cent. Gabon became independent Aug. 17, 1960. A multiparty political system was introduced in 1990, and a new constitution was enacted Mar. 14, 1991. However, the reelection of longtime Pres. Omar Bongo, on Dec. 5, 1993, prompted rioting and charges of vote fraud. International observers also found fault with the presidential elections of Dec. 6, 1998, and Nov. 27, 2005, which Bongo won by lopsided margins.

Gabon is one of the most prosperous black African countries, thanks to abundant natural resources, foreign private investment, and government development programs.

The Gambia
Republic of The Gambia

People: Population: 1,641,564. **Age distrib.** (%) <15: 44.3; 65+: 2.7. **Pop. density:** 425 per sq mi, 164 per sq km. **Urban:** 26.1%. **Ethnic groups:** Mandinka 42%, Fula 18%, Wolof 16%, Jola 10%, Serahuli 9%. **Principal languages:** English (official), Mandinka, Wolof, Fula, other native dialects. **Chief religions:** Muslim 90%, Christian 9%.

Geography: Total area: 4,363 sq mi, 11,300 sq km; **Land area:** 3,861 sq mi, 10,000 sq km. **Location:** On Atlantic coast near W tip of Africa. **Neighbors:** Surrounded on 3 sides by Senegal. **Topography:** A narrow strip of land on each side of the lower Gambia R. **Capital:** Banjul 381,000.

Government: Type: Republic. **Head of state and gov.:** Yahya Jammeh; b. May 25, 1965; in office: July 23, 1994. **Local divisions:** 5 divisions, 1 city. **Defense budget** (2005): $2.3 mil. **Active troops:** 800.

Economy: Industries: peanuts, fish, hides, tourism, beverages, agric. machinery, woodworking, metalworking, clothing. **Chief crops:** peanuts, millet, sorghum, rice, corn, sesame, cassava, palm kernels. **Natural resources:** fish. **Livestock** (2005): cattle: 330,000; chickens: 650,000; goats: 270,000; pigs: 19,000; sheep: 148,000. **Fish catch** (2004): 31,423 metric tons. **Electricity prod.** (2004): 150 mil kWh. **Labor force:** agriculture 75%, industry 19%, services 6%.

Finance: Monetary unit: Dalasi (GMD) (Sept. 2006: 28.33 = $1 U.S.). **GDP** (2005 est.): $3 bil; **per capita GDP:** $1,900; **GDP growth:** 5.5%. **Imports** (2005 est.): $197 mil; partners (2004): China 25.1%, Senegal 9.2%, UK 6.3%, Brazil 6%, Netherlands 4.9%, U.S. 4.8%. **Exports** (2005 est.): $140.3 mil; partners (2004): Thailand 16.6%, UK 15.5%, France 14.2%, India 12.3%, Germany 9.2%, Italy 8.3%, Malaysia 4.1%. **Tourism** (1995): $28 mil. **Budget** (2005 est.): $62.7 mil. **Intl. reserves less gold:** $69 mil. **Consumer prices:** 3.17%.

Transport: Motor vehicles (1998): 6,400 pass. cars, 3,500 comm. vehicles. **Civil aviation:** NA; 1 airport. **Chief port:** Banjul.

Communications: TV Sets: 3 per 1,000 pop. Radios: 394 per 1,000 pop. **Telephone lines:** 44,000. **Daily newspaper circ.:** 1.7 per 1,000 pop. **Internet:** 49,000 users.

Health: Life expect.: 52.3 male; 56 female. **Births** (per 1,000 pop.): 39.4. **Deaths** (per 1,000 pop.): 12.2. **Natural inc.:** 2.71%. **Infant mortality** (per 1,000 live births): 71.6. **AIDS rate:** 2.4%.

Education: Free: ages 6-12. **Literacy:** 40.1%.

Major Intl. Organizations: UN (FAO, IBRD, ILO, IMF, IMO, WHO, WTO), the Commonwealth, AU.

Embassy: 1155 15th St. NW, Ste. 1000, 20005.

Website: www.statehouse.gm/index.html

The peoples of Gambia were at one time associated with the West African empires of Ghana, Mali, and Songhay. The area became Britain's first African possession in 1588.

Independence came Feb. 18, 1965; republic status within the Commonwealth was achieved in 1970. The country suffered from severe famine in the 1970s. Senegambia, a confederation with Senegal, lasted from 1982 to 1989.

On July 23, 1994, after 24 years in power, Pres. Dawda K. Jawara was deposed in a bloodless coup by a military officer, Yahya Jammeh. Jammeh barred political activity, detained potential opponents, and governed by decree. A new constitution was approved by referendum, Aug. 8, 1996. On Sept. 27 Jammeh won the presidential election. Parliamentary balloting on Jan. 2, 1997, completed the nominal return to civilian rule, but Jammeh retained a firm grip on power. He followed his reelection win on Oct. 18, 2001, with a new crackdown on dissidents. Security forces suppressed an alleged coup plot by army officers Mar. 2006. Pres. Jammeh won reelection to a 3rd term Sept. 24, 2006.

Georgia

People: Population: 4,661,473. **Age distrib.** (%) <15: 17.3; 65+: 16.5. **Pop. density:** 173 per sq mi, 66 per sq km. **Urban:** 51.9%. **Ethnic groups:** Georgian 70%, Armenian 8%, Russian 6%, Azeri 6%. **Principal languages:** Georgian (official), Russian, Armenian, Azeri, Abkhaz (official in Abkhazia). **Chief religions:** Georgian Orthodox 84%, Muslim 10%.

Geography: Total area: 26,911 sq mi, 69,700 sq km; **Land area:** 26,911 sq mi, 69,700 sq km. **Location:** SW Asia, on E coast of Black Sea. **Neighbors:** Russia on N and NE, Turkey and Armenia on S, Azerbaijan on SE. **Topography:** Separated from Russia on NE by main range of the Caucasus Mts. **Capital:** Tbilisi, 1,047,000.

Government: Type: Republic. **Head of state:** Pres. Mikhail Saakashvili; b. Dec. 21, 1967; in office: Jan. 25, 2004. **Head of gov.:** Prime Min. Zurab Noghaideli; b. Oct. 22, 1964; in office: Feb. 17, 2005. **Local divisions:** 53 rayons, 9 cities, and 2 autonomous republics. **Defense budget** (2005): $44 mil. **Active troops:** 11,320.

Economy: Industries: steel, aircraft, machine tools, appliances, mining, chemicals. **Chief crops:** citrus, grapes, tea, vegetables, potatoes. **Natural resources:** timber, hydropower, mang., iron ore, copper, coal, oil. **Crude oil reserves** (2005): 35 mil bbls. **Arable land:** 9%. **Livestock** (2005): cattle: 1.3 mil; chickens: 9.1 mil; goats: 115,700; pigs: 483,900; sheep: 689,200. **Fish catch** (2004): 3,023 metric tons. **Electricity prod.** (2004): 6.8 bil kWh. **Labor force** (1999 est.): agriculture 40%, industry 20%, services 40%.

Finance: Monetary unit: Lari (GEL) (Sept. 2006: 1.73 = $1 U.S.). **GDP** (2005 est.): $15.6 bil; **per capita GDP:** $3,300; **GDP growth:** 7%. **Imports** (2005 est.): $2.5 bil; partners (2004): U.S.

14.8%, Turkey 13.6%, Russia 11%, Germany 7.5%, UK 6.5%, Azerbaijan 6.2%, Ukraine 5.3%, Italy 4.1%. **Exports** (2005 est.): $1.4 bil; partners (2004): Turkey 28.1%, Russia 9.7%, Spain 7.9%, Turkmenistan 7.5%, U.S. 7.1%, Armenia 5.3%, Greece 5%. **Tourism:** $177 mil. **Budget** (2005 est.): $1.6 bil. **Intl. reserves less gold:** $331 mil. **Consumer prices:** 8.23%.

Transport: Railroad: Length: 1,002 mi. **Motor vehicles:** 255,200 pass. cars, 68,600 comm. vehicles. **Civil aviation:** NA; 19 airports. **Chief ports:** Batumi, Sukhumi.

Communications: TV sets: 516 per 1,000 pop. **Radios:** 590 per 1,000 pop. **Telephone lines:** 683,200. **Daily newspaper circ.:** NA. **Internet:** 175,600 users.

Health: Life expect.: 72.8 male; 79.9 female. **Births** (per 1,000 pop.): 10.4. **Deaths** (per 1,000 pop.): 9.2. **Natural inc.:** 0.12%. **Infant mortality** (per 1,000 live births): 18. **AIDS rate:** 0.2%.

Education: Compulsory: ages 6-12. **Literacy:** 99%.

Major Intl. Organizations: UN (FAO, IBRD, ILO, IMF, IMO, WHO, WTO), CIS, OSCE.

Embassy: 1101 15th St. NW, Ste. 602, 20005; 387-2390.

Website: www.parliament.ge

The region, which contained the ancient kingdoms of Colchis and Iberia, was Christianized in the 4th cent. and conquered by Arabs in the 8th cent. Annexed by Russia in 1801, Georgia was forcibly incorporated into the USSR in 1922.

Georgia declared independence Apr. 9, 1991. It became an independent state when the Soviet Union disbanded Dec. 26, 1991. There was fighting during 1991 between rebel forces and loyalists of Pres. Zviad Gamsakhurdia, who fled the capital Jan. 6, 1992. The ruling Military Council picked former Soviet Foreign Minister Eduard A. Shevardnadze to chair a newly created State Council. An attempted coup by forces loyal to Gamsakhurdia was crushed June 24, 1992. Shevardnadze was later elected president. Gamsakhurdia died Jan. 1994, reportedly by suicide.

Since the country gained independence, rebel movements have challenged the Tbilisi government. In Abkhazia, an autonomous republic within Georgia, ethnic Abkhazis, reportedly aided by Russia, launched a bloody military campaign and, by late 1993, had gained control of much of the region. A cease-fire providing for Russian peacekeepers was signed in Moscow May 14, 1994, but intermittent clashes continued. Georgian government troops also fought South Ossetia secessionists. Chechen rebels based in Pankisi Gorge, northeast of Tbilisi, launched attacks against Russian troops in Chechnya, heightening tensions with Russia.

Shevardnadze was wounded by a car bomb Aug. 29, 1995, while on his way to Parliament to sign a new constitution. He was reelected president Nov. 5. Shevardnadze escaped another assassination attempt, Feb. 9, 1998, when gunmen ambushed his motorcade. A mutiny by more than 200 soldiers was crushed Oct. 19.

Shevardnadze won another 5-year presidential term Apr. 9, 2000. But parliamentary elections Nov. 2, 2003, denounced as fraudulent by opposition groups and international observers, sparked massive antigovernment protests, causing him to resign Nov. 23. Opposition leader Mikhail Saakashvili won the presidential election of Jan. 4, 2004. Prime Min. Zurab Zhvania died Feb. 3, 2005, apparently by carbon-monoxide poisoning from a faulty gas heater; he was succeeded by Zurab Noghaideli. While U.S. Pres. George W. Bush addressed a large crowd in Tbilisi May 10, a live grenade was thrown toward the stage but failed to detonate. The grenade thrower, Vladimir Arutyunian, was convicted Jan. 11, 2006, of trying to assassinate Bush and Saakashvili. Another alleged coup plot was suppressed Sept. 6.

Germany
Federal Republic of Germany

People: Population: 82,422,299. **Age distrib.** (%) <15: 14.1; 65+: 19.4. **Pop. density:** 611 per sq mi, 236 per sq km. **Urban:** 88.1%. **Ethnic groups:** German 92%, Turkish 2%. **Principal languages:** German (official), Turkish, Italian, Greek, English, Danish, Dutch, Slavic languages. **Chief religions:** Protestant 34%, Roman Catholic 34%, Muslim 4%.

Geography: Total area: 137,847 sq mi, 357,021 sq km; **Land area:** 134,836 sq mi, 349,223 sq km. **Location:** In central Europe. **Neighbors:** Denmark on N; Netherlands, Belgium, Luxembourg, France on W; Switzerland, Austria on S; Czech Rep., Poland on E. **Topography:** Germany is flat in N, hilly in center and W, and mountainous in Bavaria in the S. Chief rivers are Elbe, Weser, Ems, Rhine, and Main, all flowing toward North Sea, and Danube, flowing toward Black Sea. **Capital:** Berlin, 3,389,000. **Cities (urban aggr., 2003):** Rhein-Ruhr North (including Essen), 6.54 mil; Rhein Main (Frankfurt am Mein), 3.68 mil; Rhein-Ruhr Middle (Dusseldorf), 3.24 mil; Rhein-Ruhr South (Cologne), 3.06 mil; Stuttgart, 2.68 mil; **Cities (proper):** Hamburg, 2.67 mil; Munich, 2.3 mil; Cologne, 963,200; Frankfurt-am-Mein, 644,700.

Government: Type: Federal republic. **Head of state:** Pres. Horst Köhler; b. Feb. 22, 1943; in office: July 1, 2004. **Head of gov.:** Chan. Angela Merkel; b. July 17, 1954; in office: Nov. 22, 2005. **Local divisions:** 16 laender (states). **Defense budget** (2005): $30.2 bil. **Active troops:** 284,500.

Economy: Industries: iron, steel, coal, cement, chemicals, machinery, vehicles, machine tools, electronics, food & beverages, shipbuilding. **Chief crops:** potatoes, wheat, barley, sugar beets, fruit, cabbages. **Natural resources:** iron ore, coal, potash, timber, lignite, uranium, copper, nat. gas, salt, nickel. **Crude oil reserves** (2005): 394 mil bbls. **Arable land:** 33%. **Livestock** (2005): cattle:

13.3 mil; chickens: 112 mil; goats: 170,000; pigs: 26.2 mil; sheep: 2.1 mil. **Fish catch** (2004): 319,336 metric tons. **Electricity prod.** (2004): 566.9 bil kWh. **Labor force** (1999): agriculture 2.8%, industry 33.4%, services 63.8%.

Finance: Monetary unit: Euro (EUR) (Sept. 2006: 0.78 = $1 U.S.). **GDP** (2005 est.): $2.5 tril; **per capita GDP:** $30,400; **GDP growth:** 0.9%. **Imports** (2005 est.): $801 bil; partners (2004): France 9.2%, Netherlands 8.7%, U.S. 6.5%, Italy 6.1%, UK 5.8%, Belgium 5.8%, China 5.3%, Austria 4.3%. **Exports** (2005 est.): $1 tril; partners (2004): France 10.2%, U.S. 8.8%, UK 8.2%, Italy 7.2%, Netherlands 6.3%, Belgium 5.7%, Austria 5.4%, Spain 5%. **Tourism:** $27.6 bil. **Budget** (2005 est.): $1.4 tril. **Intl. reserves less gold:** $31.58 bil. **Gold:** 110.21 mil oz t. **Consumer prices:** 1.95%. **Transport: Railroad: Length:** 28,686 mi. **Motor vehicles:** 44.66 mil pass. cars, 3.46 mil comm. vehicles. **Civil aviation:** 77.2 bil pass.-mi; 332 airports. **Chief ports:** Hamburg, Bremen, Bremerhaven, Lubeck, Rostock.

Communications: TV sets: 581 per 1,000 pop. **Radios:** 948 per 1,000 pop. **Telephone lines:** 55 mil. **Daily newspaper circ.:** 291 per 1,000 pop. **Internet:** 48.7 mil users.

Health: Life expect.: 75.8 male; 82 female. **Births** (per 1,000 pop.): 8.2. **Deaths** (per 1,000 pop.): 10.6. **Natural inc.:** −0.24%. **Infant mortality** (per 1,000 live births): 4.1. **AIDS rate:** 0.1%.

Education: Compulsory: ages 6-18. **Literacy:** 99%.

Major Intl. Organizations: UN and all of its specialized agencies, EU, NATO, OECD, OSCE.

Embassy: 4645 Reservoir Rd. NW 20007; 298-4000.

Website: www.germany-info.org

Germany is a central European nation originally composed of numerous states, with a common language and traditions, that were united in one country in 1871; Germany was split into 2 countries from the end of WWII until 1990, when it was reunified.

History and government. Germanic tribes were defeated by Julius Caesar, 55 and 53 BCE, but Roman expansion north of the Rhine was stopped in 9 CE. Charlemagne, ruler of the Franks, consolidated Saxon, Bavarian, Rhenish, Frankish, and other lands; after him the eastern part became the German Empire. The Thirty Years' War, 1618-48, split Germany into small principalities and kingdoms. After Napoleon, Austria contended with Prussia for dominance, but lost the Seven Weeks' War to Prussia, 1866. Otto von Bismarck, Prussian chancellor, formed the North German Confederation, 1867.

In 1870 Bismarck maneuvered Napoleon III into declaring war. After the quick defeat of France, Bismarck formed the **German Empire** and on Jan. 18, 1871, in Versailles, proclaimed King Wilhelm I of Prussia German emperor (Deutscher kaiser).

The German Empire reached its peak before WWI in 1914, with 208,780 sq mi, plus a colonial empire. After that war Germany ceded Alsace-Lorraine to France; West Prussia and Posen (Poznan) province to Poland; part of Schleswig to Denmark; lost all colonies and ports of Memel and Danzig.

Republic of Germany, 1919-33, adopted the Weimar constitution; met reparation payments and elected Friedrich Ebert and Gen. Paul von Hindenburg presidents.

Third Reich, 1933-45, Adolf Hitler led the National Socialist German Workers' (Nazi) party after WWI. In 1923 he attempted to unseat the Bavarian government and was imprisoned. Pres. von Hindenburg named Hitler chancellor Jan. 30, 1933; on Aug. 3, 1934, the day after Hindenburg's death, the cabinet joined the offices of president and chancellor and made Hitler fuehrer (leader). Hitler abolished freedom of speech and assembly, and began a long series of persecutions climaxed by the murder of millions of Jews and others.

He repudiated the Versailles treaty and reparations agreements, remilitarized the Rhineland (1936), and annexed Austria (Anschluss, 1938). At Munich he made an agreement with Neville Chamberlain, British prime minister, which permitted Germany to annex part of Czechoslovakia. He signed a nonaggression treaty with the USSR, 1939, and declared war on Poland Sept. 1, 1939, precipitating WWII. With total defeat near, Hitler committed suicide in Berlin Apr. 1945. The victorious Allies voided all acts and annexations of Hitler's Reich.

Division of Germany. Germany was sectioned into 4 zones of occupation, administered by the Allied Powers (U.S., USSR, UK, and France). The USSR took control of many E German states. The territory E of the so-called Oder-Neisse line was assigned to, and later annexed by, Poland. Northern East Prussia (now Kaliningrad) was annexed by the USSR. Greater Berlin, within but not part of the Soviet zone, was administered by the 4 occupying powers under the Allied Command. In 1948 the USSR withdrew, established its single command in East Berlin, and cut off supplies. The Western Allies utilized a gigantic airlift to bring food to West Berlin, 1948-49.

In 1949, 2 separate German states were established; in May the zones administered by the Western Allies became West Germany; in Oct. the Soviet sector became East Germany. West Berlin was considered an enclave of West Germany, although its status was disputed by the Soviet bloc.

East Germany. The German Democratic Republic (East Germany) was proclaimed in the Soviet sector of Berlin Oct. 7, 1949. It was

declared fully sovereign in 1954, but Soviet troops remained on grounds of security and the 4-power Potsdam agreement.

Coincident with the entrance of West Germany into the European defense community in 1952, the East German government decreed a prohibited zone 3 mi deep along its 600-mi border with West Germany and cut Berlin's telephone system in two. Berlin was further divided by erection of a fortified wall in 1961, after over 3 mil East Germans had fled to the West.

East Germany suffered severe economic problems at least until the mid-1960s. Then a "new economic system" was introduced, easing central planning controls and allowing factories to make profits provided they were reinvested in operations or redistributed to workers as bonuses. By the early 1970s, the economy of East Germany was highly industrialized, and the nation was credited with the highest standard of living among Warsaw Pact countries. But growth slowed in the late 1970s, because of shortages of natural resources and labor, and a huge debt to lenders in the West. Comparison with the lifestyle in the West caused many young people to emigrate.

The government firmly resisted following the USSR's policy of *glasnost*, but by Oct. 1989, was faced with nationwide demonstrations demanding reform. Pres. Erich Honecker, in office since 1976, was forced to resign Oct. 18. On Nov. 4, the border with Czechoslovakia was opened and permission granted for refugees to travel to the West. On Nov. 9, the East German government announced its decision to open the border with the West, signaling the end of the "Berlin Wall," which was the supreme emblem of the cold war. On Aug. 23, 1990, the East German parliament agreed to formal unification with West Germany; this occurred Oct. 3.

West Germany. The Federal Republic of Germany (West Germany) was proclaimed May 23, 1949, in Bonn. The occupying powers, the U.S., Britain, and France, restored civil status, Sept. 21. The Western Allies ended the state of war with Germany in 1951 (the U.S. resumed diplomatic relations July 2), while the USSR did so in 1955. The powers lifted controls, and the republic became fully independent May 5, 1955.

Dr. Konrad Adenauer, Christian Democrat, was made chancellor Sept. 15, 1949, and reelected 1953, 1957, 1961. Willy Brandt, heading a coalition of Social Democrats and Free Democrats, became chancellor Oct. 21, 1969, and pursued a policy of *Ostpolitik*, or rapprochement with East Germany and the USSR. Brandt resigned May 1974 because of a spy scandal. Terrorist acts on German soil in the 1970s included activities of the Baader-Meinhof gang and the murder of Israeli athletes by Palestinian commandos at the Olympic Games in Munich, Sept. 5, 1972.

Helmut Kohl became chancellor in 1982 and led Christian Democrats to victory in 1983 and 1987. In 1989, changes in the East German government and the opening of the Berlin Wall sparked talk of reunification of the 2 Germanys. In 1990, under Kohl's leadership, West Germany moved rapidly to reunite with East Germany.

A New Era. As Communism was being rejected in East Germany, talks began concerning German reunification. At a meeting in Ottawa, Feb. 1990, the foreign ministers of the WWII "Big Four" Allied nations and of East Germany and West Germany reached agreement on a format for high-level talks on German reunification.

In May 1990, NATO ministers adopted a package of proposals on reunification, including the inclusion of the united Germany as a full member of NATO and the barring of the new Germany from having its own nuclear, chemical, or biological weapons. In July, the USSR agreed to conditions that would allow Germany to become a member of NATO.

The 2 nations agreed to monetary unification under the West German mark beginning in July. The merger of the 2 Germanys took place Oct. 3, and the first all-German elections since 1932 were held Dec. 2. Eastern Germany received over $1 trillion in public and private funds from western Germany between 1990 and 1995. In 1991, Berlin again became the capital of Germany; the legislature, most administrative offices, and most foreign embassies had shifted from Bonn to Berlin by late 1999.

Germany's highest court ruled, July 12, 1994, that German troops could participate in international military missions abroad, when approved by Parliament. Ceremonies were held marking the final withdrawal of Russian troops from Germany, Aug. 31. Ceremonies were held the following week marking the final withdrawal of American, British, and French troops from Berlin. General elections Oct. 16 left Chancellor Helmut Kohl's governing coalition with a slim parliamentary majority. On Oct. 31, 1996, after more than 14 years in office, Kohl surpassed Adenauer as Germany's longest-serving chancellor in the 20th cent.

Unemployment hit a postwar high of 12.6% in Jan. 1998. The Kohl era ended with the defeat of the Christian Democrats in parliamentary elections Sept. 27; Gerhard Schröder, of the Social Democratic Party, became chancellor. Germany contributed 8,500 troops to the NATO-led security force (KFOR) that entered Kosovo in June 1999. Kohl resigned as honorary party chairman Jan. 18, 2000, amid allegations of illegal fund-raising. Kohl reached an agreement with prosecutors Feb. 8, 2001, in which he acknowledged committing a "breach of trust" and agreed to pay a fine, but did not plead guilty to any criminal charges.

> **IT'S A FACT:** The European Union has 20 official languages: Czech, Danish, Dutch, English, Estonian, Finnish, French, German, Greek, Hungarian, Italian, Latvian, Lithuanian, Maltese, Polish, Portuguese, Slovak, Slovenian, Spanish, and Swedish. Upon joining, each member state stipulates which language or languages it wants to list as an EU official language.

Despite a stagnant economy, Schröder's coalition of Social Democrats and Greens retained a slim majority in the elections of Sept. 22, 2002; the chancellor was apparently aided by his government's response to devastating summer floods and by his criticism of U.S. policy toward Iraq. In early 2003, Germany worked with France and Russia to block the UN Security Council from endorsing the U.S.-led invasion of Iraq. However, polls showed Schröder's support sharply falling. Schröder's coalition did poorly in elections for the European Parliament, June 13. When his party lost its stronghold of North Rhine-Westphalia in regional voting, May 22, 2005, Schröder called for early elections for Sept. 18. The Christian Democrats, led by Angela Merkel, won a razor-thin plurality, and after prolonged negotiations she became chancellor Nov. 22, heading a "grand coalition" that included the Socialists.

As of mid-2006, about 2,850 German troops were serving in Afghanistan as part of a NATO peacekeeping force and about 2,000 troops were set to serve a similar role in Lebanon.

Helgoland, an island of 130 acres in the North Sea, was taken from Denmark by a British Naval Force in 1807 and later ceded to Germany to become part of Schleswig-Holstein province in return for rights in East Africa. The heavily fortified island was surrendered to UK, May 23, 1945, demilitarized in 1947, and returned to West Germany, Mar. 1, 1952. It is a free port.

Ghana
Republic of Ghana

People: Population: 22,478,658. **Age distrib.** (%) <15: 38.7; 65+: 3.5. **Pop. density:** 252 per sq mi, 97 per sq km. **Urban:** 45.4%. **Ethnic groups:** Akan 44%, Moshi-Dagomba 16%, Ewe 13%, Ga 8%, Gurma 3%, Yoruba 1%. **Principal languages:** English (official); about 75 African languages incl. Akan, Moshi-Dagomba, Ewe, and Ga. **Chief religions:** Christian 63%, indigenous beliefs 21%, Muslim 16%.

Geography: Total area: 92,456 sq mi, 239,460 sq km; **Land area:** 89,166 sq mi, 230,940 sq km. **Location:** On southern coast of W Africa. **Neighbors:** Côte d'Ivoire on W, Burkina Faso on N, Togo on E. **Topography:** Most of Ghana consists of low fertile plains and scrubland, cut by rivers and by the artificial Lake Volta. **Capital:** Accra, 1,981,000. **City (urban aggr.):** Kumasi, 1,517,000.

Government: Type: Republic. **Head of state and gov.:** Pres. John Agyekum Kufuor; b. Dec. 8, 1938; in office: Jan. 7, 2001. **Local divisions:** 10 regions. **Defense budget** (2005): $49.5 mil. **Active troops:** 7,000.

Economy: Industries: mining, lumbering, light mfg., aluminum smelting, food proc. **Chief crops:** cocoa, rice, coffee, cassava, peanuts, corn, shea nuts, bananas. **Natural resources:** gold, timber, diamonds, bauxite, mang., fish, rubber, hydropower. **Crude oil reserves** (2005): 16.5 mil bbls. **Arable land:** 12%. **Livestock** (2005): cattle: 1.4 mil; chickens: 30 mil; goats: 3.6 mil; pigs: 305,000; sheep: 3.2 mil. **Fish catch** (2004): 400,320 metric tons. **Electricity prod.** (2004): 6.5 bil kWh. **Labor force** (1999 est.): agriculture 60%, industry 15%, services 25%.

Finance: Monetary unit: Cedi (GHC) (Sept. 2006: 9,172.00 = $1 U.S.). **GDP** (2005 est.): $54.5 bil; **per capita GDP:** $2,500; **GDP growth:** 4.3%. **Imports** (2005 est.): $4.3 bil; partners (2004): Nigeria 12.8%, China 10.1%, UK 7%, U.S. 6.7%, France 5.3%, South Africa 4.2%, Netherlands 4.2%, Germany 4.1%. **Exports** (2005 est.): $2.9 bil; partners (2004): Netherlands 11.1%, UK 10.9%, France 6.9%, U.S. 6%, Belgium 4.8%, Germany 4.4%, Japan 4.3%. **Tourism:** $466 mil. **Budget** (2005 est.): $3.5 bil. **Intl. reserves less gold:** $1.23 bil. **Gold:** 280,000 oz t. **Consumer prices:** 15.12%.

Transport: Railroad: Length: 592 mi. **Motor vehicles:** 91,900 pass. cars, 124,300 comm. vehicles. **Civil aviation:** 566.7 mil pass.-mi; 7 airports. **Chief ports:** Tema, Takoradi.

Communications: TV sets: 115 per 1,000 pop. **Radios:** 680 per 1,000 pop. **Telephone lines:** 313,300. **Daily newspaper circ.:** 13.9 per 1,000 pop. **Internet:** 368,000 users.

Health: Life expect.: 58 male; 59.5 female. **Births** (per 1,000 pop.): 30.5. **Deaths** (per 1,000 pop.): 9.7. **Natural inc.:** 2.08%. **Infant mortality** (per 1,000 live births): 54.9. **AIDS rate:** 2.3%.

Education: Compulsory: ages 6-14. **Literacy:** 57.9%.

Major Intl. Organizations: UN and all of its specialized agencies, the Commonwealth, AU.

Embassy: 3512 International Dr. NW 20008; 686-4520.

Website: www.ghana.gov.gh

Named for an African empire along the Niger River, 400-1240 CE, Ghana was ruled by Britain for 113 years as the Gold Coast. The UN in 1956 approved merger with the British Togoland trust territory. Independence came Mar. 6, 1957, and republic status within the Commonwealth in 1960.

Pres. Kwame Nkrumah built hospitals and schools, promoted development projects like the Volta R. hydroelectric and aluminum plants but ran the country into debt, jailed opponents, and was accused of corruption. A 1964 referendum gave Nkrumah dictatorial powers and set up a one-party socialist state. Nkrumah was overthrown in 1966 by a police-army coup, which expelled Chinese and East German teachers and technicians. Elections were held in 1969, but 4 further coups occurred in 1972, 1978, 1979, and 1981. The 1979 and 1981 coups, led by Flight Lieut. Jerry Rawlings, were followed by suspension of the constitution and banning of political parties. A new constitution, allowing multiparty politics, was approved in April 1992.

In Feb. 1993 more than 1,000 people were killed in ethnic clashes in northern Ghana. Rawlings won the presidential election of Dec.

7, 1996. Kofi Annan, a career UN diplomat from Ghana, became UN secretary general on Jan. 1, 1997. Opposition leader John Agyekum Kufuor won a runoff vote Dec. 28, 2000, and was sworn in Jan. 7, 2001, marking Ghana's first peaceful transfer of power from one elected president to another. He was reelected Dec. 7, 2004.

Greece
Hellenic Republic

People: Population: 10,688,058. **Age distrib.** (%) <15: 14.3; 65+: 19. **Pop. density:** 211 per sq mi, 81 per sq km. **Urban:** 60.8%. **Ethnic groups:** Greek 98%. **Principal languages:** Greek (official), English, French. **Chief religions:** Greek Orthodox 98% (official), Muslim 1%.

Geography: Total area: 50,942 sq mi, 131,940 sq km; **Land area:** 50,502 sq mi, 130,800 sq km. **Location:** Occupies southern end of Balkan Peninsula in SE Europe. **Neighbors:** Albania, Macedonia, Bulgaria on N; Turkey on E. **Topography:** About three-quarters of Greece is nonarable, with mountains in all areas. Pindus Mts. run through the country N to S. The heavily indented coastline is 9,385 mi. long. Of over 2,000 islands, only 169 are inhabited, among them Crete, Rhodes, Milos, Kerkira (Corfu), Chios, Lesbos, Samos, Euboea, Delos, Mykonos. **Capital:** Athens, 3,230,000 (1999 city proper: 748,110).

Government: Type: Parliamentary republic. **Head of state:** Pres. Karolos Papoulias; b. June 4, 1929; in office: Mar. 10, 2005. **Head of gov.:** Prime Min. Konstantinos (Costas) Karamanlis; b. Sept. 14, 1956; in office: Mar. 10, 2004. **Local divisions:** 13 regions comprising 51 prefectures. **Defense budget** (2005): $4.5 bil. **Active troops:** 163,850.

Economy: Industries: tourism, food & tobacco proc., textiles, chemicals, metal products, mining, oil. **Chief crops:** wheat, corn, barley, sugar beets, olives, tomatoes, grapes. **Natural resources:** bauxite, lignite, magnesite, oil, marble, hydropower potential. **Crude oil reserves** (2005): 7 mil bbls. **Arable land:** 19%. **Livestock** (2005): cattle: 600,000; chickens: 28 mil; goats: 5.4 mil; pigs: 1 mil; sheep: 9 mil. **Fish catch** (2004): 190,288 metric tons. **Electricity prod.** (2004): 55.5 bil kWh. **Labor force** (2004 est.): agriculture 12%, industry 20%, services 68%.

Finance: Monetary unit: Euro (EUR) (Sept. 2006: 0.78 = $1 U.S.). **GDP** (2005 est.): $236.8 bil; **per capita GDP:** $22,200; **GDP growth:** 3.7%. **Imports** (2005 est.): $48.2 bil; partners (2004): Germany 13.3%, Italy 12.6%, France 6.6%, Russia 5.4%, Netherlands 5.4%, South Korea 4.6%, U.S. 4.4%, UK 4.1%. **Exports** (2005 est.): $18.5 bil; partners (2004): Germany 13.3%, Italy 10.2%, UK 7.6%, Bulgaria 6.5%, U.S. 5.2%, Cyprus 4.6%, Turkey 4.6%, France 4.2%. **Tourism:** $12.7 bil. **Budget** (2005 est.): $103.4 bil. **Intl. reserves less gold:** $354 mil. **Gold:** 3.47 mil oz t. **Consumer prices:** 3.56%.

Transport: Railroad: Length: 1,598 mi. **Motor vehicles:** 3.84 mil pass. cars, 1.16 mil comm. vehicles. **Civil aviation:** 5.3 bil pass.-mi; 66 airports. **Chief ports:** Piraeus, Thessaloníki, Patrai.

Communications: TV sets: 480 per 1,000 pop. **Radios:** 475 per 1,000 pop. **Telephone lines:** 6.3 mil. **Daily newspaper circ.:** NA. **Internet:** 3.8 mil users.

Health: Life expect.: 76.7 male; 81.9 female. **Births** (per 1,000 pop.): 9.7. **Deaths** (per 1,000 pop.): 10.2. **Natural inc.:** −0.06%. **Infant mortality** (per 1,000 live births): 5.4. **AIDS rate:** 0.2%.

Education: Compulsory: ages 6-14. **Literacy:** 96%.

Major Intl. Organizations: UN (FAO, IBRD, ILO, IMF, IMO, WHO, WTO), EU, NATO, OECD, OSCE.

Embassy: 2221 Massachusetts Ave. NW 20008; 939-1300.

Website: www.primeminister.gr/gr/

The achievements of ancient Greece in art, architecture, science, mathematics, philosophy, drama, literature, and democracy became legacies for succeeding ages. Greece reached the height of its glory and power, particularly in the Athenian city-state, in the 5th cent. BCE. Greece fell under Roman rule in the 2nd and 1st centuries BCE. In the 4th cent. CE it became part of the Byzantine Empire and, after the fall of Constantinople to the Turks in 1453, part of the Ottoman Empire.

Greece won its war of independence from Turkey 1821-29, and became a kingdom. A republic was established 1924; the monarchy was restored, 1935, and George II, King of the Hellenes, resumed the throne. In Oct. 1940, Greece rejected an ultimatum from Italy. Nazi support resulted in its defeat and occupation by Germans, Italians, and Bulgarians. By the end of 1944 the invaders withdrew. Communist resistance forces were defeated by Royalist and British troops. A plebiscite again restored the monarchy.

Communists waged guerrilla war 1947-49 against the government but were defeated with the aid of the U.S. A period of reconstruction and rapid development followed, mainly with conservative governments under Premier Constantine Karamanlis. The Center Union, led by George Papandreou, won elections in 1963 and 1964, but King Constantine, who acceded in 1964, forced Papandreou to resign. A period of political maneuvers ended in the military takeover of April 21, 1967, by Col. George Papadopoulos. King Constantine tried to reverse the consolidation of the harsh dictatorship Dec. 13, 1967, but failed and fled to Italy. Papadopoulos was ousted Nov. 25, 1973.

Greek army officers serving in the National Guard of Cyprus staged a coup on the island July 15, 1974. Turkey invaded Cyprus a week later, precipitating the collapse of the Greek junta, which was implicated in the Cyprus coup. Democratic government returned (and in 1975 the monarchy was abolished).

The 1981 electoral victory of the Panhellenic Socialist Movement (Pasok) of Andreas Papandreou brought substantial changes in

Greece's internal and external policies. A scandal centered on George Kostokas, a banker and publisher, led to the arrest or investigation of leading Socialists, implicated Papandreou, and contributed to the defeat of the Socialists at the polls in 1989. However, Papandreou, who was narrowly acquitted Jan. 1992 of corruption charges, led the Socialists to a comeback victory in general elections Oct. 10, 1993.

Tensions between Greece and the Former Yugoslav Republic of Macedonia eased when the 2 countries agreed to normalize relations Sept. 13, 1995. The ailing Papandreou was replaced as prime minister by Costas Simitis, Jan. 18, 1996. Simitis led the Socialists to victory in the election of Sept. 22.

An earthquake that shook Athens Sept. 7, 1999, killed at least 143 people and left over 60,000 homeless. The Socialists retained power by a narrow margin in the elections of Apr. 9, 2000. Police in 2002 cracked down on the November 17 terrorist movement, blamed for 23 killings since the mid-1970s.

The conservative New Democracy Party won parliamentary elections, Mar. 7, 2004, and Konstantinos (Costas) Karamanlis became prime minister. Athens hosted the Olympic Summer Games, Aug. 13-29. A Cypriot jetliner crashed near Athens, Aug. 14, 2005, killing all 121 people on board.

Grenada

People: Population: 89,703. **Age distrib.** (%) <15: 33.4; 65+: 3.3. **Pop. density:** 674 per sq mi, 260 per sq km. **Urban:** 40.7%. **Ethnic groups:** Black 82%, Creole 13%. **Principal languages:** English (official), French patois. **Chief religions:** Roman Catholic 53%, Anglican 14%, other Protestant 33%.

Geography: Total area: 133 sq mi, 344 sq km; **Land area:** 133 sq mi, 344 sq km. **Location:** In Caribbean, 90 mi. N of Venezuela. **Neighbors:** Venezuela, Trinidad & Tobago to S; St. Vincent & the Grenadines to N. **Topography:** Main island is mountainous; country includes Carriacou and Petit Martinique islands. **Capital:** Saint George's, 33,000.

Government: Type: Parliamentary democracy. **Head of state:** Queen Elizabeth II, represented by Gov.-Gen. Daniel Williams; b. Nov. 4, 1935; in office: Aug. 8, 1996. **Head of gov.:** Prime Min. Keith Mitchell; b. Nov. 12, 1946; in office: June 22, 1995. **Local divisions:** 6 parishes, 1 dependency.

Economy: Industries: food, beverages, textiles, light assembly operations, tourism, constr. **Chief crops:** bananas, cocoa, nutmeg, mace, citrus, avocados. **Natural resources:** timber. **Arable land:** 15%. **Livestock** (2005): cattle: 4,450; chickens: 268,000; goats: 7,200; pigs: 2,650; sheep: 13,200. **Fish catch** (2004): 2,039 metric tons. **Electricity prod.** (2004): 170 mil kWh. **Labor force** (1999 est.): agriculture 24%, industry 14%, services 62%.

Finance: Monetary unit: East Caribbean Dollar (XCD) (Sept. 2006: 2.67 = $1 U.S.). **GDP** (2002 est.): $440 mil; **per capita GDP:** $5,000; **GDP growth:** 2.5%. **Imports** (2004 est.): $276 mil; partners (2004): U.S. 27.7%, Trinidad and Tobago 25.4%, UK 5.2%. **Exports** (2004 est.): $40 mil; partners (2004): Saint Lucia 11.8%, U.S. 11.6%, Netherlands 8.1%, Antigua and Barbuda 8%, Germany 7.7%, Saint Kitts and Nevis 7.2%, Dominica 7.2%, France 4.5%. **Tourism:** $104 mil. **Budget** (1997): $102.1 mil. **Intl. reserves less gold:** $66 mil. **Consumer prices** (changed in 2002): 1.1%.

Transport: Motor vehicles: 15,800 pass. cars, 4,200 comm. vehicles. **Civil aviation:** NA; 3 airports. **Chief ports:** Saint George's, Grenville.

Communications: TV sets: 376 per 1,000 pop. **Radios:** 613 per 1,000 pop. **Telephone lines:** 32,700. **Internet:** 8,000 users.

Health: Life expect.: 63.1 male; 66.7 female. **Births** (per 1,000 pop.): 22.1. **Deaths** (per 1,000 pop.): 6.9. **Natural inc.:** 1.52%. **Infant mortality** (per 1,000 live births): 14.3. **AIDS rate:** NA.

Education: Compulsory: ages 5-16. **Literacy:** 98%.

Major Intl. Organizations: UN (FAO, IBRD, ILO, IMF, IMO, WHO, WTO), Caricom, the Commonwealth, OAS, OECS.

Embassy: 1701 New Hampshire Ave. NW 20009; 265-2561.

Website: www.gov.gd

Columbus sighted Grenada in 1498. First European settlers were French, 1650. The island was held alternately by France and England until final British occupation, 1784. Grenada became fully independent Feb. 7, 1974, during a general strike. It is the smallest independent nation in the Western Hemisphere.

On Oct. 14, 1983, a military coup ousted Prime Min. Maurice Bishop, who was put under house arrest, later freed by supporters, rearrested, and, finally, on Oct. 19, executed. U.S. forces, with a token force from 6 other nations, invaded Grenada, Oct. 25. Resistance from the Grenadian army and Cuban advisors was quickly overcome as most people welcomed the invading forces. U.S. troops left Grenada in June 1985. Hurricane Ivan slammed into Grenada, Sept. 7, 2004, killing 39 people and damaging an estimated 90% of the buildings on the island.

Guatemala
Republic of Guatemala

People: Population: 12,454,747. **Age distrib.** (%) <15: 41.5; 65+: 3.6. **Pop. density:** 297 per sq mi, 114 per sq km. **Urban:** 46.3%. **Ethnic groups:** Mestizo 55%, Amerindian 43%. **Principal languages:** Spanish (official); more than 20 Amerindian languages, incl. Quiche, Cakchiquel, Kekchi, Mam, Garifuna, and Xinca. **Chief religions:** Mostly Roman Catholic; some Protestant, indigenous Mayan beliefs.

Geography: Total area: 42,043 sq mi, 108,890 sq km; **Land area:** 41,865 sq mi, 108,430 sq km. **Location:** In Central America. **Neighbors:** Mexico on N and W, El Salvador on S, Honduras and Belize on E. **Topography:** The central highland and mountain areas are bordered by the narrow Pacific coast and the lowlands and fertile river valleys on the Caribbean. There are numerous volcanoes in S, more than half a dozen over 11,000 ft. **Capital:** Guatemala City, 984,000.

Government: Type: Republic. **Head of state and gov.:** Pres. Oscar Berger Perdomo; b. Aug. 11, 1946; in office: Jan. 14, 2004. **Local divisions:** 22 departments. **Defense budget** (2004): $101 mil. **Active troops:** 29,200

Economy: Industries: sugar, textiles, clothing, furniture, chemicals, oil, metals, rubber, tourism. **Chief crops:** sugarcane, corn, bananas, coffee, beans, cardamom. **Natural resources:** oil, nickel, rare woods, fish, chicle, hydropower. **Crude oil reserves** (2005): 526 mil bbls. **Arable land:** 12%. **Livestock** (2005): cattle: 2.5 mil; chickens: 27 mil; goats: 112,000; pigs: 212,000; sheep: 260,000. **Fish catch** (2004): 18,339 metric tons. **Electricity prod.** (2004): 7.6 bil kWh. **Labor force** (1999 est.): agriculture 50%, industry 15%, services 35%.

Finance: Monetary unit: Quetzal (GTQ) (Sept. 2006: 7.60 = $1 U.S.). **GDP** (2005 est.): $56.9 bil; **per capita GDP:** $4,700; **GDP growth:** 3.2%. **Imports** (2005 est.): $7.744 bil; partners (2004): U.S. 33.3%, Mexico 8.5%, South Korea 7.5%, El Salvador 5.2%, China 5%, Venezuela 4%. **Exports** (2005 est.): $3.9 bil; partners (2004): U.S. 55.6%, El Salvador 9.7%, Mexico 3.5%. **Tourism:** $776 mil. **Budget** (2005 est.): $4 bil. **Intl. reserves less gold:** $2.56 bil. **Gold:** 220,000 oz t. **Consumer prices:** 8.42%.

Transport: Railroad: Length: 551 mi. **Motor vehicles:** 646,500 pass. cars, 21,200 comm. vehicles. **Civil aviation:** 212.5 mil pass.-mi; 11 airports. **Chief ports:** Puerto Barrios, San Jose.

Communications: TV sets: 61 per 1,000 pop. **Radios:** 79 per 1,000 pop. **Telephone lines:** 1.1 mil.. **Daily newspaper circ.:** NA. **Internet:** 756,000 users.

Health: Life expect.: 67.7 male; 71.2 female. **Births** (per 1,000 pop.): 29.6. **Deaths** (per 1,000 pop.): 5.4. **Natural inc.:** 2.43%. **Infant mortality** (per 1,000 live births): 30.8. **AIDS rate:** 0.9%.

Education: Compulsory: ages 7-15. **Literacy:** 69.1%.

Major Intl. Organizations: UN (FAO, IBRD, ILO, IMF, IMO, WHO, WTO), OAS.

Embassy: 2220 R St. NW 20008; 745-4952.

Website: www.guatemala-embassy.org

The old Mayan Indian empire flourished in what is today Guatemala for over 1,000 years before Spaniards came. Guatemala was a Spanish colony 1524-1821. A republic was established in 1839.

Since 1945 when a liberal government was elected to replace the long-term dictatorship of Jorge Ubico, the country has seen a variety of military and civilian governments and periods of civil war. Dissident army officers seized power Mar. 23, 1982, denouncing a presidential election as fraudulent and pledging to restore "authentic democracy" to the nation. Political violence caused large numbers of Guatemalans to seek refuge in Mexico. Another military coup occurred Oct. 8, 1983. The nation returned to civilian rule in 1986.

The crisis-ridden government of Pres. Jorge Serrano Elías was ousted by the military June 1, 1993. Ramiro de León Carpio was elected president by Congress June 6. A conservative businessman, Alvaro Arzú Irigoyen, won the presidency, Jan. 7, 1996. On Sept. 19 the Guatemalan government and leftist rebels approved a peace accord; the final agreement was signed Dec. 29. During more than 35 years of armed conflict, some 200,000 people were killed or "disappeared" (and are presumed dead); most of these casualties were attributed to the government and its paramilitary allies.

Violent episodes in 1998 included the daylight ambush of a busload of U.S. college students, Jan. 16, resulting in the rape of five young women, and the murder of Bishop Juan José Gerardi, a human rights activist, Apr. 26. U.S. Pres. Bill Clinton, on a visit to Guatemala Mar. 10, 1999, apologized for aid the U.S. had given to forces which he said "engaged in violence and widespread repression." Candidates of the right-wing populist Guatemalan Republican Front won control of Congress, Nov. 7, 1999, and the presidency, Dec. 26.

Drought and weak export prices during 2001-02 worsened the plight of Guatemala's poor, who make up 80% of the population. Oscar Berger Perdomo, the conservative former mayor of Guatemala City, won a presidential runoff election Dec. 28, 2003. Floods and mudslides from Tropical Storm Stan, Oct. 2005, killed at least 669 people; another 844 were missing and presumed dead.

Guinea
Republic of Guinea

People: Population: 9,690,222. **Age distrib.** (%) <15: 44.4; 65+: 3.2. **Pop. density:** 102 per sq mi, 39 per sq km. **Pop. density:** 100 per sq mi, 38 per sq km. **Urban:** 34.9%. **Ethnic groups:** Peuhl 40%, Malinke 30%, Soussou 20%. **Principal languages:** French (official); many African languages. **Chief religions:** Muslim 85%, Christian 8%, indigenous beliefs 7%.

Geography: Total area: 94,926 sq mi, 245,857 sq km; **Land area:** 94,926 sq mi, 245,857 sq km. **Location:** On Atlantic coast of W Africa. **Neighbors:** Guinea-Bissau, Senegal, Mali on N; Côte d'Ivoire on E; Liberia on S. **Topography:** A narrow coastal belt leads to the mountainous middle region, the source of the Gambia, Senegal, and Niger rivers. Upper Guinea, farther inland, is a cooler upland. The SE is forested. **Capital:** Conakry, 1,425,000.

Government: Type: Republic. **Head of state:** Pres. Gen. Lansana Conté; b. 1934; in office: Apr. 5, 1984. **Head of gov.:** Vanct from Apr. 5, 2006. **Local divisions:** 33 prefectures, 1 special zone. **Defense budget** (2005): $72 mil. **Active troops:** 9,700.

Economy: Industries: bauxite, gold, diamonds, aluminum refining, light mfg., agric. proc. **Chief crops:** rice, coffee, pineapples, palm kernels, cassava, bananas, sweet potatoes. **Natural resources:** bauxite, iron ore, diamonds, gold, uranium, hydropower, fish. **Arable land:** 2%. **Livestock** (2005): cattle: 3.4 mil; chickens: 15 mil; goats: 1.4 mil; pigs: 67,500; sheep: 1.1 mil. **Fish catch** (2004): 92,550 metric tons. **Electricity prod.** (2004): 790 mil kWh. **Labor force** (2000 est.): agriculture 80%, industry and services 20%.

Finance: Monetary unit: Franc (GNF) (Sept. 2006: 5,569.80 = $1 U.S.). **GDP** (2005 est.): $19 bil; **per capita GDP:** $2,000; **GDP growth:** 2%. **Imports** (2005 est.): $680 mil; partners (2004): France 14.6%, China 9.6%, Netherlands 6.8%, Belgium 6%, U.S. 5.9%, Italy 5%, South Africa 4.6%, Côte d'Ivoire 4.3%, India 4%. **Exports** (2005 est.): $612.1 mil; partners (2004): South Korea 15.6%, Russia 13.1%, Spain 12.3%, Ireland 9.1%, U.S. 7.5%, Germany 6.2%, France 5.9%, Ukraine 5.6%, Belgium 5.2%. **Tourism:** $30 mil. **Budget** (2005 est.): $590.4 mil. **Intl. reserves less gold:** $67 mil.

Transport: Railroad: Length: 520 mi. **Motor vehicles:** 23,200 pass. cars, 13,000 comm. vehicles. **Civil aviation:** 58.4 mil pass.-mi; 5 airports. **Chief port:** Conakry.

Communications: TV sets: 47 per 1,000 pop. **Radios:** 52 per 1,000 pop. **Telephone lines:** 26,200. **Internet:** 46,000 users.

Health: Life expect.: 48.3 male; 50.7 female. **Births** (per 1,000 pop.): 41.8. **Deaths** (per 1,000 pop.): 15.5. **Natural inc.:** 2.63%. **Infant mortality** (per 1,000 live births): 90. **AIDS rate:** 1.5%.

Education: Compulsory: ages 7-12. **Literacy:** 29.5%.

Major Intl. Organizations: UN and most of its specialized agencies, AU.

Embassy: 2112 Leroy Pl. NW 20008; 483-9420.

Website: guinea.usembassy.gov

Sékou Touré, Guinea's first president (1958-84), turned to Communist nations for support and set up a one-party state. Thousands of opponents were jailed in the 1970s, after an unsuccessful Portuguese invasion. Many were tortured and killed.

The military took control in a bloodless coup after the March 1984 death of Touré. A new constitution was approved in 1991, but movement toward democracy was slow. When presidential elections were finally held, in Dec. 1993, the incumbent, Gen. Lansana Conté, was the official winner; outside monitors called the elections flawed. Parliamentary elections June 11, 1995, raised similar complaints. Conté suppressed an army mutiny in Conakry, Feb. 2-3, 1996, and won reelection in Dec. 1998.

Fighting in early 2001 along the border with Liberia and Sierra Leone created a refugee crisis in Guinea; efforts to repatriate the Liberians were ongoing in 2006. Major opposition parties boycotted the presidential election Dec. 21, 2003, in which the ailing Conté won 95.6% of the vote. After 2 months in office, Prime Min. François Fall resigned, Apr. 30, 2004, charging Conté with thwarting reform efforts. His successor, Cellou Dalein Diallo, was fired in a power struggle, Apr. 5, 2006.

Guinea-Bissau
Republic of Guinea-Bissau

People: Population: 1,442,029. **Age distrib.** (%) <15: 41.4; 65+: 3. **Pop. density:** 133 per sq mi, 51 per sq km. **Urban:** 34.0%. **Ethnic groups:** Balanta 30%, Fula 20%, Manjaca 14%, Mandinga 13%, Papel 7%. **Principal languages:** Portuguese (official), Crioulo, African languages. **Chief religions:** Indigenous beliefs 50%, Muslim 45%, Christian 5%.

Geography: Total area: 13,946 sq mi, 36,120 sq km; **Land area:** 10,811 sq mi, 28,000 sq km. **Location:** On Atlantic coast of W Africa. **Neighbors:** Senegal on N, Guinea on E and S. **Topography:** A swampy coastal plain covers most of the country; to the east is a low savanna region. **Capital:** Bissau, 367,000.

Government: Type: Republic. **Head of state:** Pres. João Bernardo Vieira; b. Apr. 27, 1939; in office: Oct. 1, 2005. **Head of gov.:** Aristides Gomes; b. Nov. 8, 1954; in office: Nov. 2, 2005. **Local divisions:** 9 regions. **Defense budget** (2005): $8.6 mil. **Active troops:** 9,250.

Economy: Industries: agric. proc., beer, soft drinks. **Chief crops:** rice, corn, beans, cassava, cashew nuts, peanuts, palm kernels, cotton. **Natural resources:** fish, timber, phosphates, bauxite, oil. **Arable land:** 11%. **Livestock** (2005): cattle: 530,000; chickens: 1.6 mil; goats: 335,000; pigs: 370,000; sheep: 300,000. **Fish catch** (2004): 6,200 metric tons. **Electricity prod.** (2004): 60 mil kWh. **Labor force** (2000 est.): agriculture 82%, industry and services 18%.

Finance: Monetary unit: CFA BCEAO Franc (XOF) (Sept. 2006: 512.27 = $1 U.S.). **GDP** (2005 est.): $1.2 bil; **per capita GDP:** $800; **GDP growth:** 2.3%. **Imports** (2004 est.): $176 mil; partners (2004): Senegal 23.4%, Portugal 20.4%, China 3%, Netherlands 5.8%. **Exports** (2004 est.): $116 mil; partners (2004): India 54.9%, U.S. 24.2%, Nigeria 12.7%, Italy 4.1%. **Tourism** (2003): $2 mil. **Intl. reserves less gold:** $56 mil. **Consumer prices:** 3.33%.

Transport: Motor vehicles: 3,500 pass. cars, 2,500 comm. vehicles. **Civil aviation:** NA; 3 airports. **Chief port:** Bissau.

Communications: Radios: 43 per 1,000 pop. **Telephone lines:** 10,600. **Daily newspaper circ.:** 4.8 per 1,000 pop. **Internet:** 26,000 users.

Health: Life expect.: 45 male; 48.8 female. **Births** (per 1,000 pop.): 37.2. **Deaths** (per 1,000 pop.): 16.5. **Natural inc.:** 2.07%. **Infant mortality** (per 1,000 live births): 105.2. **AIDS rate:** 3.8%.

Education: Compulsory: ages 7-12. **Literacy:** 42.4%.

Major Intl. Organizations: UN (FAO, IBRD, ILO, IMF, IMO, WHO, WTO), AU.

Embassy: 15929 Yukon Lane, Rockville, MD 20855; 301-947-3958.

Website: www.state.gov/p/af/ci/pu

Portuguese mariners explored the area in the mid-15th cent.; the slave trade flourished in the 17th and 18th centuries, and colonization began in the 19th.

Beginning in the 1960s, an independence movement waged a guerrilla war and formed a government in the interior that had international support. Independence came Sept. 10, 1974, after the Portuguese regime was overthrown.

A November 1980 coup gave army chief João Bernardo Vieira absolute power. Vieira eventually initiated political liberalization; multiparty elections were held July 3, 1994. An army uprising June 7, 1998, triggered a civil war with Senegal and Guinea aiding the Vieira regime. After a peace accord signed on Nov. 2 broke down, rebel troops ousted Vieira on May 7, 1999. Elections Nov. 28-29, 1999, and Jan. 16, 2000, brought a return of civilian rule. Top military officers staged an apparently bloodless coup Sept. 14, 2003. A caretaker government was installed Sept. 28, and legislative elections were held Mar. 2004. Vieira won a presidential runoff election, July 24, 2005, and returned to power Oct. 1.

Guyana
Co-operative Republic of Guyana

People: Population: 767,245. **Age distrib.** (%) <15: 26.2; 65+: 5.2. **Pop. density:** 10 per sq mi, 3 per sq km. **Urban:** 37.6%. **Ethnic groups:** East Indian 50%, black 36%, Amerindian 7%. **Principal languages:** English (official), Amerindian dialects, Creole, Hindi, Urdu. **Chief religions:** Christian 50%, Hindu 35%, Muslim 10%.

Geography: Total area: 83,000 sq mi, 214,970 sq km; **Land area:** 76,004 sq mi, 196,850 sq km. **Location:** On N coast of South America. **Neighbors:** Venezuela on W, Brazil on S, Suriname on E. **Topography:** Dense tropical forests cover much of the land, although a flat coastal area up to 40 mi. wide, where 90% of the population lives, provides rich alluvial soil for agriculture. A grassy savanna divides the 2 zones. **Capital:** Georgetown, 134,000.

Government: Type: Republic. **Head of state:** Pres. Bharrat Jagdeo; b. Jan. 23, 1964; in office: Aug. 11, 1999. **Head of gov.:** Prime Min. Samuel Hinds; b. Dec. 27, 1943; in office: Dec. 22, 1997. **Local divisions:** 10 regions. **Defense budget** (2005): $5.9 mil. **Active troops:** 1,100.

Economy: Industries: bauxite, sugar, rice milling, timber, textiles, gold mining. **Chief crops:** sugar, rice, wheat, vegetable oils. **Natural resources:** bauxite, gold, diamonds, hardwood timber, shrimp, fish. **Arable land:** 2%. **Livestock** (2005): cattle: 110,000; chickens: 20 mil; goats: 79,000; pigs: 13,000; sheep: 130,000. **Fish catch** (2004): 57,325 metric tons. **Electricity prod.** (2004): 820 mil kWh.

Finance: Monetary unit: Dollar (GYD) (Sept. 2006: 189.50 = $1 U.S.). **GDP** (2005 est.): $3.5 bil; **per capita GDP:** $4,600; **GDP growth:** -2.5%. **Imports** (2005 est.): $681.6 mil; partners (2004): U.S. 26.2%, Trinidad and Tobago 21.6%, UK 6.4%, Cuba 5.9%, China 4.7%. **Exports** (2005 est.): $587.2 mil; partners (2004): Canada 22.8%, U.S. 19%, UK 12.1%, Portugal 8.2%, Jamaica 6.6%, Belgium 6.3%. **Tourism:** $28 mil. **Budget** (2005 est.): $362.6 mil. **Intl. reserves less gold:** $176 mil. **Consumer prices:** 6.34%.

Transport: Railroad: Length: 116 mi. **Motor vehicles:** 61,300 pass. cars, 15,500 comm. vehicles. **Civil aviation:** 108.7 mil pass.-mi; 9 airports. **Chief port:** Georgetown.

Communications: TV sets: 70 per 1,000 pop. **Radios:** 468 per 1,000 pop. **Telephone lines:** 110,100. **Daily newspaper circ.:** 74.8 per 1,000 pop. **Internet:** 145,000 users.

Health: Life expect.: 63.2 male; 68.7 female. **Births** (per 1,000 pop.): 18.3. **Deaths** (per 1,000 pop.): 8.3. **Natural inc.:** 1%. **Infant mortality** (per 1,000 live births): 32.2. **AIDS rate:** 2.4%.

Education: Compulsory: ages 6-15. **Literacy:** 98.8%.

Major Intl. Organizations: UN (FAO, IBRD, ILO, IMF, IMO, WHO, WTO), Caricom, the Commonwealth, OAS.

Embassy: 2490 Tracy Place NW 20008; 265-6900.

Website: www.op.gov.gy

Guyana became a Dutch possession in the 17th cent., but sovereignty passed to Britain in 1815. Indentured servants from India soon outnumbered African slaves. Ethnic tension has affected political life.

Guyana became independent May 26, 1966. A Venezuelan claim to the western half of Guyana was suspended in 1970 but renewed in 1982; an agreement was reached in 1989. The Suriname border is disputed. The government has nationalized most of the economy, which has remained severely depressed.

The Port Kaituma ambush of U.S. Rep. Leo J. Ryan and others investigating mistreatment of American followers of the Rev. Jim Jones's People's Temple cult triggered a mass suicide-execution of 911 cultists at Jonestown in the jungle, Nov. 18, 1978.

The People's National Congress, the party in power since Guyana became independent, was voted out of office with the election of Cheddi Jagan in Oct. 1992. When Pres. Jagan died Mar. 6, 1997, Prime Min. Samuel Hinds succeeded him. Jagan's widow, Janet, became prime min. Mar. 17. She won the presidency in a disputed election Dec. 15. She resigned because of ill health Aug. 11, 1999, and was succeeded by Bharrat Jagdeo, then 35, who became the youngest head of state in the Americas. He won reelection Mar. 19, 2001, and Aug. 28, 2006.

Floods from torrential rains, Jan. 2005, affected about 40% of the population. Gunmen in Georgetown killed Agric. Min. Satyadeow Sawh and 2 members of his family, Apr. 22, 2006.

Haiti
Republic of Haiti
People: Population: 8,497,543. **Age distrib.** (%) <15: 42.3; 65+: 3.5. **Pop. density:** 798 per sq mi, 308 per sq km. **Urban:** 37.5%. **Ethnic groups:** Black 95%, Creole and other 5%. **Principal languages:** French, Creole (both official). **Chief religions:** Roman Catholic 80%, Protestant 16%; Voodoo widely practiced.

Geography: Total area: 10,714 sq mi, 27,750 sq km; **Land area:** 10,641 sq mi, 27,560 sq km. **Location:** In Caribbean, occupies western third of Isl. of Hispaniola. **Neighbors:** Dominican Republic on E, Cuba to W. **Topography:** About two-thirds of Haiti is mountainous. Much of the rest is semiarid. Coastal areas are warm and moist. **Capital:** Port-au-Prince, 2,129,000.

Government: Type: In transition. **Head of state:** Pres. René Préval; b. Jan. 17, 1943; in office May 14, 2006. **Head of gov.:** Prime Min. Jacques Édouard Alexis; b. Sept. 21, 1947; in office: June 9, 2006. **Local divisions:** 9 departments. **Defense budget:** NA. **Active troops:** None.

Economy: Industries: sugar refining, flour milling, textiles, cement, light assembly. **Chief crops:** coffee, mangoes, sugarcane, rice, corn, sorghum. **Natural resources:** bauxite, copper, calcium carbonate, gold, marble, hydropower. **Arable land:** 20%. **Livestock** (2005): cattle: 1.5 mil; chickens: 5.5 mil; goats: 1.9 mil; pigs: 1 mil; sheep: 153,500. **Fish catch** (2004): 8,300 metric tons. **Electricity prod.** (2004): 540 mil kWh. **Labor force** (2004): agriculture 66%, industry 9%, services 25%.

Finance: Monetary unit: Gourde (HTG) (Sept. 2006: 38.20 = $1 U.S.). **GDP** (2005 est.): $14.2 bil; **per capita GDP:** $1,700; **GDP growth:** 2%. **Imports** (2005 est.): $1.5 bil; partners (2004): U.S. 52.9%, Dominican Republic 6%, Japan 2.9%. **Exports** (2005 est.): $390.7 mil; partners (2004): U.S. 81.8%, Dominican Republic 7.2%, Canada 4.2%. **Tourism** (2003): $93 mil. **Budget** (2005 est.): $600.8 mil. **Intl. reserves less gold:** $93 mil. **Consumer prices:** 15.83%.

Transport: Railroad: Length: 25 mi. **Motor vehicles:** 93,000 pass. cars, 61,600 comm. vehicles. **Civil aviation:** NA; 4 airports. **Chief ports:** Port-au-Prince, Les Cayes, Cap-Haitien.

Communications: TV sets: 5 per 1,000 pop. **Radios:** 53 per 1,000 pop. **Telephone lines:** 140,000. **Daily newspaper circ.:** NA. **Internet:** 500,000 users.

Health: Life expect.: 54.8 male; 58 female. **Births** (per 1,000 pop.): 36. **Deaths** (per 1,000 pop.): 10.7. **Natural inc.:** 2.53%. **Infant mortality** (per 1,000 live births): 65.4. **AIDS rate:** 3.8%.

Education: Compulsory: ages 6-11. **Literacy:** 52.9%.

Major Intl. Organizations: UN and most of its specialized agencies, OAS, Caricom.

Embassy: 2311 Massachusetts Ave. NW 20008; 332-4090. **Website:** www.haiti.org

Haiti, visited by Columbus, 1492, and a French colony from 1697, attained its independence, 1804, following the rebellion led by former slave Toussaint L'Ouverture. After a period of political violence, the U.S. occupied the country 1915-34.

François Duvalier, known as Papa Doc, was elected president in Sept. 1957; in 1964 he was named president for life. Upon his death in 1971, he was succeeded by his son, Jean Claude Duvalier, known as Baby Doc. Following weeks of unrest, Jean Claude fled Haiti aboard a U.S. Air Force jet Feb. 7, 1986. His departure ended the Duvalier family's brutal 28-year dictatorship, but political violence, government corruption, poverty, AIDS and other health problems, and deteriorating environmental quality have continued to plague Haiti.

Father Jean-Bertrand Aristide was elected president Dec. 1990, but in Sept. 1991, he was arrested by the military and expelled from the country. Some 35,000 Haitian refugees were intercepted by the U.S. Coast Guard as they tried to enter the U.S., 1991-92. Most were returned to Haiti. There was a new upsurge of refugees starting in late 1993.

The UN authorized, July 31, 1994, an invasion of Haiti by a multinational force. With U.S. troops already en route, a full-scale invasion was averted, Sept. 18, when military leaders agreed to step down. Aristide returned to Haiti and was restored to office Oct. 15. A UN peacekeeping force exercised responsibility in Haiti from Mar. 31, 1995 to Nov. 30, 1997. Aristide transferred power to his elected successor, René Préval, on Feb. 7, 1996.

At least 140 people died and more than 160,000 became homeless when Hurricane Georges struck Haiti Sept. 22, 1998. Aristide won the presidency Nov. 26, 2000, in an election boycotted by opposition groups. An armed uprising in early 2004 and pressure from France and the U.S. toppled Aristide, who went into exile Feb. 29. A US-led contingent, sent in after the upheaval, yielded authority June 1 to a UN stabilization force (MINUSTAH); as of mid-2006, MINUSTAH had 8,700 uniformed personnel.

Flooding in late May 2004 killed more than 1,000 people, and more than 2,400 were killed in Tropical Storm Jeanne in Sept. Presidential elections Feb. 7, 2006, restored Préval to power. Meeting July 25 in Port-au-Prince, international donors pledged $750 mil in aid.

Honduras
Republic of Honduras
People: Population: 7,326,496. **Age distrib.** (%) <15: 39.9; 65+: 3.4. **Pop. density:** 169 per sq mi, 65 per sq km. **Urban:** 45.6%. **Ethnic groups:** Mestizo 90%, Amerindian 7%, Black 2%, White 1%. **Principal languages:** Spanish (official), Garífuna, Amerindian dialects. **Chief religion:** Roman Catholic 97%.

Geography: Total area: 43,278 sq mi, 112,090 sq km; **Land area:** 43,201 sq mi, 111,890 sq km. **Location:** In Central America. **Neighbors:** Guatemala on W, El Salvador and Nicaragua on S. **Topography:** The Caribbean coast is 500 mi. long. Pacific coast, on Gulf of Fonseca, is 40 mi. long. Honduras is mountainous, with wide fertile valleys and rich forests. **Capital:** Tegucigalpa, 927,000.

Government: Type: Republic. **Head of state and gov.:** Pres. José Manuel Zelaya Rosales; b. Sept. 20, 1952; in office: Jan. 27, 2006. **Local divisions:** 18 departments. **Defense budget** (2005): $52 mil. **Active troops:** 12,000.

Economy: Industries: sugar, coffee, textiles, clothing, wood products. **Chief crops:** bananas, coffee, citrus. **Natural resources:** timber, gold, silver, copper, lead, zinc, iron ore, antimony, coal, fish, hydropower. **Arable land:** 15%. **Livestock** (2005): cattle: 2.5 mil; chickens: 18.7 mil; goats: 24,207; pigs: 490,000; sheep: 14,877. **Fish catch** (2004): 37,459 metric tons. **Electricity prod.** (2004): 4.8 bil kWh. **Labor force** (2001 est.): agriculture 34%, industry 21%, services 45%.

Finance: Monetary unit: Lempira (HNL) (Sept. 2006: 18.95 = $1 U.S.). **GDP** (2005 est.): $20.6 bil; **per capita GDP:** $2,900; **GDP growth:** 4.2%. **Imports** (2005 est.): $4.2 bil; partners (2005): U.S. 51.3%, El Salvador 3.3%, Mexico 2.9%. **Exports** (2005 est.): $1.7 bil; partners (2004): U.S. 63.3%, El Salvador 2.8%, Guatemala 2.6%. **Tourism:** $396 mil. **Budget** (2005 est.): $1.9 bil. **Intl. reserves less gold:** $1.63 bil. **Gold:** 20,000 oz t. **Consumer prices:** 8.81%.

Transport: Railroad: Length: 434 mi. **Motor vehicles:** 46,000 pass. cars, 39,300 comm. vehicles. **Civil aviation:** NA; 11 airports. **Chief ports:** Puerto Cortes, La Ceiba.

Communications: TV sets: 95 per 1,000 pop. **Radios:** 410 per 1,000 pop. **Telephone lines:** 494,400. **Daily newspaper circ.:** NA. **Internet:** 223,000 users.

Health: Life expect.: 67.8 male; 71 female. **Births** (per 1,000 pop.): 28.2. **Deaths** (per 1,000 pop.): 5.3. **Natural inc.:** 2.3%. **Infant mortality** (per 1,000 live births): 25.8. **AIDS rate:** 1.5%.

Education: Compulsory: ages 6-11. **Literacy:** 80%.

Major Intl. Organizations: UN (FAO, IBRD, ILO, IMF, IMO, WHO, WTO), OAS.

Embassy: 3007 Tilden St. NW, Suite 4M, 20008; 966-7702. **Website:** www.hondurasemb.org

Mayan civilization flourished in Honduras in the 1st millennium CE. Columbus arrived in 1502. Honduras became independent after freeing itself from Spain, 1821, and from the Fed. of Central America, 1838.

Gen. Oswaldo Lopez Arellano, president for most of the period 1963-75 by virtue of one election and 2 coups, was ousted by the army in 1975 over charges of pervasive bribery by United Brands Co. of the U.S. An elected civilian government took power in 1982. Some 3,200 U.S. troops were sent to Honduras after the Honduran border was violated by Nicaraguan forces, Mar. 1988.

Already one of the poorest countries in the Western Hemisphere, Honduras was devastated in late Oct. 1998 by Hurricane Mitch, which killed at least 5,600 people and caused more than $850 mil in damage to crops and livestock.

Ricardo Maduro, a businessman who pledged to crack down on crime, won the presidency Nov. 25, 2001. A fire May 17, 2004, killed 104 inmates at an overcrowded prison in San Pedro Sula. Gunmen in that city Dec. 23 killed 28 passengers on a bus. In mid-Nov. 2005, floods and mudslides from Tropical Storm Gamma left 32 dead. José Manuel Zelaya Rosales of the opposition Liberal Party won the presidential election held Nov. 27.

Hungary
Republic of Hungary
People: Population: 9,981,334. **Age distrib.** (%) <15: 15.6; 65+: 15.2. **Pop. density:** 279 per sq mi, 108 per sq km. **Urban:** 65.1%. **Ethnic groups:** Hungarian 90%, Roma 4%, German 3%, Serb 2%. **Principal languages:** Hungarian (official), Romani, German, Slavic languages, Romanian. **Chief religions:** Roman Catholic 52%, Calvinist 16%.

Geography: Total area: 35,919 sq mi, 93,030 sq km; **Land area:** 35,653 sq mi, 92,340 sq km. **Location:** In E central Europe. **Neighbors:** Slovakia, Ukraine on N; Austria on W; Slovenia, Yugoslavia, Croatia on S; Romania on E. **Topography:** The Danube R. forms the Slovak border in the NW, then swings S to bisect the country. The eastern half of Hungary is mainly a great fertile plain, the Alfold; the W and N are hilly. **Capital:** Budapest, 1,693,000.

Government: Type: Parliamentary democracy. **Head of state:** Pres. László Sólyom; b. Jan. 3, 1942; in office: Aug. 5, 2005. **Head of gov.:** Prime Min. Ferenc Gyurcsány; b. June 4, 1961; in office: Sept. 29, 2004. **Local divisions:** 19 counties, 20 urban counties, 1 capital. **Defense budget** (2005): $1.4 bil. **Active troops:** 32,300.

Economy: Industries: mining, metallurgy, constr. materials, proc. foods, textiles, pharm., auto. **Chief crops:** wheat, corn, sunflower seed, potatoes, sugar beets. **Natural resources:** bauxite, coal, nat. gas, fertile soils. **Crude oil reserves** (2005): 102 mil bbls. **Arable land:** 51%. **Livestock** (2005): cattle: 723,000; chickens: 32.8

mil; goats: 78,000; pigs: 4.1 mil; sheep: 1.4 mil. **Fish catch** (2004): 19,986 metric tons. **Electricity prod.** (2004): 31.8 bil kWh. **Labor force** (2002): agriculture 6.2%, industry 27.1%, services 66.7%.

Finance: Monetary unit: Forint (HUF) (Sept. 2006: 216.53 = $1 U.S.). **GDP** (2005 est.): $162.6 bil; **per capita GDP:** $16,300; **GDP growth:** 4.1%. **Imports** (2005 est.): $64.8 bil; partners (2004): Germany 29.2%, Austria 8.3%, Russia 5.7%, Italy 5.5%, Netherlands 4.9%, China 4.8%, France 4.7%. **Exports** (2005 est.): $61.8 bil; partners (2004): Germany 31.4%, Austria 6.8%, France 5.7%, Italy 5.6%, UK 5.1%. **Tourism:** $4.1 bil. **Budget** (2005 est.): $58.3 bil. **Intl. reserves less gold:** $12.97 bil. **Gold:** 100,000 oz t. **Consumer prices:** 3.55%.

Transport: Railroad: Length: 4,931 mi. **Motor vehicles** 2.78 mil pass. cars, 409,900 comm. vehicles. **Civil aviation:** 1.9 bil pass.-mi; 20 airports.

Communications: TV sets: 447 per 1,000 pop. **Radios:** 690 per 1,000 pop. **Telephone lines:** 3.4 mil. **Daily newspaper circ.:** 162.3 per 1,000 pop. **Internet:** 3.05 mil users.

Health: Life expect.: 68.5 male; 77.1 female. **Births** (per 1,000 pop.): 9.7. **Deaths** (per 1,000 pop.): 13.1. **Natural inc.:** −0.34%. **Infant mortality** (per 1,000 live births): 8.4. **AIDS rate:** 0.1%.

Education: Compulsory: ages 7-16. **Literacy:** 99.4%.

Major Intl. Organizations: UN (FAO, IBRD, ILO, IMF, IMO, WHO, WTO), EU, NATO, OECD, OSCE.

Embassy: 3910 Shoemaker St. NW 20008; 362-6730.

Website: www.hungary.hu

Earliest settlers, chiefly Slav and Germanic, were overrun by Magyars from the E. Stephen I (997-1038) was made king by Pope Sylvester II in 1000 CE. The country suffered repeated Turkish invasions in the 15th-17th centuries. After the defeats of the Turks, 1686-97, Austria dominated, but Hungary obtained concessions until it regained internal independence in 1867, under a dual monarchy with the emperor of Austria. Defeated with the Central Powers in 1918, Hungary lost Transylvania to Romania, Croatia and Bacska to Yugoslavia, and Slovakia and Carpatho-Ruthenia to Czechoslovakia, all of which had large Hungarian minorities. A republic under Michael Karolyi and a Bolshevist revolt under Bela Kun were followed by a vote for a monarchy in 1920 with Admiral Nicholas Horthy as regent.

Hungary joined Germany in WWII, and was allowed to annex most of its lost territories. Russian troops captured the country, 1944-45. By terms of an armistice with the Allied powers Hungary agreed to give up territory acquired by the 1938 dismemberment of Czechoslovakia and to return to its borders of 1937.

A republic was declared Feb. 1, 1946; Zoltan Tildy was elected president. In 1947 the Communists forced Tildy out, and a hardline, pro-Soviet government was installed. Imre Nagy, who became premier in mid-1953, favored less rigid policies, but he was ousted Apr. 18, 1955. In 1956, popular demands to restore Nagy were heeded Oct. 23. Demonstrations against Communist rule then developed into open revolt. On Nov. 4 Soviet forces launched a massive attack against Budapest with 200,000 troops, 2,500 tanks and armored cars. About 200,000 persons fled the country. Thousands were arrested and executed, including Nagy in June 1958. In spring 1963 the regime freed many captives from the 1956 revolt.

Hungarian troops participated in the 1968 Warsaw Pact invasion of Czechoslovakia. Major economic reforms were launched early in 1968, switching from a central planning system to one based on market forces and profit.

In 1989 Parliament legalized freedom of assembly and association as Hungary shifted away from Communism. In Oct. the Communist Party was formally dissolved. The last Soviet troops left Hungary June 19, 1991. Hungary became a full member of NATO Mar. 12, 1999, and of the EU May 1, 2004. A leaked recording in which Prime Min. Ferenc Gyurcsány admitted lying "morning, evening, and night" about the economy before Apr. 2006 elections sparked mass protests calling for his resignation in Sept.

Iceland
Republic of Iceland

People: Population: 299,388. **Age distrib.** (%) <15: 21.7; 65+: 11.7. **Pop. density:** 7 per sq mi, 2 per sq km. **Urban:** 92.8%. **Ethnic groups:** Icelandic 94%. **Principal languages:** Icelandic (official) **Chief religion:** Evangelical Lutheran 86% (official).

Geography: Total area: 39,769 sq mi, 103,000 sq km; **Land area:** 38,707 sq mi, 100,250 sq km. **Location:** Isl. at N end of Atlantic O. **Neighbors:** Nearest is Greenland (Den.), to W. **Topography:** Recent volcanic origin. Three-quarters of the surface is wasteland: glaciers, lakes, a lava desert. There are geysers and hot springs, and the climate is moderated by the Gulf Stream. **Capital:** Reykjavík, 185,000.

Government: Type: Constitutional republic. **Head of state:** Pres. Olafur Ragnar Grímsson; b. May 14, 1943; in office: Aug. 1, 1996. **Head of gov.:** Prime Min. Geir H. Haarde; b. Apr. 8, 1951; in office: June 15, 2006. **Local divisions:** 23 counties, 14 independent towns. **Defense budget:** Icelandic Defense Force provided by the U.S.

Economy: Industries: fish proc., aluminum smelting, ferrosilicon prod., tourism. **Chief crops:** potatoes, turnips. **Natural resources:** fish, hydropower, geothermal power, diatomite. **Livestock** (2005): cattle: 64,000; chickens: 190,000; goats: 410; pigs: 35,000; sheep: 454,000. **Fish catch** (2004): 1,736,953 metric tons. **Electricity prod.** (2004): 8.5 bil kWh. **Labor force** (2003): agriculture 10.3%, industry 18.3%, services 71.4%.

Finance: Monetary unit: Krona (ISK) (Sept. 2006: 70.57 = $1 U.S.). (2005 est.): $10.6 bil; **per capita GDP:** $35,600; **GDP growth:** 5.7%. **Imports** (2005 est.): $4.6 bil; partners (2004): Germany 12.3%, U.S. 10%, Norway 9.8%, Denmark 7.6%, UK 6.9%, Sweden 6.4%, Netherlands 5.7%. **Exports** (2005 est.): $3.2 bil; partners (2004): UK 19.1%, Germany 17.1%, Netherlands 11%, U.S. 10.2%, Spain 6.9%, Denmark 4.6%. **Tourism:** $370 mil. **Budget** (2005 est.): $6.8 bil. **Intl. reserves less gold:** $725 mil. **Gold:** 60,000 oz t. **Consumer prices:** 4.16%

Transport: Motor vehicles: 166,900 pass. cars, 22,900 comm. vehicles. **Civil aviation:** 2 bil pass.-mi; 5 airports. **Chief port:** Reykjavík.

Communications: TV sets: 505 per 1,000 pop. **Radios:** 1,075 per 1,000 pop. **Telephone lines:** 193,900. **Daily newspaper circ.:** 322.3 per 1,000 pop. **Internet:** 225,000 users.

Health: Life expect.: 78.2 male; 82.5 female. **Births** (per 1,000 pop.): 13.6. **Deaths** (per 1,000 pop.): 6.7. **Natural inc.:** 0.69%. **Infant mortality** (per 1,000 live births): 3.3. **AIDS rate:** 0.2%.

Education: Compulsory: ages 6-16. **Literacy:** 99.9%.

Major Intl. Organizations: UN (FAO, IBRD, ILO, IMF, IMO, WHO, WTO), EFTA, NATO, OECD, OSCE.

Embassy: 1156 15th St. NW, Ste. 1200, 20005; 265-6653.

Website: www.iceland.is

Iceland was an independent republic from 930 to 1262, when it joined with Norway. Its language has maintained its purity for 1,000 years. Danish rule lasted from 1380-1918; the last ties with the Danish crown were severed in 1941. The Althing, or assembly, is the world's oldest surviving parliament.

India
Republic of India

People: Population: 1,111,713,910. **Age distrib.** (%) <15: 32.1; 65+: 5. **Pop. density:** 968 per sq mi, 373 per sq km. **Urban:** 28.3%. **Ethnic groups:** Indo-Aryan 72%, Dravidian 25%. **Principal languages:** Hindi, English, Bengali, Telugu, Marathi, Tamil, Urdu, Gujarati, Malayalam, Kannada, Oriya, Punjabi, Assamese, Kashmiri, Sindhi, and Sanskrit (all official); Hindustani, a mix of Hindi and Urdu spoken in the north, is popular but not official. **Chief religions:** Hindu 81%, Muslim 13%, Christian 2%, Sikh 2%.

Geography: Total area: 1,269,346 sq mi, 3,287,590 sq km; **Land area:** 1,147,955 sq mi, 2,973,190 sq km. **Location:** Occupies most of the Indian subcontinent in S Asia. **Neighbors:** Pakistan on W; China, Nepal, Bhutan on N; Myanmar, Bangladesh on E. **Topography:** The Himalaya Mts., highest in world, stretch across India's northern borders. Below, the Ganges Plain is wide, fertile, among the most densely populated regions of the world. The area below includes the Deccan Peninsula. Close to one quarter of the area is forested. The climate varies from tropical heat in S to near-Arctic cold in N. Rajasthan Desert is in NW; NE Assam Hills get 400 in. of rain a year. **Capital:** Delhi 15,048,000. **Cities (urban aggr.):** Ahmadabad 5,120,000; Bangalore 6,462,000; Chennai (Madras) 6,916,000; Hyderabad 6,115,000; Kolkata (Calcutta) 14,277,000; Mumbai (Bombay) 18,196,000.

Government: Type: Federal republic. **Head of state:** Pres. A. P. J. Abdul Kalam; b. Oct. 15, 1931; in office: July 25, 2002. **Head of gov.:** Prime Min. Manmohan Singh; b. Sept. 26, 1932; in office May 22, 2004. **Local divisions:** 28 states, 6 union territories, 1 national capital territory. **Defense budget** (2005): $22 bil. **Active troops:** 1,325,000.

Economy: Industries: textiles, chemicals, food proc., steel, transp. equip., cement, mining, oil, machinery, software. **Chief crops:** rice, wheat, oilseed, cotton, jute, tea, sugarcane, potatoes. **Natural resources:** coal, iron ore, mang., mica, bauxite, titanium ore, chromite, nat. gas, diamonds, oil, limestone. **Crude oil reserves** (2005): 5.4 bil bbls. **Arable land:** 56%. **Livestock** (2005): cattle: 185 mil; chickens: 430 mil; goats: 120 mil; pigs: 14.3 mil; sheep: 62.5 mil **Fish catch** (2004): 6,088,059 metric tons. **Electricity prod.** (2004): 630.6 bil kWh. **Labor force** (1999): agriculture 60%, industry 17%, services 23%.

Finance: Monetary unit: Rupee (INR) (Sept. 2006: 45.82 = $1 U.S.). **GDP** (2005 est.): $3.6 tril; **per capita GDP:** $3,300; **GDP growth:** 7.6%. **Imports** (2005 est.): $113.1 bil; partners (2004): U.S. 7%, Belgium 6.1%, China 5.9%, Singapore 4.8%, Australia 4.6%, UK 4.6%, Germany 4.5%. **Exports** (2005 est.): $76.2 bil; partners (2004): U.S. 18.4%, China 7.8%, UAE 6.7%, UK 4.8%, Hong Kong 4.3%, Germany 4%. **Tourism** (2003): $3.9 bil. **Budget** (2005 est.): $135.8 bil. **Intl. reserves less gold:** $92.3 bil. **Gold:** 11.5 mil oz t. **Consumer prices:** 4.25%.

Transport: Railroad: Length: 39,289 mi. **Motor vehicles:** 7.57 mil pass. cars, 9.81 mil comm. vehicles. **Civil aviation:** 17.1 bil pass.-mi; 243 airports. **Chief ports:** Kolkata (Calcutta), Mumbai (Bombay), Chennai (Madras), Vishakhapatnam, Kandla.

Communications: TV sets: 75 per 1,000 pop. **Radios:** 120 per 1,000 pop. **Telephone lines:** 48.8 mil. **Daily newspaper circ.:** 60 per 1,000 pop. **Internet:** 50.6 mil users.

Health: Life expect.: 65.7 male; 70.4 female. **Births** (per 1,000 pop.): 23.2. **Deaths** (per 1,000 pop.): 6.8. **Natural inc.:** 1.64%. **Infant mortality** (per 1,000 live births): 37.1. **AIDS rate:** 0.9%.

Education: Compulsory: ages 6-14. **Literacy:** 61.0%.

Major Intl. Organizations: UN (FAO, IBRD, ILO, IMF, IMO, WHO, WTO), the Commonwealth.

Embassy: 2107 Massachusetts Ave. NW 20008; 939-7000.

Website: www.india.gov.in

India has one of the oldest civilizations in the world. Excavations trace the Indus Valley civilization back for at least 5,000 years. Paintings in the mountain caves of Ajanta, richly carved temples, the Taj Mahal in Agra, and the Kutab Minar in Delhi are among relics of the past.

Aryan tribes, speaking Sanskrit, invaded from the northwest around 1500 BCE. Asoka ruled most of the Indian subcontinent in the 3rd cent. BCE, and established Buddhism. But Hinduism revived and eventually predominated. Under the Guptas, 4th-6th cent. CE, science, literature, and the arts enjoyed a "golden age."

Arab invaders established a Muslim foothold in the west in the 8th cent., and Turkish Muslims gained control of North India by 1200. The Mogul emperors ruled 1526-1857.

Vasco da Gama established Portuguese trading posts 1498-1503. The Dutch followed. The British East India Co. sent Capt. William Hawkins, 1609, to get concessions from the Mogul emperor for spices and textiles. Operating as the East India Co. the British gained control of most of India. The British parliament assumed political direction; under Lord Bentinck, 1828-35, rule by rajahs was curbed. After the Sepoy troops mutinied, 1857-58, the British supported the native rulers.

Nationalism grew rapidly after WWI. The Indian National Congress and the Muslim League demanded constitutional reform. A leader emerged in Mohandas K. Gandhi (called Mahatma, or Great Soul), b. Oct. 2, 1869, assassinated Jan. 30, 1948. He advocated self-rule, nonviolence, and removal of the caste system of untouchability. In 1930 he launched a program of civil disobedience, including a boycott of British goods and rejection of taxes without representation.

In 1935 Britain gave India a constitution providing a bicameral federal congress. Muhammad Ali Jinnah, head of the Muslim League, sought creation of a Muslim nation, Pakistan.

The British government partitioned British India into the dominions of India and Pakistan. India became a member of the UN in 1945, a self-governing member of the Commonwealth in 1947, and a democratic republic, Jan. 26, 1950. More than 12 mil Hindu and Muslim refugees crossed the India-Pakistan borders in a mass transferal of some of the 2 peoples during 1947; about 200,000 were killed in communal fighting.

After Pakistan troops began attacks on Bengali separatists in East Pakistan, Mar. 25, 1971, some 10 mil refugees fled into India. India and Pakistan went to war Dec. 3, 1971, on both the east and west fronts. Pakistan troops in the east surrendered Dec. 16; Pakistan agreed to a cease-fire in the west Dec. 17.

Indira Gandhi, India's prime minister since Jan. 1966, invoked emergency powers in June 1975. Thousands of opponents were arrested and press censorship imposed. These and other actions, including enforcement of coercive birth control measures in some areas, were widely resented. Opposition parties, united in the Janata coalition, turned Gandhi's New Congress Party from power in federal and state parliamentary elections in 1977.

Gandhi became prime minister for the second time, Jan. 14, 1980. She was assassinated by 2 of her Sikh bodyguards Oct. 31, 1984, in response to the government suppression of a Sikh uprising in Punjab in June 1984, which included an assault on the Golden Temple at Amritsar, the holiest Sikh shrine. Widespread rioting followed the assassination; thousands of Sikhs were killed and some 50,000 left homeless. Rajiv, Indira Gandhi's son, replaced her as prime minister. He was swept from office in 1989 amid charges of incompetence and corruption, and assassinated May 21, 1991, while campaigning to regain power.

A gas leak at a Union Carbide chemical plant in Bhopal, in Dec. 1984, eventually killed an estimated 14,000 people. A lawsuit settled in 1989 provided $470 mil in compensation to victims; in 2002 an Indian High Court upheld a culpable homicide conviction against former UC chairman Warren Anderson.

Many died in religious, ethnic, and political conflicts during the 1980s and '90s. To suppress the Sikh insurgency in Punjab, Indian government troops attacked the Golden Temple again in 1988. Nationwide riots followed the destruction of a 16th-cent. mosque by Hindu militants in Dec. 1992. Ethnic clashes in Assam in northwest India, killed thousands in Feb. 1993. In the biggest wave of criminal violence in Indian history, a series of bombs jolted Bombay and Calcutta, Mar. 12-19, 1993, killing over 300.

Mother Teresa of Calcutta, renowned for her work among the poor, died Sept. 5, 1997. India's first lowest-caste president, K. R. Narayanan, took office July 25. The Hindu nationalist Bharatiya Janata Party (BJP) won enough seats in parliamentary elections, Feb. 1998, to form a government. Atal Bihari Vajpayee was sworn in as prime minister Mar. 19. India conducted a series of nuclear tests in mid-May, drawing wide condemnation and raising tensions with Pakistan.

An alliance led by Vajpayee won a majority in legislative elections, Sept. 5-Oct. 3, 1999. A cyclone that hit the state of Orissa, East India, on Oct. 29, 1999, left some 10,000 people dead. A powerful earthquake in Gujarat state on Jan. 26, 2001, claimed more than 20,000 lives. India blamed Pakistani-sponsored terrorist groups for an Oct. 1 suicide attack on the state legislature in Jammu and Kashmir (see below), in which at least 40 people died, and a Dec. 13 assault on the Indian parliament in New Delhi Dec. 13, which left 13 people dead. Hindu-Muslim clashes in Gujarat Feb. 27-Mar. 11, 2002, claimed more than 700 lives. A. P. J. Abdul Kalam, a Muslim scientist who spearheaded India's nuclear weapons program, became president July 25.

Two bombs in Mumbai, Aug. 25, 2003, killed more than 50 people; Indian authorities blamed Muslim militants. Led by Rajiv Gandhi's Italian-born widow, Sonia, the Congress Party won the most seats in parliamentary elections Apr.-May 2004. When Hindu nationalists objected to her candidacy, she chose not to become prime minister, and Manmohan Singh, a Sikh economist, took office instead.

The Indian Ocean tsunami of Dec. 26, 2004, left more than 10,700 people dead, some 5,600 missing, and over 647,000 displaced. An agreement reached during U.S. Pres. Bush's visit to New Delhi, Mar. 2, 2006, called for the U.S. to allow India to buy nuclear fuel and reactor components, and for India to permit inspections at 14 civilian nuclear plants (but not 8 military nuclear reactors). Islamic extremists were suspected in 3 bombings in New Delhi, Oct. 29, 2005, that killed more than 60 people, and 8 blasts in Mumbai, July 11, 2006, that killed 183 on commuter trains. Monsoon rains in Aug. 2006 left more than 300 dead and forced 4.5 mil to flee their homes. In Muslim-dominated Malegaon, western India, 3 bombs near a mosque and cemetery Sept. 8 killed at least 37.

Despite robust economic growth since the 1990s, especially in high-technology industries, nearly 80% of India's population still earns less than $2 per day. According to UN estimates, 5.7 mil people in India have HIV/AIDS, the most of any country.

Sikkim, bordered by Tibet, Bhutan, and Nepal, formerly British protected, became a protectorate of India in 1950. Area, 2,740 sq mi; pop. (2001 census): 540,493; capital: Gangtok. In Sept. 1974, India's parliament voted to make Sikkim an associate Indian state, absorbing it into India.

Kashmir is a predominantly Muslim region in the NW that borders India, Pakistan, Afghanistan, and China. Originally a Hindu kingdom, Muslim rule began in 1341; after almost 200 years under the Moguls, the area was incorporated into British India in 1846. Fighting broke out in the region between India and Pakistan in 1947 following independence from Britain. A cease-fire was negotiated by the UN Jan. 1, 1949; it gave Pakistan control of one-third of the area as Azad Kashmir, in the west and northwest, and India the remaining two-thirds, as the Indian state of Jammu and Kashmir. It is India's only Muslim-majority state. Area: 39,146 sq mi.; pop. (2001 census): 10,000,000; capitals: Srinagar (summer) and Jammu (winter). Fighting returned to the area during the 1965 and 1971 wars with Pakistan. China occupied about 14,000 sq mi in the Ladakh district after a war with India in 1962.

In the 1990s there were repeated clashes between Indian army troops and separatist fighters triggered by India's decision to impose central government rule. The clashes strained relations between India and Pakistan, which India charged was aiding the separatists; fighting was especially heavy in May-June 1999. As 2002 began, some 1 mil Indian and Pakistani troops faced each other across the "line of control" that divides Kashmir. Tensions escalated when Muslim gunmen May 14 killed 34 people, many of them women and children, at an army base near Jammu, and Pakistan conducted missile tests May 25-28. U.S. mediation in June helped ease the crisis. Legislative elections were held Sept.-Oct. 2002.

A cease-fire between Indian and Pakistani troops along the line of control took effect Nov. 25, 2003, but clashes between Indian forces and Islamic militants continued. Estimates of conflict-related deaths since 1989 range from 40,000 to over 80,000. A powerful earthquake Oct. 8, 2005, killed about 80,000 and left up to 3 mil homeless in Pakistani-held Kashmir and northern Pakistan.

France, 1952-54, peacefully yielded to India its 5 colonies, former French India, comprising Pondicherry, Karikal, Mahe, Yanaon (which became **Pondicherry Union Territory,** area 190 sq mi; pop. (2001 census): 973,829 and Chandernagor (which was incorporated into the state of **West Bengal**).

Indonesia

Republic of Indonesia

People: Population: 231,820,243. **Age distrib.** (%) <15: 29.1; 65+: 5.6. **Pop. density:** 328 per sq mi, 126 per sq km. **Urban:** 45.6%. **Ethnic groups:** Javanese 45%, Sundanese 14%, Madurese 8%, Malay 8%. **Principal languages:** Bahasa Indonesia (official, modified form of Malay), English, Dutch, Javanese, other dialects. **Chief religions:** Muslim 88%, Protestant 5%, Roman Catholic 3%, Hindu 2%, Buddhist 1%.

Geography: Total area: 741,100 sq mi, 1,919,440 sq km; **Land area:** 705,192 sq mi, 1,826,440 sq km. **Location:** Archipelago SE of Asian mainland along the Equator. **Neighbors:** Malaysia on N, Papua New Guinea on E. **Topography:** Indonesia comprises over 13,500 islands (6,000 inhabited), including Java (one of the most densely populated areas in the world with over 2,000 persons per sq. mi.), Sumatra, Kalimantan (most of Borneo), Sulawesi (Celebes), and West Irian (Irian Jaya, the W half of New Guinea). Also: Bangka, Billiton, Madura, Bali, Timor. The mountains and plateaus on the major islands have a cooler climate than the tropical lowlands. **Capital:** Jakarta, 13,215,000. **Cities (urban aggr.):** Bandung, 4,126,000; Surabaja, 2,992,000.

Government: Type: Republic. **Head of state and gov.:** Susilo Bambang Yudhoyono; b. Sept. 9, 1949; in office: Oct. 20, 2004. **Local divisions:** 30 provinces, 2 special regions, 1 capital district. **Defense budget** (2005): $2.5 bil. **Active troops:** 302,000.

Economy: Industries: oil & nat. gas, textiles, apparel & footwear, mining, cement, fertilizers, plywood, rubber. **Chief crops:** rice, cassava, peanuts, rubber, cocoa, coffee, palm oil, copra. **Natural resources:** oil, tin, nat. gas, nickel, timber, bauxite, copper, coal, gold, silver. **Crude oil reserves** (2005): 4.7 bil bbls. **Arable land:** 10%. **Livestock** (2005): cattle: 11.5 mil; chickens: 1.2 bil; goats: 13.2 mil; pigs: 6.3 mil; sheep: 8.3 mil. **Fish catch** (2004): 5,856,371 metric tons. **Electricity prod.** (2004): 112.6 bil kWh. **Labor force** (1999 est.): agriculture 46.5%, industry 11.8%, services 41.7%.

Finance: Monetary unit: Rupiah (IDR) (Sept. 2006: 9,152.14 = $1 U.S.). **GDP** (2005 est.): $865.6 bil; **per capita GDP:** $3,600; **GDP growth:** 5.6%. **Imports** (2005 est.): $62 bil; partners (2004): Japan 19.3%, China 11%, Singapore 9.2%, Thailand 6.8%, Malaysia 6.5%, U.S. 5.7%, Australia 5%, Germany 4.2%. **Exports** (2005 est.): $83.6 bil; partners (2004): Japan 21.8%, U.S. 13.5%, China 7.5%, Singapore 7.4%, South Korea 5.9%, Malaysia 4.9%. **Tourism:** $4.8 bil. **Budget** (2005 est.): $57.7 bil. **Intl. reserves less gold:** $23.08 bil. **Gold:** 3.1 mil oz t. **Consumer prices:** 10.45%.

Transport: Railroad: Length: 4,013 mi. **Motor vehicles:** 3.40 mil pass. cars, 2.58 mil comm. vehicles. **Civil aviation:** 11.4 bil pass.-mi; 159 airports. **Chief ports:** Jakarta, Surabaya, Palembang, Semarang, Ujungpandang.

Communications: TV sets: 143 per 1,000 pop. **Radios:** 155 per 1,000 pop. **Telephone lines:** 12.8 mil. **Daily newspaper circ.:** 22.9 per 1,000 pop. **Internet:** 18 mil users.

Health: Life expect.: 67.4 male; 72.4 female. **Births** (per 1,000 pop.): 20.1. **Deaths** (per 1,000 pop.): 6.3. **Natural inc.:** 1.38%. **Infant mortality** (per 1,000 live births): 33.3. **AIDS rate:** 0.1%.

Education: Compulsory: ages 7-15. **Literacy:** 90.4%.

Major Intl. Organizations: UN and all of its specialized agencies, APEC, ASEAN, OPEC.

Embassy: 2020 Massachusetts Ave. NW 20036; 775-5200.

Website: www.embassyofindonesia.org

Hindu and Buddhist civilization from India reached Indonesia nearly 2,000 years ago, taking root especially in Java. Islam spread along the maritime trade routes in the 15th cent., and became predominant by the 16th cent. The Dutch replaced the Portuguese as the area's most important European trade power in the 17th cent., securing territorial control over Java by 1750. The outer islands were not finally subdued until the early 20th century, when the full area of present-day Indonesia was united under one rule for the first time.

Following Japanese occupation, 1942-45, nationalists led by Sukarno and Hatta declared independence. The Netherlands ceded sovereignty Dec. 27, 1949, after 4 years of fighting. A republic was declared, Aug. 17, 1950, with Sukarno as president. West Irian, on New Guinea, remained under Dutch control. After the Dutch in 1957 rejected proposals for new negotiations over West Irian, Indonesia stepped up the seizure of Dutch property. In 1963 the UN turned the area (later renamed Irian Jaya and now known as Papua) over to Indonesia, which promised a plebiscite. In 1969, voting by tribal chiefs favored staying with Indonesia, despite an uprising and widespread opposition.

Sukarno suspended Parliament in 1960 and was named president for life in 1963. He made close alliances with Communist governments. In Sept. 1965 an attempted coup in which several military officers were murdered was successfully put down, but Sukarno was forced to cede power to the army, led by Gen. Suharto, who became acting president in 1967 and ruled Indonesia for the next 31 years. The regime blamed the coup on the Communist Party; more than 300,000 alleged Communists were killed in army-initiated massacres.

Parliament reelected Suharto to a 7th consecutive 5-year term Mar. 10, 1998, as a severe economic downturn focused public anger on nepotism, cronyism, and corruption in the Suharto regime. Price increases in May sparked mass protests and then mob violence in Jakarta and other cities, claiming some 500 lives. Suharto resigned May 21 and was succeeded by his vice-president, Bacharuddin Jusuf Habibie. Abdurrahman Wahid, leader of Indonesia's largest Muslim organization, was elected president Oct. 20, 1999. In Aug. 2000, under pressure from the legislature, he agreed to share power with Vice Pres. Megawati Sukarnoputri, the daughter of the late Pres. Sukarno. Charging Wahid with incompetence and corruption, the legislature ousted him July 23, 2001, and Megawati became Indonesia's first woman president.

Clashes between Muslims and Christians in the Maluku (Molucca) Is., 1999-2002, claimed about 5,000 lives. Ethnic violence in Kalimantan, Borneo, killed more than 400 in Feb. 2001. East Timor, a former Portuguese colony that Indonesia invaded in Dec. 1975 and controlled until Oct. 1999, became a fully independent country May 20, 2002, as Timor-Leste. Separatists in Aceh, NW Sumatra, fought repeatedly against government troops during the 1980s and 90s; peace accords were announced in Dec. 2002 and, after that deal unraveled, in July 2005. The last of 24,000 Indonesian government troops pulled out of Aceh, Dec. 29, 2005.

Investigators blamed Islamic terrorists affiliated with al-Qaeda for bombings that killed 202 people, mostly foreign tourists, at nightclubs in Bali, Oct. 12, 2002, and 12 people at a Marriott hotel in Jakarta, Aug. 5, 2003. A car bomb attack outside the Australian embassy in Jakarta, Sept. 9, 2004, killed 9 people and injured more than 180. Susilo Bambang Yudhoyono, a retired general, defeated Megawati Sept. 20 in a direct presidential runoff vote.

A massive earthquake off northwest Sumatra, Dec. 26, 2004, triggered tsunamis that wreaked havoc in the Indian Ocean region. The death toll in Indonesia alone exceeded 125,000, not counting almost 40,000 missing. Another large quake off northwest Sumatra, Mar. 28, 2005, left at least 1,300 dead. On Java in 2006, an earthquake May 27 killed 5,800, left 1.5 mil homeless, and caused property damage estimated at $3.1 bil; a tsunami July 17 claimed at least 650 lives.

Iran
Islamic Republic of Iran

People: Population: 65,025,373. **Age distrib.** (%) <15: 24.3; 65+: 5.3. **Pop. density:** 102 per sq mi, 39 per sq km. **Urban:** 66.7%. **Ethnic groups:** Persian 51%, Azeri 24%, Gilaki/Mazandarani 8%, Kurd 7%, Arab 3%, Lur 2%, Balochi 2%, Turkmen 2%. **Principal languages:** Farsi/Persian (official), Kurdish, Pashto, Luri, Balochi, Gilaki, Mazandarami; Azeri and Turkic languages; Arabic, Turkish. **Chief religion:** Muslim (official; Shi'a 89%, Sunni 10%).

Geography: Total area: 636,296 sq mi, 1,648,000 sq km; **Land area:** 631,663 sq mi, 1,636,000 sq km. **Location:** Between the Middle East and S Asia. **Neighbors:** Turkey, Iraq on W; Armenia, Azerbaijan, Turkmenistan on N; Afghanistan, Pakistan on E. **Topography:** Interior highlands and plains surrounded by high mountains, up to 18,000 ft. Large salt deserts cover much of area, but there are many oases and forest areas. Most of the population inhabits the N and NW. **Capital:** Tehran, 7,314,000. **Cities (urban aggr.):** Esfahan, 1,535,000; Mashhad, 2,134,000.

Government: Type: Islamic republic. **Religious head:** Ayatollah Sayyed Ali Khamenei; b. 1939; in office: June 4, 1989. **Head of state and gov.:** Pres. Mahmoud Ahmadinejad; b. Oct. 28, 1956; in office: Aug. 3, 2005. **Local divisions:** 28 provinces. **Defense budget** (2005): $4.4 bil. **Active troops:** 420,000.

Economy: Industries: oil, petrochems., textiles, constr. materials, food proc., metal fabricating, armaments. **Chief crops:** wheat, rice, other grains, sugar beets, fruits, nuts, cotton. **Natural resources:** oil, nat. gas, coal, chromium, copper, iron ore, lead, mang., zinc, sulfur. **Crude oil reserves** (2005): 125.8 bil bbls. **Arable land:** 10%. **Livestock** (2005): cattle: 8.8 mil; chickens: 280 mil; goats: 26.5 mil; sheep: 54 mil. **Fish catch** (2004): 474,320 metric tons. **Electricity prod.** (2004): 155.7 bil kWh. **Labor force** (2001 est.): agriculture 30%, industry 25%, services 45%.

Finance: Monetary unit: Rial (IRR) (Sept. 2006: 9,238.50 = $1 U.S.). **GDP** (2005 est.): $561.6 bil; **per capita GDP:** $8,300; **GDP growth:** 6.1%. **Imports** (2005 est.): $42.5 bil; partners (2004): Germany 13%, France 8.9%, Italy 8%, China 7.7%, UAE 6.4%, South Korea 6.3%, Russia 4.9%. **Exports** (2005 est.): $55.4 bil; partners (2004): Japan 20%, China 9.9%, Italy 6.3%, South Africa 6.3%, Taiwan 4.8%, Turkey 4.7%, South Korea 4.7%, France 4.3%, Netherlands 4.3%. **Tourism:** $1.1 bil. **Budget** (2005 est.): $60.4 bil. **Consumer prices:** 13.43%.

Transport: Railroad: Length: 4,476 mi. **Motor vehicles:** 1.35 mil pass. cars, 384,900 comm. vehicles. **Civil aviation:** 5.4 bil pass.-mi; 129 airports. **Chief port:** Bandar-e Abbas.

Communications: TV sets: 154 per 1,000 pop. **Radios:** 265 per 1,000 pop. **Telephone lines:** 19 mil. **Daily newspaper circ.:** NA. **Internet:** 7.5 mil users.

Health: Life expect.: 68.8 male; 71.7 female. **Births** (per 1,000 pop.): 16.3. **Deaths** (per 1,000 pop.): 5.6. **Natural inc.:** 1.07%. **Infant mortality** (per 1,000 live births): 39.3. **AIDS rate:** 0.2%.

Education: Compulsory: ages 6-10. **Literacy:** 77%.

Major Intl. Organizations: UN (FAO, IBRD, ILO, IMF, IMO, WHO), OPEC.

Iranian Interests Section: 2209 Wisconsin Ave. NW, 20007; 965-4990.

Website: www.spk-gov.ir

Iran was once called Persia. The Iranians, who supplanted an earlier agricultural civilization, came from the east during the 2nd millennium BCE; they were an Indo-European group related to the Aryans of India. In 549 BCE Cyrus the Great united the Medes and Persians in the Persian Empire; he conquered Babylonia in 538 BCE, and restored Jerusalem to the Jews. Alexander the Great conquered Persia in 333 BCE, but Persians regained independence in the next century under the Parthians, themselves succeeded by Sassanian Persians in 226 CE. Arabs brought Islam to Persia in the 7th cent., replacing the indigenous Zoroastrian faith. After Persian political and cultural autonomy was reasserted in the 9th cent., arts and sciences flourished.

Turks and Mongols ruled Persia in turn from the 11th cent. to 1502, when Ismael I established the Iranian Safavid dynasty and made Shiite Islam the offical religion. The dynasty lasted until 1722. The British and Russian empires vied for influence in the 19th cent.; Afghanistan was severed from Iran by Britain in 1857.

Reza Khan, a military officer, became prime min., 1923, and shah in 1925. He began modernization, curbed foreign influence, and officially changed the country's name from Persia to Iran in 1935. Fearing the shah's Axis sympathies, British and Soviet troops forced him to abdicate, 1941; he was succeeded by his son, Mohammad Reza Pahlavi. With U.S. backing, he brought economic and social change to Iran (the "White Revolution"), but repression, often severe, of opposition groups intensified. Violent protests in 1978 eventually forced the shah to depart, Jan. 16, 1979. Shiite leader Ayatollah Ruhollah Khomeini, exiled by the shah in 1963, returned to Tehran, Feb. 1, and by Feb. 11 pro-Khomeini forces had defeated government troops. Khomeini established an Islamic theocracy.

Iranian militants seized the U.S. embassy Nov. 4, 1979 and took hostages including 62 Americans. Despite international condemnations and U.S. efforts, including an abortive Apr. 1980 rescue attempt, the crisis continued. The U.S. broke diplomatic relations with Iran, Apr. 7. The shah died in Egypt, July 27. The hostage drama ended Jan. 20, 1981, when an accord, involving the release of frozen Iranian assets, was reached.

A dispute over the Shatt al-Arab waterway situated between Iran and Iraq led to a long and costly war between the 2 countries, 1980-88, killing hundreds of thousands of people. In Nov. 1986 it became known that the U.S., which had generally sided with Iraq during the war, had secretly shipped arms to Iran to gain that country's help in obtaining the release of U.S. hostages held in Lebanon. The revelation sparked a major scandal in the U.S.. A U.S. Navy warship shot down an Iranian airliner, July 3, 1988, after mistaking it for an F-14 fighter jet; all 290 aboard the plane died.

An earthquake struck northern Iran June 21, 1990, killing more than 45,000, injuring 100,000, and leaving 400,000 homeless. Some 1 mil Kurdish refugees fled from Iraq to Iran following the Persian Gulf War of 1991. To curb Iran's alleged support for international terrorism, the U.S. in 1996 authorized sanctions on foreign companies that invest there.

Mohammad Khatami, a moderate Shiite Muslim cleric, was elected president on May 23, 1997, winning nearly 70% of the vote. During the next 3 years, hardline Islamists clashed repeatedly and sometimes violently with reformers, who won a majority in parliamentary elections Feb. 18 and May 5, 2000. Inviting rapprochement with Iran, the U.S. eased some sanctions Mar. 18. Khatami was reelected June 8, 2001, with a 77% majority but continued to face resistance from religious conservatives.

The U.S.-led war in Iraq, beginning Mar. 2003, contributed to a new period of instability in Iran. In June, armed Islamist vigilantes harassed students who were holding pro-democracy protests in Tehran and other cities. An earthquake Dec. 26 in Bam, southeast Iran, killed about 26,000 people. After the Guardian Council, dominated by religious conservatives, disqualified some 2,400 reformist candidates, hardliners won legislative elections Feb. 20, 2004.

The Guardian Council, May 22, 2005, selected 6 candidates out of 1,014 presidential aspirants. The mayor of Tehran, Mahmoud Ahmadinejad, a religious conservative who campaigned as an economic reformer, defeated former Pres. Hashemi Rafsanjani in a runoff election June 24 and took office Aug. 3. The Bush administration, which in 2002 had called Iran part of an "axis of evil," accused the Iranian regime of seeking to build nuclear weapons, aiding Shiite militias in Iraq, and supplying rockets to Hezbollah fighters in Lebanon for use against Israel. The UN Security Council threatened to impose sanctions if Iran did not halt uranium enrichment and reprocessing by Aug. 31, 2006. Iran let the UN deadline pass while agreeing to hold nuclear talks with the European Union.

Iraq
Republic of Iraq

People: Population: 26,783,383. **Age distrib.** (%) <15: 39.7; 65+: 3. **Pop. density:** 160 per sq mi, 61 per sq km. **Urban:** 67.2%. **Ethnic groups:** Arab 75%-80%, Kurdish 15%-20%. **Principal languages:** Arabic (official), Kurdish (official in Kurdish regions), Assyrian, Armenian. **Chief religion:** Muslim (official; Shi'a 60%-65%, Sunni 32%-37%)

Geography: Total area: 168,754 sq mi, 437,072 sq km; **Land area:** 166,859 sq mi, 432,162 sq km. **Location:** In the Middle East, occupying most of historic Mesopotamia. **Neighbors:** Jordan and Syria on W, Turkey on N, Iran on E, Kuwait and Saudi Arabia on S. **Topography:** Mostly an alluvial plain, including the Tigris and Euphrates rivers, descending from mountains in N to desert in SW. Persian Gulf region is marshland. **Capital:** Baghdad, 5,904,000. **Cities (urban aggr.):** Basra 837,000; Mosul 1,234,000; Erbil 925,000

Government: Type: In transition. **Head of state:** Pres. Jalal Talabani; b. 1933; in office: Apr. 7, 2005. **Head of gov.:** Prime Min. Nouri Kamel al-Maliki; b. 1950; in office: May 20, 2006. **Local divisions:** 18 governorates (3 in Kurdish Autonomous Region). **Defense budget** (2005): NA. **Active troops:** 179,800.

Economy: Industries: oil, chemicals, textiles, constr. materials, food proc. **Chief crops:** wheat, barley, rice, vegetables, dates, cotton. **Natural resources:** oil, nat. gas, phosphates, sulfur. **Arable land:** 12%. **Crude oil reserves** (2005): 115 bil bbls. **Fish catch** (2004): 26,883 metric tons. **Electricity prod.** (2004): 29.3 bil kWh.

Finance: Monetary unit: Dinar (IQD) (Sept. 2006: 1,477.55 = $1 U.S.). **GDP** (2005 est.): $94.1 bil; **per capita GDP:** $3,400; **GDP growth:** -3%. **Imports** (2004 est.): $19.6 bil; partners (2004): Turkey 25%, U.S. 11.1%, Jordan 10%, Vietnam 7.7%, Germany 5.6%, Australia 4.8%. **Exports** (2004 est.): $17.8 bil; partners (2004): U.S. 55.8%, Spain 8%, Japan 7.3%, Italy 6.5%, Canada 5.8%. **Tourism** (2002): $45 mil. **Budget** (2005 est.): $24 bil.

Transport: Railroad: Length: 1,367 mi. **Motor vehicles:** 754,130 pass. cars, 372,230 comm. vehicles; **Civil aviation:** NA; 77 airports. **Chief port:** Basra.

Communications: TV sets: 82 per 1,000 pop. **Radios:** 229 per 1,000 pop. **Telephone lines:** 1 mil. **Daily newspaper circ.:** NA. **Internet:** 36,000 users.

Health: Life expect.: 67.8 male; 70.3 female. **Births** (per 1,000 pop.): 32. **Deaths** (per 1,000 pop.): 5.4. **Natural inc.:** 2.66%. **Infant mortality** (per 1,000 live births): 48.6. **AIDS rate:** NA.

Education: Compulsory: ages 6-11. **Literacy:** 74.1%.

Major Intl. Organizations: UN (FAO, IBRD, ILO, IMF, IMO, WHO), AL, OPEC.

Iraqi Interests Section: 1801 P St., NW, 20036; 483-7500.

Website: www.iraqigovernment.org

The Tigris-Euphrates valley, formerly called Mesopotamia, was the site of one of the earliest civilizations in the world. Mesopotamia ceased to be a separate entity after the Persian, Greek, and Arab conquests. The Arabs founded Baghdad, from where the caliph ruled a vast Islamic empire in the 8th and 9th centuries. Mongol and Turkish conquests led to a decline in the region's population, economy, cultural life, and irrigation system.

Britain secured a League of Nations mandate over Iraq after WWI. Independence under a king came in 1932. Rebellious army officers killed King Faisal II, July 14, 1958, and established a leftist, pan-Arab republic, which pursued close ties with the USSR. Successive regimes were increasingly dominated by the Baath Arab Socialist Party. A Baath leader, Saddam Hussein, became president of Iraq, July 16, 1979. After purging his enemies, he ruled as a dictator for more than 2 decades, repressing Iraq's Kurds and Shiites and launching disastrous wars against 2 neighboring nations, Iran and Kuwait. Hussein sought weapons of mass destruction: Israeli planes destroyed a nuclear reactor near Baghdad June 7, 1981, claiming it could be used to produce nuclear weapons.

After skirmishing intermittently for 10 months over the sovereignty of the disputed Shatt al-Arab waterway that divides the two countries, Iraq and Iran entered into open warfare on Sept. 22, 1980. Iran repulsed early Iraqi advances, producing a long and costly stalemate; hundreds of thousands of Iraqis lost their lives during the 8-year conflict. Hussein used poison gas against Iraqi Kurds in 1988, killing up to 5,000 people in Halabja, the first mass use of poison gas against civilians since the Holocaust.

Iraq attacked and overran Kuwait Aug. 2, 1990. Backed by the UN, a U.S.-led coalition launched air and missile attacks on Iraq, Jan. 16, 1991. The coalition began a ground attack to retake Kuwait Feb. 23. Iraqi forces showed little resistance and were soundly defeated in 4 days. Some 175,000 Iraqis were taken prisoner, and Iraqi casualties were estimated at over 85,000. As part of the cease-fire agreement, Iraq agreed to scrap all poison gas and germ weapons and allow UN observers to inspect the sites. UN trade sanctions would remain in effect until Iraq complied with all terms.

In Feb. 1991, Iraqi troops drove Kurdish insurgents and civilians to the borders of Iran and Turkey, causing a refugee crisis. The U.S. and allies established havens inside Iraq for the Kurds. The U.S. launched a missile attack aimed at Iraq's intelligence headquarters in Baghdad June 26, 1993, citing evidence that Iraq had sponsored a plot to kill former Pres. George Bush. Iraqi cooperation with UN weapons inspection teams was intermittent throughout the 1990s. On Dec. 9, 1996, the UN began a programintended to allow Baghdad to sell limited amounts of oil for food and medicine. An independant panel later concluded that there was massive corruption in UN administration of the program allowing the Iraqi regime to reap huge profits (aside from the large profits through oil smuggling).

Iraqi resistance to UN access to suspected weapons sites touched off diplomatic crises during 1997-98, culminating in intensive U.S. and British aerial bombardment of Iraqi military targets, Dec. 16-19, 1998. After 2 years of sporadic activity, U.S. and British warplanes struck harder at sites near Baghdad on Feb. 16, 2001.

In a speech before the UN, Sept. 12, 2002, Pres. George W. Bush demanded that Iraq eliminate weapons of mass destruction, refrain from supporting terrorism, and end repression. Under Security Council Resolution 1441, approved Nov. 8, Iraq allowed UN inspectors to search for banned weapons, while the U.S. and Britain built up troops in the Persian Gulf. Despite opposition from some countries, including France, Germany, and Russia, a U.S.-led coalition launched an invasion of Iraq on the evening of Mar. 19, 2003. By Apr. 6 the British controlled Basra and other areas in the south, and the U.S. entered Baghdad Apr. 7. Hussein had disappeared, the Iraqi government had collapsed, and most of Iraq's armed forces had dissolved into the civilian population. On May 1, Pres. Bush declared that major combat there was over. Continuing searches failed to find evidence of usable chemical, biological, or nuclear weapons the U.S. and other countries claimed Iraq had stockpiled.

The U.S. initially governed Iraq through a Coalition Provisional Authority, headed by L. Paul Bremer. A 25-member Iraqi Governing Council was appointed and named a cabinet Sept. 1, 2003. Reconstruction efforts continued but were hampered by guerrilla attacks from Baath remnants, Islamic extremists, and others. Iraqi resistance activities widened with the bombings of the Jordanian embassy, Aug. 7; the UN headquarters in Baghdad, Aug. 19, killing UN special envoy Sergio Vieira de Mello and 21 others; and a blast in Najaf Aug. 29 that killed at least 83 people, including Ayatollah Mohammad Bakir al-Hakim, a Shiite leader. After a second bombing at its Baghdad headquarters Sept. 22, the UN scaled back its presence in Iraq.

Photographs released in Apr. 2004 graphically showed instances of physical abuse and sexual humiliation of Iraqi inmates by U.S. military personnel at Baghdad's Abu Ghraib prison in fall 2003. The images sparked widespread condemnation and U.S. criminal proceedings against some individuals.

Coalition forces succeeded in neutralizing many leaders of the former regime. Two of Hussein's sons, Uday and Qusay, were killed July 22, 2003, by U.S. troops in Mosul. Saddam Hussein was captured in an underground hideout Dec. 13; he appeared before an Iraqi tribunal July 1, 2004, and was charged with crimes against humanity committed in 1982 at the Shiite village of Dujail. His trial, which began Oct. 19, 2005, was marred by murders of several lawyers representing him and his co-defendants; the trial ended July 27, 2006, with a verdict expected Oct. 16. In a second trial, which began Aug. 21, 2006, he faced charges of genocide for crimes against the Kurds in the late 1980s.

The insurgency continued to mount attacks that killed large numbers of Iraqi civilians as well as many foreign troops and civilians participating in reconstruction. The U.S. blamed Jordanian militant Abu Musab al-Zarqawi, leader of the terrorist group Al Qaeda in Iraq, for directing a series of kidnappings, beheadings, and suicide bombings. He was killed by a U.S. air strike, June 7, 2006.

On June 28, 2004, U.S. authorities officially transferred sovereignty to a transitional Iraqi government led by Prime Min. Iyad Allawi. Despite threats by insurgents, an estimated 8 mil people in Iraq, mostly Shiites and Kurds, cast ballots Jan. 30, 2005, for a 275-member transitional national assembly. On Apr. 6, the assembly elected Jalal al-Talabani, a Kurd, as president; Ibrahim al-Jaafari, a Shiite, became prime minister. The insurgents launched new waves of attacks, killing hundreds of police and army recruits. Rumors of a suicide bomber set off a stampede by Shiite pilgrims in northern Baghdad Aug. 31, killing close to 1,000 people. A new constitution, favored by Kurds and Shiites but opposed by Sunnis, was adopted by the assembly Aug. 28 and approved by referendum Oct. 15.

Legislative elections were held Dec. 15, 2005, and official results announced Jan. 20, 2006, but political wrangling delayed installation of a new government, headed by Shiite leader Nouri Kamel al-Maliki, until May 20. Meanwhile, a bomb Feb. 22 that destroyed the dome of Samarra's Golden Mosque, a Shiite shrine, triggered a wave of revenge killings; between May and mid-July at least 6,000 civilians died in sectarian violence between Sunnis and Shiites, much of it in Baghdad. A survey conducted at midyear by the *Los Angeles Times* concluded that the overall civilian death toll since the 2003 invasion exceeded 50,000.

More than 140,000 U.S. troops remained in Iraq, along with 19,000 allied forces and thousands of foreign civilian advisers and contractors. By Sept. 2006, more than 2,600 U.S. service members had been killed and about 20,000 wounded during the war and occupation. British troop losses were put at more than 100; Italy, Ukraine, Poland, and other countries had smaller losses.

Ireland

People: Population: 4,062,235. **Age distrib.** (%) <15: 20.9; 65+: 11.6. **Pop. density:** 152 per sq mi, 58 per sq km. **Urban:** 59.9%. **Ethnic groups:** Celtic; English minority. **Principal languages:** English, Irish Gaelic (both official); Irish Gaelic spoken by small number in western areas. **Chief religions:** Roman Catholic 88%, Anglican 3%.

Geography: Total area: 27,135 sq mi, 70,280 sq km; **Land area:** 26,599 sq mi, 68,890 sq km. **Location:** In the Atlantic O. just W of Great Britain. **Neighbors:** United Kingdom (Northern Ireland) on E. **Topography:** Ireland consists of a central plateau surrounded by isolated groups of hills and mountains. The coastline is heavily indented by the Atlantic O. **Capital:** Dublin, 1,037,000.

Government: Type: Parliamentary republic. **Head of state:** Pres. Mary McAleese; b. June 27, 1951; in office: Nov. 11, 1997. **Head of gov.:** Prime Min. Bertie Ahern; b. Sept. 12, 1951; in office: June 26, 1997. **Local divisions:** 26 counties. **Defense budget** (2005): $959 mil. **Active troops:** 10,460.

Economy: Industries: food products, brewing, textiles, clothing, pharm., chemicals. **Chief crops:** turnips, barley, potatoes, sugar beets; wheat. **Natural resources:** zinc, lead, nat. gas, barite, copper, gypsum, limestone, dolomite, peat, silver. **Arable land:** 13%. **Livestock** (2005): cattle: 7 mil; chickens: 12.7 mil; goats: 7,700; pigs: 1.8 mil; sheep: 4.6 mil. **Fish catch** (2004): 338,588 metric tons. **Electricity prod.** (2004): 23.3 bil kWh. **Labor force** (2002 est.): agriculture 8%, industry 29%, services 64%.

Finance: Monetary unit: Euro (EUR) (Sept. 2006: 0.78 = $1 U.S.). **GDP** (2005 est.): $164.6 bil; **per capita GDP:** $41,000; **GDP growth:** 4.7%. **Imports** (2005 est.): $65.5 bil; $60.7 bil; partners (2004): UK 35.2%, U.S. 13.5%, Germany 8.9%, France 4.3%, Netherlands 4.3%. **Exports** (2005 est.): $102 bil; partners (2004): U.S. 20.2%, UK 17.5%, Belgium 14.8%, Germany 7.5%, France 5.9%, Italy 4.5%, Netherlands 4.4%. **Tourism:** $4.3 bil. **Budget** (2005 est.): $69.4 bil. **Intl. reserves less gold:** $545 mil. **Gold:** 180,000 oz t. **Consumer prices:** 2.43%.

Transport: Railroad: Length: 2,058 mi. **Motor vehicles:** 1.40 mil pass. cars, 231,700 comm. vehicles. **Civil aviation:** 11.5 bil pass.-mi; 15 airports. **Chief ports:** Dublin, Cork.

Communications: TV sets: 406 per 1,000 pop. **Radios:** 697 per 1,000 pop. **Telephone lines:** 2 mil. **Daily newspaper circ.:** 335.7 per 1,000 pop. **Internet:** 2.1 mil users.

Health: Life expect.: 75.1 male; 80.5 female. **Births** (per 1,000 pop.): 14.4. **Deaths** (per 1,000 pop.): 7.8. **Natural inc.:** 0.66%. **Infant mortality** (per 1,000 live births): 5.3. **AIDS rate:** 0.2%.

Education: Compulsory: ages 6-15. **Literacy:** 98%.

Major Intl. Organizations: UN (FAO, IBRD, ILO, IMF, IMO, WHO, WTO), EU, OECD, OSCE.

Embassy: 2234 Massachusetts Ave. NW 20008; 462-3939.

Website: www.irlgov.ie

Celtic tribes invaded the islands about the 4th cent. BCE; their Gaelic culture and literature flourished and spread to Scotland and elsewhere in the 5th cent. CE, the same century in which St. Patrick converted the Irish to Christianity. Invasions by Norsemen began in the 8th cent., ended with defeat of the Danes by the Irish King Brian Boru in 1014. English invasions started in the 12th cent.; for over 700 years Anglo-Irish struggle continued with bitter rebellions and savage repressions.

The Easter Monday Rebellion in 1916 failed but was followed by guerrilla warfare and harsh reprisals by British troops called the "Black and Tans." The Dail Eireann (Irish parliament) reaffirmed independence in Jan. 1919. The British offered dominion status to Ulster (6 counties) and southern Ireland (26 counties) Dec. 1921. The constitution of the Irish Free State, a British dominion, was adopted Dec. 11, 1922. Northern Ireland remained part of the United Kingdom.

A new constitution adopted by plebiscite came into operation Dec. 29, 1937. It declared the name of the state Eire in the Irish language (Ireland in the English) and declared it a sovereign democratic state. On Dec. 21, 1948, an Irish law declared the country a republic rather than a dominion and withdrew it from the Commonwealth. The British Parliament recognized both actions, 1949, but reasserted its claim to incorporate the 6 northeastern counties in the UK.

Irish governments have favored peaceful unification of all Ireland and cooperated with Britain against terrorist group. After negotiators in Northern Ireland approved a peace settlement on Good Friday, April 10, 1998, voters in the Irish Republic endorsed the accord, on May 22; the agreement required the removal from the Irish constitution of territorial claims on the north. Irish voters rejected, June 7, 2001, then reversed themselves and approved, Oct. 19, 2002, a plan calling for EU expansion.

Ireland's first woman president, Mary Robinson, resigned Sept. 12, 1997, to become UN high commissioner for human rights. She was succeeded by Mary McAleese, a law professor from Northern Ireland and the first northerner to hold the office. Expansion of educational opportunities and foreign investment in high-tech industries have helped make Ireland one of Europe's most prosperous countries in recent years.

Israel
State of Israel

People: Population: 6,352,117. **Age distrib.** (%) <15: 26.3; 65+: 9.8. **Pop. density:** 809 per sq mi, 312 per sq km. **Urban:** 51.8%. **Ethnic groups:** Jewish 80%, Arab and other 20%. **Principal languages:** Hebrew, Arabic (both official), English. **Chief religions:** Jewish 77%, Muslim (mostly Sunni) 15%, Christian 2%.

Geography: Total area: 8,019 sq mi, 20,770 sq km; **Land area:** 7,849 sq mi, 20,330 sq km. **Location:** Middle East, on E end of Mediterranean Sea. **Neighbors:** Lebanon on N; Syria, West Bank, and Jordan on E; Gaza Strip and Egypt on W. **Topography:** The Mediterranean coastal plain is fertile and well-watered. In the center is the Judean Plateau. A triangular-shaped semi-desert region, the Negev, extends from south of Beersheba to an apex at the head of the Gulf of Aqaba. The E border drops sharply into the Jordan Rift Valley, including Lake Tiberias (Sea of Galilee) and the Dead Sea, which is c.1,300 ft. below sea level, lowest point on the earth's surface. **Capital:** Jerusalem (most countries maintain their embassies in Tel Aviv), 711,000. **Cities (urban aggr.):** Tel Aviv-Yafo, 3,012,000; Haifa, 992,000.

Government: Type: Republic. **Head of state:** Pres. Moshe Katsav; b. 1945; in office: Aug. 1, 2000. **Head of gov.:** Prime Min. Ehud Olmert; b. Sept. 30, 1945; in office: Apr. 14, 2006 (acting from Jan. 4). **Local divisions:** 6 districts. **Defense budget** (2005): $7.9 bil. **Active troops:** 168,300.

Economy: Industries: high-tech products, wood & paper products, potash & phosphates, food, beverages, tobacco. **Chief crops:** citrus, vegetables, cotton. **Natural resources:** timber, potash, copper ore, nat. gas, phosphate rock, magnesium bromide, clays, sand. **Crude oil reserves** (2005): 2 mil bbls. **Arable land:** 17%. **Livestock** (2005): cattle: 400,000; chickens: 30 mil; goats: 65,000; pigs: 195,000; sheep: 390,000. **Fish catch** (2004): 25,643 metric tons. **Electricity prod.** (2004): 46.1 bil kWh. **Labor force** (1996): agriculture, forestry, and fishing 2.6%, manufacturing 20.2%, construction 7.5%, commerce 12.8%, transport, storage, and communications 6.2%, finance and business 13.1%, personal and other services 6.4%, public services 31.2%.

Finance: Monetary unit: New Shekel (ILS) (Sept. 2006: 4.32 = $1 U.S.). **GDP** (2005 est.): $154.5 bil; **per capita GDP:** $24,600; **GDP growth:** 5.2%. **Imports** (2005 est.): $43.2 bil; partners (2004): U.S. 15%, Belgium 10.1%, Germany 7.5%, Switzerland 6.5%, UK 6.1%. **Exports** (2005 est.): $40.1 bil; partners (2004): U.S. 36.8%, Belgium 7.5%, Hong Kong 4.9%. **Tourism:** $2.4 bil. **Budget** (2005 est.): $58 bil. **Intl. reserves less gold:** $19.63 bil. **Consumer prices:** 1.33%.

Transport: Railroad: Length: 398 mi. **Motor vehicles:** 1.55 mil pass. cars, 356,600 comm. vehicles. **Civil aviation:** 7.6 bil pass.-mi; 30 airports. **Chief ports:** Haifa, Ashdod, Elat.

Communications: TV sets: 328 per 1,000 pop. **Radios:** 524 per 1,000 pop. **Telephone lines:** 3 mil. **Daily newspaper circ.:** NA. **Internet:** 3.2 mil users.

Health: Life expect.: 77.3 male; 81.7 female. **Births** (per 1,000 pop.): 18. **Deaths** (per 1,000 pop.): 6.2. **Natural inc.:** 1.18%. **Infant mortality** (per 1,000 live births): 6.9. **AIDS rate:** NA.

Education: Compulsory: ages 5-15. **Literacy:** 97.1%.

Major Intl. Organizations: UN (FAO, IBRD, ILO, IMF, IMO, WHO, WTO).

Embassy: 3514 International Dr. NW 20008; 364-5500.

Website: www.mfa.gov.il

Occupying the southwest corner of the ancient Fertile Crescent, Israel contains some of the oldest known evidence of agriculture and of primitive town life. The Hebrews probably arrived early in the 2nd millennium BCE. Under King David and his successors (c. 1000 BCE-597 BCE), Judaism was developed and secured. After conquest by Babylonians, Persians, and Greeks, an independent Jewish kingdom was revived, 168 BCE, but Rome took effective control in the next century, suppressed Jewish revolts in 70 CE and 135 CE, and renamed Judea Palestine, after the earlier coastal inhabitants, the Philistines.

Arab invaders conquered Palestine in 636. The Arabic language and Islam prevailed within a few centuries, but a Jewish minority remained. The land was ruled from the 11th cent. as a part of non-Arab empires by Seljuks, Mamluks, and Ottomans (with a Crusader interval, 1098-1291).

After 4 centuries of Ottoman rule, the land was taken in 1917 by Britain, which pledged in the Balfour Declaration to support a Jewish homeland there. In 1920 a British Palestine Mandate was recognized; in 1922 the land east of the Jordan was detached.

Jewish immigration, begun in the late 19th cent., swelled in the 1930s with refugees from the Nazis; heavy Arab immigration from Syria and Lebanon also occurred. Arab opposition to Jewish immigration turned violent in 1920, 1921, 1929, and 1936. The UN General Assembly voted in 1947 to partition Palestine into an Arab and a Jewish state. Britain withdrew in May 1948.

Israel was declared an independent state May 14, 1948; the Arabs rejected partition. Egypt, Jordan, Syria, Lebanon, Iraq, and Saudi Arabia invaded but failed to destroy the Jewish state, which gained territory. Separate armistices with the Arab nations were signed in 1949; Jordan occupied the West Bank, Egypt occupied Gaza. Neither granted Palestinian autonomy.

After persistent terrorist raids, Israel invaded Egypt's Sinai, Oct. 29, 1956, aided briefly by British and French forces. A UN cease-fire was arranged Nov. 6.

An uneasy truce between Israel and the Arab countries lasted until 1967, when Egypt reoccupied the Gaza Strip and closed the Gulf of Aqaba to Israeli shipping. In a 6-day war that started June 5, the Israelis took the Gaza Strip, occupied the Sinai Peninsula to the Suez Canal, and captured East Jerusalem, Syria's Golan Heights, and Jordan's West Bank. Together, the West Bank and Gaza comprise the Palestinian territories, now represented by the Palestinian Authority (see below).

Egypt and Syria attacked Israel, Oct. 6, 1973 (on Yom Kippur, the most solemn day on the Jewish calendar). Israel counter-attacked, driving the Syrians back, and crossed the Suez Canal. A cease-fire took effect Oct. 24 and a UN peacekeeping force went to the area. Under a disengagement agreement signed Jan. 18, 1974, Israel withdrew from the canal's west bank. Israeli forces raided Entebbe, Uganda, July 3, 1976, and rescued 103 hostages who had been seized by Arab and German terrorists.

Israel's prime ministers, including David Ben-Gurion, Golda Meir, and Yitzhak Rabin, pursued a moderate socialist program, 1948-77. In 1977, the conservative opposition, led by Menachem Begin, was voted into office for the first time. Egypt's Pres. Anwar al-Sadat visited Jerusalem Nov. 1977, and on Mar. 26, 1979, Egypt and Israel signed a formal peace treaty, ending 30 years of war. Israel returned the Sinai to Egypt in 1982.

On June 7, 1981, Israeli jets destroyed an Iraqi atomic reactor near Baghdad that, Israel claimed, would have enabled Iraq to manufacture nuclear weapons. Israeli forces invaded Lebanon, June 6, 1982, to destroy Palestine Liberation Organization (PLO) strongholds there. After massive Israeli bombing of West Beirut, the PLO agreed to evacuate the city. Israeli troops entered West Beirut after newly elected Lebanese Pres. Bashir Gemayel was assassinated on Sept. 14. Israel drew widespread condemnation when Lebanese Christian forces, Sept. 16, entered two West Beirut refugee camps and slaughtered hundreds of Palestinians.

In 1989, violence escalated over the Israeli military occupation of the West Bank and Gaza Strip. In a series of uprisings known as the first intifada, Palestinian protesters defied Israeli troops, who forcibly retaliated. During the Persian Gulf War, 1991, Iraq fired Scud missiles at Israel. The Labor Party of Yitzhak Rabin won parliamentary elections, June 23, 1992.

Ongoing peace talks led to historic agreements between Israel and the PLO, Sept. 1993. The PLO recognized Israel's right to exist; Israel recognized the PLO as the Palestinians' representative. The two sides then signed, Sept. 13, an agreement for limited Palestinian self-rule in the West Bank and Gaza. Israel and Jordan signed, July 25, 1994, in Washington, DC, a declaration ending their 46-year state of war.

Arab and Jewish extremists repeatedly challenged the peace process. A Jewish gunman opened fire on Arab worshippers at a mosque in Hebron, Feb. 25, 1994, killing at least 29 before he himself was killed. On Nov. 4, 1995, an Orthodox Jewish Israeli assassinated Rabin as he left a peace rally in Tel Aviv. Support for Rabin's successor, Shimon Peres, was shaken by a series of suicide bombings and rocket attacks against Israel by Islamic militants. Emphasizing security issues, the candidate of the conservative Likud bloc, Benjamin Netanyahu, was elected prime minister on May 29, 1996.

Under an interim accord brokered by Pres. Bill Clinton and signed by Netanyahu and PLO leader Yasir Arafat at the White House, Oct. 23, 1998, Israel yielded more West Bank territory to the Palestinians, in exchange for new security guarantees. Negotiations bogged down, however, and full implementation did not begin until Sept. 1999. In the interim, Netanyahu lost by a landslide to the Labor candidate, Ehud Barak, in the election of May 17, 1999.

Israel pulled virtually all its troops out of southern Lebanon by May 24, 2000. Marathon summit talks in the U.S. between Barak and Arafat, July 11-25, failed. A second intifada began in late Sept. in Israel and the Palestinian territories. Barak called new elections for prime minister but lost Feb. 6, 2001, to Ariel Sharon, a hardliner. The bloodshed intensified during the summer, as Palestinian suicide bombers launched attacks on Israeli civilians and Israel struck at Palestinian-controlled territory and carried out an assassination campaign against suspected terrorists.

Israel launched a major West Bank offensive Mar. 29, 2002, 2 days after a suicide bomber killed 26 Israeli Jews at a Passover celebration in Netanya. Fighting was particularly fierce at the Jenin refugee camp, where 23 Israeli troops and at least 50 Palestinians were killed. Israel withdrew in early May but, after another wave of suicide bombings, reoccupied much of the West Bank June 21-27.

A U.S.-sponsored "road map" to Middle East peace, unveiled Apr. 30, 2003, made little headway. Israel Sept. 1 vowed "all-out war" against Hamas terrorists. Israeli missile strikes in Gaza City killed Hamas founder and leader Sheikh Ahmed Yassin Mar. 22, 2004, and his successor, Abdel Aziz al-Rantisi, Apr. 17. Hamas suicide bombers Aug. 31 blew up 2 buses in Beersheba, killing 16.

Sharon's decision to pull all Israeli settlers and troops out of Gaza (see below), approved by the cabinet Feb. 20, 2005, led to a realignment in Israeli politics. When right-wing Likud members opposed the plan, Sharon and Deputy Prime Min. Ehud Olmert broke with them and formed the centrist Kadima Party. Sharon suffered a massive stroke Jan. 4, 2006. With Sharon incapacitated, Olmert became prime minister, led Kadima to victory in Mar. 28 elections, and formed a broad coalition government.

Border clashes in which Hamas militants from Gaza (June 25) and Hezbollah fighters from Lebanon (July 12) killed and captured Israeli soldiers rapidly escalated into full-scale war. Israeli air and ground forces hit hard in Gaza, but the fiercest fighting raged on the northern front. Hezbollah (aided by Syria and Iran) bombarded northern Israel with nearly 4,000 rockets, while Israeli forces (backed by the U.S.) blockaded Lebanon, knocked out bridges, roads, and other infrastructure, and pounded southern Lebanon and southern Beirut, damaging Hezbollah but also killing many civilians. By Aug. 14, when a UN-sponsored cease-fire took hold, the estimated death toll from the war included nearly 1,150 Lebanese, almost 200 Gaza Palestinians, and 150 Israelis. To police the truce, 15,000 Lebanese govt. troops began moving into southern Lebanon, and expansion of the UN force in Lebanon (UNIFIL) to 15,000 was authorized.

Palestinian Territories

The Palestinian territories comprise the Gaza Strip, often called Gaza, and the West Bank, both occupied by Israel in 1967. Since 1996 the Palestinian Authority has been responsible for civil government in the territories. Elected president Jan. 20, 1996, PLO leader Yasir Arafat headed the Palestinian Authority until his death Nov. 11, 2004. Mahmoud Abbas (also called Abu Mazen), who had succeeded Arafat as PLO chairman, was elected president Jan. 9, 2005. A victory by Hamas militants in legislative elections Jan. 25, 2006, led to a power struggle with Abbas, who favored a negotiated settlement with Israel; agreement on a unity government was announced Sept. 11. Since Sept. 2000, when the second intifada began, the Israeli-Palestinian conflict has claimed the lives of more than 1,000 Israelis and at least 4,000 Palestinians.

The Gaza Strip extends northeast from the Sinai Peninsula for 40 km (25 mi), with the Mediterranean Sea to the west and Israel to the east. The Palestinian Authority is responsible for civil government. Nearly all the inhabitants are Palestinian Arabs, more than 35% of whom live in refugee camps. Population (2006 est.) 1,428,757. Area: 139 sq mi.

Israel captured Gaza from Egypt in the 1967 war. It remained under Israeli occupation until May 1994, when the Israeli Defense Forces withdrew. Agreements between Israel and the PLO in 1993 and 1994 provided for interim self-rule in Gaza, but Israel retained control over security. Israel forcibly evacuated all 9,000 Jewish settlers from Gaza by Aug. 22, 2005, and the last remaining Israeli soldiers pulled out Sept. 12. Israel established a fortified barrier on its Gaza border to block Palestinian infiltrators.

Located west of the Jordan R. and Dead Sea, the West Bank is bounded by Jordan on the east and by Israel on the north, west, and south. The Palestinian Authority administers several major cities, but Israel retains control over much land, including Jewish settlements. Population (2006 est.) 2,460,492. Area: 2,263 sq mi.

Israel captured the West Bank from Jordan in the 1967 war. A 1974 Arab summit conference designated the PLO as sole representative of West Bank Arabs. In 1988 Jordan cut legal and administrative ties with the territory. Jericho was returned to Palestinian control in May 1994. An accord between Israel and the PLO expanding Palestinian self-rule in the West Bank was signed Sept. 28, 1995. Later agreements gave Palestinians full or shared control of 40% of West Bank territory.

In June 2002 the Israeli government began building a controversial security barrier in the West Bank to restrict Palestinian access to Israel; in a nonbinding ruling, July 9, 2004, the World Court said the barrier violated international law.

Italy
Italian Republic

People: Population: 58,133,509. **Age distrib.** (%) <15: 13.8; 65+: 19.7. **Pop. density:** 512 per sq mi, 197 per sq km. **Urban:** 91.6%. **Ethnic groups:** Mostly Italian; small minorities of German, Slovene, Albanian. **Principal languages:** Italian (official), German, French, Slovenian, Albanian. **Chief religion:** Predominately Roman Catholic.

Geography: Total area: 116,306 sq mi, 301,230 sq km; **Land area:** 113,522 sq mi, 294,020 sq km. **Location:** In S Europe, jutting into Mediterranean Sea. **Neighbors:** France on W, Switzerland and Austria on N, Slovenia on E. **Topography:** Occupies a long boot-shaped peninsula, extending SE from the Alps into the Mediterranean, with the islands of Sicily and Sardinia offshore. The alluvial Po Valley drains most of N. The rest of the country is rugged and mountainous, except for intermittent coastal plains, like the Campania, S of Rome. Apennine Mts. run down through center of peninsula. **Capital:** Rome, 3,348,000. **Cities (urban aggr.):** Milan, 2,953,000; Naples, 2,245,000; Turin, 1,660,000.

Government: Type: Republic. **Head of state:** Pres. Giorgio Napolitano; b. June 29, 1925; in office: May 15, 2006. **Head of gov.:** Prime Min. Romano Prodi; b. Aug. 9, 1939; in office: May 17, 2006. **Local divisions:** 20 regions divided into 103 provinces. **Defense budget** (2005): $17.2 bil. **Active troops:** 191,875.

Economy: Industries: tourism, machinery, iron & steel, chemicals, food proc., textiles, autos. **Chief crops:** fruits, vegetables, grapes, potatoes, sugar beets, soybeans, grain, olives. **Natural resources:** mercury, potash, marble, sulfur, nat. gas, oil, fish, coal. **Crude oil reserves** (2005): 622 mil bbls. **Arable land:** 31%. **Livestock** (2005): cattle: 6.3 mil; chickens: 100 mil; goats: 985,000; pigs: 9.3 mil; sheep: 8.2 mil. **Fish catch** (2004): 404,870 metric tons. **Electricity prod.** (2004): 277.6 bil kWh. **Labor force** (2001): agriculture 5%, industry 32%, services 63%.

Finance: Monetary unit: Euro (EUR) (Sept. 2006: 0.78 = $1 U.S.). **GDP** (2005 est.): $1.7 tril; **per capita GDP:** $29,200; **GDP growth:** 0.1%. **Imports** (2005 est.): $369.2 bil; partners (2004): Germany 18.1%, France 10.7%, Netherlands 5.8%, Spain 4.7%, Belgium 4.4%, UK 4.3%, China 4.1%. **Exports** (2005 est.): $371.9 bil; partners (2004): Germany 13.7%, France 12.1%, U.S. 8%, Spain 7.3%, UK 6.9%, Switzerland 4.1%. **Tourism** $35.4 bil. **Budget** (2005): $861.5 bil. **Intl. reserves less gold:** $17.85 bil. **Gold:** 78.83 mil oz t. **Consumer prices:** 1.99%.

Transport: Railroad: Length: 12,004 mi. **Motor vehicles:** 33.13 mil pass. cars, 3.75 mil comm. vehicles. **Civil aviation:** 21.3 bil pass.-mi; 98 airports. **Chief ports:** Genoa, Venice, Trieste, Palermo, Naples, La Spezia.

Communications: TV sets: 492 per 1,000 pop. **Radios:** 880 per 1,000 pop. **Telephone lines:** 25 mil. **Daily newspaper circ.:** 109 per 1,000 pop. **Internet:** 28.9 mil.users.

Health: Life expect.: 76.9 male; 82.9 female. **Births** (per 1,000 pop.): 8.7. **Deaths** (per 1,000 pop.): 10.4. **Natural inc.:** −0.17%. **Infant mortality** (per 1,000 live births): 5.8. **AIDS rate:** 0.5%.

Education: Compulsory: ages 6-14. **Literacy:** 98.4%.

Major Intl. Organizations: UN and all of its specialized agencies, EU, NATO, OECD, OSCE.

Embassy: 3000 Whitehaven St. NW 20008; 612-4400.

Website: www.italyemb.org

Rome emerged as the major power in Italy after 500 BCE, dominating the Etruscans to the north and Greeks to the south. Under the Empire, which lasted until the 5th cent. CE, Rome ruled most of Western Europe, the Balkans, the Middle East, and North Africa.

After the Germanic invasions, lasting several centuries, a high civilization arose in the city-states of the north, culminating in the Renaissance. But German, French, Spanish, and Austrian intervention prevented the unification of the country. In 1859 Lombardy came under the crown of King Victor Emmanuel II of Sardinia. By plebiscite in 1860, Parma, Modena, Romagna, and Tuscany joined, followed by Sicily and Naples, and by the Marches and Umbria. The first Italian Parliament declared Victor Emmanuel king of Italy Mar. 17, 1861. Mantua and Venetia were added in 1866 as an outcome of the Austro-Prussian war. The Papal States were taken by Italian troops Sept. 20, 1870, on the withdrawal of the French garrison. The states were annexed to the kingdom by plebiscite. Italy recognized Vatican City as independent Feb. 11, 1929.

Fascism appeared in Italy Mar. 23, 1919, led by Benito Mussolini, who took over the government at the invitation of the king Oct. 28, 1922. Mussolini acquired dictatorial powers. He made war on Ethiopia and proclaimed Victor Emmanuel III emperor, defied the sanctions of the League of Nations, sent troops to fight for Franco against the Republic of Spain, and joined Germany in WWII.

After Fascism was overthrown in 1943, Italy declared war on Germany and Japan and contributed to the Allied victory. It surrendered conquered lands and lost its colonies. Mussolini was killed by partisans Apr. 28, 1945. Victor Emmanuel III abdicated May 9, 1946; his son Humbert II was king until June 10, when Italy became a republic after a referendum, June 2-3.

Christian Democratic leader and former Prime Min. Aldo Moro was abducted and murdered in 1978 by Red Brigade terrorists. The wave of left-wing political violence, including other kidnappings and assassinations, continued into the 1980s.

In the early 1990s, scandals implicated some of Italy's most prominent politicians. In Mar. 1994 voting, under reformed election rules, right-wing parties won a majority, dislodging Italy's long-powerful Christian Democratic Party. After a series of short-lived governments, a coalition of center-left parties won the election of Apr. 21, 1996. Italy led a 7,000-member peacekeeping force in Albania, Apr.-Aug. 1997, and contributed 2,000 troops to the NATO-led security force (KFOR) that entered Kosovo in June 1999.

Supporters of Silvio Berlusconi, a multibillionaire media magnate, won the parliamentary elections of May 13, 2001. In 2003, Berlusconi backed the U.S.-led war in Iraq, and Italian troops served in the coalition. On trial for bribing judges in the 1980s, he was helped when Parliament passed a bill in June immunizing top government leaders from prosecution while they held office. Over 4,100 elderly Italians died because of a severe summer heat wave.

Public opposition to Berlusconi's Iraq policy intensified after U.S. troops at a Baghdad checkpoint fired on a car carrying a freed hostage, Mar. 4, 2005, wounding her and killing the Italian agent who was protecting her. Turin hosted the Winter Olympics, Feb. 10-26, 2006. A coalition of center-left parties led by Romano Prodi scored a narrow win over Berlusconi in parliamentary elections, Apr. 9-10. The national soccer team took the World Cup, July 9. Italy's contingent of 2,600 troops was scheduled to leave Iraq by December. Italian troops would be heading the UN peacekeeping force in Lebanon.

Sicily, 9,926 sq mi, pop. (2001 est.) 4,866,200 is an island 180 by 120 mi, seat of a region that embraces the island of **Pantelleria**, 32 sq mi, and the **Lipari** group, 44 sq mi, including 2 active volcanoes: **Vulcano,** 1,637ft, and **Stromboli,** 3,038 ft. From prehistoric times Sicily has been settled by various peoples; a Greek state had its capital at Syracuse. Rome took Sicily from Carthage 215 BCE. **Mt. Etna,** an 11,053-ft active volcano, is its tallest peak.

Sardinia, 9,301 sq mi, pop. (2001 est.) 1,599,500, lies in the Mediterranean, 115 mi W of Italy and 7½ mi S of Corsica. It is 160 mi long, 68 mi wide, and mountainous, with mining of coal, zinc, lead, copper. In 1720 Sardinia was added to the possessions of the Dukes of Savoy in Piedmont and Savoy to form the Kingdom of Sardinia. Giuseppe Garibaldi is buried on the nearby isle of Caprera. **Elba,** 86 sq mi, lies 6 mi W of Tuscany. Napoleon I lived in exile on Elba 1814-15.

Jamaica

People: Population: 2,758,124. **Age distrib.** (%) <15: 33.1; 65+: 7.3. **Pop. density:** 659 per sq mi, 254 per sq km. **Urban:** 67.4%. **Ethnic groups:** Black 91%, mixed 7%, East Indian and other 2%. **Principal languages:** English, patois English. **Chief religions:** Protestant 61%, spiritual cults and other 35%, Roman Catholic 4%.

Geography: Total area: 4,244 sq mi, 10,991 sq km; **Land area:** 4,182 sq mi, 10,831 sq km. **Location:** In West Indies. **Neighbors:** Nearest are Cuba to N, Haiti to E. **Topography:** Four-fifths of Jamaica is covered by mountains. **Capital:** Kingston, 576,000

Government: Type: Parliamentary democracy. **Head of state:** Queen Elizabeth II, represented by Gov.-Gen. Kenneth Hall; b. Apr. 24, 1941; in office: Feb. 15, 2006. **Head of gov.:** Prime Min. Portia Simpson Miller; b. Dec. 12, 1945; in office: Mar. 30, 2006. **Local divisions:** 14 parishes. **Defense budget** (2005): $58 mil. **Active troops:** 2,830.

Economy: Industries: tourism, bauxite, textiles, food proc., light manufactures, rum, cement, metal, paper, chemical products. **Chief crops:** sugarcane, bananas, coffee, citrus, potatoes. **Natural resources:** bauxite, gypsum, limestone. **Arable land:** 14%. **Livestock** (2005): cattle: 430,000; chickens: 12.5 mil; goats: 440,000; pigs: 85,000; sheep: 1,280. **Fish catch** (2004): 17,613 metric tons. **Electricity prod.** (2004): 6.9 bil kWh. **Labor force** (2004): agriculture 19.3%, industry 16.6%, services 64.1%.

Finance: Monetary unit: Jamaican Dollar (JMD) (Sept. 2006: 65.75 = $1 U.S.). **GDP** (2005 est.): $12.2 bil; **per capita GDP:** $4,400; **GDP growth:** 1.5%. **Imports** (2004 est.): $4.1 bil; partners (2004): U.S. 38.3%, Trinidad and Tobago 10.3%, Venezuela 5.6%, France 5.5%, Japan 4.6%. **Exports** (2004 est.): $1.6 bil; partners (2004): U.S. 17.2%, Canada 14.3%, France 12.6%, China 11.4%, UK 8.6%, Netherlands 7%, Norway 5.8%, Germany 5.6%. **Tourism:** $1.4 bil. **Budget** (2005 est.): $3.2 bil. **Intl. reserves less gold:** $1.52 bil.

Transport: Railroad: Length: 169 mi. **Motor vehicles:** 129,400 pass. cars, 65,200 comm. vehicles. **Civil aviation:** 3.1 bil pass.-mi; 11 airports. **Chief ports:** Kingston, Montego Bay.

Communications: TV sets: 191 per 1,000 pop. **Radios:** 796 per 1,000 pop. **Telephone lines:** 342,000. **Daily newspaper circ.:** NA. **Internet** 1.1 mil users.

Health: Life expect.: 71.5 male; 75 female. **Births** (per 1,000 pop.): 20.8. **Deaths** (per 1,000 pop.): 6.5. **Natural inc.:** 1.43%. **Infant mortality** (per 1,000 live births): 16. **AIDS rate:** 1.5%.

Education: Compulsory: ages 6-11. **Literacy:** 79.9%.

Major Intl. Organizations: UN (FAO, IBRD, ILO, IMF, IMO, WHO, WTO), Caricom, the Commonwealth, OAS.
Embassy: 1520 New Hampshire Ave. NW 20036; 452-0660.
Website: www.jis.gov.jm

Jamaica was visited by Columbus, 1494, and ruled by Spain (under whom Arawak Indians died out) until seized by Britain, 1655. Jamaica won independence Aug. 6, 1962. The island's rich musical innovations include ska and reggae. Rastafarianism is an influential religious movement.

In 1974 Jamaica sought an increase in taxes paid by U.S. and Canadian bauxite mines. The socialist government acquired 50% ownership of the companies' Jamaican interests in 1976, and was reelected that year. Rudimentary welfare state measures were passed. Relations with the U.S. improved in the 1980s when Jamaican politics entered a more conservative phase. Violence between government forces and West Kingston slum residents claimed at least 20 lives July 7-10, 2001.

At least 17 died when Hurricane Ivan hit southern Jamaica Sept. 10-11, 2004. Portia Simpson Miller, leader of the People's National Party, became Jamaica's first female prime minister, Mar. 30, 2006.

Japan

People: Population: 127,463,611. **Age distrib.** (%) <15: 14.2; 65+: 20. **Pop. density:** 880 per sq mi, 340 per sq km. **Urban:** 52.1%. **Ethnic groups:** Japanese 99%; Korean, Chinese, and other 1%. **Principal languages:** Japanese (official), Ainu, Korean. **Chief religions:** Shinto and Buddhist, observed together by 84%.

Geography: Total area: 145,883 sq mi, 377,835 sq km; **Land area:** 144,689 sq mi, 374,744 sq km. **Location:** Archipelago off E coast of Asia. **Neighbors:** Russia to N, South Korea to W. **Topography:** Japan consists of 4 main islands: Honshu ("mainland"), 87,805 sq. mi.; Hokkaido, 30,144 sq. mi.; Kyushu, 14,114 sq. mi.; and Shikoku, 7,049 sq. mi. The coast, deeply indented, measures 16,654 mi. The northern islands are a continuation of the Sakhalin Mts. The Kunlun range of China continues into southern islands, the ranges meeting in the Japanese Alps. In a vast transverse fissure crossing Honshu E-W rises a group of volcanoes, mostly extinct or inactive, including 12,388 ft. Mt. Fuji (Fujiyama) near Tokyo. **Capital:** Tokyo, 35,197,000. **Cities (urban aggr.):** Osaka, 11,268,000, (1998 city proper: 2,599,642); Nagoya, 3,179,000; Sapporo, 2,530,000.

Government: Type: Parliamentary democracy. **Head of state:** Emp. Akihito; b. Dec. 23, 1933; in office: Jan. 7, 1989. **Head of gov.:** Prime Min. Shinzo Abe; b. Sept. 21, 1954; in office: Sept. 26, 2006. **Local divisions:** 47 prefectures. **Defense budget** (2005): $44.7 bil. **Active troops:** 239,900.

Economy: Industries: motor vehicles, electronic equip., machine tools, steel & nonferrous metals, ships, chemicals, textiles, proc. foods. **Chief crops:** rice, sugar beets, vegetables, fruit. **Natural resources:** fish. **Crude oil reserves** (2005): 58.5 mil bbls. **Arable land:** 11%. **Livestock** (2005): cattle: 4.4 mil; chickens: 283 mil; goats: 34,000; pigs: 9.6 mil; sheep: 11,000. **Fish catch** (2004): 5,177,762 metric tons. **Electricity prod.** (2004): 974.4 bil kWh. **Labor force** (2004 est.): agriculture 4.6%, industry 27.8%, services 67.7%.

Finance: Monetary unit: Yen (JPY) (Sept. 2006: 116.34 = $1 U.S.). **GDP** (2005 est.): $4 tril; **per capita GDP:** $31,500; **GDP growth:** 2.7%. **Imports** (2005 est.): $451.1 bil; partners (2004): China 20.7%, U.S. 14%, South Korea 4.9%, Australia 4.3%, Indonesia 4.1%, Saudi Arabia 4.1%, UAE 4%. **Exports** (2005 est.): $550.5 bil; partners (2004): U.S. 22.7%, China 13.1%, South Korea 7.8%, Taiwan 7.4%, Hong Kong 6.3%. **Tourism:** $11.3 bil. **Budget** (2005 est.): $1.8 tril. **Intl. reserves less gold:** $583.71 bil. **Gold:** 24.6 mil oz t. **Consumer prices:** -0.29%.

Transport: Railroad: Length: 14,650 mi. **Motor vehicles:** 55.21 mil pass. cars, 17.31 mil comm. vehicles. **Civil aviation:** 102 bil pass.-mi; 145 airports. **Chief ports:** Tokyo, Kobe, Osaka, Nagoya, Chiba, Kawasaki, Hakodate.

Communications: TV sets: 719 per 1,000 pop. **Radios:** 956 per 1,000 pop. **Telephone lines:** 58.8 mil. **Daily newspaper circ.:** 566 per 1,000 pop. **Internet:** 86.3 mil users.

Health: Life expect.: 78 male; 84.7 female. **Births** (per 1,000 pop.): 9.4. **Deaths** (per 1,000 pop.): 9.2. **Natural inc.:** 0.02%. **Infant mortality** (per 1,000 live births): 3.2. **AIDS rate:** <0.1%.

Education: Compulsory: ages 6-15. **Literacy:** 99%.
Major Intl. Organizations: UN and all its specialized agencies, APEC, OECD.
Embassy: 2520 Massachusetts Ave. NW 20008; 238-6700.
Website: www.kantei.go.jp/foreign/index-e.html

According to Japanese legend, the empire was founded by Emperor Jimmu, 660 BCE, but earliest records of a unified Japan date from 1,000 years later. Chinese influence was strong in the formation of Japanese civilization. Buddhism was introduced before the 6th cent. CE.

A feudal system, with locally powerful noble families and their samurai warrior retainers, dominated from 1192. Central power was held by successive families of shoguns (military dictators), 1192-1867, until recovered by Emperor Meiji, 1868. The Portuguese and Dutch had minor trade with Japan in the 16th and 17th centuries; U.S. Commodore Matthew C. Perry opened the country to U.S. trade in a treaty dated 1854. Industrialization was begun in the late 19th century. Japan fought China, 1894-95, gaining Taiwan. After war with Russia, 1904-05, Russia ceded southern half of Sakhalin and gave concessions in China. Japan annexed Korea 1910.

In WWI Japan ousted Germany from Shandong in China and took over German Pacific islands. Japan took Manchuria in 1931 and launched full-scale war in China in 1937. Japan launched war against the U.S. by attacking Pearl Harbor Dec. 7, 1941. The U.S. dropped atomic bombs on Hiroshima, Aug. 6, and Nagasaki, Aug. 9, 1945. Japan surrendered Aug. 14, 1945.

In a new constitution adopted May 3, 1947, Japan renounced the right to wage war; the emperor gave up claims to divinity; the Diet became the sole law-making authority. The U.S. and 48 other non-Communist nations signed a peace treaty and the U.S. a bilateral defense agreement with Japan, in San Francisco Sept. 8, 1951, restoring Japan's sovereignty as of April 28, 1952.

Rebuilding after WWII, Japan emerged as one of the most powerful economies in the world, and as a leader in technology. The U.S. and Western Europe criticized Japan for its restrictive policy on imports, which eventually allowed Japan to accumulate huge trade surpluses.

On June 26, 1968, the U.S. returned to Japanese control the Bonin Isls., Volcano Isls. (including Iwo Jima), and Marcus Isls. On May 15, 1972, Okinawa, the other Ryukyu Isls., and the Daito Isls. were returned by the U.S.; it was agreed the U.S. would continue to maintain military bases on Okinawa.

The Recruit scandal, the nation's worst political scandal since WWII, which involved illegal political donations and stock trading, led to the resignation of Premier Noboru Takeshita in May 1989. Following new political and economic scandals, the ruling Liberal Democratic Party (LDP) was denied a majority in general elections July 18, 1993. On June 29, 1994, Tomiichi Murayama became Japan's first Socialist premier since 1947-48.

An earthquake in the Kobe area in Jan. 1995 claimed more than 5,000 lives, injured nearly 35,000, and caused over $90 bil in property damage. On Mar. 20, a nerve gas attack in the Tokyo subway (blamed on a religious cult) killed 12 and injured thousands. Public anger at the rape of a 12-year-old Okinawa schoolgirl by 3 U.S. servicemen, Sept. 4, led the U.S. to begin reducing its military presence there.

Murayama resigned as prime minister, Jan. 5, 1996, and was replaced by Ryutaro Hashimoto of the LDP. Hashimoto signed a joint security declaration with U.S. Pres. Bill Clinton in Tokyo, Apr. 17, 1996. Nagano hosted the Winter Olympics, Feb. 7-22, 1998.

Murayama resigned as prime minister, Jan. 5, 1996, and was replaced by Ryutaro Hashimoto of the LDP. Nagano hosted the Winter Olympics, Feb. 7-22, 1998.

With the country mired in a lengthy recession, a series of weak LDP governments led Japan. In Apr. 2001 Junichiro Koizumi, a populist reformer, became LDP leader and prime minister. In Sept. 2002, Koizumi became the first Japanese leader to visit N. Korea; during the meeting N. Korean Prem. Kim Jong-Il apologized for abducting Japanese citizens. Five of these abductees returned to Japan in Oct. 2002.

Koizumi's coalition retained power in the elections of Nov. 9, 2003. A commuter train crash at Amagasaki, western Japan Apr. 25, 2005, killed over 100 people. Voters in legislative elections Sept. 11 gave Koizumi a mandate to restructure the economy. About 600 noncombatant troops were in Iraq Feb. 2004-July 2006, the first time since WWII that Japanese forces served in an overseas war zone. Shinzo Abe, a Koizumi protégé, succeeded him in Sept. 2006 as LDP leader and prime minister.

Jordan
Hashemite Kingdom of Jordan

People: Population: 5,906,760. **Age distrib.** (%) <15: 33.8; 65+: 3.9. **Pop. density:** 166 per sq mi, 64 per sq km. **Urban:** 79.0%. **Ethnic groups:** Arab 98%, Armenian 1%, Circassian 1%. **Principal languages:** Arabic (official), English. **Chief religions:** Muslim (official; mostly Sunni) 92%, Christian 6%.

Geography: Total area: 35,637 sq mi, 92,300 sq km; **Land area:** 35,510 sq mi, 91,971 sq km. **Location:** In Middle East. **Neighbors:** Israel and West Bank on W, Saudi Arabia on S, Iraq on E, Syria on N. **Topography:** About 88% of Jordan is arid. Fertile areas are in W. Only port is on short Aqaba Gulf coast. Country shares Dead Sea (about 1,300 ft. below sea level) with Israel. **Capital:** Amman, 1,292,000.

Government: Type: Constitutional monarchy. **Head of state:** King Abdullah II; b. Jan. 30, 1962; in office: Feb. 7, 1999. **Head of gov.:** Prime Min. Marouf al-Bakhit; b. 1947; in office: Nov. 27, 2005. **Local divisions:** 12 governorates. **Defense budget** (2005): $956 mil. **Active troops:** 100,500.

Economy: Industries: phosphates, oil refining, cement, potash, light mfg. **Chief crops:** wheat, barley, citrus, tomatoes, melons, olives. **Natural resources:** phosphates, potash, shale oil. **Crude oil reserves** (2005): 1 mil bbls. **Arable land:** 4%. **Livestock** (2005): cattle: 69,100; chickens: 25 mil; goats: 444,450; sheep: 1.7 mil. **Fish catch** (2004): 981 metric tons. **Electricity prod.** (2004): 8.4 bil kWh. **Labor force** (2001 est.): agriculture 5%, industry 12.5%, services 82.5%.

Finance: Monetary unit: Dinar (JOD) (Sept. 2006: 0.71 = $1 U.S.). **GDP** (2005 est.): $26.8 bil; **per capita GDP:** $4,700; **GDP growth:** 6.1%. **Imports** (2005 est.): $8.7 bil; partners (2004): Saudi Arabia 19.9%, China 8.4%, Germany 6.8%, U.S. 6.7%. **Exports** (2005 est.): $4.2 bil; partners (2004): U.S. 25.8%, Iraq 18%, India 6.4%, Saudi Arabia 5.2%. **Tourism:** $1.3 bil. **Budget** (2005 est.): $4.7 bil. **Intl. reserves less gold:** $3.67 bil. **Gold:** 410,000 oz t. **Consumer prices:** 3.51%.

Transport: Railroad: Length: 314 mi. **Motor vehicles:** 329,000 pass. cars, 163,000 comm. vehicles. **Civil aviation:** 2.6 bil pass.-mi; 15 airports. **Chief port:** Al Aqabah.

Communications: TV sets: 83 per 1,000 pop. **Radios:** 271 per 1,000 pop. **Telephone lines:** 617,300. **Daily newspaper circ.:** 74.2 per 1,000 pop. **Internet:** 600,000 users.

Health: Life expect.: 75.9 male; 81 female. **Births** (per 1,000 pop.): 21.2. **Deaths** (per 1,000 pop.): 2.6. **Natural inc.:** 1.86%. **Infant mortality** (per 1,000 live births): 16.8. **AIDS rate:** NA.

Education: Compulsory: ages 6-15. **Literacy:** 89.9%.

Major Intl. Organizations: UN (FAO, IBRD, ILO, IMF, IMO, WHO, WTO), AL.

Embassy: 3504 International Dr. NW 20008; 966-2664.

Website: www.jordanembassyus.org

From ancient times to 1922 the lands to the east of the Jordan R. were culturally and politically united with the lands to the W. Arabs conquered the area in the 7th cent.; the Ottomans took control in the 16th. Britain's 1920 Palestine Mandate covered both sides of the Jordan. In 1921, Abdullah, son of the ruler of Hejaz in Arabia, was installed by Britain as emir of an autonomous Transjordan, covering two-thirds of Palestine. An independent kingdom was proclaimed, 1946.

During the 1948 Arab-Israeli war the West Bank and East Jerusalem were added to the kingdom, which changed its name to Jordan. All these territories were lost to Israel in the 1967 war, which swelled the number of Arab refugees on the East Bank.

Some 700,000 refugees entered Jordan following Iraq's invasion of Kuwait, Aug. 1990. Jordan was viewed as supporting Iraq during the 1990-91 Persian Gulf crisis.

Jordan and Israel officially agreed, July 25, 1994, to end their state of war; a formal peace treaty was signed Oct. 26. Following a prolonged bout with cancer, King Hussein died Feb. 7, 1999; his eldest son and designated successor immediately assumed the throne as Abdullah II.

Jordanian authorities Apr. 2004 said they had foiled a possible chemical attack against the U.S. embassy and other Amman targets; the plot was traced to Abu Musab al-Zarqawi, a high-ranking Jordanian member of al-Qaeda whom the U.S. accused of leading guerrilla activities in Iraq. Zarqawi was also linked to a rocket attack at Aqaba, Aug. 19, 2005, that narrowly missed a U.S. warship. He was killed in Iraq by a U.S. air strike, June 7, 2006.

Kazakhstan
Republic of Kazakhstan

People: Population: 15,233,244. **Age distrib.** (%) <15: 23; 65+: 8.2. **Pop. density:** 14 per sq mi, 5 per sq km. **Urban:** 55.8%. **Ethnic groups:** Kazakh 53%, Russian 30%, Ukrainian 4%, Uzbek 3%, German 2%, Uighur 1%. **Principal languages:** Kazakh, Russian (both official); Ukrainian, German, Uzbek. **Chief religions:** Muslim 47%, Russian Orthodox 44%.

Geography: Total area: 1,049,155 sq mi, 2,717,300 sq km; **Land area:** 1,030,816 sq mi, 2,669,800 sq km. **Location:** In Central Asia. **Neighbors:** Russia on N; China on E; Kyrgyzstan, Uzbekistan, Turkmenistan on S; Caspian Sea on W. **Topography:** Extends from the lower reaches of Volga in Europe to the Altay Mts. on the Chinese border. **Capital:** Astana, 331,000. **Cities (urban aggr.):** Alma-Ata, 1,156,000.

Government: Type: Republic. **Head of state:** Pres. Nursultan A. Nazarbayev; b. July 6, 1940; in office: Apr. 1990. **Head of gov.:** Prime Min. Daniyal Akhmetov; b. June 15, 1954; in office: June 13, 2003. **Local divisions:** 14 oblystar, 3 cities. **Defense budget** (2005): $419 mil. **Active troops:** 65,800.

Economy: Industries: mining and oil producer, agric. machinery, electric motors, constr. materials. **Chief crops:** wheat, cotton, wool. **Natural resources:** oil, nat. gas, coal, iron ore, mang., chrome ore, nickel, cobalt, copper, molybd., lead, zinc, bauxite, gold, uranium. **Crude oil reserves** (2005): 9 bil bbls. **Arable land:** 12%. **Livestock** (2005): cattle: 5.2 mil; chickens: 25.5 mil; goats: 2 mil; pigs: 1.3 mil; sheep: 11.3 mil. **Fish catch** (2004): 34,485 metric tons. **Electricity prod.** (2004): 63.3 bil kWh. **Labor force** (2002 est.): agriculture 20%, industry 30%, services 50%.

Finance: Monetary unit: Tenge (KZT) (Sept. 2006: 127.18 = $1 U.S.). **GDP** (2005 est.): $124.3 bil; **per capita GDP:** $8,200; **GDP growth:** 9.2%. **Imports** (2005 est.): $17.5 bil; partners (2004): Russia 33.9%, China 13.6%, Germany 9.6%, France 6.8%. **Exports** (2005 est.): $30.1 bil; partners (2004): Russia 13.5%, Bermuda 13.4%, China 10.4%, Germany 9.2%, Switzerland 9.1%, France 6.7%. **Tourism:** $708 mil. **Budget** (2005 est.): $12.4 bil. **Intl. reserves less gold:** $4.26 bil. **Gold:** 1.92 mil oz t. **Consumer prices:** 7.58%.

Transport: Railroad: Length: 8,513 mi. **Motor vehicles:** 1.06 mil pass. cars, 280,300 comm. vehicles. **Civil aviation:** 1.1 bil pass.-mi; 67 airports. **Chief ports:** Aqtau, Atyrau.

Communications: TV sets: 240 per 1,000 pop. **Radios:** 395 per 1,000 pop. **Telephone lines:** 2.5 mil. **Internet** (2002): 400,000 users.

Health: Life expect.: 61.6 male; 72.5 female. **Births** (per 1,000 pop.): 16. **Deaths** (per 1,000 pop.): 9.4. **Natural inc.:** 0.66%. **Infant mortality** (per 1,000 live births): 28.3. **AIDS rate:** 0.1%.

Education: Compulsory: ages 7-17. **Literacy:** 99.5%.

Major Intl. Organizations: UN (FAO, IBRD, ILO, IMF, IMO, WHO), CIS, OSCE.

Embassy: 1401 16th St. NW 20036; 232-5488.

Website: www.government.kz

The region came under the Mongols' rule in the 13th cent. and gradually came under Russian rule, 1730-1853. It was admitted to the USSR as a constituent republic in 1936.

Kazakhstan declared independence Dec. 16, 1991. It became an independent state when the Soviet Union dissolved Dec. 26, 1991. The party chief, Nursultan Nazarbayev, was elected president unopposed. He boosted the economy by encouraging Western investment in the oil industry. Dissent was suppressed.

Kazakhstan agreed, Feb. 14, 1994, to dismantle nuclear missiles. Private land ownership was legalized Dec. 26, 1995. Astana (formerly Akmola) became the nation's new capital, June 9, 1998. Reelected in 1999, Pres. Nazarbayev further tightened political controls before the Dec. 4, 2005, election, which he won by 91%.

Kenya
Republic of Kenya

People: Population: 35,890,645. **Age distrib.** (%) <15: 42; 65+: 2.6. **Pop. density:** 163 per sq mi, 63 per sq km. **Urban:** 39.4%. **Ethnic groups:** Kikuyu 22%, Luhya 14%, Luo 13%, Kalenjin 12%, Kamba 11%, Kisii 6%, Meru 6%. **Principal languages:** English, Swahili (both official); numerous indigenous languages. **Chief religions:** Protestant 45%, Roman Catholic 33%, indigenous beliefs 10%, Muslim 10%.

Geography: Total area: 224,962 sq mi, 582,650 sq km; **Land area:** 219,789 sq mi, 569,250 sq km. **Location:** E Africa, on coast of Indian O. **Neighbors:** Uganda on W, Tanzania on S, Somalia on E, Ethiopia on N, Sudan on NW. **Topography:** The northern three-fifths of Kenya is arid. To the S, a low coastal area and a plateau varying from 3,000 to 10,000 ft. The Great Rift Valley enters the country N-S, flanked by high mountains. **Capital:** Nairobi, 2,773,000. **Cities (urban aggr.):** Mombasa: 817,000.

Government: Type: Republic. **Head of state and gov.:** Pres. Mwai Kibaki; b. Nov. 15, 1931; in office: Dec. 30, 2002. **Local divisions:** 7 provinces and Nairobi area. **Defense budget** (2005): $288 mil. **Active troops:** 24,120.

Economy: Industries: light consumer goods, agric. proc., oil refining, cement, tourism. **Chief crops:** coffee, tea, corn, wheat, sugarcane, fruit. **Natural resources:** gold, limestone, soda ash, salt barites, rubies, fluorspar, garnets, wildlife, hydropower. **Arable land:** 7%. **Livestock** (2005): cattle: 12 mil; chickens: 26 mil; goats: 12 mil; pigs: 415,000; sheep: 10 mil. **Fish catch** (2004): 127,902 metric tons. **Electricity prod.** (2004): 5.7 bil kWh. **Labor force** (2003 est.): agriculture 75%, industry and services 25%.

Finance: Monetary unit: Shilling (KES) (Sept. 2006: 72.72 = $1 U.S.). **GDP** (2005 est.): $37.2 bil; **per capita GDP:** $1,100; **GDP growth:** 5.2%. **Imports** (2005 est.): $5.1 bil; partners (2004): UAE 13.2%, Saudi Arabia 9.6%, South Africa 9.3%, U.S. 8%, UK 7.2%, China 6.7%, Japan 5.4%, India 4.9%. **Exports** (2005 est.): $3.2 bil; partners (2004): Uganda 12.8%, UK 11.6%, U.S. 10.4%, Netherlands 8.3%, Pakistan 5.1%, Egypt 4.7%, Tanzania 4.3%. **Tourism:** $495 mil. **Budget** (2005 est.): $3.9 bil. **Intl. reserves less gold:** $1.26 bil. **Consumer prices:** 10.31%.

Transport: Railroad: Length: 1,726 mi. **Motor vehicles:** 255,400 pass. cars, 263,700 comm. vehicles. **Civil aviation:** 2.4 bil pass.-mi; 15 airports. **Chief ports:** Mombasa, Kisumu, Lamu.

Communications: TV sets: 22 per 1,000 pop. **Radios:** 216 per 1,000 pop. **Telephone lines:** 281,800. **Daily newspaper circ.:** 8.3 per 1,000 pop. **Internet:** 1.5 mil.users.

Health: Life expect.: 54.3 male; 54.2 female. **Births** (per 1,000 pop.): 39.8. **Deaths** (per 1,000 pop.): 11.5. **Natural inc.:** 2.83%. **Infant mortality** (per 1,000 live births): 59. **AIDS rate:** 6.1%.

Education: Compulsory: ages 6-13. **Literacy:** 73.6%.

Major Intl. Organizations: UN and all of its specialized agencies, the Commonwealth, AU.

Embassy: 2249 R St. NW 20008; 387-6101.

Website: www.kenyaembassy.com

Arab colonies exported spices and slaves from the Kenya coast as early as the 8th cent. Britain obtained control in the 19th century. Kenya won independence Dec. 12, 1963, 4 years after the end of the violent Mau Mau uprising.

Kenya had steady growth in industry and agriculture under a modified private enterprise system, and enjoyed a relatively free political life. But stability was shaken in 1974-75, with opposition charges of corruption and oppression. Jomo Kenyatta, the country's leader since independence, died Aug. 22, 1978. He was succeeded by his vice president, Daniel arap Moi.

During the first half of the 1990s, Kenya suffered widespread unemployment and high inflation. Tribal clashes in the western provinces claimed thousands of lives and left tens of thousands homeless. Pres. Moi won a 3rd term in Dec. 1992 elections, which were marred by violence and fraud. Clashes in the Mombasa region, Aug. 1997, left more than 40 people dead. Pres. Moi was reelected Dec. 29, in an election again plagued by irregularities.

A truck bomb explosion at the U.S. embassy in Nairobi, Aug. 7, 1998, killed more than 200 people and injured about 5,000. The U.S. blamed the attack and a near-simultaneous embassy bombing in Tanzania on al-Qaeda. After a trial in New York City, 4 conspirators were convicted May 29, 2001. In Mombasa, Nov. 28, 2002, terrorists linked with al-Qaeda killed 12 Kenyans and 3 Israeli tourists at an Israeli-owned hotel and narrowly missed shooting down an Israeli-bound jet.

Constitutionally barred from seeking another term, Pres. Moi was succeeded Dec. 30, 2002, by Mwai Kibaki, the candidate of the opposition Democratic Party. Kibaki's top anticorruption official, John

Githongo, resigned and fled to the UK in Feb. 2005 after his life was reportedly threatened. Violence triggered by a cattle-rustling raid in northern Kenya July 12, 2005, left 65 people dead.

Kiribati
Republic of Kiribati

People: Population: 105,432. **Age distrib.** (%) <15: 38.6; 65+: 3.4. **Pop. density:** 336 per sq mi, 130 per sq km. **Urban:** 47.3%. **Ethnic groups:** Micronesian. **Principal languages:** English (official), I-Kiribati. **Chief religions:** Roman Catholic 52%, Protestant 40%.

Geography: Total area: 313 sq mi, 811 sq km; **Land area:** 313 sq mi, 811 sq km. **Location:** 33 Micronesian islands (the Gilbert, Line, and Phoenix groups) in the mid-Pacific scattered in a 2-mil sq. mi. chain around the point where the International Date Line formerly cut the Equator. In 1997 the Date Line was moved to follow Kiribati's E border. **Neighbors:** Nearest are Nauru to SW, Tuvalu and Tokelau Isls. to S. **Topography:** Except Banaba (Ocean) Isl., all are low-lying, with soil of coral sand and rock fragments, subject to erratic rainfall. **Capital:** South Tarawa, 42,000.

Government: Type: Republic. **Head of state and gov.:** Pres. Anote Tong; b. June 11, 1952; in office: July 10, 2003. **Local divisions:** 3 units, 6 districts.

Economy: Industries: fishing, handicrafts. **Chief crops:** copra, taro, breadfruit, sweet potatoes. **Natural resources:** phosphates. **Livestock** (2005): chickens: 460,000; pigs: 12,400. **Fish catch** (2004): 31,609 metric tons. **Electricity prod.** (2004): 10 mil kWh.

Finance: Monetary unit: Australian Dollar (AUD) (Sept. 2006: 1.33 = $1 U.S.). **GDP** (2001 est.): $79 mil; **per capita GDP:** $800; **GDP growth:** 1.5%. **Imports** (2004 est.): $62 mil; $83.0 mil; partners (2004): Australia 36%, Fiji 24.8%, Japan 11%, New Zealand 8.7%, France 4.4%. **Exports** (2004 est.): $17 mil; partners (2004): France 45.1%, Japan 28.9%, U.S. 9%, Thailand 5.4%. **Tourism** (2001): $3 mil. **Budget** (2000 est.): $37.2 mil.

Transport: Civil aviation: NA; 3 airports. **Chief port:** Tarawa.

Communications: TV sets: 23 per 1,000 pop. **Radios:** 341 per 1,000 pop. **Telephone lines:** 4,500. **Internet** (2004): 2,000 users.

Health: Life expect.: 59.1 male; 65.2 female. **Births** (per 1,000 pop.): 30.6. **Deaths** (per 1,000 pop.): 8.3. **Natural inc.:** 2.24%. **Infant mortality** (per 1,000 live births): 47.3. **AIDS rate:** NA.

Education: Compulsory: ages 6-15. **Literacy:** NA.

Major Intl. Organizations: UN (FAO, IBRD, ILO, IMF, IMO, WHO), the Commonwealth.

Website: www.state.gov/p/eap/ci/kr

A British protectorate since 1892, the Gilbert and Ellice Islands colony was completed with the inclusion of the Phoenix Islands, 1937. Tarawa Atoll was the scene of some of the bloodiest fighting in the Pacific during WWII.

Self-rule was granted 1971; the Ellice Islands separated from the colony 1975 and became independent Tuvalu, 1978. Kiribati (pronounced *Kiribass)* independence was attained July 12, 1979. Under a treaty of friendship the U.S. relinquished its claims to several Line and Phoenix islands, including Christmas (Kiritimati), Canton, and Enderbury. Kiribati was admitted to the UN Sept. 14, 1999.

Korea, North
Democratic People's Republic of Korea

People: Population: 23,113,019. **Age distrib.** (%) <15: 23.8; 65+: 8.2. **Pop. density:** 497 per sq mi, 191 per sq km. **Urban:** 61.1%. **Ethnic group:** Korean. **Principal languages:** Korean (official). **Chief religions:** Activities almost non-existent; traditionally Buddhist, Confucianist, Chondogyo.

Geography: Total area: 46,541 sq mi, 120,540 sq km; **Land area:** 46,491 sq mi, 120,410 sq km. **Location:** In northern E Asia. **Neighbors:** China and Russia on N, South Korea on S. **Topography:** Mountains and hills cover nearly all the country, with narrow valleys and small plains in between. The N and the E coasts are the most rugged areas. **Capital:** Pyongyang, 3,351,000. **Cities (urban aggr.):** Nampo, 1,102,000.

Government: Type: Communist state. **Leader:** Kim Jong Il; b. Feb. 16, 1942; officially assumed post Oct. 8, 1997. **Local divisions:** 9 provinces, 4 special cities. **Defense budget** (2005): $1.9 bil. **Active troops:** 1,106,000.

Economy: Industries: armaments, machine building, electric power, chemicals, mining, metallurgy, textiles. **Chief crops:** rice, corn, potatoes, soybeans. **Natural resources:** coal, lead, tungsten, zinc, graphite, magnesite, iron ore, copper, gold, pyrites, salt, fluorspar, hydropower. **Arable land:** 14%. **Livestock** (2005): cattle: 578,000; chickens: 21 mil; goats: 2.8 mil; pigs: 3.2 mil; sheep: 172,000. **Fish catch** (2004): 268,700 metric tons. **Electricity prod.** (2004): 21.7 bil kWh. **Labor force:** agricultural 36%, industry and services 64%.

Finance: Monetary unit: Won (KPW) (Sept. 2006: 170.00 = $1 U.S.). **GDP** (2005 est.): $40 bil; **per capita GDP:** $1,700; **GDP growth:** 1%. **Imports** (2004 est.): $2.8 bil; partners (2004): China 32.9%, Thailand 10.7%, Japan 4.8%. **Exports** (2004 est.): $1.3 bil; partners (2004): China 29.9%, South Korea 24.1%, Japan 13.2%. **Tourism** (2002): $150 mil.

Transport: Railroad: Length: 3,184 mi. **Civil Aviation:** 21.7 mil pass.-mi; 36 airports. **Chief ports:** Chongjin, Hamhung, Nampo.

Communications: TV sets: 55 per 1,000 pop. **Radios:** 146 per 1,000 pop. **Telephone lines:** 980,000. **Daily newspaper circ.:** NA.

Health: Life expect.: 68.9 male; 74.5 female. **Births** (per 1,000 pop.): 15.5. **Deaths** (per 1,000 pop.): 7.1. **Natural inc.:** 0.84%. **Infant mortality** (per 1,000 live births): 23.3. **AIDS rate:** NA.

Labor force: agri. 36%, other 64%.

Education: Compulsory: ages 6-15. **Literacy:** 99%.

Major Intl. Organizations: UN (FAO, ILO, IMO, WHO).

Permanent UN Representative: 820 Second Ave., 13th Floor, New York, NY 10017; (212) 972-3105.

Website: www.korea-dpr.com/menu.htm

The Democratic People's Republic of Korea was founded May 1, 1948, in the zone occupied by Russian troops after WWII. Its armies tried to conquer the south, 1950. After 3 years of fighting, with Chinese and U.S. intervention, a cease-fire was proclaimed.

For the next 4 decades, a hardline Communist regime headed by Kim Il Sung kept tight control over the nation's political, economic, and cultural life. The nation used its abundant mineral and hydroelectric resources to develop its military strength and heavy industry. By the early 1990s, North Korea was widely believed to be developing nuclear weapons. The U.S. and North Korea signed an agreement, Oct. 21, 1994, providing for phased dismantling of North Korea's nuclear development program in return for U.S. energy aid and improved ties with the U.S.

Kim Il Sung died July 8, 1994. He was succeeded by his son, Kim Jong Il. Defections by high officials, a deteriorating economy, and severe food shortages plagued North Korea in the late 1990s.

On Sept. 17, 1999, the U.S. eased travel and trade restrictions on North Korea after Pyongyang agreed to suspend long-range missile testing. A first-ever summit conference in Pyongyang between North and South Korean leaders, June 13-15, 2000, marked an unexpected improvement in relations between the 2 Koreas, and brought an end to many U.S. sanctions. In Sept. 2002, Japanese Prime Min. Junichiro Koizumi became the first Japanese prime minister to visit North Korea; in a landmark summit, North Korea and Japan agreed to begin normalizing relations.

Pres. George W. Bush, in a speech Jan. 31, 2002, included North Korea with Iraq and Iran as part of an "axis of evil." In Oct. 2002, N. Korea admitted to pursuing a secret nuclear weapons program, in violation of past agreements, and, in Jan. 2003, withdrew from the Nuclear Non-Proliferation Treaty. The U.S. insisted that North Korea dismantle its nuclear weapons program, while North Korea demanded a nonaggression treaty and economic aid from the U.S. Six-nation talks sponsored by China in 2003 and 2004 failed to produce an agreement. A huge explosion in the Ryongchon railway station Apr. 22, 2004, killed 161 people.

North Korea declared Feb. 10, 2005, that it had produced nuclear weapons. In a draft accord reached at 6-nation talks Sept. 19, 2005, Pyongyang agreed in principle to scrap its nuclear weapons program in exchange for aid, but little progress was made in a follow-up meeting, Nov. 9-11. North Korea missile tests July 5, 2006, included the long-range Taepodong-2, which failed. The UN Security Council condemned the tests, July 15, but omitted the sanctions threat requested by Japan and the U.S.

Korea, South
Republic of Korea

People: Population: 48,846,823. **Age distrib.** (%) <15: 18.9; 65+: 9.2. **Pop. density:** 1,288 per sq mi, 497 per sq km. **Urban:** 80.3%. **Ethnic group:** Korean. **Principal languages:** Korean (official). **Chief religions:** no affliiation 46%, Christian 26%, Buddhist 47%.

Geography: Total area: 38,023 sq mi, 98,480 sq km; **Land area:** 37,911 sq mi, 98,190 sq km. **Location:** In northern E Asia. **Neighbors:** North Korea on N. **Topography:** The country is mountainous, with a rugged east coast. The western and southern coasts are deeply indented, with many islands and harbors. **Capital:** Seoul, 9,645,000. **Cities (urban aggr.):** Pusan, 3,554,000; Inch'on, 2,620,000; Taegu, 2,511,000.

Government: Type: Republic. **Head of state:** Pres. Roh Moo Hyun; b. Aug. 6, 1946; in office: Feb. 25, 2003. **Head of gov.:** Prime Min. Han Myung Sook; b. Mar. 24, 1944; in office: Apr. 19, 2006. **Local divisions:** 9 provinces, 7 special cities. **Defense budget** (2005): $20.7 bil. **Active troops:** 687,700.

Economy: Industries: electronics, autos, chemicals, shipbuilding, steel, textiles, clothing, footwear, food proc. **Chief crops:** rice, root crops, barley, vegetables, fruit. **Natural resources:** coal, tungsten, graphite, molybd., lead, hydropower potential. **Arable land:** 19%. **Livestock** (2005): cattle: 2.3 mil; chickens: 110 mil; goats: 570,000; pigs: 9 mil; sheep: 1,100. **Fish catch** (2004): 1,981,085 metric tons. **Electricity prod.** (2004): 345.2 bil kWh. **Labor force** (2005 est.): agriculture 6.4%, industry 26.4%, services 67.2%.

Finance: Monetary unit: Won (KRW) (Sept. 2006: 944.40 = $1 U.S.). **GDP** (2005 est.): $965.3 bil; **per capita GDP:** $20,400; **GDP growth:** 3.9%. **Imports** (2005 est.): $256 bil; partners (2004): Japan 21.6%, U.S. 12.7%, China 12.3%, Saudi Arabia 5.1%. **Exports** (2005 est.): $288.2 bil; partners (2004): China 22.4%, U.S. 17.8%, Japan 8.3%, Hong Kong 4.8%. **Tourism:** $5.7 bil. **Budget** (2005 est.): $189 bil. **Intl. reserves less gold:** $147.15 bil. **Gold:** 460,000 oz t. **Consumer prices:** 2.72%.

Transport: Railroad: Length: 2,157 mi. **Motor vehicles:** 10.28 mil pass. cars, 4.26 mil comm. vehicles. **Civil aviation:** 40.9 bil pass.-mi; 69 airports. **Chief ports:** Pusan, Inchon.

Communications: TV sets: 364 per 1,000 pop. **Radios:** 1,039 per 1,000 pop. **Telephone lines:** 23.7 mil. **Daily newspaper circ.:** NA. **Internet:** 33.9 mil users.

Health: Life expect.: 73.6 male; 80.8 female. **Births** (per 1,000 pop.): 10. **Deaths** (per 1,000 pop.): 5.8. **Natural inc.:** 0.41%. **Infant mortality** (per 1,000 live births): 6.2. **AIDS rate:** <0.1%.

Education: Compulsory: ages 6-14. **Literacy:** 97.9%.

Major Intl. Organizations: UN (FAO, IBRD, ILO, IMF, IMO, WHO, WTO), APEC, OECD.

Embassy: 2450 Massachusetts Ave. NW 20008; 939-5600.

Website: www.korea.net

Korea, once called the Hermit Kingdom, has a recorded history since the 1st cent. BCE. It was united in a kingdom under the Silla Dynasty, 668 CE. It was at times associated with the Chinese empire; the treaty that concluded the Sino-Japanese war of 1894-95 recognized Korea's complete independence. In 1910 Japan forcibly annexed Korea as Chosun.

At the Potsdam conference, July 1945, the 38th parallel was designated as the line dividing the Soviet and the American occupation. Russian troops entered Korea Aug. 10, 1945; U.S. troops entered Sept. 8, 1945.

The South Koreans formed the Republic of Korea in May 1948 with Seoul as the capital. Dr. Syngman Rhee was chosen president. A separate, Communist regime was formed in the north; its army attacked the south in June 1950, initiating the Korean War. UN troops, under U.S. command, supported the S in the war, which ended in an armistice (July 1953) leaving Korea divided by a "no-man's land" along the 38th parallel.

Rhee's authoritarian rule became increasingly unpopular, and a movement spearheaded by college students forced his resignation Apr. 26, 1960. In an army coup May 16, 1961, Gen. Park Chung Hee became chairman of a ruling junta. He was elected president, 1963; a 1972 referendum allowed him to be reelected for an unlimited series of 6-year terms. Park was assassinated by the chief of the Korean CIA, Oct. 26, 1979.

In May 1980, Gen. Chun Doo Hwan, head of military intelligence, ordered the brutal suppression of pro-democracy demonstrations in Kwangju. On July 1, 1987, following weeks of antigovernment protests, some of them violent, Chun agreed to permit election of the next president by direct popular vote and other democratic reforms. In Dec., Roh Tae Woo was elected president. In 1990, the nation's 3 largest political parties merged; some 100,000 students protested the merger as undemocratic.

Pres. Kim Young Sam took office in 1993. Convicted of mutiny, treason, and corruption, Chun was sentenced to death by a Seoul court, Aug. 26, 1996, for his role in the 1979 coup and 1980 Kwangju massacre; Roh received a 22-1/2 year prison sentence. On Dec. 16, Chun's term was reduced to life in prison, and Roh's to 17 years.

The collapse in Jan. 1997 of the Hanbo steel firm triggered a series of corruption scandals. With currency and stock values plummeting, the nation averted default by agreeing, Dec. 4, on a $57 bil bailout from the IMF. Kim Dae Jung, a longtime dissident, won the presidential election Dec. 18. Chun and Roh were released and pardoned Dec. 22, 1997.

At an unprecedented summit meeting in Pyongyang, June 13-15, 2000, Pres. Kim Dae Jung and North Korean leader Kim Jong Il agreed to work for reconciliation and eventual reunification of their 2 countries. On Oct. 13, 2000, Kim Dae Jung was named the winner of the 2000 Nobel Peace Prize. Roh Moo Hyun won a presidential election Dec. 19.

A subway fire in Taegu, Feb. 18, 2003, killed 198 people; the arsonist was given a life term, and 8 subway officials charged with negligence also received prison sentences. Typhoon Maemi battered Pusan and other areas Sept. 12-13, 2003, leaving about 130 people dead and causing at least $4.1 bil in damage.

The National Assembly, Mar. 12, 2004, impeached Pres. Roh Moo Hyun for violating political neutrality and urging voters to support the Uri Party in upcoming legislative elections; voters backed Roh Apr. 15 by electing a Uri majority, and the Constitutional Court May 14 restored Roh to office. The IAEA Sept. 2 said South Korea had acknowledged having secretly processed a small amount of uranium to near weapons-grade level in 2000, violating the Nuclear Non-Proliferation Treaty and a bilateral accord with North Korea.

As of mid-2006, the U.S. had about 30,000 troops stationed in South Korea, and 3,300 Korean troops were participating in the U.S.-led coalition in Iraq.

Kuwait
State of Kuwait

People: Population: 2,418,393. **Age distrib.** (%) <15: 26.9; 65+: 2.8. **Pop. density:** 351 per sq mi, 135 per sq km. **Urban:** 96.3%. **Ethnic groups:** Arab 80%, South Asian 9%, Iranian 4%. **Principal languages:** Arabic (official), English. **Chief religion:** Muslim 85% (official; Sunni 70%, Shi'a 30%).

Geography: Total area: 6,880 sq mi, 17,820 sq km; **Land area:** 6,880 sq mi, 17,820 sq km. **Location:** In Middle East, at N end of Persian Gulf. **Neighbors:** Iraq on N, Saudi Arabia on S. **Topography:** The country is flat, very dry, and extremely hot. **Capital:** Kuwait City, 1,810,000.

Government: Type: Constitutional monarchy. **Head of state:** Emir Sheikh Sabah al-Ahmad al-Jabir as-Sabah; b. June 6, 1929; in office: Jan. 29, 2006. **Head of gov.:** Prime Min. Sheikh Nasser al-Muhammad al-Ahmad as-Sabah; b. 1940; in office: Feb. 7, 2006. **Local divisions:** 5 governorates. **Defense budget** (2005): $4.3 bil. **Active troops:** 15,500.

Economy: Industries: oil, petrochems., desalination, food proc., constr. materials. **Natural resources:** oil, fish, shrimp, nat. gas.

Crude oil reserves (2005): 101.5 bil bbls. **Livestock** (2005): cattle: 28,000; chickens: 32.5 mil; goats: 150,000; sheep: 900,000. **Fish catch** (2004): 5,208 metric tons. **Electricity prod.** (2004): 40.4 bil kWh.

Finance: Monetary unit: Dinar (KWD) (Sept. 2006: 0.29 = $1 U.S.). **GDP** (2005 est.): $44.8 bil; **per capita GDP:** $19,200; **GDP growth:** 4.8%. **Imports** (2005 est.): $12.2 bil; partners (2004): U.S. 13.1%, Germany 12.7%, Japan 8.2%, China 5.9%, Italy 5.4%, UK 5.4%, Saudi Arabia 4.7%, France 4.6%. **Exports** (2005 est.): $44.4 bil; partners (2004): Japan 22.6%, U.S. 13.4%, South Korea 13.4%, Singapore 12.4%, Taiwan 8.4%, Netherlands 4.1%. **Tourism:** $180 mil. **Budget** (2005 est.): $20.8 bil. **Intl. reserves less gold:** $6.2 bil. **Gold:** 2.54 mil oz t. **Consumer prices:** 4.1%.

Transport: Motor vehicles: 715,000 pass. cars, 226,000 comm. vehicles. **Civil aviation:** 4.2 bil pass.-mi; 4 airports. **Chief port:** Mina al-Ahmadi.

Communications: TV sets: 480 per 1,000 pop. **Radios:** 633 per 1,000 pop. **Telephone lines:** 510,300. **Daily newspaper circ.:** NA. **Internet:** 600,000 users.

Health: Life expect.: 76.1 male; 78.3 female. **Births** (per 1,000 pop.): 21.9. **Deaths** (per 1,000 pop.): 2.4. **Natural inc.:** 1.95%. **Infant mortality** (per 1,000 live births): 9.7. **AIDS rate:** NA.

Education: Compulsory: ages 6-13. **Literacy:** 93.3%.

Major Intl. Organizations: UN (FAO, IBRD, ILO, IMF, IMO, WHO, WTO), AL, OPEC.

Embassy: 2940 Tilden St. NW 20008; 966-0702.

Website: www.kuwait-info.org

Kuwait is ruled by the Sabah dynasty, founded 1759. Britain ran foreign relations and defense from 1899 until independence in 1961. The majority of the population is non-Kuwaiti, with many Palestinians, and cannot vote.

Oil is the fiscal mainstay, providing most of Kuwait's income. Oil pays for free medical care, education, and social security. There are no taxes, except customs duties.

Kuwait was attacked and overrun by Iraqi forces Aug. 2, 1990. The emir and senior members of the ruling family fled to Saudi Arabia to establish a government in exile. On Aug. 28, Iraq announced that Kuwait was its 19th province. Following several weeks of aerial attacks on Kuwait and Iraqi forces in Kuwait, a U.S.-led coalition began a ground attack Feb. 23, 1991. By Feb. 27, Iraqi forces were routed and Kuwait liberated.

Former U.S. Pres. George Bush visited Kuwait, Apr. 14-16, 1993. Kuwaiti authorities arrested 14 Iraqis and Kuwaitis for allegedly plotting to assassinate him during his visit; 13 were convicted and sentenced to prison or death, June 4, 1994. The UN Security Council ruled, Sept. 27, 2000, that Iraq had to pay the Kuwait Petroleum Corp. $15.9 bil for damage to Kuwaiti oil fields during the Persian Gulf War. Iraq recognized Kuwait's territorial integrity Mar. 28, 2002. Northern Kuwait was used by U.S. and British troops as a staging area prior to the Mar. 2003 invasion of Iraq.

Political rights were extended to women, May 16, 2005; the nation's first female cabinet member was appointed June 12. After Emir Sheikh Jabir al-Ahmad al-Jabir as-Sabah died Jan. 15, 2006, an ailing successor was ousted, and Prime Min. Sheikh Sabah al-Ahmad al-Jabir as-Sabah became the new emir Jan. 29.

Kyrgyzstan
Kyrgyz Republic

People: Population: 5,213,898. **Age distrib.** (%) <15: 30.9; 65+: 6.2. **Pop. density:** 70 per sq mi, 27 per sq km. **Urban:** 33.9%. **Ethnic groups:** Kyrgyz 52%, Russian 18%, Uzbek 13%, Ukrainian 3%, German 2%. **Principal languages:** Kyrgyz, Russian (both official); Uzbek. **Chief religions:** Muslim 75%, Russian Orthodox 20%.

Geography: Total area: 76,641 sq mi, 198,500 sq km; **Land area:** 73,861 sq mi, 191,300 sq km. **Location:** In Central Asia. **Neighbors:** Kazakhstan on N, China on E, Uzbekistan on W, Tajikistan on S. **Topography:** Kyrgystan is a landlocked country nearly covered by Tien Shan and Pamir Mts.; avg. elevation 9,020 ft. A large lake, Issyk-Kul, in NE is 1 mi. above sea level. **Capital:** Bishkek, 798,000.

Government: Type: Republic. **Head of state:** Pres. Kurmanbek Bakiyev; b. Aug. 1, 1949; in office: Aug. 14, 2005 (acting from Mar. 25). **Head of gov.:** Prime Min. Feliks Kulov; b. Oct. 29, 1948; in office: Sept. 1, 2005 (acting from Aug. 15). **Local divisions:** 7 oblasts and Bishkek. **Defense budget** (2005): $73 mil. **Active troops:** 12,500.

Economy: Industries: small machinery, textiles, food proc., cement, shoes, timber, refrigerators, furniture, electric motors. **Chief crops:** tobacco, cotton, potatoes, vegetables, grapes, fruits & berries. **Natural resources:** hydropower, gold, rare earth metals, coal, oil, nat. gas, nepheline, mercury, bismuth, lead, zinc. **Crude oil reserves** (2005): 40 mil bbls. **Arable land:** 7%. **Livestock** (2005): cattle: 1 mil; chickens: 4 mil; goats: 808,397; pigs: 82,659; sheep: 3 mil. **Fish catch** (2004): 27 metric tons. **Electricity prod.** (2004): 14.1 bil kWh. **Labor force** (2000 est.): agriculture 55%, industry 15%, services 30%.

Finance: Monetary unit: Som (KGS) (Sept. 2006: 39.32 = $1 U.S.). **GDP** (2005 est.): $10.7 bil; **per capita GDP:** $2,100; **GDP growth:** 2%. **Imports** (2005 est.): $937.4 mil; partners (2004): Russia 23.1%, China 22.9%, Kazakhstan 19.3%, Turkey 7.2%, Germany 4.5%, Uzbekistan 4.4%, U.S. 4.2%. **Exports** (2005 est.): $759 mil; partners (2004): UAE 23.8%, Switzerland 16.9%, Russia 16.9%, Kazakhstan 10.1%, China 9.8%. **Tourism:** $76 mil. **Budget**

(2005 est.): **$539.9** mil. **Intl. reserves less gold:** $399 mil. **Gold:** 80,000 oz t. **Consumer prices:** 4.35%.

Transport: Railroad: Length: 292 mi. **Motor vehicles:** 188,700 pass. cars. **Civil aviation:** 195.7 mil pass.-mi; 18 airports. **Chief port:** Ysyk-Kol.

Communications: TV sets: 49 per 1,000 pop. **Radios:** 113 per 1,000 pop. **Telephone lines:** 438,200. **Daily newspaper circ.:** NA. **Internet:** 263,000 users.

Health: Life expect.: 64.5 male; 72.7 female. **Births** (per 1,000 pop.): 22.8. **Deaths** (per 1,000 pop.): 7.1. **Natural inc.:** 1.57%. **Infant mortality** (per 1,000 live births): 34.5. **AIDS rate:** 0.1%.

Education: Compulsory: ages 7-15. **Literacy:** 98.7%.

Major Intl. Organizations: UN (FAO, IBRD, ILO, IMF, WHO, WTO), CIS, OSCE.

Embassy: 1001 Pennsylvania Avenue, Suite #600, NW Washington, DC 20004 338 5141

Website: www.president.kg

The region was inhabited around the 13th cent. by the Kyrgyz. It was annexed to Russia, 1864, and became a constituent republic of the USSR in 1936. Kyrgyzstan declared independence Aug. 31, 1991. It became an independent state when the USSR disbanded Dec. 26, 1991. A constitution was adopted May 5, 1993.

Reelected Dec. 24, 1995, Pres. Askar Akayev gained approval by referendum of a constitutional amendment expanding his presidential powers, Feb. 10, 1996. Amendments restricting the powers of parliament and allowing private ownership of land were ratified by referendum Oct. 17, 1998. Akayev won a 3rd 5-year term in the Oct. 29, 2000, election. The U.S. military presence in Kyrgyzstan expanded from Dec. 2001.

Fraud by Akayev loyalists in parliamentary elections Feb.-Mar. 2005 sparked protests. Akayev fled the country, Mar. 24, and formally resigned, Apr. 4. His interim successor, former Prime Min. Kurmanbek Bakiyev, a leader of the "tulip revolution," won by a landslide in the July 10 presidential vote. A prominent imam, Muhammad Rafik Kamalov, was killed Aug. 6, 2006, in what Kyrgyz security forces described as a shootout with Islamic extremists.

Laos
Lao People's Democratic Republic

People: Population: 6,368,481. **Age distrib.** (%) <15: 41.4; 65+: 3.1. **Pop. density:** 71 per sq mi, 27 per sq km. **Urban:** 20.7%. **Ethnic groups:** Lao Loum 68%, Lao Theung 22%, Lao Soung (incl. Hmong and Yao) 9%. **Principal languages:** Lao (official), French, English, and various ethnic languages. **Chief religions:** Buddhist 60%, animist and other 40%.

Geography: Total area: 91,429 sq mi, 236,800 sq km; **Land area:** 89,112 sq mi, 230,800 sq km. **Location:** In Indochina Peninsula in SE Asia. **Neighbors:** Myanmar and China on N, Vietnam on E, Cambodia on S, Thailand on W. **Topography:** Landlocked, dominated by jungle. High mountains along eastern border are the source of the E-W rivers slicing across the country to the Mekong R., which defines most of the western border. **Capital:** Vientiane, 702,000.

Government: Type: Communist. **Head of state:** Pres. Choummaly Sayasone; b. Mar. 6, 1936; in office: June 8, 2006. **Head of gov.:** Prime Min. Bouasone Bouphavanh; b. 1954; in office: June 8, 2006. **Local divisions:** 16 provinces, 1 municipality, 1 special zone. **Defense budget** (2005): NA. **Active troops:** 29,100.

Economy: Industries: mining, timber, electric power, agric. proc., constr., garments, tourism. **Chief crops:** sweet potatoes, vegetables, corn, coffee, sugarcane. **Natural resources:** timber, hydropower, gypsum, tin, gold, gemstones. **Arable land:** 3%. **Livestock** (2005): cattle: 1.3 mil; chickens: 21 mil; goats: 143,000; pigs: 1.8 mil. **Fish catch** (2004): 94,700 metric tons. **Electricity prod.** (2004): 3.9 bil kWh. **Labor force** (1997 est.): agriculture 80%, industry and services 20%.

Finance: Monetary unit: Kip (LAK) (Sept. 2006: 10,053.35 = $1 U.S.). **GDP** (2005 est.): $12.1 bil; **per capita GDP:** $1,900; **GDP growth:** 7.2%. **Imports** (2005 est.): $541 mil; partners (2004): Thailand 60.5%, China 9.2%, Vietnam 8.7%. **Exports** (2005 est.): $379 mil; partners (2004): Thailand 19%, Vietnam 16.4%, France 7.9%, Germany 5.6%, UK 4.9%. **Tourism:** $119 mil. **Budget** (2005 est.): $434.6 mil. **Intl. reserves less gold:** $164 mil. **Gold:** 150,000 oz t. **Consumer prices:** 7.17%.

Transport: Motor vehicles: 9,000 pass. cars, 9,000 comm. vehicles. **Civil aviation:** 56.5 mil pass.-mi; 9 airports.

Communications: TV sets: 10 per 1,000 pop. **Radios:** 145 per 1,000 pop. **Telephone lines:** 75,300. **Daily newspaper circ.:** NA. **Internet:** 20,900 users.

Health: Life expect.: 53.5 male; 57.6 female. **Births** (per 1,000 pop.): 35.5. **Deaths** (per 1,000 pop.): 11.6. **Natural inc.:** 2.39%. **Infant mortality** (per 1,000 live births): 83.3. **AIDS rate:** 0.1%.

Education: Compulsory: ages 6-10. **Literacy:** 68.7%.

Major Intl. Organizations: UN (FAO, IBRD, ILO, IMF, WHO), ASEAN.

Embassy: 2222 S St. NW 20008; 332-6416.

Website: www.tourismlaos.gov.la

Laos became a French protectorate in 1893, but regained independence as a constitutional monarchy July 19, 1949.

Conflicts among neutralist, Communist, and conservative factions created a chaotic political situation. Armed conflict increased after 1960.

The 3 factions formed a coalition government in June 1962, with neutralist Prince Souvanna Phouma as premier. A 14-nation conference in Geneva signed agreements, 1962, guaranteeing neutrality and independence. By 1964 the Pathet Lao had withdrawn from the coalition, and, with aid from North Vietnamese troops, renewed sporadic attacks. U.S. planes bombed the Ho Chi Minh trail, a supply line from North Vietnam to Communist forces in Laos and South Vietnam.

In 1970 the U.S. stepped up air support and military aid. After Pathet Lao military gains, Souvanna Phouma in May 1975 ordered government troops to cease fighting; the Pathet Lao took control. The Lao People's Democratic Republic was proclaimed Dec. 3, 1975.

From the mid-1970s through the 1980s, Laos relied on Vietnam for military and financial aid. Since easing its foreign investment laws in 1988, Laos has attracted more than $5 bil from Thailand, the U.S., and other nations. Laos was admitted to ASEAN on July 23, 1997. The U.S. Congress, Nov. 19, 2004, approved normalization of trade with Laos. The 8th congress of the Communist Party, Mar. 2006, marked the transition to a younger generation of leaders.

Latvia
Republic of Latvia

People: Population: 2,274,735. **Age distrib.** (%) <15: 14; 65+: 16.4. **Pop. density:** 92 per sq mi, 35 per sq km. **Urban:** 66.2%. **Ethnic groups:** Latvian 58%, Russian 30%, Belarusian 4%, Ukrainian 3%, Polish 2%, Lithuanian 1%. **Principal languages:** Latvian (official), Russian, Belorusian, Ukrainian, Polish. **Chief religions:** Lutheran, Roman Catholic, Russian Orthodox.

Geography: Total area: 24,938 sq mi, 64,589 sq km; **Land area:** 24,552 sq mi, 63,589 sq km. **Location:** E Europe, on the Baltic Sea. **Neighbors:** Estonia on N, Lithuania and Belarus on S, Russia on E. **Topography:** Latvia is a lowland with numerous lakes, marshes and peat bogs. Principal river, W. Dvina (Daugava), rises in Russia. There are glacial hills in E. **Capital:** Riga, 729,000.

Government: Type: Republic. **Head of state:** Pres. Vaira Vike-Freiberga; b. Dec. 1, 1937; in office: July 8, 1999. **Head of gov.:** Prime Min. Aigars Kalvitis; b. June 27, 1966; in office: Dec. 2, 2004. **Local divisions:** 26 counties, 7 municipalities. **Defense budget** (2005): $278 mil. **Active troops:** 5,238.

Economy: Industries: vehicles, railroad cars, synthetics, agric. machinery, fertilizers, washing machines. **Chief crops:** grain, sugar beets, potatoes, other vegetables. **Natural resources:** peat, limestone, dolomite, hydropower, wood, amber. **Arable land:** 27%. **Livestock** (2005): cattle: 371,100; chickens: 3.5 mil; goats: 14,700; pigs: 435,700; sheep: 38,600. **Fish catch** (2004): 125,936 metric tons. **Electricity prod.** (2004): 4.6 bil kWh. **Labor force** (2000 est.): agriculture 15%, industry 25%, services 60%.

Finance: Monetary unit: Lat (LVL) (Sept. 2006: 0.55 = $1 U.S.). **GDP** (2005 est.): $30.3 bil; **per capita GDP:** $13,200; **GDP growth:** 10.2%. **Imports** (2005 est.): $8.6 bil; partners (2004): Germany 16.1%, Russia 14.4%, Lithuania 7.6%, Finland 6.5%, Sweden 5.6%, Estonia 5.1%, Italy 4.2%, Poland 4%. **Exports** (2005 est.): $5.7 bil; partners (2004): UK 22.1%, Germany 9.9%, U.S. 8.2%, Sweden 7.3%, France 6.6%, Lithuania 6.4%, Estonia 5.2%, Denmark 4.2%, Russia 4.1%. **Tourism:** $267 mil. **Budget** (2005 est.): $5.9 bil. **Intl. reserves less gold:** $1.56 bil. **Gold:** 250,000 oz t. **Consumer prices:** 6.76%.

Transport: Railroad: Length: 1,431 mi. **Motor vehicles:** 648,900 pass. cars, 115,600 comm. vehicles. **Civil aviation:** 114.3 mil pass.-mi; 24 airports. **Chief port:** Riga.

Communications: TV sets: 757 per 1,000 pop. **Radios:** 701 per 1,000 pop. **Telephone lines:** 640,100. **Daily newspaper circ.:** 137.8 per 1,000 pop. **Internet:** 810,000 users.

Health: Life expect.: 66.1 male; 76.8 female. **Births** (per 1,000 pop.): 9.2. **Deaths** (per 1,000 pop.): 13.7. **Natural inc.:** −0.44%. **Infant mortality** (per 1,000 live births): 9.3. **AIDS rate:** 0.8%.

Education: Compulsory: ages 7-15. **Literacy:** 99.7%.

Major Intl. Organizations: UN (FAO, IBRD, ILO, IMF, IMO, WHO), EU, NATO, OSCE.

Embassy: 4325 17th St. NW 20011; 726-8213.

Website: www.lv

Prior to 1918, Latvia was occupied by the Russians and Germans. It was an independent republic, 1918-39. The Aug. 1939 Soviet-German agreement assigned Latvia to the Soviet sphere of influence. It was officially accepted as part of the USSR on Aug. 5, 1940. It was overrun by the German army in 1941, but retaken in 1945.

During an abortive Soviet coup, Latvia declared independence, Aug. 21, 1991. The Soviet Union recognized Latvia's independence in Sept. 1991. The last Russian troops in Latvia withdrew by Aug. 31, 1994. Responding to international pressure, Latvian voters on Oct. 3, 1998, eased citizenship laws that had discriminated against some 500,000 ethnic Russians. On June 17, 1999, the legislature elected Vaira Vike-Freiberga as Latvia's first woman president. Latvia joined the EU and NATO in 2004. Latvia ratified a proposed EU constitution, June 2, 2005.

Lebanon
Lebanese Republic

People: Population: 3,874,050. **Age distrib.** (%) <15: 26.5; 65+: 7. **Pop. density:** 980 per sq mi, 378 per sq km. **Urban:** 87.5%. **Ethnic groups:** Arab 95%, Armenian 4%. **Principal languages:** Arabic (official), French, English, Armenian. **Chief religions:** Muslim 60%, Christian 39%.

Geography: Total area: 4,015 sq mi, 10,400 sq km; **Land area:** 3,950 sq mi, 10,230 sq km. **Location:** In Middle East, on E end of Mediterranean Sea. **Neighbors:** Syria on E, Israel on S. **Topography:** There is a narrow coastal strip, and 2 mountain ranges running N-S enclosing the fertile Beqaa Valley. The Litani R. runs S through the valley, turning W to empty into the Mediterranean. **Capital:** Beirut, 1,777,000.

Government: Type: Republic. **Head of state:** Pres. Emile Lahoud; b. Jan. 12, 1936; in office: Nov. 24, 1998. **Head of gov.:** Prime Min. Fouad Siniora; b. 1943; in office: July 19, 2005. **Local divisions:** 6 governorates. **Defense budget** (2005): $530 mil. **Active troops:** 72,100.

Economy: Industries: banking, food proc., jewelry, cement, textiles, mineral & chemical products. **Chief crops:** citrus, grapes, tomatoes, apples, vegetables, potatoes, olives, tobacco. **Natural resources:** limestone, iron ore, salt, water. **Arable land:** 21%. **Livestock** (2005): cattle: 90,000; chickens: 35 mil; goats: 430,000; pigs: 15,000; sheep: 340,000. **Fish catch** (2004): 4,656 metric tons. **Electricity prod.** (2004): 9.8 bil kWh.

Finance: Monetary unit: Pound (LBP) (Sept. 2006: 1,510.30 = $1 U.S.). **GDP** (2005 est.): $23.7 bil; **per capita GDP:** $6,200; **GDP growth:** 0.5%. **Imports** (2005 est.): $8.9 bil; partners (2004): Italy 12.2%, France 11.2%, Germany 8.9%, China 6.3%, U.S. 6%, Syria 5.1%, UK 5%. **Exports** (2005 est.): $1.8 bil; partners (2004): Switzerland 10%, UAE 9.5%, Turkey 9.3%, Saudi Arabia 7.1%, France 5.1%, U.S. 5.1%. **Tourism:** $5.4 bil. **Budget** (2005 est.): $6.6 bil. **Intl. reserves less gold:** $8.32 bil. **Gold:** 9.22 mil oz t.

Transport: Railroad: Length: 249 mi. **Motor vehicles:** 1.37 mil pass. cars, 102,400 comm. vehicles. **Civil aviation:** 1.1 bil pass.-mi; 5 airports. **Chief ports:** Beirut, Tripoli, Sidon.

Communications: TV sets: 355 per 1,000 pop. **Radios:** 907 per 1,000 pop. **Telephone lines:** 990,000. **Newspaper circ.:** 63.3 per 1,000 pop. **Internet:** 600,000 users.

Health: Life expect.: 70.4 male; 75.5 female. **Births** (per 1,000 pop.): 18.5. **Deaths** (per 1,000 pop.): 6.2. **Natural inc.:** 1.23%. **Infant mortality** (per 1,000 live births): 24.5. **AIDS rate:** 0.1%.

Education: Compulsory: ages 6-15. **Literacy:** 87.4%.

Major Intl. Organizations: UN (FAO, IBRD, ILO, IMF, IMO, WHO), AL.

Embassy: 2560 28th St. NW 20008; 939-6300.

Website: www.lebanonembassyus.org

Formed from 5 former Turkish Empire districts, Lebanon became an independent state Sept. 1, 1920, administered under French mandate 1920-41. French troops withdrew in 1946.

Under the 1943 National Covenant, all public positions were divided among the various religious communities, with Christians in the majority. By the 1970s, Muslims became the majority and demanded a larger political and economic role.

U.S. Marines intervened, May-Oct. 1958, during a Syrian-aided revolt. Continued raids against Israeli civilians, 1970-75, brought Israeli retaliation in southern Lebanon.

An estimated 60,000 were killed and billions of dollars in damage inflicted in a 1975-76 civil war. Palestinian units and leftist Muslims fought against the Maronite militia, the Phalange, and other Christians. Several Arab countries provided political and arms support to the various factions, while Israel aided Christian forces. Up to 15,000 Syrian troops intervened in 1976 to fight Palestinian groups. A cease-fire was mainly policed by Syria.

Israeli forces invaded Lebanon June 6, 1982, attacking strongholds of the Palestine Liberation Organization (PLO). Israeli and Syrian forces engaged in the Bekaa Valley. On Aug. 21, the PLO evacuated west Beirut after massive Israeli bombings there. Israeli troops entered west Beirut following the Sept. 14 assassination of newly elected Lebanese Pres. Bashir Gemayel. On Sept. 16, Lebanese Christian troops entered 2 refugee camps and massacred hundreds of Palestinian refugees. An agreement May 17, 1983, between Lebanon, Israel, and the U.S. (but not Syria) provided for the withdrawal of Israeli troops; at least 30,000 Syrian troops remained in Lebanon, and Israel held onto a "security zone" in the south.

In 1983, terrorist bombings became a way of life in Beirut as some 50 people were killed in an explosion at the U.S. Embassy, Apr. 18; 241 U.S. servicemen and 58 French soldiers died in separate Muslim suicide attacks, Oct. 23. The 1980s also witnessed kidnappings of U.S., British, French, and Soviet citizens by Islamic militants. All hostages were released by 1992.

A treaty signed May 22, 1991, between Lebanon and Syria recognized Lebanon as a separate state for the first time since the 2 countries gained independence in 1943.

Israeli forces conducted air raids and artillery strikes against guerrilla bases and villages in southern Lebanon, causing over 200,000 to flee their homes July 25-29, 1993. Some 500,000 civilians fled their homes in Apr. 1996 when Israel again struck suspected guerrilla bases in the south. The economy revived in the 1990s, but Syria continued to dominate Lebanon's political affairs. Israel withdrew virtually all its troops from S Lebanon by May 24, 2000,

leaving Hezbollah, an Iranian-backed guerrilla group, in control of much of the region.

Rafik al-Hariri, a former prime minister (1992-98, 2000-04), was killed by truck bomb, Feb. 14, 2005. Many Lebanese blamed Syria, which denied involvement. As anti-Syrian protests mounted, Syria pulled nearly all its troops out of Lebanon, although some intelligence agents may have remained. An anti-Syrian bloc won parliamentary elections held in May and June. A new cabinet, installed July 19, was headed by Fouad Siniora, a friend and aide to Hariri, and included a Hezbollah member.

A rocket attack and border raid by Hezbollah, July 12, 2006, in which 3 Israeli soldiers were killed and 2 captured, triggered a massive escalation of hostilities. Hezbollah, led by Sheikh Hassan Nasrallah, bombarded northern Israel with nearly 4,000 rockets, while Israeli air and ground forces assaulted suspected Hezbollah strongholds in southern Lebanon and southern Beirut. Roads, bridges, and other installations were destroyed, and hundreds of civilians were caught in the crossfire; at least 28 civilians were killed by an Israeli air strike July 30 at Qana, where more than 100 in a UN compound had died from an Israeli artillery barrage 10 years earlier. By Aug. 14, when a UN-sponsored cease-fire took hold, the war dead included nearly 1,150 Lebanese. To enforce the truce, 15,000 Lebanese govt. troops began moving into southern Lebanon, and expansion to 15,000 of the small UN force already in Lebanon (UNIFIL) was approved.

Lesotho
Kingdom of Lesotho

People: Population: 2,022,331. **Age distrib.** (%) <15: 36.8; 65+: 4.9. **Pop. density:** 172 per sq mi, 66 per sq km. **Urban:** 17.9%. **Ethnic groups:** Sotho 99%. **Principal languages:** Sesotho, English (both official), Zulu, Xhosa. **Chief religions:** Christian 80%, indigenous beliefs 20%.

Geography: Total area: 11,720 sq mi, 30,355 sq km; **Land area:** 11,720 sq mi, 30,355 sq km. **Location:** In southern Africa. **Neighbors:** Completely surrounded by Republic of South Africa. **Topography:** Landlocked and mountainous, altitudes from 5,000 to 11,000 ft. **Capital:** Maseru, 172,000.

Government: Type: Modified constitutional monarchy. **Head of state:** King Letsie III; b. July 17, 1963; in office: Feb. 7, 1996. **Head of gov.:** Pakalitha Mosisili; b. Mar. 14, 1945; in office: May 29, 1998. **Local divisions:** 10 districts. **Defense budget** (2005): $32.3 mil. **Active troops:** 2,000.

Economy: Industries: food, beverages, textiles, apparel, handicrafts. **Chief crops:** corn, wheat, sorghum, barley. **Natural resources:** water, diamonds, other minerals. **Arable land:** 11%. **Livestock** (2005): cattle: 540,000; chickens: 1.8 mil; goats: 650,000; pigs: 65,000; sheep: 850,000. **Fish catch** (2004): 47 metric tons. **Electricity prod.** (2004): 250 mil kWh. **Labor force:** 86% of resident population engaged in subsistence agriculture; roughly 35% of the active male wage earners work in South Africa, industry and services 14%.

Finance: Monetary unit: Loti (LSL) (Sept. 2006: 7.63 = $1 U.S.). **GDP** (2005 est.): $5.1 bil; **per capita GDP:** $2,500; **GDP growth:** 0.8%. **Imports** (2005 est.): $1.2 bil; partners (2004): Hong Kong 34.2%, Taiwan 33.9%, China 11.2%, Germany 9.2%. **Exports** (2005 est.): $602.8 mil; partners (2004): U.S. 96%, Canada 1.5%, Belgium/Luxembourg 1.1%. **Tourism:** $34 mil. **Budget** (2005 est.): $792.1 mil. **Intl. reserves less gold:** $364 mil. **Consumer prices:** 3.44%.

Transport: Railroad: Length: 2 mi. **Motor vehicles:** 5,000 pass. cars, 18,000 comm. vehicles. **Civil aviation:** NA; 3 airports.

Communications: TV sets: 16 per 1,000 pop. **Radios:** 52 per 1,000 pop. **Telephone lines:** 48,000. **Daily newspaper circ.:** NA. **Internet:** 43,000 users.

Health: Life expect.: 35.5 male; 33.2 female. **Births** (per 1,000 pop.): 24.8. **Deaths** (per 1,000 pop.): 28.7. **Natural inc.:** −0.4%. **Infant mortality** (per 1,000 live births): 87.2. **AIDS rate:** 23.2%.

Education: Compulsory: ages 6-12. **Literacy:** 82.2%.

Major Intl. Organizations: UN (FOA, IBRD, ILO, IMF, WHO, WTO), the Commonwealth, AU.

Embassy: 2511 Massachusetts Ave. NW 20008; 797-5533.

Website: www.lesotho.gov.ls

Lesotho (once called Basutoland) became a British protectorate in 1868 when Chief Moshesh sought protection against the Boers. Independence came Oct. 4, 1966. Most of Lesotho's GNP is provided by citizens working in South Africa. Livestock raising is the chief industry; diamonds are the chief export.

South Africa imposed a blockade, Jan. 1, 1986, because Lesotho had given sanctuary to anti-apartheid groups. The blockade sparked a Jan. 20 military coup and was lifted, Jan. 25, when the new leaders agreed to expel the rebels.

In Mar. 1990, King Moshoeshoe was exiled by the military government. Letsie III became king Nov. 12. In Mar. 1993, Ntsu Mokhehle, a civilian, was elected prime minister, ending 23 years of military rule. After a series of violent disturbances, the king dismissed the Mokhehle government Aug. 17, 1994; constitutional rule was restored Sept. 14.

Letsie abdicated and Moshoeshoe was reinstated Jan. 25, 1995. Moshoeshoe died in an automobile accident, Jan. 15, 1996. Letsie was reinstated Feb. 7. South Africa and Botswana sent troops Sept. 22, 1998, to help suppress violent antigovernment protests.

According to UN estimates, more than 20% of the adult population has HIV/AIDS.

Liberia
Republic of Liberia

People: Population: 3,042,004. **Age distrib.** (%) <15: 43.1; 65+: 2.8. **Pop. density:** 81 per sq mi, 31 per sq km. **Urban:** 46.7%. **Ethnic groups:** Kpelle, Bassa, Dey, and other tribes 95%; Americo-Liberians 2.5%, Caribbean 2.5%. **Principal languages:** English (official); Mande, West Atlantic, and Kwa languages. **Chief religions:** Indigenous beliefs 40%, Christian 40%, Muslim 20%.

Geography: Total area: 43,000 sq mi, 111,370 sq km; **Land area:** 37,189 sq mi, 96,320 sq km. **Location:** On SW coast of W Africa. **Neighbors:** Sierra Leone on W, Guinea on N, Côte d'Ivoire on E. **Topography:** Marshy Atlantic coastline rises to low mountains and plateaus in the forested interior; 6 major rivers flow in parallel courses to the ocean. **Capital:** Monrovia, 936,000.

Government: Type: Republic. **Head of state and gov.:** Pres. Ellen Johnson-Sirleaf; b. Oct. 29, 1938; in office: Jan. 16, 2006. **Local divisions:** 15 counties. **Defense budget:** $1 mil. **Active troops:** 15,000.

Economy: Industries: rubber & palm oil proc., timber, diamonds. **Chief crops:** rubber, coffee, cocoa, rice, cassava, palm oil, sugarcane, bananas. **Natural resources:** iron ore, timber, diamonds, gold, hydropower. **Arable land:** 1%. **Livestock** (2005): cattle: 36,000; chickens: 5.3 mil; goats: 220,000; pigs: 130,000; sheep: 210,000. **Fish catch** (2004): 10,359 metric tons. **Electricity prod.** (2004): 330 mil kWh. **Labor force** (2000 est.): agriculture 70%, industry 8%, services 22%.

Finance: Monetary unit: Liberian Dollar (LRD) (Sept. 2006: 49.00 = $1 U.S.). **GDP** (2005 est.): $2.8 bil; **per capita GDP:** $1,000; **GDP growth:** 8%. **Imports** (2004 est.): $4.8 bil; partners (2004): South Korea 38.1%, Japan 21.9%, Singapore 12.6%, Croatia 4.8%. **Exports** (2004 est.): $910 mil; partners (2004): Germany 36.9%, Poland 18.6%, U.S. 11.4%, Greece 10.6%. **Tourism:** NA. **Budget** (2000 est.): $90.5 mil. **Intl. reserves less gold:** $18 mil.

Transport: Railroad: Length: 304 mi. **Motor vehicles:** 17,100 pass. cars, 12,800 comm. vehicles; 2 airports. **Civil aviation:** NA; 2 airports **Chief ports:** Monrovia, Buchanan, Greenville, Harper.

Communications: TV sets: 26 per 1,000 pop. **Radios:** 329 per 1,000 pop. **Telephone lines:** 6,900 main lines. **Daily newspaper circ.:** 14.2 per 1,000 pop. **Internet** (2002): 1,000 users.

Health: Life expect.: 38 male; 41.4 female. **Births** (per 1,000 pop.): 44.8. **Deaths** (per 1,000 pop.): 23.1. **Natural inc.:** 2.17%. **Infant mortality** (per 1,000 live births): 155.8. **AIDS rate:** NA.

Education: Compulsory: ages 6-15. **Literacy:** 57.5%.

Major Intl. Organizations: UN and most of its specialized agencies, AU.

Embassy: 5201 16th St. NW 20011; 723-0437.

Website: www.embassyofliberia.org

Liberia was founded in 1822 by U.S. black freedmen who settled at Monrovia with the aid of colonization societies. It became a republic July 26, 1847, with a constitution modeled on that of the U.S. Descendants of freedmen dominated politics.

Under Pres. William V. S. Tubman, Liberia was a founding member of the UN in 1945. Tubman died in 1971 and was succeeded by his vice president, William R. Tolbert Jr. Charging rampant corruption, an Army Redemption Council of enlisted men staged a bloody predawn coup, Apr. 12, 1980, in which Pres. Tolbert was killed and replaced as head of state by Sgt. Samuel Doe. In 1985, Doe was chosen president in a disputed election.

A civil war began Dec. 1989. In Sept. 1990, Pres. Doe was captured and put to death. Despite the introduction of peacekeeping forces from several countries, the conflict intensified. Factional fighting devastated Monrovia in Apr. 1996. On Sept. 3, Ruth Perry became modern Africa's first female head of state, leading a transitional government. By then, the civil war had claimed more than 150,000 lives and uprooted over half the population.

Former rebel leader Charles Taylor was elected president July 19, 1997, in Liberia's first national election in 12 years. The UN imposed sanctions May 4, 2001, to punish Liberia for aiding the Revolutionary United Front (RUF) insurgency in Sierra Leone. Taylor declared a state of emergency Feb. 8, 2002, after Liberian rebels launched raids near Monrovia.

A UN-sponsored war crimes tribunal indicted Taylor June 4, 2003, for his role in Sierra Leone. With rebels again threatening Monrovia, Taylor resigned Aug. 11 and went into exile. The UN authorized a 15,000-member peacekeeping force (UNMIL) Sept. 19 to help stabilize the nation. A businessman, Charles Gyude Bryant, was sworn in Oct. 14 to head a power-sharing interim government. Ellen Johnson-Sirleaf won a presidential runoff election Nov. 8, 2005, and took office Jan. 16, 2006. Captured Mar. 29 while trying to flee Nigeria, Taylor was transferred to the Netherlands, June 20, for trial at the Hague.

Libya
Great Socialist People's Libyan Arab Jamahiriya

People: Population: 5,900,754. **Age distrib.** (%) <15: 33.6; 65+: 4.2. **Pop. density:** 8 per sq mi, 3 per sq km. **Urban:** 86.3%. **Ethnic groups:** Arab-Berber 97%. **Principal languages:** Arabic (official), Italian, English. **Chief religion:** Muslim (official; mostly Sunni) 97%.

Geography: Total area: 679,362 sq mi, 1,759,540 sq km; **Land area:** 679,362 sq mi, 1,759,540 sq km. **Location:** On Mediterranean coast of N Africa. **Neighbors:** Tunisia, Algeria on W; Niger, Chad on S; Sudan, Egypt on E. **Topography:** Desert and semidesert regions cover 92% of the land, with low mountains in N, high-

er mountains in S, and a narrow coastal zone. **Capital**, Tripoli, 2,098,000. **Cities (urban aggr.):** Benghazi, 912,000.

Government: Type: Islamic Arabic Socialist "Mass-State." **Head of state and gov.:** Col. Muammar al-Qaddafi; b. Sept. 1942; in power: Sept. 1969. **Local divisions:** 25 municipalities. **Defense budget** (2005): $620 mil. **Active troops:** 76,000.

Economy: Industries: oil, food proc., textiles, handicrafts, cement. **Chief crops:** wheat, barley, olives, dates, citrus, vegetables, peanuts, soybeans. **Natural resources:** oil, nat. gas, gypsum. **Crude oil reserves** (2005): 39 bil bbls. **Arable land:** 1%. **Livestock** (2005): cattle: 130,000; chickens: 25 mil; goats: 1.3 mil; sheep: 4.5 mil. **Fish catch** (2004): 46,339 metric tons. **Electricity prod.** (2004): 19.4 bil kWh. **Labor force** (2004 est.): agriculture 17%, industry 23%, services 59%.

Finance: Monetary unit: Dinar (LYD) (Sept. 2006: 1.30 = $1 U.S.). **GDP** (2005 est.): $65.8 bil; **per capita GDP:** $11,400; **GDP growth:** 8.5%. **Imports** (2005 est.): $10.8 bil; partners (2004): Italy 28.2%, Germany 11.1%, Tunisia 6%, UK 5.8%, Turkey 5%, France 4.1%. **Exports** (2005 est.): $30.8 bil; partners (2004): Italy 37.7%, Germany 16.7%, Spain 11.6%, Turkey 7.5%, France 6.5%. **Tourism:** $218 mil. **Budget** (2005 est.): $15.5 bil. **Intl. reserves less gold:** $27.64 bil. **Gold:** 4.62 mil oz t.

Transport: Motor vehicles: 552,700 pass. cars, 195,500 comm. vehicles. **Civil aviation:** 254.1 mil. pass.-mi; 60 airports. **Chief ports:** Tripoli, Banghazi.

Communications: TV sets: 139 per 1,000 pop. **Radios:** 259 per 1,000 pop. **Telephone lines:** 750,000. **Daily newspaper circ.:** 14.1 per 1,000 pop. **Internet:** 205,000 users.

Health: Life expect.: 74.5 male; 79 female. **Births** (per 1,000 pop.): 26.5. **Deaths** (per 1,000 pop.): 3.5. **Natural inc.:** 2.3%. **Infant mortality** (per 1,000 live births): 23.7. **AIDS rate:** NA.

Education: Compulsory: ages 6-14. **Literacy:** 82.6%.

Major Intl. Organizations: UN (FAO, IBRD, ILO, IMF, IMO, WHO), AL, AU, OPEC.

Permanent UN Representative: 309-315 E. 48th St., New York, NY 10017; (212) 752-5775.

Website: www.libya-un.org

First settled by Berbers, Libya was ruled in succession by Carthage, Rome, the Vandals, and the Ottomans. Italy ruled from 1912, and Britain and France after WWII. Libya became an independent constitutional monarchy Jan. 2, 1952. In 1969 a junta led by Col. Muammar al-Qaddafi seized power.

Libya and Egypt fought several air and land battles along their border in July 1977. Chad charged Libya with military occupation of its uranium-rich northern region in 1977. Libyan troops were driven from their last major stronghold by Chad forces in 1987, leaving over $1 bil in military equipment behind.

Libya reportedly helped arm violent revolutionary groups in Egypt and Sudan and aided terrorists of various nationalities, and was blamed for aiding the attacks on the Rome and Vienna airports in Dec. 1985. The U.S. and Libya clashed, Jan.-Mar. 1986, over access to the Gulf of Sidra, which Libya claimed as territorial waters. The U.S. accused Qaddafi of ordering the Apr. 5, bombing of a West Berlin discotheque, which killed 3, including a U.S. serviceman. In response, the U.S. sent warplanes to attack what it called "terrorist-related targets" in Tripoli and Banghazi, Libya, Apr. 14; the targets included Qaddafi's barracks.

Libyan agents were accused of planting bombs that blew up Pan Am Flight 103 over Lockerbie, Scotland, killing 270 people Dec. 21, 1988, and UTA Flight 772 over Niger, killing 170 people Sept. 19, 1989. The UN imposed sanctions, Apr. 15, 1992, for Libya's failure to cooperate in the Lockerbie and UTA cases.

Libya agreed in 2003 to renounce terrorism and settle compensation cases for the families of the Lockerbie and UTA bombing victims. The UN lifted sanctions, Sept. 12. Secret talks with the U.S. and UK led to Libya's announcement Dec. 19 that it would stop developing nuclear, chemical, and biological weapons and long-range missiles. The U.S. ended most economic sanctions Apr. 23, 2004. Libya pledged Aug. 10 to compensate non-U.S. victims of the 1986 Berlin disco bombing. EU sanctions were lifted Oct. 11, 2004, and the U.S. restored full diplomatic relations May 15, 2006.

Liechtenstein
Principality of Liechtenstein

People: Population: 33,987. **Age distrib.** (%) <15: 17.4; 65+: 12.4. **Pop. density:** 548 per sq mi, 212 per sq km. **Urban:** 21.6%. **Ethnic groups:** Alemannic 86%; Italian, Turkish, and other 14%. **Principal languages:** German (official), Alemannic dialect. **Chief religions:** Roman Catholic 76%, Protestant 7%.

Geography: Total area: 62 sq mi, 160 sq km; **Land area:** 62 sq mi, 160 sq km. **Location:** Central Europe, in the Alps. **Neighbors:** Switzerland on W, Austria on E. **Topography:** The Rhine Valley occupies one-third of the country, the Alps cover the rest. **Capital:** Vaduz, 5,053.

Government: Type: Hereditary constitutional monarchy. **Head of state:** Prince Hans-Adam II; b Feb. 14, 1945; in office: Nov. 13, 1989. **Head of gov.:** Otmar Hasler; b Sept. 28, 1953; in office: Apr. 5, 2001. **Local divisions:** 11 communes.

Economy: Industries: electronics, metallurgy, textiles, ceramics, pharm., food products, precision instruments, tourism. **Chief crops:** wheat, barley, corn, potatoes. **Natural resources:** hydropower. **Arable land:** 24%. **Livestock** (2005): cattle: 6,000; goats: 280; pigs: 3,000; sheep: 2,900. **Labor force** (2001 est.): agriculture 2%, industry 47%, services 51%.

Finance: Monetary unit: Switzerland Franc (CHF) (Sept. 2006: 1.24 = $1 U.S.). **GDP** (1999 est.): $1.8 bil; **per capita GDP:** $25,000; **GDP growth:** 11%. **Imports** (1996 est.): $917.3 mil; partners: EU, Switzerland. **Exports** (1996 est.): $2.5 bil; partners : EU 62.6%, (Germany 24.3%, Austria 9.5%, France 8.9%, Italy 6.6%, UK 4.6%), U.S. 18.9%, Switzerland 15.7%. **Tourism:** NA. **Budget** (1998 est.): $414.1 mil.

Transport: Railroad: Length: 11 mi.

Communications: TV sets: 469 per 1,000 pop. **Radios:** 656 per 1,000 pop. **Daily newspaper circ.:** NA. **Internet** (2002): 20,000 users.

Health: Life expect.: 76.1 male; 83.3 female. **Births** (per 1,000 pop.): 10.2. **Deaths** (per 1,000 pop.): 7.2. **Natural inc.:** 0.3%. **Infant mortality** (per 1,000 live births): 4.6. **AIDS rate:** NA.

Education: Compulsory: ages 7-16. **Literacy:** 100%.

Major Intl. Organizations: UN (WTO), EFTA, OSCE.

Permanent UN Representative: 1300 I St NW, Washington, DC 20005 216-0460; (212) 599-0220.

Embassy: 888 17th St. NW, Ste. 1250, 20006; 331-0590

Website: www.liechtenstein.li/en

Liechtenstein became sovereign in 1806. Austria administered Liechtenstein's ports up to 1920; Switzerland has administered its postal services since 1921. Liechtenstein is united with Switzerland by a customs and monetary union. Taxes are low; many international corporations have headquarters there. Foreign workers comprise 2/3 of the labor force. On Aug. 15, 2004, Prince Hans-Adam II assigned day-to-day responsibilities for running the tiny country to his son, Crown Prince Alois.

Lithuania
Republic of Lithuania

People: Population: 3,585,906. **Age distrib.** (%) <15: 15.5; 65+: 15.5. **Pop. density:** 142 per sq mi, 54 per sq km. **Urban:** 66.7%. **Ethnic groups:** Lithuanian 81%, Russian 9%, Polish 7%, Belarusian 2%. **Principal languages:** Lithuanian (official), Belorusian, Russian, Polish. **Chief religion:** Roman Catholic 79%, none 9.5%.

Geography: Total area: 25,174 sq mi, 65,200 sq km. **Land area:** 25,174 sq mi, 65,200 sq km. **Location:** In E Europe, on SE coast of Baltic. **Neighbors:** Latvia on N, Belarus on E, S, Poland and Russia on W. **Topography:** Lithuania is a lowland with hills in W and S; fertile soil; many small lakes and rivers, with marshes espec. in N and W. **Capital:** Vilnius, 553,000.

Government: Type: Republic. **Head of state:** Pres. Valdas Adamkus; b. Nov. 3, 1926; in office: July 12, 2004. **Head of gov.:** Prime Min. Gediminas Kirkilas; b. Aug. 30, 1951; in office: July 4, 2006. **Local divisions:** 10 provinces. **Defense budget** (2005): $333 mil. **Active troops:** 13,510.

Economy: Industries: machine tools, electric motors, large appliances, oil refining, shipbuilding. **Chief crops:** grain, potatoes, sugar beets, flax, vegetables. **Natural resources:** peat. **Crude oil reserves** (2005): 12 mil bbls. **Arable land:** 35%. **Livestock** (2005): cattle: 792,000; chickens: 8.2 mil; goats: 26,900; pigs: 1.1 mil; sheep: 22,100. **Fish catch** (2004): 160,837 metric tons. **Electricity prod.** (2004): 17.8 bil kWh. **Labor force** (1997 est.): agriculture 20%, industry 30%, services 50%.

Finance: Monetary unit: Litas (LTL) (Sept. 2006: 2.70 = $1 U.S.). **GDP** (2005 est.): $49.2 bil; **per capita GDP:** $13,700; **GDP growth:** 7.5%. **Imports** (2005 est.): $13.3 bil; partners (2004): Russia 23.1%, Germany 18.1%, Poland 4.7%, Italy 4.6%. **Exports** (2005 est.): $11 bil; partners (2004): Switzerland 10.7%, Latvia 10%, Germany 9.5%, Russia 7.9%, France 7.5%, U.S. 5.2%, UK 5.1%, Estonia 4.5%, Denmark 4.3%. **Tourism:** $776 mil. **Budget** (2005 est.): $9.1 bil. **Intl. reserves less gold:** $2.6 bil. **Gold:** 190,000 oz t. **Consumer prices:** 2.66%.

Transport: Railroad: Length: 1,241 mi. **Motor vehicles:** 1.3 mil pass. cars, 126,100 comm. vehicles. **Civil aviation:** 220.6 mil pass.-mi; 34 airports. **Chief port:** Klaipeda.

Communications: TV sets: 422 per 1,000 pop. **Radios:** 502 per 1,000 pop. **Telephone lines:** 801,100. **Daily newspaper circ.:** 30.9 per 1,000 pop. **Internet:** 968,000 users.

Health: Life expect.: 69.2 male; 79.5 female. **Births** (per 1,000 pop.): 8.8. **Deaths** (per 1,000 pop.): 11. **Natural inc.:** −0.22%. **Infant mortality** (per 1,000 live births): 6.8. **AIDS rate:** 0.2%.

Education: Compulsory: ages 7-15. **Literacy:** 99.6%.

Major Intl. Organizations: UN (FAO, IBRD, ILO, IMF, IMO, WHO, WTO), EU, NATO, OSCE.

Embassy: 2622 16th St. NW 20009; 234-5860.

Website: www.president.lt/en

Lithuania was occupied by the German army, 1914-18. It was annexed by the Soviet Russian army, but the Soviets were overthrown, 1919. Lithuania was a democratic republic until 1926, when the regime was ousted by a coup. In 1939 the Soviet-German treaty assigned most of Lithuania to the Soviet sphere of influence. Lithuania was annexed by the USSR Aug. 3, 1940.

Lithuania formally declared its independence from the Soviet Union Mar. 11, 1990. During an abortive Soviet coup in Aug., the Western nations recognized Lithuania's independence, which was ratified by the Soviet Union in Sept. 1991.

The last Russian troops withdrew on Aug. 31, 1993. The conservative Homeland Union defeated the former Communists in parliamentary elections OCt.-Nov. 10, 1996. A Lithuanian-American, Valdas Adamkus, won the presidency in a runoff election Jan. 4, 1998. He lost to Rolandas Paksas in a runoff, Jan. 5, 2003. But after the legislature impeached and removed Paksas from office, Apr. 6, 2004, Adamkus regained the presidency in a runoff vote June 27. Lithuania joined the EU and NATO in 2004.

Luxembourg
Grand Duchy of Luxembourg

People: Population: 474,413. **Age distrib.** (%) <15: 18.9; 65+: 14.6. **Pop. density:** 475 per sq mi, 183 per sq km. **Urban:** 91.9%. **Ethnic groups:** Mixture of French and German. **Principal languages:** Luxembourgish (national), German, French (official). **Chief religion:** Roman Catholic 87%, 13% Protestant, Jewish, and Muslim.

Geography: Total area: 998 sq mi, 2,586 sq km; **Land area:** 998 sq mi, 2,586 sq km. **Location:** In W Europe. **Neighbors:** Belgium on W, France on S, Germany on E. **Topography:** Heavy forests (Ardennes) cover N, S is a low, open plateau. **Capital:** Luxembourg-Ville, 77,000.

Government: Type: Constitutional monarchy. **Head of state:** Grand Duke Henri; b. Apr. 16, 1955; in office: Oct. 7, 2000. **Head of gov.:** Prime Min. Jean-Claude Juncker; b. Dec. 9, 1954; in office: Jan. 20, 1995. **Local divisions:** 3 districts. **Defense budget** (2005): $264 mil. **Active troops:** 900.

Economy: Industries: banking, iron & steel, food proc., chemicals, metal products, engineering, tires, glass, aluminum. **Chief crops:** barley, oats, potatoes, wheat, fruits, grapes. **Natural resources:** iron ore. **Arable land:** 24%. **Livestock** (2005): cattle: 184,172; chickens: 72.8 mil; goats: 2,000; pigs: 75,000; sheep: 7,500. **Electricity prod.** (2004): 2.8 bil kWh. **Labor force** (2004 est.): agriculture 1%, industry 13%, services 86%.

Finance: Monetary unit: Euro (EUR) (Sept. 2006: 0.78 = $1 U.S.). **GDP** (2005 est.): $30.7 bil; **per capita GDP:** $55,600; **GDP growth:** 3.7%. **Imports** (2005 est.): $18.7 bil; partners (2004): Belgium 30%, Germany 21.8%, France 12.5%, China 11.9%, Netherlands 4.5%. **Exports** (2005 est.): $13.4 bil; partners (2004): Germany 21.8%, France 20.1%, Belgium 10.5%, UK 9.3%, Italy 7.1%, Spain 5.6%, Netherlands 4.3%. **Tourism:** $3.7 bil. **Budget** (2005 est.): $9.6 bil. **Intl. reserves less gold:** $169 mil. **Gold:** 70,000 oz t. **Consumer prices:** 2.49%.

Transport: Railroad: Length: 170 mi. **Motor vehicles:** 293,400 pass. cars, 51,700 comm. vehicles. **Civil aviation:** 271.5 mil pass.-mi; 1 airport. **Chief port:** Mertert.

Communications: TV sets: 599 per 1,000 pop. **Radios:** 683 per 1,000 pop. **Telephone lines:** 360,100. **Daily newspaper circ.:** 275.7 per 1,000 pop. **Internet:** 270,800 users.

Health: Life expect.: 75.6 male; 82.4 female. **Births** (per 1,000 pop.): 11.9. **Deaths** (per 1,000 pop.): 8.4. **Natural inc.:** 0.35%. **Infant mortality** (per 1,000 live births): 4.7. **AIDS rate:** 0.2%.

Education: Compulsory: ages 6-15. **Literacy:** 100%.

Major Intl. Organizations: UN (FAO, IBRD, ILO, IMF, IMO, WHO, WTO), EU, NATO, OECD, OSCE.

Embassy: 2200 Massachusetts Ave. NW 20008; 265-4171.

Website: www.luxembourg-usa.org

Luxembourg, founded about 963, was ruled by Burgundy, Spain, Austria, and France from 1448 to 1815. It left the Germanic Confederation in 1866. Overrun by Germany in 2 world wars, Luxembourg ended its neutrality in 1948, when a customs union with Belgium and Netherlands was adopted.

Luxembourg was one of the 6 founding members (1951) of what became the European Union. Its voters ratified the EU constitution in July 2005.

Macedonia
Former Yugoslav Republic of Macedonia

People: Population: 2,050,554. **Age distrib.** (%) <15: 20.1; 65+: 11. **Pop. density:** 213 per sq mi, 82 per sq km. **Urban:** 59.5%. **Ethnic groups:** Macedonian 67%, Albanian 23%, Turkish 4%, Roma 2%, Serb 2%. **Principal languages:** Macedonian (official), Albanian, Turkish, Romani, Serbo-Croatian. **Chief religions:** unspecified 51%, Macedonian Orthodox 32%, Muslim 17%.

Geography: Total area: 9,781 sq mi, 25,333 sq km; **Land area:** 9,597 sq mi, 24,856 sq km. **Location:** In SE Europe. **Neighbors:** Bulgaria on E, Greece on S, Albania on W, Serbia on N. **Topography:** Macedonia is a landlocked, mostly mountainous country, with deep river valleys, 3 large lakes; country is bisected by Vardar R. **Capital:** Skopje, 475,000.

Government: Type: Republic. **Head of state:** Pres. Branko Crvenkovski; b. Oct. 12, 1962; in office: May 12, 2004. **Head of gov.:** Prime Min. Nikola Gruevski; b. Aug. 31, 1970; in office: Aug. 27, 2006. **Local divisions:** 123 municipalities. **Defense budget** (2005): $129 mil. **Active troops:** 10,890.

Economy: Industries: mining, textiles, wood products, tobacco, food proc., buses. **Chief crops:** rice, tobacco, wheat, corn, millet, cotton, sesame. **Natural resources:** chromium, lead, zinc, mang., tungsten, nickel, iron ore, asbestos, sulfur, timber. **Arable land:** 24%. **Livestock** (2005): cattle: 265,000; chickens: 3 mil; pigs: 200,000; sheep: 1.2 mil. **Fish catch** (2004): 1,172 metric tons. **Electricity prod.** (2004): 6.4 bil kWh.

Finance: Monetary unit: Denar (MKD) (Sept. 2006: 48.06 = $1 U.S.). **GDP** (2005 est.): $16 bil; **per capita GDP:** $7,800; **GDP growth:** 3.7%. **Imports** (2005 est.): $3.2 bil; partners (2004): Greece 18%, Germany 14.4%, Serbia and Montenegro 9.3%, Slovenia 8.1%, Bulgaria 7.6%, Turkey 7%. **Exports** (2005 est.): $2 bil; partners (2004): Serbia and Montenegro 30.8%, Germany 20.1%,

Greece 9%, Croatia 7%, U.S. 4.8%. **Tourism:** $72 mil. **Budget** (2005 est.): $2.2 bil. **Intl. reserves less gold:** $860 mil. **Gold:** 220,000 oz t. **Consumer prices:** 0.04%.

Transport: Railroad: Length: 434 mi. **Motor vehicles:** 307,600 pass. cars, 33,000 comm. vehicles. **Civil aviation:** 146.6 mil pass.-mi; 10 airports.

Communications: TV sets: 273 per 1,000 pop. **Radios:** 550 per 1,000 pop. **Telephone lines:** 537,000. **Daily newspaper circ.:** NA. **Internet** (2004): 392,671.

Health: Life expect.: 71.5 male; 76.6 female. **Births** (per 1,000 pop.): 12. **Deaths** (per 1,000 pop.): 8.8. **Natural inc.:** 0.33%. **Infant mortality** (per 1,000 live births): 9.8. **AIDS rate:** <0.1%.

Education: Compulsory: ages 7-14. **Literacy:** 96.1%.

Major Intl. Organizations: UN (FAO, IBRD, ILO, IMF, IMO, WHO, WTO, OSCE).

Embassy: 1101 30th St., NW, Ste., 302, 20007; 337-3063.

Website: www.vlada.mk/english/index_en.htm

Macedonia, as part of a larger region also called Macedonia, was ruled by Muslim Turks from 1389 to 1912, when native Greeks, Bulgarians, and Slavs won independence. Serbia received the largest part of the territory, the rest going to Greece and Bulgaria. In 1913, the area was incorporated into Serbia, which in 1918 became part of the Kingdom of Serbs, Croats, and Slovenes (later Yugoslavia). In 1946, Macedonia became a constituent republic of Yugoslavia.

Macedonia declared its independence Sept. 8, 1991, and was admitted to the UN under a provisional name in 1993. A UN force, which included several hundred U.S. troops, was deployed there to deter the warring factions in Bosnia from carrying their dispute into other areas of the Balkans.

In Feb. 1994 both Russia and the U.S. recognized Macedonia. Greece, which objected to Macedonia's use of what it considered a Hellenic name and symbols, imposed a trade blockade on the landlocked nation; the 2 countries agreed to normalize relations Sept. 13, 1995. A car bombing, Oct. 3, seriously injured Pres. Kiro Gligorov. Macedonia and Yugoslavia signed a treaty normalizing relations Apr. 8, 1996.

By the end of NATO's air war against Yugoslavia, Mar.-June 1999, Macedonia had a Kosovar refugee population of more than 250,000; over 90% had been repatriated by Sept. 1. Boris Trajkovski, candidate of the ruling center-right coalition, won a presidential runoff vote Nov. 14.

Ethnic Albanian guerrillas launched an offensive Mar. 2001 in NW Macedonia. An accord signed Aug. 13 paved the way for the introduction of a NATO peacekeeping force. A law broadening the rights of ethnic Albanians was enacted Jan. 24, 2002. A 320-member EU force replaced the NATO peacekeepers Mar. 31, 2003. After Trajkovski died in a plane crash Feb. 26, 2004, Prime Min. Branko Crvenkovski won a presidential runoff vote Apr. 28, 2004.

Madagascar
Republic of Madagascar

People: Population: 18,872,164. **Age distrib.** (%) <15: 44.1; 65+: 3.1. **Pop. density:** 84 per sq mi, 32 per sq km. **Urban:** 26.5%. **Ethnic groups:** Mainly Malagasy (Indonesian-African); also Cotiers, French, Indian, Chinese. **Principal languages:** Malagasy, French (both official). **Chief religions:** Indigenous beliefs 52%, Christian 41%, Muslim 7%.

Geography: Total area: 226,657 sq mi, 587,040 sq km; **Land area:** 224,534 sq mi, 581,540 sq km. **Location:** In the Indian O., off the SE coast of Africa. **Neighbors:** Comoro Isls. to NW, Mozambique to W. **Topography:** Humid coastal strip in the E, fertile valleys in the mountainous center plateau region, and a wider coastal strip on the W. **Capital:** Antananarivo, 1,585,000.

Government: Type: Republic. **Head of state:** Pres. Marc Ravalomanana; b. Dec. 12, 1949; in office: Feb. 22, 2002. **Head of gov.:** Prime Min. Jacques Sylla; b. 1946; in office: Feb. 26, 2002. **Local divisions:** 6 provinces. **Defense budget** (2005): $275 mil. **Active troops:** 13,500.

Economy: Industries: meat proc., soap, brewing, hides, sugar, textiles, glassware, cement, autos. **Chief crops:** coffee, vanilla, sugarcane, cloves, cocoa, rice, cassava, beans, bananas, peanuts. **Natural resources:** graphite, chromite, coal, bauxite, salt, quartz, tar sands, gemstones, mica, fish, hydropower. **Arable land:** 4%. **Livestock** (2005): cattle: 10.5 mil; chickens: 24 mil; goats: 1.2 mil; pigs: 1.6 mil; sheep: 650,000. **Fish catch** (2004): 137,701 metric tons. **Electricity prod.** (2004): 980 mil kWh.

Finance: Monetary unit: Ariary (MGA) (Sept. 2006: 2,120.00 = $1 U.S.). **GDP** (2005 est.): $16.4 bil; **per capita GDP:** $900; **GDP growth:** 5.1%. **Imports** (2005 est.): $1.4 bil; partners (2004): France 17.6%, China 11.1%, Hong Kong 6.7%, Iran 6.2%, South Africa 5.8%. **Exports** (2005 est.): $951 mil; partners (2004): U.S. 35.7%, France 30.7%, Germany 7.1%, Mauritius 4.4%. **Tourism:** $105 mil. **Budget** (2005 est.): $853 mil. **Intl. reserves less gold:** $337 mil. **Consumer prices:** 18.51%.

Transport: Railroad: Length: 455 mi. **Motor vehicles** 64,000 pass. cars, 9,100 comm. vehicles. **Civil aviation:** 198.2 mil pass.-mi; 29 airports. **Chief ports:** Toamasina, Antsiranana, Mahajanga, Toliara, Antsohimbondrona.

Communications: TV sets: 23 per 1,000 pop. **Radios:** 209 per 1,000 pop. **Telephone lines:** 66,900. **Daily newspaper circ.:** 4.5 per 1,000 pop. **Internet:** 90,000 users.

Health: Life expect.: 59.9 male; 63.7 female. **Births** (per 1,000 pop.): 38.8. **Deaths** (per 1,000 pop.): 8.7. **Natural inc.:** 3.01%. **Infant mortality** (per 1,000 live births): 58.5. **AIDS rate:** 0.5%.

Education: Compulsory: ages 6-14. **Literacy:** 70.7%.

Major Intl. Organizations: UN (FAO, IBRD, ILO, IMF, IMO, WHO, WTO), AU.

Embassy: 2374 Massachusetts Ave. NW 20008; 265-5525.

Website: www.madagascar-consulate.org

Madagascar was settled 2,000 years ago by Malayan-Indonesian people, whose descendants still predominate. A unified kingdom ruled the 18th and 19th centuries. The island became a French protectorate, 1885, and a colony 1896. Independence came June 26, 1960.

Discontent with inflation and French domination led to a coup in 1972. The new regime nationalized French-owned financial interests, closed French bases and a U.S. space-tracking station, and obtained Chinese aid. The government conducted a program of arrests, expulsion of foreigners, and repression of strikes, 1979.

In 1990, Madagascar ended a ban on multiparty politics that had been in place since 1975. Albert Zafy was elected president in 1993, ending the 17-year rule of Adm. Didier Ratsiraka. After Zafy was impeached by the legislature, Madagascar's constitutional court removed him from office, Sept. 5, 1996. Prime Min. Norbert Ratsirahonana then became interim president pending national elections, Nov. 3 and Dec. 29, in which Ratsiraka edged Zafy. A cholera epidemic, exacerbated by cyclones in Feb. and Apr. 2000, claimed at least 1,600 lives.

Marc Ravalomanana won a power struggle with Ratsiraka that followed a disputed presidential election Dec. 16, 2001. Presidential and parliamentary elections are scheduled for Dec. 2006.

Malawi
Republic of Malawi

People: Population: 13,283,755. **Age distrib.** (%) <15: 46.3; 65+: 2.7. **Pop. density:** 365 per sq mi, 141 per sq km. **Urban:** 16.3%. **Ethnic groups:** Chewa, Nyanja, Tumbuka, Yao, Lomwe, Sena, Tonga, Ngoni, Ngonde. **Principal languages:** Chichewa, English (both official), several African languages. **Chief religions:** Protestant 39%, Roman Catholic 25%, Muslim 15%.

Geography: Total area: 45,745 sq mi, 118,480 sq km; **Land area:** 36,324 sq mi, 94,080 sq km. **Location:** In SE Africa. **Neighbors:** Zambia on W, Mozambique on S and E, Tanzania on N. **Topography:** Malawi stretches 560 mi. N-S along Lake Malawi (Lake Nyasa), most of which belongs to Malawi. High plateaus and mountains line the Rift Valley the length of the nation. **Capital:** Lilongwe, 676,000. **Cities (urban aggr., 1998 est.):** Blantyre, 2,000,000.

Government: Type: Republic. **Head of state and gov.:** Pres. Bingu wa Mutharika; b. Feb. 24, 1934; in office: May 24, 2004. **Local divisions:** 3 regions, 26 districts. **Defense budget** (2005): $12.8 mil. **Active troops:** 5,300.

Economy: Industries: tobacco, tea, sugar, wood products, cement, consumer goods. **Chief crops:** tobacco, sugarcane, cotton, tea, corn, potatoes, cassava, sorghum. **Natural resources:** limestone, hydropower, uranium, coal, bauxite. **Arable land:** 18%. **Livestock** (2005): cattle: 750,000; chickens: 15.2 mil; goats: 1.9 mil; pigs: 456,300; sheep: 115,000. **Fish catch** (2004): 57,196 metric tons. **Electricity prod.** (2004): 1.3 bil kWh. **Labor force** (2003 est.): agriculture 90% industry and services 10%.

Finance: Monetary unit: Kwacha (MWK) (Sept. 2006: 138.63 = $1 U.S.). **GDP** (2005 est.): $7.5 bil; **per capita GDP:** $600; **GDP growth:** –3%. **Imports** (2005 est.): $645 mil; partners (2004): South Africa 43.5%, India 6.8%, Tanzania 4.1%. **Exports** (2005 est.): $364 mil; partners (2004): South Africa 13.8%, U.S. 12.3%, Germany 11.8%, Egypt 8.2%, UK 6.8%. **Tourism:** $24 mil. **Budget** (2005 est.): $913.9 mil. **Intl. reserves less gold:** $111 mil. **Gold:** 10,000 oz t. **Consumer prices:** 15.41%.

Transport: Railroad: Length: 495 mi. **Motor vehicles:** 22,500 pass. cars, 57,600 comm. vehicles. **Civil aviation:** 87 mil pass.-mi; 6 airports

Communications: TV sets: 3 per 1,000 pop. **Radios:** 476 per 1,000 pop. **Telephone lines:** 102,700. **Daily newspaper circ.:** 2.4 per 1,000 pop. **Internet:** 46,100 users.

Health: Life expect.: 42.8 male; 41.9 female. **Births** (per 1,000 pop.): 42.4. **Deaths** (per 1,000 pop.): 18.7. **Natural inc.:** 2.37%. **Infant mortality** (per 1,000 live births): 93.7. **AIDS rate:** 14.1%.

Education: Compulsory: ages 6-13. **Literacy:** 64.1%.

Major Intl. Organizations: UN (FAO, IBRD, ILO, IMF, IMO, WHO, WTO), the Commonwealth, AU.

Embassy: 2408 Massachusetts Ave. NW 20008; 797-1007.

Website: www.malawi.gov.mw

Bantus came to the land in the 16th cent., Arab slavers in the 19th. The area became the British protectorate Nyasaland in 1891. It became independent July 6, 1964, and a republic in 1966.

After 3 decades as a one-party state under Pres. Hastings Kamuzu Banda, Malawi adopted a new constitution and, in multiparty elections held May 17, 1994, chose a new leader, Bakili Muluzi. Banda was acquitted, Dec. 23, 1995, of complicity in the deaths of 4 political opponents in 1983; he died Nov. 25, 1997.

Bingu wa Mutharika, candidate of the ruling United Democratic Front, won a disputed presidential election May 20, 2004. In an ongoing power struggle, an effort by Mutharika's former political allies to impeach him was halted by Malawi's Constitutional Court, Oct. 26, 2005. He fired Vice Pres. Cassim Chilumpha but was forced to reinstate him, Feb. 2006; he then had Chilumpha arrested on treason charges, Apr. 28. Former Pres. Muluzi was arrested on corruption charges, July 27, then released 4 days later.

Malaysia

People: Population: 24,385,858. **Age distrib.** (%) <15: 32.6; 65+: 4.7. **Pop. density:** 192 per sq mi, 74 per sq km. **Urban:** 63.9%. **Ethnic groups:** Malay and other indigenous 58%, Chinese 24%, Indian 8%. **Principal languages:** Malay (official), English, Chinese dialects, Tamil, Telugu, Malayalam, Panjabi, Thai, Iban, and Kadazan in East. **Chief religions:** Muslim (official) 60%, Buddhist 19%, Christian 9%, Hindu 6%, Confucianist/Taoist 3%.

Geography: Total area: 127,317 sq mi, 329,750 sq km; **Land area:** 126,854 sq mi, 328,550 sq km. **Location:** On the SE tip of Asia, plus the N coast of the island of Borneo. **Neighbors:** Thailand on N, Indonesia on S. **Topography:** Most of W Malaysia is covered by tropical jungle, including the central mountain range that runs N-S through the peninsula. The western coast is marshy, the eastern, sandy. E Malaysia has a wide, swampy coastal plain, with interior jungles and mountains. **Capital:** Kuala Lumpur, 1,405,000.

Government: Type: Constitutional monarchy. **Head of state:** Paramount Ruler Syed Sirajuddin Syed Putra Jamalullail; b May 16, 1943; in office: Dec. 13, 2001. **Head of gov.:** Prime Min. Datuk Seri Abdullah Ahmad Badawi; b Nov. 26, 1939; in office: Oct. 31, 2003. **Local divisions:** 13 states, 3 federal territories. **Defense budget** (2005): $2.5 bil. **Active troops:** 110,000.

Economy: Industries: rubber & palm oil proc., light mfg., electronics, tin, mining, timber, oil. **Chief crops:** rubber, palm oil, cocoa, rice, coconuts, pepper. **Natural resources:** tin, oil, timber, copper, iron ore, nat. gas, bauxite. **Crude oil reserves** (2005): 3 bil bbls. **Arable land:** 3%. **Livestock** (2005): cattle: 755,000; chickens: 185 mil; goats: 225,000; pigs: 2.2 mil; sheep: 119,000. **Fish catch** (2004): 1,507,034 metric tons. **Electricity prod.** (2004): 78.2 bil kWh. **Labor force** (2000 est.): agriculture 14.5%, industry 36%, services 49.5%.

Finance: Monetary unit: Ringgits (MYR) (Sept. 2006: 3.68 = $1 U.S.). **GDP** (2005 est.): $290.2 bil; **per capita GDP:** $12,100; **GDP growth:** 5.3%. **Imports** (2005 est.): $118.7 bil; partners (2004): Japan 16.1%, U.S. 14.6%, Singapore 11.2%, China 9.9%, Thailand 5.6%, Taiwan 5.5%, South Korea 5%, Germany 4.5%, Indonesia 4%. **Exports** (2005 est.): $147.1 bil; partners (2004): U.S. 18.8%, Singapore 15%, Japan 10.1%, China 6.7%, Hong Kong 6%, Thailand 4.8%. **Tourism:** $8.2 bil. **Budget** (2005 est.): $34.6 bil. **Intl. reserves less gold:** $48.88 bil. **Gold:** 1.17 mil oz t. **Consumer prices:** 2.99%.

Transport: Railroad: Length: 1,502 mi. **Motor vehicles:** 431,500 pass. cars, 48,000 comm. vehicles. **Civil aviation:** 22.9 bil pass.-mi; 37 airports. **Chief ports:** Kuantan, Kelang, Kota Kinabalu, Kuching.

Communications: TV sets: 174 per 1,000 pop. **Radios:** 434 per 1,000 pop. **Telephone lines:** 4.4 mil. **Daily newspaper circ.:** 95.3 per 1,000 pop. **Internet:** 10 mil users.

Health: Life expect.: 69.8 male; 75.4 female. **Births** (per 1,000 pop.): 22.9. **Deaths** (per 1,000 pop.): 5. **Natural inc.:** 1.78%. **Infant mortality** (per 1,000 live births): 17.2. **AIDS rate:** 0.5%.

Education: Compulsory: ages 6-11. **Literacy:** 88.7%.

Major Intl. Organizations: UN (FAO, IBRD, ILO, IMF, IMO, WHO, WTO), APEC, ASEAN, the Commonwealth.

Embassy: 3516 International Court NW 20008; 572-9700.

Website: www.gov.my

European traders appeared in the 16th century; Britain established control in 1867. Malaysia was created Sept. 16, 1963. It included Malaya (which had become independent in 1957 after the suppression of Communist rebels), plus the formerly British Singapore, Sabah (N Borneo), and Sarawak (NW Borneo). Singapore was separated in 1965, in order to end tensions between Chinese, the majority in Singapore, and Malays in control of the Malaysian government.

A monarch is elected by a council of hereditary rulers of the Malayan states every 5 years.

Abundant natural resources have bolstered prosperity, and foreign investment has aided industrialization. Work on a new federal capital at Putrajaya, south of Kuala Lumpur, began in 1995. However, sagging stock and currency prices forced the postponement of major development projects in Sept. 1997.

Mahathir bin Mohamad dominated Malaysian politics as prime minister, 1981-2003. His successor, Abdullah Ahmad Badawi, took office Oct. 31, 2003, and led his National Front coalition to a resounding win in parliamentary elections Mar. 21, 2004. The Indian Ocean tsunami of Dec. 26 left at least 68 people dead and 8,000 displaced in Malaysia.

Maldives

Republic of Maldives

People: Population: 359,008. **Age distrib.** (%) <15: 43.4; 65+: 3.1. **Pop. density:** 3,094 per sq mi, 1,196 per sq km. **Urban:** 28.8%. **Ethnic groups:** Dravidian, Sinhalese, Arab. **Principal languages:** Divehi (Sinhala dialect, Arabic script; official), English. **Chief religion:** Muslim (official; mostly Sunni).

Geography: Total area: 116 sq mi, 300 sq km; **Land area:** 116 sq mi, 300 sq km. **Location:** In the Indian O., SW of India. **Neighbors:** Nearest is India on N. **Topography:** 19 atolls with 1,190 islands, 198 inhabited. None of the islands are over 5 sq. mi. in area, and all are nearly flat. **Capital:** Male, 89,000.

Government: Type: Republic. **Head of state and gov.:** Pres. Maumoon Abdul Gayoom; b. Dec. 29, 1937; in office: Nov. 11, 1978.

Local divisions: 19 atolls and Male capital atoll. **Defense budget:** $36 mil. **Active troops:** NA.

Economy: Industries: fish proc., tourism, shipping, boat building, coconut proc., garments. **Chief crops:** coconuts, corn, sweet potatoes. **Natural resources:** fish. **Arable land:** 10%. **Fish catch** (2004): 158,576 metric tons. **Electricity prod.** (2004): 150 mil kWh. **Labor force** (1995 est.): agriculture 22%, industry 18%, services 60%.

Finance: Monetary unit: Rufiyaa (MVR) (Sept. 2006: 12.80 = $1 U.S.). **GDP** (2002 est.): $1.3 bil; **per capita GDP:** $3,900; **GDP growth:** -5.5%. **Imports** (2004 est.): $567 mil; partners (2004): Singapore 32.9%, Sri Lanka 11%, India 8.2%, UAE 7.2%, Malaysia 6.4%, Thailand 5.2%. **Exports** (2005 est.): $123 mil; partners (2004): U.S. 40.4%, Thailand 14.6%, Sri Lanka 9.5%, Japan 8.6%, UK 8.2%. **Tourism:** $471 mil. **Budget** (2004 est.): $362 mil. **Intl. reserves less gold:** $130 mil. **Consumer prices:** 3.29%.

Transport: Motor vehicles: 1,900 pass. cars, 1,400 comm. vehicles. **Civil aviation:** 16.2 mil pass.-mi; 2 airports. **Chief ports:** Male, Gan.

Communications: TV sets: 38 per 1,000 pop. **Radios:** 129 per 1,000 pop. **Telephone lines:** 32,300. **Daily newspaper circ.:** NA. **Internet:** 19,000 users.

Health: Life expect.: 63.1 male; 65.8 female. **Births** (per 1,000 pop.): 34.8. **Deaths** (per 1,000 pop.): 7.1. **Natural inc.:** 2.77%. **Infant mortality** (per 1,000 live births): 54.9. **AIDS rate:** NA.

Education: Compulsory: ages 6-12. **Literacy:** 96.3%.

Major Intl. Organizations: UN (FAO, IBRD, IMF, IMO, WHO, WTO), the Commonwealth.

Permanent UN Representative: 800 Second Ave., Ste. 400E, New York, NY 10017; 212-599-6194.

Website: www.maldivesinfo.gov.mv

A British protectorate since 1887, the nation achieved independence July 26, 1965; long a sultanate, the Maldives became a republic in 1968. Tourism and fishing are the most important sectors of the economy. Pres. Gayoom has held power since 1978; political parties are suppressed. The Indian Ocean tsunami of Dec. 26, 2004, killed at least 82 people and displaced more than 21,600 in Maldives. Rising sea levels threaten the country, which comprises at least 1,200 small, low-lying coral islands.

Mali

Republic of Mali

People: Population: 11,680,646. **Age distrib.** (%) <15: 48.1; 65+: 3.1. **Pop. density:** 24 per sq mi, 9 per sq km. **Urban:** 32.3%. **Ethnic groups:** Mande 50% (Bambara, Malinke, Soninke), Peul 17%, Voltaic 12%, Tuareg and Moor 10%, Songhai 6%. **Principal languages:** French (official); Bambara and other African languages. **Chief religions:** Muslim 90%, indigenous beliefs 9%.

Geography: Total area: 478,767 sq mi, 1,240,000 sq km; **Land area:** 471,045 sq mi, 1,220,000 sq km. **Location:** In the interior of W Africa. **Neighbors:** Mauritania, Senegal on W; Guinea, Côte d'Ivoire, Burkina Faso on S; Niger on E; Algeria on N. **Topography:** A landlocked grassy plain in the upper basins of the Senegal and Niger rivers, extending N into the Sahara. **Capital:** Bamako, 1,368,000.

Government: Type: Republic. **Head of state:** Pres. Amadou Toumani Touré; b Nov. 4, 1948; in office: June 8, 2002. **Head of gov.:** Prime Min. Ousmane Issoufi Maïga; b. 1946; in office: Apr. 30, 2004. **Local divisions:** 8 regions, 1 capital district. **Defense budget** (2005): $101 mil. **Active troops:** 7,350.

Economy: Industries: food proc., constr., phosphates, gold. **Chief crops:** cotton, millet, rice, corn, vegetables, peanuts. **Natural resources:** gold, phosphates, kaolin, salt, limestone, uranium, hydropower. **Arable land:** 2%. **Livestock** (2005): cattle: 7.7 mil; chickens: 31 mil; goats: 12.1 mil; pigs: 68,000; sheep: 8.4 mil. **Fish catch** (2004): 101,008 metric tons. **Electricity prod.** (2004): 410 mil kWh. **Labor force** (2001 est.): agriculture 80%, industry and services 20%.

Finance: Monetary unit: CFA BCEAO Franc (XOF) (Sept. 2006: 512.27 = $1 U.S.). **GDP** (2005 est.): $13.6 bil; **per capita GDP:** $1,200; **GDP growth:** 6%. **Imports** (2004 est.): $1.9 bil; partners (2004): France 15.4%, Senegal 7.2%, Côte d'Ivoire 6.6%, Germany 4.1%. **Exports** (2004 est.): $323 mil; partners (2004): China 32%, India 10.3%, Italy 7.6%, Bangladesh 6.8%, Thailand 5.9%, Germany 5.2%, Taiwan 4%. **Tourism:** $130 mil. **Budget** (2002 est.): $828 mil. **Intl. reserves less gold:** $598 mil. **Consumer prices:** 6.4%.

Transport: Railroad: Length: 453 mi. **Motor vehicles:** 18,900 pass. cars, 31,700 comm. vehicles. **Civil aviation** (2001): 80.8 mil pass.-mi; 9 airports. **Chief port:** Koulikoro.

Communications: TV sets: 13 per 1,000 pop. **Radios:** 55 per 1,000 pop. **Telephone lines:** 75,000. **Daily newspaper circ.:** 1.1 per 1,000 pop. **Internet:** 50,000 users.

Health: Life expect.: 47.2 male; 51 female. **Births** (per 1,000 pop.): 49.9. **Deaths** (per 1,000 pop.): 16.9. **Natural inc.:** 3.3%. **Infant mortality** (per 1,000 live births): 107.5. **AIDS rate:** 1.7%.

Education: Compulsory: ages 7-15. **Literacy:** 19%.

Major Intl. Organizations: UN and most of its specialized agencies, AU.

Embassy: 2130 R St. NW 20008; 332-2249.

Website: www.maliembassy.us

Until the 15th cent. the area was part of the great Mali Empire. Timbuktu (Tombouctou) was a center of Islamic study. French rule was secured, 1898. The Sudanese Rep. and Senegal became independent as the Mali Federation June 20, 1960, but Senegal withdrew, and the Sudanese Rep. was renamed Mali.

Mali signed economic agreements with France and, in 1963, with Senegal. A socialist regime led, 1960-68, by Pres. Modibo Keita, was toppled by a coup. Famine struck in 1973-74, killing as many as 100,000 people. Drought conditions returned in the 1980s.

The military, Mar. 26, 1991, overthrew the government of Pres. Moussa Traoré, who had been in power since 1968. Oumar Konare, a coup leader, was elected president, Apr. 26, 1992. A peace accord between the government and a Tuareg rebel group was signed in June 1994. Konare and his party won a series of flawed elections, Apr.-Aug. 1997. Twice condemned to death for crimes committed in office, Traoré had his sentences commuted to life imprisonment in Dec. 1997 and Sept. 1999.

Amadou Toumani Touré, who led the 1991 coup, won a presidential runoff election May 12, 2002.

Malta
Republic of Malta

People: Population: 400,214. **Age distrib.** (%) <15: 17.1; 65+: 13.7. **Pop. density:** 3,280 per sq mi, 1,266 per sq km. **Urban:** 91.7%. **Ethnic group:** Maltesde, other Mediterranean. **Principal languages:** Maltese (a Semitic dialect), English (both official). **Chief religion:** Roman Catholic 98% (official).

Geography: Total area: 122 sq mi, 316 sq km; **Land area:** 122 sq mi, 316 sq km. **Location:** In center of Mediterranean Sea. **Neighbors:** Nearest is Italy on N. **Topography:** Island of Malta is 95 sq. mi.; other islands in the group: Gozo, 26 sq. mi.; Comino, 1 sq. mi. The coastline is heavily indented. Low hills cover the interior. **Capital:** Valletta, 210,000.

Government: Type: Parliamentary democracy. **Head of state:** Pres. Edward (Eddie) Fenech-Adami; b. Feb. 7, 1934; in office: Apr. 4, 2004. **Head of gov.:** Prime Min. Lawrence Gonzi; b. July 1, 1953; in office: Mar. 23, 2004. **Local divisions:** 3 regions comprising 67 local councils. **Defense budget** (2005): $49 mil. **Active troops:** 2,237.

Economy: Industries: tourism, electronics, shipbuilding, food & beverages, textiles. **Chief crops:** potatoes, cauliflower, grapes, wheat, barley, tomatoes, citrus. **Natural resources:** limestone, salt. **Arable land:** 38%. **Livestock** (2005): cattle: 17,900; chickens: 1 mil; goats: 5,400; pigs: 73,000; sheep: 14,900. **Fish catch** (2004): 2,002 metric tons. **Electricity prod.** (2004): 2.3 bil kWh. **Labor force** (2005 est.): agriculture 3%, industry 22%, services 75%.

Finance: Monetary unit: Liri (MTL) (Sept. 2006: 0.34 = $1 U.S.). **GDP** (2005 est.): $7.9 bil; **per capita GDP:** $19,900; **GDP growth:** 1%. **Imports** (2005 est.): $3.9 bil; partners (2004): Italy 18.2%, France 17.9%, UK 9.7%, Germany 9.2%, Singapore 6.9%, China 5.7%. **Exports** (2005 est.): $2.7 bil; partners (2004): Singapore 15.5%, U.S. 12%, France 10.5%, UK 10.1%, Germany 9%, China 5.8%. **Tourism:** $780 mil. **Budget** (2005 est.): $2.7 bil. **Intl. reserves less gold:** $1.8 bil. **Consumer prices:** 3.01%.

Transport: Motor vehicles: 235,900 pass. cars, 54,600 comm. vehicles. **Civil aviation:** 1.4 bil pass.-mi; 1 airport. **Chief ports:** Valletta, Marsaxlokk.

Communications: TV sets: 549 per 1,000 pop. **Radios:** 669 per 1,000 pop. **Telephone lines:** 202,100. **Daily newspaper circ.:** NA. **Internet:** 301,000 users.

Health: Life expect.: 76.8 male; 81.3 female. **Births** (per 1,000 pop.): 10.2. **Deaths** (per 1,000 pop.): 8.1. **Natural inc.:** 0.21%. **Infant mortality** (per 1,000 live births): 3.9. **AIDS rate:** 0.1%.

Education: Compulsory: ages 5-15. **Literacy:** 87.9%.

Major Intl. Organizations: UN (FAO, IBRD, ILO, IMF, IMO, WHO, WTO), the Commonwealth, EU,OSCE.

Embassy: 2017 Connecticut Ave. NW 20008; 462-3611.

Website: www.gov.mt

Malta was ruled by Phoenicians, Romans, Arabs, Normans, the Knights of Malta, France, and Britain (since 1814). It became independent Sept. 21, 1964. Malta became a republic in 1974. The withdrawal of the last British sailors, Apr. 1, 1979, ended 179 years of British military presence on the island.

From 1971 to 1987 and again from 1996 to 1998, Malta was governed by the socialist Labour Party; the Nationalist Party, which pressed for Malta's entry into the EU, held office 1987-96 and won the elections of Sept. 5, 1998, and Apr. 12, 2003. Malta became a full member of the EU May 1, 2004.

Marshall Islands
Republic of the Marshall Islands

People: Population: 60,422. **Age distrib.** (%) <15: 38.1; 65+: 2.7. **Pop. density:** 863 per sq mi, 333 per sq km. **Urban:** 66.3%. **Ethnic groups:** Micronesian. **Principal languages:** English, Marshallese (both official); Malay-Polynesian dialects, Japanese. **Chief religion:** Protestant 55%, Assembly of God 26%.

Geography: Total area: 70 sq mi, 181 sq km; **Land area:** 70 sq mi, 181 sq km. **Location:** In N Pacific Ocean; composed of two 800-mi-long parallel chains of coral atolls. **Neighbors:** Nearest are Micronesia to W, Nauru and Kiribati to S. **Topography:** Marshall Islands are low coral limestone and sand islands. **Capital** (2003): Majuro, 25,000.

Government: Type: Republic. **Head of state and gov.:** Pres. Kessai Note; b. Aug. 7, 1950; in office: Jan. 10, 2000. **Local divisions:** 33 municipalities.

Economy: Industries: copra, fish, tourism, handicrafts, wood, pearls. **Chief crops:** coconuts, tomatoes, melons, taro, breadfruit, fruits. **Natural resources:** fish, minerals. **Fish catch** (2004): 47,172 metric tons. **Labor force:** agriculture 21.4%, industry 20.9%, services 57.7%.

Finance: Monetary unit: U.S. Dollar. **GDP**(2001 est.): $115 mil; **per capita GDP:** $2,300; **GDP growth:** 1%. **Imports** (2000 est.): $54.7 mil; partners (2000): US, Japan, Australia, NZ, Singapore, Fiji, China, Philippines. **Exports** (2000 est.): $9.1 mil; partners (2000): US, Japan, Australia, China. **Tourism** (2002): $4 mil. **Budget** (1999): $40 mil.

Transport: Civil aviation: 19.9 mil pass.-mi; 4 airports. **Chief port:** Majuro.

Communications: Telephone lines: 4,500. **Internet:** 2,000 users.

Health: Life expect.: 68.3 male; 72.4 female. **Births** (per 1,000 pop.): 33. **Deaths** (per 1,000 pop.): 4.8. **Natural inc.:** 2.83%. **Infant mortality** (per 1,000 live births): 28.4. **AIDS rate:** NA.

Education: Compulsory: ages 6-14. **Literacy:** (93.7%.

Major Intl. Organizations: UN (FAO, IBRD, IMF, IMO, WHO).

Embassy: 2433 Massachusetts Ave. NW 20008; 234-5414.

Website: www.rmiembassyus.org

The Marshall Islands were a German possession until WWI and were administered by Japan between the World Wars. After WWII, they were administered as part of the UN Trust Territory of the Pacific Islands by the U.S. From 1946-58, Bikini and Enewetak atolls were used as test sites for the U.S. nuclear weapons program, including the hydrogen bomb.

The Compact of Free Association, ratified by the U.S. on Oct. 21, 1986, gave the islands their independence. In the compact, the U.S. agreed to provide financial aid to the islands, maintain their defense, and compensate victims of nuclear testing; it was renewed Dec. 2003. The Marshall Islands joined the UN Sept. 17, 1991. Amata Kabua, the islands' first and only president since 1979, died Dec. 19, 1996. His cousin Imata Kabua, elected president Jan. 13, 1997, was succeeded by Kessai Note on Jan. 10, 2000; he began a 2nd term Jan. 5, 2004.

Mauritania
Islamic Republic of Mauritania

People: Population: 3,177,388. **Age distrib.** (%) <15: 45.6; 65+: 2.2. **Pop. density:** 7 per sq mi, 3 per sq km. **Urban:** 61.8%. **Ethnic groups:** Mixed Maur/Black 40%, Maur 30%, Black 30%. **Principal languages:** Hassaniya Arabic, Wolof (both official); Fulani, Pulaar, Soninke (all national); French. **Chief religion:** Predominantly Muslim (official). inti bbls

Geography: Total area: 397,956 sq mi, 1,030,700 sq km; **Land area:** 397,840 sq mi, 1,030,400 sq km. **Location:** In NW Africa. **Neighbors:** Morocco on N, Algeria and Mali on E, Senegal on S. **Topography:** The fertile Senegal R. valley in the S gives way to a wide central region of sandy plains and scrub trees. The N is arid and extends into the Sahara. **Capital:** Nouakchott, 637,000.

Government: Type: In transition. **Head of state:** Col. Ely Ould Mohamed Vall; b. 1952; in office: Aug. 3, 2005. **Head of gov.:** Prime Min. Sidi Mohamed Ould Boubacar; b. May 31, 1957; in office: Aug. 7, 2005. **Local divisions:** 12 regions, 1 capital district. **Defense budget** (2005): $20 mil. **Active troops:** 15,870.

Economy: Industries: fish production, iron ore, gypsum. **Chief crops:** dates, millet, sorghum, rice, corn. **Natural resources:** iron ore, gypsum, copper, phosphate, diamonds, gold, oil, fish. **Livestock** (2005): cattle: 1.6 mil; chickens: 4.2 mil; goats: 5.6 mil; sheep: 8.9 mil. **Fish catch** (2004): 199,380 metric tons. **Electricity prod.** (2004): 180 bil kWh. **Labor force** (2001 est.): agriculture 50%, industry 10%, services 40%.

Finance: Monetary unit: Ouguiya (MRO) (Sept. 2006: 266.60 = $1 U.S.). **GDP** (2005 est.): $6.9 bil; **per capita GDP:** $2,200; **GDP growth:** 5.5%. **Imports** (2004 est.): $1.1 bil; partners (2004): France 14.5%, U.S. 7.7%, China 7.4%, Spain 5.9%, Belgium 4.3%, UK 4.3%. **Exports** (2004 est.): $784 mil; partners (2004): Japan 13%, France 10.9%, Spain 9.6%, Italy 9.5%, Germany 8.7%, Belgium 7.4%, China 5.8%, Russia 4.8%. **Tourism** (1995): $11 mil. **Budget** (2002 est.): $378 mil. **Gold** (2003): 10,000 oz t. **Consumer prices:** 12.13%.

Transport: Railroad: Length: 446 mi. **Motor vehicles:** 12,200 pass. cars, 18,200 comm. vehicles. **Civil aviation:** 28 mil pass.-mi; 8 airports. **Chief ports:** Nouakchott, Nouadhibou.

Communications: TV sets: 95 per 1,000 pop. **Radios:** 146 per 1,000 pop. **Telephone lines:** 39,000. **Daily newspaper circ.:** NA. **Internet:** 14,000 users.

Health: Life expect.: 50.9 male; 55.4 female. **Births** (per 1,000 pop.): 41. **Deaths** (per 1,000 pop.): 12.2. **Natural inc.:** 2.88%. **Infant mortality** (per 1,000 live births): 69.5. **AIDS rate:** 0.7%.

Education: Compulsory: ages 6-14. **Literacy:** 51.2%.

Major Intl. Organizations: UN (FAO, IBRD, ILO, IMF, IMO, WHO, WTO), AL, AU.

Embassy: 2129 Leroy Pl. NW 20008; 232-5700.

Website: www.mauritania.mr

Mauritania was a French protectorate from 1903. It became independent Nov. 28, 1960 and annexed the south of former Spanish Sahara (now Western Sahara) in 1976. Saharan guerrillas of the Polisario Front stepped up attacks in 1977; 8,000 Moroccan troops and French bomber raids aided the government. Mauritania signed a peace treaty with the Polisario Front, 1979, and renounced sovereignty over its share of Western Sahara.

Maaouiya Ould Sid Ahmed Taya took power in a military coup in 1984. Taya, a U.S. ally, was toppled in a bloodless coup, Aug. 3, 2005. Voters approved a new constitution limiting presidential powers, June 25, 2006. Major oil finds have recently been developed.

Although slavery has been repeatedly abolished, most recently in 1980, thousands of Mauritanians continued to live under conditions of servitude. During Jan.-June 2006, up to 10,000 people tried to emigrate in handmade boats from Mauritania to Spain's Canary Islands; more than 1,700 died.

Mauritius
Republic of Mauritius

People: Population: 1,240,827. **Age distrib.** (%) <15: 23.9; 65+: 6.6. **Pop. density:** 1,582 per sq mi, 611 per sq km. **Urban:** 43.3%. **Ethnic groups:** Indo-Mauritian 68%, Creole 27%, Sino-Mauritian 3%, Franco-Mauritian 2%. **Principal languages:** English (official), Creole, French, Hindi, Urdu, Hakka, Bhojpuri. **Chief religions:** Hindu 48%, Roman Catholic 24%, Muslim 17%.

Geography: Total area: 788 sq mi, 2,040 sq km; **Land area:** 784 sq mi, 2,030 sq km. **Location:** In the Indian O., 500 mi. E of Madagascar. **Neighbors:** Nearest is Madagascar to W. **Topography:** A volcanic island nearly surrounded by coral reefs. A central plateau is encircled by mountain peaks. **Capital:** Port Louis, 146,000.

Government: Type: Republic. **Head of state:** Pres. Anerood Jugnauth; b. Mar. 29, 1930; in office: Oct. 7, 2003. **Head of gov.:** Prime Min. Navin Ramgoolam; b. July 1947; in office: July 5, 2005. **Local divisions:** 9 districts, 3 dependencies. **Defense budget** (2005): $21.4 mil. **Active troops:** None.

Economy: Industries: sugar & food proc., textiles, clothing, chemicals. **Chief crops:** sugarcane, tea, corn, potatoes, bananas. **Natural resources:** fish. **Arable land:** 49%. **Livestock** (2005): cattle: 28,000; chickens: 9.8 mil; goats: 93,000; pigs: 12,925; sheep: 11,500. **Fish catch** (2004): 10,577 metric tons. **Electricity prod.** (2004): 2.1 bil kWh. **Labor force** (1995): agriculture and fishing 14%, construction and industry 36%, transportation and communication 7%, trade, restaurants, hotels 16%, finance 3%, other services 24%.

Finance: Monetary unit: Rupee (MUR) (Sept. 2006: 32.90 = $1 U.S.). **GDP** (2005 est.): $16.1 bil; **per capita GDP:** $13,100; **GDP growth:** 3%. **Imports** (2005 est.): $2.5 bil; partners (2004): France 13.1%, South Africa 10.8%, India 7.6%, China 5.9%, Germany 4.5%, Singapore 4%. **Exports** (2005 est.): $1.9 bil; partners (2004): UK 30.6%, France 22.7%, U.S. 13.7%, Madagascar 7.7%. **Tourism:** $856 mil. **Budget** (2005 est.): $1.8 bil. **Intl. reserves less gold:** $937 mil. **Gold:** 60,000 oz t. **Consumer prices:** 4.91%.

Transport: Motor vehicles: 105,300 pass. cars, 39,300 comm. vehicles. **Civil aviation:** 3.2 bil pass.-mi; 2 airports. **Chief port:** Port Louis.

Communications: TV sets: 248 per 1,000 pop. **Radios:** 371 per 1,000 pop. **Telephone lines:** 359,000. **Daily newspaper circ.:** NA. **Internet:** 180,000 users.

Health: Life expect.: 68.7 male; 76.7 female. **Births** (per 1,000 pop.): 15.4. **Deaths** (per 1,000 pop.): 6.9. **Natural inc.:** 0.86%. **Infant mortality** (per 1,000 live births): 14.6. **AIDS rate:** 0.6%.

Education: Compulsory: ages 6-11. **Literacy:** 84.4%.

Major Intl. Organizations: UN and all of its specialized agencies, the Commonwealth, AU.

Embassy: 4301 Connecticut Ave. NW, Suite 441, 20008; 244-1491.

Website: www.gov.mu

Mauritius was uninhabited when settled in 1638 by the Dutch, who introduced sugarcane. France took over in 1721, bringing African slaves. Britain ruled from 1810 to Mar. 12, 1968, bringing Indian workers for the sugar plantations.

Mauritius formally severed its association with the British crown Mar. 12, 1992.

Mexico
United Mexican States

People: Population: 107,449,525. **Age distrib.** (%) <15: 30.6; 65+: 5.8. **Pop. density:** 144 per sq mi, 55 per sq km. **Urban:** 75.5%. **Ethnic groups:** Mestizo 60%, Amerindian 30%, White 9%. **Principal languages:** Spanish (official), Náhuatl, Maya, Zapotec, Otomi, Mixtec, other indigenous. **Chief religions:** Roman Catholic 89%, Protestant 6%.

Geography: Total area: 761,606 sq mi, 1,972,550 sq km; **Land area:** 742,490 sq mi, 1,923,040 sq km. **Location:** In southern North America. **Neighbors:** U.S. on N, Guatemala and Belize on S. **Topography:** The Sierra Madre Occidental Mts. run NW-SE near the west coast; the Sierra Madre Oriental Mts. run near the Gulf of Mexico. They join S of Mexico City. Between the 2 ranges lies the dry central plateau, 5,000 to 8,000 ft. alt., rising toward the S, with temperate vegetation. Coastal lowlands are tropical. About 45% of land is arid. **Capital:** Mexico City, 19,411,000. **Cities (urban aggr.):** Guadalajara, 3,968,000 Monterrey, 3,596,000; Puebla, 1,824,000.

Government: Type: Federal republic. **Head of state and gov.:** Pres. Vicente Fox Quesada; b. July 2, 1942; in office: Dec. 1, 2000. **Local divisions:** 31 states, 1 federal district. **Defense budget** (2005): $3.1 bil. **Active troops:** 192,770.

Economy: Industries: food & beverages, tobacco, chemicals, iron & steel, oil, mining, textiles, clothing, autos, consumer durables, tourism. **Chief crops:** corn, wheat, soybeans, rice, beans, cotton, coffee, fruit, tomatoes. **Natural resources:** oil, silver, copper, gold, lead, zinc, nat. gas, timber. **Crude oil reserves** (2005): 14.8 bil bbls. **Arable land:** 12%. **Livestock** (2005): cattle: 31.5 mil; chickens: 425 mil; goats: 9 mil; pigs: 14.6 mil; sheep: 6.8 mil. **Fish catch** (2004): 1,539,100 metric tons. **Electricity prod.** (2005): 242.4 bil kWh. **Labor force** (2003): agriculture 18%, industry 24%, services 58%.

Finance: Monetary unit: Pesos (MXN) (Sept. 2006: 11.07 = $1 U.S.). **GDP** (2005 est.): $1.1 tril; **per capita GDP:** $10,000; **GDP growth:** 3%. **Imports** (2005 est.): $223.7 bil; partners (2004): U.S. 65.8%, Germany 3.8%, China 3.7%. **Exports** (2005 est.): $213.7 bil; partners (2004): U.S. 81%, Canada 5.9%, Japan 1.1%. **Tourism:** $10.8 bil. **Budget** (2005): $184 bil. **Intl. reserves less gold:** $51.81 bil. **Gold:** 110,000 oz t. **Consumer prices:** 3.99%.

Transport: Railroad: Length: 10,957 mi. **Motor vehicles:** 13.37 mil pass. cars, 6.29 mil comm. vehicles. **Civil aviation:** 17.6 bil pass.-mi; 228 airports. **Chief ports:** Coatzacoalcos, Mazatlan, Tampico, Veracruz.

Communications: TV sets: 272 per 1,000 pop. **Radios:** 329 per 1,000 pop. **Telephone lines:** 19.5 mil. **Daily newspaper circ.:** 93.5 per 1,000 pop. **Internet:** 17 mil users.

Health: Life expect.: 72.6 male; 78.3 female. **Births** (per 1,000 pop.): 20.7. **Deaths** (per 1,000 pop.): 4.7. **Natural inc.:** 1.59%. **Infant mortality** (per 1,000 live births): 20.3. **AIDS rate:** 0.3%.

Education: Compulsory: ages 6-15. **Literacy:** 91%.

Major Intl. Organizations: UN (FAO, IBRD, ILO, IMF, IMO, WHO, WTO), APEC, OAS, OECD.

Embassy: 1911 Pennsylvania Ave. NW 20006; 728-1600.

Website: www.presidencia.gob.mx

Mexico was the site of advanced Indian civilizations. The Mayas, an agricultural people, moved up from Yucatan, built immense stone pyramids, and invented a calendar. The Toltecs were overcome by the Aztecs, who founded Tenochtitlan 1325 CE, now Mexico City. Hernán Cortés, Spanish conquistador, destroyed the Aztec empire, 1519-21. After 3 centuries of Spanish rule the people rose, under Fr. Miguel Hidalgo y Costilla, 1810, Fr. Morelos y Pavón, 1812, and Gen. Agustín Iturbide, who made himself emperor as Agustín I, 1821. A republic was declared in 1823.

Mexican territory extended into the present American Southwest and California until Texas revolted and established a republic in 1836; the Mexican legislature refused recognition but was unable to enforce its authority there. After numerous clashes, the U.S.-Mexican War, 1846-48, resulted in the loss by Mexico of the lands north of the Rio Grande.

French arms supported an Austrian archduke on the throne of Mexico as Maximilian I, 1864-67, but pressure from the U.S. forced France to withdraw. Dictatorial rule by Porfirio Díaz, president 1877-80, 1884-1911, led to a period of rebellion and factional fighting. A new constitution, Feb. 5, 1917, brought social reform.

The Institutional Revolutionary Party (PRI) dominated politics from 1929 until the late 1990s. Radical opposition, including some guerrilla activity, was contained by strong measures. Some gains in agriculture, industry, and social services were achieved, but much of the work force remained jobless or underemployed. Although prospects brightened with the discovery of vast oil reserves, inflation and a drop in world oil prices aggravated Mexico's economic problems in the 1980s. Mexico reached agreement with the U.S. and Canada on the North American Free Trade Agreement (NAFTA) Aug. 12, 1992; it took effect Jan. 1, 1994.

Guerrillas of the Zapatista National Liberation Army (EZLN) launched an uprising, Jan. 1, 1994, in southern Mexico. A tentative peace accord was reached Mar. 2. The presidential candidate of the governing PRI, Luis Donaldo Colosio Murrieta, was assassinated at a political rally in Tijuana, Mar. 23. The new PRI candidate, Ernesto Zedillo Ponce de León, won election Aug. 21 and was inaugurated Dec. 1, 1994.

An austerity plan and pledges of aid from the U.S. saved Mexico's currency from collapse in early 1995. Popular Revolutionary Army guerrillas launched coordinated attacks on government targets in Aug. 1996. In elections July 6, 1997, the PRI failed to win a congressional majority for the first time since 1929. An armed gang massacred 45 peasants in Chiapas on Dec. 22, 1997.

In the presidential election of July 2, 2000, the PRI lost for the first time in over 7 decades; the winner, opposition candidate Vicente Fox Quesada, took office Dec. 1, 2000. Fox's National Action Party (PAN) suffered a setback in midterm elections, July 6, 2003. Hurricane Wilma hit Cancún Oct. 21, 2005, causing $2 bil damage.

Results of the July 2, 2006, presidential vote gave the PAN candidate, conservative Felipe Calderón Hinojosa, a slim margin over former Mexico City mayor Andrés Manuel López Obrador, nominee of the leftist Democratic Revolutionary Party. The Federal Electoral Tribunal proclaimed Calderón the winner Sept. 5, but López Obrador and his supporters continued to challenge the outcome.

Micronesia
Federated States of Micronesia

People: Population: 108,004. **Age distrib.** (%) <15: 36.6; 65+: 3. **Pop. density:** 398 per sq mi, 153 per sq km. **Urban:** 29.3%. **Ethnic groups:** Nine distinct Micronesian and Polynesian groups. **Principal languages:** English (official), Trukese, Pohnpeian, Yapese, Kosrean, Ulithian, Woleaian, Nukuoro, Kapingamaran. **Chief religions:** Roman Catholic 50%, Protestant 47%.

Geography: Total area: 271 sq mi, 702 sq km; **Land area:** 271 sq mi, 702 sq km. **Location:** Consists of 607 islands in the W Pacific Ocean. **Topography:** The country includes both high mountainous islands and low coral atolls; volcanic outcroppings on Pohnpei, Kosrae, and Truk. Climate is tropical. **Capital:** Palikir, on Pohnpei, 7,000 (1994 island pop.) 33,372.

Government: Type: Republic. **Head of state and gov.:** Pres. Joseph J. Urusemal; b Mar. 19, 1952; in office: May 11, 2003. **Local divisions:** 4 states.

Economy: Industries: tourism, constr., fish proc., handicrafts. **Chief crops:** black pepper, fruits & vegetables, coconuts, cassava, sweet potatoes. **Natural resources:** timber, fish, minerals. **Livestock** (2005): cattle: 13,900; chickens: 185,000; goats: 4,000; pigs: 32,000. **Fish catch** (2004): 29,234 metric tons. **Labor force:** two-thirds are government employees.

Finance: Monetary unit: U.S. Dollar (USD) (Sept. 2006: 1.00 = $1 U.S.); **per capita GDP:** $3,900; **GDP growth:** 1%. **Imports** (FY99/00 est.): $82.5 mil; partners (2000): US, Australia, Japan. **Exports** (FY99/00 est.): $22 mil; partners (2000): Japan, US, Guam. **Tourism** (2003): $17 mil. **Budget** (1998 est.): $160 mil. **Intl. reserves less gold:** $35 mil.

Transport: Civil aviation: NA; 6 airports. **Chief ports:** Colonia (Yap), Kolonia (Pohnpei), Lele, Moen.

Communications: TV sets: 20 per 1,000 pop. **Radios:** 70 per 1,000 pop. **Telephone lines:** 12,000. **Internet:** 12,000 users.

Health: Life expect.: 68.2 male; 72 female. **Births** (per 1,000 pop.): 24.7. **Deaths** (per 1,000 pop.): 4.8. **Natural inc.:** 1.99%. **Infant mortality** (per 1,000 live births): 29.2. **AIDS rate:** NA.

Education: Compulsory: ages 6-13. **Literacy:** 89%.

Major Intl. Organizations: UN (FAO, IBRD, IMF, WHO).

Embassy: 1725 N St. NW 20036; 223-4383.

Website: www.fsmgov.org

The Federated States of Micronesia, formerly known as the Caroline Islands, was ruled successively by Spain, Germany, Japan, and the U.S. The nation gained independence under a compact of free association with the U.S., Nov. 1986 and was admitted to the UN, Sept. 17, 1991. Tropical Storm Chata'an July 1-2, 2002, left 47 people dead and over 1,000 homeless in Chuuk. Typhoon Sudal battered Yap Apr. 9, 2004, leaving at least 1,500 homeless.

Moldova
Republic of Moldova

People: Population: 4,325,682. **Age distrib.** (%) <15: 17; 65+: 10.7. **Pop. density:** 128 per sq mi, 332 per sq km. **Urban:** 46.0%. **Ethnic groups:** Moldovan/Romanian 65%, Ukrainian 14%, Russian 13%. **Principal languages:** Moldovan (official,), Russian, Gagauz (a Turkish dialect). **Chief religion:** Eastern Orthodox 98%.

Geography: Total area: 13,067 sq mi, 33,843 sq km; **Land area:** 12,885 sq mi, 33,371 sq km. **Location:** In E Europe. **Neighbors:** Romania on W; Ukraine on N, E, and S. **Topography:** The country is landlocked; mainly hilly plains, with steppelands in S near the Black Sea. **Capital:** Chisinau, 598,000.

Government: Type: Republic. **Head of state:** Pres. Vladimir Voronin; b. May 25, 1941; in office: Apr. 7, 2001. **Head of gov.:** Prime Min. Vasile Tarlev; b. Oct. 9, 1963; in office: Apr. 19, 2001. **Local divisions:** 9 counties, 1 municipality, 1 autonomous territory. **Defense budget** (2005): $9.2 mil. **Active troops:** 6,750.

Economy: Industries: food proc., agric. machinery, foundry equip. **Chief crops:** vegetables, grapes, grain, sunflower seed, tobacco. **Natural resources:** lignite, phosphorite, gypsum, limestone. **Arable land:** 53%. **Livestock** (2005): cattle: 331,000; chickens: 17.4 mil; goats: 119,000; pigs: 397,000; sheep: 823,000. **Fish catch** (2004): 4,957 metric tons. **Electricity prod.** (2004): 3.5 bil kWh. **Labor force** (1998): agriculture 40%, industry 14%, services 46%.

Finance: Monetary unit: Leu (MDL) (Sept. 2006: 13.29 = $1 U.S.). **GDP** (2005 est.): $8.2 bil; **per capita GDP:** $1,800; **GDP growth:** 7.1%. **Imports** (2005 est.): $2.2 bil; partners (2004): Ukraine 16.8%, Russia 14.7%, Germany 12.5%, France 9.9%, Italy 8%, Romania 5.3%. **Exports** (2005 est.): $1 bil; partners (2004): Russia 31.4%, Italy 10.7%, Germany 9.5%, Romania 9.4%, France 6.9%, Ukraine 5.8%, Belarus 4.3%. **Tourism:** $113 mil. **Budget** (2005 est.): $1.1 bil. **Intl. reserves less gold:** $418 mil. **Consumer prices:** 13.11%.

Transport: Railroad: Length: 707 mi. **Motor vehicles:** 268,900 pass. cars, 57,000 comm. vehicles. **Civil aviation:** 100 mil pass.-mi; 6 airports.

Communications: TV sets: 297 per 1,000 pop. **Radios:** 742 per 1,000 pop. **Telephone lines:** 929,400. **Daily newspaper circ.:** NA. **Internet:** 406,000 users.

Health: Life expect.: 66.2 male; 73.8 female. **Births** (per 1,000 pop.): 10.7. **Deaths** (per 1,000 pop.): 10.9. **Natural inc.:** −0.02%. **Infant mortality** (per 1,000 live births): 14.3. **AIDS rate:** 1.1%.

Education: Compulsory: ages 7-16. **Literacy:** 98.4%.

Major Intl. Organizations: UN (FAO, IBRD, ILO, IMF, IMO, WHO, WTO), CIS, OSCE.

Embassy: 2101 S St. NW 20008; 667-1130.

Website: www.moldova.org

In 1918, Romania annexed all of Bessarabia that Russia had acquired from Turkey in 1812 by the Treaty of Bucharest. In 1924, the Soviet Union established the Moldavian Autonomous Soviet Socialist Republic on the eastern bank of the Dniester. It was merged with the Romanian-speaking districts of Bessarabia in 1940 to form the Moldavian SSR.

During WWII, Romania, allied with Germany, occupied the area. It was recaptured by the USSR in 1944. Moldova declared independence Aug. 27, 1991. It became an independent state when the USSR disbanded Dec. 26, 1991.

Fighting erupted Mar. 1992 in the Trans-Dniester region between Moldovan security forces and Slavic separatists—ethnic Russians and ethnic Ukrainians—who feared Moldova would merge with neighboring Romania. In a plebiscite on Mar. 6, 1994, voters in Moldova supported independence, without unification with Romania.

Defying the Moldovan government, voters in the breakaway Trans-Dniester region held legislative elections and approved a separatist constitution Dec. 24, 1995. A peace accord with Trans-Dniester separatists was signed in Moscow May 8, 1997.

Communists won the most seats in Moldovan parliamentary elections Mar. 22, 1998, but a coalition of three center-right parties formed the government. The Communists gained legislative majorities in elections Feb. 25, 2001, and Mar. 6, 2005. In a referendum Sept. 17, 2006, Trans-Dniester voters overwhelmingly supported independence from Moldova and eventual union with Russia.

Monaco
Principality of Monaco

People: Population: 32,543. **Age distrib.** (%) <15: 15.2; 65+: 22.6. **Pop. density:** 32543 per sq mi, 16271 per sq km. **Urban:** 100.0%. **Ethnic groups:** French 47%, Monegasque 16%, Italian 16%. **Principal languages:** French (official), English, Italian, Monegasque. **Chief religion:** Roman Catholic 90% (official).

Geography: Total area: <1 sq mi, 2 sq km; **Land area:** <1 sq mi, 2 sq km. **Location:** On the NW Mediterranean coast. **Neighbors:** France to W, N, E. **Topography:** Monaco-Ville sits atop a high promontory, the rest of the principality rises from the port up the hillside. **Capital** (2003): Monaco-ville, 34,000.

Government: Type: Constitutional monarchy. **Head of state:** Prince Albert II; b. Mar. 14, 1958; in office: Apr. 6, 2005. **Head of gov.:** Min. of State Jean-Paul Proust; b. Mar. 3, 1940; in office: June 1, 2005. **Local divisions:** 4 quarters.

Economy: Industries: tourism, constr., light industrial products. **Chief crops:** none. **Natural resources:** none. **Fish catch** (2004): 3 metric tons.

Finance: Monetary unit: Euro (EUR) (Sept. 2006: 0.78 = $1 U.S.). **GDP** (2000 est.): $870 mil; **per capita GDP:** $27,000; **GDP growth:** 0.9%. **Tourism:** NA. **Budget** (2004): $864.1 mil.

Transport: Railroad: Length: 1 mi. **Motor vehicles:** 17,000 pass. cars, 4,000 comm. vehicles. **Civil aviation:** 4.3 mil pass.-mi; NA. **Chief port:** Monaco.

Communications: TV sets: 758 per 1,000 pop. **Radios:** 1,030 per 1,000 pop. **Daily newspaper circ.:** NA. **Internet** (2002): 16,000 users.

Health: Life expect.: 75.8 male; 83.7 female. **Births** (per 1,000 pop.): 9.2. **Deaths** (per 1,000 pop.): 12.9. **Natural inc.:** −0.37%. **Infant mortality** (per 1,000 live births): 5.3. **AIDS rate:** NA.

Education: Compulsory: ages 6-16. **Literacy:** 99%.

Major Intl. Organizations: UN (FAO, IMO, WHO), OSCE.

Consulate General: 565 Fifth Ave., 23rd Fl. New York, NY 10017; (212) 286-0500.

Website: www.gouv.mc

An independent principality for over 300 years, Monaco has belonged to the House of Grimaldi since 1297, except during the French Revolution. It was placed under the protectorate of Sardinia in 1815, and under France, 1861. The Prince of Monaco was an absolute ruler until the 1911 constitution. Monaco was admitted to the UN on May 28, 1993.

Monaco is noted for its mild climate, magnificent scenery, and elegant casinos. Prince Rainier III, who ruled Monaco, 1949-2005, and turned it into one of Europe's top tourist spots, died Apr. 6 and was succeeded by his son, Albert II.

Mongolia

People: Population: 2,832,224. **Age distrib.** (%) <15: 27.9; 65+: 3.7. **Pop. density:** 4 per sq mi, 1 per sq km. **Urban:** 56.7%. **Ethnic groups:** Mongol 85%, Turkic 7%, Tungusic 5%. **Principal languages:** Khalkha Mongol, Turkic, Russian. **Chief religion:** Tibetan Buddhist Lamaism 50%, none 40%.

Geography: Total area: 603,909 sq mi, 1,564,116 sq km; **Location:** In E Central Asia. **Neighbors:** Russia on N, China on E, W, and S. **Topography:** Mostly a high plateau with mountains, salt lakes, and vast grasslands. Arid lands in the S are part of the Gobi Desert. **Capital:** Ulaanbaatar, 863,000.

Government: Type: Republic. **Head of state:** Pres. Nambaryn Enkhbayar; b. June 1, 1958; in office: June 24, 2005. **Head of gov.:** Prime. Min. Miyeegombo Enkhbold; b. 1964; in office: Jan. 25,

2006. **Local divisions:** 18 provinces, 3 municipalities. **Defense budget** (2005): $17.6 mil. **Active troops:** 8,600.

Economy: Industries: constr. materials, mining, oil, food, beverages. **Chief crops:** wheat, barley, potatoes, forage crops. **Natural resources:** oil, coal, copper, molybd., tungsten, phosphates, tin, nickel, zinc, fluorspar, gold, silver, iron. **Arable land:** 1%. **Livestock** (2005): cattle: 1.8 mil; chickens: 30,000; goats: 12.2 mil; pigs: 6,000; sheep: 11.7 mil. **Fish catch** (2004): 305 metric tons. **Electricity prod.** (2004): 3.8 bil kWh. **Labor force** (2003): herding/agriculture 42%, mining 4%, manufacturing 6%, trade 14%, services 29%, public sector 5%, other 3.7%.

Finance: Monetary unit: Tughrik (MNT) (Sept. 2006: 1,167.00 = $1 U.S.). **GDP**(2005 est.): $5.2 bil; **per capita GDP:** $1,900; **GDP growth:** 6.2%. **Imports** (2004 est.): $1 bil; partners (2004): Russia 31%, China 23.1%, Japan 8.4%, South Korea 6.7%. **Exports** (2004 est.): $852 mil; partners (2004): China 50.7%, U.S. 26.3%, Canada 5.3%, UK 4.3%, Russia 4.2%. **Tourism:** $185 mil. **Budget** (2005 est.): $651 mil. **Intl. reserves less gold:** $301 mil. **Consumer prices:** 12.72%.

Transport: Railroad: Length: 1,125 mi. **Motor vehicles:** 21,000 pass. cars, 27,000 comm. vehicles. **Civil aviation:** 410.7 mil pass.-mi; 12 airports.

Communications: TV sets: 58 per 1,000 pop. **Radios:** 142 per 1,000 pop. **Telephone lines:** 156,000. **Daily newspaper circ.:** 17.6 per 1,000 pop. **Internet:** 200,000 users.

Health: Life expect.: 62.6 male; 67.2 female. **Births** (per 1,000 pop.): 21.6. **Deaths** (per 1,000 pop.): 7. **Natural inc.:** 1.46%. **Infant mortality** (per 1,000 live births): 52.1. **AIDS rate:** <0.1%.

Education: Compulsory: ages 8-15. **Literacy:** 97.8%.

Major Intl. Organizations: UN (FAO, IBRD, ILO, IMF, IMO, WHO, WTO).

Embassy: 2833 M St. NW 20007; 333-7117.

Website: www.pmis.gov.mn

One of the world's oldest countries, Mongolia reached the zenith of its power in the 13th cent. when Genghis Khan and his successors conquered all of China and extended their influence as far west as Hungary and Poland. In later centuries, the empire dissolved and Mongolia became a province of China.

With the advent of the 1911 Chinese revolution, Mongolia, with Russian backing, declared its independence. A Communist regime was established July 11, 1921.

In 1990, the Mongolian Communist Party yielded its monopoly on power but won election in July. A new constitution took effect Feb. 12, 1992. Natsagiyn Bagabandi, a former Communist, won the presidential election of May 18, 1997. A protracted political crisis took a violent turn Oct. 2, 1998, with the murder of Sanjaasuregiyn Zorig, a popular cabinet member seeking to become prime minister. Pres. Bagabandi was reelected May 20, 2001. Nambaryn Enkhbayar, a former prime minister (2000-04), won the presidential election of May 22, 2005.

Mongolia contributed troops to U.S.-led operations in Afghanistan and Iraq. On Nov. 21, 2005, Pres. George W. Bush became the first sitting U.S. president to visit Mongolia.

Montenegro
Republic of Montenegro

People: Population: (2004 est.) 691,871. **Age distrib.** NA. **Pop. density:** 50 per sq mi, 129 per sq km. **Urban:** NA. **Ethnic groups:** Montenegrin 43%, Serbian 32%, Bosniak 8%, Albanian 5%. **Principal languages:** Serbian (official). **Chief religions:** Orthodox, Muslim, Roman Catholic.

Geography: Total area: 5,415 sq mi, 14,026 sq km; **Land area:** 5,333 sq mi; 13,812 sq km. **Location:** On the Balkan Peninsula in SE Europe. **Neighbors:** Bosnia and Herzegovina on N and W; Serbia on E; Albania on SE; Adriatic Sea on SW; Croatia on W. **Topography:** Most terrain is rugged and mountainous, with few arable regions, mostly along the Zeta R.; the narrow coastline is highly indented. **Capital** (2003): Podgorica (administrative), 139,724; Cetinje (official).

Government: Type: Republic. **Head of state:** Pres. Filip Vujanovic; b. Sept. 1, 1954; in office: May 22, 2003. **Head of gov.** Prime. Min. Milo Djukanovic; b. Feb. 15, 1962; in office: Jan. 8, 2003. **Local divisions:** 21 municipalities. **Defense budget:** NA. **Active troops:** NA.

Economy: Industries: aluminum, steel, consumer goods, tourism, agriculture, animal husbandry. **Chief crops:** cereals, tobacco, potatoes, plums, citrus, olives, grapes. **Natural resources:** lignite, bauxite, hydropower, sea salt. **Livestock** (2005): cattle: 169,000; chickens: 800,000; sheep: 254,000. **Fish catch** (2005): 1,236 metric tons. **Electricity prod.** (2005): 2.9 bil kWh.

Finance: Monetary unit: Euro (EUR) (Sept. 2006: 0.78 = $1 U.S.). **GDP** (2005 est.): $1.1 bil; **per capita GDP:** $3,800; **GDP growth:** NA. **Imports** (2003): $601.7 mil; partners: Italy 12.2%, Greece 10.2%, Germany 9.6%, Bosnia and Herzegovina 9.2%. **Exports** (2003): $171.3 mil; partners: Switzerland 83.9%, Italy 6.1%, Bosnia and Herzegovina 1.3%. **Tourism:** NA. **Budget:** NA.

Transport: Railroad: Length: 155 mi. **Motor vehicles:** NA. **Civil aviation:** NA; 3 airports. **Chief port:** Bar.

Communications: TV sets: NA. **Radios:** NA. **Telephone lines:** 178,000. **Daily newspaper circ.:** NA. **Internet** (2004): 50,000 users.

Health: Life expect.: 73.9 male; 79.9 female. **Births** (per 1,000 pop.): 11.2. **Deaths** (per 1,000 pop.): 8.3. **Natural inc.:** 0.29% (per 1,000 pop.). **Infant mortality** (per 1,000 live births):10.9. **AIDS rate:** NA.

Education: Compulsory: ages 7-15. **Literacy:** 98%.

Major Intl. Organizations: UN (FAO, ILO, WHO), OSCE.

Embassy: NA.

Website: www.montenegro.yu

Part of the medieval Serbian Kingdom, Montenegro preserved its autonomy for centuries because of its mountainous terrain. It was ruled by Orthodox prince-bishops from the 16th to the 19th centuries, but became a secular principality in 1852. After WWI, it was part of the Kingdom of Serbs, Croats, and Slovenes, later renamed Yugoslavia. Italian forces occupied parts of Montenegro during WWII. In 1945, with the establishment of a federal Yugoslavia under Communist rule, Montenegro became one of 6 constituent republics.

In Apr. 1992, after 4 other republics had declared independence, Montenegro and Serbia reconstituted themselves as the Federal Republic of Yugoslavia. Because of its ties with Serbia, Montenegro was a target of NATO air strikes during the Kosovo war, Mar.-June 1999. The republic sought closer ties with the West, however, and worked to reduce its political and economic dependence on Serbia. Under a charter that took effect Feb. 4, 2003, the name Yugoslavia was dropped in favor of the new union of Serbia and Montenegro. The charter allowed Montenegro to hold a referendum on independence, which passed May 21, 2006, with barely more than the 55% majority required. Montenegro declared independence June 3 and was admitted as a UN member June 28.

Morocco
Kingdom of Morocco

People: Population: 33,241,259. **Age distrib.** (%) <15: 31.6; 65+: 5. **Pop. density:** 192 per sq mi, 74 per sq km. **Urban:** 57.5%. **Ethnic groups:** Arab-Berber 99%. **Principal languages:** Arabic (official), Berber dialects, French, Spanish, English. **Chief religion:** Muslim 99% (official).

Geography: Total area: 172,414 sq mi, 446,550 sq km; **Land area:** 172,317 sq mi, 446,300 sq km. **Location:** On NW coast of Africa. **Neighbors:** Western Sahara on S, Algeria on E. **Topography:** Consists of 5 natural regions: mountain ranges (Riff in the N, Middle Atlas, Upper Atlas, and Anti-Atlas); rich plains in the W; alluvial plains in SW; well-cultivated plateaus in the center; a pre-Sahara arid zone extending from SE. **Capital:** Rabat, 1,647,000. **Cities (urban aggr.):** Casablanca, 3,138,000; Fes, 963,000.

Government: Type: Constitutional monarchy. **Head of state:** King Mohammed VI; b. Aug. 21, 1963; in office: July 23, 1999. **Head of gov.:** Prime Min. Driss Jettou; b. May 24, 1945; in office: Oct. 9, 2002. **Local divisions:** 16 regions. **Defense budget** (2005): $2 bil. **Active troops:** 200,800.

Economy: Industries: mining, food proc., leather goods, textiles, constr., tourism. **Chief crops:** barley, wheat, citrus, grapes, vegetables, olives. **Natural resources:** phosphates, iron ore, mang., lead, zinc, fish, salt. **Crude oil reserves** (2005): 1.6 mil bbls. **Arable land:** 21%. **Livestock** (2005): cattle: 2.7 mil; chickens: 137 mil; goats: 5.4 mil; pigs: 8,000; sheep: 17 mil. **Fish catch** (2005): 896,326 metric tons. **Electricity prod.** (2004): 18.5 bil kWh. **Labor force** (2003 est.): agriculture 40%, industry 15%, services 45%.

Finance: Monetary unit: Dirham (MAD) (Sept. 2006: 8.64 = $1 U.S.). **GDP** (2005 est.): $138.3 bil; **per capita GDP:** $4,200; **GDP growth:** 1.8%. **Imports** (2005 est.): $18.2 bil; partners (2004): France 21.2%, Spain 14.9%, Germany 7.3%, Italy 6.9%, Saudi Arabia 4.8%, China 4.8%. **Exports** (2005 est.): $9.5 bil; partners (2004): France 25.3%, Spain 18.4%, UK 8%, Italy 4.9%, Germany 4.6%, U.S. 4.6%. **Tourism:** $3.9 bil. **Budget** (2005 est.): $16.8 bil. **Intl. reserves less gold:** $11.33 bil. **Gold:** $710,000 oz t. **Consumer prices:** 0.98%.

Transport: Railroad: Length: 1,185 mi. **Motor vehicles** 1.3 mil pass. cars, 444,000 comm. vehicles. **Civil aviation:** 3.8 bil pass.-mi; 26 airports. **Chief ports:** Tangier, Casablanca, Kenitra.

Communications: TV sets: 165 per 1,000 pop. **Radios:** 247 per 1,000 pop. **Telephone lines:** 1.3 mil. **Daily newspaper circ.:** NA. **Internet:** 3.5 mil users.

Health: Life expect.: 68.6 male; 73.4 female. **Births** (per 1,000 pop.): 22. **Deaths** (per 1,000 pop.): 5.6. **Natural inc.:** 1.64%. **Infant mortality** (per 1,000 live births): 40.2. **AIDS rate:** 0.1%.

Education: Compulsory: ages 6-14. **Literacy:** 52.3%.

Major Intl. Organizations: UN (FAO, IBRD, ILO, IMF, IMO, WHO, WTO), AL.

Embassy: 1601 21st St. NW 20009; 462-7979.

Website: www.mincom.gov.ma

Berbers were the original inhabitants, followed by Carthaginians and Romans. Arabs conquered in 683. In the 11th and 12th centuries, a Berber empire ruled all northwest Africa and most of Spain from Morocco.

Part of Morocco came under Spanish rule in the 19th cent.; France controlled the rest in the early 20th. Tribal uprisings lasted from 1911 to 1933. The country became independent Mar. 2, 1956. Tangier, an internationalized seaport, was turned over to Morocco, 1956. Ifni, a Spanish enclave, was ceded in 1969. Morocco annexed the disputed territory of Western Sahara during the second half of the 1970s.

King Hassan II assumed the throne in 1961, reigning until his death on July 23, 1999; he was immediately succeeded by his eldest son. Political reforms in the 1990s included the establishment of a bicameral legislature in 1997.

Five terrorist attacks in Casablanca May 16, 2003, left about 40 people dead, including 10 suicide bombers; the government blamed Salafia Jihadia, an extremist group connected with al-Qaeda. An earthquake Feb. 24, 2004, killed at least 629 people in the vicinity of al-Hoceima, northern coastal Morocco.

Western Sahara

Western Sahara, formerly the protectorate of Spanish Sahara, is bounded the in N by Morocco, the NE by Algeria, the E and S by Mauritania, and on the W by the Atlantic Ocean. Phosphates are the major resource. Population (2006 est.): 273,008; capital: Laayoune (El Aaiun). Area: 102,600 sq mi.

Spain withdrew from its protectorate in Feb. 1976. On Apr. 14, 1976, Morocco annexed over 70,000 sq mi, with the remainder annexed by Mauritania. A guerrilla movement, the Polisario Front, which had proclaimed the region independent Feb. 27, launched attacks with Algerian support. After Mauritania signed a treaty with Polisario on Aug. 5, 1979, Morocco occupied Mauritania's portion of Western Sahara.

After years of bitter fighting, Morocco controlled the main urban areas, but Polisario guerrillas moved freely in the vast, sparsely populated deserts. The 2 sides implemented a cease-fire in 1991, when a UN peacekeeping force was deployed. Former U.S. Sec. of State James A. Baker III served as UN envoy 1997-2004 but was unable to resolve the dispute.

Mozambique
Republic of Mozambique

People: Population: 20,530,023. **Age distrib.** (%) <15: 44.8; 65+: 2.8. **Pop. density:** 67 per sq mi, 26 per sq km. **Urban:** 35.6%. **Ethnic groups:** Shangaan, Chokwe, Manyika, Sena, Makua. **Principal languages:** Portuguese (official) and dialects, English. **Chief religions:** Indigenous beliefs 50%, Christian 38%, Muslim 11%.

Geography: Total area: 309,496 sq mi, 801,590 sq km; **Land area:** 302,739 sq mi, 784,090 sq km. **Location:** On SE coast of Africa. **Neighbors:** Tanzania on N; Malawi, Zambia, Zimbabwe on W; South Africa, Swaziland on S. **Topography:** Coastal lowlands comprise nearly half the country with plateaus rising in steps to the mountains along the western border. **Capital:** Maputo, 1,320,000.

Government: Type: Republic. **Head of state:** Pres. Armando Guebuza; b. Jan. 20, 1943; in office: Feb. 2, 2005. **Head of gov.:** Prime Min. Luisa Diogo; b. Apr. 11, 1958; in office: Feb. 17, 2004. **Local divisions:** 10 provinces and Maputo municipality. **Defense budget** (2005): $116 mil. **Active troops:** 11,200.

Economy: Industries: food, beverages, chemicals, oil products, textiles, cement. **Chief crops:** cotton, cashews, sugarcane, tea, cassava, corn, coconuts, sisal, trop. fruits. **Natural resources:** coal, titanium, nat. gas, hydropower, tantalum, graphite. **Arable land:** 4%. **Livestock** (2005): cattle: 1.3 mil; chickens: 28 mil; goats: 392,000; pigs: 180,000; sheep: 125,000. **Fish catch** (2004): 45,129 metric tons. **Electricity prod.** (2004): 11.6 bil kWh. **Labor force** (1997 est.): agriculture 81%, industry 6%, services 13%.

Finance: Monetary unit: Metical (MZN) (Sept. 2006: 27.03 = $1 U.S.). **GDP** (2005 est.): $26 bil; **per capita GDP:** $1,300; **GDP growth:** 7%. **Imports** (2005 est.): $2 bil; partners (2004): South Africa 35.7%, Australia 10.9%, U.S. 3.7%. **Exports** (2005 est.): $1.7 bil; partners (2004): Belgium 32%, Italy 13.9%, Spain 12.6%, Germany 9.8%, Zimbabwe 4.7%. **Tourism:** $95 mil. **Budget** (2005 est.): $1.9 bil. **Intl. reserves less gold:** $737 mil. **Gold:** $100,000 oz t. **Consumer prices:** 7.17%.

Transport: Railroad: Length: 1,941 mi. **Motor vehicles:** 81,600 pass. cars, 76,000 comm. vehicles. **Civil aviation:** 246.7 mil pass.-mi; 22 airports. **Chief ports:** Maputo, Beira, Nacala, Inhambane.

Communications: TV sets: 5 per 1,000 pop. **Radios:** 40 per 1,000 pop. **Telephone lines:** 69,700. **Daily newspaper circ.:** 2.5 per 1,000 pop. **Internet:** 138,000 users.

Health: Life expect.: 41.2 male; 40.4 female. **Births** (per 1,000 pop.): 39. **Deaths** (per 1,000 pop.): 20.7. **Natural inc.:** 1.83%. **Infant mortality** (per 1,000 live births): 112.1. **AIDS rate:** 16.1%.

Education: Compulsory: ages 6-12. **Literacy:** 47.8%.

Major Intl. Organizations: UN (FAO, IBRD, ILO, IMF, IMO, WHO, WTO), the Commonwealth, AU.

Embassy: 1990 M St. NW, Suite 570, 20036; 293-7146.

Website: www.embamoc-usa.org

The first Portuguese post on the Mozambique coast was established in 1505, on the trade route to the East. Mozambique became independent June 25, 1975, after a 10-year war against Portuguese colonial domination. The 1974 revolution in Portugal had paved the way for the orderly transfer of power to Frelimo (Front for the Liberation of Mozambique). Frelimo took over local administration Sept. 20, 1974.

The new Frelimo government, headed by Pres. Samora Machel, a former guerrilla commander, provided for a gradual transition to a Communist system. Most of the country's whites emigrated. In the 1980s, severe drought and civil war caused famine and heavy loss of life. Pres. Machel was killed i a plane crash just inside the South African border, Oct. 19, 1986. Frelimo formally abandoned Marxist-Leninism in 1989, and a new constitution, effective Nov. 30, 1990, provided for multiparty elections and a free-market economy.

On Oct. 4, 1992, a peace agreement was signed aimed at ending hostilities between the government and the rebel Mozambique National Resistance (MNR). Repatriation of 1.7 mil Mozambican refugees officially ended June 1995. In Mar. 1999 the heaviest floods in

4 decades left nearly 200,000 people stranded. Even worse flooding in Feb.-Mar. 2000 claimed more than 600 lives, displaced over 1 mil people, and devastated the economy. A train crash May 25, 2002, in southern Mozambique killed 196 people. Frelimo retained its hold under Pres. Joaquim Chissano (in office 1986-2005) and his successor, Pres. Armando Guebuza, elected Dec. 1-2, 2004.

Myanmar *(formerly* Burma)
Union of Myanmar

People: Population: 46,986,207. **Age distrib.** (%) <15: 26.5; 65+: 5.2. **Pop. density:** 185 per sq mi, 71 per sq km. **Urban:** 29.4%. **Ethnic groups:** Burman 68%, Shan 9%, Karen 7%, Rakhine 4%, Chinese 3%, Indian 2%, Mon 2%. **Principal languages:** Burmese (official); many ethnic minority languages. **Chief religions:** Buddhist 89%, Christian 4%, Muslim 4%, Animist 1%.

Geography: Total area: 261,970 sq mi, 678,500 sq km; **Land area:** 253,955 sq mi, 657,740 sq km. **Location:** Between S and SE Asia, on Bay of Bengal. **Neighbors:** Bangladesh, India on W; China, Laos, Thailand on E. **Topography:** Mountains surround Myanmar on W, N, and E, and dense forests cover much of the nation. N-S rivers provide habitable valleys and communications, especially the Irrawaddy, navigable for 900 miles. The country has a tropical monsoon climate. **Capital:** Yangon (Rangoon) 4,107,000. **Cities (urban aggr.):** Mandalay, 924,000.

Government: Type: Military. **Head of state:** Gen. Than Shwe; b. Feb. 2, 1933; in office: Apr. 23, 1992. **Head of gov.:** Lt. Gen. Soe Win; b. 1949; in office: Oct. 19, 2004. **Local divisions:** 7 states, 7 divisions. **Defense budget** (2005): $6.9 bil. **Active troops:** 428,000.

Economy: Industries: agric. proc., apparel, wood & wood products, mining, constr. materials. **Chief crops:** rice, beans, sesame, peanuts, sugarcane. **Natural resources:** oil, timber, tin, antimony, zinc, copper, tungsten, lead, coal, marble, limestone, gemstones, nat. gas, hydropower. **Crude oil reserves** (2005): 50 mil bbls. **Arable land:** 15%. **Livestock** (2005): cattle: 12 mil; chickens: 88 mil; goats: 1.8 mil; pigs: 5.2 mil; sheep: 492,000. **Fish catch** (2004): 1,987,020 metric tons. **Electricity prod.** (2004): 6.3 bil kWh. **Labor force** (2001 est.): agriculture 70%, industry 7%, services 23%.

Finance: Monetary unit: Kyat (MMK) (Sept. 2006: 6.43 = $1 U.S.). **GDP** (2005 est.): $78.7 bil; **per capita GDP:** $1,700; **GDP growth:** 2.9%. **Imports:** $3.5 bil; partners (2004): China 28.3%, Singapore 20.6%, Thailand 19.1%, South Korea 6.2%, Malaysia 4.7%. **Exports** (2004 est.): $3.1 bil; partners (2004): Thailand 37%, India 14%, China 6.2%, Japan 5.1%, UK 4%. **Tourism:** $84 mil. **Budget** (2005 est.): $716.6 mil. **Intl. reserves less gold:** $539 mil. **Gold:** 230,000 oz t. **Consumer prices:** 9.37%.

Transport: Railroad: Length: 2,458 mi. **Motor vehicles** 175,400 pass. cars, 98,900 comm. vehicles. **Civil aviation:** 717.1 mil pass.-mi; 21 airports. **Chief ports:** Bassein, Moulmein.

Communications: TV sets: 7 per 1,000 pop. **Radios:** 72 per 1,000 pop. **Telephone lines:** 476,200. **Daily newspaper circ.:** 8.7 per 1,000 pop. **Internet:** 63,700 users.

Health: Life expect.: 59.9 male; 64.4 female. **Births** (per 1,000 pop.): 17.7. **Deaths** (per 1,000 pop.): 9.4. **Natural inc.:** 0.83%. **Infant mortality** (per 1,000 live births): 52.3. **AIDS rate:** 1.3%.

Education: Compulsory: ages 5-9. **Literacy:** 89.9%.

Major Intl. Organizations: UN (FAO, IBRD, ILO, IMF, IMO, WHO, WTO), ASEAN.

Embassy: 2300 S St. NW 20008; 332-3344.

Website: www.myanmar.gov.mm

The Burmese arrived from Tibet before the 9th cent., displacing earlier cultures, and a Buddhist monarchy was established by the 11th. Burma was conquered by the Mongol dynasty of China in 1272, then ruled by Shans as a Chinese tributary, until the 16th cent.. Britain subjugated Burma in 3 wars, 1824-84, and ruled the country as part of India until 1937, when it became self-governing. Independence outside the Commonwealth was achieved Jan. 4, 1948.

Gen. Ne Win dominated politics from 1962 to 1988, first as military ruler, then as constitutional president. His regime drove Indians from the civil service and Chinese from commerce. Economic socialization was advanced, isolation from foreign countries enforced. In 1987 Burma, once the richest nation in Southeast Asia, was granted less-developed status by the UN.

Ne Win resigned July 1988, following antigovernment riots. In Sept. the military seized power, under Gen. Saw Maung. In 1989 the country's name was changed to Myanmar.

The first free multiparty elections in 30 years took place May 27, 1990, with the main opposition party winning a decisive victory, but the military refused to hand over power. A key opposition leader, Aung San Suu Kyi, awarded the Nobel Peace Prize in 1991, was held under house arrest, 1989-95, 2000-02, and again from 2003. Because of the regime's poor human rights record and continued harassment of Aung San Suu Kyi and her supporters, the U.S. has imposed sanctions. The Indian Ocean tsunami of Dec. 26, 2004, killed at least 61 people in Myanmar.

The country was admitted to ASEAN July 23, 1997. Yielding to pressure from critics of the regime, Myanmar announced July 26, 2005, that it would forgo its turn to chair ASEAN in 2006. In Sept. a human rights investigator reported to the UN that Myanmar held more than 1,100 political prisoners, who were subject to torture. Beginning Nov. 6, the government moved to Naypyidaw, a fortified inland capital near the town of Pyinmana.

Namibia
Republic of Namibia

People: Population:2,044,147. **Age distrib.** (%) <15: 38.2; 65+: 3.7. **Pop. density:** 6 per sq mi, 2 per sq km. **Urban:** 32.4%. **Ethnic groups:** Ovambo 50%, Kavangos 9%, Herero 7%, Damara 7% White 6%, mixed 7%. **Principal languages:** English (official), Afrikaans, German, Oshivambo, Herero, Nama. **Chief religions:** Lutheran 50%, other Christian 30%, indigenous beliefs 10-20%.

Geography: Total area: 318,696 sq mi, 825,418 sq km; **Land area:** 318,696 sq mi, 825,418 sq km. **Location:** In S Africa on the coast of the Atlantic Ocean. **Neighbors:** Angola on N, Botswana on E, South Africa on S. **Topography:** Three distinct regions incl. Namib desert along the Atlantic coast, a mountainous central plateau with woodland savanna, and Kalahari desert in E. True forests are found in NE. There are 4 rivers, but little other surface water. **Capital:** Windhoek, 289,000.

Government: Type: Republic. **Head of state:** Pres. Hifikepunye Pohamba; b. Aug. 18, 1935; in office: Mar. 21, 2005. **Head of gov.:** Prime Min. Nahas Angula; b. Aug. 22, 1943; in office: Mar. 21, 2005. **Local divisions:** 13 regions. **Defense budget** (2005): $160 mil. **Active troops:** 9,200.

Economy: meatpacking, fish proc., dairy products, mining. **Chief crops:** millet, sorghum, peanuts. **Natural resources:** diamonds, copper, uranium, gold, lead, tin, lithium, cadmium, zinc, salt, vanadium, nat. gas, hydropower, fish. **Arable land:** 1%. **Livestock** (2005): cattle: 2.5 mil; chickens: 3.5 mil; goats: 2.1 mil; pigs: 28,000; sheep: 2.9 mil. **Fish catch** (2004): 570,758 metric tons. **Electricity prod.** (2004): 1.4 bil kWh. **Labor force** (1999 est.): agriculture 47%, industry 20%, services 33%.

Finance: Monetary unit: Namibia Dollar (NAD) (Sept. 2006: 7.62 = $1 U.S.). **GDP** (2005 est.): $14.2 bil; **per capita GDP:** $7,000; **GDP growth:** 4.8%. **Imports** (2005 est.): $2.4 bil; partners (2001): U.S. 50%, EU 31%. **Exports** (2005 est.): $2 bil; partners (2001): EU 79%, U.S. 4%. **Tourism:** $405 mil. **Budget** (2005 est.): $2 bil. **Intl. reserves less gold:** $218 mil. **Consumer prices:** 2.26%.

Transport: Railroad: Length: 1,480 mi. **Motor vehicles:** 62,500 pass. cars, 66,500 comm. vehicles. **Civil aviation:** 472.2 mil pass.-mi; 21 airports. **Chief ports:** Luderitz, Walvis Bay.

Communications: TV sets: 38 per 1,000 pop. **Radios:** 143 per 1,000 pop. **Telephone lines:** 127,900 **Daily newspaper circ.:** 17.2 per 1,000 pop. **Internet:** 75,000 users.

Health: Life expect.: 44.5 male; 42.3 female. **Births** (per 1,000 pop.): 24.3. **Deaths** (per 1,000 pop.): 18.9. **Natural inc.:** 0.55%. **Infant mortality** (per 1,000 live births): 48.1. **AIDS rate:** 19.6%.

Education: Compulsory: ages 6-15. **Literacy:** 85%.

Major Intl. Organizations: UN (FAO, IBRD, ILO, IMF, IMO, WHO, WTO), the Commonwealth, AU.

Embassy: 1605 New Hampshire Ave. NW 20009; 986-0540.

Website: www.grnnet.gov.na

Namibia was declared a German protectorate in 1890 and officially called South-West Africa. South Africa seized the territory from Germany in 1915 during WWI; the League of Nations gave South Africa a mandate over the territory in 1920. In 1966, the Marxist South-West Africa People's Organization (SWAPO) launched a guerrilla war for independence. The UN General Assembly named the area Namibia in 1968.

After many years of guerrilla warfare, South Africa, Angola, and Cuba signed a U.S.-mediated agreement Dec. 22, 1988, to end South African administration of Namibia and provide for a cease-fire and transition to independence, in accordance with a 1978 UN plan. A separate accord between Cuba and Angola provided for a phased withdrawal of Cuban troops from Namibia. A constitution providing for multiparty government was adopted Feb. 9, 1990, and Namibia gained independence Mar. 21. SWAPO has remained the dominant political group.

Walvis Bay, the principal deepwater port, had been turned over to South African administration in 1922. It remained in South African hands after independence, but South Africa turned control of the port back to Namibia, as of Mar. 1, 1994. Separatist violence flared in the Caprivi Strip in the late 1990s.

Nauru
Republic of Nauru

People: Population: 13,287. **Age distrib.** (%) <15: 36.9; 65+: 2. **Pop. density:** 1660 per sq mi, 632 per sq km. **Urban:** 100.0%. **Ethnic groups:** Nauruan 58%, other Pacific Islander 26%, Chinese 8%, European 8%. **Principal languages:** Nauruan (official), English. **Chief religions:** Protestant 66%, Roman Catholic 33%.

Geography: Total area: 8 sq mi, 21 sq km; **Land area:**8 sq mi, 21 sq km. **Location:** In W Pacific O. just S of the Equator. **Neighbors:** Nearest is Kiribati to E. **Topography:** Mostly a plateau bearing high-grade phosphate deposits, surrounded by a sandy shore and coral reef in concentric rings. **Capital** (2003): Nauru, 13,000.

Government: Type: Republic. **Head of state and gov.:** Pres. Ludwig Scotty; b. 1948; in office June 22, 2004. **Local divisions:** 14 districts.

Economy: Industries: phosphate mining, offshore banking, coconut products. **Chief crops:** coconuts. **Natural resources:** phosphates, fish. **Livestock** (2005): chickens: 5,000; pigs: 2,800. **Fish catch** (2004): 18 metric tons. **Electricity prod.** (2004): 30 mil kWh. **Labor force:** employed in mining phosphates, public administration, education, and transportation.

Finance: Monetary unit: Australian Dollar (AUD) (Sept. 2006: 1.33 = $1 U.S.). **GDP** (2005 est.): $60.0 mil; **per capita GDP:** $5,000; **GDP growth:** NA. **Imports** (2004 est.): $20 mil; partners (2004): Australia 59.1%, Indonesia 16.7%, UK 4.3%, Germany 4.1%. **Exports** (2005 est.): $64,000 ; partners (2004): South Africa 37.6%, India 19.7%, Germany 17.9%, South Korea 10.2%, Japan 6.3%. **Tourism:** NA. **Budget** (2005): $13.5 mil.

Transport: Railroad: Length: 3 mi. **Civil aviation:** 187.7 mil. pass.-mi; 1 airport. **Chief port:** Nauru.

Communications: TV sets: 1 per 1,000 pop. **Radios:** 45 per 1,000 pop. **Internet:** (2002): 300 users.

Health: Life expect.: 59.5 male; 66.8 female. **Births** (per 1,000 pop.): 24.8. **Deaths** (per 1,000 pop.): 6.7. **Natural inc.:** 1.81%. **Infant mortality** (per 1,000 live births): 9.8. **AIDS rate:** NA.

Education: Compulsory: ages 6-16. **Literacy:** NA.

Major Intl. Organizations: UN (FAO, WHO), the Commonwealth.

Permanent UN Representative: 800 Second Avenue, Ste. 400D New York, NY 10017; (212) 937-0074.

Website: www.un.int/nauru

The island was discovered in 1798 by the British but was formally annexed to the German Empire in 1886. After WWI, Nauru became a League of Nations mandate administered by Australia. During WWII the Japanese occupied the island. In 1947 Nauru was made a UN trust territory, administered by Australia. It became an independent republic Jan. 31, 1968, and was admitted to the UN Sept. 14, 1999.

Phosphate exports provided Nauru with per capita revenues that were among the highest in the Third World. Phosphate reserves, however, are nearly depleted, and environmental damage from strip-mining has been severe. Lax banking practices have made Nauru a haven for money laundering; the country has also raised funds by selling passports to noncitizens, possibly to some with terrorist connections. Nauru defaulted on a loan payment for its real estate holdings in Australia and was virtually bankrupt in 2004.

Nepal
Kingdom of Nepal

People: Population: 28,287,147. **Age distrib.** (%) <15: 38.7; 65+: 3.7. **Pop. density:** 535 per sq mi, 206 per sq km. **Urban:** 15.0%. **Ethnic groups:** Newar, Indian, Gurung, Magar, Tamang, Rai, Limbu, Sherpa, Tharu. **Principal languages:** Nepali (official); about 30 dialects and 12 other languages. **Chief religions:** Hinduism 81% (official), Buddhism 11%, Muslim 4%.

Geography: Total area: 54,363 sq mi, 140,800 sq km; **Land area:** 52,819 sq mi, 136,800 sq km. **Location:** Astride the Himalaya Mts. **Neighbors:** China on N, India on S. **Topography:** The Himalayas stretch across the N, the hill country with its fertile valleys extends across the center, while the S border region is part of the flat, subtropical Ganges Plain. **Capital:** Capital: Kathmandu 815,000.

Government: Type: In transition. **Head of state:** King Gyanendra Bir Bikram Shah Dev; b. July 7, 1947; in office: June 4, 2001. **Head of gov.:** Girija Prasad Koirala; b. 1925; in office: Apr. 30, 2006. **Local divisions:** 5 regions subdivided into 14 zones. **Defense budget** (2005): $151 mil. **Active troops:** 69,000.

Economy: Industries: tourism, carpets, textiles, rice, jute, sugar, oilseed. **Chief crops:** rice, corn, wheat, sugarcane. **Natural resources:** quartz, water, timber, hydropower, lignite, copper, cobalt, iron ore. **Arable land:** 17%. **Livestock** (2005): cattle: 7 mil; chickens: 22.8 mil; goats: 7.2 mil; pigs: 947,711; sheep: 816,727. **Fish catch** (2004): 39,947 metric tons. **Electricity prod.** (2004): 2.4 bil kWh. **Labor force:** agriculture 76%, industry 6%, services 8%.

Finance: Monetary unit: Rupee (NPR) (Sept. 2006: 73.44 = $1 U.S.). **GDP** (2005 est.): $39.9 bil; **per capita GDP:** $1,400; **GDP growth:** 2.7%. **Imports** (2005 est.): $2 bil; partners (2004): India 43%, UAE 10%, China 10%, Saudi Arabia 4.4%, Singapore 4%. **Exports** (2005 est.): $822 mil; partners (2004): India 48.8%, US 22.3%, Germany 8.5%. **Tourism:** $230 mil. **Budget** (2006 est.): $1.8 bil. **Intl. reserves less gold:** $1.05 bil. **Gold:** 130,000 oz t. **Consumer prices:** 6.84%.

Transport: Railroad: Length: 37 mi. **Motor vehicles:** 63,500 pass. cars, 72,700 comm. vehicles. **Civil aviation:** 752.5 mil pass.-mi; 10 airports.

Communications: TV sets: 6 per 1,000 pop. **Radios:** 38 per 1,000 pop. **Telephone lines:** 448,600. **Daily newspaper circ.:** NA. **Internet:** 175,000 users.

Health: Life expect.: 60.4 male; 59.9 female. **Births** (per 1,000 pop.): 31. **Deaths** (per 1,000 pop.): 9.3. **Natural inc.:** 2.17%. **Infant mortality** (per 1,000 live births): 65.3. **AIDS rate:** 0.5%.

Education: Compulsory: ages 6-10. **Literacy:** 48.6%.

Major Intl. Organizations: UN (FAO, IBRD, ILO, IMF, IMO, WHO, WTO).

Embassy: 2131 Leroy Pl. NW 20008; 667-4550.

Website: www.nepalgov.gov.np

Nepal was originally a group of petty principalities, the inhabitants of one of which, the Gurkhas, became dominant about 1769. In 1951 King Tribhubana Bir Bikram, member of the Shah family, ended the system of rule by hereditary premiers of the Ranas family, who had kept the kings virtual prisoners, and established a cabinet system of government.

Virtually closed to the outside world for centuries, Nepal is now linked to India and Pakistan by roads and air service and to Tibet by road. Polygamy, child marriage, and the caste system were officially abolished in 1963.

The government announced the legalization of political parties in 1990. Elections on Nov. 15, 1994, led to the installation of Nepal's first Communist government, which held power until a no-confidence vote Sept. 10, 1995.

Nine members of Nepal's royal family, including King Birendra and Queen Aishwarya, died as the result of a massacre on the night of June 1, 2001. An official inquiry blamed the carnage on a 10th family member, Crown Prince Dipendra, who reportedly shot himself that night and died 3 days later, allowing Birendra's brother Gyanendra to assume the throne.

Citing the government's failure to stop a Maoist insurgency that had claimed 11,000 lives since 1996, King Gyanendra assumed absolute authority, Feb. 1, 2005. A state of emergency ended Apr. 29, but curbs on civil liberties remained in effect. After weeks of pro-democracy demonstrations, in which police killed at least 12 protesters, the king agreed Apr. 24, 2006, to reinstate parliament, which had not met for 4 years. A new government, led by Prime Min. Girija Prasad Koirala, reduced the king's powers and declared a permanent truce with Maoist rebels.

Netherlands
Kingdom of the Netherlands

People: Population: 16,491,461. **Age distrib.** (%) <15: 18; 65+: 14.2. **Pop. density:** 1,260 per sq mi, 486 per sq km. **Urban:** 65.8%. **Ethnic groups:** Dutch 83%. **Principal languages:** Dutch (official), Frisian, Flemish. **Chief religions:** Roman Catholic 31%, Protestant 21%, Muslim 4%.

Geography: Total area: 16,033 sq mi, 41,526 sq km; **Land area:** 13,082 sq mi, 33,883 sq km. **Location:** In NW Europe on North Sea. **Neighbors:** Germany on E, Belgium on S. **Topography:** The land is flat, an average alt. of 37 ft. above sea level, with much land below sea level reclaimed and protected by some 1,500 miles of dikes. Since 1920 the government has been draining the IJsselmeer, formerly the Zuider Zee. **Capital:** Amsterdam (official), 1,147,000, The Hague (administrative, 2003), 705,000. **Cities (urban aggr.):** Rotterdam, 1,101,000.

Government: Type: Parliamentary democracy under a constitutional monarch. **Head of state:** Queen Beatrix; b. Jan. 31, 1938; in office: Apr. 30, 1980. **Head of gov.:** Prime Min. Jan Peter Balkenende; b. May 7, 1956; in office: July 22, 2002. **Seat of govt.:** The Hague. **Local divisions:** 12 provinces. **Defense budget** (2005): $9.7 bil. **Active troops:** 53,130.

Economy: Industries: agro industries, metal & engineering products, electrical machinery & equip., chemicals, oil, constr., microelectronics, fishing. **Chief crops:** grains, potatoes, sugar beets, fruits, vegetables. **Natural resources:** nat. gas, oil. **Crude oil reserves** (2005): 106 mil bbls. **Livestock** (2005): cattle: 3.9 mil; chickens: 86 mil; goats: 282,000; pigs: 11.2 mil; sheep: 1.2 mil. **Fish catch** (2004): 600,561 metric tons. **Electricity prod.** (2004): 92.7 bil kWh. **Labor force** (2004 est.): agriculture 2%, industry 19%, services 79%.

Finance: Monetary unit: Euro (EUR) (Sept. 2006: 0.78 = $1 U.S.). **GDP** (2005 est.): $499.8 bil; **per capita GDP:** $30,500; **GDP growth:** 1.1%. **Imports** (2005 est.): $326.6 bil; partners (2004): Germany 17.7%, Belgium 10.2%, US 7.8%, China 7.1%, UK 6.6%, France 4.9%. **Exports** (2005 est.): $365.1 bil; partners (2004): Germany 25%, Belgium 12.6%, UK 10.1%, France 9.8%, Italy 6%, US 4.2%. **Tourism:** $10.3 bil. **Budget** (2005 est.): $303.7 bil. **Intl. reserves less gold:** $6.38 bil. **Gold:** 22.34 mil. oz t. **Consumer prices:** 1.67%.

Transport: Railroad: Length: 1,745 mi. **Motor vehicles:** 6.12 mil pass. cars, 806,000 comm. vehicles. **Civil aviation:** 42.9 bil pass.-mi; 20 airports. **Chief ports:** Rotterdam, Amsterdam, Ijmuiden.

Communications: TV sets: 540 per 1,000 pop. **Radios:** 980 per 1,000 pop. **Telephone lines:** 7.6 mil. **Daily newspaper circ.:** 280 per 1,000 pop. **Internet** (2004): 10.8 mil users.

Health: Life expect.: 76.4 male; 81.7 female. **Births** (per 1,000 pop.): 10.9. **Deaths** (per 1,000 pop.): 8.7. **Natural inc.:** 0.22%. **Infant mortality** (per 1,000 live births): 5. **AIDS rate:** 0.2%.

Education: Compulsory: ages 6-18. **Literacy** (2005): 99%.

Major Intl. Organizations: UN and all of its specialized agencies, EU, NATO, OECD, OSCE.

Embassy: 4200 Linnean Ave. NW 20008; 244-5300.

Website: www.government.nl

Julius Caesar conquered the region in 55 BCE, when it was inhabited by Celtic and Germanic tribes. After the empire of Charlemagne fell apart, the Netherlands (Holland, Belgium, Flanders) split among counts, dukes, and bishops, passed to Burgundy and thence to Spain. William the Silent, prince of Orange, led a confederation of the northern provinces, called Estates, in the Union of Utrecht, 1579; in 1581 they repudiated allegiance to Spain. The rise of the Dutch republic to naval, economic, and artistic eminence came in the 17th cent.

The United Dutch Republic ended 1795 when the French formed the Batavian Republic. Napoleon made his brother Louis king of Holland, 1806; Louis abdicated 1810 when Napoleon annexed Holland. In 1813 the French were expelled. In 1815 the Congress of Vienna formed a kingdom of the Netherlands, including Belgium, under William I. In 1830, the Belgians seceded and formed a separate kingdom.

The constitution, promulgated 1814, and subsequently revised, provides for a hereditary constitutional monarchy.

The Netherlands maintained its neutrality in WWI, but was invaded and brutally occupied by Germany, 1940-45. In 1949, after several years of fighting, the Netherlands granted independence to Indonesia.

The murder May 6, 2002, of right-wing populist leader Pim Fortuyn, 9 days before legislative elections, marked the first political assassination in modern Dutch history. The killing of filmmaker Theo van Gogh, Nov. 2, 2004, by an Islamic extremist also shocked many Dutch. Concerns about immigration contributed to the defeat of a proposed EU constitution by 62% to 38% in a referendum, June 1, 2005.

Netherlands Dependencies

The **Netherlands Antilles**, constitutionally on a level of equality with the Netherlands homeland within the kingdom, consist of 2 groups of islands in the West Indies. **Curaçao** and **Bonaire** are near the coast of Venezuela; **St. Eustatius, Saba,** and the southern part of **St. Maarten** are southeast of Puerto Rico. The northern two-thirds of St. Maarten belongs to French Guadeloupe; the French call the island St. Martin. Total area of the 2 groups is 370.7 sq mi., including Bonaire (111), Curaçao (171), St. Eustatius (8), Saba (5), St. Maarten (Dutch part) (13). St. Maarten suffered extensive damage from Hurricane Luis, Sept. 1995. Total pop. of the Netherlands Antilles (2005 est.) was 219,958. Willemstad, on Curaçao, is the capital. The principal industry is the refining of crude oil from Venezuela. Tourism is also an important industry, as is shipbuilding.

Aruba, about 26 mi west of Curaçao, was separated from the Netherlands Antilles on Jan. 1, 1986; it is an autonomous member of the Netherlands, the same status as the Netherland Antilles. Area 74.5 sq mi.; pop. (2005 est.): 71,566; capital: Oranjestad. Chief industries are oil refining and tourism.

New Zealand

People: Population: 4,076,140. **Age distrib.** (%) <15: 21.1; 65+: 11.8. **Pop. density:** 39 per sq mi, 15 per sq km. **Urban:** 85.9%. **Ethnic groups:** New Zealand European 75%, Maori 10%, other European 5%, Pacific Islander 4%. **Principal languages:** English, Maori (both official). **Chief religions:** none 26%, unspecified 17%, Anglican 15%, Roman Catholic 13%.

Geography: Total area: 103,738 sq mi, 268,680 sq km. **Land area:** 103,484 sq mi, 268,021 sq km. **Location:** In SW Pacific O. **Neighbors:** Nearest are Australia on W, Fiji and Tonga on N. **Topography:** Each of the 2 main islands (North and South Isls.) is mainly hilly and mountainous. The east coasts consist of fertile plains, especially the broad Canterbury Plains on South Isl. A volcanic plateau is in center of North Isl. South Isl. has glaciers and 15 peaks over 10,000 ft. **Capital:** Wellington, 346,000. **Cities (urban aggr.):** Auckland, 1,148,000; Christchurch, 331,443.

Government: Type: Parliamentary democracy. **Head of state:** Queen Elizabeth II, represented by Gov.-Gen. Dame Silvia Cartwright; b. Nov. 7, 1943; in office: Apr. 4, 2001. **Head of gov.:** Prime Min. Helen Clark; b. Feb. 26, 1950; in office: Dec. 10, 1999. **Local divisions:** 16 regions. **Defense budget** (2005): $1.4 bil. **Active troops:** 8,660.

Economy: Industries: food proc., wood & paper products, textiles, machinery, transp. equip., banking & insurance, tourism, mining. **Chief crops:** wheat, barley, potatoes, fruits, vegetables. **Natural resources:** nat. gas, iron ore, sand, coal, timber, hydropower, gold, limestone. **Crude oil reserves** (2005): 52 mil bbls. **Arable land:** 9%. **Livestock** (2005): cattle: 9.4 mil; chickens: 20 mil; goats: 155,000; pigs: 390,000; sheep: 40 mil. **Fish catch** (2004): 631,806 metric tons. **Electricity prod.** (2004): 41.1 bil kWh. **Labor force** (1995): agriculture 10%, industry 25%, services 65%.

Finance: Monetary unit: New Zealand Dollar (NZD) (Sept. 2006: 1.50 = $1 U.S. **GDP** (2005 est.): $101.8 bil; **per capita GDP:** $25,200; **GDP growth:** 2.2%. **Imports** (2005 est.): $24.6 bil; partners (2004): Australia 28.6%, Japan 10.7%, US 10%, China 6.6%, Germany 4.2%, Singapore 4.1%. **Exports** (2005 est.): $22.2 bil; partners (2004): Australia 19.6%, US 14.3%, Japan 11.4%, China 6.3%, UK 5.1%. **Tourism:** $4.7 bil. **Budget** (2005 est.): $37.6 bil. **Intl. reserves less gold:** $6.2 bil. **Consumer prices:** 3.04%.

Transport: Railroad: Length: 2,422 mi. **Motor vehicles:** 6.12 mil pass. cars, 806,000 comm. vehicles. **Civil aviation:** 14.5 bil pass.-mi; 45 airports. **Chief ports:** Auckland, Christchurch, Wellington, Dunedin, Tauranga.

Communications: TV sets: 516 per 1,000 pop. **Radios:** 997 per 1,000 pop. **Telephone lines:** 1.8 mil. **Daily newspaper circ.:** 202.2 per 1,000 pop. **Internet:** 3.2 mil users.

Health: Life expect.: 75.8 male; 81.9 female. **Births** (per 1,000 pop.): 13.8. **Deaths** (per 1,000 pop.): 7.5. **Natural inc.:** 0.62%. **Infant mortality** (per 1,000 live births): 5.8. **AIDS rate:** 0.1%.

Education: Compulsory: ages 5-16. **Literacy** (2005): 99%.

Major Intl. Organizations: UN (FAO, IBRD, ILO, IMF, IMO, WHO, WTO), APEC, the Commonwealth, OECD.

Embassy: 37 Observatory Cir. NW 20008; 328-4800.

Website: www.govt.nz

The Maoris, a Polynesian group from the eastern Pacific, reached New Zealand before and during the 14th cent. The first European to sight New Zealand was Dutch navigator Abel Janszoon Tasman, but Maoris refused to allow him to land. British Capt. James Cook explored the coasts, 1769-70.

British sovereignty was proclaimed and Maori land rights were recognized in the Treaty of Waitangi, 1840, with organized settlement beginning in the same year. Representative institutions were granted in 1853. Maori Wars ended in 1870 with British victory. The colony became a dominion in 1907 and gained full independence in 1947. It is a member of the Commonwealth. Maoris make up nearly

15% of the population. Six of 120 members of the House of Representatives are elected directly by the Maori people.

A progressive tradition in politics dates back to the 19th cent., when New Zealand was internationally known for social experimentation; much of the nation's economy has been deregulated in recent years. Jenny Shipley of the National Party became the nation's first female prime minister, Dec. 8, 1997. The Labour Party, led by Helen Clark, won the general elections of Nov. 27, 1999, and July 27, 2002.

The legislature legalized prostitution June 2003. In July, New Zealand contributed troops to the Australian-led force in the Solomon Islands. A measure establishing a Supreme Court and ending appeals to the UK Privy Council passed Oct. 14.

Prime Min. Clark, May 4, 2004, survived a no-confidence vote on a plan to nationalize the coastline. The plan was opposed by some Maoris, who claimed it infringed their land rights under the Waitangi Treaty. Clark formed a new coalition government after elections Sept. 17, 2005, that gave the Labour Party a thin plurality.

New Zealand comprises **North Island**, 44,702 sq mi.; **South Island**, 58,384 sq mi.; **Stewart Island**, 674 sq mi.; **Chatham Islands**, 372 sq mi.; and several groups of smaller islands.

In 1965, the **Cook Islands** (pop. [2004 est.]: 21,200; area: 92.7 sq mi, halfway between New Zealand and Hawaii, became self-governing. New Zealand retains responsibility for defense and foreign affairs. **Niue** attained the same status in 1974; it lies 400 mi W (pop. [2004 est.]: 2,156; area: 100 sq mi). Cyclone Heta devastated Niue Jan. 6, 2004. **Tokelau** (pop. [2004 est.]: 1,405; area: 4 sq mi) comprises 3 atolls 300 mi N of Samoa. A referendum on Tokelau self-government, held Feb. 13-15, 2006, failed to gain the required two-third majority.

Ross Dependency, administered by New Zealand since 1923, comprises 160,000 sq mi of Antarctic territory.

Nicaragua
Republic of Nicaragua
People: Population: 5,570,129. **Age distrib.** (%) <15: 36.4; 65+: 3.1. **Pop. density:** 119 per sq mi, 46 per sq km. **Urban:** 57.3%. **Ethnic groups:** Mestizo 69%, White 17%, Black 9%, Amerindian 5%. **Principal languages:** Spanish (official); indigenous languages, English on Atlantic coast. **Chief religion:** Roman Catholic 73%, Evangelical 15%.

Geography: Total area: 49,998 sq mi, 129,494 sq km; **Land area:** 46,430 sq mi, 120,254 sq km. **Location:** In Central America. **Neighbors:** Honduras on N, Costa Rica on S. **Topography:** Both Caribbean and Pacific coasts are over 200 mi. long. The Cordillera Mts., with many volcanic peaks, run NW-SE through the middle of the country. Between this and a volcanic range to the E lie Lakes Managua and Nicaragua. **Capital:** Managua, 1,165,000.

Government: Type: Republic. **Head of state and gov.:** Pres. Enrique Bolaños Geyer; b. May 13, 1928; in office Jan. 10, 2002. **Local divisions:** 15 departments, 2 autonomous regions. **Defense budget** (2005): $35 mil. **Active troops:** 14,000.

Economy: Industries: food proc., chemicals, machinery & metal products, textiles, clothing, oil refining & distribution, beverages, footwear, wood. **Chief crops:** coffee, bananas, sugarcane, cotton, rice, corn, tobacco, sesame, soya. **Natural resources:** gold, silver, copper, tungsten, lead, zinc, timber, fish. **Arable land:** 9%. **Livestock** (2005): cattle: 3.5 mil; chickens: 18 mil; goats: 7,100; pigs: 123,000; sheep: 4,500. **Fish catch** (2004): 27,177 metric tons. **Electricity prod.** (2004): 2.8 bil kWh. **Labor force** (2003 est.): agriculture 30.5%, industry 17.3%, services 52.2%.

Finance: Monetary unit: Cordoba (NIO) (Sept. 2006: 17.73 = $1 U.S.). **GDP** (2005 est.): $16.1 bil; **per capita GDP:** $2,900; **GDP growth:** 4%. **Imports** (2005 est.): $2.9 bil; partners (2004): US 26.3%, Venezuela 9.6%, Costa Rica 7.5%, Mexico 7.1%, Guatemala 6.1%, El Salvador 4.1%. **Exports** (2005 est.): $1.6 bil; partners (2004): US 63.5%, El Salvador 9%, Costa Rica 4.2%. **Tourism** $192 mil. **Budget** (2005 est.): $1.4 bil. **Intl. reserves less gold:** $509 mil. **Consumer prices:** 9.42%.

Transport: Railroad: Length: 4 mi. **Motor vehicles:** 82,200 pass. cars, 107,700 comm. vehicles. **Civil aviation** (2000): 44.7 mil pass.-mi; 11 airports. **Chief ports:** Corinto, Puerto Sandino, San Juan del Sur.

Communications: TV sets: 69 per 1,000 pop. **Radios:** 270 per 1,000 pop. **Telephone lines:** 220,900. **Daily newspaper circ.:** NA. **Internet:** 125,000 users.

Health: Life expect.: 68.5 male; 72.8 female. **Births** (per 1,000 pop.): 24.5. **Deaths** (per 1,000 pop.): 4.5. **Natural inc.:** 2.01%. **Infant mortality** (per 1,000 live births): 28.1. **AIDS rate:** 0.2%.

Education: Compulsory: ages 7-12. **Literacy:** 76.7%.

Major Intl. Organizations: UN and most of its specialized agencies, OAS.

Embassy: 1627 New Hampshire Ave. NW 20009; 939-6570.

Website: www.consuladodenicaragua.com

Nicaragua, inhabited by various Indian tribes, was conquered by Spain in 1552. After gaining independence from Spain, 1821, Nicaragua was united for a short period with Mexico, then with the United Provinces of Central America, finally becoming an independent republic, 1838. U.S. Marines occupied the country at times in the early 20th cent., the last time from 1926 to 1933.

Gen. Anastasio Somoza Debayle was elected president in 1967. He resigned in 1972, but was re-elected president in 1974. Martial law was imposed in Dec. 1974, after officials were kidnapped by the Marxist Sandinista guerrillas. Violent opposition spread to nearly all classes in 1978; nationwide strikes called against the government touched off a civil war, which ended when Somoza fled Nicaragua and the Sandinistas took control of Managua in July 1979. Somoza was assassinated in Paraguay, Sept. 17, 1980.

Relations with the U.S. were strained as a result of Nicaragua's aid to leftist guerrillas in El Salvador and U.S. backing of anti-Sandinista contra guerrilla groups. In 1983 the contras launched a major offensive; the Sandinistas imposed rule by decree. In 1985 the U.S. House rejected Pres. Reagan's request for military aid to the contras. The subsequent diversion of funds to the contras from the proceeds of a secret arms sale to Iran caused a major scandal in the U.S.

In a stunning upset, Violeta Barrios de Chamorro defeated Sandinista leader Daniel Ortega Saavedra in national elections, Feb. 25, 1990. Arnoldo Alemán Lacayo, a conservative former mayor of Managua, defeated Ortega in the presidential election of Oct. 20, 1996. Up to 2,000 people died in western Nicaragua Oct. 30, 1998, in a mudslide caused by rains from Hurricane Mitch.

Drought and a drop in coffee prices plunged Nicaragua into an economic crisis in 2001. Enrique Bolaños Geyer, a conservative businessman, won the presidency that year. The corruption trial of former Pres. Alemán ended with a guilty verdict, Dec. 7, 2003; he was fined $10 mil and sentenced to 20 years in prison. After a medical review, Alemán was allowed to serve the sentence under house arrest. Bolaños, backed by the U.S., thwarted efforts by allied supporters of Alemán and Ortega to impeach him or curb his powers. Presidential elections are scheduled for Nov. 5, 2006.

Niger
Republic of Niger
People: Population: 12,525,094. **Age distrib.** (%) <15: 46.9; 65+: 2.4. **Pop. density:** 25 per sq mi, 9 per sq km. **Urban:** 22.2%. **Ethnic groups:** Hausa 56%, Djerma 22%, Fula 9%, Tuareg 8%, Beri Beri (Kanouri) 4%. **Principal languages:** French (official); Hausa, Djerma, Fulani (all national). **Chief religion:** Muslim 80%.

Geography: Total area: 489,192 sq mi, 1,267,000 sq km; **Land area:** 489,076 sq mi, 1,266,700 sq km. **Location:** In the interior of N Africa. **Neighbors:** Libya, Algeria on N; Mali, Burkina Faso on W; Benin, Nigeria on S; Chad on E. **Topography:** Mostly arid desert and mountains. A narrow savanna in the S and the Niger R. basin in the SW contain most of the population. **Capital:** Niamey, 850,000.

Government: Type: Republic. **Head of state:** Pres. Mamadou Tandja; b. 1938; in office: Dec. 22, 1999. **Head of gov.:** Prime Min. Hama Amadou; b. 1950; in office: Jan. 3, 2000. **Local divisions:** 7 departments, 1 capital district. **Defense budget** (2005): $30.6 mil. **Active troops:** 5,300.

Economy: Industries: uranium mining, cement, brick, textiles, food proc., chemicals. **Chief crops:** cowpeas, cotton, peanuts, millet, sorghum, cassava, rice. **Natural resources:** uranium, coal, iron ore, tin, phosphates, gold, oil. **Arable land:** 3%. **Livestock** (2005): cattle: 2.3 mil; chickens: 25 mil; goats: 6.9 mil; pigs: 39,500; sheep: 4.5 mil. **Fish catch** (2004): 51,506 metric tons. **Electricity prod.** (2004): 230 mil kWh. **Labor force:** agriculture 90%, industry 6%, services 4%.

Finance: Monetary unit: CFA BCEAO Franc (XOF) (Sept. 2006: 512.27 = $1 U.S.). **GDP** (2005 est.): $11.3 bil; **per capita GDP:** $900; **GDP growth:** 4.5%. **Imports** (2004 est.): $588 mil; partners (2004): France 17.4%, Côte d'Ivoire 11.3%, Italy 8.4%, Nigeria 7.3%, Germany 6.5%, US 5.5%, China 4.8%. **Exports** (2004 est.): $222 mil; partners (2004): France 47.1%, Nigeria 22.7%, Japan 8.6%, US 5.4%. **Tourism** (2003): $28 mil. **Budget** (2002 est.): $320 mil. **Intl. reserves less gold:** $175 mil. **Consumer prices:** 7.8.

Transport: Motor vehicles: 57,800 pass. cars, 41,000 comm. vehicles. **Civil aviation** (2001): 80.8 mil pass.-mi; 9 airports.

Communications: TV sets: 15 per 1,000 pop. **Radios:** 36 per 1,000 pop. **Telephone lines:** 24,100. **Daily newspaper circ.:** 0.2 per 1,000 pop. **Internet:** 24,000 users.

Health: Life expect.: 43.8 male; 43.7 female. **Births** (per 1,000 pop.): 50.7. **Deaths** (per 1,000 pop.): 20.9. **Natural inc.:** 2.98%. **Infant mortality** (per 1,000 live births): 118.2. **AIDS rate:** 1.1%.

Education: Compulsory: ages 7-12. **Literacy:** 28.7%.

Major Intl. Organizations: UN (FAO, IBRD, ILO, IMF, WHO, WTO), AU.

Embassy: 2204 R St. NW 20008; 483-4224.

Website: www.nigerembassyusa.org

Niger was part of ancient and medieval African empires. European explorers reached the area in the late 18th cent. The French colony of Niger was established 1900-22, after the defeat of Tuareg fighters, who had invaded the area from the north a century before. The country became independent Aug. 3, 1960.

In 1993, Niger held its first free and open elections since independence; an opposition leader, Mahamane Ousmane, won the presidency. A peace accord Apr. 24, 1995, ended a Tuareg rebellion that began in 1990. A coup, Jan. 27, 1996, followed by a disputed presidential election in July, left the military in control of Niger. On Apr. 9, 1999, Gen. Ibrahim Bare Mainassara, Niger's president since 1996, was assassinated, apparently by members of his security team. Elections were held Oct. 17 and Nov. 24, 1999, under a new constitution, approved by referendum July 18, that restored civilian rule. One of the world's poorest countries, Niger experienced severe food shortages in 2005 after locusts and drought ruined the grain harvest.

Nigeria
Federal Republic of Nigeria

People: Population: 131,859,731. **Age distrib.** (%) <15: 42.3; 65+: 3.1. **Pop. density:** 374 per sq mi, 144 per sq km. **Urban:** 46.7%. **Ethnic groups:** More than 250; Hausa and Fulani 29%, Yoruba 21%, Igbo (Ibo) 18%, Ijaw 10%. **Principal languages:** English (official), Hausa, Yoruba, Igbo (Ibo), Fulani. **Chief religions:** Muslim 50%, Christian 40%, indigenous beliefs 10%.

Geography: Total area: 356,669 sq mi, 923,768 sq km; **Land area:** 351,650 sq mi, 910,768 sq km. **Location:** On the S coast of W Africa. **Neighbors:** Benin on W, Niger on N, Chad and Cameroon on E. **Topography:** 4 E-W regions divide Nigeria: a coastal mangrove swamp 10-60 mi. wide, a tropical rain forest 50-100 mi. wide, a plateau of savanna and open woodland, and semidesert in the N. **Capital:** Abuja, 612,000. **Cities (urban aggr.):** Lagos, 10,886,000; Kano 2,993,000; Ibadan, 2,437,000.

Government: Type: Republic. **Head of state and gov.:** Pres. Olusegun Obasanjo; b. Mar. 5, 1937; in office: May 29, 1999. **Local divisions:** 36 states, 1 capital territory. **Defense budget** (2005): $841 mil. **Active troops:** 78,500.

Economy: Industries: crude oil, mining, palm oil, peanuts, cotton, rubber. **Chief crops:** cocoa, peanuts, palm oil, corn, rice, sorghum, millet, cassava, yams, rubber. **Natural resources:** nat. gas, oil, tin, columbite, iron ore, coal, limestone, lead, zinc. **Crude oil reserves** (2005): 35.3 bil bbls. **Arable land:** 33%. **Livestock** (2005): cattle: 15.2 mil; chickens: 140 mil; goats: 28 mil; pigs: 6.7 mil; sheep: 23 mil. **Fish catch** (2004): 509,201 metric tons. **Electricity prod.** (2004): 19.1 bil kWh. **Labor force** (1999 est.): agriculture 70%, industry 10%, services 20%.

Finance: Monetary unit: Naira (NGN) (Sept. 2006: 128.52 = $1 U.S.). **GDP** (2005 est.): $174.1 bil; **per capita GDP:** $1,400; **GDP growth:** 6.2%. **Imports** (2005 est.): $26 bil; partners (2004): US 9.1%, China 8.8%, UK 8.7%, Netherlands 6.3%, France 6.1%, Germany 5.7%, Italy 4.7%. **Exports** (2005 est.): $52.2 bil; partners (2004): US 48.2%, India 8.1%, Spain 7.4%, Brazil 5.5%, Japan 4.1%. **Tourism:** $21 mil. **Budget** (2005): $13.5 bil. **Intl. reserves less gold:** $119.79 bil. **Gold:** 690,000 oz t. **Consumer prices:** 13.51%.

Transport: Railroad: Length: 2,210 mi. **Motor vehicles:** 52,300 pass. cars, 13,500 comm. vehicles. **Civil aviation:** 324.4 mil pass.-mi; 36 airports. **Chief ports:** Port Harcourt, Lagos, Warri, Calabar.

Communications: TV sets: 69 per 1,000 pop. **Radios:** 226 per 1,000 pop. **Telephone lines:** 1.2 mil. **Daily newspaper circ.:** 25.4 per 1,000 pop. **Internet:** 1.8 mil users.

Health: Life expect.: 46.5 male; 47.7 female. **Births** (per 1,000 pop.): 40.4. **Deaths** (per 1,000 pop.): 16.9. **Natural inc.:** 2.35%. **Infant mortality** (per 1,000 live births): 97.1. **AIDS rate:** 3.9%.

Education: Compulsory: ages 6-14. **Literacy** (2005): 68%.

Major Intl. Organizations: UN (FAO, IBRD, ILO, IMF, IMO, WHO, WTO), the Commonwealth, AU, OPEC.

Embassy: 1333 16th St. NW 20036; 986-8400.

Website: www.nigeria.gov.ng

Early cultures in Nigeria date back to at least 700 BCE. From the 12th to the 14th centuries, more advanced cultures developed in the Yoruba area, at Ife, and in the north, where Muslim influence prevailed. Portuguese and British slavers appeared from the 15th-16th centuries. Britain seized Lagos, 1861, and gradually extended control inland until 1900. Nigeria became independent Oct. 1, 1960, and a republic Oct. 1, 1963.

On May 30, 1967, the Eastern Region seceded, proclaiming itself the Republic of Biafra, plunging the country into civil war. Casualties in the war were estimated at over 1 mil, including many "Biafrans" (mostly Ibos) who died of starvation despite international efforts to provide relief. The secessionists, after steadily losing ground, capitulated Jan. 12, 1970.

Nigeria emerged as one of the world's leading oil exporters in the 1970s, but much of the revenue has been squandered through corruption and mismanagement. After 13 years of military rule, the nation made a peaceful return to civilian government, Oct. 1979. Military rule resumed, Dec. 31, 1983; a second coup came in 1985.

Headed by Gen. Ibrahim Babangida, the military regime held elections June 12, 1993, but annulled the vote June 23 when it appeared that Moshood Abiola would win. Riots followed and many were killed. Babangida resigned and appointed a civilian to head an interim government, Aug. 26, but that government was ousted Nov. 17 in a coup led by Gen. Sani Abacha. On June 11, 1994, Abiola declared himself president; he was jailed June 23.

Abacha's brutal rule ended June 8, 1998, when he died of an apparent heart attack. Abiola died in prison July 7, as Abacha's successor, Gen. Abdulsalam Abubakar, was reportedly preparing to free him. Abiola's death sparked riots in Lagos and other cities; on July 20, Abubakar promised elections and a return to civilian rule. Olusegun Obasanjo (a former military ruler) won the presidential vote Feb. 27, 1999, Nigeria's first civilian government in 15 years.

An oil fire that exploded from a ruptured pipeline in southern Nigeria, Oct. 17, 1998, killed at least 700 people who were scavenging for fuel. The imposition of strict Islamic law in northern states led to clashes, Jan.-Mar. 2000, in which at least 800 people died. Clashes between Muslims and Christians Sept. 7-12 and Oct. 13-14 claimed an estimated 600 lives; another 200 people died when soldiers went on a rampage in southeast Nigeria Oct. 22-24.

At least 1,000 people were killed Jan. 27, 2002, when an army weapons depot in Lagos exploded; many of the victims drowned in a drainage canal while fleeing the blasts.

By 2002, the strict Islamic legal code of sharia had been adopted by about one-third of Nigeria's 36 states. Controversy over Nigeria's plans to host a Miss World pageant sparked sectarian riots in Kaduna, Nov. 20-24, leaving more than 200 people dead and 1,100 injured. Obasanjo won reelection Apr. 19, 2003.

Christian militia members massacred about 630 Muslims at Yelwa, central Nigeria, May 2, 2004. Although the World Court awarded the oil-rich Bakassi peninsula to Cameroon in 2002 and the handover was scheduled for Sept. 2004, final agreement on a Nigerian troop pullout was not reached until June 12, 2006. Rebel activities in the Niger Delta region in 2006 led to cutbacks in Nigeria's petroleum output and upward pressure on worldwide oil prices.

Norway
Kingdom of Norway

People: Population: 4,610,820. **Age distrib.** (%) <15: 19.3; 65+: 14.8. **Pop. density:** 38 per sq mi, 14 per sq km. **Urban:** 78.6%. **Ethnic groups:** Norwegian, Sami. **Principal languages:** Norwegian (official), Sami, Finnish. **Chief religion:** Evangelical Lutheran 86% (official).

Geography: Total area: 125,182 sq mi, 324,220 sq km; **Land area:** 118,865 sq mi, 307,860 sq km. **Location:** W part of Scandinavian peninsula in NW Europe (extends farther north than any European land). **Neighbors:** Sweden, Finland, Russia on E. **Topography:** A highly indented coast is lined with tens of thousands of islands. Mountains and plateaus cover most of the country, which is only 25% forested. **Capital:** Oslo, 802,000.

Government: Type: Hereditary constitutional monarchy. **Head of state:** King Harald V; b. Feb. 21, 1937; in office: Jan. 17, 1991. **Head of gov.:** Prime Min. Jens Stoltenberg; b. Mar. 16, 1959; in office: Oct. 17, 2005. **Local divisions:** 19 provinces. **Defense budget** (2005): $4.7 bil. **Active troops:** 25,800.

Economy: Industries: oil & gas, food proc., shipbuilding, pulp & paper products, metals, chemicals, timber, mining, textiles, fishing. **Chief crops:** barley, wheat, potatoes. **Natural resources:** oil, copper, nat. gas, pyrites, nickel, iron ore, zinc, lead, fish, timber, hydropower. **Crude oil reserves** (2005): 8.5 bil bbls. **Arable land:** 3%. **Livestock** (2005): cattle: 920,300; chickens: 3.3 mil; goats: 64,500; pigs: 515,400; sheep: 2.4 mil. **Fish catch** (2004): 3,160,218 metric tons. **Electricity prod.** (2004): 108.9 bil kWh. **Labor force** (1995): agriculture, forestry, and fishing 4%, industry 22%, services 74%.

Finance: Monetary unit: Krone (NOK) (Sept. 2006: 6.54 = $1 U.S.). **GDP** (2005 est.): $194.1 bil; **per capita GDP:** $42,300; **GDP growth:** 3.9%. **Imports** (2005 est.): $58.1 bil; partners (2004): Sweden 15.7%, Germany 13.6%, Denmark 7.3%, UK 6.5%, China 5%, US 4.9%, Netherlands 4.4%, France 4.3%, Finland 4.1%. **Exports** (2005 est.): $111.2 bil; partners (2004): UK 22.4%, Germany 12.9%, Netherlands 9.9%, France 9.6%, US 8.4%, Sweden 6.7%. **Tourism:** $2.9 bil. **Budget** (2005 est.): $131.3 bil. **Intl. reserves less gold:** $32.87 bil. **Consumer prices:** 1.52%.

Transport: Railroad: Length: 2,533 mi. **Motor vehicles** 1.93 mil pass. cars, 470,300 comm. vehicles. **Civil aviation:** 6.6 bil pass.-mi; 67 airports. **Chief ports:** Bergen, Stavanger, Oslo, Kristiansand.

Communications: TV sets: 653 per 1,000 pop. **Radios:** 917 per 1,000 pop. **Telephone lines:** 2.1 mil. **Daily newspaper circ.:** 569 per 1,000 pop. **Internet:** 3.1 mil users.

Health: Life expect.: 76.9 male; 82.3 female. **Births** (per 1,000 pop.): 11.5. **Deaths** (per 1,000 pop.): 9.4. **Natural inc.:** 0.21%. **Infant mortality** (per 1,000 live births): 3.7. **AIDS rate:** 0.1%.

Education: Compulsory: ages 6-16. **Literacy** (2005): 100%.

Major Intl. Organizations: UN and all of its specialized agencies, EFTA, NATO, OECD, OSCE.

Embassy: 2720 34th St. NW 20008; 333-6000.

Website: www.norway.no

The first ruler of Norway was Harald the Fairhaired, who came to power in 872 CE. Between 800 and 1000, Norway's Vikings raided and occupied widely dispersed parts of Europe.

The country was united with Denmark 1381-1814, and with Sweden, 1814-1905. In 1905, the country became independent with Prince Charles of Denmark as king.

Norway remained neutral during WWI. Germany attacked Norway Apr. 9, 1940, and held it until liberation May 8, 1945. The country abandoned its neutrality after the war, and joined NATO. In a referendum Nov. 28, 1994, Norwegian voters rejected European Union membership.

Abundant hydroelectric resources provided the base for industrialization, giving Norway one of the highest living standards in the world. The country is a leading producer and exporter of crude oil, with extensive reserves in the North Sea. Norway's merchant marine is one of the world's largest.

A center-left bloc led by Jens Stoltenberg won parliamentary elections Sept. 12, 2005, and took office Oct. 17.

Svalbard is a group of mountainous islands in the Arctic O., area 23,957.2 sq mi, pop. (2004 est.) 2,756. The largest, Spitsbergen (formerly called West Spitsbergen), 15,060 sq mi, seat of the governor, is about 370 mi N of Norway. By a treaty signed in Paris, 1920, major European powers recognized the sovereignty of Norway, which incorporated it in 1925.

Jan Mayen, area 144 sq mi, is a volcanic island located about 565 mi W-NW of Norway; it was annexed in 1929.

Oman
Sultanate of Oman

People: Population: 3,102,229. **Age distrib.** (%) <15: 42.7; 65+: 2.6. **Pop. density:** 37 per sq mi, 14 per sq km. **Urban:** 77.6%. **Ethnic groups:** Arab, Baluchi, South Asian, African. **Principal languages:** Arabic (official), English, Baluchi, Urdu, Indian dialects. **Chief religion:** Muslim 75% (official; mostly Ibadhi).

Geography: Total area: 82,031 sq mi, 212,460 sq km; **Land area:** 82,031 sq mi, 212,460 sq km. **Location:** On SE coast of Arabian peninsula. **Neighbors:** United Arab Emirates, Saudi Arabia, Yemen on W. **Topography:** Oman has a narrow coastal plain up to 10 mi wide, a range of barren mountains reaching 9,900 ft, and a wide, stony, mostly waterless plateau, avg. alt. 1,000 ft. Also, an exclave at the tip of the Musandam peninsula controls access to the Persian Gulf. **Capital:** Muscat, 565,000.

Government: Type: Absolute monarchy. **Head of state and gov.:** Sultan Qabus bin Said; b. Nov. 18, 1940; in office: July 23, 1970 (also prime min. since Jan. 2, 1972). **Local divisions:** 6 regions and 2 governorates. **Defense budget** (2005): $3 bil. **Active troops:** 41,700.

Economy: Industries: oil, gas, constr., cement, copper. **Chief crops:** dates, limes, bananas, alfalfa, vegetables. **Natural resources:** oil, copper, asbestos, marble, limestone, chromium, gypsum, nat. gas. **Crude oil reserves** (2005): 5.5 bil bbls. **Livestock** (2005): cattle: 335,000; chickens: 4.2 mil; goats: 1.1 mil; sheep: 375,000. **Fish catch** (2004): 165,532 metric tons. **Electricity prod.** (2004): 14.3 bil kWh.

Finance: Monetary unit: Rial (OMR) (Sept. 2006: 0.38 = $1 U.S.). **GDP** (2005 est.): $39.7 bil; **per capita GDP:** $13,200; **GDP growth:** 4.3%. **Imports** (2005 est.): $8.7 bil; partners (2004): UAE 17.5%, Japan 16.6%, UK 8.5%, Italy 6.4%, Germany 5.2%, US 4.7%, India 4.3%. **Exports** (2005 est.): $19 bil; partners (2004): China 27.6%, South Korea 17.8%, Japan 12.7%, Thailand 11.7%, UAE 6.6%. **Tourism:** $518 mil. **Budget** (2005 est.): $10.6 bil. **Intl. reserves less gold:** $3.11 bil. **Consumer prices:** 1.22%.

Transport: Motor vehicles: 324,000 pass. cars, 109,100 comm. vehicles. **Civil aviation:** 2.6 bil pass.-mi; 6 airports. **Chief ports:** Matrah, Mina' al Fahl.

Communications: TV sets: 575 per 1,000 pop. **Radios:** 607 per 1,000 pop. **Telephone lines:** 265,200. **Daily newspaper circ.:** NA. **Internet:** 245,000 users.

Health: Life expect.: 71.1 male; 75.7 female. **Births** (per 1,000 pop.): 36.2. **Deaths** (per 1,000 pop.): 3.8. **Natural inc.:** 3.24%. **Infant mortality** (per 1,000 live births): 18.9. **AIDS rate:** NA.

Education: Literacy: 81.4%.

Major Intl. Organizations: UN (FAO, IBRD, ILO, IMF, IMO, WHO, WTO), AL.

Embassy: 2535 Belmont Rd. NW 20008; 387-1980.

Website: www.omanet.org.

Oman was originally called Muscat and Oman. A long history of rule by other lands, including Portugal in the 16th cent., ended with the ouster of the Persians in 1744. By the early 19th cent., Muscat and Oman was one of the most important countries in the region, controlling much of the Persian and Pakistan coasts, and also ruling far-away Zanzibar, which was separated in 1861 under British mediation.

British influence was confirmed in a 1951 treaty, and Britain helped suppress an uprising by traditionally rebellious interior tribes against control by Muscat in the 1950s.

On July 23, 1970, Sultan Said bin Taimur was overthrown by his son, who changed the nation's name to Sultanate of Oman.

Oil is the major source of income.

Oman opened its air bases to Western forces following the Iraqi invasion of Kuwait on Aug. 2, 1990, and was a base for U.S. aircraft in the Afghanistan war, 2001. After a secret trial, 31 suspected Islamists received prison sentences, May 2, 2005, for plotting a coup. A free trade agreement with the U.S. was signed Jan. 19, 2006.

Pakistan
Islamic Republic of Pakistan

People: Population: 165,803,560. **Age distrib.** (%) <15: 39; 65+: 4.1. **Pop. density:** 551 per sq mi, 212 per sq km. **Urban:** 34.1%. **Ethnic groups:** Punjabi, Sindhi, Pashtun, Balochi. **Principal languages:** English, Urdu (both official); Punjabi, Sindhi, Siraiki, Pashtu, Balochi, Hindko, Brahui, Burushaski. **Chief religions:** Muslim 97% (official; Sunni 77%, Shi'a 20%).

Geography: Total area: 310,403 sq mi, 803,940 sq km; **Land area:** 300,666 sq mi, 778,720 sq km. **Location:** In W part of South Asia. **Neighbors:** Iran on W, Afghanistan and China on N, India on E. **Topography:** The Indus R. rises in the Hindu Kush and Himalaya Mts. in the N (highest is K2, or Godwin Austen, 28,250 ft, 2nd highest in world), then flows over 1,000 mi. through fertile valley and empties into Arabian Sea. Thar Desert, Eastern Plains flank Indus Valley. **Capital:** Islamabad, 736,000. **Cities (urban aggr.):** Karachi, 11,608,000; Lahore, 6,289,000; Faisalabad, 2,494,000.

Government: Type: Republic with strong military influence. **Head of state:** Pres. Pervez Musharraf; b Aug. 11,1943; in office: Oct. 5, 1999 (as pres. from June 20, 2001). **Head of gov.:** Shaukat Aziz; b Mar. 6, 1949; in office: Aug. 28, 2004. **Local divisions:** 4 provinces and 1 capital territory, plus federally administered tribal areas. **Defense budget** (2005): $3.7 bil. **Active troops:** 619,000.

Economy: Industries: textiles, food proc., beverages, constr. materials, clothing, paper products. **Chief crops:** cotton, wheat, rice, sugarcane, fruits. **Natural resources:** nat. gas, oil, coal, iron ore, copper, salt, limestone. **Crude oil reserves** (2005): 289 mil bbls. **Arable land:** 27%. **Livestock** (2005): cattle: 24.2 mil; chickens: 166 mil; goats: 56.7 mil; sheep: 24.9 mil. **Fish catch** (2004): 569,995 metric tons. **Electricity prod.** (2004): 80.2 bil kWh. **Labor force** (2004 est.): agriculture 42%, industry 20%, services 38%.

Finance: Monetary unit: Rupee (PKR) (Sept. 2006: 60.57 = $1 U.S.). **GDP** (2005 est.): $393.4 bil; **per capita GDP:** $2,400; **GDP growth:** 6.9%. **Imports** (2005 est.): $21.3 bil; partners (2004): China 10.8%, US 10.2%, UAE 9.3%, Saudi Arabia 9%, Japan 7%, Kuwait 5.3%, Germany 4.2%. **Exports** (2005 est.): $14.9 bil; partners (2004): US 21.3%, UAE 9.8%, UK 7.1%, Germany 5.2%, Hong Kong 4.2%, Saudi Arabia 4.1%. **Tourism:** $178 mil. **Budget** (2005 est.): $20.1 bil. **Intl. reserves less gold:** $7.02 bil. **Gold:** 2.1 mil. oz t. **Consumer prices:** 9.06%.

Transport: Railroad: Length: 5,072 mi. **Motor vehicles** 1.17 mil pass. cars, 488,600 comm. vehicles. **Civil aviation:** 6.6 bil pass.-mi; 91 airports. **Chief port:** Karachi.

Communications: TV sets: 105 per 1,000 pop. **Radios:** 94 per 1,000 pop. **Telephone lines:** 5.3 mil. **Daily newspaper circ.:** 39.3 per 1,000 pop. **Internet:** 7.5 mil users.

Health: Life expect.: 62.4 male; 64.4 female. **Births** (per 1,000 pop.): 29.7. **Deaths** (per 1,000 pop.): 8.2. **Natural inc.:** 2.15%. **Infant mortality** (per 1,000 live births): 70.5. **AIDS rate:** 0.1%.

Education: Compulsory: ages 5-9. **Literacy:** 49.9%.

Major Intl. Organizations: UN (FAO, IBRD, ILO, IMF, IMO, WHO, WTO), the Commonwealth.

Embassy: 3517 International Ct., NW Washington DC 20008; 243-6500.

Website: www.pakistan.gov.pk

Pakistan shares the 5,000-year history of the India-Pakistan subcontinent. At present-day Harappa and Mohenjo Daro, the Indus Valley Civilization, with large cities and elaborate irrigation systems, flourished c. 4,000-2,500 BCE. Aryan invaders from the northwest conquered the region around 1,500 BCE, forging the Vedic civilization that dominated the region for over a thousand years. Other invaders from the west followed. The first Arab invasion, 712 CE, introduced Islam. Present-day Pakistan and India were part of the Mogul empire from 1526 to 1857. Muslim power faded by the end of the 19th cent. as the British gained control of the north and northwest areas of the subcontinent.

After WWI, the Muslims of British India began agitation for minority rights in elections. Muhammad Ali Jinnah (1876-1948) was the principal architect of Pakistan. When the British withdrew Aug. 14, 1947, the Islamic majority areas of India acquired self-government as Pakistan, with dominion status in the Commonwealth. Pakistan was divided into 2 sections, West Pakistan and East Pakistan. The 2 areas were nearly 1,000 mi apart on opposite sides of India.

The Awami League, which had sought regional autonomy for East Pakistan for several years, won a majority in Dec. 1970 elections to a constituent assembly. In Mar. 1971, Pakistan's military-dominated government postponed the assembly. Rioting and strikes broke out in the East. On Mar. 25, 1971, government troops launched attacks in the East. The Easterners, aided by India, proclaimed the independent nation of Bangladesh. In months of widespread fighting, countless thousands were killed. Some 10 mil Easterners fled into India. Full-scale war between India and Pakistan had spread to both the East and West fronts by Dec. 3. Pakistan troops in the East surrendered Dec. 16; Pakistan agreed to a cease-fire in the West Dec. 17. On July 3, 1972, Pakistan and India signed a pact agreeing to withdraw troops from their borders and resolve problems peacefully.

Zulfikar Ali Bhutto, leader of the Pakistan People's Party, which had won the most West Pakistan votes in Dec. 1970 elections, became president Dec. 20, 1971. Bhutto was overthrown in a military coup July 1977. Convicted of complicity in a 1974 political murder, he was executed Apr. 4, 1979. Millions of Afghan refugees flooded into Pakistan after the USSR invaded Afghanistan Dec. 1979; by 2006, nearly 2.9 mil refugees had been repatriated, but up to 2.5 mil remained.

Pres. Mohammad Zia ul-Haq was killed when his plane exploded in Aug. 1988. Following Nov. elections, Benazir Bhutto, daughter of Zulfikar Ali Bhutto, was named prime minister, becoming the first woman leader of a Muslim nation. She was accused of corruption and dismissed by the president, Aug. 1990. Bhutto returned to power Oct. 1993 but was dismissed again, Nov. 1996, amid further corruption charges. Responding to nuclear weapons tests by India,

Pakistan conducted its own tests, May 28-30, 1998; the U.S. imposed economic sanctions on both countries.

In mid-1999, Muslim infiltrators, apparently including Pakistani troops, seized Indian-held positions in the disputed territory of Kashmir, which witnessed its heaviest fighting in over 2 decades (see Kashmir). After meeting with Pres. Bill Clinton on July 4, Prime Min. Nawaz Sharif agreed to a Pakistani pullback. Growing conflict between Sharif and the military climaxed in his firing on Oct. 12 of army chief Gen. Pervez Musharraf, whose supporters staged a bloodless coup. Musharraf assumed the presidency June 20, 2001.

Following the Sept. 11, 2001, terrorist attacks on the U.S., Pres. Musharraf, Sept. 19, pledged cooperation with the U.S. in fighting Taliban and al-Qaeda militants within its own tribal areas and in neighboring Afghanistan. In return, the U.S. waived its 1998 sanctions and offered Pakistan financial aid and debt relief. Guerrilla violence in Kashmir and Pakistani missile tests May 25-28, 2002, heightened fears of war with India, but the crisis was eased in June with U.S. mediation. A referendum Apr. 30, 2002, extended Musharraf's rule for 5 years; many observers called the vote rigged.

During 2002-04 there was evidence of growing al-Qaeda and Taliban activity within Pakistan. Militants kidnapped *Wall Street Journal* reporter Daniel Pearl Jan. 23, 2002, and eventually killed him; 4 Islamic extremists were convicted July 15. Several alleged al-Qaeda operatives, including Ramzi bin al-Shibh, believed to have been a close associate of Sept. 11 ringleader Mohamed Atta, were captured in a shootout in Karachi, Sept. 11, 2002. The alleged mastermind of the Sept. 11 attacks, Khalid Sheikh Mohammed, was apprehended in Rawalpindi, Mar. 1, 2003. Islamic extremists carried out bombings in Rawalpindi Dec. 14 and 25, in unsuccessful attempts to assassinate Musharraf. A top al-Qaeda figure implicated in those attempts, Amjad Hussain Farooqi, was killed by security forces in late Sept. 2004.

Accused of selling atomic secrets to Iran, Libya, and North Korea, Pakistan's top nuclear scientist, Abdul Qadeer Khan, made a televised apology, Feb. 4, 2004, and said his actions were unauthorized. He received a pardon from Musharraf Feb. 5. A joint U.S.-Pakistani raid July 25 broke up an al-Qaeda cell in Gujrat, revealing possible evidence of planned attacks against U.S. financial institutions. Shaukat Aziz, who survived a suicide bomb attack July 30, was elected prime min. Aug. 27.

On Oct. 1, at least 30 worshippers were killed in the bombing of a Shiite mosque in Sialkot. Earlier bombings and other attacks on Shiite religious targets in Karachi and Quetta had killed more than 100. A car bomb, Oct. 7, at a Sunni religious gathering in Multan left more than 40 people dead. British ties with Pakistan were frayed by reports that 3 of 4 suspects in the London train and bus bombings, July 7, 2005, were of Pakistani ancestry, and that 2 had recently been to Pakistan. Musharraf pledged July 29 to arrest leaders of banned Islamist groups and to expel foreign students from Islamic schools, or *madrassas*.

An earthquake that rocked Pakistan and the Pakistani-held region of Kashmir Oct. 8 , 2005, killed about 80,000 people and left up to 3 mil homeless. In 2006, Pakistani authorities assisted the British in foiling an alleged plot to blow up jets on transatlantic routes between the UK and the U.S.; many of the suspects arrested the night of Aug. 9-10 had ties to Pakistan.

Palau
Republic of Palau
People: Population: 20,579. **Age distrib.** (%) <15: 26.3; 65+: 4.6. **Pop. density:** 116 per sq mi, 44 per sq km. **Urban:** 68.6%. **Ethnic groups:** Palauan (Micronesian/Malayan/Melanesian mix) 70%, Asian 28%, White 2%. **Principal languages:** English (official); Palauan, Sonsorolese, Tobi, Angaur, Japanese (all official in certain states). **Chief religions:** Roman Catholic 42%, Protestant 23%, Modekngei 9%.

Geography: Total area: 177 sq mi, 458 sq km; **Land area:** 177 sq mi, 458 sq km. **Location:** Archipelago (26 islands, more than 300 islets) in the W Pacific Ocean, about 530 mi SE of the Philippines. **Neighbors:** Micronesia to E, Indonesia to S. **Topography:** Palau is comprised of a mountainous main island and low coral atolls, usually fringed with large barrier reefs. **Capital:** Koror, 14,000. (Note: a new capital is being built in Babelthuap.)

Government: Type: Republic. **Head of state and gov.:** Pres. Tommy Esang Remengesau, Jr.; b. Feb. 28, 1956; in office: Jan. 19, 2001. **Local divisions:** 16 states.

Economy: Industries: tourism, handicrafts, constr., garment making. **Chief crops:** coconuts, copra, cassava, sweet potatoes. **Natural resources:** timber, gold & other minerals, fish. **Fish catch** (2004): 1,084 metric tons. **Labor force** (1990): agriculture 20%.

Finance: Monetary unit: U.S. Dollar (USD) (Sept. 2006: 1.00 = $1 U.S.). **GDP** (2001 est.): $174 mil; **per capita GDP:** $5,800; **GDP growth:** 1%. **Imports** (2001 est.): $96.8 mil; $99.0 mil; partners (2000): US, Guam, Japan, Singapore, South Korea. **Exports** (2001 est.): $33.6 mil; partners (2000): US, Japan, Singapore. **Tourism** (2002): $59 mil. **Budget** (1999 est.): $80.8 mil.

Transport: Civil aviation: NA; 1 airport.

Communications: TV sets: 98 per 1,000 pop. **Radios:** 550 per 1,000 pop. **Telephone lines:** NA. **Internet:** NA.

Health: Life expect.: 67.3 male; 73.8 female. **Births** (per 1,000 pop.): 18. **Deaths** (per 1,000 pop.): 6.8. **Natural inc.:** 1.12%. **Infant mortality** (per 1,000 live births): 14.5. **AIDS rate:** NA.

Education: Compulsory: ages 6-14. **Literacy** (2005): 92%.
Major Intl. Organizations: UN (FAO, IBRD, ILO, IMF, WHO).
Embassy: 1700 Pennsylvania Ave 20006 452-6814
Website: www.palaugov.net

Spain acquired the Palau Islands in 1886 and sold them to Germany in 1899. Japan seized them in 1914. American forces occupied the islands in 1944; in 1947, they became part of the U.S.-administered UN Trust Territory of the Pacific Islands. In 1981 Palau became an autonomous republic; in 1993 the republic ratified a compact of free association with the U.S., which provides financial aid in return for U.S. use of Palauan military facilities over 15 years. Palau became an independent nation on Oct. 1, 1994. Vice Pres. Tommy Remengesau won the presidential election held Nov. 7, 2000, and was reelected Nov. 2, 2004.

Panama
Republic of Panama
People: Population: 3,191,319. **Age distrib.** (%) <15: 30.3; 65+: 6.3. **Pop. density:** 108 per sq mi, 41 per sq km. **Urban:** 57.1%. **Ethnic groups:** Mestizo 70%, Amerindian-West Indian 14%, White 10%, Amerindian 6%. **Principal languages:** Spanish (official), English. **Chief religions:** Roman Catholic 85%, Protestant 15%.

Geography: Total area: 30,193 sq mi, 78,200 sq km; **Land area:** 29,340 sq mi, 75,990 sq km. **Location:** In Central America. **Neighbors:** Costa Rica on W, Colombia on E. **Topography:** 2 mountain ranges run the length of the isthmus. Tropical rain forests cover the Caribbean coast and eastern Panama. **Capital:** Panama City, 1,216,000.

Government: Type: Republic. **Head of state and gov.:** Pres. Martin Torrijos Espino; b. July 18, 1963; in office: Sept. 1, 2004. **Local divisions:** 9 provinces, 5 territories. **Defense budget:** 158 mil. **Active troops:** Nil. (11,800 paramilitary).

Economy: Industries: constr., oil refining, brewing, constr. materials, sugar milling. **Chief crops:** bananas, rice, corn, coffee, sugarcane. **Natural resources:** copper, mahogany, shrimp, hydropower. **Arable land:** 7%. **Livestock** (2005): cattle: 1.6 mil; chickens: 14 mil; goats: 6,300; pigs: 272,000. **Fish catch** (2004): 199,533 metric tons. **Electricity prod.** (2004): 7.5 bil kWh. **Labor force** (1995 est.): agriculture 20.8%, industry 18%, services 61.2%.

Finance: Monetary unit: Balboa (PAB) (Sept. 2006: 1.00 = $1 U.S.). **GDP** (2005 est.): $22.8 bil; **per capita GDP:** $7,200; **GDP growth:** 6.4%. **Imports** (2005 est.): $8.7 bil; partners (2004): Japan 32.9%, China 10.6%, US 9.8%, South Korea 7.2%, Singapore 7.1%, Italy 4.5%. **Exports** (2005 est.): $7.5 bil; partners (2004): US 12.2%, Nigeria 9.4%, Germany 8.4%, South Korea 8.2%, El Salvador 5.7%, Peru 5.1%, Costa Rica 5.1%, Japan 4.1%. **Tourism:** $651 mil. **Budget** (2005 est.): $4 bil. **Intl. reserves less gold:** $847 mil. **Consumer prices:** 3.26%.

Transport: Railroad: Length: 221 mi. **Motor vehicles:** 219,400 pass. cars, 70,300 comm. vehicles. **Civil aviation:** 1.8 bil pass.-mi; 53 airports. **Chief ports:** Balboa, Cristobal.

Communications: TV sets: 192 per 1,000 pop. **Radios:** 299 per 1,000 pop. **Telephone lines:** 440,100. **Daily newspaper circ.:** NA. **Internet:** 300,000 users.

Health: Life expect.: 72.7 male; 77.9 female. **Births** (per 1,000 pop.): 21.7. **Deaths** (per 1,000 pop.): 5.4. **Natural inc.:** 1.64%. **Infant mortality** (per 1,000 live births): 16.4. **AIDS rate:** 0.9%.

Education: Compulsory: ages 6-11. **Literacy:** 91.9%.
Major Intl. Organizations: UN (FAO, IBRD, ILO, IMF, IMO, OAS, WHO, WTO).
Embassy: 2862 McGill Terrace NW 20008; 483-1407.
Website: www.visitpanama.com

The coast of Panama was sighted by Rodrigo de Bastidas, sailing with Columbus for Spain in 1501, and was visited by Columbus in 1502. Vasco Nunez de Balboa crossed the isthmus and "discovered" the Pacific Ocean, Sept. 13, 1513. Spanish colonies were ravaged by Francis Drake, 1572-95, and Henry Morgan, 1668-71. Morgan destroyed the old city of Panama which had been founded in 1519. Freed from Spain, Panama joined Colombia in 1821.

Panama declared its independence from Colombia Nov. 3, 1903, with U.S. recognition. In support of Panama, U.S. naval forces deterred action by Colombia. Panama granted use, occupation, and control of the Canal Zone to the U.S. by treaty, ratified Feb. 26, 1904. In 1978, a new treaty provided for a gradual takeover by Panama of the canal, and withdrawal of U.S. troops, to be completed before the end of the century. U.S. payments were substantially increased in the interim.

President Delvalle was ousted by the National Assembly, Feb. 26, 1988, after he tried to fire the head of the Panama Defense Forces, Gen. Manuel Antonio Noriega, who was under U.S. federal indictment on drug charges. U.S. troops invaded Panama Dec. 20, 1989, and Noriega surrendered Jan. 3, 1990.

Mireya Moscoso, widow of former Pres. Arnulfo Arias, was elected president May 2, 1999, becoming Panama's first female head of state. The U.S. handed over control of the Panama Canal to Panama Dec. 31, 1999. Martin Torrijos Espino, son of Brig. Gen. Omar Torrijos Herrera (dictator of Panama, 1968-81), won the presidential election of May 2, 2004. A $5.3-bil plan to widen the canal won legislative approval, pending a national referendum Oct. 22, 2006.

War in Iraq

ZARQAWI KILLED
The leader of al-Qaeda in Iraq, Abu Musab al-Zarqawi, was killed by a U.S. bomb strike June 7, 2006.

SECTARIAN VIOLENCE
An explosion in Samarra, in Feb., damaged the golden dome of one of Iraq's most prominent Shiite shrines.

ON TRIAL
Saddam Hussein's trial continued in 2006 for his alleged role in the killings of more than 148 Shiite Muslims in the town of Dujail in 1982.

BUSH IN IRAQ
President Bush visited Iraqi Prime Minister Nouri al-Maliki (right) at the U.S. Embassy in Baghdad, June 13, 2006.

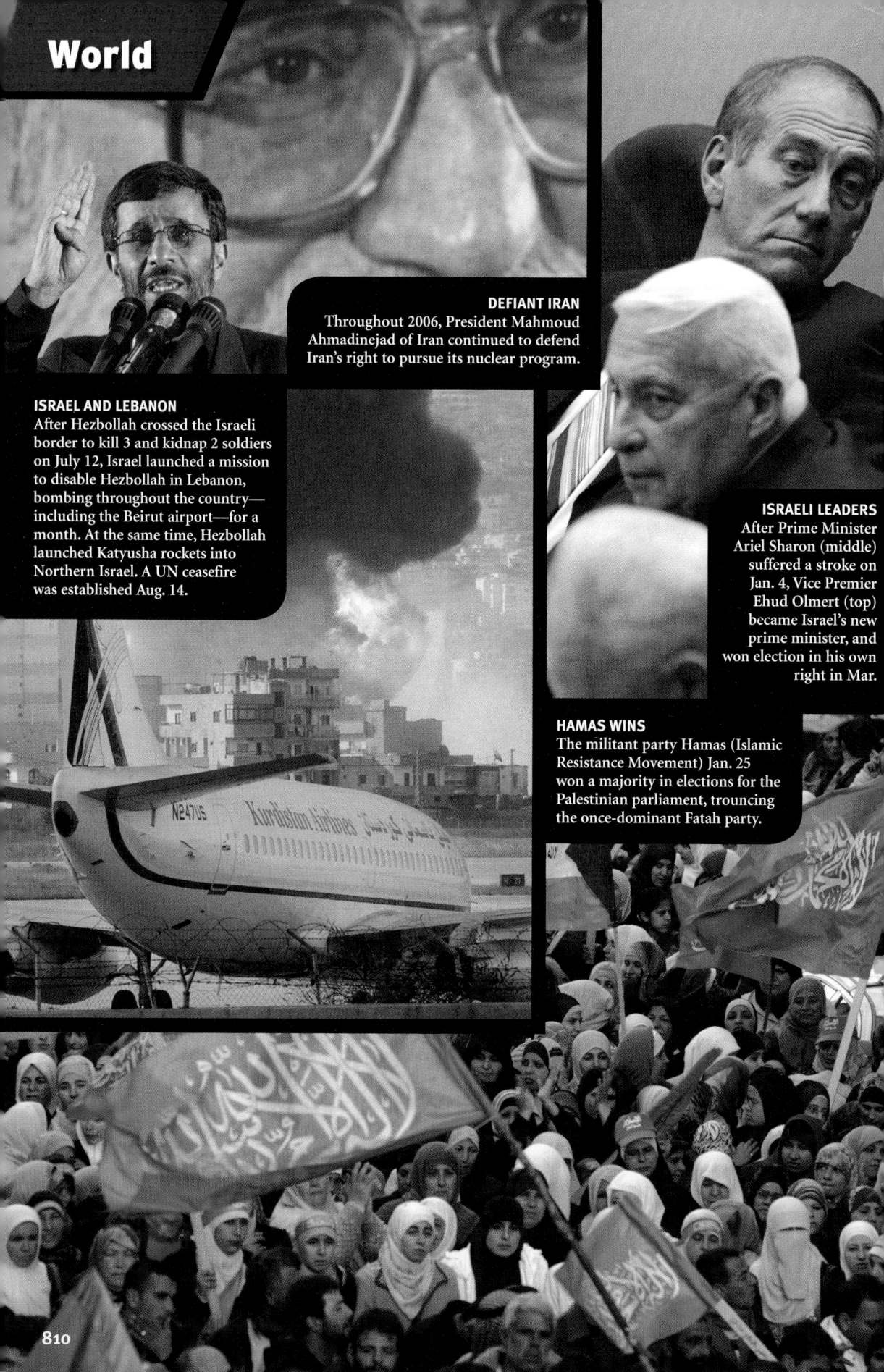

DEFIANT IRAN
Throughout 2006, President Mahmoud Ahmadinejad of Iran continued to defend Iran's right to pursue its nuclear program.

ISRAEL AND LEBANON
After Hezbollah crossed the Israeli border to kill 3 and kidnap 2 soldiers on July 12, Israel launched a mission to disable Hezbollah in Lebanon, bombing throughout the country—including the Beirut airport—for a month. At the same time, Hezbollah launched Katyusha rockets into Northern Israel. A UN ceasefire was established Aug. 14.

ISRAELI LEADERS
After Prime Minister Ariel Sharon (middle) suffered a stroke on Jan. 4, Vice Premier Ehud Olmert (top) became Israel's new prime minister, and won election in his own right in Mar.

HAMAS WINS
The militant party Hamas (Islamic Resistance Movement) Jan. 25 won a majority in elections for the Palestinian parliament, trouncing the once-dominant Fatah party.

TERRORISM IN INDIA
Train bombings during rush hour in Mumbai on July 11, 2006, killed 207 and injured 700.

LIQUID BOMB SCARE
The Aug. 9 arrest of 24 people suspected in an airplane bomb plot led to delays and cancellations of flights in and out of the U.K.

SUDANESE SUFFERING
As of Aug. 2006, the death toll in the Darfur conflict was around 200,000, and more than 2 million were estimated to have been driven from their homes. Sudan's government continued to resist the deployment of UN peacekeeping troops.

HOSTILE NORTH KOREA
South Koreans protested North Korea's July 2006 test-launching of six missiles.

World

PRESIDENT CALDERON
A close and hotly contested presidential election in Mexico resulted in victory for Felipe Calderon of the National Action Party, who was to begin his 6-year term Dec. 1.

AVIAN FLU
The Centers for Disease Control and the World Health Organization continue to monitor the H5N1 virus. Known as Avian Flu, it has been transmitted from human to human in Asia.

CARTOON PROTESTS
A set of cartoons first published in Danish and then Norwegian newspapers depicting the Prophet Muhammad set off protests worldwide (Srinagar, India, in picture) in Feb. Rioters set fire to the Danish and Norwegian embassies in Damascus, and more than 100 people were killed during protests in Nigeria.

CHANGE IN CUBA
Raul Castro (right) assumed the role of president of Cuba on July 31, after longtime president (and older brother) Fidel Castro announced that he would be having surgery due to intestinal bleeding.

WORLD CUP VICTORS
Fabio Cannavaro hoists the World Cup trophy after Italy beat France 5-3 in a penalty shootout in the final game in Berlin, July 9. One of France's star players (above on right), Zinedine Zidane, was ejected late in the second half of the final game, after he head-butted Italy's Marco Materazzi.

DOPING SCANDAL
Floyd Landis of the U.S. won the Tour de France in July, but then a positive drug test resulted in his dismissal from Swiss cycling team Phonak, on Aug. 5, and may lead to the revocation of his victory.

FALLEN CHAMPION
The winner of the Kentucky Derby, Barbaro, with jockey Edgar Prado, suffered a leg injury after the start of the Preakness Stakes May 20.

TOPPING THE BABE
Barry Bonds, who continued to be dogged by allegations of steroid use, hit home run number 715 on May 28, surpassing Babe Ruth for second on the all-time list.

STEELERS VICTORIOUS
Pittsburgh Steelers MVP Hines Ward (left) and Jerome Bettis (who retired soon after the game) celebrated their Superbowl XL victory over the Seattle Seahawks.

FIRST TO GOLD
Shani Davis of the United States became the first black athlete to win an individual Winter Olympic gold medal, for the men's 1000-meter speed-skating.

GATORS BITE BRUINS
The University of Florida Gators beat the UCLA Bruins in the men's NCAA Final Four in April to win their first NCAA basketball title.

DOMINANT DUO
Tiger Woods won the British Open (shown) and the PGA Championship, his 11th and 12th major championships. Roger Federer (left) of Switzerland won his ninth Grand Slam tennis title by beating Andy Roddick at the U.S. Open Sept. 10.

Farewells

CORETTA SCOTT KING
Jan. 31, 2006

DON KNOTTS
Feb. 25, 2006

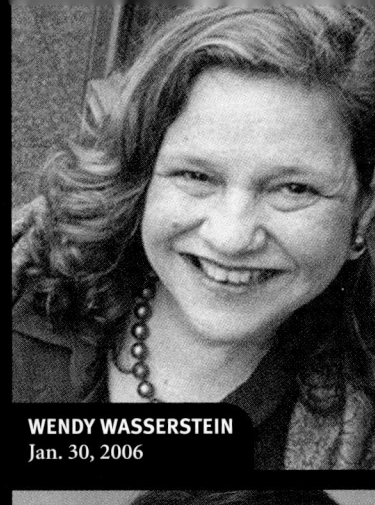

WENDY WASSERSTEIN
Jan. 30, 2006

GORDON PARKS
Mar. 7, 2006

STEPHEN IRWIN
Sept. 4, 2006

CASPAR WEINBERGER
Mar. 28, 2006

OLEG CASSINI
Mar. 17, 2006

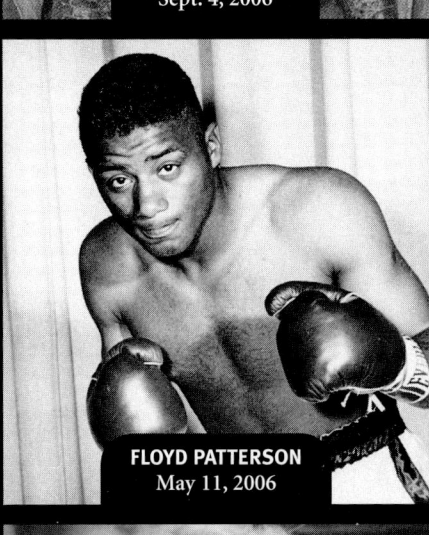

FLOYD PATTERSON
May 11, 2006

AARON SPELLING
June 23, 2006

BETTY FRIEDAN
Feb. 4, 2006

SHELLEY WINTERS
Jan. 14, 2006

CHRISTOPHER REEVE
Oct. 10, 2004

DANA REEVE
Mar. 6, 2006

Papua New Guinea
Independent State of Papua New Guinea

People: Population: 5,670,544. **Age distrib.** (%) <15: 37.8; 65+: 3.9. **Pop. density:** 32 per sq mi, 12 per sq km. **Urban:** 13.2%. **Ethnic groups:** Melanesian, Papuan, Negrito, Micronesian, Polynesian. **Principal languages:** English (official), pidgin English, Motu; 715 indigenous languages. **Chief religions:** Indigenous beliefs 34%, Roman Catholic 22%, Protestant 44%.

Geography: Total area: 178,704 sq mi, 462,840 sq km; **Land area:** 174,850 sq mi, 452,860 sq km. **Location:** SE Asia, occupying E half of island of New Guinea and about 600 nearby islands. **Neighbors:** Indonesia (West Irian) on W, Australia on S. **Topography:** Thickly forested mts. cover much of the center of the country, with lowlands along the coasts. Included are some islands of Bismarck and Solomon groups, such as the Admiralty Isls., New Ireland, New Britain, and Bougainville. **Capital:** Port Moresby, 289,000.

Government: Type: Parliamentary democracy. **Head of state:** Queen Elizabeth II, represented by Gov.-Gen. Sir Paulias Matane; b. 1931; in office: June 29, 2004. **Head of gov.:** Prime Min. Sir Michael Somare; b. Apr. 9, 1936; in office: Aug. 5, 2002. **Local divisions:** 20 provinces. **Defense budget** (2005): $27 mil. **Active troops:** 3,100.

Economy: Industries: copra & palm oil proc., wood products, mining. **Chief crops:** coffee, cocoa, coconuts, palm kernels, tea, rubber, sweet potatoes. **Natural resources:** gold, copper, silver, nat. gas, timber, oil, fish. **Crude oil reserves** (2005): 240 mil bbls. **Livestock** (2005): cattle: 91,500; chickens: 4 mil; goats: 2,700; pigs: 1.8 mil; sheep: 7,500. **Fish catch** (2004): 233,800 metric tons. **Electricity prod.** (2004): 3.4 bil kWh. **Labor force:** agriculture 85%.

Finance: Monetary unit: Kina (PGK) (Sept. 2006: 2.96 = $1 U.S.). **GDP** (2005 est.): $14.4 bil; **per capita GDP:** $2,600; **GDP growth:** 2.9%. **Imports** (2005 est.): $1.7 bil; partners (2004): Australia 45.2%, Singapore 21.1%, New Zealand 7.5%, Japan 4.2%, China 4.2%. **Exports** (2005 est.): $2.8 bil; partners (2004): Australia 27.7%, China 5.8%, Japan 5.7%, Germany 5%. **Tourism** (2001): $5 mil. **Budget** (2005 est.): $1.4 bil. **Intl. reserves less gold:** $502 mil. **Gold:** 60,000 oz t. **Consumer prices:** 1.7%.

Transport: Motor vehicles: 24,900 pass. cars, 87,800 comm. vehicles. **Civil aviation:** 730.1 mil pass.-mi; 21 airports. **Chief ports:** Port Moresby, Lae.

Communications: TV sets: 13 per 1,000 pop. **Radios:** 91 per 1,000 pop. **Telephone lines:** 62,000. **Daily newspaper circ.:** NA. **Internet:** 170,000 users.

Health: Life expect.: 63.1 male; 67.6 female. **Births** (per 1,000 pop.): 29.4. **Deaths** (per 1,000 pop.): 7.2. **Natural inc.:** 2.21%. **Infant mortality** (per 1,000 live births): 50. **AIDS rate:** 1.8%.

Education: Compulsory: ages 6-14. **Literacy:** 57.3%.

Major Intl. Organizations: UN (FAO, IBRD, ILO, IMF, IMO, WHO, WTO), the Commonwealth, APEC.

Embassy: 1779 Massachusetts Ave NW, Ste. 805, 20036; 745-3680.

Website: www.pngonline.gov.pg

Human remains have been found in the interior of New Guinea dating back at least 10,000 years and possibly much earlier. Successive waves of peoples probably entered the country from Asia through Indonesia. The indigenous population consists of a huge number of tribes, many living in almost complete isolation with mutually unintelligible languages.

Europeans visited in the 15th cent., but actual land claims did not begin until the 19th cent., when the Dutch took control of the island's western half. The southern half of eastern New Guinea was first claimed by Britain in 1884, and transferred to Australia in 1905. The northern half was claimed by Germany in 1884, but captured in WWI by Australia, which was first granted a League of Nations mandate and then a UN trusteeship over the area. The 2 territories were administered jointly after 1949, given self-government Dec. 1, 1973, and became independent Sept. 16, 1975.

Secessionist rebels clashed with government forces on Bougainville beginning in 1988; a truce signed Oct. 10, 1997, brought a halt to the fighting, which had claimed an estimated 20,000 lives. The country suffered from a severe drought in 1997. A tsunami killed at least 3,000 people July 17, 1998. A Bougainville autonomy agreement was signed Aug. 30, 2001. Army mutinies were suppressed in Mar. 2001 and Mar. 2002.

The country has extensive energy resources; a proposed pipeline would transport natural gas to Queensland, Australia.

Paraguay
Republic of Paraguay

People: Population: 6,506,464. **Age distrib.** (%) <15: 37.7; 65+: 4.8. **Pop. density:** 42 per sq mi, 16 per sq km. **Urban:** 57.2%. **Ethnic groups:** Mestizo 95%. **Principal languages:** Spanish, Guaraní (both official). **Chief religions:** Roman Catholic 90%.

Geography: Total area: 157,047 sq mi, 406,750 sq km; **Land area:** 153,398 sq mi, 397,300 sq km. **Location:** Landlocked country in central South America. **Neighbors:** Bolivia on N, Argentina on S, Brazil on E. **Topography:** Paraguay R. bisects the country. To E are fertile plains, wooded slopes, grasslands. To W is the Gran Chaco plain, with marshes and scrub trees. Extreme W is arid. **Capital:** Asunción, 1,858,000.

Government: Type: Republic. **Head of state and gov.:** Pres. Nicanor Duarte Frutos; b. Oct. 11, 1956; in office: Aug. 15, 2003. **Local divisions:** 17 departments and capital city. **Defense budget** (2005): $58 mil. **Active troops:** 10,300.

Economy: Industries: sugar, cement, textiles, beverages, wood products. **Chief crops:** cotton, sugarcane, soybeans, corn, wheat, tobacco, cassava. **Natural resources:** hydropower, timber, iron ore, mang., limestone. **Arable land:** 6%. **Livestock** (2005): cattle: 9.6 mil; chickens: 17 mil; goats: 155,000; pigs: 1.6 mil; sheep: 500,000. **Fish catch** (2004): 24,100 metric tons. **Electricity prod.** (2004): 51.8 bil kWh. **Labor force:** agriculture 45%.

Finance: Monetary unit: Guarani (PYG) (Sept. 2006: 5,348.95 = $1 U.S.). **GDP** (2005 est.): $29.1 bil; **per capita GDP:** $4,900; **GDP growth:** 2.7%. **Imports** (2005 est.): $3.8 bil; partners (2004): Brazil 24.3%, U.S. 22.3%, Argentina 16.2%, China 9.9%, Hong Kong 5%. **Exports** (2005 est.): $3.1 bil; partners (2004): Brazil 27.8%, Uruguay 15.9%, Italy 7.1%, Switzerland 5.6%, Argentina 4.3%, Netherlands 4.2%. **Tourism:** $70 mil. **Budget** (2005 est.): $1.4 bil. **Intl. reserves less gold:** $908 mil. **Consumer prices:** 6.79%.

Transport: Railroad: Length: 274 mi. **Motor vehicles** 243,600 pass. cars, 37,200 comm. vehicles. **Civil aviation:** 173.4 mil pass.-mi; 12 airports. **Chief port:** Asunción.

Communications: TV sets: 205 per 1,000 pop. **Radios:** 182 per 1,000 pop. **Telephone lines:** 320,300. **Daily newspaper circ.:** NA. **Internet:** 150,000 users.

Health: Life expect.: 72.6 male; 77.8 female. **Births** (per 1,000 pop.): 29.1. **Deaths** (per 1,000 pop.): 4.5. **Natural inc.:** 2.46%. **Infant mortality** (per 1,000 live births): 24.8. **AIDS rate:** 0.4%.

Education: Compulsory: ages 6-14. **Literacy:** 94%.

Major Intl. Organizations: UN (FAO, IBRD, ILO, IMF, IMO, WHO, WTO), OAS.

Embassy: 2400 Massachusetts Ave. NW, 20008; 483-6960.

Website: www.paraguayconsulatela.com

The Guarani Indians were settled farmers speaking a common language before the arrival of Europeans. Visited by Sebastian Cabot in 1527 and settled as a Spanish possession in 1535, Paraguay gained its independence from Spain in 1811. It lost much of its territory to Brazil, Uruguay, and Argentina in the War of the Triple Alliance, 1865-70. Large areas were won from Bolivia in the Chaco War, 1932-35.

Gen. Alfredo Stroessner, who had ruled since 1954, was ousted in a military coup led by Gen. Andrés Rodríguez on Feb. 3, 1989. Rodríguez was elected president May 1. Juan Carlos Wasmosy was elected president May 9, 1993, becoming the nation's first civilian head of state in many years.

A prolonged power struggle involving a popular military leader, Gen. Lino César Oviedo, who was accused of insubordination, culminated in his surrender Dec. 12, 1997. He was freed Aug. 18, 1998, following the inauguration of Pres. Raúl Cubas Grau, Oviedo's successor as Colorado Party nominee.

The assassination of Vice Pres. Luis María Argaña, Mar. 23, 1999, by an unidentified gunman, was widely attributed to Cubas and triggered protests and an impeachment vote; Cubas resigned Mar. 28 and was succeeded by Senate leader Luis Angel González Macchi. An attempted military coup was suppressed May 18, 2000.

Mass protests over the depressed economy led to the proclamation of a state of emergency July 15, 2002. Nicanor Duarte Frutos won the presidency, Apr. 27, 2003, maintaining 55 years of uninterrupted Colorado Party rule.

A supermarket fire in Asunción Aug. 1, 2004, killed more than 400 people. Paraguayan authorities blamed a leftist group, Patria Libre, for the Sept. 2004 kidnapping and subsequent murder of Cecilia Cubas, daugher of former Pres. Cubas.

Peru
Republic of Peru

People: Population: 28,302,603. **Age distrib.** (%) <15: 30.9; 65+: 5.3. **Pop. density:** 57 per sq mi, 22 per sq km. **Urban:** 73.9%. **Ethnic groups:** Amerindian 45%, Mestizo 37%, White 15%. **Principal languages:** Spanish, Quechua (both official); Aymara. **Chief religions:** Roman Catholic 81% (official), unspecified, none 16%.

Geography: Total area: 496,226 sq mi, 1,285,220 sq km; **Land area:** 494,211 sq mi, 1,280,000 sq km. **Location:** On the Pacific coast of South America. **Neighbors:** Ecuador, Colombia on N; Brazil, Bolivia on E; Chile on S. **Topography:** An arid coastal strip, 10 to 100 mi. wide, supports much of the population thanks to widespread irrigation. The Andes cover 27% of land area. The uplands are well-watered, as are the eastern slopes reaching the Amazon basin, which covers half the country with its forests and jungles. **Capital:** Lima, 7,186,000. **Cities (urban aggr.):** Arequipa, 819,000; Callao, 424,294.

Government: Type: Republic. **Head of state:** Pres. Alan García; b. May 23, 1949; in office: July 28, 2006. **Head of gov.:** Prime Min. Jorge del Castillo; b. July 2, 1950; in office: July 28, 2006. **Local divisions:** 12 regions, 24 departments, 1 constitutional province. **Defense budget** (2005): $1.1 bil. **Active troops:** 80,000.

Economy: Industries: mining, oil, fishing, textiles, clothing, food proc. **Chief crops:** coffee, cotton, sugarcane, rice, wheat, potatoes, corn, plantains, coca. **Natural resources:** copper, silver, gold, oil, timber, fish, iron ore, coal, phosphate, potash, hydropower, nat. gas. **Crude oil reserves** (2005): 953 mil bbls. **Arable land:** 3%. **Livestock** (2005): cattle: 5.1 mil; chickens: 95 mil; goats: 2 mil; pigs:

2.9 mil; **sheep:** 14 mil. **Fish catch** (2004): 9,635,379 metric tons. **Electricity prod.** (2004): 24 bil kWh. **Labor force** (2001): agriculture 9%, industry 18%, services 73%.

Finance: Monetary unit: Nuevos Sol (PEN) (Sept. 2006: 3.25 = $1 U.S.). (2005 est.): $164.5 bil; **per capita GDP:** $5,900; **GDP growth:** 6.7%. **Imports** (2005 est.): $12.2 bil; partners (2004): U.S. 29.2%, Spain 8.5%, Chile 6.9%, Brazil 5.6%, Colombia 5.2%, China 4%. **Exports** (2005 est.): $16 bil; partners (2004): U.S. 29.5%, China 9.8%, UK 8%, Chile 5.3%, Japan 4.7%, Switzerland 4.4%. **Tourism:** $1.1 bil. **Budget** (2005 est.): $22.5 bil. **Intl. reserves less gold:** $9.52 bil. **Gold:** 1.11 mil. oz t. **Consumer prices:** 1.62%.

Transport: Railroad: Length: 2,151 mi. **Motor vehicles:** 906,600 pass. cars, 555,300 comm. vehicles. **Civil aviation:** 1.5 bil pass.-mi; 54 airports. **Chief ports:** Callao, Chimbote, Matarani, Salaverry.

Communications: TV sets: 147 per 1,000 pop. **Radios:** 273 per 1,000 pop. **Telephone lines:** 2.3 mil. **Daily newspaper circ.:** 22.7 per 1,000 pop. **Internet:** 4.6 mil users.

Health: Life expect.: 68 male; 71.7 female. **Births** (per 1,000 pop.): 20.5. **Deaths** (per 1,000 pop.): 6.2. **Natural inc.:** 1.43%. **Infant mortality** (per 1,000 live births): 30.9. **AIDS rate:** 0.6%.

Education: Compulsory: ages 6-16. **Literacy:** 87.7%.

Major Intl. Organizations: UN and all of its specialized agencies, APEC, OAS.

Embassy: 1700 Massachusetts Ave. NW 20036; 833-9860.

Website: www.peru.info/perueng.asp

The powerful Inca empire had its seat at Cuzco in the Andes and covered much of South America. A civil war had weakened the empire when Francisco Pizarro, Spanish conquistador, began raiding Peru for its wealth, 1532. In 1533 he executed the Inca ruler, Atahualpa, and enslaved the people.

Lima was the seat of Spanish viceroys until the Argentine liberator, José de San Martin, captured it in 1821; Spanish forces were ultimately routed by Simón Bolívar, 1824. For much of the 19th cent., the country was governed by military leaders. Chile defeated Peru in the War of the Pacific (1879-83). The first half of the 20th cent. was dominated by political conflict between right-wing groups allied with the military and the leftist APRA party.

After 12 years of military rule, Peru returned to democratic leadership in 1980 but was plagued by economic problems and by leftist Shining Path (Sendero Luminoso) guerrillas. Conflict between guerrillas and government troops, 1980-2000, killed more than 69,000 people, mostly Andean Indians.

Elected president in June 1990, Alberto Fujimori, the son of Japanese immigrants, dissolved the National Congress, suspended parts of the constitution, and initiated press censorship, Apr. 5, 1992. The leader of Shining Path was captured Sept. 12.

With the economy booming and signs of significant progress in curtailing guerrilla activity, Fujimori won reelection Apr. 9, 1995. Repressive antiterrorism tactics, however, drew international criticism. On Dec. 17, 1996, leftist Tupac Amaru guerrillas infiltrated a reception at the Japanese ambassador's residence in Lima and took hundreds of hostages, most of whom were later released. Peruvian soldiers stormed the embassy Apr. 22, 1997, rescuing 71 of the remaining hostages; 1 hostage, 2 soldiers, and all 14 guerrillas were killed. Fujimori's path to a 3rd term was cleared when his lone remaining challenger withdrew, charging electoral fraud, 6 days before a runoff vote on May 28, 2000. Scandals involving his top aide and intelligence chief, Vladimiro Montesinos, led Fujimori to resign his office Nov. 20 while on a visit to Japan; instead of accepting his resignation, Congress ousted him as "morally unfit."

Alejandro Toledo won a presidential runoff election June 3, 2001. Montesinos was captured in Venezuela June 23 and extradited to Peru and sentenced on abuse of power charges July 1, 2002. Charges were filed Sept. 5 against the exiled Fujimori, alleging his complicity in the killings by a paramilitary death squad of at least 25 people during 1991-92.

Fireworks explosions killed 291 people in a crowded Lima commercial district Dec. 29, 2001. A sagging economy, resurgent rebel activity, and a series of scandals eroded Toledo's popularity during 2003-05. Alan García, whose 1st term as president (1985-90) had ended with the country facing hyperinflation and guerrilla war, won a presidential runoff election June 4, 2006, and took office July 28.

Philippines
Republic of the Philippines

People: Population: 89,468,677. **Age distrib.** (%) <15: 35; 65+: 4.1. **Pop. density:** 777 per sq mi, 300 per sq km. **Urban:** 61.0%. **Ethnic groups:** Christian Malay 91.5%, Muslim Malay 4%, Chinese 1.5%. **Principal languages:** Filipino, English (both official); many dialects. **Chief religions:** Roman Catholic 81%, Muslim 5%.

Geography: Total area: 115,831 sq mi, 300,000 sq km; **Land area:** 115,124 sq mi, 298,170 sq km. **Location:** An archipelago off the SE coast of Asia. **Neighbors:** Nearest are Malaysia and Indonesia on S, Taiwan on N. **Topography:** The country consists of some 7,100 islands stretching 1,100 mi. N-S. About 95% of area and population are on 11 largest islands, which are mountainous, except for the heavily indented coastlines and for the central plain

on Luzon. **Capital:** Manila, 10,686,000. **Cities (urban aggr.):** Quezon City, 2,160,000; Davao, 1,327,000; Cebu 799,000.

Government: Type: Republic. **Head of state and gov.:** Pres. Gloria Macapagal Arroyo; b. Apr. 5, 1947; in office: Jan. 20, 2001. **Local divisions:** 79 provinces. **Defense budget** (2005): $844 mil. **Active troops:** 106,000.

Economy: Industries: textiles, pharm., chemicals, wood products, food proc., electronics. **Chief crops:** rice, coconuts, corn, sugarcane, bananas, pineapples. **Natural resources:** timber, oil, nickel, cobalt, silver, gold, salt, copper. **Crude oil reserves** (2005): 152 mil bbls. **Arable land:** 19%. **Livestock** (2005): cattle: 2.6 mil; chickens: 136 mil; goats: 6.5 mil; pigs: 12.1 mil; sheep: 30,000. **Fish catch** (2004): 2,723,790 metric tons. **Electricity prod.** (2004): 53.1 bil kWh. **Labor force** (2004 est.): agriculture 36%, industry 16%, services 48%.

Finance: Monetary unit: Peso (PHP) (Sept. 2006: 50.34 = $1 U.S.). **GDP** (2005 est.): $451.3 bil; **per capita GDP:** $5,100; **GDP growth:** 5.1%. **Imports** (2005 est.): $42.7 bil; partners (2004): Japan 20.6%, U.S. 16%, Singapore 8.4%, China 7.4%, Hong Kong 5.3%, South Korea 5.2%, Taiwan 4.5%, Malaysia 4.4%. **Exports** (2005 est.): $41.3 bil; partners (2004): U.S. 17.5%, Japan 15.8%, China 11.4%, Hong Kong 8.3%, Singapore 7.7%, Taiwan 6.4%, Netherlands 6%, Malaysia 5.5%, Germany 4.2%. **Tourism:** $2 bil. **Budget** (2005 est.): $15.8 bil. **Intl. reserves less gold:** $11.14 bil. **Gold:** 4.97 mil. oz t. **Consumer prices:** 7.63%.

Transport: Railroad: Length: 557 mi. **Motor vehicles:** 2.4 mil pass. cars, 291,700 comm. vehicles. **Civil aviation:** 8.8 bil pass.-mi; 83 airports. **Chief ports:** Cebu, Manila, Iloilo, Davao.

Communications: TV sets: 110 per 1,000 pop. **Radios:** 161 per 1,000 pop. **Telephone lines:** 3.4 mil. **Daily newspaper circ.:** 66.1 per 1,000 pop. **Internet:** 7.8 mil.mil users.

Health: Life expect.: 67.3 male; 73.2 female. **Births** (per 1,000 pop.): 24.9. **Deaths** (per 1,000 pop.): 5.4. **Natural inc.:** 1.95%. **Infant mortality** (per 1,000 live births): 22.8. **AIDS rate:** <0.1%.

Education: Compulsory: ages 6-12. **Literacy:** 92.6%.

Major Intl. Organizations: UN (FAO, IBRD, ILO, IMF, IMO, WHO, WTO), APEC, ASEAN.

Embassy: 1600 Massachusetts Ave. NW 20036; 467-9300.

Website: www.gov.ph

Originally inhabited by Malay peoples, the archipelago was visited by Magellan, 1521. The Spanish founded Manila, 1571. The islands, named for King Philip II of Spain, were ceded by Spain to the U.S. for $20 mil, 1898, following the Spanish-American War. U.S. troops suppressed a guerrilla uprising in a brutal 6-year war, 1899-1905.

Japan attacked the Philippines Dec. 8, 1941, and occupied the islands during WWII. On July 4, 1946, independence was proclaimed in accordance with an act passed by the U.S. Congress in 1934. A republic was established.

The repressive and corrupt regime of Pres. Ferdinand Marcos and his wife, Imelda, ruled the Philippines 1965-86. The assassination of prominent opposition leader Benigno S. Aquino Jr. Aug. 21, 1983, sparked demonstrations calling for Marcos's resignation. After a bitter presidential campaign, amid allegations of widespread election fraud, Marcos was declared the victor Feb. 16, 1986, over Corazon Aquino, widow of the slain opposition leader. With his support collapsing, Marcos fled the country Feb. 25, and Corazon Aquino became president.

Her government was plagued by a weak economy, widespread poverty, Communist and Muslim insurgencies, and lukewarm military support. Rebel troops seized military bases and TV stations and bombed the presidential palace, Dec. 1, 1989. Government forces, with U.S. air support, defeated the attempted coup. Aquino endorsed Fidel Ramos in the May 1992 presidential election, which he won. The U.S. vacated the Subic Bay Naval Station in late 1992, ending its long military presence in the Philippines. The government signed a cease-fire agreement, Jan. 30, 1994, with Muslim separatist guerrillas, but some rebels refused to abide by the accord. A new treaty providing for expansion and development of an autonomous Muslim region on Mindanao was signed Sept. 2, 1996, formally ending a rebellion that had claimed more than 120,000 lives since 1972.

Running as a populist, Joseph (Erap) Estrada, a former movie actor, won the presidential election of May 11, 1998. Charged with bribery and corruption, he was impeached Nov. 13, 2000. When the Supreme Court ruled the presidency vacant Jan. 20, 2001, Vice Pres. Gloria Macapagal Arroyo became president.

As part of the war on terrorism, the U.S. assisted Filipino troops in combating Abu Sayyaf, an Islamic guerrilla group; the leader of the extremists, Abu Sabaya, was killed June 21, 2002. A resurgence of terrorism on Mindanao in 2003 included bombings at Davao's airport, Mar. 4, and ferry terminal, Apr. 2. A mutiny by some 300 troops in Manila, July 27, was suppressed.

Pres. Arroyo won reelection May 10, 2004. Flooding and mudslides from tropical storms, Nov.-Dec. 2004, left at least 1,060 people dead, more than 560 missing, and 880,000 displaced. Arroyo's supporters in the legislature beat back, Sept. 6, 2005. A landslide on the island of Leyte, Feb. 17, 2006, killed at least 139 people, with 973 missing and presumed dead. Citing the threat of a coup, Arroyo imposed a state of emergency, Feb. 24-Mar. 3, including a ban on rallies that would have marked the 20th anniversary of the 1986 uprising against Marcos.

Poland
Republic of Poland

People: Population: 38,536,869. **Age distrib.** (%) <15: 15.9; 65+: 13.3. **Pop. density:** 327 per sq mi, 126 per sq km. **Urban:** 61.9%. **Ethnic groups:** Polish 98%, German 1%. **Principal languages:** Polish (official), Ukrainian, German. **Chief religion:** Roman Catholic 90%, unspecified 8%.

Geography: Total area: 120,728 sq mi, 312,685 sq km; **Land area:** 117,555 sq mi, 304,465 sq km. **Location:** On the Baltic Sea in E central Europe. **Neighbors:** Germany on W; Czech Rep., Slovakia on S; Lithuania, Belarus, Ukraine on E; Russia on N. **Topography:** Mostly lowlands forming part of the Northern European Plain. The Carpathian Mts. along the S border rise to 8,200 ft. **Capital:** Warsaw, 1,680,000. **Cities:** Katowice, 3,069,000; Lodz, 776,000; Krakow, 763,000.

Government: Type: Republic. **Head of state:** Pres. Lech Kaczynski; b. June 18, 1949; in office: Dec. 23, 2005. **Head of gov.:** Prime Min. Jaroslaw Kaczynski; b. June 18, 1949; in office: July 14, 2006. **Local divisions:** 16 provinces. **Defense budget** (2005): $5.2 bil. **Active troops:** 141,500.

Economy: Industries: machinery, iron & steel, coal, chemicals, shipbuilding, food proc., glass, beverages, textiles. **Chief crops:** potatoes, fruits, vegetables, wheat. **Natural resources:** coal, sulfur, copper, nat. gas, silver, lead, salt. **Crude oil reserves** (2005): 96 mil bbls. **Arable land:** 47%. **Livestock** (2005): cattle: 5.5 mil; chickens: 90 mil; pigs: 18.1 mil; sheep: 315,963. **Fish catch** (2004): 227,367 metric tons. **Electricity prod.** (2004): 143.5 bil kWh. **Labor force** (2002): agriculture 16.1%, industry 29%, services 54.9%.

Finance: Monetary unit: Zloty (PLN) (Sept. 2006: 3.10 = $1 U.S.). **GDP** (2005 est.): $514 bil; **per capita GDP:** $13,300; **GDP growth:** 3.2%. **Imports** (2005 est.): $95.7 bil; partners (2004): Germany 29.8%, Italy 8%, France 7%, Russia 6.9%, Netherlands 5.3%, Belgium 4.2%. **Exports** (2005 est.): $92.7 bil; partners (2004): Germany 29.8%, Italy 6.3%, France 5.4%, UK 4.7%, Czech Republic 4.4%. **Tourism:** $5.8 bil.. **Budget** (2005 est.): $63.2 bil. **Intl. reserves less gold:** $28.59 bil. **Gold:** 3.31 mil. oz t. **Consumer prices:** 2.11%.

Transport: Railroad: Length: 14,820 mi. **Motor vehicles:** 11.24 mil pass. cars, 2.33 mil comm. vehicles. **Civil aviation:** 3.2 bil pass.-mi; 83 airports. **Chief ports:** Gdansk, Gdynia, Ustka, Szczecin.

Communications: TV sets: 387 per 1,000 pop. **Radios:** 522 per 1,000 pop. **Telephone lines:** 12.5 mil. **Daily newspaper circ.:** 101.6 per 1,000 pop. **Internet:** 10.6 mil users.

Health: Life expect.: 71 male; 79.2 female. **Births** (per 1,000 pop.): 9.8. **Deaths** (per 1,000 pop.): 9.9. **Natural inc.:** 0%. **Infant mortality** (per 1,000 live births): 7.2. **AIDS rate:** 0.1%.

Education: Compulsory: ages 7-15. **Literacy:** 99.8%.

Major Intl. Organizations: UN (FAO, IBRD, ILO, IMF, IMO, WHO, WTO), EU, NATO, OECD, OSCE.

Embassy: 2640 16th St. NW 20009; 234-3800.

Website: www.poland.pl

Slavic tribes in the area were converted to Latin Christianity in the 10th cent. Poland was a great power from the 14th to the 17th centuries. In 3 partitions (1772, 1793, 1795) it was apportioned among Prussia, Russia, and Austria. Overrun by the Austro-German armies in WWI, it declared its independence on Nov. 11, 1918, and was recognized as independent by the Treaty of Versailles, June 28, 1919. Large territories to the east were taken in a war with Russia, 1921.

Germany and the USSR invaded Poland Sept. 1-27, 1939, and divided the country. During the war, some 6 mil Polish citizens, half of them Jews, were killed by the Nazis. With Germany's defeat, a Polish government-in-exile in London was recognized by the U.S., but the USSR pressed the claims of a rival group. The election of 1947 was completely dominated by the Communists.

In compensation for 69,860 sq mi ceded to the USSR, in 1945 Poland received approx. 40,000 sq mi of German territory east of the Oder-Neisse line comprising Silesia, Pomerania, West Prussia, and part of East Prussia.

In 12 years of rule by Stalinists, large estates were abolished, industries nationalized, schools secularized, and Roman Catholic prelates jailed. Farm production fell off. Harsh working conditions caused a riot in Poznan, June 28-29, 1956. A new Politburo, committed to a more independent Polish Communism, was named Oct. 1956, with Wladyslaw Gomulka as first secretary of the party. Collectivization of farms was ended. Gomulka agreed to permit religious liberty and religious publications, provided the church kept out of politics.

In Dec. 1970 workers in port cities rioted because of price rises and new incentive wage rules. On Dec. 20 Gomulka resigned as party leader; he was succeeded by Edward Gierek. The rules were dropped and price rises revoked.

After 2 months of labor turmoil had crippled the country, the Polish government, Aug. 30, 1980, met the demands of striking workers at the Lenin Shipyard, Gdansk. Government concessions included the right to form independent trade unions and the right to strike. By 1981, 9.5 mil workers had joined the independent trade union (Solidarity). As Solidarity's demands grew bolder, the government, spurred by fear of Soviet intervention, imposed martial law Dec. 13. Lech Walesa and other Solidarity leaders were arrested.

On Apr. 5, 1989, an accord was reached between the government and opposition factions on political and economic reforms, including free elections. Candidates endorsed by Solidarity swept the parliamentary elections, June 4. Lech Walesa became president Dec. 22, 1990.

A radical economic program designed to transform the economy into a free-market system led to inflation and unemployment. In Sept. 1993, former Communists and other leftists won a majority in the lower house of Parliament. Walesa lost to a former Communist, Aleksander Kwasniewski, in a presidential runoff election, Nov. 19, 1995.

A new constitution was approved by referendum May 25, 1997. Flooding in July caused more than $1 bil in property damage. Solidarity won parliamentary elections held Sept. 21. Poland became a full member of NATO on Mar. 12, 1999. Pres. Kwasniewski was reelected Oct. 8, 2000. The former Communists won a plurality in parliamentary voting Sept. 23, 2001; in elections 4 years later, however, a center-right coalition prevailed. Lech Kaczynski, the conservative mayor of Warsaw, won a presidential runoff election Oct. 23, 2005. In July 2006 he appointed his identical twin brother Jaroslaw as prime minister.

Poland entered the European Union May 1, 2004. The country, a close U.S. ally, had about 900 troops in Iraq as of mid-2006.

Portugal
Portuguese Republic

People: Population: 10,605,870. **Age distrib.** (%) <15: 16.5; 65+: 17.2. **Pop. density:** 298 per sq mi, 115 per sq km. **Urban:** 54.6%. **Ethnic groups:** Mainly Portuguese. **Principal languages:** Portuguese (official). **Chief religion:** Roman Catholic 94%.

Geography: Total area: 35,672 sq mi, 92,391 sq km; **Land area:** 35,502 sq mi, 91,951 sq km. **Location:** At SW extreme of Europe. Neighbors: Spain on N, E. **Topography:** Portugal N of Tajus R., which bisects the country NE-SW, is mountainous, cool and rainy. To the S there are drier, rolling plains, and a warm climate. **Capital:** Lisbon, 2,761,000. **Cities (urban agg.):** Porto, 1,309,000.

Government: Type: Republic. **Head of state:** Pres. Aníbal Cavaco Silva; b. July 15, 1939; in office: Mar. 9, 2006. **Head of gov.:** Prime Min. José Sócrates Carvalho Pinto de Sousa; b. Sept. 6, 1957; in office: Mar. 12, 2005. **Local divisions:** 18 districts, 2 autonomous regions. **Defense budget** (2005): $2.4 bil. **Active troops:** 44,900.

Economy: Industries: textiles, footwear, wood and paper products, metalworking, oil refining, chemicals, fish proc, wine, tourism. **Chief crops:** grain, potatoes, olives, grapes. **Natural resources:** fish, cork, tungsten, iron ore, uranium ore, marble, hydropower. **Arable land:** 26%. **Livestock** (2005): cattle: 1.4 mil; chickens: 35 mil; goats: 547,000; pigs: 2.3 mil; sheep: 5.5 mil. **Fish catch** (2004): 228,129 metric tons. **Electricity prod.** (2004): 42.5 bil kWh. **Labor force** (1999 est.): agriculture 10%, industry 30%, services 60%.

Finance: Monetary unit: Euro (EUR) (Sept. 2006: 0.78 = $1 U.S.). **GDP** (2005 est.): $204.4 bil; **per capita GDP:** $19,300; **GDP growth:** 0.3%. **Imports** (2005 est.): $60.4 bil; partners (2004): Spain 29.3%, Germany 14.4%, France 9.7%, Italy 6.1%, Netherlands 4.6%, UK 4.5%. **Exports** (2005 est.): $38.8 bil; partners (2004): Spain 24.8%, France 14%, Germany 13.5%, UK 9.6%, U.S. 6%, Italy 4.3%, Belgium 4.1%. **Tourism:** $7.8 bil. **Budget** (2005 est.): $90.3 bil. **Intl. reserves less gold:** $2.43 bil. **Gold:** 13.42 mil. oz t. **Consumer prices:** 2.29%.

Transport: Railroad: Length: 1,771 mi. **Motor vehicles:** 6 mil pass. cars, 1.97 mil comm. vehicles. **Civil aviation:** 7.5 bil pass.-mi; 43 airports. **Chief ports:** Lisbon, Setubal, Leixoes.

Communications: TV sets: 567 per 1,000 pop. **Radios:** 306 per 1,000 pop. **Telephone lines:** 4.2 mil. **Daily newspaper circ.:** 102.4 per 1,000 pop. **Internet:** 6.1 mil users.

Health: Life expect.: 74.4 male; 81.2 female. **Births** (per 1,000 pop.): 10.7. **Deaths** (per 1,000 pop.): 10.5. **Natural inc.:** 0.02%. **Infant mortality** (per 1,000 live births): 5. **AIDS rate:** 0.4%.

Education: Compulsory: ages 6-14. **Literacy:** 93.3%.

Major Intl. Organizations: UN (FAO, IBRD, ILO, IMF, IMO, WHO, WTO), EU, NATO, OECD, OSCE.

Embassy: 2125 Kalorama Rd. NW 20008; 328-8610.

Website: www.portugal.gov.pt

Portugal, an independent state since the 12th cent., was a kingdom until a revolution in 1910 drove out King Manoel II and a republic was proclaimed. From 1932 a strong, repressive government was headed by Premier Antonio de Oliveira Salazar. Illness forced his retirement in Sept. 1968.

On Apr. 25, 1974, the government was seized by a military junta led by Gen. Antonio de Spinola, who became president. The new government reached agreements providing independence for Guinea-Bissau, Mozambique, Cape Verde Islands, Angola, and São Tomé and Príncipe. Banks, insurance companies, and other industries were nationalized.

Parliament approved, June 1, 1989, a program to denationalize industries. Portugal returned Macao to China on Dec. 20, 1999. With the economy lagging, opposition Socialists won a parliamentary majority in elections Feb. 20, 2005. The conservative Aníbal Cavaco Silva, a former prime minister (1985-95) defeated two Socialist candidates to win the presidential election of Jan. 22, 2006.

Azores Islands, in the Atlantic, 740 mi W of Portugal, have an area of 868 sq mi and a pop. (1993 est.) of 238,000. A 1951 agreement gave the U.S. rights to use defense facilities in the Azores. The **Madeira Islands**, 350 mi off the NW coast of Africa, have an area of 306 sq mi and a pop. (1993 est.) of 437,312. Both groups were offered partial autonomy in 1976.

Qatar
State of Qatar

People: Population: 885,359. **Age distrib.** (%) <15: 23.4; 65+: 3.7. **Pop. density:** 200 per sq mi, 77 per sq km. **Urban:** 92.0%. **Ethnic groups:** Arab 40%, Pakistani 18%, Indian 18%, Iranian 10%. **Principal languages:** Arabic (official), English. **Chief religion:** Muslim 95% (official).

Geography: Total area: 4,416 sq mi, 11,437 sq km; **Land area:** 4,416 sq mi, 11,437 sq km. **Location:** Middle East, occupying peninsula on W coast of Persian Gulf. **Neighbors:** Saudi Arabia on S. **Topography:** Mostly a flat desert, with some limestone ridges; vegetation of any kind is scarce. **Capital:** Doha, 357,000.

Government: Type: Traditional monarchy. **Head of state:** Emir Hamad bin Khalifa ath-Thani; b. 1952; in office: June 27, 1995. **Head of gov.:** Prime Min. Abdullah bin Khalifa ath-Thani; b. Dec. 25, 1959; in office: Oct. 29, 1996. **Local divisions:** 9 municipalities. **Defense budget** (2005): $2.2 bil. **Active troops:** 12,400.

Economy: Industries: oil prod. & refining, fertilizers, petrochems., constr. materials. **Chief crops:** fruits, vegetables. **Natural resources:** oil, nat. gas, fish. **Crude oil reserves** (2005): 15.2 bil bbls. **Livestock** (2005): cattle: 11,000; chickens: 4.5 mil; goats: 150,000; sheep: 200,000. **Fish catch** (2004): 11,134 metric tons. **Electricity prod.** (2004): 12.4 bil kWh.

Finance: Monetary unit: Riyal (QAR) (Sept. 2006: 3.64 = $1 U.S.). **GDP** (2005 est.): $23.6 bil; **per capita GDP:** $27,400; **GDP growth:** 8.8%. **Imports** (2005 est.): $6.7 bil; partners (2004): France 24.4%, UK 8.9%, Germany 8.8%, Japan 8.7%, U.S. 6.2%, Italy 5.5%, UAE 4.1%. **Exports** (2005 est.): $24.9 bil; partners (2004): Japan 43.8%, South Korea 16.1%, Singapore 10.8%. **Tourism:** $498 mil. **Budget** (2005 est.): $11.3 bil. **Intl. reserves less gold:** $3.18 bil. **Gold:** 20,000 oz t. **Consumer prices:** 8.81%.

Transport: Motor vehicles: 230,100 pass. cars, 109,700 comm. vehicles. **Civil aviation:** 5.3 bil pass.-mi; 3 airports. **Chief ports:** Doha, Umm Sáid.

Communications: TV sets: 866 per 1,000 pop. **Radios:** 450 per 1,000 pop. **Telephone lines:** 205,400. **Daily newspaper circ.:** NA. **Internet:** 165,000 users.

Health: Life expect.: 71.4 male; 76.6 female. **Births** (per 1,000 pop.): 15.6. **Deaths** (per 1,000 pop.): 4.7. **Natural inc.:** 1.08%. **Infant mortality** (per 1,000 live births): 18. **AIDS rate:** NA.

Education: Compulsory: ages 6-17. **Literacy:** 89.0%.

Major Intl. Organizations: UN (FAO, IBRD, ILO, IMF, IMO, WHO, WTO), AL, OPEC.

Embassy: 2555 M St. NW 20037; 274-1600.

Website: english.mofa.gov.qa

Qatar was under Bahrain's control until the Ottoman Turks took power, 1872 to 1915. In a treaty signed 1916, Qatar gave Great Britain responsibility for its defense and foreign relations. After Britain announced it would remove its military forces from the Persian Gulf area by the end of 1971, Qatar sought a federation with other British-protected states in the area; this failed and Qatar declared itself independent, Sept. 1, 1971. Crown Prince Hamad bin Khalifa ath-Thani ousted his father, Emir Khalifa bin Hamad ath-Thani, June 27, 1995. In municipal elections held Mar. 8, 1999, women participated for the 1st time as candidates and voters.

Oil and natural gas revenues give Qatar a per capita income among the world's highest. Military ties with the U.S. have been expanding; Camp As-Sayliyah, a base near Doha, served as a command center for the U.S.-led invasion of Iraq, Mar. 2003. The influential Arab news network Al-Jazeera is based in Qatar.

Romania

People: Population: 22,303,552. **Age distrib.** (%) <15: 15.7; 65+: 14.7. **Pop. density:** 250 per sq mi, 96 per sq km. **Urban:** 54.5%. **Ethnic groups:** Romanian 90%, Hungarian, Roma, and others 10%. **Principal languages:** Romanian (official), Hungarian, German, Romani. **Chief religions:** Romanian Orthodox 87%, Protestant 8%, Roman Catholic 5%.

Geography: Total area: 91,699 sq mi, 237,500 sq km; **Land area:** 88,935 sq mi, 230,340 sq km. **Location:** SE Europe, on the Black Sea. **Neighbors:** Moldova on E, Ukraine on N, Hungary and Serbia and Montenegro on W, Bulgaria on S. **Topography:** The Carpathian Mts. encase the north-central Transylvanian plateau. There are wide plains S and E of the mountains, through which flow the lower reaches of the rivers of the Danube system. **Capital:** Bucharest, 1,934,000.

Government: Type: Republic. **Head of state:** Pres. Traian Basescu; b. Nov. 4, 1951; in office: Dec. 20, 2004. **Head of gov.:** Prime Min. Calin Constantin Anton Popescu-Tariceanu; b. Jan. 14, 1952; in office: Dec. 29, 2004. **Local divisions:** 41 counties and Bucharest. **Defense budget** (2005): $2.1 bil. **Active troops:** 97,200.

Economy: Industries: textiles & footwear, light machinery, auto assembly, mining, timber. **Chief crops:** wheat, corn, sugar beets, sunflower seed, potatoes, grapes. **Natural resources:** oil, timber, nat. gas, coal, iron ore, salt, hydropower. **Crude oil reserves** (2005): 956 mil bbls. **Arable land:** 41%. **Livestock** (2005): cattle: 3 mil; chickens: 87.5 mil; goats: 661,000; pigs: 6.5 mil; sheep: 7.4 mil. **Fish catch** (2004): 13,223 metric tons. **Electricity prod.** (2004): 54.5 bil kWh. **Labor force** (2004): agriculture 31.6%, industry 30.7%, services 37.7%.

Finance: Monetary unit: New Leu (RON) (Sept. 2006: 2.76 = $1 U.S.). **GDP** (2005 est.): $183.6 bil; **per capita GDP:** $8,200; **GDP growth:** 4.5%. **Imports** (2005 est.): $38.2 bil; partners (2004): Italy 18.3%, Germany 17.9%, France 7.2%, Hungary 6.1%, Russia 5.7%, Austria 5.5%, Turkey 4.3%. **Exports** (2005 est.): $27.7 bil; partners (2004): Italy 20.9%, Germany 15.4%, France 7.3%, Turkey 7%, UK 6.1%, Austria 5%. **Tourism:** $503 mil. **Budget** (2005 est.): $31.4 bil. **Intl. reserves less gold:** $13.9 bil. **Gold:** 3.37 mil. oz t. **Consumer prices:** 8.99%.

Transport: Railroad: Length: 7,074 mi. **Motor vehicles:** 3.23 mil pass. cars, 504,000 comm. vehicles. **Civil aviation:** 989.8 mil pass.-mi; 25 airports. **Chief ports:** Constanta, Braila.

Communications: TV sets: 312 per 1,000 pop. **Radios:** 335 per 1,000 pop. **Telephone lines:** 4.4 mil. **Daily newspaper circ.:** NA. **Internet** (2004): 4.5 mil users.

Health: Life expect.: 68.1 male; 75.3 female. **Births** (per 1,000 pop.): 10.7. **Deaths** (per 1,000 pop.): 11.8. **Natural inc.:** −0.11%. **Infant mortality** (per 1,000 live births): 25.5. **AIDS rate:** <0.1%.

Education: Compulsory: ages 7-14. **Literacy:** 97.3%.

Major Intl. Organizations: UN (FAO, IBRD, ILO, IMF, IMO, WHO, WTO), NATO, OSCE.

Embassy: 1607 23rd St. NW 20008; 332-4846.

Website: www.guv.ro/engleza/index.php

Romania's earliest known people merged with invading Proto-Thracians, preceding by centuries the Dacians. The Dacian kingdom was occupied by Rome, 106-271 CE; people and language were Romanized. The principalities of Wallachia and Moldavia, dominated by Turkey, were united in 1859, became Romania in 1861, and gained recognition as an independent kingdom, 1881.

After WWI, Romania acquired Bessarabia, Bukovina, Transylvania, and Banat. In 1940 it ceded Bessarabia and Northern Bukovina to the USSR, part of southern Dobrudja to Bulgaria, and northern Transylvania to Hungary. In 1941, Prem. Marshal Ion Antonescu led Romania in support of Germany against the USSR. In 1944 he was overthrown, and Romania joined the Allies. After occupation by Soviet troops, a People's Republic was proclaimed, Dec. 30, 1947.

On Aug. 22, 1965, a new constitution proclaimed Romania a Socialist Republic. Pres. Nicolae Ceausescu maintained an independent course in foreign affairs, but his domestic policies were repressive. All industry was state-owned, and state farms and cooperatives owned almost all arable land. Ceausescu's security forces fired on antigovernment demonstrators in Dec. 1989, killing hundreds, but when the army sided with the protesters, his regime fell. Ceausescu and his wife were captured and, following a trial in which they were found guilty of genocide, were executed Dec. 25, 1989.

Former Communists dominated the government in succeeding years. A new constitution providing for a multiparty system took effect Dec. 8, 1991. Many of Romania's state-owned companies were privatized in 1996. The former Communists lost in elections Nov. 3 and Nov. 17, 1996, but made a comeback in balloting Nov. 26 and Dec. 10, 2000. Opposition leader Traian Basescu, the mayor of Bucharest, won a presidential runoff vote, Dec. 12, 2004.

Floods in Jul.-Aug. 2005 left more than 50 people dead. Romania, a firm U.S. ally, had about 860 troops in Iraq and 700 in Afghanistan in mid-2006. Romania became a full NATO member in 2004 and is expected to enter the EU in Jan. 2007.

Russia
Russian Federation

People: Population: 142,069,494. **Age distrib.** (%) <15: 14.6; 65+: 14.2. **Pop. density:** 21 per sq mi, 8 per sq km. **Urban:** 73.3%. **Ethnic groups:** Russian 82%, Tatar 4%, Ukrainian 3%, Chuvash 1%, Bashkir 1%, Belarusian 1%, Moldavian 1%. **Principal languages:** Russian (official), many others. **Chief religions:** Russian Orthodox, Muslim.

Geography: Total area: 6,592,772 sq mi, 17,075,200 sq km; **Land area:** 6,562,116 sq mi, 16,995,800 sq km., more than 76% of total area of the former USSR and the largest country in the world. **Location:** Stretches from E Europe across N Asia to the Pacific O. **Neighbors:** Finland, Norway, Estonia, Latvia, Belarus, Ukraine on W; Georgia, Azerbaijan, Kazakhstan, China, Mongolia, North Korea on S; Kaliningrad exclave bordered by Poland on the S, Lithuania on the N and E. **Topography:** Russia contains every type of climate except the distinctly tropical, and has a varied topography. The European portion is a low plain, grassy in S, wooded in N, with Ural Mts. on the E, and Caucasus Mts. on the S. Urals stretch N-S for 2,500 mi. The Asiatic portion is also a vast plain, with mountains on the S and in the E; tundra covers extreme N, with forest belt below; plains, marshes are in W, desert in SW. **Capital:** Moscow, 10,654,000. **Cities (urban aggr.):** St. Petersburg, 5,312,000; Nizhniy Novgorod, 1,289,000; Novosibirsk, 1,425,000.

Government: Type: Federal republic. **Head of state:** Pres. Vladimir Putin; b. Oct. 7, 1952; in office: May 7, 2000. **Head of gov.:** Prime Min. Mikhail Fradkov; b. Sept. 1, 1950; in office: Mar. 5, 2004. **Local divisions:** 7 federal districts incl. 49 provinces, 21 autonomous republics, 6 territories, 1 autonomous region, 10 autonomous districts, 2 federal cities. **Defense budget** (2004): $18.8 bil. **Active troops:** 1,037,000.

Economy: Industries: coal, oil, gas, chemicals, metals; light machinery, shipbuilding; transp., communic. equip., agric. machinery, constr. equip., electric power equip., medical & scientific instruments, consumer durables, textiles. **Chief crops:** grain, sugar beets, sunflower seed, vegetables, fruits. **Natural resources:** oil, nat. gas, coal, minerals, timber. **Crude oil reserves** (2005): 60 bil bbls. **Arable land:** 8%. **Livestock** (2005): cattle: 23 mil; chickens:

328.9 mil; goats: 2.3 mil; pigs: 13.4 mil; sheep: 15.5 mil. **Fish catch** (2004): 3,051,335 metric tons. **Electricity prod.** (2004): 881.6 bil kWh. **Labor force** (2004 est.): agriculture 10.3%, industry 21.4%, services 68.3%.

Finance: Monetary unit: Ruble (RUB) (Sept. 2006: 26.74 = $1 U.S.) NOTE: On Jan 1, 1998, Russia eliminated 3 digits from the ruble.) **GDP** (2005 est.): $1.6 tril; **per capita GDP:** $11,100; **GDP growth:** 6.4%. **Imports** (2005 est.): $125 bil; partners (2004): Germany 16.7%, China 7.1%, Ukraine 6.7%, Italy 5.9%, Finland 5%, France 4.5%, Japan 4.5%. **Exports** (2005 est.): $245 bil; partners (2004): Germany 8.4%, Netherlands 6.7%, China 6.4%, U.S. 5.8%, Ukraine 5.7%, Italy 5.4%, Turkey 4.5%. **Tourism:** $5.2 bil. **Budget** (2005 est.): $125.6 bil. **Intl. reserves less gold:** $123.06 bil. **Gold:** 12.44 mil. oz t. **Consumer prices:** 12.68%.

Transport: Railroad: Length: 54,157 mi **Motor vehicles:** 23.27 mil pass. cars, 4.36 mil comm. vehicles. **Civil aviation:** 31 bil pass.-mi; 616 airports. **Chief ports:** St. Petersburg, Murmansk, Arkhangelsk.

Communications: TV sets: 421 per 1,000 pop. **Radios:** 417 per 1,000 pop. **Telephone lines:** 40.1 mil. **Daily newspaper circ.:** NA. **Internet:** 23.7 mil users.

Health: Life expect.: 59.1 male; 72.9 female. **Births** (per 1,000 pop.): 10.8. **Deaths** (per 1,000 pop.): 16. **Natural inc.:** –0.52%. **Infant mortality** (per 1,000 live births): 11.3. **AIDS rate:** 1.1%.

Education: Compulsory: ages 6-15. **Literacy:** 99.4%.

Major Intl. Organizations: UN (FAO, IBRD, ILO, IMF, IMO, WHO), APEC, CIS, OSCE.

Embassy: 2650 Wisconsin Ave. NW 20007; 298-5700.

Website: www.gov.ru

History. Slavic tribes began migrating into Russia from the west in the 5th cent. The first Russian state, founded by Scandinavian chieftains, was established in the 9th cent., centering in Novgorod and Kiev. In the 13th cent. the Mongols overran the country. It recovered under the grand dukes and princes of Muscovy, or Moscow, and by 1480 freed itself from the Mongols. Ivan the Terrible was the first to be formally proclaimed Tsar (1547). Peter the Great (1682-1725) extended the domain and, in 1721, founded the Russian Empire.

Western ideas and the beginnings of modernization spread through the huge Russian empire in the 19th and early 20th centuries. But political evolution failed to keep pace.

Military reverses in the 1905 war with Japan and in WWI led to the breakdown of the Tsarist regime. The 1917 Revolution began in March with a series of sporadic strikes for higher wages by factory workers. A provisional democratic government under Prince Georgi Lvov was established but was quickly followed in May by the second provisional government, led by Alexander Kerensky. The Kerensky government and the freely-elected Constituent Assembly were overthrown in a Communist coup led by Vladimir Ilyich Lenin Nov. 7.

Soviet Union

Lenin's death Jan. 21, 1924, resulted in an internal power struggle from which Joseph Stalin eventually emerged on top. Stalin secured his position at first by exiling opponents, but from the 1930s to 1953, he resorted to a series of "purge" trials, mass executions, and mass exiles to work camps. These measures resulted in millions of deaths, according to most estimates.

Germany and the Soviet Union signed a non-aggression pact Aug. 1939; Germany launched a massive invasion of the Soviet Union, June 1941. A notable heroic episode was the "900 days" siege of Leningrad (now St. Petersburg), lasting to Jan. 1944, and causing a million deaths; the city was never taken. Russian winter counterthrusts, 1941-42 and 1942-43, stopped the German advance. Turning point was the failure of German troops to take and hold Stalingrad (now Volgograd), Sept. 1942 to Feb. 1943. With British and U.S. Lend-Lease aid and sustaining great casualties, the Russians drove the German forces from eastern Europe and the Balkans in the next 2 years.

After Stalin died, Mar. 5, 1953, Nikita Khrushchev was elected first secretary of the Central Committee. In 1956 he condemned Stalin and "de-Stalinization" began.

Under Khrushchev the open antagonism of Poles and Hungarians toward domination by Moscow was brutally suppressed in 1956. He advocated peaceful co-existence with the capitalist countries, but continued arming the Soviet Union with nuclear weapons. He aided the Cuban revolution under Fidel Castro but withdrew Soviet missiles from Cuba during confrontation by U.S. Pres. Kennedy, Sept.-Oct. 1962. Khrushchev was suddenly deposed, Oct. 1964, and replaced by Leonid I. Brezhnev.

In Aug. 1968 Russian, Polish, East German, Hungarian, and Bulgarian military forces invaded Czechoslovakia to put a curb on liberalization policies of the Czech government.

Massive Soviet military aid to North Vietnam in the late 1960s and early 1970s helped assure Communist victories throughout Indo-China. Soviet arms aid and advisers were sent to several African countries in the 1970s.

In Dec. 1979, Soviet forces entered Afghanistan to support that government against rebels. In Apr. 1988, the Soviets agreed to withdraw their troops, ending a futile 8-year war.

Mikhail Gorbachev was chosen gen. secy. of the Communist Party, Mar. 1985. He held 4 summit meetings with U.S. Pres. Ronald Reagan. In 1987 he initiated a program of political and economic reforms, through openness (*glasnost*) and restructuring (*perestroika*). Gorbachev faced economic problems as well as ethnic and nationalist unrest in the republics. An apparent coup by Communist hardliners Aug. 1991, was foiled with help from the pres. of the Russian Republic, Boris Yeltsin. On Aug. 24, Gorbachev resigned as leader of the Communist Party. Several republics declared their independence, including Russia, Ukraine, and Kazakhstan. On Aug. 29, the Soviet Parliament voted to suspend all activities of the Communist Party.

The Soviet Union officially broke up Dec. 26, 1991. The Soviet hammer and sickle flying over the Kremlin was lowered and replaced by the flag of Russia, ending the domination of the Communist Party over all areas of national life since 1917.

Russian Federation

Led by Pres. Yeltsin, Russia took steps toward privatization; immediate effects were inflation and a severe economic downturn. In June 1992, Yeltsin and U.S. Pres. George H. W. Bush agreed to massive arms reductions. A power struggle between Yeltsin and the Congress of People's Deputies, which was dominated by conservatives and former Communists, reached a climax Oct. 3, 1993, when anti-Yeltsin forces attacked some facilities in Moscow and broke into the Parliament building. Yeltsin ordered the army to seize the building; about 140 people were killed in the fighting.

Yeltsin remained in power, and in a referendum Dec. 12, 1993, a new constitution was approved. In Dec. 1994 the Russian government sent troops into the breakaway republic of Chechnya. Grozny, the Chechen capital, fell in Feb. 1995 after heavy fighting, but Chechen rebels continued to resist.

Despite poor health, Yeltsin won a presidential runoff election over a Communist opponent, July 3, 1996. On Aug. 14, after rebels embarrassed the Russian military by retaking Grozny, Yeltsin gave his security chief, Alexander Lebed, broad powers to negotiate an end to the Chechnya war. Lebed and Chechen leaders signed a peace accord Aug. 31. On Oct. 17, Yeltsin dismissed Lebed for insubordination. Russian troops remaining in Chechnya were pulled out Jan. 1997. On May 27, Yeltsin signed a "founding act" increasing cooperation with NATO and paving the way for NATO to admit Eastern European nations.

Russia's economic crisis deepened in the late 1990s, heightening tensions between Yeltsin and parliament. Russia moved forcibly in Aug. 1999 to suppress Islamic rebels in Dagestan; the conflict soon spread to neighboring Chechnya, where Russia launched a full-scale assault. A series of 5 bombings in Moscow and Dagestan, which the Russian government attributed to Chechen rebels, killed over 300 people.

Yeltsin unexpectedly resigned Dec. 31, 1999, naming Prime Min. Vladimir Putin as his interim successor. Russian troops took control of Grozny in early Feb. 2000. Putin defeated 10 opponents in a presidential election Mar. 26. The Russian nuclear submarine *Kursk* sank in the Barents Sea Aug. 12, killing 118 sailors.

As Russian forces continued their campaign against Islamic separatists in Chechnya, some 50 Chechen guerrillas seized more than 800 hostages in a Moscow theater, Oct. 23, 2002; 129 hostages and nearly all the guerrillas were killed Oct. 26 when Russian special forces used knockout gas in retaking the theater. Russia, which supported the U.S.-led war in Afghanistan in 2001, sided with France and Germany in blocking UN Security Council endorsement of the U.S.-led invasion of Iraq, Mar. 2003.

Putin's allies won legislative elections, Dec. 7, 2003, and the president was reelected Mar. 14, 2004, with 71% of the vote; international election monitors cited flaws on both occasions. Putin blamed Chechen terrorists for a blast on a Moscow subway car, Feb. 6, that killed at least 39 people. A bomb in Grozny, May 9, killed Chechnya's pro-Moscow president, Akhmad Kadyrov, and at least 6 others. Putin's choice for the Chechen presidency, Maj. Gen. Alu Alkhanov, was elected Aug. 29.

The Chechnya conflict unleashed a wave of terrorism elsewhere during Aug.-Sept. 2004. After taking off the night of Aug. 24 from Moscow's Domodedovo airport, 2 passenger planes exploded in midair, killing 90 people. A suicide bombing in a Moscow subway station Aug. 31 left 11 dead. Chechen rebels Sept. 1 seized control of a school in Beslan, North Ossetia, taking more than 1,100 hostages; Russian troops stormed the school Sept. 3; in the end more than 330 people died, including 186 children. Putin cited the terrorist threat Sept. 13 in proposing a government overhaul that would tighten his control over parliament and regional officeholders.

On Nov. 5, 2004, Russia ratified the Kyoto Protocol, which aims to curb greenhouse gas emissions and global warming. Russian forces killed Chechen rebel leader Aslan Maskhadov, Mar. 8, 2005. Mikhail Khodorkovsky, an oil tycoon whose political agenda had rivaled Putin's, was convicted of fraud and tax evasion, May 31, and sentenced to 9 years in prison. Chechen guerrilla leader Shamil Basayev, who had organized the terrorist attack at Beslan, was killed July 10, 2006. Putin and U.S. Pres. George W. Bush, in Russia for a Group of 8 summit meeting, failed to resolve differences in trade talks July 15 aimed at Russia's joining the WTO.

Rwanda
Republic of Rwanda

People: Population: 9,638,170. **Age distrib.** (%) <15: 41.9; 65+: 2.5. **Pop. density:** 1,000 per sq mi, 386 per sq km. **Urban:** 18.3%. **Ethnic groups:** Hutu 84%, Tutsi 15%, Twa (Pygmy) 1%. **Principal languages:** Kinyarwanda, French, English (all official); Swahili. **Chief religions:** Roman Catholic 57%, Protestant 26%, Adventist 11%, Muslim 5%.

Geography: Total area: 10,169 sq mi, 26,338 sq km; **Land area:** 9,632 sq mi, 24,948 sq km. **Location:** In E central Africa. **Neighbors:** Uganda on N, Congo (formerly Zaire) on W, Burundi on S, Tanzania on E. **Topography:** Grassy uplands and hills cover most of the country, with a chain of volcanoes in the NW. The source of the Nile R. has been located in the headwaters of the Kagera (Akagera) R., SW of Kigali. **Capital:** Kigali, 779,000.

Government: Type: Republic. **Head of state:** Pres. Paul Kagame; b. Oct. 1957; in office: Apr. 22, 2000 (de facto from Mar. 24). **Head of gov.:** Prime Min. Bernard Makuza; b. 1961; in office: Mar. 8, 2000. **Local divisions:** 12 prefectures subdivided into 155 communes. **Defense budget** (2005): $56.8 mil. **Active troops:** 51,000.

Economy: Industries: cement, agric. products. **Chief crops:** coffee, tea, pyrethrum (insecticide made from chrysanthemums), bananas. **Natural resources:** gold, tin, tungsten, methane, hydropower. **Crude oil reserves** (2002): 48.6 bil bbls. **Arable land:** 35%. **Livestock** (2005): cattle: 1 mil; chickens: 2 mil; goats: 1.3 mil; pigs: 346,922; sheep: 464,330. **Fish catch** (2004): 8,427 metric tons. **Electricity prod.** (2004): 90 mil kWh. **Labor force:** agriculture 90%, industry and services 10%.

Finance: Monetary unit: Franc (RWF) (Sept. 2006: 552.07 = $1 U.S.). **GDP** (2005 est.): $12.7 bil; **per capita GDP:** $1,500; **GDP growth:** 5.2%. **Imports** (2005 est.): $243 mil; partners (2004): Kenya 21.9%, Germany 7.8%, Belgium 7.7%, Uganda 5.9%, France 5.9%. **Exports** (2005 est.): $98 mil; partners (2004): Indonesia 35.4%, China 7.1%, Germany 3.4%. **Tourism:** $44 mil. **Budget** (2005 est.): $584.6 mil. **Intl. reserves less gold:** $284 mil. **Consumer prices:** 9.13%.

Transport: Motor vehicles: 10,700 pass. cars, 16,300 comm. vehicles. **Civil aviation:** NA; 4 airports. **Chief ports:** Gisenyi, Cyangugu.

Communications: TV sets: .09 per 1,000 pop. **Radios:** 101 per 1,000 pop. **Telephone lines:** 23,000. **Daily newspaper circ.:** 0.1 per 1,000 pop. **Internet:** 38,000 users.

Health: Life expect.: 47.2 male; 49.3 female. **Births** (per 1,000 pop.): 40.3. **Deaths** (per 1,000 pop.): 15.4. **Natural inc.:** 2.49%. **Infant mortality** (per 1,000 live births): 87.2. **AIDS rate:** 3.1%.

Education: Compulsory: ages 7-12. **Literacy:** 64.9%.

Major Intl. Organizations: UN (FAO, IBRD, ILO, IMF, WHO, WTO), AU.

Embassy: 1714 New Hampshire Ave. NW 20009; 232-2882.

Website: www.gov.rw

For centuries, the Tutsi (an extremely tall people) dominated the Hutu (90% of the population). A civil war broke out in 1959 and Tutsi power was ended. Many Tutsi went into exile. A referendum in 1961 abolished the monarchic system. Rwanda, which had been part of the Belgian UN trusteeship of Rwanda-Urundi, became independent July 1, 1962.

In 1963 Tutsi exiles invaded in an unsuccessful coup; a large-scale massacre of Tutsi followed. Rivalries among Hutu led to a bloodless coup July 1973 in which Juvénal Habyarimana took power. After an invasion and coup attempt by Tutsi exiles in 1990, a multiparty democracy was established.

Renewed ethnic strife led to an Aug. 1993 peace accord between the government and rebels of the Tutsi-led Rwandan Patriotic Front (RPF). But after Habyarimana and the president of Burundi were killed Apr. 6, 1994, in a suspicious plane crash, massive violence broke out. More than 1 mil may have died in massacres, mostly of Tutsi by Hutu militias, and in civil warfare as the RPF sought power. About 2 mil Tutsi and Hutu fled to camps in Zaire (now Congo) and other countries, where many died of cholera and other natural causes. French troops under a UN mandate moved into southwest Rwanda June 23 to establish a so-called safe zone. The RPF claimed victory, installing a government in July led by a moderate Hutu president. French troops pulled out Aug. 22. A UN peacekeeping mission ended Mar. 8, 1996, but the Rwandan government and a UN-sponsored tribunal in Tanzania continued to gather evidence against those responsible for genocide. More than 1 mil refugees (mostly Hutu) flooded back to Rwanda from Tanzania and Zaire in Nov. and Dec. 1996.

Firing squads in Rwanda on Apr. 24, 1998, executed 22 people convicted of genocide. Former Prime Min. Jean Kambanda pleaded guilty May 1 before the UN tribunal and received a life sentence Sept. 4, 1998. Maj. Gen. Paul Kagame, leader of the RPF, was sworn in as Rwanda's 1st Tutsi president Apr. 22, 2000. A Belgian court June 8, 2001, convicted 2 Roman Catholic nuns and 2 other Rwandans for their role in the 1994 genocide.

Rwanda and the Congo signed an accord July 30, 2002, in which Rwanda agreed to withdraw troops from the Congo and the Congo agreed to stop harboring Hutu guerrillas. Rwandans in 2003 approved a new constitution, May 26, reelected Pres. Kagame, Aug. 25, and chose a new parliament, Sept. 29-30. Former Pres. Bizimungu was sentenced to 15 years for embezzlement, June 2004. Village tribunals have also begun trying genocide suspects, who may number in the hundreds of thousands.

Saint Kitts and Nevis
Federation of Saint Kitts and Nevis

People: Population: 39,129. **Age distrib.** (%) <15: 27.5; 65+: 8.1. **Pop. density:** 387 per sq mi, 149 per sq km. **Urban:** 32.2%. **Ethnic group:** Black, British, Portuguese, Lebanese. **Principal languages:** English (official). **Chief religions:** Anglican, other Protestant, Roman Catholic.

Geography: Total area: 101 sq mi, 261 sq km; **Land area:** 101 sq mi, 261 sq km. **Location:** In the N part of the Leeward group of the Lesser Antilles in the E Caribbean Sea. **Neighbors:** Antigua and Barbuda to E. **Topography:** St. Kitts has forested volcanic slopes; Nevis rises from beaches to central peak. Climate is tropical moderated by sea breezes. **Capital** (2001): Basseterre, 13,033.

Government: Type: Constitutional monarchy. **Head of state:** Queen Elizabeth II, represented by Gov-Gen. Sir Cuthbert M. Sebastian; b. Oct. 22, 1921; in office: Jan. 1, 1996. **Head of gov.:** Prime Min. Denzil Llewellyn Douglas; b. Jan. 14, 1953; in office: July 7, 1995. **Local divisions:** 14 parishes.

Economy: Industries: sugar proc., tourism, cotton, salt, copra, clothing, footwear, beverages. **Chief crops:** sugarcane, rice, yams, vegetables, bananas. **Arable land:** 22%. **Livestock** (2005): cattle: 4,800; chickens: 70,000; goats: 16,000; pigs: 2,000; sheep: 12,500. **Fish catch** (2004): 477 metric tons. **Electricity prod.** (2004): 130 mil kWh.

Finance: Monetary unit: East Caribbean Dollar (XCD) (Sept. 2006: 2.67 = $1 U.S.). **GDP** (2002 est.): $339 mil; **per capita GDP:** $8,800; **GDP growth:** −1.9%. **Imports** (2004 est.): $405 mil; partners (2004): U.S. 33.1%, Italy 19.4%, Trinidad and Tobago 10.5%, UK 9.8%, Denmark 6%. **Exports** (2004 est.): $70 mil; partners (2004): U.S. 58%, Canada 9%, Portugal 8.3%, UK 6.9%. **Tourism:** $107 mil. **Budget** (2003 est.): $128.2 mil. **Intl. reserves less gold:** 50 mil. **Consumer prices:** 1.8%.

Transport: Railroad: Length: 31 mi. **Motor vehicles:** 7,700 pass. cars, 3,900 comm. vehicles. **Civil aviation:** NA; 2 airports. **Chief ports:** Basseterre, Charlestown.

Communications: TV sets: 256 per 1,000 pop. **Radios:** 718 per 1,000 pop. **Telephone lines:** 25,000. **Internet** (2002): 10,000 users.

Health: Life expect.: 69.6 male; 75.4 female. **Births** (per 1,000 pop.): 18. **Deaths** (per 1,000 pop.): 8.3. **Natural inc.:** 0.97%. **Infant mortality** (per 1,000 live births): 14.1. **AIDS rate:** NA.

Education: Compulsory: ages 5-16. **Literacy:** 97%.

Major Intl. Organizations: UN (FAO, IBRD, ILO, IMF, IMO, WHO, WTO), Caricom, the Commonwealth, OAS, OECS.

Embassy: 3216 New Mexico Ave., NW 20016; 686-2636.

Website: www.stkittsnevis.net

St. Kitts (formerly St. Christopher; known by indigenous peoples as Liamuiga) and Nevis were reached (and named) by Columbus in 1493. They were settled by Britain in 1623, but ownership was disputed with France until 1713. They were part of the Leeward Islands Federation, 1871-1956, and the Federation of the West Indies, 1958-62. The colony achieved self-government as an Associated State of the UK in 1967, and became fully independent Sept. 19, 1983. A secession referendum on Nevis, Aug. 10, 1998, fell short of the two-thirds majority required.

Saint Lucia

People: Population: 168,458. **Age distrib.** (%) <15: 29.8; 65+: 5.2. **Pop. density:** 719 per sq mi, 277 per sq km. **Urban:** 30.5%. **Ethnic groups:** Black 90%, mixed 6%, East Indian 3%, White 1%. **Principal languages:** English (official), French patois. **Chief religions:** Roman Catholic 68%, Protestant 8%.

Geography: Total area: 238 sq mi, 616 sq km; **Land area:** 234 sq mi, 606 sq km. **Location:** In E Caribbean, 2d largest of the Windward Isls. **Neighbors:** Martinique to N, St. Vincent to S. **Topography:** Mountainous, volcanic in origin; Soufriere, a volcanic crater, in the S. Wooded mountains run N-S to Mt. Gimie, 3,145 ft, with streams through fertile valleys. **Capital:** Castries, 13,000.

Government: Type: Parliamentary democracy. **Head of state:** Queen Elizabeth II, represented by Gov.-Gen. Dame Calliopa Pearlette Louisy; b. June 8, 1946; in office: Sept. 17, 1997. **Head of gov.:** Prime Min. Kenny Anthony; b. Jan. 8, 1951; in office: May 24, 1997. **Local divisions:** 11 quarters.

Economy: Industries: clothing, electronic components, beverages, cardboard, tourism, lime & coconut proc. **Chief crops:** bananas, coconuts, vegetables, citrus, root crops, cocoa. **Natural resources:** timber, pumice, mineral springs, geothermal areas. **Arable land:** 8%. **Livestock** (2005): cattle: 12,400; chickens: 270,000; goats: 9,800; pigs: 10,000; sheep: 12,500. **Fish catch** (2004): 1,509 metric tons. **Electricity prod.** (2004): 290 mil kWh. **Labor force** (2002 est.): agriculture 21.7%, industry, commerce, and manufacturing 24.7%, services 53.6%.

Finance: Monetary unit: East Caribbean Dollar (XCD) (Sept. 2006: 2.67 = $1 U.S.). **GDP** (2002 est.): $866 mil; **per capita GDP:** $5,400; **GDP growth:** 3.3%. **Imports** (2004 est.): $410 mil; partners (2004): U.S. 30%, Trinidad and Tobago 17.5%, UK 8.5%, Venezuela 8.4%. **Exports** (2004 est.): $82 mil; partners (2004): UK 49.3%, U.S. 19.9%, Antigua and Barbuda 5.4%, Dominica 5.2%, Trinidad and Tobago 4.4%. **Tourism:** $326 mil. **Budget** (2000 est.): $146.7 mil. **Intl. reserves less gold:** 81 mil. **Consumer prices:** 3.91%.

Transport: Motor vehicles 13,500 pass. cars, 10,800 comm. vehicles. **Civil aviation:** NA; 2 airports. **Chief ports:** Castries, Vieux Fort.

Communications: TV sets: 368 per 1,000 pop. **Radios:** 750 per 1,000 pop. **Telephone lines:** 51,100. **Internet:** 55,000 users.

Health: Life expect.: 70.3 male; 77.7 female. **Births** (per 1,000 pop.): 19.7. **Deaths** (per 1,000 pop.): 5.1. **Natural inc.:** 1.46%. **Infant mortality** (per 1,000 live births): 13.2. **AIDS rate:** NA.

Education: Compulsory: ages 5-15. **Literacy:** 67%.

Major Intl. Organizations: UN (FAO, IBRD, ILO, IMF, IMO, WHO, WTO), Caricom, the Commonwealth, OAS, OECS.

Embassy: 3216 New Mexico Ave. NW 20016; 364-6792.

Website: www.stlucia.gov.lc

St. Lucia was ceded to Britain by France at the Treaty of Paris, 1814. Self-government was granted with the West Indies Act, 1967. Independence was attained Feb. 22, 1979.

Saint Vincent and the Grenadines

People: Population: 117,848. **Age distrib.** (%) <15: 26.7; 65+: 6.4. **Pop. density:** 785 per sq mi, 302 per sq km. **Urban:** 58.3%. **Ethnic groups:** Black 66%, mixed 19%, East Indian 6%, Carib Amerindian 2%. **Principal languages:** English (official), French patois. **Chief religions:** Anglican 47%, Methodist 28%, Roman Catholic 13%.

Geography: Total area: 150 sq mi, 389 sq km; **Land area:** 150 sq mi, 389 sq km. **Location:** In the E Caribbean, St. Vincent (133 sq mi) and the northern islets of the Grenadines form a part of the Windward chain. **Neighbors:** St. Lucia to N, Barbados to E, Grenada to S. **Topography:** St. Vincent is volcanic, with a ridge of thickly wooded mountains running its length. **Capital:** Kingstown, 26,000.

Government: Constitutional monarchy. **Head of state:** Queen Elizabeth II, represented by Sir Frederick Ballantyne; b. July 5, 1936; in office: Sept. 2, 2002. **Head of gov.:** Prime Min. Ralph Gonsalves; b. Aug. 8, 1946; in office: Mar. 29, 2001. **Local divisions:** 6 parishes.

Economy: Industries: food proc., cement, furniture, clothing, starch. **Chief crops:** bananas, coconuts, sweet potatoes, spices. **Natural resources:** hydropower. **Arable land:** 10%. **Livestock** (2005): cattle: 5,000; chickens: 125,000; goats: 7,200; pigs: 9,150; sheep: 12,000. **Fish catch** (2004): 8,625 metric tons. **Electricity prod.** (2004): 0.11 bil kWh. **Labor force** (1980 est.): agriculture 26%, industry 17%, services 57%.

Finance: Monetary unit: East Caribbean Dollar (XCD) (Sept. 2006: 2.67 = $1 U.S.). **GDP** (2002 est.): $342 mil; **per capita GDP:** $2,900; **GDP growth:** 0.7%. **Imports** (2004 est.): $225 mil; partners (2004): France 21%, Italy 12.4%, Singapore 11.2%, U.S. 10.9%, Trinidad and Tobago 9.9%, Japan 7.3%, Spain 4.9%. **Exports** (2004 est.): $37.0 mil; partners (2004): France 30.5%, Spain 19.6%, Italy 17.7%, Greece 11.7%, UK 7.8%. **Tourism:** $96 mil. **Budget** (2000 est.): $85.8 mil. **Intl. reserves less gold:** 49 mil. **Consumer prices:** 3.74%.

Transport: Motor vehicles: 9,900 pass. cars, 4,000 comm. vehicles. **Civil aviation:** NA; 5 airports. **Chief port:** Kingstown.

Communications: TV sets: 230 per 1,000 pop. **Radios:** 688 per 1,000 pop. **Telephone lines:** 22,500. **Daily newspaper circ.:** NA. **Internet:** 8,000 users.

Health: Life expect.: 72 male; 75.8 female. **Births** (per 1,000 pop.): 16.2. **Deaths** (per 1,000 pop.): 6. **Natural inc.:** 1.02%. **Infant mortality** (per 1,000 live births): 14.4. **AIDS rate:** NA.

Education: Compulsory: ages 5-15. **Literacy:** 96%.

Major Intl. Organizations: UN (FAO, IBRD, ILO, IMF, IMO, WHO, WTO), Caricom, the Commonwealth, OAS, OECS.

Embassy: 3216 New Mexico Ave. NW 20016; 364-6730.

Website: www.embsvg.com

Columbus landed on St. Vincent on Jan. 22, 1498 (St. Vincent's Day). Britain and France both laid claim to the island in the 17th and 18th centuries; the Treaty of Versailles, 1783, finally ceded it to Britain. Associated State status was granted 1969; independence was attained Oct. 27, 1979.

Samoa *(formerly* Western Samoa)
Independent State of Samoa

People: Population: 176,908. **Age distrib.** (%) <15: 26.1; 65+: 6.6. **Pop. density:** 156 per sq mi, 60 per sq km. **Urban:** 22.3%. **Urban:** 22%. **Ethnic groups:** Samoan 92.5%, Euronesians 7%. **Principal languages:** Samoan, English (both official). **Chief religion:** Christian 99.7%.

Geography: Total area: 1,137 sq mi, 2,944 sq km; **Land area:** 1,133 sq mi, 2,934 sq km. **Location:** In the S Pacific O. **Neighbors:** Nearest are Fiji to SW, Tonga to S. **Topography:** Main islands, Savaii (659 sq mi) and Upolu (432 sq mi), both ruggedly mountainous, and small islands Manono and Apolima. **Capital:** Apia, 41,000.

Government: Type: Constitutional monarchy. **Head of state:** Malietoa Tanumafili II; b. Jan. 4, 1913; in office: Jan. 1, 1962. **Head of gov.:** Prime Min. Tuilaepa Sailele Malielegaoi; b. Apr. 14, 1945; in office: Nov. 23, 1998. **Local divisions:** 11 districts.

Economy: Industries: food proc., building materials, auto parts. **Chief crops:** coconuts, bananas, taro, yams. **Natural resources:** timber, fish, hydropower. **Arable land:** 19%. **Livestock** (2005): cattle: 29,000; chickens: 450,000; pigs: 201,000. **Fish catch** (2004): 4,719 metric tons. **Electricity prod.** (2004): 110 mil kWh.

Finance: Monetary unit: Tala (WST) (Sept. 2006: 2.84 = $1 U.S.). **GDP** (2002 est.): $1 bil; **per capita GDP:** $5,600; **GDP growth:** 5%. **Imports** (2004 est.): $285 mil; partners (2004): New Zealand 23.1%, Fiji 17.9%, Taiwan 10.7%, Australia 9.6%, Singapore 9.1%, Japan 8.1%, U.S. 5.3%. **Exports** (2004 est.): $94 mil; partners (2004): Australia 60.7%, Indonesia 17.1%, U.S. 4.9%. **Tourism:** $70 mil. **Budget** (2002): $119.0 mil. **Intl. reserves less gold:** 65 mil. **Consumer prices:** 1.85%.

Transport: Motor vehicles: 6,200 pass. cars, 700 comm. vehicles. **Civil aviation:** 190.1 mil pass.-mi; 3 airports. **Chief ports:** Apia, Asau.

Communications: TV sets: 56 per 1,000 pop. **Radios:** 1,035 per 1,000 pop. **Telephone lines:** 13,300. **Internet** (2004): 6,000 users.

Health: Life expect.: 68.2 male; 73.9 female. **Births** (per 1,000 pop.): 16.4. **Deaths** (per 1,000 pop.): 6.6. **Natural inc.:** 0.98%. **Infant mortality** (per 1,000 live births): 26.9. **AIDS rate:** NA.

Education: Compulsory: ages 5-14. **Literacy:** 99.7%.

Major Intl. Organizations: UN (FAO, IBRD, ILO, IMF, IMO, WHO), the Commonwealth.

Embassy: 800 Second Ave., Ste. 400J, New York, NY 10017; 212-599-6196.

Website: www.govt.ws

Samoa (formerly known as Western Samoa to distinguish it from American Samoa, a small U.S. territory) was a German colony, 1899 to 1914, when New Zealand landed troops and took over. It became a New Zealand mandate under the League of Nations and, in 1945, a New Zealand UN Trusteeship.

An elected local government took office in Oct. 1959, and the country became fully independent Jan. 1, 1962.

San Marino
Republic of San Marino

People: Population: 29,251. **Age distrib.** (%) <15: 16.8; 65+: 17. **Pop. density:** 1,218 per sq mi, 479 per sq km. **Urban:** 88.7%. **Ethnic groups:** Sammarinese, Italian **Principal language:** Italian (official). **Chief religion:** Predominantly Roman Catholic.

Geography: Total area: 24 sq mi, 61 sq km; **Land area:** 24 sq mi, 61 sq km. **Location:** In N central Italy near Adriatic coast. **Neighbors:** Completely surrounded by Italy. **Topography:** The country lies on the slopes of Mt. Titano. **Capital** (2003): San Marino, 5,000.

Government: Type: Republic. **Heads of state and gov.:** Two co-regents appt. every 6 months. **Local divisions:** 9 castelli.

Economy: Industries: tourism, banking, textiles, electronics, ceramics, cement, wine. **Chief crops:** wheat, grapes, corn, olives. **Natural resources:** building stone. **Arable land:** 17%. **Labor force** (2000 est.): agriculture 1%, industry 42%, services 57%.

Finance: Monetary unit: Euro (EUR) (Sept. 2006: 0.78 = $1 U.S.). **GDP** (2001 est.): $940 mil; **per capita GDP:** $34,600; **GDP growth:** 7.5%. **Intl. reserves less gold:** $248 mil. **Tourism:** NA. **Budget** (2000 est.): $400 mil.

Transport: Motor vehicles (1997): 24,825 pass. cars, 4,149 comm. vehicles.

Communications: TV sets: 875 per 1,000 pop. **Radios:** 1,346 per 1,000 pop. **Daily newspaper circ.:** NA. **Internet** (2002): 14,300 users.

Health: Life expect.: 78.2 male; 85.5 female. **Births** (per 1,000 pop.): 10. **Deaths** (per 1,000 pop.): 8.2. **Natural inc.:** 0.18%. **Infant mortality** (per 1,000 live births): 5.6. **AIDS rate:** NA.

Education: Compulsory: ages 6-14. **Literacy:** 96%.

Major Intl. Organizations: UN (FAO, IBRD, ILO, IMF, IMO, WHO), OSCE.

Website: sanmarino.usvpp.gov

San Marino claims to be the oldest state in Europe and to have been founded in the 4th cent. A Communist-led coalition ruled 1947-57; a similar coalition ruled 1978-86. San Marino has had a treaty of friendship with Italy since 1862.

São Tomé and Príncipe
Democratic Republic of São Tomé and Príncipe

People: Population: 193,413. **Age distrib.** (%) <15: 47.5; 65+: 3.8. **Pop. density:** 501 per sq mi, 193 per sq km. **Urban:** 37.8%. **Ethnic groups:** Mestizo, Black, Portuguese. **Principal languages:** Portuguese (official), Creole, Fang. **Chief religions:** Predominantly Roman Catholic.

Geography: Total area: 386 sq mi, 1,001 sq km; **Land area:** 386 sq mi, 1,001 sq km. **Location:** In the Gulf of Guinea about 125 miles off W central Africa. **Neighbors:** Gabon, Equatorial Guinea to E. **Topography:** São Tomé and Príncipe islands, part of an extinct volcano chain, are both covered by lush forests and croplands. **Capital:** São Tomé, 57,000.

Government: Type: Republic. **Head of state:** Pres. Fradique Melo de Menezes; b. Mar. 21, 1942; in office: Sept. 3, 2001. **Head of gov.:** Prime Min. Tomé Vera Cruz; in office: Apr. 21, 2006. **Local divisions:** 2 provinces.

Economy: Industries: light constr., textiles, soap, beer; fish proc. **Chief crops:** cocoa, coconuts, palm kernels, cinnamon, pepper, coffee. **Natural resources:** fish, hydropower. **Arable land:** 2%. **Livestock** (2005): cattle: 4,600; chickens: 350,000; goats: 5,000; pigs: 2,500; sheep: 3,000. **Fish catch** (2004): 4,141 metric tons.

Electricity prod. (2004): 20 mil kWh. **Labor force:** population mainly engaged in subsistence agriculture and fishing.

Finance: Monetary unit: Dobra (STD) (Sept. 2006: 6,857.55 = $1 U.S.). **GDP** (2003 est.): $214 mil; **per capita GDP:** $1,200; **GDP growth:** 6%. **Imports** (2005 est.): $38 mil; partners (2004): Portugal 50.5%, Germany 10%, U.S. 5.1%, Netherlands 4.5%, South Africa 4.2%. **Exports** (2005 est.): $8 mil; partners (2004): Netherlands 39.1%, China 11.8%, Germany 8.6%, Belgium 6.9%, Philippines 6.7%, France 4.5%. **Tourism** (2002): $10 mil. **Budget** (2004 est.): $59.5 mil. **Intl. reserves less gold** (2003): $19 mil.

Transport: Civil aviation: 8.7 mil pass.-mi; 2 airports. **Chief ports:** São Tomé, Santo Antonio.

Communications: TV sets: 229 per 1,000 pop. **Radios:** 319 per 1,000 pop. **Telephone lines:** 7,000. **Internet:** 20,000 users.

Health: Life expect.: 65.7 male; 69 female. **Births** (per 1,000 pop.): 40.2. **Deaths** (per 1,000 pop.): 6.5. **Natural inc.:** 3.38%. **Infant mortality** (per 1,000 live births): 41.8. **AIDS rate:** NA.

Education: Compulsory: ages 7-12. **Literacy:** 79.3%.

Major Intl. Organizations: UN (FAO, IBRD, ILO, IMF, IMO, WHO), AU.

Permanent UN Representative: 400 Park Ave., 7th Floor, New York, NY 10022; (212) 317-0580.

Website: www.saotome.org

The islands were discovered in 1471 by the Portuguese, who brought the first settlers—convicts and exiled Jews. Sugar planting was replaced by the slave trade as the chief economic activity until coffee and cocoa were introduced in the 19th century.

Portugal agreed, 1974, to turn the colony over to the Gabon-based Movement for the Liberation of São Tomé and Príncipe, which proclaimed as first president its East German-trained leader, Manuel Pinto da Costa. Independence came July 12, 1975. Democratic reforms were instituted in 1987. In 1991 Miguel Trovoada won the first free presidential election following da Costa's withdrawal. A military coup that ousted Trovoada Aug. 15, 1995, was reversed a week later after Angolan mediation. Trovoada defeated da Costa in a presidential runoff election, July 21, 1996.

Fradique de Menezes, a wealthy cocoa exporter, easily beat da Costa in the presidential election of July 29, 2001. The government was ousted in a military coup July 16, 2003, but was restored to power July 23 and relected July 30, 2006. The country, long one of the world's poorest, is expected to reap billions of dollars from oil development in the Gulf of Guinea.

Saudi Arabia
Kingdom of Saudi Arabia

People: Population: 27,019,731. **Age distrib.** (%) <15: 38.2; 65+: 2.4. **Pop. density:** 35 per sq mi, 13 per sq km. **Urban:** 87.7%. **Ethnic groups:** Arab 90%, Afro-Asian 10% **Principal languages:** Arabic (official). **Chief religion:** Muslim (official).

Geography: Total area: 756,985 sq mi, 1,960,582 sq km; **Land area:** 756,985 sq mi, 1,960,582 sq km. **Location:** Occupies most of Arabian Peninsula in Mid-East. **Neighbors:** Kuwait, Iraq, Jordan on N; Yemen, Oman on S; United Arab Emirates, Qatar on E. **Topography:** Bordered by Red Sea on the W. The highlands on W, up to 9,000 ft., slope as an arid, barren desert to the Persian Gulf on the E. **Capital:** Riyadh, 4,193,000. **Cities (urban aggr.):** Jeddah, 2,860,000; Mecca, 1,319,000.

Government: Type: Monarchy with council of ministers. **Head of state and gov.:** King Abdullah bin Abdul Aziz; b. 1924; in office: Aug. 1, 2005. **Local divisions:** 13 provinces. **Defense budget** (2005): $21 bil. **Active troops:** 199,500.

Economy: Industries: oil prod. & refining, petrochems., cement, construction, fertilizers, plastics. **Chief crops:** wheat, barley, tomatoes, melons, dates, citrus. **Natural resources:** oil, nat. gas, iron ore, gold, copper. **Crude oil reserves** (2005): 261.9 bil bbls. **Arable land:** 2%. **Livestock** (2005): cattle: 350,000; chickens: 141 mil; goats: 2.2 mil; sheep: 7 mil. **Fish catch** (2004): 66,590 metric tons. **Electricity prod.** (2004): 155.3 bil kWh. **Labor force** (1999 est.): agriculture 12%, industry 25%, services 63%.

Finance: Monetary unit: Riyal (SAR) (Sept. 2006: 3.75 = $1 U.S.). **GDP** (2005 est.): $338 bil; **per capita GDP:** $12,800; **GDP growth:** 6.1%. **Imports** (2005 est.): $44.9 bil; partners (2004): U.S. 9.3%, Germany 6.8%, Japan 6.7%, UK 5.4%, China 5%. **Exports** (2005 est.): $165 bil; partners (2004): U.S. 19.3%, Japan 16.4%, South Korea 8.7%, China 5.8%, Singapore 4.5%. **Tourism** (2002): $3.4 bil. **Budget** (2005 est.): $89.7 bil. **Intl. reserves less gold:** $17.57 bil. **Gold:** $18.56 bil. **Gold:** 4.6 mil. oz t. **Consumer prices:** 0.72%.

Transport: Railroad: Length: 865 mi. **Motor vehicles:** 7.55 mil pass. cars. **Civil aviation:** 12.9 bil pass.-mi; 73 airports. **Chief ports:** Jiddah, Ad Dammam.

Communications: TV sets: 263 per 1,000 pop. **Radios:** 321 per 1,000 pop. **Telephone lines:** 3.8 mil. **Daily newspaper circ.:** NA. **Internet:** 2.5 mil users.

Health: Life expect.: 73.7 male; 77.8 female. **Births** (per 1,000 pop.): 29.3. **Deaths** (per 1,000 pop.): 2.6. **Natural inc.:** 2.68%. **Infant mortality** (per 1,000 live births): 12.8. **AIDS rate:** NA.

Education: Compulsory: ages 6-11. **Literacy:** 79.4%.

Major Intl. Organizations: UN (FAO, IBRD, ILO, IMF, IMO, WHO, WTO), AL, OPEC.

Embassy: 601 New Hampshire Ave. NW 20037; 342-3800.

Website: www.saudiembassy.net

Before Muhammad, Arabia was divided among numerous warring tribes and small kingdoms. It was united for the first time by Muhammad, in the early 7th cent. His successors conquered the entire Near East and North Africa, bringing Islam and the Arabic language. But Arabia itself soon returned to its former status.

Nejd, in central Arabia, long an independent state and center of the Wahhabi sect, fell under Turkish rule in the 18th cent. In 1913 Ibn Saud, founder of the Saudi dynasty, overthrew the Turks and captured the Turkish province of Hasa in eastern Arabia; he took the Hejaz region in western Arabia in 1925 and most of Asir, in southwest Arabia, by 1926. The discovery of oil in the 1930s transformed the nation.

Ibn Saud reigned until his death, Nov. 1953. Subsequent kings have been sons of Ibn Saud. The king exercises authority together with a Council of Ministers. The Islamic religious code is the law of the land. Alcohol and public entertainments are restricted, and women have an inferior legal status.

Saudi Arabia has often allied itself with the U.S. and other Western nations, and billions of dollars of advanced arms have been purchased from Britain, France, and the U.S.; however, Western support for Israel has often strained relations. Saudi units fought against Israel in the 1948 and 1973 Arab-Israeli wars. Beginning with the 1967 Arab-Israeli war, Saudi Arabia provided large annual financial gifts to Egypt; aid was later extended to Syria, Jordan, and Palestinian groups.

King Faisal played a leading role in the 1973-74 Arab oil embargo against the U.S. and other nations. Crown Prince Khalid was proclaimed king on Mar. 25, 1975, after the assassination of Faisal. Fahd became king on June 13, 1982, following Khalid's death.

The Hejaz contains the holy cities of Islam—Medina, where the Mosque of the Prophet enshrines the tomb of Muhammad, and Mecca, his birthplace. More than 2 mil Muslims make pilgrimage to Mecca annually. In 1987, Iranians making a pilgrimage to Mecca clashed with anti-Iranian pilgrims and Saudi police; more than 400 were killed. Some 1,426 Muslim pilgrims died July 2, 1990, in a stampede in a pedestrian tunnel leading to Mecca. Nearly 300 pilgrims were killed in a stampede in Mecca, May 26, 1994. More than 340 pilgrims died in a tent fire near Mecca, Apr. 15, 1997. A stampede at Mina killed more than 250, Feb. 1, 2004; another stampede at Mina killed at least 363 pilgrims, Jan. 12, 2006.

Following Iraq's attack on Kuwait, Aug. 2, 1990, Saudi Arabia accepted the Kuwait royal family and more than 400,000 Kuwaiti refugees. King Fahd invited Western and Arab troops to deploy on its soil in support of Saudi defense forces. During the 1991 Persian Gulf War, 28 U.S. soldiers were killed when an Iraqi missile hit their barracks in Dhahran, Feb. 25, 1991. Islamic extremists were blamed for truck bombs that killed 7 (5 from the U.S.) at a military training center in Riyadh, Nov. 13, 1995, and 19 Americans at a base in Dhahran, June 25, 1996.

The presence of 15 Saudis among the 19 al-Qaeda hijackers who took part in the Sept. 11, 2001, attacks on the U.S. raised new tensions between the U.S. and Saudi governments, and some blamed the Saudi government for allowing Muslim extremism to flourish in Saudi Arabia. Policy differences over Iraq and the Israeli-Palestinian dispute were further irritants. The U.S. completed a pullout of its combat forces in Sept. 2003. Alarmed at guerrilla attacks that killed more than 100 people, mostly foreigners, in Saudi Arabia during 2003-04, the Saudi government stepped up antiterrorist activities in cooperation with the U.S. Islamist candidates on a "golden list" circulated by conservative clerics fared well in municipal council elections, Feb.-Apr. 2005; women were barred from voting in the elections, the country's first since 1963.

King Fahd, on the throne since 1982, died Aug. 1, 2005. He was succeeded by his half-brother, Abdullah, who had in effect ruled the Kingdom since Fahd suffered a stroke in Nov. 1995. Security guards thwarted an attack by suicide bombers, Feb. 24, 2006, at the huge Abqaiq oil and gas facility.

Senegal
Republic of Senegal

People: Population: 12,191,150. **Age distrib.** (%) <15: 42.2; 65+: 3. **Pop. density:** 164 per sq mi, 63 per sq km. **Urban:** 49.6%. **Ethnic groups:** Wolof 43%, Pular 24%, Serer 15%, Jola 4%, Mandinka 3%, Soninke 1%. **Principal languages:** French (official), Wolof, Pulaar, Jola, Mandinka. **Chief religions:** Muslim 94%, Christian 5%.

Geography: Total area: 75,749 sq mi, 196,190 sq km; **Land area:** 74,132 sq mi, 192,000 sq km. **Location:** At W extreme of Africa. **Neighbors:** Mauritania on N, Mali on E, Guinea and Guinea-Bissau on S; surrounds Gambia on three sides. **Topography:** Low rolling plains cover most of Senegal, rising somewhat in the SE. Swamp and jungles are in SW. **Capital:** Dakar, 2,159,000.

Government: Type: Republic. **Head of state:** Pres. Abdoulaye Wade; b. May 29, 1926; in office: Apr. 1, 2000. **Head of gov.:** Prime Min. Macky Sall; b. Dec. 11, 1961; in office: Apr. 21, 2004. **Local divisions:** 11 regions. **Defense budget** (2005): $99.6 mil. **Active troops:** 13,620.

Economy: Industries: food & fish proc., phosphate mining, fertilizer. **Chief crops:** peanuts, millet, corn, sorghum, rice, cotton. **Natural resources:** fish, phosphates, iron ore. **Arable land:** 12%. **Livestock** (2005): cattle: 3.1 mil; chickens: 46 mil; goats: 4.1 mil; pigs: 313,700; sheep: 4.8 mil. **Fish catch** (2004): 445,467 metric tons. **Electricity prod.** (2004): 1.5 bil kWh. **Labor force** (1990 est.): agriculture 77%, industry and services 23%.

Finance: Monetary unit: CFA BCEAO Franc (XOF) (Sept. 2006: 512.27 = $1 U.S.). **GDP** (2005 est.): $20.5 bil; **per capita GDP:** $1,800; **GDP growth:** 6.1%. **Imports** (2005 est.): $2.4 bil; partners (2004): France 26.2%, Nigeria 12.1%, Thailand 5.3%, Belgium 5%, Spain 4.2%. **Exports** (2005 est.): $1.5 bil; partners (2004): India 13.8%, France 10.6%, Mali 10%, Italy 6%, Côte d'Ivoire 5.7%, Spain 4%. **Tourism**(2003): $209 mi. **Budget** (2005 est.): $1.9 bil. **Intl. reserves less gold:** $833 mil. **Consumer prices:** 1.7%.

Transport: Railroad: Length: 563 mi. **Motor vehicles:** 193,000 pass. cars, 79,000 comm. vehicles. **Civil aviation:** 355.4 mil pass.-mi; 9 airports. **Chief ports:** Dakar, Saint-Louis.

Communications: TV sets: 41 per 1,000 pop. **Radios:** 141 per 1,000 pop. **Telephone lines:** 266,600. **Daily newspaper circ.:** 5.3 per 1,000 pop. **Internet:** 482,000 users.

Health: Life expect.: 55 male; 57.7 female. **Births** (per 1,000 pop.): 38.3. **Deaths** (per 1,000 pop.): 11.2. **Natural inc.:** 2.71%. **Infant mortality** (per 1,000 live births): 61.4. **AIDS rate:** 0.9%.

Education: Compulsory: ages 7-12. **Literacy:** 39.3%.

Major Intl. Organizations: UN and all of its specialized agencies, AU.

Embassy: 2112 Wyoming Ave. NW 20008; 234-0540.

Website: www.senegal-tourism.com

Portuguese settlers arrived in the 15th cent., but French control grew from the 17th cent. The last independent Muslim state was subdued in 1893. Senegal became an independent republic Aug. 20, 1960, but French political and economic influence remained strong. Senegambia, a loose confederation of Senegal and The Gambia, was established in 1982 but dissolved 7 years later.

Forty years of Socialist Party rule ended when Abdoulaye Wade, leader of the Senegalese Democratic Party, won a presidential run-off election Mar. 19, 2000. A Senegalese ferry capsized off the coast of The Gambia Sept. 26, 2002, killing at least 1,863 people. A peace accord signed Dec. 30, 2004, with separatists in Cassamance Province, S Senegal, sought to end a 22-year insurgency.

Serbia

People: Population: 10,140,311. **Age distrib.** (%) <15: 17.9; 65+: 15.2. **Pop. density:** 115 per sq mi, 297 per sq km. **Urban:** 52.0%. **Ethnic groups:** Serb 63%, Albanian 17%, Montenegrin 5%, Hungarian 3%. **Principal languages:** Serbian (official), Albanian. **Chief religions:** Orthodox 65%, Muslim 19%, Roman Catholic 4%.

Geography: Total area: 39,518 sq mi, 102,350 sq km; **Land area:** 39,435 sq mi, 102,136 sq km. **Location:** On the Balkan Peninsula in SE Europe. **Neighbors:** Croatia, Bosnia and Herzegovina on W; Hungary on N; Romania, Bulgaria on E; Albania, on S. Topography: Terrain varies widely, with fertile plains drained by the Danube and other rivers in N, limestone basins in E, ancient mountains and hills in SE, and very high coastline in Montenegro along SW. **Capital:** Belgrade, 1,106,000.

Government: Type: Republic. **Head of state:** Pres. Boris Tadic; b. Jan. 15, 1958; in office: July 11, 2004. **Head of gov.:** Vojislav Kostunica; b. Mar. 24, 1944; in office: Mar. 3, 2004. **Local divisions:** 1 republic with 2 autonomous provinces. **Defense budget** NA. **Active troops:** NA.

Economy: Industries: aircraft, vehicle, & other machine building; metallurgy, mining, consumer goods, electronics, oil products, chemicals. **Chief crops:** cereals, fruits, vegetables, tobacco, olives. **Natural resources:** oil, gas, coal, antimony, copper, lead, zinc, nickel, gold, pyrite, chrome, hydropower. **Crude oil reserves** (2005): 78 mil bbls. **Livestock** (2005): cattle: 1.2 mil; chickens: 15.2 mil; goats: 182,000; pigs: 3.6 mil; sheep: 1.8 mil. **Fish catch** (2004): 5,390 metric tons. **Electricity prod.** (2004): 38.3 bil kWh. **Labor force** (2002): agriculture 30%, industry 46%, services 24%.

Finance: Monetary unit: Dinar (CSD) (Sept. 2006: 63.90 = $1 U.S.). **GDP** (2005 est.): $43.6 bil; **per capita GDP:** $5,000; **GDP growth:** 5.9%. **Imports** (2005 est.): $10.58 bil; partners (2004): Germany 20.2%, Italy 18.1%, Austria 9%, Slovenia 6.1%, France 5.1%, Netherlands 4.4%, Bulgaria 4.3%, Greece 4.2%. **Exports** (2005 est.): $4.6 bil; partners (2004): Italy 30.1%, Germany 16.6%, Austria 7.4%, Greece 7.1%, France 5.3%, Slovenia 4.2%, U.S. 4.1%. **Tourism:** NA. **Budget** (2005 est.): $11.1 bil.

Transport: Railroad: Length: 2,569 mi. **Motor vehicles:** 1.48 mil pass. cars, 330,500 comm. vehicles. **Civil aviation:** NA; 16 airports. **Chief ports:** Bar, Novi Sad.

Communications: TV sets: 277 per 1,000 pop. **Radios:** 296 per 1,000 pop. **Telephone lines:** 2.7 mil. **Daily newspaper circ.:** NA. **Internet** (2006): 1.4 mil users.

Health: Life expect.: 72.3 male; 77.6 female. **Births** (per 1,000 pop.): 12.2. **Deaths** (per 1,000 pop.): 10.7. **Natural inc.:** 0.15%. **Infant mortality** (per 1,000 live births): 12.6. **AIDS rate:** 0.2% (figure is for Serbia and Montenegro).

Education: Compulsory: ages 7-14. **Literacy:** 96.4%.

Major Intl. Organizations: UN (FAO, IBRD, ILO, IMF, IMO, WHO), OSCE.

Embassy: 2134 Kalorama Rd. NW 20008; 332-0333.

Website: www.gov.yu

Serbia, which had since 1389 been a vassal principality of Turkey, was established as an independent kingdom by the Treaty of Berlin, 1878. After the Balkan wars, Serbia's boundaries were enlarged by the annexation of Old Serbia and Macedonia, 1913.

When the Austro-Hungarian empire collapsed after WWI, the Kingdom of Serbs, Croats, and Slovenes was formed from the former provinces of Croatia, Dalmatia, Bosnia, Herzegovina, Slovenia, Vojvodina, and the independent state of Montenegro. The name became Yugoslavia in 1929.

Nazi Germany invaded in 1941. After the Nazis were driven out in 1945, Yugoslavia became a federal republic, headed by Josip Broz, a Communist, known as Marshal Tito. He rejected Stalin's policy of dictating to all Communist nations, and he accepted economic and military aid from the West. Pres. Tito died May 4, 1980. Yugoslavia held together for a decade, then broke apart. Croatia and Slovenia declared independence in 1991. In Croatia, fighting began between Croats and ethnic Serbs. Serbia sent arms and medical supplies to the Serb rebels in Croatia. Croatian forces clashed with Yugoslav army units and their Serb supporters.

The republics of Serbia and Montenegro proclaimed a new "Federal Republic of Yugoslavia" Apr. 17, 1992. Serbia, under Pres. Slobodan Milosevic, was the main arms supplier to ethnic Serb fighters in Bosnia and Herzegovina. The UN imposed sanctions May 30 on the newly reconstituted Yugoslavia as a means of ending the bloodshed in Bosnia.

A peace agreement initialed in Dayton, OH, Nov. 21, 1995, was signed in Paris, Dec. 14, by Milosevic and leaders of Bosnia and Croatia. In May 1996, a UN tribunal in the Netherlands began trying suspected war criminals from the former Yugoslavia. The UN lifted sanctions against Yugoslavia Oct. 1, 1996, after elections were held in Bosnia. Mass protests erupted when Milosevic refused to accept opposition victories in local elections Nov. 17; non-Communist governments took office in Belgrade and other cities in Feb. 1997. Barred from running for a 3rd term as Serbian president, Milosevic had himself inaugurated as president of Yugoslavia on July 23, 1997.

Defeated in a presidential election Sept. 24, 2000, by opposition leader Vojislav Kostunica, Milosevic initially refused to accept the result. A rising tide of mass demonstrations forced him to resign Oct. 6, and Kostunica was sworn in the next day. Charged with corruption and abuse of power, Milosevic surrendered to Serbian authorities Apr. 1, 2001. He was extradited June 28 to The Hague, Netherlands, where a UN tribunal had indicted him for war crimes. His trial began Feb. 12, 2002, but proceeded slowly. He was found dead in his prison cell Mar. 11, 2006, before a verdict was reached.

A pact to reconstitute Yugoslavia as a new union of Serbia and Montenegro took effect Feb. 4, 2003. Zoran Djindjic, premier of the Republic of Serbia, was assassinated Mar. 12 in Belgrade; the murder triggered a roundup of more than 4,500 people associated with organized crime and the Milosevic regime. Serbia's union with Montenegro disintegrated in 2006, as Montenegrins voted support for separation in a referendum May 21, and Montenegro became an independent republic June 3.

Kosovo: A nominally autonomous province in southern Serbia (4,203 sq mi), with a population of about 2 mil, mostly Albanians. The capital is Pristina. Revoking provincial autonomy, Serbia began ruling Kosovo by force in 1989. Albanian secessionists proclaimed an independent Republic of Kosovo in July 1990. Guerrilla attacks by the Kosovo Liberation Army in 1997 brought a ferocious counteroffensive by Serbian authorities.

Fearful that the Serbs were employing "ethnic cleansing" tactics, as they had in Bosnia, the U.S. and its NATO allies sought to pressure the Yugoslav government. When Milosevic refused to comply, NATO launched an air war against Yugoslavia, Mar.-June 1999; the Serbs retaliated by terrorizing the Kosovars and forcing hundreds of thousands to flee, mostly to Albania and Macedonia. A 50,000-member multinational force (KFOR) entered Kosovo in June, and most of the Kosovar refugees had returned by Sept. 1. In the worst fighting there since 1999, Albanians and Serbs clashed in Mar. 2004, killing about 30 people, and injuring 500+, incl. UN/NATO troops. As of 2006, Kosovo was under UN administration (UNMIK), with a NATO-led security force of more than 17,000, pending the outcome of negotiations on Kosovo's final status.

Vojvodina: A nominally autonomous province in northern Serbia (8,304 sq. mi.), with a population of about 2 mil, mostly Serbian. The capital is Novi Sad.

▶ *IT'S A FACT:* After WWII, the English Royal Navy abandoned an artificial island sea fort seven miles off the Suffolk Coast. In 1967, Major Paddy Roy Bates declared himself Prince of the 30 ft wide platform which he named Sealand. When the Essex Crown Court declared the platform out of British jurisdiction a year later, Bates held the decision to be a *de facto* recognition of his nation's independence. One of a handful of so-called "micronations," Sealand is not recognized by any country. Although Britain extended its territorial waters to encompass Sealand, it has not tried to reclaim the island since 1968 or forced it to pay taxes. As of 2004, there were only about 300 legitimate Sealand passports (mostly those of Bates' family and friends) in existence. Sealand has a constitution, a national anthem, a football (soccer) team, banknotes, and stamps. Sealand rarely has a resident population of more than 10, and also suffered from a severe fire in June, 2006. It is now governed by Michael Bates, who runs an internet company from the platform.

Seychelles
Republic of Seychelles

People: Population: 81,541. **Age distrib.** (%) <15: 25.9; 65+: 6.1. **Pop. density:** 463 per sq mi, 179 per sq km. **Urban:** 49.9%. **Ethnic groups:** Mainly Seychellois (mix of French, African, and Asian). **Principal languages:** English, French, Creole (all official). **Chief religions:** Roman Catholic 83%, Anglican 7%.

Geography: Total area: 176 sq mi, 455 sq km; **Land area:** 176 sq mi, 455 sq km. **Location:** In the Indian O. 700 miles NE of Madagascar. **Neighbors:** Nearest are Madagascar on SW, Somalia on NW. **Topography:** A group of 86 islands, about half of them composed of coral, the other half granite, the latter predominantly mountainous. **Capital** (2004): Victoria 25,500.

Government: Type: Republic. **Head of state and gov.:** Pres. James Michel, b. Aug. 18, 1944; in office: Apr. 14, 2004. **Local divisions:** 23 districts. **Defense budget** (2005): $12.6 mil. **Active troops:** 450.

Economy: Industries: fishing, tourism, coconut & vanilla proc., rope, boats. **Chief crops:** coconuts, cinnamon, vanilla, sweet potatoes, cassava, bananas. **Natural resources:** fish, copra, cinnamon. **Arable land:** 2%. **Livestock** (2005): cattle: 1,400; chickens: 570,000; goats: 5,150; pigs: 18,500. **Fish catch** (2004): 94,915 metric tons. **Electricity prod.** (2004): 210 mil kWh. **Labor force** (1989): agriculture 10%, industry 19%, services 71%.

Finance: Monetary unit: Rupee (SCR) (Sept. 2006: 5.42 = $1 U.S.). **GDP** (2002 est.): $626 mil; **per capita GDP:** $7,800; **GDP growth:** -3%. **Imports** (2005 est.): $459.9 mil; partners (2004): Saudi Arabia 15.6%, Spain 14.1%, France 11%, Singapore 7.5%, Italy 7.3%, South Africa 7.3%, UK 5%. **Exports** (2005 est.): $312.1 mil; partners (2004): UK 29.1%, France 17.1%, Spain 11.8%, Japan 9.2%, Italy 8.1%, Germany 6.2%, Netherlands 4.3%. **Tourism:** $172 mil. **Budget** (2005 est.): $332.2 mil. **Intl. reserves less gold:** $39 mil. **Consumer prices:** 0.91%.

Transport: Motor vehicles: 6,200 pass. cars, 2,400 comm. vehicles. **Civil aviation:** 868.1 mil pass.-mi; 8 airports. **Chief port:** Victoria.

Communications: TV sets: 214 per 1,000 pop. **Radios:** 560 per 1,000 pop. **Telephone lines:** 21,400. **Daily newspaper circ.:** NA. **Internet:** 20,000 users.

Health: Life expect.: 66.7 male; 77.6 female. **Births** (per 1,000 pop.): 16. **Deaths** (per 1,000 pop.): 6.3. **Natural inc.:** 0.97%. **Infant mortality** (per 1,000 live births): 15.1. **AIDS rate:** NA.

Education: Compulsory: ages 6-15. **Literacy:** 91.8%.

Major Intl. Organizations: UN (FAO, IBRD, ILO, IMF, IMO, WHO), the Commonwealth, AU.

Embassy: 800 2nd Ave., Ste. 400C, New York, NY 10017; 212-687-9766.

Website: www.virtualseychelles.sc

The islands were occupied by France in 1768 and seized by Britain in 1794. Ruled as part of Mauritius from 1814, the Seychelles became a separate colony in 1903. Independence was declared June 29, 1976. The first president was ousted in a coup a year later by a socialist leader, France Albert René. A new constitution, approved June 1993, provided for a multiparty state. After nearly 27 years in power, Pres. René resigned Apr. 14, 2004, and was succeeded by Vice Pres. James Michel, who won a full 5-year term in elections July 28-30, 2006.

Sierra Leone
Republic of Sierra Leone

People: Population: 6,005,250. **Age distrib.** (%) <15: 44.8; 65+: 3.2. **Pop. density:** 217 per sq mi, 83 per sq km. **Urban:** 38.8%. **Ethnic groups:** Temne 30%, Mende 30%, other tribes 30%; Creole 10%. **Principal languages:** English (official), Mende in S, Temne in N, Krio (English Creole). **Chief religions:** Muslim 60%, indigenous beliefs 30%, Christian 10%.

Geography: Total area: 27,699 sq mi, 71,740 sq km; **Land area:** 27,653 sq mi, 71,620 sq km. **Location:** On W coast of W Africa. **Neighbors:** Guinea on N and E, Liberia on S. **Topography:** The heavily-indented, 210-mi coastline has mangrove swamps. Behind are wooded hills, rising to a plateau and mountains in the E. **Capital:** Freetown, 799,000.

Government: Type: Republic. **Head of state and gov.:** Pres. Ahmad Tejan Kabbah; b. Feb. 16, 1932; in office: Mar. 10, 1998. **Local divisions:** 3 provinces, 1 area. **Defense budget** (2005): $26.1 mil. **Active troops:** 12,000-13,000.

Economy: Industries: diamonds, light mfg., oil refining. **Chief crops:** rice, coffee, cocoa, palm kernels & oil, peanuts. **Natural resources:** diamonds, titanium ore, bauxite, iron ore, gold, chromite. **Arable land:** 7%. **Livestock** (2005): cattle: 400,000; chickens: 7.5 mil; goats: 220,000; pigs: 52,000; sheep: 375,000. **Fish catch** (2004): 134,440 metric tons. **Electricity prod.** (2004): 240 mil kWh.

Finance: Monetary unit: Leone (SLL) (Sept. 2006: 2,952.00 = $1 U.S.). **GDP** (2005 est.): $4.9 bil; **per capita GDP:** $800; **GDP growth:** 6.3%. **Imports** (2004 est.): $531 mil; partners (2004): Germany 17.3%, UK 9.2%, Côte d'Ivoire 8%, U.S. 8%, Ukraine 4.9%, Netherlands 4.7%, China 4.5%, Denmark 4.2%. **Exports** (2004 est.): $185 mil; partners (2004): Belgium 63.1%, Germany 11.9%, U.S. 5.8%. **Tourism:** $58 mil. **Budget** (2000 est.): $351 mil. **Intl. reserves less gold:** $119 mil. **Consumer prices:** 12.05%.

Transport: Railroad: Length: 52 mi. **Motor vehicles:** 20,100 pass. cars, 15,800 comm. vehicles. **Civil aviation:** 46 mil pass.-mi; 1 airport. **Chief ports:** Freetown, Bonthe.

Communications: TV sets: 13 per 1,000 pop. **Radios:** 274 per 1,000 pop. **Telephone lines** 24,000. **Daily newspaper circ.:** NA. **Internet:** 2,005 users.

Health: Life expect.: 38 male; 42.5 female. **Births** (per 1,000 pop.): 45.8. **Deaths** (per 1,000 pop.): 23. **Natural inc.:** 2.27%. **Infant mortality** (per 1,000 live births): 160.4. **AIDS rate:** 1.6%.

Education: Compulsory: ages 6-12. **Literacy:** 35.1%.

Major Intl. Organizations: UN (FAO, IBRD, ILO, IMF, IMO, WHO, WTO), the Commonwealth, AU.

Embassy: 1701 19th St. NW 20009; 939-9261.

Website: www.statehouse-sl.org

Freetown was founded in 1787 by the British government as a haven for freed slaves. Their descendants, known as Creoles, number more than 60,000.

Successive steps toward independence followed the 1951 constitution. Ten years later, full independence arrived Apr. 27, 1961. Sierra Leone declared itself a republic Apr. 19, 1971. A one-party state approved by referendum in 1978 brought political stability, but mismanagement and corruption plagued the economy.

Mutinous soldiers ousted Pres. Joseph Momoh Apr. 30, 1992. Another coup, Jan. 16, 1996, paved the way for multiparty elections and a return to civilian rule. A peace accord, signed Nov. 30 with the Revolutionary United Front (RUF), brought a temporary halt to a civil war that had claimed over 10,000 lives in 5 years.

A coup on May 25, 1997, was met with widespread international opposition. Armed intervention by Nigeria restored Pres. Ahmad Tejan Kabbah to power on Mar. 10, 1998, but RUF rebels mounted a guerrilla counteroffensive, reportedly killing thousands of civilians and mutilating thousands more. The Kabbah government signed a power-sharing agreement with the RUF on July 7, 1999. A UN mission (UNAMSIL) was established in Oct. to help maintain the agreement. The accord collapsed in early May 2000, as RUF guerrillas took more than 500 UN peacekeepers hostage. Rebel leader Foday Sankoh was captured in Freetown May 17. The hostages were freed by the end of May, and 233 more UN personnel behind rebel lines were rescued July 15.

A UN-sponsored disarmament program in 2001 reduced the level of violence. On Jan. 16, 2002, the government and the UN signed an agreement creating the Sierra Leone Special Court to try war crimes that had occurred from Nov. 1996 onwards. Government and rebel leaders declared an official end to the war Jan. 18. Kabbah won the May 14 presidential election.

Sankoh, an indicted war criminal, died in UN custody July 29, 2003. A UN helicopter crashed June 29, 2004, in eastern Sierra Leone, killing all 24 people on board. UNAMSIL, which ended Dec. 31, 2005, was succeeded by UNIOSIL, a UN mission intended to strengthen political institutions and oversee July 2007 elections.

Singapore
Republic of Singapore

People: Population: 4,492,150. **Age distrib.** (%) <15: 15.6; 65+: 8.3. **Pop. density:** 17,015 per sq mi, 6,577 per sq km. **Urban:** 100.0%. **Ethnic groups:** Chinese 77%, Malay 14%, Indian 8%. **Principal languages:** Chinese, Malay, Tamil, English (all official). **Chief religions:** Buddhist 43%, Muslim 15%, Christian 15%, Taoist 9%.

Geography: Total area: 267 sq mi, 693 sq km; **Land area:** 264 sq mi, 683 sq km. **Location:** Off tip of Malayan Peninsula in SE Asia. **Neighbors:** Nearest are Malaysia on N, Indonesia on S. **Topography:** Singapore is a flat, formerly swampy island. The nation includes 40 nearby islets. **Capital:** Singapore, 4,326,000.

Government: Type: Republic. **Head of state:** Pres. S. R. Nathan; b. July 3, 1924; in office: Sept. 1, 1999. **Head of gov.:** Prime Min. Lee Hsien Loong; b. Feb. 10, 1952; in office: Aug. 12, 2004. **Defense budget** (2005): $5.6 bill. **Active troops:** 72,500.

Economy: Industries: electronics, chemicals, financial services, oil drilling equip., oil refining, rubber proc. **Chief crops:** rubber, copra, fruit, orchids, vegetables. **Natural resources:** fish. **Arable land:** 2%. **Livestock** (2005): cattle: 200; chickens: 2 mil; goats: 600; pigs: 250,000. **Fish catch** (2004): 7,579 metric tons. **Electricity prod.** (2004): 32.6 bil kWh. **Labor force** (2003): manufacturing 18%, construction 6%, transportation and communication 11%, financial, business, and other services 39%, other 26%.

Finance: Monetary unit: Dollar (SGD) (Sept. 2006: 1.58 = $1 U.S.). **GDP** (2005 est.): $124.3 bil; **per capita GDP:** $28,100; **GDP growth:** 6.4%. **Imports** (2005 est.): $188.3 bil; partners (2004): Malaysia 15.3%, U.S. 12.7%, Japan 11.7%, China 9.9%, Taiwan 5.7%, South Korea 4.3%, Thailand 4.1%. **Exports** (2005 est.): $204.8 bil; partners (2004): Malaysia 15.2%, U.S. 13%, Hong Kong 9.8%, China 8.6%, Japan 6.4%, Taiwan 4.6%, Thailand 4.3%, South Korea 4.1%. **Tourism:** $5.1 bil. **Budget** (2005 est.): $18.2 bil. **Intl. reserves less gold:** $81.02 bil. **Consumer prices:** 0.47%.

Transport: Railroad: Length: 24 mi. **Motor vehicles:** 427,100 pass. cars, 137,700 comm. vehicles. **Civil aviation:** 47 bil pass.-mi; 9 airports. **Chief port:** Singapore.

Communications: TV sets: 341 per 1,000 pop. **Radios:** 744 per 1,000 pop. **Telephone lines:** 1.8 mil. **Daily newspaper circ.:** 272.9 per 1,000 pop. **Internet:** 2.4 mil users.

Health: Life expect.: 79.1 male; 84.5 female. **Births** (per 1,000 pop.): 9.3. **Deaths** (per 1,000 pop.): 4.3. **Natural inc.:** 0.51%. **Infant mortality** (per 1,000 live births): 2.3. **AIDS rate:** 0.3%.

Education: Compulsory: ages 6-16. **Literacy:** 92.5%.

Major Intl. Organizations: UN (IBRD, ILO, IMF, IMO, WHO, WTO), the Commonwealth, APEC, ASEAN.

Embassy: 3501 International Pl. NW 20008; 537-3100.
Website: www.gov.sg

Founded in 1819 by Sir Thomas Stamford Raffles, Singapore was a British colony until 1959, when it became autonomous within the Commonwealth. On Sept. 16, 1963, it joined with Malaya, Sarawak, and Sabah to form the Federation of Malaysia. Tensions between Malayans, dominant in the federation, and ethnic Chinese, dominant in Singapore, led to an accord under which Singapore became a separate nation, Aug. 9, 1965.

Singapore is one of the world's largest ports and a major center of manufacturing, banking, and commerce. Standards in health, education, and housing are generally high. The government, dominated by a single party, has taken strong actions to keep order and suppress dissent.

In Dec. 2001, the government thwarted an alleged plot to blow up the U.S. Embassy; in Sept. 2002, authorities reported arrests of 21 militants identified as members of Jemaah Islamiah, a radical Muslim group active in Southeast Asia.

Singapore has had only 3 prime ministers: Lee Kuan Yew, who dominated national politics, 1959-90; Goh Chok Tong, 1990-2004; and Lee Kuan Yew's son, Lee Hsien Loong, who took office Aug. 12, 2004. At the White House, July 12, 2005, the prime minister and Pres. George W. Bush signed an agreement tightening U.S.-Singapore defense ties.

Slovakia
Slovak Republic

People: Population: 5,439,448. **Age distrib.** (%) <15: 16.7; 65+: 12. **Pop. density:** 288 per sq mi, 111 per sq km. **Urban:** 57.4%. **Ethnic groups:** Slovak 86%, Hungarian 11%, Roma 2%. **Principal languages:** Slovak (official), Hungarian. **Chief religions:** Roman Catholic 69%, Protestant 11%.

Geography: Total area: 18,859 sq mi, 48,845 sq km; **Land area:** 18,842 sq mi, 48,800 sq km. **Location:** In E central Europe. **Neighbors:** Poland on N, Hungary on S, Austria and Czech Rep. on W, Ukraine on E. **Topography:** Mountains (Carpathians) in N, fertile Danube plane in S. **Capital:** Bratislava, 424,000.

Government: Type: Republic. **Head of state:** Pres. Ivan Gasparovic; b. Mar. 27, 1941; in office: June 15, 2004. **Head of gov.:** Prime Min. Robert Fico; b. Sept. 15, 1964; in office: July 4, 2006. **Local divisions:** 8 departments. **Defense budget** (2005): $828 mil. **Active troops:** 20,195.

Economy: Industries: metals; food & beverages; electricity, gas, coke, oil, nuclear fuels. **Chief crops:** grains, potatoes, sugar beets, hops, fruit. **Natural resources:** coal, lignite, iron ore, copper, mang., salt. **Crude oil reserves** (2005): 9 mil bbls. **Arable land:** 31%. **Livestock** (2005): cattle: 580,000; chickens: 5.6 mil; goats: 40,000; pigs: 1.3 mil; sheep: 316,000. **Fish catch** (2004): 2,783 metric tons. **Electricity prod.** (2004): 28.8 bil kWh. **Labor force** (2003): agriculture 5.8%, industry 29.3%, construction 9%, services 55.9%.

Finance: Monetary unit: Koruna (SKK) (Sept. 2006: 29.27 = $1 U.S.). **GDP** (2005 est.): $87.3 bil; **per capita GDP:** $16,100; **GDP growth:** 5.5%. **Imports** (2005 est.): $34.5 bil; partners (2004): Germany 29.6%, Czech Republic 17.1%, Russia 9.5%, Austria 7.1%, Italy 5.4%, Hungary 4.3%. **Exports** (2005 est.): $32.4 bil; partners (2004): Germany 35.7%, Czech Republic 13.4%, Austria 8.6%, Italy 5.6%, U.S. 4.8%, Poland 4.8%, Hungary 4.3%. **Tourism:** $901 mil. **Budget** (2005 est.): $23.2 bil. **Intl. reserves less gold:** $10.43 bil. **Gold:** 1.13 mil. oz t. **Consumer prices:** 2.71%.

Transport: Railroad: Length: 2,275 mi. **Motor vehicles:** 1.35 mil pass. cars, 183,000 comm. vehicles. **Civil aviation:** 58.4 mil pass.-mi; 18 airports. **Chief ports:** Bratislava, Komarno.

Communications: TV sets: 418 per 1,000 pop. **Radios:** 967 per 1,000 pop. **Telephone lines:** 1.2 mil. **Daily newspaper circ.:** 130.8 per 1,000 pop. **Internet:** 2.3 mil users.

Health: Life expect.: 70.8 male; 78.9 female. **Births** (per 1,000 pop.): 10.7. **Deaths** (per 1,000 pop.): 9.4. **Natural inc.:** 0.12%. **Infant mortality** (per 1,000 live births): 7.3. **AIDS rate:** <0.1%.

Education: Compulsory: ages 6-15. **Literacy:** NA.

Major Intl. Organizations: UN (FAO, IBRD, ILO, IMF, IMO, WHO, WTO), EU, NATO, OECD, OSCE.

Embassy: 3523 International Ct. NW 20008; 237-1054.
Website: www.sigov.si

Slovakia was originally settled by Illyrian, Celtic, and Germanic tribes and was incorporated into Great Moravia in the 9th cent. It became part of Hungary in the 11th cent. Overrun by Czech Hussites in the 15th cent., it was restored to Hungarian rule in 1526. The Slovaks disassociated themselves from Hungary after WWI and joined the Czechs of Bohemia to form the Republic of Czechoslovakia, Oct. 28, 1918.

Germany invaded Czechoslovakia, 1939, and declared Slovakia independent. Slovakia rejoined Czechoslovakia in 1945.

Czechoslovakia split into 2 separate states—the Czech Republic and Slovakia—on Jan. 1, 1993. A prolonged parliamentary standoff left the country without a president for much of 1998.

Prime Min. Vladimir Meciar, a nationalist, suffered a setback in legislative elections Sept. 25-26, 1998, and was defeated in a presidential runoff vote by Rudolf Schuster, May 29, 1999. A center-right coalition governed Slovakia after parliamentary elections Sept. 20-21, 2002. Meciar lost another bid for the presidency to his former ally, Ivan Gasparovic, Apr. 17, 2004. Slovakia became a full member of the EU and NATO in 2004. Robert Fico, a leftist, became prime minister July 4, 2006, in a coalition that included Meciar.

Slovenia
Republic of Slovenia

People: Population: 2,010,347. **Age distrib.** (%) <15: 13.8; 65+: 15.7. **Pop. density:** 258 per sq mi, 99 per sq km. **Urban:** 50.8%. **Ethnic groups:** Slovene 88%, Croat 3%, Serb 2%, Bosniak 1%. **Principal languages:** Slovenian (official), Serbo-Croatian. **Chief religion:** Roman Catholic 58%, other, unspecified 23%.

Geography: Total area: 7,827 sq mi, 20,273 sq km; **Land area:** 7,780 sq mi, 20,151 sq km. **Location:** In SE Europe. **Neighbors:** Italy on W, Austria on N, Hungary on NE, Croatia on SE, S. **Topography:** Mostly hilly; 42% of the land is forested. **Capital:** Ljubljana, 263,000.

Government: Type: Republic. **Head of state:** Pres. Janez Drnovsek; b. May 17, 1950; in office: Dec. 22, 2002. **Head of gov.:** Prime Min. Janez Jansa; b. Sept. 17, 1958; in office: Nov. 9, 2004. **Local divisions:** 183 municipalities, 11 urban municipalities. **Defense budget** (2005): $580 mil. **Active troops:** 6,550.

Economy: Industries: metallurgy, electronics, trucks, electric power equip., wood products, textiles, chemicals, machine tools. **Chief crops:** potatoes, hops, wheat, sugar beets, corn, grapes. **Natural resources:** lignite, lead, zinc, mercury, uranium, silver, hydropower, timber. **Livestock** (2005): cattle: 451,136; chickens: 4.8 mil; goats: 22,000; pigs: 533,998; sheep: 94,000. **Fish catch** (2004): 2,591 metric tons. **Electricity prod.** (2004): 14.5 bil kWh. **Labor force** (2002): agriculture 6%, industry 40%, services 55%.

Finance: Monetary unit: Tolar (SIT) (Sept. 2006: 187.12 = $1 U.S.) (Will switch to the Euro Jan. 1, 2007). **GDP** (2005 est.): $43.4 bil; **per capita GDP:** $21,600; **GDP growth:** 3.9%. **Imports** (2005 est.): $19.6 bil; partners (2004): Germany 20.1%, Italy 17%, Austria 14.1%, France 10.4%. **Exports** (2005 est.): $18.5 bil; partners (2004): Germany 18.4%, Austria 11.4%, Italy 11.1%, Croatia 7.6%, France 7.5%, Bosnia and Herzegovina 4.6%. **Tourism:** $1.6 bil. **Budget** (2005 est.): $16.7 bil. **Intl. reserves less gold:** $5.65 bil. **Gold:** 160,000 oz t. **Consumer prices:** 2.48%.

Transport: Railroad: Length: 746 mi. **Motor vehicles:** 913,700 pass. cars, 56,100 comm. vehicles. **Civil aviation:** 421.3 mil pass.-mi; 6 airports. **Chief ports:** Izola, Koper, Piran.

Communications: TV sets: 362 per 1,000 pop. **Radios:** 404 per 1,000 pop. **Telephone lines:** 816,400. **Daily newspaper circ.:** 168.4 per 1,000 pop. **Internet:** 950,000 users.

Health: Life expect.: 72.6 male; 80.3 female. **Births** (per 1,000 pop.): 9. **Deaths** (per 1,000 pop.): 10.3. **Natural inc.:** –0.13%. **Infant mortality** (per 1,000 live births): 4.4. **AIDS rate:** <0.1%.

Education: Compulsory: ages 6-14. **Literacy:** 99.7%.

Major Intl. Organizations: UN (FAO, IBRD, ILO, IMF, IMO, WHO, WTO), EU, NATO, OSCE.

Embassy: 1525 New Hampshire Ave. NW 20036; 667-5363.
Website: e-uprava.gov.si/e-uprava/en/portal.euprava

The Slovenes settled in their current territory during the period from the 6th to the 8th cent. They fell under German domination as early as the 9th cent. Modern Slovenian political history began after 1848 when the Slovenes, who were divided among several Austrian provinces, began their struggle for political and national unification. In 1918 a majority of Slovenes became part of the Kingdom of Serbs, Croats, and Slovenes, later renamed Yugoslavia.

Slovenia declared independence June 25, 1991, and joined the UN May 22, 1992. The country attained full membership in the EU and NATO in 2004. Slovenia has met EU requirements for adoption of the euro currency on Jan. 1, 2007.

Solomon Islands

People: Population: 552,438. **Age distrib.** (%) <15: 41.3; 65+: 3.3. **Pop. density:** 51 per sq mi, 20 per sq km. **Urban:** 16.5%. **Ethnic groups:** Melanesian 93%, Polynesian 4%, Micronesian, European, and others 3%. **Principal languages:** English (official), Melanesian pidgin, and 120 indigenous languages. **Chief religions:** Protestant 74%, Roman Catholic 11%.

Geography: Total area: 10,985 sq mi, 28,450 sq km; **Land area:** 10,633 sq mi, 27,540 sq km. **Location:** Melanesian Archipelago in the W Pacific O. **Neighbors:** Nearest is Papua New Guinea to W. **Topography:** 10 large volcanic and rugged islands and 4 groups of smaller ones. **Capital:** Honiara, 61,000.

Government: Type: In transition. **Head of state:** Queen Elizabeth II, represented by Gov.-Gen. Sir Nathaniel Waena; in office: July 7, 2004. **Head of gov.:** Prime Min. Manasseh Sogavare; b. 1954; in office: May 4, 2006. **Local divisions:** 9 provinces and Honiara.

Economy: Industries: tuna, mining, timber. **Chief crops:** cocoa, beans, coconuts, palm kernels, rice, potatoes. **Natural resources:** fish, timber, gold, bauxite, phosphates, lead, zinc, nickel. **Arable land:** 1%. **Crude oil reserves:** NA. **Livestock** (2005): cattle: 13,500; chickens: 230,000; pigs: 53,000. **Fish catch** (2004): 36,563 metric tons. **Electricity prod.** (2004): 0.06 bil kWh. **Labor force** (2000 est.): agriculture 75%, industry 5%, services 20%.

Finance: Monetary unit: Dollar (SBD) (Sept. 2006: 7.29 = $1 U.S.). **GDP** (2002 est.): $800 mil; **per capita GDP:** $1,700; **GDP growth:** 5.8%. **Imports** (2004 est.): $159 mil; partners (2004): Australia 25.3%, Singapore 23.8%, New Zealand 5.3%, India 4.8%. **Exports** (2004 est.): $171 mil; partners (2004): China 28.2%, Thailand 15.7%, South Korea 15.7%, Japan 9.7%, Philippines 5.1%. **Tourism:** $4 mil. **Budget** (2003): $75.1 mil. **Intl. reserves less gold:** $67 mil. **Consumer prices:** 7.17%.

Transport: Civil aviation: 34.2 mil pass.-mi; 2 airports. **Chief port:** Honiara.

Communications: TV sets: 16 per 1,000 pop. **Radios:** 141 per 1,000 pop. **Telephone lines:** 7,400. **Internet:** 8,400 users.

Health: Life expect.: 70.4 male; 75.5 female. **Births** (per 1,000 pop.): 30. **Deaths** (per 1,000 pop.): 3.9. **Natural inc.:** 2.61%. **Infant mortality** (per 1,000 live births): 20.6. **AIDS rate:** NA.

Education: NA. **Literacy:** NA.

Major Intl. Organizations: UN (FAO, IBRD, ILO, IMF, IMO, WHO, WTO), the Commonwealth.

Embassy: 800 Second Avenue, Suite 8008, New York, NY 10017; 212-599-6192

Website: www.pmc.gov.sb

The Solomon Islands were sighted in 1568 by an expedition from Peru. Britain established a protectorate in the 1890s over most of the group, inhabited by Melanesians. The islands saw major WWII battles. Self-government came Jan. 2, 1976, and independence was formally attained July 7, 1978.

A coup attempt June 5, 2000, sparked factional fighting in Honiara. During the next 3 years, violence, lawlessness, and corruption became widespread. To restore order, a 2,225-member intervention force, led by Australia and authorized by the Pacific Islands Forum, began arriving in Honiara July 24, 2003; nearly all foreign troops had been removed by mid-2005. Following elections Apr. 5, 2006, parliament's choice of Snyder Rini as prime minister led to 2 days of rioting in Honiara over alleged influence-buying by the ethnic Chinese business community. Rini resigned Apr. 26 rather than face a no-confidence vote, and Manasseh Sogavare replaced him.

Somalia

People: Population: 8,863,338. **Age distrib.** (%) <15: 44.4; 65+: 2.6. **Pop. density:** 36 per sq mi, 14 per sq km. **Urban:** 34.8%. **Ethnic groups:** Somali 85%, Bantu and other 15%. **Principal languages:** Somali, Arabic (both official); Italian, English. **Chief religion:** Sunni Muslim (official).

Geography: Total area: 246,201 sq mi, 637,657 sq km; **Land area:** 242,216 sq mi, 627,337 sq km. **Location:** Occupies the eastern horn of Africa. **Neighbors:** Djibouti, Ethiopia, Kenya on W. **Topography:** The coastline extends for 1,700 mi. Hills cover the N; the center and S are flat. **Capital:** Mogadishu, 1,320,000.

Government: Type: In transition. **Head of state:** Abdullahi Yusuf Ahmed; b. Dec. 15, 1934; in office: Oct. 14, 2004. **Head of gov.:** Prime Min. Ali Muhammad Ghedi; b. 1952; in office: Nov. 3, 2004. **Local divisions:** 18 regions. **Defense budget:** NA. **Active troops:** Nil.

Economy: Industries: a few light industries, incl. sugar refining, textiles, wireless communication. **Chief crops:** bananas, sorghum, corn, coconuts, rice. **Natural resources:** uranium, iron ore, tin, gypsum, bauxite, copper, salt, nat. gas, oil. **Arable land:** 2%. **Livestock** (2002): cattle: 5.30 mil; chickens: 3.30 mil; goats: 12.50 mil; pigs: 4,000; sheep: 13.20 mil. **Fish catch** (2004): 27,500 metric tons. **Electricity prod.** (2004): 270 mil kWh. **Labor force:** agriculture (mostly pastoral nomadism) 71%, industry and services 29%.

Finance: Monetary unit: Shilling (SOS) (Sept. 2006: 1,376.05 = $1 U.S.). **GDP** (2005 est.): $4.8 bil; **per capita GDP:** $600; **GDP growth:** 2.4%. **Imports** (2004 est.): $576 mil; partners (2004): Djibouti 28.8%, Kenya 13.1%, India 9.3%, Brazil 5.4%, Oman 5.2%, UAE 5.1%. **Tourism:** NA. **Exports** (2004 est.): $241 mil; partners (2004): Thailand 31.3%, UAE 22.8%, Yemen 14.9%, India 8.5%, Oman 5.4%, China 4.1%.

Transport: Motor vehicles: 12,000 pass. cars, 12,000 comm. vehicles. **Civil aviation:** NA; 7 airports. **Chief ports:** Mogadishu, Berbera.

Communications: TV sets: 14 per 1,000 pop. **Radios:** 53 per 1,000 pop. **Telephone lines:** 100,000 main lines. **Daily newspaper circ.:** NA. **Internet:** (2002): 89,000 users.

Health: Life expect.: 46.7 male; 50.3 female. **Births** (per 1,000 pop.): 45.1. **Deaths** (per 1,000 pop.): 16.6. **Natural inc.:** 2.85%. **Infant mortality** (per 1,000 live births): 114.9. **AIDS rate:** 0.9%.

Education: Compulsory: ages 6-13. **Literacy** (2005): 37.8%.

Major Intl. Organizations: UN (FAO, IBRD, ILO, IMF, IMO, WHO), AL, AU.

Website: www.state.gov/p/af/ci/so/

British Somaliland (present-day North Somalia) was formed in the 19th cent., as was Italian Somaliland (now central and South Somalia). Italy lost its African colonies in WWII. British Somaliland gained independence, June 26, 1960, and by prearrangement, merged July 1 with the UN Trust Territory of Somalia to create the independent Somali Republic.

On Oct. 16, 1969, Pres. Abdi Rashid Ali Shirmarke was assassinated. On Oct. 21, a military group led by Maj. Gen. Muhammad Siad Barre seized power. In 1970, Barre declared the country a socialist state—the Somali Democratic Republic.

Somalia has laid claim to Ogaden, the huge eastern region of Ethiopia, peopled mostly by Somalis. Ethiopia battled Somali rebels in 1977. Some 11,000 Cuban troops with Soviet arms defeated Somali army troops and ethnic Somali rebels in Ethiopia, 1978. As many as 1.5 mil refugees entered Somalia. Guerrilla fighting in Ogaden continued until 1988, when a peace agreement was reached with Ethiopia.

The civil war intensified again and Barre was forced to flee the capital, Jan. 1991. Fighting between rival factions caused 40,000 casualties in 1991 and 1992, and by mid-1992 the civil war, drought, and banditry combined to produce a famine that threatened some 1.5 mil people with starvation.

In Dec. 1992 the UN accepted a U.S. offer of troops to safeguard food delivery to the starving. The UN took control of the multinational relief effort from the U.S. May 4, 1993. While the operation helped alleviate the famine, there were significant U.S. and other casualties; a failed mission Oct. 3-4 left 18 U.S. troops and more than 500 Somalis dead. The U.S. withdrew its peacekeeping forces Mar. 25, 1994.

When the last UN troops pulled out Mar. 3, 1995, Mogadishu had no functioning central government, and armed factions controlled different regions. By 1999 a joint police force was operating in the capital, but much of the country, especially in southern Somalia, faced continued violence and food shortages. After political and factional leaders signed a peace deal Jan. 29, 2004, a transitional parliament, Somalia's first legislature in 13 yrs, was inaugurated Aug. 22. Meeting in Nairobi, Kenya, the parliament chose Abdullahi Yusuf Ahmed as president; he was sworn in Oct. 14. The Indian Ocean tsunami of Dec. 26, 2004, killed at least 150 people and displaced about 5,000 in Somalia.

Because Mogadishu was held by his rivals, Pres. Yusuf moved, July 26, 2005, to make his transitional capital at Jowhar; an interim parliament convened Feb. 26, 2006, at Baidoa. On June 5, after months of fighting, an Islamist militia took over Mogadishu, defeating secular warlords who reportedly were backed by the U.S. The Islamists, calling themselves the Supreme Islamic Courts Council, also held much of the central and southern regions. The African Union Sept. 13 approved a plan to send 8,000 troops to support the transitional government. Yusuf escaped assassination, Sept. 18, but 8 others died in a car bomb explosion at Baidoa 5 days later.

South Africa
Republic of South Africa

People: Population: 44,187,637. **Age distrib.** (%) <15: 29.7; 65+: 5.3. **Pop. density:** 93 per sq mi, 36 per sq km. **Urban:** 56.9%. **Ethnic groups:** Black 75%, White 14%, mixed 8%, Indian 3%. **Principal languages:** Afrikaans, English, Ndebele, Pedi, Sotho, Swazi, Tsonga, Tswana, Venda, Xhosa, Zulu (all official). **Chief religions:** Christian 68%, indigenous beliefs and animist 29%.

Geography: Total area: 471,011 sq mi, 1,219,912 sq km; **Land area:** 471,011 sq mi, 1,219,912 sq km. **Location:** At the southern extreme of Africa. **Neighbors:** Namibia, Botswana, Zimbabwe on N; Mozambique, Swaziland on E; surrounds Lesotho. **Topography:** The large interior plateau reaches close to the country's 1,739-mi coastline. There are few major rivers or lakes; rainfall is sparse in W, more plentiful in E. **Capitals:** Cape Town (legislative), 3,083,000; Pretoria (administrative), 1,271,000, and Bloemfontein (judicial), 400,000. **Cities (urban aggr.):** Durban, 2,631,000; Johannesburg, 3,254,000; Ekurhuleni, 2,817,000.

Government: Type: Republic. **Head of state and gov.:** Pres. Thabo Mvuyelwa Mbeki; b. June 18, 1942; in office: June 16, 1999. **Local divisions:** 9 provinces. **Defense budget** (2005): $3.4 bil. **Active troops:** 55,750.

Economy: Industries: mining (espec. platinum, gold, chromium), auto assembly, metalworking, machinery, textiles, chemicals, fertilizer, foodstuffs. **Chief crops:** corn, wheat, sugarcane, fruits, vegetables. **Natural resources:** gold, chromium, antimony, coal, iron ore, mang., nickel, phosphates, tin, uranium, diamonds, platinum, copper, vanadium, salt, nat. gas. **Crude oil reserves** (2005): 16 mil bbls. **Arable land:** 10%. **Livestock** (2005): cattle: 13.8 mil; chickens: 121 mil; goats: 6.4 mil; pigs: 1.6 mil; sheep: 25.3 mil. **Fish catch** (2004): 885,106 metric tons. **Electricity prod.** (2004): 227.2 bil kWh. **Labor force** (1999 est.): agriculture 30%, industry 25%, services 45%.

Finance: Monetary unit: Rand (ZAR) (Sept. 2006: 7.63 = $1 U.S.). **GDP** (2005 est.): $533.2 bil; **per capita GDP:** $12,000; **GDP growth:** 4.9%. **Imports** (2005 est.): $53 bil; partners (2004): Germany 14.2%, U.S. 8.5%, China 7.5%, Japan 6.9%, UK 6.9%, France 6%, Saudi Arabia 5.6%, Iran 5%. **Exports** (2005 est.): $50.9 bil; partners (2004): U.S. 10.2%, UK 9.2%, Japan 9%, Germany 7.1%, Netherlands 4%. **Tourism:** $6.3 bil. **Budget** (2005 est.): $70.6 bil. **Intl. reserves less gold:** $13 bil. **Gold:** 3.99 mil. oz t. **Consumer prices:** 3.4%.

Transport: Railroad: Length: 12,969 mi. **Motor vehicles:** 3.97 mil pass. cars, 2.25 mil comm. vehicles. **Civil aviation:** 14.2 bil pass.-mi; 146 airports. **Chief ports:** Durban, Cape Town, East London, Port Elizabeth.

Communications: TV sets: 138 per 1,000 pop. **Radios:** 355 per 1,000 pop. **Telephone lines:** 4.8 mil. **Daily newspaper circ.:** 25.4 per 1,000 pop. **Internet:** 3.6 mil users.

Health: Life expect.: 43.2 male; 42.2 female. **Births** (per 1,000 pop.): 18.2. **Deaths** (per 1,000 pop.): 22. **Natural inc.:** −0.38%. **Infant mortality** (per 1,000 live births): 60.7. **AIDS rate:** 18.8%.

Education: Compulsory: ages 7-15. **Literacy:** 82.4%.

Major Intl. Organizations: UN (FAO, IBRD, ILO, IMF, IMO, WHO, WTO), the Commonwealth, AU.

Embassy: 3051 Massachusetts Ave. NW 20008; 232-4400.

Website: www.gov.za

Bushmen and KhoiKhoi were the original inhabitants. Bantus, including Zulu, Xhosa, Swazi, and Sotho, had occupied the area from northeastern to southern South Africa before the 17th cent.

The Cape of Good Hope area was settled by the Dutch, beginning in the 17th cent. Britain seized the Cape in 1806. Many Dutch trekked north and founded 2 republics, Transvaal and Orange Free State. Diamonds were discovered, 1867, and gold, 1886. The Dutch (Boers) resented encroachments by the British and others; the Anglo-Boer War followed, 1899-1902. Britain won and, effective May

31, 1910, created the Union of South Africa, incorporating 2 British colonies (Cape and Natal) with Transvaal and Orange Free State. After a referendum, the Union became the Republic of South Africa, May 31, 1961, and withdrew from the Commonwealth.

With the election victory of Daniel Malan's National Party in 1948, the policy of separate development of the races, or apartheid, already existing unofficially, became official. Under apartheid, blacks were severely restricted to certain occupations, and paid far lower wages than whites for similar work. Only whites could vote or run for public office. Persons of Asian Indian ancestry and those of mixed race (Coloureds) had limited political rights. In 1959 the government passed acts providing for the eventual creation of several Bantu nations, or Bantustans.

Protests against apartheid were brutally suppressed. At Sharpeville on Mar. 21, 1960, 69 black protesters were killed by government troops. At least 600 persons, mostly Bantus, were killed in 1976 riots protesting apartheid. In 1981, South Africa launched military operations in Angola and Mozambique to combat guerrilla groups. Meanwhile, the apartheid system slowly began to crumble.

In 1986, Nobel Peace Prize winner Bishop Desmond Tutu called for Western nations to apply sanctions against South Africa to force an end to apartheid. Pres. P. W. Botha announced in Apr. the end to the nation's system of racial pass laws and offered blacks an advisory role in government. On May 19, South Africa attacked 3 neighboring countries—Zimbabwe, Botswana, Zambia—to strike at guerrilla strongholds of the black nationalist African National Congress (ANC). A nationwide state of emergency was declared June 12, giving almost unlimited power to the security forces.

Some 2 mil South African black workers staged a massive strike, June 6-8, 1988. Pres. Botha, head of the government since 1978, resigned Aug. 14, 1989, and was replaced by F. W. de Klerk. In 1990 the government lifted its ban on the ANC. Black nationalist leader Nelson Mandela was freed Feb. 11 after more than 27 years in prison. In Feb. 1991, Pres. de Klerk pledged to end all apartheid laws.

In 1993 negotiators agreed on basic principles for a new democratic constitution. South Africa's partially self-governing black territories, or "homelands," were dissolved and incorporated into a national system of 9 provinces. In elections Apr. 26-29, 1994, the ANC won 62.7% of the vote, making Mandela president. The National Party won 20.4%. The Inkatha Freedom Party won 10.5% and control of the legislature in a mainly Zulu province. By then, fighting between the ANC and Inkatha (aided, during the apartheid era, by South African defense forces) had killed more than 14,000 people in the Zulu region since the mid-1980s.

In 1995, Mandela appointed a truth commission, led by Desmond Tutu, to document human rights abuses under apartheid. A post-apartheid constitution became law Dec. 10, 1996. The ANC won a landslide victory in elections held June 2, 1999. ANC leader Thabo Mbeki thus became South Africa's second popularly elected president. Led by Mbeki, the ANC won almost 70% of the vote in elections Apr. 14, 2004. In a farewell address before parliament, Nelson Mandela, 85, retired from public life, May 10.

The UN recently estimated that 5.5 mil South Africans, including about 20% of all adults, have HIV/AIDS.

Spain
Kingdom of Spain

People: Population: 40,397,842. **Age distrib.** (%) <15: 14.4; 65+: 17.7. **Pop. density:** 209 per sq mi, 80 per sq km. **Urban:** 76.5%. **Ethnic groups:** Castilian, Catalan, Basque, Galician. **Principal languages:** Castilian Spanish (official), Catalan, Galician, Basque. **Chief religion:** Roman Catholic 94%.

Geography: Total area: 194,897 sq mi, 504,782 sq km; **Land area:** 192,874 sq mi, 499,542 sq km. **Location:** In SW Europe. **Neighbors:** Portugal on W, France on N. **Topography:** The interior is a high, arid plateau broken by mountain ranges and river valleys. The NW is heavily watered, the S has lowlands and a Mediterranean climate. **Capital:** Madrid, 5,608,000. **Cities (urban agg.):** Barcelona, 4,795,000; Valencia, 797,000.

Government: Type: Constitutional monarchy. **Head of state:** King Juan Carlos I de Borbon y Borbon; b. Jan. 5, 1938; in office: Nov. 22, 1975. **Head of gov.:** Prime Min. José Luis Rodríguez Zapatero; b. Aug. 4, 1960; in office: Apr. 17, 2004. **Local divisions:** 17 autonomous communities and two autonomous cities. **Defense budget** (2005): $8.8 bil. **Active troops:** 147,255.

Economy: Industries: textiles & apparel, food & beverages, metals, chemicals, shipbuilding, autos, machine tools, tourism. **Chief crops:** grain, vegetables, olives, grapes, sugar beets, citrus. **Natural resources:** coal, lignite, iron ore, uranium, mercury, pyrites, fluorspar, gypsum, zinc, lead, tungsten, copper, kaolin, potash, hydropower. **Crude oil reserves** (2005): 158 mil bbls. **Arable land:** 30%. **Livestock** (2005): cattle: 6.7 mil; chickens: 130 mil; goats: 2.8 mil; pigs: 25.3 mil; sheep: 22.5 mil. **Fish catch** (2004): 1,166,517 metric tons. **Electricity prod.** (2004): 263.3 bil kWh. **Labor force** (2004 est.): agriculture 5.3%, industry 30.1%, services 64.6%.

Finance: Monetary unit: Euro (EUR) (Sept. 2006: 0.78 = $1 U.S.) **GDP** (2005 est.): $1 tril; **per capita GDP:** $25,500; **GDP growth:** 3.4%. **Imports** (2005 est.): $271.8 bil; partners (2004): Germany 16.5%, France 15.7%, Italy 8.8%, UK 6.3%, Netherlands 4.8%. **Exports** (2005 est.): $194.3 bil; partners (2004): France

19.3%, Germany 11.7%, Portugal 9.6%, UK 9.1%, Italy 9.1%. **Tourism:** $45.2 bil. **Budget** (2005 est.): $448.4 bil. **Intl. reserves less gold:** $6.77 bil. **Gold:** 14.72 mil. oz t. **Consumer prices:** 3.37%.

Transport: Railroad: Length: 9,184 mi. **Motor vehicles:** 18.73 mil pass. cars, 4.31 mil. comm. vehicles. **Civil aviation:** 33.6 bil pass.-mi; 96 airports. **Chief ports:** Barcelona, Bilbao, Valencia, Cartagena.

Communications: TV sets: 555 per 1,000 pop. **Radios:** 331 per 1,000 pop. **Telephone lines:** 18.3 mil. **Daily newspaper circ.:** 98.2 per 1,000 pop. **Internet:** 17.1 mil users.

Health: Life expect.: 76.3 male; 83.2 female. **Births** (per 1,000 pop.): 10.1. **Deaths** (per 1,000 pop.): 9.7. **Natural inc.:** 0.03%. **Infant mortality** (per 1,000 live births): 4.4. **AIDS rate:** 0.6%.

Education: Compulsory: ages 6-16. **Literacy:** 97.9%.

Major Intl. Organizations: UN and all of its specialized agencies, EU, NATO, OECD, OSCE.

Embassy: 2375 Pennsylvania Ave. NW 20037; 452-0100.

Website: www.la-moncloa.es

Initially settled by Iberians, Basques, and Celts, Spain was successively ruled (wholly or in part) by Carthage, Rome, and the Visigoths. Muslims invaded Iberia from North Africa in 711. Reconquest of the peninsula by Christians from the N laid the foundations of modern Spain. In 1469 the kingdoms of Aragon and Castile were united by the marriage of Ferdinand II and Isabella I. Moorish rule ended with the fall of the kingdom of Granada, 1492. Spain's large Jewish community was expelled the same year.

Spain obtained a colonial empire with the "discovery" of America by Columbus, 1492, the conquest of Mexico by Cortes, and Peru by Pizarro. It also controlled the Netherlands and parts of Italy and Germany. Spain lost its American colonies in the early 19th century. It lost Cuba, the Philippines, and Puerto Rico during the Spanish-American War, 1898.

Primo de Rivera became dictator in 1923. King Alfonso XIII revoked the dictatorship, 1930, but was forced to leave the country in 1931. A republic was proclaimed, which disestablished the church, curtailed its privileges, and secularized education. During 1936-39 a Popular Front composed of socialists, Communists, republicans, and anarchists governed Spain.

Army officers under Francisco Franco revolted against the government, 1936. In a destructive 3-year war, in which some one million died, Franco received massive help and troops from Italy and Germany, while the USSR, France, and Mexico supported the republic. The war ended Mar. 28, 1939. Franco was named caudillo, leader of the nation. Spain was officially neutral in World War II, but its cordial relations with fascist countries caused its exclusion from the UN until 1955.

In July 1969, Franco and the Cortes (Parliament) designated Prince Juan Carlos as the future king and chief of state. After Franco's death, Nov. 20, 1975, Juan Carlos was sworn in as king. In free elections June 1977, moderates and democratic socialists emerged as the largest parties.

In 1981 a coup attempt by right-wing military officers was thwarted by the king. The Socialist Workers' Party, under Felipe González Márquez, won 4 consecutive general elections, from 1982 to 1993, but lost to a coalition of conservative and regional parties in the election of Mar. 3, 1996.

The Popular Party of conservative Prime Min. José María Aznar won a majority in the parliamentary election of Mar. 12, 2000. Aznar, going against Spanish public opinion, openly supported the U.S.-led invasion of Iraq, Mar. 2003.

Four commuter trains were bombed in central Madrid, Mar. 11, 2004, killing 191 people. Aznar's govt. initially blamed the attacks on ETA, but evidence pointed to Islamic extremists angered by Spain's role in Iraq. The opposition Socialist Workers Party won elections 3 days later, and Socialist leader José Luis Rodríguez Zapatero, who became prime min. Apr. 17, fulfilled a campaign pledge to remove the 1,300 Spanish troops stationed in Iraq. Spanish authorities arrested several suspects in the bombing, mainly from Morocco. In April, 4 other suspects, including the leader of the terrorist cell, blew themselves up in their Madrid apartment.

Same-sex marriage became legal in Spain, July 3, 2005. The move was opposed by the Roman Catholic Church and by Pope Benedict SVI, who addressed a huge rally in Valencia July 9, 2006.

Catalonia and the Basque country were granted autonomy, Jan. 1980, following overwhelming approval in home-rule referendums. Basque extremists, however, pushed for independence. Bombings carried out by the militant Basque separatist group ETA have killed about 800 people since 1968. ETA declared a permanent cease-fire effective Mar. 24, 2006, after which the Spanish govt. agreed to begin formal peace talks. On June 18, voters in Catalonia approved a plan for expanded home-rule powers.

The **Balearic Islands** in the W Mediterranean, 1,927 sq mi, are a province of Spain; they include **Majorca** (Mallorca; capital Palma de Mallorca), **Minorca, Cabrera, Ibiza,** and **Formentera**. The **Canary Islands,** 2,807 sq mi, in the Atlantic W of Morocco, form 2 provinces, and include the islands of **Tenerife, Palma, Gomera, Hierro, Grand Canary, Fuerteventura,** and **Lanzarote;** Las Palmas and Santa Cruz are thriving ports. More than 1,700 people died trying to get from Mauritania to the Canary Islands in rickety boats, Jan.-June 2006.

Ceuta and **Melilla,** small Spanish enclaves on Morocco's Mediterranean coast, gained limited autonomy in Sept. 1994. Spain has sought the return of Gibraltar, in British hands since 1704.

Sri Lanka
Democratic Socialist Republic of Sri Lanka

People: Population: 20,717,932. **Age distrib.** (%) <15: 24.6; 65+: 7.6. **Pop. density:** 828 per sq mi, 320 per sq km. **Urban:** 21.0%. **Ethnic groups:** Sinhalese 74%, Tamil 18%, Moor 7%. **Principal languages:** Sinhala, Tamil (both official); English. **Chief religions:** Buddhist 77%, Hindu 8%, Christian 7%, Muslim 9%.

Geography: Total area: 25,332 sq mi, 65,610 sq km; **Land area:** 24,996 sq mi, 64,740 sq km. **Location:** In Indian O. off SE coast of India. **Neighbors:** India on NW. **Topography:** The coastal area and the northern half are flat; the S-central area is hilly and mountainous. **Capital:** Colombo, 652,000; Sri Jayewardenepura Kotte (legislative) 117,000.

Government: Type: Republic. **Head of state:** Pres. Mahinda Rajapaksa; b. Nov. 18, 1945; in office: Nov. 19, 2005. **Head of gov.:** Prime Min. Ratnasiri Wickremanayake; b. May 5, 1933; in office: Nov. 21, 2005. **Local divisions:** 9 provinces with 25 districts. **Defense budget** (2005): $564 mil. **Active troops:** 111,000.

Economy: Industries: rubber proc., tea & coconut prod., clothing, cement, oil refining, textiles, tobacco. **Chief crops:** rice, sugarcane, grains, oilseed, spices, tea, rubber. **Natural resources:** limestone, graphite, mineral sands, gems, phosphates, clay, hydropower. **Arable land:** 14%. **Livestock** (2005): cattle: 1.2 mil; chickens: 11.6 mil; goats: 425,000; pigs: 83,000; sheep: 12,000. **Fish catch** (2004): 286,373 metric tons. **Electricity prod.** (2004): 7.7 bil kWh. **Labor force** (1998 est.): agriculture 38%, industry 17%, services 45%.

Finance: Monetary unit: Rupee (LKR) (Sept. 2006: 102.49 = $1 U.S.). **GDP** (2005 est.): $85.3 bil; **per capita GDP:** $4,300; **GDP growth:** 5.6%. **Imports** (2005 est.): $8.37 bil; partners (2004): India 14%, Singapore 8%, China 7.6%, Hong Kong 5.9%, Malaysia 4.6%, Japan 4.6%. **Exports** (2005 est.): $6.4 bil; partners (2004): U.S. 31%, UK 12.9%, India 5.1%, Belgium 4.9%, Germany 4.9%. **Tourism:** $513 mil. **Budget** (2005 est.): $5.5 bil. **Intl. reserves less gold:** $1.86 bil. **Gold:** 170,000 oz t. **Consumer prices:** 11.64%.

Transport: Railroad: Length: 900 mi. **Motor vehicles:** 443,900 pass. cars, 268,400 comm. vehicles. **Civil aviation:** 3.9 bil pass.-mi; 14 airports. **Chief ports:** Colombo, Trincomalee, Galle.

Communications: TV sets: 102 per 1,000 pop. **Radios:** 211 per 1,000 pop. **Telephone lines:** 1.2 mil. **Daily newspaper circ.:** 28.8 per 1,000 pop. **Internet:** 280,000 users.

Health: Life expect.: 72.7 male; 76.7 female. **Births** (per 1,000 pop.): 17.3. **Deaths** (per 1,000 pop.): 6. **Natural inc.:** 1.14%. **Infant mortality** (per 1,000 live births): 19.9. **AIDS rate:** <0.1%.

Education: Compulsory: ages 5-13. **Literacy:** 90.7%.

Major Intl. Organizations: UN (FAO, IBRD, ILO, IMF, IMO, WHO, WTO), the Commonwealth.

Embassy: 2148 Wyoming Ave. NW 20008; 483-4025.

Website www.priu.gov.lk

The island was known to the ancient world as Taprobane (Greek for copper-colored) and later as Serendip (from Arabic). Colonists from northern India subdued the indigenous Veddahs about 543 BCE; their descendants, the Buddhist Sinhalese, still form most of the population. Hindu descendants of Tamil immigrants from S India account for about one-fifth of the population.

Parts were occupied by the Portuguese in 1505 and the Dutch in 1658. The British seized the island in 1796. As Ceylon it became an independent member of the Commonwealth in 1948, and the Republic of Sri Lanka May 22, 1972.

Prime Min. W. R. D. Bandaranaike was assassinated Sept. 25, 1959. His widow, Mrs. Sirimavo Bandaranaike, served as prime minister 1960-65, 1970-77, 1994-2000. In 1971 the nation suffered economic problems and terrorist activities by ultra-leftists, thousands of whom were executed. Massive land reform and nationalization of foreign-owned plantations took place in the mid-1970s.

Tensions between Sinhalese and Tamil separatists erupted into violence in the early 1980s. More than 65,000 have died in the civil war, which has continued for over 2 decades; another 20,000, mostly young Tamils, "disappeared" after they were taken into custody by government security forces.

Pres. Ranasinghe Premadasa was assassinated May 1, 1993, by a Tamil rebel. Mrs. Bandaranaike's daughter, Chandrika Bandaranaike Kumaratunga, became prime minister after the Aug. 16, 1994, general elections. Elected president Nov. 9, Kumaratunga appointed her mother prime minister. Kumaratunga, who was injured in a suicide bomb attack at a campaign rally Dec. 18, 1999, won a 2nd 6-year term 3 days later. In failing health, Mrs. Bandaranaike resigned Aug. 10 and died Oct. 10, 2000.

Facing a possible no-confidence motion, Pres. Kumaratunga suspended parliament July 10, 2001. Elections Dec. 5 resulted in a victory for the United National Party, headed by Ranil Wickremesinghe. A truce accord intended to bring an end to the civil war was signed Feb. 22, 2002. Severe monsoon flooding in the S and SW, May 2003, killed at least 265 people.

A dispute with Wickremesinghe over how to negotiate with rebel Tamils led Kumaratunga again to suspend parliament, Nov. 4, 2003. Her United People's Freedom Alliance won a plurality in legislative elections Apr. 2, 2004, and formed a coalition govt. The Indian Ocean tsunami of Dec. 26 left more than 31,100 dead, 4,100 missing, and 519,000 displaced in Sri Lanka.

Foreign Min. Lakshman Kadirgamar, a Tamil who took a hard line against the rebels, died Aug. 12, 2005, after he was shot by a sniper. Prime Min. Mahinda Rajapaksa of the United People's Freedom Alliance won the presidential election of Nov. 17. An upsurge of rebel attacks and military and paramilitary retailiation beginning Apr. 2006 claimed more than 500 lives.

Sudan
Republic of the Sudan

People: Population: 41,236,378. **Age distrib.** (%) <15: 42.7; 65+: 2.4. **Pop. density:** 44 per sq mi, 17 per sq km. **Urban:** 38.9%. **Ethnic groups:** Black 52%, Arab 39%, Beja 6%. **Principal languages:** Arabic (official), Nubian, Ta Bedawie; Nilotic, Sudanic dialects; English. **Chief religions:** Sunni Muslim 70%, indigenous beliefs 25%, Christian 5%.

Geography: Total area: 967,499 sq mi, 2,505,810 sq km; **Land area:** 917,379 sq mi, 2,376,000 sq km. **Location:** At the E end of Sahara desert zone. **Neighbors:** Egypt on N; Libya, Chad, Central African Republic on W; Congo (formerly Zaire), Uganda, Kenya on S; Ethiopia, Eritrea on E. **Topography:** The N consists of the Libyan Desert in the W, and the mountainous Nubia Desert in E, with narrow Nile valley between. The center contains large, fertile, rainy areas with fields, pasture, and forest. The S has rich soil, heavy rain. **Capital:** Khartoum, 4,518,000.

Government: Type: Republic with strong military influence. **Head of state and gov.:** Pres. Gen. Omar Hassan Ahmad Al-Bashir; b. Jan. 1, 1944; in office: June 30, 1989. **Local divisions:** 26 states. **Defense budget** (2005): $483 mil. **Active troops:** 104,800.

Economy: Industries: oil, cotton ginning, textiles, cement, edible oils, sugar. **Chief crops:** cotton, peanuts, sorghum, millet, wheat, gum arabic, sugarcane. **Natural resources:** oil, iron ore, copper, chromium ore, zinc, tungsten, mica, silver, gold, hydropower. **Crude oil reserves** (2005): 563 mil bbls. **Arable land:** 5%. **Livestock** (2005): cattle: 38.3 mil; chickens: 37 mil; goats: 42 mil; sheep: 48 mil. **Fish catch** (2004): 60,600 metric tons. **Electricity prod.** (2004): 3.8 bil kWh. **Labor force** (1998 est.): agriculture 80%, industry 7%, services 13%.

Finance: Monetary unit: Dinar (SDD) (Sept. 2006: 212.59 = $1 U.S.). **GDP** (2005 est.): $85.7 bil; **per capita GDP:** $2,100; **GDP growth:** 7%. **Imports** (2005 est.): $5 bil; partners (2004): Saudi Arabia 11.7%, China 10.7%, UAE 6.2%, Egypt 5.2%, Germany 4.9%, India 4.6%, Australia 4.1%, UK 4%. **Exports** (2005 est.): $7 bil; partners (2004): China 64.3%, Japan 13.8%, Saudi Arabia 3.7%. **Tourism:** $21 mil. **Budget** (2005 est.): $5.8 bil. **Intl. reserves less gold:** $1.71 bil. **Consumer prices:** 8.5%.

Transport: Railroad: Length: 3,725 mi. **Motor vehicles:** 46,000 pass. cars, 60,500 comm. vehicles. **Civil aviation:** 476.6 mil pass.-mi; 15 airports. **Chief port:** Port Sudan.

Communications: TV sets: 173 per 1,000 pop. **Radios:** 480 per 1,000 pop. **Telephone lines:** 1 mil. **Daily newspaper circ.:** NA. **Internet:** 1.1 mil users.

Health: Life expect.: 57.7 male; 60.2 female. **Births** (per 1,000 pop.): 34.5. **Deaths** (per 1,000 pop.): 9. **Natural inc.:** 2.56%. **Infant mortality** (per 1,000 live births): 61. **AIDS rate:** 1.6%.

Education: Compulsory: ages 6-13. **Literacy:** 60.9%.

Major Intl. Organizations: UN (FAO, IBRD, ILO, IMF, IMO, WHO), AL, AU.

Embassy: 2210 Massachusetts Ave. NW 20008; 338-8565.

Website: www.sudan.gov.sd/english.htm

Northern Sudan, ancient Nubia, was settled by Egyptians in antiquity. The population was converted to Coptic Christianity in the 6th cent. Arab conquests brought Islam to the area in the 15th cent. In the 1820s Egypt took over Sudan, defeating the last of earlier empires, including the Fung. In the 1880s a revolution was led by Muhammad Ahmad, who called himself the Mahdi (leader of the faithful), and his followers, the dervishes.

In 1898 an Anglo-Egyptian force crushed the Mahdi's successors. In 1951 the Egyptian Parliament abrogated its 1899 and 1936 treaties with Great Britain and amended its constitution to provide for a separate Sudanese constitution. Sudan voted for complete independence effective Jan. 1, 1956. In 1969, a Revolutionary Council took power, but a civilian premier and cabinet were appointed. The government announced it would create a socialist state.

Economic problems plagued the nation in the 1980s and 1990s, aggravated by civil war and influxes of refugees from neighboring countries. After 16 years in power, Pres. Jaafar al-Nimeiry was overthrown in a bloodless coup, Apr. 6, 1985. Sudan held its first democratic parliamentary elections in 18 years in 1986, but the elected government was toppled in a bloodless coup June 30, 1989.

In the mid-1980s, rebels in the south (populated largely by black Christians and followers of tribal religions) took up arms against government domination by northern Sudan, mostly Arab-Muslim. War and related famine cost an estimated 2 mil lives and displaced millions of southerners. In 1993, Amnesty International accused the Sudanese government of "ethnic cleansing."

A new constitution based on Islamic law took effect June 30, 1998. On Aug. 20, in retaliation for bombings in Kenya and Tanzania, U.S. missiles destroyed a Khartoum pharmaceutical plant the U.S. alleged was associated with terrorist activities; independent inquiries later cast some doubt on the U.S. claim.

An accord to end the rebellion in the south was signed Jan. 9, 2005. Under a power-sharing constitution with autonomy for southern Sudan, former rebel leader John Garang became first vice pres., July 9. His death 3 weeks later in a helicopter crash sparked riots in Khartoum and other cities, Aug. 1-3, killing at least 130 people. A national unity government was installed Sept. 20.

During 2003-06, a rebellion in the Darfur region of western Sudan led to a new crisis. Marauding Arab militias, known as the *janjaweed*, retaliated by attacking black African villagers, looting and burning homes, and killing inhabitants, reportedly in collusion with Sudanese government troops. The African Union sent more than 7,000 peacekeepers, but fighting continued. A peace deal reached with a major rebel faction May 5, 2006, also failed to halt the conflict, which had killed at least 200,000 people and forced more than 2 mil to flee to refugee camps. Rebel and militia activities in both Sudan and Chad led to border clashes and further attacks on civilians. The UN Security Council Aug. 31 authorized over 20,000 peacekeepers (UNMIS) to take over the African Union mission in Darfur, but the Sudanese government said it would refuse to allow them to deploy.

Suriname
Republic of Suriname

People: Population: 465,610. **Age distrib.** (%) <15: 28.5; 65+: 6.2. **Pop. density:** 7 per sq mi, 2 per sq km. **Urban:** 76.1%. **Ethnic groups:** East Indians 37%, Creole 31%, Javanese 15%, Maroons 10%, Amerindian 2%, Chinese 2%, White 1%. **Principal languages:** Dutch (official), English, Sranang Tongo (an English Creole), Hindustani, Javanese. **Chief religions:** Hindu 27%, Protestant 25%, Roman Catholic 23%, Muslim 20%.

Geography: Total area: 63,039 sq mi, 163,270 sq km; **Land area:** 62,344 sq mi, 161,470 sq km. **Location:** On N shore of South America. **Neighbors:** Guyana on W, Brazil on S, French Guiana on E. **Topography:** A flat Atlantic coast, where dikes permit agriculture. Inland is a forest belt; to the S, largely unexplored hills cover 75% of the country. **Capital:** Paramaribo, 268,000.

Government: Type: Republic. **Head of state and gov.:** Pres. Runaldo Ronald Venetiaan; b. June 18, 1936; in office: Aug. 12, 2000. **Local divisions:** 10 districts. **Defense budget:** 8 mil. **Active troops:** 1,840.

Economy: Industries: mining, oil, lumber, food proc., fishing. **Chief crops:** rice, bananas, palm kernels, coconuts, plantains, peanuts. **Natural resources:** timber, hydropower, fish, kaolin, shrimp, bauxite, gold, nickel, copper, platinum, iron ore. **Crude oil reserves** (2005): 111 mil bbls. **Livestock** (2005): cattle: 137,000; chickens: 3.8 mil; goats: 7,100; pigs: 24,500; sheep: 7,700. **Fish catch** (2004): 33,065 metric tons. **Electricity prod.** (2004): 1.5 bil kWh. **Labor force:** agriculture 8%, industry 14%, services 78%.

Finance: Monetary unit: Dollar (SRD) (Sept. 2006: 2.74 = $1 U.S.). **GDP** (2005 est.): $2.8 bil; **per capita GDP:** $4,100; **GDP growth:** 2%. **Imports** (2004 est.): $750 mil; partners (2004): U.S. 28.2%, Netherlands 21.1%, Trinidad and Tobago 11.4%, Japan 7.2%, China 4.3%. **Exports** (2004 est.): $881.0 mil; partners (2004): Norway 31.1%, U.S. 16%, Canada 13.2%, Belgium 10.8%, France 8.8%, Iceland 4.6%. **Tourism:** $17 mil. **Budget** (2004): $425.9 mil. **Intl. reserves less gold:** $88 mil. **Gold:** 30,000 oz t. **Consumer prices:** 9.95%.

Transport: Railroad: Length: 103 mi. **Motor vehicles:** 71,400 pass. cars, 29,300 comm. vehicles. **Civil aviation:** 552.4 mil pass.-mi; 5 airports. **Chief ports:** Paramaribo, New Nickerie, Albina.

Communications: TV sets: 241 per 1,000 pop. **Radios:** 728 per 1,000 pop. **Telephone lines:** 81,100. **Daily newspaper circ.:** NA. **Internet:** 30,000 users.

Health: Life expect.: 70.3 male; 75.8 female. **Births** (per 1,000 pop.): 17.6. **Deaths** (per 1,000 pop.): 5.5. **Natural inc.:** 1.21%. **Infant mortality** (per 1,000 live births): 20.8. **AIDS rate:** 1.9%.

Education: Compulsory: ages 6-11. **Literacy:** 89.6%.

Major Intl. Organizations: UN (FAO, IBRD, ILO, IMF, IMO, WHO, WTO), Caricom, OAS.

Embassy: 4301 Connecticut Ave., Suite 460, NW 20008; 244-7488.

Website: www.surinameembassy.org

The Netherlands acquired Suriname in 1667 from Britain, in exchange for New Netherlands (New York). The 1954 Dutch constitution raised the colony to a level of equality with the Netherlands and the Netherlands Antilles. Independence was granted Nov. 25, 1975, despite objections from East Indians. Some 40% of the population (mostly East Indians) immigrated to the Netherlands in the months before independence.

The National Military Council took control of the government Feb. 1982. Civilian rule was restored in 1987, but political turmoil continued until 1992, disrupting the nation's economy. A special assembly, convened after parliament deadlocked, reelected Pres. Runaldo Ronald Venetiaan on Aug. 3, 2005.

Swaziland
Kingdom of Swaziland

People: Population: 1,136,334. **Age distrib.** (%) <15: 40.7; 65+: 3.6. **Pop. density:** 171 per sq mi, 66 per sq km. **Urban:** 23.5%. **Ethnic groups:** African 97%, European 3% **Principal languages:** English, siSwati (both official). **Chief religions:** Christian 60%, Muslim 10%, indigenous and other 30%.

Geography: Total area: 6,704 sq mi, 17,363 sq km; **Land area:** 6,642 sq mi, 17,203 sq km. **Location:** In southern Africa, near Indian O. coast. **Neighbors:** South Africa on N, W, S; Mozambique on E. **Topography:** The country descends from W-E in broad belts, becoming more arid in the low veld region, then rising to a plateau in the E. **Capitals:** Mbabane (administrative), 73,000; Lobamba (legislative).

Government: Type: Constitutional monarchy. **Head of state:** King Mswati III; b. Apr. 19, 1968; in office: Apr. 25, 1986. **Head of gov.:** Prime Min. Absalom Themba Dlamini; b. Dec. 1, 1950; in office: Nov. 26, 2003. **Local divisions:** 4 districts.

Economy: Industries: coal mining, pulp, sugar, soft drinks, textiles, apparel. **Chief crops:** sugarcane, cotton, corn, tobacco, rice, citrus. **Natural resources:** asbestos, coal, clay, cassiterite, hydropower, timber, gold, diamonds, quarry stone, talc. **Arable land:** 11%. **Livestock** (2005): cattle: 580,000; chickens: 3.2 mil; goats: 274,000; pigs: 30,000; sheep: 27,000. **Fish catch** (2004): 70 metric tons. **Electricity prod.** (2004): 460 mil kWh.

Finance: Monetary unit: Lilangeni (SZL) (Sept. 2006: 7.66 = $1 U.S.). **GDP** (2005 est.): $5.7 bil; **per capita GDP:** $5,000; **GDP growth:** 1.8%. **Imports** (2005 est.): $2.1 bil; partners (2004): South Africa 95.6%, EU 0.9%, Japan 0.9%, Singapore 0.3%. **Exports** (2005 est.): $2 bil; partners (2004): South Africa 59.7%, EU 8.8%, U.S. 8.8%, Mozambique 6.2%. **Tourism:** $95 mil. **Budget** (2005 est.): $957.1 mil. **Intl. reserves less gold:** $171 mil. **Consumer prices** (2003): 7.3%.

Transport: Railroad: Length: 187 mi. **Motor vehicles:** 46,400 pass. cars, 56,200 comm. vehicles. **Civil aviation:** 42.3 mil pass.-mi; 1 airport.

Communications: TV sets: 112 per 1,000 pop. **Radios:** 168 per 1,000 pop. **Telephone lines:** 35,000. **Daily newspaper circ.:** NA. **Internet:** 36,000 users.

Health: Life expect.: 32.1 male; 33.2 female. **Births** (per 1,000 pop.): 27.4. **Deaths** (per 1,000 pop.): 29.7. **Natural inc.:** −0.23%. **Infant mortality** (per 1,000 live births): 71.8. **AIDS rate:** 33.4%.

Education: Compulsory: ages 6-12. **Literacy:** 79.6%.

Major Intl. Organizations: UN (FAO, IBRD, ILO, IMF, WHO, WTO), the Commonwealth, AU.

Embassy: 1712 New Hampshire Ave. NW 20009; 234-5002.

Website: www.gov.sz

The royal house of Swaziland traces back 400 years, and is one of Africa's last ruling dynasties. The Swazis, a Bantu people, were driven to Swaziland from lands to the north by the Zulus in 1820. Their autonomy was later guaranteed by Britain and Transvaal (later part of South Africa), with Britain assuming control after 1903. Independence came Sept. 6, 1968. In 1973 the king repealed the constitution and assumed full powers.

A new constitution banning political parties took effect Oct. 13, 1978. A shrinking economy and the AIDS crisis have fueled student and labor unrest in recent years. The UN in 2005 estimated that about one-third of the adult population has HIV/AIDS.

Sweden
Kingdom of Sweden

People: Population: 9,016,596. **Age distrib.** (%) <15: 16.7; 65+: 47.3. **Pop. density:** 56 per sq mi, 21 per sq km. **Urban:** 83.4%. **Ethnic groups:** Swedish 89%, Finnish 2%; Sami and others 9%. **Principal languages:** Swedish (official), Sami, Finnish. **Chief religion:** Lutheran 87%.

Geography: Total area: 173,732 sq mi, 449,964 sq km; **Land area:** 158,663 sq mi, 410,934 sq km. **Location:** On Scandinavian Peninsula in N Europe. **Neighbors:** Norway on W, Denmark on S (across Kattegat), Finland on E. **Topography:** Mountains along NW border cover 25% of Sweden, flat or rolling terrain covers the central and southern areas, which include several large lakes. **Capital:** Stockholm, 1,708,000. **Cities (urban aggr.):** Göteborg, 827,000.

Government: Type: Constitutional monarchy. **Head of state:** King Carl XVI Gustaf; b. Apr. 30, 1946; in office: Sept. 19, 1973. **Head of gov.:** Prime Min.-designate Fredrik Reinfeldt; b. Aug. 4, 1965; in office: designated Sept. 19, 2006. **Local divisions:** 21 counties. **Defense budget** (2005): $5.6 bil. **Active troops:** 27,600.

Economy: Industries: iron & steel, precision equip., wood & paper products, proc. foods, autos. **Chief crops:** barley, wheat, sugar beets. **Natural resources:** zinc, iron ore, lead, copper, silver, timber, uranium, hydropower. **Arable land:** 7%. **Livestock** (2005): cattle: 1.6 mil; chickens: 6.6 mil; pigs: 1.8 mil; sheep: 479,400. **Fish catch** (2004): 275,911 metric tons. **Electricity prod.** (2004): 150.5 bil kWh. **Labor force** (2000 est.): agriculture 2%, industry 24%, services 74%.

Finance: Monetary unit: Krona (SEK) (Sept. 2006: 7.24 = $1 U.S.). **GDP** (2005 est.): $268 bil; **per capita GDP:** $29,800; **GDP growth:** 2.7%. **Imports** (2005 est.): $104.4 bil; partners (2004): Germany 20.2%, Denmark 8.2%, UK 7.9%, Netherlands 7.2%, Finland 7%, France 6.1%, Norway 5.9%, Belgium 4.5%. **Exports** (2005 est.): $126.6 bil; partners (2004): U.S. 10.7%, Germany 10.3%, UK 7.2%, Denmark 6.6%, Norway 6.2%, Finland 5.9%, Belgium 5.1%, Netherlands 4.8%, France 4.7%. **Tourism:** $6.1 bil. **Budget** (2005 est.): $205.9 bil. **Intl. reserves less gold:** $15.44 bil. **Gold:** 5.41 mil. oz t. **Consumer prices:** 0.45%.

Transport: Railroad: Length: 7,134 mi. **Motor vehicles:** 4.07 mil pass. cars, 435,300 comm. vehicles. **Civil aviation:** 7.2 bil pass.-mi; 155 airports. **Chief ports:** Göteborg, Stockholm, Malmö.

Communications: TV sets: 551 per 1,000 pop. **Radios:** 932 per 1,000 pop. **Telephone lines** 6.4 mil. **Daily newspaper circ.:** 409.5 per 1,000 pop. **Internet:** 6.8 mil users.

Health: Life expect.: 78.3 male; 82.9 female. **Births** (per 1,000 pop.): 10.3. **Deaths** (per 1,000 pop.): 10.3. **Natural inc.:** 0%. **Infant mortality** (per 1,000 live births): 2.8. **AIDS rate:** 0.2%.

Education: Compulsory: ages 7-16. **Literacy:** 99%.

Major Intl. Organizations: UN and all of its specialized agencies, EU, OECD, OSCE.
Embassy: 1501 M St. NW 20005; 467-2600.
Website: www.sweden.gov.se

The Swedes have lived in present-day Sweden for at least 5,000 years, longer than nearly any other European people. Gothic tribes from Sweden played a major role in the disintegration of the Roman Empire. Other Swedes helped create the first Russian state in the 9th cent.

The Swedes were Christianized from the 11th cent., and a strong centralized monarchy developed. A parliament, the Riksdag, was first called in 1435, the earliest parliament on the European continent, with all classes of society represented.

Swedish independence from rule by Danish kings (dating from 1397) was secured by Gustavus I in a revolt, 1521-23; he built up the government and military and established the Lutheran Church. In the 17th cent. Sweden was a major European power, gaining most of the Baltic seacoast, but its international position subsequently declined. The Napoleonic wars, 1799-1815, in which Sweden acquired Norway (it became independent 1905), were the last in which Sweden participated. Armed neutrality was maintained in both world wars.

More than 4 decades of Social Democratic rule ended in the 1976 parliamentary elections; the party returned to power in the 1982 elections. After Prime Min. Olof Palme was shot to death in Stockholm, Feb. 28, 1986, Ingvar Carlsson took office. Carl Bildt, a non-Socialist, became prime minister Oct. 1991, with a mandate to restore Sweden's economic competitiveness. The Social Democrats returned to power following 1994 elections.

Swedish voters approved membership in the European Union Nov. 13, 1994, and Sweden entered the EU as of Jan. 1, 1995. Carlsson retired and was succeeded by Goran Persson in Mar. 1996. Persson and his Social Democrats led coalition governments after the elections of Sept. 20, 1998, and Sept. 15, 2002. Foreign Min. Anna Lindh died Sept. 11, 2003, after being stabbed in a Stockholm department store. Her killer, Mijailo Mijailovic, was sentenced to life in prison Mar. 2004; an appeals court later deemed him mentally ill and sent him to a psychiatric ward.

Swedish voters Sept. 14, 2003, rejected adoption of the euro currency. Foreign Min. Laila Freivalds resigned Mar. 21, 2006, after press reports cited her role in shutting down an Internet political site that was about to post cartoons of the prophet Muhammad; the caricatures, originally published in Denmark, had already sparked worldwide Muslim protests. A center-right alliance led by Fredrik Reinfeldt defeated the Social Democrats in Sept. 17 elections.

Switzerland
Swiss Confederation

People: Population: 7,523,934. **Age distrib.** (%) <15: 16.3; 65+: 15.6. **Pop. density:** 489 per sq mi, 189 per sq km. **Urban:** 67.5%. **Ethnic groups:** German 65%, French 18%, Italian 10%, Romansch 1%. **Principal languages:** German, French, Italian (all official); Romansch (semi-official). **Chief religions:** Roman Catholic 42%, Protestant 35%.

Geography: Total area: 15,942 sq mi, 41,290 sq km; **Land area:** 15,355 sq mi, 39,770 sq km. **Location:** In the Alps Mts. in central Europe. **Neighbors:** France on W, Italy on S, Austria on E, Germany on N. **Topography:** The Alps cover 60% of the land area; the Jura, near France, 10%. Running between, from NE to SW, are midlands, 30%. **Capitals:** Bern (administrative), 357,000; Lausanne (judicial). **Cities (urban aggr.):** Zurich, 1,144,000; Basel, 166,700; Geneva, 398,910.

Government: Type: Federal republic. **Head of state and gov.:** The president is elected by the Federal Assembly to a nonrenewable 1-year term. **Local divisions:** 20 full cantons, 6 half cantons. **Defense budget** (2005): $3.8 bil. **Active troops:** 4,300.

Economy: Industries: machinery, chemicals, watches, textiles, precision instruments. **Chief crops:** grains, fruits, vegetables. **Natural resources:** hydropower, timber, salt. **Arable land:** 10%. **Livestock** (2005): cattle: 1.5 mil; chickens: 8.1 mil; goats: 74,000; pigs: 1.6 mil; sheep: 443,000. **Fish catch** (2004): 2,807 metric tons. **Electricity prod.** (2004): 62 bil kWh. **Labor force** (1998): agriculture 4.6%, industry 26.3%, services 69.1%

Finance: Monetary unit: Franc (CHF) (Sept. 2006: 1.23 = $1 U.S.). **GDP** (2005 est.): $241.8 bil; **per capita GDP:** $32,300; **GDP growth:** 1.8%. **Imports** (2005 est.): $135 bil; partners (2004): Germany 29%, Italy 11.8%, France 11.1%, U.S. 7.6%, Austria 4.5%, UK 4.5%, Netherlands 4.3%. **Exports** (2005 est.): $148.6 bil; partners (2004): Germany 20%, U.S. 9.1%, France 9.1%, Italy 8.8%, UK 4.9%. **Tourism:** $10.6 bil. **Budget** (2005 est.): $143.6 bil. **Intl. reserves less gold:** $25.4 bil. **Gold:** 41.48 mil. oz t. **Consumer prices:** 1.17%.

Transport: Railroad: Length: 2,813 mi. **Motor vehicles:** 3.7 mil pass. cars, 332,500 comm. vehicles. **Civil aviation:** 16.6 bil pass.-mi; 42 airports. **Chief port:** Basel.

Communications: TV sets: 457 per 1,000 pop. **Radios:** 979 per 1,000 pop. **Telephone lines:** 5.1 mil. **Daily newspaper circ.:** 371.7 per 1,000 pop. **Internet:** 4.9 mil users.

Health: Life expect.: 77.7 male; 83.5 female. **Births** (per 1,000 pop.): 9.7. **Deaths** (per 1,000 pop.): 8.5. **Natural inc.:** 0.12%. **Infant mortality** (per 1,000 live births): 4.3. **AIDS rate:** 0.4%.

Education: Compulsory: ages 7-15. **Literacy:** 99%.

Major Intl. Organizations: UN and most of its specialized agencies, EFTA, OECD, OSCE.

Embassy: 2900 Cathedral Ave. NW 20008; 745-7900.
Website: www.swissemb.org

Switzerland, the former Roman province of Helvetia, traces its modern history to 1291, when 3 cantons created a defensive league. Other cantons were subsequently admitted to the Swiss Confederation, which obtained its independence from the Holy Roman Empire through the Peace of Westphalia (1648). The cantons were joined under a federal constitution in 1848, with large powers of local control retained by each.

Switzerland has maintained an armed neutrality since 1815 and has not been involved in a foreign war since 1515. It is the seat of many UN and other international agencies but did not become a full member of the UN until Sept. 10, 2002.

Switzerland is a world banking center. Stung by charges that assets seized by the Nazis and deposited in Swiss banks in WWII had not been properly returned, the government announced, Mar. 5, 1997, a $4.7 bil fund to compensate victims of the Holocaust and other catastrophies. Swiss banks agreed Aug. 12, 1998, to pay $1.25 bil in reparations. Abortion was decriminalized by a June 2, 2002 referendum. The rightist Swiss People's Party topped Oct. 2003 parlimentary voting and entered a coalition government. In referendums June 5 and Sept. 25, 2005, voters backed plans harmonizing travel, asylum, law enforcement, and labor policies with the EU; more rights for same-sex couples were also endorsed June 5.

Syria
Syrian Arab Republic

People: Population: 18,881,361. **Age distrib.** (%) <15: 37; 65+: 3.3. **Pop. density:** 265 per sq mi, 102 per sq km. **Urban:** 50.1%. **Ethnic groups:** Arab 90%, Kurds, Armenians, and other 10%. **Principal languages:** Arabic (official); Kurdish, Armenian. **Chief religions:** Sunni Muslim 74%, other Muslims 16%, Christian 10%.

Geography: Total area: 71,498 sq mi, 185,180 sq km; **Land area:** 71,062 sq mi, 184,050 sq km. **Location:** Middle East, at E end of Mediterranean Sea. **Neighbors:** Lebanon and Israel on W, Jordan on S, Iraq on E, Turkey on N. **Topography:** Syria has a short Mediterranean coastline, then stretches E and S with fertile lowlands and plains, alternating with mountains and large desert areas. **Capital:** Damascus, 2,272,000. **Cities (urban aggr.):** Aleppo, 2,520,000; Homs,923,000.

Government: Type: Republic (under military regime). **Head of state:** Pres. Bashar al-Assad; b. Sept. 11, 1965; in office: July 17, 2000. **Head of gov.:** Prime Min. Muhammad Naji al-Otari; b. 1944; in office: Sept. 10, 2003. **Local divisions:** 14 provinces. **Defense budget** (2005): $1.7 bil. **Active troops:** 307,600.

Economy: Industries: oil, textiles, food proc., beverages, tobacco, phosphate mining. **Chief crops:** wheat, barley, cotton, lentils, chickpeas, olives, sugar beets. **Natural resources:** oil, phosphates, chrome, mang., asphalt, iron ore, salt, marble, gypsum, hydropower. **Crude oil reserves** (2005): 2.5 bil bbls. **Arable land:** 28%. **Livestock** (2005): cattle: 940,000; chickens: 30 mil; goats: 1 mil; sheep: 15.3 mil. **Fish catch** (2004): 17,210 metric tons. **Electricity prod.** (2004): 29.6 bil kWh. **Labor force** (2002 est.): agriculture 30%, industry 27%, services 43%.

Finance: Monetary unit: Pound (SYP) (Sept. 2006: 52.31 = $1 U.S.). **GDP** (2005 est.): $72.3 bil; **per capita GDP:** $3,900; **GDP growth:** 4.5%. **Imports** (2005 est.): $6 bil; partners (2004): Italy 7.7%, China 7.6%, Germany 7.4%, Turkey 4.5%, France 4.4%. **Exports** (2005 est.): $6.3 bil; partners (2004): Germany 16.5%, Italy 13.5%, UAE 8.6%, Lebanon 7.7%, France 6.3%, Turkey 5.1%. **Tourism:** $1.8 bil. **Budget** (2005 est.): $7.6 bil. **Gold** (2003): 830,000 oz t. **Consumer prices** (changed in 2002): 1.0%.

Transport: Railroad: Length: 1,685 mi. **Motor vehicles:** 227,660 pass. cars, 367,100 comm. vehicles. **Civil aviation:** 999.8 mil pass.-mi; 26 airports. **Chief ports:** Latakia, Tartus.

Communications: TV sets: 68 per 1,000 pop. **Radios:** 278 per 1,000 pop. **Telephone lines:** 2.9 mil. **Daily newspaper circ.:** NA. **Internet:** 800,000 users.

Health: Life expect.: 69 male; 71.7 female. **Births** (per 1,000 pop.): 27.8. **Deaths** (per 1,000 pop.): 4.8. **Natural inc.:** 2.29%. **Infant mortality** (per 1,000 live births): 28.6. **AIDS rate:** NA.

Education: Compulsory: ages 6-14. **Literacy:** 79.6%.

Major Intl. Organizations: UN (FAO, IBRD, ILO, IMF, IMO, WHO), AL.

Embassy: 2215 Wyoming Ave. NW 20008; 232-6313.
Website: www.syrianembassy.us

Syria was the center of the Seleucid empire, but later became absorbed in the Roman and Arab empires. Ottoman rule prevailed for 4 cents., until the end of WWI.

The state of Syria was formed from former Turkish districts, separated by the Treaty of Sevres, 1920, and divided into the states of Syria and Greater Lebanon. Both were administered under a French League of Nations mandate 1920-41.

Syria was proclaimed a republic by the occupying French Sept. 16, 1941, and exercised full independence Apr. 17, 1946. Syria joined the Arab invasion of Israel in 1948.

Syria joined Egypt Feb. 1958 in the United Arab Republic but seceded Sept. 1961. The Socialist Baath party and military leaders seized power Mar. 1963. The Baath, a pan-Arab organization, became the only legal party. The government has been dominated by the Alawite minority.

In the Arab-Israeli war of June 1967, Israel seized and occupied the Golan Heights, from which Syria had shelled Israeli settlements. On Oct. 6, 1973, Syria joined Egypt in an attack on Israel. Syrian troops entered Lebanon in 1976, during the Lebanese civil war, and remained a strong presence in the country. They fought Palestinian guerrillas and, later, Christian militiamen. Syria sided with Iran during the Iran-Iraq war, 1980-88.

Following Israel's invasion of Lebanon, June 6, 1982, Israeli planes destroyed 17 Syrian antiaircraft missile batteries in the Bekaa Valley, June 9. Some 25 Syrian planes were downed during the engagement. Israel and Syria agreed to a cease-fire June 11. Syria's alleged role in promoting international terrorism led to strained relations with the U.S. and Great Britain.

Syria condemned the Aug. 1990 Iraqi invasion of Kuwait and sent troops to help Allied forces in the Gulf War. In 1991, Syria accepted U.S. proposals for the terms of an Arab-Israeli peace conference. Syria subsequently participated in negotiations with Israel, but progress toward peace was slow.

Former Prime Min. Mahmoud al-Zoubi killed himself May 21, 2000, after being charged with corruption. Hafez al-Assad, president of Syria since 1971, died June 10, 2000, and was succeeded by his son Bashar al-Assad.

Following the invasion of Iraq, Mar. 2003, the U.S. pressured Syria to rein in extremists and deny safe haven to fugitive Iraqi leaders. Israeli planes hit an alleged terrorist camp near Damascus Oct. 4, 2003. The U.S. imposed limited sanctions on Syria, May 11, 2004.

The killing of former Lebanese Prime Min. Rafik al-Hariri by a truck bomb in Beirut, Feb. 14, 2005, was a catalyst for massive anti-Syrian protests in Lebanon. Syria denied responsibility for the blast but pulled nearly all its troops out of Lebanon by Apr. 26; some Syrian intelligence agents may have remained. Syria aided Hezbollah fighters in their conflict with Israel. When Israeli armed forces struck hard at Lebanon, July-Aug. 2006, in an effort to cripple Hezbollah, about 180,000 Lebanese found temporary refuge in Syria. Four suspected Islamic militants stormed the U.S. embassy in Damascus Sept. 12 but were gunned down by Syrian security guards.

provided military aid to deter a Communist invasion. In 1971, the UN expelled Taiwan from its seat and recognized the mainland government. The U.S. officially recognized the People's Republic, Dec. 15, 1978, and severed ties with Taiwan. However, the U.S. and Taiwan have continued a strong trading relationship and maintain contact via quasi-official agencies.

Land reform, government planning, U.S. aid and investment, and free universal education brought huge advances in industry, agriculture, and living standards. In 1987 martial law was lifted after 38 years, and in 1991 the 43-year period of emergency rule ended. Taiwan held its first direct presidential election Mar. 23, 1996. An earthquake on Sept. 21, 1999, killed more than 2,300 people and injured thousands more.

Five decades of Nationalist Party rule ended with the presidential election of Mar. 18, 2000, won by Chen Shui-bian, leader of the pro-independence Democratic Progressive Party. Chen was wounded in an apparent assassination attempt Mar. 19, 2004, one day before he narrowly won a 2nd term as president; police said Mar, 7, 2005, that Chen's assailant drowned himself 10 days after the shooting. Beleaguered by corruption scandals involving his family and aides, Chen yielded some of his powers to Prime Min. Su Tseng-chang, May 31, 2006; an attempt to remove the president June 27 failed to gain the required two-thirds majority in the legislature.

Since 1949, the People's Republic has considered Taiwan a rebel province of the mainland, while, until 1991, Taiwan claimed to be the sole government of both. Beijing and Taipei increased economic cooperation in the 1990s. In 1999, relations between the 2 soured, when Taiwan redefined its relationship with mainland China as "state to state." China has warned that any Taiwan move toward independence could provoke military action.

Taiwan has one of the world's strongest economies and is among the 10 leading capital exporters.

The **Penghu Isls.** (Pescadores), 49 sq mi, pop. (1996 est.) 90,142, lie between Taiwan and the mainland. **Quemoy** and **Matsu**, pop. (1996 est.) 53,286, lie just off the mainland.

Taiwan
Republic of China

People: Population: 23,036,087. **Age distrib.** (%) <15: 19.4; 65+: 9.8. **Pop. density:** 1,849 per sq mi, 714 per sq km. **Ethnic groups:** Taiwanese 84%, mainland Chinese 14%, Aborigine 2%. **Principal languages:** Mandarin Chinese (official), Taiwanese (Min), Hakka dialects. **Chief religions:** Buddhist, Confucian, and Taoist 93%; Christian 5%.

Geography: Total area: 13,892 sq mi, 35,980 sq km; **Land area:** 12,456 sq mi, 32,260 sq km. **Location:** Off SE coast of China, between East and South China seas. **Neighbors:** Nearest is China. **Topography:** A mountain range forms the backbone of the island; the eastern half is very steep and craggy, the western slope is flat, fertile, and well cultivated. **Capital:** Taipei, 2,606,000. **Cities:** Kaohsiung, 1,512,677; Taichung, 1,021,292.

Government: Type: Democracy. **Head of state: Pres.** Chen Shui-bian; b. 1950; in office: May 20, 2000. **Head of gov.: Prime Min.** Su Tseng-chang; b. July 28, 1947; in office: Jan. 25, 2006. **Local divisions:** 16 counties, 5 municipalities, 2 special municipalities (Taipei, Kaohsiung). **Defense budget** (2005): 8.3 bil. **Active troops:** 290,000.

Economy: Industries: electronics, oil refining, chemicals, textiles, iron & steel, machinery, cement, food proc. **Chief crops:** rice, corn, vegetables, fruit, tea. **Natural resources:** coal, nat. gas, limestone, marble, asbestos. **Crude oil reserves** (2005): 4 mil bbls. **Arable land:** 24%. **Fish catch** (2003): 1,486,291 metric tons. **Electricity prod.** (2004): 173 bil kWh. **Labor force** (2005 est.): agriculture 6%, industry 35.8%, services 58.2%.

Finance: Monetary unit: New Dollar (TWD) (Sept. 2006: 32.93 = $1 U.S.). **GDP** (2005 est.): $631.2 bil; **per capita GDP:** $27,600; **GDP growth:** 3.8%. **Imports** (2005 est.): $181.6 bil; partners (2004): Japan 26%, U.S. 13%, China, including Hong Kong 11%, South Korea 6.9%. **Exports** (2005 est.): $189.4 bil; partners (2004): China, including Hong Kong 37%, U.S. 16%, Japan 7.7%. **Tourism:** $4.1 bil. **Budget** (2005 est.): $50.3 bil. **Intl. reserves less gold:** $177.22 bil.

Transport: Railroad: Length: 1,551 mi. **Motor vehicles** (1997): 4.40 mil pass. cars, 833,545 comm. vehicles. **Civil aviation:** NA; 38 airports. **Chief ports:** Kaohsiung, Chilung (Keelung), Hualien, Taichung.

Communications: TV sets: 327 per 1,000 pop. **Radios:** 402 per 1,000 pop. **Telephone lines:** 13.6 mil. **Daily newspaper circ.:** NA. **Internet:** 13.8 mil users.

Health: Life expect.: 74.7 male; 80.5 female. **Births** (per 1,000 pop.): 12.6. **Deaths** (per 1,000 pop.): 6.5. **Natural inc.:** 0.61%. **Infant mortality** (per 1,000 live births): 6.3. **AIDS rate:** NA.

Education: Compulsory: ages 6-15. **Literacy:** 96.1%.

Major Intl. Organizations: APEC.

Embassy: 4201 Wisconsin Ave. NW, 20016; 895-1800.

Website: www.gov.tw

Large-scale Chinese immigration began in the 17th cent. The island came under mainland control after an interval of Dutch rule, 1620-62. Taiwan (also called Formosa) was ruled by Japan 1895-1945. The Kuomintang (Chinese nationalist govt) fled to Taiwan in 1949 and established the Republic of China under Chiang Kai-shek, who ruled for over 20 years with increasingly broad power. The U.S.

Tajikistan
Republic of Tajikistan

People: Population: 6,944,062. **Age distrib.** (%) <15: 35.6; 65+: 3.8. **Pop. density:** 126 per sq mi, 48 per sq km. **Urban:** 24.7%. **Ethnic groups:** Tajik 65%, Uzbek 25%, Russian 4%. **Principal languages:** Tajik (official), Russian. **Chief religions:** Sunni Muslim 85%, Shi'a Muslim 5%.

Geography: Total area: 55,251 sq mi, 143,100 sq km; **Land area:** 55,097 sq mi, 142,700 sq km. **Location:** Central Asia. **Neighbors:** Uzbekistan on N and W, Kyrgyzstan on N, China on E, Afghanistan on S. **Topography:** Mountainous region that contains the Pamirs, Trans-Alai mountain system. **Capital:** Dushanbe, 549,000.

Government: Type: Republic. **Head of state: Pres.** Imomali Rakhmonov; b. Oct. 5, 1952; in office: Nov. 6, 1994. **Head of gov.: Prime Min.** Akil Akilov; b. 1944; in office: Dec. 20, 1999. **Local divisions:** 2 vilóyats, 1 autonomous vilóyat. **Defense budget** (2005): $50.3 mil. **Active troops:** 7,600.

Economy: Industries: metals, chemicals & fertilizers, cement, vegetable oil, machine tools. **Chief crops:** cotton, grain, fruits, grapes, vegetables. **Natural resources:** hydropower, oil, uranium, mercury, lignite, lead, zinc, antimony, tungsten, silver, gold. **Crude oil reserves** (2005): 12 mil bbls. **Arable land:** 6%. **Livestock** (2005): cattle: 1.3 mil; chickens: 2.3 mil; goats: 975,000; pigs: 700; sheep: 1.8 mil. **Fish catch** (2004): 210 metric tons. **Electricity prod.** (2004): 16.5 bil kWh. **Labor force** (2000 est.): agriculture 67.2%, industry 7.5%, services 25.3%.

Finance: Monetary unit: Somoni (TJS) (Sept. 2006: 2.79 = $1 U.S.). **GDP** (2005 est.): $8.7 bil; **per capita GDP:** $1,200; **GDP growth:** 8%. **Imports** (2005 est.): $1.3 bil; partners (2004): Russia 17.8%, Uzbekistan 13.4%, Kazakhstan 9.7%, Ukraine 6.3%, Azerbaijan 6.3%, U.S. 5.8%, Turkey 4.3%. **Exports** (2005 est.): $950 mil; partners (2004): Latvia 13.1%, Switzerland 11.5%, Uzbekistan 11.3%, Norway 9.9%, Russia 8.2%, Iran 7.9%, Turkey 7.7%, Italy 6.6%, Hungary 4.4%. **Tourism:** $1 mil. **Budget** (2005 est.): $542.6 mil. **Intl. reserves less gold:** $118 mil. **Gold:** 40,000 oz t.

Transport: Railroad: Length: 300 mi. **Motor vehicles:** 117,100 pass. cars, 16,800 comm. vehicles. **Civil aviation:** 536.9 mil pass.-mi; 17 airports.

Communications: TV sets: 328 per 1,000 pop. **Radios:** 143 per 1,000 pop. **Telephone lines:** 245,200. **Daily newspaper circ.:** NAs. **Internet:** 5,000 users.

Health: Life expect.: 61.2 male; 67.4 female. **Births** (per 1,000 pop.): 27.4. **Deaths** (per 1,000 pop.): 7.2. **Natural inc.:** 2.02%. **Infant mortality** (per 1,000 live births): 45. **AIDS rate:** 0.1%.

Education: Compulsory: ages 7-15. **Literacy:** 99.5%.

Major International Organizations: UN (FAO, IBRD, ILO, IMF, WHO), CIS, OSCE.

Embassy: 1005 New Hampshire Avenue, 20037 223-6090.

Website: www.tjus.org

There were settled societies in the region from about 3000 BCE. Invaders have included Iranians, Arabs (who converted the population to Islam), Mongols, Uzbeks, Afghans, and Russians. The USSR gained control 1918-25. In 1924, the Tajik ASSR was created within the Uzbek SSR. The Tajik SSR was proclaimed in 1929.

Tajikistan declared independence Sept. 9, 1991. Factional fighting led to the installation of a pro-Communist regime, Jan. 1993. A new constitution establishing a presidential system was approved by referendum Nov. 6, 1994.

Clashes between Muslim rebels, reportedly armed by Afghanistan, and troops loyal to the government and supported by Russia, claimed an estimated 55,000 lives by mid-1997, despite a series of peace accords. Constitutional changes including legalization of Islamic political parties were approved by referendum Sept. 26, 1999. Pres. Imomali Rakhmonov won a Nov. 6 election called "a farce" by human-rights observers. Voters approved, June 22, 2003, constitutional changes giving Rakhmonov the right to serve as president until 2020.

Tanzania
United Republic of Tanzania

People: Population: 37,445,392. **Age distrib.** (%) <15: 43.7; 65+: 2.6. **Pop. density:** 109 per sq mi, 42 per sq km. **Urban:** 35.4%. **Ethnic groups:** Mainland: Bantu 95%; Zanzibar: Arab, African, mixed. **Principal languages:** Swahili, English (both official); Arabic, many local languages. **Chief religions:** Christian 30%, Muslim 35%, indigenous beliefs 35%; Zanzibar is 99% Muslim.

Geography: Total area: 364,900 sq mi, 945,087 sq km; **Land area:** 342,101 sq mi, 886,037 sq km. **Location:** On coast of E Africa. **Neighbors:** Kenya, Uganda on N; Rwanda, Burundi, Congo (formerly Zaire) on W; Zambia, Malawi, Mozambique on S. **Topography:** Hot, arid central plateau, surrounded by the lake region in the W, temperate highlands in N and S, the coastal plains. Mt. Kilimanjaro, 19,340 ft., is highest in Africa. **Capital:** Dodoma, 168,000. **Cities (urban aggr.):** Dar-es-Salaam, 2,676,000.

Government: Type: Republic. **Head of state:** Pres. Jakaya Mrisho Kikwete; b. Oct. 7, 1950; in office: Dec. 21, 2005. **Head of gov.:** Prime Min. Edward Lowassa; b. Aug. 26, 1953; in office: Dec. 30, 2005. **Local divisions:** 25 regions. **Defense budget** (2005): NA. **Active troops:** 27,000.

Economy: Industries: agric. proc., diamond & gold mining, oil refining, shoes. **Chief crops:** coffee, sisal, tea, cotton, pyrethrum (insecticide from chrysanthemums), cashews. **Natural resources:** hydropower, tin, phosphates, iron ore, coal, diamonds, gemstones, gold, nat. gas, nickel. **Arable land:** 3%. **Livestock** (2005): cattle: 17.8 mil; chickens: 30 mil; goats: 12.6 mil; pigs: 455,000; sheep: 3.5 mil. **Fish catch** (2004): 347,806 metric tons. **Electricity prod.** (2004): 2.6 bil kWh. **Labor force** (2002 est.): agriculture 80%, industry and services 20%.

Finance: Monetary unit: Shilling (TZS) (Sept. 2006: 1,282.35 = $1 U.S.). **GDP** (2005 est.): $27.1 bil; **per capita GDP:** $700; **GDP growth:** 0%. **Imports** (2005 est.): $2.4 bil; partners (2004): South Africa 13.1%, China 8.8%, India 6.6%, Zambia 5.4%, UAE 5.4%, U.S. 4.8%, UK 4.8%, Kenya 4.3%. **Exports** (2005 est.): $1.6 bil; partners (2004): India 10.2%, Netherlands 6.8%, Japan 6.1%, UK 5.3%, China 5.2%, Kenya 4.8%, Germany 4.4%. **Tourism:** $594 mil. **Budget** (2005 est.): $2.7 bil. **Intl. reserves less gold:** $1.43 bil. **Consumer prices:** 8.63%.

Transport: Railroad: Length: 2,293 mi. **Motor vehicles:** 35,600 pass. cars, 98,800 comm. vehicles. **Civil aviation:** 84.5 mil pass.-mi; 11 airports. **Chief ports:** Dar-es-Salaam, Mtwara, Tanga.

Communications: TV sets: 21 per 1,000 pop. **Radios:** 280 per 1,000 pop. **Telephone lines:** 148,400. **Daily newspaper circ.:** NA. **Internet:** 333,000 users.

Health: Life expect.: 44.9 male; 46.4 female. **Births** (per 1,000 pop.): 37.7. **Deaths** (per 1,000 pop.): 16.4. **Natural inc.:** 2.13%. **Infant mortality** (per 1,000 live births): 96.5. **AIDS rate:** 6.5%.

Education: Compulsory: ages 6-12. **Literacy:** 69.4%.

Major Intl. Organizations: UN and all of its specialized agencies, the Commonwealth, AU.

Embassy: 2139 R St. NW 20008; 939-6125.

Website: www.tanzania.go.tz/index2E.html

The Republic of Tanganyika in East Africa and the island Republic of Zanzibar, off the coast of Tanganyika, both of which had recently gained independence, joined into a single nation, the United Republic of Tanzania, Apr. 26, 1964. Zanzibar retains internal self-government.

Until resigning as president in 1985, Julius K. Nyerere, a former Tanganyikan independence leader, dominated Tanzania's politics, which emphasized government planning and control of the economy, with single-party rule. In 1992 the constitution was amended to establish a multiparty system. Privatization of the economy was undertaken in the 1990s.

At least 500 people died when an overcrowded Tanzanian ferry sank in Lake Victoria, May 21, 1996. About 460,000 Rwandan refugees, mostly Hutu, returned from Tanzania to Rwanda in Dec. 1996. A bomb at the U.S. embassy in Dar-es-Salaam, Aug. 7, 1998, killed 11 people and injured at least 70 others. The U.S. blamed the attack and a near-simultaneous embassy bombing in Kenya on Islamic terrorists associated with Osama bin Laden. After a trial in New York City, 4 conspirators were convicted May 29, 2001.

Former Pres. Nyerere died in London Oct. 14, 1999. President since 1995, Benjamin Mkapa was reelected Oct. 29, 2000. Over 280 people died in a train wreck June 24, 2002, southeast of Dodoma. Jakaya Mrisho Kikwete of the ruling Chama Cha Mapinduzi (Party of the Revolution) won the Dec. 14, 2005, presidential election.

Tanganyika. Arab colonization and slaving began in the 8th cent. CE; Portuguese sailors explored the coast by about 1500. Other Europeans followed.

In 1885 Germany established German East Africa of which Tanganyika formed the bulk. It became a League of Nations mandate and, after 1946, a UN trust territory, both under Britain. It became independent Dec. 9, 1961, and a republic within the Commonwealth a year later.

Zanzibar, the Isle of Cloves, lies 23 mi off mainland Tanzania; area 640 sq mi and pop. (2002) 622,459. The island of **Pemba**, 25 mi to the NE, area 380 sq mi and pop. (2002) 362,166 is included in the administration.

Chief industry is cloves and clove oil production, of which Zanzibar and Pemba produce most of the world's supply.

Zanzibar was for centuries the center for Arab slave traders. Portugal ruled the region for 2 centuries until ousted by Arabs around 1700. Zanzibar became a British Protectorate in 1890; independence came Dec. 10, 1963. Revolutionary forces overthrew the Sultan Jan. 12, 1964. The new government ousted Western diplomats and newsmen, slaughtered thousands of Arabs, and nationalized farms. Union with Tanganyika followed.

Thailand
Kingdom of Thailand

People: Population: 64,631,595. **Age distrib.** (%) <15: 22; 65+: 8. **Pop. density:** 327 per sq mi, 126 per sq km. **Urban:** 31.9%. **Ethnic groups:** Thai 75%, Chinese 14%. **Principal languages:** Thai, Chinese, Malay, Khmer. **Chief religions:** Buddhism 95% (official), Muslim 5%.

Geography: Total area: 198,457 sq mi, 514,000 sq km; **Land area:** 197,596 sq mi, 511,770 sq km. **Location:** On Indochinese and Malayan peninsulas in SE Asia. **Neighbors:** Myanmar on W and N, Laos on N, Cambodia on E, Malaysia on S. **Topography:** A plateau dominates the NE third of Thailand, dropping to the fertile alluvial valley of the Chao Phraya R. in the center. Forested mountains are in the N, with narrow fertile valleys. The S peninsula region is covered by rain forests. **Capital:** Bangkok, 6,593,000. **Cities (urban aggr.)** (1999): Chiang-Mai, 160,200

Government: Type: In transition. **Head of state:** King Bhumibol Adulyadej; b. Dec. 5, 1927; in office: June 9, 1946. **Head of gov.:** Gen. Surayud Chulanont; b. 1943; in office: Oct. 1, 2006. **Local divisions:** 76 provinces. **Defense budget** (2005): $2.0 bil. **Active troops:** 306,600.

Economy: Industries: tourism; textiles & garments, agric. proc., beverages, tobacco, cement, light mfg.; electric appliances & components, computers & parts. **Chief crops:** rice, cassava, rubber, corn, sugarcane, coconuts, soybeans. **Natural resources:** tin, rubber, nat. gas, tungsten, tantalum, timber, lead, fish, gypsum, lignite, fluorite. **Crude oil reserves** (2005): 583.4 mil bbls. **Arable land:** 34%. **Livestock** (2005): cattle: 5.5 mil; chickens: 260 mil; goats: 270,000; pigs: 7.2 mil; sheep: 50,000. **Fish catch** (2004): 4,017,954 metric tons. **Electricity prod.** (2004): 121.7 bil kWh. **Labor force** (2000 est.): agriculture 49%, industry 14%, services 37%.

Finance: Monetary unit: Baht (THB) (Sept. 2006: 37.41 = $1 U.S.). **GDP** (2005 est.): $560.7 bil; **per capita GDP:** $8,300; **GDP growth:** 4.5%. **Imports** (2005 est.): $107 bil; partners (2004): Japan 23.6%, China 8.6%, U.S. 7.6%, Malaysia 5.8%, Singapore 4.4%, Taiwan 4.1%. **Exports** (2005 est.): $105.8 bil; partners (2004): U.S. 15.9%, Japan 13.9%, China 7.3%, Singapore 7.2%, Malaysia 5.4%, Hong Kong 5.1%. **Tourism:** $10.0 bil. **Budget** (2005 est.): $31.8 bil. **Intl. reserves less gold:** $35.47 bil. **Gold:** 2.7 mil. oz t. **Consumer prices:** 4.54%.

Transport: Railroad: Length: 2,530 mi. **Motor vehicles:** 3.4 mil pass. cars, 4.68 mil comm. vehicles. **Civil aviation:** 30 bil pass.-mi; 66 airports. **Chief ports:** Bangkok, Sattahip.

Communication: TV sets: 274 per 1,000 pop. **Radios:** 234 per 1,000 pop. **Telephone lines:** 7 mil. **Daily newspaper circ.:** 196.9 per 1,000 pop. **Internet:** 8.4 mil users.

Health: Life expect.: 70 male; 74.7 female. **Births** (per 1,000 pop.): 13.9. **Deaths** (per 1,000 pop.): 7. **Natural inc.:** 0.68% **Infant mortality** (per 1,000 live births): 19.5. **AIDS rate:** 1.4%.

Education: Compulsory: ages 6-14. **Literacy:** 92.6%.

Major Intl. Organizations: UN (FAO, IBRD, ILO, IMF, IMO, WHO, WTO), ASEAN, APEC.

Embassy: 1024 Wisconsin Ave., Suite 401, NW 20007; 944-3600.

Website: www.thaiembdc.org

Thais began migrating from southern China during the 11th cent. A unified Thai kingdom was established in 1350. Known as Siam until 1939, Thailand is the only country in Southeast Asia never taken over by a European power, thanks to King Mongkut and his son King Chulalongkorn. Ruling successively from 1851 to 1910, they modernized the country and signed trade treaties with Britain and France. A bloodless revolution in 1932 limited the monarchy. Thailand was an ally of Japan during WWII and of the U.S. during the postwar period. For decades, the military had a dominant role in governing the country.

A steep downturn in the economy forced Thailand to seek more than $15 bil in emergency international loans in Aug. 1997. A new constitution won legislative approval Sept. 27. By the end of the 1990s, according to UN estimates, more than 750,000 people in Thailand had HIV/AIDS; a nationwide prevention campaign has reduced the number of new infections.

Following elections in Jan. 2001, Thaksin Shinawatra, a wealthy former telecommunications executive, became prime minister. On Feb. 1, 2003, Thaksin launched a nationwide crackdown on methamphetamines; human rights observers criticized police tactics in the drug war, which killed more than 2,200 people by Apr. 30. The Indian Ocean tsunami of Dec. 26, 2004, left about 5,400 people dead and more than 2,800 missing in Thailand.

Elections Feb. 6, 2005, gave Thaksin's party a huge majority in parliament. He assumed emergency powers July 15 to deal with an Islamic insurgency in southern Thailand that had claimed more than 800 lives since Jan. 2004. Facing rising opposition and accused of benefiting improperly from the sale of his familiy's telecom business, Thaksin called snap elections for Apr. 2, 2006, 3 years ahead of schedule; the vote, which major parties boycotted, was later ruled unconstitutional. A military junta took power in a bloodless coup Sept. 19 while Thaksin was in New York City preparing to address the UN.

Timor-Leste
(East Timor)
Democratic Republic of Timor-Leste

People: Population: 1,062,777. **Age distrib.** (%) <15: 36.3; 65+: 3.1. **Pop. density:** 183 per sq mi, 70 per sq km. **Urban:** 7.6%. **Ethnic groups:** Austronesian, Papuan. **Principal languages:** Tetum, Portuguese (both official); Indonesian, English, other native languages. **Chief religions:** Roman Catholic 90%, Muslim 4%, Protestant 3%.

Geography: Total area: 5,794 sq mi, 15,007 sq km. **Land area:** 5,641 sq mi, 14,609 sq km. **Location:** E half of Timor Is. in the SW Pacific O. **Neighbors:** Indonesia (West Timor) on W. **Topography:** Terrain is rugged, rising to 9,721 ft at Mt. Ramelau. **Capital:** Dili, 156,000.

Government: Type: Republic. **Head of state:** Pres. Xanana Gusmão; b. June 20, 1946; in office: May 20, 2002. **Head of gov.:** Prime Min. José Ramos-Horta; b. Dec. 26, 1949; in office: July 10, 2006. **Local divisions:** 13 districts. **Defense budget** (2005): $39 mil. **Active troops:** 3,500.

Economy: Industries: printing, soap, handicrafts, clothing. **Chief crops:** coffee, rice, maize, cassava, sweet potatoes. **Natural resources:** gold, oil, nat. gas, mang., marble. **Livestock** (2005): cattle: 171,000; chickens: 2.2 mil; goats: 80,000; pigs: 346,000; sheep: 25,000. **Fish catch** (2004): 350 metric tons.

Finance: Monetary unit: U.S. Dollar (USD) (Sept. 2006: 1.00 = $1 U.S.). **GDP** (2004 est.): $370 mil; **per capita GDP:** $400; **GDP growth:** 1%. **Imports** (2004 est.): $202 mil; partners: Indonesia, Australia, Singapore, Vietnam, Portugal, Malaysia, China. **Exports** (2005 est.): $10 mil; partners : Portugal, Taiwan, Germany, U.S., Indonesia, Australia. **Tourism:** NA. **Budget** (2004 est.): $73 mil.

Transport: Civil aviation: NA; 3 airports. **Chief port:** Dili.

Communication: Internet (2004): 1,000 users.

Health: Life expect.: 64 male; 68.7 female. **Births** (per 1,000 pop.): 27. **Deaths** (per 1,000 pop.): 6.2. **Natural inc.:** 2.08%. **Infant mortality** (per 1,000 live births): 45.9. **AIDS rate:** NA.

Education: Compulsory: ages 7-15. **Literacy:** 58.6%.

Major Intl. Organizations: UN (FAO, IBRD, ILO, IMF, IMO, WHO).

Embassy: 4201 Conn. Ave., NW, 20008; 202-966-3202

Website: www.timor-leste.gov.tl

The collapse of Portuguese rule in East Timor led to an outbreak of factional fighting in Aug. 1975 and an invasion by Indonesia in Dec. Indonesia annexed East Timor as a 27th province in 1976, despite international condemnation. In over 2 decades some 200,000 Timorese died as a result of civil war, famine, and persecution by Indonesian authorities. In a referendum held Aug. 30, 1999, under UN auspices, Timorese voted overwhelmingly for independence. Pro-Indonesian militias then went on a rampage, terrorizing the population. Under pressure, the government allowed entrance of an international peacekeeping force, which began arriving in Sept.; a UN interim administration formally took command Oct. 26, 1999.

Pro-independence forces won elections for a constituent assembly Aug. 30, 2001. Xanana Gusmão, a former guerrilla leader, won the presidential election Apr. 14, 2002. As Timor-Leste, the territory became independent May 20 and entered the UN Sept. 27. A sovereignty dispute with Australia over the oil-rich Timor Sea was resolved in Aug. 2004. Australia and other nations sent peacekeepers to suppress a wave of gang violence that engulfed Dili in May 2006.

Togo
Togolese Republic

People: Population: 5,548,702. **Age distrib.** (%) <15: 42.3; 65+: 2.6. **Pop. density:** 264 per sq mi, 102 per sq km. **Urban:** 35.1%. **Ethnic groups:** 37 African tribes; largest are Ewe, Mina, and Kabre. **Principal languages:** French (official); Ewe, Mina in S; Kabye, Dagomba in N. **Chief religions:** Indigenous beliefs 51%, Christian 29%, Muslim 20%.

Geography: Total area: 21,925 sq mi, 56,785 sq km; **Land area:** 20,998 sq mi, 54,385 sq km. **Location:** On S coast of W Africa. **Neighbors:** Ghana on W, Burkina Faso on N, Benin on E. **Topography:** A range of hills running SW-NE splits Togo into 2 savanna plains regions. **Capital:** Lomé, 1,337,000.

Government: Type: Republic. **Head of state:** Pres. Faure Gnassingbé; b. June 6, 1966; in office: May 4, 2005. **Head of gov.:** Prime Min. Yawovi Agboyibo; b. Dec. 31, 1943; in office: Sept. 20, 2006. **Local divisions:** 5 regions. **Defense budget** (2005): $38.3 mil. **Active troops:** 8,550.

Economy: Industries: phosphates mining, agric. proc., cement, handicrafts. **Chief crops:** coffee, cocoa, cotton, yams, cassava, corn. **Natural resources:** phosphates, limestone, marble. **Arable land:** 38%. **Livestock** (2005): cattle: 280,000; chickens: 9 mil; goats: 1.5 mil; pigs: 320,000; sheep: 1.9 mil. **Fish catch** (2004): 29,538 metric tons. **Electricity prod.** (2004): 290 mil kWh. **Labor force** (1998 est.): agriculture 65%, industry 5%, services 30%.

Finance: Monetary unit: CFA BCEAO Franc (XOF) (Sept. 2006: 512.27 = $1 U.S.). **GDP** (2005 est.): $9 bil; **per capita GDP:** $1,700; **GDP growth:** 1%. **Imports** (2005 est.): $1 bil; partners (2004): China 24.7%, France 16.1%, Malaysia 5.3%, Italy 4.6%, Germany 4.6%, UK 4.3%, Netherlands 4.2%, Thailand 4.2%, Belgium 4.2%. **Exports** (2005 est.): $768 mil; partners (2004): Burkina Faso 16%, Ghana 14.7%, Benin 9.2%, China 8.1%, Mali 7.5%, Netherlands 6.6%, Taiwan 4.2%. **Tourism** (2003): $15 mil. **Budget** (2005 est.): $292.9 mil. **Intl. reserves less gold:** $136 mil. **Consumer prices:** 6.8%.

Transport: Railroad: Length: 326 mi. **Motor vehicles:** 51,400 pass. cars, 24,500 comm. vehicles. **Civil aviation:** 80.8 mil pass.-mi; 2 airports. **Chief port:** Lomé.

Communications: TV sets: 22 per 1,000 pop. **Radios:** 244 per 1,000 pop. **Telephone lines:** 60,600. **Daily newspaper circ.:** 2.2 per 1,000 pop. **Internet:** 221,000 users.

Health: Life expect.: 55.4 male; 59.5 female. **Births** (per 1,000 pop.): 37. **Deaths** (per 1,000 pop.): 9.8. **Natural inc.:** 2.72%. **Infant mortality** (per 1,000 live births): 60.6. **AIDS rate:** 3.2%.

Education: Compulsory: ages 6-15. **Literacy:** 53.2%.

Major Intl. Organizations: UN (FAO, IBRD, ILO, IMF, IMO, WHO, WTO), AU.

Embassy: 2208 Massachusetts Ave. NW, 20008; 234-4212.

Website: www.state.gov/p/af/ci/to

Togoland was administered by Germany and then by France and Britain. The French sector became the republic of Togo Apr. 27, 1960. In office since 1967, Pres. Gnassingbé Eyadéma was Africa's longest-serving head of state until his death Feb. 5, 2005. His son, Faure Gnassingbé, was immediately installed as president, but other African leaders pressured Togo to hold an election, which Gnassingbé won Apr. 24. Opposition parties disputed the result, and protests led to violent clashes in Lomé.

Tonga
Kingdom of Tonga

People: Population: 114,689. **Age distrib.** (%) <15: 35.3; 65+: 4.2. **Pop. density:** 414 per sq mi, 159 per sq km. **Urban:** 33.4%. **Ethnic groups:** Polynesian. **Principal languages:** Tongan, English (both official). **Chief religions:** Wesleyan 41%, Roman Catholic 16%, Mormon 14%.

Geography: Total area: 289 sq mi, 748 sq km; **Land area:** 277 sq mi, 718 sq km. **Location:** In western South Pacific O. **Neighbors:** Nearest are Fiji to W, Samoa to NE. **Topography:** Tonga comprises 170 volcanic and coral islands, 36 inhabited. **Capital:** Nuku'alofa, 25,000.

Government: Type: Constitutional monarchy. **Head of state:** King George Tupou V; b. May 4, 1948; in office: Sept. 11, 2006. **Head of gov.:** Prime Min. Prince Ulukalala Lavaka Ata; b. July 12, 1959; in office: Jan. 3, 2000. **Local divisions:** 3 island groups.

Economy: Industries: tourism, fishing. **Chief crops:** squash, coconuts, copra, bananas, vanilla, cocoa. **Natural resources:** fish. **Arable land:** 24%. **Livestock** (2005): cattle: 11,250; chickens: 300,000; goats: 12,500; pigs: 81,000. **Fish catch** (2004): 1,673 metric tons. **Electricity prod.** (2004): 40 mil kWh. **Labor force** (1997 est.): agriculture 65%, industry and services 35%.

Finance: Monetary unit: Pa'anga (TOP) (Sept. 2006: 2.03 = $1 U.S.). **GDP** (2002 est.): $244 mil; **per capita GDP:** $2,300; **GDP growth:** 1.4%. **Imports** (2004 est.): $122 mil; partners (2004): New Zealand 46.7%, Fiji 21.1%, Australia 10.3%, U.S. 6.7%. **Exports** (2004 est.): $34 mil; partners (2004): Japan 51.4%, U.S. 24.9%, India 4.1%. **Tourism** $15 mil. **Budget** (2000 est.): $52.4 mil. **Intl. reserves less gold:** $33 mil. **Consumer prices:** 8.32%.

Transport: Motor vehicles: 5,900 pass. cars, 5,900 comm. vehicles. **Civil aviation:** 8.7 mil pass.-mi; 1 airport. **Chief port:** Nuku'alofa.

Communications: TV sets: 61 per 1,000 pop. **Radios:** 663 per 1,000 pop. **Telephone lines:** 11,200. **Daily newspaper circ.:** NA. **Internet** (2004): 3,000 users.

Health: Life expect.: 67.3 male; 72.5 female. **Births** (per 1,000 pop.): 25.4. **Deaths** (per 1,000 pop.): 5.3. **Natural inc.:** 2.01%. **Infant mortality** (per 1,000 live births): 12.3. **AIDS rate:** NA.

Education: Compulsory: ages 6-14. **Literacy:** 98.9%.

Major Intl. Organizations: UN (FAO, IBRD, ILO, IMF, IMO, WHO), the Commonwealth.

Embassy: 250 E. 51st St. New York, NY 10022; (917) 369-1025.

Website: pmo.gov.to

The islands were first visited by the Dutch in the early 17th cent. A series of civil wars ended in 1845 with establishment of the Tupou dynasty. In 1900 Tonga became a British protectorate. On June 4, 1970, Tonga became independent and a member of the Commonwealth. It joined the UN on Sept. 14, 1999. Prince Tu'ipelehake, a democratic reformer, and his wife Princess Kaimana died July 5, 2006, after a highway accident while visiting California. George Tupou V became king Sept. 11, following the death of his father, Taufa'ahau Tupou IV, who had reigned since 1965.

Trinidad and Tobago
Republic of Trinidad and Tobago

People: Population:1,065,842. **Age distrib.** (%) <15: 20.1; 65+: 8.6. **Pop. density:** 538 per sq mi, 207 per sq km. **Urban:** 75.4%. **Ethnic groups:** Black 40%, East Indian 40%, mixed 18%. **Principal languages:** English (official), Hindi, French, Spanish, Chinese. **Chief religions:** Roman Catholic 26%, Hindu 23%, Protestant 14%, Muslim 6%.

Geography: Total area: 1,980 sq mi, 5,128 sq km; **Land area:** 1,980 sq mi, 5,128 sq km. **Location:** In Caribbean, off E coast of Venezuela. **Neighbors:** Nearest is Venezuela to SW. **Topography:** Three low mountain ranges cross Trinidad E-W, with a well-watered plain between N and central ranges. Parts of E and W coasts are swamps. Tobago, 116 sq mi, lies 20 mi NE. **Capital:** Port-of-Spain, 52,000.

Government: Type: Parliamentary democracy. **Head of state:** Pres. George Maxwell Richards; b. 1931; in office: Mar. 17, 2003. **Head of gov.:** Prime Min. Patrick Augustus Mervyn Manning; b. Aug. 17, 1946; in office: Dec. 24, 2001. **Local divisions:** 8 counties, 3 municipalities, 1 ward. **Defense budget** (2005): $32 mil. **Active troops:** 2,700.

Economy: Industries: oil, chemicals, tourism, food proc. **Chief crops:** cocoa, sugarcane, rice, citrus, coffee, vegetables. **Natural resources:** oil, nat. gas, asphalt. **Crude oil reserves** (2005): 990 mil bbls. **Arable land:** 15%. **Livestock** (2005): cattle: 29,000; chickens: 28.2 mil; goats: 59,300; pigs: 43,000; sheep: 3,400. **Fish catch** (2004): 9,709 metric tons. **Electricity prod.** (2004): 1 bil kWh. **Labor force** (1997 est.): agriculture 9.5%, manufacturing, mining, and quarrying 14%, construction and utilities 12.4%, services 64.1%.

Finance: Monetary unit: Tobago Dollar (TTD) (Sept. 2006: 6.25 = $1 U.S.). **GDP** (2005 est.): $18 bil; **per capita GDP:** $16,700; **GDP growth:** 7%. **Imports** (2005 est.): $6 bil; partners (2004): U.S. 24.6%, Venezuela 12%, Germany 10.8%, Spain 7%, Italy 5.5%, Brazil 5%. **Exports** (2005 est.): $9.2 bil; partners (2004): U.S. 66.7%, Jamaica 5.7%, France 3.5%. **Tourism:** $341 mil. **Budget** (2005 est.): $4.1 bil. **Intl. reserves less gold:** $3.4 bil. **Gold:** 60,000 oz t. **Consumer prices:** 6.89%.

Transport: Motor vehicles: 229,400 pass. cars, 53,900 comm. vehicles. **Civil aviation:** 1.8 bil pass.-mi; 3 airports. **Chief ports:** Port-of-Spain, Scarborough.

Communications: TV sets: 337 per 1,000 pop. **Radios:** 532 per 1,000 pop. **Telephone lines:** 323,500. **Daily newspaper circ.:** NA. **Internet** 160,000 users.

Health: Life expect.: 65.7 male; 67.9 female. **Births** (per 1,000 pop.): 12.9. **Deaths** (per 1,000 pop.): 10.6. **Natural inc.:** 0.23%. **Infant mortality** (per 1,000 live births): 25.1. **AIDS rate:** 2.6%.

Education: Compulsory: ages 5-11. **Literacy:** 98.6%.

Major Intl. Organizations: UN (FAO, IBRD, ILO, IMF, IMO, WHO, WTO), Caricom, the Commonwealth, OAS.

Embassy: 1708 Massachusetts Ave. NW 20036; 467-6490.

Website: www.gov.tt

Columbus sighted Trinidad in 1498. A British possession since 1802, Trinidad and Tobago won independence Aug. 31, 1962. It became a republic in 1976.

The nation is one of the most prosperous in the Caribbean. Oil production has increased with offshore finds. Middle Eastern oil is refined and exported, mostly to the U.S.

In July 1990, some 114 Muslim extremists captured the Parliament building and TV station and took about 50 hostages, including Prime Min. Arthur N. R. Robinson, who was beaten, shot in the legs, and tied to explosives. After a 6-day siege, the rebels surrendered.

Basdeo Panday, the country's first prime minister of East Indian ancestry, took office Nov. 9, 1995. Robinson became president on Mar. 19, 1997. Patrick Manning of the People's National Movement became prime minister after elections Dec. 10, 2001. George Maxwell Richards, a former university dean, succeeded Robinson as president, Mar. 17, 2003. On Apr. 24, 2006, Panday was convicted of bank fraud for failing to report an overseas account while in office.

Tunisia
Tunisian Republic

People: Population: 10,175,014. **Age distrib.** (%) <15: 24.6; 65+: 6.7. **Pop. density:** 169 per sq mi, 65 per sq km. **Urban:** 63.7%. **Ethnic groups:** Arab 98%, European 1%, Jewish and other 1%. **Principal languages:** Arabic (official), French prevalent. **Chief religion:** Muslim 98% (official; mostly Sunni).

Geography: Total area: 63,170 sq mi, 163,610 sq km; **Land area:** 59,985 sq mi, 155,360 sq km. **Location:** On N coast of Africa. **Neighbors:** Algeria on W, Libya on E. **Topography:** The N is wooded and fertile. The central coastal plains are given to grazing and orchards. The S is arid, approaching Sahara Desert. **Capital:** Tunis, 734,000.

Government: Type: Republic. **Head of state:** Pres. Gen. Zine al-Abidine Ben Ali; b. Sept. 3, 1936; in office: Nov. 7, 1987. **Head of gov.:** Prime Min. Mohamed Ghannouchi; b. Aug. 18, 1941; in office: Nov. 17, 1999. **Local divisions:** 24 governorates. **Defense budget** (2005): $436 mil. **Active troops:** 35,300.

Economy: Industries: oil, mining, tourism, textiles, footwear, agribusiness. **Chief crops:** olives, grain, tomatoes, citrus, sugar beets, dates, almonds. **Natural resources:** oil, phosphates, iron ore, lead, zinc, salt. **Crude oil reserves** (2005): 307.6 mil bbls. **Arable land:** 19%. **Livestock** (2005): cattle: 750,000; chickens: 64

mil; goats: 1.4 mil; pigs: 6,000; sheep: 6.7 mil. **Fish catch** (2004): 112,796 metric tons. **Electricity prod.** (2004): 11.8 bil kWh. **Labor force** (1995 est.): agriculture 55%, industry 23%, services 22%.

Finance: Monetary unit: Dinar (TND) (Sept. 2006: 1.32 = $1 U.S.). **GDP** (2005 est.): $83.5 bil; **per capita GDP:** $8,300; **GDP growth:** 4.3%. **Imports** (2005 est.): $12.9 bil; partners (2004): France 27.5%, Italy 20.8%, Germany 9.2%, Spain 5.7%. **Exports** (2005 est.): $10.3 bil; partners (2004): France 30%, Italy 23.3%, Germany 9.3%, Spain 5.3%, Belgium 4.3%, Libya 4.2%. **Tourism:** $2.0 bil. **Budget** (2005 est.): $8.3 bil. **Intl. reserves less gold:** $3.06 bil. **Gold:** 220,000 oz t. **Consumer prices:** 2.02%.

Transport: Railroad: Length: 1,337 mi. **Motor vehicles:** 552,900 pass. cars, 281,500 comm. vehicles. **Civil aviation:** 1.6 bil pass.-mi; 14 airports. **Chief ports:** Tunis, Sfax, Bizerte.

Communications: TV sets: 190 per 1,000 pop. **Radios:** 158 per 1,000 pop. **Telephone lines:** 1.3 mil. **Daily newspaper circ.:** 18.9 per 1,000 pop. **Internet:** 835,000 users.

Health: Life expect.: 73.4 male; 77 female. **Births** (per 1,000 pop.): 15.5. **Deaths** (per 1,000 pop.): 5.1. **Natural inc.:** 1.04%. **Infant mortality** (per 1,000 live births): 23.8. **AIDS rate:** 0.1%.

Education: Compulsory: ages 6-16. **Literacy:** 74.3%.

Major Intl. Organizations: UN (FAO, IBRD, ILO, IMF, IMO, WHO, WTO), AL, AU.

Embassy: 1515 Massachusetts Ave. NW 20005; 862-1850.

Website: www.tourismtunisia.com

Site of ancient Carthage and a former Barbary state under the suzerainty of Turkey, Tunisia became a protectorate of France under a treaty signed May 12, 1881. The nation became independent Mar. 20, 1956, and ended the monarchy the following year. Habib Bourguiba, an independence leader, served as president until 1987, when he was deposed by his prime minister, Zine al-Abidine Ben Ali, who then won 4 presidential elections, 1989-2004, all tightly controlled by the ruling party.

Tunisia has actively repressed Islamic fundamentalism. A synagogue blast on Djerba Is., Apr. 11, 2002, apparently set off by al-Qaeda, killed 17 people, including 12 German tourists.

Turkey
Republic of Turkey

People: Population: 70,413,958. **Age distrib.** (%) <15: 25.5; 65+: 6.8. **Pop. density:** 236 per sq mi, 91 per sq km. **Urban:** 66.3%. **Ethnic groups:** Turkish 80%, Kurdish 20%. **Principal languages:** Turkish (official), Kurdish, Arabic, Armenian, Greek. **Chief religion:** Muslim 99.8% (mostly Sunni).

Geography: Total area: 301,384 sq mi, 780,580 sq km; **Land area:** 297,592 sq mi, 770,760 sq km. **Location:** Occupies Asia Minor, stretches into continental Europe; borders on Mediterranean and Black seas. **Neighbors:** Bulgaria, Greece on W; Georgia, Armenia on N; Iran on E; Iraq, Syria on S. **Topography:** Central Turkey has wide plateaus, with hot, dry summers and cold winters. High mountains ring the interior on all but W, with more than 20 peaks over 10,000 ft. Rolling plains are in W; mild, fertile coastal plains are in S, W. **Capital:** Ankara, 3,573,000. **Cities (urban aggr.):** Istanbul, 3,573,000; Izmir, 2,487,000.

Government: Type: Republic. **Head of state:** Pres. Ahmet Necdet Sezer; b. Sept. 13, 1941; in office: May 16, 2000. **Head of gov.:** Prime Min. Recep Tayyip Erdogan; b. Feb. 26, 1954; in office: Mar. 14, 2003. **Local divisions:** 81 provinces. **Defense budget** (2005): $9.8 bil. **Active troops:** 514,850.

Economy: Industries: textiles, food proc., autos, mining, steel, oil, constr. **Chief crops:** tobacco, cotton, grain, olives, sugar beets, citrus. **Natural resources:** antimony, coal, chromium, mercury, copper, borate, sulfur, iron ore, hydropower. **Crude oil reserves** (2005): 300 mil bbls. **Arable land:** 32%. **Livestock** (2005): cattle: 10.1 mil; chickens: 296.9 mil; goats: 6.6 mil; pigs: 4,399; sheep: 25.2 mil. **Fish catch** (2004): 644,492 metric tons. **Electricity prod.** (2004): 143.3 bil kWh. **Labor force** (3rd qtr, 2004): agriculture 35.9%, industry 22.8%, services 41.2%.

Finance: Monetary unit: New Lira (TRY) (Sept. 2006: 1.52 = $1 U.S.). **GDP** (2005 est.): $572 bil; **per capita GDP:** $8,200; **GDP growth:** 5.6%. **Imports** (2005 est.): $101.2 bil; partners (2004): Germany 12.9%, Russia 9.3%, Italy 7.1%, France 6.4%, U.S. 4.8%, China 4.6%, UK 4.4%. **Exports** (2005 est.): $72.5 bil; partners (2004): Germany 13.9%, UK 8.8%, U.S. 7.7%, Italy 7.4%, France 5.8%, Spain 4.2%. **Tourism:** $15.9 bil. **Budget** (2005 est.): $115.3 bil. **Intl. reserves less gold:** $35.39 bil. **Gold:** 3.73 mil. oz t. **Consumer prices:** 8.18%.

Transport: Railroad: Length: 5,404 mi. **Motor vehicles:** 4.7 mil pass. cars, 1.79 mil comm. vehicles. **Civil aviation:** 10.4 bil pass.-mi; 89 airports. **Chief ports:** Istanbul, Izmir, Mersin.

Communications: TV sets: 328 per 1,000 pop. **Radios:** 510 per 1,000 pop. **Telephone lines:** 19 mil. **Daily newspaper circ:** NA. **Internet** (2003): 5.5 mil users.

Health: Life expect.: 70.2 male; 75.2 female. **Births** (per 1,000 pop.): 16.6. **Deaths** (per 1,000 pop.): 6. **Natural inc.:** 1.06%. **Infant mortality** (per 1,000 live births): 39.7. **AIDS rate:** NA.

Education: Compulsory: ages 6-14. **Literacy:** 87.4%.

Major Intl. Organizations: UN (FAO, IBRD, ILO, IMF, IMO, WHO, WTO), NATO, OECD, OSCE.

Embassy: 2525 Massachusetts Ave. NW 20008; 612-6700.

Website: www.turkishembassy.org

Ancient inhabitants of Turkey were among the world's first agriculturalists. Such civilizations as the Hittite, Phrygian, and Lydian flourished in Asiatic Turkey (Asia Minor), as did much of Greek civilization. After the fall of Rome in the 5th cent., Constantinople (now Istanbul) was the capital of the Byzantine Empire for 1,000 years. It fell in 1453 to Ottoman Turks, who ruled a vast empire for over 400 years.

Just before WWI, Turkey, or the Ottoman Empire, ruled what is now Syria, Lebanon, Iraq, Jordan, Israel, Saudi Arabia, Yemen, and islands in the Aegean Sea. Turkey joined Germany and Austria in WWI, and its defeat resulted in the loss of much territory and the fall of the sultanate. A republic was declared Oct. 29, 1923, with Mustafa Kemal (later Kemal Ataturk) as its first president. Ataturk led Turkey until his death in 1938.

Turkey kept neutral during most of WWII. The country became a full member of NATO in 1952 and remained a Western ally despite domestic political instability. Military coups overthrew civilian governments in 1960 and 1980. Turkey invaded nearby Cyprus July 20, 1974, to prevent that country from being united with Greece; since then, Cyprus has been divided into Greek and Turkish zones.

In recent decades, Turkish governments have contended with Kurdish separatism and the rise of militant Islam. Turkey was a member of the U.S.-led force that ousted Iraq from Kuwait, 1991. In the aftermath of the war, millions of Kurdish refugees fled to Turkey's border to escape Iraqi forces. Turkish offensives against the Kurds caused heavy casualties among guerrillas and civilians. Kurdish militants raided Turkish diplomatic missions in some 25 Western European cities June 24, 1993.

Tansu Ciller officially became Turkey's first woman prime minister July 5, 1993. The Welfare Party, an Islamic group, gained strength in the 1990s but was unable to form a government until June 1996, when it came to power in coalition with Ciller's True Path Party. The pro-Islamic government resigned June 18, 1997, under pressure from the military, which stepped up its campaign against Islamic fundamentalism in 1998.

Kurdish rebel leader Abdullah Öcalan was captured Feb. 15, 1999; convicted of terrorism June 29, he was sentenced to death by a Turkish security court. His organization, the Kurdistan Workers' Party, announced Aug. 5, 1999, that it would abandon its 14-year-old armed insurgency, in which more than 30,000 people died.

A major earthquake Aug. 17, 1999, in northwest Turkey killed over 17,000 people and injured thousands more. Another quake in the same region Nov. 12 claimed at least 675 lives. The IMF announced $7.5 bil in emergency loans Dec. 6, 2000, to help Turkey cope with a severe financial crisis. The death penalty was abolished Aug. 3, 2002, and Öcalan's sentence was commuted to life in prison Oct. 3. The Justice and Development Party, an Islamic group headed by Recep Tayyip Erdogan, won elections Nov. 3.

During the U.S.-led invasion of Iraq, Mar.-Apr. 2003, Turkey, a NATO ally, refused to allow coalition forces to launch attacks on northern Iraq from Turkish soil. Suicide bombings by Islamic extremists Nov. 15-20, 2003, killed 58 people and wounded about 750 at 2 synagogues, the British consulate, and the offices of a London-based bank, all in Istanbul. Renewed clashes in Mar.-Apr. 2006 between Kurds and Turkish security forces claimed at least 15 lives.

Turkey has long sought to become a full member of the European Union, but the EU has deferred talks on accession until economic, human rights, and immigration issues are resolved.

Turkmenistan

People: Population: 5,042,920. **Age distrib.** (%) <15: 35.2; 65+: 4.1. **Pop. density:** 26 per sq mi, 10 per sq km. **Urban:** 45.3%. **Ethnic groups:** Turkmen 77%, Uzbek 9%, Russian 7%, Kazakh 2%. **Principal languages:** Turkmen, Russian, Uzbek. **Chief religions:** Muslim 89%, Eastern Orthodox 9%.

Geography: Total area: 188,457 sq mi, 488,100 sq km; **Land area:** 188,457 sq mi, 488,100 sq km. **Neighbors:** Kazakhstan on N, Uzbekistan on N and E, Afghanistan and Iran on S. **Topography:** The Kara Kum Desert occupies 80% of the area. Bordered on W by Caspian Sea. **Capital:** Ashgabat, 711,000.

Government: Type: Republic with authoritarian rule. **Head of state and gov.:** Pres. Saparmurad Niyazov; b. Feb. 18, 1940; in office: Oct. 27, 1990. **Local divisions:** 5 regions. **Defense budget** (2005): $173 mil. **Active troops:** 26,000.

Economy: Industries: nat. gas, oil, oil products, textiles, food proc. **Chief crops:** cotton, grain. **Natural resources:** oil, nat. gas, coal, sulfur, salt. **Crude oil reserves** (2005): 546 mil bbls. **Arable land:** 3%. **Livestock** (2005): cattle: 2 mil; chickens: 7 mil; goats: 822,000; pigs: 30,000; sheep: 14.3 mil. **Fish catch** (2004): 15,008 metric tons. **Electricity prod.** (2004): 10.8 bil kWh. **Labor force** (2003 est.): agriculture 48.2%, industry 13.8%, services 37%.

Finance: Monetary unit: Manat (TMM) (Sept. 2006: 5,200.05 = $1 U.S.). **GDP** (2005 est.): $39.5 bil; **per capita GDP:** $8,000; **GDP growth:** (IMF est.) 4%. **Imports** (2005 est.): $4.2 bil; partners (2004): Russia 14%, Ukraine 13.8%, U.S. 11.1%, UAE 8.1%, Turkey 8%, Germany 6.8%, France 4.6%. **Exports** (2005 est.): $4.7 bil; partners (2004): Ukraine 49.8%, Iran 17.2%, Italy 5.3%, Turkey 4.7%. **Tourism** (2002): $292 mil. **Budget** (2005 est.): $1.5 bil.

Transport: Railroad: Length: 1,516 mi. **Civil aviation:** 999.2 mil pass.-mi; 22 airports. **Chief port:** Turkmenbashi.

Communications: TV sets: 198 per 1,000 pop. **Radios:** 289 per 1,000 pop. **Telephone lines:** 376,100. **Daily newspaper circ.:** 6.8 per 1,000 pop. **Internet:** 36,000 users.

Health: Life expect.: 58.4 male; 65.4 female. **Births** (per 1,000 pop.): 27.6. **Deaths** (per 1,000 pop.): 8.6. **Natural inc.:** 1.9%. **Infant mortality** (per 1,000 live births): 72.6. **AIDS rate:** <0.1%.

Education: Compulsory: ages 7-15. **Literacy:** 98.8%.

Major Intl. Organizations: UN (FAO, IBRD, ILO, IMF, IMO, WHO), CIS, OSCE.

Embassy: 2207 Massachusetts Ave., NW 20008; 588-1500.

Website: www.turkmenistanembassy.org

The region has been inhabited by Turkic tribes since the 10th cent. It became part of Russian Turkestan in 1881, and a constituent republic of the USSR in 1925. Turkmenistan declared independence Oct. 27, 1991, and became an independent state when the USSR disbanded Dec. 26, 1991.

Extensive oil and gas reserves place Turkmenistan in a more favorable economic position than other former Soviet republics. A new rail line linking Iran and Turkmenistan was inaugurated May 13, 1996. Political power centered around the former Communist Party apparatus, and Pres. Saparmurad Niyazov became the object of a personality cult. An alleged coup plot Nov. 25, 2002, triggered a crackdown on Niyazov's political opponents.

Tuvalu

People: Population: 11,810. **Age distrib.** (%) <15: 30.2; 65+: 5.1. **Pop. density:** 1,181 per sq mi, 454 per sq km. **Urban:** 55.2%. **Ethnic group:** Polynesian 96%, Micronesian 4%. **Principal languages:** Tuvaluan, English, Samoan, Kiribati (on the island of Nui). **Chief religions:** Church of Tuvalu (Congregationalist) 97%.

Geography: Total area: 10 sq mi, 26 sq km; **Land area:** 10 sq mi, 26 sq km. **Location:** 9 islands forming a NW-SE chain 360 mi. long in the SW Pacific O. **Neighbors:** Nearest are Kiribati to N, Fiji to S. **Topography:** The islands are all low-lying atolls, nowhere rising more than 15 ft above sea level, composed of coral reefs. **Capital:** Funafuti, 6,000.

Government: Type: Parliamentary democracy. **Head of state:** Queen Elizabeth II, represented by Gov.-Gen. Filoimea Telito; in office: Apr. 15, 2005. **Head of gov.:** Prime Min. Apisai Ielemia; in office: Aug. 14, 2006.

Economy: Industries: fishing, tourism, copra. **Chief crops:** coconuts. **Natural resources:** fish. **Livestock:** (2005): chickens: 45,000; pigs: 13,500. **Fish catch** (2004): 2,081 metric tons. **Electricity prod.** (2003): 0.00 bil kWh. **Labor force:** people make a living mainly through exploitation of the sea, reefs, and atolls and from wages sent home by those abroad (mostly workers in the phosphate industry and sailors).

Finance: Monetary unit: Australian Dollar (TVD) (Sept. 2006: 1.33 = $1 U.S.). **GDP** (2000 est.): $12.2 mil; **per capita GDP:** $1,100; **GDP growth:** 3%. **Imports** (2004 est.): $31 mil; partners (2004): Fiji 43.1%, Japan 20%, Australia 10.6%, Poland 9.9%. **Exports** (2004 est.): $1 mil; partners (2004): Germany 34.6%, Poland 25.9%, Philippines 12.5%, Fiji 8.4%, Italy 6.7%, UK 4.7%. **Tourism:** NA. **Budget** (2000 est.): $11.2 mil.

Transport: Civil aviation: 1 airport. **Chief port:** Funafuti.

Communications: TV sets: 9 per 1,000 pop. **Radios:** 364 per 1,000 pop. **Internet** (2002): 1,300 users.

Health: Life expect.: 66.1 male; 70.7 female. **Births** (per 1,000 pop.): 22.2. **Deaths** (per 1,000 pop.): 7.1. **Natural inc.:** 1.51%. **Infant mortality** (per 1,000 live births): 19.5. **AIDS rate:** NA.

Education: Compulsory: ages 7-14. **Literacy:** NA.

Major Intl. Organizations: UN (FAO, ILO, IMO, WHO), the Commonwealth.

UN Mission: 800 Second Ave., Ste. 400D, New York, NY 10017; 212-490-0534.

Website: www.timelesstuvalu.com

The Ellice Islands separated from the British Gilbert and Ellice Islands Colony in 1975 and became Tuvalu; independence came Oct. 1, 1978. In 2000, Tuvalu joined the United Nations.

Uganda
Republic of Uganda

People: Population: 29,206,503. **Age distrib.** (%) <15: 50.3; 65+: 2.2. **Pop. density:** 378 per sq mi, 146 per sq km. **Urban:** 12.2%. **Ethnic groups:** Baganda 17%, Ankole 8%, Basoga 8%, Iteso 8%, Bakiga 7%; many other groups. **Principal languages:** English (official), Swahili, Ganda, many Bantu and Nilotic languages, Arabic. **Chief religions:** Roman Catholic 33%, Protestant 33%, Muslim 16%, indigenous beliefs 18%.

Geography: Total area: 91,136 sq mi, 236,040 sq km; **Land area:** 77,108 sq mi, 199,710 sq km. **Location:** In E Central Africa. **Neighbors:** Sudan on N, Congo (formerly Zaire) on W, Rwanda and Tanzania on S, Kenya on E. **Topography:** Most of Uganda is a high plateau 3,000-6,000 ft high, with high Ruwenzori range in W (Mt. Margherita 16,763 ft), volcanoes in SW; NE is arid, W and SW rainy. Lakes Victoria, Edward, Albert form much of borders. **Capital:** Kampala, 1,319,000.

Government: Type: Republic. **Head of state:** Pres. Yoweri Kaguta Museveni; b. Aug. 15, 1944; in office: Jan. 29, 1986. **Head of gov.:** Prime Min. Apolo Nsibambi; b. Nov. 27, 1938; in office: Apr. 5, 1999. **Local divisions:** 56 districts. **Defense budget** (2005): $196 mil. **Active troops:** 45,000 (1,800 paramilitary).

Economy: Industries: sugar, brewing, tobacco, cotton textiles, cement. **Chief crops:** coffee, tea, cotton, tobacco, cassava, potatoes. **Natural resources:** copper, cobalt, hydropower, limestone, salt. **Arable land:** 25%. **Livestock** (2005): cattle: 6.1 mil; chickens: 33 mil; goats: 7.7 mil; pigs: 1.3 mil; sheep: 1.2 mil. **Fish catch** (2004): 377,328 metric tons. **Electricity prod.** (2004): 1.9 bil kWh. **Labor force** (1999 est.): agriculture 82%, industry 5%, services 13%.

Finance: Monetary unit: Shilling (UGX) (Sept. 2006: 1,845.50 = $1 U.S.). **GDP** (2005 est.): $48.7 bil; **per capita GDP:** $1,800; **GDP growth:** 4%. **Imports** (2005 est.): $1.6 bil; partners (2004): Kenya 27.9%, India 8%, UAE 7.4%, South Africa 6.9%, UK 5.9%, China 5.6%, Japan 5.1%, U.S. 4.6%. **Exports** (2005 est.): $768 mil; partners (2004): Kenya 13.6%, Switzerland 11.2%, Netherlands 9.8%, Belgium 8.6%, France 4.2%. **Tourism:** $266 mil. **Budget** (2005 est.): $1.9 bil. **Intl. reserves less gold:** $940 mil. **Consumer prices:** 8.15%.

Transport: Railroad: Length: 771 mi. **Motor vehicles:** 56,800 pass. cars, 87,600 comm. vehicles. **Civil aviation:** 147.3 mil pass.-mi; 5 airports. **Chief ports:** Entebbe, Jinja.

Communications: TV sets: 28 per 1,000 pop. **Radios:** 130 per 1,000 pop. **Telephone lines:** 100,800. **Daily newspaper circ.:** 2.7 per 1,000 pop. **Internet:** 200,000 users.

Health: Life expect.: 50.1 male; 51.9 female. **Births** (per 1,000 pop.): 48.1. **Deaths** (per 1,000 pop.): 13. **Natural inc.:** 3.51%. **Infant mortality** (per 1,000 live births): 68.5. **AIDS rate:** 6.7%.

Education: Compulsory: ages 6-12. **Literacy:** 66.8%..

Major Intl. Organizations: UN (FAO, IBRD, ILO, IMF, WHO, WTO), the Commonwealth, AU.

Embassy: 5911 16th St. NW 20011; 726-7100.

Websites: www.statehouse.go.ug

Britain obtained a protectorate over Uganda in 1894. The country became independent Oct. 9, 1962, and a republic within the Commonwealth a year later. In 1967, the traditional kingdoms, including the powerful Buganda state, were abolished.

Gen. Idi Amin seized power from Prime Min. Milton Obote in 1971. During his 8 years of dictatorial rule, he was responsible for the deaths of up to 300,000 of his opponents. In 1972 he expelled nearly all of Uganda's 45,000 Asians. Tanzanian troops and Ugandan exiles and rebels ousted Amin, Apr. 11, 1979.

Obote held the presidency from Dec. 1980 until his ouster in a military coup July 27, 1985. Guerrilla war and rampant human rights abuses plagued Uganda under Obote's regime.

Conditions improved after Yoweri Museveni took power in Jan. 1986. In 1993 the government authorized restoration of the Buganda and other monarchies but only for ceremonial purposes. Uganda helped Laurent Kabila seize power in the Congo (formerly Zaire) in 1997 but sent troops in 1998 to aid insurgents seeking his ouster. A withdrawal accord was signed Sept. 6, 2002.

At least 330 members of the Movement for the Restoration of the Ten Commandments of God died in a church fire in Kanungu, Mar. 17, 2000; in all, over 900 deaths were linked to the cult.

Pres. Museveni won reelection Mar. 12, 2001, and Feb. 23, 2006; opponents disputed the latter result, citing what they claimed were trumped-up charges of treason, terrorism, and rape lodged against Museveni's main rival, Kizza Besigye.

An ongoing insurgency against Museveni in northern Uganda has killed more than 100,000 people and forced up to 2 mil to flee their homes. The Lord's Resistance Army, a rebel group, has fought the government since 1986 and has abducted some 30,000 children over the last decade to serve as soldiers and sex slaves. Peace talks brokered by Sudan began July 2006.

Ukraine

People: Population: 46,620,334. **Age distrib.** (%) <15: 14.3; 65+: 16.4. **Pop. density:** 200 per sq mi, 77 per sq km. **Urban:** 67.2%. **Ethnic groups:** Ukrainian 78%, Russian 17%. **Principal languages:** Ukrainian (official), Russian, Romanian, Polish, Hungarian. **Chief religions:** Ukrainian Orthodox (Kiev patriarchate and Russian patriarchate), Autocephalous Orthodox, Ukrainian Greek Catholic.

Geography: Total area: 233,090 sq mi, 603,700 sq km; **Land area:** 233,090 sq mi, 603,700 sq km. **Location:** In E Europe. **Neighbors:** Belarus on N; Russia on NE and E; Moldova and Romania on SW; Hungary, Slovakia, and Poland on W. **Topography:** Part of the E European plain. Mountainous areas include the Carpathians in the SW and Crimean chain in the S. Arable black soil constitutes a large part of the country. **Capital:** Kiev, 2,672,000. **Cities (urban aggr.):** Kharkov, 1,436,000, Odesa, 1,010,000.

Government: Type: Republic. **Head of state:** Pres. Viktor Andriyovych Yushchenko; b. Feb. 23, 1954; in office: Jan. 23, 2005. **Head of gov.:** Prime Min. Viktor Yanukovych; b. July 9, 1950; in office: Aug. 4, 2006. **Local divisions:** 24 oblasts, 2 municipalities, 1 autonomous republic. **Defense budget** (2005): $1.1 bil. **Active troops:** 187,600.

Economy: Industries: coal, electric power, metals, machinery & transp. equip., chemicals, sugar. **Chief crops:** grain, sugar beets, sunflower seeds, vegetables. **Natural resources:** iron ore, coal, mang., nat. gas, oil, salt, sulfur, graphite, titanium, magnesium, kaolin, nickel, mercury, timber. **Crude oil reserves** (2005): 395 mil bbls. **Arable land:** 58%. **Livestock** (2005): cattle: 7 mil; chickens: 130.3 mil; goats: 894,300; pigs: 6.5 mil; sheep: 875,200. **Fish catch** (2004): 228,899 metric tons. **Electricity prod.** (2004): 177.3 bil

kWh. **Labor force** (1996): agriculture 24%, industry 32%, services 44%.

Finance: Monetary unit: Hryvna (UAH) (Sept. 2006: 5.02 = $1 U.S.). **GDP** (2005 est.): $340.4 bil; **per capita GDP:** $7,200; **GDP growth:** 2.4%. **Imports** (2005 est.): $37.2 bil; partners (2004): Russia 31.9%, Germany 11.9%, Turkmenistan 5.8%, Italy 4.5%. **Exports** (2005 est.): $38.2 bil; partners (2004): Russia 17.4%, Turkey 7.1%, Italy 5.7%. **Tourism:** $1.1 bil. **Budget** (2005 est.): $23 bil. **Intl. reserves less gold:** $13.37 bil. **Gold:** 530,000 oz t. **Consumer prices:** 13.52%.

Transport: Railroad: Length: 13,964 mi. **Motor vehicles:** 5.31 mil pass. cars. **Civil aviation:** 980.5 mil pass.-mi; 193 airports. **Chief ports:** Odesa, Kiev, Berdiansk.

Communications: TV sets: 433 per 1,000 pop. **Radios:** 882 per 1,000 pop. **Telephone lines:** 12.1 mil. **Daily newspaper circ.:** 174.8 per 1,000 pop. **Internet:** 5.3 mil users.

Health: Life expect.: 62.1 male; 73.6 female. **Births** (per 1,000 pop.): 9.3. **Deaths** (per 1,000 pop.): 16.2. **Natural inc.:** –0.69%. **Infant mortality** (per 1,000 live births): 9.7. **AIDS rate:** 1.4%.

Education: Compulsory: ages 6-17. **Literacy:** 99.4%.

Major Intl. Organizations: UN (FAO, IBRD, ILO, IMF, IMO, WHO), CIS, OSCE.

Embassy: 3350 M St. NW 20007; 333-0606.

Website: www.kmu.gov.ua/control/en

Ukrainians' Slavic ancestors inhabited modern Ukrainian territory well before the 1st cent. CE. In the 9th cent., the princes of Kiev established a strong state called Kievan Rus, which included much of present-day Ukraine. Internal conflicts led to the disintegration of the Ukrainian state by the 13th cent. Mongol rule was supplanted by Poland and Lithuania in the 14th and 15th centuries. The north Black Sea coast and Crimea came under Turkish control in 1478. Ukrainian Cossacks, starting in the late 16th cent., rebelled against the occupiers of Ukraine: Russia, Poland, and Turkey.

An independent Ukrainian National Republic was proclaimed on Jan. 22, 1918. In 1921, Ukraine's neighbors occupied and divided Ukrainian territory. In 1922, Ukraine became a constituent republic of the USSR as the Ukrainian SSR. In 1932-33, the Soviet government engineered a famine in eastern Ukraine, resulting in the deaths of 6-7 mil Ukrainians. During WWII the Ukrainian nationalist underground fought both Nazi and Soviet forces. Over 5 mil Ukrainians died in the war. With the reoccupation of Ukraine by Soviet troops in 1944 came a renewed wave of mass arrests, executions, and deportations.

The world's worst nuclear power plant disaster occurred in Chernobyl, Ukraine, in April 1986; many thousands were killed or disabled as a result of the radiation leak. The plant was finally shut down Dec. 15, 2000.

Ukrainian independence was restored in Dec. 1991 with the dissolution of the Soviet Union. In the post-Soviet period Ukraine was burdened with a deteriorating economy. Following a 1994 accord with Russia and the U.S., Ukraine's large nuclear arsenal was transferred to Russia for destruction.

President since 1994, Leonid Kuchma attempted to engineer the election in 2004 of his handpicked successor, Prime Min. Viktor Yanukovych, also favored by Russia. The main challenger, Viktor Yushchenko, a former prime min., was poisoned in Sept. with dioxin, but continued to campaign. Official results of a runoff vote Nov. 21 showed a win for Yanukovych. Yushchenko supporters, calling the election fraudulent, staged massive protests (the "orange revolution"), and the vote was annulled. An election rerun Dec. 26 gave the victory to Yushchenko. Inaugurated Jan. 23, 2005, he dismissed his cabinet Sept. 8, amid allegations of infighting and corruption among his top aides. His Our Ukraine party fared poorly in parliamentary elections Mar. 26, 2006, and the resurgent Yanukovych, whose party won the vote, returned as prime minister Aug. 4.

United Arab Emirates

People: Population: 2,602,713. **Age distrib.** (%) <15: 24.9; 65+: 3.9. **Pop. density:** 80 per sq mi, 31 per sq km. **Urban:** 85.1%. **Ethnic groups:** Arab and Iranian 42%, Indian 50%. **Principal languages:** Arabic (official), Persian, English, Hindi, Urdu. **Chief religion:** Muslim 96% (official); Shi'a 16%).

Geography: Total area: 32,000 sq mi, 82,880 sq km; **Land area:** 32,000 sq mi, 82,880 sq km. **Location:** Middle East, on the S shore of the Persian Gulf. **Neighbors:** Saudi Arabia on W and S, Oman on E. **Topography:** A barren, flat coastal plain gives way to uninhabited sand dunes on the S. Hajar Mts. are on E. **Capital:** Abu Dhabi, 597,000. **Cites (urban aggr.):** Dubai, 1,330,000.

Government: Type: Federation of emirates. **Head of state:** Pres. Sheikh Khalifa ibn Zaid an-Nahayan; b. 1948; in office: Nov. 3, 2004. **Head of gov.:** Prime Min. Sheikh Muhammad ibn Rashid al-Maktum; b. 1949; in office: Jan. 5, 2006. **Local divisions:** 7 autonomous emirates: Abu Dhabi, Ajman, Dubai, Fujaira, Ras al-Khaimah, Sharjah, Umm al-Qaiwain. **Defense budget** (2005): $2.7 bil. **Active troops:** 50,500.

Economy: Industries: oil, fishing, petrochems., constr. materials, boat building, handicrafts, chemical. **Chief crops:** dates, vegetables, watermelons. **Natural resources:** oil, nat. gas. **Crude oil reserves** (2005): 97.8 bil bbls. **Livestock** (2005): cattle: 115,000; chickens: 15 mil; goats: 1.5 mil; sheep: 580,000. **Fish catch** (2004): 90,570 metric tons. **Electricity prod.** (2004): 49.5 bil kWh. **Labor force** (2000 est.): agriculture 7%, industry 15%, services 78%.

Finance: Monetary unit: Dirham (AED) (Sept. 2006: 3.67 = $1 U.S.). **GDP** (2005 est.): $111.3 bil; **per capita GDP:** $43,400; **GDP growth:** 6.7%. **Imports** (2005 est.): $60.2 bil; partners (2004): China 10.4%, India 8.3%, Japan 7.2%, Germany 6.6%, France 6.4%, UK 6.2%, U.S. 6%, Italy 4.1%. **Exports** (2005 est.): $103.1 bil; partners (2004): Japan 28.5%, South Korea 9.5%, Thailand 5.9%. **Tourism:** $1.4 bil. **Budget** (2005 est.): $29.4 bil. **Intl. reserves less gold:** $14.7 bil. **Gold** (2002): 40,000 oz t.

Transport: Motor vehicles: 794,110 pass. cars, 477,910 comm. vehicles. **Civil aviation:** 20.6 bil pass.-mi; 22 airports. **Chief ports:** Ajman, Das Island.

Communications: TV sets: 309 per 1,000 pop. **Radios:** 355 per 1,000 pop. **Telephone lines:** 1.2 mil. **Daily newspaper circ.:** NA. **Internet:** 1.4 mil users.

Health: Life expect.: 72.9 male; 78.1 female. **Births** (per 1,000 pop.): 19. **Deaths** (per 1,000 pop.): 4.4. **Natural inc.:** 1.46%. **Infant mortality** (per 1,000 live births): 14.1. **AIDS rate:** NA.

Education: Compulsory: ages 6-14. **Literacy:** 77.9%.

Major Intl. Organizations: UN (FAO, IBRD, ILO, IMF, IMO, WHO, WTO), AL, OPEC.

Embassy: 3522 International Ct. NW, Suite 400, 20008; 243-2400.

Website: www.government.ae/gov/en/index.jsp

The 7 "Trucial Sheikdoms" gave Britain control of defense and foreign relations in the 19th cent. They merged to become an independent state Dec. 2, 1971.

The Abu Dhabi Petroleum Co. was fully nationalized in 1975. Oil revenues have given the UAE one of the highest per capita GDPs in the world. International banking and investment have grown. In 2006, emirate-owned Dubai Ports World's management takeover of 6 major U.S. ports spurred controversy in the U.S.; the firm then pledged to sell the port operations to a wholly American company.

United Kingdom
United Kingdom of Great Britain and Northern Ireland

People: Population: 60,609,153. **Age distrib.** (%) <15: 17.5; 65+: 15.8. **Pop. density:** 649 per sq mi, 250 per sq km. **Urban:** 89.1%. **Ethnic groups:** English 81.5%, Scottish 9.6%, Irish 2.4%, Welsh 1.9%, Ulster 1.9%, West Indian, Indo-Pakistani, and other 2.8%. **Principal languages:** English (official), Welsh and Scottish Gaelic. **Chief religions:** Christian 72%, Muslim 3%, many others.

Geography: Total area: 94,526 sq mi, 244,820 sq km; **Land area:** 93,278 sq mi, 241,590 sq km. **Location:** Off the NW coast of Europe, across English Channel, Strait of Dover, and North Sea. **Neighbors:** Ireland to W, France to SE. **Topography:** England is mostly rolling land, rising to Uplands of southern Scotland; Lowlands are in center of Scotland, granite Highlands are in N. Coast is heavily indented, especially on W. British Isles have milder climate than N Europe due to the Gulf Stream and ample rainfall. Severn, 220 mi, and Thames, 215 mi, are longest rivers. **Capital:** London, 8,505,000. **Cities** (urban aggr.): Birmingham, 2,280,000; Manchester, 2,228,000; West Yorkshire, 1,519,000; Glasgow, 1,159,000.

Government: Type: Constitutional monarchy. **Head of state:** Queen Elizabeth II; b. Apr. 21, 1926; in office: Feb. 6, 1952. **Head of gov.:** Prime Min. Tony Blair; b. May 6, 1953; in office: May 2, 1997. **Local divisions:** 467 local authorities, including England: 387; Wales: 22; Scotland: 32; Northern Ireland: 26. **Defense budget** (2005): $51.1 bil. **Active troops:** 205,890

Economy: Industries: machine tools, electric power equip., automation equip., railroad equip., shipbuilding, aircraft, vehicles, electronics & comm. equip., metals, chemicals, coal, oil. **Chief crops:** cereals, oilseed, potatoes, vegetables. **Natural resources:** coal, oil, nat. gas, tin, limestone, iron ore, salt, clay, chalk, gypsum, lead, silica. **Crude oil reserves** (2005): 4.5 bil bbls. **Arable land:** 25%. **Livestock** (2005): cattle: 10.4 mil; chickens: 157 mil; pigs: 4.9 mil; sheep: 35.3 mil. **Fish catch** (2004): 859,608 metric tons. **Electricity prod.** (2004): 363.2 bil kWh. **Labor force** (2004): agriculture 1.5%, industry 19.1%, services 79.5%.

Finance: Monetary unit: Pound (GBP) (Sept. 2006: 0.53 = $1 U.S.). **GDP** (2005 est.): $1.8 tril; **per capita GDP:** $30,300; **GDP growth:** 1.8%. **Imports** (2005 est.): $483.7 bil; partners (2004): Germany 13%, U.S. 9.2%, France 7.5%, Netherlands 6.6%, Belgium 5%, Italy 4.3%, China 4.2%. **Exports** (2005 est.): $372.7 bil; partners (2004): U.S. 15%, Germany 10.7%, France 9.2%, Ireland 6.8%, Netherlands 6%, Belgium 5.2%, Spain 4.5%, Italy 4.2%. **Tourism:** $28.2 bil. **Budget** (2005 est.): $951 bil. **Intl. reserves less gold:** $26.92 bil. **Gold:** 9.99 mil. oz t. **Consumer prices:** 2.83%.

Transport: Railroad: Length: 10,733 mi. **Motor vehicles:** 26.46 mil pass. cars, 3.55 mil comm. vehicles. **Civil aviation:** 97.3 bil pass.-mi; 334 airports. **Chief ports:** London, Liverpool, Cardiff, Belfast.

Communications: TV sets: 661 per 1,000 pop. **Radios:** 1,437 per 1,000 pop. **Telephone lines** 33.7 mil. **Daily newspaper circ.:** 326.4 per 1,000 pop. **Internet:** 37.8 mil users.

Health: Life expect.: 76.1 male; 81.1 female. **Births** (per 1,000 pop.): 10.7. **Deaths** (per 1,000 pop.): 10.1. **Natural inc.:** 0.06%. **Infant mortality** (per 1,000 live births): 5.1. **AIDS rate:** 0.2%.

Education: Compulsory: ages 5-16. **Literacy:** 99%.

Major Intl. Organizations: UN and all of its specialized agencies, the Commonwealth, EU, NATO, OECD, OSCE.

Embassy: 3100 Massachusetts Ave. NW 20008; 588-6500.
Website: www.direct.gov.uk

The United Kingdom of Great Britain and Northern Ireland comprises England, Wales, Scotland, and Northern Ireland.

Queen and Royal Family. The ruling sovereign is Elizabeth II of the House of Windsor, b. Apr. 21, 1926, elder daughter of King George VI. She succeeded to the throne Feb. 6, 1952, and was crowned June 2, 1953. She was married Nov. 20, 1947, to Lt. Philip Mountbatten, b. June 10, 1921, former Prince of Greece. He was created Duke of Edinburgh, and given the title H.R.H., Nov. 19, 1947; he was named Prince of the United Kingdom and Northern Ireland Feb. 22, 1957. Prince Charles Philip Arthur George, b. Nov. 14, 1948, is the Prince of Wales and heir apparent. His first son, William Philip Arthur Louis, b. June 21, 1982, is second in line to the throne.

Parliament is the legislative body for the UK, with certain powers over dependent units. It consists of 2 houses: The **House of Commons** has 646 members, elected by direct ballot and divided as follows: England, 529; Wales, 40; Scotland, 59; Northern Ireland, 18. Following a drastic reduction in 1999 in the number of hereditary peerages, the **House of Lords** (July 2006) comprised 92 hereditary peers, 635 life peers, and 2 archbishops and 24 bishops of the Church of England, for a total of 753.

Resources and Industries. Great Britain's major occupations are manufacturing and trade. Metals and metal-using industries contribute more than 50% of exports. Of about 60 mil acres of land in England, Wales, and Scotland, 46 mil are farmed, of which 17 mil are arable, the rest pastures.

Large oil and gas fields have been found in the North Sea. Commercial oil production began in 1975. There are large deposits of coal.

Britain imports all of its cotton, rubber, sulphur, about 80% of its wool, half of its food and iron ore, also certain amounts of paper, tobacco, chemicals. Manufactured goods made from these basic materials have been exported since the industrial age began. Main exports are machinery, chemicals, textiles, clothing, autos and trucks, iron and steel, locomotives, ships, jet aircraft, farm machinery, drugs, radio, TV, radar and navigation equipment, scientific instruments, arms, whisky.

Religion and Education. The Church of England is Protestant Episcopal. The queen is its temporal head, with rights of appointments to archbishoprics, bishoprics, and other offices. There are 2 provinces, Canterbury and York, each headed by an archbishop. The most famous church is Westminster Abbey (1050-1760), site of coronations, tombs of Elizabeth I, Mary, Queen of Scots, kings, poets, and of the Unknown Warrior.

The most celebrated British universities are Oxford and Cambridge, each dating to the 13th cent. There are about 70 other universities.

History. Britain was part of the continent of Europe until about 6,000 BCE, but migration across the English Channel continued long afterward. Celts arrived 2,500 to 3,000 years ago. Their language survives in Welsh, and Gaelic enclaves.

England was added to the Roman Empire in 43 CE. After the withdrawal of Roman legions in 410, waves of Jutes, Angles, and Saxons arrived from German lands. They contended with Danish raiders for control from the 8th through 11th centuries. The last successful invasion was by French speaking Normans in 1066, who united the country with their dominions in France.

Opposition by nobles to royal authority forced King John to agree to the Magna Carta in 1215, a guarantee of rights and the rule of law. In the ensuing decades, the foundations of the parliamentary system were laid.

English dynastic claims to large parts of France led to the Hundred Years War, 1338-1453, and the defeat of England. A long civil war, the War of the Roses, lasted 1455-85, and ended with the establishment of the powerful Tudor monarchy. A distinct English civilization flourished. The economy prospered over long periods of domestic peace unmatched in continental Europe. Religious independence was secured when the Church of England was separated from the authority of the pope in 1534.

Under Queen Elizabeth I, England became a major naval power, leading to the founding of colonies in the new world and the expansion of trade with Europe and the Orient. Scotland was united with England when James VI of Scotland was crowned James I of England in 1603.

A struggle between Parliament and the Stuart kings led to a bloody civil war, 1642-49, and the establishment of a republic under the Puritan Oliver Cromwell. The monarchy was restored in 1660, but the "Glorious Revolution" of 1688 confirmed the sovereignty of Parliament: a Bill of Rights was granted 1689.

In the 18th cent., parliamentary rule was strengthened. Technological and entrepreneurial innovations led to the Industrial Revolution. The 13 North American colonies were lost but replaced by growing empires in Canada and India. Britain's role in the defeat of Napoleon, 1815, strengthened its position as the leading world power.

The extension of the franchise in 1832 and 1867, the formation of trade unions, and the development of universal public education were among the drastic social changes that accompanied the spread of industrialization and urbanization in the 19th cent. Large parts of Africa and Asia were added to the empire during the reign of Queen Victoria, 1837-1901.

Though victorious in WWI, Britain suffered huge casualties and economic dislocation. Ireland became independent in 1921, and independence movements became active in India and other colonies.

The country suffered major bombing damage in WWII, but held out against Germany single-handedly for a year after France fell in 1940.

Industrial growth continued in the postwar period, but Britain lost its leadership position to other powers. Labor governments passed socialist programs nationalizing some basic industries and expanding social security. Prime Min. Margaret Thatcher's Conservative government, however, tried to increase the role of private enterprise. In 1987, Thatcher became the first British leader in 160 years to be elected to a 3rd consecutive term as prime minister. Falling on unpopular times, she resigned as prime minister in Nov. 1990. Her successor, John Major, led Conservatives to an upset victory at the polls, Apr. 9, 1992.

The UK supported the UN resolutions against Iraq and sent military forces to the Persian Gulf War. The Channel Tunnel linking Britain to the Continent was inaugurated May 6, 1994.

On May 1, 1997, the Labour Party swept into power in a landslide victory, the largest of any party since 1935. Labour Party leader Tony Blair, 43, became Britain's youngest prime minister since 1812. Diana, Princess of Wales, died in a car crash in Paris, Aug. 31. Britain played a leading role in the NATO air war against Yugoslavia, Mar.-June 1999, and contributed 12,000 troops to the multinational security force in Kosovo (KFOR).

Blair led Labour to another landslide election victory June 7, 2001. After the Sept. 11 attacks on the U.S., Britain took an important role in the U.S.-led war against terrorism. The UK participated in the bombing of Afghanistan that began Oct. 7. Overcoming dissent within his own cabinet, Blair committed British troops to the U.S.-led invasion of Iraq, Mar.-Apr. 2003. Forces from the UK (7,200 in mid-2006) remained to occupy southern Iraq.

In elections May 5, 2005, Blair became the first Labour prime minister to win 3 consecutive terms, but continued controversy over Iraq reduced his parliamentary majority. Suicide bombings on 3 London underground trains and a bus, July 7, left 56 people dead and hundreds injured; police identified the bombers as 4 British Muslim men (3 of Pakistani origin). New measures to crack down on extremism and terrorism were enacted. A law providing "civil partnership" rights for same-sex couples took effect Dec. 2005.

British authorities announced Aug. 10, 2006, that they had thwarted a terrorist plot to use liquid explosives to blow up passenger aircraft flying between the U.S. and UK. Some 2 dozen suspects were arrested in Britain; many had ties to Pakistan, which assisted in cracking the case. Facing rising dissension in his own party, Prime Min. Blair pledged Sept. 7 to step down within a year.

Wales

The Principality of Wales in western Britain has an area of 8,019 sq mi and a population (2003 est.) of 2,938,200. Cardiff is the capital, pop. (2001 est., city proper) 305,000.

Less than 20% of Wales residents speak English and Welsh; about 32,000 speak Welsh solely. A 1979 referendum rejected, 4-1, the creation of an elected Welsh assembly; a similar proposal passed by a thin margin on Sept. 18, 1997. Elections for the 60-seat assembly were held May 6, 1999, and May 1, 2003.

Early Anglo-Saxon invaders drove Celtic peoples into the mountains of Wales, terming them Waelise (Welsh, or foreign). There they developed a distinct nationality. Members of the ruling house of Gwynedd in the 13th cent. fought England but were crushed, 1283. Edward of Caernarvon, son of Edward I of England, was created Prince of Wales, 1301.

Scotland

Scotland, a kingdom now united with England and Wales in Great Britain, occupies the northern 37% of the main British island, and the Hebrides, Orkney, Shetland, and smaller islands. Length 275 mi, breadth approx. 150 mi, area 30,418 sq mi, pop. (2003 est) 5,057,400.

The Lowlands, a belt of land approximately 60 mi wide from the Firth of Clyde to the Firth of Forth, divide the farming region of the Southern Uplands from the granite Highlands of the North; they contain 75% of the population and most of the industry. The Highlands, famous for hunting and fishing, have been opened to industry by many hydroelectric power stations.

Edinburgh, pop. (2001 est., city proper) 449,000, is the capital. Glasgow, pop. (2001 est.; city proper) 579,000, is Britain's greatest industrial center. It is a shipbuilding complex on the Clyde and an ocean port. Aberdeen, pop. (1996 est.) 227,430, NE of Edinburgh, is a major port, center of granite industry, fish-processing, and North Sea oil exploration. Dundee, pop. (1996 est.) 150,250, NE of Edinburgh, is an industrial and fish-processing center. About 90,000 persons speak Gaelic as well as English.

History. Scotland was called Caledonia by the Romans who battled early Celtic tribes and occupied southern areas from the 1st to the 4th centuries. Missionaries from Britain introduced Christianity in the 4th cent.; St. Columba, an Irish monk, converted most of Scotland in the 6th cent.

The Kingdom of Scotland was founded in 1018. William Wallace and Robert Bruce both defeated English armies 1297 and 1314, respectively.

In 1603 James VI of Scotland, son of Mary, Queen of Scots, succeeded to the throne of England as James I, and effected the Union of the Crowns. In 1707 Scotland received representation in the British Parliament, resulting from the union of former separate Parliaments. Its executive is in the British cabinet the Secretary of State for Scotland. The growing Scottish National Party urges independence. A 1979 referendum on the creation of an elected Scottish as-

sembly was defeated, but a proposal to create a regional legislature with limited taxing authority passed by a landslide Sept. 11, 1997. Elections for the 129-seat parliament were held May 6, 1999, and May 1, 2003.

Memorials of Robert Burns, Sir Walter Scott, John Knox, and Mary, Queen of Scots, draw many tourists, as do the beauties of the Trossachs, Loch Katrine, Loch Lomond, and abbey ruins.

Industries. Engineering products are the most important industry, with growing emphasis on office machinery, autos, electronics, and other consumer goods. Oil has been discovered offshore in the North Sea, stimulating on-shore support industries.

Scotland produces fine woolens, worsteds, tweeds, silks, fine linens, and jute. It is known for its special breeds of cattle and sheep. Fisheries have large hauls of herring, cod, whiting. Whisky is the biggest export.

The Hebrides are a group of c. 500 islands, 100 inhabited, off the W coast. The Inner Hebrides include **Skye, Mull**, and **Iona**, the last famous for the arrival of St. Columba, 563 CE. The Outer Hebrides include **Lewis** and **Harris**. Industries include sheep raising and weaving. The **Orkney Islands**, c. 90, are to the NE. The capital is Kirkwall, on Pomona Isl. Fish curing, sheep raising, and weaving are occupations. NE of the Orkneys are the 200 **Shetland Islands**, 24 inhabited, home of Shetland ponies. The Orkneys and Shetlands are centers for the North Sea oil industry.

Northern Ireland

Northern Ireland was constituted in 1920 from 6 of the 9 counties of Ulster, the NE corner of Ireland. Area 5,452 sq mi, pop. (2003 est) 1,702,600. Capital and chief industrial center, Belfast, pop. (2001 est., city proper) 277,000.

Industries. Shipbuilding, including large tankers, has long been an important industry, centered in Belfast, the largest port. Linen manufacture is also important, along with apparel, rope, and twine. Growing diversification has added engineering products, synthetic fibers, and electronics. There are large numbers of cattle, hogs, and sheep. Potatoes, poultry, and dairy foods are also produced.

Government. An act of the British Parliament, 1920, divided Northern from Southern Ireland, each with a parliament and government. When Ireland became a dominion, 1921, and later a republic, Northern Ireland chose to remain a part of the United Kingdom. It elects 18 members to the House of Commons.

During 1968-69, large demonstrations were conducted by Roman Catholics who charged they were discriminated against in voting rights, housing, and employment. The Catholics, a minority comprising about a third of the population, demanded abolition of property qualifications for voting in local elections. Violence and terrorism intensified, involving branches of the Irish Republican Army (outlawed in the Irish Republic), Protestant groups, police, and British troops.

A succession of Northern Ireland prime ministers pressed reform programs but failed to satisfy extremists on both sides. Between 1969 and 1994 more than 3,000 were killed in sectarian violence, many in England itself. Britain suspended the Northern Ireland parliament Mar. 30, 1972, and imposed direct British rule. A coalition government was formed in 1973 when moderates won election to a new one-house Assembly. But a Protestant general strike overthrew the government in 1974 and direct rule was resumed.

The agony of Northern Ireland was dramatized in 1981 by the deaths of 10 Irish nationalist hunger strikers in Maze Prison near Belfast. In 1985 the Hillsborough agreement gave the Rep. of Ireland a voice in the governing of Northern Ireland; the accord was strongly opposed by Ulster loyalists. On Dec. 12, 1993, Britain and Ireland announced a declaration of principles to resolve the Northern Ireland conflict.

A settlement reached on Good Friday, April 10, 1998, provided for restoration of home rule and election of a 108-member assembly with safeguards for minority rights. Both Ireland and Great Britain agreed to give up their constitutional claims on Northern Ireland. The accord was approved May 22 by voters in Northern Ireland and the Irish Republic, and elections to the assembly were held June 25. IRA dissidents seeking to derail the agreement were responsible for a bomb at Omagh Aug. 15 that killed 29 people and injured over 330.

London transferred authority to a Northern Ireland power-sharing government Dec. 2, 1999. Delays in IRA disarmament led to several suspensions of self-government. The IRA stated July 28, 2005, that it had renounced violence and ordered all units to disarm. In response, the British began reducing their military presence in the region. On Sept. 26, an international monitoring group reported that the IRA had apparently scrapped its entire arsenal. The Northern Ireland legislature, suspended for 3 1/2 years, reconvened May 15, 2006.

Education and Religion. Northern Ireland is about 58% Protestant, 42% Roman Catholic. Education is compulsory between the ages of 5 and 16 years.

Channel Islands

The Channel Islands, area 75 sq mi, pop. (2003 est.) 145,000, off the NW coast of France, the only parts of the one-time Dukedom of Normandy belonging to England, are Jersey, Guernsey and the dependencies of Guernsey—Alderney, Brechou, Great Sark, Little Sark, Herm, Jethou and Lihou. Jersey, pop. (2004 est.) 90,502, and Guernsey, pop. (2004 est.) 65,031, have separate legal existences and lieutenant governors named by the Crown. The islands were the only British soil occupied by German troops in WWII.

Isle of Man

The Isle of Man, area 220.9 sq mi, pop. (2004 est.) 74,655, is in the Irish Sea, 20 mi from Scotland, 30 mi from Cumberland. It is rich in lead and iron. The island has its own laws and a lieutenant governor appointed by the Crown. The Tynwald (legislature) consists of the Legislative Council, partly elected, and House of Keys, elected. Capital: Douglas. Farming, tourism, and fishing (kippers, scallops) are chief occupations. Man is famous for the Manx tailless cat.

Gibraltar

Gibraltar, a dependency on the southern coast of Spain, guards the entrance to the Mediterranean. The Rock of Gibraltar has been in British possession since 1704. The Rock is 2.5 mi long, 3/4 of a mi wide and 1,396 ft in height; a narrow isthmus connects it with the mainland. Pop. (2004 est.) 27,833.

Gibraltar has historically been an object of contention between Britain and Spain. Residents voted with near unanimity to remain under British rule, in a 1967 referendum held in pursuance of a UN resolution on decolonization. A new constitution, May 30, 1969, increased Gibraltarian control of domestic affairs (the UK continues to handle defense and internal security matters). Following a 1984 agreement between Britain and Spain, the border, closed by Spain in 1969, was fully reopened in Feb. 1985. A UN General Assembly resolution requested Britain to end Gibraltar's colonial status by Oct. 1, 1996. A plan for the U.K. and Spain to share sovereignty was rejected by Gibraltar voters, Nov. 7, 2002.

British West Indies

Swinging in a vast arc from the coast of Venezuela NE, then N and NW toward Puerto Rico are the Leeward Islands, forming a coral and volcanic barrier sheltering the Caribbean from the open Atlantic. Many of the islands are self-governing British possessions. Universal suffrage was instituted 1951-54; ministerial systems were set up 1956-60.

The **Leeward Islands** still associated with the UK are **Montserrat**, area 39.4 sq mi, pop. (2004 est.) 9,245, capital Plymouth; **British Virgin Islands**, 59.1 sq mi, pop. (2004 est.) 22,187, capital Road Town; and **Anguilla**, the most northerly of the Leeward Islands, 39.4 sq mi, pop. (2004 est.) 13,008, capital The Valley. Montserrat has been devastated by the Soufrière Hills volcano, which began erupting July 18, 1995.

The three **Cayman Islands**, a dependency, lie S of Cuba, NW of Jamaica. Pop. (2004 est.) 43,103, most of it on Grand Cayman. It is a free port; in the 1970s Grand Cayman became a tax-free refuge for foreign funds and branches of many Western banks opened there. Total area 101.2 sq mi, capital Georgetown.

The **Turks and Caicos Islands** are a dependency at the SE end of the Bahama Islands. Of about 30 islands, only 6 are inhabited; area 166 sq mi, pop. (2004 est.) 19,956; capital Grand Turk. Salt, shellfish, and conch shells are the main exports.

Bermuda

Bermuda is a British dependency governed by a royal governor and an assembly, dating from 1620, the oldest legislative body among British dependencies. Capital is Hamilton.

It is a group of about 150 small islands of coral formation, 20 inhabited, comprising 20.6 sq mi in the western Atlantic, 580 mi E of North Carolina. Pop. (2004 est.) 64,935 (about 61% of African descent). Pop. density is high.

The U.S. maintains a NASA tracking facility; a U.S. naval air base was closed in 1995.

Tourism is the major industry; Bermuda boasts many resort hotels. Bermuda is also a haven for the offshore insurance industry. Exports include petroleum products, medicine. In a referendum Aug. 15, 1995, voters rejected independence by nearly a 3-to-1 majority.

Hurricane Fabian, the most potent storm to reach Bermuda in 50 years, struck Sept. 5, 2003; 4 people were missing and presumed dead, and damage was estimated at over $300 mil.

South Atlantic

The **Falkland Islands**, a dependency, lie 300 mi E of the Strait of Magellan at the southern end of South America.

The Falklands, or Islas Malvinas, include 2 large islands and about 200 smaller ones, area 4,700 sq mi, pop. (2004 est.) 2,967, capital Stanley. The licensing of foreign fishing vessels has become the major source of revenue. Sheep-grazing is a main industry; wool is the principal export. There are indications of large oil and gas deposits. The islands are also claimed by Argentina, though 97% of inhabitants are of British origin. Argentina invaded the islands Apr. 2, 1982. The British responded by sending a task force to the area, landing their main force on the Falklands, May 21, and forcing an Argentine surrender at Port Stanley, June 14. A pact resuming commercial air service with Argentina was signed July 14, 1999.

British Antarctic Territory, south of 60° S lat., formerly a dependency of the Falkland Isls., was made a separate colony in 1962 and includes the **South Shetland Islands**, the **South Orkneys**, and the Antarctic Peninsula. A chain of meteorological stations is maintained.

South Georgia and the South Sandwich Islands, formerly administered by the Falkland Isls., became a separate dependency in 1985. South Georgia, 1507 sq mi, with no permanent population, is about 800 mi SE of the Falklands; the South Sandwich Isls., 130 sq mi, are uninhabited, about 470 mi SE of South Georgia.

St. Helena, an island 1,200 mi off the W coast of Africa and 1,800 mi E of South America, 158 sq mi and pop. (2004 est.) 7,415. Flax, lace, and rope-making are the chief industries. After Napoleon Bonaparte was defeated at Waterloo the Allies exiled him to St. Helena, where he lived from Oct. 16, 1815, to his death, May 5, 1821. Capital is Jamestown.

Tristan da Cunha is the principal island in a group of islands of volcanic origin, total area 40 sq mi, halfway between the Cape of Good Hope and South America. A volcanic peak 6,760 ft high erupted in 1961. The 262 inhabitants were removed to England, but most returned in 1963. The islands are dependencies of St. Helena. Pop. (2002) 284.

Ascension is an island of volcanic origin, 34 sq mi in area, 700 mi NW of St. Helena, through which it is administered. It is a communications relay center for Britain, and has a U.S. satellite tracking center. Pop. (2002) was 1,050, half of them communications workers. The island is noted for sea turtles.

Hong Kong
(*See* China/Hong Kong)

British Indian Ocean Territory

Formed Nov. 1965, embracing islands formerly dependencies of Mauritius or Seychelles: the Chagos Archipelago (including Diego Garcia), Aldabra, Farquhar, and Des Roches. The latter 3 were transferred to Seychelles, which became independent in 1976. Area 23 sq. mi. No permanent civilian population remains; the U.K. and the U.S. maintain a military presence.

Pacific Ocean

Pitcairn Island is in the Pacific, halfway between South America and Australia. The island was discovered in 1767 by Philip Carteret but was not inhabited until 23 years later when the mutineers of the *Bounty* landed there. The area is 18 sq mi and 2004 pop. was 46. It is a British dependency and is administered by a British High Commissioner in New Zealand and a local Council. The uninhabited islands of **Henderson, Ducie,** and **Oeno** are in the Pitcairn group.

United States
United States of America

People: Population: 298,444,215. (incl. 50 states & Dist. of Columbia). (Note: U.S. pop. figures may differ elsewhere in *The World Almanac*.) **Age distrib. (%)** <15: 20.4; 65+: 12.5. **Pop. density:** 84 per sq mi, 32 per sq km. **Urban:** 80.1%. **Ethnic groups:** White 75.1%, Black 12.3%, Asian 3.6%, Amerindian and Alaska native 0.9%. (Hispanics of any race or group 12.5%.) **Principal languages:** English, Spanish. **Chief religions:** Protestant 52%, Roman Catholic 24%, Jewish 1%.

Geography: Total area: 3,718,712 sq mi, 9,631,418 sq km. **Land area:** 3,537,439 sq mi, 9,161,923 sq km. **Topography:** Vast central plain, mountains in west, hills and low mountains in east. **Capital:** Washington, DC, 4,238,000.

Government: Federal republic, strong democratic tradition. **Head of state and gov.:** Pres. George W. Bush; b. July 6, 1946; in office: Jan. 20, 2001. **Local divisions:** 50 states and Dist. of Columbia. **Defense budget** (2004): $460.5 bil. **Active troops:** 1,433,600.

Economy: Industries: oil, steel, motor vehicles, aerospace, telecom., chemicals, electronics, food proc., consumer goods, lumber, mining. **Chief crops:** wheat, corn, fruits, vegetables, cotton. **Natural resources:** coal, copper, lead, molybd., phosphates, uranium, bauxite, gold, iron, mercury, nickel, potash, silver, tungsten, zinc, oil, nat. gas, timber. **Crude oil reserves** (2005): 21.4 bil bbls. **Arable land:** 19%. **Livestock** (2005): cattle: 95.8 mil; chickens: 2 bil; goats: 2.5 mil; pigs: 60.6 mil; sheep: 6.1 mil. **Fish catch** (2004): 5,566,375 metric tons. **Electricity prod.** (2004): 3,979 bil kWh. **Labor force** (2005): farming, forestry, and fishing 0.7%, manufacturing, extraction, transportation, and crafts 22.9%, managerial, professional., and technical 34.7%, sales and office 25.4%, other services 16.3%.

Finance: Dollar (USD) (Sept. 2006: 1.00 = $1 U.S.) GDP (2005 est.): $12.4 tril.; **per capita GDP:** $41,800; **GDP growth:** 3.5%. **Imports** (2005 est.): $1.7 tril; partners (2004): Canada 17.1%, China 13.7%, Mexico 10.4%, Japan 8.8%, Germany 5.2%. **Exports** (2005 est.): $927.5 bil; partners (2004): Canada 23%, Mexico 13.6%, Japan 6.7%, UK 4.4%, China 4.3%. **Tourism:** $93.9 bil. **Budget** (2005 est.): $2.5 tril. **Intl. reserves less gold:** $37.84 bil. **Gold:** 261.55 mil. oz t. **Consumer prices:** 3.39%.

Transport: Railroad: Length: 141,508 mi. **Motor vehicles**: 220.93 mil pass. cars, 8.69 mil comm. vehicles. **Civil aviation:** 630.2 bil pass.-mi; 5,119 airports.

Communications: TV sets: 844 per 1,000 pop. **Radios:** 2,116 per 1,000 pop. **Telephone lines:** 177.9 mil. **Daily newspaper circ.:** 196.3 per 1,000 pop. **Internet:** 203.8 mil users.

Health: Life expect.: 75 male; 80.8 female. **Births** (per 1,000 pop.): 14.1. **Deaths** (per 1,000 pop.): 8.3. **Natural inc.:** 0.59%. **Infant mortality** (per 1,000 live births): 6.4. **AIDS rate:** 0.6%.

Education: Compulsory: ages 6-17. **Literacy:** 97%.

Major Intl. Organizations: UN (FAO, IBRD, ILO, IMF, IMO, WHO, WTO), APEC, NATO, OAS, OECD, OSCE.

Website: www.firstgov.gov

See also U.S. History chapter; Chronology of the Year's Events.

Uruguay
Oriental Republic of Uruguay

People: Population: 3,431,932. **Age distrib.** (%) <15: 22.9; 65+: 13.3. **Pop. density:** 51 per sq mi, 19 per sq km. **Urban:** 92.6%. **Ethnic groups:** White 88%, Mestizo 8%, Black 4%. **Principal languages:** Spanish (official), Portunol/Brazilero (Portuguese-Spanish). **Chief religion:** Roman Catholic 66%.

Geography: Total area: 68,039 sq mi, 176,220 sq km; **Land area:** 67,035 sq mi, 173,620 sq km. **Location:** In southern South America, on the Atlantic O. **Neighbors:** Argentina on W, Brazil on N. **Topography:** Uruguay is composed of rolling, grassy plains and hills, well watered by rivers flowing W to Uruguay R. **Capital:** Montevideo, 1,264,000.

Government: Type: Republic. **Head of state and gov.:** Pres. Tabaré Ramón Vázquez Rosas; b. Jan. 17, 1940; in office: Mar. 1, 2005. **Local divisions:** 19 departments. **Defense budget** (2005): $163 mil. **Active troops:** 24,000.

Economy: Industries: food proc., electrical machinery, transp. equip., oil products, textiles. **Chief crops:** rice, wheat, corn, barley. **Natural resources:** hydropower, minor minerals, fisheries. **Arable land:** 7%. **Livestock** (2005): cattle: 11.7 mil; chickens: 13.3 mil; goats: 16,000; pigs: 240,000; sheep: 9.7 mil. **Fish catch** (2004): 123,010 metric tons. **Electricity prod.** (2004): 8.2 bil kWh. **Labor force:** agriculture 14%, industry 16%, services 70%.

Finance: Monetary unit: Peso (UYU) (Sept. 2006: 23.89 = $1 U.S.). **GDP** (2005 est.): $33 bil; **per capita GDP:** $9,600; **GDP growth:** 6.5%. **Imports** (2005 est.): $3.5 bil; partners (2004): Argentina 21.3%, Brazil 17.1%, U.S. 12.3%, China 6.9%, Russia 5.1%. **Exports** (2005 est.): $3.6 bil; partners (2004): Brazil 19.4%, U.S. 18%, Germany 6.6%, Argentina 6.4%. **Tourism:** $494 mil. **Budget** (2005 est.): $4.8 bil. **Intl. reserves less gold:** $2.15 bil. **Gold:** 10,000 oz t. **Consumer prices:** 4.7%.

Transport: Railroad: Length: 1,288 mi. **Motor vehicles:** 636,900 pass. cars, 57,300 comm. vehicles. **Civil aviation:** 358.5 mil pass.-mi; 8 airports. **Chief port:** Montevideo.

Communications: TV sets: 531 per 1,000 pop. **Radios:** 603 per 1,000 pop. **Telephone lines:** 1 mil. **Daily newspaper circ.:** NA. **Internet:** 680,000 users.

Health: Life expect.: 73.1 male; 79.7 female. **Births** (per 1,000 pop.): 13.9. **Deaths** (per 1,000 pop.): 9.1. **Natural inc.:** 0.49%. **Infant mortality** (per 1,000 live births): 11.6. **AIDS rate:** 0.5%.

Education: Compulsory: ages 6-15. **Literacy:** 98%.

Major Intl. Organizations: UN (FAO, IBRD, ILO, IMF, IMO, WHO, WTO), OAS.

Embassy: 1913 I St. NW, 20006; 331-1313.

Website: www.uruwashi.org

Spanish settlers began to supplant the indigenous Charrua Indians in 1624. Portuguese from Brazil arrived later, but Uruguay was attached to the Spanish Viceroyalty of Rio de la Plata in the 18th cent. Rebels fought against Spain beginning in 1810. An independent republic was declared Aug. 25, 1825.

Socialist measures were adopted in the early 1900s. The state retains a dominant role in the power, telephone, railroad, cement, oil-refining, and other industries, although some privatization began in the early 2000s. Uruguay's standard of living remains one of the highest in South America, and political and labor conditions among the freest. A leftist, Tabaré Vázquez, was elected president Oct. 31, 2004, and took office Mar. 1, 2005.

Uzbekistan
Republic of Uzbekistan

People: Population: 27,307,134. **Age distrib.** (%) <15: 32.9; 65+: 4.8. **Pop. density:** 166 per sq mi, 64 per sq km. **Urban:** 36.6%. **Ethnic groups:** Uzbek 80%, Russian 6%, Tajik 5%, Kazakh 3%, Karakalpak 3%, Tatar 2%. **Principal languages:** Uzbek (official), Russian, Tajik. **Chief religions:** Muslim 88% (mostly Sunni), Eastern Orthodox 9%.

Geography: Total area: 172,742 sq mi, 447,400 sq km; **Land area:** 164,248 sq mi, 425,400 sq km. **Location:** Central Asia. **Neighbors:** Kazakhstan on N and W, Kyrgyzstan and Tajikistan on E, Afghanistan and Turkmenistan on S. **Topography:** Mostly plains and desert. **Capital:** Tashkent, 2,181,000.

Government: Type: Republic. **Head of state:** Pres. Islam A. Karimov; b Jan. 30, 1938; in office: Mar. 24, 1990. **Head of gov.:** Prime Min. Shavkat Mirziyaev; b 1957; in office: Dec. 11, 2003. **Local divisions:** 12 regions, 1 autonomous republic, 1 city. **Defense budget** (2005): $60 mil. **Active troops:** 55,000.

Economy: Industries: textiles, food proc., machine building, metallurgy, nat. gas, chemicals. **Chief crops:** cotton, vegetables, fruits, grain. **Natural resources:** nat. gas, oil, coal, gold, uranium, silver, copper, lead, zinc, tungsten, molybd. **Crude oil reserves** (2005): 594 mil bbls. **Arable land:** 9%. **Livestock** (2005): cattle: 5.4 mil; chickens: 18 mil; goats: 1 mil; pigs: 90,000; sheep: 9.5 mil. **Fish catch** (2004): 4,323 metric tons. **Electricity prod.** (2004): 46.5 bil kWh. **Labor force** (1995): agriculture 44%, industry 20%, services 36%.

Finance: Monetary unit: Som (UZS) (Sept. 2006: 1,231.28 = $1 U.S.). **GDP** (2005 est.): $48.2 bil; **per capita GDP:** $1,800; **GDP growth:** 7.2%. **Imports** (2005 est.): $3.8 bil; partners (2004): Russia 26.4%, South Korea 10.8%, Germany 9.4%, China 8.3%, Kazakhstan 6%, Turkey 6%. **Exports** (2005 est.): $5 bil; partners (2004): Russia 21.2%, China 14%, Ukraine 7%, Turkey 6.3%, Tajikistan

5.8%, Bangladesh 4.2%. **Tourism:** $28 mil. **Budget** (2005 est.): $2.9 bil.

Transport: Railroad: Length: 2,454 mi. **Motor vehicles:** 865,000 pass. cars, 14,500 comm. vehicles. **Civil aviation:** 2.4 bil pass.-mi; 34 airports. **Chief port:** Termiz.

Communications: TV sets: 280 per 1,000 pop. **Radios:** 465 per 1,000 pop. **Telephone lines:** 1.7 mil. **Daily newspaper circ.:** NA. **Internet:** 880,000 users.

Health: Life expect.: 61.2 male; 68.1 female. **Births** (per 1,000 pop.): 26.4. **Deaths** (per 1,000 pop.): 7.8. **Natural inc.:** 1.85%. **Infant mortality** (per 1,000 live births): 70. **AIDS rate:** 0.2%.

Education: Compulsory: ages 7-16. **Literacy:** 99.3%.

Major Intl. Organizations: UN (FAO, IBRD, ILO, IMF, WHO), CIS, OSCE.

Embassy: 1746 Massachusetts Ave. NW 20036; 887-5300.

Website: www.gov.uz

The region was overrun by the Mongols under Genghis Khan in 1220. In the 14th cent., Uzbekistan became the center of a native Timurid empire. In later centuries Muslim feudal states emerged. Russian military conquest began in the 19th cent. Uzbek SSR became a Soviet republic in 1925.

Uzbekistan declared independence Aug. 29, 1991. It became an independent republic when the Soviet Union disbanded Dec. 26, 1991. Since then, the authoritarian government of Uzbekistan has been led by a former Communist, Islam A. Karimov.

Attacks by Islamic militants, Mar.-July 2004, killed more than 50 people. In June 2004, Russia's 2nd largest oil producer, OAO Lukoil, signed a $1 bil agreement with the govt to develop its natural gas fields. Militants bombed the U.S. and Israeli embassies in Tashkent, July 30.

After armed dissidents at Andizhan, east Uzbekistan, attacked government buildings and freed hundreds of prisoners, May 12-13, 2005, Uzbek security forces opened fire on rebels and unarmed demonstrators, killing many. Karimov then launched a general crackdown on human rights activists. Irritated by U.S. human rights pressures, Karimov ordered the U.S. to vacate an airbase used to support operations in Afghanistan; the U.S. pullout was completed Nov. 21. Meeting in Moscow a week earlier, Karimov and Russian Pres. Vladimir Putin signed a military cooperation agreement.

Vanuatu
Republic of Vanuatu

People: Population: 208,869. **Age distrib.** (%) <15: 32.6; 65+: 3.7. **Pop. density:** 44 per sq mi, 17 per sq km. **Urban:** 22.8%. **Ethnic groups:** Melanesian 98%, French, Vietnamese, Chinese, other Pacific Islanders. **Principal languages:** Bislama, English, French (all official); more than 100 local languages. **Chief religions:** Presbyterian 37%, Anglican 15%, Roman Catholic 15%, indigenous beliefs 8%, other Christian 10%.

Geography: Total area: 4,710 sq mi, 12,200 sq km; **Land area:** 4,710 sq mi, 12,200 sq km. **Location:** SW Pacific, 1,200 mi. NE of Brisbane, Australia. **Neighbors:** Fiji to E, Solomon Isls. to NW. **Topography:** Dense forest with narrow coastal strips of cultivated land. **Capital:** Port-Vila, 36,000.

Government: Type: Republic. **Head of state:** Pres. Kalkot Mataskelekele; in office: Aug. 16, 2004. **Head of gov.:** Prime Min. Ham Lini; b. 1951; in office: Dec. 11, 2004. **Local divisions:** 6 provinces.

Economy: Industries: food & fish freezing, wood proc., meat canning. **Chief crops:** copra, coconuts, cocoa, coffee, taro, yams. **Natural resources:** mang., timber, fish. **Arable land:** 2%. **Livestock** (2005): cattle: 152,000; chickens: 340,000; goats: 12,000; pigs: 62,000. **Fish catch** (2004): 94,788 metric tons. **Electricity prod.** (2004): 40 mil kWh. **Labor force** (2000 est.): agriculture 65%, industry 5%, services 30%.

Finance: Monetary unit: Vatu (VUV) (Sept. 2006: 111.45 = $1 U.S.). **GDP** (2003 est.): $580 mil; **per capita GDP:** $2,900; **GDP growth:** 1.1%. **Imports** (2004 est.): $233 mil; partners (2004): Taiwan 34.6%, Australia 15.5%, Japan 10.7%, Singapore 8%, New Zealand 6%, Fiji 4.6%. **Exports** (2004 est.): $205 mil; partners (2004): Thailand 46.3%, Malaysia 18.1%, Japan 7.4%, Belgium 5.3%, Indonesia 5.3%. **Tourism** (2003): $52 mil. **Budget** (2003): $54.3 mil. **Intl. reserves less gold:** $47 mil. **Consumer prices** (changed in 2002): 2.0%.

Transport: Motor vehicles: 2,600 pass. cars, 4,400 comm. vehicles. **Civil aviation:** 138.6 mil pass.-mi; 3 airports. **Chief ports:** Forai, Port-Vila.

Communications: TV sets: 12 per 1,000 pop. **Radios:** 350 per 1,000 pop. **Telephone lines:** 6,800 **Internet** (2004): 7,500 users.

Health: Life expect.: 61.3 male; 64.4 female. **Births** (per 1,000 pop.): 22.7. **Deaths** (per 1,000 pop.): 7.8. **Natural inc.:** 1.49%. **Infant mortality** (per 1,000 live births): 53.8. **AIDS rate:** NA.

Education: Compulsory: ages 6-12. **Literacy:** 74.0%.

Major Intl. Organizations: UN (FAO, IBRD, ILO, IMF, IMO, WHO), the Commonwealth.

Website: www.vanuatu.gov.ru

The Anglo-French condominium of the New Hebrides, administered jointly by France and Great Britain since 1906, became the independent Republic of Vanuatu on July 30, 1980. Mt. Manaro volcano on Ambae Is. began spewing steam and ash Nov. 27, 2005, forcing thousands to seek temporary refuge in emergency shelters.

Vatican City (The Holy See)

People: Population: 932. **Urban:** 100%. **Ethnic groups:** Italian, Swiss, other. **Principal languages:** Latin (official), Italian, French, Monastic Sign Language, various others. **Chief religion:** Roman Catholic.

Geography: Total area: 108.7 acres. **Location:** In Rome, Italy. **Neighbors:** Completely surrounded by Italy. Note: Dignitaries, priests, nuns, guards, and 3,000 lay workers live outside the Vatican.

Finance: Euro (EUR) (Sept. 2006: 0.78 = $1 U.S.). **Budget** (2002): $260.4 mil.

Transport: Railroad: Length: 1 mi.

Labor force: Essentially services with a small amount of industry.

Apostolic Nunciature in U.S.: 3339 Massachusetts Ave. NW 20008; 333-7121.

Website: www.vatican.va/phome_en.htm

The popes for many centuries, with brief interruptions, held temporal sovereignty over mid-Italy (the so-called Papal States), comprising an area of some 16,000 sq. mi., with a population in the 19th cent. of more than 3 mil. This territory was incorporated in the new Kingdom of Italy (1861), the sovereignty of the pope being confined to the palaces of the Vatican and the Lateran in Rome and the villa of Castel Gandolfo, by an Italian law, May 13, 1871. This law also guaranteed to the pope and his successors a yearly indemnity of over $620,000. The allowance, however, remained unclaimed.

A Treaty of Conciliation, a concordat, and a financial convention were signed Feb. 11, 1929, by Cardinal Gasparri and Premier Mussolini. The documents established the independent state of Vatican City and gave the Roman Catholic church special status in Italy. The treaty (Lateran Agreement) was made part of the Constitution of Italy (Article 7) in 1947. Italy and the Vatican signed an agreement in 1984 on revisions of the concordat; the accord eliminated Roman Catholicism as the state religion and ended required religious education in Italian schools.

Vatican City includes the Basilica of Saint Peter, the Vatican Palace and Museum covering over 13 acres, the Vatican gardens, and neighboring buildings between Viale Vaticano and the church. Thirteen buildings in Rome, outside the boundaries, enjoy extraterritorial rights; these buildings house congregations or officers necessary for the administration of the Holy See.

The legal system is based on the code of canon law, the apostolic constitutions, and laws especially promulgated for the Vatican City by the pope. The Secretariat of State represents the Holy See in its diplomatic relations. By the Treaty of Conciliation the pope is pledged to a perpetual neutrality unless his mediation is specifically requested. This, however, does not prevent the defense of the Church whenever it is persecuted.

The present sovereign of the State of Vatican City is the Supreme Pontiff Benedict XVI, born Joseph Ratzinger in Marktl am Inn, Germany, Apr. 16, 1927, elected Apr. 19, 2005.

The U.S. restored formal relations in 1984 after the U.S. Congress repealed an 1867 ban on diplomatic relations with the Vatican. The Vatican and Israel agreed to establish formal relations Dec. 30, 1993.

Venezuela
Bolivarian Republic of Venezuela

People: Population: 25,730,435. **Age distrib.** (%) <15: 29.1; 65+: 5.2. **Pop. density:** 75 per sq mi, 29 per sq km. **Urban:** 87.7%. **Ethnic groups:** Spanish, Italian, Portuguese, Arab, German, Black, indigenous. **Principal languages:** Spanish (official), numerous indigenous dialects. **Chief religion:** Roman Catholic 96%.

Geography: Total area: 352,145 sq mi, 912,050 sq km; **Land area:** 340,561 sq mi, 882,050 sq km. **Location:** On Caribbean coast of South America. **Neighbors:** Colombia on W, Brazil on S, Guyana on E. **Topography:** Flat coastal plain and Orinoco Delta are bordered by Andes Mts. and hills. Plains, called llanos, extend between mountains and Orinoco. Guiana Highlands and plains are S of Orinoco, which stretches 1,600 mi. and drains 80% of Venezuela. **Capital:** Caracas, 2,913,000. **Cities (urban aggr.):** Maracaibo, 2,255,000; Valencia, 2,451,000.

Government: Type: Federal republic. **Head of state and gov.:** Pres. Hugo Rafael Chávez Frías; b July 28, 1954; in office: Feb. 2, 1999. **Local divisions:** 23 states, federal district (Caracas), 1 federal dependency (72 islands). **Defense budget** (2005): NA. **Active troops:** 82,300.

Economy: Industries: oil, iron, constr. materials, food proc., textiles, steel, aluminum, auto assembly. **Chief crops:** corn, sorghum, sugarcane, rice, bananas, vegetables, coffee. **Natural resources:** oil, nat. gas, iron ore, gold, bauxite, other minerals, hydropower, diamonds. **Crude oil reserves** (2005): 77.2 bil bbls. **Arable land:** 4%. **Livestock** (2005): cattle: 16.3 mil; chickens: 110 mil; goats: 1.3 mil; pigs: 3.1 mil; sheep: 530,000. **Fish catch** (2004): 512,210 metric tons. **Electricity prod.** (2004): 93 bil kWh. **Labor force** (1997 est.): agriculture 13%, industry 23%, services 64%.

Finance: Monetary unit: Bolivares (VEB) (Sept. 2006: 2,145.00 = $1 U.S.). **GDP** (2005 est.): $153.7 bil; **per capita GDP:** $6,100; **GDP growth:** 9.3%. **Imports** (2005 est.): $24.6 bil; partners (2004): U.S. 33.2%, Colombia 5.7%, Brazil 5%, Germany 4%. **Exports** (2005 est.): $52.7 bil; partners (2004): U.S. 58.7%, Netherlands Antilles 4.1%, Canada 2.5%. **Tourism:** $477 mil. **Budget** (2005 est.):

$41.3 bil. Intl. reserves less gold: $16.74 bil. **Gold:** 11.48 mil oz t. **Consumer prices:** 15.95%.

Transport: Railroad: Length: 424 mi. **Motor vehicles:** 1.37mil pass. cars, 1.11 mil comm. vehicles. **Civil aviation:** 2.5 bil pass.-mi; 129 airports. **Chief ports:** Maracaibo, La Guaira, Puerto Cabello.

Communications: TV sets: 185 per 1,000 pop. **Radios:** 296 per 1,000 pop. **Telephone lines:** 3.6 mil. **Daily newspaper circ.:** NA. **Internet:** 3 mil users.

Health: Life expect.: 71.5 male; 77.8 female. **Births** (per 1,000 pop.): 18.7. **Deaths** (per 1,000 pop.): 4.9. **Natural inc.:** 1.38%. **Infant mortality** (per 1,000 live births): 21.5. **AIDS rate:** 0.7%.

Education: Compulsory: ages 6-15. **Literacy:** 93.0%.

Major Intl. Organizations: UN (FAO, IBRD, ILO, IMF, IMO, WHO, WTO), OAS, OPEC.

Embassy: 1099 30th St. NW 20007; 342-2214.

Website: www.embavenez-us.org

Columbus first set foot on the South American continent on the peninsula of Paria, Aug. 1498. Alonso de Ojeda, 1499, was the first European to see Lake Maracaibo. He called the land Venezuela, or Little Venice, because the Indians had houses on stilts. Spanish colonialists dominated Venezuela until Simón Bolívar's victory near Carabobo in June 1821. The republic was formed after secession from the Colombian Federation in 1830. Military strongmen ruled Venezuela for much of its history. Since 1959, the country has had democratically elected governments.

Oil accounts for more than 75% of export earnings and about half of government revenues. Venezuela helped found the Organization of Petroleum Exporting Countries (OPEC) in 1960. The government, Jan. 1, 1976, nationalized the oil industry with compensation. The economy suffered a cash crisis in the 1980s and 1990s as a result of depressed oil revenues. Government attempts to reduce dependence on oil have met with limited success.

An attempted coup by midlevel military officers was thwarted by loyalist troops Feb. 4, 1992. A second coup attempt was thwarted in Nov. Pres. Carlos Andrés Pérez was removed from office on corruption charges, May 1993; he was convicted, May 1996, of mismanaging a $17 mil secret government fund. A 1992 coup leader, Hugo Chávez, who ran as a populist, was elected president Dec. 6, 1998. Voters on Dec. 15 approved a new constitution greatly increasing his powers. Floods and mudslides in Dec. 1999 killed, by official estimates, at least 30,000.

Popular among the poor, Chávez alienated some middle- and upper-class Venezuelans with his program of economic and political reform, and his foreign policy antagonized the U.S. Gunfire erupted at a mass protest Apr. 11, 2002, in Caracas, killing at least 17 people. Chávez was forced to relinquish power, but when an interim government issued decrees suspending democratic institutions, Chávez loyalists rebelled; the coup fell apart, and the president reclaimed his office Apr. 14. Opponents of Chávez mounted a crippling general strike, Dec. 2002-Feb. 2003, which ended after mediation by the OAS and former U.S. Pres. Jimmy Carter. Several dissidents were killed later that month. The Colombian and Spanish embassies in Caracas were bombed Feb. 25. Chávez and opposition groups pledged, May 29, 2003, to halt political violence.

Opponents presented petitions with over 3 mil signatures Aug. 20, 2003, demanding a vote to recall Chávez. After prolonged legal wrangling, the recall election was set for Aug. 15, 2004. The referendum was monitored by Carter and the OAS, and Chávez won with 59% of the vote. Elections Dec. 4, 2005, boycotted by major opposition parties, strengthened Chávez's control over the legislature.

Chávez countered U.S. efforts to isolate him diplomatically and militarily by solidifying ties with other Latin American leftist leaders and with Iran and Russia; an agreement in July 2006 to buy fighter jets and helicopters brought Venezuela's arms purchases from Russia to over $3 bil in 18 months. Parties opposing Chávez called off a primary vote set for Aug. 13 and agreed to back a state governor, Manuel Rosales, in the Dec. 3 presidential election.

Vietnam
Socialist Republic of Vietnam

People: Population: 84,402,966. **Age distrib.** (%) <15: 27; 65+: 5.8. **Pop. density:** 671 per sq mi, 259 per sq km. **Urban:** 25.7%. **Ethnic groups:** Vietnamese 85%-90%, Chinese, Hmong, Thai, Khmer, Cham. **Principal languages:** Vietnamese (official), French, Chinese, English. **Chief religions:** Buddhist, Taoist, Roman Catholic, indigenous beliefs.

Geography: Total area: 127,244 sq mi, 329,560 sq km; **Land area:** 125,622 sq mi, 325,360 sq km. **Location:** SE Asia, on the E coast of the Indochinese Peninsula. **Neighbors:** China on N, Laos and Cambodia on W. **Topography:** Vietnam is long and narrow, with a 1,400-mi coast. About 22% of country is readily arable, including the densely settled Red R. valley in the N, narrow coastal plains in center, and the wide, often marshy Mekong R. Delta in the S. The rest consists of semi-arid plateaus and barren mountains, with some stretches of tropical rain forest. **Capital:** Hanoi, 4,164,000. **Cities (urban aggr.):** Ho Chi Minh City, 5,065,000; Hai Phong, 1,873,000.

Government: Type: Communist. **Head of state:** Pres. Nguyen Minh Triet; b. 1942; in office: June 27, 2006. **Head of gov.:** Prime Min. Nguyen Tan Dung; b. 1949; in office: June 27, 2006. **Local divisions:** 58 provinces, 3 cities, 1 capital region. **Defense budget** (2004): $3.5 bil. **Active troops:** 484,000.

Economy: Industries: food proc., garments, shoes, machinery, mining. **Chief crops:** rice, corn, potatoes, rubber, soybeans, coffee, tea. **Natural resources:** phosphates, coal, mang., bauxite, chromate, oil, nat. gas, timber, hydropower. **Crude oil reserves** (2005): 600 mil bbls. **Arable land:** 17%. **Livestock** (2005): cattle: 5.3 mil; chickens: 195 mil; goats: 1.2 mil; pigs: 27 mil. **Fish catch** (2004): 3,078,105 metric tons. **Electricity prod.** (2004): 40.1 bil kWh. **Labor force** (2005 est.): agriculture 56.8%, industry 37%, services 6.2%.

Finance: Monetary unit: Dong (VND) (Sept. 2006: 16,045.00 = $1 U.S.). **GDP** (2005 est.): $232.2 bil; **per capita GDP:** $2,800; **GDP growth:** 8.4%. **Imports** (2005 est.): $36.9 bil; partners (2004): China 13.6%, Japan 11.5%, Singapore 11.5%, Taiwan 10.2%, South Korea 9.8%, Thailand 6.7%, Hong Kong 4.4%, U.S. 4.1%, Malaysia 4.1%. **Exports** (2005 est.): $32.2 bil; partners (2004): U.S. 19.8%, Japan 13.7%, China 8.4%, Australia 7%, Germany 5.7%, Singapore 4.8%, UK 4.6%. **Tourism** (1990): $85 mil. **Budget** (2005 est.): $13 bil. **Intl. reserves less gold:** $6.33 bil. **Consumer prices:** 8.25%.

Transport: Railroad: Length: 1,615 mi. **Motor vehicles:** 69,900 comm. vehicles. **Civil aviation:** 4.1 bil pass.-mi; 26 airports. **Chief ports:** Ho Chi Minh City, Haiphong, Da Nang.

Communications: TV sets: 184 per 1,000 pop. **Radios:** 107 per 1,000 pop. **Telephone lines:** 15.8 mil. **Daily newspaper circ.:** 5.8 per 1,000 pop. **Internet:** 5.9 mil users.

Health: Life expect.: 68 male; 73.8 female. **Births** (per 1,000 pop.): 16.9. **Deaths** (per 1,000 pop.): 6.2. **Natural inc.:** 1.06%. **Infant mortality** (per 1,000 live births): 25.1. **AIDS rate:** 0.5%.

Education: Compulsory: ages 6-14. **Literacy:** 90.3%.

Major Intl. Organizations: UN (FAO, IBRD, ILO, IMF, IMO, WHO), APEC, ASEAN.

Embassy: 1233 20th St. NW, Ste. 400, 20036; 861-0737.

Website: www.na.gov.vn/english/index.html

Vietnam's recorded history began in Tonkin before the Christian era. Settled by Viets from central China, Vietnam was held by China, 111 BCE-939 CE, and was a vassal state during subsequent periods. Vietnam defeated the armies of Kublai Khan, 1288. Conquest by France began in 1858 and ended in 1884 with the protectorates of Tonkin and Annam in the north and the colony of Cochin-China in the south.

Japan occupied Vietnam in 1940; nationalist aims gathered force. A number of groups formed the Vietminh (Independence) League, headed by Ho Chi Minh, Communist guerrilla leader. In Aug. 1945 the Vietminh forced out Bao Dai, former emperor of Annam, head of a Japan-sponsored regime. France, seeking to reestablish colonial control, battled Communist and nationalist forces, 1946-54, and was defeated at Dienbienphu, May 8, 1954. Meanwhile, on July 1, 1949, Bao Dai had formed a State of Vietnam, with himself as chief of state, with French approval. China backed Ho Chi Minh.

A cease-fire signed in Geneva July 21, 1954, provided for a buffer zone, withdrawal of French troops from the North, and elections to determine the country's future. Under the agreement the Communists gained control of territory north of the 17th parallel, with its capital at Hanoi and Ho Chi Minh as president. South Vietnam came to comprise the 39 southern provinces. Some 900,000 North Vietnamese fled to South Vietnam. On Oct. 26, 1955, Ngo Dinh Diem proclaimed the Republic of Vietnam and became its president.

Communists in the North sought to take over South Vietnam beginning in 1954. The North provided aid to Vietcong guerrillas in the South; the Soviet Union and China supplied weapons for the Communist cause. The U.S. began sending military advisers to help the anti-Communist South. Northern aid to Vietcong guerrillas was intensified in 1959, and large-scale troop infiltration began in 1964, with Soviet and Chinese arms assistance. Large Northern forces were stationed in border areas of Laos and Cambodia.

During 1963, Buddhists in the South denounced the Diem government's authoritarianism and brutality. This paved the way for a military coup Nov. 1-2, 1963, which overthrew Diem. Several other military coups followed.

In 1964, the U.S. launched air strikes against North Vietnam. Beginning in 1965, the raids were stepped up and U.S. troops became combatants. U.S. troop strength in Vietnam reached a high of 543,400 in Apr. 1969, but the North Vietnamese and Vietcong continued to mount new offensives. In response to a growing antiwar movement in the U.S., Pres. Nixon gradually withdrew U.S. ground troops. U.S. warplanes conducted massive bombing raids on the Northern cities of Hanoi and Haiphong in Dec. 1972.

A cease-fire agreement was signed in Paris Jan. 27, 1973 by the U.S., North and South Vietnam, and the Vietcong. It was never implemented. North Vietnamese forces attacked remaining government outposts in the Central Highlands in the first months of 1975. Government retreats turned into a rout, and the Saigon regime surrendered April 30. North Vietnam assumed control, and began transforming society along Communist lines. The country was officially reunited July 2, 1976. The war's toll are as follows—Combat deaths: U.S. 47,369; South Vietnam more than 200,000; other allied forces 5,225. Total U.S. fatalities numbered more than 58,000. Vietnamese civilian casualties were more than a million. Displaced war refugees in South Vietnam totaled more than 6.5 mil.

Conditions in the region remained unstable after the Vietnam War ended. Heavy fighting with Cambodia took place, 1977-80. Relations with China soured as 140,000 ethnic Chinese left Vietnam charging discrimination; China cut off economic aid. Reacting to Vietnam's invasion of Cambodia, China attacked 4 Vietnamese border provinces, Feb. 1979. Vietnam launched an offensive against

Cambodian refugee strongholds along the Thai-Cambodian border in 1985; they also engaged Thai troops.

Vietnam announced reforms aimed at reducing central control of the economy in 1987, as many of the old revolutionary followers of Ho Chi Minh were removed from office.

Citing Vietnamese cooperation in returning remains of U.S. soldiers killed in the Vietnam War, the U.S. announced an end, Feb. 3, 1994, to a 19-year-old U.S. embargo on trade with Vietnam. The U.S. extended full diplomatic recognition to Vietnam July 11, 1995. The Communist Party replaced the country's ill and aging leadership in Sept. 1997.

Floods in central Vietnam, Oct.-Nov. 1999, killed some 550 people and left over 600,000 families homeless. U.S. Pres. Bill Clinton made a historic visit to Vietnam Nov. 17-19, 2000. Nong Duc Manh, a moderate, was named to head the Communist Party Apr. 22, 2001. The U.S. has become Vietnam's top export market, with total annual trade over $6 bil; the 2 countries agreed June 5, 2006, to strengthen defense ties. Communists reputed to be economic reformers became president and prime ministers June 27.

Western Samoa
See Samoa.

Yemen
Republic of Yemen

People: Population: 21,456,188. **Age distrib.** (%) <15: 46.4; 65+: 2.6. **Pop. density:** 105 per sq mi, 40 per sq km. **Urban:** 25.6%. **Ethnic groups:** Mainly Arab; Afro-Arab, South Asian, European. **Principal languages:** Arabic (official). **Chief religion:** Muslim (official; Sunni 60% and Shi'a 40%).

Geography: Total area: 203,850 sq mi, 527,970 sq km; **Land area:** 203,850 sq mi, 527,970 sq km. **Location:** Middle East, on the S coast of the Arabian Peninsula. **Neighbors:** Saudi Arabia on N, Oman on the E. **Topography:** A sandy coastal strip leads to well-watered fertile mountains in interior. **Capital:** Sana'a, 1,801,000.

Government: Type: Republic. **Head of state:** Pres. Ali Abdullah Saleh; b. 1942; in office: July 17, 1978. **Head of gov.:** Prime Min. Abd-al-Qadir Bajamal; b. 1946; in office: Apr. 4, 2001. **Local divisions:** 19 governorates and capital region. **Defense budget** (2005): $942 mil. **Active troops:** 66,700

Economy: Industries: oil prod. & refining, cotton textiles, leather goods, food proc. **Chief crops:** grain, fruits, vegetables, pulses, coffee, cotton. **Natural resources:** oil, fish, salt, marble, coal, gold, lead, nickel, copper. **Crude oil reserves** (2005): 4 bil bbls. **Arable land:** 3%. **Livestock** (2005): cattle: 1.4 mil; chickens: 37 mil; goats: 7.3 mil; sheep: 6.6 mil. **Fish catch** (2004): 256,300 metric tons. **Electricity prod.** (2004): 4.1 bil kWh. **Labor force:** most people are employed in agriculture and herding; services, construction, industry, and commerce account for less than one-fourth of the labor force.

Finance: Monetary unit: Rial (YER) (Sept. 2006: 196.75 = $1 U.S.). **GDP** (2005 est.): $19.4 bil; **per capita GDP:** $900; **GDP growth:** 2.4%. **Imports** (2005 est.): $4.2 bil; partners (2004): UAE 12.8%, Saudi Arabia 10.2%, China 9%, France 7.9%, Kuwait 4.4%, U.S. 4.4%, India 4.3%, Turkey 4.1%. **Exports** (2005 est.): $6.4 bil; partners (2004): China 33.5%, Thailand 31.4%, Singapore 7.2%, South Korea 6.1%. **Tourism:** $214 mil. **Budget** (2005 est.): $5.7 bil. **Intl. reserves less gold:** $4.28 bil. **Gold:** 50,000 oz t. **Consumer prices** (2003): 10.8%.

Transport: Motor vehicles: 346,600 pass. cars, 587,900 comm. vehicles. **Civil aviation:** 993 mil pass.-mi; 16 airports. **Chief ports:** Al Hudaydah, Al Mukalla, Aden.

Communications: TV sets: 286 per 1,000 pop. **Radios:** 64 per 1,000 pop. **Telephone lines:** 798,100. **Daily newspaper circ.:** NA. **Internet:** 220,000 users.

Health: Life expect.: 60.2 male; 64.1 female. **Births** (per 1,000 pop.): 42.9. **Deaths** (per 1,000 pop.): 8.3. **Natural inc.:** 3.46%. **Infant mortality** (per 1,000 live births): 59.9. **AIDS rate:** NA.

Education: Compulsory: ages 6-14. **Literacy:** 50.2%.

Major Intl. Organizations: UN (FAO, IBRD, ILO, IMF, IMO, WHO), AL.

Embassy: 2319 Wyoming Ave. NW 20008; 965-4760.

Website: www.nic.gov.ye

Yemen's territory once was part of the ancient biblical Kingdom of Sheba, or Saba, a prosperous link in trade between Africa and India. Yemen became independent in 1918, after centuries of Ottoman Turkish rule, but remained politically and economically backward.

Imam Ahmed ruled 1948-62. Army officers headed by Brig. Gen. Abdullah al-Salal declared the country to be the Yemen Arab Republic, Sept. 1962. Ahmed's heir, the Imam Mohamad al-Badr, fled to the mountains where tribesmen joined royalist forces, aided by the Saudi monarchy. Fighting between royalists and republicans killed about 150,000 people until hostilities ended in 1970.

Meanwhile, South Yemen, formed from the British colony of Aden and the British protectorate of South Arabia, became independent Nov. 1967. A Marxist state and a Soviet ally, it took the name People's Democratic Republic of Yemen in 1970. More than 300,000 Yemenis fled from the South to the North after independence, contributing to 2 decades of hostility between the 2 states that flared into warfare twice in the 1970s.

The 2 countries were formally united May 21, 1990, but regional clan-based rivalries led to full-scale civil war in 1994. Secessionists declared a breakaway state in South Yemen, May 21, 1994, but northern troops captured the former southern capital of Aden in July. A new constitution was approved Sept. 28.

Yemen, the ancestral home of Osama bin Laden, has been caught in a crossfire between the U.S. and Islamic extremists. While on a refueling stop in Aden, Oct. 12, 2000, the destroyer U.S.S. *Cole* was bombed, leaving 17 Americans dead and more than 3 dozen injured; the U.S. government blamed the attack on terrorists associated with bin Laden. The U.S. sent troops in 2002 to help track down members of al-Qaeda.

A missile fired Nov. 3, 2002, from an unmanned CIA surveillance aircraft killed 6 suspected al-Qaeda members, including an American. Three U.S. missionaries were slain at a Baptist hospital in Jibla, Dec. 30; the gunman, an Islamic militant, was executed Feb. 27, 2006. Clashes beginning in June 2004 between Yemeni government forces and rebels led by an anti-U.S. cleric, Hussein al-Houthi, left more than 200 people dead. The government announced Sept. 10, 2004, that Yemeni troops had killed al-Houthi. Incumbent Pres. Ali Abdullah Saleh was reelected Sept. 20, 2006.

Yugoslavia

See Montenegro and Serbia.

Zaire

See Congo.

Zambia
Republic of Zambia

People: Population: 11,288,253. **Age distrib.** (%) <15: 46; 65+: 2.4. **Pop. density:** 39 per sq mi, 15 per sq km. **Urban:** 35.7%. **Ethnic groups:** More than 70 groups; largest are Bemba, Tonga, Ngoni, and Lozi. **Principal languages:** English (official), Bemba, Kaonda, Lozi, Lunda, Luvale, Nyanja, Tonga, 70 others. **Chief religions:** Christian 50%-75%, Muslim and Hindu 24%-49%.

Geography: Total area: 290,586 sq mi, 752,614 sq km; **Land area:** 285,995 sq mi, 740,724 sq km. **Location:** In S central Africa. **Neighbors:** Congo (formerly Zaire) on N; Tanzania, Malawi, Mozambique on E; Zimbabwe, Namibia on S; Angola on W. **Topography:** Zambia is mostly high plateau country covered with thick forests, and drained by several important rivers, including the Zambezi. **Capital:** Lusaka, 1,260,000.

Government: Type: Republic. **Head of state and gov.:** Pres. Levy Patrick Mwanawasa; b. Sept. 3, 1948; in office: Jan. 2, 2002. **Local divisions:** 9 provinces. **Defense budget** (2005): $48.1 mil. **Active troops:** 15,100.

Economy: Industries: copper mining & proc., constr., foodstuffs. **Chief crops:** corn, sorghum, rice, peanuts, sunflower seeds. **Natural resources:** copper, cobalt, zinc, lead, coal, emeralds, gold, silver, uranium, hydropower. **Arable land:** 7%. **Livestock** (2005): cattle: 2.6 mil; chickens: 30 mil; goats: 1.3 mil; pigs: 340,000; sheep: 150,000. **Fish catch** (2004): 70,125 metric tons. **Electricity prod.** (2004): 10 bil kWh. **Labor force:** agriculture 85%, industry 6%, services 9%.

Finance: Monetary unit: Kwacha (ZMK) (Sept. 2006: 3,900.00 = $1 U.S.). **GDP** (2005 est.): $10.6 bil; **per capita GDP:** $900; **GDP growth:** 5.1%. **Imports** (2005 est.): $1.934 bil; partners (2004): South Africa 50.3%, Zimbabwe 13.2%, UAE 5.3%. **Exports** (2005 est.): $1.9 bil; partners (2004): Tanzania 14.1%, South Africa 13.2%, China 9.1%, Japan 7.9%, Thailand 7.9%, Switzerland 7.3%, Belgium 6.7%, Malaysia 4%. **Tourism** (2003): $149 mil. **Budget** (2005 est.): $1.9 bil. **Intl. reserves less gold:** $392 mil. **Consumer prices:** 18.32%.

Transport: Railroad: Length: 1,350 mi. **Motor vehicles:** 3,700 pass. cars, 3,900 comm. vehicles. **Civil aviation:** 9.9 mil pass.-mi; 10 airports. **Chief port:** Mpulungu.

Communications: TV sets: 145 per 1,000 pop. **Radios:** 160 per 1,000 pop. **Telephone lines:** 91,700. **Daily newspaper circ.:** 21.9 per 1,000 pop. **Internet:** 231,000 users.

Health: Life expect.: 38 male; 38.1 female. **Births** (per 1,000 pop.): 41. **Deaths** (per 1,000 pop.): 21.8. **Natural inc.:** 1.93%. **Infant mortality** (per 1,000 live births): 100.5. **AIDS rate:** 17%.

Education: Compulsory: ages 7-13. **Literacy:** 68.0%.

Major Intl. Organizations: UN (FAO, IBRD, ILO, IMF, WHO, WTO), the Commonwealth, AU.

Embassy: 2419 Massachusetts Ave. NW 20008; 265-9717.

Website: www.statehouse.gov.zm

Ruled by the British as Northern Rhodesia, the country became the independent republic of Zambia within the Commonwealth Oct. 24, 1964. Independence leader Kenneth Kaunda governed the country as president, 1964-91. A Zambian government corporation in 1970 took over 51% of 2 foreign-owned copper-mining companies. Privately-held land and other enterprises were nationalized in 1975. In the 1980s and 1990s lowered copper prices hurt the economy and severe drought caused famine.

Food riots erupted in June 1990, as the nation suffered its worst violence since independence. Elections held Oct. 1991 brought an end to Kaunda's one-party rule. The new government sought to sell state enterprises, including the copper industry. Pres. Frederick Chiluba won reelection Nov. 18, 1996, but international observers cited harassment of opposition parties. A coup attempt was suppressed Oct. 28, 1997.

Thwarted in his effort to change the constitution to allow himself to run for a 3rd term, Chiluba endorsed Levy Patrick Mwanawasa, who won a disputed election Dec. 27, 2001. Chiluba was arrested Feb. 24, 2003, on charges that he stole government funds while he was president; his trial began Dec. 9 but was slowed by prosecution delays.

Food shortages threatened more than 2 mil Zambians in 2002; the government refused to distribute shipments of U.S. grain because it was genetically modified. Zambia has made progress in treating HIV/AIDS, which afflicts about $1/_6$ of the adult population.

Zimbabwe
Republic of Zimbabwe

People: Population: 12,236,805. **Age distrib.** (%) <15: 37.4; 65+: 3.5. **Pop. density:** 81 per sq mi, 31 per sq km. **Urban:** 34.9%. **Ethnic groups:** Shona 82%, Ndebele 14%. **Principal languages:** English (official), Shona, Sindebele, numerous dialects. **Chief religions:** Syncretic (Christian-indigenous mix) 50%, Christian 25%, indigenous beliefs 24%.

Geography: Total area: 150,804 sq mi, 390,580 sq km; **Land area:** 149,294 sq mi, 386,670 sq km. **Location:** In southern Africa. **Neighbors:** Zambia on N, Botswana on W, South Africa on S, Mozambique on E. **Topography:** Zimbabwe is high plateau country, rising to mountains on eastern border, sloping down on the other borders. **Capital:** Harare, 1,515,000.

Government: Type: Republic. **Head of state and gov.:** Pres. Robert Mugabe; b. Feb. 21, 1924; in office: Dec. 31, 1987. **Local divisions:** 8 provinces, 2 cities. **Defense budget** (2005): $255 mil. **Active troops:** 29,000.

Economy: Industries: mining, steel, wood products, cement, chemicals. **Chief crops:** corn, cotton, tobacco, wheat, coffee. **Natural resources:** coal, chromium ore, asbestos, gold, nickel, copper, iron ore, vanadium, lithium, tin, platinum. **Arable land:** 7%. **Livestock** (2005): cattle: 5.4 mil; chickens: 23 mil; goats: 3 mil; pigs: 610,000; sheep: 610,000. **Fish catch** (2004): 15,955 metric tons. **Electricity prod.** (2004): 9.4 bil kWh. **Labor force** (1996): agriculture 66%, industry 10%, services 24%.

Finance: Monetary unit: Dollar (ZWN) (Sept. 2006: 250.67 = $1 U.S.). **GDP** (2005 est.): $28.4 bil; **per capita GDP:** $2,300; **GDP growth:** -7%. **Imports** (2005 est.): $2.1 bil; partners (2004): South Africa 47.2%, Democratic Republic of the Congo 6.2%, China 4.4%. **Exports** (2005 est.): $1.6 bil; partners (2004): South Africa 11.9%, Zambia 6.3%, China 3.4%. **Tourism** (2003): $44 mil. **Budget** (2005 est.): $1.9 bil. **Intl. reserves less gold** (2002): $61 mil. **Gold** (2002): 140,000 oz t. **Consumer prices** (changed in 2002): 140.1%.

Transport: Railroad: Length: 1,912 mi. **Motor vehicles:** 567,300 pass. cars, 83,500 comm. vehicles. **Civil aviation:** 418.8 mil pass.-mi; 17 airports. **Chief ports:** Binga, Kariba.

Communications: TV sets: 35 per 1,000 pop. **Radios:** 389 per 1,000 pop. **Telephone lines:** 328,000. **Daily newspaper circ.:** NA. **Internet:** 820,000 users.

Health: Life expect.: 40.4 male; 38.2 female. **Births** (per 1,000 pop.): 28. **Deaths** (per 1,000 pop.): 21.8. **Natural inc.:** 0.62%. **Infant mortality** (per 1,000 live births): 51.7. **AIDS rate:** 20.1%.

Education: Compulsory: ages 6-12. **Literacy:** 90.7%.

Major Intl. Organizations: UN (FAO, IBRD, ILO, IMF, IMO, WHO, WTO), AU.

Embassy: 1608 New Hampshire Ave. NW 20009; 332-7100.

Website: www.zim.gov.zw

Britain took over the area as Southern Rhodesia in 1923 from the British South Africa Co. (which, under Cecil Rhodes, had conquered it by 1897) and granted internal self-government. Under a 1961 constitution, voting was restricted to keep whites in power. On Nov. 11, 1965, Prime Min. Ian D. Smith announced his country's unilateral declaration of independence.

Britain termed the act illegal and demanded that the country (known as Rhodesia until 1980) broaden voting rights to provide for eventual rule by the black African majority. The UN imposed sanctions and, in May 1968, a trade embargo. Intermittent negotiations between the government and various black nationalist groups failed to prevent increasing guerrilla warfare.

In the country's first universal-franchise election, Apr. 21, 1979, Bishop Abel Muzorewa's United African National Council gained a bare majority of the black-dominated Parliament. A cease-fire was accepted by all parties, Dec. 5. Independence as Zimbabwe was finally achieved Apr. 18, 1980.

On Mar. 6, 1992, Pres. Robert Mugabe declared a national disaster because of drought and appealed to foreign donors for food, money, and medicine. An economic adjustment program caused widespread hardship. Mugabe was reelected Mar. 1996 after opposition candidates withdrew. A land redistribution campaign launched by Mugabe triggered violent attacks in Apr. 2000 against some white farmers; whites made up less than 1% of the population but held 70% of the land. Mugabe's opponents gained in legislative elections June 24-25, 2000.

International observers criticized Mugabe for relying on fraud and intimidation to win the presidential election of Mar. 9-11, 2002. The EU, the U.S., and the Commonwealth imposed sanctions on the Mugabe regime. Zimbabwe withdrew from the Commonwealth as of Dec. 7, 2003. In May 2005, Mugabe launched Operation Murambatsvina ("Drive out rubbish"), razing shanty dwellings and illegal street markets in urban areas and leaving some 700,000 people homeless. The currency was devalued in Aug. 2006 to deal with an annual inflation rate of more than 1,000%. In 2005, the UN estimated that about 20% of the adult population has HIV/AIDS.

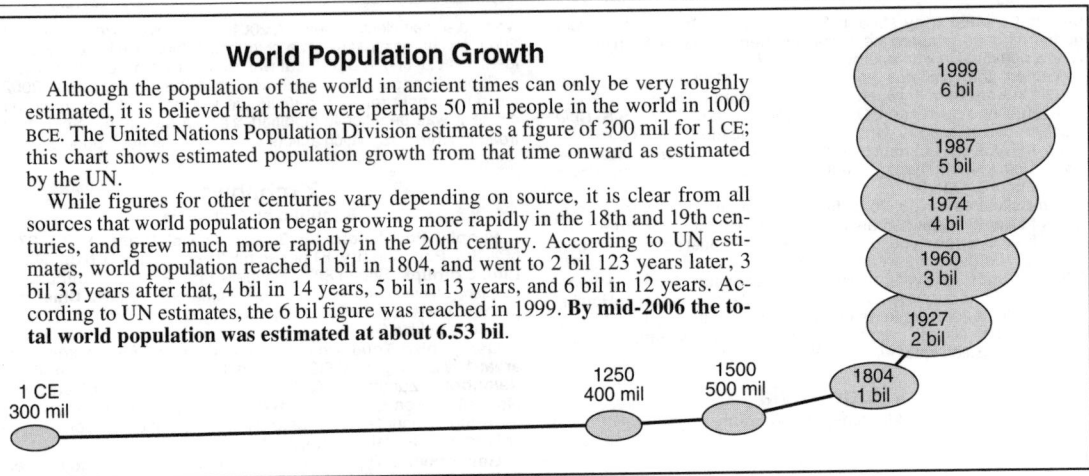

World Population Growth

Although the population of the world in ancient times can only be very roughly estimated, it is believed that there were perhaps 50 mil people in the world in 1000 BCE. The United Nations Population Division estimates a figure of 300 mil for 1 CE; this chart shows estimated population growth from that time onward as estimated by the UN.

While figures for other centuries vary depending on source, it is clear from all sources that world population began growing more rapidly in the 18th and 19th centuries, and grew much more rapidly in the 20th century. According to UN estimates, world population reached 1 bil in 1804, and went to 2 bil 123 years later, 3 bil 33 years after that, 4 bil in 14 years, 5 bil in 13 years, and 6 bil in 12 years. According to UN estimates, the 6 bil figure was reached in 1999. **By mid-2006 the total world population was estimated at about 6.53 bil**.

Area and Population of the Continents

Source: International Programs Center, U.S. Census Bureau, U.S. Dept. of Commerce

Continent or region	AREA[1] (sq km)	AREA[1] (sq mi)	% of Earth	% World total, 2006	2006	POPULATION (est., mid-year) 1950	1975	2000	2025[2]
Asia	30,757,714	11,875,620	23.6	60.6	3,957,661,498	1,437,201,723	2,412,691,104	3,677,535,065	4,812,175,242
Africa	29,807,200	11,508,624	22.8	14.0	915,722,298	228,182,746	410,728,579	801,053,965	1,338,106,036
Europe	22,738,372	8,779,335	17.4	11.1	727,656,706	546,415,793	677,127,418	729,623,640	706,757,000
N. America . .	21,261,439	8,209,087	16.3	7.9	518,249,404	220,857,588	346,216,831	485,968,142	619,720,426
S. America . .	17,522,371	6,765,425	13.4	5.8	375,667,668	111,384,890	215,772,736	348,339,764	447,305,516
Oceania, incl. Australia . .	8,426,638	3,253,543	6.5	0.5	33,131,988	12,476,128	21,220,574	30,744,658	39,685,917
Antarctica[3] . .	14,000,000	5,405,430	10.7	—	—	—	—	—	—
WORLD	**130,513,734**	**50,391,635**			**6,528,089,562**	**2,556,518,868**	**4,083,757,242**	**6,073,265,234**	**7,963,750,137**

Note: (1) Areas are as defined by the U.S. Census Bureau. Area for Europe includes all of Russia. Figures may not add to totals because of rounding. (2) Projected. (3) Antarctica has no indigenous inhabitants; researchers stay for various periods of time.

Current Population and Projections for All Countries and Territories: 2006, 2025, and 2050

Source: International Programs Center, U.S. Census Bureau, U.S. Dept. of Commerce
(mid-year figures)

	2006	2025	2050		2006	2025	2050
Afghanistan	31,056,997	50,252,227	81,933,479	Burkina Faso	13,902,972	23,995,152	43,656,786
Albania	3,581,655	3,944,360	4,016,945	Burma	46,986,207	52,995,497	54,430,334
Algeria	32,930,091	40,254,833	43,983,870	Burundi	8,090,068	13,912,642	22,852,556
American Samoa	57,794	51,752	35,129	Cambodia	13,881,427	19,289,143	25,089,909
Andorra	71,201	77,973	69,129	Cameroon	17,657,856	25,522,447	34,908,839
Angola	11,992,807	17,418,643	24,746,652	Canada	33,098,932	38,164,606	41,429,579
Anguilla	13,477	15,672	15,921	Cape Verde	420,979	451,021	380,614
Antigua and				Cayman Islands	45,436	67,308	90,230
Barbuda	69,108	75,116	69,259	Central African			
Argentina	39,921,833	45,757,375	48,740,060	Republic	4,303,356	5,486,686	6,502,151
Armenia	2,976,372	3,044,164	2,943,441	Chad	9,944,201	16,979,059	29,547,665
Aruba	71,891	75,402	69,990	Chile	16,134,219	18,521,153	19,244,843
Australia	20,264,082	23,022,980	24,175,783	China[1]	1,313,973,713	1,453,123,817	1,424,161,948
Austria	8,192,880	8,189,560	7,520,950	Colombia	43,593,035	55,064,507	64,534,230
Azerbaijan	8,066,157	9,352,531	9,955,428	Comoros	690,948	1,127,194	1,835,099
Bahamas, The	303,770	327,317	324,052	Congo (Kinshasa)	62,660,551	107,981,867	183,177,415
Bahrain	698,585	865,890	973,412	Congo Rep.			
Bangladesh	147,365,352	204,538,715	279,955,405	(Brazzaville)	3,702,314	6,165,891	9,618,358
Barbados	279,912	293,744	274,523	Cook Islands	21,571	24,025	24,930
Belarus	9,765,736	9,033,301	7,738,613	Costa Rica	4,075,261	5,074,472	5,696,700
Belgium	10,379,067	10,453,261	9,882,599	Cote d'Ivoire	17,654,843	24,381,767	32,400,664
Belize	287,730	410,468	541,734	Croatia	4,494,749	4,374,007	3,864,201
Benin	7,862,944	11,911,838	16,356,458	Cuba	11,382,820	11,668,658	10,477,677
Bermuda	65,773	70,683	66,025	Cyprus	784,301	851,733	841,102
Bhutan	2,279,723	3,294,556	4,653,447	Czech Republic	10,235,455	9,844,275	8,540,221
Bolivia	8,989,046	11,369,857	13,772,819	Denmark	5,450,661	5,697,913	5,575,147
Bosnia and				Djibouti	486,530	681,030	993,011
Herzegovina	4,498,976	4,535,296	3,891,669	Dominica	68,910	77,936	81,961
Botswana	1,639,833	1,582,776	1,411,662	Dominican			
Brazil	188,078,227	217,825,222	228,426,737	Republic	9,226,157	11,922,144	14,657,962
Brunei	379,444	505,644	600,998	Ecuador	13,547,510	17,099,305	20,332,088
Bulgaria	7,385,367	6,257,716	4,651,477	Egypt	78,887,007	103,352,882	126,920,512

	2006	2025	2050
El Salvador	6,822,378	9,107,608	12,039,149
Equatorial Guinea	540,109	768,236	1,063,071
Eritrea	4,786,994	7,244,126	10,164,076
Estonia	1,324,333	1,149,245	861,913
Ethiopia	74,777,981	107,804,235	144,716,331
Faroe Islands	47,246	51,765	53,050
Fiji	905,949	1,153,122	1,447,573
Finland	5,231,372	5,251,272	4,819,615
France	60,876,136	63,085,101	61,017,122
French Guiana	199,509	259,123	317,377
French Polynesia	274,578	343,745	390,581
Gabon	1,424,906	2,059,662	3,221,749
Gambia, The	1,641,564	2,624,964	4,068,861
Gaza Strip	1,428,757	2,588,747	4,209,026
Georgia	4,661,473	4,341,061	3,784,724
Germany	82,422,299	80,637,451	73,607,121
Ghana	22,478,658	30,536,326	38,735,638
Gibraltar	27,928	28,001	25,617
Greece	10,688,058	10,670,697	10,035,935
Greenland	56,361	56,473	56,644
Grenada	89,703	96,253	87,136
Guadeloupe	452,776	512,604	528,062
Guam	171,019	213,329	242,692
Guatemala	12,454,747	17,564,073	22,995,434
Guernsey	65,409	67,016	60,606
Guinea	9,690,222	15,806,084	28,713,509
Guinea-Bissau	1,442,029	2,060,522	2,895,666
Guyana	767,245	755,884	597,806
Haiti	8,497,543	13,254,108	19,807,275
Honduras	7,326,496	10,004,876	12,641,869
Hong Kong S.A.R.	6,940,432	7,354,531	6,172,725
Hungary	9,981,334	9,437,569	8,374,619
Iceland	299,388	337,632	350,922
India	1,111,713,910	1,448,821,234	1,807,878,574
Indonesia	231,820,243	278,502,882	313,020,847
Iran	65,025,373	76,779,032	81,490,039
Iraq	26,783,383	40,418,381	56,360,779
Ireland	4,062,235	4,842,255	5,396,215
Isle of Man	75,441	81,694	80,131
Israel	6,352,117	7,612,022	8,516,835
Italy	58,133,509	56,234,163	50,389,841
Jamaica	2,758,124	3,128,416	3,499,068
Japan	127,463,611	120,001,048	99,886,568
Jersey	91,084	93,281	84,077
Jordan	5,906,760	8,651,714	11,772,789
Kazakhstan	15,233,244	16,041,146	15,099,700
Kenya	35,890,645	51,261,167	65,175,864
Kiribati	105,432	158,047	235,342
Korea, North	23,113,019	25,755,007	26,363,688
Korea, South	48,846,823	50,560,956	45,224,224
Kuwait	2,418,393	4,175,172	6,374,800
Kyrgyzstan	5,213,898	6,678,722	8,237,623
Laos	6,368,481	9,450,131	13,176,153
Latvia	2,274,735	1,992,516	1,544,073
Lebanon	3,874,050	4,564,539	4,940,731
Lesotho	2,022,331	1,806,490	1,448,643
Liberia	3,042,004	4,745,521	7,072,402
Libya	5,900,754	8,322,662	10,817,176
Liechtenstein	33,987	37,567	35,776
Lithuania	3,585,906	3,355,985	2,787,516
Luxembourg	474,413	586,296	720,603
Macao S.A.R.	453,125	519,108	487,488
Macedonia	2,050,554	2,119,511	1,990,728
Madagascar	18,872,164	32,431,146	56,513,827
Malawi	13,283,755	20,244,055	29,820,957
Malaysia	24,385,858	33,064,523	43,122,397
Maldives	359,008	563,760	815,031
Mali	11,680,646	20,386,013	40,002,414
Malta	400,214	421,239	395,639
Marshall Islands	60,422	83,105	102,761
Martinique	436,131	479,148	478,627
Mauritania	3,177,388	5,291,845	8,635,801
Mauritius	1,240,827	1,406,809	1,451,156
Mayotte	201,234	356,898	592,627
Mexico	107,449,525	130,198,692	147,907,650

	2006	2025	2050
Micronesia, Federated States of	108,004	98,879	74,296
Moldova	4,325,682	4,194,262	3,620,416
Monaco	32,543	34,590	32,964
Mongolia	2,832,224	3,576,128	4,086,025
Montenegro	691,871	635,537	577,654
Montserrat	9,439	11,014	11,908
Morocco	33,241,259	42,553,182	50,871,553
Mozambique	20,530,023	28,893,271	41,842,274
Namibia	2,044,147	2,061,106	1,795,852
Nauru	13,287	17,887	22,696
Nepal	28,287,147	39,917,760	53,293,874
Netherlands	16,491,461	17,539,636	17,334,090
Netherlands Antilles	221,736	248,682	252,578
New Caledonia	219,246	263,151	290,682
New Zealand	4,076,140	4,672,537	4,842,397
Nicaragua	5,570,129	7,510,206	9,437,504
Niger	12,525,094	20,951,836	34,419,502
Nigeria	131,859,731	206,165,946	356,523,597
Northern Mariana Islands	82,459	116,270	143,132
Norway	4,610,820	4,916,787	4,966,385
Oman	3,102,229	5,294,475	8,337,734
Pakistan	165,803,560	228,822,199	294,995,104
Palau	20,579	24,320	26,300
Panama	3,191,319	4,109,552	5,038,122
Papua New Guinea	5,670,544	8,001,357	10,670,394
Paraguay	6,506,464	9,880,421	14,635,743
Peru	28,302,603	34,476,469	38,300,067
Philippines	89,468,677	118,685,776	147,630,852
Poland	38,536,869	37,349,696	32,084,570
Portugal	10,605,870	10,806,202	9,933,334
Puerto Rico	3,928,447	4,095,850	3,770,496
Qatar	885,359	1,153,966	1,239,216
Reunion	787,584	981,122	1,132,283
Romania	22,303,552	21,260,138	18,678,226
Russia	142,069,494	128,180,396	109,187,353
Rwanda	9,638,170	15,699,855	25,128,735
Saint Helena	7,502	7,868	7,247
Saint Kitts and Nevis	39,129	46,486	52,348
Saint Lucia	168,458	209,064	235,420
Saint Pierre and Miquelon	7,026	7,079	6,355
Saint Vincent and the Grenadines	117,848	118,308	92,335
Samoa	176,908	177,452	170,739
San Marino	29,251	34,565	35,335
Sao Tome and Principe	193,413	328,825	502,489
Saudi Arabia	27,019,731	35,668,686	49,706,851
Senegal	12,191,150	18,717,375	27,519,852
Serbia	10,140,311	10,027,056	9,274,767
Seychelles	81,541	88,071	89,713
Sierra Leone	6,005,250	9,140,077	13,998,936
Singapore	4,492,150	5,100,929	4,635,110
Slovakia	5,439,448	5,458,581	4,943,616
Slovenia	2,010,347	1,907,560	1,596,947
Solomon Islands	552,438	815,582	1,110,514
Somalia	8,863,338	14,861,596	25,499,605
South Africa	44,187,637	39,905,523	33,002,952
Spain	40,397,842	39,578,066	35,564,293
Sri Lanka	20,717,932	23,707,228	24,920,558
Sudan	41,236,378	61,338,891	84,192,309
Suriname	465,610	560,061	617,249
Swaziland	1,136,334	1,008,990	751,328
Sweden	9,016,596	9,315,507	9,084,788
Switzerland	7,523,934	7,774,334	7,296,092
Syria	18,881,361	26,547,725	34,437,235
Taiwan	23,036,087	24,635,783	23,203,650
Tajikistan	6,944,062	9,510,130	12,132,365
Tanzania	37,445,392	53,015,251	71,949,135
Thailand	64,631,595	70,523,958	69,268,817
Timor-Leste	1,062,777	1,493,841	1,942,734

	2006	2025	2050		2006	2025	2050
Togo	5,548,702	8,986,546	14,714,623	Uruguay	3,431,932	3,675,259	3,728,264
Tonga	114,689	150,787	188,340	Uzbekistan	27,307,134	36,947,068	48,597,111
Trinidad and				Vanuatu	208,869	263,267	310,486
Tobago	1,065,842	881,713	622,011	Vatican City	932	NA	NA
Tunisia	10,175,014	11,931,451	12,462,798	Venezuela	25,730,435	32,060,880	37,106,394
Turkey	70,413,958	82,204,623	86,473,786	Vietnam	84,402,966	99,977,731	107,772,641
Turkmenistan	5,042,920	7,052,993	9,626,193	Virgin Islands	108,605	107,559	103,303
Turks and Caicos				Virgin Islands,			
Islands	21,152	32,242	42,384	British	23,098	30,695	34,038
Tuvalu	11,810	15,821	20,018	Wallis and Futuna	16,168	18,502	20,434
Uganda	29,206,503	56,744,814	128,007,514	West Bank	2,460,492	3,882,966	5,580,321
Ukraine	46,620,334	41,037,583	33,573,842	Western Sahara	371,567	616,533	996,674
United Arab				Yemen	21,456,188	39,643,901	71,119,251
Emirates	2,602,713	3,269,743	3,696,962	Zambia	11,288,253	14,829,985	18,435,053
United Kingdom	60,609,153	63,818,586	63,977,435	Zimbabwe	12,236,805	12,915,433	12,221,257
United States	298,444,215	349,666,199	420,080,587				

NA = not available. (1) Excludes Hong Kong, population 6,940,432, and Macao, population 453,125.

Population of the World's Largest Cities

Source: *World Population Prospects, World Urbanization Prospects,* Dept. of Economic and Social Affairs of the United Nations Secretariat

Population figures are UN estimates and projections for "urban agglomerations"—i.e., contiguous densely populated urban areas, not demarcated by administrative boundaries, as revised in 2005. Data may differ from figures elsewhere in *The World Almanac.*

Rank[1] City, Country	Pop. (thousands) 2000	Pop. (thousands) 2015[2]	Annual growth rate % 1995-2000	Pop. (thousands) 1975	Total Growth % 1975-2000	2000-15[2]	Pop. of city as percentage of nation's 2000 pop.
1. Tokyo, Japan	34,450	35,494	0.51	26,615	29.4	3.0	27.1
2. Mexico City, Mexico	18,066	21,568	1.47	10,690	69.0	19.4	18.1
3. New York, NY, U.S.	17,846	19,876	1.04	15,880	12.4	11.4	6.3
4. São Paulo, Brazil	17,099	20,535	1.39	9,614	77.9	20.1	9.8
5. Mumbai (Bombay), India	16,086	21,869	2.62	7,082	127.1	36.0	1.6
6. Shanghai, China	13,243	17,225	4.79	7,326	80.8	30.1	1.0
7. Kolkata (Calcutta), India	13,058	16,980	1.82	7,888	65.5	30.0	1.3
8. Delhi, India	12,441	18,604	4.18	4,426	181.1	49.5	1.2
9. Buenos Aires, Argentina	11,847	13,396	1.21	8,745	35.5	13.1	32.1
10. Los Angeles, CA, U.S.	11,814	13,095	0.82	8,926	32.4	10.8	4.2
11. Osaka, Japan	11,165	11,309	0.20	9,844	13.4	1.3	8.8
12. Jakarta, Indonesia	11,065	16,822	3.78	4,813	129.9	52.0	5.3
13. Rio de Janeiro, Brazil	10,803	12,770	1.20	7,557	43.0	18.2	6.2
14. Cairo, Egypt	10,391	13,138	1.36	6,450	61.1	26.4	15.4
15. Beijing, China	9,782	12,850	2.84	6,034	62.1	31.4	0.8

(1) Ranked by 2000 population. (2) Projected.

National Rankings by Population, Area, Population Density, 2006

Source: International Programs Center, U.S. Census Bureau, U.S. Dept. of Commerce

As of mid-2006, according to U.S. Census Bureau projections, the world had an estimated population of 6,528,089,562. China was the most populous nation, with ⅕ of the world total. India, the second largest, passed the 1-bil mark in 1999. Russia is the largest country in land area.

Largest Populations

Rank	Country	Population
1.	China[1]	1,313,973,713
2.	India	1,111,713,910
3.	United States	298,444,215
4.	Indonesia	231,820,243
5.	Brazil	188,078,227
6.	Pakistan	165,803,560
7.	Bangladesh	147,365,352
8.	Russia	142,069,494
9.	Nigeria	131,859,731
10.	Japan	127,463,611

Largest Populations

Rank	Country	Population
11.	Mexico	107,449,525
12.	Philippines	89,468,677
13.	Vietnam	84,402,966
14.	Germany	82,422,299
15.	Egypt	78,887,007
16.	Ethiopia	74,777,981
17.	Turkey	70,413,958
18.	Iran	65,025,373
19.	Thailand	64,631,595
20.	Congo (Kinshasa)	62,660,551

Smallest Populations

Rank	Country	Population
1.	Vatican City	932
2.	Tuvalu	11,810
3.	Nauru	13,287
4.	Palau	20,579
5.	San Marino	29,251
6.	Monaco	32,543
7.	Liechtenstein	33,987
8.	Saint Kitts and Nevis	39,129
9.	Marshall Islands	60,422
10.	Dominica	68,910

Largest Land Areas[2]

Rank	Country	Area (sq km)	Area (sq mi)
1.	Russia	16,995,800	6,562,112
2.	China	9,326,410	3,600,946
3.	United States	9,161,923	3,537,437
4.	Canada	9,093,507	3,511,023
5.	Brazil	8,456,510	3,265,077
6.	Australia	7,617,930	2,941,299
7.	India	2,973,190	1,147,955
8.	Argentina	2,736,690	1,056,642
9.	Kazakhstan	2,669,800	1,030,816
10.	Algeria	2,381,740	919,595

Most Densely Populated[3]

Rank	Country	Persons per sq km	Persons per sq mi
1.	Monaco	16,271.5	32,543.0
2.	Singapore	6,577.1	17,015.7
3.	Vatican City	5,482.4	2,118.2
4.	Malta	1,266.5	3,280.4
5.	Maldives	1,196.7	3,094.9
6.	Bangladesh	1,100.5	2,850.2
7.	Bahrain	1,050.5	2,718.2
8.	Taiwan	714.1	1,849.4
9.	Barbados	649.4	1,686.2
10.	Nauru	632.7	1,660.9

	Smallest Land Areas[2]				Most Sparsely Populated[3]		
Rank	Country	Area (sq km)	Area (sq mi)	Rank	Country	Persons per sq km	Persons per sq mi
1.	Vatican City	0.17	0.44	1.	Mongolia	1.8	4.7
2.	Monaco	2	1	2.	Namibia............	2.5	6.4
3.	Nauru...............	21	8	3.	Australia	2.7	6.9
4.	Tuvalu	26	10	4.	Botswana..........	2.8	7.3
5.	San Marino..........	61	24	5.	Suriname...........	2.9	7.5
6.	Liechtenstein	160	62	6.	Iceland............	3.0	7.7
7.	Marshall Islands......	181	70	7.	Mauritania	3.1	8.0
8.	Saint Kitts and Nevis ...	261	101	8.	Libya	3.4	8.7
9.	Maldives.............	300	116	9.	Canada	3.6	9.4
10.	Malta	316	122	10.	Guyana	3.9	10.1

(1) Excluding Hong Kong, pop. 6,940,432, and Macau, population 453,125. (2) Land area of a country does not include inland water. Rankings by total area, including inland water, may differ from these. For national total area figures, see the countries entries in this chapter. (3) Density is calculated here according to land area.

Countries With Highest & Lowest Gross Domestic Product and Per Capita GDP[1]

Source: *The World Factbook 2006*, Central Intelligence Agency

	GDP, in millions				Per capita GDP[8]		
	Highest		Lowest		Highest		Lowest
1. U.S.	$12,360,000	1. Tuvalu[4]	$12	1. Luxembourg	$55,600	1. Timor-Leste[7] ..	$400
2. China[2]	8,859,000	2. Nauru	60	2. Equatorial Guinea..	50,200	2. Malawi.......	600
3. Japan......	4,018,000	3. Kiribati[3]	79	3. United Arab Emirates	43,400	Somalia......	600
4. India.......	3,611,000	4. Marshall Islands[3]	115	4. Norway	42,300	Comoros	600
5. Germany ...	2,504,000	5. Palau[3]	174	5. U.S.............	41,800	5. Congo, Dem. (Kinshasa)..	700
6. UK........	1,830,000	6. São Tomé and Príncipe[5]	214	6. Ireland...........	41,000	Tanzania	700
7. France	1,816,000	7. Tonga[6]	244	7. Iceland	35,600	Burundi	700
8. Italy	1,698,000	8. Micronesia[6]........	277	8. Denmark..........	34,600	8. Sierra Leone ..	800
9. Russia	1,589,000	9. St. Kitts and Nevis[6]....	339	San Marino[3]	34,600	Guinea-Bissau.	800
10. Brazil	1,556,000	10. St. Vincent and the Grenadines[6]	342	10. Canada..........	34,000	Kiribati[3]	800
11. Canada	1,114,000	11. Timor-Leste[7]	370	11. Austria	32,700	Afghanistan[7] ..	800
12. Mexico.....	1,067,000	12. Dominica[5]	384	12. Switzerland.......	32,300	12. Madagascar...	900
13. Spain......	1,029,000	13. Grenada[6]	440	13. Australia	31,900	Yemen.......	900
14. Korea, South	965,300	14. Comoros	441	14. Japan	31,500	Zambia	900
15. Indonesia...	865,600	15. Vanuatu[5]	580	15. Belgium.........	31,400	Niger	900
16. Australia....	640,100	16. Djibouti[6]	619	16. Finland	30,900	Ethiopia	900
17. Taiwan	631,200	17. Seychelles[6]..........	626	17. Netherlands......	30,500	17. Liberia	1,000
18. Turkey	572,000	18. Antigua and Barbuda[6]..	750	18. Germany........	30,400	Eritrea	1,000
19. Iran	561,600	19. Solomon Islands[6]	800	19. UK.............	30,300	19. Tuvalu[4]	1,100
20. Thailand....	560,700	20. St. Lucia[6]	866	20. France..........	29,900	Benin........	1,100

(1) All figures are for 2005, unless otherwise indicated. Data may differ from estimates by the U.S. Bureau of Economic Analysis. International GDP estimates derive from purchasing power parity calculations, which involve the use of intl. dollar price weights applied to quantities of goods and services produced in a given economy. Countries do not include some territories or former territories. (2) Does not include Hong Kong, which had a GDP of $227.3 mil and a per capita GDP of $32,900 in 2005, or Macao, which had a GDP of $10 bil and a per capita GDP of $22,000 in 2004. (3) 2001 est. (4) 2000 est. (5) 2003 est. (6) 2002 est. (7) 2004 est. (8) Per capita GDP calculated using U.S. census population figures for the year each GDP was available.

Gold Reserves of Central Banks and Governments

Source: *International Financial Statistics*, International Monetary Fund

(in million fine troy ounces)

Year end	All countries[1]	United States	China	Canada	France	Germany[2]	Italy	Japan	Netherlands	Switzerland	United Kingdom
1975	1,018.71	274.71	NA	21.95	100.93	117.61	82.48	21.11	54.33	83.20	21.03
1980	952.99	264.32	12.80	20.98	81.85	95.18	66.67	24.23	43.94	83.28	18.84
1985	949.39	262.65	12.70	20.11	81.85	95.18	66.67	24.33	43.94	83.28	19.03
1990	939.01	261.91	12.70	14.76	81.85	95.18	66.67	24.23	43.94	83.28	18.94
1995	908.79	261.70	12.70	3.41	81.85	95.18	66.67	24.23	34.77	83.28	18.43
1996	906.10	261.66	12.70	3.09	81.85	95.18	66.67	24.23	34.77	83.28	18.43
1997	890.57	261.64	12.70	3.09	81.89	95.18	66.67	24.23	27.07	83.28	18.42
1998	966.15	261.61	12.70	2.49	102.37	118.98	83.36	24.23	33.83	83.28	23.00
1999	967.07	261.67	12.70	1.81	97.25	111.52	78.83	24.23	31.57	83.28	20.55
2000	952.09	261.61	12.70	1.18	97.25	111.52	78.83	24.55	29.32	77.79	15.67
2001	942.76	262.00	16.10	1.05	97.25	111.13	78.83	24.60	28.44	70.68	11.42
2002	931.18	262.00	19.29	0.60	97.25	110.79	78.83	24.60	27.38	61.62	10.09
2003	913.29	261.55	19.29	0.11	97.25	110.58	78.83	24.60	25.00	52.51	10.07
2004	900.58	261.59	19.29	0.11	95.98	110.38	78.83	24.60	25.00	43.54	10.04
2005	881.69	261.55	19.29	0.11	90.85	110.21	78.83	24.60	22.34	41.48	9.99

NA = not available. (1) Covers IMF members with reported gold holdings. For countries not listed above, see International Monetary Fund's *International Financial Statistics* report. (2) West Germany prior to 1991.

IT'S A RECORD: South Africa has been the world's top gold producer since the early 20th century. The nation supplied 77.8% of the world's annual gold production in 1970, its high point. Though the country still leads in gold production, its share had dropped to 12% (296 tonnes) by 2005 due to aging mines and increased production costs. Since records were first kept in the 1880s, South Africa has produced about 40% of all mined gold. South Africa still has the largest gold ore reserves, with an estimated 40,000 tonnes, or 40% of the world total.

Consumer Price Changes in Selected Countries, 1975-2005

Source: *International Financial Statistics*, International Monetary Fund

(annual averages)

COUNTRY	1975-80	1980-85	1992-93	1993-94	1994-95	1995-96	1996-97	1997-98	1998-99	1999-2000	2000-01	2001-02	2002-03	2003-04	2004-05
Canada............	8.7	7.4	1.8	0.2	2.2	1.6	1.6	1.0	1.7	2.7	2.3	2.2	2.8	1.8	2.2
China	NA	NA	14.6	24.2	16.9	8.3	2.8	-.9	-1.4	0.3	0.5	-0.8	1.2	4.0	1.8
France	10.5	9.6	2.1	1.7	1.8	2.0	1.2	0.7	0.5	1.7	1.6	1.9	2.1	2.1	1.8
Germany	4.1	3.9	4.1	3.0	1.8	1.5	1.8	1.0	0.6	1.5	2.0	1.4	1.1	1.7	2.0
Italy..............	16.3	13.7	4.5	4.0	5.2	4.0	2.0	2.0	1.7	2.5	2.8	2.5	2.7	2.2	2.0
Japan	6.5	2.7	1.3	0.7	-0.1	0.1	1.7	0.6	-0.3	-0.7	-0.7	-0.9	-0.3	-0.1	-0.3
Spain	18.6	12.2	4.6	4.7	4.7	3.6	2.0	1.8	2.3	3.4	3.6	3.1	3.0	3.0	3.4
Sweden	10.5	9.0	4.6	2.2	2.5	0.5	0.5	-0.1	0.5	0.9	2.4	2.2	1.9	0.4	0.5
Switzerland.......	2.3	4.3	3.3	0.8	1.8	0.8	0.5	0.1	0.7	1.5	1.0	0.6	0.6	0.8	1.2
United Kingdom	14.4	7.2	1.6	2.5	3.4	2.4	3.1	3.4	1.6	2.9	1.8	1.6	2.9	3.0	2.8
United States	8.9	5.5	3.0	2.6	2.8	3.0	2.3	1.6	2.2	3.4	2.8	1.6	2.3	2.7	3.4

NA = not available.

Hourly Compensation Costs[1], by Selected Country, 1975-2004

Source: Bureau of Labor Statistics, U.S. Dept. of Labor

(in U.S. dollars, compensation for production workers in manufacturing)

Country/Territory	1975	1985	1995	2002	2003	2004	Country/Territory	1975	1985	1995	2002	2003	2004
Australia........	5.60	8.18	15.36	15.41	19.78	23.09	Luxembourg	6.22	7.48	23.36	18.71	23.12	26.57
Austria	4.50	7.57	25.26	20.69	25.32	28.29	Mexico.........	1.45	1.58	1.47	2.60	2.49	2.50
Belgium	5.77	8.29	25.64	21.74	26.52	29.98	New Zealand	3.10	4.30	9.78	8.60	11.04	12.89
Brazil	—	—	—	2.56	2.74	3.03	Norway	6.90	10.47	24.84	27.29	31.56	34.64
Denmark........	6.24	8.10	25.28	24.25	30.15	33.75	Portugal.........	1.52	1.46	5.09	5.07	6.24	7.02
Finland	4.63	8.20	24.31	21.78	27.10	30.67	Singapore	0.83	2.53	7.58	6.71	7.18	7.45
France	4.50	7.48	19.26	17.12	21.14	23.89	South Korea	0.32	1.23	7.28	8.77	10.03	11.52
Germany[2]......	—	—	30.09	24.20	29.63	32.53	Spain...........	2.52	4.64	12.70	11.92	14.97	17.10
Greece	1.69	3.67	9.07	—	—	—	Sri Lanka........	0.28	0.28	0.48	0.49	0.51	—
Hong Kong[3]	0.75	1.73	4.80	5.66	5.54	5.51	Sweden	7.14	9.61	21.68	20.23	25.19	28.42
Ireland	3.06	6.00	13.75	15.26	19.09	21.94	Switzerland	6.03	9.55	28.99	23.81	27.83	30.26
Israel	2.03	3.66	9.50	11.03	11.66	12.18	Taiwan..........	0.37	1.49	5.87	5.64	5.69	5.97
Italy............	4.64	7.56	15.69	14.75	18.11	20.48	United Kingdom...	3.35	6.22	13.79	18.25	21.20	24.71
Japan	2.97	6.27	23.55	18.65	20.32	21.90	United States.....	6.16	12.71	17.21	21.40	22.27	23.17

— Data not available. (1) Compensation includes all direct pay (including bonuses, etc.), paid benefits, and for some countries, labor taxes. (2) 1975 and 1985 data are for area covered by the former West Germany. 1995-2004 are unified Germany. (3) Part of China since 1997.

Unemployment Rates, by Selected Country, 1970-2005[1]

Source: Bureau of Labor Statistics, U.S. Dept. of Labor

Year	U.S.	Australia	Canada	France	Germany[2]	Italy	Japan	Sweden	UK
1970	4.9	1.6	5.7	2.5	0.5	3.2	1.2	1.5	3.1
1975	8.5	4.9	6.9	4.2	3.4	3.4	1.9	1.6	4.5
1980	7.1	6.1	7.3	6.5	2.8	4.4	2.0	2.0	6.9
1981	7.6	5.8	7.3	7.6	4.0	4.9	2.2	2.5	9.7
1982	9.7	7.2	10.7	8.3	5.6	5.4	2.4	3.1	10.8
1983	9.6	10.0	11.6	8.6	6.9	5.9	2.7	3.5	11.5
1984	7.5	9.0	10.9	10.0	7.1	5.9	2.8	3.1	11.8
1985	7.2	8.3	10.2	10.5	7.2	6.0	2.7	2.8	11.4
1986	7.0	7.9	9.3	10.6	6.6	7.5	2.8	2.6	11.4
1987	6.2	7.9	8.4	10.8	6.3	7.9	2.9	2.2	10.5
1988	5.5	7.0	7.4	10.3	6.3	7.9	2.5	1.9	8.6
1989	5.3	6.0	7.1	9.6	5.7	7.8	2.3	1.6	7.3
1990	5.6	6.7	7.7	8.6	5.0	7.0	2.1	1.8	7.1
1991	6.8	9.3	9.8	9.1	5.6	6.9	2.1	3.1	8.9
1992	7.5	10.5	10.6	10.0	6.7	7.3	2.2	5.6	10.0
1993	6.9	10.6	10.8	11.3	8.0	9.8	2.5	9.4	10.4
1994	6.1	9.4	9.6	11.9	8.5	10.7	2.9	9.6	8.7
1995	5.6	8.2	8.6	11.3	8.2	11.3	3.2	9.1	8.7
1996	5.4	8.2	8.9	11.8	9.0	11.3	3.4	9.9	8.1
1997	4.9	8.3	8.4	11.7	9.9	11.4	3.4	10.1	7.0
1998	4.5	7.7	7.7	11.2	9.3	11.5	4.1	8.4	6.3
1999	4.2	6.9	7.0	10.5	8.5	11.0	4.7	7.1	6.0
2000	4.0	6.3	6.1	9.1	7.8	10.2	4.8	5.8	5.5
2001	4.7	6.8	6.5	8.4	7.9	9.2	5.1	5.0	5.1
2002	5.8	6.4	7.0	9.0	8.7	8.7	5.4	5.1	5.2
2003	6.0	6.1	6.9	9.6	9.7	8.5	5.3	5.8	5.0
2004	5.5	5.5	6.4	9.8	9.8	8.1	4.8	6.6	4.8
2005	5.1	5.1	6.0	9.7	9.7	7.8	4.5	6.3[3]	4.8

NOTE: Civilian labor force, seasonally adjusted. For the sake of comparisons, U.S. unemployment rate concepts were applied to unemployment data for other countries. NA = not available. (1) As a result of revisions in survey methodology, there are breaks in the data series for the U.S. (1990, 1994), France (1982, 1990), Germany (1983, 1991, 1999), Italy (1986, 1991, 1993), Sweden (1987), and Australia (1986, 2001); data prior to a survey change are not fully comparable to data after a survey change. (2) For former West Germany only, through 1990; from 1991 on figures are for unified Germany and not adjusted by the Bureau of Labor Statistics. (3) The EU harmonized labor force survey for Sweden was introduced in April 2005. Seasonally adjusted data for new series not yet available. This figure is from the first quarter of 2005.

Tax Burden in Selected Countries[1]

Source: Organization for Economic Cooperation and Development, 2005

Country[2]	Income tax	Social Security	Total payment[3]	Country[2]	Income tax	Social Security	Total payment[3]
Belgium	28%	14%	42%	Iceland	25%	0%	25%
Germany	21	21	42	Czech Rep.	12	13	24
Denmark	30	11	41	Australia	24	0	24
Hungary	19	14	33	U.S.	16	8	24
Netherlands	11	22	32	Canada	17	7	24
Austria	14	18	32	Slovakia	9	13	22
Poland	6	26	32	Switzerland	11	11	22
Finland	25	6	31	Greece	6	16	22
Sweden	24	7	31	Portugal	10	11	21
Turkey	15	15	30	New Zealand	21	0	21
France	15	14	29	Spain	14	6	20
Norway	21	8	29	Japan	7	12	19
Italy	18	9	27	Ireland	13	5	18
Luxembourg	13	14	27	Korea	3	7	10
UK	17	9	27	Mexico	6	2	8

(1) Does not include taxes not listed, such as sales tax or VAT. Rates shown apply to a single person without children with average earnings. (2) Ranked by total payment %. Ties ranked by income tax % where different. (3) Totals may not add due to rounding.

The World's Refugees, 2005

Source: *World Refugee Survey 2006*, U.S. Committee for Refugees, a nonprofit corp.

These estimates are conservative and have been rounded. Totals include individuals granted asylum and those who had pending asylum claims as of year-end 2005. Figures do not include Internally Displaced Persons (IDPs), who are displaced within their own country due to persecution or armed conflict and are not protected by international refugee law. The global figure for IDPs is 21 mil. Figures generally do not include those who have achieved permanent resettlement. Region totals include nations not listed.

(as of Dec. 31, 2005; only countries estimated to host 50,000 or more refugees are listed)

Place of asylum	Origin of most refugees	Number
AFRICA		**3,176,100**
Algeria	Morocco, Palestinians	94,500
Cameroon	Chad, Nigeria, Dem. Rep. of Congo	58,900
Chad	Sudan, Central African Republic	275,500
Dem. Rep. of the Congo	Angola, Burundi, Uganda, Rwanda	204,500
Rep. of the Congo	Dem. Rep. of Congo, Rwanda	69,600
Egypt	Palestinians, Sudan, Somalia	86,700
Ethiopia	Sudan, Somalia, Eritrea	101,100
Ghana	Liberia, Togo	59,000
Guinea	Liberia, Sierra Leone, Côte d'Ivoire	67,300
Kenya	Somalia, Sudan, Ethiopia	314,600
Sierra Leone	Liberia	60,100
South Africa	Dem. Rep. of the Congo, Somalia, Zimbabwe	169,800
Sudan	Eritrea, Ethiopia, Uganda	231,700
Tanzania	Burundi, Dem. Rep. of the Congo, Somalia	549,100
Uganda	Sudan, Rwanda, Dem. Rep. of the Congo	254,400
Zambia	Angola, Dem. Rep. of the Congo, Rwanda	155,900
EUROPE		**530,200**
*Germany	Serbia and Montenegro (Kosovo), Turkey, Iraq, Afghanistan, Iran	64,200
Russia	Afghanistan, Georgia	149,200
Serbia and Montenegro[1]	Croatia, Bosnia and Herzegovina	78,600

Place of asylum	Origin of most refugees	Number
AMERICAS AND THE CARIBBEAN		**475,000**
*United States	Cuba, Colombia, Haiti, China, Somalia	176,700
Venezuela	Colombia	180,100
EAST ASIA AND THE PACIFIC		**1,029,400**
China	Vietnam, North Korea	352,700
Malaysia	Philippines, Myanmar, Indonesia	152,700
Thailand	Myanmar, Laos	477,500
SOUTH AND CENTRAL ASIA		**1,953,600**
Bangladesh	Myanmar	150,100
India	Nepal, China, Sri Lanka, Myanmar, Bangladesh, Afghanistan	515,100
Nepal	Bhutan, China	130,600
Pakistan	Afghanistan	1,088,100
MIDDLE EAST		**4,855,400**
Gaza Strip	Palestinians	986,000
Iran	Afghanistan, Iraq	994,000
Iraq	Palestinians, Iran, Turkey	63,400
Jordan	Iraq, Palestinians	609,500
Lebanon	Palestinians, Iraq, Sudan	296,800
Saudi Arabia	Palestinians	240,800
Syria	Palestinians, Iraq	866,300*
West Bank	Palestinians	699,800
Yemen	Somalia	82,700
TOTAL		**12,019,700**

* Estimates vary widely in number reported. (1) Figures compiled before Montenegro declared independence.

Principal Sources of Refugees, 2005

Sources: *World Refugee Survey 2006*, U.S. Committee for Refugees

(as of Dec. 31, 2005)

Former Palestine	2,971,600*	Vietnam	305,500	Bhutan	122,300
Afghanistan	2,192,100	Colombia	257,900	Rwanda	102,500
Iraq	888,700*	Liberia	219,800*	Sri Lanka	79,100
Myanmar	727,100*	Eritrea	215,900	Philippines	67,700
Sudan	670,900	Angola	213,500	Ethiopia	63,900
Dem. Rep. of the Congo	450,800	Nepal	201,800	Tajikistan	54,200
Burundi	438,500	China	156,300	North Korea	51,400
Somalia	328,000				

*Estimates from different sources may vary significantly.

Estimated HIV Infection and Reported AIDS Cases, Year-end 2005

Source: Joint United Nations Program on HIV/AIDS, World Health Organization

The spread of AIDS (acquired immune deficiency syndrome) has had a major impact on life expectancies in sub-Saharan Africa. Life expectancy at birth has dropped to 40 years or less in nine African countries-Botswana, Central African Republic, Lesotho, Malawi, Mozambique, Rwanda, Swaziland, Zambia, and Zimbabwe, primarily as a result of AIDS.

Global HIV prevalence, or the percentage of people living with HIV/AIDS, has leveled off somewhat, due to changes in behavior and prevention programs. The numbers of people living with HIV/AIDS have continued to rise, however, because of population growth and antiretroviral therapy extending the lives of those affected. At year-end 2005, an estimated 38.6 mil worldwide were living with HIV/AIDS, up from 36.2 mil at year-end 2003. Children under age 15 accounted for 2.3 mil of those living with HIV/AIDS. HIV prevalence is increasing in certain parts of East Asia, notably China and Vietnam. In those countries, the number of adults (defined as all those over 15, per new reporting methods) and children living with HIV/AIDS rose by about one-fifth between 2003 and 2005. Sub-Saharan Africa, though, was still by far the worst affected, with about 64% of the world's total HIV/AIDS-infected population living in this region.

The Caribbean had an HIV prevalence of 1.6% among adults 15-49—the second-highest of all regions, after sub-Saharan Africa (6.1%). In the Caribbean, AIDS was the leading cause of death among adults 15-49.

Globally, just under half of all adults (+15) living with HIV/AIDS are female. However, in many regions the percentage of the HIV/AIDS infected population that is female is expected to grow, especially in Eastern Europe and Central Asia, South and South-East Asia, and Sub-Saharan Africa.

In 2005, there were an estimated total of 4.1 mil new AIDS cases. About 2.8 mil adults and children living with AIDS died in 2005.

Global spending has nearly quadrupled since 2001. In 2001, about $2.1 bil was spent on the response to HIV/AIDS (including all spending by affected people, national spending, and international and nonprofit spending). Spending increased to $8.3 bil in 2005.

Current and New HIV/AIDS Cases and Deaths by Region, Year-end 2005

Region	Current cases[1]	Percent[2]	New cases 2005	Est. deaths 2005
Sub-Saharan Africa	24,500,000	63.5	2,700,000	2,000,000
North Africa and Middle East	440,000	1.1	64,000	37,000
South and South-East Asia	7,600,000	19.7	(4)	560,000
East Asia	680,000	1.8	(4)	33,000
Oceania	78,000	0.2	7,200	3,400
Latin America	1,600,000	4.1	140,000	59,000
Caribbean	330,000	0.9	37,000	27,000
Eastern Europe and Central Asia	1,500,000	3.9	220,000	53,000
Western and Central Europe	720,000	1.9	(5)	12,000
North America	1,300,000	3.4	(5)	18,000
WORLD[3]	**38,600,000**	**100.0**	**4,100,000**	**2,800,000**

(1) Adults (+15) and children (<15) living with HIV/AIDS. (2) Percentage of total number of people worldwide living with HIV/AIDS. (3) Figures do not add to total because of rounding. (4) There were 930,000 new cases in Asia. Figures for individual regions currently not available. (5) There were 65,000 new cases in Western and Central Europe and North America. Figures for individual regions currently not available.

Top 10 Recipients of U.S. Development Aid, 2003-04

Source: Development Assistance Committee, Organization for Economic Cooperation and Development

(in millions of U.S. dollars)

Country	Avg. 2003-04	Country	Avg. 2003-04	Country	Avg. 2003-04
1. Iraq	$2,286	5. Jordan	$666	8. Colombia	$536
2. Congo, Dem. Rep.	804	6. Afghanistan	632	9. Israel	525
3. Egypt	767	7. Pakistan	590	10. Ethiopia	500
4. Russia	737				

Note: Total outlays shared by other recipient nations averaged $11.5 bil over the two-year period.

Major Foreign Development Aid Donors, 2004-05

Source: Organization for Economic Cooperation and Development; ranked by percent of GNI (Gross National Income) in 2005.

In 2005, the U.S. gave the highest total amount of development aid but ranked 21st by percent of GNI.

Country	ODA[1], as % of GNI		ODA[1] in U.S. dollars (millions)		Country	ODA[1], as % of GNI		ODA[1] in U.S. dollars (millions)	
	2005	2004	2005	2004		2005	2004	2005	2004
1. Norway	0.93	0.87	2,775	2,199	13. Germany	0.35	0.28	9,915	7,534
2. Sweden	0.92	0.78	3,280	2,722	14. Canada	0.34	0.27	3,731	2,599
3. Luxembourg	0.87	0.83	264	236	15. Spain	0.29	0.24	3,123	2,437
4. Netherlands	0.82	0.73	5,115	4,204	(G7 Nations)	0.29	0.22	78,920	57,978
5. Denmark	0.81	0.85	2,107	2,037	Italy	0.29	0.15	5,053	2,462
6. Belgium	0.53	0.41	1,975	1,463	17. Japan	0.28	0.19	13,101	8,923
7. Austria	0.52	0.23	1,552	678	18. New Zealand	0.27	0.23	274	212
8. United Kingdom	0.48	0.36	10,754	7,883	19. Australia	0.25	0.25	1,666	1,460
9. France	0.47	0.41	10,059	8,473	20. Greece	0.24	0.23	535	465
Finland	0.47	0.37	897	680	21. United States	0.22	0.17	27,457	19,705
11. Switzerland	0.44	0.41	1,771	1,545	22. Portugal	0.21	0.63	367	1,031
12. Ireland	0.41	0.39	692	607					

(1) ODA = Official Development Assistance.

Nuclear Powers of the World

As of Oct. 2006, 8 countries were acknowledged nuclear powers: **Britain, France, China, India, Pakistan, Russia, North Korea,** and the **United States**. In addition, the Defense Intelligence Agency estimates **Israel** to have a nuclear arsenal of 60 to 80 warheads, and **Iran** was suspected of developing nuclear weapons, despite strong international pressure for it to desist. More than 40 nations have the knowledge or technology needed to produce nuclear weapons. All have signed the Nuclear Non-Proliferation Treaty (NPT) except for Israel, India, and Pakistan. North Korea withdrew in Jan. 2003.

In a draft accord reached at 6-party talks with China, Japan, Russia, South Korea, and the U.S. on Sept. 19, 2005, North Korea agreed to scrap its nuclear weapons program in exchange for aid. Left unresolved was Pyongyang's continuing demand for international donors to provide light-water nuclear reactors for "peaceful uses." North Korea has re-fused to resume six-nation talks, however, citing financial restrictions placed on it by banks under pressure from the U.S. North Korea test-fired 7 ballistic missiles, July 5, 2006, including a long-range Taepodong-2 missile that failed less than 2 minutes into its flight, and 6 short- and medium-range rockets that fell into the Sea of Japan. In Oct., the country said that it was preparing to conduct its first nuclear test.

Several countries have abandoned their nuclear ambitions. **South Africa** announced in 1993 that it had built 7 fission weapons (1 was under construction) but had dismantled all of them. In the 1980s, **Argentina** and **Brazil** had active nuclear weapons programs, but they abandoned them by mutual treaty and signed the NPT. After the Soviet Union dissolved in 1993, **Belarus, Kazakhstan**, and **Ukraine** joined the NPT and allowed Russia to remove its nuclear weapons located there.

Estimated Numbers of Nuclear Weapons by Country, 1945-2006[1]

Source: Natural Resources Defense Council; Carnegie Endowment for Intl. Peace; *Bulletin of the Atomic Scientists*

End Year	United States	U.S.S.R. Russia	United Kingdom	France	China	India	Pakistan	Total
1945	6	—	—	—	—	—	—	6
1950	369	5	—	—	—	—	—	374
1960	20,434	1,605	30	—	—	—	—	22,069
1970	26,662	11,643	280	36	75	—	—	38,696
1980	24,304	30,062	350	250	280	—	—	55,246
1990	21,004	37,000	300	505	430	—	—	59,239
1995	12,144	27,000	300	500	400	—	—	40,344
2000	10,577	21,000	185	470	400	—	—	32,632
2006	10,104[2]	16,000[3]	200	350	200	50-60	40-50	26,854

(1) In addition to these nations, Israel and North Korea are believed to have nuclear weapons. (2) Only about 5,735 are considered active or operational. The rest are categorized as reserve or inactive. (3) Only about 5,830 are considered operational. The rest are marked for dismantlement.

Major International Organizations

African Union (AU), inaugurated July 9, 2002, in Durban, South Africa, following disbanding of the Organization of African Unity, and consisting of the same 53 members, i.e., all countries of Africa except Morocco, which left the OAU after it admitted Western Sahara, a territory claimed by Morocco. The new organization is intended to focus on achieving greater socioeconomic integration and unity among its member states. The founders provided for a peer review committee to oversee member states' adherence to standards of good government, respect for human rights, and financial transparency. The AU's founding document authorized the organization to intervene to stop genocide, war crimes, or human rights abuses within individual member nations. **Headquarters:** Addis Ababa, Ethiopia. **Website:** www.africa-union.org

Asia-Pacific Economic Cooperation (APEC), founded Nov. 1989 as a forum to further cooperation on trade and investment between nations of the region and the rest of the world. Members in 2006 were Australia, Brunei, Canada, Chile, China, Hong Kong, Indonesia, Japan, Malaysia, Mexico, New Zealand, Papua New Guinea, Peru, Philippines, Russia, Singapore, South Korea, Taiwan, Thailand, the U.S., and Vietnam. **Headquarters:** Singapore. **Website:** www.apec.org

Association of Southeast Asian Nations (ASEAN), formed Aug. 8, 1967, to promote economic, social, and cultural cooperation and development among states of the Southeast Asian region. Members in 2006 were Brunei, Cambodia, Indonesia, Laos, Malaysia, Myanmar, Philippines, Singapore, Thailand, and Vietnam. **Headquarters:** Jakarta, Indonesia. **Website:** www.aseansec.org

Caribbean Community and Common Market (CARICOM), established Aug. 1, 1973. Its aim is to increase cooperation in economics, health, education, culture, science and technology, and tax administration, as well as the coordination of foreign policy. Members in 2006 were Antigua and Barbuda, Bahamas, Barbados, Belize, Dominica, Grenada, Guyana, Haiti, Jamaica, Montserrat, Saint Kitts and Nevis, Saint Lucia, Saint Vincent and the Grenadines, Suriname, and Trinidad and Tobago. Associate members in 2006 were Anguilla, Bermuda, British Virgin Islands, Cayman Islands, and Turks and Caicos Islands. **Headquarters:** Georgetown, Guyana. **Website:** www.caricom.org

The Commonwealth, originally called the British Commonwealth of Nations, then the Commonwealth of Nations is an association of nations and dependencies that were once parts of the former British Empire. The British monarch is the symbolic head of the Commonwealth.

There are 53 independent nations in the Commonwealth. As of 2006, regular members included the United Kingdom and 15 other nations recognizing the British monarch, represented by a governor-general, as their head of state: Antigua and Barbuda, Australia, The Bahamas, Barbados, Belize, Canada, Grenada, Jamaica, New Zealand, Papua New Guinea, Saint Kitts and Nevis, Saint Lucia, Saint Vincent and the Grenadines, the Solomon Islands, and Tuvalu. Also members in good standing were 37 countries with their own heads of state: Bangladesh, Botswana, Brunei, Cameroon, Cyprus, Dominica, Fiji, The Gambia, Ghana, Guyana, India, Kenya, Kiribati, Lesotho, Malawi, Malaysia, Maldives, Malta, Mauritius, Mozambique (the only member never part of the British Empire), Namibia, Nauru, Nigeria, Pakistan, Samoa, Seychelles, Sierra Leone, Singapore, South Africa, Sri Lanka, Swaziland, Tanzania, Tonga, Trinidad and Tobago, Uganda, Vanuatu, and Zambia.

Pakistan was suspended from the councils of the Commonwealth in Oct. 1999, following a military coup, but regained its member status Mar. 22, 2004. Zimbabwe was suspended in Mar. 2002, following election and land redistribution controversies; Zimbabwe withdrew from the Commonwealth, Dec. 7, 2003. The Commonwealth facilitates consultation among members through meetings of ministers and through a permanent secretariat. **Headquarters:** London, UK. **Website:** www.thecommonwealth.org

Commonwealth of Independent States (CIS), an alliance established in Dec. 1991, made up of former Soviet constituent republics. Members in 2006 were Armenia, Azerbaijan, Belarus, Georgia, Kazakhstan, Kyrgyzstan, Moldova, Russia, Tajikistan, Turkmenistan, Ukraine, and Uzbekistan. Policy is set through coordinating bodies such as the Council of the Heads of States and Council of the

Heads of Governments. **Headquarters:** Minsk, Belarus. **Website:** www.cis.minsk.by

European Free Trade Association (EFTA), created May 3, 1960, to promote expansion of free trade. By Dec. 31, 1966, tariffs and quotas between member nations had been eliminated. Members entered into free trade agreements with the EU in 1972 and 1973. In 1992, EFTA and EU agreed to create a single market—with free flow of goods, services, capital, and labor—among nations of the 2 organizations. Members in 2006 were Iceland, Liechtenstein, Norway, and Switzerland. Many former EFTA members are now EU members. **Headquarters:** Geneva, Switzerland. **Website:** www.efta.int

European Union (EU), known as the European Community (EC) until 1994; the name covers 3 organizations with common membership: the European Economic Community (Common Market), the European Coal and Steel Community, and the European Atomic Energy Community (Euratom). A merger of the 3 communities' executives went into effect July 1, 1967. As of Sept. 2006, there were 25 EU members. These included the 12 original members (Belgium, Denmark, France, Germany, Greece, Ireland, Italy, Luxembourg, Netherlands, Portugal, Spain, and UK), 3 states that entered Jan. 1, 1995 (Austria, Finland, and Sweden), and 10 members that joined on May 1, 2004 (Cyprus, Czech Republic, Estonia, Hungary, Latvia, Lithuania, Malta, Poland, Slovakia, and Slovenia.). Some 70 nations in Africa, the Caribbean, and the Pacific are affiliated under the Lomé Convention. **Headquarters:** Brussels, Belgium. **Website:** europa.eu.int

The EU aims to integrate the economies, coordinate social developments, and bring about political union of the member states. The Council of the Union, European Commission, European Parliament, and European Courts of Justice and of Auditors comprise the permanent structure. Effective Dec. 31, 1992, there are no restrictions on the movement of goods, services, capital, workers, and tourists within the EU. There are also common agricultural, fisheries, and nuclear research policies.

Leaders of the member nations (12 at the time), meeting Dec. 9-11, 1991, in Maastricht, the Netherlands, committed the organization to launching a common currency (the euro) by 1999; sought to establish common foreign policies; laid the groundwork for a common defense policy; gave the organization a leading role in social policy (Britain was not included in this plan); pledged increased aid for poorer member nations; and slightly increased the powers of the 567-member European Parliament. The treaties went into effect Nov. 1, 1993, following ratification by all 12 members.

In June 1998 the European Central Bank was established. In Jan. 1999, 11 of the then-15 EU countries began using the euro for some purposes: Austria, Belgium, Finland, France, Germany, Ireland, Italy, Luxembourg, Netherlands, Portugal, and Spain. By Feb. 2002, national currencies in these 11 countries and Greece were removed from circulation and replaced with the euro as the only currency of legal tender. EU peacekeeping forces replaced NATO troops in Macedonia, Mar. 31, 2003, the first such mission for the organization.

In July 2005, Luxembourg became the 13th EU member to ratify the EU constitution, but the constitution was rejected in May and June by voters in France and the Netherlands. Some other EU nations were deferring action on ratifying it. In June 2006, formal membership talks began with Turkey and Croatia; the EU signed a preliminary agreement with Albania regarding the path to membership. Slovenia will enter the 12-member euro currency zone in 2007. Lithuania's application to join, however, was rejected in June.

Group of Eight (G-8), established Sept. 22, 1985; forum of 7 major industrial democracies (Canada, France, Germany, Italy, Japan, the UK, and U.S.) and (later) Russia, which meet periodically to discuss economic and other issues. At its annual summit in May 1998, the name was changed to G-8 from G-7. The 7 were still free to meet without Russia on some issues, especially those relating to global finance. The presidency rotates yearly among the members. The 2004 summit was hosted in the U.S. at Sea Island, GA, June 8-10. The 2005 summit was held July 6-8 in Perthshire,

Scotland. It was interrupted by the July 7 bombings in London but concluded as scheduled. The 2006 summit was in St. Petersburg, Russia, July 15-17. The 2007 summit will take place in Heiligendamm, Germany.

International Criminal Police Organization (Interpol), created June 13, 1956, to promote mutual assistance among all police authorities within the limits of the law existing in the different countries. There were 186 members (independent nations), plus 11 sub-bureaus (dependencies) in 2006. **Headquarters:** Lyon, France. **Website:** www.interpol.com

League of Arab States (Arab League), created Mar. 22, 1945. The League promotes economic, social, political, and military cooperation, mediates disputes, and represents Arab states in certain international negotiations. Members in 2006 were Algeria, Bahrain, Comoros, Djibouti, Egypt, Iraq, Jordan, Kuwait, Lebanon, Libya, Mauritania, Morocco, Oman, Palestine (considered an independent state by the League), Qatar, Saudi Arabia, Somalia, Sudan, Syria, Tunisia, United Arab Emirates, and Yemen. **Headquarters:** Cairo, Egypt. **Website:** www.arableagueonline.org

North Atlantic Treaty Organization (NATO), created by treaty (signed Apr. 4, 1949; in effect Aug. 24, 1949). Members in 2006 included Belgium, Bulgaria, Canada, Czech Republic, Denmark, Estonia, France, Germany, Greece, Hungary, Iceland, Italy, Latvia, Lithuania, Luxembourg, Netherlands, Norway, Poland, Portugal, Romania, Slovakia, Slovenia, Spain, Turkey, UK, and U.S. Of these, 7 states—Bulgaria, Estonia, Latvia, Lithuania, Romania, Slovakia, and Slovenia—joined the alliance in 2004. All are former Warsaw Pact nations from Eastern Europe. That marked the fifth time NATO increased its membership and was the single largest expansion.

Members have agreed to settle disputes by peaceful means, to develop their capacity to resist armed attack, to regard an attack on one as an attack on all, and to take necessary action to repel an attack under Article 51 of the UN Charter. **Headquarters:** Brussels, Belgium. **Website:** www.nato.int

The NATO structure consists of the North Atlantic Council (NAC), the Defense Planning Committee, the Military Committee (realigned in June 2003 and consisting of 2 commands: Allied Command Operations and Allied Command Transformation), the Nuclear Planning Group, and the Canada-U.S. Regional Planning Group. France detached itself from the military command structure in 1966.

With the end of the cold war in the early 1990s, members put greater stress on political action and on creating a rapid deployment force to react to local crises. By the mid-1990s, 27 nations, including Russia and other former Soviet republics, had joined with NATO in the so-called Partnership for Peace (PfP; drafted Dec. 1993), which provided for limited joint military exercises, peace-keeping missions, and information exchange. NATO has proceeded gradually toward extending full membership to former Eastern bloc nations. On Mar. 12, 1999, 3 former Warsaw Pact members, Hungary, Poland, and the Czech Republic, formally became members. NATO and Russia signed a cooperation pact May 28, 2002, forming a NATO-Russia Council, and NATO invited 7 former eastern-bloc nations to join the alliance, Nov. 21.

In Dec. 1995, a NATO-led multinational force (SFOR) was deployed to help keep the peace in Bosnia and Herzegovina; in 1999, another force (KFOR) was deployed in Kosovo.

Following the terrorist attacks on the U.S., the NATO Council agreed, Sept. 12, 2001, to invoke for the first time Article 5 of the treaty, which stipulates mutual defense of alliance members. NATO assumed control of the International Security Assistance Force in Afghanistan (ISAF), Aug. 2003, marking the first time NATO led a mission outside Europe. As of Sept. 2006, ISAF troops from 37 countries numbered about 20,000.

Organization of American States (OAS), formed in Bogotá, Colombia, Apr. 30, 1948. It has a Permanent Council, Inter-American Council for Integral Development, Juridical Committee, and Commission on Human Rights. The Permanent Council can call meetings of foreign ministers to deal with urgent security matters. A General Assembly meets annually.

Members in 2006 were Antigua and Barbuda, Argentina, The Bahamas, Barbados, Belize, Bolivia, Brazil, Canada, Chile, Colombia, Costa Rica, Cuba, Dominica, Dominican Republic, Ecuador, El Salvador, Grenada, Guatemala, Guyana, Haiti, Honduras, Jamaica, Mexico, Nicaragua, Panama, Paraguay, Peru, Saint Kitts and Nevis, Saint Lucia, Saint Vincent and the Grenadines, Suriname, Trinidad and Tobago, U.S., Uruguay, and Venezuela. In 1962, the OAS barred Cuba from participation in activities though it retains membership. **Headquarters:** Washington, DC. **Website:** www.oas.org

Organization for Economic Cooperation and Development (OECD), established Dec. 14, 1960, to promote the economic and social welfare of all its member countries and to stimulate efforts on behalf of developing nations. The OECD also collects and disseminates economic and environmental information. Members in 2006 were Australia, Austria, Belgium, Canada, Czech Republic, Denmark, Finland, France, Germany, Greece, Hungary, Iceland, Ireland, Italy, Japan, Luxembourg, Mexico, Netherlands, New Zealand, Norway, Poland, Portugal, Slovakia, South Korea, Spain, Sweden, Switzerland, Turkey, UK, and the U.S. **Headquarters:** Paris, France. **Website:** www.oecd.org

Organization of Petroleum Exporting Countries (OPEC), created Sept. 14, 1960. This group made up of most—but not all—the major petroleum exporting nations seeks to stabilize the oil market and set world oil prices by controlling production. Members in 2006 were Algeria, Indonesia, Iran, Iraq, Kuwait, Libya, Nigeria, Qatar, Saudi Arabia, United Arab Emirates, and Venezuela. **Headquarters:** Vienna, Austria. **Website:** www.opec.org

Organization for Security and Cooperation in Europe (OSCE), established in 1972 as the Conference on Security and Cooperation in Europe; name adopted Jan. 1, 1995. The group, formed by NATO and Warsaw Pact members, seeks improved East-West relations through a commitment to nonaggression and human rights as well as cooperation in economics, science and technology, cultural exchange, and environmental protection. There were 56 member states in 2006. **Headquarters:** Vienna, Austria. **Website:** www.osce.org

United Nations

The 61st regular session of the United Nations General Assembly opened Sept. 12, 2006, attended by world leaders and other delegates from 192 nations.

The UN headquarters is in New York, NY, between First Ave. and Roosevelt Dr. and E. 42nd St. and E. 48th St.

The UN consists of 6 main organs: the General Assembly, Security Council, Secretariat, Economic and Social Council, Trusteeship Council, and the International Court of Justice. The UN family is much larger, encompassing 15 agencies and several programs and bodies.

The UN Dept. of Public Information maintains a news service, available online at www.un.org/news. It also publishes the *UN Chronicle*, available at www.un.org/Pubs/chronicle. The UN has a post office originating its own stamps.

Proposals to establish an organization of nations for maintenance of world peace led to the convening of the United Nations Conference on International Organization in San Francisco, Apr. 25-June 26, 1945, where the UN charter was drawn. It was signed June 26 by 50 nations and by Poland, one of the original 51 members, on Oct. 15, 1945. It went into effect Oct. 24, 1945, upon ratification by the permanent members of the Security Council and a majority of the other signatories.

Purposes. To maintain international peace and security; to develop friendly relations among nations; to achieve international cooperation in solving economic, social, cultural, and humanitarian problems and in promoting respect for human rights and basic freedoms; to be a center for harmonizing the actions of nations in attaining these common ends.

Visitors to the UN. The headquarters are open to the public every day except Thanksgiving, Christmas, New Year's holidays, Eid al-Fitr (Oct. 24, 2006), and Eid al-Adha (observance, Dec. 29, 2006). Guided tours are given about every half hour from 9:30 AM to 4:45 PM weekdays; 10 AM to 4:30 PM weekends. The UN is closed weekends in Jan. and Feb.

Groups of 12 or more should write to the Group Programmes Unit, Room GA-56, United Nations, New York, NY 10017, e-mail unitg@un.org, or telephone (212) 963-TOUR. Children under 5 not permitted on tours.

Six Main Organs of the United Nations

The United Nations consists of 6 principal organs, 15 agencies, and many programs and other bodies. The 6 principal organs are the General Assembly, the Security Council, the Secretariat, the Economic and Social Council, the Trusteeship Council, and the Intl. Court of Justice.

General Assembly. The General Assembly is composed of representatives of all the member nations. Each nation is entitled to one vote. The General Assembly meets in regular annual sessions and in special session when convoked at the request of the Security Council or a majority of UN members. On important questions a two-thirds majority of members present and voting is required; on other questions a simple majority is sufficient.

The General Assembly must approve the UN budget and apportion expenses among members. A member in arrears can lose its vote if the amount of arrears equals or exceeds the amount of the contributions due for the preceding 2 full years. The General Assembly approved a total budget for the biennium 2006-07 of $3.79 bil. **Website:** www.un.org/ga

Security Council. The Security Council consists of 15 members, 5 with permanent seats. The remaining 10 are elected for 2-year terms by the General Assembly.

The permanent members of the Council are China, France, Russia, United Kingdom, and the United States. Nonpermanent members with terms expiring Dec. 31, 2006, are Argentina, Denmark, Greece, Japan, Tanzania; those with terms expiring Dec. 31, 2007, are Republic of Congo, Ghana, Peru, Qatar, Slovakia.

The Security Council has the primary responsibility within the UN for maintaining international peace and security. The Council may investigate any dispute that threatens international peace and security.

Any member of the UN at UN headquarters may, if invited by the Council, participate in its discussions, and a nation not a member of the UN may appear if it is a party to a dispute. Decisions on procedural questions are made by an affirmative vote of 9 members. On all other matters the affirmative vote of 9 members must include the concurring votes of all permanent members (giving them veto power). A party to a dispute must refrain from voting.

The Security Council directs the various peacekeeping forces deployed throughout the world. **Website:** www.un.org/docs/sc

Secretariat. The Secretariat has an international staff of about 8,900 that carries out the day-to-day operations of the UN and is headed by the secretary general. The secretary general is the chief administrative officer of the UN, and is appointed by the General Assembly, on the recommendation of the Security Council, for a five-year, renewable term. The Secretary General reports to the General Assembly and may bring to the attention of the Security Council any matter that threatens international peace. **Website:** www.un.org/documents/st.htm

Economic and Social Council. The Economic and Social Council consists of 54 members elected by the General Assembly for 3-year terms. The council is responsible for carrying out UN functions with regard to international economic, social, cultural, educational, health, and related matters. It meets once a year. **Website:** www.un.org/esa

Trusteeship Council. Made up of the 5 permanent members of the Security Council. The administration of trust territories was under UN supervision; however, all 11 Trust Territories have attained their right to self-determination. The Council formally suspended its work Nov. 1, 1994.

International Court of Justice (World Court). The International Court of Justice is the principal judicial organ of the UN. All members are ipso facto parties to the statute of the Court. The Court has jurisdiction over cases the parties submit to it and matters especially provided for in the charter or in treaties. It gives advisory opinions and renders judgments. In disputes between nations, the Court's decisions are binding only between parties concerned and in respect to a particular dispute. If any party to a case fails to heed a judgment, the other party may have recourse to the Security Council.

The 15 judges are elected for 9-year terms by the General Assembly and the Security Council. Retiring judges are eligible for reelection. The Court remains permanently in session, except during vacations. All questions are decided by a majority. The International Court of Justice sits in The Hague, Netherlands. **Website:** www.icj-cij.org

The text of the **UN Charter** may be obtained from the Public Inquiries Unit, Department of Public Information, United Nations, New York, NY 10017. (212) 963-4475. **Website:** www.un.org/aboutun/charter/index.html

United Nations Secretaries General

Took Office	Secretary, Nation	Took Office	Secretary, Nation	Took Office	Secretary, Nation
1946	Trygve Lie, Norway	1972	Kurt Waldheim, Austria	1992	Boutros Boutros-Ghali, Egypt
1953	Dag Hammarskjöld, Sweden	1982	Javier Pérez de Cuéllar, Peru	1997	Kofi Annan, Ghana
1961	U Thant, Burma				

Selected Specialized and Related Agencies

These specialized and related agencies are autonomous, with their own memberships and organs, and at the same time have a functional relationship or working agreement with the UN (headquarters), except for UNICEF and UNHCR, which report directly to the Economic and Social Council and to the General Assembly.

Food and Agriculture Organization (FAO) helps developing countries modernize farms, forests, and fisheries; improves food distribution and marketing; and educates on nutrition. (Viale delle Terme di Caracalla, 00100 Rome, Italy) **Website:** www.fao.org

International Atomic Energy Agency (IAEA) aims to promote safe, peaceful uses of atomic energy. (P.O. Box 100, Wagramer Strasse 5, A-1400, Vienna, Austria) **Website:** www.iaea.org

International Civil Aviation Org. (ICAO) promotes international civil aviation standards and regulations. (999 University St., Montreal, Quebec H3C 5H7, Canada) **Website:** www.icao.int

International Fund for Agricultural Development (IFAD) seeks to alleviate poverty in rural areas in developing countries. (Via del Serafico, 107, 00142 Rome, Italy) **Website:** www.ifad.org

International Labor Org. (ILO) aims to promote employment practices, the improvement of labor conditions, social security, and vocational training. (4, route des Morillons, CH-1211 Geneva 22, Switzerland) **Website:** www.ilo.org

International Maritime Org. (IMO) aims to promote cooperation on technical matters affecting international shipping. (4 Albert Embankment, London, SE1 7SR, UK) **Website:** www.imo.org

International Monetary Fund (IMF) aims to promote international monetary cooperation, currency stabilization, and the expansion of international trade. (700 19th St. NW, Washington, DC 20431) **Website:** www.imf.org

International Telecommunication Union (ITU) regulates all aspects of global communication, including setting standards for radio, telegraph, telephone, and space radio-communications, and allocating radio frequencies. (Place des Nations, 1211 Geneva 20, Switzerland) **Website:** www.itu.int

Office of the High Commissioner for Human Rights (OHCHR) seeks to uphold human rights standards by monitoring areas of concern, investigating abuses, and working with gov. institutions to improve conditions. (1211 Geneva 10, Switzerland) **Website:** www.ohchr.org

United Nations Children's Fund (UNICEF) provides financial aid and development assistance to programs for children and mothers in developing countries. (3 United Nations Plaza, New York, NY 10017) **Website:** www.unicef.org

United Nations Educational, Scientific, and Cultural Org. (UNESCO) aims to promote collaboration among nations through education, science, and culture. After a 19-year boycott, the United States rejoined the organization on Sept. 29, 2003. (7, Place de Fontenoy, 75352 Paris 07 SP, France) **Website:** www.unesco.org

United Nations High Commissioner for Refugees (UNHCR) provides essential assistance to refugees. (Case Postale 2500, CH-1211 Genève 2 Dépôt, Switzerland) **Website:** www.unhcr.ch

United Nations Industrial Development Org. (UNIDO) helps developing nations and those in transition pursue sustainable industrial development while promoting international industrial cooperation. (Vienna Intl. Centre, P.O. Box 300, Wagramerstr. 5, A-1400 Vienna, Austria) **Website:** www.unido.org

Universal Postal Union (UPU) aims to perfect postal services and promote international collaboration. (Case Postale 13, 3000 Berne 15, Switzerland) **Website:** www.upu.int

World Bank Group encompasses 2 development institutions and 3 affiliates focused on worldwide poverty reduction. The **International Bank for Reconstruction and Development (IBRD)** provides loans and technical assistance for projects in developing member countries and encourages cofinancing for projects from other public and private sources. The **International Development Association (IDA)** provides funds for development projects on concessionary terms to the poorer developing member countries. The **International Finance Corporation (IFC)** promotes the growth of the private sector in developing member countries; encourages the development of local capital markets; and stimulates the international flow of private capital. The **Multilateral Investment Guarantee Agency (MIGA)** promotes investment in developing countries; guarantees investments to protect investors from noncommercial risks, such as nationalization; and advises governments on attracting private investment. The **International Center for Settlement of Investment Disputes (ICSID)** provides conciliation and arbitration services for disputes between foreign investors and host governments that arise out of an investment. (1818 H St. NW, Washington, DC 20433) **Website:** www.worldbank.org

World Health Org. (WHO) aims to aid the attainment of the highest possible level of health. (Avenue Appia 20, CH-1211 Geneva 27, Switzerland) **Website:** www.who.int

World Intellectual Property Org. (WIPO) seeks to protect, through international cooperation, literary, industrial, scientific, and artistic works. (34, Chemin des Colombettes, 1211 Geneva 20, Switzerland) **Website:** www.wipo.int

World Meteorological Org. (WMO) aims to coordinate and improve world meteorological work. (7bis, Avenue de la Paix, CP 2300, CH-1211 Geneva 2, Switzerland) **Website:** www.wmo.ch

World Tourism Org. (UNWTO) promotes responsible, sustainable, and universally accessible tourism with the aim of fostering economic development and international understanding. (Capitán Haya 42, 28020 Madrid, Spain) **Website:** www.unwto.org

World Trade Org. (WTO) replaces the General Agreement on Tariffs and Trade (GATT). It administers trade agreements and treaties between nations, examines the trade regimes of members, keeps track of various trade measures and statistics, and attempts to settle trade disputes. (Centre William Rappard, Rue de Lausanne 154, CH-1211 Geneva 21, Switzerland) **Website:** www.wto.org

Roster of the United Nations

The 192 members of the United Nations, with the years in which they became members; as of June 2006.

Member	Year	Member	Year	Member	Year	Member	Year
Afghanistan	1946	Dominica	1978	Libya	1955	Saint Vincent and the	
Albania	1955	Dominican Republic	1945	Liechtenstein	1990	Grenadines	1980
Algeria	1962	Ecuador	1945	Lithuania	1991	Samoa (formerly	
Andorra	1993	Egypt[3]	1945	Luxembourg	1945	Western Samoa)	1976
Angola	1976	El Salvador	1945	Macedonia[5]	1993	San Marino	1992
Antigua and Barbuda	1981	Equatorial Guinea	1968	Madagascar	1960	São Tomé and Príncipe	1975
Argentina	1945	Eritrea	1993	Malawi	1964	Saudi Arabia	1945
Armenia	1992	Estonia	1991	Malaysia[6]	1957	Senegal	1960
Australia	1945	Ethiopia	1945	Maldives	1965	Serbia[8,9]	1945
Austria	1955	Fiji	1970	Mali	1960	Seychelles	1976
Azerbaijan	1992	Finland	1955	Malta	1964	Sierra Leone	1961
Bahamas	1973	France	1945	Marshall Islands	1991	Singapore[6]	1965
Bahrain	1971	Gabon	1960	Mauritania	1961	Slovakia[2]	1993
Bangladesh	1974	Gambia, The	1965	Mauritius	1968	Slovenia	1992
Barbados	1966	Georgia	1992	Mexico	1945	Solomon Islands	1978
Belarus	1945	Germany	1973	Micronesia	1991	Somalia	1960
Belgium	1945	Ghana	1957	Moldova	1992	South Africa[10]	1945
Belize	1981	Greece	1945	Monaco	1993	Spain	1955
Benin	1960	Grenada	1974	Mongolia	1961	Sri Lanka	1955
Bhutan	1971	Guatemala	1945	Montenegro[8,9]	2006	Sudan	1956
Bolivia	1945	Guinea	1958	Morocco	1956	Suriname	1975
Bosnia & Herzegovina	1992	Guinea-Bissau	1974	Mozambique	1975	Swaziland	1968
Botswana	1966	Guyana	1966	Myanmar (Burma)	1948	Sweden	1946
Brazil	1945	Haiti	1945	Namibia	1990	Switzerland	2002
Brunei	1984	Honduras	1945	Nauru	1999	Syria[3]	1945
Bulgaria	1955	Hungary	1955	Nepal	1955	Tajikistan	1992
Burkina Faso	1960	Iceland	1946	Netherlands	1945	Tanzania[11]	1961
Burundi	1962	India	1945	New Zealand	1945	Thailand	1946
Cambodia	1955	Indonesia[4]	1950	Nicaragua	1945	Timor-Leste	2002
Cameroon	1960	Iran	1945	Niger	1960	Togo	1960
Canada	1945	Iraq	1945	Nigeria	1960	Tonga	1999
Cape Verde	1975	Ireland	1955	Norway	1945	Trinidad and Tobago	1962
Central African Rep.	1960	Israel	1949	Oman	1971	Tunisia	1956
Chad	1960	Italy	1955	Pakistan	1947	Turkey	1945
Chile	1945	Jamaica	1962	Palau	1994	Turkmenistan	1992
China[1]	1945	Japan	1956	Panama	1945	Tuvalu	2000
Colombia	1945	Jordan	1955	Papua New Guinea	1975	Uganda	1962
Comoros	1975	Kazakhstan	1992	Paraguay	1945	Ukraine	1945
Congo, Democratic	1960	Kenya	1963	Peru	1945	United Arab Emirates	1971
Rep. of the (Zaire)		Kiribati	1999	Philippines	1945	United Kingdom	1945
Congo, Republic of the	1960	Korea, North	1991	Poland	1945	United States	1945
Costa Rica	1945	Korea, South	1991	Portugal	1955	Uruguay	1945
Côte d'Ivoire	1960	Kuwait	1963	Qatar	1971	Uzbekistan	1992
Croatia	1992	Kyrgyzstan	1992	Romania	1955	Vanuatu	1981
Cuba	1945	Laos	1955	Russia[7]	1945	Venezuela	1945
Cyprus	1960	Latvia	1991	Rwanda	1962	Vietnam	1977
Czech Republic[2]	1993	Lebanon	1945	Saint Kitts and Nevis	1983	Yemen[12]	1947
Denmark	1945	Lesotho	1966	Saint Lucia	1979	Zambia	1964
Djibouti	1977	Liberia	1945			Zimbabwe	1980

(1) The General Assembly voted in 1971 to expel the Chinese government in Taiwan and admit the Beijing government. (2) Czechoslovakia, which split into Czech Republic and Slovakia on Jan. 1, 1993, was a UN member from 1945 to 1992. (3) Egypt and Syria were original members. In 1958, the United Arab Republic was established by a union of Egypt and Syria and continued as one single member of the UN. In 1961, Syria resumed its separate membership. (4) Indonesia withdrew from the UN in 1965 and rejoined in 1966. (5) Admitted under the provisional name of The Former Yugoslav Republic of Macedonia. (6) Malaya joined the UN in 1957. In 1963, its name was changed to Malaysia following the accession of Singapore, Sabah, and Sarawak. Singapore became an independent UN member in 1965. (7) The USSR was an original member from 1945. After the USSR's dissolution in 1991, Russia informed the UN it would be continuing the USSR's membership in the Security Council and all other UN organs with the support of the Commonwealth of Independent States (comprising most of the former Soviet republics). (8) The Socialist Federal Republic of Yugoslavia became a member in 1945. After 4 of its 6 republics (Bosnia and Herzegovina, Croatia, Macedonia, and Slovenia) declared independence in 1991-92, the 2 remaining republics, Montenegro and Serbia, reconstituted themselves as the Federal Republic of Yugoslavia, which assumed Yugoslavia's UN seat Apr. 8, 1992. In Sept. 1992, the General Assembly decided the Federal Republic of Yugoslavia could not automatically take the seat of the former Yugoslavia. Membership was granted in Nov. 2000 by a vote of the General Assembly. In Feb. 2003, Yugoslavia changed its name to Serbia and Montenegro. (9) After Montenegro declared independence in June 2006, Serbia continued the membership of the State Union of Serbia and Montenegro. Montenegro was admitted as a UN member later the same month. (10) In June 1994, the General Assembly admitted the South African delegation, after it was suspended from participation in 1974 because of apartheid. (11) Tanganyika was a member from 1961 and Zanzibar from 1963. Following the ratification in 1964 of Articles of Union between Tanganyika and Zanzibar, the United Republic of Tanganyika and Zanzibar continued as a single member of the UN, later changing its name to United Republic of Tanzania. (12) The Yemen Arab Republic was admitted in 1947; the People's Republic of Yemen, in 1967. The 2 nations merged in 1990.
NOTE: Vatican City and China (Taiwan) are not members. Vatican City is a permanent observer. Taiwan's bid for UN membership was rejected for the 14th consecutive year on Sept. 12, 2006.

U.S. Representatives to the United Nations

The U.S. Representative to the United Nations is the chief of the U.S. Mission to the United Nations in New York and holds the rank and status of Ambassador Extraordinary and Plenipotentiary (A.E.P.). Year given is the year each took office.

Year	Representative	Year	Representative	Year	Representative	Year	Representative
1946	Edward R. Stettinius, Jr.	1968	James Russell Wiggins	1981	Jeane J. Kirkpatrick	2001	James B. Cunningham
1946	Herschel V. Johnson (act.)	1969	Charles W. Yost	1985	Vernon A. Walters		(act.)
1947	Warren R. Austin	1971	George H. W. Bush	1989	Thomas R. Pickering	2001	John D. Negroponte
1953	Henry Cabot Lodge, Jr.	1973	John A. Scali	1992	Edward J. Perkins	2004	John C. Danforth
1960	James J. Wadsworth	1975	Daniel P. Moynihan	1993	Madeleine K. Albright	2005	Anne W. Patterson (act.)
1961	Adlai E. Stevenson	1976	William W. Scranton	1997	Bill Richardson	2005	John R. Bolton
1965	Arthur J. Goldberg	1977	Andrew Young	1998	A. Peter Burleigh (act.)		
1968	George W. Ball	1979	Donald McHenry	1999	Richard C. Holbrooke		

Ongoing UN Peacekeeping Missions, 2006

Source: United Nations Cartographic Section

(Year given is the year each mission began operation)

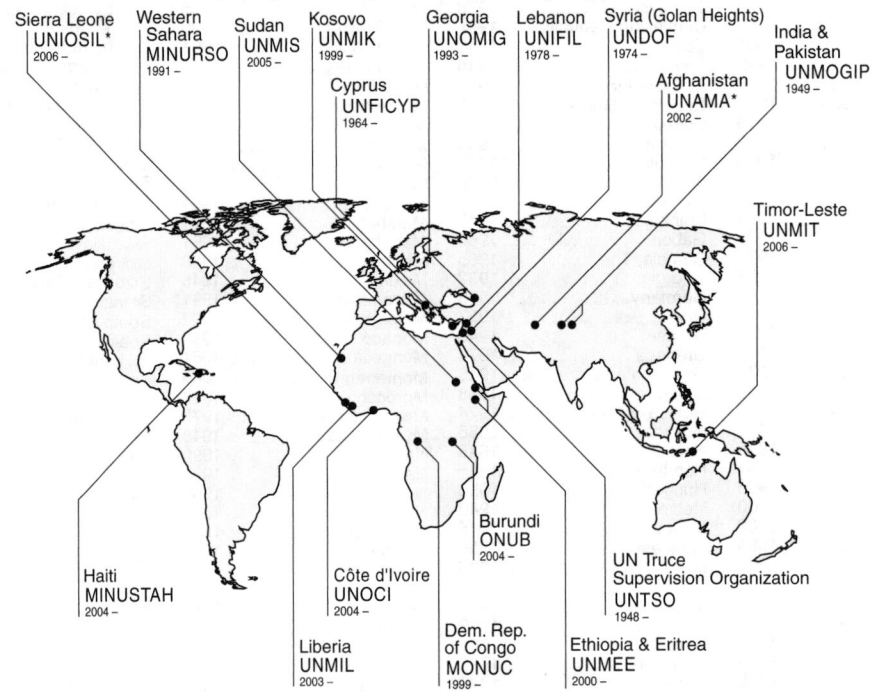

*Political mission directed and supported by the Department of Peacekeeping Operations.

Peacekeeping Personnel

As of Aug. 31, 2006

Military personnel and civilian police serving in peacekeeping operations	71,841[1]
Countries contributing military personnel and civilian police	108[1]
International civilian personnel	4,530[1]
Local civilian personnel	9,074[1]
Total number of fatalities in peacekeeping operations since 1948	2,298[2]

(1) Not including statistics for 2 special political and/or peacebuilding missions (the UNAMA and UNIOSIL). (2) Inc. fatalities for all UN peace operations.

International Criminal Court (ICC)

The International Criminal Court was created when 120 nations signed the Rome Statute on July 17, 1998. Its mission is to try individuals accused of genocide, war crimes, or other crimes against humanity, as has been undertaken in the past by temporary tribunals. The statute came into force July 1, 2002, 60 days after the 60th nation ratified it. As of Jan. 1, 2006, 100 nations were members of the ICC, although China, Japan, Russia, and the U.S. had not joined. (Ratification by Comoros and Saint Kitts and Nevis will bring the total number of parties to the statute to 102 on Nov. 1, 2006). The U.S. expressed opposition to some provisions of the ICC, mainly regarding liability of its military in peacekeeping situations.

The ICC, unlike the World Court, is not part of the UN, but an independent international agency with its own budget and administration. It consists of 18 judges elected by member na-tions. An absolute majority of these 18 judges elect three from among themselves to serve as president, 1st vice president, and 2nd vice president in 3-year, renewable terms. A Registry handles the nonjudicial aspects of administration. The Office of the Prosecutor reviews, investigates, and, prosecutes cases referred to it by a state or by the UN Security Council.

The ICC prosecutor has opened investigations into the situations in Uganda, the Dem. Republic of the Congo, and Darfur, Sudan. In July 2005, the court issued the first arrest warrants in connection to war crimes committed in Uganda.

Jurisdiction is limited to member nations and only when their courts are deemed either inoperable or unfit for fair trial. The court is based in The Hague, Netherlands, although it may also sit elsewhere. **Website:** www.icc-cpi.int

See also coverage of genocide in the Crime chapter.

Geneva Conventions

The Geneva Conventions are four international treaties governing the protection of civilians in time of war, the treatment of prisoners of war, and the care of the wounded and sick in the armed forces. The first convention, covering the sick and wounded in war, was concluded in Geneva, Switzerland, in 1864; it was amended and expanded in 1906. In 1929, two more conventions covering the wounded and prisoners of war were signed. Outrage at the treatment of prisoners and civilians during WWII by some belligerents, notably Germany and Japan, prompted the conclusion, in Aug. 1949, of 4 new conventions. Three of these restated and strengthened the previous conventions, and the fourth codified general principles of international law governing the treatment of civilians in wartime.

The 1949 convention for civilians provided for special safeguards for wounded persons, children under 15 years of age, pregnant women, and the elderly. Discrimination on racial, religious, national, or political grounds was forbidden. Torture, collective punishment, reprisals, unwarranted destruction of property, and forced use of civilians for an occupier's armed forces were also prohibited. Also included was a pledge to treat prisoners humanely, feed them adequately, and deliver relief supplies to them. They were not to be forced to disclose more than minimal information. Two additional protocols were adopted in June 1977 dealing with the protection of victims, especially civilians, in international and non-international armed conflicts.

Most countries have formally accepted all or most of the humanitarian conventions as binding. However, there is no permanent machinery in place to apprehend, try, or punish violators.

SPORTS

SPORTS HIGHLIGHTS OF 2006

The Univ. of **Texas** Longhorns claimed the **NCAA Division I-A football title** Jan. 4, beating the Univ. of Southern California Trojans, 41-38, to win the Rose Bowl in Pasadena, CA. With the Rose Bowl victory, Texas, which finished the season with a 13-0 record, was automatically ranked atop the *USA Today* final poll of college football coaches, under the rules of the Bowl Championship Series. The Longhorns were also ranked 1st in the Associated Press poll of media members.

The **Pittsburgh Steelers** defeated the Seattle Seahawks, 21-10, in Detroit, MI, Feb. 5 to win **Super Bowl XL**. The Steelers, coached by Bill Cowher, won the 5th Super Bowl in franchise history. Pittsburgh wide receiver Hines Ward, who caught 5 passes for 123 yards and a touchdown, was named the game's MVP.

The **XX Winter Olympic Games** were held Feb. 10-26 in Turin, Italy. Germany won the most medals, with 11 golds, 12 silvers and 6 bronzes for a total of 29. The U.S. was 2nd, with 25, and Canada was 3rd, with 24. Speed skater Cindy Klassen of Canada won the most medals of any athlete, with 1 gold, 2 silvers and 2 bronzes. U.S. speed skater Shani Davis won gold in the 1,000 meters Feb. 18, becoming the 1st black athlete to win an individual Winter Olympic gold medal.

Japan beat Cuba, 10-6, March 20 to win the inaugural **World Baseball Classic** in San Diego, CA. The event, a World Cup-style tournament featuring 16 nations, was held March 3-20. The U.S., a pretournament favorite, did not make it out of the second round of pool play, and ended with a 3-3 record.

The Univ. of **Florida** Gators beat the UCLA Bruins, 73-57, April 3 in Indianapolis, IN, to win the team's 1st **NCAA Division I men's basketball title**. The Univ. of **Maryland** Terrapins beat the Duke Univ. Blue Devils, 78-75, in overtime April 4 in Boston, MA, to win the **women's tournament**. Florida center Joakim Noah, who had a record 6 blocks in the title game, was named the most outstanding player of the men's Final Four. Maryland forward Laura Harper was named the top player of the women's Final Four.

Racehorse **Barbaro**, with Edgar Prado aboard, won the **Kentucky Derby** in Louisville, KY, May 6 by 6 lengths, the largest winning margin in the race since 1946. However, the colt suffered a **life-threatening injury** to his right hind leg May 20 in the **Preakness Stakes** in Baltimore, MD, which was won by Bernardini. Barbaro underwent surgery May 21, and, after a setback in July, as of Oct. 1 continued to make progress toward recovery.

San Francisco Giants left fielder **Barry Bonds** hit the 715th home run of his MLB career May 28, surpassing Babe Ruth to move into 2nd place on MLB's career home run list, behind Hank Aaron (755). However, his pursuit of the **home-run record** was dogged by accusations of performance-enhancing drug use. Bonds, 42, ended the 2006 season Oct. 1 with 734 home runs.

The **Carolina Hurricanes** beat the Edmonton Oilers, 3-1, June 19 in Raleigh, NC, to win the **Stanley Cup** finals, 4 games to 3. The Hurricanes, coached by Peter Laviolette,

won their 1st Stanley Cup. Carolina rookie goaltender Cam Ward won the Conn Smythe Trophy as the postseason MVP.

The **Miami Heat** beat the Dallas Mavericks, 95-92, in Dallas, TX, to win the **NBA title** June 20. The Heat, coached by Pat Riley, won the series 4 games to 2. Miami guard Dwayne Wade, who averaged 34.7 points in the Finals, was named series MVP.

Italy won the final of soccer's **World Cup** July 9 in Berlin, Germany, beating France. Italy won, 5-3, on penalty kicks, after the teams played to a 1-1 draw in 90 minutes of regulation and 30 minutes of extra time. Italy won its 4th World Cup. French captain Zinedine Zidane received a red card near the end of extra time in the final for head-butting Italian defender Marco Materazzi in the chest. Despite that incident, Zidane on July 10 won the Golden Ball award as the best player of the World Cup.

U.S. cyclist **Floyd Landis** won the **Tour de France** on July 23. Landis's team, Phonak, announced July 27 that he had tested positive for impermissibly high levels of testosterone in a drug test after stage 17 of the race which Landis won in a spectacular performance a day after falling precipitously out of the lead. (The race had already been overshadowed by the ouster of 13 riders in a doping scandal June 30, on the eve of its start, including several favorites.) The International Cycling Union said Aug. 5 that a backup test of a urine sample from Landis confirmed the positive result, though Landis repeatedly asserted his innocence. The U.S. Anti-Doping Association would hold a hearing on his case in early 2007, in a process that could result in him losing the title.

On July 23, defending champion **Tiger Woods** of the U.S. won the **British Open**. Woods won the **PGA Championship** Aug. 20 to claim his 12th professional major tournament. Woods, 30, moved into 2nd place in all-time major titles, behind only Jack Nicklaus (18). Woods captured the American Express Championship Oct. 1 to win his 6th straight PGA Tour event—tying a record for the 2nd-longest winning streak—and his 54th Tour title.

Switzerland's **Roger Federer** won his 3rd Grand Slam tournament of 2006 when he claimed the U.S. Open title Sept. 10, beating the U.S.'s Andy Roddick. Federer earned his 9th Grand Slam title, moving him into 6th place on the men's career list. He had won the **Australian Open** Jan. 29, beating Cyprus's Marcos Baghdatis, and took **Wimbledon** July 9 for the 4th straight year, topping Spain's Rafael Nadal.

The European team won the **Ryder Cup** Sept. 24, soundly beating the U.S. team, 18½ points to 9½ points, at the K Club in Straffan, Ireland. Europe, captained by Welshman Ian Woosnam, won the 3-day match-play competition by a record-tying margin. It was their 3rd straight Ryder Cup victory, the first time the Europeans had won 3 in a row.

On Sept. 25, the **New Orleans Saints** played their 1st game in the **Louisiana Superdome** since it had been seriously damaged in Hurricane Katrina and its aftermath in August 2005. The Saints, who had been forced to relocate for the entire 2005 season, trounced the Atlanta Falcons, 23-3, before a sellout crowd of 70,003.

World Almanac Editors' Picks
"Unbreakable" Sports Records

The editors of *The World Almanac* have selected the following as sports records unlikely to be broken.

National Football League Records

Longest streak of throwing at least 1 touchdown pass per game	Johnny Unitas, 47 games (12/9/56-12/4/60)
Most career receiving yards	Jerry Rice, 22,895 (1985-2004)
Most seasons leading the NFL in rushing yards	Jim Brown, 8 (1957-61, 1963-65)
Most career rushing yards	Emmitt Smith, 18,355 (1990-2004)
Most consecutive games played by a non-kicker	Jim Marshall, 282 (1960-79)
Perfect season and post season	Miami Dolphins, 17-0 (1972)
Most consecutive games won	New England Patriots, 18 (2003-04)
Most interceptions in a season	Dick "Night Train" Lane, 14 (1952)
Most sacks in a single game	Derrick Thomas, 7.0 (Nov. 11, 1990)
Most touchdown passes thrown in a season	Peyton Manning, 49 (2004)

National Basketball Association Records

Best regular-season team winning percentage	Chicago Bulls, 72-10, .878 (1995-96)
Most regular season games played, career	Robert Parish, 1,611 (1976-97)
Most NBA championships, player	Bill Russell, 11 (1957, 1959-66, 1968-69)
Most career assists	John Stockton, 15,806 (1984-2003)
Most career 3-point field goals	Reggie Miller, 2,560 (1987-2005)
Most seasons leading the league in scoring	Michael Jordan, 10 (1987-93, 1996-98)
Highest scoring average, single season	Wilt Chamberlain, 50.4 (1961-62)
Most points, single game	Wilt Chamberlain, 100 (March 2, 1962)
Most rebounds single game	Wilt Chamberlain, 55 (Nov. 24, 1960)
Most career points scored	Kareem Abdul-Jabbar, 38,387 (1969-89)

Major League Baseball Records

Most career wins	Cy Young, 511 (1890-1911)
Most career strikeouts	Nolan Ryan, 5,714 (1966, 1968-93)
Most career stolen bases	Rickey Henderson, 1,406 (1979-2003)
Most runs batted in (season)	Lewis Robert "Hack" Wilson, 191 (1930)
Most career shutouts	Walter Johnson, 110 (1907-27)
Longest hitting streak	Joe DiMaggio, 56 games (May 15-July 16, 1941)
Highest season batting average (after modern era began, 1901)	Nap Lajoie, .426 (1901)
Most career hits	Pete Rose, 4,256 (1963-86)
Back-to-back no hitters	Johnny Vander Meer (June 11 & June 15, 1938)
Most consecutive games played	Cal Ripken, 2,632 (May 30, 1982-Sept. 19, 1998)

Miscellaneous Sports Record Holders

UCLA Bruins: 7 consecutive NCAA basketball titles (1967-73)

Wayne Gretzky: 2,857 NHL career points (1979-99)

Martina Navratilova: 167 career tennis singles titles (1974-94)

Lance Armstrong: 7 consecutive Tour de France titles (1999-2005)

Oklahoma Sooners: 47 consecutive NCAA Division 1-A football victories (Oct. 10, 1953–Nov. 9, 1957)

Byron Nelson: 11 consecutive PGA tour victories (1945)

Sadaharu Oh: 868 career home runs in Japanese Pro Baseball (1959-80)

Just Fontaine: 13 goals for France in one FIFA World Cup finals tournament (June 8-28, 1958)

Oscar Swahn: Oldest person to win an Olympic Medal (72), (Sweden) taking silver in the running deer double-shot team event at the 1920 Antwerp Games

Montreal Canadiens: 10 straight Stanley Cup Finals (1951-60) (w/ 5 straight wins (1956-60)

Richard Petty: Winning 27 NASCAR races in one season (1967)

Rocky Marciano: Undefeated streak, retiring as heavyweight champ, 49-0 (Mar. 17, 1947-Sept. 21, 1955)

Margaret Smith Court: 62 Grand Slam wins in tennis (singles, doubles, mixed double) (1960-75)

UNC Women's Soccer: 103 consecutive games without a loss (Sept. 30, 1986-Sept. 17, 1990)

Gerald Ford: Most NFL contracts declined by a future President: 2 (Detroit Lions and Green Bay Packers)

OLYMPICS
Winter Olympic Games in 2006—Highlights
Turin (Torino), Italy, Feb. 10-26, 2006

The XX Winter Olympic Games opened Feb. 10, 2006, in Turin—Italy's 4th largest city and the largest ever to host the Winter Games—with a dramatic opening ceremony that concluded with a performance by Italian tenor Luciano Pavarotti. Retired cross-country skier Stefania Belmondo, Italy's most successful Winter Games medalist, lit the Olympic flame. More than 2,500 athletes from 84 countries competed in 84 medal events over 16 days in Turin.

A new rating system was implemented for figure skating events following a scoring controversy in the 2002 games. Favored skaters Sasha Cohen (2006 U.S. champion) and Russian Irina Slutskaya (2005 world champion) fell during their routines and had to settle for silver and bronze, respectively, as Shizuka Arakawa became the first Japanese gold medalist in that event. Speedskater Shani Davis won the men's 1,000-meter event, becoming the first African American to claim gold in a Winter Games individual event. Canadian speedskater Cindy Klassen won the most medals of any athlete in the games, with 1 gold, 2 silver and 2 bronze. The U.S. curling team won bronze after defeating Britain; it was the first curling medal for the U.S. Snowboarding events were dominated by the U.S. as the team won 3 of 6 golds. But the celebrated U.S. alpine ski team, which had given itself the motto "Best in the World," managed to claim just 2 medals in competition (both gold). The Austrian team dominated alpine competition, winning 14 of 30 medals up for grabs. In hockey, the U.S. women's team was upset in a 3-2 shootout in the semifinals by Sweden and had to settle for bronze, while the U.S. men's team did not medal and Sweden defeated Finland for the gold.

As in 1998 and 2002, Germany led the medal count, with 29, and the U.S. claimed 25, the second highest nation total. It was the highest medal count for the U.S. in Winter Games not held on U.S. soil.

2006 Final Medal Standings

	Gold	Silver	Bronze	Total		Gold	Silver	Bronze	Total
Germany	11	12	6	29	Finland	0	6	3	9
United States	9	9	7	25	Czech Republic	1	2	1	4
Canada	7	10	7	24	Estonia	3	0	0	3
Austria	9	7	7	23	Croatia	1	2	0	3
Russia	8	6	8	22	Australia	1	0	1	2
Norway	2	8	9	19	Poland	0	1	1	2
Sweden	7	2	5	14	Ukraine	0	0	2	2
Switzerland	5	4	5	14	Japan	1	0	0	1
South Korea	6	3	2	11	Belarus	0	1	0	1
Italy	5	0	6	11	Great Britain	0	1	0	1
China	2	4	5	11	Bulgaria	0	1	0	1
France	3	2	4	9	Slovakia	0	1	0	1
Netherlands	3	2	4	9	Latvia	0	0	1	1
					TOTAL	**84**	**84**	**84**	**252**

2006 Winter Olympics Medal Winners

Alpine Skiing
Men
Combined—G-Ted Ligety, U.S.; S-Ivica Kostelic, Croatia; B-Rainer Schoenfelder, Austria

Downhill—G-Antoine Deneriaz, France; S-Michael Walchhofer, Austria; B-Bruno Kernen, Switzerland

Slalom—G-Benjamin Raich, Austria; S-Reinfried Herbst, Austria; B-Rainer Schoenfelder, Austria

Giant Slalom—G-Benjamin Raich, Austria; S-Joel Chenal, France; B-Hermann Maier, Austria

Super Giant Slalom—G-Kjetil Andre Aamodt, Norway; S-Hermann Maier, Austria; B-Ambrosi Hoffmann, Switzerland

Women
Combined—G-Janica Kostelic, Croatia; S-Marlies Schild, Austria; B-Anja Paerson, Sweden

Downhill—G-Michaela Dorfmeister, Austria; S-Martina Schild, Switzerland; B-Anja Paerson, Sweden

Slalom—G-Anja Paerson, Sweden; S-Nicole Hosp, Austria; B-Marlies Schild, Austria

Giant Slalom—G-Julia Mancuso, U.S.; S-Tanja Poutianinen, Finland; B-Anna Ottosson, Sweden

Super Giant Slalom—G-Michaela Dorfmeister, Austria; S-Janica Kostelic, Croatia; B-Alexandra Meissnitzer, Austria

Biathlon
Men
10-Kilometer Sprint—G-Sven Fischer, Germany; S-Halvard Hanevold, Norway; B-Frode Andresen, Norway

20 Kilometers—G-Michael Greis, Germany; S-Ole Einar Bjoerndalen, Norway; B-Halvard Hanevold, Norway

4x7.5-Kilometer Relay—G-Germany; S-Russia; B-France

12.5-Kilometer Pursuit—G-Vincent Defrasne, France; S-Ole Einar Bjoerndalen, Norway; B-Sven Fischer, Germany

15-Kilometer Mass Start—G-Michael Greis, Germany; S-Tomasz Sikora, Poland; B-Ole Einar Bjoerndalen, Norway

Women
7.5-Kilometer Sprint—G-Florence Baverel-Robert, France; S-Anna Carin Olofsson, Sweden; B-Lilia Efremova, Ukraine

15 Kilometers—G-Svetlana Ishmouratova, Russia; S-Martina Glagow, Germany; B-Albina Akhatova, Russia

4x6-Kilometer Relay—G-Russia; S-Germany; B-France

10-Kilometer Pursuit—G-Kati Wilhelm, Germany; S-Martina Glagow, Germany; B-Albina Akhatova, Russia

12.5-Kilometer Mass Start—G-Anna Carin Olofsson, Sweden; S-Kati Wilhelm, Germany; B-Uschi Disl, Germany

Bobsledding
Two-Man—G-Germany; S-Canada; B-Switzerland
Four-Man—G-Germany; S-Russia; B-Switzerland
Two-Woman—G-Germany; S-U.S.; B-Italy

Curling
Men's—G-Canada; S-Finland; B-U.S.
Women's—G-Sweden; S-Switzerland; B-Canada

Figure Skating
Men's—G-Yevgeny Plushenko, Russia; S-Stephane Lambiel, Switzerland; B-Jeffrey Buttle, Canadal

Women's—G-Shizuka Arakawa, Japan; S-Sasha Cohen, U.S.; B-Irina Slutskaya, Russia

Pairs—G-Tatiana Totmianina & Maxim Marinin, Russia; S-Zhang Dan & Zhang Hao, China; B-Shen Xue & Zhao Hongbo, China

Ice Dancing—G-Tatiana Navka & Roman Kostomarov, Russia; S-Tanith Belbin & Benjamin Agosto, U.S.; B-Yelena Grushina & Ruslan Goncharov, Ukraine

Freestyle Skiing
Men
Moguls—G-Dale Begg-Smith, Australia; S-Mikko Ronkainen, Finland; B-Toby Dawson, U.S.

Aerials—G-Han Xiaopeng, China; S-Dmitri Dashinski, Belarus; B-Vladimir Lebedev, Russia

Women
Moguls—G-Jennifer Heil, Canada; S-Kari Traa, Norway; B-Sandra Laoura, France

Aerials—G-Evelyne Leu, Switzerland; S-Nina Li, China; B-Alisa Camplin, Australia

Ice Hockey
Men's—G-Sweden; S-Finland; B-Czech Republic
Women's—G-Canada; S-Sweden; B-U.S.

Luge
Men's Singles—G-Armin Zoeggeler, Italy; S-Albert Demtschenko, Russia; B-Martins Rubenis, Latvia

Men's Doubles—G-Andreas Linger & Wolfgang Linger, Austria; S-Andre Florschuetz & Torsten Wustlich, Germany; B-Gerhard Plankensteiner & Oswald Haselrieder, Italy

Women's Singles—G-Sylke Otto, Germany; S-Silke Kraushaar, Germany; B-Tatjana Huefner, Germany

Nordic Skiing
Men
Men's Sprint—G-Bjoern Lind, Sweden; S-Roddy Darragon, France; B-Thobias Fredriksson, Sweden
Men's 15-Kilometer Classical—G-Andrus Veerpalu, Estonia; S-Lukas Bauer, Czech Republic; B-Tobias Angerer, Germany
Men's Team Sprint—G-Sweden; S-Norway; B-Russia
Men's 50-Kilometer Freestyle—G-Giorgio di Centa, Italy; S-Eugeni Dementiev, Russia; B-Mikhail Botwinov, Austria
Men's 30-Kilometer Pursuit—G-Eugeni Dementiev, Russia; S-Frode Estil, Norway; B-Pietro Piller Cottrer, Italy
Men's 4x10-Kilometer Relay—G-Italy; S-Germany; B-Sweden

Women
Sprint—G-Chandra Crawford, Canada; S-Claudia Kuenzel, Germany; B-Alena Sidko, Russia
10-Kilometer Classical—G-Kristina Smigun, Estonia; S-Marit Bjorgen, Norway; B-Hilde G. Pedersen, Norway
Team Sprint—G-Sweden; S-Canada; B-Finland
30-Kilometer Freestyle—G-Katerina Neumannova, Czech Republic; S-Yuliya Tchepalova, Russia; B-Justyna Kowalczyk, Poland
15-Kilometer Pursuit—G-Kristina Smigun, Estonia; S-Katerina Neumannova, Czech Republic; B-Evgenia Medvedeva-Abruzova, Russia
4x5-Kilometer Relay—G-Russia; S-Germany; B-Italy

Nordic Combined
Individual 15 Kilometers—G-Georg Hettich, Germany; S-Felix Gottwald, Austria; B-Magnus-H. Moan, Norway
Individual 7.5-Kilometer Sprint—G-Felix Gottwald, Austria; S-Magnus-H. Moan, Norway; B-Georg Hettich, Germany
Team 4x5 Kilometers—G-Austria; S-Germany; B-Finland

Skeleton
Men's—G-Duff Gibson, Canada; S-Jeff Pain, Canada; B-Gregor Staehli, Switzerland
Women's—G-Maya Pedersen, Switzerland; S-Shelley Rudman, Great Britain; B-Melissa Hollingsworth-Richards, Canada

Ski Jumping
Normal (90-Meter) Hil—G-Lars Bystoel, Norway; S-Matti Hautamaeki, Finland; B-Roar Ljoekelsoey, Norway
Large (120-Meter) Hill—G-Thomas Morgenstern, Austria; S-Andreas Kofler, Austria; B-Lars Bystoel, Norway
Team (Large Hill)—G-Austria; S-Finland; B-Norway

Snowboarding
Men
Halfpipe—G-Shaun White, U.S.; S-Danny Kass, U.S.; B-Markku Koski, Finland
Parallel Giant Slalom—G-Philipp Schoch, Switzerland; S-Simon Schoch, Switzerland; B-Siegfried Grabner, Austria
Snowboard Cross—G-Seth Wescott, U.S.; S-Radoslav Zidek, Slovakia; B-Paul-Henri Delerue, France

Women
Halfpipe—G-Hannah Teter, U.S.; S-Gretchen Bleiler, U.S.; B-Kjersti Buaas, Norway
Parallel Giant Slalom—G-Daniela Meuli, Switzerland; S-Amelie Kober, Germany; B-Rosey Fletcher, U.S.
Snowboard Cross—G-Tanja Frieden, Switzerland; S-Lindsey Jacobellis, U.S.; B-Dominique Maltais, Canada

Speedskating
Men
500 Meters—G-Joey Cheek, U.S.; S-Dmitry Dorofeyev, Russia; B-Kang Soek Lee, South Korea
1,000 Meters—G-Shani Davis, U.S.; S-Joey Cheek, U.S.; B-Erben Wennemars, Netherlands
1,500 Meters—G-Enrico Fabris, Italy; S-Shani Davis, U.S.; B-Chad Hedrick, U.S.
5,000 Meters—G-Chad Hedrick, U.S.; S-Sven Kramer, Netherlands; B-Enrico Fabris, Italy
10,000 Meters—G-Bob de Jong, Netherlands; S-Chad Hedrick, U.S.; B-Carl Verheijen, Netherlands
Team Pursuit—G-Italy; S-Canada; B-Netherlands

Women
500 Meters—G-Svetlana Zhurova, Russia; S-Wang Manli, China; B-Hui Ren, China
1,000 Meters—G-Marianne Timmer, Netherlands; S-Cindy Klassen, Canada; B-Anni Friesinger, Germany
1,500 Meters—G-Cindy Klassen, Canada; S-Kristina Groves, Canada; B-Ireen Wust, Netherlands
3,000 Meters—G-Ireen Wust, Netherlands; S-Renate Groenewold, Netherlands; B-Cindy Klassen, Canada
5,000 Meters—G-Clara Hughes, Canada; S-Claudia Pechstein, Germany; B-Cindy Klassen, Canada
Team Pursuit—G-Germany; S-Canada; B-Russia

Short-Track Speedskating
Men
500 Meters—G-Apolo Anton Ohno, U.S.; S-Francois-Louis Tremblay, Canada; B-Ahn Hyun Soo, South Korea
1,000 Meters—G-Ahn Hyun Soo, South Korea*; S-Lee Ho Suk, South Korea; B-Apolo Anton Ohno, U.S.
1,500 Meter—G-Ahn Hyun Soo, South Korea; S-Lee Ho Suk, South Korea; B-Li Jiajun, China
5,000-Meter Relay—G-South Korea*; S-Canada; B-U.S.

Women
500 Meters—G-Wang Meng, China; S-Evgenia Radanova, Bulgaria; B-Anouk Leblanc-Boucher, Canada
1,000 Meters—G-Jin Sun Yu, South Korea; S-Wang Meng, China; B-Yang Yang (A), China
1,500 Meters—G-Jin Sun Yu, South Korea; S-Choi Eun Kyung, South Korea; B-Wang Meng, China
3,000-Meter Relay—G-South Korea; S-Canada; B-Italy
*=Olympic Record

Winter Olympic Games Champions, 1924-2006

In 1992, the Unified Team represented the former Soviet republics of Russia, Ukraine, Belarus, Kazakhstan, and Uzbekistan.

Alpine Skiing

Men's Downhill	Time
1948 Henri Oreiller, France	2:55.0
1952 Zeno Colo, Italy	2:30.8
1956 Toni Sailer, Austria	2:52.2
1960 Jean Vuarnet, France	2:06.0
1964 Egon Zimmermann, Austria	2:18.16
1968 Jean-Claude Killy, France	1:59.85
1972 Bernhard Russi, Switzerland	1:51.43
1976 Franz Klammer, Austria	1:45.73
1980 Leonhard Stock, Austria	1:45.50
1984 Bill Johnson, United States	1:45.49
1988 Pirmin Zurbriggen, Switzerland	1:59.63
1992 Patrick Ortlieb, Austria	1:50.37
1994 Tommy Moe, United States	1:45.75
1998 Jean-Luc Cretier, France	1:50.11
2002 Fritz Strobl, Austria	1:39.13
2006 Antoine Deneriaz, France	1:48.80

Men's Super Giant Slalom	Time
1988 Franck Piccard, France	1:39.66
1992 Kjetil-Andre Aamodt, Norway	1:13.04
1994 Markus Wasmeier, Germany	1:32.53
1998 Hermann Maier, Austria	1:34.82
2002 Kjetil Andre Aamodt, Norway	1:21.58
2006 Kjetil Andre Aamodt, Norway	1:30.65

Men's Giant Slalom	Time
1952 Stein Eriksen, Norway	2:25.0
1956 Toni Sailer, Austria	3:00.1
1960 Roger Staub, Switzerland	1:48.3
1964 Francois Bonlieu, France	1:46.71
1968 Jean-Claude Killy, France	3:29.28
1972 Gustavo Thoeni, Italy	3:09.62
1976 Heini Hemmi, Switzerland	3:26.97
1980 Ingemar Stenmark, Sweden	2:40.74
1984 Max Julen, Switzerland	2:41.18
1988 Alberto Tomba, Italy	2:06.37
1992 Alberto Tomba, Italy	2:06.98
1994 Markus Wasmeier, Germany	2:52.46
1998 Hermann Maier, Austria	2:38.51
2002 Stephan Eberharter, Austria	2:23.28
2006 Benjamin Raich, Austria	2:35.00

Men's Slalom	Time
1948 Edi Reinalter, Switzerland	2:10.3
1952 Othmar Schneider, Austria	2:00.0
1956 Toni Sailer, Austria	3:14.7
1960 Ernst Hinterseer, Austria	2:08.9
1964 Josef Stiegler, Austria	2:11.13
1968 Jean-Claude Killy, France	1:39.73
1972 Francisco Fernandez-Ochoa, Spain	1:49.27
1976 Piero Gros, Italy	2:03.29
1980 Ingemar Stenmark, Sweden	1:44.26
1984 Phil Mahre, United States	1:39.41
1988 Alberto Tomba, Italy	1:39.47
1992 Finn Christian Jagge, Norway	1:44.39
1994 Thomas Stangassinger, Austria	2:02.02
1998 Hans-Petter Buraas, Norway	1:49.31
2002 Jean-Pierre Vidal, France	1:41.06
2006 Benjamin Raich, Austria	1:43.14

Men's Combined

		Time
1936	Franz-Pfnuer, Germany	99.25 (pts.)
1948	Henri Oreiller, France	3.27 (pts.)
1988	Hubert Strolz, Austria	36.55 (pts.)
1992	Josef Polig, Italy	14.58 (pts.)
1994	Lasse Kjus, Norway	3:17.53
1998	Mario Reiter, Austria	3:08.06
2002	Kjetil Andre Aamodt, Norway	3:17.56
2006	Ted Ligety, United States	3:09.35

Women's Downhill

		Time
1948	Hedi Schlunegger, Switzerland	2:28.3
1952	Trude Beiser-Jochum, Austria	1:47.1
1956	Madeleine Berthod, Switzerland	1:40.7
1960	Heidi Biebl, Germany	1:37.6
1964	Christl Haas, Austria	1:55.39
1968	Olga Pall, Austria	1:40.87
1972	Marie-Theres Nadig, Switzerland	1:36.68
1976	Rosi Mittermaier, W. Germany	1:46.16
1980	Annemarie Moser-Proell , Austria	1:37.52
1984	Michela Figini, Switzerland	1:13.36
1988	Marina Kiehl, W. Germany	1:25.86
1992	Kerrin Lee-Gartner, Canada	1:52.55
1994	Katja Seizinger, Germany	1:35.93
1998	Katja Seizinger, Germany	1:28.89
2002	Carole Montillet, France	1:39.56
2006	Michaela Dorfmeister, Austria	1:56.49

Women's Super Giant Slalom

		Time
1988	Sigrid Wolf, Austria	1:19.03
1992	Deborah Compagnoni, Italy	1:21.22
1994	Diann Roffe (Steinrotter), United States	1:22.15
1998	Picabo Street, United States	1:18.02
2002	Daniela Ceccarelli, Italy	1:13.59
2006	Michaela Dorfmeister, Austria	1:32.47

Women's Giant Slalom

		Time
1952	Andrea Mead Lawrence, United States	2:06.8
1956	Ossi Reichert, Germany	1:56.5
1960	Yvonne Ruegg, Switzerland	1:39.9
1964	Marielle Goitschel, France	1:52.24
1968	Nancy Greene, Canada	1:51.97
1972	Marie-Theres Nadig, Switzerland	1:29.90
1976	Kathy Kreiner, Canada	1:29.13
1980	Hanni Wenzel, Liechtenstein (2 runs)	2:41.66
1984	Debbie Armstrong, United States	2:20.98
1988	Vreni Schneider, Switzerland	2:06.49
1992	Pernilla Wiberg, Sweden	2:12.74
1994	Deborah Compagnoni, Italy	2:30.97
1998	Deborah Compagnoni, Italy	2:50.59
2002	Janica Kostelic, Croatia	2:30.01
2006	Julia Mancuso, United States	2:09.19

Women's Slalom

		Time
1948	Gretchen Fraser, United States	1:57.2
1952	Andrea Mead Lawrence, United States	2:10.6
1956	Renee Colliard, Switzerland	1:52.3
1960	Anne Heggtveit, Canada	1:49.6
1964	Christine Goitschel, France	1:29.86
1968	Marielle Goitschel, France	1:25.86
1972	Barbara Ann Cochran, United States	1:31.24
1976	Rosi Mittermaier, W. Germany	1:30.54
1980	Hanni Wenzel, Liechtenstein	1:25.09
1984	Paoletta Magoni, Italy	1:36.47
1988	Vreni Schneider, Switzerland	1:36.69
1992	Petra Kronberger, Austria	1:32.68
1994	Vreni Schneider, Switzerland	1:56.01
1998	Hilde Gerg, Germany	1:32.40
2002	Janica Kostelic, Croatia	1:46.10
2006	Anja Paerson, Sweden	1:29.04

Women's Combined

		Time
1936	Christl Cranz, Germany	97.06 (pts.)
1948	Trude Beiser-Jochum, Austria	6.58 (pts.)
1988	Anita Wachter, Austria	29.25 (pts.)
1992	Petra Kronberger, Austria	2.55 (pts.)
1994	Pernilla Wiberg, Sweden	3:05.16
1998	Katja Seizinger, Germany	2:40.74
2002	Janica Kostelic, Croatia	2:43.28
2006	Janica Kostelic, Croatia	2:51.08

Biathlon

Men's 10 Kilometers

		Time
1980	Frank Ullrich, E. Germany	32:10.69
1984	Eirik Kvalfoss, Norway	30:53.80
1988	Frank-Peter Roetsch, E. Germany	25:08.10
1992	Mark Kirchner, Germany	26:02.30
1994	Serguei Tchepikov, Russia	28:07.00

Men's 10 Kilometers

		Time
1998	Ole Einar Bjoerndalen, Norway	27:16.20
2002	Ole Einar Bjoerndalen, Norway	24:51.30
2006	Sven Fischer, Germany	26:11.6

Men's 12.5 Kilometers

		Time
2002	Ole Einar Bjoerndalen, Norway	32:34.6
2006	Vincent Defrasne, France	35:20.2

Men's 15 Kilometers

		Time
2006	Michael Greis, Germany	47:20.0

Men's 20 Kilometers

		Time
1960	Klas Lestander, Sweden	1:33:21.6
1964	Vladimir Melanin, USSR	1:20:26.8
1968	Magnar Solberg, Norway	1:13:45.9
1972	Magnar Solberg, Norway	1:15:55.50
1976	Nikolai Kruglov, USSR	1:14:12.26
1980	Anatoly Aljabiev, USSR	1:08:16.31
1984	Peter Angerer, W. Germany	1:11:52.7
1988	Frank-Peter Roetsch, E. Germany	0:56:33.33
1992	Yevgeny Redkine, Unified Team	0:57:34.4
1994	Serguei Tarasov, Russia	0:57:25.3
1998	Halvard Hanevold, Norway	0:56:16.4
2002	Ole Einar Bjoerndalen, Norway	0:51:03.03
2006	Michael Greis, Germany	0:54:23.0

Men's 30-Kilometer Relay

		Time
1968	USSR, Norway, Sweden (40 km)	2:13:02.4
1972	USSR, Finland, E. Germany (40 km)	1:51:44.92
1976	USSR, Finland, E. Germany (40 km)	1:57:55.64
1980	USSR, E. Germany, W. Germany	1:34:03.27
1984	USSR, Norway, W. Germany	1:38:51.70
1988	USSR, W. Germany, Italy	1:22:30.00
1992	Germany, Unified Team, Sweden	1:24:43.50
1994	Germany, Russia, France	1:30:22.1
1998	Germany, Norway, Russia	1:19:43.3
2002	Norway, Germany, France	1:23:42.3
2006	Germany, Russia, France	1:21:51.5

Women's 7.5 Kilometers

		Time
1992	Anfissa Restsova, Unified Team	24:29.2
1994	Myriam Bedard, Canada	26:08.8
1998	Galina Koukleva, Russia	23:08.0
2002	Kati Wilhelm, Germany	20:41.4
2006	Florence Baverel-Robert, France	22:31.4

Women's 10 Kilometers

		Time
2002	Olga Pyleva, Russia	31:07.7
2006	Kati Wilhelm, Germany	36:43.6

Women's 12.5 Kilometers

		Time
2006	Anna Carin Olofsson, Sweden	40:36.5

Women's 15 Kilometers

		Time
1992	Antje Misersky, Germany	51:47.2
1994	Myriam Bedard, Canada	52:06.6
1998	Ekaterina Dafovska, Bulgaria	54:52.0
2002	Andrea Henkel, Germany	47:30.0
2006	Svetlana Ishmouratova, Russia	49:24.1

Women's 24-Kilometer Relay

		Time
1992	France, Germany, Unified Team (22.5 km)	1:15:55.6
1994	Russia, Germany, France (30 km)	1:47:19.5
1998	Germany, Russia, Norway (30 km)	1:40:13.6
2002	Germany, Norway, Russia (30 km)	1:27:55.0
2006	Russia, Germany, France	1:16:12.5

Bobsledding

(Driver in parentheses)

4-Man Bob

		Time
1924	Switzerland (Eduard Scherrer)	5:45.54
1928	United States (William Fiske) (5-man)	3:20.50
1932	United States (William Fiske)	7:53.68
1936	Switzerland (Pierre Musy)	5:19.85
1948	United States (Francis Tyler)	5:20.10
1952	Germany (Andreas Ostler)	5:07.84
1956	Switzerland (Franz Kapus)	5:10.44
1964	Canada (Victor Emery)	4:14.46
1968	Italy (Eugenio Monti) (2 races)	2:17.39
1972	Switzerland (Jean Wicki)	4:43.07
1976	E. Germany (Meinhard Nehmer)	3:40.43
1980	E. Germany (Meinhard Nehmer)	3:59.92
1984	E. Germany (Wolfgang Hoppe)	3:20.22
1988	Switzerland (Ekkehard Fasser)	3:47.51
1992	Austria (Ingo Appelt)	3:53.90
1994	Germany (Wolfgang Hoppe)	3:27.28
1998	Germany II (Christoph Langen)	2:39.41
2002	Germany II (Andre Lange)	3:07.51
2006	Germany (Andre Lange)	3:40.42

2-Man Bob	Time
1932 United States (Hubert Stevens)	8:14.74
1936 United States (Ivan Brown)	5:29.29
1948 Switzerland (F. Endrich)	5:29.20
1952 Germany (Andreas Ostler)	5:24.54
1956 Italy (Dalla Costa)	5:30.14
1964 Great Britain (Anthony Nash)	4:21.90
1968 Italy (Eugenio Monti)	4:41.54
1972 W. Germany (Wolfgang Zimmerer)	4:57.07
1976 E. Germany (Meinhard Nehmer)	3:44.42
1980 Switzerland (Erich Schaerer)	4:09.36
1984 E. Germany (Wolfgang Hoppe)	3:25.56
1988 USSR (Janis Kipours)	3:54.19
1992 Switzerland (Gustav Weber)	4:03.26
1994 Switzerland (Gustav Weber)	3:30.81
1998 Canada (Pierre Lueders),	
Italy (Guenther Huber) (tie)	3:37.24
2002 Germany II (Christoph Langen)	3:10.11
2006 Germany (Andre Lange)	3:43.38

2-Woman Bob	Time
2002 United States II (Jill Bakken)	1:37.76
2006 Germany (Sandra Kiriasis)	3:49.98

Curling

Men
1998 Switzerland, Canada, Norway
2002 Norway, Canada, Switzerland
2006 Canada, Finland, United States

Women
1998 Canada, Denmark, Sweden
2002 Britain, Switzerland, Canada
2006 Sweden, Switzerland, Canada

Figure Skating

Men's Singles
1908[1] Ulrich Salchow, Sweden
1920[1] Gillis Grafstrom, Sweden
1924 Gillis Grafstrom, Sweden
1928 Gillis Grafstrom, Sweden
1932 Karl Schaefer, Austria
1936 Karl Schaefer, Austria
1948 Richard Button, United States
1952 Richard Button, United States
1956 Hayes Alan Jenkins, United States
1960 David W. Jenkins, United States
1964 Manfred Schnelldorfer, Germany
1968 Wolfgang Schwartz, Austria
1972 Ondrej Nepela, Czechoslovakia
1976 John Curry, Great Britain
1980 Robin Cousins, Great Britain
1984 Scott Hamilton, United States
1988 Brian Boitano, United States
1992 Viktor Petrenko, Unified Team
1994 Aleksei Urmanov, Russia
1998 Ilya Kulik, Russia
2002 Alexei Yagudin, Russia
2006 Yevgeny Plushenko, Russia

(1) Event held during Summer Olympic Games.

Women's Singles
1908[1] Madge Syers, Great Britain
1920[1] Magda Julin-Mauroy, Sweden
1924 Herma von Szabo-Planck, Austria
1928 Sonja Henie, Norway
1932 Sonja Henie, Norway
1936 Sonja Henie, Norway
1948 Barbara Ann Scott, Canada
1952 Jeanette Altwegg, Great Britan
1956 Tenley Albright, United States
1960 Carol Heiss, United States
1964 Sjoukje Dijkstra, Netherlands
1968 Peggy Fleming, United States
1972 Beatrix Schuba, Austria
1976 Dorothy Hamill, United States
1980 Anett Poetzsch, E. Germany
1984 Katarina Witt, E. Germany
1988 Katarina Witt, E. Germany
1992 Kristi Yamaguchi, United States
1994 Oksana Baiul, Ukraine
1998 Tara Lipinski, United States
2002 Sarah Hughes, United States
2006 Shizuka Arakawa, Japan

(1) Event held during Summer Olympic Games.

Pairs
1908[1] Anna Hubler & Heinrich Burger, Germany
1920[1] Ludovika & Walter Jakobsson, Finland

Pairs
1924 Helene Engelman & Alfred Berger, Austria
1928 Andree Joly & Pierre Brunet, France
1932 Andree Joly & Pierre Brunet, France
1936 Maxi Herber & Ernst Baier, Germany
1948 Micheline Lannoy & Pierre Baugniet, Belgium
1952 Ria and Paul Falk, Germany
1956 Elisabeth Schwartz & Kurt Oppelt, Austria
1964 Ludmila Beloussova & Oleg Protopopov, USSR
1968 Ludmila Beloussova & Oleg Protopopov, USSR
1972 Irina Rodnina & Alexei Ulanov, USSR
1976 Irina Rodnina & Aleksandr Zaitzev, USSR
1980 Irina Rodnina & Aleksandr Zaitzev, USSR
1984 Elena Valova & Oleg Vassiliev, USSR
1988 Ekaterina Gordeeva & Sergei Grinkov, USSR
1992 Natalia Mishkutienok & Artur Dimitriev, Unified Team
1994 Ekaterina Gordeeva & Sergei Grinkov, Russia
1998 Oksana Kazakova & Artur Dmitriev, Russia
2002 Elena Berezhnaya & Anton Sikharulidze, Russia;
         Jamie Sale & David Pelletier, Canada (tie)
2006 Tatyana Totmianina & Maxim Marinin, Russia

(1) Event held during Summer Olympic Games.

Ice Dancing
1976 Ludmila Pakhomova & Aleksandr Gorschkov, USSR
1980 Natalya Linichuk & Gennadi Karponosov, USSR
1984 Jayne Torvill & Christopher Dean, Great Britain
1988 Natalia Bestemianova & Andrei Bukin, USSR
1992 Marina Klimova & Sergei Ponomarenko, Unified Team
1994 Pasha Grishuk & Evgeny Platov, Russia
1998 Pasha Grishuk & Evgeny Platov, Russia
2002 Marina Anissina & Gwendal Peizerat, France
2006 Tatyana Navka & Roman Kostomarov, Russia

Freestyle Skiing

Men's Moguls	Points
1992 Edgar Grospiron, France	25.81
1994 Jean-Luc Brassard, Canada	27.24
1998 Jonny Moseley, United States	26.93
2002 Janne Lahtela, Finland	27.97
2006 Dale Begg-Smith, Australia	26.77

Men's Aerials	Points
1994 Andreas Schoenbaechler, Switzerland	234.67
1998 Eric Bergoust, United States	255.64
2002 Ales Valenta, Czech Republic	257.02
2006 Xiaopeng Han, China	250.77

Women's Moguls	Points
1992 Donna Weinbrecht, United States	23.69
1994 Stine Lise Hattestad, Norway	25.97
1998 Tae Satoya, Japan	25.06
2002 Kari Traa, Norway	25.94
2006 Jennifer Heil, Canada	26.50

Women's Aerials	Points
1994 Lina Tcherjazova, Uzbekistan	166.84
1998 Nikki Stone, United States	193.00
2002 Alisa Camplin, Australia	193.47
2006 Evelyne Leu, Switzerland	202.55

Ice Hockey

Men
1920[1] Canada, United States, Czechoslovakia
1924 Canada, United States, Great Britain
1928 Canada, Sweden, Switzerland
1932 Canada, United States, Germany
1936 Great Britain, Canada, United States
1948 Canada, Czechoslovakia, Switzerland
1952 Canada, United States, Sweden
1956 USSR, United States, Canada
1960 United States, Canada, USSR
1964 USSR, Sweden, Czechoslovakia
1968 USSR, Czechoslovakia, Canada
1972 USSR, United States, Czechoslovakia
1976 USSR, Czechoslovakia, W. Germany
1980 United States, USSR, Sweden
1984 USSR, Czechoslovakia, Sweden
1988 USSR, Finland, Sweden
1992 Unified Team, Canada, Czechoslovakia
1994 Sweden, Canada, Finland
1998 Czech Republic, Russia, Finland
2002 Canada, United States, Russia
2006 Sweden, Finland, Czech Republic

(1) Event held during Summer Olympic Games

Women
1998 United States, Canada, Finland
2002 Canada, United States, Sweden
2006 Canada, Sweden, United States

Luge

Men's Singles	Time
1964 Thomas Keohler, E. Germany	3:27.77
1968 Manfred Schmid, Austria	2:52.48
1972 Wolfgang Scheidel, E. Germany	3:27.58
1976 Detlef Guenther, E. Germany	3:27.688
1980 Bernhard Glass, E. Germany	2:54.796
1984 Paul Hildgartner, Italy	3:04.258
1988 Jens Mueller, E. Germany	3:05.548
1992 Georg Hackl, Germany	3:02.363
1994 Georg Hackl, Germany	3:21.571
1998 Georg Hackl, Germany	3:18.436
2002 Armin Zoeggeler, Italy	2:57.941
2006 Armin Zoeggeler, Italy	3:26.088

Women's Singles	Time
1964 Ortun Enderlein, Germany	3:24.67
1968 Erica Lechner, Italy	2:28.66
1972 Anna M. Muller, E. Germany	2:59.18
1976 Margit Schumann, E. Germany	2:50.621
1980 Vera Zozulya, USSR	2:36.537
1984 Steffi Martin, E. Germany	2:46.570
1988 Steffi Walter, E. Germany	3:03.973
1992 Doris Neuner, Austria	3:06.696
1994 Gerda Weissensteiner, Italy	3:15.517
1998 Silke Kraushaar, Germany	3:23.779
2002 Sylke Otto, Germany	2:52.464
2006 Sylke Otto, Germany	3:07.979

Men's Doubles	Time
1964 Austria	1:41.62
1968 E. Germany	1:35.85
1972 Italy, E. Germany (tie)	1:28.35
1976 E. Germany	1:25.604
1980 E. Germany	1:19.331
1984 W. Germany	1:23.620
1988 E. Germany	1:31.940
1992 Germany	1:32.053
1994 Italy	1:36.720
1998 Germany	1:41.105
2002 Germany	1:26.082
2006 Austria	1:34.497

Nordic Skiing

Cross-Country Events

Men's Sprint	Time
2002 Tor Arne Hetland, Norway (1.5 kms)	2:56.9
2006 Bjoern Lind, Sweden (1.3 kms)	2:26.5

Men's Team Sprint	Time
2006 Bjoern Lind & Thobias Fredriksson, Sweden	17:02.9

Men's 10 Kilometers (6.2 miles)	Time
1992 Vegard Ulvang, Norway	27:36.0
1994 Bjoern Daehlie, Norway	24:20.1
1998 Bjoern Daehlie, Norway	27:24.5
2002 Thomas Alsgaard, Norway;	
Frode Estil, Norway (tie) (a)	49:48.9

(a) Awarded gold after Johann Muehlegg of Spain was stripped of gold for a drug offense.

Men's 15 Kilometers (9.3 miles)	Time
1924 Thorleif Haug, Norway	1:14:31
1928 Johan Grottumsbraaten, Norway	1:37:01
1932 Sven Utterstrom, Sweden	1:23:07
1936 Erik-August Larsson, Sweden	1:14:38
1948 Martin Lundstrom, Sweden	1:13:50
1952 Hallgeir Brenden, Norway	1:01:34
1956 Hallgeir Brenden, Norway	0:49:39.0
1960 Haakon Brusveen, Norway	0:51:55.5
1964 Eero Maentyranta, Finland	0:50:54.1
1968 Harald Groenningen, Norway	0:47:54.2
1972 Sven-Ake Lundback, Sweden	0:45:28.24
1976 Nikolai Balukov, USSR	0:43:58.47
1980 Thomas Wassberg, Sweden	0:41:57.63
1984 Gunde Svan, Sweden	0:41:25.6
1988 Mikhail Deviatiarov, USSR	0:41:18.9
1992 Bjoern Daehlie, Norway	0:38:01.9
1994 Bjoern Daehlie, Norway	0:35:48.8
1998 Thomas Alsgaard, Norway	1:07:01.7
2002 Andrus Veerpalu, Estonia	0:37:07.4
2006 Andrus Veerpalu, Estonia	0:38:01.3

(Note: approx. 18-km course 1924-1952)

Men's 30 Kilometers (18.6 miles)	Time
1956 Veikko Hakulinen, Finland	1:44:06.0
1956 Veikko Hakulinen, Finland	1:44:06.0
1960 Sixten Jernberg, Sweden	1:51:03.9
1964 Eero Maentyranta, Finland	1:30:50.7
1968 Franco Nones, Italy	1:35:39.2
1972 Vyacheslav Vedenine, USSR	1:36:31.15

Men's 30 Kilometers (18.6 miles)	Time
1976 Sergei Saveliev, USSR	1:30:29.38
1980 Nikolai Zimyatov, USSR	1:27:02.80
1984 Nikolai Zimyatov, USSR	1:28:56.3
1988 Aleksei Prokourorov, USSR	1:24:26.3
1992 Vegard Ulvang, Norway	1:22:27.8
1994 Thomas Alsgaard, Norway	1:12:26.4
1998 Mika Myllylae, Finland	1:33:55.8
2002 Christian Hoffmann, Austria (a)	1:11:31.0
2006 Eugeni Dementiev	1:17:00.8

(a) Awarded gold after Johann Muehlegg of Spain was stripped of gold for a drug offense.

Men's 50 Kilometers (31.2 miles)	Time
1924 Thorleif Haug, Norway	3:44:32.0
1928 Per Erik Hedlund, Sweden	4:52:03.0
1932 Veli Saarinen, Finland	4:28:00.0
1936 Elis Wiklund, Sweden	3:30:11.0
1948 Nils Karlsson, Sweden	3:47:48.0
1952 Veikko Hakulinen, Finland	3:33:33.0
1956 Sixten Jernberg, Sweden	2:50:27.0
1960 Kalevi Hamalainen, Finland	2:59:06.3
1964 Sixten Jernberg, Sweden	2:43:52.6
1968 Ole Ellefsaeter, Norway	2:28:45.8
1972 Paal Tyldum, Norway	2:43:14.75
1976 Ivar Formo, Norway	2:37:30.05
1980 Nikolai Zimyatov, USSR	2:27:24.60
1984 Thomas Wassberg, Sweden	2:15:55.8
1988 Gunde Svan, Sweden	2:04:30.9
1992 Bjoern Daehlie, Norway	2:03:41.5
1994 Vladimir Smirnov, Kazakhstan	2:07:20.3
1998 Bjoern Daehlie, Norway	2:05:08.2
2002 Mikhail Ivanov, Russia	2:06:20.8
2006 Giorgio di Centa, Italy	2:06:11.8

Men's 40-Kilometer Relay	Time
1936 Finland, Norway, Sweden	2:41:33.0
1948 Sweden, Finland, Norway	2:32:08.0
1952 Finland, Norway, Sweden	2:20:16.0
1956 USSR, Finland, Sweden	2:15:30.0
1960 Finland, Norway, USSR	2:18:45.6
1964 Sweden, Finland, USSR	2:18:34.6
1968 Norway, Sweden, Finland	2:08:33.5
1972 USSR, Norway, Switzerland	2:04:47.94
1976 Finland, Norway, USSR	2:07:59.72
1980 USSR, Norway, Finland	1:57:03.46
1984 Sweden, USSR, Finland	1:55:06.30
1988 Sweden, USSR, Czechoslovakia	1:43:58.60
1992 Norway, Italy, Finland	1:39:26.00
1994 Italy, Norway, Finland	1:41:15.00
1998 Norway, Italy, Finland	1:40:55.70
2002 Norway, Italy, Germany	1:32:45.5
2006 Italy, Germany, Sweden	1:43:45.7

Women's Sprint	Time
2002 Julia Tchepalova, Russia (1.5 km)	3:10.6
2006 Chandra Crawford, Canada (1.1. km)	2:12.3

Women's Team Sprint	Time
2006 Lina Andersson & Anna Dahlberg, Sweden	16:36.9

Women's 5 Kilometers (3.1 miles)	Time
1964 Claudia Boyarskikh, USSR	17:50.5
1968 Toini Gustafsson, Sweden	16:45.2
1972 Galina Koulacova, USSR	17:00.50
1976 Helena Takalo, Finland	15:48.69
1980 Raisa Smetanina, USSR	15:06.92
1984 Marja-Liisa Haemaelainen, Finland	17:04.0
1988 Marjo Matikainen, Finland	15:04.0
1992 Marjut Lukkarinen, Finland	14:13.8
1994 Ljubov Egorova, Russia	14:08.8
1998 Larissa Lazutina, Russia	17:37.9
2002 Beckie Scott, Canada (a)	25:09.9

(a) Awarded gold after Olga Danilova of Russia was stripped of gold and Larissa Lazutina of Russia was stripped of silver for drug offenses.

Women's 10 Kilometers (6.2 miles)	Time
1952 Lydia Wideman, Finland	41:40.0
1956 Lyubov Kosyreva, USSR	38:11.0
1960 Maria Gusakova, USSR	39:46.6
1964 Claudia Boyarskikh, USSR	40:24.3
1968 Toini Gustafsson, Sweden	36:46.5
1972 Galina Koulacova, USSR	34:17.82
1976 Raisa Smetanina, USSR	30:13.41
1980 Barbara Petzold, E. Germany	30:31.54
1984 Marja-Liisa Haemaelainen, Finland	31:44.2
1988 Vida Ventsene, USSR	30:08.3
1992 Lyubov Egorova, Unified Team	25:53.7
1994 Lyubov Egorova, Russia	27:30.1
1998 Larissa Lazutina, Russia	46.06.9
2002 Bente Skari, Norway	28:05.6
2006 Kristina Smigun, Estonia	27:51.4

Women's 15 Kilometers (9.3 miles)

		Time
1992	Lyubov Egorova, Unified Team	42:20.8
1994	Manuela Di Centa, Italy	39:44.5
1998	Olga Danilova, Russia	46:55.4
2002	Stefania Belmondo, Italy	39:54.4
2006	Kristina Smigun, Estonia	42:48.7

Women's 30 Kilometers (18.6 miles)

		Time
1992	Stefania Belmondo, Italy	1:22:30.1
1994	Manuela Di Centa, Italy	1:25:41.6
1998	Julija Tchepalova, Russia	1:22:01.5
2002	Gabriella Paruzzi, Italy	1:30:57.1
2006	Katerina Neumannova, Czech Republic	1:22:25.4

Women's 20-Kilometer Relay

		Time
1956	Finland, USSR, Sweden (15 km)	1:09:01.0
1960	Sweden, USSR, Finland (15 km)	1:04:21.4
1964	USSR, Sweden, Finland (15 km)	0:59:20.2
1968	Norway, Sweden, USSR (15 km)	0:57:30.0
1972	USSR, Finland, Norway (15 km)	0:48:46.15
1976	USSR, Finland, E. Germany	1:07:49.75
1980	E. Germany, USSR, Norway	1:02:11.1
1984	Norway, Czechoslovakia, Finland	1:06:49.7
1988	USSR, Norway, Finland	0:59:51.1
1992	United Team, Norway, Italy	0:59:34.8
1994	Russia, Norway, Italy	0:57:12.5
1998	Russia, Norway, Italy	0:55:13.5
2002	Germany, Norway, Switzerland	0:49:30.6
2006	Russia, Germany, Italy	0:54:47.7

Nordic Combined (Men)

7.5 Kilometer Nordic Combined

2002	Samppa Lajunen, Finland
2006	Felix Gottwald, Austria

15 Kilometer Nordic Combined

1924	Thorleif Haug, Norway
1928	Johan Grottumsbraaten, Norway
1932	Johan Grottumsbraaten, Norway
1936	Oddbjorn Hagen, Norway
1948	Heikki Hasu, Finland
1952	Simon Slattvik, Norway
1956	Sverre Stenersen, Norway
1960	Georg Thoma, W. Germany
1964	Tormod Knutsen, Norway
1968	Franz Keller, W. Germany
1972	Ulrich Wehling, E. Germany
1976	Ulrich Wehling, E. Germany
1980	Ulrich Wehling, E. Germany
1984	Tom Sandberg, Norway
1988	Hippolyt Kempf, Switzerland
1992	Fabrice Guy, France
1994	Fred Barre Lundberg, Norway
1998	Bjarte Engen Vik, Norway
2002	Samppa Lajunen, Finland
2006	Georg Hettich, Germany

Team Nordic Combined

1988	W. Germany, Switzerland, Austria
1992	Japan, Norway, Austria
1994	Japan, Norway, Switzerland
1998	Norway, Finland, France
2002	Finland, Germany, Austria
2006	Austria, Germany, Finland

Skeleton

Men		Time
1928	Jennison Heaton, United States	3:01.8
1948	Nino Bibbia, Italy	5:23.2
2002	Jim Shea, United States	1:41.96
2006	Duff Gibson, Canada	1:55.88

Women		Time
2002	Tristan Gale, United States	1:45.11
2006	Maya Pedersen, Switzerland	1:59.83

Ski Jumping (Men)

Normal Hill		Points
1964	Veikko Kankkonen, Finland	229.9
1968	Jiri Raska, Czechoslovakia	216.5
1972	Yukio Kasaya, Japan	244.2
1976	Hans-Georg Aschenbach, E. Germany	252.0
1980	Toni Innauer, Austria	266.3
1984	Jens Weissflog, E. Germany	215.2
1988	Matti Nykaenen, Finland	230.5
1992	Ernst Vettori, Austria	222.8
1994	Espen Bredesen, Norway	282.0
1998	Jani Soininen, Finland	234.5
2002	Simon Ammann, Switzerland	269.0
2006	Lars Bystoel, Norway	266.5

Large Hill		Points
1924	Jacob Tullin Thams, Norway	18.960
1928	Alfred Andersen, Norway	19.208
1932	Birger Ruud, Norway	228.1
1936	Birger Ruud, Norway	232.0
1948	Petter Hugsted, Norway	228.1
1952	Arnfinn Bergmann, Norway	226.0
1956	Antti Hyvarinen, Finland	227.0
1960	Helmut Recknagel, E. Germany	227.2
1964	Toralf Engan, Norway	230.7
1968	Vladimir Beloussov, USSR	231.3
1972	Wojciech Fortuna, Poland	219.9
1976	Karl Schnabl, Austria	234.8
1980	Jouko Tormanen, Finland	271.0
1984	Matti Nykaenen, Finland	231.2
1988	Matti Nykaenen, Finland	224.0
1992	Toni Nieminen, Finland	239.5
1994	Jens Weissflog, Germany	274.5
1998	Kazuyoshi Funaki, Japan	272.3
2002	Simon Ammann, Switzerland	281.4
2006	Thomas Morgenstern, Austria	276.9

Team Large Hill		Points
1988	Finland, Yugoslavia, Norway	634.4
1992	Finland, Austria, Czechoslovakia	644.4
1994	Germany, Japan, Austria	970.1
1998	Japan, Germany, Austria	933.0
2002	Germany, FInland, Slovenia	974.1
2006	Austria, Finland, Norway	984.0

Snowboarding

Men's Parallel Giant Slalom

		Time
1998	Ross Rebagliati, Canada	2:03.96
2002	Philipp Schoch, Switzerland	NA
2006	Philipp Schoch, Switzerland	NA

In 2002, the Giant Slalom became the Parallel Giant Slalom.

Men's Halfpipe

		Points
1998	Gian Simmen, Switzerland	85.2
2002	Ross Powers, United States	46.1
2006	Shaun White, United States	46.8

Men's Snowboard Cross

2006	Seth Wescott, United States

Women's Parallel Giant Slalom

		Time
1998	Karine Ruby, France	2:17.34
2002	Isabelle Blanc, France	NA
2006	Daniela Meuli, Switzerland	NA

In 2002, the Giant Slalom became the Parallel Giant Slalom.

Women's Halfpipe

		Points
1998	Nicola Thost, Germany	74.6
2002	Kelly Clark, United States	47.9
2006	Hannah Teter, United States	46.4

Women's Snowboard Cross

2006	Tanja Frieden, Switzerland

Speed Skating

*indicates Olympic record

Men's 500 Meters		Time
1924	Charles Jewtraw, United States	0:44.0
1928	Thunberg, Finland & Evensen, Norway (tie)	0:43.4
1932	John A. Shea, United States	0:43.4
1936	Ivar Ballangrud, Norway	0:43.4
1948	Finn Helgesen, Norway	0:43.1
1952	Kenneth Henry, United States	0:43.2
1956	Evgeniy Grishin, USSR	0:40.2
1960	Evgeniy Grishin, USSR	0:40.2
1964	Terry McDermott, United States	0:40.1
1968	Erhard Keller, W. Germany	0:40.3
1972	Erhard Keller, W. Germany	0:39.44
1976	Evgeny Kulikov, USSR	0:39.17
1980	Eric Heiden, United States	0:38.03
1984	Sergei Fokichev, USSR	0:38.19
1988	Uwe-Jens Mey, E. Germany	0:36.45
1992	Uwe-Jens Mey, Germany	0:37.14
1994	Aleksandr Golubev, Russia	0:36.33
1998	Hiroyasu Shimizu, Japan	0:35.59
2002	Casey FitzRandolph, United States	0:34.42*
2006	Joey Cheek, United States	0:34.82

Men's 1,000 Meters		Time
1976	Peter Mueller, U.S	1:19.32
1980	Eric Heiden, United States	1:15.18
1984	Gaetan Boucher, Canada	1:15.80
1988	Nikolai Guliaev, USSR	1:13.03
1992	Olaf Zinke, Germany	1:14.85
1994	Dan Jansen, United States	1:12.43
1998	Ids Postma, Netherlands	1:10.64
2002	Gerard van Velde, Netherlands	1:07.18*
2006	Shani Davis, United States	1:08.89

Men's 1,500 Meters

Year	Champion	Time
1924	Clas Thunberg, Finland	2:20.8
1928	Clas Thunberg, Finland	2:21.1
1932	John A. Shea, United States	2:57.5
1936	Charles Mathiesen, Norway	2:19.2
1948	Sverre Farstad, Norway	2:17.6
1952	Hjalmar Andersen, Norway	2:20.4
1956	Grishin, & Mikhailov, both USSR (tie)	2:08.6
1960	Aas, Norway & Grishin, USSR (tie)	2:10.4
1964	Ants Anston, USSR	2:10.3
1968	Cornetis Verkerk, Netherlands	2:03.4
1972	Ard Schenk, Netherlands	2:02.96
1976	Jan Egil Storholt, Norway	1:59.38
1980	Eric Heiden, United States	1:55.44
1984	Gaetan Boucher, Canada	1:58.36
1988	Andre Hoffmann, E. Germany	1:52.06
1992	Johann Koss, Norway	1:54.81
1994	Johann Koss, Norway	1:51.29
1998	Aadne Sondral, Norway	1:47.87
2002	Derek Parra, United States	1:43.95*
2006	Enrico Fabris, Italy	1:45.97

Men's 5,000 Meters

Year	Champion	Time
1924	Clas Thunberg, Finland	8:39.0
1928	Ivar Ballangrud, Norway	8:50.5
1932	Irving Jaffee, United States	9:40.8
1936	Ivar Ballangrud, Norway	8:19.6
1948	Reidar Liaklev, Norway	8:29.4
1952	Hjalmar Andersen, Norway	8:10.6
1956	Boris Shilkov, USSR	7:48.7
1960	Viktor Kosichkin, USSR	7:51.3
1964	Knut Johannesen, Norway	7:38.4
1968	F. Anton Maier, Norway	7:22.4
1972	Ard Schenk, Netherlands	7:23.61
1976	Sten Stensen, Norway	7:24.48
1980	Eric Heiden, United States	7:02.29
1984	Sven Tomas Gustafson, Sweden	7:12.28
1988	Tomas Gustafson, Sweden	6:44.63
1992	Geir Karlstad, Norway	6:59.97
1994	Johann Koss, Norway	6:34.96
1998	Gianni Romme, Netherlands	6:22.20
2002	Jochem Uytdehaage, Netherlands	6:14.66*
2006	Chad Hedrick, United States	6:14.68

Men's 10,000 Meters

Year	Champion	Time
1924	Julius Skutnabb, Finland	18:04.8
1928	Event not held because of thawing of ice	
1932	Irving Jaffee, United States	19:13.6
1936	Ivar Ballangrud, Norway	17:24.3
1948	Ake Seyffarth, Sweden	17:26.3
1952	Hjalmar Andersen, Norway	16:45.8
1956	Sigvard Ericsson, Sweden	16:35.9
1960	Knut Johannesen, Norway	15:46.6
1964	Jonny Nilsson, Sweden	15:50.1
1968	Jonny Hoeglin, Sweden	15:23.6
1972	Ard Schenk, Netherlands	15:01.35
1976	Piet Kleine, Netherlands	14:50.59
1980	Eric Heiden, United States	14:28.13
1984	Igor Malkov, USSR	14:39.90
1988	Tomas Gustafson, Sweden	13:48.20
1992	Bart Veldkamp, Netherlands	14:12.12
1994	Johann Koss, Norway	13:30.55
1998	Gianni Romme, Netherlands	13:15.33
2002	Jochem Uytdehaage, Netherlands	12:58.92*
2006	Bob de Jong, Netherlands	13:01.57

Women's 500 Meters

Year	Champion	Time
1960	Helga Haase, Germany	0:45.9
1964	Lydia Skoblikova, USSR	0:45.0
1968	Ludmila Titova, USSR	0:46.1
1972	Anne Henning, United States	0:43.33
1976	Sheila Young, United States	0:42.76
1980	Karin Enke, E. Germany	0:41.78
1984	Christa Rothenburger, E. Germany	0:41.02
1988	Bonnie Blair, United States	0:39.10
1992	Bonnie Blair, United States	0:40.33
1994	Bonnie Blair, United States	0:39.25
1998	Catriona Le May-Doan, Canada	0:38.21
2002	Catriona Le May Doan, Canada	0:37.30*
2006	Svetlana Zhurova, Russia	0:38.23

Women's 1,000 Meters

Year	Champion	Time
1960	Klara Guseva, USSR	1:34.1
1964	Lydia Skoblikova, USSR	1:33.2
1968	Carolina Geijssen, Netherlands	1:32.6
1972	Monika Pflug, W. Germany	1:31.40
1976	Tatiana Averina, USSR	1:28.43
1980	Natalya Petruseva, USSR	1:24.10
1984	Karin Enke, E. Germany	1:21.61
1988	Christa Rothenburger, E. Germany	1:17.65
1992	Bonnie Blair, United States	1:21.90
1994	Bonnie Blair, United States	1:18.74

Women's 1,000 Meters

Year	Champion	Time
1998	Marianne Timmer, Netherlands	1:16.51
2002	Chris Witty, United States	1:13.83*
2006	Marianne Timmer, Netherlands	1:16.05

Women's 1,500 Meters

Year	Champion	Time
1960	Lydia Skoblikova, USSR	2:52.2
1964	Lydia Skoblikova, USSR	2:22.6
1968	Kaija Mustonen, Finland	2:22.4
1972	Dianne Holum, United States	2:20.85
1976	Galina Stepanskaya, USSR	2:16.58
1980	Anne Borckink, Netherlands	2:10.95
1984	Karin Enke, E. Germany	2:03.42
1988	Yvonne van Gennip, Netherlands	2:00.68
1992	Jacqueline Boerner, Germany	2:05.87
1994	Emese Hunyady, Austria	2:02.19
1998	Marianne Timmer, Netherlands	1:57.58
2002	Anni Friesinger, Germany	1:54.02*
2006	Cindy Klassen, Canada	1:55.27

Women's 3,000 Meters

Year	Champion	Time
1960	Lydia Skoblikova, USSR	5:14.3
1964	Lydia Skoblikova, USSR	5:14.9
1968	Johanna Schut, Netherlands	4:56.2
1972	Christina Baas-Kaiser, Netherlands	4:52.14
1976	Tatiana Averina, USSR	4:45.19
1980	Bjoerg Eva Jensen, Norway	4:32.13
1984	Andrea Schoene, E. Germany	4:24.79
1988	Yvonne van Gennip, Netherlands	4:11.94
1992	Gunda Niemann, Germany	4:19.90
1994	Svetlana Bazhanova, Russia	4:17.43
1998	Gunda Niemann-Stirnemann, Germany	4:07.29
2002	Claudia Pechstein, Germany,	3:57.70*
2006	Ireen Wust, Netherlands	4:02.43

Women's 5,000 Meters

Year	Champion	Time
1988	Yvonne van Gennip, Netherlands	7:14.13
1992	Gunda Niemann, Germany	7:31.57
1994	Claudia Pechstein, Germany	7:14.37
1998	Claudia Pechstein, Germany	6:59.61
2002	Claudia Pechstein, Germany	6:46.91*
2006	Clara Hughes, Canada	6:59.07

Men's Team Pursuit

Year	Champion	Time
2006	Italy, Canada, Netherlands	3:44.46

Women's Team Pursuit

Year	Champion	Time
2006	Germany, Canada, Russia	3:01.25

Short-Track Speed Skating
* indicates Olympic record

Men's 500 Meters

Year	Champion	Time
1998	Takafumi Nishitani, Japan	42.862
2002	Marc Gagnon, Canada	41.802*
2006	Apolo Anton Ohno, United States	41.935

Men's 1,000 Meters

Year	Champion	Time
1992	Kim Ki-Hoon, S. Korea	1:30.76
1994	Kim Ki-Hoon, S. Korea	1:34.57
1998	Dong-Sung Kim, S. Korea	1:32.375
2002	Steven Bradbury, Australia	1:29.109
2006	Hyun-Soo Ahn, S. Korea	1:26.739*

Men's 1,500 Meters

Year	Champion	Time
2002	Apolo Anton Ohno, United States	2:18.541
2006	Hyun-Soo Ahn, S. Korea	2:25.341

Men's 5,000-Meter Relay

Year	Champion	Time
1992	S. Korea, Canada, Japan	7:14.02
1994	Italy, United States, Australia	7:11.74
1998	Canada, S. Korea, China	7:06.075
2002	Canada, Italy, China	6:51.579
2006	S. Korea, Canada, United States	6:43.376*

Women's 500 Meters

Year	Champion	Time
1992	Cathy Turner, United States	47.04
1994	Cathy Turner, United States	45.98
1998	Annie Perreault, Canada	46.568
2002	Yang Yang (A), China	44.187
2006	Meng Wang, China	44.345

Women's 1,000 Meters

Year	Champion	Time
1998	Chun Lee-Kyung, S. Korea	1:42.776
2002	Yang Yang (A), China	1:36.391
2006	Sun-Yu Jin, S. Korea	1:32.859

Women's 1,500 Meters

Year	Champion	Time
2002	Gi-Hyun Ko, S. Korea	2:31.581
2006	Sun-Yu Jin, S. Korea	2:23.494

Women's 3,000 Meter Relay

Year	Champion	Time
1992	Canada, United States, Unified Team	4:36.62
1994	S. Korea, Canada, United States	4:26.64
1998	S. Korea, China, Canada	4:16.26
2002	S. Korea, China, Canada	4:12.793*
2006	S. Korea, Canada, Italy	4:17.040

Highlights of the 2004 Summer Olympic Games

Athens, Greece, Aug. 13-29, 2004

The Olympic Games were born in ancient Greece and the first modern Games were held in Athens in 1896. In 2004, 10,500 athletes representing 202 nations gathered in Athens to compete in 301 events in 28 sports at the 28th Olympiad. Women competed for the first time in freestyle wrestling and the sabre event in fencing.

American swimmer Michael Phelps captured 8 medals—6 gold and 2 bronze—in individual and relay events, tying a record for the number of medals won in a single Olympics. American gymnasts Paul Hamm and Carly Patterson claimed gold medals in the individual all-around gymnastics competitions, but controversy erupted when it emerged that judges had erred in scoring Yang Tae Young (S. Kor.), who won the men's bronze medal, on his parallel bar routine. The International Gymnastics Federation admitted that the gold medal had been awarded to Hamm in error, but allowed the results to stand. The U.S. also fared well in women's team sports, with the soccer, softball, and basketball teams all capturing golds.

Many track and field stars were absent because of doping scandals or failure to qualify. A record 24 athletes were expelled for drug violations as of the closing ceremony. Medals in 7 events, including 3 golds, were taken away for doping violations.

Summer Olympic Games Champions, 1896-2004

(*indicates Olympic record; w indicates wind-aided)

The 1980 games were boycotted by 62 nations, including the U.S. The 1984 games were boycotted by the USSR and most Eastern bloc nations. E and W Germany competed separately, 1968-88. The 1992 Unified Team consisted of 12 former Soviet republics. The 1992 Independent Olympic Participants (I.O.P.) were from Serbia, Montenegro, and Macedonia.

Track and Field—Men

100-Meter Run — Time
1896	Thomas Burke, United States	12.0s
1900	Francis W. Jarvis, United States	11.0s
1904	Archie Hahn, United States	11.0s
1908	Reginald Walker, South Africa	10.8s
1912	Ralph Craig, United States	10.8s
1920	Charles Paddock, United States	10.8s
1924	Harold Abrahams, Great Britain	10.6s
1928	Percy Williams, Canada	10.8s
1932	Eddie Tolan, United States	10.3s
1936	Jesse Owens, United States	10.3s
1948	Harrison Dillard, United States	10.3s
1952	Lindy Remigino, United States	10.4s
1956	Bobby Morrow, United States	10.5s
1960	Armin Hary, Germany	10.2s
1964	Bob Hayes, United States	10.0s
1968	Jim Hines, United States	9.95s
1972	Valery Borzov, USSR	10.14s
1976	Hasely Crawford, Trinidad	10.06s
1980	Allan Wells, Great Britain	10.25s
1984	Carl Lewis, United States	9.99s
1988	Carl Lewis, United States	9.92s
1992	Linford Christie, Great Britain	9.96s
1996	Donovan Bailey, Canada	9.84s*
2000	Maurice Greene, United States	9.87s
2004	Justin Gatlin, United States	9.85s

200-Meter Run — Time
1900	Walter Tewksbury, United States	22.2s
1904	Archie Hahn, United States	21.6s
1908	Robert Kerr, Canada	22.6s
1912	Ralph Craig, United States	21.7s
1920	Allan Woodring, United States	22.0s
1924	Jackson Scholz, United States	21.6s
1928	Percy Williams, Canada	21.8s
1932	Eddie Tolan, United States	21.2s
1936	Jesse Owens, United States	20.7s
1948	Mel Patton, United States	21.1s
1952	Andrew Stanfield, United States	20.7s
1956	Bobby Morrow, United States	20.6s
1960	Livio Berruti, Italy	20.5s
1964	Henry Carr, United States	20.3s
1968	Tommie Smith, United States	19.83s
1972	Valeri Borzov, USSR	20.00s
1976	Donald Quarrie, Jamaica	20.23s
1980	Pietro Mennea, Italy	20.19s
1984	Carl Lewis, United States	19.80s
1988	Joe DeLoach, United States	19.75s
1992	Mike Marsh, United States	20.01s
1996	Michael Johnson, United States	19.32s*
2000	Konstantinos Kenteris, Greece	20.09s
2004	Shawn Crawford, United States	19.79s

400-Meter Run — Time
1896	Thomas Burke, United States	54.2s
1900	Maxey Long, United States	49.4s
1904	Harry Hillman, United States	49.2s
1908	Wyndham Halswelle, Great Brit., walkover	50.0s
1912	Charles Reidpath, United States	48.2s
1920	Bevil Rudd, South Africa	49.6s
1924	Eric Liddell, Great Britain	47.6s
1928	Ray Barbuti, United States	47.8s
1932	William Carr, United States	46.2s
1936	Archie Williams, United States	46.5s
1948	Arthur Wint, Jamaica	46.2s
1952	George Rhoden, Jamaica	45.9s
1956	Charles Jenkins, United States	46.7s

400-Meter Run — Time
1960	Otis Davis, United States	44.9s
1964	Michael Larrabee, United States	45.1s
1968	Lee Evans, United States	43.86s
1972	Vincent Matthews, United States	44.66s
1976	Alberto Juantorena, Cuba	44.26s
1980	Viktor Markin, USSR	44.60s
1984	Alonzo Babers, United States	44.27s
1988	Steven Lewis, United States	43.87s
1992	Quincy Watts, United States	43.50s
1996	Michael Johnson, United States	43.49s*
2000	Michael Johnson, United States	43.84s
2004	Jeremy Wariner, United States	44.00s

800-Meter Run — Time
1896	Edwin Flack, Australia	2m.11s
1900	Alfred Tysoe, Great Britain	2m.1.2s
1904	James Lightbody, United States	1m. 56s
1908	Mel Sheppard, United States	1m. 52.8s
1912	James Meredith, United States	1m. 51.9s
1920	Albert Hill, Great Britain	1m. 53.4s
1924	Douglas Lowe, Great Britain	1m. 52.4s
1928	Douglas Lowe, Great Britain	1m. 51.8s
1932	Thomas Hampson, Great Britain	1m. 49.8s
1936	John Woodruff, United States	1m. 52.9s
1948	Mal Whitfield, United States	1m. 49.2s
1952	Mal Whitfield, United States	1m. 49.2s
1956	Thomas Courtney, United States	1m. 47.7s
1960	Peter Snell, New Zealand	1m. 46.3s
1964	Peter Snell, New Zealand	1m. 45.1s
1968	Ralph Doubell, Australia	1m. 44.3s
1972	Dave Wottle, United States	1m. 45.9s
1976	Alberto Juantorena, Cuba	1m. 43.50s
1980	Steve Ovett, Great Britain	1m. 45.40s
1984	Joaquim Cruz, Brazil	1m. 43.00s
1988	Paul Ereng, Kenya	1m. 43.45s
1992	William Tanui, Kenya	1m. 43.66s
1996	Vebjoern Rodal, Norway	1m. 42.58s*
2000	Nils Schumann, Germany	1m. 45.08s
2004	Yuriy Borzakovskiy, Russia	1m. 44.45s

1,500-Meter Run — Time
1896	Edwin Flack, Australia	4m. 33.2s
1900	Charles Bennett, Great Britain	4m. 6.2s
1904	James Lightbody, United States	4m. 5.4s
1908	Mel Sheppard, United States	4m. 3.4s
1912	Arnold Jackson, Great Britain	3m. 56.8s
1920	Albert Hill, Great Britain	4m. 1.8s
1924	Paavo Nurmi, Finland	3m. 53.6s
1928	Harry Larva, Finland	3m. 53.2s
1932	Luigi Beccali, Italy	3m. 51.2s
1936	Jack Lovelock, New Zealand	3m. 47.8s
1948	Henri Eriksson, Sweden	3m. 49.8s
1952	Joseph Barthel, Luxembourg	3m. 45.2s
1956	Ron Delany, Ireland	3m. 41.2s
1960	Herb Elliott, Australia	3m. 35.6s
1964	Peter Snell, New Zealand	3m. 38.1s
1968	Kipchoge Keino, Kenya	3m. 34.9s
1972	Pekka Vasala, Finland	3m. 36.3s
1976	John Walker, New Zealand	3m. 39.17s
1980	Sebastian Coe, Great Britain	3m. 38.4s
1984	Sebastian Coe, Great Britain	3m. 32.53s
1988	Peter Rono, Kenya	3m. 35.96s
1992	Fermin Cacho Ruiz, Spain	3m. 40.12s
1996	Noureddine Morceli, Algeria	3m. 35.78s
2000	Noah Ngeny, Kenya	3m. 32.07s*
2004	Hicham el-Guerrouj, Morocco	3m. 34.18s

5,000-Meter Run

		Time
1912	Hannes Kolehmainen, Finland	14m. 36.6s
1920	Joseph Guillemot, France	14m. 55.6s
1924	Paavo Nurmi, Finlands	14m. 31.2s
1928	Willie Ritola, Finland	14m. 38s
1932	Lauri Lehtinen, Finland	14m. 30s
1936	Gunnar Hockert, Finland	14m. 22.2s
1948	Gaston Reiff, Belgium	14m. 17.6s
1952	Emil Zatopek, Czechoslovakia	14m. 6.6s
1956	Vladimir Kuts, USSR	13m. 39.6s
1960	Murray Halberg, New Zealand	13m. 43.4s
1964	Bob Schul, United States	13m. 48.8s
1968	Mohamed Gammoudi, Tunisia	14m. 05.0s
1972	Lasse Viren, Finland	13m. 26.4s
1976	Lasse Viren, Finland	13m. 24.76s
1980	Miruts Yifter, Ethiopia	13m. 21.0s
1984	Said Aouita, Morocco	13m. 05.59s*
1988	John Ngugi, Kenya	13m. 11.70s
1992	Dieter Baumann, Germany	13m. 12.52s
1996	Venuste Niyongabo, Burundi	13m. 07.96s
2000	Millon Wolde, Ethiopia	13m. 35.49s
2004	Hicham el-Guerrouj, Morocco	13m. 14.39s

10,000-Meter Run

		Time
1912	Hannes Kolehmainen, Finland	31m. 20.8s
1920	Paavo Nurmi, Finland	31m. 45.8s
1924	Willie Ritola, Finland	30m. 23.2s
1928	Paavo Nurmi, Finland	30m. 18.8s
1932	Janusz Kusocinski, Poland	30m. 11.4s
1936	Ilmari Salminen, Finland	30m. 15.4s
1948	Emil Zatopek, Czechoslovakia	29m. 59.6s
1952	Emil Zatopek, Czechoslovakia	29m. 17.0s
1956	Vladimir Kuts, USSR	28m. 45.6s
1960	Pyotr Bolotnikov, USSR	28m. 32.2s
1964	Billy Mills, United States	28m. 24.4s
1968	Naftali Temu, Kenya	29m. 27.4s
1972	Lasse Viren, Finland	27m. 38.4s
1976	Lasse Viren, Finland	27m. 40.4s
1980	Miruts Yifter, Ethiopia	27m. 42.7s
1984	Alberto Cova, Italy	27m. 47.54s
1988	Brahim Boutaib, Morocco	27m. 21.46s
1992	Khalid Skah, Morocco	27m. 46.70s
1996	Haile Gebrselassie, Ethiopia	27m. 07.34s
2000	Haile Gebrselassie, Ethiopia	27m. 18.20s
2004	Kenenisa Bekele, Ethiopia	27m. 05.10s*

110-Meter Hurdles

		Time
1896	Thomas Curtis, United States	17.6s
1900	Alvin Kraenzlein, United States	15.4s
1904	Frederick Schule, United States	16.0s
1908	Forrest Smithson, United States	15.0s
1912	Frederick Kelly, United States	15.1s
1920	Earl Thomson, Canada	14.8s
1924	Daniel Kinsey, United States	15.0s
1928	Sydney Atkinson, South Africa	14.8s
1932	George Saling, United States	14.6s
1936	Forrest Towns, United States	14.2s
1948	William Porter, United States	13.9s
1952	Harrison Dillard, United States	13.7s
1956	Lee Calhoun, United States	13.5s
1960	Lee Calhoun, United States	13.8s
1964	Hayes Jones, United States	13.6s
1968	Willie Davenport, United States	13.33s
1972	Rod Milburn, United States	13.24s
1976	Guy Drut, France	13.30s
1980	Thomas Munkelt, E. Germany	13.39s
1984	Roger Kingdom, United States	13.20s
1988	Roger Kingdom, United States	12.98s
1992	Mark McCoy, Canada	13.12s
1996	Allen Johnson, United States	12.95s
2000	Anier Garcia, Cuba	13.00s
2004	Liu Xiang, China	12.91s*

400-Meter Hurdles

		Time
1900	J.W.B. Tewksbury, United States	57.6s
1904	Harry Hillman, United States	53.0s
1908	Charles Bacon, United States	55.0s
1920	Frank Loomis, United States	54.0s
1924	F. Morgan Taylor, United States	52.6s
1928	Lord Burghley, Great Britain	53.4s
1932	Robert Tisdall, Ireland	51.7s
1936	Glenn Hardin, United States	52.4s
1948	Roy Cochran, United States	51.1s
1952	Charles Moore, United States	50.8s
1956	Glenn Davis, United States	50.1s
1960	Glenn Davis, United States	49.3s
1964	Rex Cawley, United States	49.6s
1968	Dave Hemery, Great Britain	48.12s
1972	John Akii-Bua, Uganda	47.82s
1976	Edwin Moses, United States	47.64s

400-Meter Hurdles

		Time
1980	Volker Beck, E. Germany	48.70s
1984	Edwin Moses, United States	47.75s
1988	Andre Phillips, United States	47.19s
1992	Kevin Young, United States	46.78s*
1996	Derrick Adkins, United States	47.54s
2000	Angelo Taylor, United States	47.50s
2004	Felix Sanchez, Dominican Republic	47.63s

400-Meter Relay

		Time
1912	Great Britain	42.4s
1920	United States	42.2s
1924	United States	41.0s
1928	United States	41.0s
1932	United States	40.0s
1936	United States	39.8s
1948	United States	40.6s
1952	United States	40.1s
1956	United States	39.5s
1960	Germany (U.S. disqualified)	39.5s
1964	United States	39.0s
1968	United States	38.24s
1972	United States	38.19s
1976	United States	38.33s
1980	USSR	38.26s
1984	United States	37.83s
1988	USSR (U.S. disqualified)	38.19s
1992	United States	37.40s*
1996	Canada	37.69s
2000	United States	37.61s
2004	Great Britain	38.07s

1,600-Meter Relay

		Time
1908	United States	3m. 29.4s
1912	United States	3m. 16.6s
1920	Great Britain	3m. 22.2s
1924	United States	3m. 16s
1928	United States	3m. 14.2s
1932	United States	3m. 8.2s
1936	Great Britain	3m. 9s
1948	United States	3m. 10.4s
1952	Jamaica	3m. 03.9s
1956	United States	3m. 04.8s
1960	United States	3m. 02.2s
1964	United States	3m. 00.7s
1968	United States	2m. 56.16s
1972	Kenya	2m. 59.8s
1976	United States	2m. 58.65s
1980	USSR	3m. 01.1s
1984	United States	2m. 57.91s
1988	United States	2m. 56.16s
1992	United States	2m. 55.74s*
1996	United States	2m. 55.99s
2000	United States	2m. 56.35s
2004	United States	2m. 55.91s

3,000-Meter Steeplechase

		Time
1920	Percy Hodge, Great Britain	10m. 0.4s
1924	Willie Ritola, Finland	9m. 33.6s
1928	Toivo Loukola, Finland	9m. 21.8s
1932	Volmari Iso-Hollo, Finland	10m. 33.4s
	(About 3,450 m; extra lap by error.)	
1936	Volmari Iso-Hollo, Finland	9m. 3.8s
1948	Thore Sjoestrand, Sweden	9m. 4.6s
1952	Horace Ashenfelter, United States	8m. 45.4s
1956	Chris Brasher, Great Britain	8m. 41.2s
1960	Zdzislaw Krzyszkowiak, Poland	8m. 34.2s
1964	Gaston Roelants, Belgium	8m. 30.8s
1968	Amos Biwott, Kenya	8m. 51s
1972	Kipchoge Keino, Kenya	8m. 23.6s
1976	Anders Garderud, Sweden	8m. 08.2s
1980	Bronislaw Malinowski, Poland	8m. 09.7s
1984	Julius Korir, Kenya	8m. 11.8s
1988	Julius Kariuki, Kenya	8m. 05.51s*
1992	Matthew Birir, Kenya	8m. 08.84s
1996	Joseph Keter, Kenya	8m. 07.12s
2000	Reuben Kosgei, Kenya	8m. 21.43s
2004	Ezekiel Kemboi, Kenya	8m. 05.81s

20-Kilometer Walk

		Time
1956	Leonid Spirin, USSR	1h. 31m. 27.4s
1960	Vladimir Golubnichy, USSR	1h. 33m. 7.2s
1964	Kenneth Mathews, Great Britain	1h. 29m. 34.0s
1968	Vladimir Golubnichy, USSR	1h. 33m. 58.4s
1972	Peter Frenkel, E. Germany	1h. 26m. 42.4s
1976	Daniel Bautista, Mexico	1h. 24m. 40.6s
1980	Maurizio Damilano, Italy	1h. 23m. 35.5s
1984	Ernesto Canto, Mexico	1h. 23m. 13.0s
1988	Josef Pribilinec, Czechoslovakia	1h. 19m. 57.0s
1992	Daniel Plaza Montero, Spain	1h. 21m. 45.0s
1996	Jefferson Perez, Ecuador	1h. 20m. 7s
2000	Robert Korzeniowski, Poland	1h. 18m. 59.0s*
2004	Ivano Brugnetti, Italy	1h. 19m. 40s

50-Kilometer Walk

Year	Champion	Time
1932	Thomas W. Green, Great Britain	4h. 50m. 10s
1936	Harold Whitlock, Great Britain	4h. 30m. 41.4s
1948	John Ljunggren, Sweden	4h. 41m. 52s
1952	Giuseppe Dordoni, Italy	4h. 28m. 07.8s
1956	Norman Read, New Zealand	4h. 30m. 42.8s
1960	Donald Thompson, Great Britain	4h. 25m. 30s
1964	Abdon Pamich, Italy	4h. 11m. 12.4s
1968	Christoph Hohne, E. Germany	4h. 20m. 13.6s
1972	Bern Kannenberg, W. Germany	3h. 56m. 11.6s
1980	Hartwig Gauter, E. Germany	3h. 49m. 24.0s
1984	Raul Gonzalez, Mexico	3h. 47m. 26.0s
1988	Vyacheslav Ivanenko, USSR	3h. 38m. 29.0s*
1992	Andrei Perlov, Unified Team	3h. 50m. 13.0s
1996	Robert Korzeniowski, Poland	3h. 43m. 30s
2000	Robert Korzeniowski, Poland	3h. 42m. 22s
2004	Robert Korzeniowski, Poland	3h. 38m. 46s

Marathon

Year	Champion	Time
1896	Spiridon Loues, Greece	2h. 58m. 50s
1900	Michel Theato, France	2h. 59m. 45s
1904	Thomas Hicks, United States	3h. 28m. 63s
1908	John J. Hayes, United States	2h. 55m. 18.4s
1912	Kenneth McArthur, South Africa	2h. 36m. 54.8s
1920	Hannes Kolehmainen, Finland	2h. 32m. 35.8s
1924	Albin Stenroos, Finland	2h. 41m. 22.6s
1928	A.B. El Ouafi, France	2h. 32m. 57s
1932	Juan Zabala, Argentina	2h. 31m. 36s
1936	Kijung Son, Japan (Korean)	2h. 29m. 19.2s
1948	Delfo Cabrera, Argentina	2h. 34m. 51.6s
1952	Emil Zatopek, Czechoslovakia	2h. 23m. 03.2s
1956	Alain Mimoun, France	2h. 25m.
1960	Abebe Bikila, Ethiopia	2h. 15m. 16.2s
1964	Abebe Bikila, Ethiopia	2h. 12m. 11.2s
1968	Mamo Wolde, Ethiopia	2h. 20m. 26.4s
1972	Frank Shorter, United States	2h. 12m. 19.8s
1976	Waldemar Cierpinski, E. Germany	2h. 09m. 55s
1980	Waldemar Cierpinski, E. Germany	2h. 11m. 03s
1984	Carlos Lopes, Portugal	2h. 09m. 21s*
1988	Gelindo Bordin, Italy	2h. 10m. 32s
1992	Hwang Young-Cho, S. Korea	2h. 13m. 23s
1996	Josia Thugwane, South Africa	2h. 12m. 36s
2000	Gezahgne Abera, Ethiopia	2h. 10m. 11s
2004	Stefano Baldino, Italy	2h. 10m. 55s

High Jump

1896	Ellery Clark, United States	1.81m.	(5'11¼")
1900	Irving Baxter, United States	1.90m.	(6' 2¾")
1904	Samuel Jones, United States	1.80m.	(5' 11")
1908	Harry Porter, United States	1.90m.	(6' 2¾")
1912	Alma Richards, United States	1.93m.	(6' 4")
1920	Richmond Landon, United States	1.93m.	(6' 4")
1924	Harold Osborn, United States	1.98m.	(6' 6")
1928	Robert W. King, United States	1.94m.	(6' 4¼")
1932	Duncan McNaughton, Canada	1.97m.	(6' 5½")
1936	Cornelius Johnson, United States	2.03m.	(6' 8")
1948	John L. Winter, Australia	1.98m.	(6' 6")
1952	Walter Davis, United States	2.04m.	(6' 8¼")
1956	Charles Dumas, United States	2.12m.	(6' 11½")
1960	Robert Shavlakadze, USSR	2.16m.	(7' 1")
1964	Valery Brumel, USSR	2.18m.	(7' 1¾")
1968	Dick Fosbury, United States	2.24m.	(7' 4¼")
1972	Jüri Tarmak, USSR	2.23m.	(7' 3¾")
1976	Jacek Wszola, Poland	2.25m.	(7' 4½")
1980	Gerd Wessig, E. Germany	2.36m.	(7' 8¾")
1984	Dietmar Mögenburg, W. Germany	2.35m.	(7' 8½")
1988	Hennady Avdeyenko, USSR	2.38m.	(7' 9¾")
1992	Javier Sotomayor Sanabria, Cuba	2.34m.	(7' 8")
1996	Charles Austin, United States	2.39m.	(7' 10")*
2000	Sergey Kliugin, Russia	2.35m.	(7' 8½")
2004	Stefen Holm, Sweden	2.63m.	(7' 8¾")

Long Jump

1896	Ellery Clark, United States	6.35m.	(20' 10")
1900	Alvin Kraenzlein, United States	7.18m.	(23' 6¾")
1904	Meyer Prinstein, United States	7.34m.	(24' 1")
1908	Frank Irons, United States	7.48m.	(24' 6½")
1912	Albert Gutterson, United States	7.60m.	(24' 11¼")
1920	William Petterssen, Sweden	7.15m.	(23' 5½")
1924	William DeHart Hubbard, United States	7.44m.	(24' 5")
1928	Edward B. Hamm, United States	7.73m.	(25' 4½")
1932	Edward Gordon, United States	7.64m.	(25' ¾")
1936	Jesse Owens, United States	8.06m.	(26' 5½")
1948	Willie Steele, United States	7.82m.	(25' 8")
1952	Jerome Biffle, United States	7.57m.	(24' 10")
1956	Gregory Bell, United States	7.83m.	(25' 8¼")
1960	Ralph Boston, United States	8.12m.	(26' 7¾")

Long Jump

1964	Lynn Davies, Great Britain	8.07m.	(26' 5¾")
1968	Bob Beamon, United States	8.90m.	(29' 2½")*
1972	Randy Williams, United States	8.24m.	(27' ½")
1976	Arnie Robinson, United States	8.35m.	(27' 4¾")
1980	Lutz Dombrowski, E. Germany	8.54m.	(28' ¼")
1984	Carl Lewis, United States	8.54m.	(28' ¼")
1988	Carl Lewis, United States	8.72m.	(28' 7½")
1992	Carl Lewis, United States	8.67m.	(28' 5½")
1996	Carl Lewis, United States	8.50m.	(27' 10¾")
2000	Ivan Pedroso, Cuba	8.55m.	(28' ¾")
2004	Dwight Phillips, United States	8.59m.	(28' 2¼")

Triple Jump

1896	James Connolly, United States	13.71m.	(44' 11¾")
1900	Meyer Prinstein, United States	14.47m.	(47' 5¾")
1904	Meyer Prinstein, United States	14.35m.	(47' 1")
1908	Timothy Ahearne, G.B.-Ireland	14.92m.	(48' 11½")
1912	Gustaf Lindblom, Sweden	14.76m.	(48' 5")
1920	Vilho Tuulos, Finland	14.50m.	(47' 7")
1924	Anthony Winter, Australia	15.52m.	(50' 11")
1928	Mikio Oda, Japan	15.21m.	(49' 11")
1932	Chuhei Nambu, Japan	15.72m.	(51' 7")
1936	Naoto Tajima, Japan	16.00m.	(52' 6")
1948	Arne Ahman, Sweden	15.40m.	(50' 6¼")
1952	Adhemar Ferreira da Silva, Brazil	16.22m.	(53' 2¾")
1956	Adhemar Ferreira da Silva, Brazil	16.35m.	(53' 7¾")
1960	Jozef Schmidt, Poland	16.81m.	(55' 1½")
1964	Jozef Schmidt, Poland	16.85m.	(55' 3½")
1968	Viktor Saneyev, USSR	17.39m.	(57' ¾")
1972	Viktor Saneyev, USSR	17.35m.	(56' 11¼")
1976	Viktor Saneyev, USSR	17.29m.	(56' 8¾")
1980	Jaak Uudmae, USSR	17.35m.	(56' 11")
1984	Al Joyner, United States	17.26m.	(56' 7½")
1988	Khristo Markov, Bulgaria	17.61m.	(57' 9½")
1992	Mike Conley, United States	18.17m.	(59' 7½")(w)
1996	Kenny Harrison, United States	18.09m.	(59' 4¼")*
2000	Jonathan Edwards, Britain	17.71m.	(58' 1¼")
2004	Christian Olsson, Sweden	17.79m.	(58' 4 ½")

Discus Throw

1896	Robert Garrett, United States	29.15m.	(95' 7")
1900	Rudolf Bauer, Hungary	36.04m.	(118' 3")
1904	Martin Sheridan, United States	39.28m.	(128' 10")
1908	Martin Sheridan, United States	40.89m.	(134' 1")
1912	Armas Taipale, Finland	45.21m.	(148' 3")
1920	Elmer Niklander, Finland	44.68m.	(146' 7")
1924	Clarence Houser, United States	46.15m.	(151' 4")
1928	Clarence Houser, United States	47.32m.	(155' 3")
1932	John Anderson, United States	49.49m.	(162' 4")
1936	Ken Carpenter, United States	50.48m.	(165' 7")
1948	Adolfo Consolini, Italy	52.78m.	(173' 2")
1952	Sim Iness, United States	55.03m.	(180' 6")
1956	Al Oerter, United States	56.36m.	(184' 11")
1960	Al Oerter, United States	59.18m.	(194' 2")
1964	Al Oerter, United States	61.00m.	(200' 1")
1968	Al Oerter, United States	64.78m.	(212' 6")
1972	Ludvik Danek, Czechoslovakia	64.40m.	(211' 3")
1976	Mac Wilkins, United States	67.50m.	(221' 5")
1980	Viktor Rashchupkin, USSR	66.64m.	(218' 8")
1984	Rolf Dannenberg, W. Germany	66.60m.	(218' 6")
1988	Jurgen Schult, E. Germany	68.82m.	(225' 9")
1992	Romas Ubartas, Lithuania	65.12m.	(213' 8")
1996	Lars Riedel, Germany	69.40m.	(227' 8")
2000	Virgilijus Alekna, Lithuania	69.30m.	(227' 4")
2004	Virgilijus Alekna, Lithuania	69.89m.	(228' 9¾")*

Hammer Throw

1900	John Flanagan, United States	49.73m.	(163' 1")
1904	John Flanagan, United States	51.22m.	(168' 0")
1908	John Flanagan, United States	51.92m.	(170' 4")
1912	Matt McGrath, United States	54.74m.	(179' 7")
1920	Pat Ryan, United States	52.86m.	(173' 5")
1924	Fred Tootell, United States	53.28m.	(174' 10")
1928	Patrick O'Callaghan, Ireland	51.38m.	(168' 7")
1932	Patrick O'Callaghan, Ireland	53.92m.	(176' 11")
1936	Karl Hein, Germany	56.48m.	(185' 4")
1948	Imre Németh, Hungary	56.06m.	(183' 11")
1952	József Csérmák, Hungary	60.34m.	(197' 11")
1956	Harold Connolly, United States	63.18m.	(207' 3")
1960	Vasily Rudenkov, USSR	67.10m.	(202' 0")
1964	Romuald Klim, USSR	69.74m.	(228' 10")
1968	Gyula Zsivótsky, Hungary	73.36m.	(240' 8")
1972	Anatoly Bondarchuk, USSR	75.50m.	(247' 8")
1976	Yuri Syedykh, USSR	77.52m.	(254' 4")
1980	Yuri Syedykh, USSR	81.80m.	(268' 4")
1984	Juha Tiainen, Finland	78.08m.	(256' 2")

Hammer Throw

1988	Sergei Litvinov, USSR	84.80m.	(278' 2")*
1992	Andrey Abduvaliyev, Unified Team.	82.54m.	(270' 9")
1996	Balázs Kiss, Hungary	81.24m.	(266' 6")
2000	Szymon Ziolkowski, Poland	80.02m.	(262' 6")
2004	Koji Murofushi, Japan	82.91m.	(272')

Javelin Throw

1908	Erik Lemming, Sweden	54.82m.	(179' 10")
1912	Erik Lemming, Sweden	60.64m.	(198' 11")
1920	Jonni Myyrä, Finland	64.78m.	(215' 10")
1924	Jonni Myyrä, Finland	62.96m.	(206' 7")
1928	Eric Lundkvist, Sweden	66.60m.	(218' 6")
1932	Matti Järvinen, Finland	72.70m.	(238' 6")
1936	Gerhard Stöck, Germany	71.84m.	(235' 8")
1948	Kai Tapio Rautavaara, Finland	69.76m.	(228' 11")
1952	Cy Young, United States	73.78m.	(242' 1")
1956	Egil Danielsen, Norway	85.70m.	(281' 2")
1960	Viktor Tsibulenko, USSR.	84.64m.	(277' 8")
1964	Pauli Nevala, Finland	82.66m.	(271' 2")
1968	Janis Lusis, USSR.	90.10m.	(295' 7")
1972	Klaus Wolfermann, W. Germany	90.48m.	(296' 10")
1976	Miklós Németh, Hungary	94.58m.	(310' 4")
1980	Dainis Kula, USSR	91.20m.	(299' 2")
1984	Arto Härkönen, Finland	86.76m.	(284' 8")
1988	Tapio Korjus, Finland	84.28m.	(276' 6")
1992	Jan Zelezny, Czechoslovakia (a)	89.66m.	(294' 2")
1996	Jan Zelezny, Czech Republic	88.16m.	(289' 3")
2000	Jan Zelezny, Czech Republic	90.17m.	(295' 9½")*
2004	Andreas Thorkildsen, Norway	86.50m.	(283' 10")

(a) New records were kept after javelin was modified in 1986.

Pole Vault

1896	William Welles Hoyt, United States	3.30m.	(10' 10")
1900	Irving Baxter, United States.	3.30m.	(10' 10")
1904	Charles Dvorak, United States	3.50m.	(11' 6")
1908	A. C. Gilbert, United States;		
	Edward Cooke Jr., United States	3.71m.	(12' 2")
1912	Harry Babcock, United States	3.95m.	(12' 11½")
1920	Frank Foss, United States	4.09m.	(13' 5")
1924	Lee Barnes, United States	3.95m.	(12' 11½")
1928	Sabin W. Carr, United States	4.20m.	(13' 9¼")
1932	William Miller, United States	4.31m.	(14' 1¾")
1936	Earle Meadows, United States	4.35m.	(14' 3¼")
1948	Guinn Smith, United States	4.30m.	(14' 1¼")
1952	Robert Richards, United States.	4.55m.	(14' 11¼")
1956	Robert Richards, United States	4.56m.	(14' 11½")
1960	Don Bragg, United States	4.70m.	(15' 5")
1964	Fred Hansen, United States	5.10m.	(16' 8¾")
1968	Bob Seagren, United States	5.40m.	(17' 8½")
1972	Wolfgang Nordwig, E. Germany	5.50m.	(18' ½")
1976	Tadeusz Slusarski, Poland	5.50m.	(18' ½")
1980	Wladyslaw Kozakiewicz, Poland	5.78m.	(18' 11½")
1984	Pierre Quinon, France	5.75m.	(18' 10¼")
1988	Sergei Bubka, USSR.	5.90m.	(19' 4¼")
1992	Maksim Tarassov, Unified Team.	5.80m.	(19' ¼")
1996	Jean Galfione, France	5.92m.	(19' 5")*
2000	Nick Hysong, United States.	5.90m.	(19' 4¼")
2004	Timothy Mack, United States	5.95m.	(19' 6¼")

16-lb. Shot Put

1896	Robert Garrett, United States	11.22m.	(36' 9¾")
1900	Richard Sheldon, United States	14.10m.	(46' 3¼")
1904	Ralph Rose, United States	14.81m.	(48' 7")
1908	Ralph Rose, United States	14.21m.	(46' 7½")
1912	Pat McDonald, United States	15.34m.	(50' 4")
1920	Ville Pörhölä, Finland	14.81m.	(48' 7¼")
1924	L. Clarence Houser, United States	14.99m.	(49' 2¼")
1928	John Kuck, United States	15.87m.	(52' ¾")
1932	Leo Sexton, United States	16.00m.	(52' 6")
1936	Hans Woellke, Germany	16.20m.	(53' 1¾")
1948	Wilbur Thompson, United States	17.12m.	(56' 2")
1952	W. Parry O'Brien, United States	17.41m.	(57' 1½")
1956	W. Parry O'Brien, United States	18.57m.	(60' 11¼")
1960	William Nieder, United States	19.68m.	(64' 6¾")
1964	Dallas Long, United States	20.33m.	(66' 8½")
1968	Randy Matson, United States	20.54m.	(67' 4¾")
1972	Wladyslaw Komar, Poland	21.18m.	(69' 6")
1976	Udo Beyer, E. Germany	21.05m.	(69' ¾")
1980	Vladimir Kyselyov, USSR	21.35m.	(70' ½")
1984	Alessandro Andrei, Italy	21.26m.	(69' 9")
1988	Ulf Timmermann, E. Germany	22.47m.	(73' 8¾")*
1992	Michael Stulce, United States	21.70m.	(71' 2½")
1996	Randy Barnes, United States	21.62m.	(70' 11¼")
2000	Arsi Harju, Finland.	21.29m.	(69' 10¼")
2004	Yuriy Bilonog, Ukraine	21.16m.	(69' 5¼")

Decathlon (not held 1908)

		Points
1904	Thomas Kiely, Ireland	6,036
1912	Hugo Wieslander, Sweden (a)	7,724.49
1920	Helge Lovland, Norway	6,804.35
1924	Harold Osborn, United States.	7,710.77
1928	Paavo Yrjola, Finland	8,053.29
1932	James Bausch, United States	8,462.23
1936	Glenn Morris, United States	7,900
1948	Robert Mathias, United States	7,139
1952	Robert Mathias, United States	7,887
1956	Milton Campbell, United States	7,937
1960	Rafer Johnson, United States.	8,392
1964	Willi Holdorf, Germany (b)	7,887
1968	Bill Toomey, United States	8,193
1972	Nikolai Avilov, USSR	8,454
1976	Bruce Jenner, United States	8,617
1980	Daley Thompson, Great Britain	8,495
1984	Daley Thompson, Great Britain (c)	8,798
1988	Christian Schenk, E. Germany	8,488
1992	Robert Zmelik, Czechoslovakia	8,611
1996	Dan O'Brien, United States	8,824
2000	Erki Nool, Estonia	8,641
2004	Roman Sebrle, Czech Republic	8,893*

(a) Jim Thorpe of the U.S. won the 1912 Decathlon with 8,413 pts. but was disqualified and had to return his medals because he had played pro baseball prior to the Olympics. The IOC in 1982 posthumously restored his decathlon and pentathlon golds. (b) Former point systems used prior to 1964. (c) Scoring change effective Apr. 1985; Thompson's readjusted score is 8,847 pts.

Track and Field—Women

100-Meter Run

		Time
1928	Elizabeth Robinson, United States	12.2s
1932	Stella Walsh, Poland (a)	11.9s
1936	Helen Stephens, United States	11.5s
1948	Francina Blankers-Koen, Netherlands.	11.9s
1952	Marjorie Jackson, Australia	11.5s
1956	Betty Cuthbert, Australia	11.5s
1960	Wilma Rudolph, United States	11.0s
1964	Wyomia Tyus, United States	11.4s
1968	Wyomia Tyus, United States	11.08s
1972	Renate Stecher, E. Germany.	11.07s
1976	Annegret Richter, W. Germany	11.08s
1980	Lyudmila Kondratyeva, USSR	11.06s
1984	Evelyn Ashford, United States	10.97s
1988	Florence Griffith-Joyner, United States	10.54s (w)
1992	Gail Devers, United States	10.82s
1996	Gail Devers, United States	10.94s
2000	Marion Jones, United States	10.75s
2004	Yuliya Nesterenko, Belarus	10.93s

(a) A 1980 autopsy determined that Walsh was a man.

200-Meter Run

		Time
1948	Francina Blankers-Koen, Netherlands.	24.4s
1952	Marjorie Jackson, Australia	23.7s
1956	Betty Cuthbert, Australia	23.4s
1960	Wilma Rudolph, United States.	24.0s
1964	Edith McGuire, United States	23.0s
1968	Irena Szewinska, Poland	22.5s
1972	Renate Stecher, E. Germany.	22.40s
1976	Barbel Eckert, E. Germany	22.37s
1980	Barbel Wockel, E. Germany	22.03s
1984	Valerie Brisco-Hooks, United States	21.81s
1988	Florence Griffith-Joyner, United States	21.34s*
1992	Gwen Torrence, United States	21.81s
1996	Marie-Jose Perec, France	22.12s
2000	Marion Jones, United States	21.84s
2004	Veronica Campbell, Jamaica	22.05s

400-Meter Run

		Time
1964	Betty Cuthbert, Australia.	52.0s
1968	Colette Besson, France	52.0s
1972	Monika Zehrt, E. Germany	51.08s
1976	Irena Szewinska, Poland	49.29s
1980	Marita Koch, E. Germany	48.88s
1984	Valerie Brisco-Hooks, United States	48.83s
1988	Olga Bryzgina, USSR.	48.65s
1992	Marie-Jose Perec, France	48.83s
1996	Marie-Jose Perec, France	48.25s*
2000	Cathy Freeman, Australia.	49.11s
2004	Tonique Williams-Darling, Bahamas	49.41s

800-Meter Run

		Time
1928	Lina Radke, Germany.	2m. 16.8s
1960	Ludmila Shevtsova, USSR.	2m. 4.3s
1964	Ann Packer, Great Britain.	2m. 1.1s
1968	Madeline Manning, United States.	2m. 0.9s
1972	Hildegard Falck, W. Germany	1m. 58.6s
1976	Tatyana Kazankina, USSR.	1m. 54.94s
1980	Nadezhda Olizarenko, USSR.	1m. 53.43s*

800-Meter Run		Time
1984	Doina Melinte, Romania	1m. 57.60s
1988	Sigrun Wodars, E. Germany	1m. 56.10s
1992	Ellen Van Langen, Netherlands	1m. 55.54s
1996	Svetlana Masterkova, Russia	1m. 57.73s
2000	Maria Mutola, Mozambique	1m. 56.15s
2004	Kelly Holmes, Great Britain	1m. 56.38s

1,500-Meter Run		Time
1972	Lyudmila Bragina, USSR	4m. 01.4s
1976	Tatyana Kazankina, USSR	4m. 05.48s
1980	Tatyana Kazankina, USSR	3m. 56.6s
1984	Gabriella Dorio, Italy	4m. 03.25s
1988	Paula Ivan, Romania	3m. 53.96s*
1992	Hassiba Boulmerka, Algeria	3m. 55.30s
1996	Svetlana Masterkova, Russia	4m. 00.83s
2000	Nouria Benida Merah, Algeria	4m. 05.10s
2004	Kelly Holmes, Great Britain	3m. 57.90s

3,000-Meter Run		Time
1984	Maricica Puica, Romania	8m. 35.96s
1988	Tatyana Samolenko, USSR	8m. 26.53s*
1992	Elena Romanova, Unified Team	8m. 46.04s

5,000-Meter Run		Time
1996	Wang Junxia, China	14m. 59.88s
2000	Gabriela Szabo, Romania	14m. 40.79s*
2004	Meseret Defar, Ethiopa	14m. 45.65s

10,000-Meter Run		Time
1988	Olga Boldarenko, USSR	31m. 44.69s
1992	Derartu Tulu, Ethiopia	31m. 06.02s
1996	Fernanda Ribeiro, Portugal	31m. 01.63s
2000	Derartu Tulu, Ethiopia	30m.17.49s*
2004	Xing Huina, China	30m. 24.36s

100-Meter Hurdles		Time
1972	Annelie Ehrhardt, E. Germany	12.59s
1976	Johanna Schaller, E. Germany	12.77s
1980	Vera Komisova, USSR	12.56s
1984	Benita Brown-Fitzgerald, United States	12.84s
1988	Jordanka Donkova, Bulgaria	12.38s
1992	Paraskevi Patoulidou, Greece	12.64s
1996	Ludmila Enquist, Sweden	12.58s
2000	Olga Shishigina, Kazakhstan	12.65s
2004	Joanna Hayes, United States	12.37s*

400-Meter Hurdles		Time
1984	Nawal el Moutawakii, Morocco	54.61s
1988	Debra Flintoff-King, Australia	53.17s
1992	Sally Gunnell, Great Britain	53.23s
1996	Deon Hemmings, Jamaica	52.82s
2000	Irina Privalova, Russia	53.02s
2004	Fani Halkia, Greece	52.82s*

400-Meter Relay		Time
1928	Canada	48.4s
1932	United States	46.9s
1936	United States	46.9s
1948	Netherlands	47.5s
1952	United States	45.9s
1956	Australia	44.5s
1960	United States	44.5s
1964	Poland	43.6s
1968	United States	42.88s
1972	West Germany	42.81s
1976	East Germany	42.55s
1980	East Germany	41.60s*
1984	United States	41.65s
1988	United States	41.98s
1992	United States	42.11s
1996	United States	41.95s
2000	Bahamas	41.95s
2004	Jamaica	41.73s

1,600-Meter Relay		Time
1972	East Germany	3m. 23s
1976	East Germany	3m. 19.23s
1980	USSR	3m. 20.02s
1984	United States	3m. 18.29s
1988	USSR	3m. 15.17s*
1992	Unified Team	3m. 20.20s
1996	United States	3m. 20.91s
2000	United States	3m. 22.62s
2004	United States	3m. 19.01s

10-Kilometer Walk		Time
1992	Chen Yueling, China	44m. 32s
1996	Elena Nikolayeva, Russia	41m. 49s*

20-Kilometer Walk		Time
2000	Wang Liping, China	1m. 29.05s*
2004	Athanasia Tsoumeleka, Greece	1m. 29.12s

Marathon		Time
1984	Joan Benoit, United States	2h. 24m. 52s
1988	Rosa Mota, Portugal	2h. 25m. 40s

Marathon		Time
1992	Valentina Yegorova, Unified Team	2h. 32m. 41s
1996	Fatuma Roba, Ethiopia	2h. 26m. 05s
2000	Naoko Takahashi, Japan	2h. 23m. 14s*
2004	Mizuki Noguchi, Japan	2h. 26m. 20s

High Jump			
1928	Ethel Catherwood, Canada	1.59m.	(5' 2½")
1932	Jean Shiley, United States	1.65m.	(5' 5")
1936	Ibolya Csák, Hungary	1.60m.	(5' 3")
1948	Alice Coachman, U. S.	1.68m.	(5' 6")
1952	Esther Brand, South Africa	1.67m.	(5' 5¾")
1956	Mildred L. McDaniel, U. S.	1.76m.	(5' 9¼")
1960	Iolanda Balas, Romania	1.85m.	(6' ¾")
1964	Iolanda Balas, Romania	1.90m.	(6' 2¾")
1968	Miloslava Resková, Czech.	1.82m.	(5' 11½")
1972	Ulrike Meyfarth, W. Germany	1.92m.	(6' 3½")
1976	Rosemarie Ackermann, E. Ger.	1.93m.	(6' 4")
1980	Sara Simeoni, Italy	1.97m.	(6' 5½")
1984	Ulrike Meyfarth, W. Germany	2.02m.	(6' 7½")
1988	Louise Ritter, United States	2.03m.	(6' 8")
1992	Heike Henkel, Germany	2.02m.	(6' 7½")
1996	Stefka Kostadinova, Bulgaria	2.05m.	(6' 8¾")*
2000	Yelena Yelesina, Russia	2.01m.	(6' 7")
2004	Yelena Slesarenko, Russia	2.06m.	(6' 9")*

Long Jump			
1948	Olga Gyarmati, Hungary	5.69m.	(18' 8")
1952	Yvette Williams, New Zealand	6.24m.	(20' 5¼")
1956	Elzbieta Krzeskinska, Poland	6.35m.	(20' 10")
1960	Vira Krepkina, USSR	6.37m.	(20' 10¾")
1964	Mary Rand, Great Britain	6.76m.	(22' 2¼")
1968	Viorica Viscopoleanu, Romania	6.82m.	(22' 4½")
1972	Heidemarie Rosendahl, W. Ger.	6.78m.	(22' 3")
1976	Angela Voigt, E. Germany	6.72m.	(22' ¾")
1980	Tatyana Kolpakova, USSR	7.06m.	(23' 2")
1984	Anisoara Cusmir-Stanciu, Rom.	6.96m.	(22' 10")
1988	Jackie Joyner-Kersee, United States	7.40m.	(24' 3½")*
1992	Heike Drechsler, Germany	7.14m.	(23' 5¼")
1996	Chioma Ajunwa, Nigeria	7.12m.	(23' 4½")
2000	Heike Drechsler, Germany	6.99m.	(22' 11¼")
2004	Tatyana Lebedeva, Russia	7.07m.	(23' 2½")

Triple Jump			
1996	Inessa Kravets, Ukraine	15.33m.	(50' 3½")*
2000	Tereza Marinova, Bulgaria	15.20m.	(49' 10½")
2004	Francoise Mbango Etone, Cameroon	15.30m.	(50' 2⅓")

Discus Throw			
1928	Halina Konopacka, Poland	39.62m.	(130' 0")
1932	Lillian Copeland, United States	40.58m.	(133' 2")
1936	Gisela Mauermayer, Germany	47.62m.	(156' 3")
1948	Micheline Ostermeyer, France	41.92m.	(137' 6")
1952	Nina Ponomareva, USSR	51.42m.	(168' 8")
1956	Olga Fikotová, Czech.	53.68m.	(176' 1")
1960	Nina Ponomareva, USSR	55.10m.	(180' 9")
1964	Tamara Press, USSR	57.26m.	(187' 10")
1968	Lia Manoliu, Romania	58.28m.	(191' 2")
1972	Faina Melnik, USSR	66.62m.	(218' 7")
1976	Evelin Jahl, E. Germany	69.00m.	(226' 4")
1980	Evelin Jahl, E. Germany	69.96m.	(229' 6")
1984	Ria Stalman, Netherlands	65.36m.	(214' 5")
1988	Martina Hellmann, E. Germany	72.30m.	(237' 2")*
1992	Maritza Martén Garcia, Cuba	70.06m.	(229' 10")
1996	Ilke Wyludda, Germany	69.66m.	(228' 6")
2000	Ellina Zvereva, Belarus	68.40m.	(224' 5")
2004	Natalya Sadova, Russia	67.02m.	(219' 9")

Hammer Throw			
2000	Kamila Skolimowska, Poland	71.16m.	(233' 5¾")*
2004	Olga Kuzenkova, Russia	75.02m.	(246' 1")

Pole Vault			
2000	Stacy Dragila, United States	4.60m.	(15' 1")*
2004	Yelena Isinbayeva, Russia	4.91m.	(16' 1⅓")

Shot Put (8 lb., 13 oz.)			
1948	Micheline Ostermeyer, France	13.75m.	(45' 1½")
1952	Galina Zybina, USSR	15.28m.	(50' 1½")
1956	Tamara Tyshkyevich, USSR	16.59m.	(54' 5¼")
1960	Tamara Press, USSR	17.32m.	(56' 10")
1964	Tamara Press, USSR	18.14m.	(59' 6¼")
1968	Margitta Gummel, E. Germany	19.61m.	(64' 4")
1972	Nadezhda Chizova, USSR	21.03m.	(69' 0")
1976	Ivanka Khristova, Bulgaria	21.16m.	(69' 5¼")
1980	Ilona Slupianek, E. Germany	22.41m.	(73' 6¼")*
1984	Claudia Losch, W. Germany	20.49m.	(67' 2¼")
1988	Natalya Lisovskaya, USSR	22.24m.	(72' 11¾")
1992	Svetlana Krivelyova, Unified Team	21.06m.	(69' 1¼")
1996	Astrid Kumbernuss, Germany	20.56m.	(67' 5½")
2000	Yanina Karolchik, Belarus	20.56m.	(67' 5½")
2004	Yumileidi Cumba Jay, Cuba	19.59m.	(64' 3¼")

Javelin Throw

1932	"Babe" Didrikson, United States	43.68m.	(143' 4")
1936	Tilly Fleischer, Germany	45.18m.	(148' 3")
1948	Herma Bauma, Austria	45.56m.	(149' 6")
1952	Dana Zátopková, Czech.	50.46m.	(165' 7")
1956	Inese Jaunzeme, USSR	53.86m.	(176' 8")
1960	Elvira Ozolina, USSR	55.98m.	(183' 8")
1964	Mihaela Penes, Romania	60.54m.	(198' 7")
1968	Angéla Németh, Hungary	60.36m.	(198' 0")
1972	Ruth Fuchs, E. Germany	63.88m.	(209' 7")
1976	Ruth Fuchs, E. Germany	65.94m.	(216' 4")
1980	Maria Colón Ruenes, Cuba	68.40m.	(224' 5")
1984	Tessa Sanderson, Great Britain	69.56m.	(228' 2")
1988	Petra Felke, E. Germany	74.68m.	(245' 0")
1992	Silke Renke, Germany	68.34m.	(224' 2")
1996	Heli Rantanen, Finland	67.94m.	(222' 11")
2000	Trine Hattestad, Norway (a)	68.91m.	(226' 1")
2004	Osleidys Menendez, Cuba	71.53m.	(234' 8")*

(a) New records were kept after javelin was modified in 1999.

Heptathlon

		Points
1984	Glynis Nunn, Australia	6,390
1988	Jackie Joyner-Kersee, United States	7,291*
1992	Jackie Joyner-Kersee, United States	7,044
1996	Ghada Shouaa, Syria	6,780
2000	Denise Lewis, Britain	6,584
2004	Carolina Kluft, Sweden	6,952

Swimming and Diving—Men

50-Meter Freestyle

		Time
1988	Matt Biondi, United States	0:22.14
1992	Aleksandr Popov, Unified Team	0:21.91*
1996	Aleksandr Popov, Russia	0:22.13
2000	Anthony Ervin, United States	0:21.98
2000	Gary Hall Jr., United States	0:21.98
2004	Gary Hall Jr., United States	0:21.93

100-Meter Freestyle

		Time
1896	Alfred Hajos, Hungary	1:22.2
1904	Zoltan de Halmay, Hungary (100 yards)	1:02.8
1908	Charles Daniels, United States	1:05.6
1912	Duke P. Kahanamoku, United States	1:03.4
1920	Duke P. Kahanamoku, United States	1:01.4
1924	John Weissmuller, United States	0:59.0
1928	John Weissmuller, United States	0:58.6
1932	Yasuji Miyazaki, Japan	0:58.2
1936	Ferenc Csik, Hungary	0:57.6
1948	Wally Ris, United States	0:57.3
1952	Clark Scholes, United States	0:57.4
1956	Jon Henricks, Australia	0:55.4
1960	John Devitt, Australia	0:55.2
1964	Don Schollander, United States	0:53.4
1968	Mike Wenden, Australia	0:52.2
1972	Mark Spitz, United States	0:51.22
1976	Jim Montgomery, United States	0:49.99
1980	Jorg Woithe, E. Germany	0:50.40
1984	Rowdy Gaines, United States	0:49.80
1988	Matt Biondi, United States	0:48.63
1992	Aleksandr Popov, Unified Team	0:49.02
1996	Aleksandr Popov, Russia	0:48.74
2000	Pieter van den Hoogenband, Netherlands	0:48.30
2004	Pieter van den Hoogenband, Netherlands	0:48.17

200-Meter Freestyle

		Time
1968	Mike Wenden, Australia	1:55.2
1972	Mark Spitz, United States	1:52.78
1976	Bruce Furniss, United States	1:50.29
1980	Sergei Kopliakov, USSR	1:49.81
1984	Michael Gross, W. Germany	1:47.44
1988	Duncan Armstrong, Australia	1:47.25
1992	Yevgeny Sadovyi, Unified Team	1:46.70
1996	Danyon Loader, New Zealand	1:47.63
2000	Pieter van den Hoogenband, Netherlands	1:45.35
2004	Ian Thorpe, Australia	1:44.71*

400-Meter Freestyle

		Time
1904	C. M. Daniels, United States (440 yards)	6:16.2
1908	Henry Taylor, Great Britain	5:36.8
1912	George Hodgson, Canada	5:24.4
1920	Norman Ross, United States	5:26.8
1924	John Weissmuller, United States	5:04.2
1928	Albert Zorilla, Argentina	5:01.6
1932	Clarence Crabbe, United States	4:48.4
1936	Jack Medica, United States	4:44.5
1948	William Smith, United States	4:41.0
1952	Jean Boiteux, France	4:30.7
1956	Murray Rose, Australia	4:27.3
1960	Murray Rose, Australia	4:18.3
1964	Don Schollander, United States	4:12.2
1968	Mike Burton, United States	4:09.0
1972	Brad Cooper, Australia	4:00.27
1976	Brian Goodell, United States	3:51.93

400-Meter Freestyle

		Time
1980	Vladimir Salnikov, USSR	3:51.31
1984	George DiCarlo, United States	3:51.23
1988	Ewe Dassler, E. Germany	3:46.95
1992	Yevgeny Sadovyi, Unified Team	3:45.00
1996	Danyon Loader, New Zealand	3:47.97
2000	Ian Thorpe, Australia	3:40.59*
2004	Ian Thorpe, Australia	3:43.10

1,500-Meter Freestyle

		Time
1908	Henry Taylor, Great Britain	22:48.4
1912	George Hodgson, Canada	22:00.0
1920	Norman Ross, United States	22:23.2
1924	Andrew Charlton, Australia	20:06.6
1928	Arne Borg, Sweden	19:51.8
1932	Kusuo Kitamura, Japan	19:12.4
1936	Noboru Terada, Japan	19:13.7
1948	James McLane, United States	19:18.5
1952	Ford Konno, United States	18:30.3
1956	Murray Rose, Australia	17:58.9
1960	Jon Konrads, Australia	17:19.6
1964	Robert Windle, Australia	17:01.7
1968	Mike Burton, United States	16:38.9
1972	Mike Burton, United States	15:52.58
1976	Brian Goodell, United States	15:02.40
1980	Vladimir Salnikov, USSR	14:58.27
1984	Michael O'Brien, United States	15:05.20
1988	Vladimir Salnikov, USSR	15:00.40
1992	Kieren Perkins, Australia	14:43.48
1996	Kieren Perkins, Australia	14:56.40
2000	Grant Hackett, Australia	14:48.33
2004	Grant Hackett, Australia	14:43.40*

100-Meter Backstroke

		Time
1904	Walter Brack, Germany (100 yds.)	1:16.8
1908	Arno Bieberstein, Germany	1:24.6
1912	Harry Hebner, United States	1:21.2
1920	Warren Kealoha, United States	1:15.2
1924	Warren Kealoha, United States	1:13.2
1928	George Kojac, United States	1:08.2
1932	Masaji Kiyokawa, Japan	1:08.6
1936	Adolph Kiefer, United States	1:05.9
1948	Allen Stack, United States	1:06.4
1952	Yoshi Oyakawa, United States	1:05.4
1956	David Thiele, Australia	1:02.2
1960	David Thiele, Australia	1:01.9
1968	Roland Matthes, E. Germany	0:58.7
1972	Roland Matthes, E. Germany	0:56.58
1976	John Naber, United States	0:55.49
1980	Bengt Baron, Sweden	0:56.33
1984	Rick Carey, United States	0:55.79
1988	Daichi Suzuki, Japan	0:55.05
1992	Mark Tewksbury, Canada	0:53.98
1996	Jeff Rouse, United States	0:54.10
2000	Lenny Krayzelburg, United States	0:53.72
2004	Aaron Peirsol, United States	0:54.06

200-Meter Backstroke

		Time
1964	Jed Graef, United States	2:10.3
1968	Roland Matthes, E. Germany	0:2:09.6
1972	Roland Matthes, E. Germany	2:02.82
1976	John Naber, United States	1:59.19
1980	Sandor Wladar, Hungary	2:01.93
1984	Rick Carey, United States	2:00.23
1988	Igor Polianski, USSR	1:59.37
1992	Martin Lopez-Zubero, Spain	1:58.47
1996	Brad Bridgewater, United States	1:58.54
2000	Lenny Krayzelburg, United States	1:56.76
2004	Aaron Peirsol, United States	1:54.95*

100-Meter Breaststroke

		Time
1968	Don McKenzie, United States	1:07.79
1972	Nobutaka Taguchi, Japan	1:04.94
1976	John Hencken, United States	1:03.11
1980	Duncan Goodhew, Great Britain	1:03.44
1984	Steve Lundquist, United States	1:01.65
1988	Adrian Moorhouse, Great Britain	1:02.04
1992	Nelson Diebel, United States	1:01.50
1996	Fred Deburghgraeve, Belgium	1:00.60
2000	Domenico Fioravanti, Italy	1:00.46
2004	Kosuke Kitajima, Japan	1:00.08

200-Meter Breaststroke

		Time
1908	Frederick Holman, Great Britain	3:09.2
1912	Walter Bathe, Germany	3:01.8
1920	Haken Malmroth, Sweden	3:04.4
1924	Robert Skelton, United States	2:56.6
1928	Yoshiyuki Tsuruta, Japan	2:48.8
1932	Yoshiyuki Tsuruta, Japan	2:45.4
1936	Tetsuo Hamuro, Japan	2:41.5
1948	Joseph Verdeur, United States	2:39.3
1952	John Davies, Australia	2:34.4

200-Meter Breaststroke

		Time
1956	Masura Furukawa, Japan	2:34.7
1960	William Mulliken, United States	2:37.4
1964	Ian O'Brien, Australia	2:27.8
1968	Felipe Munoz, Mexico	2:28.7
1972	John Hencken, United States	2:21.55
1976	David Wilkie, Great Britain	2:15.11
1980	Robertas Zhulpa, USSR	2:15.85
1984	Victor Davis, Canada	2:13.34
1988	Jozsef Szabo, Hungary	2:13.52
1992	Mike Barrowman, United States	2:10.16
1996	Norbert Rozsa, Hungary	2:12.57
2000	Domenico Fioravanti, Italy	2:10.87
2004	Kosuke Kitajima, Japan	2:09.44*

100-Meter Butterfly

		Time
1968	Doug Russell, United States	0:55.9
1972	Mark Spitz, United States	0:54.27
1976	Matt Vogel, United States	0:54.35
1980	Par Arvidsson, Sweden	0:54.92
1984	Michael Gross, W. Germany	0:53.08
1988	Anthony Nesty, Suriname	0:53.00
1992	Pablo Morales, United States	0:53.32
1996	Denis Pankratov, Russia	0:52.27
2000	Lars Froelander, Sweden	0:52.00
2004	Michael Phelps, United States	0:51.25*

200-Meter Butterfly

		Time
1956	William Yorzyk, United States	2:19.3
1960	Michael Troy, United States	2:12.8
1964	Kevin J. Berry, Australia	2:06.6
1968	Carl Robie, United States	2:08.7
1972	Mark Spitz, United States	2:00.70
1976	Mike Bruner, United States	1:59.23
1980	Sergei Fesenko, USSR	1:59.76
1984	Jon Sieben, Australia	1:57.04
1988	Michael Gross, W. Germany	1:56.94
1992	Mel Stewart, United States	1:56.26
1996	Denis Pankratov, Russia	1:56.51
2000	Tom Malchow, United States	1:55.35
2004	Michael Phelps, United States	1:54.04*

200-Meter Individual Medley

		Time
1968	Charles Hickcox, United States	2:12.0
1972	Gunnar Larsson, Sweden	2:07.17
1984	Alex Baumann, Canada	2:01.42
1988	Tamas Darnyi, Hungary	2:00.17
1992	Tamas Darnyi, Hungary	2:00.76
1996	Attila Czene, Hungary	1:59.91
2000	Massimiliano Rosolino, Italy	1:58.98
2004	Michael Phelps, United States	1:57.14*

400-Meter Individual Medley

		Time
1964	Dick Roth, United States	4:45.4
1968	Charles Hickcox, United States	4:48.4
1972	Gunnar Larsson, Sweden	4:31.98
1976	Rod Strachan, United States	4:23.68
1980	Aleksandr Sidorenko, USSR	4:22.89
1984	Alex Baumann, Canada	4:17.41
1988	Tamas Darnyi, Hungary	4:14.75
1992	Tamas Darnyi, Hungary	4:14.23
1996	Tom Dolan, United States	4:14.90
2000	Tom Dolan, United States	4:11.76
2004	Michael Phelps, United States	4:08.26*

400-Meter Freestyle Relay

		Time
1964	United States	3:31.2
1968	United States	3:31.7
1972	United States	3:26.42
1984	United States	3:19.03
1988	United States	3:16.53
1992	United States	3:16.74
1996	United States	3:15.41
2000	Australia	3:13.67
2004	South Africa	3:13.17*

800-Meter Freestyle Relay

		Time
1908	Great Britain	10:55.6
1912	Australia	10:11.6
1920	United States	10:04.4
1924	United States	9:53.4
1928	United States	9:36.2
1932	Japan	8:58.4
1936	Japan	8:51.5
1948	United States	8:46.0
1952	United States	8:31.1
1956	Australia	8:23.6
1960	United States	8:10.2
1964	United States	7:52.1
1968	United States	7:52.33
1972	United States	7:35.78
1976	United States	7:23.22

800-Meter Freestyle Relay

		Time
1980	USSR	7:23.50
1984	United States	7:15.69
1988	United States	7:12.51
1992	Unified Team	7:11.95
1996	United States	7:14.84
2000	Australia	7:07.05*
2004	United States	7:07.33

400-Meter Medley Relay

		Time
1960	United States	4:05.4
1964	United States	3:58.4
1968	United States	3:54.9
1972	United States	3:48.16
1976	United States	3:42.22
1980	Australia	3:45.70
1984	United States	3:39.30
1988	United States	3:36.93
1992	United States	3:36.93
1996	United States	3:34.84
2000	United States	3:33.73
2004	United States	3:30.68*

Springboard Diving

		Points
1908	Albert Zurner, Germany	85.50
1912	Paul Guenther, Germany	79.23
1920	Louis Kuehn, U.S	675.40
1924	Albert White, United States	97.46
1928	Pete Desjardins, United States	185.04
1932	Michael Galitzen, United States	161.38
1936	Richard Degener, United States	163.57
1948	Bruce Harlan, United States	163.64
1952	David Browning, United States	205.29
1956	Robert Clotworthy, United States	159.56
1960	Gary Tobian, United States	170.00
1964	Kenneth Sitzberger, United States	159.90
1968	Bernie Wrightson, United States	170.15
1972	Vladimir Vasin, USSR	594.09
1976	Phil Boggs, United States	619.52
1980	Aleksandr Portnov, USSR	905.02
1984	Greg Louganis, United States	754.41
1988	Greg Louganis, United States	730.80
1992	Mark Lenzi, United States	676.53
1996	Xiong Ni, China	701.46
2000	Xiong Ni, China	708.72
2004	Peng Bo, China	787.30

Platform Diving

		Points
1904	Dr. G.E. Sheldon, United States	112.75
1908	Hjalmar Johansson, Sweden	183.75
1912	Erik Adlerz, Sweden	73.94
1920	Clarence Pinkston, United States	100.67
1924	Albert White, United States	97.46
1928	Pete Desjardins, United States	98.74
1932	Harold Smith, United States	124.80
1936	Marshall Wayne, United States	113.58
1948	Sammy Lee, United States	130.05
1952	Sammy Lee, United States	156.28
1956	Joaquin Capilla, Mexico	152.44
1960	Robert Webster, United States	165.56
1964	Robert Webster, United States	148.58
1968	Klaus Dibiasi, Italy	164.18
1972	Klaus Dibiasi, Italy	504.12
1976	Klaus Dibiasi, Italy	600.51
1980	Falk Hoffmann, E. Germany	835.65
1984	Greg Louganis, United States	710.91
1988	Greg Louganis, United States	638.61
1992	Sun Shuwei, China	677.31
1996	Dmitri Sautin, Russia	692.34
2000	Tian Liang, China	724.53
2004	Hu Jia, China	748.08

Synchronized Platform

		Points
2004	Tian Liang and Yang Jinghui, China	383.88

Synchronized Springboard

		Points
2004	Nikolaos Siranidis and Thomas Bimis, Greece	353.34

Swimming and Diving—Women

50-Meter Freestyle

		Time
1988	Kristin Otto, E. Germany	0:25.49
1992	Yang Wenyi, China	0:24.76
1996	Amy Van Dyken, United States	0:24.87
2000	Inge de Bruijn, Netherlands	0:24.32
2004	Inge de Bruijn, Netherlands	0:24.58

100-Meter Freestyle

		Time
1912	Fanny Durack, Australia	1:22.2
1920	Ethelda Bleibtrey, United States	1:13.6
1924	Ethel Lackie, United States	1:12.4
1928	Albina Osipowich, United States	1:11.0
1932	Helene Madison, United States	1:06.8
1936	Hendrika Mastenbroek, Holland	1:05.9

100-Meter Freestyle	Time
1948 Greta Andersen, Denmark	1:06.3
1952 Katalin Szoke, Hungary	1:06.8
1956 Dawn Fraser, Australia	1:02.0
1960 Dawn Fraser, Australia	1:01.2
1964 Dawn Fraser, Australia	0:59.5
1968 Jan Henne, United States	1:00.0
1972 Sandra Neilson, United States	0:58.59
1976 Kornelia Ender, E. Germany	0:55.65
1980 Barbara Krause, E. Germany	0:54.79
1984 Carrie Steinseifer, United States	0:55.92
Nancy Hogshead, United States (tie)	0:55.92
1988 Kristin Otto, E. Germany	0:54.93
1992 Zhuang Yong, China	0:54.64
1996 Li Jingyi, China	0:54.50
2000 Inge de Bruijn, Netherlands	0:53.83
2004 Jodie Henry, Australia	0:53.84

200-Meter Freestyle	Time
1968 Debbie Meyer, United States	2:10.5
1972 Shane Gould, Australia	2:03.56
1976 Kornelia Ender, E. Germany	1:59.26
1980 Barbara Krause, E. Germany	1:58.33
1984 Mary Wayte, United States	1:59.23
1988 Heike Friedrich, E. Germany	1:57.65*
1992 Nicole Haislett, United States	1:57.90
1996 Claudia Poll, Costa Rica	1:58.16
2000 Susie O'Neill, Australia	1:58.24
2004 Camelia Potec, Romania	1:58.03

400-Meter Freestyle	Time
1924 Martha Norelius, United States	6:02.2
1928 Martha Norelius, United States	5:42.8
1932 Helene Madison, United States	5:28.5
1936 Hendrika Mastenbroek, Netherlands	5:26.4
1948 Ann Curtis, United States	5:17.8
1952 Valerie Gyenge, Hungary	5:12.1
1956 Lorraine Crapp, Australia	4:54.6
1960 Susan Chris von Saltza, United States	4:50.6
1964 Virginia Duenkel, United States	4:43.3
1968 Debbie Meyer, United States	4:31.8
1972 Shane Gould, Australia	4:19.44
1976 Petra Thuemer, E. Germany	4:09.89
1980 Ines Diers, E. Germany	4:08.76
1984 Tiffany Cohen, United States	4:07.10
1988 Janet Evans, United States	4:03.85*
1992 Dagmar Hase, Germany	4:07.18
1996 Michelle Smith, Ireland	4:07.25
2000 Brooke Bennett, United States	4:05.80
2004 Laure Manaudou, France	4:05.34

800-Meter Freestyle	Time
1968 Debbie Meyer, United States	9:24.0
1972 Keena Rothhammer, United States	8:53.68
1976 Petra Thuemer, E. Germany	8:37.14
1980 Michelle Ford, Australia	8:28.90
1984 Tiffany Cohen, United States	8:24.95
1988 Janet Evans, United States	8:20.20
1992 Janet Evans, United States	8:25.52
1996 Brooke Bennett, United States	8:27.89
2000 Brooke Bennett, United States	8:19.67*
2004 Ai Shibata, Japan	8:24.54

100-Meter Backstroke	Time
1924 Sybil Bauer, United States	1:23.2
1928 Marie Braun, Netherlands	1:22.0
1932 Eleanor Holm, United States	1:19.4
1936 Dina Senff, Netherlands	1:18.9
1948 Karen Harup, Denmark	1:14.4
1952 Joan Harrison, South Africa	1:14.3
1956 Judy Grinham, Great Britain	1:12.9
1960 Lynn Burke, United States	1:09.3
1964 Cathy Ferguson, United States	1:07.7
1968 Kaye Hall, United States	1:06.2
1972 Melissa Belote, United States	1:05.78
1976 Ulrike Richter, E. Germany	1:01.83
1980 Rica Reinisch, E. Germany	1:00.86
1984 Theresa Andrews, United States	1:02.55
1988 Kristin Otto, E. Germany	1:00.89
1992 Krisztina Egerszegi, Hungary	1:00.68
1996 Beth Botsford, United States	1:01.19
2000 Diana Mocanu, Romania	1:00.21
2004 Natalie Coughlin, United States	1:00.37

200-Meter Backstroke	Time
1968 Pokey Watson, United States	2:24.8
1972 Melissa Belote, United States	2:19.19
1976 Ulrike Richter, E. Germany	2:13.43
1980 Rica Reinisch, E. Germany	2:11.77
1984 Jolanda De Rover, Netherlands	2:12.38
1988 Krisztina Egerszegi, Hungary	2:09.29
1992 Krisztina Egerszegi, Hungary	2:07.06*
1996 Krisztina Egerszegi, Hungary	2:07.83

200-Meter Backstroke	Time
2000 Diana Mocanu, Romania	2:08.16
2004 Kirsty Coventry, Zimbabwe	2:09.19

100-Meter Breaststroke	Time
1968 Djurdjica Bjedov, Yugoslavia	1:15.8
1972 Cathy Carr, United States	1:13.58
1976 Hannelore Anke, E. Germany	1:11.16
1980 Ute Geweniger, E. Germany	1:10.22
1984 Petra Van Staveren, Netherlands	1:09.88
1988 Tania Dangalakova, Bulgaria	1:07.95
1992 Elena Roudkovskaia, Unified Team	1:08.00
1996 Penny Heyns, South Africa	1:07.73
2000 Megan Quann, United States	1:07.05
2004 Luo Xuejuan, China	1:06.64*

200-Meter Breaststroke	Time
1924 Lucy Morton, Great Britain	3:33.2
1928 Hilde Schrader, Germany	3:12.6
1932 Clare Dennis, Australia	3:06.3
1936 Hideko Maehata, Japan	3:03.6
1948 Nelly Van Vliet, Netherlands	2:57.2
1952 Eva Szekely, Hungary	2:51.7
1956 Ursula Happe, Germany	2:53.1
1960 Anita Lonsbrough, Great Britain	2:49.5
1964 Galina Prozumenschikova, USSR	2:46.4
1968 Sharon Wichman, United States	2:44.4
1972 Beverly Whitfield, Australia	2:41.71
1976 Marina Koshevaia, USSR	2:33.35
1980 Lina Kachushite, USSR	2:29.54
1984 Anne Ottenbrite, Canada	2:30.38
1988 Silke Hoerner, E. Germany	2:26.71
1992 Kyoko Iwasaki, Japan	2:26.65
1996 Penny Heyns, South Africa	2:25.41
2000 Agnes Kovacs, Hungary	2:24.35
2004 Amanda Beard, United States	2:23.37*

100-Meter Butterfly	Time
1956 Shelley Mann, United States	1:11.0
1960 Carolyn Schuler, United States	1:09.5
1964 Sharon Stouder, United States	1:04.7
1968 Lynn McClements, Australia	1:05.5
1972 Mayumi Aoki, Japan	1:03.34
1976 Kornelia Ender, E. Germany	1:00.13
1980 Caren Metschuck, E. Germany	1:00.42
1984 Mary T. Meagher, United States	0:59.26
1988 Kristin Otto, E. Germany	0:59.00
1992 Qian Hong, China	0:58.62
1996 Amy Van Dyken, United States	0:59.13
2000 Inge de Bruijn, Netherlands	50:6.61*
2004 Petria Thomas, Australia	0:57.72

200-Meter Butterfly	Time
1968 Ada Kok, Netherlands	2:24.7
1972 Karen Moe, United States	2:15.57
1976 Andrea Pollack, E. Germany	2:11.41
1980 Ines Geissler, E. Germany	2:10.44
1984 Mary T. Meagher, United States	2:06.90
1988 Kathleen Nord, E. Germany	2:09.51
1992 Summer Sanders, United States	2:08.67
1996 Susan O'Neill, Australia	2:07.76
2000 Misty Hyman, United States	2:05.88*
2004 Otylia Jedrzejczak, Poland	0:2:06.05

200-Meter Individual Medley	Time
1968 Claudia Kolb, United States	2:24.7
1972 Shane Gould, Australia	2:23.07
1984 Tracy Caulkins, United States	2:12.64
1988 Daniela Hunger, E. Germany	2:12.59
1992 Lin Li, China	2:11.65
1996 Michelle Smith, Ireland	2:13.93
2000 Yana Klochkova, Ukraine	2:10.68*
2004 Yana Klochkova, Ukraine	2:11.14

400-Meter Individual Medley	Time
1964 Donna de Varona, United States	5:18.7
1968 Claudia Kolb, United States	5:08.5
1972 Gail Neall, Australia	5:02.97
1976 Ulrike Tauber, E. Germany	4:42.77
1980 Petra Schneider, E. Germany	4:36.29
1984 Tracy Caulkins, United States	4:39.24
1988 Janet Evans, United States	4:37.76
1992 Krisztina Egerszegi, Hungary	4:36.54
1996 Michelle Smith, Ireland	4:39.18
2000 Yana Klochkova, Ukraine	4:33.59*
2004 Yana Klochkova, Ukraine	4:34.83

400-Meter Freestyle Relay	Time
1912 Great Britain	5:52.8
1920 United States	5:11.6
1924 United States	4:58.8
1928 United States	4:47.6
1932 United States	4:38.0
1936 Netherlands	4:36.0
1948 United States	4:29.2

400-Meter Freestyle Relay	Time
1952 Hungary	4:24.4
1956 Australia	4:17.1
1960 United States	4:08.9
1964 United States	4:03.8
1968 United States	4:02.5
1972 United States	3:55.19
1976 United States	3:44.82
1980 East Germany	3:42.71
1984 United States	3:43.43
1988 East Germany	3:40.63
1992 United States	3:39.46
1996 United States	3:39.29
2000 United States	3:36.61
2004 Australia	3:35.94*

800-Meter Freestyle Relay	Time
1996 United States	7:59.87
2000 United States	7:57.80
2004 United States	7:53.42*

400-Meter Medley Relay	Time
1960 United States	4:41.1
1964 United States	4:33.9
1968 United States	4:28.3
1972 United States	4:20.75
1976 East Germany	4:07.95
1980 East Germany	4:06.67
1984 United States	4:08.34
1988 East Germany	4:03.74
1992 United States	4:02.54
1996 United States	4:02.88
2000 United States	3:58.30
2004 Australia	3:57.32*

Springboard Diving	Points
1920 Aileen Riggin, United States	539.90
1924 Elizabeth Becker, United States	474.50
1928 Helen Meany, United States	78.62
1932 Georgia Coleman United States	87.52
1936 Marjorie Gestring, United States	89.27
1948 Victoria M. Draves, United States	108.74
1952 Patricia McCormick, United States	147.30

Springboard Diving	Points
1956 Patricia McCormick, United States	142.36
1960 Ingrid Kramer, Germany	155.81
1964 Ingrid Engel-Kramer, Germany	145.00
1968 Sue Gossick, United States	150.77
1972 Micki King, United States	450.03
1976 Jenni Chandler, United States	506.19
1980 Irina Kalinina, USSR	725.91
1984 Sylvie Bernier, Canada	530.70
1988 Gao Min, China	580.23
1992 Gao Min, China	572.40
1996 Fu Mingxia, China	547.68
2000 Fu Mingxia, China	609.42
2004 Guo Jingjing, China	633.15

Platform Diving	Points
1912 Greta Johansson, Sweden	39.90
1920 Stefani Fryland-Clausen, Denmark	34.60
1924 Caroline Smith, United States	33.20
1928 Elizabeth B. Pinkston, United States	31.60
1932 Dorothy Poynton, United States	40.26
1936 Dorothy Poynton Hill, United States	33.93
1948 Victoria M. Draves, United States	8.87
1952 Patricia McCormick, United States	79.37
1956 Patricia McCormick, United States	84.85
1960 Ingrid Kramer, Germany	91.28
1964 Lesley Bush, United States	99.80
1968 Milena Duchkova, Czech.	109.59
1972 Ulrika Knape, Sweden	390.00
1976 Elena Vaytsekhouskaya, USSR	406.59
1980 Martina Jaschke, E. Germany	596.25
1984 Zhou Jihong, China	435.51
1988 Xu Yanmei, China	445.20
1992 Fu Mingxia, China	461.43
1996 Fu Mingxia, China	521.58
2000 Laura Wilkinson, United States	543.75
2004 Chantelle Newbery, Australia	590.31

Synchronized Platform	Points
2004 Lao Lishi and Li Ting, China	352.14

Synchronized Springboard	Points
2004 Wu Minxia and Guo Jingjing, China	336.90

BOXING

Lt. Flyweight (48 kg/106 lbs)
1968 Francisco Rodriguez, Venezuela
1972 Gyorgy Gedo, Hungary
1976 Jorge Hernandez, Cuba
1980 Shamil Sabyrov, USSR
1984 Paul Gonzalez, United States
1988 Ivailo Hristov, Bulgaria
1992 Rogelio Marcelo, Cuba
1996 Daniel Petrov, Bulgaria
2000 Brahim Asloum, France
2004 Yan Bhartelemy Varela, Cuba

Flyweight (51 kg/112 lbs)
1904 George Finnegan, United States
1920 William Di Gennara, United States
1924 Fidel LaBarba, United States
1928 Antal Kocsis, Hungary
1932 Istvan Enekes, Hungary
1936 Willi Kaiser, Germany
1948 Pascual Perez, Argentina
1952 Nathan Brooks, United States
1956 Terence Spinks, Great Britain
1960 GyulaTorok, Hungary
1964 Fernando Atzori, Italy
1968 Ricardo Delgado, Mexico
1972 Georgi Kostadinov, Bulgaria
1976 Leo Randolph, United States
1980 Peter Lessov, Bulgaria
1984 Steve McCrory, United States
1988 Kim Kwang Sun, S. Korea
1992 Su Choi Choi, N. Korea
1996 Maikro Romero, Cuba
2000 Wijan Ponlid, Thailand
2004 Yuriorkis Gamboa Toledano, Cuba

Bantamweight (54 kg/119 lbs)
1904 Oliver Kirk, United States
1908 A. Henry Thomas, Great Britain
1920 Clarence Walker, South Africa
1924 William Smith, South Africa
1928 Vittorio Tamagnini, Italy
1932 Horace Gwynne, Canada
1936 Ulderico Sergo, Italy
1948 Tibor Csik, Hungary
1952 Pentti Hamalainen, Finland
1956 Wolfgang Behrendt, E. Germany

1960 Oleg Grigoryev, USSR
1964 Takao Sakurai, Japan
1968 Valery Sokolov, USSR
1972 Orlando Martinez, Cuba
1976 Yong-Jo Gu, N. Korea
1980 Juan Hernandez, Cuba
1984 Maurizio Stecca, Italy
1988 Kennedy McKinney, United States
1992 Joel Casamayor, Cuba
1996 Istvan Kovacs, Hungary
2000 Guillermo Rigondeaux, Cuba
2004 Guillermo Rigondeaux, Cuba

Featherweight (57 kg/125 lbs)
1904 Oliver Kirk, United States
1908 Richard Gunn, Great Britain
1920 Paul Fritsch, France
1924 John Fields, United States
1928 Lambertus van Klaveren, Netherlands
1932 Carmelo Robledo, Argentina
1936 Oscar Casanovas, Argentina
1948 Ernesto Formenti, Italy
1952 Jan Zachara, Czechoslovakia
1956 Vladimir Safronov, USSR
1960 Francesco Musso, Italy
1964 Stanislav Stephashkin, USSR
1968 Antonin Roldan, Mexico
1972 Boris Kousnetsov, USSR
1976 Angel Herrera, Cuba
1980 Rudi Fink, E. Germany
1984 Meldrick Taylor, United States
1988 Giovanni Parisi, Italy
1992 Andreas Tews, Germany
1996 Somluck Kamsing, Thailand
2000 Bekzat Sattarkhanov, Kazakhstan
2004 Alexei Tichtchenko, Russia

Lightweight (60 kg/132 lbs)
1904 Harry Spanger, United States
1908 Frederick Grace, Great Britain
1920 Samuel Mosberg, United States
1924 Hans Nielsen, Denmark
1928 Carlo Orlandi, Italy
1932 Lawrence Stevens, South Africa
1936 Imre Harangi, Hungary

1948 Gerald Dreyer, South Africa
1952 Aureliano Bolognesi, Italy
1956 Richard McTaggart, Great Britain
1960 Kazimierz Pazdzior, Poland
1964 Jozef Grudzien, Poland
1968 Ronald Harris, United States
1972 Jan Szczepanski, Poland
1976 Howard Davis, United States
1980 Angel Herrera, Cuba
1984 Pernell Whitaker, United States
1988 Andreas Zuelow, E. Germany
1992 Oscar De La Hoya, United States
1996 Hocine Soltani, Algeria
2000 Mario Kindelan, Cuba
2004 Mario Kindelan, Cuba

Lt. Welterweight (63.5 kg/139 lbs)
1952 Charles Adkins, United States
1956 Vladimir Yengibaryan, USSR
1960 Bohumil Nemecek, Czechoslovazkia
1964 Jerzy Kulej, Poland
1968 Jerzy Kulej, Poland
1972 Ray Seales, United States
1976 Ray Leonard, United States
1980 Patrizio Oliva, Italy
1984 Jerry Page, United States
1988 Viatcheslav Janovski, USSR
1992 Hector Vinent, Cuba
1996 Hector Vinent, Cuba
2000 Mahamadkadyz Abdullaev, Uzbekistan
2004 Manus Boonjumnong, Thailand

Welterweight (67 kg/147 lbs)
1904 Albert Young, United States
1920 Albert Schneider, Canada
1924 Jean Delarge, Belgium
1928 Edward Morgan, New Zealand
1932 Edward Flynn, United States
1936 Sten Suvio, Finland
1948 Julius Torma, Czechoslovakia
1952 Zygmunt Chychia, Poland
1956 Nicolae Linca, Romania
1960 Giovanni Benvenuti, Italy
1964 Marian Kasprzyk, Poland

1968	Manfred Wolke, E. Germany	1956	Gennady Schatkov, USSR		
1972	Emilio Correa, Cuba	1960	Edward Crook, United States		
1976	Jochen Bachfeld, E. Germany	1964	Valery Popenchenko, USSR		
1980	Andres Aldama, Cuba	1968	Christopher Finnegan, Great		
1984	Mark Breland, United States		Britain		
1988	Robert Wangila, Kenya	1972	Vyacheslav Lemechev, USSR		
1992	Michael Carruth, Ireland	1976	Michael Spinks, United States		
1996	Oleg Saitov, Russia	1980	Jose Gomez, Cuba		
2000	Oleg Saitov, Russia	1984	Joon-Sup Shin, S. Korea		
2004	Artayev Bakhtiyar, Kazakhstan	1988	Henry Maske, E. Germany		

Heavyweight (91 kg/201 lbs)

1984	Henry Tillman, United States
1988	Ray Mercer, United States
1992	Felix Savon, Cuba
1996	Felix Savon, Cuba
2000	Felix Savon, Cuba
2004	Odlanier Solis Fonte, Cuba

Lt. Middleweight (71 kg/156 lbs)

1952	Laszlo Papp, Hungary
1956	Laszlo Papp, Hungary
1960	Wilbert McClure, United States
1964	Boris Lagutin, USSR
1968	Boris Lagutin, USSR
1972	Dieter Kottysch, W. Germany
1976	Jerzy Rybicki, Poland
1980	Armando Martinez, Cuba
1984	Frank Tate, United States
1988	Park Si Hun, S. Korea
1992	Juan Lemus, Cuba
1996	David Reid, United States
2000	Yermakhan Ibraimov, Kazakhstan

1992	Ariel Hernandez, Cuba
1996	Ariel Hernandez, Cuba
2000	Jorge Gutierrez, Cuba
2004	Gaydarbek Gaydarbekov, Russia

Lt. Heavyweight (81 kg/178 lbs)

1920	Edward Eagan, United States
1924	Harry Mitchell, Great Britain
1928	Victor Avendano, Argentina
1932	David Carstens, South Africa
1936	Roger Michelot, France
1948	George Hunter, South Africa
1952	Norvel Lee, United States
1956	James Boyd, United States
1960	Cassius Clay, United States
1964	Cosimo Pinto, Italy
1968	Dan Poznyak, USSR
1972	Mate Parlov, Yugoslavia
1976	Leon Spinks, United States
1980	Slobodan Kacar, Yugoslavia
1984	Anton Josipovic, Yugoslavia
1988	Andrew Maynard, United States
1992	Torsten May, Germany
1996	Vassili Jirov, Kazakhstan
2000	Alexander Lebziak, Russia
2004	Andre Ward, United States

Super Heavyweight (91+ kg/201+ lbs)
(known as heavyweight, 1904-80)

1904	Samuel Berger, United States
1908	Albert Oldham, Great Britain
1920	Ronald Rawson, Great Britain
1924	Otto von Porat, Norway
1928	Arturo Rodriguez Jurado, Argentina
1932	Santiago Lovell, Argentina
1936	Herbert Runge, Germany
1948	Rafael Iglesias, Argentina
1952	H. Edward Sanders, United States
1956	T. Peter Rademacher, United States
1960	Franco De Piccoli, Italy
1964	Joe Frazier, United States
1968	George Foreman, United States
1972	Teofilo Stevenson, Cuba
1976	Teofilo Stevenson, Cuba
1980	Teofilo Stevenson, Cuba
1984	Tyrell Biggs, United States
1988	Lennox Lewis, Canada
1992	Roberto Balado, Cuba
1996	Vladimir Klitchko, Ukraine
2000	Audley Harrison, Britain
2004	Alexander Povetkin, Russia

Middleweight (75 kg/165 lbs)

1904	Charles Mayer, United States
1908	John Douglas, Great Britain
1920	Harry Mallin, Great Britain
1924	Harry Mallin, Great Britain
1928	Piero Toscani, Italy
1932	Carmen Barth, United States
1936	Jean Despeaux, France
1948	Laszlo Papp, Hungary
1952	Floyd Patterson, United States

Olympic Information

The modern Olympic Games, first held in Athens, Greece, in 1896, were the result of efforts by Baron Pierre de Coubertin, a French educator, to promote interest in education and culture and to foster better international understanding through love of athletics. His inspiration was the ancient Greek Olympic Games, most notable of the 4 Panhellenic celebrations. The games were combined patriotic, religious, and athletic festivals held every 4 years. The first such recorded festival was held in 776 BCE, which the Greeks began to keep their calendar by "Olympiads," or 4-year spans between the games.

Baron de Coubertin enlisted 13 nations to send athletes to the first modern Olympics in 1896; now athletes from nearly 200 nations and territories compete in the Summer Olympics. The Winter Olympic Games were started in 1924.

Symbol: Five rings or circles, linked together to represent the sporting friendship of all peoples. They also symbolize 5 geographic areas—Europe, Asia, Africa, Australia, and America. Each ring is a different color—blue, yellow, black, green, or red.

Flag: The symbol of the 5 rings on a plain white background.

Creed: "The most important thing in the Olympic Games is not to win but to take part, just as the most important thing in life is not the triumph but the struggle. The essential thing is not to have conquered but to have fought well."

Motto: "Citius, Altius, Fortius." Latin meaning "swifter, higher, stronger."

Oath: "In the name of all competitors I promise that we will take part in these Olympic Games, respecting and abiding by the rules which govern them, in the true spirit of sportsmanship for the glory of sport and the honor of our teams."

Flame: The modern version of the flame was adopted in 1936. The torch used to kindle it is first lit by the sun's rays at Olympia, Greece, then carried to the site of the Games by relays of runners. Ships and planes are used when necessary.

Sites of Winter Olympic Games

1924	Chamonix, France	1952	Oslo, Norway	1976	Innsbruck, Austria	1994	Lillehammer, Norway
1928	St. Moritz, Switzerland	1956	Cortina d'Ampezzo, Italy	1980	Lake Placid, NY	1998	Nagano, Japan
1932	Lake Placid, NY	1960	Squaw Valley, CA	1984	Sarajevo, Yugoslavia	2002	Salt Lake City, UT
1936	Garmisch-Partenkirchen, Germany	1964	Innsbruck, Austria	1988	Calgary, Canada	2006	Turin, Italy
1948	St. Moritz, Switzerland	1968	Grenoble, France	1992	Albertville, France	2010	Vancouver, B.C., Canada
		1972	Sapporo, Japan				

Sites of Summer Olympic Games

1896	Athens, Greece	1924	Paris, France	1960	Rome, Italy	1988	Seoul, South Korea
1900	Paris, France	1928	Amsterdam, Netherlands	1964	Tokyo, Japan	1992	Barcelona, Spain
1904	St. Louis, MO	1932	Los Angeles, CA	1968	Mexico City, Mexico	1996	Atlanta, GA
1906	Athens, Greece*	1936	Berlin, Germany	1972	Munich, W. Germany	2000	Sydney, Australia
1908	London, England	1948	London, England	1976	Montreal, Canada	2004	Athens, Greece
1912	Stockholm, Sweden	1952	Helsinki, Finland	1980	Moscow, USSR	2008	Beijing, China
1920	Antwerp, Belgium	1956	Melbourne, Australia	1984	Los Angeles, CA	2012	London, England

*Games not recognized by International Olympic Committee. Games VI (1916), XII (1940), and XIII (1944) were not celebrated.

Paralympics

The first Olympic games for the disabled were held in Rome after the 1960 Summer Olympics; use of the name "paralympic" began with the 1964 games in Tokyo. The Paralympics are held by the Olympic host country in the same year and usually the same city or venue. A goal of the Paralympics is to provide elite competition to athletes with functional disabilities that prevent their involvement in the Olympics. In 1976 the first Winter Paralympics were held, in Ornskoldsvik, Sweden.

The IX Paralympic Winter Games were held Mar. 10-19, 2006, in Turin, Italy. About 1,300 athletes from a 39 nations competed in 5 sports including, for the first time, wheelchair curling. Russia won the most medals, with 33, and the most golds, with 13. Ukraine landed at 2nd in the medal count after finishing in 18th place in 2002, with 25 medals. Germany was 3rd, with 18 medals; the U.S. won 12 and was ranked 7th.

The XII Paralympic Summer Games were held Sept. 17-28, 2004, in Athens, Greece. A record 3,969 athletes from a record 136 nations competed, and set 304 world and 448 Paralympic records in their events.

Special Olympics

Special Olympics is an international program of year-round sports training and athletic competition for people with intellectual disabilities. All 50 U.S. states, Washington, DC, and Guam have chapter offices. In addition, there are accredited Special Olympics programs in nearly 150 countries. Persons wishing to volunteer or find out more can contact Special Olympics International Headquarters, 1325 G St. NW, Suite 500, Washington, DC 20005, or access the Special Olympics website at www.specialolympics.org

The 11th Special Olympics World Summer Games were held June 21-29, 2003, in Dublin, Ireland. More than 7,000 athletes, 3,000 coaches and delegates, and 28,000 others attended the first Special Olympic World Games outside the U.S. Competition included aquatics, athletics, badminton, bocce, bowling, cycling, equestrian sports, golf, gymnastics (artistic and rhythmic), power lifting, rollerskating, table tennis, and tennis. Scheduled team sports were basketball, handball, sailing, soccer, and volleyball. Kayaking and pitch-and-putt (a form of golf) were included as demonstration sports. The 12th Special Olympics World Summer Games were scheduled to take place in Shanghai, China, Oct. 10-19, 2007.

The 8th Special Olympics World Winter Games were held Feb. 26-Mar. 5, 2005, in Nagano, Japan's Olympic venues. More than 1,800 athletes from 80 countries competed in alpine skiing, cross-country skiing, floor hockey, figure skating, speed skating, snowshoeing, and snowboarding events. The 9th Special Olympic Winter World Games were to be held in Boise, ID, Jan. 31-Feb. 7, 2009.

TRACK AND FIELD
World Track and Field Outdoor Records
As of Oct. 1, 2006

The International Association of Athletics Federations, the world body of track and field, recognizes only records in metric distances, except for the mile. *Pending ratification.

Men's Records

Running

Event	Record	Holder	Country	Date	Where made
100 meters	9.77 s.	Asafa Powell	Jamaica	June 14, 2005	Athens, Greece
200 meters	19.32 s.	Michael Johnson	U.S.	Aug. 1, 1996	Atlanta, GA
400 meters	43.18 s.	Michael Johnson	U.S.	Aug. 26, 1999	Seville, Spain
800 meters	1 m., 41.11 s.	Wilson Kipketer	Denmark	Aug. 24, 1997	Cologne, Germany
1,000 meters	2 m., 11.96 s.	Noah Ngeny	Kenya	Sept. 5, 1999	Rieti, Italy
1,500 meters	3 m., 26.00 s.	Hicham El Guerrouj	Morocco	July 14, 1998	Rome, Italy
1 mile	3 m., 43.13 s.	Hicham El Guerrouj	Morocco	July 7, 1999	Rome, Italy
2,000 meters	4 m., 44.79 s.	Hicham El Guerrouj	Morocco	Sept. 7, 1999	Berlin, Germany
3,000 meters	7 m., 20.67 s.	Daniel Komen	Kenya	Sept. 1, 1996	Rieti, Italy
5,000 meters	12 m., 37.35 s.	Kenenisa Bekele	Ethiopia	May 31, 2004	Hengelo, Netherlands
10,000 meters	26 m., 17.53 s.	Kenenisa Bekele	Ethiopia	Aug. 26, 2005	Brussels, Belgium
20,000 meters	56 m., 55.6 s.	Arturo Barrios	Mexico	Mar. 30, 1991	La Fléche, France
25,000 meters	1 hr., 13 m., 55.8 s.	Toshihiko Seko	Japan	Mar. 22, 1981	Christchurch, NZ
3,000 meter stpl.	7 m., 53.63 s.	Saif Saaeed Shaheen	Qatar	Sept. 3, 2004	Brussels, Belgium
Marathon	2 hr., 4 m., 55 s.	Paul Tergat	Kenya	Sept. 28, 2003	Berlin, Germany

Hurdles

Event	Record	Holder	Country	Date	Where made
110 meters	12.88 s.	Xiang Liu	China	July 11, 2006	Lausanne, Switzerland
400 meters	46.78 s.	Kevin Young	U.S.	Aug. 6, 1992	Barcelona, Spain

Relay Races

Event	Record	Holder	Country	Date	Where made
400 mtrs. (4x100)	37.40 s.	(Marsh, Burrell, Mitchell, Lewis)	U.S.	Aug. 8, 1992	Barcelona, Spain
800 mtrs. (4×200)	1 m., 18.68 s.	(Drummond, Cason, Mitchell, Burrell)	U.S.	Aug. 21, 1993	Stuttgart, Germany
		(Marsh, Burrell, Heard, Lewis)	U.S.	Apr. 17, 1994	Walnut, CA
1,600 mtrs. (4×400)	2 m., 54.20 s.	(Young, Pettigrew, Washington, Johnson)	U.S.	July 22, 1998	Long Island, NY
3,200 mtrs. (4×800)	7 m., 02.43 s.*	(Mutua, Yiampoy, Kombich, Bungei)	Kenya	Aug. 25, 2006	Brussels, Belgium

Field Events

Event	Record	Holder	Country	Date	Where made
High jump	2.45m (8' ½")	Javier Sotomayor	Cuba	July 27, 1993	Salamanca, Spain
Long jump	8.95m (29' 4½")	Mike Powell	U.S.	Aug. 30, 1991	Tokyo, Japan
Triple jump	18.29m (60' ¼")	Jonathan Edwards	Gr. Britain	Aug. 7, 1995	Göteborg, Sweden
Pole vault	6.14m (20' 1¾")	Sergei Bubka	Ukraine	July 31, 1994	Sestriere, Italy
16-lb. shot put	23.12m (75' 10¼")	Randy Barnes	U.S.	May 20, 1990	Los Angeles, CA
Discus	74.08m (243' 0")	Juergen Schult	E. Germany	June 6, 1986	Neubrandenburg, Germany
Javelin	98.48m (323' 1")	Jan Zelezny	Czech Rep.	May 25, 1996	Jena, Germany
16-lb. hammer	86.74m (284' 7")	Yuri Sedykh	USSR	Aug. 30, 1986	Stuttgart, W. Germany
Decathlon	9,026 pts.	Roman Šebrle	Czech Rep.	May 27, 2001	Götzis, Austria

Women's Records

Running

Event	Record	Holder	Country	Date	Where made
100 meters	10.49 s.	Florence Griffith-Joyner	U.S.	July 16, 1988	Indianapolis, IN
200 meters	21.34 s.	Florence Griffith-Joyner	U.S.	Sept. 29, 1988	Seoul, S. Korea
400 meters	47.60 s.	Marita Koch	E. Germany	Oct. 6, 1985	Canberra, Australia
800 meters	1 m., 53.28 s.	Jarmila Kratochvilova	Czech Rep.	July 26, 1983	Munich, Germany
1,000 meters	2 m., 28.98 s.	Svetlana Masterkova	Russia	Aug. 23, 1996	Brussels, Belgium
1,500 meters	3 m., 50.46 s.	Qu Yunxia	China	Sept. 11, 1993	Beijing, China
1 mile	4 m., 12.56 s.	Svetlana Masterkova	Russia	Aug. 14, 1996	Zurich, Switzerland
2,000 meters	5 m., 25.36 s.	Sonia O'Sullivan	Ireland	July 8, 1994	Edinburgh, Scotland
3,000 meters	8 m., 06.11 s.	Wang Junxia	China	Sept. 13, 1993	Beijing, China
3,000 meter stpl.	9 m., 1.59 s.	Gulnara Samitova	Russia	July 4, 2004	Iraklio, Greece
5,000 meters	14 m., 24.53 s.	Meseret Defar	Ethiopia	June 3, 2006	New York, NY
10,000 meters	29 m., 31.78 s.	Wang Junxia	China	Sept. 8, 1993	Beijing, China
20,000 meters	1 h., 05m. 26.6 s.	Tegla Loroupe	Kenya	Sept. 3, 2000	Borgholzhausen, Germany
30,000 meters	1 h., 45 m., 50 s.	Tegla Loroupe	Kenya	June 6, 2003	Warstein, Germany
Marathon	2 h., 15 m., 25 s.	Paula Radcliffe	Gr. Britain	April 13, 2003	London, England

Hurdles

Event	Record	Holder	Country	Date	Where made
100 meters	12.21 s.	Yordanka Donkova	Bulgaria	Aug. 20, 1988	Stara Zagora, Bulgaria
400 meters	52.34 s.	Yuliya Pechenkina	Russia	Aug. 10, 2003	Tula, Russia

Relay Races

Event	Record	Holder	Country	Date	Where made
400 mtrs. (4×100)	41.37 s.	(Gladisch, Rieger, Auerswald, Goehr)	E. Germany	Oct. 6, 1985	Canberra, Australia
800 mtrs. (4×200)	1 m., 27.46 s.	U.S. "Blue" (Jenkins, Clarke, Richardson, Jamieson)	U.S.	Sept. 28, 2000	Philadelphia, PA
1,600 mtrs. (4×400)	3 m., 15.17 s.	(Ledovskaya, Nazarova, Pinigina, Bryzgina)	USSR	Oct. 1, 1988	Seoul, S. Korea
3,200 mtrs. (4×800)	7 m., 50.17 s.	(Olizarenko, Gurina, Borisova, Podyalovskaya)	USSR	Aug. 5, 1984	Moscow, USSR

Field Events

Event	Record	Holder	Country	Date	Where made
High jump	2.09m (6' 10¼")	Stefka Kostadinova	Bulgaria	Aug. 30, 1987	Rome, Italy
Long jump	7.52m (24' 8¼")	Galina Chistyakova	USSR	June 11, 1988	Leningrad, Russia
Triple jump	15.50m (50' 10¼")	Inessa Kravets	Ukraine	Aug. 10, 1995	Göteborg, Sweden
Pole vault	5.01m (16' 5¼")*	Yelena Isinbaeva	Russia	Aug. 12, 2005	Helsinki, Finland
Shot put	22.63m (74' 3")	Natalya Lisovskaya	USSR	June 7, 1987	Moscow, Russia
Discus	76.80m (252' 0")	Gabriele Reinsch	E. Germany	July 9, 1988	Neubrandenburg, Germany
Hammer	77.80m (255' 3")*	Tatyana Lysenko	Russia	Aug. 15, 2006	Tallinn, Estonia
Javelin	71.70m (235' 3")	Osleidys Menéndez	Cuba	Aug. 14, 2005	Helsinki, Finland
Heptathlon	7,291 pts.	Jackie Joyner-Kersee	U.S.	Sept. 24, 1988	Seoul, S. Korea

World Track and Field Indoor Records

As of Oct. 1, 2006

The International Association of Athletics Federations first recognized world indoor track and field records on Jan. 1, 1987. World indoor bests set prior to Jan. 1, 1987, were subject to approval as world records providing they met the IAAF world records criteria, including drug testing. Criteria for indoor and outdoor records are the same, except that a track performance cannot be set on an indoor track longer than 200 meters. (a)=altitude.

Men's Records

Event	Record	Holder	Country	Date	Where made
50 meters	5.56 s.(a)	Donovan Bailey	Canada	Feb. 9, 1996	Reno, NV
60 meters	6.39 s.	Maurice Greene	U.S.	Mar. 3, 2001	Atlanta, GA
	6.39 s.	Maurice Greene	U.S.	Feb. 3, 1998	Madrid, Spain
200 meters	19.92 s.	Frank Fredericks	Namibia	Feb. 18, 1996	Lievin, France
400 meters	44.57 s.	Kerron Clement	U.S.	Mar. 12, 2005	Fayetteville, AR
800 meters	1:42.67 min.	Wilson Kipketer	Denmark	Mar. 9, 1997	Paris, France
1,000 meters	2:14.96 min.	Wilson Kipketer	Denmark	Feb. 20, 2000	Birmingham, England
1,500 meters	3:31.18 min.	Hicham El Guerrouj	Morocco	Feb. 2, 1997	Stuttgart, Germany
1 mile	3:48.45 min.	Hicham El Guerrouj	Morocco	Feb. 12, 1997	Ghent, Belgium
3,000 meters	7:24.90 min.	Daniel Komen	Kenya	Feb. 6, 1998	Budapest, Hungary
5,000 meters	12:49.60 min.	Kenenisa Bekele	Ethiopia	Feb. 20, 2004	Birmingham, England
50-meter hurdles	6.25 s.	Mark McKoy	Canada	Mar. 5, 1986	Kobe, Japan
60-meter hurdles	7.30 s.	Colin Jackson	Gr. Britain	Mar. 6, 1994	Sindelfingen, Germany
High jump	2.43m (7' 11½")	Javier Sotomayor	Cuba	Mar. 4, 1989	Budapest, Hungary
Pole vault	6.15m (20' 2")	Sergey Bubka	Ukraine	Feb. 21, 1993	Donyetsk, Ukraine
Long jump	8.79m (28' 10¼")	Carl Lewis	U.S.	Jan. 27, 1984	New York, NY
Triple jump	17.83 (58' 6")	Aliecer Urrutia	Cuba	Mar. 1, 1997	Sindelfingen, Germany
		Christian Olsson	Sweden	Mar. 7, 2004	Budapest, Hungary
Shot put	22.66m (74' 4¼")	Randy Barnes	U.S.	Jan. 20, 1989	Los Angeles, CA

Women's Records

Event	Record	Holder	Country	Date	Where made
50 meters	5.96 s.	Irina Privalova	Russia	Feb. 9, 1995	Madrid, Spain
60 meters	6.92 s.	Irina Privalova	Russia	Feb. 9, 1995	Madrid, Spain
		Irina Privalova	Russia	Feb. 11, 1993	Madrid, Spain
200 meters	21.87 s.	Merlene Ottey	Jamaica	Feb. 13, 1993	Lievin, France
400 meters	49.59 s.	Jarmila Kratochvílová	Czechoslovakia	Mar. 7, 1982	Milan, Italy
800 meters	1:55.82 s.	Jolanda Ceplak	Slovenia	Mar. 3, 2002	Vienna, Austria
1,000 meters	2:30.94 min.	Maria Mutola	Mozambique	Feb. 25, 1999	Stockholm, Sweden
1,500 meters	3:58.28 min.	Yelena Soboleva	Russia	Feb. 18, 2006	Moscow, Russia
1 mile	4:17.14 min.	Doina Melinte	Romania	Feb. 9, 1990	E. Rutherford, NJ
3,000 meters	8:29.15 min.	Berhane Adere	Ethiopia	Mar. 3, 2002	Stuttgart, Germany
5,000 meters	14:32.93 min.	Tirunesh Dibaba	Ethiopia	Jan. 29, 2005	Boston, MA
50-meter hurdles	6.58 s.	Cornelia Oschkenat	E. Germany	Feb. 20, 1988	Berlin, Germany
60-meter hurdles	7.69 s.	Ludmila Engquist	USSR	Feb. 4, 1990	Chelyabinsk, USSR
High jump	2.08m (6' 10")	Kajsa Bergqvist	Sweden	Feb. 4, 2006	Arnstadt, Germany
Pole vault	4.91m (16' 1¼")	Yelena Isinbaeva	Russia	Feb. 12, 2006	Donetsk, Ukraine
Long jump	7.37m (24' 2¼")	Heike Drechsler	E. Germany	Feb. 13, 1988	Vienna, Austria
Triple jump	15.36m (50' 4¾")	Tatyana Lebedeva	Russia	Mar. 3, 2004	Budapest, Hungary
Shot put	22.50m (73' 10")	Helena Fibingerova	Czechoslovakia	Feb. 19, 1977	Jablonec, Czechoslovakia

▶ **IT'S A FACT:** On May 12, 2006, U.S. sprinter Justin Gatlin ran the 100-meter dash in a reported time of 9.76 seconds, setting a new world record by one-hundredth of a second. The record was revoked five days later: official timers announced that they had mistakenly rounded Gatlin's time of 9.766 down, and Gatlin had merely tied the standing record. Gatlin forfeited the performance—and the tied record—altogether on Aug. 22, 2006, when the U.S. Anti-Doping Agency handed him an 8-year ban for testing positive for elevated testosterone levels in a sample taken shortly before his not quite record-setting performance.

BASEBALL

Cardinals Open New Park; Bonds Tops Ruth; Hoffman Sets Saves Record; Braves Streak Ends

The St. Louis Cardinals played their Apr. 10 home-opener at their new ballpark, New Busch Stadium, which replaced old Busch Stadium, their previous home of 40 years. Barry Bonds cracked his 715th career home run on May 29 and surpassed Babe Ruth on the all-time career home run list. Bonds ended the season with 734 home runs, just 21 short of Hank Aaron's all-time record of 755. There was renewed controversy surrounding Bonds after the March release of the book *Game of Shadows*, which chronicled Bonds' alleged performance-enhancing drug use. The Los Angeles Dodgers during a Sept. 19 game against the San Diego Padres hit four consecutive home runs in the 9th inning, a feat which had not been done since 1964, to tie the game before winning in the 10th, 11-10. San Diego closer Trevor Hoffman Sept. 24 notched save number 479 in a 2-1 win over Pittsburgh and became the all-time career saves leader. He finished the season with 482.

The New York Mets won the NL East for the first time since 1988, going 97-65, and ended the Atlanta Braves' 14-year NL division championship streak. St. Louis fought off Houston and won the NL Central. San Diego just barely took the NL West over a surging Los Angeles, who ended up grabbing the NL wild card. The New York Yankees overcame injuries and won the AL East title. Minnesota took the AL Central in the final week over Detroit, who clinched the AL wild card and made the playoffs for the first time since 1987. Oakland won the AL West.

National League Final Standings, 2006

Eastern Division

	W	L	Pct.	GB	Home	Road	vs. East	vs. Central	vs. West	vs. AL
New York	97	65	.599	—	50-31	47-34	45-29	23-17	23-10	6-9
Philadelphia	85	77	.525	12.0	41-40	44-37	41-34	20-17	19-13	5-13
Atlanta	79	83	.488	18.0	40-41	39-42	35-38	22-17	17-18	5-10
Florida	78	84	.481	19.0	42-39	36-45	33-42	22-17	14-16	9-9
Washington	71	91	.438	26.0	41-40	30-51	31-42	20-19	13-19	7-11

Central Division

	W	L	Pct.	GB	Home	Road	vs. East	vs. Central	vs. West	vs. AL
St. Louis	83	78	.516	—	49-31	34-47	16-15	39-42	23-11	5-10
Houston	82	80	.506	1.5	44-37	38-43	16-18	45-32	14-19	7-11
Cincinnati	80	82	.494	3.5	42-39	38-43	17-15	46-38	11-20	6-9
Milwaukee	75	87	.463	8.5	48-33	27-54	13-18	37-45	19-15	6-9
Pittsburgh	67	95	.414	16.5	43-38	24-57	15-19	34-44	15-20	3-12
Chicago	66	96	.407	17.5	36-45	30-51	10-22	42-42	10-21	4-11

Western Division

	W	L	Pct.	GB	Home	Road	vs. East	vs. Central	vs. West	vs. AL
San Diego	88	74	.543	—	43-38	45-36	16-18	26-12	39-36	7-8
Los Angeles*	88	74	.543	—	49-32	39-42	19-13	21-20	43-31	5-10
San Francisco	76	85	.472	11.5	43-38	33-47	12-19	19-21	37-38	8-7
Arizona	76	86	.469	12.0	39-42	37-44	11-21	24-16	37-38	4-11
Colorado	76	86	.469	12.0	44-37	32-49	18-15	16-23	31-44	11-4

* Wild Card team.

American League Final Standings, 2006

Eastern Division

	W	L	Pct.	GB	Home	Road	vs. East	vs. Central	vs. West	vs. NL
New York	97	65	.599	—	50-31	47-34	46-28	23-12	18-17	10-8
Toronto	87	75	.537	10.0	50-31	37-44	43-31	18-17	17-18	9-9
Boston	86	76	.531	11.0	48-33	38-43	40-35	15-19	15-20	16-2
Baltimore	70	92	.432	27.0	40-41	30-51	31-44	17-17	13-22	9-9
Tampa Bay	61	101	.377	36.0	41-40	20-61	26-48	13-21	11-25	11-7

Central Division

	W	L	Pct.	GB	Home	Road	vs. East	vs. Central	vs. West	vs. NL
Minnesota	96	66	.593	—	54-27	42-39	22-13	41-35	17-16	16-2
Detroit*	95	67	.586	1.0	46-35	49-32	16-17	45-30	19-17	15-3
Chicago	90	72	.556	6.0	49-32	41-40	17-17	40-36	19-15	14-4
Cleveland	78	84	.481	18.0	44-37	34-47	19-14	35-40	16-20	8-10
Kansas City	62	100	.383	34.0	34-47	28-53	12-25	27-47	13-20	10-8

Western Division

	W	L	Pct.	GB	Home	Road	vs. East	vs. Central	vs. West	vs. NL
Oakland	93	69	.574	—	49-32	44-37	29-15	22-21	34-23	8-10
Los Angeles	89	73	.549	4.0	45-36	44-37	26-19	24-18	32-25	7-11
Texas	80	82	.494	13.0	39-42	41-40	22-21	22-22	29-28	7-11
Seattle	78	84	.481	15.0	44-37	34-47	25-19	20-23	19-38	14-4

* Wild Card team.

National League Statistics, 2006

(Individual Statistics: Batting—at least 150 at-bats; Pitching—at least 70 innings or 10 saves; *changed teams within NL during season; entry includes statistics for more than 1 team; # changed teams to or from AL during season; entry includes only NL stats)

Team Batting

Team	BA	AB	R	H	HR	RBI
Los Angeles Dodgers	.276	5628	820	1552	153	787
Colorado Rockies	.270	5562	813	1504	157	761
Atlanta Braves	.270	5583	849	1510	222	818
St. Louis Cardinals	.269	5522	781	1484	184	745
Chicago Cubs	.268	5587	716	1496	166	677
Arizona Diamondbacks	.267	5645	773	1506	160	743
Philadelphia Phillies	.267	5687	865	1518	216	823
New York Mets	.264	5558	834	1469	200	800
Florida Marlins	.264	5502	758	1454	182	713
Pittsburgh Pirates	.263	5558	691	1462	141	656
San Diego Padres	.263	5576	731	1465	161	698
Washington Nationals	.262	5495	746	1437	164	695
San Francisco Giants	.259	5472	746	1418	163	711
Milwaukee Brewers	.258	5433	730	1400	180	695
Cincinnati Reds	.257	5515	749	1419	217	718
Houston Astros	.255	5521	735	1407	174	708

Team Pitching

Team	ERA	IP	H	SO	BB	SV
San Diego Padres	3.87	1463.2	1385	1097	468	50
Houston Astros	4.08	1468.2	1425	1160	480	42
New York Mets	4.14	1461.1	1402	1161	527	43
Los Angeles Dodgers	4.23	1460.1	1524	1068	492	40
Florida Marlins	4.37	1433.1	1465	1088	622	41
Arizona Diamondbacks	4.48	1459.2	1503	1115	536	34
Cincinnati Reds	4.51	1445.2	1576	1053	464	36
Pittsburgh Pirates	4.52	1435.0	1545	1060	620	39
St. Louis Cardinals	4.54	1429.2	1475	970	504	38
Philadelphia Phillies	4.60	1460.1	1561	1138	512	42
Atlanta Braves	4.60	1441.1	1529	1049	572	38
San Francisco Giants	4.63	1429.2	1422	992	584	37
Colorado Rockies	4.66	1447.1	1549	952	553	34
Chicago Cubs	4.74	1439.0	1396	1250	687	29
Milwaukee Brewers	4.82	1425.2	1454	1145	514	43
Washington Nationals	5.03	1436.1	1535	960	584	32

Arizona Diamondbacks

BATTERS	AVG	AB	R	H	HR	RBI	SO	SB
S Drew	.316	209	27	66	5	23	50	2
J Estrada	.302	414	43	125	11	71	40	0
C Jackson	.291	485	75	141	15	79	73	1
J DaVanon	.290	221	38	64	5	35	42	10
O Hudson	.287	579	87	166	15	67	78	9
C Tracy	.281	597	91	168	20	80	129	5
C Snyder	.277	184	19	51	6	32	39	0
L Gonzalez	.271	586	93	159	15	73	58	0
E Byrnes	.267	562	82	150	26	79	88	25
C Counsell	.255	372	56	95	4	30	47	15
C. Quentin	.253	166	23	42	9	32	34	1
D Easley	.233	189	24	44	9	28	30	1

PITCHERS	W-L	ERA	IP	H	BB	SO	SV
B Webb	16-8	3.10	235.0	216	50	178	0
B Medders	5-3	3.64	71.2	76	28	47	0
J Cruz	5-6	4.18	94.2	80	47	88	0
J Julio*	2-4	4.23	66.0	52	35	88	16
M Batista	11-8	4.58	206.1	231	84	110	0
L Hernandez	13-13	4.83	216.0	246	78	128	0
C Vargas	12-10	4.83	167.2	185	52	123	0
E Gonzalez	3-7	5.67	106.1	114	34	66	0
J Valverde	2-3	5.84	49.1	50	22	69	18

Manager-Bob Melvin

Atlanta Braves

BATTERS	AVG	AB	R	H	HR	RBI	SO	SB
B McCann	.333	442	61	147	24	93	54	2
M Diaz	.327	297	37	97	7	32	49	5
C Jones	.324	411	87	133	26	86	73	6
E Renteria	.293	598	100	175	14	70	89	17
A LaRoche	.285	492	89	140	32	90	128	0
W Aybar*	.280	243	32	68	4	30	36	1
A Jones	.262	565	107	148	41	129	127	4
M Giles	.262	550	87	144	11	60	105	10
J Francoeur	.260	651	83	169	29	103	132	1
P Orr	.253	154	22	39	1	8	30	2
R Langerhans	.241	315	46	76	7	28	91	1

PITCHERS	W-L	ERA	IP	H	BB	SO	SV
B Wickman	0-2	1.04	26.0	24	2	25	18
J Smoltz	16-9	3.49	232.0	221	55	211	0
O Villarreal	9-1	3.61	92.1	93	27	55	0
C James	11-4	3.78	119.0	101	47	91	0
H Ramirez	5-5	4.48	76.1	85	31	37	0
J Thomson	2-7	4.82	80.1	93	32	46	0
T Hudson	13-12	4.86	218.1	235	79	141	0
L Cormier	4-5	4.89	73.2	90	39	43	0

Manager-Bobby Cox

Chicago Cubs

BATTERS	AVG	AB	R	H	HR	RBI	SO	SB
M Barrett	.307	375	54	115	16	53	41	0
M Murton	.297	455	70	135	13	62	62	5
J Pierre	.292	699	87	204	3	40	38	58
A Ramirez	.291	594	93	173	38	119	63	2
D Lee	.286	175	30	50	8	30	41	8
J Jones	.285	533	73	152	27	81	116	9
P Nevin#	.274	179	26	49	12	33	52	0
H Blanco	.266	241	23	64	6	37	38	0
N Perez#	.254	236	27	60	2	24	21	0
A Pagan	.247	170	28	42	5	18	28	4
R Cedeno	.245	534	51	131	6	41	109	8
C Izturis*	.245	192	14	47	1	18	14	1
J Mabry	.205	210	16	43	5	25	57	0

PITCHERS	W-L	ERA	IP	H	BB	SO	SV
B Howry	4-5	3.17	76.2	70	17	71	5
C Zambrano	16-7	3.41	214.0	162	115	210	0
R Hill	6-7	4.17	99.1	83	39	90	0
R Novoa	2-1	4.26	76.0	77	32	53	0
R Dempster	1-9	4.80	75.0	77	36	67	24
S Marshall	6-9	5.59	125.2	132	59	77	0
C Marmol	5-7	6.08	77.0	71	59	59	0

Manager-Dusty Baker

Cincinnati Reds

BATTERS	AVG	AB	R	H	HR	RBI	SO	SB
R Aurilia	.300	440	61	132	23	70	51	3
S Hatteberg	.289	456	62	132	13	51	41	2
B Phillips	.276	536	65	148	17	75	88	25
E Encarnacion	.276	406	60	112	15	72	78	6
R Freel	.271	454	67	123	8	27	98	37
J Valentin	.269	186	24	50	8	27	29	0
R Clayton*	.258	454	49	117	4	40	85	14
D Ross	.255	247	37	63	21	52	75	0
K Griffey	.252	428	62	108	27	72	78	0
A Dunn	.234	561	99	131	40	92	194	7
J LaRue	.194	191	22	37	8	21	51	1

PITCHERS	W-L	ERA	IP	H	BB	SO	SV
B Arroyo	14-11	3.29	240.2	222	64	184	0
D Weathers	4-4	3.54	73.2	61	34	50	12
T Coffey	6-7	3.58	78.0	85	27	60	8
A Harang	16-11	3.76	234.1	242	56	216	0
R Franklin*	6-7	4.54	77.1	86	33	43	0
G Majewski*	4-4	4.61	70.1	79	29	43	0
E Milton	8-8	5.19	152.2	163	42	90	0
E Ramirez	4-9	5.37	104.0	123	29	69	0
B Claussen	3-8	6.19	77.0	93	28	57	0

Manager-Dave Miley, Jerry Narron

Colorado Rockies

BATTERS	AVG	AB	R	H	HR	RBI	SO	SB
G Atkins	.329	602	117	198	29	120	76	4
M Holliday	.326	602	119	196	34	114	110	10
T Helton	.302	546	94	165	15	81	64	3
J Carroll	.300	463	84	139	5	36	66	10
B Hawpe	.293	499	67	146	22	84	123	5
C Sullivan	.267	386	47	103	2	30	100	10
K Matsui*	.267	243	32	65	3	26	46	10
Y Torrealba	.247	223	23	55	7	43	49	4
C Freeman	.237	173	24	41	2	18	42	5
V Castilla	.229	275	26	63	5	27	49	0
C Barmes	.220	478	57	105	7	56	72	5

PITCHERS	W-L	ERA	IP	H	BB	SO	SV
B Fuentes	3-4	3.44	65.1	50	26	73	30
J Jennings	9-13	3.78	212.0	206	85	142	0
J Mesa	1-5	3.86	72.1	73	36	39	1
J Francis	13-11	4.16	199.0	187	69	117	0
A Cook	9-15	4.23	212.2	242	55	92	0
J Fogg	11-9	5.49	172.0	206	60	93	0
B Kim	8-12	5.57	155.0	179	61	129	0

Manager-Clint Hurdle

Florida Marlins

BATTERS	AVG	AB	R	H	HR	RBI	SO	SB
M Cabrera	.339	576	112	195	26	114	108	9
W Helms	.329	240	30	79	10	47	55	0
H Ramirez	.292	633	119	185	17	59	128	51
D Uggla	.282	611	105	172	27	90	123	6
J Willingham	.277	502	62	139	26	74	109	2
M Olivo	.263	430	52	113	16	58	103	2
M Jacobs	.262	469	54	123	20	77	105	3
A Amezaga	.260	334	42	87	3	19	46	20
J Hermida	.251	307	37	77	5	28	70	4
J Borchard	.230	230	30	53	10	28	66	0
M Treanor	.229	157	12	36	2	14	34	0
C Ross	.227	269	34	61	13	46	65	1
R Abercrombie	.212	255	40	54	5	24	78	6

PITCHERS	W-L	ERA	IP	H	BB	SO	SV
A Sanchez	10-3	2.83	114.1	90	46	72	0
J Johnson	12-7	3.10	157.0	136	68	133	0
J Borowski	3-3	3.75	69.2	63	33	64	36
D Willis	12-12	3.87	223.1	234	83	160	0
S Olsen	12-10	4.04	180.2	160	75	166	0
M Herges	2-3	4.31	71.0	94	28	36	0
R Nolasco	11-11	4.82	140.0	157	41	99	0
B Moehler	7-11	6.57	122.0	164	38	58	0

Manager-Joe Girardi

Houston Astros

BATTERS	AVG	AB	R	H	HR	RBI	SO	SB
L Scott	.336	214	31	72	10	37	43	2
L Berkman	.315	536	95	169	45	136	106	3
M Lamb	.307	381	70	117	12	45	55	2
W Taveras	.278	529	83	147	1	30	88	33
C Burke	.276	366	58	101	9	40	77	11
A Huff#	.250	224	31	56	13	38	39	0
C Biggio	.246	548	79	135	21	62	84	3
A Everett	.239	514	52	123	6	59	71	9
M Ensberg	.235	387	67	91	23	58	96	1
B Ausmus	.230	439	37	101	2	39	71	3
J Lane	.201	288	44	58	15	45	75	1

PITCHERS	W-L	ERA	IP	H	BB	SO	SV
R Clemens	7-6	2.30	113.1	89	29	102	0
D Wheeler	3-5	2.52	71.1	58	24	68	9
R Oswalt	15-8	2.98	220.2	220	38	166	0
C Qualls	7-3	3.76	88.2	76	28	56	0
A Pettitte	14-13	4.20	214.1	238	70	178	0
F Nieve	3-3	4.20	96.1	87	41	70	0
D Borkowski	3-2	4.69	71.0	70	23	52	0
B Lidge	1-5	5.28	75.0	69	36	104	32
W Rodriguez	9-10	5.64	135.2	154	63	98	0
T Buchholz	6-10	5.89	113.0	107	34	77	0

Manager-Phil Garner

Los Angeles Dodgers

BATTERS	AVG	AB	R	H	HR	RBI	SO	SB
A Ethier	.308	396	50	122	11	55	77	5
N Garciaparra	.303	469	82	142	20	93	30	3
K Lofton	.301	469	79	141	3	41	42	32
R Furcal	.300	654	113	196	15	63	98	37
M Anderson*	.297	279	43	83	12	38	49	4
O Saenz	.296	179	30	53	11	48	47	0
J Kent	.292	407	61	119	14	68	69	1
J Drew	.283	494	84	140	20	100	106	2
R Martin	.282	415	65	117	10	65	57	10
R Martinez	.278	176	20	49	2	24	20	0
W Betemit*	.263	373	49	98	18	53	102	3
M Kemp	.253	154	30	39	7	23	53	6
J Cruz	.233	223	34	52	5	17	54	5

PITCHERS	W-L	ERA	IP	H	BB	SO	SV
T Saito	6-2	2.07	78.1	48	23	107	24
J Broxton	4-1	2.59	76.1	61	33	97	3
J Beimel	2-1	2.96	70.0	70	21	30	2
D Lowe	16-8	3.63	218.0	221	55	123	0
C Billingsley	7-4	3.80	90.0	92	58	59	0
G Maddux*	15-14	4.20	210.0	219	37	117	0
B Penny	16-9	4.33	189.0	206	54	148	0
A Sele	8-6	4.53	103.1	120	30	57	0
M Hendrickson#	2-7	4.68	75.0	92	28	48	0
B Tomko	8-7	4.73	112.1	123	29	76	0

Manager-Grady Little

Milwaukee Brewers

BATTERS	AVG	AB	R	H	HR	RBI	SO	SB
J Cirillo	.319	263	33	84	3	23	33	1
C Lee#	.286	388	60	111	28	81	39	12
C Hart	.283	237	32	67	9	33	58	5
T Graffanino	.280	236	34	66	2	27	37	2
R Weeks	.279	359	73	100	8	34	92	19
G Gross	.274	208	42	57	9	38	60	1
P Fielder	.271	569	82	154	28	81	125	7
G Jenkins	.271	484	62	131	17	70	129	4
B Hall	.270	537	101	145	35	85	162	8
D Bell	.270	504	60	136	10	63	68	3
B Clark	.263	415	51	109	4	29	60	3
C Koskie	.261	257	29	67	12	33	58	1
D Miller	.251	331	34	83	6	38	86	0

PITCHERS	W-L	ERA	IP	H	BB	SO	SV
F Cordero#	3-1	1.69	26.2	20	16	30	16
B Sheets	6-7	3.82	106.0	105	11	116	0
C Capuano	11-12	4.03	221.1	229	47	174	0
J Capellan	4-2	4.40	71.2	65	31	58	0
D Bush	12-11	4.41	210	201	38	166	0
T Ohka	4-5	4.82	97.0	98	35	50	0
D Davis	11-11	4.91	203.1	206	102	159	0
D Turnbow	4-9	6.87	56.1	56	39	69	24

Manager-Ned Yost

New York Mets

BATTERS	AVG	AB	R	H	HR	RBI	SO	SB
P Lo Duca	.318	512	80	163	5	49	38	3
D Wright	.311	582	96	181	26	116	113	20
E Chavez	.306	353	48	108	4	42	44	12
J Reyes	.300	647	122	194	19	81	81	64
S Green*	.277	530	73	147	15	66	82	4
C Beltran	.275	510	127	140	41	116	99	18
J Valentin	.271	384	56	104	18	62	71	6
C Delgado	.265	524	89	139	38	114	120	0
C Floyd	.244	332	45	81	11	44	58	6
C Woodward	.216	222	25	48	3	25	55	1

PITCHERS	W-L	ERA	IP	H	BB	SO	SV
B Wagner	3-2	2.24	72.1	59	21	94	40
D Oliver	4-1	3.44	81.0	70	21	60	0
J Maine	6-5	3.60	90.0	69	33	71	0
A Heilman	4-5	3.62	87.0	73	28	73	0
T Glavine	15-7	3.82	198.0	202	62	131	0
P Martinez	9-8	4.48	132.2	108	39	137	0
O Hernandez*	11-11	4.66	162.1	155	61	164	0
S Trachsel	15-8	4.97	164.2	185	78	79	0
O Perez*	3-13	6.55	112.2	129	68	102	0

Manager-Willie Randolph

Philadelphia Phillies

BATTERS	AVG	AB	R	H	HR	RBI	SO	SB
R Howard	.313	581	104	182	58	149	181	0
C Utley	.309	658	131	203	32	102	132	15
S Victorino	.287	415	70	119	6	46	54	4
J Rollins	.277	689	127	191	25	83	80	36
B Abreu#	.277	339	61	94	8	65	86	20
A Rowand	.262	405	59	106	12	47	76	10
P Burrell	.258	462	80	119	29	95	131	0
A Nunez	.211	322	42	68	2	32	58	1

Pittsburgh Pirates

PITCHERS	W-L	ERA	IP	H	BB	SO	SV
G Geary	7-1	2.96	91.1	103	20	60	1
T Gordon	3-4	3.34	59.1	53	22	68	34
B Myers	12-7	3.91	198.0	194	63	189	0
C Hamels	9-8	4.08	132.1	117	48	145	0
A Fultz	3-1	4.54	71.1	80	28	62	0
C Lidle#	8-7	4.74	125.1	132	39	98	0
J Lieber	9-11	4.93	168.0	196	24	100	0
R Madson	11-9	5.69	134.1	176	50	99	2

Manager-Charlie Manuel

Pittsburgh Pirates

BATTERS	AVG	AB	R	H	HR	RBI	SO	SB
F Sanchez	.344	582	85	200	6	85	52	3
R Paulino	.310	442	37	137	6	55	79	0
S Casey#	.296	213	30	63	3	29	22	0
J Bay	.286	570	101	163	35	109	156	11
X Nady*	.280	468	57	131	17	63	85	3
J Wilson	.273	543	70	148	8	35	65	4
C Wilson	.267	255	38	68	13	41	88	1
J Randa	.267	206	23	55	4	28	26	0
C Duffy	.255	314	46	80	2	18	71	26
J Castillo	.253	518	54	131	14	65	98	6
J Bautista	.235	400	58	94	16	51	110	2
N McLouth	.233	270	50	63	7	16	59	10
J Burnitz	.230	313	35	72	16	49	74	1

PITCHERS	W-L	ERA	IP	H	BB	SO	SV
M Gonzalez	3-4	2.17	54.0	42	31	64	24
S Torres	3-6	3.28	93.1	98	38	72	12
M Capps	9-1	3.79	80.2	81	12	56	1
Z Duke	10-15	4.47	215.1	255	68	117	0
I Snell	14-11	4.74	186.0	198	74	169	0
P Maholm	8-10	4.76	176.0	202	81	117	0
V Santos	5-9	5.70	115.1	150	42	81	0

Manager-Jim Tracy

St. Louis Cardinals

BATTERS	AVG	AB	R	H	HR	RBI	SO	SB
A Pujols	.331	535	119	177	49	137	50	7
J Rodriguez	.301	183	31	55	2	19	45	0
S Rolen	.296	521	94	154	22	95	69	7
C Duncan	.293	280	60	82	22	43	69	0
D Eckstein	.292	500	68	146	2	23	41	7
H Luna	.291	223	27	65	4	21	34	5
J Encarnacion	.278	557	74	155	19	79	86	6
S Spiezio	.272	276	44	75	13	52	66	1
S Taguchi	.266	316	46	84	2	31	48	11
A Miles	.263	426	48	112	2	30	42	2
P Wilson	.263	501	58	132	17	72	121	12
J Edmonds	.257	350	52	90	19	70	101	4
R Belliard#	.237	194	20	46	5	23	36	0
G Bennett	.223	157	13	35	4	22	30	0
Y Molina	.216	417	29	90	6	49	41	1

PITCHERS	W-L	ERA	IP	H	BB	SO	SV
C Carpenter	15-8	3.09	221.2	194	43	184	0
A Wainwright	2-1	3.12	75.0	64	22	72	3
J Isringhausen	4-8	3.55	58.1	47	38	52	33
B Looper	9-3	3.56	73.1	76	20	41	0
J Hancock	3-3	4.09	77.0	70	23	50	1
J Suppan	12-7	4.12	190.0	207	69	104	0
A Reyes	5-8	5.06	85.1	84	34	72	0
J Weaver#	5-4	5.18	83.1	99	26	45	0
J Sosa*	3-11	5.42	118.0	138	40	75	4
J Marquis	14-16	6.02	194.1	221	75	96	0
M Mulder	6-7	7.14	93.1	124	35	50	0

Manager-Tony La Russa

San Diego Padres

BATTERS	AVG	AB	R	H	HR	RBI	SO	SB
J Bard#	.338	231	28	78	9	40	39	1
A Gonzalez	.304	570	83	173	24	82	113	0
D Roberts	.293	499	80	146	2	44	61	49
M Piazza	.283	399	39	113	22	68	66	0
J Barfield	.280	539	72	151	13	58	81	21
T Walker*	.278	442	56	123	9	53	38	2
M Cameron	.268	552	88	148	22	83	142	25
B Giles	.263	604	87	159	14	83	60	9
G Blum	.254	276	27	70	4	34	51	0
K Greene	.245	412	56	101	15	55	87	5
M Bellhorn	.190	253	26	48	8	27	90	0

PITCHERS	W-L	ERA	IP	H	BB	SO	SV
T Hoffman	0-2	2.14	63.0	48	13	50	46
C Young	11-5	3.46	179.1	134	69	164	0
S Linebrink	7-4	3.57	75.2	70	22	68	2
W Williams	12-5	3.65	145.1	152	35	72	0
C Hensley	11-12	3.71	187.0	174	76	122	0
J Peavy	11-14	4.09	202.1	187	62	215	0
C Park	7-7	4.81	136.2	146	44	96	0
M Thompson	4-5	4.99	92.0	103	30	35	0

Manager-Bruce Bochy

San Francisco Giants

BATTERS	AVG	AB	R	H	HR	RBI	SO	SB
M Alou	.301	345	52	104	22	74	31	2
O Vizquel	.295	579	88	171	4	58	51	24
R Durham	.293	498	79	146	26	93	61	7
T Greene	.289	159	16	46	2	17	45	0
B Bonds	.270	367	74	99	26	77	51	3
E Alfonzo	.266	286	27	76	12	39	74	1
R Winn	.262	573	82	150	11	56	63	10
M Sweeney	.251	259	32	65	5	37	50	0
S Hillenbrand#	.248	234	33	58	9	29	40	0
S Finley	.246	426	66	105	6	40	55	7
L Niekro	.246	199	27	49	5	31	32	0
P Feliz	.244	603	75	147	22	98	112	1
M Matheny	.231	160	10	37	3	18	30	0

PITCHERS	W-L	ERA	IP	H	BB	SO	SV
A Benitez	4-2	3.52	38.1	39	21	31	17
J Schmidt	11-9	3.59	213.1	189	80	180	0
M Cain	13-12	4.15	190.2	157	87	179	0
B Hennessey	5-6	4.26	99.1	92	42	42	1
N Lowry	7-10	4.74	159.1	166	56	84	0
M Morris	10-15	4.98	207.2	218	63	117	0
J Wright	6-10	5.19	156.0	167	64	79	0

Manager-Felipe Alou

Washington Nationals

BATTERS	AVG	AB	R	H	HR	RBI	SO	SB
N Johnson	.290	500	100	145	23	77	99	10
J Vidro	.289	463	52	134	7	47	48	1
R Zimmerman	.287	614	84	176	20	110	120	11
A Soriano	.277	647	119	179	46	95	160	41
R Church	.276	196	22	54	10	35	60	6
F Lopez*	.274	617	98	169	11	52	126	44
A Kearns*	.264	537	86	142	24	86	135	9
B Schneider	.256	410	30	105	4	55	67	2
M Byrd	.223	197	28	44	5	18	47	3
J Guillen	.216	241	28	52	9	40	48	1

PITCHERS	W-L	ERA	IP	H	BB	SO	SV
C Cordero	7-4	3.19	73.1	59	22	69	29
J Rauch	4-5	3.35	91.1	78	36	86	2
M O'Connor	3-8	4.80	105.0	96	45	59	0
T Armas	9-12	5.03	154.0	167	64	97	0
R Ortiz	11-16	5.57	190.2	230	64	104	0
P Astacio	5-5	5.98	90.1	109	31	42	0

Manager-Frank Robinson

American League Team Statistics, 2006

(Individual Statistics: Batting—at least 150 at-bats; Pitching—at least 70 innings or 10 saves; *changed teams within AL during season, entry includes statistics for more than one team; # changed teams to or from NL during season, entry includes only AL stats)

TEAM BATTING

Team	AVG	AB	R	H	HR	RBI
Minnesota Twins	.287	5602	801	1608	143	754
New York Yankees	.285	5651	930	1608	210	902
Toronto Blue Jays	.284	5596	809	1591	199	778
Cleveland Indians	.280	5619	870	1576	196	839
Chicago White Sox	.280	5657	868	1586	236	839
Texas Rangers	.278	5659	835	1571	183	799
Baltimore Orioles	.277	5610	768	1556	164	727
Los Angeles Angels	.274	5609	766	1539	159	737
Detroit Tigers	.274	5642	822	1548	203	785
Seattle Mariners	.272	5670	756	1540	172	703
Kansas City Royals	.271	5589	757	1515	124	718
Boston Red Sox	.269	5619	820	1510	192	777
Oakland Athletics	.260	5500	771	1429	175	735
Tampa Bay Devil Rays	.255	5474	689	1395	190	650

TEAM PITCHING

Team	ERA	IP	H	SO	BB	SV
Detroit Tigers	3.84	1448.0	1420	1003	489	46
Minnesota Twins	3.95	1439.1	1490	1164	356	40
Los Angeles Angels	4.04	1452.2	1410	1164	471	50
Oakland Athletics	4.21	1451.2	1525	1003	529	54
Toronto Blue Jays	4.37	1428.1	1447	1076	504	42
Cleveland Indians	4.41	1423.1	1583	948	429	24
New York Yankees	4.41	1443.2	1463	1019	496	43
Seattle Mariners	4.60	1446.2	1500	1067	560	47
Texas Rangers	4.60	1431.1	1558	972	496	42
Chicago White Sox	4.61	1449.0	1534	1012	433	46
Boston Red Sox	4.83	1441.1	1570	1070	509	46
Tampa Bay Devil Rays	4.96	1420.1	1600	979	606	33
Baltimore Orioles	5.35	1419.0	1579	1016	613	35
Kansas City Royals	5.65	1426.1	1648	904	637	35

Baltimore Orioles

BATTERS	AVG	AB	R	H	HR	RBI	SO	SB
M Tejada	.330	648	99	214	24	100	79	6
N Markakis	.291	491	72	143	16	62	72	2
B Roberts	.286	563	85	161	10	55	66	36
J Gibbons	.277	343	34	95	13	46	48	0
C Patterson	.276	463	75	128	16	53	94	45
R Hernandez	.275	501	66	138	23	91	79	1
M Mora	.274	624	96	171	16	83	99	11
K Millar	.272	430	64	117	15	64	74	1
J Conine	.265	389	43	103	9	49	53	3
B Fahey	.235	251	36	59	2	23	48	3

PITCHERS	W-L	ERA	IP	H	BB	SO	SV
C Ray	4-4	2.73	66.0	45	27	51	33
E Bedard	15-11	3.76	196.1	196	69	171	0
D Cabrera	9-10	4.74	148.0	130	104	157	0
K Benson	11-12	4.82	183.0	199	58	88	0
A Loewen	6-6	5.37	112.1	111	62	98	0
R Lopez	9-18	5.90	189.0	234	59	136	0
B Chen	0-7	6.93	98.2	137	35	70	0

Manager-Lee Mazzilli, Sam Perlozzo

Boston Red Sox

BATTERS	AVG	AB	R	H	HR	RBI	SO	SB
M Ramirez	.321	449	79	144	35	102	102	0
D Ortiz	.287	558	115	160	54	137	117	1
M Loretta	.285	635	75	181	5	59	63	4
M Lowell	.284	573	79	163	20	80	61	2
K Youkilis	.279	569	100	159	13	72	120	5
E Hinske*	.271	277	43	75	13	34	79	2
T Nixon	.268	381	59	102	8	52	56	0
C Crisp	.264	413	58	109	8	36	67	22
A Gonzalez	.255	388	48	99	9	50	67	1
J Lopez*	.251	342	36	86	8	35	76	0
J Varitek	.238	365	46	87	12	55	87	1

Chicago White Sox

BATTERS	AVG	AB	R	H	HR	RBI	SO	SB
J Dye	.315	539	103	170	44	120	118	7
P Konerko	.313	566	97	177	35	113	104	1
A Pierzynski	.295	509	65	150	16	64	72	1
R Mackowiak	.290	255	31	74	5	23	59	5
J Thome	.288	490	108	141	42	109	147	0
A Cintron	.285	288	35	82	5	41	35	10
J Crede	.283	544	76	154	30	94	58	0
T Iguchi	.281	555	97	156	18	67	110	11
S Podsednik	.261	524	86	137	3	45	96	40
J Uribe	.235	463	53	109	21	71	82	1
B Anderson	.225	365	46	82	8	33	90	4

PITCHERS	W-L	ERA	IP	H	BB	SO	SV
B Jenks	3-4	4.00	69.2	66	31	80	41
J Contreras	13-9	4.27	196.0	194	55	134	0
J Garland	18-7	4.51	211.1	247	41	112	0
F Garcia	17-9	4.53	216.1	228	48	135	0
B McCarthy	4-7	4.68	84.2	77	33	69	0
J Vazquez	11-12	4.84	202.2	206	56	184	0
M Buehrle	12-13	4.99	204.0	247	48	98	0

Manager-Ozzie Guillen

(Red Sox Pitchers:)

PITCHERS	W-L	ERA	IP	H	BB	SO	SV
J Papelbon	4-2	0.92	68.1	40	13	75	35
C Schilling	15-7	3.97	204.0	220	28	183	0
J Tavarez	5-4	4.47	98.2	110	44	56	1
T Wakefield	7-11	4.63	140.0	135	51	90	0
J Lester	7-2	4.76	81.1	91	43	60	0
J Beckett	16-11	5.01	204.2	191	74	158	0
J Johnson*	3-12	6.35	106.1	149	35	50	0

Manager-Terry Francona

Cleveland Indians

BATTERS	AVG	AB	R	H	HR	RBI	SO	SB
V Martinez	.316	572	82	181	16	93	78	0
T Hafner	.308	454	100	140	42	117	111	0
R Garko	.292	185	28	54	7	45	37	0
R Belliard#	.291	350	43	102	8	44	45	2
G Sizemore	.290	655	134	190	28	76	153	22
J Inglett	.284	201	26	57	2	21	39	5
C Blake	.282	401	63	113	19	68	93	6
J Michaels	.267	494	77	132	9	55	101	9
J Peralta	.257	569	84	146	13	68	152	0
A Boone	.251	354	50	89	7	46	62	5

PITCHERS	W-L	ERA	IP	H	BB	SO	SV
C Sabathia	12-11	3.22	192.2	182	44	172	0
J Sowers	7-4	3.57	88.1	85	20	35	0
J Westbrook	15-10	4.17	211.1	247	55	109	0
B Wickman	1-4	4.18	28.0	29	11	17	15
C Lee	14-11	4.40	200.2	224	58	129	0
P Byrd	10-9	4.88	179.0	232	38	88	0
F Carmona	1-10	5.42	74.2	88	31	58	0

Manager-Eric Wedge

Detroit Tigers

BATTERS	AVG	AB	R	H	HR	RBI	SO	SB
C Guillen	.320	543	100	174	19	85	87	20
I Rodriguez	.300	547	74	164	13	69	86	8
M Ordonez	.298	593	82	177	24	104	87	1
P Polanco	.295	461	58	136	4	52	27	1
O Infante	.277	224	35	62	4	25	45	3
C Shelton	.273	373	50	102	16	47	107	1
C Granderson	.260	596	90	155	19	68	174	8
M Thames	.256	348	61	89	26	60	92	1
C Monroe	.255	541	89	138	28	92	126	2
B Inge	.253	542	83	137	27	83	128	7
D Young	.250	172	19	43	7	23	39	1
M Stairs	.247	348	42	86	13	51	86	0
S Casey#	.245	184	17	45	5	30	21	0

PITCHERS	W-L	ERA	IP	H	BB	SO	SV
J Verlander	17-9	3.63	186.0	187	60	124	0
K Rogers	17-8	3.84	204.0	195	62	99	0
N Robertson	13-13	3.84	208.2	206	67	137	0
J Bonderman	14-8	4.08	214.0	214	64	202	0
Z Miner	7-6	4.84	93.0	100	32	59	0

Manager-JimLeyland

Kansas City Royals

BATTERS	AVG	AB	R	H	HR	RBI	SO	SB
M Grudzielanek	.297	548	85	163	7	52	69	3
D DeJesus	.295	491	83	145	8	56	70	6
M Teahen	.290	393	70	114	18	69	85	10
E Brown	.287	527	77	151	15	81	95	6
D Mientkiewicz	.283	314	37	89	4	43	50	3
R Sanders	.246	325	45	80	11	49	86	7
J Buck	.245	371	37	91	11	50	84	0
J Gathright	.238	383	59	91	1	41	75	22
A Berroa	.234	474	45	111	9	54	88	3
E German	.326	279	44	91	3	34	49	7

PITCHERS	W-L	ERA	IP	H	BB	SO	SV
J Peralta	1-3	4.40	73.2	74	17	57	1
L Hudson	7-6	5.12	102.0	109	38	64	0
J Gobble	4-6	5.14	84.0	95	29	80	2
S Elarton	4-9	5.34	114.2	117	52	49	0
A Burgos	4-5	5.52	73.1	83	37	72	18
M Redman	11-10	5.71	167.0	202	63	76	0
J Affeldt	4-6	5.91	70.0	71	42	28	0
R Hernandez	6-10	6.48	109.2	145	48	50	0

Manager-Buddy Bell

Los Angeles Angels

BATTERS	AVG	AB	R	H	HR	RBI	SO	SB
V Guerrero	.329	607	92	200	33	116	68	15
R Quinlan	.321	234	28	75	9	32	28	2
J Rivera	.310	448	65	139	23	85	59	0
M Izturis	.293	352	64	103	5	44	35	14
H Kendrick	.285	267	25	76	4	30	44	6
O Cabrera	.282	607	95	171	9	72	58	27
G Anderson	.280	543	63	152	17	85	95	1
A Kennedy	.273	451	50	123	4	55	72	16
C Figgins	.267	604	93	161	9	62	100	52
T Salmon	.265	211	30	56	9	27	44	0
J Molina	.240	225	18	54	4	22	49	1
K Morales	.234	197	21	46	5	22	28	1
M Napoli	.228	268	47	61	16	42	90	2

PITCHERS	W-L	ERA	IP	H	BB	SO	SV
J Weaver	11-2	2.56	123.0	94	33	105	0
S Shields	7-7	2.87	87.2	70	24	84	2
H Carrasco	7-3	3.41	100.1	93	27	72	1
J Lackey	13-11	3.56	217.2	203	72	190	0
K Escobar	11-14	3.61	189.1	192	50	147	0
E Santana	16-8	4.28	204.0	181	70	141	0
J Weaver#	3-10	6.29	88.2	114	21	62	0

Manager-Mike Scioscia

Minnesota Twins

BATTERS	AVG	AB	R	H	HR	RBI	SO	SB
J Mauer	.347	521	86	181	13	84	54	8
M Redmond	.341	179	20	61	0	23	18	0
J Morneau	.321	592	97	190	34	130	93	3
J Tyner	.312	218	29	68	0	18	18	4
J Bartlett	.309	333	44	103	2	32	46	10
L Castillo	.296	584	84	173	3	49	58	25
N Punto	.290	459	73	133	1	45	68	17
M Cuddyer	.284	557	102	158	24	109	130	6
T Hunter	.278	557	86	155	31	98	108	12
R White	.246	337	32	83	7	38	54	1
J Kubel	.241	220	23	53	8	26	45	2
T Batista	.236	178	24	42	5	21	27	0
L Ford	.226	234	40	53	4	18	43	9
P Nevin#	.211	218	28	46	10	35	54	0

PITCHERS	W-L	ERA	IP	H	BB	SO	SV
J Nathan	7-0	1.58	68.1	38	16	95	36
F Liriano	12-3	2.16	121.0	89	32	144	1
J Santana	19-6	2.77	233.2	186	47	245	0
J Rincon	3-1	2.91	74.1	76	24	65	1
J Crain	4-5	3.52	76.2	79	18	60	1
B Bonser	7-6	4.22	100.1	104	24	84	0
B Radke	12-9	4.32	162.1	197	32	83	0
C Silva	11-15	5.94	180.1	246	32	70	0
S Baker	5-8	6.37	83.1	114	16	62	0

Manager-Ron Gardenhire

New York Yankees

BATTERS	AVG	AB	R	H	HR	RBI	SO	SB
D Jeter	.343	623	118	214	14	97	102	34
R Cano	.342	482	62	165	15	78	54	5
B Abreu#	.330	209	37	69	7	42	52	10
H Matsui	.302	172	32	52	8	29	23	1
A Rodriguez	.290	572	113	166	35	121	139	15
J Damon	.285	593	115	169	24	80	85	25
B Williams	.281	420	65	118	12	61	53	2
M Cabrera	.280	460	75	129	7	50	59	12
J Posada	.277	465	65	129	23	93	97	3
J Giambi	.253	446	92	113	37	113	106	2
A Phillips	.240	246	30	59	7	29	56	3
M Cairo	.239	222	28	53	0	30	31	13

PITCHERS	W-L	ERA	IP	H	BB	SO	SV
M Rivera	5-5	1.80	75.0	61	11	55	34
M Mussina	15-7	3.51	197.1	184	35	172	0
S Proctor	6-4	3.52	102.1	89	33	89	1
C Wang	19-6	3.63	218.0	233	52	76	1
J Wright	11-7	4.49	140.1	157	57	84	0
R Johnson	17-11	5.00	205.0	194	60	172	0
R Villone	3-3	5.04	80.1	75	51	72	0

Manager-Joe Torre

Oakland Athletics

BATTERS	AVG	AB	R	H	HR	RBI	SO	SB
J Payton	.296	557	78	165	10	59	52	8
J Kendall	.295	552	76	163	1	50	54	11
M Bradley	.276	351	53	97	14	52	65	10
M Kotsay	.275	502	57	138	7	59	55	6
F Thomas	.270	466	77	126	39	114	81	0
B Kielty	.270	270	35	73	8	36	49	2
M Scutaro	.266	365	52	97	5	41	66	5
N Swisher	.254	556	106	141	35	95	152	1
M Ellis	.249	441	64	110	11	52	76	4
E Chavez	.241	485	74	117	22	72	100	3
D Johnson	.234	286	30	67	9	37	45	0
B Crosby	.229	358	42	82	9	40	76	8

PITCHERS	W-L	ERA	IP	H	BB	SO	SV
H Street	4-4	3.31	70.2	64	13	67	37
B Zito	16-10	3.83	221	211	99	151	0
D Haren	14-13	4.12	223	224	45	176	0
B Halsey	5-4	4.67	94.1	108	46	53	0
K Saarloos	7-7	4.75	121.1	149	53	52	2
J Blanton	16-12	4.82	194.1	241	58	107	0
E Loaiza	11-9	4.89	154.2	179	40	97	0

Manager-Ken Macha

Seattle Mariners

BATTERS	AVG	AB	R	H	HR	RBI	SO	SB
I Suzuki	.322	695	110	224	9	49	71	45
K Johjima	.291	506	61	147	18	76	46	3
R Ibanez	.289	626	103	181	33	123	115	2
Y Betancourt	.289	558	68	161	8	47	54	11
B Broussard*	.289	432	61	125	21	63	103	2
J Lopez	.282	603	78	170	10	79	80	5
A Beltre	.268	620	88	166	25	89	118	11
R Sexson	.264	591	75	156	34	107	154	1
W Bloomquist	.247	251	36	62	1	15	40	16
C Everett	.227	308	37	70	11	33	57	1
J Reed	.217	212	27	46	6	17	31	2

PITCHERS	W-L	ERA	IP	H	BB	SO	SV
J Putz	4-1	2.30	78.1	59	13	104	36
J Woods	7-4	4.02	105.0	115	53	66	1
J Moyer#	6-12	4.39	160.0	179	44	82	0
G Meche	11-8	4.48	186.2	183	84	156	0
F Hernandez	12-14	4.52	191.0	195	60	176	0
J Washburn	8-14	4.67	187.0	198	55	103	0
J Pineiro	8-13	6.36	165.2	209	64	87	1

Manager-Mike Hargrove

Tampa Bay Devil Rays

BATTERS	AVG	AB	R	H	HR	RBI	SO	SB
J Lugo*	.308	289	53	89	12	27	47	18
C Crawford	.305	600	89	183	18	77	85	58
R Baldelli	.302	364	59	110	16	57	70	10
G Norton	.296	294	47	87	17	45	69	1
A Huff#	.283	230	26	65	8	28	25	0
T Wigginton	.275	444	55	122	24	79	97	4
J Cantu	.249	413	40	103	14	62	91	1
B Upton	.246	175	20	43	1	10	40	11
D Navarro#	.244	193	23	47	4	20	33	1
T Hall	.231	221	15	51	8	23	17	0
D Hollins	.228	333	37	76	15	33	64	3
T Lee	.224	343	35	77	11	31	73	5
B Zobrist#	.224	183	10	41	2	18	26	2
J Gomes	.216	385	53	83	20	59	116	1
T Perez	.212	241	31	51	2	16	44	1

PITCHERS	W-L	ERA	IP	H	BB	SO	SV
S Kazmir	10-8	3.24	144.2	132	52	163	0
M Hendrickson	4-8	3.81	89.2	81	34	51	0
R Lugo	2-4	3.81	85.0	75	37	48	0
T Corcoran	5-9	4.38	90.1	92	48	59	0
S Camp	7-4	4.68	75.0	93	19	53	4
J Shields	6-8	4.84	124.2	141	38	104	0
T Walker	1-3	4.95	20.0	18	7	16	10
J Seo#	1-8	5.00	90.0	122	31	39	0
C Fossum	6-6	5.33	130.0	136	63	88	0
S McClung	6-12	6.29	103.0	120	68	59	6

Manager-Joe Maddon

Texas Rangers

BATTERS	AVG	AB	R	H	HR	RBI	SO	SB
C Lee#	.322	236	42	76	9	35	26	7
M Young	.314	691	93	217	14	103	96	7
G Matthews	.313	620	102	194	19	79	99	10
M DeRosa	.296	520	78	154	13	74	102	4

BATTERS	AVG	AB	R	H	HR	RBI	SO	SB
G Laird	.296	243	46	72	7	22	54	3
I Kinsler	.286	423	65	121	14	55	64	11
K Mench	.284	320	36	91	12	50	42	1
M Teixeira	.282	628	99	177	33	110	128	2
H Blalock	.266	591	76	157	16	89	98	1
R Barajas	.256	344	49	88	11	41	51	0
B Wilkerson	.222	320	56	71	15	44	116	3

PITCHERS	W-L	ERA	IP	H	BB	SO	SV
A Otsuka	2-4	2.11	59.2	53	11	47	32
R Bauer	3-1	3.55	71.0	73	25	35	2
R Tejeda	5-5	4.28	73.2	83	32	40	0
V Padilla	15-10	4.50	200.0	206	70	156	0
K Millwood	16-12	4.52	215.0	228	53	157	0
J Benoit	1-1	4.86	79.2	68	38	85	0
J Koronka	7-7	5.69	125.0	145	47	61	0
K Loe	3-6	5.86	78.1	105	22	34	0
J Rheinecker	4-6	5.86	70.2	104	19	28	0

Manager-Buck Showalter

Toronto Blue Jays

BATTERS	AVG	AB	R	H	HR	RBI	SO	SB
R Johnson	.319	461	86	147	12	49	81	8
L Overbay	.312	581	82	181	22	92	96	5
V Wells	.303	611	91	185	32	106	90	17
A Rios	.302	450	68	136	17	82	89	15
S Hillenbrand#	.301	296	40	89	12	39	40	1
F Catalanotto	.300	437	56	131	7	56	37	1
A Hill	.291	546	70	159	6	50	66	5
B Molina	.284	433	44	123	19	57	47	1
G Zaun	.272	290	39	79	12	40	42	0
T Glaus	.252	540	105	136	38	104	134	3
J McDonald	.223	260	35	58	3	23	41	7
R Adams	.219	251	31	55	3	28	41	1

PITCHERS	W-L	ERA	IP	H	BB	SO	SV
B Ryan	2-2	1.37	72.1	42	20	86	38
R Halladay	16-5	3.19	220.0	208	34	132	0
A Burnett	10-8	3.98	135.2	138	39	118	0
S Downs	6-2	4.09	77.0	73	30	61	1
T Lilly	15-13	4.31	181.2	179	81	160	0
G Chacin	9-4	5.05	87.1	90	38	47	0
S Marcum	3-4	5.06	78.1	87	38	65	0
C Janssen	6-10	5.07	94.0	103	21	44	0

Manager-John Gibbons

Major League Leaders in 2006
American League

Batting: Joe Mauer, Minnesota, .347; Derek Jeter, New York, .343; Robinson Cano, New York, .342; Miguel Tejada, Baltimore, .330; Vladimir Guerrero, Los Angeles, .329.

Runs: Grady Sizemore, Cleveland, 134; Derek Jeter, New York, 118; Johnny Damon, New York; 115; David Ortiz, Boston, 115; Alex Rodriguez, New York, 113.

Runs Batted In: David Ortiz, Boston, 137; Justin Morneau, Minnesota, 130; Raul Ibanez, Seattle, 123; Alex Rodriguez, New York, 121; Jermaine Dye, Chicago, 120.

Hits: Ichiro Suzuki, Seattle, 224; Michael Young, Texas, 217; Derek Jeter, New York, 214; Miguel Tejada, Baltimore, 214; Vladimir Guerrero, Los Angeles, 200.

Doubles: Grady Sizemore, Cleveland, 53; Michael Young, Texas, 52; Mike Lowell, Boston, 47; Lyle Overbay, Toronto, 46; Orlando Cabrera, Los Angeles, 45; Mark Teixeira, Texas, 45.

Triples: Carl Crawford, Tampa Bay, 16; Grady Sizemore, Cleveland, 11; Curtis Granderson, Detroit, 9; Ichiro Suzuki, Seattle, 9; Chone Figgins, Los Angeles, 8.

Home Runs: David Ortiz, Boston, 54; Jermaine Dye, Chicago, 44; Travis Hafner, Cleveland, 42; Jim Thome, Chicago, 42; Frank Thomas, Oakland, 39.

Stolen Bases: Carl Crawford, Tampa Bay, 58; Chone Figgins, Los Angeles, 52; Corey Patterson, Baltimore, 45; Ichiro Suzuki, Seattle, 45; Scott Podsednik, Chicago, 40.

Pitching Wins: Johann Santana, Minnesota, 19-6; Chien-Ming Wang, New York, 19-6; Jon Garland, Chicago, 18-7; Freddy Garcia, Chicago, 17-9; Randy Johnson, New York, 17-11; Kenny Rogers, Detroit, 17-8; Justin Verlander, Detroit, 17-9.

Earned Run Average: Johan Santana, Minnesota, 2.77; Roy Halladay, Toronto, 3.19; C.C. Sabathia, Cleveland, 3.22; Mike Mussina, New York, 3.51; John Lackey, Los Angeles, 3.56.

Strikeouts: Johan Santana, Minnesota, 245; Jeremy Bonderman, Detroit, 202; John Lackey, Los Angeles, 190; Javier Vasquez, Chicago, 184; Curt Schilling, Boston, 183.

Saves: Francisco Rodriguez, Los Angeles, 47; Bobby Jenks, Chicago, 41; B.J. Ryan, Toronto, 38; Todd Jones, Detroit, 37; Huston Street, Oakland, 37.

National League

Batting: Freddy Sanchez, Pittsburgh, .344; Miguel Cabrera, Florida, .339; Albert Pujols, St. Louis, .331; Garrett Atkins, Colorado, .329; Matt Holliday, Colorado, .326.

Runs: Chase Utley, Philadelphia, 131; Carlos Beltran, New York, 127; Jimmy Rollins, Philadelphia, 127; Jose Reyes, New York, 122; Matt Holliday, Colorado, 119.

Runs Batted In: Ryan Howard, Philadelphia, 149; Albert Pujols, St. Louis, 137; Lance Berkman, Houston, 136; Andruw Jones, Atlanta, 129; Garrett Atkins, Colorado, 120.

Hits: Juan Pierre, Chicago, 204; Chase Utley, Philadelphia, 203; Freddy Sanchez, Pittsburgh, 200; Garrett Atkins, Colorado, 198; Rafael Furcal, Los Angeles, 198

Doubles: Freddy Sanchez, Pittsburgh, 53; Luis Gonzalez, Arizona, 52; Miguel Cabrera, Florida, 50; Garrett Atkins, Colorado, 48; Scott Rolen, St. Louis, 48

Triples: Jose Reyes, New York, 17; Juan Pierre, Chicago, 13; Dave Roberts, San Diego, 13; Steve Finley, San Francisco, 12; Kenny Lofton, Los Angeles, 12.

Home Runs: Ryan Howard, Philadelphia, 58; Albert Pujols, St. Louis, 49; Alfonso Soriano, Washington, 46; Lance Berkman, Houston, 45; Carlos Beltran, New York, 41

Stolen Bases: Jose Reyes, New York, 64; Juan Pierre, Chicago, 58; Hanley Ramirez, Florida, 51; Dave Roberts, San Diego, 49; Felipe Lopez, Washington, 44

Pitching Wins: Aaron Harang, Cincinnati, 16-11; Derek Lowe, Los Angeles, 16-8; Brad Penny, Los Angeles, 16-9; John Smoltz, Atlanta, 16-9; Brandon Webb, Arizona, 16-8

Earned Run Average: Roy Oswalt, Houston, 2.98; Chris Carpenter, St. Louis, 3.09; Brandon Webb, Arizona, 3.10; Bronson Arroyo, Cincinnati, 3.29; Carlos Zambrano, Chicago, 3.41

Strikeouts: Aaron Harang, Cincinnati, 216; Jake Peavy, San Diego, 215; John Smoltz, Atlanta, 211; Carlos Zambrano, Chicago, 210; Brett Myers, Philadelphia, 189

Saves: Trevor Hoffman, San Diego, 46; Billy Wagner, New York, 40; Joe Borowski, Florida, 36; Tom Gordon, Philadelphia, 34; Jason Isringhausen, St. Louis, 33

All-Time Major League Single-Season Leaders

(Source: www.mlb.com; *player active in 2006 season; records for "modern" era beginning 1901)

Home Runs
Barry Bonds* (2001)	73
Mark McGwire (1998)	70
Sammy Sosa* (1998)	66
Mark McGwire (1999)	65
Sammy Sosa (2001)	64

Runs
Babe Ruth (1921)	177
Lou Gehrig (1936)	167
Lou Gehrig (1931)	163
Babe Ruth (1928)	163
Chuck Klein (1930)	158
Babe Ruth (1920, 1927)	158

Hits
Ichiro Suzuki* (2004)	262
George Sisler (1920)	257
Lefty O'Doul (1929)	254
Bill Terry (1930)	254
Al Simmons (1925)	253

Runs Batted In
Hack Wilson (1930)	191
Lou Gehrig (1931)	184
Hank Greenberg (1937)	183
Jimmie Foxx (1938)	175
Lou Gehrig (1927)	175

Batting Average
Nap Lajoie (1901)	.426
Rogers Hornsby (1924)	.424
George Sisler (1922)	.420
Ty Cobb (1911)	.420
Ty Cobb (1912)	.410

Stolen Bases
Rickey Henderson (1982)	130
Lou Brock (1974)	118
Vince Coleman (1985)	110
Vince Coleman (1987)	109
Rickey Henderson (1983)	108

Walks (Batter)
Barry Bonds* (2004)	232
Barry Bonds* (2002)	198
Barry Bonds* (2001)	177
Babe Ruth (1923)	170
Mark McGwire (1998)	162
Ted Williams (1947, 1949)	162

Strikeouts (Batter)
Adam Dunn* (2004)	195
Adam Dunn* (2006)	194
Bobby Bonds (1970)	189
Jose Hernandez* (2002)	188
Bobby Bonds (1969)	187
Preston Wilson* (2000)	187

Earned Run Average
Dutch Leonard (1914)	0.96
Mordecai Brown (1906)	1.04
Bob Gibson (1968)	1.12
Walter Johnson (1913)	1.14
Christy Mathewson (1909)	1.14

Wins
Jack Chesbro (1904)	41
Ed Walsh (1908)	40
Christy Mathewson (1908)	37
Walter Johnson (1913)	36
Joe McGinnity (1904)	35

Strikeouts
Nolan Ryan (1973)	383
Sandy Koufax (1965)	382
Randy Johnson* (2001)	372
Nolan Ryan (1974)	367
Randy Johnson* (1999)	364

Saves
Bobby Thigpen (1990)	57
Eric Gagne* (2003)	55
John Smoltz* (2002)	55
Trevor Hoffman* (1998)	53
Randy Myers (1993)	53
Mariano Rivera* (2004)	53

All-Time Major League Leaders

(Source: www.mlb.com; *player active in 2006 season)

Games
Pete Rose	3,562
Carl Yastrzemski	3,308
Hank Aaron	3,298
Rickey Henderson	3,081
Ty Cobb	3,035
Eddie Murray	3,026
Stan Musial	3,026
Cal Ripken Jr.	3,001
Willie Mays	2,992
Dave Winfield	2,973

Stolen Bases
Rickey Henderson	1,406
Lou Brock	938
Billy Hamilton	912
Ty Cobb	892
Tim Raines	808
Vince Coleman	752
Eddie Collins	745
Max Carey	738
Honus Wagner	722
Joe Morgan	689

Strikeouts
Nolan Ryan	5,714
Roger Clemens*	4,604
Randy Johnson*	4,544
Steve Carlton	4,136
Bert Blyleven	3,701
Tom Seaver	3,640
Don Sutton	3,574
Gaylord Perry	3,534
Walter Johnson	3,508
Phil Niekro	3,342

At Bats
Pete Rose	14,053
Hank Aaron	12,364
Carl Yastrzemski	11,988
Cal Ripken Jr.	11,551
Ty Cobb	11,429
Eddie Murray	11,336
Robin Yount	11,008
Dave Winfield	11,003
Stan Musial	10,972
Rickey Henderson	10,961

Triples
Sam Crawford	309
Ty Cobb	297
Honus Wagner	252
Jake Beckley	243
Roger Connor	233
Tris Speaker	222
Fred Clarke	220
Dan Brouthers	205
Joe Kelley	194
Paul Waner	191

Saves
Trevor Hoffman*	482
Lee Smith	478
John Franco	424
Mariano Rivera*	413
Dennis Eckersley	390
Jeff Reardon	367
Randy Myers	347
Rollie Fingers	341
John Wetteland	330
Roberto Hernandez	*326

Runs Batted In
Hank Aaron	2,297
Babe Ruth	2,213
Cap Anson	2,076
Lou Gehrig	1,995
Stan Musial	1,951
Ty Cobb	1,938
Barry Bonds*	1,930
Jimmie Foxx	1,922
Eddie Murray	1,917
Willie Mays	1,903

Batting Average
Ty Cobb	.367
Rogers Hornsby	.358
Ed Delahanty	.346
Tris Speaker	.345
Billy Hamilton	.344
Ted Williams	.344
Dan Brouthers	.342
Harry Heilmann	.342
Babe Ruth	.342
Willie Keeler	.341
Bill Terry	.341

Shutouts
Walter Johnson	110
Grover Alexander	90
Christy Mathewson	79
Cy Young	76
Eddie Plank	69
Warren Spahn	63
Nolan Ryan	61
Tom Seaver	61
Bert Blyleven	60
Don Sutton	58

Runs
Rickey Henderson	2,295
Ty Cobb	2,245
Hank Aaron	2,174
Babe Ruth	2,174
Pete Rose	2,165
Barry Bonds*	2,152
Willie Mays	2,062
Cap Anson	1,996
Stan Musial	1,949
Lou Gehrig	1,888

Walks
Barry Bonds*	2,426
Rickey Henderson	2,190
Babe Ruth	2,062
Ted Williams	2,019
Joe Morgan	1,865
Carl Yastrzemski	1,845
Mickey Mantle	1,733
Mel Ott	1,708
Eddie Yost	1,614
Darrell Evans	1,605

Losses
Cy Young	316
Jim Galvin	310
Nolan Ryan	292
Walter Johnson	279
Phil Niekro	274
Gaylord Perry	265
Don Sutton	256
Jack Powell	254
Eppa Rixey	251
Bert Blyleven	250

All-Time Home Run Leaders

(Source: www.mlb.com; *player active in 2006 season)

Hank Aaron	755	Mike Schmidt	548	Frank Thomas*	487	Jeff Bagwell*	449	Andres Galarraga	399
Barry Bonds*	734	Mickey Mantle	536	Stan Musial	475	Dave Kingman	442	Al Kaline	399
Babe Ruth	714	Jimmie Foxx	534	Willie Stargell	475	Andre Dawson	438	Dale Murphy	398
Willie Mays	660	Willie McCovey	521	Jim Thome*	472	Juan Gonzalez	434	Joe Carter	396
Sammy Sosa	588	Ted Williams	521	Manny Ramirez*	470	Cal Ripken Jr.	431	Graig Nettles	390
Frank Robinson	586	Ernie Banks	512	Dave Winfield	465	Billy Williams	426	Johnny Bench	389
Mark McGwire	583	Ed Mathews	512	Alex Rodriguez*	464	Mike Piazza*	419	Dwight Evans	385
Harmon Killebrew	573	Mel Ott	511	Jose Canseco	462	Darrell Evans	414	Harold Baines	384
Rafael Palmeiro	569	Eddie Murray	504	Gary Sheffield*	455	Carlos Delgado*	407	Frank Howard	382
Ken Griffey Jr*	563	Lou Gehrig	493	Carl Yastrzemski	452	Duke Snider	407	Jim Rice	382
Reggie Jackson	563	Fred McGriff	493				

Players With 3,000 Major League Hits

(Source: www.mlb.com; *player active in 2006 season)

Pete Rose	4,256	Cap Anson	3,418	Eddie Murray	3,255	Robin Yount	3,142	Lou Brock	3,023
Ty Cobb	4,189	Honus Wagner	3,415	Nap Lajoie	3,242	Tony Gwynn	3,141	Rafael Palmeiro	3,020
Hank Aaron	3,771	Paul Molitor	3,319	Cal Ripken Jr.	3,184	Dave Winfield	3,110	Wade Boggs	3,010
Stan Musial	3,630	Eddie Collins	3,315	George Brett	3,154	Rickey Henderson	3,055	Al Kaline	3,007
Tris Speaker	3,514	Willie Mays	3,283	Paul Waner	3,152	Rod Carew	3,053	Roberto Clemente	3,000
Carl Yastrzemski	3,419					

50 Home Run Club

Only Mark McGwire and Barry Bonds have ever hit 70 or more home runs in a season. Five players—including Babe Ruth and Roger Maris—have hit 60 or more, a feat Sammy Sosa accomplished for the 3rd time in 2001. Those 5 are at the pinnacle of a select group of players to have hit 50 or more homers in a season. The following list shows each time a player achieved this mark.

HR	Player, team	Year	HR	Player, team	Year
73	Barry Bonds, San Francisco Giants	2001	54	Babe Ruth, N.Y. Yankees	1928
70	Mark McGwire, St. Louis Cardinals	1998	54	Ralph Kiner, Pittsburgh Pirates	1949
66	Sammy Sosa, Chicago Cubs	1998	54	Mickey Mantle, N.Y. Yankees	1961
65	Mark McGwire, St. Louis Cardinals	1999	52	Mickey Mantle, N.Y. Yankees	1956
64	Sammy Sosa, Chicago Cubs	2001	52	Willie Mays, San Francisco Giants	1965
63	Sammy Sosa, Chicago Cubs	1999	52	George Foster, Cincinnati Reds	1977
61	Roger Maris, N.Y. Yankees	1961	52	Mark McGwire, Oakland A's	1996
60	Babe Ruth, N.Y. Yankees	1927	52	Alex Rodriguez, Texas Rangers	2001
59	Babe Ruth, N.Y. Yankees	1921	52	Jim Thome, Cleveland Indians	2002
58	Jimmie Foxx, Philadelphia Athletics	1932	51	Andruw Jones, Atlanta Braves	2005
58	Hank Greenberg, Detroit Tigers	1938	51	Ralph Kiner, Pittsburgh Pirates	1947
58	Ryan Howard, Philadelphia Phillies	2006	51	Johnny Mize, N.Y. Giants	1947
58	Mark McGwire, Oakland A's/St. Louis Cardinals	1997	51	Willie Mays, N.Y. Giants	1955
57	Luis Gonzalez, Arizona Diamondbacks	2001	51	Cecil Fielder, Detroit Tigers	1990
57	Alex Rodriguez, Texas Rangers	2002	50	Jimmie Foxx, Boston Red Sox	1938
56	Hack Wilson, Chicago Cubs	1930	50	Albert Belle, Cleveland Indians	1995
56	Ken Griffey Jr., Seattle Mariners	1997	50	Brady Anderson, Baltimore Orioles	1996
56	Ken Griffey Jr., Seattle Mariners	1998	50	Greg Vaughn, San Diego Padres	1998
54	David Ortiz, Boston Red Sox	2006	50	Sammy Sosa, Chicago Cubs	2000
54	Babe Ruth, N.Y. Yankees	1920			

Pitchers With 300 Major League Wins

(**Source:** www.mlb.com; *player active in 2006 season)

Cy Young	511	Kid Nichols	361	Eddie Plank	326	Tom Seaver	311
Walter Johnson	417	Roger Clemens*	348	Nolan Ryan	324	Charley Radbourn	309
Grover Alexander	373	Tim Keefe	342	Don Sutton	324	Mickey Welch	307
Christy Mathewson	373	Greg Maddux*	333	Phil Niekro	318	Lefty Grove	300
Jim Galvin	365	Steve Carlton	329	Gaylord Perry	314	Early Wynn	300
Warren Spahn	363	John Clarkson	328				

Official Major League Perfect Games Since 1900

Date	Pitcher	Teams	Date	Pitcher	Teams
5/5/04	Cy Young	Boston 3 vs. Phil. 0 (AL)	9/30/84	Mike Witt	Calif.1 at Texas 0 (AL)
10/2/08	Addie Joss	Clev. 1 vs. Chicago 0 (AL)	9/16/88	Tom Browning	Cincinnati 1 vs. L.A. 0 (NL)
4/30/22	Charlie Robertson	Chicago 2 at Detroit 0 (AL)	7/28/91	Dennis Martinez	Montreal 2 vs. L.A. 0 (NL)
10/8/56	Don Larsen	N.Y. 2 vs. Brooklyn 0 (AL)*	7/28/94	Kenny Rogers	Texas 4 vs. California 0 (AL)
6/21/64	Jim Bunning	Phil. 6 at N.Y. 0 (NL)	5/17/98	David Wells	N.Y. 4 vs. Minn. 0 (AL)
9/9/65	Sandy Koufax	L.A. 1 vs. Chicago 0 (NL)	7/18/99	David Cone	N.Y. 6 vs. Montreal 0 (AL)
5/8/68	Catfish Hunter	Oakland 4 vs. Minn.0 (AL)	5/18/04	Randy Johnson	Ariz. 2 vs. Atlanta 0 (NL)
5/15/81	Len Barker	Clev. 3 vs. Toronto 0 (AL)			

*World Series game

Most Career Major League No-Hitters

No.	Pitcher
7	Nolan Ryan
4	Sandy Koufax
3	Larry Corcoran, Bob Feller, Cy Young
	Jim Bunning, Steve Busby, Carl Erskine, Bob Forsch, Pud Galvin, Ken Holtzman, Randy Johnson, Addie Joss, Dutch Leonard, Jim Maloney, Christy Mathewson, Hideo Nomo, Allie Reynolds, Frank Smith, Warren Spahn, Bill Stoneman, Virgil Trucks,
2	Johnny Vander Meer, Ed Walsh, Don Wilson

Home Run Leaders, by Season

Note: Asterisk (*) indicates the all-time single-season record for each league.

	National League			American League	
Year	Player, Team	HR	Year	Player, Team	HR
1901	Sam Crawford, Cincinnati	16	1901	Napoleon Lajoie, Philadelphia	13
1902	Thomas Leach, Pittsburgh	6	1902	Socks Seybold, Philadelphia	16
1903	James Sheckard, Brooklyn	9	1903	Buck Freeman, Boston	13
1904	Harry Lumley, Brooklyn	9	1904	Harry Davis, Philadelphia	10
1905	Fred Odwell, Cincinnati	9	1905	Harry Davis, Philadelphia	8
1906	Timothy Jordan, Brooklyn	12	1906	Harry Davis, Philadelphia	12
1907	David Brain, Boston	10	1907	Harry Davis, Philadelphia	8
1908	Timothy Jordan, Brooklyn	12	1908	Sam Crawford, Detroit	7
1909	Red Murray, New York	7	1909	Ty Cobb, Detroit	9
1910	Fred Beck, Boston; Frank Schulte, Chicago	10	1910	Jake Stahl, Boston	10
1911	Frank Schulte, Chicago	21	1911	J. Franklin Baker, Philadelphia	9
1912	Henry Zimmerman, Chicago	14	1912	J. Franklin Baker, Philadelphia; Tris Speaker, Boston	10
1913	Gavvy Cravath, Philadelphia	19	1913	J. Franklin Baker, Philadelphia	13
1914	Gavvy Cravath, Philadelphia	19	1914	J. Franklin Baker, Philadelphia	9
1915	Gavvy Cravath, Philadelphia	24	1915	Robert Roth, Chicago-Cleveland	7
1916	Dave Robertson, N.Y.; Fred (Cy) Williams, Chi.	12	1916	Wally Pipp, New York	12
1917	Dave Robertson, N.Y.; Gavvy Cravath, Phi.	12	1917	Wally Pipp, New York	9
1918	Gavvy Cravath, Philadelphia	8	1918	Babe Ruth, Boston; Tilly Walker, Philadelphia	11
1919	Gavvy Cravath, Philadelphia	12	1919	Babe Ruth, Boston	29
1920	Cy Williams, Philadelphia	15	1920	Babe Ruth, New York	54
1921	George Kelly, New York	23	1921	Babe Ruth, New York	59
1922	Rogers Hornsby, St. Louis	42	1922	Ken Williams, St. Louis	39
1923	Cy Williams, Philadelphia	41	1923	Babe Ruth, New York	41
1924	Jacques Fournier, Brooklyn	27	1924	Babe Ruth, New York	46

	National League			American League	
Year	Player, Team	HR	Year	Player, Team	HR
1925	Rogers Hornsby, St. Louis	39	1925	Bob Meusel, New York	33
1926	Hack Wilson, Chicago	21	1926	Babe Ruth, New York	47
1927	Hack Wilson, Chicago; Cy Williams, Philadelphia	30	1927	Babe Ruth, New York	60
1928	Hack Wilson, Chicago; Jim Bottomley, St. Louis	31	1928	Babe Ruth, New York	54
1929	Chuck Klein, Philadelphia	43	1929	Babe Ruth, New York	46
1930	Hack Wilson, Chicago	56	1930	Babe Ruth, New York	49
1931	Chuck Klein, Philadelphia	31	1931	Babe Ruth, Lou Gehrig, both New York	46
1932	Chuck Klein, Philadelphia; Mel Ott, New York	38	1932	Jimmie Foxx, Philadelphia	58
1933	Chuck Klein, Philadelphia	28	1933	Jimmie Foxx, Philadelphia	48
1934	Rip Collins, St. Louis; Mel Ott, New York	35	1934	Lou Gehrig, New York	49
1935	Walter Berger, Boston	34	1935	Jimmie Foxx, Philadelphia; Hank Greenberg, Detroit	36
1936	Mel Ott, New York	33	1936	Lou Gehrig, New York	49
1937	Mel Ott, New York; Joe Medwick, St. Louis	31	1937	Joe DiMaggio, New York	46
1938	Mel Ott, New York	36	1938	Hank Greenberg, Detroit	58
1939	John Mize, St. Louis	28	1939	Jimmie Foxx, Boston	35
1940	John Mize, St. Louis	43	1940	Hank Greenberg, Detroit	41
1941	Dolph Camilli, Brooklyn	34	1941	Ted Williams, Boston	37
1942	Mel Ott, New York	30	1942	Ted Williams, Boston	36
1943	Bill Nicholson, Chicago	29	1943	Rudy York, Detroit	34
1944	Bill Nicholson, Chicago	33	1944	Nick Etten, New York	22
1945	Tommy Holmes, Boston	28	1945	Vern Stephens, St. Louis	24
1946	Ralph Kiner, Pittsburgh	23	1946	Hank Greenberg, Detroit	44
1947	Ralph Kiner, Pittsburgh; John Mize, New York	51	1947	Ted Williams, Boston	32
1948	Ralph Kiner, Pittsburgh; John Mize, New York	40	1948	Joe DiMaggio, New York	39
1949	Ralph Kiner, Pittsburgh	54	1949	Ted Williams, Boston	43
1950	Ralph Kiner, Pittsburgh	47	1950	Al Rosen, Cleveland	37
1951	Ralph Kiner, Pittsburgh	42	1951	Gus Zernial, Chicago-Philadelphia	33
1952	Ralph Kiner, Pittsburgh; Hank Sauer, Chicago	37	1952	Larry Doby, Cleveland	32
1953	Ed Mathews, Milwaukee	47	1953	Al Rosen, Cleveland	43
1954	Ted Kluszewski, Cincinnati	49	1954	Larry Doby, Cleveland	32
1955	Willie Mays, New York	51	1955	Mickey Mantle, New York	37
1956	Duke Snider, Brooklyn	43	1956	Mickey Mantle, New York	52
1957	Hank Aaron, Milwaukee	44	1957	Roy Sievers, Washington	42
1958	Ernie Banks, Chicago	47	1958	Mickey Mantle, New York	42
1959	Ed Mathews, Milwaukee	46	1959	Rocky Colavito, Cleve.; Harmon Killebrew, Wash.	42
1960	Ernie Banks, Chicago	41	1960	Mickey Mantle, New York	40
1961	Orlando Cepeda, San Francisco	46	1961	Roger Maris, New York	*61
1962	Willie Mays, San Francisco	49	1962	Harmon Killebrew, Minnesota	48
1963	Hank Aaron, Milwaukee; Willie McCovey, S.F.	44	1963	Harmon Killebrew, Minnesota	45
1964	Willie Mays, San Francisco	47	1964	Harmon Killebrew, Minnesota	49
1965	Willie Mays, San Francisco	52	1965	Tony Conigliaro, Boston	32
1966	Hank Aaron, Atlanta	44	1966	Frank Robinson, Baltimore	49
1967	Hank Aaron, Atlanta	39	1967	Carl Yastrzemski, Boston; Harmon Killebrew, Minn.	44
1968	Willie McCovey, San Francisco	36	1968	Frank Howard, Washington	44
1969	Willie McCovey, San Francisco	45	1969	Harmon Killebrew, Minnesota	49
1970	Johnny Bench, Cincinnati	45	1970	Frank Howard, Washington	44
1971	Willie Stargell, Pittsburgh	48	1971	Bill Melton, Chicago	33
1972	Johnny Bench, Cincinnati	40	1972	Dick Allen, Chicago	37
1973	Willie Stargell, Pittsburgh	44	1973	Reggie Jackson, Oakland	32
1974	Mike Schmidt, Philadelphia	36	1974	Dick Allen, Chicago	32
1975	Mike Schmidt, Philadelphia	38	1975	George Scott, Milwaukee; Reggie Jackson, Oakland	36
1976	Mike Schmidt, Philadelphia	38	1976	Graig Nettles, New York	32
1977	George Foster, Cincinnati	52	1977	Jim Rice, Boston	39
1978	George Foster, Cincinnati	40	1978	Jim Rice, Boston	46
1979	Dave Kingman, Chicago	48	1979	Gorman Thomas, Milwaukee	45
1980	Mike Schmidt, Philadelphia	48	1980	Reggie Jackson, New York; Ben Oglivie, Milwaukee	41
1981	Mike Schmidt, Philadelphia	31	1981	Bobby Grich, California; Tony Armas, Oakland; Dwight Evans, Boston; Eddie Murray, Baltimore	22
1982	Dave Kingman, New York	37	1982	Gorman Thomas, Milwaukee; Reggie Jackson, Cal.	39
1983	Mike Schmidt, Philadelphia	40	1983	Jim Rice, Boston	39
1984	Mike Schmidt, Phi.; Dale Murphy, Atlanta	36	1984	Tony Armas, Boston	43
1985	Dale Murphy, Atlanta	37	1985	Darrell Evans, Detroit	40
1986	Mike Schmidt, Philadelphia	37	1986	Jesse Barfield, Toronto	40
1987	Andre Dawson, Chicago	49	1987	Mark McGwire, Oakland	49
1988	Darryl Strawberry, New York	39	1988	Jose Canseco, Oakland	42
1989	Kevin Mitchell, San Francisco	47	1989	Fred McGriff, Toronto	36
1990	Ryne Sandberg, Chicago	40	1990	Cecil Fielder, Detroit	51
1991	Howard Johnson, New York	38	1991	Cecil Fielder, Detroit; Jose Canseco, Oakland	44
1992	Fred McGriff, San Diego	35	1992	Juan Gonzalez, Texas	43
1993	Barry Bonds, San Francisco	46	1993	Juan Gonzalez, Texas	46
1994	Matt Williams, San Francisco	43	1994	Ken Griffey Jr., Seattle	40
1995	Dante Bichette, Colorado	40	1995	Albert Belle, Cleveland	50
1996	Andres Galarraga, Colorado	47	1996	Mark McGwire, Oakland	52
1997[1]	Larry Walker, Colorado	49	1997[1]	Ken Griffey Jr., Seattle	56
1998	Mark McGwire, St. Louis	70	1998	Ken Griffey Jr., Seattle	56
1999	Mark McGwire, St. Louis	65	1999	Ken Griffey Jr., Seattle	48
2000	Sammy Sosa, Chicago	50	2000	Troy Glaus, Anaheim	47
2001	Barry Bonds, San Francisco	*73	2001	Alex Rodriguez, Texas	52
2002	Sammy Sosa, Chicago	49	2002	Alex Rodriguez, Texas	57
2003	Jim Thome, Philadelphia	47	2003	Alex Rodriguez, Texas	47
2004	Adrian Beltre, Los Angeles	48	2004	Manny Ramirez, Boston	43
2005	Andruw Jones, Atlanta	51	2005	Alex Rodriguez, New York	48
2006	Ryan Howard, Philadelphia	58	2006	David Ortiz, Boston	54

(1) In 1997, Mark McGwire hit 58 home runs; 34 with the Oakland Athletics (AL) and 24 with the St. Louis Cardinals (NL).

Runs Batted In Leaders, by Season

Note: Asterisk (*) indicates the all-time single-season record for each league since beginning of "modern" era in 1901.

National League Year	Player, Team	RBI	American League Year	Player, Team	RBI
1907	Sherwood Magee, Philadelphia	85	1907	Ty Cobb, Detroit	116
1908	Honus Wagner, Pittsburgh	109	1908	Ty Cobb, Detroit	108
1909	Honus Wagner, Pittsburgh	100	1909	Ty Cobb, Detroit	107
1910	Sherwood Magee, Philadelphia	123	1910	Sam Crawford, Detroit	120
1911	Frank Schulte, Chicago	121	1911	Ty Cobb, Detroit	144
1912	Henry Zimmerman, Chicago	103	1912	J. Franklin Baker, Philadelphia	133
1913	Gavvy Cravath, Philadelphia	128	1913	J. Franklin Baker, Philadelphia	126
1914	Sherwood Magee, Philadelphia	103	1914	Sam Crawford, Detroit	104
1915	Gavvy Cravath, Philadelphia	115	1915	Sam Crawford, Detroit; Robert Veach, Detroit	112
1916	Henry Zimmerman, Chicago-New York	83	1916	Del Pratt, St. Louis	103
1917	Henry Zimmerman, New York	102	1917	Robert Veach, Detroit	103
1918	Sherwood Magee, Philadelphia	76	1918	Robert Veach, Detroit	78
1919	Hi Myers, Boston	73	1919	Babe Ruth, Boston	114
1920	George Kelly, N.Y.; Rogers Hornsby, St. Louis	94	1920	Babe Ruth, New York	137
1921	Rogers Hornsby, St. Louis	126	1921	Babe Ruth, New York	171
1922	Rogers Hornsby, St. Louis	152	1922	Ken Williams, St. Louis	155
1923	Emil Meusel, New York	125	1923	Babe Ruth, New York	131
1924	George Kelly, New York	136	1924	Goose Goslin, Washington	129
1925	Rogers Hornsby, St. Louis	143	1925	Bob Meusel, New York	138
1926	Jim Bottomley, St. Louis	120	1926	Babe Ruth, New York	145
1927	Paul Waner, Pittsburgh	131	1927	Lou Gehrig, New York	175
1928	Jim Bottomley, St. Louis	136	1928	Babe Ruth, New York; Lou Gehrig, New York	142
1929	Hack Wilson, Chicago	159	1929	Al Simmons, Philadelphia	157
1930	Hack Wilson, Chicago	*191	1930	Lou Gehrig, New York	174
1931	Chuck Klein, Philadelphia	121	1931	Lou Gehrig, New York	*184
1932	Don Hurst, Philadelphia	143	1932	Jimmie Foxx, Philadelphia	169
1933	Chuck Klein, Philadelphia	120	1933	Jimmie Foxx, Philadelphia	163
1934	Mel Ott, New York	135	1934	Lou Gehrig, New York	165
1935	Walter Berger, Boston	130	1935	Hank Greenberg, Detroit	170
1936	Joe Medwick, St. Louis	138	1936	Hal Trosky, Cleveland	162
1937	Joe Medwick, St. Louis	154	1937	Hank Greenberg, Detroit	183
1938	Joe Medwick, St. Louis	122	1938	Jimmie Foxx, Boston	175
1939	Frank McCormick, Cincinnati	128	1939	Ted Williams, Boston	145
1940	John Mize, St. Louis	137	1940	Hank Greenberg, Detroit	150
1941	Adolph Camilli, Brooklyn	120	1941	Joe DiMaggio, New York	125
1942	John Mize, New York	110	1942	Ted Williams, Boston	137
1943	Bill Nicholson, Chicago	128	1943	Rudy York, Detroit	118
1944	Bill Nicholson, Chicago	122	1944	Vern Stephens, St. Louis	109
1945	Dixie Walker, Brooklyn	124	1945	Nick Etten, New York	111
1946	Enos Slaughter, St. Louis	130	1946	Hank Greenberg, Detroit	127
1947	John Mize, New York	138	1947	Ted Williams, Boston	114
1948	Stan Musial, St. Louis	131	1948	Joe DiMaggio, New York	155
1949	Ralph Kiner, Pittsburgh	127	1949	Ted Williams, Bos.; Vern Stephens, Bos.	159
1950	Del Ennis, Philadelphia	126	1950	Walt Dropo, Bos.; Vern Stephens, Bos.	144
1951	Monte Irvin, New York	121	1951	Gus Zernial, Chicago-Philadelphia	129
1952	Hank Sauer, Chicago	121	1952	Al Rosen, Cleveland	105
1953	Roy Campanella, Brooklyn	142	1953	Al Rosen, Cleveland	145
1954	Ted Kluszewski, Cincinnati	141	1954	Larry Doby, Cleveland	126
1955	Duke Snider, Brooklyn	136	1955	Ray Boone, Detroit; Jackie Jensen, Boston	116
1956	Stan Musial, St. Louis	109	1956	Mickey Mantle, New York	130
1957	Hank Aaron, Milwaukee	132	1957	Roy Sievers, Washington	114
1958	Ernie Banks, Chicago	129	1958	Jackie Jensen, Boston	122
1959	Ernie Banks, Chicago	143	1959	Jackie Jensen, Boston	112
1960	Hank Aaron, Milwaukee	126	1960	Roger Maris, New York	112
1961	Orlando Cepeda, San Francisco	142	1961	Roger Maris, New York	142
1962	Tommy Davis, Los Angeles	153	1962	Harmon Killebrew, Minnesota	126
1963	Hank Aaron, Milwaukee	130	1963	Dick Stuart, Boston	118
1964	Ken Boyer, St. Louis	119	1964	Brooks Robinson, Baltimore	118
1965	Deron Johnson, Cincinnati	130	1965	Rocky Colavito, Cleveland	108
1966	Hank Aaron, Atlanta	127	1966	Frank Robinson, Baltimore	122
1967	Orlando Cepeda, St. Louis	111	1967	Carl Yastrzemski, Boston	121
1968	Willie McCovey, San Francisco	105	1968	Ken Harrelson, Boston	109
1969	Willie McCovey, San Francisco	126	1969	Harmon Killebrew, Minnesota	140
1970	Johnny Bench, Cincinnati	148	1970	Frank Howard, Washington	126
1971	Joe Torre, St. Louis	137	1971	Harmon Killebrew, Minnesota	119
1972	Johnny Bench, Cincinnati	125	1972	Dick Allen, Chicago	113
1973	Willie Stargell, Pittsburgh	119	1973	Reggie Jackson, Oakland	117
1974	Johnny Bench, Cincinnati	129	1974	Jeff Burroughs, Texas	118
1975	Greg Luzinski, Philadelphia	120	1975	George Scott, Milwaukee	109
1976	George Foster, Cincinnati	121	1976	Lee May, Baltimore	109
1977	George Foster, Cincinnati	149	1977	Larry Hisle, Minnesota	119
1978	George Foster, Cincinnati	120	1978	Jim Rice, Boston	139
1979	Dave Winfield, San Diego	118	1979	Don Baylor, California	139
1980	Mike Schmidt, Philadelphia	121	1980	Cecil Cooper, Milwaukee	122
1981	Mike Schmidt, Philadelphia	91	1981	Eddie Murray, Baltimore	78
1982	Dale Murphy, Atlanta; Al Oliver, Montreal	109	1982	Hal McRae, Kansas City	133
1983	Dale Murphy, Atlanta	121	1983	Cecil Cooper, Milwaukee; Jim Rice, Boston	126
1984	Gary Carter, Montreal; Mike Schmidt, Phi.	106	1984	Tony Armas, Boston	123
1985	Dave Parker, Cincinnati	125	1985	Don Mattingly, New York	145
1986	Mike Schmidt, Philadelphia	119	1986	Joe Carter, Cleveland	121
1987	Andre Dawson, Chicago	137	1987	George Bell, Toronto	134
1988	Will Clark, San Francisco	109	1988	Jose Canseco, Oakland	124
1989	Kevin Mitchell, San Francisco	125	1989	Ruben Sierra, Texas	119
1990	Matt Williams, San Francisco	122	1990	Cecil Fielder, Detroit	132
1991	Howard Johnson, New York	117	1991	Cecil Fielder, Detroit	133
1992	Darren Daulton, Philadelphia	109	1992	Cecil Fielder, Detroit	124

	National League				American League		
Year	Player, Team		RBI	Year	Player, Team		RBI
1993	Barry Bonds, San Francisco		123	1993	Albert Belle, Cleveland		129
1994	Jeff Bagwell, Houston		116	1994	Kirby Puckett, Minnesota		112
1995	Dante Bichette, Colorado		128	1995	Albert Belle, Cleveland; Mo Vaughn, Boston		126
1996	Andres Galarraga, Colorado		150	1996	Albert Belle, Cleveland		148
1997	Andres Galarraga, Colorado		140	1997	Ken Griffey Jr., Seattle		147
1998	Sammy Sosa, Chicago		158	1998	Juan Gonzalez, Texas		157
1999	Mark McGwire, St. Louis		147	1999	Manny Ramirez, Cleveland		165
2000	Todd Helton, Colorado		147	2000	Edgar Martinez, Seattle		145
2001	Sammy Sosa, Chicago		160	2001	Bret Boone, Seattle		141
2002	Lance Berkman, Houston		128	2002	Alex Rodriguez, Texas		142
2003	Preston Wilson, Colorado		141	2003	Carlos Delgado, Toronto		145
2004	Vinny Castilla, Colorado		131	2004	Miguel Tejada, Baltimore		150
2005	Andruw Jones, Atlanta		128	2005	David Ortiz, Boston		148
2006	Ryan Howard, Philadelphia		149	2006	David Ortiz, Boston		137

Batting Champions, by Season

Note: Asterisk (*) indicates the all-time single-season record for each league since the beginning of the "modern" era in 1901.

	National League				American League		
Year	Player	Team	Avg.	Year	Player	Team	Avg.
1901	Jesse C. Burkett	St. Louis	.382	1901	Napoleon Lajoie	Philadelphia	*.426
1902	Clarence Beaumont	Pittsburgh	.357	1902	Ed Delahanty	Washington	.376
1903	Honus Wagner	Pittsburgh	.355	1903	Napoleon Lajoie	Cleveland	.355
1904	Honus Wagner	Pittsburgh	.349	1904	Napoleon Lajoie	Cleveland	.381
1905	James Seymour	Cincinnati	.377	1905	Elmer Flick	Cleveland	.306
1906	Honus Wagner	Pittsburgh	.339	1906	George Stone	St. Louis	.358
1907	Honus Wagner	Pittsburgh	.350	1907	Ty Cobb	Detroit	.350
1908	Honus Wagner	Pittsburgh	.354	1908	Ty Cobb	Detroit	.324
1909	Honus Wagner	Pittsburgh	.339	1909	Ty Cobb	Detroit	.377
1910	Sherwood Magee	Philadelphia	.331	1910[1]	Ty Cobb	Detroit	.385
1911	Honus Wagner	Pittsburgh	.334	1911	Ty Cobb	Detroit	.420
1912	Henry Zimmerman	Chicago	.372	1912	Ty Cobb	Detroit	.410
1913	Jacob Daubert	Brooklyn	.350	1913	Ty Cobb	Detroit	.390
1914	Jacob Daubert	Brooklyn	.329	1914	Ty Cobb	Detroit	.368
1915	Larry Doyle	New York	.320	1915	Ty Cobb	Detroit	.369
1916	Hal Chase	Cincinnati	.339	1916	Tris Speaker	Cleveland	.386
1917	Edd Roush	Cincinnati	.341	1917	Ty Cobb	Detroit	.383
1918	Zach Wheat	Brooklyn	.335	1918	Ty Cobb	Detroit	.382
1919	Edd Roush	Cincinnati	.321	1919	Ty Cobb	Detroit	.384
1920	Rogers Hornsby	St. Louis	.370	1920	George Sisler	St. Louis	.407
1921	Rogers Hornsby	St. Louis	.397	1921	Harry Heilmann	Detroit	.394
1922	Rogers Hornsby	St. Louis	.401	1922	George Sisler	St. Louis	.420
1923	Rogers Hornsby	St. Louis	.384	1923	Harry Heilmann	Detroit	.403
1924	Rogers Hornsby	St. Louis	*.424	1924	Babe Ruth	New York	.378
1925	Rogers Hornsby	St. Louis	.403	1925	Harry Heilmann	Detroit	.393
1926	Eugene Hargrave	Cincinnati	.353	1926	Henry Manush	Detroit	.378
1927	Paul Waner	Pittsburgh	.380	1927	Harry Heilmann	Detroit	.398
1928	Rogers Hornsby	Boston	.387	1928	Goose Goslin	Washington	.379
1929	Lefty O'Doul	Philadelphia	.398	1929	Lew Fonseca	Cleveland	.369
1930	Bill Terry	New York	.401	1930	Al Simmons	Philadelphia	.381
1931	Chick Hafey	St. Louis	.349	1931	Al Simmons	Philadelphia	.390
1932	Lefty O'Doul	Brooklyn	.368	1932	Dale Alexander	Detroit-Boston	.367
1933	Chuck Klein	Philadelphia	.368	1933	Jimmie Foxx	Philadelphia	.356
1934	Paul Waner	Pittsburgh	.362	1934	Lou Gehrig	New York	.363
1935	Arky Vaughan	Pittsburgh	.385	1935	Buddy Myer	Washington	.349
1936	Paul Waner	Pittsburgh	.373	1936	Luke Appling	Chicago	.388
1937	Joe Medwick	St. Louis	.374	1937	Charlie Gehringer	Detroit	.371
1938	Ernie Lombardi	Cincinnati	.342	1938	Jimmie Foxx	Boston	.349
1939	John Mize	St. Louis	.349	1939	Joe DiMaggio	New York	.381
1940	Debs Garms	Pittsburgh	.355	1940	Joe DiMaggio	New York	.352
1941	Pete Reiser	Brooklyn	.343	1941	Ted Williams	Boston	.406
1942	Ernie Lombardi	Boston	.330	1942	Ted Williams	Boston	.356
1943	Stan Musial	St. Louis	.357	1943	Luke Appling	Chicago	.328
1944	Dixie Walker	Brooklyn	.357	1944	Lou Boudreau	Cleveland	.327
1945	Phil Cavarretta	Chicago	.355	1945	George Stirnweiss	New York	.309
1946	Stan Musial	St. Louis	.365	1946	Mickey Vernon	Washington	.353
1947	Harry Walker	St.L.-Phi.	.363	1947	Ted Williams	Boston	.343
1948	Stan Musial	St. Louis	.376	1948	Ted Williams	Boston	.369
1949	Jackie Robinson	Brooklyn	.342	1949	George Kell	Detroit	.343
1950	Stan Musial	St. Louis	.346	1950	Billy Goodman	Boston	.354
1951	Stan Musial	St. Louis	.355	1951	Ferris Fain	Philadelphia	.344
1952	Stan Musial	St. Louis	.336	1952	Ferris Fain	Philadelphia	.327
1953	Carl Furillo	Brooklyn	.344	1953	Mickey Vernon	Washington	.337
1954	Willie Mays	New York	.345	1954	Roberto Avila	Cleveland	.341
1955	Richie Ashburn	Philadelphia	.338	1955	Al Kaline	Detroit	.340
1956	Hank Aaron	Milwaukee	.328	1956	Mickey Mantle	New York	.353
1957	Stan Musial	St. Louis	.351	1957	Ted Williams	Boston	.388
1958	Richie Ashburn	Philadelphia	.350	1958	Ted Williams	Boston	.328
1959	Hank Aaron	Milwaukee	.355	1959	Harvey Kuenn	Detroit	.353
1960	Dick Groat	Pittsburgh	.325	1960	Pete Runnels	Boston	.320
1961	Roberto Clemente	Pittsburgh	.351	1961	Norm Cash	Detroit	.361
1962	Tommy Davis	Los Angeles	.346	1962	Pete Runnels	Boston	.326
1963	Tommy Davis	Los Angeles	.326	1963	Carl Yastrzemski	Boston	.321
1964	Roberto Clemente	Pittsburgh	.339	1964	Tony Oliva	Minnesota	.323
1965	Roberto Clemente	Pittsburgh	.329	1965	Tony Oliva	Minnesota	.321
1966	Matty Alou	Pittsburgh	.342	1966	Frank Robinson	Baltimore	.316
1967	Roberto Clemente	Pittsburgh	.357	1967	Carl Yastrzemski	Boston	.326
1968	Pete Rose	Cincinnati	.335	1968	Carl Yastrzemski	Boston	.301
1969	Pete Rose	Cincinnati	.348	1969	Rod Carew	Minnesota	.332

	National League				American League		
Year	Player	Team	Avg.	Year	Player	Team	Avg.
1970	Rico Carty	Atlanta	.366	1970	Alex Johnson	California	.329
1971	Joe Torre	St. Louis	.363	1971	Tony Oliva	Minnesota	.337
1972	Billy Williams	Chicago	.333	1972	Rod Carew	Minnesota	.318
1973	Pete Rose	Cincinnati	.338	1973	Rod Carew	Minnesota	.350
1974	Ralph Garr	Atlanta	.353	1974	Rod Carew	Minnesota	.364
1975	Bill Madlock	Chicago	.354	1975	Rod Carew	Minnesota	.359
1976	Bill Madlock	Chicago	.339	1976	George Brett	Kansas City	.333
1977	Dave Parker	Pittsburgh	.338	1977	Rod Carew	Minnesota	.388
1978	Dave Parker	Pittsburgh	.334	1978	Rod Carew	Minnesota	.333
1979	Keith Hernandez	St. Louis	.344	1979	Fred Lynn	Boston	.333
1980	Bill Buckner	Chicago	.324	1980	George Brett	Kansas City	.390
1981	Bill Madlock	Pittsburgh	.341	1981	Carney Lansford	Boston	.336
1982	Al Oliver	Montreal	.331	1982	Willie Wilson	Kansas City	.332
1983	Bill Madlock	Pittsburgh	.323	1983	Wade Boggs	Boston	.361
1984	Tony Gwynn	San Diego	.351	1984	Don Mattingly	New York	.343
1985	Willie McGee	St. Louis	.353	1985	Wade Boggs	Boston	.368
1986	Tim Raines	Montreal	.334	1986	Wade Boggs	Boston	.357
1987	Tony Gwynn	San Diego	.370	1987	Wade Boggs	Boston	.363
1988	Tony Gwynn	San Diego	.313	1988	Wade Boggs	Boston	.366
1989	Tony Gwynn	San Diego	.336	1989	Kirby Puckett	Minnesota	.339
1990	Willie McGee	St. Louis	.335	1990	George Brett	Kansas City	.329
1991	Terry Pendleton	Atlanta	.319	1991	Julio Franco	Texas	.341
1992	Gary Sheffield	San Diego	.330	1992	Edgar Martinez	Seattle	.343
1993	Andres Galarraga	Colorado	.370	1993	John Olerud	Toronto	.363
1994	Tony Gwynn	San Diego	.394	1994	Paul O'Neill	New York	.359
1995	Tony Gwynn	San Diego	.368	1995	Edgar Martinez	Seattle	.356
1996	Tony Gwynn	San Diego	.353	1996	Alex Rodriguez	Seattle	.358
1997	Tony Gwynn	San Diego	.372	1997	Frank Thomas	Chicago	.347
1998	Larry Walker	Colorado	.363	1998	Bernie Williams	New York	.339
1999	Larry Walker	Colorado	.379	1999	Nomar Garciaparra	Boston	.357
2000	Todd Helton	Colorado	.372	2000	Nomar Garciaparra	Boston	.372
2001	Larry Walker	Colorado	.350	2001	Ichiro Suzuki	Seattle	.350
2002	Barry Bonds	San Francisco	.370	2002	Manny Ramirez	Boston	.349
2003	Albert Pujols	St. Louis	.359	2003	Bill Mueller	Boston	.326
2004	Barry Bonds	San Francisco	.362	2004	Ichiro Suzuki	Seattle	.372
2005	Derrek Lee	Chicago	.335	2005	Michael Young	Texas	.331
2006	Freddy Sanchez	Pittsburgh	.344	2006	Joe Mauer	Minnesota	.347

(1) Some baseball researchers have concluded that Ty Cobb actually hit .382 in 1910 while Napoleon Lajoie, Cleveland, hit .383.

Earned Run Average Leaders, by Season

	National League					American League			
Year	Player, team	G	IP	ERA	Year	Player, team	G	IP	ERA
1977	John Candelaria, Pittsburgh	33	231	2.34	1977	Frank Tanana, California	31	241	2.54
1978	Craig Swan, New York	29	207	2.43	1978	Ron Guidry, New York	35	274	1.74
1979	J. R. Richard, Houston	38	292	2.71	1979	Ron Guidry, New York	33	236	2.78
1980	Don Sutton, Los Angeles	32	212	2.21	1980	Rudy May, New York	41	175	2.47
1981	Nolan Ryan, Houston	21	149	1.69	1981	Steve McCatty, Oakland	22	186	2.32
1982	Steve Rogers, Montreal	35	277	2.40	1982	Rick Sutcliffe, Cleveland	34	216	2.96
1983	Atlee Hammaker, San Francisco	23	172	2.25	1983	Rick Honeycutt, Texas	25	174	2.42
1984	Alejandro Pena, Los Angeles	28	199	2.48	1984	Mike Boddicker, Baltimore	34	261	2.79
1985	Dwight Gooden, New York	35	276	1.53	1985	Dave Stieb, Toronto	36	265	2.48
1986	Mike Scott, Houston	37	275	2.22	1986	Roger Clemens, Boston	33	254	2.48
1987	Nolan Ryan, Houston	34	211	2.76	1987	Jimmy Key, Toronto	36	261	2.76
1988	Joe Magrane, St. Louis	24	165	2.18	1988	Allan Anderson, Minnesota	30	202	2.45
1989	Scott Garrelts, San Francisco	30	193	2.28	1989	Bret Saberhagen, Kansas City	36	262	2.16
1990	Danny Darwin, Houston	48	162	2.21	1990	Roger Clemens, Boston	31	228	1.93
1991	Dennis Martinez, Montreal	31	222	2.39	1991	Roger Clemens, Boston	35	271	2.62
1992	Bill Swift, San Francisco	30	164	2.08	1992	Roger Clemens, Boston	32	246	2.41
1993	Greg Maddux, Atlanta	36	267	2.36	1993	Kevin Appier, Kansas City	34	238	2.56
1994	Greg Maddux, Atlanta	25	202	1.56	1994	Steve Ontiveros, Oakland	27	115	2.65
1995	Greg Maddux, Atlanta	28	209	1.63	1995	Randy Johnson, Seattle	30	214	2.48
1996	Kevin Brown, Florida	32	233	1.89	1996	Juan Guzman, Toronto	27	187	2.93
1997	Pedro Martinez, Montrea	31	241	1.90	1997	Roger Clemens, Toronto	34	264	2.05
1998	Greg Maddux, Atlanta	34	251	2.22	1998	Roger Clemens, Toronto	33	234	2.65
1999	Randy Johnson, Arizona	35	271	2.48	1999	Pedro Martinez, Boston	31	213	2.07
2000	Kevin K. Brown, Los Angeles	33	230	2.58	2000	Pedro Martinez, Boston	29	217	1.74
2001	Randy Johnson, Arizona	35	249	2.49	2001	Freddy Garcia, Seattle	34	238	3.05
2002	Randy Johnson, Arizona	35	260	2.32	2002	Pedro Martinez, Boston	30	199	2.26
2003	Jason Schmidt, San Francisco	29	207	2.34	2003	Pedro Martinez, Boston	29	186	2.22
2004	Jake Peavy, San Diego	27	166.1	2.27	2004	Johan Santana, Minnesota	34	228	2.61
2005	Roger Clemens, Houston	32	211.1	1.87	2005	Kevin Millwood, Cleveland	30	192	2.86
2006	Roy Oswalt, Houston	33	220.2	2.98	2006	Johan Santana, Minnesota	34	233.2	2.77

ERA is computed by multiplying earned runs allowed by 9, then dividing by innings pitched.

Strikeout Leaders, by Season

Note: Asterisk (*) indicates the all-time single-season record for each league.

	National League			American League	
Year	Pitcher, Team	SO	Year	Pitcher, Team	SO
1901	Noodles Hahn, Cincinnati	239	1901	Cy Young, Boston	158
1902	Vic Willis, Boston	225	1902	Rube Waddell, Philadelphia	210
1903	Christy Mathewson, New York	267	1903	Rube Waddell, Philadelphia	302
1904	Christy Mathewson, New York	212	1904	Rube Waddell, Philadelphia	349
1905	Christy Mathewson, New York	206	1905	Rube Waddell, Philadelphia	287
1906	Fred Beebe, Chicago-St. Louis	171	1906	Rube Waddell, Philadelphia	196
1907	Christy Mathewson, New York	178	1907	Rube Waddell, Philadelphia	232
1908	Christy Mathewson, New York	259	1908	Ed Walsh, Chicago	269
1909	Orval Overall, Chicago	205	1909	Frank Smith, Chicago	177
1910	Earl Moore, Philadelphia	185	1910	Walter Johnson, Washington	313

	National League			American League	
Year	Pitcher, Team	SO	Year	Pitcher, Team	SO
1911	Rube Marquard, New York	237	1911	Ed Walsh, Chicago	255
1912	Grover Alexander, Philadelphia	195	1912	Walter Johnson, Washington	303
1913	Tom Seaton, Philadelphia	168	1913	Walter Johnson, Washington	243
1914	Grover Alexander, Philadelphia	214	1914	Walter Johnson, Washington	225
1915	Grover Alexander, Philadelphia	241	1915	Walter Johnson, Washington	203
1916	Grover Alexander, Philadelphia	167	1916	Walter Johnson, Washington	228
1917	Grover Alexander, Philadelphia	201	1917	Walter Johnson, Washington	188
1918	Hippo Vaughn, Chicago	148	1918	Walter Johnson, Washington	162
1919	Hippo Vaughn, Chicago	141	1919	Walter Johnson, Washington	147
1920	Grover Alexander, Chicago	173	1920	Stan Coveleski, Cleveland	133
1921	Burleigh Grimes, Brooklyn	136	1921	Walter Johnson, Washington	143
1922	Dazzy Vance, Brooklyn	134	1922	Urban Shocker, St. Louis	149
1923	Dazzy Vance, Brooklyn	197	1923	Walter Johnson, Washington	130
1924	Dazzy Vance, Brooklyn	262	1924	Walter Johnson, Washington	158
1925	Dazzy Vance, Brooklyn	221	1925	Lefty Grove, Philadelphia	116
1926	Dazzy Vance, Brooklyn	140	1926	Lefty Grove, Philadelphia	194
1927	Dazzy Vance, Brooklyn	184	1927	Lefty Grove, Philadelphia	174
1928	Dazzy Vance, Brooklyn	200	1928	Lefty Grove, Philadelphia	183
1929	Pat Malone, Chicago	166	1929	Lefty Grove, Philadelphia	170
1930	Bill Hallahan, St. Louis	177	1930	Lefty Grove, Philadelphia	209
1931	Bill Hallahan, St. Louis	159	1931	Lefty Grove, Philadelphia	175
1932	Dizzy Dean, St. Louis	191	1932	Red Ruffing, New York	190
1933	Dizzy Dean, St. Louis	199	1933	Lefty Gomez, New York	163
1934	Dizzy Dean, St. Louis	195	1934	Lefty Gomez, New York	158
1935	Dizzy Dean, St. Louis	190	1935	Tommy Bridges, Detroit	163
1936	Van Lingle Mungo, Brooklyn	238	1936	Tommy Bridges, Detroit	175
1937	Carl Hubbell, New York	159	1937	Lefty Gomez, New York	194
1938	Clay Bryant, Chicago	135	1938	Bob Feller, Cleveland	240
1939	Claude Passeau, Philadelphia-Chicago	137	1939	Bob Feller, Cleveland	246
	Bucky Walters, Cincinnati				
1940	Kirby Higbe, Philadelphia	137	1940	Bob Feller, Cleveland	261
1941	John Vander Meer, Cincinnati	202	1941	Bob Feller, Cleveland	260
1942	John Vander Meer, Cincinnati	186	1942	Tex Hughson, Boston	113
				Bobo Newsom, Washington	
1943	John Vander Meer, Cincinnati	174	1943	Allie Reynolds, Cleveland	151
1944	Bill Voiselle, New York	161	1944	Hal Newhouser, Detroit	187
1945	Preacher Roe, Pittsburgh	148	1945	Hal Newhouser, Detroit	212
1946	Johnny Schmitz, Cincinnati	135	1946	Bob Feller, Cleveland	348
1947	Ewell Blackwell, Cincinnati	193	1947	Bob Feller, Cleveland	196
1948	Harry Brecheen, St. Louis	149	1948	Bob Feller, Cleveland	164
1949	Warren Spahn, Boston	151	1949	Virgil Trucks, Detroit	153
1950	Warren Spahn, Boston	191	1950	Bob Lemon, Cleveland	170
1951	Warren Spahn, Boston	164	1951	Vic Raschi, New York	164
	Don Newcombe, Brooklyn				
1952	Warren Spahn, Boston	183	1952	Allie Reynolds, New York	160
1953	Robin Roberts, Philadelphia	198	1953	Billy Pierce, Chicago	186
1954	Robin Roberts, Philadelphia	185	1954	Bob Turley, Baltimore	185
1955	Sam Jones, Chicago	198	1955	Herb Score, Cleveland	245
1956	Sam Jones, Chicago	176	1956	Herb Score, Cleveland	263
1957	Jack Sanford, Philadelphia	188	1957	Early Wynn, Cleveland	184
1958	Sam Jones, St. Louis	225	1958	Early Wynn, Chicago	179
1959	Don Drysdale, Los Angeles	242	1959	Jim Bunning, Detroit	201
1960	Don Drysdale, Los Angeles	246	1960	Jim Bunning, Detroit	201
1961	Sandy Koufax, Los Angeles	269	1961	Camilo Pacual, Minnesota	221
1962	Don Drysdale, Los Angeles	232	1962	Camilo Pacual, Minnesota	206
1963	Sandy Koufax, Los Angeles	306	1963	Camilo Pacual, Minnesota	202
1964	Bob Veale, Pittsburgh	250	1964	Al Downing, New York	217
1965	Sandy Koufax, Los Angeles	382*	1965	Sam McDowell, Cleveland	325
1966	Sandy Koufax, Los Angeles	317	1966	Sam McDowell, Cleveland	225
1967	Jim Bunning, Philadelphia	253	1967	Jim Lonborg, Boston	246
1968	Bob Gibson, St. Louis	268	1968	Sam McDowell, Cleveland	283
1969	Ferguson Jenkins, Chicago	273	1969	Sam McDowell, Cleveland	279
1970	Tom Seaver, New York	283	1970	Sam McDowell, Cleveland	304
1971	Tom Seaver, New York	289	1971	Mickey Lolich, Detroit	308
1972	Steve Carlton, Philadelphia	310	1972	Nolan Ryan, California	329
1973	Tom Seaver, New York	251	1973	Nolan Ryan, California	383*
1974	Steve Carlton, Philadelphia	240	1974	Nolan Ryan, California	367
1975	Tom Seaver, New York	243	1975	Frank Tanana, California	269
1976	Tom Seaver, New York	235	1976	Nolan Ryan, California	327
1977	Phil Niekro, Atlanta	262	1977	Nolan Ryan, California	341
1978	J.R. Richard, Houston	303	1978	Nolan Ryan, California	260
1979	J.R. Richard, Houston	313	1979	Nolan Ryan, California	223
1980	Steve Carlton, Philadelphia	286	1980	Len Barker, Cleveland	187
1981	Fernando Valenzuela, Los Angeles	180	1981	Len Barker, Cleveland	127
1982	Steve Carlton, Philadelphia	286	1982	Floyd Bannister, Seattle	209
1983	Steve Carlton, Philadelphia	275	1983	Jack Morris, Detroit	232
1984	Dwight Gooden, New York	276	1984	Mark Langston, Seattle	204
1985	Dwight Gooden, New York	268	1985	Bert Blyleven, Cleveland-Minnesota	206
1986	Mike Scott, Houston	306	1986	Mark Langston, Seattle	245
1987	Nolan Ryan, Houston	270	1987	Mark Langston, Seattle	262
1988	Nolan Ryan, Houston	228	1988	Roger Clemens, Boston	291
1989	Jose DeLeon, St. Louis	201	1989	Nolan Ryan, Texas	301
1990	David Cone, New York	233	1990	Nolan Ryan, Texas	232
1991	David Cone, New York	241	1991	Roger Clemens, Boston	241
1992	John Smoltz, Atlanta	215	1992	Randy Johnson, Seattle	241
1993	Jose Rijo, Cincinnati	227	1993	Randy Johnson, Seattle	308
1994	Andy Benes, San Diego	189	1994	Randy Johnson, Seattle	204
1995	Hideo Nomo, Los Angeles	236	1995	Randy Johnson, Seattle	294
1996	John Smoltz, Atlanta	276	1996	Roger Clemens, Boston	257

	National League		
Year	Pitcher, Team		SO
1997	Curt Schilling, Philadelphia		319
1998	Curt Schilling, Philadelphia		300
1999	Randy Johnson, Arizona		364
2000	Randy Johnson, Arizona		347
2001	Randy Johnson, Arizona		372
2002	Randy Johnson, Arizona		334
2003	Kerry Wood, Chicago		266
2004	Randy Johnson, Arizona		290
2005	Jake Peavy, San Diego		216
2006	Aaron Harang, Cincinnati		216

	American League		
Year	Pitcher, Team		SO
1997	Roger Clemens, Toronto		292
1998	Roger Clemens, Toronto		271
1999	Pedro Martinez, Boston		313
2000	Pedro Martinez, Boston		284
2001	Hideo Nomo, Boston		220
2002	Pedro Martinez, Boston		239
2003	Esteban Loaiza, Chicago		207
2004	Johan Santana, Minnesota		265
2005	Johan Santana, Minnesota		238
2006	Johan Santana, Minnesota		245

Victory Leaders by Season

Note: Asterisk (*) indicates the all-time single-season record for each league in the "modern" era beginning in 1901.

	National League	Wins		American League	Wins
Year	Pitcher, Team		Year	Pitcher, Team	
1901	Bill Donavan, Brooklyn	25	1901	Cy Young, Boston	33
1902	Jack Chesbro, Pittsburgh	28	1902	Cy Young, Boston	32
1903	Joe McGinnity, New York	31	1903	Cy Young, Boston	28
1904	Joe McGinnity, New York	35	1904	Jack Chesbro, New York	41*
1905	Christy Mathewson, New York	31	1905	Rube Waddell, Philadelphia	27
1906	Joe McGinnity, New York	27	1906	Al Orth, New York	27
1907	Christy Mathewson, New York	24	1907	Doc White, Chicago	27
1908	Christy Mathewson, New York	37*	1908	Ed Walsh, Chicago	40
1909	Mordecai Brown, Chicago	27	1909	George Mullin, Detroit	29
1910	Christy Mathewson, New York	27	1910	Jack Coombs, Philadelphia	31
1911	Grover Alexander, Chicago	28	1911	Jack Coombs, Philadelphia	28
1912	Rube Marquard, New York	26	1912	Joe Wood, Boston	34
1913	Tom Seaton, Philadelphia	27	1913	Walter Johnson, Washington	36
1914	Grover Alexander, Philadelphia	27	1914	Walter Johnson, Washington	28
1915	Grover Alexander, Philadelphia	31	1915	Walter Johnson, Washington	27
1916	Grover Alexander, Philadelphia	33	1916	Walter Johnson, Washington	25
1917	Grover Alexander, Philadelphia	30	1917	Eddie Cicotte, Chicago	28
1918	Hippo Vaughn, Chicago	22	1918	Walter Johnson, Washington	23
1919	Jesse Barnes, New York	25	1919	Eddie Cicotte, Chicago	29
1920	Grover Alexander, Philadelphia	27	1920	Jim Bagby, Cleveland	31
1921	Burleigh Grimes, Brooklyn	22	1921	Urban Shocker, St. Louis	27
1922	Eppa Rixey, Cincinnati	25	1922	Eddie Rommel, Philadelphia	27
1923	Dolf Luque, Cincinnati	27	1923	George Uhle, Cleveland	26
1924	Dazzy Vance, Brooklyn	28	1924	Walter Johnson, Washington	23
1925	Dazzy Vance, Brooklyn	22	1925	Eddie Rommel, Philadelphia	21
1926	Flint Rhem, St. Louis	20	1926	George Uhle, Cleveland	27
1927	Charlie Root, Chicago	26	1927	Ted Lyons, Chicago	22
1928	Burleigh Grimes, Pittsburgh	25	1928	George Pipgras, New York	24
1929	Pat Malone, Chicago	22	1929	George Earnshaw, Philadelphia	24
1930	Pat Malone, Chicago	20	1930	Lefty Grove, Philadelphia	28
1931	Heine Meine, Pittsburgh	19	1931	Lefty Grove, Philadelphia	31
1932	Lon Warneke, Chicago	22	1932	Alvin Crowder, Washington	26
1933	Carl Hubbell, New York	23	1933	Lefty Grove, Philadelphia	24
1934	Dizzy Dean, St. Louis	30	1934	Lefty Gomez, New York	26
1935	Dizzy Dean, St. Louis	28	1935	Wes Ferrell, Boston	25
1936	Carl Hubbell, New York	26	1936	Tommy Bridges, Detroit	23
1937	Carl Hubbell, New York	22	1937	Lefty Gomez, New York	21
1938	Bill Lee, Chicago	22	1938	Red Ruffing, New York	21
1939	Bucky Walters, Cincinnati	27	1939	Bob Feller, Cleveland	24
1940	Bucky Walters, Cincinnati	22	1940	Bob Feller, Cleveland	27
1941	Whit Wyatt, Brooklyn	22	1941	Bob Feller, Cleveland	25
1942	Mort Cooper, St. Louis	22	1942	Tex Hughson, Boston	22
1943	Rip Sewell, Pittsburgh	21	1943	Dizzy Trout, Detroit	20
1944	Bucky Walters, Cincinnati	23	1944	Hal Newhouser, Detroit	29
1945	Red Barrett, Boston-St. Louis	23	1945	Hal Newhouser, Detroit	25
1946	Howie Pollet, St. Louis	21	1946	Hal Newhouser, Detroit	26
1947	Ewell Blackwell, Cincinnati	22	1947	Bob Feller, Cleveland	20
1948	Johnny Sain, Boston	24	1948	Hal Newhouser, Detroit	21
1949	Warren Spahn, Boston	21	1949	Mel Parnell, Boston	25
1950	Warren Spahn, Boston	21	1950	Bob Lemon, Cleveland	23
1951	Sal Maglie, New York	23	1951	Bob Feller, Cleveland	22
1952	Robin Roberts, Philadelphia	28	1952	Bobby Shantz, Philadelphia	24
1953	Warren Spahn, Milwaukee	23	1953	Bob Porterfield, Washington	22
1954	Robin Roberts, Philadelphia	23	1954	Early Wynn, Cleveland	23
1955	Robin Roberts, Philadelphia	23	1955	Frank Sullivan, Boston	18
1956	Don Newcombe, Brooklyn	27	1956	Frank Lary, Detroit	21
1957	Warren Spahn, Milwaukee	21	1957	Billy Pierce, Chicago	20
1958	Warren Spahn, Milwaukee	22	1958	Bob Turley, New York	21
1959	Warren Spahn, Milwaukee	21	1959	Early Wynn, Chicago	22
1960	Warren Spahn, Milwaukee	21	1960	Jim Perry, Cleveland	18
1961	Warren Spahn, Milwaukee	21	1961	Whitey Ford, New York	25
1962	Don Drysdale, Los Angeles	25	1962	Ralph Terry, New York	23
1963	Juan Marichal, San Francisco	25	1963	Whitey Ford, New York	24
1964	Larry Jackson, Chicago	24	1964	Gary Peters, Chicago	20
1965	Sandy Koufax, Los Angeles	26	1965	Mudcat (Jim) Grant, Minnesota	21
1966	Sandy Koufax, Los Angeles	27	1966	Jim Kaat, Minnesota	25
1967	Mike McCormick, San Francisco	22	1967	Earl Wilson, Detroit	22
1968	Juan Marichal, San Francisco	26	1968	Denny McLain, Detroit	31
1969	Tom Seaver, New York	25	1969	Denny McLain, Detroit	24
1970	Gaylord Perry, San Francisco	23	1970	Jim Perry, Minnesota	24
1971	Fergie Jenkins, Chicago	24	1971	Mickey Lolich, Detroit	25
1972	Steve Carlton, Philadelphia	27	1972	Wilbur Wood, Chicago	24
1973	Ron Bryant, San Francisco	24	1973	Wilbur Wood, Chicago	24
1974	Phil Niekro, Atlanta	20	1974	Fergie Jenkins, Texas	25

National League			American League		
Year	Pitcher, Team	Wins	Year	Pitcher, Team	Wins
1975	Tom Seaver, New York	22	1975	Jim Palmer, Baltimore	23
1976	Randy Jones, San Diego	22	1976	Jim Palmer, Baltimore	22
1977	Steve Carlton, Philadelphia	23	1977	Jim Palmer, Baltimore	20
1978	Gaylord Perry, San Diego	21	1978	Ron Guidry, New York	25
1979	Phil Niekro, Atlanta	21	1979	Mike Flanagan, Baltimore	23
1980	Steve Carlton, Philadelphia	24	1980	Steve Stone, Baltimore	25
1981	Tom Seaver, Cincinnati	14	1981	Pete Vuckovich, Milwaukee	14
1982	Steve Carlton, Philadelphia	23	1982	La Marr Hoyt, Chicago	19
1983	John Denny, Philadelphia	19	1983	La Marr Hoyt, Chicago	24
1984	Joaquin Andujar, St. Louis	20	1984	Mike Boddicker, Baltimore	20
1985	Dwight Gooden, New York	24	1985	Ron Guidry, New York	22
1986	Fernando Valenzuela, Los Angeles	21	1986	Roger Clemens, Boston	24
1987	Rick Sutcliffe, Chicago	18	1987	Dave Stewart, Oakland; Roger Clemens, Boston	20
1988	Danny Jackson, Cincinnati	23	1988	Frank Viola, Minnesota	24
1989	Mike Scott, Houston	20	1989	Bret Saberhagen, Kansas City	23
1990	Doug Drabek, Pittsburgh	22	1990	Bob Welch, Oakland	27
1991	John Smiley, Pittsburgh	20	1991	Bill Gullickson, Detroit	20
1992	Greg Maddux, Chicago	20	1992	Jack Morris, Toronto	21
1993	Tom Glavine, Atlanta	22	1993	Jack McDowell, Chicago	22
1994	Greg Maddux, Atlanta	16	1994	Jimmy Key, New York	17
1995	Greg Maddux, Atlanta	19	1995	Mike Mussina, Baltimore	19
1996	John Smoltz, Atlanta	24	1996	Andy Pettitte, New York	21
1997	Denny Neagle, Atlanta	20	1997	Roger Clemens, Toronto	21
1998	Tom Glavine, Atlanta	20	1998	Rick Helling, Texas; Roger Clemens, Toronto	20
1999	Mike Hampton, Houston	22	1999	Pedro Martinez, Boston	23
2000	Tom Glavine, Atlanta	21	2000	David Wells, Toronto	20
2001	Matt Morris, St. Louis; Curt Schilling, Arizona	22	2001	Mark Mulder, Oakland	21
2002	Randy Johnson, Arizona	24	2002	Barry Zito, Oakland	23
2003	Russ Ortiz, Atlanta	21	2003	Roy Halladay, Toronto	22
2004	Roy Oswalt, Houston	20	2004	Curt Schilling, Boston	21
2005	Dontrelle Willis, Florida	22	2005	Bartolo Colon, Los Angeles	21
2006	Aaron Harang, Cincinnati; Derek Lowe, Los Angeles; Brad Penny, Los Angeles; John Smoltz, Atlanta; Brandon Webb, Arizona; Carlos Zambrano, Chicago	16	2006	Johan Santana, Minnesota; Chien-Ming Wang, New York	19

Cy Young Award Winners

Year	Player, Team	Year	Player, Team	Year	Player, Team
1956	Don Newcombe, Dodgers	1977	(NL) Steve Carlton, Phillies	1993	(NL) Greg Maddux, Braves
1957	Warren Spahn, Braves		(AL) Sparky Lyle, Yankees		(AL) Jack McDowell, White Sox
1958	Bob Turley, Yankees	1978	(NL) Gaylord Perry, Padres	1994	(NL) Greg Maddux, Braves
1959	Early Wynn, White Sox		(AL) Ron Guidry, Yankees		(AL) David Cone, Royals
1960	Vernon Law, Pirates	1979	(NL) Bruce Sutter, Cubs	1995	(NL) Greg Maddux, Braves
1961	Whitey Ford, Yankees		(AL) Mike Flanagan, Orioles		(AL) Randy Johnson, Mariners
1962	Don Drysdale, Dodgers	1980	(NL) Steve Carlton, Phillies	1996	(NL) John Smoltz, Braves
1963	Sandy Koufax, Dodgers		(AL) Steve Stone, Orioles		(AL) Pat Hentgen, Blue Jays
1964	Dean Chance, Angels	1981	(NL) Fernando Valenzuela, Dodgers	1997	(NL) Pedro Martinez, Expos
1965	Sandy Koufax, Dodgers		(AL) Rollie Fingers, Brewers		(AL) Roger Clemens, Blue Jays
1966	Sandy Koufax, Dodgers	1982	(NL) Steve Carlton, Phillies	1998	(NL) Tom Glavine, Braves
1967	(NL) Mike McCormick, Giants		(AL) Pete Vuckovich, Brewers		(AL) Roger Clemens, Blue Jays
	(AL) Jim Lonborg, Red Sox	1983	(NL) John Denny, Phillies	1999	(NL) Randy Johnson, Diamondbacks
1968	(NL) Bob Gibson, Cardinals		(AL) LaMarr Hoyt, White Sox		(AL) Pedro Martinez, Red Sox
	(AL) Dennis McLain, Tigers	1984	(NL) Rick Sutcliffe, Cubs	2000	(NL) Randy Johnson, Diamondbacks
1969	(NL) Tom Seaver, Mets		(AL) Willie Hernandez, Tigers		(AL) Pedro Martinez, Red Sox
	(AL) (tie) Dennis McLain, Tigers Mike Cuellar, Orioles	1985	(NL) Dwight Gooden, Mets	2001	(NL) Randy Johnson, Diamondbacks
			(AL) Bret Saberhagen, Royals		(AL) Roger Clemens, Yankees
1970	(NL) Bob Gibson, Cardinals	1986	(NL) Mike Scott, Astros	2002	(NL) Randy Johnson, Diamondbacks
	(AL) Jim Perry, Twins		(AL) Roger Clemens, Red Sox		(AL) Barry Zito, A's
1971	(NL) Ferguson Jenkins, Cubs	1987	(NL) Steve Bedrosian, Phillies	2003	(NL) Eric Gagne, Dodgers
	(AL) Vida Blue, A's		(AL) Roger Clemens, Red Sox		(AL) Roy Halladay, Blue Jays
1972	(NL) Steve Carlton, Phillies	1988	(NL) Orel Hershiser, Dodgers	2004	(NL) Roger Clemens, Astros
	(AL) Gaylord Perry, Indians		(AL) Frank Viola, Twins		(AL) Johan Santana, Twins
1973	(NL) Tom Seaver, Mets	1989	(NL) Mark Davis, Padres	2005	(NL) Chris Carpenter, Cardinals
	(AL) Jim Palmer, Orioles		(AL) Bret Saberhagen, Royals		(AL) Bartolo Colon, Angels
1974	(NL) Mike Marshall, Dodgers	1990	(NL) Doug Drabek, Pirates		
	(AL) Jim (Catfish) Hunter, A's		(AL) Bob Welch, A's		
1975	(NL) Tom Seaver, Mets	1991	(NL) Tom Glavine, Braves		
	(AL) Jim Palmer, Orioles		(AL) Roger Clemens, Red Sox		
1976	(NL) Randy Jones, Padres	1992	(NL) Greg Maddux, Cubs		
	(AL) Jim Palmer, Orioles		(AL) Dennis Eckersley, A's		

WORLD ALMANAC EDITORS' PICKS
2006 All-World Baseball Team

The editors of The World Almanac have chosen the following as the best players at each position based on 2006 regular season performance.

Position	World Almanac 2006 Best	Position	World Almanac 2006 Best
Catcher	Joe Mauer (Minnesota Twins)	Right Field	Jermaine Dye (Chicago White Sox)
1st base	Albert Pujols (St. Louis Cardinals)	Designated hitter	David Ortiz (Boston Red Sox)
2nd base	Chase Utley (Philadelphia Phillies)	Right-handed starting pitcher	Roy Halladay (Toronto Blue Jays)
3rd base	David Wright (New York Mets)	Left-handed starting pitcher	Johan Santana (Minnesota Twins)
Shortstop	Derek Jeter (New York Yankees)	Right-handed relief pitcher	Jonathan Papelbon (Boston Red Sox)
Left field	Alfonso Soriano (Washington Nationals)	Left-handed relief pitcher	BJ Ryan (Toronto Blue Jays)
Center field	Carlos Beltran (New York Mets)		

Most Valuable Players

(As selected by the Baseball Writers' Assoc. of America. Prior to 1931, MVP honors were named by various sources.)

National League

Year	Player, team	Year	Player, team	Year	Player, team
1931	Frank Frisch, St. Louis	1956	Don Newcombe, Brooklyn	1981	Mike Schmidt, Philadelphia
1932	Chuck Klein, Philadelphia	1957	Hank Aaron, Milwaukee	1982	Dale Murphy, Atlanta
1933	Carl Hubbell, New York	1958	Ernie Banks, Chicago	1983	Dale Murphy, Atlanta
1934	Dizzy Dean, St. Louis	1959	Ernie Banks, Chicago	1984	Ryne Sandberg, Chicago
1935	Gabby Hartnett, Chicago	1960	Dick Groat, Pittsburgh	1985	Willie McGee, St. Louis
1936	Carl Hubbell, N.Y.	1961	Frank Robinson, Cincinnati	1986	Mike Schmidt, Philadelphia
1937	Joe Medwick, St. Louis	1962	Maury Wills, L.A.	1987	Andre Dawson, Chicago
1938	Ernie Lombardi, Cincinnati	1963	Sandy Koufax, L.A.	1988	Kirk Gibson, L.A.
1939	Bucky Walters, Cincinnati	1964	Ken Boyer, St. Louis	1989	Kevin Mitchell, San Francisco
1940	Frank McCormick, Cincinnati	1965	Willie Mays, San Francisco	1990	Barry Bonds, Pittsburgh
1941	Dolph Camilli, Brooklyn	1966	Roberto Clemente, Pittsburgh	1991	Terry Pendleton, Atlanta
1942	Mort Cooper, St. Louis	1967	Orlando Cepeda, St. Louis	1992	Barry Bonds, Pittsburgh
1943	Stan Musial, St. Louis	1968	Bob Gibson, St. Louis	1993	Barry Bonds, San Francisco
1944	Martin Marion, St. Louis	1969	Willie McCovey, San Francisco	1994	Jeff Bagwell, Houston
1945	Phil Cavarretta, Chicago	1970	Johnny Bench, Cincinnati	1995	Barry Larkin, Cincinnati
1946	Stan Musial, St. Louis	1971	Joe Torre, St. Louis	1996	Ken Caminiti, San Diego
1947	Bob Elliott, Boston	1972	Johnny Bench, Cincinnati	1997	Larry Walker, Colorado
1948	Stan Musial, St. Louis	1973	Pete Rose, Cincinnati	1998	Sammy Sosa, Chicago
1949	Jackie Robinson, Brooklyn	1974	Steve Garvey, L.A.	1999	Chipper Jones, Atlanta
1950	Jim Konstanty, Philadelphia	1975	Joe Morgan, Cincinnati	2000	Jeff Kent, San Francisco
1951	Roy Campanella, Brooklyn	1976	Joe Morgan, Cincinnati	2001	Barry Bonds, San Francisco
1952	Hank Sauer, Chicago	1977	George Foster, Cincinnati	2002	Barry Bonds, San Francisco
1953	Roy Campanella, Brooklyn	1978	(tie) Dave Parker, Pittsburgh	2003	Barry Bonds, San Francisco
1954	Willie Mays, N.Y.		Keith Hernandez, St. Louis	2004	Barry Bonds, San Francisco
1955	Roy Campanella, Brooklyn	1980	Mike Schmidt, Philadelphia	2005	Albert Pujols, St. Louis

American League

Year	Player, team	Year	Player, team	Year	Player, team
1931	Lefty Grove, Philadelphia	1956	Mickey Mantle, N.Y.	1981	Rollie Fingers, Milwaukee
1932	Jimmie Foxx, Philadelphia	1957	Mickey Mantle, N.Y.	1982	Robin Yount, Milwaukee
1933	Jimmie Foxx, Philadelphia	1958	Jackie Jensen, Boston	1983	Cal Ripken, Jr., Baltimore
1934	Mickey Cochrane, Detroit	1959	Nellie Fox, Chicago	1984	Willie Hernandez, Detroit
1935	Hank Greenberg, Detroit	1960	Roger Maris, N.Y.	1985	Don Mattingly, N.Y.
1936	Lou Gehrig, N.Y.	1961	Roger Maris, N.Y.	1986	Roger Clemens, Boston
1937	Charley Gehringer, Detroit	1962	Mickey Mantle, N.Y.	1987	George Bell, Toronto
1938	Jimmie Foxx, Boston	1963	Elston Howard, N.Y.	1988	Jose Canseco, Oakland
1939	Joe DiMaggio, N.Y.	1964	Brooks Robinson, Baltimore	1989	Robin Yount, Milwaukee
1940	Hank Greenberg, Detroit	1965	Zoilo Versalles, Minnesota	1990	Rickey Henderson, Oakland
1941	Joe DiMaggio, N.Y.	1966	Frank Robinson, Baltimore	1991	Cal Ripken, Jr., Baltimore
1942	Joe Gordon, N.Y.	1967	Carl Yastrzemski, Boston	1992	Dennis Eckersley, Oakland
1943	Spurgeon Chandler, N.Y.	1968	Denny McLain, Detroit	1993	Frank Thomas, Chicago
1944	Hal Newhouser, Detroit	1969	Harmon Killebrew, Minnesota	1994	Frank Thomas, Chicago
1945	Hal Newhouser, Detroit	1970	John (Boog) Powell, Baltimore	1995	Mo Vaughn, Boston
1946	Ted Williams, Boston	1971	Vida Blue, Oakland	1996	Juan Gonzalez, Texas
1947	Joe DiMaggio, N.Y.	1972	Dick Allen, Chicago	1997	Ken Griffey Jr., Seattle
1948	Lou Boudreau, Cleveland	1973	Reggie Jackson, Oakland	1998	Juan Gonzalez, Texas
1949	Ted Williams, Boston	1974	Jeff Burroughs, Texas	1999	Ivan Rodriguez, Texas
1950	Phil Rizzuto, N.Y.	1975	Fred Lynn, Boston	2000	Jason Giambi, Oakland
1951	Yogi Berra, N.Y.	1976	Thurman Munson, N.Y.	2001	Ichiro Suzuki, Seattle
1952	Bobby Shantz, Philadelphia	1977	Rod Carew, Minnesota	2002	Miguel Tejada, Oakland
1953	Al Rosen, Cleveland	1978	Jim Rice, Boston	2003	Alex Rodriguez, Texas
1954	Yogi Berra, N.Y.	1979	Don Baylor, California	2004	Vladimir Guerrero, L.A.
1955	Yogi Berra, N.Y.	1980	George Brett, Kansas City	2005	Alex Rodriguez, New York

Rookies of the Year

(As selected by the Baseball Writers' Assoc. of America)

1947—Combined selection—Jackie Robinson, Brooklyn, 1B; 1948—Combined selection—Alvin Dark, Boston, N.L., SS

National League

Year	Player, team	Year	Player, team	Year	Player, team
1949	Don Newcombe, Brooklyn, P	1969	Ted Sizemore, L.A., 2B	1987	Benito Santiago, San Diego, C
1950	Sam Jethroe, Boston, OF	1970	Carl Morton, Montreal, P	1988	Chris Sabo, Cincinnati, 3B
1951	Willie Mays, N.Y., OF	1971	Earl Williams, Atlanta, C	1989	Jerome Walton, Chicago, OF
1952	Joe Black, Brooklyn, P	1972	Jon Matlack, N.Y., P	1990	Dave Justice, Atlanta, 1B
1953	Jim Gilliam, Brooklyn, 2B	1973	Gary Matthews, S.F., OF	1991	Jeff Bagwell, Houston, 1B
1954	Wally Moon, St. Louis, OF	1974	Bake McBride, St. Louis, OF	1992	Eric Karros, L.A., 1B
1955	Bill Virdon, St. Louis, OF	1975	John Montefusco, S.F., P	1993	Mike Piazza, L.A., C
1956	Frank Robinson, Cincinnati, OF	1976	Butch Metzger, San Diego, P	1994	Raul Mondesi, L.A., OF
1957	Jack Sanford, Philadelphia, P	(tie)	Pat Zachry, Cincinnati, P	1995	Hideo Nomo, L.A., P
1958	Orlando Cepeda, S.F., 1B	1977	Andre Dawson, Montreal, OF	1996	Todd Hollandsworth, L.A., OF
1959	Willie McCovey, S.F., 1B	1978	Bob Horner, Atlanta, 3B	1997	Scott Rolen, Philadelphia, 3B
1960	Frank Howard, L.A., OF	1979	Rick Sutcliffe, L.A., P	1998	Kerry Wood, Chicago, P
1961	Billy Williams, Chicago, OF	1980	Steve Howe, L.A., P	1999	Scott Williamson, Cincinnati, P
1962	Ken Hubbs, Chicago, 2B	1981	Fernando Valenzuela, L.A., P	2000	Rafael Furcal, Atlanta, SS
1963	Pete Rose, Cincinnati, 2B	1982	Steve Sax, L.A., 2B	2001	Albert Pujols, St. Louis, OF
1964	Richie Allen, Philadelphia, 3B	1983	Darryl Strawberry, N.Y., OF	2002	Jason Jennings, Colorado, P
1965	Jim Lefebvre, L.A., 2B	1984	Dwight Gooden, N.Y., P	2003	Dontrelle Willis, Florida, P
1966	Tommy Helms, Cincinnati, 2B	1985	Vince Coleman, St. Louis, OF	2004	Jason Bay, Pittsburgh, OF
1967	Tom Seaver, N.Y., P	1986	Todd Worrell, St. Louis, P	2005	Ryan Howard, Philadelphia, 1B
1968	Johnny Bench, Cincinnati, C				

American League

Year	Player, team
1949	Roy Sievers, St. Louis, OF
1950	Walt Dropo, Boston, 1B
1951	Gil McDougald, N.Y., 3B
1952	Harry Byrd, Philadelphia, P
1953	Harvey Kuenn, Detroit, SS
1954	Bob Grim, N.Y., P
1955	Herb Score, Cleveland, P
1956	Luis Aparicio, Chicago, SS
1957	Tony Kubek, N.Y., IF-OF
1958	Albie Pearson, Washington, OF
1959	Bob Allison, Washington, OF
1960	Ron Hansen, Baltimore, SS
1961	Don Schwall, Boston, P
1962	Tom Tresh, N.Y.,IF-OF
1963	Gary Peters, Chicago, P
1964	Tony Oliva, Minnesota, OF
1965	Curt Blefary, Baltimore, OF
1966	Tommie Agee, Chicago, OF
1967	Rod Carew, Minnesota, 2B
1968	Stan Bahnsen, N.Y., P

Year	Player, team
1969	Lou Piniella, Kansas City, OF
1970	Thurman Munson, N.Y., C
1971	Chris Chambliss, Cleveland, 1B
1972	Carlton Fisk, Boston, C
1973	Al Bumbry, Baltimore, OF
1974	Mike Hargrove, Texas, 1B
1975	Fred Lynn, Boston, OF
1976	Mark Fidrych, Detroit, P
1977	Eddie Murray, Baltimore, DH
1978	Lou Whitaker, Detroit, 2B
1979	John Castino, Minnesota, 3B
(tie)	Alfredo Griffin, Toronto, SS
1980	Joe Charboneau, Cleveland, OF
1981	Dave Righetti, N.Y., P
1982	Cal Ripken, Jr., Baltimore, SS
1983	Ron Kittle, Chicago, OF
1984	Alvin Davis, Seattle, 1B
1985	Ozzie Guillen, Chicago, SS
1986	Jose Canseco, Oakland, OF

Year	Player, team
1987	Mark McGwire, Oakland, 1B
1988	Walt Weiss, Oakland, SS
1989	Gregg Olson, Baltimore, P
1990	Sandy Alomar, Jr., Cleveland, C
1991	Chuck Knoblauch, Minnesota, 2B
1992	Pat Listach, Milwaukee, SS
1993	Tim Salmon, California, OF
1994	Bob Hamelin, Kansas City, DH
1995	Marty Cordova, Minnesota, OF
1996	Derek Jeter, N.Y., SS
1997	Nomar Garciaparra, Boston, SS
1998	Ben Grieve, Oakland, OF
1999	Carlos Beltran, Kansas City, OF
2000	Kazuhiro Sasaki, Seattle, P
2001	Ichiro Suzuki, Seattle, OF
2002	Eric Hinske, Toronto, 3B
2003	Angel Berroa, Kansas City, SS
2004	Bobby Crosby, Oakland, SS
2005	Huston Street, Oakland, P

The Rawlings Gold Glove Awards: 2005 and All-Time Leaders

American League

Kenny Rogers, Texas, P
Jason Varitek, Boston, C
Mark Teixeira, Texas, 1B
Orlando Hudson, Toronto, 2B
Eric Chavez, Oakland, 3B
Derek Jeter, New York, SS
Torii Hunter, Minnesota, OF
Ichiro Suzuki, Seattle, OF
Vernon Wells, Toronto, OF

National League

Greg Maddux, Chicago, P
Mike Matheny, San Francisco, C
Derrek Lee, Chicago, 1B
Luis Castillo, Florida, 2B
Mike Lowell, Florida, 3B
Omar Vizquel, San Francisco, SS
Andruw Jones, Atlanta, OF
Jim Edmonds, St. Louis, OF
Bobby Abreu, Philadelphia, OF

The following are the players at each position who have won the most Gold Gloves since the award was instituted in 1957.

Position	Player		Position	Player		Position	Player	
Pitcher:	Jim Kaat	16	Second base:	Roberto Alomar	10	Shortstop:	Ozzie Smith	13
	Greg Maddux	15		Ryne Sandberg	9		Luis Aparicio	9
Catcher:	Ivan Rodriguez	11		Bill Mazeroski	8	Outfield:	Roberto Clemente	12
	Johnny Bench	10		Frank White	8		Willie Mays	12
First base:	Keith Hernandez	11	Third base:	Brooks Robinson	16		Al Kaline	10
	Don Mattingly	9		Mike Schmidt	10		Ken Griffey Jr.	10

Manager of the Year

1983	(NL) Tommy Lasorda, L.A.
	(AL) Tony La Russa, Chicago
1984	(NL) Jim Frey, Chicago
	(AL) Sparky Anderson, Detroit
1985	(NL) Whitey Herzog, St. Louis
	(AL) Bobby Cox, Toronto
1986	(NL) Hal Lanier, Houston
	(AL) John McNamara, Boston
1987	(NL) Buck Rodgers, Montreal
	(AL) Sparky Anderson, Detroit
1988	(NL) Tommy Lasorda, L.A.
	(AL) Tony La Russa, Oakland
1989	(NL) Don Zimmer, Chicago
	(AL) Frank Robinson, Baltimore
1990	(NL) Jim Leyland, Pittsburgh
	(AL) Jeff Torborg, Chicago

1991	(NL) Bobby Cox, Atlanta
	(AL) Tom Kelly, Minnesota
1992	(NL) Jim Leyland, Pittsburgh
	(AL) Tony La Russa, Oakland
1993	(NL) Dusty Baker, San Francisco
	(AL) Gene Lamont, Chicago
1994	(NL) Felipe Alou, Montreal
	(AL) Buck Showalter, N.Y.
1995	(NL) Don Baylor, Colorado
	(AL) Lou Piniella, Seattle
1996	(NL) Bruce Bochy, San Diego
	(AL) (tie) Joe Torre, N.Y.,
	Johnny Oates, Texas
1997	(NL) Dusty Baker, San Francisco
	(AL) Davey Johnson, Baltimore
1998	(NL) Larry Dierker, Houston
	(AL) Joe Torre, N.Y.

1999	(NL) Jack McKeon, Cincinnati
	(AL) Jimy Williams, Boston
2000	(NL) Dusty Baker, San Francisco
	(AL) Jerry Manuel, Chicago
2001	(NL) Larry Bowa, Philadelphia
	(AL) Lou Piniella, Seattle
2002	(NL) Tony La Russa, St. Louis
	(AL) Mike Scioscia, Anaheim
2003	(NL) Jack McKeon, Florida
	(AL) Tony Pena, Kansas City
2004	(NL) Bobby Cox, Atlanta
	(AL) Buck Showalter, Texas
2005	(NL) Bobby Cox, Atlanta
	(AL) Ozzie Guillen, Chicago

Major League Pennant Winners, 1901–1975

	National League						American League				
Year	Winner	Won	Lost	Pct	Manager	Year	Winner	Won	Lost	Pct	Manager
1901	Pittsburgh	90	49	.647	Clarke	1901	Chicago	83	53	.610	Griffith
1902	Pittsburgh	103	36	.741	Clarke	1902	Philadelphia	83	53	.610	Mack
1903	Pittsburgh	91	49	.650	Clarke	1903	Boston	91	47	.659	Collins
1904	New York	106	47	.693	McGraw	1904	Boston	95	59	.617	Collins
1905	New York	105	48	.686	McGraw	1905	Philadelphia	92	56	.622	Mack
1906	Chicago	116	36	.763	Chance	1906	Chicago	93	58	.616	Jones
1907	Chicago	107	45	.704	Chance	1907	Detroit	92	58	.613	Jennings
1908	Chicago	99	55	.643	Chance	1908	Detroit	90	63	.588	Jennings
1909	Pittsburgh	110	42	.724	Clarke	1909	Detroit	98	54	.645	Jennings
1910	Chicago	104	50	.675	Chance	1910	Philadelphia	102	48	.680	Mack
1911	New York	99	54	.647	McGraw	1911	Philadelphia	101	50	.669	Mack
1912	New York	103	48	.682	McGraw	1912	Boston	105	47	.691	Stahl
1913	New York	101	51	.664	McGraw	1913	Philadelphia	96	57	.627	Mack
1914	Boston	94	59	.614	Stallings	1914	Philadelphia	99	53	.651	Mack
1915	Philadelphia	90	62	.592	Moran	1915	Boston	101	50	.669	Carrigan
1916	Brooklyn	94	60	.610	Robinson	1916	Boston	91	63	.591	Carrigan
1917	New York	98	56	.636	McGraw	1917	Chicago	100	54	.649	Rowland
1918	Chicago	84	45	.651	Mitchell	1918	Boston	75	51	.595	Barrow
1919	Cincinnati	96	44	.686	Moran	1919	Chicago	88	52	.629	Gleason
1920	Brooklyn	93	60	.604	Robinson	1920	Cleveland	98	56	.636	Speaker
1921	New York	94	56	.614	McGraw	1921	New York	98	55	.641	Huggins
1922	New York	93	61	.604	McGraw	1922	New York	94	60	.610	Huggins
1923	New York	95	58	.621	McGraw	1923	New York	98	54	.645	Huggins
1924	New York	93	60	.608	McGraw	1924	Washington	92	62	.597	Harris
1925	Pittsburgh	95	58	.621	McKechnie	1925	Washington	96	55	.636	Harris
1926	St. Louis	89	65	.578	Hornsby	1926	New York	91	63	.591	Huggins

	National League						American League				
Year	Winner	Won	Lost	Pct	Manager	Year	Winner	Won	Lost	Pct	Manager
1927	Pittsburgh	94	60	.610	Bush	1927	New York	110	44	.714	Huggins
1928	St. Louis	95	59	.617	McKechnie	1928	New York	101	53	.656	Huggins
1929	Chicago	98	54	.645	McCarthy	1929	Philadelphia	104	46	.693	Mack
1930	St. Louis	92	62	.597	Street	1930	Philadelphia	102	52	.662	Mack
1931	St. Louis	101	53	.656	Street	1931	Philadelphia	107	45	.704	Mack
1932	Chicago	90	64	.584	Grimm	1932	New York	107	47	.695	McCarthy
1933	New York	91	61	.599	Terry	1933	Washington	99	53	.651	Cronin
1934	St. Louis	95	58	.621	Frisch	1934	Detroit	101	53	.656	Cochrane
1935	Chicago	100	54	.649	Grimm	1935	Detroit	93	58	.616	Cochrane
1936	New York	91	62	.597	Terry	1936	New York	102	51	.667	McCarthy
1937	New York	95	57	.625	Terry	1937	New York	102	52	.662	McCarthy
1938	Chicago	89	63	.586	Hartnett	1938	New York	99	53	.651	McCarthy
1939	Cincinnati	97	57	.630	McKechnie	1939	New York	106	45	.702	McCarthy
1940	Cincinnati	100	53	.654	McKechnie	1940	Detroit	90	64	.584	Baker
1941	Brooklyn	100	54	.649	Durocher	1941	New York	101	53	.656	McCarthy
1942	St. Louis	106	48	.688	Southworth	1942	New York	103	51	.669	McCarthy
1943	St. Louis	105	49	.682	Southworth	1943	New York	98	56	.636	McCarthy
1944	St. Louis	105	49	.682	Southworth	1944	St. Louis	89	65	.578	Sewell
1945	Chicago	98	56	.636	Grimm	1945	Detroit	88	65	.575	O'Neill
1946	St. Louis	98	58	.628	Dyer	1946	Boston	104	50	.675	Cronin
1947	Brooklyn	94	60	.610	Shotton	1947	New York	97	57	.630	Harris
1948	Boston	91	62	.595	Southworth	1948	Cleveland	97	58	.626	Boudreau
1949	Brooklyn	97	57	.630	Shotton	1949	New York	97	57	.630	Stengel
1950	Philadelphia	91	63	.591	Sawyer	1950	New York	98	56	.636	Stengel
1951	New York	98	59	.624	Durocher	1951	New York	98	56	.636	Stengel
1952	Brooklyn	96	57	.627	Dressen	1952	New York	95	59	.617	Stengel
1953	Brooklyn	105	49	.682	Dressen	1953	New York	99	52	.656	Stengel
1954	New York	97	57	.630	Durocher	1954	Cleveland	111	43	.721	Lopez
1955	Brooklyn	98	55	.641	Alston	1955	New York	96	58	.623	Stengel
1956	Brooklyn	93	61	.604	Alston	1956	New York	97	57	.630	Stengel
1957	Milwaukee	95	59	.617	Haney	1957	New York	98	56	.636	Stengel
1958	Milwaukee	92	62	.597	Haney	1958	New York	92	62	.597	Stengel
1959	Los Angeles	88	68	.564	Alston	1959	Chicago	94	60	.610	Lopez
1960	Pittsburgh	95	59	.617	Murtaugh	1960	New York	97	57	.630	Stengel
1961	Cincinnati	93	61	.604	Hutchinson	1961	New York	109	53	.673	Houk
1962	San Francisco	103	62	.624	Dark	1962	New York	96	66	.593	Houk
1963	Los Angeles	99	63	.611	Alston	1963	New York	104	57	.646	Houk
1964	St. Louis	93	69	.574	Keane	1964	New York	99	63	.611	Berra
1965	Los Angeles	97	65	.599	Alston	1965	Minnesota	102	60	.630	Mele
1966	Los Angeles	95	67	.586	Alston	1966	Baltimore	97	63	.606	Bauer
1967	St. Louis	101	60	.627	Schoendienst	1967	Boston	92	70	.568	Williams
1968	St. Louis	97	65	.599	Schoendienst	1968	Detroit	103	59	.636	Smith
1969	N.Y. Mets	100	62	.617	Hodges	1969	Baltimore	100	53	.673	Weaver
1970	Cincinnati	102	60	.630	Anderson	1970	Baltimore	108	54	.667	Weaver
1971	Pittsburgh	97	65	.599	Murtaugh	1971	Baltimore	101	57	.639	Weaver
1972	Cincinnati	95	59	.617	Anderson	1972	Oakland	93	62	.600	Williams
1973	N.Y. Mets	82	79	.509	Berra	1973	Oakland	94	68	.580	Williams
1974	Los Angeles	102	60	.630	Alston	1974	Oakland	90	72	.556	Dark
1975	Cincinnati	108	54	.667	Anderson	1975	Boston	97	65	.594	Johnson

Major League Pennant Winners, 1976-2006

National League

		East					West					Pennant
Year	Winner	W	L	Pct	Manager	Winner	W	L	Pct	Manager		Winner
1976	Philadelphia	101	61	.623	Ozark	Cincinnati	102	60	.630	Anderson		Cincinnati
1977	Philadelphia	101	61	.623	Ozark	Los Angeles	98	64	.605	Lasorda		Los Angeles
1978	Philadelphia	90	72	.556	Ozark	Los Angeles	95	67	.586	Lasorda		Los Angeles
1979	Pittsburgh	98	64	.605	Tanner	Cincinnati	90	71	.559	McNamara		Pittsburgh
1980	Philadelphia	91	71	.562	Green	Houston	93	70	.571	Virdon		Philadelphia
1981(a)	Philadelphia	34	21	.618	Green	Los Angeles	36	21	.632	Lasorda		(c)
1981(b)	Montreal	30	23	.566	Williams, Fanning	Houston	33	20	.623	Virdon		Los Angeles
1982	St. Louis	92	70	.568	Herzog	Atlanta	89	73	.549	Torre		St. Louis
1983	Philadelphia	90	72	.556	Corrales, Owens	Los Angeles	91	71	.562	Lasorda		Philadelphia
1984	Chicago	96	65	.596	Frey	San Diego	92	70	.568	Williams		San Diego
1985	St. Louis	101	61	.623	Herzog	Los Angeles	95	67	.586	Lasorda		St. Louis
1986	N.Y. Mets	108	54	.667	Johnson	Houston	96	66	.593	Lanier		New York
1987	St. Louis	95	67	.586	Herzog	San Francisco	90	72	.556	Craig		St. Louis
1988	N.Y. Mets	100	60	.625	Johnson	Los Angeles	94	67	.584	Lasorda		Los Angeles
1989	Chicago	93	69	.571	Zimmer	San Francisco	92	70	.568	Craig		San Francisco
1990	Pittsburgh	95	67	.586	Leyland	Cincinnati	91	71	.562	Piniella		Cincinnati
1991	Pittsburgh	98	64	.605	Leyland	Atlanta	94	68	.580	Cox		Atlanta
1992	Pittsburgh	96	66	.593	Leyland	Atlanta	98	64	.605	Cox		Atlanta
1993	Philadelphia	97	65	.599	Fregosi	Atlanta	104	58	.642	Cox		Philadelphia

Year	Division	Winner	W	L	Pct	Manager	Playoffs	Pennant Winner
1994 (d)	East	Montreal	74	40	.649	Alou	—	—
	Central	Cincinnati	66	48	.579	Johnson		
	West	Los Angeles	58	56	.509	Lasorda		
1995	East	Atlanta	90	54	.625	Cox	Atlanta 3, Colorado* 1	Atlanta
	Central	Cincinnati	85	59	.590	Johnson	Cincinnati 3, Los Angeles 0	
	West	Los Angeles	78	66	.542	Lasorda	Atlanta 4, Cincinnati 0	
1996	East	Atlanta	96	66	.593	Cox	Atlanta 3, Los Angeles* 0	Atlanta
	Central	St. Louis	88	74	.543	La Russa	St. Louis 3, San Diego 0	
	West	San Diego	91	71	.562	Bochy	Atlanta 4, St. Louis 3	

Year	Division	Winner	W	L	Pct	Manager	Playoffs	Pennant Winner
1997	East	Atlanta	101	61	.623	Cox	Atlanta 3, Houston 0	Florida* (e)
	Central	Houston	84	78	.519	Dierker	Florida* 3, San Francisco 0	
	West	San Francisco	90	72	.556	Baker	Florida* 4, Atlanta 2	
1998	East	Atlanta	106	56	.654	Cox	Atlanta 3, Chicago* 0	San Diego
	Central	Houston	102	60	.630	Dierker	San Diego 3, Houston 1	
	West	San Diego	97	64	.602	Bochy	San Diego 4, Atlanta 2	
1999	East	Atlanta	103	59	.636	Cox	Atlanta 3, Houston 1	Atlanta
	Central	Houston	97	65	.599	Dierker	New York* 3, Arizona 1	
	West	Arizona	100	62	.617	Showalter	Atlanta 4, New York 2	
2000	East	Atlanta	95	67	.586	Cox	St. Louis 3, Atlanta 0	New York* (f)
	Central	St. Louis	95	67	.586	La Russa	New York* 3, San Francisco 1	
	West	San Francisco	97	65	.599	Baker	New York* 4, St. Louis 1	
2001	East	Atlanta	88	74	.543	Cox	Atlanta 3, Houston 0	Arizona
	Central	Houston	93	69	.574	Dierker	Arizona 3, St. Louis* 2	
	West	Arizona	92	70	.568	Brenly	Arizona 4, Atlanta 1	
2002	East	Atlanta	101	59	.631	Cox	St. Louis 3, Arizona 0	San Francisco* (g)
	Central	St. Louis	97	65	.599	La Russa	San Francisco* 3, Atlanta 2	
	West	Arizona	98	64	.605	Brenly	San Francisco 4, St. Louis 1	
2003	East	Atlanta	101	61	.623	Cox	Chicago 3, Atlanta 2	Florida*(i)
	Central	Chicago	88	74	.543	Baker	Florida* 3, San Francisco 2	
	West	San Francisco	100	61	.621	Alou	Florida* 4, Chicago 3	
2004	East	Atlanta	96	66	.593	Cox	Houston* 3, Atlanta 2	St. Louis
	Central	St. Louis	105	57	.648	La Russa	St. Louis 3, Dodgers 1	
	West	Los Angeles	93	69	.594	Tracy	St. Louis 4, Houston 3	
2005	East	Atlanta	90	72	.556	Cox	St. Louis 3, San Diego 0	Houston* (j)
	Central	St. Louis	100	62	.617	La Russa	Houston* 3, Atlanta 1	
	West	San Diego	82	80	.506	Bochy	Houston* 4, St. Louis 2	
2006	East	N.Y. Mets	97	65	.599	Randolf	N.Y. Mets 3, *Los Angeles 0	(l)
	Central	St. Louis	83	78	.516	La Russa	St. Louis 3, San Diego 1	
	West	San Diego	88	74	.543	Bochy		

American League

	East						West				Pennant
Year	Winner	W	L	Pct	Manager	Winner	W	L	Pct	Manager	Winner
1976	New York	97	62	.610	Martin	Kansas City	90	72	.556	Herzog	New York
1977	New York	100	62	.617	Martin	Kansas City	102	60	.630	Herzog	New York
1978	New York	100	63	.613	Martin, Lemon	Kansas City	92	70	.568	Herzog	New York
1979	Baltimore	102	57	.642	Weaver	California	88	74	.543	Fregosi	Baltimore
1980	New York	103	59	.636	Howser	Kansas City	97	65	.599	Frey	Kansas City
1981(a)	New York	34	22	.607	Michael	Oakland	37	23	.617	Martin	(c)
1981(b)	Milwaukee	31	22	.585	Rodgers	Kansas City	30	23	.566	Frey, Howser	New York
1982	Milwaukee	95	67	.586	Rodgers, Kuenn	California	93	69	.574	Mauch	Milwaukee
1983	Baltimore	98	64	.605	Altobelli	Chicago	99	63	.611	La Russa	Baltimore
1984	Detroit	104	58	.642	Anderson	Kansas City	84	78	.519	Howser	Detroit
1985	Toronto	99	62	.615	Cox	Kansas City	91	71	.562	Howser	Kansas City
1986	Boston	95	66	.590	McNamara	California	92	70	.568	Mauch	Boston
1987	Detroit	98	64	.605	Anderson	Minnesota	85	77	.525	Kelly	Minnesota
1988	Boston	89	73	.549	McNamara, Morgan	Oakland	104	58	.642	La Russa	Oakland
1989	Toronto	89	73	.549	Williams, Gaston	Oakland	99	63	.611	La Russa	Oakland
1990	Boston	88	74	.543	Morgan	Oakland	103	59	.636	La Russa	Oakland
1991	Toronto	91	71	.562	Gaston	Minnesota	95	67	.586	Kelly	Minnesota
1992	Toronto	96	66	.593	Gaston	Oakland	96	66	.593	La Russa	Toronto
1993	Toronto	95	67	.586	Gaston	Chicago	94	68	.580	Lamont	Toronto

Year	Division	Winner	W	L	Pct	Manager	Playoffs	Pennant Winner
1994(d)	East	New York	70	43	.619	Showalter	—	—
	Central	Chicago	67	46	.593	Lamont		
	West	Texas	52	62	.456	Kennedy		
1995	East	Boston	86	58	.597	Kennedy	Cleveland 3, Boston 0	Cleveland
	Central	Cleveland	100	44	.694	Hargrove	Seattle 3, New York* 2	
	West	Seattle	79	66	.545	Piniella	Cleveland 4, Seattle 2	
1996	East	New York	92	70	.568	Torre	Baltimore* 3, Cleveland 1	New York
	Central	Cleveland	99	62	.615	Hargrove	New York 3, Texas 1	
	West	Texas	90	72	.556	Oates	New York 4, Baltimore* 1	
1997	East	Baltimore	98	64	.605	Johnson	Baltimore 3, Seattle 1	Cleveland
	Central	Cleveland	86	75	.534	Hargrove	Cleveland 3, New York* 2	
	West	Seattle	90	72	.556	Piniella	Cleveland 4, Baltimore 2	
1998	East	New York	114	48	.704	Torre	New York 3, Texas 0	New York
	Central	Cleveland	89	73	.549	Hargrove	Cleveland 3, Boston* 1	
	West	Texas	88	74	.543	Oates	New York 4, Cleveland 2	
1999	East	New York	98	64	.605	Torre	New York 3, Texas 0	New York
	Central	Cleveland	97	65	.599	Hargrove	Boston* 3, Cleveland 2	
	West	Texas	95	67	.586	Oates	New York 4, Boston* 1	
2000	East	New York	87	74	.540	Torre	New York 3, Oakland 2	New York
	Central	Chicago	95	67	.586	Manuel	Seattle* 3, Chicago 0	
	West	Oakland	91	70	.565	Howe	New York 4, Seattle* 2	
2001	East	New York	95	65	.594	Torre	Seattle 3, Cleveland 2	New York
	Central	Cleveland	91	71	.562	Manuel	New York 3, Oakland 2	
	West	Seattle	116	46	.716	Piniella	New York 4, Seattle* 1	
2002	East	New York	103	58	.640	Torre	Anaheim* 3, New York 1	Anaheim* (h)
	Central	Minnesota	94	67	.584	Gardenhire	Minnesota 3, Oakland 2	
	West	Oakland	103	59	.636	Howe	Anaheim* 4, Minnesota 1	
2003	East	New York	101	61	.623	Torre	New York 3, Minnesota 1	New York
	Central	Minnesota	90	72	.556	Gardenhire	Boston* 3, Oakland 2	
	West	Oakland	96	66	.593	Macha	New York 4, Boston* 3	
2004	East	New York	101	61	.623	Torre	New York 3, Minnesota 1	Boston (k)
	Central	Minnesota	92	70	.568	Gardenhire	Boston* 3, Anaheim 0	
	West	Anaheim	92	70	.568	Scioscia	Boston 4, New York 3	

Year	Division	Winner	W	L	Pct	Manager	Playoffs	Pennant Winner
2005	East	New York	95	67	.586	Torre	Chicago 3, Boston* 0	Chicago
	Central	Chicago	99	63	.611	Guillen	Los Angeles 3, New York 2	
	West	Los Angeles	95	67	.586	Scioscia	Chicago 4, Los Angeles 1	
2006	East	New York	97	65	.599	Torre	Oakland 3, Minnesota 0	Detroit
	Central	Minnesota	96	66	.593	Gardenhire	*Detroit 3, N.Y. Yankees 1	
	West	Oakland	93	69	.574	Macha		

*Wild card team. (a) First half. (b) Second half. (c) Montreal, L.A., N.Y. Yankees, and Oakland won the divisional playoffs. (d)   In   Aug. 1994, a players' strike began that caused the cancellation of the remainder of the season, the playoffs, and the World Series. Teams listed as division "winners" for 1994 were leading their divisions at the time of the strike. (e) Florida manager: Jim Leyland. (f) New York manager: Bobby Valentine. (g) San Francisco manager: Dusty Baker. (h) Anaheim manager: Mike Scioscia. (i) Florida manager: Jack McKeon. (j) Houston manager: Phil Garner. (k) Boston manager: Terry Francona. (l) Not decided at press time.

World Series Results, 1903-2005

1903 Boston AL 5, Pittsburgh NL 3	1938 New York AL 4, Chicago NL 0	1972 Oakland AL 4, Cincinnati NL 3
1904 No series	1939 New York AL 4, Cincinnati NL 0	1973 Oakland AL 4, New York NL 3
1905 New York NL 4, Philadelphia AL 1	1940 Cincinnati NL 4, Detroit AL 3	1974 Oakland AL 4, Los Angeles NL 1
1906 Chicago AL 4, Chicago NL 2	1941 New York AL 4, Brooklyn NL 1	1975 Cincinnati NL 4, Boston AL 3
1907 Chicago NL 4, Detroit AL 0, 1 tie	1942 St. Louis NL 4, New York AL 1	1976 Cincinnati NL 4, New York AL 0
1908 Chicago NL 4, Detroit AL 1	1943 New York AL 4, St. Louis NL 1	1977 New York AL 4, Los Angeles NL 2
1909 Pittsburgh NL 4, Detroit AL 3	1944 St. Louis NL 4, St. Louis AL 2	1978 New York AL 4, Los Angeles NL 2
1910 Philadelphia AL 4, Chicago NL 1	1945 Detroit AL 4, Chicago NL 3	1979 Pittsburgh NL 4, Baltimore AL 3
1911 Philadelphia AL 4, New York NL 2	1946 St. Louis NL 4, Boston AL 3	1980 Philadelphia NL 4, Kansas City AL 2
1912 Boston AL 4, New York NL 3, 1 tie	1947 New York AL 4, Brooklyn NL 3	1981 Los Angeles NL 4, New York AL 2
1913 Philadelphia AL 4, New York NL 1	1948 Cleveland AL 4, Boston NL 2	1982 St. Louis NL 4, Milwaukee AL 3
1914 Boston NL 4, Philadelphia AL 0	1949 New York AL 4, Brooklyn NL 1	1983 Baltimore AL 4, Philadelphia NL 1
1915 Boston AL 4, Philadelphia NL 1	1950 New York AL 4, Philadelphia NL 0	1984 Detroit AL 4, San Diego NL 1
1916 Boston AL 4, Brooklyn NL 1	1951 New York AL 4, New York NL 2	1985 Kansas City AL 4, St. Louis NL 3
1917 Chicago AL 4, New York NL 2	1952 New York AL 4, Brooklyn NL 3	1986 New York NL 4, Boston AL 3
1918 Boston AL 4, Chicago NL 2	1953 New York AL 4, Brooklyn NL 2	1987 Minnesota AL 4, St. Louis NL 3
1919 Cincinnati NL 5, Chicago AL 3	1954 New York NL 4, Cleveland AL 0	1988 Los Angeles NL 4, Oakland AL 1
1920 Cleveland AL 5, Brooklyn NL 2	1955 Brooklyn NL 4, New York AL 3	1989 Oakland AL 4, San Francisco NL 0
1921 New York NL 5, New York AL 3	1956 New York AL 4, Brooklyn NL 3	1990 Cincinnati NL 4, Oakland AL 0
1922 New York NL 4, New York AL 0, 1 tie	1957 Milwaukee NL 4, New York AL 3	1991 Minnesota AL 4, Atlanta NL 3
1923 New York AL 4, New York NL 2	1958 New York AL 4, Milwaukee NL 3	1992 Toronto AL 4, Atlanta NL 2
1924 Washington AL 4, New York NL 3	1959 Los Angeles NL 4, Chicago AL 2	1993 Toronto AL 4, Philadelphia NL 2
1925 Pittsburgh NL 4, Washington AL 3	1960 Pittsburgh NL 4, New York AL 3	1994 No series
1926 St. Louis NL 4, New York AL 3	1961 New York AL 4, Cincinnati NL 1	1995 Atlanta NL 4, Cleveland AL 2
1927 New York AL 4, Pittsburgh NL 0	1962 New York AL 4, San Francisco NL 3	1996 New York AL 4, Atlanta NL 2
1928 New York AL 4, St. Louis NL 0	1963 Los Angeles NL 4, New York AL 0	1997 Florida NL 4, Cleveland AL 3
1929 Philadelphia AL 4, Chicago NL 1	1964 St. Louis NL 4, New York AL 3	1998 New York AL 4, San Diego NL 0
1930 Philadelphia AL 4, St. Louis NL 2	1965 Los Angeles NL 4, Minnesota AL 3	1999 New York AL 4, Atlanta NL 0
1931 St. Louis NL 4, Philadelphia AL 3	1966 Baltimore AL 4, Los Angeles NL 0	2000 New York AL 4, New York NL 1
1932 New York AL 4, Chicago NL 0	1967 St. Louis NL 4, Boston AL 3	2001 Arizona NL 4, New York AL 3
1933 New York NL 4, Washington AL 1	1968 Detroit AL 4, St. Louis NL 3	2002 Anaheim AL 4, San Francisco NL 3
1934 St. Louis NL 4, Detroit AL 3	1969 New York NL 4, Baltimore AL 1	2003 Florida NL 4, New York AL 2
1935 Detroit AL 4, Chicago NL 2	1970 Baltimore AL 4, Cincinnati NL 1	2004 Boston AL 4, St. Louis NL 0
1936 New York AL 4, New York NL 2	1971 Pittsburgh NL 4, Baltimore AL 3	2005 Chicago AL 4, Houston NL 0
1937 New York AL 4, New York NL 1		

World Series Most Valuable Player

Year	Player, Position, Team	Year	Player, Position, Team	Year	Player, Position, Team
1955	Johnny Podres, P, Brooklyn	1973	Reggie Jackson, OF, Oakland	1989	Dave Stewart, P, Oakland
1956	Don Larsen, P, New York, AL	1974	Rollie Fingers, P, Oakland	1990	Jose Rijo, P, Cincinnati
1957	Lew Burdette, P, Milwaukee, NL	1975	Pete Rose, 3B, Cincinnati	1991	Jack Morris, P, Minnesota
1958	Bob Turley, P, NY AL	1976	Johnny Bench, C, Cincinnati	1992	Pat Borders, C, Toronto
1959	Larry Sherry, P, LA	1977	Reggie Jackson, OF, NY, AL	1993	Paul Molitor, DH, Toronto
1960[1]	Bobby Richardson, 2B, NY, AL	1978	Bucky Dent, SS, NY, AL	1994	no series
1961	Whitey Ford, P, NY, AL	1979	Willie Stargell, 1B, Pittsburgh	1995	Tom Glavine, P, Atlanta
1962	Ralph Terry, P, NY, AL	1980	Mike Schmidt, 3B, Philadelphia	1996	John Wetteland, P, NY, AL
1963	Sandy Koufax, P, Los Angeles, NL	1981	Ron Cey, 3B, LA	1997	Livan Hernandez, P, Florida
1964	Bob Gibson, P, St. Louis		Pedro Guerrero, OF, LA	1998	Scott Brosius, 3B, NY, AL
1965	Sandy Koufax, P, Los Angeles, NL		Steve Yeager, C, LA	1999	Mariano Rivera, P, NY, AL
1966	Frank Robinson, of, Baltimore	1982	Darrell Porter, C, St. Louis	2000	Derek Jeter, SS, NY, AL
1967	Bob Gibson, P, St. Louis	1983	Rick Dempsey, C, Baltimore	2001	Curt Schilling, P, Arizona
1968	Mickey Lolich, P, Detroit	1984	Alan Trammell, SS, Detroit		Randy Johnson, P, Arizona
1969	Donn Clendenon, 1B, NY, NL	1985	Bret Saberhagen, P, Kansas City	2002	Troy Glaus, 3B, Anaheim
1970	Brooks Robinson, 3B, Baltimore	1986	Ray Knight, 3B, NY, NL	2003	Josh Beckett, P, Florida
1971	Roberto Clemente, OF, Pittsburgh	1987	Frank Viola, P, Minnesota	2004	Manny Ramirez, OF, Boston
1972	Gene Tenace, C, Oakland	1988	Orel Hershiser, P, LA	2005	Jermaine Dye, OF, Chicago

(1) Bobby Richardson won the MVP although Pittsburgh beat New York.

World Series Won-Lost Records, by Franchise[1]

Team	Wins	Losses	Team	Wins	Losses
New York Yankees	26	13	Toronto Blue Jays	2	0
Philadelphia/Kansas City/Oakland A's	9	5	New York Mets	2	2
St. Louis Cardinals	9	8	Chicago White Sox	3	2
Boston Red Sox	7	4	Cleveland Indians	2	3
Brooklyn/Los Angeles Dodgers	6	12	Chicago Cubs	2	8
Pittsburgh Pirates	5	2	LA/California/Anaheim/LA Angels	1	0
Cincinnati Reds	5	4	Arizona Diamondbacks	1	0
New York/San Francisco Giants	5	12	Kansas City Royals	1	1
Detroit Tigers	4	5	Philadelphia Phillies	1	4
Washington Senators/Minnesota Twins	3	3	Seattle Pilots/Milwaukee Brewers	0	1
St. Louis Browns/Baltimore Orioles	3	4	San Diego Padres	0	2
Boston/Milwaukee/Atlanta Braves	3	6	Houston Astros	0	1
Florida Marlins	2	10			

(1) Through 2005.

All-Time World Series Career Leaders
(Through 2005)

Batting Leaders

Batter	Hits	AB	Avg.	Batter	Hits	AB	Avg.
1. Bobby Brown	18	41	.439	6. Lou Brock	34	87	.391
2. Paul Molitor	23	55	.418	7. Marquis Grissom	30	77	.390
3. Pepper Martin	23	55	.418	8. Troy Glaus	10	26	.385
4. J.T. Snow	11	27	.407	9. George Brett	19	51	.373
5. Hal McRae	18	45	.400	10. Thurman Munson	25	67	.373

Games Played

Yogi Berra	75
Mickey Mantle	65
Elston Howard	54
Hank Bauer	53
Gil McDougald	53
Phil Rizzuto	52
Joe DiMaggio	51
Frankie Frisch	50
Pee Wee Reese	44
Roger Maris	41
Babe Ruth	41

Hits

Yogi Berra	71
Mickey Mantle	59
Frankie Frisch	58
Joe DiMaggio	54
Hank Bauer	46
PeeWee Reese	46
Phil Rizzuto	45
Gil McDougald	45
Lou Gehrig	43
Elston Howard	42
Babe Ruth	42
Eddie Collins	42

Runs

Mickey Mantle	42
Yogi Berra	41
Babe Ruth	37
Lou Gehrig	30
Joe DiMaggio	27
Derek Jeter	27
Roger Maris	26
Elston Howard	25
Gil McDougald	23
Jackie Robinson	22

Runs Batted In

Mickey Mantle	40
Yogi Berra	39
Lou Gehrig	35
Babe Ruth	33
Joe DiMaggio	30
Bill Skowron	29
Duke Snider	26
Reggie Jackson	24
Hank Bauer	24
Bill Dickey	24
Gil McDougald	24

Home Runs

Mickey Mantle	18
Babe Ruth	15
Yogi Berra	12
Duke Snider	11
Reggie Jackson	10
Lou Gehrig	10
Joe DiMaggio	8
Bill Skowron	8
Frank Robinson	8
Hank Bauer	7
Gil McDougald	7
Goose Goslin	7

Stolen Bases

Lou Brock	14
Eddie Collins	14
Frank Chance	10
Dave Lopes	10
Phil Rizzuto	10
Frank Frisch	9
Honus Wagner	9
Johnny Evers	8
Roberto Alomar	7
Rickey Henderson	7
Pepper Martin	7
Joe Morgan	7
Joe Tinker	7

Pitching Leaders

Games Pitched

Whitey Ford	22
Mariano Rivera	20
Rollie Fingers	16
Jeff Nelson	16
Allie Reynolds	15
Mike Stanton	15
Bob Turley	15
Clay Carroll	14
Clem Labine	13
Mark Wohlers	13
Waite Hoyt	12
Catfish Hunter	12
Art Nehf	12

Wins

Whitey Ford	10
Bob Gibson	7
Allie Reynolds	7
Red Ruffing	7
Chief Bender	6
Lefty Gomez	6
Waite Hoyt	6
Three Finger Brown	5
Jack Coombs	5
Catfish Hunter	5
Herb Pennock	5
Vic Raschi	5
Christy Mathewson	5

Strikeouts

Whitey Ford	94
Bob Gibson	92
Allie Reynolds	62
Sandy Koufax	61
Red Ruffing	61
Chief Bender	59
George Earnshaw	56
John Smoltz	52
Waite Hoyt	49
Christy Mathewson	48

Saves

Mariano Rivera	9
Rollie Fingers	6
Johnny Murphy	4
Allie Reynolds	4
John Wetteland	4
Robb Nen	4

All-Star Baseball Games, 1933-2006

Year	Winner, Score	Host team	Year	Winner, Score	Host team	Year	Winner, Score	Host team
1933*	American, 4-2	Chicago (AL)	1959*	National, 5-4	Pittsburgh	1981	National, 5-4	Cleveland
1934*	American, 9-7	New York (NL)	1959*	American, 5-3	Los Angeles	1982	National, 4-1	Montreal
1935*	American, 4-1	Cleveland	1960*	National, 5-3	Kansas City	1983	American, 13-3	Chicago (AL)
1936*	National, 4-3	Boston (NL)	1960*	National, 6-0	New York (AL)	1984	National, 3-1	San Francisco
1937*	American, 8-3	Washington	1961*	National, 5-4[3]	San Francisco	1985	National, 6-1	Minnesota
1938*	National, 4-1	Cincinnati	1961*	Called–rain, 1-1	Boston	1986	American, 3-2	Houston
1939*	American, 3-1	New York (AL)	1962*	National, 3-1[3]	Washington	1987	National, 2-0[5]	Oakland
1940*	National, 4-0	St. Louis (NL)	1962*	American, 9-4	Chicago (NL)	1988	American, 2-1	Cincinnati
1941*	American, 7-5	Detroit	1963*	National, 5-3	Cleveland	1989	American, 5-3	California
1942	American, 3-1	New York (NL)	1964*	National, 7-4	New York (NL)	1990	American, 2-0	Chicago (NL)
1943	American, 5-3	Philadelphia (AL)	1965*	National, 6-5	Minnesota	1991	American, 4-2	Toronto
1944	National, 7-1	Pittsburgh	1966*	National, 2-1[3]	St. Louis	1992	American, 13-6	San Diego
1945	(Not played)		1967*	National, 2-1[4]	California	1993	American, 9-3	Baltimore
1946*	American, 12-0	Boston (AL)	1968	National, 1-0	Houston	1994	National, 8-7[3]	Pittsburgh
1947*	American, 2-1	Chicago (NL)	1969*	National, 9-3	Washington	1995	National, 3-2	Texas
1948*	American, 5-2	St. Louis (AL)	1970	National, 5-4[2]	Cincinnati	1996	National, 6-0	Philadelphia
1949*	American, 11-7	Brooklyn	1971	American, 6-4	Detroit	1997	American, 3-1	Cleveland
1950*	National, 4-3[1]	Chicago (AL)	1972	National, 4-3[3]	Atlanta	1998	American, 13-8	Colorado
1951*	National, 8-3	Detroit	1973	National, 7-1	Kansas City	1999	American, 4-1	Boston
1952*	National, 3-2	Philadelphia (NL)	1974	National, 7-2	Pittsburgh	2000	American, 6-3	Atlanta
1953*	National, 5-1	Cincinnati	1975	National, 6-3	Milwaukee	2001	American, 4-1	Seattle
1954*	American, 11-9	Cleveland	1976	National, 7-1	Philadelphia	2002	Tie, 7-7[6]	Milwaukee
1955*	National, 6-5[2]	Milwaukee	1977	National, 7-5	New York (AL)	2003	American, 7-6[7]	Chicago (AL)
1956*	National, 7-3	Washington	1978	National, 7-3	San Diego	2004	American, 9-4	Houston
1957*	American, 6-5	St. Louis	1979	National, 7-6	Seattle	2005	American, 7-5	Detroit
1958*	American, 4-3	Baltimore	1980	National, 4-2	Los Angeles	2006	American, 3-2	Pittsburgh

*Denotes day game. (1) 14 innings. (2) 12 innings. (3) 10 innings. (4) 15 innings. (5) 13 innings. (6) Commissioner's decision, game called in the 11th inning when both teams ran out of pitchers. (7) Under rule change beginning in 2003, league winning All-Star games earned World Series home-field advantage.

Baseball Stadiums[1]

National League

Team	Stadium (year opened)	Surface	Home run distances (ft.)			Seating capacity
			LF	Center	RF	
Arizona Diamondbacks	Chase Field (1998)	Grass	330	407	334	49,033
Atlanta Braves	Turner Field (1997)	Grass	335	401	330	50,096
Chicago Cubs	Wrigley Field (1914)	Grass	355	400	353	38,902
Cincinnati Reds	Great American Ballpark (2003)	Grass	328	404	325	42,059
Colorado Rockies	Coors Field (1995)	Grass	347	415	350	50,445
Florida Marlins	Dolphins Stadium (1987)	Grass	330	434	345	47,662
Houston Astros	Minute Maid Park (2000)	Grass	315	435	326	40,950
Los Angeles Dodgers	Dodger Stadium (1962)	Grass	330	395	330	56,000
Milwaukee Brewers	Miller Park (2001)	Grass	344	400	345	42,400
New York Mets	Shea Stadium (1964)	Grass	338	410	338	55,601
Philadelphia Phillies	Citizens Bank Park (2004)	Grass	329	401	330	43,500
Pittsburgh Pirates	PNC Park (2001)	Grass	325	399	320	38,365
St. Louis Cardinals	New Busch Stadium (2006)	Grass	336	400	335	46,861
San Diego Padres	PETCO Park (2004)	Grass	334	396	322	42,500
San Francisco Giants	SBC Park (2000)	Grass	335	404	307	41,584
Washington Nationals	Robert F. Kennedy Memorial Stadium (1961)	Grass	335	410	335	56,000

American League

Team	Stadium (year opened)	Surface	LF	Center	RF	Seating
Baltimore Orioles	Oriole Park at Camden Yards (1992)	Grass	333	400	318	48,876
Boston Red Sox	Fenway Park (1912)	Grass	310	420	302	35,095
Chicago White Sox	U.S. Cellular Field (1991)	Grass	330	400	335	47,098
Cleveland Indians	Jacobs Field (1994)	Grass	325	405	325	43,368
Detroit Tigers	Comerica Park (2000)	Grass	345	420	330	40,000
Kansas City Royals	Kauffman Stadium (1973)	Grass	330	410	330	40,793
Los Angeles Angels	Angel Stadium of Anaheim (1966)	Grass	330	406	330	45,050
Minnesota Twins	Hubert H. Humphrey Metrodome (1982)	Artificial	343	408	327	48,678
New York Yankees	Yankee Stadium (1923)	Grass	318	408	314	57,478
Oakland A's	McAfee Coliseum (1968)	Grass	330	400	330	43,662
Seattle Mariners	Safeco Field (1999)	Grass	331	405	327	47,116
Tampa Bay Devil Rays	Tropicana Field (1990)	Artificial	315	404	322	45,000
Texas Rangers	Ameriquest Field in Arlington (1994)	Grass	332	400	325	49,200
Toronto Blue Jays	Rogers Centre (1989)	Artificial	328	400	328	50,516

(1) As of 2006 season.

Major League Franchise Shifts and Additions

1953—Boston Braves (NL) became Milwaukee Braves.

1954—St. Louis Browns (AL) became Baltimore Orioles.

1955—Philadelphia Athletics (AL) became Kansas City Athletics.

1958—New York Giants (NL) became San Francisco Giants.

1958—Brooklyn Dodgers (NL) became L.A. Dodgers.

1961—Washington Senators (AL) became Minnesota Twins.

1961—L.A. Angels (renamed California Angels in 1965 and Anaheim Angels in 1997) enfranchised by the American League.

1961—Washington Senators enfranchised by the American League (a new team, replacing the former Washington club, whose franchise was moved to Minneapolis-St. Paul).

1962—Houston Colt .45's (renamed the Houston Astros in 1965) enfranchised by the National League.

1962—New York Mets enfranchised by the National League.

1966—Milwaukee Braves (NL) became Atlanta Braves.

1968—Kansas City Athletics (AL) became Oakland Athletics.

1969—Kansas City Royals and Seattle Pilots enfranchised by the American League; Montreal Expos and San Diego Padres enfranchised by the National League.

1970—Seattle Pilots became Milwaukee Brewers.

1971—Washington Senators became Texas Rangers (Dallas-Fort Worth area).

1977—Toronto Blue Jays and Seattle Mariners enfranchised by the American League.

1993—Colorado Rockies (Denver) and Florida Marlins (Miami) enfranchised by the National League.

1998—Tampa Bay Devil Rays began play in the American League; Arizona Diamondbacks (Phoenix) began play in the National League (both teams enfranchised in 1995). Milwaukee Brewers moved from the AL to the NL.

2005—Montreal Expos (NL) became Washington Nationals; Anaheim Angels became Los Angeles Angels of Anaheim.

NCAA Baseball Division I Champions

1947 California	1959 Oklahoma St.	1972 USC	1984 Cal. St.-Fullerton	1996 LSU	
1948 Southern California	1960 Minnesota	1973 USC	1985 Miami (FL)	1997 LSU	
	1961 USC	1974 USC	1986 Arizona	1998 USC	
1949 Texas	1962 Michigan	1975 Texas	1987 Stanford	1999 Miami (FL)	
1950 Texas	1963 USC	1976 Arizona	1988 Stanford	2000 LSU	
1951 Oklahoma	1964 Minnesota	1977 Arizona St.	1989 Wichita St.	2001 Miami (FL)	
1952 Holy Cross	1965 Arizona St.	1978 USC	1990 Georgia	2002 Texas	
1953 Michigan	1966 Ohio St.	1979 Cal. St.-Fullerton	1991 LSU	2003 Rice	
1954 Missouri	1967 Arizona St.	1980 Arizona	1992 Pepperdine	2004 Cal. St.-Fullerton	
1955 Wake Forest	1968 USC	1981 Arizona St.	1993 LSU	2005 Texas	
1956 Minnesota	1969 Arizona St.	1982 Miami (FL)	1994 Oklahoma	2006 Oregon State	
1957 California	1970 USC	1983 Texas	1995 Cal. St.-Fullerton		
1958 USC	1971 USC				

NCAA Women's Softball Division I Champions

1982 UCLA	1987 Texas A&M	1992 UCLA	1997 Arizona	2002 California	
1983 Texas A&M	1988 UCLA	1993 Arizona	1998 Fresno St.	2003 UCLA	
1984 UCLA	1989 UCLA	1994 Arizona	1999 UCLA	2004 UCLA	
1985 UCLA	1990 UCLA	1995 UCLA	2000 Oklahoma	2005 Michigan	
1986 Cal St. Fullerton	1991 Arizona	1996 Arizona	2001 Arizona	2006 Arizona	

Little League World Series

The Little League World Series is played annually in Williamsport, PA.

Year	Winning / Losing Team	Score	Year	Winning / Losing Team	Score
1947	Williamsport, PA; Lock Haven, PA	16-7	1953	Birmingham, AL; Schenectady, NY	1-0
1948	Lock Haven, PA; St. Petersburg, FL	6-5	1954	Schenectady, NY; Colton, CA	7-5
1949	Hammonton, NJ; Pensacola, FL	5-0	1955	Morrisville, PA; Merchantville, NJ	4-3
1950	Houston, TX; Bridgeport, CT	2-1	1956	Roswell, NM; Delaware, NJ	3-1
1951	Stamford, CT; Austin, TX	3-0	1957	Mexico; La Mesa, CA	4-0
1952	Norwalk, CT; Monongahela, PA	4-3	1958	Mexico; Kankakee, IL	10-1

Year	Winning / Losing Team	Score	Year	Winning / Losing Team	Score
1959	Hamtramck, MI; Auburn, CA	12-0	1983	Marietta, GA; Dominican Rep.	3-1
1960	Levittown, PA; Ft. Worth, TX	5-0	1984	South Korea; Altamonte Springs, FL	6-2
1961	El Cajon, CA; El Campo, TX	4-2	1985	South Korea; Mexico	7-1
1962	San Jose, CA; Kankakee, IL	3-0	1986	Taiwan; Tucson, AZ	12-0
1963	Granada Hills, CA; Stratford, CT	2-1	1987	Chinese Taipei; Irvine, CA.	21-1
1964	Staten Island, NY; Mexico	4-0	1988	Chinese Taipei; Pearl City, HI	10-0
1965	Windsor Locks, CT; Ontario, Canada	3-1	1989	Trumbull, CT; Chinese Taipei	5-2
1966	Houston, TX; W. New York, NJ	8-2	1990	Chinese Taipei; Shippensburg, PA	9-0
1967	Tokyo, Japan; Chicago, IL	4-1	1991	Chinese Taipei; Danville, CA.	11-0
1968	Osaka, Japan; Richmond, VA	1-0	1992	Long Beach, CA; Philippines*	6-0
1969	Taiwan; Santa Clara, CA	5-0	1993	Long Beach, CA; Panama	3-2
1970	Wayne, NJ; Campbell, CA	2-0	1994	Venezuela; Northridge, CA	4-3
1971	Taiwan; Gary, IN	12-3	1995	Taiwan; Spring, TX	17-3
1972	Taiwan; Hammond, IN	6-0	1996	Taiwan; Cranston, RI.	13-3
1973	Taiwan; Tucson, AZ	12-0	1997	Mexico; Mission Viejo, CA	5-4
1974	Taiwan; Red Bluff, CA	12-1	1998	Toms River, NJ; Japan	12-9
1975	Lakewood, NJ; Tampa, FL.	4-3	1999	Japan; Phenix City, AL	5-0
1976	Tokyo, Japan; Campbell, CA	10-3	2000	Venezuela; Bellaire, TX.	3-2
1977	Taiwan; El Cajon, CA.	7-2	2001	Japan; Apopka, FL	2-1
1978	Taiwan; Danville, CA	11-1	2002	Louisville, KY; Japan.	1-0
1979	Taiwan; Campbell, CA	2-1	2003	Japan; East Boynton Beach, FL	10-1
1980	Taiwan; Tampa, FL	4-3	2004	Curacao; Conejo Valley of Thousand Oaks, CA	5-2
1981	Taiwan; Tampa, FL	4-2	2005	Ewa Beach HI; Curacao	7-6
1982	Kirkland, WA; Taiwan.	6-0	2006	Columbus, GA; Japan.	2-1

*Philippines won 15-4, but was disqualified for using ineligible players. Long Beach was awarded title by forfeit 6-0 (1 run per inning).

National Baseball Hall of Fame and Museum, Cooperstown, NY[1]

#Aaron, Hank (The Hammer)
Alexander, Grover Cleveland (Old Pete)
Alston, Walt
Anderson, Sparky
Anson, Cap
Aparicio, Luis
Appling, Luke
Ashburn, Richie
Averill, Earl
Baker, Frank (Home Run)
Bancroft, Dave
#Banks, Ernie
Barlick, Al
Barrow, Edward G.
Beckley, Jake
Bell, Cool Papa
#Bench, Johnny
Bender, Chief
Berra, Yogi
#Boggs, Wade
Bottomley, Jim
Boudreau, Lou
Bresnahan, Roger
#Brett, George
#Brock, Lou
Brouthers, Dan
Brown, Mordecai (Three Finger)
*Brown, Ray
*Brown, Willard
Bulkeley, Morgan C.
Bunning, Jim
Burkett, Jesse C.
Campanella, Roy
#Carew, Rod
Carey, Max
#Carlton, Steve
Carter, Gary
Cartwright, Alexander
Cepeda, Orlando
Chadwick, Henry
Chance, Frank
Chandler, Happy
Charleston, Oscar
Chesbro, John
Chylak, Nestor
Clarke, Fred
Clarkson, John
#Clemente,Roberto
Cobb, Ty2
Cochrane, Mickey
Collins, Eddie
Collins, James
Combs, Earle
Comiskey, Charles A.

Conlan, Jocko
Connolly, Thomas H.
Connor, Roger
*Cooper, Andy
Coveleski, Stan
Crawford, Sam
Cronin, Joe
Cummings, Candy
Cuyler, Kiki
Dandridge, Ray
Davis, George (Gorgeous)
Day, Leon
Dean, Dizzy
Delahanty, Ed
Dickey, Bill
Dihigo, Martín
DiMaggio, Joe
*Doby, Larry
Doerr, Bobby
Drysdale, Don
Duffy, Hugh
Durocher, Leo
#Eckersly, Dennis
Evans, Billy
Evers, John
Ewing, Buck
Faber, Urban (Red)
#Feller, Bob
Ferrell, Rick
Fingers, Rollie
Fisk, Carlton
Flick, Elmer H.
Ford, Whitey
Foster, Andrew (Rube)
Foster, Bill
Fox, Nellie
Foxx, Jimmie
Frick, Ford
Frisch, Frank
Galvin, Pud
#Gehrig, Lou
Gehringer, Charles
#Gibson, Bob
Gibson, Josh
Giles, Warren
Gomez, Lefty
Goslin, Goose
*Grant, Frank
Greenberg, Hank
Griffith, Clark
Grimes, Burleigh
Grove, Lefty
Hafey, Chick
Haines, Jesee
Hamilton, Bill
Hanlon, Ned

Harridge, Will
Harris, Bucky
Hartnett, Gabby
Heilmann, Harry
Herman, Billy
*Hill, Pete
Hooper, Harry
Hornsby, Rogers
Hoyt, Waite
Hubbard, Cal
Hubbell, Carl
Huggins, Miller
Hulbert, William
Hunter, Catfish
Irvin, Monte
#Jackson, Reggie
Jackson, Travis
Jenkins, Ferguson
Jennings, Hugh
Johnson, Byron (Ban)
Johnson, William (Judy)
Johnson, Walter2
Joss, Addie
#Kaline, Al
Keefe, Timothy
Keeler, William
Kell, George
Kelley, Joe
Kelly, George
Kelly, King
Killebrew, Harmon
Kiner, Ralph
Klein, Chuck
Klem, Bill
#Koufax, Sandy
Lajoie, Napoleon
Landis, Kenesaw M.
Lasorda, Tom
Lazzeri, Tony
Lemon, Bob
Leonard, Buck
Lindstrom, Fred
Lloyd, Pop
Lombardi, Ernie
Lopez, Al
Lyons, Ted
Mack, Connie
*Mackey, Biz
MacPhail, Larry
MacPhail, Lee
*Manley, Effa
#Mantle, Mickey
Manush, Henry
Maranville, Rabbit
Marichal, Juan
Marquard, Rube
Mathews, Eddie

Mathewson, Christy2
#Mays, Willie
Mazeroski, Bill
McCarthy, Joe
McCarthy, Thomas
#McCovey, Willie
McGinnity, Joe
McGowan, Bill
McGraw, John
McKechnie, Bill
McPhee, John (Bid)
Medwick, Joe
*Mendez, Jose
Mize, Johnny
#Molitor, Paul
#Morgan, Joe
#Murray, Eddie
#Musial, Stan
Newhouser, Hal
Nichols, Kid
Niekro, Phil
O'Rourke, James
Ott, Mel
Paige, Satchel
#Palmer, Jim
Pennock, Herb
Perez, Tony
Perry, Gaylord
Plank, Ed
*Pompez, Alex
*Posey, Cum
#Puckett, Kirby
Radbourn, Charlie
Reese, Pee Wee
Rice, Sam
Rickey, Branch
Rixey, Eppa
Rizzuto, Phil (Scooter)
Roberts, Robin
#Robinson, Brooks
#Robinson, Frank
#Robinson, Jackie
Robinson, Wilbert
Rogan, Joe (Bullet)
Roush, Edd
Ruffing, Red
Rusie, Amos
#Ruth, Babe2
#Ryan, Nolan
Sandberg, Ryne
*Santop, Louis
Schalk, Ray
#Schmidt, Mike
Schoendienst, Red
#Seaver, Tom
Selee, Frank
Sewell, Joe

Simmons, Al
Sisler, George
Slaughter, Enos
Smith, Hilton
#Smith, Ozzie
Snider, Duke
#Spahn, Warren
Spalding, Albert
Speaker, Tris
#Stargell, Willie
Stearnes, Norman (Turkey)
Stengel, Casey
*Sutter, Bruce
*Suttles, Mule
Sutton, Don
*Taylor, Ben
Terry, Bill
Thompson, Sam
Tinker, Joe
*Torriente, Cristobal
Traynor, Pie
Vance, Dazzy
Vaughan, Arky
Veeck, Bill
Waddell, Rube
Wagner, Honus2
Wallace, Roderick (Bobby)
Walsh, Ed
Waner, Lloyd
Waner, Paul
Ward, John
Weaver, Earl
Weiss, George
Welch, Mickey
Wells, Willie
Wheat, Zach
*White, Sol
Wilhelm, Hoyt
*Wilkinson, J.L.
Williams, Billy
Williams, Joe (Smokey Joe)
#Williams, Ted
Willis, Vic
Wilson, Hack
*Wilson, Jud
#Winfield, Dave
Wright, George
Wright, Harry
Wynn, Early
#Yastrzemski, Carl
Yawkey, Tom
Young, Cy
Youngs, Ross
#Yount, Robin

(1) Player must generally be retired for 5 complete seasons before being eligible for induction. (2) Players inducted in 1936 (the year the Hall of Fame began). # Denotes players chosen in first year of Hall of Fame eligibility or under special circumstances earlier. *Denotes 2006 inductees. **Note:** Four players, Babe Ruth (1936), Lou Gehrig (1939), Joe DiMaggio (1955), and Roberto Clemente (1973), were inducted less than 5 years after retirement or, in Clemente's case, death.

NATIONAL BASKETBALL ASSOCIATION
2005–06 Season: Heat Win 1st Title; Brown Leads Knicks to Losing Season, Bryant Scores 81 Points

The Miami Heat, June 20, defeated the Dallas Mavericks, 4 games to 2, to win the 2006 NBA Finals—the first NBA championship in the history of the franchise. Although the Mavericks took a 2-0 lead, the Heat came back to win four straight games, including the deciding game in Dallas, where they pulled out a close 95-92 victory.

The first two games were one-sided wins, with the Mavericks dominating at home. Game 3 was a turning point: the Mavericks blew a 13-point lead in the 3rd quarter and lost at the last minute, 98-96. In game 4, the Heat were led by guard Dwyane Wade's 36 points to a 98-74 victory. Game 5 came down to a critical moment: Mavericks forward Josh Howard burned the Mavericks' last time-out as Wade made two free throws with 1.9 seconds left in overtime. Though Howard denied that he had signaled for a time-out, the Mavericks were put into the situation of having to inbound from under their own basket after Wade's second free throw. Mavericks guard Devin Harris missed a desperate 50-ft shot to end the game with another close Heat win, 101-100. In the 6th and final game, Wade exploded with 36 points. Mavericks point guard Jason Terry missed the last shot, capping the Heat's championship. The Heat were led by Wade, who averaged 34.7 points per game in the series; legendary center Shaquille O'Neal, who raked in 13.7 points and 10.2 rebounds per game and gave a strong performance in game 4; and Gary Payton, who made the deciding shot in game 3.

Twenty-four-year-old Wade was named MVP, making him the fourth-youngest player to have earned the award. Heat head coach Pat Riley won his fourth championship, after taking over the Miami team midway through the season. The young Mavericks team, which won a franchise-record 60 regular season games, was led by Dirk Nowitzki.

In the regular season, on Jan. 22, 2006, Kobe Bryant of the L.A. Lakers scored 81 points in a game against the Toronto Raptors—the second-highest single-game scoring total in NBA history, behind a 1962 game in which Wilt Chamberlain of the Philadelphia Warriors scored 100 points against the New York Knicks. Other regular season highlights included: the Phoenix Suns' Steve Nash winning his second straight MVP award; Avery Johnson, in his first full season as head coach, winning Coach of the Year for leading the Mavericks to the NBA Finals; and the New York Knicks, led by Coach Larry Brown, finishing up at 23-59, one game short of their worst season in franchise history. Brown was fired after the season's end. A dress code for all NBA players was implemented by Commissioner David Stern, the first rule of its kind in any major professional sport. The code, which went into effect Nov. 1, 2005, mandated that players, when not in uniform, wear "business casual" clothing during team and NBA functions and activities.

Final Standings, 2005-06 Season

(Playoff seedings in parentheses; in each conference the 3 division winners automatically get the number 1, 2, and 3 seeds.)

Eastern Conference					Western Conference				
Atlantic Division					**Northwest Division**				
	W	L	Pct	GB		W	L	Pct	GB
New Jersey (3)	49	33	.598	—	Denver (3)	44	38	.537	—
Philadelphia	38	44	.463	11	Utah	41	41	.500	3
Boston	33	49	.402	16	Seattle	35	47	.427	9
Toronto	27	55	.329	22	Minnesota	33	49	.402	11
New York	23	59	.280	26	Portland	21	61	.256	23
Central Division					**Pacific Division**				
Detroit (1)	64	18	.780	—	Phoenix (2)	54	28	.659	—
Cleveland (4)	50	32	.610	14	L.A. Clippers (6)	47	35	.573	7
Indiana (6)	41	41	.500	23	L.A. Lakers (7)	45	37	.549	9
Chicago (7)	41	41	.500	23	Sacramento (8)	44	38	.537	10
Milwaukee (8)	40	42	.488	24	Golden State	34	48	.415	20
Southeast Division					**Southwest Division**				
Miami (2)	52	30	.634	—	San Antonio (1)	63	19	.768	—
Washington (5)	42	40	.512	10	Dallas (4)	60	22	.732	3
Orlando	36	46	.439	16	Memphis (5)	49	33	.598	14
Charlotte	26	56	.317	26	New Orleans/Oklahoma City	38	44	.463	25
Atlanta	26	56	.317	26	Houston	34	48	.415	29

2005–06 NBA Regular Season Individual Highs

Minutes, game: 60, Shawn Marion, Phoenix v. New York, Jan. 2
Points, game: 81, Kobe Bryant, L.A. Lakers v. Toronto, Jan. 22
Field goals, game: 28, Kobe Bryant, L.A. Lakers v. Toronto, Jan. 22
FG attempts, game: 46, Kobe Bryant, L.A. Lakers v. Toronto, Jan. 22
3-pointers, game: 9, Ben Gordon, Chicago v. Phoenix, Feb. 4; Ben Gordon, Chicago v. Washington, Apr. 14
3-pt. attempts, game: 16, Ray Allen, Seattle v. Phoenix, Jan. 22
Free throws, game: 24, LeBron James, Cleveland v. Miami, Mar. 12
FT attempts, game: 28, LeBron James, Cleveland v. Miami, Mar. 12

Rebounds, game: 26, Dwight Howard, Orlando v. Philadelphia, Apr. 15
Assists, game: 22, Steve Nash, Phoenix v. New York, Jan. 2
Steals, game: 8, Gerald Wallace, Charlotte v. Milwaukee, Jan. 13; Shawn Marion, Phoenix v. Minnesota, Feb. 6; Morris Peterson, Toronto v. Charlotte, Feb. 10
Blocks, game: 10, Andrei Kirilenko, Utah v. Sacramento, Mar. 25
Minutes, season: 3,384, Gilbert Arenas, Washington
Off. rebounds, season: 301, Ben Wallace, Detroit
Def. rebounds, season: 752, Kevin Garnett, Minnesota
Personal fouls, season: 301, Al Harrington, Atlanta

2006 NBA Playoff Results

Eastern Conference
Cleveland defeated Washington 4 games to 2.
New Jersey defeated Indiana 4 games to 2.
Miami defeated Chicago 4 games to 2.
Detroit defeated Milwaukee 4 games to 1.
Miami defeated New Jersey 4 games to 1.
Detroit defeated Cleveland 4 games to 3.
Miami defeated Detroit 4 games to 2.

Western Conference
Dallas defeated Memphis 4 games to 0.
L.A. Clippers defeated Denver 4 games to 1.
Phoenix defeated L.A. Lakers 4 games to 3.
San Antonio defeated Sacramento 4 games to 2.
Phoenix defeated L.A. Clippers 4 games to 3.
Dallas defeated San Antonio 4 games to 3.
Dallas defeated Phoenix 4 games to 2.

Championship
Miami defeated Dallas 4 games to 2 [80-90, 85-99, 96-98, 74-98, 100-101, 95-92].

NBA Finals Composite Box Scores

Miami	FG M-A	FT M-A	Reb O-T	Ast	Avg
Dwyane Wade	65-139	75-97	12-47	23	34.7
Antoine Walker	34-87	5-9	4-33	13	13.8
Shaquille O'Neal	34-56	14-48	15-61	17	13.7
Jason Williams	18-50	7-11	0-11	28	8.8
James Posey	13-31	10-13	6-36	2	7.3
Udonis Haslem	18-36	3-10	17-37	2	6.5
Alonzo Mourning	9-13	8-12	4-19	0	4.3
Gary Payton	7-19	1-3	3-12	12	2.7
Shandon Anderson	2-6	2-4	2-7	3	1.5
Jason Kapono	0-0	0-0	0-0	0	0.0
Michael Doleac	0-0	0-0	0-0	0	0.0

Dallas	FG M-A	FT M-A	Reb O-T	Ast	Avg
Dirk Nowitzki	41-105	49-55	9-65	15	22.8
Jason Terry	54-113	11-15	1-13	21	22.0
Josh Howard	31-80	21-26	10-49	11	14.7
Jerry Stackhouse	22-62	13-14	5-17	15	12.8
Devin Harris	16-44	12-16	3-5	17	7.3
Erick Dampier	13-18	8-16	16-49	2	5.7
Adrian Griffin	9-16	0-0	8-19	5	3.0
Marquis Daniels	6-11	4-5	2-3	8	2.8
DeSagana Diop	3-6	4-8	5-20	1	1.7
Keith Van Horn	3-11	0-0	-6	0	1.4
Josh Powell	0-1	0-0	1-1	0	0.0
Didier Ilunga-Mbenga	0-0	0-0	0-3	0	0.0
Darrell Armstrong	0-2	0-0	0-1	0	0.0

NBA Finals MVP

1969 Jerry West, Los Angeles	1981 Cedric Maxwell, Boston	1994 Hakeem Olajuwon, Houston
1970 Willis Reed, New York	1982 Magic Johnson, Los Angeles	1995 Hakeem Olajuwon, Houston
1971 Lew Alcindor (Kareem Abdul-Jabbar), Milwaukee	1983 Moses Malone, Philadelphia	1996 Michael Jordan, Chicago
	1984 Larry Bird, Boston	1997 Michael Jordan, Chicago
1972 Wilt Chamberlain, Los Angeles	1985 Kareem Abdul-Jabbar, L.A. Lakers	1998 Michael Jordan, Chicago
1973 Willis Reed, New York	1986 Larry Bird, Boston	1999 Tim Duncan, San Antonio
1974 John Havlicek, Boston	1987 Magic Johnson, L.A. Lakers	2000 Shaquille O'Neal, L.A. Lakers
1975 Rick Barry, Golden State	1988 James Worthy, L.A. Lakers	2001 Shaquille O'Neal, L.A. Lakers
1976 JoJo White, Boston	1989 Joe Dumars, Detroit	2002 Shaquille O'Neal, L.A. Lakers
1977 Bill Walton, Portland	1990 Isiah Thomas, Detroit	2003 Tim Duncan, San Antonio
1978 Wes Unseld, Washington	1991 Michael Jordan, Chicago	2004 Chauncey Billups, Detroit
1979 Dennis Johnson, Seattle	1992 Michael Jordan, Chicago	2005 Tim Duncan, San Antonio
1980 Magic Johnson, Los Angeles	1993 Michael Jordan, Chicago	2006 Dwyane Wade, Miami

NBA Finals All-Time Statistical Leaders

(At the end of the 2006 NBA season finals. *Player active in 2005-06 season.)

Scoring Average (Minimum 10 games)

	G	FG	FT	Pts	Avg
Rick Barry	10	138	87	363	36.3
Michael Jordan	35	438	258	1,176	33.6
Jerry West	55	612	455	1,679	30.5
*Shaquille O'Neal	30	340	185	865	28.8
Bob Pettit	25	241	227	709	28.4

Scoring Average (Minimum 10 games)

	G	FG	FT	Pts	Avg
Hakeem Olajuwon	17	187	91	467	27.5
Elgin Baylor	44	442	277	1,161	26.4
Julius Erving	22	216	128	561	25.5
Joe Fulks	11	84	104	272	24.7
Clyde Drexler	15	126	108	367	24.5

Games Played

Bill Russell	70
Sam Jones	64
Kareem Abdul-Jabbar	56
Jerry West	55
Tom Heinsohn	52

Rebounds

Bill Russell	1,718
Wilt Chamberlain	862
Elgin Baylor	593
Kareem Abdul-Jabbar	507
Tom Heinsohn	473

Assists

Magic Johnson	584
Bob Cousy	400
Bill Russell	315
Jerry West	306
Dennis Johnson	228

NBA Scoring Leaders

Year	Scoring Champion	Pts	Avg
1947	Joe Fulks, Philadelphia	1,389	23.2
1948	Max Zaslofsky, Chicago	1,007	21.0
1949	George Mikan, Minneapolis	1,698	28.3
1950	George Mikan, Minneapolis	1,865	27.4
1951	George Mikan, Minneapolis	1,932	28.4
1952	Paul Arizin, Philadelphia	1,674	25.4
1953	Neil Johnston, Philadelphia	1,564	22.3
1954	Neil Johnston, Philadelphia	1,759	24.4
1955	Neil Johnston, Philadelphia	1,631	22.7
1956	Bob Pettit, St. Louis	1,849	25.7
1957	Paul Arizin, Philadelphia	1,817	25.6
1958	George Yardley, Detroit	2,001	27.8
1959	Bob Pettit, St. Louis	2,105	29.2
1960	Wilt Chamberlain, Philadelphia	2,707	37.9
1961	Wilt Chamberlain, Philadelphia	3,033	38.4
1962	Wilt Chamberlain, Philadelphia	4,029	50.4
1963	Wilt Chamberlain, San Francisco	3,586	44.8
1964	Wilt Chamberlain, San Francisco	2,948	36.5
1965	Wilt Chamberlain, San Francisco, Phil.	2,534	34.7
1966	Wilt Chamberlain, Philadelphia	2,649	33.5
1967	Rick Barry, San Francisco	2,775	35.6
1968	Dave Bing, Detroit	2,142	27.1
1969	Elvin Hayes, San Diego	2,327	28.4
1970	Jerry West, Los Angeles	2,309	31.2
1971	Lew Alcindor (Abdul-Jabbar), Milw.	2,596	31.7
1972	Kareem Abdul-Jabbar, Milwaukee	2,822	34.8
1973	Nate Archibald, Kans. City-Omaha	2,719	34.0
1974	Bob McAdoo, Buffalo	2,261	30.6
1975	Bob McAdoo, Buffalo	2,831	34.5
1976	Bob McAdoo, Buffalo	2,427	31.1

Year	Scoring Champion	Pts	Avg
1977	Pete Maravich, New Orleans	2,273	31.1
1978	George Gervin, San Antonio	2,232	27.2
1979	George Gervin, San Antonio	2,365	29.6
1980	George Gervin, San Antonio	2,585	33.1
1981	Adrian Dantley, Utah	2,452	30.7
1982	George Gervin, San Antonio	2,551	32.3
1983	Alex English, Denver	2,326	28.4
1984	Adrian Dantley, Utah	2,418	30.6
1985	Bernard King, New York	1,809	32.9
1986	Dominique Wilkins, Atlanta	2,366	30.3
1987	Michael Jordan, Chicago	3,041	37.1
1988	Michael Jordan, Chicago	2,868	35.0
1989	Michael Jordan, Chicago	2,633	32.5
1990	Michael Jordan, Chicago	2,753	33.6
1991	Michael Jordan, Chicago	2,580	31.5
1992	Michael Jordan, Chicago	2,404	30.1
1993	Michael Jordan, Chicago	2,541	32.6
1994	David Robinson, San Antonio	2,383	29.8
1995	Shaquille O'Neal, Orlando	2,315	29.3
1996	Michael Jordan, Chicago	2,465	30.4
1997	Michael Jordan, Chicago	2,431	29.6
1998	Michael Jordan, Chicago	2,357	28.7
1999	Allen Iverson, Philadelphia	1,284	26.8
2000	Shaquille O'Neal, L.A. Lakers	2,344	29.7
2001	Allen Iverson, Philadelphia	2,207	31.1
2002	Allen Iverson, Philadelphia	1,883	31.4
2003	Tracy McGrady, Orlando	2,407	32.1
2004	Tracy McGrady, Orlando	1,878	28.0
2005	Allen Iverson, Philadelphia	2,302	30.7
2006	Kobe Bryant, L.A. Lakers	2,832	35.4

NBA Most Valuable Player

1956 Bob Pettit, St. Louis	1961 Bill Russell, Boston	1966 Wilt Chamberlain, Philadelphia
1957 Bob Cousy, Boston	1962 Bill Russell, Boston	1967 Wilt Chamberlain, Philadelphia
1958 Bill Russell, Boston	1963 Bill Russell, Boston	1968 Wilt Chamberlain, Philadelphia
1959 Bob Pettit, St. Louis	1964 Oscar Robertson, Cincinnati	1969 Wes Unseld, Baltimore
1960 Wilt Chamberlain, Philadelphia	1965 Bill Russell, Boston	1970 Willis Reed, New York

1971 Lew Alcindor (Abdul-Jabbar), Milw.	1983 Moses Malone, Philadelphia	1995 David Robinson, San Antonio
1972 Kareem Abdul-Jabbar, Milwaukee	1984 Larry Bird, Boston	1996 Michael Jordan, Chicago
1973 Dave Cowens, Boston	1985 Larry Bird, Boston	1997 Karl Malone, Utah
1974 Kareem Abdul-Jabbar, Milwaukee	1986 Larry Bird, Boston	1998 Michael Jordan, Chicago
1975 Bob McAdoo, Buffalo	1987 Magic Johnson, L.A. Lakers	1999 Karl Malone, Utah
1976 Kareem Abdul-Jabbar, Los Angeles	1988 Michael Jordan, Chicago	2000 Shaquille O'Neal, L.A. Lakers
1977 Kareem Abdul-Jabbar, Los Angeles	1989 Magic Johnson, L.A. Lakers	2001 Allen Iverson, Philadelphia
1978 Bill Walton, Portland	1990 Magic Johnson, L.A. Lakers	2002 Tim Duncan, San Antonio
1979 Moses Malone, Houston	1991 Michael Jordan, Chicago	2003 Tim Duncan, San Antonio
1980 Kareem Abdul-Jabbar, Los Angeles	1992 Michael Jordan, Chicago	2004 Kevin Garnett, Minnesota
1981 Julius Erving, Philadelphia	1993 Charles Barkley, Phoenix	2005 Steve Nash, Phoenix
1982 Moses Malone, Houston	1994 Hakeem Olajuwon, Houston	2006 Steve Nash, Phoenix

NBA Champions, 1947-2006

	Regular Season		Playoffs		
Year	Eastern Conference	Western Conference	Champion	Coach	Runner-Up
1947	Washington Capitols	Chicago Stags	Philadelphia	Ed Gottlieb	Chicago
1948	Philadelphia Warriors	St. Louis Bombers	Baltimore	Buddy Jeannette	Philadelphia
1949	Washington Capitols	Rochester	Minneapolis	John Kundla	Washington
1950	Syracuse	Minneapolis	Minneapolis	John Kundla	Syracuse
1951	Philadelphia Warriors	Minneapolis	Rochester	Lester Harrison	New York
1952	Syracuse	Rochester	Minneapolis	John Kundla	New York
1953	New York	Minneapolis	Minneapolis	John Kundla	New York
1954	New York	Minneapolis	Minneapolis	John Kundla	Syracuse
1955	Syracuse	Ft. Wayne	Syracuse	Al Cervi	Ft. Wayne
1956	Philadelphia Warriors	Ft. Wayne	Philadelphia	George Senesky	Ft. Wayne
1957	Boston	St. Louis	Boston	Red Auerbach	St. Louis
1958	Boston	St. Louis	St. Louis	Alex Hannum	Boston
1959	Boston	St. Louis	Boston	Red Auerbach	Minneapolis
1960	Boston	St. Louis	Boston	Red Auerbach	St. Louis
1961	Boston	St. Louis	Boston	Red Auerbach	St. Louis
1962	Boston	Los Angeles	Boston	Red Auerbach	Los Angeles
1963	Boston	Los Angeles	Boston	Red Auerbach	Los Angeles
1964	Boston	San Francisco	Boston	Red Auerbach	San Francisco
1965	Boston	Los Angeles	Boston	Red Auerbach	Los Angeles
1966	Philadelphia	Los Angeles	Boston	Red Auerbach	Los Angeles
1967	Philadelphia	San Francisco	Philadelphia	Alex Hannum	San Francisco
1968	Philadelphia	St. Louis	Boston	Bill Russell	Los Angeles
1969	Baltimore	Los Angeles	Boston	Bill Russell	Los Angeles
1970	New York	Atlanta	New York	Red Holzman	Los Angeles

Year	Atlantic	Central	Midwest	Pacific	Champion	Coach	Runner-Up
1971	New York	Baltimore	Milwaukee	Los Angeles	Milwaukee	Larry Costello	Baltimore
1972	Boston	Baltimore	Milwaukee	Los Angeles	Los Angeles	Bill Sharman	New York
1973	Boston	Baltimore	Milwaukee	Los Angeles	New York	Red Holzman	Los Angeles
1974	Boston	Capital	Milwaukee	Los Angeles	Boston	Tom Heinsohn	Milwaukee
1975	Boston	Washington	Chicago	Golden State	Golden State	Al Attles	Washington
1976	Boston	Cleveland	Milwaukee	Golden State	Boston	Tom Heinsohn	Phoenix
1977	Philadelphia	Houston	Denver	Los Angeles	Portland	Jack Ramsay	Philadelphia
1978	Philadelphia	San Antonio	Denver	Portland	Washington	Dick Motta	Seattle
1979	Washington	San Antonio	Kansas City	Seattle	Seattle	Len Wilkens	Washington
1980	Boston	Atlanta	Milwaukee	Los Angeles	Los Angeles	Paul Westhead	Philadelphia
1981	Boston	Milwaukee	San Antonio	Phoenix	Boston	Bill Fitch	Houston
1982	Boston	Milwaukee	San Antonio	Los Angeles	Los Angeles	Pat Riley	Philadelphia
1983	Philadelphia	Milwaukee	San Antonio	Los Angeles	Philadelphia	Billy Cunningham	Los Angeles
1984	Boston	Milwaukee	Utah	Los Angeles	Boston	K.C. Jones	Los Angeles
1985	Boston	Milwaukee	Denver	L.A. Lakers	L.A. Lakers	Pat Riley	Boston
1986	Boston	Milwaukee	Houston	L.A. Lakers	Boston	K.C. Jones	Houston
1987	Boston	Atlanta	Dallas	L.A. Lakers	L.A. Lakers	Pat Riley	Boston
1988	Boston	Detroit	Denver	L.A. Lakers	L.A. Lakers	Pat Riley	Detroit
1989	New York	Detroit	Utah	L.A. Lakers	Detroit	Chuck Daly	L.A. Lakers
1990	Philadelphia	Detroit	San Antonio	L.A. Lakers	Detroit	Chuck Daly	Portland
1991	Boston	Chicago	San Antonio	Portland	Chicago	Phil Jackson	L.A. Lakers
1992	Boston	Chicago	Utah	Portland	Chicago	Phil Jackson	Portland
1993	New York	Chicago	Houston	Phoenix	Chicago	Phil Jackson	Phoenix
1994	New York	Atlanta	Houston	Seattle	Houston	Rudy Tomjanovich	New York
1995	Orlando	Indiana	San Antonio	Phoenix	Houston	Rudy Tomjanovich	Orlando
1996	Orlando	Chicago	San Antonio	Seattle	Chicago	Phil Jackson	Seattle
1997	Miami	Chicago	Utah	Seattle	Chicago	Phil Jackson	Utah
1998	Miami	Chicago	Utah	L.A. Lakers	Chicago	Phil Jackson	Utah
1999	Miami	Indiana	San Antonio	Portland	San Antonio	Gregg Popovich	New York
2000	Miami	Indiana	Utah	L.A. Lakers	L.A. Lakers	Phil Jackson	Indiana
2001	Philadelphia	Milwaukee	San Antonio	L.A. Lakers	L.A. Lakers	Phil Jackson	Philadelphia
2002	New Jersey	Detroit	San Antonio	Sacramento	L.A. Lakers	Phil Jackson	New Jersey
2003	New Jersey	Detroit	San Antonio	Sacramento	San Antonio	Gregg Popovich	New Jersey
2004	New Jersey	Indiana	Minnesota	L.A. Lakers	Detroit	Larry Brown	L.A. Lakers

Year	Atlantic	Central	Southeast	Northwest	Pacific	Southwest	Champion	Coach	Runner-Up
2005	Boston	Detroit	Miami	Seattle	Phoenix	San Antonio	San Antonio	Gregg Popovich	Detroit
2006	New Jersey	Detroit	Miami	Denver	Phoenix	San Antonio	Miami	Pat Riley	Dallas

All-NBA and All-Defensive Teams, 2005-06

All-NBA Team			All-Defensive Team	
First Team	Second Team	Position	First Team	Second Team
LeBron James, Cleveland	Elton Brand, L.A. Clippers	Forward	Andrei Kirilenko, Utah	Tim Duncan, San Antonio
Dirk Nowitzki, Dallas	Tim Duncan, San Antonio	Forward	Ron Artest, Sacramento	Kevin Garnett, Minnesota
		Forward		Tayshaun Prince, Detroit
Shaquille O'Neal, Miami	Ben Wallace, Detroit	Center	Ben Wallace, Detroit	Marcus Camby, Denver
Kobe Bryant, L.A. Lakers	Chauncey Billups, Detroit	Guard	Bruce Bowen, San Antonio	Chauncey Billups, Detroit
Steve Nash, Phoenix	Dwyane Wade, Miami	Guard	Kobe Bryant[1], L.A. Lakers	
		Guard	Jason Kidd[1], New Jersey	

(1) Bryant and Kidd tied in votes received, with 28 points each.

NBA Coach of the Year, 1963-2006

Year	Coach	Year	Coach	Year	Coach
1963	Harry Gallatin, St. Louis	1978	Hubie Brown, Atlanta	1993	Pat Riley, New York
1964	Alex Hannum, San Francisco	1979	Cotton Fitzsimmons, Kansas City	1994	Lenny Wilkens, Atlanta
1965	Red Auerbach, Boston	1980	Bill Fitch, Boston	1995	Del Harris, L.A. Lakers
1966	Dolph Schayes, Philadelphia	1981	Jack McKinney, Indiana	1996	Phil Jackson, Chicago
1967	Johnny Kerr, Chicago	1982	Gene Shue, Washington	1997	Pat Riley, Miami
1968	Richie Guerin, St. Louis	1983	Don Nelson, Milwaukee	1998	Larry Bird, Indiana
1969	Gene Shue, Baltimore	1984	Frank Layden, Utah	1999	Mike Dunleavy, Portland
1970	Red Holzman, New York	1985	Don Nelson, Milwaukee	2000	Glenn "Doc" Rivers, Orlando
1971	Dick Motta, Chicago	1986	Mike Fratello, Atlanta	2001	Larry Brown, Philadelphia
1972	Bill Sharman, L.A. Lakers	1987	Mike Schuler, Portland	2002	Rick Carlisle, Detroit
1973	Tom Heinsohn, Boston	1988	Doug Moe, Denver	2003	Gregg Popovich, San Antonio
1974	Ray Scott, Detroit	1989	Cotton Fitzsimmons, Phoenix	2004	Hubie Brown, Memphis
1975	Phil Johnson, Kansas City-Omaha	1990	Pat Riley, L.A. Lakers	2005	Mike D'Antoni, Phoenix
1976	Bill Fitch, Cleveland	1991	Don Chaney, Houston	2006	Avery Johnson, Dallas
1977	Tom Nissalke, Houston	1992	Don Nelson, Golden State		

NBA Statistical Leaders, 2005-06

Scoring Average
(Minimum 70 games or 1,400 pts)

	G	FG	FT	Pts	Avg
Kobe Bryant, L.A. Lakers	80	978	696	2,832	35.4
Allen Iverson, Philadelphia	72	814	675	2,375	33.0
LeBron James, Cleveland	79	875	601	2,478	31.4
Gilbert Arenas, Washington	80	746	655	2,346	29.3
Dwyane Wade, Miami	75	699	629	2,040	27.2
Paul Pierce, Boston	79	689	627	2,116	26.8
Dirk Nowitzki, Dallas	81	751	539	2,151	26.6
Carmelo Anthony, Denver	80	756	573	2,122	26.5
Michael Redd, Milwaukee	80	682	501	2,028	25.4
Ray Allen, Seattle	78	681	324	1,955	25.1

3-Point Field Goal Percentage
(Minimum 55 3-point field goals made)

	3-FGM	3-FGA	Pct
Richard Hamilton, Detroit	55	120	.458
Tyronn Lue, Atlanta	58	127	.457
Leandro Barbosa, Phoenix	87	196	.444
Mike James, Toronto	169	382	.442
Raja Bell, Phoenix	196	445	.440
Steve Nash, Phoenix	150	342	.439
Ben Gordon, Chicago	166	382	.435
Chauncey Billups, Detroit	184	425	.433
Bruce Bowen, San Antonio	104	245	.424
Jameer Nelson, Orlando	70	165	.424

Rebounds per Game
(Minimum 70 games or 800 rebounds)

	G	Off	Def	Tot	Avg
Kevin Garnett, Minnesota	76	214	752	966	12.7
Dwight Howard, Orlando	82	288	734	1,022	12.5
Shawn Marion, Phoenix	81	249	710	959	11.8
Ben Wallace, Detroit	82	301	622	923	11.3
Tim Duncan, San Antonio	80	231	650	881	11.0
Troy Murphy, Golden State	74	195	548	743	10.0
Elton Brand, L.A. Clippers	79	236	554	790	10.0
Chris Webber, Philadelphia	75	184	557	741	9.9
Chris Kaman, L.A. Clippers	78	187	563	750	9.6
Jamaal Magloire, Milwaukee	82	220	558	778	9.5

Assists per Game
(Minimum 70 games or 400 assists)

	G	Ast	Avg
Steve Nash, Phoenix	79	823	10.4
Baron Davis, Golden State	54	480	8.9
Brevin Knight, Charlotte	69	610	8.8
Chauncey Billups, Detroit	81	699	8.6
Jason Kidd, New Jersey	80	672	8.4
Andre Miller, Denver	82	674	8.2
Chris Paul, New Orleans/Oklahoma City	78	611	7.8
Allen Iverson, Philadelphia	72	532	7.4
Luke Ridnour, Seattle	79	550	7.0
Rafer Alston, Houston	63	425	6.7

Field Goal Percentage
(Minimum 300 field goals made)

	FGM	FGA	Pct
Shaquille O'Neal, Miami	480	800	.600
Eddy Curry, New York	336	597	.563
Tony Parker, San Antonio	623	1,136	.548
Gerald Wallace, Charlotte	317	589	.538
Andrew Bogut, Milwaukee	323	606	.533
Dwight Howard, Orlando	468	881	.531
Elton Brand, L.A. Clippers	756	1,435	.527
Boris Diaw, Phoenix	449	853	.526
Kevin Garnett, Minnesota	626	1,191	.526
Shareef Abdur-Rahim, Sacramento	332	632	.526

Steals per Game
(Minimum 70 games or 125 steals)

	G	Stl	Avg
Gerald Wallace, Charlotte	55	138	2.51
Brevin Knight, Charlotte	69	157	2.28
Chris Paul, New Orleans/Oklahoma City	78	175	2.24
Gilbert Arenas, Washington	80	161	2.01
Shawn Marion, Phoenix	81	160	1.98
Dwyane Wade, Miami	75	146	1.95
Allen Iverson, Philadelphia	72	140	1.94
Jason Kidd, New Jersey	80	150	1.88
Kobe Bryant, L.A. Lakers	80	147	1.84
Ben Wallace, Detroit	82	146	1.78

Free Throw Percentage
(Minimum 125 free throws made)

	FTM	FTA	Pct
Steve Nash, Phoenix	257	279	.921
Peja Stojakovic, Indiana-Sacramento	238	260	.915
Ray Allen, Seattle	324	359	.903
Dirk Nowitzki, Dallas	539	598	.901
Wally Szczerbiak, Boston-Minnesota	278	310	.897
Chauncey Billups, Detroit	465	520	.894
Jerry Stackhouse, Dallas	195	221	.882
Michael Redd, Milwaukee	501	571	.877
Luke Ridnour, Seattle	199	227	.877
Earl Boykins, Denver	152	174	.874

Blocked Shots per Game
(Minimum 70 games or 100 blocked shots)

	G	Blk	Avg
Marcus Camby, Denver	56	184	3.29
Andrei Kirilenko, Utah	69	220	3.19
Alonzo Mourning, Miami	65	173	2.66
Josh Smith, Atlanta	80	208	2.60
Elton Brand, L.A. Clippers	79	201	2.54
Samuel Dalembert, Philadelphia	66	160	2.42
Joel Przybilla, Portland	56	130	2.32
Jermaine O'Neal, Indiana	51	117	2.29
Ben Wallace, Detroit	82	181	2.21
Eddie Griffin, Minnesota	70	148	2.11

NBA Defensive Player of the Year

1983	Sidney Moncrief, Milwaukee	1992	David Robinson, San Antonio	2000	Alonzo Mourning, Miami
1984	Sidney Moncrief, Milwaukee	1993	Hakeem Olajuwon, Houston	2001	Dikembe Mutombo, Philadelphia-Atlanta
1985	Mark Eaton, Utah	1994	Hakeem Olajuwon, Houston		
1986	Alvin Robertson, San Antonio	1995	Dikembe Mutombo, Denver	2002	Ben Wallace, Detroit
1987	Michael Cooper, L.A. Lakers	1996	Gary Payton, Seattle	2003	Ben Wallace, Detroit
1988	Michael Jordan, Chicago	1997	Dikembe Mutombo, Atlanta	2004	Ron Artest, Indiana
1989	Mark Eaton, Utah	1998	Dikembe Mutombo, Atlanta	2005	Ben Wallace, Detroit
1990	Dennis Rodman, Detroit	1999	Alonzo Mourning, Miami	2006	Ben Wallace, Detroit
1991	Dennis Rodman, Detroit				

NBA Rookie of the Year

1953	Don Meineke, Ft. Wayne	1971	Dave Cowens, Boston;	1989	Mitch Richmond, Golden State	
1954	Ray Felix, Baltimore		Geoff Petrie, Portland (tie)	1990	David Robinson, San Antonio	
1955	Bob Pettit, Milwaukee	1972	Sidney Wicks, Portland	1991	Derrick Coleman, New Jersey	
1956	Maurice Stokes, Rochester	1973	Bob McAdoo, Buffalo	1992	Larry Johnson, Charlotte	
1957	Tom Heinsohn, Boston	1974	Ernie DiGregorio, Buffalo	1993	Shaquille O'Neal, Orlando	
1958	Woody Sauldsberry, Philadelphia	1975	Keith Wilkes, Golden State	1994	Chris Webber, Golden State	
1959	Elgin Baylor, Minneapolis	1976	Alvan Adams, Phoenix	1995	Grant Hill, Detroit;	
1960	Wilt Chamberlain, Philadelphia	1977	Adrian Dantley, Buffalo		Jason Kidd, Dallas (tie)	
1961	Oscar Robertson, Cincinnati	1978	Walter Davis, Phoenix	1996	Damon Stoudamire, Toronto	
1962	Walt Bellamy, Chicago	1979	Phil Ford, Kansas City	1997	Allen Iverson, Philadelphia	
1963	Terry Dischinger, Chicago	1980	Larry Bird, Boston	1998	Tim Duncan, San Antonio	
1964	Jerry Lucas, Cincinnati	1981	Darrell Griffith, Utah	1999	Vince Carter, Toronto	
1965	Willis Reed, New York	1982	Buck Williams, New Jersey	2000	Elton Brand, Chicago;	
1966	Rick Barry, San Francisco	1983	Terry Cummings, San Diego		Steve Francis, Houston (tie)	
1967	Dave Bing, Detroit	1984	Ralph Sampson, Houston	2001	Mike Miller, Orlando	
1968	Earl Monroe, Baltimore	1985	Michael Jordan, Chicago	2002	Pau Gasol, Memphis	
1969	Wes Unseld, Baltimore	1986	Patrick Ewing, New York	2003	Amaré Stoudemire, Phoenix	
1970	Lew Alcindor (Abdul-Jabbar), Milw.	1987	Chuck Person, Indiana	2004	LeBron James, Cleveland	
		1988	Mark Jackson, New York	2005	Emeka Okafor, Charlotte	
				2006	Chris Paul, New Or./Okla. City	

NBA Sixth Man Award

1983	Bobby Jones, Philadelphia	1991	Detlef Schrempf, Indiana	1999	Darrell Armstrong, Orlando
1984	Kevin McHale, Boston	1992	Detlef Schrempf, Indiana	2000	Rodney Rogers, Phoenix
1985	Kevin McHale, Boston	1993	Clifford Robinson, Portland	2001	Aaron McKie, Philadelphia
1986	Bill Walton, Boston	1994	Dell Curry, Charlotte	2002	Corliss Williamson, Detroit
1987	Ricky Pierce, Milwaukee	1995	Anthony Mason, New York	2003	Bobby Jackson, Sacramento
1988	Roy Tarpley, Dallas	1996	Toni Kukoc, Chicago	2004	Antawn Jamison, Dallas
1989	Eddie Johnson, Phoenix	1997	John Starks, New York	2005	Ben Gordon, Chicago
1990	Ricky Pierce, Milwaukee	1998	Danny Manning, Phoenix	2006	Mike Miller, Memphis

2006 NBA Player Draft, First-Round Picks
(held June 28, 2006)

Team	Player, College/Team	Team	Player, College/Team
1. Toronto	Andrea Bargnani, F, Benetton Treviso (Italy)	16. Chicago[8]	Rodney Carney[8], G-F, Memphis
2. Chicago[1]	LaMarcus Aldridge[2], F-C, Texas	17. Indiana	Shawne Williams, F, Memphis
3. Charlotte	Adam Morrison, F, Gonzaga	18. Washington	Oleksiy Pecherov, C, Paris Basket Racing (France)
4. Portland	Tyrus Thomas[3], F, Louisiana State	19. Sacramento	Quincy Douby, G, Rutgers
5. Atlanta	Shelden Williams, F, Duke	20. New York[9]	Renaldo Balkman, F, South Carolina
6. Minnesota	Brandon Roy[4], G, Washington	21. Phoenix[10]	Rajon Rondo[11], G, Kentucky
7. Boston	Randy Foye[5], G, Villanova	22. New Jersey[12]	Marcus Williams, G, Connecticut
8. Houston	Rudy Gay, F, Connecticut	23. New Jersey	Josh Boone, F, Connecticut
9. Golden State	Patrick O'Bryant, C, Bradley	24. Memphis	Kyle Lowry, G, Villanova
10. Seattle	Saer Sene, F, Verviers-Pepinster (Belgium)	25. Cleveland	Shannon Brown, G, Michigan State
11. Orlando	J.J. Redick, G, Duke	26. L.A. Lakers[13]	Jordan Farmar, G, UCLA
12. New Orleans/ Oklahoma City	Hilton Armstrong, C, Connecticut	27. Phoenix	Sergio Rodriguez[14], G, Adecco Estudiantes Madrid (Spain)
13. Philadelphia	Thabo Sefolosha[6], G, Angelico Biella (Italy)	28. Dallas	Maurice Ager, G, Michigan State
14. Utah	Ronnie Brewer, G, Arkansas	29. New York[15]	Mardy Collins, G, Temple
15. New Orleans/ Oklahoma City[7]	Cedric Simmons, F, North Carolina State	30. Portland[16]	Joel Freeland, F, Gran Canaria Fadesa (Spain)

(1) From New York. (2) Rights traded to Portland. (3) Rights traded to Chicago. (4) Rights traded to Portland. (5) Rights traded to Minnesota via Portland. (6) Rights traded to Chicago. (7) From Milwaukee. (8) Rights traded to Philadelphia. (9) From Denver via Toronto and New Jersey. (10) From L.A. Lakers via Atlanta and Boston. (11) Rights traded to Boston. (12) From L.A. Clippers via Denver and Orlando. (13) From Miami. (14) Rights traded to Portland. (15) From San Antonio. (16) From Detroit via Utah.

Number-One First-Round NBA Draft Picks, 1966-2006

Year	Team	Player, College/Team	Year	Team	Player, College/Team
1966	New York	Cazzie Russell, Michigan	1987	San Antonio	David Robinson, Navy
1967	Detroit	Jimmy Walker, Providence	1988	L.A. Clippers	Danny Manning, Kansas
1968	San Diego	Elvin Hayes, Houston	1989	Sacramento	Pervis Ellison, Louisville
1969	Milwaukee	Lew Alcindor (Kareem Abdul-Jabbar), UCLA	1990	New Jersey	Derrick Coleman, Syracuse
1970	Detroit	Bob Lanier, St. Bonaventure	1991	Charlotte	Larry Johnson, UNLV
1971	Cleveland	Austin Carr, Notre Dame	1992	Orlando	Shaquille O'Neal, LSU
1972	Portland	LaRue Martin, Loyola-Chicago	1993	Orlando	Chris Webber[2], Michigan
1973	Philadelphia	Doug Collins, Illinois State	1994	Milwaukee	Glenn Robinson, Purdue
1974	Portland	Bill Walton, UCLA	1995	Golden State	Joe Smith, Maryland
1975	Atlanta	David Thompson[1], N.C. State	1996	Philadelphia	Allen Iverson, Georgetown
1976	Houston	John Lucas, Maryland	1997	San Antonio	Tim Duncan, Wake Forest
1977	Milwaukee	Kent Benson, Indiana	1998	L.A. Clippers	Michael Olowokandi, Pacific
1978	Portland	Mychal Thompson, Minnesota	1999	Chicago	Elton Brand, Duke
1979	L.A. Lakers	Earvin "Magic" Johnson, Michigan State	2000	New Jersey	Kenyon Martin, Cincinnati
1980	Golden State	Joe Barry Carroll, Purdue	2001	Washington	Kwame Brown, Glynn Academy (HS)
1981	Dallas	Mark Aguirre, DePaul	2002	Houston	Yao Ming, Shanghai Sharks (China)
1982	L.A. Lakers	James Worthy, North Carolina	2003	Cleveland	LeBron James, St. Vincent-St. Mary (HS)
1983	Houston	Ralph Sampson, Virginia	2004	Orlando	Dwight Howard, Southwest Atlanta Christian Academy (HS)
1984	Houston	Akeem Olajuwon, Houston			
1985	New York	Patrick Ewing, Georgetown	2005	Milwaukee	Andrew Bogut, Utah
1986	Cleveland	Brad Daugherty, North Carolina	2006	Toronto	Andrea Bargnani, Benneton Treviso (Italy)

(1) Signed with Denver of the ABA. (2) Traded to Golden State for rights to Anfernee Hardaway and three future first-round draft choices.

All-Time NBA Statistical Leaders
(At the end of the 2005-06 season. *Player active in 2005-06 season.)

Scoring Average
(Minimum 400 games or 10,000 points)

	G	Pts	Avg
Michael Jordan	1,072	32,292	30.1
Wilt Chamberlain	1,045	31,419	30.1
*Allen Iverson	682	19,115	28.0
Elgin Baylor	846	23,149	27.4
Jerry West	932	25,192	27.0
Bob Pettit	792	20,880	26.4
*Shaquille O'Neal	941	24,764	26.3
George Gervin	791	20,708	26.2
Oscar Robertson	1,040	26,710	25.7
Karl Malone	1,476	36,928	25.0

Field Goal Percentage
(Minimum 2,000 field goals made)

	FGA	FGM	Pct
Artis Gilmore	9,570	5,732	.599
Mark West	4,356	2,528	.580
*Shaquille O'Neal	16,915	9,808	.580
Steve Johnson	4,965	2,841	.572
Darryl Dawkins	6,079	3,477	.572
James Donaldson	5,442	3,105	.571
Jeff Ruland	3,734	2,105	.564
Kareem Abdul-Jabbar	28,307	15,837	.559
Kevin McHale	12,334	6,830	.554
Bobby Jones	6,199	3,412	.550

Free Throw Percentage
(Minimum 1,200 free throws made)

	FTA	FTM	Pct
Mark Price	2,362	2,135	.904
Rick Barry	4,243	3,818	.900
*Steve Nash	1,926	1,726	.896
*Peja Stojakovic	2,086	1,864	.894
Calvin Murphy	3,864	3,445	.892
Scott Skiles	1,741	1,548	.889
Reggie Miller	7,026	6,237	.888
*Ray Allen	3,273	2,901	.886
Larry Bird	4,471	3,960	.886
Bill Sharman	3,559	3,143	.883

3-Point Field Goal Percentage
(Minimum 250 3-point field goals made)

	3-FGA	3-FGM	Pct
Steve Kerr	1,599	726	.454
Hubert Davis	1,651	728	.441
Drazen Petrovic	583	255	.437
Tim Legler	603	260	.431
B. J. Armstrong	1,026	436	.425
*Steve Nash	2,178	917	.421
*Ben Gordon	713	300	.421
Wesley Person	2,754	1,150	.418
*Raja Bell	844	347	.411
Dana Barros	2,652	1,090	.411

Games Played

Robert Parish	1,611
Kareem Abdul-Jabbar	1,560
John Stockton	1,504
Karl Malone	1,476
Kevin Willis	1,419
Reggie Miller	1,389
*Clifford Robinson	1,330
Moses Malone	1,329
Buck Williams	1,307
Elvin Hayes	1,303

Field Goals Attempted

Kareem Abdul-Jabbar	28,307
Karl Malone	26,210
Michael Jordan	24,537
Elvin Hayes	24,272
John Havlicek	23,930
Wilt Chamberlain	23,497
Dominique Wilkins	21,589
Alex English	21,036
Hakeem Olajuwon	20,991
Elgin Baylor	20,171

Points

Kareem Abdul-Jabbar	38,387
Karl Malone	36,928
Michael Jordan	32,292
Wilt Chamberlain	31,419
Moses Malone	27,409
Elvin Hayes	27,313
Hakeem Olajuwon	26,946
Oscar Robertson	26,710
Dominique Wilkins	26,668
John Havlicek	26,395

Minutes Played

Kareem Abdul-Jabbar	57,446
Karl Malone	54,852
Elvin Hayes	50,000
Wilt Chamberlain	47,859
John Stockton	47,764
Reggie Miller	47,619
John Havlicek	46,471
Robert Parish	45,704
Gary Payton	45,614
Moses Malone	45,071

Field Goals Made

Kareem Abdul-Jabbar	15,837
Karl Malone	13,528
Wilt Chamberlain	12,681
Michael Jordan	12,192
Elvin Hayes	10,976
Hakeem Olajuwon	10,749
Alex English	10,659
John Havlicek	10,513
Dominique Wilkins	9,963
*Shaquille O'Neal	9,808

Rebounds

Wilt Chamberlain	23,924
Bill Russell	21,620
Kareem Abdul-Jabbar	17,440
Elvin Hayes	16,279
Moses Malone	16,212
Karl Malone	14,968
Robert Parish	14,715
Nate Thurmond	14,464
Walt Bellamy	14,241
Wes Unseld	13,769

Personal Fouls

Kareem Abdul-Jabbar	4,657
Karl Malone	4,578
Robert Parish	4,443
Charles Oakley	4,421
Hakeem Olajuwon	4,383
Buck Williams	4,267
Elvin Hayes	4,193
*Kevin Willis	4,161
Otis Thorpe	4,146
James Edwards	4,042

3-Point Field Goals Attempted

Reggie Miller	6,486
*Ray Allen	4,396
Tim Hardaway	4,345
*Nick Van Exel	4,278
Dale Ellis	4,266
Vernon Maxwell	3,931
Glen Rice	3,896
*Eddie Jones	3,809
Dan Majerle	3,798
Antoine Walker	3,771

Assists

John Stockton	15,806
Mark Jackson	10,334
Magic Johnson	10,141
Oscar Robertson	9,887
Isiah Thomas	9,061
*Gary Payton	8,765
Rod Strickland	7,987
*Jason Kidd	7,955
Maurice Cheeks	7,392
Lenny Wilkens	7,211

Blocks

Hakeem Olajuwon	3,830
Kareem Abdul-Jabbar	3,189
*Dikembe Mutombo	3,154
Mark Eaton	3,064
David Robinson	2,954
Patrick Ewing	2,894
Tree Rollins	2,542
*Shaquille O'Neal	2,377
Robert Parish	2,361
*Alonzo Mourning	2,136

3-Point Field Goals Made

Reggie Miller	2,560
*Ray Allen	1,755
Dale Ellis	1,719
Glen Rice	1,559
Tim Hardaway	1,542
*Nick Van Exel	1,528
*Eddie Jones	1,434
Dan Majerle	1,360
Mitch Richmond	1,326
Allan Houston	1,305

Steals

John Stockton	3,265
Michael Jordan	2,514
*Gary Payton	2,402
Maurice Cheeks	2,310
Scottie Pippen	2,307
Clyde Drexler	2,207
Hakeem Olajuwon	2,162
Alvin Robertson	2,112
Karl Malone	2,085
Mookie Blaylock	2,075

All-Time NBA Regular Season Coaching Victories
(At the end of the 2005-06 season, ranked by wins. *Active through 2005-06 season.)

Coach	W-L	Pct	Coach	W-L	Pct	Coach	W-L	Pct
Lenny Wilkens	1,315-1,133	.537	Dick Motta	935-1,017	.479	John MacLeod	707-657	.518
Don Nelson	1,190-880	.575	*Phil Jackson	877-353	.713	Red Holzman	696-604	.535
*Pat Riley	1,151-589	.661	Jack Ramsay	864-783	.525	*Mike Fratello	661-524	.558
*Larry Brown	1,010-800	.558	Cotton Fitzsimmons	832-775	.518	Chuck Daly	638-437	.593
*Jerry Sloan	984-658	.599	Gene Shue	784-861	.477	Doug Moe	628-529	.543
Bill Fitch	944-1,106	.460	*George Karl	784-545	.590	Alvin Attles	557-518	.518
Red Auerbach	938-479	.662	*Rick Adelman	752-481	.610			

Basketball Hall of Fame, Springfield, MA

(*2006 inductees. **Enshrined as both a player and coach.)

PLAYERS

Abdul-Jabbar, Kareem
Archibald, Nate
Arizin, Paul
*Barkley, Charles
Barlow, Thomas
Barry, Rick
Baylor, Elgin
Beckman, John
Bellamy, Walt
Belov, Sergei
Bing, Dave
Bird, Larry
Blazejowski, Carol
Borgmann, Bennie
Bradley, Bill
Brennan, Joseph
Cervi, Al
Chamberlain, Wilt
Cooper, Charles
Cosic, Kresimir
Cousy, Bob
Cowens, Dave
Crawford, Joan
Cunningham, Billy
Curry, Denise
Dalipagic, Drazen
Davies, Bob
DeBernardi, Forrest
DeBusschere, Dave
Dehnert, Dutch
Donovan, Anne
Drexler, Clyde
*Dumars, Joe
Endacott, Paul
English, Alex
Erving, Julius
Foster, Bud
Frazier, Walt
Friedman, Max
Fulks, Joe
Gale, Lauren
Gallatin, Harry
Gates, Pop
Gervin, George
Gola, Tom
Goodrich, Gail
Greer, Hal
Gruenig, Ace
Hagan, Cliff
Hanson, Victor
Harris-Stewart, Lusia
Havlicek, John
Hawkins, Connie
Hayes, Elvin
Haynes, Marques
Heinsohn, Tom

Holman, Nat
Houbregs, Bob
Howell, Bailey
Hyatt, Chuck
Issel, Dan
Jeannette, Buddy
Johnson, Earvin "Magic"
Johnson, William
Johnston, Neil
Jones, K.C.
Jones, Sam
Krause, Moose
Kurland, Bob
Lanier, Bob
Lapchick, Joe
Lieberman, Nancy
Lovellette, Clyde
Lucas, Jerry
Luisetti, Hank
Macauley, Ed
Malone, Moses
Maravich, Pete
Marcari, Hortencia
Martin, Slater
McAdoo, Bob
McCracken, Branch
McCracken, Jack
McDermott, Bobby
McGuire, Dick
McHale, Kevin
Meneghin, Dino
Meyers, Ann
Mikan, George
Mikkelsen, Vern
Miller, Cheryl
Monroe, Earl
Murphy, Calvin
Murphy, Stretch
Page, Pat
Parish, Robert
Petrovic, Drazen
Pettit, Bob
Phillip, Andy
Pollard, Jim
Ramsey, Frank
Reed, Willis
Risen, Arnie
Robertson, Oscar
Roosma, John
Russell, Bill
Russell, Honey
Schayes, Adolph
Schmidt, Ernest
Schommer, John
Sedran, Barney
Semjonova, Uljana
**Sharman, Bill

Steinmetz, Christian
Stokes, Maurice
Thomas, Isiah
Thompson, Cat
Thompson, David
Thurmond, Nate
Twyman, Jack
Unseld, Wes
Vandivier, Fuzzy
Wachter, Edward
Walton, Bill
Wanzer, Bobby
West, Jerry
White, Nera
**Wilkens, Lenny
*Wilkins, Dominique
Woodard, Lynette
**Wooden, John
Worthy, James
Yardley, George

COACHES

Allen, Phog
Anderson, Harold
Auerbach, Red
*Auriemma, Geno
Barmore, Leon
Barry, Sam
Blood, Ernest
Boeheim, Jim
Brown, Hubie
Brown, Larry
Calhoun, Jim
Cann, Howard
Carlson, Clifford
Carnesecca, Lou
Carnevale, Ben
Carril, Pete
Case, Everett
Chaney, John
Conradt, Jody
Crum, Denny
Daly, Chuck
Dean, Everett
Diaz-Miguel, Antonio
Diddle, Edgar
Drake, Bruce
Gaines, Clarence
*Gamba, Sandro
Gardner, Jack
Gill, Slats
Gomelsky, Aleksandr
Gunter, Sue
Hannum, Alex
Harshman, Marv
Haskins, Don
Hickey, Edgar

Hobson, Howard
Holzman, Red
Iba, Hank
Julian, Alvin
Keaney, Frank
Keogan, George
Knight, Bob
Krzyzewski, Mike
Kundla, John
Lambert, Ward
Litwack, Harry
Loeffler, Kenneth
Lonborg, Dutch
McCutchan, Arad
McGuire, Al
McGuire, Frank
McLendon, John
Meanwell, Dr. Walter
Meyer, Ray
Miller, Ralph
Moore, Billie
Newell, Pete
Nikolic, Aleksandar
Olson, Lute
Ramsay, Jack
Rubini, Cesare
Rupp, Adolph
Sachs, Leonard
**Sharman, Bill
Shelton, Everett
Smith, Dean
Summitt, Pat
Taylor, Fred
Thompson, John
Wade, Margaret
Watts, Stan
**Wilkens, Lenny
**Wooden, John
Woolpert, Phil
Wootten, Morgan
Yow, Kay

TEAMS

First Team

Original Celtics
Buffalo Germans
NY Renaissance
Harlem Globetrotters

REFEREES

Enright, James
Hepbron, George
Hoyt, George
Kennedy, Matthew
Leith, Lloyd
Mihalik, Red
Nucatola, John
Quigley, Ernest

Shirley, J. Dallas
Strom, Earl
Tobey, David
Walsh, David

CONTRIBUTORS

Abbott, Senda Berenson
Bee, Clair
Biasone, Danny
Brown, Walter
Bunn, John
Colangelo, Jerry
Douglas, Bob
Duer, Al
Embry, Wayne
Fagan, Cliff
Fisher, Harry
Fleisher, Larry
*Gavitt, David
Gottlieb, Edward
Gulick, Dr. Luther
Harrison, Lester
Hearn, Chick
Hepp, Dr. Ferenc
Hickox, Edward
Hinkle, Tony
Irish, Ned
Jones, R. William
Kennedy, Walter
Lemon, Meadowlark
Liston, Emil
Lloyd, Earl
Mokray, Bill
Morgan, Ralph
Morgenweck, Frank
Naismith, Dr. James
Newton, C.M.
O'Brien, John
O'Brien, Larry
Olsen, Harold
Podoloff, Maurice
Porter, Henry V.
Reid, William
Ripley, Elmer
St. John, Lynn
Saperstein, Abe
Schabinger, Arthur
Stagg, Alonzo
Stankovic, Boris
Steitz, Edward
Taylor, Chuck
Teague, Bertha
Tower, Oswald
Trester, Arthur
Wells, Clifford
Wilke, Lou
Zollner, Fred

NBA Home Courts[1]

Team	Name (built)	Capacity	Team	Name (built)	Capacity
Atlanta	Philips Arena (1999)	18,729	Milwaukee	Bradley Center (1988)	18,717
Boston	TD Banknorth Garden[2] (1995)	18,854	Minnesota	Target Center (1990)	19,006
Charlotte	Charlotte Bobcats Arena (2005)	19,026	New Jersey	Continental Airlines Arena[4] (1981)	20,049
Chicago	United Center (1994)	21,711	New Orleans[5]	New Orleans Arena (1999)	18,500
Cleveland	Quicken Loans Arena (1994)	20,562	New York	Madison Square Garden (IV) (1968)	19,763
Dallas	American Airlines Center (2001)	19,200	Orlando	TD Waterhouse Centre[6] (1989)	17,248
Denver	Pepsi Center (1999)	19,099	Philadelphia	Wachovia Center[7] (1996)	20,444
Detroit	The Palace of Auburn Hills (1988)	22,076	Phoenix	U.S. Airways Center (1992)	19,023
Golden State	Arena in Oakland[3] (1966)	19,596	Portland	Rose Garden (1995)	19,980
Houston	Toyota Center (2003)	18,300	Sacramento	ARCO Arena (1988)	17,317
Indiana	Conseco Fieldhouse (1999)	18,345	San Antonio	AT&T Center[8] (2002)	18,500
L.A. Clippers	Staples Center (1999)	19,060	Seattle	KeyArena at Seattle Center[9] (1962)	17,072
L.A. Lakers	Staples Center (1999)	18,997	Toronto	Air Canada Centre (1999)	19,800
Memphis	FedExForum (2004)	18,400	Utah	Delta Center (1991)	19,911
Miami	American Airlines Arena (1999)	19,600	Washington	Verizon Center[10] (1997)	20,674

(1) At the end of the 2005-06 season. (2) Fleet Center, 1995-2005. (3) Oakland Coliseum Arena, 1966-96; renovated and renamed in 1997. (4) Brendan Byrne/Meadowlands Arena, 1981-96. (5) Due to Hurricane Katrina, the Hornets played 6 games of the 2005-06 season at the Pete Maravich Center on the campus of Louisiana State University in Baton Rouge and 35 games at the Ford Center (built 2002; capacity 19,599) in Oklahoma City, OK. The Hornets are expected to play the majority of their 2006-07 season games at the Ford Center and 6 games at the New Orleans Arena. (6) Orlando Arena, 1989-2000. (7) CoreStates Center, 1996-98; First Union Center, 1998-2003. (8) SBC Center, 2002-06. (9) Seattle Center Coliseum, 1962-94; renovated, expanded, and renamed in 1995. (10) MCI Center, 1997-2006.

WOMEN'S PROFESSIONAL BASKETBALL

WNBA 2006: Detroit Shock Defeat Sacramento Monarchs for Second Title

The Detroit Shock defeated the Sacramento Monarchs, 80-75, in Detroit, MI, in the 5th and deciding game of the 2006 WNBA Finals, Sept. 9. Detroit guard Deanna Nolan scored 24 points in the final game, including 10 to lead the Shock's second-half rally. Nolan, who averaged 17.8 points and shot 44.6% from the field in the finals, was named the series' most valuable player.

The Shock had appeared to be on the ropes after trading hard-earned wins in games 1 and 2 and losing decisively to the defending champion Monarchs in game 3. But the Shock, led by Katie Smith's 22 points, bounced back to win game 4 by 20 points, tying the series 2-2. The Shock, which celebrated its second WNBA title in 4 years, were coached by former Detroit Pistons center Bill Laimbeer. The Shock joined the Houston Comets (1997-2000) and Los Angeles Sparks (2001-02) as the only WNBA teams to have won multiple championships. A sellout crowd (19,671) watched game 5 in Detroit's Joe Louis Arena. The WNBA finals attendance record (22,076) was set in 2003 when the Shock hosted the Sparks at the Palace of Auburn Hills in game 3.

WNBA Final Standings, 2006 Season

x-clinched playoff berth; y-clinched top seed

Eastern Conference

	W	L	Pct	GB
y-Connecticut	26	8	0.765	—
x-Detroit	23	11	0.676	3.0
x-Indiana	21	13	0.618	5.0
x-Washington	18	16	0.529	8.0
Charlotte	11	23	0.324	15.0
New York	11	23	0.324	15.0
Chicago	5	29	0.147	21.0

Western Conference

	W	L	Pct	GB
y-Los Angeles	25	9	0.735	—
x-Sacramento	21	13	0.618	4.0
x-Houston	18	16	0.529	7.0
x-Seattle	18	16	0.529	7.0
Phoenix	18	16	0.529	7.0
San Antonio	13	21	0.382	12.0
Minnesota	10	24	0.294	15.0

2006 WNBA Playoffs

(Playoff seeding in parentheses; conference winner automatically gets top seed)

Eastern Conference

Connecticut (1) defeated Washington (4), 2 games to 0
Detroit (2) defeated Indiana (3), 2 games to 0
Detroit (2) defeated Connecticut (1), 2 games to 1

Western Conference

Los Angeles (1) defeated Seattle (4), 2 games to 1
Sacramento (2) defeated Houston (3), 2 games to 0
Sacramento (2) defeated Los Angeles (1), 2 games to 0

WNBA Championship (Best of 5)

Detroit defeated Sacramento 3 games to 2 [71-95, 73-63, 69-89, 72-52, 80-75]

2006 All-WNBA Teams

First Team	Position	Second Team
Tamika Catchings, Indiana	Forward	Taj McWilliams-Franklin, Connecticut
Lauren Jackson, Seattle	Forward	Sheryl Swoopes, Houston
Diana Taurasi, Phoenix	Guard	Alana Beard, Washington
Katie Douglas, Connecticut	Guard	Seimone Augustus, Minnesota
Lisa Leslie, Los Angeles	Center	Cheryl Ford, Detroit

WNBA Statistical Leaders and Awards in 2006

Minutes played — 1,134, Diana Taurasi, Phoenix
Total points — 860, Diana Taurasi, Phoenix
Points per game — 25.3, Diana Taurasi, Phoenix
Highest field goal % — .537, Erin Buescher, Sacramento
Highest 3-pt. field goal % — .431, Erin Thorn, New York
Highest free throw % — .960, Becky Hammon, New York
Total rebounds — 363, Cheryl Ford, Detroit
Rebounds per game — 11.3, Cheryl Ford, Detroit

Total assists — 183, Nikki Teasley, Washington
Assists per game — 5.38, Nikki Teasley, Washington
Total steals — 94, Tamika Catchings, Indiana
Steals per game — 2.94, Tamika Catchings, Indiana
Total blocked shots — 85, Margo Dydek, Connecticut
Coach of the year — Mike Thibault, Connecticut
Defensive player of year — Tamika Catchings, Indiana
Most improved player — Erin Buescher, Sacramento

WNBA Champions

Year	Regular Season Eastern Conference	Western Conference	Champion	Coach	Runner-Up
1997	Houston Comets	Phoenix Mercury	Houston	Van Chancellor	New York
1998	Cleveland Rockers	Houston Comets	Houston	Van Chancellor	Phoenix
1999	New York Liberty	Houston Comets	Houston	Van Chancellor	New York
2000	New York Liberty	Los Angeles Sparks	Houston	Van Chancellor	New York
2001	Cleveland Rockers	Los Angeles Sparks	Los Angeles	Michael Cooper	Charlotte
2002	New York Liberty	Los Angeles Sparks	Los Angeles	Michael Cooper	New York
2003	Detroit Shock	Los Angeles Sparks	Detroit	Bill Laimbeer	Los Angeles
2004	Connecticut Sun	Los Angeles Sparks	Seattle	Ann Donovan	Connecticut
2005	Connecticut Sun	Sacramento Monarchs	Sacramento	John Whisenant	Connecticut
2006	Connecticut Sun	Sacramento Monarchs	Detroit	Bill Laimbeer	Sacramento

WNBA Scoring Leaders

Year	Scoring Champion	Pts	Avg	Year	Scoring Champion	Pts	Avg
1997	Cynthia Cooper, Houston	621	22.2	2002	Chamique Holdsclaw, Washington	397	19.9
1998	Cynthia Cooper, Houston	680	22.7	2003	Lauren Jackson, Seattle	698	21.2
1999	Cynthia Cooper, Houston	686	22.1	2004	Lauren Jackson, Seattle	634	20.5
2000	Sheryl Swoopes, Houston	643	20.7	2005	Sheryl Swoopes, Houston	614	18.6
2001	Katie Smith, Minnesota	739	23.1	2006	Diana Taurasi, Phoenix	860	25.3

WNBA Finals MVP

Year	Player
1997	Cynthia Cooper, Houston
1998	Cynthia Cooper, Houston
1999	Yolanda Griffith, Sacramento
2000	Sheryl Swoopes, Houston
2001	Lisa Leslie, Los Angeles
2002	Sheryl Swoopes, Houston
2003	Lauren Jackson, Seattle
2004	Lisa Leslie, Los Angeles
2005	Sheryl Swoopes, Houston
2006	Deanna Nolan, Detroit

WNBA Most Valuable Player

Year	Player
1997	Cynthia Cooper, Houston
1998	Cynthia Cooper, Houston
1999	Cynthia Cooper, Houston
2000	Cynthia Cooper, Houston
2001	Lisa Leslie, Los Angeles
2002	Lisa Leslie, Los Angeles
2003	Ruth Riley, Detroit
2004	Betty Lennox, Seattle
2005	Yolanda Griffith, Sacramento
2006	Lisa Leslie, Los Angeles

WNBA Rookie of the Year

Year	Player
1997	no award
1998	Tracy Reid, Charlotte
1999	Chamique Holdsclaw, Washington
2000	Betty Lennox, Minnesota
2001	Jackie Stiles, Portland
2002	Tamika Catchings, Indiana
2003	Cheryl Ford, Detroit
2004	Diana Taurasi, Phoenix
2005	Temeka Johnson, Washington
2006	Seimone Augustus, Minnesota

COLLEGE BASKETBALL
Men's Final NCAA Division I Conference Standings, 2005-06
(*conference tournament champion)

America East

	Conf. W	Conf. L	All W	All L
Albany*	13	3	21	11
Binghamton	12	4	16	13
Hartford	9	7	13	15
Boston Univ.	9	7	12	16
New Hampshire	8	8	12	17
Vermont	7	9	13	17
Maine	7	9	12	16
MD Baltimore Co.	5	11	10	19
Stony Brook	2	14	4	24

Atlantic Coast[1]

	Conf. W	Conf. L	All W	All L
Duke*	14	2	32	4
North Carolina	12	4	23	8
Boston College	11	5	28	8
NC State	10	6	22	10
Florida State	9	7	20	10
Maryland	8	8	19	3
Clemson	7	9	19	13
Miami (FL)	7	9	18	16
Virginia	7	9	15	15
Virginia Tech	4	12	14	16
Georgia Tech	4	12	11	17
Wake Forest	3	13	17	17

Atlantic Sun

	Conf. W	Conf. L	All W	All L
Lipscomb	15	5	21	11
Belmont*	15	5	20	11
Florida Atlantic	14	6	15	13
Gardner-Webb	13	7	15	13
E. Tennessee State	12	8	15	13
Stetson	11	9	14	18
Kennesaw State	10	10	12	17
Campbell	9	11	10	18
Mercer	7	13	9	19
North Florida	3	17	6	22
Jacksonville	1	19	1	26

Atlantic 10[1]

	Conf. W	Conf. L	All W	All L
George Washington	16	0	27	3
Charlotte	11	5	19	13
La Salle	10	6	18	10
St. Louis	10	6	16	13
St. Joseph's	9	7	19	14
Fordham	9	7	16	16
Xavier*	8	8	21	11
Temple	8	8	17	15
Rhode Island	8	8	14	14
Massachusetts	8	8	13	15
Dayton	6	10	14	17
Richmond	6	10	13	17
St. Bonaventure	2	14	8	19
Duquesne	1	15	3	24

Big East[1]

	Conf. W	Conf. L	All W	All L
Connecticut	14	2	30	4
Villanova	14	2	28	5
West Virginia	11	5	22	11
Pittsburgh	10	6	25	8
Georgetown	10	6	23	10
Marquette	10	6	20	11
Seton Hall	9	7	18	12
Cincinnati	8	8	21	13
Syracuse*	7	9	23	12
Rutgers	7	9	19	14
Louisville	6	10	21	13
Notre Dame	6	10	23	12
Providence	5	11	12	15
DePaul	5	11	12	15
St. John's	5	11	12	15
South Florida	1	15	7	22

Big Sky

	Conf. W	Conf. L	All W	All L
Northern Arizona*	12	2	21	11
Montana	10	4	24	7
Eastern Wash.	9	5	15	15
Montana State	7	7	15	15
Sacramento St.	5	9	15	15
Portland State	5	9	12	16
Idaho State	4	10	13	14
Weber State	4	10	10	17

Big South

	Conf. W	Conf. L	All W	All L
Winthrop*	13	3	23	8
Birmingham South	12	4	19	9
Coastal Carolina	12	4	20	10
Radford	9	7	16	13
High Point	8	8	16	13
Charleston Southern	7	9	13	16
NC Asheville	6	10	9	19
Liberty	3	13	7	23
VA Military Institute	2	14	7	20

Big 10

	Conf. W	Conf. L	All W	All L
Ohio State	12	4	26	6
Illinois	11	5	26	7
Iowa*	11	5	25	9
Wisconsin	9	7	19	12
Indiana	9	7	19	12
Michigan	8	8	22	11
Michigan State	8	8	22	12
Penn State	6	10	15	15
Northwestern	6	10	14	15
Minnesota	5	11	16	15
Purdue	3	13	9	19

Big 12

	Conf. W	Conf. L	All W	All L
Kansas*	14	3	25	8
Texas	13	4	30	7
Oklahoma	11	5	20	9
Texas A&M	10	6	22	9
Colorado	9	7	20	10
Nebraska	7	9	19	14
Kansas State	6	10	15	13
Iowa State	6	10	16	14
Oklahoma State	6	10	17	16
Texas Tech	6	10	15	17
Missouri	5	11	12	16
Baylor	4	12	4	13

Big West

	Conf. W	Conf. L	All W	All L
Pacific*	12	2	24	8
UC Irvine	10	4	16	13
Long Beach State	9	5	18	12
Cal. Poly.	7	7	10	19
UC Santa Barbara	6	8	15	14
CSU Fullerton	5	9	16	13
CSU Northridge	4	10	11	17
UC Riverside	3	11	5	23

Colonial Athletic Association[1]

	Conf. W	Conf. L	All W	All L
George Mason	15	3	27	8
UNC Wilmington*	15	3	25	8
Hofstra	14	4	26	7
Old Dominion	13	5	24	10
Northeastern	12	6	19	11
VA Commonwealth	11	7	19	10
Drexel	8	10	15	16
Towson	8	10	12	16
Delaware	4	14	9	21
William & Mary	3	15	8	20
Georgia State	3	15	7	22
James Madison	2	16	5	23

Conference USA

	Conf. W	Conf. L	All W	All L
Memphis*	13	1	33	4
UAB	12	2	24	7
UTEP	11	3	21	10
Houston	9	5	21	10
Central Florida	7	7	14	15
Rice	6	8	12	16
Tulane	6	8	12	17
Tulsa	6	8	11	17
Marshall	5	9	12	16
SMU	4	10	13	16
Southern Miss	3	11	10	21
East Carolina	2	12	8	20

Horizon League

	Conf. W	Conf. L	All W	All L
Wisc.-Milwaukee*	12	4	22	9
Butler	11	5	20	13
Loyola (Chicago)	8	8	19	11
Illinois-Chicago	8	8	16	15
Detroit	8	8	16	16
Wisc.-Green Bay	8	8	16	16
Wright State	8	8	13	15
Cleveland State	5	11	10	18
Youngstown State	4	12	7	21

Ivy League[2]

	Conf. W	Conf. L	All W	All L
Penn	12	2	20	9
Princeton	10	4	12	15
Cornell	8	6	13	15
Yale	7	7	15	14
Brown	6	8	10	17
Harvard	5	9	13	14
Columbia	4	10	11	16
Dartmouth	4	10	6	21

Metro Atlantic Athletic

	Conf. W	Conf. L	All W	All L
Manhattan	14	4	20	11
Iona*	13	5	23	8
Marist	12	6	19	10
Siena	10	8	15	13
St. Peter's	9	9	17	15
Loyola (Maryland)	8	10	15	13
Niagara	7	11	11	18
Fairfield	7	11	9	19
Canisius	6	12	9	20
Rider	4	14	8	20

Mid-American
East Division

	Conf. W	Conf. L	All W	All L
Kent State	15	3	25	9
Akron	14	4	23	10
Miami (OH)*	14	4	18	11
Ohio	11	8	19	11
Buffalo	8	10	19	13
Bowling Green	5	13	9	21

West Division

	Conf. W	Conf. L	All W	All L
Northern Illinois	12	6	17	11
Toledo	10	8	20	11
Western Michigan	10	8	14	17
Ball St.	6	12	10	18
Eastern Michigan	3	15	7	21
Central Michigan	1	17	4	24

Mid-Continent

	Conf. W	Conf. L	All W	All L
Indiana-Purdue	13	3	19	10
Oral Roberts*	13	3	21	12
Missouri-Kansas City	11	5	14	14
Valparaiso	8	8	17	12
Chicago State	8	8	11	19
Southern Utah	8	8	10	20
Oakland	6	10	11	18
Western Illinois	3	13	7	21
Centenary	2	14	4	23

Mid-Eastern Athletic

	Conf. W	Conf. L	All W	All L
Delaware State	16	2	21	14
Coppin State	12	6	12	18
Bethune-Cookman	11	7	15	15
South Carolina St.	11	7	14	16
Hampton*	10	8	16	16
Florida A&M	10	8	14	17
Norfolk State	10	8	13	18
North Carolina A&T	6	12	6	23
Howard	5	13	7	22
MD-Eastern Shore	4	14	7	22
Morgan State	4	14	4	26

Missouri Valley

	Conf. W	Conf. L	All W	All L
Wichita State	14	4	26	9
Missouri State	12	6	22	9
Southern Illinois*	12	6	22	11
Creighton	12	6	20	10
Northern Iowa	11	7	23	10
Bradley	11	7	22	11
Drake	5	13	12	19
Evansville	5	13	10	19
Indiana State	4	14	13	16
Illinois State	4	14	9	29

Mountain West

	Conf. W	Conf. L	All W	All L
San Diego State*	13	3	24	9
Air Force	12	4	26	7
Brigham Young	12	4	20	9
UNLV	10	6	17	13
New Mexico	8	8	17	15
Utah	6	10	14	15
Wyoming	5	11	14	18
Colorado State	4	12	16	15
TCU	2	14	6	25

Northeast

	Conf. W	Conf. L	All W	All L
Fairleigh Dickinson	14	4	20	12
Central Conn. State	13	5	18	11
Monmouth*	12	6	19	15
Mount St. Mary's	11	7	13	17
Robert Morris	10	8	15	14
Long Island	9	9	12	16
Sacred Heart	8	10	11	17

	Conf. W	L	All W	L
Quinnipiac	7	11	12	16
St. Francis (NY)	7	11	10	17
Wagner	6	12	13	14
St. Francis (PA)	2	16	4	24
Ohio Valley				
Murray State*	17	3	24	7
Samford	14	7	20	11
Tennessee Tech	13	7	19	12
Jacksonville State	12	8	16	13
Austin Peay	11	9	17	14
Eastern Kentucky	11	9	14	16
Tennessee State	11	9	13	15
Tennessee-Martin	9	11	13	15
Eastern Illinois	5	15	6	21
SE Missouri State	4	16	7	20
Morehead State	3	17	4	23
Pacific-10				
UCLA*	14	4	32	7
Washington	13	5	26	7
California	12	6	20	11
Arizona	11	7	20	13
Stanford	11	7	16	14
USC	8	10	17	13
Oregon	7	11	15	18
Oregon State	5	13	13	18
Arizona State	5	13	11	17
Washington State	4	14	11	17
Patriot				
Bucknell*	14	0	27	5
Holy Cross	11	3	20	12
Lehigh	11	3	19	12
American	7	7	12	17
Lafayette	5	9	11	17
Colgate	4	10	10	19
Army	3	11	10	18
Navy	1	13	5	22
Southeastern				
East Division				
Tennessee	12	4	22	8
Florida*	10	6	33	6
Kentucky	9	7	22	13
Vanderbilt	7	9	17	13
South Carolina	6	10	23	15
Georgia	5	11	15	15

	Conf. W	L	All W	L
West Division				
LSU	14	2	27	9
Arkansas	10	6	22	10
Alabama	10	6	18	13
Ole Miss	5	11	15	15
Mississippi State	4	12	14	16
Auburn	4	12	12	16
Southern				
North Division				
Elon	10	4	15	14
Chattanooga	8	6	19	13
Western Carolina	7	7	13	17
Appalachian State	6	8	14	16
NC Greensboro	4	10	12	19
South Division				
Georgia Southern	11	4	20	10
Davidson*	10	5	20	11
Charleston	9	6	17	11
Furman	8	7	15	13
Wofford	6	9	11	18
Citadel	1	14	10	21
Southland				
Northwestern State*	15	1	26	8
Sam Houston State	11	5	22	9
SE Louisiana	10	6	16	12
Stephen F. Austin	9	7	17	12
Lamar	9	7	17	14
McNeese State	9	7	14	14
Texas-Arlington	7	9	14	16
Texas-San Antonio	6	10	11	17
Louisiana-Monroe	6	10	10	18
Nicholls State	5	11	9	18
Texas State	1	15	3	24
Southwestern Athletic				
Southern*	15	3	19	13
Grambling St.	11	7	14	13
Alabama A&M	11	7	13	13
Jackson State	10	8	15	17
Alabama State	10	8	12	18
Miss. Valley State	9	9	9	19
Ark.-Pine Bluff	8	10	13	16
Alcorn State	8	10	8	20
Texas Southern	6	12	8	22
Prairie View A&M	2	16	5	24

	Conf. W	L	All W	L
Sun Belt				
East Division				
Western Kentucky	12	2	23	8
Middle Tenn. State	8	6	16	12
Arkansas State	7	7	12	18
Ark.-Little Rock	5	9	14	15
Florida Intl.	4	10	8	20
West Division				
South Alabama*	12	3	24	7
Denver	7	8	16	15
Lou.-Lafayette	7	8	13	16
North Texas	6	9	14	14
Troy	6	9	14	15
New Orleans	6	9	10	19
West Coast				
Gonzaga*	14	0	29	4
St. Mary's (CA)	8	6	17	12
Loyola Marymount	8	6	12	18
San Francisco	7	7	11	17
San Diego	6	8	18	12
Santa Clara	5	9	13	16
Portland	5	9	11	18
Pepperdine	3	11	7	20
Western Athletic				
Nevada*	16	2	27	6
Utah State	11	5	23	9
Louisiana Tech	11	5	20	13
Hawaii	10	6	17	11
New Mexico State	10	6	16	14
Fresno State	8	8	15	13
Boise State	6	10	14	15
San Jose State	2	14	6	25
Idaho	1	15	4	25
Independents				
TX A&M-Corp. Christi	—	—	20	8
North Dakota State	—	—	16	12
Utah Valley State	—	—	16	13
I-P Fort Wayne	—	—	10	18
Longwood	—	—	10	20
South Dakota State	—	—	9	20
UC Davis	—	—	8	20
TX Pan American	—	—	7	24
Northern Colorado	—	—	5	24
Savannah State	—	—	2	28

(1) Conference changes in 2005 included: Boston College to ACC; E. Tennessee State, Kennesaw State, and North Florida to Atlantic Sun; Charlotte and St. Louis to Atlantic 10; Cincinnati, DePaul, Louisville, Marquette, and South Florida to Big East; Northeastern and Georgia State to Colonial Athletic Association; Central Florida, Marshall, Rice, SMU, Tulsa, and UTEP to Conference USA; Troy to Sun Belt. (2) Conference does not hold a tournament.

All-Time Winningest Division I College Teams by Percentage

(through 2005-06 season)

TEAM	Yrs	Won	Lost	Pct.	TEAM	Yrs	Won	Lost	Pct.
Kentucky	103	1,926	596	0.764	St. John's-NY	99	1,689	817	0.674
N. Carolina	96	1,883	689	0.732	W. Kentucky	87	1,526	753	0.670
UNLV	48	980	403	0.724	Utah	98	1,584	814	0.661
UCLA	87	1,580	708	0.709	Illinois	101	1,546	812	0.656
Kansas	108	1,873	777	0.707	Louisville	92	1,505	806	0.651
Duke	101	1,796	791	0.694	Arizona	101	1,508	818	0.648
Syracuse	105	1,680	771	0.685	Indiana	106	1,589	865	0.648

Major College Basketball Tournaments

The National Invitation Tournament (NIT), first played in 1938, is the oldest U.S. basketball tournament. The first National Collegiate Athletic Association (NCAA) national championship tournament was played one year later. In Aug. 2005, the NCAA agreed to purchase the NIT from the five New York City area colleges that had run the NIT, and administer its pre- and post-season tournaments.

National Invitation Tournament Champions

Year	Champion	Year	Champion	Year	Champion	Year	Champion	Year	Champion
1938	Temple	1952	LaSalle	1966	Brigham Young	1980	Virginia	1994	Villanova
1939	Long Island Univ.	1953	Seton Hall	1967	Southern Illinois	1981	Tulsa	1995	Virginia Tech
1940	Colorado	1954	Holy Cross	1968	Dayton	1982	Bradley	1996	Nebraska
1941	Long Island Univ.	1955	Duquesne	1969	Temple	1983	Fresno State	1997	Michigan
1942	West Virginia	1956	Louisville	1970	Marquette	1984	Michigan	1998	Minnesota
1943	St. John's	1957	Bradley	1971	North Carolina	1985	UCLA	1999	California
1944	St. John's	1958	Xavier (Ohio)	1972	Maryland	1986	Ohio State	2000	Wake Forest
1945	De Paul	1959	St. John's	1973	Virginia Tech	1987	So. Mississippi	2001	Tulsa
1946	Kentucky	1960	Bradley	1974	Purdue	1988	Connecticut	2002	Memphis
1947	Utah	1961	Providence	1975	Princeton	1989	St. John's	2003	St. John's
1948	St. Louis	1962	Dayton	1976	Kentucky	1990	Vanderbilt	2004	Michigan
1949	San Francisco	1963	Providence	1977	St. Bonaventure	1991	Stanford	2005	South Carolina
1950	CCNY	1964	Bradley	1978	Texas	1992	Virginia	2006	South Carolina
1951	Brigham Young	1965	St. John's	1979	Indiana	1993	Minnesota		

2006 MEN'S NCAA BASKETBALL TOURNAMENT

ATLANTA REGIONALS

(1) Duke 70
(16) Southern U. 54
Duke 74
(8) George Washington 88
(9) UNC Wilmington 85 (OT)
George Washington 61
Duke 54
(5) Syracuse 58
(12) Texas A&M 66
Texas A&M 57
LSU 62
(4) LSU 80
(13) Iona 64
LSU 58
LSU 70(OT)
(6) West Virginia 64
(11) Southern Ill. 46
West Virginia 67
(3) Iowa 63
(14) Northwestern St. 64
Northwestern St. 54
West Virginia 71
LSU 45
(7) California 52
(10) North Carolina St. 58
North Carolina St. 54
Texas 74
Texas 60
(2) Texas 60
(15) Pennsylvania 52
Texas 75

OAKLAND REGIONALS

(1) Memphis 94
(16) Oral Roberts 78
Memphis 72
(8) Arkansas 55
(9) Bucknell 59
Bucknell 56
Memphis 80
(5) Pittsburgh 79
(12) Kent St. 64
Pittsburgh 66
Bradley 64
Memphis 45
(4) Kansas 73
(13) Bradley 77
Bradley 72
(6) Indiana 87
(11) San Diego St. 83
Indiana 80
(3) Gonzaga 79
(14) Xavier 75
Gonzaga 90
Gonzaga 71
UCLA 59
(7) Marquette 85
(10) Alabama 90
Alabama 59
UCLA 73
UCLA 50
(2) UCLA 78
(15) Belmont 44
UCLA 62

WASHINGTON, DC REGIONALS

(1) Connecticut 72
(16) Albany (NY) 59
Connecticut 87
(8) Kentucky 69
(9) UAB 64
Kentucky 83
Connecticut 98 (OT)
(5) Washington 75
(12) Utah St. 61
Washington 67
Washington 92
Connecticut 84
(4) Illinois 78
(13) Air Force 69
Illinois 64
(6) Michigan St. 65
(11) George Mason 75
George Mason 65
(3) North Carolina 69
(14) Murray St. 65
North Carolina 60
George Mason 63
George Mason 58
(7) Wichita St. 86
(10) Seton Hall 66
Wichita St. 80
Wichita St. 55
George Mason 86
(2) Tennessee 63
(15) Winthrop 61
Tennessee 73

UCLA 57
Florida 73

MINNEAPOLIS REGIONALS

(1) Villanova 58
(16) Monmouth* 45
Villanova 82
(8) Arizona 94
(9) Wisconsin 75
Arizona 78
Villanova 60
(5) Nevada 79
(12) Montana 87
Montana 56
Boston College 59
Villanova 62
(4) Boston College 88
(13) Pacific 76 (2OT)
Boston College 69
(6) Oklahoma 74
(11) Wis.-Milwaukee 82
Wis.-Milwaukee 60
(3) Florida 76
(14) South Ala. 50
Florida 82
Florida 57
Florida 73
(7) Georgetown 54
(10) Northern Iowa 49
Georgetown 70
Georgetown 53
Florida 75
(2) Ohio St. 70
(15) Davidson 62
Ohio St. 52

*Monmouth defeated Hampton 71-49 in the opening-round game on March 14, 2006.

2006 Men's NCAA Tournament: Florida Gators Beat UCLA Bruins for Title

The Univ. of Florida Gators (33-6) defeated the Univ. of California Los Angeles (32-7), 75-70, to win its first Division I national basketball title Apr. 3, 2006, in Indianapolis, IN. Traditionally a football powerhouse, Florida dominated 11-time champion UCLA for most of the game. Forty-year-old Coach Billy Donovan earned his first NCAA title in his second NCAA Finals appearance as a head coach. Sophomore Joakim Noah, the son of tennis champion Yannick Noah, scored 16 points with 9 rebounds and 6 blocks to be named the most outstanding player of the Final Four.

NCAA Division I Champions

Year	Champion	Coach	Final opponent	Score	Outstanding player	Site
1939	Oregon	Howard Hobson	Ohio St.	46-33	None	Evanston, IL
1940	Indiana	Branch McCracken	Kansas	60-42	Marvin Huffman, Indiana	Kansas City, MO
1941	Wisconsin	Harold Foster	Washington St.	39-34	John Kotz, Wisconsin	Kansas City, MO
1942	Stanford	Everett Dean	Dartmouth	53-38	Howard Dallmar, Stanford	Kansas City, MO
1943	Wyoming	Everett Shelton	Georgetown	46-34	Ken Sailors, Wyoming	New York, NY
1944	Utah	Vadal Peterson	Dartmouth	42-40[1]	Arnold Ferrin, Utah	New York, NY
1945	Oklahoma St.[2]	Henry Iba	NYU	49-45	Bob Kurland, Oklahoma St.	New York, NY
1946	Oklahoma St.[2]	Henry Iba	North Carolina	43-40	Bob Kurland, Oklahoma St.	New York, NY
1947	Holy Cross	Alvin Julian	Oklahoma	58-47	George Kaftan, Holy Cross	New York, NY
1948	Kentucky	Adolph Rupp	Baylor	58-42	Alex Groza, Kentucky	New York, NY
1949	Kentucky	Adolph Rupp	Oklahoma St.	46-36	Alex Groza, Kentucky	Seattle, WA
1950	CCNY	Nat Holman	Bradley	71-68	Irwin Dambrot, CCNY	New York, NY
1951	Kentucky	Adolph Rupp	Kansas St.	68-58	None	Minneapolis, MN
1952	Kansas	Forrest Allen	St. John's	80-63	Clyde Lovellette, Kansas	Seattle, WA
1953	Indiana	Branch McCracken	Kansas	69-68	B.H. Born, Kansas	Kansas City, MO
1954	La Salle	Kenneth Loeffler	Bradley	92-76	Tom Gola, La Salle	Kansas City, MO
1955	San Francisco	Phil Woolpert	LaSalle	77-63	Bill Russell, San Francisco	Kansas City, MO
1956	San Francisco	Phil Woolpert	Iowa	83-71	Hal Lear, Temple	Evanston, IL
1957	North Carolina	Frank McGuire	Kansas	54-53[1]	Wilt Chamberlain, Kansas	Kansas City, MO
1958	Kentucky	Adolph Rupp	Seattle	84-72	Elgin Baylor, Seattle	Louisville, KY
1959	California	Pete Newell	West Virginia	71-70	Jerry West, West Virginia	Louisville, KY
1960	Ohio St.	Fred Taylor	California	75-55	Jerry Lucas, Ohio St.	San Francisco, CA
1961	Cincinnati	Edwin Jucker	Ohio St.	70-65[1]	Jerry Lucas, Ohio St.	Kansas City, MO
1962	Cincinnati	Edwin Jucker	Ohio St.	71-59	Paul Hogue, Cincinnati	Louisville, KY
1963	Loyola (IL)	George Ireland	Cincinnati	60-58[1]	Art Heyman, Duke	Louisville, KY
1964	UCLA	John Wooden	Duke	98-83	Walt Hazzard, UCLA	Kansas City, MO
1965	UCLA	John Wooden	Michigan	91-80	Bill Bradley, Princeton	Portland, OR
1966	Texas-El Paso[3]	Don Haskins	Kentucky	72-65	Jerry Chambers, Utah	College Park, MD
1967	UCLA	John Wooden	Dayton	79-64	Lew Alcindor, UCLA	Louisville, KY
1968	UCLA	John Wooden	North Carolina	78-55	Lew Alcindor, UCLA	Los Angeles, CA
1969	UCLA	John Wooden	Purdue	92-72	Lew Alcindor, UCLA	Louisville, KY
1970	UCLA	John Wooden	Jacksonville	80-69	Sidney Wicks, UCLA	College Park, MD
1971	UCLA	John Wooden	Villanova*	68-62	Howard Porter, Villanova*	Houston, TX
1972	UCLA	John Wooden	Florida St.	81-76	Bill Walton, UCLA	Los Angeles, CA
1973	UCLA	John Wooden	Memphis St.	87-66	Bill Walton, UCLA	St. Louis, MO
1974	North Carolina St.	Norm Sloan	Marquette	76-64	David Thompson, N.C. St.	Greensboro, NC
1975	UCLA	John Wooden	Kentucky	92-85	Richard Washington, UCLA	San Diego, CA
1976	Indiana	Bob Knight	Michigan	86-68	Kent Benson, Indiana	Philadelphia, PA
1977	Marquette	Al McGuire	North Carolina	67-59	Butch Lee, Marquette	Atlanta, GA
1978	Kentucky	Joe Hall	Duke	94-88	Jack Givens, Kentucky	St. Louis, MO
1979	Michigan St.	Jud Heathcote	Indiana St.	75-64	Magic Johnson, Michigan St.	Salt Lake City, UT
1980	Louisville	Denny Crum	UCLA*	59-54	Darrell Griffith, Louisville	Indianapolis, IN
1981	Indiana	Bob Knight	North Carolina	63-50	Isiah Thomas, Indiana	Philadelphia, PA
1982	North Carolina	Dean Smith	Georgetown	63-62	James Worthy, N. Carolina	New Orleans, LA
1983	North Carolina St.	Jim Valvano	Houston	54-52	Hakeem Olajuwon, Houston	Albuquerque, NM
1984	Georgetown	John Thompson	Houston	84-75	Patrick Ewing, Georgetown	Seattle, WA
1985	Villanova	Rollie Massimino	Georgetown	66-64	Ed Pinckney, Villanova	Lexington, KY
1986	Louisville	Denny Crum	Duke	72-69	Pervis Ellison, Louisville	Dallas, TX
1987	Indiana	Bob Knight	Syracuse	74-73	Keith Smart, Indiana	New Orleans, LA
1988	Kansas	Larry Brown	Oklahoma	83-79	Danny Manning, Kansas	Kansas City, MO
1989	Michigan	Steve Fisher	Seton Hall	80-79[1]	Glen Rice, Michigan	Seattle, WA
1990	UNLV	Jerry Tarkanian	Duke	103-73	Anderson Hunt, UNLV	Denver, CO
1991	Duke	Mike Krzyzewski	Kansas	72-65	Christian Laettner, Duke	Indianapolis, IN
1992	Duke	Mike Krzyzewski	Michigan	71-51	Bobby Hurley, Duke	Minneapolis, MN
1993	North Carolina	Dean Smith	Michigan	77-71	Donald Williams, N. Carolina	New Orleans, LA
1994	Arkansas	Nolan Richardson	Duke	76-72	Corliss Williamson, Arkansas	Charlotte, NC
1995	UCLA	Jim Harrick	Arkansas	89-78	Ed O'Bannon, UCLA	Seattle, WA
1996	Kentucky	Rick Pitino	Syracuse	76-67	Tony Delk, Kentucky	E. Rutherford, NJ
1997	Arizona	Lute Olson	Kentucky	84-79[1]	Miles Simon, Arizona	Indianapolis, IN
1998	Kentucky	Tubby Smith	Utah	78-69	Jeff Sheppard, Kentucky	San Antonio, TX
1999	Connecticut	Jim Calhoun	Duke	77-74	Richard Hamilton, Connecticut	St. Petersburg, FL
2000	Michigan St.	Tom Izzo	Florida	89-76	Mateen Cleaves, Michigan St.	Indianapolis, IN
2001	Duke	Mike Krzyzewski	Arizona	82-72	Shane Battier, Duke	Minneapolis, MN
2002	Maryland	Gary Williams	Indiana	64-52	Juan Dixon, Maryland	Atlanta, GA
2003	Syracuse	Jim Boeheim	Kansas	81-78	Carmelo Anthony, Syracuse	New Orleans, LA
2004	Connecticut	Jim Calhoun	Georgia Tech	82-73	Emeka Okafor, Connecticut	San Antonio, TX
2005	North Carolina	Roy Williams	Illinois	75-70	Sean May, North Carolina	St. Louis, MO
2006	Florida	Billy Donovan	UCLA	73-57	Joakim Noah, Florida	Indianapolis, IN

*Declared ineligible after the tournament. (1) Overtime. (2) Then known as Oklahoma A&M. (3) Then known as Texas Western.

Top Division I Career Scorers

(minimum 1,500 points; ranked by average, points per game)

Player, school	Years	Points	Avg	Player, school	Years	Points	Avg
Pete Maravich, LSU	1968-70	3,667	44.2	Dwight Lamar, SW Louisiana	1972-73	1,862	32.7
Austin Carr, Notre Dame	1969-71	2,560	34.6	Frank Selvy, Furman	1952-54	2,538	32.5
Oscar Robertson, Cincinnati	1958-60	2,973	33.8	Rick Mount, Purdue	1968-70	2,323	32.3
Calvin Murphy, Niagara	1968-70	2,548	33.1	Darrell Floyd, Furman	1954-56	2,281	32.1

John R. Wooden Award

Awarded to the nation's outstanding college basketball player by the Los Angeles Athletic Club.

1977	Marques Johnson, UCLA	1987	David Robinson, Navy	1997	Tim Duncan, Wake Forest
1978	Phil Ford, North Carolina	1988	Danny Manning, Kansas	1998	Antawn Jamison, North Carolina
1979	Larry Bird, Indiana State	1989	Sean Elliott, Arizona	1999	Elton Brand, Duke
1980	Darrell Griffith, Louisville	1990	Lionel Simmons, La Salle	2000	Kenyon Martin, Cincinnati
1981	Danny Ainge, Brigham Young	1991	Larry Johnson, UNLV	2001	Shane Battier, Duke
1982	Ralph Sampson, Virginia	1992	Christian Laettner, Duke	2002	Jay Williams, Duke
1983	Ralph Sampson, Virginia	1993	Calbert Cheaney, Indiana	2003	T.J. Ford, Texas
1984	Michael Jordan, North Carolina	1994	Glenn Robinson, Purdue	2004	Jameer Nelson, St. Joseph's
1985	Chris Mullin, St. John's	1995	Ed O'Bannon, UCLA	2005	Andrew Bogut, Utah
1986	Walter Berry, St. John's	1996	Marcus Camby, Massachusetts	2006	J.J. Redick, Duke

Most Coaching Victories in the NCAA Tournament Through 2006

(Coaches active in 2005-06 season in **bold**)

Coach, School(s), First/Last appearance	Wins	Tournaments	Championships
Mike Krzyzewski, Duke, 1984/2006	68	22	3
Dean Smith, North Carolina, 1967/1997	65	27	2
John Wooden, UCLA, 1950/1975	47	16	10
Bob Knight, Indiana, Texas Tech, 1973/2005	45	27	3
Lute Olson, Iowa, Arizona, 1979/2006	46	26	1
Denny Crum, Louisville, 1972/2000	42	23	2
Roy Williams, Kansas, N. Carolina, 1990/2006	41	17	1
Jim Boeheim, Syracuse, 1977/2006	40	25	1
Jim Calhoun, Northeastern, Connecticut, 1981/2006	38	18	2
Eddie Sutton, Creighton, Arkansas, Kentucky, Oklahoma St., 1974/2005	37	25	0

WOMEN'S COLLEGE BASKETBALL

2006 Women's NCAA Tournament: Terrapins Top Blue Devils

The Maryland Terrapins beat Duke's Blue Devils, 78-75, in overtime to win the women's Division I championship Apr. 4 in Boston, MA. Down by 13 points at the end of the first half, Coach Brenda Frese led the Terps to the second-largest comeback in women's NCAA Finals history. Maryland sophomore forward Laura Harper scored 16 points with 7 rebounds and was named the most outstanding player of the Final Four.

NCAA Division I Women's Champions

Year	Champion	Coach	Final opponent	Score	Outstanding player	Site
1982	Louisiana Tech	Sonja Hogg	Cheyney	76-62	Janice Lawrence, La. Tech	Norfolk, VA
1983	USC	Linda Sharp	Louisiana Tech	69-67	Cheryl Miller, USC	Norfolk, VA
1984	USC	Linda Sharp	Tennessee	72-61	Cheryl Miller, USC	Los Angeles, CA
1985	Old Dominion	Marianne Stanley	Georgia	70-65	Tracy Claxton, Old Dominion	Austin, TX
1986	Texas	Jody Conradt	USC	97-81	Clarissa Davis, Texas	Lexington, KY
1987	Tennessee	Pat Summitt	Louisiana Tech	67-44	Tonya Edwards, Tennessee	Austin, TX
1988	Louisiana Tech	Leon Barmore	Auburn	56-54	Erica Westbrooks, La. Tech	Tacoma, WA
1989	Tennessee	Pat Summitt	Auburn	76-60	Bridgette Gordon, Tennessee	Tacoma, WA
1990	Stanford	Tara VanDerveer	Auburn	88-81	Jennifer Azzi, Stanford	Knoxville, TN
1991	Tennessee	Pat Summitt	Virginia	70-67 (OT)	Dawn Staley, Virginia	New Orleans, LA
1992	Stanford	Tara VanDerveer	W. Kentucky	78-62	Molly Goodenbour, Stanford	Los Angeles, CA
1993	Texas Tech	Marsha Sharp	Ohio St.	84-82	Sheryl Swoopes, Texas Tech	Atlanta, GA
1994	North Carolina	Sylvia Hatchell	Louisiana Tech	60-59	Charlotte Smith, North Carolina	Richmond, VA
1995	Connecticut	Geno Auriemma	Tennessee	70-64	Rebecca Lobo, Connecticut	Minneapolis, MN
1996	Tennessee	Pat Summitt	Georgia	83-65	Michelle Marciniak, Tennessee	Charlotte, NC
1997	Tennessee	Pat Summitt	Old Dominion	68-59	Chamique Holdsclaw, Tennessee	Cincinnati, OH
1998	Tennessee	Pat Summitt	Louisiana Tech	93-75	Chamique Holdsclaw, Tennessee	Kansas City, MO
1999	Purdue	Carolyn Peck	Duke	62-45	Ukari Figgs, Purdue	San Jose, CA
2000	Connecticut	Geno Auriemma	Tennessee	71-52	Shea Ralph, Connecticut	Philadelphia, PA
2001	Notre Dame	Muffet McGraw	Purdue	68-66	Ruth Riley, Notre Dame	St. Louis, MO
2002	Connecticut	Geno Auriemma	Oklahoma	82-70	Swin Cash, Connecticut	San Antonio, TX
2003	Connecticut	Geno Auriemma	Tennessee	73-68	Diana Taurasi, Connecticut	Atlanta, GA
2004	Connecticut	Geno Auriemma	Tennessee	70-61	Diana Taurasi, Connecticut	New Orleans, LA
2005	Baylor	Kim Mulkey-Robertson	Michigan State	84-62	Sophia Young, Baylor	Indianapolis, IN
2006	Maryland	Brenda Frese	Duke	78-75 (OT)	Laura Harper, Maryland	Boston, MA

Wade Trophy

Awarded by National Assn. for Girls and Women in Sport for academics, community service, and player performance.

Year	Player, school	Year	Player, school	Year	Player, school
1978	Carol Blazejowski, Montclair St.	1988	Teresa Weatherspoon, Louisiana Tech	1997	DeLisha Milton, Florida
1979	Nancy Lieberman, Old Dominion	1989	Clarissa Davis, Texas	1998	Chamique Holdsclaw, Tennessee
1980	Nancy Lieberman, Old Dominion	1990	Jennifer Azzi, Stanford	1999	Stephanie White-McCarty, Purdue
1981	Lynette Woodard, Kansas	1991	Daedra Charles, Tennessee	2000	Edwina Brown, Texas
1982	Pam Kelly, Louisiana Tech	1992	Susan Robinson, Penn St.	2001	Jackie Stiles, SW Missouri St.
1983	LaTaunya Pollard, Long Beach St.	1993	Karen Jennings, Nebraska	2002	Sue Bird, Connecticut
1984	Janice Lawrence, Louisiana Tech	1994	Carol Ann Shudlick, Minnesota	2003	Diana Taurasi, Connecticut
1985	Cheryl Miller, USC	1995	Rebecca Lobo, Connecticut	2004	Alana Beard, Duke
1986	Kamie Ethridge, Texas	1996	Jennifer Rizzotti, Connecticut	2005	Seimone Augustus, LSU
1987	Shelly Pennefeather, Villanova			2006	Seimone Augustus, LSU

Top Division I Women's Career Scorers

(Minimum 1,500 points; ranked by average)

Player, school	Years	Points	Avg	Player, school	Years	Points	Avg
Patricia Hoskins, Miss. Valley St.	1985-89	3,122	28.4	Andrea Congreaves, Mercer	1989-93	2,796	25.9
Sandra Hodge, New Orleans	1981-84	2,860	26.7	Cindy Blodgett, Maine	1994-98	3,005	25.5
Jackie Stiles, SW Missouri St.	1997-2001	3,393	26.3	Valorie Whiteside, Appalachian St.	1984-88	2,944	25.4
Lorri Bauman, Drake	1981-84	3,115	26.0				

2006 WOMEN'S NCAA BASKETBALL TOURNAMENT

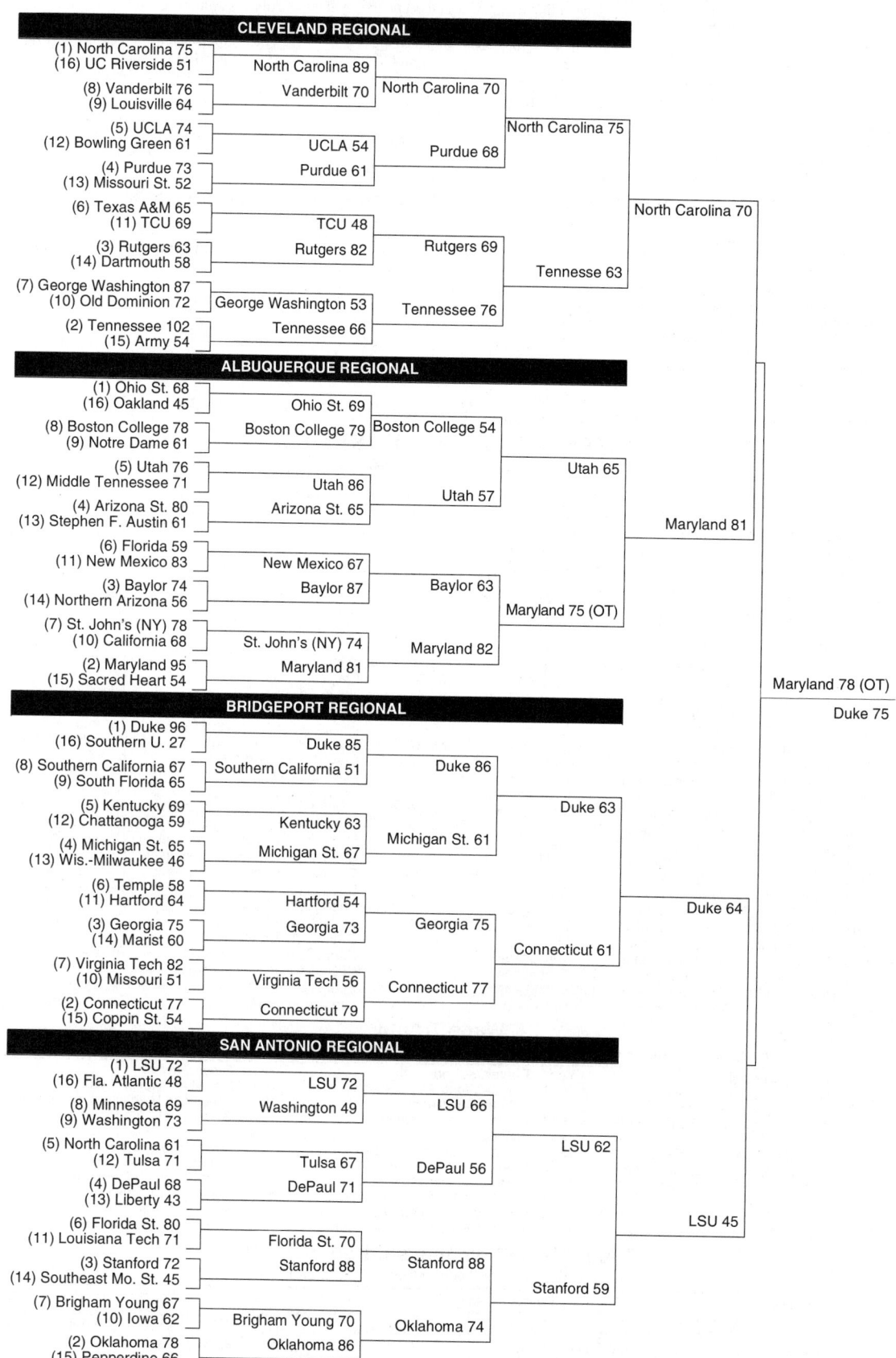

CLEVELAND REGIONAL

(1) North Carolina 75
(16) UC Riverside 51
North Carolina 89
(8) Vanderbilt 76
(9) Louisville 64
Vanderbilt 70
North Carolina 70
(5) UCLA 74
(12) Bowling Green 61
UCLA 54
Purdue 68
(4) Purdue 73
(13) Missouri St. 52
Purdue 61
North Carolina 75
(6) Texas A&M 65
(11) TCU 69
TCU 48
Rutgers 69
(3) Rutgers 63
(14) Dartmouth 58
Rutgers 82
North Carolina 70
(7) George Washington 87
(10) Old Dominion 72
George Washington 53
Tennesse 63
(2) Tennessee 102
(15) Army 54
Tennessee 66
Tennessee 76

ALBUQUERQUE REGIONAL

(1) Ohio St. 68
(16) Oakland 45
Ohio St. 69
(8) Boston College 78
(9) Notre Dame 61
Boston College 79
Boston College 54
(5) Utah 76
(12) Middle Tennessee 71
Utah 86
Utah 65
(4) Arizona St. 80
(13) Stephen F. Austin 61
Arizona St. 65
Utah 57
Maryland 81
(6) Florida 59
(11) New Mexico 83
New Mexico 67
Baylor 63
(3) Baylor 74
(14) Northern Arizona 56
Baylor 87
Maryland 75 (OT)
(7) St. John's (NY) 78
(10) California 68
St. John's (NY) 74
Maryland 82
(2) Maryland 95
(15) Sacred Heart 54
Maryland 81

BRIDGEPORT REGIONAL

(1) Duke 96
(16) Southern U. 27
Duke 85
(8) Southern California 67
(9) South Florida 65
Southern California 51
Duke 86
(5) Kentucky 69
(12) Chattanooga 59
Kentucky 63
Duke 63
(4) Michigan St. 65
(13) Wis.-Milwaukee 46
Michigan St. 67
Michigan St. 61
(6) Temple 58
(11) Hartford 64
Hartford 54
Duke 64
(3) Georgia 75
(14) Marist 60
Georgia 73
Georgia 75
(7) Virginia Tech 82
(10) Missouri 51
Virginia Tech 56
Connecticut 61
(2) Connecticut 77
(15) Coppin St. 54
Connecticut 79
Connecticut 77

SAN ANTONIO REGIONAL

(1) LSU 72
(16) Fla. Atlantic 48
LSU 72
(8) Minnesota 69
(9) Washington 73
Washington 49
LSU 66
(5) North Carolina 61
(12) Tulsa 71
Tulsa 67
LSU 62
(4) DePaul 68
(13) Liberty 43
DePaul 71
DePaul 56
LSU 45
(6) Florida St. 80
(11) Louisiana Tech 71
Florida St. 70
Stanford 88
(3) Stanford 72
(14) Southeast Mo. St. 45
Stanford 88
Stanford 59
(7) Brigham Young 67
(10) Iowa 62
Brigham Young 70
Oklahoma 74
(2) Oklahoma 78
(15) Pepperdine 66
Oklahoma 86

Maryland 78 (OT)
Duke 75

NATIONAL FOOTBALL LEAGUE

NFL 2005-2006: Steelers Win 5th Super Bowl in Team History; Alexander breaks TD Running Record and Earns League MVP Honors

The Pittsburgh Steelers beat the Seattle Seahawks, 21-10, in Detroit, MI, Feb. 5, 2006, in Super Bowl XL, winning their 5th Super Bowl in franchise history. Pittsburgh's Ben Roethlisberger, at 23 years old, became the youngest quarterback to win a Super Bowl.

During the regular season the Indianapolis Colts won 13 straight games, becoming only the fourth team ever to do so. NFL MVP Shaun Alexander, running back for the Seattle Seahawks, set the NFL record for touchdowns in a season with 28 and became the only player in NFL history to score 15 touchdowns for five straight seasons. Arizona Cardinals kicker Neil Rackers set a record for most field goals made in a season with 40. Former Auburn University star, and Tampa Bay Buccaneers running back Carnell "Cadillac" Williams won rookie of the year honors. Due to Hurricane Katrina, the New Orleans Saints had to play their entire season away from home, in San Antonio, Texas.

Final 2005 Standings

American Football Conference								National Football Conference						
	W	L	T	Pct	Pts	Opp	Div		W	L	T	Pct	Pts	Opp	Div
East Division								**East Division**						
New England	10	6	0	0.625	379	338	5-1	N.Y. Giants	11	5	0	0.688	422	314	4-2
Miami	9	7	0	0.562	318	317	3-3	*Washington	10	6	0	0.625	359	293	5-1
Buffalo	5	11	0	0.312	271	367	2-4	Dallas	9	7	0	0.562	325	308	3-3
N.Y. Jets	4	12	0	0.250	240	355	2-4	Philadelphia	6	10	0	0.375	310	388	0-6
North Division								**North Division**						
Cincinnati	11	5	0	0.688	421	350	5-1	Chicago	11	5	0	0.688	260	202	5-1
*Pittsburgh	11	5	0	0.688	389	258	4-2	Minnesota	9	7	0	0.562	306	344	5-1
Baltimore	6	10	0	0.375	265	299	2-4	Detroit	5	11	0	0.312	254	345	1-5
Cleveland	6	10	0	0.375	232	301	1-5	Green Bay	4	12	0	0.250	298	344	1-5
South Division								**South Division**						
Indianapolis	14	2	0	0.875	439	247	6-0	Tampa Bay	11	5	0	0.688	300	274	5-1
*Jacksonville	12	4	0	0.750	361	269	4-2	*Carolina	11	5	0	0.688	391	259	4-2
Tennessee	4	12	0	0.250	299	421	2-4	Atlanta	8	8	0	0.500	351	341	2-4
Houston	2	14	0	0.125	260	431	0-6	New Orleans	3	13	0	0.188	235	398	1-5
West Division								**West Division**						
Denver	13	3	0	0.812	395	258	5-1	Seattle	13	3	0	0.812	452	271	6-0
Kansas City	10	6	0	0.625	403	325	4-2	St. Louis	6	10	0	0.375	363	429	1-5
San Diego	9	7	0	0.562	418	312	3-3	Arizona	5	11	0	0.312	311	387	3-3
Oakland	4	12	0	0.250	290	383	0-6	San Francisco	4	12	0	0.250	239	428	2-4

* Wild card team.

AFC Playoffs—New England 28, Jacksonville 3; Pittsburgh 31, Cincinnati 17; Denver 27, New England 13; Pittsburgh 21, Indianapolis 18; Pittsburgh 34, Denver 17.

NFC Playoffs—Washington 17, Tampa Bay 10; Carolina 23, N.Y. Giants 0; Seattle 20, Washington 10; Carolina 29, Chicago 21; Seattle 34, Carolina 14

Super Bowl—Pittsburgh 21, Seattle 10.

American Football League Champions 1960-1969

Year	Eastern Division	Western Division	Championship
1960	Houston Oilers (10-4-0)	Los Angeles Chargers (10-4-0)	Houston 24, Los Angeles 16
1961	Houston Oilers (10-3-1)	San Diego Chargers (12-2-0)	Houston 10, San Diego 3
1962	Houston Oilers (11-3-0)	Dallas Texans (11-3-0)	Dallas 20, Houston 17 (2 overtimes)
1963	Boston Patriots (7-6-1) (a)	San Diego Chargers (11-3-0)	San Diego 51, Boston 10
1964	Buffalo Bills (12-2-0)	San Diego Chargers (8-5-1)	Buffalo 20, San Diego 7
1965	Buffalo Bills (10-3-1)	San Diego Chargers (9-2-3)	Buffalo 23, San Diego 0
1966	Buffalo Bills (9-4-1)	Kansas City Chiefs (11-2-1)	Kansas City 31, Buffalo 7
1967	Houston Oilers (9-4-1)	Oakland Raiders (13-1-0)	Oakland 40, Houston 7
1968	New York Jets (11-3-0)	Oakland Raiders (12-2-0) (b)	New York 27, Oakland 23
1969	New York Jets (10-4-0)	Oakland Raiders (12-1-1)	Kansas City 17, Oakland 7 (c)

(a) Defeated Buffalo Bills in divisional playoff. (b) Defeated Kansas City Chiefs in divisional playoff. (c) Kansas City Chiefs defeated N.Y. Jets and Oakland Raiders defeated Houston Oilers in divisional playoffs.

National Football League Champions 1933-1969

Year	East Winner (W-L-T)	West Winner (W-L-T)	Championship
1933	New York Giants (11-3-0)	Chicago Bears (10-2-1)	Chicago Bears 23, New York 21
1934	New York Giants (8-5-0)	Chicago Bears (13-0-0)	New York 30, Chicago Bears 13
1935	New York Giants (9-3-0)	Detroit Lions (7-3-2)	Detroit 26, New York 7
1936	Boston Redskins (7-5-0)	Green Bay Packers (10-1-1)	Green Bay 21, Boston 6
1937	Washington Redskins (8-3-0)	Chicago Bears (9-1-1)	Washington 28, Chicago Bears 21
1938	New York Giants (8-2-1)	Green Bay Packers (8-3-0)	New York 23, Green Bay 17
1939	New York Giants (9-1-1)	Green Bay Packers (9-2-0)	Green Bay 27, New York 0
1940	Washington Redskins (9-2-0)	Chicago Bears (8-3-0)	Chicago Bears 73, Washington 0
1941	New York Giants (8-3-0)	Chicago Bears (10-1-1)(a)	Chicago Bears 37, New York 9
1942	Washington Redskins (10-1-1)	Chicago Bears (11-0-0)	Washington 14, Chicago Bears 6
1943	Washington Redskins (6-3-1)	Chicago Bears (8-1-1)	Chicago Bears, 41, Washington 21
1944	New York Giants (8-1-1)	Green Bay Packers (8-2-0)	Green Bay 14, New York 7
1945	Washington Redskins (8-2-0)	Cleveland Rams (9-1-0)	Cleveland 15, Washington 14
1946	New York Giants (7-3-1)	Chicago Bears (8-2-1)	Chicago Bears 24, New York 14
1947	Philadelphia Eagles (8-4-0)(a)	Chicago Cardinals (9-3-0)	Chicago Cardinals 28, Philadelphia 21
1948	Philadelphia Eagles (9-2-1)	Chicago Cardinals (11-1-0)	Philadelphia 7, Chicago Cardinals 0
1949	Philadelphia Eagles (11-1-0)	Los Angeles Rams (8-2-2)	Philadelphia 14, Los Angeles 0
1950	Cleveland Browns (10-2-0)(a)	Los Angeles Rams (9-3-0) (a)	Cleveland 30, Los Angeles 28
1951	Cleveland Browns (11-1-0)	Los Angeles Rams (8-4-0)	Los Angeles 24, Cleveland 17
1952	Cleveland Browns (8-4-0)	Detroit Lions (9-3-0)(a)	Detroit 17, Cleveland 7
1953	Cleveland Browns (11-1-0)	Detroit Lions (10-2-0)	Detroit 17, Cleveland 16
1954	Cleveland Browns (9-3-0)	Detroit Lions (9-2-1)	Cleveland 56, Detroit 10
1955	Cleveland Browns (9-2-1)	Los Angeles Rams (8-3-1)	Cleveland 38, Los Angeles 14
1956	New York Giants (8-3-1)	Chicago Bears (9-2-1)	New York 47, Chicago Bears 7
1957	Cleveland Browns (9-2-1)	Detroit Lions (8-4-0)(a)	Detroit 59, Cleveland 14
1958	New York Giants (9-3-0)(a)	Baltimore Colts (9-3-0)	Baltimore 23, New York 17 (b)

Year	East Winner (W-L-T)	West Winner (W-L-T)	Championship
1959	New York Giants (10-2-0)	Baltimore Colts (9-3-0)	Baltimore 31, New York 16
1960	Philadelphia Eagles (10-2-0)	Green Bay Packers (8-4-0)	Philadelphia 17, Green Bay 13
1961	New York Giants (10-3-1)	Green Bay Packers (11-3-0)	Green Bay 37, New York 0
1962	New York Giants (12-2-0)	Green Bay Packers (13-1-0)	Green Bay 16, New York 7
1963	New York Giants (11-3-0)	Chicago Bears (11-1-2)	Chicago 14, New York 10
1964	Cleveland Browns (10-3-1)	Baltimore Colts (12-2-0)	Cleveland 27, Baltimore 0
1965	Cleveland Browns (11-3-0)	Green Bay Packers (10-3-1)(a)	Green Bay 23, Cleveland 12
1966	Dallas Cowboys (10-3-1)	Green Bay Packers (12-2-0)	Green Bay 34, Dallas 27
1967	Dallas Cowboys (9-5-0)	Green Bay Packers (9-4-1)	Green Bay 21, Dallas 17
1968	Cleveland Browns (10-4-0)	Baltimore Colts (13-1-0)	Baltimore 34, Cleveland 0
1969	Cleveland Browns (10-3-1)	Minnesota Vikings (12-2-0)	Minnesota 27, Cleveland 7

(a) Won divisional playoff. (b) Won at 8:15 of sudden death overtime period.

NFL Divisional Champions and Wild Cards 1970-1994

The American Football League and National Football League officially merged in 1966. At the beginning of the 1970 season, the two leagues became the AFC and NFC conferences in the new NFL. Regular-season records are in parentheses.

American Football Conference

Year	Eastern	Central	Western	Wild Card
1970	Baltimore Colts (11-2-1)	Cincinnati Bengals (8-6-0)	Oakland Raiders (8-4-2)	Miami Dolphins (10-4-0)
1971	Miami Dolphins (10-3-1)	Cleveland Browns (9-5-0)	Kansas City Chiefs (10-3-1)	Baltimore Colts (10-4-0)
1972	Miami Dolphins (14-0-0)	Pittsburgh Steelers (11-3-0)	Oakland Raiders (10-3-1)	Cleveland Browns (10-4-0)
1973	Miami Dolphins (12-2-0)	Cincinnati Bengals (10-4-0)	Oakland Raiders (9-4-1)	Cincinnati Bengals (10-4-0)
1974	Miami Dolphins (11-3-0)	Pittsburgh Steelers (10-3-1)	Oakland Raiders (12-2-0)	Buffalo Bills (9-5-0)
1975	Baltimore Colts (10-4-0)	Pittsburgh Steelers (12-2-0)	Oakland Raiders (11-3-0)	Cincinnati Bengals (11-3-0)
1976	Baltimore Colts (11-3-0)	Pittsburgh Steelers (10-4-0)	Oakland Raiders (13-1-0)	New England Patriots (11-3-0)
1977	Baltimore Colts (10-4-0)	Pittsburgh Steelers (9-5-0)	Denver Broncos (12-2-0)	Oakland Raiders (11-3-0)
1978	New England Patriots (11-5-0)	Pittsburgh Steelers (14-2-0)	Denver Broncos (10-6-0)	Houston Oilers (10-6-0) Miami Dolphins (11-5-0))
1979	Miami Dolphins (10-6-0)	Pittsburgh Steelers (12-4-0)	San Diego Chargers (12-4-0)	Houston Oilers (11-5-0) Denver Broncos (10-6-0)
1980	Buffalo Bills (11-5-0)	Cleveland Browns (11-5-0)	San Diego Chargers (11-5-0)	Houston Oilers (11-5-0) Oakland Raiders (11-5-0)
1981	Miami Dolphins (11-4-1)	Cincinnati Bengals (12-4-0)	San Diego Chargers (10-6-0)	Buffalo Bills (10-6-0) N.Y. Jets (10-5-1)
1982	Strike abbreviated season. See note.			
1983	Miami Dolphins (12-4-0)	Pittsburgh Steelers (10-6-0)	L.A. Raiders (12-4-0)	Denver Broncos (9-7-0) Seattle Seahawks (9-7-0)
1984	Miami Dolphins (14-2-0)	Pittsburgh Steelers (9-7-0)	Denver Broncos (13-3-0)	L.A. Raiders (11-5-0) Seattle Seahawks (12-4-0)
1985	Miami Dolphins (12-4-0)	Cleveland Browns (8-8-0)	L.A. Raiders (12-4-0)	New England Patriots (11-5-0) N.Y. Jets (11-5-0)
1986	New England Patriots (11-5-0)	Cleveland Browns (12-4-0)	Denver Broncos (11-5-0)	K.C. Chiefs (10-6-0) N.Y. Jets (10-6-0)
1987	Indianapolis Colts (9-6-0)	Cleveland Browns (10-5-0)	Buffalo Bills (12-4-0)	Houston Oilers (9-6-0) Seattle Seahawks (9-6-0)
1988	Buffalo Bills (12-4-0)	Cincinnati Bengals (12-4-0)	Seattle Seahawks (9-7-0)	Cleveland Browns (10-6-0) Houston Oilers (10-6-0)
1989	Buffalo Bills (9-7-0)	Cleveland Browns (9-6-1)	Denver Broncos (11-5-0)	Houston Oilers (9-7-0) Pittsburgh Steelers (9-7-0)
1990	Buffalo Bills (13-3-0)	Cincinnati Bengals (9-7-0)	L.A. Raiders (12-4-0)	Houston Oilers (9-7-0) Kansas City Chiefs (11-5-0) Miami Dolphins (12-4-0)
1991	Buffalo Bills (13-3-0)	Houston Oilers (11-5-0)	Denver Broncos (12-4-0)	Kansas City Chiefs (11-5-0) Miami Dolphins (12-4-0) N.Y. Jets (8-8-0)
1992	Miami Dolphins (11-5-0)	Pittsburgh Steelers (11-5-0)	San Diego Chargers (11-5-0)	Buffalo Bills (11-5-0) Houston Oilers (10-6-0) Kansas City Chiefs (10-6-0)
1993	Buffalo Bills (12-4-0)	Houston Oilers (12-4-0)	Kansas City Chiefs (11-5-0)	Denver Broncos (9-7-0) L.A. Raiders (10-6-0) Pittsburgh Steelers (9-7-0)
1994	Miami Dolphins (10-6-0)	Pittsburgh Steelers (12-4-0)	San Diego Chargers (11-5-0)	Cleveland Browns (11-5-0) Kansas City Chiefs (9-7-0) New England Patriots (10-6-0)

National Football Conference

Year	Eastern	Central	Western	Wild Card
1970	Dallas Cowboys (10-4-0)	Minnesota Vikings (12-2-0)	San Francisco 49ers (10-3-1)	Detroit Lions (10-4-0)
1971	Dallas Cowboys (11-3-0)	Minnesota Vikings (11-3-0)	San Francisco 49ers (9-5-0)	Washington Redskins (9-4-1)
1972	Washington Redskins (11-3-0)	Green Bay Packers (10-4-0)	San Francisco 49ers (8-5-1)	Dallas Cowboys (10-4-0)
1973	Dallas Cowboys (10-4-0)	Minnesota Vikings (12-2-0)	L.A. Rams (12-2-0)	Washington Redskins (10-4-0)
1974	St. Louis Cardinals (10-4-0)	Minnesota Vikings (10-4-0)	L.A. Rams (10-4-0)	Washington Redskins (10-4-0)
1975	St. Louis Cardinals (11-3-0)	Minnesota Vikings (12-2-0)	L.A. Rams (12-2-0)	Dallas Cowboys (10-4-0)
1976	Dallas Cowboys (11-3-0)	Minnesota Vikings (11-2-1)	L.A. Rams (10-3-1)	Washington Redskins (10-4-0)
1977	Dallas Cowboys (12-2-0)	Minnesota Vikings (9-5-0)	L.A. Rams (10-4-0)	Chicago Bears (9-5-0)
1978	Dallas Cowboys (12-4-0)	Minnesota Vikings (8-7-1)	L.A. Rams (12-4-0)	Atlanta Falcons (9-7-0) Philadelphia Eagles (9-7-0)
1979	Dallas Cowboys (11-5-0)	Tampa Bay Buccaneers (10-6-0)	L.A. Rams (9-7-0)	Chicago Bears (10-6-0) Philadelphia Eagles (11-5-0)
1980	Philadelphia Eagles (12-4-0)	Minnesota Vikings (9-7-0)	Atlanta Falcons (12-4-0)	Dallas Cowboys (12-4-0) L.A. Rams (11-5-0)
1981	Dallas Cowboys (12-4-0)	Tampa Bay Buccaneers (9-7-0)	San Francisco 49ers (13-3-0)	N.Y. Giants (9-7-0) Philadelphia Eagles (10-6-0)
1982	Strike abbreviated season. See note.			
1983	Washington Redskins (14-2-0)	Detroit Lions (9-7-0)	San Francisico 49ers (10-6-0)	Dallas Cowboys (12-4-0) L.A. Rams (9-7-0)
1984	Washington Redskins (11-5-0)	Chicago Bears (10-6-0)	San Francisco 49ers (15-1-0)	L.A. Rams (10-6-0) N.Y. Giants (9-7-0)

National Football Conference

Year	Eastern	Central	Western	Wild Card
1985	Dallas Cowboys (10-6-0)	Chicago Bears (15-1-0)	L.A. Rams (11-5-0)	N.Y. Giants (10-6-0) San Francisco 49ers (10-6-0)
1986	N.Y. Giants (14-2-0)	Chicago Bears (14-2-0)	San Francisco 49ers (10-5-1)	L.A. Rams (10-6-0) Washington Redskins (12-4-0)
1987	Washington Redskins (11-4-0)	Chicago Bears (11-4-0)	San Francisco 49ers (13-2-0)	Minnesota Vikings (8-7-0) New Orleans Saints (12-3-0)
1988	Philadelphia Eagles (10-6-0)	Chicago Bears (12-4-0)	San Francisco 49ers (10-6-0)	L.A. Rams (10-6-0) Minnesota Vikings (11-5-0)
1989	N.Y. Giants (12-4-0)	Minnesota Vikings (10-6-0)	San Francisco 49ers (14-2-0)	L.A. Rams (11-5-0) Philadelphia Eagles (11-5-0)
1990	N.Y. Giants (13-3-0)	Chicago Bears (11-5-0)	San Francisco 49ers (14-2-0)	New Orleans Saints (8-8-0) Philadelphia Eagles (10-6-0) Washington Redskins (10-6-0)
1991	Washington Redskins (14-2-0)	Detroit Lions (12-4-0)	New Orleans Saints (11-5-0)	Atlanta Falcons (10-6-0) Chicago Bears (11-5-0) Dallas Cowboys (11-5-0)
1992	Dallas Cowboys (13-3-0)	Minnesota Vikings (11-5-0)	San Francisco 49ers (14-2-0)	New Orleans Saints (12-4-0) Philadelphia Eagles (11-5-0) Washington Redskins (9-7-0)
1993	Dallas Cowboys (12-4-0)	Detroit Lions (10-6-0)	San Francisco 49ers (10-6-0)	Green Bay Packers (9-7-0) Minnesota Vikings (9-7-0) N.Y. Giants (11-5-0)
1994	Dallas Cowboys (12-4-0)	Minnesota Vikings (10-6-0)	San Francisco 49ers (13-3-0)	Chicago Bears (9-7-0) Detroit Lions (9-7-0) Green Bay Packers (9-7-0)

Note: A strike shortened the 1982 season from 16 to 9 games. The top 8 teams in each conference played in a tournament to determine the conference champion. AFC—Miami Dolphins, New England New England Patriots, L.A. Raiders, Cleveland Browns, N.Y. Jets, Cincinnati Bengals, San Diego Chargers, Pittsburgh Steelers. NFC—Washington Redskins, Detroit Lions, Green Bay Packers, St. Louis Cardinals, Dallas Cowboys, Tampa Bay Buccaneers, Minnesota Vikings, Atlanta Falcons.

NFL Playoff Results, 1995-2005

Year	Conference	Division	Winner (W-L-T)	Playoffs (a)	Year
1995	American	Eastern	Buffalo Bills (10-6-0)	Indianapolis* 10, Kansas City 7	1995
		Central	Pittsburgh Steelers (11-5-0)	Pittsburgh 40, Buffalo 21	
		Western	Kansas City Chiefs (13-3-0)	Pittsburgh 20, Indianapolis* 16	
	National	Eastern	Dallas Cowboys (12-4-0)	Dallas 30, Philadelphia* 11	
		Central	Green Bay Packers (11-5-0)	Green Bay 27, San Francisco 17	
		Western	San Francisco 49ers (11-5-0)	Dallas 38, Green Bay 27	
1996	American	Eastern	New England Patriots (11-5-0)	Jacksonville* 30, Denver 27	1996
		Central	Pittsburgh Steelers (10-6-0)	New England 28, Pittsburgh 3	
		Western	Denver Broncos (13-3-0)	New England 20, Jacksonville* 6	
	National	Eastern	Dallas Cowboys (10-6-0)	Green Bay 35, San Francisco* 14	
		Central	Green Bay Packers (13-3-0)	Carolina 26, Dallas 17	
		Western	Carolina Panthers (12-4-0)	Green Bay 30, Carolina 13	
1997	American	Eastern	New England Patriots (10-6-0)	Pittsburgh 7, New England 6	1997
		Central	Pittsburgh Steelers (11-5-0)	Denver* 14, Kansas City 10	
		Western	Kansas City Chiefs (13-3-0)	Denver* 24, Pittsburgh 21	
	National	Eastern	New York Giants (10-5-1)	San Francisco 38, Minnesota* 22	
		Central	Green Bay Packers (13-3-0)	Green Bay 21, Tampa Bay* 7	
		Western	San Francisco 49ers (13-3-0)	Green Bay 23, San Francisco 10	
1998	American	Eastern	N.Y. Jets (12-4-0)	Denver 38, Miami* 3	1998
		Central	Jacksonville Jaguars (11-5-0)	N.Y. Jets 34, Jacksonville 24	
		Western	Denver Broncos (14-2-0)	Denver 23, N.Y. Jets 10	
	National	Eastern	Dallas Cowboys (10-6-0)	Atlanta 20, San Francisco* 18	
		Central	Minnesota Vikings (15-1-0)	Minnesota 41, Arizona* 21	
		Western	Atlanta Falcons (14-2-0)	Atlanta 30, Minnesota 27 (OT)	
1999	American	Eastern	Indianapolis Colts (13-3-0)	Jacksonville 62, Miami* 7	1999
		Central	Jacksonville Jaguars (14-2-0)	Tennessee* 19, Indianapolis 16	
		Western	Seattle Seahawks (9-7-0)	Tennessee* 33, Jacksonville 14	
	National	Eastern	Washington Redskins (10-6-0)	Tampa Bay 14, Washington 13	
		Central	Tampa Bay Buccaneers (11-5-0)	St. Louis 49, Minnesota* 37	
		Western	St. Louis Rams (13-3-0)	St. Louis 11, Tampa Bay 6	
2000	American	Eastern	Miami Dolphins (11-5-0)	Oakland 27, Miami 0	2000
		Central	Tennessee Titans (13-3-0)	Baltimore* 24, Tennessee 10	
		Western	Oakland Raiders (12-4-0)	Baltimore* 16, Oakland 3	
	National	Eastern	N.Y. Giants (12-4-0)	Minnesota 34, New Orleans 16	
		Central	Minnesota Vikings (11-5-0)	N.Y. Giants 20, Philadelphia* 10	
		Western	New Orleans Saints (10-6-0)	N.Y. Giants 41, Minnesota 0	
2001	American	Eastern	New England Patriots (11-5-0)	New England 16, Oakland 13	2001
		Central	Pittsburgh Steelers (13-3-0)	Pittsburgh 27, Baltimore* 10	
		Western	Oakland Raiders (10-6-0)	New England 24, Pittsburgh 17	
	National	Eastern	Philadelphia Eagles (11-5-0)	Philadelphia 33, Chicago 19	
		Central	Chicago Bears (13-3-0)	St. Louis 45, Green Bay* 17	
		Western	St. Louis Rams (14-2-0)	St. Louis 29, Philadelphia 24	
2002	American	East	N.Y. Jets (9-7-0)		2002
		North	Pittsburgh Steelers (10-5-1)	Oakland 30, N.Y. Jets 10	
		South	Tennessee Titans (11-5-0)	Tennessee 34, Pittsburgh 31	
		West	Oakland Raiders (11-5-0)	Oakland 41, Tennessee 24	
	National	East	Philadelphia Eagles (12-4-0)		
		North	Green Bay Packers (12-4-0)	Philadelphia 20, Atlanta* 6	
		South	Tampa Bay Buccaneers (12-4-0)	Tampa Bay 31, San Francisco 6	
		West	San Francisco 49ers (10-6-0)	Tampa Bay 27, Philadelphia 10	
2003	American	East	New England Patriots (14-2-0)		2003
		North	Baltimore Ravens (10-6-0)	Indianapolis 38, Kansas City 31	
		South	Indianapolis Colts (12-4-0)	New England 17, Tennessee* 14	
		West	Kansas City Chiefs (13-3-0)	New England 24, Indianapolis 14	
	National	East	Philadelphia Eagles (12-4-0)		
		North	Green Bay Packers (10-6-0)	Carolina 29, St. Louis 23	
		South	Carolina Panthers (11-5-0)	Philadelphia 20, Green Bay 17	
		West	St. Louis Rams (12-4-0)	Carolina 14, Philadelphia 3	

Year	Conference	Division	Winner (W-L-T)	Playoffs (a)	Year
2004	American	East	New England Patriots (14-2-0)		2004
		North	Pittsburgh Steelers(15-1-0)	Pittsburgh 20, N.Y. Jets 17* (OT)	
		South	Indianapolis Colts (12-4-0)	New England 20, Indianapolis 3	
		West	San Diego Chargers (12-4-0)	New England 41, Pittsburgh 27	
	National	East	Philadelphia Eagles (13-3-0)		
		North	Green Bay Packers (10-6-0)	Atlanta 47, St.Louis* 17	
		South	Atlanta Falcons (11-5-0)	Philidelphia 27, Minnesota* 14	
		West	Seattle Seahawks (9-7-0)	Philidelphia 27, Atlanta 10	
2005	American	East	New England (10-6-0)		2005
		North	Cincinnati (11-5-0)	Denver 27, New England 13	
		South	Indianapolis (14-2-0)	Pittsburgh* 21, Indianapolis 18	
		West	Denver (13-3-0)	Pittsburgh* 34, Denver 17	
	National	East	N.Y Giants (11-5-0)		
		North	Chicago (11-5-0)	Seattle 20, Washington* 10	
		South	Tampa Bay (11-5-0)	Carolina* 29, Chicago 21	
		West	Seattle (13-3-0)	Seattle 34, Carolina* 14	

*Wild card team. (a) Only the final 2 conference playoff rounds are shown.

Super Bowl XL: Pittsburgh 21, Seattle 10

The Pittsburgh Steelers on Feb. 5, 2006, defeated the Seattle Seahawks, 21-10, at Ford Field in Detroit, MI, to win Super Bowl XL. It was the Steelers first Super Bowl win since 1980, and the first for head coach Bill Cowher who has been Steelers' head coach for 14 seasons, the longest current tenure in the NFL. Ben Roethlisberger, 24, became the youngest quarterback ever to lead his team to a Super Bowl victory. Steelers wide receiver Hines Ward was named Super Bowl MVP. He finished the day with 5 catches for 123 yards and a touchdown. For the Seahawks, Matt Hasselbeck threw for 273 yards and a touchdown. Running back Shaun Alexander, the league leader in rushing, did not score. Seattle took issue with several questionable calls during the game, notably Ben Roethlisberger's goal-line touchdown. After the game, longtime Steelers running back Jerome (The Bus) Bettis announced his retirement after 13 years in the NFL. Pittsburgh tied San Francisco and Dallas for the most Super Bowl wins with five.

Score by Quarters

Team	1	2	3	4	Total
Pittsburgh	0	7	7	7	21
Seattle	3	0	7	0	10

Scoring

Seattle — Josh Brown 47 yd. field goal
Pittsburgh — Ben Roethlisberger 1 yd run (Reed PAT)
Pittsburgh — Willie Parker 75 yd run (Reed PAT)
Seattle — Jerramy Stevens 16 yd pass from Matt Hasselbeck (Brown PAT)
Pittsburgh — Hines Ward, 43 yd pass from Antwaan Randle El (Reed PAT)

Individual Statistics

Rushing — Pittsburgh: Parker 10-93, 1 TD, Bettis 14-43, Roethlisberger 7-25, 1 TD, Ward 1-18, Haynes 1-2. Seattle: Alexander 20-95, Hasselbeck 3-35, Strong 2-7.

Passing — Pittsburgh: Roethlisberger 9-21, 123 yds, 0 TD, 2 Int, Randle El 1-1, 43 yds, 1 TD, 0 Int. Seattle: Hasselbeck 26-49, 273 yds, 1 TD, 1 Int.

Receiving — Pittsburgh: Ward 5-123, 1 TD, Randle El 3-22, Wilson 1020, Parker 1-1. Seattle: Jurevicius 5-93, Engram 6-70, Jackson 5-50, Stevens 3-25, 1 TD, Strong 2-15, Hannam 2-12, Morris 1-6, Alexander 2-2.

Team Statistics	SEA	PIT
1st downs	20	14
Total net yards	396	339
Rushes-yards	25-137	33-181
Passing yards, net	259	158
Punt returns-yards	4-27	2-32
Kickoff returns-yards	4-71	2-43
Interception return-yards	2-76	1-24
Field goals made-attempts	1-3	0-0
Att.-comp.-int.	26-49-1	10-22-2
Sacked-yards lost	3-14	1-8
Punts-average	6-50.2	6-48.7
Fumbles-lost	0-0	0-0
Penalties-yards	7-70	3-20
Time of possession	33:02	26:58

Attendance — 68,206. **Game Length** — 3:36.

Super Bowl Results

	Year	Winner	Loser	Winning coach	Site
I	1967	*Green Bay Packers, 35	Kansas City Chiefs, 10	Vince Lombardi	Los Angeles Coliseum, CA
II	1968	Green Bay Packers, 33	*Oakland Raiders, 14	Vince Lombardi	Orange Bowl, Miami, FL
III	1969	*New York Jets, 16	Baltimore Colts, 7	Weeb Ewbank	Orange Bowl, Miami, FL
IV	1970	Kansas City Chiefs, 23	*Minnesota Vikings, 7	Hank Stram	Tulane Stadium, New Orleans, LA
V	1971	Baltimore Colts, 16	*Dallas Cowboys, 13	Don McCafferty	Orange Bowl, Miami, FL
VI	1972	Dallas Cowboys, 24	*Miami Dolphins, 3	Tom Landry	Tulane Stadium, New Orleans, LA
VII	1973	*Miami Dolphins, 14	Washington Redskins, 7	Don Shula	Los Angeles Coliseum, CA
VIII	1974	*Miami Dolphins, 24	Minnesota Vikings, 7	Don Shula	Rice Stadium, Houston, TX
IX	1975	*Pittsburgh Steelers, 16	Minnesota Vikings, 6	Chuck Noll	Tulane Stadium, New Orleans, LA
X	1976	Pittsburgh Steelers, 21	*Dallas Cowboys, 17	Chuck Noll	Orange Bowl, Miami, FL
XI	1977	*Oakland Raiders, 32	Minnesota Vikings, 14	John Madden	Rose Bowl, Pasadena, CA
XII	1978	*Dallas Cowboys, 27	Denver Broncos, 10	Tom Landry	Superdome, New Orleans, LA
XIII	1979	Pittsburgh Steelers, 35	*Dallas Cowboys, 31	Chuck Noll	Orange Bowl, Miami, FL
XIV	1980	Pittsburgh Steelers, 31	*Los Angeles Rams, 19	Chuck Noll	Rose Bowl, Pasadena, CA
XV	1981	Oakland Raiders, 27	*Philadelphia Eagles, 10	Tom Flores	Superdome, New Orleans, LA
XVI	1982	*San Francisco 49ers, 26	Cincinnati Bengals, 21	Bill Walsh	Silverdome, Pontiac, MI
XVII	1983	Washington Redskins, 27	*Miami Dolphins, 17	Joe Gibbs	Rose Bowl, Pasadena, CA
XVIII	1984	*Los Angeles Raiders, 38	Washington Redskins, 9	Tom Flores	Tampa Stadium, FL
XIX	1985	*San Francisco 49ers, 38	Miami Dolphins, 16	Bill Walsh	Stanford Stadium, Palo Alto, CA
XX	1986	*Chicago Bears, 46	New England Patriots, 10	Mike Ditka	Superdome, New Orleans, LA
XXI	1987	New York Giants, 39	*Denver Broncos, 20	Bill Parcells	Rose Bowl, Pasadena, CA
XXII	1988	*Washington Redskins, 42	Denver Broncos, 10	Joe Gibbs	San Diego Stadium, CA
XXIII	1989	*San Francisco 49ers, 20	Cincinnati Bengals, 16	Bill Walsh	Joe Robbie Stadium, Miami, FL
XXIV	1990	San Francisco 49ers, 55	*Denver Broncos, 10	George Seifert	Superdome, New Orleans, LA
XXV	1991	New York Giants, 20	*Buffalo Bills, 19	Bill Parcells	Tampa Stadium, FL
XXVI	1992	*Washington Redskins, 37	Buffalo Bills, 24	Joe Gibbs	Metrodome, Minneapolis, MN
XXVII	1993	Dallas Cowboys, 52	*Buffalo Bills, 17	Jimmy Johnson	Rose Bowl, Pasadena, CA
XXVIII	1994	*Dallas Cowboys, 30	Buffalo Bills, 13	Jimmy Johnson	Georgia Dome, Atlanta, GA
XXIX	1995	*San Francisco 49ers, 49	San Diego Chargers, 26	George Seifert	Joe Robbie Stadium, Miami, FL
XXX	1996	*Dallas Cowboys, 27	Pittsburgh Steelers, 17	Barry Switzer	Sun Devil Stadium, Tempe, AZ
XXXI	1997	Green Bay Packers, 35	*New England Patriots, 21	Mike Holmgren	Superdome, New Orleans, LA
XXXII	1998	Denver Broncos, 31	*Green Bay Packers, 24	Mike Shanahan	Qualcomm Stadium, San Diego, CA
XXXIII	1999	Denver Broncos, 34	*Atlanta Falcons, 19	Mike Shanahan	Pro Player Stadium, Miami, FL
XXXIV	2000	*St. Louis Rams, 23	Tennessee Titans, 16	Dick Vermeil	Georgia Dome, Atlanta, GA
XXXV	2001	Baltimore Ravens, 34	*New York Giants, 7	Brian Billick	Raymond James Stad., Tampa, FL

It's a Record! Former Pittsburgh Steelers head coach Chuck Noll holds the record for the most Super Bowl coaching victories with four. Don Shula's six Super Bowl trips is the most for any coach. Bud Grant (0-4), Don Shula (2-4), Marv Levy (0-4), and Dan Reeves (0-4) have each lost four Super Bowls.

	Year	Winner	Loser	Winning coach	Site
XXXVI	2002	New England Patriots, 20	*St. Louis Rams, 17	Bill Belichick	Superdome, New Orleans, LA
XXXVII	2003	*Tampa Bay Buccaneers, 48	Oakland Raiders, 21	Jon Gruden	Qualcomm Stadium, San Diego, CA
XXXVIII	2004	New England Patriots, 32	*Carolina Panthers, 29	Bill Belichick	Reliant Stadium, Houston, TX
XXXIX	2005	*New England Patriots, 24	Philadelphia Eagles, 21	Bill Belichick	Alltel Stadium, Jacksonville, FL
XL	2006	Pittsburgh Steelers, 21	*Seattle Seahawks, 10	Bill Cowher	Ford Field, Detroit, MI

*Team that won the coin toss. All teams that won the toss elected to receive.

Super Bowl Single-Game Statistical Leaders

Passing Yards

	Year	Att/Comp	Yds	TDs
Kurt Warner, Rams	2000	45/24	414	2
Kurt Warner, Rams	2002	44/28	365	1
Joe Montana, 49ers	1989	36/23	357	2

Receiving Yards

	Year	Recept.	Yds	TDs
Jerry Rice, 49ers	1989	11	215	1
Ricky Sanders, Redskins	1988	9	193	2
Isaac Bruce, Rams	2000	6	162	1

Rushing Yards

	Year	Attempts	Yds	TDs
Timmy Smith, Redskins	1988	22	204	2
Marcus Allen, Raiders	1984	20	191	2
John Riggins, Redskins	1983	38	166	1

Passing Touchdowns

	Year	Att/Comp	Yds	TDs
Steve Young, 49ers	1995	36/24	325	6
Joe Montana, 49ers	1990	29/22	297	5
Troy Aikman, Cowboys	1993	30/22	273	4
Doug Williams, Redskins	1988	29/18	340	4
Terry Bradshaw, Steelers	1979	30/17	318	4

Scoring

	Year	Points	
Terrell Davis, Broncos	1998	18	3 TDs
Jerry Rice, 49ers	1995	18	3 TDs
Ricky Watters, 49ers	1995	18	3 TDs
Jerry Rice, 49ers	1990	18	3 TDs
Roger Craig, 49ers	1985	18	3 TDs
Don Chandler, Packers	1968	15	4 FG, 3PATs

Super Bowl MVPs

1967	Bart Starr, Green Bay	1980	Terry Bradshaw, Pittsburgh	1993	Troy Aikman, Dallas
1968	Bart Starr, Green Bay	1981	Jim Plunkett, Oakland	1994	Emmitt Smith, Dallas
1969	Joe Namath, N.Y. Jets	1982	Joe Montana, San Francisco	1995	Steve Young, San Francisco
1970	Len Dawson, Kansas City	1983	John Riggins, Washington	1996	Larry Brown, Dallas
1971	Chuck Howley, Dallas	1984	Marcus Allen, L.A. Raiders	1997	Desmond Howard, Green Bay
1972	Roger Staubach, Dallas	1985	Joe Montana, San Francisco	1998	Terrell Davis, Denver
1973	Jake Scott, Miami	1986	Richard Dent, Chicago	1999	John Elway, Denver
1974	Larry Csonka, Miami	1987	Phil Simms, N.Y. Giants	2000	Kurt Warner, St. Louis
1975	Franco Harris, Pittsburgh	1988	Doug Williams, Washington	2001	Ray Lewis, Baltimore
1976	Lynn Swann, Pittsburgh	1989	Jerry Rice, San Francisco	2002	Tom Brady, New England
1977	Fred Biletnikoff, Oakland	1990	Joe Montana, San Francisco	2003	Dexter Jackson, Tampa Bay
1978	Randy White, Harvey Martin, Dallas	1991	Ottis Anderson, N.Y. Giants	2004	Tom Brady, New England
1979	Terry Bradshaw, Pittsburgh	1992	Mark Rypien, Washington	2005	Deion Branch, New England
				2006	Hines Ward, Pittsburgh

American Football Conference Leaders

(American Football League, 1960-69)

Passing[1]					Year	Receptions			
Player, team	Att	Com	YG	TD		Player, team	Rec.	YG	TD
Jack Kemp, L.A. Chargers	406	211	3,018	20	1960	Lionel Taylor, Denver	92	1,235	12
George Blanda, Houston	362	187	3,330	36	1961	Lionel Taylor, Denver	100	1,176	4
Len Dawson, Dallas Texans	310	189	2,759	29	1962	Lionel Taylor, Denver	77	908	4
Tobin Rote, San Diego	286	170	2,510	20	1963	Lionel Taylor, Denver	78	1,101	10
Len Dawson, Kansas City	354	199	2,879	30	1964	Charley Hennigan, Houston	101	1,546	8
John Hadl, San Diego	348	174	2,798	20	1965	Lionel Taylor, Denver	85	1,131	6
Len Dawson, Kansas City	284	159	2,527	26	1966	Lance Alworth, San Diego	73	1,383	13
Daryle Lamonica, Oakland	425	220	3,228	30	1967	George Sauer, N.Y. Jets	75	1,189	6
Len Dawson, Kansas City	224	131	2,109	17	1968	Lance Alworth, San Diego	68	1,312	10
Greg Cook, Cincinnati	197	106	1,854	15	1969	Lance Alworth, San Diego	64	1,003	4
Daryle Lamonica, Oakland	356	179	2,516	22	1970	Marlin Briscoe, Buffalo	57	1,036	8
Bob Griese, Miami	263	145	2,089	19	1971	Fred Biletnikoff, Oakland	61	929	9
Earl Morrall, Miami	150	83	1,360	11	1972	Fred Biletnikoff, Oakland	58	802	7
Ken Stabler, Oakland	260	163	1,997	14	1973	Fred Willis, Houston	57	371	1
Ken Anderson, Cincinnati	328	213	2,667	18	1974	Lydell Mitchell, Baltimore Colts	72	544	2
Ken Anderson, Cincinnati	377	228	3,169	21	1975	Reggie Rucker, Cleveland	60	770	3
						Lydell Mitchell, Baltimore Colts	60	554	4
Ken Stabler, Oakland	291	194	2,737	27	1976	MacArthur Lane, Kansas City	66	686	1
Bob Griese, Miami	307	180	2,252	22	1977	Lydell Mitchell, Baltimore Colts	71	620	4
Terry Bradshaw, Pittsburgh	368	207	2,915	28	1978	Steve Largent, Seattle	71	1,168	8
Dan Fouts, San Diego	530	332	4,082	24	1979	Joe Washington, Baltimore Colts	82	750	3
Brian Sipe, Cleveland	554	337	4,132	30	1980	Kellen Winslow, San Diego	89	1,290	9
Ken Anderson, Cincinnati	479	300	3,754	29	1981	Kellen Winslow, San Diego	88	1,075	10
Ken Anderson, Cincinnati	309	218	2,495	12	1982	Kellen Winslow, San Diego	54	721	6
Dan Marino, Miami	296	173	2,210	20	1983	Todd Christensen, L.A. Raiders	92	1,247	12
Dan Marino, Miami	564	362	5,084	48	1984	Ozzie Newsome, Cleveland	89	1,001	5
Ken O'Brien, N.Y. Jets	488	297	3,888	25	1985	Lionel James, San Diego	86	1,027	6
Dan Marino, Miami	623	378	4,746	44	1986	Todd Christensen, L.A. Raiders	95	1,153	8
Bernie Kosar, Cleveland	389	241	3,033	22	1987	Al Toon, N.Y. Jets	68	976	5
Boomer Esiason, Cincinnati	388	223	3,572	28	1988	Al Toon, N.Y. Jets	93	1,067	5
Boomer Esiason, Cincinnati	455	258	3,525	28	1989	Andre Reed, Buffalo	88	1,312	9
Jim Kelly, Buffalo	346	219	2,829	24	1990	Haywood Jeffires, Houston	74	1,048	8
						Drew Hill, Houston	74	1,019	5
Jim Kelly, Buffalo	474	304	3,844	33	1991	Haywood Jeffires, Houston	100	1,181	7
Warren Moon, Houston	346	224	2,521	18	1992	Haywood Jeffires, Houston	90	913	9

Passing[1]

Player, team	Att	Com	YG	TD	Year
John Elway, Denver	551	348	4,030	25	1993
Dan Marino, Miami	615	385	4,453	30	1994
Jim Harbaugh, Indianapolis	314	200	2,575	17	1995
John Elway, Denver	466	287	3,328	26	1996
Mark Brunell, Jacksonville	435	264	3,281	18	1997
Vinny Testaverde, N.Y. Jets	421	259	3,256	29	1998
Peyton Manning, Indianapolis	533	331	4,135	26	1999
Brian Griese, Denver	336	216	2,688	19	2000
Rich Gannon, Oakland	549	361	3,828	27	2001
Chad Pennington, N.Y. Jets	399	275	3,120	22	2002
Steve McNair, Tennessee	400	250	3,215	24	2003
Peyton Manning, Indianapolis	497	336	4,557	49	2004
Peyton Manning, Indianapolis	453	305	3747	28	2005

Receptions

Player, team	Rec.	YG	TD	Year
Reggie Langhorne, Indianapolis	85	1,038	3	1993
Ben Coates, New England	96	1,174	7	1994
Carl Pickens, Cincinnati	99	1,234	17	1995
Carl Pickens, Cincinnati	100	1,180	12	1996
Tim Brown, Oakland	104	1,408	5	1997
O.J. McDuffie, Miami	90	1,050	7	1998
Jimmy Smith, Jacksonville	116	1,636	6	1999
Marvin Harrison, Indianapolis	102	1,413	14	2000
Marvin Harrison, Indianapolis	109	1,524	15	2001
Marvin Harrison, Indianapolis	143	1,722	11	2002
LaDainian Tomlinson, San Diego	100	725	4	2003
Tony Gonzalez, Kansas City	102	1,258	9	2004
Chad Johnson, Cincinnati	97	1,432	9	2005

Scoring

Player, team	TD	PAT	FG	Pts	Year
Gene Mingo, Denver	6	33	18	123	1960
Gino Cappelletti, Boston	8	48	17	147	1961
Gene Mingo, Denver	4	32	27	137	1962
Gino Cappelletti, Boston	2	35	22	113	1963
Gino Cappelletti, Boston	7	36	25	155	1964
Gino Cappelletti, Boston	9	27	17	132	1965
Gino Cappelletti, Boston	6	35	16	119	1966
George Blanda, Oakland	0	56	20	116	1967
Jim Turner, N.Y. Jets	0	43	34	145	1968
Jim Turner, N.Y. Jets	0	33	32	129	1969
Jan Stenerud, Kansas City	0	26	30	116	1970
Garo Yepremian, Miami	0	33	28	117	1971
Bobby Howfield, N.Y. Jets	0	40	27	121	1972
Roy Gerela, Pittsburgh	0	36	29	123	1973
Roy Gerela, Pittsburgh	0	33	20	93	1974
O.J. Simpson, Buffalo	23	0	0	138	1975
Toni Linhart, Baltimore Colts	0	49	20	109	1976
Errol Mann, Oakland	0	39	20	99	1977
Pat Leahy, N.Y. Jets	0	41	22	107	1978
John Smith, New England	0	46	23	115	1979
John Smith, New England	0	51	26	129	1980
Jim Breech, Cincinnati	0	49	22	115	1981
Nick Lowery, Kansas City	0	37	26	115	
Marcus Allen, L.A. Raiders	14	0	0	84	1982
Gary Anderson, Pittsburgh	0	38	27	119	1983
Gary Anderson, Pittsburgh	0	45	24	117	1984
Gary Anderson, Pittsburgh	0	40	33	139	1985
Tony Franklin, New England	0	44	32	140	1986
Jim Breech, Cincinnati	0	25	24	97	1987
Scott Norwood, Buffalo	0	33	32	129	1988
David Treadwell, Denver	0	39	27	120	1989
Nick Lowery, Kansas City	0	37	34	139	1990
Pete Stoyanovich, Miami	0	28	31	121	1991
Pete Stoyanovich, Miami	0	34	30	124	1992
Jeff Jaeger, L.A. Raiders	0	27	35	132	1993
John Carney, San Diego	0	33	34	135	1994
Norm Johnson, Pittsburgh	0	39	34	141	1995
Cary Blanchard, Indianapolis	0	27	36	135	1996
Mike Hollis, Jacksonville	0	41	31	134	1997
Steve Christie, Buffalo	0	41	33	140	1998
Mike Vanderjagt, Indianapolis	0	43	34	145	1999
Matt Stover, Baltimore	0	30	35	135	2000
Mike Vanderjagt, Indianapolis	0	41	28	125	2001
Priest Holmes, Kansas City	24	0	0	144	2002
Priest Holmes, Kansas City	27	0	0	162	2003
Adam Vinatieri, New England	0	48	31	141	2004
Shayne Graham, Cincinnati	0	47	28	131	2005

Rushing

Player, team	Yds	Att	TD	Year
Abner Haynes, Dallas Texans	875	156	9	1960
Billy Cannon, Houston	948	200	6	1961
Cookie Gilchrest, Buffalo	1,096	214	13	1962
Clem Daniels, Oakland	1,099	215	3	1963
Cookie Gilchrest, Buffalo	981	230	6	1964
Paul Lowe, San Diego	1,121	222	7	1965
Jim Nance, Boston	1,458	299	11	1966
Jim Nance, Boston	1,216	269	7	1967
Paul Robinson, Cincinnati	1,023	238	8	1968
Dick Post, San Diego	873	182	6	1969
Floyd Little, Denver	901	209	3	1970
Floyd Little, Denver	1,133	284	6	1971
O.J. Simpson, Buffalo	1,251	292	6	1972
O.J. Simpson, Buffalo	2,003	332	12	1973
Otis Armstrong, Denver	1,407	263	9	1974
O.J. Simpson, Buffalo	1,817	329	16	1975
O.J. Simpson, Buffalo	1,503	290	8	1976
Mark van Eeghen, Oakland	1,273	324	7	1977
Earl Campbell, Houston	1,450	302	13	1978
Earl Campbell, Houston	1,697	368	19	1979
Earl Campbell, Houston	1,934	373	13	1980
Earl Campbell, Houston	1,376	361	10	1981
Freeman McNeil, N.Y. Jets	786	151	6	1982
Curt Warner, Seattle	1,446	335	13	1983
Earnest Jackson, San Diego	1,179	296	8	1984
Marcus Allen, L.A. Raiders	1,759	380	11	1985
Curt Warner, Seattle	1,481	319	13	1986
Eric Dickerson, L.A. Rams-Ind.	1,288*	283	6	1987
Eric Dickerson, Indianapolis	1,659	388	14	1988
Christian Okoye, Kansas City	1,480	370	12	1989
Thurman Thomas, Buffalo	1,297	271	11	1990
Thurman Thomas, Buffalo	1,407	288	7	1991
Barry Foster, Pittsburgh	1,690	390	11	1992
Thurman Thomas, Buffalo	1,315	355	6	1993
Chris Warren, Seattle	1,545	333	9	1994
Curtis Martin, New England	1,487	368	14	1995
Terrell Davis, Denver	1,538	345	13	1996
Terrell Davis, Denver	1,750	369	15	1997
Terrell Davis, Denver	2,008	392	21	1998
Edgerrin James, Indianapolis	1,553	369	13	1999
Edgerrin James, Indianapolis	1,709	387	13	2000
Priest Holmes, Kansas City	1,555	325	8	2001
Ricky Williams, Miami	1,853	383	16	2002
Jamal Lewis, Baltimore	2,066	387	14	2003
Curtis Martin, N.Y. Jets	1,697	371	12	2004
Larry Johnson, Kansas City	1,750	336	20	2005

*Includes 277 yards after being traded to NFC; 1,011 yards led AFC. (1) Based on quarterback rating points.

National Football Conference Leaders

(National Football League, 1960-69)

Passing[1]

Player, team	Att	Com	YG	TD	Year
Milt Plum, Cleveland	250	151	2,297	21	1960
Milt Plum, Cleveland	302	177	2,416	18	1961
Bart Starr, Green Bay	285	178	2,438	12	1962
Y.A. Tittle, N.Y. Giants	367	221	3,145	36	1963
Bart Starr, Green Bay	272	163	2,144	15	1964
Rudy Bukich, Chicago	312	176	2,641	20	1965
Bart Starr, Green Bay	251	156	2,257	14	1966
Sonny Jurgensen, Washington	508	288	3,747	31	1967
Earl Morrall, Baltimore Colts	317	182	2,909	26	1968
Sonny Jurgensen, Washington	442	274	3,102	22	1969
John Brodie, San Francisco	378	223	2,941	24	1970
Roger Staubach, Dallas	211	126	1,882	15	1971
Norm Snead, N.Y. Giants	325	196	2,307	17	1972
Roger Staubach, Dallas	286	179	2,428	23	1973
Sonny Jurgensen, Washington	167	107	1,185	11	1974
Fran Tarkenton, Minnesota	425	273	2,994	25	1975
James Harris, L.A. Rams	158	91	1,460	8	1976
Roger Staubach, Dallas	361	210	2,620	18	1977

Receptions

Player, team	Rec.	YG	TD	Year
Raymond Berry, Baltimore Colts	74	1,298	10	1960
Jim Phillips, L.A. Rams	78	1,092	5	1961
Bobby Mitchell, Washington	72	1,384	11	1962
Bobby Joe Conrad, St. Louis Cardinals	73	967	10	1963
Johnny Morris, Chicago	93	1,200	10	1964
Dave Parks, San Francisco	80	1,344	12	1965
Charley Taylor, Washington	72	1,119	12	1966
Charley Taylor, Washington	70	990	9	1967
Clifton McNeil, San Francisco	71	994	7	1968
Dan Abramowicz, New Orleans	73	1,015	7	1969
Dick Gordon, Chicago	71	1,026	13	1970
Bob Tucker, N.Y. Giants	59	791	4	1971
Harold Jackson, Philadelphia	62	1,048	4	1972
Harold Carmichael, Philadelphia	67	1,116	9	1973
Charles Young, Philadelphia	63	696	3	1974
Chuck Foreman, Minnesota	73	691	9	1975
Drew Pearson, Dallas	58	806	6	1976
Ahmad Rashad, Minnesota	51	681	2	1977

Passing[1] / Receptions

Player, team	Att	Com	YG	TD	Year	Player, team	Rec.	YG	TD
Roger Staubach, Dallas	413	231	3,190	25	1978	Rickey Young, Minnesota	88	704	5
Roger Staubach, Dallas	461	267	3,586	27	1979	Ahmad Rashad, Minnesota	80	1,156	9
Ron Jaworski, Philadelphia	451	257	3,529	27	1980	Earl Cooper, San Francisco	83	567	4
Joe Montana, San Francisco	488	311	3,565	19	1981	Dwight Clark, San Francisco	85	1,105	4
Joe Thiesmann, Washington	252	161	2,033	13	1982	Dwight Clark, San Francisco	60	913	5
Steve Bartkowski, Atlanta	432	274	3,167	22	1983	Roy Green, St. Louis Cardinals	78	1,227	14
						Charlie Brown, Washington	78	1,225	8
						Earnest Gray, N.Y. Giants	78	1,139	5
Joe Montana, San Francisco	432	279	3,630	28	1984	Art Monk, Washington	106	1,372	7
Joe Montana, San Francisco	494	303	3,653	27	1985	Roger Craig, San Francisco	92	1,016	6
Tommy Kramer, Minnesota	372	208	3,000	24	1986	Jerry Rice, San Francisco	86	1,570	15
Joe Montana, San Francisco	398	266	3,054	31	1987	J.T. Smith, St. Louis Cardinals	91	1,117	8
Wade Wilson, Minnesota	332	204	2,746	15	1988	Henry Ellard, L.A. Rams	86	1,414	10
Joe Montana, San Francisco	386	271	3,521	26	1989	Sterling Sharpe, Green Bay	90	1,423	12
Phil Simms, N.Y. Giants	311	184	2,284	15	1990	Jerry Rice, San Francisco	100	1,502	13
Steve Young, San Francisco	279	180	2,517	17	1991	Michael Irvin, Dallas	93	1,523	8
Steve Young, San Francisco	402	268	3,465	25	1992	Sterling Sharpe, Green Bay	108	1,461	13
Steve Young, San Francisco	462	314	4,023	29	1993	Sterling Sharpe, Green Bay	112	1,274	11
Steve Young, San Francisco	461	324	3,969	35	1994	Cris Carter, Minnesota	122	1,256	7
Brett Favre, Green Bay	570	359	4,413	38	1995	Herman Moore, Detroit	123	1,686	14
Steve Young, San Francisco	316	214	2,410	14	1996	Jerry Rice, San Francisco	108	1,254	8
Steve Young, San Francisco	356	241	3,029	19	1997	Herman Moore, Detroit	104	1,293	8
Randall Cunningham, Minnesota	425	259	3,704	34	1998	Frank Sanders, Arizona	89	1,145	3
Kurt Warner, St. Louis	499	325	4,353	41	1999	Muhsin Muhammad, Carolina	96	1,253	8
Trent Green, St. Louis	240	145	2,063	16	2000	Muhsin Muhammad, Carolina	102	1,183	6
Kurt Warner, St. Louis	546	375	4,830	36	2001	David Boston, Arizona	98	1,598	8
Brad Johnson, Tampa Bay	451	281	3,049	22	2002	Randy Moss, Minnesota	106	1,347	7
Daunte Culpepper, Minnesota	454	295	3,479	25	2003	Torry Holt, St. Louis	117	1,696	12
Daunte Culpepper, Minnesota	548	379	4,717	39	2004	Joe Horn, New Orleans	94	1,399	11
						Torry Holt, St. Louis	94	1,372	10
Matt Hasselbeck, Seattle	449	294	3,459	24	2005	Steve Smith, Carolina	103	1,563	12
						Larry Fitzgerald, Arizona	103	1,409	10

Scoring / Rushing

Player, team	TD	PAT	FG	Pts	Year	Player, team	Yds	Att	TD
Paul Hornung, Green Bay	15	41	15	176	1960	Jim Brown, Cleveland	1,257	215	9
Paul Hornung, Green Bay	10	41	15	146	1961	Jim Brown, Cleveland	1,408	305	8
Jim Taylor, Green Bay	19	0	0	114	1962	Jim Taylor, Green Bay	1,474	272	19
Don Chandler, N.Y. Giants	0	52	18	106	1963	Jim Brown, Cleveland	1,863	291	12
Lenny Moore, Baltimore Colts	20	0	0	120	1964	Jim Brown, Cleveland	1,446	280	7
Gale Sayers, Chicago	22	0	0	132	1965	Jim Brown, Cleveland	1,544	289	17
Bruce Gossett, L.A. Rams	0	29	28	113	1966	Gale Sayers, Chicago	1,231	229	8
Jim Bakken, St. Louis Cardinals	0	36	27	117	1967	Leroy Kelly, Cleveland	1,205	235	11
Leroy Kelly, Cleveland	20	0	0	120	1968	Leroy Kelly, Cleveland	1,239	248	16
Fred Cox, Minnesota	0	43	26	121	1969	Gale Sayers, Chicago	1,032	236	8
Fred Cox, Minnesota	0	35	30	125	1970	Larry Brown, Washington	1,125	237	5
Curt Knight, Washington	0	27	29	114	1971	John Brockington, Green Bay	1,105	216	4
Chester Marcol, Green Bay	0	29	33	128	1972	Larry Brown, Washington	1,216	285	8
David Ray, L.A. Rams	0	40	30	130	1973	John Brockington, Green Bay	1,144	265	3
Chester Marcol, Green Bay	0	19	25	94	1974	Lawrence McCutcheon, L.A. Rams	1,109	236	3
Chuck Foreman, Minnesota	22	0	0	132	1975	Jim Otis, St. Louis Cardinals	1,076	269	5
Mark Moseley, Washington	0	31	22	97	1976	Walter Payton, Chicago	1,390	311	13
Walter Payton, Chicago	16	0	0	96	1977	Walter Payton, Chicago	1,852	339	14
Frank Corral, L.A. Rams	0	31	29	118	1978	Walter Payton, Chicago	1,395	333	11
Mark Moseley, Washington	0	39	25	114	1979	Walter Payton, Chicago	1,610	369	14
Ed Murray, Detroit	0	35	27	116	1980	Walter Payton, Chicago	1,460	317	6
Ed Murray, Detroit	0	46	25	121	1981	George Rogers, New Orleans	1,674	378	13
Rafael Septien, Dallas	0	40	27	121					
Wendell Tyler, L.A. Rams	13	0	0	78	1982	Tony Dorsett, Dallas	745	177	5
Mark Moseley, Washington	0	62	33	161	1983	Eric Dickerson, L.A. Rams	1,808	390	18
Ray Wersching, San Francisco	0	56	25	131	1984	Eric Dickerson, L.A. Rams	2,105	379	14
Kevin Butler, Chicago	0	51	31	144	1985	Gerald Riggs, Atlanta	1,719	397	10
Kevin Butler, Chicago	0	36	28	120	1986	Eric Dickerson, L.A. Rams	1,821	404	11
Jerry Rice, San Francisco	23	0	0	138	1987	Charles White, L.A. Rams	1,374	324	11
Mike Cofer, San Francisco	0	40	27	121	1988	Herschel Walker, Dallas	1,514	361	5
Mike Cofer, San Francisco	0	49	29	136	1989	Barry Sanders, Detroit	1,470	280	14
Chip Lohmiller, Washington	0	41	30	131	1990	Barry Sanders, Detroit	1,304	255	13
Chip Lohmiller, Washington	0	56	31	149	1991	Emmitt Smith, Dallas	1,563	365	12
Morten Andersen, New Orleans	0	33	29	120	1992	Emmitt Smith, Dallas	1,713	373	18
Chip Lohmiller, Washington	0	30	30	120					
Jason Hanson, Detroit	0	28	34	130	1993	Emmitt Smith, Dallas	1,486	283	9
Fuad Reveiz, Minnesota	0	30	34	132	1994	Barry Sanders, Detroit	1,883	331	7
Emmitt Smith, Dallas	22	0	0	132					
Emmitt Smith, Dallas	25	0	0	150	1995	Emmitt Smith, Dallas	1,773	377	25
John Kasay, Carolina	0	34	37	145	1996	Barry Sanders, Detroit	1,553	307	11
Richie Cunningham, Dallas	0	24	34	126	1997	Barry Sanders, Detroit	2,053	335	11
Gary Anderson, Minnesota	0	59	35	164	1998	Jamal Anderson, Atlanta	1,846	410	14
Jeff Wilkins, St. Louis	0	64	20	124	1999	Stephen Davis, Washington	1,405	290	17
Marshall Faulk, St. Louis	26	0	0	156	2000	Robert Smith, Minnesota	1,521	295	7
Marshall Faulk, St. Louis	21	0	0	128	2001	Stephen Davis, Washington	1,432	356	5
Jay Feely, Atlanta	0	42	32	138	2002	Deuce McAllister, New Orleans	1,388	325	13
Jeff Wilkins, St. Louis	0	46	39	163	2003	Ahman Green, Green Bay	1,883	355	15
David Akers, Philadelphia	0	41	27	122	2004	Shaun Alexander, Seattle	1,696	353	16
Shaun Alexander, Seattle	28	0	0	168	2005	Shaun Alexander, Seattle	1,880	370	27

(1) Based on quarterback rating points.

> **IT'S A FACT:** The American Professional Football Association changed its name to the National Football League in 1922. That year the 18 NFL teams were: Canton Bulldogs, Chicago Bears, Chicago Cardinals, Toledo Maroons, Rock Island Independents, Racine Legion, Dayton Triangles, Green Bay Packers, Buffalo All-Americans, Akron Pros, Milwaukee Badgers, Oorang Indians, Minneapolis Marines, Louisville Brecks, Rochester Jeffersons, Hammond Pros, Columbus Panhandles, and the Evansville Crimson Giants.

2005 NFL Individual Leaders
American Football Conference

PASSING	Att	Comp	Pct Comp	Yds	Yds/Att	Long	TD	Pct TD	Int	Rating Points
Peyton Manning, Indianapolis	453	305	67.3	3,747	8.27	80	28	6.2	10	104.1
Carson Palmer, Cincinnati	509	345	67.8	3,836	7.54	70	32	6.3	12	101.1
Ben Roethlisberger, Pittsburgh	268	168	62.7	2,385	8.90	85	17	6.3	9	98.6
Tom Brady, New England	530	334	63.0	4,110	7.76	71	26	4.9	14	92.3
Jake Plummer, Denver	456	277	60.7	3,366	7.38	72	18	3.9	7	90.2
Trent Green, Kansas City	507	317	62.5	4,014	7.92	60	17	3.4	10	90.1
Byron Leftwich, Jacksonville	302	175	57.9	2,123	7.03	45	15	5.0	5	89.3
Drew Brees, San Diego	500	323	64.6	3,576	7.15	54	24	4.8	15	89.2
Kelly Holcomb, Buffalo	230	155	67.4	1,509	6.56	65	10	4.3	8	85.6
Steve McNair, Tennessee	476	292	61.3	3,161	6.64	57	16	3.4	11	82.4

RUSHING	Yds	Att	Avg	Long	TD
Larry Johnson, Kansas City	1,750	336	5.2	49	20
Edgerrin James, Indianapolis	1,506	360	4.2	33	13
LaDainian Tomlinson, San Diego	1,462	339	4.3	62	18
Rudi Johnson, Cincinnati	1,458	337	4.3	33	12
Willis McGahee, Buffalo	1,247	325	3.8	27	5
Reuben Droughns, Cleveland	1,232	309	4.0	75	2
Willie Parker, Pittsburgh	1,202	255	4.7	80	4
LaMont Jordan, Oakland	1,025	272	3.8	26	9
Mike Anderson, Denver	1,014	239	4.2	44	12
Domanick Davis, Houston	976	230	4.2	44	2

RECEIVING	Rec	Yds	Avg	Long	TD
Chad Johnson, Cincinnati	97	1,432	14.8	70	9
Antonio Gates, San Diego	89	1,101	12.4	38	10
Derrick Mason, Baltimore	86	1,073	12.5	39	3
Rod Smith, Denver	85	1,105	13.0	72	6
Reggie Wayne, Indianapolis	83	1,055	12.7	66	5
M. Harrison, Indianapolis	82	1,146	14.0	80	12
C. Chambers, Miami	82	1,118	13.6	77	11
Eric Moulds, Buffalo	81	816	10.1	55	4
Deion Branch, New England	78	998	12.8	51	5
T. Houshmandzadeh, Cincinnati	78	956	12.3	43	7
Tony Gonzalez, Kansas City	78	905	11.6	39	2

SCORING—KICKERS	PAT	FG	Long	Pts
S. Graham, Cincinnati	47/47	28/32	49	131
L. Tynes, Kansas City	44/45	27/33	52	125
M. Vanderjagt, Indianapolis	52/52	23/25	48	121
J. Reed, Pittsburgh	45/45	24/29	44	117
J. Elam, Denver	43/44	24/32	51	115

SCORING—NON-KICKERS	TD	Rush	Rec	2 Pt	Pts
Larry Johnson, Kansas City	21	20	1	0	126
LaDainian Tomlinson, San Diego	20	18	2	0	120
Edgerrin James, Indianapolis	14	13	1	0	84
Corey Dillon, New England	13	12	1	0	78
Mike Anderson, Denver	13	12	1	0	78

INTERCEPTIONS	No.	Yds	Avg	Long	TD
Ty Law, N.Y. Jets	10	195	19.5	74	1
Deltha O'Neal, Cincinnati	10	103	10.3	37	0
Champ Bailey, Denver	8	139	17.4	65	2
Greg Wesley, Kansas City	6	106	17.7	51	0
Cato June, Indianapolis	5	115	23.0	36	2
David Barrett, N.Y. Jets	5	28	5.6	13	0
Tory James, Cincinnati	5	5	1.0	5	0
Odell Thurman, Cincinnati	5	59	11.8	30	1
Rashean Mathis, Jacksonville	5	79	15.8	41	1
Nick Ferguson, Denver	5	59	11.8	30	0

KICKOFF RETURNS	No.	Yds	Avg	Long	TD
Terrence McGee, Buffalo	46	1,391	30.2	99	1
Jerome Mathis, Houston	54	1,542	28.6	99	2
Justin Miller, N.Y. Jets	60	1,577	26.3	95	1
Pacman Jones, Tennessee	43	1,127	26.2	85	0
Quincy Morgan, Pittsburgh	23	583	25.3	74	0

PUNT RETURNS	No.	Yds	Avg	Long	TD
B.J. Sams, Baltimore	33	401	12.2	51	0
Dennis Northcutt, Cleveland	35	368	10.5	62	1
Antwaan Randle El, Pittsburgh	44	448	10.2	81	2
Pacman Jones, Tennessee	29	272	9.4	52	1
Wes Welker, Miami	43	390	9.1	47	0

PUNTING	No.	Yds	Long	Avg
Brian Moorman, Buffalo	71	3,242	68	45.7
Shane Lechler, Oakland	82	3,744	64	45.7
Josh Miller, New England	76	3,431	59	45.1
Hunter Smith, Indianapolis	52	2,301	58	44.3
Todd Sauerbrun, Denver	72	3,157	66	43.8

Sacks: Derrick Burgess, Oakland,16.0; Kyle Vanden Bosch, Tennessee, 12.5; Aaron Schobel, Buffalo, 12.0; Jason Taylor, Miami, 12.0; Robert Mathis, Indianapolis, 11.5; Dwight Freeney, Indianapolis, 11.0; Jared Allen, Kansas City, 11.0; John Abraham, N.Y. Jets, 10.5; Joey Porter, Pittsburgh, 10.5; Shawne Merriman, San Dieg, 10.0.

National Football Conference

PASSING	Att	Comp	Pct Comp	Yds	Yds/Att	Long	TD	Pct TD	Int	Rating Points
Matt Hasselbeck, Seattle	449	294	65.5	3,459	7.70	56	24	5.3	9	98.2
Marc Bulger, St. Louis	287	192	66.9	2,297	8.00	57	14	4.9	9	94.4
Brad Johnson, Minnesota	294	184	62.6	1,885	6.41	80	12	4.1	4	88.9
Jake Delhomme, Carolina	435	262	60.2	3,421	7.86	80	24	5.5	16	88.1
Mark Brunell, Washington	454	262	57.7	3,050	6.72	78	23	5.1	10	85.9
Kurt Warner QB, Arizona	375	242	64.5	2,713	7.24	63	11	2.9	9	85.8
Donovan McNabb, Philadelphia	357	211	59.1	2,507	7.02	91	16	4.5	9	85.0
Drew Bledsoe, Dallas	499	300	60.1	3,639	7.29	71	23	4.6	17	83.7
Chris Simms, Tampa Bay	313	191	61.0	2,035	6.50	78	10	3.2	7	81.4
Eli Manning, N.Y. Giants	557	294	52.8	3,762	6.75	78	24	4.3	17	75.9

RUSHING	Att	Yds	Avg	Long	TD
Shaun Alexander, Seattle	370	1,880	5.1	88	27
Tiki Barber, N.Y. Giants	357	1,860	5.2	95	9
Clinton Portis, Washington	352	1,516	4.3	47	11
Warrick Dunn, Atlanta	280	1,416	5.1	65	3
Thomas Jones, Chicago	314	1,335	4.3	42	9
Cadillac Williams, Tampa Bay	290	1,178	4.1	71	6
Steven Jackson, St. Louis	254	1,046	4.1	51	8
Julius Jones, Dallas	257	993	3.9	51	5
DeShaun Foster, Carolina	205	879	4.3	70	2
Kevin Jones, Detroit	186	664	3.6	40	5

RECEIVING	Rec	Yds	Avg	Long	TD
Larry Fitzgerald, Arizona	103	1,409	13.7	47	10
Steve Smith, Carolina	103	1,563	15.2	80	12
Anquan Boldin, Arizona	102	1,402	13.7	54	7
Torry Holt, St. Louis	102	1,331	13.0	44	9
Donald Driver, Green Bay	86	1,221	14.2	59	5
Santana Moss, Washington	84	1,483	17.7	78	9
Joey Galloway, Tampa Bay	83	1,287	15.5	80	10
Plaxico Burress, N.Y. Giants	76	1,214	16.0	78	7
Keyshawn Johnson, Dallas	71	839	11.8	34	6
Chris Cooley, Washington	71	774	10.9	32	7

SCORING—KICKERS	PAT	FG	Long	Pts
Jay Feely, N.Y. Giants	43/43	35/42	52	148
Neil Rackers, Arizona	20/20	40/42	54	140
John Kasay, Carolina	43/44	26/34	52	121
Jeff Wilkins, St. Louis	36/36	27/31	53	117
Josh Brown, Seattle	56/57	18/25	55	110

SCORING—NON-KICKERS	TD	Rush	Rec	Ret	Pts
Shaun Alexander, Seattle	28	27	1	0	168
Steve Smith, Carolina	13	1	12	0	78
Stephen Davis, Carolina	12	12	0	0	72
Tiki Barber, N.Y. Giants	11	9	2	0	68
Clinton Portis, Washington. . . .	11	11	0	0	68

INTERCEPTIONS	No.	Yds	Avg	Long	TD
Darren Sharper, Minnesota . . .	9	276	30.7	92	2
Nathan Vasher, Chicago	8	145	18.1	46	1
Chris Gamble, Carolina	7	157	22.4	61	1
Dre' Bly, Detroit	6	54	9.0	28	0
DeAngelo Hall, Atlanta.	6	177	29.5	65	0
Ken Lucas, Carolina.	6	70	11.7	32	0

KICKOFF RETURNS	No.	Yds	Avg	Long	TD
Koren Robinson, Minnesota . . .	47	1,221	26.0	86	1
Willie Ponder, N.Y. Giants	35	905	25.9	95	1
Ladell Betts, Washington	24	621	25.9	94	1
Tyson Thompson, Dallas	57	1,399	24.5	49	0
Roderick Hood, Philadelphia . . .	38	900	23.7	53	0

PUNT RETURNS	No.	Yds	Avg	Long	TD
Reno Mahe, Philadelphia	21	269	12.8	44	0
Mewelde Moore, Minnesota . . .	21	245	11.7	71	1
Steve Smith, Carolina	27	286	10.6	44	0
Chad Morton, N.Y. Giants	47	453	9.6	58	1
Mark Jones, Tampa Bay	51	492	9.6	31	0
Bobby Wade, Chicago.	33	317	9.6	73	1

PUNTING	No.	Yds	Long	Avg
Josh Bidwell, Tampa Bay	90	4,101	61	45.6
Chris Kluwe, Minnesota.	71	3,130	62	44.1
Scott Player, Arizona.	73	3,206	60	43.9
Nick Harris, Detroit	84	3,656	60	43.5
Jason Baker, Carolina.	72	3,118	59	43.3

Sacks: Osi Umenyiora, N.Y. Giants, 14.5; Simeon Rice, Tampa Bay, 14.0; Michael Strahan, N.Y. Giants, 11.5; Rod Coleman, Atlanta, 10.5; Julius Peppers, Carolina, 10.5; Adewale Ogunleye, Chicago, 10.0; Leonard Little, St. Louis, 9.5; Bryce Fisher, Seattle, 9.0; Rocky Bernard, Seattle, 8.5; Will Smith, New Orleans, 8.5

First-Round Selections in the 2006 NFL Draft

Team	Player	Pos	College	Team	Player	Pos	College
1. Houston	Williams, Mario	DE	NC State	17. Minnesota	Greenway, Chad	OLB	Iowa
2. New Orleans	Bush, Reggie	RB	USC	18. Dallas	Carpenter, Bobby	OLB	Ohio State
3. Tennessee	Young, Vince	QB	Texas	19. San Diego	Cromartie, Antonio	CB	Florida State
4. N.Y. Jets	Ferguson, D'Brickashaw	OT	Virginia	20. Kansas City	Hali, Tamba	DE	Penn State
5. Green Bay	Hawk, A.J.	OLB	Ohio State	21. New England	Maroney, Laurence	RB	Minnesota
6. San Francisco	Davis, Vernon	TE	Maryland	22. San Francisco[5]	Lawson, Manny	OLB	NC State
7. Oakland	Huff, Michael	SS	Texas	23. Tampa Bay	Joseph, Davin	G	Oklahoma
8. Buffalo	Whitner, Donte	SS	Ohio State	24. Cincinnati	Joseph, Johnathan	CB	South Carolina
9. Detroit	Sims, Ernie	OLB	Florida State	25. Pittsburgh[6]	Holmes, Santonio	WR	Ohio State
10. Arizona	Leinart, Matt	QB	USC	26. Buffalo[7]	McCargo, John	DT	NC State
11. Denver[1]	Cutler, Jay	QB	Vanderbilt	27. Carolina	Williams, DeAngelo	RB	Memphis
12. Baltimore[2]	Ngata, Haloti	DT	Oregon	28. Jacksonville	Lewis, Marcedes	TE	UCLA
13. Cleveland[3]	Wimbley, Kamerion	DE	Florida State	29. N.Y. Jets[8]	Mangold, Nick	C	Ohio State
14. Philadelphia	Bunkley, Brodrick	DT	Florida State	30. Indianapolis	Addai, Joseph	RB	LSU
15. St. Louis[4]	Hill, Tye	CB	Clemson	31. Seattle	Jennings, Kelly	CB	Miami (Fla.)
16. Miami	Allen, Jason	CB	Tennessee	32. N.Y. Giants[9]	Kiwanuka, Mathias	DE	Boston College

(1) From St. Louis. (2) From Cleveland. (3) From Baltimore. (4) From Atlanta through Denver. (5) From Washington through Denver. (6) From N.Y. Giants. (7) From Chicago. (8) From Denver. (9) From Pittsburgh.

Number One NFL Draft Choices, 1936-2006

Year	Team	Player, Pos., College	Year	Team	Player, Pos., College
1936	Philadelphia	Jay Berwanger, HB, Chicago	1972	Buffalo	Walt Patulski, DE, Notre Dame
1937	Philadelphia	Sam Francis, FB, Nebraska	1973	Houston	John Matuszak, DE, Tampa
1938	Cleveland Rams	Corbett Davis, FB, Indiana	1974	Dallas	Ed "Too Tall" Jones, DE, Tenn. St.
1939	Chicago Cards	Ki Aldrich, C, TCU	1975	Atlanta	Steve Bartkowski, QB, Cal.
1940	Chicago Cards	George Cafego, HB, Tennessee	1976	Tampa Bay	Lee Roy Selmon, DE, Oklahoma
1941	Chicago Bears	Tom Harmon, HB, Michigan	1977	Tampa Bay	Ricky Bell, RB, USC
1942	Pittsburgh	Bill Dudley, HB, Virginia	1978	Houston	Earl Campbell, RB, Texas
1943	Detroit	Frank Sinkwich, HB, Georgia	1979	Buffalo	Tom Cousineau, LB, Ohio St.
1944	Boston Yanks	Angelo Bertelli, QB, Notre Dame	1980	Detroit	Billy Sims, RB, Oklahoma
1945	Chicago Cards	Charley Trippi, HB, Georgia	1981	New Orleans	George Rogers, RB, S.Carolina
1946	Boston Yanks	Frank Dancewicz, QB, Notre Dame	1982	New England	Kenneth Sims, DT, Texas
1947	Chicago Bears	Bob Fenimore, HB, Okla. A&M	1983	Baltimore Colts	John Elway, QB, Stanford
1948	Washington	Harry Gilmer, QB, Alabama	1984	New England	Irving Fryar, WR, Nebraska
1949	Philadelphia	Chuck Bednarik, C, Penn	1985	Buffalo	Bruce Smith, DE, Va.Tech
1950	Detroit	Leon Hart, E, Notre Dame	1986	Tampa Bay	Bo Jackson, RB, Auburn
1951	N.Y. Giants	Kyle Rote, HB, SMU	1987	Tampa Bay	Vinny Testaverde, QB, Miami (FL)
1952	L.A. Rams	Bill Wade, QB, Vanderbilt	1988	Atlanta	Aundray Bruce, LB, Auburn
1953	San Francisco	Harry Babcock, E, Georgia	1989	Dallas	Troy Aikman, QB, UCLA
1954	Cleveland	Bobby Garrett, QB, Stanford	1990	Indianapolis	Jeff George, QB, Illinois
1955	Baltimore Colts	George Shaw, QB, Oregon	1991	Dallas	Russell Maryland, DL, Miami (FL)
1956	Pittsburgh	Gary Glick, DB, Col. A&M	1992	Indianapolis	Steve Emtman, DL, Washington
1957	Green Bay	Paul Hornung, QB, Notre Dame	1993	New England	Drew Bledsoe, QB, Washington St.
1958	Chicago Cards	King Hill, QB, Rice	1994	Cincinnati	Dan Wilkinson, DT, Ohio St.
1959	Green Bay	Randy Duncan, QB, Iowa	1995	Cincinnati	Ki-Jana Carter, RB, Penn State
1960	L.A. Rams	Billy Cannon, HB, LSU	1996	N.Y. Jets	Keyshawn Johnson, WR, USC
1961	Minnesota	Tommy Mason, HB, Tulane	1997	St. Louis	Orlando Pace, T, Ohio St.
1962	Washington	Ernie Davis, HB, Syracuse	1998	Indianapolis	Peyton Manning, QB, Tennessee
1963	L.A. Rams	Terry Baker, QB, Oregon St.	1999	Cleveland	Tim Couch, QB, Kentucky
1964	San Francisco	Dave Parks, E, Texas Tech	2000	Cleveland	Courtney Brown, DE, Penn State
1965	N.Y. Giants	Tucker Frederickson, HB, Auburn	2001	Atlanta	Michael Vick, QB, Virginia Tech
1966	Atlanta	Tommy Nobis, LB, Texas	2002	Houston	David Carr, QB, Fresno St.
1967	Baltimore Colts	Bubba Smith, DT, Michigan St.	2003	Cincinnati	Carson Palmer, QB, USC
1968	Minnesota	Ron Yary, T, USC	2004	San Diego	Eli Manning, QB, Mississippi
1969	Buffalo	O.J. Simpson, RB, USC	2005	San Francisco	Alex D. Smith, QB, Utah
1970	Pittsburgh	Terry Bradshaw, QB, La.Tech	2006	Houston	Mario Williams, DE, NC State
1971	New England	Jim Plunkett, QB, Stanford			

NFL MVP, Defensive Player of the Year, and Rookie of the Year

The Most Valuable Player and Defensive Player of the Year are two of many awards given out annually by the Associated Press. Rookie of the Year is one of many awards given out annually by *The Sporting News*. Many other organizations give out annual awards honoring the NFL's best players.

Most Valuable Player

1957	Jim Brown, Cleveland
1958	Gino Marchetti, Baltimore Colts
1959	Charley Conerly, N.Y. Giants
1960	(tie) Norm Van Brocklin, Philadelphia; Joe Schmidt, Detroit
1961	Paul Hornung, Green Bay
1962	Jim Taylor, Green Bay
1963	Y.A. Tittle, N.Y. Giants
1964	John Unitas, Baltimore Colts
1965	Jim Brown, Cleveland
1966	Bart Starr, Green Bay
1967	John Unitas, Baltimore Colts
1968	Earl Morrall, Baltimore Colts
1969	Roman Gabriel, L.A. Rams
1970	John Brodie, San Francisco
1971	Alan Page, Minnesota
1972	Larry Brown, Washington
1973	O.J. Simpson, Buffalo
1974	Ken Stabler, Oakland
1975	Fran Tarkenton, Minnesota
1976	Bert Jones, Baltimore
1977	Walter Payton, Chicago
1978	Terry Bradshaw, Pittsburgh
1979	Earl Campbell, Houston
1980	Brian Sipe, Cleveland
1981	Ken Anderson, Cincinnati
1982	Mark Moseley, Washington
1983	Joe Theismann, Washington
1984	Dan Marino, Miami
1985	Marcus Allen, L.A. Raiders
1986	Lawrence Taylor, N.Y. Giants
1987	John Elway, Denver
1988	Boomer Esiason, Cincinnati
1989	Joe Montana, San Francisco
1990	Joe Montana, San Francisco
1991	Thurman Thomas, Buffalo
1992	Steve Young, San Francisco
1993	Emmitt Smith, Dallas
1994	Steve Young, San Francisco
1995	Brett Favre, Green Bay
1996	Brett Favre, Green Bay
1997	(tie) Brett Favre, Green Bay; Barry Sanders, Detroit
1998	Terrell Davis, Denver
1999	Kurt Warner, St. Louis
2000	Marshall Faulk, St. Louis
2001	Kurt Warner, St. Louis
2002	Rich Gannon, Oakland
2003	(tie) Peyton Manning, Indianapolis; Steve McNair, Tennessee
2004	Peyton Manning, Indianapolis
2005	Shaun Alexander, Seattle

Defensive Player of the Year

1966	Larry Wilson, St. Louis
1967	Deacon Jones, Los Angeles
1968	Deacon Jones, Los Angeles
1969	Dick Butkus, Chicago
1970	Dick Butkus, Chicago
1971	Carl Eller, Minnesota
1972	Joe Greene, Pittsburgh
1973	Alan Page, Minnesota
1974	Joe Greene, Pittsburgh
1975	Curley Culp, Houston
1976	Jerry Sherk, Cleveland
1977	Harvey Martin, Dallas
1978	Randy Gradishar, Denver
1979	Lee Roy Selmon, Tampa Bay
1980	Lester Hayes, Oakland
1981	Joe Klecko, N.Y. Jets
1982	Mark Gastineau, N.Y. Jets
1983	Jack Lambert, Pittsburgh
1984	Mike Haynes, L.A. Raiders
1985	(tie) Howie Long, L.A. Raiders; Andre Tippett, New England
1986	Lawrence Taylor, N.Y. Giants
1987	Reggie White, Philadelphia
1988	Mike Singletary, Chicago
1989	Tim Harris, Green Bay
1990	Bruce Smith, Buffalo
1991	Pat Swilling, New Orleans
1992	Junior Seau, San Diego
1993	Bruce Smith, Buffalo
1994	Deion Sanders, San Francisco
1995	Bryce Paup, Buffalo
1996	Bruce Smith, Buffalo
1997	Dana Stubblefield, San Francisco
1998	Reggie White, Green Bay
1999	Warren Sapp, Tampa Bay
2000	Ray Lewis, Baltimore
2001	Michael Strahan, NY Giants
2002	Derrick Brooks, Tampa Bay
2003	Ray Lewis, Baltimore
2004	Ed Reed, Baltimore
2005	Brian Urlacher, Chicago

Rookie of the Year

1964	Charley Taylor, Washington
1965	Gale Sayers, Chicago
1966	Tommy Nobis, Atlanta
1967	Mel Farr, Detroit
1968	Earl McCullouch, Detroit
1969	Calvin Hill, Dallas
1970	NFC: Bruce Taylor, San Francisco; AFC: Dennis Shaw, Buffalo
1971	NFC: John Brockington, Green Bay; AFC: Jim Plunkett, New England
1972	NFC: Chester Marcol, Green Bay; AFC: Franco Harris, Pittsburgh
1973	NFC: Chuck Foreman, Minnesota; AFC: Boobie Clark, Cincinnati
1974	NFC: Wilbur Jackson, San Francisco; AFC: Don Woods, San Diego
1975	NFC: Steve Bartkowski, Atlanta; AFC: Robert Brazile, Houston
1976	NFC: Sammy White, Minnesota; AFC: Mike Haynes, New England
1977	NFC: Tony Dorsett, Dallas; AFC: A. J. Duhe, Miami
1978	NFC: Al Baker, Detroit; AFC: Earl Campbell, Houston
1979	NFC: Ottis Anderson, St. Louis; AFC: Jerry Butler, Buffalo
1980	Billy Sims, Detroit
1981	George Rogers, New Orleans
1982	Marcus Allen, L.A. Raiders
1983	Dan Marino, Miami
1984	Louis Lipps, Pittsburgh
1985	Eddie Brown, Cincinnati
1986	Rueben Mayes, New Orleans
1987	Robert Awalt, St. Louis
1988	Keith Jackson, Philadelphia
1989	Barry Sanders, Detroit
1990	Richmond Webb, Miami
1991	Mike Croel, Denver
1992	Santana Dotson, Tampa Bay
1993	Jerome Bettis, L.A. Rams
1994	Marshall Faulk, Indianapolis
1995	Curtis Martin, New England
1996	Eddie George, Houston
1997	Warrick Dunn, Tampa Bay
1998	Randy Moss, Minnesota
1999	Edgerrin James, Indianapolis
2000	Brian Urlacher, Chicago
2001	Kendrell Bell, Pittsburgh
2002	Clinton Portis, Denver
2003	Anquan Boldin, Arizona
2004	Ben Roethlisberger, Pittsburgh
2005	Carnell "Cadillac" Williams, Tampa Bay

The Sporting News 2005 NFL All-Pro Team

Offense—Quarterback: Peyton Manning, Indianapolis. Running Backs: Shaun Alexander, Seattle; LaDainian Tomlinson, San Diego. Wide Receivers: Chad Johnson, Cincinnati; Steve Smith, Carolina. Tight End: Antonio Gates, San Diego. Tackles: Walter Jones, Seattle; Willie Roaf, Kansas City. Guards: Alan Faneca, Pittsburgh; Steve Hutchinson, Seattle. Center: Olin Kreutz, Chicago.

Defense—Linebackers: Shawne Merriman, San Diego; Brian Urlacher, Chicago; Al Wilson, Denver. Defensive Ends: Dwight Freeney, Indianapolis; Michael Strahan, N.Y. Giants. Defensive Tackles: Marcus Stroud, Jacksonville; Jamal Williams, San Diego. Cornerbacks: Champ Bailey, Denver; Deltha O'Neal, Cincinnati. Safeties: Troy Polamalu, Pittsburgh; Darren Sharper, Minnesota.

Special Teams—Kicker: Neil Rackers, Phoenix; Brian Moorman, Buffalo. Punt Returner: B.J. Sams, Baltimore. Kick Returner: Jerome Mathis, Houston.

All-Time NFL Coaching Victories

(at end of 2005 season; ranked by overall career wins; *active in 2005)

Coach	Team	Yrs.	Regular Season				Overall			
			W	L	T	Pct.	W	L	T	Pct.
Don Shula	Colts, Dolphins	33	328	156	6	0.677	347	173	6	0.677
George Halas	Bears	40	318	148	31	0.682	324	151	31	0.682
Tom Landry	Cowboys	29	250	162	6	0.607	270	178	6	0.603
Earl "Curly" Lambeau	Packers, Cardinals, Redskins	33	226	132	22	0.631	229	134	22	0.631
Chuck Noll	Steelers	23	193	148	1	0.566	209	156	1	0.572
Dan Reeves	Broncos, Giants, Falcons	23	190	165	2	0.535	201	174	2	0.536
Chuck Knox	Rams, Bills, Seahawks	22	186	147	1	0.558	193	158	1	0.550
Marty Schottenheimer*	Browns, Chiefs, Redskins, Chargers	20	186	124	1	0.600	191	136	1	0.584
Bill Parcells*	Giants, Patriots, Jets, Cowboys	18	163	123	1	0.570	174	130	1	0.572
Paul Brown	Browns, Bengals	21	166	100	6	0.624	170	108	6	0.612

Coach	Team	Yrs.	Regular Season W	L	T	Pct.	Overall W	L	T	Pct.
Bud Grant............	Vikings...................	18	158	96	5	0.621	168	108	5	0.608
Joe Gibbs*..........	Redskins.................	14	140	76	0	0.648	157	82	0	0.657
Marv Levy..........	Chiefs, Bills.............	17	143	112	0	0.561	154	120	0	0.562
Bill Cowher*.........	Steelers................	14	141	82	1	0.632	153	91	1	0.627
Steve Owen..........	Giants..................	23	151	100	17	0.602	153	108	17	0.586
Mike Holmgren*......	Packers, Seahawks........	14	138	86	0	0.616	149	95	0	0.611
Hank Stram..........	Chiefs, Saints............	17	131	97	10	0.574	136	100	10	0.576
Weeb Ewbank........	Colts, Jets..............	20	130	129	7	0.502	134	130	7	0.508
Mike Shanahan*......	Raiders, Broncos..........	13	122	74	0	0.622	130	79	0	0.622
Mike Ditka	Bears, Saints...........	14	121	95	0	0.560	127	101	0	0.557

All-Time Professional (NFL and AFL) Football Records
(at the end of the 2005 season)

Leading Lifetime Scorers

Player	Yrs.	TD	PAT	FG	Total
Gary Anderson......	23	0	820	538	2,434
Morten Anderson.....	23	0	798	520	2,358
George Blanda (a)	26	9	943	335	2,002
Norm Johnson	18	0	638	366	1,736
Nick Lowery	18	0	562	383	1,711
Jan Stenerud (a)	19	0	580	373	1,699
John Carney*........	18	0	464	390	1,634
Lou Groza (a)........	21	1	810	264	1,608
Eddie Murray	19	0	538	352	1,594
Matt Stover*.........	15	0	454	380	1,594
Al Del Greco	17	0	543	347	1,584
Jason Elam*.........	13	0	534	341	1,557
Steve Christie*......	15	0	468	336	1,476
Pat Leahy	18	0	558	304	1,470
Jim Turner (a).......	16	1	521	304	1,439
Matt Bahr..........	17	0	522	300	1,422
Jason Hanson*......	14	0	439	327	1,420
Mark Moseley.......	16	0	482	300	1,382
Jim Bakken.........	17	0	534	282	1,380
Fred Cox	15	0	519	282	1,365

Leading Lifetime Touchdown Scorers

Player	Yrs.	Rush	Rec.	Ret.	TD
Jerry Rice	20	10	197	1	208
Emmitt Smith........	15	164	11	0	175
Marcus Allen	16	123	21	1	145
Marshal Faulk*	12	100	36	0	136
Cris Carter..........	16	0	130	1	131
Jim Brown	9	106	20	0	126
Walter Payton	13	110	15	0	125
John Riggins	14	104	12	0	116
Lenny Moore	12	63	48	2	113
Marvin Harrison*......	10	0	110	0	110
Barry Sanders	10	99	10	0	109
Tim Brown	17	1	100	4	105
Don Hutson	11	3	99	3	105
Terrell Owens*.......	10	2	101	0	103
Steve Largent	14	1	100	0	101
Shaun Alexander*.....	6	89	11	0	100
Franco Harris.......	13	91	9	0	100
Curtis Martin*........	11	90	10	0	100
Randy Moss*.........	8	0	98	1	99
Eric Dickerson	11	90	6	0	96

*Active in 2005. (a) Includes AFL statistics.

Most Points, Season — 176, Paul Hornung, Green Bay Packers, 1960 (15 TDs, 41 PATs, 15 FGs).
Most Points, Game — 40, Ernie Nevers, Chicago Cardinals vs. Chicago Bears, Nov. 28, 1929 (6 TDs, 4 PATs).
Most Touchdowns, Season — 28, Shaun Alexander, Seattle Seahawks, 2005.
Most Touchdowns, Game — 6, Ernie Nevers, Chicago Cardinals vs. Chicago Bears, Nov. 28, 1929 (6 rushing); Dub Jones, Cleveland Browns vs. Chicago Bears, Nov. 25, 1951 (4 rushing, 2 pass receptions); Gale Sayers, Chicago Bears vs. San Francisco 49ers, Dec. 12, 1965 (4 rushing, 1 pass reception, 1 punt return).
Most Points After TD, Season — 66, Uwe von Schamann, Miami Dolphins, 1984.
Most Consecutive Points After TD — 371, Jason Elam, Denver Broncos, 1993-2002.
Most Field Goals, Season — 40, Neil Rackers, Arizona Cardinals, 2005
Most Field Goals, Game — 7, Jim Bakken, St. Louis Cardinals vs. Pittsburgh Steelers, Sept. 24, 1967; Rich Karlis, Minnesota Vikings vs. L.A. Rams, Nov. 5, 1989 (OT); Chris Boniol, Dallas Cowboys vs. Green Bay Packers, Nov. 18, 1996; Billy Cundiff, Dallas Cowboys vs. N.Y. Giants, Sept. 15, 2003 (OT).
Most Field Goals, Career — 538, Gary Anderson, Pittsburgh Steelers-Philadelphia Eagles-San Francisco 49ers-Minnesota Vikings-Tennessee Titans, 1982-2004.
Longest Field Goal — 63 yds., Tom Dempsey, New Orleans Saints vs. Detroit Lions, Nov. 8, 1970; Jason Elam, Denver Broncos vs. Jacksonville Jaguars, Oct. 25, 1998.

Defensive Records

Most Interceptions, Career — 81, Paul Krause, Washington Redskins-Minnesota Vikings, 1964-79.
Most Interceptions, Season — 14, Dick "Night Train" Lane, L. A. Rams, 1952.
Most Touchdowns, Career — 12, Rod Woodson, Pittsburgh Steelers-San Francisco 49ers-Baltimore Ravens-Oakland Raiders, 1987-2003.
Most Touchdowns, Season — 4, Ken Houston, Houston Oilers, 1971; Jim Kearney, Kansas City Chiefs, 1972; Eric Allen, Philadelphia Eagles, 1993.
Most Sacks, Career (Since 1982) — 200, Bruce Smith, Buffalo Bills-Washington Redskins, 1985-2003.
Most Sacks, Season (Since 1982) — 22.5, Michael Strahan, N.Y. Giants, 2001.
Most Sacks, Game (Since 1982) — 7, Derrick Thomas, Kansas City Chiefs vs. Seattle Seahawks, Nov. 11, 1990.

Leading Lifetime Rushers
(ranked by rushing yards)

Player	Yrs.	Att.	Yards	Avg.	Long	TD
Emmitt Smith	15	4,409	18,355	4.2	75	164
Walter Payton.......	13	3,838	16,726	4.4	76	110
Barry Sanders	10	3,062	15,269	5.0	85	99
Curtis Martin*.......	11	3,518	14,101	4.0	70	90
Jerome Bettis*	13	3,479	13,662	3.9	71	91
Eric Dickerson	11	2,996	13,259	4.4	85	90
Tony Dorsett........	12	2,936	12,739	4.3	99	77
Jim Brown	9	2,359	12,312	5.2	80	106
Marshall Faulk*	12	2,836	12,279	4.3	71	100
Marcus Allen	16	3,022	12,243	4.1	61	123

Player	Yrs.	Att.	Yards	Avg.	Long	TD
Franco Harris.......	13	2,949	12,120	4.1	75	91
Thurman Thomas ...	13	2,877	12,074	4.2	80	65
John Riggins	14	2,916	11,352	3.9	66	104
O.J. Simpson (a)	11	2,404	11,236	4.7	94	61
Ricky Watters	10	2,622	10,643	4.1	57	78
Eddie George	9	2,865	10,441	3.6	76	68
Corey Dillon*	9	2,419	10,429	4.3	96	69
Otis Anderson	14	2,562	10,273	4.0	76	81
Earl Campbell	9	2,187	9,407	4.3	81	74
Edgerrin James*	7	2,188	9,226	4.2	72	64

*Active in 2005. (a) Includes AFL statistics.

Most Yards Gained, Season — 2,105, Eric Dickerson, L.A. Rams, 1984.
Most Yards Gained, Game — 295, Jamal Lewis, Baltimore Ravens vs. Cleveland Browns, Sept. 14, 2003.
Most Touchdowns Rushing, Career — 164, Emmitt Smith, Dallas Cowboys-Arizona Cardinals, 1990-2004.
Most Touchdowns Rushing, Season — 27, Priest Holmes, Kansas City Chiefs, 2003.
Most Touchdowns Rushing, Game — 6, Ernie Nevers, Chicago Cardinals vs. Chicago Bears, Nov. 28, 1929.
Most Rushing Attempts, Game — 45, Jamie Morris, Washington Redskins vs. Cincinnati Bengals, Dec. 17, 1988 (overtime).
Longest Run From Scrimmage — 99 yds., Tony Dorsett, Dallas Cowboys vs. Minnesota Vikings, Jan. 3, 1983 (touchdown).

Leading Lifetime Receivers
(ranked by number of receptions)

Player	Yrs.	No.	Yards	Avg.	Long	TD	Player	Yrs.	No.	Yards	Avg.	Long	TD
Jerry Rice.........	20	1,549	23,546	14.8	96	197	Steve Largent.....	14	819	13,089	16.0	74	100
Cris Carter	16	1,101	13,899	12.6	80	130	Shannon Sharpe...	14	815	10,060	12.3	82	62
Tim Brown	17	1,094	14,934	13.7	80	100	Henry Ellard.......	16	814	13,777	16.9	81	65
Andre Reed	16	951	13,198	13.9	83	87	Isaac Bruce	12	813	12,278	15.1	80	77
Art Monk..........	16	940	12,721	13.5	79	68	Rod Smith*	11	797	10,877	13.6	85	65
Marvin Harrison* ...	10	927	12,331	13.3	80	110	Marshall Faulk*	12	767	6,875	9.0	85	36
Jimmy Smith*......	12	862	12,287	14.3	75	67	James Lofton......	16	764	14,004	18.3	80	75
Irving Fryar........	17	851	12,785	15.0	80	84	Michael Irvin......	12	750	11,904	15.9	87	65
Larry Centers......	14	827	6,797	8.2	54	28	Charlie Joiner (a)...	18	750	12,146	16.2	87	65
Keenan McCardell* ..	14	825	10,680	12.9	76	62	Keyshawn Johnson*	10	744	9,756	13.1	76	60

*Active in 2005. (a) Includes AFL statistics.
Most Yards Gained, Career — 22,895, Jerry Rice, San Francisco 49ers-Oakland Raiders-Seattle Seahawks, 1985-2004.
Most Yards Gained, Season — 1,848, Jerry Rice, San Francisco 49ers, 1995.
Most Yards Gained, Game — 336, Willie "Flipper" Anderson, L. A. Rams vs. New Orleans, Nov. 26, 1989 (overtime).
Most Pass Receptions, Season — 143, Marvin Harrison, Indianapolis Colts, 2002.
Most Pass Receptions, Game — 20, Terrell Owens, San Francisco 49ers vs. Chicago Bears, Dec. 17, 2000 (283 yards).
Most Touchdown Receptions, Career — 197, Jerry Rice, San Francisco 49ers-Oakland Raiders-Seattle Seahawks, 1985-2004.
Most Touchdown Receptions, Season — 22, Jerry Rice, San Francisco 49ers, 1987.
Most Touchdown Receptions, Game — 5, Bob Shaw, Chicago Cardinals vs. Baltimore Colts, Oct. 2, 1950; Kellen Winslow, San Diego Chargers vs. Oakland Raiders, Nov. 22, 1981; Jerry Rice, San Francisco 49ers vs. Atlanta Falcons, Oct. 14, 1990.

Leading Lifetime Passers
(minimum 1,500 attempts; ranked by quarterback rating points)

Player	Yrs.	Att.	Comp.	Yards	TD	Int.	Pts.[1]	Player	Yrs.	Att.	Comp.	Yards	TD	Int.	Pts.[1]
Steve Young....	15	4,149	2,667	33,124	232	107	96.8	Dan Marino.....	17	8,358	4,967	61,361	420	252	86.4
Kurt Warner*	8	2,340	1,537	19,214	119	78	94.1	Brett Favre*.....	15	7,610	4,678	53,615	396	255	86.0
Peyton Manning* .	8	4,333	2,769	33,189	244	130	93.5	Jeff Garcia*.....	7	2,785	1,695	19,076	126	71	85.8
Joe Montana	15	5,391	3,409	40,551	273	139	92.3	Drew Brees*.....	5	1,809	1,125	12,348	80	53	84.9
Daunte Culpepper*	7	2,607	1,678	20,162	135	86	91.5	Brian Griese*....	8	2,318	1,463	16,344	103	78	84.8
Marc Bulger*	4	1,518	987	11,932	71	51	90.6	Rich Gannon....	16	4,206	2,533	28,743	180	104	84.7
Tom Brady*	6	2,548	1,577	18,035	123	66	88.5	Jake Delhomme*.	5	1,503	888	11,160	75	52	84.5
Trent Green*	8	3,329	2,022	25,621	150	92	88.3	Jim Kelly	11	4,779	2,874	35,467	237	175	84.4
Otto Graham (a)..	10	2,626	1,464	23,584	174	135	86.6	Brad Johnson*...	12	3,798	2,350	25,798	155	102	84.4
Matt Hasselbeck*.	7	2,205	1,342	15,925	96	57	86.6	Donovan McNabb*	7	2,943	1,718	19,433	134	66	84.1

*Active in 2005. (a) Includes AFL statistics. (1) Rating points based on performances in the following categories: Percentage of completions, percentage of touchdown passes, percentage of interceptions, and average gain per pass attempt.
Most Yards Gained, Career — 61,361, Dan Marino, Miami Dolphins, 1983-99.
Most Yards Gained, Season — 5,084, Dan Marino, Miami Dolphins, 1984.
Most Yards Gained, Game — 554, Norm Van Brocklin, L. A. Rams vs. N.Y. Yanks, Sept. 28, 1951 (27 completions in 41 attempts).
Most Touchdowns Passing, Career — 420, Dan Marino, Miami Dolphins, 1983-99.
Most Touchdowns Passing, Season — 49, Peyton Manning, Indianapolis Colts, 2004.
Most Touchdowns Passing, Game — 7, Sid Luckman, Chicago Bears vs. N.Y. Giants, Nov. 14, 1943; Adrian Burk, Phil. Eagles vs. Washington Redskins, Oct. 17, 1954; George Blanda, Houston Oilers vs. N.Y. Titans, Nov. 19, 1961; Y.A. Tittle, N.Y. Giants vs. Washington Redskins, Oct. 28, 1962; Joe Kapp, Minnesota Vikings vs. Baltimore Colts, Sept. 28, 1969.
Most Passes Completed, Career — 4,967, Dan Marino, Miami Dolphins, 1983-99.
Most Passes Completed, Season — 418, Rich Gannon, Oakland Raiders, 2002.
Most Passes Completed, Game — 45, Drew Bledsoe, New England Patriots vs. Minnesota Vikings, Nov. 13, 1994 (OT).

National Football League Franchise Origins
(founding year, league; home stadium location; subsequent history)

Arizona Cardinals—1920, American Professional Football Association (APFA)[1]. Chicago, 1920-59; St. Louis, 1960-87; Tempe, AZ, 1988-present.
Atlanta Falcons—1996, NFL. Atlanta, 1966-present.
Baltimore Ravens—1996, NFL. Baltimore, 1996-present.
Buffalo Bills—1969, American Football League (AFL)[2]. Buffalo, 1960-72; Orchard Park, NY, 1972-present.
Carolina Panthers—1995, NFL. Clemson, SC, 1995; Charlotte, NC, 1996-present.
Chicago Bears—1920 APFA. Decatur, IL, 1920; Chicago, 1921-present.
Cincinnati Bengals—1968, AFL. Cincinnati, 1968-present.
Cleveland Browns—1946, All-America Football Conference (AAFC)[3]. Cleveland, 1946-95; 1999-present.
Dallas Cowboys—1960, NFL. Dallas, 1960-70; Irving, TX, 1971-present.
Denver Broncos—1960, AFL. Denver, 1960-present.
Detroit Lions—1930, NFL. Portsmouth, OH, 1930-33; Detroit, 1934-74; Pontiac, MI, 1975-present.
Green Bay Packers—1921, APFA. Green Bay, WI, 1921-present.
Houston Texans—2002, NFL. Houston 2002-present.
Indianapolis Colts—1953, NFL. Baltimore, 1953-83; Indianapolis, 1984-present.
Jacksonville Jaguars—1995, NFL. Jacksonville, FL, 1995-present.
Kansas City Chiefs—1960, AFL. Dallas, 1960-62; Kansas City, 1963-present.
Miami Dolphins—1966, AFL. Miami, 1966-present.
Minnesota Vikings—1961, NFL. Bloomington, MN, 1961-81; Minneapolis, 1982-present.
New England Patriots—1960, AFL. Boston, 1960-70; Foxboro, MA, 1971-present.
New Orleans Saints—1967, NFL. New Orleans, 1967-2004; Baton Rouge and San Antonio, 2005.
New York Giants—1925, NFL. New York, 1925-73, 1975; New Haven, CT, 1973-74; E. Rutherford, NJ, 1976-present.
New York Jets—1960, AFL. New York, 1960-83; E. Rutherford, NJ, 1984-present.
Oakland Raiders—1960, AFL. Oakland, CA, 1960-81, 1995-present; Los Angeles, 1982-94.
Philadelphia Eagles—1933, NFL. Philadelphia, 1933-present.
Pittsburgh Steelers—1933, NFL. Pittsburgh, 1933-present.
St. Louis Rams—1937, NFL. Cleveland, 1936-45; Los Angeles, 1946-79; Anaheim, 1980-94; St. Louis, 1995-present.
San Diego Chargers—1960, AFL. Los Angeles, 1960; San Diego, 1961-present.
Seattle Seahawks—1976, NFL. Seattle, 1976-present.
San Francisco 49ers—1946, AAFC. San Francisco, 1946-present.
Tampa Bay Buccaneers—1976, NFL. Tampa, 1976-present.
Tennessee Titans—1960, AFL. Houston, 1969-96; Memphis, 1997; Nashville, 1998-present.
Washington Redskins—1932, NFL. Boston, 1932-36; Washington, DC, 1937-96; Landover, MD, 1997-present.

(1) The American Professional Football Association (APFA) was formed in 1920 to standardize the rules of professional football. In 1922, the name was changed to the National Football League. (2) The most successful of 4 separate leagues called the "American Football League" (1926; 1936-37; 1940-41, 1960-69). Congress approved an NFL/AFL merger in 1966. Baltimore, Cleveland, and Pittsburgh agreed to join the 10 incoming AFL teams to form the American Football Conference. The NFL began play in 1970 with 26 teams. (3) The All-America Football Conference, 1946-49. In 1950, 3 of its teams joined the NFL (Baltimore, Cleveland, and San Francisco). The Baltimore franchise failed, but the NFL awarded the city a 2nd one, also called the Colts, in 1953.

Pro Football Hall of Fame, Canton, Ohio

(Asterisks indicate 2006 inductees.)

Herb Adderley
*Troy Aikman
George Allen
Marcus Allen
Lance Alworth
Doug Atkins
Morris "Red" Badgro
Lem Barney
Cliff Battles
Sammy Baugh
Chuck Bednarik
Bert Bell
Bobby Bell
Raymond Berry
Elvin Bethea
Charles Bidwill
Fred Biletnikoff
George Blanda
Mel Blount
Terry Bradshaw
Bob Brown
Jim Brown
Paul Brown
Roosevelt Brown
Willie Brown
Buck Buchanan
Nick Buoniconti
Dick Butkus
Earl Campbell
Tony Canadeo
Joe Carr
*Harry Carson
Dave Casper
Guy Chamberlin
Jack Christiansen
Earl "Dutch" Clark
George Connor
Jim Conzelman
Lou Creekmur
Larry Csonka
Al Davis
Willie Davis
Len Dawson
Joe DeLamielleure
Eric Dickerson
Dan Dierdorf
Mike Ditka
Art Donovan

Tony Dorsett
John "Paddy" Driscoll
Bill Dudley
Glen "Turk" Edwards
Carl Eller
John Elway
Weeb Ewbank
Tom Fears
Jim Finks
Ray Flaherty
Len Ford
Dr. Daniel Fortmann
Dan Fouts
Benny Friedman
Frank Gatski
Bill George
Joe Gibbs
Frank Gifford
Sid Gillman
Otto Graham
Red Grange
Bud Grant
Joe Greene
Forrest Gregg
Bob Griese
Lou Groza
Joe Guyon
George Halas
Jack Ham
Dan Hampton
John Hannah
Franco Harris
Mike Haynes
Ed Healey
Mel Hein
Ted Hendricks
Wilbur "Pete" Henry
Arnold Herber
Bill Hewitt
Clarke Hinkle
Elroy "Crazylegs" Hirsch
Paul Hornung
Ken Houston
Cal Hubbard
Sam Huff
Lamar Hunt
Don Hutson

Jimmy Johnson
John Henry Johnson
Charlie Joiner
David "Deacon" Jones
Stan Jones
Henry Jordan
Sonny Jurgensen
Jim Kelly
Leroy Kelly
Walt Kiesling
Frank "Bruiser" Kinard
Paul Krause
Earl "Curly" Lambeau
Jack Lambert
Tom Landry
Dick "Night Train" Lane
Jim Langer
Willie Lanier
Steve Largent
Yale Lary
Dante Lavelli
Bobby Layne
Alphonse "Tuffy" Leemans
Marv Levy
Bob Lilly
Larry Little
James Lofton
Vince Lombardi
Howie Long
Ronnie Lott
Sid Luckman
Roy "Link" Lyman
Tom Mack
John Mackey
*John Madden
Tim Mara
Wellington Mara
Gino Marchetti
Dan Marino
George Preston Marshall
Ollie Matson
Don Maynard
George McAfee
Mike McCormack
Tommy McDonald
Hugh McElhenny

Johnny "Blood" McNally
Mike Michalske
Wayne Millner
Bobby Mitchell
Ron Mix
Joe Montana
*Warren Moon
Lenny Moore
Marion Motley
Mike Munchak
Anthony Munoz
George Musso
Bronko Nagurski
Joe Namath
Earle "Greasy" Neale
Ernie Nevers
Ozzie Newsome
Ray Nitschke
Chuck Noll
Leo Nomellini
Merlin Olsen
Jim Otto
Steve Owen
Alan Page
Clarence "Ace" Parker
Jim Parker
Walter Payton
Joe Perry
Pete Pihos
Fritz Pollard
Hugh "Shorty" Ray
Dan Reeves
Mel Renfro
John Riggins
Jim Ringo
Andy Robustelli
Art Rooney
Dan Rooney
Pete Rozelle
Bob St. Clair
Barry Sanders
Gale Sayers
Joe Schmidt
Tex Schramm
Lee Roy Selmon
Billy Shaw
Art Shell

Don Shula
O.J. Simpson
Mike Singletary
Jackie Slater
Jackie Smith
John Stallworth
Bart Starr
Roger Staubach
Ernie Stautner
Jan Stenerud
Dwight Stephenson
Hank Stram
Ken Strong
Joe Stydahar
Lynn Swann
Fran Tarkenton
Charley Taylor
Jim Taylor
Lawrence "LT" Taylor
Jim Thorpe
Y.A. Tittle
George Trafton
Charley Trippi
Emlen Tunnell
Clyde "Bulldog" Turner
Johnny Unitas
Gene Upshaw
Norm Van Brocklin
Steve Van Buren
Doak Walker
Bill Walsh
Paul Warfield
Bob Waterfield
Mike Webster
Arnie Weinmeister
Randy White
*Reggie White
Dave Wilcox
Bill Willis
Larry Wilson
Kellen Winslow
Alex Wojciechowicz
Willie Wood
*Rayfield Wright
Ron Yary
Steve Young
Jack Youngblood

NFL Stadiums[1]

Team—Stadium, Location, Turf (Year Built)	Capacity
Bears—New Soldier Field[2], Chicago, IL, G (1924)	61,500
Bengals—Paul Brown Stad., Cincinnati, OH, G (2000)	65,600
Bills—Ralph Wilson Stad., Orchard Park, NY, A (1973)	73,967
Broncos—Invesco Field at Mile High, Denver, CO, G (2001)	76,125
Browns—Cleveland Browns Stad., Cleveland, OH, G (1999)	73,200
Buccaneers—Raymond James Stad., Tampa, FL, G (1998)	65,647
Cardinals—Arizona Cardinals Stad., Glendale, AZ, G (2006)	63,000
Chargers—Qualcomm Stad.[3], San Diego, CA, G (1967)	71,500
Chiefs—Arrowhead Stad., Kansas City, MO, G (1972)	79,451
Colts—RCA Dome [4], Indianapolis, IN, A (1983)	60,272
Cowboys—Texas Stad., Irving, TX, A (1971)	65,675
Dolphins—Dolphins Stad.[5], Miami, FL, G (1987)	75,192
Eagles—Lincoln Financial Field, Philadelphia, PA, G (2003)	68,532
Falcons—Georgia Dome, Atlanta, GA, A (1992)	71,228
49ers—Monster Park[6], San Francisco, CA, G (1960)	69,734
Giants—Giants Stad., E. Rutherford, NJ, G (1976)	78,741
Jaguars—ALLTEL Stad.[7], Jacksonville, FL, G (1946)	67,164
Jets—Giants Stad., E. Rutherford, NJ, G (1976)	78,741
Lions—Ford Field, Detroit, MI, A (2002)	65,000
Packers—Lambeau Field[8], Green Bay, WI, G (1957)	72,515
Panthers—Bank of America Stad.[9], Charlotte, NC, G (1996)	73,400
Patriots—Gillette Stad., Foxboro, MA, G (2002)	68,756
Raiders—McAfee Coliseum[10], Oakland, CA, G (1966)	63,132
Rams—Edward Jones Dome[11], St. Louis, MO, A (1995)	66,000
Ravens—M & T Bank Stad.[12], Baltimore, MD, SG (1998)	70,107
Redskins—FedEx Field[13], Landover, MD, G (1997)	91,000
Saints—Louisiana Superdome, New Orleans, LA (1975)	69,703
Seahawks—Qwest Field[14], Seattle, WA, A (2002)	67,000
Steelers—Heinz Field, Pittsburgh, PA, A (2001)	64,450
Texans—Reliant Stadium, Houston, TX, G (2002)	69,500
Titans—The Coliseum[15], Nashville, TN, G (1999)	67,000
Vikings—Hubert H. Humphrey Metrodome, Minn., MN, A (1982)	63,000

G=Grass. A=Artificial turf. SG=Sport Grass (hybrid of artificial and natural turf). (1) As of the start of the 2006 season. (2) Renovation in 2002 replaced interior of stadium (1967-80). (3) Formerly San Diego Stadium (1967-80); San Diego Jack Murphy Stadium (1981-97). (4) Formerly the Hoosier Dome (1983-94). (5) Formerly Joe Robbie Stadium (1987-96). (6) Formerly Candlestick Park (1960-94); 3Com Park at Candlestick Point (1995-2004). (7) Formerly Jacksonville Municipal Stadium (1946-97). (8) Formerly City Stadium (1957-65). Renovation completed in 2003, added 11,625 seats. (9) Formerly Ericsson Stadium (1996-2003). (10) Formerly Oakland/Alameda County Coliseum until 1998; Network Associates Coliseum until 2005. (11) Formerly Trans World Dome (1995-2001); full name: Edward Jones Dome at America's Center. (12) Formerly PSINet Stadium (1998-2002); Ravens Stadium (2002-03). (13) Formerly Jack Kent Cooke Stadium (1997-99). (14) Formerly Seahawks Stadium (2002-04). (15) Formerly Adelphia Col. (1999-2002).

Future Sites of the Super Bowl

(Information subject to change.)

No.	Site	Date	No.	Site	Date
XLI	Dolphins Stadium, Miami, FL	Feb. 4, 2007	XLIII	Raymond James Stadium, Tampa, FL	Feb. 1, 2009
XLII	Cardinals Stadium, Glendale, AZ	Feb. 3, 2008	XLIV	Dolphins Stadium, Miami, FL	Feb. 2010

COLLEGE FOOTBALL

Texas Longhorns Squeak Past USC Trojans to Win National Title

The Univ. of Texas Longhorns beat the Univ. of Southern California Trojans, 41-38, to win the Rose Bowl in Pasadena, CA, Jan. 4. With their win, the second-ranked Longhorns, under coach Mack Brown, claimed the NCAA Division I-A football title and snapped the 34-game winning streak of the top-ranked Trojans. The Trojans and Longhorns had swapped the lead several times during the game, and USC was winning, 38-26, with less than 7 minutes remaining. Texas quarterback Vince Young then led the Longhorns on two successful touchdown drives, claiming the lead with only 19 seconds to play. Young ran for 200 yards and passed for 267 more, and was named the Rose Bowl's Most Valuable Player (MVP).

National College Football Champions, 1936-2005

The unofficial champion as selected by the AP poll of writers and USA Today/ESPN (until 1991, UPI; 1991-1996 USA Today/CNN) poll of coaches. Where the polls disagreed, both teams are listed (AP winner first). The AP poll started in 1936; the UPI poll in 1950.

1936 Minnesota	1951 Tennessee	1966 Notre Dame	1980 Georgia	1993 Florida St.
1937 Pittsburgh	1952 Michigan St.	1967 USC	1981 Clemson	1994 Nebraska
1938 Texas Christian	1953 Maryland	1968 Ohio St.	1982 Penn St.	1995 Nebraska
1939 Texas A&M	1954 Ohio St., UCLA	1969 Texas	1983 Miami (FL)	1996 Florida
1940 Minnesota	1955 Oklahoma	1970 Nebraska, Texas	1984 Brigham Young	1997 Michigan,
1941 Minnesota	1956 Oklahoma	1971 Nebraska	1985 Oklahoma	Nebraska
1942 Ohio St.	1957 Auburn, Ohio St.	1972 USC	1986 Penn St.	1998 Tennessee
1943 Notre Dame	1958 Louisiana St.	1973 Notre Dame,	1987 Miami (FL)	1999 Florida St.
1944 Army	1959 Syracuse	Alabama	1988 Notre Dame	2000 Oklahoma
1945 Army	1960 Minnesota	1974 Oklahoma, USC	1989 Miami (FL)	2001 Miami (FL)
1946 Notre Dame	1961 Alabama	1975 Oklahoma	1990 Colorado,	2002 Ohio State
1947 Notre Dame	1962 USC	1976 Pittsburgh	GA Tech	2003 LSU, USC
1948 Michigan	1963 Texas	1977 Notre Dame	1991 Miami (FL),	2004 USC
1949 Notre Dame	1964 Alabama	1978 Alabama, USC	Washington	2005 Texas
1950 Oklahoma	1965 Alabama, Mich. St.	1979 Alabama	1992 Alabama	

2005 Final AP and USA Today/ESPN Rankings

Associated Press Poll

1. Texas....... 13-0	6. LSU 11-2	11. TCU........ 11-1	16. UCLA........10-2	21. Clemson 8-4
2. USC........ 12-1	7. Virginia Tech 11-2	12. Florida...... 9-3	17. Miami (FL) ... 9-3	22. Oklahoma... 8-4
3. Penn St...... 11-1	8. Alabama.... 10-2	12. Oregon 10-2	18. Boston College 9-3	23. Florida St.... 8-5
4. Ohio St...... 10-2	9. Notre Dame . 9-3	14. Auburn 9-3	19. Louisville 9-3	24. Nebraska ... 8-4
5. West Virginia . 11-1	10. Georgia 10-3	15. Wisconsin ... 10-3	20. Texas Tech .. 9-3	25. California ... 8-4

USA Today/ESPN Coaches' Poll

1. Texas....... 13-0	6. West Virginia . 11-1	11. Notre Dame.. 9-3	16. Florida...... 9-3	21. Clemson 8-4
2. USC........ 12-1	7. Virginia Tech . 11-2	12. Oregon 10-2	17. Boston College 9-3	22. Oklahoma... 8-4
3. Penn St...... 11-1	8. Alabama.... 10-2	13. UCLA 10-2	18. Miami (FL) ... 9-3	23. Florida St.... 8-5
4. Ohio St...... 10-2	9. TCU 11-1	14. Auburn 9-3	19. Texas Tech .. 9-3	24. Nebraska ... 8-4
5. LSU 11-2	10. Georgia 10-3	15. Wisconsin ... 10-3	20. Louisville 9-3	25. California ... 8-4

Note: Team records include bowl games. The American Football Coaches Assn. prohibits coaches from voting for schools on major NCAA probation.

Annual Results of Major Bowl Games

(Dates indicate year the game was played; bowl games are generally played in late December or early January.)

Rose Bowl, Pasadena, CA

1902	(Jan.) Michigan 49, Stanford 0	1947	Illinois 45, UCLA 14	1977	USC 14, Michigan 6
1916	Washington St. 14, Brown 0	1948	Michigan 49, USC 0	1978	Washington 27, Michigan 20
1917	Oregon 14, Pennsylvania 0	1949	Northwestern 20, California 14	1979	USC 17, Michigan 10
1918-19	Service teams	1950	Ohio St. 17, California 14	1980	USC 17, Ohio St. 16
1920	Harvard 7, Oregon 6	1951	Michigan 14, California 6	1981	Michigan 23, Washington 6
1921	California 28, Ohio St. 0	1952	Illinois 40, Stanford 7	1982	Washington 28, Iowa 0
1922	Wash. & Jeff. 0, California 0	1953	USC 7, Wisconsin 0	1983	UCLA 24, Michigan 14
1923	USC 14, Penn St. 3	1954	Mich. St. 28, UCLA 20	1984	UCLA 45, Illinois 9
1924	Navy 14, Washington 14	1955	Ohio St. 20, USC 7	1985	USC 20, Ohio St. 17
1925	Notre Dame 27, Stanford 10	1956	Mich. St. 17, UCLA 14	1986	UCLA 45, Iowa 28
1926	Alabama 20, Washington 19	1957	Iowa 35, Oregon St. 19	1987	Arizona St. 22, Michigan 15
1927	Alabama 7, Stanford 7	1958	Ohio St. 10, Oregon 7	1988	Mich. St. 20, USC 17
1928	Stanford 7, Pittsburgh 6	1959	Iowa 38, California 12	1989	Michigan 22, USC 14
1929	Georgia Tech 8, California 7	1960	Washington 44, Wisconsin 8	1990	USC 17, Michigan 10
1930	USC 47, Pittsburgh 14	1961	Washington 17, Minnesota 7	1991	Washington 46, Iowa 34
1931	Alabama 24, Wash. St. 0	1962	Minnesota 21, UCLA 3	1992	Washington 34, Michigan 14
1932	USC 21, Tulane 12	1963	USC 42, Wisconsin 37	1993	Michigan 38, Washington 31
1933	USC 35, Pittsburgh 0	1964	Illinois 17, Washington 7	1994	Wisconsin 21, UCLA 16
1934	Columbia 7, Stanford 0	1965	Michigan 34, Oregon St. 7	1995	Penn St. 38, Oregon 20
1935	Alabama 29, Stanford 13	1966	UCLA 14, Mich. St. 12	1996	USC 41, Northwestern 32
1936	Stanford 7, SMU 0	1967	Purdue 14, USC 13	1997	Ohio St. 20, Arizona St. 17
1937	Pittsburgh 21, Washington 0	1968	USC 14, Indiana 3	1998	Michigan 21, Wash. St. 16
1938	California 13, Alabama 0	1969	Ohio St. 27, USC 16	1999	Wisconsin 38, UCLA 31
1939	USC 7, Duke 3	1970	USC 10, Michigan 3	2000	Wisconsin 17, Stanford 9
1940	USC 14, Tennessee 0	1971	Stanford 27, Ohio St. 17	2001	Washington 34, Purdue 24
1941	Stanford 21, Nebraska 13	1972	Stanford 13, Michigan 12	2002	Miami (FL) 37, Nebraska 14
1942*	Oregon St. 20, Duke 16	1973	USC 42, Ohio St. 17	2003	Oklahoma, 34, Washington St. 14
1943	Georgia 9, UCLA 0	1974	Ohio St. 42, USC 21	2004	USC 28, Michigan 14
1944	USC 29, Washington 0	1975	USC 18, Ohio St. 17	2005	Texas 38, Michigan 37
1945	USC 25, Tennessee 0	1976	UCLA 23, Ohio St. 10	2006	Texas 41, USC 38
1946	Alabama 34, USC 14				

*Played in Durham, NC.

Orange Bowl, Miami, FL

1935	(Jan.) Bucknell 26, Miami (FL) 0	1941	Mississippi St. 14, Georgetown 7	1947	Rice 8, Tennessee 0
1936	Catholic U. 20, Mississippi 19	1942	Georgia 40, TCU 26	1948	Georgia Tech 20, Kansas 14
1937	Duquesne 13, Mississippi St. 12	1943	Alabama 37, Boston Coll. 21	1949	Texas 41, Georgia 28
1938	Auburn 6, Michigan St. 0	1944	LSU 19, Texas A&M 14	1950	Santa Clara 21, Kentucky 13
1939	Tennessee 17, Oklahoma 0	1945	Tulsa 26, Georgia Tech 12	1951	Clemson 15, Miami (FL) 14
1940	Georgia Tech 21, Missouri 7	1946	Miami (FL) 13, Holy Cross 6	1952	Georgia Tech 17, Baylor 14

1953 Alabama 61, Syracuse 6
1954 Oklahoma 7, Maryland 0
1955 Duke 34, Nebraska 7
1956 Oklahoma 20, Maryland 6
1957 Colorado 27, Clemson 21
1958 Oklahoma 48, Duke 21
1959 Oklahoma 21, Syracuse 6
1960 Georgia 14, Missouri 0
1961 Missouri 21, Navy 14
1962 LSU 25, Colorado 7
1963 Alabama 17, Oklahoma 0
1964 Nebraska 13, Auburn 7
1965 Texas 21, Alabama 17
1966 Alabama 39, Nebraska 28
1967 Florida 27, Georgia Tech 12
1968 Oklahoma 26, Tennessee 24
1969 Penn St. 15, Kansas 14
1970 Penn St. 10, Missouri 3

1971 Nebraska 17, LSU 12
1972 Nebraska 38, Alabama 6
1973 Nebraska 40, Notre Dame 6
1974 Penn St. 16, LSU 9
1975 Notre Dame 13, Alabama 11
1976 Oklahoma 14, Michigan 6
1977 Ohio St. 27, Colorado 10
1978 Arkansas 31, Oklahoma 6
1979 Oklahoma 31, Nebraska 24
1980 Oklahoma 24, Florida St. 7
1981 Oklahoma 18, Florida St. 17
1982 Clemson 22, Nebraska 15
1983 Nebraska 21, LSU 20
1984 Miami (FL) 31, Nebraska 30
1985 Washington 28, Oklahoma 17
1986 Oklahoma 25, Penn St. 10
1987 Oklahoma 42, Arkansas 8
1988 Miami (FL) 20, Oklahoma 14

1989 Miami (FL) 23, Nebraska 3
1990 Notre Dame 21, Colorado 6
1991 Colorado 10, Notre Dame 9
1992 Miami (FL) 22, Nebraska 0
1993 Florida St. 27, Nebraska 14
1994 Florida St. 18, Nebraska 16
1995 Nebraska 24, Miami (FL) 17
1996 Florida St. 31, Notre Dame 26
1996 (Dec.) Nebraska 41, Virginia Tech 21
1998 (Jan.) Nebraska 42, Tennessee 17
1999 Florida 31, Syracuse 10
2000 Michigan 35, Alabama 34 (OT)
2001 Oklahoma 13, Florida St. 2
2002 Florida 56, Maryland 23
2003 USC 38, Iowa 17
2004 Miami 16, Florida State 14
2005 USC 55, Oklahoma 19
2006 Penn St. 26, Florida St. 23 (3 OT)

Sugar Bowl, New Orleans, LA

1935 (Jan.) Tulane 20, Temple 14
1936 TCU 3, LSU 2
1937 Santa Clara 21, LSU 14
1938 Santa Clara 6, LSU 0
1939 TCU 15, Carnegie Tech 7
1940 Texas A&M 14, Tulane 13
1941 Boston Col. 19, Tennessee 13
1942 Fordham 2, Missouri 0
1943 Tennessee 14, Tulsa 7
1944 Georgia Tech 20, Tulsa 18
1945 Duke 29, Alabama 26
1946 Oklahoma A&M 33, St. Mary's 13
1947 Georgia 20, N. Carolina 10
1948 Texas 27, Alabama 7
1949 Oklahoma 14, N. Carolina 6
1950 Oklahoma 35, LSU 0
1951 Kentucky 13, Oklahoma 7
1952 Maryland 28, Tennessee 13
1953 Georgia Tech 24, Mississippi 7
1954 Georgia Tech 42, West Virginia 19
1955 Navy 21, Mississippi 0
1956 Georgia Tech 7, Pittsburgh 0
1957 Baylor 13, Tennessee 7
1958 Mississippi 39, Texas 7
*Played in Atlanta, GA.

1959 LSU 7, Clemson 0
1960 Mississippi 21, LSU 0
1961 Mississippi 14, Rice 6
1962 Alabama 10, Arkansas 3
1963 Mississippi 17, Arkansas 13
1964 Alabama 12, Mississippi 7
1965 LSU 13, Syracuse 10
1966 Missouri 20, Florida 18
1967 Alabama 34, Nebraska 7
1968 LSU 20, Wyoming 13
1969 Arkansas 16, Georgia 2
1970 Mississippi 27, Arkansas 22
1971 Tennessee 34, Air Force 13
1972 Oklahoma 40, Auburn 22
1972 (Dec.) Oklahoma 14, Penn St. 0
1973 Notre Dame 24, Alabama 23
1974 Nebraska 13, Florida 10
1975 Alabama 13, Penn St. 6
1977 (Jan.) Pittsburgh 27, Georgia 3
1978 Alabama 35, Ohio St. 6
1979 Alabama 14, Penn St. 7
1980 Alabama 24, Arkansas 9
1981 Georgia 17, Notre Dame 10
1982 Pittsburgh 24, Georgia 20

1983 Penn St. 27, Georgia 23
1984 Auburn 9, Michigan 7
1985 Nebraska 28, LSU 10
1986 Tennessee 35, Miami (FL) 7
1987 Nebraska 30, LSU 15
1988 Syracuse 16, Auburn 16
1989 Florida St. 13, Auburn 7
1990 Miami (FL) 33, Alabama 25
1991 Tennessee 23, Virginia 22
1992 Notre Dame 39, Florida 28
1993 Alabama 34, Miami (FL) 13
1994 Florida 41, West Virginia 7
1995 Florida St. 23, Florida 17
1995 (Dec.) Virginia Tech 28, Texas 10
1997 (Jan.) Florida 52, Florida St. 20
1998 Florida St. 31, Ohio St. 14
1999 Ohio St. 24, Texas A&M 14
2000 Florida St. 46, Virginia Tech 29
2001 Miami (FL) 37, Florida 20
2002 LSU 47, Illinois 34
2003 Georgia 26, Florida St. 13
2004 LSU 21, Oklahoma 14
2005 Auburn 16, Virginia Tech 13
2006 West Virginia 38, Georgia 35*

Cotton Bowl, Dallas, TX

1937 (Jan.) TCU 16, Marquette 6
1938 Rice 28, Colorado 14
1939 St. Mary's 20, Texas Tech 13
1940 Clemson 6, Boston Coll. 3
1941 Texas A&M 13, Fordham 12
1942 Alabama 29, Texas A&M 21
1943 Texas 14, Georgia Tech 7
1944 Randolph Field 7, Texas 7
1945 Oklahoma A&M 34, TCU 0
1946 Texas 40, Missouri 27
1947 Arkansas 0, LSU 0
1948 SMU 13, Penn St. 13
1949 SMU 21, Oregon 13
1950 Rice 27, North Carolina 13
1951 Tennessee 20, Texas 14
1952 Kentucky 20, TCU 7
1953 Texas 16, Tennessee 0
1954 Rice 28, Alabama 6
1955 Georgia Tech 14, Arkansas 6
1956 Mississippi 14, TCU 13
1957 TCU 28, Syracuse 27
1958 Navy 20, Rice 7
1959 TCU 0, Air Force 0
1960 Syracuse 23, Texas 14

1961 Duke 7, Arkansas 6
1962 Texas 12, Mississippi 7
1963 LSU 13, Texas 0
1964 Texas 28, Navy 6
1965 Arkansas 10, Nebraska 7
1966 LSU 14, Arkansas 7
1966 (Dec.) Georgia 24, SMU 9
1968 (Jan.) Texas A&M 20, Alabama 16
1969 Texas 36, Tennessee 13
1970 Texas 21, Notre Dame 17
1971 Notre Dame 24, Texas 11
1972 Penn St. 30, Texas 6
1973 Texas 17, Alabama 13
1974 Nebraska 19, Texas 3
1975 Penn St. 41, Baylor 20
1976 Arkansas 31, Georgia 10
1977 Houston 30, Maryland 21
1978 Notre Dame 38, Texas 10
1979 Notre Dame 35, Houston 34
1980 Houston 17, Nebraska 14
1981 Alabama 30, Baylor 2
1982 Texas 14, Alabama 12
1983 SMU 7, Pittsburgh 3

1984 Georgia 10, Texas 9
1985 Boston Coll. 45, Houston 28
1986 Texas A&M 36, Auburn 16
1987 Ohio St. 28, Texas A&M 12
1988 Texas A&M 35, Notre Dame 10
1989 UCLA 17, Arkansas 3
1990 Tennessee 31, Arkansas 27
1991 Miami (FL) 46, Texas 3
1992 Florida St. 10, Texas A&M 2
1993 Notre Dame 28, Texas A&M 3
1994 Notre Dame 24, Texas A&M 21
1995 USC. 55, Texas Tech 14
1996 Colorado 38, Oregon 6
1997 Brigham Young 19, Kansas St. 15
1998 UCLA 29, Texas A&M 23
1999 Texas 38, Mississippi St. 11
2000 Arkansas 27, Texas 6
2001 Kansas St. 35, Tennessee 21
2002 Oklahoma 10, Arkansas 3
2003 Texas 35, LSU 20
2004 Mississippi 31, Oklahoma St. 28
2005 Tennessee 38, Texas A&M 7
2006 Alabama 13, Texas Tech 10

Capital One Bowl, Orlando, FL
(Florida Citrus Bowl 1984-2002, Tangerine Bowl, 1947-1983)

1947 (Jan.) Catawba 31, Maryville 6
1948 Catawba 7, Marshall 0
1949 Murray St. 21, Sul Ross St. 21
1950 St. Vincent 7, Emory & Henry 6
1951 Morris Harvey 35, Emory & Henry 14
1952 Stetson 35, Arkansas St. 20
1953 East Texas St. 33, Tenn. Tech 0
1954 East Texas St. 7, Arkansas St. 7
1955 Neb.-Omaha 7, E. Kentucky 6
1956 Juniata 6, Missouri Valley 6
1957 West Texas St. 20, So. Miss. 13
1958 East Texas St. 10, So. Miss. 9
1958 (Dec.) East Texas St. 26,
      Missouri Valley 7
1960 (Jan.) Middle Tennessee 21,
      Presbyterian 12
1960 (Dec.) Citadel 27, Tenn. Tech 0
1961 Lamar 21, Middle Tennessee 14
1962 Houston 49, Miami (OH) 21
1963 Western Ky. 27, Coast Guard 0
1964 E. Carolina 14, Massachusetts 13

1965 E. Carolina 31, Maine 0
1966 Morgan St. 14, West Chester 6
1967 Tenn.-Martin 25, West Chester 8
1968 Richmond 49, Ohio U. 42
1969 Toledo 56, Davidson 33
1970 Toledo 40, William & Mary 12
1971 Toledo 28, Richmond 3
1972 Tampa 21, Kent St. 18
1973 Miami (OH) 16, Florida 7
1974 Miami (OH) 21, Georgia 10
1975 Miami (OH) 20, S. Carolina 7
1976 Okla. St. 49, Brigham Young 21
1977 Florida St. 40, Texas Tech 17
1978 N. Carolina St. 30, Pittsburgh 17
1979 LSU 34, Wake Forest 10
1980 Florida 35, Maryland 20
1981 Missouri 19, So. Mississippi 17
1982 Auburn 33, Boston College 26
1983 Tennessee 30, Maryland 23
1984 Georgia 17, Florida St. 17
1985 Ohio St. 10, Brigham Young 7

1987 (Jan.) Auburn 16, USC 7
1988 Clemson 35, Penn St. 10
1989 Clemson 13, Oklahoma 6
1990 Illinois 31, Virginia 21
1991 Georgia Tech 45, Nebraska 21
1992 California 37, Clemson 13
1993 Georgia 21, Ohio St. 14
1994 Penn St. 31, Tennessee 13
1995 Alabama 24, Ohio St. 17
1996 Tennessee 20, Ohio St. 14
1997 Tennessee 48, Northwestern 28
1998 Florida 21, Penn St. 6
1999 Michigan 45, Arkansas 31
2000 Michigan St. 37, Florida 34
2001 Michigan 31, Auburn 28
2002 Tennessee 45, Michigan 17
2003 Auburn 13, Penn St. 9
2004 Georgia 34, Purdue 27 (OT)
2005 Iowa 30, LSU 25
2006 Wisconsin 24, Auburn 10

Fiesta Bowl, Tempe, AZ

1971 (Dec.) Arizona St. 45, Florida St. 38	1984 Ohio St. 28, Pittsburgh 23	1996 Nebraska 62, Florida 24
1972 Arizona St. 49, Missouri 35	1985 UCLA 39, Miami (FL) 37	1997 Penn St. 38, Texas 15
1973 Arizona St. 28, Pittsburgh 7	1986 Michigan 27, Nebraska 23	1997 (Dec.) Kansas St. 35, Syracuse 18
1974 Okla. St. 16, Brigham Young 6	1987 Penn St. 14, Miami (FL) 10	1999 (Jan.) Tennessee 23, Florida St. 16
1975 Arizona St. 17, Nebraska 14	1988 Florida St. 31, Nebraska 28	2000 Nebraska 31, Tennessee 21
1976 Oklahoma 41, Wyoming 7	1989 Notre Dame 34, W. Virginia 21	2001 Oregon St. 41, Notre Dame 9
1977 Penn St. 42, Arizona St. 30	1990 Florida St. 41, Nebraska 17	2002 Oregon 38, Colorado 16
1978 UCLA 10, Arkansas 10	1991 Louisville 34, Alabama 7	2003 Ohio St. 31, Miami 24 (2 OT)
1979 Pittsburgh 16, Arizona 10	1992 Penn St. 42, Tennessee 17	2004 Ohio St. 35, Kansas St. 28
1980 Penn St. 31, Ohio St. 19	1993 Syracuse 26, Colorado 22	2005 Utah 35, Pittsburgh 7
1982 (Jan.) Penn St. 26, USC 10	1994 Arizona 29, Miami (FL) 0	2006 Ohio St. 34, Notre Dame 20
1983 Arizona St. 32, Oklahoma 21	1995 Colorado 41, Notre Dame 24	

Gator Bowl, Jacksonville, FL

1946 (Jan.) Wake Forest 26, S. Carolina 14	1966 Tennessee 18, Syracuse 12	1986 Clemson 27, Stanford 21
1947 Oklahoma 34, N. Carolina St. 13	1967 Penn St. 17, Florida St. 17	1987 LSU 30, S. Carolina 13
1948 Maryland 20, Georgia 20	1968 Missouri 35, Alabama 10	1989 (Jan.) Georgia 34, Michigan St. 27
1949 Clemson 24, Missouri 23	1969 Florida 14, Tennessee 13	1989 (Dec.) Clemson 27, W. Virginia 7
1950 Maryland 20, Missouri 7	1971 (Jan.) Auburn 35, Mississippi 28	1991 (Jan.) Michigan 35, Mississippi 3
1951 Wyoming 20, Washington & Lee 7	1971 (Dec.) Georgia 7, N. Carolina 3	1991 (Dec.) Oklahoma 48, Virginia 14
1952 Miami (FL) 14, Clemson 0	1972 Auburn 24, Colorado 3	1992 Florida 27, N. Carolina St. 10
1953 Florida 14, Tulsa 13	1973 Texas Tech 28, Tennessee 19	1993 Alabama 24, N. Carolina 10
1954 Texas Tech 35, Auburn 13	1974 Auburn 27, Texas 3	1994 Tennessee 45, Virginia Tech 23
1954 (Dec.) Auburn 33, Baylor 13	1975 Maryland 13, Florida 0	1996 (Jan.) Syracuse 41, Clemson 0
1955 Vanderbilt 25, Auburn 13	1976 Notre Dame 20, Penn St. 9	1997 N. Carolina 20, W. Virginia 13
1956 Georgia Tech 21, Pittsburgh 14	1977 Pittsburgh 34, Clemson 3	1998 N. Carolina 42, Virginia Tech 3
1957 Tennessee 3, Texas A&M 0	1978 Clemson 17, Ohio St. 15	1999 Georgia Tech 35, Notre Dame 28
1958 Mississippi 7, Florida 3	1979 N. Carolina 17, Michigan 15	2000 Miami (FL) 28, Georgia Tech 13
1960 (Jan.) Arkansas 14, Georgia Tech 7	1980 Pittsburgh 37, S. Carolina 9	2001 Virginia Tech 41, Clemson 20
1960 (Dec.) Florida 13, Baylor 12	1981 N. Carolina 31, Arkansas 27	2002 Florida St. 30, Virginia Tech 17
1961 Penn St. 30, Georgia Tech 15	1982 Florida St. 31, West Virginia 12	2003 N. Carolina St. 28, Notre Dame 6
1962 Florida 17, Penn St. 7	1983 Florida 14, Iowa 6	2004 Maryland 41, West Virginia 7
1963 N. Carolina 35, Air Force 0	1984 Oklahoma St. 21, S. Carolina 14	2005 Florida St. 30, West Virginia 18
1965 (Jan.) Florida St. 36, Okla.19	1985 Florida St. 34, Oklahoma St. 23	2006 Virginia Tech 35, Louisville 24
1965 (Dec.) GA Tech 31, Texas Tech 21		

Liberty Bowl, Memphis, TN

1959 (Dec.) Penn St. 7, Alabama 0	1975 USC 20, Texas A&M 0	1991 Air Force 38, Mississippi St. 15
1960 Penn St. 41, Oregon 12	1976 Alabama 36, UCLA 6	1992 Mississippi 13, Air Force 0
1961 Syracuse 15, Miami (FL) 14	1977 Nebraska 21, N. Carolina 17	1993 Louisville 18, Michigan St. 7
1962 Oregon St. 6, Villanova 0	1978 Missouri 20, LSU 15	1994 Illinois 30, East Carolina 0
1963 Mississippi 16, N. Carolina St. 12	1979 Penn St. 9, Tulane 6	1995 East Carolina 19, Stanford 13
1964 Utah 32, West Virginia 6	1980 Purdue 28, Missouri 25	1996 Syracuse 30, Houston 17
1965 Mississippi 13, Auburn 7	1981 Ohio St. 31, Navy 28	1997 So. Mississippi 41, Pittsburgh 7
1966 Miami (FL) 14, Virginia Tech 7	1982 Alabama 21, Illinois 15	1998 Tulane 41, Brigham Young 27
1967 N. Carolina St. 14, Georgia 7	1983 Notre Dame 19, Boston Coll. 18	1999 So. Mississippi 23, Colorado St. 17
1968 Mississippi 34, Virginia Tech 17	1984 Auburn 21, Arkansas 15	2000 Colorado St. 22, Louisville 17
1969 Colorado 47, Alabama 33	1985 Baylor 21, LSU 7	2001 Louisville 28, BYU 10
1970 Tulane 17, Colorado 3	1986 Tennessee 21, Minnesota 14	2002 TCU 17, Colorado St. 3
1971 Tennessee 14, Arkansas 13	1987 Georgia 20, Arkansas 17	2003 Utah 17, So. Mississippi 0
1972 Georgia Tech 31, Iowa St. 30	1988 Indiana 34, S. Carolina 10	2004 Louisville 44, Boise St. 40
1973 N. Carolina St. 31, Kansas 18	1989 Mississippi 42, Air Force 29	2005 Tulsa 31, Fresno St. 24
1974 Tennessee 7, Maryland 3	1990 Air Force 23, Ohio St. 11	

Peach Bowl, Atlanta, GA

1968 (Dec.) LSU 31, Florida St. 27	1981 (Dec.) W. Virginia 26, Florida 6	1995 (Jan.) N. Carolina St. 28, Miss. St. 24
1969 W. Virginia 14, S. Carolina 3	1982 Iowa 28, Tennessee 22	1995 (Dec.) Virginia 34, Georgia 27
1970 Arizona St. 48, N. Carolina 26	1983 Florida St. 28, N. Carolina 3	1996 LSU 10, Clemson 7
1971 Mississippi 41, Georgia Tech 18	1984 Virginia 27, Purdue 22	1998 (Jan.) Auburn 21, Clemson 17
1972 N. Carolina St. 49, W. Virginia 13	1985 Army 31, Illinois 29	1998 (Dec.) Georgia 35, Virginia 33
1973 Georgia 17, Maryland 16	1986 Va. Tech 25, N. Carolina St. 24	1999 Mississippi St. 27, Clemson 7
1974 Vanderbilt 6, Texas Tech 6	1988 (Jan.) Tennessee 28, Indiana 22	2000 LSU 28, Georgia Tech 14
1975 W. Virginia 13, N. Carolina St. 10	1988 (Dec.) N. Carolina St. 28, Iowa 23	2001 North Carolina 16, Auburn 10
1976 Kentucky 21, N. Carolina 0	1989 Syracuse 19, Georgia 18	2002 Maryland 30, Tennessee 3
1977 N. Carolina St. 24, Iowa St. 14	1990 Auburn 27, Indiana 23	2003 Clemson 27, Tennessee 14
1978 Purdue 41, Georgia Tech. 21	1992 (Jan.) E. Carolina 37, NC St. 34	2004 Miami (FL) 27, Florida 10
1979 Baylor 24, Clemson 18	1993 N. Carolina 21, Mississippi St. 17	2005 LSU 40, Miami (FL) 3
1981 (Jan.) Miami (FL) 20, Virginia Tech 10	1993 (Dec.) Clemson 14, Kentucky 13	

Sun Bowl, El Paso, TX (John Hancock Bowl, 1989-93)

1936 (Jan.) Hardin-Simmons 14, New Mexico St. 14	1958 (Dec.) Wyoming 14, Hardin-Simmons 6	1981 Oklahoma 40, Houston 14
1937 Hardin-Simmons 34, Texas Mines 6	1959 New Mexico St. 28, N. Texas St. 8	1982 North Carolina 26, Texas 10
1938 West Virginia 7, Texas Tech 6	1960 New Mexico St. 20, Utah St. 13	1983 Alabama 28, SMU 7
1939 Utah 26, New Mexico 0	1961 Villanova 17, Wichita 9	1984 Maryland 28, Tennessee 27
1940 Catholic U. 0, Arizona St. 0	1962 West Texas St. 15, Ohio U. 14	1985 Georgia 13, Arizona 13
1941 Western Reserve 26, Arizona St. 13	1963 Oregon 21, SMU 14	1986 Alabama 28, Washington 6
1942 Tulsa 6, Texas Tech 0	1964 Georgia 7, Texas Tech 0	1987 Oklahoma St. 35, West Virginia 33
1943 2d Air Force 13, Hardin-Simmons 7	1965 Texas Western 13, TCU 12	1988 Alabama 29, Army 28
1944 Southwestern (TX) 7, New Mexico 0	1966 Wyoming 28, Florida St. 20	1989 Pittsburgh 31, Texas A&M 28
1945 Southwestern (TX) 35, Univ. of Mexico 0	1967 UTEP 14, Mississippi 7	1990 Michigan St. 17, USC 16
1946 New Mexico 34, Denver 24	1968 Auburn 34, Arizona 10	1991 UCLA 6, Illinois 3
1947 Cincinnati 18, Virginia Tech 6	1969 Nebraska 45, Georgia 6	1992 Baylor 20, Arizona 15
1948 Miami (OH) 13, Texas Tech 12	1970 Georgia Tech. 17, Texas Tech 9	1993 Oklahoma 41, Texas Tech 10
1949 West Virginia 21, Texas Mines 12	1971 LSU 33, Iowa St. 15	1994 Texas 35, North Carolina 31
1950 Texas Western 33, Georgetown 20	1972 North Carolina 32, Texas Tech 28	1995 Iowa 38, Washington 18
1951 West Texas St. 14, Cincinnati 13	1973 Missouri 34, Auburn 17	1996 Stanford 38, Michigan St. 0
1952 Texas Tech 25, Pacific (CA) 14	1974 Mississippi St. 26, North Carolina 24	1997 Arizona St. 17, Iowa 7
1953 Pacific (CA) 26, S. Mississippi 7		1998 TCU 28, USC 19
1954 Texas Western 37, S. Miss. 14	1975 Pittsburgh 33, Kansas 19	1999 Oregon 24, Minnesota 20
1955 Texas Western 47, Florida St. 20	1977 (Jan.) Texas A&M 37, Florida 14	2000 Wisconsin 21, UCLA 20
1956 Wyoming 21, Texas Tech 14	1977 (Dec.) Stanford 24, LSU 14	2001 Washington St. 33, Purdue 27
1957 Geo. Washington 13, TX Western 0	1978 Texas 42, Maryland 0	2002 Purdue 34, Washington 24
1958 Louisville 34, Drake 20	1979 Washington 14, Texas 7	2003 Minnesota 31, Oregon 30
	1980 Nebraska 31, Mississippi St. 17	2004 Arizona St. 27, Purdue 23
		2005 UCLA 50, Northwestern 39

Other Bowl Results, Late 2005 - Early 2006

Alamo Bowl, San Antonio, TX: Nebraska 32, Michigan 28
Champs Sports Bowl, Orlando, FL: Clemson 19, Colorado 10
Meineke Car Care Bowl, Charlotte, NC: NC State 14, South Florida 0
Emerald Bowl, San Francisco, CA: Utah 38, Georgia Tech 10
Fort Worth Bowl, Ft. Worth, TX: Kansas 42, Houston 13
GMAC Bowl, Mobile, AL: Toledo 45, UTEP 13
Hawaii Bowl, Honolulu, HI: Nevada 49, UCF 48 (OT)
Holiday Bowl, San Diego, CA: Oklahoma 17, Oregon 14
Houston Bowl, Houston, TX: TCU 27, Iowa State 24
Independence Bowl, Shreveport, LA: Missouri 38, South Carolina 31

Insight Bowl, Phoenix, AZ: Arizona State 45, Rutgers 40
Las Vegas Bowl, Las Vegas, NV: California 35, BYU 28
Motor City Bowl, Detroit, MI: Memphis 38, Akron 31
MPC Computers (formerly Humanitarian) Bowl, Boise, ID: Boston College 27, Boise State 21
Music City Bowl, Nashville, TN: Virginia 34, Minnesota 31
New Orleans Bowl: Southern Miss 31, Arkansas State 19 (played in Lafayette, LA)
Outback Bowl, Tampa, FL: Florida 31, Iowa 24
Poinsettia Bowl, San Diego, CA: Navy 51, Colorado State 30

All-Time NCAA Division I-A Statistical Leaders

(At end of 2005 season. Prior to 2002, postseason games were not included in NCAA final football statistics or records. Beginning with the 2002 season, all postseason games were included. Career rushing yards per game rankings do not include active players.)

Career Rushing Yards

Player, team	Yrs	Carries	Yds	Avg
Ron Dayne, Wisconsin	1996-99	1,115	6,397	5.74
Ricky Williams, Texas	1995-98	1,011	6,279	6.21
Tony Dorsett, Pittsburgh	1973-76	1,074	6,082	5.66
DeAngelo Williams, Memphis	2002-05	969	6,026	6.22
Charles White, USC	1976-79	1,023	5,598	5.47

Career Passing Yards

Player, team	Yrs	Comp/Att	Yds
Timmy Chang, Hawaii	2000-04	1,388/2,436	17,072
Ty Detmer, BYU	1988-91	958/1,530	15,031
Tim Rattay, Louisiana Tech	1997-99	1,015/1,552	12,746
Chris Redman, Louisville	1996-99	1,031/1,679	12,541
Kliff Kingsbury, Texas Tech	1999-02	1,231/1,883	12,429

Career Rushing Yard/Game (min. 2,500 yds.)

Player, team	Yrs	Carries	Yds	Avg/Game
Ed Marinaro, Cornell	1969-71	918	4,715	174.6
O.J. Simpson, USC	1967-68	621	3,124	164.4
Herschel Walker, Georgia	1980-82	994	5,259	159.4
LeShon Johnson, N. Illinois	1992-93	592	3,314	150.6
Ron Dayne, Wisconsin	1996-99	1,115	6,397	148.8

Career Receiving Yards

Player, team	Yrs	Rec	Yds	Avg
Trevor Insley, Nevada	1996-99	298	5,005	16.8
Marcus Harris, Wyoming	1993-96	259	4,518	17.4
Ryan Yarborough, Wyoming	1990-93	229	4,357	19.0
Troy Edwards, Louisiana Tech	1996-98	280	4,352	15.5
Aaron Turner, Pacific (CA)	1989-92	266	4,345	16.3

All-Time Team Won-Lost Records*

	Years	Won	Lost	Tied	Total	Pct.		Years	Won	Lost	Tied	Total	Pct.
Notre Dame	117	811	266	42	1,119	.744	Miami (FL)	79	525	291	19	835	.640
Michigan	126	849	280	36	1,165	.744	Miami (OH)	117	639	352	44	1,035	.639
Texas	113	800	310	33	1,143	.714	LSU	112	669	374	47	1,090	.635
Oklahoma	111	757	289	53	1,099	.713	Washington	116	641	372	50	1,063	.631
Alabama	111	774	301	43	1,118	.712	Auburn	113	656	382	47	1,085	.626
Ohio St.	116	774	300	53	1,127	.710	Arizona St.	93	523	318	24	865	.618
Nebraska	116	794	321	40	1,155	.705	Florida	99	606	367	40	1,013	.618
USC	113	732	298	54	1,084	.700	Colorado	116	650	402	36	1,088	.614
Tennessee	109	751	312	53	1,116	.697	South Fla. (2000)	9	61	39	0	100	.610
Penn St.	119	771	339	41	1,151	.688	Central Michigan	105	532	338	36	906	.607
Boise St (1996)	38	304	140	2	446	.684	Texas A&M	111	639	415	48	1,102	.602
Florida St.	59	436	205	17	658	.676	Syracuse	116	665	444	49	1,158	.595
Georgia	112	693	375	54	1,122	.642							

*As of 2005 season. Includes records as senior college only. Bowl and playoff games are included, and each tie game is computed as half won and half lost. Teams listed with years in parentheses indicates reclassification to Division I-A. The year in parentheses is the first year of Division I-A membership. Tiebreaker rule began with 1996 season.

Heisman Trophy Winners

Awarded annually to the nation's outstanding college football player by the Downtown Athletic Club.

1935	Jay Berwanger, Chicago, HB	1959	Billy Cannon, LSU, HB	1983	Mike Rozier, Nebraska, RB
1936	Larry Kelley, Yale, E	1960	Joe Bellino, Navy, HB	1984	Doug Flutie, Boston College, QB
1937	Clinton Frank, Yale, HB	1961	Ernest Davis, Syracuse, HB	1985	Bo Jackson, Auburn, RB
1938	David O'Brien, Texas Christian, QB	1962	Terry Baker, Oregon St., QB	1986	Vinny Testaverde, Miami, QB
1939	Nile Kinnick, Iowa, HB	1963	Roger Staubach, Navy, QB	1987	Tim Brown, Notre Dame, WR
1940	Tom Harmon, Michigan, HB	1964	John Huarte, Notre Dame, QB	1988	Barry Sanders, Oklahoma St., RB
1941	Bruce Smith, Minnesota, HB	1965	Mike Garrett, USC, HB	1989	Andre Ware, Houston, QB
1942	Frank Sinkwich, Georgia, HB	1966	Steve Spurrier, Florida, QB	1990	Ty Detmer, BYU, QB
1943	Angelo Bertelli, Notre Dame, QB	1967	Gary Beban, UCLA, QB	1991	Desmond Howard, Michigan, WR
1944	Leslie Horvath, Ohio St., QB	1968	O. J. Simpson, USC, RB	1992	Gino Torretta, Miami, QB
1945	Felix Blanchard, Army, FB	1969	Steve Owens, Oklahoma, RB	1993	Charlie Ward, Florida St., QB
1946	Glenn Davis, Army, HB	1970	Jim Plunkett, Stanford, QB	1994	Rashaan Salaam, Colorado, RB
1947	John Lujack, Notre Dame, QB	1971	Pat Sullivan, Auburn, QB	1995	Eddie George, Ohio St., RB
1948	Doak Walker, SMU, HB	1972	Johnny Rodgers, Nebraska, RB-WR	1996	Danny Wuerffel, Florida, QB
1949	Leon Hart, Notre Dame, E	1973	John Cappelletti, Penn St., RB	1997	Charles Woodson, Michigan, CB
1950	Vic Janowicz, Ohio St., HB	1974	Archie Griffin, Ohio St., RB	1998	Ricky Williams, Texas, RB
1951	Richard Kazmaier, Princeton, HB	1975	Archie Griffin, Ohio St., RB	1999	Ron Dayne, Wisconsin, RB
1952	Billy Vessels, Oklahoma, HB	1976	Tony Dorsett, Pittsburgh, RB	2000	Chris Weinke, Florida St., QB
1953	John Lattner, Notre Dame, HB	1977	Earl Campbell, Texas, RB	2001	Eric Crouch, Nebraska, QB
1954	Alan Ameche, Wisconsin, FB	1978	Billy Sims, Oklahoma, RB	2002	Carson Palmer, USC, QB
1955	Howard Cassady, Ohio St., HB	1979	Charles White, USC, RB	2003	Jason White, Oklahoma, QB
1956	Paul Hornung, Notre Dame, QB	1980	George Rogers, S. Carolina, RB	2004	Matt Leinart, USC, QB
1957	John Crow, Texas A & M, HB	1981	Marcus Allen, USC, RB	2005	Reggie Bush, USC, TB
1958	Pete Dawkins, Army, HB	1982	Herschel Walker, Georgia, RB		

All-Time Division I-A Coaching Victories (Including Bowl Games)

Bobby Bowden 359	Bo Schembechler 234	Dan McGugin 197	Johnny Majors 185
Joe Paterno 354	Hayden Fry 232	Fielding Yost 196	**Jim Tressel** 185
Paul "Bear" Bryant 323	Jess Neely 207	Howard Jones 194	Darrell Royal 184
Glenn "Pop" Warner ... 319	Warren Woodson 203	John Cooper 192	Gil Dobie 180
Amos Alonzo Stagg 314	Eddie Anderson 201	John Vaught 190	Jackie Sherrill 180
LaVell Edwards 257	Vince Dooley 201	George Welsh 189	Carl Snavely 180
Tom Osborne 255	Jim Sweeney 200	**Frank Beamer** 188	Jerry Claiborne 179
Lou Holtz 249	Dana X. Bible 198	John Heisman 185	Ben Schwartzwalder 178
Woody Hayes 238			

Coaches active in 2005 shown in bold. Total victories through 2006 bowl games. John Gagliardi of St. John's Univ. (MN) (Div. III) holds the record for most college football victories, with 429.

College Football Coach of the Year

The Division I-A Coach of the Year has been selected by the American Football Coaches Assn. since 1935 and selected by the Football Writers Assn. of America since 1957. When polls disagree, both winners are indicated.

1935 Lynn Waldorf, Northwestern	1965 Tommy Prothro, UCLA (AFCA);	1984 LaVell Edwards, Brigham Young
1936 Dick Harlow, Harvard	Duffy Daugherty, Mich. St. (FWAA)	1985 Fisher De Berry, Air Force
1937 Edward Mylin, Lafayette	1966 Tom Cahill, Army	1986 Joe Paterno, Penn St.
1938 Bill Kern, Carnegie Tech	1967 John Pont, Indiana	1987 Dick MacPherson, Syracuse
1939 Eddie Anderson, Iowa	1968 Joe Paterno, Penn St. (AFCA);	1988 Don Nehlen, W. Virginia (AFCA);
1940 Clark Shaughnessy, Stanford	Woody Hayes, Ohio St. (FWAA)	Lou Holtz, Notre Dame (FWAA)
1941 Frank Leahy, Notre Dame	1969 Bo Schembechler, Michigan	1989 Bill McCartney, Colorado
1942 Bill Alexander, Georgia Tech	1970 Charles McClendon, LSU, &	1990 Bobby Ross, Georgia Tech
1943 Amos Alonzo Stagg, Pacific	Darrell Royal, Texas (AFCA);	1991 Don James, Washington
1944 Carroll Widdoes, Ohio St.	Alex Agase, Northwestern (FWAA)	1992 Gene Stallings, Alabama
1945 Bo McMillin, Indiana	1971 Paul "Bear" Bryant, Alabama	1993 Barry Alvarez, Wisconsin (AFCA);
1946 Earl "Red" Blaik, Army	(AFCA); Bob Devaney, Nebraska	Terry Bowden, Auburn (FWAA)
1947 Fritz Crisler, Michigan	(FWAA)	1994 Tom Osborne, Nebraska (AFCA);
1948 Bennie Oosterbaan, Michigan	1972 John McKay, USC	Rich Brooks, Oregon (FWAA)
1949 Bud Wilkinson, Oklahoma	1973 Paul "Bear" Bryant, Alabama	1995 Gary Barnett, Northwestern
1950 Charlie Caldwell, Princeton	(AFCA); Johnny Majors, Pittsburgh	1996 Bruce Snyder, Arizona St.
1951 Chuck Taylor, Stanford	(FWAA)	1997 Mike Price, Washington St.
1952 Biggie Munn, Michigan St.	1974 Grant Teaff, Baylor	1998 Phillip Fulmer, Tennessee
1953 Jim Tatum, Maryland	1975 Frank Kush, Arizona St. (AFCA);	1999 Frank Beamer, Virginia Tech
1954 Henry "Red" Sanders, UCLA	Woody Hayes, Ohio St. (FWAA)	2000 Bob Stoops, Oklahoma
1955 Duffy Daugherty, Michigan St.	1976 Johnny Majors, Pittsburgh	2001 Larry Coker, Miami (FL) & Ralph
1956 Bowden Wyatt, Tennessee	1977 Don James, Washington (AFCA);	Friedgen, Maryland (AFCA); Ralph
1957 Woody Hayes, Ohio St.	Lou Holtz, Arkansas (FWAA)	Friedgen, Maryland (FWAA)
1958 Paul Dietzel, LSU	1978 Joe Paterno, Penn St.	2002 Jim Tressel, Ohio St.
1959 Ben Schwartzwalder, Syracuse	1979 Earle Bruce, Ohio St.	2003 Pete Carroll, USC (AFCA); Nick
1960 Murray Warmath, Minnesota	1980 Vince Dooley, Georgia	Saban, LSU (FWAA)
1961 Paul "Bear" Bryant, Ala. (AFCA);	1981 Danny Ford, Clemson	2004 Tommy Tuberville, Auburn (AFCA);
Darrell Royal, Texas (FWAA)	1982 Joe Paterno, Penn St.	Urban Meyer, Utah (FWAA)
1962 John McKay, USC	1983 Ken Hatfield, Air Force (AFCA);	2005 Joe Paterno, Penn State (AFCA);
1963 Darrell Royal, Texas	Howard Schnellenberger,	Charlie Weis, Notre Dame (FWAA)
1964 Ara Parseghian, Notre Dame, &	Miami (FL) (FWAA)	
Frank Broyles, Arkansas (AFCA);		
Ara Parseghian (FWAA)		

NCAA Div. I-A Football Conference Champions (1980-2005)

Atlantic Coast [1]	**Big East** [2]	1999 Wisconsin	2002 Cincinnati, TCU
1980 North Carolina	1991 Miami (FL), Syracuse	2000 Michigan, Northwestern,	2003 So. Mississippi
1981 Clemson	1992 Miami (FL)	Purdue	2004 Louisville
1982 Clemson	1993 West Virginia	2001 Illinois	2005 Tulsa
1983 Maryland	1994 Miami (FL)	2002 Iowa, Ohio St.	
1984 Maryland	1995 Virginia Tech, Miami (FL)	2003 Michigan	**Mid-American Athletic**
1985 Maryland	1996 Virginia Tech, Miami	2004 Iowa, Michigan	1980 Central Michigan
1986 Clemson	(FL), Syracuse	2005 Penn St., Ohio St.	1981 Toledo
1987 Clemson	1997 Syracuse		1982 Bowling Green
1988 Clemson	1998 Syracuse	**Big West** [3]	1983 Northern Illinois
1989 Virginia, Duke	1999 Virginia Tech	1980 Long Beach St.	1984 Toledo
1990 Georgia Tech	2000 Miami (FL)	1981 San Jose St.	1985 Bowling Green
1991 Clemson	2001 Miami (FL)	1982 Fresno St.	1986 Miami (OH)
1992 Florida St.	2002 Miami (FL)	1983 Cal St.-Fullerton	1987 E. Michigan
1993 Florida St.	2003 Miami (FL)	1984 Cal St.-Fullerton	1988 W. Michigan
1994 Florida St.	2004 Pittsburgh, W. Virginia,	1985 Fresno St.	1989 Ball St.
1995 Virginia, Florida St.	Boston, Syracuse	1986 San Jose St.	1990 Central Michigan
1996 Florida St.	2005 West Virginia	1987 San Jose St.	1991 Bowling Green
1997 Florida St.	**Big Ten**	1988 Fresno St.	1992 Bowling Green
1998 Florida St.,	1980 Michigan	1989 Fresno St.	1993 Ball St.
Georgia Tech	1981 Iowa, Ohio St.	1990 San Jose St.	1994 Central Michigan
1999 Florida St.	1982 Michigan	1991 San Jose St., Fresno St.	1995 Toledo
2000 Florida St.	1983 Illinois	1992 Nevada	1996 Ball St.
2001 Maryland	1984 Ohio St.	1993 SW Louisiana, Utah St.	1997 Marshall
2002 Florida St.	1985 Iowa	1994 Nevada, SW Louisiana,	1998 Marshall
2003 Florida St.	1986 Michigan, Ohio St.	UNLV	1999 Marshall
2004 Virginia Tech	1987 Michigan St.	1995 Nevada	2000 Marshall
2005 Florida St.	1988 Michigan	1996 Nevada, Utah St.	2001 Toledo
	1989 Michigan	1997 Nevada, Utah St.	2002 Marshall
Big 12	1990 Iowa, Ill., Mich., Mich. St.	1998 Idaho	2003 Miami (OH)
1996 Texas	1991 Michigan	1999 Boise St.	2004 Toledo
1997 Nebraska	1992 Michigan	2000 Boise St.	2005 Akron
1998 Texas A&M	1993 Ohio St., Wisconsin		
1999 Nebraska	1994 Penn St.	**Conference USA** [3]	**Mountain West** [4]
2000 Oklahoma	1995 Northwestern	1996 So. Mississippi, Houston	1999 BYU, Colorado St., Utah
2001 Colorado	1996 Ohio St., Northwestern	1997 So. Mississippi	2000 Colorado St.
2002 Oklahoma	1997 Michigan	1998 Tulane	2001 BYU
2003 Kansas St.	1998 Ohio St., Wisconsin,	1999 So. Mississippi	2002 Colorado St.
2004 Oklahoma	Michigan	2000 Louisville	2003 Utah
2005 Texas		2001 Louisville	2004 Utah
			2005 TCU

Pacific Ten
1980 Washington
1981 Washington
1982 UCLA
1983 UCLA
1984 USC
1985 UCLA
1986 Arizona St.
1987 UCLA, USC
1988 USC
1989 USC
1990 Washington
1991 Washington
1992 Washington, Stanford
1993 UCLA, Arizona, USC
1994 Oregon
1995 USC, Washington
1996 Arizona St.
1997 Washington St., UCLA
1998 UCLA
1999 Stanford
2000 Washington, Oregon St., Oregon

2001 Oregon
2002 USC, Washington St.
2003 USC
2004 USC
2005 USC

Southeastern
1980 Georgia
1981 Georgia, Alabama
1982 Georgia
1983 Auburn
1984 Florida (title vacated)
1985 Tennessee
1986 LSU
1987 Auburn
1988 Auburn, LSU
1989 Ala., Tenn., Auburn
1990 Tennessee
1991 Florida
1992 Alabama
1993 Florida
1994 Florida
1995 Florida
1996 Florida

1997 Tennessee
1998 Tennessee
1999 Alabama
2000 Florida
2001 LSU
2002 Georgia
2003 LSU
2004 Auburn
2005 Georgia

Sun Belt[5]
2001 Middle Tenn. St., North Texas
2002 North Texas
2003 North Texas
2004 North Texas
2005 Arkansas St., LA-Lafayette, LA-Monroe

Western Athletic[6]
1980 Brigham Young (BYU)
1981 Brigham Young
1982 Brigham Young
1983 Brigham Young

1984 Brigham Young
1985 BYU, Air Force
1986 San Diego St.
1987 Wyoming
1988 Wyoming
1989 Brigham Young
1990 Brigham Young
1991 Brigham Young
1992 Hawaii, BYU, Fresno St.
1993 Wyoming, Fresno St., BYU
1994 Colorado St.
1995 Colorado St., Air Force, Utah, BYU
1996 Brigham Young
1997 Colorado St.
1998 Air Force
1999 Fresno St., Hawaii, TCU
2000 Texas Christian, UTEP
2001 Louisiana Tech
2002 Boise St.
2003 Boise St.
2004 Boise St.
2005 Boise State, Nevada

(1) Boston Coll. joined the Atlantic Coast Conf. in 2005. (2) Former Conf. USA teams Cincinnati, Louisville, and South Florida joined the Big East Conf. in 2005. (3) In 2005, former Mid-American teams Marshall and UCF, and former Western Athletic teams Rice, SMU, Tulsa, and UTEP, joined Conf. USA. (4) In 2005, former Western Athletic team TCU joined the Mountain West Conference. (5) Florida Atlantic joined the Sun Belt Conf. in 2005. (6) In 2005, former Sun Belt teams Idaho, New Mexico St., and Utah St. joined the Western Athletic Conf.

NCAA Div. I-AA Football Conference Champions (1990-2005)

Atlantic 10
1990 Massachusetts
1991 Delaware, Villanova
1992 Delaware
1993 Boston U.
1994 New Hampshire
1995 Delaware
1996 William & Mary
1997 Villanova
1998 Richmond
1999 J. Madison, Mass.
2000 Delaware, Richmond
2001 Hofstra, Maine, Villanova, Will. & Mary
2002 Maine, Northeastern
2003 Delaware, Mass.
2004 Delaware, J. Madison, New Hampshire, William & Mary
2005 New Hampshire, Richmond

Big Sky
1990 Nevada
1991 Nevada
1992 Idaho, Eastern Wash.
1993 Montana
1994 Boise St.
1995 Montana
1996 Montana
1997 Eastern Wash.
1998 Montana
1999 Montana
2000 Montana
2001 Montana
2002 Idaho St., Montana, Montana St.
2003 Montana St., Montana, No. Arizona
2004 Montana, Eastern Wash.
2005 Eastern Wash., Montana, Montana St.

Big South
2002 Gardner-Webb
2003 Gardner-Webb
2004 Coastal Carolina
2005 Coastal Carolina, Charleston Southern

Gateway
1990 Northern Iowa
1991 Northern Iowa
1992 Northern Iowa
1993 Northern Iowa
1994 Northern Iowa
1995 N. Iowa, Eastern Ill.
1996 Northern Iowa
1997 Western Illinois
1998 Western Illinois
1999 Illinois St.
2000 Western Illinois

2001 Northern Iowa
2002 W. Illinois, W. Kentucky
2003 No. Iowa, So. Illinois
2004 So. Illinois
2005 No. Iowa, So. Illinois, Youngstown St.

Great West
2004 Cal. Poly
2005 Cal. Poly, UC Davis

Ivy League
1990 Cornell, Dartmouth
1991 Dartmouth
1992 Dartmouth, Princeton
1993 Penn
1994 Penn
1995 Princeton
1996 Dartmouth
1997 Harvard
1998 Penn
1999 Brown, Yale
2000 Penn
2001 Harvard
2002 Pennsylvania
2003 Pennsylvania
2004 Harvard
2005 Brown

Metro Atlantic
1993 Iona
1994 Marist, St. John's (NY)
1995 Duquesne
1996 Duquesne
1997 Georgetown
1998 Fairfield, Georgetown
1999 Duquesne
2000 Duquesne
2001 Duquesne
2002 Duquesne
2003 Duquesne
2004 Duquesne
2005 Duquesne

Mid-Eastern Athletic
1990 Florida A&M
1991 North Carolina A&T
1992 North Carolina A&T
1993 Howard
1994 South Carolina St.
1995 Florida A&M
1996 Florida A&M
1997 Hampton
1998 Florida A&M, Hampton
1999 North Carolina A&T
2000 Florida A&M
2001 Florida A&M
2002 Bethune-Cookman
2003 North Carolina A&T
2004 Hampton, South Carolina St.
2005 Hampton

Northeast
1996 R. Morris, Monmouth
1997 Robert Morris
1998 R.Morris, Monmouth
1999 Robert Morris
2000 Robert Morris
2001 Sacred Heart
2002 Albany (NY)
2003 Albany, Monmouth
2004 Central Conn. St., Monmouth
2005 Central Conn. St., Stony Brook

Ohio Valley
1990 E. Kentucky., Middle Tenn.
1991 Eastern Kentucky
1992 Middle Tennessee
1993 Eastern Kentucky
1994 Eastern Kentucky
1995 Murray St.
1996 Murray St.
1997 Eastern Kentucky
1998 Tennessee St.
1999 Tennessee St.
2000 Western Kentucky
2001 Eastern Illinois
2002 E. Illinois, Murray St.
2003 Jacksonville St.
2004 Jacksonville St.
2005 Eastern Illinois

Patriot
1990 Holy Cross
1991 Holy Cross
1992 Lafayette
1993 Lehigh
1994 Lafayette
1995 Lehigh
1996 Bucknell
1997 Colgate
1998 Lehigh
1999 Colgate, Lehigh
2000 Lehigh
2001 Lehigh
2002 Colgate, Fordham
2003 Colgate
2004 Lafayette, Lehigh
2005 Colgate, Lafayette

Pioneer
1993 Dayton
1994 Dayton, Butler
1995 Drake
1996 Dayton
1997 Dayton
1998 Drake
1999 Dayton
2000 Dayton, Drake, Valparaiso
2001 Dayton

2002 Dayton
2003 Valparaiso
2004 Drake
2005 San Diego

Southern
1990 Furman
1991 Appalachian St.
1992 Citadel
1993 Georgia Southern
1994 Marshall
1995 Appalachian St.
1996 Marshall
1997 Georgia Southern
1998 Georgia Southern
1999 Appalachian St., GA Southern, Furman
2000 Georgia Southern
2001 Georgia Southern
2002 Georgia Southern
2003 Wofford
2004 Furman, GA Southern
2005 Appalachian St.

Southland
1990 La.-Monroe
1991 McNeese St.
1992 La.-Monroe
1993 McNeese St.
1994 North Texas
1995 McNeese St.
1996 Troy St.
1997 McNeese St., Northwestern St.
1998 Northwestern St.
1999 Troy St., S. F. Austin
2000 Troy St.
2001 Sam Houston St., McNeese St.
2002 McNeese St.
2003 McNeese St.
2004 Northwestern St., Sam Houston St.
2005 Texas St., Nicholls St.

Southwestern Athletic
1990 Jackson St.
1991 Alabama St.
1992 Alcorn St.
1993 Southern
1994 Grambling St., Alcorn St.
1995 Jackson St.
1996 Jackson St.
1997 Southern
1998 Southern
1999 Southern
2000 Grambling St.
2001 Grambling St.
2002 Grambling St.
2003 Southern
2004 Alabama St.
2005 Grambling St.

Selected College Division I Football Teams

(W-L records in last column are for 2005-06 season and include bowl games and Division I-AA playoff games. Conferences and coaches listed are as of July 2006.)

Team	Nickname	Team colors	Conference	Coach	(W-L)
Air Force	Falcons	Blue & silver	Mountain West	Fisher DeBerry	4-7
Akron	Zips	Blue & gold	Mid-American	J.D. Brookhart	7-6
Alabama	Crimson Tide	Crimson & white	Southeastern	Mike Shula	10-2
*Appalachian State	Mountaineers	Black & gold	Southern	Jerry Moore	12-3
Arizona	Wildcats	Cardinal & navy	Pacific Ten	Mike Stoops	3-8
Arizona State	Sun Devils	Maroon & gold	Pacific Ten	Dirk Koetter	7-5
Arkansas	Razorbacks	Cardinal & white	Southeastern	Gus Malzahn	4-7
Arkansas State	Indians	Scarlet & black	Sun Belt	Steve Roberts	6-6
Army	Cadets, Black Knights	Black, gold, gray	Independent	Bobby Ross	4-7
Auburn	Tigers	Burnt orange & navy	Southeastern	Tommy Tuberville	9-3
Ball State	Cardinals	Cardinal & white	Mid-American	Brady Hoke	4-7
Baylor	Bears	Green & gold	Big Twelve	Guy Morriss	5-6
Boise State	Broncos	Blue & orange	Western Athletic	Chris Petersen	9-4
Boston College	Eagles	Maroon & gold	Atlantic Coast	Tom O'Brien	9-3
Bowling Green	Falcons	Orange & brown	Mid-American	Gregg Brandon	6-5
Brigham Young (BYU)	Cougars	Royal blue, white, tan	Mountain West	Bronco Mendenhall	6-6
*Brown	Bears	Brown, cardinal, white	Ivy League	Phil Estes	9-1
California	Golden Bears	Blue & gold	Pacific Ten	Jeff Tedford	8-4
Central Michigan	Chippewas	Maroon & gold	Mid-American	Brian Kelly	6-5
Cincinnati	Bearcats	Red & black	Big East	Mark Dantonio	4-7
*Citadel	Bulldogs	Blue & white	Southern	Kevin Higgins	4-7
Clemson	Tigers	Purple & orange	Atlantic Coast	Tommy Bowden	8-4
*Colgate	Red Raiders	Maroon, gray, & white	Patriot League	Dick Biddle	8-4
Colorado	Buffaloes	Silver, gold, & black	Big Twelve	Dan Hawkins	7-6
Colorado State	Rams	Green & gold	Mountain West	Sonny Lubick	6-6
*Columbia	Lions	Columbia blue & white	Ivy League	Norries Wilson	2-8
Connecticut	Huskies	Blue & white	Big East	Randy Edsall	5-6
*Cornell	Big Red	Carnelian & white	Ivy League	Jim Knowles	6-4
*Dartmouth	Big Green	Dartmouth green & white	Ivy League	Buddy Teevens	2-8
*Delaware	Fightin' Blue Hens	Blue & gold	Atlantic Ten	K.C. Keeler	6-5
*Delaware State	Hornets	Red & blue	Mid-Eastern Athletic	Alton Lavan	7-4
Duke	Blue Devils	Royal blue & white	Atlantic Coast	Ted Roof	1-10
East Carolina	Pirates	Purple & gold	Conference USA	Skip Holtz	5-6
*Eastern Illinois	Panthers	Blue & gray	Ohio Valley	Bob Spoo	9-3
*Eastern Kentucky	Colonels	Maroon & white	Ohio Valley	Danny Hope	7-4
Eastern Michigan	Eagles	Dark green & white	Mid-American	Jeff Genyk	4-7
*Eastern Washington	Eagles	Red & white	Big Sky	Paul Wulff	7-5
Florida	Gators	Orange & blue	Southeastern	Urban Meyer	9-3
*Florida A&M	Rattlers	Orange & green	Mid-Eastern Athletic	Rubin Carter	6-5
Florida State	Seminoles	Garnet & gold	Atlantic Coast	Bobby Bowden	8-5
Fresno State	Bulldogs	Cardinal & blue	Western Athletic	Pat Hill	8-5
*Furman	Paladins	Purple & white	Southern	Bobby Lamb	11-3
Georgia	Bulldogs	Red & black	Southeastern	Mark Richt	10-3
*Georgia Southern	Eagles	Blue & white	Southern	Brian VanGorder	8-4
Georgia Tech	Yellow Jackets	Old gold & white	Atlantic Coast	Chan Gailey	7-5
*Grambling State	Tigers	Black & gold	Southwestern Athletic	Melvin Spears	11-1
*Harvard	Crimson	Crimson, black, white	Ivy League	Tim Murphy	7-3
Hawaii	Warriors	Green, black, white, silver	Western Athletic	June Jones	5-7
*Holy Cross	Crusaders	Royal purple	Patriot League	Tom Gilmore	6-5
Houston	Cougars	Scarlet & white	Conference USA	Art Briles	6-6
*Howard	Bison	Blue, white & red	Mid-Eastern Athletic	Rayford Petty	4-7
Idaho	Vandals	Silver & gold	Western Athletic	Nick Holt	2-9
*Idaho State	Bengals	Orange & black	Big Sky	Larry Lewis	5-6
Illinois	Fighting Illini	Orange & blue	Big Ten	Ron Zook	2-9
*Illinois State	Redbirds	Red & white	Gateway	Denver Johnson	7-4
Indiana	Hoosiers	Cream & crimson	Big Ten	Terry Hoeppner	4-7
*Indiana State	Sycamores	Blue & white	Gateway	Lou West	0-11
Iowa	Hawkeyes	Old gold & black	Big Ten	Kirk Ferentz	7-5
Iowa State	Cyclones	Cardinal & gold	Big Twelve	Dan McCarney	7-5
*Jackson State	Tigers	Blue & white	Southwestern Athletic	Rick Comegy	2-9
*James Madison	Dukes	Purple & gold	Atlantic Ten	Mickey Matthews	7-4
Kansas	Jayhawks	Crimson & blue	Big Twelve	Mark Mangino	7-5
Kansas State	Wildcats	Purple & white	Big Twelve	Ron Prince	5-6
Kent State	Golden Flashes	Navy blue & gold	Mid-American	Doug Martin	1-10
Kentucky	Wildcats	Blue & white	Southeastern	Rich Brooks	3-8
*Lafayette	Leopards	Maroon & white	Patriot League	Frank Tavani	8-4
*Lehigh	Mountain Hawks	Brown & white	Patriot League	Andy Coen	8-3
*Liberty	Flames	Red, white, blue	Big South	Danny Rocco	1-10
Louisiana-Lafayette	Ragin' Cajuns	Vermilion & white	Sun Belt	Rickey Bustle	6-5
Louisiana-Monroe	Indians	Maroon & gold	Sun Belt	Charlie Weatherbie	5-6
Louisiana State (LSU)	Fighting Tigers	Purple & gold	Southeastern	Les Miles	11-2
Louisiana Tech	Bulldogs	Red & blue	Western Athletic	Jack Bicknell	7-4
Louisville	Cardinals	Red, black, white	Big East	Bobby Petrino	9-3
*Maine	Black Bears	Blue & white	Atlantic Ten	Jack Cosgrove	5-6
Marshall	Thundering Herd	Green & white	Conference USA	Mark Snyder	4-7
Maryland	Terrapins	Red, white, black, gold	Atlantic Coast	Ralph Friedgen	5-6
*Massachusetts	Minutemen	Maroon & white	Atlantic Ten	Don Brown	7-4
*McNeese State	Cowboys	Blue & gold	Southland	Tommy Tate	5-4
Memphis	Tigers	Blue & gray	Conference USA	Tommy West	7-5
Miami (Florida)	Hurricanes	Orange, green, white	Atlantic Coast	Larry Coker	9-3
Miami (Ohio)	RedHawks	Red & white	Mid-American	Shane Montgomery	7-4
Michigan	Wolverines	Maize & blue	Big Ten	Lloyd Carr	7-5
Michigan State	Spartans	Green & white	Big Ten	John L. Smith	5-6
Mid. Tennessee State	Blue Raiders	Blue & white	Sun Belt	Rick Stockstill	4-7
Minnesota	Golden Gophers	Maroon & gold	Big Ten	Glen Mason	7-5
Mississippi	Rebels	Cardinal red & navy	Southeastern	Ed Orgeron	3-8
Mississippi State	Bulldogs	Maroon & white	Southeastern	Sylvester Croom	3-8

Team	Nickname	Team colors	Conference	Coach	(W-L)
*Mississippi Valley State	Delta Devils	Green & white	Southwestern Athletic	Willie Totten	6-5
Missouri	Tigers	Old gold & black	Big Twelve	Gary Pinkel	7-5
*Montana	Grizzlies	Copper, silver, gold	Big Sky	Bobby Hauck	8-4
*Montana State	Bobcats	Blue & gold	Big Sky	Mike Kramer	7-4
*Morehead State	Eagles	Blue & gold	Pioneer	Matt Ballard	8-4
*Morgan State	Bears	Blue & orange	Mid-Eastern Athletic	Donald Hill-Eleyl	2-9
*Murray State	Racers	Blue & gold	Ohio Valley	Matt Griffin	2-9
Navy	Midshipmen	Navy blue & gold	Independent	Paul Johnson	8-4
Nebraska	Cornhuskers	Scarlet & cream	Big Twelve	Bill Callahan	8-4
Nevada	Wolf Pack	Silver & blue	Western Athletic	Chris Ault	9-3
Nev.-Las Vegas (UNLV)	Runnin' Rebels	Scarlet & gray	Mountain West	Mike Sanford	2-9
*New Hampshire	Wildcats	Blue & white	Atlantic Ten	Sean McDonnell	11-2
New Mexico	Lobos	Cherry & silver	Mountain West	Rocky Long	6-5
New Mexico State	Aggies	Crimson & white	Western Athletic	Hal Mumme	0-12
*Nicholls State	Colonels	Red & gray	Southland	Jay Thomas	6-4
North Carolina	Tar Heels	Carolina blue & white	Atlantic Coast	John Bunting	5-6
North Carolina State	Wolfpack	Red & white	Atlantic Coast	Chuck Amato	7-5
North Texas	Mean Green	Green & white	Sun Belt	Darrell Dickey	2-9
*Northeastern	Huskies	Red & black	Atlantic Ten	Rocky Hager	2-9
*Northern Arizona	Lumberjacks	Blue & gold	Big Sky	Jerome Souers	3-8
Northern Illinois	Huskies	Cardinal & black	Mid-American	Joe Novak	7-5
*Northern Iowa	Panthers	Purple & old gold	Gateway	Mark Farley	11-4
Northwestern	Wildcats	Purple & white	Big Ten	Pat Fitzgerald	7-5
*Northwestern State	Demons	Purple, white, & orange	Southland	Scott Stoker	5-5
Notre Dame	Fighting Irish	Gold & blue	Independent	Charlie Weis	9-3
Ohio	Bobcats	Hunter green & white	Mid-American	Frank Solich	4-7
Ohio State	Buckeyes	Scarlet & gray	Big Ten	Jim Tressel	10-2
Oklahoma	Sooners	Crimson & cream	Big Twelve	Bob Stoops	8-4
Oklahoma State	Cowboys	Orange & black	Big Twelve	Mike Gundy	4-7
Oregon	Ducks	Green & yellow	Pacific Ten	Dennis Erickson	10-2
Oregon State	Beavers	Orange & black	Pacific Ten	Mike Riley	5-6
Penn State	Nittany Lions	Blue & white	Big Ten	Joe Paterno	11-1
*Pennsylvania	Quakers	Red & blue	Ivy League	Al Bagnoli	5-5
Pittsburgh	Panthers	Blue & gold	Big East	Dave Wannstedt	5-6
*Princeton	Tigers	Orange & black	Ivy League	Roger Hughes	7-3
Purdue	Boilermakers	Old gold & black	Big Ten	Joe Tiller	5-6
*Rhode Island	Rams	Light & dark blue, white	Atlantic Ten	Tim Stowers	4-7
Rice	Owls	Blue & gray	Conference USA	Todd Graham	1-10
*Richmond	Spiders	Red & white	Atlantic Ten	Dave Clawson	9-4
Rutgers	Scarlet Knights	Scarlet	Big East	Greg Schiano	7-5
*Sam Houston State	Bearkats	Orange & white	Southland	Todd Whitten	3-7
*Samford	Bulldogs	Crimson & blue	Ohio Valley	Bill Gray	5-6
San Diego State	Aztecs	Scarlet & black	Mountain West	Chuck Long	5-7
San Jose State	Spartans	Gold, white, blue	Western Athletic	Dick Tomey	3-8
South Carolina	Gamecocks	Garnet & black	Southeastern	Steve Spurrier	7-5
*South Carolina State	Bulldogs	Garnet & blue	Mid-Eastern Athletic	Oliver Pough	9-2
*SE Missouri State	Redhawks	Red & white	Ohio Valley	Tony Samuel	2-9
Southern California (USC)	Trojans	Cardinal & gold	Pacific Ten	Pete Carroll	12-1
South Florida	Bulls	Green & gold	Big East	Jim Leavitt	6-6
*Southern Illinois	Salukis	Maroon & white	Gateway	Jerry Kill	9-4
Southern Methodist (SMU)	Mustangs	Red & blue	Conference USA	Phil Bennett	5-6
Southern Mississippi	Golden Eagles	Black & gold	Conference USA	Jeff Bower	7-5
Stanford	Cardinal	Cardinal & white	Pacific Ten	Walt Harris	5-6
*Stephen F. Austin	Lumberjacks	Purple & white	Southland	Robert McFarland	5-6
Syracuse	Orange	Orange	Big East	Greg Robinson	1-10
Temple	Owls	Cherry & white	Independent	Al Golden	0-11
Tennessee	Volunteers	Orange & white	Southeastern	Phillip Fulmer	5-6
*Tennessee-Martin	Skyhawks	Orange, white, blue	Ohio Valley	Jason Simpson	6-5
*Tennessee State	Tigers	Royal blue & white	Ohio Valley	James Webster	2-9
*Tennessee Tech	Golden Eagles	Purple & gold	Ohio Valley	Mike Hennigan	4-7
Texas	Longhorns	Burnt orange & white	Big Twelve	Mack Brown	13-0
Texas A & M	Aggies	Maroon & white	Big Twelve	Dennis Franchione	5-6
Texas Christian (TCU)	Horned Frogs	Purple & white	Mountain West	Gary Patterson	11-1
*Texas Southern	Tigers	Maroon & gray	Southwestern Athletic	Steve Wilson	1-10
*Texas State	Bobcats	Maroon & gold	Southland	David Bailiff	11-3
Texas Tech	Red Raiders	Scarlet & black	Big Twelve	Mike Leach	9-3
Toledo	Rockets	Blue & gold	Mid-American	Tom Amstutz	9-3
Troy	Trojans	Cardinal & black	Sun Belt	Larry Blakeney	4-7
Tulane	Green Wave	Olive green & sky blue	Conference USA	Chris Scelfo	2-9
Tulsa	Golden Hurricane	Blue, gold, crimson	Conference USA	Steve Kragthorpe	9-4
UCLA	Bruins	Blue & gold	Pacific Ten	Karl Dorrell	10-2
Utah	Utes	Crimson & white	Mountain West	Kyle Whittingham	7-5
Utah State	Aggies	Navy blue & white	Western Athletic	Brent Guy	3-8
UTEP (Texas-El Paso)	Miners	Orange, blue, silver	Conference USA	Mike Price	8-4
Vanderbilt	Commodores	Black & gold	Southeastern	Bobby Johnson	5-6
*Villanova	Wildcats	Blue & white	Atlantic Ten	Andy Talley	4-7
Virginia	Cavaliers	Burnt orange & blue	Atlantic Coast	Al Groh	7-5
Virginia Tech	Hokies	Burnt orange & maroon	Atlantic Coast	Frank Beamer	11-2
Wake Forest	Demon Deacons	Old gold & black	Atlantic Coast	Jim Grobe	4-7
Washington	Huskies	Purple & gold	Pacific Ten	Tyrone Willingham	2-9
Washington State	Cougars	Crimson & gray	Pacific Ten	Bill Doba	4-7
*Weber State	Wildcats	Royal purple & white	Big Sky	Ron McBride	6-5
West Virginia	Mountaineers	Old gold & blue	Big East	Rich Rodriguez	11-1
*Western Carolina	Catamounts	Purple & gold	Southern	Kent Briggs	5-4
*Western Illinois	Leathernecks	Purple & gold	Gateway	Don Patterson	5-6
*Western Kentucky	Hilltoppers	Red & white	Gateway	David Elson	6-5
Western Michigan	Broncos	Brown & gold	Mid-American	Bill Cubit	7-4
*William & Mary	Tribe	Green, gold, silver	Atlantic Ten	Jimmye Laycock	5-6
Wisconsin	Badgers	Cardinal & white	Big Ten	Barry Alvarez	10-3
Wyoming	Cowboys	Brown & gold	Mountain West	Joe Glenn	4-7
*Yale	Bulldogs, Elis	Yale blue & white	Ivy League	Jack Siedlecki	4-6
*Youngstown State	Penguins	Red & white	Gateway	Jon Heacock	8-3

* I-AA

NATIONAL HOCKEY LEAGUE

2005-2006: NHL Play Resumes; Carolina Wins 1st Stanley Cup

After a lockout by team owners forced the cancellation of the 2004-2005 season, the NHL resumed play on Oct. 5, 2005. The Carolina Hurricanes, under coach Peter Laviolette, won their first NHL title in their 27-year history, defeating the Edmonton Oilers, 3-1, in Game 7 of the Stanley Cup Finals in Raleigh, NC, on June 19, 2006. The Hurricanes, who had re-located from Hartford, CT, in 1997, held on to win after the Oilers came back to even the series from being down 3-1. Hurricanes rookie goalie Cam Ward, who was a backup during the regular season, had 22 saves in the playoffs and won the Conn Smythe Trophy as MVP of the NHL postseason. San Jose Sharks center Joe Thornton, the NHL's regular-season points leader with 125, won the Hart Trophy as MVP of the 2005-2006 season.

In other hockey news, the N.Y. Rangers and the Washington Capitals played the longest shootout in NHL history on Nov. 26, ending the game with a shot from Rangers defenseman Marek Malik in the 15th round. The All-Star game was cancelled so that NHL players could participate in the Winter Olympics in Turin, Italy.

Final NHL Standings 2005-2006

(Playoff seeding in parentheses; division winners automatically seeded 1, 2, or 3; teams tied at the end of regulation time are each awarded 1 point, an additional point is awarded to the overtime winner)

Eastern Conference

Atlantic Division	W	L	OTL	GF	GA	PTS
New Jersey Devils (3)	46	27	9	242	229	101
Philadelphia Flyers (5)	45	26	11	267	259	101
N.Y. Rangers (6)	44	26	12	257	215	100
N.Y. Islanders	36	40	6	230	278	78
Pittsburgh Penguins	22	46	14	244	316	58

Northeast Division	W	L	OTL	GF	GA	PTS
Ottawa Senators (1)	52	21	9	314	211	113
Buffalo Sabres (4)	52	24	6	281	239	110
Montreal Canadiens (7)	42	31	9	243	247	93
Toronto Maple Leafs	41	33	8	257	270	90
Boston Bruins	29	37	16	230	266	74

Southeast Division	W	L	OTL	GF	GA	PTS
Carolina Hurricanes (2)	52	22	8	294	260	112
Tampa Bay Lightning (8)	43	33	6	252	260	92
Atlanta Thrashers	41	33	8	281	275	90
Florida Panthers	37	34	11	240	257	85
Washington Capitals	29	41	12	237	306	70

Western Conference

Central Division	W	L	OTL	GF	GA	PTS
Detroit Red Wings (1)	58	16	8	305	209	124
Nashville Predators (4)	49	25	8	259	227	106
Columbus Blue Jackets	35	43	4	223	279	74
Chicago Blackhawks	26	43	13	211	285	65
St. Louis Blues	21	46	15	197	292	57

Northwest Division	W	L	OTL	GF	GA	PTS
Calgary Flames (3)	46	25	11	218	200	103
Colorado Avalanche (7)	43	30	9	283	257	95
Edmonton Oilers (8)	41	28	13	256	251	95
Vancouver Canucks	42	32	8	256	255	92
Minnesota Wild	38	36	8	231	215	84

Pacific Division	W	L	OTL	GF	GA	PTS
Dallas Stars (2)	53	23	6	265	218	112
San Jose Sharks (5)	44	27	11	266	242	99
Anaheim Ducks (6)	43	27	12	254	229	98
Los Angeles Kings	42	35	5	249	270	89
Phoenix Coyotes	38	39	5	246	271	81

2006 Stanley Cup Playoff Results

Eastern Conference
Buffalo defeated Philadelphia 4 games to 2
New Jersey defeated N.Y. Rangers 4 games to 0
Carolina defeated Montreal 4 games to 2
Ottawa defeats Buffalo 4 games to 1
Carolina defeated Tampa Bay 4 games to 1
Buffalo defeated Ottawa 4 games to 1
Carolina defeated Buffalo 4 games to 3

Western Conference
San Jose defeated Nashville 4 games to 1
Anaheim defeated Calgary 4 games to 1
Colorado defeated Dallas 4 games to 1
Edmonton defeated Detroit 4 games to 2
Edmonton defeated San Jose 4 games to 2
Edmonton defeated Anaheim 4 games to 1

Finals
Carolina defeated Edmonton 4 games to 3 [5-4, 5-0, 1-2, 2-1, 3-4 (OT), 0-4, 3-1]

Stanley Cup Champions Since 1927

Year	Champion	Coach	Final opponent	Year	Champion	Coach	Final opponent
1927	Ottawa	Dave Gill	Boston	1958	Montreal	Toe Blake	Boston
1928	N.Y. Rangers	Lester Patrick	Montreal	1959	Montreal	Toe Blake	Toronto
1929	Boston	Cy Denneny	N.Y. Rangers	1960	Montreal	Toe Blake	Toronto
1930	Montreal	Cecil Hart	Boston	1961	Chicago	Rudy Pilous	Detroit
1931	Montreal	Cecil Hart	Chicago	1962	Toronto	Punch Imlach	Chicago
1932	Toronto	Dick Irvin	N.Y. Rangers	1963	Toronto	Punch Imlach	Detroit
1933	N.Y. Rangers	Lester Patrick	Toronto	1964	Toronto	Punch Imlach	Detroit
1934	Chicago	Tommy Gorman	Detroit	1965	Montreal	Toe Blake	Chicago
1935	Montreal Maroons	Tommy Gorman	Toronto	1966	Montreal	Toe Blake	Detroit
1936	Detroit	Jack Adams	Toronto	1967	Toronto	Punch Imlach	Montreal
1937	Detroit	Jack Adams	N.Y. Rangers	1968	Montreal	Toe Blake	St. Louis
1938	Chicago	Bill Stewart	Toronto	1969	Montreal	Claude Ruel	St. Louis
1939	Boston	Art Ross	Toronto	1970	Boston	Harry Sinden	St. Louis
1940	N.Y. Rangers	Frank Boucher	Toronto	1971	Montreal	Al MacNeil	Chicago
1941	Boston	Cooney Weiland	Detroit	1972	Boston	Tom Johnson	N.Y. Rangers
1942	Toronto	Hap Day	Detroit	1973	Montreal	Scotty Bowman	Chicago
1943	Detroit	Jack Adams	Boston	1974	Philadelphia	Fred Shero	Boston
1944	Montreal	Dick Irvin	Chicago	1975	Philadelphia	Fred Shero	Buffalo
1945	Toronto	Hap Day	Detroit	1976	Montreal	Scotty Bowman	Philadelphia
1946	Montreal	Dick Irvin	Boston	1977	Montreal	Scotty Bowman	Boston
1947	Toronto	Hap Day	Montreal	1978	Montreal	Scotty Bowman	Boston
1948	Toronto	Hap Day	Detroit	1979	Montreal	Scotty Bowman	N.Y. Rangers
1949	Toronto	Hap Day	Detroit	1980	N.Y. Islanders	Al Arbour	Philadelphia
1950	Detroit	Tommy Ivan	N.Y. Rangers	1981	N.Y. Islanders	Al Arbour	Minnesota
1951	Toronto	Joe Primeau	Montreal	1982	N.Y. Islanders	Al Arbour	Vancouver
1952	Detroit	Tommy Ivan	Montreal	1983	N.Y. Islanders	Al Arbour	Edmonton
1953	Montreal	Dick Irvin	Boston	1984	Edmonton	Glen Sather	N.Y. Islanders
1954	Detroit	Tommy Ivan	Montreal	1985	Edmonton	Glen Sather	Philadelphia
1955	Detroit	Jimmy Skinner	Montreal	1986	Montreal	Jean Perron	Calgary
1956	Montreal	Toe Blake	Detroit	1987	Edmonton	Glen Sather	Philadelphia
1957	Montreal	Toe Blake	Boston	1988	Edmonton	Glen Sather	Boston

Year	Champion	Coach	Final opponent	Year	Champion	Coach	Final opponent
1989	Calgary	Terry Crisp	Montreal	1998	Detroit	Scotty Bowman	Washington
1990	Edmonton	John Muckler	Boston	1999	Dallas	Ken Hitchcock	Buffalo
1991	Pittsburgh	Bob Johnson	Minnesota	2000	New Jersey	Larry Robinson	Dallas
1992	Pittsburgh	Scotty Bowman	Chicago	2001	Colorado	Bob Hartley	New Jersey
1993	Montreal	Jacques Demers	Los Angeles	2002	Detroit	Scotty Bowman	Carolina
1994	N.Y. Rangers	Mike Keenan	Vancouver	2003	New Jersey	Pat Burns	Anaheim
1995	New Jersey	Jacques Lemaire	Detroit	2004	Tampa Bay	John Tortorella	Calgary
1996	Colorado	Marc Crawford	Florida	2005	No competition		
1997	Detroit	Scotty Bowman	Philadelphia	2006	Carolina	Peter Laviolette	Edmonton

Most NHL Goals in a Season

Player	Team	Season	Goals	Player	Team	Season	Goals
Wayne Gretzky	Edmonton	1981-82	92	Jari Kurri	Edmonton	1984-85	71
Wayne Gretzky	Edmonton	1983-84	87	Brett Hull	St. Louis	1991-92	70
Brett Hull	St. Louis	1990-91	86	Mario Lemieux	Pittsburgh	1987-88	70
Mario Lemieux	Pittsburgh	1988-89	85	Bernie Nicholls	Los Angeles	1988-89	70
Phil Esposito	Boston	1971-72	76	Mike Bossy	N.Y. Islanders	1978-79	69
Alexander Mogilny	Buffalo	1992-93	76	Mario Lemieux	Pittsburgh	1992-93	69
Teemu Selanne	Winnipeg	1992-93	76	Mario Lemieux	Pittsburgh	1995-96	69
Wayne Gretzky	Edmonton	1984-85	73	Mike Bossy	N.Y. Islanders	1980-81	68
Brett Hull	St. Louis	1989-90	72	Phil Esposito	Boston	1973-74	68
Wayne Gretzky	Edmonton	1982-83	71	Jari Kurri	Edmonton	1985-86	68

All-Time Regular Season Leading Scorers

Player	Goals	Assists	Points	Player	Goals	Assists	Points	Player	Goals	Assists	Points
Wayne Gretzky	894	1,963	2,857	Phil Esposito	717	873	1,590	Adam Oates	341	1,079	1,420
Mark Messier	694	1,193	1,887	Ray Bourque	410	1,169	1,579	Doug Gilmour	450	964	1,414
Gordie Howe	801	1,049	1,850	Paul Coffey	396	1,135	1,531	Dale Hawerchuk	518	891	1,409
Ron Francis	549	1,249	1,798	Joe Sakic*	574	915	1,489	Jari Kurri	601	797	1,398
Marcel Dionne	731	1,040	1,771	Stan Mikita	541	926	1,467	Luc Robitaille*	668	726	1,394
Steve Yzerman*	692	1,063	1,755	Jaromir Jagr*	591	841	1,432	Brett Hull*	741	650	1,391
Mario Lemieux*	690	1,033	1,723	Bryan Trottier	524	901	1,425				

Note: Through end of 2005-2006 season. *Active in the 2005-2006 season.

Hart Memorial Trophy (MVP)

1927	Herb Gardiner, Montreal		1954	Al Rollins, Chicago		1980	Wayne Gretzky, Edmonton
1928	Howie Morenz, Montreal		1955	Ted Kennedy, Toronto		1981	Wayne Gretzky, Edmonton
1929	Roy Worters, N.Y. Americans		1956	Jean Beliveau, Montreal		1982	Wayne Gretzky, Edmonton
1930	Nels Stewart, Montreal Maroons		1957	Gordie Howe, Detroit		1983	Wayne Gretzky, Edmonton
1931	Howie Morenz, Montreal		1958	Gordie Howe, Detroit		1984	Wayne Gretzky, Edmonton
1932	Howie Morenz, Montreal		1959	Andy Bathgate, N.Y. Rangers		1985	Wayne Gretzky, Edmonton
1933	Eddie Shore, Boston		1960	Gordie Howe, Detroit		1986	Wayne Gretzky, Edmonton
1934	Aurel Joliat, Montreal		1961	Bernie Geoffrion, Montreal		1987	Wayne Gretzky, Edmonton
1935	Eddie Shore, Boston		1962	Jacques Plante, Montreal		1988	Mario Lemieux, Pittsburgh
1936	Eddie Shore, Boston		1963	Gordie Howe, Detroit		1989	Wayne Gretzky, Los Angeles
1937	Babe Siebert, Montreal		1964	Jean Beliveau, Montreal		1990	Mark Messier, Edmonton
1938	Eddie Shore, Boston		1965	Bobby Hull, Chicago		1991	Brett Hull, St. Louis
1939	Toe Blake, Montreal		1966	Bobby Hull, Chicago		1992	Mark Messier, N.Y. Rangers
1940	Ebbie Goodfellow, Detroit		1967	Stan Mikita, Chicago		1993	Mario Lemieux, Pittsburgh
1941	Bill Cowley, Boston		1968	Stan Mikita, Chicago		1994	Sergei Fedorov, Detroit
1942	Tom Anderson, N.Y. Americans		1969	Phil Esposito, Boston		1995	Eric Lindros, Philadelphia
1943	Bill Cowley, Boston		1970	Bobby Orr, Boston		1996	Mario Lemieux, Pittsburgh
1944	Babe Pratt, Toronto		1971	Bobby Orr, Boston		1997	Dominik Hasek, Buffalo
1945	Elmer Lach, Montreal		1972	Bobby Orr, Boston		1998	Dominik Hasek, Buffalo
1946	Max Bentley, Chicago		1973	Bobby Clarke, Philadelphia		1999	Jaromir Jagr, Pittsburgh
1947	Maurice Richard, Montreal		1974	Phil Esposito, Boston		2000	Chris Pronger, St. Louis
1948	Buddy O'Connor, N.Y. Rangers		1975	Bobby Clarke, Philadelphia		2001	Joe Sakic, Colorado
1949	Sid Abel, Detroit		1976	Bobby Clarke, Philadelphia		2002	Jose Theodore, Montreal
1950	Chuck Rayner, N.Y. Rangers		1977	Guy Lafleur, Montreal		2003	Peter Forsberg, Colorado
1951	Milt Schmidt, Boston		1978	Guy Lafleur, Montreal		2004	Martin St. Louis, Tampa Bay
1952	Gordie Howe, Detroit		1979	Bryan Trottier, N.Y. Islanders		2006	Joe Thornton, San Jose
1953	Gordie Howe, Detroit						

Conn Smythe Trophy (MVP in Playoffs)

1965	Jean Beliveau, Montreal		1979	Bob Gainey, Montreal		1993	Patrick Roy, Montreal
1966	Roger Crozier, Detroit		1980	Bryan Trottier, N.Y. Islanders		1994	Brian Leetch, N.Y. Rangers
1967	Dave Keon, Toronto		1981	Butch Goring, N.Y. Islanders		1995	Claude Lemieux, New Jersey
1968	Glenn Hall, St. Louis		1982	Mike Bossy, N.Y. Islanders		1996	Joe Sakic, Colorado
1969	Serge Savard, Montreal		1983	Billy Smith, N.Y. Islanders		1997	Mike Vernon, Detroit
1970	Bobby Orr, Boston		1984	Mark Messier, Edmonton		1998	Steve Yzerman, Detroit
1971	Ken Dryden, Montreal		1985	Wayne Gretzky, Edmonton		1999	Joe Nieuwendyk, Dallas
1972	Bobby Orr, Boston		1986	Patrick Roy, Montreal		2000	Scott Stevens, New Jersey
1973	Yvan Cournoyer, Montreal		1987	Ron Hextall, Philadelphia		2001	Patrick Roy, Colorado
1974	Bernie Parent, Philadelphia		1988	Wayne Gretzky, Edmonton		2002	Nicklas Lidstrom, Detroit
1975	Bernie Parent, Philadelphia		1989	Al MacInnis, Calgary		2003	Jean-Sebastien Giguere, Anaheim
1976	Reg Leach, Philadelphia		1990	Bill Ranford, Edmonton		2004	Brad Richards, Tampa Bay
1977	Guy Lafleur, Montreal		1991	Mario Lemieux, Pittsburgh		2006	Cam Ward, Carolina
1978	Larry Robinson, Montreal		1992	Mario Lemieux, Pittsburgh			

Calder Memorial Trophy (Rookie of the Year)

1933	Carl Voss, Detroit	1958	Frank Mahovlich, Toronto	1982	Dale Hawerchuk, Winnipeg
1934	Russ Blinco, Montreal Maroons	1959	Ralph Backstrom, Montreal	1983	Steve Larmer, Chicago
1935	Dave Schriner, N.Y. Americans	1960	Bill Hay, Chicago	1984	Tom Barrasso, Buffalo
1936	Mike Karakas, Chicago	1961	Dave Keon, Toronto	1985	Mario Lemieux, Pittsburgh
1937	Syl Apps, Toronto	1962	Bobby Rousseau, Montreal	1986	Gary Suter, Calgary
1938	Cully Dahlstrom, Chicago	1963	Kent Douglas, Toronto	1987	Luc Robitaille, Los Angeles
1939	Frank Brimsek, Boston	1964	Jacques Laperriere, Montreal	1988	Joe Nieuwendyk, Calgary
1940	Kilby Macdonald, N.Y. Rangers	1965	Roger Crozier, Detroit	1989	Brian Leetch, N.Y. Rangers
1941	John Quilty, Montreal	1966	Brit Selby, Toronto	1990	Sergei Makarov, Calgary
1942	Grant Warwick, N.Y. Rangers	1967	Bobby Orr, Boston	1991	Ed Belfour, Chicago
1943	Gaye Stewart, Toronto	1968	Derek Sanderson, Boston	1992	Pavel Bure, Vancouver
1944	Gus Bodnar, Toronto	1969	Danny Grant, Minnesota	1993	Teemu Selanne, Winnipeg
1945	Frank McCool, Toronto	1970	Tony Esposito, Chicago	1994	Martin Brodeur, New Jersey
1946	Edgar Laprade, N.Y. Rangers	1971	Gilbert Perreault, Buffalo	1995	Peter Forsberg, Quebec
1947	Howie Meeker, Toronto	1972	Ken Dryden, Montreal	1996	Daniel Alfredsson, Ottawa
1948	Jim McFadden, Detroit	1973	Steve Vickers, N.Y. Rangers	1997	Bryan Berard, N.Y. Islanders
1949	Pentti Lund, N.Y. Rangers	1974	Denis Potvin, N.Y. Islanders	1998	Sergei Samsonov, Boston
1950	Jack Gelineau, Boston	1975	Eric Vail, Atlanta	1999	Chris Drury, Colorado
1951	Terry Sawchuk, Detroit	1976	Bryan Trottier, N.Y. Islanders	2000	Scott Gomez, New Jersey
1952	Bernie Geoffrion, Montreal	1977	Willi Plett, Atlanta	2001	Evgeni Nabokov, San Jose
1953	Gump Worsley, N.Y. Rangers	1978	Mike Bossy, N.Y. Islanders	2002	Dany Heatley, Atlanta
1954	Camille Henry, N.Y. Rangers	1979	Bobby Smith, Minnesota	2003	Barret Jackman, St. Louis
1955	Ed Litzenberger, Chicago	1980	Ray Bourque, Boston	2004	Andrew Raycroft, Boston
1956	Glenn Hall, Detroit	1981	Peter Stastny, Quebec	2006	Alexander Overchkin, Washington
1957	Larry Regan, Boston				

Lady Byng Memorial Trophy (Most Gentlemanly Player)

1925	Frank Nighbor, Ottawa	1952	Sid Smith, Toronto	1979	Bob MacMillan, Atlanta
1926	Frank Nighbor, Ottawa	1953	Red Kelly, Detroit	1980	Wayne Gretzky, Edmonton
1927	Billy Burch, N.Y. Americans	1954	Red Kelly, Detroit	1981	Rick Kehoe, Pittsburgh
1928	Frank Boucher, N.Y. Rangers	1955	Sid Smith, Toronto	1982	Rick Middleton, Boston
1929	Frank Boucher, N.Y. Rangers	1956	Earl Reibel, Detroit	1983	Mike Bossy, N.Y. Islanders
1930	Frank Boucher, N.Y. Rangers	1957	Andy Hebenton, N.Y. Rangers	1984	Mike Bossy, N.Y. Islanders
1931	Frank Boucher, N.Y. Rangers	1958	Camille Henry, N.Y. Rangers	1985	Jari Kurri, Edmonton
1932	Joe Primeau, Toronto	1959	Alex Delvecchio, Detroit	1986	Mike Bossy, N.Y. Islanders
1933	Frank Boucher, N.Y. Rangers	1960	Don McKenney, Boston	1987	Joe Mullen, Calgary
1934	Frank Boucher, N.Y. Rangers	1961	Red Kelly, Toronto	1988	Mats Naslund, Montreal
1935	Frank Boucher, N.Y. Rangers	1962	Dave Keon, Toronto	1989	Joe Mullen, Calgary
1936	Doc Romnes, Chicago	1963	Dave Keon, Toronto	1990	Brett Hull, St. Louis
1937	Marty Barry, Detroit	1964	Ken Wharram, Chicago	1991	Wayne Gretzky, Los Angeles
1938	Gordie Drillon, Toronto	1965	Bobby Hull, Chicago	1992	Wayne Gretzky, Los Angeles
1939	Clint Smith, N.Y. Rangers	1966	Alex Delvecchio, Detroit	1993	Pierre Turgeon, N.Y. Islanders
1940	Bobby Bauer, Boston	1967	Stan Mikita, Chicago	1994	Wayne Gretzky, Los Angeles
1941	Bobby Bauer, Boston	1968	Stan Mikita, Chicago	1995	Ron Francis, Pittsburgh
1942	Syl Apps, Toronto	1969	Alex Delvecchio, Detroit	1996	Paul Kariya, Anaheim
1943	Max Bentley, Chicago	1970	Phil Goyette, St. Louis	1997	Paul Kariya, Anaheim
1944	Clint Smith, Chicago	1971	John Bucyk, Boston	1998	Ron Francis, Pittsburgh
1945	Bill Mosienko, Chicago	1972	Jean Ratelle, N.Y. Rangers	1999	Wayne Gretzky, N.Y. Rangers
1946	Toe Blake, Montreal	1973	Gil Perreault, Buffalo	2000	Pavol Demitra, St. Louis
1947	Bobby Bauer, Boston	1974	John Bucyk, Boston	2001	Joe Sakic, Colorado
1948	Buddy O'Connor, N.Y. Rangers	1975	Marcel Dionne, Detroit	2002	Ron Francis, Carolina
1949	Bill Quackenbush, Detroit	1976	Jean Ratelle, N.Y.R.-Boston	2003	Alexander Mogilny, Toronto
1950	Edgar Laprade, N.Y. Rangers	1977	Marcel Dionne, Los Angeles	2004	Brad Richards, Tampa Bay
1951	Red Kelly, Detroit	1978	Butch Goring, Los Angeles	2006	Pavel Datsyuk, Detroit

James Norris Memorial Trophy (Outstanding Defenseman)

1954	Red Kelly, Detroit	1972	Bobby Orr, Boston	1989	Chris Chelios, Montreal
1955	Doug Harvey, Montreal	1973	Bobby Orr, Boston	1990	Ray Bourque, Boston
1956	Doug Harvey, Montreal	1974	Bobby Orr, Boston	1991	Ray Bourque, Boston
1957	Doug Harvey, Montreal	1975	Bobby Orr, Boston	1992	Brian Leetch, N.Y. Rangers
1958	Doug Harvey, Montreal	1976	Denis Potvin, N.Y. Islanders	1993	Chris Chelios, Chicago
1959	Tom Johnson, Montreal	1977	Larry Robinson, Montreal	1994	Ray Bourque, Boston
1960	Doug Harvey, Montreal	1978	Denis Potvin, N.Y. Islanders	1995	Paul Coffey, Detroit
1961	Doug Harvey, Montreal	1979	Denis Potvin, N.Y. Islanders	1996	Chris Chelios, Chicago
1962	Doug Harvey, N.Y. Rangers	1980	Larry Robinson, Montreal	1997	Brian Leetch, N.Y. Rangers
1963	Pierre Pilote, Chicago	1981	Randy Carlyle, Pittsburgh	1998	Rob Blake, Los Angeles
1964	Pierre Pilote, Chicago	1982	Doug Wilson, Chicago	1999	Al MacInnis, St. Louis
1965	Pierre Pilote, Chicago	1983	Rod Langway, Washington	2000	Chris Pronger, St. Louis
1966	Jacques Laperriere, Montreal	1984	Rod Langway, Washington	2001	Nicklas Lidstrom, Detroit
1967	Harry Howell, N.Y. Rangers	1985	Paul Coffey, Edmonton	2002	Nicklas Lidstrom, Detroit
1968	Bobby Orr, Boston	1986	Paul Coffey, Edmonton	2003	Nicklas Lidstrom, Detroit
1969	Bobby Orr, Boston	1987	Ray Bourque, Boston	2004	Scott Niedermayer, New Jersey
1970	Bobby Orr, Boston	1988	Ray Bourque, Boston	2006	Nicklas Lidstrom, Detroit
1971	Bobby Orr, Boston				

Art Ross Trophy (Leading Points Scorer)

1927	Bill Cook, N.Y. Rangers	1931	Howie Morenz, Montreal	1935	Charlie Conacher, Toronto
1928	Howie Morenz, Montreal	1932	Harvey Jackson, Toronto	1936	Dave Schriner, N.Y. Americans
1929	Ace Bailey, Toronto	1933	Bill Cook, N.Y. Rangers	1937	Dave Schriner, N.Y. Americans
1930	Cooney Weiland, Boston	1934	Charlie Conacher, Toronto	1938	Gordie Drillon, Toronto

1939	Toe Blake, Montreal	1962	Bobby Hull, Chicago	1984	Wayne Gretzky, Edmonton
1940	Milt Schmidt, Boston	1963	Gordie Howe, Detroit	1985	Wayne Gretzky, Edmonton
1941	Bill Cowley, Boston	1964	Stan Mikita, Chicago	1986	Wayne Gretzky, Edmonton
1942	Bryan Hextall, N.Y. Rangers	1965	Stan Mikita, Chicago	1987	Wayne Gretzky, Edmonton
1943	Doug Bentley, Chicago	1966	Bobby Hull, Chicago	1988	Mario Lemieux, Pittsburgh
1944	Herbie Cain, Boston	1967	Stan Mikita, Chicago	1989	Mario Lemieux, Pittsburgh
1945	Elmer Lach, Montreal	1968	Stan Mikita, Chicago	1990	Wayne Gretzky, Los Angeles
1946	Max Bentley, Chicago	1969	Phil Esposito, Boston	1991	Wayne Gretzky, Los Angeles
1947	Max Bentley, Chicago	1970	Bobby Orr, Boston	1992	Mario Lemieux, Pittsburgh
1948	Elmer Lach, Montreal	1971	Phil Esposito, Boston	1993	Mario Lemieux, Pittsburgh
1949	Roy Conacher, Chicago	1972	Phil Esposito, Boston	1994	Wayne Gretzky, Los Angeles
1950	Ted Lindsay, Detroit	1973	Phil Esposito, Boston	1995	Jaromir Jagr, Pittsburgh
1951	Gordie Howe, Detroit	1974	Phil Esposito, Boston	1996	Mario Lemieux, Pittsburgh
1952	Gordie Howe, Detroit	1975	Bobby Orr, Boston	1997	Mario Lemieux, Pittsburgh
1953	Gordie Howe, Detroit	1976	Guy Lafleur, Montreal	1998	Jaromir Jagr, Pittsburgh
1954	Gordie Howe, Detroit	1977	Guy Lafleur, Montreal	1999	Jaromir Jagr, Pittsburgh
1955	Bernie Geoffrion, Montreal	1978	Guy Lafleur, Montreal	2000	Jaromir Jagr, Pittsburgh
1956	Jean Beliveau, Montreal	1979	Bryan Trottier, N.Y. Islanders	2001	Jaromir Jagr, Pittsburgh
1957	Gordie Howe, Detroit	1980	Marcel Dionne, Los Angeles	2002	Jarome Iginla, Calgary
1958	Dickie Moore, Montreal	1981	Wayne Gretzky, Edmonton	2003	Peter Forsberg, Colorado
1959	Dickie Moore, Montreal	1982	Wayne Gretzky, Edmonton	2004	Martin St. Louis, Tampa Bay
1960	Bobby Hull, Chicago	1983	Wayne Gretzky, Edmonton	2006	Joe Thornton, San Jose
1961	Bernie Geoffrion, Montreal				

Vezina Trophy (Outstanding Goalie)*

1927	George Hainsworth, Montreal	1954	Harry Lumley, Toronto	1980	Sauve, Edwards, Buffalo
1928	George Hainsworth, Montreal	1955	Terry Sawchuk, Detroit	1981	Sevigny, Larocque, Herron, Montreal
1929	George Hainsworth, Montreal	1956	Jacques Plante, Montreal		
1930	Tiny Thompson, Boston	1957	Jacques Plante, Montreal	1982	Bill Smith, N.Y. Islanders
1931	Roy Worters, N.Y. Americans	1958	Jacques Plante, Montreal	1983	Pete Peeters, Boston
1932	Charlie Gardiner, Chicago	1959	Jacques Plante, Montreal	1984	Tom Barrasso, Buffalo
1933	Tiny Thompson, Boston	1960	Jacques Plante, Montreal	1985	Pelle Lindbergh, Philadelphia
1934	Charlie Gardiner, Chicago	1961	John Bower, Toronto	1986	John Vanbiesbrouck, N.Y. Rangers
1935	Lorne Chabot, Chicago	1962	Jacques Plante, Montreal	1987	Ron Hextall, Philadelphia
1936	Tiny Thompson, Boston	1963	Glenn Hall, Chicago	1988	Grant Fuhr, Edmonton
1937	Normie Smith, Detroit	1964	Charlie Hodge, Montreal	1989	Patrick Roy, Montreal
1938	Tiny Thompson, Boston	1965	Sawchuk, Bower, Toronto	1990	Patrick Roy, Montreal
1939	Frank Brimsek, Boston	1966	Worsley, Hodge, Montreal	1991	Ed Belfour, Chicago
1940	Dave Kerr, N.Y. Rangers	1967	Hall, DeJordy, Chicago	1992	Patrick Roy, Montreal
1941	Turk Broda, Toronto	1968	Worsley, Vachon, Montreal	1993	Ed Belfour, Chicago
1942	Frank Brimsek, Boston	1969	Hall, Plante, St. Louis	1994	Dominik Hasek, Buffalo
1943	Johnny Mowers, Detroit	1970	Tony Esposito, Chicago	1995	Dominik Hasek, Buffalo
1944	Bill Durnan, Montreal	1971	Giacomin, Villemure, N.Y. Rangers	1996	Jim Carey, Washington
1945	Bill Durnan, Montreal	1972	Esposito, Smith, Chicago	1997	Dominik Hasek, Buffalo
1946	Bill Durnan, Montreal	1973	Ken Dryden, Montreal	1998	Dominik Hasek, Buffalo
1947	Bill Durnan, Montreal	1974	Bernie Parent, Philadelphia;	1999	Dominik Hasek, Buffalo
1948	Turk Broda, Toronto		Tony Esposito, Chicago	2000	Olaf Kolzig, Washington
1949	Bill Durnan, Montreal	1975	Bernie Parent, Philadelphia	2001	Dominik Hasek, Buffalo
1950	Bill Durnan, Montreal	1976	Ken Dryden, Montreal	2002	Jose Theodore, Montreal
1951	Al Rollins, Toronto	1977	Dryden, Larocque, Montreal	2003	Martin Brodeur, New Jersey
1952	Terry Sawchuk, Detroit	1978	Dryden, Larocque, Montreal	2004	Martin Brodeur, New Jersey
1953	Terry Sawchuk, Detroit	1979	Dryden, Larocque, Montreal	2006	Miikka Kiprusoff, Calgary

*Before 1982, awarded to the goalie or goalies who played a minimum of 25 games for the team that allowed the fewest goals; since 1982, awarded to the outstanding goalie, as determined by a vote of NHL general managers.

NHL Home Ice[1]

Team	Name (built)	Capacity	Team	Name (built)	Capacity
Anaheim	The Arrowhead Pond of Anaheim (1993)	17,174	Montreal	Le Centre Bell[7] (1996)	21,273
Atlanta	Philips Arena (1999)	18,750	Nashville	Gaylord Entertainment Center[8] (1996)	17,500
Boston	TD Banknorth Garden[2] (1995)	17,565	New Jersey	Continental Airlines Arena[9] (1981)	19,040
Buffalo	HSBC Arena[3] (1996)	18,595	N.Y. Islanders	Nassau Veterans Memorial Col. (1972)	16,297
Calgary	Pengrowth Saddledome (1983)	17,104	N.Y. Rangers	Madison Square Garden (1968)	18,200
Carolina	RBC Center[4] (1999)	18,730	Ottawa	Corel Centre (1996)	18,500
Chicago	United Center (1994)	20,500	Philadelphia	Wachovia Center[10] (1996)	19,519
Colorado	Pepsi Center (1999)	18,007	Phoenix	Glendale Arena (2003)	17,500
Columbus	Nationwide Arena (2000)	18,500	Pittsburgh	Mellon Arena[11] (1961)	17,537
Dallas	American Airlines Center (2001)	18,000	St. Louis	Savvis Center[12] (1994)	21,000
Detroit	Joe Louis Arena (1979)	20,066	San Jose	HP Pavilion[13] (1993)	17,483
Edmonton	Rexall Place[5] (1974)	17,100	Tampa Bay	St. Pete Times Forum[14] (1996)	19,758
Florida	Office Depot Center[6] (1998)	19,250	Toronto	Air Canada Centre (1999)	18,800
Los Angeles	Staples Center (1999)	18,118	Vancouver	GM Place (1995)	18,422
Minnesota	Xcel Energy Arena (2000)	18,604	Washington	MCI Center (1997)	19,700

(1) At the end of the 2005-06 season. (2) Fleet Center 1995-2005. (3) Marine Midland Arena, 1996-2000. (4) Entertainment & Sports Arena, 1999-2002. (5) Northlands Col., 1974-79; Edmonton Col., 1979-98; Skyreach Centre, 1998-2003. (6) National Car Rental Center, 1998-2002. (7) Le Centre Molson, 1996-2002. (8) Nashville Arena, 1997-99. (9) Brendan Byrne/Meadowlands Arena, 1981-96. (10) First Union Center, 1996-2003. (11) Civic Arena, 1961-99. (12) Kiel Center, 1994-2000. (13) San Jose Arena, 1993-2000; Compaq Center, 2001. (14) Ice Palace, 1996-2002.

National Hockey Hall of Fame, Toronto, Ontario

(2006 inductees have an asterisk*)

PLAYERS

Abel, Sid
Adams, Jack
Apps, Syl
Armstrong, George
Bailey, Ace
Bain, Dan
Baker, Hobey
Barber, Bill
Barry, Marty
Bathgate, Andy
Bauer, Bobby
Beliveau, Jean
Benedict, Clint
Bentley, Doug
Bentley, Max
Blake, Toe
Boivin, Leo
Boon, Dickie
Bossy, Mike
Bouchard, Butch
Boucher, Frank
Boucher, George
Bourque, Ray
Bower, Johnny
Bowie, Dubbie
Brimsek, Frank
Broadbent, Punch
Broda, Turk
Bucyk, John
Burch, Billy
Cameron, Harry
Bucyk, John
Burch, Billy
Cameron, Harry
Cheevers, Gerry
Clancy, King
Clapper, Dit
Clarke, Bobby
Cleghorn, Sprague
Coffey, Paul
Colville, Neil
Conacher, Charlie
Conacher, Lionel
Conacher, Roy
Connell, Alex
Cook, Bill
Cook, Bun
Coulter, Art
Cournoyer, Yvan
Cowley, Bill
Crawford, Rusty
Darragh, Jack
Davidson, Scotty
Day, Hap
Delvecchio, Alex
Denneny, Cy
Dionne, Marcel
Drillon, Gordie
Drinkwater, Graham
Dryden, Ken
*Duff, Terrance "Dick"
Dumart, Woody
Dunderdale, Tommy
Durnan, Bill
Dutton, Red
Dye, Babe
Esposito, Phil
Esposito, Tony
Farrel, Arthur
Federko, Bernie

Fetisov, Viacheslav
Flaman, Fernie
Foyston, Frank
Fredrickson, Frank
Fuhr, Grant
Gadsby, Bill
Gainey, Bob
Gardiner, Chuck
Gardiner, Herb
Gardiner, Jimmy
Gartner, Mike
Geoffrion, Bernie
Gerard, Eddie
Giacomin, Eddie
Gilbert, Rod
Gillies, Clark
Gilmour, Billy
Goheen, Moose
Goodfellow, Ebbie
Goulet, Michel
Grant, Mike
Green, Shorty
Gretzky, Wayne
Griffis, Si
Hainsworth, George
Hall, Glenn
Hall, Joe
Harvey, Doug
Hawerchuk, Dale
Hay, George
Hern, Riley
Hextall, Bryan
Holmes, Hap
Hooper, Tom
Horner, Red
Horton, Tim
Howe, Gordie
Howe, Syd
Howell, Harry
Hull, Bobby
Hutton, Bouse
Hyland, Harry
Irvin, Dick
Jackson, Busher
Johnson, Ching
Johnson, Ernie
Johnson, Tom
Joliat, Aurel
Kharlamov, Valeri
Keats, Duke
Kelly, Red
Kennedy, Ted
Keon, Dave
Kurri, Jari
Lach, Elmer
Lafleur, Guy
LaFontaine, Pat
Lalonde, Newsy
Langway, Rod
Laperriere, Jacques
Lapointe, Guy
Laprade, Edgar
Laviolette, Jack
LeSueur, Percy
Lehman, Hughie
Lemaire, Jacques
Lemieux, Mario
Lewis, Herbie
Lindsay, Ted
Lumley, Harry
MacKay, Mickey

Mahovlich, Frank
Malone, Joe
Mantha, Sylvio
Marshall, Jack
Maxwell, Fred
McDonald, Lanny
McGee, Frank
McGimsie, Billy
McNamara, George
Mikita, Stan
Moore, Dickie
Moran, Paddy
Morenz, Howie
Mosienko, Bill
Mullen, Joe
Murphy, Larry
Neely, Cam
Nighbor, Frank
Noble, Reg
O'Connor, Buddy
Oliver, Harry
Olmstead, Bert
Orr, Bobby
Parent, Bernie
Park, Brad
Patrick, Lester
Patrick, Lynn
Perreault, Gilbert
Phillips, Tom
Pilote, Pierre
Pitre, Didier
Plante, Jacques
Potvin, Denis
Pratt, Babe
Primeau, Joe
Pronovost, Marcel
Pulford, Bob
Pulford, Harvey
Quackenbush, Bill
Rankin, Frank
Ratelle, Jean
Rayner, Chuck
Reardon, Kenny
Richard, Henri
Richard, Maurice
Richardson, George
Roberts, Gordie
Robinson, Larry
Ross, Art
*Roy, Patrick
Russel, Blair
Russell, Ernie
Ruttan, Jack
Salming, Borje
Savard, Denis
Savard, Serge
Sawchuk, Terry
Scanlan, Fred
Schmidt, Milt
Schriner, Sweeney
Seibert, Earl
Seibert, Oliver
Shore, Eddie
Shutt, Steve
Siebert, Babe
Simpson, Joe
Sittler, Darryl
Smith, Alf
Smith, Billy
Smith, Clint
Smith, Hooley

Smith, Tommy
Stanley, Allan
Stanley, Barney
Stastny, Peter
Stewart, Jack
Stewart, Nels
Stuart, Bruce
Stuart, Hod
Taylor, Cyclone
Thompson, Tiny
Tretiak, Vladislav
Trihey, Harry
Trottier, Bryan
Ullman, Norm
Vezina, Georges
Walker, Jack
Walsh, Marty
Watson, Harry (Moose)
Watson, HarryPercival
Weiland, Cooney
Westwick, Harry
Whitcroft, Fred
Wilson, Phat
Worsley, Gump
Worters, Roy

BUILDERS

Adams, Charles
Adams, Weston
Ahearn, Bunny
Ahearn, Frank
Allan, Sir Montagu
Allen, Keith
Arbour, Al
Ballard, Harold
Bauer, Father David
Bickell, J.P.
Bowman, Scotty
*Brooks, Herbert
Brown, George
Brown, Walter
Buckland, Frank
Bush, Walter, Jr.
Butterfield, Jack
Calder, Frank
Campbell, Angus
Campbell, Clarence
Cattarinich, Joseph
Costello, Murray
Dandurand, Leo
Dilio, Frank
Dudley, George
Dunn, James
Fletcher, Cliff
Francis, Emile
Gibson, Jack
Gorman, Tommy
Griffiths, Frank
Hanley, Bill
Hay, Charles
Hendy, Jim
Hewitt, Foster
Hewitt, William
*Hotchkiss, Harley
Hume, Fred
Ilitch, Mike
Imlach, Punch
Ivan, Tommy
Jennings, William
Johnson, Bob
Juckes, Gordon
Kilpatrick, John

Kilrea, Brian
Knox, Seymour
LeBel, Robert
Leader, Al
Lockhart, Thomas
Loicq, Paul
Mariucci, John
Mathers, Frank
McLaughlin, Frederic
Milford, Jake
Molson, Sen. Hartland
Morrison, Ian "Scotty"
Murray, Pere Athol
Neilson, Roger
Nelson, Francis
Norris, Bruce
Norris, James
Norris, James Sr.
Northey, William
O'Brien, J. Ambrose
O'Neill, Brian Francis
Page, Frederick
Patrick, Craig
Patrick, Frank
Pickard, Allan
Pilous, Rudy
Poile, Bud
Pollock, Sam
Raymond,
   Sen. Donat
Robertson,
   John Ross
Robinson, Claude
Ross, Phillip
Sabetzki, Gunther
Sather, Glen
Selke, Frank
Sinden, Harry
Smith, Frank
Smythe, Conn
Snider, Ed
Stanley, Lord (of
   Preston)
Sutherland, Capt.
   James T.
Tarasov, Anatoli
Torrey, Bill
Turner, Lloyd
Tutt, William
Voss, Carl
Waghorne, Fred
Wirtz, Arthur
Wirtz, Bill
Ziegler, John A., Jr.

**REFEREES
AND LINESMEN**

Armstrong, Neil
Ashley, John
Chadwick, Bill
D'Amico, John
Elliott, Chaucer
Hayes, George
Hewiston, Bobby
Ion, Mickey
Pavelich, Matt
Rodden, Mike
Smeaton, Cooper
Storey, Red
Udvari, Frank
Van Hellemond, Andy

NCAA Hockey Champions

1948 Michigan	1960 Denver	1972 Boston Univ.	1984 Bowling Green	1996 Michigan
1949 Boston College	1961 Denver	1973 Wisconsin	1985 RPI	1997 North Dakota
1950 Colorado College	1962 Michigan Tech	1974 Minnesota	1986 Michigan State	1998 Michigan
1951 Michigan	1963 North Dakota	1975 Michigan Tech	1987 North Dakota	1999 Maine
1952 Michigan	1964 Michigan	1976 Minnesota	1988 Lake Superior St.	2000 North Dakota
1953 Michigan	1965 Michigan Tech	1977 Wisconsin	1989 Harvard	2001 Boston College
1954 RPI	1966 Michigan State	1978 Boston Univ.	1990 Wisconsin	2002 Minnesota
1955 Michigan	1967 Cornell	1979 Minnesota	1991 N. Michigan	2003 Minnesota
1956 Michigan	1968 Denver	1980 North Dakota	1992 Lake Superior St.	2004 Denver
1957 Colorado College	1969 Denver	1981 Wisconsin	1993 Maine	2005 Denver
1958 Denver	1970 Cornell	1982 North Dakota	1994 Lake Superior St.	2006 Wisconsin
1959 North Dakota	1971 Boston Univ.	1983 Wisconsin	1995 Boston Univ.	

SOCCER

Italy Wins 2006 FIFA World Cup

Italy defeated France, 5-3 on penalty kicks July 9, after a 1-1 draw continued through 30 minutes of extra time, to win the final match of the 2006 World Cup in Berlin, Germany. The tournament set records for the total number of yellow cards (345) and red cards (28) issued by referees, including France midfielder Zinedine Zidane's red card, received for head-butting Italy's Marco Materazzi in the chest in the Final. Italy, coached by Marcello Lippi and captained by defender Fabio Cannavaro, won its fourth World Cup. Zidane nevertheless received the Golden Ball award as the tournament's best player. German striker Miroslav Klose, who scored 5 goals during the tournament—including the 80th-minute goal that tied Germany's quarterfinal match, enabling the home team to win in penalty kicks—was awarded the Golden Boot as the tournament's top scorer.

First Round Results

Group A	W	L	T	GF	GA	Pts		Group E	W	L	T	GF	GA	Pts
Germany	3	0	0	8	2	9		Italy	2	0	1	5	1	7
Ecuador	2	1	0	5	3	6		Ghana	2	1	0	4	3	6
Poland	1	2	0	2	4	3		Czech Republic	1	2	0	3	4	3
Costa Rica	0	3	0	3	9	0		USA	0	2	1	2	6	1
Group B								**Group F**						
England	2	0	1	5	2	7		Brazil	3	0	0	7	1	9
Sweden	1	0	2	3	2	5		Australia	1	1	1	5	5	4
Paraguay	1	2	0	2	2	3		Croatia	0	1	2	2	3	2
Trinidad and Tobago	0	2	1	0	4	1		Japan	0	2	1	2	7	1
Group C								**Group F**						
Argentina	2	0	1	8	1	7		Switzerland	2	0	1	4	0	7
Netherlands	2	0	1	3	1	7		France	1	0	2	3	1	5
Côte d'Ivoire	1	2	0	5	6	3		Korea Republic	1	1	1	3	4	4
Serbia and Montenegro	0	3	0	2	10	0		Togo	0	3	0	1	6	0
Group D								**Group G**						
Portugal	3	0	0	5	1	9		Spain	3	0	0	8	1	9
Mexico	1	1	1	4	3	4		Ukraine	2	1	0	5	4	6
Angola	0	1	2	1	2	2		Tunisia	0	2	1	3	6	1
Iran	0	2	1	2	6	1		Saudi Arabia	0	2	1	2	7	1

Final Round Results

June 24: Munich
Germany 2, Sweden 0

June 24: Leipzig
Argentina 2, Mexico 1 (extra time)

June 30: Berlin
Germany 1, Argentina 1
(Germany won 4-2 in penalty kicks)

June 26: Kaiserslautern
Italy 1, Australia 0

June 26: Cologne
Ukraine 0, Switzerland 0
(Ukraine won 3-0 in penalty kicks)

June 30: Hamburg
Italy 3, Ukraine 0

July 4: Dortmund
Italy 2, Germany 0 (extra time)

July 9: Berlin
Italy 1, France 1
(Italy won 5-3 in penalty kicks)

June 25: Stuttgart
England 1, Ecuador 0

June 25: Nuremberg
Portugal 1, Netherlands 0

July 1: Gelsenkirchen
Portugal 0, England 0
(Portugal won 3-1 in penalty kicks)

July 5: Munich
France 1, Portugal 0

June 27: Dortmund
Brazil 3, Ghana 0

July 1: Frankfurt
France 1, Brazil 0

June 27: Hanover
France 3, Spain 1

Third Place Final
July 8: Stuttgart
Germany 3, Portugal 1

Men's World Cup, 1930-2006

Year	Winner	Final opponent	Score	Site		Year	Winner	Final opponent	Score	Site
1930	Uruguay	Argentina	4-2	Uruguay		1974	W. Germany	Netherlands	2-1	W. Germany
1934	Italy	Czechoslovakia	2-1*	Italy		1978	Argentina	Netherlands	3-1*	Argentina
1938	Italy	Hungary	4-2	France		1982	Italy	W. Germany	3-1	Spain
1950	Uruguay	Brazil	2-1	Brazil		1986	Argentina	W. Germany	3-2	Mexico
1954	W. Germany	Hungary	3-2	Switzerland		1990	W. Germany	Argentina	1-0	Italy
1958	Brazil	Sweden	5-2	Sweden		1994	Brazil	Italy	0-0[1]	U.S.
1962	Brazil	Czechoslovakia	3-1	Chile		1998	France	Brazil	3-0	France
1966	England	W. Germany	4-2*	England		2002	Brazil	Germany	2-0	Japan/S. Korea
1970	Brazil	Italy	4-1	Mexico		2006	Italy	France	1-1[2]	Germany

*Extra time. (1) Brazil won 3-2 on penalty kicks. (2) Italy won 5-3 on penalty kicks.

Women's World Cup

The Women's World Cup was scheduled to be held Sept. 10-30, 2007, in China, which hosted the first Women's World Cup in 1991. Teams from 16 nations will compete in 5 cities, with the opening and closing matches to be held in Shanghai.

Previous Women's World Cup Finals: 2003 – Germany 2-1 (extra time) over Sweden in Carson, CA; 1999 – U.S., 0-0 (5-4 in penalty kicks), over China in Pasadena, CA; 1995 – Norway, 2-0, over Germany in Sweden; 1991 – U.S., 2-1, over Norway in China.

UEFA (European) Champions League
UEFA Championship League Winners and Runners-Up, 1956-2006

Year	Winner	Runner Up	Score	Year	Winner	Runner Up	Score
1956	Real Madrid	Reims	4-3	1982	Villa	Bayern Munich	1-0
1957	Real Madrid	Fiorentina	2-0	1983	Hamburg	Juventus	1-0
1958	Real Madrid	AC Milan	3-2#	1984	Liverpool	Roma	1-1 (4-2)*
1959	Real Madrid	Reims	2-0	1985	Juventus	Liverpool	1-0
1960	Real Madrid	Eintracht	7-3	1986	Steaua	Barcelona	0-0 (2-0)*
1961	Benfica	Barcelona	3-2	1987	Porto	Bayern Munich	2-1
1962	Benfica	Real Madrid	5-3	1988	PSV	Benfica	0-0 (6-5)*
1963	AC Milan	Benfica	2-1	1989	AC Milan	Steaua	4-0
1964	Inter Milan	Real Madrid	3-1	1990	AC Milan	Benfica	1-0
1965	Inter Milan	Benfica	1-0	1991	Crvena zvezda	Marseille	0-0 (5-3)*
1966	Real Madrid	Partizan	2-1	1992	Barcelona	Sampdoria	1-0#
1967	Celtic	Inter Milan	2-1	1993	Marseille	AC Milan	1-0
1968	Man. United	Benfica	4-1#	1994	AC Milan	Barcelona	4-0
1969	AC Milan	Ajax	4-1	1995	Ajax	AC Milan	1-0
1970	Feyenoord	Celtic	2-1#	1996	Juventus	Ajax	1-1 (4-2)*
1971	Ajax	Panathinaikos	2-0	1997	Dortmund	Juventus	3-1
1972	Ajax	Inter Milan	2-0	1998	Real Madrid	Juventus	1-0
1973	Ajax	Juventus	1-0	1999	Man. United	Bayern Munich	2-1
1974	Bayern Munich	Atlético	5-11	2000	Real Madrid	Valencia	3-0
1975	Bayern Munich	Leeds	2-0	2001	Bayern Munich	Valencia	1-1 (5-4)*
1976	Bayern Munich	St-Etienne	1-0	2002	Real Madrid	Leverkusen	2-1
1977	Liverpool	Mönchen-gladbach	3-1	2003	AC Milan	Juventus	0-0 (3-2)*
1978	Liverpool	Club Brugge	1-0	2004	Porto	Monaco	3-0
1979	Notts Forest	Malmö	1-0	2005	Liverpool	AC Milan	3-3 (3-2)*
1980	Notts Forest	Hamburg	1-0	2006	Barcelona	Arsenal	2-1
1981	Liverpool	Real Madrid	1-0				

*Match decided in penalty kicks (shootout score in parentheses). (#) Match decided in extra time. (1) Aggregate score. First game 1-1; 4-0.

European Championships, 1960-2004

The final rounds of the 2008 UEFA European Championships will be jointly hosted by Austria and Switzerland, and were scheduled to open June 7, 2008, in Basel, Switzerland, with the final match to be played at Ernst Happle Stadium in Vienna, Austria, on June 29, 2008.

Year	Winner	Final opponent	Score	Site
1960	USSR	Yugoslavia	2-1 (extra time)	France
1964	Spain	USSR	2-1	Spain
1968	Italy	Yugoslavia	2-0	Italy
1972	W. Germany	USSR	3-0	Belgium
1976	Czechoslovakia	W. Germany	2-2 (Czech. won 5-3 on pens.)	Yugoslavia
1980	W. Germany	Belgium	2-1	Italy
1984	France	Spain	2-0	France
1988	Netherlands	USSR	2-0	W. Germany
1992	Denmark	Germany	2-0	Sweden
1996	Germany	Czech Rep.	2-1 (extra time)	England
2000	France	Italy	2-1 (extra time)	Belgium/Neth.
2004	Greece	Portugal	1-0	Portugal

Major League Soccer

The Los Angeles Galaxy won its 2nd Major League Soccer (MLS) championship on Nov. 13, 2005, with a 1-0 victory over the New England Revolution in Frisco, TX. The victory was an unlikely upset: the Galaxy finished 4th in the Western Division and has the honor of having the worst regular season record (13-13-6) of any MLS champion. Galaxy midfielder Guillermo (Pando) Ramirez, a 66th-minute substitute with the worst shooting efficiency in MLS history (1 goal in 62 attempted shots going into the match), scored the game's only goal in overtime and was named the championship game's MVP.

Major League Soccer (MLS) Cup Champions, 1996-2005

Year	Winner	Final opponent	Score	Site	MVP
1996	D.C. United	Los Angeles Galaxy	3-2 (OT)	Foxboro, MA	Marco Etcheverry
1997	D.C. United	Colorado Rapids	2-1	Washington, DC	Jaime Moreno
1998	Chicago Fire	D.C. United	2-0	Pasadena, CA	Peter Nowak
1999	D.C. United	Los Angeles Galaxy	2-0	Foxboro, MA	Ben Olsen
2000	Kansas City Wizards	Chicago Fire	1-0	Washington, DC	Tony Meola
2001	San Jose Earthquakes	Los Angeles Galaxy	2-1 (OT)	Columbus, OH	Dwayne DeRosario
2002	Los Angeles Galaxy	New England Revolution	1-0 (OT)	Foxboro, MA	Carlos Ruiz
2003	San Jose Earthquakes	Chicago Fire	4-2	Carson, CA	Landon Donovan
2004	D.C. United	Kansas City Wizards	3-2	Carson, CA	Alecko Eskandarian
2005	Los Angeles Galaxy	New England Revolution	1-0 (OT)	Frisco, TX	Guillermo Ramirez

NCAA Soccer Champions, 1982-2005

Year[1]	Men	Women	Year[1]	Men	Women
1982	Indiana	North Carolina	1994	Virginia	North Carolina
1983	Indiana	North Carolina	1995	Wisconsin	Notre Dame
1984	Clemson	North Carolina	1996	St. John's (NY)	North Carolina
1985	UCLA	George Mason	1997	UCLA	North Carolina
1986	Duke	North Carolina	1998	Indiana	Florida
1987	Clemson	North Carolina	1999	Indiana	North Carolina
1988	Indiana	North Carolina	2000	Connecticut	North Carolina
1989	Santa Clara (tie, 2 OT) Virginia	North Carolina	2001	North Carolina	Santa Clara
1990	UCLA	North Carolina	2002	UCLA	Portland
1991	Virginia	North Carolina	2003	Indiana	North Carolina
1992	Virginia	North Carolina	2004	Indiana	Notre Dame
1993	Virginia	North Carolina	2005	Maryland	Portland

(1) NCAA Championships began in 1959 for men, in 1982 for women.

GOLF
Men's All-Time Major Professional Championship Leaders
(Through the 2006 season; *active PGA player; (a)=amateur.)

Player	Masters	U.S. Open	British Open	PGA	Total
Jack Nicklaus	1963, '65-66, '72, '75, '86	1962, '67, '72, '80	1966, '70, '78	1963, '71, '73, '75, '80	18
Tiger Woods*	1997, 2001, 2002, 2005	2000, 2002	2000, 2005-06	1999, 2000, 2006	12
Walter Hagen	—	1914, '19	1922, '24, '28-29	1921, '24-27	11
Ben Hogan	1951, '53	1948, '50-51, '53	1953	1946, '48	9
Gary Player	1961, '74, '78	1965	1959, '68, '74	1962, '72	9
Tom Watson*	1977, '81	1982	1975, '77, '80, '82-83	—	8
Bobby Jones (a)	—	1923, '26, '29-30	1926-27, '30	—	7
Arnold Palmer	1958, '60, '62, '64	1960	1961-62	—	7
Gene Sarazen	1935	1922, '32	1932	1922-23, '33	7
Sam Snead	1949, '52, '54	—	1946	1942, '49, '51	7
Harry Vardon	—	1900	1896, '98-99, 1903, '11, '14	—	7
Nick Faldo	1989-90, '96	—	1987, '90, '92	—	6
Lee Trevino	—	1968, '71	1971-72	1974, '84	6

Professional Golfers' Association Leading Money Winners, by Year

Year	Player	Earnings	Year	Player	Earnings	Year	Player	Earnings
1946	Ben Hogan	$42,556	1966	Billy Casper	$121,944	1986	Greg Norman	$653,296
1947	Jimmy Demaret	27,936	1967	Jack Nicklaus	188,988	1987	Curtis Strange	925,941
1948	Ben Hogan	36,812	1968	Billy Casper	205,168	1988	Curtis Strange	1,147,644
1949	Sam Snead	31,593	1969	Frank Beard	175,223	1989	Tom Kite	1,395,278
1950	Sam Snead	35,758	1970	Lee Trevino	157,037	1990	Greg Norman	1,165,477
1951	Lloyd Mangrum	26,088	1971	Jack Nicklaus	244,490	1991	Corey Pavin	979,430
1952	Julius Boros	37,032	1972	Jack Nicklaus	320,542	1992	Fred Couples	1,344,188
1953	Lew Worsham	34,002	1973	Jack Nicklaus	308,362	1993	Nick Price	1,478,557
1954	Bob Toski	65,819	1974	Johnny Miller	353,201	1994	Nick Price	1,499,927
1955	Julius Boros	65,121	1975	Jack Nicklaus	323,149	1995	Greg Norman	1,654,959
1956	Ted Kroll	72,835	1976	Jack Nicklaus	266,438	1996	Tom Lehman	1,780,159
1957	Dick Mayer	65,835	1977	Tom Watson	310,653	1997	Tiger Woods	2,066,833
1958	Arnold Palmer	42,407	1978	Tom Watson	362,429	1998	David Duval	2,591,031
1959	Art Wall, Jr.	53,167	1979	Tom Watson	462,636	1999	Tiger Woods	6,616,585
1960	Arnold Palmer	75,262	1980	Tom Watson	530,808	2000	Tiger Woods	9,188,321
1961	Gary Player	64,540	1981	Tom Kite	375,699	2001	Tiger Woods	5,687,777
1962	Arnold Palmer	81,448	1982	Craig Stadler	446,462	2002	Tiger Woods	6,912,625
1963	Arnold Palmer	128,230	1983	Hal Sutton	426,668	2003	Vijay Singh	7,573,907
1964	Jack Nicklaus	113,284	1984	Tom Watson	476,260	2004	Vijay Singh	10,905,166
1965	Jack Nicklaus	140,752	1985	Curtis Strange	542,321	2005	Tiger Woods	10,628,024

Masters Golf Tournament Winners

Year	Winner	Year	Winner	Year	Winner	Year	Winner
1934	Horton Smith	1954	Sam Snead	1972	Jack Nicklaus	1990	Nick Faldo
1935	Gene Sarazen	1955	Cary Middlecoff	1973	Tommy Aaron	1991	Ian Woosnam
1936	Horton Smith	1956	Jack Burke	1974	Gary Player	1992	Fred Couples
1937	Byron Nelson	1957	Doug Ford	1975	Jack Nicklaus	1993	Bernhard Langer
1938	Henry Picard	1958	Arnold Palmer	1976	Ray Floyd	1994	Jose Maria Olazabal
1939	Ralph Guldahl	1959	Art Wall Jr.	1977	Tom Watson	1995	Ben Crenshaw
1940	Jimmy Demaret	1960	Arnold Palmer	1978	Gary Player	1996	Nick Faldo
1941	Craig Wood	1961	Gary Player	1979	Fuzzy Zoeller	1997	Tiger Woods
1942	Byron Nelson	1962	Arnold Palmer	1980	Seve Ballesteros	1998	Mark O'Meara
1943-45	not played	1963	Jack Nicklaus	1981	Tom Watson	1999	Jose Maria Olazabal
1946	Herman Keiser	1964	Arnold Palmer	1982	Craig Stadler	2000	Vijay Singh
1947	Jimmy Demaret	1965	Jack Nicklaus	1983	Seve Ballesteros	2001	Tiger Woods
1948	Claude Harmon	1966	Jack Nicklaus	1984	Ben Crenshaw	2002	Tiger Woods
1949	Sam Snead	1967	Gay Brewer, Jr.	1985	Bernhard Langer	2003	Mike Weir
1950	Jimmy Demaret	1968	Bob Goalby	1986	Jack Nicklaus	2004	Phil Mickelson
1951	Ben Hogan	1969	George Archer	1987	Larry Mize	2005	Tiger Woods
1952	Sam Snead	1970	Billy Casper	1988	Sandy Lyle	2006	Phil Mickelson
1953	Ben Hogan	1971	Charles Coody	1989	Nick Faldo		

United States Open Winners
(First contested in 1895)

Year	Winner	Year	Winner	Year	Winner	Year	Winner
1934	Olin Dutra	1955	Jack Fleck	1973	Johnny Miller	1990	Hale Irwin
1935	Sam Parks, Jr.	1956	Cary Middlecoff	1974	Hale Irwin	1991	Payne Stewart
1936	Tony Manero	1957	Dick Mayer	1975	Lou Graham	1992	Tom Kite
1937	Ralph Guldahl	1958	Tommy Bolt	1976	Jerry Pate	1993	Lee Janzen
1938	Ralph Guldahl	1959	Billy Casper	1977	Hubert Green	1994	Ernie Els
1939	Byron Nelson	1960	Arnold Palmer	1978	Andy North	1995	Corey Pavin
1940	Lawson Little	1961	Gene Littler	1979	Hale Irwin	1996	Steve Jones
1941	Craig Wood	1962	Jack Nicklaus	1980	Jack Nicklaus	1997	Ernie Els
1942-45	not played	1963	Julius Boros	1981	David Graham	1998	Lee Janzen
1946	Lloyd Mangrum	1964	Ken Venturi	1982	Tom Watson	1999	Payne Stewart
1947	L. Worsham	1965	Gary Player	1983	Larry Nelson	2000	Tiger Woods
1948	Ben Hogan	1966	Billy Casper	1984	Fuzzy Zoeller	2001	Retief Goosen
1949	Cary Middlecoff	1967	Jack Nicklaus	1985	Andy North	2002	Tiger Woods
1950	Ben Hogan	1968	Lee Trevino	1986	Ray Floyd	2003	Jim Furyk
1951	Ben Hogan	1969	Orville Moody	1987	Scott Simpson	2004	Retief Goosen
1952	Julius Boros	1970	Tony Jacklin	1988	Curtis Strange	2005	Michael Campbell
1953	Ben Hogan	1971	Lee Trevino	1989	Curtis Strange	2006	Geoff Ogilvy
1954	Ed Furgol	1972	Jack Nicklaus				

IT'S A RECORD: With his 2006 PGA Championship win, Tiger Woods claimed his 12th major tournament victory—6 titles behind Jack Nicklaus on the all-time list—at the age of 30. Nicklaus was 33 when he claimed his 12th Major in 1973, also at the PGA Championship. Woods also holds or has tied the record low scores (in relation to par) for every major tournament: he won the 2000 British Open with a score 19 under par, claimed his first Masters in 18 under par (1997), scored 18 under par twice (2000, 2006) at the PGA, and shot 12 under par at the 2000 U.S. Open.

British Open Winners
(First contested in 1860)

Year	Winner	Year	Winner	Year	Winner	Year	Winner
1934	Henry Cotton	1956	Peter Thomson	1973	Tom Weiskopf	1990	Nick Faldo
1935	Alf Perry	1957	Bobby Locke	1974	Gary Player	1991	Ian Baker-Finch
1936	Alf Padgham	1958	Peter Thomson	1975	Tom Watson	1992	Nick Faldo
1937	T.H. Cotton	1959	Gary Player	1976	Johnny Miller	1993	Greg Norman
1938	R.A. Whitcombe	1960	Kel Nagle	1977	Tom Watson	1994	Nick Price
1939	Richard Burton	1961	Arnold Palmer	1978	Jack Nicklaus	1995	John Daly
1940-45	not played	1962	Arnold Palmer	1979	Seve Ballesteros	1996	Tom Lehman
1946	Sam Snead	1963	Bob Charles	1980	Tom Watson	1997	Justin Leonard
1947	Fred Daly	1964	Tony Lema	1981	Bill Rogers	1998	Mark O'Meara
1948	Henry Cotton	1965	Peter Thomson	1982	Tom Watson	1999	Paul Lawrie
1949	Bobby Locke	1966	Jack Nicklaus	1983	Tom Watson	2000	Tiger Woods
1950	Bobby Locke	1967	Roberto de Vicenzo	1984	Seve Ballesteros	2001	David Duval
1951	Max Faulkner	1968	Gary Player	1985	Sandy Lyle	2002	Ernie Els
1952	Bobby Locke	1969	Tony Jacklin	1986	Greg Norman	2003	Ben Curtis
1953	Ben Hogan	1970	Jack Nicklaus	1987	Nick Faldo	2004	Todd Hamilton
1954	Peter Thomson	1971	Lee Trevino	1988	Seve Ballesteros	2005	Tiger Woods
1955	Peter Thomson	1972	Lee Trevino	1989	Mark Calcavecchia	2006	Tiger Woods

PGA Championship Winners
(First contested in 1916)

Year	Winner	Year	Winner	Year	Winner	Year	Winner
1934	Paul Runyan	1953	Walter Burkemo	1971	Jack Nicklaus	1989	Payne Stewart
1935	Johnny Revolta	1954	Melvin Harbert	1972	Gary Player	1990	Wayne Grady
1936	Denny Shute	1955	Doug Ford	1973	Jack Nicklaus	1991	John Daly
1937	Denny Shute	1956	Jack Burke	1974	Lee Trevino	1992	Nick Price
1938	Paul Runyan	1957	Lionel Hebert	1975	Jack Nicklaus	1993	Paul Azinger
1939	Henry Picard	1958	Dow Finsterwald	1976	Dave Stockton	1994	Nick Price
1940	Byron Nelson	1959	Bob Rosburg	1977	Lanny Wadkins	1995	Steve Elkington
1941	Victor Ghezzi	1960	Jay Hebert	1978	John Mahaffey	1996	Mark Brooks
1942	Sam Snead	1961	Jerry Barber	1979	David Graham	1997	Davis Love III
1943	not played	1962	Gary Player	1980	Jack Nicklaus	1998	Vijay Singh
1944	Bob Hamilton	1963	Jack Nicklaus	1981	Larry Nelson	1999	Tiger Woods
1945	Byron Nelson	1964	Bob Nichols	1982	Ray Floyd	2000	Tiger Woods
1946	Ben Hogan	1965	Dave Marr	1983	Hal Sutton	2001	David Toms
1947	Jim Ferrier	1966	Al Geiberger	1984	Lee Trevino	2002	Rich Beem
1948	Ben Hogan	1967	Don January	1985	Hubert Green	2003	Shaun Micheel
1949	Sam Snead	1968	Julius Boros	1986	Bob Tway	2004	Vijay Singh
1950	Chandler Harper	1969	Ray Floyd	1987	Larry Nelson	2005	Phil Mickelson
1951	Sam Snead	1970	Dave Stockton	1988	Jeff Sluman	2006	Tiger Woods
1952	James Turnesa						

Women's All-Time Major Professional Championship Leaders
(Through the 2006 season; *active in 2006 LPGA season.)

Player	Nabisco[1]	LPGA	U.S. Women's Open	du Maurier/ British Open[2]	Titleholders[3]	Western Open[4]	Total
Patty Berg	—	—	1946	—	1937-39, '48, '53, '55, '57	1941, '43, '48, '51, '55, '57-58	15
Mickey Wright	—	1958, '60-61, '63	1958-59, '61, '64	—	1961-62	1962-63, '66	13
Louise Suggs	—	1957	1949, '52	—	1946, '54, '56, '59	1946-47, '49, '53	11
Babe Zaharias	—	—	1948, '50, '54	—	1947, '50, '52	1940, '44-45, '50	10
Annika Sorenstam*	2001-02, '05	2003-05	1995-96, 2006	2003	—	—	10
Betsy Rawls	—	1959, '69	1951, '53, '57, '60	—	—	1952, '59	8
Juli Inkster*	1984, '89	1999, 2000	1999, 2002	1984	—	—	7
Pat Bradley	1986	1986	1981	1980, '85-86	—	—	6
Betsy King*	1987, '90, '97	1992	1989-90	—	—	—	6
Patty Sheehan	1996	1983-84, '93	1992, '94	—	—	—	6
Kathy Whitworth	—	1967, '71, '75	—	—	1965-66	1967	6
Karrie Webb*	2000, 2006	2001	2000-01	1999, 2002	—	—	7

(1) Nabisco Championship, formerly Nabisco Dinah Shore (1982-99), designated major in 1983. (2) In 2001, the British Open replaced the du Maurier Classic as the LPGA's 4th major. (3) Title holders Championship was a major from 1930 to 1972. (4) Western Open was a major from 1937 to 1967.

Ladies Professional Golf Association Leading Money Winners

Year	Player	Earnings	Year	Player	Earnings	Year	Player	Earnings
1954	Patty Berg	$16,011	1972	Kathy Whitworth	$65,063	1989	Betsy King	$654,132
1955	Patty Berg	16,492	1973	Kathy Whitworth	82,854	1990	Beth Daniel	863,578
1956	Marlene Hagge	20,235	1974	JoAnne Carner	87,094	1991	Pat Bradley	763,118
1957	Patty Berg	16,272	1975	Sandra Palmer	94,805	1992	Dottie Mochrie	693,335
1958	Beverly Hanson	12,629	1976	Judy Rankin	150,734	1993	Betsy King	595,992
1959	Betsy Rawls	26,774	1977	Judy Rankin	122,890	1994	Laura Davies	687,201
1960	Louise Suggs	16,892	1978	Nancy Lopez	189,813	1995	Annika Sorenstam	666,533
1961	Mickey Wright	22,236	1979	Nancy Lopez	215,987	1996	Karrie Webb	1,002,000
1962	Mickey Wright	21,641	1980	Beth Daniel	231,000	1997	Annika Sorenstam	1,236,789
1963	Mickey Wright	31,269	1981	Beth Daniel	206,977	1998	Annika Sorenstam	1,092,748
1964	Mickey Wright	29,800	1982	JoAnne Carner	310,399	1999	Karrie Webb	1,591,959
1965	Kathy Whitworth	28,658	1983	JoAnne Carner	291,404	2000	Karrie Webb	1,876,853
1966	Kathy Whitworth	33,517	1984	Betsy King	266,771	2001	Annika Sorenstam	2,105,868
1967	Kathy Whitworth	32,937	1985	Nancy Lopez	416,472	2002	Annika Sorenstam	2,863,904
1968	Kathy Whitworth	48,379	1986	Pat Bradley	492,021	2003	Annika Sorenstam	2,029,506
1969	Carol Mann	49,152	1987	Ayako Okamoto	466,034	2004	Annika Sorenstam	2,544,707
1970	Kathy Whitworth	30,235	1988	Sherri Turner	347,255	2005	Annika Sorenstam	2,588,240
1971	Kathy Whitworth	41,181						

Kraft Nabisco Championship Winners[1]

Year	Winner	Year	Winner	Year	Winner	Year	Winner
1983	Amy Alcott	1989	Juli Inkster	1995	Nanci Bowen	2001	Annika Sorenstam
1984	Juli Inkster	1990	Betsy King	1996	Patty Sheehan	2002	Annika Sorenstam
1985	Alice Miller	1991	Amy Alcott	1997	Betsy King	2003	Patricia Meunier-Lebouc
1986	Pat Bradley	1992	Dottie Pepper	1998	Pat Hurst	2004	Grace Park
1987	Betsy King	1993	Helen Alfredsson	1999	Dottie Pepper	2005	Annika Sorenstam
1988	Amy Alcott	1994	Donna Andrews	2000	Karrie Webb	2006	Karrie Webb

(1) Formerly the Colgate Dinah Shore (1972-81), the Nabisco Dinah Shore (1982-99), the Nabisco Championship (2000-01). Designated as a major championship in 1983.

LPGA Championship Winners

Year	Winner	Year	Winner	Year	Winner	Year	Winner
1955	Beverly Hanson	1968	Sandra Post	1981	Donna Caponi	1994	Laura Davies
1956	Marlene Hagge	1969	Betsy Rawls	1982	Jan Stephenson	1995	Kelly Robbins
1957	Louise Suggs	1970	Shirley Englehorn	1983	Patty Sheehan	1996	Laura Davies
1958	Mickey Wright	1971	Kathy Whitworth	1984	Patty Sheehan	1997	Chris Johnson
1959	Betsy Rawls	1972	Kathy Ahern	1985	Nancy Lopez	1998	Se Ri Pak
1960	Mickey Wright	1973	Mary Mills	1986	Pat Bradley	1999	Juli Inkster
1961	Mickey Wright	1974	Sandra Haynie	1987	Jane Geddes	2000	Juli Inkster
1962	Judy Kimball	1975	Kathy Whitworth	1988	Sherri Turner	2001	Karrie Webb
1963	Mickey Wright	1976	Betty Burfeindt	1989	Nancy Lopez	2002	Se Ri Pak
1964	Mary Mills	1977	Chako Higuchi	1990	Beth Daniel	2003	Annika Sorenstam
1965	Sandra Haynie	1978	Nancy Lopez	1991	Meg Mallon	2004	Annika Sorenstam
1966	Gloria Ehret	1979	Donna Caponi	1992	Betsy King	2005	Annika Sorenstam
1967	Kathy Whitworth	1980	Sally Little	1993	Patty Sheehan	2006	Se Ri Pak

U.S. Women's Open Winners

Year	Winner	Year	Winner	Year	Winner	Year	Winner
1946	Patty Berg	1962	Murle Lindstrom	1977	Hollis Stacy	1992	Patty Sheehan
1947	Betty Jameson	1963	Mary Mills	1978	Hollis Stacy	1993	Lauri Merten
1948	Babe Zaharias	1964	Mickey Wright	1979	Jerilyn Britz	1994	Patty Sheehan
1949	Louise Suggs	1965	Carol Mann	1980	Amy Alcott	1995	Annika Sorenstam
1950	Babe Zaharias	1966	Sandra Spuzich	1981	Pat Bradley	1996	Annika Sorenstam
1951	Betsy Rawls	1967	Catherine Lacoste	1982	Janet Alex	1997	Alison Nicholas
1952	Louise Suggs		(amateur)	1983	Jan Stephenson	1998	Se Ri Pak
1953	Betsy Rawls	1968	Susie Maxwell Berning	1984	Hollis Stacy	1999	Juli Inkster
1954	Babe Zaharias	1969	Donna Caponi	1985	Kathy Baker	2000	Karrie Webb
1955	Fay Crocker	1970	Donna Caponi	1986	Jane Geddes	2001	Karrie Webb
1956	Mrs. K. Cornelius	1971	JoAnne Carner	1987	Laura Davies	2002	Juli Inkster
1957	Betsy Rawls	1972	Susie Maxwell Berning	1988	Liselotte Neumann	2003	Hilary Lunke
1958	Mickey Wright	1973	Susie Maxwell Berning	1989	Betsy King	2004	Meg Mallon
1959	Mickey Wright	1974	Sandra Haynie	1990	Betsy King	2005	Birdie Kim
1960	Betsy Rawls	1975	Sandra Palmer	1991	Meg Mallon	2006	Annika Sorenstam
1961	Mickey Wright	1976	JoAnne Carner				

Women's British Open Winners[1]

Year	Winner	Year	Winner	Year	Winner	Year	Winner
1979	Amy Alcott	1986	Pat Bradley	1993	Brandie Burton	2000	Meg Mallon
1980	Pat Bradley	1987	Jody Rosenthal	1994	Martha Nause	2001	Se Ri Pak
1981	Jan Stephenson	1988	Sally Little	1995	Jenny Lidback	2002	Karrie Webb
1982	Sandra Haynie	1989	Tammie Green	1996	Laura Davies	2003	Annika Sorenstam
1983	Hollis Stacy	1990	Cathy Johnston	1997	Colleen Walker	2004	Karen Stupples
1984	Juli Inkster	1991	Nancy Scranton	1998	Brandie Burton	2005	Jeong Jang
1985	Pat Bradley	1992	Sherri Steinhauer	1999	Karrie Webb	2006	Sherri Steinhauer

(1) First held as the Ladies' British Open in 1976; became the LPGA's 4th major championship in 2001, replacing the du Maurier Classic. Winners listed 1979-2000 are for the du Maurier Classic (Peter Jackson Classic, 1979-82).

International Golf

Ryder Cup

Began as a biennial team competition between pro golfers from the U.S. and Great Britain. The British team was expanded in 1973 to include players from Ireland and in 1979 from the rest of Europe. The Ryder Cup moved to even years after being postponed following the terrorist attacks of Sept. 11, 2001. Europe routed the Americans for its 3rd-straight victory at the 2006 match up, Sept. 22-24 at the K Club in Straffan, Ireland. The 2008 Ryder Cup was scheduled to be held Sept. 19-21 at the Valhalla Golf Club in Louisville, KY.

Year	Winner	Year	Winner	Year	Winner	Year	Winner
1927	U.S., 9½-2½	1953	U.S., 6½-5½	1971	U.S., 18½-13½	1989	Draw, 14-14
1929	Britain-Ireland, 7-5	1955	U.S., 8-4	1973	U.S., 19-13	1991	U.S., 14½-13½
1931	U.S., 9-3	1957	Britain-Ireland, 7½-4½	1975	U.S., 21-11	1993	U.S., 15-13
1933	Britain, 6½-5½	1959	U.S., 8½-3½	1977	U.S., 12½-7½	1995	Europe, 14½-13½
1935	U.S., 9-3	1961	U.S., 14½-9½	1979	U.S., 17-11	1997	Europe, 14½-13½
1937	U.S., 8-4	1963	U.S., 23-9	1981	U.S., 18½-9½	1999	U.S., 14½-13½
1939-45	Not played	1965	U.S., 19½-12½	1983	U.S., 14½-13½	2002	Europe, 15½-12½
1947	U.S., 11-1	1967	U.S., 23½-8½	1985	Europe, 16½-11½	2004	Europe, 18½-9½
1949	U.S., 7-5	1969	Draw, 16-16	1987	Europe, 15-13	2006	Europe, 18½-9½
1951	U.S., 9½-2½						

Solheim Cup

Began in 1990 as a biennial team competition between pro women golfers from Europe and the U.S. Competition moved to odd years in 2003 to alternate with the Ryder Cup, which had been postponed and moved to even years after the Sept. 2001 terrorist attacks. In 2005 the U.S. team defeated Europe at the Crooked Stick Golf Club in Carmel, IN, in the Sept. 11 final, after the first 2 days of competition ended with an 8-8 tie. The next Solheim Cup was scheduled for Sept. 14-16, 2007, at Halmstad Golfklubb in Sweden.

Year	Winner	Year	Winner	Year	Winner	Year	Winner
1990	U.S., 11½-4½	1996	U.S., 17-11	2000	Europe, 14½-11½	2003	Europe, 17½-12½
1992	Europe, 11½-6½	1998	U.S., 16-12	2002	U.S., 15½-12½	2005	U.S., 15½-12½
1994	U.S., 13-7						

TENNIS
Australian Open Singles Champions, 1969-2006
(First contested 1905 for men, 1922 for women. Became an Open Championship in 1969.)
*2 tournaments held in 1977 (Jan. & Dec.). **In 1986 tournament moved to Jan. 1987; no championship in 1986.

Men's Singles

Year	Champion	Final Opponent
1969	Rod Laver	Andres Gimeno
1970	Arthur Ashe	Dick Crealy
1971	Ken Rosewall	Arthur Ashe
1972	Ken Rosewall	Mal Anderson
1973	John Newcombe	Onny Parun
1974	Jimmy Connors	Phil Dent
1975	John Newcombe	Jimmy Connors
1976	Mark Edmondson	John Newcombe
1977*	Roscoe Tanner	Guillermo Vilas
	Vitas Gerulaitis	John Lloyd
1978	Guillermo Vilas	John Marks
1979	Guillermo Vilas	John Sadri
1980	Brian Teacher	Kim Warwick
1981	Johan Kriek	Steve Denton
1982	Johan Kriek	Steve Denton
1983	Mats Wilander	Ivan Lendl
1984	Mats Wilander	Kevin Curren
1985**	Stefan Edberg	Mats Wilander
1987	Stefan Edberg	Pat Cash
1988	Mats Wilander	Pat Cash
1989	Ivan Lendl	Miloslav Mecir
1990	Ivan Lendl	Stefan Edberg
1991	Boris Becker	Ivan Lendl
1992	Jim Courier	Stefan Edberg
1993	Jim Courier	Stefan Edberg
1994	Pete Sampras	Todd Martin
1995	Andre Agassi	Pete Sampras
1996	Boris Becker	Michael Chang
1997	Pete Sampras	Carlos Moya
1998	Petr Korda	Marcelo Rios
1999	Yevgeny Kafelnikov	Thomas Enqvist
2000	Andre Agassi	Yevgeny Kafelnikov
2001	Andre Agassi	Arnaud Clement
2002	Thomas Johansson	Marat Safin
2003	Andre Agassi	Rainer Schuettler
2004	Roger Federer	Marat Safin
2005	Marat Safin	Lleyton Hewitt
2006	Roger Federer	Marcos Baghdatis

Women's Singles

Year	Champion	Final Opponent
1969	Margaret Smith Court	Billie Jean King
1970	Margaret Smith Court	Kerry Melville Reid
1971	Margaret Smith Court	Evonne Goolagong
1972	Virginia Wade	Evonne Goolagong
1973	Margaret Smith Court	Evonne Goolagong
1974	Evonne Goolagong	Chris Evert
1975	Evonne Goolagong	Martina Navratilova
1976	Evonne Goolagong	Renata Tomanova
1977*	Kerry Reid	Dianne Balestrat
	Evonne Goolagong	Helen Gourlay
1978	Chris O'Neill	Betsy Nagelsen
1979	Barbara Jordan	Sharon Walsh
1980	Hana Mandlikova	Wendy Turnbull
1981	Martina Navratilova	Chris Evert Lloyd
1982	Chris Evert Lloyd	Martina Navratilova
1983	Martina Navratilova	Kathy Jordan
1984	Chris Evert Lloyd	Helena Sukova
1985**	Martina Navratilova	Chris Evert Lloyd
1987	Hana Mandlikova	Martina Navratilova
1988	Steffi Graf	Chris Evert
1989	Steffi Graf	Helena Sukova
1990	Steffi Graf	Mary Joe Fernandez
1991	Monica Seles	Jana Novotna
1992	Monica Seles	Mary Joe Fernandez
1993	Monica Seles	Steffi Graf
1994	Steffi Graf	Arantxa Sánchez Vicario
1995	Mary Pierce	Arantxa Sánchez Vicario
1996	Monica Seles	Anke Huber
1997	Martina Hingis	Mary Pierce
1998	Martina Hingis	Conchita Martínez
1999	Martina Hingis	Amelie Mauresmo
2000	Lindsay Davenport	Martina Hingis
2001	Jennifer Capriati	Martina Hingis
2002	Jennifer Capriati	Martina Hingis
2003	Serena Williams	Venus Williams
2004	Justine Henin-Hardenne	Kim Clijsters
2005	Serena Williams	Lindsay Davenport
2006	Amelie Mauresmo	Justine Henin-Hardenne

French Open Singles Champions, 1968-2006
(First contested 1891 for men, 1897 for women. Became an Open Championship in 1968.)

Men's Singles

Year	Champion	Final Opponent
1968	Ken Rosewall	Rod Laver
1969	Rod Laver	Ken Rosewall
1970	Jan Kodes	Zeljko Franulovic
1971	Jan Kodes	Ilie Nastase
1972	Andres Gimeno	Patrick Proisy
1973	Ilie Nastase	Nikki Pilic
1974	Bjorn Borg	Manuel Orantes
1975	Bjorn Borg	Guillermo Vilas
1976	Adriano Panatta	Harold Solomon
1977	Guillermo Vilas	Brian Gottfried
1978	Bjorn Borg	Guillermo Vilas
1979	Bjorn Borg	Victor Pecci
1980	Bjorn Borg	Vitas Gerulaitis
1981	Bjorn Borg	Ivan Lendl
1982	Mats Wilander	Guillermo Vilas
1983	Yannick Noah	Mats Wilander
1984	Ivan Lendl	John McEnroe
1985	Mats Wilander	Ivan Lendl
1986	Ivan Lendl	Mikael Pernfors
1987	Ivan Lendl	Mats Wilander
1988	Mats Wilander	Henri Leconte
1989	Michael Chang	Stefan Edberg
1990	Andres Gomez	Andre Agassi
1991	Jim Courier	Andre Agassi
1992	Jim Courier	Petr Korda
1993	Sergi Bruguera	Jim Courier
1994	Sergi Bruguera	Alberto Berasategui
1995	Thomas Muster	Michael Chang
1996	Yevgeny Kafelnikov	Michael Stich
1997	Gustavo Kuerten	Sergei Bruguera
1998	Carlos Moya	Alex Corretja
1999	Andre Agassi	Andrei Medvedev
2000	Gustavo Kuerten	Magnus Norman
2001	Gustavo Kuerten	Alex Corretja
2002	Albert Costa	Juan Carlos Ferrero
2003	Juan Carlos Ferrero	Martin Verkerk
2004	Gaston Gaudio	Guillermo Coria
2005	Rafael Nadal	Mariano Puerta
2006	Rafael Nadal	Roger Federer

Women's Singles

Year	Champion	Final Opponent
1968	Nancy Richey	Ann Jones
1969	Margaret Smith Court	Ann Jones
1970	Margaret Smith Court	Helga Niessen
1971	Evonne Goolagong	Helen Gourlay
1972	Billie Jean King	Evonne Goolagong
1973	Margaret Smith Court	Chris Evert
1974	Chris Evert	Olga Morozova
1975	Chris Evert	Martina Navratilova
1976	Sue Barker	Renata Tomanova
1977	Mima Jausovec	Florenza Mihai
1978	Virginia Ruzici	Mima Jausovec
1979	Chris Evert Lloyd	Wendy Turnbull
1980	Chris Evert Lloyd	Virginia Ruzici
1981	Hana Mandlikova	Sylvia Hanika
1982	Martina Navratilova	Andrea Jaeger
1983	Chris Evert Lloyd	Mima Jausovec
1984	Martina Navratilova	Chris Evert Lloyd
1985	Chris Evert Lloyd	Martina Navratilova
1986	Chris Evert Lloyd	Martina Navratilova
1987	Steffi Graf	Martina Navratilova
1988	Steffi Graf	Natalia Zvereva
1989	Arantxa Sánchez Vicario	Steffi Graf
1990	Monica Seles	Steffi Graf
1991	Monica Seles	Arantxa Sánchez Vicario
1992	Monica Seles	Steffi Graf
1993	Steffi Graf	Mary Joe Fernandez
1994	Arantxa Sánchez Vicario	Mary Pierce
1995	Steffi Graf	Arantxa Sánchez Vicario
1996	Steffi Graf	Arantxa Sánchez Vicario
1997	Iva Majoli	Martina Hingis
1998	Arantxa Sánchez Vicario	Monica Seles
1999	Steffi Graf	Martina Hingis
2000	Mary Pierce	Conchita Martinez
2001	Jennifer Capriati	Kim Clijsters
2002	Serena Williams	Venus Williams
2003	Justine Henin-Hardenne	Kim Clijsters
2004	Anastasia Myskina	Elena Dementieva
2005	Justine Henin-Hardenne	Mary Pierce
2006	Justine Henin-Hardenne	Svetlana Kuznetsova

U.S. Open Champions, 1925-2006

(Became an Open Championship in 1970)

Men's Singles

(First contested 1881)

Year	Champion	Final Opponent
1925	Bill Tilden	William Johnston
1926	Rene Lacoste	Jean Borotra
1927	Rene Lacoste	Bill Tilden
1928	Henri Cochet	Francis Hunter
1929	Bill Tilden	Francis Hunter
1930	John Doeg	Francis Shields
1931	H. Ellsworth Vines	George Lott
1932	H. Ellsworth Vines	Henri Cochet
1933	Fred Perry	John Crawford
1934	Fred Perry	Wilmer Allison
1935	Wilmer Allison	Sidney Wood
1936	Fred Perry	Don Budge
1937	Don Budge	Baron G. von Cramm
1938	Don Budge	C. Gene Mako
1939	Robert Riggs	S. Welby Van Horn
1940	Don McNeill	Robert Riggs
1941	Robert Riggs	F. L. Kovacs
1942	F. R. Schroeder Jr.	Frank Parker
1943	Joseph Hunt	Jack Kramer
1944	Frank Parker	William Talbert
1945	Frank Parker	William Talbert
1946	Jack Kramer	Thomas Brown Jr.
1947	Jack Kramer	Frank Parker
1948	Pancho Gonzales	Eric Sturgess
1949	Pancho Gonzales	F. R. Schroeder Jr.
1950	Arthur Larsen	Herbert Flam
1951	Frank Sedgman	E. Victor Seixas Jr.
1952	Frank Sedgman	Gardnar Mulloy
1953	Tony Trabert	E. Victor Seixas Jr.
1954	E. Victor Seixas Jr.	Rex Hartwig
1955	Tony Trabert	Ken Rosewall
1956	Ken Rosewall	Lewis Hoad
1957	Malcolm Anderson	Ashley Cooper
1958	Ashley Cooper	Malcolm Anderson
1959	Neale A. Fraser	Alejandro Olmedo
1960	Neale A. Fraser	Rod Laver
1961	Roy Emerson	Rod Laver
1962	Rod Laver	Roy Emerson
1963	Rafael Osuna	F. A. Froehling 3rd
1964	Roy Emerson	Fred Stolle
1965	Manuel Santana	Cliff Drysdale
1966	Fred Stolle	John Newcombe
1967	John Newcombe	Clark Graebner
1968	Arthur Ashe	Tom Okker
1969	Rod Laver	Tony Roche
1970	Ken Rosewall	Tony Roche
1971	Stan Smith	Jan Kodes
1972	Ilie Nastase	Arthur Ashe
1973	John Newcombe	Jan Kodes
1974	Jimmy Connors	Ken Rosewall
1975	Manuel Orantes	Jimmy Connors
1976	Jimmy Connors	Bjorn Borg
1977	Guillermo Vilas	Jimmy Connors
1978	Jimmy Connors	Bjorn Borg
1979	John McEnroe	Vitas Gerulaitis
1980	John McEnroe	Bjorn Borg
1981	John McEnroe	Bjorn Borg
1982	Jimmy Connors	Ivan Lendl
1983	Jimmy Connors	Ivan Lendl
1984	John McEnroe	Ivan Lendl
1985	Ivan Lendl	John McEnroe
1986	Ivan Lendl	Miloslav Mecir
1987	Ivan Lendl	Mats Wilander
1988	Mats Wilander	Ivan Lendl
1989	Boris Becker	Ivan Lendl
1990	Pete Sampras	Andre Agassi
1991	Stefan Edberg	Jim Courier
1992	Stefan Edberg	Pete Sampras
1993	Pete Sampras	Cedric Pioline
1994	Andre Agassi	Michael Stich
1995	Pete Sampras	Andre Agassi
1996	Pete Sampras	Michael Chang
1997	Patrick Rafter	Greg Rusedski
1998	Patrick Rafter	Mark Philippoussis
1999	Andre Agassi	Todd Martin
2000	Marat Safin	Pete Sampras
2001	Lleyton Hewitt	Pete Sampras
2002	Pete Sampras	Andre Agassi
2003	Andy Roddick	Juan Carlos Ferrero
2004	Roger Federer	Lleyton Hewitt
2005	Roger Federer	Andre Agassi
2006	Roger Federer	Andy Roddick

Women's Singles

(First contested 1887)

Year	Champion	Final Opponent
1925	Helen Willis	Kathleen McKane
1926	Molla B. Mallory	Elizabeth Ryan
1927	Helen Wills	Betty Nuthall
1928	Helen Wills	Helen Jacobs
1929	Helen Wills	M. Watson
1930	Betty Nuthall	L. A. Harper
1931	Helen Wills Moody	E. B. Whittingstall
1932	Helen Jacobs	Carolin A. Babcock
1933	Helen Jacobs	Helen Wills Moody
1934	Helen Jacobs	Sarah H. Palfrey
1935	Helen Jacobs	Sarah Palfrey Fabyan
1936	Alice Marble	Helen Jacobs
1937	Anita Lizana	Jadwiga Jedrzejowska
1938	Alice Marble	Nancye Wynne
1939	Alice Marble	Helen Jacobs
1940	Alice Marble	Helen Jacobs
1941	Sarah Palfrey Cooke	Pauline Betz
1942	Pauline Betz	Louise Brough
1943	Pauline Betz	Louise Brough
1944	Pauline Betz	Margaret Osborne
1945	Sarah Palfrey Cooke	Pauline Betz
1946	Pauline Betz	Doris Hart
1947	Louise Brough	Margaret Osborne
1948	Margaret Osborne duPont	Louise Brough
1949	Margaret Osborne duPont	Doris Hart
1950	Margaret Osborne duPont	Doris Hart
1951	Maureen Connolly	Shirley Fry
1952	Maureen Connolly	Doris Hart
1953	Maureen Connolly	Doris Hart
1954	Doris Hart	Louise Brough
1955	Doris Hart	Patricia Ward
1956	Shirley Fry	Althea Gibson
1957	Althea Gibson	Louise Brough
1958	Althea Gibson	Darlene Hard
1959	Maria Bueno	Christine Truman
1960	Darlene Hard	Maria Bueno
1961	Darlene Hard	Ann Haydon
1962	Margaret Smith	Darlene Hard
1963	Maria Bueno	Margaret Smith
1964	Maria Bueno	Carole Graebner
1965	Margaret Smith	Billie Jean Moffitt
1966	Maria Bueno	Nancy Richey
1967	Billie Jean King	Ann Haydon Jones
1968	Virginia Wade	Billie Jean King
1969	Margaret Smith Court	Nancy Richey
1970	Margaret Smith Court	Rosemary Casals
1971	Billie Jean King	Rosemary Casals
1972	Billie Jean King	Kerry Melville
1973	Margaret Smith Court	Evonne Goolagong
1974	Billie Jean King	Evonne Goolagong
1975	Chris Evert	Evonne Goolagong
1976	Chris Evert	Evonne Goolagong
1977	Chris Evert	Wendy Turnbull
1978	Chris Evert	Pam Shriver
1979	Tracy Austin	Chris Evert Lloyd
1980	Chris Evert Lloyd	Hana Mandlikova
1981	Tracy Austin	Martina Navratilova
1982	Chris Evert Lloyd	Hana Mandlikova
1983	Martina Navratilova	Chris Evert Lloyd
1984	Martina Navratilova	Chris Evert Lloyd
1985	Hana Mandlikova	Martina Navratilova
1986	Martina Navratilova	Helena Sukova
1987	Martina Navratilova	Steffi Graf
1988	Steffi Graf	Gabriela Sabatini
1989	Steffi Graf	Martina Navratilova
1990	Gabriela Sabatini	Steffi Graf
1991	Monica Seles	Martina Navratilova
1992	Monica Seles	Arantxa Sanchez Vicario
1993	Steffi Graf	Helena Sukova
1994	Arantxa Sanchez Vicario	Steffi Graf
1995	Steffi Graf	Monica Seles
1996	Steffi Graf	Monica Seles
1997	Martina Hingis	Venus Williams
1998	Lindsay Davenport	Martina Hingis
1999	Serena Williams	Martina Hingis
2000	Venus Williams	Lindsay Davenport
2001	Venus Williams	Serena Williams
2002	Serena Williams	Venus Williams
2003	Justine Henin-Hardenne	Kim Clijsters
2004	Svetlana Kuznetsova	Elena Dementieva
2005	Kim Clijsters	Mary Pierce
2006	Maria Sharapova	Justine Henin-Hardenne

All-England Champions, Wimbledon, 1925-2006

(First contested 1877 for men, 1884 for women. Became an Open Championship in 1968. Not held 1940-45)

Men's Singles

Year	Champion	Final Opponent
1925	Rene Lacoste	Jean Borotra
1926	Jean Borotra	Howard Kinsey
1927	Henri Cochet	Jean Borotra
1928	Rene Lacoste	Henri Cochet
1929	Henri Cochet	Jean Borotra
1930	Bill Tilden	Wilmer Allison
1931	Sidney B. Wood	Francis X. Shields
1932	Ellsworth Vines	Henry Austin
1933	Jack Crawford	Ellsworth Vines
1934	Fred Perry	Jack Crawford
1935	Fred Perry	Gottfried von Cramm
1936	Fred Perry	Gottfried von Cramm
1937	Donald Budge	Gottfried von Cramm
1938	Donald Budge	Henry Austin
1939	Bobby Riggs	Elwood Cooke
1946	Yvon Petra	Geoff E. Brown
1947	Jack Kramer	Tom P. Brown
1948	Bob Falkenburg	John Bromwich
1949	Ted Schroeder	Jaroslav Drobny
1950	Budge Patty	Frank Sedgman
1951	Dick Savitt	Ken McGregor
1952	Frank Sedgman	Jaroslav Drobny
1953	Vic Seixas	Kurt Nielsen
1954	Jaroslav Drobny	Ken Rosewall
1955	Tony Trabert	Kurt Nielsen
1956	Lew Hoad	Ken Rosewall
1957	Lew Hoad	Ashley Cooper
1958	Ashley Cooper	Neale Fraser
1959	Alex Olmedo	Rod Laver
1960	Neale Fraser	Rod Laver
1961	Rod Laver	Chuck McKinley
1962	Rod Laver	Martin Mulligan
1963	Chuck McKinley	Fred Stolle
1964	Roy Emerson	Fred Stolle
1965	Roy Emerson	Fred Stolle
1966	Manuel Santana	Dennis Ralston
1967	John Newcombe	Wilhelm Bungert
1968	Rod Laver	Tony Roche
1969	Rod Laver	John Newcombe
1970	John Newcombe	Ken Rosewall
1971	John Newcombe	Stan Smith
1972	Stan Smith	Ilie Nastase
1973	Jan Kodes	Alex Metreveli
1974	Jimmy Connors	Ken Rosewall
1975	Arthur Ashe	Jimmy Connors
1976	Bjorn Borg	Ilie Nastase
1977	Bjorn Borg	Jimmy Connors
1978	Bjorn Borg	Jimmy Connors
1979	Bjorn Borg	Roscoe Tanner
1980	Bjorn Borg	John McEnroe
1981	John McEnroe	Bjorn Borg
1982	Jimmy Connors	John McEnroe
1983	John McEnroe	Chris Lewis
1984	John McEnroe	Jimmy Connors
1985	Boris Becker	Kevin Curren
1986	Boris Becker	Ivan Lendl
1987	Pat Cash	Ivan Lendl
1988	Stefan Edberg	Boris Becker
1989	Boris Becker	Stefan Edberg
1990	Stefan Edberg	Boris Becker
1991	Michael Stich	Boris Becker
1992	Andre Agassi	Goran Ivanisevic
1993	Pete Sampras	Jim Courier
1994	Pete Sampras	Goran Ivanisevic
1995	Pete Sampras	Boris Becker
1996	Richard Krajicek	MaliVai Washington
1997	Pete Sampras	Cedric Pioline
1998	Pete Sampras	Goran Ivanisevic
1999	Pete Sampras	Andre Agassi
2000	Pete Sampras	Patrick Rafter
2001	Goran Ivanisevic	Patrick Rafter
2002	Lleyton Hewitt	David Nalbandian
2003	Roger Federer	Mark Philippoussis
2004	Roger Federer	Andy Roddick
2005	Roger Federer	Andy Roddick
2006	Roger Federer	Rafael Nadal

Women's Singles

Year	Champion	Final Opponent
1925	Suzanne Lenglen	Joan Fry
1926	Kathleen McKane Godfree	Lili de Alvarez
1927	Helen Wills	Lili de Alvarez
1928	Helen Wills	Lili de Alvarez
1929	Helen Wills	Helen Jacobs
1930	Helen Wills Moody	Elizabeth Ryan
1931	Cilly Aussem	Hilde Kranwinkel
1932	Helen Wills Moody	Helen Jacobs
1933	Helen Wills Moody	Dorothy Round
1934	Dorothy Round	Helen Jacobs
1935	Helen Wills Moody	Helen Jacobs
1936	Helen Jacobs	Hilde Kranwinkel Sperling
1937	Dorothy Round	Jadwiga Jedrzejowska
1938	Helen Wills Moody	Helen Jacobs
1939	Alice Marble	Kay Stammers
1946	Pauline Betz	Louise Brough
1947	Margaret Osborne	Doris Hart
1948	Louise Brough	Doris Hart
1949	Louise Brough	Margaret Osborne duPont
1950	Louise Brough	Margaret Osborne duPont
1951	Doris Hart	Shirley Fry
1952	Maureen Connolly	Louise Brough
1953	Maureen Connolly	Doris Hart
1954	Maureen Connolly	Louise Brough
1955	Louise Brough	Beverly Fleitz
1956	Shirley Fry	Angela Buxton
1957	Althea Gibson	Darlene Hard
1958	Althea Gibson	Angela Mortimer
1959	Maria Bueno	Darlene Hard
1960	Maria Bueno	Sandra Reynolds
1961	Angela Mortimer	Christine Truman
1962	Karen Hantze-Susman	Vera Sukova
1963	Margaret Smith	Billie Jean Moffitt
1964	Maria Bueno	Margaret Smith
1965	Margaret Smith	Maria Bueno
1966	Billie Jean King	Maria Bueno
1967	Billie Jean King	Ann Haydon Jones
1968	Billie Jean King	Judy Tegart
1969	Ann Haydon-Jones	Billie Jean King
1970	Margaret Smith Court	Billie Jean King
1971	Evonne Goolagong	Margaret Smith Court
1972	Billie Jean King	Evonne Goolagong
1973	Billie Jean King	Chris Evert
1974	Chris Evert	Olga Morozova
1975	Billie Jean King	Evonne Goolagong Cawley
1976	Chris Evert	Evonne Goolagong Cawley
1977	Virginia Wade	Betty Stove
1978	Martina Navratilova	Chris Evert
1979	Martina Navratilova	Chris Evert Lloyd
1980	Evonne Goolagong	Chris Evert Lloyd
1981	Chris Evert Lloyd	Hana Mandlikova
1982	Martina Navratilova	Chris Evert Lloyd
1983	Martina Navratilova	Andrea Jaeger
1984	Martina Navratilova	Chris Evert Lloyd
1985	Martina Navratilova	Chris Evert Lloyd
1986	Martina Navratilova	Hana Mandlikova
1987	Martina Navratilova	Steffi Graf
1988	Steffi Graf	Martina Navratilova
1989	Steffi Graf	Martina Navratilova
1990	Martina Navratilova	Zina Garrison
1991	Steffi Graf	Gabriela Sabatini
1992	Steffi Graf	Monica Seles
1993	Steffi Graf	Jana Novotna
1994	Conchita Martinez	Martina Navratilova
1995	Steffi Graf	Arantxa Sánchez Vicario
1996	Steffi Graf	Arantxa Sánchez Vicario
1997	Martina Hingis	Jana Novotna
1998	Jana Novotna	Nathalie Tauziat
1999	Lindsay Davenport	Steffi Graf
2000	Venus Williams	Lindsay Davenport
2001	Venus Williams	Justine Henin
2002	Serena Williams	Venus Williams
2003	Serena Williams	Venus Williams
2004	Maria Sharapova	Serena Williams
2005	Venus Williams	Lindsay Davenport
2006	Amelie Mauresmo	Justine Henin-Hardenne

> **IT'S A FACT:** The 2006 U.S. Open was the final tournament for 8-Grand Slam winner Andre Agassi—one of only 5 men to win every Grand Slam tournament at least once. Agassi lost in the 3rd round and retired at the age of 36. The tournament was also the last for 49-year-old tennis legend Martina Navratilova, who won her 59th Grand Slam title, her 10th in mixed doubles, at this year's U.S. Open. Navratilova had previously retired in 1994, having won 18 Grand Slam singles titles and 31 women's doubles titles, but returned to the sport in 2000.

Davis Cup, 1900-2005*

Year	Result	Year	Result	Year	Result
1900	U.S. 3, British Isles 0	1936	Great Britain 3, Australia 2	1974	South Africa (default by India)
1901	Not held	1937	U.S. 4, Great Britain 1	1975	Sweden 3, Czechoslovakia 2
1902	U.S. 3, British Isles 2	1938	U.S. 3, Australia 2	1976	Italy 4, Chile 1
1903	British Isles 4, U.S. 1	1939	Australia 3, U.S. 2	1977	Australia 3, Italy 1
1904	British Isles 5, Belgium 0	1940-45	Not held	1978	U.S. 4, Great Britain 1
1905	British Isles 5, U.S. 0	1946	U.S. 5, Australia 0	1979	U.S. 5, Italy 0
1906	British Isles 5, U.S. 0	1947	U.S. 4, Australia 1	1980	Czechoslovakia 4, Italy 1
1907	Australia 3, British Isles 2	1948	U.S. 5, Australia 0	1981	U.S. 3, Argentina 1
1908	Australasia 3, U.S. 2	1949	U.S. 4, Australia 1	1982	U.S. 4, France, 1
1909	Australasia 5, U.S. 0	1950	Australia 4, U.S. 1	1983	Australia 3, Sweden 2
1910	Not held	1951	Australia 3, U.S. 2	1984	Sweden 4, U.S. 1
1911	Australasia 5, U.S. 0	1952	Australia 4, U.S. 1	1985	Sweden 3, W. Germany 2
1912	British Isles 3, Australasia 2	1953	Australia 3, U.S. 2	1986	Australia 3, Sweden 2
1913	U.S. 3, British Isles 2	1954	U.S. 3, Australia 2	1987	Sweden 5, India 0
1914	Australasia 3, U.S. 2	1955	Australia 5, U.S. 0	1988	W. Germany 4, Sweden 1
1915-18	Not held	1956	Australia 5, U.S. 0	1989	W. Germany 3, Sweden 2
1919	Australasia 4, British Isles 1	1957	Australia 3, U.S. 2	1990	U.S. 3, Australia 2
1920	U.S. 5, Australasia 0	1958	U.S. 3, Australia 2	1991	France 3, U.S. 1
1921	U.S. 5, Japan 0	1959	Australia 3, U.S. 2	1992	U.S. 3, Switzerland 1
1922	U.S. 4, Australasia 1	1960	Australia 4, Italy 1	1993	Germany 4, Australia 1
1923	U.S. 4, Australasia 1	1961	Australia 5, Italy 0	1994	Sweden 4, Russia 1
1924	U.S. 5, Australasia 0	1962	Australia 5, Mexico 0	1995	U.S. 3, Russia 2
1925	U.S. 5, France 0	1963	U.S. 3, Australia 2	1996	France 3, Sweden 2
1926	U.S. 4, France 1	1964	Australia 3, U.S. 2	1997	Sweden 5, U.S. 0
1927	France 3, U.S. 2	1965	Australia 4, Spain 1	1998	Sweden 4, Italy 1
1928	France 4, U.S. 1	1966	Australia 4, India 1	1999	Australia 3, France 2
1929	France 3, U.S. 2	1967	Australia 4, Spain 1	2000	Spain 3, Australia 1
1930	France 4, U.S. 1	1968	U.S. 4, Australia	2001	France 3, Australia 2
1931	France 3, Great Britain 2	1969	U.S. 5, Romania 0	2002	Russia 3, France 2
1932	France 3, U.S. 2	1970	U.S. 5, W. Germany 0	2003	Australia 3, Spain 1
1933	Great Britain 3, France 2	1971	U.S. 3, Romania 2	2004	Spain 3, U.S. 2
1934	Great Britain 4, U.S. 1	1972	U.S. 3, Romania 2	2005	Croatia 3, Slovakia 2
1935	Great Britain 5, U.S. 0	1973	Australia 5, U.S. 0		

*The challenge round format, which guaranteed the previous year's winner a spot in the finals at home, was eliminated in 1972.

All-Time Grand Slam Singles Titles Leaders

Men	Australian Open	French Open[2]	Wimbledon	U.S. Open	Total
Pete Sampras	1994, '97	—	1993-95, 1997-2000	1990, '93, '95-96, 2002	14
Roy Emerson	1961, '63-67	1963, '67	1964-65	1961, '64	12
Bjorn Borg	—	1974-75, 1978-81	1976-80	—	11
Rod Laver	1960, '62, '69	1962, '69	1961-62, '68-69	1962, '69	11
Bill Tilden	—	—	1920-21, '30	1920-25, '29	10
Roger Federer[1]	2004, '06	—	2003-06	2004-06	9
Andre Agassi[1]	1995, 2000, '01, '03	1999	1992	1994, '99	8
Jimmy Connors	1974	—	1974, '82	1974, '76, '78, '82-83	8
Ivan Lendl	1989-90	1984, '86-87	—	1985-87	8
Fred Perry	1934	1935	1934-36	1933-34, '36	8
Ken Rosewall	1953, '55, '71-72	1953, '68	—	1956, '70	8
Women					
Margaret Smith Court	1960-66, '69-71, '73	1962, '64, '69-70, '73	1963, '65, '70	1962, '65, '69-70, '73	24
Steffi Graf	1988-90, '94	1987-88, '93, '95-96, '99	1988-89, '91-93, '95-96	1988-89, '93, '95-96	22
Helen Wills Moody	—	1928-30, '32	1927-30, '32-33, '35, '38	1923-25, '27-29, '31	19
Chris Evert Lloyd	1982, '84	1974-75, '79-80, '83, '85-86	1974, '76, '81	1975-78, '80, '82	18
Martina Navratilova	1981, '83, '85	1982, '84	1978-79, '82-87, '90	1983-84, '86-87	18
Billie Jean King	1968	1972	1966-68, '72-73, '75	1967, '71-72, '74	12
Suzanne Lenglen	—	1920-23, '25-26	1919-23, '25	—	12
Maureen Connolly	1953	1953-54	1952-54	1951-53	9
Monica Seles[1]	1991-93, '96	1990-92	—	1991-92	9

(1) Active player in 2006. (2) Prior to 1925, French Open entry was limited to members of French clubs.

RIFLE AND PISTOL INDIVIDUAL CHAMPIONSHIPS

Source: National Rifle Association

NRA Bianchi Cup National Action Pistol Championships in 2006

Action Pistol—Bruce Piatt, Montvale, NJ, 1920-177x
Woman Action Pistol—Vera Koo, Atherton, CA, 1897-143x

Junior Action Pistol—Jordan Dick, Hutchinson, KS, 1880-147x

National Outdoor Rifle and Pistol Championships in 2006

Pistol—SSG James M. Henderson, USA, Festus, MO 2643-134x
Civilian Pistol—David I. Lange, Glen Rock, NJ, 2630-116x
Woman Pistol—Judy Tant, East Lansing, MI, 2576-93x
Smallbore Rifle Prone—Paul T. Gideon, Gambier, OH, 6388-464x
Civilian Smallbore Rifle Prone—Paul T. Gideon, Gambier, OH, 6388-464x
Woman Smallbore Rifle Prone—Edie Reynolds, Raleigh, NC 6370-437x
Smallbore Rifle NRA 3-Position—MAJ Michael E. Anti, Ft. Benning, GA, 2311-96x

Civilian Smallbore Rifle NRA 3-Position—Vincent P. Pestilli, Lebanon, PA, 2262-81x
Woman Smallbore Rifle NRA 3-Position—Kimberly M. Chrostowski, Rockvile, RI 2263-71x
High Power Rifle—Norman G. Houle, Warwick, RI, 2382-125x
Civilian High Power Rifle—Norman G. Houle, Warwick, RI, 2382-125x
Woman High Power Rifle—Michelle Gallagher, Prescott, AZ, 2346-89x
High Power Rifle Long Range—Kent R. Reeve, Cary, NC, 1436-73x
Woman High Power Rifle Long Range—Michelle Gallagher, Prescott, AZ, 1424-64x

National Indoor Rifle and Pistol Championships in 2006

Smallbore Rifle 4-Position—Shane Barnhart, Phenix City, AL, 797-72x

Woman Smallbore Rifle 4-Position—Michelle Bohren, Taylor, MI, 792-55x

Smallbore Rifle NRA 3-Position—Michael McPhail, Phenix City, AL, 1181-85x

Woman Smallbore Rifle NRA 3-Position—Ashley Lane, Grand Rapids, MN, 1175-44x

International Smallbore Rifle—Michael Anti, Fort Benning, GA, 1175-80x

Woman International Smallbore Rifle—Danielle Langfield, Orlando, FL, 1161-83x

Air Rifle—Amanda Jeffries, Norman, OK, 587-50x

Woman Air Rifle—Amanda Jeffries, Norman, OK, 587-50x

Conventional Pistol—Jack Adams, Bethel, OH, 889-41x

Woman Conventional Pistol—Judy Tant, East Lansing, MI, 869-24x

International Free Pistol—John Zurek, Phoenix, AZ, 552-50x

Woman International Free Pistol—Ashley Davis, Salt Lake City, UT, 488-20x

International Standard Pistol—Bruce Martindale, Charlton, NY, 565-50x

Woman International Standard Pistol—Kathy Chatterton, Glen Rock, NJ, 529-20x

Air Pistol—Dwaine Hurt, Red Oak, IA, 575-50x

Woman Air Pistol—Frances Spear, Harpursville, NY, 554-20x

AUTO RACING

Indianapolis 500 Winners, 1911-2006

(At Indianapolis Motor Speedway in Indianapolis, IN)

Year	Winner, Car (Chassis-Engine)	MPH[1]	Year	Winner, Car (Chassis-Engine)	MPH[1]
1911	Ray Harroun, Marmon	74.602	1961	A.J. Foyt Jr., Trevis-Offy	139.130
1912	Joe Dawson, National	78.719	1962	Rodger Ward, Watson-Offy	140.293
1913	Jules Goux, Peugeot	75.933	1963	Parnelli Jones, Watson-Offy	143.137
1914	Rene Thomas, Delage	82.474	1964	A.J. Foyt Jr., Watson-Offy	147.350
1915	Ralph DePalma, Mercedes	89.840	1965	Jim Clark, Lotus-Ford	150.686
1916	Dario Resta, Peugeot	84.001	1966	Graham Hill, Lola-Ford	144.317
1917-18—Not held			1967	A.J. Foyt Jr., Coyote-Ford	151.207
1919	Howdy Wilcox, Peugeot	88.050	1968	Bobby Unser, Eagle-Offy	152.882
1920	Gaston Chevrolet, Frontenac	88.618	1969	Mario Andretti, Hawk-Ford	156.867
1921	Tommy Milton, Frontenac	89.621	1970	Al Unser, P.J. Colt-Ford	155.749
1922	Jimmy Murphy, Duesenberg-Miller	94.484	1971	Al Unser, P.J. Colt-Ford	157.735
1923	Tommy Milton, Miller	90.954	1972	Mark Donohue, McLaren-Offy	162.962
1924	L.L. Corum-Joe Boyer, Duesenberg	98.234	1973	Gordon Johncock, Eagle-Offy	159.036
1925	Peter DePaolo, Duesenberg	101.127	1974	Johnny Rutherford, McLaren-Offy	158.589
1926	Frank Lockhart, Miller	95.904	1975	Bobby Unser, Eagle-Offy	149.213
1927	George Souders, Duesenberg	97.545	1976	Johnny Rutherford, McLaren-Offy	148.725
1928	Louie Meyer, Miller	99.482	1977	A.J. Foyt Jr., Coyote-Foyt	161.331
1929	Ray Keech, Miller	97.585	1978	Al Unser, Lola-Cosworth	161.363
1930	Billy Arnold, Summers-Miller	100.448	1979	Rick Mears, Penske-Cosworth	158.899
1931	Louis Schneider, Stevens-Miller	96.629	1980	Johnny Rutherford, Chaparral-Cosworth	142.862
1932	Fred Frame, Wetteroth-Miller	104.144	1981	Bobby Unser, Penske-Cosworth	139.084
1933	Louie Meyer, Miller	104.162	1982	Gordon Johncock, Wildcat-Cosworth	162.029
1934	Bill Cummings, Miller	104.863	1983	Tom Sneva, March-Cosworth	162.117
1935	Kelly Petillo, Wetteroth-Offy	106.240	1984	Rick Mears, March-Cosworth	163.612
1936	Louie Meyer, Stevens-Miller	109.069	1985	Danny Sullivan, March-Cosworth	152.982
1937	Wilbur Shaw, Shaw-Offy	113.580	1986	Bobby Rahal, March-Cosworth	170.722
1938	Floyd Roberts, Wetteroth-Miller	117.200	1987	Al Unser, March-Cosworth	162.175
1939	Wilbur Shaw, Maserati	115.035	1988	Rick Mears, Penske-Chevy V8	144.809
1940	Wilbur Shaw, Maserati	114.277	1989	Emerson Fittipaldi, Penske-Chevy Indy V8	167.581
1941	Floyd Davis-Mauri Rose, Wetteroth-Offy	115.117	1990	Arie Luyendyk, Lola-Chevy Indy V8	185.981*
1942-45—Not held			1991	Rick Mears, Penske-Chevy Indy V8	176.457
1946	George Robson, Adams-Sparks	114.820	1992	Al Unser Jr., Galmer-Chevy Indy V8A	134.477
1947	Mauri Rose, Deidt-Offy	116.338	1993	Emerson Fittipaldi, Penske-Chevy Indy V8C	157.207
1948	Mauri Rose, Deidt-Offy	119.814	1994	Al Unser Jr., Penske-Mercedes Benz	160.872
1949	Bill Holland, Deidt-Offy	121.327	1995	Jacques Villeneuve, Reynard-Ford Cosworth XB	153.616
1950	Johnnie Parsons, Kurtis-Offy	124.002	1996	Buddy Lazier, Reynard-Ford Cosworth	147.956
1951	Lee Wallard, Kurtis-Offy	126.244	1997	Arie Luyendyk, G Force-Aurora	145.827
1952	Troy Ruttman, Kuzma-Offy	128.922	1998	Eddie Cheever, Dallara-Aurora	145.155
1953	Bill Vukovich, KK500A-Offy	128.740	1999	Kenny Brack, Dallara-Aurora	153.176
1954	Bill Vukovich, KK500A-Offy	130.840	2000	Juan Montoya, G Force-Aurora	167.607
1955	Bob Sweikert, KK500C-Offy	128.213	2001	Helio Castroneves, Reynard-Honda	131.294
1956	Pat Flaherty, Watson-Offy	128.490	2002	Helio Castroneves, Reynard-Honda	166.499
1957	Sam Hanks, Salih-Offy	135.601	2003	Gil de Ferran, G Force-Toyota	156.291
1958	Jimmy Bryan, Salih-Offy	133.791	2004	Buddy Rice, G Force-Honda	138.518
1959	Rodger Ward, Watson-Offy	135.857	2005	Dan Wheldon, Dallara-Honda	157.603
1960	Jim Rathmann, Watson-Offy	138.767	2006	Sam Hornish Jr., Dallara-Honda	157.085

(1) Average speed. *Race record. **Note:** The race was less than 500 mi in the following years: 1916 (300 mi), 1926 (400 mi), 1950 (345 mi), 1973 (332.5 mi), 1975 (435 mi), 1976 (255 mi), 2004 (450 mi).

Champ Car World Series Vanderbilt Cup Winners, 1959-2005

(U.S. Auto Club Champions prior to 1979; Championship Auto Racing Teams [CART] Champions, 1979-2003; Champ Car World Series Champion, 2004-present. The Vanderbilt Cup became the series' championship trophy in 2000.)

Year	Driver	Year	Driver	Year	Driver	Year	Driver
1959	Roger Ward	1971	Joe Leonard	1983	Al Unser	1995	Jacques Villeneuve
1960	A. J. Foyt	1972	Joe Leonard	1984	Mario Andretti	1996	Jimmy Vasser
1961	A. J. Foyt	1973	Roger McCluskey	1985	Al Unser	1997	Alex Zanardi
1962	Rodger Ward	1974	Bobby Unser	1986	Bobby Rahal	1998	Alex Zanardi
1963	A. J. Foyt	1975	A. J. Foyt	1987	Bobby Rahal	1999	Juan Montoya
1964	A. J. Foyt	1976	Gordon Johncock	1988	Danny Sullivan	2000	Gil de Ferran
1965	Mario Andretti	1977	Tom Sneva	1989	Emerson Fittipaldi	2001	Gil de Ferran
1966	Mario Andretti	1978	Tom Sneva	1990	Al Unser Jr.	2002	Cristiano da Matta
1967	A. J. Foyt	1979	Rick Mears	1991	Michael Andretti	2003	Paul Tracy
1968	Bobby Unser	1980	Johnny Rutherford	1992	Bobby Rahal	2004	Sebastien Bourdais
1969	Mario Andretti	1981	Rick Mears	1993	Nigel Mansell	2005	Sebastien Bourdais
1970	Al Unser	1982	Rick Mears	1994	Al Unser Jr.		

Indy Racing League (IRL) Winners, 1996-2005

(The Indy Racing League was begun in 1994 by a break-away group of CART drivers; its first championship was awarded in 1996)

Year	Driver	Year	Driver	Year	Driver	Year	Driver	Year	Driver
1996	(tie) Scott Sharp, Buzz Calkins	1998	Kenny Brack	2000	Buddy Lazier	2002	Sam Hornish Jr.	2004	Tony Kanaan
1997	Tony Stewart	1999	Greg Ray	2001	Sam Hornish Jr.	2003	Scott Dixon	2005	Dan Wheldon

NASCAR Racing
Nextel Cup Champions, 1949-2005
(Strictly Stock, 1949; Grand National, 1950-1970; Winston Cup 1971-2003)

Year	Driver	Year	Driver	Year	Driver	Year	Driver	Year	Driver
1949	Red Byron	1961	Ned Jarrett	1973	Benny Parsons	1984	Terry Labonte	1995	Jeff Gordon
1950	Bill Rexford	1962	Joe Weatherly	1974	Richard Petty	1985	Darrell Waltrip	1996	Terry Labonte
1951	Herb Thomas	1963	Joe Weatherly	1975	Richard Petty	1986	Dale Earnhardt	1997	Jeff Gordon
1952	Tim Flock	1964	Richard Petty	1976	Cale Yarborough	1987	Dale Earnhardt	1998	Jeff Gordon
1953	Herb Thomas	1965	Ned Jarrett	1977	Cale Yarborough	1988	Bill Elliott	1999	Dale Jarrett
1954	Lee Petty	1966	David Pearson	1978	Cale Yarborough	1989	Rusty Wallace	2000	Bobby Labonte
1955	Tim Flock	1967	Richard Petty	1979	Richard Petty	1990	Dale Earnhardt	2001	Jeff Gordon
1956	Buck Baker	1968	David Pearson	1980	Dale Earnhardt	1991	Dale Earnhardt	2002	Tony Stewart
1957	Buck Baker	1969	David Pearson	1981	Darrell Waltrip	1992	Alan Kulwicki	2003	Matt Kenseth
1958	Lee Petty	1970	Bobby Isaac	1982	Darrell Waltrip	1993	Dale Earnhardt	2004	Kurt Busch
1959	Lee Petty	1971	Richard Petty	1983	Bobby Allison	1994	Dale Earnhardt	2005	Tony Stewart
1960	Rex White	1972	Richard Petty						

NASCAR Rookie of the Year, 1958-2005

Year	Driver	Year	Driver	Year	Driver	Year	Driver	Year	Driver
1958	Shorty Rollins	1968	Pete Hamilton	1978	Ronnie Thomas	1988	Ken Bouchard	1997	Mike Skinner
1959	Richard Petty	1969	Dick Brooks	1979	Dale Earnhardt	1989	Dick Trickle	1998	Kenny Irwin
1960	David Pearson	1970	Bill Dennis	1980	Jody Riley	1990	Rob Moroso	1999	Tony Stewart
1961	Woodie Wilson	1971	Walter Ballard	1981	Ron Bouchard	1991	Bobby Hamilton	2000	Matt Kenseth
1962	Tom Cox	1972	Larry Smith	1982	Geoff Bodine	1992	Jimmy Hensley	2001	Kevin Harvick
1963	Billy Wade	1973	Lennie Pond	1983	Sterling Marlin	1993	Jeff Gordon	2002	Ryan Newman
1964	Doug Cooper	1974	Earl Ross	1984	Rusty Wallace	1994	Jeff Burton	2003	Jamie McMurray
1965	Sam McQuagg	1975	Bruce Hill	1985	Ken Schrader	1995	Ricky Craven	2004	Kasey Kahne
1966	James Hylton	1976	Skip Manning	1986	Alan Kulwicki	1996	Johnny Benson	2005	Kyle Busch
1967	Donnie Allison	1977	Ricky Rudd	1987	Davey Allison				

Daytona 500 Winners, 1959-2006
(At Daytona International Speedway in Daytona Beach, FL)

Year	Driver, car	Avg. MPH	Year	Driver, car	Avg. MPH	Year	Driver, car	Avg. MPH
1959	Lee Petty, Oldsmobile	135.521	1975	Benny Parsons, Chevrolet	153.649	1991	Ernie Irvan, Chevrolet	148.148
1960	Junior Johnson, Chevrolet	124.740	1976	David Pearson, Mercury	152.181	1992	Davey Allison, Ford	160.256
1961	Marvin Panch, Pontiac	149.601	1977	Cale Yarborough, Chevrolet	153.218	1993	Dale Jarrett, Chevrolet	154.972
1962	Fireball Roberts, Pontiac	152.529	1978	Bobby Allison, Ford	159.730	1994	Sterling Marlin, Chevrolet	156.931
1963	Tiny Lund, Ford	151.566	1979	Richard Petty, Oldsmobile	143.977	1995	Sterling Marlin, Chevrolet	141.710
1964	Richard Petty, Plymouth	154.334	1980	Buddy Baker, Oldsmobile	177.602	1996	Dale Jarrett, Ford	154.308
1965	Fred Lorenzen, Ford (a)	141.539	1981	Richard Petty, Buick	169.651	1997	Jeff Gordon, Chevrolet	148.295
1966	Richard Petty, Plymouth (b)	160.627	1982	Bobby Allison, Buick	153.991	1998	Dale Earnhardt, Chevrolet	172.712
1967	Mario Andretti, Ford	146.926	1983	Cale Yarborough, Pontiac	155.979	1999	Jeff Gordon, Chevrolet	161.551
1968	Cale Yarborough, Mercury	143.251	1984	Cale Yarborough, Chevrolet	150.994	2000	Dale Jarrett, Ford	155.669
1969	LeeRoy Yarbrough, Ford	160.875	1985	Bill Elliott, Ford	172.265	2001	Michael Waltrip, Chevrolet	161.783
1970	Pete Hamilton, Plymouth	149.601	1986	Geoff Bodine, Chevrolet	148.124	2002	Ward Burton, Dodge	142.971
1971	Richard Petty, Plymouth	144.456	1987	Bill Elliott, Ford	176.263	2003	Michael Waltrip, Chevrolet (d)	133.870
1972	A. J. Foyt, Mercury	161.550	1988	Bobby Allison, Buick	137.531	2004	Dale Earnhardt Jr., Chevrolet	156.345
1973	Richard Petty, Dodge	157.205	1989	Darrell Waltrip, Chevrolet	148.466	2005	Jeff Gordon, Chevrolet	135.173
1974	Richard Petty, Dodge (c)	140.894	1990	Derrike Cope, Chevrolet	165.761	2006	Jimmie Johnson, Chevrolet	142.667

(a) 322.5 mi. (b) 495 mi. (c) 450 mi. (d) 272.5 mi.

Coca-Cola 600 Winners, 1960-2006
(At Lowe's Motor Speedway in Concord, NC. Known as World 600, 1960-85. *=rain-shortened.)

Year	Driver, car	Avg. MPH	Year	Driver, car	Avg. MPH	Year	Driver, car	Avg. MPH
1960	Joe Lee Johnson, Chevrolet	107.735	1976	David Pearson, Mercury	137.352	1992	Dale Earnhardt, Chevrolet	132.980
1961	David Pearson, Pontiac	111.633	1977	Richard Petty, Dodge	137.676	1993	Dale Earnhardt, Chevrolet	145.504
1962	Nelson Stacy, Ford	125.552	1978	Darrell Waltrip, Chevrolet	138.355	1994	Jeff Gordon, Chevrolet	139.445
1963	Fred Lorenzen, Ford	132.418	1979	Darrell Waltrip, Chevrolet	136.674	1995	Bobby Labonte, Chevrolet	151.952
1964	Jim Paschal, Plymouth	125.772	1980	Benny Parsons, Chevrolet	119.265	1996	Dale Jarrett, Ford	147.581
1965	Fred Lorenzen, Ford	121.772	1981	Bobby Allison, Buick	129.326	1997	Jeff Gordon, Chevrolet*	136.745
1966	Marvin Panch, Plymouth	135.042	1982	Neil Bonnett, Ford	130.058	1998	Jeff Gordon, Chevrolet	136.424
1967	Jim Paschal, Plymouth	135.832	1983	Neil Bonnett, Chevrolet	140.707	1999	Jeff Burton, Ford	151.367
1968	Buddy Baker, Dodge*	104.207	1984	Bobby Allison, Buick	129.233	2000	Matt Kenseth, Ford	142.640
1969	LeeRoy Yarborough, Mercury	134.361	1985	Darrell Waltrip, Chevrolet	141.807	2001	Jeff Burton, Ford	138.107
1970	Donnie Allison, Ford	129.680	1986	Dale Earnhardt, Chevrolet	140.406	2002	Mark Martin, Ford	137.729
1971	Bobby Allison, Mercury	140.422	1987	Kyle Petty, Ford	131.483	2003	Jimmie Johnson, Chevrolet*	126.198
1972	Buddy Baker, Dodge	142.255	1988	Darrell Waltrip, Chevrolet	124.460	2004	Jimmie Johnson, Chevrolet	142.763
1973	Buddy Baker, Dodge	134.890	1989	Darrell Waltrip, Chevrolet	144.077	2005	Jimmie Johnson, Chevrolet	114.698
1974	David Pearson, Mercury	135.720	1990	Rusty Wallace, Pontiac	137.650	2006	Kasey Kahne, Dodge	128.840
1975	Richard Petty, Dodge	145.327	1991	Davey Allison, Ford	138.951			

Allstate Brickyard 400 Winners, 1994-2006
(At Indianapolis Motor Speedway in Indianapolis, IN)

Year	Driver, car	Avg. MPH	Year	Driver, car	Avg. MPH	Year	Driver, car	Avg. MPH
1994	Jeff Gordon, Chevrolet	131.977	1999	Dale Jarrett, Ford	148.194	2003	Kevin Harvick, Chevrolet	134.554
1995	Dale Earnhardt, Chevrolet	155.206	2000	Bobby Labonte, Pontiac	155.912	2004	Jeff Gordon, Chevrolet	115.037
1996	Dale Jarrett, Ford	139.508	2001	Jeff Gordon, Chevrolet	130.790	2005	Tony Stewart, Chevrolet	118.782
1997	Ricky Rudd, Ford	130.814	2002	Bill Elliott, Dodge	125.033	2006	Jimmie Johnson, Chevrolet	137.180
1998	Jeff Gordon, Chevrolet	126.772						

Sharpie 500 Winners, 1961-2006

(At Bristol Motor Speedway in Bristol, TN. Known as the Volunteer 500, 1961-75, '78-79; Volunteer 400, 1976-77; Busch 500, 1980-90; Bud 500, 1991-93; Goody's 500, 1994-99; goracing.com 500, 2000. * = rain-shortened)

Year	Driver, car	Avg. MPH	Year	Driver, car	Avg. MPH	Year	Driver, car	Avg. MPH
1961	Jack Smith, Pontiac	68.37	1977	Cale Yarborough, Chevrolet	79.726	1992	Darrell Waltrip, Chevrolet	91.198
1962	Bobby Johns, Pontiac	73.32	1978	Cale Yarborough, Oldsmobile	88.628	1993	Mark Martin, Ford	88.172
1963	Fred Lorenzen, Ford	74.844	1979	Darrell Waltrip, Chevrolet	91.493	1994	Rusty Wallace, Ford	91.363
1964	Fred Lorenzen, Ford	78.044	1980	Cale Yarborough, Chevrolet	86.973	1995	Terry Labonte, Chevrolet	81.979
1965	Ned Jarrett, Ford	61.826	1981	Darrell Waltrip, Buick	84.723	1996	Rusty Wallace, Ford	91.267
1966	Paul Goldsmith, Plymouth	77.963	1982	Darrell Waltrip, Buick	94.318	1997	Dale Jarrett, Ford	80.013
1967	Richard Petty, Plymouth	78.705	1983	Darrell Waltrip, Chevrolet*	89.43	1998	Mark Martin, Ford	86.949
1968	David Pearson, Ford	76.31	1984	Terry Labonte, Chevrolet	85.365	1999	Dale Earnhardt, Chevrolet	91.276
1969	David Pearson, Ford	79.737	1985	Dale Earnhardt, Chevrolet	81.388	2000	Rusty Wallace, Ford	85.394
1970	Bobby Allison, Dodge	84.88	1986	Darrell Waltrip, Chevrolet	86.934	2001	Tony Stewart, Pontiac	85.106
1971	Charlie Glotzbach, Chevrolet	101.074	1987	Dale Earnhardt, Chevrolet	90.373	2002	Jeff Gordon, Chevrolet	77.097
1972	Bobby Allison, Chevrolet	92.735	1988	Dale Earnhardt, Chevrolet	78.775	2003	Kurt Busch, Ford	77.421
1973	Benny Parsons, Chevrolet	91.342	1989	Darrell Waltrip, Chevrolet	85.554	2004	Dale Earnhardt, Jr., Chevrolet	88.538
1974	Cale Yarborough, Chevrolet	75.43	1990	Ernie Irvan, Chevrolet	91.782	2005	Matt Kenseth, Ford	84.678
1975	Richard Petty, Dodge	97.016	1991	Alan Kulwicki, Ford	82.028	2006	Matt Kenseth, Ford	90.025
1976	Cale Yarborough, Chevrolet	99.175						

NASCAR Nextel All-Star Race

(at Lowe's Motor Speedway in Concord, NC. Known as The Winston, 1985-2003; The Winston Select, 1995-96.)

Year	Driver	Year	Driver	Year	Driver
1985	Darrell Waltrip, Chevrolet	1993	Dale Earnhardt, Chevrolet	2000	Dale Earnhardt Jr., Chevrolet
1986	Bill Elliott, Ford	1994	Geoffrey Bodine, Ford	2001	Jeff Gordon, Chevrolet
1987	Dale Earnhardt, Chevrolet	1995	Jeff Gordon, Chevrolet	2002	Ryan Newman, Ford
1988	Terry Labonte, Chevrolet	1996	Michael Waltrip, Chevrolet	2003	Jimmie Johnson, Chevrolet
1989	Rusty Wallace, Ford	1997	Jeff Gordon, Chevrolet	2004	Matt Kenseth, Ford
1990	Dale Earnhardt, Chevrolet	1998	Mark Martin, Ford	2005	Mark Martin, Ford
1991	Davey Allison, Ford	1999	Terry Labonte, Chevrolet	2006	Jimmie Johnson, Chevrolet
1992	Davey Allison, Ford				

Formula One Racing
World Grand Prix Champions, 1950-2005

Year	Driver	Year	Driver	Year	Driver
1950	Nino Farini, Italy	1969	Jackie Stewart, Scotland	1988	Ayrton Senna, Brazil
1951	Juan Manuel Fangio, Argentina	1970	Jochen Rindt, Austria	1989	Alain Prost, France
1952	Alberto Ascari, Italy	1971	Jackie Stewart, Scotland	1990	Ayrton Senna, Brazil
1953	Alberto Ascari, Italy	1972	Emerson Fittipaldi, Brazil	1991	Ayrton Senna, Brazil
1954	Juan Manuel Fangio, Argentina	1973	Jackie Stewart, Scotland	1992	Nigel Mansell, Britain
1955	Juan Manuel Fangio, Argentina	1974	Emerson Fittipaldi, Brazil	1993	Alain Prost, France
1956	Juan Manuel Fangio, Argentina	1975	Niki Lauda, Austria	1994	Michael Schumacher, Germany
1957	Juan Manuel Fangio, Argentina	1976	James Hunt, England	1995	Michael Schumacher, Germany
1958	Mike Hawthorne, England	1977	Niki Lauda, Austria	1996	Damon Hill, England
1959	Jack Brabham, Australia	1978	Mario Andretti, United States	1997	Jacques Villeneuve, Canada
1960	Jack Brabham, Australia	1979	Jody Scheckter, South Africa	1998	Mika Hakkinen, Finland
1961	Phil Hill, United States	1980	Alan Jones, Australia	1999	Mika Hakkinen, Finland
1962	Graham Hill, England	1981	Nelson Piquet, Brazil	2000	Michael Schumacher, Germany
1963	Jim Clark, Scotland	1982	Keke Rosberg, Finland	2001	Michael Schumacher, Germany
1964	John Surtees, England	1983	Nelson Piquet, Brazil	2002	Michael Schumacher, Germany
1965	Jim Clark, Scotland	1984	Niki Lauda, Austria	2003	Michael Schumacher, Germany
1966	Jack Brabham, Australia	1985	Alain Prost, France	2004	Michael Schumacher, Germany
1967	Denis Hulme, New Zealand	1986	Alain Prost, France	2005	Fernando Alonso, Spain
1968	Graham Hill, England	1987	Nelson Piquet, Brazil		

2006 Le Mans 24 Hours Race

The Audi Sport Team Joest—led by drivers Frank Biela and Marco Werner (Germany) and Emanuele Pirro (Italy)—won the 74th Le Mans 24 Hours Race on June 18, 2006. Werner had also been on the winning Le Mans team the previous year. The Audi R10 became the first ever diesel-engine-powered sports car to win the endurance race. Audi teams have won 6 of the last 7 Le Mans 24 Hours Races. Following the race, Peugeot announced their decision to field a diesel-run model in next year's Le Mans.

Notable One-Mile Land Speed Records

Andy Green, a Royal Air Force pilot, broke the sound barrier and set the first supersonic world speed record on land, Oct. 15, 1997, in Black Rock Desert, NV. Green, driving a car built by Richard Noble, had 2 runs at an average speed of 763.035 mph, as calculated under the rules of the Fédération Internationale de l'Automobile (FIA). This record and speed exceeded the speed of sound, calculated at 751.251 mph for that place and time.

Date	Driver	Car	MPH	Date	Driver	Car	MPH
1/26/1906	Marriott	Stanley (Steam)	127.659	11/19/37	Eyston	Thunderbolt 1	311.42
3/16/10	Oldfield	Benz	131.724	9/16/38	Eyston	Thunderbolt 1	357.5
4/23/11	Burman	Benz	141.732	8/23/39	Cobb	Railton	368.9
2/12/19	DePalma	Packard	149.875	9/16/47	Cobb	Railton-Mobil	394.2
4/27/20	Milton	Dusenberg	155.046	8/05/63	Breedlove	Spirit of America	407.45
4/28/26	Parry-Thomas	Thomas Spl.	170.624	10/27/64	Arfons	Green Monster	536.71
3/29/27	Seagrave	Sunbeam	203.790	11/15/65	Breedlove	Spirit of America	600.601
4/22/28	Keech	White Triplex	207.552	10/23/70	Gabelich	Blue Flame	622.407
3/11/29	Seagrave	Irving-Napier	231.446	10/09/79	Barrett	Budweiser Rocket	638.637*
2/05/31	Campbell	Napier-Campbell	246.086	10/04/83	Noble	Thrust 2	633.468
2/24/32	Campbell	Napier-Campbell	253.96	9/25/97	Green	Thrust SSC	714.144
2/22/33	Campbell	Napier-Campbell	272.109	10/15/97	Green	Thrust SSC	763.035
9/03/35	Campbell	Bluebird Special	301.13				

*Not recognized as official by sanctioning bodies.

BOXING

There are many boxing governing bodies, including the World Boxing Council, World Boxing Assn., International Boxing Fed., World Boxing Org., U.S. Boxing Assn., N. American Boxing Fed., and European Boxing Union. All have their own champions and divisions.

Champions by Classes*

Class (weight limit)	WBA	WBC	IBF
Heavyweight	Nicolay Valuev, Russia	Oleg Maskaev, Kazakhstan	Wladimir Klitschko, Ukraine
Cruiserweight (200 lb)	O'Neil Bell, Jamaica[1]	O'Neil Bell, Jamaica	Vacant
Light Heavyweight (175 lb)	Fabrice Tiozzo, France	Tomasz Adamek, Poland	Clinton Woods, England
Super Middleweight (168 lb)	Mikkel Kessler, Denmark	Markus Beyer, Germany	Joe Calzaghe, England
Middleweight (160 lb)	Jermain Taylor, U.S.[2]	Jermain Taylor, U.S.	Arthur Abraham, Germany
Jr. Middleweight (154 lb)	Jose Rivera, U.S.	Oscar de la Hoya, U.S.	Cory Spinks, U.S.
Welterweight (147 lb)	Ricky Hatton, England	Carlos Baldomir, Argentina	Vacant
Jr. Welterweight (140 lb)	Souleymane M'baye, France	Junior Witter, England	Juan Urango, Colombia
Lightweight (135 lb)	Juan Diaz, U.S.	Joel Casamayor, Cuba	Vacant
Jr. Lightweight (130 lb)	Edwin Velero, Venezuela	Marco Antonio Barrera, Mexico	Gairy St. Clair, Australia
Featherweight (126 lb)	Chris John, Indonesia	Rodolfo Lopez, Mexico	Robert Guerrero, U.S.
Jr. Featherweight (122 lb)	Celestino Caballero, Panama	Israel Vazquez, Mexico	Vacant
Bantamweight (118 lb)	Wladimir Sidorenko, Ukraine	Hozumi Hasegawa, Japan	Rafael Márquez, Mexico
Jr. Bantamweight (115 lb)	Nabuo Nashiro, Japan	Masamori Tokuyama, Japan	Luis Perez, Nicaragua
Flyweight (112 lb)	Lorenzo Parra, Venezuela	Pongsaklek Wonjongkam, Thailand	Vic Darchinyan, Australia
Jr. Flyweight (108 lb)	Koki Kameda, Japan	Omar Niño Romero, Mexico	Ulises Solis, Mexico
Strawweight (105 lb)	Yukata Niida, Japan	Eagle Kyowa, Thailand	Muhammad Rachman, Indo.

*As of Oct. 10, 2006. **Note:** Interim champions not listed. The WBA and WBC designate certain title holders as "Super World Champs" (listed above) and permit concurrent "World" champions in those classes. Following are the "World" champions: (1) Virgil Hill, U.S., cruiserweight. (2) Javier Castillejo, Spain, middleweight.

Ring Champions by Years

(*abandoned the title or was stripped of it; IBF champions listed only for heavyweight division)

Heavyweights

1882-1892	John L. Sullivan (a)	1973-1974	George Foreman	1992-1994	Lennox Lewis (WBC)
1892-1897	James J. Corbett (b)	1974-1978	Muhammad Ali	1993-1994	Evander Holyfield (WBA, IBF)
1897-1899	Robert Fitzsimmons	1978-1979	Muhammad Ali* (WBA)	1994	Michael Moorer (WBA, IBF)
1899-1905	James J. Jeffries* (c)	1978	Leon Spinks (WBC*, WBA) (e);	1994-1995	Oliver McCall (WBC);
1905-1906	Marvin Hart		Ken Norton (WBC)		George Foreman (WBA*, IBF*)
1906-1908	Tommy Burns	1978-1983	Larry Holmes* (WBC) (f)	1995	Frans Botha* (IBF)
1908-1915	Jack Johnson	1979-1980	John Tate (WBA)	1995-1996	Bruce Seldon (WBA);
1915-1919	Jess Willard	1980-1982	Mike Weaver (WBA)		Frank Bruno (WBC)
1919-1926	Jack Dempsey	1982-1983	Michael Dokes (WBA)	1996	Mike Tyson (WBC*, WBA)
1926-1928	Gene Tunney*	1983-1984	Gerrie Coetzee (WBA)	1996-1997	Michael Moorer (IBF)
1928-1930	Vacant	1983-1985	Larry Holmes (IBF) (f)	1996-1997	Evander Holyfield (WBA, IBF)
1930-1932	Max Schmeling	1984	Tim Witherspoon (WBC)	1997-2001	Lennox Lewis (WBC)
1932-1933	Jack Sharkey	1984-1985	Greg Page (WBA)	1999-2001	Lennox Lewis (WBA*, WBC, IBF)
1933-1934	Primo Carnera	1984-1986	Pinklon Thomas (WBC)	2000-2001	Evander Holyfield (WBA)
1934-1935	Max Baer	1985-1986	Tony Tubbs (WBA)	2001-2004	John Ruiz (WBA)
1935-1937	James J. Braddock	1985-1987	Michael Spinks* (IBF)	2001	Hasim Rahman (WBC, IBF)
1937-1949	Joe Louis*	1986	Tim Witherspoon (WBA);	2001-2002	Lennox Lewis (IBF*)
1949-1951	Ezzard Charles		Trevor Berbick (WBC)	2001-2004	Lennox Lewis (WBC)
1951-1952	Joe Walcott	1986-1987	Mike Tyson (WBC); James	2002-2006	Chris Byrd (IBF)
1952-1956	Rocky Marciano*		"Bonecrusher" Smith (WBA)	2003	Roy Jones Jr. (WBA)
1956-1959	Floyd Patterson	1987	Tony Tucker (IBF)	2004-2005	Vitali Klitschko (WBC*);
1959-1960	Ingemar Johansson	1987-1990	Mike Tyson (WBC, WBA, IBF)		John Ruiz (WBA)
1960-1962	Floyd Patterson	1990	"Buster" Douglas (WBA, WBC,	2005-2006	Hasim Rahman (WBC)
1962-1964	Sonny Liston		IBF)		James Toney (WBA)(g)*;
1964-1967	Cassius Clay (Muhammad Ali) (d)	1990-1992	Evander Holyfield (WBA, WBC,		Nicolay Valuev (WBA)
1970-1973	Joe Frazier		IBF)	2006	Oleg Maskaev (WBC)
		1992-1993	Riddick Bowe (WBA, IBF,WBC*)		Wladimir Klitschko (IBF)

(a) London Prize Ring (bare knuckle champion). (b) First Marquis of Queensberry champion. (c) Jeffries vacated title (1905), designated Marvin Hart and Jack Root as logical contenders. Hart defeated Root in 12 rounds (1905), in turn was defeated by Tommy Burns (1906), who claimed the title. Jack Johnson def. Burns (1908) and was recognized as champ. Johnson won the title by defeating Jeffries in the latter's attempted comeback (1910). (d) Title declared vacant by the WBA and others in 1967 after Ali refused military induction. Joe Frazier recognized as champ by 6 states, Mexico, and S. America. Jimmy Ellis declared champ by the WBA. Frazier KOd Ellis, Feb. 16, 1970. (e) After Spinks defeated Ali, the WBC recognized Ken Norton as champ. Ali defeated Spinks in 1978 rematch for WBA title, retired in 1979. (f) Holmes relinquished WBC title in Dec. 1983, to fight as champ of the new IBF. (g) Toney defeated Ruiz to claim the title, but it was rescinded when Toney tested positive for steroids.

Light Heavyweights

1903	Jack Root, George Gardner	1963-1965	Willie Pastrano	1987	Thomas Hearns* (WBC)
1903-1905	Bob Fitzsimmons	1965-1966	Jose Torres	1987-1988	Don Lalonde (WBC)
1905-1912	Philadelphia Jack O'Brien*	1966-1968	Dick Tiger	1988	Sugar Ray Leonard* (WBC)
1912-1916	Jack Dillon	1968-1974	Bob Foster*	1989	Dennis Andries (WBC)
1916-1920	Battling Levinsky	1974-1977	John Conteh (WBC)	1989-1990	Jeff Harding (WBC)
1920-1922	George Carpentier	1974-1978	Victor Galindez (WBA)	1990-1991	Dennis Andries (WBC)
1922-1923	Battling Siki	1977-1978	Miguel Cuello (WBC)	1991-1994	Jeff Harding (WBC)
1923-1925	Mike McTigue	1978	Mate Parlov (WBC)	1991-1992	Thomas Hearns (WBA)
1925-1926	Paul Berlenbach	1978-1979	Mike Rossman (WBA);	1992	Iran Barkley* (WBA)
1926-1927	Jack Delaney*		Marvin Johnson (WBC)	1992-1997	Virgil Hill (WBA)
1927-1929	Tommy Loughran*	1979-1981	Matthew Saad Muhammad	1994-1995	Mike McCallum (WBC)
1930-1934	Maxey Rosenbloom		(WBC)	1995-1996	Fabrice Tiozzo* (WBC)
1934-1935	Bob Olin	1979-1980	Marvin Johnson (WBA)	1996-1997	Roy Jones Jr. (WBC)
1935-1939	John Henry Lewis*	1980-1981	Eddie Mustafa Muhammad	1997	Montell Griffin (WBC);
1939	Melio Bettina		(WBA)		Roy Jones Jr. (WBC);
1939-1941	Billy Conn*	1981-1983	Michael Spinks (WBA);		Darius Michalczewski* (WBA)
1941	Anton Christoforidis (won NBA		Dwight Braxton (WBC)	1997-1998	Lou Del Valle (WBA)
	title)	1983-1985	Michael Spinks*	1998-2003	Roy Jones Jr. (WBA*, WBC*)
1941-1948	Gus Lesnevich, Freddie Mills	1985-1986	J. B. Williamson (WBC)	2003	Mehdi Sahnoune (WBA)
1948-1950	Freddie Mills	1986-1987	Marvin Johnson (WBA);	2003-2004	Antonio Tarver (WBC)
1950-1952	Joey Maxim		Dennis Andries (WBC)	2004-2006	Fabrice Tiozzo (WBA)
1952-1962	Archie Moore	1987	Leslie Stewart (WBA)	2005-2006	Tomasz Adamek (WBC)
1962-1963	Harold Johnson	1987-1991	Virgil Hill (WBA)		

Middleweights

1884-1891	Jack "Nonpareil" Dempsey	1955-1957	Ray Robinson	1980-1987	Marvin Hagler
1891-1897	Bob Fitzsimmons*	1957	Gene Fullmer; Ray Robinson	1987	Sugar Ray Leonard* (WBC)
1897-1907	Tommy Ryan*	1957-1958	Carmen Basilio	1987-1989	Sumbu Kalambay (WBA)
1907-1908	Stanley Ketchel; Billy Papke	1958	Ray Robinson	1987-1988	Thomas Hearns (WBC)
1908-1910	Stanley Ketchel	1959	Gene Fullmer (NBA);	1988-1989	Iran Barkley (WBC)
1911-1913	vacant		Ray Robinson (NY)	1989-1990	Roberto Duran* (WBC)
1913	Frank Klaus; George Chip	1960	Gene Fullmer (NBA);	1989-1991	Mike McCallum (WBA)
1914-1917	Al McCoy		Paul Pender (NY and MA)	1990-1993	Julian Jackson (WBC)
1917-1920	Mike O'Dowd	1961	Gene Fullmer (NBA); Terry	1992-1993	Reggie Johnson (WBA)
1920-1923	Johnny Wilson		Downes (NY, MA, Europe)	1993-1995	Gerald McClellan* (WBC)
1923-1926	Harry Greb	1962	Gene Fullmer; Dick Tiger (NBA);	1993-1994	John David Jackson (WBA)
1926-1931	Tiger Flowers; Mickey Walker		Paul Pender (NY and MA)*	1994-1997	Jorge Castro (WBA)
1931-1932	Gorilla Jones (NBA)	1963	Dick Tiger (universal)	1995	Julian Jackson (WBA)
1932-1937	Marcel Thil	1963-1965	Joey Giardello	1995-1996	Quincy Taylor (WBC);
1938	Al Hostak (NBA);	1965-1966	Dick Tiger		Shinji Takehara (WBA)
	Solly Krieger (NBA)	1966-1967	Emile Griffith	1996-1998	Keith Holmes (WBC)
1939-1940	Al Hostak (NBA)	1967	Nino Benvenuti	1996-1997	William Joppy (WBA)
1941-1947	Tony Zale	1967-1968	Emile Griffith	1997	Julio Cesar Green (WBA)
1947-1948	Rocky Graziano	1968-1970	Nino Benvenuti	1998-2001	William Joppy (WBA)
1948	Tony Zale; Marcel Cerdan	1970-1977	Carlos Monzon*	1998-1999	Hassine Cherifi (WBC)
1949-1951	Jake LaMotta	1977-1978	Rodrigo Valdez	1999-2001	Keith Holmes (WBC)
1951	Ray Robinson; Randy Turpin;	1978-1979	Hugo Corro	2001	Felix Trinidad (WBA)
	Ray Robinson*	1979-1980	Vito Antuofermo	2001-2004	Bernard Hopkins (WBC, WBA)
1953-1955	Carl (Bobo) Olson	1980	Alan Minter	2005-2006	Jermain Taylor (WBC, WBA)

Welterweights

1892-1894	Mysterious Billy Smith	1951-1954	Kid Gavilan	1986-1987	Lloyd Honeyghan (WBC)
1894-1896	Tommy Ryan	1954-1955	Johnny Saxton	1987	Mark Breland (WBA)
1896	Kid McCoy*	1955	Tony De Marco	1987-1988	Marlon Starling (WBA);
1900	Rube Ferns; Matty Matthews	1955-1956	Carmen Basilio		Jorge Vaca (WBC)
1901	Rube Ferns	1956	Johnny Saxton	1988-1989	Tomas Molinares (WBA);
1901-1904	Joe Walcott	1956-1957	Carmen Basilio*		Lloyd Honeyghan (WBC)
1904-1906	Dixie Kid; Joe Walcott;	1958	Virgil Akins	1989-1990	Marlon Starling (WBC);
	Honey Mellody	1958-1960	Don Jordan		Mark Breland (WBA)
1907-1911	Mike Sullivan	1960-1961	Benny Paret	1990-1991	Maurice Blocker (WBC);
1911-1915	Vacant	1961	Emile Griffith		Aaron Davis (WBA)
1915-1919	Ted Lewis	1961-1962	Benny Paret	1991	Simon Brown (WBC)
1919-1922	Jack Britton	1962-1963	Emile Griffith	1991-1992	Meldrick Taylor (WBA)
1922-1926	Mickey Walker	1963	Luis Rodriguez	1991-1993	Buddy McGirt (WBC)
1926	Pete Latzo	1963-1966	Emile Griffith*	1992-1994	Crisanto Espana (WBA)
1927-1929	Joe Dundee	1966-1969	Curtis Cokes	1993-1997	Pernell Whitaker (WBC)
1929	Jackie Fields	1969-1970	Jose Napoles	1994-1998	Ike Quartey (WBA*)
1930	Jack Thompson; Tommy Freeman	1970-1971	Billy Backus	1997-1999	Oscar De La Hoya (WBC*)
1931	Tommy Freeman;	1971-1975	Jose Napoles	1998	James Page (WBA*)
	Jack Thompson;	1975-1976	John Stracey (WBC);	1999-2000	Felix Trinidad (WBC*)
	Lou Brouillard		Angel Espada (WBA)	2000	Oscar De La Hoya (WBC*)
1932	Jackie Fields	1976-1979	Carlos Palomino (WBC)	2000-2002	Shane Mosley (WBC)
1933	Young Corbett; Jimmy McLarnin	1976-1980	Jose Cuevas (WBA)	2001-2002	Andrew Lewis (WBA)
1934	Barney Ross; Jimmy McLarnin	1979	Wilfredo Benitez (WBC)	2002	Ricardo Mayorga (WBA)
1935-1938	Barney Ross	1979-1980	Sugar Ray Leonard (WBC)	2002-2003	Vernon Forrest (WBC)
1938-1940	Henry Armstrong	1980	Roberto Duran (WBC)	2003	Ricardo Mayorga (WBA, WBC)
1940-1941	Fritzie Zivic	1980-1981	Thomas Hearns (WBA)	2003-2005	Cory Spinks (WBA, WBC)
1941-1946	Fred Cochrane	1980-1982	Sugar Ray Leonard*	2005-2006	Zab Judah (WBA, WBC)
1946	Marty Servo*	1983-1985	Donald Curry (WBA);	2006	Ricky Hatton (WBA); Carlos
1946-1951	Ray Robinson* (a)		Milton McCrory (WBC)		Baldomir (WBC)
1951	Johnny Bratton (NBA)	1985-1986	Donald Curry		

(a) Robinson gained the title by defeating Tommy Bell in an elimination agreed to by the New York Commission and the National Boxing Association. Both claimed Robinson waived his title when he won the middleweight crown from LaMotta in 1951.

Lightweights

1896-1899	Kid Lavigne	1956	Bud Smith; Joe Brown	1987-1988	Julio Cesar Chavez (WBA);
1899-1902	Frank Erne	1956-1962	Joe Brown		Jose Luis Ramirez (WBC)
1902-1908	Joe Gans	1962-1965	Carlos Ortiz	1988-1989	Julio Cesar Chavez (WBA, WBC)
1908-1910	Battling Nelson	1965	Ismael Laguna	1989-1990	Edwin Rosario (WBA);
1910-1912	Ad Wolgast	1965-1968	Carlos Ortiz		Pernell Whitaker (WBC)
1912-1914	Willie Ritchie	1968-1969	Teo Cruz	1990	Juan Nazario (WBA)
1914-1917	Freddie Welsh	1969-1970	Mando Ramos	1990-1992	Pernell Whitaker*
1917-1925	Benny Leonard*	1970	Ismael Laguna	1992	Joey Gamache (WBA)
1925	Jimmy Goodrich;	1970-1972	Ken Buchanan (WBA)	1992-1996	Miguel Angel Gonzalez* (WBC)
	Rocky Kansas	1971-1972	Pedro Carrasco (WBC)	1992-1993	Tony Lopez (WBA)
1926-1930	Sammy Mandell	1972-1979	Roberto Duran* (WBA)	1993	Dingaan Thobela (WBA)
1930	Al Singer; Tony Canzoneri	1972	Mando Ramos (WBC);	1993-1998	Orzubek Nazarov (WBA)
1930-1933	Tony Canzoneri		Chango Carmona (WBC)	1996-1997	Jean-Baptiste Mendy (WBC)
1933-1935	Barney Ross*	1972-1974	Rodolfo Gonzalez (WBC)	1997-1999	Steve Johnston (WBC)
1935-1936	Tony Canzoneri	1974-1976	Ishimatsu Suzuki (WBC)	1998-1999	Jean-Baptiste Mendy (WBA);
1936-1938	Lou Ambers	1976-1978	Esteban De Jesus (WBC)		Cesar Bazan (WBC)
1938	Henry Armstrong	1979-1981	Jim Watt (WBC)	1999	Julian Lorcy (WBA);
1939	Lou Ambers	1979-1980	Ernesto Espana (WBA)		Stefano Zoff (WBA)
1940	Lew Jenkins	1980-1981	Hilmer Kenty (WBA)	1999-2000	Gilberto Serrano (WBA);
1941-1943	Sammy Angott	1981	Sean O'Grady (WBA);		Steve Johnston (WBC)
1944	S. Angott (NBA); J. Zurita (NBA)		Claude Noel (WBA)	2000-2001	Takanori Hatakeyama (WBA);
1945-1951	Ike Williams (NBA: later	1981-1983	Alexis Arguello* (WBC)	2000-2002	Jose Luis Castillo (WBC)
	universal)	1981-1982	Arturo Frias (WBA)	2001	Julien Lorcy (WBA)
1951-1952	James Carter	1982-1984	Ray Mancini (WBA)	2001-2002	Raul Balbi (WBA)
1952	Lauro Salas; James Carter	1983-1984	Edwin Rosario (WBC)	2002-2003	Leonard Dorin (WBA)
1953-1954	James Carter	1984-1986	Livingstone Bramble (WBA)	2002-2004	Floyd Mayweather (WBC)
1954	Paddy De Marco;	1984-1985	Jose Luis Ramirez (WBC)	2004-2006	Juan Diaz (WBA)
	James Carter	1985-1986	Hector (Macho) Camacho (WBC)	2005-2006	Diego Corrales (WBC)
1955	James Carter; Bud Smith	1986-1987	Edwin Rosario (WBA)	2006	Joel Casamayor (WBC)

Featherweights

1892-1900	George Dixon (disputed)	1968	Paul Rojas (WBA)	1986-1987	Steve Cruz (WBA)
1900-1901	Terry McGovern;	1968-1969	Jose Legra (WBC)	1987-1991	Antonio Esparragoza (WBA)
	Young Corbett*	1968-1971	Shozo Saijyo (WBA)	1988-1990	Jeff Fenech* (WBC)
1901-1912	Abe Attell	1969-1970	Johnny Famechon (WBC)	1990-1991	Marcos Villasana (WBC)
1912-1923	Johnny Kilbane	1970	Vicente Salvidar (WBC)	1991-1993	Park Yung Kyun (WBA);
1923	Eugene Criqui; Johnny Dundee	1970-1972	Kuniaki Shibata (WBC)		Paul Hodkinson (WBC)
1923-1925	Johnny Dundee*	1971-1972	Antonio Gomez (WBA)	1993	Goyo Vargas (WBC)
1925-1927	Kid Kaplan*	1972	Clemente Sanchez* (WBC)	1993-1995	Kevin Kelley (WBC)
1927-1928	Benny Bass; Tony Canzoneri	1972-1974	Ernesto Marcel* (WBA)	1993-1996	Eloy Rojas (WBA)
1928-1929	Andre Routis	1972-1973	Jose Legra (WBC)	1995	Alejandro Gonzalez (WBC)
1929-1932	Battling Battalino*	1973-1974	Eder Jofre* (WBC)	1995-1996	Manuel Medina (WBC)
1932-1934	Tommy Paul (NBA)	1974	Ruben Olivares (WBA)	1995-1999	Luisito Espinosa (WBC)
1933-1936	Freddie Miller	1974-1975	Bobby Chacon (WBC)	1996-1997	Wilfredo Vasquez* (WBA)
1936-1937	Petey Sarron	1974-1976	Alexis Arguello* (WBA)	1998	Freddie Norwood (WBA)
1937-1938	Henry Armstrong*	1975	Ruben Olivares (WBA)	1998-1999	Antonio Cermeno (WBA)
1938-1940	Joey Archibald	1975-1976	David Kotey (WBC)	1999	Cesar Soto (WBC);
1940-1941	Harry Jeffra	1976-1980	Danny Lopez (WBC)		Naseem Hamed* (WBC);
1942-1948	Willie Pep	1977	Rafael Ortega (WBA)		Freddie Norwood (WBA)
1948-1949	Sandy Saddler	1977-1978	Cecilio Lastra (WBA)	2000-2001	Guty Espadas (WBC)
1949-1950	Willie Pep	1978-1985	Eusebio Pedrosa (WBA)	2000-2003	Derrick Gainer (WBA)
1950-1957	Sandy Saddler*	1980-1982	Salvador Sanchez (WBC)	2001-2004	Erik Morales (WBC)(a)
1957-1959	Hogan (Kid) Bassey	1982-1984	Juan LaPorte (WBC)	2003-2005	Juan Manuel Marquez (WBA)
1959-1963	Davey Moore	1984	Wilfredo Gomez (WBC)	2004-2005	In-jin Chi (WBC)
1963-1964	Sugar Ramos	1984-1988	Azumah Nelson (WBC)	2006	Chris John (WBA);
1964-1967	Vicente Saldivar*	1985-1986	Barry McGuigan (WBA)		Rodolfo Lopex (WBC)

(a) Marco Antonio Barrera won unan. decision over Morales, June 22, 2002, but refused WBC title. Morales regained WBC title with unan. decision over Paulie Ayala, Nov. 16, 2002. Morales moved up to Junior Lightweight div. in 2004.

History of Title-Changing Heavyweight Championship Bouts

1889: July 8, John L. Sullivan def. Jake Kilrain, 75, Richburg, MS.

1892: Sept. 7, James J. Corbett def. John L. Sullivan, 21, New Orleans.

1897: Mar. 17, Bob Fitzsimmons def. James J. Corbett, 14, Carson City, NV.

1899: June 9, James J. Jeffries def. Bob Fitzsimmons, 11, Coney Island, NY. (Jeffries retired as champion in 1905.)

1905: July 3, Marvin Hart KOd Jack Root, 12, Reno, NV. (Jeffries refereed, gave title to Hart. Jack O'Brien also claimed the title.)

1906: Feb. 23, Tommy Burns def. Marvin Hart, 20, Los Angeles.

1908: Dec. 26, Jack Johnson KOd Tommy Burns, 14, Sydney, Australia. (Police halted contest.)

1915: April 5, Jess Willard KOd Jack Johnson, 26, Havana.

1919: July 4, Jack Dempsey KOd Jess Willard, Toledo. (Willard failed to answer bell for 4th round.)

1926: Sept. 23, Gene Tunney def. Jack Dempsey, 10, Philadelphia. (Tunney retired as champion in 1928.)

1930: June 12, Max Schmeling def. Jack Sharkey, 4, NY. (Resulted in the election of a successor to Tunney.)

1932: June 21, Jack Sharkey def. Max Schmeling, 15, NY.

1933: June 29, Primo Carnera KOd Jack Sharkey, 6, NY.

1934: June 14, Max Baer KOd Primo Carnera, 11, NY.

1935: June 13, James J. Braddock def. Max Baer, 15, NY.

1937: June 22, Joe Louis KOd James J. Braddock, 8, Chicago. (Louis retired as champion in 1949.)

1949: June 22, Ezzard Charles def. Joe Walcott, 15, Chicago; NBA recognition only.

1951: July 18, Joe Walcott KOd Ezzard Charles, 7, Pittsburgh.

1952: Sept. 23, Rocky Marciano KOd Joe Walcott, 13, Philadelphia. (Marciano retired as champion in 1956.)

1956: Nov. 30, Floyd Patterson KOd Archie Moore, 5, Chicago.

1959: June 26, Ingemar Johansson KOd Floyd Patterson, 3, NY.

1960: June 20, Floyd Patterson KOd Ingemar Johansson, 5, NY.

1962: Sept. 25, Sonny Liston KOd Floyd Patterson, 1, Chicago.

1964: Feb. 25, Cassius Clay (Muhammad Ali) KOd Sonny Liston, 7, Miami Beach, FL. (In 1967, Ali was stripped of his title by the WBA and others for refusing military service.)

1970: Feb. 16, Joe Frazier KOd Jimmy Ellis, 5, NY. (Frazier def. Ali in 15 rounds, Mar. 8, 1971, in NY.)

1973: Jan. 22, George Foreman KOd Joe Frazier, 2, Jamaica.

1974: Oct. 30, Muhammad Ali KOd George Foreman, 8, Kinshasa, Zaire.

1978: Feb. 15, Leon Spinks def. Muhammad Ali, 15, Las Vegas. (WBC recognized Ken Norton as champion after Spinks refused to fight him before his rematch with Ali.); June 9, (WBC) Larry Holmes def. Ken Norton, 15, Las Vegas; Sept. 15, (WBA) Muhammad Ali def. Leon Spinks, 15, New Orleans. (Ali retired as champion in 1979.)

1979: Oct. 20, (WBA) John Tate def. Gerrie Coetzee, 15, Pretoria, South Africa.

1980: Mar. 31, (WBA) Mike Weaver KOd John Tate, 15, Knoxville.

1982: Dec. 10, (WBA) Michael Dokes KOd Mike Weaver, 1, Las Vegas.

1983: Sept. 23, (WBA) Gerrie Coetzee KOd Michael Dokes, 10, Richfield, OH; in Dec., Larry Holmes relinquished the WBC title and was named champion of the newly formed IBF.

1984: Mar. 9, (WBC) Tim Witherspoon def. Greg Page, 12, Las Vegas; Aug. 31, (WBC) Pinklon Thomas def. Tim Witherspoon, 12, Las Vegas; Dec. 2, (WBA) Greg Page KOd Gerrie Coetzee, 8, Sun City, Bophuthatswana, South Africa.

1985: Apr. 29, (WBA) Tony Tubbs def. Greg Page, 15, Buffalo; Sept. 21, (IBF) Michael Spinks def. Larry Holmes, 15, Las Vegas. (Spinks relinquished title in Feb. 1987.)

1986: Jan. 17, (WBA) Tim Witherspoon def. Tony Tubbs, 15, Atlanta, GA; Mar. 23, (WBC) Trevor Berbick def. Pinklon Thomas, 12, Miami; Nov. 22, (WBC) Mike Tyson KOd Trevor Berbick, 2, Las Vegas; Dec. 12, (WBA) James "Bonecrusher" Smith KOd Tim Witherspoon, 1, NY.

1987: Mar. 7, (WBA, WBC) Mike Tyson def. James "Bonecrusher" Smith, 12, Las Vegas; May 30, (IBF) Tony Tucker KOd James "Buster" Douglas, 10, Las Vegas; Aug. 1, (WBA, WBC, IBF) Mike Tyson def. Tony Tucker, 12, Las Vegas. (Tyson became undisputed champion.)

1990: Feb. 11, (WBA, WBC, IBF) James "Buster" Douglas KOd Mike Tyson, 10, Tokyo; Oct. 25, (WBA, WBC, IBF) Evander Holyfield KOd James "Buster" Douglas, 3, Las Vegas.

1992: Nov. 13, (WBA, WBC, IBF) Riddick Bowe def. Evander Holyfield, 12, Las Vegas. (Lennox Lewis was later named WBC champion when Bowe refused to fight him.)

1993: Nov. 6, (WBA, IBF) Evander Holyfield def. Riddick Bowe, 12, Las Vegas.

1994: Apr. 22, (WBA, IBF) Michael Moorer def. Evander Holyfield, 12, Las Vegas; Sept. 24, (WBC) Oliver McCall KOd Lennox Lewis, 2, London; Nov. 5, (WBA, IBF) George Foreman KOd Michael Moorer, 10, Las Vegas. (In Mar. 1995, Foreman was stripped of the WBA title; he relinquished the IBF title in June.)

1995: Sept. 2, (WBC) Frank Bruno def. Oliver McCall, 12, London; Dec. 9, (IBF) Frans Botha def. Axel Schulz, 12, Las Vegas. (Botha was subsequently stripped of title.)

1996: Mar. 16, (WBC) Mike Tyson KOd Frank Bruno, 3, Las Vegas; June 22, (IBF) Michael Moorer def. Axel Schulz, 12, Dortmund, Germany; Sept. 7, (WBA, WBC) Mike Tyson KOd Bruce Seldon, 1, Las Vegas. (Tyson was subsequently stripped of WBC title.); Nov. 9, (WBA) Evander Holyfield KOd Mike Tyson, 11, Las Vegas.

1997: Feb. 7, (WBC) Lennox Lewis KOd Oliver McCall, 5, Las Vegas; Nov. 8, (IBF) Evander Holyfield def. Michael Moorer, 8, Las Vegas.

1999: Nov. 13, (WBA, WBC, IBF) Lennox Lewis def. Evander Holyfield, 12, Las Vegas. (Lewis became undisputed champion. In April 2000, Lewis was stripped of his WBA title.)

2000: Aug. 12, (WBA) Evander Holyfield def. John Ruiz, 12, Las Vegas.

2001: Mar. 3, (WBA) John Ruiz def. Evander Holyfield, 12, Las Vegas; Apr. 21, (IBF) Hasim Rahman KOd Lennox Lewis, 5, Brakpan, South Africa; Nov. 17, (WBC, IBF) Lennox Lewis KOd Hasim Rahman, 4, Las Vegas.

2002: Dec. 14, (IBF) Chris Byrd def. Evander Holyfield, 12, Atl. City.

2003: Mar. 1, (WBA) Roy Jones Jr. def. John Ruiz, 12, Las Vegas; Dec. 13.

2004: Feb. 20, (WBA) Ruiz gained title when Roy Jones, Jr. relinquished it; Apr. 24, (WBC) Vitali Klitschko TKOd Corrie Sanders, 8, Los Angeles, to win title vacated when champ Lennox Lewis retired in Feb.

2005: Apr. 30, (WBA) James Toney def. John Ruiz, 12, NYC (Toney tested positive for steroids; title returned to Ruiz); Nov. 9, (WBC) Hasim Rahman gained title when Vitali Klitschko retired; Dec. 17, (WBA) Nicolay Valuev def. John Ruiz, 12, Berlin, Ger.

2006: Aug. 12, (WBC) Oleg Maskaev TKOd Hasim Rahman, 12, Las Vegas.; Apr. 22, (IBF) Wladimir Klitschko TKOd Chris Byrd, 7, Mannheim, Ger.

THOROUGHBRED RACING
Triple Crown Winners
Since 1920, colts have carried 126 lb. in triple crown events; fillies, 121 lb.
(Kentucky Derby, Preakness, and Belmont Stakes)

Year	Horse	Jockey	Trainer	Year	Horse	Jockey	Trainer
1919	Sir Barton	J. Loftus	H. G. Bedwell	1946	Assault	W. Mehrtens	M. Hirsch
1930	Gallant Fox	E. Sande	J. Fitzsimmons	1948	Citation	E. Arcaro	H. A. Jones
1935	Omaha	W. Sanders	J. Fitzsimmons	1973	Secretariat	R. Turcotte	L. Laurin
1937	War Admiral	C. Kurtsinger	G. Conway	1977	Seattle Slew	J. Cruguet	W. H. Turner Jr.
1941	Whirlaway	E. Arcaro	B. A. Jones	1978	Affirmed	S. Cauthen	L. S. Barrera
1943	Count Fleet	J. Longden	G. D. Cameron				

Kentucky Derby
Churchill Downs, Louisville, KY; inaug. 1875; distance 1-1/4 mi; 1-1/2 mi until 1896. 3-year-olds.
Best time: 1:59 2/5, by Secretariat, 1973; 2006 time: 2:01.36.

Year	Winner	Jockey	Year	Winner	Jockey	Year	Winner	Jockey
1875	Aristides	O. Lewis	1919	Sir Barton	J. Loftus	1963	Chateaugay	B. Baeza
1876	Vagrant	R. Swim	1920	Paul Jones	T. Rice	1964	Northern Dancer	W. Hartack
1877	Baden Baden	W. Walker	1921	Behave Yourself	C. Thompson	1965	Lucky Debonair	W. Shoemaker
1878	Day Star	Carter	1922	Morvich	A. Johnson	1966	Kauai King	D. Brumfield
1879	Lord Murphy	C. Schauer	1923	Zev	E. Sande	1967	Proud Clarion	R. Ussery
1880	Fonso	G. Lewis	1924	Black Gold	J. D. Mooney	1968	Dancer's Image#	R. Ussery
1881	Hindoo	J. McLaughlin	1925	Flying Ebony	E. Sande	1969	Majestic Prince	W. Hartack
1882	Apollo	B. Hurd	1926	Bubbling Over	A. Johnson	1970	Dust Commander	M. Manganello
1883	Leonatus	W. Donohue	1927	Whiskery	L. McAtee	1971	Canonero II	G. Avila
1884	Buchanan	I. Murphy	1928	Reigh Count	C. Lang	1972	Riva Ridge	R. Turcotte
1885	Joe Cotton	E. Henderson	1929	Clyde Van Dusen	L. McAtee	1973	Secretariat	R. Turcotte
1886	Ben Ali	P. Duffy	1930	Gallant Fox	E. Sande	1974	Cannonade	A. Cordero
1887	Montrose	I. Lewis	1931	Twenty Grand	C. Kurtsinger	1975	Foolish Pleasure	J. Vasquez
1888	Macbeth II	G. Covington	1932	Burgoo King	E. James	1976	Bold Forbes	A. Cordero
1889	Spokane	T. Kiley	1933	Brokers Tip	D. Meade	1977	Seattle Slew	J. Cruguet
1890	Riley	I. Murphy	1934	Cavalcade	M. Garner	1978	Affirmed	S. Cauthen
1891	Kingman	I. Murphy	1935	Omaha	W. Saunders	1979	Spectacular Bid	R. Franklin
1892	Azra	A. Clayton	1936	Bold Venture	I. Hanford	1980	Genuine Risk*	J. Vasquez
1893	Lookout	E. Kunze	1937	War Admiral	C. Kurtsinger	1981	Pleasant Colony	J. Velasquez
1894	Chant	F. Goodale	1938	Lawrin	E. Arcaro	1982	Gato del Sol	E. Delahoussaye
1895	Halma	J. Perkins	1939	Johnstown	J. Stout	1983	Sunny's Halo	E. Delahoussaye
1896	Ben Brush	W. Simms	1940	Gallahadion	C. Bierman	1984	Swale	L. Pincay
1897	Typhoon II	F. Garner	1941	Whirlaway	E. Arcaro	1985	Spend a Buck	A. Cordero
1898	Plaudit	W. Simms	1942	Shut Out	W. D. Wright	1986	Ferdinand	W. Shoemaker
1899	Manuel	F. Taral	1943	Count Fleet	J. Longden	1987	Alysheba	C. McCarron
1900	Lieut. Gibson	J. Boland	1944	Pensive	C. McCreary	1988	Winning Colors*	G. Stevens
1901	His Eminence	J. Winkfield	1945	Hoop, Jr.	E. Arcaro	1989	Sunday Silence	P. Valenzuela
1902	Alan-a-Dale	J. Winkfield	1946	Assault	W. Mehrtens	1990	Unbridled	C. Perret
1903	Judge Himes	H. Booker	1947	Jet Pilot	E. Guerin	1991	Strike the Gold	C. Antley
1904	Elwood	F. Prior	1948	Citation	E. Arcaro	1992	Lil E. Tee	P. Day
1905	Agile	J. Martin	1949	Ponder	S. Brooks	1993	Sea Hero	J. Bailey
1906	Sir Huon	R. Troxler	1950	Middleground	W. Boland	1994	Go for Gin	C. McCarron
1907	Pink Star	A. Minder	1951	Count Turf	C. McCreary	1995	Thunder Gulch	G. Stevens
1908	Stone Street	A. Pickens	1952	Hill Gail	E. Arcaro	1996	Grindstone	J. Bailey
1909	Wintergreen	V. Powers	1953	Dark Star	H. Moreno	1997	Silver Charm	G. Stevens
1910	Donau	F. Herbert	1954	Determine	R. York	1998	Real Quiet	K. Desormeaux
1911	Meridian	G. Archibald	1955	Swaps	W. Shoemaker	1999	Charismatic	C. Antley
1912	Worth	C.H. Shilling	1956	Needles	D. Erb	2000	Fusaichi Pegasus	K. Desormeaux
1913	Donerail	R. Goose	1957	Iron Liege	W. Hartack	2001	Monarchos	J. Chavez
1914	Old Rosebud	J. McCabe	1958	Tim Tam	I. Valenzuela	2002	War Emblem	V. Espinoza
1915	Regret*	J. Notter	1959	Tomy Lee	W. Shoemaker	2003	Funny Cide	J. Santos
1916	George Smith	J. Loftus	1960	Venetian Way	W. Hartack	2004	Smarty Jones	S. Elliot
1917	Omar Khayyam	C. Borel	1961	Carry Back	J. Sellers	2005	Giacomo	M. Smith
1918	Exterminator	W. Knapp	1962	Decidedly	W. Hartack	2006	Barbaro	E. Prado

*Regret, Genuine Risk, and Winning Colors are the only fillies to have won the Derby. # Dancer's Image was disqualified from purse money after tests disclosed that he had run with a pain-killing drug, phenylbutazone, in his system. All wagers were paid on Dancer's Image. Forward Pass was awarded first place money. The Kentucky Derby has been won 5 times by 2 jockeys: Eddie Arcaro, 1938, 1941, 1945, 1948, and 1952; and Bill Hartack, 1957, 1960, 1962, 1964, and 1969. It was won 4 times by Willie Shoemaker, 1955, 1959, 1965, and 1986; and 3 times by each of 4 jockeys: Isaac Murphy, 1884, 1890, and 1891; Earle Sande, 1923, 1925, and 1930; Angel Cordero, 1974, 1976, and 1985; and Gary Stevens, 1988, 1995, and 1997.

Fastest Winning Times for the Kentucky Derby
(Kentucky Derby times measured in fifths of a second according to tradition.)

Time	Horse	Jockey	Year	Time	Horse	Jockey	Year
1m. 59 2/5 s.	Secretariat	Ron Turcotte	1973	2m. 1 1/5 s.	Thunder Gulch	Gary Stevens	1995
1m. 59 4/5 s.	Monarchos	Jorge Chavez	2001		Affirmed	Steve Cauthen	1978
2m.	Northern Dancer	Bill Hartack	1964		Lucky Debonair	Bill Shoemaker	1965
2m. 1/5 s.	Spend a Buck	Angel Cordero Jr.	1985	2m. 1 2/5 s.	Whirlaway	Eddie Arcaro	1941
2m. 2/5 s.	Decidedly	Bill Hartack	1962		Barbaro	Edgar Prado	2006
2m. 3/5 s.	Proud Clarion	Robert Ussery	1967	2m. 1 3/5 s.	Bold Forbes	Angel Cordero Jr.	1976
2m. 1 s.	Funny Cide	Jose Santos	2003		Hill Gail	Eddie Arcaro	1952
	War Emblem	Victor Espinoza	2002		Middleground	William Boland	1950
	Fusaichi Pegasus	Kent Desormeaux	2000				
	Grindstone	Jerry Bailey	1996				

Preakness Stakes

Pimlico Race Course, Baltimore, MD; inaug. 1873; distance 1-3/16 mi. 3-year-olds.
Best time: 1:53 2/5, by Tank's Prospect (1985) and Louis Quatorze (1996); 2006 time: 1:54.65.

Year	Winner	Jockey	Year	Winner	Jockey	Year	Winner	Jockey
1873	Survivor	G. Barbee	1919	Sir Barton	J. Loftus	1963	Candy Spots	W. Shoemaker
1874	Culpepper	M. Donohue	1920	Man o' War	C. Kummer	1964	Northern Dancer	W. Hartack
1875	Tom Ochiltree	L. Hughes	1921	Broomspun	F. Coltiletti	1965	Tom Rolfe	R. Turcotte
1876	Shirley	G. Barbee	1922	Pillory	L. Morris	1966	Kauai King	D. Brumfield
1877	Cloverbrook	C. Holloway	1923	Vigil	B. Marinelli	1967	Damascus	W. Shoemaker
1878	Duke of Magenta	C. Holloway	1924	Nellie Morse	J. Merimee	1968	Forward Pass	I. Valenzuela
1879	Harold	L. Hughes	1925	Coventry	C. Kummer	1969	Majestic Prince	W. Hartack
1880	Grenada	L. Hughes	1926	Display	J. Malben	1970	Personality	E. Belmonte
1881	Saunterer	W. Costello	1927	Bostonian	A. Abel	1971	Canonero II	G. Avila
1882	Vanguard	W. Costello	1928	Victorian	R. Workman	1972	Bee Bee Bee	E. Nelson
1883	Jacobus	G. Barbee	1929	Dr. Freeland	L. Schaefer	1973	Secretariat	R. Turcotte
1884	Knight of Ellerslie	S. H. Fisher	1930	Gallant Fox	E. Sande	1974	Little Current	M. Rivera
1885	Tecumseh	J. McLaughlin	1931	Mate	G. Ellis	1975	Master Derby	D. McHargue
1886	The Bard	S. H. Fisher	1932	Burgoo King	E. James	1976	Elocutionist	J. Lively
1887	Dunboyne	W. Donohue	1933	Head Play	C. Kurtsinger	1977	Seattle Slew	J. Cruguet
1888	Refund	F. Littlefield	1934	High Quest	R. Jones	1978	Affirmed	S. Cauthen
1889	Buddhist	G. Anderson	1935	Omaha	W. Saunders	1979	Spectacular Bid	R. Franklin
1890	Montague	W. Martin	1936	Bold Venture	G. Woolf	1980	Codex	A. Cordero
1894	Assignee	F. Taral	1937	War Admiral	C. Kurtsinger	1981	Pleasant Colony	J. Velasquez
1895	Belmar	F. Taral	1938	Dauber	M. Peters	1982	Aloma's Ruler	J. Kaenel
1896	Margrave	H. Griffin	1939	Challedon	G. Seabo	1983	Deputed Testamony	D. Miller
1897	Paul Kauvar	C. Thorpe	1940	Bimelech	F.A. Smith	1984	Gate Dancer	A. Cordero
1898	Sly Fox	W. Simms	1941	Whirlaway	E. Arcaro	1985	Tank's Prospect	P. Day
1899	Half Time	R. Clawson	1942	Alsab	B. James	1986	Snow Chief	A. Solis
1900	Hindus	H. Spencer	1943	Count Fleet	J. Longden	1987	Alysheba	C. McCarron
1901	The Parader	F. Landry	1944	Pensive	C. McCreary	1988	Risen Star	E. Delahoussaye
1902	Old England	L. Jackson	1945	Polynesian	W.D. Wright	1989	Sunday Silence	P. Valenzuela
1903	Flocarline	W. Gannon	1946	Assault	W. Mehrtens	1990	Summer Squall	P. Day
1904	Bryn Mawr	E. Hildebrand	1947	Faultless	D. Dodson	1991	Hansel	J. Bailey
1905	Cairngorm	W. Davis	1948	Citation	E. Arcaro	1992	Pine Bluff	C. McCarron
1906	Whimsical	W. Miller	1949	Capot	T. Atkinson	1993	Prairie Bayou	M. Smith
1907	Don Enrique	G. Mountain	1950	Hill Prince	E. Arcaro	1994	Tabasco Cat	P. Day
1908	Royal Tourist	E. Dugan	1951	Bold	E. Arcaro	1995	Timber Country	P. Day
1909	Effendi	W. Doyle	1952	Blue Man	C. McCreary	1996	Louis Quatorze	P. Day
1910	Layminster	R. Estep	1953	Native Dancer	E. Guerin	1997	Silver Charm	G. Stevens
1911	Watervale	E. Dugan	1954	Hasty Road	J. Adams	1998	Real Quiet	K. Desormeaux
1912	Colonel Holloway	C. Turner	1955	Nashua	E. Arcaro	1999	Charismatic	C. Antley
1913	Buskin	J. Butwell	1956	Fabius	W. Hartack	2000	Red Bullet	J. Bailey
1914	Holiday	A. Schuttinger	1957	Bold Ruler	E. Arcaro	2001	Point Given	G. Stevens
1915	Rhine Maiden	D. Hoffman	1958	Tim Tam	I. Valenzuela	2002	War Emblem	V. Espinoza
1916	Damrosch	L. McAtee	1959	Royal Orbit	W. Harmatz	2003	Funny Cide	J. Santos
1917	Kalitan	E. Haynes	1960	Bally Ache	R. Ussery	2004	Smarty Jones	S. Elliot
1918*	War Cloud	J. Loftus	1961	Carry Back	J. Sellers	2005	Afleet Alex	J. Rose
	Jack Hare Jr.	C. Peak	1962	Greek Money	J.L. Rotz	2006	Bernardini	J. Castellano

*Horses ran in 2 divisions.

Belmont Stakes

Belmont Park, Elmont, NY; inaug. 1867; distance 1-1/2 mi. 3-year-olds. Best time: 2:24, Secretariat, 1973; 2006 time: 2:27.86.

Year	Winner	Jockey	Year	Winner	Jockey	Year	Winner	Jockey
1867	Ruthless	J. Gilpatrick	1904	Delhi	G. Odom	1943	Count Fleet	J. Longden
1868	General Duke	R. Swim	1905	Tanya	E. Hildebrand	1944	Bounding Home	G. L. Smith
1869	Fenian	C. Miller	1906	Burgomaster	L. Lyne	1945	Pavot	E. Arcaro
1870	Kingfisher	W. Dick	1907	Peter Pan	G. Mountain	1946	Assault	W. Mehrtens
1871	Harry Bassett	W. Miller	1908	Colin	J. Notter	1947	Phalanx	R. Donoso
1872	Joe Daniels	J. Rowe	1909	Joe Madden	E. Dugan	1948	Citation	E. Arcaro
1873	Springbok	J. Rowe	1910	Sweep	J. Butwell	1949	Capot	T. Atkinson
1874	Saxon	G. Barbee	1913	Prince Eugene	R. Troxler	1950	Middleground	W. Boland
1875	Calvin	R. Swim	1914	Luke McLuke	M. Buxton	1951	Counterpoint	D. Gorman
1876	Algerine	W. Donohue	1915	The Finn	G. Byrne	1952	One Count	E. Arcaro
1877	Cloverbrook	C. Holloway	1916	Friar Rock	E. Haynes	1953	Native Dancer	E. Guerin
1878	Duke of Magenta	L. Hughes	1917	Hourless	J. Butwell	1954	High Gun	E. Guerin
1879	Spendthrift	S. Evans	1918	Johren	F. Robinson	1955	Nashua	E. Arcaro
1880	Grenada	L. Hughes	1919	Sir Barton	J. Loftus	1956	Needles	D. Erb
1881	Saunterer	T. Costello	1920	Man o' War	C. Kummer	1957	Gallant Man	W. Shoemaker
1882	Forester	J. McLaughlin	1921	Grey Lag	E. Sande	1958	Cavan	P. Anderson
1883	George Kinney	J. McLaughlin	1922	Pillory	C. H. Miller	1959	Sword Dancer	W. Shoemaker
1884	Panique	J. McLaughlin	1923	Zev	E. Sande	1960	Celtic Ash	W. Hartack
1885	Tyrant	P. Duffy	1924	Mad Play	E. Sande	1961	Sherluck	B. Baeza
1886	Inspector	B.J. McLaughlin	1925	American Flag	A. Johnson	1962	Jaipur	W. Shoemaker
1887	Hanover	J. McLaughlin	1926	Crusader	A. Johnson	1963	Chateaugay	B. Baeza
1888	Sir Dixon	J. McLaughlin	1927	Chance Shot	E. Sande	1964	Quadrangle	M. Ycaza
1889	Eric	W. Hayward	1928	Vito	C. Kummer	1965	Hail to All	J. Sellers
1890	Burlington	S. Barnes	1929	Blue Larkspur	M. Garner	1966	Amberoid	W. Boland
1891	Foxford	E. Garrison	1930	Gallant Fox	E. Sande	1967	Damascus	W. Shoemaker
1892	Patron	W. Hayward	1931	Twenty Grand	C. Kurtsinger	1968	Stage Door Johnny	H. Gustines
1893	Comanche	W. Simms	1932	Faireno	T. Malley	1969	Arts and Letters	B. Baeza
1894	Henry of Navarre	W. Simms	1933	Hurryoff	M. Garner	1970	High Echelon	J. L. Rotz
1895	Belmar	F. Taral	1934	Peace Chance	W. D. Wright	1971	Pass Catcher	W. Blum
1896	Hastings	H. Griffin	1935	Omaha	W. Saunders	1972	Riva Ridge	R. Turcotte
1897	Scottish Chieftain	J. Scherrer	1936	Granville	J. Stout	1973	Secretariat	R. Turcotte
1898	Bowling Brook	F. Littlefield	1937	War Admiral	C. Kurtsinger	1974	Little Current	M. Rivera
1899	Jean Bereaud	R. R. Clawson	1938	Pasteurized	J. Stout	1975	Avatar	W. Shoemaker
1900	Ildrim	N. Turner	1939	Johnstown	J. Stout	1976	Bold Forbes	A. Cordero
1901	Commando	H. Spencer	1940	Bimelech	F. A. Smith	1977	Seattle Slew	J. Cruguet
1902	Masterman	J. Bullman	1941	Whirlaway	E. Arcaro	1978	Affirmed	S. Cauthen
1903	Africander	J. Bullman	1942	Shut Out	E. Arcaro	1979	Coastal	R. Hernandez

Year	Winner	Jockey	Year	Winner	Jockey	Year	Winner	Jockey
1980	Temperence Hill	E. Maple	1989	Easy Goer	P. Day	1998	Victory Gallop	G. Stevens
1981	Summing	G. Martens	1990	Go and Go	M. Kinane	1999	Lemon Drop Kid	J. Santos
1982	Conquistador Cielo	L. Pincay	1991	Hansel	J. Bailey	2000	Commendable	P. Day
1983	Caveat	L. Pincay	1992	A.P. Indy	E. Delahoussaye	2001	Point Given	G. Stevens
1984	Swale	L. Pincay	1993	Colonial Affair	J. Krone	2002	Sarava	E. Prado
1985	Creme Fraiche	E. Maple	1994	Tabasco Cat	P. Day	2003	Empire Maker	J. Bailey
1986	Danzig Connection	C. McCarron	1995	Thunder Gulch	G. Stevens	2004	Birdstone	E. Prado
1987	Bet Twice	C. Perret	1996	Editor's Note	R. Douglas	2005	Afleet Alex	J. Rose
1988	Risen Star	E. Delahoussaye	1997	Touch Gold	C. McCarron	2006	Jazil	F. Jara

Annual Leading Jockey — Money Won[1]
(as of Dec. 22, 2005)

Year	Jockey	Earnings	Year	Jockey	Earnings	Year	Jockey	Earnings
1957	Bill Hartack	$3,060,501	1974	Laffit Pincay, Jr.	$4,251,060	1990	Gary Stevens	$13,881,198
1958	Willie Shoemaker	2,961,693	1975	Braulio Baeza	3,695,198	1991	Chris McCarron	14,441,083
1959	Willie Shoemaker	2,843,133	1976	Angel Cordero, Jr.	4,709,500	1992	Kent Desormeaux	14,193,006
1960	Willie Shoemaker	2,123,961	1977	Steve Cauthen	6,151,750	1993	Mike Smith	14,024,815
1961	Willie Shoemaker	2,690,819	1978	Darrel McHargue	6,029,885	1994	Mike Smith	15,979,820
1962	Willie Shoemaker	2,916,844	1979	Laffit Pincay, Jr.	8,193,535	1995	Jerry Bailey	16,311,876
1963	Willie Shoemaker	2,526,925	1980	Chris McCarron	7,663,300	1996	Jerry Bailey	19,465,376
1964	Willie Shoemaker	2,649,553	1981	Chris McCarron	8,397,604	1997	Jerry Bailey	18,320,743
1965	Braulio Baeza	2,582,702	1982	Angel Cordero, Jr.	9,483,590	1998	Gary Stevens	19,622,855
1966	Braulio Baeza	2,951,022	1983	Angel Cordero, Jr.	10,116,697	1999	Pat Day	18,092,845
1967	Braulio Baeza	3,088,888	1984	Chris McCarron	12,045,813	2000	Pat Day	17,479,838
1968	Braulio Baeza	2,835,108	1985	Laffit Pincay, Jr.	13,353,299	2001	Jerry Bailey	22,597,720
1969	Jorge Velasquez	2,542,315	1986	Jose Santos	11,329,297	2002	Jerry Bailey	22,871,814
1970	Laffit Pincay, Jr.	2,626,526	1987	Jose Santos	12,375,433	2003	Jerry Bailey	22,829,570
1971	Laffit Pincay, Jr.	3,784,377	1988	Jose Santos	14,877,298	2004	John R. Velazquez	22,248,661
1972	Laffit Pincay, Jr.	3,225,827	1989	Jose Santos	13,838,389	2005	John R. Velazquez	20,770,272
1973	Laffit Pincay, Jr.	4,093,492						

(1) Total earnings for all horses that jockey raced in year listed; does not reflect jockey's earnings.

Breeders' Cup World Thoroughbred Championships

The Breeders' Cup was inaugurated in 1984 and consists of 7 races at one track on one day late in the year to determine Thoroughbred racing's champion contenders. It has been held at the following locations:

1984 Hollywood Park, CA	1990 Belmont Park, NY	1996 Woodbine Racetrack, Ontario	2001 Belmont Park, NY
1985 Aqueduct Racetrack, NY	1991 Churchill Downs, KY	1997 Hollywood Park, CA	2002 Arlington Park, IL
1986 Santa Anita Park, CA	1992 Gulfstream Park, FL	1998 Churchill Downs, KY	2003 Santa Anita Park, CA
1987 Hollywood Park, CA	1993 Santa Anita Park, CA	1999 Gulfstream Park, FL	2004 Lone Star Park, TX
1988 Churchill Downs, KY	1994 Churchill Downs, KY	2000 Churchill Downs, KY	2005 Belmont Park, NY
1989 Gulfstream Park, FL	1995 Belmont Park, NY		

Juvenile
Distances: 1 mi 1984-85, 1987; 1-1/16 mi 1986 and since 1988

Year	Horse	Jockey	Year	Horse	Jockey	Year	Horse	Jockey
1984	Chief's Crown	D. MacBeth	1992	Gilded Time	C. McCarron	1999	Anees	G. Stevens
1985	Tasso	L. Pincay, Jr.	1993	Brocco	G. Stevens	2000	Macho Uno	J. Bailey
1986	Capote	L. Pincay, Jr.	1994	Timber Country	P. Day	2001	Johannesburg	M. Kinane
1987	Success Express	J. Santos	1995	Unbridled's Song	M. Smith	2002	Vindication	M. Smith
1988	Is It True	L. Pincay, Jr.	1996	Boston Harbor	J. Bailey	2003	Action This Day	D. Flores
1989	Rhythm	C. Perret	1997	Favorite Trick	P. Day	2004	Wilko	F. Dettori
1990	Fly So Free	J. Santos	1998	Answer Lively	J. Bailey	2005	Stevie Wonderboy	G. Gomez
1991	Arazi	P. Valenzuela						

Juvenile Fillies
Distances: 1 mi 1984-85, 1987; 1-1/16 mi 1986 and since 1988

Year	Horse	Jockey	Year	Horse	Jockey	Year	Horse	Jockey
1984	*Outstandingly	W. Guerra	1992	Eliza	P. Valenzuela	1999	Cash Run	J. Bailey
1985	Twilight Ridge	J. Velasquez	1993	Phone Chatter	L. Pincay, Jr.	2000	Caressing	J. Velazquez
1986	Brave Raj	P. Valenzuela	1994	Flanders	P. Day	2001	Tempera	D. Flores
1987	Epitome	P. Day	1995	My Flag	J. Bailey	2002	Storm Flag Flying	J. Velazquez
1988	Open Mind	A. Cordero, Jr.	1996	Storm Song	C. Perret	2003	Halfbridled	J. Krone
1989	Go for Wand	R. Romero	1997	Countess Diana	S. Sellers	2004	Sweet Catomine	C. Nakatani
1990	Meadow Star	J. Santos	1998	Silverbulletday	G. Stevens	2005	Folklore	E. Prado
1991	Pleasant Stage	E. Delahoussaye						

*By disqualification.

Sprint
Distance: 6 furlongs

Year	Horse	Jockey	Year	Horse	Jockey	Year	Horse	Jockey
1984	Eillo	C. Perret	1992	Thirty Slews	E. Delahoussaye	1999	Artax	J. Chaves
1985	Precisionist	C. McCarron	1993	Cardmania	E. Delahoussaye	2000	Kona Gold	A. Solis
1986	Smile	J. Vasquez	1994	Cherokee Run	M. Smith	2001	Squirtle Squirt	J. Bailey
1987	Very Subtle	P. Valenzuela	1995	Desert Stormer	K. Desormeaux	2002	Orientate	J. Bailey
1988	Gulch	A. Cordero, Jr.	1996	Lit De Justice	C. Nakatani	2003	Cajun Beat	C. Velasquez
1989	Dancing Spree	A. Cordero, Jr.	1997	Elmhurst	C. Nakatani	2004	Speightstown	J. Velazquez
1990	Safely Kept	C. Perret	1998	Reraise	C. Nakatani	2005	Silver Train	E. Prado
1991	Sheikh Albadou	P. Eddery						

Mile

Year	Horse	Jockey	Year	Horse	Jockey	Year	Horse	Jockey
1984	Royal Heroine	F. Toro	1992	Lure	M. Smith	1999	Silic	C. Nakatani
1985	Cozzene	W. Guerra	1993	Lure	M. Smith	2000	War Chant	G. Stevens
1986	Last Tycoon	Y. St.-Martin	1994	Barathea	L. Dettori	2001	Val Royal	J. Valdivia Jr.
1987	Miesque	F. Head	1995	Ridgewood Pearl	J. Murtagh	2002	Domedriver	T. Thulliez
1988	Miesque	F. Head	1996	Da Hoss	G. Stevens	2003	Six Perfections	J. Bailey
1989	Steinlen	J. Santos	1997	Spinning World	C. Asmussen	2004	Singletary	D. Flores
1990	Royal Academy	L. Piggott	1998	Da Hoss	J. Velazquez	2005	Artie Schiller	G. Gomez
1991	Opening Verse	P. Valenzuela						

Filly & Mare Turf
Distances: 1-3/8 mi 1999-2000, 2004; 1-1/4 mi 2001-03, 2005

Year	Horse	Jockey	Year	Horse	Jockey	Year	Horse	Jockey
1999	Soaring Softly	J. Bailey	2002	Starine	J. Velazquez	2004	Ouija Board	K. Fallon
2000	Perfect Sting	J. Bailey	2003	Islington	K. Fallon	2005	Intercontinental	R. Bejarano
2001	Banks Hill	O. Peslier						

Distaff
Distances: 1-1/4 mi 1984-87; 1-1/8 mi since 1988

Year	Horse	Jockey	Year	Horse	Jockey	Year	Horse	Jockey
1984	Princess Rooney	E. Delahoussaye	1992	Paseana	C. McCarron	1999	Beautiful Pleasure	J. Chaves
1985	Life's Magic	A. Cordero, Jr.	1993	Hollywood Wildcat	E. Delahoussaye	2000	Spain	V. Espinoza
1986	Lady's Secret	P. Day	1994	One Dreamer	G. Stevens	2001	Unbridled Elaine	P. Day
1987	Sacahuista	R. Romero	1995	Inside Information	M. Smith	2002	Azeri	M. Smith
1988	Personal Ensign	R. Romero	1996	Jewel Princess	C. Nakatani	2003	Adoration	P. Valenzuela
1989	Bayakoa	L. Pincay, Jr.	1997	Ajina	M. Smith	2004	Ashado	J. Velazquez
1990	Bayakoa	L. Pincay, Jr.	1998	Escena	G. Stevens	2005	Pleasant Home	C. Velasquez
1991	Dance Smartly	P. Day						

Turf
Distance: 1-1/2 mi

Year	Horse	Jockey	Year	Horse	Jockey	Year	Horse	Jockey
1984	Lashkari	Y. St.-Martin	1991	Miss Alleged	E. Legrix	1999	Daylami	L. Dettori
1985	Pebbles	P. Eddery	1992	Fraise	P. Valenzuela	2000	Kalanisi	J. Murtagh
1986	Manila	J. Santos	1993	Kotashaan	K. Desormeaux	2001	Fantastic Light	L. Dettori
1987	Theatrical	P. Day	1994	Tikkanen	M. Smith	2002	High Chaparral	M. Kinane
1988	Great Communicator	R. Sibille	1995	Northern Spur	C. McCarron	2003	tie-High Chaparral	M. Kinane
			1996	Pilsudski	W. Swinburn		Johar	A. Solis
1989	Prized	E. Delahoussaye	1997	Chief Bearhart	J. Santos	2004	Better Talk Now	R. Dominguez
1990	In The Wings	G. Stevens	1998	Buck's Boy	S. Sellers	2005	Shirocco	C. Soumillon

Classic
Distance: 1-1/4 mi

Year	Horse	Jockey	Year	Horse	Jockey	Year	Horse	Jockey
1984	Wild Again	P. Day	1992	A.P. Indy	E. Delahoussaye	1999	Cat Thief	P. Day
1985	Proud Truth	J. Velasquez	1993	Arcangues	J. Bailey	2000	Tiznow	C. McCarron
1986	Skywalker	L. Pincay, Jr.	1994	Concern	J. Bailey	2001	Tiznow	C. McCarron
1987	Ferdinand	W. Shoemaker	1995	Cigar	J. Bailey	2002	Volponi	P. Johnson
1988	Alysheba	C. McCarron	1996	Alphabet Soup	C. McCarron	2003	Pleasantly Perfect	A. Solis
1989	Sunday Silence	C. McCarron	1997	Skip Away	M. Smith	2004	Ghostzapper	J. Castellano
1990	Unbridled	P. Day	1998	Awesome Again	P. Day	2005	Saint Liam	J. Bailey
1991	Black Tie Affair	J. Bailey						

Eclipse Awards

The Eclipse Awards, honoring the Horse of the Year and other champions of the sport, began in 1971 and are sponsored by the *Daily Racing Form,* the National Thoroughbred Racing Association, and the National Turf Writers Assn. Prior to 1971, the *DRF* (1936-70) and the TRA (1950-70) issued separate selections for Horse of the Year.

Eclipse Awards for 2005

Horse of the Year—Saint Liam
2-year-old male—Stevie Wonderboy
2-year-old female—Folklore
3-year-old male—Afleet Alex
3-year-old female—Smuggler
Older female (4-year-olds & up)—Ashado

Older male (4-year-olds & up)—Saint Liam
Male turf horse—Leroidesanimaux
Female turf horse—Intercontinental
Sprinter—Lost in the Fog
Steeplechase horse—McDynamo

Trainer—Todd Pletcher
Jockey—John R. Velazquez
Apprentice jockey—Emma-Jayne Wilson
Breeder—Adena Springs
Owner—Michael Gill

Horse of the Year

Year	Horse	Year	Horse	Year	Horse	Year	Horse
1936	Granville	1954	Native Dancer	1970	Fort Marcy (DRF)	1988	Alysheba
1937	War Admiral	1955	Nashua		Personality (TRA)	1989	Sunday Silence
1938	Seabiscuit	1956	Swaps	1971	Ack Ack	1990	Criminal Type
1939	Challedon	1957	Bold Ruler (DRF)	1972	Secretariat	1991	Black Tie Affair
1940	Challedon		Dedicate (TRA)	1973	Secretariat	1992	A.P. Indy
1941	Whirlaway	1958	Round Table	1974	Forego	1993	Kotashaan
1942	Whirlaway	1959	Sword Dancer	1975	Forego	1994	Holy Bull
1943	Count Fleet	1960	Kelso	1976	Forego	1995	Cigar
1944	Twilight Tear	1961	Kelso	1977	Seattle Slew	1996	Cigar
1945	Busher	1962	Kelso	1978	Affirmed	1997	Favorite Trick
1946	Assault	1963	Kelso	1979	Affirmed	1998	Skip Away
1947	Armed	1964	Kelso	1980	Spectacular Bid	1999	Charismatic
1948	Citation	1965	Roman Brother (DRF)	1981	John Henry	2000	Tiznow
1949	Capot		Moccasin (TRA)	1982	Conquistador Cielo	2001	Point Given
1950	Hill Prince			1983	All Along	2002	Azeri
1951	Counterpoint	1966	Buckpasser	1984	John Henry	2003	Mineshaft
1952	One Count (DRF)	1967	Damascus	1985	Spend A Buck	2004	Ghostzapper
	Native Dancer (TRA)	1968	Dr. Fager	1986	Lady's Secret	2005	Saint Liam
1953	Tom Fool	1969	Arts and Letters	1987	Ferdinand		

HARNESS RACING
Harness Horse of the Year
(Chosen by the U.S. Trotting Assn. and the U.S. Harness Writers Assn.)

Year	Horse	Year	Horse	Year	Horse	Year	Horse
1947	Victory Song	1956	Scott Frost	1965	Bret Hanover	1974	Delmonica Hanover
1948	Rodney	1957	Torpid	1966	Bret Hanover	1975	Savoir
1949	Good Time	1958	Emily's Pride	1967	Nevele Pride	1976	Keystone Ore
1950	Proximity	1959	Bye Bye Byrd	1968	Nevele Pride	1977	Green Speed
1951	Pronto Don	1960	Adios Butler	1969	Nevele Pride	1978	Abercrombie
1952	Good Time	1961	Adios Butler	1970	Fresh Yankee	1979	Niatross
1953	Hi Lo's Forbes	1962	Su Mac Lad	1971	Albatross	1980	Niatross
1954	Stenographer	1963	Speedy Scot	1972	Albatross	1981	Fan Hanover
1955	Scott Frost	1964	Bret Hanover	1973	Sir Dalrae	1982	Cam Fella

1983	Cam Fella	1989	Matt's Scooter	1995	CR Kay Suzie	2001	Bunny Lake
1984	Fancy Crown	1990	Beach Towel	1996	Continentalvictory	2002	Real Desire
1985	Nihilator	1991	Precious Bunny	1997	Malabar Man	2003	No Pan Intended
1986	Forrest Skipper	1992	Artsplace	1998	Moni Maker	2004	Rainbow Blue
1987	Mack Lobell	1993	Staying Together	1999	Moni Maker	2005	Rocknroll Hanover
1988	Mack Lobell	1994	Cam's Card Shark	2000	Gallo Blue Chip		

The Hambletonian (3-year-old trotters)

Year	Winner	Driver	Year	Winner	Driver
1965	Egyptian Candor	Del Cameron	1986	Nuclear Kosmos	Ulf Thoresen
1966	Kerry Way	Frank Ervin	1987	Mack Lobell	John Campbell
1967	Speedy Streak	Del Cameron	1988	Armbro Goal	John Campbell
1968	Nevele Pride	Stanley Dancer	1989	Park Avenue Joe	Ron Waples
1969	Lindy's Pride	Howard Beissinger	1990	Harmonious	John Campbell
1970	Timothy T	John Simpson, Sr.	1991	Giant Victory	Jack Moiseyev
1971	Speedy Crown	Howard Beissinger	1992	Alf Palema	Mickey McNicholl
1972	Super Bowl	Stanley Dancer	1993	American Winner	Ron Pierce
1973	Flirth	Ralph Baldwin	1994	Victory Dream	Michel Lachance
1974	Christopher T	Bill Haughton	1995	Tagliabue	John Campbell
1975	Bonefish	Stanley Dancer	1996	Continental-victory	Michel Lachance
1976	Steve Lobell	Bill Haughton	1997	Malabar Man	Malvern Burroughs
1977	Green Speed	Bill Haughton	1998	Muscles Yankee	John Campbell
1978	Speedy Somolli	Howard Beissinger	1999	Self Possessed	Mike Lachance
1979	Legend Hanover	George Sholty	2000	Yankee Paco	Trevor Ritchie
1980	Burgomeister	Bill Haughton	2001	Scarlet Knight	Stefan Melander
1981	Shiaway St. Pat	Ray Remmen	2002	Chip Chip Hooray	Eric Ledford
1982	Speed Bowl	Tommy Haughton	2003	Amigo Hall	Mike Lachance
1983	Duenna	Stanley Dancer	2004	Windsong's Legacy	Trond Smedshammer
1984	Historic Freight	Ben Webster	2005	Vivid Photo	Roger Hammer
1985	Prakas	Bill O'Donnell	2006	Glidemaster	John Campbell

BOWLING
Professional Bowlers Association
Hall of Fame

PERFORMANCE

Bill Allen	Buzz Fazio	Mark Roth
Glenn Allison	Dave Ferraro	Carmen Salvino
Earl Anthony	Jim Godman	Ernie Schlegel
Mike Aulby	Billy Hardwick	Harry Smith
Joe Berardi	Marshall Hollman	Dave Soutar
Ray Bluth	Tommy Hudson	Jim Stefanich
Parker Bohn III	Dave Husted	Brian Voss
Roy Buckley	Don Johnson	Wayne Webb
Nelson Burton Jr.	Joe Joseph	Dick Weber
Don Carter	Larry Laub	Pete Weber
Pat Colwell	Amleto Monacelli	Billy Welu
Steve Cook	David Ozio	Mark Williams
Dave Davis	George Pappas	Walter Ray
Gary Dickinson	Johnny Petraglia	Williams Jr.
Mike Durbin	Dick Ritger	Wayne Zahn

MERITORIOUS SERVICE

Glenn Allison	Skee Foremsky	Steve Nagy
Joe Antenora	Lou Frantz	Keijiro Nakano
John Archibald	Harry Golden	Chuck Pezzano
Barry Asher	John Guenther	Jack Reichert
Tom Baker	Ted Hoffman Jr.	Joe Richards
Chuck Clemens	Joe Joseph	Jim St. John
Eddie Elias	John Jowdy	Chris Schenkel
Frank Esposito	Joe Kelley	Ernie Schlegel
Dick Evans	Larry Lichstein	Teata Semiz
Matt Fiorito	Mike Limongello	Lorraine Stilzlein
Raymond	Mort Luby Jr.	Bob Strampe
Firestone	Andy Marzich	Al Thompson
E. A. "Bud" Fisher	Don McCune	Roger Zeller
Jim Fitzgerald	Mike McGrath	

PBA Tournament of Champions, 1965-2006[1]

Year	Winner	Year	Winner	Year	Winner	Year	Winner
1965	Billy Hardwick	1975	Dave Davis	1985	Mark Williams	1996	Dave D'Entremont
1966	Wayne Zahn	1976	Marshall Holman	1986	Marshall Holman	1997	John Gant
1967	Jim Stefanich	1977	Mike Berlin	1987	Pete Weber	1998	Bryan Goebel
1968	Dave Davis	1978	Earl Anthony	1988	Mark Williams	1999	Jason Couch
1969	Jim Godman	1979	George Pappas	1989	Del Ballard, Jr.	2000	Jason Couch
1970	Don Johnson	1980	Wayne Webb	1990	Dave Ferraro	2002	Jason Couch
1971	Johnny Petraglia	1981	Steve Cook	1991	David Ozio	2003	Patrick Healey Jr
1972	Mike Durbin	1982	Mike Durbin	1992	Marc McDowell	2005	Steve Jaros
1973	Jim Godman	1983	Joe Berardi	1993	George Branham, 3rd	2006	Chris Barnes
1974	Earl Anthony	1984	Mike Durbin	1994	Norm Duke		

(1) No tournament held in 2001 because of schedule changes; the tournament now takes place in Apr. at the end of the PBA season (previously held in Dec.).

PBA Leading Money Winners

Total winnings are from PBA, ABC Masters, and BPAA All-Star tournaments only and do not include numerous other tournaments or earnings from special television shows and matches. In 2001, the PBA began an Oct.-Apr. season schedule. After 2000, year shown is year the season ended.

Year	Bowler	Amount	Year	Bowler	Amount	Year	Bowler	Amount
1962	Don Carter	$49,972	1977	Mark Roth	$105,583	1992	Marc McDowell	$174,215
1963	Dick Weber	46,333	1978	Mark Roth	134,500	1993	Walter Ray Williams Jr.	296,370
1964	Bob Strampe	33,592	1979	Mark Roth	124,517	1994	Norm Duke	273,753
1965	Dick Weber	47,674	1980	Wayne Webb	116,700	1995	Mike Aulby	219,792
1966	Wayne Zahn	54,720	1981	Earl Anthony	164,735	1996	Walter Ray Williams Jr.	241,330
1967	Dave Davis	54,165	1982	Earl Anthony	134,760	1997	Walter Ray Williams Jr.	240,544
1968	Jim Stefanich	67,377	1983	Earl Anthony	135,605	1998	Walter Ray Williams Jr.	238,225
1969	Billy Hardwick	64,160	1984	Mark Roth	158,712	1999	Parker Bohn III	240,912
1970	Mike McGrath	52,049	1985	Mike Aulby	201,200	2000	Norm Duke	143,325
1971	Johnny Petraglia	85,065	1986	Walter Ray Williams Jr.	145,550	2002	Parker Bohn III	245,200
1972	Don Johnson	56,648	1987	Pete Weber	175,491	2003	Walter Ray Williams Jr.	419,700
1973	Don McCune	69,000	1988	Brian Voss	225,485	2004	Mika Koivuniemi	238,590
1974	Earl Anthony	99,585	1989	Mike Aulby	298,237	2005	Patrick Allen	350,740
1975	Earl Anthony	107,585	1990	Amleto Monacelli	204,775	2006	Tommy Jones	301,700
1976	Earl Anthony	110,833	1991	David Ozio	225,585			

Leading PBA Averages by Year

Year	Bowler	Average	Year	Bowler	Average	Year	Bowler	Average
1962	Don Carter	212.84	1977	Mark Roth	218.17	1992	Dave Ferraro	219.70
1963	Billy Hardwick	210.34	1978	Mark Roth	219.83	1993	Walter Ray Williams Jr.	222.98
1964	Ray Bluth	210.51	1979	Mark Roth	221.66	1994	Norm Duke	222.83
1965	Dick Weber	211.89	1980	Earl Anthony	218.53	1995	Mike Aulby	225.49
1966	Wayne Zahn	208.66	1981	Mark Roth	216.69	1996	Walter Ray Williams Jr.	225.37
1967	Wayne Zahn	212.34	1982	Marshall Holman	212.84	1997	Walter Ray Williams Jr.	222.00
1968	Jim Stefanich	211.89	1983	Earl Anthony	216.64	1998	Walter Ray Williams Jr.	226.13
1969	Bill Hardwick	212.95	1984	Marshall Holman	213.91	1999	Parker Bohn III	228.04
1970	Nelson Burton Jr.	214.90	1985	Mark Baker	213.71	2000	Chris Barnes	220.93
1971	Don Johnson	213.97	1986	John Gant	214.37	2002	Parker Bohn III	221.54
1972	Don Johnson	215.29	1987	Marshall Holman	216.80	2003	Walter Ray Williams Jr.	224.94
1973	Earl Anthony	215.79	1988	Mark Roth	218.03	2004	Mika Koivuniemi	222.73
1974	Earl Anthony	219.39	1989	Pete Weber	215.43	2005	Walter Ray Williams Jr.	227.07
1975	Earl Anthony	219.06	1990	Amleto Monacelli	218.15	2006	Norm Duke	224.29
1976	Mark Roth	215.97	1991	Norm Duke	218.20			

United States Bowling Congress

Formed Jan. 1, 2005, from a merger of the American Bowling Congress, Women's International Bowling Congress, the Young American Bowling Alliance, and USA Bowling. Before 2006, sanctioned games and champions are for ABC only.

Most Sanctioned 300 Games — Men

Jeff Carter, Springfield, IL	83	Frank Massengale Jr., Hixon, TN	71

Jeff Carter, Springfield, IL 83
Joe Jimenez, Saginaw, MI 79
Chris Hayward, Toledo, OH 75
Jeff Ripic, Endicott, NY 75
John Delp III, West Lawn, PA 73
Dean Wolf, Reading, PA 73
Jerry Kessler, Dayton, OH 71

Frank Massengale Jr., Hixon, TN . . . 71
Gordon Childers, Benton, AR 66
Jim Hosier, Wayne, NJ 66
Randy Choat, Granite City, IL 64
Jack Kurent, Luzerne, PA 64
Jim Tomek Jr., Camp Hill, PA 63
David Bingham, Brainard, NY 62

John Chacko Jr., Larksville, PA 61
Robert Faragon, Albany, NY 61
Jeff Jensen, Wichita, KS 60
Bob Learn Jr., Erie, PA 60
Leonard Reynoldt, Catskill, NY 60
Dale Strike, Saginaw, MI 56
John Wilcox Jr., Lewisburg, PA 55

USBC Masters Tournament Champions

Year	Winner	Year	Winner	Year	Winner
1980	Neil Burton, St. Louis, MO	1989	Mike Aulby, Indianapolis, IN	1999	Brian Boghosian, Middletown, CT
1981	Randy Lightfoot, St. Charles, MO	1990	Chris Warren, Dallas, TX	2000	Mika Koivuniemi, Finland
1982	Joe Berardi, Brooklyn, NY	1991	Doug Kent, Canandaigua, NY	2001	Parker Bohn III, Jackson, NJ
1983	Mike Lastowski, Havre de Grace, MD	1992	Ken Johnson, N. Richmond Hills, TX	2002	Brett Wolfe, Reno, NV
1984	Earl Anthony, Dublin, CA	1993	Norm Duke, Oklahoma City, OK	2003	Bryon Smith, Roseburg, OR
1985	Steve Wunderlich, St. Louis, MO	1994	Steve Fehr, Cincinnati, OH	2004	Walter Ray Williams Jr., FL
1986	Mark Fahy, Chicago, IL	1995	Mike Aulby, Indianapolis, IN	2005	Walter Ray Williams Jr., FL (Jan.)
1987	Rick Steelsmith, Wichita, KS	1996	Ernie Schlegel, Vancouver, WA		Danny Wiseman, MD (Oct.)
1988	Del Ballard, Jr., Richardson, TX	1997	Jason Queen, Decatur, IL	2006	Mike Scroggins, Amarillo, TX
		1998	Mike Aulby, Indianapolis, IN		

Open Champions, 2006

Regular Singles: Wendy Macpherson, Henderson, NV
Regular Doubles: Bobby Stives, El Paso, TX & Paul Yoder, Albuquerque, NM
Regular All-Events: Dave Mitchell, Farmington, MN
Regular Team: Browning Pontiac, Cincinnati, OH
Team All-Events: Linds Lakers, Minneapolis, MN

Classified Singles: Shawn Fisher, Albuquerque, NM
Classified Doubles: Robert Tukker Jr., Mt. Prospect, IL & David Clauss, Chicago, IL
Classified All-Events: Kirby Lomax, Gainesville, GA
Classified Team: Torkelson Construction, Clarion, IA

USBC Queens and Open Champions, 2006
Note: Formerly WIBC Queens.

Queens Tournament: Shannon Pluhowsky, Phoenix, AZ
Classic Singles: Karen Stroud, Victoria, TX
Classic Doubles: Leanne Barrette, Elk Grove, CA & Lauren Takahashi, Woodland Hills, CA
Classic All-Events: Karen Stroud, Victoria, TX
Classic Team: Together Once Again, North Richland Hills, TX

Div. I Singles: Kathy Woessner, Euless, TX
Div. I Doubles: Pam Schulz, Longview, WA & Valery Hubbard, Kelso, WA
Div. I All-Events: Maika Winkler, Antelope, CA
Div. I Team: 5 Hot Mamas, Orland, CA

Most Sanctioned 300 Games — Women

Jodi Musto, Schenectady, NY 36
Altramese Webb, Detroit, MI 36
Tish Johnson, Panorama City, CA 35
Dede Davidson, Woodland Hills, CA . . 29
Shannon Duplantis, New Orleans, LA . . 27
Debbie McMullen, Denver, CO 27
Aleta Sill, Dearborn, MI 27
Leanne Barrette, Yukon, OK 26
Marianne DiRupo, Succasunna, NJ . . . 26

Anne-Marie Duggan, Edmond, OK . . . 25
Vicki Fischel, Wheat Ridge, CO 23
Tammy Jones, Decatur, IL 23
Jeanne Naccarato, Tacoma, WA 23
Cheryl Daniels, Detroit, MI 22
Jeanette Menacho, Sacramento, CA 22
Kim Terrell, San Francisco, CA 22

Carolyn Dorin-Ballard, N. Richland Hills, TX 21
Jodi Hughes, Greenville, SC 21
Mandy Wilson, Dayton, OH 21
Jackie Mitskavich 19
Kim Adler, Palm City, FL 18
Cindy Coburn-Carroll, Tonawanda, NY 18

NCAA WRESTLING CHAMPIONS

Year	Champion	Year	Champion	Year	Champion	Year	Champion	Year	Champion
1964	Oklahoma State	1973	Iowa State	1982	Iowa	1991	Iowa	1999	Iowa
1965	Iowa State	1974	Oklahoma	1983	Iowa	1992	Iowa	2000	Iowa
1966	Oklahoma State	1975	Iowa	1984	Iowa	1993	Iowa	2001	Minnesota
1967	Michigan State	1976	Iowa	1985	Iowa	1994	Oklahoma State	2002	Minnesota
1968	Oklahoma State	1977	Iowa State	1986	Iowa	1995	Iowa	2003	Oklahoma State
1969	Iowa State	1978	Iowa	1987	Iowa State	1996	Iowa	2004	Oklahoma State
1970	Iowa State	1979	Iowa	1988	Arizona State	1997	Iowa	2005	Oklahoma State
1971	Oklahoma State	1980	Iowa	1989	Oklahoma State	1998	Iowa	2006	Oklahoma State
1972	Iowa State	1981	Iowa	1990	Oklahoma State				

CHESS
World Chess Champions
Sources: U.S. Chess Federation; International Chess Federation (FIDE)
Official world champions since the title was first used are as follows:

1886-1894	Wilhelm Steinitz, Austria	1969-1972	Boris Spassky, USSR
1894-1921	Emanuel Lasker, Germany	1972-1975	Bobby Fischer, U.S. (b)
1921-1927	Jose R. Capablanca, Cuba	1975-1985	Anatoly Karpov, USSR
1927-1935	Alexander Alekhine, France	1985-2000	Garry Kasparov, USSR/Russia (c)
1935-1937	Max Euwe, Netherlands	1993-1999	Anatoly Karpov, Russia (FIDE)
1937-1946	Alexander Alekhine, France (a)	1999-2000	Alexander Khalifman, Russia (FIDE)
1948-1957	Mikhail Botvinnik, USSR	2000-2002	Viswanathan Anand, India (FIDE)
1957-1958	Vassily Smyslov, USSR	2000-2006	Vladimir Kramnik, Russia (classical) (d,e)
1958-1959	Mikhail Botvinnik, USSR	2002-2004	Ruslan Ponomariov, Ukraine (FIDE)
1960-1961	Mikhail Tal, USSR	2004-2005	Rustam Kasimdzhanov, Uzbekistan (FIDE)
1961-1963	Mikhail Botvinnik, USSR	2005-2006	Veselin Topalov, Bulgaria (FIDE)
1963-1969	Tigran Petrosian, USSR	2006-	Vladimir Kramnik, Russia (e)

(a) After Alekhine died in 1946, the title was vacant until 1948, when Botvinnik won the 1st world championship event sanctioned by FIDE. (b) Defaulted championship after refusing to accept FIDE rules for a championship match, Apr. 1975. (c) Kasparov broke with FIDE, Feb. 26, 1993. FIDE stripped Kasparov of his FIDE title Mar. 23. Kasparov then defeated Nigel Short of Great Britain in a world championship match played Sept.-Oct. 1993 under the auspices of a new organization the two had founded, the Professional Chess Association. FIDE held a replacement championship match between Anatoly Karpov (Russia) and Jan Timman (the Netherlands), which Karpov won in Nov. 1993. The PCA folded in 1995, but Kasparov was still considered the "classical" world champion. (d) In Nov. 2000, Vladimir Kramnik (Russia) defeated Garry Kasparov (Russia), for the classical world championship title in London. (e) Vladimir Kramnik, the classical world champion since 2000, and Veselin Topalov, FIDE champion since 2005, met at the world chess championship match in Elista, Russia, to compete for a unified championship, which Kramnik won Oct. 13, 2006. **Further information:** www.fide.com

FIGURE SKATING
U.S. and World Individual Champions, 1952-2006

U.S. Champions			World Champions	
MEN	**WOMEN**	**YEAR**	**MEN**	**WOMEN**
Dick Button	Tenley Albright	1952	Dick Button, U.S.	Jacqueline du Bief, France
Hayes Jenkins	Tenley Albright	1953	Hayes Jenkins, U.S.	Tenley Albright, U.S.
Hayes Jenkins	Tenley Albright	1954	Hayes Jenkins, U.S.	Gundi Busch, W. Germany
Hayes Jenkins	Tenley Albright	1955	Hayes Jenkins, U.S.	Tenley Albright, U.S.
Hayes Jenkins	Tenley Albright	1956	Hayes Jenkins, U.S.	Carol Heiss, U.S.
Dave Jenkins	Carol Heiss	1957	Dave Jenkins, U.S.	Carol Heiss, U.S.
Dave Jenkins	Carol Heiss	1958	Dave Jenkins, U.S.	Carol Heiss, U.S.
Dave Jenkins	Carol Heiss	1959	Dave Jenkins, U.S.	Carol Heiss, U.S.
Dave Jenkins	Carol Heiss	1960	Alain Giletti, France	Carol Heiss, U.S.
Bradley Lord	Laurence Owen	1961	none	none
Monty Hoyt	Barbara Roles Pursley	1962	Don Jackson, Canada	Sjoukje Dijkstra, Netherlands
Tommy Litz	Lorraine Hanlon	1963	Don McPherson, Canada	Sjoukje Dijkstra, Netherlands
Scott Allen	Peggy Fleming	1964	Manfred Schnelldorfer, W. Germany	Sjoukje Dijkstra, Netherlands
Gary Visconti	Peggy Fleming	1965	Alain Calmat, France	Petra Burka, Canada
Scott Allen	Peggy Fleming	1966	Emmerich Danzer, Austria	Peggy Fleming, U.S.
Gary Visconti	Peggy Fleming	1967	Emmerich Danzer, Austria	Peggy Fleming, U.S.
Tim Wood	Peggy Fleming	1968	Emmerich Danzer, Austria	Peggy Fleming, U.S.
Tim Wood	Janet Lynn	1969	Tim Wood, U.S.	Gabriele Seyfert, E. Germany
Tim Wood	Janet Lynn	1970	Tim Wood, U.S.	Gabriele Seyfert, E. Germany
John Misha Petkevich	Janet Lynn	1971	Ondrej Nepela, Czechoslovakia	Beatrix Schuba, Austria
Ken Shelley	Janet Lynn	1972	Ondrej Nepela, Czechoslovakia	Beatrix Schuba, Austria
Gordon McKellen, Jr.	Janet Lynn	1973	Ondrej Nepela, Czechoslovakia	Karen Magnussen, Canada
Gordon McKellen, Jr.	Dorothy Hamill	1974	Jan Hoffmann, E. Germany	Christine Errath, E. Germany
Gordon McKellen, Jr.	Dorothy Hamill	1975	Sergei Volkov, USSR	Dianne de Leeuw, Neth.-U.S.
Terry Kubicka	Dorothy Hamill	1976	John Curry, Gr. Britain	Dorothy Hamill, U.S.
Charles Tickner	Linda Fratianne	1977	Vladimir Kovalev, USSR	Linda Fratianne, U.S.
Charles Tickner	Linda Fratianne	1978	Charles Tickner, U.S.	Anett Poetzsch, E. Germany
Charles Tickner	Linda Fratianne	1979	Vladimir Kovalev, USSR	Linda Fratianne, U.S.
Charles Tickner	Linda Fratianne	1980	Jan Hoffmann, E. Germany	Anett Poetzsch, E. Germany
Scott Hamilton	Elaine Zayak	1981	Scott Hamilton, U.S.	Denise Biellmann, Switzerland
Scott Hamilton	Rosalynn Sumners	1982	Scott Hamilton, U.S.	Elaine Zayak, U.S.
Scott Hamilton	Rosalynn Sumners	1983	Scott Hamilton, U.S.	Rosalynn Sumners, U.S.
Scott Hamilton	Rosalynn Sumners	1984	Scott Hamilton, U.S.	Katarina Witt, E. Germany
Brian Boitano	Tiffany Chin	1985	Aleksandr Fadeev, USSR	Katarina Witt, E. Germany
Brian Boitano	Debi Thomas	1986	Brian Boitano, U.S.	Debi Thomas, U.S.
Brian Boitano	Jill Trenary	1987	Brian Orser, Canada	Katarina Witt, E. Germany
Brian Boitano	Debi Thomas	1988	Brian Boitano, U.S.	Katarina Witt, E. Germany
Christopher Bowman	Jill Trenary	1989	Kurt Browning, Canada	Midori Ito, Japan
Todd Eldredge	Jill Trenary	1990	Kurt Browning, Canada	Jill Trenary, U.S.
Todd Eldredge	Tonya Harding	1991	Kurt Browning, Canada	Kristi Yamaguchi, U.S.
Christopher Bowman	Kristi Yamaguchi	1992	Viktor Petrenko, Ukraine	Kristi Yamaguchi, U.S.
Scott Davis	Nancy Kerrigan	1993	Kurt Browning, Canada	Oksana Baiul, Ukraine
Scott Davis	vacant[1]	1994	Elvis Stojko, Canada	Yuka Sato, Japan
Todd Eldredge	Nicole Bobek	1995	Elvis Stojko, Canada	Chen Lu, China
Rudy Galindo	Michelle Kwan	1996	Todd Eldredge, U.S.	Michelle Kwan, U.S.
Todd Eldredge	Tara Lipinski	1997	Elvis Stojko, Canada	Tara Lipinski, U.S.
Todd Eldredge	Michelle Kwan	1998	Alexei Yagudin, Russia	Michelle Kwan, U.S.
Michael Weiss	Michelle Kwan	1999	Alexei Yagudin, Russia	Maria Butyrskaya, Russia
Michael Weiss	Michelle Kwan	2000	Alexei Yagudin, Russia	Michelle Kwan, U.S.
Timothy Goebel	Michelle Kwan	2001	Yevgeny Plushchenko, Russia	Michelle Kwan, U.S.
Todd Eldredge	Michelle Kwan	2002	Alexei Yagudin, Russia	Irina Slutskaya, Russia
Michael Weiss	Michelle Kwan	2003	Yevgeny Plushchenko, Russia	Michelle Kwan, U.S.
Johnny Weir	Michelle Kwan	2004	Yevgeny Plushchenko, Russia	Shizuka Arakawa, Japan
Johnny Weir	Michelle Kwan	2005	Stephane Lambiel, Switzerland	Irina Slutskaya, Russia
Johnny Weir	Sasha Cohen	2006	Stephane Lambiel, Switzerland	Kimmie Meissner, U.S.

(1) Tonya Harding was stripped of title.

SKIING
World Cup Alpine Champions, 1967-2006

Men		Women	
1967	Jean Claude Killy, France	1994	Kjetil Andre Aamodt, Norway
1968	Jean Claude Killy, France	1995	Alberto Tomba, Italy
1969	Karl Schranz, Austria	1996	Lasse Kjus, Norway
1970	Karl Schranz, Austria	1997	Luc Alphand, France
1971	Gustavo Thoeni, Italy	1998	Hermann Maier, Austria
1972	Gustavo Thoeni, Italy	1999	Lasse Kjus, Norway
1973	Gustavo Thoeni, Italy	2000	Hermann Maier, Austria
1974	Piero Gros, Italy	2001	Hermann Maier, Austria
1975	Gustavo Thoeni, Italy	2002	Stephan Eberharter, Austria
1976	Ingemar Stenmark, Sweden	2003	Stephan Eberharter, Austria
1977	Ingemar Stenmark, Sweden	2004	Hermann Maier, Austria
1978	Ingemar Stenmark, Sweden	2005	Bode Miller, U.S.
1979	Peter Luescher, Switzerland	2006	Benjamin Raich, Austria

Women (Men column continued / Women)

1980	Andreas Wenzel, Liechtenstein	1967	Nancy Greene, Canada
1981	Phil Mahre, U.S.	1968	Nancy Greene, Canada
1982	Phil Mahre, U.S.	1969	Gertrud Gabl, Austria
1983	Phil Mahre, U.S.	1970	Michele Jacot, France
1984	Pirmin Zurbriggen, Switzerland	1971	Annemarie Proell, Austria
1985	Marc Girardelli, Luxembourg	1972	Annemarie Proell, Austria
1986	Marc Girardelli, Luxembourg	1973	Annemarie Proell, Austria
1987	Pirmin Zurbriggen, Switzerland	1974	Annemarie Proell, Austria
1988	Pirmin Zurbriggen, Switzerland	1975	Annemarie Proell, Austria
1989	Marc Girardelli, Luxembourg	1976	Rose Mittermaier, W. Germany
1990	Pirmin Zurbriggen, Switzerland	1977	Lise-Marie Morerod, Switzerland
1991	Marc Girardelli, Luxembourg	1978	Hanni Wenzel, Liechtenstein
1992	Paul Accola, Switzerland	1979	Annemarie Proell Moser, Austria
1993	Marc Girardelli, Luxembourg		

1980	Hanni Wenzel, Liechtenstein
1981	Marie-Theres Nadig, Switzerland
1982	Erika Hess, Switzerland
1983	Tamara McKinney, U.S.
1984	Erika Hess, Switzerland
1985	Michela Figini, Switzerland
1986	Maria Walliser, Switzerland
1987	Maria Walliser, Switzerland
1988	Michela Figini, Switzerland
1989	Vreni Schneider, Switzerland
1990	Petra Kronberger, Austria
1991	Petra Kronberger, Austria
1992	Petra Kronberger, Austria
1993	Anita Wachter, Austria
1994	Vreni Schneider, Switzerland
1995	Vreni Schneider, Switzerland
1996	Katja Seizinger, Germany
1997	Pernilla Wiberg, Sweden
1998	Katja Seizinger, Germany
1999	Alexandra Meissnitzer, Austria
2000	Renate Goetschl, Austria
2001	Janica Kostelic, Croatia
2002	Michaela Dorfmeister, Austria
2003	Janica Kostelic, Croatia
2004	Anja Paerson, Sweden
2005	Anja Paerson, Sweden
2006	Janica Kostelic, Croatia

CYCLING
2006 Tour de France

On July 23, 2006, Floyd Landis won the 103rd Tour de France, cycling's premier event, making it the 8th straight year the event had been won by an American. The 2,267-mi Tour began July 1, in Strasbourg, France, and ended 21 stages later in Paris. Landis, riding for the Swiss-based Phonak team, finished the race in 89 hours, 39 minutes, and 30 seconds. Spain's Oscar Pereiro came in 2nd, 57 seconds behind Landis. Landis's performance over the last few days of the tour was heralded as one of the great comebacks in cycling history: just a few days earlier, on July 19, he was 8 min., 8 sec. behind Pereiro and in 11th place overall.

Landis's victory celebration was shortlived. Phonak announced July 27, 2006, that a 17th-stage drug test showed Landis to have impermissibly high testosterone levels. A second test of the sample confirmed the finding, Aug. 5, and noted that the sample contained traces of synthetic testosterone. Landis asserted his innocence, pointing out that the other drug tests he had taken during the tour had been negative. The International Cycling Union referred the case to the U.S. Anti-Doping Agency and USA Cycling, which was to be responsible for formally stripping Landis of his title if proceedings determined Landis was guilty of the charges.

Tour de France Winners, 1980-2006

Year	Winner	Year	Winner	Year	Winner	Year	Winner
1980	Zoop Zoetemelk, The Netherlands	1986	Greg LeMond, U.S.	1993	Miguel Indurain, Spain	2000	Lance Armstrong, U.S.
		1987	Stephen Roche, Ireland	1994	Miguel Indurain, Spain	2001	Lance Armstrong, U.S.
1981	Bernard Hinault, France	1988	Pedro Delgado, Spain	1995	Miguel Indurain, Spain	2002	Lance Armstrong, U.S.
1982	Bernard Hinault, France	1989	Greg LeMond, U.S.	1996	Bjarne Riis, Denmark	2003	Lance Armstrong, U.S.
1983	Laurent Fignon, France	1990	Greg LeMond, U.S.	1997	Jan Ullrich, Germany	2004	Lance Armstrong, U.S.
1984	Laurent Fignon, France	1991	Miguel Indurain, Spain	1998	Marco Pantani, Italy	2005	Lance Armstrong, U.S.
1985	Bernard Hinault, France	1992	Miguel Indurain, Spain	1999	Lance Armstrong, U.S.	2006	Floyd Landis, U.S.*

*Landis's title stood in jeopardy as of Sept. 2006 due to doping allegations (see above).

LACROSSE
Lacrosse Champions in 2006

Major League Lacrosse—Carson, CA, Aug. 27: Philadelphia Barrage 23, Denver Outlaws 12.
U.S. Club Lacrosse Association Championship—New Hyde Park, NY, June 11: MAB Philly Paints 14, North Hempstead LC 13.
National Lacrosse League Championship—Buffalo, NY, May 13: Colorado Mammoth 16, Buffalo Bandits 9.
NCAA Men's Division I Championship—Philadelphia, PA, May 29: Virginia 15, Massachusetts 7.
NCAA Women's Division I Championship—Annapolis, MD, May 28: Northwestern 7, Dartmouth 4.

2006 Men's NCAA Division I All-America Team

Attack: Sean Morris, Massachusetts; Chris Unterstein, Hofstra; Joe Walters, Maryland; Matt Ward, Virginia
Midfield: Joe Boulukos, Cornell; Kyle Dixon, Virginia; Bill McGlone, Maryland; Paul Rabil, Johns Hopkins.
Defense: Mike Culver, Virginia; Brett Moyer, Hofstra; Jack Reid, Massachusetts.
Goal: Alex Hewit, Princeton.

2006 Women's NCAA Division I All-America Team

Attack: Katie Chrest, Duke; Crysti Foote, Notre Dame; Mary Key, Johns Hopkins; Tyler Leachman, Virginia; Lindsey Munday, Northwestern; Coco Stanwick, Georgetown.
Midfield: Sarah Albrecht, Northwestern; Kelly Berger, James Madison; Kristen Kjellman, Northwestern; Nikki Lieb, Virginia; Rachel Sanford, Duke; Kristen Zimmer, Dartmouth.
Defense: Jenn Cook, North Carolina; Lizzy Cuneo, Dartmouth; Lauren Vance, Princeton.
Goal: Maggie Koch, Georgetown.

NCAA Division I Lacrosse Champions 1982-2006

Year[1]	Men	Women	Year[1]	Men	Women	Year[1]	Men	Women
1982	North Carolina	Massachusetts	1991	North Carolina	Virginia	1999	Virginia	Maryland
1983	Syracuse	Delaware	1992	Princeton	Maryland	2000	Syracuse	Maryland
1984	Johns Hopkins	Temple	1993	Syracuse	Virginia	2001	Princeton	Maryland
1985	Johns Hopkins	New Hampshire	1994	Princeton	Princeton	2002	Syracuse	Princeton
1986	North Carolina	Maryland	1995	Syracuse	Maryland	2003	Virginia	Princeton
1987	Johns Hopkins	Penn St.	1996	Princeton	Maryland	2004	Syracuse	Virginia
1988	Syracuse	Temple	1997	Princeton	Maryland	2005	Johns Hopkins	Northwestern
1989	Syracuse	Penn St.	1998	Princeton	Maryland	2006	Virginia	Northwestern
1990	vacated	Harvard						

(1) NCAA Championships began in 1971 for men, in 1982 for women.

SWIMMING
World Swimming Records
(Long course (50 m), as of Oct. 2006)
Men's Records

Freestyle

Distance	Time	Holder	Country	Where made	Date
50 meters	0:21.64	Alexander Popov	Russia	Moscow, Russia	June 16, 2000
100 meters	0:47.84	Pieter van den Hoogenband	Netherlands	Sydney, Australia	Sept. 19, 2000
200 meters	1:44.06	Ian Thorpe	Australia	Fukuoka, Japan	July 25, 2001
400 meters	3:40.08	Ian Thorpe	Australia	Manchester, England	July 30, 2002
800 meters	7:38.65	Grant Hackett	Australia	Montreal, Canada	July 27, 2005
1,500 meters	14:34.56	Grant Hackett	Australia	Fukuoka, Japan	July 29, 2001

Breaststroke

Distance	Time	Holder	Country	Where made	Date
50 meters	0:27.18	Oleg Lisogor	Ukraine	Berlin, Germany	Aug. 2, 2002
100 meters	0:59.30	Brendan Hansen	U.S.	Long Beach, CA	July 8, 2004
200 meters	2:09.04	Brendan Hansen	U.S.	Long Beach, CA	July 11, 2004

Butterfly

Distance	Time	Holder	Country	Where made	Date
50 meters	0:22.96	Roland Schoeman	Russia	Montreal, Canada	July 25, 2005
100 meters	0:50.40	Ian Crocker	U.S.	Montreal, Canada	July 30, 2005
200 meters	1:53.93	Michael Phelps	U.S.	Barcelona, Spain	July 22, 2003

Backstroke

Distance	Time	Holder	Country	Where made	Date
50 meters	0:24.80	Thomas Rupprath	Germany	Barcelona, Spain	July 27, 2003
100 meters	0:53.17	Aaron Peirsol	U.S.	Indianapolis, IN	Apr. 2, 2005
200 meters	1:54.66	Aaron Peirsol	U.S.	Montreal, Canada	July 29, 2005

Individual Medley

Distance	Time	Holder	Country	Where made	Date
200 meters	1:55.94	Michael Phelps	U.S.	College Park, MD	Aug. 9, 2003
400 meters	4:08.26	Michael Phelps	U.S.	Athens, Greece	Aug. 14, 2004

Medley Relay

Distance	Time	Holder	Country	Where made	Date
400 m. (4×100)	3:30.68	(Peirsol, Hansen, Crocker, Lezak)	U.S.	Athens, Greece	Aug. 21, 2004

Freestyle Relays

Distance	Time	Holder	Country	Where made	Date
400 m. (4×100)	3:13.17	(Schoeman, Ferns, Townsend, Neethling)	South Africa	Athens, Greece	Aug. 15, 2004
800 m. (4×200)	7:04.66	(Hackett, Klim, Kirby, Thorpe)	Australia	Fukuoka, Japan	July 27, 2001

Women's Records

Freestyle

Distance	Time	Holder	Country	Where made	Date
50 meters	0:24.13	Inge de Bruijn	Netherlands	Sydney, Australia	Sept. 22, 2000
100 meters	0:53.42	Lisbeth Lenton	Australia	Melbourne, Australia	Jan. 31, 2006
200 meters	1:56.64	Franziska Van Almsick	Germany	Berlin, Germany	Aug. 3, 2002
400 meters	4:03.03	Laure Manaudou	France	Tours, France	May 12, 2006
800 meters	8:16.22	Janet Evans	U.S.	Tokyo, Japan	Aug. 20, 1989
1,500 meters	15:52.10	Janet Evans	U.S.	Orlando, FL	Mar. 26, 1988

Breaststroke

Distance	Time	Holder	Country	Where made	Date
50 meters	0:30.31	Jade Edmistone	Australia	Melbourne, Australia	Jan. 30, 2006
100 meters	1:05.09	Leisel Jones	Australia	Melbourne, Australia	Mar. 20, 2006
200 meters	2:20.54	Leisel Jones	Australia	Melbourne, Australia	Feb. 1, 2006

Butterfly

Distance	Time	Holder	Country	Where made	Date
50 meters	0:25.57	Anna-Karin Kammerling	Sweden	Berlin, Germany	July 30, 2000
100 meters	0:56.61	Inge de Bruijn	Netherlands	Sydney, Australia	Sept. 17, 2000
200 meters	2:05.61	Otylia Jedrejczak	Poland	Montreal, Canada	July 28, 2005

Backstroke

Distance	Time	Holder	Country	Where made	Date
50 meters	0:28.19	Janine Pietsch	Germany	Berlin, Germany	May 25, 2005
	0:28.19*	Aleksandra Herasimenia	Belarus	Minsk, Belarus	May 31, 2006
100 meters	0:59.58	Natalie Coughlin	U.S.	Ft. Lauderdale, FL	Aug. 13, 2002
200 meters	2:06.62	Kristina Egerszegi	Hungary	Athens, Greece	Aug. 25, 1991

Individual Medley

Distance	Time	Holder	Country	Where made	Date
200 meters	2:09.72	Yanyan Wu	China	Shanghai, China	Oct. 17, 1997
400 meters	4:33.59	Yana Klochkova	Ukraine	Sydney, Australia	Sept. 16, 2000

Freestyle Relays

Distance	Time	Holder	Country	Where made	Date
400 m. (4×100)	3:35.94	(Mills, Lenton, Thomas, Henry)	Australia	Athens, Greece	Aug. 14, 2004
800 m. (4×200)	7:53.42	(Coughlin, Piper, Vollmer, Sandeno)	U.S.	Athens, Greece	Aug. 18, 2004

Medley Relay

Distance	Time	Holder	Country	Where made	Date
400 m. (4×100)	3:56.30	(Edington, Jones, Schipper, Lenton)	Australia	Melbourne, Australia	Mar. 21, 2006

*Pending FINA approval.

RODEO
Pro Rodeo Cowboy All-Around Champions, 1977-2005

Year	Winner	Money won	Year	Winner	Money won
1977	Tom Ferguson, Miami, OK	$76,730	1992	Ty Murray, Stephenville, TX	$225,992
1978	Tom Ferguson, Miami, OK	103,734	1993	Ty Murray, Stephenville, TX	297,896
1979	Tom Ferguson, Miami, OK	96,272	1994	Ty Murray, Stephenville, TX	246,170
1980	Paul Tierney, Rapid City, SD	105,568	1995	Joe Beaver, Huntsville, TX	141,753
1981	Jimmie Cooper, Monument, NM	105,862	1996	Joe Beaver, Huntsville, TX	166,103
1982	Chris Lybbert, Coyote, CA	123,709	1997	Dan Mortensen, Manhattan, MT	184,559
1983	Roy Cooper, Durant, OK	153,391	1998	Ty Murray, Stephenville, TX	264,673
1984	Dee Pickett, Caldwell, ID	122,618	1999	Fred Whitfield, Hockley, TX	217,819
1985	Lewis Feild, Elk Ridge, UT	130,347	2000	Joe Beaver, Huntsville, TX	225,396
1986	Lewis Feild, Elk Ridge, UT	166,042	2001	Cody Ohl, Stephensville, TX	296,419
1987	Lewis Feild, Elk Ridge, UT	144,335	2002	Trevor Brazile, Anson, TX	273,997
1988	Dave Appleton, Arlington, TX	121,546	2003	Trevor Brazile, Anson, TX	294,839
1989	Ty Murray, Odessa, TX	134,806	2004	Trevor Brazile, Decatur, TX	253,170
1990	Ty Murray, Stephenville, TX	213,772	2005	Ryan Jarrett, Summerville, GA	263,665
1991	Ty Murray, Stephenville, TX	244,230			

POWER BOATING
American Power Boat Assn. Gold Cup Champions, 1978-2006

Year	Boat	Driver	Year	Boat	Driver
1978	Atlas Van Lines	Bill Muncey	1993	Miss Budweiser	Chip Hanauer
1979	Atlas Van Lines	Bill Muncey	1994	Smokin' Joe's	Mark Tate
1980	Miss Budweiser	Dean Chenoweth	1995	Miss Budweiser	Chip Hanauer
1981	Miss Budweiser	Dean Chenoweth	1996	Pico American Dream	Dave Villwock
1982	Atlas Van Lines	Chip Hanauer	1997	Miss Budweiser	Dave Villwock
1983	Atlas Van Lines	Chip Hanauer	1998	Miss Budweiser	Dave Villwock
1984	Atlas Van Lines	Chip Hanauer	1999	Miss PICO	Chip Hanauer
1985	Miller American	Chip Hanauer	2000	Miss Budweiser	Dave Villwock
1986	Miller American	Chip Hanauer	2001	Miss Tubby's Subs	Mike Hanson
1987	Miller American	Chip Hanauer	2002	Miss Budweiser	Dave Villwock
1988	Circus Circus	Chip Hanauer	2003	Miss Fox Hills	Mitch Evans
1989	Miss Budweiser	Tom D'Eath	2004	Miss Detroit Yacht Club	Nate Brown
1990	Miss Budweiser	Tom D'Eath	2005	Miss Al Deeby Dodge	Terry Troxell
1991	Winston Eagle	Mark Tate	2006	Miss Beacon Plumbing	Jean Theoret
1992	Miss Budweiser	Chip Hanauer			

YACHTING
The America's Cup

In the 31st America's Cup, the Swiss boat *Alinghi* swept 2-time defending champion *Team New Zealand,* 5-0, in the best-of-nine series, held in the Hauraki Gulf off the coast of Auckland, New Zealand in Feb. and Mar. 2003. *Alinghi* was skippered by New Zealander Russell Coutts, who had helped guide New Zealand to victory in 1995 and 2000. For the 1st time in its 152-year history, the Cup resides on the European continent, in landlocked Switzerland.

The *Alinghi* team announced on Nov. 26, 2003, that the next America's Cup would be held in Valencia, on Spain's Mediterranean coast, in 2007. However, Coutts was unlikely to be involved in *Alinghi*'s title defense—he was fired on July 26, 2004, after reportedly clashing with syndicate owner Ernesto Bertarelli.

Competition for the America's Cup grew out of the first contest to establish a world yachting championship, one of the carnival features of the London Exposition of 1851. The race covered a 60-mile course around the Isle of Wight; the prize was a cup worth about $500, donated by the Royal Yacht Squadron of England, known as the "America's Cup" because it was first won by the U.S. yacht *America*. It was held by American yachts until 1983.

Winners of the America's Cup

1851 America	1958 Columbia defeated Sceptre, England, (4-0)
1870 Magic defeated Cambria, England, (1-0)	1962 Weatherly defeated Gretel, Australia, (4-1)
1871 Columbia (first three races) and Sappho (last two races) defeated Livonia, England, (4-1)	1964 Constellation defeated Sovereign, England, (4-0)
1876 Madeline defeated Countess of Dufferin, Canada, (2-0)	1967 Intrepid defeated Dame Pattie, Australia, (4-0)
1881 Mischief defeated Atalanta, Canada, (2-0)	1970 Intrepid defeated Gretel II, Australia, (4-1)
1885 Puritan defeated Genesta, England, (2-0)	1974 Courageous defeated Southern Cross, Australia, (4-0)
1886 Mayflower defeated Galatea, England, (2-0)	1977 Courageous defeated Australia, Australia, (4-0)
1887 Volunteer defeated Thistle, Scotland, (2-0)	1980 Freedom defeated Australia, Australia, (4-1)
1893 Vigilant defeated Valkyrie II, England, (3-0)	1983 Australia II, Australia, defeated Liberty, (4-3)
1895 Defender defeated Valkyrie III, England, (3-0)	1987 Stars & Stripes defeated Kookaburra III, Australia, (4-0)
1899 Columbia defeated Shamrock, England, (3-0)	1988 Stars & Stripes defeated New Zealand, New Zealand, (2-0)
1901 Columbia defeated Shamrock II, England, (3-0)	1992 America³ defeated Il Moro di Venezia, Italy, (4-1)
1903 Reliance defeated Shamrock III, England, (3-0)	1995 Black Magic 1, New Zealand, defeated Young America, (5-0)
1920 Resolute defeated Shamrock IV, England, (3-2)	
1930 Enterprise defeated Shamrock V, England, (4-0)	2000 New Zealand, NZ, defeated Luna Rossa, Italy, (5-0)
1934 Rainbow defeated Endeavour, England, (4-2)	2003 Alinghi, Switzerland, defeated Team New Zealand, NZ, (5-0)
1937 Ranger defeated Endeavour II, England, (4-0)	

DOGS
Westminster Kennel Club, 1989-2006

Year	Best-in-show	Breed	Owner(s)
1989	Ch. Royal Tudor's Wild As The Wind	Doberman	Sue & Art Kemp, Richard & Carolyn Vida, Beth Wilhite
1990	Ch. Wendessa Crown Prince	Pekingese	Ed Jenner
1991	Ch. Whisperwind on a Carousel	Poodle	Joan & Frederick Hartsock
1992	Ch. Registry's Lonesome Dove	Fox Terrier	Marion & Sam Lawrence
1993	Ch. Salilyn's Condor	English Springer Spaniel	Donna & Roger Herzig
1994	Ch. Chidley Willum	Norwich Terrier	Ruth Cooper & Patricia Lussier
1995	Ch. Gaelforce Post Script	Scottish Terrier	Dr. Vandra Huber & Dr. Joe Kinnarney
1996	Ch. Clussexx Country Sunrise	Clumber Spaniel	Judith & Richard Zaleski
1997	Ch. Parsifal Di Casa Netzer	Standard Schnauzer	Rita Holloway & Gabrio Del Torre
1998	Ch. Fairewood Frolic	Norwich Terrier	Sandina Kennels
1999	Ch. Loteki Supernatural Being	Papillon	John Oulton
2000	Ch. Salilyn 'N Erin's Shameless	English Springer Spaniel	Carl Blain, Fran Sunseri, & Julia Gasow
2001	Ch. Special Times Just Right	Bichons Frises	Cecilia Ruggles, E. McDonald, & F. Werneck
2002	Ch. Surrey Spice Girl	Poodle (Miniature)	Ron L. & Barbara Scott
2003	Ch. Torum's Scarf Michael	Kerry Blue Terrier	Marilu Hanson
2004	Ch. Darbydale's All Rise Pouchcove	Newfoundland	Peggy Helming & Carol A. Bernard Bergmann
2005	Ch. Kan-Point's VJK Autumn Roses	German Shorthaired Pointer	Linda & Richard Stark, Carol Cronk, Valerie Nunes-Atkinson
2006	Ch. Rocky Top's Sundance Kid	Bull Terrier (colored)	Barbara Bishop, W. F. Poole, N. Shepherd, & R. P. Poole

2006 Iditarod Trail Sled Dog Race

Jeff King won the 34th annual Iditarod Trail Sled Dog Race from Anchorage to Nome, Alaska, for the 4th time on Mar. 15, 2006. King, a 50-year-old resident of Denali, Alaska, finished the 1,112-mile course along the northern Iditarod route in 9 days, 11 hours, 11 minutes, and 36 seconds. In all, 71 mushers completed the race to Nome. The 2007 race was scheduled to begin Mar. 3 in Anchorage and follow the 1,131-mile southern route to Nome.

MARATHONS
World Marathon Majors

Five of the world's leading marathons (Berlin, Boston, Chicago, London, and New York) agreed Jan. 23, 2006, to form a series called the World Marathon Majors. Marathon runners will be awarded points relative to their finish in each race in the series, and in Olympic and other world championship marathons. The male and female runners with the most points at the end of each 2-year cycle will win $500,000.

Boston Marathon Winners, 1972-2006

All times in hour:minute:second format. *Course records

Men's Winner	Time	Year	Women's Winner	Time
Olavi Suomalainen, Finland	2:15:39	1972	Nina Kuscsik, U.S.	3:10:26
Jon Anderson, U.S.	2:16:03	1973	Jacqueline Hansen, U.S.	3:05:59
Neil Cusack, Ireland	2:13:39	1974	Michiko Gorman, U.S.	2:47:11
Bill Rodgers, U.S.	2:09:55	1975	Liane Winter, West Germany	2:42:24
Jack Fultz, U.S.	2:20:19	1976	Kim Merritt, U.S.	2:47:10
Jerome Drayton, Canada	2:14:46	1977	Michiko Gorman, U.S.	2:48:33
Bill Rodgers, U.S.	2:10:13	1978	Gayle S. Barron, U.S.	2:44:52
Bill Rodgers, U.S.	2:09:27	1979	Joan Benoit, U.S.	2:35:15
Bill Rodgers, U.S.	2:12:11	1980	Jacqueline Gareau, Canada	2:34:28
Toshihiko Seko, Japan	2:09:26	1981	Allison Roe, N. Zealand	2:26:46
Alberto Salazar, U.S.	2:08:52	1982	Charlotte Teske, West Germany	2:29:33
Greg Meyer, U.S.	2:09:00	1983	Joan Benoit, U.S.	2:22:43
Geoff Smith, Great Britain	2:10:34	1984	Lorraine Moller, New Zealand	2:29:28
Geoff Smith, Great Britain	2:14:05	1985	Lisa Larsen Weidenbach, U.S.	2:34:06
Robert de Castella, Australia	2:07:51	1986	Ingrid Kristiansen, Norway	2:24:55
Toshihiko Seko, Japan	2:11:50	1987	Rosa Mota, Portugal	2:25:21
Ibrahim Hussein, Kenya	2:08:43	1988	Rosa Mota, Portugal	2:24:30
Abebe Mekonnen, Ethiopia	2:09:06	1989	Ingrid Kristiansen, Norway	2:24:33
Gelindo Bordin, Italy	2:08:19	1990	Rosa Mota, Portugal	2:25:24
Ibrahim Hussein, Kenya	2:11:06	1991	Wanda Panfil, Poland	2:24:18
Ibrahim Hussein, Kenya	2:08:14	1992	Olga Markova, Russia	2:23:43
Cosmas Ndeti, Kenya	2:09:33	1993	Olga Markova, Russia	2:25:27
Cosmas Ndeti, Kenya	2:07:15	1994	Uta Pippig, Germany	2:21:45
Cosmas Ndeti, Kenya	2:09:22	1995	Uta Pippig, Germany	2:25:11
Moses Tanui, Kenya	2:09:15	1996	Uta Pippig, Germany	2:27:12
Lameck Aguta, Kenya	2:10:34	1997	Fatuma Roba, Ethiopia	2:26:23
Moses Tanui, Kenya	2:07:34	1998	Fatuma Roba, Ethiopia	2:23:21
Joseh Chebet, Kenya	2:09:52	1999	Fatuma Roba, Ethiopia	2:23:25
Elijah Lagat, Kenya	2:09:47	2000	Catherine Ndereba, Kenya	2:26:11
Lee Bong-ju, S. Korea	2:09:43	2001	Catherine Ndereba, Kenya	2:23:53
Rodgers Rop, Kenya	2:09:02	2002	Margaret Okayo, Kenya	2:20:43*
Robert K. Cheruiyot, Kenya	2:10:11	2003	Svetlana Zakharova, Russia	2:25:20
Timothy Cherigat, Kenya	2:10:37	2004	Catherine Ndereba, Kenya	2:24:27
Hailu Negussie, Ethiopia	2:11:45	2005	Catherine Ndereba, Kenya	2:25:13
Robert Cheruiyot, Kenya	2:07:14*	2006	Rita Jeptoo, Kenya	2:23:38

Boston Marathon Winners, 1897-1971

The 1st Boston Marathon was held in 1897. Women were officially accepted into the race in 1972.

Year	Winner	Time	Year	Winner	Time
1897	John J. McDermott, New York	2:55:10	1935	John A. Kelley, Massachusetts	2:32:07
1898	Ronald J. MacDonald, Canada	2:42:00	1936	Ellison M. Brown, Rhode Island	2:33:40
1899	Lawrence Brignolia, Massachusetts	2:54:38	1937	Walter Young, Canada	2:33:20
1900	John Caffery, Canada	2:39:44	1938	Leslie S. Pawson, Rhode Island	2:35:34
1901	John Caffery, Canada	2:29:23	1939	Ellison M. Brown, Rhode Island	2:28:51
1902	Sammy Mellor, New York	2:43:12	1940	Gerard Cote, Canada	2:28:28
1903	John Lorden , Massachusetts	2:41:29	1941	Leslie S. Pawson, Rhode Island	2:30:38
1904	Michael Spring, New York	2:38:04	1942	Joe Smith, Massachusetts	2:26:51
1905	Frederick Lorz, New York	2:38:25	1943	Gerard Cote, Canada	2:28:25
1906	Tim Ford, Massachusetts	2:45:45	1944	Gerard Cote, Canada	2:31:50
1907	Thomas Longboat, Canada	2:24:24	1945	John A. Kelley, Massachusetts	2:30:40
1908	Thomas Morrissey, New York	2:25:43	1946	Stylianos Kyriakides, Greece	2:29:27
1909	Henri Renaud, New Hampshire	2:53:36	1947	Yun Bok Suh, Korea	2:25:39
1910	Fred Cameron, Canada	2:28:52	1948	Gerard Cote, Canada	2:31:02
1911	Clarence DeMar, Massachusetts	2:21:39	1949	Karl Leandersson, Sweden	2:31:50
1912	Michael Ryan, New York	2:21:18	1950	Kee Yong Ham, Korea	2:32:39
1913	Fritz Carlson, Minnesota	2:25:14	1951	Shigeki Tanaka, Japan	2:27:45
1914	James Duffy, Canada	2:25:14	1952	Doroteo Flores, Guatemala	2:31:53
1915	Edouard Fabre, Canada	2:31:41	1953	Keizo Yamada, Japan	2:18:51
1916	Arthur Roth, Massachusetts	2:27:16	1954	Veikko Karvonen, Finland	2:20:39
1917	Bill Kennedy, New York	2:28:37	1955	Hideo Hamamura, Japan	2:18:22
1918	Military Relay, Camp Devens	2:29:53	1956	Antti Viskari, Finland	2:14:14
1919	Carl Linder, Massachusetts	2:29:13	1957	John J. Kelley, Connecticut	2:20:05
1920	Peter Trivoulides, New York	2:29:31	1958	Franjo Mihalic, Yugoslavia	2:25:54
1921	Frank Zuna, New York	2:18:57	1959	Eino Oksanen, Finland	2:22:42
1922	Clarence DeMar, Massachusetts	2:18:10	1960	Paavo Kotila, Finland	2:20:54
1923	Clarence DeMar, Massachusetts	2:23:47	1961	Eino Oksanen, Finland	2:23:39
1924	Clarence DeMar, Massachusetts	2:29:40	1962	Eino Oksanen, Finland	2:23:48
1925	Charles Mellor, Illinois	2:33:00	1963	Aurele Vandendriessche, Belgium	2:18:58
1926	John C. Miles, Canada	2:25:40	1964	Aurele Vandendriessche, Belgium	2:19:59
1927	Clarence DeMar, Massachusetts	2:40:22	1965	Morio Shigematsu, Japan	2:16:33
1928	Clarence DeMar, Massachusetts	2:37:07	1966	Kenji Kemihara, Japan	2:17:11
1929	John C. Miles, Canada	2:33:08	1967	David McKenzie, New Zealand	2:15:45
1930	Clarence DeMar, Massachusetts	2:34:48	1968	Amby Burfoot, Connecticut	2:22:17
1931	James P. Henigan, Massachusetts	2:46:45	1969	Yoshiaki Unetani, Japan	2:13:49
1932	Paul DeBruyn, Germany	2:33:36	1970	Ron Hill, Great Britain	2:10:30
1933	Leslie S. Pawson, Rhode Island	2:31:01	1971	Alvaro Mejia, Colombia	2:18:45
1934	Dave Komonen, Canada	2:32:53			

New York City Marathon Winners, 1970-2005

All time in hour:minute:second format; *Course records.

Men's Winner	Time	Year	Women's Winner	Time
Gary Muhrcke, U.S.	2:31:38	1970	no finisher	—
Norman Higgins, U.S.	2:22:54	1971	Beth Bonner, U.S.	2:55:22
Sheldon Karlin, U.S.	2:27:52	1972	Nina Kuscsik, U.S.	3:08:41
Tom Fleming, U.S.	2:19:25	1973	Nina Kuscsik, U.S.	2:57:07
Norbert Sander, U.S.	2:26:30	1974	Katherine Switzer, U.S.	3:07:29
Tom Fleming, U.S.	2:19:27	1975	Kim Merritt, U.S.	2:46:14
Bill Rodgers, U.S.	2:10:10	1976	Miki Gorman, U.S.	2:39:11
Bill Rodgers, U.S.	2:11:28	1977	Miki Gorman, U.S.	2:43:10
Bill Rodgers, U.S.	2:12:12	1978	Grete Waitz, Norway	2:32:30
Bill Rodgers, U.S.	2:11:42	1979	Grete Waitz, Norway	2:27:33
Alberto Salazar, U.S.	2:09:41	1980	Grete Waitz, Norway	2:25:42
Alberto Salazar, U.S.	2:08:13	1981	Allison Roe, New Zealand	2:25:29
Alberto Salazar, U.S.	2:09:29	1982	Grete Waitz, Norway	2:27:14
Rod Dixon, New Zealand	2:08:59	1983	Grete Waitz, Norway	2:27:00
Orlando Pizzolato, Italy	2:14:53	1984	Grete Waitz, Norway	2:29:30
Orlando Pizzolato, Italy	2:11:34	1985	Grete Waitz, Norway	2:28:34
Gianni Poli, Italy	2:11:06	1986	Grete Waitz, Norway	2:28:06
Ibrahim Hussein, Kenya	2:11:01	1987	Priscilla Welch, England	2:30:17
Steve Jones, Great Britain	2:08:20	1988	Grete Waitz, Norway	2:28:07
Juma Ikangaa, Tanzania	2:08:01	1989	Ingrid Kristiansen, Norway	2:25:30
Douglas Wakiihuri, Kenya	2:12:39	1990	Wanda Panfil, Poland	2:30:45
Salvador Garcia, Mexico	2:09:28	1991	Liz McColgan, Great Britain	2:27:32
Willie Mtolo, South Africa	2:09:29	1992	Lisa Ondieki, Australia	2:24:40
Andres Espinosa, Mexico	2:10:04	1993	Uta Pippig, Germany	2:26:24
German Silva, Mexico	2:11:21	1994	Tegla Loroupe, Kenya	2:27:37
German Silva, Mexico	2:11:00	1995	Tegla Loroupe, Kenya	2:28:06
Giacomo Leone, Italy	2:09:54	1996	Anuta Catuna, Romania	2:28:43
John Kagwe, Kenya	2:08:12	1997	F. Rochat-Moser, Switzerland	2:28:43
John Kagwe, Kenya	2:08:45	1998	Franca Fiacconi, Italy	2:25:17
Joseph Chebet, Kenya	2:09:14	1999	Adriana Fernandez, Mexico	2:25:06
Abdelkhader El Mouaziz, Morocco	2:10:09	2000	Ludmila Petrova, Russia	2:25:45
Tesfaye Jifar, Ethiopia	2:07:43*	2001	Margaret Okayo, Kenya	2:24:21
Rodgers Rop, Kenya	2:08:07	2002	Joyce Chepchumba, Kenya	2:25:56
Martin Lel, Kenya	2:10:30	2003	Margaret Okayo, Kenya	2:22:31*
Hendrik Ramaala, South Africa	2:09:28	2004	Paula Radcliffe, England	2:23:10
Paul Tergat, Kenya	2:09:30	2005	Jelena Prokopcuka, Latvia	2:24:41

Other Marathon Results in 2006

Los Angeles Marathon—Mar. 19. *Men:* Benson Cherono, Kenya, 2:08:40. *Women:* Lidiya Grigoryeva, Russia, 2:25:10.
Paris Marathon—Apr. 9. *Men:* Gashaw Melese, Ethiopia, 2:08:03. *Women:* Irina Timofeyeva, Russia, 2:27:22.
Rotterdam Marathon—Apr. 9. *Men:* Sammy Korir, Kenya, 2:06:38. *Women:* Mindaye Gishu, Ethiopia, 2:28:30.
London Marathon—Apr. 23. *Men:* Felix Limo, Kenya, 2:06:39. *Women:* Deena Kastor, U.S., 2:19:36.
Berlin Marathon—Sept. 24. *Men:* Haile Gebrselassie, Ethiopia, 2:05:56. *Women:* Gete Wami, Ethiopia, 2:21:34.
Chicago Marathon—Oct. 9, 2005. *Men:* Felix Limo, Kenya, 2:07:04. *Women:* Deena Kastor, U.S., 2:21:24.

Ironman Triathlon World Championships

The Ironman Triathlon World Championships—a 2.4-mile ocean swim, 112-mile bike ride, and 26.2-mile run—are held annually at Kailua-Kona, Hawaii. On Oct. 15, 2005, the men's race was won by Germany's Faris al-Sultan in 8:14:17. Switzerland's Natascha Badmann won the women's race for the sixth time in her career, with a time of 9:09:30.

All times in hour:minute:second format. *Course records.

Men's Winner	Time	Year	Women's Winner	Time
Gordon Haller, U.S.	11:46:58	1978	no finisher	—
Tom Warren, U.S.	11:15:56	1979	Lyn Lemaire, U.S.	12:55:00
Dave Scott, U.S.	9:24:33	1980	Robin Beck, U.S.	11:21:24
John Howard, U.S.	9:38:29	1981	Linda Sweeney, U.S.	12:00:32
Dave Scott, U.S.	9:08:23	1982	Julie Leach, U.S.	10:54:08
Dave Scott, U.S.	9:05:57	1983	Sylviane Puntous, Canada	10:43:36
Dave Scott, U.S.	8:54:20	1984	Sylvanie Puntous, Canada	10:25:13
ScottTinley, U.S.	8:50:54	1985	Joanne Ernst, U.S.	10:25:22
Dave Scott, U.S.	8:28:37	1986	Paula Newby-Fraser, Zimbabwe	9:49:14
Dave Scott, U.S.	8:34:13	1987	Erin Baker, New Zealand	9:35:25
Scott Molina, U.S.	8:31:00	1988	Paula Newby-Fraser, Zimbabwe	9:01:01
Mark Allen, U.S.	8:09:15	1989	Paula Newby-Fraser, Zimbabwe	9:00:56
Mark Allen, U.S.	8:28:17	1990	Erin Baker, New Zealand	9:13:42
Mark Allen, U.S.	8:18:32	1991	Paula Newby-Fraser, Zimbabwe	9:07:52
Mark Allen, U.S.	8:09:08	1992	Paula Newby-Fraser, Zimbabwe	8:55:28*
Mark Allen, U.S.	8:07:45	1993	Paula Newby-Fraser, Zimbabwe	8:58:23
Greg Welch, Australia	8:20:27	1994	Paula Newby-Fraser, Zimbabwe	9:20:14
Mark Allen, U.S.	8:20:34	1995	Karen Smyers, U.S.	9:16:46
Luc Van Lierde, Belgium	8:04:08*	1996	Paula Newby-Fraser, Zimbabwe	9:06:49
Thomas Hellriegel, Germany	8:33:01	1997	Heather Fuhr, Canada	9:31:43
Peter Reid, Canada	8:24:20	1998	Natascha Badmann, Switz.	9:24:16
Luc Van Lierde, Belgium	8:17:17	1999	Lori Bowden, U.S.	9:13:02
Peter Reid, Canada	8:21:01	2000	Natascha Badmann, Switz.	9:26:16
Timothy Deboom, U.S.	8:31:18	2001	Natascha Badmann, Switz.	9:28:37
Timothy Deboom, U.S.	8:29:56	2002	Natascha Badmann, Switz.	9:07:54
Peter Reid, Canada	8:22:35	2003	Lori Bowden, Canada	9:11:55
Norman Stadler, Germany	8:33:29	2004	Natascha Badmann, Switz.[1]	9:50:04
Faris al-Sultan, Germany	8:14:17	2005	Natascha Badmann, Switz.	9:09:30

(1) First place finisher Nina Kraft (Germany) admitted to using performance enhancing drugs and was disqualified, Nov. 15, 2004.

SULLIVAN AWARD
James E. Sullivan Memorial Trophy Winners

The James E. Sullivan Memorial Trophy, named after the former president of the Amateur Athletic Union (AAU) and inaugurated in 1930, is awarded annually by the AAU to the athlete who "by his or her performance, example and influence as an amateur, has done the most during the year to advance the cause of sportsmanship."

Year	Winner	Sport	Year	Winner	Sport	Year	Winner	Sport
1930	Bobby Jones	Golf	1958	Glenn Davis	Track	1985	Joan Benoit Samuelson	Marathon
1931	Barney Berlinger	Track	1959	Parry O'Brien	Track	1986	Jackie Joyner-Kersee	Track
1932	Jim Bausch	Track	1960	Rafer Johnson	Track	1987	Jim Abbott	Baseball
1933	Glenn Cunningham	Track	1961	Wilma Rudolph Ward	Track	1988	Florence Griffith Joyner	Track
1934	Bill Bonthron	Track	1962	James Beatty	Track	1989	Janet Evans	Swimming
1935	Lawson Little	Golf	1963	John Pennel	Track	1990	John Smith	Wrestling
1936	Glenn Morris	Track	1964	Don Schollander	Swimming	1991	Mike Powell	Track
1937	Don Budge	Tennis	1965	Bill Bradley	Basketball	1992	Bonnie Blair	Speed Skating
1938	Don Lash	Track	1966	Jim Ryun	Track	1993	Charlie Ward	Football, Basketball
1939	Joe Burk	Rowing	1967	Randy Matson	Track			
1940	Greg Rice	Track	1968	Debbie Meyer	Swimming	1994	Dan Jansen	Speed Skating
1941	Leslie MacMitchell	Track	1969	Bill Toomey	Track			
1942	Cornelius Warmerdam	Track	1970	John Kinsella	Swimming	1995	Bruce Baumgartner	Wrestling
1943	Gilbert Dodds	Track	1971	Mark Spitz	Swimming	1996	Michael Johnson	Track
1944	Ann Curtis	Swimming	1972	Frank Shorter	Track	1997	Peyton Manning	Football
1945	Doc Blanchard	Football	1973	Bill Walton	Basketball	1998	Chamique Holdsclaw	Basketball
1946	Arnold Tucker	Football	1974	Rick Wohlhutter	Track	1999	Coco Miller and Kelly Miller	Basketball
1947	John Kelly, Jr.	Rowing	1975	Tim Shaw	Swimming			
1948	Robert Mathias	Track	1976	Bruce Jenner	Track	2000	Rulon Gardner	Wrestling
1949	Dick Button	Skating	1977	John Naber	Swimming	2001	Michelle Kwan	Figure Skating
1950	Fred Wilt	Track	1978	Tracy Caulkins	Swimming			
1951	Rev. Robert Richards	Track	1979	Kurt Thomas	Gymnastics	2002	Sarah Hughes	Figure Skating
1952	Horace Ashenfelter	Track	1980	Eric Heiden	Speed Skating			
1953	Dr. Sammy Lee	Diving				2003	Michael Phelps	Swimming
1954	Mal Whitfield	Track	1981	Carl Lewis	Track	2004	Paul Hamm	Gymnastics
1955	Harrison Dillard	Track	1982	Mary Decker	Track	2005	J. J. Redick	Basketball
1956	Patricia McCormick	Diving	1983	Edwin Moses	Track			
1957	Bobby Joe Morrow	Track	1984	Greg Louganis	Diving			

FISHING
Selected IGFA Saltwater & Freshwater All-Tackle World Records
Source: International Game Fish Association; based on records granted as of Oct. 2005

Saltwater Fish Records

Species	Weight	Where caught	Date	Angler
Albacore	88 lbs. 2 oz.	Canary Islands, Spain	Nov. 19, 1977	Siegfried Dickemann
Amberjack, greater	155 lbs. 12 oz.	Bermuda	Aug. 16, 1992	Larry Trott
Barracuda, great	85 lbs.	Christmas Island, Kiribati	Apr. 11, 1992	John Helfrich
Barracuda, Mexican	21 lbs.	Phantom Isle, Costa Rica	Mar. 27, 1987	E. Kent
Barracuda, Pacific	26 lbs. 8 oz.	Playa Matapalo, Costa Rica	Jan. 3, 1999	Doug Hettinger
Bass, barred sand	13 lbs. 3 oz.	Huntington Beach, CA	Aug. 29, 1988	Robert Halal
Bass, black sea	10 lbs. 4 oz.	Virginia Beach, VA	Jan. 1, 2000	Allan Paschall
Bass, giant sea	563 lbs. 8 oz.	Anacapa Island, CA	Aug. 20, 1968	James McAdam Jr.
Bass, striped	78 lbs. 8 oz.	Atlantic City, NJ	Sept. 21, 1982	Albert McReynolds
Bluefish	31 lbs. 12 oz.	Hatteras, NC	Jan. 30, 1972	James Hussey
Bonefish	19 lbs.	Zululand, South Africa	May 26, 1962	Brian Batchelor
Bonito, Atlantic	18 lbs. 4 oz.	Faial Island, Azores	July 8, 1953	D. Higgs
Bonito, Pacific	21 lbs. 5 oz.	181 Spot, CA	Oct. 19, 2003	Kim Larson
Cabezon	23 lbs.	Juan De Fuca Strait, WA	Aug. 4, 1990	Wesley Hunter
Cobia	135 lbs. 9 oz.	Shark Bay, Australia	July 9, 1985	Peter Goulding
Cod, Atlantic	98 lbs. 12 oz.	Isle of Shoals, NH	June 8, 1969	Alphonse Bielevich
Cod, Pacific	38 lbs. 9 oz.	Kawashiro, Kamoenai, Hokkaido, Japan	Jan. 16, 2005	Atsunori Takahira
Conger	133 lbs. 4 oz.	Berry Head, S. Devon, England	June 5, 1995	Vic Evans
Dolphinfish	87 lbs.	Papagallo Gulf, Costa Rica	Sept. 25, 1976	Manuel Salazar
Drum, black	113 lbs. 1 oz.	Lewes, DE	Sept. 15, 1975	Gerald Townsend
Drum, red	94 lbs. 2 oz.	Avon, NC	Nov. 7, 1984	David Deuel
Eel, American	9 lbs. 4 oz.	Cape May, NJ	Nov. 9, 1995	Jeff Pennick
Eel, marbled	36 lbs. 1 oz.	Hazelmere Dam, South Africa	June 10, 1984	Ferdie Van Nooten
Flounder, southern	20 lbs. 9 oz.	Nassau Sound, FL	Dec. 23, 1983	Larenza Mungin
Flounder, summer	22 lbs. 7 oz.	Montauk, NY	Sept. 15, 1975	Charles Nappi
Grouper, Goliath	680 lbs.	Fernandina Beach, FL	May 20, 1961	Lynn Joyner
Grouper, Warsaw	436 lbs. 12 oz.	Gulf of Mexico, Destin, FL	Dec. 22, 1985	Steve Haeusler
Halibut, Atlantic	418 lbs. 13 oz.	Vannaya Troms, Norway	July 28, 2004	Thomas Nielsen
Halibut, California	58 lbs. 9 oz.	Santa Rosa Island, CA	June 26, 1999	Roger W. Borrell
Halibut, Pacific	459 lbs.	Dutch Harbor, AK	June 11, 1996	Jack Tragis
Jack, crevalle	58 lbs. 6 oz.	Barra do Kwanza, Angola	Dec. 10, 2000	Nuno Abohbot
Jack, horse-eye	29 lbs. 8 oz.	Ascencion Island, South Atlantic	May 28, 1993	Mike Hanson
Jack, Pacific crevalle	39 lbs.	Playa Zancudo, Costa Rica	Mar. 3, 1997	Ingrid Callaghan
Kawakawa	29 lbs.	Clarion Island, Mexico	Dec. 17, 1986	Ronald Nakamura
Lingcod	76 lbs. 9 oz.	Gulf of Alaska, AK	Aug. 11, 2001	Antwan Tinsley
Mackerel, cero	17 lbs. 2 oz.	Islamorada, FL	Apr. 5, 1986	G. Michael Mills
Mackerel, king	93 lbs.	San Juan, PR	Apr. 18, 1999	Steve Perez Graulau
Mackerel, Spanish	13 lbs.	Ocracoke Inlet, NC	Nov. 4, 1987	Robert Cranton
Marlin, Atlantic blue	1,402 lbs. 2 oz.	Vitoria, Brazil	Feb. 29, 1992	Paulo Amorim
Marlin, black	1,560 lbs.	Cabo Blanco, Peru	Aug. 4, 1953	Alfred Glassell Jr.
Marlin, Pacific blue	1,376 lbs.	Kaaiwi Pt., Kona, HI	May 31, 1982	Jay deBeaubien
Marlin, striped	494 lbs.	Tutukaka, New Zealand	Jan. 16, 1986	Bill Boniface
Marlin, white	181 lbs. 14 oz.	Vitoria, Brazil	Dec. 8, 1979	Evandro Coser
Permit	60 lbs. 0 oz.	Ilha do Mel, Paranagua, Brazil	Dec. 14, 2002	Renato Fiedler
Pollack, European	27 lbs. 6 oz.	Salcombe, Devon, England	Jan. 16, 1986	Robert Milkins
Pollock	50 lbs.	Salstraumen, Norway	Nov. 30, 1995	Thor-Magnus Lekang
Pompano, African	50 lbs. 8 oz.	Daytona Beach, FL	Apr. 21, 1990	Tom Sargent

Species	Weight	Where caught	Date	Angler
Roosterfish	114 lbs.	La Paz, Baja Cal., Mexico	June 1, 1960	Abe Sackheim
Runner, blue	11 lbs. 2 oz.	Dauphin Isl., AL	June 28, 1997	Stacey Moiren
Runner, rainbow	37 lbs. 9 oz.	Clarion Island, Mexico	Nov. 21, 1991	Tom Pfleger
Sailfish, Atlantic	141 lbs. 1 oz.	Luanda, Angola	Feb. 19, 1994	Alfredo de Sousa Neves
Sailfish, Pacific	221 lbs.	Santa Cruz Island, Ecuador	Feb. 12, 1947	Carl Stewart
Seabass, white	83 lbs. 12 oz.	San Felipe, Mexico	Mar. 31, 1953	Lyal Baumgardner
Seatrout, spotted	17 lbs. 7 oz.	Ft. Pierce, FL	May 11, 1995	Craig Carson
Shark, bigeye thresher	802 lbs.	Tutukaka, New Zealand	Feb. 8, 1981	Dianne North
Shark, bignose	369 lbs. 14 oz.	Markham R., Papua New Guinea	Oct. 23, 1993	Lester Rohrlach
Shark, blue	528 lbs.	Montauk Point, NY	Aug. 9, 2001	Joe Seidel
Shark, great hammerhead	991 lbs.	Sarasota, FL	May 30, 1982	Allen Ogle
Shark, Greenland	1,708 lbs. 9 oz.	Trondheimsfjord, Norway	Oct. 18, 1987	Terje Nordtvedt
Shark, porbeagle	507 lbs.	Caithness, Scotland	Mar. 9, 1993	Christopher Bennett
Shark, shortfin mako	1,221 lbs.	Chatham, MA	July 21, 2001	Luke Sweeney
Shark, tiger	1,785 lbs. 11oz.	Ulladulla, Australia	Mar. 28, 2004	Kevin Clapson
Shark, white	2,664 lbs.	Ceduna, Australia	Apr. 21, 1959	Alfred Dean
Sheepshead	21 lbs. 4 oz.	New Orleans, LA	Apr. 16, 1982	Wayne Desselle
Skipjack, black	26 lbs.	Thetis Bank, Baja Cal., Mexico	Oct. 23, 1991	Clifford Hamaishi
Snapper, cubera	121 lbs. 8 oz.	Cameron, LA	July 5, 1982	Mike Hebert
Snapper, red	50 lbs. 4 oz.	Gulf of Mexico, LA	June 23, 1996	Capt. Doc Kennedy
Snook, common	53 lbs. 10 oz.	Parismina Ranch, Costa Rica	Oct. 18, 1978	Gilbert Ponzi
Spearfish, Mediterranean	90 lbs. 13 oz.	Madeira Island, Portugal	June 2, 1980	Joseph Larkin
Swordfish	1,182 lbs.	Iquique, Chile	May 7, 1953	Louis Marron
Tarpon	286 lbs. 9 oz.	Rubane, Guinea-Bissau	Mar. 20, 2003	Max Domecq
Tautog	25 lbs.	Ocean City, NJ	Jan. 20, 1998	Anthony Monica
Trevally, bigeye	31 lbs. 8 oz.	Poivre Isl., Seychelles	Apr. 23, 1997	Les Sampson
Trevally, giant	145 lbs. 8 oz.	Makena, Maui, HI	Mar. 28, 1991	Russell Mori
Tuna, Atlantic bigeye	392 lbs. 6 oz.	Canary Islands, Spain	July 25, 1996	Dieter Vogel
Tuna, blackfin	45 lbs. 8 oz.	Key West, FL	May 4, 1996	Sam Burnett
Tuna, bluefin	1,496 lbs.	Aulds Cove, Nova Scotia	Oct. 26, 1979	Ken Fraser
Tuna, longtail	79 lbs. 2 oz.	Montague Isl., Australia	Apr. 12, 1982	Tim Simpson
Tuna, Pacific bigeye	435 lbs.	Cabo Blanco, Peru	Apr. 17, 1957	Dr. Russel Lee
Tuna, skipjack	45 lbs. 4 oz.	Flathead Bank, Baja Cal., Mexico	Nov. 16, 1996	Brian Evans
Tuna, southern bluefin	348 lbs. 5 oz.	Whakatane, New Zealand	Jan. 16, 1981	Rex Wood
Tuna, yellowfin	388 lbs. 12 oz.	San Benedicto Island, Mexico	Apr. 1, 1977	Curt Wiesenhutter
Tunny, little	35 lbs. 2 oz.	Cap de Garde, Algeria	Dec. 14, 1988	Jean Chatard
Wahoo	158 lbs. 8 oz.	Loreto, Baja Cal., Mexico	June 10, 1996	Keith Winter
Weakfish	19 lbs. 2 oz.	Jones Beach Inlet, NY	Oct. 11, 1984	Dennis Rooney
		Delaware Bay, DE	May 20, 1989	William Thomas
Yellowtail, California	92 lbs. 1 oz.	Guadelupe Isl., Mexico	Aug. 4, 2004	Kevin Pfeif
Yellowtail, southern	114 lbs. 10 oz.	Tauranga, New Zealand	Feb. 5, 1984	Mike Godfrey
		White Island, New Zealand	Jan. 9, 1987	David Lugton

Freshwater Fish Records

Species	Weight	Where caught	Date	Angler
Barramundi	83 lbs. 7 oz.	Lake Tinaroo, N. Queensland, Australia	Sept. 23, 1999	David Powell
Bass, largemouth	22 lbs. 4 oz.	Montgomery Lake, GA	June 2, 1932	George Perry
Bass, rock	3 lbs.	York River, Ontario	Aug. 1, 1974	Peter Gulgin
	3 lbs.	Lake Erie, PA	June 18, 1998	Herbert Ratner Jr.
Bass, shoal	8 lbs. 12 oz.	Apalachicola River, FL	Jan. 28, 1995	Carl Davis
Bass, smallmouth	10 lbs. 14 oz.	Dale Hollow, TN	Apr. 24, 1969	John Gorman
Bass, white	6 lbs. 13 oz.	Lake Orange, VA	July 31, 1989	Ronald Sprouse
Bass, whiterock	27 lbs. 5 oz.	Greers Ferry Lake, AR	April 24, 1997	Jerald Shaum
Bass, yellow	2 lbs. 9 oz.	Duck River, Waverly, TN	Feb. 27, 1998	John Chappell
Bluegill	4 lbs. 12 oz.	Ketona Lake, AL	Apr. 9, 1950	T. Hudson
Bowfin	21 lbs. 8 oz.	Florence, SC	Jan. 29, 1980	Robert Harmon
Bream	13 lbs. 3 oz.	Hagbyan Creek, Sweden	May 11, 1984	Luis Kilian Rasmussen
Buffalo, bigmouth	70 lbs. 5 oz.	Bastrop, LA	Apr. 21, 1980	Delbert Sisk
Buffalo, black	63 lbs. 6 oz.	Mississippi River, IA	Aug. 14, 1999	Jim Winters
Buffalo, smallmouth	82 lbs. 3 oz.	Athens Lake, AL	June 6, 1993	Randy Collins
Bullhead, brown	6 lbs. 5 oz.	Lake Mahopac, NY	Sept. 8, 2002	Ray Lawrence
Bullhead, yellow	4 lbs. 15 oz.	Ogeechee R., GA	Oct. 12, 2003	Glenn Settles
Burbot	18 lbs. 11 oz.	Angenmanalren, Sweden	Oct. 22, 1996	Margit Agren
Carp, common	75 lbs. 11 oz.	Lac de St. Cassien, France	May 21, 1987	Leo van der Gugten
Catfish, blue	124 lbs.	Mississippi R., IL	May 21, 2005	Timothy Pruitt.
Catfish, channel	58 lbs.	Santee-Cooper Res., SC	July 7, 1964	W. B. Whaley
Catfish, flathead	123 lbs.	Independence, KS	May 14, 1998	Ken Paulie
Catfish, white	19 lbs. 5 oz.	Oakdale, CA	May 7, 2005	Russell Price
Char, Arctic	32 lbs. 9 oz.	Tree River, Canada	July 30, 1981	Jeffrey Ward
Crappie, white	5 lbs. 3 oz.	Enid Dam, MS	July 31, 1957	Fred Bright
Dolly Varden	20 lbs. 14 oz.	Wulik R., AK	July 7, 2001	Raz Reid
Dorado	51 lbs. 5 oz.	Toledo (Corrientes), Argentina	Sept. 27, 1984	Armando Giudice
Drum, freshwater	54 lbs. 8 oz.	Nickajack Lake, TN	Apr. 20, 1972	Benny Hull
Gar, alligator	279 lbs.	Rio Grande, TX	Dec. 2, 1951	Bill Valverde
Gar, Florida	10 lbs.	Everglades, FL	Jan. 28, 2002	Herbert Ratner Jr.
Gar, longnose	50 lbs. 5 oz.	Trinity River, TX	July 30, 1954	Townsend Miller
Gar, shortnose	5 lbs. 12 oz.	Rend Lake, IL	July 16, 1995	Donna Willmert
Gar, spotted	9 lbs. 12 oz.	Lake Mexia, TX	Apr. 7, 1994	Rick Rivard
Grayling, Arctic	5 lbs. 15 oz.	Katseyedie River, NT	Aug. 16, 1967	Jeanne Branson
Inconnu	53 lbs.	Pah River, AK	Aug. 20, 1986	Lawrence Hudnall
Kokanee	9 lbs. 6 oz.	Okanagan Lake, BC	June 18, 1988	Norm Kuhn
Muskellunge	67 lbs. 8 oz.	Lake Court Oreilles, WI	July 24, 1949	Cal Johnson
Muskellunge, tiger	51 lbs. 3 oz.	Lac Vieux-Desert, MI	July 16, 1919	John Knobla
Perch, Nile	230 lbs.	Lake Nasser, Egypt	Dec. 20, 2000	William Toth
Perch, white	3 lbs. 1 oz.	Forest Hill Park, NJ	May 6, 1989	Edward Tango
Perch, yellow	4 lbs. 3 oz.	Bordentown, NJ	May, 1865	Dr. C. C. Abbot
Pickerel, chain	9 lbs. 6 oz.	Homerville, GA	Feb. 17, 1961	Baxley McQuaig Jr.
Pike, northern	55 lbs. 1 oz.	Lake of Grefeern, W. Germany	Oct. 16, 1986	Lothar Louis
Redhorse, greater	9 lbs. 3 oz.	Salmon River, Pulaski, NY	May 11, 1985	Jason Wilson
Redhorse, silver	11 lbs. 7 oz.	Plum Creek, WI	May 29, 1985	Neal Long
Salmon, Atlantic	79 lbs. 2 oz.	Tana River, Norway	Jan. 1, 1928	Henrik Henriksen

Species	Weight	Where caught	Date	Angler
Salmon, chinook	97 lbs. 4 oz.	Kenai River, AK	May 17, 1985	Les Anderson
Salmon, chum	35 lbs.	Edye Pass, BC	July 11, 1995	Todd Johansson
Salmon, coho	33 lbs. 4 oz.	Salmon River, Pulaski, NY	Sept. 27, 1989	Jerry Lifton
Salmon, pink	14 lbs. 13 oz.	Monroe, WA	Sept. 30, 2001	Alexander Minerich
Salmon, sockeye	15 lbs. 3 oz.	Kenai River, AK	Aug. 9, 1987	Stan Roach
Sauger	8 lbs. 12 oz.	Lake Sakakawea, ND	Oct. 6, 1971	Mike Fischer
Shad, American	11 lbs. 4 oz.	Connecticut River, MA	May 19, 1986	Bob Thibodo
Sturgeon, beluga	224 lbs. 13 oz.	Guryev, Kazakhstan	May 3, 1993	Merete Lehne
Sturgeon, white	468 lbs.	Benicia, CA	July 9, 1983	Joey Pallotta III
Sunfish, green	2 lbs. 2 oz.	Stockton Lake, MO	June 18, 1971	Paul Dilley
Sunfish, redbreast	1 lb. 12 oz.	Suwannee River, FL	May 29, 1984	Alvin Buchanan
Sunfish, redear	5 lbs. 7oz.	Diverson Canal, SC	Nov. 6, 1998	Amos Gay
Tigerfish, giant	97 lbs.	Zaire River, Kinshasa, Zaire (Congo)	July 9, 1988	Raymond Houtmans
Tilapia, Nile	13 lbs. 3 oz.	Antelope Isl., Kariba, Zimbabwe	July 5, 2002	Sarel van Rooyen
Trout, Apache	5 lb. 3 oz.	Apache Res., AZ	May 29, 1991	John Baldwin
Trout, brook	14 lbs. 8 oz.	Nipigon River, ON	July 1916	Dr. W. J. Cook
Trout, bull	32 lbs.	Lake Pend Oreille, ID	Oct. 27, 1949	N. L. Higgins
Trout, cutthroat	41 lbs.	Pyramid Lake, NV	Dec. 1925	John Skimmerhorn
Trout, golden	11 lbs.	Cooks Lake, WY	Aug. 5, 1948	Charles Reed
Trout, lake	72 lbs.	Great Bear Lake, NT	Aug. 19, 1995	Lloyd Bull
Trout, rainbow	42 lbs. 2 oz.	Bell Island, AK	June 22, 1970	David White
Trout, tiger	20 lbs. 13 oz.	Lake Michigan, WI	Aug. 12, 1978	Pete Friedland
Walleye	25 lbs.	Old Hickory Lake, TN	Aug. 2, 1960	Mabry Harper
Warmouth	2 lbs. 7 oz.	Yellow River, Holt, FL	Oct. 19, 1985	Tony Dempsey
Whitefish, lake	14 lbs. 6 oz.	Meaford, ON	May 21, 1984	Dennis Laycock
Whitefish, mountain	5 lbs. 8 oz.	Elbow River, Calgary, AB	Aug. 1, 1995	Randy Woo
Whitefish, round	6 lbs.	Putahow R., MB	June 14, 1984	Allan Ristori
Zander	25 lbs. 2 oz.	Trosa, Sweden	June 12, 1986	Harry Lee Tennison

DIRECTORY OF SPORTS ORGANIZATIONS

Major League Baseball

Office of the Commissioner, 245 Park Ave., 31st Fl., New York, NY 10167. **Website:** www.mlb.com

American League

Baltimore Orioles
333 W. Camden St.
Baltimore, MD 21201

Boston Red Sox
4 Yawkey Way
Boston, MA 02215

Chicago White Sox
333 W. 35th St.
Chicago, IL 60616

Cleveland Indians
2401 Ontario St.
Cleveland, OH 44115-4003

Detroit Tigers
2100 Woodward Ave.
Detroit, MI 48201

Kansas City Royals
One Royal Way
Kansas City, MO 64141

Los Angeles Angels of Anaheim
2000 Gene Autry Way
Anaheim, CA 92806

Minnesota Twins
34 Kirby Puckett Place
Minneapolis, MN 55415

New York Yankees
161st St. and River Ave.
Bronx, NY 10451

Oakland Athletics
7000 Coliseum Way
Oakland, CA 94621

Seattle Mariners
P.O. Box 4100
Seattle, WA 98104

Tampa Bay Devil Rays
One Tropicana Dr.
St. Petersburg, FL 33705

Texas Rangers
1000 Ballpark Way
Arlington, TX 76011

Toronto Blue Jays
One Blue Jays Way
Toronto, ON M5V 1J1

National League

Arizona Diamondbacks
401 E. Jefferson St.
Phoenix, AZ 85001

Atlanta Braves
755 Hank Aaron Drive
Atlanta, GA 30315

Chicago Cubs
1060 W. Addison St.
Chicago, IL 60613

Cincinnati Reds
100 Main St.
Cincinnati, OH 45202

Colorado Rockies
2001 Blake St.
Denver, CO 80205

Florida Marlins
2269 Dan Marino Blvd.
Miami, FL 33056

Houston Astros
501 Crawford St.
Houston, TX 77002

Los Angeles Dodgers
1000 Elysian Park Ave.
Los Angeles, CA 90012

Milwaukee Brewers
One Brewers Way
Milwaukee, WI 53214

New York Mets
123-01 Roosevelt Ave.
Flushing, NY 11368

Philadelphia Phillies
One Citizens Bank Way
Philadelphia, PA 19148

Pittsburgh Pirates
115 Federal St.
Pittsburgh, PA 15212

St. Louis Cardinals
420 S. 8th St.
St. Louis, MO 63102

San Diego Padres
100 Park Blvd.
San Diego, CA 92101

San Francisco Giants
24 Willie Mays Plaza
San Francisco, CA 94107

Washington Nationals
2400 E. Capitol St. SE
Washington, DC 20003

National Basketball Association

League Office, Olympic Tower, 645 5th Ave., New York, NY 10022. **Website:** www.nba.com

Atlanta Hawks
101 Marietta St. SW, Ste. 1900
Atlanta, GA 30303

Boston Celtics
226 Causeway St.
Boston, MA 02114

Charlotte Bobcats
333 E. Trade St.
Charlotte, NC 28202

Chicago Bulls
1901 W. Madison St.
Chicago, IL 60612

Cleveland Cavaliers
One Center Court
Cleveland, OH 44115

Dallas Mavericks
2500 Victory Ave.
Dallas, TX 75219

Denver Nuggets
1000 Chopper Circle
Denver, CO 80204

Detroit Pistons
Four Championship Dr.
Auburn Hills, MI 48326

Golden State Warriors
1011 Broadway
Oakland, CA 94607

Houston Rockets
1510 Polk St.
Houston, TX 77002

Indiana Pacers
125 S. Pennsylvania St.
Indianapolis, IN 46204

Los Angeles Clippers
1111 S. Figueroa St., Ste. 1100
Los Angeles, CA 90015

Los Angeles Lakers
555 N. Nash St.
El Segundo, CA 90245

Memphis Grizzlies
191 Beale St.
Memphis, TN 38103

Miami Heat
601 Biscayne Blvd.
Miami, FL 33132

Milwaukee Bucks
1001 N. 4th St.
Milwaukee, WI 53203

Minnesota Timberwolves
600 1st Ave. North
Minneapolis, MN 55403

New Jersey Nets
390 Murray Hill Parkway
E. Rutherford, NJ 07073

New Orleans Hornets[1]
1501 Girod St.
New Orleans, LA 70113

New York Knickerbockers
Two Pennsylvania Plaza
New York, NY 10121

Orlando Magic
8701 Maitland Summit Blvd.
Orlando, FL 32810

Philadelphia 76ers
3601 S. Broad St.
Philadelphia, PA 19148

Phoenix Suns
201 E. Jefferson St.
Phoenix, AZ 85004

Portland Trail Blazers
One Center Ct.
Portland, OR 97227

Sacramento Kings
One Sports Parkway
Sacramento, CA 95834

San Antonio Spurs
One SBC Center
San Antonio, TX 78219

Seattle SuperSonics
305 Harrison St.
Seattle, WA 98109

Toronto Raptors
40 Bay St.
Toronto, ON M5J 2X2

Utah Jazz
301 W. South Temple
Salt Lake City, UT 84101

Washington Wizards
601 F St. NW
Washington, DC 20004

(1) Most of the New Orleans Hornets' home games in the 2005-06 and 2006-07 seasons were relocated to the Ford Center in Oklahoma City.

National Hockey League

League Headquarters, 1251 Ave. of the Americas, 47th Fl., New York, NY 10020. **Website:** www.nhl.com

Anaheim Ducks
2695 E. Katella Ave.
Anaheim, CA 92806

Atlanta Thrashers
Centennial Tower
101 Marietta St. NW
Atlanta, GA 30303

Boston Bruins
100 Legends Way
Boston, MA 02114

Buffalo Sabres
One Seymour H. Knox III Plaza
Buffalo, NY 14203

Calgary Flames
P.O. Box 1540, Station M
Calgary, AB T2P 3B9

Carolina Hurricanes
1400 Edwards Mill Rd.
Raleigh, NC 27607

Chicago Blackhawks
1901 W. Madison St.
Chicago, IL 60612

Colorado Avalanche
1000 Chopper Circle
Denver, CO 80204

Columbus Blue Jackets
200 W. Nationwide Blvd.
Columbus, OH 43215

Dallas Stars
2601 Avenue of the Stars
Frisco, TX 75034

Detroit Red Wings
600 Civic Center Dr.
Detroit, MI 48226

Edmonton Oilers
11230 110 St.
Edmonton, AB T5G 3H7

Florida Panthers
One Panther Parkway
Sunrise, FL 33323

Los Angeles Kings
1111 S. Figueroa St.
Los Angeles, CA 90015

Minnesota Wild
317 Washington St.
St. Paul, MN 55102

Montreal Canadiens
1275 St. Antonie St. W
Montreal, QC H3C 5L2

Nashville Predators
501 Broadway
Nashville, TN 37203

New Jersey Devils
50 Rte. 120 North
E. Rutherford, NJ 07073

New York Islanders
1255 Hempstead Tpke.
Uniondale, NY 11553

New York Rangers
Two Pennsylvania Plaza
New York, NY 10121

Ottawa Senators
1000 Palladium Dr.
Kanata, ON K2V 1A5

Philadelphia Flyers
3601 South Broad St.
Philadelphia, PA 19148

Phoenix Coyotes
5800 W. Glenn Dr., Ste. 350
Glendale, AZ 85301

Pittsburgh Penguins
66 Mario Lemieux Place
Pittsburgh, PA 15219

St. Louis Blues
1401 Clark Ave.
St. Louis, MO 63103

San Jose Sharks
525 W. Santa Clara St.
San Jose, CA 95113

Tampa Bay Lightning
401 Channelside Dr.
Tampa, FL 33602

Toronto Maple Leafs
40 Bay St.
Toronto, ON M5J 2X2

Vancouver Canucks
800 Griffiths Way
Vancouver, BC V6B 6G1

Washington Capitals
401 9th St. NW, Ste. 750
Washington, DC 20004

National Football League

League Office, 280 Park Ave., New York, NY 10017 **Website:** www.nfl.com

Arizona Cardinals
P.O. Box 888
Phoenix AZ 85001

Atlanta Falcons
4400 Falcon Parkway
Flowery Branch, GA 30542

Baltimore Ravens
1101 Russel St.
Baltimore, MD 21230

Buffalo Bills
One Bills Drive
Orchard Park, NY 14127

Carolina Panthers
800 S. Mint St.
Charlotte, NC 28202

Chicago Bears
1000 Football Dr.
Lake Forest, IL 60045

Cincinnati Bengals
One Paul Brown Stadium
Cincinnati, OH 45202

Cleveland Browns
100 Alfred Lerner Way
Cleveland, OH 44114

Dallas Cowboys
2401 E. Airport Fwy.
Irving, TX 75062

Denver Broncos
13655 Broncos Pkwy.
Englewood, CO 80112

Detroit Lions
222 Republic Dr.
Allen Park, MI 48101

Green Bay Packers
1265 Lombardi Ave.
Green Bay, WI 54304

Houston Texans
Two Reliant Park
Houston, TX 77054

Indianapolis Colts
7001 W. 56th St.
Indianapolis, IN 46254

Jacksonville Jaguars
One Alltel Stadium Place
Jacksonville, FL 32202

Kansas City Chiefs
One Arrowhead Drive
Kansas City, MO 64129

Miami Dolphins
7500 SW 30th St.
Davie, FL 33314

Minnesota Vikings
9520 Viking Dr.
Eden Prairie, MN 55344

New England Patriots
One Patriot Pl.
Foxboro, MA 02035

New Orleans Saints
1500 Podyras St.
New Orleans, LA 70112

New York Giants
Giants Stadium
E. Rutherford, NJ 07073

New York Jets
1000 Fulton Ave.
Hempstead, NY 11550

Oakland Raiders
1220 Harbor Bay Pkwy.
Alameda, CA 94502

Philadelphia Eagles
One NovaCare Way
Philadelphia, PA 19145

Pittsburgh Steelers
100 Art Rooney Ave.
Pittsburgh, PA 15212

St. Louis Rams
One Rams Way
St. Louis, MO 63045

San Diego Chargers
4020 Murphy Canyon Rd.
San Diego, CA 92123

San Francisco 49ers
4949 Centennial Blvd.
Santa Clara, CA 95054

Seattle Seahawks
800 Occidental Ave. South
Seattle, WA 98134

Tampa Bay Buccaneers
One Buccaneer Place
Tampa, FL 33607

Tennessee Titans
One Titans Way
Nashville, TN 37228

Washington Redskins
21300 Redskin Park Dr.
Ashburn, VA 20147

Other North American Sports Organizations

Amateur Athletic Union,
P.O. Box 22409,
Lake Buena Vista, FL 32830
www.aausports.org

Amateur Softball Assn.
2801 NE 50th St.
Oklahoma City, OK 73111
www.softball.org

American Kennel Club
260 Madison Ave.
New York, NY 10016
www.akc.org

Canadian Football League
50 Wellington St. E., 3rd Fl.
Toronto, Ont. M5E 1C8
www.cfl.ca

CART (Championship Auto Racing Teams)
5350 Lakeview Pkwy. S. Dr.
Indianapolis, IN 46268
www.champcarworldseries.com

Intl. Game Fish Assn.
300 Gulf Stream Way
Dania Beach, FL 33004
www.igfa.org

LPGA
100 International Golf Dr.
Daytona Beach, FL 32124
www.lpga.com

Little League Baseball
PO Box 3485
Williamsport, PA 17701
www.littleleague.org

Major League Soccer
420 5th Ave.
New York, NY 10018
www.mlsnet.com

NASCAR
P.O. Box 2875
Daytona Beach, FL 32120
www.nascar.com

NCAA
700 W. Washington St.
P.O. Box 6222
Indianapolis, IN 46206
www.ncaa.org

National Rifle Assn.
11250 Waples Mill Rd.
Fairfax, VA 22030
www.nra.org

Pro Bowlers Assn.
719 2nd Ave., Ste. 701
Seattle, WA 98104
www.pbatour.com

PGA
112 PGA Tour Blvd.
Ponte Vedra Beach, FL 32082
www.pga.com

Pro Rodeo Cowboys Assn.
101 Pro Rodeo Dr.
Colorado Springs, CO 80919
www.prorodeo.org

Special Olympics
1133 19th St. NW
Washington, DC 20036
www.specialolympics.org

Thoroughbred Racing Assn.
420 Fair Hill Dr.
Elkton, MD 21921
www.tra-online.com

US Equestrian Federation
4047 Iron Works Pkwy.
Lexington, KY 40511
www.usef.org

USA Rugby
1033 Walnut St., Suite 200
Boulder, CO 80302
www.usarugby.org

USA Swimming
One Olympic Plaza
Colorado Springs, CO 80909
www.usa-swimming.org

USA Track & Field
One RCA Dome, Ste. 140
Indianapolis, IN 46225
www.usatf.org

U.S. Auto Club
4910 W. 16th St.
Speedway, IN 46224
www.usacracing.com

U.S. Figure Skating Assn.
20 First St.
Colorado Springs, CO 80906
www.usfigureskating.org

U.S. Olympic Committee
One Olympic Plaza
Colorado Springs, CO 80909
www.usoc.org

U.S. Ski and Snowboard Assn.
1500 Kearns Blvd.
P.O. Box 100
Park City, UT 84060
www.ussa.org

U.S. Soccer Federation
1801 S. Prairie Ave.
Chicago, IL 60616
www.ussoccer.com

U.S. Tennis Assn.
70 W. Red Oak Lane
White Plains, NY 10604
www.usta.com

U.S. Trotting Assn.
750 Michigan Ave.
Columbus, OH 43215
www.ustrotting.com

WNBA
Olympic Tower
645 5th Ave.
New York, NY 10022
www.wnba.com

NOTABLE SPORTS PERSONALITIES

Henry (Hank) Aaron, b. 1934, Milwaukee-Atlanta outfielder; hit record 755 home runs, led NL 4 times; record 2,297 RBI.

Kareem Abdul-Jabbar, b. 1947, Milwaukee, L.A. Lakers center; MVP 6 times; all-time leading NBA scorer, 38,387 points.

Freddy Adu, b. 1989, D.C. United midfielder; youngest player ever to play in the MLS at 14 years, 308 days, in 2004.

Andre Agassi, b. 1970, won: Wimbledon, '92; U.S. Open, '94, '99, '99; Aust. Open, '95, 2000-01, 2003; French Open, '99.

Troy Aikman, b. 1966, quarterback; led Dallas Cowboys to Super Bowl wins in 1993-94, 1996; Super Bowl MVP, 1993.

Amy Alcott, b. 1956, golfer; 29 career wins (5 majors), inducted into World Golf Hall of Fame in 1999.

Shawn Alexander, b. 1977, Seattle Seahawks running back; NFL record for touchdowns in a season, 28.

Grover Cleveland "Pete" Alexander, 1887-1950, pitcher; won 373 NL games; pitched 16 shutouts, 1916.

Muhammad Ali, b. 1942, 3-time heavyweight champion.

Fernando Alonso,, b. 1981, Spanish Formula 1 racer; youngest ever to win a World Grand Prix championship, 2005.

Gary Anderson, b. 1959, kicker; NFL's career points leader, with 2,434 through the end of the 2003 season.

Sparky Anderson, b. 1934, only manager to win World Series in the NL (Cincinnati, 1975-76) and the AL (Detroit, 1984).

Mario Andretti, b. 1940, race-car driver; won Daytona 500 (1967), Indy 500 (1969); Formula 1 world title (1978).

Earl Anthony, 1938-2001, bowler; won record 6 PBA Championships (1973-75, 1981-83), 41 career PBA tournaments.

Eddie Arcaro, 1916-97, only jockey to win racing's Triple Crown twice, 1941,1948; rode to 4,779 wins in his career.

Lance Armstrong, b. 1971, cyclist; record 7-time winner of the Tour de France (1999-2005).

Arthur Ashe, 1943-93, tennis player; won U.S. Open (1968); Wimbledon (1975); died of AIDS.

Evelyn Ashford, b. 1957, sprinter; won 100m gold (1984) and silver (1988); member of 5 U.S. Olympic teams (1976-1992).

Red Auerbach, b. 1917, coached Boston to 9 NBA titles.

Tracy Austin, b. 1962: youngest player to win U.S. Open tennis title (age 16 in 1979), 2-time AP Female Athlete of the Year.

Ernie Banks, b. 1931, Chicago Cubs slugger; hit 512 NL homers; never played in World Series.

Roger Bannister, b. 1929, British physician; ran first sub 4-minute mile, May 6, 1954 (3 min. 59.4 sec.).

Charles Barkely, b. 1963, NBA MVP, 1993; 4th player ever to surpass 20,000 pts, 10,000 rebounds, and 4,000 assists.

Rick Barry, b. 1944: NBA scoring leader, 1967; ABA, 1969.

Sammy Baugh, b. 1914: Washington Redskins quarterback; held numerous records upon retirement after 16 seasons.

Elgin Baylor, b. 1934, L.A. Lakers forward; 11-time all-star.

Bob Beamon, b. 1946, Olympic long jump gold medalist in 1968; world record jump of 29' 2½" stood until 1991.

Boris Becker, b. 1967, German tennis star; won U.S. Open 1989; Wimbledon champ 3 times.

David Beckham, b. 1975, English soccer star; captain of 2002 World Cup team.

Bill Belichick, b. 1952, NFL coach; led New England Patriots to Super Bowl wins in 2001, 2003, 2004; best all-time post-season coaching record.

Jean Beliveau, b. 1931, Montreal Canadiens center; scored 507 goals; twice MVP.

Johnny Bench, b. 1947, Cincinnati Reds catcher; MVP twice; led league in home runs twice, RBIs 3 times.

Patty Berg, b. 1918, won more than 80 golf tournaments; AP Woman Athlete of the Year 3 times.

Yogi Berra, b. 1925, Yankee catcher (1946-63); 3-time MVP.

Abebe Bikila, 1932-73, Ethiopian runner; won consecutive Olympic marathon gold medals in 1960 (barefoot), 1964.

Matt Biondi, b. 1965, swimmer; won 5 golds, 1988 Olympics.

Larry Bird, b. 1956, Boston Celtics forward; NBA MVP, 1984-86; 1998 coach of the year with Indiana Pacers.

Bonnie Blair, b. 1964, speed skater; won 5 individual gold medals in 3 Olympics (1988, '92, '94).

George Blanda, b. 1927, quarterback, kicker; 26 years as active player, scored 2,002 career points.

Fanny Blankers-Koen, 1918-2004, track; won 4 golds in 1948 Olympics.

Wade Boggs, b. 1958, AL batting champ, 1983, 1985-88; reached 3,000 career hits, 1999 (3,010).

Barry Bonds, b. 1964, outfielder; hit record 73 homers in 2001; NL MVP 1990, 1992-93, 2001-04; 2nd all-time in HRs (734).

Bjorn Borg, b. 1956, led Sweden to first Davis Cup, 1975; Wimbledon champion 5 times.

Ray Bourque, b. 1960, Boston defenseman,1979-2000; 5-time Norris Trophy winner; won Stanley Cup with Colorado, 2001.

Bill Bradley, b. 1943, All-America at Princeton; led N.Y. Knicks to 2 NBA titles (1970, '73); U.S. senator, 1979-97.

Donald Bradman, 1908-2001, Australian widely regarded as the greatest cricketer ever; set several batting records.

Terry Bradshaw, b. 1948, quarterback; led Pittsburgh to 4 Super Bowl wins (1975-76, 1979-80); NFL MVP, 1978.

Tom Brady, b. 1977, quarterback; led New England Patriots to 3 Super Bowl titles, 2002, 2004, 2005; MVP 2002, 2004.

George Brett, b. 1953, Kansas City Royals infielder; led AL in batting, 1976, 1980, 1990; MVP, 1980.

Lou Brock, b. 1939, St. Louis Cardinals outfielder; stole NL single-season record 118 bases, 1974; led NL 8 times.

Jim Brown, b. 1936, Clev. fullback; 12,312 career yds.; 2-time Associated Press MVP.

Paul Brown, 1908-91, football owner, coach; led eponymous Cleveland Browns to 3 NFL championships.

Kobe Bryant, b. 1978, guard; won 3 straight titles with Lakers (2000-02).

Paul "Bear" Bryant, 1913-83, college football coach with 323 wins; led Alabama to 5 national titles (1961, '64, '65, '78, '79).

Sergei Bubka, b. 1963, Ukrainian pole vaulter; first to clear 20 feet; gold medal, 1988 Olympics.

Don Budge, 1915-2000, won numerous amateur and pro tennis titles; Grand Slam, 1938.

Reggie Bush, b. 1985, New Orleans Saints running back drafted 2nd overall in 2006; helped USC to 2 National Titles (2003-04); Heisman Trophy winner (2005).

Dick Butkus, b. 1942, Chicago Bears linebacker; twice chosen NFL defensive player of the year.

Dick Button, b. 1929, figure skater; won 1948, 1952 Olympic gold medals; world titlist, 1948-52.

Walter Camp, 1859-1925, Yale football player, coach, athletic director; established many rules for modern football.

Roy Campanella, 1921-93, Hall of Fame catcher for the Brooklyn Dodgers (1948-57); 3-time NL MVP.

Earl Campbell, b. 1955, NFL running back; MVP 1978-79.

Jose Canseco, b. 1964, outfielder; led Oakland A's to the World Series, 1988; wrote book about steroids in baseball, 2005.

Eric Cantona, b. 1966, French soccer star; Manchester United 1992-97; named Premier League Overseas Player of the Decade (to mark the 1st 10 years of the Premiere League, 1993-2003) in 2003.

Jennifer Capriati, b. 1976, won Aust. (2001-02) and French Opens (2001), at 14 in 1990 was youngest top-10 player.

Rod Carew, b. 1945, AL infielder; 7 batting titles, 1977 MVP.

Steve Carlton, b. 1944, NL pitcher; won 20 games 6 times, Cy Young award 4 times; 4,136 career strikeouts.

Pete Carroll, b. 1951, college football coach; coached the USC Trojans to 2 championships (2003-4).

Billy Casper, b. 1931, PGA Player of the Year 3 times; U.S. Open champ twice .

Wilt Chamberlain, 1936-99, center; was NBA leading scorer 7 times, MVP 4 times; scored 100 pts. in a game, 1962.

Fred Chapman, 1872-1957, pitcher, Philadelphia A's; became the youngest ever U.S. pro athlete on July 22, 1887 when he pitched against the Cleveland Spiders; he was 14 years, 7 months, 29 days old.

Bobby Clarke, b. 1949, Philadelphia Flyers center; led team to 2 Stanley Cup championships; MVP 3 times.

Roger Clemens, b. 1962, pitcher; 1986 AL MVP; only 7-time Cy Young winner (1986-87, '91, '97-98, 2001, '04); twice recorded record 20 Ks in a game; 348 wins, 4,604 Ks (2nd all-time).

Roberto Clemente, 1934-72, Pittsburgh Pirates outfielder; won 4 batting titles; MVP, 1966; killed in plane crash.

Ty Cobb, 1886-1961, Detroit Tigers outfielder; had record .367 lifetime batting average, 12 batting titles.

Sebastian Coe, b. 1956, British runner; won Olympic 1,500m gold medal and 800m silver medal in 1980 and 1984.

Nadia Comaneci, b. 1961, Romanian gymnast; won 3 gold medals, achieved 7 perfect scores, 1976 Olympics.

Maureen Connolly, 1934-69, won tennis Grand Slam, 1953; AP Woman-Athlete-of-the-Year 3 times.

Jimmy Connors, b. 1952, tennis; 5 U.S. titles, 2 Wimbledon.

Cynthia Cooper, b. 1963, basketball; 4-time MVP of the WNBA finals and 2-time league MVP for the Houston Comets.

James J. Corbett, 1866-1933, heavyweight champion, 1892-97; credited with being the first "scientific" boxer.

Angel Cordero Jr., b. 1942, jockey; leading money winner, 1976, 1982-83; rode 3 Kentucky Derby winners.

Margaret Smith Court, b. 1942, Australian tennis great; won 24 Grand Slam events.

Bob Cousy, b. 1928, Boston guard; 6 NBA titles; 1957 MVP.

Mark Cuban, b. 1958, Dallas Mavericks owner; known for outspoken criticism of NBA.

Al Davis, b. 1929, Oakland Raiders owner and former coach.

Bjoern Daehlie, b. 1967, Norwegian cross-country skier; won record 8 Winter Olympic gold medals.

Lindsay Davenport, b. 1976, tennis; won Olympic gold (1996), U.S. Open (1998), Wimbledon (1999), Aust. Open (2000).

Dizzy Dean, 1910-74, pitcher; St. Louis Cardinals' "Gashouse Gang" in the 30s.

Mary Decker Slaney, b. 1958, runner; has held 6 separate American records from the 800m to 10,000m.

Oscar De La Hoya, b. 1972, won IBF lightweight (1995); WBC super lightweight (1996) and welterweight (1997, 2000) titles.

Donna de Varona, b. 1947, 2 Olympic swimming golds,1964; 1st female sportscaster at a major network (ABC), 1965.

Jack Dempsey, 1895-1983, heavyweight champ, 1919-26.

Gail Devers, b. 1966, Olympic 100m gold medalist, 1992, '96.

Eric Dickerson, b. 1960, NFL record 2,105 rushing yds.,1984.

Joe DiMaggio, 1914-99, N.Y. Yankees outfielder; hit safely in record 56 consecutive games, 1941; AL MVP 3 times.

Tony Dorsett, b. 1954, Heisman winner who led the Dallas Cowboys to an NFL title in his rookie year (1977).

Tim Duncan, b. 1976, San Antonio center; 3-time NBA Finals MVP (1999, 2003, 2005); NBA MVP, 2002-03.

Roberto Duran, b. 1951, Panamanian boxer, held titles at 3 weights; lost 1980 "no mas" fight to Sugar Ray Leonard.

Leo Durocher, 1905-91, manager; won 3 NL pennants (Brooklyn-1941, N.Y. Giants-1951, '54) and 1954 World Series.

Dale Earnhardt, 1951-2001, 7-time NASCAR Winston Cup champ; died in a last-lap crash at 2001 Daytona 500.

Stefan Edberg, b. 1966, Swedish tennis player; U.S. Open champ, 1991, 1992; Wimbledon champ, 1988, 1990.

Gertrude Ederle, 1906-2003, first woman to swim English Channel, broke existing men's record, 1926.

Teresa Edwards, b. 1964, basketball; 5-time Olympian; gold medalist in 1984, '88, '96, 2000 and bronze medal in 1992.

Hicham El Guerrouj, b. 1974, Moroccan runner; holds world records in mile (3:43.13) and 1,500m (3:26); won gold medals in 1,500m and 5,000m in 2004 Olympics.

John Elway, b. 1960, quarterback; led Denver Broncos to 2 Super Bowl wins, 1998, 1999; regular-season MVP, 1987.

Julius "Dr. J" Erving, b. 1950, 3-time ABA MVP, 1981 NBA MVP.

Phil Esposito, b. 1942, NHL scoring leader 5 times.

Janet Evans, b. 1971, 4 Olympic swimming golds, 1988-92.

Lee Evans, b. 1947, Olympic 400m gold medalist in 1968 with a 43.86 sec. world record not broken until 1988.

Chris Evert, b. 1954, U.S. Open tennis champ 6 times, Wimbledon champ 3 times.

Ray Ewry, 1873-1937, track-and-field star; won 8 gold medals, 1900, 1904, and 1908 Olympics.

Nick Faldo, b. 1957, British golfer; won Masters, British Open 3 times each.

Juan Manuel Fangio, 1911-95, Argentinian; 5-time World Grand Prix driving champ (1951, 1954-57).

Marshall Faulk, b. 1973, 2000 NFL MVP; scored then-record 26 TDs in 2001; 3-time Off. Player of the Year (1999-2001).

Brett Favre, b. 1969, quarterback; led Green Bay to Super Bowl win, 1997; NFL MVP, 1995, 1996; co-MVP, 1997.

Roger Federer, b. 1981, Swiss tennis star; won Aust. Open (2004, 2006), Wimbledon (2003-06), U.S. Open (2004-06).

Bob Feller, b. 1918, Cleveland Indians pitcher; won 266 games; pitched 3 no-hitters, 12 one-hitters.

Rollie Fingers, b. 1946, pitcher; 341 career saves; AL MVP, Cy Young Award, 1981; World Series MVP, 1974.

Peggy Fleming, b. 1948, world figure skating champion, 1966-68; gold medalist, 1968 Olympics.

Whitey Ford, b. 1928, N.Y. Yankees pitcher; won record 10 World Series games.

George Foreman, b. 1949, heavyweight champion, 1973-74, 1994-95; at 45, the oldest to win a heavyweight title.

Dick Fosbury, b. 1947, high jumper; won 1968 Olympic gold medal; developed the "Fosbury Flop."

Jimmie Foxx, 1907-67, Red Sox, Athletics slugger; MVP 3 times; triple crown, 1933.

A.J. Foyt, b. 1935, won Indy 500 4 times; U.S. Auto Club champ 7 times.

Joe Frazier, b. 1944, heavyweight champion, 1970-73.

Walt Frazier, b. 1945, Hall of Fame guard for N.Y. Knicks' NBA championship teams (1970, '73).

Lou Gehrig, 1903-41, N.Y. Yankees 1st baseman; MVP, 1927, 1936; triple crown, 1934; AL record 184 RBIs, 1931; played in 2,130 straight games (1925-39), a record that stood until 1995.

Althea Gibson,1927-2003, 2-time U.S. and Wimbledon champ.

Bob Gibson, b. 1935, St. Louis Cardinals pitcher; won Cy Young award twice; struck out 3,117 batters.

Josh Gibson, 1911-47, Hall of Fame catcher; known as "Babe Ruth of the Negro Leagues"; credited with as many as 84 homers in 1 season and about 800 in his career.

Marc Girardelli, b. 1963, skier (Lux.); won 5 World Cup titles.

Raul Gonzalez, b. 1977, Spanish soccer player; led Real Madrid to 3 Champions League titles 1998, 2000, 2002.

Jeff Gordon, b. 1971, race car driver; youngest to win NASCAR title 4 times (1995, 1997-98, 2001).

Steffi Graf, b. 1969, German; won tennis Grand Slam, 1988; U.S. champ 5 times; Wimbledon champ 7 times.

Otto Graham, 1921-2003, Cleveland quarterback; 4-time all-pro.

Red Grange, 1903-91, All-American at Univ. of Illinois, 1923-25; played for Chicago Bears, 1925-35.

"Mean" Joe Greene, b. 1946, Pittsburgh Steelers lineman; twice NFL outstanding defensive player.

Wayne Gretzky, b. 1961, top scorer in NHL history with record 894 goals, 1,963 assists, 2,857 points; MVP, 1980-87, 1989.

Bob Griese, b. 1945, All-Pro quarterback; led Miami Dolphins to 17-0 season (1972) and 2 Super Bowl titles (1973-74).

Ken Griffey Jr., b. 1969, outfielder; led AL in homers 1994, 1997-1999; 1997 AL MVP; 10 gold gloves.

Archie Griffin, b. 1954, Ohio State running back; only 2-time winner of the Heisman Trophy (1974-75).

Florence Griffith Joyner, 1959-98, sprinter; won 3 gold medals at 1988 Olympics; world and Olympic record for 100m.

Lefty Grove, 1900-75, pitcher; won 300 AL games.

Janet Guthrie, b. 1938, 1st woman driver in Indy 500 (1977).

Tony Gwynn, b. 1960, 8-time NL batting champ, 1984, 1987-89, 1994-97; 3,141 career hits.

Walter Hagen, 1892-1969, golfer; 5 PGA, 4 British Open titles.

Mika Hakkinen, b. 1968, Finnish Formula One racing driver; Formula One champion 1998, 1999.

George Halas, 1895-1983, founder/player/coach of Chicago Bears; won 6 NFL championships as a coach.

Dorothy Hamill, b. 1956, figure skater; gold medalist at the Olympics and World championships in 1976.

Scott Hamilton, b. 1958, U.S. and world figure skating champion, 1981-84; Olympic gold medalist, 1984.

Mia Hamm, b. 1972, led U.S. to World Cup (1991, '99) and Olympic ('96, 2004) titles; most career internat. goals (144).

Franco Harris, b. 1950, running back; 4 Super Bowls with Steelers (1975-76, 1979-80); 1,000+ yds. in a season 8 times.

Marvin Harrison, b. 1972, Indianapolis Colts wide receiver; holds NFL record for single-season receptions, 143, 2002

Bill Hartack, b. 1932, jockey; rode 5 Kentucky Derby winners.

Dominik Hasek, b. 1965, NHL goaltender; won Vezina Trophy, 1994-95, 1997-99, 2001; NHL MVP, 1997-98.

John Havlicek, b. 1940, Boston Celtics forward; scored 26,395 career pts.

Eric Heiden, b. 1958, speed skater; won 5 Olympic golds, 1980.

Rickey Henderson, b. 1958, outfielder; 1990 AL MVP; record 130 stolen bases, 1982; all-time leader in steals, runs.

Sonja Henie, 1912-69, Norwegian world champion figure skater, 1927-36; Olympic gold medalist, 1928, 1932, 1936.

Martina Hingis, b. 1980, Swiss; won Aust. and U.S. Opens, Wimbledon; youngest No. 1 player (16 yrs., 6 m.), 1997.

Trevor Hoffman, b. 1967; San Diego Padres relief pitcher; set a new all-time career saves record in 2006 with 482.

Ben Hogan, 1912-97, golfer; won 4 U.S. Open titles, 2 PGA Championships, 2 Masters.

Chamique Holdsclaw, b. 1977, L.A. Sparks forward.

Evander Holyfield, b. 1962, 4-time heavyweight champion.

Rogers Hornsby, 1896-1963, NL 2nd baseman; batted record .424 in 1924; twice won triple crown.

Paul Hornung, b. 1935, Green Bay Packers running back, placekicker; scored record 176 points, 1960.

Gordie Howe, b. 1928, hockey forward; NHL MVP 6 times; scored 801 goals in 26 NHL seasons.

Carl Hubbell, 1903-88, N.Y. Giants pitcher; 20-game winner 5 consecutive years, 1933-37.

Bobby Hull, b. 1939, NHL all-star 10 times; MVP, 1965-66.

Brett Hull, b. 1964: St. Louis Blues forward; led NHL in goals, 1990-92; MVP, 1991.

Catfish Hunter, 1946-99, pitched perfect game, 1968; 20-game winner 5 times.

Don Hutson, 1913-97, Packers receiver; caught 99 TD passes; 2-time NFL MVP.

Juli Inkster, b. 1960, Hall of Fame golfer; 2nd to win all 4 of LPGA's modern majors; won 7 career major titles.

Phil Jackson, b. 1945, won 9 NBA titles as coach of Bulls and Lakers; 1973 title as a player with N.Y Knicks.

Reggie Jackson, b. 1946, slugger; led AL in home runs 4 times; MVP, 1973; hit 5 World Series home runs, 1977.

"Shoeless" Joe Jackson, 1889-1951, outfielder; 3rd highest career batting average (.356); one of the "Black Sox" banned for allegedly throwing 1919 World Series.

Jaromir Jagr, b. 1972, Czech hockey player; NHL MVP in 1999; Art Ross Trophy (leading scorer) 1995, 1998-2001.

Lebron James, b. 1984, Cleveland Cavaliers forward; won Rookie of the Year, 2004.

Bruce Jenner, b. 1949, Olympic decathlon gold medalist, 1976.

Lynn Jennings, b. 1960, runner; 3-time World and 9-time U.S. cross country champ; bronze at 1992 Olympics (10,000m).

Derek Jeter, b. 1974, shortstop; 7-time All-Star; led NY Yankees to 4 World Series titles; World Series MVP, 2000.

Earvin "Magic" Johnson, b. 1959, NBA MVP, 1987, 1989, 1990; Playoff MVP, 1980, 1982, 1987; 2nd in career assists.

Jack Johnson, 1878-1946, heavyweight champion, 1908-15.

Michael Johnson, b. 1967, 5-time Olympic gold medalist (1996, 2000); world and Olympic record, 200m and 400m.

Randy Johnson, b. 1963, 5-time Cy Young winner; strikeout leader: 1992-95, 1999-2004; 4,544 strikeouts (3rd all-time); pitched perfect game, 2004.

Walter Johnson, 1887-1946, Washington Senators pitcher; won 416 games; record 110 shutouts.

Bobby Jones, 1902-71, won golf's Grand Slam, 1930; U.S. Amateur champ 5 times, U.S. Open champ 4 times.

Cobi Jones, b. 1970, soccer; most U.S. national team appearances with 164.

David "Deacon" Jones, b. 1938, 5-time All-Pro with L.A. Rams (1965-69); "sack" specialist credited with inventing the term.

Marion Jones, b. 1975, 2000 Olympic 100m, 200m, 1,600m relay gold medalist, bronze in long jump and 400m relay.

Roy Jones Jr., b. 1969, light heavyweight champ, 1999-2004.

Michael Jordan, b. 1963, guard; leading NBA scorer, 1987-93, 1996-98; MVP, 1988, 1991-92, '96, '98; playoff MVP, 1991-93, 1996-98; ESPN Athlete of the Century.

Dorothy Kamenshek, b. 1925, led Rockford (IL) Peaches to 4 All-American Girls Baseball League titles in the 1940s.

Kasey Keller, b. 1969, U.S. goalkeeper; U.S. record for most career international victories, 39.

Jackie Joyner-Kersee, b. 1962, Olympic gold medalist in heptathlon (1988,'92) and long jump (1988).

Harmon Killebrew, b. 1936, Minnesota Twins slugger; led AL in home runs 6 times; 573 lifetime.

Jean Claude Killy, b. 1943, French skier; 3 Olympic golds, 1968.

Ralph Kiner, b. 1922, Pittsburgh Pirates slugger; led NL in home runs 7 consecutive years, 1946-52.

Billie Jean King, b. 1943, U.S. singles champ 4 times; Wimbledon champ 6 times; beat Bobby Riggs, 1973.

Bob Knight, b. 1940, basketball coach; led Indiana U. to NCAA title in 1976, '81, '87.

Olga Korbut, b. 1955, Soviet gymnast; 3 1972 Olympic golds.

Sandy Koufax, b. 1935, 3-time Cy Young winner; lowest ERA in NL, 1962-66; pitched 4 no-hitters, one a perfect game.

Ingrid Kristiansen, b. 1956, Norwegian; only runner to have held world records in 5,000m, 10,000m, and marathon.

Julie Krone, b. 1963, winningest female jockey; only woman to ride a winner in a Triple Crown race (Belmont, 1993).

Michelle Kwan, b.1980, figure skater; 9 U.S. and 5 World titles; silver medalist at 1998 Olympics, bronze in 2002.

Guy Lafleur, b. 1951, 3-time NHL scoring leader; 1977-78 MVP.

Alexi Lalas, b. 1970, soccer player; first American to play in Italian League Serie A.

Kennesaw Mountain Landis, 1866-1944, 1st commissioner of baseball (1920-44); banned the 8 "Black Sox" involved in fixing 1919 World Series.

Tom Landry, 1924-2000, Dallas Cowboys head coach, 1960-88; won 2 Super Bowls (1972, '78); 3rd in career wins (270).

Dick "Night Train" Lane, 1928-2002, Hall of Fame defensive back, intercepted an NFL season record 14 passes (1952).

Don Larsen, b. 1929, As N.Y. Yankee, pitched only World Series perfect game, Oct. 8, 1956—a 2-0 win over Brooklyn.

Rod Laver, b. 1938, Australian; won tennis Grand Slam twice, 1962, 1969; Wimbledon champ 4 times.

Mario Lemieux, b. 1965, 6-time NHL leading scorer; MVP, 1988, 1993, 1996; playoff MVP 1991-92.

Greg Lemond, b. 1961, cyclist; 3-time Tour de France winner (1986, '89-90); first American to win the event.

Ivan Lendl, b. 1960, Czech; U.S. Open tennis champ, 1985-87.

Sugar Ray Leonard, b. 1956: boxer; held titles in 5 different weight classes.

Carl Lewis, b. 1961, track-and-field star; won 9 Olympic gold medals in sprinting and the long jump.

Lennox Lewis, b. 1965, Brit.; heavyweight champ, 1997-2004.

Ray Lewis, b. 1975: Ravens linebacker; 5-time Pro Bowler; NFL Defensive Player of the Year (2000, '03); Super Bowl MVP, 2001.

Tara Lipinski, b. 1982, youngest figure skater to win U.S. and world championships, 1997, and Winter Olympic gold, 1998.

Vince Lombardi, 1913-70, Green Bay Packers coach; led team to 5 NFL championships and 2 Super Bowl victories.

Nancy Lopez, b. 1957, Hall of Fame golfer; 4-time LPGA Player of the Year, 3-time winner of the LPGA Championship.

Greg Louganis, b. 1960, won Olympic gold medals in both springboard and platform diving, 1984, 1988.

Joe Louis, 1914-81, heavyweight champion, 1937-49.

Sid Luckman, 1916-98, Chicago Bears quarterback; led team to 4 NFL championships; MVP, 1943.

Connie Mack, 1862-1956, Philadelphia Athletics manager, 1901-50; won 9 pennants, 5 championships.

John Madden, b. 1936, won Super Bowl as coach of the Oakland Raiders (1977); NFL TV analyst since 1982.

Greg Maddux, b. 1966, NL pitcher, won 4 consecutive Cy Young awards, 1992-95; 333 career wins.

Karl Malone, b. 1963, Utah Jazz, L.A. Laker forward; MVP, 1997, 1999; 14-time All-Star; 36,928 career points (2nd all-time).

Moses Malone, b. 1955, NBA center; MVP, 1979, 1982-83.

Peyton Manning, b. 1976, Indianapolis Colts quarterback; MVP, 2004; NFL single-season record 49 TD passes, 121.1 passer rating, 2004.

Mickey Mantle, 1931-95, N.Y. Yankees outfielder; triple crown, 1956; 18 World Series home runs; MVP 3 times.

Diego Maradona, b. 1960, soccer player; led Argentina to World Cup in 1986.

"Pistol" Pete Maravich, 1947-88, guard; scored NCAA record 44.2 ppg during collegiate career; led NBA in scoring, 1977.

Rocky Marciano, 1923-69, heavyweight champion, 1952-56; retired undefeated.

Dan Marino, b. 1961, Miami quarterback; NFL record 5,084 yds passing and 48 TDs, 1984; career leader, TDs, yds passing.

Roger Maris, 1934-85, N.Y. Yankees outfielder; hit AL record 61 home runs, 1961; MVP, 1960 and 1961.

Curtis Martin, b. 1973: Jets running back; 5-time Pro-Bowler; 4th all-time in rushing yards with 14,101.

Eddie Mathews, 1931-2001, Milwaukee-Atlanta Braves 3rd baseman; hit 512 career home runs.

Christy Mathewson, 1880-1925, pitcher; won 373 games.

Bob Mathias, b. 1930, decathlon gold, 1948, 1952 Olympics.

Willie Mays, b. 1931, N.Y.-S.F. Giants center fielder; hit 660 home runs, led NL 4 times; had 3,283 hits; twice MVP.

Willie McCovey, b. 1938, S.F. Giants slugger; hit 521 home runs; led NL 3 times; MVP, 1969.

John McEnroe, b. 1959, U.S. Open tennis champ, 1979-81, 1984; Wimbledon champ, 1981, 1983-84.

John McGraw, 1873-1934, N.Y. Giants manager; led team to 10 pennants, 3 championships.

Mark McGwire, b. 1963, hit then-record 70 home runs in 1998; 583 career home runs (6th).

Tamara McKinney, b. 1962, 1st U.S. skier to win overall Alpine World Cup championship (1983).

Andrea Mead Lawrence, b. 1932, skier; only woman to win 2 gold medals in alpine skiing at one Olympics (1952).

Mark Messier, b. 1961, center; NHL MVP, 1990, 1992; Conn Smythe Trophy, 1984.

Debbie Meyer, b. 1952, 1st swimmer to win 3 individual Olympic golds (1968).

George Mikan, (1924-2005), Minn. Lakers center; considered the best basketball player of the first half of the 20th century.

Stan Mikita, b. 1940, Chicago Blackhawks center; led NHL in scoring 4 times; MVP twice.

Billy Mills, b. 1938, runner; upset winner of the 1964 Olympic 10,000m; only American man ever to win the event.

Joe Montana, b. 1956, S.F. 49ers quarterback; Super Bowl MVP, 1982, 1985, 1990.

Archie Moore, 1913-98, light-heavyweight champ, 1952-62.

Howie Morenz, 1902-37, Montreal Canadiens forward; considered best hockey player of first half of the 20th century.

Edwin Moses, b. 1955, undefeated in 122 consecutive 400m hurdles races, 1977-87; Olympic gold medalist, 1976, '84.

Shirley Muldowney, b. 1940, 1st woman to race National Hot Rod Assoc. Top Fuel dragsters; 3-time NHRA points champ.

Eddie Murray, b. 1956, 3rd player to combine 3,000+ hits with 500+ home runs.

Stan Musial, b. 1920, St. Louis Cardinals star; won 7 NL batting titles; MVP 3 times.

Bronko Nagurski, 1908-90, Chicago Bears fullback and tackle; gained more than 4,000 yds. rushing.

Joe Namath, b. 1943, Jets quarterback; 1969 Super Bowl MVP.

Steve Nash, b. 1974, Phoenix Suns point guard; NBA MVP, in 2005, 2006.

Martina Navratilova, b. 1956, Wimbledon champ 9 times, U.S. Open champ 1983-84, 1986-87.

Byron Nelson, b. 1912-2006, won 11 consecutive golf tournaments in 1945; twice Masters and PGA titlist.

Ernie Nevers, (1903-76), Stanford football star; selected as best college fullback to play between 1919-69.

Paula Newby-Fraser, b. 1972, 8-time Ironman Triathlon World Champ; holds women's course record.

John Newcombe, b. 1943, Australian; twice U.S. Open tennis champ; Wimbledon titlist 3 times.

Jack Nicklaus, b. 1940, PGA Player of the Year, 1967, 1972; leading money winner 8 times; won 18 majors (6 Masters).

Chuck Noll, b. 1932, Pittsburgh coach; won 4 Super Bowls.

Paavo Nurmi, 1897-1973, Finnish distance runner; won 6 Olympic gold medals, 1920, 1924, 1928.

Al Oerter, b. 1936, discus thrower; won gold medal at 4 consecutive Olympics, 1956-68.

Hakeem Olajuwon, b. 1963, Houston center; NBA MVP, 1994, playoffs MVP, 1994-95; career blocked shots leader.

Barney Oldfield, 1878-1946, pioneer auto racer; was first to drive a car 60 mph (1903).

Shaquille O'Neal, b. 1972, center; led L.A. Lakers to NBA titles, 2000-2002; and Miami Heat to NBA title, 2006; Finals MVP 2000, 2002; NBA MVP 2000 .

Bobby Orr, b. 1948, Boston Bruins defenseman; 8-time Norris Trophy winner; led NHL in scoring twice, assists 5 times.

Mel Ott, 1909-1958, N.Y. Giants rightfielder; hit 511 home runs; led NL 6 times.

Jesse Owens, 1913-1980, track and field; 4 1936 Olympic golds.

Terrell Owens, b 1973; Dallas Cowboys wide receiver; NFL record for single-game receptions with 20 in 2000.

Satchel Paige, 1906-1982, pitcher; starred in Negro leagues, 1924-48; entered major leagues at age 42.

Arnold Palmer, b. 1929, golf's first $1 million winner; won 4 Masters, 2 British Opens.

Jim Palmer, b. 1945, Baltimore Orioles pitcher; won Cy Young award 3 times; 20-game winner 8 times.

Joe Paterno, b. 1926, football coach; 2nd-most wins in NCAA Div. I-A (343 through 2004); led Penn St. to titles, 1982, 1986.

Danica Patrick, b. 1982, racecar driver; 4th woman to race at Indy 500, and 1st to lead (2005).

Floyd Patterson, 1935-2006, 2-time heavyweight champion; first to ever regain the title after losing it.

Walter Payton, 1954-1999, Chicago Bears running back; most rushing yards in NFL history; top NFC rusher, 1976-80.

Pelé (Edson Arantes do Nascimento), b. 1940, Brazilian soccer player; led Brazil to 3 World Cups (1958, '62, '70); scored 1,281 goals.

Bob Pettit, b. 1932, first NBA player to score 20,000 points; twice NBA scoring leader.

Richard Petty, b. 1937, NASCAR national champ 7 times; 7-time Daytona 500 winner.

Michael Phelps, b. 1985, swimmer; won 8 medals (6 gold, 2 bronze) at 2004 Olympics; set numerous world records.

Picabo Street, b. 1971, skier; 2-time World Cup downhill champion (1995-96); Olympic super G gold medalist, 1998.

Laffit Pincay Jr., b. 1946, jockey; leading money-winner, 1970-74, 1979, 1985.

Jacques Plante, 1929-86, NHL goaltender; 7 Vezina trophies; first goalie to wear a mask in a game.

Gary Player, b. 1936, South African golfer; won 3 Masters, 3 British Opens, 2 PGA Championships, and the U.S. Open.

Steve Prefontaine, 1951-75, runner; 1st to win 4 NCAA titles in same event (5,000m, 1970-73); died in auto accident.

Kirby Puckett, 1960-2006, Minnesota Twins center fielder (1984-95); led team to World Series titles in 1987 and 1991.

Albert Pujols, b. 1980, St. Louis first baseman; NL MVP, 2005.

Paula Radcliffe, b. 1973, British runner; set marathon world record of 2:15:25 in London, 2003.

Manny Ramirez, b. 1972, Boston Red Sox slugger; 2004 World Series champs.

Willis Reed, b. 1942, N.Y. Knicks center; MVP, 1970; playoff MVP, 1970, 1973.

Mary Lou Retton, b. 1968, gymnast; won all-around gold medal at 1984 Olympics; also won 2 silvers and 2 bronzes.

Claudio Reyna, b. 1973, midfielder; U.S. National Team; named to the FIFA World Cup All-Star team in 2002.

Jerry Rice, b. 1962, receiver; 1989 Super Bowl MVP; NFL record for career touchdowns (208) and receptions (1,549).

Maurice Richard, 1921-2000, Montreal Canadiens forward; scored 544 regular season goals, 82 playoff goals.

Branch Rickey, 1881-1965, MLB executive; helped break baseball's color barrier, 1947; initiated farm system, 1919.

Cal Ripken Jr., b. 1960, Baltimore shortstop; AL MVP 1983, 1991; most consecutive games played (2,632).

Mariano Rivera, b. 1969; relief pitcher; helped NY Yankees to 4 World Series titles; World Series MVP, 1999; all-time MLB leader in post-season saves with 34.

Oscar Robertson, b. 1938, NBA guard; averaged career 25.7 points per game; 4th in career assists (9,887); MVP, 1964.

Brooks Robinson, b. 1937, Baltimore Orioles 3rd baseman; played in 4 World Series; MVP, 1964; 16 gold gloves.

Frank Robinson, b. 1935, MVP in both NL and AL; triple crown, 1966; 586 career home runs; first black manager in majors.

Jackie Robinson, 1919-72, broke baseball's color barrier with Brooklyn Dodgers, 1947; MVP, 1949.

Sugar Ray Robinson, 1920-89, boxer; middleweight champion 5 times, welterweight champion.

Knute Rockne, 1888-1931, Notre Dame football coach, 1918-31; revolutionized game by stressing forward pass.

Bill Rodgers, b. 1947, runner; won Boston and New York City marathons 4 time each, 1975-80.

Alex Rodriguez, b. 1975, New York Yankees third baseman; A.L. MVP in 2003 and 2005; 10-time All Star.

Juan "Chi Chi" Rodriguez, b. 1935, champion golfer; 8 PGA tour wins and 22 Champions tour wins.

Ben Roethlisberger, b. 1982, quarterback, led Pittsburgh Steelers to Super Bowl, 2005; youngest Super Bowl winning quarterback with Pittsburgh Steelers in 2005.

Ronaldinho, b. 1980, soccer midfielder; led Brazil to World Cup Finals in 2006; FIFA World Player of the Year, 2004, 2005.

Ronaldo (Ronaldo Luiz Nazario de Lima), b. 1976, soccer forward; led Brazil to 2002 World Cup title; 3-time FIFA world player of the year (1996-97, 2002); most World Cup goals, 15.

Art Rooney, 1901-88, famous NFL owner; bought Pittsburgh Pirates in 1933, renamed Steelers in 1940.

Pete Rose, b. 1941, won 3 NL batting titles; hit in 44 consecutive games, 1978; most career hits, 4,256; banned for gambling, 1989; admitted betting on his team, 2004.

Ken Rosewall, b. 1934, Australian tennis player; 2-time U.S. champ, 8 Grand Slam singles titles.

Patrick Roy, b. 1965, Montreal-Colorado goalie; only 3-time NHL Playoffs MVP (Conn Smythe Trophy), 1986, '93, 2001.

Wilma Rudolph, 1940-94, sprinter; won 3 1960 Olympic golds.

Adolph Rupp, 1901-77, NCAA basketball coach; led Kentucky to 4 national titles, 1948-49, 1951, 1958.

Bill Russell, b. 1934, Boston Celtics center; led team to 11 NBA titles; MVP 5 times; first black coach of major pro sports team.

Babe Ruth, 1895-1948, N.Y. Yankees outfielder; hit 60 home runs, 1927; 714 lifetime (2nd all-time); led AL 12 times.

Johnny Rutherford, b. 1938, auto racer; won 3 Indy 500s.

Nolan Ryan, b. 1947, pitcher; holds season (383), career (5,714) strikeout records; won 324 games (7 no-hitters).

Pete Sampras, b. 1971, tennis star; 1st man in Open era to win 7 Wimbledons; most career Grand Slam wins (14).

Joan Benoit Samuelson, b. 1968, won 1st Olympic women's marathon (1984), Boston Marathon (1979, '83).

Barry Sanders, b. 1968, rushed for 2,053 yards in 1997; led NFL in rushing, 1990, 1994, 1996, 1997.

Gale Sayers, b. 1943, Chicago back; twice led NFL in rushing.

Mike Schmidt, b. 1949, Phillies 3rd baseman; led NL in home runs 8 times; 548 lifetime; NL MVP, 1980, 1981, 1986.

Michael Schumacher, b. 1969, German race-car driver; 7-time Formula 1 world champ (1994-95, 2000-2004).

Tom Seaver, b. 1944, pitcher; won NL Cy Young award 3 times; won 311 major league games.

Monica Seles, b. 1973, tennis; won U.S. ('91-92), Aust. ('91-93, '96), French ('90-92) Opens; stabbed on court by fan, 1993.

Maria Sharapova, b.1987, Russian tennis star; won Wimbledon 2004, U.S. Open 2006.

Patty Sheehan, b. 1956, Hall of Fame golfer; 3 LPGA Championships (1983-84, '93).

Willie Shoemaker, 1931-2003, jockey; rode 4 Kentucky Derby and 5 Belmont Stakes winners; leading career money winner.

Frank Shorter, b. 1947, runner, only American to win men's Olympic marathon (1972) since 1908; silver medalist in 1976.

Don Shula, b. 1930, all-time winningest NFL coach (347 games).

Al Simmons, 1902-56, AL outfielder; lifetime .334 batting avg.

O.J. Simpson, b. 1947, running back; rushed for 2,003 yds., 1973; AFC leading rusher 4 times; acquitted of murder, 1995.

George Sisler, 1893-1973, St. Louis Browns 1st baseman; had then-record 257 hits, 1920; batted .340 lifetime.

Dean Smith, b. 1931, basketball coach; most career Division I wins (879); led North Carolina to 2 NCAA titles (1982, '93).

Emmitt Smith, b. 1969, running back; NFL and Super Bowl MVP, 1993.

Conn Smythe, 1895-1980, won 7 Stanley Cups as Toronto GM (1929-1961); playoff MVP award named in his honor.

Sam Snead, 1912-2002, PGA and Masters champ 3 times each, record 82 PGA tournament victories.

Annika Sorenstam, b. 1970, Swedish golfer; set LPGA 18-hole record of 59 (−13) and 72-hole record of 27-under-par, 2001; won 9 LPGA majors, including career Grand Slam.

Sammy Sosa, b. 1968, Cubs outfielder; 66 homers, NL MVP, 1998; 1st to hit 60+ homers 3 times (1998, 1999, 2001).

Warren Spahn, 1921-2003, pitcher; won 363 NL games; 20-game winner 13 times; Cy Young award, 1957.

Tris Speaker, 1888-1958, AL outfielder; batted .345 over 22 seasons; hit record 793 career doubles.

Mark Spitz, b. 1950, swimmer; won 7 golds at 1972 Olympics.

Amos Alonzo Stagg, (1862-1965), football innovator; Univ. of Chicago football coach for 41 years, 5 undefeated seasons.

Bart Starr, b. 1934, Green Bay Packers quarterback; led team to 5 NFL titles and 2 Super Bowl victories.

Roger Staubach, b. 1942, Dallas Cowboys quarterback; leading NFC passer 5 times.

Casey Stengel, 1890-1975, managed Yankees to 10 pennants, 7 championships, 1949-60.

Jackie Stewart, b. 1939, Scot auto racer; 27 Grand Prix wins.

John Stockton, b. 1962, Utah Jazz guard; NBA career leader in assists, steals; NBA assists leader, 1988-96.

Louise Suggs, b. 1923, golfer; U.S. Women's Open champ., 1949, '52; 11 major victories, ranks 3rd all-time.

John L. Sullivan, 1858-1918, last bareknuckle heavyweight champion, 1882-1892.

Pat Summit, b. 1952, women's basketball coach; led Tennessee Lady Vols to 6 NCAA titles (1987, '89, '91, '96-98).

Ichiro Suzuki, b. 1973, Japanese right fielder, Seattle Mariners; MLB record for hits in a season, 262, in 2004.

Fran Tarkenton, b. 1940, Minnesota, N.Y. Giants quarterback; 3rd in career TD passes (342); 1975 Player of the Year.

Lawrence Taylor, b. 1959, linebacker; led N.Y. Giants to 2 Super Bowl titles; played in 10 Pro Bowls.

Jenny Thompson, b. 1973, swimmer; most decorated U.S. female Olympian; 12 medals (8 gold) in 1992, '96, 2000, '04.

Daley Thompson, b. 1958, British decathlete; Olympic gold medalist in 1980, '84.

Jim Thorpe, 1888-1953, football All-America, 1911, 1912; won pentathlon and decathlon, 1912 Olympics.

Bill Tilden, 1893-1953, won 7 U.S. tennis titles, 3 Wimbledon.

Y. A. Tittle, b. 1926, N.Y. Giants quarterback; MVP, 1961, 1963.

Alberto Tomba "La Bomba", b. 1966, Italian skier; 5 Olympic alpine medals (3 golds, 2 silver) in 1988, 1992.

Lee Trevino, b. 1939, golfer; won U.S., British Open twice.

Bryan Trottier, b. 1956, Islanders, Penguins center for 6 Stanley Cup champs.

Gene Tunney, 1897-1978, heavyweight champion, 1926-28.

Mike Tyson, b. 1966, undisputed heavyweight champ, 1987-1990; at 20, youngest to win a heavyweight title (WBC, 1986).

Wyomia Tyus, b. 1945, Olympic 100m gold medalist, 1964, '68.

Johnny Unitas, 1933-2002, Baltimore Colts quarterback; passed for more than 40,000 yds; MVP, 1957, 1967.

Al Unser, b. 1939, Indy 500 winner 5 times.

Bobby Unser, b. 1934, Indy 500 winner 3 times.

Brian Urlacher, b.1978, Chicago Bears linebacker; Defensive Rookie of the Year, 2000; 5-time Pro Bowler.

Norm Van Brocklin, 1926-83, quarterback; passed for game record 554 yds., 1951; MVP, 1960.

Amy Van Dyken, b. 1973, swimmer, first American woman to win 4 gold medals in one Olympics (1996).

Lasse Viren, b. 1949, Finnish runner; Olympic 5,000m and 10,000m gold medalist in 1972 and 1976.

Dwayne Wade, b.1982, guard; led Miami Heat to NBA title in 2006; finals MVP 2006.

Honus Wagner, 1874-1955, Pirates shortstop; 8 NL batting titles.

Grete Waitz, b. 1953, Norwegian; 9-time winner of the New York City Marathon (1978-80, 1982-86, '88).

"Jersey" Joe Walcott, 1914-94, boxer; became heavyweight champion at age 37, 1951-52.

Bill Walton, b. 1952, center; led Portland Trail Blazers to 1977 NBA title; MVP, 1978; NBA TV commentator.

Kurt Warner, b. 1971, Rams, Giants, Cardinals quarterback; NFL MVP 1999, 2001; Super Bowl MVP, 2000.

Tom Watson, b. 1949, golfer; 6-time PGA Player of the Year, won 5 British Opens, 2 Masters, U.S. Open.

Karrie Webb, b. 1974, Australian golfer; youngest woman (26 yrs. 6 mos.) to win career Grand Slam, 1999-2001.

Johnny Weissmuller, 1903-84, swimmer; won 52 national championships, 5 Olympic gold medals; set 67 world records.

Jerry West, b. 1938, L.A. Lakers guard; had career average 27 points per game; first team all-star 10 times.

Byron "Whizzer" White, 1917-2002, running back; led NCAA in scoring and rushing at Colorado (1937); led NFL in rushing twice (1938, '40); Supreme Court justice, 1962-93.

Kathy Whitworth, b. 1939, 7-time LPGA Player of the Year (1966-69, 1971-73); 88 tour wins most on LPGA or PGA tour.

Michelle Wie, b. 1989, golfer; in 2002 became youngest-ever qualifier for an LPGA event; turned pro at age 15.

Lenny Wilkens, b. 1937, winningest coach in NBA history; in Hall of Fame as player and coach.

Serena Williams, b. 1981, tennis; Wimbledon (2002, 2003), U.S. Open champ; Australian Open (2003, 2005); French Open (2002).

Ted Williams, 1918-2002, Boston Red Sox outfielder; won 6 batting titles, 2 triple crowns; hit .406 in 1941.

Venus Williams, b. 1980, champ at Wimbledon (2000, 2001, 2005), Australian Open (2003), French Open (2002).

Helen Wills Moody, 1905-98, tennis star; won U.S. Open 7 times, Wimbledon 8 times.

Katarina Witt, b. 1965, German figure skater; won Olympic gold medal, 1984, 1988; world champ, 1984-84, 1987-88.

John Wooden, b. 1910, UCLA basketball coach; 10 NCAA titles.

Tiger Woods, b. 1975, golfer; youngest to win career Grand Slam, at age 24 (1997-2000); 12 career major titles.

Mickey Wright, b. 1935, golfer; won LPGA and U.S. Open championship 4 times; 82 career wins, including 13 majors.

Eric Wynalda, b. 1969, soccer; all-time leading U.S. international goal scorer with 33.

Kristi Yamaguchi, b. 1971, figure skater; won national, world, and Olympic titles in 1992.

Carl Yastrzemski, b. 1939, Boston Red Sox slugger; won 3 batting titles; triple crown, 1967.

Cy Young, 1867-1955, pitcher; won record 511 games.

Steve Young, b. 1961, 49ers quarterback; led NFL in passing, 1991-94, 1996, 1997; Super Bowl MVP, 1995.

Babe Didrikson Zaharias, 1911-56, all-around athlete; 3 track & field medals (2 golds), 1932 Olympics; won 10 golf majors; also played baseball; 6-time AP Female Athlete of the Year.

Emil Zátopek, 1922-2000, Czech runner; won 3 gold medals at 1952 Olympics (5,000m, 10,000m, and marathon).

Zinedine Zidane, b. 1972, soccer midfielder; led France to 1998 World Cup title; named top player in 2006; 3-time FIFA world player of the year (1998, 2000, 2003).

GENERAL INDEX

Note: Page numbers in **boldface** indicate key reference. Page numbers in *italics* indicate photos.

CROSSWORD PUZZLE ANSWERS

ACROSS: 1 OMAHA, 6 DAMN, 10 CATS, 14 REHAB, 15 ESAI, 16 AGRA, 17 FROMRUSSIA, 19 NEAL, 20 FEY, 21 ASIA, 22 MINCE, 23 HERMAJESTYS, 26 DAYCARE, 30 SOO, 31 INARMS, 32 THEWORLD, 37 ETNA, 38 OBE, 39 LIEU, 40 DIAMONDS, 43 BEACON, 45 DYE, 46 HEAVENS, 47 FORYOUREYES, 52 LAYER, 53 TACT, 54 ESP, 57 USDA, 58 ANOTHERDAY, 61 BEER, 62 RENT, 63 ROGUE, 64 SSRS, 65 PASS, 66 NEEDS

DOWN: 1 ORFF, 2 MERE, 3 AHOY, 4 HAM, 5 ABRAHAM, 6 DESIRE, 7 ASSAM, 8 MAI, 9 NIA, 10 CANIS, 11 AGENT, 12 TRACY, 13 SALES, 18 USERS, 22 MEOW, 24 ASHE, 25 JOE, 26 DIED, 27 ANTI, 28 YANA, 29 CRAM, 32 TBS, 33 OLAV, 34 RICE, 35 LEON, 36 DUNS, 38 ODER, 41 ODOR, 42 NYU, 43 BEECH, 44 EASTERN, 46 HYATTS, 47 FLUBS, 48 OASES, 49 RYDER, 50 YEARS, 51 ETONS, 54 EDGE, 55 SAUD, 56 PYES, 58 ARP, 59 NEA, 60 ROE

SPORTS QUICK REFERENCE INDEX

FOR COMPLETE INDEX, SEE PAGES 979-1007.

WORLD ALMANAC QUICK QUIZ ANSWERS

83—d, c, a, b; **137**—b; **142**—c; **169**—b, c, d, a; **213**— a, d, b; **235**—d; **245**—d; **262**—b; **284**—a; **343**—a; **355**—a; **401**—c; **451**—d; **460**—a—3, b—4, c—1, d—2; **527**—c; **553**— b, c, a, d; **570**—a; **585**—d; **606**—d; **649**—b; **659**—b; **673**—d, a, c, b.; **693**—b; **694**—c; **706**—c; **720**—c; **730**—b; **738**—c, d, b, a; **787**—c; **807**—d.